REVISED AND UPDATED

VARIETY MOVIE GUIDE 2001

Edited by
The Editors of *Variety*

A PERIGEE BOOK

Most Perigee Books are available at special quantity discounts for bulk purchases for sales promotions, premiums, fund-raising, or educational use. Special books, or book excerpts, can also be created to fit specific needs.

For details, write: Special Markets, The Berkley Publishing Group, 375 Hudson Street, New York, New York 10014.

Cover photographs credits are as follows: *American Beauty* Kevin Spacey, Annette Bening photograph: © 1999 Dreamworks LLC / Lorey Sebastian, photographer; *American Beauty* Thora Birch photograph: © 1999 Dreamworks LLC / Lorey Sebastian, photographer; *The Sixth Sense* Haley Joel Osment photograph: © 1999 Hollywood Pictures / Lorey Sebastian, photographer; *All About My Mother* photograph: © 1999 Sony Classic Pictures / Teresa Isasi, photographer; *Gladiator* Russell Crowe photograph: © 2000 Dreamworks LLC / Jaap Buitendijk, photographer; *The Graduate* Dustin Hoffman photograph: Embassy Pictures (courtesy Kobal); *Godzilla* (1998) photograph: Columbia Tri-Star (courtesy Kobal) / Centropolis Effects, photographer; *Saving Private Ryan* Tom Hanks, Tom Sizemore, Matt Damon, Adam Goldberg photograph: Dreamworks (courtesy Kobal) / Davis James, photographer; *Austin Powers: International Man of Mystery* Elizabeth Hurley, Mike Myers photograph: New Line Cinema (courtesy Kobal) / K. Wright, photographer; *Life Is Beautiful* Roberto Benigni, Giorgio Cantarini photograph: Miramax (courtesy Kobal) / Sergio Strizzi, photographer; *Shakespeare in Love* Gwyneth Paltrow photograph: Miramax (courtesy Kobal)

A Perigee Book
Published by The Berkley Publishing Group
A division of Penguin Putnam Inc.
375 Hudson Street
New York, New York 10014

Book design by Pauline Neuwirth, Neuwirth & Associates, Inc.
Cover design by Miguel Santana, adapted by Dawn Velez Le Bron

This book is a revised and updated edition of *Variety Movie Guide '97*, originally published by Hamlyn, an imprint of Reed Consumer Books Limited.

First Perigee edition: March 2001

ISBN: 0-399-52657-9
ISSN: 1523-1666

Published simultaneously in Canada.

The Penguin Putnam Inc. World Wide Web site address is http://www.penguinputnam.com

Printed in the United States of America

10 9 8 7 6 5 4 3 2 1

INTRODUCTION

Welcome to the ninth edition of *Variety Movie Guide*, the only one of its kind to combine a you-were-there-at-the-time feel with an unrivalled "trade" orientation to the reviews.

The current volume contains some 8,600 reviews selected from the 57,000-plus published by *Variety* over the past 94 years, from January 1907 to December 2000. The earliest review included is of D. W. Griffith's *Judith of Bethulia* (1914). Although *Variety* stopped publishing film reviews for a short spell—between March 1911 and January 1913—the paper is still the longest unbroken source of film criticism in existence.

The *Guide* does not pretend to supplant the 24-volume *Variety Film Reviews* (1907–1996), which reprints the original texts in full, nor to compete with pocket guides which offer a couple of sentences of opinion on up to 20,000 movies. What it does do, in the space of a single volume, is provide the guts of the original reviews along with key technical and creative credits. As such it's a practical guide first, not a pure reference work for scholars or archivists—and, one hopes, a fascinating browse.

The present edition includes around 100 extra reviews selected from the period since the last edition closed, i.e., December 1999. That's a much tighter selection (due to space constraints) than in earlier editions, and has meant deleting some relatively obscure films and selecting very few foreign-language ones. But we hope most of your favorites are here.

This edition has again been corrected as part of the ongoing process of checking all credits against actual prints of the movies. (Uncredited personnel are listed in square brackets.) Foreign-language movies—only some 420, due to lack of space—are entered under their original title(s), cross-referenced by English title(s). The emphasis is on accepted classics, both old and new. Especially in the early days, many of these were reviewed in a hard-nosed trade style very different to criticism from the '60s onward. When a film was reviewed twice (a common practice in *Variety*'s early history), preference has been given to the first, reflecting opinion at its original unspooling.

Reviewers' now-meaningless box-office predictions ("Fort Knox, move over"—*A Star Is Born*) have been cut out, as well as plot revelations. Minor changes to tenses have been made so that reviews "read" from a modern viewpoint, and any obscure contemporary references or pointless prejudices (especially during the two world wars and the McCarthy period) have been toned down or deleted. Until the mid-'30s, when *Variety* reviews began to take on their unique shape and structure, editing has been considerably heavier. Early reviews were more like scattergun essays: "film criticism" as we now know it did not arrive until the '30s.

Although *Variety* has occasionally included accents on foreign names, this book adheres to tradition by omitting them.

Variety only started regularly to publish cast lists and limited technical credits in the mid-'30s; fuller credits began from the late '30s. So, assembling this data for each film has often involved separate research. Mistakes and misprints in the original reviews have been corrected where possible; real names put in square brackets after pseudonyms; and the latest version of people's names used throughout for consistency in the present format.

The following are the main criteria used:

★ **FILM TITLE.** The original title in country of origin ("majority" country in the case of coproductions) or, for foreign productions shot in English, the English title (e.g., Bergman's *The Touch*, Leone's *The Good, the Bad and the Ugly*). When a film has subsequently had a title change, and is now better known under that title, the latter is used (e.g., *Murder My Sweet*, originally released out-of-town in 1944 as *Farewell, My Lovely*). The form of the title is that used on the print itself, not the officially registered one nor that on secondary material like posters or press handouts. So-called "possessory credits" are omitted (e.g., *Billy Rose's Jumbo* is listed as *Jumbo*), but are cross-indexed.

A film's subsidiary title ("handle"), a growing trend since the '80s and the habit of sequels, is put on a separate line. A.k.a. ("also known as") is a general dumping ground for other release titles, video titles and TV titles, but not production titles.

The book is self-indexing, with entries in strict letter-by-letter A–Z order; those starting with numerals are positioned as if the figures were spelled out. To be included, a film has to have received a theatrical showing somewhere at some time in its life. Direct-to-video and TV movies are not included.

★ **YEAR.** The year of first press release in its country of origin (or, with coproductions, "majority" country). Sneaks and out-of-town tryouts don't count; end-of-year Oscar-qualifying runs do. If a film never got a proper theatrical release, we've used the year of its first showing on the festival circuit, which nowadays is virtually an alternative exhibition chain. Establishing some films' opening dates is still problematic.

★ **RUNNING TIME.** The hardest nut to crack, as secondary materials (press handouts, festival catalogues, producers' claims) are often wildly inaccurate, and during the era of roadshow epics the intermission was often permed into the running time. *Variety* reviewers now time all films themselves, but no running time should be taken as gospel. Movies are trimmed, speeded up by projectionists, cut for TV and generally mangled; more recently there has been a trend toward issuing longer versions for TV and home video (the so-called "director's cut").

★ **COUNTRY OF ORIGIN.** The second hardest nut. The rule here has been where the money actually came from, rather than where a film was shot, what passport the director had, what language the cast spoke in, or a movie's "cultural identity." With coproductions, the first country listed is the "majority" one (which decides its official title—see above). In the case of many British and American movies, especially since the '50s, whether some are UK/US, US/UK or even UK or US is virtually impossible to define.

★ **VIDEO.** A nightmare keeping track of. Films which have been released on video (at one time or another, or are expected to be released during the lifetime of this edition) carry the symbol Ⓥ.

★ **LASERDISC AND DVD.** The symbol ⊙ denotes that the film has been released, or should be released shortly, on laserdisc and/or DVD. In text annotations, the term "home video" includes video, laser and DVD.

★ **WIDESCREEN.** Films originally shown in an aspect ratio of 2:1 or greater—such as CinemaScope, Panavision widescreen, Todd-AO, etc.—are marked ▭. (Standard American so-called "widescreen" is only 1.85:1, and does not qualify; and almost all films in VistaVision—a variable ratio—were projected in less than 2:1.)

★ **SILENT.** Films originally shown without a synchronized dialog track are indicated with the symbol ⊗ .

★ **COLOR/BLACK & WHITE.** Movies mostly, or all, in color are marked "col." Black-and-white films that include some bits in processed color are marked "b/w & col." Silent movies that were originally tinted (i.e., most of them) are still marked "b&w."

★ **DIRECTOR.** The film's officially credited director or co-directors. Some productions are in fact the work of several hands (especially during Hollywood's studio era); only well-known uncredited contributions are listed in square parentheses. Second-unit or dance-number directors are occasionally included up top or in the text, if their contribution merits it.

★ **PRODUCER.** This does not include co-producers, associate, executive or line producers. If no producer is credited on a film's print, the executive or associate producer is included instead (and noted as such).

★ **SCRIPT.** The officially credited scriptwriters, dialog writers and additional dialog writers; not adaptors, story writers or authors of the original novel, play or musical (their names generally appear in the review, or have been added in square brackets). Because of changes in terminology over the years, deciding the scriptwriter credit for films up to the early '30s is especially difficult; when in doubt, a name has been included.

★ **PHOTOGRAPHY.** The director of photography, also known as "lighting cameraman." Occasionally includes those credited with "additional photography" but not camera operators or (apart from rare instances) second-unit directors of photography.

★ **EDITOR.** Also includes supervising and associate editors, but not assistant or assembly editors.

★ **MUSIC.** The composer who contributed the dramatic score, not the one who wrote the songs or show music. With musicals/song movies, the musical director/arranger/adaptor is listed rather than those who wrote the original stage musical or songs (their names generally appear in the review, or have been added in square brackets). Dates against titles of musicals in the text are those of their first stage production.

★ **ART DIRECTOR.** When a film has a production designer as well as an art director, the former is chosen. In productions from the studio era, "associates" are also included as these, rather than the first-listed heads of department, did most of the actual work. Does not include set decorators, costume designers or any other artistic types. *Variety* only began to list art directors from the late '60s, so establishing the credit on earlier films is sometimes difficult.

★ **CAST LISTS.** For space consideration, these have been limited to a maximum of six—ideally, in their original order of billing, with the sixth slot sometimes used for an interesting name hidden way down in the cast. For consistency, actors who later changed names are listed by their most recent moniker.

★ **PRODUCTION COMPANY.** More and more difficult, thanks to the growing complexity of production credits ("A so-and-so presentation, in association with so-and-so, of a so-and-so production, with the participation of so-and-so," etc.). The general rule, as in deciding the country of origin, has been to list those companies that actually stumped up the cash, but in a world of pre-buys and lengthy development periods, that too is often difficult to decide. For space reasons, an abbreviated version of companies' names is used. Companies that simply distributed the finished product are not included (unless, in the case of major studios, they basically funded it via the producer's private shingle), nor those credited as "in association with."

★ **ACADEMY AWARDS/NOMINATIONS.** Includes winners and nominations in all feature categories. The date is of the Oscar award, not of the actual ceremony (generally held the following spring).

—THE EDITORS
December 2000

GLOSSARY

The following is a guide to 93 years of *Variety* "slanguage" as occurs in the reviews selected. It is not exhaustive and is intended especially for non-American and more general readers.

Variety's snazzy coinages and neologisms are a goulash of publishing and showbiz/movie jargon, foreign words, Yiddish, street slang, contractions and acronyms that since the mid-'30s (when the reviews took on a recognizable style) have acquired a reputation and life of their own (e.g., "whodunit," "helmer," "chopsocky").

Many of the words have long vanished from use in the paper (along with the slang that inspired them); new ones are still being invented. The only rule is that they sound "right" and carry on the tradition of sharp, compressed, flavorful prose. As a further aid for general readers, we have also included some words that are just movie jargon or archaic slang rather than pure *Variety* slanguage.

a.d.	assistant director
a.k.	ass-kisser
a.k.a.	also known as
alky	alcoholic
ancillary	non-theatrical business, i.e., home video, TV
ankle	leave, quit
anent	regarding
anklebiter	child
auds	audiences
avoirdupois	weight
back-to-back	(two or more films shot) at the same time or without a break between
beaucoup	much
b.b.	big business
beer stube	bar
belter	boxer
b.f.	boyfriend
Big Apple	New York
Blighty	U.K.
burley	burlesque, music hall
b.o.	box office (income)
bow	debut, praise
b.r.	bankroll, sum of money
cannon	gun
carny	carnival
Chi	Chicago
chick	girl
chili	Mexican
chirp(er)	sing(er)
chopsocky	martial arts (film)
chore	job, routine assignment
chump	crazy (in love)
cleff(er)	compose(r)
click	hit, success
coin	money, finance
contempo	contemporary
coprod	coproduction
d.a.	district attorney
dick	detective
doughboy	infantry soldier
d.p.	director of photography
dualer	double-billed feature film
femme	female, woman
fest	festival
filmer	filmmaker
flap	flapper
flivver	car
f/x	special effects
G	$1,000
gat	gun
g.f.	girlfriend
g.m.	general manager
gob	sailor
gorefest	orgy of violence
Gotham	New York
gyp	swindler, cheat
habiliments	clothing
helm(er)	direct(or)
histrionics	performance(s)
hoke	hokum
hoke-up	overact
hoofology	dancing
hotcha	excellent
hoyden(ish)	tomboy(ish)
h.s.	high school
indie	independent (production or company), i.e., not by an established major studio
ink	sign
i.r.	inquiring reporter, investigative reporter
Italoater	spaghetti western
j.d.	juvenile delinquent
jitterbug	(1940s) jazz dance(r), nervous person
kayo	knockout
keptive	"kept" woman
legit(imate)	theatrical, theater, stage
legiter	stage play
legituner	stage musical
lens(er)	photograph(er)
limn	portray
lingo	language, dialogue
longhair	highbrow, intellectual
lower case	minor (quality)
LST	landing ship tank (a WWII landing craft)
manse	mansion
medico	doctor
meg(aphoner)	direct(or)
megger	director
meller	melodrama(tic)
Milquetoast	meek man
m.o.	modus operandi
moniker	name
moppet	child
nabes	suburbs
negative cost	production cost
newshen	female reporter
nitery	night club
oater	Western
ofay	white man
oke	okay
one-shot	one-off
o.o.	once-over
opp	opposite
org	organization, large company
Oz	Australia(n)
ozoner	drive-in theater
p.a.	press agent
pactee	contract player
Par	Paramount
p.d.	production designer
pen	penitentiary, prison
Pennsy	Pennsylvania
perf	performance
photog	photographer
p.i.	private investigator
pic	picture, movie
pix	pictures, movies
plat	platinum blonde
p.m.	professional model
pol	politician

p.o.v.	point of view
p.r.	public relations
prexy	(company) president
prez	president
profesh	profession
programmer	B-movie fodder
pug	boxer
quondam	one time
ridic	ridiculous
rod-man	gunman
RR	railroad
s.a.	sex appeal
sagebrush saga	Western
sauce	alcohol
Scandi	Scandinavia(n)
schtick	comic routine(s)
scripter	scriptwriter
sec	secretary
seg	segment
segue	link, follow on
sheet	screen, newspaper
shingle	production company (often attached to a major studio)
shutterbug	photographer
single	single woman
slugfest	fight
smokeater	fireman
sock(eroo)	excellent, powerful
solon	lawmaker
speak	speakeasy
spec	spectacle
stepping	dancing
stew	drinking bout
stock	repertory theater
sudser	soap opera
super	super-production
switcheroo	(plot) twist
tab	tabloid
tapster	tap-dancer
tech credits	technical credits, i.e., photography, editing, art direction, etc.
ten-twent-thirt	10-20-30/amateurish (acting)
terp(ing)	danc(ing)
terpsichore	dancing
thesp(ing)	actor, act(ing)
thespically	performance-wise
thespics	acting
tint(ed)	color(ed)
tintuner	showbiz musical
topkick	boss
topper	boss
topline(r)	star
trick work	special effects
troubadour	singer
trouping	acting
tube	TV
tuner	musical
20th	20th Century-Fox
U	Universal
unreel	play
unspool	play
upper case	major (quality)
vaude	vaudeville
vet	veteran
vignetting	describing
vis-a-vis	(romantic/sexual/billing) partner
v.o.	voiceover
warbling	singing
WB	Warner Bros.
w.k.	well-known
yahoo	redneck
yak	joke
yclept	played by
yegg	thief
yock	joke
zaftig	luscious, juicy

ABBA
THE MOVIE
1977, 94 mins, Sweden/Australia Ⓥ col
Dir Lasse Hallstrom ***Prod*** Stig Anderson, Reg Grundy ***Scr*** Lasse Hallstrom, Bob Caswell ***Ph*** Jack Churchill, Paul Onorato ***Ed*** Lasse Hallstrom, Malou Hallstrom, Ulf Neidemar
Act Anni-Frid Lyngstad, Agnetha Faltskog, Benny Andersson, Bjorn Ulvaeus, Bruce Barry, Robert Hughes (Polar Music/Grundy)

ABBA The Movie is a handsomely produced, smooth, fast and wittily edited musical entertainment that, in Lasse Hallstrom's script and direction, is both a bit of a documentary of Swedish group ABBA's Australian tour and of its four personable performers' backgrounds and work methods. There is also a slight but funny story about an Aussie disk-jockey's chasing of the group and being most of the way thwarted in his attempts to do a taped interview with the Swedes.

The Australian actors perform with obvious gusto. So does ABBA as a group whereas they have not wished to attempt any acting.

Apart from glimpses of them receiving adoring crowds of fans, they are seen mostly doing their stage work.

•

ABBOTT AND COSTELLO IN HOLLYWOOD
1945, 83 mins, US Ⓥ b/w
Dir S. Sylvan Simon ***Prod*** Martin A. Gosch ***Scr*** Nat Perrin, Lou Breslow ***Ph*** Charles Schoenbaum ***Ed*** Ben Lewis ***Mus*** George Bassman (dir.) ***Art*** Cedric Gibbons, Wade B. Rubottom
Act Bud Abbott, Lou Costello, Frances Rafferty, Robert Stanton, Jean Porter, Warner Anderson (M-G-M)

An Abbott and Costello picture may not be an artistic triumph, but the duo certainly try hard enough to make audiences laugh. *Abbott and Costello in Hollywood* is no exception. Duo portrays the role of barber and shineboy in a tonsorial establishment, who get the yen to be actors' agents when they see the easy life one of the latter has. When the agent turns down a youngster with a nice voice, they take him on, and before the film unwinds they have him set in a picture, but not before they almost wreck the studio and upset the personnel therein.

Despite the 83 minutes running time, this one [from a story by Nat Perrin and producer Martin A. Gosch] moves rapidly, aided by direction of S. Sylvan Simon.

•

ABBOTT AND COSTELLO MEET DR. JEKYLL AND MR. HYDE
1953, 76 mins, US Ⓥ b/w
Dir Charles Lamont ***Prod*** Howard Christie ***Scr*** Lee Loeb, John Grant ***Ph*** George Robinson ***Ed*** Russell Schoengarth ***Mus*** Joseph Gershenson ***Art*** Bernard Herzbrun, Eric Orbom
Act Bud Abbott, Lou Costello, Boris Karloff, Craig Stevens, Helen Westcott, Reginald Denny (Universal)

A rousing good time for Abbott and Costello fans is contained in this spoof on fiction's classic bogeyman [from stories by Sidney Fields and Grant Garrett]. The fat and thin comics combat Boris Karloff as the fictional dual personality in the very broad doings, and Karloff's takeoff on the character adds to the chuckles dished out by A & C.

Helen Westcott, ward of, and coveted by, the good Dr. Jekyll, supplies excellent femme appeal in a romance with Craig Stevens, a reporter; while Reginald Denny, harassed Scotland Yard inspector, and John Dierkes, the doctor's zombie-like assistant, help the fun.

Bounced off Denny's police force because of their bungling, Abbott and Costello figure they might be able to get their jobs back if they catch the monster that is terrorizing Hyde Park. Comedic chills and thrills ensue as the pair track down the monster and wind up with its alter ego, Dr. Jekyll.

•

ABBOTT AND COSTELLO MEET FRANKENSTEIN
1948, 82 mins, US Ⓥ ⦿ b/w
Dir Charles T. Barton ***Prod*** Robert Arthur ***Scr*** Robert Lees, Frederic I. Rinaldo, John Grant ***Ph*** Charles Van Enger ***Ed*** Frank Gross ***Mus*** Frank Skinner ***Art*** Bernard Herzbrun, Hilyard Brown
Act Bud Abbott, Lou Costello, Lon Chaney, Bela Lugosi, Glenn Strange, Lenore Aubert (Universal)

The comedy team battles it out with the studio's roster of bogeymen in a rambunctious fracas that is funny and, at the same time, spine-tingling. Stalking through the piece to add menace are such characters as the Frankenstein Monster, the Wolf Man and Dracula.

Loosely knit script depicts the Monster growing weak. His master, Dracula, decides to transfer Costello's brain to the Frankenstein creation. As a lure, the batman uses wiles of Lenore Aubert to soften the fat man and maneuver him into a proper setup.

Through it all runs the Wolf Man as a sympathetic character who tries to warn the heroes against the plot but, unfortunately, proves a bit of a menace himself whenever the moon rises and changes him into a killer.

•

ABBOTT AND COSTELLO . . . MEET THE INVISIBLE MAN
1951, 82 mins, US b/w
Dir Charles Lamont ***Prod*** Howard Christie ***Scr*** Robert Lees, Frederic I. Rinaldo, John Grant ***Ph*** George Robinson ***Ed*** Virgil Vogel ***Mus*** Joseph Gershenson (dir.) ***Art*** Bernard Herzbrun, Richard H. Riedel
Act Bud Abbott, Lou Costello, Nancy Guild, Arthur Franz, Adele Jergens, Sheldon Leonard (Universal)

Team's stock double-takes and bewhiskered gags are still fulsome, but the hackneyed quips achieve a new gloss in this entry. Credit for the comics' renaissance goes primarily to the story that Hugh Wedlock, Jr., and Howard Snyder fashioned from H. G. Wells's *The Invisible Man*. With three other writers screenplaying, the yarn is tied around the efforts of fighter Arthur Franz to clear himself of a murder rap. He hires private eyes Abbott and Costello to help him in his mission. When Franz injects himself with a serum possessing powers of invisibility, a flock of amusing sequences are touched off. Best of these is a scene in which Costello kayoes the champ (with the Invisible Man's help).

Franz does a crisp job as the "invisible" boxer, while Sheldon Leonard is well cast as the heavy. Nancy Guild portrays Franz's girl with a tender affection. In contrast to her demureness, is the blowziness Adele Jergens injects into her role as a come-on for the fixers.

•

ABDICATION, THE
1974, 103 mins, UK col
Dir Anthony Harvey ***Prod*** Robert Fryer, James Cresson ***Scr*** Ruth Wolff ***Ph*** Geoffrey Unsworth ***Ed*** John Bloom ***Mus*** Nino Rota ***Art*** Alan Tomkins
Act Liv Ullmann, Peter Finch, Cyril Cusack, Graham Crowden, Michael Dunn, Paul Rogers (Warner)

The Abdication is a period film in more ways than one. The Ruth Wolff script, from her play based on the 17th-century abdication of Queen Christina of Sweden, has been directed by Anthony Harvey, like a trite 1930s sob-sister meller, with dainty debauchery and titillating tease straight from 1920s women's pulp magazines.

Peter Finch plays a Vatican-based Cardinal assigned to investigate the background and the motivations of Liv Ullmann, who has quit her throne after converting to Roman Catholicism late in 1655.

Ullmann's early life was a mess: Her kindly father (Edward Underdown) died when she was six; her mother (Kathleen Byron) was a horror; she was reared as a boy; and chancellor Cyril Cusack keeps chiding her on her queenly duties.

Michael Dunn, engaged as Queen Ullmann's dwarf companion, died during Pinewood Studios shooting, and the covering substitute is too different to escape casual notice.

•

ABIE'S IRISH ROSE
1928, 129 mins, US ⊗ b/w
Dir Victor Fleming ***Scr*** Julian Johnson, Herman Mankiewicz ***Ph*** Harold Rosson
Act Jean Hersholt, Charles Rogers, Nancy Carroll, J. Farrell MacDonald, Bernard Gorcey (Paramount)

Anne Nichols's play has been translated literally from the stage, and the picture adds nothing, while it does detract a good deal.

Some fine production has gone into the war sequences and a few of the sentimental passages have been shrewdly intensified. The picture takes a good deal of interest from dramatic tricks—for example, the bit early in the picture that covers a lapse of time in a graphic way.

Abie Levy is growing up in the great melting pot of New York's East Side. He is among the schoolchildren in the schoolyard. They are assembled in lines reciting the school pledge to the flag; a bell rings, and they march in many files to their classrooms. While the kids go tramp, tramp across the yard, the scene dissolves slowly and the marching children become the American soldiers marching down Fifth Avenue in 1917.

The picture takes over two hours to lead up to what in substance is a rather feeble gag, when the antagonistic fathers, Jewish and Irish, at length come around on Christmas Eve to see the offspring of their cast-off children.

The outstanding performance is that of Jean Hersholt as Solomon Levy, an eloquent and sincere performance. Nancy Carroll and Charles Rogers make a charming pair of young people, J. Farrell MacDonald is just a comic Irishman, while Bernard Gorcey as Solomon's attorney friend is a strong asset in his low-comedy role.

•

ABIE'S IRISH ROSE
1928, 80 mins, US b/w
Dir Victor Fleming ***Scr*** Julian Johnson, Herman Mankiewicz ***Ph*** Harold Rosson ***Mus*** J. B. Zamencnik
Act Jean Hersholt, Charles Rogers, Nancy Carroll, J. Farrell MacDonald, Bernard Gorcey (Paramount)

Use of added sound makes *Abie* a different matter. Most of the serious religious material is eliminated and the story treatment greatly lightened. Accompanying score is skillfully done, an accompaniment that holds to the action in its varying moods and introduces a certain humor with its switch from Irish to Jewish themes, military ideas in the war scenes and the like.

The schoolyard scene has been retained in its old form, except that in the new version the children all recite the pledge to the flag and march into the schoolhouse, the camera being trained on Abie for this passage.

The sequence where Abie plays in the entertainment hut for a gang of soldiers is splendidly built up in the love passage for the hero and heroine. Back to America and into the Irish-Jewish love, story proceeds without dialog. Dialog comes in again after the wedding, when both fathers have cast off the two young lovers.

Generally speaking, the footage, sound heightens the effect of the picture. Also the footage has been cut 49 minutes and the story moves much faster.

•

ABIE'S IRISH ROSE
1946, 96 mins, US b/w
Dir A. Edward Sutherland ***Prod*** Bing Crosby ***Scr*** Anne Nichols ***Ph*** William Mellor ***Mus*** John Scott Trotter ***Art*** William Flannery
Act Joanne Dru, Richard Norris, Michael Chekhov, J. M. Kerrigan (United Artists/Crosby)

The essence of film fare is obviously to entertain. This one doesn't. It can't, when the fundamentals are as meretricious as unwind in these hokey 96 minutes.

Fundamentally the story is a topical misfit. It opens with ultra-modern young Abie Levy meeting USO–Camp Shows entertainer Rosemary Murphy in a V-E Day London mixup, resulting in their marriage by an army chaplain (incidentally Protestant, so as to get in all the three faiths, which didn't exist in the original play by Anne Nichols).

Papa Levy is patently a prosperous Bronx department store owner; his place of business, his household and his friends bespeak prosperity. But thereafter this premise falls apart for he has the prejudices of a pushcart peddler; and barrister Isaac Cohen (George E. Stone) and Mrs. Levy (Vera Gordon, who somehow manages a slightly more restrained characterization) are depicted as narrow-minded nitwits.

•

ABILENE TOWN
1946, 91 mins, US Ⓥ b/w
Dir Edwin L. Marin ***Prod*** Jules Levy ***Scr*** Harold Shumate ***Ph*** Archie J. Stout ***Ed*** Otho Lovering, Richard Heermance ***Mus*** Fred Spielman, Kermit Goell
Act Randolph Scott, Ann Dvorak, Edgar Buchanan, Rhonda Fleming, Lloyd Bridges (United Artists)

Fundamentally a story about the violent conflict of interests between the cattlemen and newly arrived homesteaders. *Abilene Town* [based on a novel by Ernest Haycox] focuses interest on the evolution of this Kansas village from the familiar reckless cowboy town into a more peaceful community.

Abilene is located where the Chisholm Trail ends. It's where cattle were placed on trains for the packinghouse cities. This was the habit back in the early 1870s, with the plot pointing up that the business men with stores there felt that without this cattle business, and the periodical visits of the cattlemen after their 90-day drive from Texas, the town would die. Arrival of homesteaders proved how wrong they were.

Randolph Scott chips in with one of his best western characterizations as the marshal, a law officer who really whips the community into line. Ann Dvorak clicks as the dancehall entertainer, equally adept at warbling and stepping.

Lloyd Bridges does a solid bit of work as the vigorous youthful leader of the homesteaders. Rhonda Fleming is the nice gal, daughter of the town's biggest storekeeper and political leader. At times, she's excellent.

•

ABOMINABLE DOCTOR PHIBES, THE

1971, 94 mins, UK Ⓥ ⦿ col

Dir Robert Fuest ***Prod*** Louis M. Heyward, Ronald S. Dunas ***Scr*** James Whiton, William Goldstein ***Ph*** Norman Warwick ***Ed*** Tristam Cones ***Mus*** Basil Kirchen, Jack Nathan ***Art*** Brian Eatwell

Act Vincent Price, Joseph Cotten, Virginia North, Terry-Thomas, Hugh Griffith, Peter Jeffrey (American International)

The Abominable Doctor Phibes stars Vincent Price as a living corpse, out for revenge on the nine medics in attendance when his wife died in surgery. Anachronistic, period horror musical camp fantasy is a fair description, loaded with comedic gore of the type that packs theaters and drives child psychologists up the walls. Joseph Cotten also stars as an intended victim who foils the plot.

James Whiton and William Goldstein wrote a well-structured screenplay, which starts in motion a series of inventive murders and later drops the requisite expository clues. Price, presumed dead until Cotten and gumshoe Peter Jeffrey discover his and the wife's coffins bare, concocts revenge on nine doctors according to the pattern of 10 curses upon the Pharaoh, from the Old Testament.

Terry-Thomas is one of the victims, all of whom die from some bizarre use of rats, bees, bats, boils, etc. Assisting Price is the silent Virginia North. Price's makeup, by Trevor Crole-Rees, is outstanding in depicting without revulsion the look of a living corpse covered with scars.

•

A BOUT DE SOUFFLE

1960, 89 mins, France Ⓥ ⦿ b/w

Dir Jean-Luc Godard ***Prod*** Georges de Beauregard ***Scr*** Jean-Luc Godard ***Ph*** Raoul Coutard ***Ed*** Cecile Decugis ***Mus*** Martial Solal

Act Jean Seberg, Jean-Paul Belmondo, Henri-Jacques Huet, Jean-Pierre Melville, Liliane David, Daniel Boulanger (SNC)

This film, a first pic by a film critic, shows the immediate influence of Yank actioners and socio-psycho thrillers but has its own personal style.

All of this adds up to a production resembling such pix as *Gun Crazy*, *They Live by Night* and *Rebel Without a Cause*. But it has local touches in candor, lurid lingo, frank love scenes, and general tale of a young childish hoodlum (Jean-Paul Belmondo) whose love for a boyish looking, semi-intellectual American girl (Jean Seberg) is his undoing.

Pic uses a peremptory cutting style that looks like a series of jump cuts. Characters suddenly shift around rooms, have different bits of clothing on within two shots, etc. But all this seems acceptable, for this unorthodox film [from an original screen story by Francois Truffaut] moves quickly and ruthlessly.

The young, mythomaniacal crook is forever stealing autos, but the slaying of a cop puts the law on his trail. The girl finally gives him up because she feels she does not really love him, and also she wants her independence.

There are too many epigrams and a bit too much palaver in all this. However, it is picaresque and has enough insight to keep it from being an out-and-out melodramatic quickie.

Seberg lacks emotive projection but it helps in her role of a dreamy little Yank abroad playing at life. Her boyish prettiness is real help. Belmondo is excellent as the cocky hoodlum.

•

ABOUT LAST NIGHT . . .

1986, 113 mins, US Ⓥ ⦿ col

Dir Edward Zwick ***Prod*** Jason Brett, Stuart Oken ***Scr*** Tim Kazurinsky, Denise DeClue ***Ph*** Andrew Dintenfass ***Ed*** Harry Keramidas ***Mus*** Miles Goodman ***Art*** Ida Random

Act Rob Lowe, Demi Moore, James Belushi, Elizabeth Perkins, George DiCenzo, Michael Alldredge (TriStar-Delphi IV & V)

About Last Night . . . has little to do with perversity, let alone *Sexual Perversity in Chicago*, the David Mamet play on which it ostensibly is based. Film lacks much of Mamet's grittiness, but is likable in its own right.

Film presents a look at the mating habits of young Americans, the ones who frequent singles bars and regard commitment as a lifelong disease.

Focus of the story is on Danny (Rob Lowe) and Debbie (Demi Moore) who meet, move in together, separate and get back together with an ease and casualness that makes it both appealing and disturbing. Ups and downs of the relationship are delivered in a series of montages that look like soft-drink commercials for the now generation.

As the sour note, James Belushi is probably the high point of the film. Performance borrows much from his late brother (John) in its outrageousness and unpredictability.

•

ABOVE SUSPICION

1943, 90 mins, US Ⓥ b/w

Dir Richard Thorpe ***Prod*** Victor Saville ***Scr*** Keith Winter, Melville Baker, Patricia Coleman ***Ph*** Robert Planck ***Ed*** George Hively ***Mus*** Bronislau Kaper

Act Joan Crawford, Fred MacMurray, Conrad Veidt, Basil Rathbone, Reginald Owen, Richard Ainley (M-G-M)

After establishing Fred MacMurray and Joan Crawford as newlywed Americans in England, planning honeymoon south of Germany just prior to outbreak of the war, yarn has British secret service drafting them for mission to secure vital confidential plans for the secret weapon—a magnetic mine. Pair pick up the trail in Paris and then hop to Salzburg, where it becomes a mysterious chase with various and sundry characters peering out of shadows and suddenly turning up in the most approved spy fashion.

Picture is filled with various incidents that crop up and then vanish, with no reason for their inclusion except to confuse the audience and by-pass straight-line exposition of the tale.

Both MacMurray and Crawford competently handle their roles, despite drawbacks of script material. Conrad Veidt clicks solidly in major supporting spot, along with brief appearances of Basil Rathbone as a Gestapo leader.

•

ABOVE THE LAW

1988, 99 mins, US ⦿ col

Dir Andrew Davis ***Prod*** Steven Seagal, Andrew Davis ***Scr*** Steven Pressfield, Ronald Shusett, Andrew Davis ***Ph*** Robert Steadman ***Ed*** Michael Brown ***Mus*** David M. Frank ***Art*** Maher Ahmad

Act Steven Seagal, Pam Grier, Henry Silva, Ron Dean, Daniel Faraldo, Sharon Stone (Warner)

Above the Law is an ultraviolent actioner with Steven Seagal playing an aikido-chopping cop on a one man crusade to clean up Chi streets. [Screen story by Seagal and director Andrew Davis.]

As Nico Toscani, Seagal is a no-nonsense cop with a cynical eye towards authority. When he's taken off the trail of a suspected drug dealer, he smells a rat or two at the top of his chain of command.

With a couple dozen stunt persons and an earthy, warm and supportive partner (Pam Grier), Seagal kicks, kills and crushes with his skillful hands one handful after another of street hoods who try and thwart his mission.

Somehow an assassination plot is worked in against the U.S. senator who's about ready to expose a drug trafficking trade in Central America and a group of Salvadoran refugees hiding out in the basement of Seagal's neighborhood Catholic church.

Henry Silva is a sicko sadist who gets off threatening to chop his victims' limbs off one by one until they talk. Quiet moments like the ones with Seagal and his emotional wife (Sharon Stone) comprise about 1 percent of the film.

•

ABRAHAM LINCOLN

1930, 93 mins, US Ⓥ ⦿ b/w

Dir D.W. Griffith ***Scr*** Stephen Vincent Benet ***Ph*** Karl Struss ***Ed*** James Smith, Hal C. Kern ***Mus*** Hugo Riesenfeld ***Art*** William Cameron Menzies, Park French

Act Walter Huston, Una Merkel, Kay Hammond, Jason Robards, Ian Keith, Hobart Bosworth (United Artists)

Abraham Lincoln is a startlingly superlative accomplishment. Next to the direction by D. W. Griffith, with only a tiny margin separating, is Walter Huston's Abraham Lincoln. Young, aging and aged, playful, fighting, grief-stricken, commanding, pleading.

A vivid prolog, with camera sweeping through dark-lit forests, hazy fields and clouded cities, brings the opening to the little log cabin and the birth of Abe. Romance of Lincoln and Ann Rutledge (Una Merkel) is slightly unconvincing in parts.

From the first fight in the country store and the passing of Ann, Huston then begins to make the personality of Lincoln heighten in realism.

The scenes at Springfield where he meets the haughty Mary Todd (Kay Hammond) have considerable comedy. The assassination of Lincoln is classically melodramatic.

•

ABSENCE OF MALICE

1981, 116 mins, US Ⓥ ⦿ ▭ col b/w

Dir Sydney Pollack ***Prod*** Sydney Pollack ***Scr*** Kurt Luedtke ***Ph*** Owen Roizman ***Ed*** Sheldon Kahn ***Mus*** Dave Grusin ***Art*** Terence Marsh

Act Paul Newman, Sally Field, Bob Balaban, Melinda Dillon, Luther Adler, Barry Primus (Columbia)

Absence of Malice is the flipside of *All the President's Men*, a splendidly disturbing look at the power of sloppy reporting to inflict harm on the innocent.

Tackling a long-standing public issue that has no resolution, producer-director Sydney Pollack neatly keeps all the points in focus while sustaining traditional entertainment values. This is, quite simply, a whale of a good story with something important to say. For that, much of the credit undoubtedly should go to writer Kurt Luedtke, a veteran newsman himself.

More typical of her trade than a Woodward or Bernstein, Sally Field is a workaday reporter on a Miami paper, trying to stay on top of a breaking story about the mysterious disappearance of a local longshore labor leader.

Paul Newman is the son of a mobster whose late father kept him straight and out of the rackets, running a legitimate business. But he still has unsavory family ties, particularly Uncle Luther Adler. Bob Balaban, the head of a federal task force investigating the case, believes a little pressure on Newman might force his help in solving the disappearance.

Though Newman has no connection with a crime, Balaban suckers Field into printing a story identifying him—with editor Josef Sommer's zealous encouragement—as a prime suspect.

Not surprisingly, the story produces tragedy, finally shaking Field's faith in her calling. It also outrages Newman and his grievous, angry confrontation with Field may be the best single scene the actor has ever performed.

1981: NOMINATIONS: Best Actor (Paul Newman), Supp. Actress (Melinda Dillon), Original Screenplay

•

ABSENT MINDED PROFESSOR, THE

1961, 90 mins, US Ⓥ ⦿ b/w

Dir Robert Stevenson ***Prod*** Bill Walsh (assoc.) ***Scr*** Bill Walsh ***Ph*** Edward Colman ***Ed*** Cotton Warburton ***Mus*** George Bruns ***Art*** Carroll Clark

Act Fred MacMurray, Nancy Olson, Keenan Wynn, Tommy Kirk, Leon Ames, Ed Wynn (Walt Disney)

On the surface, Walt Disney's *The Absent Minded Professor* is a comedy-fantasy of infectious absurdity, a natural follow-up to the studio's *Shaggy Dog*. But deeply rooted within the screenplay [from a story by Samuel W. Taylor] is a subtle protest against the detached, impersonal machinery of modern progress.

The Professor (Fred MacMurray) is an easygoing, likeable small-town practical chemist who comes up with a practical discovery—a gooey substance endowed with the elusive quality of antigravity. He dubs it "flubber" (flying rubber) and proceeds to put it to use in incongruous ways.

In the film's most hilarious passage, he applies it at halftime to the gym shoes of a basketball team hopelessly outclassed by its opponents' height, whereupon the beaten boys promptly stage a bouncy aerial second half ballet.

MacMurray is ideally cast as the car-hopping prof, and plays the role with warmth and gusto. Nancy Olson attractively supplies romantic interest. Keenan Wynn is a delight in a delicious satirical role—that of a money-man loan tycoon who would sell his own alma mater for a buck.

1961: NOMINATIONS: Best B&W Cinematography, B&W Art Direction, Special Effects

•

ABSOLUTE BEGINNERS

1986, 107 mins, UK Ⓥ ⦿ ▭ col

Dir Julien Temple ***Prod*** Stephen Woolley, Chris Brown ***Scr*** Richard Burridge, Christopher Wicking, Don MacPherson ***Ph*** Oliver Stapleton ***Ed*** Michael Bradsell, Gerry Hambling,

Richard Bedford, Russell Lloyd ***Mus*** Gil Evans (arr.) ***Art*** John Beard
Act Eddie O'Connell, Patsy Kensit, David Bowie, James Fox, Ray Davies, Steven Berkoff (Virgin/Goldcrest/Palace)

Absolute Beginners is a terrifically inventive original musical for the screen. Daring attempt to portray the birth of teenagedom in London 1958, almost exclusively through song is based upon Colin MacInnes's cult novel about teen life and pop fashion in the percolating moments just before the youth cultural explosion in the early 1960s.

Tenuous storyline is a typical one of teen love achieved, lost and regained, and is used as a mere string to which a constant parade of musical numbers and flights of fancy are attached. Aspiring photographer Colin (Eddie O'Connell) and tyro fashion designer Suzette (Patsy Kensit) seem a perfect match, but when the latter begins getting ahead and becomes engaged to a snooty couturier played by James Fox, Colin decides to sell out and make the most of his connections in a last-ditch effort to win back his lady love.

In creating a stylized view of 1950s culture, director Julien Temple and lenser Oliver Stapleton have made great use of fabulous sets fashioned by production designer John Beard. An astonishing moving camera take throughout the Soho set in the early going represents a fully worthy homage to the opening shot of Orson Welles's *Touch of Evil*.

•

ABSOLUTE POWER
1997, 120 mins, US Ⓥ ⦿ ▭ col
Dir Clint Eastwood ***Prod*** Clint Eastwood, Karen Spiegel ***Scr*** William Goldman ***Ph*** Jack N. Green ***Ed*** Joel Cox ***Mus*** Lennie Niehaus ***Art*** Henry Bumstead
Act Clint Eastwood, Gene Hackman, Ed Harris, Laura Linney, Judy Davis, Scott Glenn (Malpaso/Castle Rock/Columbia)

Absolute Power is a high-toned potboiler, a reasonably engrossing and entertaining suspenser for most of its running time, but one that is undercut by too many coincidences and some whoppingly far-fetched developments in the home stretch. Venturing away from Warner Bros. for only the second time in eighteen years, Clint Eastwood has delivered a clean, unfussy and straightforward piece of old-style narrative filmmaking.

A strong cast and stellar production values lend a tony feel to novelist David Baldacci's scummy tale of capital crime and outrageous coverups at the top levels of American government. Account of a veteran master thief's (Eastwood) dilemma after witnessing a murder of a woman participated in by the U.S. president (Gene Hackman) represents melodrama of a juicy nature.

The woman was the wife of the prez's prime backer, eighty-year-old Walter Sullivan (E. G. Marshall), in whose home the crime took place, and the two gunmen (Scott Glenn, Dennis Haysbert) were the commander in chief's personal Secret Service agents. Also on the scene was the chief of staff (Judy Davis), organizer of the coverup. While senior homicide detective Seth Frank (Ed Harris) analyzes the perplexing evidence, Luther decides to turn the tables on the all-powerful establishment.

No-frills direction seems almost charmingly old-fashioned at times, and produces some genuine satisfactions, as in an excellent, very simply shot tête-à- tête between Luther and Seth in a cafe, in which the thief adroitly deflects the detective's suspicions of him.

Eastwood is in good, sly form. Harris and Laura Linney (as Luther's estranged daughter) make the most decisive contributions, and Davis is a bit of a hoot as the seethingly neurotic chief of staff.

•

ABSOLUTION
1981, 95 mins, UK Ⓥ ⦿ col
Dir Anthony Page ***Prod*** Elliott Kastner, Danny O'Donovan ***Scr*** Anthony Shaffer ***Ph*** John Coquillon ***Ed*** John Victor Smith ***Mus*** Stanley Myers ***Art*** Natasha Kroll
Act Richard Burton, Dominic Guard, Billy Connolly, Dai Bradley, Andrew Keir, Willoughby Gray (Kastner-O'Donovan (Kastner-O'Donovan)

Absolution is a dull, gloomy, nasty, contrived marketplace misfit, apparently designed to ride on Richard Burton's shirttails.

Or in this case his cassock since the actor portrays a stern, super devout priest-teacher in a Catholic boarding school for boys. Gist of Anthony Shaffer's melodramatic plot has to do with a catch-22 test of Burton's faith as two embittered students, taking advantage of the secrecy of the confessional box, conspire to drive him round the bend and to an unwitting killing.

It's heavy, artless going, with an abrupt, embarrassing (for Burton) conclusion. Anthony Page's direction is routine, perhaps unavoidably.

•

ABYSS, THE
1989, 140 mins, US Ⓥ ⦿ ▭ col
Dir James Cameron ***Prod*** Gale Anne Hurd ***Scr*** James Cameron ***Ph*** Mikael Salomon ***Ed*** Joel Goodman ***Mus*** Alan Silvestri ***Art*** Leslie Dilley
Act Ed Harris, Mary Elizabeth Mastrantonio, Michael Biehn, Leo Burmester, Todd Graff, Kimberly Scott (20th Century-Fox)

A first-rate underwater suspenser with an otherworldly twist, *The Abyss* suffers from a payoff unworthy of its buildup. Same sensibilities that enable writer-director James Cameron to deliver riveting, supercharged action segments get soggy when the "aliens" turn out to be friendly.

Action is launched when a Navy nuclear sub suffers a mysterious power failure and crashes into a rock wall. Bud Brigman (Ed Harris) and his gamy crew of undersea oil-rig workers are hired to dive for survivors.

At the last minute Brigman's flinty estranged wife, Lindsey (Mary Elizabeth Mastrantonio), who designed their submersible oil rig, insists on coming aboard to lend an uninvited hand.

Crew finds nothing but a lot of corpses floating eerily in the water-filled sub, but meanwhile, Lindsey has a close encounter with a kind of swift-moving neon-lit jellyfish she's convinced is a friendly alien.

When turbulence from a hurricane rocking the surface cuts off the crew's ties to their command ship, their underwater stay is perilously extended.

The Abyss has plenty of elements in its favor, not least the performances by Harris as the compassionate crewleader and Mastrantonio as his steel-willed counterpart. Not even the $50 million–plus pic's elaborate technical achievements can overshadow these two.

[In 1993 a 171-min. *Special Edition*—later renamed *Extended Version*—was released on home video. Restored footage was spread throughout the pic but primarily during the final two reels, including the original ending.]

1989: Best Visual Effects.

NOMINATIONS: Best Cinematography, Art Direction, Sound

•

ACCATTONE
1961, 116 mins, Italy Ⓥ ⦿ col
Dir Pier Paolo Pasolini ***Prod*** Alfredo Bini ***Scr*** Pier Paolo Pasolini ***Ph*** Tonino Delli Colli ***Ed*** Nino Baragli ***Mus*** Carlo Rustichelli (adapt.)
Act Franco Citti, Silvana Corsini, Franca Pasut, Paola Guidi, Adele Cambria, Mario Cipriani (Arco/Cino Del Duca)

This is a fascinating debut by writer-director Pier Paolo Pasolini, who has scripted some interesting pix. Tale is essentially about Accattone, a sort of Roman rebel without a cause who lives from hand to mouth in the daily pursuit of the wherewithal to live—preferably accomplished without manual labor, and sometimes with the unsavory financial support of local prostitutes.

This world of men and women who skirt legality, often flaunting laws and mores, is particular to Pasolini. It's naturally repellent, but has a certain earthy poetry.

Pic's story recounts Accattone's way of life, then introduces a new love (he's married, but has abandoned wife and kids), which influences him for the better, drives him to work for a living, but ironically brings about his final demise and death just as he's determined to go straight.

Pasolini's actors, practically every one of them taken from life (many are reenacting their slum selves), are all excellent. Franco Citti is especially standout as the sleepy-eyed Accattone, a definite find. Dozens of others fill out the picture with almost equal ability, though here and there a naive stint tips its non-pro origins.

Pic needs some trimming to heighten effect and tighten story. A Bach musical adaptation effectively counterpoints action, especially in a fight scene.

•

ACCIDENT
1967, 105 mins, UK Ⓥ ⦿ col
Dir Joseph Losey ***Prod*** Joseph Losey, Norman Priggen ***Scr*** Harold Pinter ***Ph*** Gerry Fisher ***Ed*** Reginald Beck ***Mus*** John Dankworth ***Art*** Carmen Dillon
Act Dirk Bogarde, Stanley Baker, Jacqueline Sassard, Michael York, Vivien Merchant, Harold Pinter (London)

The team that turned *The Servant* into a success took another novel as their plot material—Nicholas Mosley's *Accident*—and jacked it into a haunting study in relationships, with Harold Pinter's flair for spare, suggestive dialog getting full scope in an adaptation which stays remarkably faithful to the book.

It starts with a car crash splitting that night air of the quiet countryside outside Oxford. A male student has been killed, and his female companion, a campus gal, is taken into the neighboring mansion, occupied by the university teacher (Dirk Bogarde) who has been instructing them both in philosophy.

The accident sparks the prolonged flashback that explores the tight-knit relationship of this enclosed community.

A first-rate cast is headed by Bogarde, who wins sympathy for his superficially cold character, and his contained way with emotion is superbly right. But the main acting surprise is contributed by Stanley Baker, unusually bespectacled as the amorous Charlie, and wittily suggesting the man's self-esteem and his lonely search for horizontal satisfaction.

•

ACCIDENTAL HERO
SEE: HERO

ACCIDENTAL TOURIST, THE
1988, 121 mins, US Ⓥ ⦿ ▭ col
Dir Lawrence Kasdan ***Prod*** Lawrence Kasdan, Charles Okun, Michael Grillo ***Scr*** Frank Galati, Lawrence Kasdan ***Ph*** John Bailey ***Ed*** Carol Littleton ***Mus*** John Williams ***Art*** Bo Welch
Act William Hurt, Kathleen Turner, Geena Davis, Amy Wright, Bill Pullman, Ed Begley, Jr. (Warner)

The Accidental Tourist is a slow, sonorous and largely satisfying adaptation of Anne Tyler's bestseller of one man's intensely self-contained passage from a state of grief to one of newfound love.

William Hurt is an uptight, travel book writer from the slightly eccentric, financially comfortable Leary family of unmarried middle-aged siblings in this essentially simple narrative story awash in warmth and wisdom about the emotional human animal.

Weighty tone is set from the opening scene where Kathleen Turner, having just made tea for Hurt upon his return from a travel-writing excursion, calmly informs him she's moving out.

Then, in a series of strange, unpredictable and out-of-character encounters with his unruly dog's trainer (Geena Davis), Hurt finds himself in another, vastly different, relationship. Davis is unabashedly forward, poor, openly vulnerable, a flamboyant dresser and most importantly, has a sickly son (Robert Gorman) who fills the parental void in Hurt's life.

That Hurt remains expressionless and speaks in a monotone, except at the very end, puts a damper on the hopefulness of his changing situation. Davis is the constant, upbeat force in the proceedings. Turner is equally compelling and sympathetic throughout.

1988: Best Supp. Actress (Geena Davis)

NOMINATIONS: Best Picture, Score, Adapted Screenplay

•

ACCUSED, THE
1949, 101 mins, US Ⓥ b/w
Dir William Dieterle ***Prod*** Hal B. Wallis ***Scr*** Ketti Frings, [Leonard Spigelgass, Barre Lyndon, Jonathan Latimer, Allen Rivkin, Charles Schnee] ***Ph*** Milton Krasner ***Ed*** Warren Low ***Mus*** Victor Young ***Art*** Hans Dreier, Earl Hedrick
Act Loretta Young, Robert Cummings, Wendell Corey, Sam Jaffe, Douglas Dick, Sara Allgood (Paramount)

The Accused exploits fear and emotional violence into a high-grade melodrama. The screenplay is based on a novel [*Be Still, My Love*] by June Truesdell and is class scripting. Director William Dieterle, with a solid story foundation and an ace cast upon which to build, marches the melodrama along with a touch that keeps punching continually at audience emotions.

An unbalanced but attractive student is on the make for his professor. By guile he induces her to ride with him to the beach. He attempts to attack her and she, in a moment of surrender to violence, bashes his head in with a tire iron. The crime is concealed to make it look like he died in a dive over the sea cliff.

Loretta Young's portrayal of the distraught professor plays strongly for sympathy. It's an intelligent delineation, gifting the role with life. She gets under the skin in bringing out the mental processes of an intelligent woman who knows she has done wrong but believes that her trail is so covered that murder will never out.

•

ACCUSED, THE
1988, 110 mins, US Ⓥ ⦿ col
Dir Jonathan Kaplan ***Prod*** Stanley R. Jaffe, Sherry Lansing ***Scr*** Tom Topor ***Ph*** Ralf Bode ***Ed*** Jerry Greenberg, O. Nicholas Brown ***Mus*** Brad Fiedel ***Art*** Richard Kent Wilcox

Act Kelly McGillis, Jodie Foster, Bernie Coulson, Leo Rossi, Ann Hearn, Carmen Argenziano (Paramount)

The Accused is a dry case study of a rape incident whose only impact comes from the sobering crime itself, not the dramatic treatment.

Inspired by, but not based upon the 1983 barroom pool-table gang rape in New Bedford, Mass., the screenplay is designed to pose questions about the thin line between sexual provocation and assault, seduction and force, and observation of and participation in a crime.

Pic begins with a bloodied, dishevelled Jodie Foster stumbling out of a roadhouse. A young patron calls the police to report an incident, and in short order three men plead guilty to the reduced charge of "reckless endangerment" (the film's original title) rather than rape.

All this takes place without the participation of the victim, who becomes furious with her lawyer (Kelly McGillis) when she learns via television of the legal deal. McGillis abruptly decides to pursue the matter much further by prosecuting some of the onlookers in the bar for criminal solicitation.

Foster is edgy and spunky but McGillis's role, as conceived, is a joke, since she exists only as a stick figure with no psychology or background offered up over the course of nearly two hours.

With British Columbia standing in for Washington State, pic looks only okay.

1988: Best Actress (Jodie Foster)

●

ACE IN THE HOLE

1951, 111 mins, US Ⓥ b/w

Dir Billy Wilder **Prod** Billy Wilder **Scr** Billy Wilder, Lesser Samuels, Walter Newman **Ph** Charles B. Lang, Jr. **Ed** Doane Harrison, Arthur Schmidt **Mus** Hugo Friedhofer **Art** Hal Pereira, Earl Hedrick

Act Kirk Douglas, Jan Sterling, Bob Arthur, Porter Hall, Frank Cady, Richard Benedict (Paramount)

The grim story of an unscrupulous reporter who wins brief fame at the expense of a cave-in victim is rather graphically unfolded in *Ace in the Hole*.

Kirk Douglas is the reportorial opportunist. He has been exiled to a small New Mexico daily after being kicked off top Eastern sheets for dishonesty, drinking and a variety of insubordination. One day he accidentally stumbles on a story that he believes can get him back in the big leagues, if he plays the yarn long enough and can keep it to himself.

A dealer in Indian curios has become trapped by a cave-in in an ancient cliff dwelling. Douglas is the first to reach the victim (Richard Benedict), sees the story possibilities and makes a deal with a crooked sheriff and a contractor to delay the rescue as long as possible while he arranges exclusive coverage.

The performances are fine. Douglas enacts the heel reporter ably, giving it color to balance its unsympathetic character. Jan Sterling also is good in a role that has no softening touches, and Benedict's victim portrayal is first-rate. Billy Wilder's direction captures the feel of morbid expectancy that always comes out in the curious that flock to scenes of tragedy.

1951: NOMINATION: Best Story & Screenplay

●

ACES HIGH

1976, 114 mins, UK/France Ⓥ col

Dir Jack Gold **Prod** S. Benjamin Fisz **Scr** Howard Barker **Ph** Gerry Fisher **Ed** Anne V. Coates **Mus** Richard Hartley **Art** Syd Cain

Act Malcolm McDowell, Christopher Plummer, Simon Ward, Peter Firth, John Gielgud, Trevor Howard (EMI/Fisz)

Pic is based on R. C. Sheriff's 1929 London and Broadway stageplay, *Journey's End*, a classic on the theme of the futility and boredom of trench warfare in which some men cracked up while others found ways—like the bottle—of averting crackup. *Aces High* packs little of the involving emotional credibility and impact of the play.

Characterization in the film is without sufficient ambiguity and dimension. Thus, the young British airmen of 76 Squadron are either bushy-tailed rookies (Peter Firth), disciplined but emotionally soft (Christopher Plummer), or scared stiff and bucking for medical discharge (Simon Ward). As their squadron leader, Malcolm McDowell is both brave and scared—and dependent on whisky to sustain him as a credible leader of machine-gun fodder.

●

ACES: IRON EAGLE III

1992, 98 mins, US Ⓥ ⊙ col

Dir John Glen **Prod** Ron Samuels **Scr** Kevin Elders **Ph** Alec Mills **Ed** Bernard Gribble **Mus** Harry Manfredini **Art** Robb Wilson King

Act Louis Gossett, Jr., Rachel McLish, Paul Freeman, Horst Buchholz, Christopher Cazenove, Sonny Chiba (Seven Arts/Carolco)

Aces is an action-packed, campy entry in Lou Gossett's *Iron Eagle* series. Best in its cartoonish moments, this follow-up helmed by James Bond director John Glen notably introduces the beautiful bodybuilder Rachel McLish.

Air Force pilot Gossett rounds up a group of fellow veteran fighter aces to fly to Peru and blow up a cocaine factory. The U.S. government won't support this mission, so the guys use vintage World War II era planes they've been flying in air shows.

Gossett fights the drug lords because a friend was killed by them and his sister (McLish) captured and tortured. He frees McLish, who turns out to be more than the equal of any of the male combatants.

When not making corny patriotic speeches, Gossett is a steadying force here. McLish is terrific in action scenes and merely needs intensive coaching on her acting.

●

ACE VENTURA, PET DETECTIVE

1994, 93 mins, US Ⓥ ⊙ col

Dir Tom Shadyac **Prod** James G. Robinson **Scr** Jack Bernstein, Tom Shadyac, Jim Carrey **Ph** Julio Macat **Ed** Don Zimmerman **Mus** Ira Newborn **Art** William Elliott

Act Jim Carrey, Courteney Cox, Sean Young, Dan Marino, Noble Winningham, Udo Kier (Morgan Creek/Warner)

Built as a slapstick vehicle for *In Living Color* star Jim Carrey, *Ace Ventura, Pet Detective* clearly follows a path carved by anarchic clowns such as Jerry Lewis and Peter Sellers. Directed with vigor if not spades of style or polish by vet TV thesp-director Tom Shadyac in his feature debut, *Ace* spoofs the detective genre by posting Carrey as a goofball private gumshoe whose speciality is finding missing pets.

Pic [from a screen story by Jack Bernstein] shifts in tone from social satire to sophomoric pranks and cop-show plotting as Ventura sets out to solve the kidnapping of the Miami Dolphins' lovable dolphin mascot, Snowflake. Along the trail he befriends and beds the Dolphins beautiful flak (Courteney Cox), perplexes top cop Einhorn (Sean Young) and stumbles onto a nefarious revenge plot that involves Dolphins quarterback Dan Marino and a mythical Super Bowl misplay of the past.

Pic scores points for its preppy, unpretentious quest to wrest laughs out of less than sparkling material. Best gags involve Ventura's menagerie-packed apartment and animal-like qualities, including high-revved senses of taste, smell and sexual appetite.

Supporting players Cox, Warhol alumnus Udo Kier as mysterious billionaire Camp and rapper Tone Loc as a sympathetic cop have little to do but watch Carrey riff. Young grimaces and growls as she is subjected to an endless barrage of indignities.

●

ACE VENTURA: WHEN NATURE CALLS

1995, 92 mins, US Ⓥ ⊙ col

Dir Steve Oedekerk **Prod** James G. Robinson **Scr** Steve Oedekerk **Ph** Donald E. Thorin **Ed** Malcolm Campbell **Mus** Robert Folk **Art** Stephen J. Lineweaver

Act Jim Carrey, Ian McNeice, Simon Callow, Maynard Eziashi, Bob Gunton, Sophie Okonedo (Morgan Creek/Warner)

Warner Bros. has a commercial ace up its sleeve with *Ace Ventura: When Nature Calls*, as fresh, brash and outrageous as the original.

On assignment to retrieve a raccoon improbably abandoned on an Everest-like slope, Ace Ventura is bowed and shaken when the critter falls to its death following a spectacular rescue. Ace responds by retreating to a Tibetan monastery to seek inner peace.

But just short of nirvana, Fulton Greenwall (Ian McNiece), a pudgy British emissary, arrives with the entreaty to recover a purloined, sacred beast that stands between harmony and bloodshed among tribes of a small African nation.

Only later does he learn that the creature's a white bat, and Ace just happens to be chiropterphobic. Allrightee!

Plot is the least of concerns in the sequel. It's your basic boy gets bat, boy loses bat, boy gets bat back yarn, an opportunity to take this unlikely screen hero into satire, spoof, utter juvenilia, total tastelessness and, believe it or not, social commentary. It's a death-defying hodgepodge anchored by the complete confidence of star Jim Carrey. Nor can one discount the better-than-yeoman-like work of screenwriter-turned-director Steve Oedekerk.

Supporting players nicely complement the antics. There's also a seamless quality to this around-the-world kook's tour that subs the Canadian Rockies and a South Carolina animal refuge, respectively, for the remote and raw Himalayan and African locales.

●

ACROSS 110TH STREET

1972, 102 mins, US Ⓥ col

Dir Barry Shear **Prod** Ralph Serpe, Fouad Said **Scr** Luther Davis **Ph** Jack Priestley **Ed** Byron Brandt **Mus** J. J. Johnson **Art** Perry Watkins

Act Anthony Quinn, Yaphet Kotto, Anthony Franciosa, Paul Benjamin, Ed Bernard, Richard Ward (Film Guarantors/United Artists)

Across 110th Street is not for the squeamish. From the beginning it is a virtual bloodbath. Those portions of it which aren't bloody violent are filled in by the squalid location sites in New York's Harlem or equally unappealing ghetto areas leaving no relief from depression and oppression. Based upon the novel *Across 110th* by Wally Ferris, it is strong and relentless in its pursuit of violence.

With the knock-over by three Harlem blacks (Paul Benjamin, Ed Bernard, Antonio Fargas) of the family's $300,000 take from the streets, Anthony Franciosa, uncool son-in-law of the org's head, goes out to "teach them a lesson".

Quinn's performance is controlled, but the character is not clearly defined.

●

ACROSS THE BRIDGE

1957, 103 mins, UK b/w

Dir Ken Annakin **Prod** John Stafford **Scr** Guy Elmes, Denis Freeman **Ph** Reginald Wyer **Ed** Alfred Roome **Mus** James Bernard **Art** Cedric Dawe

Act Rod Steiger, David Knight, Marla Landi, Noel Willman, Bernard Lee, Eric Pohlmann (IFP)

Across the Bridge, based on Graham Greene's story, unfolds slowly. But this is strong on situation and acting stints and winds up with a surefire climax. In essence, it is a gripping character study of an arrogant man who, through his own crooked folly and greed, topples from power to degrading death as a gutter outcast.

Rod Steiger is a shady international financier who is on the lam from Scotland Yard and the FBI. On the train he meets up with a gabby Mexican stranger and, by skullduggery, assumes the stranger's identity and acquires his passport. In Mexico, he is caught between the Scotland Yard man, trying to lure him into American territory, and the Mexican police chief, who withholds Steiger's own passport in order to indulge in a spot of astute blackmail.

These complicated goings-on are background to a remarkable study of mental and physical decay by Steiger. At times it is irritatingly over-fussy and mannered, but he dominates the screen.

Aided by skillful lensing, director Ken Annakin has excellently built up the atmosphere of a sleepy, brooding Mexican border town. Exteriors were shot in Spain.

As the Mexican police chief, Noel Willman gives a wily, subtle performance which, because of its very restraint, contrasts admirably with the Steiger technique. The scenes between the two are filmic highlights.

●

ACROSS THE PACIFIC

1942, 86 mins, US Ⓥ b/w

Dir John Huston **Prod** Jerry Wald, Jack Saper **Scr** Richard Macauley **Ph** Arthur Edeson **Ed** Frank Magee **Mus** Adolph Deutsch

Act Humphrey Bogart, Sydney Greenstreet, Mary Astor, Victor Sen Yung, Keye Luke, Richard Loo (Warner)

Warners had a problem in transferring the Robert Carson *Sat. Eve Post* serial to the screen. Original, under title of *Aloha Means Goodbye*, depicted a spy melodrama on ship that finally reached Hawaii but after the war's start and studio purchase scripter Richard Macauley had to change things around.

Result is switch of locale from the West to East Coast—and the yarn never gets into the Pacific Ocean, despite the title.

After Humphrey Bogart is court-martialed out of the army coast artillery, he shifts to Canada in attempt to enlist in the Dominion artillery. Turned down, he gets passage on a Jap freighter bound for Panama and the Orient.

Although the picture does not quite hit the edge-of-seat tension engendered by *Maltese Falcon*, it's a breezy and fast-paced melodrama. Huston directs deftly from thrill-packed script by Macauley.

●

ACROSS THE WIDE MISSOURI

1951, 78 mins, US Ⓥ col

Dir William A. Wellman **Prod** Robert Sisk **Scr** Talbot Jennings **Ph** William C. Mellor **Ed** John Dunning **Mus** David Raksin **Art** Cedric Gibbons, James Basevi

Act Clark Gable, Ricardo Montalban, John Hodiak, Adolphe Menjou, Maria Elena Marques, J. Carrol Naish (M-G-M)

There's much that will seize audience attention in *Missouri*. The color lensing of the rugged outdoor locations backgrounding the story of beaver trappers and Indians in the early West brings the sites to the screen with breathtaking beauty. Critically, though, the presentation is choppy and episodic, and the device of having the Indian dialog lengthily translated, is dull and boring.

Story [by Talbot Jennings and Frank Cavett] is narrated by an unseen voice (Howard Keel) identified as the son of Clark Gable and his Indian wife, played by Mexican film star Maria Elena Marques.

Plot finds Gable, a rough and ready trapper, taking Marques as a bride because he believes it will help him get into some untouched beaver country controlled by an Indian tribe led by the bride's grandfather (Jack Holt). Gable, the wife and other trappers make the long trek and, upon arrival, are temporarily repulsed by young Indians led by Ricardo Montalban.

Wellman's direction clicks when he has the story on the move in the battle and trekking sequences. He's not able to do much when the script requires the actors to sit down and talk out the long translations.

•

ACT OF VIOLENCE
1949, 82 mins, US b/w
Dir Fred Zinnemann *Prod* William H. Wright *Scr* Robert L. Richards *Ph* Robert Surtees *Ed* Conrad A. Nervig *Mus* Bronislau Kaper *Art* Cedric Gibbons, Hans Peters
Act Van Heflin, Robert Ryan, Janet Leigh, Phyllis Thaxter, Mary Astor, Berry Kroeger (M-G-M)

The grim melodrama implied by its title is fully displayed in *Act of Violence*. It is strong meat for the heavy drama addicts, tellingly produced and played to develop tight excitement.

Story concerns two vets. Van Heflin has come out of the war with honors while his comrades, all but one, were killed in a Nazi prison camp. Robert Ryan, crippled and vengeful, pursues Heflin to make him answer for betraying his buddies.

The playing and direction catch plot aims and the characterizations are all topflight thesping. Heflin and Ryan deliver punchy performances that give substance to the menacing terror of the Robert L. Richards script, taken from a story by Collier Young.

It's grim business, unrelieved by lightness, and the players belt over their assignments under Zinnemann's knowing direction. Janet Leigh points up her role as Heflin's worried but courageous wife, while Phyllis Thaxter does well by a smaller part as Ryan's girl. A standout is the brassy, blowzy femme created by Mary Astor—a woman of the streets who gives Heflin shelter during his wild flight from fate.

•

ACTORS AND SIN
1952, 85 mins, US Ⓥ b/w
Dir Ben Hecht *Prod* Sid Kuller *Scr* Ben Hecht *Ph* Lee Garmes *Ed* Otto Ludwig *Mus* George Antheil *Art* Howard Bristol
Act Edward G. Robinson, Marsha Hunt, Dan O'Herlihy, Eddie Albert, Tracey Roberts, Jenny Hecht (Hecht/United Artists)

Written, produced and directed by Ben Hecht, *Actors and Sin* is an overall title for two stories separately tagged *Actor's Blood* and *Woman of Sin*. First is a creaky yarn while the second is a racy, tradey satire on Hollywood.

Actor's Blood largely wastes the talents of Edward G. Robinson and Marsha Hunt. At the peak of her stage career, Hunt is shown slipping downward on a rope of poor plays, an uneven temperament and a variety of pointless affairs with male acquaintances. Robinson, her doting father and an actor of the old school, decides to take revenge upon those who have cast his daughter aside by making her suicide appear as murder.

Woman of Sin is a genuinely, amusing burlesque of prewar Hollywood.

•

ACTOR'S REVENGE, AN
SEE: YUKINOJO HENGE

•

ACTRESS, THE
1953, 89 mins, US b/w
Dir George Cukor *Prod* Lawrence Weingarten *Scr* Ruth Gordon *Ph* Harold Rosson *Ed* George Boemler *Mus* Bronislau Kaper *Art* Cedric Gibbons, Arthur Lonergan
Act Spencer Tracy, Jean Simmons, Teresa Wright, Anthony Perkins, Ian Wolfe, Kay Williams (M-G-M)

A warm, humorous motion picture has been made from Ruth Gordon's chronicle of her New England girlhood and burning desire for a legit career. Presented on the stage as *Years Ago*, it engagingly puts over the characters taken from real life, as well as the feel of the early 1900 period in which the plot is laid.

Jean Simmons plays the title role, and portrays perfectly the teenage agonies and joys of a girl who must become an actress at all cost, yet stands in awe of a papa who, though seeming to have no sympathy for such youthful ambitions, is the one who comes through to make them possible at the finale.

Spencer Tracy is fine as the father, a man who easily becomes a bore at times, who lives quite a bit in his seafaring past, and desires better things for his family than he can provide on the miserly stipend he makes as a clerk. As a balance wheel in the family, Teresa Wright's mother is top-notch.

Actually, the script is a series of incidents establishing Miss Simmons's stage yen and it's told with solid heart, some drama and humor that spills honestly from the family types seen. Anthony Perkins's impresses as Simmons's swain, and their scenes together have a nostalgic flavor.

1950: NOMINATION: B&W Costume Design

•

ADAM HAD FOUR SONS
1941, 108 mins, US Ⓥ b/w
Dir Gregory Ratoff *Prod* Robert Sherwood *Scr* William Hurlbut, Michael Blankfort *Ph* Peverell Marley *Ed* Francis D. Lyon *Mus* W. Franke Harling
Act Ingrid Bergman, Warner Baxter, Susan Hayward, Fay Wray (Columbia)

This is a film version of Charles Bonner's novel, *Legacy*, which details the decade history of a typical American family kept intact by the father through the panic of 1907 and the World War. The unanimous loyalties of the group, through prosperity and vicissitudes, are broadly etched to result in moderately satisfactory entertainment.

Under able guidance of Gregory Ratoff, Ingrid Bergman turns in a persuasive and sympathetic performance. Warner Baxter does well as the head of the household, steeped in good old American tradition that family bonds are unbreakable.

In 1907, young Bergman arrives from abroad to assume charge of the four young boys as governess. She soon becomes one of the family, but the sudden death of the wife, followed by the family's financial collapse necessitate the girl returning home.

Ten years later Baxter recoups his fortunes, reacquires the old home, and sends for Bergman to return. With the boys grown to near-manhood, and all enlisting in various branches of the service, she is pitted against the attempts of unscrupulous Susan Hayward to disrupt the family happiness.

•

ADAM'S RIB
1950, 103 mins, US Ⓥ ⊙ b/w
Dir George Cukor *Prod* Lawrence Weingarten *Scr* Ruth Gordon, Garson Kanin *Ph* George J. Folsey *Ed* George Boemler *Mus* Miklos Rozsa *Art* Cedric Gibbons, William Ferrari
Act Spencer Tracy, Katharine Hepburn, Judy Holliday, Tom Ewell, David Wayne, Jean Hagen (M-G-M)

Adam's Rib is a bright comedy success, belting over a succession of sophisticated laughs. Ruth Gordon and Garson Kanin have fashioned their amusing screenplay around the age-old battle of the sexes.

Setup has Spencer Tracy as an assistant D.A., married to femme attorney Katharine Hepburn. He believes no woman has the right to take shots at another femme. Hepburn believes a woman has the same right to invoke the unwritten law as a man. They do courtroom battle over their theories when Tracy is assigned to prosecute Judy Holliday.

This is the sixth Metro teaming of Tracy and Hepburn, and their approach to marital relations around their own hearth is delightfully saucy. A better realization on type than Holliday's portrayal of a dumb Brooklyn femme doesn't seem possible.

1950: NOMINATION: Best Story & Screenplay

•

ADDAMS FAMILY, THE
1991, 99 mins, US Ⓥ ⊙ col
Dir Barry Sonnenfeld *Prod* Scott Rudin *Scr* Caroline Thompson, Larry Wilson *Ph* Owen Roizman *Ed* Dede Allen, Jim Miller *Mus* Marc Shaiman *Art* Richard MacDonald
Act Anjelica Huston, Raul Julia, Christopher Lloyd, Dan Hedaya, Elizabeth Wilson, Christina Ricci (Paramount)

Despite inspired casting and nifty visual trappings, the eagerly awaited *Addams Family* figures as a major disappointment. First-time director Barry Sonnenfeld never really gets past the skeletal plot, which plays like a collection of sitcom one-liners augmented by feature-film special effects. Script is one visual joke or pun after another based on the decidedly different family Charles Addams created in his New Yorker cartoons. The ABC-TV series ran from 1964 to 1966.

The performers work gamely, but how many times are we expected to laugh at Morticia (Anjelica Huston) speaking wistfully about torture or Gomez (Raul Julia) imploring the disembodied digits Thing to "lend a hand?"

The disjointed plot turns on the long-missing Uncle Fester and an attempt by the family lawyer (Dan Hedaya) to cash in on Fester's absence—and gain access to Gomez's hidden fortune—by passing off the son of a loan-sharking client (Elizabeth Wilson) as Fester. After becoming acclimated to the ooky-kooky-spooky clan, the son (Christopher Lloyd) grows increasingly fond of them, prompting his conspirators to engage in drastic tactics.

The only moment that lives up to the film's potential involves tots Wednesday (Christina Ricci) and Pugsley (Jimmy Workman) enacting a scene from *Hamlet* for the school talent show. Huston is properly ethereal as Morticia, and Julia makes a swashbuckling Gomez, though neither can do much with the roles. Ricci is a perfect, somber Wednesday.

1991: NOMINATION: Best Costume Design

•

ADDAMS FAMILY VALUES
1993, 93 mins, US Ⓥ ⊙ col
Dir Barry Sonnenfeld *Prod* Scott Rudin *Scr* Paul Rudnick *Ph* Donald Peterman *Ed* Arthur Schmidt, Jim Miller *Mus* Marc Shaiman *Art* Ken Adam
Act Anjelica Huston, Raul Julia, Christopher Lloyd, Joan Cusack, Christina Ricci, Carol Kane (Paramount)

They're back!!! Yes, Charles Addams gloriously macabre characters have returned in *Addams Family Values*, and the big-screen sequel shares many of the pluses and minuses of the 1991 excursion. It remains perilously slim in the story department, but glides over the thin ice with technical razzle-dazzle and an exceptionally winning cast. Chief among its virtues is an anarchic spirit that embraces and delights in all that is politically incorrect.

The screen equivalent of a Rube Goldberg invention kicks into action as Morticia (Anjelica Huston) informs devoted hubby Gomez (Raul Julia) that they are expecting a child—right now. The new spawn, the cuddly, mustachioed Pubert (Kaitlyn and Kristen Hooper), immediately becomes the object of offspring Wednesday (Christina Ricci) and Pugsley Addams (Jimmy Workman) lethal jealousy.

So the couple recruit a nanny, the nauseatingly perky Debbie Jellinsky (Joan Cusack). Her bottomless taste for the bizarre is promoted by a desire to woo, wed and murder hapless, lovesick Fester Addams (Christopher Lloyd) and abscond with his considerable financial assets.

Huston and Julia are one of the truly magical screen couples; it is a sublime pairing of effortless grace. Cusack is a lively addition, playing her black widow character as a princess with an attitude. Also notable is Peter MacNicol as the suitably loopy, vain, misguided camp leader.

1993: NOMINATION: Best Art Direction

•

ADDICTION, THE
1995, 82 mins, US Ⓥ ⊙ b/w
Dir Abel Ferrara *Prod* Denis Hann, Fernando Sulichin *Scr* Nicholas St. John *Ph* Ken Kelsch *Ed* Mayin Lo *Mus* Joe Delia *Art* Charlie Lagola
Act Lili Taylor, Christopher Walken, Annabella Sciorra, Edie Falco, Paul Calderon, Fredro Star (Fast)

Vampires go for their Ph.D.s in *The Addiction*, a horror show that's heady in both senses of the word. Abel Ferrara's maverick entry in the never-dead genre is dramatically surprising, stylishly made in black-and-white and well acted, especially by Lili Taylor in the leading role.

Pic dives off the board right into the deep end as Kathleen Conklin (Lili Taylor), a doctoral candidate in philosophy at NYU, is pursued and attacked in a dark alley by a fierce woman who looks like a hooker (Annabella Sciorra). Result is two bloody holes in her neck, followed by agonizing pain and inability to eat. Once she's passed through to the other side, Kathleen commences her nocturnal rounds.

Punctuating the action with glimpses of such atrocities as the Holocaust, the My Lai massacre and other historical mass slaughters, and loading up the dialogue with references to Nietzsche, Heidegger and other philosophers, filmmakers equate vampirism with the imposition of one's will on the human race. Raising this line of enquiry to another level is a fellow vampire (Christopher Walken).

Even when the narrative road turns bumpy, what holds the picture together is Taylor. Stalking around in shades most of the time, Taylor makes palpable her character's intense suffering at the outset as well as, later on, her superhuman strength and resolve. A terrific vampire, Walken is on all too briefly. Ken Kelsch's monochrome lensing is grittily moody.

•

ADJUSTER, THE
1991, 102 mins, Canada Ⓥ ⦿ ▭ col
Dir Atom Egoyan ***Prod*** Camelia Frieberg, Atom Egoyan ***Scr*** Atom Egoyan ***Ph*** Paul Sarossy ***Ed*** Susan Shipton ***Mus*** Mychael Danna ***Art*** Linda Del Rosario, Richard Paris
Act Elias Koteas, Arsinee Khanjian, Maury Chaykin, Gabrielle Rose, Jennifer Dale, David Hemblen (Alliance/Ego)

In an escalating quest for eccentricity, Atom Egoyan's analysis of voyeurism is becoming profoundly shallow. Trying to streamline his radical and visionary *Family Viewing*, his follow-up pic, *Speaking Parts*, xeroxed the theme and polished the images but lost its edge in the process. Ditto for *The Adjuster*, with its cast of superbly photographed, eclectic characters who take an aimless walk on the wild side.

Noah (Elias Koteas), an insurance adjuster, is a wedded philanderer who exploits the vulnerability of female clients who've lost their homes to fires. His mate, Hera (played by Egoyan's mate, Arsinee Khanjian), is a film censor who secretly videotapes porn flicks for her sister Sete (Rose Sarkisyan), a matron with betwixt desires.

These frigid spouses rent their model home to a couple (Maury Chaykin, Gabrielle Rose) who stiffly stage their sexual fantasies in absurd and eventually violent acts. Their characters have potential that the script never develops.

At no point does the viewer ever gain in-depth knowledge of any character in the film. Visuals are gorgeous.

•

ADMIRABLE CRICHTON, THE
1957, 93 mins, UK col
Dir Lewis Gilbert ***Prod*** Ian Dalrymple ***Scr*** Vernon Harris, Lewis Gilbert ***Ph*** Wilkie Cooper ***Ed*** Peter Hunt ***Mus*** Douglas Gamley ***Art*** William Kellner
Act Kenneth More, Diane Cilento, Cecil Parker, Sally Ann Howes, Martita Hunt, Jack Watling (Modern Screen Play)

Staged many times since its original production in London in 1902, and filmed in the silent days (1919) as *Male and Female*, this [J. M. Barrie] story of a butler who becomes master on a desert island is a sound starrer for Kenneth More.

A peer of one of England's stately homes takes his three daughters off on a yachting cruise with a few friends and domestic staff. They are shipwrecked and marooned on an uncharted island, and dig themselves in awaiting rescue. Crichton (More), the impeccable butler, is obliged to take complete control, because of the inefficiency of the other castaways. He now gives, not takes orders, and establishes himself as benevolent dictator.

Although More lacks the accepted stature of an English butler, his personality makes a more human and sympathetic figure of the servant who has a firmer sense of snob values than his master. Cecil Parker, alternately genial and pompous as the father, is perhaps more in keeping with the period.

•

ADVENTURE
1945, 130 mins, US b/w
Dir Victor Fleming ***Prod*** Sam Zimbalist ***Scr*** Frederick Hazlitt Brennan, Vincent Lawrence ***Ph*** Joseph Ruttenberg ***Ed*** Frank Sullivan ***Mus*** Herbert Stothart ***Art*** Cedric Gibbons, Urie McCleary
Act Clark Gable, Greer Garson, Joan Blondell, Thomas Mitchell, Tom Tully, Richard Haydn (M-G-M)

Clark Gable is bos'n mate on a Merchant Marine vessel, and as tough as the toughest sailor on board. Handy with his dukes, he has a femme in every port. That is until he meets Greer Garson, the librarian, who finally decides that the venturesome traits displayed by Gable are just what she has been missing in life. So, it s a hurried wedding, a honeymoon in Reno. Then the romance collapses on the pair. He decides the sea is still for him and she decides on a divorce. The payoff is trite.

Film shows a new Gable. He has many of the old mannerisms, but director Victor Fleming (from a novel by Clyde Brion Davis), makes him overly boisterous and stubborn, a seafaring man who would toss aside his new bride of a few days like she was another girl in port. Garson dominates every scene even when being browbeaten by the obstinate mate. She effects the transition from the prim, standoffish office gal into a life-loving femme who refuses to let her man get away.

Joan Blondell, as her girlfriend, who likes Gable from the start, and even better after a drinking session, seems almost a reborn actress in this role. Thomas Mitchell, who is the God-fearing sailor and particular pal of Gable, has a powerful characterization, and does it up brown.

•

ADVENTURE FOR TWO
SEE: THE DEMI-PARADISE

•

ADVENTURE OF SHERLOCK HOLMES' SMARTER BROTHER, THE
1975, 91 mins, UK Ⓥ col
Dir Gene Wilder ***Prod*** Richard A. Roth ***Scr*** Gene Wilder ***Ph*** Gerry Fisher ***Ed*** Jim Clark ***Mus*** John Morris ***Art*** Terence Marsh
Act Gene Wilder, Madeline Kahn, Marty Feldman, Dom DeLuise, Leo McKern, Roy Kinnear (20th Century-Fox)

Gene Wilder joins Mel Brooks in that elusive pantheon of madcap humor, by virtue of Wilder's script, title characterization and directorial debut, all of which are outstanding.

Wilder's script sends the famous Holmes (played by Douglas Wilmer) and Dr. Watson (Thorley Walters) ostensibly out of England, in order to fool Prof. Moriarty (Leo McKern). Latter has a plot going with Dom DeLuise, the most unlikely blackmailing opera freak of the season, to obtain some official state papers stolen from nobleman John Le Mesurier.

Holmes's strategy is to use his younger brother, played by Wilder, as a decoy, backstopped by Feldman, a policeman blessed with a photographic memory. Together, this fearless duo fumbles their way to ultimate success.

•

ADVENTURERS, THE
1970, 171 mins, US Ⓥ ▭
Dir Lewis Gilbert ***Prod*** Lewis Gilbert ***Scr*** Michael Hastings, Lewis Gilbert ***Ph*** Claude Renoir ***Ed*** Anne Coates ***Mus*** Antonio Carlos Jobim ***Art*** Tony Masters
Act Bekim Fehmiu, Charles Aznavour, Alan Badel, Candice Bergen, Thommy Berggren, Ernest Borgnine (Paramount)

The Adventurers is a classic monument to bad taste. Film is marked by profligate and squandered production opulence; inferior, imitative and curiously old-hat direction; banal, ludicrous dialog; substandard, lifeless and embarrassing acting; cornball music; indulgent, gratuitous and boring violence; and luridly nonerotic sex.

Harold Robbins's guess-who novel about the jet set and South American politics was as commercial as it was trashy; film version may be fairly said to make the novel look better. Story depicts the life of a South American playboy who, if one were to swallow the specious sociology, was a victim of childhood traumas which crystalized revolutionary violence and brutal rape.

On the romantic front there is Candice Bergen, about the only principal to salvage anything from the film, playing a fabulously wealthy girl who marries the hero, but loses their baby in a swing accident, becomes barren, and eventually turns lesbian.

•

ADVENTURES AT RUGBY
SEE: TOM BROWN'S SCHOOLDAYS

•

ADVENTURES IN BABYSITTING
1987, 99 mins, US Ⓥ ⦿ col
Dir Chris Columbus ***Prod*** Debra Hill, Lynda Obst ***Scr*** David Simkins ***Ph*** Ric Waite ***Ed*** Fredric Steinkamp, William Steinkamp ***Mus*** Michael Kamen ***Art*** Todd Hallowell
Act Elisabeth Shue, Maia Brewton, Keith Coogan, Anthony Rapp, Vincent D'Onofrio, Penelope Ann Miller (Touchstone)

Ferris Bueller meets *Risky Business* in this teen-dream set in (where else?) the suburbs of Chicago. Chris Columbus weighs in adequately in his directorial debut, thanks to a fresh, solid lead performance from Elisabeth Shue. Yet the film can never rise above the leaden script.

Chris Parker (Shue) takes an assignment babysitting for two kids, the 15-year-old Brad (Keith Coogan), who has a crush on her, and Sara (Maia Brewton), a little brat who idolizes comicbook hero Thor. Trouble starts when Chris gets a call from her best friend Brenda (Penelope Ann Miller), who had decided to run away from home but thought better of it upon reaching the bus station in downtown Chicago.

Chris heads down to the city with Brad, his best friend Daryl (Anthony Rapp) and Sara in tow and, in short order, blows out a tire, realizes she's left her purse back in the 'burbs, gets a tow from a one-armed man who drives by his house to find his wife cheating on him, sneaks into the car that's being hotwired by professional car thief Joe Gipp (Calvin Levels), and winds up in the headquarters of a national car-theft ring.

The only party not guilty of overacting is Levels, who gives a sweetly controlled performance in his bit as the young thief with a conscience.

•

ADVENTURES OF BARON MUNCHAUSEN, THE
1989, 125 mins, UK/W. Germany Ⓥ ⦿ col
Dir Terry Gilliam ***Prod*** Thomas Schuhly ***Scr*** Charles McKeown, Terry Gilliam ***Ph*** Giuseppe Rotunno ***Ed*** Peter Hollywood ***Mus*** Michael Kamen ***Art*** Dante Ferretti
Act John Neville, Eric Idle, Jonathan Pryce, Oliver Reed, Sting, Robin Williams (Prominent/Laura)

A fitting final installment in Terry Gilliam's trilogy begun with *Time Bandits* and continued with *Brazil*, *The Adventures of Baron Munchausen* shares many of those films strengths and weaknesses, but doesn't possess the visionary qualities of the latter.

The film offers a continual feast for the eyes, and not enough for the funnybone or the heart. Set in Europe in the 18th century, tale begins with a city under intense siege by the Turks. An elderly gent who purports to be the Baron begins relating the true story of how he caused the war.

With this, Gilliam takes the viewer into the exquisite palace of the sultan, whose ferocity is aroused when he loses a bet to the visiting baron (John Neville). With the help of his variously and superhumanly gifted gang of four, which consists of the fastest runner in the world, a dwarf who can exhale with hurricane force, an expert sharpshooter and an immeasurably strong black man, the Baron makes off with the sultan s entire treasure, but his city is left to suffer the consequences.

Promising to save the city from the renewed attack, the Baron escapes in a gigantic hot-air balloon fashioned out of ladies' underwear, and goes in search of his four comrades. This journey takes the unlikely pair to some unlikely places where they meet some unlikely people.

1989: NOMINATIONS: Best Art Direction, Costume Design, Makeup, Visual Effects

•

ADVENTURES OF BARRY MCKENZIE, THE
1972, 117 mins, Australia col
Dir Bruce Beresford ***Prod*** Phillip Adams ***Scr*** Bruce Beresford, Barry Humphries ***Ph*** Don McAlpine ***Ed*** John Scott ***Mus*** Peter Best ***Art*** John Stoddart
Act Barry Crocker, Barry Humphries, Paul Bertram, Dennis Price, Avice Landon, Peter Cook (Longford)

Satirist Barry Humphries has put his talents to a film, as coauthor and costar. The result is what one would expect if the Marx Brothers were put into an Aussie-brand *Carry On* pic. It's based on a comic strip (*The Wonderful World of Barry McKenzie*), written by Humphries, around a very Aussie character in London known as Bazza.

Barry Crocker plays title role of the gauche young Aussie visiting Britain for the first time. His turns of phrases are witty and original, often with a bawdy twinge, and although much is in the Australian vernacular (frequently invented by Humphries), few are likely to miss the drift of the remarks.

•

ADVENTURES OF BUCKAROO BANZAI ACROSS THE EIGHTH DIMENSION, THE
1984, 103 mins, US Ⓥ ⦿ ▭ col
Dir W. D. Richter ***Prod*** Neil Canton, W. D. Richter ***Scr*** Earl Mac Rauch ***Ph*** Fred J. Koenekamp ***Ed*** Richard Marks, George Bowers ***Mus*** Michael Boddicker ***Art*** J. Michael Riva
Act Peter Weller, John Lithgow, Ellen Barkin, Jeff Goldblum, Christopher Lloyd, Rosalind Cash (Sherwood)

The Adventures of Buckaroo Banzai plays more like an experimental film than a Hollywood production aimed at a mass audience. It violates every rule of storytelling and narrative structure in creating a self-contained world of its own.

First-time director W. D. Richter and writer Earl Mac Rauch have created a comic-book world chock-full of references, images, pseudoscientific ideas and plain mumbo jumbo.

Buried within all this Banzai trivia is an indecipherable plot involving a modern band of Robin Hoods who go to battle with enemy aliens released accidentally from the eighth dimension as a result of Buckaroo's experiments with particle physics.

Buckaroo is a world-class neurosurgeon, physicist, racecar driver and, with his band of merry pranksters, the Hong Kong Cavaliers, a rock'n'roll star.

As the great one (Buckaroo), Peter Weller presents a moving target that is tough to hit. Also very funny is Jeff Goldblum, coming as if from another dimension as every mother's Jewish son. Ellen Barkin does a turn as Buckaroo's mysterious girlfriend and looks great but is another emotionless character.

•

ADVENTURES OF DON JUAN
1949, 110 mins, US Ⓥ ⦿ col
Dir Vincent Sherman *Prod* Jerry Wald *Scr* George Oppenheimer, Harry Kurnitz *Ph* Elwood Bredell *Ed* Alan Crosland, Jr. *Mus* Max Steiner *Art* Edward Carrere
Act Errol Flynn, Viveca Lindfors, Robert Douglas, Raymond Burr, Alan Hale, Ann Rutherford (Warner)

The loves and escapades of the fabulous Don Juan are particularly adapted to the screen abilities of Errol Flynn and he gives them a flair that pays off strongly.

Plot depicts Don Juan adventuring in England. Opening has him escaping an angry husband, only to become immediately involved again with another femme. This time his wooing ruins a state-arranged wedding and he s shipped off to Spain to face his angry monarch. The queen assigns him to post of instructor in the royal fencing academy, he discovers a plot against her majesty, instigated by a conniving prime minister. Viveca Lindfors co-stars as the queen and she brings a compelling beauty to the role.

Top action is reached in the deadly duel between Flynn and Robert Douglas, the crooked prime minister, climaxing with a long leap down a huge flight of castle stairs.

1949: Best Color Costume Design

NOMINATION: Best Color Art Direction

•

ADVENTURES OF FORD FAIRLANE, THE
1990, 101 mins, US Ⓥ ⦿ ▭ col
Dir Renny Harlin *Prod* Joel Silver, Steve Perry *Scr* Daniel Waters, James Cappe, David Arnott *Ph* Oliver Wood *Ed* Michael Tronick *Mus* Yello *Art* John Vallone
Act Andrew Dice Clay, Wayne Newton, Priscilla Presley, Morris Day, Lauren Holly, Robert Englund (20th Century-Fox/Silver)

Surprisingly funny and expectedly rude, this first starring vehicle by vilified stand-up comic Andrew Dice Clay has a decidedly lowbrow humor that is a sort of modern equivalent to that of the Three Stooges.

Clay plays Ford Fairlane, a private eye specializing in cases involving rock acts (hence his overused nickname, "the rock & roll detective"). He gets drawn into a murder mystery linked to a shock-radio deejay (Gilbert Gottfried, in a hilarious cameo), and a sleazy record executive (Wayne Newton) and his ex-wife (Priscilla Presley).

With its heavy rock bent and the direction of Renny Harlin (*Die Hard 2*), much of the film resembles a music video.

Aside from his appeal to rednecks and high-school boys overly impressed by certain four-letter words, Clay's chain-smoking goombah in many ways self-parodies the macho ethic that prizes rock 'n' roll, fast cars and cheap bimbos above all else.

The film's most significant find, undoubtedly, is Lauren Holly, who brings a lot of flash and charisma to a difficult role as Fairlane's longing girl Friday. Also, Robert Englund (aka Freddy Krueger) plays a sadistic killer, sans makeup.

•

ADVENTURES OF HUCK FINN, THE
1993, 108 mins, US Ⓥ ⦿ col
Dir Stephen Sommers *Prod* Laurence Mark *Scr* Stephen Sommers *Ph* Janusz Kaminski *Ed* Bob Ducsay *Mus* Bill Conti *Art* Richard Sherman
Act Elijah Wood, Courtney B. Vance, Robbie Coltrane, Jason Robards, Ron Perlman, Dana Ivey (Walt Disney)

Disney's remake of Mark Twain's classic *The Adventures of Huckleberry Finn* is a timely, literate and handsome film. However, the acting of the two leads fails to provide the electrifying and stirring mood that the tale deserves.

Elijah Wood stars as the roguish Huck Finn, living with the Widow Douglas (Dana Ivey). The film improves considerably once Huck encounters Jim (Courtney B. Vance), the runaway slave whose goal is to escape to the North and buy his family's freedom. The two drifters strike up a unique friendship as they start their fateful journey down the Mississippi.

Scripter-director Sommers centers his narrative on the interracial friendship, providing a thorough examination of a morally complex bond. His direction, however, is uneven; the first half-hour is oddly flat and not very engaging. But helmer's work improves as the film progresses.

Fortunately, the two central roles are surrounded by a marvelous ensemble of supporting actors: the brilliant Jason Robards and Robbie Coltrane as the King and the Duke, respectively, Ron Perlman as the nasty Pap Finn, Ivey as the Widow Douglas and Laura Bundy as the precocious Susan Wilks.

Despite its faults, *Huck Finn* is superior to Michael Curtiz's 1960 or J. Lee Thompson's 1974 efforts.

•

ADVENTURES OF HUCKLEBERRY FINN, THE
1960, 90 mins, US Ⓥ ▭ col
Dir Michael Curtiz *Prod* Samuel Goldwyn, Jr. *Scr* James Lee *Ph* Ted McCord *Ed* Freeric Steinkamp *Mus* Jerome Moross *Art* George W. Davis, McClure Capps
Act Tony Randall, Eddie Hodges, Archie Moore, Patty McCormack, Neville Brand, Mickey Shaughnessy (M-G-M)

Mark Twain's Huckleberry Finn is all boy. Eddie Hodges Huck isn't. Therein lurks the basic reason this production of the Twain classic is not all it could, and should, be.

There is something artificial and self-conscious about young Hodges's all-important portrayal of Huck, a lack of actor-character chemistry for which he's certainly not wholly responsible. An equal share of the rap must be shouldered by director Michael Curtiz, not only for the youthful star's shortcomings in the role, but for a general slack, a disturbing shortage of vitality noticeable at several key junctures.

James Lee's screenplay simplifies Twain's episodic tale, erasing some of the more complex developments and relationships, presumably for the benefit of the young audience. Some of the more sinister, frightening aspects of the story have been forgotten.

On the brighter side of the ledger, there are some stimulating performances and the handsome physical production itself. An extremely colorful and experienced cast has been assembled. These include Tony Randall, whose work as the roguish "King" is a delightful balance of whimsy and threat. And Archie Moore, the light heavyweight champion of the world, who brings the story its only moments of real warmth and tenderness.

•

ADVENTURES OF MARCO POLO, THE
1938, 100 mins, US b/w
Dir Archie Mayo *Prod* Samuel Goldwyn *Scr* Robert E. Sherwood *Ph* Rudolph Mate *Ed* Fred Allen *Mus* Hugo Friedhofer *Art* Richard Day
Act Gary Cooper, Sigrid Gurie, Basil Rathbone, George Barbier, Binnie Barnes, Ernest Truex (Goldwyn/United Artists)

A glamorous figure in history, which places him in the 13th century as the first European to visit the Orient, Marco Polo has been portrayed in as many different guises as imagination permits: as traveler, adventurer, merchant, diplomat. He probably was all of these and a first-class liar besides. Robert E. Sherwood, who penned the screenscript [from a story by N. A. Pogson], conceives him also as an ardent lover and politician. Gary Cooper fits the character to the apex of his six feet two.

The plot is strictly meller, starting with Ahmed (Basil Rathbone) as a conniving prime minister to the Chinese ruler Kublai Kahn (George Barbier). Schemer has his eye on the throne and a desire for the dynastic princess for his queen. Into such a vortex of beauty and villainy come Marco Polo and his business agent.

Marco Polo is admitted to the court and there glimpses the beautiful princess, who is much taken with his six feet two and easy manner of love-making behind the Chinese fountain.

It is all played on the dead level by a fine cast. Rathbone is an excellent plotter, and Sigrid Gurie, a Norwegian actress who makes her American film debut in the picture, possesses beauty of a kind to start civil war in any country.

•

ADVENTURES OF MARK TWAIN, THE
1944, 130 mins, US b/w
Dir Irving Rapper *Prod* Jesse L. Lasky *Scr* Alan LeMay, Harry Chandlee *Ph* Sol Polito *Ed* Ralph Dawson *Mus* Max Steiner *Art* John Hughes
Act Fredric March, Alexis Smith, Donald Crisp, Alan Hale, C. Aubrey Smith, John Carradine (Warner)

So rich and full was the life of Mark Twain, born Sam Clemens, that it requires two hours–plus to tell the full tale [adapted from Twain's works, and Harold M. Sherman's play *Mark Twain*, by Alan LeMay and Sherman]. It is a film that has its measure of symbolism: linking the humorist's lifetime of 75 years to appearances of Halley's Comet. The astronomical display was visible when Sam Clemens was born in Hannibal, MO, on the banks of the Mississippi, and 75 years later, when the Chancellor of Oxford extols the great American writer, at a time when the famed university is also paying honor to Rudyard Kipling with an honorary doctorate of literature, it again makes its astral appearance.

In between Clemens has adventured as a river boatman, journeyman reporter, and Western goldrusher, only to find sudden fame with his saga of the jumping frogs. Soon follow renown and fortune as Tom Sawyer, Huck Finn and the rest of his "funny books" capture the hearts and the minds of all America, only to be dissipated in abortive attempts with an automatic printing press, extravagant publishing ventures and the like.

1944: NOMINATIONS: Best B&W Art Direction, Scoring of a Dramatic Picture, Special Effects

•

ADVENTURES OF PRISCILLA, QUEEN OF THE DESERT, THE
1994, 102 mins, Australia Ⓥ ⦿ col
Dir Stephan Elliott *Prod* Al Clark, Michael Hamlyn *Scr* Stephan Elliott *Ph* Brian J. Breheny *Ed* Sue Blainey *Mus* Guy Grosse *Art* Owen Patterson
Act Terence Stamp, Hugo Weaving, Guy Pearce, Bill Hunter, Sarah Chadwick, Mark Holmes (PFE/Latent Image/Specific)

If ever a film flaunted itself, it's *The Adventures of Priscilla, Queen of the Desert.* A cheerfully vulgar and bitchy, but essentially warmhearted, road movie with a difference, which boasts an amazing star turn by Terence Stamp as a transsexual, Stephan Elliott's second feature is a lot of fun.

Stamp plays Bernadette, whose lover has recently died. She decides to team up with gay friends Tick (Hugo Weaving) and Adam (Guy Pearce), who are heading to the central Australian town of Alice Springs to perform a drag act at a casino. The invitation to perform has been offered by Tick's ex-wife. The trio purchases a not-very-reliable second-hand bus they name Priscilla, and set out from Sydney on the long journey across the desert.

The plot of *Priscilla* isn't as important as the outlandish, wicked dialogue, the wild costumes and makeup, and the general high spirits of the entire enterprise. Dressed in femme clothes throughout, Stamp gives one of his best perfs as the bereaved woman whose latent masculinity occasionally shows through her graciously elegant exterior.

Pic is just a smidge long, but it would be unfair to say it drags.

1994: Best Costume Design

•

ADVENTURES OF QUENTIN DURWARD, THE
SEE: QUENTIN DURWARD

•

ADVENTURES OF ROBIN HOOD, THE
1938, 104 mins, US Ⓥ ⦿ col
Dir Michael Curtiz, William Keighley *Prod* Henry Blanke *Scr* Norman Reilly Raine, Seton I. Miller *Ph* Tony Gaudio, Sol Polito, W. Howard Greene *Ed* Ralph Dawson *Mus* Erich Wolfgang Korngold *Art* Carl Jules Weyl
Act Errol Flynn, Olivia de Havilland, Basil Rathbone, Claude Rains, Patric Knowles, Eugene Pallette (Warner)

Warner revives the legend with Errol Flynn in the role that Douglas Fairbanks, Sr., scored his first big success in 1922. It is cinematic pageantry at its best, a highly imaginative telling of folklore in all the hues of Technicolor.

Film is done in the grand manner of silent-day spectacles with sweep and breadth of action, swordplay and hand-to-hand battles between Norman and Saxon barons. Superlative on the production side.

Played with intensity by an excellent company of actors, an illusion of fairy-story quality is retained throughout. Michael Curtiz and William Keighley are credited as co-directors, the former having picked up the story soon after its filming started when Keighley was incapacitated by illness. There is skillful blending of their joint work.

Flynn makes the heroic Robin a somewhat less agile savior of the poor than Fairbanks portrayed him, but the Warner version emphasizes the romance. Teamed with Olivia de Havilland as Marian, Flynn is an ardent suitor and a gallant courtier. There are some convincing histrionics by Basil Rathbone, Claude Rains, Patric Knowles, Eugene Palette, Alan Hale and Melville Cooper. Lighter moments are furnished by Una O'Connor and Herbert Mundin.

1938: Best Interior Decoration (Carl Jules Weyl), Original Score, Editing

NOMINATION: Best Picture

•

ADVENTURES OF SADIE, THE
SEE: OUR GIRL FRIDAY

•

ADVENTURES OF SHERLOCK HOLMES, THE
1939, 71 mins, US Ⓥ ⦿ b/w
Dir Alfred Werker ***Prod*** Gene Markey ***Scr*** Edwin Blum, William Drake ***Ph*** Leon Shamroy ***Ed*** Robert Bischoff ***Mus*** Cyril J. Mockridge (dir.) ***Art*** Richard Day, Hans Peters
Act Basil Rathbone, Nigel Bruce, Ida Lupino, Alan Marshal, E. E. Clive, George Zucco (20th Century-Fox)

Choice of Basil Rathbone as Sherlock was a wise one. Nigel Bruce as Doctor Watson is equally expert. With the two key characters thus capably handled, the film has the additional asset of being well conceived and grippingly presented.

Plenty of ingenuity is concentrated into two concurrent mysteries with the impossible clues not made too absurd or too obvious for mystery devotees. The "Elementary, my dear Watson" type of dialog is soft-pedalled for more modern phrases or understandable patter.

George Zucco offers a splendid characterization as the arch-criminal and Ida Lupino is highly competent as the sole romantic figure in the mystery fable.

•

ADVENTURES OF THE ROCKETEER, THE
SEE: THE ROCKETEER

•

ADVENTURES OF TOM SAWYER, THE
1938, 93 mins, US Ⓥ col
Dir Norman Taurog ***Prod*** David O. Selznick ***Scr*** John V. A. Weaver ***Ph*** James Wong Howe, Wilfrid M. Cline ***Ed*** Hal C. Kern, Margaret Clancey ***Mus*** Lou Forbes ***Art*** Lyle Wheeler, William Cameron Menzies, Casey Roberts
Act Tommy Kelly, Jackie Moran, Ann Gillis, May Robson, Walter Brennan, Victor Jory (Selznick/United Artists)

The Adventures of Tom Sawyer is in Technicolor and contains visual beauty and appeal in addition to a faithful and nearly literal adaptation of the Mark Twain story.

The story of the boy in an isolated Missouri community of the 1880s, who made fence-painting an enviable art, who attended his own funeral services, who was the cynosure of all eyes in the witness chair at an exciting murder trial, who teased and plagued his elders and melted in tears at the slightest kindness, is imperishable.

Casting of the picture was reported a laborious job, in the course of which hundreds of boys were tested before Tommy Kelly, from the Bronx, NY, was selected for the role of Tom. His early scenes show self-consciousness but in the final sequences when he is being pursued by Injun Joe, Kelly performs like a veteran.

Walter Brennan is a standout among the adult players. He is the village drunkard, Muff Potter, accused of the graveyard murder.

May Robson loses no opportunities as Aunt Polly, whose life by turn is celestial and hellish depending upon the vagaries of Tom's vivid imagination.

Injun Joe is played by Victor Jory with all the fiendish villainy in the part.

1938: NOMINATION: Art Direction

•

ADVISE & CONSENT
1962, 140 mins, US Ⓥ ⦿ ▭ b/w
Dir Otto Preminger ***Prod*** Otto Preminger ***Scr*** Wendell Mayes ***Ph*** Sam Leavitt ***Ed*** Louis Loeffler ***Mus*** Jerry Fielding ***Art*** Lyle R. Wheeler
Act Henry Fonda, Charles Laughton, Don Murray, Walter Pidgeon, Gene Tierney, Peter Lawford (Columbia)

Allen Drury's big-selling novel has also served as a stage play. There are recognizable projections of character assassination, McCarthy-like demagoguery and use of the two hard-to-answer smears of this ill-natured generation: "Are you now or were you once a homosexual and/or a communist?"

As interpreted by producer-director Otto Preminger and scripter Wendell Mayes, *Advise & Consent* is intermittently well dialogued and too talky, and, strangely, arrested in its development and illogical.

Preminger has endowed his production with wholly capable performers. Henry Fonda as the Secretary of State nominee, Charles Laughton as a Southern-smooth rebellious Solon, Don Murray as the focal point of the homo-suicidal scandal and Walter Pidgeon as a Majority leader fighting in best stentorian tradition in Fonda's behalf all register firmly. The characterizations come through with fine clarity.

Disturbing is lack of sufficiently clear motivation for the nub of the action. Why are Pidgeon and Laughton so pro and con about confirmation of the Presidential appointee? And isn't the Murray character too strong to kill himself?

The settings are powerfully like real. A Senate hearing room, the Senate itself, a party home in immediate Washington and varying apartments plus a place in D.C. suburbia all have the look of genuineness.

•

AFFAIRS OF SUSAN, THE
1945, 110 mins, US b/w
Dir William A. Seiter ***Prod*** Hal B. Wallis ***Scr*** Thomas Monroe, Laszlo Gorog, Richard Flournoy ***Ph*** David Abel ***Ed*** Eda Warren ***Mus*** Frederick Hollander ***Art*** Hans Dreier, Franz Bachelin
Act Joan Fontaine, George Brent, Dennis O'Keefe, Don DeFore, Walter Abel, Rita Johnson (Paramount)

In this tale [from an original story by Thomas Monroe and Laszlo Gorog] about the four loves of Susan Darell (Joan Fontaine), producer Hal B. Wallis has invested the picture with considerable production values, while making the story and action the thing.

Fontaine, as Susan, legit actress just back from a USO camp tour, accepts Walter Abel's proposal of marriage. He soon learns that there have been three men in her life previously. Abel tosses a bachelor dinner party for the three, her ex-husband and stage producer, a young lumber millionaire, and the ardent author. They recite how they figured in Susan s life, with most of flashback sequences devoted to her contact with producer George Brent, her lone marriage.

Fontaine's sparkle in this first comedienne role is impressive. She swings easily from plain Jane to the seasoned actress type, then to the glamorous, and finally to the intellectual. Top male contribution is Brent, as the producer. He's a fine combination of the hard-boiled showman and admiring husband.

1945: NOMINATION: Best Original Story

•

AFFAIR TO REMEMBER, AN
1957, 115 mins, US Ⓥ ⦿ ▭ col
Dir Leo McCarey ***Prod*** Jerry Wald ***Scr*** Delmer Daves, Leo McCarey ***Ph*** Milton Krasner ***Ed*** James B. Clark ***Mus*** Hugo Friedhofer ***Art*** Lyle R. Wheeler, Jack Martin Smith
Act Cary Grant, Deborah Kerr, Richard Denning, Neva Patterson, Cathleen Nesbitt, Robert Q. Lewis (20th Century-Fox)

Adding comedy lines, music, color and CinemaScope, Jerry Wald and Leo McCarey turn this remake of the 1939 *Love Affair* into a winning film that is alternately funny and tenderly sentimental. *An Affair to Remember*, using plenty of attractive settings (on and off the USS *Constitution*), is still primarily a film about two people; and since those two happen to be Cary Grant and Deborah Kerr the bittersweet romance sparkles and crackles with high spirits.

Story [by McCarey and Mildred Cram] has Grant and Kerr fall in love aboard ship, though both are engaged to other people. They decide to meet in six months atop the Empire State Building. Meanwhile, Grant, a faintly notorious bachelor, is to change his life in a more useful direction. He shows up for the rendezvous, but she is struck by a car on her way to the meeting and may never walk again.

McCarey, who with Delmer Daves wrote the screenplay, has done a fine job, and has gotten the most out of his players' talents. Both are experts in restrained, sophisticated comedy. Both are able to get a laugh by waving a hand or raising an eyebrow. The Grant-Kerr romance is never maudlin, not even at the end.

1957: NOMINATIONS: Best Cinematography, Costume Design, Score of a Dramatic Picture, Song ("An Affair to Remember")

•

AFRAID OF THE DARK
1992, 91 mins, UK/France Ⓥ ⦿ col
Dir Mark Peploe ***Prod*** Simon Bosanquet ***Scr*** Mark Peploe ***Ph*** Bruno de Keyzer ***Ed*** Scott Thomas ***Mus*** Richard Hartley ***Art*** Caroline Amies
Act James Fox, Fanny Ardant, Paul McGann, Clare Holman, Robert Stephens, Susan Wooldridge (Telescope/Ariane/Cine Cinq)

Bernardo Bertolucci scripter Mark Peploe makes an ambitious bow behind the lens with Afraid of the Dark, a tricky mix of slasher movie and psychodrama that's strong on tease but weak on final delivery.

Double-headed plot centers on an 11-year-old (Ben Keyworth), whose dad (James Fox) is a cop and mother (Fanny Ardant) is blind. With a sicko terrorizing their west London nabe, kid is concerned for the safety of mom's blind friend (Clare Holman). Worse, he reckons the razor-man is someone he knows—the local window cleaner, locksmith or photog (Paul McGann), who has a sideline in nudie portraits.

At exact halfway point, Peploe springs his main surprise, and rest of pic has trouble building up a matching head of steam. But for pure technique (and Hitchcock Michael Powell homework), Peploe can't be faulted.

As the scarily introverted boy, young Keyworth is on the money throughout. Holman handles her key role with style and shading, well matched by McGann. Fox is surprisingly flat as the moppet's dad, and Ardant (who only seems to be there because of French co-prod coin) makes a linguistically shaky British bow in a smallish part.

•

AFRICAN FURY
SEE: CRY, THE BELOVED COUNTRY

•

AFRICAN QUEEN, THE
1951, 104 mins, UK Ⓥ ⦿ col
Dir John Huston ***Prod*** S. P. Eagle [=Sam Spiegel] ***Scr*** James Agee, John Huston ***Ph*** Jack Cardiff ***Ed*** Ralph Kemplen ***Mus*** Allan Gray ***Art*** Wilfrid Shingleton
Act Humphrey Bogart, Katharine Hepburn, Robert Morley, Peter Bull, Theodore Bikel, Walter Gotell (Horizon/Romulus)

This story of adventure and romance, experienced by a couple in Africa just as World War I got underway, is an engrossing motion picture. Just offbeat enough in story, locale and star teaming of Humphrey Bogart and Katharine Hepburn to stimulate the imagination. It is a picture with an unassuming warmth and naturalness.

The independent production unit took stars and cameras to Africa to film C. S. Forester's novel *African Queen*, against its actual background. Performance-wise, Bogart has never been seen to better advantage. Nor has he ever had a more knowing, talented film partner than Hepburn.

The plot concerns a man and woman, completely incongruous as to coupling, who are thrown together when the war news comes to German East Africa in 1914. The man, a sloven, gin-swilling, ne'er-do-well pilot of a steam-driven river launch, teams with the angular, old-maid sister of a dead English missionary to contribute a little to the cause of the Empire. The impossible deed they plan is taking the little, decrepit 30-foot launch known as *African Queen* down uncharted rivers to a large Central Africa lake and then use the small boat as a torpedo to sink a German gunboat that is preventing invasion by British forces.

John Huston's scripting and direction, and the playing, leaven the storytelling with a lot of good humor. Unfoldment has a leisureness that goes with the characters and situations.

1951: Best Actor (Humphrey Bogart)

NOMINATIONS: Best Director, Actress (Katharine Hepburn), Screenplay

•

AFRICA— TEXAS STYLE
1967, 110 mins, US Ⓥ col
Dir Andrew Marton ***Prod*** Andrew Marton ***Scr*** Andy White ***Ph*** Paul Beeson ***Ed*** Henry Richardson ***Mus*** Malcolm Arnold ***Art*** Maurice Fowler
Act Hugh O'Brian, John Mills, Nigel Green, Tom Nardini, Adrienne Corri (Paramount/Ivan Tors)

Africa—Texas Style is a slick and exceptionally well-turned-out piece of adventure picture-making, its title the only weight of heaviness about it.

Shot entirely in Kenya, director Andrew Marton, scripter Andy White and cameraman Paul Beeson have thoroughly caught feeling of Africa. They make effective use of the terrain as an atmospheric setting and thousands of animals of all descriptions to lend authenticity.

Story twirls about the subject of game ranching, the domestication and breeding of wild animal life as a potentially huge source of meat and as a means of preserving many of Africa's rapidly vanishing species of wild beasts.

Premise is given punch via its human story of rancher John Mills importing Texas cowboys Hugh O'Brian and his Navajo pal Tom Nardini to rope and corral as many animals as they can ride down.

•

AFTER DARK, MY SWEET
1990, 114 mins, US Ⓥ ⦿ ▭ col
Dir James Foley ***Prod*** Robert Redlin, Ric Kidney ***Scr*** Robert Redlin, James Foley ***Ph*** Mark Plummer ***Ed*** Howard Smith ***Mus*** Maurice Jarre ***Art*** David Brisbin
Act Jason Patric, Rachel Ward, Bruce Dern, George Dickerson, James Cotton, Corey Carrier (Avenue)

Director-cowriter James Foley has given this near-perfect adaptation of a Jim Thompson novel a contempo setting and emotional realism that make it as potent as a snakebite.

Foley's take on *After Dark, My Sweet* feels right from the first frame, as ex-boxer and nuthouse escapee "Kid" Collins (Jason Patric) shambles into a desert town with a cardboard bundle under his arm, accompanied by his own desultory narration of Thompson's pungent first-person prose. In a bar he meets Fay Anderson (Rachel Ward), who tortures and tests him with her wit before taking him home.

She puts him to work as a handyman on the rambling estate, while both provoking and fending off their sensual attraction. In a country-western joint, the two are joined by a wily ex-detective (Bruce Dern), who immediately gets designs on Collie, as Fay calls him, as a partner in a kidnaping scheme. Kid gets sucked into it, but as he keeps telling Fay, he's not stupid.

The detached point of view in this suspense thriller leaves audience as much twisted by doubt as Collie. One is never sure how much is certain, or what is really going on.

Ward is at her direct and provocative best as the lonely widow who can never give a straight answer, and Patric is enigmatic and affecting as the bruised drifter. Dern has his best role in years as the grasping con man Uncle Bud, and actually evokes some sympathy for the weasely character.

Lensed in the arid and existential sun-blasted landscape of Indio, CA, the pungently seedy film creates a kind of genre unto itself, a film soleil, perhaps.

●

AFTERGLOW
1997, 113 mins, US Ⓥ ⦿ col
Dir Alan Rudolph ***Prod*** Robert Altman ***Scr*** Alan Rudolph ***Ph*** Toyomichi Kurita ***Ed*** Suzy Elmiger ***Mus*** Mark Isham ***Art*** Francois Seguin
Act Julie Christie, Nick Nolte, Lara Flynn Boyle, Jonny Lee Miller (Sand Castle 5/Elysian Dreams)

Followers of Alan Rudolph's career will rejoice at *Afterglow*, an incurably romantic comedy-drama that perceptively dissects the delicate imbalances of two very modern but very different marriages

Jeffrey Byron (Jonny Lee Miller) is a self-centered twentysomething careerist who's convinced that "everything's working quite well on many levels." His sexually frustrated wife, Marianne (Lara Flynn Boyle), believes that "nothing is working," least of all her burning wish to become a mother. Amorous Lucy Mann (Nick Nolte), a repair contractor, experiences his own marital problems with longtime spouse, Phyllis (Julie Christie), a former B-movie actress.

Both marriages are sexually and emotionally barren. The quartet is thrown off balance when Lucy arrives at the Byrons' ultra-designed apartment to do some minor repairs and Marianne becomes instantly infatuated with him.

This modern fairy tale needed four spectacular performers; unfortunately, it has only two. Christie dominates every scene she is in, rendering the witty, often wickedly funny lines with a suave irony. She is ably supported by Nolte, in a flashy, equally demanding role. Boyle is too harsh and one-dimensional, and Miller is pale and a bit stiff. Still, whatever is wrong with the acting is compensated for by the fluid staging and leisurely pacing.

1997: NOMINATION: Best Actress (Julie Christie)

●

AFTER HOURS
1985, 97 mins, US Ⓥ ⦿ col
Dir Martin Scorsese ***Prod*** Amy Robinson, Griffin Dunne, Robert F. Colesberry ***Scr*** Joseph Minion ***Ph*** Michael Ballhaus ***Ed*** Thelma Schoonmaker ***Mus*** Howard Shore ***Art*** Jeffrey Townsend
Act Griffin Dunne, Rosanna Arquette, Verna Bloom, Thomas Chong, Linda Fiorentino, Teri Garr (Geffen/Double Play)

The cinema of paranoia and persecution reaches an apogee in *After Hours*, a nightmarish black comedy from Martin Scorsese. Anxiety-ridden picture would have been pretty funny if it didn't play like a confirmation of everyone's worst fears about contemporary urban life.

A description of one rough night in the life of a mild-mannered New York computer programmer, film is structured like a *Pilgrim's Progress* through the anarchic, ever-treachous streets of SoHo. Every corner represents a turn for the worse, and by the end of the night, he's got to wonder, like Kafka's K, if he might not actually be guilty of something.

It all starts innocently enough, as Griffin Dunne gets a come-on from Rosanna Arquette and ends up visiting her in the loft of avant-garde sculptress Linda Fiorentino. Both girls turn out to be too weird for Dunne, but he can't get home for lack of cash, so he veers from one stranger to another in search of the most mundane salvation and finds nothing but trouble.

This was Scorsese's first fictional film in a decade without Robert De Niro in the leading part, and Dunne, who doubled as co-producer, plays a mostly reactive role, permitting easy identification of oneself in his place. Supporting roles are filled by uniformly vibrant and interesting thesps.

●

AFTER THE FOX
1966, 102 mins, UK/Italy Ⓥ ⦿ ▭ col
Dir Vittorio De Sica ***Prod*** John Bryan ***Scr*** Neil Simon, Cesare Zavattini ***Ph*** Leonida Barboni ***Ed*** Russell Lloyd ***Mus*** Burt Bacharach ***Art*** Mario Garbugha
Act Peter Sellers, Britt Ekland, Lidia Brazzi, Paola Stoppa, Victor Mature, Martin Balsam (Delagate/Nancy)

Peter Sellers is in nimble, lively form in this whacky comedy which, though sometimes strained, has a good comic idea and gives the star plenty of scope for his usual range of impersonations.

Neil Simon's screenplay is uneven but naturally has a good quota of wit, and Vittorio De Sica's direction plays throughout for laughs. The Fox is a quick-witted crook who nevertheless manages to find himself in the cooler seven times in nine years. But he's equally adroit at getting out. This time he makes the break (a) because he's worried about his sister who, he has a hunch, is getting into bad habits as a film starlet, and (b) to arrange for the smuggling into Rome of the loot from a $3-million Cairo bullion robbery. He hits on the idea of pretending to make a film on an Italian beach and conning the local villagers and the police into landing the gold ashore as part of the "film script."

The filming parody is better in promise than when start of shooting is actually being made, but even these sequences are good for plenty of yocks. Much of this is created by Victor Mature, roped into the film within the film as an aging, corseted film star fighting the wrinkles and still living in the past.

●

AFTER THE THIN MAN
1936, 107 mins, US Ⓥ b/w
Dir W. S. Van Dyke ***Prod*** Hunt Stromberg ***Scr*** Frances Goodrich, Albert Hackett ***Ph*** Oliver T. Marsh ***Ed*** Robert J. Kern ***Mus*** Herbert Stothart, Edward Ward ***Art*** Cedric Gibbons, Harry McAfee
Act William Powell, Myrna Loy, James Stewart, Elissa Landi, Joseph Calleia, Jessie Ralph (M-G-M)

First thing everyone will want to know about this one is whether it is as good as *The Thin Man*, and the answer is that it is—and it isn't. It has the same stars, William Powell and Myrna Loy; the same style of breezy direction by W. S. Van Dyke; almost as many sparkling lines of dialog and amusing situations; but it hasn't, and probably couldn't have, the same freshness and originality of its predecessor.

The same author, Dashiell Hammett, wrote it, and the same screenwriters, Frances Goodrich and Albert Hackett, did the adaptation. It's the "same" all the way through, and while that's a guarantee of a certain general excellence, it's the reason why it does not shine so brightly.

Powell as the amateur detective—with Loy tagging along and getting herself tangled up in the plot—eventually gets his man. The two leading players seem to have a swell time throughout. They do a bedroom scene that is packed with laughs, but that's topped by a subsequent sequence when, having slept through an entire day, they have their breakfast in the evening and appear unable, or unwilling, to adjust themselves to the passing of time.

1936: NOMINATION: Best Screenplay

●

AGAINST ALL ODDS
1984, 128 mins, US Ⓥ ⦿ col
Dir Taylor Hackford ***Prod*** Taylor Hackford, William S. Gilmore ***Scr*** Eric Hughes ***Ph*** Donald Thorin ***Ed*** Fredric Steinkamp, William Steinkamp ***Mus*** Michel Colombier ***Art*** Richard James Lawrence
Act Rachel Ward, Jeff Bridges, James Woods, Alex Karras, Jane Greer, Richard Widmark (Columbia)

If not for a somewhat murky and misanthropic ending, *Against All Odds* would stand as a well-engineered secondtry at 1947's *Out of the Past*.

Jeff Bridges is a fading pro footballer with shady connections to James Woods, a small-time LA bookie-hood who has been keeping house with Rachel Ward until she stabbed him and got away.

Jane Greer, who played Ward's role in the earlier version of the Daniel Mainwaring yarn, is now Ward's mean mother, who owns the team Bridges is cut from. Greer is allied with suave, sinister Richard Widmark, lawyer in arapacious real-estate deal who will turn out to be more than suspected at first.

The action ranges all the way to remote Mexican areas whose scenic moods are captured nicely by cinematographer Donald Thorin, heating up the #2 love affair between Bridges and Ward. All the performances are first-rate.

1984: NOMINATION: Best Song ("Against All Odds [Take a Look at Me Now]")

●

AGATHA
1979, 98 mins, UK Ⓥ ▭ col
Dir Michael Apted ***Prod*** Jarvis Astaire, Gavrik Losey ***Scr*** Kathleen Tynan, Arthur Hopcraft ***Ph*** Vittorio Storaro ***Ed*** Jim Clark ***Mus*** Johnny Mandel ***Art*** Shirley Russell
Act Dustin Hoffman, Vanessa Redgrave, Timothy Dalton, Helen Morse, Celia Gregory, Paul Brooke (Warner/First Artists)

Billed as "an imaginary solution to an authentic mystery," Kathleen Tynan's original story fills in the gaps of Agatha Christie's well-publicized disappearance in 1926.

Christie, portrayed by Vanessa Redgrave in superlative fashion, is confronted with the breakdown of her marriage to war hero Timothy Dalton, who is prepared to marry his secretary (Celia Gregory). She flees to a remote health spa, where she sets in motion a unique form of revenge, while thousands scour the British countryside for some sign of her.

Enter Dustin Hoffman as a celebrated American journalist. He, too, joins the search, at first with the idea of a story, and then pursuing more romantic notions.

Director Michael Apted has perfectly recaptured the mood of post–World War I Britain, and the film is gorgeously photographed by Italian cinematographer Vittorio Storaro.

Agatha packs a surprise twist that the real Agatha Christie might have envied.

1979: NOMINATION: Best Costume Design

●

AGE D'OR, L'
1930, 65 mins, France Ⓥ b/w
Dir Luis Bunuel ***Prod*** Charles Vicomte de Noailles ***Scr*** Luis Bunuel, Salvador Dali ***Ph*** Albert Dubergen ***Ed*** Luis Bunuel ***Mus*** Georges van Parys ***Art*** Schilzneck
Act Gaston Modot, Lya Lys, Max Ernst, Pierre Prevert, Jose Artigas, Jacques Brunius (Vicomte de Noailles)

Made two years after his surrealistic *Le Chien Andalou*, director Luis Bunuel's second effort created such a furor when first shown in Paris [on Oct. 28, 1930] that, after a stormy run, it was finally banned by the French government. Bunuel's film was offensive to both society and church. Establishment teamed up to "eradicate" this impudent upstart.

Although Salvador Dali is co-credited with the screenplay, there's little evidence of his contribution to the film beyond the occasional surrealistic treatment of an incident or a visual image indicative of his pictorial style.

Bunuel's anger at society, particularly its attitude on morality, seems not only dated today, but laugh provoking. [Review is of a 1964 screening at Lincoln Center, NY, first showing of pic in the U.S.] The behavior of his libidinous hero and heroine, played by Gaston Modot and Lya Lys in a style straight out of *A Fool There Was*, wouldn't cause raised eyebrows today at a Flatbush cocktail party.

As antique as his comments on morality now seem, those he makes against religion are still marked by violence, blasphemy and vilification. This Jesuit-educated Spaniard uses for closing a sequence based on an excerpt from the writings of Marquis de Sade. It's a particularly brutal comment with a Jesus Christ–like figure staggering out of a sin castle. There are some intentional moments of humor, some so broad that they were obviously influenced by the earlier American slapstick films. Others, while subtler, are also effective.

●

AGENT 8¾
SEE: HOT ENOUGH FOR JUNE

●

AGE OF CONSENT
1932, 80 mins, US b/w
Dir Gregory La Cava ***Scr*** Sarah Y. Mason, Francis Cockrell ***Ph*** J. Roy Hunt ***Ed*** Jack Kitchin
Act Dorothy Wilson, Richard Cromwell, Eric Linden, Arline Judge, John Halliday (Radio)

Picture marks the first release of Dorothy Wilson, the stenographer in the Radio coast studio offices who was skyrocketed from her typewriter into semi-stardom.

Wilson turns out to be a highly interesting young type, suggesting in appearance a flapper Norma Shearer. The part of a college coed does not call for any histrionic fireworks, but the newcomer reveals a remarkable aptitude for natural acting.

Story is a sexy tale [based on the play *Cross Roads* by Martin Flavin, adapted by H. N. Swanson], dealing in often sprightly manner with the adolescent amours of a coed campus and its environs, this angle being insidiously exploited under cover of being a sympathetic study of the love problems of the young.

Cast is made up of young people, with just the leavening in the professor character, deftly handled as usual by John Halliday. Central male characters are played by Richard Cromwell, an excellent choice as the young hero, and Eric Linden, once more a philandering student high-flyer.

●

AGE OF CONSENT
1969, 103 mins, Australia Ⓥ col
Dir Michael Powell ***Prod*** Michael Powell, James Mason ***Scr*** Peter Yeldham ***Ph*** Hannes Staudinger ***Ed*** Anthony Buckley ***Mus*** Stanley Myers ***Art*** Dennis Gentle
Act James Mason, Helen Mirren, Jack MacGowran, Neva Carr-Glyn, Antonia Katsaros, Frank Thring (Nautilus)

Bradley Morahan (James Mason) is a famous Australian painter, paying a lot of alimony and about to return to his homeland.

He proceeds to the Great Barrier Reef to settle in a broken-down shack on a dream island, close to the mainland. The only other inhabitants are a gin-sodden old hag, her granddaughter Cora (Helen Mirren) and Isabel Marley (Antonia Katsaros), a man-hungry spinster living on annuity, but also rearing chickens and growing vegetables.

The film [from a novel by Norman Lindsay] has plenty of corn, is sometimes too slow, repetitious and badly edited, almost as if scenes had been deleted. Yet the picture has immense charm and the actual photography (particularly underwater scenes) and superb scenery make it a good travelog ad for the Great Barrier Reef area where most of it was filmed.

●

AGE OF GOLD
SEE: L'AGE D'OR

●

AGE OF INNOCENCE, THE
1993, 136 mins, US Ⓥ ⊙ ▭ col
Dir Martin Scorsese ***Prod*** Barbara De Fina ***Scr*** Jay Cocks, Martin Scorsese ***Ph*** Michael Ballhaus ***Ed*** Thelma Schoonmaker ***Mus*** Elmer Bernstein ***Art*** Dante Ferretti
Act Daniel Day-Lewis, Michelle Pfeiffer, Winona Ryder, Miriam Margolyes, Richard E. Grant, Alec McCowen (Columbia)

An extraordinarily sumptuous piece of filmmaking, *The Age of Innocence* is a faithful adaptation of Edith Wharton's classic 1921 Pulitzer Prize–winning novel, which is both a blessing and a bit of a curse. The material remains cloaked by the very propriety, stiff manners and emotional starchiness the picture delineates in such copious detail in its portrait of an impossible romance set in the upper reaches of New York society in the 1870s. Prestige entry has a $40-million-plus price tag.

Present rendition (Irene Dunne and John Boles starred in a forgotten 1934 version) plunges the viewer into the hotbed of high society—the opera, where the real action is in the boxes, not onstage. The focus of most lorgnettes this evening is Ellen Olenska (Michelle Pfeiffer), a beautiful American recently returned from Europe after leaving her aristocratic husband.

Ellen is a cousin of lovely young May Welland (Winona Ryder), who is just now announcing her engagement to socially prominent lawyer Newland Archer (Daniel Day-Lewis). Just as he is urging May to move up the date of their wedding, Newland becomes entranced by the bewitching Ellen, who is tantalizingly different from everyone else in his sphere.

The real subject of the film is Newland's adhering to his prescribed role rather than following his heart, and while this is apparent, the emotion is, crucially, not deeply felt or conveyed. The picture's other subject is the re-creation of an era, and in this the film is almost overwhelmingly successful.

In his attempt to define an era through a thwarted romance set among the trappings of the very rich, director Martin Scorsese conjures up the cinematic worlds of Max Ophuls, notably *Madame de . . .*, and Luchino Visconti, particularly *Senso* and *The Leopard*. For a director previously associated mostly with the violence of the lower classes of New York, it's a notable attempt to stretch, and admirable in many ways.

Day-Lewis cuts an impressive figure as Newland, and the two principal female roles are superbly filled. A great roster of superior actors fills out the supporting roles. Thesps generally affect a mid-Atlantic accent that would seem appropriate to the time. Elmer Bernstein's score is full-bodied and richly romantic.

1993: Best Costume Design

NOMINATIONS: Best Supp. Actress (Winona Ryder), Adapted Screenplay, Art Direction, Original Score

●

AGNES OF GOD
1985, 98 mins, US Ⓥ ⊙ ▭ col
Dir Norman Jewison ***Prod*** Patrick Palmer, Norman Jewison ***Scr*** John Pielmeier ***Ph*** Sven Nykvist ***Ed*** Antony Gibbs ***Mus*** Georges Delerue ***Art*** Ken Adam
Act Jane Fonda, Anne Bancroft, Meg Tilly, Anne Pitoniak, Winston Rekert, Gratien Gelinas (Columbia-Delphi IV)

John Pielmeier penned the screenplay from his own 1982 play about a young nun who is found to have given birth and then strangled the baby at an isolated convent. A psychiatrist, played by Jane Fonda, is appointed by the court to determine whether or not the young woman (Meg Tilly) is fit to stand trial, and is assured that the seemingly innocent, naive girl has no recollection of the child or conception.

In her aggressive quest for the facts in the case, Fonda goes head-to-head with Mother Superior Anne Bancroft, a cagey, very hip woman of God whose past as a wife and mother gives her a strong knowledge of the real world values represented by Fonda.

Fonda's relentless interrogating, mannered chain-smoking and enforced two-dimensionality cause her to become tiresome very early on. She remains a brittle cliche of a modern professional woman.

Bancroft gives a generally highly engaging performance as a religious woman too knowledgeable to be one-upped by even the craftiest layman.

Tilly is angelically beautiful as the troubled youngster and brings a convincing innocence and sincerity to the role that would be hard to match.

1985: NOMINATIONS: Best Actress (Anne Bancroft), Supp. Actress (Meg Tilly), Original Score

●

AGONY AND THE ECSTASY, THE
1965, 136 mins, US Ⓥ ⊙ ▭ col
Dir Carol Reed ***Prod*** Carol Reed ***Scr*** Philip Dunne ***Ph*** Leon Shamroy ***Ed*** Samuel E. Beetley ***Mus*** Alex North, Franco Potenza ***Art*** John DeCuir
Act Charlton Heston, Rex Harrison, Diane Cilento, Harry Andrews, Alberto Lupo, Adolfo Celi (International Classics/20th Century-Fox)

Against a backdrop of political-religious upheaval during the Italian Renaissance, *The Agony and the Ecstasy* focuses on the personal conflict between sculptor-painter Michelangelo and his patron, Pope Julius II.

Scripter Philip Dunne has zeroed in on a four-year span during which the painter labored on the ceiling frescoes for the Sistine Chapel. The potent seeds in Dunne's excellent treatment [of the novel by Irving Stone] are the artistic arrogance of Michelangelo and equally stubborn mind of the soldier Pontiff Julius.

Rex Harrison is outstanding as the Pope, from the moment of his striking entrance as a hooded soldier leading the suppression of a pocket of revolt, to his later scenes as an urbane, yet sensitive, pragmatic ruler of a worldly kingdom.

Charlton Heston's Michelangelo is, in its own way, also outstanding. Combination of austere garb, thinned face, short hair and beard, plus underplaying in early scenes, effectively submerge the Heston image fostered by his earlier epix.

Assisting Harrison's verbal whiplashes are the grandiose engineering plans of the architect Bramante, then engaged in building the new basilica of St. Peter. Harry Andrews excels in the role, while his protege, the painter Raphael, played by Tomas Milian, projects very well as Heston's possible replacement.

[Prior to roadshow presentations of the pic, a 12½-minute documentary prologue was included, featuring the sculpture of Michelangelo and scored by Jerry Goldsmith.]

1965: NOMINATIONS: Best Color Cinematography, Color Costume Design, Color Art Direction, Original Music Score, Sound

●

AGUIRRE, DER ZORN GOTTES
1973, 95 mins, West Germany Ⓥ ⊙ col
Dir Werner Herzog ***Prod*** Werner Herzog ***Scr*** Werner Herzog ***Ph*** Thomas Mauch ***Ed*** Beate Mainka-Jellinghaus ***Mus*** Popol Vuh
Act Klaus Kinski, Cecilia Rivera, Ruy Guerra, Helena Rojo, Del Negro, Peter Berling (Herzog)

Independent West German filmmaker Werner Herzog has explored military psychology, the irony of revolt, colonialism and the lack of scientific reliability in some of his previous films. Here he has trekked down a river in Peru to resurrect the ancient conquistadores of Spain in a sort of parable on human need for power and warping of the best intentions when they are by the sword or by fanatics.

No preaching here, but a rivetingly shot odyssey as a group of the conqueror Pizarro's men are sent to find the fabled city of gold, El Dorado. The head of the expedition tags himself "The Wrath of God." He sets up his own Emperor and pushes on to win power and glory for himself in the name of God. Their trek turns out a voyage to extinction.

The acting is properly larger than life, especially Klaus Kinski as the title character, a lean, driven but imposing man who has heads lopped off when in any way interfered with in his task of destruction and exploration. Visuals are exciting without distracting from the harsh theme.

●

AGUIRRE, WRATH OF GOD
SEE: AGUIRRE, DER ZORN GOTTES

●

AI NO CORRIDA
SEE: L'EMPIRE DES SENS

●

AIR AMERICA
1990, 112 mins, US Ⓥ ⊙ ▭ col
Dir Roger Spottiswoode ***Prod*** Daniel Melnick ***Scr*** John Eskow, Richard Rush ***Ph*** Roger Deakins ***Ed*** John Bloom, Lois Freeman-Fox ***Mus*** Charles Gross ***Art*** Allan Cameron
Act Mel Gibson, Robert Downey, Jr., Nancy Travis, Ken Jenkins, David Marshall Grant, Lane Smith (Carolco)

Spectacular action sequences and engaging perfs by Mel Gibson and Robert Downey, Jr., make this big-budgeter entertaining and provocative.

It's probably news to most even at this late date that the CIA, through its proprietary Air America, was using drug money to finance the war in Southeast Asia and condoning the refining and exportation of heroin both to GIs in that part of the world and to the American public. Air America became known as a dope airline, as Christopher Robbins's 1979 source book puts it, and the filmmakers don't shrink from showing Gibson knowingly flying opium and cynically justifying it as essential to the U.S. war effort.

Starting off as a reckless radio station helicopter pilot in a wild stunt sequence on an LA freeway in 1969, Downey is recruited by the CIA to perform his hair-raising flying feats for Uncle Sam in Laos, where oxymoronic military intelligence officer David Marshall Grant insists, "We're not actually here."

With his reported $35-million budget and a vast army of tech assistants to help carry out the stunt flying and crashes on the atmospheric Thailand locations, director Roger Spottiswoode does an efficient job in marshaling his forces and walking the thin line required to keep a black comedy from becoming gruesome or flippant.

●

AIR FORCE
1943, 124 mins, US Ⓥ b/w
Dir Howard Hawks ***Prod*** Hal B. Wallis ***Scr*** Dudley Nichols ***Ph*** James Wong Howe ***Ed*** George Amy ***Mus*** Franz Waxman ***Art*** John Hughes
Act John Ridgely, Gig Young, Arthur Kennedy, Harry Carey, Charles Drake, John Garfield (Warner)

Air Force is the saga of a Flying Fortress (the *Mary Ann*, a Boeing B-17). It is gripping, informative, entertaining, thrilling. It is a patriotic heartthrob in celluloid without preaching; it is inspirational without being phoney in its emotions.

Perhaps the best-known cast component is John Garfield and it's the more effective that the principals are not as well-known. John Ridgley is Capt. Quincannon and Gig Young his co-pilot, both capital. Arthur Kennedy plays the bombardier; Charles Drake gives new and usually not suspected importance to the navigator's role in a Flying Fortress. Harry Carey gives a corking performance as the veteran crew chief, a career sgt. from way back.

Ray Montgomery is the asst. radio operator, and the surly Sgt. Winocki, aerial gunner, is excellently played by John Garfield. Having flunked out as a flying officer, Garfield looks forward to three weeks hence, when his enlistment is over, but of course the Pearl Harbor debacle regenerates him into a vindictive American who stays on indef.

1943: Best Editing

NOMINATIONS: Best Original Screenplay, B&W Cinematography, Special Effects

•

AIR FORCE ONE
1997, 124 mins, US Ⓥ ⦿ ▭ col
Dir Wolfgang Petersen *Prod* Wolfgang Petersen, Gail Katz, Armyan Bernstein, Jon Shestack *Scr* Andrew W. Marlowe *Ph* Michael Ballhaus *Ed* Richard Francis-Bruce *Mus* Jerry Goldsmith, Joel McNeely *Art* William Sandell
Act Harrison Ford, Gary Oldman, Glenn Close, Wendy Crewson, Paul Guilfoyle, William H. Macy (Radiant/ Beacon/Columbia)

Seeing the president of the United States as a kick-butt action hero pretty much sums up the appeal of this preposterously pulpy but quite entertaining suspense meller. Tale of the hijacking of the world's most security-laden plane comes as far more "realistic" simply because everything in it is meant to be physically possible in the real world, rather than being rooted in the credibility of the effects themselves.

The search for possible villains in the post–Cold War era this time leads to Kazakhstan, where a prologue shows a Yank-Russian commando raid snaring fascistic leader Gen. Radek (Jurgen Prochnow). No sooner has Air Force One taken off for the trip home [after a celebratory dinner in Moscow by U.S. President James Marshall] than it is taken over by a bunch of Radek faithful led by the fanatical Ivan (Gary Oldman).

Ivan's plan to take the president (Harrison Ford) hostage is thwarted when the latter seems to escape in an emergency pod. Marshall, however—Vietnam vet and Medal of Honor winner that he is—has not jumped ship, but has become a guerrilla fighter on board his own aircraft.

The pilot's attempt to land the 747 at a German airbase makes for a terrific action setpiece that can genuinely be called nerve-wracking. Second boffo sequence involves dozens of passengers parachuting out of the plane's belly during an attempted refueling. Unfortunately, pic shares with many of its companions the sin of excess endings.

All the key scenes are shot and edited to pulse-quickening effect, which casts into shadow the numerous objections one can easily raise to the film: that it is a wildly jingoistic American imperialist exercise, a more covert *Rambo*-like fantasy projection for Vietnam-era men, or that first-time screenwriter Andrew W. Marlowe's admittedly clever scenario could have sorely used some wit and humor.

The film succeeds despite a monotone, physically unexciting performance from Ford.

1997: NOMINATIONS: Best Editing, Sound

•

AIRHEADS
1994, 91 mins, US Ⓥ ⦿ col
Dir Michael Lehmann *Prod* Robert Simonds, Mark Burg *Scr* Rich Wilkes *Ph* John Schwartzman *Ed* Stephen Semel *Mus* Carter Burwell *Art* David Nichols
Act Brendan Fraser, Steve Buscemi, Adam Sandler, Joe Mantegna, Chris Farley, Amy Loncane (20th Century-Fox/Island World)

There's plenty of sound and fury in *Airheads*, and while it would be extreme to say it adds up to nothing, the antic musical lark certainly doesn't have a lot on its mind. An absurdist variation on *Dog Day Afternoon*, the picture is a rather good-natured view of Generation X and the pursuit of rock 'n' roll stardom.

The slim premise finds a trio of "we don't want to be labelled" musicians desperately trying to get a little bit of attention. Attempts to get music execs to listen to a demo tape have landed on deaf ears.

So, after ringleader Chazz (Brendan Fraser) gets turfed out by his girlfriend, Kayla (Amy Locane), he tells cronies Rex (Steve Buscemi) and Pip (Adam Sandler) that it's time to be more aggressive. His plan is to storm rebel radio station KPPX and get their tape played on the air. But execution proves more troublesome.

Though it's little more than a one-joke premise, director Michael Lehmann gets maximum mileage from the low-octane script. Though Fraser looks the role, his attitude is a tad too earnest to effect the kind of whacky vision called for in the material. Cohorts Buscemi and Sandler drift more naturally to the required zaniness.

•

AIR MAIL
1932, 85 mins, US b/w
Dir John Ford *Prod* Carl Laemmle, Jr. *Scr* Dale Van Every, Frank W. Wead *Ph* Karl Freund
Act Pat O'Brien, Ralph Bellamy, Russell Hopton, Slim Summerville, Gloria Stuart, Lilian Bond (Universal)

Picture is a fund of interesting atmosphere about the air mail service. Radio exchanges are coming in and going out all the time, couched in technical language such as "Visibility zero, ceiling zero. Caution to all planes." It's interesting enough, but in essence the producer has dramatized the air mail service first and slipped in a human story as a second thought.

Duke Talbot (Pat O'Brien) is a great flyer and the bravest of the brave, in the air or on the ground. But he's a vainglorious show-off for one thing and a double-crossing lover. His disreputable affair with the wife of one of his service mates earns him the enmity of Mike Miller (Ralph Bellamy), in charge of the Desert Station post in the heart of the Rocky Mountains. When the betrayed husband is killed during a flight through a violent storm, Duke declines to take his mail on to the next stage, in order to elope with the wife, now free. Instead he allows Mike to take the trip, although Mike has eye trouble that makes the journey especially hazardous.

The stunt stuff is breathtaking. There are long sequences of Duke surveying the terrain from a plane, vast stretches of jagged mountains involving hair-raising stunt flying, apparently within scant feet of peaks and rugged cliffs.

Slim Summerville turns in a capable performance in a comedy relief role while O'Brien and Bellamy give strong, simple handling to the main roles. Gloria Stuart is a pale heroine in a pale part. Lilian Bond does the more spirited playing in an unsympathetic role.

•

AIRPLANE!
1980, 88 mins, US Ⓥ ⦿ col
Dir Jim Abrahams, David Zucker, Jerry Zucker *Prod* Jon Davison *Scr* Jim Abrahams, David Zucker, Jerry Zucker *Ph* Joseph Biroc *Ed* Patrick Kennedy *Mus* Elmer Bernstein *Art* Ward Preston
Act Robert Hays, Julie Hagerty, Lloyd Bridges, Peter Graves, Leslie Nielsen, Robert Stack (Paramount)

Airplane! is what they used to call a laff-riot. Made by team which turned out *Kentucky Fried Movie*, this spoof of disaster features beats any other film for sheer number of comic gags.

Writer-directors leave no cliche unturned as they lay waste to the *Airport*-style disaster cycle, among other targets. From the clever *Jaws* takeoff opening to the final, irreverent title card, laughs come thick and fast.

Plot has former pilot Robert Hays, now terrified of flying due to wartime malfeasance, boarding an LA-to-Chicago flight in pursuit of ex-girlfriend stewardess Julie Hagerty.

When flight personnel, including sexually deviant pilot Peter Graves and co-pilot Kareem Abdul-Jabbar, contract food poisoning on board, Hays is called upon to land the craft safely, an effort not made easier by fact that air controller Lloyd Bridges is completely crazed.

•

AIRPLANE II: THE SEQUEL
1982, 85 mins, US Ⓥ ⦿ Col
Dir Ken Finkleman *Prod* Howard W. Koch *Scr* Ken Finkleman *Ph* Joseph Biroc *Ed* Dennis Virkler *Mus* Elmer Bernstein *Art* William Sandell
Act Robert Hays, Julie Hagerty, Lloyd Bridges, Peter Graves, William Shatner, Chad Everett (Paramount)

It can't be said that *Airplane II* is no better or worse than its predecessor. It is far worse, but might seem funnier had there been no original.

In the first *Airplane*, Jim Abrahams, David Zucker and Jerry Zucker had a fresh satirical crack at that hoary old genre, the airborne disaster film. But they wisely chose not to tackle a sequel, leaving incoming writer-director Ken Finkleman a tough task for his feature debut.

Robert Hays is still solid as the fearful pilot destined to take the controls. Ditto his daffy girlfriend Julie Hagerty. But instead of their hilariously earnest efforts the first time around, they seem (perhaps subconsciously) too aware what they're doing is supposed to be funny.

Peter Graves remains amusing as the captain with a fondness for naughty talk with young boys. Among those with nothing much to do are Raymond Burr, Sonny Bono, Chuck Connors, John Dehner, Rip Torn and Chad Everett. Among those with too much to do is William Shatner.

•

AIRPORT
1970, 137 mins, US Ⓥ ⦿ ▭ col
Dir George Seaton *Prod* Ross Hunter *Scr* George Seaton *Ph* Ernest Laszlo *Ed* Stuart Gilmore *Mus* Alfred Newman *Art* Alexander Golitzen, Preston Ames
Act Burt Lancaster, Dean Martin, Jean Seberg, Jacqueline Bisset, George Kennedy, Helen Hayes (Universal)

Based on the novel by Arthur Hailey, over-produced by Ross Hunter with a cast of stars as long as a jet runway, and adapted and directed by George Seaton in a glossy, slick style, *Airport* is a handsome, often dramatically involving $10-million epitaph to a bygone brand of filmmaking.

However, the ultimate dramatic situation of a passenger-loaded jetliner with a psychopathic bomber aboard that has to be brought into a blizzard-swept airport with runway blocked by a snow-stalled plane actually does not create suspense because the audience knows how it's going to end.

As the cigar chomping, bull boss of the maintenance men, George Kennedy gives a strong portrayal. But here again there's not a moment of plot doubt that he is going to get that stuck plane cleared off the runway in time for the emergency landing.

1970: Best Supporting Actress (Helen Hayes)

NOMINATIONS: Best Picture, Supp. Actress (Maureen Stapleton), Screenplay, Cinematography, Costume Design, Art Direction, Editing, Original Score, Sound

•

AIRPORT '80—THE CONCORD
SEE: THE CONCORDE—AIRPORT '79, THE

•

AIRPORT 1975
1974, 106 mins, US Ⓥ ▭ col
Dir Jack Smight *Prod* William Frye *Scr* Don Ingalls *Ph* Philip Lathrop *Ed* J. Terry Williams *Mus* John Cacavas *Art* George C. Webb
Act Charlton Heston, Karen Black, George Kennedy, Efrem Zimbalist, Jr., Susan Clark, Gloria Swanson (Universal)

Airport 1975 gathers its specimens into a 747 jetliner that collides midair with a private plane, precipitating a complicated rescue effort. Charlton Heston's formula characterization is, quite literally, Messiah-exmachina.

Don Ingalls is credited with the scripture, "inspired" (as the crawl says) by Ross Hunter's 1970 pic which, in turn, came from Arthur Hailey's novel. Jack Smight's direction has the refreshing pace of a filmmaker who knows his plot can crash unless he hurries.

The redundant script-massaging of the 747's elaborate backup controls, safety features and all those other yum-yum goodies that airlines keep yacking about would suggest that some of the dialog was written by Boeing.

•

AIRPORT '77
1977, 113 mins, US Ⓥ ⦿ ▭ col
Dir Jerry Jameson *Prod* William Frye *Scr* Michael Scheff, David Spector *Ph* Philip Lathrop *Ed* J. Terry Williams, Robert Watts *Mus* John Cacavas *Art* George C. Webb
Act Jack Lemmon, Lee Grant, Brenda Vaccaro, Joseph Cotten, Olivia de Havilland, James Stewart (Universal)

With Charlton Heston either busy elsewhere or exhausted from earthquakes, World War II and previous aerial disasters, Jack Lemmon assumed the Noah lead in *Airport* '77. This time around, a giant private jet gets hijacked and crashes off the Florida coast.

The story's formula banality is credible most of the time and there's some good actual U.S. Navy search-and-rescue procedure interjected in the plot.

The story peg here [by H.A.L. Craig and Charles Kuenstle] has James Stewart, billionaire who has converted his home to museum status, loading his private plane with priceless paintings and a broader quality of people for a junket to the estate. However, Lemmon's co-pilot, Robert Foxworth, has joined with Monte Markham and Michael Pataki to hijack the plane for the artwork.

1977: NOMINATIONS: Best Costume Design, Art Direction

•

AIRPORT '79
SEE: CONCORDE—AIRPORT '79, THE

•

AIRPORT III
SEE: AIRPORT '77

•

AKAHIGE
1965, 188 mins, Japan Ⓥ ⦿ ▭ b/w
Dir Akira Kurosawa *Prod* Tomoyuki Tanaka, Ryuzo Kikushima *Scr* Ryuzo Kikushima, Masato Ide, Hideo Oguni, Akira Kurosawa *Ph* Asakazu Nakai, Takao Saito *Mus* Masaru Sato *Art* Yoshiro Muraki
Act Toshiro Mifune, Yuzo Kayama, Tsutomu Yamazaki, Kyoko Kagawa, Miyuki Kuwano, Kinuyo Tanaka (Kurosawa/Toho)

Take a season of *Doctor Kildare* TV skeins, throw in a half-dozen classic Hollywood hospital perennials, but do them all up with great taste and visual, cinematic flair, and you have the Akira Kurosawa pic *Red Beard*. It's hokum lifted to the highest denominator, the banal made into near art by great skill and craftsmanship by the Japanese master.

The over three-hour running time is an undeniable but adjustable defect: Much of the film's initial footage could be elegantly elided for major effect.

The main plot [from Shugoro Yamamoto's novel] is the old chestnut about the enterprising young doctor and the misunderstood old curmudgeon, in this case "Red Beard" (Toshiro Mifune). Slowly, as Kurosawa interweaves several plots, understanding for his methods grows as human relations triumph over sheer medical know-how. [Pic is set in 1822, in Endo.]

Here and there, as noted, the plot drifts into over-familiar waters, but elsewhere it soars to stylistic and heartwarming heights, which show that this is not just the routine ward drama, but has higher scope and targets. Kurosawa has blended handkerchief elements with drama shock (there's a harrowing anesthetic operation scene), humor and lively action (a knock-down, drag-out fight).

Thesping is uniformly good, with Mifune and Yuzo Kayama standout in the two leads.

•

AKENFIELD

1975, 95 mins, UK Ⓥ col

Dir Peter Hall ***Prod*** Peter Hall, Rex Pyke ***Scr*** Ronald Blythe ***Ph*** Ivan Strasberg ***Mus*** Michael Tippett ***Art*** Ian Whittaker, Roger Christian

Act Garrow Shand, Peggy Cole, Barbara Tilney, Lyn Brooks, Ida Page, Ted Dedman (Angle Films)

Adapted from Ronald Blythe's social study of a Suffolk village, this is the story of three generations of farm laboring, intercutting flashbacks with present day to demonstrate that the more things change, the more they remain the same. It is funny and touching and seldom less than engrossing.

A virtue is that Hall has not idealized the subject. Throughout there's a strong current of melancholy, of dreams crushed and human potential stunted. Though it's not a despairing film, one is apt to feel that Suffolk's a lovely place to visit only.

Ivan Strasberg's color photography, using only natural light (even indoors), is one of the conspicuous delights. His composition of the rolling English countryside is often lyrical, sometimes magical.

•

AKIRA

1988, 124 mins, Japan Ⓥ ⊙ col

Dir Katsuhiro Otomo (sup.) ***Prod*** Ryohei Suzuki, Shunzo Kato ***Scr*** Katsuhiro Otomo, Izo Hashimoto ***Ph*** Katsuji Misawa ***Ed*** Takeshi Seyama ***Mus*** Shoji Yamashiro ***Art*** Toshiharu Mizutani (Akira Committee)

A lavish animation extravaganza produced at a cost of $8 million, this futuristic exploration is a followup by author-director Katsuhiro Otomo to his tremendously popular comic books.

The action takes place 30 years from now, in Neo-Tokyo, the reconstructed version of the Japanese capital, previously destroyed in a 1988 nuclear war. The shape of the city has changed but not its problems, as the social fabric is falling to pieces, students organize demonstrations, unemployment generates constant unrest and terrorists conspire to overthrow the government.

The military is developing a new and more powerful source of energy, ESP. The problem is that they don't quite know how to control it, and when a young biker with natural talents refuses to cooperate, the entire world is in a lot of trouble.

A remarkable technical achievement in every respect, from the imaginative and detailed design of tomorrow to the booming Dolby effects on the soundtrack, pic's only drawback is the slight stiffness in the drawing of human movement.

•

ALADDIN

1992, 90 mins, US Ⓥ ⊙ col

Dir John Musker, Ron Clements ***Prod*** John Musker, Ron Clements ***Scr*** Ron Clements, John Musker, Ted Elliott, Terry Rossio ***Ed*** H. Lee Peterson ***Mus*** Alan Menken ***Art*** R. S. Vander Wende (Walt Disney)

Floridly beautiful, shamelessly derivative and infused with an irreverent, sophisticated comic flair thanks to Robin Williams's vocal calisthenics, *Aladdin* represents the ultimate synthesis of filmmaking and marketing, extracting winning elements from Disney's last two animated hits (*The Little Mermaid* and *Beauty and the Beast*) as well as more venerable sources, particularly the 1940 *Thief of Bagdad*.

Lyricist Tim Rice filled in seamlessly on three of the six songs after Howard Ashman's death, and while Alan Menken's score may not be as instantly hummable as *Beauty*'s, it's still impressive, with two show-stoppingly elaborate numbers.

Aladdin (voiced by Scott Weinger, sung by Brad Kane) is a thief and a street urchin who stumbles across the defiant and anachronistically liberated Princess Jasmine (Linda Larkin/Lea Salonga), who flees the palace to escape a law dictating that she must marry a prince.

The bad guy, functional if not one of the great Disney villains, is the Sultan's adviser Jafar (Jonathan Freeman), a sorcerer who recruits Aladdin to help claim the magic lamp from a huge cave hidden in the desert. The narrative moves somewhat unevenly before the kid uncorks Williams, at which point things kick into another level.

1992: Best Original Score, Song ("A Whole New World")

NOMINATIONS: Best Song ("Friends Like Me"), Sound, Sound Effects Editing

•

ALAMO, THE

1960, 192 mins, US Ⓥ ⊙ ▭ col

Dir John Wayne [John Ford] ***Prod*** John Wayne ***Scr*** James Edward Grant ***Ph*** William H. Clothier ***Ed*** Stuart Gilmore ***Mus*** Dimitri Tiomkin ***Art*** Alfred Ybarra

Act John Wayne, Richard Widmark, Laurence Harvey, Frankie Avalon, Richard Boone, Linda Cristal (Batjac)

The Alamo, which was shot in 91 days at a stated cost of $12 million, has a good measure of mass appeal in its 192 minutes. But to get it, producer-director-star John Wayne has loaded the telling of the tale with happy homilies on American virtues and patriotic platitudes under life-and-death fire, which smack of yesteryear theatricalism rather than the realism of modern battle drama.

Obviously Wayne and James Edward Grant, who penned the original screenplay, had an entertainment, not a history lesson, in mind. But in their zeal to reproduce a colorful, homespun account of what went on in the course of those 13 remarkable days in 1836, they have somehow shrouded some of the fantastic facts of the original with some of the frivolous fancies of their re-creation.

In spite of the painstaking attempts to explore the characters of the picture's three principal heroes (Bowie, Crockett, Travis), there is an absence of emotional feeling, of a sense of participation. It is almost as if the writer is willing to settle for the popular conception of familiar heroes such as Davy Crockett and Jim Bowie as sufficient explanation of their presence and activities.

With the rousing battle sequence at the climax (for which a goodly share of credit must go to second unit director Cliff Lyons) the picture really commands rapt attention.

It is as actor that Wayne functions under his own direction in his least successful capacity. Generally playing with one expression on his face, he seems at times to be acting like a man with $12 million on his conscience. Both Widmark and Harvey suffer minor lapses in their performances but there is vigor and color in them. Younger players Frankie Avalon and Patrick Wayne show spirit.

1960: Best Sound (Samuel Goldwyn Studio Sound Dept., Todd-AO Sound Dept.)

NOMINATIONS: Best Picture, Supp. Actor (Chill Wills), Color Cinematography, Editing, Score of a Dramatic Picture, Song ("The Green Leaves of Summer")

•

ALAMO BAY

1985, 98 mins, US Ⓥ ⊙ col

Dir Louis Malle ***Prod*** Louis Malle, Vincent Malle ***Scr*** Alice Arlen ***Ph*** Curtis Clark ***Ed*** James Bruce ***Mus*** Ry Cooder ***Art*** Trevor Williams

Act Amy Madigan, Ed Harris, Ho Nguyen, Donald Moffat, Truyen V. Tran, Rudy Young (Tri-Star/Delphi III)

Alamo Bay is a failed piece of social consciousness. The peripatetic Louis Malle hasn t managed to shed any meaningful light on his current subject, that of the conflict between refugee Vietnamese and local fisherfolk around Galveston Bay, Texas, circa 1979–81.

Malle dared to place an exceedingly unsympathetic character at the center of his drama. Here it is Ed Harris, a bruising, philandering, unreflective lout who resents the intrusion of Vietnamese into his community and finally resorts to the easiest method of dealing with them, i.e., brutal, illegal violence.

Scene-setting is devoted to the native whites and newcomer Asians trying to fish the same waters, with the whites becoming increasingly irritated as the Vietnamese, in their view, horn in on their traditional territory, and work for lower wages to boot.

Mixed in with this is a reignition of a romance between Harris and Amy Madigan, latter being the daughter of controversial fish factory operator Donald Moffat and now at odds politically with her former boyfriend.

On the other side of the fence is new arrival Ho Nguyen, who at first wears a permanent, subservient smile in hopes of ingratiating himself, but later refuses to be intimidated along with the rest of his people.

•

ALAN SMITHEE FILM—BURN, HOLLYWOOD, BURN, AN

1997, 86 mins, US Ⓥ ⊙ col

Dir Arthur Hiller ***Prod*** Ben Myron ***Scr*** Joe Eszterhas ***Ph*** Reynaldo Villalobos ***Ed*** Jim Langlois ***Mus*** Gary G-Wiz, Chuck D ***Art*** David L. Snyder

Act Ryan O'Neal, Coolio, Chuck D, Eric Idle, Harvey Weinstein, Richard Jeni (Cinergi/Hollywood)

One of the industry's longest-standing in-jokes has been turned into one of its more elaborate home movies, a caustic but under-funny "expose" of the venality of the motion picture business by scriptwriter Joe Eszterhas.

The Alan Smithee name, the all-purpose pseudonym used by the Directors Guild of America when a filmmaker wants to decline credit, has popped up on more than 30 films in as many years. [At the time of its preem at the Mill Valley fest in October 1997, pic also carried the Smithee moniker, following a supposed dispute over the cutting. By the time of its release on homevideo in 1998, Arthur Hiller's name was restored.] New effort is extremely consistent with the Smithee oeuvre to date.

The cut negative of a $212 million action extravaganza called *Trio*, starring Sylvester Stallone, Whoopi Goldberg and Jackie Chan, produced by blowhard producer James Edmunds (Ryan O'Neal) and backed by spineless studio exec Jerry Glover (Richard Jeni), has been destroyed by its director, Smithee (Eric Idle), after the film was taken away from him by Edmunds. With Smithee now interned in the Keith Moon Psychiatric Institute in his native England, what is promised is an "autopsy" of the film.

Docu-like approach, in which things are described more than shown, quickly becomes tiresome and prevents the picture from developing a rhythm of its own. Five days before its release date, gruff detective Sam Rizzo (Miramax honcho Harvey Weinstein) is put on the case, while Smithee recruits cutting-edge black filmmakers the Brothers Brothers (Coolio, Chuck D) to serve as intermediaries in his quest for final cut.

Film teems with minor in-jokes, few of which will mean anything to people outside of Hollywood. The best one can say for the film is that it does nail the self-justifying, rationalizing, smug and arrogant posturing not hard to find among Hollywood's power class, production values are routine.

[Others appearing as themselves are Larry King, Billy Bob Thornton, Dominick Dunne, Joe Eszterhas, Naomi Eszterhas, Robert Evans, Peter Bart, Shane Black, Robert Shapiro and Arthur Hiller.]

•

ALBERT, R.N.

1953, 88 mins, UK b/w

Dir Lewis Gilbert ***Prod*** Daniel M. Angel ***Scr*** Vernon Harris, Guy Morgan ***Ph*** Jack Asher ***Ed*** Charles Hasse ***Mus*** Malcolm Arnold ***Art*** Bernard Robinson

Act Anthony Steel, Jack Warner, Robert Beatty, William Sylvester, Guy Middleton, Anton Diffring (Eros)

The setting is a German camp for Allied naval officers, the action taking place late in 1944. The camp is regarded by its German masters as escape-proof and admittedly various attempts to breakout have been frustrated by alert prison guards. That is, until one of the internees hits on the idea of making a dummy to cover up for an absentee. The result is "Albert, R.N." with a papier mache head and a wire-framed body.

Camp atmosphere is effective. There is plenty of talk about women but it is an all-male cast. The main problem is the battle against monotony and for liberty.

A solid all-round cast admirably fits into the plot [from the play by Guy Morgan and Edward Sammis]. Anthony Steel handsomely suggests the young artist responsible for the creation of Albert and Jack Warner is reliably cast as the senior British officer who maintains discipline with understanding in the camp. Frederick Valk is a sympathetic camp commandant, but Anton Diffring suggests the typical ruthless Nazi type.

•

AL CAPONE

1959, 105 mins, US Ⓥ b/w

Dir Richard Wilson ***Prod*** John Burrows, Leonard Ackerman ***Scr*** Malvin Wald, Henry F. Greenberg ***Ph*** Lucien Ballard ***Ed*** Walter Hannemann ***Mus*** David Raksin ***Art*** Hilyard Brown

Act Rod Steiger, Fay Spain, James Gregory, Martin Balsam, Nehemiah Persoff, Murvyn Vye (Allied Artists)

A tough, ruthless and generally unsentimental account of the most notorious gangster of the prohibition-repeal era, *Al Capone* is also a very well-made picture. There isn't much "motivation" given for Capone, at least not in the usual sense. But the screenplay does supply reasons and they are more logical than the usual once-over-lightly on the warped youth bit.

Capone, played by Rod Steiger, is shown as an amoral personality with a native genius for leadership and organization. He became rich and famous in a way that seemed to him dandy. Nobody was more genuinely surprised than Capone when the revulsion his acts caused finally overwhelmed him.

The story picks up when Steiger is brought to Chicago as a low-grade torpedo by a fellow countryman (Nehemiah Persoff) to act as bouncer in his gambling establishment. Capone begins his rise when he murders the local political boss (Joe DeSantis), and eventually takes over Persoff's territory, on the latter's retirement. He teams with Bugs Moran and Dion O'Banion to divide Chicago into territories.

Steiger's performance is mostly free of obvious technique, getting inside the character both physically and emotionally. Fay Spain has a role—the romantic attachment of Capone's life—that is probably more distracting than helpful. But she plays well. James Gregory as the honest cop, Martin Balsam as the dishonest reporter and Persoff as Capone's mentor, give skillful performances.

•

ALEKSANDR NYEVSKI
1938, 87 mins, Russia Ⓥ ⊙ b/w
Dir Sergei Eisenstein, Dmitri Vasiliev ***Scr*** Pyotr Pavlenko, Sergei Eisenstein ***Ph*** Eduard Tisse ***Ed*** Sergei Eisenstein ***Mus*** Sergei Prokofiev ***Art*** Isaak Shpinel, N. Solovyov
Act Nikolai Cherkassov, Nikolai Okhlopkov, Andrei Abrikosov, Valentina Ivashova, Dmitri Orlov, Varvara Massalitinova (Mosfilm)

Huge reservoirs of manpower and materials have been thrown into this epic production, which is lavish in scope, theme, performance and wealth of production detail, but despite its magnificence and scale the picture lacks the qualities that first impressed director Sergei Eisenstein's technique. Analogy is drawn to present-day politics, and meaning and purpose of the entire production are shaped toward threats against any Russian invader.

Saga relates of times in the early 1200s when Russia was overrun by Tartars in the east and Teutonic Knights from Germany on the west. Prince Alexander, whose fighting fame had spread throughout the land and even beyond, is summoned from peaceful occupations by popular acclaim. He exhorts and arouses the peasantry to bear arms in defense of Russia. At Lake Peipus, in 1242, Alexander's strategy defeats a superior German force. It is an utter rout, with fleeing Teutons perishing beneath the icy waters of the lake.

The Teutonic Knights are portrayed as ancient forerunners of the Ku Klux Klan. While there is a slight romantic tale paralleling major events, it is not seriously developed and serves merely to relieve the stern character of the warlike tale. First half of the picture is expository and deals with attempts of Alexander to arouse his followers to action. In the latter half of the picture great masses of troops move onward toward the crucial battle.

At times, Eisenstein's direction of battle movements appears extremely stilted and unreal. Groups of soldiers stand about static and uncertain as to where to go or what to do with their weapons.

Of the numerous "honored artists" in the film, Nikolai Cherkassov, as Prince Alexander, fulfills the requirements of the part in every respect. He is kingly, commanding, human and gives a performance not easily forgotten.

•

ALEXANDER NEVSKY
SEE: ALEKSANDR NYEVSKI

•

ALEXANDER'S RAGTIME BAND
1938, 105 mins, US b/w
Dir Henry King ***Prod*** Harry Joe Brown (assoc.) ***Scr*** Kathryn Scola, Lamar Trotti ***Ph*** Peverell Marley ***Ed*** Barbara McLean ***Mus*** Alfred Newman (dir.) ***Art*** Bernard Herzbrun, Boris Leven
Act Tyrone Power, Alice Faye, Don Ameche, Ethel Merman, Jack Haley, Jean Hersholt (20th Century-Fox)

Irving Berlin's *Alexander's Ragtime Band* is a grand filmusical that stirs and thrills, a medley of more than 30 pieces, selected from some 600 that Berlin has composed.

Although the story opens back in 1911, the narrative moves swiftly through the years. None of the characters ages a single gray hair in 25 years.

Richard Sherman conceived the story idea with a central figure, a San Francisco bandmaster who adopts the name of Alexander. It is strictly fiction with only slight similarity to the Berlin biog. The screenplay is a fine piece of work in its subtle and logical inclusions of the Berlin ballads. Henry King directs with humor and sentiment, letting loose with an occasional broadside of mass movement.

Berlin supervised the musical angles and, in addition, tossed off three new numbers, "Now It Can Be Told," "My Walking Stick" and "Marching Along with Time."

In the foreground are Tyrone Power, as Alexander; Alice Faye; and Don Ameche, who carries most of the story with an occasional song number of his own. Cast is heavy with featured names. Although Ethel Merman is a late entry into the proceedings, she sings and acts excellently. Jack Haley shows advantageously in comedy.

1938: Best Score (Alfred Newman)

NOMINATIONS: Best Picture, Original Story (Irving Berlin), Art Direction, Editing, Song ("Now It Can Be Told")

•

ALEXANDER THE GREAT
1956, 143 mins, US Ⓥ ▭ col
Dir Robert Rossen ***Prod*** Robert Rossen ***Scr*** Robert Rossen ***Ph*** Robert Krasker ***Ed*** Ralph Kemplen ***Mus*** Mario Nascimbene ***Art*** Andre Andrejew
Act Richard Burton, Fredric March, Claire Bloom, Danielle Darrieux, Harry Andrews, Stanley Baker (Rossen/United Artists)

It took Alexander the Great some 10 years to conquer the known world back in the fourth century B.C. It seems to take Robert Rossen almost as long to recreate on film this slice of history. Despite the length, however, he has fashioned a spectacle of tremendous size.

Written, produced and directed by Rossen, the presentation is neither niggardly in the coin lavished on its physical makeup nor in the outlay for the talented international cast that enacts the historical saga of a man who believed both that he was a god and in his destiny to unite the world.

Rossen is not always able to hold interest in his story and action, resulting in some long, dull stretches.

Nor do the players have much chance to be more than puppets against the giant sweep of the spectacle. There are a number of single scenes that give the individual characters a chance to grow.

Alexander's romance with Barsine (Claire Bloom) is more implied than realized, but she does have some fine, expressive moments.

•

ALEX IN WONDERLAND
1970, 110 mins, US col
Dir Paul Mazursky ***Prod*** Larry Tucker ***Scr*** Paul Mazursky ***Ph*** Laszlo Kovacs ***Ed*** Stuart H. Pappe ***Mus*** Tom O'Horgan ***Art*** Pato Guzman
Act Donald Sutherland, Ellen Burstyn, Meg Mazursky, Glenna Sargent, Viola Spolin, Federico Fellini (M-G-M)

This fictional account of the personal and professional travails of a hotshot film director, played by Donald Sutherland, is partly admirable, partly realized, but also partly dull and somewhat deja vu to boot.

Sutherland is brought to a big studio after what must be presumed to be the sort of flop d'estime that has uncovered many a real-life counterpart. With wife, played superbly by Ellen Burstyn, and children, Meg Mazursky and Glenna Sargent, Sutherland attempts to retain his integrity amid the trappings of fame and too-expensive Beverly Hills living accommodations.

Shortly into the film, however, Sutherland's character becomes as secondary as the various vignettes become all-too-overpowering. Perhaps Sutherland's man never had much to begin with.

•

ALFIE
1966, 113 mins, UK Ⓥ ▭ col
Dir Lewis Gilbert ***Prod*** Lewis Gilbert ***Scr*** Bill Naughton ***Ph*** Otto Heller ***Ed*** Thelma Connell ***Mus*** Sonny Rollins ***Art*** Peter Mullins
Act Michael Caine, Shelley Winters, Vivien Merchant, Millicent Martin, Julia Foster, Jane Asher (Sheldrake)

Alfie pulls few punches. With Michael Caine giving a powerfully strong performance as the woman-mad anti-hero, and with dialog and situations that are humorous, tangy, raw and, ultimately, often moving, the film may well shock. But behind its alley-cat philosophy, there's some shrewd sense, some pointed barbs and a sharp moral.

One of the biggest chances that the film takes is in its frequent use of the direct speech approach to the audience. This does not always come off in the picture as well as it used to do with Groucho in the old Marx Bros films. But the device served well enough in Bill Naughton's play, and does here.

Story concerns a glib, cynical young Cockney whose passion in life is chasing dames of all shapes, sizes, and dispositions, providing they are accommodating. The film traces the promiscuous path of this energetic young amoralist as he flits from one to the other without finding much lasting pleasure. In fact, he finishes up as a somewhat jaded, cut-price Lothario, disillusioned but still on the chase.

Caine brings persuasiveness, and a sardonic, thoroughly shabby and humorous charm to the role. The two best performances among the women come from Julia Foster, becomingly wistful throughout, and Vivien Merchant as the married woman who suffers an abortion.

1966: NOMINATIONS: Best Picture, Actor (Michael Caine), Supp. Actress (Vivien Merchant), Screenplay, Song ("Alfie")

•

ALFRED THE GREAT
1969, 122 mins, UK Ⓥ ▭ col
Dir Clive Donner ***Prod*** Bernard Smith, James R. Webb ***Scr*** Ken Taylor, James R. Webb ***Ph*** Alex Thomson ***Ed*** Fergus McDonell ***Mus*** Raymond Leppard ***Art*** Michael Stringer
Act David Hemmings, Michael York, Prunella Ransome, Colin Blakely, Julian Glover, Ian McKellen (M-G-M)

Idea was to show that Alfred, Prince of Wessex, who became the first and only British King to be called "Great," was not just a guy who burned the cakes.

He was the man who wanted to be a priest and only became a warrior against his will. He "invented" the British Navy. He raised the standards of education and brought new laws to his subjects. But most of these facts have gotten lost in heavy-handed script.

Result is a film that hasn't the power or the passion to be a lavish historical film saga. Hints of the man's personality are given but they are sandwiched between two or three well staged hand-to-hand battles between Alfred's troops and the marauding Danes.

David Hemmings plays the title role with intelligence, and does his best to suggest the inner complexities of the man, but he is underage for the role and rarely matches the stature of the man he is portraying.

•

ALGIERS
1938, 93 mins, US Ⓥ b/w
Dir John Cromwell ***Prod*** Walter Wanger ***Scr*** John Howard Lawson, James M. Cain ***Ph*** James Wong Howe ***Ed*** Otho Lovering, William Reynolds ***Mus*** Vincent Scott, Mohammed Igorbouchen ***Art*** Alexander Toluboff
Act Charles Boyer, Hedy Lamarr, Sigrid Gurie, Joseph Calleia, Gene Lockhart, Alan Haleei (Wanger/United Artists)

Charles Boyer creates an interesting portrait of a continental gangster, jewel thief and tough guy in *Algiers*. Other meritorious aspects include John Cromwell's direction and the first appearance in an American-made film of Hedy Lamarr, the alluring natatorial star of the much-censored *Ecstasy*.

Film is a remake of *Pepe le Moko* (1937), a French picture directed by Julien Duvivier in which Jean Gabin starred. Wanger purchased the world rights, retired the prints from the domestic field, and assigned John Howard Lawson to write the English adaptation.

Boyer is a Parisian youth who is hunted by police and finally located in the native section of Algiers. So long as he stays within the prescribed area and lives and moves among the natives, without attempting escape to the European section, he is allowed his liberty. Police informants report his whereabouts; an inspector of detectives is his confidante; yet he dares not show himself outside.

At this juncture Boyer meets Lamarr, a beautiful Parisian girl who falls madly in love with him. She cannot remain in the restricted section; to possess her he must escape and return to Paris.

In performances by a fine cast, Lamarr comes next to Boyer in a photo finish. On the side of the unrelenting police is Joseph Calleia, as the inspector. Gene Lockhart is a stand-out as one of the informers.

1938: NOMINATIONS: Best Actor (Charles Boyer), Supp. Actor (Gene Lockhart), Cinematography, Art Direction

•

ALI
SEE: ANGST ESSEN SEELE AUF

•

ALIBI
1929, 90 mins, US b/w
Dir Roland West ***Prod*** Roland West ***Scr*** Roland West, C. Gardner Sullivan ***Ph*** Ray June ***Mus*** Hugo Riesenfeld

Act Chester Morris, Harry Stubbs, Mae Busch, Eleanor Griffith, Irma Harrison, Regis Toomey (United Artists/Roland West)

Jolt-packed crook melodrama in dialog. Lots of reliable excitement, deluxe production values and general audience satisfaction.

From the human interest standpoint picture belongs to Chester Morris, virile stage juvenile. In this picture he is a cruel, cold-blooded gangster.

Alibi starts out to give the cops the losing end of an expository tract on brutality. It winds up by hinting that the gendarmes have to be tough. Morris impersonates a clever young rodent with the instincts of a Chinese brigand. Picture is dedicated to the proposition that the man with a gun is a dirty name to start with.

There are loose ends and desultory passages in *Alibi*, but in general it has tempo and is punched with some gripping sequences. Police atmosphere and detail have realism and the ring of authenticity.

Roland West is the only entirely independent producer releasing through United Artists. He can sleep in peace in the security that his investment is safe and his picture there.

1928/29: NOMINATIONS: Best Picture, Actor (Chester Morris)

•

ALICE

1990, 106 mins, US Ⓥ col

Dir Woody Allen ***Prod*** Robert Greenhut ***Scr*** Woody Allen ***Ph*** Carlo Di Palma ***Ed*** Susan E. Morse ***Art*** Santo Loquasto

Act Mia Farrow, Joe Mantegna, Alec Baldwin, Blythe Danner, Judy Davis, William Hurt (Orion)

If *Stardust Memories* was Woody Allen's *8½* and *Radio Days* his *Amarcord*, then *Alice* is his *Juliet of the Spirits*. It's a subtler, gentler retelling of Federico Fellini's tale of a pampered but unappreciated housewife who learns to shed her illusions by giving in to her fantasies. In quick, hilarious strokes, Allen introduces Alice (Mia Farrow), who's been married 16 years to ultra-successful businessman (William Hurt). Though her deepest daily concerns are gossip, decorators, fitness trainers, Bergdorf Goodman and pedicures, she feels a kinship with Mother Theresa.

But sudden fantasies about a divorced father (Joe Mantegna) at her kids' school and a trip to an unorthodox herbalist-acupuncturist (Keye Luke) set off a chain of sexual, mystical, frequently comic events.

Performances are strong all around, with a succession of top actors making the most of their brief turns. Alec Baldwin is Farrow's first love, who turns up in a surprising way; Bernadette Peters does some of her best film work in about two minutes on screen; Luke is the gruff-voiced, chain-smoking healer; and Gwen Verdon and Blythe Danner are Farrow's mom and sister, respectively. But the center of the pic is Farrow, who's funny and touching.

1990: NOMINATION: Best Original Screenplay

•

ALICE ADAMS

1935, 95 mins, US Ⓥ ⦿ b/w

Dir George Stevens ***Prod*** Pandro S. Berman ***Scr*** Dorothy Yost, Mortimer Offner, Jane Murfin ***Ph*** Robert De Grasse ***Ed*** [uncredited] ***Mus*** Roy Webb (dir.) ***Art*** Van Nest Polglase, Perry Ferguson

Act Katharine Hepburn, Fred MacMurray, Fred Stone, Evelyn Venable, Frank Albertson, Ann Shoemaker (RKO)

Translating Booth Tarkington's sometimes poignant and pathetic 1921 novel of the pretending, wistful Alice, whose economic background almost proves too much of a hurdle to surmount, must have been a yeoman task. That George Stevens's direction captures the wistfulness of Katharine Hepburn's superb histrionism, and yet has not sacrificed audience values at the altar of too much drabness and prosaic realism, is an achievement of no small order.

The star's own performance is uncompromising and unvacillating. If she's a silly little ninny in her pretenses and simple pretexts, she is permitted to run almost berserk on the petty inanities of small-town aspirations.

Ann Shoemaker, as the ambitious but firm and understanding mother, is effective contrast to Fred Stone's cinematic debut performance as the thankful-for-small-favors head of the Adams household.

Likewise, good taste in Evelyn Venable's rich girl's aspirant for Fred MacMurray, principal juve, is shown in not toughening up the role unnecessarily.

1935: NOMINATIONS: Best Picture, Actress (Katharine Hepburn)

•

ALICE DOESN'T LIVE HERE ANYMORE

1974, 112 mins, US Ⓥ ⦿ col

Dir Martin Scorsese ***Prod*** David Susskind, Audrey Maas ***Scr*** Robert Getchell ***Ph*** Kent L. Wakeford ***Ed*** Marcia Lucas ***Mus*** Richard LaSalle ***Art*** Toby Carr Rafelson

Act Ellen Burstyn, Kris Kristofferson, Billy Green Bush, Diane Ladd, Lelia Goldoni, Harvey Keitel (Warner)

Alice Doesn't Live Here Anymore takes a group of well-cast film players and largely wastes them on a smaller-than-life film—one of those "little people" dramas that make one despise little people.

Script establishes Ellen Burstyn as the lovingly slovenly wife of Billy Green Bush, who gets killed near their New Mexico tract home. Burstyn decides to return to her long-ago Monterey origins.

Burstyn's young fatherless child is played to excruciating repulsiveness by Alfred Lutter. The pair wander westward through the story. Burstyn resumes her singing career as a saloon entertainer, then a waitress, as assorted minor characters come and go.

Eventually, just over an hour into the proceedings, enter Kris Kristofferson. The last half of the film is, indeed, a picture; but as a whole it's a distended bore.

1974: Best Actress (Ellen Burstyn)

NOMINATIONS: Best Supp. Actress (Diane Ladd), Original Screenplay

•

ALICE IN WONDERLAND

1951, 74 mins, US Ⓥ ⦿ col

Dir Clyde Geronimi, Hamilton Luske, Wilfred Jackson ***Prod*** Ben Sharpsteen (sup.) ***Scr*** Winston Hibler, Bill Peet, Joe Rinaldi, Bill Cottrell, Joe Grant, Del Connell, Ted Sears, Erdman Penner, Milt Banta, Dick Kelsey, Dick Huemer, Tom Oreb, John Walbridge ***Ed*** Lloyd Richardson ***Mus*** Oliver Wallace (Walt Disney)

Walt Disney has gone a long way toward tightening the leisurely, haphazard adventure of Alice in the wonderland of her imagination. He has dropped some characters and sequences in the interest of a better picture, but the deletions are not missed.

The Mad Hatter, the March Hare, the Caterpillar, the Cheshire Cat, Tweedle Dee and Tweedle Dum, the White Rabbit, the Walrus and the Carpenter, the Queen of Hearts and other remembered characters are enchantingly projected as Alice strolls through her dream world to the accompaniment of ballads and musical nonsense.

Young Kathryn Beaumont enchants as the voice of Alice, Ed Wynn (Mad Hatter), Jerry Colonna (March Hare), Richard Haydn (Caterpillar—a particular standout in his smoke-ring alphabet scene with Alice), Sterling Holloway (Cheshire Cat), Bill Thompson (White Rabbit), Pat O'Malley (Tweedle Twins) and Verna Felton (Queen of Hearts) are among those whose tonal tricks help sell the pen-and-ink people.

1951: NOMINATION: Scoring of a Musical Picture

•

ALICE'S ADVENTURES IN WONDERLAND

1972, 96 mins, UK Ⓥ ▭ col

Dir William Sterling ***Prod*** Derek Horne ***Scr*** William Sterling ***Ph*** Geoffrey Unsworth ***Ed*** Peter Weatherley ***Mus*** John Barry ***Art*** Michael Stringer

Act Fiona Fullerton, Michael Crawford, Ralph Richardson, Flora Robson, Peter Sellers, Robert Helpmann (Fox-Rank)

Alice's Adventures in Wonderland, from the Lewis Carroll classic, is a major disappointment. Superior stylistic settings and often terrific process effects are largely wasted by the limp, lifeless pacing of adapter-director William Sterling.

The secret of family-film conception is providing interest to all age groups. Some such films forget teenagers and adults in favor of catering strictly to moppets. This film largely forgets all audience segments in favor of static tableaux and one-two-three-kick direction, and even the John Barry–Don Black score of 16 tunes is confined to key largo.

Fiona Fullerton is a pleasantly bland Alice as are all other players. The film just lies there, and dies there, for 96 minutes.

•

ALICE'S RESTAURANT

1969, 111 mins, US Ⓥ ▭ col

Dir Arthur Penn ***Prod*** Hillard Elkins, Joe Manduke ***Scr*** Venable Herndon, Arthur Penn ***Ph*** Michael Nebbia ***Ed*** Dede Allen ***Mus*** Arlo Guthrie, Garry Sherman (sup.), Fred Hellerman (dir.) ***Art*** Warren Clymer

Act Arlo Guthrie, Pat Quinn, James Broderick, Michael McClanathan, Geoff Outlaw, Tina Chen (United Artists/Florin)

Alice's Restaurant is the phantasmagorical account of the misadventures of a young folk singer in his brushes with the law and his draft board. Based on folk singer Arlo Guthrie's 18-minute, 20-second hit recording, "The Alice's Restaurant Massacree," in which he limned some of his real-life experiences, the whole is a rather weird collection of episodes losely strung together. There are occasional flashes of wry humor and some rib-tickling sequences. But they are all too few.

The opening sequences particularly are too wispily contrived to rivet full attention, their sole purpose seemingly to introduce Arlo as a very odd fellow indeed. Plotline is virtually nil. Some of the acting is very good, but Arlo's performance is of the uncertain type and he appears to be living in a world of his own.

1969: NOMINATION: Best Director

•

ALIEN

1979, 124 mins, US Ⓥ ⦿ ▭ col

Dir Ridley Scott ***Prod*** Gordon Carroll, David Giler, Walter Hill ***Scr*** Dan O'Bannon ***Ph*** Derek Vanlint ***Ed*** Terry Rawlings ***Mus*** Jerry Goldsmith ***Art*** Michael Seymour

Act Tom Skerritt, Sigourney Weaver, Veronica Cartwright, Harry Dean Stanton, John Hurt, Ian Holm (20th Century-Fox/Brandywine)

Plainly put, *Alien* is an old-fashioned scary movie set in a highly realistic sci-fi future, made all the more believable by expert technical craftmanship. Picture isn't quite good enough to be a combination of *The Exorcist* and *Star Wars*, but both titles are likely to come to mind.

Script [from a story by Dan O'Bannon and Ronald Shusett] has more loose ends than the Pittsburgh Steelers but that doesn't matter as director Ridley Scott, cameraman Derek Vanlint and composer Jerry Goldsmith propel the emotions relentlessly from one visual surprise—and horror—to the next. [Plot has several parallels with the 1958 lowbudgeter *It! The Terror from Beyond Space*.]

The price paid for the excitement, and it's a small one, is very little involvement with the characters themselves. But it really doesn't matter when the screaming starts. In contrast to the glamorous, adventurous outerspace life often depicted in sci-fi, *Alien* initially presents a mundane commercial spacecraft with crew members like Yaphet Kotto bitching and moaning about wages and working conditions.

The tedium is shared by Captain Tom Skerritt, his aide Sigourney Weaver and the rest of the crew, played by a generally good cast in cardboard roles. Eventually, it will be Weaver who gets the biggest chance in her film debut, and she carries it off well.

Since they were doomed to get an R rating for gore, anyway, the filmmakers have thrown in some 20th-century swearing for Weaver, which seems odd and awkward in the context, plus a bit of a skin show that's fetching but a little far-fetched.

[In 1992, a *Collector's Edition* on laserdisc included 18 mins of discarded scenes among its supplementary materials.]

1979: Best Visual Effects

NOMINATION: Best Art Direction

•

ALIEN NATION

1988, 94 mins, US Ⓥ ⦿ ▭ col

Dir Graham Baker ***Prod*** Gale Anne Hurd, Richard Kobritz ***Scr*** Rockne S. O'Bannon ***Ph*** Adam Greenberg ***Ed*** Kent Beyda, Don Brochu ***Mus*** Curt Sobel ***Art*** Jack T. Collis

Act James Caan, Mandy Patinkin, Terence Stamp, Kevyn Major Howard, Leslie Bevis, Peter Jason (20th Century-Fox)

Solid performances by leads James Caan and his humanoid buddy-cop partner Mandy Patinkin move this production beyond special effects, clever alien makeup and car chases. A whole culture of aliens, called "newcomers," land in the Mojave desert in the 1990s and are allowed refuge by the U.S. government as if they were Salvadorans or Vietnamese boat people. Some are good, decent upstanding citizen types, others are just the opposite. They find America a land of ideological confusion. Americans speak of equality yet aren't consistent when it comes to acting on those beliefs.

Pic is handled by British director Graham Baker on a slightly more serious than comic book level. There's a lot of violence and noise in this futuristic adaptation of a drug pusher story, but also a compelling human-humanoid drama. Pic doesn't quite sustain a heart-pounding, eerie tone throughout.

●

ALIEN RESURRECTION

1997, 108 mins, US Ⓥ ⊙ ▭ col

Dir Jean-Pierre Jeunet ***Prod*** Bill Badalato, Gordon Carroll, David Giler, Walter Hill ***Scr*** Joss Whedon ***Ph*** Darius Khondji ***Ed*** Herve Schneid ***Mus*** John Frizzell ***Art*** Nigel Phelps

Act Sigourney Weaver, Winona Ryder, Ron Perlman, Dominique Pinon, Michael Wincott, Dan Hedaya (Brandywine/20th Century-Fox)

Tiptoeing into weird Freudian areas and moments of grotesquerie new even to this series, *Alien Resurrection*, the fourth entry in Fox's almost 20-year-old franchise, is a generally cold, though sometimes wildly imaginative and surprisingly jokey, $70 million scarefest held back by a lack of emotional engagement at its center and a pottage of half-assimilated, European-flavored quirks.

Jean-Pierre Jeunet (the more directorial half of the duo behind *Delicatessen* and *The City of Lost Children*), scripter Joss Whedon and an ace visual team have appropriated elements from all three previous pics while giving some a fresh spin.

On board the United Systems Military's colossal *Auriga* spaceship, led by obsessive Gen. Perez (Dan Hedaya), is Ellen Ripley (Sigourney Weaver), from whose chest surgeons delicately remove a baby alien Queen. It's 200 years on from *Alien³*, and the USM plans to raise tame aliens for some nefarious purpose. Ripley was cloned from preserved blood samples in order to birth the Queen with which she was impregnated in the last picture. Since alien DNA also was in the cloning process, Perez would like to see her disposed of.

Then arrives the *Betty*, a grungy commercial freighter crewed by six hardnosed mercenaries, including its captain (Michael Wincott), a grunt (Ron Perlman) and junior mechanic Call (Winona Ryder), who hides a secret or two. As soon as the crew have delivered their load—alien eggs with human hosts attached—things start to go wrong, the aliens break out of captivity, and it becomes clear the Queen has been a busy bee breeding.

Only a half-hour in, the storyline settles into a more or less straightforward escape drama as Ripley and the mercenaries try to reach the *Betty*. Movie is frequently gripping and always highly watchable, but its interest in Ripley's split, half-human personality and her maternal bond with the Queen leads to some of the most intriguing—and cheesiest—stuff in the picture.

It's almost as if the pic is afraid to enter the darkened rooms whose doors it keeps opening, though if it had, a truly original movie could have resulted. Pic is the first to be shot on U.S. stages rather than in the U.K. and effects (done in California and Paris) are tip-top.

●

ALIENS

1986, 137 mins, US Ⓥ ⊙ col

Dir James Cameron ***Prod*** Gale Anne Hurd ***Scr*** James Cameron ***Ph*** Adrian Biddle ***Ed*** Ray Lovejoy ***Mus*** James Horner ***Art*** Peter Lamont

Act Sigourney Weaver, Carrie Henn, Michael Biehn, Lance Henriksen, Paul Reiser, Jenette Goldstein (20th Century-Fox/Brandywine)

Aliens proves a very worthy follow-up to Ridley Scott's 1979 sci-fi shocker, *Alien*. James Cameron's vault into the big-time after scoring with the exploitation actioner *The Terminator* makes up for lack of surprise with sheer volume of thrills and chills—emphasis is decidedly on the plural aspect of the title.

Cameron [working from a story by him, David Giler and Walter Hill] picks up the thread 57 years later, when Sigourney Weaver and her cat (who have been in hibernation) are rescued by a deep-space salvage team. The authorities ask her to accompany a team of marines back to the planet to investigate why all contact with the colony has suddenly been lost. Group sent this time consists of a bunch of tough grunts with a sour attitude about having been sent on such a dippy mission.

Weaver finds one human survivor on the planet—a cute, tough, terrified little girl played by Carrie Henn.

The odds against the crew are, in a word, monstrous, and unsurprisingly, its members are dispatched one by one until it once again comes down to a battle royal between Weaver and one last monster.

Although film accomplishes everything it aims to do, overall impression is of a film made by an expert craftsman, while Scott clearly had something of an artist in him.

Weaver does a smashing job as Ripley. Henn is very appealing as the little girl and Jenette Goldstein makes a striking impression as a body-building recruit who is tougher than any of the guys in the outfit.

[A 1992 video release, with the handle *Special Edition*, featured an extra 17 mins of footage.]

1986: Best Visual Effects, Sound Effects Editing

NOMINATIONS: Best Actress (Sigourney Weaver), Art Direction, Editing, Original Music Score, Sound

●

ALIEN³

1992, 115 mins, US Ⓥ ⊙ ▭ col

Dir David Fincher ***Prod*** Gordon Carroll, David Giler, Walter Hill ***Scr*** David Giler, Walter Hill, Larry Ferguson ***Ph*** Alex Thomson ***Ed*** Terry Rawlings ***Mus*** Elliot Goldenthal ***Art*** Norman Reynolds

Act Sigourney Weaver, Charles S. Dutton, Charles Dance, Paul McGann, Brian Glover, Ralph Brown (20th Century-Fox/Brandywine)

The shape-shifting *Alien* trilogy reverts back to the form of the first film in this third close encounter, a muddled effort offering little more than visual splendor to recommend it.

The action picks up in the opening credits where *Aliens* left off, as Ripley's hibernation pod crash-lands on a grim, all-male penal colony planet. It seems an alien egg was still on the shuttle (how is anybody's guess). In any event, Ripley (Weaver) finds herself stranded on a planet with a bunch of converted convicts who've embraced religion, led by Charles S. Dutton. The colony's kindly doctor (Charles Dance), with whom Ripley shares another kind of close encounter, suspects something is wrong.

Musicvideo director David Fincher doesn't reveal much finesse with actors in his big-screen debut, and the screenplay [based on a story by Vincent Ward, who was originally to have directed] proves fraught with lapses in reason, motivation and logic. Weaver's character is so encumbered with baggage that she can't really showcase the qualities (particularly evident in the second film) that made the audience empathize with her.

1992: NOMINATION: Best Visual Effects

●

ALIVE

1993, 127 mins, US Ⓥ ⊙ col

Dir Frank Marshall ***Prod*** Robert Watts, Kathleen Kennedy ***Scr*** John Patrick Shanley ***Ph*** Peter James ***Ed*** Michael Kahn, William Goldenberg ***Mus*** James Newton Howard ***Art*** Norman Reynolds

Act Ethan Hawke, Vincent Spano, Josh Hamilton, Bruce Ramsay, John Haymes Newton, David Kriegel (Touchstone/Paramount)

Producer-turned-director Frank Marshall and producer-partner-spouse Kathleen Kennedy have chosen the true story (already told by 1976 Par release *Survive!*) of a 1970s plane crash in which the survivors, a rugby team, held on for more than two months in the subfreezing Andes largely by eating the corpses of the victims.

Marshall and writer John Patrick Shanley [adapting Piers Paul Read's book] deal with the topic seriously, exploring the survivors desperation as well as their reluctance, down to an ethical debate prior to the initial meal, to engage in cannibalism.

It doesn't help that character personalities generally aren't distinct enough to keep track of who's who throughout the story, leaving the audience to empathize only generally. Heightening the problem is a strong resemblance among actors, including leads Ethan Hawke and Josh Hamilton.

For all its action elements, *Alive* also puts on some rather pretentious airs, among them a musical coda of *Ave Maria* and bookending an uncredited John Malkovich as one of the survivors, 20 years later.

●

ALL ABOUT EVE

1950, 138 mins, US Ⓥ ⊙ b/w

Dir Joseph L. Mankiewicz ***Prod*** Darryl F. Zanuck ***Scr*** Joseph L. Mankiewicz ***Ph*** Milton Krasner ***Ed*** Barbara McLean ***Mus*** Alfred Newman ***Art*** Lyle Wheeler, George Davis

Act Bette Davis, Anne Baxter, George Sanders, Celeste Holm, Gary Merrill, Thelma Ritter (20th Century-Fox)

Anne Baxter, in the title role, is the radiant newcomer who has attained the thespic heights. And as she mounts the podium to receive the supreme accolade, the intimates who figured in her breathless success story project their own vignettes on what made this hammy glammy run.

Baxter plays a starry-eyed would-be actress who, by extraordinary design, finally meets Bette Davis, her histrionic idol (through the kind offices of Celeste Holm). She is taken into the household, machinates an understudy chore—and in return is ruthless in her pitch for both the beau and the husband of the two women who most befriended her.

The basic story is garnished with exceedingly well-cast performances wherein Davis does not spare herself, makeup-wise, in the aging star assignment. Baxter gives the proper shading to her cool and calculating approach in the process of ingratiation and ultimate opportunities.

Backgrounding are Gregory Ratoff, as the producer, and George Sanders as the debonair, machiavellian dramatic critic who knows the angles—plus.

It is obvious author-director Joe Mankiewicz knew what he wanted his cast to say and how he wanted them to interpret it.

1950: Best Picture, Director, Supp. Actor (George Sanders), Screenplay, Sound Recording, B&W Costume Design

NOMINATIONS: Best Actress (Anne Baxter, Bette Davis), Supp. Actress (Celeste Holm, Thelma Ritter), B&W Cinematography, Art Direction, Editing, Original Music Score

●

ALL ABOUT MY MOTHER

SEE: TODO SOBRE MI MADRE

●

ALLAN QUATERMAIN AND THE LOST CITY OF GOLD

1987, 99 mins, US Ⓥ ⊙ ▭ col

Dir Gary Nelson, Newt Arnold ***Prod*** Menahem Golan, Yoram Globus ***Scr*** Gene Quintano ***Ph*** Alex Phillips, Frederick Elmes ***Ed*** Alain Jakubowicz ***Mus*** Michael Linn [Jerry Goldsmith] ***Art*** Trevor Williams, Leslie Dilley

Act Richard Chamberlain, Sharon Stone, James Earl Jones, Henry Silva, Robert Donner, Aileen Marson (Cannon)

Pic is a remake of Harry Alan Towers's 1977 film *King Solomon's Treasure*, which starred John Colicos as H. Rider Haggard's adventure hero Allan Quatermain (from the book by that name).

Embarrassing screenplay jettisons Haggard's enduring fantasy and myth-making in favor of a back-of-the-envelope plotline and anachronistic jokes about Cleveland. Quatermain (Richard Chamberlain) receives a gold piece from a dying man that inspires him to trek to East Africa in search of his brother Robeson (Martin Rabbett). Joining him are his archeologist girlfriend (Sharon Stone) and African warrior (James Earl Jones), a comic relief mystic (Robert Donner camping it up) and five expendable bearers.

After considerable filler, they find the lost race of Phoenicians, ruled by bland beauty-contest queen Nyleptha (Aileen Marson).

A poor followup to the same producers' 1985 *King Solomon's Mines*, film relies frequently on a very phony gimmick of a spear-proof tunic and story completely runs out of gas once the heroes arrive at their destination.

●

ALL FALL DOWN

1962, 111 mins, US b/w

Dir John Frankenheimer ***Prod*** John Houseman ***Scr*** William Inge ***Ph*** Lionel Lindon ***Ed*** Fredric Steinkamp ***Mus*** Alex North ***Art*** George W. Davis, Preston Ames

Act Eva Marie Saint, Warren Beatty, Karl Malden, Angela Lansbury, Brandon de Wilde (M-G-M)

Within John Houseman's production of *All Fall Down* there are some truly memorable passages—moments and scenes of great pith, poignance, truth and sensitivity. How disheartening it is, then, that the sum total is an artfully produced, cinematically rich, historically noteworthy, dramatically uneven near-miss.

A 16-year-old boy (Brandon de Wilde), who idolizes his emotionally unstable older brother (Warren Beatty), is the pivotal figure in William Inge's screenplay based on James Leo Herlihy's novel. The important issue is that the adolescent matures into a decent young man. But his path to maturity is threatened by his adulation for this brother, a selfish, irrational free spirit who survives on odd jobs and loose women. When the older boy proceeds to destroy a young spinster (Eva Marie Saint), whom de Wilde adores in a hopeless, adolescent fashion, the latter has his moment of reckoning.

Angela Lansbury and Karl Malden, as the tragicomic elders, create indelible, dimensional and deeply affecting people.

●

ALL I DESIRE
1953, 79 mins, US b/w
Dir Douglas Sirk *Prod* Ross Hunter *Scr* James Gunn, Robert Blees *Ph* Carl Guthrie *Ed* Milton Carruth *Mus* Joseph Gershenson *Art* Bernard Herzbrun, Alexander Golitzen
Act Barbara Stanwyck, Richard Carlson, Lyle Bettger, Marcia Henderson, Maureen O'Sullivan, Lori Nelson (Universal)

Plot [from the novel *Stopover* by Carol Brink, adapted by Gina Kaus] concerns the return of a mother to the family she ran away from 10 years previously for a fling at the stage. Homecoming is to see her daughter in the high school graduation play, but, secretly, the mother hopes for a reconciliation. Things are moving to this end, until the small-town lothario, who had figured in her previous flight, tries to renew the affair.

The Ross Hunter production and Douglas Sirk's direction pull all stops to make the picture a 79-minute excursion into sentimentality. With help of Barbara Stanwyck's performance, the soap-operish tear-jerking is palatable. Richard Carlson plays the stiff-necked husband character straight to make it acceptable. Lyle Bettger is sadly misused as the former lover. Maureen O'Sullivan does what she can with the role of a school teacher hopelessly in love with Carlson.

•

ALLIGATOR
1980, 94 mins, US Ⓥ col
Dir Lewis Teague *Prod* Brandon Chase *Scr* John Sayles *Ph* Joseph Mangine *Ed* Larry Bock, Ronald Medico *Mus* Craig Hundley *Art* Michael Erler
Act Robert Forster, Robin Riker, Michael Gazzo, Dean Jagger, Henry Silva, Jack Carter (Group 1)

Alligator is bloody and boisterous, featuring the only maneating monster in memory named Ramone.

First seen, Ramone is a little baby alligator on a reptile farm in Florida, soon to be bought as a pet and taken to Missouri by sweet little Marisa. Bud dad gets mad and dumps Ramone down the toilet.

Fast forward 12 years and Marisa (Robin Riker) has grown up to be a world-famous herpatologist, while down below in the sewer Ramone has grown up unnoticed to be a 36-foot, one-ton, mean-tempered alligator.

Ramone developed his size and personality eating dead dogs thrown into the sewer by a chemical company experimenting on them in search of growth-inducing hormones. Ultimately tired of dog meat, the alligator starts to eat sewer workers and pet-store owners and policemen and finally a newspaper reporter.

Dumb as it is, director Lewis Teague brings some plusses to the pic. Robert Forster, as a detective, and Riker are amiable leads, never taking the film too seriously. Tech credits are cheap but serviceable. Exploitation fans will be glad to see Sue Lyon and Angel Tompkins, cameoed as news reporters.

•

ALL MY SONS
1948, 98 mins, US b/w
Dir Irving Reis *Prod* Chester Erskine *Scr* Chester Erskine *Ph* Russell Metty *Ed* Ralph Dawson *Mus* Leith Stevens *Art* Bernard Herzbrun, Hilyard Brown
Act Edward G. Robinson, Burt Lancaster, Mady Christians, Howard Duff, Louisa Horton, Arlene Francis (Universal)

All My Sons comes to the screen with a potent impact. Whatever message may have been in the stage presentation has been resolved to the more fundamental one of man's duty to man, and gains strength by that switch. It's a serious, thoughtful study, loaded with dramatic dynamite.

Chester Erskine's approach to the Arthur Miller play benefits from the broader movement permitted by the screen. It's an ace scripting and production job that carefully measures every value to be found in the plot.

Script makes the point that we all are our brothers' keepers with a responsibility that can't be shunted aside for purely personal desires. Rather than hammering the point over, it is gradually brought out in telling of a man who, in a desire for success, becomes responsible for the death of 21 fliers during the war.

Edward G. Robinson gives an effective performance as the small-town manufacturer who sends defective parts to the Army Air Forces. It's a humanized study that rates among his best and lends the thought behind the film much strength. Burt Lancaster, as his war-embittered son, shades the assignment with just the right amount of intensity. His love and belief in his dad, whom he must betray to right the wrong done, cloaks the role with that human touch that marks all of the characters.

•

ALL NIGHT LONG
1981, 88 mins, US Ⓥ col
Dir Jean-Claude Tramont *Prod* Leonard Goldberg, Jerry Weintraub *Scr* W. D. Richter *Ph* Philip Lathrop *Ed* Marion Rothman *Mus* Ira Newborn *Art* Peter Jamison
Act Gene Hackman, Barbra Streisand, Diane Ladd, Dennis Quaid, Annie Girardot, William Daniels (Universal)

A weary premise and a hackneyed theme are given some wry, offbeat twists in *All Night Long*. Film has the distinction of being one of the few—if not the only—Barbra Streisand starrers which was not designed as a vehicle for her.

Plot is the same old middle-age-blues song, with Hackman chucking his dreary job, wife and lifestyle in favor of a younger woman and new reputation as a goofy, carefree iconoclast. Familiar targets, such as uptight career businessmen, frivolous middle-class society ladies and sterile suburbia are knocked with easy precision.

With just one French feature, *Focal Point*, behind him, director Jean-Claude Tramont makes a good American debut here. Even though he has lived off-and-on in the U.S. for years, he lends an appealingly different eye to the Southern California lifestyle.

Hackman brings even more to his role than might have been apparent in the script.

Playing a clearly subordinate role, which she took over from Lisa Eichhorn shortly after lensing began, Streisand is more subdued than usual and effective as such.

•

ALL OF ME
1984, 93 mins, US Ⓥ ⦿ col
Dir Carl Reiner *Prod* Stephen Friedman *Scr* Phil Alden Robinson *Ph* Richard H. Kline *Ed* Bud Molin *Mus* Patrick Williams *Art* Edward Carfagno
Act Steve Martin, Lily Tomlin, Victoria Tennant, Madolyn Smith, Richard Libertini, Dana Elcar (Kings Road)

All of Me plays more like an old-fashioned screwball comedy than a contempo film, its premise of a woman dying and her soul inhabiting half of another person's body in the same vein as *Here Comes Mr. Jordan*. When he is not arranging divorce settlements for rich husbands, Roger Cobb (Steve Martin) is a jazz guitarist. Martin's troubles really start on his 38th birthday when he inherits the soul of departing heiress and first-rank crank Edwina Cutwater (Lily Tomlin). Circumstances under which this occurs, assisted by guru Prahka Lasa (Richard Libertini), are patently ridiculous, but acceptable because of the charm of the characters.

Screenwriter Phil Alden Robinson [working from Ed Davis's novel *Me Two*, adapted by Henry Olek] has created enough interesting situations for the Martin-Tomlin mismatch. Urinating, shaving and making love take on new proportions when a man and woman are trying to do it in the same body.

For all its clowning, *All of Me* makes some good points about taking chances and doing what you want in life. Tomlin undergoes a transformation from a crabby, sheltered, poor little rich girl to a compassionate woman. It's a measure of her performance that even as a sourpuss she's irresistible.

•

ALL QUIET ON THE WESTERN FRONT
1930, 152 mins, US Ⓥ ⦿ b/w
Dir Lewis Milestone *Prod* Carl Laemmle, Jr. *Scr* Maxwell Anderson, Del Andrews, George Abbott *Ph* Arthur Edeson, Karl Freund, Tony Gaudio *Ed* Edgar Adams, Milton Carruth *Mus* David Broekman *Art* Charles D. Hall, William R. Schmidt
Act Lew Ayres, Louis Wolheim, John Wray, Raymond Griffith, Slim Summerville, Russell Gleason (Universal)

A harrowing, gruesome, morbid tale of war, compelling in its realism, bigness and repulsiveness.

Driving men and boys to their certain finish before murderous machine guns, dodging all kinds of missiles from the air, living with rats, starving while fighting, forgetting country and home, just becoming a fighting machine—that's the story and picture.

The story carries a group of German school boys, enthused by their professor's plea for fealty to country, from their training days through warfare to their deaths. In performance one might say it's due to Lewis Milestone's direction and let it go at that. But there are standout performances, even in bits. *All Quiet on the Western Front* [from the novel by Erich Maria Remarque] cost Universal $1.2 million.

1929/30: Best Picture, Director

NOMINATIONS: Best Writing, Cinematography (Arthur Edeson)

•

ALL THAT HEAVEN ALLOWS
1955, 89 mins, US col
Dir Douglas Sirk *Prod* Ross Hunter *Scr* Peg Fenwick *Ph* Russell Metty *Ed* Frank Gross *Mus* Frank Skinner *Art* Alexander Golitzen, Eric Orbom
Act Jane Wyman, Rock Hudson, Agnes Moorehead, Conrad Nagel, Virginia Grey, Gloria Talbott (Universal)

Although this story of a long-suffering woman who, at 40 or so, finds romance with a man between 10 and 15 years her junior, is hardly designed to ignite prairie fires, scripter Peg Fenwick nevertheless has managed to turn the Edna L. and Harry Lee story into a slightly offbeat yarn with some interesting overtones that accent the social prejudices of a small town.

Jane Wyman is appealing and properly long-suffering. The script makes her into a rather weak character and it's difficult, after a while, to rouse much sympathy for her plight.

Hudson is handsome and somewhat wooden. Laconic of speech, and imbued with an angel's patience and understanding, it's at times hard to understand his passion for the widow, what with pretty girls just spoiling for his attention.

Standout performance is delivered by a young newcomer, Gloria Talbott, playing Wyman's teenage daughter.

•

ALL THAT JAZZ
1979, 123 mins, US Ⓥ ⦿ col
Dir Bob Fosse *Prod* Robert Alan Aurthur *Scr* Bob Fosse, Robert Alan Aurthur *Ph* Giuseppe Rotunno *Ed* Alan Heim *Mus* Ralph Burns *Art* Philip Rosenberg
Act Roy Scheider, Jessica Lange, Ann Reinking, Cliff Gorman, John Lithgow, Erzebet Foldi (20th Century-Fox/Columbia)

All That Jazz is a self-important, egomaniacal, wonderfully choreographed, often compelling film that portrays the energetic life, and preoccupation with death, of a director-choreographer who ultimately suffers a heart attack.

The picture, reportedly based heavily on aspects of the real life of its director, Bob Fosse, deals with the director-choreographer Joe Gideon's career and his involvements with women.

Roy Scheider gives a superb performance as Gideon, creating a character filled with nervous energy. Running from project to project, the film portrays Gideon completing work on one film while working simultaneously on another project.

The film's major flaw lies in its lack of real explanation of what, beyond ego, really motivates Gideon.

1979: Best Art Direction, Adapted Score, Editing, Costume Design

NOMINATIONS: Best Picture, Director, Actor (Roy Scheider), Original Screenplay, Cinematography

•

ALL THAT MONEY CAN BUY
SEE: THE DEVIL AND DANIEL WEBSTER

•

ALL THE BROTHERS WERE VALIANT
1953, 94 mins, US Ⓥ col
Dir Richard Thorpe *Prod* Pandro S. Berman *Scr* Harry Brown *Ph* George Folsey *Ed* Ferris Webster *Mus* Miklos Rozsa *Art* Cedric Gibbons, Randall Duell
Act Robert Taylor, Stewart Granger, Ann Blyth, Betta St. John, Keenan Wynn, James Whitmore (M-G-M)

Special effects are used to advantage to spotlight the high romance of adventuring on the bounding main. Film's big moments include the excitement stirred up by the dangers of 19th-century whaling and the climactic mass battle with mutineers aboard a sailing vessel.

Directorial vigor of Richard Thorpe helps picture through its faltering spots. The latter come from shallow character development in the script [from a novel by Ben Ames Williams] and a rambling storyline. Stars Robert Taylor, Stewart Granger and Ann Blyth are competent but the people they portray haven't enough depth or reality to come robustly alive.

Taylor and Granger are brothers in a seafaring family. When Granger, the elder, disappears on a whaling voyage, Taylor takes over his ship and, with his bride (Blyth) sails off to find him. At a South Seas stopover he finds Granger who goes for his brother's bride and incites a mutiny aboard ship, which he wants to use to recover a fortune in pearls he had found during his disappearance.

1953: NOMINATION: Best Color Cinematography

•

ALL THE FINE YOUNG CANNIBALS
1960, 112 mins, US ▭ col
Dir Michael Anderson ***Prod*** Pandro S. Berman ***Scr*** Robert Thom ***Ph*** William H. Daniels ***Ed*** John McSweeney ***Mus*** Jeff Alexander ***Art*** George W. Davis, Edward Carfagno
Act Robert Wagner, Natalie Wood, Susan Kohner, George Hamilton, Pearl Bailey (M-G-M)

The handsome production surrounds a ludicrous *Modern Romances* sort of screenplay that was suggested by Rosamond Marshall's novel *The Bixby Girls*. Under scrutiny is the accelerated world of troubled youth, where a one-night stand invariably results in pregnancy, fame or attempted suicide.

More specifically, the scenario explores the affairs of two young couples, (Natalie Wood–George Hamilton and Robert Wagner–Susan Kohner) who eventually learn to live with the fact that they share a mutual tax-deduction in the form of a bouncing babe who bounced out of the premarital union of one-half of each partnership (Wagner and Wood).

Director Michael Anderson attempts to establish and link the individual personalities of the central foursome by flashing rapidly to and fro from family to family. The technique backfires in that, by attempting to take in too much too swiftly, it leaves the audience out of focus on all four individual sets of motivations.

Wood is very pleasant to behold, even though a pained expression is about all she is required to project here. Kohner is not very convincing in her efforts to appear alternately gay, bored and distressed. Even less at ease are Wagner and Hamilton in a pair of incredibly unmasculine roles. Best emoting is done by Pearl Bailey, but even she can barely cope with a preposterous role of a celebrated blues singer who dies of a broken heart when jilted by the man who played horn for her.

●

ALL THE KING'S MEN
1949, 109 mins, US Ⓥ ⦿ b/w
Dir Robert Rossen ***Prod*** Robert Rossen ***Scr*** Robert Rossen ***Ph*** Burnett Guffey ***Ed*** Al Clark, Robert Parrish ***Mus*** Louis Gruenberg ***Art*** Sturges Carne
Act Broderick Crawford, John Derek, Joanne Dru, John Ireland, Mercedes McCambridge, Shepperd Strudwick (Columbia)

The rise and fall of a backwoods political messiah, and the mark he left on the American scene, is given graphic celluloid treatment in *All the King's Men*.

Robert Rossen has produced and directed from his own script, based upon the Pulitzer Prize novel by Robert Penn Warren.

As a great man using the opinionless, follow-the-leader instinct of the more common voter, Broderick Crawford does a standout performance.

The story is told through the eyes of John Ireland, newspaperman. He becomes a devotee pursuing the Crawford career from small-time into big-time.

Joanne Dru appears to advantage as a friend of Ireland's, but the most compelling of the femme players is Mercedes McCambridge, the mistress to the great man.

1949: Best Picture, Actor (Broderick Crawford), Supp. Actress (Mercedes McCambridge)

NOMINATIONS: Best Director, Supp. Actor (John Ireland), Screenplay, Editing

●

. . . ALL THE MARBLES
1981, 113 mins, US Ⓥ col
Dir Robert Aldrich ***Prod*** William Aldrich ***Scr*** Mel Frohman ***Ph*** Joseph Biroc ***Ed*** Irving C. Rosenblum, Richard Lane ***Mus*** Frank DeVol ***Art*** Carl Anderson
Act Peter Falk, Vicki Frederick, Laurene Landon, Burt Young, Tracy Reed, Richard Jaeckel (M-G-M/Aldrich)

By any measure *Marbles* is a major disappointment, given the deft casting of Peter Falk as a seedy, selfish and demanding manager of a couple of tag-team women wrestlers (Vicki Frederick and Laurene Landon).

The lead trio does get solid help from Burt Young as a crooked promoter and John Hancock as the decent manager of the opposing team consisting of Tracy Reed and Ursaline Bryant-Young.

For some odd reason, however, director Robert Aldrich and writer Mel Frohman have chosen to portray women's wrestling as a serious sport, aiming for another *Rocky*-like climb from obscurity to triumph. It never works for a minute. Except for a busted lip occasionally and a bruise or two, Frederick and Landon are always sprightly, pretty and ready for the road again after each bout.

Though Aldrich sometimes hints of hanky-panky and collusion among the teams, he generally insists that each match is won or lost on ability alone, building the "California Dolls" up to a legitimate contest for the championship in Reno.

●

ALL THE PRESIDENT'S MEN
1976, 138 mins, US Ⓥ ⦿ col
Dir Alan J. Pakula ***Prod*** Walter Coblenz ***Scr*** William Goldman ***Ph*** Gordon Willis ***Ed*** Robert L. Wolfe ***Mus*** David Shire ***Art*** George Jenkins
Act Dustin Hoffman, Robert Redford, Jack Warden, Martin Balsam, Hal Holbrook, Jason Robards (Wildwood/Warner)

Some ingenious direction by Alan J. Pakula and scripting by William Goldman remove much of the inherent dramatic lethargy in any story of reporters running down a story.

Thus, *All the President's Men*, from the Bob Woodward and Carl Bernstein book about their experiences uncovering the Watergate coverup for *The Washington Post*, emerges close to being an American *Z*. Robert Redford and especially Dustin Hoffman excel in their starring roles.

Besides the stars, many of the featured players contribute mightily. As Deep Throat, the official who assisted the reporters in filtering out the facts, Hal Holbrook is outstanding; this actor, herein in near-total shadow, is as compelling as he is in virtually every role played. Jason Robards, as *Post* exec editor Ben Bradlee, provides an excellent characterization, backed up strongly by Jack Warden and Martin Balsam as senior editors.

1976: Best Supp. Actor (Jason Robards), Adapted Screenplay, Art Direction, Sound

NOMINATIONS: Best Picture, Director, Supp. Actress (Jane Alexander), Editing

●

ALL THE PRETTY HORSES
2000, 117 mins, US Ⓥ ⦿ ▭ col
Dir Billy Bob Thornton ***Prod*** Robert Salerno, Billy Bob Thornton ***Scr*** Ted Tally ***Ph*** Barry Markowitz ***Ed*** Sally Menke ***Mus*** Marty Stuart ***Art*** Clark Hunter
Act Matt Damon, Henry Thomas, Lucas Black, Penelope Cruz, Ruben Blades, Robert Patric (Miramax/Columbia)

All the Pretty Horses is a half-broken adaptation of Cormac McCarthy's great modern Western novel. Neither dull nor exciting, this tale of two Texas boys who get all the trouble they can handle down Mexico way boasts a faithful script that is underserved by director Billy Bob Thornton's lack of a coherent visual style and inability to catch a proper rhythm.

Young John Grady Cole (Matt Damon) and his best buddy, Lacey Rawlins (Henry Thomas), ride for Mexico, where they figure they can find work as top hands and live the life of "real cowboys" that they have always imagined was their destiny. No sooner have they set off on their trek than they run into Jimmy Blevins (Lucas Black), an uncouth but cocky 16-year-old who is riding a horse so fine they have to suspect it is stolen.

The film hopscotches from one condensed scene from the book to another, without ever sweeping one up in the journey or tapping into the mother lode of rich comedy that exists in McCarthy's brilliant dialogue, good chunks of which have been wisely retained. Splitting off from Blevins, Cole and Rawlins hire on as hands at the ranch of the aristocratic Rocha (Ruben Blades), whose saucy daughter, Alejandra (Penelope Cruz), gives Cole the eye. Pierced through the heart even after one of the most uneventful courtship scenes in memory, Cole ignores the friendship he's cemented with Rocha, the dictates of Alejandra's watchful aunt Alfonsa (Miriam Colon) and Alejandra's need to retain her reputation by bedding down with the sultry senorita. But no one can doubt that there will be a price to pay. Cole and Rawlins are hauled off to a rural jail where they encounter, of all people, Blevins, who's in for horse thieving and murder.

Damon is responsive to the physical and attitudinal demands of the leading role, but he just doesn't quite seem like a young man who's spent his life amidst the dust and dung of a Texas cattle ranch. Nor does he strike any sparks with Cruz, the dark Iberian beauty who still hasn't registered in English with the effectiveness that she does in her Spanish films. Young Black is the actor here who best captures the dialect and cadences of cowboy speech.

●

ALL THE RIGHT MOVES
1983, 91 mins, US Ⓥ ⦿ col
Dir Michael Chapman ***Prod*** Stephen Deutsch ***Scr*** Michael Kane ***Ph*** Jan De Bont ***Ed*** David Garfield ***Mus*** David Campbell ***Art*** Mary Ann Biddle
Act Tom Cruise, Craig T. Nelson, Lea Thompson, Charles Cioffi, Paul Carafotes, Christopher Penn (20th Century-Fox)

A smash directorial debut by well-known cinematographer Michael Chapman, *All the Right Moves* crackles with authenticity. The story is centered on characters fighting to get out of a dying Pennsylvania mill town to make a better life for themselves.

In a nice twist on expectations, the driven include Tom Cruise's girlfriend, sharply played by newcomer Lea Thompson, whose own aspirations take the frill out of the coed image, and the hard-nosed high school coach, superbly portrayed by Craig T. Nelson, who wants the big time as much as Cruise, his star safety.

Another welcome surprise is the touching relationship between high school senior Cruise and his father. For once, here's a pop in a redneck town who treats his son like a human being, and Charles Cioffi, however brief his screentime, conveys a durable dignity.

●

ALL THE WAY
SEE: THE JOKER IS WILD

●

ALL THIS, AND HEAVEN TOO
1940, 140 mins, US Ⓥ b/w
Dir Anatole Litvak ***Prod*** Hal B. Wallis, David Lewis ***Scr*** Casey Robinson ***Ph*** Ernest Haller ***Ed*** Warren Low ***Mus*** Max Steiner ***Art*** Carl Jules Weyl
Act Bette Davis, Charles Boyer, Jeffrey Lynn, Barbara O'Neil, Virginia Weidler, Helen Westley (Warner)

Heaven is film theatre at its best. In the two starring roles are Bette Davis, as the young French governess, Henriette Deluzy-Desportes, and Charles Boyer, projecting one of his best performances as Duc de Praslin. The tragedy of their love affair, which resulted in the murder of the Duchesse de Praslin (Barbara O'Neil), the suicide of the Duc and the subsequent glimpse of some happiness for Henriette in her marriage to the American theological student, Henry Martyn Field (Jeffrey Lynn), is strong fare, involving delicate psychological shadings and understandings.

Casey Robinson in the scripting captures the quaintness of the manners and customs of Paris in 1848, and succeeds admirably in retaining both spirit and characters of Rachel Field's novel, despite much deletion of material. Anatole Litvak's direction is outstanding. Film throughout bears the mark of earnest and expert workmanship in all departments.

There are unusually effective performances of four youthful players as the de Praslin children. Every progressive step in the story is built around these youngsters, a bit of plot unfolding that takes the film far from conventional grooves. The children roles are played with fine emotional results by Virginia Weidler, June Lockhart, Ann Todd and Richard Nichols.

As for Davis, she is off the screen during the briefest interludes. In her scenes with Boyer, she retains an outward composure that only intensifies her real feelings, never completely expressed. It is acting so restrained that a single overdrawn passage or expression would shatter the illusion.

1940 : NOMINATIONS: Best Picture, Supp. Actress (Barbara O'Neil), B&W Cinematography

●

ALL THROUGH THE NIGHT
1942, 107 mins, US Ⓥ b/w
Dir Vincent Sherman ***Prod*** Hal B. Wallis (exec.) ***Scr*** Leonard Spigelgass, Edwin Gilbert ***Ph*** Sid Hickox ***Ed*** Rudi Fehr ***Mus*** Adolph Deutsch ***Art*** Max Parker
Act Humphrey Bogart, Conrad Veidt, Kaaren Verne, Jane Darwell, Frank McHugh, Peter Lorre (Warner)

Gripping espionage meller [from a screen story by Leonard Q. Ross and Leonard Spigelgass] highlights three bad boys, with Humphrey Bogart this time working on the side of the law, order and liberty in trying to clean up a nest of Nazi spies and fifth-columnists. Two other toughies are sinister, soft-spoken Peter Lorre and immaculate, iron-fist-in-velvet-glove Nazi agent Conrad Veildt, both first-rate. Locale is New York City.

Bogart, as retired mobster turned big-time gambler, is easy to take. Protected against background of Nazi beatings and murders, U.S. gangsters look like Sunday school kids fighting over marbles. Chase and gun battle in Central Park, scraps in the warehouse district, the mystery girl in distress, emphasis on danger to American institutions from foreign conspirators add up to elementary but surefire audience appeal.

Casting is a big asset, with Jane Darwell as Bogart's mother, Frank McHugh, Judith Anderson and William Demarest prominent. Kaaren Verne, femme lead, fills the bill nicely and pleasantly warbles two songs in a nitery sequence.

●

ALMOST AN ANGEL
1990, 95 mins, US Ⓥ ⊙ ⌑ col

Dir John Cornell ***Prod*** John Cornell ***Scr*** Paul Hogan ***Ph*** Russell Boyd ***Ed*** David Stiven ***Mus*** Maurice Jarre ***Art*** Henry Bumstead

Act Paul Hogan, Elias Koteas, Linda Kozlowski, Charlton Heston, Doreen Lang, Joe Dallesandro (Paramount/Ironbark)

Almost an Angel is simply a no-effort vanity project with only Paul Hogan's easygoing charm to fill the space between the sprocket holes.

Instead of stretching his acting muscles, Hogan assigns himself the comfortable role of an electronics expert/cracksman just released from prison who turns into an inveterate do-gooder. In between bank heists, he instinctively saves a guy from a traffic accident and is himself run down.

Hospital scene has him dreaming of (or actually) floating to the clouds where uncredited guest star Charlton Heston as God reads him the riot act. He sends Hogan back to Earth for a second chance as an angel of mercy on probation.

Trekking to the small town of Fillmore, California, he sets about being kind to people. Chief recipients of his largesse are Elias Koteas, a bitter young man suffering from a terminal illness confining him to a wheelchair, and his self-sacrificing sister, Hogan's real-life wife and inevitable co-star Linda Kozlowski.

Koteas is affecting as the cripple with a chip on his shoulder. Kozlowski, styled plain with dark hair, is wasted as the mildest of romantic interests.

•

ALMOST FAMOUS
2000, 122 mins, US Ⓥ ⊙ col

Dir Cameron Crowe ***Prod*** Cameron Crowe, Ian Bryce ***Scr*** Cameron Crowe ***Ph*** John Toll ***Ed*** Joe Hutshing, Saar Klein ***Mus*** Nancy Wilson ***Art*** Clay A. Griffith, Clayton R. Hartley, Virginia Randolph-Weaver

Act Billy Crudup, Frances McDormand, Kate Hudson, Jason Lee, Patrick Fugit, Anna Paquin, Fairuza Balk (Vinyl/DreamWorks)

Almost Famous is a sweetly amiable memoir of one boy's coming of age with rock 'n' roll that's more gentle and modestly insightful than it is exhilarating or revelatory. Cameron Crowe's heartfelt, semifictionalized spin on his own remarkable personal and professional entry into the music scene as a wide-eyed teenager in the early '70s is eager to please and does just that, but it's neither as outright funny nor as resonant as it seems to want to be.

As a purely fictional yarn, this would probably be too far-fetched to swallow—a green 15-year-old from San Diego is granted total access to a rising rock band for weeks as he preps a piece for Rolling Stone. But the combination of the fluid, hang-loose nature of the period, the inherent craziness of the music world and, above all, the credibility of the personal observations makes it all go down very easily, just as the affection with which the film views even the most ridiculous behavior will make most viewers warm to it without resistance.

Most of the picture's elements—the crazed rock scene, raging musician egos, easy sex and drugs, the now amusing fashions and behavior at the tail end of the hippie era—have been seen plenty of times before. The one new angle introduced here is that of the protag's mother (Frances McDormand), a somewhat eccentric intellectual who abhors rock, and particularly drugs, is far from being a standard-issue moralistic prig. Character hovers over her son, and the entire film, in an often funny, sobering way, but, among other things, the fact that McDormand is so much better an actor than almost everyone else in the picture makes the others seem rather spineless in comparison.

Pic strangely deflates a bit whenever it has the chance to get outrageous and score laughs at the expense of the scene's unchecked behavioral norms. It's not that Crowe should have been expected to compete with *This Is Spinal Tap* in this area, but how can anyone consider rockers on tour and hanging out in hotels anything other than comic bait waiting to be swallowed whole? Pic ribs them, to be sure, but never goes for the kill, resulting in a sense of missed hilarity, which, if delivered, would have given the film a needed kick.

•

ALMOST PERFECT AFFAIR, AN
1979, 93 mins, US Ⓥ col

Dir Michael Ritchie ***Prod*** Terry Carr ***Scr*** Walter Bernstein, Don Peterson ***Ph*** Henri Decae ***Ed*** Richard A. Harris ***Mus*** Georges Delerue ***Art*** Willy Holt

Act Keith Carradine, Monica Vitti, Raf Vallone, Christian De Sica, Dick Anthony Williams (Paramount)

The emotions director Michael Ritchie is parlaying in this slim fable, which revolves around tender egos and unlimited ambition, are universal. But the details are so specific, and so grounded in film industry reality, that the larger implications may be lost.

Keith Carradine is a young filmmaker, who wraps up two years of devotion to a film about executed murderer Gary Gilmore, *Choice of Ending*, by sinking all his remaining funds into a trip to Cannes. His film is seized at French customs until the censor can see it, an unlikely possibility until Monica Vitti intercedes on his behalf.

Carradine mirrors lotsa nouveau helmers adrift in their initial dealings with industry salesmanship.

Focus is the intriguing relationship between Vitti and Carradine, which starts out as a one-nighter, and turns into a brief, but ill-fated romance.

•

ALONG CAME JONES
1945, 90 mins, US b/w

Dir Stuart Heisler ***Prod*** Gary Cooper ***Scr*** Nunnally Johnson ***Ph*** Milton Krasner ***Ed*** Thomas Neff ***Mus*** Arthur Lange ***Art*** Wiard B. Ihnen

Act Gary Cooper, Loretta Young, William Demarest, Dan Duryea, Frank Sully, Russell Simpson (International/Cinema Artists)

For his first independent production, Gary Cooper turned out a better-than-average Western [from the novel by Alan LeMay]. Cooper is not only the producer but also the star, along with Loretta Young. Without Cooper and Young *Jones* would be just another horse opera.

Cooper plays a mild-mannered cowpoke who drifts into a small town with his sidekick (William Demarest), thus precipitating a situation in which he's mistaken for a notorious road agent. Cooper, actually, can't even handle a gun, but the inevitable result finds him the unwitting and indirect cause of the holdup man's slaying. And, of course, he gets the latter's girl (Young).

Cooper plays his usually languid self impressively, while Young is decorative and photographed well. Demarest is in for some comedy relief, of which there is too little, while Dan Duryea is properly menacing as the killer.

•

ALONG THE GREAT DIVIDE
1951, 88 mins, US Ⓥ b/w

Dir Raoul Walsh ***Prod*** Anthony Veiller ***Scr*** Walter Doniger, Lewis Meltzer ***Ph*** Sid Hickox ***Ed*** Thomas Reilly ***Mus*** David Buttolph ***Art*** Edward Carrere

Act Kirk Douglas, Virginia Mayo, John Agar, Walter Brennan, Ray Teal, Hugh Sanders (Warner)

In his first Western, Kirk Douglas is a U.S. marshall, interested only in enforcing the letter of the law. Plot [from a story by Walter Doniger] is concerned with Douglas bringing in a prisoner charged with rustling and murder, and the efforts of a cattle baron to take justice in his own hands.

The prisoner (Walter Brennan) has been rescued from a lynching when Douglas and his two deputies stumble onto the necktie party being arranged by Morris Ankrum, who has accused Brennan of killing his son.

The law group, by now having Brennan's daughter (Virginia Mayo) in the party, flees across a desert from Ankrum's men, is attacked and deputy John Agar is killed. Douglas manages to capture Ankrum's other son (James Anderson) as hostage, and the dry, thirsty desert trek continues.

Douglas tries hard with his characterization and would have brought it off successfully had the scripting stuck to straight Western action and not gone off in mental maneuverings. Mayo's character has several good scenes but mostly misses. Her dialect isn't consistent.

•

ALPHABET MURDERS, THE
1966, 85 mins, UK b/w

Dir Frank Tashlin ***Prod*** Lawrence P. Bachmann ***Scr*** David Pursall, Jack Seddon ***Ph*** Desmond Dickinson ***Ed*** John Victor Smith ***Mus*** Ron Goodwin ***Art*** Bill Andrews

Act Tony Randall, Anita Ekberg, Robert Morley, Maurice Denham, Guy Rolfe, Sheila Allen (M-G-M British)

This British translation of one of Agatha Christie's better-known whodunits, *The A.B.C. Murders*, gets the broad comedy treatment. Much of the suspence of Christie's writing is lost in converting to comedy, and as a result is no more than a parody of the original, insufficiently clever to be outstanding.

Tony Randall, as Hercule Poirot, introduces himself in the opening scene with remark, I'm a Belgian snoop. But he delivers a very definite characterization in making his way through the plot haze of a series of murders that has for its victims people with the initials A.A., B.B., C.C.

Lawrence P. Bachmann, who previously brought to screen four Christie mysteries with Margaret Rutherford, is responsible for excellent production values, making handsome use at times of London street backgrounds.

Robert Morley, as a British Intelligence agent whose sole duty here is to see that Poirot remains unharmed while in England, like Randall clowns the part in a dippy sort of way. Anita Ekberg is mostly lost in her fleeting appearances bundled up in trench coat. Maurice Denham as the familiar Inspector Japp of Scotland Yard plays it straight as does Guy Rolfe as the psychiatrist treating Ekberg.

•

ALPHAVILLE
UNE ETRANGE AVENTURE DE LEMMY CAUTION
1965, 98 mins, France/Italy Ⓥ b/w

Dir Jean-Luc Godard ***Prod*** Andre Michelin ***Scr*** Jean-Luc Godard ***Ph*** Raoul Coutard ***Ed*** Agnes Guillemot ***Mus*** Paul Misraki ***Art*** [uncredited]

Act Eddie Constantine, Anna Karina, Akim Tamiroff, Laszlo Szabo, Howard Vernon, Jean-Louis Comolli (Chaumiane/Filmstudio)

The most prolific of French filmmakers and ex–New Wavers, Jean-Luc Godard has come up with an adventurous philosophical pic with this one. He takes a popular actor and uses his screen personage in a new way.

That Yank who became a star over here [in France] playing in parody G-man pix, Eddie Constantine is shown in some future city where human feelings have all but been done away with and where the powerful leader is a super computer.

Though supposed to be some city 30 years hence, Godard has shot strictly on location in Paris. But he has managed to give it a depressing aspect in choosing grubby, large tourist hotels as well as canny use of many modern buildings. This builds up a sort of no-man's-land between totalitarian drabness and super-modern garishness.

Constantine is secret agent Lemmy Caution masquerading as a newsman authorized to bring back a scientist from the old American part of the universe termed Nueva York. He meets his daughter, now an automaton without much human feeling, whom he makes feel again as he destroys the computer and takes off with the girl.

Anna Karina has the right doll-like appearance as the robot who slowly feels long-forgotten human feelings coming back. Akim Tamiroff is outstanding in one seg as an ex-agent who has been humanly destroyed by the system. Godard again shows his uncompromising, intellectual, unorthodox methods for a pic that is both piquant and sketchy.

•

ALTERED STATES
1980, 102 mins, US Ⓥ ⊙ col

Dir Ken Russell ***Prod*** Howard Gottfried ***Scr*** Sidney Aaron [=Paddy Chayefsky] ***Ph*** Jordan Cronenweth ***Ed*** Eric Jenkins ***Mus*** John Corigliano ***Art*** Richard McDonald

Act William Hurt, Blair Brown, Bob Balaban, Charles Haid, Drew Barrymore (Warner)

Altered States is an exciting combo science fiction–horror film [from the novel by Paddy Chayefsky]. Direction by Ken Russell has energy to spare, with appropriate match-up of his baroque visual style to special effects intensive material.

Producers weathered stormy pre-production problems, including the ankling of director Arthur Penn late in 1978, departure soon after of special effects wiz John Dykstra, and transfer of project from Columbia to Warner as proposed budget grew to $15 million.

Tall tale concerns a young psychophysiologist, Edward Jessup (William Hurt), working in New York and later at Harvard on dangerous experiments involving human consciousness.

Using himself as the subject, Jessup makes use of a sensory deprivation tank to hallucinate back to the event of his birth and beyond, regressing into primitive stages of human evolution. Shattering use of Dolby stereo effects conspires with the images to give the viewer a vicarious LSD-type experience sans drugs. Hurt's feature film debut is arresting, especially during the grueling climactic sequence.

1980: NOMINATIONS: Best Original Score, Sound

•

ALVAREZ KELLY
1966, 110 mins, US Ⓥ ⌑ col

Dir Edward Dmytryk ***Prod*** Sol C. Siegel ***Scr*** Franklin Coen, Elliott Arnold ***Ph*** Joseph MacDonald ***Ed*** Harold F. Kress ***Mus*** John Green ***Art*** Walter M. Simonds

Act William Holden, Richard Widmark, Janice Rule, Patrick O'Neal, Victoria Shaw, Roger C. Carmel (Columbia)

Based on a true U.S. Civil War incident, *Alvarez Kelly* concerns successful cattle grab engineered by Southern forces and executed under the noses of Northern troops. Outdoor action sequences, including an exciting stampede, enliven a tame script, routinely directed and performed erratically.

Franklin Coen and Elliott Arnold scripted Coen's story, which pits Mexican-Irish William Holden (hence, the title) against Confederate officer Richard Widmark, eyeing Holden's cattle as food for a starving South.

A lot of double-crossing takes place, with Victoria Shaw, mistress of a captured mansion, causing Holden's kidnapping by Widmark, who forces the former to teach his troops how to handle cattle. Janice Rule, Widmark's faithful sweetie, gives up her marriage hopes, and Holden helps her escape to NY with Scottish sea captain Roger C. Carmel. Patrick O'Neal is the Northern officer who is depicted in unsympathetic hues.

Director Edward Dmytryk has achieved uneven response from his players, in part due to scripting that overdevelops some characters and situations, and underdevelops others.

•

ALVIN PURPLE
1973, 97 mins, Australia Ⓥ col
Dir Tim Burstall **Prod** Tim Burstall **Scr** Alan Hopgood **Ph** Robin Copping **Ed** Edward McQueen Mason **Mus** Brian Cadd **Art** Leslie Binns
Act Graeme Blundell, George Whaley, Penne Hackforth-Jones, Elli Maclure, Jacki Weaver, Jenny Hagen (Hexagon)

Alvin Purple is a young man whom women find irresistible. At 16 he flees from schoolgirls right into the clutches of his school teacher's wife. At 21, still running from the opposite sex, Alvin becomes a waterbed salesman and discovers it isn't only the waterbed a bored housewife, body-painting fanatic, kinky woman, and a drag queen are after. Exhausted and bewildered by these multiple activities Alvin confesses to his girlfriend, Tina (with whom his relationship is utterly platonic), he is unable to resist sex.

This comedy, made in Melbourne with local actors, is beautifully scripted by Aussie playwright Alan Hopgood with double entendres and situations abounding. Pace is slick and the pic never sags.

In the title role Graeme Blundell gives a thoroughly convincing performance.

•

ALWAYS
1985, 105 mins, US Ⓥ ⊙ ▭ col
Dir Henry Jaglom **Prod** Henry Jaglom **Scr** Henry Jaglom **Ph** Hanania Baer **Ed** [Henry Jaglom], Francesca Riviere **Mus** Miles Kreuger (consult.) **Art** Dennis Boses
Act Patrice Townsend, Henry Jaglom, Joanna Frank, Alan Rachins, Melissa Leo, Bob Rafelson (Jagtown/International Rainbow)

Always is writer-director-producer Henry Jaglom's confessional comedy about his divorce from actress Patrice Townsend. The two star, more or less, as themselves, and are joined by two other couples who are, respectively, near the beginning and toward the middle of the marriage process for an alternately awkward, painful, loving and farcical July Fourth weekend. Pic's subject matter is at once highly personal and utterly universal.

Jaglom frames the proceedings with ruminations directed straight at the viewer, then jumps into a telling of how Townsend showed up one night at Jaglom's home to sign the divorce papers and ended up staying on for a weekend of emotional confrontations, recriminations, joyful reminiscences and partial reconciliation.

In French farce style, two unexpected flings take place, but mainly, picture is wall-to-wall talk about what went wrong between Jaglom and Townsend, about emotional happiness and lack of same, about sexual matters, and many related topics.

•

ALWAYS
1989, 121 mins, US Ⓥ ⊙ col
Dir Steven Spielberg **Prod** Steven Spielberg, Frank Marshall, Kathleen Kennedy, Richard Vane **Scr** Jerry Belson **Ph** Mikael Salomon **Ed** Michael Kahn **Mus** John Williams **Art** James Bissell
Act Richard Dreyfuss, Holly Hunter, Brad Johnson, John Goodman, Audrey Hepburn, Keith David (Universal/United Artists/Amblin)

Always is a relatively small scale, engagingly casual, somewhat silly, but always entertaining fantasy.

Richard Dreyfuss charmingly inherits the lead role of a pilot returned from the dead in this remake of the 1943 Spencer Tracy pic *A Guy Named Joe* set among fire-fighters in national parks.

Steven Spielberg's transposition of the fondly remembered original to the spectacularly burning Montana forests—incorporating footage shot during the devastating 1988 fires at Yellowstone National Park—is a valid equivalent, for the most part, especially since his action sequences using old World War II-era planes are far more thrilling than those of *A Guy Named Joe*.

Holly Hunter's dispatcher and semi-skilled aspiring pilot, lacking the womanly grace Irene Dunne brought to the part, comes off as gawky and ditzy in the early parts of *Always*. Bereavement seems to visibly mature the actress, whose emotional struggle between the memory of Dreyfuss and new love Brad Johnson becomes spirited and gripping.

•

AMADEUS
1984, 158 mins, US Ⓥ ⊙ ▭ col
Dir Milos Forman **Prod** Saul Zaentz **Scr** Peter Shaffer **Ph** Miroslav Ondricek **Ed** Nena Danevic, Michael Chandler **Mus** John Strauss (coord.) **Art** Patrizia Von Brandenstein
Act F. Murray Abraham, Tom Hulce, Elizabeth Berridge, Simon Callow, Roy Dotrice, Christine Ebersole (Zaentz)

On a production level and as an evocation of a time and place, *Amadeus* is loaded with pleasures, the greatest of which derive from the on-location filming in Prague, the most 18th-century of all European cities.

With great material and themes to work with, and such top talent involved, film nevertheless arrives as a disappointment. Although Peter Shaffer adapted his own outstanding play for the screen, the stature and power the work possessed onstage have been noticeably diminished, and Milos Forman's handling is perhaps too naturalistic for what was conceived as a highly stylized piece.

Amadeus is Shaffer's fictionalized account, based on well-informed speculation, of the relationship between Viennese court composer Antonio Salieri and Wolfgang Amadeus Mozart, during the 10 final years of the latter's life. It is a caustic study of the collision between mediocrity and genius; it is based on the provocative premise that the manipulative Salieri may have intentionally caused Mozart's death in 1791.

Shaffer has drawn Salieri as a character of Mephistophelian proportions, a man who needs to drag Mozart down in order to cope with his awareness of his own shortcomings.

Fueling the fire of Salieri's fury is Mozart's offensive personality. In opposition to the idealized, romanticized 19th-century view of the composer, the character is an outlandish vulgarian. As played by Tom Hulce, Mozart emerges as the John McEnroe of classical music.

1984: Best Picture, Director, Actor (F. Murray Abraham), Adapted Screenplay, Art Direction, Sound, Costume Design, Makeup

NOMINATIONS: Best Actor (Tom Hulce), Cinematography, Editing

•

AMANTS, LES
1958, 90 mins, France Ⓥ ⊙ ▭ b/w
Dir Louis Malle **Scr** Louis Malle, Louise de Vilmorin **Ph** Henri Decae **Ed** Leonide Azar **Art** Bernard Evein, Jacques Saulnier
Act Jeanne Moreau, Alain Cluny, Jean-Marc Bory, Judith Magre, Jose-Luis Villalonga, Gaston Modot (NEF)

A comedy of manners is mixed with an attempt at outright eroticism in this film [from Dominique Vivant's *Point de lendemain*]. Neither is completely successful; only exploitation chances are its 20-minute love scene between a young wife and a young man in the house and grounds of the husband who happens to be at home during the tryst. The lovers snuggle, moan and even take a bath together, but the lack of dimension in the characters dissipates the impact.

The wife, married to an older man who seems to think more of his newspaper than her, spends weekends in Paris where she has taken a lover, an effeminate polo-playing playboy. On the way home from Paris, her car breaks down and she is picked up by a simple young man who hates what her rich, smug set stands for. Love comes quickly.

Fairly banal dialog, and a narration imposed over the action, diminishes its needed early vitality. It limps along until the sex scenes.

Direction dwells on too many unessential points and lacks the true feel for this woman's plight to make her emotional release effective drama. Jeanne Moreau displays some insight into her character, which is more than most of the men can do.

•

AMARCORD
1973, 125 mins, Italy/France Ⓥ col
Dir Federico Fellini **Prod** Franco Cristaldi **Scr** Federico Fellini, Tonino Guerra **Ph** Giuseppe Rotunno **Ed** Ruggero Mastroianni **Mus** Nino Rota **Art** Danilo Donati
Act Pupella Maggio, Magali Noel, Armando Brancia, Ciccio Ingrassia, Nandino Orfei, Luigi Rossi (FC/PECF)

Amarcord is probably the first time an established film director went before cameras with one concept in mind and then created an almost entirely different picture. Instead of lensing a nostalgic look at the past to recapture the happy simplicity of existence before mechanization, the maestro did just the opposite.

With a loose reference to his boyhood years in the very Italian province of Romagna (Fellini was born in Rimini), he has looked back as much in anger as in sorrow and has recreated provincial life in the early 1930s with unsparing emphasis on the inadequacies of man and existence.

Amarcord unrolls in a four-season span—opening and closing in a sky full of thistledown (harbinger of spring). From spring to midsummer, the provincial town (symbolic of all small towns) is the throbbing cauldron of human activity.

The young adolescent schoolboy, Titta (Bruno Zanin), and his family constitute the script thread in the screenplay. Titta is both victim and rebel.

In production almost a year and costly (around $3.5 million), this Fellini opus is his most accessible to mass audiences since *La Dolce Vita*. Elements of earthiness and sentiment are relevant to his purpose. Fellini's traditionally generous dosage of fantasy and poetry are subordinated to the grotesque, the macabre, the sentimental.

1974: Best Foreign Language Film

•

AMATEUR
1994, 105 mins, US/UK/France Ⓥ ⊙ col
Dir Hal Hartley **Prod** Hal Hartley, Ted Hope **Scr** Hal Hartley **Ph** Michael Spiller **Ed** Steven Hamilton **Mus** Ned Rifle, Jeffrey Taylor **Art** Steve Rosenzweig
Act Isabelle Huppert, Martin Donovan, Elina Lowensohn, Damian Young, Chuck Montgomery, David Simonds (True Fiction/Zenith/UGC)

A former nun who writes erotic stories, an amnesiac with a criminal past and "the most notorious porno actress in the world" bounce off each other with tasty results in Hal Hartley's *Amateur*. Just as quirky and idiosyncratic as the Gotham-based writer/director's earlier efforts, this one pushes the spiky humor a bit more to the fore.

Isabelle Huppert, who wrote Hartley a fan letter offering to act in one of his films, plays Isabelle, who recently checked out of convent life after 15 years. A failure at writing about sex, she also claims to be a nymphomaniac to Thomas (Martin Donovan), a man who awakens on a downtown New York street with no memory and is trustingly taken in by Isabelle.

Before long, it becomes clear that Thomas has been pushed out a window (and is presumed dead) by his wife, Sofia (Elina Lowensohn), a porno queen whose desperate financial straits lead her to deal with a powerful arms merchant. This sends the film onto an unexpected tangent involving Thomas's accountant, Edward (Damian Young).

Viewers not in tune with the filmmaker's approach may find the comic elements forced and contrived, since they are often based on absurd conceits. But Hartley s technique is now so refined and precise that he easily achieves his desired effects.

Donovan can't do much with a character who basically doesn't exist, but remainder of the cast is excellent. Huppert has a sweet gravity underlaid with quietly suggestive humor. Lowensohn makes the most of the sexpot goddess in an eye-catching turn.

•

AMAZING DR. CLITTERHOUSE, THE
1938, 87 mins, US b/w
Dir Anatole Litvak **Prod** Robert Lord **Scr** John Wexley, John Huston **Ph** Tony Gaudio **Ed** Warren Low **Mus** Max Steiner **Art** Carl Jules Weyl
Act Edward G. Robinson, Claire Trevor, Humphrey Bogart, Allen Jenkins, Donald Crisp, Gale Page (Warner)

The Amazing Dr. Clitterhouse was successful on the London stage and mildly so in New York. The producers have retained the basic idea from the play [by Barre Lyndon]—that of a veteran physician whose study of the physiological effects of crime on its habitues takes him on a series of ventures with a skilled gang of crooks. This thread has been followed even to the deliberate poisoning of the gangster chief by the doctor when he learns of a hoodlum's blackmailing scheme.

But in many respects it is an outright gangster film with the medico's study of criminals as the excuse for carefully diagraming the gang's operations. In addition, the feature inculcates a bit of the sherlocking theme and modified romance. Claire Trevor, the ace fence for the thieves, is the sole romance that enters the doctor's life.

Edward G. Robinson, in the role of the criminal medico, is at his best. Humphrey Bogart's interpretation of the gangster chief, whose jealousy of Clitterhouse eventually builds to the blackmail scheme, is topflight.

●

AMAZING GRACE AND CHUCK

1987, 115 mins, US Ⓥ ⊙ col

Dir Mike Newell ***Prod*** David Field ***Scr*** David Field ***Ph*** Robert Elswit ***Ed*** Peter Hollywood ***Mus*** Elmer Bernstein ***Art*** Dena Roth

Act Jamie Lee Curtis, Alex English, Gregory Peck, William L. Petersen, Joshua Zuehlke (Tri-Star/Rastar/Turnstar)

Amazing Grace and Chuck is destined to go down in history as the camp classic of the anti-nuke genre. As amazingly bad as it is audacious, film will live forever in the hearts of connoisseurs of Hollywood's most memorably outrageous moments.

Little League baseball pitcher Chuck Murdock, having been shown a Minuteman missile under the Montana prairie, announces, "I can't play because of nuclear weapons." Who should read a news report of the incident but Boston Celtics star Amazing Grace Smith (played by Denver Nuggets great Alex English), who promptly gives up his $1-million-per-year salary to join Chuck in protest of nukes. In no time, hundreds of athletes on both sides of the Iron Curtain are refusing to play until the ultimate weapon is eliminated.

When it looks as though the upcoming baseball season will have to be cancelled, the President of the United States (an impressive Gregory Peck) summons young Chuck to the White House to drum some sense into him.

●

AMAZING PANDA ADVENTURE, THE

1995, 84 mins, US Ⓥ ⊙ ▭ col

Dir Christopher Cain ***Prod*** Lee Rich, John Wilcox, Gary Foster, Dylan Sellers ***Scr*** Jeff Rothberg, Laurice Elehwany ***Ph*** Jack N. Green ***Ed*** Jack Hofstra ***Mus*** William Ross ***Art*** John Willett

Act Stephen Lang, Ryan Slater, Yi Ding, Huang Fei (Warner)

The script [from a screen story by John Wilcox and Steven Alldredge] is a mix of the trite and the true. Ryan (Ryan Slater) is off on spring break to see his dad (Stephen Lang), an American working on a preserve in China to rescue the panda population. To save the preserve, its staffers must come up with a panda cub to show that they're accomplishing something, but the only known cub has been captured by poachers. Through various plot twists, Ryan, a young Chinese girl (Yi Ding), who works at the preserve, and the cub are separated from the adults and pursued by the poachers. Pic, which was shot in Sichuan province, follows their adventures until the inevitable reunion and happy ending.

Lang earns his pay as the father, but the bulk of the film is carried by Slater (brother of Christian) and Ding. It is enough to say they are upstaged both by the locations and by the pandas, a mix of real animals and the special effects work of Rick Baker and his crew.

●

AMAZON

1992, 91 mins, Finland/US Ⓥ ▭ col

Dir Mika Kaurismaki ***Prod*** Mika Kaurismaki, Pentti Kouri ***Scr*** Mika Kaurismaki, Richard Reitinger ***Ph*** Timo Salminen ***Ed*** Michael Chandler ***Mus*** Nana Vasconcelos ***Art*** Tony de Castro

Act Kari Vaananen, Robert Davi, Rae Dawn Chong, Minna, Aili Sovio, Rui Polanah (Villealfa/Noema)

Shot in CinemaScope with an international B-movie cast playing foreigners at the ends of their ropes in the Brazilian jungle, *Amazon* plays like a dualer that might have been made in the 1960s by Sam Fuller or Gordon Douglas starring Burt Reynolds or Stuart Whitman.

Opening with the nearly surreal sight of a Finnish man and his two daughters attempting to travel on the hellish Trans-Amazonian Highway to the accompaniment of some noirish narration, pic briefly flashes back to explain that banker Kari Vaananen has fled Finland with the girls upon his wife's accidental death.

But, lo and behold, they run out of gas, as does, in an amusing scene, their would-be saviour, a bitter American bush pilot named Dan (Robert Davi). A mercenary and treasure hunter of the old school, Dan speaks of searching for gold using a debilitated bulldozer he's found, and eventually Kari joins him in his quest.

Visually film is always stimulating but storytelling is wildly uneven, and director Mika Kaurismaki has an uncertain command of pic's tone. Acting is okay.

●

AMAZON WOMEN ON THE MOON

1987, 85 mins, US Ⓥ ⊙ col

Dir Joe Dante, Carl Gottlieb, Peter Horton, John Landis ***Prod*** Robert K. Weiss ***Scr*** Michael Barrie, Jim Malholland ***Ph*** Daniel Pearl ***Ed*** Bert Lovitt, Marshall Harvey, Malcolm Campbell ***Art*** Alex Hajdu

Act Rosanna Arquette, Ralph Bellamy, Carrie Fisher, Griffin Dunne, Steve Guttenberg, Russ Meyer (Universal)

Amazon Women on the Moon is irreverent, vulgar and silly and has some hilarious moments and some real groaners too. John Landis & Co. have found some 1980s things to satirize—like yuppies, the videocassette biz, dating, condoms, done up in a way that's not particularly shocking anymore.

Besides Landis, directors Joe Dante, Carl Gottlieb, Peter Horton and producer Robert K. Weiss take turns doing sketches—Weiss's *Amazon Women on the Moon* 1950s parody of bad sci-fi pics being the one that was stretched piecemeal throughout the film in a semi-successful attempt to hold this anthology together as one comedic work.

Eighteen other segs fill up the pic's 85 minutes, some mercifully short like Weiss's *Silly Pate* while Landis's *Hospital* is one of those slow-building, totally zany bits where the chuckles grow as the situation gets more ridiculous and you wish there was more.

●

AMBUSHERS, THE

1968, 101 mins, US Ⓥ ⊙ col

Dir Henry Levin ***Prod*** Irving Allen ***Scr*** Herbert Baker ***Ph*** Burnett Guffey ***Ed*** Harold F. Kress ***Mus*** Hugo Montenegro

Act Dean Martin, Senta Berger, Janice Rule, James Gregory, Albert Salmi, Kurt Kasznar (Columbia/Meadway-Claude)

This third Matt Helm pic starts out with silly double entendre, then shifts for last half to tedious plot resolution. While production values remain strong, acting, writing and direction are pedestrian.

Plot is simple: U.S. flying sauceress Janice Rule is kidnapped by despicable beast Albert Salmi; James Gregory sends Dean Martin to find out why; Senta Berger reps another foreign government (lucky place too); Kurt Kasznar is a funny bad guy—a Mexican beer baron; assorted heavies get their desserts.

Although visual aspects—the Oleg Cassini wardrobe and overall fashion supervision—are very good, pic at same time has that slapdash quickie look.

●

AMERICA AMERICA

1963, 177 mins, US b/w

Dir Elia Kazan ***Prod*** Elia Kazan ***Scr*** Elia Kazan ***Ph*** Haskell Wexler ***Ed*** Dede Allen ***Mus*** Manos Hadjidakis ***Art*** Gene Callahan

Act Stathis Giallelis, Frank Wolf, Harry Davis, Linda Marsh, Paul Mann, Lou Antonio (Warner)

Elia Kazan gives a penetrating, thorough and profoundly affecting account of the hardships endured and surmounted at the turn of the century by a young Greek lad in attempting to fulfill his cherished dream—getting to America from the old country.

Kazan's film stems from his book of the same title, which evidently was inspired by tales of the experiences of his own ancestors that sifted down through the family grapevine. The picture begins with the young Greek hero witnessing Turkish oppression of Greek and Armenian minorities, circa 1896. It follows him to Constantinople, to which he has been sent by his family with its entire fortune to pave their way. He finally arrives in the promised land—America—where, as a lowly shoeshine boy, he painstakingly earns and saves the money that will bring the other members of his large family across the sea.

The acting is incredibly good. In the all-important focal role of the young man with the dream, Stathis Giallelis, an unknown, makes a striking screen debut. Virtually everyone is memorable, perhaps the three most vivid are Linda Marsh as the plain and unassuming maiden to whom the hero is treacherously betrothed, Paul Mann as her sybaritic, self-indulgent father and Lou Antonio as a thoroughly detestable crook.

1963: Best B&W Art Direction

NOMINATIONS: Best Picture, Director, Original Story & Screenplay

●

AMERICAN BEAUTY

1999, 122 mins, US Ⓥ ⊙ ▭ col

Dir Sam Mendes ***Prod*** Bruce Cohen, Dan Jinks ***Scr*** Alan Ball ***Ph*** Conrad L. Hall ***Ed*** Tariq Anwar, Christopher Greenbury ***Mus*** Thomas Newman ***Art*** Naomi Shohan

Act Kevin Spacey, Annette Bening, Thora Birch, Wes Bentley, Mena Suvari, Peter Gallagher (Jinks-Cohen/Dream-Works)

An acerbic, darkly comic critique of how social conventions can lead people into false, sterile and emotionally stunted lives, *American Beauty* is a real American original. This independent-minded feature represents a stunning card of introduction for two cinematic freshmen, screenwriter Alan Ball (a playwright and TV writer) and director Sam Mendes (the hottest young British theater director of recent years).

The landscape of Ball's story is the familiar one of small-town America, of houses with white picket fences wracked by hostility, tension, noncommunication and perversity. Fortunately, this view is intended not as a revelation but as a given, a starting point for a tale in which nearly every important character metamorphoses in an utterly unpredictable way.

Lester Burnham (Kevin Spacey) is a self-described loser, having lost interest in his job, his beautiful, high-strung wife, Carolyn (Annette Bening), and sullen school-age daughter, Jane (Thora Birch). Lester becomes smitten by Jane's best friend, Angela (Mena Suvari), and begins obsessively pumping iron and smoking dope with a strange young man, Ricky Fitts (Wes Bentley), who has just moved into the house next door.

Pic clicks into high gear midway when Lester and Carolyn finally have it out. They don't declare war, exactly, but Lester decides to let down any pretense to responsibility or normalcy in order to do his own thing as he did when he was 20.

The ensemble of actors could not be better. Spacey hums along with droll line readings before jump-starting to antic life. Bening goes well beyond the expected, while Bentley is sensational as the creepy kid living a complex life.

1999: Best Picture, Director, Actor (Kevin Spacey), Original Screenplay, Cinematography

NOMINATIONS: Best Actress (Annette Bening), Editing, Original Score

●

AMERICAN FLYERS

1985, 114 mins, US Ⓥ ⊙ ▭ col

Dir John Badham ***Prod*** Gareth Wigan, Paula Weinstein ***Scr*** Steve Tesich ***Ph*** Don Peterman ***Ed*** Frank Morriss ***Mus*** Lee Ritenour, Greg Mathieson ***Art*** Lawrence G. Paull

Act Kevin Costner, David Grant, Rae Dawn Chong, Alexandra Paul, Janice Rule, Luca Bercovici (Warner)

Story of two brothers who untangle their mixed emotions as they compete in a grueling bicycle race, *American Flyers* is most entertaining when it rolls along unencumbered by big statements. Unfortunately, overblown production just pumps hot air in too many directions and comes up limp.

Basic conflict between underachiever David (David Grant) and older brother Marcus (Kevin Costner), a fierce competitor and no-nonsense sports doctor, is crammed into a hotbed of family problems including a career-woman mother (Janice Rule) who emotionally abandoned her dying husband.

If this isn't enough, one of the boys is destined for the same fate as the father. So, with the shadow of death hanging over them, the brothers set off for Colorado for "the toughest bicycle race in America."

Combativeness between brothers yields to comaraderie, but true nature of their conflict is difficult to get a handle on.

Performances are adequate considering that overproduction makes the characters seem larger than life without being lifelike.

●

AMERICAN FRIENDS

1991, 95 mins, UK Ⓥ ⊙ col

Dir Tristram Powell ***Prod*** Patrick Cassavetti, Steve Abbott ***Scr*** Michael Palin, Tristram Powell ***Ph*** Philip Bonham-Carter ***Ed*** George Akers ***Mus*** Georges Delerue ***Art*** Andrew McAlpine

Act Michael Palin, Connie Booth, Trini Alvarado, Alfred Molina, David Calder (Millenium/Mayday)

Easy on the eyes and on the emotions, *American Friends* is a slim vignette about two Yank women who fall for a reserved Oxford don.

Pic opens in the 1860s at a stuffy Oxford college where

bachelor classics don Francis Ashby (Michael Palin) is setting off for a walking vacation in Switzerland. Atop the Alps, he meets two Americans, Caroline (Connie Booth) and her doe-eyed ward, Elinor (Trini Alvarado). Emotions are stirred, and Elinor gets the first kiss.

Back in Oxford, Ashby is one of two candidates lined up to take over as college president when the current one dies. Ashby rival Oliver Syme (Alfred Molina) has hyperactive hormones, so if Ashby can stay respectably celibate, the job's virtually his. Enter, en route to Philadelphia, the two Yanks—and much trouble for Ashby.

There's a lot going on beneath the surface, but not much of it reaches the screen. Lack of dramatic tension can be blamed, in part, on the ex–Monty Python trouper's performance.

Although yarn is based on an actual event discovered in his great-grandfather Edward's travel diaries, Palin is too lightweight for such a key role. His crusty, middle-aged bachelor doesn't ring true. Thesping otherwise is crisp and reliable.

•

AMERICAN GIGOLO

1980, 117 mins, US Ⓥ ⊙ col

Dir Paul Schrader ***Prod*** Jerry Bruckheimer ***Scr*** Paul Schrader ***Ph*** John Bailey ***Ed*** Richard Halsey ***Mus*** Giorgio Moroder ***Art*** Fernando Scarfiotti

Act Richard Gere, Lauren Hutton, Hector Elizondo, Nina Van Pallandt, Bill Duke, Brian Davies (Paramount)

A hot subject, cool style and overly contrived plotting don't all mesh in *American Gigolo*. Paul Schrader's third outing as a director is betrayed by a curious, uncharacteristic evasiveness at its core.

Things begin to go awry, both for Richard Gere and the picture, when senator's wife Lauren Hutton begins taking more than a passing interest in her man-for-hire and when a kinky sex murder is laid at his door. Gere's character has been portrayed with moral and emotional ambivalence, which makes caring about his predicament and ultimate fate difficult.

As with several of Schrader's other scripts, this one charts the course of a loner, a solo driver navigating in a sea of sharks ready to eat him alive. Rarely offscreen, Gere is notably convincing in look and manner. Very low-keyed, Hutton is not quite up to the difficult part of a woman-with-everything who throws it all over for her questionable lover.

•

AMERICAN GRAFFITI

1973, 109 mins, US Ⓥ ⊙ ▭ col

Dir George Lucas ***Prod*** Francis Coppola, Gary Kurtz ***Scr*** George Lucas, Gloria Katz, Willard Huyck ***Ph*** Haskell Wexler ***Ed*** Verna Fields, Marcia Lucas ***Mus*** Karin Green (sup.) ***Art*** Dennis Clark

Act Richard Dreyfuss, Ron Howard, Paul Le Mat, Charles Martin Smith, Cindy Williams, Candy Clark (Universal)

Set in 1962 but reflecting the culmination of the 1950s, the film is a most vivid recall of teenage attitudes and mores, told with outstanding empathy and compassion through an exceptionally talented cast.

Design consultant Al Locatelli, art director Dennis Clark and set director Douglas Freeman have brilliantly reconstructed the fabric and texture of the time, while Walter Murch's outstanding sound collage—an unending stream of early rock platter hits—complements in the aural department.

Against this chrome and neon backdrop is told the story of one long summer night in the lives of four school chums: Richard Dreyfuss, on his last night before leaving for an Eastern college; Ron Howard, less willing to depart the presence of Cindy Williams; Charles Martin Smith, a bespectacled fumbler whose misadventures with pubescent swinger Candy Clark are as touching as they are hilarious; and Paul Le Mat, 22 years old on a birth certificate but still strutting as he did four years earlier.

[Pic was reissued in 1978 in a 112-min. version featuring three extra scenes.]

1973: NOMINATIONS: Best Picture, Director, Supp. Actress (Candy Clark), Original Screenplay, Editing

•

AMERICAN GUERRILLA IN THE PHILIPPINES

1950, 104 mins, US col

Dir Fritz Lang ***Prod*** Lamar Trotti ***Scr*** Lamar Trotti ***Ph*** Harry Jackson ***Ed*** Robert Simpson ***Mus*** Cyril J. Mockridge ***Art*** Lyle Wheeler, J. Russell Spencer

Act Tyrone Power, Micheline Presle, Tom Ewell, Bob Patten, Jack Elam, Robert Barrat (20th Century-Fox)

20th Fox has made an interesting, if somewhat long, film version of Ira Wolfert's [novel] *American Guerrilla in the Philippines*. A story of the Second World War in the Pacific, from the spring of 1942 up to General MacArthur's return to the islands, it is neatly staged.

The Philippine locales supply a lush tropical dressing to brighten the heroics of a small band of Americans and natives who fight the U.S. cause against the invading Japs. Tyrone Power and Tom Ewell escape into the jungle after the sinking of their P-T boat. They join the natives to fight guerrilla fashion against the Japs.

Footage has some good, male humor mixed in with the derring-do, and Fritz Lang's direction develops a strong sense of expectancy and suspense in the story-telling.

•

AMERICAN HEART

1992, 113 mins, US Ⓥ ⊙ col

Dir Martin Bell ***Prod*** Rosilyn Heller, Jeff Bridges ***Scr*** Peter Silverman ***Ph*** James Bagdonas ***Ed*** Nancy Baker ***Mus*** James Newton Howard ***Art*** Joel Schiller

Act Jeff Bridges, Edward Furlong, Lucinda Jenney, Don Harvey, Tracey Kapinsky, Maggie Welsh (Avenue/Asis-Heller)

A long-in-the-works labor of love for all concerned, first fictional feature from Martin Bell is rooted in an elemental story about an irresponsible, ex-con father and his teenage son, who is so ignored he must fend for himself on the streets. Around the edges are a host of observations about the sorry state of urban America, and grafted on is a bit of crime melodrama that provides some conventional chase and shoot-em-up action.

Released from prison on a work furlough program, Jack Keely (Jeff Bridges) reunites in Seattle with his 14-year-old son Nick (Edward Furlong), who has been staying with his aunt in the country. Bright, resourceful Nick is discouraged from signing up at school and increasingly hangs around with other dispossessed kids. Jack has trouble assuming the responsibilities of fatherhood, preferring to spend time with his g.f. (Lucinda Jenney).

Peter Silverman's screenplay (based on a story by himself, director Bell and associate producer Mary Ellen Mark, a photographer who is also Bell's wife) offers many honest, reality-grappling scenes, but it could have used a dash of reality-heightening poetry to lift the pic out of the ordinary.

•

AMERICAN IN PARIS, AN

1951, 113 mins, US Ⓥ ⊙ col

Dir Vincente Minnelli ***Prod*** Arthur Freed ***Scr*** Alan Jay Lerner ***Ph*** Alfred Gilks, John Alton ***Ed*** Adrienne Fazan ***Mus*** Johnny Green, Saul Chaplin (dirs.) ***Art*** Cedric Gibbons, Preston Ames

Act Gene Kelly, Leslie Caron, Oscar Levant, Georges Guetary, Nina Foch, Eugene Borden (M-G-M)

An American in Paris is one of the most imaginative musical confections turned out by Hollywood, spotlighting Gene Kelly, Oscar Levant, Nina Foch, and a pair of bright newcomers (Leslie Caron and Georges Guetary) against a cavalcade of George and Ira Gershwin's music.

Kelly is the picture's top star and rates every inch of his billing. His diversified dancing is great as ever and his thesping is standout. But he reveals new talents in this one with his choreography. There's a lengthy ballet to the film's title song for the finale, which is a masterpiece of design, lighting, costumes and color photography. It's a unique blending of classical and modern dance with vaude-style tapping.

Caron is a beauteous, lissome number with an attractively pert personality and plenty of s.a. She scores neatly with her thesping, particularly in the appealing love scenes with Kelly, and displays standout dancing ability. Guetary demonstrates a socko musicomedy tenor and okay acting talents. He's cast neatly as the older man whom Caron almost marries out of gratitude. Story is a sprightly yarn about an American GI (Kelly) who stayed on in Paris after the war to further his art study. Foch, as a wealthy American playgal, "discovers" his art talents and takes him on as her protege to add him to her retinue of lovers. Kelly accepts the idea warily but then meets and falls for Caron.

Gershwin's music gets boffo treatment throughout. While some 10 songs get special handling, true Gershwin fans will recognize strains of most of his other tunes in the background score.

1951: Best Picture, Story & Screenplay, Color Cinematography, Color Art Direction, Score for a Musical Picture, Color Costume Design

NOMINATIONS: Director, Editing

•

AMERICANIZATION OF EMILY, THE

1964, 115 mins, US Ⓥ b/w

Dir Arthur Hiller ***Prod*** Martin Ransohoff ***Scr*** Paddy Chayefsky ***Ph*** Philip Lathrop ***Ed*** Tom McAdoo ***Mus*** Johnny Mandel ***Art*** George W. Davis, Hans Peters, Elliot Scott

Act James Garner, Julie Andrews, Melvyn Douglas, James Coburn, Joyce Grenfell, Edward Binns (M-G-M)

Emily, with Julie Andrews in title role as an English motor pool driver in World War II, takes place immediately before the Normandy invasion. Most of the action unspools in London where Garner, a lieutenant commander who makes avowed cowardice his career, is "dog robber" to Melvyn Douglas, an erratic admiral and one of the heads of the oncoming onslaught on the French coast.

Most of Garner's duties consist of rounding up delicacies and services, impossible to get, for his boss, until the admiral orders him to make a film showing activities of Navy demolition on their landing at Omaha Beach.

Basic idea builds around the admiral being beset with an obsession to have the first man killed on Omaha Beach a sailor, to show the Navy can have no peer in the service, and the script takes it from there.

Pic [based on the novel by William Bradford Huie] is primarily interesting for the romance between Andrews and Garner, the former struggling against being Americanized through her contact with the outgoing and freewheeling Garner.

Garner generally delivers a satisfactory performance. Douglas plays his admiral strictly for laughs. James Coburn as a Navy officer is outstanding particularly for his comedy scenes. Joyce Grenfell as femme star's mother and Keenan Wynn, a salty old salt, likewise handle their roles well.

1964: NOMINATIONS: Best B&W Cinematography, B&W Art Direction

•

AMERICAN ME

1992, 125 mins, US Ⓥ col

Dir Edward James Olmos ***Prod*** Sean Daniel, Robert M. Young, Edward James Olmos ***Scr*** Floyd Mutrux, Desmond Nakano ***Ph*** Reynaldo Villalobos ***Ed*** Arthur R. Coburn, Richard Candib ***Mus*** Dennis Lambert, Claude Gaudette ***Art*** Joe Aubel

Act Edward James Olmos, William Forsythe, Pepe Serna, Danny De La Paz, Evelina Fernandez, Cary-Hiroyuki Tagawa (Universal/YOY)

The criminal life is portrayed with all the glamour of a mugshot in *American Me*, a powerful indictment of the cycle of violence bred by the prisons and street culture. Project has been gestating since 1973, when Floyd Mutrux wrote the script. Al Pacino was once slated to star.

In a punchy prologue, the central figure of Santana (played as an adult by Edward James Olmos) is shown to be, literally, a child of the Pachuco riots of 1943. Pushed along by some incantatory, poetic narration, pic jumps to 1959, when the 16-year-old Santana forms a gang with his buddies Mundo (Pepe Serno) and J. D. (William Forsythe).

Long section detailing life at Folsom State Prison (where the company shot for three weeks) is as fascinating as it is disturbing. Film sketches racial divisions within the pen, the rise of the so-called Mexican Mafia, how drugs are smuggled inside, the scams that can make life there safer and how men inside control things outside. Olmos makes for a mesmerizing, implacable Santana, one of the least romanticized film gangsters since Paul Muni's Scarface.

•

AMERICAN NINJA

1985, 95 mins, US Ⓥ ⊙ col

Dir Sam Firstenberg ***Prod*** Menahem Golan, Yoram Globus ***Scr*** Paul de Mielche ***Ph*** Hanania Baer ***Ed*** Michael J. Duthie ***Mus*** Michael Linn ***Art*** Adrian Gorton

Act Michael Dudikoff, Steve James, Judie Aronson, Guich Koock, John Fujioka, Don Stewart (Cannon)

Michael Dudikoff is the titular hero, a sullen GI named Joe who arrives at U.S. Army base Fort Sonora with a chip on his shoulder. He quickly alienates everyone except the pretty daughter of the commanding officer, Patricia Hickock (Judie Aronson), by singlehandedly saving her from the deadly ninjas working for corrupt arms dealer Ortega (Don Stewart).

Director Sam Firstenberg stages the numerous action scenes well, but engenders little interest in the non-story [by Avi Kleinberger and Gideon Amir].

Dudikoff comes off awkwardly as a new James Dean clone who's been pumping iron. Most winning performance is turned in by Steve James, Joe's sole pal on the base.

•

AMERICAN NINJA 2: THE CONFRONTATION

1987, 89 mins, US Ⓥ ⊙ col

Dir Sam Firstenberg ***Prod*** Menahem Golan, Yoram Globus ***Scr*** Gary Conway, James Booth ***Ph*** Gideon Porath ***Ed*** Michael J. Duthie ***Mus*** George S. Clinton ***Art*** Holger Gross

Act Michael Dudikoff, Steve James, Larry Poindexter, Gary Conway, Jeff Weston, Michelle Botes (Golan-Globus)

This time out, after *American Ninja* (1985) and *Avenging Force* (1986), globe-trotting army hardbodies Michael Dudikoff and Steve James arrive on a small Caribbean island to investigate the disappearance of four U.S. Marines. It turns out that a local drug kingpin is kidnaping soldiers and others to turn them into genetically reengineered ninja assassins who will do his bidding worldwide.

All this merely provides an excuse for an ample number of martial arts showdowns between the heroes and the black-robed baddies who swarm from all directions only to be dispatched in tidy fashion by the good guys.

Script by actors Gary Conway (who plays the narcotics overlord) and James Booth trades heavily upon the notion of Americans inherent mental and physical superiority to native warriors, who are a dime a dozen, but in such a comic way that the viewer can laugh with it rather than at it.

Pic was lensed in South Africa, and is extremely picturesque despite the modest means.

•

AMERICAN NINJA 3: BLOOD HUNT
1989, 90 mins, US Ⓥ ⦿ col
Dir Cedric Sundstrom ***Prod*** Harry Alan Towers ***Scr*** Cedric Sundstrom ***Ph*** George Bartels ***Ed*** Michael J. Duthie ***Mus*** George S. Clinton ***Art*** Ruth Strimling
Act David Bradley, Steve James, Marjoe Gortner, Michele Chan, Yehuda Efroni, Calvin Yung (Breton)

With karate expert David Bradley replacing Michael Dudikoff in the leading role, series continues with a rehash of the enjoyable second entry, as top international martial arts combatants gather on a tropical isle for a tournament.

As before, the island plays host to an evil entrepreneur (Marjoe Gortner), who is on the verge of perfecting a virus that will become the ultimate terrorist weapon. Ridiculously, he is looking for the perfect specimen on whom to test the germ, and finds him in the hunky Bradley, who is prepared for a "designer death."

For his part, Bradley is determined to rescue his Japanese master, whom he believes has been kidnapped by the baddies. This provokes him and his fearless partners into an assault on the fortresslike laboratory.

Even for this level of by-the-numbers action filmmaking, Cedric Sundstrom's script is incredibly lame, and his staging of chopsocky violence is little better. Cheap-looking pic was produced in South Africa.

•

AMERICAN PIE
1999, 95 mins, US Ⓥ ⦿ col
Dir Paul Weitz ***Prod*** Warren Zide, Craig Perry, Chris Moore, Chris Weitz ***Scr*** Adam Herz ***Ph*** Richard Crudo ***Ed*** Priscilla Nedd-Friendly ***Mus*** David Lawrence ***Art*** Paul Peters
Act Jason Biggs, Shannon Elizabeth, Alyson Hannigan, Chris Klein, Natasha Lyonne, Thomas Ian Nicholas (Universal)

A film with a one-track mind, *American Pie* has but a single ambition—to be the king of gross-out comedy.

The nothing-fancy, just-get-to-the-point approach continues throughout, and follows neatly off the simple premise: Four semi-out-of-it seniors, sick of their virginity and determined not to carry their burden with them to college, resolve to divest themselves of their innocence by prom night—and it has to be for real, not purchased.

In addition to Jim (Jason Biggs), who's something of an oaf, the buddies include Kevin (Thomas Ian Nicholas), who's already reached third base with his blond g.f., Vicky (Tara Reid); skinny Finch (Eddie Kaye Thomas), who has no apparent prospects; and Oz (Chris Klein), whose advantageous great looks and jock status are mitigated by an underlying propriety and shyness.

Jim places all his chips on exotic Czech student, Nadia (Shannon Elizabeth); a slapstick bedroom encounter between these two, witnessed by the entire student body via computer, is a particularly wild comic highlight.

Film succeeds in its elementary mission due to its relentless bluntness and fundamental realism about human teenage behavior. Largely no-name cast is game and gangy. Klein, discovered in *Election*, stands out once again as the sensitive stud; and Elizabeth will set thousands of boys drooling as the statuesque Euro who could no doubt teach the whole graduating class a few tricks.

Set in Michigan, but shot mostly around Long Beach, CA, film is technically very low end except for the jam-packed soundtrack of 30-plus tunes.

•

AMERICAN PRESIDENT, THE
1995, 113 mins, US Ⓥ ⦿ ▭ col
Dir Rob Reiner ***Prod*** Rob Reiner ***Scr*** Aaron Sorkin ***Ph*** John Seale ***Ed*** Robert Leighton ***Mus*** Marc Shaiman ***Art*** Lilly Kilvert
Act Michael Douglas, Annette Bening, Martin Sheen, Michael J. Fox, David Paymer, Richard Dreyfuss (Wildwood/Castle Rock/Universal)

A romantic comedy about the dating problems of the world's most powerful man, *The American President* is genial middlebrow fare that coasts a long way on the charm of its two stars.

Michael Douglas plays the embodiment of every liberal's dream—an attractive, dashing, sensitive, humane and smart president of the United States. A widower with a young daughter, he has his attention diverted to his personal life when he meets crack lobbyist Sydney Ellen Wade (Annette Bening), hired to make sure an environmental bill retains its teeth. It takes Ellen a while to come to grips with the nature of the president's interest in her, and some of Bening's best comic moments are in her embarrassed but flattered reactions to his admiring advances.

Republican meanie and presidential hopeful Sen. Bob Rumson (Richard Dreyfuss) brands Ellen "the First Mistress" and helps drag the Shepherd's approval rating down to precarious levels. This, in turn, weakens the president's hand on Capitol Hill, placing his legislation, and his status with Ellen, in jeopardy.

Working with Reiner again after their successful teaming on *A Few Good Men*, screenwriter Aaron Sorkin has cooked up some reasonably engaging banter for his two bright, quick-witted, hard-driving leading characters without letting it get too artificial. Douglas and Bening are more than up to the challenge, delivering winning turns as A-plus personality types.

Supporting roles have been adroitly filled, with Martin Sheen as the prez's chief of staff and longtime best friend, and Anna Deavere Smith, Samantha Mathis and David Paymer as other staffers. Production designer Lilly Kilvert brings the White House to life with lavish, full-scale sets.

Pic was originally developed as *The President Elopes* with Robert Redford long set to star, which accounts for the production involvement of Wildwood and Universal.

1995: NOMINATION: Original Musical or Comedy Score

•

AMERICAN PSYCHO
2000, 97 mins, US Ⓥ ⦿ ▭ col
Dir Mary Harron ***Prod*** Edward R. Pressman, Chris Hanley, Christian Halsey Solomon ***Scr*** Mary Harron, Guinevere Turner ***Ph*** Andrzej Sekula ***Ed*** Andrew Marcus ***Mus*** John Cale ***Art*** Gideon Ponte
Act Christian Bale, Willem Dafoe, Jared Leto, Reese Witherspoon, Samantha Mathis, Chloe Sevigny (Pressman/Lions Gate)

Literary Brat Packer Bret Easton Ellis' controversial 1991 tome—arguably one of the most-loathed and least-read novels in recent memory—undergoes a rather startling transformation via Mary Harron's razored adaptation. She and co-scenarist Guinevere Turner have liberally reframed Ellis' book as a satire of conspicuous consumption and moral bankruptcy amid the giddy excesses of High Reaganomics, and Harron's *Psycho* represent an impressive reclaiming of dubious material.

Ellis' protag remains the quintessential "soulless yuppie" Patrick Bateman (as in Bates Motel, presumably), a Trump-worshipping, coke-snorting, insider-trading, cash-hemorrhaging monster of materialistic vacuity. With his past erased to an even greater extent than in the novel, Bateman is a chillingly amoral blank slate for whom emotions register only when he does "bad things"—and even then he's not so sure that his actions are real rather than delusional.

Tightly wound screenplay mercifully substitutes a propulsive structure and relatively restrained images for the book's genuinely pornographic longueurs—the sex and sadism here are both largely offscreen. Still, *American Psycho* begs an unsettling question: If its hero is such a zero, what exactly is being satirized? Does he serve to amplify an amoral era's more callous aspects, or does the film, like the book before it, merely inventory them? To the extent that it's harrowing, *American Psycho* remains indefensible as critique; only in the marginal details—disposable pop soundtrack, fussed-over decor and cuisine, prostitutes numbered by their commodity status—does it achieve anything approaching satire.

Welsh-born Christian Bale is perfectly cast as Bateman. He verges on caricature at times (particularly in a silly dance sequence), but arguably that approach makes the role bearable, at times almost human. Pic sports an impressive widescreen palette, with cold, formal compositions and glittering Manhattan nightscapes predominant. Feature is a clear triumph of design as content—to be enjoyed (or analyzed) at one's own risk.

•

AMERICAN ROMANCE, AN
1944, 151 mins, US col
Dir King Vidor ***Prod*** King Vidor ***Scr*** Herbert Delmas, William Ludwig ***Ph*** Harold Rosson ***Ed*** Conrad A. Nervig ***Mus*** Louis Gruenberg ***Art*** Cedric Gibbons, Urie McCleary
Act Brian Donlevy, Ann Richards, Walter Abel, John Qualen, Horace McNally (M-G-M)

One of Metro's greatest efforts (claimed to be two years in the making and costing over $3 million), this film is Brian Donlevy's baby from opening to closing, as the Czech immigrant who runs the gamut from poverty to become a wealthy industrialist.

King Vidor's story, coupled with his forthright direction and the excellent acting, are assets that add up to a winning total. The one fault with *Romance* is that it is much too long in the telling. Yarn takes more than an hour to get down to business. During that hour, true, Vidor lays the setting for the rest of the film, showing how Donlevy, who is held up at Ellis Island on landing in America because he did not own the equivalent of $25 in U.S. money, overcomes this poverty by hard work in the Mesabi iron ore pits of Minnesota, and meets the girl whom he is to marry (Ann Richards).

Photographed in beautiful Technicolor, this romantic drama is notable for the documented montage shots of the intricate mining and shipping of iron ore; the making of steel in the huge mills of the Midwest; films showing the way autos are made; and the excellent details of airplane-making.

•

AMERICAN SUCCESS
SEE: THE AMERICAN SUCCESS COMPANY

•

AMERICAN SUCCESS COMPANY, THE
1979, 94 mins, US/W. Germany col
Dir William Richert ***Prod*** Daniel H. Blatt, Edgar J. Scherrick ***Scr*** William Richert, Larry Cohen ***Ph*** Anthony Richmond ***Ed*** Ralph E. Winters ***Mus*** Maurice Jarre ***Art*** Rolf Zehetbauer
Act Jeff Bridges, Belinda Bauer, Ned Beatty, Bianca Jagger, Steven Keats, John Glover (Columbia/Geria)

Although almost everything that happens on screen is done with considerable style and a morbid sense of humor, lack of overall point ultimately sinks the picture.

Jeff Bridges here plays the mild-mannered son-in-law of international credit card tycoon Ned Beatty. Called a loser by his boss and under the thumb of gorgeous wife Belinda Bauer, youth decides to turn the tables on them by assuming the guise of a gangsterish tough-guy, then commencing to push them around to get his way.

Undeniable is William Richert's visual flair and sometimes startling sense of the absurd. Billed as "A William Richert-Larry Cohen Film," pic was to have been helmed by Cohen, writer of the original story, and was known during production as *The Ringer*.

[Pic was later released in re-edited versions as *American Success* and *Success*.]

•

AMERICAN TAIL, AN
1986, 80 mins, US Ⓥ ⦿ col
Dir Don Bluth ***Prod*** Don Bluth, John Pomeroy, Gary Goldman ***Scr*** Judy Freudberg, Tony Geiss ***Mus*** James Horner (Amblin)

The film endeavors to tell the story of Russian immigrants, who happen in this case to be mice of the Mousekewitz clan, and their flight in the late 1800s to the United States, where, Papa Mousekewitz insists, there are no cats.

Cartoons with ambitions even this noble are as rare as Steven Spielberg films that lose money, but every character and every situation presented herein have been seen a thousand times before.

The mouse-vs-cat standoff is as old as animation itself, Dom DeLuise's friendly feline is uncomfortably close to the Cowardly Lion in concept, a little bug smacks directly of Jiminy Cricket, and assorted villains are straight out of Dickens by way of Damon Runyon.

1986: NOMINATION: Best Song ("Somewhere Out There")

•

AMERICAN TAIL: FIEVEL GOES WEST, AN
1991, 74 mins, US Ⓥ ⦿ col
Dir Phil Nibbelink, Simon Wells ***Prod*** Steven Spielberg, Robert Watts ***Scr*** Flint Dille ***Ed*** Nick Fletcher ***Mus*** James Horner ***Art*** Neil Ross (Amblin)

Complete with legendary James Stewart voicing broken-down lawdog Wylie Burp, *An American Tail: Fievel Goes West* is an amiable sequel to the 1986 animated smash featuring the Russian immigrant mouse.

The story picks up the plucky Fievel and family living in grim, turn-of-the-century Bronx, menaced by omnipresent cats. The expansive shift to the Old West is welcome, as is the slowing of the pace to accommodate the relaxed, drawling and almost comatose personality of Fievel's hero/mentor Wylie Burp.

Fievel Goes West cleverly draws on the oft-expressed

thought that the mythic West was largely an immigrant's wide-eyed dream of what America should be, in opposition to hellish big-city reality and the old country left behind.

Phillip Glasser's sweet rendition of the mouse's voice is a major asset, as are the voice parts of Dom DeLuise, as Fievel's scene-stealing companion, a scaredy-cat who turns brave; John Cleese, as the unctuously villainous Cat R. Waul; and Amy Irving, as the brassy saloon entertainer Miss Kitty. There isn't much of a plot to speak of.

•

AMERICAN TRAGEDY, AN

1931, 96 mins, US b/w

Dir Josef von Sternberg ***Scr*** Samuel Hoffenstein ***Ph*** Lee Garmes ***Art*** Hans Dreier

Act Phillips Holmes, Sylvia Sidney, Francis Dee, Irving Pichel, Frederick Burton, Claire McDowell (Paramount)

An American Tragedy unreels as an ordinary program effort with an unhappy ending. Its relations to the book [by Theodore Dreiser] upon which it is based are decidedly strained. As von Sternberg has seen fit to present it this celluloid structure is slow, heavy and not always interesting drama.

There is not a performance in the cast of any real interest. Histrionic honors belong to the elegantly voiced Irving Pichel, a veteran of the legit stage and one of the original founders of The Theatre Guild, as the district attorney.

The film spends a third or more of its 96 minutes on the trial. It's a big and theatrically good atmospheric scene, but has the handicap of involving neither of the girls, as Roberta (for whose murder Clyde is convicted) is already dead, and Sondra escapes through the influence of a wealthy father. So the entire burden is on Phillips Holmes, as the floundering victim, which he is incapable of upholding for the camera.

On the sympathetic end there's Sylvia Sidney acting as the trusting Roberta, which she mainly accomplishes by means of a wistful smile. Frances Dee, as Sondra, merely registers as the Hollywood conception of a debutante and is not important, except as the brusque motivation for Clyde's reversal of his relations with Roberta and his longing to become one of the younger social set of the small town.

It's questionable if even the admirers of this author's work condone the evident publicity complex he had developed, so it shouldn't be a matter of inflamed indignation by the minority in defense of the writer over the picture as an illustrated interpretation of the novel. Dreiser complained that the script first prepared by Sergei Eisenstein, to have directed, was entirely satisfactory. This, however was not the treatment finally used, with von Sternberg replacing the Russian in the directorial chair.

•

AMERICAN WEREWOLF IN LONDON, AN

1981, 97 mins, US Ⓥ ⦿ col

Dir John Landis ***Prod*** George Folsey, Jr. ***Scr*** John Landis ***Ph*** Robert Paynter ***Ed*** Malcolm Campbell ***Mus*** Elmer Bernstein ***Art*** Leslie Dilley

Act David Naughton, Jenny Agutter, Griffin Dunne, John Woodvine, Brian Glover, Frank Oz (Universal/Lycanthrope)

A clever mixture of comedy and horror that succeeds in being both funny and scary, *An American Werewolf in London* possesses an overriding eagerness to please that prevents it from becoming off-putting, and special effects freaks get more than their money's worth. Bumming around Europe, two American students (David Naughton and Griffin Dunne) seek refuge from the nasty North England elements in the Slaughtered Lamb pub. Natives there are uncommonly hostile, to the point of forcing the lads out into the night despite indications that there's trouble in these parts.

In short order, they're attacked by a fierce beast and, after the good-natured humor of this prelude, audience is instantly sobered up when Dunne is killed and Naughton is heavily gashed and gored.

Recovering in a London Hospital and, later, in the flat of amorous nurse Jenny Agutter, Naughton experiences some disturbing and visually outrageous nightmares and is visited by the Undead Dunne, who urges his friend to commit suicide or turn into a werewolf with the next full moon.

Naughton ignores the advice and, sure enough, undergoes a complete transformation on camera, a highlight in which talents of special makeup effects designer Rick Baker are shown in full flower.

1981: Best Makeup

•

AMISTAD

1997, 152 mins, US Ⓥ ⦿ ⊏⊐ col

Dir Steven Spielberg ***Prod*** Steven Spielberg, Debbie Allen, Colin Wilson ***Scr*** David Franzoni ***Ph*** Janusz Kaminski ***Ed*** Michael Kahn ***Mus*** John Williams ***Art*** Rick Carter

Act Morgan Freeman, Anthony Hopkins, Matthew McConaughey, Nigel Hawthorne, Djimon Hounsou, Pete Postlethwaite (DreamWorks)

Amistad is an artistically solid, if not always dramatically exciting, chronicle of the 1839 rebellion on board the Spanish slave ship of the title. True story is presented as an international intrigue of a high order, one that involved the governments of pre–civil War U.S., Great Britain, Spain and, of course, the 53 Africans held captive in the cramped cargo off the Cuban coast

Boasting a high-voltage cast, led by Brits Anthony Hopkins and Nigel Hawthorne, Americans Morgan Freeman and Matthew McConaughey and, most impressively, West African Djimon Hounsou as the rebels' leader, this second release from DreamWorks touches on the very fabric of the American social system

Steven Spielberg's second foray into African-American history is far more effective and moving than *The Color Purple*. Aiming to instruct as well as entertain—and often struggling to reconcile these two goals—pic lacks the subtlety of tone and simplicity of form that made his *Schindler's List* so special.

Though there are a number of trials, Spielberg shrewdly avoids the routine format of courtroom drama, instead seamlessly integrating the numereous characters and their particular stands on the case. Occasionally, the film sucumbs to the level of an anthropological survey, viewing the Africans and their rituals as exotic curiosity, though Hounsou's dignified portrayal of Cinque as a man of outer strength and inner peace successfully counters this weakness. Freeman is totally wasted as former slave Joadson, a fictional character that's a composite of several historical figures.

McConaughey renders a passable performance as a shady lawyer. Hopkins, as John Quincy Adams, former president and son of founding father John Adams, shines throughout.

1997: NOMINATIONS: Best Supp. Actor (Anthony Hopkins), Cinematography, Original Dramatic Score, Costume Design

•

AMITYVILLE 3-D

1983, 105 mins, US Ⓥ ⦿ col

Dir Richard Fleischer ***Prod*** Stephen F. Kesten ***Scr*** William Wales ***Ph*** Fred Schuler ***Ed*** Frank J. Urioste ***Mus*** Howard Blake ***Art*** Giorgio Postiglione

Act Tony Roberts, Tess Harper, Robert Joy, Candy Clark, John Beal, Meg Ryan (De Laurentiis)

Amityville 3-D proudly announces that it is not a sequel to *The Amityville Horror* or *Amityville II*. Even so, there is hardly anything original about the picture. A new cast of characters and the addition of 3-D does little to pump new life, supernatural or otherwise, into this tired genre. This time around a doubting Tom journalist (Tony Roberts) and his partner (Candy Clark) expose an occult hoax only to have their intervention literally backfire on them.

Roberts ignores the warnings of Clark and his estranged wife (Tess Harper) and thinks nothing of the sudden death of the realtor (John Harkins). His teenage daughter (Lori Loughlin) and her friend (Meg Ryan) can't resist the temptations of the house either, despite a series of strange occurrences.

The story itself, involving the daughter being swallowed up by the forces that apparently live in a well in the basement of the house, moves along at a snail's pace enlivened from time to time by some nice special effects and 3-D images. Images tossed about by the ArriVision 3-D process include a man being engulfed by flies, a pole impaling a car and a free-floating Frisbee. The film would have worked better played for laughs.

•

AMITYVILLE HORROR, THE

1979, 117 mins, US Ⓥ ⦿ col

Dir Stuart Rosenberg ***Prod*** Ronald Saland, Elliot Geisinger ***Scr*** Sandor Stern ***Ph*** Fred J. Koenekamp ***Ed*** Robert Brown ***Mus*** Lalo Schifrin ***Art*** Kim Swados

Act James Brolin, Margot Kidder, Rod Steiger, Don Stroud, Natasha Ryan (American International)

Taken from the Jay Anson tome, Sandor Stern's script deals faithfully with the supposedly true (but since challenged) story of the Lutz family, who move into a home in Amityville, NY, at a knocked-down price because of its bloody history. The Lutz fled 28 days later in terror. Stepfather James Brolin, mother Margot Kidder and moppets Natasha Ryan, Meeno Peluce and K. C. Martel sympathetically play the happy, innocent family and director Stuart Rosenberg—ably aided by efex specialists William Cruse and Delwyn Rheaume—have the house all ready for them.

Flies swarm where they shouldn't, pipes and walls ooze ick, doors fly open, and priests and psychic sensitives cringe and flee in panic. It's definitely a house that audiences will enjoy visiting, especially if unfamiliar with the ending.

1979: NOMINATION: Best Original Score

•

AMITYVILLE: THE DEMON

SEE: AMITYVILLE 3-D

•

AMITYVILLE II: THE POSSESSION

1982, 104 mins, US Ⓥ ⦿ col

Dir Damiano Damiani ***Prod*** Ira N. Smith, Stephen R. Greenwald ***Scr*** Tommy Lee Wallace ***Ph*** Franco DiGiacomo ***Ed*** Sam O'Steen ***Mus*** Lalo Schifrin ***Art*** Pierluigi Basile

Act Burt Young, Rutanya Alda, James Olson, Jack Magner, Diane Franklin, Andrew Prine (Orion/De Laurentiis)

It is never quite explained in the context of the film whether this is a prequel, sequel or entirely new version of the Amityville story. No matter. We still have the same house of horrors about to be occupied by a family who, as usual, never think to leave the house once it starts taking on a personality of its own.

Of course, this is not the typical American family. Burt Young, who gives new meaning to the word one-dimensional in his portrait of the father, loves beating the daylights out of his wife and kids. Jack Magner, a screen newcomer saddled with the plum role of the troubled oldest son, begins finding his sister sexually attractive. And Rutanya Alda, who does a lot of screaming as the spineless mother, spends a lot of time praying her problem will go away.

There are actually two films meandering in this mess—one a second-rate horror flick about a family in peril, and another that is a slight variation on the demon-possessed *Exorcist* theme.

•

AMOROUS ADVENTURES OF MOLL FLANDERS, THE

1965, 123 mins, UK Ⓥ ⦿ ⊏⊐ col

Dir Terence Young ***Prod*** Marcel Hellman ***Scr*** Denis Cannan, Roland Kibbee ***Ph*** Ted Moore ***Ed*** Frederick Wilson ***Mus*** John Addison ***Art*** Syd Cain

Act Kim Novak, Richard Johnson, Angela Lansbury, George Sanders, Leo McKern, Vittorio De Sica (Paramount)

Moll Flanders—The Amorous Adventures of—is a sprawling, brawling, gaudy, bawdy, tongue-in-cheek comedy that seeks to caricature an 18th-century London wench's desire to be a gentlewoman and her varying exploits thereof. Starring Kim Novak in title role, it has sex and color, slapstick and lusty, busty characterization, action which is sometimes very funny and, again, equally unfunny.

The foreword slyly states: "Any similarity between this film and any other film is purely coincidental." However that may be, it was a natural that the success scored by *Tom Jones* should be followed by a femme counterpart in this adaptation of Daniel Defoe's novel.

Director Terence Young seems constantly to keep in mind the comic potentialities of his subject and his helming is always broad, leavened with old-fashioned sight gags. The screenplay follows Moll as she goes to London, to seek her goal through a variety of affairs and marriages that culminate in a ceremony with a highwayman whom she mistook to be a wealthy landowner.

Richard Johnson (whom Novak wed after pic ended) gives colorful and romantic enactment to the highwayman character. George Sanders's portrayal of a rich banker wed to Moll is robust and comical. Leo McKern, as Johnson's outlaw henchman, also scores a comedy hit.

•

AMOROUS PRAWN, THE

1962, 89 mins, UK b/w

Dir Anthony Kimmins ***Prod*** Leslie Gilliat ***Scr*** Anthony Kimmins, Nicholas Phipps ***Ph*** Wilkie Cooper ***Ed*** Thelma Connell ***Mus*** John Barry ***Art*** Albert Witherick

Act Ian Carmichael, Joan Greenwood, Cecil Parker, Dennis Price, Robert Beatty, Liz Fraser (British Lion/Covent Garden)

Anthony Kimmins's comedy, *The Amorous Prawn*, chalked up well over 1,000 performances on the stage. Now, directed by the author, it shapes up as non-demanding light entertainment, cheerfully put over by a reliable cast of popular British thesps.

General Fitzadam (Cecil Parker) is on the eve of retirement but is a bit short of cash. His wife hits on the idea of converting his military headquarters in Scotland into a guest house. The general's army staff is brought into the scheme.

Two major complications develop. One is the sudden,

unexpected return of the general which, at first, calls for a considerable amount of repetitious camouflage by the conspirators. The second is when an unexpected guest turns up who is revealed as the Minister of State for War.

Parker produces one of his typical, bumbly performances, but Joan Greenwood, as his wife, is not so peppily in character as she normally is in this sort of drawing room farce. Ian Carmichael does a shrewd job as the wily corporal who becomes maitre d'hotel in the scheme while Liz Fraser and Bridget Armstrong provide some pulchritude.

•

AMOUR DE SWANN, UN

1984, 110 mins, France/W. Germany b/w

Dir Volker Schlondorff ***Prod*** Margaret Menegoz ***Scr*** Peter Brook, Jean-Claude Carriere, Marie-Helene Estienne, Volker Schlondorff ***Ph*** Sven Nykvist ***Ed*** Francoise Bonnot ***Mus*** Hans-Werner Henze ***Art*** Jacques Saulnier

Act Jeremy Irons, Ornella Muti, Alain Delon, Fanny Ardant, Marie-Christine Barrault, Anne Bennent

Volker Schlondorff's film is not sacrilege—merely a disappointment. One did not really expect a miracle, but the makers of the adaptation seemed to have their sights held at a reasonable level—only *Swann in Love*, the second part of the first volume of Marcel Proust's monumental book. Schlondorff fails because he has no substantial style of his own. His fastidious application makes for a film of attractive surfaces and little depth or feeling. In other words, it's fairly dull.

In *Swann in Love*, Proust created a sort of blueprint for the rest of his *Remembrances of Things Past* with the story of a Parisian dandy, Charles Swann, who falls in love with and pursues a social-climbing demi-mondaine, Odette de Crecy. His passion becomes so obsessive and his jealousy so overpowering that he gradually cuts himself off from the brilliant high society circles—the time is the mid-1880s—that he has succeeded in penetrating, despite his Jewish origins.

Scripters do a cut-and-paste job on the text, lifting, transposing and dovetailing episodes and dialog from all over the novel and concentrating them into a single 24-hour period. The performances might have salvaged the film, but Jeremy Irons is not up to the difficult central role. One tires of his foppish single-mindedness and tends to side with poor Odette, lusciously but vaguely incarnated by Ornella Muti. (Both are dubbed into French.)

Alain Delon is both marvelously comic and touching as Charlus, the middle-aged homosexual aristocrat, whose own vain amorous pursuit of a young man is a parallel to Swann's actions.

•

AMOUR, L'APRES-MIDI, L'

1972, 95 mins, France col

Dir Eric Rohmer ***Prod*** Pierre Cottrell ***Scr*** Eric Rohmer ***Ph*** Nestor Almendros ***Ed*** Cecile Decugis ***Mus*** Arie Dzierlatka

Act Bernard Verley, Zouzou, Francoise Verley, Daniel Ceccaldi, Malvina Penne, Barbette Ferrier (Films du Losange/Barbet Schroeder)

Late starter in the New Wave, Eric Rohmer adds another plus to his record with this latest "moral tale" [the last of his series of six]. His shrewdly knowing dialogue, asides and insight into the vagaries of love come across without verbosity or preciosity. To this add the knowing counterpoint of fine visual nuances, expert acting, bright editing and delicate lensing. It's a witty tale of a self-satisfied, middle-class, white-collar man (Bernard Verley) who almost gives into Chloe, a free-living, impulsive woman (Zouzou), who barges in on him and whom he has not seen in years. Actually, she was a girlfriend of a friend and almost drove that man to suicide. She is a bit marked by life but still attractive and with the élan, unpredictability and direct emotional charm that Rohmer can exact so well.

Zouzou has heretofore played only in fringe experimental films but with this pic should be sought after. Verley is right as the slightly puffy but still good-looking architect who has found a good relationship with his wife, Helene (Francoise Verley). It is his free afternoons that lead to his problems with the woman and his near seduction.

All the pro and non-pro actors are effectively used by Rohmer. The nearest thing to a love scene is Verley drying Zouzou when he arrives and she is taking a shower, or when he holds her and rubs her naked back.

•

ANACONDA

1997, 89 mins, US col

Dir Luis Llosa ***Prod*** Verna Harrah, Leonard Rabinowitz, Carole Little ***Scr*** Hans Bauer, Jim Cash, Jack Epps, Jr. ***Ph*** Bill Butler ***Ed*** Michael R. Miller ***Mus*** Randy Edelman ***Art*** Kirk M. Petruccelli

Act Jennifer Lopez, Ice Cube, Jon Voight, Eric Stoltz, Jonathan Hyde, Owen Wilson (Cinema Line/Columbia)

Despite some game efforts by a fine cast dominated by a brazenly over-the-top Jon Voight, *Anaconda* is a silly and plodding *Jaws* rip-off about a 40-foot, man-eating snake on the prowl in the Brazilian rain forest.

A documentary crew sets out on a river journey to find the Shirishama Indians, a legendary tribe. Anthropologist Steve Cale (Eric Stoltz) heads a team that includes director Terri Flores (Jennifer Lopez), cameraman Danny (Ice Cube), sound mixer Gary (Owen Wilson), production manager Denise (Kari Wuhrer) and narrator Warren (Jonathan Hyde). Early on, they bring abroad an unexpected guest: Paul Sarone (Voight), an aggressively charismatic fellow who offers to guide his rescuers but has a very different agenda in mind.

Sporting a scarred face, an arrogant leer and a tricky accent that's meant to identify him as a Paraguayan, Voight gives a performance that could be labeled Swift's Premium and sold by the pound. Voight is a lot more fun, and more convincing, than the Animatronic anaconda, which comes off looking like a cartoonish bit player from *Who Framed Roger Rabbit?*

Stoltz spends nearly three-quarters of the pic off camera while his character is asleep below deck, recovering from injuries. It's hard to shake the suspicion that, while his costars continued to labor, Stoltz was free to go off and do two or three indie movies.

There is an amusing undercurrent to the scene in which Lopez's character, a first-time filmmaker, bitterly surveys her situation. "I thought this movie would be my first big break," she says. "Instead, it's turned into a disaster." Amen, sister.

•

ANALYZE THIS

1999, 103 mins, US col

Dir Harold Ramis ***Prod*** Paula Weinstein, Jane Rosenthal ***Scr*** Peter Tolan, Harold Ramis, Kenneth Lonergan ***Ph*** Stuart Dryburgh ***Ed*** Christopher Tellefsen ***Mus*** Howard Shore ***Art*** Wynn Thomas

Act Robert De Niro, Billy Crystal, Lisa Kudrow, Joe Viterelli, Chazz Palminteri, Bill Macy

A shrink pushes a mobster to get in touch with the good fella inside him in *Analyze This*, a sometimes funny situation comedy in which the mechanics of the situation eventually overwhelm the comedy. Robert De Niro and Billy Crystal both have moments to shine in this farcical concoction.

Paul Vitti (De Niro), one of New York's two mob kingpins, is suffering from a modern malady entirely alien to the gangland ethos: anxiety attacks. Could anyone ever imagine Scarface, Little Caesar or Vito Corleone stressing out? Vitti coyly pretends to his recruited shrink, "family" therapist Ben Sobel (Crystal), that he's only there on behalf of a friend before coercing the doc into being on 24-hour call to attend to his crises.

The timing is inconvenient for Sobel, as he's headed for Miami to marry broadcaster Laura MacNamara (Lisa Kudrow). Vitti heads for Florida, precipitating a gangland hit that aborts Sobel's wedding, ups the ante between Vitti and his New York rival Primo Sindone (Chazz Palminteri) and wreaks havoc on Sobel's personal life.

De Niro's precise comic timing and colorful line readings constitute pic's greatest pleasure, and script [from a screen story by Kenneth Lonergan and Peter Tolan] takes every opportunity to inject shrinky jargon into the mouth of a man much more at ease with four-letter expletives.

Once the action returns to Gotham, however, the plot machinery starts becoming far too visible, to the detriment of the steady laughs.

•

ANASTASIA

1956, 105 mins, US col

Dir Anatole Litvak ***Prod*** Buddy Adler ***Scr*** Arthur Laurents ***Ph*** Jack Hildyard ***Ed*** Bert Bates ***Mus*** Alfred Newman ***Art*** Andrei Andrejew, Bill Andrews

Act Ingrid Bergman, Yul Brynner, Helen Hayes, Akim Tamiroff, Martita Hunt, Felix Aylmer (20th Century-Fox)

The legit hit *Anastasia* has been made into a wonderfully moving and entertaining motion picture from start to finish, and the major credit inevitably must go to Ingrid Bergman who turns in a great performance.

Yet the picture is by no means all Bergman. Yul Brynner as General Bounine, the tough Russian exile, etches a strong and convincing portrait that stands up perfectly to Bergman's Anastasia, and Helen Hayes has great dignity as the Empress.

Story basically is the one from the French play of Marcelle Maurette adapted by Guy Bolton. Brynner and a group of conspirators are working in Paris to produce an Anastasia who might help them collect the ú10 million deposited in England by the Czar's family. Brynner keeps the destitute Bergman from suicide, then grooms her to play Anastasia's part.

Bergman bears an amazing resemblance to the Czar's youngest daughter who was supposed to have been killed by the Reds in 1918. Desperate to forget the past, Bergman first resists, then begins to recover her regal bearing—and her memories.

Director Anatole Litvak and producer Buddy Adler imbue the story with realistic settings.

1956: Best Actress (Ingrid Bergman)

NOMINATION: Best Scoring of a Dramatic Picture

•

ANASTASIA

1997, 94mins, US col

Dir Don Bluth, Gary Goldman ***Prod*** Don Bluth, Gary Goldman ***Scr*** Susan Gauthier, Bruce Graham, Bob Tzudiker, Noni White ***Ed*** Fiona Trayler ***Mus*** David Newman (Fox Family)

The much-anticipated debut offering of Fox's new animation unit in Phoenix reps an ambitious, serious but not particularly stimulating musical feature [from the play by Marcelle Maurette as adapted by Guy Bolton, and the screenplay by Arthur Laurents] that attempts to graft warm and cuddly family-film motifs onto turbulent aspects of modern history. Ninth effort from the Don Bluth–Gary Goldman team seems poised to appeal most to girls between seven and 12.

Pre-credits prologue establishes Anastasia (voiced by Kirsten Dunst, sung by Lacey Chabert) as the beloved daughter of Czar Nicholas in 1916, but stumbles as it essentially attributes Russia's social unrest entirely to the sinister sorcerer Rasputin (Christopher Lloyd, sung by Jim Cummings). She and her grandmother (Angela Lansbury) escape the curse that Rasputin lowers upon the rest of the Romanovs, and Anastasia is next seen as a beautiful young woman named Anya (Meg Ryan, sung by Liz Callaway) emerging from a People's Orphanage a decade later.

Needing a supreme villain, the filmmakers resurrect Rasputin, who has his evil powers restored by his chatty pet bat. He unleashes his demons upon the train carrying Anastasia and her mentors to Paris [to meet her grandmother], making for an action-packed railway setpiece.

The mid-$50 million film's physical specifications are sumptuous enough, and picture reps a rare animated feature produced in widescreen, the first in CinemaScope since Disney's *Sleeping Beauty* in 1959. Nonetheless, the impact is moderate at best: animation style is variable, with characters' body movements sometimes jerky. Facial expressions don't measure up to the best Disney standards.

A stellar cast delivers mostly good readings, particularly Lansbury as the Dowager Empress, but Ryan's accent comes across as extremely modern American.

1997: NOMINATIONS: Best Original Musical Score, Original Song ("Journey to the Past")

•

ANATOLIAN SMILE, THE

SEE: AMERICA AMERICA

•

ANATOMY OF A MURDER

1959, 160 mins, US b/w

Dir Otto Preminger ***Prod*** Otto Preminger ***Scr*** Wendell Mayes ***Ph*** Sam Leavitt ***Ed*** Louis R. Loeffler ***Mus*** Duke Ellington ***Art*** Boris Leven

Act James Stewart, Lee Remick, George C. Scott, Ben Gazzara, Arthur O'Connell, Eve Arden, Kathryn Grant (Columbia/Carlyle)

Director Otto Preminger got his film on the screen for preview only 21 days after the final shooting on Michigan location. This dispatch may be one reason why *Anatomy* is overlong. Wendell Mayes's screenplay otherwise is a large reason for the film's general excellence. In swift, brief strokes it introduces a large number of diverse characters and sets them in motion. An army lieutenant (Ben Gazzara) has killed a tavern operator whom he suspects of attempting to rape his wife (Lee Remick). James Stewart, former district attorney and now a privately practicing attorney in a small Michigan city, is engaged for the defense.

Mayes's screenplay differs in some respects from the novel by the Michigan judge who uses the nom de plume Robert Traver. Partly through casting, there is considerable doubt about the real innocence of Gazzara and Remick. This handsome young couple astray of the law are far from admirable.

Preminger purposely creates situations that flicker with uncertainty and may be evaluated in different ways. Motives are mixed and dubious, and therefore sustain interest. Balancing the fascinating nastiness of the younger players, there is the warmth and intelligence of Stewart and Arthur

O'Connell. O'Connell, a bright, but booze-prone Irishman of great charm, is his ally. Joseph N. Welch, Boston attorney, is tremendous as the trial judge. George C. Scott, as the prosecution attorney, has the suave menace of a small-time Torquemada.

1959: NOMINATIONS: Best Picture, Actor (James Stewart), Supp. Actor (Arthur O'Connell, George C. Scott), Screenplay, B&W Cinematography, Editing

•

ANCHORS AWEIGH

1945, 138 mins, US Ⓥ ⦿ col

Dir George Sidney ***Prod*** Joe Pasternak ***Scr*** Isobel Lennart ***Ph*** Robert Planck, Charles Boyle ***Ed*** Adrienne Fazan ***Mus*** Georgie Stoll (dir.) ***Art*** Cedric Gibbons, Randall Duell

Act Frank Sinatra, Kathryn Grayson, Gene Kelly, Jose Iturbi, Dean Stockwell, Pamela Britton (M-G-M)

Anchors Aweigh is solid musical fare. The production numbers are zingy; the songs are extremely listenable; the color treatment outstanding.

Two of the potent entertainment factors are the tunes and Gene Kelly's hoofing. Jule Styne and Sammy Cahn cleffed five new numbers, three of which are given the Frank Sinatra treatment for boff results.

In the dance department Kelly sells top terping. There is a clever Tom and Jerry sequence combining Kelly's live action with a cartoon fairy story. Kelly also combines three Spanish tunes into another sock number executed with little Sharon McManus. His third is a class tango.

Kathryn Grayson, one of the three co-stars, figures importantly in the score with her vocaling. Jose Iturbi plays and conducts *Donkey Serenade*, Piano Concerto and *Hungarian Rhapsody No. 2* for additional potent musical factor.

Sinatra and Kelly are sailors on liberty. They come to Hollywood. Sinatra is a shy Brooklynite who's being instructed in the art of pickups by Kelly, the traditional gob with a gal in every port. [Screenplay was "suggested" by a story by Natalie Marcin.]

1945: Best Score for a Musical Picture

NOMINATIONS: Best Picture, Actor (Gene Kelly), Color Cinematography, Song ("I Fall in Love Too Easily")

•

AND BABY MAKES THREE

1949, 83 mins, US b/w

Dir Henry Levin ***Prod*** Robert Lord ***Scr*** Lou Breslow, Joseph Hoffman ***Ph*** Burnett Guffey ***Ed*** Viola Lawrence ***Mus*** George Duning

Act Robert Young, Barbara Hale, Robert Hutton, Janis Carter, Billie Burke (Columbia/Santana)

Fun starts confusingly but mood warms up as footage unfolds and plot line becomes clear. Robert Young has been divorced by Barbara Hale after being caught in a compromising spot. It's a hurry-up Reno untying and Hale is ready to do a quick rebound marriage when she faints on the way to the altar. Pregnancy is the diagnosis. This upsets wedding plans with Robert Hutton and complications also develop when Young announces he'll fight for partial custody.

Young is his usual able self in taking care of his part of the footage. Hale delights as the would-be mother. Henry Levin's direction gets good movement into the script and comedy touches are neatly devised.

•

ANDERSON TAPES, THE

1971, 98 mins, US Ⓥ ⦿ col

Dir Sidney Lumet ***Prod*** Robert M. Weitman ***Scr*** Frank R. Pierson ***Ph*** Arthur J. Ornitz ***Ed*** Joanne Burke ***Mus*** Quincy Jones ***Art*** Benjamin J. Kasazkow

Act Sean Connery, Dyan Cannon, Martin Balsam, Alan King, Ralph Meeker, Christopher Walken (Columbia)

Sean Connery plays an ex-con who schemes to burglarize an entire apartment house on Manhattan's plush Upper East Side. With backing from a new breed of organized mobster, led by Alan King, Connery recruits a band of diverse helpmates ranging from a homosexual antique dealer (Martin Balsam) to a fellow ex-con just released after 40 years in prison (Stan Gottlieb).

Overriding the machinations of the plot are the Anderson tapes themselves. Lawrence Sanders's novel was composed of snippets of surreptitious recordings compiled by local police, FBI agents, private investigators, treasury spies, etc., all snooping on the activities for various reasons, and all unable to piece together what they're overhearing.

Scripter Frank Pierson—with director Sidney Lumet—has injected broadly comic aspects and the laughs work without reducing suspense.

Essentially miscast but trying mightily to keep his accent under control, Connery's presence is strong. As a high-priced mistress, frigid until Connery melts her, Dyan Cannon has little to do but look appetizing.

With the flashiest role, Martin Balsam swishes off with the honors, although gay activists will take umbrage at the abundance of conventional fag jokes.

•

AND GOD CREATED WOMAN

1988, 94 mins, US Ⓥ ⦿ col

Dir Roger Vadim ***Prod*** George C. Braunstein, Ron Hamady ***Scr*** R. J. Stewart ***Ph*** Stephen M. Katz ***Ed*** Suzanne Petit ***Mus*** Thomas Chase, Steve Rucker ***Art*** Victor Kempster

Act Rebecca DeMornay, Vincent Spano, Frank Langella, Donovan Leitch, Judith Chapman (Crow/Vestron)

A remake in name only of his first feature, made 32 years earlier, Roger Vadim's new film is considerably more legitimate dramatically than one might expect.

Vadim tells a modestly involving tale about how a woman with two strikes against her gives herself a shot at life through a combination of sex, imagination, energy and plenty of scheming.

Attention-grabbing opening has inmate Rebecca De-Mornay escaping from prison and hitching a ride in a limo belonging to New Mexico gubernatorial candidate Frank Langella, only to be deposited right back where she came from.

In the picture's hottest scene, she then gets it on with carpenter Vincent Spano and wins early parole by convincing this earnest young single father to marry her. DeMornay lays a major surprise on her husband when she announces that their marriage contract does not include sex.

DeMornay throws herself deeply into the part as a lifelong loser determined to win at all costs. Spano's macho exterior is nicely modified as the story progresses with considerable emotional shading, and Langella is just right as the politico who is most intrigued by DeMornay but knows he could get burned by her.

•

. . . AND GOD CREATED WOMAN

SEE: ET DIEU . . . CREA LA FEMME

•

. . . AND JUSTICE FOR ALL

1979, 120 mins, US Ⓥ ⦿ col

Dir Norman Jewison ***Prod*** Norman Jewison, Patrick Palmer ***Scr*** Valerie Curtin, Barry Levinson ***Ph*** Victor J. Kemper ***Ed*** John F. Burnett ***Mus*** Dave Grusin ***Art*** Richard MacDonald

Act Al Pacino, Jack Warden, John Forsythe, Lee Strasberg, Christine Lahti, Jeffrey Tambor (Columbia)

. . . And Justice for All is a film that attempts to alternate between comedy and drama, handling neither one incompetently, but also not excelling at either task.

Centering on the impossible circumstances a sensitive lawyer encounters when dealing with the complexities and corruption of the American judicial system, pic is another good vehicle for Al Pacino.

Pic begins on a serious note with Pacino, jailed for contempt of court, witnessing jailers and inmates terrify a transvestite being locked up for robbery.

Mood quickly changes to comedy with Pacino going off to the scene of a car accident to aid an overemotional client.

The story most explored, that of John Forsythe's judge accused of brutally raping a young girl, is compelling but never fully fleshed out to satisfaction.

1979: NOMINATIONS: Best Actor (Al Pacino), Original Screenplay

•

ANDREI ROUBLEV

1966, 180 mins, USSR ▭ col

Dir Andrei Tarkovsky ***Scr*** Andrei Mikhalkov-Konchalovsky, Andrei Tarkovsky ***Ph*** Vadim Yusov ***Mus*** Vyacheslav Ovchinnikov ***Art*** Yevgeni Chernayev

Act Anatoli Solonitsyn, Ivan Lapikov, Nikolai Grinko, Nikolai Sergeyev, Irma Raush, Nikolai Burlyayev (Mosfilm)

Film is a brilliantly fashioned fresco of 15th-century Russia built around the life of noted icon painter Andrei Roublev. It catches the medieval brutality and man's awakening cognizance of a need for change.

The icon painter, Roublev (Anatoli Solonitsyn), is a monk invited to paint at the house of a lord. But his cognizance of the treatment of peasants who are trying to free themselves, the many noblemen fighting each other by enlisting the help of the occupying Tartars, and one raid in which he is forced to kill a man to save a woman, has him renouncing his work.

In an extraordinary segment of the pic, when a young man oversees the making of a giant bell by saying he knows the secret of his late, great, bell-making father (though he does not), Roublev decides he will paint again.

In black and white, the film suddenly bursts into color to show Rublev's actual icons. It avoids an academic aspect and displays a director of exceptional talent in Andrei Tarkovsky, whose second film this is after *My Name Is Ivan*.

[Pic was completed in 1966, shown at the Cannes festival in 1969, but not released in Russia until 1971.]

•

ANDROCLES AND THE LION

1952, 98 mins, US Ⓥ b/w

Dir Chester Erskine ***Prod*** Gabriel Pascal ***Scr*** Chester Erskine, Ken Englund ***Ph*** Harry Stradling ***Ed*** Roland Cross ***Mus*** Frederick Hollander

Act Jean Simmons, Alan Young, Victor Mature, Robert Newton, Maurice Evans, Elsa Lanchester (RKO)

Bernard Shaw's satirical comedy on Romans and Christians provides the basis for a fair film offering. Picture is a curious mixture of basic comedy and Shavian wit. The romance between the Christian girl and the Roman captain is the most effective part of the film, differing from the original play.

The first filming of a Shaw play in Hollywood, the presentation has the confined feeling of having been made indoors. There's an amusing superficiality to some of the sequences involving the decadent Roman court, its customs and reactions, with real wit in the Shaw dialog.

Director Chester Erskine's strongest guidance is evidenced in the scenes with Jean Simmons and Victor Mature as the Christian girl and the Roman captain.

The familiar story deals with Androcles's love of animals, a feeling that saves the Greek tailor when he frees a lion from a thorn and later meets that lion in the Roman arena.

•

ANDROID

1982, 80 mins, US Ⓥ ⦿ col

Dir Aaron Lipstadt ***Prod*** Mary Ann Fisher ***Scr*** James Reigle, Don Opper ***Ph*** Tim Suhrstedt ***Ed*** R. J. Kizer, Andy Horvitch ***Mus*** Don Preston ***Art*** K. C. Scheibel, Wayne Springfield

Act Klaus Kinski, Brie Howard, Norbert Weisser, Crofton Hardester, Kendra Kirchner, Don Opper (New World)

Obsessed researcher Klaus Kinski inhabits a remote space station in the year 2036 with his android assistant, Max 404, played by co-writer Don Opper. Doctor is on the verge of perfecting his masterpiece, a perfect robot who happens to be a beautiful blonde, and who will render Max obsolete.

Onto the craft from a prison ship come three escaped convicts with no precise plans but with dangerous personalities. One way or another, they intend to make their way back to Earth, where a revolt by androids proved of sufficient magnitude to make them illegal.

Although there are the obligatory fight scenes and nudity, film works mainly due to the unusual interaction between the all-too-human Max robot and those around him. Most pics of this ilk offer nothing but cardboard characters, so it's commendable that not only Max but the three fugitives come across with strong personalities. Kinski has relatively little to do, but is nevertheless plausible as a Dr. Frankenstein type.

•

ANDROMEDA STRAIN, THE

1971, 130 mins, US Ⓥ ⦿ ▭ col

Dir Robert Wise ***Prod*** Robert Wise ***Scr*** Nelson Gidding ***Ph*** Richard H. Kline ***Ed*** Stuart Gilmore, John W. Holmes ***Mus*** Gil Melle ***Art*** Boris Leven

Act Arthur Hill, David Wayne, James Olson, Kate Reid, Paula Kelly, George Mitchell (Universal)

The Andromeda Strain is a high-budget "science-fact" melodrama, marked by superb production, an excellent score, an intriguing story premise and an exciting conclusion. But Nelson Gidding's adaptation of the Michael Crichton novel is too literal and talky. In four acts representing days, a team of civilian medics attempt to find and isolate an unknown phenomenon that has killed most of a desert town near the place where a space satellite has fallen to earth. Arthur Hill, David Wayne, James Olson and Kate Reid are the specialists racing against time to determine why the town's only survivors are an old wino (George Mitchell) and an infant.

In the first half hour, the plot puzzle and eerie mood are well established, and in the final half hour there is a dramatically exciting climax with massive self-destruction machinery. The middle hour, however, drags proceedings numbingly. The four scientists repeatedly get into long-winded discussions. There are times when one wants to shout at the players to get on with it.

The glacial internal plot evolution is not at all relieved by the performances. Hill is dull; Wayne is dull; Olson caroms from another dull character to a petulant kid; and Reid's unexplained-until-later epilepsy condition does not generate much interest. Mitchell and nurse Paula Kelly are most refreshing changes of pace.

1971: NOMINATIONS: Best Art Direction, Editing

•

AND THEN THERE WERE NONE

1945, 97 mins, US Ⓥ b/w

Dir Rene Clair ***Prod*** Harry M. Popkin ***Scr*** Dudley Nichols ***Ph*** Lucien Andriot ***Ed*** Harvey Manger ***Mus*** Mario Castelnuovo-Tedesco

Act Barry Fitzgerald, Walter Huston, Louis Hayward, Roland Young, June Duprez, C. Aubrey Smith (20th Century-Fox)

This screen version of Agatha Christie's [novel and stage play *Ten Little Niggers*] mystery is a dull whodunit. The Christie mag yarn [serialized in *The Saturday Evening Post*] was a fair mystery story and a Broadway hit as a stage adaptation, called *10 Little Indians*, but the film version adds no laurels to the original.

Plot concerns itself with 10 assorted characters, each with a bad spot in his past, who are marooned on a lonely island off the English coast. Like the nursery rhyme, the number is decimated by sudden death until only two leave the island alive. Victims are mysteriously gathered in the spot by a mad judge who fancies himself a dispenser of justice.

Picture rarely rises to moments of suspense and despite the killings it gives the appearance of nothing ever happening as directed by Rene Clair.

Barry Fitzgerald is only fair. Walter Huston, Louis Hayward, Roland Young, June Duprez, C. Aubrey Smith and others appear equally out of place. Production is first venture by Harry M. Popkin, burlesque and film theater operator.

•

AND WOMAN . . . WAS CREATED

SEE: ET DIEU . . . CREA LA FEMME

•

ANDY WARHOL'S FRANKENSTEIN

SEE: FLESH FOR FRANKENSTEIN

•

ANGEL

1937, 98 mins, US b/w

Dir Ernst Lubitsch ***Prod*** Ernst Lubitsch ***Scr*** Samson Raphaelson, Guy Bolton, Russell Medcraft ***Ph*** Charles Lang ***Ed*** William Shea ***Mus*** Boris Morros (dir.) ***Art*** Hans Dreier, Robert Usher

Act Marlene Dietrich, Herbert Marshall, Melvyn Douglas, Edward Everett Horton, Herbert Mundin, Ernest Cossart (Paramount)

Angel is a rich Hollywood dish that copies foreign recipes. It is Ernest Lubitsch, with Continental delight, tackling a plot to his liking [from a play by Melchior Lengyel] in a far more serious manner than is his custom.

Angel is drama more than it is comedy, laugh lines being restricted almost to servants, who include Edward Everett Horton, Ernest Cossart and Herbert Mundin. Cossart gets the biggest chance to make good. He is a particularly engaging butler in the swank household of a British diplomat. Lubitsch has used a comparatively small cast, keeping the action almost entirely to three people: Marlene Dietrich, Herbert Marshall and Melvyn Douglas.

The story seriously portrays a girl of the old world who loves her husband and home, yet must graze around in strange pastures. Authors seek to accentuate that a woman can love two men at the same time. It also sets out to prove that a husband is willing to recognize this on evidence and take chances on the consequences.

Dietrich is glamour in double dress. This time she is wearing eyelashes you could hang your hat on and every now and then the star flicks 'em as though a dust storm was getting in her way. Marshall is excellent as the duped husband. The usual, smooth performance is obtained from Douglas as the persistent lover.

•

ANGEL

1982, 90 mins, Ireland Ⓥ ⦿ col

Dir Neil Jordan ***Prod*** Barry Blackmore ***Scr*** Neil Jordan ***Ph*** Chris Menges ***Ed*** Pat Duffner ***Mus*** Paddy Meegan ***Art*** John Lucas

Act Stephen Rea, Alan Devlin, Veronica Quilligan, Peter Caffrey, Honor Heffernan, Ray McAnally (MPCI)

Angel carries knockout power. A story of retribution set against the troubles in Northern Ireland, which are kept way in the background, it's an impressive pic debut for director-scripter Neil Jordan.

A saxophonist with a traveling band unwittingly observes the murder of the band's manager (involved in extortion payoffs) and that of a deaf and dumb girl witness. The musician, vigorously played by Stephen Rea, is obsessed to hunt down the murderers and does so, becoming a murderer himself several times over.

Played out with a minimum of violence, despite its theme, *Angel* contrasts the sweetness of dance music and the dark side of daily life. The acting is strong.

Camerawork by Chris Menges (the only non-Irish native involved in the production) is striking as are other credits.

•

ANGEL AND THE BADMAN

1947, 100 mins, US Ⓥ ⦿ B/W

Dir James Edward Grant ***Prod*** John Wayne ***Scr*** James Edward Grant ***Ph*** Archie J. Stout ***Ed*** Harry Keller ***Mus*** Richard Hageman ***Art*** Ernst Fegte

Act John Wayne, Gail Russell, Harry Carey, Bruce Cabot, Irene Rich, Lee Dixon (Republic)

Big-time western drama has resulted from John Wayne's first production effort. *Angel and the Badman* is solid entertainment way above what might be expected from its western locale and characters. It's loaded with sharp performances, honest writing and direction.

Story essentials deal with a hot gunman of the early West who is succored by a family of Quakers when he falls wounded on its doorstep. There is a gradual absorption of the family's formula for living by the bad man, and in the end he turns to the soil and the religion in a perfectly believable manner. Reformation is achieved not only through his love for the daughter of the Quaker family but through gradual realization that the faith of the Friends is a solid basis for achievement of happiness.

Wayne does his best job since *Stagecoach* as the gunman. Gail Russell has never been seen to better advantage as the frank and honest Quaker girl who falls in love and actually pursues the gunman. Role is played with an intelligent interpretation of the attraction between the sexes. Harry Carey makes his sheriff role a stout contributer to the general worth of this feature.

Archie J. Stout's camera takes full advantages of the wide-open western scenery and other production dress.

•

ANGELA'S ASHES

1999, 145 mins, US Ⓥ ⦿ col

Dir Alan Parker ***Prod*** Scott Rudin, David Brown, Alan Parker ***Scr*** Laura Jones, Alan Parker ***Ph*** Michael Seresin ***Ed*** Gerry Hambling ***Mus*** John Williams ***Art*** Geoffrey Kirkland

Act Emily Watson, Robert Carlyle, Joe Breen, Ciaran Owens, Michael Legge, Ronnie Masterson (Dirty Hands/Universal/Paramount)

Like a stone skipping across the surface of the book, Alan Parker's film version of *Angela's Ashes* artfully evokes the physical realities of Irish poverty, but mostly misses the humor, lyricism and emotional charge of Frank McCourt's magical and magnificent memoir.

The book's entire opening section, detailing the McCourts' miserable lives in Brooklyn during the Depression, is disposed of in a quick five minutes, just long enough to establish the unemployability of alcoholic Dad (Robert Carlyle), the inability of his perennially pregnant wife, Angela (Emily Watson), to cope, and the resourcefulness of five-year-old Frank (Joe Breen) and his younger brother, Malachy. When baby Margaret dies, Angela hits the wall, making them about the only family to emigrate back to Ireland from the U. S. in the '30s.

After a futile stop in Dublin, the penniless family proceeds to Limerick, Angela's hometown and the poverty capital of Ireland. At the 50-minute mark, action jumps ahead to find the 10-year-old Frank (Ciaran Owens) being felled by typhoid but also having his literary ability recognized for the first time. By the time he turns 16, Frank (Michael Legge) realizes he's got to return to New York at all costs.

The leavening that young Frank's humorous outlook provided in the book is seldom evident, making the tale considerably grimmer onscreen than it was on the page. Watson and Carlyle take their leading roles as far as they can. Aside from Frank, the other kids are mere ciphers. Picture gives a strong sense of a place physically defined by heavy gray skies, acrid smoke and water dripping, pouring and flooding everywhere.

1999: NOMINATION: Best Original Score

•

ANGEL AT MY TABLE, AN

1990, 156 mins, New Zealand/Australia Ⓥ ⦿ col

Dir Jane Campion ***Prod*** Bridget Ikin ***Scr*** Laura Jones ***Ph*** Stuart Dryburgh ***Ed*** Veronica Haussler ***Mus*** Don McGlashan ***Art*** Grant Major

Act Kerry Fox, Alexia Keogh, Karen Fergusson, Melina Bernecker, Glynis Angell, William Brandt (Hibiscus)

Jane Campion comes up with a touching and memorable biography of New Zealand author Janet Frame, originally made as a three-part TV miniseries (each part 52 minutes). In the 1950s, Frame spent eight years in a mental home undergoing shock treatment for wrongly diagnosed schizophrenia.

Part one, *To the Island*, deals with the writer's childhood in a rural community in the country's South Island. Tragedy strikes early when Janet's beloved older sister, Myrtle (Melina Bernecker), drowns in a swimming accident. As a teen (Karen Fergusson), Janet undergoes a painful puberty and becomes exceptionally shy.

In part two, *An Angel at My Table*, Janet (Kerry Fox) goes to university but is unable to cope with practical teaching. Further tragedy enters her life when her younger sister and best friend, Isabel (Glynis Angell), also drowns. She spends the next eight years in shock treatment.

With her first novel also published, Janet, in part three (*The Envoy from Mirror City*), travels on a literary grant to London and then Spain. She rents a room in a fishing village and has her first (and only?) love affair with a young poet (William Brandt).

A potentially painful and harrowing film is imbued with gentle humor and great compassion, which makes every character come vividly alive. Campion constructs the film in a series of short, sometimes elliptical scenes.

•

ANGEL EXTERMINADOR, EL

1962, 95 mins, Mexico Ⓥ b/w

Dir Luis Bunuel ***Prod*** Gustavo Alatriste ***Scr*** Luis Bunuel ***Ph*** Gabriel Figueroa ***Ed*** Carlos Savage, Jr. ***Art*** Jesus Bracho

Act Silvia Pinal, Enrique Rambal, Jacqueline Andere, Jose Baviera, Augusto Benedico, Luis Beristain (Uninci/Films 59)

Unusual offbeater could be pegged a parable, social satire as a dream film. It has power and solidity.

A group of rich people go to a friend's home for late supper after the opera. The servants leave and the group notices suddenly that they lack the will or the ability to get out of the house. Problems of privacy, food, water and human association and comportment come up. People outside can't get into the house and it is put under quarantine.

Drugs, cabalistic signs, and attempts to marshall the people into action all seem to fail as they slowly sink into near violence. Pic may be a razor-sharp look at purgatory. The symbols may have or not have any true, clear meaning, but do have shock value.

Acting is of a piece and brilliantly utilized by director Luis Bunuel, while Gabriel Figueroa's crystal-like lensing is another asset.

[Script is from a 1957 scenario, *Los naufragos de la calle de la Providencia*, by Bunuel and Luis Alcoriza, suggested by the unpublished play *Los naufragos* by Jose Bergamin.]

•

ANGEL FACE

1953, 91 mins, US b/w

Dir Otto Preminger ***Prod*** Otto Preminger ***Scr*** Frank Nugent, Oscar Millard ***Ph*** Harry Stradling ***Ed*** Frederic Knudtson ***Mus*** Dimitri Tiomkin ***Art*** Albert S. D'Agostino, Carroll Clark

Act Robert Mitchum, Jean Simmons, Mona Freeman, Herbert Marshall, Leon Ames, Barbara O'Neil (RKO)

Jean Simmons portrays the title role of a young lady behind whose beautiful face is a diseased mind that plots to murder her wealthy stepmother (Barbara O'Neil). Drawn into this scheme, although innocently, is Robert Mitchum, an ambulance driver who attends the stepmother when Simmons's first murder attempt backfires. Attracted to Mitchum, she gets him a chauffeur job with the family.

Mitchum and Simmons make a good team, both delivering the demands of the script [from a story by Chester Erskine] and Preminger's direction ably. Co-starred are Mona Freeman, the girl Mitchum casts off for Simmons, and Herbert Marshall, but neither has much to do in the footage.

•

ANGEL HEART

1987, 113 mins, US Ⓥ ⦿ col

Dir Alan Parker ***Prod*** Alan Marshall, Elliott Kastner ***Scr*** Alan Parker ***Ph*** Michael Seresin ***Ed*** Gerry Hambling ***Mus*** Trevor Jones ***Art*** Brian Morris

Act Mickey Rourke, Robert De Niro, Lisa Bonet, Charlotte Rampling (Carolco/Winkast-Union)

Even if it may be a specious work at its core, *Angel Heart* still proves a mightily absorbing mystery, a highly exotic telling of a small-time detective's descent into hell, with Faustian theme, heavy bloodletting and pervasive grimness.

Based on William Hjortsberg's novel *Falling Angel*, Alan Parker's screenplay, set in 1955, has seedy Gotham gumshoe Mickey Rourke engaged by mysterious businessman Robert De Niro to locate a certain Johnny Favorite, a big band singer from the pre-war days who, De Niro says, failed to live up to the terms of a contract.

Rourke as Harry Angel, quickly discovers that Favorite, a war casualty and reportedly a vegetable, was removed years earlier from the nursing home where he was supposedly under care, and follows his leads to New Orleans, and particularly the jazz and voodoo elements within its black community.

Rourke is a commanding lead, putting everyone around him (except De Niro) on edge. Charlotte Rampling is in very briefly as an elegant fortune teller, while Lisa Bonet's striking looks are rather undercut by her Valley Girl accent, not terribly convincing for a poor black girl from bayou country.

Controversial lovemaking scene between Rourke and Bonet becomes rather rough but, probably more to the point, involves torrents of blood leaking down on them from the ceiling, all of this being intercut with glimpses of voodoo rituals.

•

ANGEL OF VENGEANCE
SEE: MS. 45

•

ANGEL ON MY SHOULDER
1946, 100 mins, US Ⓥ ⊙ b/w
Dir Archie Mayo ***Prod*** Charles R. Rogers ***Scr*** Harry Segall, Roland Kibbee ***Ph*** James Van Trees ***Ed*** George Arthur, Asa Clark ***Mus*** Dimitri Tiomkin ***Art*** Bernard Herzbrun
Act Paul Muni, Anne Baxter, Claude Rains, George Cleveland, Onslow Stevens (United Artists)

Angel on My Shoulder deals with Satan's efforts to best his Heavenly adversary at least once. He uses as a tool for the attempt a gangster who wants revenge on the pal who bumped him off.

Paul Muni is the murdered gangster, turning in performance that measures up to past credits and giving film plenty of zip. Awakening in hell after being bumped, Muni wants out so he can get revenge on his killer. Claude Rains, as Satan, sees chance to even things with a crime-busting earthly judge who's the double for Muni. Old Nick offers Muni opportunity to get his killer if he'll queer the judge's political halo. It's a deal, the two take off for earth and the fun starts.

Rains shines as the Devil, shading the character with a likeable puckishness good for both sympathy and chuckles. Anne Baxter is excellent as the troubled fiancée.

•

ANGELS AND INSECTS
1995, 117 mins, US/UK Ⓥ ⊙ col
Dir Philip Haas ***Prod*** Joyce Herlihy, Belinda Haas ***Scr*** Belinda Haas, Philip Haas ***Ph*** Bernard Zitzerman ***Ed*** Belinda Haas ***Mus*** Alexander Balanescu ***Art*** Jennifer Kernke
Act Mark Rylance, Kristin Scott Thomas, Patsy Kensit, Jeremy Kemp, Douglas Henshall, Annette Badland (Samuel Goldwyn/Playhouse)

A curious, vastly uneven analysis of the early cracking in the armor of Victorian society, *Angels and Insects* gets off the ground only when the warped and weird final moves of A. S. Byatt's story come into play. Awkwardly filmed and erratically acted, this English-lensed second feature by U.S. director Philip Haas begins poorly but develops a degree of narrative and thematic interest in the final reels.

Set in 1862, entire narrative is played out at the lovely country estate of Rev. Harald Alabaster (Jeremy Kemp), an aging thinking man whose enduring faith has been called into question by the recently published theories of Charles Darwin. He has taken in naturalist William Adamson (Mark Rylance), who in a shipwreck lost the invaluable specimens he collected during a decade in the Amazon.

Utterly impoverished, William has no hope of gaining the favor of Alabaster's beautiful blonde daughter, Eugenia (Patsy Kensit), until he boldly proposes marriage to her upon learning that her fiancé has committed suicide. Once married, they launch a feverish sexual relationship. Things pick up a bit when William undertakes a research project with an intellectual equal, Matty Crompton (Kristin Scott Thomas). As the screw turns further, it becomes evident that William and Matty aren't the only ones in the house with a secret. An eye-opening sex scene reveals the true reason for Eugenia's fiancé's demise.

Thomas steals the acting honors with the thespian equivalent of a home run in the bottom of the ninth. Rylance slowly comes into his own, although William is far too pallid and passive to make for a compelling protagonist. On the downside, Kensit can't provide the subtle hints of the dark, twisted side of Eugenia.

1996: NOMINATION: Best Costume Design (Paul Brown)

•

ANGELS AND THE PIRATES
SEE: ANGELS IN THE OUTFIELD

•

ANGELS IN THE OUTFIELD
1951, 99 mins, US b/w
Dir Clarence Brown ***Prod*** Clarence Brown ***Scr*** Dorothy Kingsley, George Wells ***Ph*** Paul C. Vogel ***Ed*** Robert J. Kern ***Mus*** Daniele Amfitheatrof
Act Paul Douglas, Janet Leigh, Keenan Wynn, Donna Corcoran, Lewis Stone, Spring Byington (M-G-M)

Clarence Brown has carved a tremendously satisfying filmization from a script [based on a story by Richard Conlin] that, from every evidence, could have gone completely haywire if handled clumsily, dealing as it does with fantasy. Religious angle also presented a delicate situation, but Brown has handled it all masterfully.

Pivotal character is Paul Douglas, who plays one of the most tyrannical, blasphemous managers in the history of baseball. His team is in seventh place and is headed into the sub-basement when somebody unknown to Douglas intercedes with the Angel Gabriel. A voice tells Douglas to look for a miracle in the third inning of a crucial game.

Janet Leigh's paper, the *Pittsburgh Messenger*, prints her interview with a little orphan girl who swears she has seen angels standing alongside the men of Douglas's team, helping them win. Douglas, accidentally conked by a line drive, admits to the press that the angels are helping him. This brings on an investigation into his sanity by the baseball commissioner. Douglas is perfect as the brawler reformed by a little girl's prayers. Leigh foils cleverly. Donna Corcoran plays the orphan.

•

ANGELS IN THE OUTFIELD
1994, 102 mins, US Ⓥ col
Dir William Dear ***Prod*** Irby Smith, Joe Roth, Roger Birnbaum ***Scr*** Dorothy Kingsley, George Wells, Holly Goldberg Sloan ***Ph*** Matthew F. Leonetti ***Ed*** Bruce Green ***Mus*** Randy Edelman ***Art*** Dennis Washington
Act Danny Glover, Tony Danza, Brenda Fricker, Christopher Lloyd, Ben Johnson, Jay O. Sanders (Walt Disney)

Angels in the Outfield shows scant devotion to the 1951 film on which it's based, changing the gender of its child lead and augmenting its implied magic with gauzily shot angels and other special effects.

Updated for non-nuclear families of the '90s, the story centers on a foster child, Roger (Joseph Gordon-Levitt), whose shiftless father says he may be able to reclaim him when the boy's favorite baseball team, the last-place California Angels, wins the pennant. Roger offers up a prayer to make it so, and the stars twinkle in response sending down a wild-eyed, honest-to-you-know-who angel, Al (Christopher Lloyd), whom only Roger can see.

Circumstances bring Roger and his friend J.P. (Milton Davis, Jr.) into contact with the Angels's sour manager, George Knox (Danny Glover), who ultimately comes to believe the boy and uses his heavenly advice to lift the team out of the cellar.

William Dear, who directed the equally warm and fuzzy *Harry and the Hendersons*, doesn't shy away from overblown sentimentality after a rather slow and grim first act, as glowing winged figures pop up all over the field.

•

ANGELS ONE FIVE
1952, 97 mins, UK b/w
Dir George More O'Ferrall ***Prod*** John W. Gossage, Derek Twist ***Scr*** Derek Twist ***Ph*** Christopher Challis ***Ed*** Daniel Birt ***Mus*** John Wooldridge (arr.) ***Art*** Fred Pusey
Act Jack Hawkins, Michael Denison, Dulcie Gray, Andrew Osborn, Cyril Raymond, John Gregson (Templar/Associated British)

Action of *Angels One Five* takes place during the period described by Winston Churchill as "Britain's finest hour," when a handful of fighter pilots (the few against the many) stemmed the air invasion by Nazi war planes.

Breaking away from the more conventional treatment, the script [from a story by Pelham Groom] watches the progress of the battle, not from the actual combats, but from the messages received by and emanating from the operational control room.

Competent acting is followed by whole cast. Jack Hawkins and Michael Denison are the two big shots of the base and their sharp discipline is tempered by a generous measure of understanding. Dulcie Gray has little more to do than appear sympathetic as the wife of the harassed control room chief.

•

ANGELS OVER BROADWAY
1940, 78 mins, US Ⓥ ⊙ B/W
Dir Ben Hecht, Lee Garmes ***Prod*** Ben Hecht ***Scr*** Ben Hecht ***Ph*** Lee Garmes ***Ed*** Gene Havlick ***Mus*** George Antheil ***Art*** Lionel Banks
Act Douglas Fairbanks, Jr., Rita Hayworth, Thomas Mitchell, John Qualen, George Watts (Columbia)

Angels over Broadway is a synthetic tale of Broadway nightlife and the characters that roam around Times Square. Aside from Thomas Mitchell, as a screwball playwright who sees a story in every individual, and who delights in plotting a finish, there's nothing much in the Hechtian tale. Picture stutters and sputters too often to carefully etch human beings, with result that it develops into an over-dramatic stage play transformed to celluloid.

Writer-director-producer Ben Hecht gets little movement in the unwinding, and depends too much on stage technique in trying to put over his points. An embezzler (John Qualen) is saved from committing suicide by the zany playwright (Mitchell) who proceeds to try and help the former out of his jam and give him a new lease on life. Douglas Fairbanks, Jr., is a slick youth who shills for a big poker game, and sets his sights for Qualen who he assumes is a rural hick. There's much byplay between the trio and a girl who moves in (Rita Hayworth) before plan is worked out to recoup the coin in the come-on game.

Characters are all overdrawn, with Mitchell providing many sharp cracks on the philosophy of life and living. Mitchell does much to hold together the minor interest retained in the running. Fairbanks fails to get much sympathy or attention as the wise young Broadwayite who knows all the angles. Hayworth is passable as the girl, while Qualen is bewildered enough as the prospective suicide.

1940: NOMINATION: Best Original Screenplay

•

ANGEL STREET
SEE: GASLIGHT (1940 B&W)

•

ANGELS WITH DIRTY FACES
1938, 97 mins, US Ⓥ ⊙ b/w
Dir Michael Curtiz ***Prod*** [Sam Bischoff] ***Scr*** John Wexley, Warren Duff ***Ph*** Sol Polito ***Ed*** Owen Marks ***Mus*** Max Steiner ***Art*** Robert Haas
Act James Cagney, Pat O'Brien, Humphrey Bogart, Ann Sheridan, George Bancroft, Billy Halop (Warner)

Another typical *Dead End* kids picture, but with the single exception that it has James Cagney and Pat O'Brien to bolster the dramatic interest.

Cagney is the tenderloin toughie who's the idol of the gutter-bred youngsters because of his criminal exploits and cocky belligerence. O'Brien is the priest who was a boyhood chum of Cagney's and who seeks to retrieve the neighborhood kids from trying to emulate their gangster hero. There's a singular ending for the story, which has Cagney pretending to turn yellow as he goes to the electric chair so he'll kill the kids' unhealthy adoration. It is a novel twist to a commonplace story [by Rowland Brown], but it's thoroughly hokey.

The screenplay contains many effective cinematic touches. However, in at least one instance the same set is used for two supposedly different locales.

Cagney and O'Brien form an irresistible team. Their personalities and acting styles offer both a blend and an eloquent contrast. Cagney has a swagger and an aw-go-to-hell pugnacity. O'Brien gives an eminently credible performance of the mild-mannered, two-fisted, compassionate priest. The *Dead End* kids are as rambunctious as usual.

1938: NOMINATIONS: Best Director, Actor (James Cagney), Original Story

•

ANGIE
1994, 107 mins, US Ⓥ ⊙ ▭ col
Dir Martha Coolidge ***Prod*** Larry Brezner, Patrick McCormick ***Scr*** Todd Graff ***Ph*** Johnny E. Jensen ***Ed*** Steven Cohen ***Mus*** Jerry Goldsmith ***Art*** Mel Bourne

Act Geena Davis, Stephen Rea, James Gandolfini, Aida Turturro, Philip Bosco, Jenny O'Hara (Hollywood)

Angie is a skin-deep feel-good movie about such less-than-breezy issues as a broken engagement, childbirth, single motherhood, infant infirmities and discovering brutal truths about your parents.

On the bright side is a star performance from Geena Davis, in which the dazzling actress remains center screen virtually at all times, as well as an appealing turn by Stephen Rea as a wry Irish suitor who sticks around as long as it suits him. On the downside, pic goes mushy soft when confronted with its assorted heavy issues.

Davis plays Angie Scacciapensieri, a spirited working girl from Bensonhurst, Brooklyn, who finds herself pregnant by her b.f., Vinnie the plumber (James Gandolfini). After a meet-cute with the raffish Noel (Rea), she dumps Vinnie and starts dating Noel.

Director Martha Coolidge is unable to successfully shift the tone to something graver and more substantial. Todd Graff's script (originally written for Madonna [and based on Avra Wing's novel *Angie, I Says*]) clearly aspires to be deeply moving and deliver a life's-arc catharsis, but the best the film manages is to hit an occasionally touching chord.

•

ANGI VERA
1979, 96 mins, Hungary col
Dir Pal Gabor ***Scr*** Pal Gabor ***Ph*** Lajos Koltai ***Ed*** Eva Karmento ***Mus*** Gyorgy Selmeczi ***Art*** Andras Gyurki
Act Veronika Pap, Erzsi Pasztor, Tamas Dunai, Eva Szabo, Laszlo Halasz, Laszlo Horvath (Objektiv)

A cool treatment of early Communist Party training of selected people to fit into various areas of the new socialist regime at its beginnings in 1948. [Based on the novel by Endre Veszi] it is mainly about an innocent 18-year-old girl and her corruption by the hard-line, puritanical, Stalinist outlooks of the day.

Vera, played with intensity by Veronika Pap, attacks the rundown methods of a hospital she works at during a party meeting. She is singled out and sent off to party school. Here she gets tied up with a rather hard-lining older woman who has her even turning in an old worker who has confided to them why he took part in a strike.

She is enamored of a married teacher and finally goes to his room for an idyllic love scene. But thinking her mentor has seen her, she renounces what she did in a confession scene before the school.

The good playing, the perceptive direction (despite its lack of more dramatic sweep) and its theme make this film an engrossing look at the period.

•

ANGRY HILLS, THE
1959, 105 mins, UK ▭ b/w
Dir Robert Aldrich ***Prod*** Raymond Stross ***Scr*** A. I. Bezzerides ***Ph*** Stephen Dade ***Ed*** Peter Tanner ***Mus*** Richard Rodney Bennett
Act Robert Mitchum, Elisabeth Mueller, Stanley Baker, Gia Scala, Theodore Bikel, Donald Wolfit (M-G-M)

The Angry Hills, set in Greece, is a rather confused yarn but has the merit of good direction by Robert Aldrich and some very competent performances.

Robert Mitchum plays an American war correspondent who is hunted by Gestapo chief Stanley Baker and fifth columnist Theodore Bikel when he arrives in Athens as Greece is about to fall to the Nazis. Baker and Bikel want Mitchum because he has a list of 16 Greek underground leaders that he is conveying to British intelligence in London. He is helped by Gia Scala and also by Elisabeth Mueller, both of whom fall in love with Mitchum.

Both Baker and Mitchum give very sound performances. Mueller brings a radiant charm to the part of the widow. A. I. Bezzerides's screenplay [from Leon Uris's book] falters toward the end when the love complications arise but he tells the story briskly and well.

•

ANGRY SILENCE, THE
1960, 95 mins, UK b/w
Dir Guy Green ***Prod*** Richard Attenborough, Bryan Forbes ***Scr*** Bryan Forbes ***Ph*** Arthur Ibbetson ***Ed*** Anthony Harvey ***Mus*** Malcolm Arnold
Act Richard Attenborough, Pier Angeli, Michael Craig, Bernard Lee, Alfred Burke, Penelope Horner (Beaver)

The Angry Silence details the impact of industrial unrest on individuals, told with passion, integrity and guts, but without false theatrical gimmicks. Apart from the message, there is a solid core of entertainment produced by taut writing, deft direction and top-notch acting.

Plot concerns a worker in a factory where there has been no trouble until a political troublemaker moves in. Insidiously he stirs up unrest, makes one of the workers his cat's-paw, creates a wildcat strike and then quietly moves on to spread his poison in other factories. The main victim of the strike is played by Richard Attenborough who, because he refuses to be pushed around, is sent to Coventry (shunned by his workmates) and is beaten up, and his family intimidated.

Original story by Richard Gregson and Michael Craig has been skilfully written for the screen by Bryan Forbes. Perhaps the end is slightly contrived, but Guy Green has directed with quiet skill, leaving the film to speak for itself.

Attenborough, as the quiet little man who just wants to be left alone to grapple with his home problems, has done nothing better on the screen for a long time. That goes, too, for Pier Angeli as his wife. Here she is a creature of flesh and blood, unhappily involved in a problem she cannot understand. Michael Craig, as Attenborough's best friend, is also in his best form.

1960: NOMINATION: Best Original Screenplay

•

ANGST ESSEN SEELE AUF
1974, 94 mins, W. Germany col
Dir Rainer Werner Fassbinder ***Scr*** Rainer Werner Fassbinder ***Ph*** Juergen Juerges ***Ed*** Thea Eymesz ***Art*** Rainer Werner Fassbinder
Act Brigitte Mira, El Hedi Ben Salem, Barbara Valentin, Irm Hermann, Peter Gauhe, Rainer Werner Fassbinder (Tango)

Racism is the theme but done in a low-profile way that creates an interior end reaction rather than easy outrage at outright racists.

A sixtyish widow one day wanders into a bar catering to Arab workers. She meets a thirtyish, handsome, bearded Arab worker who asks her to dance. They sympathize and somehow their mutual loneliness makes them friends. He takes her home and stays. It is not sex, but respect and finally love that binds this strange couple together.

Her grown children are outraged; people she works with as a cleaning woman also shun her, as do tradespeople. They go off on a vacation and suddenly people seem transformed on their return. But it is only because they need her.

Film is played with reserve. Technically flawless, deceptively simple and avoiding excesses, it is about problems that are timely and timeless in implications.

•

ANIMAL CRACKERS
1930, 97 mins, US Ⓥ ⦿ b/w
Dir Victor Heerman ***Prod*** [uncredited] ***Scr*** Morrie Ryskind ***Ph*** George Folsey ***Ed*** [uncredited] ***Mus*** [uncredited] ***Art*** [uncredited]
Act Groucho Marx, Harpo Marx, Chico Marx, Zeppo Marx, Lillian Roth, Margaret Dumont (Paramount)

First give Paramount extreme credit for reproducing *Animal Crackers* intact from the stage [musical written by George S. Kaufman, Morrie Ryskind, Harry Ruby and Bert Kalmar], without too much of the songs and musical numbers.

Among the Marx boys there is no preference. Groucho shines; Harpo remains a pantomimic clown who ranks with the highest; Chico adds an unusual comedy sense to his dialog as well as business and piano playing; and Zeppo, if in on a split, is lucky.

Lillian Roth may have been cast here to work out a contract. She can't hurt because the Marxes are there, but if Roth is in for any other reason it doesn't appear. She sings one song in the ingenue role. That song is useless. Opposite is Hal Thompson, a juve who doesn't prove it here.

•

ANIMAL FARM
1954, 72 mins, UK Ⓥ ⦿ col
Dir John Halas, Joy Batchelor (animation), John F. Reed ***Prod*** John Halas, Joy Batchelor ***Scr*** Lothar Wolff, Borden Mace, Philip Stapp, John Halas, Joy Batchelor ***Ph*** S. G. Griffiths, J. Gurr, W. Traylor, R. Turk ***Mus*** Matyas Seiber (Halas & Batchelor)

Human greed, selfishness and conniving are lampooned in *Animal Farm* with the pigs behaving in a piglike manner and the head pig, named Napoleon, corrupting and perverting an honest revolt against evil social conditions into a new tyranny as bad as, and remarkably similar to, the old regime. In short, this cartoon feature [from the novel by George Orwell] is a sermon against all that is bestial in politics and rotten in the human will to live in luxury at the expense of slaves.

Made in Britain, the cartoon is vividly realized pictorially. The musical score, the narration, the sound effects and the editing all are of impressive imaginative quality.

•

ANNA AND THE KING
1999, 147 mins, US Ⓥ ⦿ ▭ col
Dir Andy Tennant ***Prod*** Lawrence Bender, Ed Elbert ***Scr*** Steve Meerson, Peter Krikes ***Ph*** Caleb Deschanel ***Ed*** Roger Bondelli ***Mus*** George Fenton ***Art*** Luciana Arrighi
Act Jodie Foster, Chow Yun-fat, Bai Ling, Tom Felton, Syed Alwi, Randall Duk Kim (Fox 2000)

Jodie Foster makes a valiant effort at bringing a contemporary edge to the role of 19th-century schoolteacher Anna Leonowens in *Anna and the King*, the third major screen version of the popular tale [based on her diaries]. But her performance is contained in a schmaltzy, ultra-elaborate, overly long production, all too consciously conceived as old-fashioned family entertainment.

The most notable element of this production is its large cast of Asian actors, beginning with the effective Hong Kong star Chow Yun-fat as King Mongkut. Foster, too, is well cast, bringing to the role of the young widow and governess a different interpretation from those by the graceful Irene Dunne in the 1946 b&w drama *Anna and the King of Siam* and the ladylike Deborah Kerr in the 1956 Rodgers & Hammerstein musical *The King and I*.

Each element of this production is designed to soothe and gratify everyone in the manner of '50s and '60s big-budget epics. Indeed, watching the movie is like leafing through a catalogue of Hollywood's popular adventures of the past four decades.

It takes 45 minutes for Anna and the King to exchange their first "meaningful" look. Thereon, romantic interludes are periodically inserted, with at least three nocturnal occasions in which the duo dance cheek-to-cheek.

Foster moves gracefully in period costumes and commands the screen charismatically. She enjoys strong chemistry with Chow, who, in his first nonaction role in an American movie, impress with his handsome presence and dignified stillness. Widescreen lensing in Malaysia (standing in for Thailand) is eye-popping.

1999: NOMINATIONS: Best Art Direction, Costume Design

•

ANNA AND THE KING OF SIAM
1946, 128 mins, US Ⓥ b/w
Dir John Cromwell ***Prod*** Louis D. Lighton ***Scr*** Talbot Jennings, Sally Benson ***Ph*** Arthur Miller ***Ed*** Harmon Jones ***Mus*** Bernard Herrmann ***Art*** Lyle R. Wheeler, William Darling
Act Irene Dunne, Rex Harrison, Linda Darnell, Lee J. Cobb, Gale Sondergaard (20th Century-Fox)

Socko adult drama. *Anna and the King of Siam* is a rather faithful screen adaptation of Margaret Landon's biography, intelligently handled to spellbind despite its long footage. *Anna* tells a straightforward narrative, bringing in the natural humor, suspense and other dramatic values of the story of an English widow who finds herself confronted with the many problems of educating the children and some of the wives of the King of Siam. The monarch, himself, needs some education, and Anna sees that he gets it.

Script builds fascinating adult interest without ever implying that relationship between teacher and pupil goes beyond the friendship stage.

Irene Dunne does a superb enactment of Anna, the woman who influenced Siamese history by being teacher and confidante to a kingly barbarian. Rex Harrison shines particularly in his American film debut. It's a sustained characterization of the King of Siam that makes the role real. Linda Darnell, third star, has little more than a bit as one of the king's wives, who incurs his displeasure and is burned at the stake. She does well.

1946: Best B&W Cinematography, B&W Interior Decoration (Lyle R. Wheeler, William Darling)

NOMINATIONS: Best Supp. Actress (Gale Sondergaard), Screenplay, Scoring of a Dramatic Picture

•

ANNA CHRISTIE
1923, 87 mins, US ⊗ b/w
Dir John Griffith Wray ***Prod*** Thomas H. Ince ***Scr*** Bradley King ***Ph*** Henry Sharp
Act Blanche Sweet, William Russell, George F. Marion, Eugenie Besserer (Ince/Associated First National)

Anna Christie is a picture that is as different to the regular runs of screen productions as the Eugene O'Neill plays are to the majority of hits and near-hits that come to the spoken stage.

There is one mistake John Griffith Wray makes in the direction. In the usual picture fashion he tries to force his leading woman to overshadow the character role. Blanche Sweet isn't the Anna Christie Pauline Lord was on the stage, but George Marion is Chris and as such he so far overshadows the leading woman that the director is undoubtedly forced to take the extremes he does to keep her in the eye of the audience. But that is not good direction.

William Russell makes Matt Burke a convincing sort of a brute Irish coal passer on a steam tramp and puts over his role with a wallop, and likewise Eugenie Besserer handles Marthy, so that in all Sweet is the only weak spot of the cast of four.

•

ANNA CHRISTIE
1930, 86 mins, US Ⓥ b/w
Dir Clarence Brown ***Scr*** Frances Marion ***Ph*** William Daniels ***Ed*** Hugh Wynn ***Mus*** [uncredited] ***Art*** Cedric Gibbons
Act Greta Garbo, George F. Marion, Marie Dressler, Charles Bickford (M-G-M)

In all departments a wow picture. Comparison is inevitable with the silent version made by Thomas Ince seven years earlier with Blanche Sweet and William Russell. In both instances Hollywood closely follows the Eugene O'Neill play.

Infinite care in developing each sequence, just the proper emphasis on characterizations and a part that exactly fits Greta Garbo put *Anna Christie* safely in the realm of the superlative.

"Garbo talks" is, beyond quarrel, an event. La Garbo's accent is nicely edged with a Norse "yah," but once the ear gets the pitch it's okay.

George Marion, in the original Ince production, again plays the old sentiment-hungry, seagoing father. Charles Bickford as the Irish sailor of massive muscles and primitive ideals is magnificent. Perhaps the greatest surprise is Marie Dressler, who steps out of her usual straight slapstick to stamp herself an actress.

1929/30: NOMINATIONS: Best Director, Actress (Greta Garbo), Cinematography

•

ANNA KARENINA
1935, 95 mins, US Ⓥ b/w
Dir Clarence Brown ***Prod*** David O. Selznick ***Scr*** Clemence Dane, Salka Viertel, S. N. Behrman ***Ph*** William Daniels ***Ed*** Robert J. Kern ***Mus*** Herbert Stothart ***Art*** Cedric Gibbons
Act Greta Garbo, Fredric March, Freddie Bartholomew, Basil Rathbone, Maureen O'Sullivan, May Robson (M-G-M)

Greta Garbo starred in this story once before in 1927. Silent film was titled *Love* and John Gilbert had the role now handled by Fredric March. March handles his assignment firmly and with understanding and the film in toto is a more honest and sincere rendition of the Tolstoy classic than the silent.

Garbo, too, seems to have grown since 1927. There is no flaw to be found in her rendition of the love-wracked Russian girl Anna.

Trimmed to its essentials the story is an extremely simple one: a married woman, hating her cold, unloving, hypocritical husband, falls in love with a young officer of the guards. Love sweeps everything from under her. Her husband won't give her a divorce. She gives up everything she has in life, including her baby, to go to her lover.

Casting throughout is excellent, although just a trifle annoying. There is a distinct clash of accents, which might have been avoided. Reginald Denny, Basil Rathbone and Reginald Owen speak Oxfordese English, as opposed to Garbo's Stockholmese.

•

ANNA KARENINA
1948, 139 mins, UK Ⓥ b/w
Dir Julien Duvivier ***Prod*** Alexander Korda ***Scr*** Jean Anouilh, Guy Morgan, Julien Duvivier ***Ph*** Henri Alekan ***Ed*** Russell Lloyd ***Mus*** Constant Lambert ***Art*** Andre Andrejeff
Act Vivien Leigh, Ralph Richardson, Kieron Moore, Hugh Dempster (London)

Fine as this fourth production of Tolstoy's novel is [Fox 1915, Metro 1927 and 1935], it misses greatness and has tedious stretches.

It would appear that far too much attention was paid to the sets and the artistic structure at the expense of the players. It would have been wise for Korda and Duvivier to realize that the story, for screen purposes, is frankly Victorian melodrama, and that there was always the danger of reducing the characters to puppets.

It speaks volumes for Leigh and Richardson that they are able to disentangle themselves from their overwhelming surroundings and become credibly human. Leigh dominates the picture, as she rightly should with her beauty, charm and skill. It isn't her fault that eyes remain dry and hearts unwrung when she moves to inevitable tragedy, as the neglected wife and discarded lover.

Richardson's portrayal of the priggish, unlikeable husband is masterly yet uneven. Sometimes he gives the impression of a Chinese philosopher with accent and staccato phrase. Incidentally, the multiplicity of pronunciations of "Karenina" by various people is a trifle distracting.

•

ANNA LUCASTA
1949, 86 mins, US b/w
Dir Irving Rapper ***Prod*** Philip Yordan ***Scr*** Philip Yordan, Arthur Laurents ***Ph*** Sol Polito ***Ed*** Charles Nelson ***Mus*** David Diamond
Act Paulette Goddard, William Bishop, Oscar Homolka, John Ireland, Broderick Crawford (Columbia/Security)

Anna Lucasta, reverting the tale from the legit Negro cast to an all-white ensemble, is no bowl of Wheaties for the kiddies.

Enduring quality of *Lucasta* is its ability to lend itself to a fast stream of quips and repartee that stems directly from the situations. Scripters Philip Yordan and Arthur Laurents [working from Yordan's play] have taken full advantage of that factor.

It's about a greedy family that has thrown out the youngest daughter believing she has sinned. She is brought back when the family sees the chance of conning some money by wedding her off to a Southern farmer.

Paulette Goddard performs competently although her physical accoutrements do not measure up to the lush requirements of the part. Her Anna is a game attempt in that direction but the lack of corporeal apparatus keeps the sparks from flying.

•

ANNE AND MURIEL
SEE: DEUX ANGLAISES ET LE CONTINENT

•

ANNEE DERNIERE A MARIENBAD, L'
1961, 93 mins, France/Italy Ⓥ ▭ b/w
Dir Alain Resnais ***Prod*** Pierre Courau, Raymond Froment ***Scr*** Alain Robbe-Grillet ***Ph*** Sacha Vierny ***Ed*** Henri Colpi, Jasmine Chasney ***Mus*** Francis Seyrig ***Art*** Jacques Saulnier
Act Delphine Seyrig, Giorgio Albertazzi, Sacha Pitoeff

This film was passed over by Culture Minister Andre Malraux for repping France at the [1961] Cannes Fest. It is a difficult, daring film that takes plenty of patience from any audience, including the most aesthetic.

A man sees a woman in a fashionable German hotel that looks like an old chateau. He keeps asking her if she remembers last year, and they are seen in different periods, mixing the present with the past and the varying versions of the past. All other characters, except a man who might be her husband, are seen as mere silhouettes, mouthing inanities or platitudes. Director Alain Resnais's aim seems to be to lay bare the impossibility of true remembrance. He has made the characters a part of the baroque surroundings of the castlelike hotel. Delphine Seyrig looks like a pre-war romantic film heroine with her slender body and studied poses. Editing is outstanding, keeping its various layers of thought, action and posing fluid and intact. Lensing too is exemplary.

•

ANNE OF GREEN GABLES
1934, 80 mins, US b/w
Dir George Nicholls, Jr. ***Prod*** Kenneth Macgowan ***Scr*** Sam Mintz ***Ph*** Lucien Andriot ***Ed*** Arthur Schmidt ***Mus*** Max Steiner (dir.) ***Art*** Van Nest Polglase, Al Herman
Act Anne Shirley, Tom Brown, O. P. Heggie, Helen Westley, Sara Haden, Murray Kinnell (RKO)

Anne of Green Gables is wholesome, sympathetic, romantic and dramatic, packing many a heart-tug and tear-jerk. It will do much to establish Anne Shirley, who has taken her professional nom-de-screen from her character in the L. M. Montgomery classic. It parallels the professional billing stunt done when Tom Brown (*Tom Brown of Culver*) was given his marquee handle [two years earlier].

Orphan Annie's influence on Green Gables is relieved by an adolescent garrulousness that is most natural and captivating. Her conversion of the dour sister (Helen Westley) is a fine screen portrait, while the already basically sympathetic brother (O. P. Heggie) mellows into another excellent celluloid characterization.

Tom Brown's adolescent beau likewise develops into a manly and matured swain as Anne outgrows her pigtails and into young womanhood.

Homespun setting is almost idyllic in a natural, bucolic Prince Edward Island (Canada) locale, which cinematographer Lucien Andriot has deftly caught in a sequence of fetching landscapes, soft shadows and the like.

•

ANNE OF THE INDIES
1951, 81 mins, US col
Dir Jacques Tourneur ***Prod*** George Jessel ***Scr*** Philip Dunne, Arthur Caesar ***Ph*** Harry Jackson ***Ed*** Robert Fritch ***Mus*** Franz Waxman ***Art*** Lyle Wheeler, Albert Hogsett
Act Jean Peters, Louis Jourdan, Debra Paget, Herbert Marshall, Thomas Gomez, James Robertson Justice (20th Century-Fox)

As the femme pirate who sailed the Caribbean seas as the dreaded Captain Providence, Jean Peters outdoes the best Ruth Roland tradition and looks good while doing it. There's nothing ludicrous about her performance in the type of action usually handed to males.

The film plays along at an imaginative pace under Jacques Tourneur's direction. Sea battles are expertly staged to make the most of such actionful moments.

Plot [from a story by Herbert Ravenal Sass] finds Louis Jourdan, a French naval officer whose ship and wife are being held by the British, volunteering to capture Captain Providence. He manages to get aboard her pirate vessel, takes advantage of a natural attraction that springs up to trick her with a phony treasure map, thus leading her into a British ambush. However, Anne escapes the trap and takes her vengeance by kidnapping the wife, played by Debra Paget.

Jourdan supplies a good hero and Thomas Gomez a colorful Blackbeard. Herbert Marshall, as a rum-sodden doctor aboard the pirate ship, James Robertson Justice, buccaneer first-mate, and the lineup of cut-throat characters all come over excellently.

•

ANNE OF THE THOUSAND DAYS
1970, 145 mins, UK Ⓥ ▭ col
Dir Charles Jarrott ***Prod*** Hal B. Wallis ***Scr*** Bridget Boland, John Hale ***Ph*** Arthur Ibbetson ***Ed*** Richard Marden ***Mus*** Georges Delerue ***Art*** Maurice Carter, Lionel Couch
Act Richard Burton, Genevieve Bujold, Irene Papas, Anthony Quayle, John Colicos, Michael Hordern (Universal)

With Richard Burton as Henry VIII and Genevieve Bujold in the title role of Anne Boleyn, *Anne of the Thousand Days* is a stunningly acted, sumptuous, grand-scale widescreen drama of the royal bed chamber and political intrigues that created the Church of England.

Although Burton's portrayal is sensitive, vivid and arresting, it is still basically an unsympathetic role.

The screenplay, as adapted by Richard Sokolove, based on Maxwell Anderson's stage play, bristles with sharp epigrammatic dialog.

In his first feature film, TV director Charles Jarrot frames his Renaissance pageant handsomely and handles the skilled cast to achieve an effective uniform period style. However, there is a basically stagey pace to the drama that makes it more static and less cinematic than it might have been.

1969: Best Costume Design

NOMINATIONS: Best Picture, Actor (Richard Burton), Actress (Genevieve Bujold), Supp. Actor (Anthony Quayle), Screenplay, Cinematography, Art Direction, Original Score, Sound

•

ANNIE
1982, 128 mins, US Ⓥ ⦿ ▭ col
Dir John Huston ***Prod*** Ray Stark ***Scr*** Carol Sobieski ***Ph*** Richard Moore ***Ed*** Margaret Booth, Michael A. Stevenson ***Mus*** Ralph Burns (arr.) ***Art*** Dale Hennesy
Act Albert Finney, Carol Burnett, Aileen Quinn, Ann Reinking, Bernadette Peters, Tim Curry (Columbia)

Many people said John Huston was an odd choice to direct *Annie* and he proves them right. In an effort to be more "realistic" *Annie* winds up exposing just how weak a story it had to start with [stage play book by Thomas Meehan], not helped here by the music [songs by Charles Strouse and Martin Charnin]. Aside from the memorable "Tomorrow" the show's songs weren't all that much in the first place and four new tunes penned for the $35 million film aren't any better.

In the title role, little Aileen Quinn acquits herself quite well. Carol Burnett gets most of what chuckles there are as the drunken Miss Hannigan who runs the orphanage.

Albert Finney is best of the bunch as Daddy Warbucks, but it's really not a test for his talents. Edward Herrman is acceptable as FDR, a part he has down pat. As the villainous phony parents, Bernadette Peters and Tim Curry add little.

1982: NOMINATIONS: Best Art Direction, Original Song Score

•

ANNIE GET YOUR GUN
1950, 107 mins, US col
Dir George Sidney ***Prod*** Arthur Freed ***Scr*** Sidney Sheldon ***Ph*** Charles Rosher ***Ed*** James F. Newcom ***Mus*** Adolph Deutsch (dir.) ***Art*** Cedric Gibbons, Paul Groesse
Act Betty Hutton, Howard Keel, Louis Calhern, J. Carrol Naish, Edward Arnold, Keenan Wynn (M-G-M)

Annie Get Your Gun is socko musical entertainment on film, just as it was on the Broadway stage [in 1946]. In many respects, the film version gets the nod over the legit piece; at least there is enough pro and con to reprise that great novelty number "Anything You Can Do." Ten of the *Annie* Irving Berlin hits are used and two are reprised.

Briefly, Annie is a backwoods gal, a deadshot who is taken into a wildwest show, soon supplants the show's male marksman, goes on to become a star and then wins her man by losing a shooting match.

Annie is Wild West, shooting, Indians, daredevil-riding and action, never slowing a minute as put together for the screen by producer Arthur Freed and director George Sidney. They will find it hard to top.

1950: Best Score for a Musical Picture

NOMINATIONS: Best Color Cinematography, Color Art Direction, Editing

•

ANNIE HALL
1977, 93 mins, US Ⓥ ⊙ col
Dir Woody Allen ***Prod*** Charles H. Joffe ***Scr*** Woody Allen, Marshall Brickman ***Ph*** Gordon Willis ***Ed*** Ralph Rosenblum ***Art*** Mel Bourne
Act Woody Allen, Diane Keaton, Tony Roberts, Carol Kane, Paul Simon, Colleen Dewhurst (United Artists)

Woody Allen's four romantic comedies with Diane Keaton strike a chord of believability that makes them nearly the 1970s equivalent of the Tracy-Hepburn films. *Annie Hall* is by far the best, a touching and hilarious three-dimensional love story.

The gags fly by in almost non-stop profusion, but there is an undercurrent of sadness and pain reflecting a maturation of style. Allen tells Keaton in the film that he has "a very pessimistic view of life," and it's true.

The script is loosely structured, virtually a two-character running conversation between Allen and Keaton as they meet, fall in love, quarrel, and break up. Meanwhile, he continues his career as a moderately successful TV nightclub comic and she develops a budding career as a singer.

1977: Best Picture, Director, Actress (Diane Keaton), Original Screenplay

NOMINATION: Best Actor (Woody Allen)

•

ANNIE OAKLEY
1935, 79 mins, US Ⓥ
Dir George Stevens ***Prod*** Cliff Reid (assoc.) ***Scr*** Joel Sayre, John Twist ***Ph*** J. Roy Hunt ***Ed*** Jack Hively ***Mus*** Alberto Colombo (dir.) ***Art*** Albert S. D'Agostino, Perry Ferguson
Act Barbara Stanwyck, Preston Foster, Melvyn Douglas, Moroni Olsen, Pert Kelton, Andy Clyde (RKO)

If the picture misses as outstanding, it's because the script and the direction are not up to the star and title combination. It sums as a swell idea that doesn't quite come through.

Comedy drama has the colorful background of Buffalo Bill's Wild West show. Show business never produced a more glamorous personality than Col. Cody and Annie Oakley, famous rifle shot, was a star attraction in his aggregation. Her name was internationally known in the 1890s. The film storytellers have sought to recount the events which led to Annie's joining Buffalo Bill (Moroni Olsen), and have told a tale of romantic interest involving Annie (Barbara Stanwyck) and two of the troupe's figures. Toby Walker (Preston Foster), famous marksman, and Jeff Hogarth (Melvyn Douglas), general manager of the outfit.

When the action moves to the Wild West show, the interest in the characters and the story picks up considerably. Nothing has been spared in production, though the background lacks distinction, to reproduce the old-time show in its original form. Splendid feats of horsemanship and roping give excitement to the performance.

After the early scenes, where she plays a backwoods girl effectively, Stanwyck does little enough for the picture, probably because the material [from a screen story by Joseph A. Fields and Ewart Adamson] gives her few opportunities.

•

ANNIVERSARY, THE
1968, 95 mins, UK Ⓥ col
Dir Roy Ward Baker ***Prod*** Jimmy Sangster ***Scr*** Jimmy Sangster ***Ph*** Harry Waxman ***Ed*** Peter Wetherley ***Mus*** Philip Martell
Act Bette Davis, Sheila Hancock, Jack Hedley, James Cossins, Elaine Taylor, Christian Roberts (Hammer)

Derived from Bill McIllwraith's legit original, this was turned into a vehicle for the extravagant tantrums of Bette Davis, in her most ghoulish mood. This, together with its modish black-comedy lines and bold situation, is its chief asset.

Because it skates near the bone of family relationships, it rouses plenty of understanding yocks, but the exaggeration of the concept doesn't wear as well on film as it did on stage. It is a highly theatrical piece, and needs remoteness, rather than closeups, for its bitter characterizations not to come across as caricature.

Davis gets her teeth into the role of the ultra-possessive ma and hurls it out with splendid panache and flamboyance, but some might find her outsized portrayal too stark to carry the conviction. She bosses it over a family of three sons, all of whom are in advanced stages of spinelessness.

The action, which little attempt has been made to transfer into the wider visual terms of a feature pic, takes place on the anniversary of Davis's husband's death, and the family gathers to do him honor.

•

ANOTHER COUNTRY
1984, 90 mins, UK Ⓥ ⊙ col
Dir Marek Kanievska ***Prod*** Alan Marshall ***Scr*** Julian Mitchell ***Ph*** Peter Biziou ***Ed*** Gerry Hambling ***Mus*** Michael Storey ***Art*** Brian Morris
Act Rupert Everett, Colin Firth, Michael Jenn, Robert Addie, Rupert Wainwright, Anna Massey (Goldcrest)

Julian Mitchell's adaptation of his successful West End play *Another Country* is an absorbing tale about life in a British public (i.e., private) boarding school in the 1930s. Story is supposedly based on the early friendship of Guy Burgess and Donald MacLean who, in the 1950s, spied for the U.S.S.R. while working for the British government, but defected to Moscow before they could be arrested.

Mitchell's contention is that the homosexuality of Burgess, called Bennett here, made him as much an outsider in the claustrophobic atmosphere of the British uppercrust as did MacLean's (Judd's) Marxism.

Film is marvelously acted down the line, with Rupert Everett a standout as the tormented Bennett.

•

ANOTHER 48 HRS.
1990, 95 mins, US Ⓥ ⊙ col
Dir Walter Hill ***Prod*** Lawrence Gordon, Robert D. Wachs ***Scr*** John Fasano, Jeb Stuart, Larry Gross ***Ph*** Matthew F. Leonetti ***Ed*** Freeman Davies, Carmel Davies, Donn Aron ***Mus*** James Horner ***Art*** Joseph C. Nemec III
Act Eddie Murphy, Nick Nolte, Brion James, Kevin Tighe, Ed O'Ross, David Anthony Marshall (Paramount/Eddie Murphy)

Pic's really misnamed, since it's not *Another 48 HRS.* but the same *48 HRS.*, the 1982 mismatched buddy action pic.

Director Walter Hill, reprising those chores, knows the terrain and tills it with all the familiar elements: bawdy humor, cannon-loud gunplay, hissable bad guys and plenty of action. Eddie Murphy and Nick Nolte manage to recapture some of their initial chemistry, but for the most part the film is curiously flat—in part due to a jumped plot that's so quickly tied up at the end it seems everyone was in a hurry to get their checks and get out of town.

The plot [by Fred Braughton] even hinges on the first film, as two hit men are dispatched to kill Murphy, one the brother of the lead baddie offed in *48 HRS.* Nolte, meanwhile, has spent the past four years chasing a faceless drug kingpin called the Iceman, who paid for the hit on Murphy. He's been thwarted at every turn, however, leading Murphy to suspect corruption within the police department.

Hill and his trio of screenwriters choose the stale and predictable route at almost every turn, the plot being strictly a slender means of allowing Murphy and Nolte to strut their stuff.

•

ANOTHER MAN ANOTHER CHANCE
SEE: UN AUTRE HOMME UNE AUTRE CHANCE

•

ANOTHER PART OF THE FOREST
1948, 106 mins, US col b/w
Dir Michael Gordon ***Prod*** Jerry Bresler ***Scr*** Vladimir Pozner ***Ph*** Hal Mohr ***Ed*** Milton Carruth ***Mus*** Daniele Amfitheatrof ***Art*** Bernard Herzbrun, Robert Boyle
Act Fredric March, Dan Duryea, Edmond O'Brien, Ann Blyth, Florence Eldridge, Dona Drake (Universal)

Another Part of the Forest backtracks 20 years from *The Little Foxes*, Lillian Hellman's play, showing the same family of Hubbards and how they got to be that way in *Foxes*. Picture opens 15 years after close of the Civil War, in a small Southern town where the Hubbards dominate the community financially but still aren't accepted socially, due to Hubbard pere (Fredric March) having run salt at $8 a pound during the war to Confederates who badly needed the commodity.

March delivers to tremendous effect as the father, and he has benefit of as fine a cast of co-stars and support as could be imagined. Florence Eldridge makes her portrayal count, particularly as the mother who in the end admits she dislikes every one of her children, because of their meanness. Edmond O'Brien, as the elder son, is seen in the best role of his career.

Dan Duryea, the weakling son, does a rare bit of character acting, and Anne Blyth, the daughter, is a vixen who elicits small sympathy as she makes up to her father for his favor until her brother takes over the household.

•

ANOTHER STAKEOUT
1993, 109 mins, US Ⓥ ⊙ ▭ col
Dir John Badham ***Prod*** Jim Kouf, Cathleen Summers, Lynn Bigelow ***Scr*** Jim Kouf ***Ph*** Roy H. Wagner ***Ed*** Frank Morriss ***Mus*** Arthur B. Rubinstein ***Art*** Lawrence G. Paull
Act Richard Dreyfuss, Emilio Estevez, Rosie O'Donnell, Dennis Farina, Marcia Strassman, Madeleine Stowe (Touchstone)

A purely escapist entertainment, John Badham's *Another Stakeout*, a sequel to his 1987 hit, is sillier and less plausible than the first movie, but it's also funnier.

Scripter Jim Kouf's new comedy-adventure picks up Chris Lecce (Richard Dreyfuss) and Bill Reimers (Emilio Estevez), the two Seattle police detectives, six years later. Estevez is now married and the father of two. Dreyfuss, who is clean-shaven, lives with Maria (Madeleine Stowe, uncredited), the woman he was assigned to observe and fell in love with the first time out.

The eternally feuding cops are appointed to locate Lu Delano (Cathy Moriarty), a missing key witness in the trial of a Las Vegas mobster. This time around, their team also includes Gina Garrett (Rosie O'Donnell), an assertive, tough-talking assistant DA, who insists on bringing along her dog. Once they situate themselves in an elegant house in an upscale neighborhood, pretending to be one big, happy family, the real movie and frolic—begins. Most of the humor revolves around comic exchanges between Dreyfuss as Dad, O'Donnell as Mom and Estevez as their grown son.

There's one hilarious scene, a dinner party hosted by Dreyfuss and O'Donnell for their neighbors (Dennis Farina, Marcia Strassman). The fluency of wisecracks and sight gags in this sequence, which would do Blake Edwards proud, overshadows everything that follows.

•

ANOTHER TIME ANOTHER PLACE
1983, 101 mins, UK Ⓥ ⊙ col
Dir Michael Radford ***Prod*** Simon Perry ***Scr*** Michael Radford ***Ph*** Roger Deakins ***Ed*** Tom Priestley ***Mus*** John McLeod ***Art*** Hayden Pearce
Act Phyllis Logan, Giovanni Mauriello, Gian Luca Favilla, Claudio Rosini, Paul Young, Gregor Fisher (Umbrella)

It's not often that a British film is realized with as much creative integrity as *Another Time Another Place*. The plot springs from the cultural difference between the inhabitants of a bleak Scottish agricultural village and a trio of Italians confined to the community during World War II. One Italian in particular, the passionate Neopolitan Luigi (Giovanni Mauriello), mesmerizes Janie (Phyllis Logan) by seeming to offer an alternative to an emotionally cold marriage and a laborious, penny-pinching life. The rest of the Scottish community remain suspicious of the strangers in their midst.

The developing relationship is narrated with a light and humorous touch, even though both parties are drawn to each other out of desperation.

Central to the film's effectiveness is the performance of Logan as the girl entranced. Eyes and gestures capture the initial longing followed by the remorse that follows surrender.

The film's impact derives also from representations of daily life and a landscape that changes with the seasons.

•

ANOTHER WOMAN
1988, 84 mins, US Ⓥ ⦿ col
Dir Woody Allen ***Prod*** Robert Greenhut ***Scr*** Woody Allen ***Ph*** Sven Nykvist ***Ed*** Susan E. Morse ***Art*** Santo Loquasto
Act Gena Rowlands, Mia Farrow, Ian Holm, Blythe Danner, Gene Hackman, Martha Plimpton (Rollins/Joffe)

Woody Allen once again explores the human condition via the inner turmoil of gifted New Yorkers.

Story deals with a very successful, often idolized character who discovers around the time of her 50th birthday that she has made many mistakes, but people have been more or less too deferential to confront her.

Gena Rowlands plays Marion Post, head of a graduate philosophy department, married to a doctor. She takes an apartment downtown in which to write a book, and begins overhearing analysis sessions from the psychiatrist's office next door. At first she's annoyed, then gets hooked as a patient (Mia Farrow) tells of her unsettling conviction that her marriage has begun to disintegrate.

Soon, she's reliving some of the turning points in her life, through dreams, flashbacks and chance encounters with family and friends. Throughout, she's haunted by the memory of a man (Gene Hackman) who once loved her passionately.

Film that emerges is brave, in many ways fascinating, and in all respects of a caliber rarely seen.

•

ANOTHER YOU
1991, 94 mins, US Ⓥ ⦿ col
Dir Maurice Phillips ***Prod*** Ziggy Steinberg ***Scr*** Ziggy Steinberg ***Ph*** Victor J. Kemper ***Ed*** Dennis M. Hill ***Mus*** Charles Gross ***Art*** Dennis Washington
Act Richard Pryor, Gene Wilder, Mercedes Ruehl, Stephen Lang, Vanessa Williams, Phil Rubenstein (Tri-Star)

Gene Wilder's frantic routines can't compensate for Richard Pryor's sadly depleted energy in *Another You*, and producer Ziggy Steinberg's feeble script is given slapdash direction by the man who replaced Peter Bogdanovich on what is billed a "film by Maurice Phillips" (the best joke in the film).

The setup isn't without promise, as the "mentally challenged" Wilder is released from a sanitarium into the dubious care of Hollywood street hustler Pryor, who's been ordered to do community service as a condition of his parole.

Some amiable, if predictable, gags about Wilder's readjustment to the sleazy outside world give way all too quickly to tiresome plot mechanics as Stephen Lang and Mercedes Ruehl maneuver to use the gullible Wilder to impersonate a missing brewery heir.

The depressing mood is worsened by the murky color scheme of production designer Dennis Washington and lenser Victor J. Kemper, who somehow manage to make Wilder's Bev Hills manse look almost as unattractive as Hollywood Boulevard.

•

A NOUS LA LIBERTE
1931, 93 mins, France Ⓥ b/w
Dir Rene Clair ***Scr*** Rene Clair ***Ph*** Georges Perinal ***Ed*** Rene Le Henaff ***Mus*** Georges Auric ***Art*** Lazare Meerson
Act Henri Marchand, Raymond Cordy, Rolla France, Paul Olivier, Jacques Shelley, Germaine Aussey (Tobis)

Rene Clair has applied a technical formula similar to that of his preceding productions, *Sous les Toits de Paris* and *Le Million*, to subject matter which constitutes social satire. That is, his film has a minimum of dialog and a good deal of accompanying music.

This film really comprises two parts. One half is social, and really the backbone of the picture. The other part, which practically constitutes an independent story, is a love affair. Like most Clair films it contains much footage devoted to chases. A distinct effort at production has been made, and cost of film is well over $100,000. A ghost chorus express in song thoughts, which the principals act.

Social half shows two prisoners attempting to break jail. The one who escapes (Raymond Cordy) secures a job as a gramophone salesman and then rises to the position of a big manufacturer. Chain system and discipline in his factories are identical to those in the prison. When the recaptured prisoner (Henri Marchand) has been liberated, he traces his former mate who gives him a job.

Love story consists of the manager's pal, as one of the workers, in love with a girl clerk (Rolla France) and finding that she already loves another man.

Cordy, who gives a fine impersonation of the industrialist, was a taxi driver [before making the film]. He is somewhat of the George Bancroft type. His pal is well played by Marchand. Balance of the cast is excellent.

•

ANTHONY ADVERSE
1936, 139 mins, US Ⓥ col
Dir Mervyn LeRoy ***Prod*** Henry Blanke ***Scr*** Sheridan Gibney ***Ph*** Tony Gaudio ***Ed*** Ralph Dawson ***Mus*** Erich Wolfgang Korngold ***Art*** Anton Grot
Act Fredric March, Olivia de Havilland, Edmund Gwenn, Claude Rains, Anita Louise, Louise Hayward, Gale Sondergaard (Warner)

In transmuting the Hervey Allen bestseller to the screen the producers were faced with the unusual problem of too much material. They have maneuvered a straightforward and comparatively logical story. It's a bit choppy and it's a bit long-winded, but it is a direct line and easy to follow.

Writer Sheridan Gibney managed to hew a straight course through the 1,200 pages of Allen's writing by concentrating on his titular character and avoiding the danger of skirting off and away. Thus he clips off the entire last portion of the book, for instance, and plenty of juicy matter in between.

Fredric March as Adverse is an ace choice, playing the role to the hilt. Much less theatrical than he occasionally becomes, March is convincing through a varied series of moods and portrayals.

Olivia de Havilland has, perhaps, the next important role as Adverse's wife, Angela. She handles it acceptably, especially in the emotional scenes. In the opera sequences she uncovers a lovely singing voice. In the supporting cast, Edmund Gwenn makes the part of John Bonyweather stand out. Claude Rains does a splendid job as Don Luis.

Pleasant, rather than exciting, is Eric Wolfang Korngold's musical accompaniment.

1936: Best Supp. Actress (Gale Sondergaard), Cinematography, Score, Editing

NOMINATIONS: Best Picture, Art Direction, Assistant Director (William Cannon)

•

ANTONIA'S LINE
1995, 93 mins, Belgium/Uk/Netherlands Ⓥ col
Dir Marleen Gorris ***Prod*** Hans De Weers ***Scr*** Marleen Gorris ***Ph*** Willy Stassen ***Ed*** Michiel Reichwein, Wim Louwrier ***Mus*** Ilona Seckaz ***Art*** Harry Ammerlaan
Act Willeke van Ammelrooy, Els Dottermans, Jan Decleir, Marina De Graaf, Mil Seghers, Jan Steen

Marleen Gorris's idealized perspective on an independent-minded woman who comes to live in a small Dutch farming community, *Antonia's Line*, is a feel-good fairy tale that will appeal to many women.

Antonia (Willeke van Ammelrooy) is a very old lady when pic opens, and she knows it is the last day of her life by a kind of magic realism that pops up sporadically throughout the film. A long flashback begins at the end of the war, when she and her teenage daughter, Danielle (Els Dottermans), return to the farm town where Antonia—now a stocky, attractive matron of 40—was born.

Willy Stassen's sensuous camerawork depicts the idyllic Dutch farm country as a lush natural paradise. In the same spirit, Gorris narrates the lives of five generations of women who work, have kids and bond with each other and some of the more decent males in the vicinity, as season follows season in a natural rhythm of birth and death.

In Antonia's magical kingdom, no woman ever makes a false step—which puts much of the story squarely in the wishful-thinking category. In the title role, van Ammelrooy provides a strong center to the rambling story, both feminine and authoritative.

1995: Best Foreign Language Film

•

ANTONY AND CLEOPATRA
1972, 158 mins, UK/Spain/Switzerland Ⓥ ⌴ col
Dir Charlton Heston ***Prod*** Peter Snell ***Scr*** Charlton Heston ***Ph*** Rafael Pacheco ***Ed*** Eric Boyd-Perkins ***Mus*** John Scott ***Art*** Maurice Pelling
Act Charlton Heston, Hildegard Neil, Eric Porter, John Castle, Fernando Rey, Freddie Jones (Folio/Izaro/Filmtransac)

Charlton Heston, whose ardor for Shakespeare goes back to his 16mm film college days in Chicago, has herein come up with a very creditable retelling of the Bard's Antony and Cleopatra passion. It is impressively mounted and well played, and though lengthy it sustains well.

The finished film is a neat balance of closeup portraiture and panoramic action; the big battle sequences on land and sea are impressive achievements [directed by Joe Canutt], and the Spanish location landscape provides a stunning backdrop.

Heston's adaptation, for the most part, succeeds in avoiding the sort of character simplification that would have produced a picture simply for the eye. Hildegard Neil proves one of Cleo's more convincing screen incarnations.

Heston himself as Antony very often succeeds in capturing the nobility of the character. The real handicap is borne by John Castle as Octavius Caesar. It's one of those monochromatic, steadily dour parts that doesn't leave the actor much room.

•

ANTZ
1998, 83 MINS, US Ⓥ ⦿ col
Dir Eric Darnell, Tim Johnson ***Prod*** Brad Lewis, Aron Warner, Patty Wooton ***Scr*** Todd Alcott, Chris Weitz, Paul Weitz ***Ed*** Stan Webb ***Mus*** Harry Gregson-Williams, John Powell ***Art*** John Bell (DreamWorks/PDI)

Antz is a dazzling delight. This initial collaboration between DreamWorks, and partial subsidiary Pacific Data Images, reps the second fully computer-animated feature, after *Toy Story*, and is a sort of *Metropolis* meets *Microcosmos* with a commoner-princess-lovers-on-the-run romance at its core. Pic beat to markey by seven weeks Disney's computer animated *A Bug's Life*.

Appropriately enough for a feature toplining Woody Allen [among the voicers], the picture starts on an analyst's couch, as a meek worker ant named Z (Allen) complains about his upbringing as "the middle child in a family of 5 million." The physical grandeur of the ants' underground totalitarian world is dazzlingly displayed in the early going, as countless workers are driven to extremes by Gen. Mandible (Gene Hackman), a martinet with dreams of even greater glory, and his aide de camp Col. Cutter (Christopher Walken).

Mandible convinces his queen (Anne Bancroft) that the colony is threatened with imminent invasion by termites and that he must launch a preemptive strike. On the night before the invasion, the queen's daughter, Princess Bala (Sharon Stone), who is unhappily engaged to Mandible, goes slumming and asks an unsuspecting Z to dance. Z convinces a friendly soldier, Weaver (Sylvester Stallone), to let him take his place in the military review, hoping this will allow him to see Bala again.

The neurotic Z is the only survivor of the massacre and is more or less forced into kidnapping Bala. Much of the remainder of the story takes place in the open air, where the pair must elude Mandible's posses, contend with the occasional human being, and encounter the unlikely paradise of Insectopia, falling in love all the while.

Vocal performances are outstanding across the board, while the backgrounds are magnificently designed with detail and bold, clear colors that continually provide feasts for the eyes.

•

ANYBODY'S WOMAN
1930, 80 mins, US b/w
Dir Dorothy Arzner ***Scr*** Zoe Akins, Doris Anderson ***Ph*** Charles Lang ***Ed*** Jane Loring
Act Ruth Chatterton, Clive Brook, Paul Lukas, Huntly Gordon (Paramount)

The picture will appeal to some and probably not to others. Its story is an old one, basically the successful efforts of the bad, bad girl to become a good wife to a lawyer far above her station.

It's mainly the unsympathetic role handed Clive Brook that takes the big punch out of the story. It starts out far more promisingly than it develops.

Brook has just become divorced from his upper-strata wife who bolts to marry a richer man. He takes to drink to dull the effects of the jolt and is tossed into the society of the chorus girl he once defended as an attorney. She falls for his philosophy that probably a bad girl like her would make the best wife in the long run.

The social ostracism angle is also overdone, as is Ruth Chatterton's interpretation of the tough one's role. Her best work is in the more dramatic scenes.

•

ANY GIVEN SUNDAY
1999, 162 mins, US Ⓥ ⦿ ⌴ col
Dir Oliver Stone ***Prod*** Lauren Shuler Donner, Clayton Townsend, Dan Halsted ***Scr*** John Logan, Oliver Stone ***Ph*** Salvatore Totino ***Ed*** Tom Nordberg, Keith Salmon, Stuart Waks, Stuart Levy ***Mus*** Robbie Robertson, Paul Kelly, Richard Horowitz ***Art*** Victor Kempster
Act Al Pacino, Cameron Diaz, Dennis Quaid, James Woods, Jamie Foxx, LL Cool J (Ixtlan/The Donners'/Warner)

A rambunctious, hyperkinetic, testosterone-and-adrenaline-drenched look at professional football, *Any Given Sunday* connects for long yardage as smart popular entertainment. Oliver Stone mixes right-minded takes on innumerable issues with his recently developed helter-skelter style on his way to making his most purely enjoyable film in years.

Nearly an hour of football action frames the story, which begins by plunging the viewer headlong into a bizarre and bitterly fought game. For 23 minutes, the contest plays out in agonizing fashion for Miami's [fictional] "Sharks." First, their aging star quarterback, Jack "Cap" Rooney (Dennis Quaid), goes down from a devastating hit, and the same fate awaits the backup. The third-stringer, the nervous and unprepared Willie Beamen (Jamie Foxx), barfs on the field and looks real bad at first.

For the remainder of the season, more crises erupt off the field than during games. The Sharks' savvy veteran coach, Tony D'Amato (Al Pacino) has sacrificed his wife and kids to his job. Christina Pagniacci (Cameron Diaz) has inherited the team with her alcoholic mother (Ann-Margret) and has the sort of ruthless bottom-line mentality entirely at odds with the old-school approach of her late father.

Main figures' private lives are sketched in quick, clear strokes. Through all the characters, Stone and co-writer John Logan [who also wrote the screen story with Daniel Pyne] are able to make plenty of sharp observations about the generational, racial and attitudinal divides in American life.

Uniforms have a bright, vaguely futuristic look. Music from myriad sources contributes further to the sensory overload. Performances are almost all shot through with electricity.

•

ANY NUMBER CAN PLAY

1949, 102 mins, US b/w

Dir Mervyn LeRoy ***Prod*** Arthur Freed ***Scr*** Richard Brooks ***Ph*** Harold Rosson ***Ed*** Ralph E. Winters ***Mus*** Lenny Hayton

Act Clark Gable, Alexis Smith, Wendell Corey, Audrey Totter, Mary Astor, Lewis Stone (M-G-M)

In attempting to sketch a portrait of a big-time casino operator, screenwriter Richard Brooks has jammed the yarn [based on a novel by Edward Harris Heth] with too many subordinate characterizations which fly off at a tangent. Director Mervyn LeRoy, however, does a creditable job in integrating the secondary roles and subplots with an atmospheric consistency.

Pic's thesis maintains that gambling is legitimate—if you're a winner. Yarn develops the point via a domestic break between Clark Gable, as the legalized gambling house operator, and his collegiate son, who is ashamed of his pappy's profession.

Gable effectively projects the hard-playing gambler with no sympathy for his son's idealistic gripings.

•

ANYTHING CAN HAPPEN

1952, 107 mins, US b/w

Dir George Seaton ***Prod*** William Perlberg ***Scr*** George Seaton, George Oppenheimer ***Ph*** Daniel L. Fapp ***Ed*** Alma Macrorie ***Mus*** Victor Young

Act Jose Ferrer, Kim Hunter, Kurt Kasznar, Eugenie Leontovich, Oscar Karlweis, Nick Dennis (Paramount)

Anything Can Happen, based on the bestselling book by George and Helen Papashvily detailing their own real-life adventures, is a heart-warming comedy, engagingly acted, slickly produced and directed.

Film concerns a loveable group of Near Eastern immigrants and their devotion for the new homeland in America. It shows Jose Ferrer's arrival in the new, strange country, his struggles with the English language, his shy courting of an American (Kim Hunter), and his eventual ownership of a California orange grove on which he is privileged to pay U.S. taxes.

Ferrer proves his versatility with a restrained, believable performance. Hunter is always convincing as the seemingly unattainable American whose friendliness and interest in the foreigner turn to real love.

•

ANYTHING GOES

1936, 90 mins, US b/w

Dir Lewis Milestone ***Prod*** Benjamin Glazer ***Scr*** [uncredited] ***Ph*** Karl Struss ***Ed*** Eda Warren

Act Bing Crosby, Ethel Merman, Charles Ruggles, Ida Lupino, Grace Bradley, Arthur Treacher (Paramount)

Cole Porter's lyrics, which were the essence and chief asset of the original [1934] stage *Anything Goes*, have been replaced by plot motion in this adaptation. Of the Porter poetical sleight-of-hand, which listened so well on Broadway for a couple of seasons, only "I Get a Kick Out of You" and "You're the Top" are used. The title song is in also, but just for thematic and strictly instrumental use. There are four new numbers, of which "My Heart and I," "Sailor Beware" and "Moonburn" are the most likely.

Ethel Merman comes from the original cast and her job in the picture equals her job in the stage version, which means aces. But Charlie Ruggles as the gag gangster is miscast. His delivery is too vigorous for the sap character, and the role calls for low comeding, which is out of Ruggles line.

With the story opening in a cabaret and finishing in a production scene, with most of the bulk in between taking place on a big ocean liner, the production is lavish, and logical most of the time. Only in the closing flash does it go beyond credibility. This occurs on the "dock" at Southampton, upon the boat landing on the other side.

Crosby is fine singing "Sailor Beware" alone. And he's also there when it comes to getting his quota of laughs.

•

ANYTHING GOES

1956, 106 mins, US col

Dir Robert Lewis ***Prod*** Robert Emmett Dolan ***Scr*** Sidney Sheldon ***Ph*** John F. Warren ***Ed*** Frank Bracht ***Mus*** Cole Porter

Act Bing Crosby, Donald O'Connor, Zizi Jeanmaire, Mitzi Gaynor, Phil Harris, Kurt Kasznar (Paramount)

Paramount's sock musical package borrows the title and songs from that yesteryear stage hit, *Anything Goes*. Male topliners Bing Crosby and Donald O'Connor go together as though born to give the zip to what scripter Sidney Sheldon has concocted.

While there are Cole Porter songs and the legit handle is still carried, that's about all that remains of what went on behind the footlights, and there's scant resemblance to Paramount's 1936 film version, in which Crosby also starred with Ethel Merman.

Choice of the two femme stars, Zizi Jeanmaire and Mitzi Gaynor, both leggy and appealing, is a click factor.

Script provides Crosby with plenty of those sotto voce, throwaway cracks he and his fans dote on. Plot, simply, has Crosby and O'Connor agreeing to do a B'way musical together after European vacations. Abroad, each signs a femme star and the remainder concerns fitting the gals in with previous plans.

Jeanmaire has two ballets that are clicks. Gaynor belts the title tune staged by Ernie Platt to score solidly in her solo showcasing.

•

ANY WEDNESDAY

1966, 109 mins, US Ⓥ col

Dir Robert Ellis Miller ***Prod*** Julius J. Epstein ***Scr*** Julius J. Epstein ***Ph*** Harold Lipstein ***Ed*** Stefan Arnsten ***Mus*** George Duning ***Art*** Al Sweeney

Act Jane Fonda, Jason Robards, Dean Jones, Rosemary Murphy, Ann Prentiss, Jack Fletcher (Warner)

Based on Muriel Resnik's popular legiter, *Any Wednesday* emerges in screen translation as an outstanding sophisticated comedy about marital infidelity. Adaptation and production by Julius J. Epstein is very strong, enhanced by solid direction and excellent performances. Epstein's zesty adaptation wisely distributes the comedy emphasis among all four principals: Jason Robards, the once-a-week philanderer; Jane Fonda, his two-year Wednesday date; Dean Jones, whose arrival rocks Robards's dreamboat; and Rosemary Murphy, recreating in superior fashion her original Broadway role as Robards's wife.

Interactions between principals are uniformly strong, both in dialog and acting as well as in very effective use of split-screen effects.

Fonda comes across quite well as the girl who can't make up her mind, although she has a tendency to overplay certain bits in what might be called an exaggerated Doris Day manner. Jones impresses as a likeable comedy performer whose underlying dramatic ability gets a good showcasing here. Robards is outstanding as the likeable lecher who winds up losing both his mistress and his wife.

•

ANYWHERE BUT HERE

1999, 114 mins, US Ⓥ ⊙ ⌑ col

Dir Wayne Wang ***Prod*** Laurence Mark ***Scr*** Alvin Sargent ***Ph*** Roger Deakins ***Ed*** Nicholas C. Smith ***Mus*** Danny Elfman ***Art*** Donald Graham, Graham Burt

Act Susan Sarandon, Natalie Portman, Eileen Ryan, Ray Baker, John Diehl, Shawn Hatosy (Fox 2000)

Centering on the turbulent but loving relationship between a single mother and her rebellious teenage daughter, *Anywhere but Here* is a sumptuously crafted but extremely old-fashioned comedy-drama, made in the manner of Hollywood weepies of yesteryear. Natalie Portman lends excellent support to Susan Sarandon's turn as her eccentric but ultimately self-sacrificing mother.

Though pic is set in 1995, and is based on Mona Simpson's 1986 novel, a good deal of the film registers as an updated version of the King Vidor version of *Stella Dallas* with Sarandon's crude working-class woman reminiscent of Barbara Stanwyck's role in the 1937 film.

In the first scene, Adele (Sarandon) and 14-year-old Ann (Portman) are zooming down the highway in their 1978 Mercedes, heading toward the promised land of Beverly Hills. Against Ann's will, they're leaving Bay City, WI, a provincial town Adele finds suffocating. Ann is furious over losing the cozy family and social life she enjoyed with her grandmother Lillian (Eileen Ryan), cousin Benny (Shawn Hatosy) and intimate friends.

Adele is pushing her daughter into acting, hoping that life in sunny Los Angeles will fulfill her dreams. Ann goes through a painful coming of age, and the tension between mom and daughter when latter decides to attend an East Coast college is particularly well handled.

The revelation here is Portman, whose casting was reportedly Sarandon's condition for making the movie. With half a dozen roles to her credit, Portman is a natural performer who brings rough edges to any role she plays. Wayne Wang directs with clarity, stressing crowd-pleasing and tear-jerking moments

•

ANY WHICH WAY YOU CAN

1980, 116 mins, US Ⓥ ⊙ col

Dir Buddy Van Horn ***Prod*** Fritz Manes ***Scr*** Stanford Sherman ***Ph*** David Worth ***Ed*** Ferris Webster, Ron Spang ***Mus*** Snuff Garrett (sup.) ***Art*** William J. Creber

Act Clint Eastwood, Sondra Locke, Ruth Gordon, William Smith, Harry Guardino, Geoffrey Lewis (Warner)

Any Which Way You Can is a benign continuation of *Every Which Way but Loose*. Clint Eastwood, Sondra Locke, Geoffrey Lewis, Ruth Gordon and numerous supporting players all repeat their characterizations from the first outing to similar effect. Main difference is that individuals this time seem almost forgiving, loving and considerate.

Eastwood's Philo Beddoe swears off his lucrative sideline career, better to settle down with Ma Gordon, a significantly tamed Locke and orangutan chum Clyde. However, the mob makes him an offer he can't refuse to battle he-man William Smith, and the two, despite having become good pals, end up in an epic brawl.

Original ape from *Loose* was not available to Eastwood here, but substitute performs heroically.

•

ANZIO

1968, 117 mins, Italy Ⓥ ⌑ col

Dir Edward Dmytryk ***Prod*** Dino De Laurentiis ***Scr*** Harry A. L. Craig ***Ph*** Giuseppe Retonno ***Ed*** Alberto Gallitti, Peter Taylor ***Mus*** Riz Ortolani ***Art*** Luigi Scaccianoce

Act Robert Mitchum, Peter Falk, Robert Ryan, Arthur Kennedy, Earl Holliman, Mark Damon (Columbia)

Anzio, based on the World War II campaign in Italy, suffers from flat writing, stock performances, uninspired direction and dull pacing. Produced by Dino De Laurentiis, film would seem to be a large-scale war epic, but it really is a pale tale of a small group of men trapped behind German lines. Robert Mitchum stars in a cast that is far better in potential than in reality.

Two U.S. generals (Arthur Kennedy and Robert Ryan) play a cautious and a headline-hungry type, respectively. But from the moment the film begins, it is apparent that the overall pace is going to limp.

Mitchum's character, a wiseguy newspaper reporter, plays off against the brass, whom he puts down, and his seven army cohorts, who put him down for not getting involved. Only Earl Holliman has any significant life.

Peter Falk overacts an overwritten part of a rough-guy-with-heart-of-tin. He and Mitchum discuss some basic philosophical points, one of several forced injections of "meaning," which not only fail to elevate the story, but actually depress it further into banality.

•

APA

1966, 96 mins, Hungary Ⓥ ⊙ b/w

Dir Istvan Szabo ***Scr*** Istvan Szabo ***Ph*** Sandor Sara ***Ed*** Janos Rozsa ***Mus*** Janos Gonda

Act Miklos Gabor, Klari Tolnay, Andras Balint, Dani Erdelyi, Kati Solyom, Zsuzsa Rathonyi (Mafilm III)

The growth of a youth into manhood is explored here via the use of real and imaginary flashbacks to life with his father, a doctor who died just after the end of the last World War, leaving his young son with a number of confused memories. As he grows, the child becomes slowly obsessed by the father's continuing influence on his life, and he unconsciously begins inventing wartime exploits with the partisans and other exaggerated achievements to further the hero image, which, he finds, rubs off on him with his fellow pupils.

In his second feature pic, young Hungarian director Istvan Szabo is especially good in his brief, sketchlike notations, either real or imagined, in which the boy recalls or constructs his father's past. This is real, solid, moving yet unsentimental stuff, and it's beautifully illustrated as well by Sandor Sara's camerawork with its nostalgic glimpses of the past.

Pic also avoids no issues, thorny or not, and its integration of the 1956 Hungarian uprising is apt and honest, as are such other topics as early befuddlement with Marxism or the problems of a Jewish minority in Budapest.

Acting is uniformly good, with Miklos Gabor lending his personality to the role of father. Andras Balint is able in the role of the youth.

•

APACHE

1954, 86 mins, US Ⓥ ⦿ col

Dir Robert Aldrich ***Prod*** Harold Hecht ***Scr*** James R. Webb ***Ph*** Ernest Laszlo ***Ed*** Alan Crosland, Jr. ***Mus*** David Raksin ***Art*** Nicolai Remisoff

Act Burt Lancaster, Jean Peters, John McIntire, Charles Bronson, John Dehner, Paul Guilfoyle (United Artists)

This initial Hecht/Lancaster release through United Artists is a rugged action saga in best Burt Lancaster style of muscle-flexing. Production is based on history, retelling the story of a die-hard Apache who waged a one-man war against the United States and thereafter became a tribal legend. While its roots are historic, the James R. Webb screenplay from Paul I. Wellman's novel, *Broncho Apache*, gives it good old outdoor action punch true to Western film tradition.

Main plot switch is viewing Indian from sympathetic angle, even though his knife, arrows, bullets often find their marks among white soldiers.

Lancaster and Jean Peters play their Indian roles understandingly without usual screen stereotyping.

Robert Aldrich, making second start as feature film director, handles cast and action well, waste movement being eliminated and only essentials to best storytelling retained, as attested by comparatively short running time.

•

APARAJITO

1957, 108 mins, India Ⓥ b/w

Dir Satyajit Ray ***Scr*** Satyajit Ray ***Ph*** Subrata Mitra ***Ed*** Dulal Dutt ***Mus*** Ravi Shankar ***Art*** Bansi Chandragupta

Act Kanu Bannerjee, Karuna Bannerjee, Pinaki Sen Gupta, Sumiran Ghosjal (Epic)

As the second in Satyajit Ray's trilogy of Indian life, *Aparajito* is a worthy successor to the first film *Pather Panchali.* It doesn't have quite the tension or quite the variety of mood but it has a special brooding quality and a more explicit conflict between East and West.

The story [from Bibhuti Bannerjee's novel] simply continues to follow the fortunes and misfortunes of one Brahman family, which has moved to the holy city of Banares, where the father, movingly played by Kanu Bannerjee, practices as a priest until he contracts a fatal illness.

The mother, played by sad-eyed Karuna Bannerjee, is forced to take work as a rich family's cook until a priestly uncle takes her and her little son, played by Pinaki Sen Gupta, back to a small village, where the 10-year-old boy becomes a priest. The little boy, however, yearns for a Western education and eventually wins a scholarship to a Calcutta university. The city tears the young man, played by Sumiran Ghosjal, from his mother and she becomes ill.

Satyajit Ray's relentless camera searches out the foibles of mankind: a half-Westernized Hindu lecher hiding a bottle of forbidden liquor, a fellow Brahman trying to put the touch on the father, a hideous railway butcher peddling religious nostrums, etc. There are moments of lightness, too, when the son and a schoolmate stretch out on a grassy slope and contemplate the Calcutta roadstead and even a voyage to England.

This is the India of the 1920s, an awakening India, an empire bound by stringent religious precepts, which slowly grows to realize its own strength.

•

APARTMENT, THE

1960, 124 mins, US Ⓥ ⦿ ▭ b/w

Dir Billy Wilder ***Prod*** Billy Wilder ***Scr*** Billy Wilder, I.A.L. Diamond ***Ph*** Joseph LaShelle ***Ed*** Daniel Mandell ***Mus*** Adolph Deutsch ***Art*** Alexander Trauner

Act Jack Lemmon, Shirley MacLaine, Fred MacMurray, Ray Walston, Edie Adams, Jack Kruschen (Mirisch/United Artists)

Billy Wilder furnishes *The Apartment* with a one-hook plot that comes out high in comedy, wide in warmth and long in running time. As with *Some Like It Hot*, the broad handling is of more consequence than the package.

The story is simple. Lemmon is a lonely insurance clerk with a convenient, if somewhat antiquated, apartment that has become the rendezvous point for five of his bosses and their amours. In return, he's promoted from the 19th-floor office pool to a 27th-floor wood-paneled office complete with key to the executive washroom. When he falls in love with Shirley MacLaine, an elevator girl who's playing Juliet to top executive Fred MacMurray's Romeo, he turns in his washroom key.

The screenplay fills every scene with touches that spring only from talented, imaginative filmmakers. But where their *Some Like It Hot* kept you guessing right up to fadeout, *Apartment* reveals its hand early in the game. Second half of the picture is loosely constructed and tends to lag.

Apartment is all Lemmon, with a strong twist of MacLaine. The actor uses comedy as it should be used, to evoke a rainbow of emotions. He's lost in a cool world, this lonely bachelor, and he is not so much the shnook as the well-meaning, ambitious young man who lets good be the ultimate victor. MacLaine, in pixie hairdo, is a prize that's consistent with the fight being waged for her affections. Her ability to play it broad where it should be broad, subtle where it must be subtle, enables the actress to effect reality and yet do much more.

1960: Best Picture, Director, Original Story & Screenplay, B&W Art Direction, Editing

NOMINATIONS: Best Actor (Jack Lemmon), Actress (Shirley MacLaine), Supp. Actor (Jack Kruschen), B&W Cinematography, Sound

•

APARTMENT FOR PEGGY

1948, 96 mins, US col

Dir George Seaton ***Prod*** William Perlberg ***Scr*** George Seaton ***Ph*** Harry Jackson ***Ed*** Robert Simpson ***Mus*** David Raksin ***Art*** Lyle Wheeler, Richard Irvine

Act Jeanne Crain, William Holden, Edmund Gwenn, Gene Lockhart, Griff Barnett, Randy Stuart (20th Century-Fox)

The producer and director-scripter combination that made *Miracle on 34th Street* an entertaining study of human behavior has repeated with *Peggy*. As a team, William Perlberg and George Seaton sell the human interest with just the right amount of believeable hokum and heartstring tugs, and the cast plays it to the hilt.

Jeanne Crain is perfect casting for the young wife of William Holden, veteran studying under the GI bill. She gives the role a thoroughly believeable reading that comes off big and Holden's work matches. *Miracle*'s Santa Claus, Edmund Gwenn, completes the star trio, socking over his professor of philosophy role with such deft understanding it's a joy to watch. Seaton endows his script [from a story by Faith Baldwin] with modern dialog and quails not from using everyday expressions that usually are skirted in pictures. Crain is pregnant, and says so. Dialog also has something to point up on postwar conditions for GIs, and says it lucidly without preaching. The same goes for ignorance as the fount of trouble—personal or world—but the writing never mounts a soapbox to make its points, remembering always its entertainment aims.

•

APARTMENT ZERO

1989, 124 mins, UK Ⓥ ⦿ col

Dir Martin Donovan ***Prod*** Martin Donovan, David Koepp ***Scr*** Martin Donovan, David Koepp ***Ph*** Miguel Rodriguez ***Ed*** Conrad M. Gonzalez ***Mus*** Elia Cmiral ***Art*** Miguel Angel Lumaldo

Act Colin Firth, Hart Bochner, Dora Bryan, Liz Smith, Fabrizio Bentivoglio, Cipe Lincovsky (Summit)

Apartment Zero emerges as a genuinely creepy, disturbing and gripping psychological piece. Story's fundamental opposition is between Colin Firth, the nervously repressed, emotionally constipated British cinephile, and Hart Bochner, a charming, loose, Yankee rascal whom Firth takes into his lovely flat as a boarder when finances demand it.

Periodically, there are reports of serial murders taking place throughout Buenos Aires, and suggestions that mercenary foreigners who came to Argentina in the employ of the Death Squads may still be active. Suspicion grows that the enigmatic Bochner may not be what he claims.

Both actors are excellent, with Firth expressing and transcending the irritating emotional constriction of a non-participant in life, and Bochner displaying hitherto unrevealed talent portraying a profoundly split personality.

•

APOCALYPSE NOW

1979, 153 mins, US Ⓥ ⦿ ▭ col

Dir Francis Coppola ***Prod*** Francis Coppola ***Scr*** John Milius, Francis Coppola ***Ph*** Vittorio Storaro ***Ed*** Richard Marks, Walter Murch, Gerald B. Greenberg, Lis Fruchtman ***Mus*** Carmine Coppola, Francis Coppola ***Art*** Dean Tavoularis

Act Marlon Brando, Robert Duvall, Martin Sheen, Frederic Forrest, Dennis Hopper, Sam Bottoms (Omni Zoetrope/United Artists)

Alternately a brilliant and bizarre film, Francis Coppola's "work in progress" offers the definitive validation to the old saw, war is hell. Coppola's vision of Hell on Earth hews closely to Joseph Conrad's novella *Heart of Darkness*, and therein lies the $40 million film's principal commercial defect.

An exhilarating action-adventure exercise for two-thirds of its 139 minutes, *Apocalypse* abruptly shifts to surrealistic symbolism for its denouement. Result will be many spectators left in the lurch. It's the first film to directly excoriate U.S. involvement in the Indochina war. *Apocalypse Now* takes realistic cinema to a new extreme—Coppola virtually creates World War III on screen. There are no models or miniatures, no tank work, nor process screens for the airborne sections. The resulting footage outclasses any war pic made to date.

Coppola's wisest decision was to narrow the focus on the members of the patrol boat crew entrusted with taking Intelligence assassin Martin Sheen on a hazardous mission upriver into Cambodia. There Sheen hopes to track down and "terminate with extreme prejudice" Marlon Brando, a megalomaniac officer whose methods and motives have become, in Pentagonese, "unsound," as he leads an army of Montagnard tribesmen on random genocide missions.

Robert Duvall appears midway as an air cavalry helicopter commander who's a surfing nut, and has his boys riding the waves in the midst of flak attacks. These and some otherworldly, nighttime river excursions seem the principal contributions of original scenarist John Milius, and they contain a wacky, manic energy that serves *Apocalypse* well. [Pic also features a narration, written by Michael Herr.]

It's when the ghost of Conrad enters the picture that *Apocalypse Now* runs aground. Final third of the pic fails to jell. [Version reviewed was a 139-min. "work in progress" shown at the 1979 Cannes festival.]

Brando's intimating but inscrutable performance doesn't clarify anything. Rest of the cast is extraordinary, with Sheen extremely effective in a laconic style. Coppola himself shows up in a brief cameo as a combat director.

Apocalypse Now is emblazoned with firsts: a 70mm version without [the 6 mins. of] credits, a director putting himself personally on the hook for the film's $18-million cost overrun, and then obtaining rights to the pic in perpetuity and a revolutionary sound system that adds immeasurably to the film's impact.

1979: Best Cinematography, Sound

NOMINATIONS: Best Picture, Director, Supp. Actor (Robert Duvall), Screenplay, Art Direction, Editing

•

APOLLO 13

1995, 140 mins, US Ⓥ ⦿ ▭ col

Dir Ron Howard ***Prod*** Brian Grazer ***Scr*** William Broyles, Jr., Al Reinert ***Ph*** Dean Cundey ***Ed*** Mike Hill, Dan Hanley ***Mus*** James Horner ***Art*** Michael Corenblith

Act Tom Hanks, Kevin Bacon, Bill Paxton, Gary Sinise, Ed Harris, Kathleen Quinlan (Universal/Imagine)

With its rah-rah, gung-ho, can-do attitude and cast full of good-looking young white men in buzz cuts, this engrossing account of NASA's most perilous moon shot embodies what many consider to be old-fashioned American virtues in a virtually pristine state.

Scarcely embellishing the story [from the book *Lost Moon* by Jim Lovell and Jeffrey Kluger] of how three astronauts barely avoided becoming the first Americans to die in outer space, director Ron Howard and his team walk a narrative line that's almost as narrow as the course of the mission itself.

A bunch of NASA personnel and their kin assemble to watch the dramatic moment on July 20,1969, when Neil Armstrong became the first man to walk on the moon. The host, family man Jim Lovell (Tom Hanks), has to wait nine more months to get his chance to become the fifth man to set foot on the lunar surface.

As the April 11, 1970, launch date approaches, command module pilot Ken Mattingly (Gary Sinise) is replaced by swinging bachelor Jack Swigert (Kevin Bacon). But by the time they and lunar module pilot Fred Haise (Bill Paxton) blast off on their trip, the public has come to regard moon missions as worthy of only passing interest.

Two-and-a-half days later, and 50 minutes into the picture, this attitude abruptly changes. During a routine "stirring" of the oxygen supply, an oxygen tank explodes, which quickly leads to three significant problems for the crew: a dissipating oxygen supply, reduced power on board and a filtering system on the blink, leaving the men susceptible to carbon dioxide poisoning.

A number of nicely individualized scientists and nerdy computer geniuses argue the merits of different courses of action, with chain-smoking flight director Kranz (Ed Harris) making the ultimate decisions through a sort of consensus by decree.

Casting Hanks as Lovell gives the film a human center, someone with whom the audience can feel at home. Bacon brings a colorful cockiness to the one *Top Gun*–style flyer in the bunch, while Paxton is obliged to suffer quietly with a high fever. Harris's coiled tension provides a strong focus of attention in the control room, and Kathleen Quinlan gives depth of feeling to the necessarily compartmentalized role of Lovell's omen-fearing wife.

1995: Best Sound, Best Film Editing

NOMINATIONS: Best Picture, Best Supp. Actor (Ed Harris), Screenplay Adaptation, Original Dramatic Score, Best Art Direction, Best Sound, Visual Effects

●

APOSTLE, THE
1997, 133 mins, US Ⓥ ⊙ col
Dir Robert Duvall ***Prod*** Rob Carliner ***Scr*** Robert Duvall ***Ph*** Barry Markowitz ***Ed*** Steve Mack ***Mus*** David Mansfield ***Art*** Linda Burton
Act Robert Duvall, Farrah Fawcett, Miranda Richardson, Todd Allen, John Beasley, June Carter Cash (Butchers Run)

A labor of love coming to fruition after 13 years, Robert Duvall's third—and best—directorial effort is a sharply observed exploration of a middle-aged preacher who embarks on a redemptive odyssey after committing a crime.

A devout Pentecostal preacher from New Boston, TX, Eulis (Sonny) Dewey (Duvall) lives a seemingly happy life with his beautiful wife, Jessie (Farrah Fawcett). But Jessie is cheating on him with a younger minister, Horace (Todd Allen), and she succeeds in wresting control of the church from Sonny. Sonny descends into an uncontrollable rage, strikes Horace with a bat at a softball game, and gets on a bus to Louisiana.

Shedding all traces of his past, he baptizes himself as "the Apostle" to God. Landing in the predominantly black town of Bayou Boutte, LA, he conquers his inner demons by fervently organizing a grass-roots church, until his estranged wife discovers his whereabouts.

Duvall renders a superlative and modulated performance, one that allows the audience to feel an immediate connection with his character, even when his motives are dubious. The other thesps do well in the same emotionally truthful vein.

Running time presents a problem; a streamlining by perhaps 20 minutes seems possible without damaging the pic's integrity. [Version reviewed ran 148 mins.; following its world preem at the Toronto fest, pic was cut by 15 min.]

1997: NOMINATION: Best Actor (Robert Duvall)

●

APPAT, L'
1995, 117 mins, France col
Dir Bertrand Tavernier ***Prod*** Rene Cleitman, Frederic Bourboulonj ***Scr*** Colo Tavernier O'Hagan, Bertrand Tavernier ***Ph*** Alain Choquart ***Ed*** Luce Grunenwaldt ***Mus*** Philippe Haim ***Art*** Emile Ghico
Act Marie Gillain, Olivier Sitruk, Bruno Putzulu, Richard Berry, Philippe Duclos, Clothilde Courau

Fresh Bait captures the twisted symbiosis whereby three reasonably nice and normal French kids become a clumsy death squad. Bertrand Tavernier's conscientious look at moral bankruptcy, as demonstrated by murders as chillingly excessive as they are pointless, does a sober, fairly suspenseful job of deglamorizing violence. *Fresh Bait* was to have been the realistic crime follow-up to *L.627*, but helmer was obliged to take up the reins on *D'Artagnan's Daughter* first. Co-scripters Tavernier and ex-wife Colo Tavernier O'Hagan [adapting Morgan Sportes's book] have updated a true story that stunned the nation in 1984.

Barely 18, fresh-faced and shapely Nathalie (Marie Gillain) works in a Paris clothing boutique and lives in a small apartment with her handsome, marginally older boyfriend, Eric (Olivier Sitruk), and Eric's none-too-bright, emotionally codependent buddy, Bruno (Bruno Putzulu). While Nat works, the guys watch American gangster and adventure pix on TV.

Nathalie methodically collects the business cards of professional men while Eric formulates a grandiose plan. Nathalie—the bait—is to get herself invited to the victim's home, presumably for sex, only to have Eric and Bruno burst in and empty the overflowing safe that they imagine all lawyers and merchants must have. Kids believe that a handful of such heists will yield the seed money they need to open a pie-in-the-sky chain of ready-to-wear boutiques in the U.S.

Tightly knit ensemble cast is good, particularly Putzulu as the dim-bulb sponger who takes things literally. Extensive use of nocturnal, roving hand-held camera renders the proceedings up-close, fluid and intimate.

●

APPLAUSE
1929, 80 mins, US Ⓥ b/w
Dir Rouben Mamoulian ***Prod*** Monta Bell ***Scr*** Garret Fort ***Ph*** George Folsey
Act Helen Morgan, Joan Peers, Fuller Mellish, Jr., Jack Cameron, Henry Wadsworth, Dorothy Cumming (Paramount)

This is the real old burlesque, in its background, people and atmosphere. So was Beth Brown's book, and Garret Fort has adapted with sufficient fidelity to hold together the odd story that makes an odd picture.

Helen Morgan is Kitty Darling, a fading star of burlesque, aging on the stage as her daughter, born in a dressing room, grows up.

Joan Peers comes to the front toward the finish as the daughter, April. Earlier and in the convent scenes she doesn't convince.

Hitch Nelson as done by Fuller Mellish, Jr., is the pi, Kitty's husband, who tries to make the daughter. A turkey burlesque chiseler with the women stuff on the side, and always bullyragging his woman. A good performance every minute by Mellish. Henry Wadsworth is the juve, opposite Peers.

The picture was made at Paramount's Long Island studio.

●

APPLEGATES, THE
SEE: MEET THE APPLEGATES

●

APPOINTMENT, THE
1969, 100 mins, US Ⓥ col
Dir Sidney Lumet ***Prod*** Martin Poll ***Scr*** James Salter ***Ph*** Carlo Di Palma ***Ed*** Thelma Connell ***Mus*** John Barry, Don Walker ***Art*** Piero Gherardi
Act Omar Sharif, Anouk Aimee, Lotte Lenya, Fausto Tozzi, Ennio Balbo (M-G-M/Marpol)

A flimsy love story that never really catches fire emerges from an Antonio Leonviola original that James Salter has shaped for the screen in this disappointing Sidney Lumet effort.

Omar Sharif plays a Roman lawyer who falls for a colleague's fiancée, a mannequin played by Anouk Aimee, and eventually marries her, undeterred by his pal's fear that she's secretly a high-priced call girl. Soon, however, suspicion begins to gnaw and he begins to tail his spouse.

Flat writing and an over-rigid performance by Sharif in a crucial role, which at times skirts the laughable, seriously flaw what might otherwise have been an intriguing love tale cum suspenser.

Instead, the love affair is never convincingly established from the start, and with the exception of a largely wasted contribution by Aimee the film drags along to its mellerish windup.

●

APPOINTMENT FOR LOVE
1941, 88 mins, US b/w
Dir William A. Seiter ***Prod*** Bruce Manning ***Scr*** Bruce Manning, Felix Jackson ***Ph*** Joseph Valentine ***Ed*** Ted Kent ***Mus*** Frank Skinner
Act Charles Boyer, Margaret Sullavan, Rita Johnson, Eugene Pallette, Ruth Terry, Cecil Kellaway (Universal)

Appointment for Love is a neatly constructed piece of bright entertainment. Producer Bruce Manning, who also collaborated on the script with Felix Jackson [from an original by Ladislas Bus-Fekete], points up the romantic adventure while injecting numerous refreshing episodes to the oft-told tale of newlywed problems.

Charles Boyer, a successful playwright, suave with the femmes, falls in love with Margaret Sullavan, seriously immersed in the practice of medicine and with very novel and unusual ideas about marriage and continuance of separate careers. Sullavan takes a separate apartment in the same building with Boyer, explaining this unusual procedure in difference in time schedules of their work.

Situation created upsets Boyer, with conflict between the pair raging in merriest mood, including setups for jealousies on both sides.

William Seiter paces the direction with an expert hand, deftly timing the smacko laugh lines and situations for brightest effect. Boyer handles his assignment with utmost assurance. Sullavan provides both charm and ability to her role of the serious medic who finally turns romantic.

1941: NOMINATION: Best Sound

●

APPOINTMENT WITH DANGER
1951, 90 mins, US b/w
Dir Lewis Allen ***Prod*** Robert Fellows ***Scr*** Richard Breen, Warren Duff ***Ph*** John F. Seitz ***Ed*** LeRoy Stone ***Art*** Victor Young
Act Alan Ladd, Phyllis Calvert, Paul Stewart, Jan Sterling, Jack Webb, Henry Morgan (Paramount)

Exploits of the Postal Inspection Service furnish Alan Ladd with a good cops-and-robbers actioner. Film deals with government detectives tracking down the killers of a fellow postal inspector and preventing a million-dollar mail robbery. Ladd is right at home as the tight-lipped, tough inspector assigned to the case. There is a neat contrasting byplay in the nun character done by Phyllis Calvert as co-star, which adds an offbeat note to the meller plot.

While investigating the murder of an inspector, Ladd comes across a plot to loot the mails of a large cash shipment during transfer from one railway station to another. He sets himself up as a cop who can be bribed by demanding money from the gang on threat of spilling the robbery plans.

Calvert's character figures importantly as she is the only witness who can tie the gang to the original murder. Paul Stewart dominates the crooks, with capable assists on menace from Jack Webb, Stacy Harris and Henry Morgan. Jan Sterling supplies the s.a. on the wrong side of the law as Stewart's moll.

●

APPOINTMENT WITH DEATH
1988, 108 mins, US Ⓥ b/w
Dir Michael Winner ***Prod*** Michael Winner ***Scr*** Anthony Shaffer, Peter Buckman, Michael Winner ***Ph*** David Gurfinkel ***Ed*** Arnold Crust (Michael Winner) ***Mus*** Pino Donaggio ***Art*** John Blezard
Act Peter Ustinov, Lauren Bacall, Carrie Fisher, John Gielgud, Piper Laurie, Hayley Mills (Cannon)

Peter Ustinov hams his way through *Appointment with Death* one more time as ace Belgian detective "Hercuool Pwarow," but neither he nor glitz can lift the pic from an impression of little more than a routine whodunit. Even the normally amusing Ustinov looks a bit jaded in his third big-screen outing as the sleuth, as well as several TV productions.

Director Michael Winner has some fine Israeli locations to play with, but his helming is only lackluster, the script and characterizations bland, and there simply are not enough murders to sustain the interest of even the most avid Agatha Christie fan.

The film opens in 1937 in a New Jersey mansion with the obligatory reading of the will, a scene that also establishes Piper Laurie as she fixes the will to get all hubby's money and for his four children to get nothing. She takes them off on a trip to Europe and the Holy Land, and it is while they are en route to Palestine by liner that they meet Ustinov, Lauren Bacall (playing a British Member of Parliament), Jenny Seagrove and Hayley Mills.

Laurie finally is poisoned while the troupe is at an archaeological dig, leaving Ustinov to twiddle his mustache and pinpoint the killer (who actually is quite easy to spot).

●

APPRENTICESHIP OF DUDDY KRAVITZ, THE
1974, 120 mins, Canada Ⓥ ▭ col
Dir Ted Kotcheff ***Prod*** John Kemeny ***Scr*** Mordecai Richler ***Ph*** Brian West ***Ed*** Thom Noble ***Mus*** Stanley Myers (sup.) ***Art*** Anne Pritchard
Act Richard Dreyfuss, Micheline Lanctot, Jack Warden, Randy Quaid, Joseph Wiseman, Denholm Elliott (International Cinemedia Center)

Director Ted Kotcheff has taken Mordecai Richler's novel by the scruff of the neck and worked a zesty but somewhat muted nostalgic look at a nervy Jewish kid on the make in the 1940s [adaptation by Lionel Chetwynd].

On screen, *Duddy Kravitz* remains as it was when first published in 1959 to outraged cries from Jewish groups across North America and more particularly from Montreal where it is authentically set. There is an at-times bitter, satiric portrayal of a 19-year-old who gets his money, women and power by emulating the richest of those around him, selling everyone, closest friends included, out.

Kravitz, played by a continually grinning, scratching, nervous-making yet vulnerable Richard Dreyfuss, comes across effectively and with force.

1974: NOMINATION: Best Adapted Screenplay

•

APRIL FOOLS, THE

1969, 95 mins, US Ⓥ ▭ col

Dir Stuart Rosenberg ***Prod*** Gordon Carroll ***Scr*** Hal Dresner ***Ph*** Michel Hugo ***Ed*** Bob Wyman ***Mus*** Marvin Hamlisch ***Art*** Richard Sylbert

Act Jack Lemmon, Catherine Deneuve, Peter Lawford, Jack Weston, Myrna Loy, Charles Boyer (Cinema Center/Jalem)

Jack Lemmon is both funny and touching as the mild-mannered stockbroker, tied to a nothing of a wife. Given a big promotion by his boss (Peter Lawford), he meets the latter's wife (Catherine Deneuve) at a stultifying cocktail party. She's bored and he doesn't know her real identity but they depart for a night of self-discovery.

In addition to Lemmon, comedians Jack Weston (as his lawyer) and Harvey Korman (as a drinking companion they encounter in the commuter train's drinking car) provide their own brand of laughs and the contrasting styles of the three actors gives the plot most of its action.

Things slow down to a mere simmer, by contrast, in the romantic segments although Deneuve, in her first American film, is worth just looking at.

•

APT PUPIL

1998, 111 MINS, US Ⓥ ⦿ ▭ col

Dir Bryan Singer ***Prod*** Jane Hamsher, Don Murphy, Bryan Singer ***Scr*** Brandon Boyce ***Ed*** John Ottman ***Mus*** John Ottman ***Art*** Richard Hoover

Act Ian McKellen, Brad Renfro, Bruce Davison, Elias Koteas, Joe Morton, Jan Triska (Bad Hat Harry/Phoenix/TriStar)

A creepy, well-acted story of contagious evil, *Apt Pupil* has more than enough chilling dramatic scenes to rivet the attention but suffers from some hokey contrivances and underlying insufficiencies of motivation. Ian McKellen and Brad Renfro excel as a Nazi war criminal and an aggressive small-town high-school student who uncovers the man's past.

Premise is deftly set up as, in 1984, 16-year-old senior Todd Bowden (Renfro) becomes fascinated by the Holocaust and, via an old photograph, recognizes a grizzled local resident as one Kurt Dussander (McKellen), a former officer at the Paten concentration camp, where 90,000 prisoners died. Under threat of turning him in, Todd commands the Nazi to tell him the brutal truth. "I want to hear about it. Everything. Everything they're afraid to show us in school."

A month later, Todd is still listening with morbid fascination to the drunken geezer, and gives Dussander a Christmas present of a pristine Nazi uniform and instructs him to put it on. His old self thus revived, Dussander warns Todd that he's playing with fire. For his part, Todd is now so preoccupied by Nazi evil that he can no longer peform sexually and sees his grades decline.

Main shortcoming is a failure to take Todd's fascination with Dussander far enough, to analyze the attraction evil has for him and, by extension, the potential anyone may have for inhuman acts under certain circumstances. As it is, Todd's motivation seems to stem from little more than a sadistic desire to humiliate the old man for his crimes.

All the same, screenwriter Brandon Boyce, in adapting Stephen King's novella, has outfitted the story with a goodly number of intense confrontations and nasty twists, and Bryan Singer has directed with a disciplined approach to maintaining tension and building malevolent mood. Modestly budgeted production is smooth in all departments.

•

APUR SANSAR

1959, 105 mins, India Ⓥ b/w

Dir Satyajit Ray ***Prod*** Satyajit Ray ***Scr*** Satyajit Ray ***Ph*** Subrata Mitra ***Ed*** Dulal Dutt ***Mus*** Ravi Shankar ***Art*** Bansi Chandragupta

Act Soumitra Chatterjee, Sharmila Tagore, Shapan Mukerjee, Alkoe Chakravarty (Ray)

Film is the final one of a trilogy on Indian life in the 1930s [from Bibhuti Bannerjee's novel], following the life of a young boy and his family. This entry compares with its predecessors in knowing insight, poetics and ability, but surpasses them in craftsmanship.

Here the boy, Apu (Soumitra Chatterjee), is seen after he has finished schooling at 23. Hazy bureaucracy keeps him from getting a decent job. In a visit to his cousin's wedding he is talked into marrying the girl himself when the bridegroom, who has been arranged for the 15-year-old girl sight unseen, has a fit during the ceremony.

Script then deals with the love that grows between the newlyweds, the wife's death in childbirth, the husband's anguish and wanderings and refusal to see his son, and finally his determination to win the boy over after some years.

Story appears simple, but its delineation of character makes this a timeless, placeless story of love and adjustment. Director Satyajit Ray, with greater technical means, makes the truth of his relationships and the revelation of India the main trumps of the film. Wit, tenderness and intrinsic human revelations illuminate this unusual film.

•

ARAB, THE

1924, 75 mins, US ⊗ b/w

Dir Rex Ingram ***Scr*** Rex Ingram ***Ph*** John F. Seitz ***Ed*** Grant Whytock

Act Ramon Novarro, Alice Terry, Maxudian, Jerrold Robertshaw, Jean De Limur (Metro-Goldwyn)

This is the finest sheik film of them all. *The Arab* is a compliment to the screen, a verification of the sterling repute of director Rex Ingram.

As a sheik, Ramon Novarro is the acme. Surrounded as he is by genuine men of the desert—for the scenes were shot in Algiers and the mobs are all natives in their natural environments—he seems as bona fide as the Arabs themselves.

Alice Terry as the wistful, frightened, assailed little Christian whose winsomeness and piety, even though they are foreign and even hostile to all that this thieving, concubinous rogue stands for, makes the presentation plausible, romantic and attractive.

The "happy ending" is wisely left open—it is asking too much for her to dismiss the handsome, noble Moslem who has saved her and her white family and flock, given up his indigenous rascalities for her and fallen in love with her.

•

ARABESQUE

1966, 107 mins, US/UK Ⓥ ▭ col

Dir Stanley Donen ***Prod*** Stanley Donen ***Scr*** Julian Mitchell, Stanley Price, Pierre Marton [=Peter Stone] ***Ph*** Christopher Challis ***Ed*** Frederick Wilson ***Mus*** Henry Mancini ***Art*** Reece Pemberton

Act Gregory Peck, Sophia Loren, Alan Badel, Kieron Moore, Carl Duering, John Merivale (Universal/Donen)

Arabesque packs the names of Gregory Peck and Sophia Loren and a foreign intrigue theme, but doesn't always progress on a true entertainment course. Fault lies in a shadowy plotline and confusing characters, particularly in the miscasting of Peck in a cute role.

Based on the Gordon Cotler novel *The Cipher*, script projects Peck as an American exchange professor of ancient languages at Oxford drawn into a vortex of hazardous endeavor. He is called upon to decipher a secret message written in hieroglyphics, a document and its translation sought by several different factions from the Middle East. He is assisted by the paradoxical character played by Loren, as an Arab sexpot who seems to be on everyone's side. There are chases, murders and attempted assassinations to whet the appetite, as well as misuses of comedy.

Peck tries valiantly with a role unsuited to him and Loren displayes her usual lush and plush presence. If her part is an enigma to Peck, it is to the spectator, too.

Menace is provided by Alan Badel and Kieron Moore, both trying to latch on to contents of the cipher and out to dispose of Peck.

•

ARABIAN NIGHT

1995, 72 mins, US/UK Ⓥ ⦿ ▭ col

Dir Richard Williams ***Prod*** Imogen Sutton ***Scr*** Richard Williams, Margaret French, Parker Bennet, Terry Runte, Bette L. Smith, Tom Towler, Stephen Zito, Eric Gilliland, Michael Hitchcock, Gary Glasberg ***Ph*** John Leatherbarrow ***Ed*** Peter Bond ***Mus*** Robert Folk (Allied Filmmakers)

As with any fable, there are forces of light and darkness at odds in the animated romantic adventure *Arabian Night*.

The good can be seen in some outstanding, complex and eye-popping animation—perhaps the last great work to be done in this area prior to the advent of computer assists. The bad news is that although its production history dates back as early as 1968, the film gives the overriding sense that animator Richard Williams finished the picture without really completing it—that there were still both visual and story refinements needed to bring the work fully to fruition.

The story is relatively straightforward. In ancient Baghdad, the realm is about to be beset by the mighty hordes of the warrior One-Eye (voiced by Kevin Dorsey). Court magician Zigzag (Vincent Price) is in league with the tyrant, for the hand of the appropriately named King Nod's daughter, Princess Yum Yum (Jennifer Beals).

Legend has it that the city will be protected as long as the three gold balls on the tallest minaret shine upon the town. Zigzag winds up with them. It then falls upon Yum Yum and the humble young cobbler Tack (Matthew Broderick) to retrieve the orbs and save the empire from doom.

Though it sounds like a ripping yarn, and runs barely more than one hour (plus credits), *Arabian Night* is slow and often awkwardly paced. The film's songs—with the exception of the comic "Bom Bom Bom Beem Bom"—are largely forgettable ballads, perfunctorily placed within the drama.

Previously known as *The Thief and the Cobbler*, Williams's labor of love has a fractious history. It was expected to premiere about two years earlier with Warner Bros. handling it in the U.S. But delivery dates could not be met, and when the banks demanded payment, the Completion Bond Co. wound up with ownership of the production.

The bond company, prior to domestic pickup by Miramax, relooped new voices for several characters and altered sections of voice-over narration, adding some new material [to the original screenplay by Williams and Margaret French].

•

ARACHNOPHOBIA

1990, 109 mins, US Ⓥ ⦿ col

Dir Frank Marshall ***Prod*** Kathleen Kennedy, Richard Vane ***Scr*** Don Jakoby, Wesley Strick ***Ph*** Mikael Salomon ***Ed*** Michael Kahn ***Mus*** Trevor Jones ***Art*** James Bissell

Act Jeff Daniels, Harley Jane Kozak, John Goodman, Julian Sands, Stuart Pankin, Brian McNamara (Tangled Web/Amblin)

Arachnophobia expertly blends horror and tongue-in-cheek comedy in the tale of a small California coastal town overrun by Venezuelan killer spiders. Frank Marshall's sophisticated feature directing debut never indulges in ultimate gross-out effects and carefully chooses both its victims and its means of depicting their dispatch.

Beginning like an *Indiana Jones* film with an 18-minute prolog of British entomologist Julian Sands's expedition in the Venezuelan jungle, *Arachnophobia* cleverly follows the route of a prehistoric male spider hitching a ride to California and escaping to the farm of newly arrived town doctor Jeff Daniels.

The droll John Goodman has a relatively small part as the town's magnificently slobby and incompetent exterminator. Daniels is the one with the arachnophobia, which, like James Stewart's trauma in Hitchcock's *Vertigo*, must be agonizingly overcome in the spectacular climax.

Marshall has the directorial confidence to allow scripters [working from a story by Don Jakoby and Al Williams] plenty of screen time to develop characters more fully than usual in a horror film. With a variety of versatile spider performers including live South American tarantulas and more than 40 mechanical creatures devised by Chris Walas, Marshall is able to do just about anything he wants in terms of creepy-crawly effects.

•

ARCH OF TRIUMPH

1948, 120 mins, US Ⓥ b/w

Dir Lewis Milestone ***Prod*** David Lewis ***Scr*** Lewis Milestone, Harry Brown ***Ph*** Russell Metty ***Ed*** Duncan Mansfield ***Mus*** Louis Gruenberg ***Art*** William Cameron Menzies

Act Charles Boyer, Ingrid Bergman, Charles Laughton, Louis Calhern, Michael Romanoff, Ruth Warrick (Enterprise)

The Erich Maria Remarque novel, by very suggestion of authorship and the Lewis Milestone association, conjures up analogy to the now classic *All Quiet*, the post–First World War film, also from a Remarque work. The analogy ends there because the character of both differs strikingly. Current entry is a frank romantic item, laid in a setting of Paris intrigue just before open war with the western allies broke out.

The surcharged atmosphere of pre-Polish aggression and its repercussions in the City of Light that suddenly grows into blackout is a dramatic background for the Boyer-Bergman romance. The very atmosphere of the boulevards, from the Eternal Light underneath the Arc de Triomphe to the gaiety of the Sheherezade and kindred boîtes on the hill (Montmartre) make for surefire appeal.

Charles Laughton is rather wasted as a Nazi menace, obviously the victim of the cutting room shears, as was Ruth Warrick, the American dilettante. There is no question but that over $1 million of this film's cost never shows on the screen. It's reported to have hit near the $4-million negative cost.

•

ARIA
1987, 98 mins, US/UK Ⓥ ⊙ col
Dir Nicolas Roeg, Charles Sturridge, Jean-Luc Godard, Julien Temple, Bruce Beresford, Robert Altman, Franc Roddam, Ken Russell, Derek Jarman, Bill Bryden ***Prod*** Don Boyd ***Ph*** Harvey Harrison, Gale Tattersall, Carolyn Champeti, Oliver Stapleton, Dante Spinotti, Pierre Mignot, Frederick Elmes, Micke Southon, Gabriel Beristain ***Ed*** Tony Lawson, Matthew Longfellow, Jean-Luc Godard, Neil Abrahamson, Marie-Therese Boiche, Robert Altman, Rick Elgood, Michael Bradsell, Peter Cartwright, Mike Cragg
Act Theresa Russell, Nicola Swain, Buck Henry, Julie Hagerty, Tilda Swinton, John Hurt (Lightyear/Virgin)

Aria, a string of selections from 10 operas illustrated by 10 directors, is a film that could not have happened without the advent of music videos.

Producer Don Boyd, who orchestrated the project, instructed the directors not to depict what was happening to the characters in the operas but to create something new out of the emotion and content expressed in the music. The arias were the starting point.

Result is both exhilaratingly successful and distractingly fragmented. Individual segments are stunning but they come in such speedy succession that overall it is not a fully satisfying film experience.

Selections also represent a variety of filmmaking styles from Bruce Beresford's rather pedestrian working of a love theme from Korngold's *Die tote Stadt* to Ken Russell's characteristically excessive treatment of an idea distilled from Puccini's *Turandot*. Structurally, the most ambitious of the selections is Jean-Luc Godard's working of Lully's *Armide*, which he transposes to a body-building gym where two naked women try to attract the attention of the men.

The most striking clash of images is achieved by Franc Roddam who moves Wagner's *Tristan und Isolde* to Las Vegas. As the lush strains of the music blare, the neon sea of the casinos has never looked more strange.

•

ARISTOCATS, THE
1970, 78 mins, US col
Dir Wolfgang Reitherman ***Prod*** Walt Disney, Wolfgang Reitherman, Winston Hibler ***Scr*** Larry Clemmons ***Ed*** Tom Acosta ***Mus*** George Bruns (Walt Disney)

The Aristocats is a good animated feature from Walt Disney Studios, an original period comedy with drama about a feline family rescued from the plans of an evil butler who would prefer his mistress not to leave her fortune to the cats.

Helped immeasurably by the voices of Phil Harris, Eva Gabor, Sterling Holloway, Scatman Crothers and others, plus some outstanding animation, songs, sentiment, some excellent dialog and even a touch of psychedelia.

Harris, who gave *Jungle Book* a lot of its punch, is even more prominent here as the voice of an alley cat who rescues Gabor and her three kittens. Gabor's voice and related animation are excellent, ditto that for two hound dogs, Pat Buttram and George Lindsey.

The technical details of the $4-million cartoon are marvelous to behold.

•

ARIZONA DREAM
1992, 142 mins, FRANCE Ⓥ ⊙ col
Dir Emir Kusturica ***Prod*** Claudie Ossard ***Scr*** David Atkins, Emir Kusturica ***Ph*** Vilko Filac ***Ed*** Andrija Zafranovic ***Mus*** Goran Bregovic ***Art*** Miljen Kljakovic
Act Johnny Depp, Jerry Lewis, Faye Dunaway, Lili Taylor, Vincent Gallo, Paulina Porizkova (Constellation/UGC/Hachette Premiere)

Despite gorgeous, sometimes surreal visuals and the valiant efforts of an interesting cast, Emir Kusturica's *Arizona Dream* is heavy going. Award-winning Sarajevo-born helmer's first English-lingo pic tackles dreams and flight only to alternately soar and crash.

Johnny Depp anchors the overlong pic as an unambitious 23-year-old fish and game warden summoned from Manhattan to Arizona. Depp's uncle (Jerry Lewis) is about to take a bride three decades his junior (Paulina Porizkova) and wants Depp to be his best man and stay on to work at his Cadillac dealership.

Depp finds himself torn between seductive, half-mad widow Faye Dunaway and Dunaway's equally unstable stepdaughter, heiress Lili Taylor. Vincent Gallo plays a womanizing, aspiring actor who sells cars between auditions.

Kusturica grafts his sometimes unwieldy Europe-inflected concerns onto brash American landscapes with mixed results. Much is made of dreams that, either spoken of at length or illustrated, are offered in lieu of character development.

Impeccably lensed in Alaska, New York and Douglas, AZ, pic remains stuck in an awkward netherworld between slapstick and pathos.

•

ARMAGEDDON
1998, 150 mins, US Ⓥ ⊙ ▭ col
Dir Michael Bay ***Prod*** Jerry Bruckheimer, Gale Anne Hurd, Michael Bay ***Scr*** Jonathan Hensleigh, J. J. Abrams, [Paul Attanasio, Ann Biderman, Scott Rosenberg, Robert Towne] ***Ph*** John Schwartzman ***Ed*** Mark Goldblatt, Chris Lebenzon, Glen Scantlebury ***Mus*** Trevor Rabin ***Art*** Michael White
Act Bruce Willis, Billy Bob Thornton, Liv Tyler, Ben Affleck, Will Patton, Steve Buscemi (Bruckheimer/Touchstone)

Bruce Willis saves the world but can't save *Armageddon*. The second of 1998's nuke-the-asteroid-or-bust pre-millenium spectaculars is so effects-obsessed and dramatically benumbed as to make *Deep Impact* [released eight weeks earlier, in early May] look like a humanistic masterpiece. Despite its frequently incoherent staging, $150 million scifi actioner nonetheless has the Willis juice and Jerry Bruckheimer–Michael Bay bad-boy ingredients.

Pic [from a screen story by Robert Roy Pool and Jonathan Hensleigh, adaptation by Tony Gilroy and Shane Salerno] plays more like *Con Air Goes to Outer Space*, with Doomsday approached like a giant videogame and a jingoistic, thank-you-America-for-saving-the-world message. Determining that the only thing to do is to implant a nuke or two in the giant hunk of rock, NASA, repped by exec director Dan Truman (Bily Bob Thornton), recruits the world's top oil driller, Harry S. Stamper (Willis), for the job. Stamper agrees on the condition that he can select his own team—mostly miscreants with bad attitudes.

Exposition, training and buildup to blastoff occupy film's first half. Pic then becomes an outer-space saga in which the two shuttles dock with a Russian space station to refuel, slingshot around the moon, endure debris from the asteroid and finally land to lay a nuke deep inside the inhospitable black rock.

Bay's cutting style resembles a machine gun stuck in the firing position for 2½ hours. Film's performance style consists of yelling above the ambient noise, which is usually considerable. Special effects are incessant and sometimes pretty groovy, but they're usually here one second, gone the next. All tech credits are predictably gigantic.

•

ARMED AND DANGEROUS
1986, 88 mins, US Ⓥ ⊙ col
Dir Mark L. Lester ***Prod*** Brian Grazer, James Keach ***Scr*** Harold Ramis, Peter Torokvei ***Ph*** Fred Schuler ***Ed*** Michael Hill, Daniel Hanley, George Pedugo ***Mus*** Bill Meyers ***Art*** David L. Snyder
Act John Candy, Eugene Levy, Robert Loggia, Kenneth McMillan, Meg Ryan, Brion James (Columbia)

Armed and Dangerous is a broad farce slightly elevated by the presence of John Candy and Eugene Levy.

Story [by Brian Grazer, Harold Ramis and James Keach] functions as little more than a fashion show for Candy. The piece de resistance is Candy in a blue tuxedo with a ruffled shirt that makes his enormous bulk look like a wrapped Christmas present.

Candy plays one of L.A.'s finest until he's wrongfully kicked off the force for corruption. He winds up at Guard Dog Security where he teams with shyster lawyer Levy on a new career. Company, it turns out, is under the thumb of the mob headed by union honcho Robert Loggia.

It's all pretty basic stuff delivered with a minimum of imagination.

•

ARMORED CAR ROBBERY
1950, 67 mins, US Ⓥ b/w
Dir Richard Fleischer ***Prod*** Herman Schlom ***Scr*** Earl Felton, Gerald Drayson Adams ***Ph*** Guy Roe ***Ed*** Desmond Marquette ***Mus*** Constantin Bakaleinikoff (dir.) ***Art*** Albert S. D'Agostino, Ralph Berger
Act Charles McGraw, Adele Jergens, William Talman, Douglas Fowley, Steve Brodie, Don McGuire (RKO)

RKO has concocted an okay cops-and-robbers melodrama [suggested by a story by Robert Angus and Robert Leeds] for the supporting market. *Armored Car Robbery* plays off at a good pace.

Charles McGraw heads the cast as Cordell, a tough cop out to run down a gang that robbed an armored car and killed his policeman buddy. Police work on closing in on the gang is interesting and believable, and there's considerable suspense in the various close escapes the crooks have.

Pervus (William Talman) masterminds the robbery, a carefully planned job executed at L.A.'s Wrigley Field, the last stop of the armored car in its cash-collecting rounds. By chance, Cordell and buddy are near the scene and fight it out with Pervus's outfit, but they still escape with the cash and a wounded crook. From then on it's a cat-and-mouse game of hide-and-seek.

McGraw, Don McGuire and James Flavin, as cops, do very well. Talman and his cohorts put plenty of color into their heavy assignments. Adele Jergens attracts as a stripteaser and Talman's romantic interest.

•

ARMS AND THE GIRL
SEE: RED SALUTE

•

ARMY OF DARKNESS
EVIL DEAD 3
1993, 95 mins, US Ⓥ ⊙ col
Dir Sam Raimi ***Prod*** Robert Tapert ***Scr*** Ivan Raimi, Sam Raimi ***Ph*** Bill Pope ***Ed*** Bob Muraski, R.O.C. Sandstorm ***Mus*** Joe Lo Duca, Danny Elfman ***Art*** Anthony Trembay
Act Bruce Campbell, Embeth Davidtz, Marcus Gilbert, Ian Abercrombie, Richard Grove, Michael Earl Reid (De Laurentiis/Renaissance)

Blending almost nonstop violence with humorous parody, Sam Raimi's latest excursion into horror-kitsch seems more like an irreverent *A Connecticut Yankee in King Arthur's Court*. The Yank, however, is equipped with a chainsaw for an arm and a '73 Oldsmobile instead of a steed.

Whisked from his country cottage by some evil force, Bruce Campbell and his car are plunked down in the midst of an Arthurian war, where Campbell is posthaste thrown into chains. He fights his way to freedom and ingratiates himself with Arthur.

The only way for him to get back to California is by retrieving a sacred book. On his quest he runs across various obstacles, including the evil dead (who turn the maiden he's sweet on into a witch). Wizardry and special effects abound.

In the version shown at Spain's Sitges festival, the hero miscalculates the time he wants to travel ahead in space and arrives at the end of the 21st century only to see a planet in ruins. This ending will be changed and the pic will lose 10 minutes for its U.S. release.

•

ARNELO AFFAIR, THE
1947, 86 mins, US b/w
Dir Arch Oboler ***Prod*** Jerry Bresler ***Scr*** Arch Oboler ***Ph*** Charles Salerno ***Ed*** Harry Komer ***Mus*** George Bassman ***Art*** Cedric Gibbons, Wade Rubottom
Act John Hodiak, George Murphy, Frances Gifford, Dean Stockwell, Eve Arden, Warner Anderson (M-G-M)

Arch Oboler, radio's master of suspense, has effectively transposed his technique into the visual medium with *The Arnelo Affair*. Strictly speaking this is not a whodunit, nor can it be catalogued as a psychological suspense picture.

Anne (Frances Gifford), a well-wedded Chicago wife on the eve of her 12th anniversary, finds herself attracted to Tony Arnelo (John Hodiak), nitery owner with a disreputable background who is a client of her lawyer husband, Ted (George Murphy). Subordinated by Ted to his work, her almost hypnotic fascination for Arnelo drives her to see him daily. When another of Arnelo's amours turns up murdered, she is involved and he uses this as a means to bring her to him. There's never a question as to who committed the murder, but the crime is secondary to its effect on the characters involved. Until the film's very climax, no hint is given to the ultimate denouement. Dialog instills the feeling of action where none exists for much of the footage, and the gab is excellent but for a couple of spots when Oboler gives vent to florid passages. Thesping of Gifford, a horse opera graduate, marks her for a top dramatic slot in Metro's future book, while Hodiak smartly underplays the nitery op's vicious nature concealed by a genteel gloss. Surprise of the pic [from a story by Jane Burr] is the slow-talking detective, limned by Warner Anderson. It's unusual that the police are shown as anything but boobs.

•

AROUND THE WORLD IN EIGHTY DAYS
1956, 175 mins, US Ⓥ ⊙ ▭ col
Dir Michael Anderson ***Prod*** Michael Todd ***Scr*** S. J. Perelman, John Farrow, James Poe ***Ph*** Lionel Lindon ***Ed*** Gene Ruggiero, Paul Weatherwax ***Mus*** Victor Young ***Art*** James Sullivan, Ken Adam
Act David Niven, Cantinflas, Robert Newton, Shirley MacLaine, Charles Boyer, Ronald Colman (Todd)

This is a long picture—two hours and 55 minutes plus intermission. Little time has been wasted and the story races on as Phileas Fogg and company proceed from London to Paris, thence via balloon to Spain and the bullfights; from there to Marseilles and India, where Fogg and Passepartout rescue beautiful Shirley MacLaine from death on a funeral pyre; to Hong Kong, Japan, San Francisco, across the country by train to New York (notwithstanding an Indian attack) and thence back to England.

Todd-AO system here, for the first time, is properly used and fills the screen with wondrous effects. Images are extraordinarily sharp and depth of focus is striking in many scenes. David Niven, as Fogg, is the perfect stereotype of the unruffled English gentleman and quite intentionally, a caricature of 19th-century British propriety. Matching him is Mexican star Cantinflas (Mario Moreno) as Passepartout. Robert Newton in the role of Mr. Fix—the detective who trails Fogg, whom he suspects of having robbed the Bank of London—is broad comic all the way through, and MacLaine is appealing as the princess.

There's rarely been a picture that can boast of so many star names in bit parts. Just to name a few in the more important roles: John Carradine as the pompous Col. Proctor; Finlay Currie, Ronald Squires, Basil Sydney, A. E. Matthews and Trevor Howard as members of the Reform Club who bet against Fogg; Robert Morley as the stodgy governor of the Bank of England; Cedric Hardwicke as a colonial militarist; Red Skelton, as a drunk; Marlene Dietrich and George Raft. There are many others, including Frank Sinatra in a flash shot as a piano player. Jose Greco, early in the footage, wows with a heel fandango.

Pic's sound is extraordinarily vivid and effective and a major asset. Saul Bass final titles are a tribute to the kind of taste and imagination, the ingenuity and the splendor that mark this entire Todd production. It's all on the screen, every penny of the $5–6 million that went into the making.

1956: Best Picture, Adapted Screenplay, Color Cinematography, Scoring of a Dramatic Picture, Editing

NOMINATIONS: Best Director, Color Costume Design, Color Art Direction

•

ARRANGEMENT, THE
1969, 125 mins, US Ⓥ ▭ col
Dir Elia Kazan ***Prod*** Elia Kazan ***Scr*** Elia Kazan ***Ph*** Robert Surtees ***Ed*** Stefan Arnsten ***Mus*** David Amram ***Art*** Gene Callahan
Act Kirk Douglas, Faye Dunaway, Deborah Kerr, Richard Boone, Hume Cronyn, Dianne Hull (Athena/Warner)

The Arrangement is a one-man production show; consequently, one man is responsible for a confused, overly contrived and overlong film peopled with a set of characters about whom the spectator couldn't care less. In a four-way plunge, Elia Kazan produced and directed from his own screenplay based upon his own 1967 novel.

Three principals in a story focusing on a man's problems and bafflements are Kirk Douglas, Deborah Kerr and Faye Dunaway.

The talents of cast are taxed but they almost rise above their assignments. Douglas plays a successful Los Angeles advertising man, apparently a wizard account exec, wed to Kerr, a long-suffering wife who tries to understand her husband's obsession for Dunaway, with whom he's been carrying on a tumultous affair.

•

ARROWHEAD
1953, 105 mins, US Ⓥ ⊙ col
Dir Charles Marquis Warren ***Prod*** Nat Holt ***Scr*** Charles Marquis Warren ***Ph*** Ray Rennahan ***Ed*** Frank Bracht ***Mus*** Paul Sawtell ***Art*** Hal Pereira, Al Roelofs
Act Charlton Heston, Jack Palance, Katy Jurado, Brian Keith, Mary Sinclair, Milburn Stone (Paramount)

The southwest frontier is the setting for this good outdoor actioner. Plot is laid in Texas during 1878 in and around Fort Clark, historical old cavalry post, and Nat Holt films his production on the actual sites described in W. R. Burnett's novel, *Adobe Walls*.

Principals involved are Charlton Heston, army scout and bitter enemy of the Apaches, particularly Jack Palance, a chief's son who has aroused the braves and is leading them on the warpath. Katy Jurado, as a Mexican-Apache attracted to Heston but spying on him, gives the story s.a. touches, while Mary Sinclair furnishes a more ladylike part as an army widow also interested in the scout.

Conflict gets underway early as Heston, raised among the Apaches as a child, warns a stubborn cavalry officer that only treachery can result from his efforts to make peace with the Indians. Heston's point is made when the cavalry is ambushed and the officer slain. The new commander also refuses to believe the scout, by now fired for his views, and it's not until he saves them from further treachery that he is allowed to lead the soldiers in the kind of combat that can whip the redskins.

Charles Marquis Warren's direction and screenplay are forthright in dealing with the masculine action and lift the plentiful mass clash sequences.

•

ARROWSMITH
1931, 108 mins, US Ⓥ b/w
Dir John Ford ***Prod*** Samuel Goldwyn ***Scr*** Sidney Howard ***Ph*** Ray June ***Ed*** Hugh Bennett ***Mus*** Alfred Newman ***Art*** Richard Day
Act Ronald Colman, Helen Hayes, Richard Bennett, A. E. Anson, Clarence Brooks, Myrna Loy (Goldwyn)

That portion of the citizenry that has read the Sinclair Lewis novel will probably be in sympathy with the filmization. Those who haven't will not be prone to deem this macabre tale entertainment. Both factions will find it hard to believe Ronald Colman in the title role.

The responsible factors include complete elimination of the novel's exposé phase as regards the medical profession; unusual length; a tendency on the part of the director, John Ford, to too often disregard or overlook tempo; and an unhappy ending. But above all these things is the inability of Colman, a romantic juvenile, to convince as the intense scientist.

Helen Hayes, as the nurse who becomes the promising physician's wife, is wholly delightful and gives an enlightening and natural performance. She is mostly responsible for the interest in the early reels. Richard Bennett, as Sondelius, a Swedish scientist, opens up impressively in the picture but eventually seems to pale. Along with Hayes, A. E. Anson is the most genuine figure in the film, although Claude King also makes a small part stand out.

1931–32: NOMINATIONS: Best Picture, Adaptation, Cinematography, Art Direction

•

ARSENE LUPIN
1932, 64 mins, US b/w
Dir Jack Conway ***Prod*** [uncredited] ***Scr*** Carey Wilson, Bayard Veiller, Lenore Coffee ***Ph*** Oliver T. Marsh ***Ed*** Hugh Wynn ***Mus*** [uncredited] ***Art*** Cedric Gibbons
Act John Barrymore, Lionel Barrymore, Karen Morley, John Miljan, Tully Marshall, Henry Armetta (M-G-M)

First screen appearance of John and Lionel Barrymore together and their fine acting lifts the production to a high artistic level.

But the action often is allowed to lapse for dangerously long intervals while the two Barrymores elaborate their interpretation of the super-thief (John) and the dogged detective (Lionel).

A neat angle of this film version [of the French play by Maurice Le Blanc and Francis de Croisset] is the fact that the audience never sees Lupin in the act of larceny itself. This literary scheme is maintained until the last episode, when the elaborate plot to steal the Mona Lisa from the Louvre is worked out in detail and in sight, a fitting climax and a well-paced and balanced sequence.

Story has a touch of discreet but sophisticated spice in the love affair between Lupin and Sonia, the girl released from prison on parole and forced to aid the police in the pursuit. Femme lead is played by Karen Morley with a beautiful balance of reticence and occasional emphasis.

•

ARSENE LUPIN RETURNS
1938, 81 mins, US b/w
Dir George Fitzmaurice ***Prod*** John W. Considine, Jr. ***Scr*** James Kevin McGuinness, Howard Emmett Rogers, George Harmon Coxe ***Ph*** George Folsey ***Ed*** Ben Lewis ***Mus*** Franz Waxman ***Art*** Cedric Gibbons, Stan Rogers, Edwin B. Willis
Act Melvyn Douglas, Virginia Bruce, Warren William, John Halliday, Nat Pendleton, Monty Woolley (M-G-M)

Supposedly killed by the police long ago, the gendarme mystifier, Lupin, a character created (and used before in films) by Maurice Leblanc, is found by the writers of this original to have merely retired and gone legit. He is played by Melvyn Douglas, whose two associates, Nat Pendleton and E. E. Clive, a couple of mugs, help him in his pseudo-crime re-entry. Whole thing is deftly handled by director and cutter, the pace fast enough to always hold the viewer, and there's enough comedy to liven nearly every situation.

The beginning of the story concerns the FBI's casting out of Warren William, a publicity hog who becomes of no use to the government because he's known everywhere. He goes into private practice and gets an insurance company protective job watching a $250,000 jewel on transport from America to France. Only after the boat docks on the other side, does Lupin begin figuring. Last half becomes very much cops-and-robbers.

•

ARSENIC AND OLD LACE
1944, 118 mins, US Ⓥ ⊙ b/w
Dir Frank Capra ***Prod*** Frank Capra ***Scr*** Julius J. Epstein, Philip G. Epstein ***Ph*** Sol Polito ***Ed*** Daniel Mandell ***Mus*** Max Steiner ***Art*** Max Parker
Act Cary Grant, Priscilla Lane, Raymond Massey, Jack Carson, Peter Lorre, Edward Everett Horton (Warner)

Despite the fact that picture runs 118 minutes, Frank Capra has expanded on the original play [by Joseph Kesselring] to a sufficient extent to maintain a steady, consistent pace. With what he has crammed into the running time, film doesn't seem that long. The majority of the action is confined to one set, that of the home of the two amiably nutty aunts who believe it's kind to poison people they come in contact with and their non-violently insane brother who thinks he's Teddy Roosevelt.

Cary Grant and Priscilla Lane are paired romantically. They open the picture getting married but are delayed in their honeymoon when Grant finds his two screwy aunts have been bumping off people in their house, burying them in the cellar and even holding thoughtful funeral ceremonies for them. The laughs that surround his efforts to get John Alexander, the "Teddy Roosevelt" of the picture, committed to an institution; troubles that come up when a maniacal long-lost brother shows up after a world tour of various murders with a phony doctor, and other plot elements make for diversion of a very agreeable character.

•

ARTHUR
1981, 117 mins, US Ⓥ ⊙ col
Dir Steve Gordon ***Prod*** Robert Greenhut ***Scr*** Steve Gordon ***Ph*** Fred Schules ***Ed*** Susan E. Morse ***Mus*** Burt Bacharach ***Art*** Stephen Hendrickson
Act Dudley Moore, Liza Minnelli, John Gielgud, Geraldine Fitzgerald, Jill Eikenberry, Stephen Elliott (Orion)

Arthur is a sparkling entertainment that attempts, with a large measure of success, to resurrect the amusingly artificial conventions of 1930s screwball romantic comedies. Dudley Moore is back in top-*10* form as a layabout drunken playboy who finds himself falling in love with working-class girl Liza Minnelli just as he's being forced into an arranged marriage with a society WASP.

Central dilemma, which dates back to Buster Keaton at least, has wastrel Moore faced with the choice of marrying white-bread heiress Jill Eikenberry or being cut off by his father from $750 million. After much procrastination, he finally agrees to the union, but situation is complicated when, in a vintage (meet cute), he protects shoplifter Minnelli from the authorities and finds himself genuinely falling for someone for the first time in his padded life.

As Moore's eternally supportive but irrepressibly sarcastic valet, John Gielgud gives a priceless performance. Minnelli fills the bill in a less showbizzy and smaller part than usual, but pic's core is really the wonderful relationship between Moore and Gielgud.

1981: Best Supp. Actor (John Gielgud), Song ("Best That You Can Do")

NOMINATION: Best Actor (Dudley Moore), Original Screenplay

•

ARTHUR 2 ON THE ROCKS
1988, 113 mins, US Ⓥ ⊙ col
Dir Bud Yorkin ***Prod*** Robert Shapiro ***Scr*** Andy Breckman ***Ph*** Stephen H. Burum ***Ed*** Michael Kahn ***Mus*** Burt Bacharach ***Art*** Gene Callahan
Act Dudley Moore, Liza Minnelli, John Gielgud, Geraldine Fitzgerald, Stephen Elliott, Paul Benedict (Warner)

Arthur 2 is not as classy a farce as the original, but still manages to be an amusing romp. Five years into their marriage and living the enviable Park Avenue lifestyle with the kind of digs photographed by *Architectural Digest*, wife Linda (Liza Minnelli) finds she's unable to conceive and goes about adopting a baby.

While Minnelli is gung ho to expand the fold, Arthur's ex-girlfriend's father (Stephen Elliott) seeks to break it apart. Vindictive over having his love-struck daughter stood up at the altar by Arthur last time around, he works up a legal trick to take away the wastrel's $750-million fortune and force him to marry his daughter after all.

Though not critical to the pleasures of watching Moore in one of his best screen roles, it does undermine his performance when he has lesser personalities to tease. Minnelli loses some of her working-class sassiness as the downtown-gone-uptown-gone-downtown wife trying to put her house in order, though credit is due her for carrying plot's best scenes.

•

ARTICLE 99
1992, 100 mins, US Ⓥ ⊙ col
Dir Howard Deutch *Prod* Michael Gruskoff, Michael I. Levy *Scr* Ron Cutler *Ph* Richard Bowen *Ed* Richard Halsey *Mus* Danny Elfman *Art* Virginia L. Randolph
Act Ray Liotta, Kiefer Sutherland, Forest Whitaker, Lea Thompson, Kathy Baker, Eli Wallach (Orion/Gruskoff-Levy)

With didactic intent behind a rabble-rousing story, filmmakers admirably draw attention to the scandalous condition of health care at the nation's Veterans' Administration hospitals while aiming for the seriocomic tone of *M*A*S*H*, *Catch-22* and *The Hospital*. Title refers to a fictional but apparently functioning regulation at the V.A. that withholds full medical benefits from vets if they can't prove their ailments are specifically related to military service.

Set almost entirely within a zoolike V.A. facility in Kansas City, screenplay presents a villainous bureaucracy ruled by hospital director John Mahoney. Opposing him are the irreverent but dedicated can-do doctors led by surgeon Ray Liotta.

Liotta and fellow medics Forest Whitaker, John C. McGinley and Lea Thompson naturally give newcomer Kiefer Sutherland a hard time, accusing him of having his sights set on a cushy private practice after a short stint in the trenches. Little by little, Sutherland's eyes are opened to the crazy methods his colleagues need to employ to do any good, and to the value of their work.

Kathy Baker enlivens every scene she's in as a warm-blooded shrink who gets right to the point when Liotta shows an interest in her. Lenser Richard Bowen has given the film a rough, vérité look.

•

ARTISTS AND MODELS
1937, 95 mins, US b/w
Dir Raoul Walsh *Prod* Lewis E. Gensler *Scr* Walter DeLeon, Francis Martin *Ph* Victor Milner *Ed* Ellsworth Hoagland
Act Jack Benny, Ida Lupino, Richard Arlen, Gail Patrick, Ben Blue, Judy Canova (Paramount)

Artists and Models holds enough variety, comedy, color, spec, flash, dash and novelty for a couple of pictures. It's so replete with a cavalcade of radio, nitery, vaudeville and revuesque ingredients that it's much to the credit of all concerned that this madcap musical [story by Sig Herzig and Gene Thackrey, adapted by Eve Greene and Harlan Ware] shapes up as well as it does.

There are a couple of misguided sequences, one of which is that "Public Melody Number One" sequence, done in a frankly Harlem setting, with Louis Armstrong tooting his trumpet against a pseudo-musical gangster idea. While Martha Raye is under cork, this intermingling of the races isn't wise, especially as she lets herself go into the extremest manifestations of Harlemania torso-twisting and gyrations.

Jack Benny, Ida Lupino, Richard Arlen and Gail Patrick are chiefly responsible for holding the film together. This is Benny's first solo starrer and it's also a departure for him in that he s assigned the major romantic interest.

Benny is cast as the advertising agency head. Arlen is his biggest (and practically only) account. Lupino is a professional model who, because she's a p.m., is at first snubbed by Arlen for a ritzy ad campaign. Lupino hies to Miami posing as a socialite, in order to impress that being a pro model isn't a liability.

1937: NOMINATION: Best Song ("Whispers in the Dark")

•

ARTISTS AND MODELS
1955, 108 mins, US Ⓥ ⊙ col b/w
Dir Frank Tashlin *Prod* Hal Wallis *Scr* Frank Tashlin, Hal Kanter, Herbert Baker *Ph* Daniel L. Fapp *Ed* Warren Low *Mus* Walter Scharf
Act Dean Martin, Jerry Lewis, Shirley MacLaine, Dorothy Malone, Eddie Mayehoff, Anita Ekberg (Paramount)

Comedic diversion in the Martin and Lewis manner has been put together in this overdone, slaphappy melange of gags and gals. Six writers [three scripters, plus adaptation by Don McGuire from a play by Michael Davidson and Norman Lessing] figure in the production and, while giving the comics a story line to follow, also worked in everything but the proverbial kitchen sink.

Co-starring with the comedy team are Shirley MacLaine and Dorothy Malone. The former tackles her role of model with a bridling cuteness but has a figure to take the viewer's mind off her facial expression. Ditto Dorothy Malone, her artist roommate.

Dean Martin is an artist and Jerry Lewis is a would-be writer of kiddie stories, both starving in NY.

•

ART OF LOVE, THE
1965, 99 mins, US col
Dir Norman Jewison *Prod* Ross Hunter *Scr* Carl Reiner *Ph* Russell Metty *Ed* Milton Carruth *Mus* Cy Coleman *Art* Alexander Golitzen, George Webb
Act James Garner, Dick Van Dyke, Elke Sommer, Angie Dickinson, Ethel Merman, Carl Reiner (Universal/Cherokee)

Ross Hunter's pic starts out as pure film satire aimed only at light, bright comedy entertainment. With the addition of a wide variety of often zesty elements it grows into a garbled mixture of coquettish comedy that has side-splitting moments, some unusually fine character performances, but so much of everything it never once settles down to a consistent point of view.

Story [by Richard Alan Simmons and William Sackheim] is of would-be American artist Dick Van Dyke who gives up to return to the rich fiancée in America who is paying his bills—and those of his roommate would-be author James Garner. Garner is so devastated at the loss of his meal ticket, he tries everything to keep Van Dyke in Paris, including a mock suicide that unwittingly backfires into what looks like the real thing. When Van Dyke reappears, he has to go into hiding because Garner has found a dead painter sells better than a live one.

Writer Carl Reiner and director Norman Jewison go aground by allowing too many bits to fill their pot. The picture looks like one that kept changing as each member of the company suggested some new cute bit.

•

AS GOOD AS IT GETS
1997, 138 mins, US Ⓥ ⊙ col
Dir James L. Brooks *Prod* James L. Brooks, Bridget Johnson, Kristi Zea *Scr* Mark Andrus, James L. Brooks *Ph* John Bailey *Ed* Richard Marks *Mus* Hans Zimmer *Art* Bill Brzeski
Act Jack Nicholson, Helen Hunt, Greg Kinnear, Cuba Gooding, Jr., Skeet Ulrich, Shirley Knight (Gracie/TriStar)

James L. Brooks's sitcom roots are all too apparent in this sporadically funny romantic comedy [from a screen story by Mark Andrus] with all the dramatic plausibility and tonal consistency of a TV variety show. The filmmaker's ability to deliver crowd-pleasing entertainment remains intact, as the outrageous one-liners of Jack Nicholson's hopelessly misanthropic, anti-p.c. leading character snap one to attention, and the various narrative zigzags will keep viewers on their toes. But this arch film changes mood and apparent intention virtually every other minute.

Middle-aged New York City curmudgeon Melvin Udall (Nicholson) defines himself as the neighbor from hell by tossing a little dog down a garbage chute and gleefully assailing Fido's gay owner, Simon (Greg Kinnear), and the latter's black friend, Frank (Cuba Gooding, Jr.). He is busy finishing his 62nd book and emerges once a day to eat at the same restaurant, barely tolerated by his favorite waitress, Carol Connelly (Helen Hunt).

From the beginning, it is clear tht the story has only one potential trajectory, the gradual humanization of Melvin. The door to his self-awakening is opened by, of all things, Simon's dog, which he comes to love and opens something in the Scrooge's heart. Ninety minutes in, pic takes a half-hour detour when Melvin is shanghaied into driving Simon and Carol down to Baltimore. The hotel stop involved provides a setting for some intimacy that may never have happened otherwise.

Nicholson's performance is wonderfully enjoyable when Melvin remains an irascible s.o.b. but becomes unfathomable in its would-be tender moments. Hunt's Carol is a more rounded and comprehensible creation, but the character isn't all that interesting. Kinnear is decent.

1997: Best Actor (Nicholson), Best Actress (Helen Hunt)

NOMINATIONS: Best Picture, Supp. Actor (Greg Kinnear), Original Screenplay, Editing, Original Comedy Score

•

ASHANTI
1979, 117 mins, Switzerland Ⓥ ▭ col
Dir Richard Fleischer *Prod* Georges-Alain Vuille *Scr* Stephen Geller *Ph* Aldo Tonti *Mus* Michael Melvoin *Art* Aurelio Crugnola
Act Michael Caine, Peter Ustinov, Beverly Johnson, Omar Sharif, Rex Harrison, William Holden (Vuille)

A polished but lackluster adventure entertainment.

Michael Caine and Beverly Johnson are World Health Organization medics on a visit to an African tribe when the lady becomes a prize catch of Arabian slave trader Peter Ustinov. Caine's retrieval odyssey thereafter is variously aided by Rex Harrison as an ambiguous go-between, William Holden as a mercenary helicopter pilot, and Indian actor Kabir Bedi as a Bedouin with his own score to settle with Ustinov. All acquit with professional grace but unremarkable impact.

No help to the film's grip on interest is director Richard Fleischer's minuet pacing. He seems to have come under the spell of those Saharan sand dunes lavishly and lengthily dwelled on as Caine and Bedi pick up Ustinov's trail. [Script is based on the novel *Ebony* by Alberto Vasquez-Figueroa.]

•

ASHES AND DIAMONDS
SEE: POPIOL I DIAMENT

•

ASH WEDNESDAY
1973, 99 mins, US Ⓥ col
Dir Larry Peerce *Prod* Dominick Dunne *Scr* Jean-Claude Tramont *Ph* Ennio Guarnieri *Ed* Marion Rothman *Mus* Maurice Jarre *Art* Philip Abramson
Act Elizabeth Taylor, Henry Fonda, Helmut Berger, Keith Baxter, Maurice Teynac, Maggie Blye (Sagittarius/Paramount)

Ash Wednesday is a jolting tearjerker about middle-age marital trauma, compounded by the superficial and spiritual uplift of cosmetic surgery. Elizabeth Taylor stars as the fiftyish wife of Henry Fonda, and Helmut Berger is featured as her brief Italian resort affair after the beautification process has restored her surface charm.

Script is essentially a three-act play, about evenly divided over the film's 99 minutes. Act 1 is a gruesome, overdone series of ugly surgical scenes. Act 2 introduces Taylor to a new world of uncertain poise, while Act 3 precipitates the powerful, neatly restrained dissolution of her marriage to Fonda.

Taylor, fashionably gowned and bejewelled, carries the film almost single-handedly. Fonda is excellent in his climatic appearance, an usually superb casting idea.

•

ASK A POLICEMAN
1939, 83 mins, UK b/w
Dir Marcel Varnel *Scr* Marriott Edgar, Val Guest *Ph* Derick Williams
Act Will Hay, Graham Moffatt, Moore Marriott, Glennis Lorimer, Peter Gawthorne, Charles Oliver (Gainsborough)

Bits of *Dr. Syn* (1937), with George Arliss, and *The Ghost Train* (1931) blend happily with amusing dialog and situations [story by Sidney Gilliatt] usually associated with Will Hay and his two stooges, the fat boy and old man.

A village police station becomes the center of interest when it's discovered there's been no crime there for over 10 years. The sergeant (Hay) in command of two subordinates (Graham Moffatt, Moore Marriott), hearing they're likely to be transferred or fired because of lack of "business," plans to frame one or two cases.

Planting a keg of brandy on the beach, to stage a smuggler's racket, they discover another, real contraband keg. From then on it's a wild chase between the three witnits and a band headed by the local squire (Charles Oliver), which is carrying on a lucrative haul.

•

AS LONG AS THEY'RE HAPPY
1955, 95 mins, UK col
Dir J. Lee Thompson *Prod* Raymond Stross *Scr* Alan Melville *Ph* Gilbert Taylor *Ed* John D. Guthridge *Mus* Stanley Black *Art* Michael Stringer
Act Jack Buchanan, Janette Scott, Jean Carson, Brenda Banzie, Diana Dors, Susan Stephen (Rank)

Generously adapted from the West End stage hit of a couple of seasons back, *As Long As They're Happy* has been embellished with high quality production values to give it broader and more popular appeal. In transferring the original Vernon Sylvaine piece to the screen, Alan Melville's screenplay takes full advantage of the opportunities of a wider canvas. Jack Buchanan repeats his original stage role as the stockbroker head of the family whose wife and three daughters are overwhelmed by the arrival of a Hollywood crooner at their suburban London home. The youngest (Janette Scott) is full of adoration; her elder sister (Jean Carson), a Parisienne existentialist, is full of adimiration, while their mother (Brenda Banzie) sees the chance of some honest fun at the expense of her staid husband. Around these characters, the plot develops into a hearty and good-humored romp, without much attention to story line.

Nine songs by Sam Coslow get full treatment and although production values are toned down, they strike an effective note. Jerry Wayne, who has the dominant role of the crooner, does four of the numbers, one of which is shared by Buchanan.

Carson, who does a couple of numbers with great effect, always looks attractive, but Scott is too repetitive as the adoring teenager. There is a delightful guest bit by Diana Dors.

●

ASPHALT JUNGLE, THE
1950, 112 mins, US Ⓥ ⊙ b/w
Dir John Huston ***Prod*** Arthur Hornblow, Jr. ***Scr*** Ben Maddow, John Huston ***Ph*** Harold Rosson ***Ed*** George Boemler ***Mus*** Miklos Rozsa ***Art*** Cedric Gibbons, Randall Duell
Act Sterling Hayden, Louis Calhern, James Whitmore, Jean Hagen, Sam Jaffe, Marilyn Monroe (M-G-M)

The Asphalt Jungle is a study in crime, hard-hitting in its exposé of the underworld. Ironic realism is striven for and achieved in the writing, production and direction. An audience will quite easily pull for the crooks in their execution of the million-dollar jewelry theft around which the plot is built.

W. R. Burnett's lusty novel about criminal types, from the cheap hood to the mastermind, provided the punchy basis for the script. The actual heist is a suspenseful piece of filming, as is the following police chase and gradual disintegration of the gang.

Sterling Hayden and Louis Calhern star as contrasting criminals, the former a mean, bitter hood who dreams of restoring an old Kentucky horse farm, and Calhern a crooked attorney who needs money to continue sating his desire for curvy blondes and high living.

1950: NOMINATIONS: Best Director, Supp. Actor (Sam Jaffe), Screenplay, B&W Cinematography

●

ASSASSIN, THE
SEE: POINT OF NO RETURN

●

ASSASSINATION BUREAU LIMITED, THE
1969, 106 mins, UK/US Ⓥ col
Dir Basil Dearden ***Prod*** Michael Relph, Basil Dearden ***Scr*** Michael Relph, Wolf Mankiewicz ***Ph*** Geoffrey Unsworth ***Ed*** Teddy Darvas ***Mus*** Ron Grainer ***Art*** Michael Relph
Act Oliver Reed, Diana Rigg, Telly Savalas, Curt Jurgens, Philippe Noiret, Warren Mitchell (Paramount)

That dry, wry humor that flavors such British films as *Kind Hearts and Coronets* is again apparent to a degree in *The Assassination Bureau Limited*. In less skillful hands its premise of a 1906 international homicide organization might have been dime-a-dozen stuff. Fused with the capable talents of Michael Relph and Basil Dearden, picture emerges as a somewhat unusual and clever comedy after an over-leisurely opening.

Producers have made handsome use of both extraordinarily fine interiors and interesting exteriors in London, Paris, Zurich, Vienna and Venice, which give added zest to yarn's unfoldment. Plotline, based on an idea from Jack London and Robert Fish's book, is escapist fare throughout.

As a comedy thriller, film stands high, if the spectator isn't too meticulous about expository details, particulary the whys and wherefores of a determined young femme reporter (Diana Rigg) who decides that a strange outbreak of highly professional, apparently motiveless killings, must be the work of a single organization.

Entire cast play their respective roles broadly and each gives a good account of himself. Curt Jurgens as a German general, also a Bureau member, and Annabella Incontrera, as the wife of the Italian member of the Bureau, are outstanding.

●

ASSASSINATION OF TROTSKY, THE
1972, 105 mins, France/Italy Ⓥ col
Dir Joseph Losey ***Prod*** Norman Priggen, Joseph Losey ***Scr*** Nicholas Mosley, Masolino D'Amico ***Ph*** Pasqualino De Santis ***Ed*** Reginald Beck ***Mus*** Egisto Macchi ***Art*** Richard Macdonald
Act Richard Burton, Alain Delon, Romy Schneider, Valentina Cortese, Luigi Vannucchi, Giorgio Albertazzi (Cinetel/CIAC/De Laurentiis)

The last days (1940) in the life of the Russian revolutionary figure Leon Trotsky are traced in this fairly cryptic film.

Intended as a sort of political thriller, the film remains cloudy vis-à-vis the Stalin menance though it works up dread, and the foreshadowed (pickax, skull-shattering) death. But there is too much forced symbolism, diffuse characterization and a sort of schematic feel sans enough interplay of people, historical perspective, or new insights into this political or psychological murder.

Richard Burton sometimes catches a cantankerous and surface aspect of the aging revolutionary, once almost as popular as Lenin in Russia.

The film rarely transcends a sort of banal look at the murder. It has little to say about political hatred and fanaticism.

●

ASSASSINS
1995, 132 mins, US Ⓥ ⊙ col
Dir Richard Donner ***Prod*** Richard Donner, Joel Silver, Bruce Evans, Raynold Gideon, Andrew Lazar, Jim Van Wyck ***Scr*** Andy Wachowski, Larry Wachowski, Brian Helgeland ***Ph*** Vilmos Zsigmond ***Ed*** Richard Marks ***Mus*** Mark Mancina ***Art*** Tom Sanders
Act Sylvester Stallone, Antonio Banderas, Julianne Moore, Anatoly Davydov (Silver/Warner)

A not-much-fun high-tech actioner, *Assassins* has a body temperature that matches those of its coldly ruthless leading characters. As steely and well-tooled as the fancy firearms that Sylvester Stallone and Antonio Banderas fire so frequently, this contrived hide-and-seek suspenser [from a screen story by Andy and Larry Wachowski] about a veteran hit man and the young hotshot who would bump him off is a simplistic reworking of *The Gunfighter* in modern dress.

Haunted by fragmentary black-and-white memories of a long-ago hit, Robert Rath (Stallone) has seen enough and wants out. But when he goes to knock off an old man at a funeral, he's beaten to the punch by one Miguel Bain (Banderas), a Latin wild man who's clearly a little loco but also has the cojones to try to knock Rath off his throne.

When Rath takes on his intended final assignment, to intercept a valuable disc and terminate the seller and buyers, he finds once again that Bain is on the same case. In an elaborate game of cat-and-mouse in a Seattle hotel, Rath makes off with both the disc and its owner, a ditzy surveillance expert named Electra (Julianne Moore), who goes nowhere without her large cat.

Stallone is playing his usual strong, morose, silent type who has an ounce of compassion and tenderness buried somewhere under the beefcake. Banderas bounces and gesticulates all over the screen, injecting some welcome humor into the proceedings. Critics' favorite Moore at first seems trapped by the cutesy, quirky traits by which her character is defined but ultimately seems to have fun with this change of pace.

An old hand at this sort of thing after the *Lethal Weapon* pics, Richard Donner handles the numerous chases, pursuits and showdowns with efficient, icy expertise, although the whole thing runs needlessly long at more than two hours.

●

ASSAULT OF THE KILLER BIMBOS
1988, 81 mins, US Ⓥ ⊙ col
Dir Anita Rosenberg ***Prod*** David DeCoteau, John Schouweiler ***Scr*** Ted Nicolaou ***Ph*** Thomas Callaway ***Ed*** Barry Zetlin ***Mus*** Fred Lapides, Marc Ellis ***Art*** Royce Mathew
Act Christina Whitaker, Elizabeth Kaitan, Tammara Souza, Nick Cassavetes, Griffin O'Neal, Jamie Bozian (Titan)

Assault of the Killer Bimbos is the kind of engagingly dumb, slyly hip pic that is tailor-made for cult enjoyment. First-timer Anita Rosenberg has fashioned an under-$1-million pic [from a story by her, Patti Astor and Ted Nicolaou] that dips and sways with its own kind of bimbotic integrity.

Chief bimbos are played by Christina Whitaker and Elizabeth Kaitan as go-go dancers in a deadend nightclub who are mistakenly taken for murderers after their boss gets bumped off by hoods. On the 1am to Mexico, they pick up a willing hostage—truckstop waitress Tammara Souza—and three cartoonish surf bums played by Jamie Bozian and movie-biz brats Nick Cassavetes and Griffin O'Neal.

Road adventures, which include a high-speed chase on the desert highway complete with a flying police car stunt, end in a low-rent Tijuana motel. Head bimbo Whitaker has the kind of unshakeable cool that makes her look like she's cruising Ocean Avenue even while driving a getaway car out of a truckstop.

●

ASSAULT ON A QUEEN
1966, 106 mins, US Ⓥ ▭ col
Dir Jack Donohue ***Prod*** William Goetz ***Scr*** Rod Serling ***Ph*** William H. Daniels ***Ed*** Archie Marshek ***Mus*** Duke Ellington ***Art*** Paul Groesse
Act Frank Sinatra, Virna Lisi, Anthony Franciosa, Richard Conte, Alf Kjellin, Errol John (Seven Arts/Sinatra)

Producer William Goetz has supervised a remarkable job of making plausible the admittedly wild-eyed adventures of an odd assortment of moral derelicts who salvage a submarine with the intent of robbing the *Queen Mary* (hence the title) [based on the novel by Jack Finney]. Virna Lisi, Anthony Franciosa and Alf Kjellin, on the hunt for a sunken treasure ship off the Bahamas, hire Frank Sinatra and his partner, Errol John, who run a fishing boat business, to help them find the treasure. Sinatra, instead, finds a small sunken German submarine. Kjellin, a former German U-boat commander, talks the group into salvaging it and holding up the *Queen Mary*.

Only Kjellin is able to create a well-rounded character and is outstanding as the apparently bland German, holding in control his diabolic intent. Sinatra and Lisi are very good in roles that make few demands on their acting ability. John, while efficient in the tenser moments, seems inhibited in scenes where he must wax sentimental over his rehabilitation by Sinatra.

●

ASSAULT ON PRECINCT 13
1976, 91 mins, US Ⓥ ▭ col
Dir John Carpenter ***Prod*** J. S. Kaplan ***Scr*** John Carpenter ***Ph*** Douglas Knapp ***Ed*** John T. Chance [=John Carpenter] ***Mus*** John Carpenter ***Art*** Tommy Vallance
Act Austin Stoker, Darwin Joston, Laurie Zimmer, Martin West, Tony Burton, Kim Richards (CKK)

Novelty of a gang swearing a blood oath to destroy a precinct station and all inside is sufficiently compelling for the gory-minded to assure acceptance.

Gang is motivated by a man who kills one of their members for the murder of his small daughter and takes refuge in the Los Angeles station so distraught he cannot explain. Assault closely follows his arrival, and it's a war.

Precinct station is within hours of closing to move to new quarters, which explains why only a single cop and a policewoman remain to hold down the fort, abetted by two prisoners who are temporarily incarcerated on their way to Death Row in Salinas.

John Carpenter's direction of his screenplay, after a pokey opening half, is responsible for realistic movement.

●

ASSIGNMENT—PARIS
1952, 84 mins, US b/w
Dir Robert Parrish ***Prod*** Samuel Marx, Jerry Bresler ***Scr*** William Bowers, Walter Goetz, Jack Palmer White ***Ph*** Burnett Guffey, Ray Cory ***Ed*** Charles Nelson ***Mus*** George Duning
Act Dana Andrews, Marta Toren, George Sanders, Audrey Totter, Sandro Giglio, Willis Bouchey (Columbia)

A topical thriller of newspaper work under the handicaps of the Iron Curtain. Dana Andrews, Marta Toren, George Sanders and Audrey Totter are newspaper people attached to the Paris office of a stateside paper, involved in the tale of intrigue. Spy-chase angles are mixed with romantic involvements, plus some speaking out against Communist rule in such countries as Hungary.

Story is from the Pauline and Paul Gallico story, serialized in the *Sat Eve Post* as *Trial by Terror*.

Andrews, a good, aggressive reporter, is sent to the Paris office, where Sanders is the editor. He immediately falls for Toren, a staff member just back from Budapest with a story of plotting between the Hungarian puppet dictator and Tito, but which she can't back up with proof. Details of radiotelephone delivery of news from correspondents to the Paris bureau, with the Red censors holding itchy fingers on the controls, its reception, interpretation and dissemination, along with typical undercover spy work, sinister characters, etc., all help hold the interest.

●

ASTRONAUT'S WIFE, THE
1999, 109 mins, US Ⓥ ⊙ col
Dir Rand Ravich ***Prod*** Andrew Lazar ***Scr*** Rand Ravich ***Ph*** Allen Daviau ***Ed*** Steve Mirkovich, Tim Alverson ***Mus*** [none] ***Art*** Jan Roelfs
Act Johnny Depp, Charlize Theron, Joe Morton, Clea DuVall, Donna Murphy, Nick Cassavetes (Mad Chance/New Line)

Rosemary's Baby gets an extraterrestrial twist in *The Astronaut's Wife*, an aggressively stylish but dramatically flaccid drama that plays like an upscale reprise of a '50s sci-fi potboiler. Topflight work by professionals on both sides of the camera can't quite disguise the predictability of the formulaic material.

Sporting peroxided hair and a good-ol'-boy drawl, Johnny Depp stars as NASA shuttle pilot Spencer Armacost, a vet space jock who's introduced during a preflight close encounter with Jillian (Charlize Theron), his beautiful schoolteacher wife. Out in space, Armacost and fellow astronaut Alex Streck (Nick Cassavetes) run into trouble during a routine repair of a malfunctioning satellite.

Ground control loses contact with the pair for two minutes after the satellite explodes. Both men survive but are unconscious when they are brought back to Earth for longterm R&R. Spencer announces his decision to quit the space program and accept a private-sector job with a New York aerospace firm.

Jillian's peace of mind is undermined by what she views as strange behavior on the part of her husband. She's also unsettled by his increased lustiness. After Jillian discovers she is pregnant with twins, Spencer may know *everything* about what's going on inside her.

Convincingly maneuvering through a wide range of emotions, Theron hits the right balance of strong-willed resilience and moist-eyed vulnerability. Her performance is more than compelling enough to sustain interest for long stretches when she's the only person onscreen. Depp is aptly ambiguous in what amounts to a supporting role.

•

ASYLUM

1972, 88 mins, UK Ⓥ ⊙ col

Dir Roy Ward Baker ***Prod*** Max J. Rosenberg, Milton Subotsky ***Scr*** Robert Bloch ***Ph*** Denys Coop ***Ed*** Peter Tanner ***Mus*** Douglas Gamley ***Art*** Tony Curtis

Act Peter Cushing, Britt Ekland, Herbert Lom, Patrick Magee, Robert Powell, Barbara Parkins (Amicus)

Herewith a dependable programmer off the Amicus belt line. It's a trim little chiller, with a moderate quota of blood and mayhem, polished performances and smooth direction. It also boasts some imaginative props—like the decapitated limbs, etc., of Sylvia Syms metaphysically killing her murderer and errant husband, Richard Todd, and his sweetie Barbara Parkins.

The plot is essentially about a young shrink's (Robert Powell) voyage of discovery in an insane asylum where he hopes to become a staffer. He arrives to find that the bossman has himself become confined as a homicidal nut case. His successor (Patrick Magee), by way of putting the young doc to the test, has him interview several psychos.

Very few of the key thesps remain robust and vertical by the windup, for which scripter Robert Bloch comes up with an effective trick ending.

•

AS YOU DESIRE ME

1932, 70 mins, US Ⓥ b/w

Dir George Fitzmaurice ***Scr*** Gene Markey ***Ph*** William Daniels ***Ed*** George Hiveley

Act Greta Garbo, Melvyn Douglas, Erich von Stroheim, Owen Moore, Hedda Hopper, Rafaela Ottiano (M-G-M)

A romantic problem play, interestingly played by the fascinating Greta Garbo, treated in a manner of high drama. The original [play by Luigi Pirandello] hasn't been broadly hoked in the manner that Metro has so often followed.

Story has to do with an Italian countess, victim of the Austrian invasion and violence from drunken soldiers and driven into a mental fog that has blotted out her past. She is recognized 10 years later in her wanderings as a music-hall singer by the painter who had done her portrait as a bride, and by him brought back to her grief-stricken husband. But she cannot recall the past and is never entirely received by the people of her former life, with the exception of the portrait painter, who sees with the eyes of faith.

Garbo's performance is always absorbing, vivid in its acting and compelling in appeal. Melvyn Douglas is a rather lukewarm actor in a stencil husband role, impeccably played but unexciting. Owen Moore grabs the acting honors among the men with his jaunty handling of a minor part, while Erich von Stroheim fails signally to make himself the man you love to hate by revealing an accent of blended Yorkville and Ninth Avenue.

•

¡ATAME!

1990, 101 mins, Spain Ⓥ ⊙ col

Dir Pedro Almodovar ***Prod*** Agustin Almodovar (exec.) ***Scr*** Pedro Almodovar ***Ph*** Jose Luis Alcaine ***Ed*** Jose Salcedo ***Mus*** Ennio Morricone ***Art*** Ferran Sanchez

Act Victoria Abril, Antonio Banderas, Loles Leon, Julieta Serrano, Francisco Rabal, Rossy de Palma (El Deseo)

In contrast to *Women on the Verge of a Nervous Breakdown*, this film harks back to Pedro Almodovar's earlier features where sexuality was a central theme. He has moved away from sight gags, shock tactics and glamorized kitsch, which have been molded into a subtler narrative.

Yarn concerns Ricki (Antonio Banderas), a 23-year-old man who is released from a mental institution. He sees a picture of Marina (Victoria Abril) in a film buff magazine. She is a hooker and porno actress he once paid to spend a night with, and Ricki decides to marry her.

Ricki forces his way into her apartment and declares his intentions. After a scuffle, he decides to tie her to the bed, certain that she will learn to love him. The relationship between the protagonists gradually shifts from that of captor and captured to lovers. Meanwhile, the elderly porno film director, who is confined to a wheelchair, teams up with Marina's sister Lola (Loles Leon) to try and find the missing thesp.

Almodovar's inventive direction, superb lensing by Jose Luis Alcaine, a fine score by Ennio Morricone and top technical credits make pic a pleasure to watch. The film has the same Spanish framework as its predecessors, reflecting the modern, amoral, sex and drug culture of modern Madrid, intertwined with long-entrenched religious and social values. Abril and Banderas are compelling to watch as the central couple.

•

AT CLOSE RANGE

1986, 111 mins, US Ⓥ ⊙ ▭ col

Dir James Foley ***Prod*** Elliott Lewitt, Don Guest ***Scr*** Nicholas Kazan ***Ph*** Juan Ruiz-Anchia ***Ed*** Howard Smith ***Mus*** Patrick Leonard ***Art*** Peter Jamison

Act Sean Penn, Christopher Walken, Mary Stuart Masterson, Christopher Penn, Millie Perkins, Candy Clark (Hemdale)

A downbeat tale [by Elliott Lewitt and Nicholas Kazan] of brutal family relations, James Foley's *At Close Range* is a very tough picture. Violent without being vicarious, this true story is set in a small Pennsylvania town in 1978. Story introduces young Brad (Sean Penn) as just another rather tough kid with an eye for a new girl (the charming Mary Stuart Masterson) and fiercely protective of his brother (Christopher Penn).

Along comes Brad's father (Christopher Walken), who has a reputation as a criminal. Intrigued by his seemingly exciting parent, Brad, Jr., is encouraged to form his own gang to carry out more modest heists.

General audiences will respond to the very strong performances of the two leads, especially Walken in one of his best roles.

•

AT FIRST SIGHT

1999, 128 mins, US Ⓥ ⊙ col

Dir Irwin Winkler ***Prod*** Irwin Winkler, Rob Cowan ***Scr*** Steve Levitt ***Ph*** John Seale ***Ed*** Julie Monroe ***Mus*** Mark Isham ***Art*** Jane Musky

Act Val Kilmer, Mira Sorvino, Kelly McGillis, Steven Weber, Bruce Davison, Nathan Lane (M-G-M)

Schmaltzy Val Kilmer–Mira Sorvino starrer about a blind man who recovers, then loses, his sight will be anathema to many men, while potentially appealing to women. In structure and tone, pic reminds of the 1990 drama *Awakenings*. No surprise there: Both tales are spun from the experiences of noted physician Dr. Oliver Sacks [his story *To See and Not See*].

An accomplished, high-strung Gotham-based architect, Amy (Sorvino) heads to a small upstate town for some spa relaxation. There she meets Virgil (Kilmer), a masseur who releases her stress and, inevitably, her passion. Over the objections of Virgil's devoted sister, Jennie (Kelly McGillis), Amy begins pushing an experimental surgery developed by Dr. Charles Aaron (Bruce Davison) aimed at restoring sight to those who, like Virgil, have been blind since childhood.

Just when it seems that Amy and Virgil have stumbled through the worst of their problems—and the story's third act feels like it has nowhere to go—Virgil relapses.

Unfortunately, Irwin Winkler is a director of little subtlety; this material could have used a lighter touch. Screenplay, moreover, leaves little to the imagination. It's a script that articulates the self-evident, telling where it should show, as in Virgil's assertion, "We don't see with our eyes; we live in darkness." Kilmer acquits himself admirably; his Virgil is a man of immense sensitivity and childlike innocence but not self-pity. Sorvino, however, frequently seems to be struggling not to appear awkward.

•

ATLANTIC CITY

1980, 104 mins, Canada/France/US Ⓥ ⊙ col

Dir Louis Malle ***Prod*** Denis Heroux ***Scr*** John Guare ***Ph*** Richard Ciupka ***Ed*** Suzanne Baron ***Mus*** Michel Legrand ***Art*** Anne Pritchard

Act Burt Lancaster, Susan Sarandon, Michel Piccoli, Kate Reid, Robert Joy, Hollis McLaren (Cine-Neighbor/Selta)

Film is blessed with a spare, intriguing script by Yank John Guare, who always skirts impending cliches and predictability by finding unusual facets in his characters and their actions.

The film is well limned by Burt Lancaster as a small-time, mythomaniacal, aging mafia hood, Susan Sarandon as an ambitious young woman, Kate Reid as a fading moll and Robert Joy and Hollis McLaren as Sarandon's husband and young sister.

Atlantic City is also a character as director Louis Malle adroitly uses decrepit old and new façades; New Jersey voted to allow gambling at this resort, which had boasted gangsters, prohibition capers and big-show attractions.

1981: NOMINATIONS: Best Picture, Director, Actor (Burt Lancaster), Actress (Susan Sarandon), Original Screenplay

•

ATLANTIS, THE LOST CONTINENT

1961, 91 mins, US Ⓥ ⊙ col

Dir George Pal ***Prod*** George Pal ***Scr*** Daniel Mainwaring ***Ph*** Harold E. Wellman ***Ed*** Ben Lewis ***Mus*** Russell Garcia ***Art*** George W. Davis, William Ferrari

Act Anthony Hall, Joyce Taylor, Frank de Kova, John Dall (M-G-M)

After establishing legendary significance via an arresting prologue in which the basis for age-old suspicion of the existence of a lost continental cultural link in the middle of the Atlantic is discussed, scenarist Daniel Mainwaring promptly proceeds to ignore the more compelling possibilities of the hypothesis in favor of erecting a tired, shopworn melodrama out of Gerald Hargreaves's play.

There is an astonishing similarity to the stevereevesian spectacles. An "ordeal by fire and water" ritual conducted in a great, crowded stadium seems almost a replica of gladiatorial combat in the Colosseum. When Atlantis is burning to a cinder at the climax, one can almost hear Nero fiddling. Even Russ Garcia's score has that pompous, martial Roman air about it. And at least several of the mob spectacle scenes have been lifted from Roman screen spectacles of the past (the 1951 version of *Quo Vadis?* looks like the source). The acting is routine.

•

AT LONG LAST LOVE

1975, 118 mins, US col

Dir Peter Bogdanovich ***Prod*** Peter Bogdanovich ***Scr*** Peter Bogdanovich ***Ph*** Laszlo Kovacs ***Ed*** Douglas Robertson ***Mus*** Artie Butler, Lionel Newman (sup.) ***Art*** Gene Allen

Act Burt Reynolds, Cybill Shepherd, Madeline Kahn, Duilio Del Prete, Eileen Brennan, John Hillerman (20th Century-Fox/Copa De Oro)

At Long Last Love, Peter Bogdanovich's experiment with a mostly singing, 1930s, upper-class romance, is a disappointing and embarrassing waste of talent.

Utilizing 16 Cole Porter songs, many of them not heard for years and all of them replete with additional lyrics hardly ever used, writer-producer-director Bogdanovich tries to float a bubble of gaiety involving three couples: bored playboy Reynolds with rent-hungry deb Cybill Shepherd; Broadway star Madeline Kahn and immigrant gambler Duilio Del Prete; and Eileen Brennan (Shepherd's maid) and John Hillerman (Reynolds's urbane valet). The customary plot crises and romantic complications, recognized and adored by vintage film buffs, eventually resolve themselves.

The principals sang their numbers while being filmed, with orchestrations dubbed in later, in an attempt to eliminate the lifelessness of post-sync when it is done poorly. On the basis of this experiment, pre-recording can rest its case.

•

AT PLAY IN THE FIELDS OF THE LORD

1991, 187 mins, US Ⓥ ⊙ col

Dir Hector Babenco ***Prod*** Saul Zaentz ***Scr*** Jean-Claude Carriere, Hector Babenco ***Ph*** Lauro Escorel ***Ed*** William Anderson ***Mus*** Zbigniew Preisner ***Art*** Clovis Bueno

Act Tom Berenger, Aidan Quinn, Kathy Bates, John Lithgow, Daryl Hannah, Tom Waits (Zaentz)

At Play in the Fields of the Lord is how half-breed Cheyenne mercenary Lewis Moon describes his location to missionaries before he parachutes into the Amazon jungle to seek his essence among a tribe called the Niaruna. Tale that follows—a challenging, cerebral and beautifully controlled take on Peter Matthiessen's revered 1965 novel—amounts to a cry of warning against interference with a delicate ecological and cultural balance.

Central to this telling are two men: a callous, brooding jungle rat (Tom Berenger) and his nemesis (Aidan Quinn), a dedicated Evangelical worker. One is in the Brazilian jungle town of Mae de Deus to bring Christianity to the Indians; the other is there to bomb them out of their habitat so the Brazilian government can seize their land. Each subverts his own mission, only to find that his presence among the natives can bring them only ill.

Film has a bracing story that hews remarkably close to the novel. Action is a bit stiff and pedantic at first as it stakes out its philosophical turf but then softens and blooms. Among the first-rate ensemble cast are Kathy Bates as Quinn's shrill, hysterically repressed wife; John Lithgow as a briskly buffoonish fellow missionary; Daryl Hannah as Lithgow's sweetly blank and dogmatic wife; and Tom Waits in his best showcase ever as Moon's sidekick and soul of self-mocking depravity.

Pic was shot over a harrowing six months in the remote jungle town of Belem, Brazil. Lauro Escorel's cinematography is spellbinding.

•

ATTACK

1956, 107 mins, US Ⓥ ◉ b/w

Dir Robert Aldrich ***Prod*** Robert Aldrich ***Scr*** James Poe ***Ph*** Joseph Biroc ***Ed*** Michael Luciano ***Mus*** Frank DeVol ***Art*** William Glasgow

Act Jack Palance, Eddie Albert, Lee Marvin, Robert Strauss, Richard Jaeckel, Buddy Ebsen (Associates & Aldrich)

Attack presents a cowardly officer who's murdered by his men. Entire film [from the play *Fragile Fox* by Norman Brooks] is treated with a hard realism that pays off in gutsy entertainment. It's a grim, extremely tough account of an infantry company during the Battle of the Bulge in World War II, brightly projected by the fine characterizations contributed by the cast.

Eddie Albert is the cowardly captain who's too yellow to back the actions attempted by his lieutenants (Jack Palance and William Smithers). Disastrous missions follow each other until Palance threatens to kill Albert if he fails on the next one.

Pic gains realism through depicting army brass and GIs as humans with different reactions to the reality of combat. Palance stands out in his portrayal of the gaunt, enraged lieutenant. Albert makes an unpleasant character quite real and understandable. Scoring exceptionally strong is Lee Marvin, the opportunistic colonel who keeps the coward in command because he will be useful after the war in politics.

•

ATTACK OF THE 50 FOOT WOMAN

1958, 65 mins, US Ⓥ ◉ b/w

Dir Nathan Hertz ***Prod*** Bernard Woolner ***Scr*** Mark Hanna ***Ph*** Jacques R. Marquette ***Ed*** Edward Mann ***Mus*** Ronald Stein ***Art*** [uncredited]

Act Allison Hayes, William Hudson, Yvette Vickers, Roy Gordon, George Douglas, Ken Terrell (Allied Artists)

Attack of the 50 Foot Woman shapes up as a minor offering for the sci-fi trade where demands aren't too great.

The production is the story of a femme who overnight grows into a murderous giantess, out to get husband who's cheating with another woman. Growth was caused by ray burns suffered when she's seized by huge monster, who lands in the desert near home in a satellite from outer space. Breaking the chains used to restrain her in her luxurious mansion, she makes her way to a tavern where spouse is with his lady love and literally squeezes him to death before the sheriff kills her with a riot gun.

Allison Hayes takes title role as a mentally disturbed woman who has been in a sanitarium, William Hudson is the husband and Yvette Vickers his girlfriend, all good enough in their respective characters.

•

ATTACK OF THE KILLER TOMATOES

1979, 87 mins, US Ⓥ col

Dir John De Bello ***Prod*** Steve Peace, John De Bello ***Scr*** Costa Dillon, Steve Peace, John De Bello ***Ph*** John K. Culley ***Ed*** John De Bello ***Mus*** Gordon Goodwin, Paul Sundfor

Act David Miller, George Wilson, Sharon Taylor, Jack Riley (Four Square)

Attack of the Killer Tomatoes, a low-budget indie production made by a group of young San Diego filmmakers, isn't even worthy of sarcasm. Plot, if it can be called that, concerns sudden growth spurt of tomatoes and their rampage.

Only saving grace is the satire pic's opening titles, a clever lampoon of theatre trailers and advertising pitches, including a mid-credit title card that boasts, "This space for rent." There's also a tongue-in-cheek parody of disaster pic music, sung in a deep basso voice, but that's over in about two minutes. Thereafter it's all downhill, rapidly.

•

AT THE CIRCUS

1939, 86 mins, US Ⓥ b/w

Dir Edward Buzzell ***Prod*** Mervyn LeRoy ***Scr*** Irving Brecher ***Ph*** Leonard M. Smith ***Ed*** William H. Terhune ***Mus*** Franz Waxman (dir.) ***Art*** Cedric Gibbons, Stan Rogers

Act Groucho Marx, Chico Marx, Harpo Marx, Margaret Dumont, Florence Rice, Kenny Baker (M-G-M)

The Marx Bros. revert to the rousing physical comedy and staccato gag dialog of their earlier pictures in *At the Circus*.

Story is slight but unimportant. Kenny Baker, owner of a circus, is harrassed by pursuing James Burke, who wants to foreclose the mortgage he holds on the outfit. When Baker's bankroll is stolen, Chico and Harpo call in Groucho to straighten out the difficulties. Groucho winds up by selling the circus for one performance to Margaret Dumont, Baker's rich aunt and Newport social leader.

Chico does his pianolog in circus car, while Harpo's turn for a harp solo is set up in the menagerie with a production and choral background. A colored kid band and adult chorus (from Hollywood company of *Swing Mikado*) are used here.

•

AT THE EARTH'S CORE

1976, 89 mins, UK Ⓥ col

Dir Kevin Connor ***Prod*** John Dark ***Scr*** Milton Subotsky ***Ph*** Alan Hume ***Ed*** John Ireland, Barry Peters ***Mus*** Mike Vickers ***Art*** Maurice Carter

Act Doug McClure, Peter Cushing, Caroline Munro, Cy Grant, Godfrey James, Sean Lynch (Amicus)

At the Earth's Core, from the Edgar Rice Burroughs novel, is an okay fantasy adventure film. Made in England, it's a fast-paced, slightly tongue-in-cheek tale about stalwart hero Doug McClure's battles with underground monsters. There's old-fashioned rooting interest in the outlandish exploits of McClure and his doddering old professor sidekick, Peter Cushing, who goes through the entire ordeal carrying his umbrella.

Pic takes place in the Victorian Era, charmingly evoked at the beginning when The Iron Mole, McClure and Cushing's experimental earth-boring contraption, embarks on a test mission. The machine goes awry, and they wind up in the land of Pellucidar, becoming slaves to a race of birdlike creatures. McClure falls in love with Caroline Munro, another captive.

Director Kevin Connor keeps the right balance of humor and straightforward adventure in the story, never making the fatal mistake of condescending to his plot or his audience.

•

AUSTIN POWERS
INTERNATIONAL MAN OF MYSTERY

1997, 89 mins, US Ⓥ ◉ ▭ col

Dir Jay Roach ***Prod*** Suzanne Todd, Demi Moore, Jennifer Todd, Mike Myers ***Scr*** Mike Myers ***Ph*** Peter Deming ***Ed*** Debra Neil-Fisher ***Mus*** George c. Clinton ***Art*** Cynthia Charette

Act Mike Myers, Elizabeth Hurley, Michael York, Mimi Rogers, Robert Wagner, Seth Green (Moving Pictures/Eric's Boys/New Line)

An all-stops-out spoof, this is one of the goofiest movies to come down the pike in a long time. A loving paean to Bond, Flint, Helm and their ilk (as well as a mountain of outlandish villains), the film knows its turf and only missteps when it ventures into more contemporary territory.

The mythic Powers (Mike Myers) is a bespectacled, mop-topped fruggin' Carnaby Street–tailored agent who calls women "baby" and is the height of fashion in a series of unnaturally colored crushed velvet suits. Back in 1967, he went toe to toe with Dr. Evil (also Myers), a bald, scarred criminal uberboss, who jumped into a cryogenic chamber. Not to be outdone, the British secret service also put their operative into deep freeze.

Thirty years later, Evil returns and the process of thawing the 000-agent begins. Both men are hopelessly out of date and therefore perfect adversaries. Back in action, Powers is teamed with Vanessa Kensington (Elizabeth Hurley), the daughter of his former partner (Mimi Rogers).

The tale barrels along with the hijack of missiles and the demand for $100 billion not to use them. There are zaftig sirens, newfangled gizmos, disco segues and a barrage of humorous nods to the heyday of secret agents on celluloid.

Tyro feature director Jay Roach makes a splashy, impressive debut. His sense of timing is generally adroit, as evidenced by a fiendishly clever sequence that hides "the naughty bits" and a hilarious dinner table sequence with all the principals.

Myers gets a real workout playing both the title role and his arch enemy. The strong supporting cast connects perfectly with the material, with Hurley displaying a true penchant for comedy. Pic's a wonderful rogue's gallery populated by the likes of vets Robert Wagner (as Evil's Number Two), Michael York, and a deft cameo from Carrie Fisher.

•

AUSTIN POWERS
THE SPY WHO SHAGGED ME

1999, 95 mins, US Ⓥ ◉ ▭ col

Dir Jay Roach ***Prod*** Suzanne Todd, Jennifer Todd, Demi Moore, Eric McLeod, John Lyons, Mike Myers ***Scr*** Mike Myers, Michael McCullers ***Ph*** Ueli Steiger ***Ed*** John Poll, Debra Neil-Fisher ***Mus*** George S. Clinton ***Art*** Rusty Smith

Act Mike Myers, Heather Graham, Michael York, Robert Wagner, Rob Lowe, Seth Green (Eric's Boy/Moving Pictures/Team Todd/New Line)

Expanded in every aspect save inspiration, the follow-up to the 1997 sleeper tickles the funny bone ably enough for 95 minutes, yet feels like a quickie where it ultimately counts most—in the writing.

Brit intelligence boss Basil Exposition (Michael York) calls in news that, natch, the world is again imperiled by arch-nemesis Dr. Evil (Myers), whose outerspace exile hasn't lasted long. Rejoining subordinates Frau Farbissina (Mindy Sterling), Number Two (Robert Wagner) and whiny teenage son, Scott (Seth Green), the doc now plans to plant a giant laser gun on the moon, picking off urban centers until his ransom demand is met.

Yea worse, he's rigged a flunky's time machine to travel to 1969, hypodermically stealing the "mojo" (viscous guck equated with Samson's hair) from our then-cryogenically frozen superhero. Soon Austin himself is tripping back to the Paisley Age, where curvaceous fellow agent Felicity Shagwell (Heather Graham) is his new ally.

Among the better new wrinkles are crybaby Scott's reunion with nefarious Dad on *The Jerry Springer Show* and a steamy chess game with bodacious enemy spy Ivana Humpalot (Kristen Johnston). It's also a hoot seeing Rob Lowe's spot-on Wagner impression as a younger Number Two. But major added characters—Dr. E's diminutive clone Mini-Me (Verne J. Troyer) and repulsive Scottish hit man Fat Bastard (Myers), who provokes far too much scatological humor—are just middling conceits.

Graham is a sexy, game partner who, like Elizabeth Hurley before her, doesn't really bring much comic flair of her own to the party.

1999: NOMINATION: Best Makeup

•

AUTUMN IN NEW YORK

2000, 103 mins, US Ⓥ ◉ col

Dir Joan Chen ***Prod*** Amy Robinson, Gary Lucchesi, Tom Rosenberg ***Scr*** Allison Burnett ***Ph*** Changwei Gu ***Ed*** Ruby Yang ***Mus*** Gabriel Yared ***Art*** Mark Friedberg

Act Richard Gere, Winona Ryder, Anthony LaPaglia, Elaine Stritch, Vera Farmiga, Sherry Stringfield, Jill Hennessy (MGM)

Autumn in New York is not a bad picture, just utterly banal. Desperately eager to register as a love affair in the mold of Hollywood's classics, Joan Chen's tediously sappy romantic meller is a kind of modern-day *Love Story* with a "new" twist: The casting of Richard Gere as a suave lover old enough to be Winona Ryder's father.

Meller's chief concession to the zeitgeist is its explicit acknowledgment of the lovers' age difference: Will (Gere) claims to be 48, and Charlotte (Ryder), 22. In actuality, both stars are older than their fictional characters, facts that shouldn't matter but somehow indicate the fake and facile nature of the entire proceedings.

At least half of the dialogue—and jokes—are about Will's age and history as a playboy. At first, Will expects yet another quick and easy fling with Charlotte. But, gradually, he realizes that Charlotte is more emotionally mature and intellectually savvy than she appears to be. The dates, which are not particularly erotic due to routine staging and weak chemistry between Gere and Ryder, serve mostly as platforms to propagate differing philosophies and intergenerational clashes.

During Hollywood's heyday, Cary Grant and Gary Cooper, to name two, played opposite alluring women who were half their age, but they didn't find the need to be defensive or apologetic about it. In this pic, however, Will Keane (Cooper's name in *High Noon* was Will Kane) is made to be an irresponsible playboy who needs to grow up. Who better to facilitate his maturation than a young woman who has limited time to live? Saccharin script is replete with movieish asides, beginning with Ryder's name, Charlotte, which recalls Bette Davis' famous heroine in *Now, Voyager*.

•

AVENGERS, THE
1998, 89 mins, US Ⓥ ⊙ col
Dir Jeremiah Chechik ***Prod*** Jerry Weintraub ***Scr*** Don MacPherson ***Ph*** Roger Pratt ***Ed*** Mick Audsley ***Mus*** Joel McNeely ***Art*** Stuart Craig
Act Ralph Fiennes, Uma Thurman, Sean Connery, Patrick Macnee, Jim Broadbent, Fiona Shaw (Warner)

While not the complete calamity that Warner Bros.' refusal to press-screen it suggested, *The Avengers* is a pretty thin cuppa Earl Grey.

Costing upward of $60 million yet running less than 90 minutes including credits, pic, which was bumped from its original June opening to a late-summer [August] dumping ground, makes a game effort at reviving the popular '60s British spy serial. What's missing is chemistry: the right blend of seriousness and whimsy, and charmingly compelling interplay between leads Ralph Fiennes and Uma Thurman, who turn in lackluster perfs.

Steed's (Fiennes) controllers, the paradoxically monikered Mother (Jim Broadbent) and Father (Fiona Shaw), bring him together with the chic, agile Emma Peel (Thurman) to combat the predation of an out-of-control project called Prospero, which threatens to wreak havoc on Britain's weather.

Mrs. Peel herself is initially suspected of being a player in Prospero's mischief, until it's revealed that she has an evil double who's working for the baddies. The chief culprit, meanwhile, is the climatologically monikered Sir August de Wynter (Sean Connery), a maniacal aristocrat who plans to reduce Britain to an arctic wasteland unless the nation agrees to fork over 10% of its GNP.

Pic's most stellar contributor is production designer Stuart Craig, who provides an imaginative look that deftly balances the '60s and the '90s, mod and postmodern, abstract and concrete. Don MacPherson's script tries for the same, but its version of the Steed-Peel pas de deux is like champagne that's lost its fizz.

Fiennes is bland and wimpy where rectitude and aplomb are needed. And Thurman does little more than give millions of guys reason to sigh, "Well, she's no Diana Rigg."

Patrick Macnee, the original Steed, provides a brief vocal cameo.

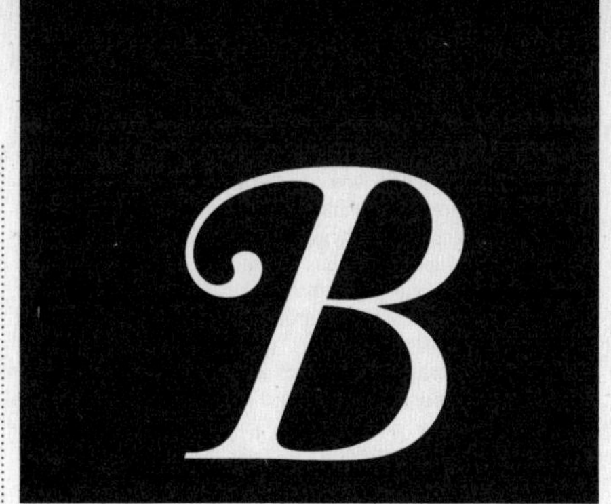

BABE, THE
1992, 113 mins, US Ⓥ ⊙ col
Dir Arthur Hiller ***Prod*** John Fusco ***Scr*** John Fusco ***Ph*** Haskell Wexler ***Ed*** Robert C. Jones ***Mus*** Elmer Bernstein ***Art*** James D. Vance
Act John Goodman, Kelly McGillis, Trini Alvarado, Bruce Boxleitner, Peter Donat, James Cromwell (Universal/Waterhorse)

Despite Haskell Wexler's alluring lensing, this thinly dramatized, overly episodic Babe Ruth biopic resembles a telepic that has lost its way onto the big screen.

Lovable TV star, erstwhile movie character actor John Goodman plays one of America's most endearing folk heroes. Though heavier with a bigger torso and thicker legs than the Bambino's incongruously spindly pins, Goodman otherwise has been made up into a remarkable likeness of the real Babe. Goodman has an exuberant, bumptious charm ideally suited to the overgrown child he's playing.

Starting in his Dickensian childhood when he's abandoned into the care of a boys' school in Baltimore, pic touchingly shows how the fat, unloved boy (Andy Voils) blossoms into an athletic marvel under the tutelage of a kindly Brother (James Cromwell). But it skips too quickly over Ruth's turbulent adolescent years. The rage and feelings of neglect that fueled Ruth's ambition aren't explored adequately.

Pic is so infatuated with the Babe, warts and all, that it fails to bring to life the feelings of his first wife (Trini Alvarado). His satisfying second marriage to a practical-minded showgirl (saucy Kelly McGillis) brings out a new strain of maturity in Ruth, but it's hardly big-league pic material.

•

BABE
1995, 94 mins, Australia/US Ⓥ ⊙ col
Dir Chris Noonan ***Prod*** George Miller, Doug Mitchell, Bill Miller ***Scr*** George Miller, Chris Noonan ***Ph*** Andrew Lesnie ***Ed*** Marcus D'Arcy, Jay Friedkin ***Mus*** Nigel Westlake ***Art*** Roger Ford
Act James Cromwell, Magda Szubanski (Kennedy Miller/Universal)

Babe is a dazzling family entertainment with enormous charm and breathtaking technical innovation. The Australia-set tale of a piglet who becomes a championship sheepdog is an unexpectedly enthralling story, relayed from the animals' perspective. It's done in a wholly unselfconscious manner with a combination of animatronic wizardry and human voice-overs.

Babe's story unfolds in a series of episodes with intriguing chapter cards such as *Crime and Punishment* and *Pigs Are Stupid*. His one-way ticket to pig paradise snatched from him by a carnival huckster, he winds up on Arthur Hoggett's (James Cromwell's) farm.

The perplexed piglet is taken under the paw of Fly, a Border collie who has just delivered a litter. But Ferdinand—a duck who lives in fear of becoming Christmas dinner—preys on his naivete and gets the oinker into sufficient trouble to make him a replacement candidate for the Yuletide platter.

Initially, it's a bit of a shocker to watch a family drama unfold in which the cast comprises real-life, fuzzy creatures and where humans get the "pet" roles. Nonetheless, you can't stop watching.

Director Chris Noonan, who co-adapted Dick King-Smith's kid lit *The Sheep-Pig* with producer George Miller (who helmed *Mad Max*), basically gives his material a serious bent, though there's plenty of comic relief. Miller apparently nursed this project along for seven years.

1995: Best Visual Effects

NOMINATIONS: Best Picture, Best Supp. Actor (James Cromwell), Director, Screenplay Adaptation, Film Editing, Best Art Direction

•

BABE
PIG IN THE CITY
1998, 97 mins, Australia/US Ⓥ ⊙ col
Dir George Miller ***Prod*** George Miller, Doug Mitchell, Bill Miller ***Scr*** George Miller, Judy Morris, Mark Lamprell ***Ph*** Andrew Lesnie ***Ed*** Jay Friedkin, Margaret Sixel ***Mus*** Nigel Westlake ***Art*** Roger Ford
Act Magda Szubanski, James Cromwell, Mary Stein, Mickey Rooney, Julie Godfrey (Kennedy Miller/Universal)

There is plenty of fun in this $80 million cinematic menagerie, consummate screen magic and a series of well-intentioned messages that sidestep the cloying and saccharine.

New chapter picks up pretty much where the young porker was last seen. Having earned his stripes as a champion sheep "dog," Babe experiences his 15 minutes of fame, which spawn myriad invitations, including one to visit the Queen of England. Back on the farm, life resumes. But a freak accident results in farmer Hoggett (James Cromwell) falling down a well and being unable to work.

Hoggett's well-meaning zaftig wife, Esme (Magda Szubanski), fails miserably at maintaining the spread, and faceless bankers arrive with a notice of foreclosure. The solution to the financial plight is to accept an invitation, with a generous fee attached, for Babe to demonstrate his herding prowess at a big fair far, far away.

Stuck in the big city, they are directed to a rooming house, the Flealands Hotel, where pets are welcome. Babe and Esme are the proverbial rubes cast adrift in this jungle, with their innate goodness allowing them not only to swim among the sharks but, eventually, to lead the pack to more noble pursuits.

Pic straddles the animal and human worlds, invests the nonhumans with emotional qualities and flips the image by turning the more traditional cast members into well-observed Hogarthian creatures with bestial qualities. Szubanski, Mary Stein as the Flealand owner and Mickey Rooney [as Fugley Floom, a human in a performing apes act] play their roles at perfect pitch.

The seamless mix of real and animatronic animals is a testament to the vision of the creative team. As with the original, it's the rare instance where one is conscious of the difference, largely because one is caught up with the characters and story.

•

BABES IN ARMS
1939, 93 mins, US Ⓥ ⊙ b/w
Dir Busby Berkeley ***Prod*** Arthur Freed ***Scr*** Jack MacGowan, Kay Van Riper ***Ph*** Ray June ***Ed*** Frank Sullivan ***Mus*** Georgie Stoll (dir.) ***Art*** Cedric Gibbons, Merrill Pye
Act Mickey Rooney, Judy Garland, Charles Winninger, Guy Kibbee, June Preisser (M-G-M)

Film version of the Rodgers and Hart [1937] musical has been considerably embellished in its transfer to the screen. Basic idea is there, and two songs are retained. Otherwise, it's a greatly enhanced piece of entertainment, with Mickey Rooney having a field day parading his versatile talents.

He sings, dances, gives out with a series of imitations including Eddie Leonard, Clark Gable, Lionel Barrymore, President Roosevelt. With Judy Garland he sings "Good Mornning," a new tune by Nacio Herb Brown and producer Arthur Freed; he pounds the ivories; he directs a kid show to provide impersonations, and a dinner table sequence, with mix-up of decision on the silverware, is an old routine but his technique and timing make for grand fun.

Direction by Busby Berkeley is enthusiastic and at a fast clip throughout.

1939: NOMINATIONS: Best Actor (Mickey Rooney), Score

•

BABES IN TOYLAND
1934, 79 mins, US Ⓥ ⊙ b/w
Dir Charles Rogers, Gus Meins ***Prod*** Hal Roach ***Scr*** Nick Grinde, Frank Butler ***Ph*** Art Lloyd, Francis Corby ***Ed*** William Terhune, Bert Jordan
Act Stan Laurel, Oliver Hardy, Charlotte Henry, Felix Knight, Henry Brandon, Marie Wilson (Roach/M-G-M)

Babes in Toyland is faraway from the Victor Herbert original operetta. The arithmetic song and "March of the Toys" are the only outstanding survivors of Herbert's score, and these are merely background. Two other lesser numbers are used. Of the original book there is no trace at all. This is not a musical brought to the screen. It is a fairy story in technique and treatment, but a gorgeous fairy tale, which gives everything to Laurel and Hardy and to which, in return, they give their happiest best.

The story is simple. Tom-Tom loves Bo-Peep, who is one of the numerous progeny of the Old Woman who lived in a shoe. Barnaby, a miser, holds the mortgage. Bo-Peep must marry him or else. Hardy promises to redeem the mortgage, but he and Laurel get fired from the toy shop when they make 100 soldiers six feet tall instead of 600 each a foot high. For this they are punished, but Bo-Peep begs them off, promising Barnaby she will marry him. Barnaby really is married to Laurel in bride's dress. He frames Tom, who is exiled to Bogeyland, whither Bo-Peep follows him. The comedians follow and help them to effect their escape. This brings a smashing climax with the soldiers marching to the strains of "March of the Toys."

All Mother Goose characters are woven into the plot, not to mention the Three Little Pigs, but it's Laurel and Hardy's picture. While they are on the story zips along, but the mistake has not been made of asking them to fill the stage continuously.

•

BABES IN TOYLAND
1961, 106 mins, US Ⓥ col
Dir Jack Donohue ***Scr*** Ward Kimball, Joe Rinaldi, Lowell S. Hawley ***Ph*** Edward Colman ***Ed*** Robert Stafford ***Mus*** George Bruns (adapt.) ***Art*** Carroll Clark, Marvin Ambrey Davis
Act Ray Bolger, Tommy Sands, Annette Funicello, Ed Wynn, Tommy Kirk, Kevin Corcoran (Walt Disney)

Walt Disney's first live-action musical, a lavish translation to the screen of Victor Herbert's operetta *Babes in Toyland*, is an expensive gift, brightly wrapped and intricately packaged. But some of the more mature patrons may be distressed to discover that quaint, charming *Toyland* has been transformed into a rather gaudy and mechanical *Fantasyland*. What actually emerges is *Babes in Disneyland*.

The Disney concept of *Toyland* falls somewhere in that never-never land where the techniques of the stage, the live action screen and the animated cartoon overlap.

Ray Bolger is the standout member of the cast. As the arch-villain out to dispose of Tommy Sands in order to wed the heiress, Annette Funicello, he delivers a sly, rollicking, congenially menacing portrayal. His rubber-legged hoofing shows to special advantge on a *Castles in Spain* number.

Sands and Funicello are rather wooden as the young lovers, but each has an opportunity to display vocal prowess and capable choreographic footwork. Ed Wynn and Tommy Kirk score as toymaker and assistant.

Modernization of Herbert's evergreen score has been accomplished smoothly by George Bruns, Mel Leven's new libretto and lyrics are clever, but some of the simple charm of the original words, such as in the delightful "I Can't Do the Sum," have been sacrificed for purposes of visual trickery. Tommy Mahoney's choreography is brisk and workable, with best results obtained in an exciting dance of gypsies.

•

BABES ON BROADWAY
1942, 121 mins, US Ⓥ ⊙ col
Dir Busby Berkeley ***Prod*** Arthur Freed ***Scr*** Fred Finklehoffe, Elaine Ryan ***Ph*** Lester White ***Ed*** Fredrick Y. Smith ***Mus*** Georgie Stoll (dir.), Roger Edens (adapt.) ***Art*** Cedric Gibbons, Malcolm Brown
Act Mickey Rooney, Judy Garland, Richard Quine, Fay Bainter (M-G-M)

If all the energy used by Mickey Rooney in making *Babes on Broadway* could be assembled in one place, there would be enough to sustain a flying fortress in the stratosphere from Hollywood to New York and return, non-stop. And there might be some left over. Teamed with Judy Garland in a filmusical which is very similar to their previous efforts, Rooney is as fresh as the proverbial daisy at the end of two hours of strenuous theatrical calisthenics. He dances, sings, acts and does imitations—dozens of them.

There isn't time to catch one's breath from the opening moment to the closing fadeout of Rooney and Garland giving their all in one of those Metro production numbers, where the stage, the scenery, the actors and some of the audience are doing a gigantic revolution around the camera. In between, there is related a story [by Fred Finklehoffe] about young performers battling for their "chance" on Broadway.

Busby Berkeley directs this sort of thing about as well as anybody. But both Rooney and Garland are fast outgrowing this type of presentation, which depends entirely on the ahs and ohs that spring from watching precocious children.

1942: NOMINATION: Best Song ("How About You")

•

BABETTE'S FEAST
SEE: BABETTE'S GÆSTEBUD

•

BABETTE'S GAESTEBUD
(BABETTE'S FEAST)
1987, 102 mins, Denmark Ⓥ ⦿ col
Dir Gabriel Axel ***Prod*** Just Betzer, Bo Christensen ***Scr*** Gabriel Axel ***Ph*** Henning Kristiansen ***Ed*** Finn Henriksen ***Mus*** Per Norgard ***Art*** Sven Wichman
Act Stephane Audran, Jean-Philippe Lafont, Gudmar Wivesson, Jarl Kulle, Bibi Andersson, Ebbe Rode (Panorama)

Isak Dinesen's most widely read work, next to *Out of Africa*, is the short novel *Babette's Feast*, a rousing yarn of delicate philosophical overtones about a French female *chef de cuisine* of five-star repute, exiled after the Paris uprisings of 1871, who survives as a maid and cook to a couple of elderly puritan and devout spinster daughters of a strict sectarian vicar-prophet, now passed away, on a remote and rugged Scandinavian North Sea coast.

Story has its title character (France's Stephane Audran) given a fling at preparing and serving up one final great dinner by blowing on it her entire 10,000 Golden Francs winnings from a lottery ticket. At the table are the villagers, sect members lately fallen to bickering among themselves, innocent and even averse to any food beyond brown bread soup and dried cod with water on the side. A visiting Swedish general and diplomat (Jarl Kulle), once a suitor to one of the vicar's daughters, has happened by, too. Now, they are all momentarily propelled spiritually heavenwards by what they eat and drink.

After a somewhat lingering start, veteran helmer Gabriel Axel succeeds where it really counts. On the screen he serves up the famous dinner with vigor and juicy detail. What bogs *Babette* down a bit at the outset is Axel's resorting to voice-over narration technique in supplying story background and motivations. Still, the overall mood of the original story is faithfully retained, and Sweden's Kulle, one of Ingmar Bergman's favorite actors, matches Audran in wit and depth although the two are never seen together.

•

BABY BOOM
1987, 103 mins, US Ⓥ ⦿ col
Dir Charles Shyer ***Prod*** Nancy Meyers ***Scr*** Nancy Meyers, Charles Shyer ***Ph*** William A. Fraker ***Ed*** Lynzee Klingman ***Mus*** Bill Conti ***Art*** Jeffrey Howard
Act Diane Keaton, Harold Ramis, Sam Wanamaker, James Spader, Pat Hingle, Sam Shepard (United Artists)

A transparent and one-dimensional parable about a power-devouring female careerist and the unwanted bundle of joy that turns her obsessive fast-track life in Gotham upside-down. Constructed almost entirely upon facile and familiar media cliches about "parenting" and the super-yuppie set, *Baby Boom* has the superficiality of a project inspired by a lame *New York* magazine cover story and sketched out on a cocktail napkin at Spago's.

J. C. Wiatt (Diane Keaton) is a dressed-for-success management consultant whose steamroller ambition has earned this workaholic the proudly flaunted nickname "Tiger Lady." She lives in trendy high-rise splendor with bland investment banker Steven Buchner (Harold Ramis), to whom she reluctantly allots a four-minute slot for lovemaking before returning to late-night paperwork.

Suddenly, J. C. learns that a cousin has died together with her husband in an accident in England. J. C. is intrigued to learn that she's inherited something from this misfortune but, to her considerable shock, this turns out to be a precious apple-cheeked 12-month-old girl, Elizabeth (Kristina and Michelle Kennedy).

Baby Boom tries to be a lot funnier than it actually is, and handsome production design and cinematography do little to compensate for its annoying over-reliance on cornball action montages and a dreadfully saccharine soundtrack score.

•

BABY DOLL
1956, 114 mins, US Ⓥ b/w
Dir Elia Kazan ***Prod*** Elia Kazan ***Scr*** Tennessee Williams ***Ph*** Boris Kaufman ***Ed*** Gene Milford ***Mus*** Kenyon Hopkins ***Art*** Richard Sylbert, Paul Sylbert
Act Karl Malden, Carroll Baker, Eli Wallach, Mildred Dunnock, Lonny Chapman (Newtown)

Except for moments of humor that are strictly inherent in the character of the principals, *Baby Doll* plays off against a sleazy, dirty, depressing Southern background. Over it hangs a feeling of decay, expertly nurtured by director Elia Kazan.

Baby Doll is based on a 1941 Tennessee Williams vignette, dramatized on Broadway in 1955 as *27 Wagons Full of Cotton.*

Story briefly has Carroll Baker, an immature teenager, married to middle-aged Karl Malden, who runs a cotton gin. When their on-credit furniture is carted away, Malden sets fire to the Syndicate cotton gin in town. Suspecting Malden, Eli Wallach—owner of the gin—carts his cotton to Malden's gin for processing but then proceeds to seduce Baker, who signs a note confessing that Malden committed the arson. Malden, who has promised not to touch his young wife until one year after their marriage, finds Baker and Wallach together in the house and goes berserk with jealousy.

Baker's performance captures all the animal charm, the naivete, the vanity, contempt and rising passion of Baby Doll.

Wallach as the vengeful Vacarro plays it to the hilt. Malden is cast to perfection and turns in a sock performance.

1956: NOMINATIONS: Best Actress (Carroll Baker), Supp. Actress (Mildred Dunnock), Adapted Screenplay, B&W Cinematography

•

BABY FACE NELSON
1957, 85 mins, US Ⓥ b/w
Dir Don Siegel ***Prod*** Al Zimbalist ***Scr*** Irving Shulman, Daniel Mainwaring ***Ph*** Hal Mohr ***Ed*** Leon Barsha ***Mus*** Van Alexander ***Art*** David Milton
Act Mickey Rooney, Carolyn Jones, Cedric Hardwicke, Leo Gordon, Anthony Caruso, Jack Elam (Fryman-ZS/United Artists)

Nelson was a member of the notorious Dillinger gang that scourged the Midwest circa 1933. The script [from a story by Robert Adler] makes him a ruthless, trigger-happy, cold-blooded killer.

The versatile Mickey Rooney is not particularly convincing as the pint-sized Nelson. He snarls, boils with hatred and is unrepentant. But he merely seems to be going through the motions and his performance never matches the acting found in gangster classics.

More impressive is Carolyn Jones's portrayal of Rooney's loyal moll. She's a plain-Jane who's attracted to him by some strange affection. But with the FBI closing in on the wounded Rooney, it is she who kills him when he admits he would even shoot down small boys.

•

BABYFEVER
1994, 110 mins, US Ⓥ ⦿ col
Dir Henry Jaglom ***Prod*** Judith Wolinsky ***Scr*** Henry Jaglom, Victoria Foyt ***Ph*** Hanania Baer ***Ed*** Henry Jaglom
Act Victoria Foyt, Matt Salinger, Dinah Lenney, Eric Roberts, Frances Fisher, Zack Norman (Jagtoria)

Henry Jaglom's *Babyfever* is to women and their biological clocks what his 1991 *Eating* was to women and their relationship with food. The indie filmmaker fashions a stylistic blend of fictional story, based on his own experience, and documentary, using interviews with many women, that emerges as overly long, fractured and only intermittently entertaining.

Victoria Foyt (Jaglom's wife) stars as Gena, an attractive middle-aged career woman who can't make up her mind whether she wants to have a baby with James (Matt Salinger), her sensitive b.f. Just when Gena is about to make a commitment, old flame Anthony (Eric Roberts) reappears with a proposition that confuses her even more.

While *Babyfever* is a more focused film, its anecdotal narrative is not as rich as that of *Eating*, where food served as both a metaphor and a substitute for love and sex.

It's too bad that lovely actresses like Frances Fisher (*Unforgiven*) are made to ask—straight-faced—about pregnancy and artificial insemination. The most disappointing element of *Babyfever* is how conventional and humorless the material is.

•

BABY, IT'S YOU
1983, 105 mins, US Ⓥ ⦿ col
Dir John Sayles ***Prod*** Griffin Dunne, Amy Robinson ***Scr*** John Sayles ***Ph*** Michael Ballhaus ***Ed*** Sonya Polonsky ***Art*** Jeffrey Townsend
Act Rosanna Arquette, Vincent Spano, Joanna Merlin, Jack Davidson, Nick Ferrari, Dolores Messina (Double Play)

Despite some strong thematic material and a vibrant central performance, *Baby, It's You* remains an essentially unfulfilled romantic drama. John Sayles's third directorial outing, penned from a story by co-producer Amy Robinson, improves as it moves along from 1966 to a slightly later time frame, but can't recoup from the ultimately unbelievable pairing of leading characters.

Film has an elegantly dressed Italian street kid with the mysterious name of Sheik pursue, win, lose and, at length, haunt the emotional life of a bright, ambitious and terribly attractive high school drama student, Jill.

When the pair split at the time of her prom, after an affectionate but still chaste courtship, the two travel radically different roads from Trenton, NJ: she to school and encroaching hippiedom, and he to Miami to follow his dream of being Frank Sinatra.

In spite of being a character that could have used more fleshing out in the writing, it's Rosanna Arquette who makes *Baby, It's You* persistently watchable. Resembling something of a more voluptuous cross between Nastassja Kinski and Andrey Hepburn, to whom her character is compared in the film, Arquette's exceedingly alive performance shows great potential. As the Sinatra idolator, Vincent Spano, with his hair greased back and clothes beautifully pressed, looks just like the poor man's idea of elegance he's supposed to embody. He does a good turn, but unavoidably suffers from miscasting of his character opposite Arquette's.

•

BABYLON
1980, 95 mins, UK Ⓥ col
Dir Franco Rosso ***Prod*** Gavrik Losey ***Scr*** Martin Stellman, Franco Rosso ***Ph*** Chris Menges ***Ed*** Thomas Schwalm ***Mus*** Denis Bovell, Aswad ***Art*** Brian Savegar
Act Brinsley Forde, Karl Howman, Trevor Laird (Diversity Music/NFFC/Chrysalis/Lee Electric)

Like the reggae music that pulses through it, *Babylon* is rich, rough and real. And like the streetlife of the young black Londoners it portrays, it's threatening, touching, violent and funny. This one seems to explode in the gut with a powerful mix of pain and pleasure. The screenplay was originally commissioned as a BBC-TV play. Subsequent rewrites, while triumphantly upgrading it to the level of big-screen fare, have at the same time sharpened rather than softened that controversial angle.

Brinsley Forde plays the dreadlocked fellow whose problems at the outset are no more than everyday irritants.

By the end, however, he's lost his job, been chased, beaten by police, discovered his precious sound equipment has been ripped to pieces at the group's backstreet base by nearby white residents, and he's plunged a screwdriver into the stomach of the man he knows is responsible.

•

BABY MAKER, THE
1970, 109 mins, US Ⓥ col
Dir James Bridges ***Prod*** Richard Goldstone ***Scr*** James Bridges ***Ph*** Charles Rosher, Jr. ***Ed*** Walter Thompson ***Mus*** Fred Karlin ***Art*** Mort Rabinowitz
Act Barbara Hershey, Collin Wilcox-Horne, Sam Groom, Scott Glenn, Jeannie Berlin, Lili Valenty (National General/Wise)

The Baby Maker is an offbeat story of a childless couple who hire a young girl to conceive by the husband.

Director James Bridges's story is stronger than his direction of players, though the physical staging is admirable.

Collin Wilcox-Horne and Sam Groom are a barren couple, who hire Barbara Hershey to bear his child. This in turn shatters the girl's relationship with Scott Glenn, both of whom are from the love generation. Development of an emotional relationship between Hershey and Groom is more than implicit.

Wilcox-Horne is excellent in a multi-faceted performance: sometimes warm and loving, occasionally on the verge of jealousy, but always sincere in her character's motivations and reactions. Hers is the film's best performance.

Glenn comes over well as the frustrated but likeable lover. His role is important if subsidiary, and he handles it very well.

1970: NOMINATION: Best Original Song Score

•

BABY OF MACON, THE
1993, 122 mins, Netherlands/France Ⓥ col
Dir Peter Greenaway ***Prod*** Kees Kasander ***Scr*** Peter Greenaway ***Ph*** Sachy Vierny ***Ed*** Chris Wyatt ***Art*** Ben Van Os, Jan Roelfs
Act Julia Ormond, Ralph Fiennes, Philip Stone, Jonathan Lacey, Don Henderson, Jeff Nuttall (Allarts/UGC)

Peter Greenaway's *The Baby of Macon* is all fluff and no filling. Visually sumptuous and laden with religious refs and Brechtian devices, this elaborate but overlong film of a play about the birth of a 17th-century miracle child and his short-lived period of grace plays like a tired rerun of the director's previous extravaganzas.

Entire film takes place in a single giant set that includes audience and performers, gathered for an elaborate theatrical masque to celebrate fertility. The community is plagued by barrenness, seen as God's punishment for letting the local cathedral fall into disrepair. The miracle child quickly becomes an icon for the region's barren mothers, and one of its sisters (Julia Ormond) uses the window of opportunity to claim to be its rightful mother. The fact she's still a virgin doesn't cramp her style.

While Greenaway's previous movies have been a cornucopia of challenging ideas and intellectual jeux, this one quickly starts going round in circles once the board has been laid out. Still, as a master of the ornate, Greenaway is firing on all cylinders.

•

BABY'S DAY OUT
1994, 98 mins, US Ⓥ ⊙ col
Dir Patrick Read Johnson ***Prod*** John Hughes, Richard Vane ***Scr*** John Hughes ***Ph*** Thomas Ackerman ***Ed*** David Rawlins ***Mus*** Bruce Broughton ***Art*** Doug Kramer
Act Joe Mantegna, Lara Flynn Boyle, Joe Pantoliano, Brian Haley, Cynthia Nixon, Fred Dalton Thompson (20th Century-Fox)

Somewhere, far too late in the plot progression of *Baby's Day Out*, one of the villains eyes the camera and declares, "This isn't funny anymore." Offering from writer-producer John Hughes is a tired retread of past comic formulas played a pitch higher, a rhythm faster. It tries too hard to please and fails miserably.

The plot is rather like a pre-pubescent spin on O. Henry's *The Ransom of Red Chief*. A trio of kidnappers (Joe Mantegna, Joe Pantoliano, Brian Haley) pose as baby photographers to gain access to the home of an old-money Chicago couple (Lara Flynn Boyle and Matthew Glave). At an opportune moment they snatch the infant son and hide out until their ransom demands are met.

The foolproof plan goes awry when 9-month-old Bennington August Cottwell IV, aka Baby Bink, crawls out of an apartment window and into the hustle bustle of downtown. For the ensuing period, the three stooges, the Cotwell household and the authorities are just a few baby steps behind the object of desire and love.

It's a simple enough premise, but neither Hughes nor director Patrick Read Johnson provides much in the way of novelty. The action is either played out for slapstick or dripping with pathos. Either tack is geared toward obvious results.

•

BABY . . .
SECRET OF THE LOST LEGEND
1985, 95 mins, US Ⓥ ⊙ ▭ col
Dir B.W.L. Norton ***Prod*** Jonathan T. Taplin ***Scr*** Clifford Green, Ellen Green ***Ph*** John Alcott ***Ed*** Howard Smith, David Bretherton ***Mus*** Jerry Goldsmith ***Art*** Raymond G. Storey
Act William Katt, Sean Young, Patrick McGoohan, Julian Fellowes, Kyalo Mativo, Hugh Quarshie (Touchstone)

A huggable prehistoric hatchling is discovered by a young American couple in an African rain forest. Story has an engaging performance from William Katt, who plays the sportswriter husband of paleontologist Sean Young. Latter, whose maternal and scientific instincts propel events, is rather bland.

Evil foil is Patrick McGoohan as a rival, ruthless paleontologist who enlists the aid of a rapacious revolutionary army to capture Baby's towering brontosaurus mama, after overzealous soldiers gun down the 70-or-so-foot-tall papa.

Katt and Young risk their lives to save the baby, who stretches 10 feet, has a kind of *E.T.* winsomeness, and once even hops like a shaggy family pooch in between the covers of Katt and Young.

Dinosaur movements derive from both cable and from operators who were inside the gargantuan structures.

•

BABY-SITTERS CLUB, THE
1995, 94 mins, US Ⓥ col
Dir Melanie Mayron ***Prod*** Jane Startz, Peter O. Almond ***Scr*** Dalene Young ***Ph*** Willy Kurant ***Ed*** Christopher Greenbury ***Mus*** David Michael Frank ***Art*** Larry Fulton
Act Schuyler Fisk, Bre Blair, Rachael Leigh Cook, Larisa Oleynik, Tricia Joe, Stacey Linn Ramsower (Scholastic/Beacon)

The popular kid lit (and cable series) *The Baby-sitters Club* [from the book series by Ann M. Martin] comes to the bigscreen as a warm, cuddly and earnest tale of modern youth. Resembling one of television's Afterschool Specials, it has the snuggly quality of a security blanket. This particular episode, so to speak, centers on the seven young girls who comprise the title group and their efforts to open up a summer day-care camp for their charges. Because of the large congregation of characters, the story is largely a series of vignettes.

The most serious plot thread involves group leader Kristy (Schuyler Fisk) and her sub-rosa relationship with her estranged father (Peter Horton). He's arrived back in the quaint Connecticut town to pursue a job opening at the local newspaper. He insists she keep mum about his presence.

The picture's problem is that it is small in every way. Tyro director Melanie Mayron does yeoman work, eliciting perky performances from a predominantly untried cast. She's slightly less effective with her adults.

•

BABY THE RAIN MUST FALL
1965, 93 mins, US Ⓥ ⊙ b/w
Dir Robert Mulligan ***Prod*** Alan J. Pakula ***Scr*** Horton Foote ***Ph*** Ernest Laszlo ***Ed*** Aaron Stell ***Mus*** Elmer Bernstein ***Art*** Roland Anderson
Act Lee Remick, Steve McQueen, Don Murray, Paul Fix, Josephine Hutchinson, Ruth White (Park Place/Solar)

Chief assets of Pakula-Mulligan's *Baby the Rain Must Fall* [from Horton Foote's play *The Traveling Lady*] are outstanding performances by its stars and an emotional punch that lingers. Steve McQueen is exactly right as irresponsible rockabilly singer, Lee Remick portrays his wife sensitively, and newcomer Kimberly Block is charming and unaffected as their six-year-old daughter.

McQueen, raised by dictatorial spinster (Georgia Simmons) who disapproves of his singing in roadhouses, is trouble-prone rebel. When story opens he is free on parole for a stabbing, and is joined by Remick and Block, wife and daughter he had kept secret.

Remick is vividly alive in spontaneous-appearing scenes with daughter. But director Robert Mulligan apparently was so determined to avoid soap-opera clichés that he did not permit actress to register negative emotion beyond look of distraught unhappiness even though sad events should have allowed room for tears.

Other cast members are adequate, but roles suffer from editorial cuts (confirmed by director) that leave subplots dangling.

•

BACHELOR, THE
1999, 101 mins, US Ⓥ ⊙ col
Dir Gary Sinyor ***Prod*** Lloyd Segan, Bing Howenstein ***Scr*** Steve Cohen ***Ph*** Simon Archer ***Ed*** Robert Reitano ***Mus*** David A. Hughes, John Murphy ***Art*** Craig Stearns
Act Chris O'Donnell, Renee Zellweger, Hal Holbrook, James Cromwell, Artie Lange, Edward Asner (Segan/New Line)

You don't have to know and love Buster Keaton's 1925 farce *Seven Chances* to dislike the modern remake *The Bachelor*, although it certainly doesn't hurt. A remarkably mirthless and inept romantic comedy about a young man who must marry within a day if he's to inherit $100 million, new pic is woefully misconceived on virtually every level.

The most memorable sight in Keaton's zippy comedy was that of dozens, if not hundreds, of prospective brides in hot pursuit of the stone-faced, would-be heir through the streets. Action climax of this new version reproduces this image and predictably magnifies it, as 1,000 bridal-gowned women race up and down the steep hills of San Francisco.

Jimmy Shannon (Chris O'Donnell, also aboard as exec producer) is a good-looking but otherwise uninteresting confirmed bachelor who, after three years with g.f. Anne (Renee Zellweger), reaches the relationships crossroads. Then the videotaped will of his grandfather (Peter Ustinov) reveals that he will receive 100 very big ones only if he marries by 6:05 P.M. on his 30th birthday. Naturally, his birthday is the very next day.

Jimmy rushes off to propose to Anne once again, this time enthusiastically. She's still not convinced, so Jimmy spends most of the remaining 27 hours tracking down some of his former girlfriends and discovering, to his distress, just how unmercenary they are.

O'Donnell's Jimmy is as bland as bland can be, and thesp lacks the comic chops to add humor. Zellweger comes off far less well here than in her other major films.

•

BACHELOR AND THE BOBBY-SOXER, THE
1947, 94 mins, US Ⓥ ⊙ b/w
Dir Irving Reis ***Prod*** Dore Schary ***Scr*** Sidney Sheldon ***Ph*** Robert de Grasse, Nicholas Musuraca ***Ed*** Frederick Knudtson ***Mus*** Leigh Harline ***Art*** Albert S. D'Agostino, Carroll Clark
Act Cary Grant, Myrna Loy, Shirley Temple, Rudy Vallee, Ray Collins, Harry Davenport (RKO)

The Bachelor and the Bobby-Soxer poses a plot easily adapted to fluffy situations. Tossed together are a lady judge, a playboy artist and an impressionable teenager. Grant, the artist, has already had a brush with the judge, Myrna Loy, so when the judge's kid sister, Shirley Temple, is found in the artist's apartment late at night, he's in plenty of trouble. Court psychiatrist proposes that, rather than make Grant a martyr in Temple's eyes, he be assigned to escort her around until she gets over her crush.

Chuckles get heartier and heartier as adult Grant plays at being a juvenile at basketball games, school picnics, etc. It's done with slapstick touch that pays off. Romance switch with Loy going for Grant is an obvious development but well done.

1947: Best Original Screenplay

•

BACHELOR FATHER
1931, 84 mins, US b/w
Dir Robert Z. Leonard ***Scr*** Laurence E. Johnson ***Ph*** Oliver T. Marsh ***Ed*** Harry Reynolds
Act Marion Davies, Ralph Forbes, C. Aubrey Smith, Ray Milland, Guinn Williams, David Torrence (M-G-M)

Marion Davies plays with debonair comedy with just the touch of rowdiness, and relieved at the other extreme with the merest suggestion of under-the-surface sentiment.

Story is pure comedy almost to the end, but late sequences weave in a neatly contrasting note of jaunty sentiment that gives the picture the touch of legit comedy drama.

Picture has a beautiful balance of pattern in the playing. C. Aubrey Smith, who created the part of the crusty British nobleman in the Belasco stage production [by Edward Childs Carpenter], is in the picture with a screen portrait that is a gem, while Ralph Forbes brings a suave gentility to the juvenile lead in admirable contrast to the flamboyant playing of the star.

Picture has a more spirited finish than the play, giving it the advantage of dramatic suspense that lasts right up to the final foot. The out-of-favor Davies has gone to the flying field desperately determined to make a transatlantic plane flight, while her lover speeds to the airfield to prevent the gamble with death. Meanwhile the old peer remains at home, listening with anxiety to a radio broadcast of the takeoff on the hop. Alternating shots of these three elements in the episode builds the climax.

•

BACHELOR FLAT
1961, 92 mins, US ▭ col
Dir Frank Tashlin ***Prod*** Jack Cummings ***Scr*** Frank Tashlin, Budd Grossman ***Ph*** Daniel L. Fapp ***Ed*** Hugh S. Fowler ***Mus*** John Williams ***Art*** Jack Martin Smith, Leland Fuller
Act Tuesday Weld, Richard Beymer, Terry-Thomas, Celeste Holm, Francesca Bellini, Howard McNear (20th Century-Fox)

Carry on Archaeologist might be an apt subtitle for this frivolous, farcical concoction about a British bone specialist (dinosaur variety) who is irresistibly attractive to the predatory, modern American female. Frank Tashlin directed from his own screenplay, written with Budd Grossman, who wrote the play. Terry-Thomas is the archaeology professor situated in California, where he is on the verge of wedlock with a roving fashion designer (Celeste Holm) who is abroad on business as the nuptial date aproaches. T-T's path to the altar is complicated by: (1) the unscheduled advent of Tuesday Weld, who is Holm's daughter, unbeknownst to the prof; (2) regular invasions of his bachelor quarters by campus cuties; (3) the irresponsible advice of cynical student-neighbor Richard Beymer, who has a crush on Tuesday; (4) the singleness-of-purpose of Beymer's dachshund, a typical bona-Fido determined to bury the professor's prize possession—a rare dinosaur bone.

Except for Terry-Thomas, whose comic intuition and creativity is responsible for most of the merriment, it is the supporting cast, rather than the principals, that comes through on the comedy end. Neither Weld nor Beymer seems comfortably at home in farce, and the strain often shows through. Holm, a formidable light comedienne, is stuck regrettably in a rather bland role. Francesca Bellini, a well-constructed ballerina, shows a flair for comedy as an oversexed lush equipped with an instant martini kit and disposition to match.

The dachshund, incidentally, is an accomplished low comedienne.

•

BACHELOR GIRL APARTMENT
SEE: ANY WEDNESDAY

•

BACHELOR IN PARADISE
1961, 109 mins, US ▭ col
Dir Jack Arnold ***Prod*** Ted Richmond ***Scr*** Valentine Davies, Hal Kanter ***Ph*** Joseph Ruttenberg ***Ed*** Richard W. Farrell ***Mus*** Henry Mancini ***Art*** George W. Davis, Hans Peters
Act Bob Hope, Lana Turner, Janis Paige, Jim Hutton, Paula Prentiss, Agnes Moorehead (M-G-M)

The screenplay, taken from a Vera Caspary story, is a no-depth (but easy to take) yarn that has Bob Hope as a writer whose business affairs are mismanaged with the result that he's in hock to Internal Revenue. He goes to a newly developed California community to indite something on what makes American women tick.

The women in town, all young marrieds and pretty, take to him, either for his counsel on marital affairs or a flirtation walk now and then. Actually, though, Hope is innocent of any romantic hanky-panky and eventually announces his love for Lana Turner, the only single girl in the vicinity.

Nothing special about the performances, but then not too much is demanded.

●

BACHELOR MOTHER
1939, 80 mins, US Ⓥ ⊙ b/w
Dir Garson Kanin ***Prod*** Buddy De Sylva ***Scr*** Norman Krasna ***Ph*** Robert de Grasse ***Ed*** Henry Berman, Robert Wise ***Mus*** Roy Webb ***Art*** Van Nest Polglase, Carroll Clark
Act Ginger Rogers, David Niven, Charles Coburn, Frank Albertson, E. E. Clive (RKO)

Story [by Felix Jackson] itself is a rather ordinary Cinderella yarn, gaining substance and strength through adroit direction, excellently tempoed lines and situations, and top-notch cast performances. Ginger Rogers blossoms forth as a most competent comedienne. David Niven delivers strongly as the romantic interest.

Picking up a baby on the steps of a foundling home, Rogers finds her excuses inadequate and she's tabbed as the unwed mother of the child. Girl easily adopts maternal love for the baby, finding the home's intervention with her boss saves her job in the department store. Niven, playboy son of the department store owner, becomes curiously interested in the foundling, and gradually generates romantic inclinations toward Rogers.

Garson Kanin's direction keeps up a breezy and steady pace.

1939: NOMINATION: Best Original Story (Felix Jackson)

●

BACHELOR OF HEARTS
1958, 94 mins, UK col
Dir Wolf Rilla ***Prod*** Vivian A. Cox ***Scr*** Leslie Bricusse, Frederic Raphael ***Ph*** Geoffrey Unsworth ***Ed*** Eric Boyd-Perkins ***Mus*** Hubert Clifford ***Art*** Edward Carrick
Act Hardy Kruger, Sylvia Syms, Ronald Lewis, Miles Malleson, Eric Barker, Barbara Steele (Independent Artists)

Bachelor of Hearts is a switch on *A Yank at Oxford*, and might have been more simply titled *A German at Cambridge*. It is a facetious, rather embarrassing glimpse of life at Cambridge University. Since the screenplay was written by two ex-Cambridge students it must be assumed to be authentic. In which case, some rather adolescent malarkey appears to go on at the university.

The thin yarn has Hardy Kruger as a German student on an exchange scholarship system. At first treated with suspicion, he proves himself a good fellow, passes his exams and falls in love. But the story is only an excuse for some predictable situations and jokes. This might have been acceptable had there been more wit, but the wisecracks mostly depend on the young German's inability to understand the English idiom or the traditional behavior at the university.

Kruger, who made a big impression with his first British pic, *The One That Got Away*, is less happy in this comedy. But he has a pleasant personality to make his slight love affair with Sylvia Syms acceptable.

●

BACHELOR PARTY, THE
1957, 92 mins, US Ⓥ b/w
Dir Delbert Mann ***Prod*** Harold Hecht ***Scr*** Paddy Chayefsky ***Ph*** Joseph LaShelle ***Ed*** William B. Murphy ***Mus*** Paul Madeira ***Art*** Ted Haworth
Act Don Murray, E. G. Marshall, Jack Warden, Philip Abbott, Carolyn Jones, Patricia Smith (United Artists/Norma)

The title tips that the comedy will come from the international institution of giving the groom-to-be his last fling as a single man. The script [from Paddy Chayefsky's own TV play] gets it all in—the drinking dinner, the stag movies, the pub crawling, the visit to a strip show, and finally, the calling on a professional lady. Each sequence is vividly etched.

Cast, mostly from television and stage, is headed by Don Murray. He's good as the bookkeeper husband of Patricia Smith, who is expecting a child. As he becomes a reluctant member of the bachelor party, the round of tawdry revelry is seen through his eyes, and revealing viewing it is, even involving him temporarily with a sexpot Greenwich Village character, played with great vitality by Carolyn Jones.

Philip Abbott scores as the frightened groom-to-be, his manly abilities as yet untried. The sequences wherein he makes an abortive attempt to go through with the introduction to sex arranged by the boys with Barbara Ames is a standout. Jack Warden shows up well as the office bachelor who masterminds the party for Abbott, as does Larry Blyden, married man who departs the festivities early.

1957: NOMINATION: Best Supp. Actress (Carolyn Jones)

●

BACHELOR PARTY
1984, 106 mins, US Ⓥ ⊙ col
Dir Neal Israel ***Prod*** Ron Moler, Bob Israel ***Scr*** Neal Israel, Pat Proft ***Ph*** Hal Trussell ***Ed*** Tom Walls ***Mus*** Robert Folk ***Art*** Kevin Colin, Martin Price
Act Tom Hanks, Tawny Kitaen, Adrian Zmed, George Grizzard, Barbara Stuart, Robert Prescott (Aspect Ratio/Twin Continental)

Bachelor Party is too contrived to capture the craziness it strains for and ultimately becomes offensive rather than funny.

Filled with cartoon caricatures instead of people, picture is built around a prenuptial celebration that seems to bring the worst out in people. Against the objections of her parents, Rick (Tom Hanks) is marrying Debbie (Tawny Kitaen) and Rick's friends decide to throw a bash for their departing pal.

While the film offers predictable shenanigans, such as a donkey snorting cocaine and an attempted suicide with an electric razor, main reason to see the pic is for Hanks's performance. Recalling a younger Bill Murray, he's all over the place, practically spilling off the screen with an overabundance of energy.

Unfortunately the writers [working from a story by producer Bob Israel] surround Hanks with a bunch of run-of-the-mill friends who act as if they have never seen a woman before. Sexual attitudes throughout have scarcely gotten out of grade school. Kitaen is the one woman who gets slightly better treatment, but even her role amounts to little more than looking good (which she does) and smiling.

●

BACKBEAT
1994, 100 mins, UK Ⓥ ⊙ col
Dir Iain Softley ***Prod*** Finola Dwyer, Stephen Woolley ***Scr*** Iain Softley, Michael Thomas, Stephen Ward ***Ph*** Ian Wilson ***Ed*** Martin Walsh ***Mus*** Don Was ***Art*** Joseph Bennett
Act Sheryl Lee, Stephen Dorff, Ian Hart, Gary Bakewell, Chris O'Neill, Scot Williams (Scala/PFE/Forthcoming)

The early, pre-fame days of the Beatles are a great subject for a film, but the potential has been only partly realized in *Backbeat*. This energetic, dramatically potent look at the band's Hamburg days, with special emphasis on the little-known original fifth Beatle, Stuart Sutcliffe, lacks a crucial, heightened artistic quality and point of view that would have given it real distinction.

Spanning 1960–62, just before Beatlemania broke out in Britain, rock video and docu director Iain Softley's first feature looks at how the world's first supergroup got it together musically, personally and image-wise during its wild days and nights in Germany.

More intensely, the screenplay focuses on John Lennon's relationship with his best friend, Sutcliffe, a young man of James Dean looks but little musical ability who left the group to pursue his muse as a painter and his love affair with Astrid Kirchherr, a young German photographer.

For the most part, pic has been well cast. Returning as Lennon after his successful outing in *The Hours and Times*, Ian Hart is again terrifically effective, catching John's rebellious attitude. American actor Stephen Dorff also scores strongly as Sutcliffe. More problematic is Sheryl Lee (Laura Palmer of *Twin Peaks*) as Astrid. Lee looks too much like the well-scrubbed Midwestern cheerleader type to be truly convincing as an alluring, off-the-map sophisticated Continental bohemian. Production values are a bit threadbare.

●

BACKDRAFT
1991, 135 mins, US Ⓥ ⊙ ▭ col
Dir Ron Howard ***Prod*** Richard B. Lewis, Pen Densham, John Watson ***Scr*** Gregory Widen ***Ph*** Mikael Salomon ***Ed*** Daniel Hanley, Michael Hill ***Mus*** Hans Zimmer ***Art*** Albert Brenner
Act Kurt Russell, William Baldwin, Robert De Niro, Scott Glenn, Jennifer Jason Leigh, Donald Sutherland (Universal/Imagine)

Director Ron Howard torches off more thrilling scenes in *Backdraft* than any Saturday matinee serial ever dared. Visually, pic often is exhilarating, but it's shapeless and dragged down by corny, melodramatic characters and situations.

Ex-fireman Gregory Widen's script about Chicago smoke eaters begins with a scene of the two central characters as boys in 1971. This provides shorthand for later formulaic conflicts between fire-fighting brothers Kurt Russell and William Baldwin.

Baldwin is ambivalent about fire-fighting as a result of a childhood experience. His older brother, the charismatic Russell, is a hardboiled sort, even more recklessly heroic than the father.

Widen uncertainly blends these tiresome family quarrels with a suspense plot involving fire department investigator Robert De Niro's search for a mysterious arsonist. His intense, obsessive characterization is a major plus for the film but isn't given enough screen time.

Though De Niro is portrayed as the Sherlock Holmes of arson investigators, script has him and Baldwin led to the truth by the airheaded assistant (Jennifer Jason Leigh) of a corrupt local alderman (J. T. Walsh) and by an institutionalized pyromaniac played by Donald Sutherland with his customary glee.

The spectacular fire scenes are done with terrifying believability (usually with the actors in the same shot as the fire effects) and a kind of sci-fi grandeur.

1991: NOMINATIONS: Best Sound, Sound Effects Editing, Visual Effects

●

BACKLASH
1956, 83 mins, US col
Dir John Sturges ***Prod*** Aaron Rosenberg ***Scr*** Borden Chase ***Ph*** Irving Glassberg ***Ed*** Sherman Todd ***Mus*** Herman Stein ***Art*** Alexander Golitzen, Eric Orbom
Act Richard Widmark, Donna Reed, William Campbell, John McIntire, Barton MacLane, Edward C. Platt (Universal)

Richard Widmark and Donna Reed add name value to this regulation Western drama. Story period is early Arizona soon after the Civil War, and most of the location lensing was done in that state for picturesque visual values.

When interest wanders from the story, the eye can always pick up scenic beauty for compensation. Interest will wander, too, because John Sturges's direction is not always sure-handed and permits some characters to wander to the ludicrous side. Such a one is the young killer played by William Campbell, who does his deadly work with an overboard Liberacean grin. When Sturges is telling the Frank Gruber novel, scripted by Borden Chase, with a straight toughness, the guidance is good; otherwise, just fair.

Identification of five white men killed in an Apache raid and of one who escaped, plus the whereabouts of $60,000 in gold the party was supposed to have had, puts the plot in gear. Jim Slater (Widmark) wants to make sure his no-good father (John McIntire) is one of the dead and not, as he secretly fears, the one who escaped with the coin. Karyl Orton (Reed) is on the search for the money, believing her husband, one of the dead, had an interest in it.

Widmark is tough enough to please those who like him best when he's mean. Reed also handles her character well, that of a girl who hasn't always been what a lady's supposed to be.

●

BACK ROADS
1981, 94 mins, US Ⓥ ▭ col
Dir Martin Ritt ***Prod*** Ronald Shedlo ***Scr*** Gary DeVore ***Ph*** John A. Alonzo ***Ed*** Sidney Levin ***Mus*** Henry Mancini ***Art*** Walter Scott Herndon
Act Sally Field, Tommy Lee Jones, Michael Gazzo, M. Emmet Walsh (Warner)

Plot focuses on Southern hooker Sally Field who meets down-on-his-luck-boxer Tommy Lee Jones in the course of a working night. Jones can't pay for his fun but is intrigued by the spunky Field—so much so that he punches out a policeman about to bust her.

Forced to move out of her temporary abode, Field spends the night at Jones's meager surroundings and sneaks out the next morning to take a look at the little boy she gave up for adoption some years ago. After the adoptive mother threatens to call the police if she persists trying to make contact, Field returns to Jones (who just lost his car-washing job) and the pair decide to leave Alabama for the promising California shores. Thrust of the film is their adventures hitchhiking along the road.

Although both stars rise above script contrivances, they are somehow never an affecting romantic pair. All of their shared troubles would seem to make a great love story but they never share enough really intimate moments to carry it off.

•

BACK STREET
1932, 86 mins, US b/w
Dir John M. Stahl ***Prod*** Carl Laemmle, Jr. ***Scr*** Gladys Lehman, Lynn Starling ***Ph*** Karl Freund ***Ed*** Milton Carruth ***Art*** Charles D. Hall
Act Irene Dunne, John Boles, June Clyde, George Meeker, ZaSu Pitts, Shirley Grey (Universal)

Just as Fannie Hurst's bestseller must have fired the imagination of readers, this saga of Ray Schmidt who lives in a shadowy "back street," and technically meretricious relationship with Walter Saxel, leaps off the screen and smacks the viewer above the gray matter and under the heart.

The sympathy for Schmidt is naturally, humanly and wallopingly developed, even unto Irene Dunne's superb characterization, winning her audience away from a slightly unconventional start where she is shown hobnobbing gaily but harmlessly with the travelling salesmen in the Over-the-Rhine beer gardens of Cincinnati.

Her ready acquiescence to every demand of her lover (John Boles) despite his own imminent marriage, "for family reasons," is as natural in its artlessness as having a cup of coffee, and yet it is packed with human interest.

Dunne is excellent as Schmidt. She is the personification of "a real woman." Boles, too, is very effective, deftly highlighting the somewhat selfish man who makes heavy demands of his mistress, and yet withal genuinely in love with the No. 2 woman in his life.

•

BACK STREET
1941, 89 mins, US b/w
Dir Robert Stevenson ***Prod*** Bruce Manning ***Scr*** Bruce Manning, Felix Jackson ***Ph*** William Daniels ***Ed*** Ted Kent ***Mus*** Frank Skinner ***Art*** Jack Otterson, Richard H. Riedel
Act Charles Boyer, Margaret Sullavan, Richard Carlson, Frank McHugh, Tim Holt, Esther Dale (Universal)

Second picturization of Fannie Hurst's novel—first turned out in 1932 with John Boles and Irene Dunne under direction of John Stahl—retains all of the tear-jerking qualities of the author's original work.

Universal has provided a class-A production background on which to weave a straightforward and logical drama of a woman's love and devotion for one man over a span of years—and her complete willingness to remain in the shadowy alleys of his life. Generating strong sympathy for the plight of a woman unable to enjoy the security of marriage, picture carries hefty dramatic punch.

Margaret Sullavan delivers a strong and sympathetic characterization as the most willing victim of love and devotion. Charles Boyer provides a deft and restrained portrayal of the man willing to share his time and affections between wife and mistress. Richard Carlson is seen briefly to advantage as the boyhood sweetheart who rises to become an automotive tycoon and just misses marrying the girl.

•

BACK TO BATAAN
1945, 95 mins, US Ⓥ ⦿ b/w
Dir Edward Dmytryk ***Prod*** Robert Fellows (exec.) ***Scr*** Ben Barzman, Richard H. Landau ***Ph*** Nicholas Musuraca ***Ed*** Marston Fay ***Mus*** Roy Webb ***Art*** Albert S. D'Agostino, Ralph Berger
Act John Wayne, Anthony Quinn, Beulah Bondi, Fely Franquelli, Richard Loo, Philip Ahn (RKO)

Events are based on fact, according to foreword, and clips of several U.S. fighting men released from Jap prison camps with the return of MacArthur's army are used both at beginning and end. Plot [from a story by Aeneas MacKenzie and William Gordon] spans time from fall of Bataan and Corregidor to the Yank landings on Leyte, and depicts adventures of John Wayne as a colonel leading Filipino patriots in undercover sabotage against the "islands" temporary conquerors.

Love interest is given over to Anthony Quinn, portraying the descendant of the Filipino hero, Bonifacio, and Fely Franquelli, Manila contact for the band of heroes. Quinn does a particularly outstanding job, as does Franquelli. Wayne makes a stalwart leader for the guerrillas, commendably underplaying the role for best results.

•

BACK TO THE FUTURE
1985, 116 mins, US Ⓥ ⦿ col
Dir Robert Zemeckis ***Prod*** Bob Gale, Neil Canton ***Scr*** Robert Zemeckis, Bob Gale ***Ph*** Dean Cundey ***Ed*** Arthur Schmidt, Harry Keramidas ***Mus*** Alan Silvestri ***Art*** Lawrence G. Paull
Act Michael J. Fox, Christopher Lloyd, Crispin Glover, Lea Thompson, Claudia Wells, Thomas F. Wilson (Amblin)

The central winning elements in the scenario are twofold: hurtling the audience back to 1955, which allows for lots of comparative, pop culture humor, and delivering a 1985 teenager (Michael J. Fox) at the doorstep of his future parents when they were 17-year-old kids. That encounter is a delicious premise, especially when the young hero's mother-to-be develops the hots for her future son and his future father is a bumbling wimp.

Film is also sharply anchored by zestful byplay between Fox's Arthurian knight figure and Christopher Lloyd's Merlinlike, crazed scientist. The latter has mounted a nuclear-powered time machine in a spaced-out DeLorean car, which spirits the bedazed Fox 30 years back in time to the same little town in which he grew up.

In the film's opening sequences, the father (wonderfully played by Crispin Glover) is an unctuous nitwit, and the mother (Lea Thompson) a plump, boozey, turtle-necked frau.

Performances by the earnest Fox, the lunatic Lloyd, the deceptively passionate Lea Thompson, and, particularly, the bumbling-to-confident Glover, who runs away with the picture, merrily keep the ship sailing.

1985: Best Sound Effects Editing

NOMINATIONS: Best Original Screenplay, Sound, Song ("Power of Love")

•

BACK TO THE FUTURE PART II
1989, 107 mins, US Ⓥ ⦿ col
Dir Robert Zemeckis ***Prod*** Bob Gale, Neil Canton ***Scr*** Bob Gale ***Ph*** Dean Cundey ***Ed*** Arthur Schmidt, Harry Keramidas ***Mus*** Alan Silvestri ***Art*** Rick Carter
Act Michael J. Fox, Christopher Lloyd, Lea Thompson, Thomas F. Wilson, Harry Waters, Jr., Elisabeth Shue (Amblin/Universal)

The energy and heart that Robert Zemeckis and story-writing partner Bob Gale (who takes solo screenplay credit this time) poured into the ingenious story of part one is diverted into narrative mechanics and camera wizardry in *Future II*.

The story starts exactly where the original left off, with Michael J. Fox's Marty McFly and Christopher Lloyd's visionary inventor Dr. Emmett Brown taking off in their flying DeLorean time machine for 2015 on an urgent mission to save Fox's children from a terrible fate.

Future II finds the McFly family living in shabby lower-middle-class digs in a world that isn't so much Orwellian as a gaudier and tackier projection of the present day.

What matters to Fox is that his son has become a wimp, just like his father was in the 1955 segment of the original film.

Then, in a curious narrative lapse, Fox picks up a sports almanac that, if taken back to the past, will enable him to get rich by gambling on future events. But villainous Biff (Thomas F. Wilson) absconds with it in the time machine to give it to his 1955 self, and the chase begins.

Zemeckis's fascination with having characters interact at different ages of their lives hurts the film visually, and strains credibility past the breaking point, by forcing him to rely on some very cheesy makeup designs.

1989: NOMINATION: Best Visual Effects

•

BACK TO THE FUTURE PART III
1990, 118 mins, US Ⓥ ⦿ col
Dir Robert Zemeckis ***Prod*** Bob Gale, Neil Canton ***Scr*** Bob Gale ***Ph*** Dean Cundey ***Ed*** Arthur Schmidt, Harry Keramidas ***Mus*** Alan Silvestri ***Art*** Rick Carter
Act Michael J. Fox, Christopher Lloyd, Mary Steenburgen, Thomas F. Wilson, Lea Thompson, Elisabeth Shue (Amblin)

Back to the Future Part III recovers the style, wit and grandiose fantasy elements of the original. The simplicity of plot, and the wide expansiveness of its use of space, are a refreshing change from the convoluted, visually cramped and cluttered second part.

Michael J. Fox's Marty McFly in his time-travelling DeLorean finds himself in the midst of a band of charging Indians in John Ford country, Monument Valley 1885. His mission is to bring back Doc (Christopher Lloyd) before he is shot in the back by Thomas F. Wilson's hilariously unhinged Buford "Mad Dog" Tannen, an ancestor of McFly's 20th-century nemesis Biff Tannen.

Fox steps into the background of the story and lets Lloyd have the chance to play the romantic lead for a change. Doc's offbeat romance with Mary Steenburgen's Clara Clayton, a spinster schoolmarm who shares his passion for Jules Verne, is funny, touching and exhilarating. Their ultimate journey through time gives the plot trajectory an unexpected and entirely satisfying resolution.

The fun of this meta-Western is partly the recognition of elements familiar from genre classics: the dance from *My Darling Clementine*, the sobering-up concoction from *El Dorado*, the costume from *Fistful of Dollars*. Fox reexperiences all this, literally flying through the screen (at an incongruous Monument Valley drive-in) into every Western fan's dream of being a character in a "real" Western.

•

BAD
1977, 105 mins, US Ⓥ col
Dir Jed Johnson ***Prod*** Jeff Tornberg ***Scr*** Pat Hackett, George Abagnalo ***Ph*** Allan Metzger ***Ed*** Franca Silvi, David McKenna ***Mus*** Mike Bloomfield ***Art*** Eugene Rudolph
Act Carroll Baker, Perry King, Susan Tyrrell, Stefania Cassini, Cyrinda Foxe, Mary Boylan (New World)

Watching Andy Warhol's *Bad* is a compellingly revolting experience. This is among the blackest of black comedies, featuring Carroll Baker as a Queens housewife who supplements her home electrolysis business by arranging for young girls to do repulsive errands for clients—killing dogs, retarded babies, etc. Don't see it after eating.

Pat Hackett and George Abagnalo wrote the script, which, on a professional level, is a good piece of craftsmanship. Jed Johnson, who has edited prior Warhol pix, handles the direction in top fashion.

Baker plays a suburban Ma Barker, cherishing her TV commercial middle-class materialistic standards, while thinking nothing about her gruesome sideline. Susan Tyrrell is Baker's slovenly and abandoned daughter-in-law, complete with sniveling infant. Baker's crew of hit-persons is mainly a gaggle of slatternly young street maidens who carry out their assignments with truly frightening aplomb.

•

BAD AND THE BEAUTIFUL, THE
1952, 116 mins, US Ⓥ ⦿ b/w
Dir Vincente Minnelli ***Prod*** John Houseman ***Scr*** Charles Schnee ***Ph*** Robert Surtees ***Ed*** Conrad A. Nervig ***Mus*** David Raksin ***Art*** Cedric Gibbons, Edward Carfagno
Act Kirk Douglas, Lana Turner, Walter Pidgeon, Dick Powell, Barry Sullivan, Gloria Grahame (M-G-M)

Contemporary Hollywood, including composites of the characters that make the town the glamour capital it is, is the setting for *The Bad and the Beautiful*.

It is the story of a first-class heel, a ruthless, driving individual whose insistent push changes a number of lives to the end that all have benefited in some way from his multiple double crosses, despite the personal sorrow or loss experienced. The screenplay of the George Bradshaw story is exceptionally well-written.

Kirk Douglas scores as the ruthless individual out to prove he is the best when it comes to making pictures. Swung along with him is Lana Turner, the drunken, inferiority-complexed daughter of a former screen great; Dick Powell, the self-satisfied Southern professor-writer who is pulled into the Hollywood mill; and Barry Sullivan, who, as an embryo director, gets Douglas his first chance and is double-crossed for the helping hand.

1952: Best Supp. Actress (Gloria Grahame), Screenplay, B&W Cinematography, B&W Art Direction, B&W Costume Design

NOMINATION: Best Actor (Kirk Douglas)

•

BAD BEHAVIOUR
1993, 100 mins, UK Ⓥ col
Dir Les Blair ***Prod*** Sarah Curtis ***Scr*** [uncredited] ***Ph*** Witold Stok ***Ed*** Martin Walsh ***Mus*** John Altman ***Art*** Jim Grant
Act Stephen Rea, Sinead Cusack, Philip Jackson, Clare Higgins, Phil Daniels, Saira Todd (Channel 4/Parallax)

Stephen Rea heads a strong cast, crisply directed, in *Bad Behaviour*, a delightful comedy of manners set among a group of north Londoners.

Rea plays a district planning officer and amateur cartoonist, whose wife Ellie (Sinead Cusack) is quietly going through a midlife crisis. In strides Ellie's greaseball ex-husband (Philip Jackson), who's operating real estate scams. Things get real complicated when Jackson tries to rip off Rea, et al., for some rebuilding work, a job done by identical twins (both played by Phil Daniels) to whom Jackson already owes money.

Working, in the style of Mike Leigh, from an improvised script, helmer Les Blair juggles his small cast with great dexterity, drawing tight playing down the line with no feel of treading water. The pic is character, not knockabout, comedy, but this is a group of mild eccentrics you want to follow to the end.

•

BAD BLOOD
1982, 105 mins, UK/New Zealand Ⓥ col
Dir Mike Newell ***Prod*** Andrew Brown ***Scr*** Andrew Brown ***Ph*** Gary Hansen ***Ed*** Peter Hollywood ***Mus*** Richard Hartley ***Art*** Kai Hawkins
Act Jack Thompson, Carol Burns, Dennis Lill, Donna Akersten, Martyn Sanderson, Marshall Napier (Southern)

Story revolves around Stan (Jack Thompson) and Dorothy Graham (Carol Burns), gun-happy dairy farmers who by 1941 have become ostracized from their neighbors in the isolated, close-knit New Zealand town of Kowhiterangi, mainly due to their own paranoia.

A gunpoint confrontation with two neighbors forces until now patient constable Ted Best (Dennis Lill) to confiscate Thompson's rifle, backed by a trio of fellow officers. When the gendarmes invade Thompson's farmhouse, his last refuge from a world of his own making, the inevitable violence ensues. Thompson then flees into the bush, and more will die before an amateurish manhunt reaches its inevitable conclusion. Direction by Mike Newell stands out for conveying more meaning with pictures than words, though the film [from the book *Manhunt: The Story of Stanley Graham* by Howard Willis] stumbles somewhat through the narrative until the carnage begins.

Thompson turns in an okay performance, and he's clearly better in the early scenes when his character is still a semi-rational being. The actor seems stretched thin once his mainspring snaps.

•

BAD BOY BUBBY
1993, 112 mins, Australia/Italy Ⓥ ⊙ col
Dir Rolf De Heer ***Prod*** Domenico Procacci, Giorgio Draskovic, Rolf De Heer ***Scr*** Rolf De Heer ***Ph*** Ian Jones, and 30 others ***Ed*** Suresh Ayyar ***Mus*** Graham Tardif ***Art*** Mark Abbott
Act Nicholas Hope, Claire Benito, Ralph Cotterill, Carmel Johnson, Natalie Carr, Norman Kaye (Bubby/Fandango)

Rolf De Heer's *Bad Boy Bubby* is a very original dramatic comedy with something to offend just about everybody. Pic starts off like a modern variation on *The Wild Child* or *Kasper Hauser*, but then veers off into the sci-fi territory of *Starman* or John McNaughton's *The Borrower*, in which an alien acquires knowledge and power from the people who cross his path.

Bubby's crazy mother (Claire Benito), a religious freak, has kept her son (Nicholas Hope) in isolation from the outside world for the first 35 years of his life. Living in a grubby, windowless room, they bathe each other and even have sex together, an act Bubby has been raised to regard as normal.

This strange existence is interrupted by the arrival of Bubby's long-lost father (Ralph Cotterill), a ragged priest heavily into booze and sex. He quickly displaces Bubby in mom's bed, and the younger man's jealousy and frustration erupts in violence.

Out in the city, Bubby encounters a number of "normal people," whose language, speech patterns and actions he memorizes and repeats, often at inappropriate moments. No less than 30 different cameramen filmed these sequences, the idea being to depict Bubby's experiences in different visual styles.

Hope gives a brave and sometimes astonishing performance as the naive "wild child."

•

BAD BOYS
1983, 123 mins, US Ⓥ ⊙ col
Dir Rick Rosenthal ***Prod*** Robert Solo ***Scr*** Richard Dilello ***Ph*** Bruce Surtees, Donald Thorin ***Ed*** Antony Gibbs ***Mus*** Bill Conti ***Art*** J. Michael Riva
Act Sean Penn, Reni Santoni, Esai Morales, Eric Gurry, Jim Moody, Ally Sheedy (EMI)

Bad Boys is a troubling and often riveting drama about juvenile delinquency. Director Rick Rosenthal does a top-notch job of bringing to life the seedy, hopeless environment of a jail for juvenile offenders and has gotten some terribly convincing performances from his young cast, notably topliner Sean Penn.

From the first scene, where 16-year-old tough guy Penn breaks the window of a car and steals a woman's purse, it's clear this is not going to be the picture of youth most people are used to.

Penn's only safety is in the love of girlfriend Ally Sheedy, the one person who has ever seemingly seen the softer side of his nature. It is in jail that the film really takes off, pitting Penn against the abuses of his fellow inmates and the inherent hopelessness of his situation.

Penn is nothing short of terrific in the key role, which, given a minimal amount of dialog, calls for him to rely primarily on his emotional and physical abilities.

•

BAD BOYS
1995, 118 mins, US Ⓥ ⊙ col
Dir Michael Bay ***Prod*** Don Simpson, Jerry Bruckheimer ***Scr*** Michael Barrie, Jim Mulholland, Doug Richardson ***Ph*** Howard Atherton ***Ed*** Christian Wagner ***Mus*** Mark Mancina ***Art*** John Vallone
Act Martin Lawrence, Will Smith, Tea Leoni, Tcheky Karyo, Theresa Randle, Joe Pantoliano (Columbia)

Beverly Hills Cop meets *Miami Vice* in *Bad Boys*, with predictably combustible results. After a dormant period, the Simpson/Bruckheimer machine is back in working order with this ultra-slick combination [from a screen story by George Gallo] of expensive action, rude attitude, sassy humor, trendy locations, fast cars, heavy soundtrack and decorous violence.

Package is designed as if to reassert the commercial credentials of one of the most successful producing partnerships of the 1980s. Simpson & Bruckheimer have gone back to the basics that worked so well for them before—a battle between irreverent (black) cops and ruthless (white) villains, with huge amounts of drugs and money hanging in the balance and some babes and nightclubbing lightly sprinkled into the mix. Marcus Burnett (Martin Lawrence) and Mike Lowrey (Will Smith) are longtime friends who have been undercover partners on the Miami police force for six years. In a zingy sequence, some dazzlingly efficient crooks penetrate the bowels of the police department to make off with $100 million in heroin the heroes recently confiscated in their "career bust."

With 72 hours to solve the case before the Feds step in, Marcus and Mike plausibly suspect a corrupt ex-cop as being in on the job, but he's knocked off by the real mastermind, cold-blooded Frenchman Fouchet (Tcheky Karyo), as is Max (Karen Alexander), a gorgeous high-class hooker and ex-girlfriend of Mike's.

A friend of Max's, Julie (Tea Leoni), is willing to help the cops, but only if she deals directly with Mike, of whom Max always spoke highly. With Mike temporarily detained, Marcus is forced to impersonate his best friend in order to advance the case. This central ruse serves as the basis of much of the humor.

Throughout, pic is punctuated by the requisite number of intimidations, beatings, shootings, explosions and chases, all staged with knowing panache by 30-year-old first-time helmer Michael Bay, who made his mark with his musicvideos and award-winning Miller Beer and milk commercials.

•

BAD COMPANY
1972, 91 mins, US Ⓥ col
Dir Robert Benton ***Prod*** Stanley R. Jaffe ***Scr*** David Newman, Robert Benton ***Ph*** Gordon Willis ***Ed*** Ralph Rosenblum, Ron Kalish ***Mus*** Harvey Schmidt ***Art*** Paul Sylbert
Act Jeff Bridges, Barry Brown, Jim Davis, David Huddleston, John Savage, Jerry Houser (Jaffilms/Paramount)

Bad Company is an excellent film that combines wry humor and gritty action with in-depth characterizations of two youths on the lam in the Civil War West. The production is generally sensitive in its treatment, though pockmarked with some incongruous "fun-and-poetic" type violence unworthy of the otherwise quality storytelling. Robert Benton, who co-wrote the fine original script, makes a noteworthy directorial debut. It's an intriguing story of the maturing-under-fire of Barry Brown, a Midwest draft dodger, but otherwise of "good" stock, who gradually develops the educated, pragmatic survival instinct necessary in the old West. In this he is influenced primarily by Jeff Bridges, a more primitive con-artist character who knows the ropes of street fighting and finagling.

Among the many highlights of the film is an outstanding performance by Brown.

•

BAD COMPANY
1995, 108 mins, US Ⓥ ⊙ ▭ col
Dir Damian Harris ***Prod*** Amedeo Ursini, Jeffrey Chernov ***Scr*** Ross Thomas ***Ph*** Jack N. Green ***Ed*** Stuart Pappe ***Mus*** Carter Burwell ***Art*** Andrew McAlpine
Act Ellen Barkin, Laurence Fishburne, Frank Langella, Michael Beach, Gia Carides, David Odgen Stiers (Touchstone)

Bad Company seemingly has no more noble ambition than to give audiences the interracial sex only hinted at in *The Pelican Brief*'s chaste pairing of Julia Roberts and Denzel Washington. But with its uninvolving story, listless delivery and unsympathetic characters played by leads Laurence Fishburne and Ellen Barkin, would-be suspenser fails even on the erotic level.

Story opens with ex-CIA troubleshooter Nelson Crowe (Fishburne) getting a new job at a company headed by Margaret Wells (Barkin) and Vic Grimes (Frank Langella). Couple's shady firm specializes in using former government sleuths to do the dirty work of corporations and other private predators.

First assignment has Crowe and new partner Tod Stapp (Michael Beach) sent to bribe a gambling-addicted judge (Odgen Stiers). Crowe finds himself facing an even more covert job when Wells asks him to join her in offing Grimes and claiming the company as their own.

Soon after comes the revelation that, rather than being the free agent he seems, Crowe remains in thrall to the CIA, which wants him to conspire with Wells in order to toss the boutique spy outfit into the agency's waiting hands.

Barkin and Fishburne do capable work in roles that require only one-note shrewishness from her, stolid taciturnity from him. Supporting performances are generally OK, with some welcome subtlety coming from Stiers and Beach.

•

BAD DAY AT BLACK ROCK
1954, 81 mins, US Ⓥ ⊙ ▭ col
Dir John Sturges ***Prod*** Dore Schary ***Scr*** Millard Kaufman ***Ph*** William C. Mellor ***Ed*** Newell P. Kimlin ***Mus*** Andre Previn ***Art*** Cedric Gibbons, Malcolm Brown
Act Spencer Tracy, Robert Ryan, Anne Francis, Dean Jagger, Walter Brennan, Ernest Borgnine (M-G-M)

Considerable excitement is whipped up in this suspense drama, and fans who go for tight action will find it entirely satisfactory. Besides telling a yarn of tense suspense, the picture is concerned with a social message on civic complacency.

Basis for the smoothly valued production is a story by Howard Breslin, adapted by Don McGuire. To the tiny town of Black Rock, one hot summer day in 1945, comes Spencer Tracy, war veteran with a crippled left arm. He wants to find a Japanese farmer and give to him the medal won by his son in an action that left the latter dead and Tracy crippled. Tracy is greeted with an odd hostility and his own life is endangered when he puts together the reason for the cold, menacing treatment.

Film is paced to draw suspense tight and keep expectancy mounting as the plot crosses the point where Tracy could have left without personal danger and plunges him into deadly menace when he becomes the hunted.

There's not a bad performance from any member of the cast, each socking their characters for full value.

1955: NOMINATIONS: Best Director, Actor (Spencer Tracy), Screenplay

•

BAD GIRL
1931, 90 mins, US b/w
Dir Frank Borzage ***Scr*** Edwin Burke ***Ph*** Chester Lyons ***Ed*** Margaret Clancy
Act Sally Eilers, James Dunn, Minna Gombell, William Pawley, Frank Darien (Fox)

Story tells of two kids (Sally Eilers and James Dunn) who meet on a Coney Island boat, delve into marriage after a night in his boardinghouse room and Dorothy (Eilers) is consequently kicked out of a parentless home by her brother. Then Eddie (Dunn) gives up his dream of a radio shop of his own to furnish a new flat for his wife with the added complication of the baby that she has kept a secret from her inarticulate husband.

After which there is the misunderstanding of both thinking the other doesn't want the child, which is not brought out as strongly here as in the stage version [based on the novel by Vina Delmar]. Minna Gombell figures as the widowed girlfriend of Dorothy and a constant source of annoyance to Eddie as his wife's advisor.

As a whole *Bad Girl* classes as a workmanlike job, with Dunn's scene with the doctor as its strong point.

1931/32: Best Director, Adaptation

NOMINATION: Best Picture

•

BAD GIRLS
SEE: LES BICHES

•

BAD GIRLS
1994, 99 mins, US Ⓥ ⊙ col
Dir Jonathan Kaplan ***Prod*** Albert S. Ruddy, Andre E. Morgan ***Scr*** Ken Friedman, Yolande Finch ***Ph*** Ralf Bode ***Ed*** Jane Kurson ***Mus*** Jerry Goldsmith ***Art*** Guy Barnes
Act Madeleine Stowe, Mary Stuart Masterson, Andie MacDowell, Drew Barrymore, James Russo, James LeGros (20th Century-Fox)

Even though the sight of four comely cowgirls strapping on six-guns and thundering across the plains has its undeniable kick, the bad news is that *Bad Girls* drinks from an empty trough of wit and style.

Tall tale starts with barroom floozy Cody Zamora (Madeleine Stowe) gunning down a prominent lawman when he starts getting too rough with her fellow prostie Anita Crown (Mary Stuart Masterson). Saved from lynching at the hands of local religious reformers, Cody hightails it out of town with Anita, self-styled Southern belle Eileen Spenser (Andie MacDowell) and blond babe Lilly Laronette (Drew Barrymore).

Just as Cody is withdrawing her life's savings from a bank to open a sawmill, old flame Kid Jarrett (James Russo) robs it, thus ensnaring the women in the world of big-stakes outlawry and treachery.

The five script and story writers [latter being Albert S. Ruddy, Charles Finch and Gray Frederickson] were unfortunately unable to come up with much interesting for the feisty femmes to do, providing director Jonathan Kaplan, who replaced original helmer Tamra Davis, with an insurmountable problem. Film looks like what it is—four Hollywood actresses duded up in Western gear, riding horses and toting pistols.

•

BAD GUYS
1986, 86 mins, US Ⓥ col
Dir Joel Silberg ***Prod*** John D. Backe, Myron A. Hyman ***Scr*** Brady W. Setwater, Joe Gillis ***Ph*** Hanania Baer ***Ed*** Peter Parasheles, Christopher Holmes ***Mus*** William Goldstein ***Art*** Ivo Cristante
Act Adam Baldwin, Mike Jolly, Michelle Nicastro, Ruth Buzzi, James Booth, Dutch Mann (Tomorrow)

Bad Guys is a poorly scripted, would-be comedy attempting to cash in on the popularity of wrestling. Merest pretext of a story has young cops Adam Baldwin and Mike Jolly suspended from the LA police after a brawl with bikers in a bar owned by Dutch Mann (who pointlessly keeps cropping up in the film as their nemesis). After tastless footage detailing their odd jobs (including a leering stint as male strippers), they turn their wrestling avocation into a full-time job under the tutelage of pretty reporter-turned-manager Michelle Nicastro.

Quickly discovering that the dirty practitioners are the stars in wrestling's firmament, the heroes don masks and become the Boston Bad Guys, tutored in illegal moves by Gene LeBell and his wife (Ruth Buzzi).

Burdened with hoary, unfunny dialog, director Joel Silberg directs in frantic, comic-strip fashion, having the lines exclaimed as if they were displayed in balloons above the actors' heads. Topliner Baldwin is unrecognizable here with blond-dyed hair. He doesn't have the body weight to be convincing as a wrestler. Co-star Jolly is bland while Nicastro looks out of place in a role better suited to a comedienne in the Cyndi Lauper style.

•

BAD INFLUENCE
1990, 99 mins, US Ⓥ ⦿ col
Dir Curtis Hanson ***Prod*** Steve Tisch ***Scr*** David Koepp ***Ph*** Robert Elswitt ***Ed*** Bonnie Koehler ***Mus*** Trevor Jones ***Art*** Ron Foreman
Act Rob Lowe, James Spader, Lisa Zane, Christian Clemenson, Kathleen Wilhoite, Tony Maggio (Epic/Sarlui-Diamant/PRO)

Bad Influence proves a reasonably taut, suspenseful thriller that provides its share of twists before straying into silliness. Rob Lowe doesn't really project enough menace or charisma to pull off his role as Alex, a baby-faced psycho who slowly leads Michael (James Spader) through a liberating fantasy that ultimately turns into a yuppie nightmare. Director and writer seem to draw their inspiration most closely from Alfred Hitchcock's *Strangers on a Train*—a chance meeting between a regular guy and an outwardly normal stranger whose hidden darkness ultimately leads to fatal complications.

Foremost, however, the film is about Michael's seduction by Alex's free-wheeling attitude, only to find that the rewards don't come cheap. Spader delivers a terrific performance, and some of the scenes have tremendous impact, especially when—via video—he discovers the depth of Alex's depravity, as fantasy turns into fatal distraction.

Director Curtis Hanson and writer David Koepp create a continued sense of tension and invest many scenes with much-needed humor.

•

BADLANDERS, THE
1958, 85 mins, US Ⓥ ▭ col
Dir Delmer Daves ***Prod*** Aaron Rosenberg ***Scr*** Richard Collins ***Ph*** John F. Seitz ***Ed*** William H. Webb, James Baiotto ***Art*** William A. Horning, Daniel B. Cathcart
Act Alan Ladd, Ernest Borgnine, Katy Jurado, Claire Kelly, Nehemiah Persoff, Kent Smith (M-G-M)

It is possible to make an adult Western without making it a psychological Western. Aaron Rosenberg proves the point with his production of *The Badlanders*, a truly original frontier drama, a suspense melodrama on one level and a huge horselaugh on another, with each element playing off on the other.

The heroes of the screenplay, based on a novel by W. R. Burnett [*The Asphalt Jungle*], are two ex-cons, released from the Nevada Territorial Prison, circa 1900, with little but revenge and larceny in their hearts. It is the plan of one of them (Alan Ladd) to do nothing less than rob a gold mine, and he enlists the other (Ernest Borgnine) in support. The problem, of course, is formidable. They must blast the ore—half a ton of it—from a spot right next to a mine full of workmen, then get the huge load away from under the noses (and shotguns) of the legal owners. Delmer Daves's direction has a facility of throwing a laugh into the midst of a suspense buildup, relieving and heightening it with flashes of humor.

Ladd is not required over-heroic, physically. His strength is emotional, and with casual grace and a way with an ironic line, he creates an effective contrast to Borgnine. Katy Jurado is handsomely colorful and alternately touching as a Mexican girl. Claire Kelly, who makes her major bow in this picture, is a stunning redhead but she is not yet a strong enough actress to hold her own with this trio.

•

BADLANDS
1973, 95 mins, US Ⓥ ⦿ col
Dir Terrence Malick ***Prod*** Terrence Malick ***Scr*** Terrence Malick ***Ph*** Brian Probyn, Tak Fujimoto, Stevan Larner ***Ed*** Robert Estrin, William Weber ***Mus*** George Tipton ***Art*** Jack Fisk, Ed Richardson
Act Martin Sheen, Sissy Spacek, Warren Oates, Alan Vint, Ramon Bieri, Gary Littlejohn (Pressman-Williams)

Badlands is a uniquely American fairy tale, a romantic account set in the late 1950s of a 15-year-old girl's journey into violence and out of love with a 25-year-old South Dakota garbageman-turned-thrill-killer. Pic is told through the girl's eyes as she narrates in dumb *Teen Romance* style the saga of her hero, a James Dean carbon, who kills her father and whisks her away on a flight into myth that ends in the badlands of Montana.

Written, produced and directed by Terrence Malick, pic is his first feature and it's an impressive debut.

The killer lead, played with cunning and charm by Martin Sheen, is a perverse Horatio Alger, a culturally deprived American boy weaned on James Dean pix who works at his rebel image and achieves success, i.e. notoriety, capture, fame and death.

His girl (Sissy Spacek) is one of those mid-teen catatonics whose life is defined in terms of Hollywood gossip and visions of white knights. Together they litter their escape route with the dead.

•

BAD LIEUTENANT
1992, 96 mins, US Ⓥ ⦿ col
Dir Abel Ferrara ***Prod*** Edward R. Pressman, Mary Kane ***Scr*** Zoe Lund, Abel Ferrara ***Ph*** Ken Kelsch ***Ed*** Anthony Redman ***Mus*** Joe Delia ***Art*** Charlie Lagola
Act Harvey Keitel, Frankie Thorn, Zoe Lund, Anthony Ruggiero, Victoria Bastel, Robin Burrows (Pressman)

Abel Ferrara's uncompromising *Bad Lieutenant* is a harrowing journey observing a corrupt NY cop sink into the depths, with an extraordinary and uninhibited perf by Harvey Keitel in the title role. Screenplay by Zoe Lund, who made her screen debut billed as Zoe Tamerlis in Ferrara's *Ms. 45*, ambitiously takes on taboo issues in looking at a degraded subculture in an era of faithlessness and despair.

Foul-mouthed cop Keitel is almost constant sniffing, smoking or injecting drugs he's stolen from police busts while also indulging in alchohol and time-outs for sex. Turning point for him is being assigned to the case of a gang-raped nun. He's a lapsed Catholic who makes light of the event, but when nun Frankie Thorn (in an unadorned, affecting performance) forgives her assailants Keitel faces a religious crisis of conscience.

Elsewhere, Keitel lets it all hang out in a nude Christlike pose, and spends the final reel in howls of despair as he hallucinates the presence of Christ in a church.

•

BAD NEWS BEARS, THE
1976, 102 mins, US Ⓥ ⦿ col
Dir Michael Ritchie ***Prod*** Stanley R. Jaffe ***Scr*** Bill Lancaster ***Ph*** John A. Alonzo ***Ed*** Richard A. Harris ***Mus*** Jerry Fielding ***Art*** Polly Platt
Act Walter Matthau, Tatum O'Neal, Vic Morrow, Joyce Van Patten, Ben Piazza, Jackie Earle Haley (Paramount)

The Bad News Bears is an extremely funny adult-child comedy film. Walter Matthau stars to perfection as a bumbling baseball coach in the sharp production about the foibles and follies of Little League athletics. Tatum O'Neal also stars as Matthau's ace pitcher. Michael Ritchie's film has the correct balance of warmth and empathy to make the gentle social commentary very effective.

Premise finds activist politico Ben Piazza having won a class-action suit to admit some underprivileged kids to an otherwise upwardly mobile WASP suburban Little League schedule.

Piazza recruits Matthau, a one-time minor leaguer now cleaning swimming pools to coach the slapdash outfit. O'Neal and Jackie Earle Haley reluctantly join their juvenile peers to spark the team to a second place win.

•

BAD NEWS BEARS GO TO JAPAN, THE
1978, 91 mins, US Ⓥ ⦿ col
Dir John Berry ***Prod*** Michael Ritchie ***Scr*** Bill Lancaster ***Ph*** Gene Polito, Kozo Okazaki ***Ed*** Richard A. Harris ***Mus*** Paul Chihara ***Art*** Walter Scott Herndon
Act Tony Curtis, Jackie Earle Haley, Tomisaburo Wakayama, Hatsune Ishihara, George Wyner, Lonny Chapman (Paramount)

The dangers inherent in sequel-making are clearly apparent in *The Bad News Bears Go to Japan*, third in the series of junior baseball antics that began with the smash *Bad News Bears* in 1976. Producer Michael Ritchie (who directed the first installment) and writer-creator Bill Lancaster encore with *Japan* resulting in a more vigorous film than the sodden *Bad News Bears in Breaking Training* [1977].

In keeping with tradition, the boys are taken in by yet another hustler (following in the steps of Walter Matthau and William Devane). This time it's Tony Curtis as a Hollywood agent out for big bucks via promoting a game between the Bears and the Japanese all-star Little Leaguers.

Formula is strictly standard, with Curtis inviting the enmity of the kids, with exception of moppet Scoody Thornton, only to be reformed before the final game, which, of course, the Bears win. Japanese locations at least add a different look, and there is much joking about language and cultural customs, humor that went out of style with *Sayonara*.

•

BAD SEED, THE
1956, 127 mins, US Ⓥ ⦿ b/w
Dir Mervyn LeRoy ***Prod*** Mervyn LeRoy ***Scr*** John Lee Mahin ***Ph*** Hal Rosson ***Ed*** Warren Low ***Mus*** Alex North
Act Nancy Kelly, Patty McCormack, Henry Jones, Eileen Heckart, Evelyn Varden, William Hopper (Warner)

This melodrama about a child with an inbred talent for homicide is pretty unpleasant stuff on its own. Taken from Maxwell Anderson's stage play, adapted from William March's novel, the film remains more of the theatre than of the motion picture field. Nonetheless, it is well done within that qualification.

With the possible exception of the Production Code–conscious ending, the screenplay varies little from the Anderson legit piece. Some of the casting is from the stage success, too, with young Patty McCormack as the innocent-looking murderess, and Nancy Kelly as her distraught mother. Both are outstanding.

Scoring also is William Hopper, the father who never sees through the evil of his little girl.

It is the story of a woman who discovers that her daughter, a sweet, innocent-faced child, is a killer. Director Mervyn LeRoy mounts sequences with shocking horror as it is brought out that the girl deliberately murdered a schoolmate because she wanted the penmanship medal he had won.

1956: NOMINATIONS: Best Actress (Nancy Kelly), Supp. Actress (Eileen Heckart, Patty McCormack), B&W Cinematography

•

BAD TIMING
1980, 123 mins, UK Ⓥ ⦿ ▭ col
Dir Nicolas Roeg ***Prod*** Jeremy Thomas ***Scr*** Yale Udoff ***Ph*** Anthony Richmond ***Ed*** Tony Lawson ***Mus*** Richard Hartley ***Art*** David Brockhurst
Act Art Garfunkel, Theresa Russell, Harvey Keitel, Denholm Elliott, Daniel Massey, Dana Gillespie (Recorded Picture/Rank)

Technically flashy, and teeming with degenerate chic, this downbeat tale of two destructively selfish lovers is unrelieved by its tacked-on thriller ending, and deals purely in despair.

Every scene is shot with at least one eye and one ear to the editing table: results are generally masterful but at times obtrusively pretentious. Director Nicolas Roeg's visual sense remains a peculiar talent.

Yale Udoff's screenplay plots the often brutal love affair exhaustively in terms of what the parties do to each other, but seldom why—beyond the fact that he is the possessive type and she isn't.

Most milestones are missing along the presumably tortuous psychological route by which Art Garfunkel's jealousy reaches such a pitch of hatred that he ravishes the girl's (Theresa Russell) drugged and senseless body instead of calling an ambulance. Alienation sets in early.

•

BAILIFF, THE
SEE: SANSHO DAYU

•

BAISERS VOLES
(STOLEN KISSES)
1968, 90 mins, France Ⓥ col
Dir Francois Truffaut ***Prod*** Marcel Bebert ***Scr*** Francois Truffaut, Claude de Givray, Bernard Revon ***Ph*** Denys Clerval ***Ed*** Agnes Guillemot ***Mus*** Antoine Duhamel ***Art*** Claude Pignot
Act Jean-Pierre Leaud, Delphine Seyrig, Claude Jade, Michel Lonsdale, Daniel Ceccaldi, Claire Duhamel (Films du Carrosse/Artistes Associes)

That timid, yet engaging, adolescent of *The 400 Blows*, played again by Jean-Pierre Leaud, is now in his 20s and cashiered out of the military. He comes home to a series of jobs that carry him through adventures that encompass his final winning of a childhood girlfriend (Claude Jade) as his wife, plus his first amorous adventure with the wife (Delphine Seyrig) of one of the men (Michel Lonsdale) he works for.

The slice-of-life pic also has neat slices of observation, tasteful presentation and easeful acting that avoid banality. Antoine Doinel (Leaud), the hero, shows a shrewdness, a harshness and even a hardheaded strength, if necessary, that balances his otherwise seemingly innocent, self-deprecating manner.

Seyrig has the knowing maturity, gentleness and yet demanding female desires that make her scenes highlights of this perceptive pic on a young man's coming-of-age. Leaud has romantic callowness, engaging directness and charm to give his character depth in spite of the film's reserved modesty.

Doinel's adventures as a private detective allow for a series of character vignettes that Francois Truffaut excels at. Especially arresting is the shoeshop boss's desire to know why people do not like him. Though he is a pompous, ruthless character, Lonsdale gives him a human aspect that makes him almost likable, as indeed are all the characters in this human comedy.

•

BALANCE, LA
1982, 102 mins, France Ⓥ col
Dir Bob Swaim ***Prod*** Alexandre Mnouchkine, Georges Dancigers ***Scr*** Bob Swaim, M. Fabiani ***Ph*** Bernard Zitzermann ***Ed*** Francoise Javet ***Mus*** Roland Bocquet, Boris Bergman ***Art*** Eric Moulard
Act Nathalie Baye, Philippe Leotard, Richard Berry, Christophe Malavoy, Maurice Ronet, Tcheky Karyo (Ariane/Films A2)

La Balance is a taut, engrossing crime drama that interweaves action and character interest to fine dramatic effect. Ironically, the film, with its purportedly factual overlay of details about contemporary Paris police and underworld mentalities, and its telling, unglossy use of the city, was written and directed by an American, Bob Swaim, 38, a former anthropology student-turned-filmmaker, based here for nearly 20 years. This is his second feature.

Swaim's tale centers on the methods of the Brigades Territoriales, plainclothes detective squads that operate in different sectors of the capital and rely heavily on a network of local informers to nip crime in the bud.

When an informer in the Belleville quarter is murdered, apparently by a local hood (Maurice Ronet), the Brigade seeks a new narc who will be able to engineer an ambush for the gangster. A young inspector (Richard Berry) decides to pressure a prostitute (Nathalie Baye) and her boyfriend (Philippe Leotard), who were once linked up with Ronet, into betraying him.

The obligatory action sequences are brought off in fine style, particularly the harrowing climactic ambush at a congested urban intersection, and the police procedural scenes are measured and credible. (Swaim had a real young inspector collaborate on the film dialog.)

The acting is especially fine, with the big surprise being Nathalie Baye, at last breaking out of a syndrome of wholesome roles. As the streetwise young whore profoundly devoted to her man, she is real and affecting.

•

BALCONY, THE
1963, 84 mins, US Ⓥ ⦿ b/w
Dir Joseph Strick ***Prod*** Ben Maddow, Joseph Strick ***Scr*** Ben Maddow ***Ph*** George Folsey ***Ed*** Chester W. Schaeffer
Act Shelley Winters, Peter Falk, Lee Grant, Peter Brocco, Jeff Corey, Ruby Dee (Walter Reade-Sterling/Allen Hodgdon)

With Jean Genet's apparent approval, Joe Strick and Ben Maddow have eliminated the play's obscene language (though it's still plenty rough) and clarified some of its obscurations. The result is a tough, vivid and dispassionate fantasy.

This is never an easy film to watch, but also it is never boring or pretentious, and often it is acidly funny. Most of the action of the film, localed in an unnamed city in the throes of a bloody revolution, takes place in a highly special kind of brothel, equipped like a movie studio with sets, costumes, rear projection devices, etc., which permit the patrons to enact their darkest fantasies (they can also pay with credit cards).

Presiding over the macabre revels is Shelley Winters, the madame who designs the illusions and is all the more ominous for her complete, almost tender detachment. The peace of the brothel is shattered with the arrival of the police chief, Peter Falk, the madame's occasional lover who is fighting a last-ditch stand outside to destroy the revolution.

Strick and Maddow have provided this fantastic film with its own reality. It is never capricious nor purposefully obscure, proceeding always with a recognizable logic. It is full of chilling detail and knife-sharp scenes, as when the police chief harangues the populace via radio from the brothel, speaking a furious jargon of nonsensical political and TV commercial cliches.

The performances are excellent, beginning with those of Winters, Falk and Lee Grant, and including the entire supporting cast.

1963: NOMINATION: B&W Cinematography

•

BALLADA O SOLDATYE
(BALLAD OF A SOLDIER)
1960, 85 mins, Russia Ⓥ ⦿ b/w
Dir Grigori Chukhrai ***Scr*** Valentin Yezhov, Grigori Chukhrai ***Ph*** Vladimir Nikolaev, Era Savelyeva ***Ed*** M. Timofeyeva ***Mus*** Mikhail Ziv ***Art*** B. Nemechek
Act Vladimir Ivashov, Zhanna Prokhorenko, Antonina Maksimova, Nikolai Kryuchkov, Yevgeni Urbanski (Mosfilm)

This film is in *The Cranes Are Flying* vein in that it is a war film done in a poetic style and a purported pacifistic outlook. It emerges a warm, simple film that is tenuous but able to be sentimental without being mawkish.

A 19-year-old Russian soldier, during the last war, is trapped by a couple of tanks that he manages to knock out in spite of his fear. He gets a four-day pass and sets out for his home to see his mother and fix the roof. But he gets into a series of adventures and manages to get home only for a few minutes to talk to his mother.

On this slim thread, the director has woven a series of tender sketches emphasizing the lurking terror, uselessness and hopelessness of war. It also shows that all Russo soldiers were not brave, that there were shirkers and that there were women who cheated on their husbands. But its main treatment is in a lyrical style with excellent camerawork, direct acting and deft character blocking.

•

BALLAD OF A SOLDIER
SEE: BALLADA O SOLDATYE

•

BALLAD OF CABLE HOGUE, THE
1970, 121 mins, US Ⓥ ⦿ col
Dir Sam Peckinpah ***Prod*** Sam Peckinpah ***Scr*** John Crawford, Edmund Penney ***Ph*** Lucien Ballard ***Ed*** Frank Santillo, Lou Lombardo ***Mus*** Jerry Goldsmith ***Art*** Leroy Coleman
Act Jason Robards, Stella Stevens, David Warner, Strother Martin, Slim Pickens, L. Q. Jones (Warner)

The Ballad of Cable Hogue is a Damon Runyonesque oater comedy from Sam Peckinpah.

Jason Robards is the title character, a charming desert rat; Stella Stevens is the cow-town harlot with the heart of gold; and David Warner is a preacher of sorts.

Robards is a grizzled prospector left to die in the desert wastes by Strother Martin and L. Q. Jones, two bumbling villains. Robards instead finds water where nobody ever had, and prospers as a rest-stop owner on a stage route owned by R. G. Armstrong, where Slim Pickens and Max Evans are the carriage drivers. Stevens becomes Robards's big romance, but exits for Frisco on her gold-digging hunt. Characterizations are fully developed.

•

BALLAD OF LITTLE JO, THE
1993, 120 mins, US Ⓥ ⦿ col
Dir Maggie Greenwald ***Prod*** Fred Berner, Brenda Goodman ***Scr*** Maggie Greenwald ***Ph*** Declan Quinn ***Ed*** Keith Reamer ***Mus*** David Mansfield ***Art*** Mark Friedberg
Act Suzy Amis, Bo Hopkins, Ian McKellen, David Chung, Carrie Snodgress, Rene Auberjonois (Fine Line/PFE/JoJo)

Suzy Amis's superlative performance dominates every frame of *The Ballad of Little Jo*, an earnest drama about a woman who disguises herself as a man to survive hardship in the Old West. But this well-intentioned, revisionist frontier saga is too solemn and dramatically unexciting.

Inspired by a true story, writer-director Maggie Greenwald's fascinating story is set in 1866, during the Gold Rush. Josephine Monaghan (Amis) is a wealthy woman from the East, cast out by her family after giving birth out of wedlock. Heading west, she meets Hollander (Rene Auberjonois), a peddler who initially befriends her but then sexually harasses her. Realizing her only chance of freedom in the West is as a man, Josephine proceeds to cut her long hair, scar her face, put on trousers—and change her name to Little Jo. She begins her new life in Ruby City, a frontier mining outpost populated by fortune-seeking adventurers. Before long, she learns how to mine, hunt and manage a self-sufficient existence. Jo's solitary life changes after she saves Tinman Wong (David Chung), an Asian outcast, from lynching.

Greenwald brings a contemporary feminist vision to the saga. But despite her efforts to demystify the Old West, she ends up mythologizing her heroine as a symbol of pioneering endurance.

•

BALLAD OF NARAYAMA, THE
SEE: NARAYAMA BUSHI-KO [1958]

•

BALLAD OF NARAYAMA, THE
SEE: NARAYAMA BUSHI-KO [1983]

•

BALLAD OF THE SAD CAFE, THE
1991, 100 mins, US/UK Ⓥ col
Dir Simon Callow ***Prod*** Ismail Merchant ***Scr*** Michael Hirst ***Ph*** Walter Lassally ***Ed*** Andrew Marcus ***Mus*** Richard Robbins ***Art*** Bruno Santini
Act Vanessa Redgrave, Keith Carradine, Cork Hubbert, Rod Steiger, Austin Pendleton, Beth Dixon (Merchant-Ivory/Film Four)

Simon Callow makes an assured feature directing debut adapting Carson McCullers's novella *The Ballad of the Sad Cafe*, a demanding, abstract fable.

Amelia (Vanessa Redgrave) is a violent, mannishly styled woman who threw out her husband (Keith Carradine) on their wedding night and has become a legendary figure in her little Southern town in the 1930s. With cropped hair and unglamorous makeup, Redgrave throws herself into the role with uncensored force.

Carradine, who replaced Sam Shepard, brings a naturalism to his embittered role as the ex-con and spurned spouse.

Catalyst in the piece is the fantasy character of Cousin Lymon (Cork Hubbert), a hunchbacked dwarf who pops up out of nowhere claiming to be Redgrave's cousin. He gets Redgrave to convert her general store into a cafe, serving the moonshine she prepares at her still. Carradine shows up midway through the pic fresh out of the state pen. He's out to avenge himself against Redgrave.

Film climaxes memorably in a bare-knuckles boxing match staged at the cafe between Carradine and Redgrave to settle their differences once and for all.

Redgrave's body English, strange accent and physical outbursts are a triumph of pure acting. Carradine's more natural approach helps bring pic closer to reality. An intense supporting performance by Rod Steiger also provides exposition as the town preacher.

•

BALL OF FIRE
1941, 110 mins, US Ⓥ ⦿ b/w
Dir Howard Hawks ***Prod*** Samuel Goldwyn ***Scr*** Charles Brackett, Billy Wilder ***Ph*** Gregg Toland ***Ed*** Daniel Mandell ***Mus*** Alfred Newman ***Art*** Perry Ferguson
Act Gary Cooper, Barbara Stanwyck, Oscar Homolka, Dana Andrews, Dan Duryea, Henry Travers (RKO/Samuel Goldwyn)

A simple gag is hardly enough on which to string 110 minutes of film. And that's all—one funny situation—that Samuel Goldwyn's director and writers have to support *Ball of Fire*. It's sufficient, however, to provide quite a few chuckles.

Gag on which the whole thing is based [from an original story by Billy Wilder and Thomas Monroe] is Gary Cooper's professorial efforts to write a learned piece on slang for an encyclopedia. He needs, for research purposes, someone who's hep to the last syllable of the lingo and brings into a sanctum, where he and seven colleagues are working on the encyclopedia, a burlesque stripper (Barbara Stanwyck). She upsets and excites the eight old men in the expected manner. Much of the dialog is rapid-fire slang, plenty labored, but frequently good for laughs.

Casting is meticulously perfect to make every character a caricature of itself. Cooper is in the familiar "Mr. Smith–John Doe" role of the brainy guy who's not quite hep to his surroundings until near the end, when he wises up in time to snatch victory from the smart boys. Stanwyck is likewise in a familiar part that she can play for maximum results.

1941: NOMINATIONS: Best Actress (Barbara Stanwyck), Original Story, Scoring of a Dramatic Picture, Sound

•

BALTIMORE BULLET, THE

1980, 103 mins, US Ⓥ col

Dir Robert Ellis Miller ***Prod*** John F. Brascia ***Scr*** John F. Brascia, Vincent O'Neill ***Ph*** James A. Crabe ***Ed*** Jerry Brady ***Mus*** Johnny Mandel ***Art*** Herman Blumenthal

Act James Coburn, Omar Sharif, Bruce Boxleitner, Ronee Blakely, Jack O'Halloran, Calvin Lockhart (Avco Embassy)

James Coburn and Bruce Boxleitner limn a kind of father-son pool hustling team who make their living traveling through the country taking advantage of local would-be billiard sharks. They do occasionally enter tournaments, one of which will enable Coburn to reunite with his arch nemesis Omar Sharif.

Coburn and Boxleitner work well together although the former looks and speaks more like someone sipping champagne aboard a yacht than a journeyman dashing through an endless array of hick towns. Ronee Blakely is picked up by the pair along the way for moral support and fulfills the limited duties asked of her.

Problem here is scrpt. Situations are just too inane to take seriously and not funny enough to be laughed at.

•

BALTO

1995, 77 mins, US Ⓥ ⦿ col

Dir Simon Wells ***Prod*** Steve Hickner ***Scr*** Cliff Ruby, Elana Lesser, David Steven Cohen, Roger S. H. Schulman ***Ed*** Nick Fletcher, Sim Evan-Jones ***Mus*** James Horner ***Art*** Hans Bacher

Act Miriam Margolyes, Lola Bates-Campbell (Amblin/Universal)

Offering a mild diversion for the youngest of kids, *Balto* is an average, at best, animated yarn based loosely on a true story from the 1920s. Live-action wraparounds help frame the story of Balto (voiced by Kevin Bacon), a stray half-dog, half-wolf who, despite being an outcast among both humans and canines due to his lineage, helps guide a sled carrying medication to a town full of sick kids in Alaska.

Taking a page from *Beauty and the Beast*, the villain, Steele (Jim Cummings), is a much-admired leader of the pack with an insidious core who deeply resents Balto, vying with him for the affection of Jenna (Bridget Fonda), whose owner, Rosy, is among the sick children. Despite being shunned by most of the dogs, Balto has an assortment of friends that includes a Russian goose named Boris (Bob Hoskins) and two landlocked polar bears, Muk and Luk (Phil Collins).

Balto doesn't miss many tricks as far as pro-social messages go, but comes up short in a number of areas, as director Simon Wells and a quartet of writers fall flat with much of the humor, only occasionally delivering laughs either with broad comedy or more sophisticated jokes capable of truly tickling adults as well as tots. James Horner's blaring score does work overtime to create a sense of excitement.

•

BAMBI

1942, 70 mins, US Ⓥ ⦿ col

Dir David Hand ***Prod*** Walt Disney ***Scr*** Larry Morey ***Mus*** Frank Churchill, Edward Plumb (Walt Disney)

Bambi is gemlike in its reflection of the color and movement of sylvan plant and animal life. The transcription of nature in its moments of turbulence and peace heightens the brilliance of the canvas. The story [by Felix Salten] is full of tenderness and the characters tickle the heart.

Thumper, the rabbit, steals the picture. His human attributes are amazing and the voice that is attached to him in the earlier sequences proves an admirable piece of casting. It's a regret that there wasn't much more of him in the picture.

In this story of Bambi, and his friends of the forest, the span of the central character is from birth to the period in which he reaches bull buckhood. The episodes in between show him learning to adapt himself to his surroundings and to outwit the biped with the gun, falling in love, entering parenthood and finally taking his place beside his proud and hoary father, prince of the forest. The dramatic highlights of Bambi's career include the death of his mother by gunshot (a scene of deep pathos), and his fight to the death with another buck over the doe, Faline.

The interplay of color and movement make their sharpest impressions on the sensibilities during the sequences depicting the advent and passing of the various seasons. The glow and texture of the Disney brush reach new heights, especially in the treatment of a summer thunderstorm and a raging snowstorm.

1942: NOMINATIONS: Best Scoring of a Dramatic Picture, Song ("Love Is a Song"), Sound

•

BAMBOOZLED

2000, 135 mins, US Ⓥ ⦿ col

Dir Spike Lee ***Prod*** Jon Kilik, Spike Lee ***Scr*** Spike Lee ***Ph*** Ellen Kuras ***Ed*** Sam Pollard ***Mus*** Terence Blanchard ***Art*** Victor Kempster

Act Damon Wayans, Savion Glover, Jada Pinkett-Smith, Tommy Davidson, Michael Rapaport, Thomas Jefferson Byrd (40 Acres and a Mule/New Line)

Spike Lee's *Bamboozled* is an ambitious satire on race and ratings, centering on the stereotypical imagery of blacks in American mass media. The topic that Lee tackles head-on here is hardly new. What is new about Lee's satire is that it's not so much about black performers as about black TV executive-writers, a profession still overwhelmingly dominated by white men. Protagonist is Pierre Delacroix (Damon Wayans), a bright, Harvard-educated writer who wants desperately to be taken seriously. As the lone black at a foundering network, Pierre is constantly under pressure to go with the flow—to predict public taste and boost dwindling ratings. Commanded by network exec Dunwitty (Michael Rapaport) to come up with a show all America will talk about, Pierre delves into the history of blacks in the arts and revives a long-popular but now taboo form of entertainment: the minstrel show, of burnt-cork blackface and dance-comedy routines.

He recruits Manray (Savion Glover), a tap-dancing street artist, and latter's partner, Womack (Tommy Davidson), to become a 21st-century minstrel duo in blackface. Pierre changes Womack's name to Sleep 'N Eat and Manray's to Mantan, after actor Mantan Moreland. *Mantan: The New Millennium Minstrel Show* is unexpectedly embraced by the press and the public as hip and funny, and becomes a top-rated program. Changing tone, text's second half is disappointingly melodramatic.

Though *Bamboozled* centers on the TV world, Lee's frame is broader, meant to rep all the arts. Obviously disappointed by the limited ways people of color have been portrayed in—and often altogether written out of—history, he provokes uneasy feelings in the audience, suggesting that the old minstrel stereotype can, and does, resurface in subtler ways, dressed in new garb to look modern, hip and politically relevant.

Bamboozled is a no-holds-barred film that skewers everybody on both sides of the racial divide; no one is a winner. And while the movie contains many emotionally effective moments, Wayans's awkward performance, in an admittedly complex role, is problematic and exerts a negative effect on the film as a whole.

•

BANANAS

1971, 82 mins, US Ⓥ ⦿ col

Dir Woody Allen ***Prod*** Jack Rollins, Charles H. Joffe ***Scr*** Woody Allen, Mickey Rose ***Ph*** Andrew M. Costikyan ***Ed*** Ron Kalish ***Mus*** Marvin Hamlisch

Act Woody Allen, Louise Lasser, Carlos Montalban, Natividad Abascal, Jacobo Morales, Miguel Suarez (United Artists)

Bananas is chockful of sight gags, one-liners and swiftly executed unnecessary excursions into vulgarity whose humor for the most part can't make up for content.

Woody Allen, as bumbling New Yorker working for an automation film, is rejected by his activist sweetheart Louise Lasser, who is involved in revolutions, particularly in fictional San Marcos where dictator Carlos Montalban has seized control. Allen, disconsolate, bids farewell to parents Charlotte Rae and Stanley Ackerman while they are performing medical operation. Landing in San Marcos, he is feted by Montalban, who is setting him up as pigeon to be erased supposedly by revolutionary Jacobo Morales's men.

Allen and Mickey Rose have written some funny stuff, and Allen, both as director and actor, knows what to do with it. Scenes between Lasser and comedian have wonderfully fresh, incisive touch. Montalban's dictator is properly arrogant. Morales performs with assurance right up to the point when, drunk with power, he proclaims Swedish the national language.

•

BANDIDO

1956, 91 mins, US ▭ col

Dir Richard Fleischer ***Prod*** Robert L. Jacks ***Scr*** Earl Felton ***Ph*** Ernest Laszlo ***Ed*** Robert Golden ***Mus*** Max Steiner ***Art*** Jack Martin Smith

Act Robert Mitchum, Ursula Thiess, Gilbert Roland, Zachary Scott, Rodolfo Acosta, Henry Brandon (Bandido/United Artists)

Gun-running in Mexico back in 1916 sets up a round of adventurous action. Robert Mitchum is a likeable, not always understandable, sort of hero-heavy who likes war because it gives him a chance to make some money gun-running, besides finding amusement in his profession.

While the yarn is a dime thriller, it is also presented with some above-average touches here and there, plus some frank birds-and-bees byplay between Mitchum and the heroine (Ursula Thiess) that adds spice to the action. Film has its slow spots, mostly due to occasionally draggy direction by Richard Fleischer and a need of tighter editing.

In addition to Mitchum, the male end of the cast draws notable help from the presence of Gilbert Roland, leader of the rebels for whom the gun-runner is trying to obtain arms by hijacking a shipment being brought in by Zachary Scott for the Regulares.

Below-the-border locationing gives the picture strikingly beautiful scenes.

•

BANDITI A ORGOSOLO
(THE BANDITS OF ORGOSOLO)

1961, 98 mins, Italy b/w

Dir Vittorio De Seta ***Scr*** Vera Gherarducci, Vittorio De Seta ***Ph*** Vittorio De Seta ***Mus*** Valentino Bucchi

Act Michele Cossu, Peppeddu Cuccu, Vittorina Pisano (Titanus)

Fine initial effort by young Italian filmmaker Vittorio De Seta, *Orgosolo* is a pic that while closely bordering on the documentary nevertheless has enough story elements to hold audience attention.

Plot tells of vain efforts of a Sardinian shepherd to escape from his fate. He is unjustly involved in a theft and murder episode, with the police hunting him and his flock of sheep over hill and valley. Animals die and the shepherd, already partly resigned, accompanies his brother to the village where they lived. Then he takes to the hills again, where circumstances now force him to steal others' sheep and become what to the outside world is merely a "bandit."

It's a director's picture all the way, and a brilliant start for De Seta who, though he doesn't entirely attain the stature of a Robert Flaherty, hits the mark with his pure treatment of elemental themes of man and nature. His choice and direction of the Sardinian back country smacks of the uncanny, and the craggy rock-hewn face of Michele Cossu, as the shepherd, is unforgettable.

The only concession to realism is that the characters speak Italian, not the original local argot. Pace is keyed to setting and people, slow and not overly talkative.

•

BANDIT OF SHERWOOD FOREST, THE

1946, 85 mins, US col

Dir George Sherman, Henry Levin ***Prod*** Leonard S. Picker, Clifford Sanforth ***Scr*** Wilfrid H. Pettitt, Melvin Levy ***Ph*** Tony Gaudio, William Snyder, George B. Meehan, Jr. ***Ed*** Richard Fanti ***Mus*** Hugo Friedhofer ***Art*** Stephen Goosson, Rudolph Sternad

Act Cornel Wilde, Anita Louise, Jill Esmond, Edgar Buchanan, George Macready, Henry Daniell (Columbia)

Technicolor spectacle of high adventure in Sherwood Forest. It's a costume Western, in effect, offering the fictional escapades of the son of Robin Hood, a hard-riding, hard-loving hombre who uses his trusty bow and arrow to right injustice and tyranny back in the days of feudal England.

There is considerable ineptness in writing, production and direction but it still stands up as okay escapist film fare for the not-too-critical.

There is a concentration of chases and "they-went-thataway" flavor about the doings that hints at the Western feature training of producers and directors.

Plot has the son of Robin Hood coming back to Sherwood Forest to save England's Magna Carta and young king from the cruel plotting of a wicked regent. With his long bow, sword and trusty horse, Wilde proves himself more than a match for the villain, saves the young king's life, the Magna Carta and wins true love and knighthood. Concocting the script, full of dialogue cliches and ten-twent-thirt dramatics, were Wilfrid H. Pettitt and Melvin Levy, working from a story by Paul A. Castleton and Pettitt, based on the novel *Son of Robin Hood* by Castleton.

Wilde is properly swashbuckling as the hero, and probably had himself a time enacting the dare-and-do.

•

BANDIT QUEEN
1994, 121 mins, India/UK Ⓥ col
Dir Shekhar Kapur ***Prod*** Sundeep Singh Bedi ***Scr*** Mala Sen ***Ph*** Ashok Mehta, Giles Nutgens ***Ed*** Renu Saluja ***Mus*** Nusrat Fateh Ali Khan, Roger White ***Art*** Eve Mavrakis
Act Seema Biswas, Nirmal Pandey, Manoj Bajpai, Rajesh Vivek, Govind Namdeo, Saurabh Shukla (Kaleidoscope/Channel 4)

True story of a femme bandit who eluded the Indian authorities for five years makes initially leisurely but finally gripping viewing in *Bandit Queen*.

Phoolan Devi finally surrendered to the police in the northern state of Uttar Pradesh in January 1983, accused of murder and kidnapping. Pic is based on the dictated prison diaries of the woman herself who, after a change of government, was finally released in February 1994 to local superstar status.

A long, 15-minute pre-credit sequence opens in 1968, with Devi a feisty young girl burdened by her low-caste background but not prepared to accept a standard rural existence. Post-main title, she's an assured young woman (Seema Biswas) living with relatives but the target of insults from local studs. One day, she comes across handsome young local bandit Vikram (Nirmal Pandey), and a spark flies.

Things get complicated when the real gang henchman, SriRam (Govind Namdeo), is released from prison and reassumes leadership. The dramatic screws tighten with a shocking sequence—all the more powerful for its visual discretion—of Devi gang-raped by SriRam's men and then stripped naked in front of the villagers. Her subsequent revenge, dubbed the Behmai Massacre of February '81, forms the dramatic climax of the pic. Comprehension isn't helped by sometimes choppy editing in the early going, but once the story moves into high gear, helmer Shekhar Kapur brings out his big guns to often stunning effect. Biswas is terrific in the title role, moving from tough to tender with natural ease.

•

BANDITS OF ORGOSOLO, THE
SEE: BANDITI A ORGOSOLO

•

BAND OF ANGELS
1957, 125 mins, US col
Dir Raoul Walsh ***Prod*** Jerry Wald ***Scr*** John Twist, Ivan Goff, Ben Roberts ***Ph*** Lucien Ballard ***Ed*** Folmar Blangsted ***Mus*** Max Steiner ***Art*** Franz Bachelin
Act Clark Gable, Yvonne De Carlo, Sidney Poitier, Efrem Zimbalist, Jr., Patric Knowles, Carolle Drake (Warner)

Subject of miscegenation is explored and developed in this colorful production of the Old South. Raoul Walsh is in top form in direction of the screenplay derived from a Robert Penn Warren novel. Screenwriters have captured the mood and spirit of the Deep South narrative, which deals with a young woman of quality discovering that her mother was a slave.

Sold on the auction block to a former slave-trader, unfoldment dwells on the pair's relations, both in New Orleans and later on a plantation up-river. Beautiful and realistic backgrounds are achieved through locationing in Louisiana.

Clark Gable's characterization is reminiscent of his Rhett Butler in *Gone with the Wind*, although there is obviously no paralleling of plot. As former slave-runner turned New Orleans gentleman, with bitter memories of his earlier days, he contributes a warm, decisive portrayal that carries tremendous authority.

Yvonne De Carlo is beautiful as the mulatto, who learns of her true status when she returns from a Cincinnati finishing school to attend her father's funeral. Sidney Poitier impresses as Gable's educated protégé, whom slaver picked up as an infant in Africa and reared as his son.

•

BANDOLERO!
1968, 107 mins, US Ⓥ ▭ col
Dir Andrew V. McLaglen ***Prod*** Robert L. Jacks ***Scr*** James Lee Barrett ***Ph*** William H. Clothier ***Ed*** Folmar Blangsted ***Mus*** Jerry Goldsmith ***Art*** Jack Martin Smith, Alfred Sweeney, Jr.
Act James Stewart, Dean Martin, Raquel Welch, George Kennedy, Andrew Prine, Will Geer (20th Century-Fox)

Bandolero! is a dull Western meller. Though competently produced, film suffers from distended scripting, routine direction and overlength. Basic story is the escape and capture of a gang of post–Civil War vagabonds. Dean Martin heads an outlaw group that includes Will Geer, Tom Heaton, Sean McClory and Clint Ritchie.

Pre-title bank heist, in which Raquel Welch's husband is killed, lands the group in George Kennedy's jail, awaiting hanging by itinerant executioner Guy Raymond. Stewart, Martin's older brother who always has rescued him from mistakes, takes Raymond's place in order to effect gang's escape. Having accomplished this, the upright Stewart then robs a bank. This opening action, well developed, takes 40 minutes.

Welch is got up to look like a Mexican Sophia Loren. Her makeup is distressingly false-looking, her accent moreso. Of Kennedy, she says at one point, "Hee ees a good mahn."

•

BAND WAGON, THE
1953, 112 mins, US Ⓥ ⦿ col
Dir Vincente Minnelli ***Prod*** Arthur Freed ***Scr*** Betty Comden, Adolph Green ***Ph*** Harry Jackson ***Ed*** Albert Akst ***Mus*** Adolph Deutsch (dir.) ***Art*** Cedric Gibbons, Preston Ames, Oliver Smith
Act Fred Astaire, Cyd Charisse, Oscar Levant, Nanette Fabray, Jack Buchanan, James Mitchell (M-G-M)

Plot is the one about a dancing film star whose pictures aren't selling. A couple of writing pals conceive a stage musical for him and the rest of the story is concerned with making the show a success after a flop tryout and weeks of rewriting and new starts.

Twelve songs [staged by Michael Kidd] from various Broadway musicals are either chirped or terped. Showing up as an imaginative highlight is "Girl Hunt," the modern jazz ballet finale done to a turn by Fred Astaire and Cyd Charisse. A takeoff in dance on the Mickey Spillane type of private eye, number is a new cleffing for the picture by Howard Dietz and Arthur Schwartz, credited with all of the songs.

Astaire, as the film star, shows his ability with a song and dance character. Oscar Levant and Nanette Fabray make up the writing team. Fabray is given enough chance to display her talent from legit musicals, and her personality is caught by the cameras. Charisse is an eye-filling filly, especially when dancing. Levant is his usual phlegmatic self. Buchanan enacts the show's director and costar and is one of the picture's strong points with his comedy moments.

1953: NOMINATIONS: Best Story & Screenplay, Color Costume Design, Scoring of a Musical Picture

•

BANK BREAKER, THE
SEE: KALEIDOSCOPE

•

BANK DETECTIVE, THE
SEE: THE BANK DICK

•

BANK DICK, THE
(U.K.: THE BANK DETECTIVE)
1940, 69 mins, US Ⓥ ⦿ b/w
Dir Edward Cline ***Prod*** [uncredited] ***Scr*** Mahatma Kane Jeeves [= W. C. Fields] ***Ph*** Milton Krasner ***Ed*** Arthur Hilton ***Mus*** Charles Previn (dir.) ***Art*** Jack Otterson, Richard Riedel
Act W. C. Fields, Cora Witherspoon, Una Merkel, Jessie Ralph, Franklin Pangborn, Grady Sutton (Universal)

Story is credited to Mahatma Kane Jeeves, Fields's own humorous nom de plume. It's a deliberate rack on which to hang the varied Fieldsian comedic routines, many of them repeats from previous pictures but with enough new material inserted to overcome the antique gags. A wild auto ride down the mountainside for the climax is an old formula dating back to the Mack Sennett days, but director Edward Cline [and "collaborating director" Ralph Ceder] has refurbished the episode with new twists that make it a thrill-laugh dash of top proportions.

Fields is the town's foremost elbow bender who injects himself into any situation without invitation. The unexpected hero of a bank robbery, he is rewarded with the job of detective to guard against future holdups. He involves his prospective son-in-law as a temporary embezzler to buy wildcat mining stock, and then holds off the bank examiner via the Mickey Finn route. Repeat bank robbery again results in Fields's accepting hero honors, the reward and sudden riches from a film directing contract.

Several times, Fields reaches into satirical pantomime reminiscent of Charlie Chaplin's best efforts during his Mutual and Essanay days. Directorial guidance by Cline (graduate of the Keystone Kop school) smacks over every gag line and situation to the fullest extent.

Fields has a field day in tabbing the various characters. His own screen name, he is careful to explain, is pronounced Soozay, and not Souse, as it appears from English pronunciation.

•

BANK HOLIDAY
(U.S.: THREE ON A WEEKEND)
1938, 86 mins, UK b/w
Dir Carol Reed ***Scr*** Rodney Ackland, Roger Burford ***Ph*** Arthur Crabtree ***Ed*** R. E. Dearing, Alfred Roome ***Mus*** Louis Levy (dir.) ***Art*** Alex Vetchinsky
Act John Lodge, Margaret Lockwood, Hugh Williams, Rene Ray, Linden Travers, Merle Tottenham (Gainsborough)

This is good entertainment. A young nurse, Catherine (Margaret Lockwood), has planned to spend an illicit weekend with a man to whom she cannot be married until their financial position improves. Her patient dies in childbirth and her pity for the forlorn husband changes her whole life.

In the hectic rush of London's termini, she joins her waiting lover. They reach the coast, only to find no rooms available; they spend the night on the beach, duly chaperoned by hundreds of others. The tragedy she has left behind mars her pleasure; she flees her lover and with the aid of the police saves the widower from suicide.

Interspersed [in the story by Hans Wilhelm and Rodney Ackland] are many rich characters: a Cockney family with squabbling kids, two young soldiers on leave, entrants for a beauty prize—one trying to get over a jilt, another aping society and making all the judges. None is overdrawn and all are depicted with human interest.

•

BARABBAS
1962, 144 mins, Italy Ⓥ ▭ col
Dir Richard Fleischer ***Prod*** Dino De Laurentiis ***Scr*** Christopher Fry [Diego Fabbri, Nigel Balchin] ***Ph*** Aldo Tonti ***Ed*** Raymond Poulton ***Mus*** Mario Nascimbene ***Art*** Mario Chiari
Act Anthony Quinn, Silvana Mangano, Arthur Kennedy, Jack Palance, Vittorio Gassman, Ernest Borgnine (De Laurentiis)

Barabbas is technically a fine job, reflecting big thinking and infinite patience on the parts of producer Dino De Laurentiis and director Richard Fleischer. In Technirama 70 and shot in Technicolor it has one or two sequences that stand up to the chariot race highlight in *Ben-Hur*.

Set in Jerusalem 2,000 years ago, the film [based on the novel by Par Lagerkvist, adapted by Giuseppe Berto and Ivo Perilli] tells the story of Barabbas, thief and murderer, who was released from prison by the will of the people and replaced, in jail and on the Cross, by Jesus Christ. Barabbas's conscience plagues him. In a struggling, almost bovine manner, he tries to find the truth about the new wave of faith that is sweeping the country.

Where the film hits the bell is in Fleischer's bold, dramatic handling of certain scenes, allied to some slick lensing by Aldo Tonti. The scenes in the Rome gladiatorial pit, sharply etched by Jack Palance as the top boy, have an urgent excitement, with Palance's sadism matched only by Quinn's bewildered concentration.

Individually, the performances are uneven. Quinn is first-class in a role that could have become monotonous after his beefy approach to his scenes with a vital Katy Jurado following his release from jail. Palance plays the sadistic gladiator with a lip-licking panache that tends to pinpoint the fact that the whole pic is a shade too violent, but certainly the thesp makes Torvald a vivid and urgent figure in the setup.

Silvana Mangano does an adequate job as Rachel, but the part never comes to life, nor does that of Ernest Borgnine as a Christian doing undercover work among the Romans.

•

BARBARELLA
(AKA: BARBARELLA—QUEEN OF THE GALAXY)
1968, 98 mins, France/Italy Ⓥ ⦿ b col
Dir Roger Vadim ***Prod*** Dino De Laurentiis ***Scr*** Terry Southern, Roger Vadim, Claude Brule, Vittorio Bonicelli, Clement Biddle Wood, Brian Degas, Tudor Gates, Jean Claude Forest ***Ph*** Claude Renoir ***Ed*** Victoria Mercanton ***Mus*** Michel Magne, Charles Fox ***Art*** Mario Garbuglia
Act Jane Fonda, John Phillip Law, Anita Pallenberg, Milo O'Shea, David Hemmings, Marcel Marceau (Marianne/De Laurentiis)

Despite a certain amount of production dash and polish and a few silly-funny lines of dialog, *Barbarella* isn't very much of a film. Based on what has been called an adult comic strip [by Jean Claude Forest], the Dino De Laurentiis production is flawed with a cast that is not particularly adept at comedy, a flat script, and direction that can't get this beached whale afloat.

Jane Fonda stars in the title role, and comes across as an ice-cold, antiseptic, wide-eyed girl who just can't say no. Fonda's abilities are stretched to the breaking point along with her clothes.

In key supporting roles, John Phillip Law is inept as a simp angel while Anita Pallenberg, as the lesbian queen, fares better because of a well-defined character.

Made at De Laurentiis's Rome studios, film can't really be called over-produced, considering the slapdash special effects, grainy process and poor calibre of the props, though put together on a massive scale so as to appear of spectacle proportions.

•

BARBARIAN AND THE GEISHA, THE

1958, 105 mins, US Ⓥ ▭ col

Dir John Huston ***Prod*** Eugene Frenke ***Scr*** Charles Grayson ***Ph*** Charles G. Clarke ***Ed*** Stuart Gilmore ***Mus*** Hugo Friedhofer ***Art*** Lyle R. Wheeler, Jack Martin Smith

Act John Wayne, Eiko Ando, Sam Jaffe, So Yamamura, Morita, Hiroshi Yamato (20th Century-Fox)

The Barbarian and the Geisha is an Oriental pageant of primitive beauty based on the "true" story of the exploits of the first U.S. consul to establish headquarters in Japan. The production is lavish but it is light in other departments.

Once opened to Christian missionaries, then closed, Japan was a Forbidden Kingdom to outsiders in 1856 when U.S. Consul-General Townsend Harris (John Wayne) arrives off the port of Shimoda, where the screenplay, based on Ellis St. Joseph's story, begins. Harris is under orders to open the door on the hermetically sealed country, and, armed only with his own personality and accompanied only by his European translator (Sam Jaffe) he prepares to do so.

After initial harrassing and setbacks, Wayne gains the confidence of the local noble (So Yamamura) who agrees to take him to the court of the Shogun to plead his case. Meantime, to make Wayne's isolation easier, Yamamura delivers a geisha (Eiko Ando) to the non-Nipponese barbarian.

The Barbarian and the Geisha (originally titled *The Townsend Harris Story*) is rich in atmosphere and in some stirringly staged scenes, such as Wayne's arrival by ship at Shimoda, his presentation to the Shogun's court and an archery meet of medieval pomp. It is less exciting in its personal delineations. Huston uses a technique of having the Japanese speak Japanese throughout. The character played by Ando acts as the narrator behind some of this action, but this device is only partially successful.

•

BARBAROSA

1982, 90 mins, US Ⓥ ⊙ ▭ col

Dir Fred Schepisi ***Prod*** Paul N. Lazarus III ***Scr*** William D. Wittliff ***Ph*** Ian Baker ***Ed*** Don Zimmerman, David Ramirez ***Mus*** Bruce Smeaton ***Art*** Michael Levesque, Leon Ericksen

Act Willie Nelson, Gary Busey, Isela Vega, Gilbert Roland, Danny De La Paz, Alma Martinez (Universal/Associated)

Australian director Fred Schepisi does a careful job of bringing the Western legend to light with endearing performances from actors Willie Nelson and Gary Busey.

Nelson limns the renowned title character, who in essence is nothing more than a "sensitive" outlaw forever eluding the assassination attempts of his wife's over-protective family. Nelson visits his spouse and daughter (who live with the family) several times a year, but past events coupled with his yearning for freedom make it impossible to live a normal life.

Busey turns in a natural portrayal of the poor, goofy farm boy the outlaw takes under his wing. While it's an honorable performance, the Busey character and his growth into a soulful human being primarily serves to point up what a nice guy Nelson is.

•

BARBARY COAST

1935, 97 mins, US Ⓥ ⊙ b/w

Dir Howard Hawks ***Prod*** Samuel Goldwyn ***Scr*** Ben Hecht, Charles MacArthur ***Ph*** Ray June ***Ed*** Edward Curtiss ***Mus*** Alfred Newman (dir.) ***Art*** Richard Day

Act Miriam Hopkins, Edward G. Robinson, Joel McCrea, Walter Brennan, Frank Craven, Brian Donlevy (Goldwyn/United Artists)

Sam Goldwyn picked *Barbary Coast* as a title and called in Ben Hecht and Charles MacArthur to write a story to fit. Result is a picture that has all it takes to get along in thoroughbred company.

Atmosphere of the period has been richly caught, even if the girl's efforts to free herself from the gambling hall proprietor aren't so sincere.

Miriam Hopkins is introduced when she arrives in Frisco to meet the man she is going to marry, admittedly because he has struck it rich. When learning he has been killed over a gambling loss, she throws herself toward Edward G. Robinson, town's underworld leader. Story makes Hopkins a partially unsympathetic character until she falls in love with a young prospector and finds herself tangled up through prior associations. It is mostly Hopkins's picture but Robinson and Joel McCrea are also strong.

Harry Carey plays the organizer of vigilantes and gives a good performance. Other standout small parts are by Walter Brennan and Frank Craven.

1935: NOMINATION: Best Cinematography

•

BARB WIRE

1996, 99 mins, US Ⓥ ⊙ col

Dir David Hogan ***Prod*** Mike Richardson, Todd Moyer, Brad Wyman ***Scr*** Chuck Pfarrer, Ilene Chaiken ***Ph*** Rick Bota ***Ed*** Peter Schink ***Mus*** Michel Colombier ***Art*** Jean Philippe Carp

Act Pamela Anderson Lee, Temuera Morrison, Victoria Rowell, Jack Noseworthy, Udo Kier, Steve Railsbeck (Propaganda/Dark Horse/PolyGram)

Despite its obvious flaws, *Barb Wire* does what it sets out to do and does it well. If not a great action film, this cartoonlike starring vehicle for Pamela Anderson Lee offers enough choreographed fight sequences, heavy artillery and fleeting glimpses of the star's august body parts to satisfy the raging hormones of its target young male audience.

Pic is set in the year 2017, in the midst of America's second civil war, in Steel Harbor, home of a seedy yet stylish joint called the Hammerhead Bar & Grille, owned by the aloof and amoral Barb Wire (Lee).

Barb is forced—inexplicably, since the club is always packed—to moonlight as a bounty hunter. The surprisingly complicated plot has a fugitive named Krebs (Loren Rubin) in possession of valuable contact lenses that allow the wearer to escape detection by the government's ubiquitous retinal scanners. The evil feds suspect he's about to pass the lenses on to a former government doctor, Cora D (Victoria Rowell), who has defected to the rebel cause. Barb eventually takes possession of the lenses.

It's all improbable, silly and full of gaping plot holes, but it matters not at all, since *Barb Wire* is a ride that is definitely fun while it lasts. Pic is based on a [screen story by Ilene Chaiken, based on a] comic book [character created by Chris Warner] from Dark Horse, which also published *The Mask*, and Lee, with her bionic bosom, wasp-thin waist and pretty, symmetrical features, is the embodiment of a comic-book super heroine, whose emotions range narrowly from homicidal to merely pissed off.

Tech credits are decent if not top-notch. Barb's showroom-perfect Triumph motorcycle gets major play.

•

BARCELONA

1994, 100 mins, US Ⓥ ⊙ col

Dir Whit Stillman ***Prod*** Whit Stillman ***Scr*** Whit Stillman ***Ph*** John Thomas ***Ed*** Christopher Tellefsen ***Mus*** Marc Suozzo ***Art*** Jose Maria Botines

Act Taylor Nichols, Chris Eigeman, Tushka Bergen, Mira Sorvino, Pep Munne, Nuria Badia (Westly/Castle Rock)

Four years after his distinctive debut feature, *Metropolitan*, Whit Stillman has delivered a superior followup in *Barcelona*. A verbal tale of two well-spoken young American men posted in the beautiful seaport city during what is described as "the last decade of the Cold War," sophisticated picture possesses a strong authorial voice and an appealing intelligence in its handling of affairs of the heart and its Yanks-abroad theme.

In a sensual, Old World setting rocked by sporadic violence directed at U.S.-identified targets, the somewhat priggish Ted (Taylor Nichols) lives a charmed existence as a sales rep for an American company. His cousin Fred (Chris Eigeman), a U.S. Navy officer, suddenly turns up and camps out in Ted's apartment. With his loud, obnoxious ways and patriotic views, Fred could easily be written off as a typical Ugly American, but he quickly shows himself to be more complex than that.

Ted meets Monserrat (Tushka Bergen), a somewhat sullen blonde who dates Ted but still continues to see a virulently anti-Yank Spanish b.f. Perhaps the film's most singular achievement is the portrayal of the manifold ways—from subtle to overt—in which anti-American sentiments were vented overseas during a certain period in the '70s and '80s. Fred himself becomes the victim of a terrorist act.

Abundant dialogue is tart, informed, often droll and as opinionated as real conversation. Pic's almost extreme literary quality and expatriate characters make one feel that Stillman could be a spiritual brother to the Lost Generation of 1920s writers. Nichols and Eigeman, both from *Metropolitan*, seem right at home in Stillman's world, and make their not always easy characters grow on one as things proceed.

•

BAREFOOT CONTESSA, THE

1954, 128 mins, US Ⓥ col

Dir Joseph L. Mankiewicz ***Prod*** Forrest E. Johnston (man.) ***Scr*** Joseph L. Mankiewicz ***Ph*** Jack Cardiff ***Ed*** William Hornbeck ***Mus*** Mario Nascimbene ***Art*** Arrigo Equini

Act Humphrey Bogart, Ava Gardner, Edmond O'Brien, Marius Goring, Valentina Cortese, Rossano Brazzi (United Artists/Figaro)

Sharpness of the characters, the high-voltage dialog, the cynicism and wit and wisdom of the story, the spectacular combination of the immorally rich and the immorally sycophantic—these add up to a click feature from writer-director Joseph L. Mankiewicz.

Ava Gardner is the contessa of the title, "discovered" in a second-rate flamenco nitery in Madrid. The trio of discoverers: Humphrey Bogart as a writer-director and determined member of Alcoholics' Anonymous; Edmond O'Brien as a glib, nervous, perspiring combination of press agent and (apparent) procurer; and Warren Stevens, the rich producer. Gardner is ideal in her spot, looking every inch the femme magnetism around which all the action revolves. Bogart is splendid throughout, taking part quietly and with maximum effectiveness in the twists and turns of the intriguing story.

At times, Mankiewicz, the writer, seems over-generous in providing his characters with words.

Mankiewicz has been quoted as saying none of his characters is for real. This was in answer to suspicion that the moneybags producer might be an only slightly distorted mirroring of Howard Hughes.

1954: Best Supp. Actor (Edmond O'Brien)

NOMINATION: Best Story & Screenplay

•

BAREFOOT IN THE PARK

1967, 104 mins, US Ⓥ ⊙ col

Dir Gene Saks ***Prod*** Hal B. Wallis ***Scr*** Neil Simon ***Ph*** Joseph LaShelle ***Ed*** William A. Lyon ***Mus*** Neal Hefti ***Art*** Hal Pereira, Walter Tyler

Act Robert Redford, Jane Fonda, Charles Boyer, Mildred Natwick, Herb Edelman, Mabel Albertson (Paramount)

Barefoot in the Park is one howl of a picture. Adapted by Neil Simon from his legit smash, retaining Robert Redford and Mildred Natwick from the original cast, and adding Jane Fonda and Charles Boyer to round out the principals, this is a thoroughly entertaining comedy delight about young marriage. Director Gene Saks makes a sock debut.

Redford is outstanding, particularly adept in light comedy. Fonda is excellent, ditto Natwick, her mother. A genuine surprise casting is Boyer, as the Bohemian who lives in the attic above the newlyweds' top-floor flat. With only one slight flagging pace—about 30 minutes from the end, when Redford and Fonda have their late-night squabble—pic moves along smartly.

1967: NOMINATION: Best Supp. Actress (Mildred Natwick)

•

BARFLY

1987, 99 mins, US Ⓥ ⊙ col

Dir Barbet Schroeder ***Prod*** Barbet Schroeder ***Scr*** Charles Bukowski ***Ph*** Robby Muller ***Ed*** Eva Gardos ***Art*** Bob Ziembicki

Act Mickey Rourke, Faye Dunaway, Alice Krige, Jack Nance, J. C. Quinn, Frank Stallone (Coppola/Cannon)

Barfly is a lowlife fairy tale, an ethereal seriocomedy about gutter existence from the pen of one who's been there, Charles Bukowski. First American fictional feature from Swiss-French director Barbet Schroeder is spiked with unexpected doses of humor, much of it due to Mickey Rourke's quirky, unpredictable, most engaging performance as the boozy hero.

Much as in a Bukowski short story, a bar is the center of the universe here. Populating the dive in a seedy section of L.A. are a floating assortment of winos and derelicts, of which one of the youngest and most volatile is Henry (Rourke), a self-styled poet of the bottle. He meets a terribly attractive fellow alcoholic, Wanda (Faye Dunaway), who immediately takes him in and keeps him well plied with drink and sex, to the extent they are both interested in and capable of the latter.

Rourke's performance is the centerpiece of the film, and keeps it buoyantly alive throughout. Dunaway also is on the right wavelength as the "distressed goddess" who grows dependent upon and loyal to the wildly unreliable Rourke.

•

BARKLEYS OF BROADWAY, THE
1949, 102 mins, US Ⓥ ⦿ col
Dir Charles Walters ***Prod*** Arthur Freed ***Scr*** Betty Comden, Adolph Green ***Ph*** Harry Stradling ***Ed*** Albert Akst ***Mus*** Lenny Hayton (dir.) ***Art*** Cedric Gibbons, Edward Carfagno
Act Fred Astaire, Ginger Rogers, Oscar Levant, Billie Burke, Gale Robbins, George Zucco (M-G-M)

With Fred Astaire and Ginger Rogers *The Barkleys of Broadway* is an ace dancefest, presenting them at their terpsichorean best against a production background that is Metro at its lushest. However, the songs are ordinary.

The screen's most complementary dance team glides through five dance numbers [staged and directed by Robert Alton] with the grace and apparent spontaneity that is their trademark when appearing together. Sixth dance number is done solo by Astaire. It is the combination of special effects and Astaire hoofing in a dance with shoes that spellbinds into standout terping.

Plot is light, but ties together neatly in depicting a more or less standard story of a Broadway star team of man and wife who have a misunderstanding, separate and then get back together for the finale. Dialog is good and the cast is very competent.

1949: NOMINATION: Best Color Cinematography

•

BARQUERO
1970, 108 mins, US col
Dir Gordon Douglas ***Prod*** Aubrey Schenk, Hal Klein ***Scr*** George Schenck ***Ph*** Jerry Finnerman ***Ed*** Charles Nelson ***Mus*** Dominic Frontiere ***Art*** Allen E. Smith
Act Lee Van Cleef, Forrest Tucker, Warren Oates, Kerwin Mathews, Mariette Hartley, Marie Gomez (United Artists)

Barquero is a taut, bloody-as-a-slaughterhouse western morality play with Lee Van Cleef as the fierce pioneering individualist against Warren Oates, the personification of evil dressed all in black.

Oates is the twitchy, sadistic leader of a band of mercenaries from the Mexican Revolution, who sweep through the countryside as merciless as the Four Horsemen of the Apocalypse.

Van Cleef is the barquero who has hand-built and operates a primitive ferry across a river. At one side of the water the first bare-boards beginnings of a town have sprung up in the center of which stands the steepled skeleton of a church. On the other side is the wilderness, hostile Indians and Mexico.

Oates plans to evacuate his men and loot on the barque and burn it behind him.

•

BARRETTS OF WIMPOLE STREET, THE
1934, 110 mins, US Ⓥ ⦿ b/w
Dir Sidney Franklin ***Prod*** [Irving G. Thalberg] ***Scr*** Claudine West, Ernest Vajda, Donald Ogden Stewart ***Ph*** William Daniels ***Ed*** Margaret Booth ***Mus*** Herbert Stothart ***Art*** Cedric Gibbons, Harry McAfee, Edwin B. Willis
Act Norma Shearer, Fredric March, Charles Laughton, Maureen O'Sullivan, Katherine Alexander, Una O'Connor (M-G-M)

The Barretts of Wimpole Street is an artistic cinematic translation of the Katherine Cornell stage success [by Rudolf Besier].

As a film it's slow. Very. The first hour is wandering, planting-the-plot stuff that has some difficulty cementing the interest, but in the final stretch it grips and holds. It's talky throughout—truly an actor's picture, with long speeches and verbose philosophical observations.

The romance between Elizabeth Barrett (Norma Shearer) and Robert Browning (Fredric March) is a beautiful exposition in its ethereal and physically rehabilitating effect on the ailing Barrett. The unnatural love of Papa Barrett is graphically depicted by Charles Laughton, as the psychopathic, hateful character whose twisted affections for his children especially daughter Elizabeth, almost proves her physical and spiritual undoing.

Not the least of the many good performances is the nifty chore turned in by Marion Clayton as the lisping Bella Hadley. Maureen O'Sullivan, Katherine Alexander, Una O'Connor (exceptional as the mincing Wilson, the maid) and Ralph Forbes all register in a long but not too involved cast which director Sidney Franklin has at all times kept well in hand and never permitted to become confusing.

The confining locale of London's Wimpole Street in 1845 limits the action to the interior of the Barretts's home, but the general persuasiveness of all the histrionics achieves much in offsetting the lack of physical action.

March's bravado style is well suited to the role of the ardent Browning, the poet. Shearer is at all times sincerely compelling in her role, even in the bedridden portions.

1934: NOMINATIONS: Best Picture, Actress (Norma Shearer)

•

BARRETTS OF WIMPOLE STREET, THE
1957, 104 mins, US/UK ⊏⊐ col
Dir Sidney Franklin ***Prod*** Sam Zimbalist ***Scr*** John Dighton ***Ph*** F. A. Young ***Ed*** Frank Clarke ***Mus*** Bronislau Kaper ***Art*** Alfred Junge
Act Jennifer Jones, John Gielgud, Bill Travers, Virginia McKenna, Jean Anderson, Vernon Gray (M-G-M)

Lovers of the classics will find *The Barretts of Wimpole Street* a reliving of the romance between Elizabeth Barrett and Robert Browning as originally plotted in Rudolf Besier's play and in a 1934 screen version, also made by Metro.

Sidney Franklin, who directed the original screen version starring Norma Shearer and Fredric March, helms this production.

Jennifer Jones, while a surprisingly healthy-looking Elizabeth, plays the invalid literary figure with great skill. Bill Travers's Browning, the vigorous, colorful poet who managed to court and win the delicate Elizabeth under the nose of her despotic father, is personable and competent enough.

John Gielgud, the father with an almost incestuous attachment for his daughter, repeats the role originally done by Charles Laughton with all the stern menace it requires. Virginia McKenna is lively and appealing as the younger sister, Henrietta, secretly in love with Vernon Gray, good as Captain Surtees Cook.

•

BARRY LYNDON
1975, 184 mins, UK Ⓥ ⦿ col
Dir Stanley Kubrick ***Prod*** Stanley Kubrick ***Scr*** Stanley Kubrick ***Ph*** John Alcott ***Ed*** Tony Lawson ***Mus*** Leonard Rosenman (sup.) ***Art*** Ken Adam
Act Ryan O'Neal, Marisa Berenson, Patrick Magee, Hardy Kruger, Gay Hamilton, Leonard Rossiter (Hawk/Warner)

Stanley Kubrick's series of film morality plays continues with *Barry Lyndon*, a most elegant and handsome adaptation of William Makepiece Thackeray's early 19th-century novel. Ryan O'Neal's excellent performance captures the shallow opportunism endemic to the title character who is brought down as much by his own flaws as by the mores of the ordered social structure of 18th-century England. Casting, concept and execution are all superb.

O'Neal's character evolves from a passive, likable Irish lad, enamored of cousin Nora (Gay Hamilton), whose eyes are fixed on the pocketbook of British officer Capt. Quin (Leonard Rossiter). Conned into fleeing his home after a fake duel, Barry learns about life from a highwayman (Arthur O'Sullivan), a Prussian captor-benefactor (Hardy Kruger) and spy (Patrick Magee).

Barry emerges from these trials as a cynical manipulator of people, instead of a life-hardened person retaining some nobility. The pile of victims grows ever larger, eventually including a wealthy widow (Marisa Berenson) whose means provide a possible avenue to Barry's social and financial security in a peerage.

The 184-minute film has two acts—102 minutes up from the back country to Berenson, 82 minutes downhill to a clouded and defeated end. Michael Hordern's excellent narration intones the Greek chorus commentary. Kubrick's outstanding external landscapes—in rich, cool tones—overpower the ant-like people crawling about; his interiors—hot, uncomfortable despite their plushness—seem unnatural in contrast. This cinematic mural bears repeated and sustained watching without ever really commanding and demanding acute attention. Could anyone else have pulled this off? Not since the days of those great David O. Selznick–George Cukor productions.

1975: Best Cinematography, Art Direction, Costume Design, Adapted Scoring.

NOMINATIONS: Best Picture, Director, Adapted Screenplay

•

BARTLEBY
1971, 78 mins, UK Ⓥ ⦿ col
Dir Anthony Friedmann ***Prod*** Rodney Carr-Smith ***Scr*** Rodney Carr-Smith, Anthony Friedmann ***Ph*** Ian Wilson ***Ed*** John S. Smith ***Mus*** Roger Webb ***Art*** Simon Holland
Act Paul Scofield, John McEnery, Thorley Walters, Colin Jeavons, Raymond Mason, Charles Kinross (Pantheon)

It's understandable that Paul Scofield, an intelligent, choosey actor, should have been intrigued by this enigmatic, short film.

Bartleby is virtually a duel between Scofield and John McEnery, who plays a young audit clerk, a fallout from society. He is no rebel or rabble-raiser; just a guy who can't adjust himself to the demands of these times. He gets a job with Scofield who patiently employs him but is astounded at the young man's attitude. Very politely he insists that "he prefers not do this or that." Baffled, Scofield does everything possible to get through to the young man but is thwarted and eventually, irritated, fires him. But Bartleby prefers not to go.

This modestly budgeted picture, from Herman Melville's story, is downbeat. But it is intriguing because of the two main performances. Scofield, who radiates thought and integrity in every speech movement and gesture is fine. McEnery underplays the incomprehensible, pitiful Bartleby with just the right note to engender sympathy but not ridicule. The film is a riddle but it should intrigue any thoughtful filmgoer.

•

BARTON FINK
1991, 116 mins, US Ⓥ ⦿ col
Dir Joel Coen ***Prod*** Ethan Coen ***Scr*** Ethan Coen, Joel Coen ***Ph*** Roger Deakins ***Ed*** Roderick Jaynes ***Mus*** Carter Burwell ***Art*** Dennis Gassner
Act John Turturro, John Goodman, Judy Davis, Michael Lerner, John Mahoney (20th Century-Fox/Circle)

Joel and Ethan Coen's hermetic tale of a "genius" playwright's brief stint as a studio contract writer is a painstakingly miniaturist work that can be read any number of ways. This film will appeal to buffs at least as much as the brothers' last, *Miller's Crossing*.

Title character, played with a creepily growing sense of dread by John Turturro, is a gravely serious New York dramatist who scores a soaring triumph on Broadway in 1941 with a deep-dish think piece about the working class. In Hollywood he is assigned a Wallace Beery wrestling programmer and told to come up with something by the end of the week. Checking into a huge, slightly frayed and weirdly underpopulated hotel, he becomes friendly with the hulking fellow bachelor next door, Charlie Meadows (John Goodman), an insurance salesman with a gift for gab. Working at home, Fink suffers from intense writer's block.

After a little more than an hour, the pic is thrown in a wholly unexpected direction. There is a shocking murder, the presence of a mysterious box in Fink's room, the revelation of another's character's sinister true identity, three more killings, a truly weird hotel fire and the humiliation of the writer after he believes he's finally turned out a fine script.

Scene after scene is filled with a ferocious strength and humor. Michael Lerner's performance as a Mayer-like studio overlord is sensational. Goodman is marvelous as the folksy neighbor, rolling his tongue around pages of wonderful dialog. Judy Davis nicely etches a woman who has a way with difficult writers, and John Mahoney turns up as a near dead ringer for William Faulkner in his Hollywood period.

1991: NOMINATIONS: Best Supp. Actor (Michael Lerner), Art Direction, Costume Design

•

BASIC INSTINCT
1992, 127 mins, US Ⓥ ⦿ ⊏⊐ col
Dir Paul Verhoeven ***Prod*** Alan Marshall ***Scr*** Joe Eszterhas ***Ph*** Jan De Bont ***Ed*** Frank J. Urioste ***Mus*** Jerry Goldsmith ***Art*** Terence Marsh
Act Michael Douglas, Sharon Stone, George Dzundza, Jeanne Tripplehorn, Denis Arndt, Leilani Sarelle (Carolco/Canal Plus)

Basic Instinct is grade-A pulp fiction. This erotically charged thriller about the search for an ice-pick murderer in San Francisco rivets attention through its sleek style, attractive cast doing and thinking kinky things, and story, which is as weirdly implausible as it is intensely visceral.

Tale gets off to a slambang start when, at the peak of mutual sexual excitement, an unidentifiable blonde ties up her lover's hands and does him in. Back on the streets of San Francisco, detective Michael Douglas and partner George Dzundza head up the coast to quiz the dead man's g.f., the fabulously wealthy and sexy Sharon Stone who has published a novel in which an identical murder is depicted. The very tough and ice-cold Stone quickly begins tantalizing Douglas, who has recently gone cold turkey off cigarettes, booze, drugs and sex.

Stone bends Douglas so out of shape that, in the first torrid sex scene, he roughly assaults his former lover and police department shrink (Jeanne Tripplehorn). Stone remains the prime suspect all the way through the tale, which includes four more killings. The extensively intertwined sexual histories of Douglas, Stone and Tripplehorn, not to mention Stone's jealous female lover (Leilani Sarelle), throws suspicion all over the place.

Douglas scores with a game and gamey portrayal of an iconoclastic cop not afraid to go over the line professionally or personally. After a decade of marking time in schlockers, Stone has a career-making role here as a beautiful, smart manipulator who is always several steps ahead of everyone else.

[Pic's uncut version, distributed outside the U.S., ran 42 seconds longer than version reviewed.]

1992: NOMINATIONS: Best Editing, Original Score

•

BASIL THE GREAT MOUSE DETECTIVE
SEE: THE GREAT MOUSE DETECTIVE

•

BASKETBALL DIARIES, THE
1995, 102 mins, US Ⓥ col
Dir Scott Kalvert ***Prod*** Liz Heller ***Scr*** Bryan Goluboff ***Ph*** David Phillips ***Ed*** Dana Congdon ***Mus*** Graeme Revell ***Art*** Christopher Nowak
Act Leonardo DiCaprio, Bruno Kirby, Lorraine Bracco, Ernie Hudson, Patrick McGaw, Juliette Lewis (Island)

The Basketball Diaries is a weak-tea rendition of Jim Carroll's much admired cult tome about his teenage drug addiction. Many screenwriters have tried over the years to give Carroll's 1978 perennial seller the narrative spine needed to make a dramatic film, but Bryan Goluboff's adaptation is pretty much a straight-line approach with an upbeat kicker at the end.

Leonardo DiCaprio's Jim Carroll is part of a mischievous quartet of boys, three of whom form the nucleus of the hottest Catholic hoopsters in Gotham. Jim's descent into mad-dog heroin addiction is presented as a road cleared by recreational cocaine indulgence and an idiotic use of downers right before a basketball game, which gets him and his buddy Mickey (Mark Wahlberg) kicked off the team and briefly expelled from school, and also leads to Jim's being booted out by his hard-working mother (Lorraine Bracco).

From there the story becomes a tour through hell that's been visited before by any number of films and often in more compelling fashion. Jim and his friends take up crime in order to support their habits, even mugging an old lady. Even more significantly skimped are aspects of Jim's personal life outside of his relationships with his druggie friends.

On camera nearly all the time, DiCaprio keeps the film interesting with a game, highly emotional performance. Marking his feature directing debut, musicvid helmer Scott Kalvert keeps the camera on the move, sometimes with precision and sometimes aimlessly, but hasn't gotten under the skin of his material.

•

BASKET CASE
1982, 90 mins, US Ⓥ ⦿ col
Dir Frank Henenlotter ***Prod*** Edgar Ievens ***Scr*** Frank Henenlotter ***Ph*** Bruce Torbet ***Ed*** Frank Henenlotter ***Mus*** Gus Russo
Act Kevin Van Hentenryck, Terri Susan Smith, Beverly Bonner, Robert Vogel, Diana Browne, Lloyd Pace (Ievens-Henenlotter)

Basket Case is an ultracheap monster film created by neophyte filmmaker Frank Henenlotter with a tongue-in-cheek approach.

Picture concerns a young man Duane (Kevin Van Hentenryck) from Glens Falls in upstate New York, who comes to the Big Apple and checks into a seedy 42nd St. hotel carrying a large wicker basket. A lengthy midfilm flashback reveals he is bent on revenge, carried out by his Siamese twin monstrous brother Belial (residing in the basket), killing off the three doctors who separated them surgically at age 10.

Acting styles vary (creating intentional camp humor), but the leads are fine: Van Hentenryck creating great sympathy as a neurotic youngster and girlfriend Terri Susan Smith (as a doctor's receptionist) emerging in a blonde wig as an ingratiating performer. Robert Vogel in the stock role of a harried hotel manager gets some big laughs by forcefully playing it straight.

Tech credits are a drawback, particularly the variable sound recording, grainy blowup from 16mm and shrill musical score.

•

BASKET CASE 2
1990, 89 mins, US Ⓥ ⦿ col
Dir Frank Henenlotter ***Prod*** Edgar Ievens ***Scr*** Frank Henenlotter ***Ph*** Robert M. Baldwin ***Ed*** Kevin Tent ***Mus*** Joe Renzetti ***Art*** Michael Moran
Act Kevin Van Hentenryck, Annie Ross, Kathryn Meisle, Heather Rattray, Matt Mitler, Ted Sorel (Shapiro-Glickenhaus)

Belated sequel to the 1982 cult horror film, *Basket Case 2* is a hilarious genre spoof. Here Frank Henenlotter's paying homage to Tod Browning's 1932 classic *Freaks*.

Annie Ross as Granny Ruth is a crusader for the rights of "unique individuals" (i.e., freaks) and welcomes the Siamese twin brothers Kevin and Belial into her home in Staten Island. Weird menagerie of youngsters, mostly crazy variations on the Elephant Man by makeup whiz Gabe Bartalos, are treated very sympathetically at first, but as in Browning's film their potential for scaring the audience also is exploited.

Pic climaxes with Belial's ultraviolent attacks on foes of freaks, namely tabloid reporter Kathryn Meisle, her shutterbug assistant Matt Mitler and cop Ted Sorel. En route is one of the oddest scenes in recent horror pics, Belial making love to Eve, a similarly grotesque Siamese twin.

Casting coup is Annie Ross, the legendary jazz singer, who is a lot of fun as the demented granny who goads her freakish charges to fight back.

•

BASKET CASE 3: THE PROGENY
1992, 90 mins, US Ⓥ col
Dir Frank Henenlotter ***Prod*** Edgar Ievens ***Scr*** Frank Henenlotter, Robert Martin ***Ph*** Bob Paone ***Ed*** Greg Sheldon ***Mus*** Joe Renzetti ***Art*** William Barclay
Act Annie Ross, Kevin Van Hentenryck, Dan Biggers, Gil Roper, Tina Louise Hilbert, James O'Doherty (Shapiro Glickenhaus)

Pic opens with a lengthy dose of footage from *Basket Case 2*, detailing sex between the two monsters Belial and Eve and the death of Eve's sister Susan. Part three begins with Eve's pregnancy.

Granny Ruth (jazz vocalist Annie Ross) takes Eve, papa-to-be Belial and a commune of unique individuals (i.e., monsters) to a small town in Georgia to stay with Uncle Hal (Dan Biggers), a doctor who will help with the mutant birth. Ross is reunited there with her grotesque monstrosity of a son (stand-up comic James O'Doherty), while Belial's "normal" twin brother (series regular Kevin Van Hentenryck) gets a crush on the sheriff's pretty daughter (Tina Louise Hilbert).

Henenlotter's mix of wild overacting, cartoon color scheme and heavy-handed message regarding tolerance is tough to take for the uninitiated. His fans will enjoy seeing the growing menagerie of creatures, including the cute/grotesque progeny.

Van Hentenryck acts way over the top, while Ross literally dominates the film with her intensity and gets to lead the monsters in a sing-a-long of the golden oldie *Personality*. Heroine Hilbert makes a good impression in a Jekyll & Hyde role. Creature effects are quite inventive.

•

BASTARD OUT OF CAROLINA
1996, 97 mins, US Ⓥ col
Dir Anjelica Huston ***Prod*** Gary Hoffman ***Scr*** Anne Meredith ***Ph*** Anthony B. Richmond ***Ed*** Eva Gardos ***Mus*** Van Dyke Parks ***Art*** Nelson Coates
Act Jennifer Jason Leigh, Ron Eldard, Jena Malone, Glenne Headly, Lyle Lovett, Dermot Mulroney (TNT)

An absorbing, sometimes wrenching tale of growing up poor and abused in the 1950s South, *Bastard out of Carolina* is a handsome, thoughtful picture that may benefit from Ted Turner's refusal to air it on TNT. Pic is a quality item, with nonexploitative handling of potent material, strong work by debuting helmer Anjelica Huston and striking perfs from young newcomer Jena Malone, Jennifer Jason Leigh and others.

Huston's pic, like the acclaimed Dorothy Allison novel on which it is based, concerns much besides child abuse. Set in Greenville, SC (though filmed in Wilmington, NC), not long after WWII, story looks behind Tobacco Road cliches to evoke the complex weave of love, hardship and family bonds that conditioned the life of poor whites in the days before New South prosperity kicked in.

Pic opens with a narrator (voiced by Laura Dern) recalling that she was born after her single mom, Anney (Jennifer Jason Leigh), was hurled through a car windshield during an accident. An uncle nicknamed the newborn Bone.

With Bone still a tyke, Anney meets and weds Lyle (Dermot Mulroney), a sweet-tempered sort who gives her a second daughter before expiring in a freak auto mishap. She eventually succumbs to the earnest courting of Glen (Ron Eldard), a laborer. Bone (Malone) and Glen are subtly at odds from the outset. But it's not until Anney loses the son she's carrying, and is declared unable to have more children, that the man starts looking for a punching bag. Bone is the nearest target.

Anne Meredith's script preserves the key ingredients of Allison's tale while skillfully imposing dramatic structure and economy. It's one drawback, a minor one, lies in not making more use of the novel's pungent humor.

•

BAT, THE
1926, 91 mins, US Ⓥ b/w
Dir Roland West ***Prod*** Roland West ***Scr*** Roland West, George Marion, Jr. ***Ph*** Arthur Edeson ***Art*** William Cameron Menzies
Act Tullio Carminati, Jewel Carmen, Louise Fazenda, Emily Fitzroy, Arthur Houseman, Jack Pickford (West/United Artists)

This picture runs 91 minutes—a long time for anybody's film, but it is interesting every minute of the way. The story is that its maker, Roland West, paid heavy money for the film rights to this long-run legit show [by Mary Roberts Rinehart and Avery Hopwood].

The mystery concerns the death of a bank president, the theft of $200,000, the disappearance of the young cashier, and the mysterious criminal whose sign is the shadow of a bat projected from the front of an electric flashlight. This mysterious criminal is behind a thousand suspicious actions but meantime, every member of the cast is suspected of having been the culprit.

An Italian actor named Tullio Carminati gives a performance as the detective that is one of the best things done by a newcomer to the screen. Everybody else is okay and Louise Fazenda draws her share of laughs with the hoke maid's part, while Eddie Gribbon is good for a giggle or so as the hick detective who knows not his intelligence from the lining of a coat pocket.

•

BATAAN
1943, 113 mins, US Ⓥ b/w
Dir Tay Garnett ***Prod*** Irving Starr ***Scr*** Robert D. Andrews ***Ph*** Sidney Wagner ***Ed*** George White ***Mus*** Bronislau Kaper
Act Robert Taylor, George Murphy, Thomas Mitchell, Lloyd Nolan, Robert Walker, Desi Arnaz (M-G-M)

Bataan is a melodramatic reenactment of the last ditch stand of an American patrol detailed to guard a road in the Philippines following the evacuation of Manila. Picture pulls no punches in displaying the realistically grim warfare.

There's a sufficient amount of jungle battle action and a couple of hand-to-hand skirmishes where bayonets are brought into play, but a major portion of the extended running time is devoted to dramatic incidents revolving around the hastily recruited patrol unit and their efforts to stave off the Jap's advance into the Bataan peninsula so that the main American and Philippine forces could dig in.

Robert Taylor gives a strong performance as the commanding sergeant, but picture focuses attention on screen debut of Robert Walker, who smacks over an arresting portrayal as the sensitive and sympathetic young sailor who attaches himself to the outfit to get a crack at the Japs.

•

BATAILLE DU RAIL, LA
(BATTLE OF THE RAILS; THE BATTLE OF THE RAILWAYS)
1946, 90 mins, France b/w
Dir Rene Clement ***Prod*** Rene Clement ***Scr*** Rene Clement, Colette Audry, Jean Daurand ***Ph*** Henri Alekan ***Ed*** Jacques Desagneaux ***Mus*** Yves Baudrier
Act Jean Daurand, Tony Laurent, Clarieux, Jacques Desagneaux, Leray, Lozach (Cooperative Generale)

A lengthy documentary recording the bitter fight which French railway workers waged against the Germans, picture originally was released in France in 1946, and for U.S. distribution an introduction and partial narration by Charles Boyer have been added. While some of the scenes are startlingly realistic, the balance of the film is inclined to be repetitious.

Rails primarily offers audiences a birds-eye view of how French transportation employees utilized sabotage to obstruct the Nazis from securing maximum advantages from the Gallic railway system. However, in an effort to overly emphasize the workers' resistance, the glorification of the trainmen frequently steps beyond the bounds of logic.

It's hard to believe that the Germans, who almost mastered the art of total war, could have neglected so vital a link to their armies' security as the French transportation system. An answer to the amazing feats of the workers, along with the relatively minor retaliatory steps on the part of the Nazis, might be in the fact that the railroad employees themselves not only conceived the film, but also partly financed it.

Action of the film sweeps through the years of the Occupation up to the triumphant landing of the Allies in Normandy. Best of the camerawork, perhaps, is the sequence showing an unsuccessful attack of the French underground on a German armored train.

•

BATHING BEAUTY

1944, 102 mins, US Ⓥ ⊙ col

Dir George Sidney ***Prod*** Jack Cummings ***Scr*** Dorothy Kingsley, Allen Boretz, Frank Waldman ***Ph*** Harry Stradling ***Ed*** Blanche Sewell ***Mus*** Johnny Green ***Art*** Cedric Gibbons, Stephen Goosson, Merrill Pye

Act Red Skelton, Esther Williams, Basil Rathbone, Bill Goodwin, Ethel Smith, Jean Porter (M-G-M)

Bathing Beauty is produced in the lush, lavish, manner which is as familiar as the Metro trademark.

Esther Williams, who formerly appeared in *Andy Hardy* films and briefly in *A Guy Named Joe*, is pulled to stardom by her swimsuit straps. Dressed in either bathing togs or street finery, she is a pretty picture indeed. The former swimming champ displays her aquatic and acting abilities in the role of a collegienne who travels the rocky road of love with songwriter Red Skelton.

Skelton is his usual effervescent self, bouncing in and out of the script, getting in and out of scrapes with his girl, and the authorities at the college she attends. His two speciality numbers are especially funny: one, where he attends a ballet dancing class with the girls of the school, dressed in a short, fluffy, pink dress with dancing slippers, endeavoring to go through the motions, and being slapped around by the instructress; the other, which he did in vaude for years prior to landing in films, is his impression of a gal getting up in the morning, prettying herself and dressing.

Unlike musicals prior to this one, Metro has invested in beautiful sequences rather than cast. Water ballet costumes by Irene Sharaff, and the water ballet, produced under the supervision of John Murray Anderson, are memorable.

•

BATMAN
(AKA: BATMAN THE MOVIE)

1966, 105 mins, US Ⓥ ⊙ col

Dir Leslie Martinson ***Prod*** William Dozier ***Scr*** Lorenzo Semple, Jr. ***Ph*** Howard Schwartz ***Ed*** Harry Gerstad ***Mus*** Nelson Riddle ***Art*** Jack Martin Smith, Serge Krizman

Act Adam West, Burt Ward, Lee Merriwether, Cesar Romero, Burgess Meredith, Frank Gorshin (20th Century-Fox)

Batman is packed with action, clever sight gags, interesting complications and goes all out on bat with batmania: batplane, batboat, batcycle, etc. etc. Humor is stretched to the limit, color is comic-strip sharp and script retrieves every trick from the highly popular teleseries' oatbag, adding a few more sophisticated touches.

It's nearly impossible to attempt to relate plot. Suffice to say that it's Batman and Robin against his four archenemies, Catwoman, The Joker, The Penguin and The Riddler. Quartet have united and are out to take over the world. They elaborately plot the dynamic duo's death again and again but in every instance duo escape by the skin of their tights.

The acting is uniformly impressively improbable. The intense innocent enthusiasm of Cesar Romero, Burgess Meredith and Frank Gorshin as the three criminals is balanced against the innocent calm of Adam West and Burt Ward, Batman and Robin respectively.

•

BATMAN

1989, 126 mins, US Ⓥ ⊙ col

Dir Tim Burton ***Prod*** Jon Peters, Peter Guber ***Scr*** Sam Hamm, Warren Skaaren ***Ph*** Roger Pratt ***Ed*** Ray Lovejoy ***Mus*** Danny Elfman ***Art*** Anton Furst

Act Michael Keaton, Jack Nicholson, Kim Basinger, Robert Wuhl, Pat Hingle, Billy Dee Williams (Guber-Peters/Warner)

Director Tim Burton effectively echoes the visual style of the original Bob Kane comics while conjuring up a nightmarish world of his own. Going back to the source elements of the cartoon figure, who made his debut in 1939 for Detective (now DC) Comics, the Jon Peters–Peter Guber production [from a story by Sam Hamm] will appeal to purists who prefer their heroes as straight as Clint Eastwood.

In a striking departure from his usual amiable comic style, Michael Keaton captures the haunted intensity of the character, and seems particularly lonely and obsessive without Robin around to share his exploits.

The gorgeous Kim Basinger takes the sidekick's place, in a determined bow to heterosexuality that nonetheless leaves Batman something less than enthusiastic.

It comes as no surprise that Jack Nicholson steals every scene in a sizable role as the hideoulsy disfigured Joker. Nicholson embellishes fascinatingly baroque designs with his twisted features, lavish verbal pirouettes and inspired excursions into the outer limits of psychosis. It's a masterpiece of sinister comic acting.

What keeps the film arresting is the visual stylization. It was a shrewd choice for Burton to emulate the jarring angles and creepy lighting of film noir.

1989: Best Art Direction

•

BATMAN & ROBIN

1997, 130 mins, US Ⓥ ⊙ col

Dir Joel Schumacher ***Prod*** Peter Macgregor-Scott ***Scr*** Akiva Goldsman ***Ph*** Stephen Goldblatt ***Ed*** Dennis Virkler ***Mus*** Elliot Goldenthal ***Art*** Barbara Ling

Act Arnold Schwarzenegger, George Clooney, Chris O'Donnell, Uma Thurman, Alicia Silverstone, Michael Gough (Warner)

Batman loses a bit of altitude and velocity in this fourth installment of Warner Bros.' hugely successful series. The villains—Arnold Schwarzenegger, and especially Uma Thurman—remain the highlights here, as the rest of the gargantuan production lacks the dash and excitement that would have given the franchise a boost in its eighth year.

George Clooney as Batman and Alicia Silverstone as Batgirl are the new arrivals, with Chris O'Donnell back for his sophomore appearance as Robin and director Joel Schumacher up to the plate for a second time as well. Unfortunately, the operative word is bland, as the newcomers don't add much to the formula. Narrative drive and humor are also in short supply.

Initial suiting up of the black-caped duo constitutes the most conspicuous fetishizing yet of the anatomically sculpted Batgear, this in preparation for their initial battle with Mr. Freeze (Schwarzenegger), a warrior bedecked in climate-controlled armor. He keeps his beautiful wife (supermodel Vendela K. Thommessen), the victim of a degenerative disease, in a state of suspended animation until he can devise a cure for her.

Meanwhile, revenge is the word, as it is for a nerdy horticulturalist (Thurman) who emerges from a near-fatal incident in the curvy form of an outrageously sexy vamp, Poison Ivy, bent on destroying the human race for its offenses to all things green.

Midsection is woefully low on conflict and incident. The climax is a protracted sequence as thunderously numbing as that of any other $100 million in recent memory. Clooney is the most ideal Batman to date, but none of the series' screenwriters has ever gotten a handle on how to make the character as interesting as those around him. Thurman's performance has comic wit conspicuously lacking elsewhere in the picture.

•

BATMAN FOREVER

1995, 121 mins, US Ⓥ ⊙ col

Dir Joel Schumacher ***Prod*** Tim Burton, Peter Macgregor-Scott ***Scr*** Lee Batchler, Janet Scott Batchler, Akiva Goldsman ***Ph*** Stephen Goldblatt ***Ed*** Dennis Virkler ***Mus*** Elliot Goldenthal ***Art*** Barbara Ling

Act Val Kilmer, Tommy Lee Jones, Jim Carrey, Nicole Kidman, Chris O'Donnell, Michael Gough (Warner)

An enormous fun-house ride, the second *Batman* sequel [from a screen story by Lee Batchler and Janet Scott Batchler] succeeds on some basic levels while coming up short on others. On the plus side, the tone has lightened up after criticism of the last outing, Val Kilmer seamlessly slides into the Dark Knight's cape, and the film boasts considerable action and visual splendor. In the negative column, that action isn't as involving as it should be, and there are so many characters the movie can't adequately service them all.

With so much ground to cover, the filmmakers cheat a bit by beginning in the middle as Two-Face (Tommy Lee Jones)—a onetime district attorney gone bad after being scarred by acid—terrorizes Gotham. After grappling with Two-Face and his minions, Batman encounters a criminal psychologist, Dr. Chase Meridian (Nicole Kidman), with her own designs on Gotham's hero. That ongoing romance overlaps with the introduction of Dick Grayson (Chris O'Donnell), a teenage circus acrobat who, after losing his family, is taken in by Batman alter-ego Bruce Wayne.

A final thread involves Jim Carrey's transformation from an addled inventor, Edward Nygma, into the villainous Riddler, eventually teaming with Two-Face to zero in on Batman's identity. That leads to a somewhat anticlimatic series of showdowns, beginning with a siege on Wayne Manor.

Screenwriters walk their own tightrope, trying to find time to depict not only Robin's origins (in a faithful homage to his comic-book roots) but also to rehash Wayne's inspiration for turning into a caped crime fighter. It's a lot to handle, and director Joel Schumacher doesn't have the luxury of pausing long enough to let those strands build momentum, with a fight or chase always just around the corner.

Carrey continues the tradition of villainous scene-stealing in the Batman movies, and overshadows Jones, who aside from a wild cackle has little to do. O'Donnell proves there is room for heroic thievery as well, and his bond with Batman provides what little emotional wallop the pic can muster. Kidman looks terrific, but her Batman fixation is clearly the least interesting element in this crowded broiler.

As for Kilmer, he gamely steps into the dual Batman/Wayne role but can't get much traction, finding, as Michael Keaton had, that beyond a stern jaw there's not much to be done with the it, since the suit does most of the work.

Technically, pic benefits from a truly spectacular production design, and the costumes add enormously to the film's look.

[Pic's title is technically *Forever*, with the word superimposed over the Batman logo.]

1995: NOMINATIONS: Cinematography, Best Sound, Best Sound Effects Editing

•

BATMAN RETURNS

1992, 126 mins, US Ⓥ ⊙ col

Dir Tim Burton ***Prod*** Denise Di Novi, Tim Burton ***Scr*** Daniel Waters ***Ph*** Stefan Czapsky ***Ed*** Chris Lebenzon ***Mus*** Danny Elfman ***Art*** Bo Welch

Act Michael Keaton, Danny DeVito, Michelle Pfeiffer, Christopher Walken, Michael Gough, Michael Murphy (Warner)

On all counts the Warner Bros. reported $80 million-plus *Batman Returns* is a monster. Follow-up has the same dark allure, but many non-fans of *Batman* will find this sequel [from a screen story by Daniel Waters and Sam Hamm] superior in several respects. Batman's new foes, Penguin and Catwoman, are both fascinating creations, wonderfully played. Much of the film is massively inventive and spiked with fresh, perverse humor.

Interest gets cranked up high immediately by a prologue that illustrates the creation of the Penguin. Playing the infant's parents, Diane Salinger and a virtually unrecognizable Paul (Pee-wee Herman) Reubens dump the cradled tot into a freezing stream in a park. Like Moses, he survives.

Disrupting a civic Christmas celebration, the adult Penguin (Danny DeVito) announces that he wants some respect. Forming an alliance with tycoon Max Shreck (Christopher Walken), a specialist in industrial waste, Penguin decides to run for mayor.

Equally intriguing character of Catwoman evolves out of the demeaning treatment dished out by Shreck to his lovely, somewhat disheveled secretary Selina Kyle. Michelle Pfeiffer becomes a kitten with a whip who can very much hold her own with Batman. In one scene, Batman gets a literal licking from her.

Lensed seemingly entirely indoors or on covered sets, pic is a magnificently atmospheric elaboration on German Expressionist design principles. All the way down the line, behind-the-scenesters can take deep bows.

On the performance side, the deck is stacked entirely in favor of the villains. Briskly waddling, cawing his rude remarks and conveying decades' worth of resentment and bitterness, DeVito makes Penguin very much his own. Endearingly klutzy initially as Selina, Pfeiffer, who replaced the pregnant Annette Bening in the role, looks amazing in her skintight, S&M-like leather skin. Wild-maned Walken has the right comic understatement and sangfroid as Shreck, an in-joke on the German actor Max Schreck (1922's *Nosferatu*).

As in the first film, Michael Keaton is encased in a role as constricting as his superhero costume, and while the actor's instincts seem right, the range he is allowed is distinctly limited.

1992: NOMINATIONS: Best Makeup, Visual Effects

•

BATTAGLIA DI ALGERI, LA
(THE BATTLE OF ALGIERS)

1966, 122 mins, Italy/Algeria Ⓥ ⊙ ▭ b/w

Dir Gillo Pontecorvo ***Prod*** Antonio Musu, Yacef Saadi ***Scr*** Franco Solinas ***Ph*** Marcello Gatti ***Ed*** Mario Serandrei, Mario Morra ***Mus*** Ennio Morricone, Gillo Pontecorvo

Act Jean Martin, Yacef Saadi, Brahim Haggiag, Tommaso Neri, Fawzia El-Kader, Michele Kerbash (Igor/Casbah)

Graphic, straightforward, realistic reenactment [from a screen story by Gillo Pontecorvo and Franco Solinas] of the events that led to the birth, in 1962, of a free Algerian nation, pic is also the first feature film ever made in Algiers by Algerians—teamed here with Italian talent, notably director Gillo Pontecorvo and producer Antonio Musu. It's a dedicated effort with importance as a "document."

Backdrop of documentary-like treatment of Algerian strife between 1954 and final liberation in 1962 is shown via restaging skillfully blended with newsreel clips. Gray reel quality gives pic an authentic flavor throughout, and adds to dramatic impact of many of its sequences.

Up front, but not as spotlit as in usual pix of this kind, are some key characters drawn from life but guided here to heighten dramatic effect. Thus the chutist general whose all-out tactics make things tough for the Algerian rebels in the city, plus a handful of rebels themselves, stoically, heroically battling seemingly unbeatable odds.

There are no stars and there is no glamour.

•

***BATTERIES NOT INCLUDED**
1987, 106 mins, US Ⓥ ⦿ col
Dir Matthew Robbins *Prod* Ronald L. Schwary *Scr* Matthew Robbins, Brad Bird, Brent Maddock, S. S. Wilson *Ph* John McPherson *Ed* Cynthia Scheider *Mus* James Horner *Art* Ted Haworth
Act Hume Cronyn, Jessica Tandy, Frank McRae, Elizabeth Pena, Michael Carmine, Dennis Boutsikaris (Universal/Amblin)

**batteries not included* could have used more imaginative juices to distinguish it from other, more enchanting Spielbergian pics where lovable mechanical things solve earthly human dilemmas. Still, it's suitable entertainment for kids.

Instead of the suburbs, Spielberg's usual haunt, scene here is in one of the crumbling neighborhoods of Manhattan where some tenants of an old and much beloved brownstone are being harassed to move out so a sleek office/residential complex can go up in its place. The most stubborn of the holdouts is an irascible cafe owner (Hume Cronyn) and his senile wife (Jessica Tandy).

Before too long, Tandy is visited in the middle of the night by a couple of—that is, a male and female—miniature flying saucers which take their energy from the electrical outlets in the building and repair their parts with the tenants' metal appliances. They also become little angels, repairing all that the local hoods have broken on any number of their rampages.

Led by the Cronyn-Tandy team, pic [based on a story by Mick Garris] has a good mix of personalities, even if perhaps Elizabeth Pena as an unwed mother may raise some questions in children's minds their parents just as soon would not answer. Tech credits are terrific.

•

BATTLE BENEATH THE EARTH
1968, 91 mins, UK Ⓥ col
Dir Montgomery Tully *Prod* Charles Reynolds *Scr* L. Z. Hargreaves *Ph* Kenneth Talbot *Ed* Sidney Stone *Mus* Ken Jones *Art* Jim Morahan
Act Kerwin Mathews, Viviane Ventura, Robert Ayres, Peter Arne, Martin Benson, Al Mulock (M-G-M)

Atomic destruction is given a new twist in this production made at M-G-M British Studios. It's a well-made film, once the premise is established after a slow opening.

Premise deals with the Chinese burrowing beneath the U.S. from Hawaii in a vast complex of tunnels that extend under all major installations and population centers. Once this system is completed and atomic warheads planted the U.S. will be virtually wiped out and a new civilization built by the Chinese. Before the plan can be put into force, but after most of the tunnels have been bored, the U.S. Navy learns the fantastic undertaking and American ingenuity blasts the project sky-high.

Montgomery Tully's direction maintains an appropriately fast pace. Kerwin Mathews as an American commander detailed to counter the danger does a good job in a straight part and Martin Benson is properly menacing as the Chinese general planning the giant scheme independent of Peking.

•

BATTLE BEYOND THE STARS
1980, 104 mins, US Ⓥ ⦿ col
Dir Jimmy T. Murakami *Prod* Ed Carlin *Scr* John Sayles *Ph* Daniel Lacambre *Ed* Allan Holzman, R. J. Kizer *Mus* James Horner *Art* John Zabrucky
Act Richard Thomas, Robert Vaughn, George Peppard, John Saxon, Darlanne Fluegel, Sybil Danning (New World)

The fascination of watching how the defenseless cope with marauding barbarians is put to the test with New World's production of *Battle Beyond the Stars*.

In unfolding its saga [by John Sayles, Anne Dyer] of how the peace-loving bunch on a small planet rebuffs a genetically deficient but vicious band of bad guys, *Battle* incorporates touches of an old-fashioned western, horror pics and even a touch of softcore.

Despite the expense involved, the pic appears not to take itself too seriously. Principal characterizations are skin deep. Dialogue takes the form of relaxed banter with a minimum of homilies.

George Peppard has fun as a Scotch-tippling cowboy from earth who turns up as one of the mercenaries hired by the planet's earnest young soldier (Richard Thomas). John Saxon is hilarious as the chief bad guy.

•

BATTLE CRY
1955, 147 mins, US Ⓥ ⦿ ▭ col
Dir Raoul Walsh *Scr* Leon M. Uris *Ph* Sid Hickox *Ed* William Zeigler *Mus* Max Steiner *Art* John Beckman
Act Van Heflin, Aldo Ray, Mona Freeman, Nancy Olson, Tab Hunter, Dorothy Malone (Warner)

Amatory, rather than military, action is the mainstay of this saga of the United States Marines. While overboard in length, this comes from the detailing of several sets of romantics, each interesting in itself, plus the necessary battle action to indicate the basis is rather grim warfare.

The latter is at a minimum, however, since Leon Uris's screen adaptation of his own novel is more concerned with the liberties and loves of the World War II Marines with whom he served, than with actually winning the fight in the Pacific. It is the story of a group of enlisted men and their officers in a communications battalion, taking them from civilian life, through training and then to New Zealand, from which base the outfit participates in Pacific action.

Of the romantic pairings, the most impression is made by Aldo Ray and Nancy Olson, not only because it occupies the main portion of the film's second half after the two other principal teamings have been completed, but also because of the grasp the two stars have on their characters.

1955: NOMINATION: Best Scoring of a Dramatic Picture

•

BATTLEFIELD EARTH
2000, 117 mins, US Ⓥ ⦿ ▭ col
Dir Roger Christian *Prod* Elie Samaha, Jonathan D. Krane, John Travolta *Scr* Corey Mandell, J. D. Shapiro *Ph* Giles Nuttgens *Ed* Robin Russell *Mus* Elia Cmiral *Art* Patrick Tatopoulos
Act John Travolta, Barry Pepper, Forest Whitaker, Kim Coates, Richard Tyson, Sabine Karsenti (Franchise/Krane/JTP/Warner)

Few career revivals have enjoyed as heartfelt a welcome as that attending John Travolta's when *Pulp Fiction* ended his long slump six years ago. But this bombastic, frantic, frequently ludicrous "dream project" of the actor (for which he takes co-producer credit with his manager, Jonathan Krane, and Elia Samaha) is truly an insta-camp idiot's delight.

The film is all too faithful to its source material, an 819-page doorstop [by L. Ron Hubbard] that reputedly sold 5 million copies. Script by Corey Mandell and J. D. Shapiro reshuffles and compacts events from the novel's first half, altering a few of the more ridiculous conceits (e.g., hero's warrior allies are no longer brogue-spaykin' Scotsmen). But haplessly clichéd dialogue, cardboard characters and dunderheaded plot logic remain.

This may be the loudest actioner yet, challenging viewer tolerance with incessant sonic-boom footfalls, detonations, gunplay and screamed dialogue. Adding to the din is Elia Cmiral's score, which ODs right away on bass-drum thunder, yet keeps on chugging till the celestial choirs come home.

Compared with those in other recent digitally enhanced pics, the visual effects are often quite blatantly mattes or computer graphics. Yet the overall look, though derivative (*The Matrix, Blade Runner, Waterworld*, etc.), rates as *Battlefield*'s one nonguilty pleasure. Wide format abets splendid views of diverse wilderness areas and ruined human cityscapes.

Travolta affects a hoity-toity mid-Atlantic accent suggesting *The Importance of Being Earnest* as performed by the Dogpatch Players. If this perf reps an indisputable Personal Worst, it is also an undeniable bull's-eye realization of Hubbard's pulp print villainy.

•

BATTLE FOR ANZIO, THE
SEE: ANZIO

•

BATTLE FOR RUSSIA, THE
1943, 80 mins, US b/w
Dir Frank Capra *Prod* Anatole Litvak *Ed* William C. Hornbeck, William A. Lyon *Mus* Dimitri Tiomkin (U.S. War Department)

In *The Battle for Russia*, Lt. Col. Frank Capra, of the Special Service Division, Army Service Forces, turns out by far the most notable in the series of *Why We Fight* army orientation pictures. Fifth of the series of seven documentaries, *Battle for Russia* is a powerful, yet simple, drama vividly depicting the greatest military achievement of all time.

As in the case of its predecessors, *Prelude to War, The Nazis Strike, Divide and Conquer* and *Battle of Britain, Russia* is a brilliant compilation of carefully edited footage culled, in the latter instance, from official Soviet sources and from newsreel and Signal Corps film, with a good part of the Russian material made available to the War Dept. exclusively for this production.

Portraying the historical background of Russia from the time of Alexander Nevsky to the present, the film explains the reasons motivating the various conquests over Russia. Effective use of animated maps helps detail its enormous resources, raw materials, manpower, etc.

Keyed to Gen. Douglas MacArthur's statement that: "The scale and grandeur of the (Russian) effort mark it as the greatest military achievement in all history," this Capra-Litvak documentary is primarily the story of the titanic struggle up to the successful defense of Stalingrad.

•

BATTLE FOR THE PLANET OF THE APES
1973, 88 mins, US Ⓥ ▭ col
Dir J. Lee Thompson *Prod* Arthur P. Jacobs *Scr* John William Corrington, Joyce Hooper Corrington *Ph* Richard H. Kline *Ed* Alan L. Jaggs, John C. Horger *Mus* Leonard Rosenman *Art* Dale Hennesy
Act Roddy McDowall, Claude Akins, Natalie Trundy, Severn Darden, Lew Ayres, John Huston (20th Century-Fox)

The fifth and last film of the series depicts the confrontation between the apes and the nuclear mutated humans inhabiting a large city destroyed in previous episode. Roddy McDowall encores as the ape's leader, having his own tribal strife with Claude Akins, a militant troublemaker.

Considering the usual fate of sequels, it's not so much that this final effort [from a story by Paul Dehn] is limp, but that the previous four pix maintained for so long a good quality level.

McDowell and Natalie Trundy head the cast, in which Paul Williams plays a philosopher-type, and Austin Soker is a black counselor, most respected of the humans who are more or less captives of the apes.

Severn Darden is leader of the mutated humans. Lew Ayres has a good bit, and John Huston appears in another pompous cameo as an aged philosopher of future generations who sets the flashback motif for the story.

•

BATTLEGROUND
1949, 118 mins, US Ⓥ b/w
Dir William A. Wellman *Prod* Dore Schary *Scr* Robert Pirosh *Ph* Paul C. Vogel *Ed* John Dunning *Mus* Lennie Hayton
Act Van Johnson, John Hodiak, Ricardo Montalban, George Murphy, James Whitmore, Leon Ames (M-G-M)

Film deals with a segment of the Battle of the Bulge and is "dedicated to the battered bastards of Bastogne," those heroic unyielding GIs who were reinspired to the ultimate victory by General McAuliffe's famous "Nuts" reply to the Krauts when they sought to negotiate a peaceful surrender by the Americans.

Through sharp focus on a group of characters it exposes all the griping disappointments and foxhole dreams and aspirations of the battle-wearied foot soldier.

The cast performs in inspired manner. Murphy is the 35-year-old "Pop" who is being discharged but finds himself a civilian in no-man's-land because Bastogne is surrounded. Johnson plays the carefree GI, and with great credibility. Other standouts include: John Hodiak as the newspaperman who enlisted; Montalban as the Mexican-American.

1949: Best Screenplay & Story, B&W Cinematography

NOMINATIONS: Best Picture, Director, Supp. Actor (James Whitmore), Editing

•

BATTLE HELL
SEE: YANGTSE INCIDENT

●

BATTLE HYMN
1956, 108 mins, US col
Dir Douglas Sirk ***Prod*** Ross Hunter ***Scr*** Charles Grayson, Vincent B. Evans ***Ph*** Russell Metty ***Ed*** Russell F. Schoengarth ***Mus*** Frank Skinner ***Art*** Alexander Golitzen, Emrich Nicholson
Act Rock Hudson, Anna Kashfi, Dan Duryea, Don DeFore, Martha Hyer, Jock Mahoney (Universal)

The inspirational story of a young clergyman is neatly integrated with fighter pilot action in *Battle Hymn*. Rock Hudson, as Col. Dean Hess, the minister whose story is told, heads the excellent cast.

Perhaps best known of Hess's deeds were his efforts on behalf of the Korean children left orphans and homeless in the wake of the fighting in that country. While quite a bit that gets on the screen may seem typical motion picture fiction, Hess served as technical advisor to assure that fact predominates.

Douglas Sirk's direction and the screenplay stirs compassion and sympathy for the personal cross Col. Hess had to bear after accidentally bombing a German orphanage during his fighting days in World War II. This incident comes to light via flashback to establish his need to again give up his pulpit for pilot wings and go to Korea with the Air Force. In Korea he finds himself via the 1,000 or more orphans he cares for and airlifts to safety.

Hudson does one of his better performances in capturing the Hess personality and character. Martha Hyer plays Mrs. Hess, the wife who waits and worries at home, with a gracious, winning appeal, although femme emphasis more naturally falls to Anna Kashfi, very effective as Miss Wong, a true Korean heroine who literally gave her life to aid Hess's work with the orphans.

●

BATTLE OF ALGIERS, THE
SEE: LA BATTAGLIA DI ALGERI

●

BATTLE OF BRITAIN
1969, 133 mins, UK col
Dir Guy Hamilton ***Prod*** Harry Saltzman, S. Benjamin Fisz ***Scr*** James Kennaway, Wilfred Greatorex ***Ph*** Freddie Young ***Mus*** Ron Goodwin, William Walton ***Art*** Maurice Carter
Act Laurence Olivier, Trevor Howard, Michael Caine, Ralph Richardson, Susannah York, Michael Redgrave (United Artists)

Battle sequences in the air are splendidly conceived and sweepingly dramatic, though sometimes repetitious.

The $12 million-plus film strikes a happy medium between action and human interest. Stressed admirably are the strained headaches of the RAF top brass as they tackled the perilous problems. The battle fatigue, the difference of opinion on tactics, the shortage of planes and pilots, and the dreadful anxiety of time running out are all revealed.

Standouts among the stars are Laurence Olivier as Sir Hugh Dowding, Fighter Command's supremo, and Trevor Howard as the tight-lipped, dedicated Air Vice-Marshall Keith Park.

Some of the star names are woefully wasted, notably Michael Caine, Patrick Wymark and Kenneth More, all playing routine parts.

●

BATTLE OF MIDWAY
SEE: MIDWAY

●

BATTLE OF THE BULGE
1965, 167 mins, US col
Dir Ken Annakin ***Prod*** Milton Sperling, Philip Yordan ***Scr*** Philip Yordan, Milton Sperling, John Nelson ***Ph*** Jack Hildyard ***Ed*** Derek Parsons ***Mus*** Benjamin Frankel ***Art*** Eugene Lourie
Act Henry Fonda, Robert Shaw, Robert Ryan, Dana Andrews, Telly Savalas, George Montgomery (Warner/United States)

Based on the pivotal action which precipitated the end of the Second World War in Europe, but otherwise fictionalized, *Battle of the Bulge* is a rousing, commercial battlefield action-drama of the emotions and activities of U.S. and German forces.

Script pits hard-charging German tank commander Robert Shaw against a U.S. military hierarchy topped by Robert Ryan, intelligence chief Dana Andrews, and latter's assistant (Henry Fonda) who is initially unpopular with the higher brass because he insists that the Germans are building toward a winter offensive.

Shaw is outstanding in a multifaceted role which demands he be a true war-lover, coolly rational under battle pressure and somewhat contemptuous of rear echelon chief Werner Peters.

On the U.S. side script is flawed in the introduction of stock military types. Ken Annakin's direction and the adroit spacing of skirmishes minimize the script softness, exemplified by Fonda's character, whose solo sleuthing and tactical analysis strains credulity. Withal, Fonda is excellent.

●

BATTLE OF THE RAILS
SEE: LA BATAILLE DU RAIL

●

BATTLE OF THE RIVER PLATE
(US: PURSUIT OF THE GRAF SPEE)
1956, 119 mins, UK b/w
Dir Michael Powell, Emeric Pressburger ***Prod*** Michael Powell, Emeric Pressburger ***Scr*** Michael Powell, Emeric Pressburger ***Ph*** Christopher Challis ***Ed*** Reginald Mills ***Mus*** Brian Easdale ***Art*** Arthur Lawson, Hein Heckroth
Act John Gregson, Anthony Quayle, Peter Finch, Ian Hunter, Jack Gwillim, Bernard Lee (Arcturus/Rank)

Defeat of the *Graf Spee* was the first major naval victory for Britain in the last big war. Apart from the strategy involved, it was also an exercise in subterfuge and diplomacy. All these points are neatly and simply brought out in the Michael Powell–Emeric Pressburger filmization. What they have failed to do is to achieve any degree of characterization for the three naval commanders who led the British cruisers to victory against the Germans' more powerful pocket battleship. The only really sympathetic character emerging from the screenplay is the skipper of the enemy ship.

The battle sequences, in which the lightweight British cruisers close in on the *Graf Spee* and force the enemy to take shelter in Montevideo harbor, are powerful, exciting and technically impressive. Story is given a neat twist by the diplomatic exchanges which take place while the *Graf Spee* is sheltering. The atmosphere in Montevideo is heightened by a series of on-the-spot dramatic broadcasts to the U.S., a device which is most effective.

The players are mostly secondary to the ships themselves. John Gregson, as the skipper of the *Exeter*; Anthony Quayle, commodore on the *Ajax*; Ian Hunter, captain on the *Ajax*, and Jack Gwillim on the *Achilles*, give forthright portrayals. Peter Finch gets the plum role as the German captain, who emerges as a warm, sincere and kindly person.

●

BATTLE OF THE SEXES, THE
1914, 60 mins, US b/w
Dir D. W. Griffith ***Scr*** Daniel Carson Goodman, Gemit J. Lloyd, D. W. Griffith ***Ph*** Billy Bitzer ***Ed*** James E. Smith, Rose Smith
Act Donald Crisp, Robert Harron, Lillian Gish, Mary Alden, Owen Moore, Fay Tincher (Reliance)

The story is a familiar but intimate tale vividly illustrated on the screen. Griffith keeps it alive every moment.

A family of four—father, mother, son and daughter—are living in an apartment house. To the same floor comes an adventuress, who is planted there to make a play for the husband (Donald Crisp). His general reputation is undisclosed, but it may be taken for granted that he is a wealthy chaser. The woman (Fay Tincher), after renting the apartment, goes to work on the head of the house in the opposite flat by leaving her door ajar and her skirt slightly lifted, as the husband starts out. From this beginning the story pictures a mistress, a broken home, a heartbroken mother (Mary Alden) and two sad children (Robert Harron and Lillian Gish).

The acting hit of the film, far and away over anything else, is the wife, played by Alden. As a middle-aged woman, called upon to pantomimically represent all the emotions, including an impulse toward insanity upon the discovery of her husband's unfaithfulness, Alden is superb. Crisp gives a competent performance, Gish is girlish and nice, Harron does exceedingly well as the son, and Owen Moore as the lover, in a somewhat slim part, plays it well.

The blot on the acting is Fay Tincher as Cleo, the adventuress.

●

BATTLE OF THE VILLA FIORITA, THE
1965, 111 mins, US col
Dir Delmer Daves ***Prod*** Delmer Daves ***Scr*** Delmer Daves ***Ph*** Oswald Morris ***Ed*** Bert Bates ***Mus*** Mischa Spoliansky ***Art*** Carmen Dillon
Act Maureen O'Hara, Rossano Brazzi, Richard Todd, Phyllis Calvert, Olivia Hussey, Maxine Audley (Warner)

The Battle of the Villa Fiorita is a beautifully photographed and well-mounted Delmer Daves production which falls short artistically by switching gears.

Daves's script (from Rumer Godden's novel) propels Maureen O'Hara into an affair with Italian composer Rossano Brazzi when latter attends English tunefest during one of hubby Richard Todd's frequent absences from home. The lovers hie to Italian villa and set up housekeeping before her divorce action jells.

At this point concept shifts to attempts by her kids (Martin Stephens and Elizabeth Dear) to break it up, joined later by Brazzi's moppet, Olivia Hussey. Idea is played for laffs, from juves' trek from England through hunger strikes, faked illness and other gambits.

O'Hara looks appropriately shook up but script does not permit much acting. Brazzi projects very well as lover, father and foil. Phyllis Calvert is on for seconds as gossipy English lady.

●

BATTLESHIP POTEMKIN
SEE: BRONENOSETS "POTYOMKIN"

●

BATTLING BUTLER
1926, 75 mins, US b/w
Dir Buster Keaton ***Scr*** Paul Gerard Smith, Al Boasberg, Charles Smith, Lex Neal ***Ph*** Dev Jennings, Bert Haines ***Art*** Fred Gabourie
Act Buster Keaton, Sally O'Neil, Snitz Edwards, Francis McDonald (Keaton/M-G-M)

"Frozen Pan" Buster's face is as rigid as ever, and he gets an abundance of laughs out of pure gag stuff. Keaton takes screen credit for having directed this one. And if so, some of his stuff is excellent.

Keaton opens up as a pampered son of wealth. A disgusted father sends him out to rough it, and he goes plus a foreign car, valet and an elaborate camping outfit. Here he meets the girl (Sally O'Neil), whose backwoods dad and brother think little of Alfred (Keaton) until the valet (Snitz Edwards) bridges the breach by explaining his young boss is "Battling" Butler, the lightweight boxer, about to fight the champ in his division.

Circumstances force the meek scion into marriage and he has to migrate to the genuine Butler's training quarters to make it look on the level. Corking support from practically all members, O'Neil and O'Brien making their dual wives stand up and Edwards getting a full quota from his valet characterization.

●

BAT 21
1988, 105 mins, US col
Dir Peter Markle ***Prod*** David Fisher, Gary A. Neill, Michael Balson ***Scr*** William C. Anderson, George Gordon ***Ph*** Mark Irwin ***Ed*** Stephen E. Rivkin ***Mus*** Christopher Young ***Art*** Vincent Cresciman
Act Gene Hackman, Danny Glover, Jerry Reed, David Marshall Grant, Clayton Rohner, Erich Anderson (Tri-Star/Vision/Eagle)

BAT 21 represents the flip side of *Rambo*. The true story of an officer forced to parachute into enemy-infested jungle during the Vietnam War and survive on his own until a rescue can be attempted, this is a straightforward, surprisingly somber picture [from William C. Anderson's book] that sticks to the facts.

Produced independently on location in Sabahn, Borneo, with the cooperation of the Malaysian military, this $10 million venture recounts the exceptional efforts of a reconnaisance flyer nicknamed Bird-Dog (Danny Glover) to keep tabs on the downed missile intelligence expert, Lt. Col. Iceal Hambleton (Gene Hackman) who has never before seen actual combat or come face-to-face with the enemy. Only Glover's personal initiative and daring gives Hackman any chance of escaping before the jungle is napalmed to smithereens. Several times, he comes within inches of being spotted by VC patrols.

Weight of the picture falls on Glover, who does most of the talking during their radio communications, squares off on occasion with his superior, nicely etched by Jerry Reed (also exec producer) and enjoys the benefit of being at the joystick for the snazzy flying scenes. Glover turns in a solid job but, as with Hackman, he remains one-dimensional.

Peter Markle's direction is dramatically sound and visually crisp, and Christopher Young's score is a plus.

●

BAT WHISPERS, THE
1931, 82 mins, US b/w
Dir Roland West ***Prod*** Roland West ***Ph*** Ray June (standard version), Robert H. Planck (65mm version) ***Ed*** James Smith ***Mus*** [uncredited] ***Art*** Paul Roe Crawley

Act Chester Morris, Una Merkel, Chance Ward, Richard Tucker, Wilson Benge, DeWitt Jennings (Art Cinema/United Artists)

Of the clutching-hand school that the stage smash, *The Bat* [by Mary Roberts Rinehart and Avery Hopwood], was probably the real parent of, *The Bat Whispers*, in its talking version, is a good picture in the class division, for shivers and smiles.

The wide-screen [Magnifilm] film, United Artists' first, is somewhat grandiloquent. Bits of direction with the camera, particularly early on, are very engaging. The same effects will come over in a lesser way on the standard size screen.

Most of the comedy is by Maude Eburne, as the lady's maid. Some more is quietly injected by Spencer Chartres. It's not the noisy kind of ghostly slapstick so long associated with haunted house stories.

Chester Morris [as Detective Anderson] has little to do. It's some time before his appearance and shortly after that he's knocked out for another lapse. At the finale the audience is halted by a cry from the screen not to leave, and, as a sort of epilog, Morris reappears to request the audience not to divulge the identity of the Bat in the picture. Other cast players take care of their portions without distinction either way. Una Merkel is the girl, with William Bakewell opposite.

•

BAWANG BIE JI
(FAREWELL TO MY CONCUBINE; FAREWELL MY CONCUBINE)

1993, 170 mins, Hong Kong Ⓥ ⦿ col

Dir Chen Kaige **Prod** Hsu Feng **Scr** Lilian Lee, Lu Wei **Ph** Gu Changwei **Ed** Pei Xiaonan **Mus** Zhao Jiping **Art** Chen Huaikai

Act Leslie Cheung, Zhang Fengyi, Gong Li, Lu Qi, Ying Da, Ge You (Tomson)

A seductively lensed but emotionally uninvolving drama about two male Peking Opera stars and the ex-prostie who comes between them. Chen Kaige's fourth feature, *Farewell to My Concubine*, reps a stylistic U-turn compared with his earlier abstract parables like *Life on a String* and *Yellow Earth*.

Production is a high-profile blending of money and talent from the three Chinese territories. Though entirely shot in Beijing, the $4 million-plus coin came entirely from the Hong Kong affil of Taiwan-based Tomson Films, run by former actress Hsu Feng (*A Touch of Zen*), with the Mainland side simply providing facilities. Cast blends Mainland stars with former Hong Kong pop singer Leslie Cheung.

Long-arced storyline [from the novel by Lilian Lee] spans 50 years of modern Chinese history, from the warlord period of the '20s, through Japanese occupation during WWII, to Communist rule and the turmoil of the Cultural Revolution. From the earliest scenes, at the Peking Opera training school, Chen's helming is consciously operatic in style.

There's a stagy, unreal quality that mirrors the tight, enclosed universe in which the homosexual Douzi's (Cheung) friendship and rift with fellow student and eventual male-roles star Shitou (Zhang Fengyi) over his marriage to Juxian (Gong Li) is played out. But there's little attempt to dig deep into the political and historical background, and the script skirts around any real examination of Douzi's sexual identity.

As the "male" half of the duo, Mainland actor Zhang anchors the movie in a powerful, shaded performance. Cheung, though well cast as the tragic gay, does his best in an underwritten part. Gong, strong in several scenes, is also shackled by a script that's too stop/go.

[Following its Hong Kong release and subsequent Cannes fest showing, pic was cut to 156 mins. on insistence of U.S. distributor, and the English title changed to *Farewell My Concubine*. Above review is of original version.]

1993: NOMINATIONS: Best Foreign Language Film, Cinematography

•

BAY BOY

1984, 104 mins, Canada Ⓥ ⦿ col

Dir Daniel Petrie **Prod** John Kemeny, Denis Heroux, Rene Cleitman **Scr** Daniel Petrie **Ph** Claude Agostini **Ed** Susan Shanks **Mus** Claude Bolling **Art** Wolf Kroeger

Act Liv Ullmann, Kiefer Sutherland, Alan Scarfe, Mathieu Carriere, Peter Donat, Isabelle Mejias (ICC)

Canadian-born director Daniel Petrie had long cherished making a film about his early days in Nova Scotia. *Bay Boy* is the realization of that dream, but it's far from the pot of gold at the end of his rainbow.

Setting is a coastal mining community circa 1937. Principals are a family of nonminers barely eking out an existence during the Depression. Kiefer Sutherland has the pivotal part of Donald Campbell, a teenager whose family envision his future with the clergy. He's more dubious about this path.

The family travails—father's precarious fortunes, brother's debilitating disease, mother's profound religious guilt, etc.—are cut with humorous vignettes and insights. However, Donald witnesses the murder of an old Jewish couple by a local policeman.

•

BEACH, THE

2000, 120 mins, UK/US Ⓥ ⦿ ▭ col

Dir Danny Boyle **Prod** Andrew Macdonald **Scr** John Hodge **Ph** Darius Khondji **Ed** Mashiro Hirakubo **Mus** Angelo Badalamenti **Art** Andrew McAlpine

Act Leonardo DiCaprio, Tilda Swinton, Virginie Ledoyen, Guillaume Canet, Paterson Joseph, Robert Carlyle (Figment/20th Century Fox)

A bunch of pleasure-seeking Westerners have no problem stirring up trouble in an Eastern paradise in this visually resplendent but dramatically uneven adaptation of Alex Garland's engaging bestseller by the Scottish *Trainspotting* crew. Anchored by a solid central theme—that of the need for children of the virtual generation to seek out real adventures and experiences—this story of a young man's intense immersion in a rarefied communal existence on a remote Thai island manages to maintain reasonable interest throughout. All the same, its narrative waters become rather muddy in the late going, and its currents finally don't run very deep.

While sticking to the tenets of the rather extravagantly praised 1997 tome by the then-27-year-old British writer, filmmakers have made some key dramatic and commercial accommodations by making the protagonist American rather than English and giving him a romance and a separate sexual tryst that don't exist in the book, as well as by moving some of the violent confrontations more center stage.

Richard (DiCaprio) is too much the American everyman and not enough of a well-defined individual to entirely capture one's interest and imagination, and DiCaprio, while perfectly watchable, does not endow him with the quirks or distinguishing marks to make this man from nowhere a dimensional character.

While the novel makes much more of how full Richard's head (and by extension, those of others in his age group) is with pop culture detritus and its related techno/virtual/faux-experiential components, and has rather more to imply about the motives for Western trespass on ever-more-exotic turf, the film is content to suggest that no earthly paradise can presume to remain immune from the mix of good and evil, and of the constructive and destructive, in the world at large. That's fair enough, but also not really enough to make *The Beach* any more than moderately compelling even at its best.

•

BEACHES

1988, 123 mins, US Ⓥ ⦿ col

Dir Garry Marshall **Prod** Bonnie Bruckheimer-Martell, Bette Midler, Margaret Jennings South, **Scr** Mary Agnes Donoghue **Ph** Dante Spinotti **Ed** Richard Halsey **Mus** Georges Delerue **Art** Albert Brenner

Act Bette Midler, Barbara Hershey, John Heard, Spalding Gray, Lainie Kazan, James Read (Touchstone/Silver Screen Partners IV/South-All Girl)

Story of this engaging tearjerker [from the novel by Iris Rainer Dart] is one of a profound friendship, from childhood to beyond the grave, between two wildly mismatched women, a lower-class Jew (Bette Midler) from the Bronx whose every breath is showbiz, and a San Francisco blueblood (Barbara Hershey) destined for a pampered but troubled life. Men, marriages and career vicissitudes come and go, but their bond ultimately cuts through it all.

Midler's strutting, egotistical, self-aware character gets off any number of zingers, but all in the context of a vulnerable woman who seems to accept, finally, that certain things in life, notably happiness in romance and family, are probably unreachable for her.

By way of contrast, Hershey plays her more emotionally untouchable part with an almost severe gravity. Hillary seems to have no real center, which in Hershey's interpretation could be part of the point, as nothing really works out for this woman who has everything—looks, intelligence, money—going for her.

1988: NOMINATION: Best Art Direction

•

BEACH PARTY

1963, 104 mins, US Ⓥ ▭ col

Dir William Asher **Prod** James H. Nicholson, Lou Rusoff **Scr** Lou Rusoff **Ph** Kay Norton **Ed** Homer Powell **Mus** Les Baxter

Act Robert Cummings, Dorothy Malone, Frankie Avalon, Annette Funicello, Harvey Lembeck, Jody McCrea (American International)

Beach Party is a bouncy bit of lightweight fluff, attractively cast, beautifully set (Malibu Beach) and scored throughout with a big twist beat. It has a kind of direct, simpleminded cheeriness.

The comparatively elderly Robert Cummings toplines the cast (with Dorothy Malone) and provides the picture with what real comic substance it has. Plot is pegged on a study of teenage sex habits undertaken by anthropologist Cummings on the beach at Malibu.

As the square professor, Cummings shows himself to be an able farceur and notably at ease in surroundings which might embarrass a less professional star. Malone is along just for the ride in a small role as the prof's longsuffering secretary. It's a waste of her talent.

What plot complications there are center around the romantic problems of a group of young surfers, principally Frankie Avalon and Annette Funicello, each of whom undertakes a campaign to make the other jealous—he with buxom Eva Six, she with the erudite professor. Story is padded out with some lovely surf-riding sequences and a whole string of Les Baxter songs.

•

BEACH RED

1967, 105 mins, US col

Dir Cornel Wilde **Prod** Cornel Wilde **Scr** Clint Johnston, Donald A. Peters, Jefferson Pascal **Ph** Cecil R. Cooney **Ed** Frank P. Keller **Mus** Elbey Vid, Antonio Buenaventura **Art** Francisco Balangue

Act Cornel Wilde, Rip Torn, Burr DeBenning, Patrick Wolfe, Jean Wallace, Jaime Sanchez (United Artists)

In contrast to many professedly antiwar films, *Beach Red* is indisputably sincere in its war is hell message. Except for brief reveries of civilian life, the film focuses entirely on a single dreary campaign by an American unit out to take a Japanese-held island in the Pacific.

Notably absent are the usual stereotypes: the tough-talking sarge with the heart of gold, the frightened kid who becomes a man in combat, etc. The trouble with the screenplay, adapted from Peter Bowman's 1945 novel, is that little is substituted for these wisely avoided cliches. The central characters are spokesmen for differing points of view, not real, full-bodied people. The acting quality suffers as a result.

The captain (Cornel Wilde) loves his wife and hates war. The sergeant (Rip Torn) derives sadistic pleasure from the war. An 18-year-old minister's son (Patrick Wolfe) remembers his girl back home and inarticulately echoes the captain's pacificism. His Southern sidekick (Burr DeBenning) is a hearty illiterate for whom the armed forces is a haven.

1967: NOMINATION: Best Editing

•

BEAN

1997, 90 mins, UK Ⓥ ⦿ col

Dir Mel Smith **Prod** Tim Bevan, Eric Fellner, Peter Bennett-Jones **Scr** Richard Curtis, Robin Driscoll, Rowan Atkinson **Ph** Francis Kenny **Ed** Chris Blunden **Mus** Howard Goodall **Art** Peter Larkin

Act Rowan Atkinson, Peter MacNicol, Pamela Reed, Harris Yulin, Burt Reynolds, John Mills (Working Title/PolyGram)

The half-hour, almost silent British comedy series *Bean* segues to the big screen, aiming squarely at the U.S. market, with mostly satisfactory results.

Rowan Atkinson's Mr. Bean, created by the actor in association with writers Richard Curtis (*Four Weddings and a Funeral*) and Robin Driscoll, is a Mr. Average who lives alone, dresses conservatively in jacket and tie, and relates better to children than he does to adults. Though possessed of a child's innocence, he has an evil streak himself, and very often deliberately provokes the catastrophes that follow inevitably in his wake.

Bean works as a kind of caretaker at Britain's formidable Royal National gallery. His employees have to find a way to get rid of him and their chance comes with a request from a small Los Angeles art gallery. Owner George Grierson (Harris Yulin) has secured a $50 million donation from army Gen. Newton (Burt Reynolds) to buy back the U.S.'s greatest painting, *Whistler's Mother.* Grierson seeks an art scholar to officiate at the unveiling and the National sends Mr. Bean. Bean's misadventures begin on the transatlantic aircraft.

Atkinson, who is in almost every scene, boasts a full-on comic personality that on the cinema screen is a bit daunting at times. Director Mel Smith marshals the material with a sure hand until near the end when he veers off into another direction with an extended sequence in an emergency hospital.

•

BEAST, THE

1988, 109 mins, US Ⓥ col

Dir Kevin Reynolds ***Prod*** John Fiedler ***Scr*** William Mastrosimone ***Ph*** Douglas Milsome ***Ed*** Peter Boyle ***Mus*** Mark Isham ***Art*** Kuli Sander

Act George Dzundza, Jason Patric, Steven Bauer, Stephen Baldwin, Don Harvey, Kabir Bedi (A & M)

A harrowing, tightly focused war film that becomes a moving, near-biblical allegory, *The Beast* represents a stellar achievement for all involved. Based on William Mastrosimone's play *Nanawatai* pic explores a single fictional incident set in 1981, the second year of the Russian occupation of Afghanistan.

A Russian tank gets trapped in a no-exit valley after its brutal decimation of a nearby Afghan village, and the surviving villagers, who've discovered a weapon capable of destroying a tank, decide to track it down for revenge.

"The Beast" is the tank, a formidably efficient war machine that becomes the center of the pic. Among its crew are Daskal (George Dzundza), a vicious, paranoid commander capable of killing his own crewmen, and Koverchenko (Jason Patric), a conscience-stricken former philosophy student. The Afghans, who see the war in religious terms, include a young man (Steven Bauer) struggling to attain a leadership role.

Performances, many of them repeated from the stage version, are remarkably evocative, particularly from the Afghans, who speak in subtitled dialect (the Russians speak English). Patric gives a resonant portrayal of the questioning Russian.

From pic's harrowing opening scene to its beautiful, meditative final stroke, director Kevin Reynolds (*Fandango*) displays remarkably mature and effective storytelling skills. Photography of Israeli desert locales is striking.

•

BEAST FROM 20,000 FATHOMS, THE

1953, 80 mins, US Ⓥ ⦿ b/w

Dir Eugene Lourie ***Prod*** Hal Chester, Jack Dietz ***Scr*** Lou Morheim, Fred Freiberger ***Ph*** Jack Russell ***Ed*** Bernard W. Burton ***Mus*** David Buttolph ***Art*** [uncredited]

Act Paul Christian, Paula Raymond, Cecil Kellaway, Kenneth Tobey, Donald Woods, Lee Van Cleef (Warner)

Producers have created a prehistoric monster that makes Kong seem like a chimpanzee. It's a gigantic amphibious beast that towers above some of New York's highest buildings. The sight of the beast stalking through Gotham's downtown streets is awesome. Special credit should go to Ray Harryhausen for the socko technical effects.

An experimental atomic blast in the Arctic region results in the "unfreezing" of the strange prehistoric reptile of the dinosaur family. Scientist Tom Nesbitt's (Paul Christian) report of the beast is attributed to hallucination resulting from Arctic exposure.

After several unsuccessful attempts, Nesbitt enlists the aid of Prof Thurgood Elson (Cecil Kellaway) and his pretty assistant Lee Hunter (Paula Raymond). Elson is killed by the monster while exploring an undersea canyon in a diving bell 150 miles from New York. The beast finally turns up in Manhattan.

Christian is first-rate as the determined scientist and Kellaway scores as the doubting professor. Raymond appears too stiff and unconvincing as the professor's assistant and Christian's romantic vis-à-vis. Screenplay [suggested by the *Saturday Evening Post* story "The Fog Horn" by Ray Bradbury] has a documentary flavor, which Jack Russell's camera captures expertly.

•

BEASTMASTER, THE

1982, 118 mins, US Ⓥ ⦿ col

Dir Don Coscarelli ***Prod*** Paul Pepperman, Sylvio Tabet ***Scr*** Don Coscarelli, Paul Pepperman ***Ph*** John Alcott ***Ed*** Roy Watts ***Mus*** Lee Holdridge ***Art*** Conrad E. Angone

Act Marc Singer, Tanya Roberts, Rip Torn, John Amos, Josh Milrad, Rod Loomis (M-G-M/United Artists)

When *The Beastmaster* begins, it is very hard to tell what it is all about. An hour later, it is very hard to care what it is all about. Another hour later, it is very hard to remember what it was all about. From the early confusion, in which it seems that a cow gives birth to a baby boy, Marc Singer emerges as Dar.

Singer's destiny is to go after the villains led by Rip Torn to revenge the destruction of the village. Along the way he teams up with two ferrets, an eagle, a panther, Tanya Roberts and John Amos and other assorted creatures of equal acting ability. Much of the time they are involved in rescuing each other from rather noninteresting situations [adapted from Andre Norton's novel].

•

BEASTMASTER 2 THROUGH THE PORTAL OF TIME

1991, 107 mins, US Ⓥ ⦿ col

Dir Sylvio Tabet ***Prod*** Sylvio Tabet ***Scr*** R.J. Robertson, Jim Wynorski, Sylvio Tabet, Ken Hauser, Doug Miles ***Ph*** Ronn Schmidt ***Ed*** Adam Bernardi ***Mus*** Robert Folk ***Art*** Allen Jones

Act Marc Singer, Kari Wuhrer, Wings Hauser, Sarah Douglas, Charles Young (Republic/Films 21)

Despite this low-budget sequel's silly dialog and cheesy special effects, *Beastmaster 2* is a mildly engaging tongue-in-cheek fantasy about mythical characters traveling through a time warp to battle it out in the mean streets of contempo L.A. Like its 1982 predecessor, pic should do well on homevid following a modest theatrical run.

Blond, lithely muscular Marc Singer returns in his loin-clothed title role as a sort of violent St. Francis figure accompanied by a tiger, an eagle and two ferrets who help him out of scrapes with the evil rulers of his desert abode. Singer maintains a winning simplicity despite all the sword-and-sorcery hokum.

The dandy bad guy is laser-wielding Wings Hauser who turns out to be Singer's long-lost brother, and a half-human creature (John Fifer) gives Singer the unpleasant task of saving the land from destruction by committing fratricide.

Goofball script is rife with contemporary slang, even in the mythical kingdom. Hauser's voluptuous witch-companion (Sarah Douglas) has visited L.A. through the time warp. Ronn Schmidt's lensing is suitably noirish.

•

BEAST WITH FIVE FINGERS, THE

1946, 90 mins, US Ⓥ b/w

Dir Robert Florey ***Prod*** William Jacobs ***Scr*** Curt Siodmak ***Ph*** Wesley Anderson ***Ed*** Frank Magee ***Mus*** Max Steiner ***Art*** Stanley Fleischer

Act Robert Alda, Andrea King, Peter Lorre, Victor Francen (Warner)

The Beast with Five Fingers is a weird, Grand Guignol–ish concoction that puts the customers strictly on their own. Till the last gasp, when J. Carrol Naish winks into the lens and gives out with a crack that "it could happen," it gives more credit for intelligence than the average thriller.

Victor Francen, as a semi-invalid concert pianist, lives in a gloomy villa in northern Italy. His companions are his secretary, Peter Lorre; his nurse, Andrea King; a composer friend, Robert Alda, and his attorney, David Hoffman.

A good deal of the plot is projected through Lorre's eyes, without any explanation of the switches from straight narration to scenes registered by Lorre's deranged mind. Best and most gruesome parts of the picture are when Lorre is alone with his vivid imagination. He chases a ghoulish hand around the library several times, catching it finally and hammering it down in a bloodcurdling scene reminiscent in mood of *The Cabinet of Dr. Caligari*. Still it pursues him, escaping at last from the burning coals into which he has thrown it.

•

BEAST WITHIN, THE

1982, 90 mins, US Ⓥ col

Dir Philippe Mora ***Prod*** Harvey Bernhard, Gabriel Katzka ***Scr*** Tom Holland ***Ph*** Jack L. Richards ***Ed*** Robert Brown, Bert Lovitt ***Mus*** Les Baxter ***Art*** David M. Haber

Act Ronny Cox, Bibi Besch, Paul Clemens, Don Gordon, R. G. Armstrong, Kitty Moffat (M-G-M/United Artists)

Honeymooning, Ronny Cox and Bibi Besch get their car stuck in the woods and while he goes for help, she gets raped by something with hairy legs.

Fast-forward 17 years to find them parents of that most dreaded of monsters—a teenager. [Film is based on the novel by Edward Levy.]

The teenager (Paul Clemens) is bad sick, and reluctantly Mom and Dad go back to the Mississippi town where she was raped to see if there could be any connection between his illness and the hairy legs. Feeling better, young Clemens follows and starts to chomp people.

There does come a time when Clemens has to get out of his body and get on with being a big-time monster. Thanks to Thomas R. Burman's makeup effects, this sequence actually creates chills as the boy's head bubbles and bursts and his skin pops and stretches.

•

BEAT THE DEVIL

1953, 100 mins, UK/Italy Ⓥ ⦿ ▭ b/w

Dir John Huston ***Scr*** John Huston, Anthony Veiller, Peter Viertel, Truman Capote ***Ph*** Oswald Morris ***Ed*** Ralph Kemplen ***Mus*** Franco Mannino ***Art*** Wilfrid Shingleton

Act Humphrey Bogart, Jennifer Jones, Gina Lollobrigida, Robert Morley, Peter Lorre, Edward Underdown (Romulus/Santana)

In an easy sort of way, the story [from a novel by James Helvick] describes the adventures of a bunch of uranium exploiteers who want to get hold of some valuable land in Africa. While they're waiting for a passage from Italy, their go-between (Humphrey Bogart) becomes involved with a young couple, played by Jennifer Jones and Edward Underdown. The way in which they get done out of their property, and the potential millions that go with it, provides the background for all the action.

All the exteriors were lensed on location in Italy, with fine matching work at Shepperton Studios. There are carefully timed laughs in the script as well as intended comedy situations that misfire. The best gag is derived from Bogart's interview with an Arab bigwig who provides a slow boat to Africa in exchange for a promised introduction to Rita Hayworth.

Under John Huston's stylish direction a fine acting standard is maintained by a front-ranking cast. Bogart's virile performance is handsomely matched by Jones's pert and vivacious study of the wife of the Englishman who pretends to status and riches which neither has enjoyed. Gina Lollobrigida gives a provocative portrayal as Bogart's wife while Edward Underdown stands out as the Englishman.

•

BEAU BRUMMELL

1924, 120 mins, US Ⓥ ⊗ b/w

Dir Harry Beaumont ***Scr*** Dorothy Farnum ***Ph*** David Abel

Act John Barrymore, Mary Astor, Willard Louis, Irene Rich, Alec B. Francis, Carmel Myers (Warner)

This has John Barrymore at the head of a cast that holds some strong picture names. The direction is not what it might have been, and the casting is also somewhat faulty. Irene Rich as the Duchess of York would have undoubtedly made a much better Lady Margery than Mary Astor, who played it. Although Astor is seen to advantage from the standpoint of beauty, she does not display any great histrionic ability.

Willard Louis as George, Prince of Wales, is one of the real outstanding figures. He walks away with practically every scene in which he appears.

Carmel Myers as a vamp is a modern vamp rather than one of the period in which the action is laid. Alec B. Francis as the servant to Beau Brummell makes a work of art of his role.

As to Barrymore, there are flashes in his characterization of the London dandy that are inspired, and there are other moments when he does not seem to get over at all.

•

BEAU GESTE

1926, 129 mins, US ⊗ b/w

Dir Herbert Brenon ***Scr*** Paul Schofield, John Russell, Herbert Brenon ***Ph*** J. Roy Hunt ***Art*** Julian Boone Fleming

Act Ronald Colman, Neil Hamilton, Ralph Forbes, Alice Joyce, Mary Brian, Noah Beery (Paramount)

Beau Geste is a "man's" picture. The story revolves around three brothers and their love for each other. And a great looking trio—Ronald Colman, Neil Hamilton and Ralph Forbes. Beyond that the love interest is strictly secondary, practically nil.

The picture is all story. In fact, only one cast member seems to get above the scenario. This is Noah Beery as the bestial sergeant-major. A part that only comes along every so often, and Beery gives it the same prominence in which P. C. Wren, the author, conceived it. It's undoubtedly one of his best portrayals.

When all is said and done, Colman, in the title role, hasn't so very much to do. Hamilton equals him for footage and Forbes exceeds him. Forbes, in his first picture, impresses all the way. Hamilton also gives a sincere performance. But there can be no question that Beery is the outstanding figure of the picture.

•

BEAU GESTE

1939, 114 mins, US Ⓥ ⦿ b/w

Dir William A. Wellman ***Prod*** William A. Wellman ***Scr*** Robert Carson ***Ph*** Theodor Sparkuhl, Archie Stout ***Ed*** Thomas Scott ***Mus*** Alfred Newman ***Art*** Hans Dreier, Robert Odell

Act Gary Cooper, Ray Milland, Robert Preston, Brian Donlevy, Susan Hayward, J. Carrol Naish (Paramount)

Beau Geste has been produced with vigorous realism and spectacular sweep. Director William Wellman has focused attention on the melodramatic and vividly gruesome aspects of the story, and skimmed lightly over the episodes and motivation that highlighted Percival Christopher Wren's original novel.

Beau employs the flashback method in unfolding the adventures of three Geste brothers in the Foreign Legion. Audience interest is gained at the start with presentation of the mystery of the desert fort with relief patrol finding the entire garrison dead and dead soldiers propped up for battle in the parapets. Confused by the weirdness of the situation, the head of the patrol pitches camp in the nearby oasis. Suddenly the fort is enveloped in flames and destroyed.

Gary Cooper is okay in the title spot. Ray Milland and Robert Preston work hard and competently to get over their respective characterizations. Trio are overshadowed, however, by the vivid Brian Donlevy as the savagely brutal sergeant of the Legion.

1939: NOMINATIONS: Best Supp. Actor (Brian Donlevy), Art Direction

•

BEAU GESTE

1966, 105 mins, US col

Dir Douglas Heyes ***Prod*** Walter Seltzer ***Scr*** Douglas Heyes ***Ph*** Bud Thackery ***Ed*** Russell F. Schoengarth ***Mus*** Hans J. Salter ***Art*** Alexander Golitzen, Henry Bumstead

Act Guy Stockwell, Doug McClure, Leslie Nielsen, Telly Savalas, David Mauro, Robert Wolders (Universal)

Third time out for one of the most memorable silent films still packs hardy entertainment. The production is an expertly-made translation of Percival Christopher Wren's novel of the French Foreign Legion in a lonely Sahara outpost, distinguished by good acting, fine photographic values and fast direction. Guy Stockwell delineates the title role.

Plot has been slightly changed. Beau and his brother, John, are now Americans instead of English, and the third brother, Digby, has been eliminated. While still a story of brother love under fire, this facet has been somewhat subordinated for a script focusing on the savagery of the sergeant, a dominant point previously but accentuated even more in this version. Basic storyline has been altered little, Beau having joined the Legion after shouldering the blame for a crime he did not commit to save another from disgrace.

Top-notch performances are contributed right down the line. Stockwell handles himself creditably and convincingly.

•

BEAU SERGE, LE
(HANDSOME SERGE)

1958, 97 mins, France b/w

Dir Claude Chabrol ***Prod*** Claude Chabrol ***Scr*** Claude Chabrol ***Ph*** Henri Decae ***Ed*** Jacques Gaillard ***Mus*** Emile Delpierre ***Art*** [uncredited]

Act Gerard Blain, Jean-Claude Brialy, Michele Meritz, Bernadette Lafont, Edmond Beauchamp, Claude Cerval (Ajym)

An important new French director, Claude Chabrol, is unveiled in this pic. Chabrol used his own money and made this feature entirely on location in his old hometown.

Recovering from an illness, a young man goes back to his hometown. Here he finds an old friend has becomes a hopeless alcoholic. He at first blames it on his wife but then finds that the boy's disorientation comes from a stillborn, idiotic first child and the general provincialism and lack of moral or spiritual strength in the small, inbred town.

Technically excellent, pic was brought in for $150,000.

•

BEAUTIFUL BLONDE FROM BASHFUL BEND, THE

1949, 76 mins, US col

Dir Preston Sturges ***Prod*** Preston Sturges ***Scr*** Preston Sturges ***Ph*** Harry Jackson ***Ed*** Robert Fritch ***Mus*** Cyril Mockridge ***Art*** Lyle Wheeler, George W. Davis

Act Betty Grable, Cesar Romero, Rudy Vallee, Olga San Juan, Sterling Holloway, Hugh Herbert (20th Century-Fox)

Blonde is basically a rather silly western farce, loosely concocted. Producer-director-writer Preston Sturges plays his script [based on a story by Earl Felton] with frantic slapstick, stressing raw, bawdy comedy rather than genuine humor, to get the laughs. The pacing is erratic, as is the film editing.

Betty Grable is the chief asset as a western dancehall gal who knows how to handle a gun—and gets into trouble because of it. The boyfriend is Cesar Romero. It's the latter that starts the trouble. Grable is out to kill him for two-timing but, in a dark room, shoots a judge in the posterior by mistake.

Cast goes about its business okay in answering Sturges's demands for burlesquing of the characters and occasionally makes the coarse humor pay off.

•

BEAUTIFUL GIRLS

1996, 110 mins, US col

Dir Ted Demme ***Prod*** Cary Woods ***Scr*** Scott Rosenberg ***Ph*** Adam Kimmel ***Ed*** Jeffrey Wolf ***Mus*** David A. Stewart ***Art*** Dan Davis

Act Matt Dillon, Noah Emmerich, Annabeth Gish, Lauren Holly, Timothy Hutton, Rosie O'Donnell (Woods)

There are several beautiful girls in *Beautiful Girls*, but they, along with the guys, are stuck making a lot of mundane moves. A great title in search of a movie to live up to it, this startlingly uneventful compendium of thick-headed boy talk and female tolerance squanders a fine cast on incredibly ordinary characters and situations.

Willie (Timothy Hutton) is a semisuccessful NYC club pianist who returns to working-class Knight's Ridge, MA, for a high school reunion. His "nice" girlfriend, Tracy (Annabeth Gish), a lawyer, will be joining him in a few days, but in the meantime he catches up with such old buddies as Tommy (Matt Dillon), Kev (Max Perlich), Paul (Michael Rapaport) and Mo (Noah Emmerich).

Tommy is going with the sweet Sharon (Mira Sorvino), but still carries on with his first love, Darian (Lauren Holly), who's married, but continues to want action on the side. Paul, who has a thing for supermodels, has just been given the heave-ho by waitress Jan (Martha Plimpton), so flaunts in front of her the fabulous Andera (Uma Thurman). Willie is intrigued by a new next-door neighbor, the precocious and tease-talking Marty (Natalie Portman), a tantalizing 13-year-old. Rounding out the main crew is Gina (Rosie O'Donnell), a brash, self-styled shrink.

The talk is almost single-mindedly about sex and relationships, redundantly and routinely so. The mesmerizing, quicksilver work of young actress Portman reps the single best reason to see the film. Hutton is easygoing and likable while Thurman has no trouble making her dazzler dazzling.

•

BEAUTIFUL THING

1996, 89 mins, UK col

Dir Hettie Macdonald ***Prod*** Tony Garnett, Bill Shapter ***Scr*** Jonathan Harvey ***Ph*** Chris Seager ***Ed*** Don Fairservice ***Mus*** John Altman ***Art*** Mark Stevenson

Act Linda Henry, Glen Berry, Scott Neal, Ben Daniels, Tameka Empson, Anna Karen (World/Channel 4)

Ken Loach meets Mike Leigh in *Beautiful Thing*, an often rough-and-ready but infectiously funny working-class comedy, with a feel-good gay theme, set in a southeast London housing project. Fresh performances from a largely unknown cast make this low-budget version of Jonathan Harvey's 1994 off–West End legit hit.

Cockney single mom Sandra (Linda Henry), manager of a local bar, is hooked up with hippie painter Tony (Ben Daniels) and trying to cope with the growing pains of her teenage son, Jamie (Glen Berry). Next door, Jamie's pal, Ste (Scott Neal), is abused by his older brother and alcoholic father. On the other side lives acid-tongued Leah (Tameka Empson), a black girl who thinks she's Mama Cass.

The plot gradually coalesces when Ste stays over one night at Jamie's flat, where the kids' initially innocent sharing of a bed turns into a life-changing homosexual encounter.

At heart, it's a working-class dramedy with a couple of gay characters, propelled by a sense of humor that comes as much from its noncorrect approach to the subject as from its one-liners.

In her first stint behind the camera, theater director Hettie Macdonald, who helmed the original stage play, doesn't bring much shape or rhythm to the material, delivering what could politely be called a *verismo*-looking TV movie. The pic has a gauche, ambling charm that's like Loach's pioneering TV dramas of the '60s with laughs.

•

BEAUTY AND THE BEAST
SEE: LA BELLE ET LA BETE

•

BEAUTY AND THE BEAST

1991, 85 mins, US col

Dir Gary Trousdale, Kirk Wise ***Prod*** Don Hahn ***Scr*** Linda Woolverton ***Ed*** John Carnochan ***Mus*** Alan Menken ***Art*** Brian McEntee (Walt Disney)

A lovely film that ranks with the best of Disney's animated classics, *Beauty and the Beast* is a tale freshly retold. Darker-hued than the usual animated feature, with a predominant brownish-gray color scheme balanced by Belle's blue dress and radiant features, *Beauty* [from the classic French fairy tale] engages the emotions with an unabashed sincerity that manages to avoid the pitfalls of triteness and corn.

The character of Belle, magnificently voiced by Paige O'Hara, is a brainy young woman scorned as a bookworm by her townsfolk and kidnapped by the Beast. She finds her initial aversion overcome by a growing appreciation of his inner beauty and sensitivity. While the usually soft-spoken Robby Benson might seem an odd choice for the voice of the Beast, his booming bass voice in the early sections and the increasingly boyish timbre of his voice in the later parts perfectly capture the character's complexity.

Howard Ashman and Alan Menken's songs are witty, charming, richly orchestrated and smoothly integrated into the plot. The first-rate animation staff bring a strikingly three-dimensional look to the film, augmented in some spots by Jim Hillin's state-of-the-art computer graphics images.

1991: Best Song ("Beauty and the Beast"), Original Score

NOMINATIONS: Best Picture, Song ("Belle," "Be Our Guest"), Sound

•

BEAUTY JUNGLE, THE
(US: CONTEST GIRL)

1964, 114 mins, UK col

Dir Val Guest ***Prod*** Val Guest ***Scr*** Robert Muller, Val Guest ***Ph*** Arthur Grant ***Ed*** Bill Lenny ***Mus*** Laurie Johnson ***Art*** Maurice Carter

Act Ian Hendry, Janette Scott, Ronald Fraser, Edmund Purdom, Jean Claudio, Kay Walsh (Rank)

There's some lively, if not over subtle, comedy in this yarn of a girl who gains quick rewards as a beauty queen, but finds the going full of disillusionment and pitfalls.

Screenplay tends to soft pedal the problems involved and the writers (Val Guest and an observant journalist-author Robert Muller, who studied the beauty queen scene) seem reluctant to come out with their views on whether such contests are degrading or even dangerous to comely damsels who take them too seriously, or whether they are just a harmless giggle.

Story concerns a pretty stenographer (Janette Scott) who is joshed by a local newspaper columnist into entering a seaside pier contest. She wins and he takes over and builds her up into a regular contestant at such junkets who progresses steadily around the familiar circuit and gets into the big-time league of big money, overblown publicity, commercialism and spurious glitter that's the magnet.

Ian Hendry, as the poor man's Svengali, is brisk and credible while Ronald Fraser, as his lenser buddy, also turns in a ripe performance.

•

BEAVIS AND BUTT-HEAD DO AMERICA

1996, 80 mins, US col

Dir Mike Judge, Yvette Kaplan (anim.) ***Prod*** Abby Terkuhle ***Scr*** Mike Judge, Joe Stillman ***Ed*** Terry Kelley, Gunter Glinka, Neil Lawrence ***Mus*** John Frizell (MTV/Paramount)

The good news is *Beavis and Butt-head Do America* doesn't suck. The bad news is it doesn't rule, either.

To stretch things out for feature length, director Mike Judge sends Beavis and Butt-head on a cross-country odyssey. It is not, strictly speaking, a journey of self-discovery. But it does manage to kill 80 minutes with reasonable efficiency.

While seeking a replacement TV at a seedy hotel, they meet a hard-drinking redneck who mistakes the boys for hired killers and offers them $10,000 to fly to Las Vegas and "do" his errant wife. The boys, figuring this may be the only way they'll ever get lucky, accept the offer. Not surprisingly, things don't go as smoothly as they hope.

Among the notables who lend their vocal talents to the enterprise: Robert Stack, as a stern ATF agent, and Cloris Leachman, as a sweet little old lady. Eric Bogosian and director Richard Linklater voice a few minor characters.

The animation is slightly more sophisticated than on the TV show, though it remains, by movie standards, minimalist at best. That, of course, is part of the joke.

•

BECAUSE OF HIM

1946, 100 mins, US b/w

Dir Richard Wallace ***Prod*** Felix Jackson ***Scr*** Edmund Beloin ***Ph*** Hal Mohr ***Ed*** Ted Kent ***Mus*** Miklos Rozsa ***Art*** John B. Goodman, Robert Clatworthy

Act Deanna Durbin, Franchot Tone, Charles Laughton (Universal)

Film is a merry melange of music, comedy and drama with a good story and a top cast. Durbin, despite the fact that she portrays a stagestruck waitress through most of the plot, is gowned to perfection and looks ditto. Music plays a minor part in the film, with the star's vocal efforts limited to three songs, but seldom has she been in finer voice.

Plot revolves around Durbin's attempt to inveigle her way into a top Broadway production, and director Richard Wallace gets the most out of the consequent wacky proceedings. Faking a letter of intro from Laughton, top legit actor, the star gets in to see producer Stanley Ridges, who's convinced she's just the gal for the lead in Sheridan's new show. Playwright Franchot Tone objects, however, and pulls his name off the credits when Laughton also goes for her.

Laughton grabs the acting honors in a sterling portrayal of the actor whose every gesture would look well between two slices of rye.

•

BECKET

1964, 148 mins, UK Ⓥ ⊙ ▭ col

Dir Peter Glenville ***Prod*** Hal Wallis ***Scr*** Edward Anhalt ***Ph*** Geoffrey Unsworth ***Ed*** Anne V. Coates ***Mus*** Laurence Rosenthal ***Art*** John Bryan

Act Richard Burton, Peter O'Toole, John Gielgud, Donald Wolfit, Gino Cervi, Paolo Stoppa (Paramount/Keep)

Made in Shepperton Studios in the U.K., this is a very fine, perhaps great, motion picture. It is costume drama but not routine, invigorated by story substance, personality clash, bright dialog and religious interest. Not least among its virtues is the pace of the narrative in the astute handing of Peter Glenville, with his advantage of having also mounted the stage play from which the film is derived.

The screenplay owes much to Jean Anouilh's orginal stage script. The modern psychology of Anouilh lends fascination to these 12th-century shenanigans by investing them with special motivational insights rare in costume drama. The basic story is, of course, historic, the murder on December 29, 1170, in the cathedral of Canterbury of its archbishop, Becket, by barons from the entourage of Henry II, great-grandson of William the Conquerer. For fictional purposes, Becket and the King had been old roustabouts together, much as, later in English history, Henry V and Falstaff were.

In the title role, Richard Burton gives a generally convincing and resourceful performance. The transition from the cold, calculating Saxon courtier of a Norman king into a duty-obsessed sincere churchman is not easily managed. Burton does manage.

As Henry II, Peter O'Toole emerges as the fatter role, and the more colorful. The king is an unhappy monarch who has known little affection in life. His only satisfying companionship has been provided by the Saxon Becket. Hating-loving, miserably lonely when deserted by his friend, O'Toole makes of the king a tormented, many-sided baffled, believable human being.

1964: Best Adapted Screenplay

NOMINATIONS: Best Picture, Director, Actor (Richard Burton, Peter O'Toole), Supp. Actor (John Gielgud), Color Cinematography, Color Costume Design, Color Art Direction, Editing, Original Music Score, Sound

•

BECKY SHARP

1935, 84 mins, US Ⓥ col

Dir Rouben Mamoulian ***Prod*** Kenneth Macgowan ***Scr*** Francis Edward Faragoh ***Ph*** Ray Rennahan ***Ed*** Archie Marshek ***Mus*** Roy Webb ***Art*** Robert Edmond Jones, Wiard B. Ihnen

Act Miriam Hopkins, Cedric Hardwicke, Nigel Bruce, Frances Dee, Alan Mowbray, G. P. Huntley, Jr. (Pioneer/RKO)

The first full-length talker in highly improved Technicolor, cinematographically it's a tribute to the new process and to Robert Edmond Jones's beautiful splashes of multitone visual values. The pastel shades of the interior properties, the faithful reproduction even of the femmes' makeup, the gay carnival splashes of color such as that in the Brussels waltz-quadrille scene (climaxed by Napoleon's Waterloo return) impress optically, but the story falls flat dramatically and the dialog is likewise fraught with too much discordant stridency of tone.

Miriam Hopkins at times fairly shrieks her way through the footage [based on Thackeray's *Vanity Fair* and the play by Langdon Mitchell]. She's basically handicapped by a negative characterization. As the calculating Becky, her role of a temptress is neither lurid nor winsome. It's a wishy-washy compromise of a gamin who annexes a sextet of masculine conquests, with the character not sufficiently definite to impress her as a great siren.

With the exceptions of G. P. Huntley, Jr., Nigel Bruce and Cedric Hardwicke, none of the support is particularly distinguished nor has it much opportunity for distinction.

1935: NOMINATION: Best Actress (Miriam Hopkins)

•

BED AND BOARD

SEE: DOMICILE CONJUGAL

•

BEDAZZLED

1967, 104 mins, UK Ⓥ ⊙ ▭ col

Dir Stanley Donen ***Prod*** Stanley Donen ***Scr*** Peter Cook, Dudley Moore ***Ph*** Austin Dempster ***Ed*** Richard Marden ***Mus*** Dudley Moore ***Art*** Terence Knight

Act Peter Cook, Dudley Moore, Eleanor Bron, Raquel Welch, Robert Russell, Barry Humphries (20th Century-Fox)

Bedazzled is smartly styled and typical of certain types of high British comedy. It's a fantasy of a London short-order cook madly in love with a waitress, who is offered seven wishes by the Devil in return for his soul.

Stanley Donen production is pretty much the work of two of its three stars, Peter Cook and Dudley Moore. Pair scripted from Cook's original story, and Moore also composed music score. Eleanor Bron is third star, plus Raquel Welch, whose brief appearance is equalled only by her scant attire.

Mephistophelean overtones are inserted in this modern-day Faust legend tacked onto Moore, who would give his soul to possess Margaret, the waitress (Bron). Cook (Mephistopheles), parading under the mundane name of George Spiggot, appears mysteriously in Moore's flat as he flubs a suicide attempt and grants all of the cook's wishes.

•

BEDAZZLED

2000, 93 mins US Ⓥ ⊙ col

Dir Harold Ramis ***Prod*** Trevor Albert, Harold Ramis ***Scr*** Harold Ramis, Larry Gelbart, Peter Tolan ***Ph*** Bill Pope ***Ed*** Craig P. Herring ***Mus*** David Newman ***Art*** Rick Heinrichs

Act Brendan Fraser, Elizabeth Hurley, Frances O'Connor, Miriam Shor, Orlando Jones, Paul Adelstein (Regency/20th Century-Fox)

Harold Ramis's spirited reprise of Stanley Donen's 1967 cult-fave farce—starring and dreamed up by Dudley Moore and the late, great Peter Cook, with the latter penning the script—is pretty damn funny on its own terms. Remake retains the original's sketch-comedy structure, but recycles only the bare bones of the Cook–Moore plot. The 2000 version is louder, broader and much, much bigger. Indeed, one particularly lavish scene, set in hell, looks like it cost more than the entire budget of the '67 comedy.

Elliot Richards (Brendan Fraser), a maladroit nerd, is at ease only while wearing a telephone headset at work, where he's a tech-support adviser. In a moment of desperate longing for Alison (Frances O'Connor), a lovely co-worker, Elliot vows that he "would give anything to have that woman" in his life. Unfortunately, his plaintive words summon the ultimate femme fatale, a shapely Satan played by Elizabeth Hurley. In return for his signature on a contract that guarantees her ultimate claim on his immortal soul, she grants him seven wishes. Elliot jumps at what seems like a foolproof chance—seven foolproof chances, actually—to win the woman he loves. Each time he makes a wish, however, the Devil springs a trap. Very quickly, a pattern emerges: Elliot wishes to become a dream lover; the Devil transforms his dreams into a nightmare.

Bedazzled allows Brendan Fraser to demonstrate his prodigious versatility by running the gamut from sweetly ingenuous to aggressively dorky, from cartoonishly boisterous (most memorably, as a frightfully huge basketball player) to suave. Exceptionally well cast as Fraser's foil, Hurley fully validates the risk of gender-bender casting with a wickedly witty performance. Hurley takes an almost unholy delight in her own naughtiness, and her saving grace is her generosity: She permits the aud to have even more fun than she does. In her first major U.S.-made pic, Aussie thesp Frances O'Connor is able to demonstrate her own considerable range as various dream girls in Elliot's orbit.

Insistently upbeat finale plays like an afterthought—or, worse, like a last-minute substitution for something marginally edgier. Closing credits offer "special thanks" to Stanley Donen. But Peter Cook and Dudley Moore are acknowledged in a more stealthy fashion. Pay close attention during a scene in which Hurley appears with a pair of ferocious pets.

•

BEDFORD INCIDENT, THE

1965, 102 mins, US Ⓥ b/w

Dir James B. Harris ***Prod*** James B. Harris, Richard Widmark ***Scr*** James Poe ***Ph*** Gilbert Taylor ***Ed*** John Jympson ***Mus*** Gerard Schurmann ***Art*** Arthur Lawson, Lionel Couch

Act Richard Widmark, Sidney Poitier, James MacArthur, Martin Balsam, Wally Cox, Eric Portman (Bedford/Columbia)

The Bedford Incident is an excellent contemporary sea drama based on a little-known but day-to-day reality of the Cold War; the monitoring of Russian submarine activity by U.S. Navy destroyers. The production, made at England's Shepperton Studios, has salty scripting and solid performances, including one of the finest in Widmark's career.

James Poe's adaptation of the Mark Rascovich novel depicts the "hunt-to-exhaustion" tactic in antisubmarine warfare, whereby a sub contact is pursued until one side or the other either gives up or eludes.

Widmark stars as the skipper of the USS *Bedford,* a modern destroyer, equipped with tactical nuclear weapons, on patrol in the North Atlantic. Widmark's skipper is that rare breed whom the crew not only follows, but worships. The character of this seadog is drawn out by the helicopter arrival of Sidney Poitier, as a wiseguy magazine writer, and Martin Balsam, a Reserve medic back on active duty.

Poitier does an excellent job in both the light and serious aspects of his role, and manages to leave a personal stamp on his scenes.

•

BEDKNOBS AND BROOMSTICKS

1971, 117 mins, US Ⓥ ⊙ col

Dir Robert Stevenson ***Prod*** Bill Walsh ***Scr*** Bill Walsh, Don DaGradi ***Ph*** Frank Phillips ***Ed*** Cotton Warburton ***Mus*** Irwin Kostal (sup.) ***Art*** John B. Mansbridge, Peter Ellenshaw

Act Angela Lansbury, David Tomlinson, Roddy McDowall, Sam Jaffe, John Ericson, Bruce Forsyth (Walt Disney)

The magic of Walt Disney lingers magnificently on in *Bedknobs and Broomsticks.*

The setting is a quaint olde-worlde English seaside village during the earlier days of World War II. Three Cockney kids (Roy Snart, Ian Weighill and Cindy O'Callaghan) are evacuated there and are as appalled by the dullness of it all as they are with the eccentricities and rules of Angela Lansbury with whom they are billetted. Then they discover she is studying witchcraft by correspondence course with the idea of using it against the Germans should they invade. Life takes on a rosier hue. They learn to perform all sorts of magic, fly to London on a bedstead and spend a joyous time in the never-never land [songs by Richard M. and Robert B. Sherman].

It is when the film [based on the book by Mary Norton] dives deeply into the realms of fantasy that it is most enjoyable. The trip with the principals on the bedstead through the underwater kingdom of the fishes and animated football match between jungle animals with a superimposed David Tomlinson refereeing are not only sheer delights but technical masterpieces.

[In 1997 a 139-min. de facto director's cut was released on home video.]

1971: Best Special Visual Effects

NOMINATIONS: Best Costume Design, Art Direction, Original Song Score, Song ("The Age of Not Believing")

•

BED OF ROSES

1996, 87 mins, US Ⓥ ⊙ col

Dir Michael Goldenberg ***Prod*** Allan Mindel, Denise Shaw ***Scr*** Michael Goldenberg ***Ph*** Adam Kimmel ***Ed*** Jane Kurson ***Mus*** Michael Convertino ***Art*** Stephen McCabe

Act Christian Slater, Mary Stuart Masterson, Pamela Segall, Josh Brolin, Ally Walker, Debra Monk (New Line)

Sweet but uninspired, *Bed of Roses* is a genial, old-fashioned romance with very little to recommend it other than earnest, likable performances by leads Christian Slater and Mary Stuart Masterson. Sprinkled with fairy-tale trappings—from the premise to Michael Convertino's score—pic proves a relatively straightforward tale about a young, career-driven woman whose life ends up being transformed by one simple act of kindness.

Masterson plays Lisa, an investment banker with no time for a personal life who receives flowers from an unknown source. She traces the gift to Lewis (Slater), a florist who had seen the woman crying through her window. Unfortunately, first-time writer-director Michael Goldenberg piles on the cliches, with both characters toting ample baggage—Lisa from a difficult childhood, Lewis from the death of his wife and his own workaholic past.

Beyond Lisa's college chum Kim (Pamela Segall), Goldenberg doesn't establish any supporting players, meaning that Slater and Masterson have to carry the entire film. As a result, the movie has a flat, rather dry feel, with little humor and only occasional romantic flourishes.

Tech credits are OK, with New York City emerging as the most utilized supporting player.

•

BEDROOM WINDOW, THE

1986, 112 mins, US Ⓥ ⊙ ▭ col

Dir Curtis Hanson ***Prod*** Martha Schumacher ***Scr*** Curtis Hanson ***Ph*** Gil Taylor ***Ed*** Scott Conrad ***Mus*** Michael Shrieve, Patrick Gleeson ***Art*** Ron Foreman

Act Steve Guttenberg, Elizabeth McGovern, Isabelle Huppert, Paul Shenar, Wallace Shawn, Carl Lumbly (De Laurentiis)

Cast against type, Steve Guttenberg plays a malleable young executive carrying on an affair with his boss' wife, the sexy Sylvia (Isabelle Huppert). During a tryst at Guttenberg's apartment one night after a party, Huppert, looking out his bedroom window, sees a girl (Elizabeth McGovern) being assaulted outside.

Guttenberg ultimately becomes a suspect in the rash of rape and murder cases, forcing him in the Hitchcock tradition to begin his own investigation in trying to prove who the real killer is.

Curtis Hanson's screenplay [from the novel *The Witnesses* by Anne Holden] involves several ingenious plot twists. Huppert carries the first half of the film, replaced by McGovern in importance in the final reels and both actresses are alluring and mysterious in keeping the piece suspenseful. Unfortunately, a lot of coincidences and just plain stupid actions by Guttenberg are relied upon to keep the pot boiling.

•

BED SITTING ROOM, THE
1970, 90 mins, UK Ⓥ col
Dir Richard Lester ***Prod*** Oscar Lewenstein, Richard Lester ***Scr*** John Antrobus, Charles Wood ***Ph*** David Watkin ***Ed*** John Victor Smith ***Mus*** Ken Thorne ***Art*** Assheton Gordon
Act Rita Tushingham, Ralph Richardson, Peter Cook, Dudley Moore, Spike Milligan, Michael Hordern (United Artists)

A play by Spike Milligan and John Antrobus serves as an ideal springboard for an offbeat antiwar film by Richard Lester which, miraculously, manages to convey its grim message with humor.

Sketch-like pic catches glimpses and comments of the 20-odd survivors of a London shredded by an A-bomb as they dig out of their holes to try and cope with the gray new world before they, too, become animals.

In the manner of vaude blackouts, they soon meld into a general mosaic of stiff-upper-lip acceptance of new conditions, some fizzlers but others very amusing.

Ralph Richardson is superb in a relatively brief stint as the diehard traditionalist who eventually "becomes" the title's bed-sitting room, but all in a carefully chosen roster of British character thesps who contribute stellar bits in almost impossibly difficult roles.

•

BEDTIME STORY
1941, 83 mins, US b/w
Dir Alexander Hall ***Prod*** B. P. Schulberg ***Scr*** Richard Flournoy ***Ph*** Joseph Walker ***Ed*** Viola Lawrence ***Mus*** Werner Heymann ***Art*** Lionel Banks, Cary Odell
Act Fredric March, Loretta Young, Robert Benchley, Allyn Joslyn, Eve Arden, Helen Westley (Columbia)

Picture is a combo of slick scripting, fast-paced direction and excellent performances. Richard Flournoy provides plenty of laugh embellishment to the original story by Horace Jackson and Grant Garrett; director Alexander Hall keeps his foot on the speed throttle from start to finish; and Fredric March teams with Loretta Young for a pair of topnotch performances in the starring spots.

Despite the light and fluffy tale unreeled, maximum entertainment is provided in the breezy exposition of the marital problems of producer-playwright March and his star-wife Young. After seven years of marriage and struggle, pair are top successes in their respective endeavors. The wife desires to retire to their farm in Connecticut, while the energetic March hatches a new play in which he wants Young to star. Both Young and the audience keep intrigued by the inventive devices concocted by the playwright in trying to swing his wife into the new play.

•

BEDTIME STORY
1964, 99 mins, US Ⓥ col
Dir Ralph Levy ***Prod*** Stanley Shapiro ***Scr*** Stanley Shapiro, Paul Henning ***Ph*** Clifford Stine ***Ed*** Milton Garruth ***Mus*** Hans J. Salter ***Art*** Alexander Golitzen, Robert Clatworthy
Act Marlon Brando, David Niven, Shirley Jones, Dody Goodman, Aram Stephan, Marie Windsor (Universal)

Bedtime Story will divert the less discriminating, although there are times when even such major league performers as Marlon Brando and David Niven have to strain to sustain the overall meager romantic comedy material.

Some of the lines snap and crackle, and several of the situations (done with slapstick overtones) in which Brando and Niven find themselves involved as con men in competition on the French Riviera are broadly funny.

The screenplay has Niven as a big-time operator and Brando a relatively petty practitioner of the confidence art who comes to challenge the "king of the mountain" in his own background. The mercenary contest centers around "American soap queen" Shirley Jones, who turns out to be merely the penniless winner of a soap queen contest.

Brando wins the girl, but he loses the histrionic contest to Niven, whose effortless flair for sophisticated comedy is not matched by his costar.

•

BEETHOVEN
1992, 88 mins, US Ⓥ ⦿ col
Dir Brian Levant ***Prod*** Joe Medjuck, Michael C. Gross ***Scr*** Edmond Dantes, Amy Holden Jones ***Ph*** Victor J. Kemper ***Ed*** Sheldon Kahn, William D. Gordean ***Mus*** Randy Edelman ***Art*** Alex Tavoularis
Act Charles Grodin, Bonnie Hunt, Dean Jones, Oliver Platt, Stanley Tucci, Nicholle Tom (Universal)

Six-year-olds and animal rights activists should warm up to the titular big slobbering dog, his perfect family and the experimentation ring that brings them together, and the pic rallies at the end to prevent chaperoning adults from feeling their time was completely wasted.

The real star is a 185-pound St. Bernard. Stolen as a puppy, he stumbles into the Newton family's life. They are a demographically perfect group, with an uptight dad (Charles Grodin) who reluctantly agrees to adopt the beast.

Beethoven grows and, as only movie dogs can, manages to help the kids' lives in various creative ways, even as he mangles the house and antagonizes Dad. Ultimately, Grodin is forced into action when the dog becomes the victim of an animal-theft ring led by an oily vet (Dean Jones), leading to a resolution so predictable that even the youngest of tots can feel smug in having guessed it.

Director Brian Levant cut his teeth directing sitcoms before turning to features with *Problem Child 2*, and the influence shows, particularly in the cartoonish perfs he gets from villains.

•

BEETHOVEN'S 2ND
1993, 88 mins, US Ⓥ ⦿ col
Dir Rod Daniel ***Prod*** Michael C. Gross, Joe Medjuck ***Scr*** Len Blum ***Ph*** Bill Butler ***Ed*** Sheldon Kahn, William D. Gordean ***Mus*** Randy Edelman ***Art*** Lawrence Miller
Act Charles Grodin, Bonnie Hunt, Nicholle Tom, Christopher Castle, Sarah Rose Karr, Debi Mazar (Universal)

The producers don't stray far thematically from their first composition, where reluctant family patriarch George Newton (Charles Grodin) had to be won over to keeping a monstrous mutt around. To its credit, though, *Beethoven's 2nd* does better than just double up its mediocre forebearer, creating what amounts to a live-action cartoon with a strong *One Hundred and One Dalmatians* riff that should play particularly well among moppets.

Pic begins with a lonely Beethoven meeting his dream dog and having puppies, only to have the pooch taken away by her evil owner, Regina (Debi Mazar), who hopes to use the St. Bernard to fleece her husband in their divorce settlement.

The Newton kids start raising the puppies, concealing them from Dad, before Regina becomes determined to cash in on a second front by selling the purebred litter. After a section based largely on kid-dog antics, the climax occurs at a mountain retreat where both the Newtons and Regina, conveniently, are vacationing.

Not surprisingly, the trainers merit the biggest kudos, as the dog actors (more than 100 play the puppies at various stages, per the production notes) out-emote their two-footed counterparts.

1993: NOMINATION: Best Song ("The Day I Fall in Love")

•

BEETLEJUICE
1988, 92 mins, US Ⓥ ⦿ col
Dir Tim Burton ***Prod*** Michael Bender, Larry Wilson, Richard Hashimoto ***Scr*** Michael McDowell, Warren Skaaren ***Ph*** Thomas Ackerman ***Ed*** Jane Kurson ***Mus*** Danny Elfman ***Art*** Bo Welch
Act Alec Baldwin, Geena Davis, Michael Keaton, Jeffrey Jones, Winona Ryder, Sylvia Sidney (Geffen)

Beetlejuice springs to life when the raucous and repulsive Betelgeuse (Michael Keaton) rises from his moribund state to wreak havoc on fellow spooks and mortal enemies.

Geena Davis and Alec Baldwin are a couple of affectionate New Englanders who live in a big barn of a house that they lovingly are restoring. But they crash over a covered bridge and drown—consigned to an afterlife that keeps them stuck at home forever invisible to anyone not similarly situated.

No sooner is their funeral over when their beloved house is sold to a rich New York financier (Jeffrey Jones) and his wife, the affected artiste (Catherine O'Hara).

Help comes via a cryptically written book for the newly deceased that takes Davis and Baldwin into the afterlife—kind of a comical holding cell for people who died of unnatural causes like themselves—but better yet, from this freak of a character named Betelgeuse that lives in the graveyard that's part of the miniature tabletop town that Baldwin built.

In the script [from a story by Michael McDowell and Larry Wilson], things above ground aren't nearly as inventive as they are below. Luckily, Keaton pops up from his grave to liven things up when the antics pitting the good ghosts against the intruders become a trite cat and mouse game.

1988: Best Makeup

•

BEFORE AND AFTER
1996, 107 mins, US Ⓥ ⦿ col
Dir Barbet Schroeder ***Prod*** Barbet Schroeder, Susan Hoffman ***Scr*** Ted Tally ***Ph*** Luciano Tovoli ***Ed*** Lee Percy ***Mus*** Howard Shore ***Art*** Stuart Wurtzel
Act Meryl Streep, Liam Neeson, Edward Furlong, Julia Weldon, Alfred Molina, Daniel Von Bargen (Hollywood)

Before and After is so afraid of violating basic pieties that it ends up saying nothing. Telling of parents put to a sudden and drastic challenge when their teenage son is accused of murdering his girlfriend, the earnest, handsomely mounted meller is marred not only by thematic waffling but also by narrative awkwardness and some unexpected weakness in the acting department.

The tough question of how solid, intelligent, well-meaning parents respond when their child commits a horrible crime is softened by a crucial qualifier: the child isn't guilty. This aspect of Ted Tally's script, however true to Rosellen Brown's source novel, immediately pushes the film away from the hardhitting toward the sentimental.

The Ryans are well-off residents of a picture-book slice of Massachusetts. Carolyn (Meryl Streep) is an established pediatrician, Ben (Liam Neeson) a successful artist. Their well-ordered life is upended one winter's eve when a local policeman brings the news that their son, Jacob (Edward Furlong), was the last person seen with a teen girl who's been murdered, and he's now missing.

After five agonizing weeks—which pass like five seconds because, evidently, a section of the story didn't make pic's final cut—the boy is apprehended in Boston. Ben attempts to skirt the law by persuading Jacob to assert that he was away from the scene when the girl died, a claim the boy relates to the high-priced lawyer the Ryans have engaged, Panos Demeris (Alfred Molina).

The script at every turn falls back on mushy affirmations of family rather than taking the risk of exploring conflicts that reveal the bitterest divisions between one family member and another, and between family and community. Apart from Molina's sharp performance as Demeris, none of the main actors come off particularly well.

•

BEFORE SUNRISE
1995, 101 mins, U.S. Ⓥ ⦿ col
Dir Richard Linklater ***Prod*** Anne Walker-McBay ***Scr*** Richard Linklater, Kim Krizan ***Ph*** Lee Daniel ***Ed*** Sandra Adair ***Art*** Florian Reichmann
Act Ethan Hawke, Julie Delpy (Castle Rock/Detour)

A lovely, rather risky concept isn't entirely fulfilled in the telling of *Before Sunrise*, the third feature by *Slacker* helmer Richard Linklater. Fragile tale concerns two kids who meet by chance on a train in Europe and decide to spend a few hours together to see what happens. While pic remains sympathetic and appealing, the endless dialogue and repetitive settings become wearing through the couple's one long night together.

As their train is speeding towards Vienna, a young American fellow, Jesse (Ethan Hawke), begins chatting with a lovely French student, Celine (Julie Delpy), who's on her way back to Paris. Jesse, who is due to fly back to the States the next day, convinces Celine to detrain with him in Vienna so they can get to know each other better.

The pair range around the city, taking in a few sights, stopping at countless cafés, exchanging backgrounds and life experiences, daring each other to reveal themselves emotionally, propounding half-baked analyses and philosophies and feeling that they might be falling in love. The morning brings the inevitable leave-taking and a sweet coda. What's commendable about Linklater's approach here, is the real-time, in-depth aspect of portraying a burgeoning relationship. But while attractive and enthusiastic, Jesse is ultimately a regular guy who lacks the quirks and distinctiveness that would make him a resonant personality. By contrast, Delpy's Celine is a beautiful creation, a young lady seemingly mature beyond her years. She quickly emerges as a far more engaging and fully drawn personality.

•

BEFORE THE RAIN
1994, 115 mins, U.K./France/Macedonia ▭ col
Dir Milcho Manchevski ***Prod*** Judy Counihan, Cedomir Kolar, Sam Taylor ***Scr*** Milcho Manchevski ***Ph*** Manuel Teran ***Ed***

Nick Gaster ***Mus*** Anastasia ***Art*** Sharon Lamofsky, David Munns
Act Katrin Cartlidge, Rade Serbedzija, Gregoire Colin, Labina Mitevska, Silvija Stojanovska (Aim/Noe/Varder)

Before the Rain is a visually and narratively stunning tale in three parts, set between modern London and the timeless hills of Macedonia in the former Yugoslavia. Through a parable of intertwined lives, it attempts to answer the tragic riddle of why the Balkan states are perpetually at war.

Rain, the first feature directed by Macedonian-born helmer Milcho Manchevski (now a New York resident and director of music vids), is also the first film made in the newly declared republic of Macedonia.

Bordering Greece (which hotly disputes its very name), Albania, Bulgaria and Serbia, the mountainous country is shown to be in danger of becoming the site of the next Balkan bloodbath. Manchevski depicts senseless ethnic hatred as endemic in the region.

Film is divided into three parts. In *Words*, the young Greek Orthodox monk Kiril (Gregoire Colin), living in an ancient monastery, shelters and hides an Albanian girl, Zamira (Labina Mitevska), even though they can't understand each other's language. A band of machine-gun wielding roughnecks bursts into the monastery looking for her, claiming she killed their brother.

The modernity of the second episode, *Faces*, comes as a shock. Anne (Katrin Cartlidge), who works in a London photo agency, is torn between her Macedonian lover, Aleksandar (Rade Serbedzija), a Pulitzer Prize–winning war photographer, and her sweet, boring husband, Nick (Jay Villiers). Before she can make up her mind between them, Aleksandar takes off for Macedonia and Nick dies in an absurd shootout in a restaurant. *Pictures* takes the story back to Macedonia and brings the threads together.

Pic owes part of its disturbing magic to its challenging structure. All the events seem to take place at the same time, until the surprising and clever ending. Actors have a strong iconic presence, in which faces are as important as speeches. Dialogue is kept to a realistic minimum.

1994: NOMINATION: Best Foreign Language Film

•

BEFORE WINTER COMES

1969, 107 mins, UK col
Dir J. Lee Thompson ***Prod*** Robert Emmett Ginns ***Scr*** Andrew Sinclair ***Ph*** Gil Taylor ***Ed*** Willy Kemplen ***Mus*** Ron Grainer ***Art*** John Blezard
Act David Niven, Topol, Anna Karina, John Hurt, Anthony Quayle, Ori Levy (Columbia/Windward)

An unevenly scripted, confusingly directed drama about the treatment of displaced persons in Austria immediately following VE Day. *Before Winter Comes* is a modestly budgeted British drama about conflict between military authority and humanistic concepts in the peacetime army.

David Niven turns in his usual competent professional job as a major assigned to run a camp for displaced persons during the spring of 1945. Topol is the multilingual magician from among the DPs whom Niven chooses to assist him in deciding who should be turned over to American and who to Russian authorities.

To its basic military story [from short story *The Interpreter* by Frederick L. Keefe] film tries to add a *Zorba the Greek* aspect, with Topol representing an earthy life-force counter to Niven's harsh rigidity.

Nothing dims Topol's impact. He exudes a romantic masculinity not without sexual charm at the same time that he shows a formidable comedic timing and grace.

•

BEGGAR'S OPERA, THE

1953, 94 mins, UK Ⓥ col
Dir Peter Brook ***Prod*** Herbert Wilcox, Laurence Olivier ***Scr*** Dennis Cannan, Christopher Fry ***Ph*** Guy Green ***Ed*** Reginald Beck ***Mus*** Arthur Bliss ***Art*** William C. Andrews
Act Laurence Olivier, Stanley Holloway, George Devine, Hugh Griffith, Athene Syler, Dorothy Tutin (British Lion)

A bold experiment which does not come off, *The Beggar's Opera* is an example of the uneasy partnership between screen and opera.

Herbert Wilcox, who promoted the production, cast his net over a wide field for new and promising talent. Peter Brook was recruited from legit to direct his first motion picture. Denis Cannan, the noted playwright, authored the screenplay and additional dialog and lyrics were penned by Christopher Fry. Most important of all was the casting of Laurence Olivier in his first singing role.

At constant intervals events are brought to a standstill by the John Gay lyrics and, attractive though they are in their own right, they do not merge too happily in the film.

Brook brings an obviously arty approach to his direction, resorting to a surplus of subdued lights. He is at his best in handling the big crowd scenes. The sequence in which Macheath is being driven from Newgate Gaol to the gallows is boldly and imaginatively presented.

Apart from Olivier and Stanley Holloway, the singing voices of the cast are dubbed by leading British vocalists and the contrast is clear and distinct. Olivier's light baritone, pleasant enough in its own way, is no match for the other voices. This apart, his performance is as robust and as lively as could be expected.

Holloway as Lockit, the jailer, is a polished singer as well as being a first-class thesper and his is one of the best individual contributions to the pic. Arthur Bliss's score is outstanding.

•

BEGINNING OR THE END, THE

1947, 110 mins, US b/w
Dir Norman Taurog ***Prod*** Samuel Marx ***Scr*** Frank Wead ***Ph*** Ray June ***Ed*** George Boemler ***Mus*** Daniele Amfitheatrof ***Art*** Cedric Gibbons, Hans Peters
Act Brian Donlevy, Robert Walker, Tom Drake, Audrey Totter, Hume Cronyn, Beverly Tyler (M-G-M)

The Beginning or the End tells its portentous tale in broad strokes of masterful scripting and production. Picture tees off with a pseudo news clip, showing the burying of a time capsule, not to be opened until A.D. 2446. In the time capsule is placed a motion-picture film which records *The Beginning or the End*. Thereafter is unfolded the nearly two-hour picture.

It brings an appreciation of how science and big business were mobilized by America to achieve the Atomic Bomb even though President Roosevelt was told it would cost a billion dollars and possibly two billion; the mobilization of big business and stout young scientists to work with their more experienced elders; the rallying around Dr. J. Robert Oppenheimer (whom Hume Cronyn expertly impersonates); the questioning by young Tom Drake whether he was doing the right thing.

Brian Donlevy is capital as Gen. Groves, eclipsed only by Godfrey Tearle's extraordinary personation of President Roosevelt.

It's to the sum credit of everybody concerned that the documentary values are sufficiently there without becoming static.

•

BEGIN THE BEGUINE

SEE: VOLVER A EMPEZAR

•

BEGUILED, THE

1971, 105 mins, US Ⓥ ⊙ col
Dir Don Siegel ***Prod*** Don Siegel ***Scr*** John B. Sherry, Grimes Grice ***Ph*** Bruce Surtees ***Ed*** Carl Pingitore ***Mus*** Lalo Schifrin ***Art*** Ted Haworth
Act Clint Eastwood, Geraldine Page, Elizabeth Hartman, Jo Ann Harris, Darleen Carr, Mae Mercer (Malpaso/Universal)

Marking a distinct change of pace for both director Don Siegel and star Clint Eastwood, *The Beguiled* doesn't come off, and cues laughter in all the wrong places.

Eastwood eschews his usual action character to portray a wounded Union soldier recuperating within the confines of a small school for Southern girls run by Geraldine Page. His presence cues a series of diverse sexual frustrations, and his wily handling of the ladies, spark jealousies of meller proportions.

Pic is essentially black comedy, but treatment is consistently heavy-handed. Script [from novel by Thomas Cullinan] resorts to tired symbolism, including that chestnut that equates Southern womanhood with incestuous dreams under the Spanish moss.

Eastwood is not called upon to do much emoting; that is left in spades to the ladies. Page, per usual, runs away with the honors, whether girlishly remembering her erotic relationship with her brother or grimly sawing off Eastwood's leg in a sequence that would be nauseating if it weren't so funny.

•

BEHIND THE GREEN DOOR

1972, 72 mins, US Ⓥ col
Dir Jim Mitchell, Art Mitchell ***Prod*** Jim Mitchell, Art Mitchell ***Scr*** Jim Mitchell ***Ph*** Jon Fontana ***Ed*** Jon Fontana
Act Marilyn Chambers, George S. McDonald, Johnny Keyes, Ben Davidson (Mitchell Brothers)

Football fans attracted to the hardcore debut of Oakland Raider pro Ben Davidson should flag him for box-office clipping. His fully clothed cameo appearance is hardly worth the time. But sports fans won't go away entirely disappointed, since ex-middleweight boxing champ Johnny Keyes is also featured—and he goes all the way.

Marilyn Chambers makes her hardcore debut in *Behind the Green Door*. Unlike the crones who used to populate pornos, Chambers may be remembered as the fresh-faced "innocent" in *Together* [1971, directed by Sean S. Cunningham]. In that one, she was bare a lot, but never went all the way. In this, she does everything, quite realistically.

Unfortunately, she never has enough to say to judge whether she qualifies as an actress.

Filmmakers lavished $50,000 on this feature, their biggest budget to date.

•

BEHIND THE RISING SUN

1943, 86 mins, US Ⓥ b/w
Dir Edward Dmytryk ***Scr*** Emnett Lavery ***Ph*** Russell Metty ***Ed*** Joseph Noriega ***Mus*** Roy Webb
Act Margo, Tom Neal, J. Carrol Naish, Robert Ryan, Gloria Holden (RKO)

Screenplay is from factual information contained in book by James R. Young, International News Service correspondent in Tokyo for several years prior to the war's outbreak at Pearl Harbor. Although foreword points out that the characters are imaginary, facts woven into the dramatics are real. Result is a good drama of inside info on Jap indoctrination and thinking.

Story is an intimate affair of a Jap family of the upper class; and the impress of the conquests in Asia and war against the United States on both father and son. Father is influential newspaper publisher (J. Carrol Naish), while son is Cornell-educated Tom Neal. When latter arrives from America after completing college education and figures to embark on career as an engineer with Don Douglas, there are family objections for a time. But when Neal further falls in love with lower-caste Jap girl (Margo) marriage is impossible.

•

BEHOLD A PALE HORSE

1964, 119 mins, US Ⓥ b/w
Dir Fred Zinnemann ***Prod*** Fred Zinnemann ***Scr*** J. P. Miller ***Ph*** Jean Badal ***Ed*** Walter Thompson ***Mus*** Maurice Jarre ***Art*** Alexandre Trauner
Act Gregory Peck, Anthony Quinn, Omar Sharif, Raymond Pellegrin, Paola Stoppa, Mildred Dunnock (Columbia)

Pale Horse [from the novel *Killing a Mouse on Sunday* by Emeric Pressburger] is rooted in the Spanish Civil War, using introductory newsreel footage and the fighting to set the background for a story that happens 20 years later and essentially concerns a Spanish guerrilla (Gregory Peck) who continues to live the war alone. He is thrown again into the fray in a personal attack against a vain and arrogant police captain (Anthony Quinn) who has vowed his death.

The one-man fight against a corrupt and powerful adversary is an obvious losing battle, but the guerrilla's last stand, he knows, can be his most effective.

Peck is a worn-out, untidy broken man who once again surges with force and energy in a characterization that ranks among the better in his long career. There also is an excellent performance from Quinn, who is coarse, crude and worldly as the arrogant police chief but shows his own insecurity beneath a physically courageous false front. Omar Sharif shows a warm, sensitive side in this film, playing the role of a young priest torn between obligations of personal morality and the official laws of government.

•

BEING HUMAN

1994, 125 mins, US/UK Ⓥ ⊙ col
Dir Bill Forsyth ***Prod*** Robert F. Colesberry, David Puttnam ***Scr*** Bill Forsyth ***Ph*** Michael Coulter ***Ed*** Michael Ellis ***Mus*** Michael Gibbs ***Art*** Norman Garwood
Act Robin Williams, John Turturro, Anna Galiena, Vincent D'Onofrio, Hector Elizondo, Lorraine Bracco (Warner/Enigma)

Being Human never comes alive. This stillborn series of little fables is so flat and ill-conceived that it could convince the uninitiated that neither Robin Williams nor the highly idiosyncratic Scottish writer/director Bill Forsyth had any talent. Warner Bros. kept this one under wraps for at least a year.

Forsyth has built this curiosity out of five historical vignettes centered upon a character named Hector (Williams). He's a caveman in the Bronze Age, a slave during the Roman Empire, a traveler fleeing war in the Middle Ages, a Portuguese adventurer during the Age of Exploration and a hapless divorced man in contempo New York—but in any era he's a meek, ineffectual wimp who can't make a decision or stand up for himself.

After more than two hours of patience-eroding tepid drama and non-comedy, the picture reveals no philosophical connective tissue, no elements that have been meaningfully placed and built so as to coalesce into rewarding meaning at the end. As entertainment, it's equally a washout. Never in the film has Williams's inspired, manic personality been so suppressed, never has he seemed to bland.

•

BEING JOHN MALKOVICH
1999, 112 mins, UK/US Ⓥ ⊙ col
Dir Spike Jonze ***Prod*** Michael Stipe, Sandy Stern, Steve Golin, Vincent Landay ***Scr*** Charlie Kaufman ***Ph*** Lance Acord ***Ed*** Eric Zumbrunnen ***Mus*** Carter Burwell ***Art*** K. K. Barrett.
Act John Cusack, Cameron Diaz, Catherine Keener, Orson Bean, Mary Kay Place, John Malkovich (Propaganda/Single Cell/Gramercy)

Hot music video and commercials creator Spike Jonze makes a bracingly original entry into the feature-film arena with *Being John Malkovich*, a metaphysical comic love story about the desire to be someone else and the urge to control another person's thoughts.

What makes it so fresh is the decision to treat even the story's most surreal inventions in real, rather than fantastical terms, placing writer Charlie Kaufman's peculiar universe in everyday New York City, with characters who register each surprise development as merely another unusual but not incredible crease in the fabric of their lives.

At the center of this world is talented but esoteric street puppeteer Craig Schwartz (John Cusack), unfulfilled in his marriage to frumpy pet-store staffer Lotte (a startlingly deglamorized Cameron Diaz). Driven to find a job, Craig answers an ad for a filing clerk in offices on a Manhattan building's low ceilinged 7½th floor, where he meets Maxine (Catherine Keener) and is immediately smitten.

The two colleagues form a business partnership when Craig stumbles on a weird discovery. Behind a cabinet in his office is a sealed door that opens onto a cramped, sticky tunnel. Exploring this, he is sucked into the head of John Malkovich, viewing the world through the actor's eyes for precisely 15 minutes before being spat out into a ditch off the New Jersey Turnpike. Complications arise when Lotte takes the trip and is instantly hooked on "the Malkovich ride," and begins to consider sex reassignment.

Kaufman's endlessly resourceful script never lets up, and Jonze draws rich, enjoyable performances from the entire cast.

1999: NOMINATIONS: Best Director, Supporting Actress (Catherine Keener), Original Screenplay

•

BEING THERE
1979, 130 mins, US Ⓥ ⊙ col
Dir Hal Ashby ***Prod*** Andrew Braunsberg ***Scr*** Jerzy Kosinski ***Ph*** Caleb Deschanel ***Ed*** Don Zimmerman ***Mus*** John Mandel ***Art*** Michael Haller
Act Peter Sellers, Shirley MacLaine, Melvyn Douglas, Jack Warden, Richard Basehart (United Artists/Lorimar)

Being There is a highly unusual and an unusually fine film. A faithful but nonetheless imaginative adaptation of Jerzy Kosinski's quirky comic novel, pic marks a significant achievement for director Hal Ashby and represents Peter Sellers's most smashing work since the mid-1960s.

Kosinski's story is a quietly outrageous fable which takes Sellers from his position as a childlike, unblinking naif who can't read or write to that of a valued advisor to an industrial giant and ultimately to the brink of a presidential nomination.

Tale possesses political, religious and consumer society undertones, but by no means is an overly symbolic affair trying to impress with its deep meanings.

Sellers's performance stands as the centerpiece of the film, and it's a beauty. Shirley MacLaine is subtle and winning, retaining her dignity despite several precarious opportunities to lose it. If such is possible in a picture dominated by Sellers, Melvyn Douglas almost steals the film with his spectacular performance as the dying financial titan.

1979: Best Supp. Actor (Melvyn Douglas)

NOMINATION: Best Actor (Peter Sellers)

•

BELL, BOOK AND CANDLE
1958, 106 mins, US Ⓥ ⊙ col
Dir Richard Quine ***Prod*** Julian Blaustein ***Scr*** Daniel Taradash ***Ph*** James Wong Howe ***Ed*** Charles Nelson ***Mus*** George Duning ***Art*** Cary Odell
Act James Stewart, Kim Novak, Jack Lemmon, Ernie Kovacs, Hermione Gingold, Elsa Lanchester (Phoenix/Columbia)

Richard Quine's direction gets everything possible out of the screenplay and the cast. But with Kim Novak as the central figure, the picture lacks the spontaneity and sparkle written in by playwright John Van Druten.

The offbeat story is concerned with witches and warlocks (male gender of the broomstick set) operating against today's world of skepticism and realism. James Stewart is the straight man thrust by chance into a group of people, headed by Novak, where incantations, spells and sorcery are accepted as realities as commonplace as processed foods. Novak literally weaves a spell on Stewart to make him fall in love with her.

There are some wonderfully weird proceedings here, including Elsa Lanchester and Hermione Gingold as rival witches, and Jack Lemmon as a clean-cut, bongo-beating warlock.

The hazard of the story is that there is really only one joke. This was sustained in the play by Van Druten's witty dialog. It is undercut in the picture by the fact that the backgrounds are too often as weird as the situations.

1958: NOMINATIONS: Best Costume Design, Art Direction

•

BELLBOY, THE
1960, 72 mins, US Ⓥ ⊙ b/w
Dir Jerry Lewis ***Prod*** Jerry Lewis ***Scr*** Jerry Lewis ***Ph*** Haskell Boggs ***Ed*** Stanley Johnson ***Mus*** Walter Scharf ***Art*** Hal Pereira, Henry Bumstead
Act Jerry Lewis, Alex Gerry, Bob Clayton, Bill Richmond, Sonny Sands, Milton Berle (Paramount)

From an artistic standpoint, *The Bellboy* is minor-league screen comedy, the victim of its energetic star's limited craftsmanship.

The picture is, as it admits in an introductory disclaimer, a "series of silly sequences," with "no story, no plot." It follows Jerry Lewis, as a bellboy at Miami's fashionable Fontainebleau Hotel, through a number of zany misadventures in which he speaks not a word of dialog. Several of the sequences are amusing, but too many are dependent upon climactic sight gags anticipated well in advance of the punch.

The film has a tendency to grow repetitious, one of the major reasons for this being Lewis's strict adherence to the sort of physical exaggertation (the palsied movement and distorted facial maneuvers) that has become his trademark.

There are latent elements of Charlie Chaplin's little tramp, Jacques Tati's "Hulot", Danny Kaye's "Mitty" and Harpo Marx's curiously tender child-man, but the execution falls far short of such inspiration. Under Lewis's direction, the Bellboy emerges as a two-dimensional portrait, a clown without a soul, a funnyman to be laughed at, but not rooted for. Lewis has surrounded himself with some exceptionally vigorous talents. Among the standouts in the large, relatively unfamilar supporting cast are Alex Gerry, Bob Clayton, Bill Richmond (in a Stan Laurel takeoff) and the Novelites, who fashion one of the picture's comedy peaks. Milton Berle puts in a surprise guest appearance.

Since all the action takes place at the actual Fontainebleau, and no well-known names other than Lewis grace its cast roster, *Bellboy* undoubtedly was brought in on an unusually small budget.

•

BELLE DE JOUR
1967, 102 mins, France/Italy Ⓥ ⊙ col
Dir Luis Bunuel ***Prod*** Robert Hakim, Raymond Hakim ***Scr*** Luis Bunuel, Jean-Claude Carriere ***Ph*** Sacha Vierny ***Ed*** Walter Spohr ***Mus*** [none] ***Art*** Robert Clavel
Act Catherine Deneuve, Jean Sorel, Michel Piccoli, Genevieve Page, Francisco Rabal, Pierre Clementi (Paris/Five)

Luis Bunuel, Mexican filmmaker of Hispano origin, comes up with a crackling look at a supposedly well-married, comely girl who begins to give way to masochistic leanings working by day in a sporting house, if a good wife by night.

Pic [from the novel by Joseph Kessel] starts in a jolting manner as she is riding with her husband in a carriage in the woods. He has his coachmen stop, string her up, strip her, whip her and then begin to make advances. This is all in her mind. When the dandyish friend talks of clandestine houses, and even drops an address of one he used, she finds herself looking up the place, and finally beginning to work there. Belle de Jour is the name she uses.

Catherine Deneuve has the fine, luminous features to help make her heroine always coherent, rigorous and forthright enough to clarify the dual life. Jean Sorel is properly attractive and weak as her husband. Michel Piccoli is an outspoken friend who sees through the heroine as effectively as the many perverted clients in her bagnio life. The color photography is also an asset as is the production dress and the well-done editing.

•

BELLE ET LA BETE, LA
(BEAUTY AND THE BEAST)
1946, 110 mins, France Ⓥ ⊙ b/w
Dir Jean Cocteau ***Prod*** Andre Paulve ***Scr*** Jean Cocteau ***Ph*** Henri Alekan ***Ed*** Claude Iberia ***Mus*** Georges Auric ***Art*** Christian Berard
Act Josette Day, Jean Marais, Mila Parely, Nane Germon, Michel Auclair, Marcel Andre (Paulve)

Unduly slow pace and repetitious use of trick sets hurts chances of this film. Story, a fairy tale [by Mme. Leprince de Beaumont] in medieval costumes, shows Josette Day in a Cinderella part falling in love with a monster who turns into a Prince Charming upon death. Picture is geared more for the arty crowd than the masses.

•

BELLE OF NEW YORK, THE
1952, 82 mins, US Ⓥ col
Dir Charles Walters ***Prod*** Arthur Freed ***Scr*** Robert O'Brien, Irving Elinson ***Ph*** Robert Planck ***Ed*** Albert Akst ***Mus*** Harry Warren ***Art*** Cedric Gibbons, Jack Martin Smith
Act Fred Astaire, Vera-Ellen, Marjorie Main, Keenan Wynn, Alice Pearce, Clinton Sundberg (M-G-M)

A film musical usually can get by with the lightest plot if the dance numbers and tunes are sock, but *Belle* has an even lighter plot than usual, and the numbers are just ordinary. It's all done pleasantly but not of a quality that rates more than passing interest.

Score contains nine songs, most of which are given some eye appeal in production staging, although not elaborately. Most pleasing is Vera-Ellen's "Naughty But Nice," which she sings and dances to fit a story situation.

Script has Astaire as an early-New York playboy who falls for a Bowery mission worker (Vera-Ellen) and changes his ways, even getting employment to prove he is worthy of her pure, honest affection. Tunes and production numbers are hung on that framework.

•

BELLE OF THE NINETIES
1934, 75 mins, US b/w
Dir Leo McCarey ***Prod*** William LeBaron ***Scr*** Mae West ***Ph*** Karl Struss ***Ed*** LeRoy Stone ***Art*** Hans Dreier, Bernard Herzbrun
Act Mae West, Roger Pryor, John Mack Brown, Katherine DeMille, John Miljan (Paramount)

Mae West's opera, *Belle of the Nineties*, is as ten-twent-thirt as its mauve decade time and locale. The melodramatics are put on a bit thick, including the arch-villain who is an arch-renegade, a would-be murderer, a welcher, an arsonist and everything else in the book of ye good old-time mellers.

The original songs by Sam Coslow and Arthur Johnston are "My Old Flame," "American Beauty" and "Troubled Waters." Duke Ellington's nifty jazzique is a natural for the Westian song delivery.

Just like she makes stooges of almost anybody assigned to bandy talk with her, West dittoes with her principal support, including Roger Pryor, the fave vis-à-vis, John Mack Brown as the good time Charlie, and John Miljan, a villyun of darkest mien. Katherine DeMille as the spurned gambler's sweetheart looks better and suggests better opportunities than the prima facie script accords her.

•

BELLE OF THE YUKON
1944, 83 mins, US col
Dir William A. Seiter ***Prod*** William A. Seiter ***Scr*** James Edward Grant ***Ph*** Ray Rennahan ***Ed*** Ernest Nims ***Mus*** Arthur Lange ***Art*** Perry Ferguson
Act Randolph Scott, Gypsy Rose Lee, Dinah Shore, Charles Winninger, William Marshall (RKO)

Belle of the Yukon is a typical backstage filmusical, utilizing a Yukon dancehall for setting. Opening title tips off that it is not to be taken seriously, and then yarn spins with tongue-in-cheek attitude and in general light vein.

Randolph Scott is a reformed confidence man who fled north from the law, and opened a successful dancehall-gambling establishment at Malamute. Gypsy Rose Lee, deserted by Scott in his flight, arrives as head of a new entertainment unit and is intrigued by his reformation to again fall in love with him.

William Seiter grooves the fragile tale in a light vein throughout, accentuating the characters to compensate for the slim plot. Screenplay [from a story by Houston Branch]

has liberal supply of chuckling dialog. Production mounting is top grade.

•

BELLES OF ST. TRINIAN'S, THE
1954, 91 mins, UK Ⓥ b/w
Dir Frank Launder ***Prod*** Frank Launder, Sidney Gilliat ***Scr*** Frank Launder, Sidney Gilliat, Val Valentine ***Ph*** Stanley Pavey ***Ed*** Thelma Connell ***Mus*** Malcolm Arnold ***Art*** Joseph Bato
Act Alastair Sim, Joyce Grenfell, George Cole, Hermione Baddeley, Betty Ann Davies, Renee Houston (British Lion/London)

Inspired by Ronald Searle's British cartoons about the little horrors of a girls' school, *The Belles of St. Trinian's* makes an excellent start but never lives up to the promise of the opening reel.

By way of a story, Frank Launder and Sidney Gilliat have concocted an involved yarn about a plot to steal the favorite horse in a big race which is foiled by the girls in the fourth form after a battle royal with the sixth form.

Unrestrained direction by Launder is matched by the lively and energetic performances by most of the cast. As both the headmistress and her bookmaker brother, Alastair Sim rarely reaches comedy heights. Joyce Grenfell, however, as a police spy posing as a games teacher, is good for plenty of laughs. Best individual contribution is by George Cole, playing a wide-shouldered wiseguy, who acts as selling agent for the homemade gin brewed in the school lab, and also as go-between for the girls and the local bookie.

•

BELL FOR ADANO, A
1945, 103 mins, US b/w
Dir Henry King ***Prod*** Louis D. Lighton, Lamar Trotti ***Scr*** Lamar Trotti, Norman Reilly Raine ***Ph*** Joseph La Shelle ***Ed*** Barbara McLean ***Mus*** Alfred Newman ***Art*** Lyle R. Wheeler, Mark-Lee Kirk
Act Gene Tierney, John Hodiak, William Bendix, Richard Conte (20th Century-Fox)

John Hersey's story of an American major's administration of a town in Sicily, and his attempts to return it to its peaceful prewar status, has not been tampered with or elaborated upon. The film begins quietly to set the simple keynote, has some very beautiful, inspired moments, and finishes off with several scenes of emotional brilliance.

John Hodiak, in the difficult role of Major Joppolo, presents the right hardboiled type of civil affairs officer, determined to bring spiritual rebirth (through the return of its city-hall bell) to the community.

Gene Tierney, too, as the blonde fisherman's daughter, has a certain quiet grace without always bringing sufficient poignancy to the role. William Bendix, as the major's orderly, plays the part in subdued fashion for the most convincing portrayal of the three leads, rising superbly to his one big scene at the end. Here Bendix goes roaring drunk at learning that the major is to be displaced.

Henry King's direction caps the story's mood superbly, because of his ability to instill the thought of movement frequently where no action actually exists.

•

BELLISSIMA
1952, 130 mins, Italy Ⓥ b/w
Dir Luchino Visconti ***Scr*** Luchino Visconti, Suso Cecchi D'Amico, Francesco Rosi ***Ph*** Piero Portalupi ***Ed*** Mario Serandrei ***Mus*** Franco Mannino
Act Anna Magnani, Walter Chiari, Tina Apicella, Gastone Renzelli, Arturo Bragaglia, Alessandro Blasetti (Bellissima)

Although having a slight plot, film gets top-drawer handling in production, thesping and direction. Anna Magnani has rarely been better. Story was suggested to writer Cesare Zavattini (*Miracle in Milan*) during the casting of recent Italian films. In telling about the attempts by a Rome worker's wife to get her little girl a film role, it launches some sharp barbs at the Roman film milieu. A screen test is finally engineered via bribes, after the unknowing child has been coached, primped, and "beautified."

In one of the cruellest scenes ever filmed, mother and child secretly watch a screening of the test, in which all present double with laughter at the girl's ugliness and ineptitude. The mother interrupts the show and tells them off, leaves with her dream shattered, dragging the girl along.

Magnani runs the thespian gamut in this one, in her colorful portrayal of the mother's role, with splendid support from comedian Walter Chiari. Latter here plays a straight part as a likeable studio profiteer. The scene In which he tries and fails to seduce her on an excursion is one of pic's highlights. Remainder of colorful cast of professionals and non-pros is given a perfect blending under Luchino Visconti's sensitive direction.

Production was shot in direct sound, an Italian rarity, and resulting realism and depth are outstanding.

•

BELL JAR, THE
1979, 107 mins, US Ⓥ col
Dir Larry Peerce ***Prod*** Jerrold Brandt, Jr. ***Scr*** Marjorie Kellogg ***Ph*** Gerald Hirschfeld ***Ed*** Marvin Wallowitz ***Mus*** Gerald Fried ***Art*** John Robert Lloyd
Act Marilyn Hassett, Julie Harris, Anne Jackson, Barbara Barrie, Donna Mitchell, Robert Klein (Avco Embassy)

The Bell Jar, based on the late poet Sylvia Plath's autobiographical novel, evokes neither understanding nor sympathy for the plight of its heroine, Esther Greenwood, the epitome of a straight-A, golden-girl overachiever, who is mentally "coming apart at the seams."

As played by Marilyn Hassett, Esther emerges as a selfish, morbid little prig. She eventually confesses to hating her mother, admirably played by Julie Harris, presumably because her mother refuses to wallow in the details of her father's death with her.

Marjorie Kellogg's screenplay seems fairly faithful to the novel's spirit. Larry Peerce's direction provides a sense of headachey dullness 15 minutes into the film.

Donald Brooks's costumes are the perfect evocation of 1950s style, the film's time period, and the color of Gerald Hirschfeld's camera is almost too pretty.

•

BELLS ARE RINGING
1960, 126 mins, U.S. Ⓥ ⦿ ▭ col
Dir Vincente Minnelli ***Prod*** Arthur Freed ***Scr*** Betty Comden, Adolph Green ***Ph*** Milton Krasner ***Ed*** Adrienne Fazan ***Mus*** Andre Previn (adapt.) ***Art*** George W. Davis, Preston Ames
Act Judy Holliday, Dean Martin, Fred Clark, Eddie Foy, Jean Stapleton, Frank Gorshin (M-G-M)

Better Broadway musicals than *Bells Are Ringing* have come to Hollywood, but few have been translated to the screen so effectively. *Bells* is ideally suited to the intimacy of the film medium. Where it might have a tendency in several passages to become dwarfed on a big stage, it's always bigger than life on-screen, which actually is a desirable factor in broad, freewheeling comedy such as this.

The Betty Comden-Adolph Green screenplay, based on their [1956] book musical, is not by any means the sturdiest facet of the picture, but it's a pleasant yarn from which several rather inspired musical numbers spring. "Just in Time" and "The Party's Over" are delivered smoothly by Dean Martin and Judy Holliday. The latter's outstanding turn, however, occurs near the end of the picture, when she demonstrates her verve and versatility on the amusing "I'm Goin' Back (Where I Can Be Me, at the Bonjour Tristesse Brassiere Factory)."

Martin has a chance to get in some solid licks on the alcoholically inspired "Do It Yourself" and in a traffic-stopping, crowd elbowing street sequence labelled "Hello." A real showstopper is a production number with symphonic overtones presided over dynamically by Eddie Foy. Vincente Minnelli's graceful, imaginative direction puts spirit and snap into the musical sequences, warmth and humor into the straight passages, and manages to knit it all together without any traces of awkwardness in transition, a frequent stumbling block in filmusicals. Jule Styne's bright score has been vibrantly adapted and conducted by Andre Previn.

Holliday, as might be expected, steals show with a performance of remarkable variety and gusto as a girl who takes her switchboard and humanity seriously, Martin is excellent as her writer friend, displaying more animation than customary.

1960: NOMINATION: Best Scoring of a Dramatic Picture

•

BELLS GO DOWN, THE
1943, 86 mins, UK b/w
Dir Basil Dearden ***Prod*** Michael Balcon ***Scr*** Roger MacDougall ***Ph*** Ernest Palmer ***Ed*** Sidney Cole, Mary Habberfield ***Mus*** Roy Douglas ***Art*** Michael Relph
Act Tommy Trinder, James Mason, Mervyn Johns, Philippa Hiatt, Finlay Currie, Beatrice Varley (Ealing)

Like *Fires Were Started* this film depicts the activities of life in the London Auxiliary Fire Service. But the first one out was more legitimate in that it was portrayed by actual members of the service.

Viewed as a mere low comedy, *The Bells Go Down* [from the book by Stephen Black] ambles along amiably. There is a running commentary patterned on the lines of those made familiar by Quentin Reynolds, and the fire scenes alternate with the wisecracking of Tommy Trinder, which are often without provocation. Thrillingly effective conflagration scenes deserve a large share of the honors.

Trinder enacts a lovable East Side young man whose mother runs a fish-and-chip shop, and who owns a racing greyhound that never wins until his comrades have gone broke backing the pooch.

The supporting cast is very well chosen, with Mervyn Johns offering a scintillating portrayal. James Mason, as a fireman, scores as usual; Beatrice Varley, as Trinder's mother, and fully a score of others can be set down as efficient support. Direction, production and photography are praiseworthy.

•

BELLS OF ST. MARY'S, THE
1945, 126 mins, US Ⓥ ⦿ b/w
Dir Leo McCarey ***Prod*** Leo McCarey ***Scr*** Dudley Nichols ***Ph*** George Barnes ***Ed*** Henry Marker ***Mus*** Robert Emmett Dolan ***Art*** William Flannery
Act Bing Crosby, Ingrid Bergman, Henry Travers, Ruth Donnelly, Rhys Williams, Una O'Connor (RKO/Rainbow)

The Bells of St. Mary's is warmly sentimental, has a simple story leavened with many laughs and bears comparison with *Going My Way*. Leo McCarey, who demonstrated his ability to combine wholesome sentiment into a potent attraction with *Going My Way*, duplicates that ability as producer-director on this one.

Bing Crosby's Father O'Malley is the same priest character seen in *Way*, and *Bells* tells of his new assignment as parish priest at the parochial school, St. Mary's.

Story tells of how he aids the nuns' prayers for a new school building with a more practical application of guidance; steers a young girl through an unhappy domestic situation, and brings the parents together again. It's all done with the natural ease that is Crosby's trademark.

Ingrid Bergman again demonstrates her versatility as the sister in charge. Her clashes with Crosby—all good-mannered—over proper methods of educating children, her venture into athletics, and coaching of a youngster to return a good left hook instead of the other cheek, are moments that will have an audience alternately laughing and sniffling.

1945: Best Sound Recording

NOMINATIONS: Best Picture, Director, Actor (Bing Crosby), Actress (Ingrid Bergman), Editing, Scoring of a Dramatic Picture, Song ("Aren't You Glad You're You")

•

BELLY OF AN ARCHITECT, THE
1987, 118 mins, UK Ⓥ ⦿ col
Dir Peter Greenaway ***Prod*** Colin Callender, Walter Donohue ***Scr*** Peter Greenaway ***Ph*** Sacha Vierny ***Ed*** John Wilson ***Mus*** Wim Mertens, Glenn Branca ***Art*** Luciana Vedovelli
Act Brian Dennehy, Chloe Webb, Lambert Wilson, Sergio Fantoni (Callender/Film Four/British Screen)

The Belly of an Architect is a visual treat, almost an homage to the style of Rome's architecture, lensed with skill and packed with esoteric nuances, but doubts about the story and the skill of the acting linger. The belly in question is the stomach of a U.S. architect, played by a suitably paunchy Brian Dennehy, who arrives in Rome with his fickle wife to set up an exhibition celebrating French architect Boullee. He becomes convinced he is being slowly poisoned by his wife (Chloe Webb) who is having an affair with a rival Italian architect (Lambert Wilson).

Dennehy, usually spotted in Yank actioners, makes an admirable effort as the troubled architect, but the rest of the cast—mostly European—turn in generally poor efforts. Webb as his wife looks okay, but her voice (apt in *Sid and Nancy*) just seems irritating, while Wilson as the rival architect/lover is little more than a clotheshorse.

•

BELOVED ENEMY
1936, 90 mins, US Ⓥ b/w
Dir H. C. Potter ***Prod*** Samuel Goldwyn ***Scr*** John L. Balderston, Rose Franken, William Brown Meloney, David Hertz ***Ph*** Gregg Toland ***Ed*** Sherman Todd ***Mus*** Alfred Newman ***Art*** Richard Day
Act Merle Oberon, Brian Aherne, Karen Morley, Jerome Cowan, David Niven, Henry Stephenson (Goldwyn/United Artists)

Beloved Enemy is a Hollywood version of how peace was restored betwen the British and Irish in 1921. The three collaborators of *Beloved Enemy* have dealt with fictional principals. They have conceived a romantic tragedy between the leader of the Irish insurrectionists and the titled daughter of a British conciliator, and the result is more fantastic than anything. G. A. Henty ever invented.

Merle Oberon and Brian Aherne are surprisingly well suited to each other, and the romantic episodes, although somewhat overlength, are charmingly played. Oberon is lovely to look upon and speaks her lines with fine enunciation. Aherne plays the young Irish rebel with humorous ease.

The strain on credulity is the implication that the armistice between the warring factions was brought about by the English girl because of her love for the Irish chief. Representatives meet in London and discuss settlement terms. Just why Aherne becomes a marked man for consenting to what is apparently a popular peace, is not made too clear, but on his return to Dublin he is assassinated by one of his own party and dies in his sweetheart's arms. A second, "happy" ending was made by the studio, but the tragic note seems consistent with the plot.

•

BELOVED INFIDEL

1959, 123 mins, US ▭ col

Dir Henry King ***Prod*** Jerry Wald ***Scr*** Sy Bartlett ***Ph*** Leon Shamroy ***Ed*** William Reynolds ***Mus*** Franz Waxman ***Art*** Lyle R. Wheeler, Maurice Ransford

Act Gregory Peck, Deborah Kerr, Eddie Albert, Philip Ober, Herbert Rudley, John Sutton (20th Century-Fox)

The protracted and stormy Sheilah Graham–F. Scott Fitzgerald romance in the 1930s is brought to the screen taking Graham's autobiographical book [cowritten with Gerold Frank] as the jumping-off point. Judging by the book, Fitzgerald, despite his drinking and his eccentricities, was a fascinating personality, a tortured genius from Princeton who ran aground in Hollywood. Graham didn't paint herself in quite so favorable a light.

In the picture, the tables have been turned. It is the columnist, played by Deborah Kerr, who suffers nobly and "serves" sympathetically. It is Fitzgerald who is portrayed as a weak, moody, spoiled child with little more to his credit than the attractive looks of Gregory Peck.

This is primarily a film about a sharp, aggressive film columnist who falls in love with a man who is her intellectual superior by miles and who, through association with him, attains a new human stature. It is also a film in which the characters go mostly unexplained and this makes for a superficiality which deprives them of sympathy. What's more, the acting, while excellent and persuasive in parts, is shallow and artificial in others.

Problem is primarily with Peck, who brings to Fitzgerald the kind of clean-cut looks and youthful appearance that conflict with the image of a has-been novelist, whacking away at a studio typewriter to make a living and to meet his family obligations. Kerr can't overcome the artificiality of the part or the situation, and after a while the affair just peters out and becomes dull.

•

BEN

1972, 83 mins, US Ⓥ col

Dir Phil Karlson ***Prod*** Mort Briskin ***Scr*** Gilbert A. Raiston ***Ph*** Russell Metty ***Ed*** Harry Gerstad ***Mus*** Walter Scharf ***Art*** Rolland M. Brooks

Act Lee H. Montgomery, Joseph Campanella, Arthur O'Connell, Rosemary Murphy, Meredith Baxter, Kaz Garas (Cinerama/Crosby)

Willard has a tension-packed sequel in *Ben*, which takes up minutes after Willard, the man who trained rats, was killed off by his rodents in original entry. Ben, the rat heavy of the other, plays the title role here.

Chief protagonist is a young boy played by Lee H. Montgomery, who befriends Ben. Latter's army of rats obey his orders, and they create a reign of terror as they indulge in a wave of killing.

Moppet plays his part to perfection and Phil Karlson's direction is responsible for mounting moments of excitement, well handled by cast headed by Joseph Campanella as a police lieutenant in charge of crisis and Meredith Baxter, Lee's sister.

1972: NOMINATION: Best Song ("Ben")

•

BEND OF THE RIVER
(UK: WHERE THE RIVER BENDS)

1952, 91 mins, US Ⓥ col

Dir Anthony Mann ***Prod*** Aaron Rosenberg ***Scr*** Borden Chase ***Ph*** Irving Glassberg ***Ed*** Russell Schoengarth ***Mus*** Hans J. Salter ***Art*** Bernard Herzbrun, Nathan Juran

Act James Stewart, Arthur Kennedy, Julie Adams, Rock Hudson, Lori Nelson, Jay C. Flippen (Universal)

Basic plot line is a simple affair, as lifted from Bill Gulick's novel, *Bend of the Snake*. It deals with a band of settlers who make a long, wagon train trek into Oregon to claim the country from the wilderness and the hardships of such pioneering.

James Stewart is the wagon train guide, leading the settlers into Oregon. He rescues Arthur Kennedy, a former Missouri raider, from a hanging and the latter joins the party for the trek to Portland, where group boards a river steamer for a journey into the back country. The summer passes and promised supplies that are to carry the settlers through the winter do not arrive. Stewart returns to Portland, finds the town gold-mad and the supplies held up for more money.

Stewart's handling of his role has punch. Kennedy socks his likeable heavy role. Julie Adams fulfills romantic demands of her top femme role, and Rock Hudson pleasantly projects the part of a young gambler who joins the settlers.

•

BENEATH THE PLANET OF THE APES

1970, 95 mins, US Ⓥ ⊙ ▭ col

Dir Ted Post ***Prod*** Arthur P. Jacobs ***Scr*** Paul Dehn ***Ph*** Milton Krasner ***Ed*** Marion Rothman ***Mus*** Leonard Rosenman ***Art*** Jack Martin Smith, William Creber

Act James Franciscus, Kim Hunter, Maurice Evans, Linda Harrison, Charlton Heston, Victor Buono (20th Century-Fox/Apjac)

This sequel to the 1968 smash, *Planet of the Apes*, is hokey and slapdash. The story [by Paul Dehn and Mort Abrahams] and Ted Post's direction fall far short of the original.

Film utilizes closing sequence of the original—where Charlton Heston and the silent Linda Harrison ride into an unknown country on the supposedly unknown planet, only to find the head of the Statue of Liberty buried in the sand. Heston's curtain cry of anguish now is followed by new footage, as he and Harrison wander the vast wasteland, in which Heston suddenly disappears.

James Franciscus is yet another space explorer who crash-lands, centuries out of time. Dialogue, acting and direction are substandard. Heston appears in some new footage, and Franciscus looks just like a twin brother by this time, in face and in voice.

•

BENEATH THE 12-MILE REEF

1953, 102 mins, US Ⓥ ▭ col

Dir Robert D. Webb ***Prod*** Robert Bassler ***Scr*** A. I. Bezzerides ***Ph*** Edward Cronjager ***Ed*** William Reynolds ***Mus*** Bernard Herrmann ***Art*** Lyle R. Wheeler, George Patrick

Act Robert Wagner, Terry Moore, Gilbert Roland, J. Carrol Naish, Richard Boone, Peter Graves (20th Century-Fox)

Set among the sponge-diving Greek colony at Tarpon Springs, Fla, the squeeze-lensing gives punch in the display of underwater wonders, the seascapes and the brilliant, beautiful sunrises and sunsets of the Florida Gulf coast.

In handling the young cast, Robert D. Webb's direction is less effective, particularly in the case of Robert Wagner and Terry Moore. Both are likable, so the shallowness of their performances is no serious handicap to the entertainment. Thesping quality is maintained by the more experienced casters. Scoring resoundingly is Gilbert Roland, colorful Greek diver and father of Wagner. Angela Clarke also clicks as the wife and mother.

The plot takes on two lines of conflict—the age-old battle between man and the sea, the more personal rivalry between the diving Greeks of Tarpon Springs and the hook-spongers of the shallow Key West waters.

Romance gets in its licks when the daring Gilbert ventures into Key West waters controlled by Boone and the young Wagner meets conch-girl Moore.

It's an instant attraction between the pair and their romance builds to a runaway marriage after Gilbert is killed diving at the dangerous 12-mile reef. Wagner then becomes the man of the family, proving his right to the title by diving where his father met death, fighting off an octopus and beating Graves in an underwater battle.

1953: NOMINATION: Best Color Cinematography

•

BENEATH THE VALLEY OF THE ULTRA VIXENS

1979, 93 mins, US Ⓥ ⊙ col

Dir Russ Meyer ***Prod*** Russ Meyer ***Scr*** R. Hyde [= Roger Ebert], B. Callum [= Russ Meyer] ***Ph*** Russ Meyer ***Ed*** Russ Meyer ***Mus*** William Tasker ***Art*** Michele Levesque

Act Francesca "Kitten" Natividad, Anne Marie, Ken Kerr, June Mack, Lola Langusta (RM International)

For the fanciers of pneumatic pulchritude, Russ Meyer is back with *Beneath the Valley of the Ultra Vixens* which as the onscreen narrator says "is a very simple story," presumably for very simple people.

Briefly, the strand of plot concerns Lavonia (Francesca "Kitten" Natividad), whose only fault is "enthusiasm" and her unsatisfactory sex relationship with her man Lamar (Ken Kerr). In the course of curing Lamar so that he will straighten up and satisfy, Lavonia has a hot time with everybody in town.

This is the umpteenth in Meyer's vixen series. But are they satire, as Meyer would have one believe, or fantasy, or both? If anything, they are funny and though a bit too long, Meyer, who does everything (directs, edits, photographs and produces), keeps the action fast and furious.

•

BENEFIT OF THE DOUBT

1993, 90 mins, US Ⓥ ⊙ col

Dir Jonathan Heap ***Prod*** Michael Spielberg, Brad M. Gilbert ***Scr*** Jeffrey Polman, Christopher Keyser ***Ph*** Johnny Jensen ***Ed*** Sharyn L. Ross ***Mus*** Hummie Mann ***Art*** Marina Kieser

Act Donald Sutherland, Amy Irving, Rider Strong, Christopher McDonald, Graham Greene, Theodore Bikel (Monument)

Suspense is not the strongest suit of *Benefit of the Doubt*, a lackluster psychological thriller that uses the format of a TV-styled family melodrama but fails to target the gut or the mind. Initially interesting setup has Frank Braswell (Donald Sutherland) paroled after 22 years in prison. Accused of killing his wife, Frank's conviction was helped by the testimony of his daughter Karen (Amy Irving), who still believes he is guilty.

A single mother working as a cocktail waitress in a strip joint, Karen dreads the return of her father to Cottonwood, a small Arizona town. The idea of seeing him again not only revives haunting childhood nightmares, but also threatens the new life she has built with young son Pete (Rider Strong) and b.f. Dan (Christopher McDonald).

The chief problem is that a half-hour into the movie, the pivotal dirty family secrets are disclosed and the story has nowhere to go. When the first murder makes its scheduled stop, one can sniff red herring a mile away.

The movie [from a story by Michael Lieber] aspires to the ambience and tonality of *The Stepfather*, with which it shares some common themes, but it lacks the nasty irony and frightening undertones of that film. Novice director Jonathan Heape doesn't possess the savvy technique or manipulative skills required for a taut thriller. Cast against type, Irving gives a startling performance. The usually reliable Sutherland is surprisingly timid and inexpressive.

•

BEN-HUR

1959, 212 mins, US Ⓥ ⊙ ▭ col

Dir William Wyler, [Andrew Marton, Richard Thorpe] ***Prod*** Sam Zimbalist ***Scr*** Karl Tunberg, [Christopher Fry, Gore Vidal, Maxwell Anderson, S. N. Behrman] ***Ph*** Robert L. Surtees ***Ed*** Ralph E. Winters, John D. Dunning ***Mus*** Miklos Rozsa ***Art*** William Horning, Edward Carfagno

Act Charlton Heston, Jack Hawkins, Stephen Boyd, Haya Harareet, Hugh Griffith, Sam Jaffe (M-G-M)

The $15 million *Ben-Hur* is a majestic achievement, representing a superb blending of the motion picture arts by master craftsmen. The big difference between *Ben-Hur* and other spectacles, biblical or otherwise, is its sincere concern for human beings. They're not just pawns reciting flowery dialog to fill gaps between the action. This has been accomplished without sacrificing the impact of the spectacle elements.

The famous chariot race between Ben-Hur, the Prince of Judea, and Messala, the Roman tribune—directed by Andrew Marton and Yakima Canutt—represents some 40 minutes of the most hair-raising excitement ever witnessed.

Wisely, however, the film does not depend wholly on sheer spectacle. The family relationship between Ben-Hur and his mother, Miriam, and his sister, Tirzah; his touching romance with Esther, the former slave; his admiration of the Roman consul, Quintus Arrius, whom he rescues after a sea battle; his association with the Arab horseowner, Sheik Ilderim; and his struggle with Messala, the boyhood friend who becomes his mortal enemy, make moving scenes. And overshadowing these personal conflicts is the deeply religious theme involving the birth and crucifixion of Christ.

Karl Tunberg receives sole screen credit, although such heavyweight writers as Maxwell Anderson, S. N. Behrman, Gore Vidal and Christopher Fry also worked on the film. Fry, a respected British poet-playwright, was present on the set throughout the production in Rome.

Charlton Heston is excellent as the brawny yet kindly Ben-Hur who survives the life of a galley slave to seek revenge of his enemy Messala. Haya Harareet, an Israeli actress making her first appearance in an American film is sensitive and revealing as Esther. Jack Hawkins, as Quintus Arrius, the Roman consul who adopts Ben-Hur, adds another fine depiction to his career. Stephen Boyd, as Ben-Hur's enemy Messala, is not the standard villain, but succeeds in giving understanding to this position in his dedication to the Roman Empire.

The film took 10 months to complete at Rome's Cinecitta Studios. The 300 sets are one of the highlights of the film, particularly the massive arena for the chariot sequence. The musical score by Miklos Rozsa also contributes to the overall excellence of the giant project.

Ben-Hur is a fitting climax to Zimbalist's career as a producer. He died of a heart attack in Rome when the film was near completion.

1959: Best Picture, Director, Actor (Charlton Heston), Supp. Actor (Hugh Griffith), Color Cinematography, Color Art Direction, Sound, Scoring of a Dramatic Picture, Editing, Special Effects, Color Costume Design

NOMINATION: Best Adapted Screenplay

●

BEN-HUR
A TALE OF THE CHRIST
1925, 128 mins, US Ⓥ ⊙ ⊗ b/w & col
Dir Fred Niblo ***Prod*** Louis B. Mayer, Irving Thalberg ***Scr*** Bess Meredyth, Carey Wilson, June Mathis, Katherine Hilliker, H. H. Caldwell ***Ph*** Rene Guissart, Percy Hilburn, Karl Struss, Clyde De Vinna ***Ed*** Lloyd Nosler ***Art*** Cedric Gibbons, Horace Jackson, Arnold Gillespie
Act Ramon Novarro, Francis X. Bushman, May McAvoy, Betty Bronson, Carmel Myers (M-G-M)

Ben Hur is a picture that rises above spectacle, even though it is spectacle. On the sceeen it isn't the chariot race or the great battle scenes between the fleet of Rome and the pirate galleys of Golthar. It is the tremendous heart throbs that one experiences leading to those scenes that make them great.

It is the story of the oppression of the Jews, the birth of the Savior, the progression of the Christus to the time of his crucifixion, the enslavement of the race from which Jesus himself sprang, and the tremendous love tale of the bond slave and a prince of Jerusalem that holds an audience spell bound.

As to individual performance: first the Mary of Betty Bronson. It is without doubt the most tremendous individual score that any actress has ever made, with but a single scene with a couple of close-ups. And in the color scenes she appears simply superb.

Then as to Ramon Novarro: anyone who sees him in this picture will have to admit that he is without doubt a man's man and 100 percent of that. Francis X. Bushman does a comeback in the role of the heavy (Messala) that makes him stand alone.

As to the women, following Bronson, May McAvoy in blonde tresses as Esther deserves a full measure of credit for her performance. While Claire McDowell, as the mother of Hur, and Kathleen Key, as his sister, both score tremendously. Carmel Myers, as the vamp Iras, looks a million dollars' worth of woman and it is hard to understand how Ben-Hur could finally resist her.

●

BENJI
1974, 85 mins, US Ⓥ col
Dir Joe Camp ***Prod*** Joe Camp ***Scr*** Joe Camp ***Ph*** Don Reddy ***Ed*** Leon Smith ***Mus*** Euel Box ***Art*** Harland Wright
Act Patsy Garrett, Allen Fiuzat, Cynthia Smith, Peter Breck, Edgar Buchanan (Mulberry Square)

Benji is a dog's picture from first to last. From the moment he pokes his head through a broken door in a deserted house where he has his pad until he's adopted by the family whose two children he saves from kidnappers, interest rests squarely on the head of this pooch, of uncertain parentage.

One of the wonders of the production, told simply and with no pretense of grandiose style, is the manner in which Benji—real name Higgins—performs. In this case, it isn't a dog performing, but a dog acting, just as humans act.

Much of the footage is shot from about 18 inches above the ground, upward from Benji's point of view, and innovation is fascinating.

1974: NOMINATION: Best Song ("I Feel Love")

●

BENNY & JOON
1993, 98 mins, US Ⓥ ⊙ col
Dir Jeremiah Chechik ***Prod*** Susan Arnold, Donna Roth ***Scr*** Barry Berman ***Ph*** John Schwartzman ***Ed*** Carol Littleton ***Mus*** Rachel Portman ***Art*** Neil Spisak
Act Johnny Depp, Mary Stuart Masterson, Aidan Quinn, Julianne Moore, Oliver Platt, C. C. H. Pounder (M-G-M)

Johnny Depp and Mary Stuart Masterson render such startling performances in the romantic fable *Benny & Joon* they almost overcome being in a not particularly well-written or directed film [from a story by Barry Berman and Leslie McNeil].

Masterson stars as Juniper ("Joon"), the mentally ill sister of Benny (Aidan Quinn), an auto mechanic who takes care of her. The quick-witted Joon spends her days at home, painting with passion.

This frail equilibrium is shattered when Sam (Depp), a modern-day clown in the mold of Chaplin and Keaton, shows up and changes the rules of the game. Quinn continues to worry, but he is also freer to pursue affairs of the heart with the charming Ruthie (Julianne Moore).

The pic's strength lies more in the nuances of the relationships than in the smooth flow of an episodic narrative. The love story is superficially placed in a frame that revolves around suspense over whether Benny will institutionalize Joon. In mood and theme, film bears some resemblance to *David and Lisa*, Frank Perry's 1963 sleeper.

As a fairy-tale clown, Depp is playing a variation on Edward Scissorhands, a misunderstood eccentric par excellence. Both Depp and Masterson, whose screen chemistry sparkles, excel in embodying the spirits of magic.

●

BENNY GOODMAN STORY, THE
1955, 116 mins, US Ⓥ col
Dir Valentine Davies ***Prod*** Aaron Rosenberg ***Scr*** Valentine Davies ***Ph*** William Daniels ***Ed*** Russell Schoengarth ***Mus*** Henry Mancini
Act Steve Allen, Donna Reed, Berta Gersten, Herbert Anderson, Robert F. Simon (Universal)

The Benny Goodman Story is of the same stripe as Universal's previously socko bandleader saga, *The Glenn Miller Story*. Both have bespectacled bandleaders with titles, both are Aaron Rosenberg productions.

If the romantics of the script and Steve Allen and Donna Reed's interpretations lack a bit, they are sufficiently glossed over because the major canvas is the saga of the Chicago youth with the licorice stick and his dedication to the cause of a new exciting tempo, later interpreted as "swing."

The unfolding is uncompromising on several fronts. The close-ups on the very poor Jewish family and Goodman's humble environments are not glossed over. In the same idiom there is no fanfare about the interracial mixing, socially or professionally.

●

BEQUEST TO THE NATION
(US: THE NELSON AFFAIR)
1973, 115 mins, UK ▭ col
Dir James Cellan Jones ***Prod*** Hal B. Wallis ***Scr*** Terence Rattigan ***Ph*** Gerry Fisher ***Ed*** Anne V. Coates ***Mus*** Michel Legrand ***Art*** Carmen Dillon
Act Glenda Jackson, Peter Finch, Michael Jayston, Anthony Quayle, Margaret Leighton, Dominic Guard (Universal)

This is a deliberate, though stylish and genteel, de-glamorizing of the affair between Lord Nelson and Lady Hamilton which scandalized England. Production is based on Terence Rattigan's adaptation of his own play, and never completely escapes its legit origins.

The plot introduces Peter Finch's Nelson just returned from a successful thwarting of Napoleon's maritime maneuvers, as executed by Andre Maranne as French Admiral Villeneuve. Begging several months' leave, Nelson repairs to his adored mistress (Glenda Jackson), who like him, is showing signs of less-than-graceful aging. Increasingly embittered by their status as social pariahs and pressed by his superiors to return to sea, Nelson engages in a series of harangues with his love, who finally urges his return to sea.

The story-as-is permits Jackson to display a variety of her dramatic abilities. Finch is slightly less effective as Nelson, though he manages to project the complex facets of character.

●

BERKELEY SQUARE
1933, 87 mins, US b/w
Dir Frank Lloyd ***Prod*** Jesse L. Lasky ***Scr*** Sonya Levien, John L. Balderston ***Ph*** Ernest Palmer ***Mus*** Louis De Francesco (dir.) ***Art*** William Darling
Act Leslie Howard, Heather Angel, Valerie Taylor, Irene Browne, Alan Mowbray, Juliette Compton (Fox)

Berkeley Square is an imaginative, beautiful and well-handled production.

The atmosphere of Berkeley Square, London, is resurrected almost perfectly, as it is today, and presumably as it was in the 18th century. There's a devotion to detail and atmospherics that is almost painfully exacting.

Leslie Howard in the same role he played on the stage (he produced the stage play [by John L. Balderston] himself) is as near perfection as can be hoped for in screen characterization. The rest of the cast is more than adequate.

Story of *Berkeley Square* is still another variation on Mark Twain's *A Connecticut Yankee in King Arthur's Court.* Where Twain used the idea of flashing a character into another century for fun. However, Balderston takes the thing very seriously. Balderston's character, Peter Standish (Howard) moves back into a spot used by one of his forefathers and falls in love with a gal of that period. It's a new kind of love story. Heather Angel, as the girl, turns in a splendid performance.

1932/33: NOMINATION: Best Actor (Leslie Howard)

●

BERLIN EXPRESS
1948, 86 mins, US Ⓥ ⊙ b/w
Dir Jacques Tourneur ***Prod*** Bert Granet ***Scr*** Harold Medford ***Ph*** Lucien Ballard ***Ed*** Sherman Todd ***Mus*** Frederick Hollander ***Art*** Albert S. D'Agostino, Alfred Herman
Act Merle Oberon, Robert Ryan, Charles Korvin, Paul Lukas, Robert Coote, Reinhold Schunzel (RKO)

Most striking feature of this production is its extraordinary background of war-ravaged Germany. With a documentary eye, this film etches a powerfully grim picture of life amidst the shambles. It makes awesome and exciting cinema.

Chief defect of the screenplay [based on a story by Curt Siodmak] is its failure to break away from the formula of anti-Nazi films. The Nazis, now underground, are still the heavies but it's difficult to get excited about such a group of ragged hoodlums. Their motivation in the pic, moreover, is never explained satisfactorily as they set about kidnapping a prominent German democrat, played by Paul Lukas.

Starting out on the Paris-to-Berlin express to an Allied conference on the unification of Germany, Lukas gets waylaid in Frankfurt despite an over-elaborate scheme of guarding him. Symbolizing the Big Four powers, other passengers on the train include an American (Robert Ryan), a Frenchwoman (Merle Oberon), an Englishman (Robert Coote), and a Russian (Roman Toporow) plus a dubious character of unknown nationality (Charles Korvin).

Ryan establishes himself as a firstrate actor in this film, demonstrating conclusively that his brilliant performance in *Crossfire* was no one-shot affair.

●

BEST FOOT FORWARD
1943, 93 mins, US Ⓥ col
Dir Edward Buzzell ***Prod*** Arthur Freed ***Scr*** Irving Brecher, Fred F. Finklehoffe ***Ph*** Leonard Smith ***Ed*** Blanche Sewell ***Mus*** Lenny Hayton (dir.)
Act Lucille Ball, Tommy Dix, Nancy Walker, June Allyson, Gloria de Haven, Chill Wills (M-G-M)

This filmusical version of George Abbott's [1941] stage production retains all of the youthful enthusiasm and spontaneity of the original, with addition of Harry James and his orchestra for generous supply of his trumpeteering and jump music.

Although picture is aimed directly at the younger generation, there's sufficient diversion and lightness to provide strong appeal for the adults. Following the lines established by Abbott with the stage presentation, Metro displays a number of new faces and teenage talent including five—Tommy Dix, Nancy Walker, June Allyson, Kenny Bowers and Jack Jordan—from the original stage cast.

Scholastic zest and pep, and the musical interludes, successfully carry the extremely fragile story premise. Annual prom and commencement ceremonies of the military prep school provides excuse for Hollywood film star to make an appearance to further her publicity efforts, and to accept wildly-made promise of stude to make her queen of the dance.

●

BEST FRIENDS
1982, 116 mins, US Ⓥ ⊙ col
Dir Norman Jewison ***Prod*** Norman Jewison ***Scr*** Valerie Curtin, Barry Levinson ***Ph*** Jordan Cronenweth ***Ed*** Don Zimmerman ***Mus*** Michel Legrand ***Art*** Joe Russo
Act Burt Reynolds, Goldie Hawn, Jessica Tandy, Barnard Hughes, Audra Lindley, Keenan Wynn (Warner)

Best Friends is probably not the light romantic comedy audiences expect from a Burt Reynolds–Goldie Hawn screen pairing but is nevertheless a very engaging film. Addressing the problems two writers in a professional and personal relationship encounter when they decide to get married, almost all of the picture's funny moments are underscored by the more serious issues they face from themselves, their families and society as a "married couple."

Both stars are tremendously aided by an intelligent screenplay from Valerie Curtin and Barry Levinson, who are said to have based at least part of this work on their own relationship. They leave Hawn and Reynolds more than enough room to inject their own nuances.

Director Norman Jewison does a capable job of moving things along and a nice balance between comedy and drama.

1982: NOMINATION: Best Original Song ("How Do You Keep the Music Playing")

•

BEST IN SHOW
2000, 90 mins, US Ⓥ ⦿ col
Dir Christopher Guest ***Prod*** Karen Murphy ***Scr*** Christopher Guest, Eugene Levy ***Ph*** Robert Schaefer ***Ed*** Robert Leighton ***Mus*** Jeffery C. J. Vanston ***Art*** Joseph T. Garrity
Act Michael Hitchcock, Parker Posey, Eugene Levy, Catherine O'Hara, Christopher Guest, John Michael Higgins (Castle Rock/Warner)

American dog clubs are no doubt full of decent, hardworking folks who balance the demands of their lives with the pleasures of their hobby. None of these people appear in *Best in Show*, a barkingly funny "mockumentary." Guest and co-writer Eugene Levy, working in concert with a large and familiar cast, walk a fine line between cruelty and affection, creating what is in essence a showcase for a series of improvisations on distinctly American types and their neuroses, strung together by a theme at one ripe for skewering and convenient for plotting.

Show introduces its diverse cast through interviews and glimpses of their treks to Philadelphia for the Mayflower Kennel Club Dog Show. Yuppie couple Meg and Hamilton Swan (Parker Posey, Michael Hitchcock) consult a doctor to find out if watching them have kinky sex has affected their Wiemaraner, Beatrice. Perky couple Gerry and Cookie Fleck (Eugene Levy, Catherine O'Hara) prepare for the drive north with their Norwich terrier, Winky. Fly-fishing shop owner Harlan Pepper (Guest) has a bloodhound named Hubert he's pretty fond of, while gay couple Scott Donlan (John Michael Higgins) and Stefan Vanderhoof (Michael McKean) just know one of their twin Shih Tzus, Miss Agnes, is ready for stardom. Competitors are rounded out by trashy blonde gold digger Sherri Ann Ward Cabot (Jennifer Coolidge), who has hired pro handler Christy Cummings (Jane Lynch) to walk the runway with Rhapsody in Blue, champion standard poodle. Setbacks dog each camp.

Tension of event itself is upstaged by nonstop and often surreal string of one-liners and non sequiturs from Buck Laughlin (Fred Willard), a sports broadcaster brought in to call the event for TV who's blissfully ignorant of the milieu.

Only cavil is a predictable rhythmic rut that the film settles into, as many segs begin with fairly normal "interviews" that soon spiral into bizarre verbal riffing.

•

BEST LITTLE WHOREHOUSE IN TEXAS, THE
1982, 114 mins, US Ⓥ ⦿ ▭ col
Dir Colin Higgins ***Prod*** Thomas L. Miller, Edward K. Milkis, Robert L. Boyett ***Scr*** Larry L. King, Peter Masterson, Colin Higgins ***Ph*** William A. Fraker ***Ed*** Pembroke J. Herring, David Bretherton, Jack Hofstra, Nicholas Eliopoulos ***Mus*** Patrick Williams ***Art*** Robert F. Boyle
Act Burt Reynolds, Dolly Parton, Dom DeLuise, Charles Durning, Jim Nabors, Robert Mandan (Universal-RKO)

The Best Little Whorehouse in Texas is just about everything it's meant to be—a couple of diverting hours in the dark. Rollicking, good-natured, a bit spicy and with just enough heart to avoid seeming totally synthetic, the $26 million adaptation of the 1978 Broadway hit [musical, book by Larry L. King and Peter Masterson, songs by Carol Hall] ideally teams powerhouse stars Burt Reynolds and Dolly Parton.

Nifty prolog sketches how the title establishment is a regular Texas institution. Modest abode is currently under the proprietorship of Miss Mona, a super lady played by Parton with all her accustomed humor, warmth and knockout charm. Local Sheriff Reynolds is her b.f. of long standing, a do-home boy technically corrupt because he protects the illegal goings-on.

But nothing is sacred to media crusader Dom DeLuise, an outrageously self-serving muckraker who "exposes" the bawdyhouse on his glitzy, song-and-dance TV news show and will stop at nothing to shut the place down.

1982: NOMINATION: Best Supp. Actor (Charles Durning)

•

BEST MAN, THE
1964, 102 mins, US Ⓥ ⦿ b/w
Dir Franklin J. Schaffner ***Prod*** Stuart Millar, Lawrence Turman ***Scr*** Gore Vidal ***Ph*** Haskell Wexler ***Ed*** Robert E. Swink ***Mus*** Mort Lindsey ***Art*** Lyle R. Wheeler
Act Henry Fonda, Cliff Robertson, Edie Adams, Margaret Leighton, Shelley Berman, Lee Tracy (United Artists)

Gore Vidal's provocative drama of political infighting on the national level has been skillfully converted to film. Although not an especially fresh or profound piece of work, it is certainly a worthwhile, lucid and engaging dramatization of a behind-the-scenes party power struggle that accompanies a contest for presidential nomination.

Vidal's straightforward, sharply drawn scenario describes the bitter struggle for a party's presidential nomination between an ambitious self-righteous character assassin (many will see him as a Nixon-McCarthy composite) and a scrupulous intellectual (of Stevensonian essence) who, ultimately faced with a choice of resorting to his opponent's smear tactics or bowing out of the race gracefully, decides he'd rather be right than president—leading to a somewhat pat and convenient conclusive development.

Between these two antagonists, portrayed with conviction and sensitivity by Cliff Robertson and Henry Fonda respectively, stands the imposing figure of the mortally ill but still politically virile expresident, a character likely to be associated with Harry S. Truman. Lee Tracy repeats his Broadway characterization in the role and just about steals the show with his expressive, colorful portrayal.

1964: NOMINATION: Best Supp. Actor (Lee Tracy)

•

BEST OF ENEMIES, THE
1961, 104 mins, UK/Italy ▭ col
Dir Guy Hamilton ***Prod*** Dino De Laurentiis ***Scr*** Jack Pulman, Incrocci Agenore, Furio Scaroelli, Suso Cecchi D'Amico ***Ph*** Giuseppe Rotunno ***Ed*** Bert Bates ***Mus*** Nino Rota
Act David Niven, Alberto Sordi, Michael Wilding, Amedeo Nazzari, Harry Andrews, David Opatoshu (Columbia)

The Best of Enemies produced by Italy's Dino De Laurentiis for Columbia, is a splendidly warm, wryly witty and amusing hybrid. Written by one Englishman and two Italians, it is directed by an Englishman (Guy Hamilton), has an Anglo-Italian star cast, with a few exceptions (one being American David Opatoshu), and an Anglo-Italian crew. It was shot mainly in Israel, with some location and studio work in Italy. Israelites were used as extras. Some Abyssinians were imported to play Abyssinians, and two trained gazelles were recruited in Frankfurt, Germany.

It's a wartime comedy, with a gently serious undertone for those who seek it. Locale is the Ethiopian desert in 1941. David Niven, a British major, and his pilot RAF officer Michael Wilding, crash on a reconnaissance trip. They are captured by an Italian patrol, led by an Italian officer (Alberto Sordi). He releases them on condition that they let his patrol move freely to a nearby fort. Back in base, Niven is ordered to attack the fort and does so reluctantly. From then on it's an hilarious, cat-and-mouse game, with captor and captive alternating as the fortunes of war sway. The serious undertone? That war is crazy.

The screenplay is peppered with brisk jokes and unexpected offbeat situations which keep the proceedings light and easy. Hamilton has directed with a sure touch which brings out the characteristics of the two opposed nations admirably. Niven, debonair, nonchalant and skilfully underplaying, is matched excellently by Sordi, playing his first English-speaking role.

•

BEST OF EVERYTHING, THE
1959, 122 mins, US Ⓥ ▭ col
Dir Jean Negulesco ***Prod*** Jerry Wald ***Scr*** Edith Sommer, Mann Rubin ***Ph*** William C. Mellor ***Ed*** Robert Simpson ***Mus*** Alfred Newman ***Art*** Lyle R. Wheeler, Jack Martin Smith, Mark-Lee Kirk
Act Hope Lange, Stephen Boyd, Suzy Parker, Martha Hyer, Diane Baker, Joan Crawford (20th Century-Fox)

The Best of Everything is slick and glossy, like a color still on coated stock, and with no more depth, yet as popular entertainment it sustains interest.

A subtitle might be *Except Men—Who Are Beasts*. Amanda (Joan Crawford), a successful career woman in the book publishing field that is the film's setting, is having an unsuccessful affair with a married man (unseen). One of her co-workers, Barbara (Martha Hyer), is also involved in an affair with another married man, fellow editor Sidney (Donald Harron). Gregg (Suzy Parker), one of the firm's secretaries, is having an affair with stage producer David (Louis Jourdan), who jilts her to take up (extramaritally, of course) with Judy (Myrna Hansen).

To continue, April (Diane Baker) becomes pregnant (out of wedlock) by Dexter (Robert Evans), who proposes they solve this problem by visiting an abortionist. Caroline (Hope Lange) is jilted by Eddie (Brett Halsey) for a rich girl, but he suggests that he and Caroline set up housekeeping on the side. Sex, it will be seen, occupies a large part of this film.

The screenplay is not as blatant as all this sounds. It has taken Rona Jaffe's novel and simmered it down somewhat. If not wit, it is still several cuts above office wisecracking.

The perfomances are generally good, although there is no real chance for developments. Parker, burdened with the most difficult emotional role, is least successful. Jean Negulesco's direction is firm-handed at keeping the overwrought story from getting overheated.

•

BEST SELLER
(AKA: HARD COVER)
1987, 110 mins, US Ⓥ ⦿ col
Dir John Flynn ***Prod*** Carter De Haven ***Scr*** Larry Cohen ***Ph*** Fred Murphy ***Ed*** David Rosenbloom ***Mus*** Jay Ferguson ***Art*** Gene Rudolf
Act James Woods, Brian Dennehy, Victoria Tennant, Allison Balson, Paul Shenar, George Coe (Hemdale)

Best Seller combines the sinister appeal of James Woods at his cold-blooded best with the gruffly lovable persona of Brian Dennehy as a literary cop; on the level of detective thriller, it's a real page-turner.

Dennehy is Dennis Meechum, a cop who writes a book based on a famous unsolved case, during which he was wounded and three other policemen were killed. Seventeen years after the incident, he is a lonely burnout case who lives at home with his meek teenage daughter (Allison Balson), trying to crank out another book.

Into the picture comes mystery man Woods, full of unctuous charm and foreboding stares. He presents himself as Cleve, a former hit man who worked for a pillar of L.A. society who, Cleve claims, ordered murders on everyone from business associates to tax auditors.

The body of the film has Cleve bringing Meechum around the country, providing different details in his story in an attempt to prove its authenticity, while Meechum takes it all down in a book.

Director John Flynn keeps things moving through action scenes but is at his best during the psychological cat-and-mouse games in which the two leads find out about one another. While the conclusion is pat, pic is ultimately carried by two lead performances.

•

BEST SHOT
SEE: HOOSIERS

•

BEST THINGS IN LIFE ARE FREE, THE
1956, 104 mins, US ▭ col
Dir Michael Curtiz ***Prod*** Henry Ephron ***Scr*** William Bowers, Phoebe Ephron ***Ph*** Leon Shamroy ***Ed*** Dorothy Spencer ***Mus*** Lionel Newman
Act Gordon MacRae, Dan Dailey, Sheree North, Ernest Borgnine, Tommy Noonan, Murvyn Vye (20th Century-Fox)

In *The Best Things in Life Are Free*, producer Henry Ephron and director Michael Curtiz went on the reasonably sound theory that, in telling the story of Tin Pan Alley's fabulous team of Buddy DeSylva, Lew Brown and Ray Henderson, all that was necessary was to fill the widescreen with a huge potpourri of their works.

Considering that John O'Hara wrote the story, this CinemaScope tinter leaves a few things to wish for in that department. It catches little of the Jazz Age feeling, except in its costumes and the frantic shimmy and Black Bottom numbers, and the songwriting trio barely come to life as real people.

It's a sparkling string of hits that's presented with all the nostalgic attention they deserve. Performances are top calibre, from Gordon MacRae's and Dan Dailey's pleasant crooning, to Ernest Borgnine's clowning and Sheree North's agile terp routines.

There are no fewer than 20 numbers in this opus. Outstanding are the big production numbers—"Birth of the Blues" and "Black Bottom"—choreographed by Rod Alexander. North, who has trouble with her diction in the speaking parts, is standout in the dance numbers.

1956: NOMINATION: Best Scoring of a Musical Picture

•

BEST YEARS OF OUR LIVES, THE
1946, 163 mins, US Ⓥ ⦿ b/w
Dir William Wyler ***Prod*** Samuel Goldwyn ***Scr*** Robert E. Sherwood ***Ph*** Gregg Toland ***Ed*** Daniel Mandell ***Mus*** Hugo Friedhofer ***Art*** Perry Ferguson, George Jenkins
Act Fredric March, Myrna Loy, Dana Andrews, Teresa Wright, Harold Russell, Cathy O'Donnell (RKO/Goldwyn)

This is the postwar saga [based on a screen treatment by MacKinley Kantor, later published as *Glory for Me*] of the soda jerk who became an army officer; the banker who was mustered out as the sergeant; and a seaman who came back to glory minus both hands.

Inspired casting has newcomer Harold Russell, a real-life amputee, pacing the seasoned trouper, and Fredric March, for personal histrionic triumphs. But all the other performances are equally good. Myrna Loy is the small town bank veepee's beauteous wife. Teresa Wright plays their daughter,who goes for the already-married Dana Andrews with full knowledge of his wife (Virginia Mayo, who does a capital job as the cheating looker). Both femmes in this triangle, along with Andrews, do their stuff convincingly.

Cathy O'Donnell does her sincerely-in-love chore with the same simplicity as Harold Russell, the $200-a-month war-pensioned hero, who, since he has lost his hands in combat, spurns O'Donnell because he never wants to be a burden. That scene, as he skillfully manages the wedding ring, is but one of several memorable highspots.

The pace of the picture is a bit leisurely. Almost a full hour is required to set the mood and the motivation, but never does it pall. Not a line or scene is spurious. The people live; they are not mere shadow etchings on a silver sheet.

1946: Best Picture, Director, Actor (Fredric March), Supp. Actor (Harold Russell), Screenplay, Scoring of a Dramatic Picture, Editing, Special Award (Harold Russell)

NOMINATION: Best Sound

•

BETE HUMAINE, LA
1939, 96 mins, France Ⓥ b/w
Dir Jean Renoir ***Scr*** Jean Renoir ***Ph*** Curt Courant ***Ed*** Marguerite Renoir ***Mus*** Joseph Kosma ***Art*** Eugene Lourie
Act Jean Gabin, Simone Simon, Fernand Ledoux, Carette, Jean Renoir, Blanchette Brunoy (Paris)

La Bete Humaine is French production at its best. Jean Renoir, in adapting and filming Emile Zola's penetrating study of a man obsessed by an irrepressible desire to kill, inherited from a long line of alcoholics, has captured that repression in all of its nuances.

Jean Gabin, as the humble locomotive engineer, knows and is haunted by his desire to strangle whoever is within reach when the urge strikes his numbed brain. Drink heightens that desire.

Ledoux is the station chief at Le Havre, Gabin's terminus, and Simone Simon is Ledoux's unfaithful wife. Ledoux, much older, is foolishly in love with his wife and murders her lover before her eyes. Gabin and Ledoux's wife become lovers, she aware that he knows who committed the murder. She tells Gabin he must kill her husband or he will kill them both.

Throughout Gabin never misses. Simon is very effective. Ledoux takes the station master in good stride. Photography is good.

•

BETHUNE
THE MAKING OF A HERO
1990, 115 mins, Canada/China/France Ⓥ col
Dir Phillip Borsos ***Prod*** Pieter Kroonenburg, Nicolas Clermont ***Scr*** Ted Allan ***Ph*** Mike Molloy, Raoul Coutard ***Ed*** Yves Langlois, Angelo Corrao ***Mus*** Alan Reeves
Act Donald Sutherland, Helen Mirren, Helen Shaver, Harrison Liu, Anouk Aimee, Ronald Pickup (Filmline/August 1st/Parmentier/Belstar

This C$18 million political saga is a thorough documenting of the life of Canadian doctor Norman Bethune, a hero in China for his medical input during the long march in Mao Tse-tung's revolution.

The film belongs to Donald Sutherland, who delivers a stunning performance as the complex and controversial surgeon. Harrison Liu delivers a fine performance as Bethune's protege, Dr. Fong, but Helen Shaver (as a missionary in China) and Helen Mirren (as Bethune's wife) pale beside Sutherland.

Bethune was at once a boozing womanizer, a loving husband, a revolutionary surgeon and an ardently committed antifascist. He made a slew of enemies among colleagues and government officials before he declared himself a "red" and headed first to Spain and then to China (the latter of which provides magnificent scenery in the film).

After several years of financial problems from both coprod partners (China and Canada), it's a relief that the film is better than expected and a disappointment that it is not as good as hoped.

•

BETRAYAL
1983, 95 mins, UK Ⓥ col
Dir David Jones ***Prod*** Sam Spiegel ***Scr*** Harold Pinter ***Ph*** Mike Fash ***Ed*** John Bloom ***Mus*** Dominic Muldowney ***Art*** Eileen Diss
Act Jeremy Irons, Ben Kingsley, Patricia Hodge (Horizon)

As it was onstage in 1978, *Betrayal* is an absorbing, quietly amusing chamber drama for those attuned to Harold Pinter's way with words. In laying out his study of a rather conventional menage a trois among two male best friends and the wife of one of them, Pinter's gambit was to present it in reverse chronological order. Tale thus starts in the present and gradually steps backwards over the course of nine years.

Kingsley comes across best, as the film only springs fully to life when he's onscreen. Irons also seems very much at home with the required style. As the fulcrum of the tale, Patricia Hodge knows her way around dialog but pales somewhat in the presence of the two men and lacks allure.

1983: NOMINATION: Best Adapted Screenplay

•

BETRAYED
SEE: WHEN STRANGERS MARRY

•

BETRAYED
1988, 127 mins, US Ⓥ ⊙ col
Dir Constantin Costa-Gavras ***Prod*** Irwin Winkler ***Scr*** Joe Eszterhas ***Ph*** Patrick Blossier ***Ed*** Joele Van Effenterre ***Mus*** Bill Conti ***Art*** Patrizia Von Brandenstein
Act Debra Winger, Tom Berenger, John Heard, Betsy Blair, John Mahoney, Ted Levine (United Artists)

Betrayed is a political thriller that is more political than thrilling but never less than absorbing due to the combustible subject matter, that of the white supremacist movement.

Clearly inspired by the murder of Denver radio talk show host Alan Berg, opening scene has abrasive Chicago broadcaster Richard Libertini followed home and gunned down by assailants who identify themselves only by spraying the letters "ZOG" on the victim's car.

Cut to the endless wheat fields of the rural Midwest, where Debra Winger has come up from Texas as a "combine girl." Local farmer Tom Berenger quickly takes a shine to the new gal in town, while she responds to the warmth of his family life. Winger soon hops back to Chicago to brief her superiors at the FBI on her progress in infiltrating the group suspected of perpetrating Libertini's murder.

Like Ingrid Bergman in *Notorious*, Winger is pushed even further in her masquerade by her chief government contact (John Heard) who from all appearances is in love with her himself.

Berenger proves forceful and properly unpredictable in his vulnerable macho role, and entire cast is nicely lowkeyed.

•

BETSY, THE
1978, 125 mins, US Ⓥ ⊙ col
Dir Daniel Petrie ***Prod*** Robert R. Weston ***Scr*** William Bast, Walter Bernstein ***Ph*** Mario Tosi ***Ed*** Rita Roland ***Mus*** John Barry ***Art*** Herman A. Blumenthal
Act Laurence Olivier, Robert Duvall, Katharine Ross, Tommy Lee Jones, Jane Alexander, Lesley-Anne Down (Allied Artists/Robbins)

It's a backhanded criticism, but there's something too classy about this version of the Harold Robbins novel. It's too tame. And too solemn. To be blunt, where's the raunch? This should be *Peyton Place* with plenty of flesh. Don't entice audiences with the name of an author associated with a long list of bestselling seamy novels and then deliver a 125-minute film you wouldn't be embarrassed to bring your mother to.

The script has four main interests: cars, sex, money and power. It's an American movie. Laurence Olivier is retired auto tycoon Loren Hardeman, Sr., founder of Bethlehem Motor Co, now interested in manufacturing a revolutionary car—one too efficient, too practical and too benevolent for American industry. It is to be called the Betsy, after his great-granddaughter.

Through a series of flashbacks, Olivier ages from 40 to 90. Complete with midwest accent, he's on target, maybe too much so. Ditto for Robert Duvall as his grandson and current president of the auto company, Jane Alexander as Duvall's wife and Katharine Ross as Olivier's daughter-in-law and lover.

Tommy Lee Jones as a daredevil race driver hired by Olivier to build the dream car plays his role with a mixture of edginess and off-handedness—a combination of Burt Reynolds and Harvey Keitel. His style—it's got a sense of humor and a campy quality to it—seems more to the point. It's almost trashy. (Now that's Harold Robbins.)

•

BETSY'S WEDDING
1990, 98 mins, US Ⓥ ⊙ col
Dir Alan Alda ***Prod*** Martin Bregman, Louis A. Stroller ***Scr*** Alan Alda ***Ph*** Kelvin Pike ***Ed*** Michael Polakow ***Mus*** Bruce Broughton ***Art*** John Jay Moore
Act Alan Alda, Madeline Kahn, Molly Ringwald, Ally Sheedy, Anthony LaPaglia, Joe Pesci (Touchstone/Silver Screen Partners IV)

From a bolt of ordinary cloth Alan Alda fashions a thoroughly engaging matrimonial romp in *Betsy's Wedding*. Most of the action comes from the clash of personalities and wills as unconventional daughter Betsy (Molly Ringwald) announces her plans to wed boyfriend Jake (Dylan Walsh), and everyone jumps into the act.

Overreaching dad (Alda) wants a big, wonderful Italian-Jewish wedding, and plans accelerate into a one-upmanship contest when Jake's wealthy WASP parents try to take the reins. To finance the bash, Alda, a contractor, unwittingly throws in with some funny-money Italian business partners, as arranged by his double-dealing brother-in-law (Joe Pesci).

Setting a buoyant, anything-could-happen tone from the outset, Alda as director creates what he's striving for: a feeling of being caught up in the warm craziness of this family, as all its vivid characters push and tug to impose their will on the proceedings. His punchy, impertinent script is equally good.

•

BETTER TOMORROW, A
SEE: YINGHUNG BUNSIK

•

BETTER TOMORROW II, A
SEE: YINGHUNG BUNSIK II

•

BETTY BLUE
SEE: 37°2 LE MATIN

•

BETWEEN HEAVEN AND HELL
1956, 94 mins, US Ⓥ ▭ col
Dir Richard Fleischer ***Prod*** David Weisbart ***Scr*** Harry Brown ***Ph*** Leo Tover ***Ed*** James B. Clark ***Mus*** Hugo Friedhofer
Act Robert Wagner, Terry Moore, Broderick Crawford, Buddy Ebsen, Robert Keith, Brad Dexter (20th Century-Fox)

Between Heaven and Hell is a good, hard-hitting action film, replete with the usual heroics but also full with the ugly realization that the men who fought World War II were far from perfect. The hero, played by Robert Wagner, is a moody Southerner in whom the camaraderie of danger awakens a social consciousness.

The Francis Gwaltney novel painted a vivid picture of battle. The film, directed by Richard Fleischer, captures the sights and sounds of the Pacific fighting and generates a good deal of tension and excitement. Not all of it is believable, and Wagner's final rushing down the Jap-infested mountain is almost ludicrous as he sideswipes one Jap party after the other.

Terry Moore is the only girl in the pic and she's adequate in a brief role. Wagner gives a good, low-key performance as the boy who gets busted to private after he hits an officer who has killed the men in his patrol. Broderick Crawford is loud and overbearing as the psycho colonel. His role is made harder since the picture fails to point out that the colonel is in charge of a group of misfits.

•

BETWEEN THE LINES
1977, 101 mins, US Ⓥ col
Dir Joan Micklin Silver ***Prod*** Raphael D. Silver ***Scr*** Fred Barron ***Ph*** Kenneth Van Sickle ***Ed*** John Carter ***Mus*** Southside Johnny and the Asbury Jukes ***Art*** Stuart Wurtzel
Act John Heard, Lindsay Crouse, Jeff Goldblum, Jill Eikenberry, Bruno Kirby, Gwen Welles (Midwest/Silver)

A fresh and uncluttered look at what goes on behind the scenes at a grubby, underpaid but undaunted little newspaper.

Where it is strong is partially due to the excellently written script, partially due to the overall first-rate acting by the entire cast.

It's a series of interrelationships, professionally and romantically, between staff photographer Lindsay Crouse and top investigative reporter John Heard; reporter-cum-book-writer Stephen Collins and staffer Gwen Welles; plus the story of underpaid and overworked rock music critic Jeff

Goldblum, copyboy and would-be reporter Bruno Kirby and the other oddballs who work for the newspaper, due to be taken over any day by a communications conglomerate.

•

BETWEEN TWO WORLDS

1944, 112 mins, US b/w

Dir Edward A. Blatt ***Prod*** Mark Hellinger ***Scr*** Daniel Fuchs ***Ph*** Carl Guthrie ***Ed*** Rudi Fehr ***Mus*** Erich Wolfgang Korngold ***Art*** Hugh Reticker

Act John Garfield, Paul Henreid, Sydney Greenstreet, Eleanor Parker, Edmund Gwenn, George Tobias (Warner)

An artistic transcription of [Sutton Vane's] *Outward Bound*, the Broadway stage hit of 1925, this film was earlier brought to the screen by Warner Bros in 1930.

A 1944 opening has been provided here, the locale being an unidentified port in England from which a small assorted group of persons is preparing to sail for America. Unable to leave because his papers aren't in order is Paul Henreid, former pianist, who recently had fought with the Free French. As result he and his wife, played with much feeling by Eleanor Parker, take to the gaspipe, both wanting to die together. Meantime, in an air raid the bus carrying others to the evacuation ship are killed.

From here the action shifts to a mystery ship which, it finally becomes evident, is bound for the Great Beyond, with Henreid, Parker and the group which had been killed in the bomb raid. Brilliant dialog and excellent performances, as well as thoughtful, imaginative direction by Edward A. Blatt, neatly sustain the interest aboard ship on the long voyage. There is no place in the story for comedy relief.

On reaching High Olympus and Judgement Day, Sydney Greenstreet enters the scene as the examiner, taking his new arrivals one by one. His performance is outstanding, and the sequence, though quite lengthy, represents a productional, directional and acting triumph.

•

BEVERLY HILLBILLIES, THE

1993, 93 mins, US Ⓥ ⊙ col

Dir Penelope Spheeris ***Prod*** Ian Bryce, Penelope Spheeris ***Scr*** Lawrence Konner, Mark Rosenthal, Jim Fisher, Jim Staahl ***Ph*** Robert Brinkmann ***Ed*** Ross Albert ***Mus*** Lalo Schifrin ***Art*** Peter Jamison

Act Diedrich Bader, Dabney Coleman, Erika Eleniak, Cloris Leachman, Rob Schneider, Lea Thompson (20th Century-Fox)

Just as corny and stupid as the long-running TV series, pic version has been cleverly cast and shrewdly skewed to appeal jointly to original fans of the show and younger viewers only vaguely familiar with it. No matter the updating, new cast and big screen—the comic effect of the Clampett clan, 1993, is nearly identical to the one it had during its heyday on CBS from 1962–71.

Taking officious control of the newly rich family's affairs when they arrive in BevHills are toadying banker Mr Drysdale and prim secretary Miss Hathaway, roles neatly filled by TV-friendly Dabney Coleman and Lily Tomlin. Latter is given the assignment of finding a suitable wife for the widowed Jed (Jim Varney), who is now one of the most eligible men in America.

Intrigue cooked up by a quartet of screenwriters involves the efforts of the nefarious Laura (Lea Thompson), assisted by bank employee Woodrow (Rob Schneider), to trick Jed into marriage and run off with his loot.

It's all pretty thin, scattershot stuff, but the ingratiating naivete of the characters and the aw-shucks friendliness of the cast are disarming. Varney feels like the genuine article and weighs his words and decisions with good comic timing. As the stubborn Granny, Cloris Leachman is a near-dead ringer for the late Irene Ryan and conveys the right antic, anarchic spirit.

•

BEVERLY HILLS COP

1984, 105 mins, US Ⓥ ⊙ ▭ col

Dir Martin Brest ***Prod*** Don Simpson, Jerry Bruckheimer ***Scr*** Daniel Petrie, Jr. ***Ph*** Bruce Surtees ***Ed*** Billy Weber, Arthur Coburn ***Mus*** Harold Faltermeyer ***Art*** Angelo Graham

Act Eddie Murphy, Judge Reinhold, Lisa Eilbacher, John Ashton, Ronny Cox, Steven Berkoff (Paramount)

Beverly Hills Cop is more cop show than comedy riot. Expectations that Eddie Murphy's street brand of rebelliousness would devastate staid and glittery Beverly Hills are not entirely met in a film that grows increasingly dramatic as Murphy's recalcitrant cop from Detroit runs down the killers of his best friend.

Film was originally tagged for Sylvester Stallone and the finished product still carries the melodramatic residue of a hard, violent property, pre-Murphy.

Strong assists come from a deceptively likable performance from Judge Reinhold as a naive Beverly Hills detective, from by-the-book chief Ronny Cox, and from the serpentine villainy of Steven Berkoff, who plays an art dealer involved in nefarious endeavors.

Best moments arrive early when Murphy, bouncy, determined and vengeful, arrives in Beverly Hills in what old Detroit friend turned Beverly Hills art dealer Lisa Eilbacher correctly calls his "crappy blue Chevy Nova."

1984: NOMINATION: Best Original Screenplay

•

BEVERLY HILLS COP II

1987, 102 mins, US Ⓥ ⊙ ▭ col

Dir Tony Scott ***Prod*** Don Simpson, Jerry Bruckheimer ***Scr*** Larry Ferguson, Warren Skaaren ***Ph*** Jeffrey L. Kimball ***Ed*** Billy Weber, Chris Lebenson, Michael Tronick ***Mus*** Harold Faltermeyer ***Art*** Ken Davis

Act Eddie Murphy, Judge Reinhold, Jurgen Prochnow, Ronny Cox, John Ashton, Brigitte Nielsen (Paramount/Murphy)

Beverly Hills Cop II is a noisy, numbing, unimaginative, heartless remake of the original film.

Getting Eddie Murphy back to Beverly Hills from his native Detroit turf is the critical wounding of police captain Ronny Cox by a group of rich baddies committing the "Alphabet Crimes," a series of violent robberies at heavily guarded locations. Once again, he goads reluctant cops Judge Reinhold and John Ashton into straying from the straight and narrow, once again the group visits a strip joint that looks like a *Flashdance* spinoff, and finally shoot it out with the villains.

Criminal element is represented by enforcer Dean Stockwell, towering hit woman Brigitte Nielsen, who looks like Max Headroom's sister, and kingpin Jurgen Prochnow.

Murphy keeps things entertainingly afloat with his sassiness, raunchy one-liners, take-charge brazenness and innate irreverence. Murphy's a hoot in numerous scenes, but less so than on other occasions because of the frosty context for his shenanigans.

1987: NOMINATION: Best Song ("Shakedown")

BEVERLY HILLS COP III

1994, 109 mins, US Ⓥ ⊙ col

Dir John Landis ***Prod*** Mace Neufeld, Robert Rehme ***Scr*** Steven E. de Souza ***Ph*** Mac Ahlberg ***Ed*** Dale Beldin ***Mus*** Nile Rodgers ***Art*** Michael Seymour

Act Eddie Murphy, Judge Reinhold, Hector Elizondo, Timothy Carhart, John Saxon, Bronson Pinchot (Paramount)

The third installment of the *Beverly Hills Cop* series boasts a return to form by Eddie Murphy and a breezy and witty first half, though the film runs out of steam before the end.

The film gets off to a brisk start with a sting-gone-bad at a Detroit stolen-car chop shop. Director John Landis gets a mighty chuckle out of two overweight thieves mimicking a vintage Supremes tune and then quickly shifts moods with an efficient St Valentine's Day-style massacre and a chase in which Murphy drives a snazzy sports car that disintegrates piece by piece.

The bad-guy trail inevitably leads to Southern California, where Murphy is reunited with an old Beverly Hills crony, Billy Rosewood (Judge Reinhold), and a new cop buddy played by Hector Elizondo. The focus of the action is a theme park called WonderWorld (actually a dressed-up Great America in Santa Clara, owned by Paramount Communications). Screenwriter Steven E. de Souza has a lark lampooning the squeaky clean Americana atmosphere of these entertainments as well as those overwrought Universal crash-bam-boom thrill rides. Unfortunately, the villains are not as interesting as the milieu in which they thrive, which dissipates the tension.

Another first-half highlight is the return of the impossibly effete Serge (Bronson Pinchot), who has moved from hawking cappuccino on Rodeo Drive to selling designer guns. There's more action in his wrists than in some of the film's climactic moments.

•

BEWITCHED

1945, 65 mins, US b/w

Dir Arch Oboler ***Prod*** Jerry Bresler ***Scr*** Arch Oboler ***Ph*** Charles Salerno, Jr. ***Ed*** Harry Komer ***Mus*** Bronislau Kaper ***Art*** Cedric Gibbons, Malcolm Brown

Act Phyllis Thaxter, Edmund Gwenn, Henry H. Daniels, Jr., Horace McNally, Minor Watson (M-G-M)

Produced on a low budget, with a sterling cast of actors' actors, this picture just oozes with class because of the excellent adaptation and direction it has been given by radio's Arch Oboler, author of the story, *Alter Ego*, on which the film is based. Climax follows climax, strong performance follows strong performance in this thrilling psychopathic study of a girl obsessed by an inner voice that drives her to murder.

Phyllis Thaxter carries the major burden in this one, and Oboler's direction guides her to new dramatic heights. She's in fast company here, with Edmund Gwenn, costarred in the role of a psychiatrist who endeavors to drive out the troubled girl's obsessions, registering tellingly.

Yarn is told in flashbacks, an eerie musical score by Bronislau Kaper adding to the suspense. Set to wed, Joan Ellis (Thaxter) hears a voice which she cannot drive away. She flees to another city, tries to escape her tormentor, even goes out with another man, a lawyer. But little words dropped at the most unexpected moments bring the voice back. It tells her to kill her hometown boyfriend who came to take her home.

Entire production consists of stock sets, narration being depended upon to do the work. Oboler, in a way, uses radio technique in pictures. He definitely has something different to offer Hollywood.

•

BEYOND A REASONABLE DOUBT

1956, 80 mins, US Ⓥ b/w

Dir Fritz Lang ***Prod*** Bert Friedlob ***Scr*** Douglas Morrow ***Ph*** William Snyder ***Ed*** Gene Fowler, Jr. ***Mus*** Herschel Burke Gilbert ***Art*** Carroll Clark

Act Dana Andrews, Joan Fontaine, Sidney Blackmer, Barbara Nichols, Philip Bourneuf, Shepperd Strudwick (RKO)

A trick ending wraps up the melodrama in *Beyond a Reasonable Doubt* but comes a little too late to revive interest in a tale that relies too often on pat contrivance rather than logical development. Fritz Lang's direction does what it can to inject suspense and interest but the melodrama never really jells.

Dana Andrews is a writer engaged to Joan Fontaine, daughter of newspaper publisher Sidney Blackmer. The latter talks Andrews into going along with his scheme for showing up the fallacy of circumstantial evidence that has given ambitious district attorney Philip Bourneuf a long string of convictions.

In brief, Blackmer plans to plant evidence that will get Andrews arrested, tried and convicted for the murder of a burlesque stripper, recently found dead without any clues to indicate the killer. Scheme works as planned, except at the crucial moment Blackmer gets himself killed.

Neither above-mentioned players nor others in the cast add much to make the events credible, seemingly performing with an almost casual air.

•

BEYOND BEDLAM

1994, 88 mins, UK Ⓥ col

Dir Vadim Jean ***Prod*** Paul Brooks ***Scr*** Rob Walker, Vadim Jean ***Ph*** Gavin Finney ***Ed*** Liz Webber ***Mus*** David A. Hughes, John Murphy ***Art*** James Helps

Act Craig Fairbrass, Elizabeth Hurley, Keith Allen, Anita Dobson, Craig Kelly, Jesse Birdsall (Metrodome)

Beyond Bedlam is an ambitious Brit horror schlocker that seems to have mislaid its script halfway. Careening, often stylish meltdown of everything from Thomas Harris shavings to Elm Street and Clive Barker offshoots starts with a bang but trails off into a whimper as the pic abandons all logic in the second half.

Biggest surprise for auteurists is that the film, based on the novel by Harry Adam Knight (*Carnosaur*), emanates from the same producer/director team (Paul Brooks, Vadim Jean) as the cheeky 1992 low-budget comedy *Leon the Pig Farmer*.

Cop Terry Hamilton (Craig Fairbrass) is still haunted by a psycho he put away seven years ago—Gilmour, dubbed the Bone Man (Keith Allen), who is the prize patient of a doctor at a research institute, Stephanie Lyell (Elizabeth Hurley).

Stephanie has been testing a mind-calming drug, BFND, on herself and Gilmour. In a long climax that takes up the whole of the picture's second half, Stephanie and Terry team up to take Gilmour out, in between being menaced by hallucinations generated by the Bone Man in his cell.

Shot largely in an abandoned sanitarium in north London, the $3 million production has an umbral, high-gloss visual style in its early going. As the leering loon, Allen comes off best.

•

BEYOND RANGOON

1995, 99 mins, US Ⓥ ⊙ ▭ col

Dir John Boorman ***Prod*** Barry Spikings, Eric Pleskow, John Boorman ***Scr*** Alex Lasker, Bill Rubenstein ***Ph*** John Seale ***Ed*** Ron Davis ***Mus*** Hans Zimmer ***Art*** Anthony Pratt

Act Patricia Arquette, Frances McDormand, Spalding Gray, Aung Ko, Victor Slezak, Adelle Lutz (Castle Rock/Columbia)

Another of John Boorman's ambitious, highly physical explorations of a remote foreign culture, *Beyond Rangoon* goes only part of the way in elucidating both its topical subject matter and tormented leading lady. Physically handsome effort was originally planned with Meg Ryan as its star. In the end, Patricia Arquette took on the role of Laura Bowman, an American doctor trying to escape the devastating memories of the murder of her husband and young son by literally getting as far away from the States as possible.

With her sister Andy (Frances McDormand), Laura is in Burma in 1988 when the peaceful protests against the military government begin reaching a crescendo. In the first of numerous melodramatic contrivances, Laura manages to lose her passport and be left behind when her sister and the rest of her touring party beat a hasty retreat from the country. Seeking a safe haven away from the capital, she escapes with ostensible guide Aung Ko, a former professor and political dissident.

The momentary excitement of the large-scale action sequences notwithstanding, the film never goes more than halfway in satisfying on all its levels of concentration—as psychological exploration of Laura's inner journey, as exposé of a little-dramatized political situation and as pure adventure tale.

Once again, the peril of a Yank on the loose in exotic territory is made to seem of rather more urgent concern than the fate of any number of anonymous Third Worlders. Matters aren't helped by the casting and central performance of Arquette, who simply doesn't have the presence and command to carry such a big picture, as the part requires her to do.

Nonpro Aung Ko, himself an exile from Burma for 20 years, acquits himself honorably as Laura's knowing, good-humored companion, while other perfs are strictly surface.

Substituting Malaysian locations for off-limits Burma, Boorman has staged some convincing set pieces of savage violence against defenseless citizens as well as some muscular action in river and thick jungle settings.

•

BEYOND REASONABLE DOUBT
1980, 127 mins, New Zealand Ⓥ ▭ col
Dir John Laing ***Prod*** John Barnett ***Scr*** David Yallop ***Ph*** Alun Bollinger ***Ed*** Michael Horton ***Mus*** Dave Fraser ***Art*** Kai Hawkins
Act David Hemmings, John Hargreaves, Martyn Sanderson, Grant Tilly, Diana Rowan, Ian Watkin (Endeavour)

For 10 years the New Zealand public lived with the murder mystery surrounding the deaths of Jeanette and Harvey Crewe. After an unprecendented two trials, Arthur Thomas was found guilty. He was pardoned late in 1979. The story had enough false trials and contradictions to interest Britain's investigative writer David Yallop, and his book, *Beyond Reasonable Doubt*, is credited with much of the final boost that led to Thomas's pardon.

Yallop has done a workmanlike job on the book's translation to screen, and if the aim was to persuade us that a tough cop, hellbent on a conviction, manipulated murder evidence even to the extent of planting a cartridge case at the scene of the crime to implicate Thomas, then it strikes a bull's-eye.

Roles have been sharply cast to have lookalikes doubling for the real-life protagonists. David Hemmings brings a chillingly vindictive venom to the role of the cop, no doubt an accurate portrayal in terms of the Yallop thesis. John Hargreaves is suitably bewildered as Thomas, the rather simple young farmer who can't believe it's happening to him. The soundtrack is noisy, drowning the dialog at times. John Laing's direction is mostly straight down the middle.

•

BEYOND THE CLOUDS
SEE: PAR-DELA LES NUAGES

•

BEYOND THE FOREST
1949, 95 mins, US Ⓥ b/w
Dir King Vidor ***Prod*** Henry Blanke ***Scr*** Lenore Coffee ***Ph*** Robert Burks ***Ed*** Rudi Fehr ***Mus*** Max Steiner ***Art*** Robert Haas
Act Bette Davis, Joseph Cotten, David Brian, Ruth Roman, Regis Toomey (Warner)

Beyond the Forest gives Bette Davis a chance to portray the neurotic femme she does so well. The character of Rosa Moline, a woman who yearns for broader vistas than those supplied by the Wisconsin mill town to which she is tied, furnishes plenty of bite for the Davis technique and she belts it across.

Character [from the novel by Stuart Engstrand] is a modern-day Madame Bovary, a woman who sets her traps for a rich man. Davis gets over the character of the black-hearted Rosa, expressing the part with a vitality and earnestness that gives it a stylized vividness.

Joseph Cotten is the small-town minded doctor married to Rosa. His chore as the doctor is quiet and effective and David Brian is colorful as the man on whom Rosa has set her sights. He and Davis make their scenes particularly red-blooded playing of illicit love.

King Vidor seldom falters in his direction.

1949: NOMINATION: Best Scoring of a Dramatic Picture

•

BEYOND THE LIMIT
SEE: THE HONORARY CONSUL

•

BEYOND THE POSEIDON ADVENTURE
1979, 122 mins, US Ⓥ ▭ col
Dir Irwin Allen ***Prod*** Irwin Allen ***Scr*** Nelson Gidding ***Ph*** Joseph Biroc ***Ed*** Bill Brame ***Mus*** Jerry Fielding ***Art*** Preston Ames
Act Michael Caine, Sally Field, Telly Savalas, Peter Boyle, Jack Warden, Karl Malden (Warner)

Beyond the Poseidon Adventure comes off as a virtual remake of the 1972 original, without that film's mounting suspense and excitement. Recap of original premise, a luxury liner turned upside down by gigantic tidal wave, is accomplished in a few seconds.

New plot turn pits salvage tug operators Michael Caine, Karl Malden and Sally Field against evildoer Telly Savalas for looting rights to the big boat. Caine and company are after hard cash, while Savalas, posing as a medico, is searching out a cargo of valuable plutonium.

The only change in this group's struggle to reach the top (really, the bottom) of the boat is a set of different faces.

Because the outcome is so predictable, the defects in the script take on greater magnitude.

•

BEYOND THE VALLEY OF THE DOLLS
1970, 109 mins, US Ⓥ ▭ col
Dir Russ Meyer ***Prod*** Russ Meyer ***Scr*** Roger Ebert ***Ph*** Fred J. Koenekamp ***Ed*** Dann Cahn, Dick Wormel ***Mus*** Stu Phillips ***Art*** Jack Martin Smith
Act Dolly Read, Cynthia Myers, Marcia McBroom, John LaZar, Michael Blodgett, David Gurian (20th Century-Fox)

This trashy, gaudy, sound-stage vulgarity about lowlife among the high life is as funny as a burning orphanage.

Dolly Read, Cynthia Myers and Marcia McBroom head a busty cast as three pop singers who come to swinging Hollywood with manager David Gurian. Read has determined to pry some inheritance money from aunt Phyllis Davis, who runs with a super-groovy set, shepherded by John La Zar, a Shakespeare-spouting effete.

Michael Blodgett plays a film hero louse, Edy Williams a sex goddess, Erica Gavin the obligatory lesbian, and Duncan McLeod an unscrupulous lawyer. The sole good running gag involves Williams and Gurian; she's ready for sex any place except in bed.

•

B. F.'S DAUGHTER
1948, 107 mins, US b/w
Dir Robert Z. Leonard ***Prod*** Edwin H. Knopf ***Scr*** Luther Davis ***Ph*** Joseph Ruttenberg ***Ed*** George White ***Mus*** Bronislau Kaper ***Art*** Cedric Gibbons, Daniel B. Cathcart
Act Barbara Stanwyck, Van Heflin, Charles Coburn, Keenan Wynn, Richard Hart, Margaret Lindsay (M-G-M)

The polished production supervision has been carefully handled to give it the expected Metro gloss, and performances are of top caliber.

Script, however, makes an even more shallow exploration of the passing of a colorful era than did the John P. Marquand novel on which it is based. It's a boy meets girl story, backgrounded against the period from the early '30s into the war years. Barbara Stanwyck has been stunningly gowned and beautifully photographed.

Stanwyck and Van Heflin, as the two principal characters, wrap up the roles with smooth performances. Heflin gives an expressive interpretation as the poor, liberal college professor and lecturer who falls in love with and marries the daughter of an industrial giant. Charles Coburn is his competent self as the industrialist. Richard Hart does well as the stuffy lawyer fiance who is tossed over for the poor prof. Keenan Wynn ably projects the opportunist newscaster.

•

BHOWANI JUNCTION
1956, 110 mins, US Ⓥ ▭ col
Dir George Cukor ***Prod*** Pandro S. Berman ***Scr*** Sonya Levien, Ivan Moffat ***Ph*** Freddie Young ***Ed*** Frank Clarke, George Boemler ***Mus*** Miklos Rozsa ***Art*** Gene Allen, John Howell
Act Ava Gardner, Stewart Granger, Bill Travers, Abraham Sofaer, Francis Matthews, Peter Illing (M-G-M)

To make *Bhowani Junction*, based on the John Masters novel, Metro went to Pakistan to shoot a film about India. The journey paid rich dividends, for the sense of realism in the film is one of the best things about it.

Bhowani Junction, starring Ava Gardner as an Anglo-Indian, and Stewart Granger as a British colonel who falls in love with her, is a horse of many colors. Picture goes off in quite a few directions, ranging from romance and action to a halfhearted attempt to explain the Indians and a more serious effort to dramatize the social twilight into which the British withdrawal from India tossed a small group of people who were of mixed Indian and British blood.

Story has Gardner as the half-caste returning home to an India seething with discontent and boiling with riots prior to the departure of the British. At Bhowani Junction, a railroad center, she meets Granger who's been sent to command a security detail to guard the rail line against Communist saboteurs.

Gardner thinks she loves Bill Travers, the local rail superintendent, also an Anglo-Indian. She's soon torn between being European and Indian, kills a British lieutenant who's trying to rape her and is temporarily saved by the Communist boss (Peter Illing).

Director George Cukor, in staging his crowd scenes, achieves some magnificent effects and Freddie Young's lensing is first-rate. The milling, sweating, shouting crowds, egged on by Red agents, are almost frighteningly real and the screen comes alive with an abundance of movement.

•

BIBLE, THE
IN THE BEGINNING . . .
1966, 174 MINS, ITALY/US Ⓥ ⦿ ▭ col
Dir John Huston ***Prod*** Dino De Laurentiis ***Scr*** Christopher Fry, Jonathan Griffin, Ivo Perilli, Vittorio Bonicelli ***Ph*** Giuseppe Rotunno ***Ed*** Ralph Kemplen ***Mus*** Toshiro Mayuzumi ***Art*** Mario Chiari, Stephen Grimes
Act Michael Parks, Ulla Bergryd, Richard Harris, John Huston, Stephen Boyd, George C. Scott (De Laurentiis/20th Century-Fox)

The world's oldest story—the origins of mankind, as told in the Book of Genesis—is put upon the screen by director John Huston and producer Dino De Laurentiis with consummate skill, taste and reverence.

Christopher Fry, who wrote the screenplay with the assistance of Biblical scholars and religious consultants, has fashioned a straightforward, sensitive and dramatic telling, through dialog and narration, of the first 22 chapters of Genesis.

A lavish, but always tasteful production—assaults and rewards the eye and ear with awe-inspiring realism.

Huston's rich voice functions in narration, and he also plays Noah with heartwarming humility, compassion and humor.

The seduction of Eve by the serpent, the latter well represented by a man reclining in a tree, cues a sudden shift of mood and pace. Richard Harris plays the jealous and remorseful Cain with a sure feeling, while Franco Nero's Abel conveys in very brief footage the image of a sensitive, obedient young man whose murder provoked a supreme outrage. The 45-minute sequence devoted to Noah and the Flood is, in itself, a triumph in filmmaking. It plays dramatically and fluidly, and belies monumental logistics of production. Huston's Noah is, again, perfect casting.

Stephen Boyd then emerges as Nimrod, the proud king, whose egocentric monument became the Tower of Babel where the languages of his people suddenly were changed. The remainder of the film is devoted to Abraham, played with depth by George C. Scott. Ava Gardner is very good as the barren Sarah who, to give her husband a male heir, urges him to conceive with her servant, Zoe Sallis.

1966: NOMINATION: Best Original Music Score

•

BICENTENNIAL MAN
1999, 131mins, US Ⓥ ⦿ col
Dir Chris Columbus ***Prod*** Wolfgang Petersen, Gail Katz, Neal Miller, Laurence Mark, Chris Columbus, Mark Radcliffe, Michael Barnathan ***Scr*** Nicholas Kazan ***Ph*** Phil Meheux ***Ed*** Neil Travis ***Mus*** James Horner ***Art*** Norman Reynolds
Act Robin Williams, Sam Neill, Embeth Davidtz, Oliver Platt, Wendy Crewson, Hallie Kate Eisenberg (1492 Pictures/Touchstone/Columbia)

An ambitious tale handled in a dawdling, sentimental way, *Bicentennial Man* filters the prescient vision of late sci-fi writer Isaac Asimov through the touchy-feely sensibility of the "new" Robin Williams. This long-arc story of a robot's 200-year journey to become a human being benefits from compelling thematic notions and wizardly visual, robotic and makeup effects, but bogs down due to slack storytelling and an insipidly conventional approach.

Based on a short story written by Asimov on the occasion of the American bicentennial in 1976 [and on the novel *The Positronic Man* by Asimov and Robert Silverberg], screenplay takes about an hour to suggest it intends to be about anything other than a futuristic tin man, or that it will have such an epic scope. The higher the stakes grow in the later stages, the more director Chris Columbus resorts to obviousness and emotional pandering.

Williams is Andrew, a genial robot, that's been acquired by the upscale Bay Area Martin family as a maid-butler-cook-nanny. The head of the family, simply called Sir (Sam Neill), suspects there might be more to Andrew than metal, fiberglass and wire, and the robot over the years also becomes the closest confidant of one of Sir's daughters, Little Miss (Embeth Davidtz).

When Sir dies, Andrew embarks upon a long odyssey to locate others of his ilk. Search concludes back in San Francisco, where he finds the bouncy femme robot Galatea and her owner, Rupert Burns (Oliver Platt), a benign Dr. Frankenstein.

With the role placing a straitjacket on his usual shtick, Williams emits expressions of personality as well as anyone could under the circumstances.

1999: NOMINATION: Best Makeup

•

BICHES, LES

(THE DOES; THE GIRLFRIENDS; BAD GIRLS)

1968, 100 mins, France/Italy Ⓥ col

Dir Claude Chabrol ***Prod*** Andre Genoves ***Scr*** Paul Gegauff, Claude Chabrol ***Ph*** Jean Rabier ***Ed*** Jacques Gaillard ***Mus*** Pierre Jansen ***Art*** Marc Berthier

Act Stephane Audran, Jacqueline Sassard, Jean-Louis Trintignant, Nane Germon, Henri Attal, Dominique Zardi (Boetie/Alexandra)

Here, director Claude Chabrol deals with lesbianism and bisexuality but still within a psychological and even suspense envelope. This one is a bit reminiscent of his *Les Cousins*, where a country cousin was overridden by a decadent city cousin. Here it treats with two women and the encroaching madness of one that leads to tragedy.

A rich and bored woman (Stephane Audran) picks up a Left Bank hippie girl (Jacqueline Sassard) who draws does on the sidewalks in Paris. She seduces her in an adroit, daring scene. Then she takes her to her villa in Saint Tropez.

There are two deadbeats living there who are her clowns. Into this setup comes a young architect (Jean-Louis Trintignant) who first seduces the hippie girl and then is seduced in turn by the rich woman.

The characters keep pic afloat until the gripping second part develops the strange relationships. Acting is a help in Audran's split rich woman and Sassard's boyish, empty drifter who lacks true identity. Trintignant is effective, if effaced, in the principal role.

•

BICYCLE THIEF, THE

SEE: LADRI DI BICICLETTE

•

BICYCLE THIEVES

SEE: LADRI DI BICICLETTE

•

BIDONE, IL

(THE SWINDLE)

1955, 100 mins, Italy/France Ⓥ ⊙ b/w

Dir Federico Fellini ***Scr*** Federico Fellini, Ennio Flaiano, Tullio Pinelli ***Ph*** Otello Martelli ***Ed*** Mario Serandrei, Giuseppe Vari ***Mus*** Nino Rota ***Art*** Dario Cecchi

Act Broderick Crawford, Richard Basehart, Franco Fabrizi, Giulietta Masina, Sue Ellen Blake, Giacomo Gabrielli (Titanus/SGC)

Controversial pic, considerably trimmed since its Venice Film Festival showing, tells of three small-time swindlers and some of their exploits in fleecing gullible Romans of their hard-earned coin.

But more than in telling these tales, some of them amusing, pic centers on the sad loneliness which characterizes the lives of these men, and especially that of Augusto (Broderick Crawford). For while Roberto (Franco Fabrizi), the youngest, progresses in the "trade" and moves on to bigger exploits in Milan, and Picasso (Richard Basehart) gives it up while he still can, Augusto is killed by his own men in his first serious attempt to go straight.

Film is full of symbolism and contains some powerful moments, as well as bitingly satirical sequences such as a cocktail party brawl in a rich swindler's apartment. Yet despite the arty slant, general audiences are bound to note a general tediousness, only here and there relieved by a humorous or human touch. It is a bitter pic on a bitter subject [from a screen story by Federico Fellini and Ennio Flaiano].

Acting is good, with Crawford turning in a somber performance as Augusto, though his choice for the role is debatable. Basehart's Picasso is unclearly defined in the script, while Fabrizi comes off best as the carefree member of the group.

•

BIG

1988, 102 mins, US Ⓥ ⊙ col

Dir Penny Marshall ***Prod*** James L. Brooks, Robert Greenhut ***Scr*** Gary Ross, Anne Spielberg ***Ph*** Barry Sonnenfeld ***Ed*** Barry Malkin ***Mus*** Howard Shore ***Art*** Santo Loquasto

Act Tom Hanks, Elizabeth Perkins, John Heard, Jared Rushton, Robert Loggia, David Moscow (20th Century-Fox/Gracie)

A 13-year-old junior high kid Josh (David Moscow) is transformed into a 35-year-old's body (Tom Hanks) by a carnival wishing machine in this pic which unspools with enjoyable genuineness and ingenuity.

Immediate dilemma, since going back to school is not an option and his mom thinks he's an intruder and doesn't buy into the explanation that he's changed into a man, is to escape to anonymous New York City and hide out in a seedy hotel.

Pretty soon, the viewer forgets that what's happening on screen has no basis in reality. The characters are having too much fun enjoying life away from responsibility, which begs the question why adults get so serious when there is fun to be had in almost any situation.

Hanks plays chopsticks on a walking piano at F.A.O. Schwarz with a man who turns out to be his boss (Robert Loggia) and as a result of this free-spirited behavior is promoted way beyond his expectations, but it's what he does with all his newfound self-worth that propels this "dramedy."

Greatest growth comes from his involvement with coworker Elizabeth Perkins, though by no means is he the only one getting an education.

1988: NOMINATIONS: Best Actor (Tom Hanks), Original Screenplay

•

BIG BAD MAMA

1974, 83 mins, US Ⓥ col

Dir Steve Carver ***Prod*** Roger Corman ***Scr*** William Norton, Frances Doel ***Ph*** Bruce Logan ***Ed*** Tina Hirsch ***Mus*** David Grisman ***Art*** Peter Jamison

Act Angie Dickinson, William Shatner, Tom Skerritt, Susan Sennett, Robbie Lee, Noble Willingham (New World)

The plotline is flimsy at best, opening circa 1932 with Angie Dickinson posturing as a hard-bitten mother, rumrunner, bank robber, jewel thief, kidnapper and queen bee in the sack. Both producer Roger Corman and director Steve Carver make a feeble attempt at social import by having Mama and true-blue lover Tom Skerritt martyr themselves so that the children may live and spend their ill-got gains. Carver's direction mostly consists of winks at the film buffs in the crowd, as he apes the wedding scene from *The Graduate* and swipes bank robbery and shootout scenes, as well as the bluegrass tempo from *Bonnie and Clyde*.

Big Bad Mama is mostly rehashed *Bonnie and Clyde*, with a bit more blood and Angie Dickinson taking off her clothes for sex scenes with the crooks in her life.

•

BIG BLUE, THE

SEE: LE GRAND BLEU

•

BIG BOSS, THE

SEE: TANG SHAN DAXIONG

•

BIG BRASS RING, THE

1999, 104 mins, US Ⓥ ⊙ col

Dir George Hickenlooper ***Prod*** Andrew Pfeffer, Donald Zuckerman ***Scr*** F. X. Feeney, George Hickenlooper ***Ph*** Kramer Morgenthau ***Ed*** Jim Makiej ***Mus*** Thomas Morse ***Art*** Jerry Fleming

Act William Hurt, Nigel Hawthorne, Miranda Richardson, Irene Jacob, Ewan Stewart, Gregg Henry (Pfilmco/Millennium)

A serious-minded, emotionally distant study of political intrigue and personal betrayal, *The Big Brass Ring* offers some interesting ideas, but is rather lacking in dramatic plausibility and decipherable character motivation. A good cast, fresh St. Louis settings, snippets of lively dialogue and some resonant themes remaining from Orson Welles's original script keep the film watchable.

Written by Welles, with contributions from his longtime collaborator Oja Kodar, in 1981–82 and published posthumously in 1987, the screenplay was seen by scholars as a fascinating companion piece to *Citizen Kane*. Director George Hickenlooper and co-scenarist, L.A.–based film critic F. X. Feeney, have departed from their source in many important ways, beginning with moving its settings from Spain and Africa to the U.S. and changing its central figure from a U.S. senator to an aspirant to the governor's mansion.

The close race between Blake Pellarin (William Hurt) and his competitor is pushing into its final week when a potential trip wire turns up in the form of Kim Mennaker (Nigel Hawthorne), a former senator who is Pellarin's unofficial stepfather. Mennaker has been living in exile in Havana for years after his gay exploits finished his political career.

Into the middle of the storm jumps an aggressive European journalist, Cela Brandini (Irene Jacob), who uses tidbits thrown to her by Mennaker to pry additional info out of Pellarin.

Hurt is plausible as an attractive political figure in the most modern opaque sense, and Hawthorne has a good time as a grand dirty old man.

•

BIG BRAWL, THE

1980, 95 mins, US/Hong Kong Ⓥ ⊏⊐ col

Dir Robert Clouse ***Prod*** Fred Weintraub, Terry Morse, Jr. ***Scr*** Robert Clouse ***Ph*** Robert Jessup ***Ed*** George Grenville ***Mus*** Lalo Schifrin ***Art*** Joe Altadonna

Act Jackie Chan, Jose Ferrer, Kristine DeBell, Mako, Rosalind Chao, Mary Ellen O'Neill (Warner/Golden Harvest)

Hong Kong martial arts star Jackie Chan makes an amiable American film debut in *The Big Brawl*, an amusing chopsocky actioner whose appeal is not limited to the usual audience for this genre. Key ingredient here is humor.

Story is set in Chicago, 1938, and filmed with engagingly artificial style that resembles vintage gangster pix. Epicene gangster lord Jose Ferrer runs his terrain with the aid of his foul-mouthed, cigar-chomping mother (Mary Ellen O'Neill).

Attempts to strong-arm a Chinese restaurateur run afoul when his son (Chan) gets into the act with chopsocky skills. Chan eventually is recruited by Ferrer to be his entrant into a Texas free for all (the "big brawl" of the title).

Chan's physical prowess grows, leaving the flashiest stuff for the finale.

•

BIG BROADCAST, THE

1932, 80 mins, US b/w

Dir Frank Tuttle ***Scr*** George Marion, Jr. ***Ph*** George Folsey

Act Stuart Erwin, Bing Crosby, George Burns, Gracie Allen, Leila Hyams (Paramount)

It's an all-star show with a flock of the biggest air favorites. Bing Crosby, Burns and Allen, Kate Smith, the Boswell Sisters, Arthur Tracy (The Street Singer), Donald Novis, and the Vincent Lopez and Cab Calloway orchestras are as varied a galaxy of radio favorites as they are ether-renowned.

Crosby and Burns and Allen alone went to the Coast to participate in the actual production, having lines and parts, with the rest shot in the east and cut in for their specialties. While disjointed in action, the cutting in of the variety interludes is skillfully accomplished.

The film is a credit to Crosby as a screen juve possibility, although he has a decidedly dizzy and uncertain role which makes him misbehave as no human being does. George Burns with his serious-miened straighting for the dumb Dora-ish Gracie Allen are a stock interlude in themselves as the station manager and dumb stenog, although it evolves into more or less a specialty routine.

The chief fault with *Broadcast* is that it's not a feature film but a succession of talking shorts. The story is rather childish.

•

BIG BROADCAST OF 1936, THE

1935, 97 mins, US b/w

Dir Norman Taurog ***Prod*** Benjamin Glazer ***Scr*** Walter DeLeon, Francis Martin, Ralph Spence ***Ph*** Leo Tover

Act Jack Oakie, George Burns, Gracie Allen, Lyda Roberti, Bing Crosby, Ethel Merman (Paramount)

Big Broadcast of 1936 is a film broadcaster of plenty of names and considerable entertainment. It hasn't much story, but the lack won't bother much.

Names are in and out as fast and as often as a firefly's taillight. There just isn't time for a "plot," and probably best that none was attempted. Jack Oakie, Burns and Allen, Lyda Roberti, Wendy Barrie, Henry Wadsworth, C. Henry

Gordon and a few others carry on whatever yarn there is and they play it lightly, as required.

You have to look quickly to see such names as Bing Crosby, Ethel Merman, Ray Noble's band, Amos 'n' Andy, Boland and Ruggles and Bill Robinson. These and other specialty turns are worked into the continuity via a crazy television gag.

Oakie is the slightly bankrupt operator of a small-time station and doubles as the outlet's "great lover." Oakie does the spieling and his partner (Henry Wadsworth) the crooning. Burns and Allen come in with an ingenious and also nutty television contraption, invented by Gracie's uncle, which can pick up any event and also send. The plot flows in between frequent "television" specialties, with the telebox the vital prop of the picture.

1935: NOMINATION: Best Dance Direction ("Elephant Number—It's the Animal in Me")

•

BIG BROADCAST OF 1937, THE

1936, 100 mins, US b/w

Dir Mitchell Leisen ***Prod*** Lewis E. Gensler ***Scr*** Edwin Gelsey, Arthur Kober, Barry Trivers, Walter DeLeon, Francis Martin ***Ph*** Theodor Sparkuhl ***Ed*** Stuart Heisler ***Art*** Hans Dreier, Robert Usher

Act Jack Benny, George Burns, Gracie Allen, Martha Raye, Shirley Ross, Ray Milland (Paramount)

The third in the *Big Broadcast* series from Paramount, this one, with its large cast of radio, stage and screen talent, far outdistances the two that precede it.

There are enough comedians of one form or another in *Broadcast* to make it a hit soley on the strength of the laughs: Jack Benny, Martha Raye, Bob Burns and Burns & Allen are the prominents poking at audience ribs. Burns's best scenes are those in which he bursts in on radio programs which are on the air, while looking for conductor Leopold Stokowski. Raye is slow to get started but finishes strong. Towards the end she socks through with the "Vote for Mr. Rhythm" number.

Benny plays the manager of the radio studios. He is mostly having his troubles with everyone from Gracie Allen down. The latter clicks from the outset, getting in for the earlier laughs built around the rehearsal of a skit under cute circumstances.

Several well-known New York niteries get their names into the footage through the director's manner of suggesting how Ray Milland and Shirley Ross make the town one night.

•

BIG BROADCAST OF 1938, THE

1938, 88 mins, US b/w

Dir Mitchell Leisen ***Prod*** Harlan Thompson ***Scr*** Walter DeLeon, Francis Martin, Ken Englund, Howard Lindsay, Russell Crouse ***Ph*** Harry Fischbeck ***Ed*** Eda Warren, Chandler House ***Mus*** Boris Morros ***Art*** Hans Dreier, Ernst Fegte

Act W. C. Fields, Martha Raye, Dorothy Lamour, Shirley Ross, Lynne Overman, Bob Hope (Paramount)

With the rejuvenated W. C. Fields at his inimitable best in a streamlined production which combines spectacle, melody and dance, *The Big Broadcast of 1938* is pictorially original and alluring.

The outstanding moment of the film, however, is a contribution by Kirsten Flagstad, of the Metropolitan opera company, singing an aria from *Die Walkure*.

Surrounding Fields and the diva is a company of players who keep alive interest in a better than usual libretto and, at the same time, turn in a full quota of laughs and musical numbers. Martha Raye, Dorothy Lamour, Shirley Ross, Lynne Overman, Bob Hope, Ben Blue, Leif Erikson, Rufe Davis and Grace Bradley are clicks. Specialties also come from Tito Guizar and Patricia Wilder. Shep Fields and his orchestra appear in a cartoon novelty.

There are half a dozen good musical numbers by Ralph Rainger and Leo Robin. The smash production number is "The Waltz Lives On," which is a fanciful bit of terp and song that carries the waltz strain through the past 100 years. Staged by LeRoy Prinz and featuring Shirley Ross and Bob Hope it is the high spot of Mitchell Leisen's direction.

Screenplay starting with Frederick Hazlitt Brennan's original story, has something to do with a transatlantic steamship race between two greyhounds of the deep, one of which is owned by Fields. Specialties are introduced as the entertainment supplied to the passengers.

1938: Best Song ("Thanks for the Memory")

•

BIG BUS, THE

1976, 88 mins, US Ⓥ ▭ col

Dir James Frawley ***Prod*** Fred Freeman, Lawrence J. Cohen ***Scr*** Fred Freeman, Lawrence J. Cohen ***Ph*** Harry Stradling, Jr. ***Ed*** Edward Warschilka ***Mus*** David Shire ***Art*** Joel Schiller

Act Joseph Bologna, Stockard Channing, John Beck, Rene Auberjonois, Ned Beatty, Jose Ferrer (Paramount)

Heading the cast of this overkill spoof is Joseph Bologna, good as a down-and-out bus driver whose chance to make a comeback is the nuclear-powered behemoth designed by Stockard Channing and father Harold Gould. The first half hour or so is devoted to preparations for boarding.

Herein is presented also John Beck, assistant driver with only one hang-up (he blacks out on the road); computerized control center; Larry Hagman, malpractice-wary doctor treating Gould for injuries from industrial sabotage efforts led by iron-lung-bound Jose Ferrer. Next comes the parade of passengers, each with their own formula destiny.

Finally come the complications, too numerous to mention. Suffice it to say that no cliché is left unattached.

•

BIG BUSINESS

1988, 97 mins, US Ⓥ ⊙ col

Dir Jim Abrahams ***Prod*** Steve Tisch, Michael Peyser ***Scr*** Dori Pierson, Marc Rubel ***Ph*** Dean Cundey ***Ed*** Harry Keramidas ***Mus*** Lee Holdridge ***Art*** William Sandell

Act Bette Midler, Lily Tomlin, Fred Ward, Edward Herrmann, Michele Placido, Barry Primus (Touchstone/Silver Screen Partners III)

Big Business is a shrill, unattractive comedy which stars Bette Midler and Lily Tomlin, who play two sets of twins mixed up at birth. They have distinctly different comic styles, with the former's loud brashness generally dominating the latter's sly skittishness.

A mishap at a rural hospital pairs off the daughters of a hick couple with the sprigs of a major industrialist and his society wife. Jump to New York today, where dynamic Moramax Corp board chairman Sadie Shelton (Midler) is forced to tolerate her scatterbrained, sentimental sister Rose (Tomlin) while trying to push through the sale of a subsidiary firm in their birthplace of Jupiter Hollow.

To try to thwart the sale at a stockholders' meeting, another Sadie and Rose, of the Ratcliff clan, leave Jupiter Hollow for the big city. As soon as they arrive at the airport, the complications begin.

Of the four performances by the two leads, the one easiest to enjoy is Midler's as venal corporate boss. Dressed to the nines and sporting a mincing but utterly determined walk, Midler tosses off her waspish one-liners with malevolent glee, stomping on everyone in her path.

There are moments of delight as well in her other characterization as a country bumpkin who has always yearned for the material pleasures of Babylon.

Tomlin has her moments, too, but her two sweetly flakey, nay-saying characters for a while seem so similar.

•

BIG CARNIVAL

SEE: ACE IN THE HOLE

•

BIG CHILL, THE

1983, 103 mins, US Ⓥ ⊙ col

Dir Lawrence Kasdan ***Prod*** Michael Shamberg ***Scr*** Lawrence Kasdan, Barbara Benedek ***Ph*** John Bailey ***Ed*** Carol Littleton ***Mus*** John Williams ***Art*** Ida Random

Act Tom Berenger, Glenn Close, Jeff Goldblum, William Hurt, Kevin Kline, JoBeth Williams (Carson/Columbia)

The Bill Chill is an amusing, splendidly acted but rather shallow look at what's happened to the generation formed by the 1960s.

Framework has seven old college friends gathering on the Southeastern seaboard for the funeral of another old pal, who has committed suicide in the home of happily married Glenn Close and Kevin Kline.

Others in attendance are: sharp-looking Tom Berenger, who has gained nationwide fame as a Tom Selleck-type private eye on TV; Jeff Goldblum, horny wiseacre who writes for *People* magazine; William Hurt, the Jake Barnes of the piece by virtue of having been strategically injured in Vietnam; Mary Kay Place, a successful career woman who just hasn't met the right man; and JoBeth Williams, whose older husband returns home to the two kids before the weekend has barely begun.

Also provocatively on hand is Meg Tilly, much younger girlfriend of the deceased who doesn't react with sufficient depth to the tragedy in the eyes of the older folk.

Except perhaps for Hurt, who still takes drugs heavily and is closest in personality to the dead man [played by Kevin Costner, but edited out of the finished film], characters are generally middle-of-the-roaders, and pic lacks a tough-minded spokesman who might bring them all up short for a moment.

1983: NOMINATIONS: Best Picture, Supp. Actress (Glenn Close), Original Screenplay

•

BIG CLOCK, THE

1948, 95 mins, US b/w

Dir John Farrow ***Prod*** Richard Maibaum ***Scr*** Jonathan Latimer ***Ph*** John F. Seitz ***Ed*** Eda Warren, Gene Ruggiero ***Mus*** Victor Young ***Art*** Hans Dreier, Roland Anderson, Albert Nozaki

Act Ray Milland, Charles Laughton, Maureen O'Sullivan, George Macready, Elsa Lanchester, Dan Tobin (Paramount)

There are weaknesses lurking in this pic [based on the novel by Kenneth Fearing, adaptation by Harold Goldman], namely a too-patly tailored yarn and some spotty acting, but these matter little. The pace is so red-hot that there's no time or inclination, during the unfolding, to question coincident or misplaced mugging.

Laughton, in this instance, is cracking the whip as the topkick in a gigantic publishing house. Toiling under him is Ray Milland, editor of a crime mag, whose peculiar value is his ability to run down concealed felons and expose them in his sheet. Goaded by insane jealousy, Laughton kills his mistress and scurries for cover. It's at this point that story's peculiar twist shoves it into high.

Laughton is aware that he's been sighted by his unknown rival. As he sees it, there's only one way out, and that's to locate the sole witness and either buy him off or cancel him in some other way. Milland, of course, is hired for that job, and his desperate efforts are directed towards covering his own tracks while pinning the goods on the real murderer.

Milland turns in a workmanlike job, polished to groove to the unrelenting speed of the plot. Laughton, unfortunately, overplays his hand so that his tycoon-sans-heart takes on the quality of parodying the real article.

•

BIG COMBO, THE

1955, 86 mins, US Ⓥ b/w

Dir Joseph H. Lewis ***Prod*** Sidney Harmon ***Scr*** Philip Yordan ***Ph*** John Alton ***Ed*** Robert Eisen ***Mus*** David Raksin ***Art*** Rudi Feld

Act Cornel Wilde, Richard Conte, Brian Donlevy, Jean Wallace, Robert Middleton, Lee Van Cleef (Security/Theodora)

This is another saga of the honest cop who lets nothing sway him from the self-appointed task of smashing a crime syndicate and its leader. It is done with grim melodramatics that are hard-hitting despite a rambling, not-too-credible plot, and is cut out to order for the meller fan who likes his action rough and raw.

One torture scene in particular will shock the sensibilities and cause near-nausia. After honest cop Diamond (Cornel Wilde) has been tormented by gangster Brown (Richard Conte) via a hearing aid plugged in his ear while the receiver is held to a radio going full blast, the cold-blooded crook forces the contents of a large bottle of hair tonic down the victim's throat.

Even after Wilde has been subjected to the indignities by Conte and his strong-arm boys (Brian Donlevy, Lee Van Cleef, Earl Holliman), pic has you believe he still can't bring the hood to justice. In addition to his desire to get Conte, Wilde also has a desire for the crook's girlfriend Susan (Jean Wallace) but it takes some doing to get her to escape the gangster.

Performances are in keeping with the bare-knuckle direction by Joseph Lewis and, on that score, are good. Low-key photography by John Alton and a noisy, jazzy score by David Raksin [with solo piano by Jacob Gimpel] are in keeping with the film's tough mood.

•

BIG COUNTRY, THE

1958, 166 mins, US Ⓥ ⊙ ▭ col

Dir William Wyler ***Prod*** William Wyler, Gregory Peck ***Scr*** James R. Webb, Sy Bartlett, Robert Wilder ***Ph*** Franz F. Planer ***Ed*** Robert Swink, Robert Belcher, John Faure ***Mus*** Jerome Moross ***Art*** Frank Hotaling

Act Gregory Peck, Jean Simmons, Carroll Baker, Charlton Heston, Burl Ives, Charles Bickford (United Artists/Anthony Worldwide)

The Big Country lives up to its title. The camera has captured a vast section of the southwest with such fidelity that the long stretches of dry country, in juxtaposition to tiny western settlements, and the giant canyon country in the arid area, have been recorded with almost three-dimensional effect.

Although the story—based on Donald Hamilton's novel, with Jessamyn West and Robert Wyler credited with the screen adaptation—is dwarfed by the scenic outpourings, *The Big Country* is nonetheless armed with a serviceable, adult western yarn.

Basically it concerns the feud between Major Henry Terrill (Charles Bickford) and Rufus Hannassey (Burl Ives), rugged individualists who covet the same watering area for their cattle. The water spot is open to both camps since it is the property of Julie Maragon (Jean Simmons) who has been willed the property by her grandfather.

Bickford is the "have" rancher of the area, with a fine home, a large head of cattle, a beautiful daughter (Carroll Baker), and a full crew of ranch hands. Ives is the "have not," with a brood of unruly and uncouth sons, a bunch of shacks, and an army of "white trash" relatives. Into the atmosphere of hate and vengeance comes Gregory Peck, a genteel eastern dude, to marry Baker. Peck arouses Baker's displeasure when he refuses to ride a wild horse and backs away from a fight with Charlton Heston, Bickford's truculent foreman who's after Baker himself.

As the peace-loving easterner, Peck gives one of his better performances. Ives is top-notch as the rough but fair-minded Hannassey; Bickford is fine as the ruthless, unforgiving rancher. Chuck Connors, a former professional baseball player, is especially convincing as Ives's uncouth son who attempts to rape Simmons. Jerome Moross's musical score is also on the plus side.

1958: Best Supp. Actor (Burl Ives)

NOMINATION: Best Score of a Dramatic Picture

•

BIG EASY, THE
1986, 108 mins, US Ⓥ ⦿ col
Dir Jim McBride ***Prod*** Stephen Friedman ***Scr*** Dan Petrie, Jr. ***Ph*** Afonso Beato ***Ed*** Mia Goldman ***Mus*** Brad Feidel ***Art*** Jeannine Claudia Oppewall
Act Dennis Quaid, Ellen Barkin, Ned Beatty, John Goodman, Ebb Roe Smith, Lisa Jane Persky (Kings Road)

Until conventional plot contrivances begin to spoil the fun, *The Big Easy* is a snappy, sassy battle of the sexes in the guise of a melodrama about police corruption.

Build up is quite engaging. In the classic screwball comedy tradition of opposites irresistibly attracting, brash New Orleans homicide detective Dennis Quaid puts the make on Ellen Barkin, a northern import assigned by the DA's office to investigate possible illegal activities in the department.

Not necessarily the likeliest of couples, Quaid and Barkin bring great energy and an offbeat wired quality to their roles. Quaid's character is always "on," always performing for effect, during most of the action, and actor's natural charm easily counterbalances character's overbearing tendencies. Barkin is sexy and convincing as the initially uptight target of Quaid's attentions.

Ned Beatty projects an appealing paternalism as the homicide chief, while top supporting turn comes from the Ridiculous Theater Co.'s Charles Ludlam as a very Tennessee Williams-ish defense attorney.

•

BIG FISHERMAN, THE
1959, 180 mins, US ▭ col
Dir Frank Borzage ***Prod*** Rowland V. Lee ***Scr*** Howard Estabrook, Rowland V. Lee ***Ph*** Lee Garmes ***Ed*** Paul Weatherwax ***Mus*** Albert Hay Malotte ***Art*** John De Cuir
Act Howard Keel, Susan Kohner, John Saxon, Martha Hyer, Herbert Lom, Ray Stricklyn (Buena Vista)

The Big Fisherman is a pious but plodding account of the conversion to Christianity of Simon-Peter, the apostle called "the fisher of men." Its treatment is reverent but far from rousing.

There is plenty of opportunity for both spectacle and sex, and it is all the more curious, considering its big budget and leisurely production schedule, that both are almost absent. Although the climax of the film is in Herod's palace where Salome served the head of John the Baptist to the tyrant, this scene, laid in a sumptuous and impressively lavish banquet hall, is done almost entirely by shadows and is swiftly over. Salome, in fact, is not only never shown, she is never mentioned.

Although the title seems to make Simon-Peter the central character, the film [from the novel by Lloyd C. Douglas] is only incidentally about him. His part in the story is his influence on two young lovers, John Saxon as an Arab prince and Susan Kohner as the daughter of Herod by an Arab princess. Saxon wants to succeed his father as chieftan of an Arab tribe and Kohner wants to kill her father for the unhappiness he has inflicted on her mother.

Kohner and Saxon make a handsome young couple. But their problems seem trivial against the turbulent era. Howard Keel is handsomely picturesque as Simon-Peter, and shows he can hold his own as a straight actor. It is not his fault that there is no suggestion of the doughty strength identified with the chief apostle.

The "Palestine" that is the film's setting was shot entirely on locations in the San Fernando Valley and the California desert. It seems entirely authentic.

•

BIG FIX, THE
1978, 108 mins, US Ⓥ col
Dir Jeremy Paul Kagan ***Prod*** Carl Borack, Richard Dreyfuss ***Scr*** Roger L. Simon ***Ph*** Frank Stanley ***Ed*** Patrick Kennedy ***Mus*** Bill Conti ***Art*** Robert F. Boyle
Act Richard Dreyfuss, Susan Anspach, Bonnie Bedelia, John Lithgow, Ofelia Medina, F. Murray Abraham (Universal)

In *The Big Fix* Richard Dreyfuss delivers what is for him a particularly relaxed and confident performance as Moses Wine, the 1970s answer to Philip Marlowe, Lew Archer and Sam Spade.

Simply as a detective thriller, *The Bix Fix* has strong appeal. As a centerpiece it has a tough, cynical, intelligent detective—an independent man with a rat hole for an apartment, a personal life in need of some investigating and a full supply of wisecracks.

Briefly, the film finds Dreyfuss employed by Susan Anspach, like Dreyfuss a former campus activist, gone straight as a campaign worker for a gubernatorial candidate. Someone is trying to sabotage the election by distributing leaflets linking the middle-of-the-road candidate with radical elements. Dreyfuss is a natural for the case because he knew people in the radical movement.

The trail leads through Los Angeles—from the Beverly Hills mansions and social clubs to the Mexican barrios. Jeremy Paul Kagan's direction is nicely paced, starting off slow with the development of Dreyfuss's character and then speeding up as the plot complications mount.

•

BIG GAMBLE, THE
1961, 98 mins, US ▭ col
Dir Richard Fleischer ***Prod*** Darryl F. Zanuck ***Scr*** Irwin Shaw ***Ph*** William Mellor ***Ed*** Roger Dwyre ***Mus*** Maurice Jarre ***Art*** Jean d'Eaubonne
Act Stephen Boyd, Juliette Greco, David Wayne, Gregory Ratoff, Fernand Ledoux, Sybil Thorndike (Zanuck/20th Century-Fox)

A short but invaluable course on how not to drive a 10-ton truck through French Equitorial Africa is offered in Darryl F. Zanuck's production of *The Big Gamble*. Outside of a heap of dramatic jeopardy and some interesting scenic views of the Dark Continent, there isn't a great deal in this picture to entice the average customer.

Irwin Shaw's original screenplay launches itself in Dublin, where newlyweds Marie (Juliette Greco) and Vic (Stephen Boyd) are seeking funds from the latter's family to finance a trucking venture in Africa. They get the money, but they also inherit Milquetoast bank clerk cousin Samuel (David Wayne) who decides to accompany them in order to "protect the family investment." Balance of the film depicts the trio's oversea and overland misadventures in reaching their destination.

Boyd amply fills the physical specifications of the iron-willed, quick-tempered character he is portraying, but he has one or two dramatic lapses. Greco, too, has some uncertain moments.

The late Gregory Ratoff is convincing and colorful in an incidental part, and Sybil Thorndike works with assurance as matriarch of Boyd's Irish brood. Supporting cast includes players from the Abbey Theatre, Ulster Theatre and Comedie Francaise.

A great portion of the film was shot on location in the Ivory Coast of Africa, with other exteriors in Dublin and France, interiors in London and Paris. African second unit was headed by director Elmo Williams and cameraman Henri Persin.

•

BIG HIT, THE
1998, 91 mins, US Ⓥ ⦿ col
Dir Che-Kirk Wong ***Prod*** Warren Zide, Wesley Snipes ***Scr*** Ben Ramsey ***Ph*** Danny Nowak ***Ed*** Robin Russell, Pietro Scalia ***Mus*** Graeme Revell ***Art*** Taavo Soodor
Act Mark Wahlberg, Lou Diamond Phillips, Christina Applegate, Avery Brooks, Bokeem Woodbine, China Chow (Amen-Ra/Zide-Perry/Lion Rock/TriStar)

Combine the high-energy pyrotechnic choreography of a Hong Kong action film with the plight of a banal sitcom schnook and you have *The Big Hit*. A fleet piece of sock-'em entertainment, its kinetic force plows through myriad plot holes and inconsistencies with game abandon.

In genre tradition, the piece opens with a take-no-prisoners slam-bang contract job. The first weird wrinkle materializes when uberboss, Paris, (Avery Brooks) doles out the dough for the contract, dropping the bonus in team workhorse Mel's (Mark Wahlberg) lap. Mel's partner Cisco (Lou Diamond Phillips) objects, saying the victim wasn't quite dead and he had to apply the finishing touches. Mel just shrugs and hands over the wad.

The conceit of *The Big Hit* is that the killer simply can't say "no." He's a big-hearted lug who wants to be liked and have a normal family life once he arrives home from "the office."

Strapped to keep up payments on his suburban tract, Mel reluctantly agrees to do a moonlighting job for Cisco. It's a snatch-and-grab of Japanese-American Jiro Nishi's (Sab Shimono) teenage daughter, Keiko (China Chow), with a cool $1 million ransom attached. But Keiko just happens to be the goddaughter of Cisco's boss, Paris, so Cisco quickly figures out a way to cover his tracks and implicate Mel as the ringleader.

Vet Hong Kong director Che-Kirk Wong—making his U.S. debut—approaches the offbeat material with the kind of boldness and blindness the Cisco character exhibits. There's a herky-jerky quality to the narrative in which plot lapses are glossed over with elaborate set pieces and bizarre asides.

The cast manages to elevate the piece several notches. Wahlberg's hangdog look and pained expression is perfectly employed for wry comic effect. Phillips glories in Cisco's flaboyance. Chow makes an impressive debut, and only the overstated roles of Christina Applegate and Lainie Kazan [as Mel's Jewish-American princess fiancée and future mother-in-law] prove cacophonous.

•

BIGGER SPLASH, A
1975, 105 mins, UK col
Dir Jack Hazan ***Scr*** Jack Hazan, David Mingay ***Ph*** Jack Hazan ***Ed*** David Mingay ***Mus*** Patrick Gowers
Act David Hockney, Peter Schlesinger, Celia Birtwell, Mo McDermott, Henry Geldzahler, Kasmin (Buzzy)

A Bigger Splash is a revealing last ripple of the so-called lifestyle of "Swinging London" invented mainly by journalists.

Jack Hazan uses painter David Hockney, his art dealer in the U.S. and his fashion creator friend and the latter's wife. It has Hockney breaking with a boyfriend and not being able to work as his friends worry and his American dealer exhorts him. He finally does begin one on a swimming pool, which eventually has a man floating in it and the one who left him standing outside and staring.

Real people play themselves around a partly fictionalized tale. Hockney was noted for his color and specialization in California subjects. The gay life around him is indicated with style and taste.

•

BIGGER THAN LIFE
1956, 95 mins, US ▭ col
Dir Nicholas Ray ***Prod*** James Mason ***Scr*** Cyril Hume, Richard Maibaum ***Ph*** Joe MacDonald ***Ed*** Louis Loeffler ***Mus*** David Raksin
Act James Mason, Barbara Rush, Walter Matthau, Robert F. Simon, Christopher Olsen, Roland Winters (20th Century-Fox)

James Mason has picked a powerful subject for his first 20th Century-Fox production and delivers it with quite a bit of dramatic distinction in carrying out the supervisory duties and as the male lead. *Bigger Than Life* exposes the good and bad in cortisone.

A great deal of care is taken in the forceful, realistically drafted screenplay [based on a *New Yorker* article by Berton Rouche] to give both sides of the case, while at the same time telling a gripping, dramatic story of people that become very real under Nicholas Ray's wonder-working direction. The performances are standout, with Barbara Rush earning particular praise as Mason's wife.

Mason is exceptionally fine as the modestly circumstanced grade school teacher who undergoes a series of experiments with cortisone in the hope he can be cured of a usually fatal disease. At first the experiments progress promisingly, but he begins to overdose himself and some startling personality changes occur.

Christopher Olsen scores with his tremendously effective study of Mason's young son.

•

BIGGEST BUNDLE OF THEM ALL, THE
1968, 105 mins, US col
Dir Ken Annakin ***Prod*** Josef Shaftel ***Scr*** Sy Salkowitz ***Ph*** Piero Portalupi ***Ed*** Ralph Sheldon ***Mus*** Riz Ortolani ***Art*** Arrigo Equini
Act Vittorio De Sica, Raquel Welch, Robert Wagner, Godfrey Cambridge, Francesco Mule, Edward G. Robinson (M-G-M)

Title refers to the theft of $5 million in platinum ingots—by a gang composed of a deported Italian mobster and four amateurs.

Screenplay by Sy Salkowitz, from an original by the producer, is amusing, although never of the belly-laugh genre, and Ken Annakin's direction is imaginative enough to maintain a light mood. Yarn has a set of characters which fit nicely into the action.

What appeals most is the general ineptitude of the would-be criminals as they seek to rob the train bearing the ingots. In need of $3,000 to buy proper equipment for the caper, all their plans go wrong.

Vittorio De Sica pumps plenty of heart and humor into his role of the erstwhile Chicago mobster who attends the funeral in Naples of a Chicago comrade-in-arms and finds himself kidnapped by four strangers, headed by American Robert Wagner.

Wagner handles himself satisfactorily, and Raquel Welch is his voluptuous girlfriend, still playing bikini queen.

•

BIG GIRLS DON'T CRY . . . THEY GET EVEN
(UK: STEPKIDS)
1992, 102 mins, US Ⓥ col
Dir Joan Micklin Silver ***Prod*** Laurie Perlman, Gerald T. Olson ***Scr*** Frank Mugavero ***Ph*** Theo Van de Sande ***Ed*** Janice Hampton ***Mus*** Patrick Williams ***Art*** Victoria Paul
Act Hillary Wolf, David Strathairn, Margaret Whitton, Griffin Dunne, Patricia Kalember, Adrienne Shelly (New Line)

This tale of a teenage girl overlooked by her parents never escapes its sitcom premise and finally gives in to an ending so hackneyed it practically defines the term. Even with the reasonably deft guidance of director Joan Micklin Silver, the film struggles under its heavy-handed screenplay, featuring a stilted narration by teen protagonist Hillary Wolf that's a mix of bad one-liners and romance-novel angst.

Wolf resides with her uncaring mother (Margaret Whitton), rich stepfather (David Strathairn) and three step-siblings, while her biological father (Griffin Dunne) is estranged from his kind second wife (Patricia Kalember) and shacked up with his pregnant, much younger New-Age g.f. (Adrienne Shelly).

Muddle gets worse when Wolf flees to the woods with her stepbrother (Dan Futterman) to escape a family trip to Hawaii, with the rest of her extended family in hot pursuit.

Most of the kids prove annoyingly precocious, and even the generally appealing Wolf gets stuck with dialogue that clearly sounds written for her by a third party and not like the ruminations of a teenage girl.

•

BIGGLES
1986, 108 mins, UK Ⓥ ⊙ col
Dir John Hough ***Prod*** Pom Oliver, Kent Walwin ***Scr*** John Groves, Kent Walwin ***Ph*** Ernest Vincze ***Ed*** Richard Trevor ***Mus*** Stanislas ***Art*** Terry Pritchard
Act Neil Dickson, Alex Hyde-White, Fiona Hutchinson, Peter Cushing, Marcus Gilbert, William Hootkins (Compact Yellowbill)

This stylish romp combining World War I heroics and the currently in-vogue plot device of time travel has all the makings of a solid draw in countries where older audiences are familiar with the fictional hero from Captain W. E. Johns's series of *Biggles* books.

Script updates the WWI set piece to 1986 Manhattan via the time travel gimmick, which has food service entrepreneur Jim Ferguson (Alex Hyde-White) inexplicably hurled across the decades. Trouble is, he doesn't know when this phenomenon will recur, which makes for some amusing (and not-so) juxtapositions of past and present. Best bit is his drop in to a French convent under siege, attired only in a bath towel.

Ferguson keeps meeting up with Biggles (Neil Dickson), a dashing, WWI British aviator who's out to stop the Hun from implementing a hi-tech secret weapon which, as they find out later, is akin to a big microwave oven for men and machinery. Ferguson is aided and advised in the present by Col. Raymond (Peter Cushing), who somehow knows what's going on. Amidst all this, Ferguson's coworker girlfriend Debbie (Fiona Hutchison) has followed him to London to learn why he's behaving so strangely.

Thesping among the supporting cast, especially Biggles's mates (Michael Siberry, Daniel Flynn and James Saxon) is uniformly lively, but Neil Dickson as Biggles steals the film. A huskier, younger version of Peter O'Toole, he evokes a Biggles who's survived on wits and more than a little luck. Technically, pic is topnotch, especially aerial sequences using vintage biplanes.

•

BIG HANGOVER, THE
1950, 82 mins, US Ⓥ b/w
Dir Norman Krasna ***Prod*** Norman Krasna ***Scr*** Norman Krasna ***Ph*** George Folsey ***Ed*** Fredrick Y. Smith ***Mus*** Adolph Deutsch
Act Van Johnson, Elizabeth Taylor, Percy Waram, Fay Holden, Leon Ames, Edgar Buchanan (M-G-M)

Norman Krasna, as writer-director-producer, does a good job. Film gets a little too cute at times, and has a few dull stretches, but neither happens often enough to be serious.

Story is that of a young idealist, graduating from law school and about to enter a rich, socialite law firm. He has a peculiar allergy—to liquor—the result of being trapped in a wine cellar during a bombing, and almost drowning in a flood of brandy.

Meantime, the daughter of the law firm's senior partner, who fancies herself an amateur psychiatrist, has taken the law grad in hand to cure him of his drink allergy, with the inevitable romantic complications.

Elizabeth Taylor is warm and appealing as the amateur psychiatrist. Van Johnson, too, is rather subdued and serious here, to just as an warming effect.

•

BIG HEART, THE
SEE: MIRACLE ON 34TH STREET

•

BIG HEAT, THE
1953, 89 mins, US Ⓥ ⊙ b/w
Dir Fritz Lang ***Prod*** Robert Arthur ***Scr*** Sydney Boehm ***Ph*** Charles Lang ***Ed*** Charles Nelson ***Mus*** Daniele Amfitheatrof ***Art*** Robert Peterson
Act Glenn Ford, Gloria Grahame, Jocelyn Brando, Alexander Scourby, Lee Marvin, Jeanette Nolan (Columbia)

The picture starts with a tight, believable screenplay by Sydney Boehm, based on the William P. McGivern *SatEvePost* serial, and goes on from there through tense, forceful direction by Fritz Lang and top-notch trouping led by Glenn Ford.

It's the story of a cop, a homicide sergeant, who busts up the crime syndicate strangling his city and its administration. Because he prefers to do his job and collect his pay honestly, he finds the going tough. So tough that his wife is murdered by an auto bomb intended for him, his child is threatened with kidnapping, and he loses his police job because of pressure from higher-ups.

Ford's portrayal of the homicide sergeant is honest and packs much wallop. Lang's direction builds taut suspense, throwing unexpected, and believable, thrills at the audience.

Gloria Grahame's character, that of a gangster's sweetie, is choice and she makes it a colorful, important part of the picture.

Alexander Scourby, the man who heads the corrupt syndicate; Lee Marvin, his chief lieutenant; and Jeanette Nolan, the widow of a crooked cop who blackmails the syndicate, turn in strong individual performances.

•

BIG HOUSE, THE
1930, 84 mins, US b/w
Dir George Hill ***Scr*** Frances Marion, Joe Farnham, Martin Flavin ***Ph*** Harold Wenstrom ***Ed*** Blanche Sewell ***Art*** Cedric Gibbons, Frederic Hope
Act Chester Morris, Wallace Beery, Lewis Stone, Robert Montgomery, Leila Hyams, Karl Dane (Cosmopolitan)

As Butch, Morgan and Kent, Wallace Beery, Chester Morris and Robert Montgomery are a great trio in "the big house," where each is serving a stretch for homicide, forgery and manslaughter, respectively.

Prison life on the half shell is plainly exposed. The big wallop is the prison revolt, resulting in several deaths and an expose of how the officials deal with foolhardy prisoners. The hand grenades, barrages, stench bombs, tractor attacks and other means to conquer rebellious prisoners, with variations in the dungeon, etc, are all graphically dovetailed into the tense story.

1929/30: Best Writing (Frances Marion), Sound

NOMINATIONS: Best Picture, Actor (Wallace Beery)

•

BIG JAKE
1971, 109 mins, US Ⓥ col
Dir George Sherman ***Prod*** Michael A. Wayne ***Scr*** Harry Julian Fink, R. M. Fink ***Ph*** William H. Clothier ***Ed*** Harry Gerstad ***Mus*** Elmer Bernstein ***Art*** Carl Anderson
Act John Wayne, Richard Boone, Maureen O'Hara, Patrick Wayne, Christopher Mitchum, Bruce Cabot (Batjac)

Big Jake is an extremely slick and commercial John Wayne starrer, this time as a long-gone husband out to rescue a grandson from kidnapper Richard Boone.

Harry Julian Fink and R. M. Fink's original story and script is well-structured and fleshed with solid dialogue. It opens with a ten-person slaughter 13 minutes into the film. Maureen O'Hara, as a strong-willed woman whose husband (Wayne) has long since departed, sends for him to track down Boone's gang which has kidnapped grandson John Ethan Wayne (the star's own eight-year-old son). Sons Patrick Wayne and Christopher Mitchum mature, in a manner of speaking, when they team up with their father. Bruce Cabot's performance as an Indian scout is excellent.

There is gore spattered all over the screen. A Wayne film doesn't have to resort to such excess. Performances are totally professional. Wayne and Boone snarl extremely well at each other. Patrick Wayne handles his role with a fine cockiness. Mitchum is very good. Bobby Vinton plays another son who has little footage.

•

BIG JIM MCLAIN
1952, 90 mins, US Ⓥ ⊙ col
Dir Edward Ludwig ***Prod*** Robert Fellows ***Scr*** James Edward Grant, Richard English, Eric Taylor ***Ph*** Archie Stout ***Ed*** Jack Murray ***Mus*** Emil Newman ***Art*** Alfred Ybarra
Act John Wayne, Nancy Olson, James Arness, Alan Napier, Veda Ann Borg, Hans Conried (Wayne-Fellows/Warner)

Honolulu forms the setting for a story of the work to expose Communist activities. The picture was rushed into the market and bears evidence of that haste. Continuity is choppy, the script sketchy and lacking in clarity.

John Wayne and James Arness are crack investigators for the House Committee on un-American Activities. When it is learned the Communists are threatening in the islands, the pair is dispatched there to get evidence against the Red cells that can be used for a documented public hearing.

The investigation is tedious and not too fruitful. During its course Wayne meets and falls for Nancy Olson, a secretary working for a suspected doctor (Gayne Whitman). He pursues Olson and the Commies, gradually making time on both counts.

•

BIG KNIFE, THE
1955, 111 mins, US b/w
Dir Robert Aldrich ***Prod*** Robert Aldrich ***Scr*** James Poe ***Ph*** Ernest Laszlo ***Ed*** Michael Luciano ***Mus*** Frank DeVol ***Art*** William Glasgow
Act Jack Palance, Ida Lupino, Wendell Corey, Shelley Winters, Jean Hagen, Rod Steiger (Associates & Aldrich)

Film is of the *Sunset Blvd.* and *A Star Is Born* genre, an inside Hollywood story. It's sometimes so brittle and brutal as to prove disturbing. It differs from the Clifford Odets stage play of 1949, when John Garfield starred.

Rod Steiger vividly interprets the Janus aspects of the studio head who knows when to con and cajole Jack Palance into a 7-year deal. He has no compunction about staging an "accidental death" of one of those "casting couch contractees" (Shelley Winters), foiled by his laconic and resourceful publicity director.

Wendell Corey is properly "the cynical Celt," Steiger's resourceful hatchet man in the clinches. Ida Lupino scores as the realistic wife who wants Palance to forget the Hollywood loot and return to his "ideals."

•

BIG LEBOWSKI, THE
1998, 127 mins, US Ⓥ ⊙ col
Dir Joel Coen ***Prod*** Ethan Coen ***Scr*** Joel Coen, Ethan Coen ***Ph*** Roger Deakins ***Ed*** Roderick Jaynes, Tricia Cooke ***Mus*** Carter Burwell ***Art*** Rick Heinrichs
Act Jeff Bridges, John Goodman, Julianne Moore, Steve Buscemi, Peter Stormare, David Huddleston (Working Title/PolyGram)

Spiked with wonderfully funny sequences and some brilliantly original notions, *The Big Lebowski* adds up to considerably less than the sum of its often scintillating parts.

Not really a detective story, but taking the form of one with its v.o. narration and plot loaded with kidnapping, missing money, convoluted twists and turns, and evocative L.A. settings, pic throws several middle-aged men still mentally stuck in the '60s into a more mercenary '90s context.

Story clicks in immediately when the Dude (Jeff Bridges), whose real name is Lebowski, is beaten up by two goons looking for a multimillionaire known as the Big

Lebowski, whose wife owes their boss money. The Dude, goaded on by his Vietnam vet bowling buddy, Walter (John Goodman), tracks down the other Jeffrey Lebowski (David Huddleston) and meets his sexpot young wife, Bunny (Tara Reid). It isn't long before the Dude is paged by Lebowski to deliver a $1 million ransom for the return of his wife, who has been kidnapped.

In the interim, snappily paced film bowls a few frames with the Dude, Walter and their clueless pal Donny (Steve Buscemi). Walter insinuates himself into his friend's ransom return, then royally screws up. In the wake, the Dude is pulled into the multiple schemes of Lebowski's smart-tongued daughter (Julianne Moore), a provocative erotic artist, and the clutches of a big-time porno publisher (Ben Gazzara).

Bridges throws himself into the leading role with glee, and as the blustery Walter, Goodman is vastly entertaining. There is an astonishing cameo by John Turturro as a flamboyant Latin sex offender who suddenly turns up at the bowling alley.

•

BIG MAN, THE
(US: CROSSING THE LINE)
1990, 115 mins, UK Ⓥ ⦿ col
Dir David Leland ***Prod*** Stephen Wooley ***Scr*** Don MacPherson ***Ph*** Ian Wilson ***Ed*** George Akers ***Mus*** Ennio Morricone ***Art*** Caroline Amies
Act Liam Neeson, Joanne Whalley-Kilmer, Ian Bannen, Billy Connolly, Maurice Roeves, Hugh Grant (Palace/Miramax/BSB/British Screen)

Though unquestionably well-intentioned and determined not to pull any punches, *The Big Man* [from the book by William McIlvanney] has a depressing theme and ultraviolent conclusion.

The early scenes, set in a depressed Scottish village where an abandoned coal mine and mass unemployment reflect the aftermath of Britain's crippling miners' strike, look promising. Liam Neeson comes on strong as the unemployed Danny, who was imprisoned during the strike for hitting a policeman and now has a middle-class wife (Joanne Whalley-Kilmer) and two bright children to support.

His best friend, Frankie (an engaging "straight" turn from Scottish comedian Billy Connolly), acts as a runner for Mason (Ian Bannen), a corrupt businessman who needs Danny to fight for him. Motives for the fight, a bareknuckle affair with no rules, are obscure.

The fight, when it comes, is one of the most grueling ever caught on film. Top marks go to the makeup team, which provided the battered and bloodied faces for the actors.

•

BIG MOMMA'S HOUSE
2000, 98 mins, US ⦿ Ⓥ col
Dir Raja Gosnell ***Prod*** David T. Friendly, Michael Green ***Scr*** Darryl Quarles, Don Rhymer ***Ph*** Michael D. O'Shea ***Ed*** Bruce Green, Kent Beyda ***Mus*** Richard Gibbs ***Art*** Craig Stearns
Act Martin Lawrence, Nia Long, Paul Giamatti, Terrence Howard, Anthony Anderson, Ella Mitchell (Friendly-Runteldat/Regency/20th Century Fox)

A drag comedy laced with numerous low-comedy set pieces, *Big Momma's House* sees Martin Lawrence follow his former co-star Eddie Murphy into the salon for a heavy prosthetic makeover. This routine slice of warm-weather entertainment, about an FBI agent who poses as a 300-pound Southern granny in order to catch the bad guy, could have been funnier and considerably better made.

The sight and sound of Lawrence in fat-lady drag remains engaging throughout; script may often let him down, forcing him to keep things afloat almost single-handedly, but he's adept enough to pull off all but the thinnest interludes. Thanks to the extremely effective special makeup created by Greg Cannom and Captive Audience, the actor's looks and personality show through all the silicone, rubber and makeup, and the difference between his Big Momma and the real one is noticeable but subtle enough to allow the viewer to accept the charade.

Director Raja Gosnell goes for the obvious target every time, and the law of averages allows him to hit it every so often. Aside from the makeup work, production values are on the skimpy side, with studio-ish interiors and Southern California locations not convincing as Deep South substitutes. Soundtrack is crammed to overflowing with hip-hop and funk tunes that are collectively too abrasive and intrusive for a comedy.

•

BIG NIGHT, THE
1951, 70 mins, US b/w
Dir Joseph Losey ***Prod*** Philip A. Waxman ***Scr*** Joseph Losey, Stanley Ellin ***Ph*** Hal Mohr ***Ed*** Edward Mann ***Mus*** Lyn Murray ***Art*** Nicholas Remisoff
Act John Barrymore, Jr., Preston Foster, Joan Lorring, Howard St. John, Dorothy Comingore, Philip Bourneuf (Waxman/United Artists)

John Barrymore, Jr., is the star of this story, ineptly scripted by Stanley Ellin and Joseph Losey from Ellin's novel, *Dreadful Summit*. Losey's direction pars the writing and the playing is in keeping.

Plotline that can be sorted out of the muddled script gets underway on Barrymore's 17th birthday. Just as he is ready to enjoy a birthday cake supplied by his father (Preston Foster), the latter is brutally caned, without resisting, by Howard St John, a disliked sports columnist. Barrymore, disturbed by the incident, later that night takes a pistol from his father's bar and goes looking for St. John. Much footage, all lensed in such low-key lighting as to be almost obscure is involved with the people he encounters and side adventures during a night of wandering.

Young Barrymore is called upon to suffer extensively during his mental travail. Joan Lorring, a girl he meets during the night; Foster, St. John, Dorothy Comingore, Philip Bourneuf and the others in the cast provide no lift or interest.

•

BIG NOISE, THE
1928, 77 mins, US ⊗ b/w
Dir Allan Dwan ***Prod*** Robert T. Kane ***Scr*** Ben Hecht, Tom Geraghty
Act Chester Conklin, Alice White, Bodil Rosing, Sam Hardy, Jack Egan, Ned Sparks (First National)

There isn't a newspaperman anywhere who won't enjoy this picture. Whether it's a slap or burlesque on a tabloid daily's methods, or a sort of satirical dreamland idea of bringing a boob into the limelight, to let him sink back into the darkness of the tenement, it's fine either way. There is much sublety to it all of the while. Chester Conklin's playing is no small part of this.

The daily tab that uses Conklin's subway worker as a mark for its mayorality candidate is a constant laugh. When the daily—after Conklin has fallen off the subway platform and is nearly run over by a train but not hurt, going to a hospital because he is sleepy—goes to Conklin's home to get the big story complete, the reporters find the wife has but a grown-up daughter. So they send for the kids in the tenement and have a group picture taken, the kids bawling "We want our daddy," with the mother in the center. When Conklin sees the picture in the paper, he rubs his head, saying to a nurse, "How long have I been here?"

•

BIG PARADE, THE
1925, 150 mins, US Ⓥ ⦿ ⊗ b/w
Dir King Vidor ***Scr*** Laurence Stallings, Harry Behn, Joseph W. Farnham ***Ph*** John Arnold ***Ed*** Hugh Wynn ***Mus*** David Mendoza, William Axt ***Art*** Cedric Gibbons, James Basevi
Act John Gilbert, Renee Adoree, Hobart Bosworth, Claire McDowell, Claire Adams, Karl Dane (M-G-M)

King Vidor had a tough subject to deal with. He knew that he would have to show the horrors of war, and therefore worked his story out in such a manner that it has plenty of comedy relief and a love sequence.

John Gilbert's performance is a superb thing, while Renée Adoree, as the little French peasant, figuratively lives the role. The same may as well be said for Karl Dane and Tom O'Brien, for it is the excellent work of all these players and the manner in which Vidor has handled them that lift this production far above the ordinary.

Teamwork has made this picture. It makes 'em laugh, cry and it thrills—plenty. Besides which the captions are an example and a lesson of how it should be done.

The continuity is replete with little things that ordinarily wouldn't draw attention. For example, while a company of infantry is advancing a German machine gun opens up and sprays the line. Four or five men drop and the middle private of the group becomes rooted to the ground in terror, with his knees trembling.

•

BIG PICTURE, THE
1989, 99 mins, US Ⓥ col
Dir Christopher Guest ***Prod*** Michael Varhol ***Scr*** Michael Varhol, Christopher Guest, Michael McKean ***Ph*** Jeff Jur ***Ed*** Marty Nicholson ***Mus*** David Nichtern ***Art*** Joseph Garrity
Act Kevin Bacon, Emily Longstreth, J. T. Walsh, Jennifer Jason Leigh, Martin Short, Michael McKean (Aspen/Columbia)

The Big Picture is a surprisingly genial, good-natured satire on contemporary Hollywood mores, one of the last pics made under the David Puttnam regime at Columbia.

Christopher Guest's debut feature as helmer is loaded with detail. Industryites will want to decide for themselves whether the spider woman studio executive is really a nasty portrait of Dawn Steel, delight in the devastating sight gags about colorization, and roar at (unbilled) Martin Short's merciless impersonation of a flaky agent.

Befitting two of the coauthors of *This Is Spinal Tap*, Guest and Michael McKean, *The Big Picture* displays a keen eye for the silliness of film biz customs, lingo and attitudes. Pic also makes the point that success in Hollywood bears only a coincidental relationship to talent and can't rationally be explained.

Kevin Bacon and Emily Longstreth are appealing enough in the leads, but it is in the supporting roles that things come alive, thanks also to Jennifer Jason Leigh, almost unrecognizable as an avant-garde hip-hoppy dancer, J. T. Walsh as the super-cool but shallow studio boss, and Teri Hatcher as the starlet with a perfect body.

Cameos by the likes of John Cleese, Elliott Gould, Eddie Albert, June Lockhart, Roddy McDowall and Stephen Collins help root the picture in its setting. Tracy Brooks Swope's icy blond studio chief appears only briefly and would seem to have little to do with Columbia's current boss.

•

BIG RED ONE, THE
1980, 111 mins, US Ⓥ ⦿ col
Dir Samuel Fuller ***Prod*** Gene Corman ***Scr*** Samuel Fuller ***Ph*** Adam Greenberg ***Ed*** David Bretherton, Morton Tubor ***Mus*** Dana Kaproff ***Art*** Peter Jamison
Act Lee Marvin, Mark Hamill, Robert Carradine, Bobby DiCicco, Stephane Audran, Kelly Ward (Lorimar)

The Big Red One was two years in the making and 35 years in Samuel Fuller's head. It's a terrific war yarn, a picture of palpable raw power which manages both intense intimacy and great scope at the same time. The story of the First Infantry Division's exploits in North Africa and Europe between 1942–45, fast-paced pic attempts to tell entire story of the European land war through the eyes of five foot soldiers and pulls it off to a great degree.

Based on the writer-director's own experiences as a GI, pic was announced as a John Wayne-starrer in the late 1950s and came close to realization on many other occasions, but only came together when producer Gene Corman found means to make it almost entirely in Israel.

Approach eschews usual sociological analysis used in many war pix. These men are there for one reason only, to survive the war.

•

BIG SKY, THE
1952, 122 mins, US Ⓥ b/w
Dir Howard Hawks ***Prod*** Howard Hawks ***Scr*** Dudley Nichols ***Ph*** Russell Harlan ***Ed*** Christian Nyby ***Mus*** Dimitri Tiomkin ***Art*** Albert S. D'Agostino, Perry Ferguson
Act Kirk Douglas, Dewey Martin, Elizabeth Threatt, Arthur Hunnicutt, Hank Worden, Jim Davis (Winchester/RKO)

Howard Hawks has spared nothing in the filming of A. B. Guthrie, Jr.'s, novel, *The Big Sky*, except the cutting shears. Pic is a gigantic outdoor epic, but its impact is dissipated by the marathon running time. [Version reviewed ran 138 mins. Pic was subsequently cut by RKO soon after initial release in major cities.]

Kirk Douglas is cast as a Kentucky mountaineer. Story involves his joining a keelboat expedition up the Missouri river in the 1830s. Story line centers on the 1,200-mile trek up the Missouri from St. Louis to the Blackfoot Indian tribe in the northwest. Expedition is headed by French fur trader, Jourdonnais, excellently played by Steven Geray. The long trip is filled with the usual obstacles, warring Indians, treacherous white men, nature's forces, etc.

Femme interest is supplied by newcomer Elizabeth Threatt, who plays the daughter of a Blackfoot chief being returned to her tribe by Geray.

1952: NOMINATIONS: Best Supp. Actor (Arthur Hunnicutt), B&W Cinematography

•

BIG SLEEP, THE
1946, 113 mins, US Ⓥ ⦿ b/w
Dir Howard Hawks ***Prod*** Howard Hawks ***Scr*** William Faulkner, Leigh Brackett, Jules Furthman, [Philip Epstein] ***Ph*** Sid Hickox ***Ed*** Christian Nyby ***Mus*** Max Steiner ***Art*** Carl Jules Weyl
Act Humphrey Bogart, Lauren Bacall, John Ridgely, Martha Vickers, Dorothy Malone, Peggy Knudsen (Warner)

Brittle Chandler characters have been transferred to the screen with punch by Howard Hawks's production and direction, providing full load of rough, tense action most of the way.

Humphrey Bogart as Philip Marlowe and Lauren Bacall as Vivian, Marlowe's chief romantic interest, make a smooth team to get over the amatory play and action in the script. Hawks has given story a staccato pace in the development, using long stretches of dialogless action and then whipping in fast talk between characters. This helps to punch home high spots of suspense, particularly in latter half of picture.

Chandler plot deals with adventures of Bogart when he takes on a case for the eccentric Sternwood family. There are six deaths to please whodunit fans, plenty of lusty action, both romantic and physical, as Bogart matches wits with dealers in sex literature, blackmail, gambling and murder. Before he closes his case he has dodged sudden death, been unmercifully beaten, threatened, fought off mad advances of one of the Sternwood females, and fallen in love with another.

Some good scenes are tossed to others in the cast. Dorothy Malone, a bookshop proprietress, has her big moment in a sequence shot with sex implications as she goes on the make for Bogart.

[In 1996 a 116-min. version, containing 18 mins. of previously unseen footage, a clearer plot, and less of Lauren Bacall, was unearthed. This had been shown to U.S. troops overseas in 1945; subsequently, in early 1946, Warner had shot extra material for the final release version.]

•

BIG SLEEP, THE
1978, 99 mins, UK Ⓥ ⦿ col
Dir Michael Winner ***Prod*** Elliott Kastner, Michael Winner ***Scr*** Michael Winner ***Ph*** Robert Paynter ***Ed*** Freddie Wilson ***Mus*** Jerry Fielding ***Art*** Harry Pottle
Act Robert Mitchum, Sarah Miles, Richard Boone, Candy Clark, Joan Collins, Edward Fox (United Artists)

Howard Hawks's lusty, if confusing, 1946 filming of Raymond Chandler's *The Big Sleep* takes on even more filmic history in light of this remake which transplants from 1940s California to 1970s London. The move denatures the Chandler environment. Robert Mitchum encores as he did in the 1975 *Farewell My Lovely* remake.

Mitchum is hired by wealthy cripple James Stewart to probe possible blackmail. This leads him into the tangled lives of the client's daughters—seminympho Candy Clark and the more mature Sarah Miles. Latter has a relationship with gambler Oliver Reed whose wife Diana Quick has disappeared. Edward Fox was once in love with Clark; he is killed by Simon Turner. Bookstore staff includes Joan Collins. Weak-willed Colin Blakely is no match for hit man Richard Boone.

As for the police, the shift to London introduces John Mills, Richard Todd and James Donald. Back at the mansion, butler Harry Andrews acts officiously, while chauffeur Martin Potter dies in attempt to help Clark avoid implication in pornographer John Justin's murder; she has been posing for nude pix.

The production is handsome, but in the updating and relocation a lot has been lost. In particular, gone is the 1940s LA feel. Only Clark seems to project the requisite spoiled-rotten youthful spark. Nearly every other principal seems beyond the point of really caring.

•

BIG SQUEEZE, THE
1996, 82 mins, US Ⓥ col
Dir Marcus De Leon ***Prod*** Zane W. Levitt, Mark Yellen, Liz McDermott ***Scr*** Marcus De Leon ***Ph*** Jacques Haitkin ***Ed*** Sonny Baskin ***Mus*** Mark Mothersbaugh ***Art*** J. Rae Fox
Act Peter Dobson, Lara Flynn Boyle, Luca Bercovici, Danny Nucci, Teresa Dispina, Sam Vlahos (Zeta)

A film noir formula is updated to modern, multicultural LA and played mostly for sophisticated laughs in *The Big Squeeze*, a well-judged ensemble piece that manages to be steamy and satirical at the same time.

Veteran cable helmer Marcus De Leon takes a stock set of characters and gives them a fresh spin with his witty, light-fingered script, which centers on a Chicano bar where Tanya (Lara Flynn Boyle) pops Coronas behind the bar while husband Henry (Luca Bercovici), once a promising baseball player, sits on his duff. Tanya really gets miffed when she accidentally discovers that he's also sitting on $130,000 in disability money he never bothered to mention.

Enter Benny (Peter Dobson), an indigent yet slick opportunist who hits on the slinky barmaid and, when rebuffed, looks to her peppery co-worker (Teresa Dispina) for a safe haven. Tanya herself bunks in, platonically, with Jesse (Danny Nucci), a soulful-eyed young gardener who's secretly in love with her. She puts out feelers to Benny to see if they can hook hubby in a handy sting. True to noir-scam form, Benny soon has Jesse drawn into his nefarious plan (unbeknownst to Tanya), and it's not long before all are at one another's throats.

What makes this work is that De Leon immediately establishes a breezy, nonviolent tone and sticks to it without sacrificing atmosphere or tension. He throws a lot of balls in the air and keeps them juggling right to the end, which offers a pleasing twist few will see coming. The cast is also carefully balanced, with their marked contrasts used to good effect.

•

BIG STEAL, THE
1949, 78 mins, US Ⓥ ⦿ b/w
Dir Don Siegel ***Prod*** Jack J. Gross ***Scr*** Geoffrey Homes, Gerald Drayson Adams ***Ph*** Harry J. Wild ***Ed*** Samuel F. Beetley ***Mus*** Leigh Harline
Act Robert Mitchum, Jane Greer, William Bendix, Patric Knowles, Ramon Novarro (RKO)

Steal was lensed on location in and around Mexico City. It gains added sight interest from this, as well as strengthened melodramatics. It takes a little time for an audience to sort out what all the shootin's about since the script dives immediately into its story without explanatory footage.

When it does become clear the interest is strong as director Don Siegel unfolds a good chase yarn. Dialog is often racy and saucy, sharpening Jane Greer's s.a. factors.

Footage is one long chase through Mexico. Robert Mitchum is chasing Patric Knowles and, in turn, is being chased by William Bendix. All are interested in a $300,000 army payroll, stolen from Mitchum by Knowles.

There's a nifty performance by Ramon Novarro as the hep Mexican police officer.

•

BIG STEAL, THE
1990, 100 mins, Australia col
Dir Nadia Tass ***Prod*** Nadia Tass, David Parker ***Scr*** David Parker ***Ph*** David Parker ***Ed*** Peter Carrodus ***Art*** Paddy Reardon
Act Ben Mendelsohn, Claudia Karvan, Steve Bisley, Marshall Napier, Tim Robertson (Cascade)

The third feature from husband-and-wife team Nadia Tass and David Parker has a low-key charm that's appealing, and a couple of riotously funny scenes.

Ben Mendelsohn is Danny, a shy 18-year-old who wants two things: to own a Jaguar and to date Joanna (Claudia Karvan). Danny's father (Marshall Napier in a rich comic performance) gives him a car for his birthday, but it's a 1963 Nissan Cedric the family has owned for years. Danny decides to trade this in for a 1973 Jag in time for his first date. Trouble is that car dealer Gordon Farkas (Steve Bisley giving a splendidly sleazy performance) is a crook who's switched engines on Danny. He and his mates decide to hit back by lifting the engine from Farkas's Jag while he's having a drunken time at a sex club.

Teens here are incredibly unsophisticated compared to 18-year-olds in Hollywood teen comedies, and that's part of the film's charm. Mendelsohn and Karvan are quite sweet in their roles.

•

BIG STORE, THE
1941, 94 mins, US Ⓥ b/w
Dir Charles Riesner ***Prod*** Louis K. Sidney ***Scr*** Sid Kuller, Hal Fimberg, Ray Golden ***Ph*** Charles Lawton ***Ed*** Conrad A. Nervig ***Mus*** Georgie Stoll (dir.), Earl Brent (adapt.) ***Art*** Cedric Gibbons, Stan Rogers
Act Groucho Marx, Chico Marx, Harpo Marx, Tony Martin, Virginia Grey, Margaret Dumont (M-G-M)

A large department store serves as background for this display of familiar Marxian comedy, the final film appearance of Groucho, Chico and Harpo as a combo [from a screen story by Nat Perrin].

Groucho gets a job as bodyguard-detective for Tony Martin, coowner of the store, when manager Douglass Dumbrille tries to get Martin out of the way. The freres Marx then proceed to romp through the store in their usual slaphappy manner, taking advantage of the numerous props available for comedy purposes. There's the ususal chase through the aisles at the finish which catches plenty of laughs with its speedy display of ribald Sennettian knockabout slapstick.

Martin is okay in the straight role, delivering his vocal assignments satisfactorily. Others in support include Margaret Dumont, who continues as femme foil for Groucho's amorous approaches.

Direction by Charles Riesner takes advantage of every opportunity for basic slapstick—the broader the better. Harp solo by Harpo, staged between mirrors to obtain unusual effects both musically and comedically, is most original.

•

BIG STREET, THE
1942, 88 mins, US Ⓥ b/w
Dir Irving Reis ***Prod*** Damon Runyon ***Scr*** Leonard Spigelgass ***Ph*** Russell Metty ***Ed*** William Hamilton ***Mus*** Roy Webb
Act Henry Fonda, Lucille Ball, Agnes Moorehead, Barton MacLane, Eugene Pallette, Sam Levene (RKO)

Taken from a *Collier* mag story [*Little Pinks*] by Damon Runyon, this is a Cinderella-like fable of a Broadway café-singing gold digger who becomes more human long after a fall cripples her for life. Scripter Leonard Spigelgass makes the transition from the grasping, selfish little beauty to a bitter disillusioned girl entirely lifelike albeit a prolonged affair. He's done a neat job of transferring the spirit of the piece to the screen, studding it with typical Runyon humor.

Lucille Ball, cast at first in an unsympathetic role, comes through with high laurels. Henry Fonda, as the mooning but intensely loyal Little Pinks, is at his best. Eugene Pallette is well teamed with Agnes Moorehead, the food-loving but realistic Violette whom he weds.

•

BIG TIME OPERATORS
SEE: THE SMALLEST SHOW ON EARTH

•

BIG TOP PEE-WEE
1988, 86 mins, US Ⓥ ⦿ col
Dir Randal Kleiser ***Prod*** Paul Reubens, Debra Hill ***Scr*** Paul Reubens, George McGrath ***Ph*** Steven Poster ***Ed*** Jeff Gourson ***Mus*** Danny Elfman ***Art*** Stephen Marsh
Act Pee-wee Herman [= Paul Reubens], Kris Kristofferson, Valeria Golino, Penelope Ann Miller, Susan Tyrrell, Terrence Mann (Paramount)

Big Top Pee-wee again demonstrates that Peewee Herman is one very strange screen personality; he previously scored with his 1985 feature debut, *Pee-wee's Big Adventure*.

Surrounded by animals as strange as himself, Herman pursues a career in agricultural extravagance with the help of his goggled talking pig Vincent (amusingly voiced by Wayne White). Together, they grow outsized vegetables and a hot dog tree while wanly romancing pretty Penelope Ann Miller.

A storm brings a broken-down circus to Herman's farm, adding a menagerie of freakish animals and people to his already curious collection. Kris Kristofferson oversees the visitors and keeps them rallied with hearty circus sayings, along with explanations of how he came to marry his miniature wife (Susan Tyrrell) whom he carries around in his pocket.

Very little of this is interesting or amusing on paper, which must have been a real challenge to director Randal Kleiser, who ably keeps all the surrounding players in tune to whatever it is that Herman's up to at any given moment.

•

BIG TRAIL, THE
1930, 125 mins, US Ⓥ ▭ b/w
Dir Raoul Walsh ***Scr*** Jack Peabody, Marie Boyle, Florence Postal ***Ph*** Lucien Andriot, Don Anderson, Bill McDonald, Roger Sherman, Bobby Mack, Henry Pollack, (35mm version) Arthur Edeson, Dave Ragin, Sol Halprin, Curt Fetters, Max Cohn ***Ed*** Jack Dennis ***Mus*** Arthur Kay ***Art*** Harold Miles, Fred Sersen
Act John Wayne, Marguerite Churchill, El Brendel, Tully Marshall, Tyrone Power, Sr., David Rollins (Fox)

A big-screen effort [based on a story by Hal G. Evarts] and an elegantly directed job by Raoul Walsh. But the recurrence of the same things, interrupted now and then by a "big scene," such as the river or cliff crossing, or El Brendel's dragged-in comedy with his mother-in-law, or the simple romance and the silly melodrama, commences to weary. This leaves the historical portion, the Oregon trail, as the single interesting part.

Young John Wayne, wholly inexperienced, shows it, but also suggests he can be built up. He certainly has a great start as the lead role in a $2 million production.

Marguerite Churchill is set much in the same key, with not a great deal to do. Hers is mostly a silent role through being continually in a scrap with her sweetheart (Wayne) and not speaking to him.

The widescreen Grandeur [process] seems to dim the photography; leaves ensemble scenes indistinct, except for figure or form.

•

BIG TROUBLE IN LITTLE CHINA
1986, 99 mins, US Ⓥ ⦿ ▭ col
Dir John Carpenter ***Prod*** Larry J. Franco ***Scr*** Gary Goldman, David Z. Weinstein, W. D. Richter ***Ph*** Dean Cundey ***Ed*** Mark Warner, Steve Mirkovich, Edward A. Warschilka ***Mus*** John Carpenter ***Art*** John J. Lloyd
Act Kurt Russell, Kim Cattrall, Dennis Dun, James Hong, Victor Wong, Kate Burton (20th Century-Fox)

Story is promising, involving an ancient Chinese magician Lo Pan (James Hong) who controls an evil empire beneath San Francisco's Chinatown while he searches to find a green-eyed Chinese beauty to mate with and make him mortal.

Director John Carpenter seems to be trying to make an action-adventure along the lines of *Indiana Jones and the Temple of Doom*. The effect goes horribly awry.

Leading the cast is Kurt Russell who looks embarrassed, and should be, playing his CB philosophizing truck driver character as a cross between a swaggering John Wayne, adventurous Harrison Ford and wacky Bill Murray.

He's caught in Hong's supposedly ghostly underworld with restaurateur friend Wang Chi (Dennis Dun) while trying to rescue Wang's green-eyed Chinese fiancée, Miao Yin (Suzee Pai), from Hong's lascivious clutches.

•

BIG WEDNESDAY

1978, 126 mins, US Ⓥ ⦿ ▭ col

Dir John Milius ***Prod*** Buzz Feitshans ***Scr*** John Milius, Dennis Aaberg ***Ph*** Bruce Surtees ***Ed*** Robert L. Wolfe, Tim O'Meara ***Mus*** Basil Poledouris ***Art*** Charles Rosen

Act Jan-Michael Vincent, William Katt, Gary Busey, Patti D'Arbanville, Lee Purcell, Robert Englund (A-Team/Warner)

A rubber stamp wouldn't do for John Milius. So he took a sledgehammer and pounded IMPORTANT all over *Big Wednesday*. This film about three Malibu surfers in the 1960s has been branded major statement and it's got Big Ideas about adolescence, friendship and the 1960s.

Big Wednesday has a character named Bear, a combination John Milius–Ernest Hemingway, played by Sam Melville. He is described this way: "He knew where the waves came from and why." Really.

But Melville is a secondary character. The film revolves around three friends, Jan-Michael Vincent, William Katt and Gary Busey. Each is a noted surfer with Vincent something of a legend. Their life is surfing, but man—not even boy—cannot live by saltwater alone. So they grow up, awkwardly.

The movie is divided into four movements with each section moving ahead a few years. It climaxes at the final segment, Big Wednesday, when the surf has swelled to unknown proportions and the three reunite as men to again conquer the ocean.

•

BILL & TED'S BOGUS JOURNEY

1991, 98 mins, US Ⓥ ⦿ col

Dir Peter Hewitt ***Prod*** Scott Kroopf ***Scr*** Chris Matheson, Ed Solomon ***Ph*** Oliver Wood ***Ed*** David Finfer ***Mus*** David Newman ***Art*** David L. Snyder

Act Keanu Reeves, Alex Winter, William Sadler, Joss Ackland, Pam Grier, George Carlin (Interscope/Nelson)

In aptly named *Bill & Ted's Bogus Journey*, the characters of the dopey, sweet-spirited dudes from San Dimas, Calif, go undeveloped in a sequel that contrives another elaborate but nonexcellent adventure. Same producing and writing team pumps much effort into production design and special effects, creating a few triumphant moments, but not enough to sustain pic's running time.

This time, evil robot versions of Bill and Ted (Alex Winter and Keanu Reeves) have been sent from the future to kill the duo before their band, Wyld Stallyns, can win a local talent contest and inspire a Bill and Ted following that changes the world.

The "evil us's," as B&T call them, throw the good dudes off a cliff, but before the Grim Reaper can claim them, they get to try to beat him in a contest, and since they pick the games (Battleship, Clue, Twister), they win. His Royal Deathness (played by William Sadler in a takeoff on Ingmar Bergman's *The Seventh Seal*) is then at their service as they embark on an odyssey to try to overcome the evil robot dudes and win the battle of the bands.

These guileless airheads with the outrageous vocabulary are obviously a beloved creation, and filmmakers might have gotten more mileage if they'd rooted their adventure a bit more in reality.

•

BILL & TED'S EXCELLENT ADVENTURE

1989, 90 mins, US Ⓥ ⦿ ▭ col

Dir Stephen Herek ***Prod*** Scott Kroopf, Michael S. Murphey, Joel Soisson ***Scr*** Chris Matheson, Ed Solomon ***Ph*** Timothy Suhrstedt ***Ed*** Larry Bock, Patrick Rand, Duwayne Dunham ***Mus*** David Newman ***Art*** Roy Forge Smith

Act Keanu Reeves, Alex Winter, George Carlin, Terry Camilleri, Dan Shor (Nelson/Interscope)

Keanu Reeves (Ted) and Alex Winter (Bill) play San Dimas "dudes" so close they seem wired together.

Preoccupied with plans for "a most triumphant video" to launch their two-man rock band, The Wyld Stallyns, they're suddenly, as Bill put it, "in danger of flunking most heinously" out of history.

George Carlin appears as a cosmic benefactor who offers them a chance to travel back through history and gather up the speakers they need for an awesome presentation.

Through brief, perilous stops here and there, they end up jamming Napoleon, Billy The Kid, Sigmund Freud, Socrates, Joan of Arc, Genghis Khan, Abraham Lincoln and Mozart into their time-traveling phone booth. Each encounter is so brief and utterly cliched that history has little chance to contribute anything to this pic's two dimensions.

Reeves, with his beguilingly blank face and loose-limbed, happy-go-lucky physical vocabulary, and Winter, with his golden curls, gleefully good vibes and "bodacious" vocabulary, propel this adventure as long as they can.

•

BILLIE

1965, 86 mins, US Ⓥ ▭ col

Dir Don Weis ***Prod*** Don Weis ***Scr*** Ronald Alexander ***Ph*** John Russell ***Ed*** Adrienne Fazan ***Mus*** Dominic Frontiere ***Art*** Arthur Lonergan

Act Patty Duke, Jim Backus, Jane Greer, Warren Berlinger, Billy De Wolfe, Charles Lane (Chrislaw/United Artists)

Patty Duke stars as *Billie*, the tomboy who complicates her family life before shedding athletic gear for maiden attire.

Ronald Alexander adapted his *Time Out for Ginger* legiter of the early 1950s, cutting some characters to focus on Duke, the younger daughter of understanding Jane Greer and bumbling Jim Backus who shines in field meets via a mental gimmick. Coach Charles Lane uses her to goad his less proficient males, including Warren Berlinger to whom the gal eventually reveals her secret and gives her heart.

Complications, pat and unreal, include a mayoralty battle between Backus and Billy De Wolfe, wasted herein as a heavy who exploits pop's platform in terms of barbs at Billie and older sister Susan Seaforth. Latter pair stand out, as does Berlinger.

Backus is good in his now-standard characterization, while Greer is radiant and charming. Duke has an infectious personality which comes across.

•

BILLION DOLLAR BRAIN

1967, 111 mins, UK Ⓥ ▭ col

Dir Ken Russell ***Prod*** Harry Saltzman ***Scr*** John McGrath ***Ph*** Billy Williams ***Ed*** Alan Osbiston ***Mus*** Richard Rodney Bennett ***Art*** Syd Cain

Act Michael Caine, Karl Malden, Ed Begley, Oscar Homolka, Francoise Dorleac, Guy Doleman (United Artists)

Plot takes too long to get moving, and when it does it is quite incredible and hard to follow. Harry Palmer (Michael Caine) is instructed by an electronic voice over the phone to take a package containing mysterious eggs to Finland, and meets up with a former American CIA man, Ed Newbigin (Karl Malden), whose life he has saved in the past.

Palmer, whose mission is known to his previous MI5 employers, pretends to join the organization, which turns out to be controlled by a crazy American General (Ed Begley) with a Senator McCarthy attitude re Commies and a determination to defeat them by fomenting revolution in satellite countries and attacking with his own private army.

It doesn't matter so much that the story line offends belief—so do the Bond gambols—but it is deployed by director Ken Russell with such abrupt speed that it doesn't make immediate sense in its own frivolous terms.

Malden and Begley, always reliable, do what they can with roles conceived as stereotypes of greed and fanaticism respectively, and Francoise Dorleac introduces a touch of glamour as an agent who might be working for anybody.

•

BILL OF DIVORCEMENT, A

1932, 75 mins, US Ⓥ b/w

Dir George Cukor ***Scr*** Howard Estabrook, Harry Wagstaff Gribble ***Ph*** Sid Hickox ***Ed*** Arthur Roberts ***Mus*** Max Steiner ***Art*** Carroll Clark

Act John Barrymore, Billie Burke, Katharine Hepburn, David Manners, Bramwell Fletcher (Radio)

Standout here is the smash impression made by Katharine Hepburn in her first picture assignment. She has a vital something that sets her apart from the picture galaxy.

The play [of the same name by Clemence Dane] has lost none of its tremendous grip in translation to celluloid. Ten years after its stage success, this peculiarly British version of the Ibsen *Ghosts* theme still has power to grip and hold.

John Barrymore distinguishes himself anew in the role of the unhappy Hilary, a part far from his accustomed range. For Billie Burke, the role of the distracted wife holds out small promise of flourish and histrionic parade, but she looks miraculously fresh and young, giving much charm to the character of the secondary femme character. David Manners as the heroine's young sweetheart is another happy choice.

•

BILL OF DIVORCEMENT, A

1940, 70 mins, US b/w

Dir John Farrow ***Prod*** Lee Marcus ***Scr*** Dalton Trumbo ***Ph*** Nicholas Musuraca ***Ed*** Harry Marker

Act Maureen O'Hara, Adolphe Menjou, Fay Bainter, Herbert Marshall, May Whitty, C. Aubrey Smith (RKO)

Clemence Dane's play, originally turned out by RKO [in 1932], skyrocketed Katharine Hepburn into prominence and marquee lights. Maureen O'Hara, a capable Irish actress imported by Erich Pommer and Charles Laughton, essays the Hepburn role in this remake with utmost confidence and ability.

Story is of a woman's sacrifice of love, marriage, and an anticipated family in order to care for her demented father. Adolphe Menjou, escaping from an institution for the insane, returns to his English manor home on Xmas to find his wife has divorced him and is ready to remarry. His appearance upsets plans, including those of his young daughter (O'Hara) who is engaged to a young Australian.

O'Hara takes fullest advantage of a meaty role which is attention-arresting and rich in acting opportunity. Menjou provides an excellent characterization of the father (previously handled by John Barrymore). Fay Bainter delivers her usual warmful and sincere performance as the wife who falls in love with Herbert Marshall and gets a new start for happiness. May Whitty commands attention as the elderly Victorian aunt of the household.

Direction by John Farrow provides dramatic power in his handling of a delicate subject. Script by Dalton Trumbo is workmanlike, although here and there are found long dialogue stretches that carry over from the stage technique of the original play.

•

BILLY BATHGATE

1991, 106 mins, US Ⓥ ⦿ col

Dir Robert Benton ***Prod*** Arlene Donovan, Robert F. Colesberry ***Scr*** Tom Stoppard ***Ph*** Nestor Almendros ***Ed*** Alan Heim, Robert Reitano, David Ray ***Mus*** Mark Isham ***Art*** Patrizia Von Brandenstein

Act Dustin Hoffman, Nicole Kidman, Loren Dean, Bruce Willis, Steven Hill, Stanley Tucci (Touchstone)

This refined, intelligent drama about thugs appeals considerably to the head but has little impact in the gut, which is not exactly how it should be with gangster films. Robert Benton's screen version of *Billy Bathgate*, E. L. Doctorow's 1988 bestseller about the last act of Dutch Shultz's life, is beautifully realized and a pleasure to watch, but its center is hard to locate.

Returning to the 1930s criminal milieu for the first time since *Bonnie & Clyde*, Benton has invested the picture with extensive class and storytelling smarts, and the $40 million-plus production bears no signs of the rumored troubles of its making.

Tom Stoppard's tight, neatly arcing screenplay kicks off powerfully with Schultz (Dustin Hoffman), arguably the king of the New York underworld in 1935, taking his once-trusted top enforcer (Bruce Willis) for a nocturnal tugboat ride, tying him up and planting his feet in cement. Observing this showdown from close range is Billy (Loren Dean), a nervy kid who (as seen in an eventful 35-minute flashback) has worked his way up from the streets of the Bronx to become one of Dutch's valued flunkies. Dutch still may be prospering, but the Feds are moving in mercilessly.

All this is a backdrop to the personal drama that mainly concerns Billy earning a place in the gang and vowing to take care of the beautiful Drew Preston (Nicole Kidman), the dead enforcer's former girlfriend.

Despite Dean's alert, open performance, Billy remains an opaque witness to events that are unfolding over his head. Hoffman's performance also is problematic. There is a stiffness that sets his impersonation apart from his best contempo characterizations. Kidman comes on strongly, showing both girlish frivolousness and steely resolve in her portrait of the opportunistic Drew.

•

BILLY BUDD

1962, 123 mins, US/UK Ⓥ ▭ b/w

Dir Peter Ustinov ***Prod*** Peter Ustinov ***Scr*** Peter Ustinov, Robert Rossen ***Ph*** Robert Krasker ***Ed*** Jack Harris ***Mus*** Anthony Hopkins ***Art*** Don Ashton

Act Robert Ryan, Peter Ustinov, Melvyn Douglas, Terence Stamp, Ronald Lewis, David McCallum (Allied Artists)

Peter Ustinov's production of *Billy Budd* is a near miss, and Ustinov, alas, is the culprit. The ubiquitous Mr. U is to be commended for spearheading the noble effort to translate Herman Melville's highly regarded, thought-provoking last story to the screen—a difficult task. But as director he is guilty of at least one major flaw of execution in which Ustinov, the actor is most prominently implicated.

Billy Budd is the allegorical tale of the clash of an incredibly good-hearted young foretopman and an inhumanly sadistic master-at-arms aboard a British fighting vessel in 1797, and the issue of moral justice vs. the wartime military code that arises when the former is condemned to hang for killing the latter, though recognized even by those who sit in judgment upon him as being spirituallly innocent.

The clash between Budd and his tormentor, Claggart—archetypes of good and evil—has been carried off well by Terence Stamp and Robert Ryan under Ustinov's guidance. Where Ustinov has slipped is in the development and delineation of the character he himself plays—the overly conscientious Captain Vere, whose judgment in favor of military over moral ramifications of the issue sends Budd to his death.

1962: NOMINATION: Best Supp. Actor (Terence Stamp)

•

BILLY ELLIOT

2000, 111 mins, UK Ⓥ ⊙ col

Dir Stephen Daldry ***Prod*** Greg Brenman, Jon Finn ***Scr*** Lee Hall ***Ph*** Brian Tufano ***Ed*** John Wilson ***Mus*** Stephen Warbeck ***Art*** Maria Djurkovic

Act Julie Walters, Jamie Bell, Jamie Driven, Gary Lewis, Jean Heywood, Stuart Wells, Nicola Blackwell (Tiger Aspect/WT2/Universal)

Stephen Daldry makes all the right moves in his delightful debut feature. Winning story of a preteen lad from a poor mining family who dreams of becoming a ballet dancer strikes a delicate balance of comedy and pathos with an uplifting final act that delivers a resoundingly satisfying emotional payoff.

The leap into filmmaking of London's Royal Court Theater artistic director Daldry may not be quite so distinctive as fellow theater fixture Sam Mendes's with *American Beauty*. But together with screenwriter Lee Hall, he takes a triumph-over-adversity tale that could have been as blandly formulaic as *Flashdance* and resolutely refuses to travel the most predictable route.

Neither director nor scripter shy away from the story's sentimental aspects, but even while it milks tears, which it does in no small quantity, the deftly handled drama maintains a sufficiently gritty edge to avoid becoming cloying or saccharine. What makes *Billy Elliot* so refreshing is the warmly compassionate view of its characters, even the most unlikely of which undertake an emotional journey that steers them through conflict and animosity, ultimately to embrace the cause of the pirouetting underdog hero.

Appealing newcomer Jamie Bell sparks vibrantly to life in his spirited, amusingly unconventional dance routines choreographed by Peter Darling. Remaining cast is solid, especially an amusing turn from Julie Walters.

•

BILLY JACK

1971, 115 mins, US Ⓥ ⊙ col

Dir T. C. Frank [= Tom Laughlin] ***Prod*** Mary Rose Solti ***Scr*** T. C. Frank, Teresa Christina [= Delores Taylor] ***Ph*** Fred Koenekamp, John Stephens ***Ed*** Larry Heath, Marion Rothman ***Mus*** Mundell Lowe

Act Tom Laughlin, Delores Taylor, Clark Howat, Bert Freed, Julie Webb, Ken Tobey (National Student)

Billy Jack appears to be a labor of love in which the plight of the American Indian, are pinpointed.

Produced by National Student Film Corp, Warners bought picture outright. Leading character is a half-breed named Billy Jack, guardian of the Redman's rights and nemesis of any white who may intrude on these rights. He finds plenty of opportunity to assert himself, what with defending wild horses on the Arizona reservation, wild kids, a school on the reservation and the actions of residents of a neighboring town violently opposed both to the school and Billy himself.

Screenplay attempts to encompass too many story facets. Result is that the action frequently drags and interest palls as some of the young people in the school, many of them white, spout their philosophy and question the behavior of the whites.

Tom Laughlin, as the invincible defender, is first-rate, handling himself effectively. So, too, does Delores Taylor, a white woman who runs the school. Clark Howat, as the sheriff who understands the Indians' problems, is convincing.

•

BILLY JACK GOES TO WASHINGTON

1977, 155 mins, US ▭ col

Dir T. C. Frank [= Tom Laughlin] ***Prod*** Frank Capra, Jr. ***Scr*** T. C. Frank, Teresa Christina [= Delores Taylor] ***Ph*** Jack Marta ***Mus*** Elmer Bernstein ***Art*** Hilyard Brown

Act Tom Laughlin, Delores Taylor, E. G. Marshall, Teresa Laughlin, Sam Wanamaker, Lucie Arnaz (Taylor-Laughlin)

Billy Jack Goes to Washington, a remake of the 1939 Frank Capra classic *Mr. Smith Goes to Washington*, compensates for its lack of subtlety with an angry, attack on governmental corruption.

The corruption of the Senate in the Capra film is changed here to the issue of nuclear plants.

In the old James Stewart role of the innocent-turned-Senator, Tom Laughlin is fighting against the scheme of political boss Sam Wanamaker and corrupt fellow Senator E. G. Marshall to exploit a planned nuclear plant for their financial gain.

Laughlin, identified with activist groups, takes the same stand against the establishment Stewart did in the original.

By comparison with the brilliance of the Capra version, the pic is much flatter and largely devoid of performing or visual nuances.

•

BILLY LIAR

1963, 98 mins, UK Ⓥ ▭ b/w

Dir John Schlesinger ***Prod*** Joseph Janni ***Scr*** Keith Waterhouse, Willis Hall ***Ph*** Denys Coop ***Ed*** Roger Cherrill ***Mus*** Richard Rodney Bennett ***Art*** Ray Simm

Act Tom Courtenay, Julie Christie, Wilfred Pickles, Mona Washbourne, Finlay Currie, Rodney Bewes (Vic/Anglo-Amalgamated)

Based on a West End hit play by Keith Waterhouse (who wrote the novel) and Willis Hall, *Billy Liar* is an imaginative, fascinating film. It is perhaps unfair to label the film as entirely realistic, since it moves into a world of Walter Mitty-like fantasy, and that is its only weakness. These scenes lack impact.

Billy Liar (Tom Courtenay) is a daydreaming young man who leads an irresponsible life as a funeral director's clerk. He fiddles the petty cash, he is at war with his parents, he has become involved with two young women who share an engagement ring. Above all, he is an incorrigible liar, dreaming dreams and, whenever possible, retreating into an invented world where he is the dictator of an imagined slice of Ruritania.

Courtenay who took over from Albert Finney in the legit version of *Billy Liar*, has a hefty part and is rarely off the screen. Of the three girls with whom he is involved, Julie Christie is the only one who really understands him. Christie turns in a glowing performance. Helen Fraser and Gwendolyn Watts provide sharply contrasting performances as the other young women in Billy Liar's complicated, muddled existence.

Mona Washbourne, as his dim mother, Wilfred Pickles, playing a hectoring, stupid father, and grandmother Ethel Griffies also lend considerable color.

•

BILLY MADISON

1995, 89 mins, US Ⓥ col

Dir Tamra Davis ***Prod*** Robert Simonds ***Scr*** Tim Herlihy, Adam Sandler ***Ph*** Victor Hammer ***Ed*** Jeffrey Wolf ***Mus*** Randy Edelman ***Art*** Perry Blake

Act Adam Sandler, Darren McGavin, Bridgette Wilson, Bradley Whitford, Josh Mostel, Norm McDonald (Universal)

Saturday Night Live grad Adam Sandler's title character is the son of a hotel magnate (Darren McGavin) who slobs around a huge estate with his friends drinking beer, lounging in the pool and staging inane pranks. When his dad decides to retire, Billy—who slid through school on bribes—must pass all 12 grades, two weeks at a time, to prevent his father from leaving the company to an insidious aide (Bradley Whitford) who, of course, seeks to sabotage Billy's plan.

Sandler (who also scripted, with Tim Herlily) delivers the expected adult-among-children scenes and, unfortunately, plenty of material on the level of bodily excretions gags and gay jokes directed at the high school principle (Josh Mostel). They tend to obscure some of the more clever bits, such as an impromptu musical number, a swipe at *The Godfather Part II* and an extended smooch planted by Billy on an 8-by-10 picture of the teacher (Bridgette Wilson) for whom he pines.

Sandler and director Tamra Davis bring a certain manic energy and no-holds-barred attitude to the proceedings but still feel like they're stretching sketch material to feature length.

•

BILLY ROSE'S JUMBO

SEE: JUMBO

•

BILLY THE KID

1930, 95 mins, US ▭ b/w

Dir King Vidor ***Scr*** Wanda Tuchock, Laurence Stallings, Charles MacArthur ***Ph*** Gordon Avil ***Ed*** Hugh Wynn ***Art*** Cedric Gibbons

Act John Mack Brown, Wallace Beery, Kay Johnson, Karl Dane, Wyndham Standing, Russell Simpson (M-G-M)

Metro turned this one out on Realife—shooting with a 70mm camera [negative] after which the result is reduced to 35mm for the projectors on which a special lens supposedly brings out all the condensed details on an enlarged screen. It spreads across the stage in the same oblong shape as Fox's Grandeur [process, used for *The Big Trail*, also 1930]. The panoramic exteriors all look good. Director King Vidor evidently wanted to impress that fact early for the initial shot is an imposing peek of what may be the Grand Canyon.

Billy the Kid [from the book *The Saga of Billy the Kid* by Walter Noble Burns] is replete with gunfights and anticlimaxes. At least on two occasions it looks as if the feature is finished—but it keeps right on going. There's little or no love interest, albeit the script intimates that the Kid would like to fall for best friend's wife. That her fiance is shot on their wedding day is the reason the Kid swears vengeance upon one-half of the State of New Mexico and they have to call in the cavalry to halt his ensuing feud with the Donovan mob.

•

BILLY TWO HATS

1974, 99 mins, US Ⓥ col

Dir Ted Kotcheff ***Prod*** Norman Jewison, Patrick Palmer ***Scr*** Alan Sharp ***Ph*** Brian West ***Mus*** John Scott ***Art*** Tony Pratt

Act Gregory Peck, Desi Arnaz, Jr., Jack Warden, Sian Barbara Allen, David Huddleston, John Pearce (Algonquin)

This is a fresh, different oater (the first filmed in Israel) that opens with violence and contains some throughout but never lingers lovingly on mayhem and gore.

A Scot and a young half-Indian (Billy Two Hats, because his white father was an important man) commit a robbery with an unintended murder that nets them only $420. They get away, but the far-off Scot is shot in the leg with a buffalo gun. The lad makes a rough stretcher and hauls him behind his horse. They stop at the home of an old rancher with a young wife he'd bought for $100 in St. Louis.

Gregory Peck, almost unrecognizable behind a broad Highland brogue and a bushy beard, is splendid. Desi Arnaz, Jr., as the "breed" treated with contempt by almost everyone, is okay and shows promise.

•

BILOXI BLUES

1988, 106 mins, US Ⓥ ⊙ ▭ col

Dir Mike Nichols ***Prod*** Ray Stark ***Scr*** Neil Simon ***Ph*** Bill Butler ***Ed*** Sam O'Steen ***Mus*** Georges Delerue ***Art*** Paul Sylbert

Act Matthew Broderick, Christopher Walken, Matt Mulhern, Michael Dolan, Penelope Ann Miller, Markus Flanagan (Rastar/Universal)

Biloxi Blues is an agreeable but hardly inspired film version of Neil Simon's second installment of his autobiographical trilogy, which bowed during the 1984–85 season. Even with high-powered talents Mike Nichols and Matthew Broderick aboard, World War II barracks comedy provokes just mild laughs and smiles rather than the guffaws Simon's work often elicits in the theater.

Film is narrated from an adult perspective by Simon's alter ego, Eugene Morris Jerome (Broderick), an aspiring writer called up for service in the waning months of the war.

With 10 weeks of boot camp ahead of them, it's not at all sure that Eugene and his cohorts will ever see action, but that doesn't prevent basic training from being a living hell relieved only by an excursion into town to party and look for ladies.

Playing a character perched precisely on the point between adolescence and manhood, Broderick is enjoyable all the way.

Penelope Ann Miller is adorable as the girl who inspires love at first sight in Eugene at a dance, while the most intriguing performance comes from Christopher Walken as the weird sergeant.

•

BINGO LONG TRAVELING ALL-STARS AND MOTOR KINGS, THE

1976, 110 mins, US Ⓥ col

Dir John Badham ***Prod*** Rob Cohen ***Scr*** Hal Barwood, Matthew Robbins ***Ph*** Bill Butler ***Ed*** David Rawlins ***Mus*** William Goldstein ***Art*** Lawrence G. Paull

Act Billy Dee Williams, James Earl Jones, Richard Pryor, Rico Dawson, Sam "Birmingham" Brison, Jophery Brown (Motown/Pan-Arts)

Billy Dee Williams and James Earl Jones are superb as leaders of a barnstorming black baseball team circa 1939. Based on a William Brashler novel, the script is an adroit mix of broad comedy and credible dramatic conflict.

Fed up with the hard-nosed ways of team owner Ted Ross, Williams quits a team in the old Negro (remember the film's period) baseball league. Shut out of the league, and not yet admitted to mainstream sports, the slap-happy crew discovers success by combining top performance with farce. But Ross's goons (Ken Force and Carl Gordon) eventually get the upper hand.

Among the standout featured players is Richard Pryor, shifting amusingly from Cuban to Indian heritages as a way to break the black barrier.

•

BIRD

1988, 161 mins, US Ⓥ ⦿ col

Dir Clint Eastwood ***Prod*** Clint Eastwood ***Scr*** Joel Oliansky ***Ph*** Jack N. Green ***Ed*** Joel Cox ***Mus*** Lennie Niehaus ***Art*** Edward C. Carfagno

Act Forest Whitaker, Diane Venora, Michael Zelniker, Samuel E. Wright, Keith David (Malpaso/Warner)

In taking on a biopic of late jazz great Charlie Parker, Clint Eastwood has had to chart bold new territory for himself as a director, and he has pulled it off in most impressive fashion.

Sensitively acted, beautifully planned visually and dynamite musically, this is a dramatic telling of the troubled life of a revolutionary artist.

That Parker (Forest Whitaker), who died in 1955 at 34, was the greatest sax man of them all is virtually undisputed, but he also lived a messy, complicated life, mixing drug addiction and a multitude of women with an ongoing attempt at a home life with his wife Chan (Diane Venora) and their two children.

Joel Oliansky's big-framed script, originally written for Richard Pryor at Columbia some years earlier jumps around considerably at the beginning, skipping strikingly from Parker's Childhood to a suicide attempt in 1954, then to some other key incidents.

Naturally, the prolific artist's music provides the continuing thread for the film, and jazzman Lennie Niehaus does a sensational job in blending Bird's actual sax solos with fresh backups by contemporary musicians.

Whitaker makes an imposing, likable, very hip genius, with an especially memorable death scene. Venora is so riveting that her occasional long absences from the story are sorely missed. The one person who could really understand Bird is presented as a feisty woman of great character, awareness and strength.

1988: Best Sound

•

BIRDCAGE, THE

1996, 119 mins, US Ⓥ ⦿ col

Dir Mike Nichols ***Prod*** Mike Nichols ***Scr*** Elaine May ***Ph*** Emmanuel Lubezki ***Ed*** Arthur Schmidt ***Mus*** Jonathan Tunick ***Art*** Bo Welch

Act Robin Williams, Gene Hackman, Nathan Lane, Dianne Wiest, Hank Azaria, Christine Baranski (United Artists)

The Birdcage is a scream. It may not have seemed that the world needed a remake of *La Cage aux Folles*, the 1978 French smash hit that spawned two sequels plus a Broadway musical, but Mike Nichols and Elaine May, in their first official screen collaboration, have scored with a riotous comedy whose irreverent topicality is one of its most refreshing components.

Armand (Robin Williams) runs the hugely successful boite, where the family-oriented drag revue is headed by "Starina," otherwise known as Albert (Nathan Lane). Although the more "masculine" Armand must frequently calm and placate the campy and often hysterical Albert, the two have enjoyed a strong personal and professional relationship for 20 years and have successfully raised Armand's son, Val (Dan Futterman). Complications click in when Val arrives to announce that he intends to get married and that Val's future father-in-law is Republican Sen. Keeley (Gene Hackman), cofounder of the Coalition for Moral Order. He and his prim and proper wife (Dianne Wiest) and daughter, Barbara (Calista Flockhart), drop in on the menagerie in Miami, and the impending visit throws the household into a tizzy.

The filmmakers have strayed from the structure and characters of the original nary at all, but have adapted it all to a contempo American context with dizzying skill. The ultratrendy and colorful South Beach setting, with toned, tanned and virtually naked bodies constantly parading along the beach front, couldn't be more appropriate.

1996: NOMINATION: Best Art Direction

•

BIRDMAN OF ALCATRAZ

1962, 147 mins, US Ⓥ ⦿ b/w

Dir John Frankenheimer ***Prod*** Stuart Millar, Guy Trosper ***Scr*** Guy Trosper ***Ph*** Burnett Guffey ***Ed*** Edward Mann ***Mus*** Elmer Bernstein ***Art*** Ferdie Carrere

Act Burt Lancaster, Karl Malden, Thelma Ritter, Neville Brand, Telly Savalas, Edmond O'Brien (United Artists/Harold Hecht)

Birdman of Alcatraz is not really a prison picture in the traditional and accepted sense of the term. *Birdman* reverses the formula and brings a new breadth and depth to the form. In telling, with reasonable objectivity but understandably deep compassion the true story of Robert Stroud, it achieves a human dimension way beyond its predecessors. Trosper's penetrating and affecting screenplay, based on the book by Thomas E. Gaddis, delicately and artfully sketches the 53-year imprisonment of the 72-year-old "Birdman," Stroud, illustrating the highlights and lowlights of that terrible, yet miraculously ennobling span. The screenplay's, and the film's only real flaw is its dismissal of Stroud's background, leaving the audience to mull over psychological ramifications and expositional data by and large denied it.

Lancaster gives a superbly natural, unaffected performance—one in which nobility and indestructibility can be seen cumulatively developing and shining from within through a weary exterior eroded by the deep scars of time and enforced privacy in a "prison within a prison." His running clash with the narrow-minded and vengeful warden Shoemaker is a highlight of the film, consummating in a powerful scene depicting their opposing views on penology. Karl Malden is excellent as the warden. Four distinguished top supporting performances light up the picture. They are those of Telly Savalas as a fellow inmate and birdkeeper, Thelma Ritter (in a change of pace from her customary characterization) as Stroud's mother (whose seemingly unselfish devotion to the cause of her son ultimately grows suspect), Neville Brand as an understanding guard, and Betty Field as the woman who married Stroud in prison, then reluctantly drifts away at his realistic request. Edmond O'Brien narrates and plays the author.

1962: NOMINATIONS: Best Actor (Burt Lancaster), Supp. Actor (Telly Savalas), Supp. Actress (Thelma Ritter), B&W Cinematography

•

BIRD OF PARADISE

1932, 80 mins, US Ⓥ b/w

Dir King Vidor ***Prod*** David O. Selznick ***Scr*** Wells Root, Leonard Praskins, Wanda Tuchock ***Ph*** Clyde DeVinna ***Mus*** Max Steiner

Act Dolores Del Rio, Joel McCrea, John Halliday, Lon Chaney, Jr., Skeets Gallagher, Bert Roach (Radio)

The old Richard Walton Tully stage perennial stands the test of the innumerable South Seas pictures that have been done since its stage production way back yonder.

Outside of its romantic side, the subject's greatest asset is the truly fine performance of Dolores Del Rio as the savage princess Luana. The punch of her performance is admirably supplemented by the playing of the stalwart Joel McCrea, who plays simply and with natural grace a romantic role that has been tested by the years for its basic appeal.

Spectacular side of the production has received handsome treatment by director King Vidor. Possibilities for stunning tropical Hawaiian scenery have been realized to the fullest.

Story gets into motion promptly aboard a pleasure yacht carrying a group of Americans on a jaunt, with one of the amateur skippers driving the ship under full canvas in a stiff wind through a tricky channel into an atoll. Yacht comes safely to anchor and the natives come out to greet it, opening the story neatly.

•

BIRD OF PARADISE

1951, 100 mins, US col

Dir Delmer Daves ***Prod*** Harmon Jones ***Scr*** Delmer Daves ***Ph*** Winton C. Hoch ***Ed*** James B. Clark ***Mus*** Daniele Amfitheatrof ***Art*** Lyle Wheeler, Albert Hogsett

Act Louis Jourdan, Debra Paget, Jeff Chandler, Everett Sloane, Jack Elam, Maurice Schwartz (20th Century-Fox)

Richard Walton Tully's old legit piece, *Bird of Paradise*, makes another trip to the screen in a refurbished version. Previous filming of the play was in 1932 and, while Delmer Daves's version deviates from the Tully form, the essentials of the drama are still there, plus a beautiful Technicolor camera job, haunting island music and the use of actual locales.

Louis Jourdan and Debra Paget play the roles of the white man and native girl. There's another strong casting in Jeff Chandler, seen in the new character of a native who returns to his island after a try at stateside living. With him comes Jourdan. There the latter meets Chandler's sister (Paget). It is love at first sight, but native courting customs must first be satisfied, as well as the medicine man, who sees evil in the white man's visit.

Paget hits a high level in her performance as the Princess Kalua. She, as well as the other players give their characters considerable sincerity. Jourdan is an excellent choice as the island visitor, as is Chandler as the prince.

•

BIRD ON A WIRE

1990, 110 mins, US Ⓥ ⦿ ▭ col

Dir John Badham ***Prod*** Rob Cohen ***Scr*** David Seltzer, Louis Venosta, Eric Lerner ***Ph*** Robert Primes ***Ed*** Frank Morriss, Dallas Puett ***Mus*** Hans Zimmer ***Art*** Philip Harrison

Act Mel Gibson, Goldie Hawn, David Carradine, Bill Duke, Joan Severance, Stephen Tobolowsky (Badham-Cohen/Interscope)

Frank Capra's *It Happened One Night* established the format, but John Badham is stuck with a terrible script on this 1990s version. Only the chemistry of Goldie Hawn and Mel Gibson makes the film watchable. Gibson plays a shnook who's been hiding out for 15 years under an FBI witness relocation program. He gave testimony on a drug deal and the man he fingered (David Carradine) is just out of prison. Contrived and thoroughly unconvincing plot cog has Gibson discovered incognito by old flame Hawn at the Detroit gas station where he works just as Carradine and partner Duke catch up with him. Resulting shootout throws Hawn and Gibson together on the lam for the rest of the pic.

Rekindling of duo's romance is best thing about the repetitive chase format, set in numerous U.S. locations but shot almost entirely in British Columbia. Main kudos goes to British designer Philip Harrison, who's allowed to run hog wild in a large-scale climax set at a zoo exhibit depicting a Brazilian rain forest.

•

BIRDS, THE

1963, 120 mins, US Ⓥ ⦿ col

Dir Alfred Hitchcock ***Prod*** Alfred Hitchcock ***Scr*** Evan Hunter ***Ph*** Robert Burks ***Ed*** George Tomasini ***Mus*** [none] ***Art*** Robert Boyle

Act Rod Taylor, Tippi Hedren, Jessica Tandy, Suzanne Pleshette, Veronica Cartwright, Charles McGraw (Universal)

Beneath all of this elaborate feather bedlam lies a Hitchcock-and-bull story that's essentially a fowl ball.

The premise is fascinating. The idea of billions of birdbrains refusing to eat crow any longer and adopting the hunt-and-peck system, with homo sapiens as their ornithological target, is fraught with potential. Cinematically, Hitchcock and Co. have done a masterful job of meeting this formidable challenge. But dramatically, *The Birds* is little more than a shocker for shock's-sake.

Evan Hunter's screenplay, from Daphne du Maurier's story, has it that a colony of our feathered "friends" over California's Bodega Bay (it's never clear how far-reaching this avian mafia extends) suddenly decides, for no apparent reason, to swoop down en masse on the human population, beaks first. These bird raids are captivatingly bizarre and terrifying.

Where the scenario and picture slip is in the sphere of the human element. An unnecessary elaborate romantic plot has been cooked up and then left suspended. It involves a young bachelor attorney (Rod Taylor), his sister (Veronica Cartwright), their mother (Jessica Tandy), and a plucky, mysterious playgirl (Tippi Hedren) whose arrival from San Francisco with a pair of caged lovebirds for Taylor coincides with the outbreak of avian hostility.

Aside from the birds, the film belongs to Hedren, who makes an auspicious screen bow. She virtually has to carry the picture alone for the first 45-minute stretch, prior to the advent of the first wave of organized attackers from the sky.

Of the others, Tandy, a first-class actress, makes the most vivid impression. Taylor emotes with strength and attractiveness.

1963: NOMINATION: Best Special Effects

•

BIRDY
1984, 120 mins, US Ⓥ ⦿ col
Dir Alan Parker ***Prod*** Alan Marshall ***Scr*** Sandy Kroopf, Jack Behr ***Ph*** Michael Seresin ***Ed*** Gerry Hambling ***Mus*** Peter Gabriel ***Art*** Geoffrey Kirkland
Act Matthew Modine, Nicolas Cage, John Harkins, Sandy Baron, Karen Young, Bruno Kirby (A&M/Tri-Star)

Belying the lightheartedness of its title, *Birdy* is a heavy adult drama about best friends and the aftereffects of war, but it takes too long to live up to its ambitious premise.

Matthew Modine stars in the adaptation of William Wharton's novel as the title character who had been missing in action and now, psychologically ill and institutionalized, spends much of his time naked, curled up in birdlike positions and speaking to no one.

These posturings stem from a childhood affinity to birds which he shared to a significant degree with Nicolas Cage, who himself is banged up from the fighting, but is brought in to try to communicate with his boyhood pal.

Alan Parker's flashback direction ultimately serves to disjoint *Birdy*.

•

BIRTHDAY PARTY, THE
1968, 123 mins, UK Ⓥ col
Dir William Friedkin ***Prod*** Max Rosenberg, Milton Subotsky ***Scr*** Harold Pinter ***Ph*** Denys Coop ***Ed*** Tony Gibbs
Act Robert Shaw, Patrick McGee, Dandy Nichols, Sydney Tafler (Continental/Palomar)

Harold Pinter's comedy of menace has been transfered to the screen as an intellectual exercise in verbal gymnastics. Its study of unreality at a dingy British seaside resort is geared for thoughtful interpretation by alert audiences.

Robert Shaw is the pivotal force in *The Birthday Party*. He is the frightened lost soul, put upon as humanity's nonconformist. It appears, and Shaw is least sure of all, that prior to vegetating the past year at Dandy Nichols's boardinghouse he may have been a piano player and a deserting member of a criminal organization. Sydney Tafler and cohort Patrick McGee are the organization men sent to get Shaw.

On these bones, Pinter fleshes out his philosophy of the complex fictions people employ. The completed film is thus an elaboration of the images of reality.

Tafler milks the role for laughs on whatever intellectual level, and comes off quite well.

Director William Friedkin has obvious respect for Pinter's written word and left the film an observation on abstract ideas.

•

BIRTH OF A NATION, THE
(AKA: THE CLANSMAN)
1915, 187 mins, US Ⓥ ⦿ ⊗ b/w
Dir D. W. Griffith ***Prod*** D. W. Griffith, [Harry E. Aitken] ***Scr*** D.W. Griffith, Frank E. Woods ***Ph*** Billy Bitzer ***Ed*** [James E. Smith] ***Mus*** Joseph Carl Breil
Act Henry B. Walthall, Miriam Cooper, Mae Marsh, Lillian Gish, Ralph Lewis, George Siegmann (Griffith/Epoch/Dixon)

The Birth of a Nation is the main title David Wark Griffith gave to his version of Thomas Dixon's story of the South, *The Clansman*. It received its first New York public presentation in the Liberty theatre, New York, March 3. The daily newspaper reviewers pronounced it as the last word in picture making.

The story involves: the Camerons of the south and the Stonemans of the north and Silas Lynch, the mulatto Lieutenant-Governor; the opening and finish of the Civil War; the scenes attendant upon the assassination of Abraham Lincoln; the period of carpetbagging days and Union reconstruction following Lee's surrender; and the terrorizing of the southern whites by the newly freed blacks and the rise of the Ku Klux Klan. All these including some wonderfully well-staged battle scenes taken at night are realistically, graphically and most superbly depicted by the camera.

Griffith took his time. Thousands of feet of celluloid were used and for some six months or so he and his codirectors worked day and night to shape the story into a thrilling, dramatic wordless play. The battle scenes are wonderfully conceived, the departure of the soldiers splendidly arranged, and the death of the famous martyred president deftly and ably handled. Henry Walthall makes a manly, straightforward character of the "Little Colonel" and handles his big scenes most effectively. Mae Marsh as the pet sister does some remarkable work as the little girl who loves the south and loves her brother. Ralph Lewis is splendid as the leader of the House who helps Silas Lynch rise to power. George Siegmann gets all there can be gotten out of the despicable character of Lynch. Walter Long makes Gus, the renegade negro, a hated, much despised type, his acting and makeup being complete.

The Birth of a Nation is said to have cost $300,000.

•

BIRTH OF A NATION, THE
1930, 108 mins, US b/w
Dir D. W. Griffith ***Mus*** Joseph Carl Breil (Griffith)

The original score, assembled by J. C. Breil, has been recorded for [this sound reissue]. But though tuneful the music seems shallow in its tenderness and short of the sweeping spectacle that's the essence of this crossroads production. The print is surprisingly clear.

There is the blare of the Klan's trumpet as the horses and men gallop, and this ride remains a big thrill. There are also battle effects.

The picture startled the world in 1915 by showing in 12 reels. It has been shorn since in running time.

The film cost around $110,000 to make and Billy Bitzer's photography and Breil's score still stand out.

•

BIRTH OF THE BLUES
1941, 80 mins, US b/w
Dir Victor Schertzinger ***Prod*** Buddy DeSylva ***Scr*** Harry Tugend, Walter DeLeon ***Ph*** William Mellor ***Ed*** Paul Weatherwax ***Mus*** Robert Emmett Dolan (arr.)
Act Bing Crosby, Mary Martin, Brian Donlevy, Carolyn Lee, Eddie "Rochester" Anderson, J. Carrol Naish (Paramount)

Birth of the Blues has everything from melody to comedy, and for the show bunch it's just so much jive history in swingtime. A saga of Basin Street, New Orleans, cradle of the Dixieland jazz idiom, it projects its story with bounce and gusto; forthright in its allegiance to a then unorthodox jazz style; plus arresting romance, a plug-ugly cabaret meanace, and a wealth of cavalcade jazzapation.

Bing Crosby is the licorice-stick disciple who adheres to his premise that the colored man's levee music, at the foot of Basin Street, was bound to sweep the country.

Mary Martin is introduced in al fresco fashion, as is Brian Donlevy, a mean man on the horn from Memphis, just what the rest of the band has been waiting for—an ofay who can toot like a Satchmo.

When Crosby, as a kid, swings Paderewski and brings down the wrath of his musicianly father, it's solid stuff for the initiate. The jailhouse jam session with the Memphis horn man (Donlevy) in the clink is another directorial highlight.

1941: NOMINATION: Best Scoring of a Musical Picture

•

BIRUMA NO TATEGOTO
(THE BURMESE HARP; HARP OF BURMA)
1956, 116 mins, Japan Ⓥ b/w
Dir Kon Ichikawa ***Prod*** Masayuki Takagi ***Scr*** Natto Wada, Michio Takeyama ***Ph*** Minoru Yokoyama ***Ed*** Masanori Tsujii ***Mus*** Akira Ifukube ***Art*** Takashi Matsuyama
Act Rentaro Mikuni, Shoji Yasui, Tatsuya Mihashi, Taniye Kitabayashi, Yunosuke Ito (Nikkatsu)

Offbeater concerns the last days of the war in Burma and is about a Japanese private who decides to stay on to bury all the Japanese dead strewn over the land. He is wounded and saved by a holy man whose robes he steals to get back to his troop. However, he runs on a whole battalion of his dead, with vultures settling, and makes his vow to stay on. Film concerns how his captive mates learn of his resolve and try to talk him into going back with them.

Film has a good narrative style, but has oversimplified storytelling and intermittently taking action. It is too downbeat.

Technical credits and acting are good and direction is restrained but lacks the power to make this an unusual plea.

•

BISHOP'S WIFE, THE
1947, 106 mins, US Ⓥ ⦿ b/w
Dir Henry Koster ***Prod*** Samuel Goldwyn ***Scr*** Robert E. Sherwood, Leonardo Bercovici ***Ph*** Gregg Toland ***Ed*** Monica Collingwood ***Mus*** Hugo Friedhofer ***Art*** George Jenkins, Perry Ferguson
Act Cary Grant, Loretta Young, David Niven, Monty Woolley, Gladys Cooper, Elsa Lanchester (RKO)

While a fantasy, there are no fantastic heavenly manifestations. There's a humanness about the characters, even the angel, that beguiles full attention. Henry Koster's sympathetic direction deftly gets over the warm humor supplied by the script, taken from Robert Nathan's novel of the same title.

Cary Grant is the angel of the piece and has never appeared to greater advantage. Role, with the exception of a minor miracle or two, is potently pointed to indicate character could have been a flesh-and-blood person, a factor that embellishes sense of reality as the angel sets about answering the troubled prayers of Episcopalian bishop (David Niven).

Plot, essentially, deals with Grant's assignment to make people act like human beings. In great need of his help is Niven, a young bishop who has lost the common touch and marital happiness because of his dream of erecting a massive cathedral.

Loretta Young gives a moving performance as the wife whose life is touched by an angel without her knowledge of his heavenly origin. Niven's cleric character is played straight but his anxieties and jealousy loosen much of the warm humor gracing the plot.

Gregg Toland's camera work and the music score by Hugo Friedhofer, directed by Emil Newman, are ace credits among the many expert contributions.

1947: Best Sound Recording.

NOMINATIONS: Best Picture, Director, Editing, Scoring of a Dramatic Picture

•

BITCH, THE
1979, 90 mins, UK Ⓥ col
Dir Gerry O'Hara ***Prod*** John Quested ***Scr*** Gerry O'Hara ***Ph*** Denis Lewiston ***Art*** Malcolm Middleton
Act Joan Collins, Michael Coby, Kenneth Haigh, Ian Hendry, Carolyn Seymour, Sue Lloyd (Brent Walker)

The Bitch offers more mock orgasm than plot as it oscillates between the disco floor and the sack—or the pool, shower, or wherever a couple can couple. Two Lesbos, at one point, are glimpsed pawing each other in a sauna.

Not to mince about, the production, scripted and feverishly directed by Gerry O'Hara, is corny and coarse, but at least mercifully brief at 90 minutes.

Between all the sex and sybaritic palaver, there's some nuisance plotting involving Michael Coby as a debonair hustler in trouble with the mob.

Pic's ending, ostensibly ironic, only seems confusing as to who done what to whom. But for disco freaks, there's plenty of their kind of action. Joan Collins does her spoiled nympho rich girl turn with assurance.

•

BITE THE BULLET
1975, 131 mins, US Ⓥ ⦿ ▭ col
Dir Richard Brooks ***Prod*** Richard Brooks ***Scr*** Richard Brooks ***Ph*** Harry Stradling, Jr. ***Ed*** George Grenville ***Mus*** Alex North ***Art*** Robert Boyle
Act Gene Hackman, Candice Bergen, James Coburn, Ben Johnson, Ian Bannen, Jan-Michael Vincent (Columbia)

Bite the Bullet is an excellent, literate action-drama probing the diverse motivations of participants in an endurance horse race. The contestants include Gene Hackman and James Coburn as ex-San Juan Hill Rough Riders; Candice Bergen as a former resident of Jean Willes frontier pleasure shanty, seeking money to help her imprisoned lover; vagabond Ben Johnson desperately wanting to "be somebody" for a brief moment in life.

After a leisurely though intriguing buildup, the race begins, and during the daily ordeals of mountain, desert, rain, sun, cold and heat, the pressures and the secrets of the characters emerge plausibly and rationally.

Bergen's ulterior motivation in particular triggers a surprise, pre-climactic turn. Effective use of slow motion in the final scene lends suspense to the outcome as the two surviving riders inch towards the ribbon.

1975: NOMINATIONS: Best Original Song Score, Sound

•

BITTER HARVEST
1963, 96 mins, UK Ⓥ col
Dir Peter Graham Scott ***Prod*** Albert Fennell ***Scr*** Ted Willis ***Ph*** Ernest Steward ***Ed*** Russell Lloyd ***Mus*** Laurie Johnson ***Art*** Alex Vetchinsky
Act Janet Munro, John Stride, Anne Cunningham, Alan Badel, William Lucas, Barbara Ferris (Independent Artists)

The story of the country innocent (Janet Munro) who gets caught up in the dizzy pitfalls of London nightlife is taken from a Patrick Hamilton novel, *Twenty Thousand Streets under the Sky.* Surprising thing is that scripter Ted Willis has not come up with any surprises or twists, and director Peter Graham Scott has been no help in this matter, either. Result is a conventional yarn.

Munro is given opportunities to portray innocence, gaiety, cupidity, depression, vanity, fear, cunning, tenderness, harshness, wonder and anger. All the emotions are fleeting but the star helps to mold them into a well-drawn picture of an innocent who learns quickly.

John Stride is solid, charming and resourceful as the infatuated bartender. Alan Badel makes a brief but telling contribution as a steely, unscrupulous theatre boss. There is also a beautifully underplayed performance by Anne Cunningham as a barmaid who has long been secretly in love with Stride.

•

BITTER MOON

1992, 139 mins, France/UK Ⓥ ⊙ col

Dir Roman Polanski ***Prod*** Roman Polanski ***Scr*** Roman Polanski, Gerard Brach, John Brownjohn, Jeff Gross ***Ph*** Tonino Delli Colli ***Ed*** Herve de Luze, Glenn Cunningham ***Mus*** Vangelis ***Art*** Willy Holt, Gerard Viard

Act Peter Coyote, Emmanuelle Seigner, Hugh Grant, Kristin Scott Thomas, Victor Bannerjee, Sophie Patel (RP/Burrill)

Four years after *Frantic*, Roman Polanski approaches rock bottom with *Bitter Moon*, a phony slice of *huis clos* drama between two couples aboard a Euroliner. Strong playing by topliner Peter Coyote can't compensate for a script [from Pascal Bruckner's novel *Lunes de fiel*] that's all over the map and a tone that veers from outré comedy to erotic game-playing.

Initial focus is on a couple of hoity-toity Brits (Hugh Grant, Kristin Scott Thomas) enjoying a seventh-anniversary Mediterranean cruise to Istanbul. Thing start to go awry when they help a distraught young femme, Mimi (Emmanuelle Seigner), who turns out to be the ship's glamorous cabaret act.

That night Grant is accosted by her American hubby (Peter Coyote), a wheelchair-bound misanthrope who lures the Englishman into a drinking session and insists on recounting his life story. Thereon, pic settles into a series of long flashbacks detailing Coyote-Seigner's tempestuous love life.

Despite its two-hour-plus length, pic holds a certain awful fascination as Polanski careens every which way with the material. Coyote gives a scenery-chewing performance as both the younger lovestruck scribe and the whisky-soaked cripple. Seigner, matured since her *Frantic* days, is eye-popping in the sex scenes, but the helmer's wife often sounds as if she's reading her dialogue off cue cards.

•

BITTER SWEET

1933, 76 mins, UK Ⓥ b/w

Dir Herbert Wilcox ***Prod*** Herbert Wilcox ***Scr*** Herbert Wilcox, Lydia Hayward, Monckton Hoffe ***Ph*** F. A. Young ***Mus*** Noel Coward ***Art*** L. P. Williams

Act Anna Neagle, Fernand Gravet, Esme Percy, Clifford Heatherly, Ivy St. Helier, Miles Mander (British & Dominions/United Artists)

Direction hampers Anna Neagle, a stunning blonde of compelling grace, but here restricted to an acting style. She is permitted no emotional range and her performance is flavorless except that she does manage to suggest that if she broke loose she might start something.

Fernand Gravet is young, dark and a vital type, a vigorous personality. Chief support role here doesn't bring out his engaging personality in full.

Clifford Heatherly does the Vienna café proprietor, Herr Schlick, contributing a splendidly flexible performance with a capital knack of legitimate comedy. Suggests something of the Charles Laughton technique in subtle villainy. Last of the quartet is Ivy St. Helier, obviously French, who plays the soubrette role to the hilt.

Continuity takes many liberties with the operetta script [by Noel Coward], usually without improving it. Story progress is jerky. Whole episode of the singer's second marriage is omitted, which is all right for economy of narrative though it does fog up the finish, which leaves the heroine rather indefinite. Love scenes are stretched out to great lengths.

Coward's score, hailed at the time of the stage presentation as brilliant, is a part of the picture and helps its classy tone. The leads handle several numbers agreeably.

•

BITTER SWEET

1940, 92 mins, US Ⓥ col

Dir W. S. Van Dyke ***Prod*** Victor Saville ***Scr*** Lesser Samuels ***Ph*** Oliver T. Marsh, Allen Davey ***Ed*** Harold F. Kress ***Mus*** Noel Coward ***Art*** Cedric Gibbons, John S. Detlie

Act Jeanette MacDonald, Nelson Eddy, George Sanders, Ian Hunter, Felix Bressart (M-G-M)

Bitter Sweet is a super-elaborate production providing a background for the fetching Noel Coward songs, in his highly successful operetta, delivered by Jeanette MacDonald and Nelson Eddy.

The story development receives minor attention. It's an obvious and static romance from the time music teacher Eddy elopes with his pupil (MacDonald); takes her to Vienna while he writes an operetta; and his tragic death just as his work is to be presented. The love scenes between the couple are staid and cold, neither providing any warmth to those proceedings which were a vital factor in the original play.

Both MacDonald and Eddy interpret Coward's numbers in excellent style. All the favorites of the operetta are here, including "Zigeuner," "Little Café," "Tokay," and "I'll See You Again."

Final production number for background of MacDonald's rendition of "Zigeuner," is most ingeniously contrived, having dancers in copper-brown and white costumes, with background in similar tones.

•

BITTER TEA OF GENERAL YEN, THE

1933, 87 mins, US Ⓥ col

Dir Frank Capra ***Prod*** Frank Capra ***Scr*** Edward Paramore ***Ph*** Joseph Walker ***Ed*** Edward Curtis ***Mus*** W. Frank Harling

Act Barbara Stanwyck, Nils Asther, Gavin Gordon, Toshia Mori, Walter Connolly, Richard Loo (Columbia)

This picture is a queer story [from a novel by Grace Zaring Stone] of a romance in China between a Chinese and a white woman. A young New England girl arrives in Shanghai to join her sweetheart missionary. They are to be married. China's unceasing civil wars are made the background of the girl's experiences from that point.

The Chinese warlord around whom the plot is built is a curious and rather questionable human composition of a poet, philosopher and bandit. He speaks rather fluent English and essays somewhat dainty American mannerisms, especially in manipulating a handkerchief. Nils Asther plays the role.

After the Chinese general goes on the make for the white girl the picture goes blah. That's before the film is even halfway.

Barbara Stanwyck is the white girl. Pleasant enough and for the first half where she repulses the Chinaman gathers some audience sympathy. Subsequently, where the photography attempts to simulate that the girl, in her dreams, loves the Chinese, the role fails her. Besides which, as a New England missionary type, Stanwyck does not fit.

A fine actor from the legit, Walter Connolly takes the acting honors as the adventurous American financial advisor of General Yen. A kind of a tramp philosopher which Connolly does admirably.

•

BITTER VICTORY

1958, 97 mins, France/US ▭ b/w

Dir Nicholas Ray ***Prod*** Paul Graetz ***Scr*** Rene Hardy, Nicholas Ray, Gavin Lambert, Paul Gallico ***Ph*** Michel Kelber ***Ed*** Leonide Azar ***Mus*** Maurice Le Roux ***Art*** Jean d'Eaubonne

Act Richard Burton, Curt Jurgens, Ruth Roman, Raymond Pellegrin, Anthony Bushell, Christopher Lee (Transcontinental/Laffont)

Rene Hardy's novel has been translated for the screen into a literary, hard-hitting screenplay which almost always manages to overcome some of the incongruities of the original story line. This sets up a deadly struggle between two British Army officers during the Second World War African campaign.

Conflict between Capt Leith and Major Brand derives from the fact that Leith knows of Brand's basic cowardice in action, and also from jealousy over Brand's wife, with whom Leith has had an affair. Returning from a dangerous mission in German-held Benghazi, Brand tries twice indirectly to bring about Leith's death, once by leaving him behind to guard two wounded Germans, again by deliberately letting a scorpion bite his rival.

Script is basically flawed by the unclearly delineated key character of the major—and Curt Jurgens's competent, straightforward performance is less successful because of it. Fine thesping by Richard Burton leads a series of top performances by other members of large cast.

•

BLACK AND WHITE IN COLOR

SEE: LA VICTOIRE EN CHANTANT

•

BLACKBEARD'S GHOST

1968, 106 mins, US Ⓥ ⊙ col

Dir Robert Stevenson ***Prod*** Bill Walsh ***Scr*** Bill Walsh, Don DaGradi ***Ph*** Edward Colman ***Ed*** Robert Stafford ***Mus*** Robert F. Brunner ***Art*** Carroll Clark, John B. Mansbridge

Act Peter Ustinov, Dean Jones, Suzanne Pleshette, Elsa Lanchester, Joby Baker, Elliott Reid (Walt Disney)

Blackbeard's Ghost, a lively and entertaining Walt Disney production, features Peter Ustinov in a tour de force title role as the restless spirit of the famed pirate. Dean Jones and Suzanne Pleshette share top billing. Robert Stevenson's direction is highlighted by several very amusing chase and special effects sequences.

Ben Stahl's novel has been adapted into an essentially one-situation script—some hoods want to take over an island for a gambling casino; Ustinov and Jones thwart the scheme—loaded with self-contained vignettes.

The inspired direction makes it all come alive via first-rate special effects and sight gags, and through a fanciful script that, in a most adroit way, is neither too literate nor too sketchy.

Ustinov plays his part to the hilt: mugging and cutting up, as the wandering spirit who must do a good deed to achieve repose.

Joby Baker is the lead heavy, and Pleshette's presence lends a romantic, also sympathetic touch to the proceedings.

•

BLACKBEARD, THE PIRATE

1952, 98 mins, US Ⓥ ⊙ col

Dir Raoul Walsh ***Prod*** Edmund Grainger ***Scr*** Alan LeMay ***Ph*** William E. Snyder ***Ed*** Ralph Dawson ***Mus*** Victor Young ***Art*** Albert S. D'Agostino, Jack Okey

Act Robert Newton, Linda Darnell, William Bendix, Keith Andes, Torin Thatcher, Richard Egan (RKO)

Blackbeard, the Pirate is a rollicking swashbuckler stacked with high adventure, extensive swordplay and all the things big pirate pictures are made of.

Alan LeMay's scripting of the DeVallon Scott story gives a neat blending to the tongue-in-cheek and on-the-level ingredients.

It's the 17th century on the Spanish Main again. Torin Thatcher, a "reformed" pirate, has been commissioned by the King of England to rid the seas of Robert ("Blackbeard") Newton. Keith Andes, a young sailor of fortune out to collect some reward money, allows himself to be shanghaied. Also going aboard, is Thatcher's adopted daughter (Linda Darnell). Once on board, the pair discover the captain has been murdered and "Blackbeard" has taken over.

Newton turns in a memorable performance.

•

BLACK BEAUTY

1933, 63 mins, US b/w

Dir Phil Rosen ***Prod*** I. E. Chadwick ***Scr*** Charles Logue ***Ph*** Charles Stumar ***Ed*** Carl Pearson

Act Esther Ralston, Alexander Kirkland, Hale Hamilton, Gavin Gordon, Don Alvardo, George Walsh (Monogram)

This is not a western, nor is it about a Harlem queen. This is a picturization of that classic juvenile story which has behind it a sale of three million copies in the U.S. It was first published in 1877 and has been printed in edition after edition ever since.

A tear element figures as the horse, hero of the tale, gets rough breaks, one after another. Not laid on with unnatural thickness but, rather, strikes a note of sympathy which stands as an asset. Two particularly sympathetic characters, as done by Esther Ralston and Alexander Kirkland, go with the animal. They are the wealthy widow and the boyish owner of Black Beauty, all of whom become united for the happy finish.

Story is fairly well and evenly told, starting with the birth of the horse that was to lose his chance as a racing champ, go down the river to a cruel buyer and later land as a dray horse for a junkman.

•

BLACK BEAUTY

1946, 74 mins, US Ⓥ b/w

Dir Max Nosseck ***Prod*** Edward L. Alperson ***Scr*** Lillie Hayward, Agnes Christine Johnston ***Mus*** Dimitri Tiomkin

Act Mona Freeman, Richard Denning, Evelyn Ankers, Charles Evans, J. M. Kerrigan, Moyna Macgill (Alson/20th Century-Fox)

Black Beauty, another of the Hollywood equine species, is none too promising. It lacks marquee names and adult entertainment values, though it's the sort of item that the youngsters would relish.

Adapted from the novel by Anna Sewell, *Beauty*, a standard among horse yarns, has been filmed twice before, once in sound. Dealing with a young girl's love for a colt that she rears, the story, backgrounded by the English countryside in the late 19th century, mostly concerns the heartaches that result when the animal, through circumstances, is forced into the hands of others and subsequently encounters the downtrail as a job horse.

Mona Freeman plays the girl and Richard Denning the American with whom she teams romantically. Freeman is properly impetuous and eager, while Denning is bedeviled by the script, as are all the others. Direction is frequently poor. Acting by some lesser characters is unusually bad.

●

BLACK BEAUTY
1971, 106 mins, UK/W. Germany/Spain Ⓥ col
Dir James Hill ***Prod*** Peter L. Andrews, Malcolm B. Heyworth ***Scr*** Art Bernd, Pedro Samu, Wolf Mankowitz ***Ph*** Fernando Arribas ***Ed*** Pablo Delano ***Mus*** Lionel Bart
Act Mark Lester, Uschi Glas, Walter Slezak, Peter Lee Lawrence, John Nettleton, Patrick Mower (Tigon British/Chilton/CCC Filmkunst/Emiliano Piedra

Anna Sewell's evergreen novel, *Black Beauty*, which has sold more than 6 million copies in 17 languages, has been made into a film several times before (1921, 1933, 1946) in England and Hollywood. Now, continental producers have taken their first crack at this bestseller.

In their attempt to please all audiences, in too many different lands, the filmmakers have ridden off in all directions at once. The heavies hamming up their parts, probably intended to suit Spanish tastes. An oversweet saccharin streak of German "heart and soul" oozes through the picture. Still another element, quite foreign to the original story, is unsuccessfully aimed at Yank preferences: to some extent, this charming horse saga emerges as a rough-riding Western.

Director James Hill, who has piloted other pix with skill and great sensitivity, does little to save this one from disintegrating into self-contradiction. An international cast does not merge with any semblance of conformity, either. Uschi Glas, easy-to-look-at star of the German screen, shows almost no reason for her popularity with Teutonic audiences which gets her six film leads every year.

It's due to the script, or a casting error, or both, that Walter Slezak's acrid brand of wit doesn't spark. Film's assets are the noble title horse with its great equestrian stunts and the appealing landscape, exquisitely color-lensed by Fernando Arribas.

●

BLACK BEAUTY
1994, 85 mins, US Ⓥ col
Dir Caroline Thompson ***Prod*** Robert Shapiro, Peter Macgregor-Scott ***Scr*** Caroline Thompson ***Ph*** Alex Thomson ***Ed*** Claire Simpson ***Mus*** Danny Elfman ***Art*** John Box
Act Sean Bean, David Thewlis, Jim Carter, Peter Davison, Alun Armstrong, John McEnery (Warner)

Although already filmed three times in the sound era, *Black Beauty* has never been put on-screen faithfully or well, a situation partially remedied by this affecting, rather grave rendition of the children's perennial. Debuting director Caroline Thompson, who penned *The Secret Garden*, has brought considerable feeling and care to this story of a fine horse's often difficult life in Victorian England.

Anna Sewell's original motivation in writing the 1877 book was to bring to light the cruel treatment of horses prevalent in the England of her day. Work's other most notable feature is its first-person narration from the point of view of Black Beauty, which soon proves charming and lends the film what world view it has.

Like an old man sitting under a tree ruminating about his long life, an aged Black Beauty (voiced enthusiastically with a light Brit accent by Alan Cumming) casts a look back to his idyllic youth on a gorgeous country estate. Illness comes, as does a horrible stable fire, but these are more easily survived than life under his aristocratic new owners. Black Beauty becomes a horse for rent and, later, a taxi horse in darkest working-class London.

By closely following the book, Thompson has had to face its extremely episodic nature, a problem that has not entirely been surmounted either in the scripting or the editing.

Demands on the performers are moderate, although David Thewlis weighs in sympathetically as Black Beauty's driver and '60s British film icons Peter Cook and Eleanor Bron are welcome presences as the snooty aristocrats.

●

BLACK BELT JONES
1974, 85 mins, US Ⓥ col
Dir Robert Clouse ***Prod*** Fred Weintraub, Paul Heller ***Scr*** Oscar Williams ***Ph*** Kent Wakeford ***Ed*** Michael Kahn ***Mus*** Luchi De Jesus, Dennis Coffy
Act Jim Kelly, Gloria Hendry, Scatman Crothers, Alan Weeks, Eric Laneuville, Andre Phillipe (Warner)

Black Belt Jones reteams the *Enter the Dragon* producing team and director Robert Clouse, also Jim Kelly, this time heading the cast. The story strand pits a group of graceful black martial arts students against some cliche white gangsters, neither side taking things seriously.

Kelly, between the thousands of body blows given and taken, has time for Gloria Hendry, equally adept at physical jousting as providing a good romantic interest. She's the daughter of Scatman Crothers, whose karate studio is on land eyed for a building project by Malik Carter and his own crime superior (Andre Phillipe), a clumsy godfather type.

The action sequences, coordinated by Robert Wall, are standard steps in the choreography of martial arts.

●

BLACK BIRD, THE
1926, 76 mins, US ⊗ b/w
Dir Tod Browning ***Scr*** Tod Browning, Waldemar Young ***Ph*** Percy Hilburn ***Ed*** Errol Taggart ***Art*** Cedric Gibbons, Arnold Gillespie
Act Lon Chaney, Renee Adoree, Owen Moore, Doris Lloyd (MGM)

In *The Black Bird* Lon Chaney plays a dual role, that of a crook and of his brother, a Limehouse missionary. Although the reverend fellow is crippled up plenty, the curse is taken off by one shot showing the crook throwing his arm and leg out of joint and then assuming the role of the man whom the world thought to be his brother. That's the basis of the story, for the crook falls in love with a music hall performer, while a flashier crook from the West End also goes for the same girl.

It's a good melodrama, excellently produced. Chaney handles his two parts well and Waldemar Young's scenario has been so constructed that the rather unique dual role is plausible at all times.

●

BLACK BIRD, THE
1975, 98 mins, US Ⓥ col
Dir David Giler ***Prod*** Saul David ***Scr*** David Giler ***Ph*** Phil Lathrop ***Ed*** Margaret Booth, Walter Thompson, Lou Lombardo ***Mus*** Jerry Fielding ***Art*** Harry Horner
Act George Segal, Stephane Audran, Lionel Stander, Lee Patrick, Elisha Cook, Jr., Felix Silla (Columbia/ Rastar)

This satirical contemporary update of Dashiell Hammett's novel *The Maltese Falcon* emerges as fair whimsy.

Basis of the plot [from a story by Don M. Mankiewitz and Gordon Cotler] is that George Segal, as Sam Spade's son, has inherited the detective agency, still in its old location, but now a run-down black neighborhood.

Lee Patrick, in a delightful recasting as Effie, the secretary, hangs in there, partly because she hasn't been paid in years, and despite an animosity towards Segal. The search for the elusive Maltese Falcon is reinstated, bringing in all sorts of mysterious characters.

The general tenor of the film shows a sentimental empathy for the original material with no heartless put-downs marring the work. There are lots of smiles, many chuckles, and a few strong laughs.

●

BLACKBOARD JUNGLE
1955, 100 mins, US Ⓥ ⊙ b/w
Dir Richard Brooks ***Prod*** Pandro S. Berman ***Scr*** Richard Brooks ***Ph*** Russell Harlan ***Ed*** Ferris Webster ***Mus*** Charles Wolcott (adapt.) ***Art*** Cedric Gibbons, Randall Duell
Act Glenn Ford, Anne Francis, Louis Calhern, Vic Morrow, Sidney Poitier, Margaret Hayes (M-G-M)

Director-scripter Richard Brooks, working from novel by Evan Hunter, has fashioned an angry picture that flares out in moral and physical rage at mental slovenliness, be it juvenile, mature, or in the pattern of society acceptance of things as they are because no one troubles to devise a better way.

The main issue is the juvenile bum who terrorizes schoolrooms and teachers.

The strong among the evil element, here represented by Vic Morrow, is already beyond any reform. The good, represented by Sidney Poitier, has had no stimulus to awaken his leadership abilities because he is a Negro. Glenn Ford, Morrow and Poitier are so real in their performances under the probing direction by Brooks that the picture alternatingly has the viewer pleading, indignant and frightened before the conclusion.

1955: NOMINATIONS: Best Screenplay, B&W Cinematography, B&W Art Direction, Editing

●

BLACK CAT, THE
(UK: HOUSE OF DOOM)
1934, 65 mins, US ⊙ b/w
Dir Edgar G. Ulmer ***Prod*** Carl Laemmle, Jr. ***Scr*** Peter Ruric ***Ph*** Jack Mescal ***Mus*** Heinz Roemheld ***Art*** Charles D. Hall
Act Boris Karloff, Bela Lugosi, David Manners, Julie Bishop, Andy Devine, John Carradine (Universal)

Story is confused and confusing, and while with the aid of heavily shadowed lighting and mausoleumlike architecture, a certain eeriness has been achieved, it's all a poor imitation of things seen before.

Boris Karloff occupies a spooky manor built over the ruins of a world war fort where 10,000 soldiers drenched the valley in blood in a terrible military defeat caused by Karloff's treachery. That is told but not shown. Bela Lugosi is a batty doctor just out of a cruel jail in which he spent 15 years. Also due to Karloff's unworthy character.

Clash of the two eyebrow-squinting nuts involves an American bridal couple temporarily caught in the manor. It is the playful notion of nasty Karloff to make the bride Exhibit A in a devil cult of which he is the head, and it is the revenge of Lugosi to torture his enemy by skinning him alive.

Corpses standing upright in glass cases and operating table murders are other tricks which the story uses. Edgar Allan Poe's name is used for publicity purposes. All that is used is the title which belongs to a Poe short story.

Karloff and Lugosi are sufficiently sinister and convincingly demented.

●

BLACK CAULDRON, THE
1985, 80 mins, US Ⓥ ▭ col
Dir Ted Berman, Richard Rich ***Prod*** Joe Hale ***Scr*** David Jonas, Vance Gerry, Ted Berman, Richard Rich, Al Wilson, Roy Morita, Peter Young, Art Stevens, Joe Hale, Rosemary Anne Sisson, Roy Edward Disney ***Ed*** James Melton, Kim Koford, Armetta Jackson ***Mus*** Elmer Bernstein (Walt Disney)

By any hard measure, the $25 million animated *Cauldron* is not very original. The characters, though cute and cuddly and sweet and mean and ugly and simply awful, don't really have much to do that would remain of interest to any but the youngest minds.

Story line [based on *The Chronicles of Prydain* series by Lloyd Alexander] is fairly stock sword-and-sorcery, with a band of likable youngsters, animals and creatures forced to tackle an evil mob of monsters to keep them from using a magic cauldron to raise an army of the dead. No need to guess who wins. [Prolog is narrated by John Huston.]

●

BLACK CHRISTMAS
1974, 93 mins, Canada Ⓥ col
Dir Bob Clark ***Prod*** Bob Clark, Gerry Arbeid ***Scr*** Roy Moore ***Ph*** Reg Morris ***Ed*** Stan Cole ***Mus*** Carl Zittrer ***Art*** Karen Bromley
Act Olivia Hussey, Keir Dullea, Margot Kidder, Andrea Martin, John Saxon, Marian Waldman (August)

Black Christmas, a bloody, senseless kill-for-kicks feature, exploits unnecessary violence in a university sorority house operated by an implausibly alcoholic ex-hoofer. Its slow-paced, murky tale involves an obscene telephone caller who apparently delights in killing the girls off one by one, even the hapless housemother.

The plot has the usual abundant cliches: a drunken girl student, played by Margot Kidder, who goes to her death much too late in the film; a housemother, who finds her hidden whiskey bottles after much swearing; a "nice" girl, who finds herself pregnant much to the horror of her psycho piano student boyfriend; and stock dumb policemen.

Only Marian Waldman as the housemother comes across with any life.

●

BLACK FURY
1935, 94 mins, US Ⓥ b/w
Dir Michael Curtiz ***Prod*** [Robert Lord] ***Scr*** Abem Finkel, Carl Erickson ***Ph*** Byron Haskin ***Ed*** Thomas Richards ***Mus*** Leo F. Forbstein (dir.) ***Art*** John Hughes
Act Paul Muni, Karen Morley, William Gargan, Barton MacLane, John Qualen, J. Carrol Naish (Warner)

Pennsy coal-mining background is basically a masculine setting for intraindustry politics [from the story *Jan Volkanik* by M. A. Musmanno and play *Bohunk* by Henry R. Irving]. The fomenting antiunionists who generate ill will for benefit of ultimate strike-breaking maneuvers is the means for bringing in the strongarm coal mine police, the scabs, etc. They become the abstract composite villain.

There are times when the footage is slow and Paul Muni's Polish brogue too thick but in the main the general result is arresting. Muni is the fulcrum of the film but there are other fine performances. J. Carrol Naish is excellent as the strike fomenter. John Qualen's hunky-pal personation is a sympathetic characterization, parred by Sarah Haden in a slavey role, that of his wife. Barton MacLane's thankless assignment as the bullying head of the muscle bunch is sufficiently hateful to impress him.

•

BLACK HOLE, THE
1979, 97 mins, US Ⓥ ⦿ ▭ col
Dir Gary Nelson ***Prod*** Ron Miller ***Scr*** Jeb Rosebrook, Gerry Day ***Ph*** Frank Phillips ***Ed*** Gregg McLaughlin ***Mus*** John Barry ***Art*** Peter Ellenshaw
Act Maximilian Schell, Anthony Perkins, Robert Forster, Joseph Bottoms, Yvette Mimieux, Ernest Borgnine (Walt Disney)

The black hole itself gets short shrift in the screenplay, based on a story by Jeb Rosebrook, Bob Barbash and Richard Landau. Most of the pic is devoted to setting up the story of mad scientist Maximilian Schell, poised on the brink of his voyage to the unknown. An exploration ship staffed by Robert Forster, Anthony Perkins, Joseph Bottoms, Yvette Mimieux and Ernest Borgnine, stumbles on both Schell and the nearby black hole, with unpredictable results.

What ensues is sometimes talky but never dull. Director Gary Nelson's pacing and visual sense are right on target.

In typical Disney fashion, the most attractive and sympathetic characters are not human at all. George F. McGinnis has constructed a bevy of robots that establish a mechanical world all their own.

1979: NOMINATIONS: Best Cinematography, Visual Effects

•

BLACK JACK
1979, 106 mins, UK col
Dir Ken Loach ***Prod*** Tony Garnett ***Scr*** Ken Loach ***Ph*** Chris Menges ***Ed*** Bill Shapter ***Mus*** Bob Pegg ***Art*** Martin Johnson
Act Jean Franval, Stephen Hirst, Louise Cooper, Andrew Bennett (Kestrel Films)

Basically an adventure yarn set in northern England in 1750, this collaboration of writer-director Kenneth Loach and producer Tony Garnett add first-rate period re-creation (more than could have been expected from the $1 million budget) to their already established talents for sharp, telling realism.

Loach's screenplay, adapted from Leon Garfield's same-title novel, suffers from a meandering plotline, but that hardly matters as it is continuously engrossing, and enlivened with a wry wit.

After miraculously surviving a hanging, Black Jack, a gigantic Frenchman with few words of English, endearingly played by Jean Franval, takes along a young boy (Stephen Hirst) with him on his escape, to "speak for him." The main plot concerns a girl (Louise Cooper) they encounter by chance, whose irrational behavior has caused her wealthy parents to commit her to a privately run madhouse for fear of possible scandal.

•

BLACK LEGION, THE
1937, 80 mins, US Ⓥ b/w
Dir Archie Mayo ***Prod*** Robert Lord ***Scr*** Abem Finkel, William Wister Haines ***Ph*** George Barnes ***Ed*** Edward Marks ***Art*** Robert Hass
Act Humphrey Bogart, Dick Foran, Erin O'Brien-Moore, Ann Sheridan, Robert Barrat, Helen Flint (Warner)

Warners has taken yesterday's headlines and fashioned a melodrama which gives the emotions a rough going over.

The action [from a story by Robert Lord] includes floggings, the burning of a chicken farm, destruction of a drugstore, a neophyte's taking of the oath of allegiance amid a woodland gathering of the clan, and the behind-the-scene machinations of the Michigan hooded order's promoters, ex-phoney stock salesmen.

Humphrey Bogart is the pacemaker of a smartly selected cast and lays down a telling performance. His is the role of a young workman in a large machine-making plant who, out of disappointment at losing the foremanship to another with a non-American name, joins the hooded order and eventually degenerates into becoming its murderous tool. His wife (Erin O'Brien-Moore) leaves him when he violently resents her probing into his marauding activities.

Almost equally impressive is the job done by Nick Foran as Bogart's factory sidekick, but antagonist of the Legion.

•

BLACKMAIL
1929, 88 mins, UK Ⓥ ⦿ b/w
Dir Alfred Hitchcock ***Prod*** John Maxwell ***Scr*** Alfred Hitchcock, Ben W. Levy, Charles Bennett ***Ph*** Jack Cox ***Ed*** Emile de Ruelle ***Mus*** Hubert Bath, Henry Stafford (arr.) ***Art*** Wilfred C. Arnold, Norman Arnold
Act Anny Ondra, Sara Allgood, Charles Paton, Donald Calthrop, John Longden, Cyril Ritchard (British International)

Blackmail is most draggy. It has no speed or pace and very little suspense. Everything's open-face. It's a story [from the play by Charles Bennett] that has been told in different disguises—the story of a girl who kills a man trying to assault her.

The girl, Anny Ondra, leaves a very lively scene in one of the Lyons feederies after flirting with a stranger and airing her steady, a regular Scotland Yard dick, to join the other half of the flirtation. The other half lives near the cigar store of her father, and asks the girl upstairs to see his studio, he being an artist. She foolishly assents, and then follows the jam.

In performance the standout is Donald Calthrop as the rat crook. He looks it. Ondra is excellent as the girl.

Dialog is ordinary but sufficient. Camerawork rather well, especially on the British Museum [in the chase finale] and the eating house scenes. A bit of comedy here and there, but not enough to be called relief.

•

BLACKMAIL
1939, 80 mins, US b/w
Dir H. C. Potter ***Prod*** John W. Considine ***Scr*** David Hertz, William Ludwig ***Ph*** Clyde DeVinna ***Ed*** Howard O'Neill ***Mus*** Edward Ward, David Snell ***Art*** Cedric Gibbons, Howard Campbell
Act Edward G. Robinson, Ruth Hussey, Gene Lockhart, Bobs Watson, Guinn Williams, John Wray (M-G-M)

Blackmail starts and finishes with spectacular oil well fires. In between there's some lusty and actionful melodrama, with moderate tincture of a wife's loyalty and sacrifice. Picture is a good programmer.

After giving promise of being a good story [by Endre Bohem and Dorothy Yost], script forgets all about its original background to take Edward G. Robinson back to a chain-gang camp to complete a sentence. This sequence, which runs through the middle of the picture, is realistically graphic in its display of physical brutality and mental torture.

Robinson rehabilitates himself after escape from a chain gang. Prospering as head of an oil well firefighting business in Oklahoma, he's a staid and happy family man. Gene Lockhart strolls into town, and after confessing to Robinson he committed the crime for which Robinson was sentenced, double-crosses Robinson, who goes back to serve his sentence. Tortured in the chain gang, and discovering his wife and son are destitute while Lockhart enjoys wealth from the oil well, Robinson escapes.

Robinson provides a vigorous characterization as the innocent victim of Lockhart's conniving and cunning. Lockhart is excellent as the nemesis. Ruth Hussey advances several notches up the film ladder with a most sympathetic and understanding portrayal of the loyal wife.

•

BLACK MARBLE, THE
1980, 112 mins, US Ⓥ ▭ col
Dir Harold Becker ***Prod*** Frank Capra, Jr. ***Scr*** Joseph Wambaugh ***Ph*** Owen Roizman ***Ed*** Maury Winetrobe ***Mus*** Maurice Jarre ***Art*** Alfred Sweeney
Act Robert Foxworth, Paula Prentiss, Harry Dean Stanton, Barbara Babcock, James Woods, Christopher Lloyd (Avco Embassy)

With *The Black Marble*, Joseph Wambaugh [adapting his own novel] at last comes close to presenting police as human, even humorous, beings, capable of balancing remorse, regret and romance without becoming total psychotics.

Transferred out of homicide after too much exposure to a string of child murders, Robert Foxworth is teamed on a burglary detail with Paula Prentiss. The crime is either terribly serious or impossibly trivial, depending on your love of animals. Barbara Babcock's show dog is kidnapped and she proves superb in the role of a lonely, sex-starved woman with her whole life wrapped up in her schnauzer.

Director Harold Becker is at his best in maneuvering carefully through the minefields of animal worship.

Much of the credit for making the picture work goes to Harry Dean Stanton as the dognapper, driven to his dirty deed by debt.

•

BLACK NARCISSUS
1947, 100 mins, UK Ⓥ ⦿ col
Dir Michael Powell, Emeric Pressburger ***Prod*** Michael Powell, Emeric Pressburger ***Scr*** Michael Powell, Emeric Pressburger ***Ph*** Jack Cardiff ***Ed*** Reginald Mills ***Mus*** Brian Easdale ***Art*** Alfred Junge
Act Deborah Kerr, Sabu, David Farrar, Kathleen Byron, Flora Robson, Jean Simmons (Archers)

Cynics may dub this lavish production *Brief Encounter in the Himalayas* and not without reason. Stripped of most of its finery, the picture [based on the novel by Rumer Godden] resolves itself into the story of two sex-starved women and a man. And since the women are nuns, there can be no happy ending except perhaps in the spiritual sense.

At the invitation of an Indian ruler, five sisters of an Anglo-Catholic order open a school and hospital in a remote Himalayan village. They occupy an ancient palace, once known as "The House of Women," built on a ledge 6,000 feet in the air. The nuns find their task overwhelming and Deborah Kerr, as the sister in charge, has to call for help on the cynical British agent, David Farrar, in spite of her instinctive antagonism.

To add to their worries, a native girl in need of a few months cloistering is boarded with the nuns by Farrar. The peace of the convent is further disturbed when the young general heir to the ruler enrolls as a pupil. Materially the work of the convent prospers, but Sister Kerr feels that spiritually most of the nuns are out of harmony. Her thoughts stray back to her girlhood sweetheart in Ireland. Another Sister is obviously thinking too much of Farrar and is taken to task.

Production has gained much through being in color. The production and camerawork atone for minor lapses in the story, Jack Cardiff's photography being outstanding.

The cast has been well chosen, but Kerr gets only occasional opportunities to reveal her talents.

Most effective acting comes from Kathleen Byron who has the picture's plum as the neurotic half-crazed Sister Ruth.

1947: Best Color Cinematography, Color Art Direction

•

BLACK ORCHID, THE
1959, 94 mins, US Ⓥ b/w
Dir Martin Ritt ***Prod*** Carlo Ponti, Marcello Girosi ***Scr*** Joseph Stefano ***Ph*** Robert Burks ***Ed*** Howard Smith ***Mus*** Alessandro Cicognini ***Art*** Hal Pereira, Roland Anderson
Act Sophia Loren, Anthony Quinn, Mark Richman, Ina Balin, Virginia Vincent, Frank Puglia (Paramount)

Orchid has a flavor of *Marty*, a touch of *Wild Is the Wind*. The story threads and changing emotions are securely locked in through Martin Ritt's honest direction. Without pushing, he tells an intricately drawn story with a smooth, authoritative hand.

As the widower who falls in love with the pretty widow, Anthony Quinn is excellent, uniting charm with strength. Sophia Loren plays with notable feeling, convincingly portraying the mother, the widow and the bride. The black orchid literally is a white rose—Rose Bianco—who is the late widow of a man she helped turn to crime to satisfy her own desires. Played by Loren, she mourns her husband and mourns what she has done when a widower (Quinn), with a daughter about to be married, comes along with a joyous manner and serious intentions.

The film technically is excellent, Robert Burks's photography standing out adeptly in black-and-white VistaVision. The musical score by Alessandro Cicognini aptly points up contrasts in the story.

•

BLACK ORPHEUS
SEE: ORFEU NEGRO

•

BLACKOUT
SEE: CONTRABAND

•

BLACK PIRATE, THE
1926, 88 mins, US Ⓥ ⦿ ⊗ col
Dir Albert Parker ***Prod*** Douglas Fairbanks ***Scr*** Elton Thomas [= Douglas Fairbanks], Jack Cunningham ***Ph*** Henry Sharp ***Ed*** William Nolan ***Art*** Karl Oscar Borg
Act Douglas Fairbanks, Billie Dove, Donald Crisp, Anders Randolf, Tempe Piggott, Sam De Grasse (Elton/United Artists)

Douglas Fairbanks's initial feature shot completely in color. It's as great a boost for the Technicolor process as for Fairbanks.

In the tale that it spins it's the weakest Fairbanks has ever had. It's simply a matter of scores of pirates in color and the Fairbanks curriculum of stunts.

Fairbanks is up and down the screen with his acrobatics, the punch being his taking of a merchant vessel singlehandedly as a pirate. His best athletic bit is the manner in which he rips the sails by mounting to the cross arms, piercing the wide sail with his sword, grabbing the hilt and descending to the deck, his momentum retarded by the sword ripping the canvas as he comes down.

•

BLACK RAIN
1989, 126 mins, US Ⓥ ⦿ ▭ col
Dir Ridley Scott ***Prod*** Stanley R. Jaffe, Sherry Lansing ***Scr*** Craig Bolotin, Warren Lewis ***Ph*** Jan DeBont ***Ed*** Tom Rolf ***Mus*** Hans Zimmer ***Art*** Norris Spencer
Act Michael Douglas, Andy Garcia, Ken Takakura, Kate Capshaw, Yusaku Matsuda, John Spencer (Paramount)

Since this is a Ridley Scott film, *Black Rain* is about 90 percent atmosphere and 10 percent story. But what atmosphere! This gripping crime thriller about hardboiled NY cop Michael Douglas tracking a *yakuza* hood in Osaka, Japan, boasts magnificent lensing and powerfully baroque production design.

Douglas is utterly believable as a reckless and scummy homicide detective who takes kickbacks from drug dealers and resorts to the most brutal methods to capture escaped counterfeiter Yusaka Matsuda.

First collaring Matsuda after a shocking outbreak of violence in a NY restaurant, Douglas is sent with him to Osaka, where he promptly loses him to the *yakuza* and watches helplessly as his partner Andy Garcia is murdered. Coming into conflict with the Japanese police, Douglas turns to the criminal underground to help bring in his prey.

Script fascinatingly depicts the growing influence of Ken Takakura's higher concepts of honor and loyalty on Douglas, who in turn causes some of his expedient lack of morality to rub off on the Japanese police inspector.

1989: Best Sound

NOMINATION: Best Sound Effects Editing

•

BLACK RAINBOW
1990, 113 mins, UK Ⓥ col
Dir Mike Hodges ***Prod*** John Quested, Geoffrey Helman ***Scr*** Mike Hodges ***Ph*** Gerry Fisher ***Ed*** Malcolm Cooke ***Mus*** John Scott ***Art*** Voytek
Act Rosanna Arquette, Jason Robards, Tom Hulce, Mark Joy, Ron Rosenthal, John Bennes (Goldcrest)

This enjoyable supernatural thriller is set in the fundamentalist society of crumbling industrial towns where folks have a deep-rooted faith in the spiritualist movement. Pic opens with journalist Tom Hulce tracking down traveling clairvoyant Rosanna Arquette to fill in the background to a story he himself was involved in some years before.

During one act Arquette receives a message from a murdered man to pass on to his wife in the audience. Unfortunately he is not dead and his wife gets rather upset. Later that night the man is killed in his home. Small-town reporter Hulce sets about uncovering the scoop, and follows Arquette and Jason Robards to their next town. There he gets drunk with Robards and sleeps with Arquette, but still doesn't believe her "gift." That night she predicts even more deaths, and again her vision comes true.

Arquette is excellent as the strange but seductive Martha. She has an ethereal quality combined with innate sexuality. Robards is in his element as the drunkard father. Hulce is intelligently restrained.

•

BLACK ROBE
1991, 100 mins, Canada/Australia Ⓥ ⦿ col
Dir Bruce Beresford ***Prod*** Robert Lantos, Stephane Reichel, Sue Milliken ***Scr*** Brian Moore ***Ph*** Peter James ***Ed*** Tim Wellburn ***Mus*** Georges Delerue ***Art*** Herbert Pinter
Act Lothaire Bluteau, Aden Young, Sandrine Holt, August Schellenberg, Tantoo Cardinal, Frank Wilson (Alliance/Samson)

First official coproduction between Canada and Australia is a magnificently staged combination of top talents delivering a gripping and tragic story about a 17th-century Jesuit priest's expedition through remote areas of "New France" (Quebec). Indian dialog is translated into English subtitles.

Saga begins in 1634 at Fort Champlain, where newly arrived French Jesuit priest Lothaire Bluteau (whom the Indians call "Black Robe" because of his austere garb), is assigned to a difficult and dangerous journey 1,500 miles north to the mission outpost of Ihonatiria. He's accompanied by a handful of friendly Algonquin Indians, led by the chief (August Schellenberg), his wife (Tantoo Cardinal), daughter (Sandrine Holt) and young son.

Also joining the party is Aden Young as a young French carpenter who develops a passionate relationship with the Algonquin girl. The travelers are captured, beaten and tortured. The priest arrives at his destination to find the priest in charge (Frank Wilson) dying and the local Indians decimated by a fever brought by the white men.

Director Bruce Beresford and writer Brian Moore [adapting his own novel] have made this intriguing yarn a small epic of endurance. The production has an austere beauty and thoughtful approach. Bluteau gives a moving performance in the central role, and Schellenberg is particularly notable as the friendly Chomina.

•

BLACK ROSE, THE
1950, 120 mins, US/UK Ⓥ col
Dir Henry Hathaway ***Prod*** Louis D. Lighton ***Scr*** Talbot Jennings ***Ph*** Jack Cardiff ***Ed*** Manuel del Campo ***Mus*** Richard Addinsell ***Art*** Paul Sherriff, W. Andrews
Act Tyrone Power, Orson Welles, Cecile Aubry, Jack Hawkins, Michael Rennie, Herbert Lom (20th Century-Fox)

Produced in England and North Africa with frozen currency, and with a supporting British cast, *Rose* is an adaptation of the Thomas B. Costain bestseller. It is 13th-century drama that seems hardly to have ignored a thing in its plotting.

Black Rose is the story of Saxon revolt against Norman domination, 200 years after the conquest. The central figure in the Saxon fight is Walter of Gurnie (Tyrone Power), the illegitimate son of a Saxon peer.

In a picture of warring, there is only the suggestion of battle. Perhaps one good scene, with some honest-to-goodness cinematic bloodletting, might have done something to increase the tempo of the picture.

Power is credible in the lead role, while Welles underplays effectively the part of Bayan.

1950: NOMINATION: Best Color Costume Design

•

BLACK STALLION, THE
1979, 118 mins, US Ⓥ ⦿ col
Dir Carroll Ballard ***Prod*** Fred Roos, Tom Sternberg ***Scr*** Melissa Mathison, Jeanne Rosenberg, William D. Wittliff ***Ph*** Caleb Deschanel ***Ed*** Robert Dalva ***Mus*** Carmine Coppola, [Shirley Walker] ***Art*** Aurelio Crugnola, Earl Preston
Act Kelly Reno, Mickey Rooney, Teri Garr (United Artists)

The Black Stallion is a perfect gem. Based on Walter Farley's 1941 novel, which spawned 16 sequels, Carroll Ballard's feature debut is rich in adventure, suspense and mythical elements and marks the prizewinning short-subjects director as a major talent. Ballard's camera eye and powers of sequence conceptualization are manifestly extraordinary. Set in 1949, pic is divided into four basic sections. Opening sees the American boy Alec (Kelly Reno) on a ship with his amiable father. Also on board is "the Black," a stallion owned by a menacing Arab.

After both end up overboard, Alec and the horse find sanctuary on a deserted Mediterranean island, filmed on unusual Sardinian locations. Ensuing half hour, in which the two gradually make contact and establish rapport is pulled off completely without dialog, backed instead by Carmine Coppola's richly complementary score.

After rescue, focus shifts Stateside. Alec's mother (Teri Garr) naturally doesn't understand her son's now nearly symbiotic relationship with Black. Horse escapes, later to be found by the boy at farm of retired racehorse trainer Mickey Rooney. Fourth act is consumed by Black's entry into a match race as a "mystery horse."

Performances are all low-keyed and right on pitch. Film went into production over two years earlier and is said to have experienced numerous problems along the way. They've all been ironed out.

1979: NOMINATIONS: Best Supp. Actor (Mickey Rooney), Editing

•

BLACK STALLION RETURNS, THE
1983, 93 mins, US Ⓥ ⦿ col
Dir Robert Dalva ***Prod*** Tom Sternberg, Fred Roos, Doug Claybourne ***Scr*** Richard Kletter, Jerome Kass ***Ph*** Carlo Di Palma, Caleb Deschanel ***Ed*** Paul Hirsch ***Mus*** Georges Delerue ***Art*** Aurelio Crugnola
Act Kelly Reno, Vincent Spano, Allen Garfield, Woody Strode, Ferdy Mayne, Teri Garr (Zoetrope)

The Black Stallion Returns is little more than a contrived, cornball story that most audiences will find to be an interminable bore. Much of the charm and innocence of the original are absent here as now young teen-hero Kelly Reno follows the unlikeliest of searches through the Sahara Desert for his devoted horse.

A band of supposed "good guy" Moroccans steal the horse in order to bring him back to his real home in the deserts of nothern Africa (where he will run in a once-every-five-years horse race) much to the chagrin of the "bad guy" Moroccans who represent a supposedly evil tribe.

Robert Dalva, who edited *The Black Stallion* serves as director here but doesn't manage to convincingly merge the feelings of fantasy and reality that made the first film so charming.

•

BLACK SUNDAY
1977, 143 mins, US Ⓥ ⦿ ▭ col
Dir John Frankenheimer ***Prod*** Robert Evans ***Scr*** Ernest Lehman, Kenneth Ross, Ivan Moffat ***Ph*** John A. Alonzo ***Ed*** Tom Rolf ***Mus*** John Williams ***Art*** Walter Tyler
Act Robert Shaw, Bruce Dern, Marthe Keller, Fritz Weaver, Steven Keats, Bekim Fehmiu (Paramount)

John Frankenheimer's film of *Black Sunday* is an intelligent and meticulous depiction of an act of outlandish terrorism—the planned slaughter of the Super Bowl stadium audience.

Strong scripting and performances elevate Robert Evans's handsome production far above the crass exploitation level, which at least mitigates subject matter that can never be completely comfortable on the minds of an audience.

Thomas Harris's novel has been adapted into a well-plotted, well-executed countdown to potential mass disaster. The motivations of stars Robert Shaw, as an Israeli guerrilla, Black September activist Marthe Keller and mentally unbalanced pilot Bruce Dern are handled with unusual dramatic depth which displays the gray areas of real life.

•

BLACK SWAN, THE
1942, 83 mins, US col
Dir Henry King ***Prod*** Robert Bassler ***Scr*** Ben Hecht, Seton I. Miller ***Ph*** Leon Shamroy ***Ed*** Barbara McLean ***Mus*** Alfred Newman ***Art*** Richard Day, James Basevi
Act Tyrone Power, Maureen O'Hara, Laird Cregar, Thomas Mitchell, George Sanders, Anthony Quinn (20th Century-Fox)

This is a lusty story [from a novel by Rafael Sabatini] of English buccaneers who plunder women and the Spanish Main with equal facility. Some of the pirates reform, while the others meet their just desserts at sword's end or the gallows. Thus chief pirate Laird Cregar, playing Henry Morgan, winds up as the honest governor of Jamaica; his chief aide (Tyrone Power) likewise turns pure, even winning the love of Maureen O'Hara, whom he previously tries to compromise; Thomas Mitchell also winds up a reformed pirate, while such brutes as George Sanders and Anthony Quinn, as a one-eyed scourge of the sea, become dead pirates.

Some of the film's action stuff is of the cliff-hanger variety, but director Henry King keeps the fantasy pretty well in hand so that it doesn't become too ludicrous. He paces the story well with the dialogue bright and peppery.

1942: Best Color Cinematography

•

BLACK WATCH, THE
1929, 91 mins, US b/w
Dir John Ford ***Scr*** John Stone, J. K. McGuinness ***Ph*** Joseph H. August ***Ed*** A. Troffey
Act Victor McLaglen, Myrna Loy, David Rollins, Roy D'Arcy, Walter Long, Mitchell Lewis (Fox)

Story is loose jointed and far from well knit, the audience being asked to take plenty for granted.

Talbot Mundy's tale is that of the Scottish Captain King (Victor McLaglen), who is ordered to India to prevent a native uprising on the eve his regiment is leaving for France. He gets into a drunken brawl, during which he supposedly kills a fellow serviceman, the ruse being an escape among the pack of fanatics planning to overthrow British rule. The natives worship a woman (Myrna Loy) as their goddess, who, in turn, succumbs to the brawn of King.

Just how King manages to get about a dozen British soldiers among the hordes, who, at a signal, throw off their robes to reveal khaki, is not explained.

Director John Ford's best work is the opening of a Scottish officers' dinner on the eve of war, with bagpipes wailing. Joseph August's camerawork is superb. McLaglen's performance is just normal. Loy sheds an attractive appearance under, at times, outstanding lighting, aided by long robes.

•

BLACK WIDOW
1954, 95 mins, US ▭ col
Dir Nunnally Johnson ***Prod*** Nunnally Johnson ***Scr*** Nunnally Johnson ***Ph*** Charles G. Clarke ***Ed*** Dorothy Spencer ***Mus*** Leigh Harline
Act Ginger Rogers, Van Heflin, Gene Tierney, George Raft, Peggy Ann Garner, Reginald Gardiner (20th Century-Fox)

The up-front reels spin off somewhat slowly as the plot groundwork is laid but, once the business of murder is gotten down to, *Black Widow* takes a firm and unrelenting grip on audience attention.

Flashbacks are worked in smoothly in relating how Nanny, a young girl (Peggy Ann Garner), comes to Gotham with a yen to break into the big time and winds up the murder victim. Brought into the web are: Lottie (Ginger Rogers), a top-rung legit actress and shallow character who finds evil delight in meddling into others' lives; Peter (Van Heflin), producer of Lottie's current play, whose assistance to Nanny backfires into odious involvement in her murder; Gene Tierney, as Heflin's wife and also a prominent stage actress; and Bruce (George Raft), the detective on the prowl for a murderer.

Under Nunnally Johnson's direction, *Widow* plays out plausibly and with some solid tense moments. The audience is kept properly confused as to who the actual murderer really is.

Music nicely underscores the dramatic high points and Chales G. Clarke's camerawork manages to achieve intimacy despite the big screen. There are a few instances, though, wherein closeup lensing of dialog exchanges between the story's characters must be followed in a fashion somewhat akin to watching a tennis match.

•

BLACK WIDOW
1987, 103 mins, US Ⓥ ⦿ col
Dir Bob Rafelson ***Prod*** Harold Schneider ***Scr*** Ronald Bass ***Ph*** Conrad L. Hall ***Ed*** John Bloom ***Mus*** Michael Small ***Art*** Gene Callahan
Act Debra Winger, Theresa Russell, Sami Frey, Dennis Hopper, Nicol Williamson, Diane Ladd (Mark/Americent/American Entertainment)

Lacking the snap and sharpness that might have made it a first-rate thriller, *Black Widow* instead plays as a moderately interesting tale of one woman's obsession for another's glamorous and criminal lifestyle.

Theresa Russell portrays an icy-hard, beautiful woman who, it quickly becomes clear, makes an exceptionally handsome living by marrying wealthy men, murdering them, then collecting the settlements from the wills.

Pattern would go unnoticed were it not for conscientious, disheveled Justice Dept agent Debra Winger, who thinks she smells a rat and begs permission to pursue the case.

Winger first takes off after her prey for purely professional reasons, but the most intriguing aspect of screenplay is the barely submerged sexual jealousy the overworked government employee feels for the sexy, utterly confident manipulator of sex and lives.

Winger and Russell are both talented and watchable young actresses, so the picture has a lot going for it thanks to their casting alone. At the same time, both play very tense, brittle women rather near the breaking point, so there is a nervousness and restraint in both performances that harnesses them slightly.

•

BLACK WINDMILL, THE
1974, 106 mins, UK Ⓥ ▭ col
Dir Don Siegel ***Prod*** Don Siegel ***Scr*** Leigh Vance ***Ph*** Ousama Rawi ***Ed*** Antony Gibbs ***Mus*** Roy Budd ***Art*** Peter Murton
Act Michael Caine, Donald Pleasence, Delphine Seyrig, Clive Revill, John Vernon, Joss Ackland (Universal)

Don Siegel's filmmaking takes a dip in *The Black Windmill*, a British espionage drama with Michael Caine as an agent whose son has been kidnapped by one of his own spy colleagues. All principal players are well cast, but the production fizzles in its final half-hour because the story premise gets clobbered by clumsy and ineffective resolution and execution.

Clive Egleton's novel, *Seven Days to a Killing*, has been adapted by Leigh Vance. Script sets Caine up well: his superior (Donald Pleasence) hates him anyway, so the kidnapping and later circumstantial evidence suggests Caine himself has arranged the snatch. Janet Suzman, estranged from Caine because of his work, returns to his side. John Vernon and Delphine Seyrig are key figures in the kidnap and concurrent entrapment of Caine.

•

BLACULA
1972, 92 mins, US Ⓥ ⦿ col
Dir William Crain ***Prod*** Joseph T. Naar ***Scr*** Joan Torres, Raymond Koenig ***Ph*** John Stevens ***Ed*** Allan Jacobs ***Mus*** Gene Page ***Art*** Walter Herndon
Act William Marshall, Vonetta McGee, Denise Nicholas, Thalmus Rasulala, Gordon Pinsent, Charles McCauley (American International)

Count Dracula has a black counterpart. Following a prolog located in Transylvania (where else?), when Count Dracula places the vampire curse upon an African prince and condemns him to the realm of the undead, plot picks up in Los Angeles nearly two centuries later. A pair of interior decorators have purchased all the furnishings of Castle Dracula and shipped them to America, including the locked coffin in which Blacula is resting.

William Marshall portrays title role with a flourish and gets first-rate support right down the line: Vonetta McGee, whom he believes to be his reincarnated wife; Thalmus Rasulala, a black doctor who hits upon mystery of the rash of murders in L.A.; and Gordon Pinsent, homicide lieutenant who learns the hard way that murders are the work of vampires.

•

BLADE
1998, 121 mins, US Ⓥ ⦿ ▭ col
Dir Stephen Norrington ***Prod*** Peter Frankfurt, Wesley Snipes, Robert Engleman ***Scr*** David S. Goyer ***Ph*** Theo Van De Sande ***Ed*** Paul Rubell ***Mus*** Mark Isham ***Art*** Kirk M. Petruccelli
Act Wesley Snipes, Stephen Dorff, Kris Kristofferson, N'Bushe Wright, Donal Logue, Udo Kier (Amen Ra/New Line)

The edge is off *Blade*, which top-lines Wesley Snipes as a Marvel Comics–derived vampire slayer. Though slick and diverting in some aspects, increasingly silly pic [based on characters created by Marv Wolfman and Gene Colan] has trouble meshing disparate elements—horror, superhero fantasy, straight-up action—into a workable whole.

Post-credits set piece is far and away the film's best. A young man [lured into a vampire dance club] is saved by the sudden appearance of Blade—Snipes in a sort of black leather RoboCop ensemble. But when the cops arrive, they take aim at Blade, revealing that certain authorities have an agreement with the vampire colony so long as they stay "underground."

Protag flees, leaving behind a charred undead man. When this figure is delivered to the morgue, he provides an unpleasant surprise for hematologist Karen (N'Bushe Wright) and her ex-boyfriend coworker (Tim Guinee). Wounded Karen is taken by Blade to the warehouse lair he shares with grizzled mortal Whistler (Kris Kristofferson), his loyal partner in creature killing.

The ghoul eatery-cum-discos are the brainchild of young Turk vampire Frost (Stephen Dorff), much frowned upon by a corporate old guard led by Dragonetti (Udo Kier). Frost wants to rock the boat and instigate a full-fledged "vampire apocalypse."

Scenarist David S. Goyer (*Dark City*) and director Stephen Norrington (*Death Machine*) create a lineup of hyperbolic action sequences that encompass everything from kickbox-y martial arts to often gory, supernatural effects. What they don't manage is much sustained atmosphere or cumulative excitement. Minimal comic relief falls flat.

Cast as a standard, iron-jawed superhero [with the characteristics of both undead and mortals], Snipes gets to show off muscular athleticism. Dorff sneers competently.

•

BLADE RUNNER
1982, 114 mins, US Ⓥ ⦿ ▭ col
Dir Ridley Scott ***Prod*** Michael Deeley ***Scr*** Hampton Fancher, David Peoples ***Ph*** Jordan Cronenweth ***Ed*** Terry Rawlings, Marsha Nakashima ***Mus*** Vangelis ***Art*** Lawrence G. Paull
Act Harrison Ford, Rutger Hauer, Sean Young, Edward James Olmos, M. Emmet Walsh, Daryl Hannah (Warner/Ladd)

Ridley Scott's reported $30 million picture is a stylistically dazzling film noir set in November 2019 in a brilliantly imagined Los Angeles marked by both technological wonders and horrendous squalor.

Basic premise taken from a novel [*Do Androids Dream of Electric Sheep?*] by Philip K. Dick provides a strong dramatic hook—replicants, robots designed to supply "Off-World" slave labor, are outlawed on earth. But a few of them have infiltrated L.A., and retired enforcer Harrison Ford is recruited to eliminate them before they can do any damage.

One of them, beautiful Sean Young, is an advanced model with implanted memories so "real" that even she doesn't know she's a replicant until she's tested by Ford.

Unfortunately, Young disappears for long stretches at a time, and at others Ford merely sits morosely around his apartment staring at photographs, which slows up the action.

Dramatically, film is virtually taken over at the midway point by top replicant Rutger Hauer. After destroying his creator, the massive, albino-looking Hauer takes off after Ford, and the villain here is so intriguing and charismatic that one almost comes to prefer him to the more stolid hero.

[In 1992, Scott's original cut, sans Ford's voice-over and final flying sequence, was released. This 117-min. version was billed on posters, but not on prints, as *The Director's Cut*.]

1982: NOMINATIONS: Best Art Direction, Visual Effects

•

BLAIR WITCH PROJECT, THE
1999, 87 mins, US Ⓥ ⦿ col
Dir Daniel Myrick, Eduardo Sanchez ***Prod*** Gregg Hale, Robin Cowie ***Scr*** Daniel Myrick, Eduardo Sanchez ***Ph*** Neal Fredericks ***Ed*** Daniel Myrick, Eduardo Sanchez ***Mus*** Tony Cora ***Art*** Ben Rock
Act Heather Donahue, Michael Williams, Joshua Leonard, Bob Griffith, Jim King, Sandra Sanchez (Haxan)

An intensely imaginative piece of conceptual filmmaking that also delivers the goods as a dread-drenched horror movie, resourceful ultra-lowbudgeter *The Blair Witch Project* puts a clever modern twist on the universal fear of the dark and things that go bump in the night.

An opening title card informs that, in October 1994, three young filmmakers hiked into the Black Hills Forest in Maryland to shoot a docu about the legend of the Blair Witch. The filmmakers were never heard of again, but a year later their footage was found, an edited version of which constitutes the present feature.

[According to pic's production notes, writer-director-editors Daniel Myrick and Eduardo Sanchez heightened the project's verisimilitude by training their actors to use cameras, then sending them out into the forest for eight days to shoot the picture themselves; certain destination points and encounters were established in advance, and notes to the thesps were left in baskets along the way.]

All the visuals are either handheld, often jittery color-video images taken by the bossy director and project organizer, Heather, or black-and-white 16mm shots lensed by the troupe's tyro cameraman, the hippie-ish Joshua; regular guy Michael is along to record sound.

The Blair Witch legend involves numerous mysterious disappearances and evidence of gruesome torture many years before. Terror sets in on the second night when they hear what sounds like people circling their tent. Thus begins an awful succession of days taken up with endless walking and periods of willed levelheadedness broken by fear-driven yelling and recriminations about how they ever got into this mess.

Climax is both intense and ambiguous. All the same, the film builds up a sense of horrific expectation that it can't quite match in its payoff. Thesps are uniformly naturalistic.

•

BLAME IT ON RIO
1984, 110 mins, US Ⓥ ⦿ col
Dir Stanley Donen ***Prod*** Stanley Donen ***Scr*** Charlie Peters, Larry Gelbart ***Ph*** Reynaldo Villalobos ***Ed*** George Hively, Richard Marden ***Mus*** Ken Wannberg, Oscar Castro Neves ***Art*** Marcos Flaksman
Act Michael Caine, Joseph Bologna, Valerie Harper, Michelle Johnson, Jose Lewgoy, Demi Moore (Sherwood/20th Century-Fox)

Central premise of a secret romance between Michael Caine and the love-smitten daughter of his best friend (Joe Bologna) while the trio vacations together in torrid Rio may be adventurous comedy. Zany comedic conflict, however, is offputting, even at times nasty, in this essentially dead-ahead comedy that sacrifices charm and a light touch for too much realism.

Newcomer Michelle Johnson comes off as callow and disagreeably spoiled in key role of buxom daughter lusting after dad's best buddy.

Caine and Bologna play colleagues in a Sao Paulo coffee company whose marriages are toppling—Bologna is getting a divorce and Caine's wife (Valerie Harper) tells Caine while couple is packing for Rio that she's splitting for Bahia in a separate vacation.

Director Stanley Donen gets sharp, comic performances from Caine and Bologna.

•

BLAME IT ON THE BELLBOY
1992, 77 mins, UK/US Ⓥ col
Dir Mark Herman ***Prod*** Jennie Howarth, Steve Abbott ***Scr*** Mark Herman ***Ph*** Andrew Dunn ***Ed*** Michael Ellis ***Mus*** Trevor Jones ***Art*** Gemma Jackson
Act Dudley Moore, Bryan Brown, Richard Griffiths, Andreas Katsulas, Patsy Kensit, Alison Steadman (Hollywood)

British farce meets the ghost of the *Carry On* series in *Blame It on the Bellboy*, a lightweight ensemble comedy in which ingenious plotting is let down by weak dialog and stop-go direction that largely squanders the talent involved.

Plot gets off to a promising start with three similarly named characters—Orton, Lawton and Horton—checking into a Venice hotel. Thanks to a bellboy who can't speak English, their mail gets mixed up. Realtor Dudley Moore gets a letter for hit man Bryan Brown, who gets a letter for blind-dater Richard Griffiths, who gets a letter for Moore.

Moore is soon wired up to a generator by local mobster Andreas Katsulas; Brown thinks his target is lonely blind-dater Penelope Wilton; and Griffiths schmoozes with sexy Patsy Kensit, who's into a real-estate scam rather than a roll in the hay.

Problem is first-time director-scripter Mark Herman couldn't decide to make a breakneck farce or goofy comedy. The Brit actors mostly phone in their performances.

•

BLAUE ENGEL, DER
(THE BLUE ANGEL)
1930, 109 mins, Germany Ⓥ ⊙ b/w
Dir Josef von Sternberg ***Prod*** Erich Pommer ***Scr*** Carl Zuckmayer, Karl Vollmueller, Robert Liebmann ***Ph*** Guenther Rittau, Hans Schneeberger ***Mus*** Friedrich Hollander ***Art*** Otto Hunte, Emil Hasler
Act Emil Jannings, Marlene Dietrich, Kurt Gerron, Rosa Valetti, Hans Albers, Eduard von Winterstein (UFA)

Producer Erich Pommer's idea of engaging Josef von Sternberg to direct Emil Jannings's first starring vehicle for UFA proved an astute calculation. On top of the drawing power of Jannings comes the discovery of a new magnet, Marlene Dietrich.

At the beginning the scenario sticks pretty closely to the novel, *Professor Unrath* by Heinrich Mann, on which it is founded. A middle-aged school teacher discovers that several of his pupils are attending a dive, the Blue Angel, and hanging around the performer Lola. He goes to the cabaret in the hope of catching them redhanded and falls for the singer himself.

Despite the jeers of his pupils and the warnings of the principal of the school, he marries Lola. As a result, he loses his position. In the novel he and the girl remain in the town and she takes on several influential citizens. At the end the two are running a well-paying gambling house patronized by all the good burghers.

Sternberg chose a more conventional twist. The teacher sinks from peddler of postcards showing his wife in seminudity to assistant in a magician's act. Despite his protests, he has to play in his native town and is featured on the bill under his real name.

Kurt Gerron and Rosa Valetti as a hard-boiled conjuror and old comedienne are perfect in their roles of rather sardonic comic relief. Dietrich as Lola has a slow-rhythmed sensuality which gets over without being in any way crude or offensive.

Sound on the whole satisfactory, especially the music. Dialog not always natural in quality and in the dramatic passages has a tendency to become distorted.

Only fault is a certain ponderousness of tempo which tends to tire. The story is not one with strong dramatic impulse and seldom grips with suspense or moves you emotionally. It is the exceptional playing of Jannings and Dietrich, and the sensitive direction of Sternberg which put it across.

[Review above is of German version. Paramount released the English version, shot at the same time, later that year, following its success with *Morocco*, Dietrich's first U.S. picture.]

•

BLAZE
1989, 108 mins, US Ⓥ ⊙ col
Dir Ron Shelton ***Prod*** Gil Friesen, Dale Pollock ***Scr*** Ron Shelton ***Ph*** Haskell Wexler ***Ed*** Robert Leighton ***Mus*** Bennie Wallace ***Art*** Armin Ganz
Act Paul Newman, Lolita Davidovich, Jerry Hardin, Gailard Sartain, Jeffrey DeMunn (Touchstone/Silver Screen Partners IV)

A bawdy and audacious tale of politics and scandal, *Blaze* delivers a good love story and a brave and marvelous character turn by Paul Newman. Newman plays Louisiana governor Earl K. Long in 1959–60 during his May-December romance with famed New Orleans stripper Blaze Starr (Lolita Davidovich).

"Ol' Earl," a self-decribed "progressive thinker," was a stump speaker extraordinaire, an advocate of black voting rights and a friend of the poor man. He was also, many believed, a tax evader, a drunk and a madman. Starr was a queen of tawdry New Orleans showbiz who'd come up from poverty in the Tennessee hills.

In Shelton's hands, their relationship, which churned up newspaper headlines and plagued Long's teetering career, is a great and comic love story.

Davidovich is impressive, taking the character from a clunky, overripe hillbilly teenager to a woman with her powers fully focused.

1989: NOMINATION: Best Cinematography

•

BLAZING SADDLES
1974, 93 mins, US Ⓥ ⊙ ▭ col
Dir Mel Brooks ***Prod*** Michael Hertzberg ***Scr*** Mel Brooks, Norman Steinberg, Andrew Bergman, Richard Pryor, Alan Uger ***Ph*** Joseph Biroc ***Ed*** John C. Howard, Danford Greene ***Mus*** John Morris ***Art*** Peter Wooley
Act Cleavon Little, Gene Wilder, Slim Pickens, David Huddleston, Mel Brooks, Madeline Kahn (Crossbow/Warner)

Blazing Saddles spoofs old-time westerns with an avalanche of one-liners, vaudeville routines, campy shticks, sight gags, satiric imitations and comic anachronisms. Pic [from a screen story by Alan Uger] is essentially a raunchy, protracted version of a television comedy skit.

Although Cleavon Little and Gene Wilder head a uniformly competent cast, pic is handily stolen by Harvey Korman and Madeline Kahn. Kahn is simply terrific doing a Marlene Dietrich lampoon.

Rest of cast is fine, although Little's black sheriff doesn't blend too well with Brooks's Jewish-flavored comic style. Wilder is amusingly low-key in a relatively small role.

1974: NOMINATIONS: Best Supp. Actress (Madeline Kahn), Editing, Song ("Blazing Saddles")

•

BLEAK MOMENTS
1972, 110 mins, UK col
Dir Mike Leigh ***Prod*** Les Blair ***Scr*** Mike Leigh ***Ph*** Bahram Manoochehri ***Ed*** Les Blair ***Mus*** Mike Bardwell ***Art*** Richard Rambant
Act Anne Raitt, Sarah Stephenson, Eric Allan, Joolia Cappleman, Mike Bradwell, Liz Smith (Autumn/Memorial)

A film with downbeat themes of solitude, difficulties of communication, coping with a retarded 29-year-old sister, it has enough human insight sans mawkishness or undue sentimentality to make it wryly funny, with its recognition of human foibles that gives it an edge, charm and warmth, tempered with compassion.

Anne Raitt, a handsome, heavyset woman, works in an office with a candy-eating friend who dreams of a possible, but not probable, marriage.

Raitt has a quiet suitor who turns out to be impotent. Their night out in a Chinese restaurant is a revealing set piece. Raitt has rented her garage to a hippie who publishes an underground newspaper. As the hippie leaves, all revert to their original bleak but never depressing lives, which will go on unless something good or better comes along or they take a more affirmative stand.

•

BLECHTROMMEL, DIE
(THE TIN DRUM)
1979, 150 mins, W. Germany/France Ⓥ ⊙ col
Dir Volker Schlondorff ***Prod*** Franz Seitz ***Scr*** Jean-Claude Carriere, Volker Schloendorff, Franz Seitz, Guenter Grass ***Ph*** Igor Luther ***Ed*** Suzanne Baron ***Mus*** Friedrich Meyer ***Art*** Nicos Perakis
Act Mario Adorf, Angela Winkler, David Bennent, Daniel Olbrychski, Katharina Thalbach, Heinz Bennent (Seitz/Bioskop/Artemis/Hallelujah/GGB/Argos

This two-and-a-half-hour adaptation of Guenter Grass's world-renowned novel, *The Tin Drum*, was made by the best craftsman on the German film scene, Volker Schloendorff, and produced at a circa $4 million budget by vet producer Franz Seitz. It was lensed partially in Poland (also in France and Yugoslavia, as well as West Germany) to fit the novel's Danzig character and adheres to the book more than enough not to disappoint avid readers of the best-seller.

The Tin Drum (published 1959) is a complex, "free association" novel, strongly antireligious and (in a positive sense) antipolitical; it is also humorous and absurd, as well as being historical and metaphoric. In short, a mudsling at the beloved *Bildungsroman* in classic German literature.

This is the tale of a Tiny Tim who is a Jack the Giant Killer at the same time. Even before his birth, Oskar Matzerath in his mother's womb realizes he has special gifts. One is breaking glass with his voice; another is the decision at three years of age not to grow another centimeter. Because of his stunted growth, he can crawl under tables and skirts to watch, with sardonic eye, the lies and hypocrisies about him. This is a chronicle on the history of Germany from the beginning of this century (the film's introductory part before Oskar is born) up to nearly the present day, i.e. 1959 (the final chapters of the book are excluded), with a special emphasis on the city of Danzig where Poles and Germans were constantly in strife. Most of all, it's about that social and political phenomenon known as Nazism.

Several scenes in *Tin Drum* are eye-catchers. The attack on the Danzig Post Office where Polish Resistance fighters have banded together is expertly handled, as well as other crowd scenes, particularly one about a Nazi Party Day during which Oskar's drum puts everything out-of-step.

As Oskar, David Bennet (a boy of 12 hindered in his own growth, so that he appears to be about five years old) has the eyes and the acting talent to carry some scenes remarkably well, but he is not the insatiable wallower in sex and religious mysticism that Grass intended.

1979: Best Foreign Language Film

•

BLIND ALLEY
1939, 68 mins, US b/w
Dir Charles Vidor ***Prod*** Fred Kohlmar (assoc.) ***Scr*** Philip MacDonald, Michael Blankfort, Albert Duffy ***Ph*** Lucien Ballard ***Ed*** Otto Meyer ***Mus*** Morris Stoloff (dir.) ***Art*** Lionel Banks
Act Chester Morris, Ralph Bellamy, Ann Dvorak, Joan Perry, Melville Cooper, Rose Stradner (Columbia)

In attempting to delve into the psychopathic reasons why a criminal carries a killer complex, *Blind Alley* holds moderate interest [pic is based on a play by James Warwick].

Chester Morris gives a vigorous portrayal of the killer, while Ralph Bellamy contrasts with a quiet and self-assured role of the professor of psychology. Balance of cast provides adequate support, and direction, by Charles Vidor, although slow in several spots, is okay.

Morris is aided in a prison break by group of former associates, and gang winds up in weekend home of Bellamy to make prisoners of the family and guests. Setup allows mental conflict between the criminal and psychologist to generate through dramatic phases while Bellamy proceeds to uncover the subconscious basis for Morris's killing mania.

•

BLIND DATE
1987, 93 mins, US Ⓥ ⊙ ▭ col
Dir Blake Edwards ***Prod*** Tony Adams ***Scr*** Dale Launer ***Ph*** Harry Stradling ***Ed*** Robert Pergament ***Mus*** Henry Mancini ***Art*** Rodger Maus
Act Kim Basinger, Bruce Willis, John Larroquette, William Daniels, Phil Hartman, Stepanie Faracy (Tri-Star)

Bruce Willis abandons his mugging TV personality in favor of playing an animated, amiable, hard-working, ambitious financial analyst in LA.

Stuck without a date for a company function, he reluctantly agrees to ask his brother's wife's cousin (Kim Basinger) to accompany him. His first impression: she's darling. His first mistake: he's not supposed to let her drink and ignores the advice. Two sips of champagne later, she's out of control.

Theme of pure mayhem works well because of chemistry between the main trio of actors, Willis, Basinger and her spurned ex-beau (John Larroquette).

Basinger is cool when sober and wacky when drunk. Her part is really secondary to Willis's, who starts out a befuddled date with the manners of a gentleman and ends up not only befuddled, but crazy for the woman.

It's really the psychotic Larroquette who drives this romp. While Willis tries to control his date (or at least figure her out), Larroquette is hot on his tail trying to get her back. Their skirmishes are hilarious. Pic is essentially a running string of gags with snippets of catchy dialog in between.

•

BLINDFOLD
1966, 102 mins, US ▭ col
Dir Philip Dunne ***Prod*** Marvin Schwartz ***Scr*** Philip Dunne, W. H. Menger ***Ph*** Joseph MacDonald ***Ed*** Ted J. Kent ***Mus*** Lalo Schifrin ***Art*** Alexander Golitzen, Henry Bumstead
Act Rock Hudson, Claudia Cardinale, Jack Warden, Guy Stockwell, Brad Dexter, Alejandro Rey (Universal/7 Pictures)

In their adaptation of Lucille Fletcher's novel, scripters have approached their task with sights set on combining romantic comedy with tome's adventurous elements. Director Philip Dunne follows through with this tenor in his visual exposition.

Hudson plays part of a famed NY psychologist treating a mentally disturbed scientist sought by an international ring, who becomes involved in a plot to kidnap scientist from a top-secret hideout. Film takes its title from his being blindfolded whenever he is to visit his patient, held for self-protection by the government in a secluded spot in the swamp country of the South, where doctor is flown every night from NY.

Hudson offers one of his customary light portrayals, sometimes on the cloyingly coy side, and is in for more physical action than usual. Claudia Cardinale, as the chorus-girl sister of the scientist, displays plenty of appeal. Jack Warden, as an American general in charge of protecting the scientist and who hires Hudson to bring him out of his despondency, knows his way through a line and Guy Stockwell heads the ring.

•

BLIND FURY
1989, 85 mins, US Ⓥ ⦿ col
Dir Phillip Noyce ***Prod*** Daniel Grodnik, Tim Matheson ***Scr*** Charles Robert Carner ***Ph*** Don Burgess ***Ed*** David Simmons ***Mus*** J. Peter Robinson ***Art*** Peter Murton
Act Rutger Hauer, Brandon Call, Terry O'Quinn, Lisa Blount, Meg Foster, Sho Kosugi (Tri-Star/Interscope)

Blind Fury is an action film with an amusing gimmick, toplining Rutger Hauer, as an apparently invincible blind Vietnam vet who wields a samurai sword with consummate skill.

Nick Parker (Hauer) is actually based on Zatoichi, the heroic blind samurai who starred in a couple of dozen popular actions films for Japanese company Daiei in the 1960s and early 1970s.

First problem for writer Charles Robert Carner [adapting a screenplay by Ryozo Kasahara] is to find a way to Americanize such a character. This is solved by having Parker blinded and lost in action in Vietnam and then trained by friendly Vietnamese to use his other senses to survive.

Twenty years later, Parker is back in Miami to look up an old army buddy, Frank Deveraux (Terry O'Quinn) who's in trouble with the mob in Reno. Parker's in time to prevent the kidnapping of Billy (Brandon Call), Frank's son, but not to stop the murder of Frank's ex-wife, Lynn (Meg Foster, in for only one scene) by the vicious Slag, played by Randall "Tex" Cobb.

The rest of the film is simply a series of fights and chases as Parker heads for Reno to reunite Billy with his father.

•

BLIND TERROR
SEE: SEE NO EVIL

•

BLINK
1994, 106 mins, US Ⓥ ⦿ ▭ col
Dir Michael Apted ***Prod*** David Blocker ***Scr*** Dana Stevens ***Ph*** Dante Spinotti ***Ed*** Rick Shaine ***Mus*** Brad Fiedel ***Art*** Dan Bishop
Act Madeleine Stowe, Aidan Quinn, Laurie Metcalf, James Remar, Peter Friedman, Bruce A. Young (New Line)

High concept blurs the bedrock of plot and plausibility in *Blink*. A thriller steeped in scientific research, its focus is too often bogged down in lab-room mumbo jumbo.

Outing is about a formerly blind woman in peril from a killer whom she may or may not have seen. Musician Emma Brody (Madeleine Stowe) has recently regained her eyesight following a corneal transplant. But the coordination between what her brain registers and what she actually sees isn't quite aligned.

One evening upon hearing noise in the hallway of her apartment building, she goes to investigate. All she can discern is a form until the next morning, when she hallucinates a man's face. As her upstairs neighbor was murdered the night before, it doesn't take a genius to figure out what the killer might look like. The only reason John Hallstrom (Aidan Quinn)—the detective in charge of investigating the presumed serial killer—begins to rely on Emma is because she's his only witness and he's sexually attracted to her.

Stowe simply is not good in the role of a somewhat dumb woman in jeopardy, though she has more range here than in *Unlawful Entry*. Quinn is just barely capable of keeping a straight face confronted with his cop steeped in cliche.

•

BLISS
1985, 135 mins, Australia Ⓥ ⦿ col
Dir Ray Lawrence ***Prod*** Anthony Buckley ***Scr*** Ray Lawrence, Peter Carey ***Ph*** Paul Murphy ***Ed*** Wayne Le Clos ***Mus*** Peter Best ***Art*** Owen Paterson
Act Barry Otto, Lynette Curran, Helen Jones, Miles Buchanan, Gia Carides, Tim Robertson (Window III/NSW Film Corp.)

Pic opens with the death of Harry Joy (Barry Otto), its central character. He runs an ad agency and leads an apparently happy life with a wife and two children. A heart attack fells him during a family gathering, and he's dead for four minutes. When he recovers, he believes he has entered Hell.

That's because everything seems to have changed. His loving wife (Lynette Curran) is having an open affair with his sleazy business partner (Jeff Truman); his son (Miles Buchanan) is a drugrunner with ambitions to join the Mafia; his daughter (Gia Carides) is an addict who gives her brother sexual favors to get free dope; and Harry discovers, too, that his biggest client manufacturers products known to cause cancer. Faced with these unexpected upheavals, Harry goes a little mad.

The biggest flaw in *Bliss* is the way the novel has been adapted by its author, Peter Carey, and director Ray Lawrence. The best films of difficult books (and *Bliss* was a difficult book) have pared down the source material while keeping the spirit and intention of the original. Carey and Lawrence have left nothing out; the film teems with characters.

•

BLISS OF MRS. BLOSSOM, THE
1968, 93 mins, UK col
Dir Joseph MacGrath ***Prod*** Josef Shaftel ***Scr*** Alec Coppel, Denis Norden ***Ph*** Geoffrey Unsworth ***Ed*** Ralph Sheldon ***Mus*** Riz Ortolani ***Art*** Assheton Gorton
Act Shirley MacLaine, Richard Attenborough, James Booth, Freddie Jones, William Rushton, Bob Monkhouse (Paramount)

The Bliss of Mrs. Blossom is a silly, campy and sophisticated marital comedy, always amusing and often hilarious in impact. Shirley MacLaine stars as a wife with two husbands—Richard Attenborough, the legal and nighttime spouse, and James Booth, who lives in the attic. Script covers the laugh spectrum from throwaway verbal and sight gags through broad comedy to satirical pokes at old-fashioned film romances.

MacLaine, bored but adoring wife, calls Attenborough, a noted brassiere manufacturer, for help when her sewing machine breaks down. Only plant worker available is the bumbling Booth, who is seduced by MacLaine. He refuses to leave the attic, and MacLaine gets to liking the cozy arrangement. Gumshoes Freddie Jones and William Rushton pursue Booth's "disappearance" over the course of many years.

Although basically a one-joke story, idea is fleshed out most satisfactorily so as to take undue attention away from the premise. Performances are all very good, Attenborough's in particular.

•

BLITHE SPIRIT
1945, 96 mins, UK Ⓥ col
Dir David Lean ***Prod*** Noel Coward ***Scr*** David Lean, Ronald Neame, Anthony Havelock-Allan ***Ph*** Ronald Neame ***Ed*** Jack Harris ***Mus*** Richard Addinsell ***Art*** C. P. Norman
Act Rex Harrison, Constance Cummings, Kay Hammond, Margaret Rutherford, Hugh Wakefield, Joyce Carey (Two Cities/Cineguild)

Inasmuch as this is largely a photographed copy of the stage play [by Noel Coward], the camerawork is outstandingly good and helps to put across the credibility of the ghost story more effectively than the flesh-and-blood performance does.

Acting honors go to Margaret Rutherford as Mme. Arcati, a trance medium who makes you believe she's on the level. There is nothing ethereal about this 200-pounder. Her dynamic personality has all the slapdash of Fairbanks, Sr., in his prime.

Kay Hammond, as dead Wife No. 1, brings to the screen a faithful repetition of the performance she has been giving in the flesh for nearly four years. As a spoiled darling with murder in her heart for Wife No. 2, she is as much a smiling menace as she is wistfully wraithlike.

As Ruth, the very much alive Wife No. 2, Constance Cummings more than holds her own in an altogether capable cast—until her death in the automobile accident engineered by Elvira. As a ghost, Cummings is not at all convincing. As Charles Condomine, twice married novelist, Rex Harrison repeats his stage performance, which is so flawless as to merit some critics' charge of underacting.

1946: Best Special Effects

•

BLOB, THE
1958, 85 mins, US Ⓥ ⦿ col
Dir Irvin S. Yeaworth, Jr. ***Prod*** Jack H. Harris ***Scr*** Theodore Simonson, Kate Phillips ***Ph*** Thomas Spalding ***Ed*** Alfred Hillman ***Mus*** Jean Yeaworth ***Art*** William Jersey, Karl Karlson
Act Steve McQueen, Aneta Corseaut, Earl Rowe, Olin Howlin (Paramount/Tonylyn)

The initial production of Jack H. Harris, a regional distrib in the Philadelphia area, *The Blob* had a reported budget of $240,000. Story, from an idea by Irvine H. Millgate, will tax the imagination of adult patrons.

A small Pennsylvania town has been plagued by teenage pranks. Hence, when high schoolers Steve McQueen and Aneta Corseaut report that a parasitic substance from outer space has eaten the local doctor and his nurse, no one will believe them. Especially when no bodies can be found. Neither the acting nor direction is particularly creditable. McQueen, who's handed star billing, makes with the old college try while Corseaut also struggles valiantly as his girlfriend.

Star performers, however, are the camerawork of Thomas Spalding and Barton Sloane's special effects. Production values otherwise are geared to economy. Intriguing is the title number, written by Burt Bacharach and Mack David. It's sung offscreen by a harmony group as the credits unreel. Picture was lensed at the Valley Forge, Pa, studios.

•

BLOB, THE
1988, 92 mins, US Ⓥ ⦿ col
Dir Chuck Russell ***Prod*** Jack H. Harris, Elliott Kastner ***Scr*** Chuck Russell, Frank Darabont ***Ph*** Mark Irwin ***Ed*** Terry Stokes, Tod Feuerman ***Mus*** Michael Hoenig ***Art*** Craig Stearns
Act Kevin Dillon, Shawnee Smith, Donovan Leitch, Jeffrey DeMunn, Candy Clark, Joe Seneca (Tri-Star)

A great B movie with an A pic budget, the Blob is back with a vengeance. Updated [from the 1958 original] with awesome, no-expense-spared special effects and a feisty female hero, horrific outing should prove thoroughly satisfying for fans of the genre.

Starting life as an aggressive glueball that creeps out of a fallen meteor and attacks a vagrant in the woods, the malevolent plasma grows to raging, ferocious proportions, gobbling unlucky locals and carrying their blood and body parts along with it. Glutinous glutton has only one weakness—ice—and that's hard to come by in this warm, weather-blighted ski town.

Director Chuck Russell (*A Nightmare on Elm Street 3*) builds suspense slowly and carefully, devoting 30 minutes to establishing apple-pie normalcy before the first grisly strike. Likewise, suspense in third-act crisis scenes is pumped for all it's worth. Weakest moments involve the creaky sci-fi explanation for Blob's presence, which is part of a germ warfare experiment run amok.

Perfs by Kevin Dillon as an outlaw kid who ends up battling the Blob and Shawnee Smith as a cheerleader who turns into a machine-gun toting she-devil to save her town are adequate for the genre, with Dillon's the more resonant.

•

BLOCKADE
1938, 73 mins, US b/w
Dir William Dieterle ***Prod*** Walter Wanger ***Scr*** John Howard Lawson ***Ph*** Rudolph Mate ***Ed*** Dorothy Spencer ***Mus*** Werner Janssen ***Art*** Alexander Toluboff
Act Madeleine Carroll, Henry Fonda, Leo Carrillo, John Halliday, Vladimir Sokoloff, Reginald Denny (Paramount)

Blockade is a film with a purpose—a plea against war. But it misses any claim to greatness because it pulls its punches.

Modern Spain in the death-grip of civil war is the background of the screenplay, an original by John Howard Lawson. Lawson is not a writer who ordinarily pussyfoots his themes, but in an apparent attempt to straddle the Spanish issues and preserve an international distribution market for the picture, he disguises the warring factions and attempts the impossible task of impersonalizing war and its helpless, starving civilian victims.

The Hays office advised radical alterations in the original script to avoid offense to foreign powers. Fact is, that the strength and power of a film of this type reside in offensiveness and partisanship.

This is a story of romance and espionage. Madeleine Carroll is the daughter of an international agent, who is the tool of a higher-up. The group profits from war. Henry Fonda is a farmer youth, now a soldier fighting for his land, and soon discovers that Carroll, despite all her blonde beauty, is his country's enemy. When she sees firsthand the suffering of innocent and helpless women and children, she confesses her part in the dirty work and leads Fonda to the rendezvous of the spies.

Werner Jenssen's special music for the film is interesting because he uses an offscreen chorus in several spots to highlight the martial mood and the happiness of the people when their ship comes in.

•

BLONDE CRAZY
1931, 78 mins, US Ⓥ ⊙ b/w
Dir Roy Del Ruth ***Scr*** Kubec Glasmon, John Bright ***Ph*** Ernest Haller, Sid Hickox ***Ed*** Ralph Dawson ***Mus*** Leo F. Forbstein (dir.) ***Art*** Esdras Hartley
Act James Cagney, Joan Blondell, Louis Calhern, Noel Francis, Guy Kibbee, Ray Milland (Warner)

Wise remarks, a fresh guy and dame stuff. Quick pace and a performance by James Cagney typically Cagney. These give *Blonde Crazy* a fast start and keep it going most of the way. Finish is weak but not enough to kill off the early impression.

Strictly a petty larceny guy is Cagney and all the way to the finish, when stretched out on a prison hospital cot, he hints he might go straight. Original yarn gives Cagney plenty of room for his customary fresh punk characterization.

Joan Blondell is Cagney's business partner—and what a business—who loves him in other ways besides biz but doesn't find that out until her marriage to a comparative nice boy proves a flop.

Everything depends on the dialogue and playing both come through satisfactorily. Cagney and Blondell make a natural pair. Louis Calhern uses his long experience to good effect in a class cheater part.

•

BLONDE FIST
1991, 100 mins, UK Ⓥ col
Dir Frank Clarke ***Prod*** Joseph D'Morais, Christopher Figg ***Scr*** Frank Clarke ***Ph*** Bruce McGowan ***Ed*** Brian Peachey ***Mus*** Alan Gill ***Art*** Colin Pocock
Act Margi Clarke, Carroll Baker, Ken Hutchison, Sharon Power, Angela Clarke, Lewis Bester (Blue Dolphin)

Margi Clarke packs a mean punch in *Blonde Fist* as a scrappy Liverpudlian and devoted mother who eventually wins in the boxing ring and at home. In a gritty *Thelma & Louise* meets *Rocky*, Clarke is a knockout and pic is punchy, but the complex story drags.

After fleeing jail and ending up in New York, Clarke befriends a fun-loving, aging ex-stripper (superbly played by Carroll Baker) who becomes her ally and "manager" in the ring.

Fight scenes are dynamically choreographed, beautifully shot and provide pic's most engaging footage. But there are too many characters and scenarios for a tight film.

•

BLONDE IN LOVE, A
SEE: JASKY JEDNE PLAVOVLASKY

•

BLONDE SINNER
SEE: YIELD TO THE NIGHT

•

BLONDE VENUS
1932, 93 mins, US Ⓥ b/w
Dir Josef von Sternberg ***Scr*** S. K. Lauren, Jules Furthman ***Ph*** Bert Glennon ***Ed*** [uncredited] ***Mus*** [uncredited] ***Art*** [Wiard Ihnen]
Act Marlene Dietrich, Herbert Marshall, Cary Grant, Dickie Moore, Gene Morgan, Robert Emmett O'Connor (Paramount)

A disappointer. Much of the blame is to be laid at director Josef von Sternberg's doorstep. In a desire to glamorously build up Marlene Dietrich he sloughs almost every other element that goes to round out a box-office production. He devotes two reels to her flight from her husband and all the drab details that went with it, as she scrams from Baltimore to Washington to Nashville to Chattanooga to Savannah to New Orleans, etc, etc. The police reports of her hunt sound like a railroad timetable.

Then in a meteoric rise, with no details whatsoever, she's suddenly again the queen of the nightclubs, this time in Paris, where Cary Grant (who had formerly maintained her) once again meets up with her. In this and previous nite club scenes, Dietrich sings two numbers in that deep, throaty manner of hers, one chorus being in French.

Herbert Marshall is sadly miscast as the radium-poisoned husband who needs funds so badly for a European cure that his devoted wife takes resource to financial succor from such a remote source as influential politician (Grant).

The 93 minutes, despite their episodic and ofttimes ragged sequences, are much too much considering the triteness of the basic story, a theme of mother love of the German-American café songstress whose child (well played by Dickie Moore, in perhaps the only convincing casting) is the sympathetic basis of it all. Otherwise there's little sympathy for any of the characters; neither the hapless husband, the faithless wife nor the other man.

•

BLONDIE OF THE FOLLIES
1932, 91 mins, US b/w
Dir Edmund Goulding ***Scr*** Frances Marion, Anita Loos ***Ph*** George Barnes
Act Marion Davies, Robert Montgomery, Billie Dove, Jimmy Durante, James Gleason, ZaSu Pitts (M-G-M)

Jimmy Durante is rushed into a house party scene for his first and only appearance after the picture has gone 70 minutes. That's the best evidence that this picture's big weakness was analyzed by the producers. In the five minutes that Durante is on, his Barrymore-Garbo takeoff with Marion Davies easily becomes the bright spot on the picture.

The story is simply the rise of two New York girls of the poor class to *Follies* girl status, their temporary enjoyment of the luxurious fancy living and then their return to normalcy.

Chief situation is love rivalry between the two girl pals, with Blondie (Davies) finally winning out.

Davies and Billie Dove are both real life Follies grads, so their backstage conduct in this picture probably is authentic. Of the two Dove is more the showgirl type in looks and manner. As usual, Davies is best in her few comedy chances, but on the whole this try is under par for her.

•

BLOOD AND SAND
1922, 110 mins, US Ⓥ ⊙ ⊗ b/w
Dir Fred Niblo ***Prod*** Jesse L. Lasky ***Scr*** June Mathis ***Ph*** Alvin Wyckoff
Act Rudolph Valentino, Lila Lee, Nita Naldi, George Field, Walter Long, Rose Rosanova (Paramount)

Rudolph Valentino's switch to a St. Anthony type comes as a shock. The essential moral conflict of the bullfighter never gets to the surface. He is just a bewildered simpleton, which makes his gaudy clothes ridiculous.

The story [from the novel by Vicente Blasco Ibanez and the play by Tom Cushing] has many picturesque elements but it is episodic and scattered. It starts with the theme of a humble shoemaker raised to eminence as a national hero of the bull ring and an idol of the people.

Soon the problem is changed to "What will be the fate of a man who lives by blood and cruelty?" Then the conflict appears to be an attack on the institution of the bullfight.

"Poor matador; poor beast," says the benign philosopher, "But the real bull is out there (the crowd around the arena). There is the beast with 10,000 heads."

•

BLOOD AND SAND
1941, 123 mins, US Ⓥ col
Dir Rouben Mamoulian ***Prod*** Darryl F. Zanuck ***Scr*** Jo Swerling ***Ph*** Ernest Palmer, Ray Rennahan ***Ed*** Robert Bischoff ***Mus*** Alfred Newman ***Art*** Richard Day, Joseph C. Wright
Act Tyrone Power, Linda Darnell, Rita Hayworth, Nazimova, Anthony Quinn, John Carradine (20th Century-Fox)

Blood and Sand [from the novel by Vicente Blasco Ibanez] is associated in the memories of theatregoers as a hot and decidedly sexy piece of merchandise, chiefly because of Valentino's silent version two decades ago. The revival follows the original as a straight drama of the bullfight ring.

Especially effective are the bullfight arena sequences, which disclose exceptional camera angles and intercutting of shots of crowds at arena in Mexico City with studio shots.

Tyrone Power is a peon kid in Seville, son of a bullfighter killed in the ring, decidedly illiterate, and with a passion for bullfighting. He has an adolescent love for Linda Darnell, and finally runs off to Madrid with a bunch of his pals. Ten years later, as a minor league matador, he returns to Seville, marries Darnell and goes on to become the most famous and widely acclaimed matador of the time. Surrounded by leeches, Power is continually in debt, but happy with his wife until fascinated by sexy Rita Hayworth, socialite flame.

Power delivers a persuasive performance as Ibanez's hero while Darnell is pretty and naive as the young wife. Hayworth is excellent as the vamp and catches major attention on a par with Nazimova, who gives a corking performance as Power's mother.

1941: Best Color Cinematography

NOMINATION: Best Color Art Direction

•

BLOOD AND SAND
1989, 117 mins, Spain Ⓥ col
Dir Javier Elorrieta ***Prod*** Jose Frade ***Scr*** Raphael Azcona, Ricardo Franco, Thomas Fucci ***Ph*** Antonio Rios ***Ed*** Jose Antonio Rojo ***Mus*** Jesus Gluck ***Art*** Luis Arguello
Act Christopher Rydell, Sharon Stone, Ana Torrent, Guillermo Montesinos, Albert Vidal, Simon Andreu (Frade)

Producer Jose Frade has claimed his *Blood and Sand* is the first truly Spanish film version of Vicente Blasco Ibanez's famous novel. Frade's claim turns out to be empty. His picture is about as Spanish as Coke spiked with Fundador brandy.

The new version was shot with English (American) dialogue and an American-Spanish cast in and around the bullrings of Madrid, Jerez and Sevilla. The bullfighting shown is cleansed of all blood except that shed by a couple of humans.

What is left to tell of Blasco Ibanez's novel is told with plodding care and brief sex scenes between Christopher Rydell's Juan Gallardo and Sharon Stone's Dona Sol. Stone appears to be not much more than a pudgy-faced teenager with a body that one might say strips well.

The beauty, symmetry and finely tuned dance of death of a bullfight at its best is sensed only via an introductory b/w newsreel clip. The rest of this *Blood and Sand* is, sad to say, pure bull. Jesus Gluck has built a strong score around excerpts from the works of Spain's best old and newer composers.

•

BLOODBROTHERS
1978, 116 mins, US Ⓥ col
Dir Robert Mulligan ***Prod*** Stephen Friedman ***Scr*** Walter Newman ***Ph*** Robert Surtees ***Ed*** Shelly Kahn ***Mus*** Elmer Bernstein ***Art*** Gene Callahan
Act Paul Sorvino, Tony Lo Bianco, Richard Gere, Lelia Goldoni, Yvonne Wilder, Kenneth McMillan (Warner)

Bloodbrothers is an ambitious, if uneven probe into the disintegration of an Italian-American family [from the novel by Richard Price]. Under Robert Mulligan's forceful direction, sharply drawn characters clash, scream and argue, but fail to resolve any of their or the film's conflicts.

Bloodbrothers delves into the steamy emotional mess known as the De Coco clan, headed by construction worker father Tony Lo Bianco, his brother Paul Sorvino, wife Lelia Goldoni, and sons Richard Gere and Michael Hershewe.

Although the focus of the film isn't clear until about halfway through, *Bloodbrothers* is concerned primarily with the plight of Gere, who is trying to make one of those crucial life decisions about whether he wants to join the men on the construction girders or opt for the job that gives him real pleasure, working with small children.

This pedestrian tale is placed against a background of vibrant machoism, with numerous scenes of boozing, whoring and fighting set in the Bronx.

1978: NOMINATION: Best Adapted Screenplay

•

BLOODFIST III: FORCED TO FIGHT
1992, 88 mins, US Ⓥ col
Dir Oley Sassone ***Prod*** Roger Corman ***Scr*** Allison Burnett, Charles Mattera ***Ph*** Rick Bota ***Ed*** Eric L. Beason ***Mus*** Nigel Holton ***Art*** James Shumaker
Act Don Wilson, Richard Roundtree, Gregory McKinney, Rick Dean, Richard Paul, John Cardone (Concorde)

This prison story is the best screen vehicle to date for kickboxing champ Don Wilson. He's a wrongly convicted guy in the state pen who continually has to prove himself against bigger and feistier convicts.

Under director Oley Sassone (a.k.a., Francis Sassone), who previously co-scripted the radically dissimilar Disney family film *Wild Hearts Can't Be Broken*, film is tightly constructed. Wilson befriends John Cardone, a nerdy prisoner shunned by the other inmates and is in turn taken under the wing of prison sage Richard Roundtree.

Racism is the key theme, as white and black cons are continually fighting, with "half-breed" (half-Japanese) Wilson caught in the middle. Per genre tradition, when the baddies attack Wilson's best friends, star whips into action and cleans up the place. In a characterstic role, Roundtree is extremely sympathetic.

•

BLOOD FOR DRACULA
1974, 90 mins, France/Italy Ⓥ ▭ col
Dir Paul Morrissey ***Prod*** Andrew Braunsberg ***Scr*** Paul Morrissey ***Ph*** Luigi Kueveillier ***Ed*** Ted Johnson ***Mus*** Claudio Gizzi

Act Joe Dallesandro, Udo Kier, Vittorio De Sica, Maxime McKendry, Arno Juerging, Milena Vukotic (CC-Champion & 1/Ponti/Yanne/Rassam)

Dracula has about been hammered to bits in hi many British incarnations. Now Paul Morrisey takes a turn at the old bloodsucker, made in Italy in English [back-to-back with *Flesh for Frankenstein*] with a mixture of nationalities acting in it.

Morrisey long showed that his films, although more implicit in sex, drugs and characterizations, were really Hollywood films at the core. Udo Kier is a youngish Dracula, in the 1930s. It seems he will die unless he gets virgin blood. So he has to leave his Transylvanian lair to go to Italy for that, since a Catholic country should have some. Accepted by a supposedly rich family, who have four pretty daughters, Dracula gets his comeuppance.

•

BLOOD FROM THE MUMMY'S TOMB

1971, 94 mins, UK col

Dir Seth Holt, [Michael Carreras] *Prod* Howard Brandy *Scr* Christopher Wicking *Ph* Arthur Grant *Ed* Peter Weatherley *Mus* Tristram Cary *Art* Scott MacGregor

Act Andrew Keir, Valerie Leon, James Villiers, Hugh Burden, George Coulouris, Mark Edwards (Hammer)

This polished and well-acted but rather tame Hammer horror entry revolves around an exploration group who discovered an ancient Egyptian tomb and brought relics, including the Princess Tera's mummy; home to England. The sacrilege is savagely avenged by Tera being reincarnated in the leader's beautiful daughter.

Valerie Leon has the dual role of the princess and the modern miss who brings a reign of terror to a quiet London suburb. Solid support comes from Andrew Keir, James Villiers, Hugh Burden, George Coulouris, Rosalie Crutchley and James Cossins who bring credence to the proceedings.

Director Seth Holt died suddenly a few days before shooting was completed and the lack of his guiding hand through post-production could explain, without justifying, certain vagaries and roughness.

•

BLOODHOUNDS OF BROADWAY

1989, 101 mins, US Ⓥ ⦿ col

Dir Howard Brookner *Prod* Howard Brookner *Scr* Howard Brookner, Colman DeKay *Ph* Elliot Davis *Ed* Camilla Toniolo *Mus* Jonathan Sheffner, Roma Baran *Art* Linda Conaway-Parsloe

Act Julie Hagerty, Randy Quaid, Madonna, Jennifer Grey, Rutger Hauer, Matt Dillon (American Playhouse)

Howard Brookner (who died after completing this first feature) and Colman DeKay interweave four of Damon Runyon's famous *Broadway* short stories [*The Bloodhound of Broadway*, *A Very Honorable Guy*, *Social Error* and *The Brain Goes Home*] about New Year's Eve on Broadway in 1928. It's a gangster's farce that falls somewhat short of true comic inspiration. Strong character acting by an all-star cast enlivens this fluffy little piece about romance and gangsters during Prohibition.

There's Harriet Mackyle (Julie Hagerty), who delivers a fine performance as a rich society babe who's throwing the party and invites some local mobsters for added color.

Randy Quaid as Feet Samuels does a satisfying job as an honorable dimwit who's madly in love with a beautiful, diamond-hungry showgirl, Hortense Hathaway, very adeptly played by Madonna.

Matt Dillon gives a rather tepid performance as Regret, Broadway's lousiest horse player, especially in comparison with Jennifer Grey, who does a good job as Lovey Lou, an angel-faced showgirl in love with Regret.

•

BLOOD IN BLOOD OUT

1993, 174 mins, US Ⓥ col

Dir Taylor Hackford *Prod* Taylor Hackford, Jerry Gershwin *Scr* Jimmy Santiago Baca, Jeremy Iacone, Floyd Mutrux *Ph* Gabriel Beristain *Ed* Fredric Steinkamp, Karl F. Steinkamp *Mus* Bill Conti *Art* Bruno Rubeo

Act Damian Chapa, Jesse Borrego, Benjamin Bratt, Enrique Castillo, Victor Rivers, Delroy Lindo (Hollywood Pictures)

Producer-director Taylor Hackford clearly wants this to be a major cinematic exploration of the Latino experience, from its ponderous near-three-hour length to its more-than-occasional sermonizing.

Unfortunately, disjointed storytelling and uneven performances undermine those aspirations.

With script help from poet and former convict Jimmy Santiago Baca, among others [from a story by Ross Thomas], Hackford—relying on a virtually unknown cast—has blended elements of *Boyz N the Hood* and *The Godfather*.

Starting in the early '70s, the plot centers on three youths and follows them into their early 30s: Paco (Benjamin Bratt), a hot-tempered boxer; Cruz (Jesse Borrego), a gifted painter seemingly destined to escape the barrio; and Miklo (Damian Chapa), their half-white cousin who ultimately becomes the focus when he's drawn into an interracial turf war in San Quentin.

Blood In Blood Out (the title refers to the code of a prison gang) seems compelled to say something profound but too often stands on a soapbox to do it. Much of the story takes place in prison, unflinchingly exploring some of the same brutal themes touched on in Edward James Olmos's *American Me*.

•

BLOODLINE

1979, 116 mins, US Ⓥ col

Dir Terence Young *Prod* David V. Picker, Sidney Beckerman *Scr* Laird Koenig *Ph* Freddie Young *Ed* Bud Molin *Mus* Ennio Morricone *Art* Ted Haworth

Act Audrey Hepburn, Ben Gazzara, James Mason, Irene Papas, Romy Schneider, Omar Sharif (Paramount/Geria)

Even for the never-never land of high chic melodrama the film inhabits, the tale of a woman who, unprepared, inherits control of her father's vast pharmaceutical empire contains wild implausibilities.

Flashback reveal papa's medical genius in a Jewish Polish slum. Audience is then asked to swallow premise that, 40-odd years later, his family, making up the company's scheming board of directors, contains Italian and French upper-crusters as well as a member of the British Parliament.

This is Terence Young's first completed film since *The Klansman* five years earlier and he's clearly out of practice, as his performers range unevenly in tone from the comic (Omar Sharif, Irene Papas, Gert Frobe) to the merely drab (James Mason, Michelle Phillips, Maurice Ronet).

•

BLOOD MONEY

SEE: REQUIEM FOR A HEAVYWEIGHT

•

BLOOD MONEY

(U.S.: CLINTON AND NADINE)

1988, 90 mins, UK/US Ⓥ ⦿ col

Dir Jerry Schatzberg *Prod* Donald March *Scr* Willard Walpole, [Robert Foster] *Ph* Isidore Mankofsky *Ed* David Ray *Mus* Jan Hammer *Art* Howard Barker

Act Andy Garcia, Ellen Barkin, Morgan Freeman, Michael Lombard, John C. McGinley, Brad Sullivan (ITC)

Clinton and Nadine are the lead couple who muddle through a murder mystery tale linked to illicit Contra fundraising.

Andy Garcia is Clinton, a parrot smuggler who stumbles onto his brother's slaying and foils murderers' attempts to escape with a backpack containing some audiocassettes.

Clinton also came away from the crime scene with a purse belonging to Nadine Powers (Ellen Barkin), a hooker on the run from the refuge of his brother's home. Lonely and confused, she is drawn reluctantly into Clinton's attempt to track down those responsible for the murders.

By the time the pair become lovers, one hardly cares and problem is compounded when the story becomes bewildering as everyone is transposed suddenly to Costa Rica for the denouement.

•

BLOOD OATH

1990, 105 mins, Australia Ⓥ ⦿ col

Dir Stephen Wallace *Prod* Charles Waterstreet, Denis Whitburn, Brian Williams *Scr* Denis Whitburn, Brian Williams *Ph* Russell Boyd *Ed* Nicholas Beauman *Mus* David McHugh, Stewart D'Arrietta, Don Miller-Robinson *Art* Bernard Hides

Act Bryan Brown, George Takei, Terry O'Quinn, Toshi Shioya, John Bach, Deborah Unger (Village Roadshow/Blood Oath)

Blood Oath is a courtroom drama that raises questions about wartime crime and punishment. The drama, based on actual incidents, takes place on the Indonesian island of Ambon in late 1945.

Ambon, site of a Japanese POW camp for Australian prisoners, was under the command of aristocratic, Oxford-educated Vice-Admiral Baron Takahashi (George Takei). Bryan Brown plays Capt. Cooper, Aussie officer assigned to prosecute Takashahi and his men for war crimes. He finds his hands tied at every turn, mainly because an American "observer" at the trial, Major Beckett (Terry O'Quinn), doesn't want Takahashi found guilty, figuring he'll be more useful in reconstructed postwar Japan.

At least half the film takes place in the courtroom, and director Stephen Wallace stages these surefire scenes with maximum tension. Brown brings sardonic humor and a wholly convincing feeling of frustration to the tenacious character of Cooper (based on the father of co-scripter/co-producer Brian A. Williams).

•

BLOOD OF A POET

SEE: LE SANG D'UN POETE

•

BLOOD OF HEROES, THE

SEE: THE SALUTE OF THE JUGGER

•

BLOOD ON MY HANDS

SEE: KISS THE BLOOD OFF MY HANDS

•

BLOOD ON THE MOON

1948, 86 mins, US Ⓥ b/w

Dir Robert Wise *Prod* Theron Warth *Scr* Lillie Hayward *Ph* Nicholas Musuraca *Ed* Samuel E. Beetley *Mus* Roy Webb *Art* Albert S. D'Agostino, Walter E. Keller

Act Robert Mitchum, Barbara Bel Geddes, Robert Preston, Walter Brennan, Phyllis Thaxter (RKO)

Blood on the Moon is a terse, tightly drawn western drama. There's none of the formula approach to its storytelling. Picture captures the crisp style used by Luke Short in writing his western novels.

Plot deals with a Texas cowpoke who rides into a section of range country where ranchers and settlers are battling. Broke, he hires out his gun to an old friend, who is scheming with an Indian agent to acquire a cattle herd by promoting the feud.

Robert Mitchum is the cowpoke, a role he handles with skill under Robert Wise's realistic direction. Barbara Bel Geddes registers strongly as the range heroine who first battles and then loves Mitchum. Robert Preston makes an oily villain, whose false charms fool Mitchum as well as the daughter of his chief rancher opponent, and the settlers.

Picture's pace has a false sense of leisureliness that points up several tough moments of action. There is a deadly knock-down-and-drag-out fist-fight between Mitchum and Preston; a long chase across snow-covered mountains and the climax gun battle between Preston's henchmen and Mitchum, Brennan and Bel Geddes that are loaded with suspense wallop.

•

BLOOD ON THE SUN

1945, 98 mins, US Ⓥ ⦿ b/w

Dir Frank Lloyd *Prod* William Cagney *Scr* Lester Cole, Nathaniel Curtis *Ph* Theodor Sparkuhl *Ed* Truman K. Wood, Walter Hannemann *Mus* Miklos Rozsa *Art* Wiard B. Ihnen

Act James Cagney, Sylvia Sidney, Porter Hall, Robert Armstrong, John Emery, Rosemary DeCamp (United Artists/Cagney)

Cagney portrays an American editor of a Tokyo newspaper who dares to print the story of the world-conquest plan formulated by Jap militarists. Naturally, the fur flies when the sheet hits the street—the police confiscating the papers, the Jap secret police demanding a retraction from the publisher, and the editor threatening to walk out if the latter does so. Quickly, Cagney finds himself in the midst of a dual murder committed by the Japs upon a U.S. newspaper pal and his wife, who were leaving Japan to bring to America the document describing the world-conquest plot in detail.

The stars of this picture [from a story by Garrett Fort, based on an idea by Frank Melford] are given plenty of opportunity to display their histrionics. Cagney is the same rough and tumble character he's always been, ready to tell the Jap big shots off at the drop of a hat.

There are a couple of overdramatic sequences, but they just add to the tension of whether they're going to get the envelope with the plot out of the country, or not.

1945: Best B&W Interior Decoration (Wiard B. Ihnen)

•

BLOOD RED

1989, 91 mins, US Ⓥ col

Dir Peter Masterson *Prod* Judd Bernard, Patricia Casey *Scr* Ron Cutler *Ph* Toyomichi Kurita *Ed* Randy Thornton *Mus* Carmine Coppola *Art* Bruno Rubeo

Act Eric Roberts, Giancarlo Giannini, Dennis Hopper, Burt Young, Carlin Glynn, Julia Roberts (Kettledrum)

Blood Red, a saga of oppressed Sicilian winegrowers in 19th century California, is an unsucessful throwback to earlier forms of filmmaking. Project was announced in 1976 by producer Judd Bernard, filmed in 1986 and given a perfunctory regional release in summer 1989. It was the first-time screen teaming of siblings Eric and Julia Roberts.

A robust Giannini is patriarch of one of two families in Brandon, Calif., and soon is warring with robber baron, railroad magnate Dennis Hopper (fitted with an unconvincing Scottish brogue here) determined to get his land for his railroad's right of way. Giannini's rebellious son (Roberts), is in love with the beautiful daughter (Lara Harris) of another winegrowing clan.

Roberts is more subdued than usual as the script fails to develop a three-dimensional character for him. His scenes with real-life sister Julia, cast as his sister, are intriguing because of the visual match. She doesn't get much chance to emote, but that nascent star quality already is evident.

•

BLOOD RELATIVES
1978, 100 mins, France/Canada Ⓥ col
Dir Claude Chabrol ***Prod*** Denis Heroux, Eugene Lepecier ***Scr*** Claude Chabrol, Sydney Banks ***Ph*** Jean Rabier ***Ed*** Yves Langlois ***Mus*** Howard Blake ***Art*** Anne Pritchard
Act Donald Sutherland, Stephane Audran, Micheline Lanctot, Aude Landry, Donald Pleasence, David Hemmings (Classic/Cinevideo/Filmel)

Made in Canada and based on a Yank police precinct novel by Ed McBain, film settles down as an inspector, played with a low profile and humanity by Donald Sutherland, probes a knife killing of a teenage girl and the wounding of another girl who was with her. At first it is felt to be the work of a psychotic but then segues into a middle-class family that might have been the crucible for the gory carryings-on.

French director Claude Chabrol has often used murder as a catalyst in his grim pix about upper-class French life. But here it is more psychosis, repression and jealousy than the more absorbing social patterns of his French work. It makes the pic somewhat ambivalent, for it is a sudden revelation of madness rather than having more depth in characterization and a harder edge focused on its police work.

Playing is generally good. Chabrol shows a narrative and atmospheric flair, ringing in some solid sidebar feel in Donald Pleasence's rendering of a middle-aged man who likes girls picked up as sex deviates and questioned, and David Hemmings as the older man falling for the victim.

•

BLOOD SIMPLE
1984, 97 mins, US Ⓥ ⊙ col
Dir Joel Coen ***Prod*** Ethan Coen ***Scr*** Joel Coen, Ethan Coen ***Ph*** Barry Sonnenfeld ***Ed*** Roderick Jaynes, Don Wiegmann ***Mus*** Carter Burwell ***Art*** Jane Musky
Act John Getz, Frances McDormand, Dan Hedaya, Samm-Art Williams, M. Emmet Walsh (River Road)

An inordinately good low-budget film noir thriller, *Blood Simple* is written, directed and produced by brothers Joel and Ethan Coen.

Aside from the subtle performances, usually lacking in a film of this size (around $1.5 million), the observant viewer will find a cornucopia of detail.

Dan Hedaya plays Marty, a brooding owner of a Texas bar. Hedaya hires a sleazy, onerous malcreant named Visser (played with appropriate malice by M. Emmet Walsh) to kill his wayward wife and her boyfriend Ray (John Getz).

Walsh takes a snapshot of the lovers asleep in bed, doctors the photo to make it appear he's fulfilled the contract, and meets Hedaya at the bar after hours to collect. Upon payment, Walsh pulls out the wife's gun and shoots Marty dead in the chest. But the victim has swapped the photo and put it in the office safe before his demise, making Walsh's perfect crime not so. Final confrontation between Walsh and the lovers is outright horrific.

Performances are top-notch all around, Walsh in particular conveying the villainy and scummy aspects of his character with convincing glee.

•

BLOODY MAMA
1970, 90 mins, US Ⓥ ⊙ col
Dir Roger Corman ***Prod*** Roger Corman ***Scr*** Robert Thorn ***Ph*** John Alonzo ***Ed*** Eve Newman ***Mus*** Don Randi
Act Shelley Winters, Pat Hingle, Don Stroud, Diane Varsi, Bruce Dern, Robert De Niro (American International)

The story of Kate (Ma) Barker, who with her four killer sons terrorized mountain country in the Depression era, *Bloody Mama* is a pseudobiopic starring Shelley Winters in one of those all-over-the-screen performances which sometimes are labelled as bravura acting.

Film was made entirely on location in Arkansas, and manifests an apparently deliberate attempt at naturalistic filming.

Story is a loosely connected string of macabre vignettes, with an emphasis on dramatic peaks but very little character development or motivation. Cast as Ma's brood are Don Stroud as the psychotic, Robert Walden as the masochistic homosexual, Robert De Niro as the drug addict and Clint Kimbrough as the quiet boy. Bruce Dern plays a sadistic homosexual, mated with Walden, and Diane Varsi is Stroud's girl, a stray hooker.

The best performance in the film, and one of the most outstanding screen portrayals in many moons, is that of Pat Hingle, playing a wealthy businessman kidnapped for high ransom.

•

BLOSSOMS IN THE DUST
1941, 98 mins, US Ⓥ col
Dir Mervyn LeRoy ***Prod*** Mervyn LeRoy ***Scr*** Anita Loos ***Ph*** Karl Freund, M. Howard Greene ***Ed*** George Boemler ***Mus*** Herbert Stothart ***Art*** Cedric Gibbons, Urie McCleary
Act Greer Garson, Walter Pidgeon, Felix Bressart, Marsha Hunt (M-G-M)

What Father Flanagan is to Boys Town in Nebraska, Edna Gladney was to an orphans' home in Texas operated entirely on a strong mother love instinct and the gracious donations of Texans. The home is the Texas Children's Home and Aid Society of Ft Worth. *Blossoms in the Dust* is a worthy production on which much care has been showered by Mervyn LeRoy and others, but the picture fails to impress as being big.

There are almost too many kids, with much attention paid to them. Result is a sentimentally sugary flavor which also extends over the romantic portions of the film. There is no comedy relief.

Pidgeon is the Texan who marries Edna Gladney of Wisconsin and worships her. The baby born to them dies and subsequently Pidgeon passes away suddenly after they have done some charity work for poor kids and foundlings. From there on Garson takes up the placement of unfortunate children as a lifetime work and ultimately is instrumental in passing a law which eliminates from public record whether orphans were born illegitimately or not.

Playing Edna Gladney, Garson spans many years but does not appreciably age.

1941: Best Color Interior Decoration

NOMINATIONS: Best Picture, Actress (Greer Garson), Color Cinematography

•

BLOWN AWAY
1994, 121 mins, US Ⓥ ⊙ ▭ col
Dir Stephen Hopkins ***Prod*** John Watson, Richard Lewis, Pen Densham ***Scr*** Joe Batteer, John Rice ***Ph*** Peter Levy ***Ed*** Timothy Wellburn ***Mus*** Alan Silvestri ***Art*** John Graysmark
Act Jeff Bridges, Tommy Lee Jones, Lloyd Bridges, Forest Whitaker, Suzy Amis, Caitlin Clarke (Trilogy/M-G-M)

The pyrotechnics are the stars of *Blown Away*, an overly complex, muddled thriller of politics and revenge. In need of some dynamite to dislodge an often unfathomable story, the film is just too cool and cynical.

The adversaries are Jimmy Dove (Jeff Bridges), a veteran of Boston's Bomb Squad, and Ryan Gaerity (Tommy Lee Jones), a mad, Irish explosives expert recently escaped from a security lockup in Northern Ireland. As a young man, Jimmy (then known as Liam) was trained by the other man in bombology. Once allies, the student thwarted one of his teacher's more diabolic efforts when it became clear innocent people would be hurt. Jimmy/Liam escaped to the U.S., while Gaerity spent 20 years waiting for a chance to escape and wreak havoc on his former pupil. Gaerity schemes to blow up Jimmy's new wife (Suzy Amis) and stepdaughter at a Boston Pops concert in which the wife plays violin.

Joe Batteer and John Rice's script [from a story by them and M. Jay Roach] operates almost exclusively on movie logic and not common sense. Its bigger sins range from sloppy dramatic shorthand and a shockingly careless attitude toward humanity. Back story of strife in Northern Ireland and its impact on the central characters has no texture.

In the absence of character development or depth, Bridges and Jones are reduced to a kind of posturing that borders on the embarrassing.

Marginally more acceptable are the supporting turns by Forest Whitaker, Lloyd Bridges, Amis and Caitlin Clarke.

•

BLOW OUT
1981, 108 mins, US Ⓥ ⊙ ▭ col
Dir Brian De Palma ***Prod*** George Litto ***Scr*** Brian De Palma ***Ph*** Vilmos Zsigmond ***Ed*** Paul Hirsch ***Mus*** Pino Donaggio ***Art*** Paul Sylbert
Act John Travolta, Nancy Allen, John Lithgow, Dennis Franz, Peter Boyden, John Aquino (Cinema 77/Geria/Filmways)

Writer-director Brian De Palma's *Blow Out* is a frequently exciting $18 million suspense thriller which suffers from a distracting emphasis upon homages to other motion pictures.

Travolta appears as a Philadelphia-based soundman working out of his studio on low-budget horror films. Film turns serious with plot of Travolta caught up in a murder and cover-up scheme when the tire of a politician's car is blown out by a rifle shot at a bridge where he is recording sounds.

Saving a young woman (Nancy Allen) from drowning in the car, Travolta's fate becomes entwined with hers as he uses his professional expertise to unravel the murder mystery while both of them dodge the assassin (John Lithgow).

With attractive leads and a stylish flair for suspense, De Palma misses sustaining involvement by his distracting allusions to prior films (ranging broadly from *Blowup* to *Touch of Evil*).

Travolta scores with a combo of intensity and naturalism in the sympathetic lead role, but costar Allen is stuck essaying a helpless loser instead of the romantic teammate favored by De Palma's avowed mentor, Alfred Hitchcock.

•

BLOWUP
1966, 110 mins, UK Ⓥ ⊙ col
Dir Michelangelo Antonioni ***Prod*** Carlo Ponti ***Scr*** Michelangelo Antonioni, Tonino Guerra, Edward Bond ***Ph*** Carlo Di Palma ***Ed*** [Frank Clarke] ***Mus*** Herbie Hancock ***Art*** Assheton Gorton
Act Vanessa Redgrave, Sarah Miles, David Hemmings, John Castle, Jane Birkin, Gillian Hills (Bridge/M-G-M)

There may be some meaning, some commentary about life being a game, beyond what remains locked in the mind of film's creator, Italian director-writer Michelangelo Antonioni. But it is doubtful that the general public will get the "message" of this film [from a short story by Julio Cortazar]. As a commentary on a sordid, confused side of humanity in this modern age it's a bust.

Filmed in England and Antonioni's first English-speaking production, interesting use is made of London backgounds. There also is certain sustained interest at times as the audience presses hopefully to piece together the significance of the story(?).

Footage centers on a topflight London fashion photographer who learns of a murder through his secret lensing of a couple he sees embracing in a park. Through a series of blowups of the many exposures he snapped he finds indications of a murder, and visiting the park again discovers the body of the man whom he had been photographing.

David Hemmings makes an interesting impression as the bulber whose studio is invaded by various femmes, and Vanessa Redgrave, as the woman involved in the park, projects another vivid impression.

1967: NOMINATIONS: Best Director, Original Story and Screenplay

•

BLUE
1968, 113 mins, US ▭ col
Dir Silvio Narizzano ***Prod*** Judd Bernard, Irwin Winkler ***Scr*** Meade Roberts ***Ph*** Stanley Cortez ***Ed*** Stewart Linder ***Mus*** Manos Hadjidakis ***Art*** Hal Pereira
Act Terence Stamp, Joanna Pettet, Karl Malden, Ricardo Montalban, Anthony Costello, Joe De Santis (Paramount/Kettledrum)

Poor writing, dull performances and pretentious direction waste the rugged physical beauty of the location area. The $5 million-plus film is neither the intellectual drama it apparently was meant to be, nor even a reasonably satisfying programmer.

Terence Stamp stars in a title role which can't amount to more than 200 words, many of them dubbed, the rest in his British accent, incongruous to plot. Basic trouble with *Blue* is that there seems to have been an attempt to make a "great" or "definitive" film.

Setting is the uneasy border between Mexico and Texas, across which bandits Ricardo Montalban, and older brother Joe de Santis come for looting raids. Stamp, raised by Montalban is supposedly torn between loyalty to Montalban and his own (undefined) kin.

Allowing for the last-minute casting of Stamp, his performance is dull. He does not speak a word for 50 minutes (though he grunts a bit), and the first sentence is "I'll do it," betraying therein his native accent.

•

BLUE
1993, 76 mins, UK Ⓥ col
Dir Derek Jarman ***Prod*** James Mackay, Takashi Asai ***Scr*** Derek Jarman ***Mus*** Simon Fisher Turner (Baselisk/Uplink/Channel 4)

Perhaps not since Andy Warhol's *Sleep* and *Empire State* has there been a film quite like Derek Jarman's *Blue*. This conceptual essay/meditation/memoir on the director's deteriorating condition with AIDS consists of a dense soundtrack accompanied visually by 76 minutes of a blue screen.

Very early on in the experience, there is a tendency to look away from the screen, as staring continually at the bright, almost glowing blue Technicolor hue proves both too boring and too intense. Joined occasionally on the track by three close collaborators and backed by Simon Fisher Turner's rich score and Marvin Black's complex sound design, Jarman ponders numerous subjects and aspects of his disease.

Blue has moments of power, but its many digressions prompt the mind to wander, giving one of the chance to think about anything—Jarman's other films, how other artists have reacted to their own AIDS, what's playing down the street.

•

BLUE ANGEL, THE
SEE: DER BLAUE ENGEL

•

BLUE ANGEL, THE
1930, 99 mins, Germany Ⓥ ⊙ b/w
Dir Josef von Sternberg ***Prod*** Erich Pommer ***Scr*** Carl Zuckmayer, Karl Vollmoller, Robert Liebmann ***Ph*** Gunther Rittau, Hans Schneeberger ***Ed*** S. K. Winston ***Mus*** Frederick Hollander ***Art*** Otto Hunte
Act Emil Jannings, Marlene Dietrich, Kurt Gerron, Rosa Valetti, Hans Albers, Karl Huszar-Puffy (UFA)

Splendid English version of a German original [released earlier the same year]. It's Emil Jannings's first talker with his name over the title and Marlene Dietrich's underneath.

It's a standout picture along typical UFA lines—meaning that the story [from the novel *Professor Unrath* by Heinrich Mann] is heavy, tends to drag and holds up more on the strength of the two principals than anything else.

Dietrich, as a cabaret girl of liberal morals with those Continental soubret costumes of much stocking, bare limb and garters, is an eyeful. She seems a bit timid as regard the dialog. This is not so when she sings. One tune carries a plaintive melody which has a tendency to linger, and Dietrich sings it better in English than in German.

Dietrich's final rendition of the main song astride a chair, as she tosses it with almost a sneer on her face at the lowbrow mob in the sailors' dive, is something of a classic.

Emil Jannings gives a fine characterization of the circumspect school teacher who falls completely for the cabaret singer whom his students have been nightly sneaking away to see. He descends to become the pantomimic clown assistant of the magician-manager of the show, with the mimicking of a rooster as his comedy punch.

Josef von Sternberg, directing, stretches the picture beyond its limit but shows high judgment in handling the dialog.

•

BLUE ANGEL, THE
1959, 107 mins, US ▭ col
Dir Edward Dmytryk ***Prod*** Jack Cummings ***Scr*** Nigel Balchin ***Ph*** Leon Shamroy ***Ed*** Jack W. Holmes ***Mus*** Hugo Friedhofer ***Art*** Lyle R. Wheeler, Maurice Ransford
Act Curt Jurgens, May Britt, Theodore Bikel, John Banner, Fabrizio Mioni (20th Century-Fox)

When UFA made *Der blaue Engel* it catapulted Emil Jannings, Marlene Dietrich, producer Erich Pommer and director Josef von Sternberg into international repute. Later that year (1930), Paramount dubbed an English version and "Legs" Dietrich was on the road to Hollywood renown. This remake is not the rocker that the Jannings-Dietrich impact made but neither Germany's Curt Jurgens nor Sweden's May Britt need be ashamed of their performances.

Perhaps counting the most against them is the somewhat familiar plot motivation—the femme fatale and the destruction of the German professor who succumbs to her wiles. But the prime shortcoming is the decision to give this saga a post-midcentury topicality in 1950s West Germany.

Britt is an eyeful as the seductress. Her shoulder-length blonde hair; her saucy mien and manner; the Dietrichesque style of straddling the chairs, showing off her saucy gams, are eyefuls in every department. She handles two vocal reprises of Frederick Hollander's "Falling in Love Again" and also projects the new thematic, "Lola Lola" which Jay Livingston and Ray Evans fashioned for her.

Jurgens proves a flexible performer. He disguises his masculine attractiveness under an authentic German academician's mien, impersonating the unworldly schoolmaster with conviction. Film was part-shot in Bavaria and the interiors in Hollywood. Support is authentic.

•

BLUEBEARD
1972, 123 mins, US Ⓥ col
Dir Edward Dmytryk ***Prod*** Alexander Salkind ***Scr*** Ennio De Concini, Edward Dmytryk, Maria Pia Fusco ***Ph*** Gabor Pogany ***Ed*** Jean Ravel ***Mus*** Ennio Morricone ***Art*** Tomas Vayer
Act Richard Burton, Raquel Welch, Joey Heatherton, Virna Lisi, Nathalie Delon, Sybil Danning (Vulcano)

Bluebeard is high camp. Richard Burton portrays title role in a modernized version of the legendary character who had a way with women—doing them in—and in dignified tread saunters through a whole phantasmagoria of murders and a veritable shower of bare bosoms to a finale which shows why he was that way, poor guy.

Joey Heatherton is the principal protagonist, who discovers all his victims in a huge refrigerator-room and who, as a result of her discovery, is to be his next victim. To her, he relates in flashback form the fate of his other wives.

One of the most entertaining sequences focuses on Nathalie Delon, who after getting nowhere with Burton in bed prevails upon a prostitute (Sybil Danning) to instruct her in the art of seduction. Lesson ends with her learning the total ways of lesbianism and Burton drops a pointed chandelier on them.

•

BLUEBEARD'S EIGHTH WIFE
1938, 83 mins, US b/w
Dir Ernst Lubitsch ***Prod*** Ernst Lubitsch ***Scr*** Charles Brackett, Billy Wilder ***Ph*** Leo Tover ***Ed*** William Shea ***Mus*** Frederick Hollander, Werner R. Heymann ***Art*** Hans Dreier, Robert Usher
Act Claudette Colbert, Gary Cooper, Edward Everett Horton, David Niven, Elizabeth Patterson, Herman Bing (Paramount)

Par's talker remake of the Alfred Savoir farce [in the American version by Charlton Andrews], a thin piece basically, isn't given much more heft under the Lubitsch touch or with the celluloid trimmings. It's a light and sometimes bright entertainment, but gets a bit tiresome, despite its comparatively moderate running time.

Once the premise is established that Claudette Colbert wants to deflate the multimillionaire Gary Cooper, who buys his wives—seven of 'em prior to her—as he buys a fancy motor car, making premarriage settlements with them, etc, it then becomes an always obvious farce.

Atmosphere is rich and French. It starts on the Riviera and wanders over the European map, focusing finally in Paris. The Brackett-Wilder scripting is ofttimes bright but illogical and fragile.

Edward Everett Horton is more or less of a bit as her father and the rest are casual. David Niven has a mild opportunity and Herman Bing, with his characteristic style, is another who makes his rather light chore stand up.

•

BLUE BIRD, THE
1976, 100 mins, US/USSR Ⓥ col
Dir George Cukor ***Prod*** Paul Maslansky, Lee Savin, Paul Radnia ***Scr*** Hugh Whitemore, Alfred Hayes, Alexei Kapler ***Ph*** Freddie Young, Ionas Gritzus ***Ed*** Ernest Walter, Tatyana Shaprio, Stanford C. Allen ***Mus*** Irwin Kostal ***Art*** Brian Wildsmith
Act Elizabeth Taylor, Jane Fonda, Ava Gardner, Cicely Tyson, Robert Morley, Harry Andrews (20th Century-Fox)

Third film version of the Maurice Maeterlinck novel (after 1918 and 1939) takes spoiled peasant children Todd Lookinland (excellent, by the way) and Patsy Kensit on a dream trip from their humble abode through a fantasy world in search of the bluebird of happiness.

Elizabeth Taylor's four roles include the dominant (and dazzling) one as (a) Light; as mother (b) she's uncomfortable; as witch (c) she's fun to guess at; as maternal love (d) she's elegantly simple and believable.

Jane Fonda does Night, the princess of darkness, with a flair, while Ava Gardner is extremely effective as Luxury.

Nobody's going to laugh in ridicule at any of it (it's that good) but nobody's going to be strongly moved (it's that bad).

•

BLUE CHIPS
1994, 108 mins, US Ⓥ ⊙ col
Dir William Friedkin ***Prod*** Michele Rappaport ***Scr*** Ron Shelton ***Ph*** Tom Priestley, Jr. ***Ed*** Robert K. Lambert, David Rosenbloom ***Mus*** Nile Rodgers, Jeff Beck, Jed Leiber ***Art*** James Bissell
Act Nick Nolte, Mary McDonnell, J. T. Walsh, Ed O'Neill, Alfre Woodard, Louis Gossett, Jr. (Paramount)

The venerable all-American pastimes of greed, cheating and winning at all costs take it on the chin in *Blue Chips*, a deafness-inducing but otherwise ho-hum would-be expose of shady recruiting practices by college basketball programs.

The combination of Nick Nolte's ranting, agitated performance as a beleaguered coach, director William Friedkin's compulsive style and the frantic pace of the basketball action itself provides an overdose of stimulation that is more numbing than exciting.

Nolte is on the verge of his first losing season and knows he's got to perform some kind of miracle. He hits the road to find those elusive low-profile greats who aren't already heading for the top Eastern schools. Nolte comes up with three winners: a Chicago sharpshooter played by Anfernee (Penny) Hardaway; a towering farmboy (Matt Nover) from Larry Bird's hometown of French Lick, Ind; and, especially, Shaquille O'Neal, playing a ne'er-do-well of monster talents.

With the exception of the cool young players, performances, led by Nolte's, are full-throttle. Pro athletes involved may not be great actors, but they're generally relaxed and likable.

•

BLUE COLLAR
1978, 110 mins, US Ⓥ ⊙ col
Dir Paul Schrader ***Prod*** Don Guest ***Scr*** Paul Schrader, Leonard Schrader ***Ph*** Bobby Byrne ***Ed*** Tom Rolf ***Mus*** Jack Nitzsche ***Art*** Lawrence G. Paull
Act Richard Pryor, Harvey Keitel, Yaphet Kotto, Ed Begley, Jr., Harry Bellaver, George Memmoli (TAT)

Paul Schrader's directorial debut is an artistic triumph. Schrader has transformed a carefully researched original screenplay penned by him and his brother Leonard into a powerful, gritty, seamless profile of three automobile assembly line workers banging their heads against the monotony and corruption that is the factory system.

It is a picture about the monotony and routine of factory life that isn't monotonous, but *is* realistic. Regardless of where individual scenes are set—at the after-work tavern, at a bowling alley, at a worker's home, in the union headquarters or in a Detroit street—the factory dominates every frame of this film.

The film's three stars—Richard Pryor, Harvey Keitel and Yaphet Kotto—all turn in outstanding and disciplined performances.

Plot centers around the three workers' attempts to confront and battle the reality of this system as Schrader views it. The three devise a plan to rob the union, which in the end turns into another helpless action.

•

BLUE DAHLIA, THE
1946, 96 mins, US b/w
Dir George Marshall ***Prod*** John Houseman ***Scr*** Raymond Chandler ***Ph*** Lionel Lindon ***Ed*** Arthur Schmidt ***Mus*** Victor Young (dir.) ***Art*** Hans Dreier, Walter Tyler
Act Alan Ladd, Veronica Lake, William Bendix, Howard da Silva, Doris Dowling, Tom Powers (Paramount)

Playing a discharged naval flier returning home from the Pacific first to find his wife unfaithful, then to find her murdered and himself in hiding as the suspect, Alan Ladd does a bang-up job. Performance has a warm appeal, while in his relentless track down of the real criminal, Ladd has a cold, steellike quality that is potent. Fight scenes are stark and brutal, and tremendously effective.

Story gets off to a slow start, but settles to an even pace that never lets down in interest. Audience may guess the killer, as the story follows several alleys of suspects, but pic always has suspense, with sufficient variations in mood. Ladd is one of trio to return from the wars, others being William Bendix and Hugh Beaumont. Ladd's path crosses Veronica Lake's, latter being separated wife of a nightclub owner who is one of the killer-suspects. Scenes between Ladd and Lake are surprisingly sensitive, with an economy of dialog and emotion doubly appealing.

1946: NOMINATION: Best Original Screenplay

•

BLUE DENIM
(UK: BLUE JEANS)
1959, 89 mins, US ▭ col
Dir Philip Dunne ***Prod*** Charles Brackett ***Scr*** Philip Dunne, Edith Sommer ***Ph*** Leo Tover ***Ed*** William Reynolds ***Mus*** Bernard Herrmann ***Art*** Lyle R. Wheeler, Leland Fuller
Act Carol Lynley, Brandon de Wilde, Macdonald Carey, Marsha Hunt, Warren Berlinger, Vaughn Taylor (20th Century-Fox)

Based on the Broadway stage play by James Leo Herlihy and William Noble, *Blue Denim* recounts, often movingly and intelligently, the torments of a pair of high school lovers who are about to become unwed parents. The desperation of these babes in the basement—a 15-year-old girl and a 16-year-old boy—is further highlighted by their inability to communicate with their parents.

The girl's father is a college professor determined to raise his only daughter to emulate his dead wife. The boy's father is a retired army officer given to reciting platitudes about the value of service life and unable to forget his moments of past glory.

The screenplay has been considerably watered down. The word "abortion" is never mentioned although it is obvious what is taking place. Moreover, the ending deteriorates to cliche melodrama.

Carol Lynley repeats her stage role with the same éclat and sensitivity. As her young lover, Brandon de Wilde gives a moving performance as the confused 16-year-old learning the realities of sex. Warren Berliner, also from the stage play, is fine as his wisecracking buddy and confidante.

•

BLUE GARDENIA, THE
1953, 90 mins, US b/w
Dir Fritz Lang ***Prod*** Alex Gottlieb ***Scr*** Charles Hoffman ***Ph*** Nicholas Musuraca ***Ed*** Edward Mann ***Mus*** Raoul Kraushaar ***Art*** Daniel Hall
Act Anne Baxter, Richard Conte, Ann Sothern, Raymond Burr, Jeff Donnell, Nat "King" Cole (Warner)

A stock story and handling keep *The Blue Gardenia* from being anything more than a regulation mystery melodrama, from a yarn by Vera Caspary. Formula development has an occasional bright spot, mostly because Ann Sothern breathes some life into a stock character and quips.

Anne Baxter is a telephone operator who believes she committed murder when she was drinking away the tears of a broken romance. Too much rum with Raymond Burr, a licentious artist, has blacked out her memory and when she reads a newspaper account of his violent death, she naturally thinks she did it while fighting for her honor. Richard Conte, all-powerful newspaper columnist, masterminds the disclosure of her identity strictly to get an exclusive, but falls in love with her and has to uncover the real killer.

Baxter and Conte do what they can but fight a losing battle with the script while Burr is a rather obvious wolf. Nat "King" Cole is spotted to sing the title tune, written by Bob Russell and Lester Lee.

•

BLUE HAWAII
1961, 103 mins, US Ⓥ ⦿ ▭ col
Dir Norman Taurog ***Prod*** Hal B. Wallis ***Scr*** Hal Kanter ***Ph*** Charles Lang, Jr. ***Ed*** Warren Low, Terry Morse ***Mus*** Joseph J. Lilley ***Art*** Hal Pereira, Walter Tyler
Act Elvis Presley, Joan Blackman, Nancy Walters, Roland Winters, Angela Lansbury, Howard McNear (Paramount)

Hal Kanter's breezy screenplay, from a story by Allan Weiss, is the slim, but convenient, foundation for a handsome, picture-postcard production crammed with typical South Seas musical hulaballoo. Plot casts Elvis Presley as the rebellious son of a pineapple tycoon who wants to make his own way in life, a project in which he succeeds after numerous romantic entanglements and misunderstandings.

Under Norman Taurog's broad direction, Presley, in essence, is playing himself. Romantic support is attractively dispatched by Joan Blackman and Nancy Walters. In a somewhat overemphasized and incompletely motivated role of an unhappy young tourist, pretty Jenny Maxwell emotes with youthful relish and spirit.

Musical numbers, about a dozen of them, are effectively staged by Charles O'Curran.

•

BLUE ICE
1992, 104 mins, UK Ⓥ ⦿ col
Dir Russell Mulcahy ***Prod*** Martin Bregman, Michael Caine ***Scr*** Ron Hutchinson ***Ph*** Denis Crossan ***Ed*** Seth Flaum ***Mus*** Michael Kamen ***Art*** Grant Hicks
Act Michael Caine, Sean Young, Ian Holm, Alun Armstrong, Sam Kelly, Bob Hoskins (M & M)

Michael Caine re-dons spy-catcher duds in *Blue Ice*, a determinedly old-fashioned actioner that's terminally light on real thrills.

Caine is Harry Anders, a retired MI6 op who's whiling away his years running a London jazz bar. When a U.S. ambassador's wife (Sean Young) literally bumps into him at a red light, he gets drawn back into espionage when she asks him to find a former b.f. (Todd Boyce) who supposedly holds old love letters.

The movie is a throwback to formula pics of the '60s, with transatlantic leads swanning around London tourist spots and an uncomplicated plot that has fewer twists than a cocktail spoon.

As the retired cockney spy who cooks a mean langoustine provencale [based on a character created by Ted Allbeury], Caine skirts close to an aging Harry Palmer. His settled, effortless performance carries the pic, but there's a lack of real electricity with Young.

Title refers to a chunk of ice falling off an airliner out of a clear blue sky and braining someone on the ground.

•

BLUE IN THE FACE
1995, 89 mins, US col
Dir Wayne Wang, Paul Auster ***Prod*** Greg Johnson, Peter Newman, Diana Phillips ***Scr*** Wayne Wang, Paul Aster ***Ph*** Adam Holender ***Ed*** Christopher Tellefsen ***Mus*** John Lurie ***Art*** Kalina Ivanov
Act Harvey Keitel, Lou Reed, Roseanne, Michael J. Fox, Jim Jarmusch, Lily Tomlin (Blue in the Face/Miramax)

During the making of *Smoke*, director Wayne Wang and screenwriter Paul Auster apparently felt unable to include all the characters and subplots originally envisaged. Money was found, via Miramax, to make another film and production commenced immediately after principal shooting of *Smoke* was completed.

Result is a piecemeal collection of barely connected scenes and characters stitched together with videotaped comments from a cross section of Brooklyn residents. It's sporadically lively and contains quite a few amusing bits and pieces.

Action again centers on the Brooklyn Cigar store, which is still managed by Auggie (Harvey Keitel), but several characters from *Smoke* don't make it back. Most notable newcomer is Roseanne, who exuberantly plays store owner Vinnie's long-suffering wife, Dot. Fed up because he never takes her anywhere, she makes a play for an unresponsive Auggie. Victor Argo's Vinnie also has a more substantial role.

Newcomers include Madonna doing a lively bit as a singing telegram girl, Michael J. Fox playing a ragged type conducting an off-beat questionnaire, and an unrecognizable Lily Tomlin as an off-the-wall street person.

A couple of familiar faces play themselves. Jim Jarmusch raps with Auggie as he smokes what he claims will be his last cigarette. And Lou Reed explains that he's never nervous in Brooklyn (Stockholm, he says, is more frightening).

•

BLUE JEANS
SEE: BLUE DENIM

•

BLUE JUICE
1995, 90 mins, UK Ⓥ col
Dir Carl Prechezer ***Prod*** Peter Salmi, Simon Relph ***Scr*** Carl Prechezer, Peter Salmi ***Ph*** Richard Greatrex ***Ed*** Michael Ellis ***Mus*** Simon Davison ***Art*** Mark Tildesley
Act Sean Pertwee, Catherine Zeta Jones, Steven Mackintosh, Ewan McGregor, Peter Gunn, Keith Allen (Film Four/Pandora/Skreba)

Absolutely charming, unabashedly offbeat *Blue Juice* is a quirky comedy billed as Britain's first surf pic. Writer-director Carl Prechezer and coscripter Peter Salmi make the most of the comic ironies inherent in a story about hapless surf bums stuck on the chilly Cornish coast of England.

Legendary local surfer JC (Sean Pertwee) is having a hard time coming to grips with the notion that his wave-riding heroics are a thing of the past, and he's having an even tougher time dealing with his sexy girlfriend, Chloe (Catherine Zeta Jones), who's unsuccessfully trying to get him to settle down.

Chloe finally kicks him out of the house when three old friends of his from London show up on his doorstep in the middle of the night. Dean (Ewan McGregor) is a drug-addled hipster, Josh (Steven Mackintosh) is a hot techno-music producer, and together they've kidnapped Terry (Peter Gunn), another old buddy who is about to be married.

At the beginning, not all that much surfing goes on for the very good reason that there doesn't seem to be a wave in sight off the picturesque Cornwall coast.

Pertwee is perfect as the impossible-to-dislike JC, Zeta Jones steams up the screen as Chloe, and McGregor, who starred in the Scottish hit *Shallow Grave*, delivers the pic's best performance as the bordering-on-psychotic Dean.

•

BLUE LAGOON, THE
1949, 103 mins, UK col
Dir Frank Launder, Sidney Gilliat ***Prod*** Frank Launder, Sidney Gilliat ***Scr*** Frank Launder, John Baines, Michael Hogan ***Ph*** Geoffrey Unsworth, Arthur Ibbetson ***Ed*** Thelma Myers ***Mus*** Clifton Parker
Act Jean Simmons, Donald Houston, Noel Purcell, James Hayter, Cyril Cusack (Individual)

Technicolor photography of a glorious South Sea setting provides appropriate romantic background for this picturization of Henry De Vere Stacpoole's novel.

There is very little plot to the film and the story of the two children, who are shipwrecked on a South Sea island, is developed by a series of incidents rather than by a woven theme.

As the production relies for its appeal mainly on its eye-filling virtues, little demand has been made on the cast. Jean Simmons displays a sarong to advantage and Donald Houston has little more to do than show off his manly torso. Noel Purcell gives a warm study as the irascible old sailor shipwrecked with them.

•

BLUE LAGOON, THE
1980, 102 mins, US Ⓥ ⦿ col
Dir Randal Kleiser ***Prod*** Randal Kleiser ***Scr*** Douglas Day Stewart ***Ph*** Nestor Almendros ***Ed*** Robert Gordon ***Mus*** Basil Poledouris ***Art*** Jon Dowding
Act Brooke Shields, Christopher Atkins, Leo McKern, William Daniels, Elva Josephson, Glenn Kohan (Columbia)

The Blue Lagoon is a beautifully mounted production, a low-keyed love story stressing the innocent eroticism of Brooke Shields and newcomer Christopher Atkins. This is the second adaptation of the 1903 novel by Henry De Vere Stacpoole about two shipwrecked children who grow from childhood in an isolated South Seas paradise.

Producer-director Randal Kleiser takes the pair through puberty and into parenthood with a charming candor that stresses natural, instinctive sexual development without leering at it.

Their romance is enhanced by Nestor Almendros's exquisite photography (and Basil Poledouris's score), as is the stunning beauty of the Fiji island where it was filmed.

1980: NOMINATION: Best Cinematography

•

BLUE LAMP, THE
1950, 82 mins, UK Ⓥ b/w
Dir Basil Dearden ***Prod*** Michael Balcon ***Scr*** T.E.B. Clarke, Alexander Mackendrick ***Ph*** Gordon Dines ***Ed*** Peter Tanner ***Mus*** Ernest Irving (dir.) ***Art*** Jim Morahan
Act Jack Warner, Jimmy Hanley, Dirk Bogarde, Robert Flemyng, Bernard Lee, Peggy Evans (Ealing)

Dedicated to the British police force, the story (from an original treatment by Jan Read and Ted Willis) describes the post-war crime wave as seen through the eyes of the man on the beat. Clear-cut direction and interesting location shots of London's back streets help the story along.

The crime wave is spotlighted on two characters. At first they are small-time crooks, but gradually become ambitious and go for the bigger stuff.

The all-round cast is topped by Jack Warner, who as always turns in a human, workmanlike performance. He takes the part of the constable and brings to that role the typical humor associated with the London copper. Jimmy Hanley plays a raw recruit to the police force with feeling, but the best performance comes from Dirk Bogarde who, with Patric Doonan, are the criminals.

•

BLUE MAX, THE
1966, 154 mins, UK Ⓥ ⦿ ▭ col
Dir John Guillermin ***Prod*** Christian Ferry ***Scr*** David Pursall, Jack Seddon, Gerald Hanley ***Ph*** Douglas Slocombe ***Ed*** Max Benedict ***Mus*** Jerry Goldsmith ***Art*** Wilfrid Shingleton
Act George Peppard, James Mason, Ursula Andress, Jeremy Kemp, Karl Michael Vogler, Anton Diffring (20th Century-Fox)

The Blue Max is a World War I drama [from a novel by Jack D. Hunter, adapted by Ben Barzman and Basilio Franchina] with some exciting aerial combat sequences [directed by Anthony Squire] helping to enliven a somewhat grounded, meller script in which no principal character engenders much sympathy.

A downbeat air prevails in the drama. The hero, a lower-class climber played by George Peppard, is a heel; his adversary in the ranks of an air squadron, also for the free affections of Ursula Andress, is also a negative character, played by Jeremy Kemp. James Mason, husband of Andress, is looking for a propaganda symbol, finds it in Peppard, and eventually causes the latter's death. Only Karl Michael Vogler, the squadron commander, evokes any sympathy as a gentleman.

Director John Guillermin, who derived the uniformly fine performances within the given plot frame, has at times an exciting visual sense. On the other hand, his technique in more intimate sequences becomes obvious and mechanical.

•

BLUE MURDER AT ST. TRINIANS

1958, 86 mins, UK Ⓥ b/w

Dir Frank Launder ***Prod*** Frank Launder, Sidney Gilliat ***Scr*** Frank Launder, Val Valentine, Sidney Gilliat ***Ph*** Gerald Gibbs ***Ed*** Geoffrey Foot ***Mus*** Malcolm Arnold ***Art*** Allan Harris

Act Terry-Thomas, George Cole, Joyce Grenfell, Lionel Jeffries, Lisa Gastoni, Sabrina (British Lion)

The pic packs in quite a lot of yocks, but the humor is a bit obvious and the string of slapstick situations pinned on to a thin, yet complicated, story line does not add up to a very satisfactory comedy film.

There are all the obvious gags, with the "awful schoolgirls" of Ronald Searle's cartoons behaving like little fiends. The school is without a headmistress and the army has been called in to keep order.

By cheating, the girls have won an Unesco essay contest with first prize a coach trip to Rome. The girls are anxious to go in order that one of them be married off to Prince Bruno of Italy. Further complications are caused by one of the girls' fathers pulling off a diamond robbery. To get him out of the country he poses as the headmistress of St. Trinians. Trip enables Lionel Jeffries to pose as a woman, Joyce Grenfell to pose as an interpreter though actually a police woman, and Terry-Thomas to steal the film as a shady boss of a coach firm. The older girls of St. Trinians are easy on the eye but it seems stupid wasting Lisa Gastoni on this sort of tripe.

•

BLUES BROTHERS, THE

1980, 133 mins, US Ⓥ ⦿ col

Dir John Landis ***Prod*** Robert K. Weiss ***Scr*** Dan Aykroyd, John Landis ***Ph*** Stephen M. Katz ***Ed*** George Folsey, Jr. ***Mus*** Ira Newborn (sup.) ***Art*** John J. Lloyd

Act John Belushi, Dan Aykroyd, James Brown, Ray Charles, Carrie Fisher, Aretha Franklin (Universal)

If Universal had made it 35 years earlier, *The Blues Brothers* might have been called *Abbott & Costello in Soul Town*. Level of inspiration is about the same now as then, the humor as basic, the enjoyment as fleeting. But at $30 million, this is a whole new ball game.

Enacting Jake and Elwood Blues roles created for their popular concert and recording act, John Belushi and Dan Aykroyd use the slenderest of stories—attempt to raise $5,000 for their childhood parish by putting their old band back together—as an excuse to wreak havoc on the entire city of Chicago and much of the Midwest.

Film's greatest pleasure comes from watching the likes of James Brown, Cab Calloway, Ray Charles and especially Aretha Franklin do their musical things.

Given all the chaos, director and, with Aykroyd, cowriter, John Landis manages to keep things reasonably controlled and in a straight line. Pic plays as a spirited tribute by white boys to black musical culture, which was inspiration for the Blues Brothers act in the first place.

[The director's original 148-min. version was issued on homevideo in 1998.]

•

BLUES BROTHERS 2000

1998, 123 mins, US Ⓥ ⦿ col

Dir John Landis ***Prod*** John Landis, Dan Aykroyd, Leslie Belzberg ***Scr*** Dan Aykroyd, John Landis ***Ph*** David Herrington ***Ed*** Dale Beldin ***Mus*** Paul Shaffer ***Art*** Bill Brodie

Act Dan Aykroyd, John Goodman, Joe Morton, J. Evan Bonifant, Nia Peeples, Kathleen Freeman (Universal)

Dan Aykroyd and director John Landis take a bumpy trip down memory lane in this sluggishly paced, fitfully funny follow-up to their 1980 musical-comedy extravaganza. It's a risky business to make a sequel to any pic that's more than a decade old, even with several members of the original cast.

Aykroyd reprises his signature role as Elwood Blues, the monotone, stiff-gaited R&B aficionado who comes fully alive only while performing on stage. New outing begins with Elwood's release from prison after 18 years, and he's devastated to learn that Jake Blues (John Belushi), his brother and collaborator, has passed away.

Undeterred, Elwood sets out to reassemble the Blues Brothers Band. However, Mother Mary Stigmata (Kathleen Freeman), the intimidating nun who operated the orphanage where the Blues Brothers were raised, demands that Elwood serve as mentor to Buster (J. Evan Bonifant), a troublesome 10-year-old orphan.

Elwood befriends Mighty Mack McTeer (John Goodman), a bartender who earns the right to replace Jake, and they take flight after they run afoul of Russian Mafia tough guys. Inevitably, this leads to another cross-country chase, as Elwood and company reassemble the original band while speeding toward a gig in Louisiana.

Landis keeps the car-crash action to a minimum. Trouble is, while restraint may be a valuable commodity in some comedies, it's hardly what audiences want or expect in a *Blues Brothers* adventure. On the plus side, the film does feature two genuine show-stoppers in its second half ("John the Revelator," "How Blue Can You Get").

•

BLUE SKIES

1946, 104 mins, US col

Dir Stuart Heisler ***Prod*** Sol C. Siegel ***Scr*** Arthur Sheekman ***Ph*** Charles Lang ***Ed*** LeRoy Stone ***Mus*** Robert Emmett Dolan ***Art*** Hans Dreier, Hal Pereira

Act Bing Crosby, Fred Astaire, Joan Caulfield, Billy De Wolfe, Olga San Juan, Frank Faylen (Paramount)

The cue sheet on *Blue Skies* lists 42 different Irving Berlin song items but some of it has been excised and the rest so skillfully arranged, orchestrated and presented that the nostalgic musical cavalcade doesn't pall. Fred Astaire's "Puttin' on the Ritz" (originally written for Harry Richman) is the musical standout of the more than 30 items which have been retained.

The story of *Blue Skies* is of familiar pattern and rather sketchily hung together by Astaire. He's cast as a disk jockey stringing the cavalcade of Berliniana together by recounting the nostalgic episodes behind the success of the platters as they are miked.

Bing Crosby is the romantic winnah throughout. Joan Caulfield is partial to the nitery troubadour (Crosby) whose unusual flair for opening and closing niteries is a plot keynote. Astaire is the suave dancing star and she's in the line of one of his shows. Astaire's romantic interest carries her along but Crosby's crooning charms her.

Mark Sandrich, who with Berlin, Crosby and Astaire whipped up *Holiday Inn* was the key man in *Blue Skies* until his sudden death interrupted production plans for the pic. Then, too, there was the emergency substitution of Astaire for Paul Draper, but with it all this film emerges a winner in every respect.

1946: NOMINATIONS: Best Scoring of a Dramatic Picture, Song ("You Keep Coming Back Like a Song")

•

BLUE SKY

1994, 101 mins, US Ⓥ ⦿ col

Dir Tony Richardson ***Prod*** Robert H. Solo ***Scr*** Rama Laurie Stagner, Arlene Sarner, Jerry Leichtling ***Ph*** Steve Yaconelli ***Ed*** Robert K. Lambert ***Mus*** Jack Nitzsche ***Art*** Timian Alsaker

Act Jessica Lange, Tommy Lee Jones, Powers Boothe, Carrie Snodgress, Amy Locane, Chris O'Donnell (Orion)

Two fine actors give among their best performances of their careers in *Blue Sky*, an old-fashioned but lively character study of a long-married military couple having midlife trouble. This long-on-the-shelf 1991 production was the last film directed by Tony Richardson, and it happens to be one of the more creditable efforts of the latter part of his career.

Jessica Lange makes the most of an opportunity at a full-blown star turn as Carly Marshall, the wife of Army scientist Hank Marshall (Tommy Lee Jones), whose irrepressible sensuality and wild spirit can't be reined in even by the military. It's the early 1960s, and at the outset she friskily teases and tempts the local officers in Hawaii with her Brigitte Bardot get-up, only to shortly move into a Marilyn Monroe phase.

When Hank, Carly and their two girls are transferred to a base in Alabama, the "litter box" they are forced to live in sends Carly into a deep funk. Her violent mood swings are alarming, especially to older daughter Alex (Amy Locane), who's just entered troublesome teendom. When Hank bows out of twirling her around at a big social, Carly gets carried away on the dance floor with the camp's commanding officer, Vince Johnson (Powers Boothe), and the seeds are surely planted for future trouble.

Rama Laurie Stagner's semi-autobiographical original story later pushes into rather more dubious territory. When Hank tries to reveal the fact that two civilians were exposed to radiation during a nuclear test explosion, Carly suddenly becomes a crusader for full disclosure of military secrets and coverups.

Richardson, who died in 1991 shortly after completing the picture, mounted the action in a visually straightforward, unflashy manner, concentrating his attention on the performances. Result is very much like a solid melodrama from the 1950s. Lange has the showy role, with almost unlimited opportunities to emote and strut her stuff, which she does magnificently and with total abandon.

1994: Best Actress (Jessica Lange)

•

BLUE STEEL

1990, 102 mins, US Ⓥ ⦿ col

Dir Kathryn Bigelow ***Prod*** Edward R. Pressman, Oliver Stone ***Scr*** Kathryn Bigelow, Eric Red ***Ph*** Amir Mokri ***Ed*** Lee Percy ***Mus*** Brad Fiedel ***Art*** Toby Corbett

Act Jamie Lee Curtis, Ron Silver, Clancy Brown, Elizabeth Pena, Louise Fletcher, Philip Bosco (United Artists/Vestron/Lightning)

A taut, relentless thriller that hums with an electric current of outrage. Director and cowriter Kathryn Bigelow makes the most of her hook—the use of a female star (Jamie Lee Curtis) in a tough action pic—by stressing the character's vulnerability in remarkable early scenes. As rookie cop Megan Turner, Curtis is hit with doubts and resistance from all corners, then suspended after she kills an armed robber (Tom Sizemore) her first night out and no gun is found at the scene. The psycho bystander who picked the gun up (Ron Silver) starts commiting serial murders with bullets he's carved her name onto, and Curtis, under deep suspicion, gets dragged back onto the force to help find him.

Curtis gives an eerily effective performance as Turner, getting across in palpable waves her shaky determination and inner steeliness.

Script is at its weakest where the villain (Silver) is concerned—his characterization as a schizophrenic nutso with violent religious hallucinations is a writeoff. Even so, pic lacks nothing for menace and suspense, and has a frightening, explosively violent second half.

•

BLUE THUNDER

1983, 108 mins, US Ⓥ ⦿ ▭ col

Dir John Badham ***Prod*** Gordon Carroll ***Scr*** Dan O'Bannan, Don Jakoby ***Ph*** John A. Alonzo ***Ed*** Frank Morriss, Edward Abroms ***Mus*** Arthur B. Rubinstein ***Art*** Sidney Z. Litwack

Act Roy Scheider, Malcolm McDowell, Warren Oates, Candy Clark, Daniel Stern, Paul Roebling (Rastar/Columbia)

Blue Thunder is a ripsnorting live-action cartoon, utterly implausible but no less enjoyable for that.

Opening 15 minutes take vet LA police helicopter pilot Roy Scheider and rookie Daniel Stern on nocturnal rounds, which encompass apprehension of some liquor store holdup men, a little voyeurism outside the window of a sexy babe and, more seriously, trying to help stem an assault on a female city councilwoman at her home.

Reprimanded by boss Warren Oates for the sex-show detour, Scheider is nevertheless invited to a demonstration of the Feds' latest creation, Blue Thunder, a top-secret antiterrorist chopper loaded with artillery and all manner of privacy invasion technology.

Craft has been brought to LA for possible use against subversives during the 1984 Olympic Games, and among those in charge of the program is cardboard villain Malcolm McDowell, with whom Scheider served in Vietnam. For sketchy reasons, they hated each other then and they hate each other now. Although brief Vietnam flashbacks punctuate the film to "explain" animosity between Scheider and McDowell, streamlined script has been shorn of almost all psychology and complexity, and it hardly matters.

1983: NOMINATION: Best Editing

•

BLUE TIGER

1994, 87 mins, US Ⓥ ⦿ col

Dir Norberto Barba ***Prod*** Michael Leahy, Aki Komine ***Scr*** Joel Soisson ***Ph*** Christopher Walling ***Ed*** Caroline Ross ***Mus*** David C. Williams ***Art*** Markus Canter

Act Virginia Madsen, Toru Nakamura, Dean Hallo, Ryo Ishibashi, Sal Lopez, Harry Dean Stanton (Neo Motion/First Look)

Packed with classy production values and performances that range from first-rate to standard action-pic dramatics, *Blue Tiger* is distinguished by real care to the lensing and main story [by co-exec producer Taka Ichise], which positions Virginia Madsen and Toru Nakamura as doomed lovers, a la *Duel in the Sun*, caught in the crossfire of a mob battle for control of a Southern California business operation. Pic announces a first-rate directing talent in first-timer Norberto Barba.

When Madsen loses her son in a bloody Yakuza hit, the all-American mother slowly disintegrates into madness. Her recovery is spurred by the memory of one detail that distinguished her son's killer—an elaborate tattoo of a blue tiger. She takes up work in a cocktail bar frequented by Japanese mobsters, flaunting her tattoo in hopes of flushing out the killer.

As long as Madsen and Nakamura are circling each other, drawn in by sexual chemistry and palpable doom, *Tiger* is fun, even riveting fare. But less effective is the Yakuza gang war.

•

BLUE VEIL, THE
1951, 113 mins, US b/w
Dir Curtis Bernhardt ***Prod*** Jerry Wald, Norman Krasna ***Scr*** Norman Corwin ***Ph*** Franz Planer ***Ed*** George J. Amy ***Mus*** Franz Waxman ***Art*** Albert S. D'Agostino, Carroll Clark
Act Jane Wyman, Charles Laughton, Joan Blondell, Richard Carlson, Agnes Moorehead, Don Taylor (Wald-Krasna/RKO)

Story [by Francois Campaux] is nothing more than a series of episodes strung together by the central character of a First World War war-widow who devotes her life to children after losing her only child. Footage opens with the child's death, a moving sequence, and carries Jane Wyman through a succession of jobs as a baby nurse until, old and worn-out physically, she is given the lifetime job of caring for the offspring of one of her former charges.

Charles Laughton, as a portly, kindly corset manufacturer, is Wyman's first costar, in the initial episode.

Romance makes a bid for Wyman in her new job in the home of wealthy Agnes Moorehead, but she is unable to leave her charge to go off to foreign lands with Richard Carlson, a tutor who courts her.

Next is the episode in which she cares for Natalie Wood, daughter of fading musical actress Joan Blondell. This sequence is considerably enlivened by the pert vivacity of Blondell and her singing of two old tunes.

Wyman experiences real heartbreak at the end of eight years of caring for the abandoned son of Audrey Totter when the latter returns from England after the Second World War, with a stepfather, and claims the boy.

Curtis Bernhardt's direction handles the drama surely, if at times a bit measured, and never strives for dramatic tricks beyond the level of the simple, warm story being told.

1951: NOMINATIONS: Best Actress (Jane Wyman; Supp. Actress Joan Blondell)

•

BLUE VELVET
1986, 120 mins, US Ⓥ ⊙ ⌴ col
Dir David Lynch ***Prod*** Fred Caruso ***Scr*** David Lynch ***Ph*** Frederick Elmes ***Ed*** Duwayne Dunham ***Mus*** Angelo Badalamenti ***Art*** Patricia Norris
Act Kyle MacLachlan, Isabella Rossellini, Dennis Hopper, Laura Dern, Hope Lange, Dean Stockwell (De Laurentiis)

Blue Velvet finds David Lynch back on familiar, strange, territory. Picture takes a disturbing and at times devastating look at the ugly underside of Middle American life.

The modest proportions of the film are just right for the writer-director's desire to investigate the inexplicable demons that drive people to deviate from expected norms of behavior and thought.

The setting, a small town called Lumberton, seems on the surface to be utterly conventional, placid, comforting and serene. The bland perfection is disrupted when a man collapses in Kyle MacLachlan's yard and is further upset when he discovers a disembodied human ear in an empty lot.

He begins investigating whose ear he might have found, and ends up spying on local roadhouse chanteuse and prostie Isabella Rossellini. Peeping through a closet keyhole, what he sees violent client Dennis Hopper do to sweet Laura Dern launches MacLachlan into another world, into an unfamiliar, dangerously provocative state of mind.

Rossellini, dressed in lingerie or less much of the time, throws herself into this mad role with complete abandon. Hopper creates a flabbergasting portrait of unrepentent, irredeemable evil.

1986: NOMINATION: Best Director

•

BLUME IN LOVE
1973, 115 mins, US Ⓥ col
Dir Paul Mazursky ***Prod*** Paul Mazursky ***Scr*** Paul Mazursky ***Ph*** Bruce Surtees ***Ed*** Donn Cambern ***Mus*** Bill Conti ***Art*** Pato Guzman
Act George Segal, Susan Anspach, Kris Kristofferson, Marsha Mason, Shelley Winters, Paul Mazursky (Warner)

Blume in Love is a technically well made, but dramatically distended comedy-drama starring George Segal as a man determined to win back the affections of Susan Anspach, the wife who divorced him for infidelity.

Needless time-juggling flashback, indulgent writing, lazy structure, and intrusive and pretentious social commentary blunt some fine performances which occasionally inject life into the plot.

It takes Segal 115 minutes to win back Anspach's affections, the road being littered with relentless footage from Venice, Italy, and lots of cutesy sidebar micro-vignette which is lingeringly set up only for a fast cut from some limp gag line. There are a few good laughs, a handful of chuckles, several smiles, and a ton of songs, some by Kris Kristofferson who is starred as Anspach's dropout lover.

•

BOARDWALK
1979, 98 mins, US Ⓥ col
Dir Stephen Verona ***Prod*** George Willoughby ***Scr*** Stephen Verona, Leigh Chapman ***Ph*** Billy Williams
Act Ruth Gordon, Lee Strasberg, Janet Leigh, Joe Silver, Eddie Barth, Kim Delgado (Atlantic Releasing)

At times genuinely affecting, at others patently manipulative, *Boardwalk* is a small, well-wrought feature that centers on the efforts of an elderly Jewish couple to survive the barrenness and dangers of their decaying Brooklyn neighborhood.

But although there's a strong emotional core (and ample talent) to its portrait of the stubbornly "youthful" eldsters (Lee Strasberg and Ruth Gordon), it's the film's chronicle of their mounting terrorization at the hands of a black youth gang that overrides its tone, shading the pic into a *Death Wish* finale.

Director and coscripter Stephen Verona quickly establishes his focal family as a tightknit, mostly loving unit.

•

BOAT, THE
SEE: DAS BOOT

•

BOB & CAROL & TED & ALICE
1969, 104 mins, US Ⓥ ⊙ col
Dir Paul Mazursky ***Prod*** Larry Tucker ***Scr*** Paul Mazursky, Larry Tucker ***Ph*** Charles E. Lang ***Ed*** Stuart Pappe ***Mus*** Quincy Jones ***Art*** Pato Guzman
Act Natalie Wood, Robert Culp, Elliott Gould, Dyan Cannon, Horst Ebersberg, Lee Bergere (Columbia/Frankovich)

The story concerns a young documentary filmmaker (Robert Culp) and his wife (Natalie Wood) who visit an institute in Southern California which supposedly helps people expand their capacities for love and understanding. When our friends are back in their swank surroundings, chatting with friends, Elliott Gould and wife Dyan Cannon, the comedy begins and never lets up until the final scenes when the sociological effects of this pseudo-liberal thinking come into play.

The acting is superb. Cannon proves an expert comedienne. She and Gould practically steal the film, although admittedly they have the best lines. Wood and Culp give equally fine performances. The film is almost flawless, presenting the issues in a pleasing, entertaining and thought-provoking manner.

1969: NOMINATIONS: Best Supp. Actor (Elliott Gould), Supp. Actress (Dyan Cannon), Original Story & Screenplay, Cinematography

•

BOBBY DEERFIELD
1977, 124 mins, US Ⓥ ⌴ col
Dir Sydney Pollack ***Prod*** Sydney Pollarck ***Scr*** Alvin Sargent ***Ph*** Henri Decae ***Ed*** Fredric Steinkamp ***Mus*** Dave Grusin ***Art*** Stephen Grimes
Act Al Pacino, Marthe Keller, Anny Duperey, Walter McGinn, Romolo Valli, Stephan Meldegg (Columbia)

Bobby Deerfield is a brilliantly unusual love story, told in a European fashion which makes the Sydney Pollack film at first irritating, then intriguing, finally most rewarding and emotionally satisfying.

Stars Al Pacino and Marthe Keller are both excellent as shallow jet-set floaters who become whole persons in their romance. Foreign location footage is lavish.

Erich Maria Remarque's novel, *Heaven Has No Favorites*, served as the basis for screenplay. Pacino plays the title character, a Newark boy whose interest in car racing has propelled him into international celeb status where he'd rather forget his origins. Keller is a wealthy and elusive character, manic in her life style because of terminal illness.

•

BOB LE FLAMBEUR
1956, 95 mins, France Ⓥ ⊙ b/w
Dir Jean-Pierre Melville ***Scr*** Auguste Le Breton, Jean-Pierre Melville ***Ph*** Henri Decae ***Ed*** Monique Bonnot ***Mus*** Eddie Barclay, Jean Boyer ***Art*** Jean-Pierre Melville, Bouxin
Act Roger Duchesne, Isabelle Corey, Daniel Cauchy, Howard Vernon, Guy Decomble, Claude Cerval (Jenner/Cyme/Play Art/OGC)

Pic is in the *Rififi* classification and is even written by the same man. It concerns the last job of an aging gangster who has been devoting himself to gambling until the final heist presents itself. However, here the similarity ends, for this lacks the suspense, characterization and deft direction of the predecessor.

This plods through its tale of the underworld without adding the needed filip to make it unusual. Otherwise, lagging direction, so-so thesping and usual femme and low-down aspects of this type production make this an ordinary entry. Production values show a tight budget and technical values are below par.

•

BOBO, THE
1967, 103 mins, US Ⓥ ⊙ col
Dir Robert Parrish ***Prod*** Jerry Gershwin, Elliott Kastner ***Scr*** David R. Schwartz ***Ph*** Gerry Turpin ***Ed*** John Jympson ***Mus*** Francis Lai ***Art*** Elven Webb
Act Peter Sellers, Britt Ekland, Rossano Brazzi, Adolfo Celi, Hattie Jacques, John Wells (Warner)

The Bobo (based by scriptwriter David Schwartz on his own play and a novel by Burt Cole) is a clever, sophisticated and charming farce. Peter Sellers is teamed here with Britt Ekland, who plays the most beauteous, capricious, frivolous and difficult femme in all Barcelona.

As a golddigger to stop all gold-digging she is at once endowed with childlike naivete and a witchiness that makes her the focal point of the entire male population. Which, of course, makes all the more beguiling the challenge offered Sellers—a matador who sings, or a singer who is a half-baked torero, take your pick—of possessing her within exactly three days by a stopwatch if he is to receive a week's enagement at the city's biggest teatro.

Sellers undertakes a change of pace as the impoverished but self-confident bullfighter from the provinces who arrives in Barcelona determined to make his debut as a singer and meets stubborn opposition from impresario Adolfo Celi.

•

BOB ROBERTS
1992, 105 mins, US Ⓥ ⊙ col
Dir Tim Robbins ***Prod*** Forrest Murray ***Scr*** Tim Robbins ***Ph*** Jean Lepine ***Ed*** Lisa Churgin ***Mus*** David Robbins ***Art*** Richard Hoover
Act Tim Robbins, Giancarlo Esposito, Ray Wise, Brian Murray, Gore Vidal, Rebecca Jenkins (PolyGram/Working Title)

A sort of political *This Is Spinal Tap*, *Bob Roberts* is both a stimulating social satire and a depressing commentary on the devolution of the U.S. political system. Caustic docudrama about a wealthy crypto-fascist folk singer who runs for U.S. Senate showcases the impressive multiple talents of Tim Robbins as director, writer, actor, singer and songwriter.

Roberts (Robbins) is a self-assured, highly successful singer who attempts to ride his popularity into public office. Castigated as yuppie scum by his detractors, he has secured his niche as an anti-1960s folk artist who blames the country's ills on liberals and the social programs of the Great Society. Roberts's aim is to unseat longtime Pennsylvania Sen. Brickley Paiste (Gore Vidal).

Entire film is framed as a British TV documentary being prepared on Roberts's campaign. Dogging Roberts's heels on the campaign trail is one Bugs Raplin (Giancarlo Esposito), a black journalist for an underground rag.

Robbins is spookily dead-on projecting the candidate's bland confidence and homogenized middle-American personality. He has cast a healthy number of w.k. thesps to enact cameos, mostly as cute, superficial and dumb TV newscasters. Largest of these roles goes to Alan Rickman, ferociously good in a part that mainly has him heatedly denying major misdeeds.

•

BOCCACCIO 70
1962, 159 mins, Italy/France Ⓥ col
Dir Vittorio De Sica, Federico Fellini, Luchino Visconti ***Prod*** Carlo Ponti, Antonio Cervi ***Scr*** Cesare Zavattini, Federico

Fellini, Ennio Flaiano, Tullio Pinelli, Brunello Rondi, Goffredo Parise, Suso Cecchi D'Amico, Luchino Visconti **Ph** Otello Martelli, Giuseppe Rotunno **Ed** Adriana Novelli, Leo Cattozzo, Mario Serandrei **Mus** Armando Trovajoli (adapt.), Nino Rota **Art** Elio Costanzi, Piero Zuffi, Mario Garbuglia
Act Sophia Loren, Luigi Giuliani, Anita Ekberg, Peppino De Filippo, Romy Schneider, Tomas Milian (Concordia/Cineriz/Francinex/Gray)

Pic differs from most sketch items by the fact that each segment was separately conceived and executed, making episodes pocket-sized feature pix on their own. There's nothing pocket-sized about the production values, however, all three being expensively mounted and lavishly lensed in Technicolor.

First item, Federico Fellini's *The Temptation of Dr Antonio* (*Le tentazioni del Dottor Antonio*), is a searing, violent denunciation of hypocrisy with special attention to bigoted censorship. Episode deals with a Doctor Antonio (Peppino De Filippo) who is carrying on a one-man campaign against external expressions of love and sex. When a provocative poster of Anita Ekberg is set up facing his apartment, Antonio tries to fight one more battle against his concept of immorality. But he is defeated when the ebullient Ekberg comes to life and drives him berserk.

Second item, *The Job* (*Il lavoro*), provides a complete change of pace via Luchino Visconti's elegant styling of a modern boudoir piece, in which nuances of dialog and acting, as well as lush sets and color, help gain the total effect. In keeping with film's title, episode deals with young count (Tomas Milian) who's mixed up in a call girl scandal and fears his wife (Romy Schneider) will divorce him.

Act Three, *The Raffle* (*La riffa*), the most completely enjoyable of the lot, has Sophia Loren as the object of a raffle among visitors to a provincial fairground in northern Italy. The winner gets to sleep with her, and the money goes toward the dowry which will allow her marriage and an independent life. Vittorio De Sica tells the tale (which has a twist ending) with a brash and earthy humor aptly keyed to the provincial setting.

[Version reviewed is three-episode one shown outside Italy. Four-episode Italian version began with the De Sica episode and concluded with a seg by director Mario Monicelli, *Renzo e Luciana/Renzo and Luciana*.]

•

BODIES, REST & MOTION

1993, 93 mins, US Ⓥ ⊙ col
Dir Michael Steinberg **Prod** Allan Mindel, Denise Shaw, Eric Stoltz **Scr** Roger Hedden **Ph** Bernd Heinl **Ed** Jay Cassidy **Mus** Michael Convertino **Art** Stephen McCabe
Act Phoebe Cates, Bridget Fonda, Tim Roth, Eric Stoltz (Fine Line/August)

Uncompelling but moderately engaging throughout due to its attractive cast and closeup look at contemporary spiritual ennui, *Bodies, Rest & Motion* is both flashy and laidback, eventful and static. Script feels as if it knows whereof it speaks.

Set in a sun-baked, fictional Arizona town called Enfield that is all malls and fast-food pit stops, the sharp-looking film looks at four young people coping with a malaise that seems neither easily diagnosable nor curable. Adapted by Roger Hedden from his own play, piece betrays its theatrical origins by taking place over one weekend mostly in a house shared by agitated, dissatisfied Tim Roth and his unfocused g.f., Bridget Fonda.

In the opening scene, Roth tells former g.f. Phoebe Cates, now Fonda's best friend, that they have decided to move to the "city of the future"—Butte, Montana—and are packing up. However, Roth hits the road on his own, leaving the distraught Fonda alone with a pile of furniture and dope-smoking housepainter Eric Stoltz, and the new couple soon get it on.

Michael Steinberg, who makes his solo debut here after codirecting *The Waterdance*, is good with the actors, and the more intimate the scene, the more effectively it registers. However, many scenes don't really have much going on in them, resulting in a relatively low-impact experience.

•

BODY AND SOUL

1947, 101 mins, US Ⓥ ⊙ b/w
Dir Robert Rossen **Prod** Bob Roberts **Scr** Abraham Polonsky **Ph** James Wong Howe **Ed** Francis Lyon, Robert Parrish **Mus** Hugo Friedhofer **Art** Nathan Juran
Act John Garfield, Lilli Palmer, Anne Revere, Canada Lee, Hazel Brooks, William Conrad (United Artists/Enterprise)

Body and Soul has a somewhat familiar title and a likewise familiar narrative. It's the telling, however, that's different.

The story concerns a youngster with a punching flair who emerges from the amateurs to ride along the knockout trail to the middleweight championship. But to get himself a crack at the title he has to sell 50 percent of himself to a bigtime gambler with a penchant for making and breaking champs at will.

There are a flock of loopholes in this story, but interest seldom lags. Some of the "inside boxing" is authentic, but the "inside gambling" is another story in itself, which this pic doesn't tell. John Garfield is convincing in the lead part, and the boxing scenes look the McCoy. Poolhall and beer stube environments are effectively captured to indicate the sordidness that backgrounds the early careers of most boxers, who turn to the ring because of a proficiency with their fists on the streetcorner.

Lilli Palmer is miscast as Garfield's sweetheart and inspiration, especially with a continental accent that even the dialog can't properly clarify.

1947: Best Editing

NOMINATIONS: Best Actor (John Garfield), Original Screenplay

•

BODY DOUBLE

1984, 109 mins, US Ⓥ ⊙ col
Dir Brian De Palma **Prod** Brian De Palma **Scr** Robert J. Avrech, Brian De Palma **Ph** Stephen H. Burum **Ed** Jerry Greenberg, Bill Pankow **Mus** Pino Donaggio **Art** Ida Random
Act Craig Wasson, Gregg Henry, Melanie Griffith, Deborah Shelton, Guy Boyd, Dennis Franz (Columbia/Delphi Prods II)

Brian De Palma lets all his obsessions hang out in *Body Double*. A voyeur's delight and a feminist's nightmare, sexpenser features an outrageously far-fetched and flimsy plot.

The first half offers up virtually no storyline. Down-on-his-luck Hollywood actor Craig Wasson is befriended by fellow actor Gregg Henry, who invites him to housesit for him at a rich man's hilltop pad.

In a house across the way a beautiful woman enacts an elaborate striptease dance at the same hour every evening. Wasson digs the lady's act so much that he follows her the next day, when she is also pursued by a hideous-looking Indian.

Pivotal murder scene occurs at about the midpoint, and it's an offensive lulu, being performed with an enormous power drill. Remainder of the film sees Wasson getting involved in the porno film world as a way of solving the murder.

Thesping by Wasson, Henry and former Miss USA Deborah Shelton, as the lady across the hill, is serviceable, while Melanie Griffith, with punky dyed hair and teensy voice, is just right as a porno queen.

•

BODYGUARD, THE

SEE: YOJIMBO

•

BODYGUARD, THE

1992, 129 mins, US Ⓥ ⊙ col
Dir Mick Jackson **Prod** Lawrence Kasdan, Jim Wilson, Kevin Costner **Scr** Lawrence Kasdan **Ph** Andrew Dunn **Ed** Richard A. Harris, Donn Cambern **Mus** Alan Silvestri **Art** Jeffrey Beecroft
Act Kevin Costner, Whitney Houston, Gary Kemp, Bill Cobbs, Ralph Waite, Michele Lamar Richards (Warner/Tig)

No wonder this Lawrence Kasdan script was on the shelf for more than a decade: in the custody of director Mick Jackson, it proves a jumbled mess with a few enjoyable moments but little continuity or flow. Those shortcomings are puzzling since the pic's core is sheer simplicity: Bodyguard-for-hire Frank Farmer (Kevin Costner), who fears becoming too attached to his clients, takes a job protecting actress-singer Rachel Marron (Whitney Houston) and ends up falling for her. Someone is trying to kill her, and it seems possible that one of the members of her entourage may be involved.

Blame it on the setting, but the collaboration of Kasdan and Jackson (the one-time BBC director who helmed *L.A. Story*) at times feels like a music video interrupted by a movie.

For all that, pic isn't without its pleasures, from Costner silently drubbing his charge's testy security chief (Mike Starr) to his bluntly deflating a predatory partygoer.

The chemistry between the leads stems more from their inherent appeal than anything the story develops. Houston makes a solid debut and looks glorious, snapping off saucy dialogue. Kasdan was inspired by Steve McQueen in *Bullitt* when he wrote the script in 1975, and Costner manages some of that quiet intensity.

1992: NOMINATIONS: Best Song ("I Have Nothing"; "Run to You")

•

BODY HEAT

1981, 113 mins, US Ⓥ ⊙ col
Dir Lawrence Kasdan **Prod** Fred T. Gallo **Scr** Lawrence Kasdan **Ph** Richard H. Cline **Ed** Carol Littleton **Mus** John Barry **Art** Bill Kenney
Act William Hurt, Kathleen Turner, Richard Crenna, Ted Danson, Mickey Rourke, J. A. Preston (Warner/Ladd)

Body Heat is an engrossing, mightily stylish meller in which sex and crime walk hand in hand down the path to tragedy, just like in the old days. Working in the imposing shadow of the late James M. Cain screenwriter Lawrence Kasdan makes an impressively confident directorial debut.

William Hurt is a spirited but struggling lawyer just getting by in a marginal Florida coast town whose persistent pursuit of sultry Kathleen Turner pays off in the way of a torrid affair, highly satisfying for both parties.

She's the young wife of loaded middle-aged businessman Richard Crenna, and it isn't long before the passion can't tolerate the limitations imposed. Just as in *Double Indemnity* it's the dame who hatches the murder plot, with the guy finally falling into line and coming up with the ingenious way to pull it off.

However familiar the elements, Kasdan has brought the drama alive by steeping it in humid, virtually oozing atmosphere. The heat of the title is palpably evident, both mundanely in the weather and in the irresistible attraction of the sexy leads.

Hurt successfully mixes both laconicism and innocence. In her film debut, Turner registers strongly as a hard gal with a past. Her deep-voiced delivery instantly recalls that of young Lauren Bacall without seeming like an imitation.

•

BODY OF EVIDENCE

1993, 99 mins, US Ⓥ ⊙ col
Dir Uli Edel **Prod** Dino De Laurentiis **Scr** Brad Mirman **Ph** Doug Milsome **Ed** Thom Noble **Mus** Graeme Revell **Art** Victoria Paul
Act Madonna, Willem Dafoe, Joe Mantegna, Anne Archer, Julianne Moore, Jurgen Prochnow (De Laurentiis)

A courtroom drama built around the charge that Madonna's body is a deadly weapon with which she "fornicated" a man to death, this showcase for the singer-thesp as femme fatale is more silly than erotic.

The ever-self-inventing one plays the g.f. of a rich older man with a heart ailment who is found dead after a night in the sack with her. That he's left her $8 million and had cocaine in his system points the finger of guilt straight to the "cokehead slut"—as the man's secretary (Anne Archer) calls her.

Defense attorney Willem Dafoe makes the unforgettable opening argument that, "It's not a crime to be a great lay," but soon discovers that Madonna isn't into old men exclusively. Dafoe just can't say no and the pair's several sex bouts are the film's main action set-pieces.

Trial begins a mere 20 minutes into the story, and most of the running time alternates between courtroom testimony—much of it racy—and Madonna-Dafoe face-offs.

Decked out in a short platinum blonde haircut and fancy clothes that rip easily, Madonna has little trouble passing as a predatory tramp whose credo would seem to be, "I f———, therefore I am." Dafoe holds his own manfully. Portland locations give the pic's exteriors an appealingly wet, cool feel.

[On homevideo and outside the U.S., pic was distributed in an uncut 101-min. version.]

•

BODY PARTS

1991, 88 mins, US Ⓥ ⊙ ▭ col
Dir Eric Red **Prod** Frank Mancuso, Jr. **Scr** Eric Red, Norman Snider **Ph** Theo Van de Sande **Ed** Anthony Redman **Mus** Loek Dikker **Art** Bill Brodie
Act Jeff Fahey, Lindsay Duncan, Kim Delaney, Brad Dourif, Zakes Mokae, Peter Murnik (Paramount)

What could have been a reasonably interesting thriller literally goes to pieces in last third, until the brain seems the most salient part missing. Pic was inspired by a novel [*Choice Cuts*, adapted by Patricia Herskovic and Joyce Taylor] by French authors Thomas Narcejac and Pierre Boileau, who wrote the novel that provided the basis for *Vertigo*. Hitchcock and others reportedly grappled with adapting this book.

Jeff Fahey plays a criminal psychologist who loses his arm in a car accident, only to have it replaced by a doctor (Lindsay Duncan) perfecting a new limb-grafting procedure. The psychologist is told that the new limb belonged to a serial killer, prompting him to wonder if the murderer's arm might be invading his own soul.

He even seeks out other donor recipients (Brad Dourif and Peter Murnik), who are initially unconcerned or unaware of any ill effects. Then, suddenly, the narrative hurriedly kicks into a slasher mode, replete with car chases, dismemberment and unintentional, if rather vulgar, hilarity.

•

BODY SNATCHER, THE
1945, 70 mins, US Ⓥ ⦿ b/w
Dir Robert Wise ***Prod*** Val Lewton ***Scr*** Philip MacDonald, Carlos Keith ***Ph*** Robert de Grasse ***Ed*** J. R. Whittredge ***Mus*** Roy Webb ***Art*** Albert S. D'Agostino, Walter E. Keller
Act Boris Karloff, Bela Lugosi, Henry Daniell, Edith Atwater, Russell Wade, Rita Corday (RKO)

Based on a short story by Robert Louis Stevenson, and given tightly scripted adaptation, *Snatcher* seldom lacks interest. Yarn deals with the traffic on dead bodies by hansom cabbie Boris Karloff. Corpses are used for study purposes in a medical school mastered by Henry Daniell. Russell Wade, young assistant to Daniell, is caught in the web of the illicit dealings, with Edith Atwater playing the wife of Daniell. Bela Lugosi is seen briefly as a handyman at the med school.

Karloff portrays his sadistic role in characteristic style, but best performance comes from Daniell. Lugosi is more or less lost, probably on the cutting floor, since he is only in for two sequences.

Body Snatcher is located in Scotland over a century ago. Settings are inexpensive but sufficient for the needs. Production values, in general, however, aid materially in making this picture a winner.

•

BODY SNATCHERS
1994, 87 mins, US Ⓥ ⦿ ▭ col
Dir Abel Ferrara ***Prod*** Robert H. Solo ***Scr*** Stuart Gordon, Dennis Paoli, Nicholas St. John ***Ph*** Bojan Bazelli ***Ed*** Anthony Redman ***Mus*** Joe Delia ***Art*** Peter Jamison
Act Gabrielle Anwar, Terry Kinney, Billy Wirth, Meg Tilly, Forest Whitaker, Christine Elise (Warner)

The third screen version of Jack Finney's 1954 novel *The Body Snatchers* is a tremendously exciting thriller that compares favorably with Don Siegel's classic 1956 original.

Producer Robert Solo effectively remade the picture in 1978 and has carried over several innovations, notably the shrieking sound effects. Improvements include having a teenage heroine and setting the film (from a screen story by Raymond Cistheri and Larry Cohen) on an Alabama military base.

Gabrielle Anwar toplines in a star-building performance as teen Marty Malone, who has moved to an army base with her EPA biologist dad (Terry Kinney), stepmom (Meg Tilly) and younger brother (Reilly Murphy). She also narrates the tale.

Anwar is befriended by the punkette daughter (Christine Elise) of the base commander, Gen. Platt (R. Lee Ermey). Unsettling events occur early: Anwar is accosted by a black man who warns her cryptically: "They get you when you sleep." Camp medical officer Forest Whitaker tells Kinney he's received many reports of delusional fixations in people afraid to sleep.

Kinney, a low-key type resembling Don Johnson, is on the money as the ambiguous father, while Billy Wirth exudes sex appeal as Anwar's b.f. and savior. Tilly is chilling.

Makeup effects eschew the genre's explicit gore, in favor of frightening tendrils snaking around the victims.

•

BOEING BOEING
1965, 102 mins, US Ⓥ col
Dir John Rich ***Prod*** Hal B. Wallis ***Scr*** Edward Anhalt ***Ph*** Lucien Ballard ***Ed*** Warren Low, Archie Marshek ***Mus*** Neal Hefti ***Art*** Hal Pereira, Walter Tyler
Act Tony Curtis, Jerry Lewis, Dany Saval, Christiane Schmidtmer, Suzanna Leigh, Thelma Ritter (Paramount)

Boeing Boeing is an excellent modern comedy about two newshawks with a yen for airline hostesses. Firstrate performances and direction make the most of a very good script.

The fanciful dream of a dedicated bachelor is realized in this adaptation of a Marc Camoletti play in which Paris-based U.S. newsman Tony Curtis has three airline gals on a string.

Director John Rich has done a topnotch job in overcoming what is essentially (except for a few Paris exteriors) a one-set, one-joke comedy. Curtis is excellent and neatly restrained as the harem keeper whose cozy scheme approaches collapse when advanced design Boeing aircraft (hence, the title) augur a disastrous overlap in femme availability.

Rich has also brought out a new dimension in Lewis, herein excellent in a solid comedy role as Curtis's professional rival who threatens to explode the plan.

The outstanding performance is delivered by Thelma Ritter, Curtis's harried housekeeper who makes the necessary domestic changes in photos, clothing and menu so that the next looker will continue to believe that she, alone, is mistress of the flat.

•

BOFORS GUN, THE
1968, 105 mins, UK col
Dir Jack Gold ***Prod*** Otto Plaschkes ***Scr*** John McGrath ***Ph*** Alan Hume ***Ed*** Anne V. Coates ***Mus*** Carl Davis ***Art*** Terence Knight
Act Nicol Williamson, Ian Holm, David Warner, Peter Vaughan, Richard O'Callaghan, Barry Jackson (Universal)

No question of the quality of this absorbing, though downbeat military pic set in a British barracks in Germany in the mid-1950s. It has all the gripping fascination of a tussle between two wily, desperate young animals. Taut, icy direction and acting flawlessly tuned to what the writer [John McGrath, from his play *Events While Guarding the Bofors Gun*] has in mind bring a faultless realism.

Clash is between David Warner as an immature, indecisive one-striper and Nicol Williamson as a half-crazy, embittered Irish rebel, alcoholic and self-tortured. Events sizzle powerfully on the night before Warner is due to go to England for an officers' course. Williamson is attached to Warner's guard and, with rebellion and anger rankling inside him, sets out to humiliate the NCO and wreck his prospects of promotion.

Williamson brings out the rebel's mood brilliantly, his features, speech and behavior veering alarmingly from good-humored cynicism to anger and viciousness. Warner is just as good as the weak young man.

•

BOILING POINT
1993, 90 mins, US/France Ⓥ ⦿ col
Dir James B. Harris ***Prod*** Marc Frydman, Leonardo de la Fuente ***Scr*** James B. Harris ***Ph*** King Baggot ***Ed*** Jerry Brady ***Mus*** Cory Lerios, John D'Andrea ***Art*** Ron Foreman
Act Wesley Snipes, Dennis Hopper, Lolita Davidovich, Viggo Mortensen, Dan Hedaya, Seymour Cassel (Hexagon)

Promoted as a hard-action film for Wesley Snipes fans, *Boiling Point* turns out to be an old-fashioned police procedural, low-key and bland in the extreme. Writer/director James B. Harris, in his zeal to re-create the mood and character acting of '40s film noir, seems to have forgotten about excitement and visual flair.

Snipes toplines as a U.S. Treasury agent partnered with Dan Hedaya. The third T-man on their stakeout is killed by ruthless thug Viggo Mortensen, who gets away with partner Dennis Hopper before the feds can close in. Snipes is reassigned from LA to Newark. He holds out for one week's time to catch the killers; coincidentally Hopper is given a week to find the $50,000 he owes gangster Tony LoBianco.

Throughout the picture, Snipes keeps running into Hopper, neither knowing one is methodically hunting the other. Because of terrific acting down to the smallest role, one's interest is maintained despite the minimalist direction and lack of story twists.

•

BOLERO
SEE: LES UNS ET LES AUTRES

•

BOLERO
1984, 104 mins, US Ⓥ ⦿ col
Dir John Derek ***Prod*** Bo Derek ***Scr*** John Derek ***Ph*** John Derek ***Ed*** John Derek ***Mus*** Peter Bernstein, Elmer Bernstein ***Art*** Alan Roderick-Jones
Act Bo Derek, George Kennedy, Andrea Occhipinti, Ana Obregon, Olivia D'Abo, Greg Bensen (Cannon/City)

Bolero is all about Bo Derek's determination to lose her virginity after graduating from an English boarding school. Accompanied by friend Ana Obregon and family retainer George Kennedy, Bo ventures first to Arabia where a sheik falls asleep in her arms.

Still unviolated, Bo moves on to Spain where she meets handsome bullfighter Andrea Occhipinti. Ready for womanhood, Bo utters the immortal lines: "Do everything to me. Show me how I can do everything to you. Is there enough I can do for you so you can give ecstasy to me?" Then the dog barks and the deed is done. But poor Bo no sooner has her initial introduction to amour than the new lover gets gored in a sensitive location, putting him out of commission.

•

BONE COLLECTOR, THE
1999, 118 mins, US Ⓥ ⦿ ▭ col
Dir Phillip Noyce ***Prod*** Martin Bregman, Louis A. Stroller, Michael Bregman ***Scr*** Jeremy Iacone ***Ph*** Dean Semler ***Ed*** William Hoy ***Mus*** Craig Armstrong ***Art*** Nigel Phelps
Act Denzel Washington, Angelina Jolie, Queen Latifah, Michael Rooker, Mike McGlone, Luis Guzman (Universal/Columbia)

The obvious difficulties in making an action thriller out of Jeffery Deaver's bestseller *The Bone Collector*—which pivots on a paralyzed protagonist solving a serial-murder case—aren't entirely surmounted in Phillip Noyce's glossy adaptation. While Denzel Washington delivers a convincing central turn, suspense is inevitably compromised by protag's physical stasis; perhaps more serious flaws, however, lie in Angelina Jolie's credulity-straining role and a narrative that keeps the killer's identity and motives unknown until a hyperbolic, contrived climax.

Brilliant NYPD criminologist Lincoln Rhyme (Washington) passes days in unhappy retirement, tended by omnipresent nurse Thelma (Queen Latifah), with occasional visits from medical technician Richard (Leland Orser). His former partner, Det. Sellitto (Ed O'Neill), thinks only Rhyme's uncanny skills can help in finding a multimillionaire and his wife who disappeared after entering an airport taxi the previous day.

Patrol cop Amelia Donaghy (Jolie) discovers the man's corpse buried beneath subway tracks, with a hand protuding upward. The kidnapped woman is presumed still alive, and Rhyme is able to pinpoint a likely hostage location. Clues eventually point toward the assailant's re-creation of crimes from the turn of the century.

Jeremy Iacone's (*One Tough Cop*) screenplay doesn't provide much in the way of backstory, or deep relationships. More poignancy should have been mined from Rhyme's isolation; dutiful Thelma appears to be his sole significant companion by choice.

Subsidiary roles are well cast, with Luis Guzman contributing comic relief as an antic forensics specialist. Production values are high grade.

•

BONFIRE OF THE VANITIES, THE
1990, 125 mins, US Ⓥ ⦿ ▭ col
Dir Brian De Palma ***Prod*** Brian De Palma ***Scr*** Michael Cristofer ***Ph*** Vilmos Zsigmond ***Ed*** David Ray, Bill Pankow ***Mus*** Dave Grusin ***Art*** Richard Sylbert
Act Tom Hanks, Bruce Willis, Melanie Griffith, Kim Cattrall, Morgan Freeman, F. Murray Abraham (Warner)

Brian De Palma's take on Tom Wolfe's *The Bonfire of the Vanities* is a misfire of inanities. Wolfe's first novel boasted rich characters and teeming incident that proved highly alluring to filmmakers. Unfortunately, De Palma was not the man for the job. It doesn't take long to turn off and tune out on this glitzy $45 million-plus dud. Early sequences of marital discord between Wall Street maestro Sherman McCoy (Tom Hanks) and wife Judy (Kim Cattrall) possess a grating, uncertain quality, and film never manages to locate a consistent tone. McCoy is having an affair with Southern bombshell Maria Ruskin (Melanie Griffith), and clearly stands as a symbol for Success, 1980s style. Monkeywrench arrives in the form of an automobile mishap one night in deepest Bronx.

Seemingly threatened by two black youths, Maria backs Sherman's Mercedes into one of them, slightly injuring him. When the kid falls into a coma, the machinery of law, politics and journalism begins grinding. The rich man's status makes him an ideal scapegoat for multifarious social ills, as well for as the personal agendas of the city's most shameless operators, most prominently, Peter Fallow (Bruce Willis), a down-and-out alcoholic reporter who parlays the McCoy story into fame and fortune. Unfortunately, the caricatures are so crude and the "revelations" so unenlightening of the human condition, that the satire is about as socially incisive as a *Police Academy* entry.

•

BONJOUR TRISTESSE
1958, 94 mins, US/UK Ⓥ ▭ col & b/w
Dir Otto Preminger ***Prod*** Otto Preminger ***Scr*** Arthur Laurents ***Ph*** Georges Perinal ***Ed*** Helga Cranston ***Mus*** Georges Auric ***Art*** Roger Furse
Act Deborah Kerr, David Niven, Jean Seberg, Mylene Demongeot, Geoffrey Horne, Juliette Greco (Wheel/Columbia)

In transplanting Francoise Sagan's thin book to the screen, producer-director Otto Preminger basically has stayed with her first-person tale of the amours of a middle-aged, charming and wealthy Frenchman within both view and earshot of his daughter who, like the author at the time, is 17. It's hardly a matter of wonder that pere's free-living escapades should prove contagious, that the girl, too, should take a fling at same.

But it is not a Class A effort. Script deficiencies and awkward reading—some lines are spoken as though just that—have static results. Detracting from the make-believe also is Jean Seberg's deportment. In her second cinematic try (her first was in Preminger's unfortunate *Saint Joan*), Seberg's

Cecile is more suggestive of a high school senior back home than the frisky, knowing, close friend and daughter of a roue living it up in the sumptious French setting. She is, of course, a selfish and malicious character to start with.

David Niven is properly affable as the father who travels with a mistress and makes no attempt to disguise his pursuits. Deborah Kerr is a standout talent as the artist whom Niven proposes to marry and who speeds away to apparent suicide upon finding him in another illicit situation, but there are instances where she, too, has difficulty with the stiltedness of the dialog.

Mylene Demongeot fits in well as a silly, sunburned blonde; Geoffrey Horne rates adequate as playmate for Cecile; and Walter Chiari comes off as something of a cariacature of a rich South American.

The Riviera villa backdrop and beach scenes are rich in eye appeal via the CinemaScope and Technicolor photography, and wardrobes make for another visual plus. Effective also is the switch to monochrome for Left Bank bistro scenes.

•

BONNIE AND CLYDE
1967, 111 mins, US Ⓥ ⦿ col
Dir Arthur Penn ***Prod*** Warren Beatty ***Scr*** David Newman, Robert Benton ***Ph*** Burnett Guffey ***Ed*** Dede Allen ***Mus*** Charles Strouse ***Art*** Dean Tavoularis
Act Warren Beatty, Faye Dunaway, Michael J. Pollard, Gene Hackman, Estelle Parsons, Denver Pyle (Warner)

Warren Beatty's *Bonnie and Clyde* incongruously couples comedy with crime, in this biopic of Bonnie Parker and Clyde Barrow, a pair of Texas desperadoes who roamed and robbed the southwest and midwest during the bleak Depression days of the early 1930s.

Conceptually, the film leaves much to be desired, because killings and the backdrop of the Depression are scarcely material for a bundle of laughs. However, the film does have some standout interludes.

Scripters David Newman and Robert Benton have depicted these real-life characters as inept, bumbling, moronic types, and if this had been true they would have been erased in their first try. It's a picture with conflicting moods, racing from crime to comedy, and intermingling genuinely moving love scenes between Faye Dunaway as Bonnie and Beatty as Clyde.

This inconsistency of direction is the most obvious fault of *Bonnie and Clyde*, which has some good ingredients, although they are not meshed together well. Like the film itself, the performances are mostly erratic. Beatty is believable at times, but his characterization lacks any consistency. Dunaway is a knockout as Bonnie Parker, registers with deep sensitivity in the love scenes, and conveys believability to her role. Michael J. Pollard and Gene Hackman are more clowns than baddies as gang members; Estelle Parsons is good.

1967: Best Supp. Actress (Estelle Parsons), Cinematography

NOMINATIONS: Best Picture, Director, Actor (Warren Beatty), Actress (Faye Dunaway), Supp. Actor (Gene Hackman, Michael J. Pollard), Original Story & Screenplay, Costume Design

•

BOOGIE NIGHTS
1997, 152 mins, US Ⓥ ⦿ ▭ col
Dir Paul Thomas Anderson ***Prod*** Lloyd Levin, Paul Thomas Anderson, John Lyons, Joanne Sellar ***Scr*** Paul Thomas Anderson ***Ph*** Robert Elswit ***Ed*** Dylan Tichenor ***Mus*** Michael Penn ***Art*** Bob Ziembicki
Act Mark Wahlberg, Burt Reynolds, Julianne Moore, John C. Reilly, Don Cheadle, Heather Graham (New Line)

Spanning the height of the disco era, 1977–84, pic offers a visually stunning exploration of the adult entertainment industry, centering on a hardcore movie outfit whose members form a close-knit extended family. Helmer Paul Thomas Anderson makes a quantum leap forward in his second feature, following *Hard Eight*, which didn't find an audience.

Story follows the rise and fall of Eddie Adams (Mark Wahlberg), a handsome, uneducated teenager who works in the kitchen of a popular San Fernando Valley nightclub. When he's spotted by Jack Horner (Burt Reynolds), a successful porn producer, Eddie is instantly lured to a promising career. Naive and gullible, he immerses himself in the new world, which offers a substitute family and the seductive lifestyle of sex-music-drugs.

Adopting a new name, Dirk Diggler, he soon becomes a hot property. However, as the yarn moves into the '80s, Diggler's endless partying and enormous ego begin to interfere with his work.

Pic's first hour, which is devoted to one year (1977), is nothing short of brilliant, both narratively and technically. But subsequent chapters, which become increasingly shorter, and numerous subplots and secondary characters make the saga a bit too messy for its own good.

Each individual is given a distinctive profile: a cuckolded husband (a touching William H. Macey) who's tormented; a blond Rollergirl (a terrific Heather Graham) who demands respect from her sex partners; a decent man whose dream is to open a stereo store (a dignified Don Cheadle); a rich druggie who's smarter than he appears (an eccentric Alfred Molina).

Wahlberg renders a splendid performance, Reynolds shines as the film's moral center, and the versatile Julianne Moore excels as Amber, the company's female star and surrogate mother.

1997: NOMINATIONS: Best Supp. Actor (Burt Reynolds), Supp. Actress (Julianne Moore), Original Screenplay

•

BOOK OF SHADOWS: BLAIR WITCH 2
2000, 90 mins, US Ⓥ ⦿ col
Dir Joe Berlinger ***Prod*** Bill Carraro ***Scr*** Dick Beebe, Joe Berlinger ***Ph*** Nancy Schreiber ***Ed*** Sarah Flack ***Mus*** Carter Burwell ***Art*** Vince Peranio
Act Kim Director, Jeffrey Donovan, Erica Leerhsen, Tristen Skyler, Stephen Turner (Haxan/Artisan)

Disappointing in every aspect, sequel fails to make good on auds' curiosity about "what really happened" in part one, while draining the concept of any residual mystique or novelty. It was a given that sequel wouldn't try to duplicate the original's no-budget, faux-docu approach. But *Book* replaces that distinctive tactio with an artillery of cliched film styles. Feature would have been vastly improved had it concentrated on the sketchy central story, reserving flashbacks, flash-forwards and "visions" for the last lap. As is, the film never has a chance to build tension, let alone credible characters or situations.

From the get-go, pic's in self-canceling overdrive mode. Vanful of prospective victims is driven by Jeff (Jeffrey Donovan), the local we've already glimpsed during his (unexplained) past mental-hospital stay and later police grilling. While most Burkittsville townies bemoan the tourists who have overrun the area since *The Blair Witch Project* was released, Jeff is determined to cash in with a "Blair Witch Hunt" enterprise. His first customers take the Blair "legend" with varying degrees of salt. Spooked by mysterious events during their first night (five hours that draw a collective blank), they watch videotapes they took during their lost night in the woods, shocked to discover themselves amid the naked participants in orgiastic pagan rites.

Drastically overloaded scenario bungles several avenues of potential fright. For one thing, flash-forwards spoil all mystery regarding who will survive. The "Book of Shadows" itself scarcely figures in the narrative, and auds who assumed *BW2* would provide face time with—or at least fuller explanation of—the Blair Witch herself will feel sorely misled.

Nothing much works, but everything is tried: multiple aspect-ratio, film, vid, color and B&W formats; in-joke flippancy and deadly earnestness. Elaborate f/x, crane shots and distorted images clash against vérité roughness. Overall atmosphere and scene rhythms never get a chance to take hold.

•

BOOM
1968, 112 mins, UK ▭ col
Dir Joseph Losey ***Prod*** John Heyman, Norman Priggen ***Scr*** Tennessee Williams ***Ph*** Douglas Slocombe ***Ed*** Reginald Beck ***Mus*** John Barry ***Art*** Richard MacDonald
Act Elizabeth Taylor, Richard Burton, Noel Coward, Joanna Shimkus, Michael Dunn, Romolo Valli (World Film Services/Moonlake/Universal)

The translation to film of Tennessee Williams's much-revised play, *The Milk Train Doesn't Stop Here Anymore*, has at least given more physical movement to the symbolic drama of not-so-dolce vita among the jaded rich. Joseph Losey directs stars Elizabeth Taylor, Richard Burton and Noel Coward in John Heyman's plush production.

Film is the uninteresting tale of a multi-married, aging shrew, played by Taylor. Coward, a neighboring swish from Capri, adds a good shot of life, unfortunately too early and too little.

Taylor's delineation of the lead role is off the mark; instead of an earthy dame, hypochondriac and hyperemotional, who has survived six wealthy husbands, she plays it like she has just lost the first, who would appear to have taken her away from a roadside truck stop job. The wealth is shown in too nouveau riche a manner. The gowns, jewels and sets only emphasize the point. Burton is far more believable as a freeloading poet working the Mediterranean circuit.

•

BOOMERANG!
1947, 87 mins, US b/w
Dir Elia Kazan ***Prod*** Louis de Rochemont ***Scr*** Richard Murphy ***Ph*** Norbert Brodine ***Ed*** Harmon Jones ***Mus*** David Buttolph ***Art*** Richard Day, Chester Gore
Act Dana Andrews, Jane Wyatt, Lee J. Cobb, Arthur Kennedy, Karl Malden, Sam Levene (20th Century-Fox)

Boomerang! is gripping, real-life melodrama, told in semi-documentary style. Lensing was done on location at Stamford, CT, the locale adding to realism. Based on a still unsolved murder case in Bridgeport, CT, plot is backed up with strong cast.

Dana Andrews heads the convincing cast. His role is realistic and a top performance job. While carrying a fictional name as state's attorney, the role, in real life, has its counterpart in Homer Cummings, who went on from the state post to become Attorney-General of the United States. Case on which plot is based deals with murder of a Bridgeport priest and how the prosecuting attorney establishes the innocence of the law's only suspect.

All the leads have the stamp of authenticities. The dialog and situations further the factual technique. Lee J. Cobb shows up strongly as chief detective, harassed by press and politicians alike while trying to carry out his duties. Arthur Kennedy is great as the law's suspect.

1947: NOMINATION: Best Screenplay

•

BOOMERANG
1992, 118 mins, US Ⓥ ⦿ col
Dir Reginald Hudlin ***Prod*** Brian Grazer ***Scr*** Barry W. Blaustein, David Sheffield ***Ph*** Woody Omens ***Ed*** Earl Watson, John Carter, Michael Jablow ***Mus*** Marcus Miller ***Art*** Jane Musky
Act Eddie Murphy, Halle Berry, Robin Givens, David Alan Grier, Grace Jones, Eartha Kitt (Paramount)

In *Boomerang* Eddie Murphy straitjackets himself in an ill-fitting comedy vehicle that's desperately in need of a reality check.

For his 11th feature film, Murphy's credited with the high-concept story, developed by scripters as a cornball tale of comeuppance. He's a marketing exec at a New York cosmetics firm that women find irresistible (all six female leads want to seduce him). After a merger with a French firm, his new departmental boss, Robin Givens, turns the tables on Murphy and treats him the way he's been treating women all his adult life.

Film works best when Murphy plays his strong suits, including a childlike innocence, flair for mimicry and self-deprecating humour. Unfortunately, his character's fat ego keeps hogging center stage. The fact that he's dominated during the middle reels by aggressive Givens doesn't make up for the blatant sexism of the script.

Only naturalistic character in a cast of caricatures is cute subordinate Halle Berry during the film's first half. Director Reginald Hudlin, making the big jump here from low budget *House Party* to major studio filmmaking, handles individual scenes well but misses the big picture.

•

BOOM TOWN
1940, 117 mins, US Ⓥ b/w
Dir Jack Conway ***Prod*** Sam Zimbalist ***Scr*** John Lee Mahin, James Edward Grant ***Ph*** Harold Rosson ***Ed*** Blanche Sewell ***Mus*** Franz Waxman ***Art*** Cedric Gibbons, Eddie Imazu
Act Clark Gable, Spencer Tracy, Claudette Colbert, Hedy Lamarr, Frank Morgan, Lionel Atwill (M-G-M)

Unlike many large-budgeted productions carrying multi-star setups that tend either to costume background or sophistication for limited appeal, this one (with an outlay of around $2 million) breaks out with a dashing, rough-and-tumble yarn of modern adventure. Interspersed is romance and love interest of more than minor importance.

Boom Town is the tale of wildcat oil drilling, with fortunes won and lost just as quickly as a roller coaster dips and rises. It centers around the partnership of Clark Gable and Spencer Tracy, a couple of tough, fighting, two-fisted oil drillers who know all the angles. After teaming up with Gable's short bankroll and Tracy's wildcat lease, and hijacking a drilling rig and equipment, they hit saltwater—but on the second try hit a gusher. They split and go separate ways, each taking the bumps of riches and poverty along the eight-year stretch.

Tracy and Gable share prominence in splitting responsibilities of carrying the picture along. Little to choose between the pair—each handles his tailor-made role in excellent fashion. Colbert catches attention as the sincere and loving wife who shares Gable's fortunes and misfortunes with courage and a smile. Hedy Lamarr is of minor importance in the overall story as the New York siren who is flagged from stealing Gable from his wife by some effective manipulations by Tracy.

•

BOOST, THE

1988, 95 mins, US Ⓥ ⦿ col

Dir Harold Becker ***Prod*** Daniel H. Blatt ***Scr*** Darryl Ponicsan ***Ph*** Howard Atherton ***Ed*** Maury Winetrobe ***Mus*** Stanley Myers ***Art*** Waldemar Kalinowski

Act James Woods, Sean Young, John Kapelos, Steven Hill, Kelle Kerr, Amanda Blake (Hemdale)

Based on Benjamin Stein's book *Ludes*, well-wrought screenplay is a cautionary tale about a couple involved in a mutually destructive, coke-dominated lifestyle.

Young and very much in love, Lenny and Linda Brown (James Woods and Sean Young) are still struggling to make ends meet in New York City when Lenny, a born hustler with financial smarts, receives an extraordinary opportunity from businessman Steven Hill to make his fortune by moving to Los Angeles and selling tax shelters.

His expanding balloon is popped by word that Congress proposed to close the tax loopholes through which he and his clients are benefiting. Lenny suddenly finds himself deep in the hole financially, as well as hooked on the cocaine he started taking only as a "boost" to get him through rough times.

For the film to work at all, the love story between Lenny and Linda must feel as overpowering as it is meant to, and Woods and Young put this over with miles to spare. Both actors are live wires, so the passion, care and commitment the characters have for one another is palpable at all times.

•

BOOT, DAS
(THE BOAT)

1981, 145 mins, W. GERMANY Ⓥ ⦿ col

Dir Wolfgang Petersen ***Prod*** Gunter Rohrbach ***Scr*** Wolfgang Petersen ***Ph*** Jost Vacano ***Ed*** Hannes Nikel ***Mus*** Klaus Doldinger ***Art*** Rolf Zehetbauer, Gotz Weidner

Act Jurgen Prochnow, Arthur Grunemeyer, Klaus Wennemann, Hubertus Bengsch, Martin Semmelrogge, Bernd Tauber (Bavaria Atelier/Radiant)

Produced at a cost of DM25 million (circa $12 million), Wolfgang Petersen's *The Boat* is far and away the most expensive German film made since World War II, possibly in the history of German cinema. It's based on a bestseller by Lothar-Gunther Buchheim and is a two hour–plus action film on the fate of a German U-Boat in 1941.

Everything described in the film is authentic: it's the story of a single mission in the Atlantic, from the departure of the boat from La Rochelle in Occupied France to its return to port some months later. In between, it's constantly a question of life or death, give and take, kill or be killed—a descent into the pit of hell with slim odds of ever returning.

When Buchheim joined one of these boats as a photojournalist during the war, he was a kid among equals. His experiences on missions were later compiled into an autobiographical book. The captain, tagged the "old man" (Jurgen Prochnow), already wears an iron cross for bravery in action. So does another drunken U-Boat officer, Thomsen (a strong cameo by Otto Sander), who nearly incites a riot in the Bar Royal by speaking his mind on both the war and its Fuhrer in vividly blunt terms. Then comes the dull, monotonous early days at sea followed by some initial skirmishes and hide-and-seek games with the enemy. At last, about midway through the film, the first opportunity to strike presents itself, and the real action begins. Then come orders to brave the Strait of Gibraltar and enter the Mediterranean for further seek-and-kill operations.

Two model subs were constructed for shooting at La Rochelle and the Bavaria Atelier in Munich. All the actors are, with a few major exceptions, unknown faces to the German film and TV scene.

[Pic was also made as a six-hour TV miniseries. A 207-min. *Director's Cut* was released theatrically and on homevideo in 1997.]

•

BOOTS MALONE

1951, 103 mins, US Ⓥ b/w

Dir William Dieterle ***Prod*** Milton Holmes ***Scr*** Milton Holmes ***Ph*** Charles Lawton, Jr. ***Ed*** Al Clark ***Mus*** Elmer Bernstein ***Art*** Cary Odell

Act William Holden, Johnny Stewart, Stanley Clements, Basil Ruysdael, Carl Benton Reid, Ed Begley (Columbia)

Plot deals with the relationship between Johnny Stewart, a 15-year-old who loves horses, and William Holden, a jockey's agent down on his luck. Story is run off against an authentic racetrack background, drawing a good picture of the less prosperous side of racing and the hanger-ons.

Stewart appears as a rich boy neglected by his career mother. He takes up with Holden, who decides to go along with the kid as long as his money holds out by pretending to teach him how to be a winning jockey. Their scenes together are very effective. Yarn picks up faster drama when the mother locates her son and tries to prevent his riding debut, while Holden is faced with the problem of talking the boy into losing or be killed by a gambling syndicate that is betting on another horse in the race.

As producer-writer, Milton Holmes has told the story with good emotional moments and sentiment without being maudlin. This handling also is reflected in the direction by William Dieterle.

•

BOPHA!

1993, 121 mins, US Ⓥ ⦿ col

Dir Morgan Freeman ***Prod*** Lawrence Taubman ***Scr*** Brian Bird, John Wierick ***Ph*** David Watkin ***Ed*** Neil Travis ***Mus*** James Horner ***Art*** Michael Philips

Act Danny Glover, Malcolm McDowell, Alfre Woodard, Marius Weyers, Maynard Eziashi, Malick Bowens (Paramount/Hall)

Percy Mtwa's contemporary saga of political/personal strife in a South African township, *Bopha!* has been transferred to the screen with tremendous emotional power and integrity. The theatrical directing debut of actor Morgan Freeman is a handsomely crafted, potently played drama that brings the issue of apartheid down to a visceral human dimension.

Set in 1980, the story revolves around the Mangena family. Micah (Danny Glover) is the senior black police officer in his township. He takes great pride in the peace and order evident in the small community. His son, Zweli (Maynard Eziashi), is cut from a different cloth. A student, his generation is striving to make a country of majority native rule. As wife and mother, Rosie Mangena (Alfre Woodard) finds herself primarily in the role of conciliator.

With growing unrest being experienced already in other townships, De Villiers (Malcolm McDowell), an officer in the country's Special Branch, is charged with keeping the Mangenas' township calm. "Bopha," from the Zulu language, means to arrest or detain. In this tale, that constraint translates into a stasis that can be resolved only by violent force. Freeman has a natural feel for environment and a not surprising facility with his performers. The only misstep comes from an all too familiarly painted depiction of bigotry as embodied by McDowell.

•

BORDER, THE

1982, 107 mins, US Ⓥ ⦿ col

Dir Tony Richardson ***Prod*** Edgar Bronfman, Jr. ***Scr*** Deric Washburn, Walon Green, David Freeman ***Ph*** Ric Waite, Vilmos Zsigmond ***Ed*** Robert K. Lambert ***Mus*** Ry Cooder ***Art*** Toby Rafelson

Act Jack Nicholson, Harvey Keitel, Valerie Perrine, Warren Oates, Elpidia Carrillo, Shannon Wilcox (Universal/RKO)

Despite Jack Nicholson's multi-leveled performance, *The Border* is a surprisingly uninvolving film. Story of the personal and professional pressures on border patrol guard Nicholson, caught between right and wrong on both fronts, becomes murky and disjointed under Tony Richardson's uninspired direction.

Nicholson etches a nice guy victimized by his surroundings instead of an eccentric. Living in depressed circumstances with whiney, materialistic wife Valerie Perrine, he is the quintessential poor working stiff. Nicholson is then befriended by Harvey Keitel, husband of Perrine's bimbo girlfriend and a fellow guard. It is their job to make sure none of the Mexicans over the border get into the U.S. a task to which the humane Nicholson is ill-suited.

This is particularly the case once Nicholson views the rampant corruption of his fellow workers. The situation escalates as the baby of a poor, beautiful Mexican girl is kidnapped for adoption and Nicholson has to decide whether to stand by or take action.

The picture was already in the can when Universal decided to go back and shoot a much more upbeat ending where Nicholson emerges as hero.

•

BORDER INCIDENT

1949, 92 mins, US b/w

Dir Anthony Mann ***Prod*** Nicholas Nayfack ***Scr*** John C. Higgins ***Ph*** John Alton ***Ed*** Conrad A. Nervig ***Mus*** Andre Previn (dir.) ***Art*** Cedric Gibbons, Hans Peters

Act Ricardo Montalban, George Murphy, Howard da Silva, James Mitchell, Arnold Moss, Alfonso Bedoya

Produced on a modest budget, pic wraps a conventional yarn within a semi-documentary casing. Film is handicapped by a screenplay which treats the important subject of illegal immigration into the U.S. with a naive cop-and-robbers approach. Anthony Mann, who was brought over to the Metro lot after his standout job on *He Walked by Night*, for Eagle Lion, succeeds in imparting some tautness to the action but the pic never breaks out of its formula framework.

Yarn [by John C. Higgins and George Zuckerman] opens strongly with a depicition of the plight of Mexican laborers who annually migrate north for work on U.S. farms. Filmed on location, this section has an authentic quality and impact. When the plot, however, switches to tracking down a ring of border-running racketeers, the film unfortunately takes on the unconvincing flavor of an old-fashioned melodrama.

Both George Murphy, as the U.S. agent, and Ricardo Montalban, as the Mexican counterpart, enter the ring to smash it from the inside. Murphy, however, is found out and is cruelly murdered under a plowing machine. Murphy and Montalban turn in effective, hard-hitting performances in a yarn that contains no romantic angles. As the chief heavy, Howard da Silva makes a menacing smoothie.

•

BORDERLINE

1980, 97 mins, US Ⓥ col

Dir Jerrold Freedman ***Prod*** Martin Starger ***Scr*** Steve Kline, Jerrold Freedman ***Ph*** Tak Fujimoto ***Ed*** John Link ***Mus*** Gil Melle ***Art*** Michael Levesque

Act Charles Bronson, Bruno Kirby, Ed Harris, Karmin Murcelo, Michael Lerner (ITC)

This Charles Bronson vehicle tackles a serious subject—the profiteering in illicit Mexican immigration—with workmanlike dramatic skill and a notable preference for realism over hokum.

The film's big name is self-effacing almost to the point of elusiveness. As a long-serving, compassionate border patrolman, Bronson is hunched and hated virtually throughout; his face is mostly masked by heavy shadow.

The professionally-honed, conventional plot pits him against a younger, ruthless racketeer who runs wetbacks across the border at an exploitative price on behalf of a U.S. business corporation.

Newcomer Ed Harris is memorable as the frontline villain, displaying screen presence to match the star's and thus injecting a powerful sense of danger.

•

BORDERTOWN

1935, 80 mins, US b/w

Dir Archie Mayo ***Prod*** Robert Lord ***Scr*** Robert Lord, Laird Doyle, Wallace Smith ***Ph*** Tony Gaudio ***Ed*** Thomas Richards ***Mus*** Bernhard Kaun ***Art*** Jack Okey

Act Paul Muni, Bette Davis, Margaret Lindsay, Eugene Pallette, Robert Barrat, Hobart Cavanaugh (Warner)

Paul Muni is a Mexican, and does it realistically and effectively. He's a kid who's worked hard in night school and finally manages to pass a legal examination in Los Angeles. But he loses his first case and his temper in the courtroom, so he's disbarred.

He hitch-hikes to a Mexican bordertown and becomes a power in the gambling sector. Eugene Pallette owns a joint and Muni is his bouncer, then his partner. Pallette's wife (Bette Davis) goes for Muni, who won't tumble. She kills her husband to get Muni, and he still won't play. So she tells the cops he did the murder. In court she goes insane, which frees him. Muni continues building up as a gambler and falls for Dale Elwell (Margaret Lindsay), a society bud. She acknowledges him temporarily and cools him off when he becomes too ambitious.

By this time 80 minutes have been used up and, seemingly, everybody wants it over with as quickly as possible. Finish is phoney, but it can't hurt the previous good work. Casting throughout the film, which is also well written [from a novel by Carrol Graham] and paced, is exceptionally good.

•

BORN FREE

1966, 95 mins, UK Ⓥ ⦿ ▭ col

Dir James Hill ***Prod*** Sam Jaffe, Paul Radin ***Scr*** Gerald L. C. Copley ***Ph*** Kenneth Talbot ***Ed*** Don Deacon ***Mus*** John Barry

Act Virginia McKenna, Bill Travers, Geoffrey Keen, Peter Lukoye, Omar Chambati, Bill Godden (Open Road/High Road)

Born Free is a heart-warming story of a British couple in Africa who, at the maturity of their pet lioness, educate the beast to survive in the bush.

It's an excellent adaptation of Joy Adamson's books (which were as much photos as text) with restraint, loving care, and solid emotional appeal that seldom becomes banal.

Gerald L. C. Copley has done a first rate adaptation of the true story of Joy Adamson, who with hubby George involuntarily domesticated several pet lions. They kept one, Elsa, until she was fully grown and then, to save her from government-ordered zoo captivity, trained her to survive as a wild animal. The apparently childless couple are portrayed in top form by real-life married couple Virginia McKenna and Bill Travers.

Geoffrey Keen is excellent as the friendly government commissioner who finally convinces them the lioness should be sent to a zoo or set free. Keen gives the role much depth via the humor engendered from his natural aversion to the lioness, balanced by his British reserve.

1966: Best Song ("Born Free"), Original Score

•

BORN LOSERS

1967, 114 mins, US Ⓥ col

Dir T. C. Frank [= Tom Laughlin] ***Prod*** Donald Henderson ***Scr*** E. James Lloyd ***Ph*** Gregory Sandor ***Ed*** John Winfield ***Mus*** Mike Curb ***Art*** Rick Beck-Meyer

Act Tom Laughlin, Elizabeth James, Jane Russell, Jeremy Slate, William Wellman, Jr., Robert Tessier (American International)

Born Losers carries the mark of authority and has been well made throughout. Pic, started as an indie, was acquired by AIP during shooting.

The Donald Henderson production points up the ruthlessness of an outlaw motorcycle gang which takes over a community. Premise of the screenplay sees peace officers stymied in steps to curb lawlessness by reluctance of the public, through fear, to testify against those who have committed crimes.

Director T. C. Frank [Tom Laughlin] builds mounting tension and suspense and draws sock performances from his entire cast, in which Jane Russell appears as a guest star.

Tom Laughlin delivers a first-rate performance in an underplayed portrayal and Jeremy Slate scores strongly as leader of cut-throats out to terrorize the community.

•

BORN ON THE FOURTH OF JULY

1989, 144 mins, US Ⓥ ⊙ ▭ col

Dir Oliver Stone ***Prod*** A. Kitman Ho ***Scr*** Ron Kovic, Oliver Stone ***Ph*** Robert Richardson ***Ed*** David Brenner ***Mus*** John Williams ***Art*** Bruno Rubeo

Act Tom Cruise, Raymond J. Barry, Caroline Kava, Kyra Sedgwick, Willem Dafoe, Jerry Levine (Ixtlan/Universal)

Oliver Stone again shows America to itself in a way it won't forget. His collaboration with Vietnam veteran Ron Kovic to depict Kovic's odyssey from teenage true believer to wheelchair-bound soldier in a very different war results in a gripping, devastating and telling film about the Vietnam era.

Stone creates a portrait of a fiercely pure-hearted boy who loved his country and believed that to serve it and to be a man was to fight a war. It turned out to be Vietnam, and that's where the belief was shattered.

In 'Nam, things go terribly wrong—young Sgt. Kovic accidentally kills a fellow marine in battle. His attempted confession is harshly denied him by a c.o. Later, he's shot in the foot, gets up for a gritty round of Sgt. Rock grandstanding, and is hit again and paralyzed.

Stone drenches the picture in visceral reality, from the agonizing chaos of a field hospital to the dead stalemate of a Bronx veteran's hospital infested with rats, drugs and the humiliation of lying helplessly in one's own excrement.

The U.S. Kovic left behind is unrecognizable, yet as he struggles uselessly to regain control of his body he remains steadfast in his ideas, shouting "Love it or leave it!" at his peacenik brother (Josh Evans).

Tom Cruise, who takes Kovic from clean-cut eager teen to impassioned long-haired activist, is stunning. Dafoe, as a disabled vet hiding out in a Mexican beach town in a haze of mescal, whores and poker, gives a startling, razor-sharp performance.

1989: Best Director, Editing

NOMINATIONS: Best Picture, Actor (Tom Cruise), Adapted Screenplay, Cinematography, Original Score, Sound

•

BORN TO DANCE

1936, 105 mins, US Ⓥ b/w

Dir Roy Del Ruth ***Prod*** Jack Cummings ***Scr*** Jack McGowan, Sid Silvers ***Ph*** Ray June ***Ed*** Blanche Sewell ***Mus*** Alfred Newman (dir.), Roger Edens (arr.) ***Art*** Cedric Gibbons, Joseph Wright, Edwin B. Willis

Act Eleanor Powell, James Stewart, Virginia Bruce, Una Merkel, Sid Silvers, Frances Langford (M-G-M)

Born to Dance is corking entertainment, more nearly approaching the revue type than most musical films, despite the presence of a "book." Cast is youthful, sight stuff is lavish, the specialties are meritorious, and as for songs, the picture is positively filthy with them. Cole Porter included at least two hits among the seven numbers delivered.

Eleanor Powell becomes a star in her second picture. She is given an opportunity to show that she's not just a good buck dancer, but an exceptionally versatile girl. As an actress she still has not arrived, as indicated in the few occasions when this plot calls for acting. James Stewart's assignment calls for a shy youth. His singing and dancing are rather painful on their own, but he's surrounded by good people, and it's all done in a spirit of fun. Frances Langford has a running part, but her big responsibility is the singing build-up to Powell's finale dance and the pretentious production topper of the picture.

Buddy Ebsen has a couple of spots for his eccentric dancing and tackles the comedy, along with Sid Silvers, Una Merkel and Raymond Walburn. It's a combination navy-backstage story [by Jack McGowan, Sid Silvers and B. G. DeSylva], with the sailors, as usual, looking for their old girlfriends while on leave in the big town, and the understudy follows the rules by stepping into the indisposed star's part at the last moment.

1934: NOMINATIONS: Best Song ("I've Got You Under My Skin"), Dance Direction ("Swingin' the Jinx")

•

BORN YESTERDAY

1950, 102 mins, US Ⓥ ⊙ b/w

Dir George Cukor ***Prod*** S. Sylvan Simon ***Scr*** Albert Mannheimer ***Ph*** Joseph Walker ***Ed*** Charles Nelson ***Mus*** Frederick Hollander

Act Broderick Crawford, Judy Holliday, William Holden, Howard St. John, Frank Otto, Larry Oliver (Columbia)

The bright, biting comedy of the Garson Kanin legit hit adapts easily to film.

Judy Holliday repeats her legit success here as femme star of the film version. Almost alone, she makes *Born Yesterday*.

Holliday delights as she tosses off the malaprops that so aptly fit the character. Even though considerable amount of the dialog is unintelligible, its sound and her artful delivery smite the risibilities. William Holden is quietly effective as the newspaperman hired to coach her in social graces so she will better fit in with her junkman's ambitious plans.

Broderick Crawford, as the selfmade dealer in junk, comes off much less successfully. The actual and implied sympathy is missing, leaving it just a loud-shouting, boorish person.

1950: Best Actress (Judy Holliday)

NOMINATIONS: Best Picture, Director, Screenplay, B&W Costume Design

•

BORN YESTERDAY

1993, 101 mins, US Ⓥ ⊙ col

Dir Luis Mandoki ***Prod*** D. Constantine Conte ***Scr*** Douglas McGrath ***Ph*** Lajos Koltai ***Ed*** Lesley Walker ***Mus*** George Fenton ***Art*** Lawrence G. Paull

Act Melanie Griffith, John Goodman, Don Johnson, Edward Herrmann, Max Perlich, Fred Dalton Thompson (Hollywood Pictures)

Updated remake of the Pygmalion-like *Born Yesterday* arrives with a credible modern resonance. The basic dynamics of the original Garson Kanin play have stood the test of time thanks to some clever contemporary tweaking. However, the verdict on the makeover is not all good news. The attractive cast, individually strong, fails to coalesce as an ensemble. There's also a problem in creating a uniform tone for the yarn of a real estate speculator and his socially awkward girlfriend who invade the power elite of Washington, DC.

Harry Brock (John Goodman), a scrap metal czar in the original, hies to DC when the evaporation of defense contracts near his super mall threaten to undo his empire. In tow is Billie Dawn (Melanie Griffith), a former showgirl with more moxie than college knowledge.

Harry asks lobbyist Ed Devery (Edward Herrmann) to 'smarten her up'. To that end he hires local reporter Paul Verrall (Don Johnson) to provide the Professor Higgins treatment and, in short order, she wises up and the sparks, romantic and otherwise, begin to fly.

Screenwriter Douglas McGrath expands his source material with the latest twists on power brokering. However, he also imbues the story with a glib, sitcom breeziness that favors cuteness over content. Griffith provides her own credible spin on Billie Dawn. The film also gives Johnson an opportunity for some effective light comic work.

•

BORSALINO

1970, 123 mins, France/US Ⓥ col

Dir Jacques Deray ***Prod*** Alain Delon ***Scr*** Jean-Claude Carriere, Claude Sautet, Jean Cau, Jacques Deray ***Ph*** Jean-Jacques Tarbes ***Ed*** Paul Cayatte ***Mus*** Claude Bolling ***Art*** Francois de Lamothe

Act Alain Delon, Jean-Paul Belmondo, Michel Bouquet, Catherine Rouvel, Corinne Marchand, Francoise Christophe (Adel/Paramount)

Paramount put a reported $2 million into this $3 million pic, produced by one of the stars (Alain Delon) via his own company, Adel. Based on the real gangster milieu of Marseille in the 1930s, pic laces together French lowlife aspects with a more probing look at organized crime in the Hollywood manner via the rise and fall of two young hoodlums. Problem is that pic [from Eugene Saccomano's novel *Bandits at Marseilles*] is more a vehicle for its stars' personalities than a more cogent insight into French pre-war organized gangsters.

Delon is a secretive, ambitious and cruel type, while Jean-Paul Belmondo is an easygoing, engaging hoodlum who is content with small jobs. They meet when Delon gets out of jail and finds his girl, a prostie, has taken up with somebody else. They join forces, the girl becomes a part of the scheme, and then begins the climb instigated by Delon.

Delon has sharp grace and poise as the handsome, more cultured, facet of the duo, while Belmondo displays his usual ease, good nature but physical deadliness with aplomb.

Others all acquit themselves well, with Corinne Marchand stately as a lawyer's wife, Michel Bouquet ironic and menacing as the lawyer with connections, and Daniel Ivernel excellent as a police inspector who only interferes when the gangsters tread on political toes.

Title refers to the big brimmed felt hats sported by the gangsters of the period manufactured by a reputable Italo firm.

•

BOSTONIANS, THE

1984, 120 mins, UK Ⓥ ⊙ col

Dir James Ivory ***Prod*** Ismail Merchant ***Scr*** Ruth Prawer Jhabvala ***Ph*** Walter Lassally ***Ed*** Katherine Wenning, Mark Potter ***Mus*** Richard Robbins ***Art*** Leo Austin

Act Christopher Reeve, Vanessa Redgrave, Madeleine Potter, Jessica Tandy, Nancy Marchand, Wesley Addy (Merchant Ivory)

Like the Merchant-Ivory-Jhabvala team's 1979 *The Europeans*, this is a classy adaptation of a Henry James novel.

From the film's opening sequence at a women's meeting in late 19th-century Boston, the dice are loaded against the feminist cause. The young Verena Tarrant offers an impassioned exposition of woman's sufferings only after being "touched" by the hands of her faith-healer father.

The emotional weight of the pic is carried by the relationship that evolves between Verena (Madeleine Potter) and Olive Chancellor (Vanessa Redgrave). Latter is a mature spinster who attempts to secure her charge to the cause with a promise that she will never marry.

Central obstacle to Olive's ambition is Basil Ransome, a persuasive lawyer from the south.

The film is ultimately convincing because of the central performance by newcomer Madeleine Potter as Verena who conveys all the dilemmas of a naive but strong-minded girl caught between her attachment to the cause and her longing for love.

1984: NOMINATIONS: Best Actress (Vanessa Redgrave), Costume Design

•

BOSTON STRANGLER, THE

1968, 116 mins, US Ⓥ ▭ col

Dir Richard Fleischer ***Prod*** Robert Fryer ***Scr*** Edward Anhalt ***Ph*** Richard H. Kline ***Ed*** Marion Rothman ***Mus*** [none] ***Art*** Jack Martin Smith, Richard Day

Act Tony Curtis, Henry Fonda, George Kennedy, Mike Kellin, Murray Hamilton (20th Century-Fox)

The Boston Strangler, based on Gerold Frank's book, emerges as a triumph of taste and restraint with a telling, low-key semi-documentary style. Adaptation is topnotch not only in structure but also in the incisive, spare dialog which defines neatly over 100 speaking parts. Among other things it makes a very strong, but implicit, comment on police sleuthing. The screenplay suggests the irony that instinctive police methods remain the rounding up of pitiable segments of society which do harm only to themselves. As told here, police got onto the prime suspect only via the fluke of an elevator ride.

Action cross-cuts between police work and off-screen depictions of the earlier murders.

Henry Fonda's performance as rep of Massachusetts Attorney-General is excellent, from his initial dislike of the task assigned through a quiet, dogged determination to break down Tony Curtis's mental barriers.

●

BOTTOM OF THE BOTTLE, THE

1956, 88 mins, US ▭ col

Dir Henry Hathaway *Prod* Buddy Adler *Scr* Sydney Boehm *Ph* Lee Garmes *Ed* David Bretherton *Mus* Leigh Harline *Art* Lyle R. Wheeler, Maurice Ransford

Act Van Johnson, Joseph Cotten, Ruth Roman, Jack Carson, Margaret Hayes, Bruce Bennett (20th Century-Fox)

An escaped convict's desperate efforts to reach his wife and three children in Mexico add up to 88 minutes of melodrama in *The Bottom of the Bottle*, based on the Georges Simenon novel.

The screenplay has an emotional field day as it touches on the Cain and Abel relationship between brothers Van Johnson and Joseph Cotten. Former, the con who's on the lam, turns to his kin to speed his flight across the border. But Cotten, a successful lawyer-rancher who's built a flourishing practice in southern Arizona, fears for his reputation. The rancher fraternity, also comprising Jack Carson, his wife Margaret Hayes, Jim Davis and Margaret Lindsay, among others, has a penchant for one party after another and the liquor flows freely. Johnson, whose yen for alcohol was indirectly responsible for his prison stretch, again becomes a victim of the bottle.

Director Henry Hathaway, an old hand at spreading mellers on a broad CinemaScope canvas, accents the action and suspense at the right moments. Although some of the plot may tax the imagination, it's to Cotten's credit that he makes his own role relatively believable under the circumstances. Good support is provided by a long list of other players.

●

BOTTOMS UP

1934, 85 mins, US b/w

Dir David Butler *Prod* B. G. DeSylva *Scr* B. G. DeSylva, David Butler, Sid Silvers *Ph* Arthur Miller *Ed* Irene Morra *Mus* Constantin Bakaleinikoff *Art* Gordon Wiles, Russell Patterson

Act Spencer Tracy, John Boles, 'Pat' Paterson, Herbert Mundin, Sid Silvers, Thelma Todd (Fox)

Bottoms Up is tiptop. It's good cinematic fare from every angle, particularly the elements of comedy and plot, of which aspects most filmusicals are singularly devoid.

Story, while light in spots, is sufficiently coherent to shape up as a mild form of the *Once in a Lifetime* school of Hollywood-kidding. That it's all humanly handled makes these elements the more arresting. "Pat" Paterson, a Fox importee from England, is assigned the Hollywood Cinderella role. John Boles is the film star whom she has secretly idolized. Through a combination of circumstances the three sympathetic sharpshooters—Spencer Tracy, Herbert Mundin and Sid Silvers—contrive to scale the Hollywood heights.

Thelma Todd as an established Hollywood satellite falls for the carefully contrived ruse that Mundin is an English lord, incognito; that Paterson is his daughter; with Tracy and Silvers abetting the entire structure, culminating in a contract for the girl, plus employment for all of them.

The picture is chiefly Tracy, Paterson, Boles, Mundin and Silvers, the latter two carrying the comedy and almost wholly and to more than average good effect. It's a personal triumph for Silvers who, while one of the script collaborators, didn't have to rely solely on the lines accorded himself for good impression.

●

BOUCHER, LE
(THE BUTCHER)

1970, 92 mins, France Ⓥ col

Dir Claude Chabrol *Prod* Andre Genoves *Scr* Claude Chabrol *Ph* Jean Rabier *Ed* Jacques Gaillard *Mus* Pierre Jansen *Art* Guy Littaye

Act Stephane Audran, Jean Yanne, Antonio Passalia, Pascal Ferone, Mario Beccara, Roger Rudel (La Boetie/Euro International)

A lucid, clear style, fine narration and expert playing make this tale of a psychopathic killer in a small French town one of ex–New Wave filmmaker Claude Chabrol's most accomplished films. But it builds suspense slowly and, perhaps, gets a bit repetitious in its denouement.

The town butcher, played with direct bonhommie and brusque humanity by Jean Yanne, is enamored of the town schoolteacher, etched with warm flair and tender dedication by Chabrol's wife, Stephane Audran. She once had an unhappy love affair and is afraid of any commitments.

Behind an extremely fine feel for the town and its everyday life comes a cloud, as policemen are seen coming in and out. It seems a little girl was found murdered in the woods and then another and finally a woman, wife of another schoolteacher.

The killer is shown as a fairly sympathetic character except for his sickness. Color is rightly bright and technical qualities fine right down the line.

●

BOUDU SAUVE DES EAUX
(BOUDU SAVED FROM DROWNING)

1932, 84 mins, France Ⓥ b/w

Dir Jean Renoir *Prod* Michel Simon, Jean Gehret *Scr* Jean Renoir *Ph* Marcel Lucien *Ed* Suzanne de Troeye *Mus* Raphael *Art* Laurent, Jean Castanier

Act Michel Simon, Charles Grandval, Marcelle Hainia, Jean Gehret, Max Dalban, Jean Daste (Simon-Gehret)

Jean Renoir's small-scale "rites of spring" [from the play by Rene Fauchois] has Michel Simon, as Boudu, saved from drowning in the Seine (where he has flung himself, despondent over the loss of his dog). A filthy, surly, ungrateful tramp, taken into the household of his rescuer (Charles Grandval), he nearly wrecks the house and lives of his benefactors. After seducing the wife (Marcelle Hainia), he wins a large amount of money in a lottery, marries the opportunistic maid (Severine Lerczynska) but at the last minute rebels.

Renoir manages to get in a few blows at the smugness of the middle-class French, the ambivalent attitudes toward sexual morality, and the less-than-heroic actions of the average human being. Technically, the film is excellent. Jacques Becker, Renoir's assistant [director] on the film, also acts a brief vignette as a kooky poet.

[Pic was reviewed on first U.S. release, in 1967.]

●

BOUDU SAVED FROM DROWNING

SEE: BOUDU SAUVE DES EAUX

●

BOUNCE

2000, 106 mins, US Ⓥ ⊙ col

Dir Don Roos *Prod* Steve Golin, Michael Besman *Scr* Don Roos *Ph* Robert Elswit *Ed* David Codron *Mus* Mychael Danna *Art* David Wasco

Act Ben Affleck, Gwyneth Paltrow, Joe Morton, Natasha Henstridge, Tony Goldwyn, Jennifer Grey (Golin-Besman/Miramax)

A sincere, teary-eyed love story is the opposite of what you'd expect from writer-director Don Roos after the rudely sarcastic *The Opposite of Sex*, but that's what he delivers in *Bounce*. Simultaneously contrived and genuinely felt, this notably straightforward and irony-free pic recounts the touchy romance between a young widow and the callow young man partially responsible for her husband's death. In a certain way, *Bounce* reps a refreshing anomaly in that it is a very modestly scaled production that nonetheless boasts a number of significant actors in large and small roles, and exerts most of its artistic energy trying to convey the emotional truth of its scenes.

Killing time at Chicago's O'Hare Airport during a snowstorm, slick ad exec Buddy Amaral (Ben Affleck) becomes chummy with writer Greg Janello (Tony Goldwyn). Buddy gives Greg his ticket and gets him on the last flight out so the man can quickly get back to his wife and sons. But the plane goes down in Kansas.

Buddy goes into an emotional tailspin over the incident. A year later, a rehab-refreshed Buddy feels compelled to meet the woman, Abby (Gwyneth Paltrow), whose life he unwittingly damaged. A physical relationship modestly begins. Buddy persists in his growing relationship with Abby and her young sons while procrastinating about dropping the bomb about why he's there and Greg isn't.

Paltrow, here deglamorized in brown tresses but looking great nonetheless as a suburban mom gamely struggling back from crushing tragedy, once again demonstrates her great skill at locating a character's emotional core and precisely expressing its many variants; the immediacy of her personality keeps one in the picture even when other elements are falling short.

Would that the same could be said of her co-star. Affleck has no trouble convincing us as the callow babe magnet to whom everything comes easily, but beyond that he's at sea. With his unfailingly casual manner, boyishly eager-to-please eyes and modest approach to every dramatic possibility, Affleck never suggests that he's been through the ringer, realized what a shallow cad he was and then found something resembling heart and soul.

●

BOUND

1996, 107 mins, US Ⓥ ⊙ col

Dir Larry Wachowski, Andy Wachowski *Prod* Andrew Lazar, Stuart Boros *Scr* Larry Wachowski, Andy Wachowski *Ph* Bill Pope *Ed* Zach Staenberg *Mus* Don Davis *Art* Eve Cauley

Act Jennifer Tilly, Gina Gershon, Joe Pantoliano, Barry Kivel, Christopher Meloni, John P. Ryan (De Laurentiis)

An attention-getting lesbians-vs-the-mob hook merely serves as a disguise for what is just another designer thriller in *Bound*, a notably unpalatable and calculated crime piece. Novelty of having two sultry babes hook up with each other while pulling a fast one on some mobsters wears thin before becoming ludicrously contrived. Debuting writer-directors Larry and Andy Wachowski come off like Coen Brothers wannabes with no sense of humor.

Corky (Gina Gershon), a tattooed hardbody with a '63 Chevy truck who would look right at home up a telephone pole, is fixing up an apartment after serving five years for robbery. Next door live the alluring Violet (Jennifer Tilly) and crude mid-level gangster Caesar (Joe Pantoliano), who specializes in money laundering.

Soon Violet is offering to show Corky her own tattoo, and once they dive into a relationship, Violet lets on that she's looking for a way out of her mob lifestyle, which entails sleeping with other tough-talking creeps.

Up to this point, pic holds at least some potential as a fresh take on standard underworld fare. But then the focus shifts to Caesar, whom Pantoliano plays as if trying to outdo Richard Widmark's cackling cretin in the original *Kiss of Death*.

Both Gershon and Tilly are initially intriguing but can't sustain interest in their superficially conceived roles. They share one passionate scene, which is covered in a single take.

●

BOUND & GAGGED
A LOVE STORY

1993, 94 mins, US Ⓥ ⊙ col

Dir Daniel Appleby *Prod* Dennis J. Mahoney *Scr* Daniel Appleby *Ph* Dean Lent, Vincent Donohue, Roger Schmitz *Ed* Kaye Davis *Mus* William Murphy *Art* Dane Pizzuti Krogman

Act Ginger Lynn Allen, Karen Black, Chris Denton, Elizabeth Saltarrelli, Mary Ella Ross, Chris Mulkey (Cinescope)

An offbeat sex comedy with serious moral overtones, *Bound & Gagged* marks a respectable feature debut for writer-helmer Daniel Appleby. Three disparate characters form the bizarre triangle of this black comedy. Cliff (Chris Denton) is a passive man, deeply depressed over the breakup of his marriage. His best friend, the bisexual Elizabeth (Elizabeth Saltarrelli), attempts to cheer him up and rescue him from his suicidal behaviour by taking him on the road with her lover Leslie (Ginger Lynn Allen), an attractive blonde trapped in a bad marriage.

It is one of the film's ironic jokes that both Cliff and Leslie are forced to go on the road. Leslie is actually kidnapped from her own home by Elizabeth, who claims she knows what's good for her friend. Believing that Leslie has been brainwashed by her macho-pig husband Steve (Chris Mulkey), Elizabeth takes her to Carla (Karen Black), a professional "deprogrammer." Once on the road, Cliff attempts a number of suicides, some funnier than others, and Leslie tries to escape back to her abusive husband.

In structure, pic approximates classical farce. In execution, however, both writing and direction suffer from the lack of crazy energy and relentless logic without which satires become square and repetitious. A strong screen presence, Saltarrelli credibly renders the extravagent, spunky woman bent on securing her lover at all costs, be they moral or immoral.

●

BOUND FOR GLORY

1976, 147 mins, US Ⓥ ⊙ col

Dir Hal Ashby *Prod* Robert F. Blumofe, Harold Leventhal *Scr* Robert Getchell *Ph* Haskell Wexler *Ed* Robert Jones, Pembroke J. Herring *Mus* Leonard Rosenman *Art* Michael Haller

Act David Carradine, Ronny Cox, Melinda Dillon, Gail Strickland, John Lehne, Ji-Tu Cumbuka (United Artists)

Bound for Glory is outstanding biographical cinema, not only of the late Woody Guthrie but also of the 1930s Depression era which served to disillusion, inspire and radicalize him and millions of other Americans. The plot [based on Guthrie's autobiography] advances smoothly and sensitively through about six major phases of Guthrie's earlier life: the natural tragedy of the southwest dust bowl; Guthrie's transit to California; his exposure to the horrors in the migrant worker valleys; his initial radio career; his political activism, finally his decision to strike out for large urban areas where his songs and experience might add some momentum to change.

Leonard Rosenman's selection of many Guthrie songs makes for discreet but effective underscoring.

1976: Best Cinematography, Original Song Score

NOMINATIONS: Best Picture, Adapted Screenplay, Costume Design, Editing

•

BOUNTY, THE

1984, 130 mins, US Ⓥ ⦿ ▭ col

Dir Roger Donaldson ***Prod*** Bernard Williams ***Scr*** Robert Bolt ***Ph*** Arthur Ibbetson ***Ed*** Tony Lawson ***Mus*** Vangelis ***Art*** John Graysmark

Act Mel Gibson, Anthony Hopkins, Laurence Olivier, Edward Fox, Daniel Day-Lewis, Bernard Hill (De Laurentiis)

The Bounty is an intelligent, firstrate, revisionist telling of the famous tale of Fletcher Christian's mutiny against Captain Bligh. The $20 million-plus film is particularly distinguished by a sensational, and startlingly human, performance by Anthony Hopkins as Bligh, heretofore one of history's most one-dimensional villains. Present third version of the yarn was initiated by director David Lean, who brought Robert Bolt aboard to write the entire *Bounty* saga [based on the book *Captain Bligh and Mr. Christian* by Richard Hough]. Lean eventually moved on, and Dino De Laurentiis paid for the construction of a replica ship.

This is a remake with a reason, that being the exoneration and rehabilitation of the reputation of William Bligh. A British Naval court-martial, which serves to frame Bolt's dramatization, ultimately absolved Bligh of blame for the mutiny, and he went on to enjoy a distinguished career.

The mutiny itself is here presented as a chaotic mess, with Christian nearly delirious. Bligh's subsequent 4,000-mile voyage to safety in an open boat is depicted as the amazing, arduous achievement that it was. Tailor-made physically to fit the mold of old-style heroes, Mel Gibson gets across Christian's melancholy and torn motivations in excellent fashion.

•

BOWERY, THE

1933, 92 mins, US b/w

Dir Raoul Walsh ***Prod*** Darryl F. Zanuck ***Scr*** Howard Estabrook, James Gleason ***Ph*** Barney McGill ***Ed*** Allen McNeil ***Mus*** Alfred Newman (dir.) ***Art*** Richard Day

Act Wallace Beery, George Raft, Jackie Cooper, Fay Wray, Pert Kelton, George Walsh (20th Century)

Two old Bowery characters, Steve Brodie and Chuck Connors, have been dramatized to a point where the only thing that's recognizable from the record books about them are the jump from Brooklyn Bridge and Bowery lingo respectively.

This script [from the novel by Michael L. Simmons and Bessie Ruth Solomon] makes them rivals for mass leadership on the old street, but the important point is that as rewritten the two practically legendary characters make good entertainment.

The Connors-Brodie honest rivalry over everything, from gals to fighting ability, giving the tale a Flagg-Quirt glow, is the story. Brodie (George Raft) gets the girl. But he takes a licking from Connors (Wallace Beery) in their private finish fight on a river barge. The fight is an exciting interlude, and it comes in handy where it's placed—under the finale. Previously, in the extremely well-staged Brodie bridge leap, the picture has reached its peak. It then stumbles until the fight arrives, but the latter brings home the bacon.

Beery is doing *The Champ* all over again to a great extent, with Jackie Cooper again as his foil. The Cooper kid, obviously outgrowing the baby type, is still a trouper and sends in another gem performance. Raft, much improved, is an okay choice as Brodie. The other meat parts are carried by Fay Wray, who plays straight to the boys, and Pert Kelton, who sings and dances as a Bowery soubrette in Connors's joint.

•

BOWFINGER

1999, 96 mins Ⓥ ⦿ col

Dir Frank Oz ***Prod*** Brian Grazer ***Scr*** Steve Martin ***Ph*** Ueli Steiger ***Ed*** Richard Pearson ***Mus*** David Newman ***Art*** Jackson Degovia

Act Steve Martin, Eddie Murphy, Heather Graham, Christine Baranski, Jamie Kennedy, Adam Alexi-Malle (Imagine/Universal)

Several scenes of explosive hilarity punctuate *Bowfinger*, a welcome first-time pairing of Steve Martin and Eddie Murphy. Screenwriter Martin's typically quirky premise—a down-and-out filmmaker surreptitiously shoots a feature toplining a huge star without the actor knowing it—provides him with an ample clothesline on which to hang innumerable jokes.

Although nearly every character here is in the movies, *Bowfinger* is not really a showbiz satire, nor is it remotely an insider's picture. The most notable element linking the characters is a sense of self-delusion that allows them to live in a state of expectant bliss, no matter how desperate their circumstances.

No one is more delusional than Bobby Bowfinger (Martin), a schlock producer-director who sets out to make his fortune with a sci-fi action script called *Chubby Rain* penned by his accountant, Afrim (Adam Alexi-Malle). He actually gets a commitment from a smarmy studio exec (a droll Robert Downey, Jr.) if he can deliver action star Kit Ramsey (Murphy).

A small and seedy group helps him out: never-has-been actress Carol (Christine Baranski), studio gofer Dave (Jamie Kennedy), handsome slacker actor Slater (Kohl Sudduth), and Daisy (Heather Graham), a straight-off-the-bus Midwestern waif who sleeps with everyone on the production.

The entire cast performs with verve and energy. Weirdest element is Martin's character, who seems disconnected from any known reality, a flipped-out zombie with nothing left but strangely channeled chutzpah. Tech credits are consummately pro.

•

BOXCAR BERTHA

1972, 88 mins, US Ⓥ ⦿ col

Dir Martin Scorsese ***Prod*** Roger Corman ***Scr*** Joyce H. Corrington, John William Corrington ***Ph*** John Stephens ***Ed*** Buzz Feitshans ***Mus*** Gib Guilbeau, Thad Maxwell

Act Barbara Hershey, David Carradine, Barry Primus, Bernie Casey, John Carradine (American International)

Whatever its intentions, *Boxcar Bertha* is not much more than an excuse to slaughter a lot of people. Barbara Hershey stars in title role as a Depression wanderer. The Roger Corman production, shot on an austere budget in Arkansas area, is routinely directed by Martin Scorsese. Joyce H. Corrington and John William Corrington adapted *Sister of the Road*, an autobiog by Boxcar Bertha Thompson. Hershey is introduced as a rural girl whose father dies in an unsafe airplane. She is upset, naturally, and suddenly begins a life of vagrancy.

Performances are dull. Whatever sociological, political or dramatic motivations may once have existed in the story have been ruthlessly stripped from the plot, leaving all characters bereft of empathy or sympathy. There's hardly a pretense toward justifying the carnage.

•

BOXING HELENA

1993, 107 mins, US Ⓥ ⦿ ▭ col

Dir Jennifer Chambers Lynch ***Prod*** Philippe Caland, Carl Mazzocone ***Scr*** Jennifer Chambers Lynch ***Ph*** Frank Byers ***Ed*** David Finfer ***Mus*** Graeme Revell ***Art*** Paul Huggins

Act Julian Sands, Sherilyn Fenn, Bill Paxton, Kurtwood Smith, Betsy Clark, Nicolette Scorsese (Main Line)

Feature debut of 24-year-old writer-director Jennifer Lynch (daughter of David) offers up Julian Sands as a top surgeon who has had a one-night stand with stunning neighbor Sherilyn Fenn and now can't get the voluptuous sexpot out of his mind.

Bitchy, condescending and cruel, Fenn tells Sands in a hundred different ways to get lost, until a horrible accident deprives her of her legs and places her forever in the sick doctor's hands.

Remainder of the warped story [by Philippe Caland] plays on the notion of whether one person can force another to love him through cumulative dependence, time and the force of his own love. Fenn remains defiantly belligerent even through Sands's unnecessary removal of her arms. The numerous sex scenes are good and steamy.

It's probably just as well that last-minute dropouts Kim Basinger or Madonna didn't take the title role, as the presence of a star lurking powerlessly on the little platform no doubt would have been distracting and more laughable than it now, on occasion, is. But the thesps give it all the overheated conviction they can muster.

•

BOY, DID I GET A WRONG NUMBER!

1966, 98 mins, US Ⓥ col

Dir George Marshall ***Prod*** Edward Small ***Scr*** Burt Styler, Albert E. Lewin, George Kennett ***Ph*** Lionel Lindon ***Ed*** Grant Whytlock ***Mus*** Richard LaSalle, "By" Dunham ***Art*** Frank Sylos

Act Bob Hope, Elke Sommer, Phyllis Diller, Cesare Danova, Marjorie Lord, Kelly Thordsen (United Artists)

Bob Hope enters the realm of near-bedroom farce as he finds a near-unclad film star on his hands in a lake cottage and his ever-loving spouse continually appearing on the scene. If the action sometimes seems to get out of hand it really doesn't matter, for Phyllis Diller is there too, to help him hide the delectable Elke Sommer from the missus.

Hope plays his role straight for the most part, making the most of the situation. George Marshall's direction sparks events in proper perspective, wisely allowing his characters to go their separate ways in their own particular styles. Sommer, who knows her way through a comedy scene either with or without clothes, elects the latter state for most of her thesping, raimented mostly in a shirt. Diller is immense as the nosy domestic responsible for the majority of the funny lines that abound throughout the fast unfoldment.

•

BOY FRIEND, THE

1971, 108 mins, UK Ⓥ ⦿ ▭ col

Dir Ken Russell ***Prod*** Ken Russell ***Scr*** Ken Russell ***Ph*** David Watkin ***Ed*** Michael Bradsell ***Mus*** Peter Maxwell Davies (arr.) ***Art*** Tony Walton

Act Twiggy, Christopher Gable, Max Adrian, Bryan Pringle, Murray Melvin, Glenda Jackson (M-G-M)

If for nothing else—but film has more—Ken Russell's screen translation of *The Boy Friend* is a beautiful vehicle for Twiggy, a clever young performer. It is delightful entertainment, novel and engaging.

Russell, who also directed and scripted the Sandy Wilson musical, has adopted a play within a play concept for the telling. Film might be a glorification of the Busby Berkeley manner of production. Russell has expanded the play into a kaleidoscope of the dance director's techniques during his heyday.

Narrative revolves around the personal lives of a group of repertory players who stage an English provincial production of *The Boy Friend*, and a film director strives to catch the performance.

Twiggy plays the unsophisticated young assistant stage manager—also errand and jack-of-all-trades girl—suddenly thrust into top role when the star injures her ankle. (Glenda Jackson unbilled, cameos as the injured "star".)

Twiggy acquits herself charmingly and professionally. There's an unspoiled charm about her, and she weaves a spell of her own both with her singing and dancing.

1971: NOMINATION: Best Adapted Score

•

BOY MEETS GIRL

1938, 86 mins, US b/w

Dir Lloyd Bacon ***Prod*** George Abbott ***Scr*** Bella Spewack, Samuel Spewack ***Ph*** Sol Polito ***Ed*** William Holmes ***Mus*** Leo F. Forbstein (dir.) ***Art*** Esdras Hartley

Act James Cagney, Pat O'Brien, Marie Wilson, Ralph Bellamy, Frank McHugh, Dick Foran (Warner)

The filmization of *Boy Meets Girl* does not approximate the ripsnorting click of the play original by the Spewacks. Whether the fault lies in some of the denaturing, or the idea of a film poking fun at the picture business, doesn't quite come out, but the fact remains that the picture version of this comedy classic is a little more than adequate but not socko.

Hollywood ribbing itself, in celluloid, sounds like a daring thing and, as the Warners have done it, it is. Director Lloyd Bacon, in fact, has out-Spewacked the dramatists in limning the madcap scenarists, as James Cagney and Pat O'Brien personate them.

Cagney eclipses the somewhat more practical O'Brien in the buffoonery, but that's a script handicap since the latter is be-plotted by the spectre of a spendthrift wife, and a practical yen to keep earning those 1,500 tears a week, whereas Cagney is devil-may-care, and scriptually quite eager to retire to his Vermont hideaway, live on $12 a week, and write that great book he has in his system.

Marie Wilson, newcomer, rates the most attention in her assignment as Susie, who has been given benefit of clergy (under Haysian mandate) in her role as the mammy of Happy (Paul Clark). The latter is the wonder-child who resurrects a has-been mustang star into big b.o. again. Ralph Bellamy, sub-featured, is adequately distrait as the studio executive whose cross in life is the fact that he's the only film producer with a college degree, hence "they despise me." Ronald Reagan, as the radio announcer, makes his brief opportunity register.

•

BOY ON A DOLPHIN

1957, 103 mins, US Ⓥ ▭ col

Dir Jean Negulesco ***Prod*** Samuel G. Engel ***Scr*** Ivan Moffat, Dwight Taylor ***Ph*** Milton Krasner ***Ed*** William Mace ***Mus*** Hugo Friedhofer ***Art*** Lyle R. Wheeler, Jack Martin Smith

Act Alan Ladd, Sophia Loren, Clifton Webb, Alexis Minotis, Laurence Naismith, Jorge Mistral (20th Century-Fox)

Shot in Greece's Aegean Sea and environs, with the interiors filmed in Rome's Cinecitta Studios, *Boy on a Dolphin* [from the novel by David Divine] develops into a "chase" that is a pleasant blend of archaeological research, quasi-cloak & dagger stuff, and earthy, primitive acquisitiveness.

Alan Ladd is the archaeologist who has been engaged on several occasions in besting Clifton Webb's passion for antiquities. He has been invariably successful in restoring them to their rightful owners. The "boy," in the same idiom, is historic Greek property. Sophia Loren's hunger for a home, the greed of an expatriate, alcohol-sotted British medico (Laurence Naismith) and the trickery of her Albanian lover (Jorge Mistral, a strong face in a chameleon role) conspire to thwart the American archaeologist and collaborate with the aesthetic, wealthy Webb in spiriting the ancient treasure from Greek waters.

Director Jean Negulesco has not overextended any of the values, playing it in the right tempo for the locale and likewise playing down the neo-melodramatics. Ladd is the all-American boy archaeologist; Webb the suave dastard (because of his dollars); Loren a lustily appealing native Greek girl whose endowments fall automatically into character.

1957: NOMINATION: Best Scoring of a Dramatic Picture

●

BOYS

1996, 89 mins, US Ⓥ ⊙ col

Dir Stacy Cochran ***Prod*** Peter Frankfurt, Paul Feldsher, Erica Huggins ***Scr*** Stacy Cochran ***Ph*** Robert Elswit ***Ed*** Camilla Tonido ***Mus*** Stewart Copeland ***Art*** Dan Bishop

Act Winona Ryder, Lukas Haas, Skeet Ulrich, John C. Reilly, Bill Sage, Wiley Wiggins (Interscope/PolyGram/Touchstone)

Stretched from a short story [from James Salter] called *Twenty Minutes*, this flat, oddly paced mystery/coming-of-age drama might have been better served sticking to that time length. As it is, *Boys*, pairing Lukas Haas with "older woman" Winona Ryder, is as vague and unfocused as its title, and Stacy Cochran's direction promises far more than her script delivers.

Haas plays John Baker, Jr., a high school senior in a not-terribly-exclusive New England boys school, bored with classes and dorky friends yet dreading the corporate life that looms ahead. A jolt of excitement arrives in the beautiful, if semiconscious, form of Ryder's Patty Vare, a mysterious, sophisticated 25-year-old found helpless after being thrown from her horse near the school grounds. Baker spirits the young woman away to his dorm room, falling headlong into love and intrigue faster than you can say "Holden Caulfield meets the Hardy Boys."

Boys essentially runs on two courses, with Patty's mystery storyline considerably more intriguing—at least until its anticlimactic climax—than Baker's run-ins with school officials, parents and nosy classmates. This is the stuff of teen comedy, played straight.

Ryder is saddled with the knowledge that the baggage her character lugs is empty. Rest of the cast is a mixed bag, with young Charlie Hofheimer the standout among the schoolboy actors.

●

BOYS DON'T CRY

1999, 116 mins, US Ⓥ ⊙ col

Dir Kimberly Peirce ***Prod*** Jeffrey Sharp, John Hart, Eva Kolodner, Christine Vachon ***Scr*** Kimberly Peirce, Andy Bienen ***Ph*** Jim Denault ***Ed*** Lee Percy, Tracy Granger ***Mus*** Nathan Larsen ***Art*** Michael Shaw

Act Hilary Swank, Chloe Sevigny, Peter Sarsgaard, Brendan Sexton III, Alison Folland, Alicia Goranson (Killer/Hart-Sharp)

This powerful tale [based on the 1993 rape and murder of Teena Brandon] of a young girl who disguised herself as a boy is anchored by two fully realized performances: Hilary Swank as the sexual misfit and Chloe Sevigny as her sensitive girlfriend.

Story begins in Lincoln, NE, with the 20-year-old Brandon (Swank) getting a boyish haircut and preparing for a night out. Though warned by close friend Lonny (Matt McGrath) that "his" behavior signals big trouble and "folks in Fall City kill fags," Brandon insists that her life—now his life—is on the right track. Brandon arrives in Fall City as a bright newcomer who enchants all those who meet him. As soon as he lays eyes on the sexually appealing Lana (Sevigny), it's love at first sight.

Second act centers on the tender love relationship that evolves: their first date, initial kiss and outdoor lovemaking. Turning point occurs when Brandon is thrown into the women's section of the local jail for cumulative traffic offenses and Lana comes to visit him. Brandon contends he's a case of "sexual identity crisis," born with some male and some female parts. With total understanding, Lana continues the affair.

Midsection is repetitive and plods a bit, but last reel is extremely powerful in chronicling the rednecks' reaction when a local newspaper breaks Brandon's story.

Stunningly accomplished in every department, this first film boasts sharp cinematography and flawless acting by the ensemble, with the two young leads contributing their best perfs to date.

1999: Best Actress (Hilary Swank)

NOMINATIONS: Best Supp. Actress (Chloe Sevigny)

●

BOYS FROM BRAZIL, THE

1978, 123 mins, US Ⓥ ⊙ col

Dir Franklin J. Schaffner ***Prod*** Martin Richards, Stanley O'Toole ***Scr*** Heywood Gould ***Ph*** Henri Decae ***Ed*** Robert E. Swink ***Mus*** Jerry Goldsmith ***Art*** Gil Parrondo

Act Gregory Peck, Laurence Olivier, James Mason, Lilli Palmer, Uta Hagen, Denholm Elliott (Producer Circle/20th Century-Fox)

With two excellent antagonists in Gregory Peck and Laurence Olivier, *The Boys from Brazil* presents a gripping, suspenseful drama for nearly all of its two hours—then lets go at the end and falls into a heap. In a fine shift from his usual roles, Peck plays the evil Josef Mengele, a real-life character who murdered thousands of Jews, including many children, carrying out bizarre genetic experiments at Auschwitz in Poland. Olivier, slipping completely into the role of an elderly Jewish gentleman, is the Nazi hunter who brings him to bay.

With the aid of James Mason, Peck is out to assassinate 94 fathers around the world. In a brief but lively part, Steven Guttenberg discovers the plot and tips Olivier, who sets out to find how the killings fit together. His search turns up three identical lads, all played menacingly by Jeremy Black, who are more than triplets.

What they are and whence they came are plausibly developed in Heywood Gould's script [from Iva Levin's novel] and director Franklin J. Schaffner builds the threatening menace well.

1978: NOMINAITONS: Best Actor (Laurence Olivier), Editing, Original Score

●

BOYS FROM SYRACUSE, THE

1940, 73 mins, US b/w

Dir A. Edward Sutherland ***Prod*** Jules Levey ***Scr*** Leonard Spigelgass, Charles Grayson ***Ph*** Joseph Valentine ***Ed*** Milton Carruth

Act Allan Jones, Joe Penner, Martha Raye, Rosemary Lane, Charles Butterworth, Irene Hervey (Mayfair/Universal)

Writers Leonard Spigelgass and Charles Grayson have transformed the legiter—which George Abbott authored in collaboration with Richard Rodgers and Lorenz Hart (with a plot copped from Bill Shakespeare's *Comedy of Errors*)—from a satire to plain burlesque.

Martha Raye and Joe Penner are particularly outstanding in the comedy leads. Penner, away from the stereotyped "wanna buy a duck?" characterization, makes a droll slave. Raye, provided with the swell Rodgers and Hart tunes, gets good opportunity to use her pipes as well as exhibit her broad comedy style. Charles Butterworth and Eric Blore, in lesser roles, turn in plenty of additional laughs, while Allan Jones capably acts and warbles his way through the top characterization.

Four of the tunes have been retained and two new ones have been provided by R&H to sub for three that were dropped. "Who Are You?," romantic ballad sung by Jones, is one of the new ones, and "The Greeks Had No Word for It," a specialty for Martha Raye, is the other. Both are equal to the originals.

Writers have done everything possible to further the basically ludicrous idea of the stage show, in which all sorts of modernisms surround the toga-clad populace of ancient Greece. It gives plenty of opportunity for gags, and none is missed, even to the checkered chariot, with a meter. Stone "newspapers" announce that "Ephesus Blitzkriegs Syracuse," while the gladiators' union pickets and a voice strangely like that of Winchell's gives gossip on station EBC.

Tale concerns twin brothers and their twin slaves. One brother and one slave are parted from the other brother and his slave as babies. One brother becomes ruler of Ephesus and conqueror of Syracuse, town in which he doesn't know he was born. The other son comes to Ephesus, also, in search of his father. Neither twin knows the other exists and the resultant mixup of identity makes plenty of base for laughs.

1940: NOMINATIONS: Best B&W Art Direction, Special Effects

●

BOYS IN COMPANY C, THE

1978, 125 mins, US Ⓥ ⊙ ⌑ col

Dir Sidney J. Furie ***Prod*** Andre Morgan ***Scr*** Rick Natkin, Sidney J. Furie ***Ph*** Godfrey A. Godar ***Ed*** Michael Berman, Frank J. Urioste, Alan Pattillo, James Benson ***Mus*** Jaime Mendoza-Nava ***Art*** Robert Lang

Act Stan Shaw, Andrew Stevens, James Canning, Michael Lembeck, Craig Wasson, Scott Hylands (Golden Harvest)

The Boys in Company C is a spotty but okay popcorn trade drama about five young Marines and how their lives were changed by duty in the Vietnam war. Laden with barracks dialog and played at the enlisted man's level, the Raymond Chow production, directed well by Sidney J. Furie, features strong performances by some very fine actors.

Not that *The Boys in Company C* is anywhere near a definitive film about the Vietnam debacle. No geopolitics or other cosmic matters intrude; instead, it's a deliberate action programmer (shot in the Philippines). Stan Shaw heads the cast as a dope pusher who sees Vietnam as a major new connection, until he matures into a natural leader. Andrew Stevens, son of Stella Stevens, is a Southern athlete who turns junkie in action. James Canning is an aspiring writer who records the bewildering and unnatural warfare.

●

BOYS IN THE BAND, THE

1970, 117 mins, US Ⓥ ⊙ col

Dir William Friedkin ***Prod*** Mart Crowley ***Scr*** Mart Crowley ***Ph*** Arthur J. Ornitz ***Ed*** Jerry Greenburg ***Art*** John Robert Lloyd

Act Kenneth Nelson, Frederick Combs, Leonard Frey, Cliff Gorman, Reuben Greene, Robert La Tourneaux (Leo/Cinema Center)

Boys in the Band drags. But despite its often tedious postulations of homosexual case histories instead of realistic dialog, and the stagey posturing of the actors, the too literately faithful adaptation of Mart Crowley's off-Broadway swish-set piece has bitchy, back-biting humor, fascinating character studies, melodrama and, most of all, perverse interest.

As queen and host of the gay birthday party that is the film's only setting, Kenneth Nelson tells straight Peter White, it's like watching an accident, one is horrified and repulsed, but can't take his eyes away.

Crowley takes the fault for the self-indulgent dialog with prolonged speeches.

●

BOYS NEXT DOOR, THE

1985, 88 mins, US Ⓥ ⊙ col

Dir Penelope Spheeris ***Prod*** Keith Rubinstein, Sandy Howard ***Scr*** Glen Morgan, James Wong ***Ph*** Arthur Albert ***Ed*** Andy Horvitch ***Mus*** George S. Clinton ***Art*** John Tarnoff

Act Maxwell Caulfield, Charlie Sheen, Christopher McDonald, Hank Garrett, Patti D'Arbanville, Paul C. Dancer (New World/Republic Entertainment)

A before-credits sequence of *The Boys Next Door* helps explain the motives for making the film. Stills are shown of notorious figures in the U.S. who, for no apparent reason, have gone on killing sprees. One commentator suggests young criminals are so brutalized by their own upbringing that they can't see other people as human beings. Unfortunately the film itself doesn't live up to the expectations. Even if intentions are worthy, it emerges glib and uninvolvingly.

Two alienated and disturbed 18-year-olds, Roy Alston (Maxwell Caulfield) and Bo Richards (Charlie Sheen), graduate from a small high school in California. Before taking up factory jobs, they decide to have a weekend in L.A. in which "anything goes."

An eruption of violence begins with the brutal beating of a gas station attendant. It ends with one boy shooting the other as the police close in on the pair in a shopping mall. In between there are beatings and killings of a homosexual, a young couple and a woman.

With conventional clean-cut good looks, Caulfield and Sheen clearly resemble the title, but they fail to adequately project the "angry stuff" within.

●

BOYS' NIGHT OUT

1962, 113 mins, US col

Dir Michael Gordon ***Prod*** Martin Ransohoff ***Scr*** Ira Wallach ***Ph*** Arthur E. Arling ***Ed*** Tom McAdoo ***Mus*** Frank DeVol ***Art*** George W. Davis, Hans Peters

Act Kim Novak, James Garner, Tony Randall, Howard Duff, Janet Blair, Anne Jeffreys (Kimco-Filmways/M-G-M)

In *Boys' Night Out*, four grown men, genus Americus Suburbicus, rent a town pad on the co-op plan for the express purpose of sharing, one by one, an illicit evening per week with a voluptuous and accommodating blonde. Red-blooded male audiences will be astonished to discover that boy one does nothing but gab, boy two nothing but putter, boy three nothing but eat, and that boy four ups and marries the girl.

Since the element of story surprise, so vital in humour, is completely absent in the Ira Wallach screenplay, adapted by Marion Hargrove from a story by Arne Sultan and Marvin Worth, the audience is forced to seek comedy rewards in isolated doses—individual gags and situations. Kim Novak slinks and purrs through the role of the object of all this extra-marital monkeyshine, an upstanding young postgrad sociology student who is secretly compiling data for a thesis on *Adolescent Sexual Fantasies in the Adult Suburban Male*. James Garner seems comfortable in the part of the number one son-of-a-gun who wins her heart. Tony Randall and Howard Morris (television funnyman in his screen bow) walk off with comedy honors.

•

BOYS ON THE SIDE
1995, 117 mins, US Ⓥ ⦿ ▭ col
Dir Herbert Ross ***Prod*** Arnon Milchan, Steven Reuther, Herbert Ross ***Scr*** Don Roos ***Ph*** Donald E. Thorin ***Ed*** Michael R. Miller ***Mus*** David Newman ***Art*** Ken Adam
Act Whoopi Goldberg, Mary-Louise Parker, Drew Barrymore, Matthew McConaughey, James Remar, Billy Wirth (New Regency/Hera/Warner)

Boasting tour-de-force performances by its three leads, *Boys on the Side* possesses a flavor similar to *Fried Green Tomatoes*. Director Herbert Ross and writer Don Roos (*Single White Female*) certainly don't shy away from the melodrama but also lighten the load with ample humor, much of that courtesy of Drew Barrymore's vivacious presence as the most unlikely side of the pic's central triangle.

Boys comes off the blocks looking like a road movie before veering into more dramatic and emotional territory. Beginning in New York, Jane (Whoopi Goldberg), a semi-employed club singer, and Robin (Mary-Louise Parker), an uptight real estate exec, meet by happenstance when they share a cross-country trip to Southern California. Along the way they detour to visit Jane's friend Holly (Barrymore), who joins the twosome. The trip comes to a screeching halt in Tuscon, however, when Robin falls ill and the three settle into a sort of non-nuclear family—one of the twists being that Jane, a lesbian, may have a romantic interest in her stricken roommate.

Though the action and tone are all over the map at first, Ross's direction and the stellar performances somehow create a real sense of tenderness and pathos. The lesbian overtones—virtually eliminated from *Tomatoes* in the movie version—may make *Boys* seem unconventional. Yet even with those slightly different chords, Ross manages to pluck the right heartstrings, in the process delivering a grade-A tearjerker.

•

BOYS TOWN
1938, 96 mins, US Ⓥ ⦿ b/w
Dir Norman Taurog ***Prod*** John W. Considine, Jr. ***Scr*** John Meehan, Dore Schary ***Ph*** Sidney Wagner ***Ed*** Elmo Veron ***Mus*** Edward Ward
Act Spencer Tracy, Mickey Rooney, Henry Hull, Leslie Fenton, Gene Reynolds, Bobs Watson (M-G-M)

The story of Father Flanagan's struggle to make a successful boy's home and then an entire community near Omaha, Neb, is the motivating theme throughout. Producers shrewdly have not made it entirely a paean of praise for Boys Town, but rather a realistic portrayal of Father Flanagan's untiring efforts to make something of wayward youngsters who otherwise might wind up in the electric chair.

With Spencer Tracy and Mickey Rooney as the priest and the incorrigible lad, in tailor-made roles, *Boys Town* is a tearjerker of the first water. Yet it has equal distribution of humorous and bitter moments. Rooney virtually takes the production away from the capable and veteran Tracy, though not appearing until feature is half-finished.

Rooney is the toughie whose repartee is as laughable as his cocky walk and mannerisms. Slow curbing of his desires as he bucks Boys Town customs and rules is a transition of character that is logically worked out. Tracy, showing necessary restraint, makes his portrayal of Flanagan sincere and human. It is not the first time he has played the role of a priest on the screen.

Henry Hull, the money-supplying pawnbroker who makes possible the boys home, builds this comparatively minor role into an impressive assignment.

1938: Best Actor (Spencer Tracy), Original Story (Eleanore Griffin, Dore Schary)

NOMINATIONS: Best Picture, Director, Screenplay

•

BOY TEN FEET TALL, A
SEE: SAMMY GOING SOUTH

•

BOY WHO COULD FLY, THE
1986, 114 mins, US Ⓥ ⦿ col
Dir Nick Castle ***Prod*** Gary Adelson ***Scr*** Nick Castle ***Ph*** Steven Poster, Adam Holender ***Ed*** Patrick Kennedy ***Mus*** Bruce Broughton ***Art*** Jim Bissell
Act Lucy Deakins, Jay Underwood, Bonnie Bedelia, Fred Savage, Colleen Dewhurst, Louise Fletcher (20th Century-Fox)

The Boy Who Could Fly is a well-intentioned film that deals with mental illness, suicide and other weighty subjects and their effects on children in a general and understanding way.

Story involves the special relationship between a sweet, patient teenage girl named Milly (Lucy Deakins) and the autistic neighbor Eric (Jay Underwood), who sits for hours on his roof directly across from her bedroom window with his arms outstretched as if ready to take off and fly.

Milly has just moved in with her recently widowed mother (Bonnie Bedelia) and precocious little brother (Fred Savage) following the suicide of their father. Milly is supersensitive and understands how lonely and misunderstood the troubled boy must be. She gets him to open up and talk; he takes her flying.

Under Nick Castle's careful direction, scenes never become maudlin, which is remarkable considering the potential of the subject matter. Deakins and Underwood handle their difficult roles with amazing grace. Near the end of the film comes the breather as the two finally become airborne—soaring over the city at night in beautifully crafted scenes by special effects wizard Richard Edlund and Boss Film Corp. Supporting cast of pros all turn in terrific performances.

•

BOY WITH GREEN HAIR, THE
1948, 82 mins, US Ⓥ col
Dir Joseph Losey ***Prod*** Stephen Ames ***Scr*** Ben Barzman, Alfred Lewis Levitt ***Ph*** George Barnes ***Ed*** Frank Doyle ***Mus*** Leigh Harline ***Art*** Albert S. D'Agostino, Ralph Berger
Act Pat O'Brien, Robert Ryan, Barbara Hale, Dean Stockwell, Richard Lyon, Walter Catlett (RKO)

RKO has turned out an absorbing, sensitive story of tolerance and child understanding in *The Boy with Green Hair*.

Story [by Betsy Beaton] is that of a war orphan, shifted around from one relative to another, who finally finds haven and security with a waiter in a small town. Then, one morning, he wakes to find his hair has turned green—and the world turns topsy-turvey about him. Other kids jeer at him; adults are perturbed; even the kindly milkman turns against him when accused of bringing it about through his product.

Film was made by Dore Schary for RKO before Howard Hughes gained control of the studio, and in its small way was one of the things that caused Schary to step out of the RKO setup. Pic had been completed, but Hughes ordered it to be re-edited and the tolerance theme taken out, on Hughes's general theory that films should entertain only and eschew social significance. Studio found that pic couldn't be re-edited, although it's reported to be toned down somewhat.

Through this parable about the unconscious cruelty of people to what is different, and the need of tolerance, runs another theme, that of anti-war preachment. When the boy meets children from war-orphan posters in a dream scene in the woods, and returns to annoy the townsfolk with the message that war is very bad—his green hair has thus acquired a meaning, to preach pacifism—the film hits a well-intentioned but false note.

•

BOYZ N THE HOOD
1991, 111 mins, US Ⓥ ⦿ col
Dir John Singleton ***Prod*** Steve Nicolaides ***Scr*** John Singleton ***Ph*** Charles Mills ***Ed*** Bruce Cannon ***Mus*** Stanley Clarke ***Art*** Bruce Bellamy
Act Larry Fishburne, Ice Cube, Cuba Gooding, Jr., Nia Long, Morris Chestnut, Tyra Ferrell (New Deal)

Boyz N The Hood is an absorbing, smartly made dramatic encyclopedia of problems and ethics in the black community, 1991. An impressive debut by 23-year-old John Singleton, sincere pic is ultra socially responsible, sometimes to the point of playing like a laundry list of difficulties faced specifically by the urban black community.

Tale principally looks at the lives of three boys in south-central L.A., beginning in '84 and then jumping, after a half-hour, to the present, when the realities of violence hit the teens.

Tre Styles (Cuba Gooding, Jr.) is a bright but rather sullen and insolent kid who moves to his father's home when his mother decides he needs a man's discipline. Dad, whose first name is Furious (Larry Fishburne), is a walking lesson in how to live the right way. Tre's best friend is Ricky (Morris Chestnut), who wants to be a football player, and they hang out with the latter's half-brother, Doughboy (Ice Cube), a roughhouser with a generally bad attitude.

Singleton constantly and effectively lays in the constant irritants and reminders of violence in the 'hood—the jets and choppers flying overhead, the ever-present dense smog, the random, easily-provoked fights, the day-and-night wailing of police sirens, the nearby gunshots. Lively dialog embraces everything from Furious's righteous sermons to Doughboy's rough, sexist diatribes. Director's skill clearly extends to handling actors, as leading players all do fine jobs of conveying various states of intensity. Produced for $6 million, pic is simple from a technical p.o.v.

1991: NOMINATIONS: Best Director, Original Screenplay

•

BRADY BUNCH MOVIE, THE
1995, 88 mins, US Ⓥ ⦿ col
Dir Betty Thomas ***Prod*** Sherwood Schwartz, Lloyd Schwartz, David Kirkpatrick ***Scr*** Laurice Elehwany, Rick Copp, Bonnie Turner, Jerry Turner ***Ph*** Mac Ahlberg ***Ed*** Peter Teschner ***Mus*** Guy Moon ***Art*** Steven Jordan
Act Shelley Long, Gary Cole, Michael McKean, Jean Smart, Henriette Mantel, Christopher Daniel Barnes (Paramount)

For five years back in the early 1970s, American TV homes were in thrall of *The Brady Bunch*. Two decades after their small screen demise, the clean-cut crew is back in mythic form as *The Brady Bunch Movie*. Part homage, part spoof, the deft balancing act is a clever, engaging adaption—albeit culled from less than pedigreed source material. With new actors in the roles, age has not withered the Brady brood. They still live in a suburban split-level house and face the travails of job, home and school. Papa Mike (Gary Cole) is hopelessly lost in a bygone era. The kids, who wear pastels, are relentlessly cute and obsessed with being popular. Mom (Shelley Long), ever smiling, is concerned about her kids without ever being less than chirpy.

Into this time capsule arrives Ditmeyer (Michael McKean), an obstreperous real estate agent who needs the Brady plot to close a massive land development deal. But no ridiculous amount of money can surmount the Bradys' love for their home and neighborhood.

The film's juxtaposition of contemporary and period realities is taken to extremes. The Brady bubble is lifted intact from a television soundstage circa 1970. Great care has been taken to replicate the artificiality of overlit, modestly furnished sets. But once out the door, director Betty Thomas opts for real locations and a natural look for a walk on the wild side of L.A. It's a truly inspired visual contrast.

Thomas has a wonderful cast of young performers who understand the gospel of groovy Greg, perfect Marcia and misunderstood Jan. But best of all is Cole.

•

BRAIN CANDY
(AKA: KIDS IN THE HALL: BRAIN CANDY)
1996, 88 mins, US Ⓥ col
Dir Kelly Makin ***Prod*** Lorne Michaels ***Scr*** Norm Hiscock, Bruce McCulloch, Kevin McDonald/Mark McKinney, Scott Thompson ***Ph*** David Makin ***Ed*** Christopher Cooper ***Mus*** Craig Northey ***Art*** Gregory P. Keen
Act David Foley, Bruce McCulloch, Kevin McDonald, Mark McKinney, Scott Thompson, Janeane Garofalo (Lakeshore/Paramount)

Television's Kids in the Hall make a relatively smooth, if offbeat, transition to the bigscreen with *Brain Candy*. The mad-scientist/corporate-heavy comedy is an odd combination of belly laughs and cerebral humor that will delight those familiar with the troupe's antics.

The simple saga, in which the Kids collectively play 32 roles, involves the fortunes of the mammoth pharmaceutical concern Roritor, in desperate need of a new hit drug. Dr. Chris Cooper (Kevin McDonald) tells the board of initial "favorable results" from his new antidepressant, which has not been fully tested. In a flash, the drug is dubbed Gleemonex, outperforms penicillin . . . and the first side effects arise.

Kids in the Hall are social satirists in an era when humor tends to be anarchic or about bowel movements. Though the story enjoys going off on tangents, it has a solid core that brings together its myriad strings. With the five Kids playing the lion's share of roles, the rest of the cast consists largely of day players and extras. (Brendan Fraser pops up in an uncredited cameo as a member of an experiment gone awry.) And while many of the troupe's characters derive from the television series, there is no attempt to tailor the film to conform to previous small-screen scenarios.

•

BRAINDEAD
1992, 101 mins, New Zealand Ⓥ ⦿ col
Dir Peter Jackson ***Prod*** Jim Booth ***Scr*** Peter Jackson, Stephen Sinclair, Frances Walsh ***Ph*** Murray Milne ***Ed*** Jamie Selkirk ***Mus*** Peter Dasent ***Art*** Kenneth Leonard-Jones
Act Timothy Balme, Diana Penalver, Elizabeth Moody, Ian Watkin, Brenda Kendall, Stuart Devenie (WingNut)

Kiwi gore specialist Peter Jackson goes for broke with an orgy of bad taste and splatter humor. Set in 1957, the standard zombie plot is played for laughs with a nerdy hero (Timothy Balme) whose domineering Mum (Elizabeth Moody) is bitten by a rare carnivorous monkey while spying on her son and his Spanish g.f. (Diana Penalver) at the Wellington Zoo.

Mum goes rabid fast and attacks a nurse, who also becomes a zombie. The poor son locks the creatures in the cellar and tries to pacify them with liberal doses of a tranquilizer administered by a giant hypo.

Comic highlights include Balme trying to pacify the zombie baby in a public park (horrified moms look on as he beats the creature into submission), and Balme literally re-entering his mother's womb in a gore-spattered end. Technically, this is Jackson's best pic to date, with state-of-the-art creature and gore effects.

•

BRAIN DONORS
1992, 79 mins, US Ⓥ ⦿ col
Dir Dennis Dugan ***Prod*** Gil Netter, James D. Brubaker ***Scr*** Pat Proft ***Ph*** David M. Walsh ***Ed*** Malcolm Campbell ***Mus*** Ira Newborn ***Art*** William J. Cassidy
Act John Turturro, Bob Nelson, Mel Smith, Nancy Marchand, John Savident, George De La Pena (Paramount/Zucker)

The title *Brain Donors* sounds like a horror film and for those expecting a comedy, it is. Patterned after *A Night at the Opera*, *Brain Donors* badly wants to be a latter-day Marx Bros pic. "Badly" is the key word.

John Turturro is Roland T. Flakfizer—a Groucho-esque, ambulance-chasing attorney out to fleece a well-heeled and well-fed widow (Nancy Marchand). Bob Nelson and Mel Smith are his equally zany aides-de-camp, the former a clear Harpo derivative and the latter a British cabbie who at least never tries to play the piano.

Hoping to land a $500,000-a-year job heading the widow's ballet company, Flakfizer and his cohorts end up at odds with a snooty attorney (John Savident) and stuck-up dancer (George De La Pena) while championing the cause of two young lovers.

Director Dennis Dugan's first feature, *Problem Child*, was a curious box office success, and so he finds himself laboring on another broad farce, again with numbingly flat results.

•

BRAINSCAN
1994, 95 mins, US Ⓥ ⦿ col
Dir John Flynn ***Prod*** Michel Roy ***Scr*** Andrew Kevin Walker ***Ph*** Francois Protat ***Ed*** Jay Cassidy ***Mus*** George S. Clinton ***Art*** Paola Ridolfi
Act Edward Furlong, Frank Langella, T. Ryder Smith, Amy Hargreaves, Jamie Marsh, Victor Ertmanis (Roy)

It's a rare teen horror pic that can be faulted for excessive restraint, but *Brainscan* may be too tame for the creature-feature fans and slasher devotees. At least one murder takes place entirely offscreen, while two other deaths are relatively bloodless and entirely accidental.

Edward Furlong of *Terminator 2* fame is well cast as Michael, a 16-year-old horror movie fan, computer whiz and social misfit who responds to an ad for Brainscan, a CD-ROM interactive virtual-reality game that promises to "interface with your unconscious."

Michael dreams of brutally stabbing a total stranger, then slicing off the dead man's foot. But when he wakes up, he finds the amputated foot is in his refrigerator. Enter Trickster (T. Ryder Smith), a sardonic bogeyman who pops out of Michael's computer and warns that if he wants to stay a few steps ahead of an inquisitive cop (Frank Langella), he must keep playing new Brainscan CDs. Once the first murder is out of the way, film [from a screen story by Brian Owens] becomes an exceedingly tame, only sporadically exciting thriller. The most elaborate special effects are saved until the end.

•

BRAINSTORM
1983, 106 mins, US Ⓥ ⦿ b col
Dir Douglas Trumbull ***Prod*** Douglas Trumbull ***Scr*** Robert Stitzel, Philip Frank Messina ***Ph*** Richard Yuricich ***Ed*** Edward Warschilka, Freeman Davies ***Mus*** James Horner ***Art*** John Vallone
Act Christopher Walken, Natalie Wood, Louise Fletcher, Cliff Robertson, Jordan Christopher, Joe Dorsey (M-G-M/ JF Prod.)

Shaken and embattled during its completion phase, and carrying the memory of Natalie Wood's death *Brainstorm* is a high-tech $18 million movie dependent on the visualization of a fascinating idea.

Producer-director Douglas Trumbull's effects wizardry—and the concept behind it—is the movie. The fetching idea (story by Bruce Joel Rubin) is a brain-wave device that gives characters the power to record and experience the physical, emotional and intellectual sensations of another human being.

On the downside, majority of players, including stars Christopher Walken and Wood as a married couple in a research environment, seem merely along for the ride. The film's acting surprise is Louise Fletcher, whose flinty, career scientist is a strong flavorful, workaholic portrait. The film offers irrefutable evidence that Natalie Wood's drowning (in November 1981) did not cause the filmmakers to drastically re-write or re-shoot scenes. Her work appears intact and, reportedly, only one scene had to be changed (with actor Joe Dorsey replacing Wood in a scene with Walken).

Cliff Robertson earnestly plays the compromising head of a vast research complex that employs colleagues Walken and Fletcher. Predictably, a government bogeyman is trying to gum up pure science for the sake of national security.

•

BRAINWAVES
1983, 81 mins, US Ⓥ col
Dir Ulli Lommel ***Prod*** Ulli Lommel ***Scr*** Ulli Lommel, Buz Alexander, Suzanna Love ***Ph*** Jon Kranhouse, Ulli Lommel ***Ed*** Richard Brummer ***Mus*** Robert O. Ragland ***Art*** Stephen E. Graff
Act Keir Dullea, Suzanna Love, Vera Miles, Percy Rodrigues, Tony Curtis, Paul Willson (CinAmerica)

Brainwaves is a briskly told, engaging psychological thriller dealing with the sci-fi concept of transferring thought processes and memories electronically between different people.

Suzanna Love toplines as Kaylie Bedford, a young San Francisco housewife who suffers a severe brain trauma (leaving her in a coma-like trance) in an auto accident. Her husband, Julian (Keir Dullea), and mother (Vera Miles) agree to an experimental medical procedure, unaware that it has not yet been tested on humans.

Designed to transfer corrective patterns by computer from a donor brain to the victim's damaged brain areas, process goes awry when the donor turns out to be a murdered girl (Corinne Alphen). Kaylie is physically and mentally rehabilitated, but plagued with traumatic first-person memories of the murder. Worse yet, the murderer is now after her.

Well-edited by Richard Brummer, picture zips along with admirable verisimilitude.

•

BRAMBLE BUSH, THE
1960, 93 mins, US col
Dir Daniel Petrie ***Prod*** Milton Sperling ***Scr*** Milton Sperling, Philip Yordan ***Ph*** Lucien Ballard ***Ed*** Folmar Blangsted ***Mus*** Leonard Rosenman ***Art*** John S. Poplin
Act Richard Burton, Barbara Rush, Jack Carson, Angie Dickinson, James Dunn, Tom Drake (Warner)

So-called mercy killing is the subject of *The Bramble Bush*, but the principals have such a brisk sex life that the subject rather gets lost in the bedclothes.

The screenplay, from a novel by Charles Mergendahl, presents the doctor who performs the mercy killing as a sympathetic character. Setting of the film is one of those New England towns that seem to be a hotbed (sic) of sex. Richard Burton is a young doctor who returns to his home town to care for his best friend, Tom Drake, who is dying of Hodgkin's disease. Burton has a brief affair with Drake's wife, Barbara Rush, who becomes pregnant.

Burton has left his home partly because his father, a doctor before him, committed suicide long before the action of the picture opens, on discovering his wife (Burton's mother) was having an affair with James Dunn. Other complications include nurse Angie Dickinson's unrequited torch for Burton.

Burton is intense and intelligent as the doctor, although he is miscast as a New Englander of laconic cast. Burton delivers a strong and sensitive performance. Dickinson's warmth overcomes some script deficiencies, and Dunn is interesting in a role not completely realized. Drake is excellent.

Art director John S. Poplin is expert at creating the New England atmosphere (out of what looks, on close inspection, to be local California coastline).

•

BRANDED
1950, 50 mins, US Ⓥ ⦿ col
Dir Rudolph Mate ***Prod*** Mel Epstein ***Scr*** Sydney Boehm, Cyril Hume ***Ph*** Charles B. Lang, Jr. ***Ed*** Doane Harrison ***Mus*** Roy Webb ***Art*** Hans Dreier, Roland Anderson
Act Alan Ladd, Mona Freeman, Charles Bickford, Robert Keith, Joseph Calleia, Peter Hansen (Paramount)

Branded is a pleasing western that has a bit more plot and appeal than the average.

Rudolph Mate, photographer-turned-director, demonstrates he has not lost his hand at his former art. He and cameraman Charles B. Lang, Jr., must be given a score for at least part of *Branded's* appeal on basis of the Technicolor scenic work along the Rio Grande.

Yarn [from a novel by Evan Evans] finds Alan Ladd a no-good who figures on stealing the fortune of a cattle family by making like he's the long-lost son who was kidnapped at five. He doesn't figure, however, on falling for his "sister" and getting right fond of mom and pop. Ladd's inability to indicate successfully a transition from scoundrel to a kid with a 24-karat heart makes the story at times harder to digest than it should be.

•

BRANNIGAN
1975, 111 mins, UK Ⓥ ⦿ ▭ col
Dir Douglas Hickox ***Prod*** Jules Levy, Arthur Gardner ***Scr*** Christopher Trumbo, Michael Butler, William P. McGivern, Michael Butler ***Ph*** Gerry Fisher ***Ed*** Malcolm Cooke ***Mus*** Dominic Frontiere ***Art*** Ted Marshall
Act John Wayne, Richard Attenborough, Judy Geeson, Mel Ferrer, John Vernon, Daniel Pilon (United Artists)

Okay John Wayne actioner, as a contemporary cop in London tracking down Chicago fugitive John Vernon, whose lawyer Mel Ferrer has concocted a bewildering escape cover. Richard Attenborough plays well against Wayne as an urbane Scotland Yard detective.

Judy Geeson, as Wayne's policewoman escort, and Daniel Pilon, as a hired gun carrying Vernon's contract on Wayne's life, round out the principal players. Car chases, booby traps, etc. round out the formula plot turns.

•

BRASSED OFF
1996, 109 mins, UK Ⓥ ⦿ col
Dir Mark Herman ***Prod*** Steve Abbott ***Scr*** Mark Herman ***Ph*** Andy Collins ***Ed*** Michael Ellis ***Mus*** Trevor Jones ***Art*** Don Taylor
Act Pete Postlethwaite, Tara Fitzgerald, Ewan McGregor, Jim Carter, Philip Jackson, Peter Martin (Prominent/Channel 4)

There's a lot to enjoy in *Brassed Off*, but most of it is in the first half. This well-played, often very sparky dramedy about the shenanigans in a northern [English] brass band composed of miners threatened with pit closure gets a bad attack of social realism in the latter stages that rocks the crowded craft. Despite its flaws, the movie is still streets ahead of writer-director Mark Herman's freshman effort, *Blame It on the Bellboy*.

Set in the fictional Yorkshire town of Grimley, film takes place during 1992, when the Conservative government launched another of its periodic programs of pit closures. Proud, stubborn Danny (Pete Postlethwaite) is determined to override his players' feelings that if the pit closes, so should the band.

On the eve of the band's entry in the national semifinals, its numbers are swollen by the arrival of looker Gloria (Tara Fitzgerald), who plays a mean flugelhorn and immediately invigorates the slightly tired, all-male ranks. Why the nattily dressed Gloria suddenly has returned to her hometown is a mystery, not least to her former b.f., Andy (Ewan McGregor).

Movie ends up a true ensemble portrait of a community, wives included. Where it doesn't quite take flight is in its early promise of music being the defining, and elevating, force of the characters' lives. Playing is excellent down the line.

•

BRASS TARGET
1978, 111 mins, US Ⓥ ⦿ ▭ col
Dir John Hough ***Prod*** Arthur Lewis ***Scr*** Alvin Boretz ***Ph*** Tony Imi ***Ed*** David Lane ***Mus*** Laurence Rosenthal ***Art*** Rolf Zehetbauer
Act Sophia Loren, John Cassavetes, George Kennedy, Robert Vaughn, Patrick McGoohan, Max von Sydow (M-G-M)

Brass Target, like *The Eagle Has Landed*, speculates on what might have happened to an historical figure in World War II had a given set of circumstances taken place.

This time, instead of Winston Churchill getting bumped off, it's General George Patton's turn. Writer Alvin Boretz has turned Frederick Nolan's speculative novel, *The Algonquin Project*, into a seemingly true-to-life revelation of how Patton actually died, not in a car accident, but at the hands of a clever paid assassin.

Robert Vaughn, Edward Herrman and Ed Bishop play three officers in Occupied Germany who concoct a plan to steal the Third Reich's gold stores with the help of OSS head Patrick McGoohan.

Patton, as played by George Kennedy, gets into a snit when the Russian Allies taunt him about the theft, and personally supervises the investigation, joined by OSS vet John Cassavetes. Gradually, just about every cast member is eliminated by one side or the other, until only Cassavetes, assassin Max von Sydow, and mutual lover Sophia Loren remain for the predictable finale.

Hough manages to interject some excitement into the action scenes, but these come few and far between. A generally competent cast is hamstrung by the material at hand.

•

BRAVE BULLS, THE

1951, 106 mins, US b/w

Dir Robert Rossen ***Prod*** Robert Rossen ***Scr*** John Bright ***Ph*** Floyd Crosby, James Wong Howe ***Ed*** Henry Batista, Philip Cook ***Art*** Cary Odell

Act Mel Ferrer, Miroslava, Anthony Quinn, Eugene Iglesias, Jose Torvay (Columbia)

Columbia has a distinctive, offbeat picture in this treatment of Tom Lea's bestseller novel. There's nothing routine in the way it has been filmed, producer-director Robert Rossen apparently preferring to sacrifice some commercial values in favor of an adult handling of the story of a Mexican matador and life and death in the bull arena.

The bullfight sequences have a shocker quality that will repel while fascinating. Script deals with a matador who rose to the fleeting status of public idol from a peasant beginning. At the top of his popularity he encounters mental confusion and fear because he doubts his real ability and believes his success comes from the mentoring of his manager-friend.

Rossen's direction and the camera work by Floyd Crosby and James Wong Howe are alive with the real flavor of Mexico, its bright, hard lights and shadows. Mel Ferrer seems the perfect choice to portray the very human matador. He has practically all of the footage and story emphasis, and dominates every bit of it.

•

BRAVEHEART

1995, 177 mins, US Ⓥ ⦿ ▭ col

Dir Mel Gibson ***Prod*** Mel Gibson, Alan Ladd, Jr., Bruce Davey ***Scr*** Randall Wallace ***Ph*** John Toll ***Ed*** Steven Rosenblum ***Mus*** James Horner ***Art*** Tom Sanders

Act Mel Gibson, Sophie Marceau, Patrick McGoohan, Catherine McCormack, Angus McFadyen, Ian Bannen (Icon/Ladd/20th Century-Fox)

A huge, bloody and sprawling epic, Mel Gibson's second directing effort, *Braveheart*, is the sort of massive vanity piece that would be easy to disparage if it didn't essentially deliver.

There are clearly elements of *Spartacus* running through the film in tone and inspiration, from the enormous battles with thousands of kilted extras to Gibson's William Wallace—a charismatic leader obsessed with freedom who rallies Scottish rebels against the tyrannical English king Edward the Longshanks (Patrick McGoohan).

Pic also engages in considerable court intrigue, from the forced marriage between Edward's gay son and a French princess (Sophie Marceau), to the inner torment of Robert the Bruce (Angus McFadyen), one of the many Scottish lords whose feuding and avarice ultimately leave Wallace's band to their own considerable devices.

There's also a strong romantic undercurrent, but even with that, the movie is not for the squeamish, demonstrating as it does in graphic detail the brutality of hand-to-hand combat—masterfully staged sequences that nevertheless become somewhat numbing after repeated exposure to all the bludgeoning and skewering.

Gibson's direction meanders at first but takes hold once the fighting starts, and while the movie is indeed a long sit, from that point on it's far from boring. The director also pulls the camera back to capture the grandeur and scope of the conflict, which, again, is diminished only through repetition.

Marceau and Catherine McCormack [as Wallace's wife Murron] both cut striking figures in limited femme roles amidst the carnage, while McGoohan perhaps overplays his hand slightly as the villainous king, a figure notable principally for his utter amorality. Gibson's central performance is also strong, and his Wallace does inspire, in both his messianic zeal and his unflinching heroism. Tech credits are roundly impressive.

1995: Best Film, Best Cinematography, Best Sound Effects Editing, Best Makeup

NOMINATIONS: Director, Best Original Screenplay, Film Editing, Original Dramatic Score, Costume Design, Best Sound

•

BRAVE ONE, THE

1956, 100 mins, US Ⓥ ▭ col

Dir Irving Rapper ***Prod*** Maurice King, Frank King ***Scr*** Harry Franklin, Merrill G. White ***Ph*** Jack Cardiff ***Ed*** Merrill G. White ***Mus*** Victor Young

Act Michel Ray, Rodolfo Hoyos, Elsa Cardenas, Carlos Navarro, Joi Lansing, Fermin Rivera (RKO)

A kid's love for his pet themes this sentimentally moving story of a small Mexican boy who raises a fighting bull. Told against some magnificent CinemaScope photography of the below-the-border setting, it's a picture of overall appeal.

The sensitive script was taken from a Robert Rich [pseudonym for blacklisted writer Dalton Trumbo] story based on an actual bullring incident that occurred in the Plaza de Toros in Barcelona in 1936 when a bull of much bravery and heart was pardoned to his young master. Plot is the touching account of a young Mexican farm boy who raises a pet bull, only to have it taken away from him when the ranch owner is accidentally killed and the stock sold off. The bull is shipped to the Plaza de Mexico to face Fermin Rivera, matador playing himself.

There's some near schmaltz, along with the sensitivity, in the screenplay, but because of the warm, tender aspects, the touches of human comedy and the exciting bullring finale, most viewers won't find the tendency to over-sentimentality objectionable. Irving Rapper's direction is sure-handed in the assorted aspects of the plot.

•

BRAZIL

1944, 91 mins, US b/w

Dir Joseph Santley ***Prod*** Robert North ***Scr*** Frank Gill, Jr., Laura Kerr ***Ph*** Jack Marta ***Ed*** Fred Allen ***Mus*** Ary Barroso ***Art*** Russell Kimball

Act Tito Guizar, Virginia Bruce, Robert Livingston, Henry Da Silva, Edward Everett Horton, Roy Rogers (Republic)

With Ary Barroso, Latin American composer who did the lilting "Brazil" song-dance number, contributing bulk of music, this is in the groove for all who like south-of-border music.

Unlike too many films with Latin American locales, this has a plot [by Richard English] that adds up. Virginia Bruce, as author of *Why Marry a Latin?* is in Rio to get material for a book on Brazil. She's hardly given a warm welcome because of that book. Otherwise, her stay in Brazil is okay because not recognized by natives. That is until she bumps into Tito Guizar. On learning she authored *Why Marry a Latin?* he decides to give her an object lesson, and prove that Latins aren't such lousy lovers. Of course, in trying to prove his point, Guizar falls in love with her.

Joseph Santley's direction is topflight throughout while Robert North has given the picture elaborate production backgrounding. Special camera crew went to Brazil for background shots, most important being the Rio carnival scenes.

1944: NOMINATIONS: Best Scoring of a Musical Picture, Sound, Song ("Rio de Janeiro")

•

BRAZIL

1985, 142 mins, UK Ⓥ ⦿ col

Dir Terry Gilliam ***Prod*** Arnon Milchan ***Scr*** Terry Gilliam, Tom Stoppard, Charles McKeown ***Ph*** Roger Pratt ***Ed*** Julian Doyle ***Mus*** Michael Kamen ***Art*** Norman Garwood

Act Jonathan Pryce, Robert De Niro, Michael Palin, Kim Greist, Katherine Helmond, Ian Holm (Embassy)

Brazil offers a chillingly hilarious vision of the near-future, set "somewhere in the 20th Century."

Director Terry Gilliam reportedly wanted to call the film *1984 1/2*. As in Orwell's classic, society is monitored by an insidious, tentacular ministry, and the film's protagonist, a diligent but unambitious civil servant, Sam Lowry—played with vibrant comic imagination by Jonathan Pryce—becomes a victim of his own romantic delusions, and is crushed by a system he had never before thought of questioning.

He sees himself as a winged super-hero, part-Icarus, part-Siegfried, soaring lyrically through the clouds to the tune of "Brazil," the old Xavier Cugat favorite, which as the film's ironic musical leitmotif, recurs in numerous mock variations.

Robert De Niro shows delightful comic flair in a small, but succulent characterization of a proletariat superhero, who disposes of some obnoxious rival repairmen in a disgustingly original manner, but meets a most bizarre end in the film's nightmare climax.

Gilliam has assembled a brilliant supporting cast of character actors, notably Ian Holm, as the edgy, paranoid ministry department chief hopelessly dependent on Pryce to untie bureaucratic knots.

1985: NOMINATIONS: Best Original Screenplay, Art Direction

•

BREAKDANCE

SEE: BREAKIN'

•

BREAKDANCE 2: ELECTRIC BOOGALOO

SEE: BREAKIN' 2: ELECTRIC BOOGALOO

•

BREAKDOWN

1997, 93 mins, US Ⓥ ⦿ ▭ col

Dir Jonathan Mostow ***Prod*** Martha De Laurentiis, Dino De Laurentiis ***Scr*** Jonathan Mostow, Sam Montgomery ***Ph*** Doug Milsome ***Ed*** Derek Brechin, Kevin Stitt ***Mus*** Basil Poledouris ***Art*** Victoria Paul

Act Kurt Russell, J. T. Walsh, Kathleen Quinlan, M. C. Gainey, Jack Noseworthy, Rex Linn (Paramount)

The fear of vast, wide-open spaces, not to mention demented redneck cowboys, fuels *Breakdown*, a tremendously tense thriller that expertly keeps tightening the screws throughout its taught running time. In his bigscreen feature debut, director and cowriter Jonathan Mostow displays real flair for visceral cinema while adroitly sidestepping many of the usual tripwires of this sort of film.

Jeff and Amy Taylor (Kurt Russell, Kathleen Quinlan) are on a drive moving from Massachusetts to California when their bright red Jeep Grand Cherokee breaks down in a particularly desolate part of the Southwest. They reluctantly accept an offer of solicitous truck driver Red (J. T. Walsh) to drive Amy to the nearest cafe where she can call for assistance.

Jeff is able to restart the car himself, but when he arrives at the diner, Amy isn't there and no one admits to having seen her. Pic skillfully maintains Jeff's p.o.v. as it presses ahead, and Mostow and cowriter Sam Montgomery neatly manage to flipflop the advantage between protagonist and villains several times before it's all over.

Mostow, who helmed the 1991 Showtime thriller *Flight of Black Angel*, generates a strong sense of foreboding without resorting to cheap tricks. Russell emphasizes the reactions of a normal man to the extreme events the story holds in store. Performance is functional, but very effective. Quinlan is offscreen most of the time, but the villains, led by the truly sinister Walsh, are all great.

•

BREAKER MORANT

1980, 106 mins, Australia Ⓥ ⦿ col

Dir Bruce Beresford ***Prod*** Matt Carroll ***Scr*** Bruce Beresford, Jonathon Hardy, David Stevens ***Ph*** Don McAlpine ***Ed*** William Anderson ***Mus*** Phil Cunneen (arr.) ***Art*** David Copping

Act Edward Woodward, Jack Thompson, John Waters, Bryan Brown, Charles Tingwell, Lewis Fitz-Gerald (South Australian Film)

Harry "The Breaker" Morant (Edward Woodward) was an Englishman who went to Australia in the last century. When Britain and the Boers squared off against each other in South Africa, he and a number of other Australians volunteered and were absorbed into the non-regular army contingent.

The nature of the war made prisoner-taking a difficult business logistically, and while the film [from a play by Kenneth Ross] in no way tries to justify the killing of them, it does make clear that the Establishment's blind-eye can become very quickly healed.

As an example to others, Morant and two other Australians, Handcock (Bryan Brown) and Witton (Lewis Fitz-Gerald) were tried by court martial. Morant and Handcock were convicted and sentenced to death by firing-squad.

The execution sequence as handled by Bruce Beresford and the two actors is profoundly affecting. Beresford then turns his audience into an unwitting jury; as a sheer exercise in manipulation, it approaches the masterful and is extremely effective.

1980: NOMINATION: Best Adapted Screenplay

•

BREAKFAST AT TIFFANY'S

1961, 115 mins, US Ⓥ ⦿ col

Dir Blake Edwards ***Prod*** Martin Jurow, Richard Shepherd ***Scr*** George Axelrod ***Ph*** Franz F. Planer ***Ed*** Howard Smith ***Mus*** Henry Mancini ***Art*** Hal Pereira, Roland Anderson

Act Audrey Hepburn, George Peppard, Patricia Neal, Buddy Ebsen, Martin Balsam, Mickey Rooney (Paramount)

Out of the elusive, but curiously intoxicating Truman Capote fiction, scenarist George Axelrod has developed a surprisingly moving film, touched up into a stunningly visual motion picture. Capote buffs may find some of Axelrod's fanciful alterations a bit too precocious, pat and glossy for comfort, but enough of the original's charm and vigor has been retained.

What makes *Tiffany's* an appealing tale is its heroine, Holly Golightly, a charming, wild and amoral "free spirit" with a latent romantic streak. Axelrod's once-over-golightly erases the amorality and bloats the romanticism, but retains the essential spirit ("a phony, but a real phony") of the character, and, in the exciting person of Audrey Hepburn, she comes vividly to life on the screen.

Hepburn's expressive, "top banana in the shock department" portrayal is complemented by the reserved, capable work of George Peppard as the young writer whose love ultimately (in the film, not the book) enables the heroine to come to realistic terms with herself.

Excellent featured characterizations are contributed by Martin Balsam as a Hollywood agent, Buddy Ebsen as Hepburn's deserted husband, and Patricia Neal as Peppard's wealthy "sponsor." Mickey Rooney as a much-harassed upstairs Japanese photographer adds an unnecessarily incongruous note to the proceedings.

The film is a sleek, artistic piece of craftsmanship, particularly notable for Franz F. Planer's haunting photography and Henry Mancini's memorably moody score. The latter's "Moon River," with lyrics by Johnny Mercer, is an enchanting tune.

1961: Best Song ("Moon River"), Scoring of a Dramatic Picture

NOMINATIONS: Best Actress (Audrey Hepburn), Adapted Screenplay, Color Art Direction

•

BREAKFAST CLUB, THE

1985, 97 mins, US Ⓥ ⊙ col

Dir John Hughes ***Prod*** Ned Tanen, John Hughes ***Scr*** John Hughes ***Ph*** Thomas Del Ruth ***Ed*** Dede Allen ***Mus*** Keith Forsey ***Art*** John W. Corso

Act Emilio Estevez, Judd Nelson, Molly Ringwald, Anthony Michael Hall, Ally Sheedy, Paul Gleason (A&M/Universal)

In typical Shermer High in Chicago, a cross-section of five students—the jock, Miss Popularity, the ruffian, the nerd and Miss Weirdo—are thrown together under adverse circumstances and cast aside all discord and unite under the sudden insight that none would be such a despicable little twit if mom or dad or both weren't so rotten. The querulous quintet are actually being forced to *spend the entire day at school on Saturday* for some previous infraction of the rules.

Coming together as strangers, none of the group initially likes thuggish loudmouth Judd Nelson, who taunts pretty Molly Ringwald, torments dorkish Anthony Michael Hall and challenges champ athlete Emilio Estevez while the odd lady, Ally Sheedy, looks on from a different space.

When the causes of the Decline of Western Civilization are finally writ, Hollywood will surely have to answer why it turned one of man's most significant art forms over to the self-gratification of high-schoolers. Or does director John Hughes really believe, as he writes here, that "when you grow up, your heart dies." It may. But not unless the brain has already started to rot with films like this.

•

BREAKFAST FOR TWO

1937, 67 mins, US b/w

Dir Alfred Santell ***Prod*** Edward Kaufman ***Scr*** Charles Kaufman, Paul Yawitz, Viola Brothers Shore, David Garth ***Ph*** Roy Hunt ***Ed*** George Hively ***Art*** Van Nest Polglase, Al Herman

Act Barbara Stanwyck, Herbert Marshall, Glenda Farrell, Eric Blore, Frank M. Thomas, Donald Meek (Kaufman/RKO)

Breakfast for Two is loaded with a wide assortment of larynx and midriff ticklers, with Barbara Stanwyck and Herbert Marshall turning in slick performances. About the only time that the zany pace bogs down is toward the end when the action overstrains itself with an awkwardly contrived mess of housewrecking and pie-tossing.

Barrage of screwy situations [story by David Garth] take their cue from the efforts of a rich dame (Stanwyck) to straighten out a tippling waster (Marshall) and make him realize his responsibilities as the inheriting head of a steamship line. Also to land him as her husband.

With such expert farceurs as Eric Blore and Glenda Farrell piling in to help keep things boiling, the plot gravitates from sly humor to fantastic goofiness.

•

BREAKFAST OF CHAMPIONS

1999, 110 mins, US Ⓥ ⊙ col

Dir Alan Rudolph ***Prod*** David Blocker, David Willis ***Scr*** Alan Rudolph ***Ph*** Elliot Davis ***Ed*** Suzy Elmiger ***Mus*** Mark Isham ***Art*** Nina Ruscio

Act Bruce Willis, Albert Finney, Nick Nolte, Barbara Hershey, Glenne Headly, Lukas Haas

File this one under "Rudolph . . . whoops." A hearty meal that starts off tickling the taste buds but ends up smothering them, *Breakfast of Champions* is a game attempt to film Kurt Vonnegut, Jr.'s 1976 satire on American greed and commercialism. Supercharged on every level, Alan Rudolph's movie is the kind of manic, social-commentary comedy that was in fashion when the source novel was written but now fits awkwardly into today's blander Hollywood panorama.

Project has a long history, starting with Robert Altman asking Rudolph to do a script when the book first came out. [In the early '90s] Bruce Willis became interested, and finally called Rudolph, bankrolling the whole production.

Relentlessly upbeat Dwayne Hoover (Willis) runs Midland City's most successful car dealership. However, Dwayne is a troubled man: He starts every day summoning up the courage to blow his brains out. His longtime sales manager, Harry (Nick Nolte), likes to wear female undies, and his secretary, the plastic Francine (Glenne Headly), is really more interested in making big bucks than making her boss. Dwayne is also under investigation by the Environmental Protection Agency.

By a series of coincidences, Dwayne becomes convinced that the man with the big solutions is Kilgore Trout (Albert Finney), a dime-store philosopher-hack, whose copious novels have mostly been turned into wood pulp. Finney, in a grouchy, hobolike role, is a major piece of miscasting, not half as funny as the picture needs him to be. Willis and Nolte are very good in the early going, but are given no chance to step beyond their caricatures as the pic progresses.

•

BREAK FOR FREEDOM

SEE: ALBERT, R.N.

•

BREAKHEART PASS

1976, 95 mins, US Ⓥ ⊙ col

Dir Tom Gries ***Prod*** Jerry Gershwin ***Scr*** Alistair MacLean ***Ph*** Lucien Ballard ***Ed*** Byron (Buzz) Brandt ***Mus*** Jerry Goldsmith ***Art*** Johannes Larsen

Act Charles Bronson, Ben Johnson, Jill Ireland, Richard Crenna, Charles Durning, Ed Lauter (United Artists)

Production has Charles Bronson as a government undercover agent who trips up a gang of gun runners, and a marvellous old steam train as setting for most of the plot.

Working from a lean Alistair MacLean script (based on his own novel), director Tom Gries forges a brisk and polished cinematic tale in which the mysteries pile up as old No. 9 steams with troops and medical supplies to an army post gripped by a killer epidemic.

Even before embarkation, a couple of officers go missing. Then, along the journey, telegraphic contact is lost, bodies hurtle out of the train into gorges, and the train's rear section containing the relief troops becomes detached.

Seasoned support in stock turns is furnished by Ben Johnson as a crooked marshal, and Ed Lauter as an honest army colonel.

•

BREAKIN'
(UK: BREAKDANCE)

1984, 87 mins, US Ⓥ ⊙ col

Dir Joel Silberg ***Prod*** Allen DeBevoise, David Zito ***Scr*** Charles Parker, Allen DeBevoise, Gerald Scaife ***Ph*** Hannania Baer ***Ed*** Mark Helfrich ***Mus*** Gary Remal, Michael Boyd ***Art*** Ivo G. Crisante

Act Lucinda Dickey, Adolfo Quinones, Michael Chambers, Ben Lokey, Christopher McDonald, Phineas Newborn III (Golan-Globus)

Breakin' is the first feature film entirely devoted to the breakdancing craze.

On a plot level, concoction is too derivative of *Flashdance* for its own good, as the premise once again is untrained, but highly skilled and imaginative, street dancers versus the stuffy, inflexible dance establishment.

Filmmakers have also played it safe in focusing the action on a nice, middle-class white girl (Lucinda Dickey), whereas breakdancing is almost exclusively the domain of blacks and Latinos.

Aside from these fainthearted choices, however, film is quite satisfactory and breezily entertaining on its own terms.

•

BREAKIN' 2: ELECTRIC BOOGALOO

1984, 94 mins, US Ⓥ ⊙ col

Dir Sam Firstenberg ***Prod*** Menahem Golan, Yoram Globus ***Scr*** Jan Ventura, Julie Reichert ***Ph*** Hanania Baer ***Ed*** Marcus Manton ***Mus*** Mike Linn ***Art*** Joseph T. Garrity

Act Lucinda Dickey, Adolfo Quinones, Michael Chambers, Susie Bono, Harry Caesar, Jo de Winter (Cannon)

Breakin' 2 is a comic book of a film, and, as in a cartoon, kids can get away with anything to have a good time.

As a phenomenon, the hip-hop, breakdancing, sidewalk graffiti and rap music culture lends itself well to a comic-book approach and to his credit director Sam Firstenberg doesn't try to interject too much reality into the picture.

This time around Ozone (Adolfo "Shabba-Doo" Quinones) and Turbo (Michael "Boogaloo Shrimp" Chambers) have turned their street dancing talents to teaching other disadvantaged youths at a rundown community club they've dubbed Miracles.

When a developer (Peter MacLean) and a corrupt politician (Ken Olfson) try to put up a shopping center where the community center stands, the kids decide to put on a show to raise the necessary $200,000.

•

BREAKING AWAY

1979, 100 mins, US Ⓥ ⊙ col

Dir Peter Yates ***Prod*** Peter Yates ***Scr*** Steve Tesich ***Ph*** Matthew F. Leonetti ***Ed*** Cynthia Scheider ***Mus*** Patrick Williams ***Art*** Patrizia Von Brandenstein

Act Dennis Christopher, Dennis Quaid, Daniel Stern, Jackie Earle Haley, Barbara Barrie, Robyn Douglass (20th Century-Fox)

Though its plot wins no points for originality, *Breaking Away* is a thoroughly delightful light comedy, lifted by fine performances from Dennis Christopher and Paul Dooley. The story is nothing more than a triumph for the underdog through sports, this time cycle racing.

Christopher, Dennis Quaid, Daniel Stern and Jackie Earle Haley are four recent high-school graduates with no particular educational ambitions, yet stuck in a small college town—and a fairly snooty college at that.

But Christopher is a heck of a bike rider and such an adulator of Italian champions that he pretends to be Italian himself, even at home. Pretending to be an Italian exchange student, Christopher meets pretty coed Robyn Douglass (an able film debut for her) and this ultimately brings the boys into conflict with the big men on campus that must finally be resolved in a big bike race.

The relationship among the four youths is warm and funny, yet full of different kinds of conflicts. Quaid is very good as the ex-quarterback facing a life with no more cheers; Haley is good as a sawed-off romantic; and Stern is superb as a gangly, wise-cracking mediator. Though pic sometimes seems padded with too much cycle footage, the climax is exciting, even though predictable.

1979: Best Original Screenplay

NOMINATIONS: Best Picture, Director, Supp. Actress (Barbara Barrie), Adaptated Score

•

BREAKING GLASS

1980, 104 mins, UK Ⓥ ▭ col

Dir Brian Gibson ***Prod*** Davina Belling, Clive Parsons ***Scr*** Brian Gibson ***Ph*** Stephen Goldblatt ***Ed*** Michael Bradsell ***Mus*** Tony Visconti (dir.) ***Art*** Evan Hercules

Act Phil Daniels, Hazel O'Connor, Jon Finch, Jonathan Pryce (Allied Stars/Film & General)

Breaking Glass presents a cynical, off-the-peg, view of the post-punk record business.

Cast opposite Hazel O'Connor, who's seen initially as a two-bit teenage performer playing a handful of her own numbers around lousy London gigs, is Phil Daniels, a hustling would-be manager who teams with O'Connor. Ensuing success undermines the pair's tentative romantic partnership and, with the arrival on the scene of Jon Finch as an overly smooth-mannered producer, their professional interdependence as well.

Relentlessly fast-paced, the yarn relates to reality in much the same way as a fashion photo—that is, it works as an image-conscious reflection of a time and milieu, but does not purport to portray life as it really is.

•

BREAKING IN
1989, 91 mins, US Ⓥ ⦿ col
Dir Bill Forsyth ***Prod*** Harry Gittes ***Scr*** John Sayles ***Ph*** Michael Coulter ***Ed*** Michael Ellis ***Mus*** Michael Gibbs ***Art*** Adrienne Atkinson
Act Burt Reynolds, Casey Siemaszko, Sheila Kelley, Lorraine Toussant, Albert Salmi, Harry Carey (Act III/Goldwyn)

Burt Reynolds plays Ernie Mullins, a 61-year-old, graying, professional burglar with a gammy leg and the beginning of a pot belly, in this charming buddy-caper movie.

He teams up with young Mike Lefebb (Casey Siemaszko), a garage hand who likes to break into houses to raid the fridge and read the mail, when they both hit the same place one night. They become partners, with the old-timer teaching the youngster the tricks of the trade.

What follows is a gentle comedy, filled with incisive observation, which builds to a wry conclusion which won't set well with action fans. Reynolds plays the old-timer with a relaxed charm that's wholly delightful. Siemaszko is fine, too, as the initially nervous and ultimately relaxed and confident young criminal. Sheila Kelley is fun as a prostie who favors colored condoms and likes to be known as an actress.

•

BREAKING THE SOUND BARRIER
SEE: THE SOUND BARRIER

•

BREAKING THE WAVES
1996, 159 mins, Denmark/France Ⓥ ▭ col
Dir Lars Von Trier ***Prod*** Vibeke Windelov, Peter Aalbaek Jensen ***Scr*** Lars Von Trier ***Ph*** Robby Muller ***Ed*** Anders Refn ***Mus*** Joachim Holbek ***Art*** Karl Juliusson
Act Emily Watson, Stellan Skarsgard, Katrin Cartlidge, Jean-Marc Barr, Adrian Rawlins, Sandra Voe (Zentropa/La Sept)

This emotionally draining new film is a complete change of pace for Danish wunderkind Lars Von Trier, whose previous work includes the florid thriller *Element of the Crime*, the brooding exploration of fascism *Zentropa* and the comically quirky hospital satire *The Kingdom*. None of these will prepare audiences for *Breaking the Waves*, a soaring story of love and devotion set in a remote, backward coastal village in north Scotland in the '70s, and which deals with such weighty subjects as faith, sacrifice and miracles. A sock performance from newcomer Emily Watson is the centerpiece of this distended spiritual journey.

Pic centers on Bess (Watson), a shy, religious girl who's lived all her life in an austere community. Bess is to marry Jan (Stellan Skarsgard), a raffish adventurer who works on a North Sea oil rig. When Jan is injured in an accident on the rig, he's confined to a hospital bed and begs Bess to entertain him by having sex with other men and telling him about her experiences.

Gradually, as her behavior becomes known, she's ostracized by the little community, including her troubled mother (Sandra Voe). The last section of the film, which is filled with savage irony, rewards the viewer's patience with its power, and few will be unmoved by the finale (pic ends with a truly memorable image).

The film wonderfully captures the atmosphere of the remote village where time seems to have stood still and a deeply conservative group of churchmen make the inflexible rules.

Watson is a major find as Bess. Graced with delicate, expressive features, she gives an extraordinary performance, never descending into conventional "mad" scenes. Skarsgard is fine as Jan and lends welcome nuance to a character he has to play mostly on his back.

1996: NOMINATIONS: Best Actress (Emily Watson)

•

BREAKOUT
1975, 96 mins, US Ⓥ ⦿ ▭ col
Dir Tom Gries ***Prod*** Robert Chartoff, Irwin Winkler ***Scr*** Howard B. Kreitsek, Marc Norman, Elliott Baker ***Ph*** Lucien Ballard ***Ed*** Bud Isaacs ***Mus*** Jerry Goldsmith ***Art*** Alfred Sweeney, Jr.
Act Charles Bronson, Robert Duvall, Jill Ireland, John Huston, Randy Quaid, Sheree North (Persky-Bright/Vista)

Breakout is a cheap exploitation pic with Charles Bronson as a carefree aviator who rescues Robert Duvall from the Mexican prison frameup engineered by his father-in-law, John Huston. Jill Ireland, Duvall's wife, wants him back badly.

The spitball plot [from the novel *The Second Jailbreak* by Warren Hinckle, William Turner and Eliot Asinof] is the sort of thing Columbia made before Frank Capra. Director Tom Gries and the entire cast perform as though they all had better things to do.

•

BREATHLESS
SEE: A BOUT DE SOUFFLE

•

BREATHLESS
1983, 100 mins, US Ⓥ ⦿ col
Dir Jim McBride ***Prod*** Martin Erlichman ***Scr*** L. M. Kit Carson, Jim McBride ***Ph*** Richard H. Kline ***Ed*** Robert Estrin ***Mus*** Jack Nitzsche ***Art*** Richard Sylbert
Act Richard Gere, Valerie Kaprisky, Art Metrano, John P. Ryan, William Tepper, Robert Dunn (Orion/Miko)

More than a little guts was required to remake such a certified film classic as Jean-Luc Godard's *Breathless*, and the generation of film critics that had their lives changed by the 1959 film will easily be able to argue on behalf of the artistic superiority of the original. But the comparison remains virtually irrelevant to youthful audiences, who should find this update a suitably jazzy, sexy, entertainment.

On his way back from Las Vegas in a stolen car, Richard Gere accidentally mortally wounds a cop, then heads for the L.A. apartment of French UCLA student Valerie Kaprisky, with whom he's had just a brief fling but whom he is also convinced he loves.

A real romantic who dreams of escaping down to Mexico with his inamorata, Gere behaves as if he's oblivious to the heat closing in on him after the cop dies.

Gere's status as a sex star is certainly reaffirmed here, and not only does he appear with his shirt off through much of the pic, but he does some full-frontal scenes. Fresh and attractive, Kaprisky also does numerous scenes semi-clad or less.

•

BREED APART, A
1984, 101 mins, US Ⓥ col
Dir Philippe Mora ***Prod*** John Daly, Derek Gibson ***Scr*** Paul Wheeler ***Ph*** Geoffrey Stephenson ***Ed*** Chris Lebenzon ***Mus*** Maurice Gibb ***Art*** Bill Barclay
Act Rutger Hauer, Powers Boothe, Kathleen Turner, Donald Pleasence, John Dennis Johnston, Brion James (Hemdale/Sagittarius)

The visual splendors of North Carolina deserve top billing in *A Breed Apart*. The tale of romance and chicanery in the backwoods simply lacks reason, dramatic tension or emotional involvement.

The core of the story centers on an obsessive bird egg collector's passion to secure specimens of a newly discovered breed of bald eagle. As the bird is protected by law, he has to hire a noted climber (Powers Boothe) to illegally pilfer the shells. However, apart from the physical danger of reaching their lofty peak, he must contend with their protector, a reclusive mystery man (Rutger Hauer) who inhabits a secluded island.

Also figuring into the story is the unstated emotional bond between Hauer and the storekeeper, played by Kathleen Turner, and her son who worships his independent ways.

•

BREEZY
1973, 106 mins, US col
Dir Clint Eastwood ***Prod*** Robert Daley ***Scr*** Jo Heims ***Ph*** Frank Stanley ***Ed*** Ferris Webster ***Mus*** Michel Legrand ***Art*** Alexander Golitzen
Act William Holden, Kay Lenz, Roger C. Carmel, Marj Dusay, Joan Hotchkis, Jamie Smith Jackson (Malpaso/Universal)

Clint Eastwood's third directorial effort is an okay contemporary drama about middle-aged William Holden falling for teenage Kay Lenz. Associate producer Jo Heims's script works the problem over with perhaps too much ironic, wry or broad humor for solid impact.

Story has divorced Holden, embittered at women (sequence with Joan Hotchkis is a dramatic highlight), falling for Lenz, a persistent overly precocious teenage drifter in the Hollywood Hills. Roger C. Carmel and wife Shelley Morrison provide sounding boards for Holden's misgivings, before and after Holden begins having sex with Lenz.

The script doesn't help Eastwood out: too much laugh/smile/chuckle sitcom patter and situation make the film more like a TV feature than a gripping and certainly relevant sudser.

•

BREWSTER MCCLOUD
1970, 104 mins, US Ⓥ ▭ col
Dir Robert Altman ***Prod*** Lou Alder ***Scr*** Doran William Cannon ***Ph*** Lamar Boren, Jordan Cronenweth ***Ed*** Louis Lombardo ***Mus*** Gene Page ***Art*** George W. Davis, Preston Ames
Act Bud Cort, Sally Kellerman, Michael Murphy, William Windom, Shelley Duvall, Rene Auberjonois (M-G-M/Lion's Gate)

Brewster McCloud spares practically nothing in contemporary society. Literate original screenplay is a sardonic fairy tale for the times, extremely well cast and directed.

Bud Cort heads the cast as a young boy, hiding in the depths of Houston's mammoth Astrodome where he is building wings. He is, or is not, in reality a bird in human form.

His guardian angel is Sally Kellerman, always in the right spot to foil some nefarious person about to take advantage of Cort. Trouble is, her protection involves a series of unexplained murders.

Michael Murphy is the sleuth brought in from Frisco to help oldfashioned gumshoe G. Wood.

Kellerman, gets sensational results from her part. She can project more ladylike sensuality and emotion in a look than most actresses can in an hour.

•

BREWSTER'S MILLIONS
1945, 79 mins, US Ⓥ b/w
Dir Allan Dwan ***Prod*** Edward Small ***Scr*** Siegfried Herzig, Charles Rogers, Wilkie Mahoney ***Ph*** Charles Lawton ***Ed*** Grant Whytock, Richard Heermance ***Mus*** Hugo Friedhofer ***Art*** Joseph Sternad
Act Dennis O'Keefe, Helen Walker, Eddie "Rochester" Anderson, June Havoc, Gail Patrick, Mischa Auer (Small/United Artists)

Play [by Winchell Smith and Byron Ongley based on the novel by George Barr McCutcheon], first produced in 1907, remains somewhat dated despite efforts to refurbish background in this screen adaptation through introduction of wartime atmosphere.

The young, handsome soldier returns home to a swell girl waiting to marry him. He finds he's inherited 8 million bucks. Now here's the problem—he's got to spend $1 million in two months, or lose the entire estate. Even with the help of a flop musical, a bankrupt banker, the stock market, the racetrack and a spending society gal he has trouble. *Millions* is a broad farce, of course, and gets over as such.

1945: NOMINATION: Best Scoring of a Dramatic Picture

•

BREWSTER'S MILLIONS
1985, 97 mins, US Ⓥ ⦿ col
Dir Walter Hill ***Prod*** Lawrence Gordon, Joel Silver ***Scr*** Herschel Weingrod, Timothy Harris ***Ph*** Ric Waite ***Ed*** Freeman Davies, Michel Ripps ***Mus*** Ry Cooder ***Art*** John Vallone
Act Richard Pryor, John Candy, Lonette McKee, Stephen Collins, Jerry Orbach, Pat Hingle (Universal)

It's hard to believe a comedy starring Richard Pryor and John Candy is not funnier than this one is, but director Walter Hill has overwhelmed the intricate genius of each with constant background action, crowd confusions and other endless distractions.

All the frenetic motion, unfortunately, never disguises the fact that the writers haven't done much of distinction with the familiar story [a 1902 novel by George Barr McCutcheon] that has been produced in many forms, dating back to a 1906 stage version. [Previous film versions were in 1914, 1921, 1935, 1945 and 1961.]

In one incarnation or another, the yarn always involves somebody who stands to inherit a huge fortune, but first must squander a small one over a short time. In order to enjoy the fantasy, the audience must be given good reason to root for the hero.

Though Pryor plays it likeably enough, he never seems particularly deserving of the fun, excitement and brief luxury he falls into in having to spend $30 million in 30 days, much less the $300 million inheritance he stands to receive if he succeeds.

•

BRIDE, THE
1985, 118 mins, US Ⓥ ⦿ col
Dir Franc Roddam ***Prod*** Victor Drai ***Scr*** Lloyd Fonvielle ***Ph*** Stephen H. Burum ***Ed*** Michael Ellis ***Mus*** Maurice Jarre ***Art*** Michael Seymour
Act Sting, Jennifer Beals, Anthony Higgins, Clancy Brown, David Rappaport, Geraldine Page (Columbia-Delphi III/Colgems)

Production departs from the host of other *Frankensteins* in its bright visual look, its lush Maurice Jarre score, its view of women, its younger characters, and its romantic scope.

Pic opens with a jolting laboratory sequence, when Sting as Baron Frankenstein brings to life the gauze-wrapped Jennifer Beals as the doctor's original monster creation looks on with frothing agitation. The ensuing fairy tale aura of the story is merely leisurely rather than enthralling. In opting to tone down the horror aspect of the genre, producer Victor Drai and his team have created another kind of monster: A *Frankenstein* movie that's not scary. The result culminates in silliness when the bride and her hulking mate-to-be (wonderfully played by Clancy Brown) collapse in each other's arms at the top of the baron's castle.

While there is deliberate humor at times, most of it successfully produced by a lilting dwarf character who steals the movie (David Rappaport), the intention of the filmmakers is not camp. That's both the pic's virtue and, at the conclusion, its downfall.

Screenwriter Lloyd Fonvielle (who collaborated with director Franc Roddam on *The Lords of Discipline*) weaves, in concept, a nice balancing act between the monster and the dwarf. Increasingly, this odd couple attracts interest while momentum flags in the Sting-Beals relationship. Lensing, largely in southern France, is a strong production value.

●

BRIDE CAME C.O.D., THE

1941, 94 mins, US Ⓥ b/w

Dir William Keighley ***Prod*** Hal B. Wallis (exec.) ***Scr*** Julius J. Epstein, Philip G. Epstein ***Ph*** Ernest Haller ***Ed*** Thomas Richards ***Mus*** Max Steiner ***Art*** Ted Smith

Act James Cagney, Bette Davis, Stuart Erwin, Jack Carson, Eugene Pallette, George Tobias (Warner)

Bette Davis is teamed with James Cagney in a broad farce that combines spontaneous gaiety and infectious humor. It's a hefty package of laugh entertainment [from the story by Kenneth Earl and M. M. Musselman]. In handing Davis a comedy assignment, Warners go all out in also making her the victim of continual physical and mental violence. She's dirtied up in a mine; acquires three doses of cacti needles in periodic falls; and even exposes her posterior as target for well-directed shots from Cagney's improvised slingshot.

Cagney is the owner of a plane about to be repossessed by the finance company. Davis is an oil heiress about to marry orchestra leader Jack Carson. Radio gossiper Stuart Erwin prevails on the pair to elope via plane to Las Vegas—and naturally Cagney's ship is chartered. Cagney grooves in a familiar role as the aggressive and two-fisted battler—manhandling the girl periodically for maximum results. Davis clicks strongly as the oil heiress, displaying a flair for comedy.

●

BRIDE COMES HOME, THE

1935, 83 mins, US b/w

Dir Wesley Ruggles ***Prod*** Wesley Ruggles ***Scr*** Claude Binyon ***Ph*** Leo Tover ***Art*** Hans Dreier, Roberet Usher

Act Claudette Colbert, Fred MacMurray, Robert Young, William Collier, Sr., Donald Meek, James Colin (Paramount)

Another galloping lithograph of the boy-and-girl-always-fighting woodblock [from a story by Elizabeth Sanxay Holding]. *It Happened One Night* (1934) is the spiritual pappy of this type of entertainment. Preaching the philosophy that a good fight (between the sexes) never hurt anybody and that a strong masculine ego is the proper consort for a snippy female ditto, *The Bride Comes Home* runs Claudette Colbert and Fred MacMurray over a not-too-serious steeplechase of minor frictions and clashes. To supply the missing apex of the triangle is Robert Young, a frankly unaggressive but beaming son of $3 million. He is almost too charming for the best interests of the story.

It's a made-to-measure framework for Colbert, presenting her in the always-attractive position of a young lady beset by two lovers, both fascinating and both collapsible at her slightest whim. Several bit parts are played for maximum values. Notably Edgar Kennedy and William Collier, Sr.

●

BRIDE FOR SALE

1949, 87 mins, US b/w

Dir William D. Russell ***Prod*** Jack H. Skirball ***Scr*** Bruce Manning, Islin Auster ***Ph*** Joseph Valentine ***Ed*** Frederic Knudtson ***Mus*** Frederick Hollander

Act Claudette Colbert, Robert Young, George Brent, Max Baer, Gus Schilling (RKO/Crest)

Bride for Sale is a lot of escapist nonsense that manages to be generally amusing, and sometimes hilariously so. Screwball angles are played up for laughs, the pacing is good and the playing enjoyable, making it entirely acceptable for light entertainment.

Kingpinning the slapstick are Claudette Colbert, Robert Young and George Brent. Colbert does glib work as a tax expert for the accounting firm conducted by Brent. She figures to find the perfect husband, with suitable bankroll, by casing the returns the firm makes out. Brent wants to keep her on the job so enlists aid of Young to make like an eligible male, and woo the maiden.

On that basis of fun, William D. Russell's direction marches the plot and the players along a broad path of antics.

●

BRIDE OF FRANKENSTEIN

1935, 73 mins, US Ⓥ ⊙ b/w

Dir James Whale ***Prod*** Carl Laemmle, Jr. ***Scr*** William Hurlbut ***Ph*** John Mescall ***Ed*** Ted Kent ***Mus*** Franz Waxman ***Art*** Charles D. Hall

Act Boris Karloff, Colin Clive, Valerie Hobson, Ernest Thesiger, Elsa Lanchester, O. P. Heggie (Universal)

In the previous Frankenstein film's finale the monster was burned in a huge fire. Here it's started off with the same fire scene, except that in a few moments he is revealed to have bored through the earth to a subterranean stream, which saved him from death. From there on, of course, it's a romp [from a story by William Hurlnut and John Balderston, "suggested" by Mary Shelley's novel].

Perhaps a bit too much time is taken up by the monster and too little by the woman created to be his bride. Frankenstein, the monster's creator, is this time sorry and tries to crawl out but Dr. Pretorious forces him to go into more life manufacturing, having conceived the idea of a woman to act as the monster's playmate. The woman is finally evolved, but she's just as horrified at him as everyone else.

Karloff manages to invest the character with some subtleties of emotion that are surprisingly real and touching. Especially is this true in the scene where he meets a blind man who, not knowing that he's talking to a monster, makes a friend of him.

Runner-up position from an acting standpoint goes to Ernest Thesiger as Dr. Pretorious, a diabolic characterization if ever there was one. Elsa Lanchester handles two assignments, being first in a preamble as author Mary Shelley and then the created woman. In latter assignment she impresses quite highly, although in both spots she has very little to do.

1935: NOMINATION: Best Sound

●

BRIDE OF RE-ANIMATOR

1991, 97 mins, US Ⓥ ⊙ col

Dir Brian Yuzna ***Prod*** Brian Yuzna ***Scr*** Woody Keith, Rick Fry ***Ph*** Rick Fichter ***Ed*** Peter Teschner ***Mus*** Richard Band ***Art*** Philip J. C. Duffin

Act Jeffrey Combs, Bruce Abbott, Claude Earl Jones, Fabiana Udenio, David Gale, Kathleen Kinmont (Wildstreet)

Fans of Stuart Gordon's 1985 *Re-Animator* will probably dig this campy gorefest sequel directed by the original's producer, Brian Yuzna. Jeffrey Combs returns in top form as H. P. Lovecraft's dotty scientist Herbert West, this time [in a story by Yuzna, Woody Keith and Rick Fry] intent on joining the trendy club of would-be Dr. Frankensteins creating a female monster (a la *Frankenhooker*, *Steel & Lace*, *Eve of Destruction*). Reluctantly assisting Combs again is fellow doctor Bruce Abbott, whose beautiful new Italian girlfriend Fabiana Udenio can't shake his grieving attachment to his true love Megan, who was killed in the first film. When Combs tells him that he's going to build his femme creation around Megan's preserved heart, Abbott joins the grisly experiment.

The over-the-top acting that Gordon encouraged in *Re-Animator* is continued here with Combs particularly adept at the darkly comic throwaway line. Overabundance of gore (an even more explicit unrated version will be made available in vidstores) will turn off mainstream viewers, however. Tall actress Kathleen Kinmont is a good choice for the monster, with her stitched together, see-through torso.

●

BRIDE OF VENGEANCE

1949, 92 mins, US b/w

Dir Mitchell Leisen ***Prod*** Richard Maibaum ***Scr*** Cyril Hume, Michael Hogan ***Ph*** Daniel L. Fapp ***Ed*** Alma Macrorie ***Mus*** Hugo Friedhofer

Act Paulette Goddard, John Lund, Macdonald Carey, Raymond Burr (Paramount)

The poisonous Borgias, who introduced the lethal mickey finn to early-day Italy, provide the highly romantic adventure basis for *Bride of Vengeance*.

It's escapist material, done with a lightness that doesn't always fit its adventuring, but with enough swagger to back up the story. It has familiar ingredients of this type of adventure costumer, and there's not much ingenuity in the way it has been filmed.

Title derives from Borgia role played by Paulette Goddard, who marries John Lund, head of an Italian state, to avenge the death of an earlier husband, whom she believes Lund had killed. Mixed in with that is a state plot by her Borgia brother to control all of Italy, including Lund's lands, and latter's efforts to cast a cannon. Plot has plenty of bloodthirsty moments.

●

BRIDE WORE BOOTS, THE

1946, 85 mins, US b/w

Dir Irving Pichel ***Prod*** Seton I. Miller ***Scr*** Dwight Mitchell Wiley ***Ph*** Stuart Thompson ***Ed*** Ellsworth Hoagland ***Mus*** Frederick Hollander ***Art*** Hans Dreier, John Meehan

Act Barbara Stanwyck, Robert Cummings, Diana Lynn, Patric Knowles, Robert Benchley, Natalie Wood (Paramount)

The Bride Wore Boots is never as funny as its makers intended. It is only in the final 10 minutes or so when the story casts off all restraint and goes slapstick with a vengeance that comedy rates a genuinely hearty response.

Barbara Stanwyck and Robert Cummings are seen as married couple with divided interests. Stanwyck loves horses, in fact operates a breeding farm. Cummings is an author and hates horses. The wife hates the stuffy Civil War relics wished off on her husband by adoring Confederate Dames societies.

Star trio, which has Diana Lynn as a young southern vamp, make frantic efforts to put the material over, but often fail. Patric Knowles has a thankless spot as near-rival for Stanwyck's attention. Peggy Wood and Robert Benchley team for more adult chuckles and Willie Best is good as Cummings's handy-man. Natalie Wood and Gregory Muradian are seen as the obnoxious offspring of the married couple.

●

BRIDGE AT REMAGEN, THE

1969, 116 mins, US Ⓥ ⊙ ⌑ col

Dir John Guillermin ***Prod*** David L. Wolper ***Scr*** Richard Yates, William Roberts ***Ph*** Stanley Cortez ***Ed*** William Cartwright ***Mus*** Elmer Bernstein ***Art*** Alfred Sweeney

Act George Segal, Robert Vaughn, Ben Gazzara, Bradford Dillman, E. G. Marshall, Peter Van Eyck (United Artists)

The taking of a bridge provides the basis for an actionful World War II melodrama. This time out it's the Ludendorff Bridge over the Rhine in the Remagen area, scene of desperate fighting for its control by both American and German forces.

Certain confusion in plot content exists, as it never appears overly clear the exact purpose of American and Nazi military thinking. Against this background chief interest rests in the performance of George Segal, a hardboiled American platoon leader, as he and his men attempt to accomplish the orders of their high command.

Director John Guillermin succeeds in realistic movement as he attempts to overcome deficiencies of script and generally manages strong characterizations from his cast.

●

BRIDGE ON THE RIVER KWAI, THE

1957, 161 mins, UK Ⓥ ⊙ ⌑ col

Dir David Lean ***Prod*** Sam Spiegel ***Scr*** Pierre Boulle [Carl Foreman, Michael Wilson, Calder Willingham] ***Ph*** Jack Hildyard ***Ed*** Peter Taylor ***Mus*** Malcolm Arnold ***Art*** Donald M. Ashton

Act William Holden, Alec Guinness, Jack Hawkins, Sessue Hayakawa, Geoffrey Horne, James Donald (Horizon)

The Bridge on the River Kwai is a gripping drama, expertly put together and handled with skill in all departments. From a technical standpoint, it reflects the care and competence that went into the $3 million-plus venture, filmed against the exotic background of the steaming jungles and mountains of Ceylon [repping Burma]. A story of the futility of war in general [adapted, uncredited, by Carl Foreman, Michael Wilson and Calder Willingham from the novel by Pierre Boulle], the underlying message is never permitted to impede.

Story is "masculine." It's about three men, William Holden, Alec Guinness and Sessue Hayakawa. Latter is the commandant of a Japanese prison camp in which Holden, a Yank sailor posing as a commander, is a prisoner. Guinness is a British colonel who commands a new group of prisoners. He's a strict rules-of-war man who clashes immediately with Hayakawa over the latter's insistence that officers as well as men must work on the railroad bridge being built over the River Kwai.

Guinness wins and then proceeds to guide his men in building a superb bridge to prove the mettle of British soldiers under any conditions. Holden, meanwhile, escapes to safety but is talked into leading Jack Hawkins and British commandos back to the bridge to blow it up.

There are notable performances from the key characters, but the film is unquestionably Guinness's. He etches an unforgettable portrait of the typical British army officer, strict, didactic and serene in his adherence to the book. It's a performance of tremendous power and dignity. Hayakawa, once a star in American silents and long absent from the screen, also is solidly impressive as the Japanese officer, limning him as an admixture of cruelty and correctness.

[In 1992 a letterboxed video reissue of the film featured a revised script credit, to Michael Wilson and Carl Foreman.]

1957: Best Picture, Director, Actor (Alec Guinness), Adapted Screenplay, Cinematography, Score, Editing

NOMINATION: Best Supp. Actor (Sessue Hayakawa)

•

BRIDGES AT TOKO-RI, THE

1955, 102 mins, US Ⓥ ⦿ col

Dir Mark Robson ***Prod*** William Perlberg, George Seaton ***Scr*** Valentine Davies ***Ph*** Loyal Griggs ***Ed*** Alma Macrorie ***Mus*** Lyn Murray ***Art*** Hal Pereira, Henry Bumstead

Act William Holden, Grace Kelly, Fredric March, Mickey Rooney, Robert Strauss, Charles McGraw (Paramount)

James A. Michener's hard-hitting novel of the Korean conflict finds slick translation in this topflight war spectacle.

In taking advantage of the navy's resources, aboard an aircraft carrier off the coast of Korea and through the use of planes and equipment, Mark Robson in his taut direction catches the spirit of the navy and what it stood for in the Korean War, never losing sight, however, of the personalized story of a Navy combat flier.

Narrative drives toward the climactic bombing by US fliers of the five bridges at Toko-Ri, which span a strategic pass in Korea's interior. Here the story of William Holden, a reserve officer recalled to service, unfolds. A fine flier, he is taken under the wing of the admiral, played by Frederic March, who understands his gripe of having been forced to leave his wife and children to return to the Navy.

Practically every principal performance is a standout. Holden lends conviction to his character, and March delivers a sock portrayal of the admiral, who is drawn to Holden beause he reminds him of his two sons lost in war. As Holden's wife who brings their two daughters to Tokyo so they may be near the flier, Grace Kelly is warmly sympathetic.

1955: Best Special Effects

NOMINATION: Best Editing

•

BRIDGES OF MADISON COUNTY, THE

1995, 135 mins, US Ⓥ ⦿ col

Dir Clint Eastwood ***Prod*** Clint Eastwood, Kathleen Kennedy ***Scr*** Richard LaGravenese ***Ph*** Jack N. Green ***Ed*** Joel Cox ***Mus*** Lennie Niehaus ***Art*** Jeannine Oppewall

Act Clint Eastwood, Meryl Streep, Annie Corley, Victor Slezak, Jim Haynie (Amblin/Malpaso/Warner)

Clint Eastwood and Co. have performed a considerable job of alchemy on *The Bridges of Madison County* turning Robert James Waller's slender, treacly romance into a handsomely crafted, beautifully acted adult love story. Readers of the book will find the sexual heat reduced, along with the author's most egregiously sentimental excesses, while longtime Clint Eastwood fans may have divided reactions to seeing their hero in his most touchy-feely role to date.

The story, which even at 171 book pages felt heavily padded, could scarcely be simpler. Photographer Robert Kincaid, on assignment in Madison County in 1965, stops at the farmhouse of Francesca Johnson (Meryl Streep), whose husband and two teenage kids are out of town, to ask directions to the area's photogenic covered bridges, and the two embark on a four-day fling that deeply marks both of them for the rest of their lives.

In contrast to the novel's chaotic structural devices, Richard LaGravenese has smartly framed the story around the confessional narrative of the affair left for Francesca's children to read after her death.

Project is well known for having gone through several writers and proposed directors, including Steven Spielberg, Sydney Pollack and Bruce Beresford, and one can only feel that it finally landed in the right hands.

All the choices made by LaGravenese represent improvements on the original text: the amplification of Francesca's children provides helpful echoes to the main drama; the addition of another adulteress in the small town of Winterset creates a parallel, and more tragic, alternative to Francesca.

It's Douglas Sirk-type women's weepie material, handled by Eastwood with the utmost tact, maturity and restraint. The attention to detail, in both character and rural atmosphere, is superb. Onscreen together a great majority of the time, the two leads come up aces.

NOMINATION: Best Actress (Meryl Streep)

•

BRIDGE TOO FAR, A

1977, 175 mins, UK Ⓥ ⦿ ▭ col

Dir Richard Attenborough ***Prod*** Joseph E. Levine, Richard P. Levine ***Scr*** William Goldman ***Ph*** Geoffrey Unsworth ***Ed*** Anthony Gibbs ***Mus*** John Addison ***Art*** Terry Marsh

Act Dirk Bogarde, James Caan, Michael Caine, Sean Connery, Edward Fox, Elliott Gould (United Artists)

Futility and frustration are the overriding emotional elements in *A Bridge Too Far*, Joseph E. Levine's sprawling Second World War production [from the novel by Cornelius Ryan] about a 1944 military operation botched by both Allied and German troops.

Film opens with some vintage black and white newsreel footage in original frame ratio, setting up the falls. 1944, attempt to expedite the end of the Second World War by an enormous paratroop operation involving a series of bridges leading to Germany. The first part of the film introduces senior officers Dirk Bogarde, Sean Connery, Gene Hackman, Michael Caine, Anthony Hopkins and Edward Fox as the plans are outlined.

Later, as operations begin, periodic appearances are made by cocky Robert Redford, wise-cracking Elliott Gould, stolid Ryan O'Neal and James Caan. On the other side of hostilities, Hardy Kruger, Maximilian Schell and Wolfgang Priess represent different levels of German military thinking about, and reaction to, the offbeat Allied strategy. In the middle Laurence Olivier and Liv Ullmann are two Dutch residents who attend to the wounded.

•

BRIEF ENCOUNTER

1945, 83 mins, UK Ⓥ b/w

Dir David Lean ***Prod*** Noel Coward ***Scr*** Noel Coward, David Lean, Ronald Neame ***Ph*** Robert Krasker ***Ed*** Jack Harris, Margery Saunders ***Mus*** Muir Mathieson (dir.) ***Art*** L. P. Williams

Act Celia Johnson, Trevor Howard, Stanley Holloway, Joyce Carey, Cyril Raymond, Valentine Dyall (Cineguild)

Based on his playlet, *Still Life from Tonight at 8:30*, *Brief Encounter* does more for Noel Coward's reputation as a skilled film producer than *In Which We Serve*. His use of express trains thundering through a village station coupled with frantic, last-minute dashes for local trains is only one of the clever touches masking the inherent static quality of the drama.

Celia Johnson as the small-town mother whose brief encounter with a doctor, encumbered with a wife and kids, plunges her into a love affair from which she struggles vainly to escape, is terrific. Co-starred with her, Trevor Howard, as the doctor, gives a performance calculated to win the sympathy of femmes of all ages. As for the dumb husband whose idea of marital happiness is summed up in his parrot-like iteration, "Have it your own way, my dear," Cyril Raymond manages to invest the stodgy character with a lovable quality.

1946: NOMINATIONS: Best Director, Actress (Celia Johnson), Screenplay

•

BRIGADOON

1954, 108 mins, US Ⓥ ⦿ ▭ col

Dir Vincente Minnelli ***Prod*** Arthur Freed ***Scr*** Alan Jay Lerner ***Ph*** Joseph Ruttenberg ***Ed*** Albert Akst ***Mus*** Johnny Green (dir.) ***Art*** Cedric Gibbons, Preston Ames

Act Gene Kelly, Van Johnson, Cyd Charisse, Elaine Stewart, Barry Jones, Hugh Laing (M-G-M)

In transferring *Brigadoon*, a click as a [1947] Broadway musical play, to the screen, Metro has medium success. It's a fairly entertaining tunefilm of mixed appeal.

Among the more noteworthy points are the score, as directed by Johnny Green, and the stage-type settings that represent the plot's Highland locale. The latter are striking, even though they are the major contribution to the feeling that this is a filmed stage show, rather than a motion picture musical.

Less noteworthy is the choreography by Gene Kelly, who also plays the lead male role, and his singing of the Alan Jay Lerner-Frederick Loewe songs.

The Lerner musical play tells of two New Yorkers who become lost while hunting in Scotland and happen on Brigadoon on the one day that it is visible every 100 years. Besides, a wedding is to take place and Kelly and Van Johnson, the modern-day males, join in the fun. Particularly Kelly, who falls for Cyd Charisse hard enough to be willing to join his sweetheart in the long ago.

1954: NOMINATIONS: Best Color Costume Design, Color Art Direction, Sound

•

BRIGHAM YOUNG

1940, 112 mins, US b/w

Dir Henry Hathaway ***Prod*** Kenneth Macgowan ***Scr*** Lamar Trotti ***Ph*** Arthur Miller ***Ed*** Robert Bischoff ***Mus*** Alfred Newman ***Art*** William Darling, Maurice Ransford

Act Tyrone Power, Linda Darnell, Dean Jagger, Brian Donlevy, Jane Darwell, John Carradine (20th Century-Fox)

Taking the favorable factual aspects of the trek of Mormons to the west, and combining them with well-concocted fictional ingredients, picture emerges as an epic filmization of early American history.

There's dramatic power in the persecution of the Mormons in their settlement at Nauvoo, Illinois; the conviction and murder of Joseph Smith; and the resultant decision of Brigham Young to lead his flock across the plains to their eventual home on the shores of Salt Lake. Adversity hits the entourage at every turn, but, despite recalcitrants in the ranks, Young commands attention with a most dominating personality which is most vividly depicted.

Through it all runs a minor romance between Tyrone Power and Linda Darnell; and a more important impress of man and wife on the parts of Young (Dean Jagger) and his first and favorite spouse, Mary Ann (Mary Astor). Latter is decidedly sympathetic and carries prominent appeal as standing solidly behind the leader through adversity.

Jagger brings to the character of the Mormon leader a personable humaneness and sympathy. Astor turns in one of the finest performances of her career. Power and Darnell are overshadowed by the above twain.

•

BRIGHT ANGEL

1990, 94 mins, US Ⓥ col

Dir Michael Fields ***Prod*** Paige Simpson, Robert MacLean ***Scr*** Richard Ford ***Ph*** Elliott Davis ***Ed*** Melody London, Clement Barclay ***Mus*** Christopher Young ***Art*** Marcia Hinds Johnson

Act Dermot Mulroney, Lili Taylor, Sam Shepard, Valerie Perrine, Sheila McCarthy, Burt Young (Hemdale-Northwood/Bright Angel)

Bright Angel is one of those films that breathe freshness and life into familiar genres. Basically a road movie about a pair of young lovers who become involved in crime, Michael Fields's first feature as a director boasts a full cast-list of near-perfect performances. The intelligent and spare screenplay is by Richard Ford, who based it on two of his short stories [*Children* and *Great Falls*].

The setting is Montana, "where the Great Plains begin." George Russell (Dermot Mulroney), 18, lives with his parents (Sam Shepard and Valerie Perrine) who separate violently when his father finds his mother with another man. George is attracted to Lucy (Lili Taylor), who has spent an afternoon in a motel with the father of his best friend, an Indian. She needs to get to the Wyoming town where her brother's in prison, and George offers to drive her.

Much of the film is taken up with the relationship between the naive and good-hearted George and the old-beyond-her-years Lucy as they journey to their destination, and with the characters they become involved with. Fields and Ford deal with a familiar genre here, but they avoid cliches: no sex scenes (but a great deal of sexual tension); no shoot-outs (but an agonizing sequence of suspense); no neat ending.

•

BRIGHT LIGHTS, BIG CITY

1988, 110 mins, US Ⓥ ⦿ col

Dir James Bridges ***Prod*** Mark Rosenberg, Sydney Pollack ***Scr*** Jay McInerney ***Ph*** Gordon Willis ***Ed*** John Bloom, George Berndt ***Mus*** Donald Fagen, Rob Mounsey ***Art*** Santo Loquasto

Act Michael J. Fox, Kiefer Sutherland, Phoebe Cates, Swoosie Kurtz, Frances Sternhagen, Tracy Pollan (United Artists/Mirage)

This novel-cum-feature film (from Jay McInerney's book) is a distinctly morose and maudlin journey through one man's destructive period of personal loss.

Opening scene establishes Michael J. Fox as a lonesome barfly with a cocaine habit in the Big Apple. First reason given is that his wife (Phoebe Cates) has dumped him to pursue modeling in Paris. It's later learned that he's also grieving over the death of his mother (Dianne Wiest) a year earlier.

Fox is cast here as Jamie, a would-be writer marking time as a fact checker for literary giant *Gotham* magazine. Jamie quickly slides so badly that he's fired during a scene with editorial chief, Frances Sternhagen—an exchange that points up the benefit of placing the youthful Fox in situations with seasoned veterans.

Jason Robards's appearance as a drunken fiction writer is all too familiar and a brief encounter with the fascinating William Hickey and a pittance of time with Wiest round out these cameos.

•

BRIGHTON BEACH MEMOIRS
1986, 108 mins, US Ⓥ ⦿ col
Dir Gene Saks ***Prod*** Ray Stark ***Scr*** Neil Simon ***Ph*** John Bailey ***Ed*** Carol Littleton ***Mus*** Michael Small ***Art*** Stuart Wurtzel
Act Blythe Danner, Bob Dishy, Brian Dillinger, Stacey Glick, Judith Ivey, Lisa Waltz (Rastar)

The first of Neil Simon's semi-autobiographical trilogy, *Brighton Beach* bowed in Los Angeles in late 1982 and opened in New York in March 1983. Set in 1937 in a lower-middle class section of Brooklyn, story details assorted life crises of members of the Jerome family, hard-working moral Jews whose problems are all taken to heart by Mama Kate, played by Blythe Danner.

Despite the assurance of verbal reprisals, all family members are expected to speak their minds and share their difficulties (there can be no secrets anyway, since nothing can escape Mama's notice). Emotions are fully felt, responsibilities accepted and decisions taken, not avoided. Performances are skilled all the way through.

•

BRIGHTON ROCK
(US: YOUNG SCARFACE)
1948, 92 mins, UK Ⓥ b/w
Dir John Boulting ***Prod*** Roy Boulting ***Scr*** Graham Greene, Terence Rattigan ***Ph*** Harry Waxman ***Ed*** Peter Graham Scott ***Mus*** Hans May ***Art*** John Howell
Act Richard Attenborough, Hermione Baddeley, William Hartnell, Carol Marsh, Harcourt Williams, Nigel Stock (Boulting Brothers)

British producers are competing with each other in rushing mobster yarns to the screen. This tends to prove that Britain can turn out a gangster picture as brutal as any Hollywood had devised.

With Graham Greene and Terence Rattigan responsible for the screenplay [based on Greene's own novel], something more exciting might reasonably have been expected. Some of blame goes to director John Boulting whose tempo is much too leisurely for this type of picture.

Story is laid in pre-war seaside resort Brighton, where two razor-slashing race gangs are feuding.

It is difficult to believe that any gang which included William Hartnell could be led by Richard Attenborough. Hartnell is so much more the gangster type than Attenborough that it is obvious that an exchange of parts would have made the film more credible.

Acting honors are collared by that seasoned actress, Hermione Baddeley. She steals every scene in which she appears, making Ida, the concert artist, a sympathetic character. Carol Marsh (formerly Norma Simpson) plays the waitress and gangster's wife with modesty.

•

BRIMSTONE & TREACLE
1982, 87 mins, UK Ⓥ col
Dir Richard Loncraine ***Prod*** Kenith Trodd ***Scr*** Dennis Potter ***Ph*** Peter Hannan ***Ed*** Paul Green ***Mus*** Sting ***Art*** Milly Burns
Act Sting, Denholm Elliott, Joan Plowright, Suzanna Hamilton, Benjamin Whitrow, Dudley Sutton (PFH/Namara)

Strong on ambiance and suggested terror, *Brimstone & Treacle* is a handsomely mounted gothic tale. Sting, rock singer from The Police, makes a strong impression in his first major film role.

Playing a young drifter, Martin Taylor, Sting has a running con game where he bumps into passersby and pretends to know them. His pigeon is Thomas Bates (Denholm Elliott), the owner of a company that prints inspirational cards. Sting pretends to be a friend of Elliott's crippled daughter (Suzanna Hamilton).

Elliott remains cynical but his wife (Joan Plowright) only sees his kindness and insists he stay with them overnight. Soon, he's wormed his way into the troubled household. He frees Plowright of her domestic chores, including the care of spastic daughter Hamilton. He molests Hamilton, who can only utter grunts and whines, and has his eyes on money and jewels in the house.

Director Richard Loncraine heightens the terror by closing in the action and using shadow to further darken the mood and obscure character intent. The script presents a devastating view of the middle-class English family. The performances, all excellent, are played slightly off-centre so one never knows whether the action will darken or veer into comedy.

•

BRINGING OUT THE DEAD
1999, 120 mins, US Ⓥ ⦿ ▭ col
Dir Martin Scorsese ***Prod*** Scott Rudin, Barbara De Fina ***Scr*** Paul Schrader ***Ph*** Robert Richardson ***Ed*** Thelma Schoonmaker ***Mus*** Elmer Bernstein ***Art*** Dante Ferretti
Act Nicolas Cage, Patricia Arquette, John Goodman, Ving Rhames, Tom Sizemore, Marc Anthony (Rudin/Cappa-De Fina/Paramount/Touchstone)

Martin Scorsese teams for the fourth time with scripter Paul Schrader for *Bringing Out the Dead*, based on Joe Connelly's novel. It's a quintessential New York nocturnal tale of the occupational hazards, joys and sorrows of a paramedic, splendidly played by Nicolas Cage, as he "routinely" goes about his job of saving people's lives. Dark humor, amusing moments, visual pyrotechnics and bravura acting from the entire ensemble make more palatable a movie that's intense and full of gory details.

British director Michael Powell once fondly described Scorsese as "the Goya of Tenth Avenue," a label that perfectly applies to this effort. More shapely than the book from a dramatic standpoint, the taut script is punctuated by much-needed romantic and comedic interludes that modulate what's fundamentally a hysterical yarn.

Like *Taxi Driver*'s Travis Bickle, Frank Pierce (Cage) is a man on the edge, an insomniac loner who works the graveyard shift and undergoes a severe spiritual crisis that may lead to either self-destruction or redemption.

Story is set in the early '90s, when New York's City's Emergency Medical Service was in disorder. The film follows Frank over the course of three days and three nights (56 crucial hours), as he threatens to collapse from exhaustion. Each night, Frank teams with a different partner (John Goodman, Tom Sizemore, Ving Rhames), and his distinctive interactions with each paramedic provide the film's texture.

With the exception of Arquette, who gives a merely adequate performance as a former druggie, rest of the cast is first-rate.

•

BRINGING UP BABY
1938, 102 mins, US Ⓥ ⦿ b/w
Dir Howard Hawks ***Prod*** Howard Hawks ***Scr*** Dudley Nichols, Hagar Wilde ***Ph*** Russell Metty ***Ed*** George Hively ***Mus*** Roy Webb (dir.)
Act Katharine Hepburn, Cary Grant, Charlie Ruggles, Barry Fitzgerald, May Robson, Walter Catlett (RKO)

This harum-scarum farce comedy, Katharine Hepburn's first of the type, is constructed for maximum of laughs. Opposite her is Cary Grant, who is perfectly at home as a farceur after his work in *The Awful Truth* (1937). Wacky developments [story by Hagar Wilde] include pursuit of an heiress after a zoology professor who expects to wed his femme assistant in the museum on the same day he plans to complete a giant brontosaurus; a pet leopard, "Nissa," who makes a playmate of "Asta," a redoubtable Scots terrier; a wealthy woman who may endow the prof's museum with $1 million; an escaped wild leopard from the circus; a stupid town con- stable; a forgetful ex-big game hunter; a scientifically minded brain specialist; and a tippling gardener.

Hepburn is invigorating as the madcap deb. Grant, who thinks more of recovering the priceless missing bone for his uncompleted brontosaurus than his impending wedding and the companionship of the playful heiress, performs his role to the hilt. Charlie Ruggles, as the former African game hunter, does wonders with a minor characterization brought in late in the picture.

Chief shortcoming is that too much time is consumed with the jail sequence. Prime reason for it, of course, is that it gives Hepburn a chance to imitate a gunmoll.

•

BRING IT ON
2000, 98 mins, US Ⓥ ⦿ col
Dir Peyton Reed ***Prod*** Marc Abraham, Thomas A. Bliss, John Ketcham ***Scr*** Jessica Bendinger ***Ph*** Shawn Maurer ***Ed*** Larry Bock ***Mus*** Christophe Beck ***Art*** Sharon Lomofsky
Act Kirsten Dunst, Eliza Dushku, Jesse Bradford, Gabrielle Union, Clare Kramer, Nicole Bilderback (Beacon/Universal)

Bring It On routinely tries to make heroes of cheerleaders, the most mocked of high school groups. There are hints here and there of a more devilish sense of humor in the script, in which cheerleading squads—one from the rich white San Diego 'burbs, another from poor black East Compton—battle like sports teams for the national cheerleading crown.

Sense of edginess appears before opening credits, as Torrance (Kirsten Dunst) has a Busby Berkeley–styled nightmare in which she loses her top during a goofy squad routine. It's all part of Torrance's anxiety about being selected captain of Rancho Carne High Toros cheer squad-reigning national champs.

Torrance wins the election against bitchy rivals Courtney (Clare Kramer) and Whitney (Nicole Bilderback). After a squad member breaks her leg, tepidly comic audition for a replacement leads to recruiting above-it-all but highly skilled transfer student Missy (Eliza Dushku). First big crisis occurs when Missy storms out of practice, telling Torrance that the Toros' routine is a total rip-off of one by the East Compton High Clovers, led by smart, competitive Isis (Gabrielle Union). A visit to Clovers' campus convinces Torrance that "my entire cheerleading career has been a lie!"; unable to persuade her squad to drop the routine, Torrance and Co. are humiliated at a game by Isis and her Clovers, who make a surprise appearance. Spunky Torrance pushes her team to come up with a whole new routine in two weeks before the nationals.

Pic succeeds in displaying the physical drive and demands of cheerleading. Tyro helmer Peyton Reed and editor Larry Bock miss a golden opportunity to make the turns, flips and dance steps into something kinetically thrilling, as if too much style would mar pic's rather plain-wrap look. Still, closing contest between Toros and Clovers reps a close facsimile of real thing.

In a disappointing comic turn, Dunst can't really hold pic together, showing too much thesping sweat in her efforts to make Torrance likable. Dushku leaves a strong impression, as does the charismatic Union, whom the camera loves.

•

BRING ME THE HEAD OF ALFREDO GARCIA
1974, 112 mins, US Ⓥ ⦿ col
Dir Sam Peckinpah ***Prod*** Martin Baum ***Scr*** Gordon Dawson, Sam Peckinpah ***Ph*** Alex Phillips ***Ed*** Garth Craven, Robbe Roberts, Sergio Ortega, Dennis E. Dolan ***Mus*** Jerry Fielding ***Art*** Agustin Ituarte
Act Warren Oates, Isela Vega, Gig Young, Robert Webber, Helmut Dantine, Kris Kristofferson (Optimus/Estudios Churubusco)

Bring Me the Head of Alfredo Garcia is turgid melodrama [from a story by Frank Kowalski and Sam Peckinpah] at its worst.

Warren Oates stars as an expatriate American piano bar musician making a stab for riches in Mexico by finding the never-seen title character sought by an outraged Mexican father. Naturally the search brings unhappiness, and, being a Peckinpah film, lots and lots of people get killed along the way, as well as audience interest.

The title derives from the command of wealthy Emilio Fernandez to find the father of his unwed daughter's child. Gig Young, Helmut Dantine and Robert Webber are the private detectives engaged. They meet Oates whose girl (Isela Vega) had been intimate with the stud. He is dead, so Oates and Vega head off to steal the guy's head from a grave.

•

BRING ON THE GIRLS
1945, 96 mins, US col
Dir Sidney Lanfield ***Prod*** Fred Kohlmar ***Scr*** Karl Tunberg, Darrell Ware ***Ph*** Karl Struss ***Ed*** William Shea ***Mus*** Robert Emmett Dolan (dir.) ***Art*** Hans Dreier, John Meehan
Act Veronica Lake, Sonny Tufts, Eddie Bracken, Marjorie Reynolds (Paramount)

Bring On the Girls is a lightweight musical with some sprightly tunes by Jimmy McHugh and Harold Adamson, and a neat production. The book [from a story by Pierre Wolff] is one of those things, but *Girls* is fast paced all the way and has the benefit of gorgeous Technicolor plus other productional accoutrements that stamp film as being top-budget.

It's the story of a young millionaire with a proclivity for becoming engaged to dames who are out only for the money. So he joins the navy, where he won't be so well-known, but he becomes linked to a gold-digging ciggie girl (Veronica Lake), and thereafter the travail concerns whether or not Lake will get him.

Story becomes pitiful at times, and it remains for Bracken's performance to salvage much of it. Sonny Tufts and Lake and Marjorie Reynolds are somewhat obscured by the story.

There are a number of neat specialties, particularly a couple of hoofing numbers, and there's some comedy by Spike Jones's orch.

•

BRITANNIA HOSPITAL

1982, 115 mins, UK Ⓥ col

Dir Lindsay Anderson ***Prod*** Davina Belling, Clive Parsons ***Scr*** David Sherwin ***Ph*** Mike Fash ***Ed*** Michael Ellis ***Mus*** Alan Price ***Art*** Norris Spencer

Act Leonard Rossiter, Graham Crowden, Malcolm McDowell, Joan Plowright, Jill Bennett, Marsha Hunt (EMI/General)

Britannia Hospital is a witty, unsparing expose of British manners and mores.

The film revolves around a strike at a hospital where a royal personage is expected. This gives rise to union complaints about privileges showered on monied notables when the National Health system was supposed to make medicine equally available for all.

Medics' own misuse of National Health funds is pilloried in no uncertain style. A mad doctor experiments, from funds meant for socialized medicine, to create Frankenstein-type creatures.

A zealous reporter with a small video camera sneaks in to tape the mad doctor's creature-building only to end up as the head of the Frankenstein figure.

Through it all, the hospital director tries to cope with typical British phlegm, assured by a Scotland Yard top cop that crowds and unions will be kept in check.

Malcolm McDowell is rightly overacting as the reporter who loses his head. Leonard Rossiter copes staunchly as the beset hospital director. Marsha Hunt, Jill Bennett and Joan Plowright do fine cameo work as nurse, doctor and the union head.

•

BRITANNIA MEWS

1949, 91 mins, UK b/w

Dir Jean Negulesco ***Prod*** William Perlberg ***Scr*** Ring Lardner, Jr. ***Ph*** Georges Perinal, Denys Coop ***Mus*** Malcolm Arnold

Act Maureen O'Hara, Dana Andrews, Sybil Thorndike, Wilfrid Hyde White, Fay Compton (20th Century-Fox)

Picture tells the simple story [from a novel by Margery Sharp] of a girl on the better side of the street who falls in love with a drunken art teacher in the mews. By marrying him she is ostracized by her family.

Production is staged almost entirely in the sordid surroundings of Britannia Mews. This main setting is a triumph for the art director as it captures the grim, degrading atmosphere necessary to indicate the gradual degradation of its inhabitants.

Dana Andrews plays husbands number one and two (an out of work lawyer), and there are obvious signs of dubbing. Much of the illusion is lost by the unnecessary resemblance which arises from the playing of both roles. Maureen O'Hara inclines to be static although looking most attractive, and the only live characterization comes from Sybil Thorndike as a repulsive hag.

•

BRITISH AGENT

1934, 75 mins, US b/w

Dir Michael Curtiz ***Scr*** Laird Doyle ***Ph*** Ernest Haller ***Ed*** Thomas Richards ***Mus*** Leo F. Forbstein (dir.) ***Art*** Anton Grot

Act Leslie Howard, Kay Francis, William Gargan, Philip Reed, Irving Pichel, J. Carrol Naish (First National/Warner)

A powerful yarn of espionage during the early days of the Russian revolution. Leslie Howard and Kay Francis handle the two chief roles tellingly. Story comes from a novel by R. H. Bruce Lockhart, with much liberty taken in the screen version.

Yarn has Howard spotted in Russia, just prior to the rebellion, as the British consul-general. Russia wants to break away from the war and sign a separate peace with Germany. England doesn't want, and here the adaptation goes on its own. In the film England also doesn't want the hero to butt in. But he is so determined in his belief that Russia must be kept in the war that he conducts a one-man campaign against Bolshevism.

Romantic element is via Francis, cast as Lenin's secretary. Howard accidentally saves her life, and they fall in love. Through the revolution the romance continues, but it is kept in check though never lost sight of.

Historical accuracy is attempted by the portrayal of Trotsky, Lenin, David Lloyd George and others. Not a perfect job but well done generally.

•

BROADCAST NEWS

1987, 131 mins, US Ⓥ ⊙ col

Dir James L. Brooks ***Prod*** James L. Brooks ***Scr*** James L. Brooks ***Ph*** Michael Ballhaus ***Ed*** Richard Marks ***Mus*** Bill Conti ***Art*** Charles Rosen

Act William Hurt, Albert Brooks, Holly Hunter, Robert Prosky, Lois Chiles, Jack Nicholson (Gracie/20th Century-Fox)

Enormously entertaining, *Broadcast News* is an inside look at the personal and professional lives of three TV journlists.

Brooks gently punctures the self-importance of his characters with a sly satrical edge. When veteran reporter Aaron Altman (Albert Brooks) and hard-nosed producer Jane Craig (Holly Hunter) go to the jungles of Central America to report on the revolution, the results are too humorous and self-serving to take seriously.

Where Craig and Altman are seasoned professionals with great talent, Tom Grunick (William Hurt) is a slick exsportscaster who knows how to turn on the charm and seduce an audience. But is it news, his colleagues wonder.

Tom loves himself and loves Jane. In short it's a case of scrambled emotions among people who heretofore have substituted work for pleasure. Hunter is simply superb barking out orders from a mouth contorted with who-knows-what emotions. As the neurotic but brilliant reporter, Brooks gives an insightful performance while communicating his character's guardedness and anguish. As the hardest of the characters to read, Hurt does a good job keeping up the mystery so one never knows when he's sincere or faking, and maybe he doesn't either.

1987: NOMINATIONS: Best Picture, Actor (William Hurt), Actress (Holly Hunter), Supp. Actor (Albert Brooks), Original Screenplay, Cinematography, Editing

•

BROADWAY

1929, 105 mins, US col

Dir Paul Fejos ***Scr*** Edward T. Lowe, Jr., Charles Furthman ***Mus*** Howard Jackson

Act Glenn Tryon, Evelyn Brent, Merna Kennedy, Thomas E. Jackson, Robert Ellis, Paul Porcash (Universal)

U paid $200,000 for the screen rights to Phil Dunning's smash. As a melodrama with music the screenplay expands way beyond the stage production as well as in the melodramatic portion with its street scenes. Finest of these is a duplicate of Broadway at Times Square, from a miniature. Through Broadway strides a big bronze Demon Rum, and the picture starts right out of this scene.

U's own film players hold the leads, with Glenn Tryon as the hick hoofer. Tryon does nobly, discounting the singing and dancing suspicion. Evelyn Brent is first choice for good acting, with Merna Kennedy doing her little bit mildly as the hoofer's partner. Robert Ellis as the heavy runs alongside Thomas Jackson for realism. Paul Porcash was wisely chosen for the hard role of the cafe proprietor.

Paul Fejos directs, with much judgment, if little novelty. His work and the cutting, however, do much to make this film. The final scene is in Technicolor, giving a corking finish to a corking picture.

•

BROADWAY

1942, 89 mins, US b/w

Dir William A. Seiter ***Prod*** Bruce Manning ***Scr*** Felix Jackson, John Bright ***Ph*** George Barnes ***Ed*** Ted Kent ***Mus*** Charles Previn

Act George Raft, Pat O'Brien, Broderick Crawford, Janet Blair, Anne Gwynne, Marjorie Rambeau (Universal)

Universal's modernized presentation of *Broadway* retains the thrilling tenseness and dramatic suspense of both the original Philip Dunning–George Abbott play and the first film version turned out by Universal in 1929.

As modernized, *Broadway* could easily be the autobiography of George Raft—and this impression is carried through the unreeling via the medium of a prolog deftly contrived. Picture opens with Raft airlining to New York with companion-bodyguard-shadow, Mack Gray, for a short visit between pictures. Wandering onto Broadway, alone, he stops at a cellar being remodelled into a bowling alley. Looking around, he starts reminiscing to the old night-watchman about the heyday of the spot as a cabaret during the lush prohibition era—when Raft got his start as a hoofer in the place.

In addition to swift dramatic pace, provided both in script and direction, picture is studded with a group of excellent performances. Raft justifies his casting for the lead, and clicks solidly. Sharing honors with him is Pat O'Brien.

•

BROADWAY BILL

1934, 90 mins, US Ⓥ b/w

Dir Frank Capra ***Prod*** Frank Capra ***Scr*** Robert Riskin ***Ph*** Joseph Walker ***Ed*** Gene Havlick

Act Warner Baxter, Myrna Loy, Walter Connolly, Helen Vinson, Douglas Dumbrille, Raymond Walburn (Columbia)

If any racetrack picture ever had a chance to beat the no-femme-draw bugaboo, *Broadway Bill* is the picture. It has a story, a tiptop cast—and Frank Capra's direction.

Capra has a fine pair of leads in Warner Baxter and Myrna Loy, and then he has a yarn [by Broadway newspaperman Mark Hellinger] in which the tempo appears to have been especially suited to his directorial talents. The rest was up to Capra, and the rest is very much okay.

The training routine, the betting machinery, the track atmosphere, the gimmicks, the muscle boys, the game's intrigue—all these things have been truly captured and charmingly presented this time.

The troubles and jams of Dan Brooks (Baxter) as hopeful owner of a stout-hearted horse, Broadway Bill, supply the action. Brooks is broke, with the entry fee unpaid and the big race a few days off. The horse gets sick, then recovers. The horse is attached for the feed bill. Brooks is jailed for fighting the sheriff. He's released just in time. The jockey is fixed by gamblers. Etcetera.

Behind the alternately humorous and sad racetrack stuff, there is an underlying romance that ties the incidentals together. The fascinating attachment of Brooks for his sister-in-law (Loy) develops after Brooks has rebelled against and walked out on his refrigeratress-wife and dominating father-in-law (Walter Connolly). Raymond Walburn is aces in the finely drawn role of a con man who touts so well he believes it himself.

•

BROADWAY DANNY ROSE

1984, 86 mins, US Ⓥ ⊙ b/w

Dir Woody Allen ***Prod*** Robert Greenhut ***Scr*** Woody Allen ***Ph*** Gordon Willis ***Ed*** Susan E. Morse ***Mus*** Dick Hyman ***Art*** Mel Bourne

Act Woody Allen, Mia Farrow, Nick Apollo Forte, Milton Berle, Sandy Baron, Corbett Monica (Orion)

Broadway Danny Rose is a delectable diversion which allows Woody Allen to present a reasonably humane, and amusing gentle character study without sacrificing himself to overly commercial concerns.

Allen's perfect as a small-time, good-hearted Broadway talent agent, giving his all for a roster of hopeless clients.

Agent's career is fondly recalled here by a group of Catskill comics (all played by themselves) sitting around over coffee, focusing mainly on Allen's attempt to revive the career of an aging, overweight, boozing lounge singer, beautifully played by Nick Apollo Forte.

One of Forte's many problems that Allen must deal with is a floozy of a girlfriend. And it's truly one of the picture's early delights that this sunglassed bimbo is actually on screen for several minutes before most of the audience catches on that she's Mia Farrow.

Through Forte and Farrow, Allen becomes the target of a couple of hit men.

1984: NOMINATIONS: Best Director, Original Screenplay

•

BROADWAY MELODY, THE

1929, 104 mins, US Ⓥ ⊙ col

Dir Harry Beaumont ***Scr*** Edmund Goulding, James Gleason, Norman Houston ***Ph*** John Arnold ***Mus*** Herb Nacio Brown, Arthur Freed ***Art*** Cedric Gibbons

Act Anita Page, Bessie Love, Charles King, Jed Prouty, Kenneth Thomson, Edward Dillon (M-G-M)

Broadway Melody, the first screen musical, tells of a vaudeville sister team coming in from the middle west, with the older girl engaged to a song-and-dance boy in a Broadway revue. Latter goes for the kid sister, now grown up, who starts playing with one of the show's backers to stand off the boy and spare the blow to her sister, despite that she, too, is in love with her prospective brother-in-law.

In between are the troubles of the femme team making the revue grade. Both girls, Bessie Love as the elder sister and Anita Page as the youngster, are great in their respective climaxes, especially Love. Charlie King looks as good as he plays and plants comedy lines as they should be delivered. Other cast support is up to the mark with the exception of Kenneth Thomson, as the chaser, who plays too slow and doesn't convince.

Excellent bits of sound workmanship are that of camera and mike following Page and the heavy along the dance floor to pick up their conversation as they glide.

1928/29: Best Picture

NOMINATIONS: Best Director, Actress (Bessie Love)

•

BROADWAY MELODY OF 1936

1935, 102 mins, US Ⓥ ⊙ b/w

Dir Roy Del Ruth ***Prod*** John W. Considine, Jr. ***Scr*** Jack McGowan, Sid Silvers, Harry Conn ***Ph*** Charles Rosher ***Ed*** Blanche Sewell ***Mus*** Alfred Newman (dir.), Roger Edens (arr.) ***Art*** Cedric Gibbons, Merrill Pye, Edwin B. Willis

Act Jack Benny, Eleanor Powell, Robert Taylor, Una Merkel, Sid Silvers, Buddy Ebsen (M-G-M)

Everything revolves about Eleanor Powell, Robert Taylor and June Knight, the menace. She's the Park Avenue bankroll ($60,000) for the forthcoming musical comedy [dance direction by Dave Gould]. Columnist Jack Benny had been building up a phoney French comedienne, and so when Taylor fails to recognize his adolescent sweetheart from Albany she (Powell) essays an accent, bizarre make-up and goals everybody with her personality and her stepping as the pseudo-French star.

Story [by Moss Hart] is a curious hodge-podge of fantasy, realism and just hokum musical comedy. When the Ebsens (Vilma and Buddy) are doing their "Sing Before Breakfast," it's quite Rene Clair-ish in the whimsical mating of the tempo with the attic time-stepping. In other spots it goes Busby Berkeley with overhead ballet shots, or the sequence in what looks like the Rainbow Room at Radio City.

Songs are all good. "Broadway Rhythm," sung by Frances Langford and with dance specialties by Powell, Nick Long, Jr., Knight and the Ebsens, is a corking creation.

1935: Best Dance Direction ("I've Got a Feeling You're Fooling")

NOMINATIONS: Best Picture, Original Story

•

BROADWAY MELODY OF 1938

1937, 115 mins, US Ⓥ ⊙ b/w

Dir Roy Del Ruth ***Prod*** Jack Cummings ***Scr*** Jack McGowan ***Ph*** William Daniels ***Ed*** Blanche Sewell ***Mus*** George Stoll (dir.)

Act Robert Taylor, Eleanor Powell, George Murphy, Binnie Barnes, Judy Garland, Sophie Tucker (M-G-M)

Much better than its predecessor of 1936, and not far behind the original 1929 *Broadway Melody.*

No use getting into the details until Sophie Tucker and Judy Garland are disposed of. Former is somewhere past 40, but when she walks on the screen something happens. Then she steps back and pushes Garland, still in her teens, into the camera foreground. Young Garland gives them "Everybody Sing," with a letter to the homefolks.

Each does numbers solo later on. Judy sings a plaint to Clark Gable's photograph which is close to great screen acting. Then, to top it off, Soph does "Your Broadway and My Broadway," with lyrics which bring in the great names of the past generation.

Most of the rest is just fill-in between the Tucker and the Garland numbers. There is a lot of plot [by Jack McGowan and Sid Silvers] about a racehorse which is owned by Eleanor Powell, and a Broadway musical show which Robert Taylor is trying to produce on a short bankroll. Buddy Ebsen handles some first-class comedy bits on his own in addition to his eccentric dancing.

Music and lyrics by Nacio Herb Brown and Arthur Freed are first rate.

•

BROADWAY MELODY OF 1940

1940, 102 mins, US Ⓥ ⊙ b/w

Dir Norman Taurog ***Prod*** Jack Cummings ***Scr*** Leon Gordon, George Oppenheimer ***Ph*** Oliver T. Marsh, Joseph Ruttenberg ***Ed*** Blanche Sewell ***Mus*** Alfred Newman (dir.), Roger Edens (arr.) ***Art*** Cedric Gibbons, John S. Detlie

Act Fred Astaire, Eleanor Powell, George Murphy, Frank Morgan, Ian Hunter, Florence Rice (M-G-M)

Long on its display of corking dance routines and numbers by Fred Astaire, Eleanor Powell and George Murphy, mounted against elaborate production backgrounds, *Broadway Melody of 1940* slides through as moderately satisfying entertainment.

The story [by Jack McGowan and Dore Schary] is a typical backstage yarn. Astaire and Murphy are an ambitious team of hoofers working in a dance hall for coffee and cakes. Mistake in names shoots Murphy instead of Astaire into the lead of a Broadway musical opposite the star (Eleanor Powell). Murphy hits the bottle for the opening night, Astaire taking his place to protect his former partner.

This is the first teaming of Astaire and Powell in a filmusical. The result is as to be expected, both presenting several new and applause-generating numbers. But the numbers are too many and too extended for general purposes. This is particularly true of the finale, a super-lavish production background in which Astaire and Powell dance tap and whirl for six minutes. It's not sufficient to maintain interest for that length of time.

Murphy gains attention with a top performance as the hoofer-partner of Astaire. Latter is adequate in the role of the dance expert who goes to town when he starts stepping out with his new routines. Powell is an eyeful in her dances, and okay for the story sequences. Frank Morgan provides plenty of laughs in characterization of the musical show producer, while Ian Hunter is his partner who really stages the shows.

•

BROADWAY RHYTHM

1944, 115 mins, US col

Dir Roy Del Ruth ***Prod*** Jack Cummings ***Scr*** Dorothy Kingsley, Harry Clork ***Ph*** Leonard Smith ***Ed*** Albert Akst ***Mus*** Johnny Green (dir) ***Art*** Cedric Gibbons, Jack Martin Smith

Act George Murphy, Ginny Simms, Charles Winninger, Gloria de Haven, Lena Horne (M-G-M)

Broadway Rhythm is a typical backstage filmusical wheeled out in the usual Metro elaborate and colorful style. Displaying group of toprank specialties and names among the entertainers, the fragile and hodge-podge yarn [based on the 1939 Kern-Hammerstein musical *Very Warm for May*] stops periodically while the guest stars appear.

Story follows run-of-mill formula for a backstager. George Murphy is a top musical comedy producer readying his next show for Broadway. Ginny Simms, Hollywood film star, hits town for a whirl at the stage after being stymied on new contract in films. Charles Winninger, veteran song-and-dance man, is Murphy's dad, while Gloria DeHaven is the young sister with stage ambitions.

Tommy Dorsey and his orchestra provide the musical backgrounds, and are spotlighted for opening number to get picture away to a good start and one other number later. Lena Horne socks over two songs—the Gershwins's "Somebody Loves Me," and "Brazilian Boogie," by Hugh Martin and Ralph Blane—and both are smartly presented for maximum effect.

•

BROADWAY TO HOLLYWOOD

1933, 88 mins, US b/w

Dir Willard Mack ***Prod*** Harry Rapf ***Scr*** Willard Mack, Edgar Allan Woolf ***Ph*** William Daniels, Norbert Brodine ***Mus*** William Axt (arr.) ***Art*** Stanford Rogers

Act Alice Brady, Frank Morgan, Madge Evans, Russell Hardie, Jackie Cooper, Mickey Rooney (M-G-M)

Little from Metro's costly *March of Time* Technicolor musical has actually been resuscitated, although Metro's now historic and costly floppo venture inspired this combined effort by Harry Rapf, Willard Mack and Edgar Allan Woolf to retrieve something from the celluloid wreckage. Patently it was primed to trace the hoofing variety Hacketts from their Tony Pastor's days until the third-generation success of grandson Ted Hackett III as a film juvenile star. Dovetailed in is all the array of venerable variety talent which Metro assembled for its *March of Time* production four years earlier.

It's all Alice Brady and Frank Morgan's picture in sterling characterizations as the original hoofing Hacketts of Tony Pastor's time and down through the years into the third generation. Madge Evans and Russell Hardie (Ted Hackett, Jr.) sustain the sub-romance interest. The third generation has Jackie Cooper as Ted III as a child, and Eddie Quillan playing the matured Ted III when he becomes an overnight Hollywood click.

Cast names which are also included are dragged in by the heels, strictly for ballyhoo value. Among 'em are Jimmy Durante, whose brief appearance in a studio anteroom, as a would-be film aspirant, is strictly a one-to-fill; Fay Templeton and May Robson in the resurrected Technicolor stuff; Una Merkel in an anonymous bit merely shown flirting with the stage actor.

•

BROKEN ARROW

1950, 92 mins, US Ⓥ col

Dir Delmer Daves ***Prod*** Julian Blaustein ***Scr*** Michael Blankfort ***Ph*** Ernest Palmer ***Ed*** J. Watson Webb, Jr. ***Mus*** Hugo Friedhofer

Act James Stewart, Jeff Chandler, Debra Paget, Basil Ruysdael, Will Geer, Joyce MacKenzie (20th Century-Fox)

Broken Arrow is a western with a little different twist—the story of the attempt of whites and Apaches to learn to live together in the Arizona of 1870. Essentially it's an appealing, sentimental Indian romance, with plenty of action.

Pic has a quality of naive charm that peculiarly fits. There are colorful Indian tribal ceremonies that ring true.

Story [from a novel by Elliott Arnold] concerns a far-sighted young frontiersman (James Stewart) who, tired of the mutual killings of whites and redskins, boldly plans a visit to the feared Apache leader Cochise (Jeff Chandler) to propose a truce. Meeting not only succeeds, but Stewart falls in love with an Indian maiden (Debra Paget). Both truce and troth are impeded by treachery on the part of whites and Indians.

1950: NOMINATIONS: Best Supp. Actor (Jeff Chandler), Screenplay, Color Cinematography

•

BROKEN ARROW

1996, 108 mins, US Ⓥ ⊙ ▭ col

Dir John Woo ***Prod*** Mark Gordon, Bill Badalato ***Scr*** Graham Yost ***Ph*** Peter Levy ***Ed*** John Wright, Steve Mirkovich, Joe Hutshing ***Mus*** Hans Zimmer ***Art*** Holger Gross

Act John Travolta, Christian Slater, Samantha Mathis, Delroy Lindo, Bob Gunton, Frank Whaley (20th Century-Fox)

A virtually nonstop actioner that's heavy on imaginative destruction but light on coherence and character, *Broken Arrow* doesn't score a direct hit but will still do the trick for thrill-seeking audiences. In a flat-out villainous portrayal, John Travolta continues his winning post-comeback ways as a duplicitous Air Force pilot who steals two nuclear bombs.

Planes, trains, boats, trucks, helicopters, Humvees—just about every mode of transportation is used as the good government guys, led by copilot Christian Slater and Park Ranger Samantha Mathis, try to outmaneuver the bad guys, masterminded by Travolta, before the latter lay waste to the Western United States. This roller-coaster ride through the Four Corners area rarely lets up, for the good reason that any pauses would give the audience time to think about the sheer improbability of many of the incidents.

Writer Graham Yost (*Speed*) and action ace John Woo play fast and loose with continuity in a way that finds Mathis's character, last seen hiding from the villains on a river raft, suddenly hopping a truck and then winding up on a train.

Still, the big set pieces just keep on coming, from the initial low-level flight of the batlike Stealth bomber and a spectacular underground explosion to the final cat-and-mouse between a helicopter and a train carrying the traitors and the bomb toward Denver, and the more intimate face-off on board the train between the two pilots.

Travolta and Slater hold their own with the hardware and scenery, delivering the kind of nifty star turns that this sort of vehicle needs. Mathis's lonely ranger gets the shortest background shrift of all, but she eventually mixes it up with some well-placed martial arts moves learned who-knows-where.

•

BROKEN BLOSSOMS OR THE YELLOW MAN AND THE GIRL

1919, 107 mins, US Ⓥ ⊙ ⊗ b/w

Dir D. W. Griffith ***Prod*** D. W. Griffith ***Scr*** D. W. Griffith ***Ph*** Billy Bitzer, Herdrik Sartor, Karl Brown ***Ed*** James E. Smith, Rose Smith ***Mus*** Louis Gottschalk, D. W. Griffith ***Art*** Charles E. Baker

Act Lillian Gish, Donald Crisp, Richard Barthelmess, Edward Peil, Arthur Howard, George Beranger (Artcraft)

Although the picture consumes only 90 minutes, it somehow seems draggy, for the reason that everything other than the scenes with the three principals seems extraneous and tends to clog the progression of the tale.

Broken Blossoms is adapted from a story by Thomas Burke entitled *The Chink and the Child.* The footage allotted the titles is a point to be commended, ample time being allowed to read them slowly and digest their meaning.

The story is a drama of pathos, culminating in tragedy. A pure-minded young Chinaman, reared in the beautiful teachings of Buddha, journeys to London with the altruistic idea of civilizing the white race.

In London there resides in his vicinity a brutish prize-fighter who beats his child into helplessness and she crawls away, half dead, falling insensible into the shop of the Mongolian. With perhaps a whiff of the lilied pipe still in his brain, he finds her on the floor, carries her to his living room above and watches over her with a love so pure as to be wholly unnatural and inconsistent.

Lillian Gish as the girl, shrinking, self-effacing, timid, fearful and wistful, has never before done anything so fine. Donald Crisp is the brutal father, as great a triumph of histrionic artistry as that registered by Gish.

Yet not one whit behind these two masterful portrayals is that of Richard Barthelmess as the young Chinaman, idealized, necessarily, in the matter of facial attractiveness, yet visualizing to the full the gentle delicacy of the idyllic Oriental youth.

•

BROKEN HARVEST
1994, 101 mins, Ireland col
Dir Maurice O'Callaghan ***Prod*** Jerry O'Callaghan ***Scr*** Maurice O'Callaghan, Kate O'Callaghan ***Ph*** Jack Conroy ***Ed*** J. Patrick Duffner ***Mus*** Patrick Cassidy ***Art*** Alan Galett
Act Colin Lane, Niall O'Brien, Marian Quinn, Darren McHugh, Joy Florish, Joe Jeffers (Destiny)

Part rites-of-passage movie, part meditation on the "new" Ireland forged from the War of Independence and subsequent Civil War, *Broken Harvest* is a beautifully lensed but dramatically static pic that falls short of its aspirations.

Story opens in present-day New York, where businessman Jimmy O'Leary (Pete O'Reilly) hears of the death of his mother, Catherine (Marian Quinn, sister of Aidan). The news cues a long flashback to growing up in rural West Cork during the '50s, where old tensions still linger from the anti-Brit struggles of the '20s and later divisions.

Young Jimmy (Darren McHugh) lives a carefree life of comic books, rock 'n' roll, escapades with pal Willie (Joe Jeffers), and growing attention from the pubescent Mary (Joy Florish). A deep-seated feud between Jimmy's dad and Willie's easygoing uncle, Josie (Niall O'Brien), leads to violence when Josie (rightly) accuses Jimmy of pilfering money from the church collection.

Director Maurice O'Callaghan's script, from his own story *The Shilling*, obstinately fails to cohere into an engaging package. Blame that mostly on dialogue that's overspare and often awkward, and a directorial style that's too first-gear and stiff.

•

BROKEN LANCE
1954, 96 mins, US Ⓥ ▭ col
Dir Edward Dmytryk ***Prod*** Sol C. Siegel ***Scr*** Richard Murphy ***Ph*** Joe MacDonald ***Ed*** Dorothy Spencer ***Mus*** Leigh Harline ***Art*** Lyle Wheeler, Maurice Ransford
Act Spencer Tracy, Robert Wagner, Jean Peters, Richard Widmark, Katy Jurado, Hugh O'Brian (20th Century-Fox)

Broken Lance is topnotch western drama. Seems too bad so much of the story [by Philip Yordan] is told via an unnecessary flashback. However, there is enough force in the trouping and direction to sustain mood and interest. This is particularly true of Spencer Tracy's performance, since he has the difficult task of making alive a character already dead when the picture opens.

Film starts with Robert Wagner's release from an Arizona prison after serving a three-year sentence. The enmity that lies between him and his three half-brothers (Richard Widmark, Hugh O'Brian and Earl Holliman) is quickly established.

The scene shifts from this strong early sequence, taking place in the office of the governor (E.G. Marshall), where they all try to get him to leave the state, to the once proud family ranch, now decayed from neglect. There Wagner recalls the events that led to his imprisonment. Within the flashback Tracy is shown as a domineering cattle baron, who rules his four sons and vast empire ruthlessly by his own laws. However, time is running out for him as civilization advances, and he takes the law into his own hands once too often in destroying mining property and injuring miners.

1954: Best Motion Picture Story

NOMINATION: Best Supp. Actress (Katy Jurado)

•

BRONCO BILLY
1980, 119 mins, US Ⓥ ⊙ col
Dir Clint Eastwood ***Prod*** Dennis E. Hackin, Neal Dobrofsky ***Scr*** Dennis E. Hackin ***Ph*** David Worth ***Ed*** Ferris Webster, Joel Cox ***Mus*** Snuff Garrett (sup.) ***Art*** Gene Lourie
Act Clint Eastwood, Sondra Locke, Geoffrey Lewis, Scatman Crothers, Bill McKinney, Sam Bottoms (Warner)

In the title role, Clint Eastwood plays an ex-NJ shoe salesman who has trained himself to live out a fantasy as a sharpshooting, knife-throwing, stunt-riding cowboy. There's no place to practice it except as the leader of a rundown Wild West show touring tank towns and county fairs. The others in the troupe are also definitive losers of varying talents.

Along the same highways, however, comes Sondra Locke, an arrogant spoiled heiress, and Geoffrey Lewis, delightful as the idiotic husband she has just married. Fed up with Locke's mistreatment, Lewis abandons her without a dime and she winds up—quite reluctantly—as Eastwood's helper.

Bronco Billy is a caricature of many of the strong heroes whom Eastwood has played in other pix and he's obviously having a wonderful time with the satire.

•

BRONCO BULLFROG
1970, 86 mins, UK col
Dir Barney Platts-Mills ***Prod*** Andrew St. John ***Scr*** Barney Platts-Mills ***Ph*** Adam Barker-Mill ***Ed*** Jonathan Gili ***Mus*** Howard Werth, Tony Connor, Keith Gemmell, Trevor Williams
Act Del Walker, Anne Gooding, Sam Shepherd, Roy Haywood, Freda Shepherd, Dick Philpott (British Lion)

Producer Andrew St. John and director-writer Barney Platts-Mills assembled a bunch of East End amateurs and, with a thin story line and dialog that seems mainly improvised, let them loose in "their own scene." Made for only $48,000, film is a praiseworthy attempt to show the drab environment of an area and to indicate how boredom in that environment can drive youngsters into being layabouts, petty thieves, etc., and how such trapped youngsters can develop into more hardened criminals.

Through the film is woven an inarticulate, but frequently touching Romeo and Juliet theme, about two minors who run away from home because there is nowhere to go and nothing to do.

It would be pointless to comment on the nonexistent acting. There is behavior, instead.

•

BRONCO BUSTER
1952, 80 mins, US Ⓥ col
Dir Budd Boetticher ***Prod*** Ted Richmond ***Scr*** Horace McCoy, Lillie Hayward ***Ph*** Clifford Stine ***Ed*** Edward Curtiss ***Mus*** Joseph Gershenson ***Art*** Bernard Herzbrun, Robert Boyle
Act John Lund, Scott Brady, Joyce Holden, Chill Wills, Casey Tibbs (Universal-International)

A satisfying round of outdoor action thrills is provided by *Bronco Buster*. A lot of actual rodeo thrill footage is used to bolster authenticity and add interest to the development of what actually is a routine plot line. Excellent scripting [from a story by Peter B. Kyne] and direction, however, gloss over and enliven the stock plot.

John Lund and Scott Brady handle the principal male roles as rodeo and romantic rivals. Brady, newcomer to the bronco-busting circuit, shows promise, so Lund, already a champion rider, takes him in hand. After Brady has benefitted from Lund's tips, he turns swellhead and grandstands so thoroughly he earns the enmity of the other performers. He makes a play for Joyce Holden, longtime sweetie of Lund and the daughter of Chill Wills's rodeo clown.

•

BRONENOSETS "POTYOMKIN"
(BATTLESHIP POTEMKIN; THE POTEMKIN; CRUISER POTEMKIN)
1925, 65 mins, USSR Ⓥ ⊙ ⊗ b/w
Dir Sergei Eisenstein ***Scr*** Nina Agadzhanova-Shutko, Sergei Eisenstein ***Ph*** Eduard Tisse ***Ed*** Sergei Eisenstein ***Mus*** Edmund Meisel ***Art*** Vasili Rakhals
Act Aleksandr Antonov, Vladimir Barsky, Levshin, Grigori Aleksandrov, Mikhail Gomorov (Goskino)

Scenario concerns an actual historical incident which has been found by the Soviet government in the czarist archives. In 1905 the armored cruiser *Potemkin* was lying off Odessa. The crew had been getting inedible rations and finally worm-ridden meat was brought on board. The sailors protested and refused to eat this.

The czarist commander, true to the principles of his regime, decided at once to make an example. He portioned off 10 of the sailors, had them covered with a sail cloth and ordered the marines to shoot them. After a moment of hesitancy the soldiers lowered their guns and mutiny broke out.

Within a few moments all the officers had either been shot or thrown overboard. The news of the mutiny spread like wildfire through the city and the oppressed citizens, in the hope that the czarist regime was about to fall, came to pay homage at the bier.

Coming from both sides of the big square and stairway leading up the hill, the Cossack troops shot down mercilessly all in the way, cripples, old men, women and children. This was only stopped by the cruiser opening fire on the city hall.

The cruiser got news the entire Russian fleet was on its way to subdue them. They decided to go to meet it and die a heroic death in battle. The fleet, however, also sympathized with them and let them pass through its lines without firing a single shot. The *Potemkin* then found refuge in a Romanian harbor, where it was interned until the end of the Russo-Japanese war.

The direction of Sergei Eisenstein is original and powerful. There are moments in the film which even the most hardened conservative could not help being thrilled. Also, the inexorable advance of the shooting Cossacks down the steps is interesting from a rhythmic angle. The photography by Eduard Tisse is fine throughout but occasionally is too "pretty" for the subject.

[Above review is of pic's first overseas showing, in Berlin in 1926.]

•

BRONX TALE, A
1993, 122 mins, US Ⓥ ⊙ col
Dir Robert De Niro ***Prod*** Jane Rosenthal, Jon Kilik, Robert De Niro ***Scr*** Chazz Palminteri ***Ph*** Reynaldo Villalobos ***Ed*** David Ray, R. Q. Lovett ***Mus*** Jeffrey Kimball (sup.), Butch Barbella (dir.) ***Art*** Wynn Thomas
Act Robert De Niro, Chazz Palminteri, Lillo Brancato, Francis Capra, Taral Hicks, Clem Caserta (Price/Tribeca)

Goodfellas with heart, *A Bronx Tale* represents a wonderfully vivid snapshot of a colorful place and time, as well as a very satisfying directorial debut by Robert De Niro. Adroitly expanded by Chazz Palminteri from the one-man play he wrote and performed successfully in Los Angeles and New York, tale charts the growing-up of a youngster named Calogero amidst the small-time hoods and wiseguys of the Bronx in the 1960s.

The neighborhood in 1960 is ruled by Sonny (Palminteri). Everything changes after 9-year-old Calogero (Francis Capra) sees Sonny shoot down a man in the street. When Calogero doesn't identify the killer to the police, Sonny takes the kid under his wing, letting him in on craps games from which he takes home more money than his bus driver father (De Niro) makes in weeks.

Eight years later, Calogero (Lillo Brancato) and his buddies have their own social club, Sonny is a much bigger shot, and black neighborhoods have edged close to Italian turf. Calogero takes a fancy to a black girl (Taral Hicks) and dares to date her against a backdrop of escalating racial tension.

Brancato is utterly believable as De Niro's son. De Niro cast himself in the script's least showy role, as the responsible, upright man amidst a carnival of flashy hoods, but he delivers some great scenes. It's also given to him to repeatedly deliver pic's theme—"The saddest thing in life is wasted talent." Palminteri is terrific as the charismatic Sonny; his quicksilver mood changes keeping everyone on their toes.

•

BROOD, THE
1979, 91 mins, Canada Ⓥ ⊙ col
Dir David Cronenberg ***Prod*** Claude Heroux ***Scr*** David Cronenberg ***Ph*** Mark Irwin ***Ed*** Alan Collins ***Mus*** Howard Shore ***Art*** Carol Spier
Act Oliver Reed, Samantha Eggar, Art Hindle, Cindy Hinds, Henry Beckman, Nuala FitzGerald (Mutuelles/Elgin)

A horror entry which casts children in the role of malevolent little monsters, *The Brood* is an extremely well made, if essentially unpleasant, shocker.

Cronenberg's helming is skillful enough to command attention even through his script's needlessly long stretches of dialog.

Action is relatively plodding stuff, with young parent Art Hindle trying to keep his daughter away from mother Samantha Eggar, who's supposedly in psychotherapy at the posh forested retreat of analyst Oliver Reed. Action is spiked with the mysterious murders of Eggar's parents. Reed registers forcefully as the egotistical doctor and Eggar is appropriately flipped out but, unfortunately, most of the running time is spent with Hindle center stage and the actor is just too morose to enlist much sympathy, despite his plight.

•

BROTHER FROM ANOTHER PLANET, THE
1984, 104 mins, US Ⓥ col
Dir John Sayles ***Prod*** Peggy Rajski, Maggie Renzi ***Scr*** John Sayles ***Ph*** Ernest R. Dickerson ***Ed*** John Sayles ***Mus*** Mason Daring ***Art*** Steve Lineweaver
Act Joe Morton, Darryl Edwards, Steve James, Leonard Jackson, Bill Cobbs, Maggie Renzi (A-Train)

John Sayles takes a turn toward offbeat fantasy in *The Brother from Another Planet*, a vastly amusing but progressively erratic look at the Harlem adventures of an alien, a black E.T.

Brother begins with a tall, mute, young black fellow seeming to be dumped unceremoniously in New York harbor. Within minutes, he makes his way to Harlem, where his unusual, but not truly bizarre, behavior raises some cackles but in most respects blends into the neighborhood.

Pic is essentially a series of behavioral vignettes, and many of them are genuinely delightful and inventive. Once the Brother discovers the Harlem drug scene, however, tale takes a rather unpleasant and, ultimately, confusing turn.

•

BROTHERHOOD, THE
1968, 96 mins, US Ⓥ ⦿ col
Dir Martin Ritt ***Prod*** Kirk Douglas ***Scr*** Lewis John Carlino ***Ph*** Boris Kaufman ***Ed*** Frank Bracht ***Mus*** Lalo Schifrin ***Art*** Tambi Larsen
Act Kirk Douglas, Alex Cord, Irene Papas, Luther Adler, Susan Strasberg, Murray Hamilton (Paramount/Bryna)

Mafia-themed story pits Kirk Douglas, as a middle-aged New Jersey syndicate chief, against Alex Cord, his ambitious younger brother not as attuned to the curious, but rigidly-structured old underworld code. Martin Ritt's top-notch direction of an excellent cast maximizes the tragedy inherent in original screenplay.

Goading Douglas to progress are syndicate partners Luther Adler, Murray Hamilton, Val Avery and Alan Hewitt, repping in dialog and acting the commingling of Irish gangsters and Jewish gangsters with Sicilian-Italian gangsters.

Cord is excellent as the product of an environment which has smoothed out not only the rough edges of immigrant assimilation into the U.S., but also the surface emotions, noble and ignoble, which marked earlier generations. Urbane, cold, ambitious, unfeeling—Cord's character is chilling.

Since a prolog telegraphs some tragic climax, there is not much suspense in the usual sense of the word.

•

BROTHERLY LOVE
SEE: COUNTRY DANCE

•

BROTHERS IN LAW
1957, 94 mins, UK Ⓥ b/w
Dir Roy Boulting ***Prod*** John Boulting ***Scr*** Frank Harvey, Jeffrey Dell, Roy Boulting ***Ph*** Max Greene ***Ed*** Anthony Harvey ***Mus*** Benjamin Frankel ***Art*** Albert Witherick
Act Richard Attenborough, Ian Carmichael, Terry-Thomas, Jill Adams, Miles Malleson, Eric Barker (Tudor/British Lion)

The three stars in *Private's Progress* are reunited in this Roy Boulting comedy. This time it's making fun of the law, doing full justice to a laugh-loaded script.

The witty and lighthearted yarn [from the novel by Henry Cecil] traces the experiences of a young lawyer from the day of his graduation until he achieves his first legal victory.

The raw legal recruit is Ian Carmichael, who through the good offices of his roommate and fellow attorney, is accepted as a pupil barrister by Miles Malleson, a distinguished but absent-minded Queen's Counsel. Within a few minutes of his appointment he accompanies his senior to the High Court, and is left to plead the case without even knowing which side he's on. This unhappy start to his career affects Carmichael's confidence. He gets his chance from Terry-Thomas, a seasoned swindler with 17 appearances at the Criminal Court to his credit—and gets his first practical lesson in how to beat the law.

•

BROTHERS KARAMAZOV, THE
1958, 149 mins, US Ⓥ col
Dir Richard Brooks ***Prod*** Pandro S. Berman ***Scr*** Richard Brooks ***Ph*** John Alton ***Ed*** John Dunning ***Mus*** Bronislau Kaper ***Art*** William A. Horning, Paul Groesse
Act Yul Brynner, Maria Schell, Claire Bloom, Lee J. Cobb, Richard Basehart, William Shatner (M-G-M/Avon)

Bold handling of crude unbridled passion, of violently conflicting ideas, and of earthy humor makes up *The Brothers Karamazov*. Sex and Salvation are the twin obsessions of the brothers and father, and they are the two themes that are hammered relentlessly home by Richard Brooks, who directs his own screenplay.

Brooks wrote his screenplay from an adaptation by Julius J. and Philip G. Epstein of the Dostoievsky novel. Lee J. Cobb is the father of the Karamazov brothers, a lecherous old buffoon who taunts, tantalizes and frustrates his sons into violence, despair and apathy. Yul Brynner is the handsome, cruel, profligate army officer, a combination of adult power and childish pleasure. He is in conflict with his father partly because they both lust after the same woman, Maria Schell as Grushenka.

Richard Basehart is in revolt because of his intellectual coldness, a rigidity brought on by revulsion at the open and untrammeled sexuality of the old rogue. The third son, William Shatner, has chosen his way of survival in contest with his father; he has retreated into the church as a monk. The explosion that these figures ignite comes when Brynner imagines Schell has gone to his father in preference to him.

Brynner succeeds in making his Dmitri a hero despite the fact that every facet of his character is against it. Schell, in her American motion picture debut, illumines her role, seemingly able to suggest innocence and depravity with the same sweet face. Claire Bloom, as the alabaster beauty who saves Brynner from debtors' prison, is very moving particularly in the court scene as her facade cracks from within, rent by bitterness and despair. It is Lee J. Cobb, however, who walks—or rather gallops—away with the picture. The part is gargantuan and it is not a bit too big for the actor. The Metrocolor used by Brooks and cameraman John Alton is rich in purples, reds and blues.

1958: NOMINATION: Best Supp. Actor (Lee J. Cobb)

•

BROTHERS RICO, THE
1957, 90 mins, US b/w
Dir Phil Karlson ***Prod*** Lewis J. Rachmil ***Scr*** Lewis Meltzer, Ben Perry ***Ph*** Burnett Guffey ***Ed*** Charles Nelson ***Mus*** George Duning ***Art*** Robert Boyle
Act Richard Conte, Dianne Foster, Kathryn Grant, Larry Gates, James Darren, Lamont Johnson (Columbia)

Screenplay [from a story by Georges Simenon] follows the efforts of a crime ring to locate one of its members who bolted after participating in a murder. Missing member's elder brother (Richard Conte), once chief accountant for the syndicate but now a reputable businessman with the promise that he can go straight, is recalled to find him. He learns too late that the gang merely wanted him to lead them to the wanted brother.

Phil Karlson forges hard action into unfoldment of film. Performances are first-class right down the line, Conte a standout as a man finally disillusioned after thinking of the syndicate leader who orders his brother's execution as a close family friend. Both femmes have comparatively little to do, Dianne Foster as Conte's wife and Kathryn Grant as the brother's, but make their work count. Larry Gates as gang chief scores smoothly and James Darren as younger brother handles character satisfactorily.

•

BROTHER SUN, SISTER MOON
1973, 121 mins, Italy/ UK Ⓥ col
Dir Franco Zeffirelli ***Prod*** Luciano Perugia ***Scr*** Suso Cecchi D'Amico, Kenneth Ross, Lina Wertmuller, Franco Zeffirelli ***Ph*** Ennio Guarnieri ***Ed*** Reginald Hills, John Rushton ***Mus*** Donovan ***Art*** Lorenzo Mongiardino
Act Graham Faulkner, Judi Bowker, Alec Guinness, Leigh Lawson, Kenneth Cranham, Michael Feast (Euro International/Vic)

Brother Sun, Sister Moon is a delicate, handsome quasi-fictional biography of one of the great saints of the Catholic Church, Francis of Assisi. Franco Zeffirelli has utilized a style of simple elegance, befitting both the period and the subject.

Graham Faulkner makes an important film debut as Francis of Assisi. Judi Bowker, cast as a young girl who eventually sheds her materialistic existence for religious poverty, is stunningly beautiful, projecting the very essence of innocence.

Evidently edited from original form, the film utilizes flashback to establish briefly Faulkner's early life as a spoiled wastrel, indulged by parents Valentina Cortese and Lee Montague until a rude spiritual awakening in the fevers of wartime pestilence.

Faulkner's character evolution slowly recruits to the humble life of his friends. The illwill of older characters against the growsing band of mystics is portrayed with strength.

1973: NOMINATION: Best Art Direction

•

BROWNING VERSION, THE
1951, 90 mins, UK Ⓥ b/w
Dir Anthony Asquith ***Prod*** Teddy Baird ***Scr*** Terence Rattigan ***Ph*** Desmond Dickinson ***Ed*** John D. Guthridge ***Art*** Carmen Dillon
Act Michael Redgrave, Jean Kent, Nigel Patrick, Wilfrid Hyde White, Brian Smith, Bill Travers (Javelin)

Terence Rattigan's play, which had a big success in the West End in 1948, has been faithfully translated to the screen. The celluloid version is crammed with emotional incidents and has two noteworthy tearjerker scenes.

The background of the story is an English public school with the action spanning barely 48 hours. It is the last day of term, and Andrew Crocker-Harris, an austere disciplinarian, is retiring because of ill health without a pension. The events leading up to the final, powerful valedictory address make up a plot which is rich in incident and human understanding.

The role of the retiring master is not an easy one, but a prize in the right hands. Michael Redgrave fills it with distinction. Almost matching this performance is the role of his wife, played with a mixture of callousness and coyness by Jean Kent.

Nigel Patrick, in a less bombastic part than usual, chalks up another personal success as the science master who becomes ashamed of the intrigue he has had with Kent. Wilfrid Hyde White is as smooth as ever as the headmaster.

•

BROWNING VERSION, THE
1994, 97 mins, UK/US Ⓥ ⦿ col
Dir Mike Figgis ***Prod*** Ridley Scott, Mimi Polk ***Scr*** Ronald Harwood ***Ph*** Jean-Francois Robin ***Ed*** Herve Schneid ***Mus*** Mark Isham ***Art*** John Beard
Act Albert Finney, Greta Scacchi, Matthew Modine, Julian Sands, Michael Gambon, Ben Silverston (Percy Main/Paramount)

The themes of Terence Rattigan's play *The Browning Version* seem curiously out of date in a modern context. It's more than four decades since Anthony Asquith's original screen adaptation, in which Michael Redgrave assayed the role of Andrew Crocker-Harris, a public school Latin teacher with a bad ticker who's facing a forced, early retirement. Albert Finney puts his unique stamp on the role, effecting a heaviness that suggests a hard crust shielding a marshmallow center.

Crocker-Harris is about to vacate his seat for a less stressful life of teaching English to foreigners. The tragedy of this sometimes ridiculous man is multifold. His marriage to Laura (Greta Scacchi) is a sham. Her extra-curricular activity is centered around Frank Hunter (Matthew Modine), the brash, well-liked Yank teaching chemistry. Hunter, however, is in awe of the man's discipline and decency.

Ronald Harwood's adaptation has abridged the original without diluting its most potent contemporary resonances. It provides Scacchi and Modine with meatier roles than they have more commonly limned. Finney is masterful at the center, and helmer Mike Figgis excels in the traditional setting.

•

BRUBAKER
1980, 130 mins, US Ⓥ ⦿ col
Dir Stuart Rosenberg ***Prod*** Ron Silverman ***Scr*** W. D. Richter ***Ph*** Bruno Nuytten ***Ed*** Robert Brown ***Mus*** Lalo Schifrin ***Art*** J. Michael Riva
Act Robert Redford, Yaphet Kotto, Jane Alexander, Murray Hamilton, David Keith, Morgan Freeman (20th Century-Fox)

Brubaker is a successfully grim and brutal drama which, unfortunately, has written its own commercial epitaph with its message: The public at large does not care about prison reform.

Even with a sharp cast topped by the star power of Robert Redford, it's hard to imagine a broad audience wanting to share the two hours of agony in this one, all the way to a downbeat ending with Redford the loser in his righteous battle.

For the squeamish, the first half hour is rough going, indeed, as Redford is inducted into a small state prison, isolated in the farmlands near a hamlet.

Joining the ranks, Redford discovers one horror after another. The prison administration is in corrupt cahoots with townspeople, leasing prisoners as slave labor; brutal trustees administer the discipline to fellow convicts, gaining good time for killing some off; minimally decent food and privileges must be bought for cash, with wormy gruel going to those who can't afford it.

Just when it seems any hope is beyond these men, Redford reveals himself as the prison's new warden, brought to the job by Lillian (Jane Alexander), good as an assistant to a reform-minded governor never seen. Stuart Rosenberg has directed W.D. Richter's thought-provoking script [from a screen story by Richter and Arthur Ross] with a sure hand after coming aboard in mid-picture.

1980: NOMINATION: Best Original Screenplay

•

BRUTE FORCE
1947, 94 mins, US b/w
Dir Jules Dassin ***Prod*** Mark Hellinger ***Scr*** Richard Brooks ***Ph*** William Daniels ***Ed*** Edward Curtiss ***Mus*** Miklos Rozsa ***Art*** Bernard Herzbrun, John F. DeCuir
Act Burt Lancaster, Hume Cronyn, Charles Bickford, Yvonne De Carlo, Ann Blyth, Howard Duff (Hellinger/Universal)

A closeup on prison life and prison methods, *Brute Force* is a showmanly mixture of gangster melodramatics, sociological exposition, and sex [from a story by Robert Patterson]. The s.a. elements are plausible and realistic, well within the bounds, but always pointing up the femme fatale. Thus Yvonne De Carlo, Ann Blyth, Ella Raines and Anita Colby are the women on the "outside" whose machinations, wiles or charms accounted for their men being on the "inside."

Burt Lancaster, Charles Bickford, Sam Levene, Howard Duff, Art Smith and Jeff Corey, along with Hume Cronyn as the machinating prison captain (later warden), are the "inside" cast.

Each of the more prominent criminals has a saga. The flashback technique shows how bookkeeper Whit Bissell embezzled $3,000 to give his ambitious wife (Raines) that mink coat; how soldier Duff got jammed with the Military Police because of his love for his Italian bride (De Carlo) and through the snivelling skullduggery of her fascistic father; how the sympathetic Lancaster is in love with the invalided Blyth.

Bristling, biting dialog by Richard Brooks paints broad cameos as each character takes shape under existing prison life. Bickford is the wise and patient prison paper editor whose trusty (Levene), has greater freedom in getting "stories" for the sheet. Cronyn is diligently hateful as the arrogant, brutal captain, with his system of stoolpigeons and bludgeoning methods.

The aspect of an audience rooting for the prisoners plotting a jailbreak is given a sharp turnabout, at the proper time, to point up that brute force by prisoners is as wrong as the brute force exercised by their keepers.

•

BUCCANEER, THE

1958, 121 mins, US Ⓥ ⦿ col

Dir Anthony Quinn ***Prod*** Henry Wilcoxon ***Scr*** Jesse L. Lasky, Jr., Bernice Mosk ***Ph*** Loyal Griggs ***Ed*** Archie Marshek ***Mus*** Elmer Bernstein ***Art*** Hal Pereira, Walter H. Tyler, Albert Nozako

Act Yul Brynner, Charlton Heston, Claire Bloom, Charles Boyer, Inger Stevens, E. G. Marshall (Paramount)

Romance is effectively brought in the Cecil B. DeMille–supervised production that focuses on the colorful historical character of Jean Lafitte. On the deficit side is a wordy script that lacks any large degree of excitement. It marks the debut for Anthony Quinn as director.

Continuity-wise, *Buccaneer* is a scrambled affair in the early reels. Open to question, also, are the story angles in the screenplay which derives from a previous *Buccaneer* scenario put out by DeMille in 1938 and, in turn, from an adaptation of the original book, *Lafitte the Pirate*, by Lyle Saxon.

It's the War of 1812 against Britain and the battle area in New Orleans. The action takes place on land except for the sinking of one ship, which is curiously underplayed, by a renegade buccaneer. Highpoint is the land battle between Andrew Jackson's forces and the British, with Jackson aided by Lafitte's personnel and ammunition. The British, like so many toy soldiers, go down in defeat as Lafitte rules the mast.

Yul Brynner is masterly as the pirate. Charlton Heston is a hard, firm Andrew Jackson, who, while mounted on horse, sees the wisdom of making a deal with the pirate Lafitte. Claire Bloom is a fiery creation who alternately hates and loves Lafitte; Charles Boyer is light as Lafitte's aide, and Inger Stevens is properly attractive as Lafitte's true love and daughter of the governor.

1958: NOMINATION: Best Costume Design

BUCHANAN RIDES ALONE

1958, 89 mins, US col

Dir Budd Boetticher ***Prod*** Harry Joe Brown ***Scr*** Charles Lang ***Ph*** Lucien Ballard ***Ed*** Al Clark ***Mus*** [uncredited] ***Art*** Robert Boyle

Act Randolph Scott, Craig Stevens, Barry Kelley, Peter Whitney, Manuel Rojas, L. Q. Jones (Columbia)

Buchanan Rides Alone is one of those workhorses of saddle opera. Turned out on a relatively modest budget, still it is an honest picture, made with skill and craftsmanship.

Well-paced screenplay, based on a novel (*The Name's Buchanan*) by Jonas Ward, has Randolph Scott as a man more or less innocently involved in the problems of a frontier western border town, as he is passing through to his home in Texas from making his stake in Mexico. He befriends a young Mexican (Manuel Rojas), who kills the town bully. Scott is thrown in jail with Rojas and both are threatened with lynching.

The plotting is tricky, with the local First Family divided among itself by greed and lust for power. Scott plays one member off against another, until the final blow-off.

Scott gives an understated performance, taciturnity relieved by humour and warmth. Craig Stevens is intriguing as a man of mystery; L. Q. Jones is picturesque as an offbeat gunman, and Rojas handles his role with finesse.

•

BUCK PRIVATES

1941, 82 mins, US Ⓥ ⦿ b/w

Dir Arthur Lubin ***Prod*** Alex Gottlieb ***Scr*** Arthur T. Horman, John Grant ***Ph*** Milton Krasner ***Ed*** Philip Cahn ***Mus*** Charles Previn

Act Lee Bowman, Alan Curtis, Bud Abbott, Lou Costello, Jane Frazee (Universal)

Geared at a zippy pace, and providing lusty and enthusiastic comedy of the broadest slapstick, *Buck Privates* is a hilarious laugh concoction. Supplied with a compact script and spontaneous direction by Arthur Lubin, Abbott and Costello have a field day in romping through a lightly frameworked yarn that makes little attempt to be serious or credible. Aiding considerably is the appearance of the Andrews Sisters, who do their regularly competent harmonizing of several tuneful melodies.

Abbott and Costello are inducted into the army and assigned to camp. The madcap and zany antics of Costello are displayed in numerous comedy and knock-about sequences that—although the material is familiar—click for solid laughs through the timing of the gags and situations. There's a light thread of romantic triangle between rich boy, Lee Bowman; comely camp hostess, Jane Frazee; and former chauffeur Alan Curtis.

•

BUCK PRIVATES COME HOME

1947, 77 mins, US Ⓥ ⦿ b/w

Dir Charles T. Barton ***Prod*** Robert Arthur ***Scr*** John Grant, Frederic I. Rinaldo, Robert Lees ***Ph*** Charles Van Enger ***Ed*** Edward Curtiss ***Mus*** Walter Schumann ***Art*** Bernard Herzbrung, Frank A. Richards

Act Bud Abbott, Lou Costello, Nat Pendleton, Tom Brown, Joan Fulton (Universal-International)

Fat and thin comics romp through familiar routines with few variations, but it's still strong laugh material with capacity to satisfy fans of rowdy slapstick. Picture opens with scene from the original *Buck Privates*, getting things going with a sure laugh. Pace is maintained throughout by Charles Barton's direction which has plenty of punch to put over the crazy brand of comedy.

Sight gags, situations and chases that always feature Abbott & Costello comedies are strung on a story line that has the boys smuggling a little French girl into this country upon their return from overseas. Efforts to conceal the kid and prevent her deportation is frantic fun, climaxing in a hilarious chase that is socko. Another high spot is version of the old heights situation wherein Costello dangles from a clothes-line between two high buildings.

Lending strong support to comedians, is Nat Pendleton as the tough top kick who is driven frantic by antics.

•

BUDDY BUDDY

1982, 96 mins, US Ⓥ ▭ col

Dir Billy Wilder ***Prod*** Jay Weston ***Scr*** Billy Wilder, I.A.L. Diamond ***Ph*** Harry Stradling, Jr. ***Ed*** Argyle Nelson ***Mus*** Lalo Schifrin ***Art*** Daniel A. Lomino

Act Jack Lemmon, Walter Matthau, Paula Prentiss, Klaus Kinski, Dana Elcar, Miles Chapin (M-G-M)

The script, based on the [1973] French Jacques Brel-Lino Ventura starrer *L'emmerdeur*, directed by Edouard Molinaro and written by Francis Veber, is one of the rare Wilder projects not initiated by the director himself, and a certain lack of care and even thought permeate the effort, from script to casting to execution.

Abandoned by wife Paula Prentiss, Jack Lemmon is a nebbishy failure who checks into a Riverside hotel to end it all. In the next room is Walter Matthau, a stone-faced grouch and heartless hit man who's preparing to knock off a squealer.

The two men's paths quickly cross and, despite Matthau's claim that "I'm nobody's friend," he allows himself to become involved in Lemmon's plight, saving him from suicide attempts and actually driving him to the nearby sex clinic where Prentiss is attempting to achieve the ultimate orgasm under the guidance of oddball therapist Klaus Kinski.

Talented thesps Prentiss and Kinski bear the brunt of hopeless miscasting. Lalo Schifrin's dippy score sounds as if it were concocted in a few minutes for a sitcom pilot.

•

BUDDY HOLLY STORY, THE

1978, 113 mins, US Ⓥ ⦿ col

Dir Steve Rash ***Prod*** Fred Bauer ***Scr*** Robert Gittler ***Ph*** Stevan Larner ***Ed*** David Blewitt ***Mus*** Joe Renzetti ***Art*** Joel Schiller

Act Gary Busey, Don Stroud, Charles Martin Smith, Bill Jordan, Maria Richwine, Conrad Janis (Innovisions/ECA)

The Buddy Holly Story smacks of realism in almost every respect, from the dramaturgy involving Holly and his backup band, The Crickets, to the verisimilitude of the musical numbers. Latter were recorded live, using 24 tracks, and there was no studio rerecording. It was a gamble that pays off in full, and the Holly repertoire (an extensive one) gives the pic its underlying structure.

Gary Busey not only imparts the driven, perfectionist side of Holly's character, but his vocal work is excellent, as is his instrumentation. Robert Gittler's screenplay [from a story by Alan Swyer] takes Holly from his early days in Lubbock, Texas, where he churns out be-bop for the roller rink crowd, through his disastrous recording career (he punches out a Nashville producer), and up through national recognition on the heels of his big hit, "That'll Be the Day."

Along the way, director Steve Rash zeroes in on the growing conflict between Busey, drummer Don Stroud and bassist Charles Martin Smith, and the love relationship of Busey and Maria Richwine as his Puerto Rican bride. All principals register strongly.

1978: Best Adapted Score

NOMINATIONS: Best Actor (Gary Busey), Sound

•

BUECHSE DER PANDORA, DIE (PANDORA'S BOX)

1929, 131 mins, Germany Ⓥ ⊗ b/w

Dir G. W. Pabst ***Prod*** Seymour Nebenzal ***Scr*** Laszlo Wajda ***Ph*** Guenther Krampf

Act Louise Brooks, Fritz Kortner, Franz Lederer, Carl Goetz, Alice Roberts, Gustav Diessl (Nero)

Louise Brooks, especially imported for the title role, does not pan out, due to no fault of hers. She is quite unsuited to the vamp type [Lulu, a temptress finally killed by Jack the Ripper] which was called for by the play from which the picture was made.

Grave mistake to try to make a film of a Franz Wedekind play. Heavy vamp stuff which he wrote is already dated. On the stage, dialog is still of sufficient interest to hold, but the mere plot outline is trivial and overdone.

G. W. Pabst, director, in an attempt to keep the whole natural and easy, succeeds merely in making it superficial and lacking in suspense or thrill. Germany's newly discovered juvenile find, Franz Lederer, doesn't have a chance to show much, nor can Fritz Kortner get anything out of the heavy.

•

BUFFALO BILL

1944, 90 mins, US Ⓥ col

Dir William A. Wellman ***Prod*** Harry A. Sherman ***Scr*** Aeneas MacKenzie, Clements Ripley, Cecile Kramer ***Ph*** Leon Shamroy ***Ed*** James B. Clark ***Mus*** David Buttolph ***Art*** James Baseri, Lewis Creber

Act Joel McCrea, Maureen O'Hara, Linda Darnell, Thomas Mitchell, Anthony Quinn (20th Century-Fox)

Primarily escapist fare, *Buffalo Bill* is a super-western and often a tear-jerker. Filming it in colorful outdoor panorama, Harry A. Sherman has made it a magnificent production.

Those familiar with the story of William F. Cody may wonder why this cinema version [based on a story by Frank Winch] does not lay more stress on his career as a showman and less on his romance and wedded life. But few residents of Cody, Wyo, Council Bluffs or the Platte river country will find fault with the sweep of the redskin-white man struggle done so skillfully by director William A. Wellman.

Head-on battle between U.S. cavalry and Cheyenne tribe at War Bonnet Gorge is the story's focal point, with Buffalo Bill, famed scout and friend of the Indian, becoming the yarn's hero in man-to-man combat with his former redskin pal.

Joel McCrea makes a realistic Buffalo Bill. Maureen O'Hara, as the daughter of a senator who goes West to push through a railroad line, and later weds McCrea, is satisfying. Linda Darnell, the Indian schoolteacher who loves Cody, has too little to do but does that little with charm. Thomas Mitchell is the Eastern newspaperman who authors books about Buffalo Bill's fame in the West and acts as his promoter when he visits the east. Per usual, a shipshape characterization.

•

BUFFALO BILL AND THE INDIANS OR SITTING BULL'S HISTORY LESSON

1976, 123 mins, US Ⓥ ⦿ ▭ col

Dir Robert Altman ***Prod*** Robert Altman ***Scr*** Alan Rudolph, Robert Altman ***Ph*** Paul Lohmann ***Ed*** Peter Appleton, Dennis Hill ***Mus*** Richard Baskin ***Art*** Tony Masters

Act Paul Newman, Joel Grey, Kevin McCarthy, Harvey Keitel, Allan Nicholls, Geraldine Chaplin (De Laurentiis/Lion's Gate)

It appears that the idea here is to expose and debunk the Buffalo Bill legend, revealing it for the promotional distortion which, in some ways, it most certainly has to have been. Project was shot completely in Alberta.

Film [based on the play *Indians* by Arthur Kopit] shows Paul Newman bumbling through the challenge of living up to a legend created by Burt Lancaster, regularly popping up with bartender Bert Remsen in scenes of verbal recall. Joel Grey is Newman's current showman partner, while Kevin McCarthy grinds out the press agent claptrap.

The serious plot note is the determination of Sitting Bull (played very well in total silence by Frank Kaquitts) and interpreter Will Sampson not to debase history through cheap carny melodrama.

•

BUFFY THE VAMPIRE SLAYER
1992, 86 mins, US Ⓥ ⦿ col
Dir Fran Rubel Kuzui ***Prod*** Kaz Kuzui, Howard Rosenman ***Scr*** Joss Whedon ***Ph*** James Hayman ***Ed*** Camilla Toniolo, Jill Savitt ***Mus*** Carter Burwell ***Art*** Lawrence Miller
Act Kristy Swanson, Donald Sutherland, Paul Reubens, Rutger Hauer, Luke Perry, Michele Abrams (20th Century-Fox/Sandollar/Kuzui)

Buffy the Vampire Slayer is a bloodless comic resurrection of the undead that goes serious just when it should get wild and woolly. The marginal buoyancy of the opening reels quickly disappears from this threadbare (reportedly only $7 million) production, more effective as a sendup of Valley girls than as a clever take on bloodsuckers.

Blond, bouncy Buffy (Kristy Swanson) is lead cheerleader and Miss Popular in the senior class at Hemery High. A dirty old man in a long overcoat (Donald Sutherland) turns up to inform Buffy that she is a female vampire slayer, and she passes her trial by fire with flying colors when she subdues two marauding cretins.

When it becomes apparent that L.A. is under threat of a serious vampire invasion led by king Rutger Hauer and cackling henchman Paul Reubens, Buffy dives into an Olympian workout regimen to sharpen her skills with a stake. After biting a few teens and menacing Buffy and her would-be b.f. (Luke Perry), the vampires crash a high school dance in a limp rehash of the big set-piece in *Carrie*.

Swanson has a robust, athletic sexiness that will keep boy viewers happy, while the amiable Perry, in his first screen appearance since hitting with *Beverly Hills, 90210*, will make this a must-see for many adolescent girls.

Director Fran Rubel Kuzui, whose previous credit was the so-so indie *Tokyo Pop*, keeps her camera subjects very close to the lens and aims to accomplish no more than one piece of action per shot.

•

BUG
1975, 99 mins, US Ⓥ col
Dir Jeannot Szwarc ***Prod*** William Castle ***Scr*** William Castle, Thomas Page ***Ph*** Michael Hugo ***Ed*** Allan Jacobs ***Mus*** Charles Fox ***Art*** Jack Martin Smith
Act Bradford Dillman, Joanna Miles, Richard Gilliland, Jamie Smith Jackson, Alan Fudge, Jesse Vint (Paramount)

Bug concerns some mutated cockroaches liberated by an earthquake from the earth's core. Adapted from Thomas Page's book, *The Hephaestus Plague*, it starts off well with an earthquake in a farmland town, after which mysterious fires begin breaking out. The bugs, being from underground areas, are hot and eat carbon.

Bradford Dillman, an animal scientist, gets intrigued with them, so much so that, after wife Miles is incinerated in a bug attack, he becomes a recluse with the creatures and communicates with them. At the same time Dillman goes into seclusion, so does the film; its last half is largely static, and the film never revives much interest.

•

BUG'S LIFE, A
1998, 96 MINS, US Ⓥ ⦿ ▭ col
Dir John Lasseter, Andrew Stanton ***Prod*** Darla K. Anderson, Kevin Reher ***Scr*** Andrew Stanton, Donald McEnery, Bob Shaw ***Ph*** Sharon Calahan ***Ed*** Lee Unkrich ***Mus*** Randy Newman, ***Art*** William Cone (Pixar/Walt Disney)

Entertaining in a very showbizzy sort of way, *A Bug's Life* is more broad based and kid friendly in its appeal than DreamWorks' more sophisticated *Antz* [released seven weeks earlier, in September].

Director John Lasseter and Pixar Animation Studios broke new technical and aesthetic ground with the computer animated *Toy Story* (1995), and here they surpass it in both the scope and complexity of movement while telling a story that overlaps with that of *Antz* in numerous ways.

Presented in CinemaScope, *A Bug's Life* bursts upon the screen with beautiful verdant hues as a legion of ants laboriously transport food to await the arrival of their terrorizers, a gang of grasshoppers. Unfortunately, the hapless Flik (voiced by Dave Foley) knocks over the offering and the grasshoppers' big bully chief, Hopper (Kevin Spacey, oozing menace), threatens the little ones' existence unless they double their donation by the end of the season.

Flik exiles himself in a search for anyone who might help. All he can find are the eccentric members of a ragtag flea circus which counts among its numbers a male ladybug (Denis Leary) obsessed with his virility, a proud old praying mantis (Jonathan Harris), a humorous German caterpillar (Joe Ranft) and an unusually friendly black widow spider (Bonnie Hunt).

Story plays out at slight over-length. But Lasseter [who cowrote the original screen story with codirector Andrew Stanton and Ranft] and his imaginative team keep the senses stimulated most of the time with boisterous action.

Colors are bold and beautiful but never gaudy; overall look is crisp, clean and invariably pretty. While the number of individually rendered players is impressive, *Antz* has the edge when it comes to sheer spectacle.

Peformances across the board are spirited. Long end credits are spiced up by some very funny faux outtakes that are well worth sticking around for.

•

BUGSY
1991, 135 mins, US Ⓥ ⦿ col
Dir Barry Levinson ***Prod*** Mark Johnson, Barry Levinson, Warren Beatty ***Scr*** James Toback ***Ph*** Allen Daviau ***Ed*** Stu Linder ***Mus*** Ennio Morricone ***Art*** Dennis Gassner
Act Warren Beatty, Annette Bening, Harvey Keitel, Ben Kingsley, Elliott Gould, Joe Mantegna (Tri-Star/Mulholland/Baltimore)

A melancholy and intimate gangster saga about a romantic dreamer with fatal flaws, *Bugsy* emerges as a smooth, safe portrait of a volatile, dangerous character. An absorbing narrative flow and a parade of colorful underworld characters vie for screen time with an unsatisfactory central romance.

Handsome pic about the inventor of Las Vegas tells how Benjamin Siegel (Warren Beatty) was sent to L.A. to take over the West Coast rackets but stayed to become one of the legendary Hollywood characters of the 1940s. Siegel is a terrific subject for a film, but only part of the story comes across in this intelligently conceived drama. In James Toback's writing and Beatty's gutsy playing, Bugsy bursts out as a fully realized, psychologically complex character endowed with very human strengths and weaknesses. Unfortunately, his great love and female counterpart, Virginia Hill (Annette Bening), remains a one-dimensional and annoying stick figure, throwing great sections of the film out of whack.

Director Barry Levinson treats this punchy, emotionally eruptive story in fluid, almost dreamy fashion, rather like a sordid fairy tale. Although ethnically wrong and lacking a street-tough attitude, Beatty gives a dynamite performance, his most vital and surprising in a long time.

Among the standouts in the impressive supporting cast are Harvey Keitel as a feisty, appealing Mickey Cohen; Ben Kingsley as the impeccably businesslike Meyer Lansky; and director Richard Sarafian as the pathetic Jack Dragna. Elliott Gould effectively underplays the weak squealer Harry Greenberg. Joe Mantegna is oddly cast as George Raft.

1991: Best Art Direction, Costume Design

NOMINATIONS: Best Picture, Director, Actor (Warren Beatty), Supp. Actor (Harvey Keitel, Ben Kingsley), Original Screenplay, Cinematography, Original Score

•

BUGSY MALONE
1976, 93 mins, UK Ⓥ ⦿ col
Dir Alan Parker ***Prod*** Alan Marshall ***Scr*** Alan Parker ***Ph*** Michael Seresin, Peter Biziou ***Ed*** Gerry Hambling ***Mus*** Dave Garland (dir.) ***Art*** Geoffrey Kirkland
Act Scott Baio, Jodie Foster, Florrie Dugger, John Cassisi, Martin Lev, Paul Murphy (Goodtimes)

Set in 1929 Gotham, pic is a compendium of gangster/Prohibition pic situations and cliches, played tongue-in-cheek by a splendid cast of juves, a veritable casting treasure trove.

Jodie Foster is outstanding as a moll, but so are Scott Baio as Bugsy, John Cassisi as Fat Sam, Florrie Dugger as Blousey, Martin Lev as Dandy Dan, Paul Murphy and Albin Jenkins as, respectively, Leroy and Fizzy. Plus many others.

Writer-director Alan Parker deserves much of the credit for concept and execution, with Paul Williams sharing the spotlight on the strength of his songs (music and lyrics), all pleasantly reminiscent and tinkly. In short, it's a brave, funny and winning pic which is nearly—but regrettably not quite—a triumph.

1976: NOMINATION: Best Adapted Score

•

BUILD MY GALLOWS HIGH
SEE: OUT OF THE PAST

•

BULLDOG BREED, THE
1960, 100 mins, UK b/w
Dir Robert Asher ***Prod*** Hugh Stewart ***Scr*** Jack Davies, Henry Blyth, Norman Wisdom ***Ph*** Jack Asher ***Ed*** Gerry Hambling ***Mus*** Philip Green ***Art*** Harry Pottle
Act Norman Wisdom, Ian Hunter, David Lodge, Robert Urquhart, Edward Chapman, Eddie Byrne (Rank)

Series of situations, pegged to a thin story line, offer a lot of yocks even at their most contrived.

Without bothering with logical reasons, Norman Puckle (Norman Wisdom) tries to commit suicide for love of a haughty cinema cashbox blonde. As in everything in life he fails horribly, is rescued and persuaded to join the navy, where he continues to make a hash of everything. For a reason known only to the admiral, he is chosen, as the newest recruit, to be the first man sent into space in the *Interplanetary Projectile Bosun*.

The film stands or falls by Wisdom and though the actor, as always, seems to be trying rather too hard, his general good humor and energy carry him through the various situations entertainingly. Whether he's flirting with a dame, getting into the hair of senior officers, pricking pomposity, suffering indignities in the gymnasium or in special training, he is always the amiable gump, who retains the audience's sympathy even when they're ribbing him.

Wisdom is surrounded by some very capable performers, notably Ian Hunter as the pompous admiral and Edward Chapman as an even more pompous character. Technically, it's a capable job.

•

BULLDOG DRUMMOND
1929, 80 mins, US Ⓥ b/w
Dir F. Richard Jones ***Prod*** Samuel Goldwyn ***Scr*** Sidney Howard ***Ph*** George S. Barnes, Gregg Toland ***Ed*** Frank Lawrence, Viola Lawrence ***Mus*** [uncredited] ***Art*** William Cameron Menzies
Act Ronald Colman, Claud Allister, Joan Bennett, Lilyan Tashman, Lawrence Grant, Montagu Love (Goldwyn)

Entertaining picture of the highly charged thriller meller kind, mostly because of the likable performance of Ronald Colman in his first screamer. As a picture it's intense, with the suspense often and sharply broken into for a laugh by a fop Englishman of the common stage type. Adapted from the English stage play, many scenes are on the screen that could not have been set upon a stage. Bulldog Drummond is an idler looking for excitement. He gets it by saving the grandfather of a strange young woman from an insane asylum's crooks.

Play appears to have been pretty faithfully followed. Samuel Goldwyn gives the story a good production in all ways, with F. Richard Jones expertly handling the direction.

Lilyan Tashman is the she-devil. She takes her whisky straight. Lawrence Grant plays the fiendish doctor and well enough. Joan Bennett, the new lead, is oke on the looks side. She seems held down here, probably through inexperience.

1929/30: NOMINATION: Best Art Direction

•

BULL DURHAM
1988, 108 mins, US Ⓥ ⦿ col
Dir Ron Shelton ***Prod*** Thom Mount, Mark Burg ***Scr*** Ron Shelton ***Ph*** Bobby Byrne ***Ed*** Robert Leighton, Adam Weiss ***Mus*** Michael Convertino ***Art*** Armin Ganz
Act Kevin Costner, Susan Sarandon, Tim Robbins, Trey Wilson, Robert Wuhl, Jenny Robertson (Mount/Orion)

Bull Durham is a fanciful and funny bush league sports story where the only foul ball is its overuse of locker-room dialog. Kevin Costner is the quintessential American male who loves romance, but loves baseball even more.

The Durham Bulls of North Carolina dream of getting called up to be "in the show" as they endure another season of riding town to town on the team bus and suffering the dubious distinction of being one of the losingest clubs in Carolina league history.

Sent over from another "A" farm team to instruct, insult and inspire the Bulls' bullet-fast pitcher Ebby Calvin "Nuke" Laloosh (Tim Robbins) is embittered veteran catcher Crash David (Kevin Costner). His job is to get the cocky kid's arm on target by game time.

Costner is a natural as the dyed-in-the-wool ballplayer. His best lines are when he's philosophizing, like on being an All-American male who hates anything by Susan Sontag.

Susan Sarandon is never believable as a community college English lit teacher who, at the start of every season, latches on to the most promising rookie—in this case Robbins.

1988: NOMINATION: Best Original Screenplay

•

BULLETS OR BALLOTS

1936, 68 mins, US Ⓥ b/w

Dir William Keighley ***Prod*** Lou Edelman ***Scr*** Seton I. Miller ***Ph*** Hal Mohr ***Ed*** Jack Killifer ***Mus*** Leo F. Forbstein (dir.) ***Art*** Carl Jules Weyl

Act Edward G. Robinson, Joan Blondell, Humphrey Bogart, Barton MacLane, Frank McHugh, Joseph Keen (Warner/Frank McHugh)

This is a fast, smooth-working action picture. Story formula is along usual lines, with news events liberally sprinkled throughout. Martin Mooney, a New York reporter who got himself some front-page attention with a series of racketeering yarns in his newspaper, [is credited with cowriting the screen story with Seton I. Miller].

Edward G. Robinson bows out on his Warner contract in this picture with one of his most virile he-man characterizations. He's Johnny Blake, a tough but honest dick, duplicating the methods and mannerisms of an actual N.Y. dick. Al Kruger (Barton MacLane), obviously based on Dutch Schultz, is the racketeer king who has everything beautifully organized.

Director William Keighley keeps the picture moving and real at all times. MacLane is tops, with the role neatly paralleled by the work of Humphrey Bogart as a first aid and a convicing menace. Joan Blondell is dragged in by the heels as a sort of minor romance note for Robinson, but not too emphasized.

•

BULLETS OVER BROADWAY

1994, 99 mins, US Ⓥ ⊙ col

Dir Woody Allen ***Prod*** Robert Greenhut ***Scr*** Woody Allen, Douglas McGrath ***Ph*** Carlo Di Palma ***Ed*** Susan E. Morse ***Art*** Santo Loquasto

Act John Cusack, Jack Warden, Chazz Palminteri, Joe Viterelli, Jennifer Tilly, Rob Reiner (Sweetland/Miramax)

Woody Allen works a clever twist on the Cyrano theme in *Bullets over Broadway*, a backstage comedy bolstered by healthy shots of prohibition gangster melodrama and romantic entanglements. Not all the characters in the colorful ensemble cast are well developed, and some of the subplots peter out, but constantly amusing confection keeps improving as it scoots along.

This is Allen's first indie venture away from his longtime studio affiliations, but longtime behind-the-scenes collaborators are still on board to turn out an unusually handsome 1920s period piece.

The neurotic, hypochondriacal Allen personality is present in the form of David Shayne (John Cusack), a young Greenwich Village playwright who swears he'll brook no compromise in the production of his new play, *God of Our Fathers*. Shayne quickly changes his tune when producer Julian Marx (Jack Warden) informs him that he's found a backer with the proviso that the man's girlfriend play a prominent role.

The "actress," Olive Neal (Jennifer Tilly), is a goo-voiced bimbo and her only qualification is that she's the mistress of bigtime mobster Nick Valenti (Joe Viterelli). Shayne must also tolerate the critical barbs of Olive's thuggish bodyguard, Cheech (Chazz Palminteri), who sits in on all rehearsals.

The shenanigans of these characters, as well as the rest of the play's cast, including Jim Broadbent, Tracey Ullman and grande dame leading lady Dianne Wiest, consume most of the seriocomic attention as the play wends its way, first to Boston, then back to New York.

A street hoodlum and hit man, Cheech begins by telling Shayne, "You don't write like people talk," and gradually makes secret contributions to the play-in-progress that end up saving it from major flopdom. In its mixing of showbiz and gangsters, this is a nice companion piece to Allen's *Broadway Danny Rose*, and about as amusing.

1995: Best Supp. Actress (Dianne Wiest)

NOMINATIONS: Director, Supp. Actor (Chazz Palminteri), Supp. Actress (Jennifer Tilly), Original Screenplay, Art Direction, Costume Design

•

BULLFIGHTER AND THE LADY

1951, 87 mins, US Ⓥ ⊙ b/w

Dir Budd Boetticher ***Prod*** John Wayne ***Scr*** James Edward Grant ***Ph*** Jack Draper ***Ed*** Richard L. Van Enger ***Mus*** Victor Young ***Art*** Alfred Ybarra

Act Robert Stack, Joy Page, Gilbert Roland, Virginia Grey, John Hubbard, Katy Jurado (Republic)

Producer John Wayne and associate producer-director Budd Boetticher evidence a fondness for the Mexican scene through care in which they bring it accurately to the screen. Use of Robert Stack as an American vacationing below the border brings the plot and development closer to the Stateside audience and gives an understanding insight into the art of bullfighting and why it is the favorite Mexican pastime.

Stack falls in love with Joy Page's high-born Mexican girl. To impress her, he induces Gilbert Roland's matador idol to instruct him in the use of the cape and sword. Stack begins to feel the urge and thrill of the art but, in a careless, showoff moment, he causes Roland's death when the latter tries to save him. To atone, Stack fights another bull in honor of his friend.

The story [by Boetticher and Ray Nazarro] comes off much better in the viewing than in the telling as Boetticher keeps it punching at all times. A particular standout is Roland. Without overplaying, he gives his matador character color and vigor, bravery without bravado, and dignity.

1951: NOMINATION: Best Motion Picture Story

•

BULLITT

1968, 113 mins, US Ⓥ ⊙ col

Dir Peter Yates ***Prod*** Philip D'Antoni ***Scr*** Alan R. Trustman, Harry Kleiner ***Ph*** William A. Fraker ***Ed*** Frank P. Keller ***Mus*** Lalo Schifrin ***Art*** Albert Brenner

Act Steve McQueen, Robert Vaughn, Jacqueline Bisset, Don Gordon, Robert Duvall, Simon Oakland (Solar/Warner)

Conflict between police sleuthing and political expediency is the essence of *Bullitt*, an extremely well-made crime melodrama [from Robert L. Pike's novel *Mute Witness*] filmed in Frisco. Steve McQueen delivers a very strong performance as a detective seeking a man whom Robert Vaughn, ambitious politico, would exploit for selfish motives. Good scripting and excellent direction by Peter Yates maintain deliberately low-key but mounting suspense.

Arrival in Frisco of a Chi hood cues assignment of McQueen, plus assistants Don Gordon and Carol Reindel, to protect his life until headline-hunting Vaughn produces him dramatically before a senate crime committee. Hood's death, at the hands of Paul Genge, provokes the primary dramatic conflict: Vaughn wants a live witness, while McQueen is interested in apprehending the killer.

Simon Oakland, McQueen's superior, lets him pursue the case independently, while Vaughn, with aid from another senior detective, Norman Fell, is after independent sleuth's scalp.

1968: Best Editing

NOMINATION: Best Sound

•

BULWORTH

1998, 107 mins, US Ⓥ ⊙ col

Dir Warren Beatty ***Prod*** Warren Beatty, Pieter Jan Brugge ***Scr*** Warren Beatty, Jeremy Pikser ***Ph*** Vittorio Storaro ***Ed*** Robert C. Jones, Billy Weber ***Mus*** Ennio Morricone ***Art*** Dean Tavoularis

Act Warren Beatty, Halle Berry, Don Cheadle, Oliver Platt, Paul Sorvino, Jack Warden (20th Century-Fox)

Warren Beatty's disarmingly blunt look at a U.S. senator who suddenly starts speaking the truth about the day's important issues—in rhyming rap cadences, no less—is an uncommonly smart, sharp and irreverent American picture, a disillusioned liberal's broadside against political sellouts, corporate deceit, media manipulation, aggravated race relations and even mediocre, cynical Hollywood filmmaking.

Pic shares with *Shampoo* a manic, borderline farcical approach to serious subjects, albeit one that abruptly shifts, like all of Beatty's best work, to rueful melancholy at the end.

On the eve of the 1996 California primary, Sen. Jay Bulworth (Beatty) is despondent over the hollow sound of his own voice and campaign slogans. Taking out a $10 million insurance policy, he orders a hit on himself that will put him out of his misery for once and for all.

At an African-American church in South Central, the neo-con Democrat begins shocking his friendly audience with brutal remarks about why politicians ignore their promises to blacks, to the chagrin of his spin-obsessed manager (Oliver Platt) and a quizzical reaction from a local fox, Nina (Halle Berry). He [later] packs Nina and two of her girlfriends into his limo and has them take him along to the wildest after-hours club in South Central.

During a long, druggy night, WASP-y Bulworth metamorphoses into an irreverent hip-hopper. After Nina comes on to him in an elevator, he phones his contact to call off the hit, but, unbeknownst to him, the word doesn't get through.

Centerscreen most of the time, Beatty rarely before has given the impression of having so much fun as he does here. In a cast selected with exceptional imagination, the one insufficiently conceived character is Berry's, whose inscrutability often serves as a drain on the action.

•

BUNNY LAKE IS MISSING

1965, 107 mins, UK Ⓥ ▭ b/w

Dir Otto Preminger ***Prod*** Otto Preminger ***Scr*** John Mortimer, Penelope Mortimer ***Ph*** Denys Coop ***Ed*** Peter Thornton ***Mus*** Paul Glass ***Art*** Don Ashton

Act Carol Lynley, Keir Dullea, Laurence Olivier, Noel Coward, Martita Hunt, Anna Massey (Columbia/Wheel)

Bunny Lake is about the only thing missing from Otto Preminger's exercise in suspense and the viewer is kept in uncertainty about her for most of the film. What Preminger has achieved is an entertaining, fast-paced exercise in the exploration of a sick mind. Evelyn Piper's 1957 novel dealt entirely with the unpredictable actions of a mother searching for her child (real or imaginary) who had disappeared. To this plot skeleton Preminger has added an equally important character whose predictable actions provide the search's principal obstacles.

Carrying much of the film on her shoulders, Carol Lynley, as the mother shoved into a state of near hysteria almost from the beginning, is outstanding.

Keir Dullea, as her brother, most effective in earlier scenes where he conveys the natural, if easily aroused, anger of a devoted brother. Laurence Olivier's police inspector, is played in the manner of a psychiatrist. While nothing more than a routine role, Olivier does give it dignity and purpose and makes it a calm and restful contrast to the highly-strung emoting of Dullea and Lynley.

•

BUONA SERA, MRS. CAMPBELL

1968, 111 mins, Italy Ⓥ ⊙ col

Dir Melvin Frank ***Prod*** Melvin Frank ***Scr*** Melvin Frank, Shelden Keller, Dennis Norden ***Ph*** Gabor Pogany ***Ed*** William Butler ***Mus*** Riz Ortolani ***Art*** Arrigo Equini

Act Gina Lollobrigida, Shelley Winters, Phil Silvers, Peter Lawford, Telly Savalas, Janet Margolin (United Artists/Connaught)

Buona Sera, Mrs. Campbell is a very entertaining comedy with solid, personal, human values. Story is about an Italian woman who has conned three American bed partners from World War II into support of her and an illegitimate daughter for more than 20 years.

Gina Lollobrigida, Shelley Winters, Phil Silvers, Peter Lawford, Telly Savalas and Lee Grant head an excellent cast.

Story is economically laid forth: Lollobrigida has fooled her neighbors into believing daughter Janet Margolin was by a deceased U.S. Air Force pilot. However, a reunion of the airmen, in the town where they were based, precipitates a potential crisis, since, in truth, the real father could have been Silvers, Lawford or Savalas. Performances are strong: Lollobrigida, no comedy actress, is one here. Winters and Grant are great; Silvers and all the others are just right.

•

'BURBS, THE

1989, 103 mins, US Ⓥ ⊙ col

Dir Joe Dante ***Prod*** Larry Brezner, Michael Finnell ***Scr*** Dana Olsen ***Ph*** Robert Stevens ***Ed*** Marshall Harvey ***Mus*** Jerry Goldsmith ***Art*** James Spencer

Act Tom Hanks, Bruce Dern, Carrie Fisher, Rick Ducommun, Corey Feldman, Henry Gibson (Imagine/Universal)

Director Joe Dante funnels his decidedly cracked view of suburban life through dark humour in *The 'Burbs*. The action never strays beyond the cozy confines of the nightmarish block everyman Ray (Tom Hanks) inhabits along with an uproarious assemblage of wacky neighbors.

Poor Ray has a week off and just wants to spend it quietly at home with his wife Carol (Carrie Fisher). Instead, he's drawn into an increasingly elaborate sleuthing game involving the mysterious Klopeks, who reside in a "Munsters"-esque house rife with indications of foul play.

Ray's more familiar neighbors are equally bizarre: the corpulent Art (Rick Ducommun), convinced the Klopeks are performing satanic sacrifices; Rumsfield (Bruce Dern), a shell-shocked ex-GI; Walter (Gale Gordon), who delights in letting his dog relieve himself on Rumsfield's lawn; and Ricky (Corey Feldman) a teenager who sees all the strange goings-on as viewing fodder for parties with his friends.

Hanks does a fine impersonation of a regular guy on the verge of a nervous breakdown, while Dern adds another memorable psychotic to his resume. The big breakthroughs, however, are Ducommun, superb in a role that would have well-suited John Candy; and Wendy Schaal as Dern's airhead wife.

•

BUREAU OF MISSING PERSONS
1933, 75 mins, US Ⓥ b/w
Dir Roy Del Ruth *Scr* Robert Presnell *Ph* Barney McGill *Ed* James Gibbon *Mus* Leo F. Forbstein (dir.) *Art* Robert M. Haas
Act Bette Davis, Lewis S. Stone, Pat O'Brien, Glenda Farrell, Allen Jenkins, Ruth Donnelly (First National)

Pretty fair entertainment. Fortunately, it's been steered clear of over sombreness or becoming too morbid; also hyperdramatic or bordering on the gangster cycle.

Preface mentions the large percentage of humans who seemingly manage to drop off the face of the earth with great success and little difficulty. Lewis Stone, as the kindly captain heading the Missing Persons Dept., is shown in sundry cross-sections how to properly pursue his duties without working too great a hardship on any of the principals.

When a playboy husband is found in his love nest he suggests not bringing extra heartaches to his family but a pseudo-amnesia disappearance and ultimate discovery instead. When a violin child prodigy of 12 runs away from his concerts and the symphony halls because he has the natural boyhood yen to be a kid and not a genius, the human equation is gotten over.

Against these colorful but rather disjointed details, scenarist Robert Presnell [adapting John H. Ayres and Carol Bird's story *Missing Men*] has wisely thrown a main romance theme involving Bette Davis and Pat O'Brien. Just when it threatens to become banal, excellent trouping and some inspired dialoging snap it back into proper gait.

•

BURGLAR, THE
1957, 90 mins, US b/w
Dir Paul Wendkos *Prod* Louis W. Kellman *Scr* David Goodis *Ph* Don Malkames *Ed* Paul Wendkos *Mus* Sol Kaplan *Art* Jim Leonard
Act Dan Duryea, Jayne Mansfield, Martha Vickers, Peter Capell, Mickey Shaughnessy, Wendell Phillips (Kellman)

Dan Duryea, Jayne Mansfield and Martha Vickers manage to overcome handicaps posed by David Goodis's scripting and Paul Wendkos's direction to rate an okay for performance. The same can't be said for other casters, most of whom are permitted to overact to the point of oldtime scenery-chewing, especially radio's Peter Capell in his role as a member of Duryea's burglar gang.

Novel opening is a newsreel-type prolog, in which Duryea spots a necklace he wants. Plot then moves into the story, goes through the heist of the jewels from the mansion of a Philadelphia spiritualist, followed by the gang's holing-up in a battered old house while the police look for clues and set law-enforcement machinery into work. Basic story idea, taken from Goodis's novel of the same title, is okay, but suspense and action are by-passed and sloughed while the assorted characters go into long soliloquizing about how they got into their various predicaments.

Don Malkames's lensing pays attention to highspots of the Philadelphia–Atlantic City locales while helping story mood.

•

BURKE & WILLS
1985, 140 mins, Australia Ⓥ ⦿ ▭ col
Dir Graeme Clifford *Prod* Graeme Clifford *Scr* Michael Thomas *Ph* Russell Boyd *Ed* Tim Wellburn *Mus* Peter Sculthorpe *Art* Ross Major
Act Jack Thompson, Nigel Havers, Greta Scacchi, Matthew Fargher, Ralph Cotterill, Drew Forsythe (Hoyts Edgley)

Big in scope, and emotionally stimulating, this Australian pic about the doomed 1860 expedition of explorers Burke and Wills to cross the continent and back, is satisfying entertainment despite its length and seemingly downbeat subject.

That the story emerges quite differently on film is very much to the credit of director Graeme Clifford and screenwriter Michael Thomas, two expatriate Australians.

Russell Boyd's superior cinematography, on the locations originally traversed by the explorers, is quite ravishing. Clifford shrewdly inserts flashbacks into the desert material evoking scenes of Wills at home in England and Burke's dalliance with a comely opera singer.

Jack Thompson, with full beard, is an imposing Burke, a fiery-tempered Irishman whose determination to succeed clouds his judgment. This is one of Thompson's best performances. British actor Nigel Havers is excellent as the scientist, Wills, stubbornly following his friend into the unknown while barely concealing his fears for the outcome.

•

BURMESE HARP, THE
SEE: BIRUMA NO TATEGOTO

•

BURNING HILLS, THE
1956, 93 mins, US Ⓥ ▭ col
Dir Stuart Heisler *Prod* Richard Whorf *Scr* Irving Wallace *Ph* Ted McCord *Ed* Clarence Kolster *Mus* David Buttolph *Art* Charles H. Clarke
Act Tab Hunter, Natalie Wood, Skip Homeier, Eduard Franz, Earl Holliman, Claude Akins (Warner)

Tab Hunter and Natalie Wood form a team of somewhat younger stars than is customarily found in sagebrush sagas and do an okay job of the outdoor assignment. The Louis L'Amour novel and screenplay by Irving Wallace pretty much follows a familiar pattern in basic ingredients and dialogue.

Story has to do with Trace Jordan's (Hunter) efforts to avenge the death of his brother, murdered by henchmen of a big cattle baron (Ray Teal) who doesn't want small operators on his range. From avenger he becomes the chased, taking off through the hills in the company of Maria Colton (Wood), Anglo-Mexican girl, with the baron's gunslingers in hot pursuit. Skip Homeier gets in his deadly licks as the son of cattle baron Teal. He's just as bloodthirsty as his old man. Eduard Franz, Indian tracker reluctantly leading the gunslingers on the trail, is good.

•

BURNING SECRET
1989, 106 mins, UK/US/W. Germany Ⓥ ⦿ col
Dir Andrew Birkin *Prod* Norma Heyman, Eberhard Junkersdorf, Carol Lynn Greene *Scr* Andrew Birkin *Ph* Ernest Day *Ed* Paul Green *Mus* Hans Zimmer *Art* Bernd Lepel
Act Faye Dunaway, Klaus Maria Brandauer, David Eberts, Ian Richardson (NFH/CLG/BA)

Burning Secret is the intriguing story of a mother's near-adultery as seen through the impressionable eyes of her 12-year-old son, coupled with the elegant setting of post-World War I Austria in winter.

First-time director Andrew Birkin (brother of France-based actress Jane Birkin) has adapted a Stefan Zweig short story [*Brennendes Geheimnis*] set in 1919 and previously filmed in Germany in 1933 by Robert Siodmak. Drama has some of the same elements found in Zweig's more famous story, *Letter from an Unknown Woman*.

The woman is Sonya (Faye Dunaway), elegant wife of a stuffy diplomat (Ian Richardson) far older than she. When their young son, who suffers severely from asthma, is sent for treatment at a sanitorium in the mountains, the mother accompanies him.

On the first morning, the son meets Baron Alexander Maria von Hauenschild (Klaus Maria Brandauer), a charming veteran of the war. Sonya is quite willing to seize the opportunity of a passionate love affair which is only constrained by the constant presence of her innocent, inquisitive son.

Although the material is a little slight, the drama works thanks to the flawless performances. Dunaway is coolly stylish and yet passionate. Brandauer brings a touch of menace to his charming character. Young David Eberts (son of former Goldcrest exec Jake Eberts) is a find as the trusting youngster. The production was filmed entirely in Czechoslovakia, on location in Prague (doubling for Vienna) and Marienbad.

•

BURNT OFFERINGS
1976, 116 mins, US Ⓥ col
Dir Dan Curtis *Prod* Dan Curtis *Scr* William F. Nolan, Dan Curtis *Ph* Jacques Marquette *Ed* Dennis Virkler *Mus* Robert Cobert *Art* Eugene Lourie
Act Karen Black, Oliver Reed, Burgess Meredith, Eileen Heckart, Lee H. Montgomery, Dub Taylor (PEA)

Most of the cliches of the Gothic genre are encompassed in the plot about Karen Black, Oliver Reed, Bette Davis, and young Lee H. Montgomery having a weird summer after moving into a home owned by batty Burgess Meredith and Eileen Heckart. The horror is expressed through sudden murderous impulses felt by Black and Reed, a premise which might have been interesting if director Dan Curtis hadn't relied strictly on formula treatment.

The plot [from the novel by Robert Marasco] is treated in mysterioso fashion but the audience can guess the ending maybe an hour before it happens. Black gives an uncertain performance, Reed grimaces and sweats a lot, but Montgomery manages to be believable in the film's best role, and Meredith is suitably creepy.

•

BUS RILEY'S BACK IN TOWN
1965, 93 mins, US col
Dir Harvey Hart *Prod* Elliott Kastner *Scr* Walter Gage *Ph* Russell Metty *Ed* Folmar Blangsted *Mus* Richard Markowitz *Art* Alexander Golitzen, Frank Arrigo
Act Ann-Margret, Michael Parks, Janet Margolin, Brad Dexter, Jocelyn Brando, Larry Storch (Universal)

Where to pinpoint the blame for this well-intended major feature's failure is difficult. Certainly some of it must be allotted to former TV-director Harvey Hart's inexperience with the bigger-screen medium, and his lack of control over several of the thespians involved, but the erratic, chopped-up screenplay is also a major fault. Originally announced as the work of William Inge, screen credit is now given to Walter Gage, evidently a pseudonym for the several studio writers who had a go at it. Bits of Inge remain.

The story centers on the title character, played by newcomer Michael Parks. He tends to rely overmuch on "method" methods—the tightly constricted gesture, the stammer, the withdrawn, hunched-shoulder, hooded-eye type of acting that is rarely effective on the wide screen. Fortunately, Parks responds to the interplay provided by a bona fide talent. His scenes with Janet Margolin are his best, those with Ann-Margret, his poorest.

A simple plot—young ex-serviceman seeking an identity and faced with the problem of succumbing to the wiles of bad girl (Ann-Margret) or meeting responsibility head on (with implied support of good girl).

•

BUS STOP
1956, 96 mins, US Ⓥ ⦿ ▭ col
Dir Joshua Logan *Prod* Buddy Adler *Scr* George Axelrod *Ph* Milton Krasner *Ed* William Reynolds *Mus* Alfred Newman, Cyril Mockridge *Art* Lyle R. Wheeler, Mark-Lee Kirk
Act Marilyn Monroe, Don Murray, Arthur O'Connell, Betty Field, Eileen Heckart, Hope Lange (20th Century-Fox)

William Inge's rowdy play about a cowboy and a lady (sic) gets a raucous screen treatment. Both the scripter and director, George Axelrod and Joshua Logan respectively, were brought from the legit field to get the Inge comedy on film and, with a few minor exceptions, bring the chore off resoundingly.

New face Don Murray is the exuberant young cowhand who comes to the city to win some rodeo money and learn about women.

Marilyn Monroe fans will find her s.a. not so positive, but still potent, in her *Bus Stop* character, but this goes with the type of well-used saloon singer and would-be actress she portrays. Monroe comes off acceptably, even though failing to maintain any kind of consistency in the Southern accent.

Murray is a 21-year-old Montana rancher who comes to Phoenix for the rodeo, meets and kisses his first girl and literally kidnaps her. The girl, a "chantoosie" in a cheap restaurant patronized by rodeo performers, is reluctant about marriage, but by the time Murray ropes her, shouts at her, and gets beat up for her, she gives in, both because love has set in, as well as physical exhaustion.

Arthur O'Connell milks everything from his spot as Murray's friend and watchdog and Betty Field clicks big as the amorous operator of the roadside bus stop.

1956: NOMINATION: Best Supp. Actor (Don Murray)

•

BUSTER
1988, 103 mins, UK Ⓥ ⦿ col
Dir David Green *Prod* Norma Heyman *Scr* David Shindler *Ph* Tony Imi *Ed* Lesley Walker *Mus* Anne Dudley *Art* Simon Holland
Act Phil Collins, Julie Walters, Larry Lamb, Stephanie Lawrence, Ellen Beaven, Michael Attwell (NFH/Movie Group/Hemdale)

Buster is part romantic comedy, part crime thriller and part moral tale, but more importantly it features a charismatic big screen bow by popster Phil Collins in the title role.

Pic opens in London of 1963 with self-proclaimed smalltime "lucky thief" Collins and Julie Walters blissfully happy. Collins gets involved in a scheme to rob a Royal Mail train of £2.6 million, and when the gang pulls off the raid, hailed as The Great Train Robbery, they find themselves regarded as folk heroes.

Collins, wife Walters and daughter Ellen Beaven go into hiding, but police pressure mounts and the family is forced to go on the run to Switzerland and finally Acapulco. In Mexico, the Collins-Walters marriage is stretched.

Buster can't seem to make up its mind what sort of film it is. It plays as a romantic comedy to begin with, then switches to a caper pic before ending with domestic drama. Helmer David Green directs all aspects well, adding nice insights into the characters, especially when in Mexico, but there is an overall feeling that the pic is slightly disjointed.

1988: NOMINATION: Best Song ("Two Hearts")

•

BUSTER AND BILLIE
1974, 98 mins, US Ⓥ col
Dir Daniel Petrie ***Prod*** Ron Silverman ***Scr*** Ron Turbeville ***Ph*** Mario Tosi ***Ed*** Michael Kahn ***Mus*** Al De Lory
Act Jan-Michael Vincent, Joan Goodfellow, Pamela Sue Martin, Clifton James, Robert Englund, Jessie Lee Fulton (Columbia)

Nostalgia gets another workout in *Buster and Billie.* Screenplay, conventionally directed by Daniel Petrie, has a good deal of charm and veristic detail until its romantic tale crashes in a last-reel melee of unmotivated violence.

On the surface pic is just 1948 Georgia graffiti. Jan-Michael Vincent and Pamela Sue Martin are the town sweethearts, petting heavily in his truck but delaying further action until their imminent wedding day. Meanwhile, the stags all get theirs from Joan Goodfellow, a rather dumpy blonde from the other side of the tracks.

Feeling more frustrated than usual, Vincent also pays the glumly obliging Goodfellow a visit one night, then finds himself falling in love with her.

The slim plot raises psychological questions that could have been profitably explored.

•

BUSTING
1974, 91 mins, US Ⓥ col
Dir Peter Hyams ***Prod*** Irwin Winkler, Robert Chartoff ***Scr*** Peter Hyams ***Ph*** Earl Rath ***Ed*** James Mitchell ***Mus*** Billy Goldenberg ***Art*** [uncredited]
Act Elliott Gould, Robert Blake, Allen Garfield, Antonio Fargas, Sid Haig, Michael Lerner (United Artists)

Elliott Gould and Robert Blake star as vagrant vice squad detectives, the kind who in real life set law and order back decades. Production is confused, compromised and clumsy.

The plot eventually gets around to blaming nearly every criminal activity in town on Allen Garfield, cast as a local crime lord. Garfield, as ever an outstanding performer, brings dignity and a sense of being totally together to the part.

Atop the script problems is overlaid some embarrassingly forced direction by debuting Peter Hyams, a former TV newsman. In particular the crutch of an incessant slowly tracking camera, as though a pile of debris looks any different (or better) from assorted angles. There are a couple of well-staged vehicle chases which for a few minutes divert attention from the story.

•

BUSTIN' LOOSE
1981, 94 mins, US Ⓥ ⦿ col
Dir Oz Scott ***Prod*** Richard Pryor, Michael S. Glick ***Scr*** Roger L. Simon ***Ph*** Dennis Dalzell ***Ed*** David Holden ***Mus*** Mark Davis ***Art*** Charles R. Davis, John Corso
Act Richard Pryor, Cicely Tyson, Robert Christian, Alphonso Alexander, Janet Wong (Universal)

Bustin' Loose is obviously a personal project for Pryor, who produced and wrote the story, which has admirable ambitions but is also the film's greatest weakness.

Still, Pryor is an infectious comedian and a master of body language, keeping the picture on the move with sheer energy. He's a bungling burglar but good mechanic whose parole officer (Robert Christian) forces him to go to the aid of Cicely Tyson, the director of a school for emotionally disturbed children about to close for lack of money. She wants to flee Philly with eight of the kids and get to her family farm near Seattle. There's a bit of the *African Queen* to this journey as the prissy, prim and dominant Tyson and vulgar, unkempt Pryor find their initial hostility turning to romance.

On the way, it's the constant breakdowns of the bus, the impatience with the kids and other obstacles—including a hilarious encounter with the Ku Klux Klan—that feed Pryor his material and he makes the most of it. This is a feature debut for Broadway director Oz Scott and he handles the chore comfortably.

•

BUTCH AND SUNDANCE: THE EARLY DAYS
1979, 110 mins, US Ⓥ ⦿ col
Dir Richard Lester ***Prod*** Gabriel Katzka, Steven Bach ***Scr*** Allan Burns ***Ph*** Laszlo Kovacs ***Ed*** Antony Gibbs, George Trirogoff ***Mus*** Patrick Williams ***Art*** Brian Eatwell
Act William Katt, Tom Berenger, Brian Dennehy, Peter Weller, Jeff Corey, Jill Eikenberry (20th Century-Fox/Pantheon)

This prequel doesn't match its progenitor in either casting or style. Without Paul Newman or Robert Redford in the title roles, it doesn't matter whether *Butch* dwells on the pair's infancy or senility—there's no star chemistry. Tom Berenger and William Katt acquit themselves admirably, but they simply can't compete with the ghosts of two superstars.

Butch is standard sagebrush material, with few of the comic misadventures that characterized the original. There are some patented Richard Lester hijinks in the first half-hour of the prequel, but these peter out surprisingly soon.

1979: NOMINATION: Best Costume Design

•

BUTCH CASSIDY AND THE SUNDANCE KID
1969, 112 mins, US Ⓥ ⦿ ▭ col
Dir George Roy Hill ***Prod*** John Foreman ***Scr*** William Goldman ***Ph*** Conrad Hill ***Ed*** John C. Howard, Richard C. Meyer ***Mus*** Burt Bacharach ***Art*** Jack Martin Smith, Philip Jefferies
Act Paul Newman, Robert Redford, Katharine Ross, Strother Martin, Jeff Corey, Cloris Leachman (20th Century-Fox/Campanile)

Lighthearted treatment of a purportedly true story of the two badmen who made Wyoming outlaw history, film emerges a near-comedy of errors. Newman plays Butch, one of the most deadly outlaws of the West whose gang variously was known as The Wild Bunch and Hole-in-the-Wall Gang. Robert Redford, portrays the Kid, wizard with a gun.

Butch is an affable, almost gay, individual who can turn on the power when he wishes but usually is a sociable, talkative sort of cuss; Redford, silent, menacing in the power of his fabled guns, displays no evidence of the evil temper which gained him his reputation. Together, they make a fine team, accompanied by frequent banter.

Narrative starts in Wyoming where Butch and his gang are involved in various train holdups and pursuits by posses after bank robberies. This leads to Butch and the Kid trying their luck in Bolivia.

1969: Best Original Story & Screenplay, Cinematography, Song ("Raindrops Keep Fallin' on My Head"), Original Score

NOMINATIONS: Best Picture, Director, Sound

•

BUTCHER, THE
SEE: LE BOUCHER

•

BUTCHER BOY, THE
1917, 30 mins, US ⊗ b/w
Dir Roscoe "Fatty" Arbuckle ***Prod*** Joseph M. Schenck
Act Roscoe "Fatty" Arbuckle, Arthur Earle, Josephine Stevens, Al St. John, Buster Keaton, Agnes Neilsen (Comique)

The Comique Film Co.'s series of Arbuckle two-reelers starts off with Fatty shaking out a bag of laugh-making tricks. The cast fits the star, and not the least important member is Luke, the bull terrier.

Arbuckle juggling with the accessories of the country store where he is an important factor, also his way of handling feminine clothes worn in his visit to the girl's boarding school, is done in such a serious, earnest way the comic effect is all the more forceful.

The butcher boy in a country store falls in love with the cashier (Josephine Stevens), the daughter of the proprietor (Arthur Earle), and when she is sent away to boarding school he goes to the school as her cousin. The first of the Arbuckle series sets a good mark to aim at.

•

BUTCHER'S WIFE, THE
1991, 104 mins, US Ⓥ ⦿ col
Dir Terry Hughes ***Prod*** Wallis Nicita, Lauren Lloyd ***Scr*** Ezra Litwak, Marjorie Schwartz ***Ph*** Frank Tidy ***Ed*** Donn Cambern ***Mus*** Michael Gore ***Art*** Charles Rosen
Act Demi Moore, Jeff Daniels, George Dzundza, Mary Steenburgen, Frances McDormand, Margaret Colin (Paramount)

A gentle romantic comedy with a distinct 1940s flavor, *The Butcher's Wife* is blessed with a fine cast working from a storybook plot. The unpretentious and simple film has a "make 'em weep like they used to" quality. Its belief in modern-day magic (in a sense similar to *Moonstruck*) softens an inherent predictability dictating that all loose ends be resolved to everyone's satisfaction in 100 minutes.

Demi Moore plays a country clairvoyant whose visions of romance are answered in the surprising form of a New York butcher (George Dzundza) whom she marries immediately, returning with him to his neighborhood. Her visions immediately start to touch all those who cross her path, in the process increasingly nettling the local psychologist (Jeff Daniels), whose patients seem to need him far less as they bathe in the comfort of Moore's future gazing.

Those who encounter Moore include the shrink's girlfriend (Margaret Colin), a dowdy patient (Mary Steenburgen) with aspirations to sing the blues, and lesbian friend (Frances McDormand), who's told romance waits just around the corner.

Helmer Terry Hughes, a TV director, and first-time screenwriters bring a fresh, uncynical eye to familiar terrain. Pic's only real revelation is Steenburgen, not for her considerable acting skills, but for her fine voice in a trio of bluesy ballads.

•

BUTLEY
1974, 129 mins, UK/US/Canada col
Dir Harold Pinter ***Prod*** Ely Landau ***Scr*** Simon Gray ***Ph*** Gerry Fisher ***Ed*** Malcolm Cooke ***Art*** Carmen Dillon
Act Alan Bates, Jessica Tandy, Richard O'Callaghan, Susan Engel, Michael Byrne, Georgina Hale (American Express/Landau)

Alan Bates's stage triumph in Simon Gray's *Butley* has been superbly recreated on the screen, with the added excellence of Harold Pinter's top-notch film directorial debut. It reunites both Richard O'Callaghan and Michael Byrne from the original London production.

The plot basically is one horrendous day in the life of an embittered teacher, who loses his estranged wife to a lesser professional colleague, his lover to another man, and his sense of superiority over a female associate whose lifelong book project has been accepted for publication while his lies unfinished.

Jessica Tandy, a middle-aged teacher who doesn't seem to understand her modern students, is excellent in projection of both a dedicated instructor and a skilled academic politician.

•

BUTTERCUP CHAIN, THE
1970, 95 mins, UK ▭ col
Dir Robert Ellis Miller ***Prod*** John Whitney, Philip Waddilove ***Scr*** Peter Draper ***Ph*** Douglas Slocombe ***Ed*** Thelma Conneli ***Mus*** Richard Rodney Bennett ***Art*** Wilfrid Shingleton
Act Hywel Bennett, Leigh Taylor-Young, Jane Asher, Sven-Bertil Taube, Clive Revill, Roy Dotrice (Columbia)

The story's somewhat contrived and over glib. Even superficial. But it is directed and written with sympathy and tact and acted by a small cast that could hardly be bettered.

Film, based on Janice Elliott's graceful novel, concerns four individualistic young people who develop as intense friendship among themselves which, during one frenzied summer, strays into dangerous ground obviously aimed for tragedy.

Hywel Bennett is the catalyst, a brooding, withdrawn young man who inevitably sets things in motion. His cousin, a disturbed wary young woman, from whom he's inseparable is Jane Asher.

Leigh Taylor-Young has a radiant personality which gives life to all her scenes. Asher is a shade less effective in a more complicated role.

•

BUTTERFIELD 8
1960, 109 mins, US Ⓥ ⦿ ▭ col
Dir Daniel Mann ***Prod*** Pandro S. Berman ***Scr*** Charles Schnee, John Michael Hayes ***Ph*** Joseph Ruttenberg, Charles Harten ***Ed*** Ralph E. Winters ***Mus*** Bronislau Kaper ***Art*** George W. Davis, Urie McCleary
Act Elizabeth Taylor, Laurence Harvey, Eddie Fisher, Dina Merrill, Mildred Dunnock, Betty Field (M-G-M/Afton-Linebrook)

Alterations made on John O'Hara's 1935 novel by the scenarists (among other things, they have updated it from the Prohibition era, spectacularized the ending and refined some of the dialog) have given *Butterfield 8* the form and pace it needs, but the story itself remains a weak one, the behavior and motivations of its characters no more tangible than in the original work.

Under director Daniel Mann's guidance it is an extremely sexy and intimate film, but the intimacy is only skin deep, the sex only a dominating behavior pattern.

B

It is the tragic tale of a young woman (Elizabeth Taylor) tormented by the contradictory impulses of flesh and conscience.

Victim of traumatic childhood experiences, a fatherless youth, a mother's refusal to face facts and, most of all, her own moral irresponsibility, she drifts from one illicit affair to another until passion suddenly blossoms into love on a six-day sex spree with Laurence Harvey, who's got the sort of "problems" (loving, devoted wife, oodles of money via marriage, soft, respectable job) non-neurotic men might envy.

The picture's major asset is Taylor. It is a torrid, stinging portrayal with one or two brilliantly executed passages within. Harvey seems ill-at-ease and has a tendency to exaggerate facial reactions. Eddie Fisher, as Taylor's longtime friend and father image, cannot unbend and get any warmth into the role. Dina Merrill's portrayal of the society wife is without animation or depth. But there is better work from Mildred Dunnock as Taylor's mother and Susan Oliver as Fisher's impatient girl friend.

1960: Best Actress (Elizabeth Taylor)

NOMINATION: Best Color Cinematography

●

BUTTERFLIES ARE FREE

1972, 109 mins, US Ⓥ col

Dir Milton Katselas ***Prod*** Mike Frankovich ***Scr*** Leonard Gershe ***Ph*** Charles B. Lang ***Ed*** David Blewitt ***Mus*** Bob Alcivar ***Art*** Robert Clatworthy

Act Goldie Hawn, Edward Albert, Eileen Heckart, Michael Glasser, Mike Warren (Columbia)

Although the setting has been changed from New York to San Francisco for no apparent reason, Leonard Gershe's screen adaptation of his successful Broadway play, is an excellent example of how to switch from one medium to another.

Several other carryovers—Eileen Heckart and director Milton Katselas—from the stage production were also brilliant moves. In the move a slight change of emphasis has resulted, moving the center of attention from the blind boy, handsomely played by Edward Albert to the girl (Goldie Hawn). What comes over with great strength is Gershe's intimate tale of the interrelationships of three individuals, all of whom gain from their contacts with each other.

Hawn, funny and touching, is a delight throughout and Heckart gets a film role that enables her to display versatility.

1972: Best Supp. Actress (Eileen Heckart)

NOMINATIONS: Best Cinematography, Sound

●

BUTTERFLY

1981, 107 mins, US Ⓥ ⊙ col

Dir Matt Cimber ***Prod*** Matt Cimber ***Scr*** John Goff, Matt Cimber ***Ph*** Eddy Van Der Enden ***Mus*** Ennio Morricone ***Art*** Dave De Carlo

Act Stacy Keach, Pia Zadora, Orson Welles, Lois Nettleton, James Franciscus, Stuart Whitman (Riklis/Par-Par)

Pia Zadora plays Kady, a nymphet who's been searching for her father in the Nevada silver mines. She tracks him down at an abandoned mine where he (Stacy Keach) is serving as a guard.

The headstrong young woman brings out incestuous desires in her God-fearing father. Eventually, his inner passions overcome his honest instincts. In an effort to keep Kady close to him, he agrees to work the almost depleted mine and cash in the remaining ore.

For Kady, the act is motivated by revenge. The mine-owner's son got her pregnant and refused to marry her. However, the son reconsiders his cowardice and agrees to marry.

Keach plays his role without shadings and this self-righteousness is difficult to swallow even with the picture's old-fashioned underpinnings. Zadora, in her screen debut, has most of the picture's best moments and registers well with her little girl looks and Lolita sensuality.

Orson Welles as a corrupt judge provides the film with a few comic but misplaced moments. The final courtroom session sinks into a farce better suited to a comedy of manners on stage. Transferring novelist James M. Cain's narrative and eroticism proves too great a task for the filmmakers and the picture remains a series of partially realized sketches.

The film, however, does not betray its modest budget. Made for $2 million, *Butterfly* has the look of a studio production of three to four times its cost.

●

BUTTERFLY KISS

1995, 85 mins, UK Ⓥ col

Dir Michael Winterbottom ***Prod*** Julie Baines ***Scr*** Frank Cottrell Boyce ***Ph*** Seamus McGarvey ***Ed*** Trevor Waite ***Mus*** John Harle ***Art*** Rupert Miles

Act Amanda Plummer, Saskia Reeves, Paul Bown, Freda Dowie, Fine Time Fontayne, Des McAleer (Dan)

An often breathtakingly original weld of road movie, lesbian love story, psychodrama and black comedy, *Butterfly Kiss* toplines Amanda Plummer and Saskia Reeves as two Northerners who hook up in a macabre, realistic fairytale of murder and romantic obsession as they travel the U.K.'s highways.

Plummer plays Eunice, a cross between a punk Harpo Marx and short-fused free spirit, who's intro'd antsily stalking a highway service station and asking the convenience store salesgirl if her name is Judith. Shortly thereafter, the clerk is seen dead on the floor.

When Eunice repeats the same "Judith" shtick at a gas station where Miriam (Reeves) works, the two women are immediately drawn to each other. After they make love—in a scene which is the first of many to spring jaw-dropping surprises—the pair set off on the road.

So totally does Miriam buy into Eunice and her little world that when she's shown the battered body of a guy Eunice has just enjoyed strenuous sex with, she hardly bats an eyelid. She later wields the instrument of death on a man in a blackly funny but shocking sequence that sets the characters up for their final apotheosis on a deserted seashore.

Despite director Michael Winterbottom's technical skills, confidently on display, and Frank Cottrell Boyce's street-poetic dialogue, it's still the easy playing of the two leads that motors the movie. In the showier role, Plummer, sporting a thick Northern English accent, dominates the early going. Reeves is seemingly outpaced at the start but finally pulls along side Plummer with a minutely observed study of a pupil who finally becomes the master.

●

BWANA DEVIL

1952, 79 mins, US col

Dir Arch Oboler ***Prod*** Arch Oboler ***Scr*** Arch Oboler ***Ph*** Joseph F. Biroc ***Ed*** John Hoffman ***Mus*** Gordon Jenkins

Act Robert Stack, Barbara Britton, Nigel Bruce, Ramsay Hill, Paul McVey (Oboler/United Artists)

This novelty feature boasts of being the first full-length film in Natural Vision 3-D. Although adding backsides to usually flat actors and depth to landscapes, the 3-D technique still needs further technical advances.

Without the paper-framed, polaroid glasses Natural Vision looks like a ghosty television picture. While watching 3-D, viewers are constantly forced to refocus their vision as the focus of the film changes, resulting in a tiring eye workout.

The Oboler production is full of tricks devised to show off the process, rather than to tell the screen story effectively. The much-ballyhooed point of a lion seemingly leaping out of the screen into the auditorium comes off very mildly. The single gasper is the throwing of a spear by a native, which has the illusion of coming right into the audience. With banal dialog, stilted sequences and impossibly directed players, Oboler tells a story, based on fact, of how two lions halt the building of a railroad in British East Africa.

●

BYE BYE BIRDIE

1963, 120 mins, US Ⓥ ⊙ ▭ col

Dir George Sidney ***Prod*** Fred Kohlmar ***Scr*** Irving Brecher ***Ph*** Joseph Biroc ***Ed*** Charles Nelson ***Mus*** Johnny Green (sup.) ***Art*** Paul Groesse

Act Janet Leigh, Dick Van Dyke, Ann-Margret, Maureen Stapleton, Bobby Rydell, Jesse Pearson (Columbia)

Credit George Sidney with directing one of the better fun and frolic tune packages. The adaptation of the successful [1960] legit musical comedy clearly called for lots of visuals, rather than just dialog and straight storytelling. Additionally, there's apparently more emphasis on the dance (interesting choreography by Onna White)—more so perhaps than in the original.

Strikingly important in *Bye Bye Birdie* is Ann-Margret. Singer, hoofer and cutie-pie, all wrapped up into one, she has the magnetism of early-vintage Judy Garland.

Story is the wacky thing about an Elvis Presley type (Jesse Pearson) who's subject to immediate army call. Goes by the name of Conrad Birdie and he swoons the girls no end, what with all that guitar and hip-notism. Songwriter Dick Van Dyke, trying to make time with Janet Leigh, while his mother, Maureen Stapleton, interferes, also is engaged in having Presley-type appear on the Ed Sullivan TV show while doing his farewell song in Sweet Apple, IA. Sullivan is on view, playing the part of Ed Sullivan with remarkable authenticity.

There's lots of talent involved. The songs as penned by Charles Strouse and Lee Adams, fit in nicely. Van Dyke displays a showbiz knowhow far more extensive than his television outings communicate. Leigh is called upon to play it straight, and does so attractively. Stapleton is a comedienne of the first order. Young songster Rydell gets the right kind of chance to warble. Ann-Margret, to repeat, is a wow.

1963: NOMINATIONS: Best Adapted Score, Sound

●

BYE BYE BRAVERMAN

1968, 94 mins, US col

Dir Sidney Lumet ***Prod*** Sidney Lumet ***Scr*** Herbert Sargent ***Ph*** Boris Kaufman ***Ed*** Gerald Greenberg ***Mus*** Peter Matz ***Art*** Ben Kasazkow

Act George Segal, Jack Warden, Joseph Wiseman, Sorrell Booke, Phyllis Newman, Jessica Walter (Warner/Seven Arts)

Bye Bye Braverman is a curious mixture of tasty and tasteless jokes, all at the expense of Jewish people. Pic describes, in padded vignette and travelog transition, the hypocritical mourning of a deceased man by four alleged friends.

Herbert Sargent has taken the "dark comedy" approach; were it black comedy, or straight comedy, it might have worked better. As it is, the curious and erratic use of Jewish ruggedness of spirit and the native non-sequitur humor makes for a plot stew which will offend the sensibilities of many, and titillate the prejudices of others. George Segal, Jack Warden, Joseph Wiseman and Sorrell Booke are the mourners of never-seen Braverman. Jessica Walter, the less-than-bereaved widow, has the yen for Segal (married to Zohra Lampert).

If the film meant to portray the four principals as basically clod characters, with some good points, it missed. If the idea was to portray them as basically good, with human frailties, insufficient depth was given along these lines, too.

●

BY HOOK OR BY CROOK

SEE: I DOOD IT

●

BY LOVE POSSESSED

1961, 115 mins, US Ⓥ col

Dir John Sturges ***Prod*** Walter Mirisch ***Scr*** John Dennis ***Ph*** Russell Metty ***Ed*** Ferris Webster ***Mus*** Elmer Bernstein ***Art*** Malcolm Brown

Act Lana Turner, Efrem Zimbalist, Jr., Jason Robards, George Hamilton, Susan Kohner, Barbara Bel Geddes (United Artists/Mirisch)

James Gould Couzzen's thoughtful novel has been reduced to a complex soap opera. In barest outline, the screenplay seems much like the source material: a look into the lives of a half-dozen socially prominent, well-to-do citizens in a small eastern town.

The focal point is a successful lawyer (Efrem Zimbalist, Jr.) who, in the course of several climactic days, finds that his perfectly ordered life is, in reality, as full of self deception and chaos as the lives of some of his less stable friends. The latter include his law partner (Jason Robards) who, after a crippling accident, refuses the love-pity of his wife (Lana Turner) who subsequently turns to double scotches and solace with Zimbalist.

Further complications involve Zimbalist's inability to understand his son (George Hamilton) who seeks release with the town hussy, who charges the boy with rape.

Turner looks beautiful in a great wardrobe, but can only suggest the ironic, gutsy dame the character might have been. Zimbalist spends most of his time looking thoughtful while chomping on his pipe, and Robards just limps and looks pained. Scoring nicely is Yvonne Craig as the town trollop who persists in talking about herself in the third person.

●

BY THE SWORD

1992, 91 mins, US Ⓥ ⊙ col

Dir Jeremy Paul Kagan ***Prod*** Peter E. Strauss, Marlon Staggs ***Scr*** John McDonald, James Donadio ***Ph*** Arthur Albert ***Ed*** David Holden ***Mus*** Bill Conti

Act F. Murray Abraham, Eric Roberts, Mia Sara, Chris Rydell, Elaine Kagan, Brett Cullen (Movie Group/Foil-Film)

Little-explored world of competitive fencing is the setting for this dramatic crowd pleaser in which F. Murray Abraham delivers a riveting performance as a complex killer, ex-con, lover, janitor and swordsman.

Pic begins in flashback, where his surreal nightmares are haunted by the trainer he skewered 20 years earlier. The dead man's son (Eric Roberts) is now an undefeated, cold-hearted champ running a fencing academy, where most of the picture takes place.

Well-choreographed fencing scenes between Roberts's promising students are kept to a minimum and used as a backdrop for the mounting tension between Roberts and his dad's murderer.

CABARET

1972, 124 mins, US Ⓥ ⊙ col

Dir Bob Fosse ***Prod*** Cy Feuer ***Scr*** Jay Presson Allen, Hugh Wheeler ***Ph*** Geoffrey Unsworth ***Ed*** David Bretherton ***Mus*** Ralph Burns (dir.) ***Art*** Rolf Zehetbauer, Jurgen Kiebach

Act Liza Minnelli, Michael York, Helmut Griem, Marisa Berenson, Fritz Wepper, Joel Grey (AA-ABC)

The film version of [the 1966 John Kander-Fred Ebb Broadway musical] *Cabaret* is most unusual: It is literate, bawdy, sophisticated, sensual, cynical, heart-warming, and disturbingly thought-provoking. Liza Minnelli heads a strong cast. Bob Fosse's generally excellent direction re-creates the milieu of Germany some 40 years ago.

The adaptation of the stage book is expertly accomplished. The basic material derives from Christopher Isherwood's Berlin stories, and a 1951 dramatic play by John Van Druten, filmed in 1955, *I Am a Camera*.

The screenplay, which never seems to talk down to an audience while at the same time making its candid points with tasteful emphasis, returns the story to a variety of settings. The sleazy cabaret remains a major recurring set.

The choice of Minnelli for the part of Sally Bowles was indeed daring. Good-hearted, quasi-sophisticated amorality and hedonism are not precisely Minnelli's professional bag, and within many scenes she seems to carom from golly-gee-whiz-down-home rusticity to something closer to the mark.

1972: Best Director, Actress (Liza Minnelli), Supp. Actor (Joel Grey), Cinematography, Art Direction, Sound, Adapted Scoring, Editing

NOMINATIONS: Best Picture, Adapted Screenplay

CABIN BOY

1994, 80 mins, US Ⓥ col

Dir Adam Resnick ***Prod*** Tim Burton, Denise Di Novi ***Scr*** Adam Resnick ***Ph*** Steve Yaconelli ***Ed*** Jon Poll ***Mus*** Steve Bartek ***Art*** Steven Legler

Act Chris Elliott, Ritch Brinkley, James Gammon, Brian Doyle-Murray, Brion James, Russ Tamblyn (Touchstone)

Obnoxious, snide and pointless, this ill-fated spoof carries the bonus of being as crude and gamy as the hold of an old fishing barge. Although Tim Burton's company produced the film, the filmmaker clearly left the creative carnage to the team of Chris Elliott and writer-director Adam Resnick, both former *Late Night with David Letterman* scribes (they share story credit here). Think of this as a bad version of an old *Saturday Night Live* sketch, stretched to an interminable 80 minutes.

Elliott plays a finishing school snob who, en route to his father's hotel in Hawaii, accidentally boards the wrong boat. He ends up on a schooner, *The Filthy Whore*, populated by a quintet of surly, grizzled fishermen who delight in abusing him.

But wait, it gets worse. The ship nears an island called Hell's Bucket, which leads to several fantasy elements lifted from old Sinbad movies, from a snow beast to the six-armed dominatrix Calli (Ann Magnuson). Elliott's character also discovers a love interest, Trina (Melora Walters), who runs afoul of the boat while seeking to swim around the world. Russ Tamblyn turns up in a silent cameo as a half-man, half-shark named Chocki.

Elliott either can't act or seems unwilling to try. Purposely shoddy sets and special effects only add to the mess.

CABINET OF DR. CALIGARI, THE

SEE: DAS CABINETT DES DR CALIGARI

CABINETT DES DR. CALIGARI, DAS *(THE CABINET OF DR. CALIGARI)*

1919, 69 mins, Germany Ⓥ ⊙ ⊗ b/w

Dir Robert Wiene ***Prod*** Erich Pommer ***Scr*** Carl Mayer, Hans Janowitz ***Ph*** Willy Hameister ***Art*** Walter Roehrig, Walter Reimann, Hermann Warm

Act Werner Krauss, Conrad Veidt, Lil Dagover, Friedrich Feher (Decla)

The German-made *Cabinet of Dr. Caligari* is a mystery story told in the Poe manner and fairly prods the interest along at a high pace. But it is morbid. The story is of a young man who is seen first relating to a visitor the peculiar reasons for the trance in which a young lady whom he points out appears to be. And then we are into the major portion of the story.

This relates how a faker came to a fair at a small town and proceeded to enliven things by having a somnambulist, Cesare, who had been asleep for 23 years foretell the future. The faker called himself Dr. Caligari. A murder is foretold

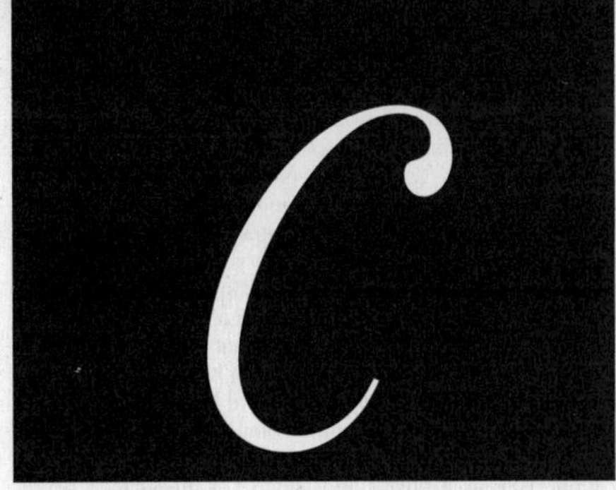

and a series of them occur. Dr. Caligari is pursued to a neighboring insane asylum, where he is revealed as Dr. Sonnow, head of the institution.

At this point we dissolve back to the young man, Francis, telling the visitor his story. Enter Dr. Sonnow. Francis promptly attacks him, protesting he is Caligari. That is the delusion of Francis, and now that he knows his delusion, the innocent Dr. Sonnow can cure him. The rest was a tale told by a madman.

Of first importance is the direction and cutting. This has resulted in a series of actions so perfectly dovetailed as to carry the story through at a perfect tempo. Robert Wiene has made perfect use of settings designed by Hermann Warm, Walter Reimann and Walter Roehrig, settings that squeeze and turn and adjust the eye and through the eye the mentality.

The best performance unquestionably is that given by Werner Krauss as Dr Caligari. The unpleasant somnambulist, Cesare, is ghoulishly made evident by Conrad Veidt. Lesser roles are competently taken.

CABIN IN THE COTTON

1932, 76 mins, US b/w

Dir Michael Curtiz ***Prod*** Jack L. Warner ***Scr*** Paul Green ***Ph*** Barney McGill ***Ed*** George Amy

Act Richard Barthelmess, Dorothy Jordan, Bette Davis, Henry B. Walthall, Berton Churchill (First National)

Picture proves that a book that attracts a good deal of attention isn't necessarily screen material. Conflict is the feud between a Southern cotton planter (landowner) and tenant farmer (here described as "peckerwoods"). It's the industrial capital vs labor wrangle in another setting, and not a particularly fascinating one at that.

Picture is not well done and it presents Richard Barthelmess in another lukewarm role, a role which he plays without vigor. Nub of the drama is that Marvin Blake (Barthelmess) belongs to the underdog tenant farmer class, but is befriended by the planter and finds himself between two fires—torn by loyalty to his class and an obligation to their enemy who also is his benefactor. Also Marvin falls in love with the planter's daughter.

Bette Davis is the naughty-naughty planter's daughter. Dorothy Jordan, as a humble farm girl, is just a shadow. Indeed, most of the people are puppet-like, including the Barthelmess character.

CABIN IN THE SKY

1943, 98 mins, US Ⓥ ⊙ b/w

Dir Vincente Minnelli ***Prod*** Arthur Freed ***Scr*** Joseph Schrank ***Ph*** Sidney Wagner ***Ed*** Harold F. Cress ***Mus*** Vernon Duke, Harold Arlen

Act Ethel Waters, Eddie "Rochester" Anderson, Lena Horne, Louis Armstrong, Rex Ingram (M-G-M)

The picture version of *Cabin in the Sky* is little changed from the original stage show. It still tells of Little Joe Jackson's weakness for dice, likker and the seductive Georgia Brown, of his mortal wound in a barroom brawl, and of his six-month period of grace obtained by his eternally-devoted wife, Petunia. It still shows the contest between Lucifer, Jr. and the General for Little Joe's soul.

In the legit version *Cabin* seemed constantly to be constricted by the limitations of the stage. But difficulty has not been solved in the present film adaptation. The yarn still appears weighed down by unimaginative conception, the few changes in the screen medium merely filling out the story, without expanding or developing its fantasy. In only one of two moments, such as the stairway to heaven finale, is there any apparent effort to utilize the facilities of the camera. There are far too many closeups, particularly in the vocal numbers.

Ethel Waters remains the one transcendant asset of the film *Cabin*, just as she was in the original. Her sincerity, compassion, personal warmth and dramatic skill, plus her unique talent as a singer make her performance as Petunia an overpowering accomplishment.

1943: NOMINATION: Best Song ("Happiness Is a Thing Called Joe")

CABLE GUY, THE

1996, 95 mins, US Ⓥ ⊙ ▭ col

Dir Ben Stiller ***Prod*** Andrew Licht, Jeffrey A. Mueller, Judd Apatow ***Scr*** Lou Holtz, Jr. ***Ph*** Robert Brinkman ***Ed*** Steven Weisberg ***Mus*** John Ottman ***Art*** Sharon Seymour

Act Jim Carrey, Matthew Broderick, Leslie Mann, Jack Black, George Segal, Diane Baker (Columbia)

Tune out, turn off, drop out . . . *The Cable Guy* is loose. A thin collection of comic constructs, this entry from Jim Carrey is a career switch attached to a dimmer board.

The premise is quite simple. Architect Steven Kovacs (Matthew Broderick) has been bounced by his girlfriend, Robin (Leslie Mann), after proposing marriage. He moves into a new apartment and waits for the cable service technician to hook him up. The cable guy, Chip Douglas (Carrey), is an electronics geek who is alternately bizarre and compassionate. Steven, in a moment of weakness, makes the mistake of agreeing to join him on a pilgrimage to the satellite dish where all electromagnetic signals converge.

It's an intriguing enough jumping-off point. But instead of a narrative progression, we are beset with a series of situations marked by mayhem. After its first surge of energy, the film goes on the blink and never recovers. Carrey's character lacks the empathy or poignance to command ongoing interest, and Broderick's role strains one's patience because he's hopelessly dimwitted and slow to react in any way vaguely resembling human behavior.

CACTUS FLOWER

1969, 103 mins, US Ⓥ ⊙ col

Dir Gene Saks ***Prod*** Mike Frankovich ***Scr*** I.A.L. Diamond ***Ph*** Charles E. Lang ***Ed*** Maury Winetrobe ***Mus*** Quincy Jones ***Art*** Robert Clatworthy

Act Walter Matthau, Ingrid Bergman, Goldie Hawn, Jack Weston, Rick Lenz, Vito Scotti (Columbia)

Cactus Flower drags, which is probably the worst thing that can be said of a light comedy. It's due to sloppy direction by Gene Saks and the miscasting of Walter Matthau opposite Ingrid Bergman.

The plot [from the play by Abe Burrows, based on a French play by Barillet & Gredy] is minimal and the lines are somewhat stilted and hollow, but if the direction was tighter and the mood kept light and airy it might have worked.

Matthau is cast as a dentist ready to marry his young mistress who enlists the aid of his stuffy but organized secretary. This too, might have worked had they found a suitable foil for him. Bergman, more believable in her role as the nurse, is too reserved and sophisticated opposite Matthau.

There are some laughs and Goldie Hawn, as the Greenwich Village kook with whom Matthau contemplates marriage, makes a credible screen debut.

1969: Best Supp. Actress (Goldie Hawn)

CADAVERI ECCELLENTI *(ILLUSTRIOUS CORPSES; THE CONTEXT)*

1976, 110 mins, Italy col

Dir Francesco Rosi ***Prod*** Alberto Grimaldi ***Scr*** Francesco Rosi, Tonino Guerra, Lino Jannuzzi ***Ph*** Pasqualino De Santis ***Ed*** Ruggero Mastroianni ***Mus*** Piero Piccioni ***Art*** Andrea Crisanti

Act Lino Ventura, Alain Cuny, Paolo Bonacelli, Marcel Bozzuffi, Tina Aumont, Max von Sydow (PEA)

Strikingly composed, well acted, with a pervasive sense of hard-to-pinpoint menace operating in its elliptical plot about political assassinations in Italy, Alberto Grimaldi's production, *Illustrious Corpses*, misses being a topnotch film only because of a certain dryness in the approach taken by director Francesco Rosi.

Lino Ventura, playing in thoughtful but colorless fashion, is an inspector uncovering a Watergate-scope conspiracy below the surface of a series of murdered officials. The film lacks visceral excitement. With an approach at times reminiscent of Francis Coppola's *The Conversation*, but without the emotional involvement that film engendered, Rosi and his scripting collaborators keep the exact nature of the conspiracy in the shadows, making the audience work along with Ventura to decipher the bizarre events.

Sequence involving Max von Sydow, as a fanatic official involved in the conspiracy, shows what the film could have been, giving a frightening and totally believable picture of obsessive approach to obliterating political dissent. Otherwise, the officials portrayed are a lackluster crew.

What keeps the film highly watchable are the crisp shooting style of Rosi and the firstrate lensing by Pasqualino De Santis, along with excellent choice of locations to give the film the texture, if not the dramatic intensity, of real-life political intrigue.

•

CADDIE
1976, 107 mins, Australia Ⓥ col
Dir Donald Crombie ***Prod*** Tony Buckley ***Scr*** Joan Long ***Ph*** Peter James ***Ed*** Tim Wellburn ***Mus*** Patrick Flynn ***Art*** Owen Williams
Act Helen Morse, Takis Emmanuel, Jack Thompson, Jacki Weaver, Melissa Jaffer, Ron Blanchard (Buckley)

Caddie is based on the autobiography of a Sydney barmaid who, adandoned by her husband, struggled through the Depression to bring up two children. It is a sensitively told story of one woman's fight—not a militant, but rather one of the masses; an unsung heroine.

Helen Morse, in the title role, maintains a wonderful dignity that is typical of the character's social class and aspirations. She never slips, and her scenes with the children are natural, especially at the fade out when despite a crushing personal disappointment, she rallies as soon as they appear.

But it is in her scenes with Takis Emmanuel that Caddie's story takes on fire. Emmanuel, a Greek actor imported for the production, registers power immediately his face hits the screen.

•

CADDY, THE
1953, 95 mins, US Ⓥ b/w
Dir Norman Taurog ***Prod*** Paul Jones ***Scr*** Edmund L. Hartmann, Danny Arnold, Ken Englund ***Ph*** Daniel L. Fapp ***Ed*** Warren Low ***Mus*** Joseph J. Lilley (dir.) ***Art*** Hal Pereira, Franz Bachelin
Act Dean Martin, Jerry Lewis, Donna Reed, Barbara Bates, Joseph Calleia, Fred Clark (Paramount)

Dean Martin and Jerry Lewis dig a lot of divots among the fairways of *The Caddy*. It's an amusing romp [from a story by Danny Arnold] that, while not always parring previous M & L successes, comes close enough. Production tells how a couple of San Francisco boys, both liking golf, team for tournament play. Since Lewis can't stand the strain of competition, he's the caddy-manager for Martin. Early successes swell Martin's head and he tries to break from Lewis. Their quarrel during a big match at Pebble Beach turns on a riot that ends with their plunge into showbiz when golf kicks them out.

Emphasis is on warm humor with heart. The comics have two femme stars as curvy contrasts for their antics. Donna Reed plays a rich society gal who sets her cap for Martin and gets him, even if Lewis's ineptness does mix up the romance for awhile. Barbara Bates, as Martin's sister, is Lewis's sweetie.

Cut into the footage are some actual mob scenes of crowds around the NY Paramount Theatre when M & L were appearing there for a stage date.

1953: NOMINATION: Best Song ("That's Amore")

•

CADDYSHACK
1980, 90 mins, US Ⓥ ⊙ col
Dir Harold Ramis ***Prod*** Douglas Kenney ***Scr*** Brian Doyle-Murray, Harold Ramis, Douglas Kenney ***Ph*** Stevan Larner ***Ed*** William Carruth ***Mus*** Johnny Mandel ***Art*** Stan Jolley
Act Chevy Chase, Rodney Dangerfield, Bill Murray, Michael O'Keefe, Ted Knight, Cindy Morgan (Orion)

In *Caddyshack*'s unabashed bid for the mammoth audience which responded to the antiestablishment outrageousness of *National Lampoon's Animal House*, this vaguely likable, too-tame comedy falls short of the mark.

This time, the thinly plotted shenanigans unfold against the manicured lawns and posh backdrop of a restricted country club, generally pitting the free-living youthful caddies against the uptight gentry who employ them.

Stock characters include Chevy Chase as resident golf-pro; club prexy and jurist Ted Knight; and Rodney Dangerfield as the perfectly cast and very funny personification of anti-social, nouveau riche grossness.

Beyond Chase, prime lure is Bill Murray as a foul-habited, semi-moronic groundskeeper, constantly aroused by the older femme golfers.

•

CADILLAC MAN
1990, 97 mins, US Ⓥ ⊙ col
Dir Roger Donaldson ***Prod*** Charles Roven, Roger Donaldson ***Scr*** Ken Friedman ***Ph*** David Gribble ***Ed*** Richard Francis-Bruce ***Mus*** J. Peter Robinson ***Art*** Gene Rudolf
Act Robin Williams, Tim Robbins, Pamela Reed, Fran Drescher, Annabella Sciorra, Zack Norman (Orion)

Denied an opportunity to showcase his deft rapid-fire comic skills, Robin Williams produces few laughs amid wreckage of the screenplay and poorly paced direction. Only Tim Robbins gets out alive as a crazed, simple-minded, cuckolded husband who ultimately makes hostages of the womanizing Joey (Williams) and everyone else in the car dealership where he works, suspecting correctly that his wife (Annabella Sciorra) is having an affair.

Williams lapses in and out of a what seems to be a New York-Italian street accent. Aside from being a smart aleck, however, he's rarely funny and shows little depth until the predictable ending. Some minor pleasures can be found in smaller roles drawn from the N.Y. street scene, especially Lauren Tom as a pushy and abusive waitress in a neighbourhood dim sum restaurant.

•

CAESAR AND CLEOPATRA
1946, 135 mins, UK Ⓥ col
Dir Gabriel Pascal ***Prod*** Gabriel Pascal ***Scr*** George Bernard Shaw ***Ph*** Freddie Young, Robert Krasker, Jack Hildyard, Jack Cardiff ***Mus*** Georges Auric ***Art*** Oliver Messel, John Bryan
Act Vivien Leigh, Claude Rains, Stewart Granger, Flora Robson, Francis L. Sullivan, Cecil Parker (Eagle Lion)

Caesar and Cleopatra is a disappointment. In spite of its prodigal magnificence, indeed because of its production values, such vague story interest as it has is hopelessly swamped.

Claude Rains's Caesar—thanks to Shaw and Gabriel Pascal, director—is accurately and succinctly pinpointed by Vivien Leigh as Cleopatra when she calls him "a nice old gentleman." As for her portrayal of the Queen of Queens—again the responsibility of author and director—Rains calls the turn when he tells her with justifiable incredulity she is not Queen of Egypt, but a queen of the gypsies.

Sketchy references to an earlier visit of a young Roman "with strong, round, gleaming arms" elicit his identification by Caesar as being Marc Antony. Apart from this vague, soft-pedal reference to the possibility of her knowing what passion means, Leigh's Cleopatra is as lacking in sex consciousness as the boy actor (Anthony Harvey) who plays the part of her brother, Ptolemy, whose throne she seizes.

Seemingly just to make things more irritating there appears halfway through the pic Stewart Granger as Apollodorus, a Sicilian with flashing eyes, dazzling white teeth and a torso of burnished bronze. But nix on anything like that, says Shaw. So Cleopatra passes Granger up as if he were a dirty deuce—instead of being what he so obviously, so vibrantly is, a grand chunk of three-quarters nude male s.a.

In a cast of more than 100 of Britain's finest stage actors individual performances of bits are all flawless. And make no mistake about it, the prodigality of this $6 million spectacle makes Griffith and DeMille and Von Stroheim look like niggards.

1946: NOMINATION: Best Color Art Direction

•

CAGE AUX FOLLES, LA
1978, 103 mins, Italy/France Ⓥ ⊙ col
Dir Edouard Molinaro ***Scr*** Francis Veber, Edouard Molinaro, Marcello Danon, Jean Poiret ***Ph*** Armando Nannuzzi ***Ed*** Robert Isnardon, Monique Isnardon ***Mus*** Ennio Morricone
Act Ugo Tognazzi, Michel Serrault, Michel Galabru, Claire Maurier, Reni Laurent, Benny Luke (Da Ma/Artistes Associes)

Jean Poiret's 1973 play of a middle-aged gay couple beset by problems when the 20-year-old son of one announces his marriage, gets uneven film treatment. Most of the characters appear stereotyped and the familiar plotting reveals the gay duo could have easily been heterosexual or an odd couple.

Though predictable, the film has one solid trump in Michel Serrault who makes the more feminine member of the happy couple a very shrewd limning of outsize campy gay attributes that avoid tastelessness. Thesp manages to comment on the queenly, demanding character to garner most of the laughs and the few insights into gay life.

Italo player Ugo Tognazzi is the one who at one time, the only time, was bisexual enough to father a child brought up by him and Serrault. He, too, shows a feel for the surface mannerisms and outlooks of the more male side of the two. The son's bride-to-be has bluenose parents and the father heads a politico party devoted to moral outlooks.

The pic revolves around fooling the parents, not letting them in on the sex of the boy's father or his running a transvestite nitery where Serrault is the drag star.

•

CAGE AUX FOLLES II, LA
1980, 100 mins, Italy/France Ⓥ col
Dir Edouard Molinaro ***Prod*** Marcello Danon ***Scr*** Francis Veber, Jean Poiret, Marcello Danon ***Ph*** Armando Nannuzzi ***Ed*** Robert Isnardon, Monique Isnardon, Carlo Della Corte ***Mus*** Ennio Morricone ***Art*** Luigi Scaccianoce
Act Ugo Tognazzi, Michel Serrault, Marcel Bozzuffi, Paola Borboni, Giovanni Vettorazzo, Michel Galabru (DaMa/Artistes Associes)

The Abbott and Costello of gaydom are back with new limp-wristed adventures. But the very title gives you an idea of the singular lack of effort that's gone into its packaging. Ironically, though the first picture was filmed theatre, it was a better film, more competently made, a neater, more satisfying commercial product.

Producer Marcello Danon and his collaborators (the same as in number one) have mechanically embroiled Michel Serrault and costar Ugo Tognazzi in a dull espionage plot that lacks surprise and comic ingenuity. It looks as if further sequels may amount to little more than genre grafts. Don't be surprised if Serrault and Tognazzi next meet Dracula, go to Mars, or become buck privates.

Story begins when a deeply offended Serrault sets out to prove to his companion that he's still got sex appeal. Pretty soon there are a couple of dead spies, and a roll of microfilm winds up in Serrault's pill case, unknown to him. With French agents trying to use them as decoys and foreign agents out to torture or kill them for the recovery of the film, Tognazzi and Serrault head for the (Italian) hills where they find temporary refuge on the farm of Tognazzi's mother, dismayed at the shabby specimen of womanhood her son has married.

Almost all the comedy rests on the splendid comic talents of Serrault. The role is a cinch for him and he's perfected it flamboyantly. Tognazzi has less to do than before and just fades into the background. Edouard Molinaro's direction is pedestrian. He did a snappier job on number one, working hard to keep the material from looking stagey. Armando Nannuzzi's lensing is ugly, washed out Technicolor.

•

CAGE AUX FOLLES 3, LA
(LA CAGE AUX FOLLES 3: THE WEDDING)
1985, 87 mins, France/Italy Ⓥ col
Dir Georges Lautner ***Prod*** Marcello Danon (exec.) ***Scr*** Michel Audiard/Jacques Audiard, Marcello Danon, Georges Lautner, Gerard Lamballe ***Ph*** Luciano Tovoli ***Ed*** Michele David ***Mus*** Ennio Morricone ***Art*** Mario Garbuglia
Act Michel Serrault, Ugo Tognazzi, Antonella Interlenghi, Saverio Vallone, Benny Luke, Stephane Audran (Columbia France/DaMa)

It took no fewer than seven—count 'em seven—credited writers to dream up the weak premise and poorly sustained consequences in which our limpwristed heroes are embroiled. Among them one can spot producer Marcello Danon and the late Michel Audiard, specifically credited with the dialog, for which he certainly will not be remembered.

Zaza (Michel Serrault) and Renato (Ugo Tognazzi) are alive and well and still living in Saint-Tropez, but their gay nightclub, where Zaza is preparing his high-flying new revue as the Queen of Bees, is in financial straits. Fortunately, Albin stands to inherit a magnificent castle and vast property in Scotland. Unfortunately, the will stipulates Zaza must marry and provide an heir within 18 months, or the inheritance will go to his virile, greedy young cousin.

Renato, pragmatic and wily, hits on a number of schemes to goad his obstinate mate into wedlock, including a pretense that an accident has restored him to heterosexuality; and a matchmaking arrangement with a lonely young beauty who has been jilted and left pregnant by her ex-lover.

The poor screenplay and indifferent direction by Georges Lautner probably won't matter to those who find a full evening's entertainment in Serrault, who is always a scream, literally and figuratively. Tognazzi resumes his role as Renato, but still looks bored. Technically, production is more handsome than the previous installment.

•

CAGED
1950, 96 mins, US b/w
Dir John Cromwell ***Prod*** Jerry Wald ***Scr*** Virginia Kellogg, Bernard C. Schoenfeld ***Ph*** Carl Guthrie ***Ed*** Owen Marks ***Mus*** Max Steiner ***Art*** Charles H. Clarke
Act Eleanor Parker, Agnes Moorehead, Ellen Corby, Hope Emerson, Jan Sterling, Jane Darwell (Warner)

Caged makes a stab at objective reporting of life in a women's prison. A grim, unrelieved study of cause and effect, it adds up to very drab entertainment, unleavened with any measure of escapism.

Plot provides Eleanor Parker with what is known as a

meaty femme role, completely deglamourized. There are other strong portrayals among the predominantly femme cast, and the most colorful is the sadistic prison matron socked over by Hope Emerson.

Script is based on actual prison life incidents. Motivation on which it is hung is the downward path taken by a first offender after she rubs up against the assorted characters who people a prison. In that respect, story's finish is realistic, stating clearly that Parker will soon be back with her old cellmates.

1950: NOMINATIONS: Best Actress (Eleanor Parker), Supp. Actress (Hope Emerson), Story & Screenplay

•

CAHILL, UNITED STATES MARSHAL
1973, 103 mins, US Ⓥ ⦿ ▭ col
Dir Andrew V. McLaglen ***Prod*** Michael Wayne ***Scr*** Harry Julian Fink, Rita M. Fink ***Ph*** Joseph Biroc ***Ed*** Robert L. Simpson ***Mus*** Elmer Bernstein ***Art*** Walter Simonds
Act John Wayne, Gary Grimes, George Kennedy, Neville Brand, Clay O'Brien, Marie Windsor (Batjac/Warner)

John Wayne combines the problems of fatherhood with his activities as a lawman in *Cahill, United States Marshal* to give different motivation from the usual western theme.

Crux of the strained relationship between Wayne and his two young sons is his continued absence tracking down criminals, which leads to the boys, 17 and 12, becoming involved in a bank robbery and murder.

Script, based on a story by Barney Slater, opens strongly with Wayne catching up to a band of outlaws and shooting it out with them. When he returns to town he finds the bank has been robbed, sheriff and deputy murdered and four new prisoners in jail, including his elder son. Boys have been lured into crime by smooth-talking outlaw George Kennedy. Wayne carries out characterization realistically and gets firm support right down the line. Kennedy is menacing.

•

CAINE MUTINY, THE
1954, 123 mins, US Ⓥ ⦿ col
Dir Edward Dmytryk ***Prod*** Stanley Kramer ***Scr*** Stanley Roberts, Michael Blankfort ***Ph*** Franz Planer ***Ed*** William A. Lyon, Henry Batista ***Mus*** Max Steiner ***Art*** Rudolph Sternad
Act Humphrey Bogart, Jose Ferrer, Van Johnson, Fred MacMurray, Robert Francis, May Wynn (Columbia)

The Caine Mutiny is highly recommendable motion picture drama, told on the screen as forcefully as it was in the Herman Wouk bestselling novel. The intelligently adapted screenplay retains all the essence of the novel.

The Caine Mutiny is the story of a war-weary destroyer-minesweeper and its personnel, over which presides—by the book—Captain Queeg, a man beginning to crack from the strain of playing hero over the years while he hides deep his inferiority complex. Lt. Tom Keefer is the first to spot the crack in Queeg's armor and he needles Maryk and the other officers into seeing it, too.

Little incidents of faulty command build until, during a raging typhoon when the tired ship is in extreme danger of foundering Maryk relieves the captain, using Navy Article 184, which permits the executive officer taking over under certain emergency conditions, to do so.

Scene after scene in the picture during the hour and one-half buildup to the court martial stand out, either for high action, drama or the beauty and grace of ships making their way proudly through the seas.

1954: NOMINATIONS: Best Picture, Actor (Humphrey Bogart), Supp. Actor (Tom Tully), Screenplay, Editing, Scoring of a Dramatic Picture, Sound

•

CAIRO ROAD
1950, 88 mins, UK Ⓥ col
Dir David Macdonald ***Prod*** Aubrey Baring ***Scr*** Robert Westerby ***Ph*** Oswald Morris ***Ed*** Peter Taylor ***Mus*** Robert Gill, Na'im al-Basri ***Art*** Duncan Sutherland
Act Eric Portman, Laurence Harvey, Maria Mauban, Camelia, Karel Stepanek, John Gregson (ABPC/Mayflower)

Cairo Road is a so-so thriller dealing with dope smugglers. Action moves slowly in the first half and much of the story is veiled so as to obscure the plot. However, it winds up with a meaty climax. Action takes place in Cairo, Port Said and along the Suez.

Principal characters are the chief of the Anti-Narcotic Bureau, suavely played by Eric Portman, and his impetuous assistant (Laurence Harvey). Police are investigating a murder which leads them to the trail of hashish peddlers. Capture of the two major criminals is the climax.

Apart from the principals, the most distinctive performance comes from Harold Lang, who plays a smuggler. New Egyptian star Camelia is a looker, but is given little chance in a small part. The only other femme role is played by Maria Mauban as the sweet and understanding wife of Harvey.

•

CALAMITY JANE
1953, 100 mins, US Ⓥ ⦿ col
Dir David Butler ***Prod*** William Jacobs ***Scr*** James O'Hanlon ***Ph*** Wilfrid M. Cline ***Ed*** Irene Morra ***Mus*** Ray Heindorf (dir.) ***Art*** John Beckman
Act Doris Day, Howard Keel, Allyn McLerie, Philip Carey, Dick Wesson, Paul Harvey (Warner)

Giving such Wild West characters as Calamity Jane and Wild Bill Hickok a workout in a tuned-in western doubtless had strong possibilities but Warners comes close to missing the stagecoach. Colorful settings and costumes add the entry some sparkle but the "book" is lacking in originality and the players simply are uneasy.

Compensating factor is the total of 11 songs (music by Sammy Fain, lyrics by Paul Francis Webster) which gives the production some entertainment wallop. [Musical numbers staged and directed by Jack Donohue.]

Doris Day works very, very hard at being Calamity and is hardly realistic at all. She'd register fine as a country girl in calico or a cutie from the chorus line but strain shows through in her essaying of the hard and dynamic Calamity character. Howard Keel handles the Bill Hickok assignment with listless amiability.

While flavorful, a number of the *Calamity* songs suggest other scores of other years. As a matter of fact, the entire film seems a little familiar, having some ingredients in common with *Annie Get Your Gun* and *Oklahoma!*. The dialog throughout is commonplace.

1953: Best Song ("Secret Love")

NOMINATIONS: Best Scoring of a Musical Picture, Sound

•

CALENDAR GIRL
1993, 90 mins, US Ⓥ ⦿ col
Dir John Whitesell ***Prod*** Debbie Robins, Gary Marsh ***Scr*** Paul W. Shapiro ***Ph*** Tom Priestley ***Ed*** Wendy Greene Bricmont ***Mus*** Hans Zimmer ***Art*** Bill Groom
Act Jason Priestley, Gabriel Olds, Jerry O'Connell, Joe Pantoliano, Steve Railsbeck, Kurt Fuller (Columbia/Parkway)

Masquerading as a wild romantic adventure, *Calendar Girl* is actually a dull, sanctimonious morality tale about the meaning of friendship and manhood in the manner of James Dean's melodramas.

Awkward narration intros the three heroes, who are fated to form a lifelong bond. Main story is set in June 1962, right after Monroe was fired from Fox's *Something's Got to Give*, with the three high school grads now experts on the star's life and career. Preying on his friends' fantasy of meeting the actress, Roy Darpinian (Jason Priestley) talks his pals (Jerry O'Connell, Gabriel Olds) into a crazy plan: Why not leave their boring Nevada town and drive to Hollywood in his father's sky blue Galaxy 500 convertible?

Regrettably, once the trio lands in Hollywood and starts a vigil outside Monroe's house, pic settles into a static mood. Staying with Priestley's uncle Harvey (Joe Pantoliano), an aspiring actor whose day job is selling bomb shelters, provides some amusing moments, but they aren't enough. Chief problem is unfunny, schematic script, which consists of the boys' interminable machinations to meet Monroe.

•

CALIFORNIA DOLLS, THE
SEE: . . . ALL THE MARBLES

•

CALIFORNIA MAN
SEE: ENCINO MAN

•

CALIFORNIA SPLIT
1974, 108 mins, US Ⓥ ▭ col
Dir Robert Altman ***Prod*** Robert Altman, Joseph Walsh ***Scr*** Joseph Walsh ***Ph*** Paul Lohmann ***Ed*** Lou Lombardo ***Mus*** Phyllis Shotwell ***Art*** Leon Ericksen
Act George Segal, Elliott Gould, Ann Prentiss, Gwen Welles, Edward Walsh, Joseph Walsh (Columbia)

California Split is an aimless, strung-out series of vignettes starring George Segal and Elliott Gould as compulsive gamblers. The film is technically and physically handsome, all the more so for being mostly location work, but lacks a cohesive and reinforced sense of story direction.

The pic is well cast—Segal and Gould contrast well, while Ann Prentiss and Gwen Welles play happy hookers to good effect. Bert Remsen, an Altman stock player, herein does a drag number. Edward Walsh (the writer's father) is very good as a mean poker adversary, and the writer himself has a good scene as Segal's loan shark.

•

CALIFORNIA SUITE
1978, 103 mins, US Ⓥ ⦿ col
Dir Herbert Ross ***Prod*** Ray Stark ***Scr*** Neil Simon ***Ph*** David M. Walsh ***Ed*** Michael A. Stevenson, Margaret Booth ***Mus*** Claude Bolling ***Art*** Albert Brenner
Act Alan Alda, Michael Caine, Bill Cosby, Jane Fonda, Walter Matthau, Elaine May (Columbia)

Neil Simon and Herbert Ross have gambled in radically altering the successful format of *California Suite* as it appeared on stage. Instead of four separate playlets, there is now one semi-cohesive narrative revolving around visitors to the Beverly Hills Hotel.

Alan Alda and Jane Fonda portray a divorced couple wrangling over possession of their child, while Michael Caine and Maggie Smith play a showbiz couple with varying sexual tastes holed up at the Bev-Hills prior to the Academy Awards. Walter Matthau has to explain his unwitting infidelity to spouse Elaine May in a third segment, and Richard Pryor and Bill Cosby, accompanied by their wives (Gloria Gifford and Sheila Frazier), manage to turn a vacation into a series of disastrous mishaps. Ross and Simon have set up as counterpoint to the more tragicomic episodes (those involved Alda and Fonda, and Caine and Smith) some farcical moments around Matthau and blitzed floozy Denise Galik, along with the Pryor-Cosby shenanigans. The technique is less than successful, veering from poignant emotionalism to broad slapstick in sudden shifts.

Fonda demonstrates yet another aspect of her amazing range, although her brittle quips with Alda seem very stage-bound. Smith and Caine interplay wonderfully, as do Pryor and Cosby. The latter duo get the worst break, however, as their seg is chopped up, spread around and generally given short shrift.

1978: Best Supp. Actress (Maggie Smith)

NOMINATIONS: Best Adapted Screenplay, Art Direction

•

CALIGULA
1979, 150 mins, Italy/US Ⓥ ⦿ col
Dir Tinto Brass ***Prod*** Bob Guccione, Franco Rossellini ***Scr*** [uncredited] ***Ph*** Silvano Ippoliti ***Ed*** Nino Baragli ***Mus*** Paul Clemente ***Art*** Danilo Donati
Act Malcolm McDowell, Teresa Ann Savoy, Helen Mirren, Peter O'Toole, John Gielgud (Penthouse/Felix)

With the biggest investment ever in porn to play with, Tinto Brass in a creative fit of paranoic obsession, sifts through the pages of first century Rome under syphilitic Tiberius and epileptic Caligula to demonstrate the unlimited baseness of the human condition [from a story by Gore Vidal].

Such established names as John Gielgud and Peter O'Toole will have to be seen to be believed. Malcolm McDowell as the sick and/or insane emperor runs the gamut of cardboard emotions from grand guignol to hapless pathos.

Paid off to yield final cut and end two years of film freeze litigation, Brass gets a kind of ambiguous director credit ('scenes directed by'). He filmed everything on screen; though some reports mention added porno inserts during the post-Brass completion period. (A 210-minute version was clandestinely screened at Cannes earlier in the year.)

•

CALL ME BWANA
1963, 93 mins, UK Ⓥ ⦿ col
Dir Gordon Douglas ***Prod*** Albert R. Broccoli ***Scr*** Nate Monaster, Johanna Harwood ***Ph*** Ted Moore ***Ed*** Peter Hunt ***Mus*** Muir Mathieson, Monty Norman ***Art*** Syd Cain
Act Bob Hope, Anita Ekberg, Edie Adams, Lionel Jeffries, Arnold Palmer, Percy Herbert (Eon)

Bob Hope's gags are tossed off in his usual slick fashion. And a great number of them are slyly but pointedly directed at Anita Ekberg's stimulating sculpture. The visual situations and incidents need spacing out a little more but they invariably crop up just in time to disguise the occasional repetition of plot.

Hope has built up a phoney reputation as an intrepid explorer of the jungles of Darkest Africa, by writing successful books based on old, secret diaries of his uncle. Actually, the nearest the timid character has ever been to Africa is to visit his aunt in Cape Cod. When an American moon-probe capsule is lost in the jungle and it's necessary to locate it before foreign powers get their thieving mitts on it, Hope is detailed for the task because of his supposed expert knowledge of the locale.

Overall, there's enough fun to keep this bubbling along merrily. There is Hope going through bravery tests to escape the native tribe, getting mixed up with a rogue elephant, a lion in his tub, having his pants repaired by Ekberg while he's wearing 'em (and with the poisoned needle from his suicide kit), and eventually becoming airborne in the moon-capsule.

Though most of the responsibility falls on Hope and his personality, Edie Adams gives a pleasantly unobtrusive performance and La Ekberg, though an unlikely Mata Hari, is a sound and decorative foil for Hope. Only the most fastidious carper will protest that the jungle often reeks of Pinewood Studio.

•

CALL ME GENIUS
SEE: THE REBEL

•

CALL ME MADAM
1953, 114 mins, US col
Dir Walter Lang *Prod* Sol C. Siegel *Scr* Arthur Sheekman *Ph* Leon Shamroy *Ed* Robert Simpson *Mus* Alfred Newman (dir.) *Art* Lyle R. Wheeler, John De Cuir
Act Ethel Merman, Donald O'Connor, Vera-Ellen, George Sanders, Billy De Wolfe, Helmut Dantine (20th Century-Fox)

A [1950] hit musical on Broadway, *Call Me Madam* scored a run of close to two years in Gotham with Ethel Merman, as Ambassador Sally Adams, the fabulous Femme diplomat, representing the U.S. in the mythical Grand Duchy of Lichtenburg. Merman still reigns in the cinematic version.

In key spots, George Sanders is the tiny country's foreign department chief, and Donald O'Connor is the U.S. press attache, Billy De Wolfe is the American charge d'affaires, Vera-Ellen plays the princess and Helmut Dantine is on hand as the prince who's spurned by the princess in favor of the American press rep.

Madam offers an ingratiating book loosely fashioned after the career of Perle Mesta, former U.S. Minister to Luxembourg. Added plusses are via the widened scope and richness of the production, lush mountains and extra trimmings for the delightful Irving Berlin score. Also, there's the fresh, inventive choreography staged by Robert Alton, with O'Connor and Vera-Ellen as a terping combo of top calibre.

The screenplay, from the Howard Lindsay-Russel Crouse book, is imaginative and whimsical. Merman is at her robust best with a tune. At the opening, she gives "Hostess with the Mostest on the Ball" a powerhouse delivery and it's a cinch to provoke heavy mitting. Her "You're Just in Love" duet with O'Connor also is standout.

1953: Best Scoring of a Musical Picture

NOMINATION: Best Color Costume Design

•

CALL ME MISTER
1951, 96 mins, US col
Dir Lloyd Bacon *Prod* Fred Kohlmar *Scr* Albert E. Lewin, Burt Styler *Ph* Arthur E. Arling *Ed* Louis Loeffler *Mus* Alfred Newman (dir.) *Art* Lyle Wheeler, Joseph C. Wright
Act Betty Grable, Dan Dailey, Danny Thomas, Dale Robertson, Richard Boone, Jeffrey Hunter (20th Century-Fox)

Drawing but lightly on its Broadway revue namesake for book and songs, *Call Me Mister* is smooth, easy-to-take screen entertainment.

Garbed in a glowing Technicolor dress and gifted with musical-wise Betty Grable and Dan Dailey, the footage sparks along through songs, dances (staged by Busby Berkeley) and a skeleton story framework with an infectious zip. Only four of the stage revue's songs are used, one with revised lyrics, and four new numbers were contributed. Book places action in Japan just after World War II's end, instead of back in the States, so the title itself is the chief suggestion of the film's legit origin.

Of the eight tunes, probably the best is "Japanese Girl Like American Boy," during which Grable works with a Japanese femme chorus, and scene then segues into a dance with the Dunhill dance team of three males. Grable, impersonating a sailor with the dance trio, does a wow job.

Film plot finds Dailey a GI ready to be shipped home from Japan. When he finds Grable, a wife from with whom he has been separated, is serving with the Civilian Actresses Technician Service, he forges an assignment paper so he can help her stage a camp show and possibly win her back.

•

CALL NORTHSIDE 777
1948, 111 mins, US b/w
Dir Henry Hathaway *Prod* Otto Lang *Scr* Jerome Cady, Jay Dratler *Ph* Joe MacDonald *Ed* J. Watson Webb, Jr. *Mus* Alfred Newman *Art* Lyle R. Wheeler, Mark-Lee Kirk
Act James Stewart, Richard Conte, Lee J. Cobb, Helen Walker, Betty Garde (20th Century-Fox)

Call Northside 777 has all the separate ingredients for a sock film but registers only with a mild impact due to a lack of integration. Among the film's principal drawbacks is James Stewart's jarring and unpersuasive performance in the key role. As a Chicago reporter who's assigned to dig up a human-interest angle out of an 11-year-old murder case, Stewart shuttles between a phoney cynicism and a sob-sister sentimentalism into a recognizable newspaperman.

Henry Hathaway's direction marks a retreat from the documentary form. Instead of consistent realism, he lapses into a hybrid technique with plenty of hokey melodramatic tones.

Based on a celebrated miscarriage of justice in 1932, when two innocent men were sentenced to 99 years apiece for killing a cop, the screenplay [based on articles by James P. McGuire, adaptation by Leonard Hoffman and Quentin Reynolds] constructs a serviceable plot on the factual groundwork. Film, however, tends to wander aimlessly in an over-sized running time.

Title is derived from a personal ad placed in the *Chicago Times-Herald* by the mother of one of the prisoners offering a $5,000 reward for information leading to the release of her son. Answering the ad, Stewart uses it as a peg for a series of human interest stories about the case. Initially skeptical, he's progressively drawn to a belief in the man's innocence. Richard Conte gives an intensely sincere performance as the young Polish-American who is railroaded to jail.

•

CALL OF THE WILD, THE
1935, 89 mins, US b/w
Dir William A. Wellman *Prod* Darryl F. Zanuck (exec.), Raymond Griffith *Scr* Gene Fowler, Leonard Praskins *Ph* Charles Rosher *Ed* Hanson Fritch *Mus* Alfred Newman (dir.) *Art* Richard Day, Alexander Golitzen
Act Clark Gable, Loretta Young, Jack Oakie, Frank Conroy, Reginald Owen, Sidney Toler (20th Century)

The lion-hearted dog that was Jack London's creation as the leading character of *Call of the Wild* emerges now as a stooge for a rather conventional pair of human love birds. Changes have made the canine classic hardly recognizable, but they have not done any damage.

The big and exceptionally wild St Bernard, known as Buck, is not entirely submerged, since such of his feats as the haul of a 1,000-pound load over the snow and his mating with a femme wolf are included, but he has been decidedly picture-house broken.

Clark Gable strong-and-silents himself expertly and Loretta Young, in the opposite corner of the revised love affair, is lovely and competent. But Jack Oakie has the laughs, and they land him on top.

It's a story of treachery, hardship, violence and unrequited love in Alaska, so anything that does away with sadness for a momentary giggle is highly welcome. Gable and Oakie's rescue of Young, whose husband has apparently lost his way and perished; their finding of the gold mine; their encounter with the villainous Reginald Owen; the return of Young's husband, lending a bitter-sweet finish to the romance, are the highlights of the story's human element.

This is the second trip for the London novel to the screen. Pathe made it silent in 1923.

•

CALL OF THE WILD, THE
1973, 100 mins, UK/France/W. Germany/Italy/Norway/Spain Ⓥ ⊙ col
Dir Ken Annakin *Prod* Harry Alan Towers *Scr* Peter Welbeck, Win Wells, Peter Yeldham *Ph* John Cabrera *Ed* Thelma Connell *Mus* Carlo Rustichelli *Art* Knut Solberg
Act Charlton Heston, Raimund Harmsdorf, Michele Mercier, George Eastman, Sancho Gracia, Maria Rohm (Towers of London)

Jack London's thrilling, often-filmed tale trails a couple of roughnecks, John and Pete, on their gold-digging, mail-hopping, and booze-deal fortune hunts in Alaska's snow-bound wilderness. Time and again, they are outsmarted and outroughed by an assorted pack of rivals.

Director Ken Annakin picked a few good actors (Charlton Heston and Italo-western hero George Eastman) and some others capable of no more than looking their parts (Raimund Harmsdorf, Michele Mercier). But everybody appears to play merely along action line on his own and create a vacuum around him.

Thus lacking the density of London's original, the picture falls to pieces with all that frozen gore, dog fights, sled chases, saloon brawls and other knock-down melodramatics.

•

CAMELOT
1967, 179 mins, US Ⓥ ⊙ ▭ col
Dir Joshua Logan *Prod* Jack L. Warner *Scr* Alan Jay Lerner *Ph* Richard H. Kline *Ed* Folmar Blangsted *Mus* Alfred Newman (dir.) *Art* John Truscott
Act Richard Harris, Vanessa Redgrave, Franco Nero, David Hemmings, Lionel Jeffries, Estelle Winwood (Warner/Seven Arts)

On the sumptuous face of it, *Camelot* qualifies as one of Hollywood's alltime great screen musicals. While most big musicals have fine production, dazzling costumes and all that, what gives *Camelot* special value is a central dramatic conflict that throbs with human anguish and compassion.

Camelot never need resort to the more obvious kind of added action. The focus is kept on the three mentally-tortured people, the cuckolded king, the cheating queen, the confused knight.

All of this is against the often exquisite sets and costumes of John Truscott, the creative use of research that is constantly visible. The fine camera work of Richard H. Kline, the clever screenplay by Alan Jay Lerner, the singular appropriateness to time and place of the Frederick Loewe score as lovingly managed by Alfred Newman are all major contributions.

Joshua Logan rates extraordinary tribute for the performances he elicits from Richard Harris as King Arthur, Vanessa Redgrave as Guinevere, and Franco Nero as the knight whose idealism succumbs to passion.

1967: Best Art Direction, Adapted Scoring, Costume Design

NOMINATION: Best Cinematography, Sound

•

CAMERAMAN, THE
1928, 68 mins, US ⊗ b/w
Dir Edward Sedgwick *Scr* Clyde Bruckman, Richard Schayer *Ph* Elgin Lessley
Act Buster Keaton, Marceline Day, Harold Goodwin, Sidney Bracy, Harry Gribbon (M-G-M)

Good laugh picture with Buster Keaton. The same old stencil about a boob that does everything wrong and cashes in finally through sheer accident.

Keaton is a problem on love interest. In the present case his cow-like adoration of the heroine (Marceline Day) is used to build up sympathy as a counter-irritant to his abysmal stupidity.

In trying to land a job with M-G-M News, Keaton, as a tintype photographer suddenly turned cinematic, goes through a series of hoke adventures. There is the comedy. One of the smartest bits is when setting up his camera to shoot an admiral leaving a hotel—Keaton mistakes the gorgeously uniformed hotel doorman for the admiral. Another clever bit is when, swimming in a public tank with women all about, Keaton loses his over-size bathing suit. The big punch is when he photographs a Chinese tong war from the center of the melee.

Day is appealing as the femme. Harold Goodwin has the only other part of consequence, as a newsreel cameraman also soft on the gal.

•

CAMILLA
1994, 95 mins, Canada/UK Ⓥ ⊙ col
Dir Deepa Mehta *Prod* Christina Jennings, Simon Relph *Scr* Paul Quarrington *Ph* Guy Dufaux *Ed* Barry Farrell *Mus* Daniel Lanois *Art* Sandra Kybartas
Act Jessica Tandy, Bridget Fonda, Elias Koteas, Maury Chaykin, Graham Greene, Hume Cronyn (Skreba/Shaftesbury)

Featuring a standout performance from Jessica Tandy in her last starring bigscreen role, *Camilla* is a warm, funny road movie. Pic opens with Freda Lopez (Bridget Fonda) strumming on her electric guitar, and it's soon clear that she's a frustrated singer/songwriter whose husband, Vincent (Elias Koteas), is more that a little skeptical of her musical talents. The less-than-happily-married couple head out from Toronto to a cottage somewhere near Savannah, GA, for a much-needed vacation.

That's where they meet neighbor Camilla Cara (Tandy), a wacky old woman prone to tall tales, tippling sherry and reminiscing about her exploits as a concert violinist. Camilla's son, Harold (Maury Chaykin), a high-strung, soft-core porn producer, convinces Vincent to help him market his films, and this partnership leaves the two women by themselves. Freda and Camilla, who hit it off immediately, decide to go back to Toronto to catch a special performance of a Brahms concerto. Film soon turns into a May-December female buddy pic over a series of rather improbable adventures that include an encounter with a suave con artist (Graham Greene).

Canuck novelist/screenwriter Paul Quarrington [from a

screen story by Al Jennings] has penned a script that neatly captures the bittersweet tone of the story without slipping into syrupy sentimentality.

•

CAMILLE
1921, 90 mins, US ⊗ b/w
Dir Ray C. Smallwood ***Prod*** Nazimova ***Scr*** June Mathis ***Ph*** Rudolph Bergquist ***Art*** Natacha Rambova
Act Nazimova, Rudolph Valentino, Arthur Hoyt, Zeffie Tilbury, Edward Connelly, Patsy Ruth Miller (Nazimova/Metro)

This production of Nazimova in *Camille* proves to be a modernized version of the story of *The Lady with the Camellias*, which fact is welcome for the major part, but not so felicitous as the concluding parts are reached. For, wonder of wonders, the director has entirely omitted the scene of Armand at the bedside of his beloved as she breathes her last. Perhaps this big moment was eliminated in the thought the picture fans, if unable to witness a happy ending, wanted one as happy as possible under the circumstances. Nothing could be further from the fact.

Nazimova totally immerses her own distinct personality into that of the famed heroine. Instead of the sinuous, clinging Nazimova, she appears an actress almost new-born for the part.

The surrounding company is excellent. Second to the star is the Armand of Rudolph Valentino. There are many opportunities for obtrusiveness in the role, but he keeps it correct to the minutest detail.

•

CAMILLE
1927, 96 mins, US ⊗ b/w
Dir Fred Niblo ***Scr*** Fred De Gresac, Olga Printzlau, Chandler Sprague, George Marion, Jr. ***Ph*** Oliver T. Marsh
Act Norma Talmadge, Gilbert Roland, Lilyan Tashman, Maurice Costello, Harvey Clark, Alec B. Francis (Talmadge/First National)

Fred Niblo and Norma Talmadge have dedicated a pretty love story [from the novel by the younger Alexandre Dumas] to the screen that lacks the punch to make it a standout. Dramatic intensity only twice arises to make an audience forget it is watching a picture. This is when Armand returns to his suburban cottage to find Camille has left him, and when he next meets her in a gambling parlor escorted by her first financial amour, the Baron.

For some reason Niblo omitted the traditional sympathy that goes with Camille's death or a pull on the heart strings where she gives up Armand at the instigation of his father. For a demi-mondaine supposedly in the throes of the first and only real love of her life. Talmadge gives in much too easily as Niblo has screened it.

And through it all Talmadge looks beautiful. Never better, besides giving a sterling performance. Opposite Talmadge is Gilbert Roland. Other than Talmadge and Roland, no one shines except Harvey Clark.

•

CAMILLE
1937, 108 mins, US Ⓥ b/w
Dir George Cukor ***Prod*** David Lewis (assoc.) ***Scr*** Zoe Akins, Frances Marion, James Hilton ***Ph*** William Daniels, Karl Freund ***Ed*** Margaret Booth ***Mus*** Herbert Stothart ***Art*** Cedric Gibbons, Fredric Hope, Edwin B. Willis
Act Greta Garbo, Robert Taylor, Lionel Barrymore, Elizabeth Allan, Jessie Ralph, Henry Daniell (M-G-M)

George Cukor directs this famous play [by Alexandre Dumas] with rare skill. Interior settings, costumes and exteriors are lavish and beautiful. The film shows the great care which went into its preparation and making.

Robert Taylor plays with surprising assurance and ease. He never seems to be striving for a point. He speaks with a moderately modulated voice, never hurriedly, and in all the familiar Armand scenes, such as the first meeting, the parting from his mistress, the accusation in the gambling hall and, finally, the death chamber sequence, Taylor holds up his end of the story with distinction.

Garbo's impersonation of Marguerite Gautier is one of her best portraits. She wears striking clothes, white usually, and while she looks older than the ardent young Armand, the disparity does not mitigate against the illusion.

The two principals play the love scenes for full worth. There is much talk of their affection for each other, but Cukor, with wisdom, shows a minimum of embrace footage.

Of the support players, Henry Daniell, as Baron de Varville, turns in a performance of unusual interest. He is the menace in the background, the lover whom Camille deserts for Armand and the one to whom she returns. Daniell is suave and properly elegant without being too obvious.

1937: NOMINATION: Best Actress (Greta Garbo)

•

CAMILLE CLAUDEL
1988, 170 mins, France Ⓥ ⦿ ▭ col
Dir Bruno Nuytten ***Prod*** Christian Fechner ***Scr*** Bruno Nuytten, Marilyn Goldin ***Ph*** Pierre Lhomme ***Ed*** Joelle Hache, Jeanne Kef ***Mus*** Gabriel Yared ***Art*** Bernard Vezat
Act Isabelle Adjani, Gerard Depardieu, Laurent Crevill, Alain Cuny, Madeleine Robinson, Katrine Boorman (Fechner/Lilith/Gaumont/A2/DD)

France's Isabelle Adjani and Gerard Depardieu find roles tailored to their considerable talents in this conscientious but dramatically conventional biopic about the gifted sculptress Camille Claudel, who was the muse and mistress of Auguste Rodin. Film was made in closed-set circumstances on a $16 million budget (cofinanced by pubcaster Antenne 2, which will get a longer miniseries version).

Though nominal producer and director are Christian Fechner and ace lenser Bruno Nuytten, in his scripting-helming debut, *Camille Claudel* is very much Adjani's picture. She bought the rights to a recent official biography, won the exclusive blessings of the Claudel estate (which effectively sank two rival film projects, including one by Claude Chabrol with Isabelle Huppert) and developed the project over a five-year period.

The screenplay attempts to reestablish Camille Claudel as an artist and woman in her own right, fighting for control of her artistic and emotional destiny and losing in the end. The film (in its theatrical cut) tends to define Claudel essentially in her tumultuous 15-year relationship with Rodin, who at the beginning of the picture is sufficiently impressed with her work (and her ambitious temperament) to take her on as assistant in his public works atelier.

As exclusive in her romantic needs as she is exacting in her artistic standards, Claudel pushes the complex liaison toward its breaking point. In the process her own mind begins to go.

As her brother, Paul Claudel (Laurent Crevill) rises to celebrity as Catholic poet and dramatist, Camille declines. Her situation between Rodin and Paul, both overbearing and pompous artists, never is seriously dramatized. Scenes with the parents (played by Madeleine Robinson and Alain Cuny, 80-year-old veteran of Paul Claudel's theater) are not the most convincing.

Adjani throws herself into a role worthy of her abilities, giving intense relief, if not enough pathos, to a strong-willed femme artist. Depardieu, sporting a thick beard, "sculpts" a massive portrait of the artist as man, lover and creator. What's missing between the two performances, however, is the evolution of feelings complicated by professional and private jealousies.

•

CAMPBELL'S KINGDOM
1957, 100 mins, UK col
Dir Ralph Thomas ***Prod*** Betty E. Box ***Scr*** Robin Estridge ***Ph*** Ernest Steward ***Ed*** Frederick Wilson ***Mus*** Clifton Parker ***Art*** Maurice Carter
Act Dirk Bogarde, Stanley Baker, Michael Craig, Barbara Murray, James Robertson Justice, Athene Seyler (Rank)

Campbell's Kingdom is virtually a British western. It is a straightforward, virile, action-packed yarn with ample excitement and mounting drama.

Story is a simple clash between a stiff-lipped hero and a glowering villain. When Dirk Bogarde, with only six months to live, arrives in the township of Come Lucky in the Rockies to take up his grandfather's inheritance, a whole train of skulduggery is unleashed. Said inheritance is Campbell's Kingdom, a valley which has been a problem child for some years. The old man obstinately insisted that it held oil. The local inhabitants invested their money in his idea. Meanwhile ruthless contractor Stanley Baker wants to flood the valley as part of a new hydro-electric scheme involving building of a new dam with inferior cement.

The plot unfolds slowly but gathers tremendous momentum, with the dam crashing a great thrill. The alleged Rockies were lensed brilliantly in Cortina by Ernest Steward. Director Ralph Thomas wisely resists the temptation to allow his characters to indulge in personal rough stuff. Film keeps fairly close to the novel [by Hammond Innes].

•

CAMP ON BLOOD ISLAND, THE
1958, 82 mins, UK ▭ b/w
Dir Val Guest ***Prod*** Anthony Hinds ***Scr*** Jon Manchip White, Val Guest ***Ph*** Jack Asher ***Ed*** Bill Lenny, James Needs ***Mus*** Gerard Schurmann ***Art*** John Stoll
Act Carl Mohner, Andre Morell, Edward Underdown, Michael Goodliffe, Barbara Shelley, Michael Gwynn (Hammer)

The yarn, based on a real-life incident, takes place in a Japanese prisoner-of-war camp, ruled over by a sadistic commandant who has sworn to massacre all the British prisoners should Japan lose the war. The British officers learn on a secret radio that the war has ended but, somewhat implausibly, they manage to keep the secret from the Nips until the end of the film.

There are as many holes in the film as there are in a fishing net. Yet it holds the attention mainly because of the frightful realization that such things did actually happen in the war. The dialog and situations have been devised on the very simple premise that all Japs are rats.

•

CANADIAN BACON
1995, 91 mins, US Ⓥ col
Dir Michael Moore ***Prod*** David Brown, Ron Rotholz, Michael Moore ***Scr*** Michael Moore ***Ph*** Haskell Wexler ***Ed*** Wendy Stanzler, Michael Berenbaum ***Mus*** Elmer Bernstein, Peter Bernstein ***Art*** Carol Spier
Act Alan Alda, John Candy, Rhea Perlman, Kevin Pollak, Rip Torn, Bill Nunn (PolyGram/Propaganda)

What do we really know about Canadians? Michael Moore's long curing *Canadian Bacon* isn't about to reveal any national secrets but it does reinforce a lot of familiar stereotypes. As the film halfheartedly asserts, it's difficult to imagine them as a malevolent force ready to sweep across the 49th parallel and seize the U.S. government at the point of a nuclear warhead. Recalling such bygone droll political comedies as *Dr. Strangelove* and *The Mouse That Roared*, *Bacon* is an amusing outing for a sophisticated crowd.

The premise paints modern-day Americans as restless for the smell of battle. The nation's rivals, however, have all been quelled, and the president (Alan Alda) is an ineffectual peacenik more mindful of his popularity rating than methods of getting the nation out of its Cold War mentality. The normally sedate hamlet of Niagara Falls, NY, is feeling the crunch because Hacker Industries, a munitions factory, is closing up shop. It's failed to convert its operation to something more practical because its owner (G. D. Spradlin) had hoped to sell the government the ultimate doomsday machine. At the White House, spin doctor Stuart Smiley (Kevin Pollak) hits on the idea of a northern scapegoat after news of a cross-border incident during a hockey tourney. He quickly gets the backing of military honcho Gen. Dick Panzer (Rip Torn). Soon phoney skirmishes are being concocted to fuel tension, and the gullible—like Niagara Falls sheriff Bud Boomer (John Candy)—not only buy it, they organize their own patriotic, gun-toting forays.

Canadian Bacon has all the makings of a funny, acidic satire. There's just enough truth in the proceedings to give the humor bite.

•

CANARY MURDER CASE
1929, 80 mins, US b/w
Dir Malcolm St. Clair ***Scr*** Florence Ryerson, Albert Shelby
Act William Powell, James Hall, Louise Brooks, Jean Arthur, Gustav von Seyffertitz, Eugene Pallette (Paramount)

A perfect program picture, wherein the principal character, Philo Vance (William Powell), detective, doesn't look at a dame without a professional motive. He's strictly a crime solver.

S. S. Van Dine's original story, from which the scenario was adapted, was a bestseller among detective novels.

The Canary is Margaret O'Dell (Louise Brooks), musical comedy star. She is a merciless little blackmailer off stage, having three prominent and wealthy men in her power for coin and young Jimmy Spotswood (James Hall) for social climbing.

On the night she was murdered, she called up the three rich suckers, informing them she would shortly marry Jimmy and advising them to deliver some hefty wedding gifts that evening in person.

Intricacies of the motive, crime and detection are intelligently directed by Malcolm St. Clair. Next to Powell in the trouping section comes Eugene Pallette as a thick-headed detective sergeant.

•

CAN-CAN
1960, 134 mins, US Ⓥ ⦿ ▭ col
Dir Walter Lang ***Prod*** Jack Cummings ***Scr*** Dorothy Kingsley, Charles Lederer ***Ph*** William H. Daniels ***Ed*** Robert Simpson ***Mus*** Nelson Riddle (arr.) ***Art*** Lyle Wheeler, Jack Martin Smith
Act Frank Sinatra, Shirley MacLaine, Maurice Chevalier, Louis Jourdan, Juliet Prowse, Marcel Dalio (20th Century-Fox)

Can-Can [based on the musical by Abe Burrows] is a serviceable musical. The more discriminating will find it wanting. It's Las Vegas, 1960; not Montmartre, 1896. The production somehow conveys the feeling that Clan members Frank Sinatra and Shirley MacLaine will soon be joined by other members of the group for another "summit" meeting.

MacLaine is bouncy, outgoing, scintillating, vivacious and appealing—but French she ain't. Sinatra is, well, Sinatra, complete with the ring-a-ding-ding vocabulary of the insiders. The juxtaposition of Sinatra and MacLaine on the one hand, and authentic Parisians Maurice Chevalier and Louis Jourdan on the other is jarring.

As the proprietor of a cafe that pays off the gendarmes so that the imbibers can witness the illegal dance, MacLaine has the opportunity to indulge in uninhibited and brash clowning and frenzied dancing. Sinatra is her wisecracking playboy-lawyer who aptly handles her legal and private affairs. Both Chevalier and Jourdan, who clicked so strongly in *Gigi*, are wasted in thankless roles as corruptible and incorruptible judges, respectively.

The musical score has been enhanced with three Cole Porter songs that were not in the original Broadway musical—"Let's Do It," "Just One of Those Things" and "You Do Something to Me." The best tune from the original, as sung by Sinatra, is still "C'est Magnifique."

The dance numbers, for the most part, are the highlights of the film, particularly MacLaine's Apache dance. The famous "Adam and Eve" ballet falls somewhat flat, although it does show off to good advantage Marc Wilder and Juliet Prowse. The can-can is fun, but about as lewd and lascivious as a Maypole dance.

1960: NOMINATIONS: Best Color Costume Design, Scoring of a Musical Picture

•

CANDIDATE, THE

1972, 109 mins, US Ⓥ ⊙ col

Dir Michael Ritchie ***Prod*** Walter Coblenz ***Scr*** Jeremy Larner ***Ph*** Victor J. Kemper ***Ed*** Richard A. Harris, Robert Estrin ***Mus*** John Rubinstein ***Art*** Gene Callahan

Act Robert Redford, Peter Boyle, Don Porter, Allen Garfield, Karen Carlson, Melvyn Douglas (Warner)

The Candidate is an excellent drama starring Robert Redford as a naive liberal political novice who wises up fast. Walter Coblenz produced the zesty, gritty film, directed and paced superbly by Michael Ritchie. Peter Boyle and Allen Garfield are tops as campaign supervisors.

The well-structured and developed screenplay takes Redford from a rural legal assistance vocation through the temptations and tortures of mass-merchandising politics, to an upset victory over longtime California Senator Don Porter. Redford's superior acting talents, which not-often-enough are tapped by the scripts he decides to do, are nearly all on display herein in a virtuoso peformance.

Intercutting of some actual political banquet footage is excellent, and the entire film often seems like a documentary special in the best sense of the word.

1972: Best Original Story & Screenplay

NOMINATION: Best Sound

•

CANDY

1968, 123 mins, US/Italy/France col

Dir Christian Marquand ***Prod*** Robert Haggiog ***Scr*** Buck Henry ***Ph*** Giuseppe Rotunno ***Ed*** Frank Santillo, Giancarlo Cappelli ***Mus*** Dave Grusin ***Art*** Dean Tavoularis

Act Charles Aznavour, Marlon Brando, Richard Burton, James Burton, John Huston, Ewa Aulin (Selmur/Dear)

Candy is a mixed bag of goodies. Based on a novel [by Terry Southern and Mason Hoffenberg] which was a successful satire on pornographic stories, film is at times hilarious, delightfully outrageous, silly, flat, and routine. Director Christian Marquand utilizes a Buck Henry adaptation, a very fine comedy sexpot newcomer (Ewa Aulin) and a strong cast of cameo stars and character thesps.

Candy tells of the unbelievably naive and innocent sexpot heroine, whose adventures were setups for the de rigeur sexual incidents found in most pornography.

The continuing characters are excellent. Aulin's performance in the title role is a delight. John Astin plays both her square father and lecherous uncle, and he is terrific. Elsa Martinelli also is excellent as Aunt Livia.

In retrospect, a prime flaw in *Candy* is the over-exposition of the vignettes. Nearly every episode suffers from the temptation to get one or two more gags out of the material before cutting.

Richard Burton, first cameo star, comes across as the most effective. Ringo Starr, as the Mexican gardener, is very good.

•

CANDYMAN

1992, 93 mins, US Ⓥ ⊙ col

Dir Bernard Rose ***Prod*** Steve Golin, Sigurjon Sighvatsson, Alan Poul ***Scr*** Bernard Rose ***Ph*** Anthony B. Richmond ***Ed*** Dan Rae ***Mus*** Philip Glass ***Art*** Jane Ann Stewart

Act Virginia Madsen, Tony Todd, Xander Berkeley, Kasi Lemmons, Vanessa Williams, DeJuan Guy (Propaganda)

Candyman is an uppper-register horror item that delivers the requisite shocks and gore but doesn't cheat or cop out.

Doctoral candidate Helen Lyle (Virginia Madsen) is studying neighborhood legends and learns that Candyman, the educated, talented son of a slave, had his hand cut off and was put to death by throwing him to a swarm of bees in revenge for impregnating a young upper-class woman.

Lyle's investigation leads her to the site of the century-old outrage, Cabrini Green, now crime-ridden housing projects in Chicago. Supposedly, Candyman (Tony Todd) has committed 21 murders thus far, and it doesn't take long for Lyle to discover his gruesome lair in the projects.

Working from a story [*The Forbidden*] originally set in Liverpool by horror meister Clive Barker, Brit helmer Bernard Rose provides plenty of jolts, both bogus and actual, along the way. Threat of Candyman bursting out from behind mirrors is ever-present, and his evisceration technique with his hook is particularly gruesome. Performances are unusually credible for this sort of fare.

•

CANDYMAN FAREWELL TO THE FLESH

1995, 94 mins, US Ⓥ ⊙ col

Dir Bill Condon ***Prod*** Sigurjon Sighvatsson, Gregg D. Fienberg ***Scr*** Rand Ravich, Mark Kruger ***Ph*** Tobias Schliessler ***Ed*** Virginia Katz ***Mus*** Philip Glass ***Art*** Barry Robison

Act Tony Todd, Kelly Rowan, Timothy Carhart, Veronica Cartwright, William O'Leary, Fay Hauser (Propaganda/PFE)

The sequel to the surprise horror hit is a case of diminishing artistic returns but not, thankfully, a victim of the terrible twos. The avenger first popped up on-screen in 1992 in Chicago's Cabrini Green housing project and now resurfaces in New Orleans's French Quarter in time for Mardi Gras. This time he appears to be taking a personal and lethal interest in the aristocratic Tarrant family.

Dad, who believes he knows how to destroy Candyman, is first to feel the power of the merciless hook. Son Ethan (William O'Leary) is fingered for the crime and daughter Annie (Kelly Rowan) winds up delving into the legend and uncovering its dark secrets.

The script [from a story by Clive Barker] is constructed too much like a novel, which slows the pace of the early, establishing sections. Director Bill Condon works too hard to tie all the plot strands into a neat bow. So, for much of the picture, the audience is way ahead of the screen characters in guessing what comes next.

Still, the story picks up speed as it proceeds and as it shifts into a visceral gear. Tech credits are extremely smooth, but flashback re-creations of the title character's 19th-century roots stand out in sharp contrast as clunky and archly melodramatic.

•

CAN HEIRONYMUS MERKIN EVER FORGET MERCY HUMPPE AND FIND TRUE HAPPINESS?

1969, 117 mins, UK col

Dir Anthony Newley ***Prod*** Anthony Newley ***Scr*** Herman Raucher, Anthony Newley ***Ph*** Otto Heller ***Ed*** Bernard Gribble ***Mus*** Anthony Newley ***Art*** William Constable

Act Anthony Newley, Joan Collins, Milton Berle, George Jessel, Connie Kreski, Bruce Forsyth (Universal/Taralex)

This film is the work of Anthony Newley, who not only produced and directed from the script on which he collabed with Herman Raucher, and wrote the music, but stars as well in the title role.

Newley plays an introspective film singing idol who relives his part-real, part-illusionary past in a movie within a movie, drawing on strange characters to people this past as well as lovelies who line up in wild expectancy as Heironymus plucks them one by one.

Milton Berle in the fetching character-name of Good Time Eddie Filth is his agent who lures him into his career of concupiscence, and George Jessel as The Presence, perhaps an advance angel of death, occasionally emerges out of the blue before disappearing again to spout shaggy jokes as pointless parables.

Married to Polyester Poontang (Joan Collins), Heironymus cannot forget Mercy Humppe, the beautiful innocent so deliciously cavorted by Connie Kreski, one-time Playboy bunny.

•

CANNERY ROW

1982, 120 mins, US Ⓥ ⊙ col

Dir David S. Ward ***Prod*** Michael Phillips ***Scr*** David S. Ward ***Ph*** Sven Nykvist ***Ed*** David Bretherton ***Mus*** Jack Nitzsche ***Art*** Richard MacDonald

Act Nick Nolte, Debra Winger, Audra Lindley, Frank McRae, M. Emmet Walsh, Tom Mahoney (M-G-M/United Artists)

Maybe Raquel Welch will have the last laugh after all. *Cannery Row*, pic from which she was ignominiously dismissed, gets somewhat better as it lurches along from vignette to vignette, but this long-in-the-works adaptation of John Steinbeck's waterfront tomes [*Cannery Row* and *Sweet Thursday*] displays more appreciation for the values inherent in the material than it does ability to breathe life into it.

Highly anecdotal in nature and tied together by some personable, literary narration by John Huston, 1940s tale centers mostly upon the sketchy activities of a self-employed marine biologist named Doc (Nick Nolte), who lives at ocean's edge, consorts with floozies, counts local bums as his best friends and conceals a troubled past behind his handsome physique.

Across the way stands the neighborhood bordello, into which comes mixed-up drifter girl Suzy (Debra Winger), who has eyes for Doc but little knowledge of how to pursue him or improve her lot in life. The two sort of get together and break up numerous times.

Nolte seems ideally cast as Doc and has no trouble carrying the film, but is nevertheless hampered by incomplete nature of the part as written. Winger's winning personality and great cracking voice carry her through here, but she relies unduly on a few pat mannerisms.

•

CANNONBALL (UK: CARQUAKE)

1976, 93 mins, US/Hong Kong Ⓥ col

Dir Paul Bartel ***Prod*** Samuel W. Gelfman ***Scr*** Paul Bartel, Donald C. Simpson ***Ph*** Tak Fujimoto ***Ed*** Morton Tubor ***Mus*** David A. Axelrod ***Art*** Michel Levesque

Act David Carradine, Bill McKinney, Veronica Hamel, Gerrit Graham, Robert Carradine, Martin Scorsese (New World/Shaws)

Cannonball will please those who won't rest until they see every car in creation destroyed and aflame.

The sophisticated story line puts David Carradine, Bill McKinney and various other drivers and characters in autos in Los Angeles and promises $100,000 to the first to arrive in New York. Surely, goodness, mercy and high octane will triumph over villainy with lead in their guns, if not in their gas.

That's not to say *Cannonball* has no appeal beyond the crash crowd. It's full of handy highway hints, like what to do when someone steals your jack and then blasts your back tire apart with a pistol.

Best of all, though, is Carradine's inspirational automotive fortitude. When frustrated, he spins in circles, kicks his wheels, mutters oaths—just like the average weekend driver.

•

CANNONBALL RUN, THE

1981, 93 mins, US Ⓥ ⊙ col

Dir Hal Needham ***Prod*** Albert S. Ruddy ***Scr*** Brock Yates ***Ph*** Michael Butler ***Ed*** Donna Cambern, William D. Gordean ***Mus*** Snuff Garrett (sup.) ***Art*** Carol Wenger

Act Burt Reynolds, Roger Moore, Farrah Fawcett, Dom DeLuise, Dean Martin, Sammy Davis, Jr. (20th Century-Fox)

Full of terribly inside showbiz jokes and populated by what could be called Burt and Hal's Rat Pack, film takes place in that redneck never-never land where most of the guys are beer-guzzling good ole boys and all the gals are fabulously built tootsies.

Cross-country race of the title comes off as almost entirely incidental to the star turns. Overall effect is akin to watching the troupe take a vacation.

Reynolds doesn't even lay a finger on Farrah Fawcett, settling instead for a nice chat in the back of his speedy ambulance. Tuxedoed Roger Moore drives around in his Aston-Martin and tries to convince everyone he's really Roger Moore and not one Seymour Goldfarb. Oriental driver Jackie Chan distracts (and almost kills) himself by putting on a videotape of *Behind the Green Door*, one way to stay awake on a coast-to-coast trip. Partner Michael Hui plays it straight.

CANNONBALL RUN II

1984, 108 mins, US Ⓥ ⦿ col

Dir Hal Needham ***Prod*** Albert S. Ruddy ***Scr*** Hal Needham, Albert S. Ruddy, Harvey Miller ***Ph*** Nick McLean ***Ed*** William Gordean, Carl Kress ***Mus*** Al Capps ***Art*** Thomas E. Azzari

Act Burt Reynolds, Dom DeLuise, Dean Martin, Sammy Davis, Jr., Telly Savalas, Shirley MacLaine (Golden Harvest/Warner)

This film is so inept that the best actor in the pic is Jilly Rizzo. But he has a great advantage: he's on screen five seconds and he doesn't have to talk.

Sequel to the all-star, 1981 hit *The Cannonball Run*, which was in turn an embellishment of Roger Corman's *Cannonball* (1976), plays as if former colleagues—producer Albert Ruddy, director Hal Needham and stars Burt Reynolds, Dom DeLuise, Dean Martin and Sammy Davis, Jr.—don't even have to make an effort any more. It's the ole boy network kind of filmmaking, joined this time by Frank Sinatra (playing himself) and Shirley MacLaine, in terms not endearing.

Again, a bunch of crazies, in a disparate collection of cars, are engaged in racing across the country to collect a lot of money. Action on the road, as encounters with most of the supporting players resemble nothing more than day work for majority of the cast, is limited to dusty, desert highway scenes (filmed in Arizona). To depict the later momentum of the race, filmmakers engaged Ralph Bakshi to show the race's progress in animation.

Execution is uninspired, laughs are hard to find, and the script is also difficult to locate. Reynold's high-pitched laugh is wearing thin.

CANNON FOR CORDOBA

1970, 104 mins, US Ⓥ ▭ col

Dir Paul Wendkos ***Prod*** Vincent M. Fennelly ***Scr*** Stephen Kandel ***Ph*** Antonio Macasoli ***Ed*** Walter Hanneman ***Mus*** Elmer Bernstein

Act George Peppard, Giovanna Ralli, Raf Vallone, Pete Duel, Don Gordon, Francine York (United Artists/Mirisch)

The story is about Mex outlaws who are a source of agony to the American military. Brig-Gen John J. Pershing (John Russell) dispatches his intelligence captain (George Peppard) to quell the disturbances. Peppard and a few friends conquer the army led by adversary Cordoba (Raf Vallone).

Interspersed are the episodes with a couple of girls, Giovanna Ralli and Francine York, whose effects are not special. Ralli, the double-dealing one, is pretty and treacherous and the observer gets to wonder about her costume changes in the heat of battle.

Director Paul Wendkos, cued by writer Stephen Kandel, might have put together a fairly arresting actioner. But they show an unsteady composite hand, for the script (if it has been adhered to) is an unorganized thing.

CAN SHE BAKE A CHERRY PIE?

1983, 90 mins, US Ⓥ col

Dir Henry Jaglom ***Prod*** M. H. Simonson ***Scr*** Henry Jaglom ***Ph*** Bob Fiore ***Mus*** Karen Black

Act Karen Black, Michael Emil, Michael Margotta, Frances Fisher, Martin Frydberg (Jagfilm)

Henry Jaglom follows his *Sitting Ducks* [1981] with a similar opus. This is once again a talky comedy, in which the scripter-director puts his characters in a number of sitcom situations, feeds them the opening lines of their scenes and lets them embroider the rest on their own. Starting from the basic premise that human beings suffer from their inability to communicate with their fellow men, Jaglom builds up a romance of sorts between a fresh divorcee who is still not emotionally rid of her husband, and a man who has been living on his own for some years.

Characters are built very much around the personality of the two main actors, Karen Black giving a beautiful performance, humorous, edgy, nervous and implying deep fears and pains hidden barely under the surface, and Michael Emil brings back many of the peculiarities of his part in *Sitting Ducks*.

CANTERBURY TALE, A

1944, 124 mins, UK Ⓥ b/w

Dir Michael Powell, Emeric Pressburger ***Prod*** Michael Powell, Emeric Pressburger ***Scr*** Michael Powell, Emeric Pressburger ***Ph*** Erwin Hillier ***Ed*** John Seabourne ***Mus*** Allan Gray ***Art*** Alfred Junge

Act Eric Portman, Sheila Sim, Dennis Price, John Sweet, Charles Hawtrey, Freda Jackson (Archers)

Sincerity and simplicity shine through every foot of this oversized modern version of the Chaucer epic tale. Here is rare beauty. Without belittling the highly imaginative genius inspiring the two directors, Michael Powell and Emeric Pressburger, first honors go to Erwin Hillier, whose camerawork is superb. Nothing more effective by way of a time transition shot has been conceived than the way he carries his audience through nine centuries in a few seconds. Beginning with a close-up of a hooded falcon on the wrist of an ancient Canterbury pilgrim (400 years before Columbus discovered America), he follows the graceful bird as it soars aloft on speedy wings. When it becomes a mere speck, it turns and comes gliding back. On coming nearer, it is seen to be a Spitfire.

Sheila Sim is the sole femme in the story. As a London shop girl, turned farmeret for the duration, she turns in a polished performance. Although giving the American GI all the best of it, there is an equally well-drawn characterization, the British tank sergeant, done so well by Dennis Price. For him the cathedral works a miracle.

Star of the film, Eric Portman, gives a splendid, restrained performance as a small-town justice of the peace. Four miracles occur in this story, one to each of the four principal characters.

CANTERVILLE GHOST, THE

1944, 95 mins, US Ⓥ ⦿ b/w

Dir Jules Dassin ***Prod*** Arthur L. Field ***Scr*** Edwin Harvey Blum ***Ph*** Robert Planck ***Ed*** Chester W. Schaeffer ***Mus*** George Bassman ***Art*** Cedric Gibbons, Edward Carfagno

Act Charles Laughton, Robert Young, Margaret O'Brien, Peter Lawford, Una O'Connor, Mike Mazurki (M-G-M)

The Canterville Ghost is entertaining comedy-drama, with the accent on comedy despite the mystery-chiller emphasis in the title. Tight scripting, nimble direction and excellent casting are about equally responsible for the satisfactory results.

Margaret O'Brien and Charles Laughton come through with topnotch performances, with the clever moppet a solid smash and topping everything. One of her outstanding bits is in a jitterbug terping number with an American soldier and her sedately demure dancing with Robert Young. Her solemn, dignified interpretation as the youthful Lady Jessica de Canterville, head of one of the great English landowning families, is terrific.

Yarn [from the Oscar Wilde short story] is about a 300-year-old ghost (Laughton), once walled up alive in the castle by his father because he proved a coward on the field of battle, who is looking for a kinsman to perform an act of bravery in his name so that he can be freed from his miserable existence.

CAN'T HELP SINGING

1944, 89 mins, US col

Dir Frank Ryan ***Prod*** Felix Jackson ***Scr*** Lewis R. Foster, Frank Ryan ***Ph*** Woody Bredell, W. Howard Greene ***Ed*** Ted J. Kent ***Mus*** Hans J. Salter ***Art*** John B. Goodman, Robert Clatworthy

Act Deanna Durbin, Robert Paige, Akim Tamiroff, David Bruce (Universal)

Can't Help Singing is a bright, colorful and gay filmusical, notable for the collection of tunes by Jerome Kern and the fine scenic mounting accentuated by the Technicolor photography. Deanna Durbin's initial color starrer, and her first filmusical comedy vehicle, picture rates as fine escapist entertainment.

Picture is set in the 1850 era, opening in Washington to introduce Durbin as the daughter of an influential senator who's determined to marry a cavalry officer. When the senator's influence ships the latter on quick notice to a California post, the girl follows but never quite catches up.

Lavish and superb production numbers frequently punctuate the proceedings for display of the Kern songs with large crowds of colorfully-costumed extras being used with apparent abandon by the production office. Frank Ryan's direction is okay, while the script inclines to loosely assembled sequences at times, and a liberal amount of corn and slapstick is sown along the route.

CAN'T STOP THE MUSIC

1980, 118 mins, US Ⓥ ▭ col

Dir Nancy Walker ***Prod*** Allan Carr, Jacques Morali, Henri Belolo ***Scr*** Bronte Woodard, Allan Carr ***Ph*** Bill Butler ***Ed*** John F. Burnett ***Mus*** Jacques Morali ***Art*** Harold Michelson

Act Valerie Perrine, Steve Guttenberg, June Havoc, Barbara Rush, Leigh Taylor-Young, The Village People (AFD/Allan Carr)

Writers have recreated the old "I know, we'll put on a show" gimmick to hinge their story on. Valerie Perrine plays the ex-model with a heart of gold. Her room-mate is an aspiring pop composer (Steve Guttenberg) whom she helps.

She recruits various friends (The Village People) to sing on a demo tape she's going to present to ex-lover and president of Marrakesh Records.

Among the standout sequences is the "Y.M.C.A." number, replete with a chorus line of young males side-diving just like in an Esther Williams aquastravaganza in the 1950s.

Director Nancy Walker clearly had trouble with the non-actors in the cast. The Village People, along with ex-Olympic decathlon champion Bruce Jenner, have a long way to go in the acting stakes.

CAPE FEAR

1962, 105 mins, US Ⓥ ⦿ b/w

Dir J. Lee Thompson ***Prod*** Sy Bartlett ***Scr*** James R. Webb ***Ph*** Samuel Leavitt ***Ed*** George Tomasini ***Mus*** Bernard Herrmann ***Art*** Alexander Golitzen, Robert Boyle

Act Gregory Peck, Robert Mitchum, Polly Bergen, Lori Martin, Martin Balsam, Telly Savalas (Melville-Talbot/Universal)

As a forthright exercise in cumulative terror *Cape Fear* is a competent and visually polished entry.

Taken from John D. MacDonald's magazine-serialized novel, *The Executioners*, the screeplay deals with the scheme of a sadistic ex-convict (Robert Mitchum) to gain revenge against a smalltown Georgia lawyer (Gregory Peck), his wife and daughter. Peck, it seems, had testified against him eight years earlier for the savage assault on a woman in a parking lot.

Mitchum's menacing omnipresence causes the family much mental anguish. Their pet dog is poisoned, the daughter has a harrowing encounter with the degenerate, and there is the culminating terror in Georgia swampland.

What ails Mitchum obviously requires violent sexual expression—the women he takes have to be clobbered as well as violated. But in the undiluted flow of evil, there is nothing in the script or J. Lee Thompson's direction which might provide audiences with some insight into Mitchum's behavior.

Peck, displaying his typical guarded self, is effective, if perhaps less distraught over the prospect of personal disaster than his character might warrant. Granting the shallowness of his motivation, Mitchum has no trouble being utterly hateful. Wearing a Panama fedora and chomping a cocky cigar, the menace of his visage has the hiss of a poised snake. Polly Bergen, breaking an eight-year screen absence, turns in a sympathetic job as Peck's wife.

CAPE FEAR

1991, 128 mins, US Ⓥ ⦿ ▭ col

Dir Martin Scorsese ***Prod*** Barbara De Fina ***Scr*** Wesley Strick ***Ph*** Freddie Francis ***Ed*** Thelma Schoonmaker ***Mus*** Elmer Bernstein (adapt.) ***Art*** Henry Bumstead

Act Robert De Niro, Nick Nolte, Jessica Lange, Juliette Lewis, Joe Don Baker, Illeana Douglas (Universal/Amblin)

Cape Fear is a smart and stylish remake of the 1962 suspenser. Sharply written adaptation follows the basic plot of J. Lee Thompson's solid black & white 1962 Universal release, which featured Robert Mitchum as a white trash ex-con who returns from prison to torment the prosecuting attorney (Gregory Peck) who sent him up.

Changes, however, enrich and blacken the material, making the characters squirm physically, morally and sexually. Instead of being a "normal" upstanding Southern family, the Bowdens (Nick Nolte, Jessica Lange and 15-year-old daughter Juliette Lewis) are troubled by father's history of infidelity and daughter's difficulties with both parents.

Enter Robert De Niro's Max Cady, a psychopath whose body is covered with a mural of threatening, religiously oriented tattoos, including the scales of "truth" and "justice" hanging off either side of a cross. Penned up for 14 years, Cady begins by just annoying the family, but soon launches his campaign of terror by killing the family dog and brutalizing a boozy young law clerk (Illeana Douglas) whom Nolte has been seeing.

In maximum souped-up style, director Martin Scorsese slams through the mandatory plot mechanics with powerful short scenes, dynamic in-your-face dollies and cranes and machine-gun editing. Director and his collaborators really cut to the quick in the disturbing sexual component, mainly between Cady and the teen.

De Niro's Cady is a memorable nasty right up there with Travis Bickle and Jake La Motta, a sickie utterly determined in his righteous cause. Nolte copes admirably with a difficult role written as somewhat unsympathetic. Lange's role plays as rather subsidiary to the others. Lewis is excellent as the troubled, tempted teen, and tale begins and ends with brief narration from her p.o.v. Robert Mitchum, Gregory Peck and Martin Balsam, all of whom appeared in the '62 version, pop up here in astutely judged roles. Bernard Herrmann's original score is adapted and rearranged by Elmer Bernstein.

1991: NOMINATIONS: Best Actor (Robert De Niro), Supp. Actress (Juliette Lewis)

•

CAPONE

1975, 101 mins, US col

Dir Steve Carver ***Prod*** Roger Corman ***Scr*** Howard Browne ***Ph*** Vilis Lapenieks ***Ed*** Richard Meyer ***Mus*** David Grisman ***Art*** Ward Preston

Act Ben Gazzara, Susan Blakely, Harry Guardino, John Cassavetes, Sylvester Stallone, Peter Maloney (20th-Century Fox)

Capone, a somewhat crude, violent and deja vu actioner, focusses on Ben Gazzara as Capone, showing his brutish, casual arrogance in a climb from neighborhood punk to a Chi rackets kingpin, then his decline via an income tax rap (arranged, it is claimed by his own aide, Frank Nitti, very well played by Sylvester Stallone).

Susan Blakely again shows her sensual sparkle as a slumming rich chick taken to Capone; while John Cassavetes has a good cameo as the N.Y. hood who discovers Capone's potential.

Gazzara has evidently gone to great lengths to attempt a full characterization of Capone, but it's hard to shoehorn developed drama between machine gun bullets.

•

CAPRICE

1967, 97 mins, US Ⓥ ▭ b/w

Dir Frank Tashlin ***Prod*** Aaron Rosenburg, Martin Melcher ***Scr*** Jay Jayson, Frank Tashlin ***Ph*** Leon Shamroy ***Ed*** Robert Simpson ***Mus*** Frank DeVol ***Art*** Jack Martin Smith, William Creber

Act Doris Day, Richard Harris, Ray Walston, Jack Kruschen, Edward Mulhare, Michael J. Pollard (20th Century-Fox)

Caprice is one of those occasional pictures about which it can be said fairly that it could have been better than it is. A timely and inventive plot—industrial espionage—is never fully developed in either writing, acting or direction.

Doris Day and Richard Harris are double-crossing double agents working, variously, for U.S. cosmetics king Jack Kruschen, British counterpart Edward Mulhare, or Interpol.

Ray Walston plays Kruschen's inventive genius, although it turns out that Lilia Skala, Walston's mother-in-law in Switzerland, is the creative brain.

Elements of comedy, murder, satire and psychology are blended uncertainly in the never-boiling pot.

•

CAPRICORN ONE

1978, 124 mins, US Ⓥ ⊙ ▭ col

Dir Peter Hyams ***Prod*** Paul N. Lazarus III ***Scr*** Peter Hyams ***Ph*** Bill Butler ***Ed*** James Mitchell ***Mus*** Jerry Goldsmith ***Art*** Albert Brenner

Act Elliott Gould, James Brolin, Brenda Vaccaro, Sam Waterston, O. J. Simpson, Hal Holbrook (Lazarus/Associated General)

Capricorn One begins with a workable, if cynical cinematic premise: the first manned space flight to Mars was a hoax and the American public was fooled through Hollywood gimmickry into believing that the phony landing happened. But after establishing the concept, Peter Hyams's script asks another audience—the one in the theatre—to accept something far more illogical, the uncovering of the hoax by reporter Elliott Gould.

The astronaut trio of James Brolin, Sam Waterston and O. J. Simpson together add up to nothing; there's no group chemistry. Still, scattershot casting means once in a while you hit and in the final scene Gould and Telly Savalas are teamed. The duo is a bullseye. Savalas, in a delightful cameo as a crop duster hired to help rescue Brolin in the desert and uncover the plot, is a marvelous complement to Gould.

Hal Holbrook plays the mission commander who calls off the Mars shot and engineers the dupe. His character must change from sincere—he believes he's doing the right thing by fooling the public—to menacing. In general, it is a script of conveniences.

•

CAPTAIN BLOOD

1935, 119 mins, US Ⓥ ⊙ b/w

Dir Michael Curtiz ***Scr*** Casey Robinson ***Ph*** Hal Mohr ***Ed*** George Amy ***Mus*** Erich Wolfgang Korngold ***Art*** Anton Grot

Act Errol Flynn, Olivia de Havilland, Basil Rathbone, Lionel Atwill, Ross Alexander, Guy Kibbee (Cosmopolitan/Warner)

Captain Blood, from the Rafael Sabatini novel, is a big picture. It's a spectacle which will establish both Errol Flynn and Olivia de Havilland. Director Michael Curtiz hasn't spared the horses. It's a lavish, swashbuckling saga of the Spanish main.

The engaging Flynn is the titular Peter Blood, erstwhile physician, later sold into West Indian slavery, to emerge thereafter as a peer among Caribbean pirates, Capt Blood, only later to be pardoned, his crew of run-away slaves likewise granted their freedom, and sworn into the King's navy.

Flynn impresses favorably from the start. One lives with him in the unfairness of a tyrant King Charles which causes him and his fellow Englishmen to be sold into slavery. One suffers with their travail; the audience roots with them in their ultimately fruitless plot for escape from the island. And then he is catapulted into leadership of a pirate ship.

De Havilland, who came to attention in Warner's *A Midsummer Night's Dream*, is romantically beauteous as the unsympathetic plantation owner's (later governor's) niece. This supplies a modicum of romantic interest, although all too paltry. It's one of the prime shortcomings of the production. Lionel Atwill is sufficiently hateful as the uncle. Basil Rathbone is an effective co-pirate captain (French brigands, this time), he and Flynn engaging in an arresting duel in the course of events.

1935: NOMINATIONS: Best Picture, Sound

•

CAPTAIN CAREY, U.S.A.

1950, 92 mins, US b/w

Dir Mitchell Leisen ***Prod*** Richard Maibaum ***Scr*** Robert Thoeren ***Ph*** John F. Seitz ***Ed*** Alma Macrorie ***Mus*** Hugo Friedhofer ***Art*** Hans Dreier

Act Alan Ladd, Wanda Hendrix, Francis Lederer, Joseph Calleia (Paramount)

Plot of the Martha Albrand novel gets its title from Alan Ladd's OSS work in Italy during the war. Action opens during that period to establish principal characters and then deals with Ladd's return to Italy to avenge the death of a girl who had aided his war work. He finds her still alive but married, plans to return to the States until a number of mysterious doings intrigue him enough to stay.

A series of knife murders, the hate of the Italian villagers for an American whom they believe had caused most of their misfortunes, and the stealth the real heavy uses to conceal his misdeeds provide plenty of melodramatic incidents.

Wanda Hendrix, as the Italian girl isn't called upon for much in the way of a performance. Francis Lederer, the war-traitor, does very well.

•

CAPTAIN FROM CASTILE

1947, 140 mins, US ⊙ col

Dir Henry King ***Prod*** Lamar Trotti ***Scr*** Lamar Trotti ***Ph*** Charles Clarke, Arthur E. Arling ***Ed*** Barbara McLean ***Mus*** Alfred Newman ***Art*** Richard Day, James Basen

Act Tyrone Power, Jean Peters, Cesar Romero, Lee J. Cobb, Antonio Moreno (20th Century-Fox)

Based on Samuel Shellaberger's 1945 bestselling historical novel, the cinema adaptation hews closely to the structure of the book, capturing the vast sweep of its story and adding to it an eye-stunning Technicolor dimension. The coin poured into this production, reported to be around $4.5 million, is visible in every inch of the footage.

For this plume-and-sabre epic of 16th-century Spanish imperial conquerors, producer and production chief have assembled a group of thespers who are cleanly tailored for the various parts. Led by Tyrone Power, who's rarely been shown to better advantage, the roster is buttressed by Cesar Romero, in a stirringly virile protrait of Cortez; Lee J. Cobb, as a fortune hunter; John Sutton, as a velvety villain, and newcomer Jean Peters, a buxom, appealing wench for the romantic byplay. From one viewpoint, this picture is constructed like a self-contained double feature. In the first half, the locale is Spain during the Inquisition, with Power and his family unjustly persecuted for heresy. Escaping from Spain, Power finds himself during the second half in Mexico as a recruit in Cortez's expedition of plunder against the Aztec empire ruled by Montezuma.

There are, however several soft spots in the story that interfere with credibility. There is, for instance, the fact that Power narrowly escapes death no less than three times under the most extreme circumstances. Sutton, likewise, cheats death two times despite his being stabbed through the heart with a foot of steel one time and near-strangled the next.

1947: NOMINATION: Best Scoring of a Dramatic Picture

•

CAPTAIN HORATIO HORNBLOWER R.N.

1951, 116 mins, UK Ⓥ ⊙ col

Dir Raoul Walsh ***Prod*** [uncredited] ***Scr*** Ivan Goff, Ben Roberts, Aeneas Mackenzie ***Ph*** Guy Green ***Ed*** Jack Harris ***Mus*** Robert Farnon ***Art*** Tom Morahan

Act Gregory Peck, Virginia Mayo, Robert Beatty, Dennis O'Dea, James Robertson Justice, Stanley Baker (Warner)

The exploits of one of Britain's greatest fictional naval adventurers have been filmed by Warner with spectacular success. *Captain Horatio Hornblower* has been brought to the screen as effervescent entertainment with action all the way.

Three C. S. Forester stories provide the basis for the pic, and the author, in preparing his own adaptation, has selected the best material. It is an incisive study of a man who is dispassionate, aloof and remote, yet often capable of finer feelings.

In his interpretation of the title role, Gregory Peck stands out as a skilled artist, capturing the spirit of the character and atmosphere of the period. Whether as the ruthless captain ordering a flogging as a face-saving act for a junior officer or tenderly nursing Virginia Mayo through yellow fever, he never fails to reflect the Forester character.

The film is divided into two halves. In the opening, Hornblower (Peck) is commanding the frigate *Lydia* throught the Pacific waters to fulfill a British mission to provide arms to enemies of Spain. On his return to England, he participates in an exiting adventure against Napoleon's fleet, eventually becoming a national hero. The major action sequences have been lensed with great skill.

•

CAPTAIN KIDD

1945, 89 mins, US Ⓥ b/w

Dir Rowland V. Lee ***Prod*** Benedict Bogeaus ***Scr*** Norman Reilly Raine ***Ph*** Archie Stout, Lee Zavitz ***Ed*** Joseph Smith ***Mus*** Werner Janssen ***Art*** Charles Odds

Act Charles Laughton, Randolph Scott, Barbara Britton, John Carradine, Gilbert Roland, John Qualen (United Artists)

Captain Kidd is a swashbuckler which will please generally, despite its minimum of feminine appeal. Barbara Britton, who is costarred with Charles Laughton and Randolph Scott, could phone her stuff into the celluloid for all its impact, coming on past midsection of the footage, but it's sufficiently adequate to inject a modicum of romance.

Story [from an original by Robert N. Lee] in the main focuses around the piratical rogues of the late 17th century when Captain Kidd (Laughton) freebooted the Spanish Main on the route of ships from England to fabulously rich India. When the king enlists Kidd as a loyal subject of the empire to give safe escort to treasury-laden vessels belonging to the crown, Kidd's doublecrossing leads him to the gallows. The footage inbetween is replete with piratical skullduggery.

Laughton is capital as the ruthless brigand of the seas, ruling his equally villainous rogues with stern cruelty.

•

CAPTAIN KRONOS—VAMPIRE HUNTER

1974, 91 mins, UK Ⓥ col

Dir Brian Clemens ***Prod*** Albert Fennell, Brian Clemens ***Scr*** Brian Clemens ***Ph*** Ian Wilson ***Ed*** James Needs ***Mus*** Laurie Johnson ***Art*** Robert Jones

Act Horst Janson, John Carson, Shane Briant, Caroline Munro, John Cater, Ian Hendry (Hammer)

Captain Kronos—Vampire Hunter, as played by Horst Janson, is a prototype blond Germanic, superstud caped like an operetta leading man. Accompanied by faithful friend John Cater, playing a hunchback professor, Kronos solves a vampire mystery with a lot of swash and buckle.

Story is unusual in that the vampire, who turns out to be an elderly woman (her ladyship in the castle, halfway up the next hill), sucks blood to get a youthful appearance. Being a new horror character, Kronos naturally has a groupie in tow (Caroline Munro) who caters to his earthier needs between random jousts with bad guys and bad vampires. Ian Hendry has one scene as a heavy, got up like an aging leather gang leader solely for the purpose of Kronos showing off his swordsmanship.

•

CAPTAIN NEWMAN, M.D.

1963, 126 mins, US Ⓥ col

Dir David Miller ***Prod*** Robert Arthur ***Scr*** Richard L. Breen, Pheobe Ephron, Henry Ephron ***Ph*** Russell Metty ***Ed*** Alma Macrorie ***Mus*** Frank Skinner ***Art*** Alexander Golitzen, Alfred Sweeney

Act Gregory Peck, Tony Curtis, Angie Dickinson, Eddie Albert, Bobby Darin, Robert Duvall (Universal/Brentwood/Reynard)

Captain Newman, M.D. oscillates between scenes of great dramatic impact and somewhat strained and contrived comedy of the heartwarming variety.

Leo Rosten's novel is the source of the hot-and-cold scenario. Hero of the story is Capt. Newman (Gregory Peck), chief of the neuro-psychiatric ward of a wartime (1944) army hospital who places his medical obligations above military duty. Newman's treatment of three cases is illustrated. One involves a decorated corporal (Bobby Darin) who believes himself a coward for having deserted a buddy in a burning aircraft. Another concerns a colonel (Eddie Albert) who has gone berserk with a sense of guilt at having sent so many men to their deaths in aerial combat. The third (Robert Duvall) feels shame over having hidden alone in a cellar for over a year in Nazi-occupied territory.

In between all of this, Newman gets his kicks in a romance with his nurse (Angie Dickinson) and by observing the antics of his number one orderly (Tony Curtis), a glib, resourceful operator from Jersey City with a streak of Bergen County larceny.

Peck's portrayal of the title figure is characteristically restrained and intelligent. Curtis has some good moments, but essentially he is the pivotal figure in the film's secondary comic shenanigans. Dickinson is sweet, sometimes too darned sweet, as the nurse.

1963: NOMINATIONS: Best Supp. Actor (Bobby Darin), Adapted Screenplay, Sound

•

CAPTAINS COURAGEOUS

1937, 115 mins, US Ⓥ ⦿ b/w

Dir Victor Fleming ***Prod*** Louis D. Lighton ***Scr*** John Lee Mahin, Marc Connolly, Dale Van Every ***Ph*** Harold Rosson ***Ed*** Elmo Vernon ***Mus*** Franz Waxman

Act Spencer Tracy, Freddie Bartholomew, Lionel Barrymore, Melvyn Douglas, Charley Grapewin, Mickey Rooney (M-G-M)

Taking this Rudyard Kipling story, written when he visited America some years earlier, the producers have made the central character of the spoiled child younger than he was in the book, and for the purposes of the screen have indulged in other slight, unimportant alterations. Spencer Tracy is a Portuguese fisherman with an accent and a flair for singing songs of the briny. Lionel Barrymore is the happy-go-lucky but stern captain of a fishing schooner while Bartholomew, of course, is the boy.

The Kipling yarn, built around a wealthy, motherless brat who accidentaly lands with a cod-fishing fleet, and undergoes regeneration during an enforced three months' piscatorial quest, has been given splendid production, performance, photography and dramatic composition. Young Bartholomew plays the spoiled kid, only son of wealthy father, who falls off a liner bound for Europe and is picked up by Tracy, the fisherman to whom the recalcitrant boy finally becomes deeply attached. Bartholomew's transition from a brat to a lovable child is done with convincing strokes.

His performance is matched by Tracy, who also doesn't seem right doing an accent and singing songs, but he, too, later gets under the skin of the character. Barrymore is himself, as usual. As the father of the boy, Melvyn Douglas gives a smooth, unctuous performance. One of the fishermen is deftly portrayed by John Carradine.

1937: Best Actor (Spencer Tracy)

NOMINATIONS: Best Picture, Screenplay, Editing

•

CAPTAINS OF THE CLOUDS

1942, 113 mins, US col

Dir Michael Curtiz ***Prod*** Hal B. Wallis (exec.) ***Scr*** Arthur T. Horman, Richard Macaulay, Norman Reilly Raine ***Ph*** Sol Polito, Wilfrid M. Cline, Elmer Dyer, Charles Marshall, Winton C. Hoch ***Ed*** George Amy ***Mus*** Max Steiner ***Art*** Ted Smith

Act James Cagney, Dennis Morgan, Brenda Marshall, Alan Hale, George Tobias, Reginald Gardiner (Warner)

Story splits into two sections—first half depicts the adventurous and rowdy experiences of a group of freelance bush flyers of northern Canada who pilot supplies to the settlers and prospectors along the lakes and rivers of the northland—and second portion outlines their adventures as members of the Royal Canadian Air Force training schools.

Cast is of topnotch calibre throughout. James Cagney holds attention throughout as the nervy, adventurous and happy-go-lucky flying expert. It's a spotlight performance for Cagney in every foot of film.

Screenplay [from a story by Arthur T. Horman and Roland Gillett] is a fine admixture of vigorous adventure with narrative insight of pilot training procedure across the border. Michael Curtiz directs with a positive straight-line objective of pointing up the sweeping drama.

•

CAPTAIN'S PARADISE, THE

1953, 93 mins, UK Ⓥ ⦿ b/w

Dir Anthony Kimmins ***Prod*** Anthony Kimmins ***Scr*** Alec Coppel, Nicholas Phipps ***Ph*** Ted Scaife ***Ed*** G. Turney-Smith ***Mus*** Malcolm Arnold ***Art*** Paul Sheriff

Act Alec Guinness, Yvonne De Carlo, Celia Johnson, Charles Goldner, Miles Malleson, Tutte Lemkow (London)

The yarn is done in an almost continuous flashback. In the opening scene Alec Guinness, a ship's captain, is facing a firing squad in North Africa. Back on his ship the first officer begins to explain the philosophy behind Guinness's mode of life. It appears that ever since his childhood Guinness has been in search of paradise, and eventually he finds it by having a wife in Gibraltar who satisfies his domestic yearning and a diversion in North Africa who panders to the more exotic things in life.

The original story by Alec Coppel has been subtly translated to celluloid by the author in conjunction with Nicholas Phipps. It takes some little time for the plot to emerge. But once the theme is established, the situation is developed with good clean fun and satire. The role of the paradise-seeking captain is a natural for Guinness while the two women in his life are admirably portrayed by Yvonne De Carlo and Celia Johnson. The former's performance as a high-spirited girl is in perfect contrast to Johnson's interpretation of the sedate British housewife.

Of the supporting cast, Charles Goldner has the prize role as the chief officer, a man anxious to emulate his chief.

•

CAPTIVE CITY, THE

1952, 91 mins, US b/w

Dir Robert Wise ***Prod*** Theron Warth ***Scr*** Karl Kamb, Alvin Josephy, Jr. ***Ph*** Lee Garmes ***Ed*** Ralph Swink ***Mus*** Jerome Moross ***Art*** Maurice Zuberano

Act John Forsythe, Joan Camden, Harold J. Kennedy, Marjorie Crossland, Victor Sutherland, Ray Teal (Aspen/United Artists)

The Captive City is a tense, absorbing drama [from a screen story by Alvin M. Josephy, Jr.] of a small town editor's fight against corruption. It has a documentary quality that rings with authenticity. Based on facts uncovered by probes of the Senate Crime Investigation Committee, it contains a cleverly interwoven epilog by Senator Estes Kefauver, who headed the latter group.

John Forsythe and Harold J. Kennedy, as former GI buddies, are co-owners of a newspaper in a city called Kennington. Then a local private detective, working on an apparently harmless divorce case, discovers the existence of a big-time gambling syndicate operating with the knowledge of the city fathers, the local police and the respectable elements of the community.

Forsythe succeeds in uncovering the whole mess. However, he is powerless to do anything.

•

CAPTIVE HEART, THE

1946, 108 mins, UK b/w

Dir Basil Dearden ***Prod*** Michael Balcon ***Scr*** Angus MacPhail, Guy Morgan ***Ph*** Douglas Slocombe ***Ed*** Charles Hasse ***Mus*** Alan Rawsthorne ***Art*** Michael Relph

Act Michael Redgrave, Rachel Kempson, Mervyn Johns, Jack Warner, Basil Radford, Gordon Jackson (Ealing)

Second only to the unrelieved grim reality of life as it was lived in Stalags, the outstanding merit of *The Captive Heart* is the number of superlatively good performances turned in. To Michael Balcon as producer must go chief credit for the newsreel fidelity of the prison camp sequences.

Michael Redgrave, as a Czech, educated in England and fleeing from the Gestapo, takes on the identity of a dead English army officer and is jailed in a Stalag with British soldiers. He escapes lynching only to find himself marked down for a visit to a Nazi gas chamber.

Even when he convinces the British of the truth of his story, and after he has won freedom through repatriation, he's up against the task of squaring himself with the wife of the dead man whose identity he has assumed. The fact that this final sequence holds one's attention says something for the writing, acting, and directing.

•

CAPTURE, THE

1950, 91 mins, US b/w

Dir John Sturges ***Prod*** Niven Busch ***Scr*** Niven Busch ***Ph*** Edward Cronjager ***Ed*** George Amy ***Mus*** Daniele Amfitheatrof

Act Lew Ayres, Teresa Wright, Victor Jory, Jacqueline White (RKO/Showtime)

The Capture is an offbeat drama, with psychological overtones, that plays off against the raw and rugged background of Mexican locales.

Picture kicks off with a wallop, depicting a desperate chase that, storywise, sets up the plot's finale. Lew Ayres is fleeing the Mexican rurales, wanted on a charge of murder. He holes up in a priest's cabin and begins to disclose his story. A year before he had killed a fugitive, wanted for a robbery. The possibility of the man's innocence haunted him, and Ayres sought out the widow. They fall in love, are married, but his guilty conscience makes full happiness impossible.

Ayres and Teresa Wright are very capable in the lead characters, adding to the general realism given the story because of the locales used. One of the interestintg touches to the film is the incidental native music hauntingly spotted with the appearance of a blind guitar player.

•

CARAVAGGIO

1986, 89 mins, UK Ⓥ col

Dir Derek Jarman ***Prod*** Sarah Radclyffe ***Scr*** Derek Jarman ***Ph*** Gabriel Beristain ***Ed*** George Akers ***Mus*** Simon Fisher Turner ***Art*** Christopher Hobbs

Act Nigel Terry, Sean Bean, Garry Cooper, Spencer Leigh, Tilda Swinton, Michael Gough (BFI)

Derek Jarman's *Caravaggio* triumphantly rises above its financial restrictions and proves, once again, that less can be a lot more.

Pic is an imagined biopic of one of the last Renaissance painters, Michelangelo Merisi da Caravaggio (1571–1610), but the inspiration seems to be Italian film director Pier Paolo Pasolini, since both artists came from poor backgrounds and used beautiful young men from the slums in their work. Both also became involved in scandal and violence.

Jarman's film, in classical tradition, is told in flashback as the artist lies dying in poverty. Story takes a backseat, however, since much of the joy of the film is to be found in the way Jarman and his team recreate the look and color of the original paintings. But film lacks a certain warmth and emotional depth.

•

CARAVANS

1978, 127 mins, US/Iran Ⓥ ▭ col

Dir James Fargo ***Prod*** Elmo Williams ***Scr*** Nancy Voyles Crawford, Thomas A. McMahon, Lorraine Williams ***Ph*** Douglas Slocombe ***Ed*** Richard Marden ***Mus*** Mike Batt ***Art*** Ted Tester, Peter Williams, Peter James

Act Anthony Quinn, Michael Sarrazin, Jennifer O'Neill, Christopher Lee, Joseph Cotten, Behrooz Vosoughi (Ibex/FIDCI)

The main trouble with this tale of 1948 Persia isn't the Iranians, it's Hollywood. Almost every fake moment in the film, and there are lots of them, has the touch of Hollywood laid on with a heavy coating. Fortunately for the average viewer, the scenic scope of the film, based on James Michener's epic story, and shot entirely on locations in Iran, is so sweeping that the tale that is told is almost palatable. But barely.

Briefly, the film deals with the search of a minor American consular employee (Michael Sarrazin) for an American woman (Jennifer O'Neill) who has married an Iranian colonel (Behrooz Vosoughi) but deserted him for a Kochi chieftain (Anthony Quinn) and has disappeared. Sarrazin finds her in short order. That's when the real trouble begins. She won't go back and he won't go back without her and off everyone goes into the desert. Sarrazin, Quinn and O'Neill carry most of the story. The other non-Persians—Christopher Lee, Barry Sullivan, Jeremy Kemp and Joseph Cotten—are seen so briefly they may have done their roles over a long weekend. Histrionically, only Quinn is believable, followed closely by Vosoughi.

1978: NOMINATION: Best Costume Design

•

CARAVAN TO VACCARES

1974, 98 mins, UK/France Ⓥ col

Dir Geoffrey Reeve ***Prod*** Geoffrey Reeve, Richard Morris-Adams ***Scr*** Paul Wheeler ***Ph*** John Cabrera, David Bevan, Ted Deason ***Mus*** Stanley Myers ***Art*** Frank White

Act Charlotte Rampling, David Birney, Michel Lonsdale, Marcel Bozzuffi, Michael Bryant, Manitas de Plata (Reeve/Prodis)

There's good, reliable stuff in this Alistair MacLean action-adventure item, colorfully location-set in Southern France's Camargue area and well acted by a carefully chosen Franco-British cast.

Plot basics involve the attempt to smuggle an East European scientist out of France and into the U.S., attempt which is hampered by repeated harassment and kidnappings by a scrupleless rival gang bent on gleaning the fugitive's secrets for resale to the highest bidder.

Principally involved are a footloose young American (David Birney), hired by a French Duke (Michel Lonsdale) to whisk the scientist onto a U.S.-bound plane, and a pretty young British photographer (Charlotte Rampling) who gets involved when she hitches a ride with Birney.

•

CARD, THE
(US: THE PROMOTER)

1952, 91 mins, UK Ⓥ b/w

Dir Ronald Neame ***Prod*** John Bryan ***Scr*** Eric Ambler ***Ph*** Oswald Morris ***Ed*** Clive Donner ***Mus*** William Alwyn ***Art*** T. Hopwell Ash

Act Alec Guinness, Petula Clark, Glynis Johns, Valerie Hobson, Edward Chapman, Gibb McLaughlin (British Film Makers/Rank)

The principal character in Arnold Bennett's novel *The Card*, depicting the progression of a washer-woman's son from poverty to wealth, from humble beginnings to the top of the civic tree, provides a made-to-measure part for Alec Guinness in a capital performance.

Set in the Potteries, without any attempt to glamorize the grimy, smoky, slum-ridden district, Eric Ambler's script keeps the focus entirely on Guinness.

The rise of the young lad is depicted in all its stages, from his dishonest beginning, when he alters examination results to ensure a place in high school. And from there he gradually makes his name in the world, advancing from a humble lawyer's clerk to rent collector and to big business as head and founder of a loan club.

1952: NOMINATION: Best Sound

•

CARDINAL, THE

1963, 175 mins, US Ⓥ ⊙ ▭ col

Dir Otto Preminger ***Prod*** Otto Preminger ***Scr*** Robert Dozier ***Ph*** Leon Shamroy ***Ed*** Louis R. Loeffler ***Mus*** Jerome Moross ***Art*** Lyle Wheeler

Act Tom Tryon, Carol Lynley, Romy Schneider, John Huston, Raf Vallone, John Saxon (Columbia)

Otto Preminger's *The Cardinal* is a long motion picture but for most of the way it is superlative drama, emotionally stirring, intellectually stimulating and scenically magnificent.

Like the Henry Morton Robinson novel that it lives up to more in spirit than plot-wise, it is a skillful, fascinating blend of fact and fiction. The story concerns the development of a Rome-educated American priest who has aspirations of clerical high office. However, he experiences shattering doubt of his ability to be a good priest and, indeed, if he ever had a true "call," having from his earliest memory been destined, according to his parents, for the priesthood.

Without faulting scenarist Robert Dozier, *The Cardinal* is Preminger's picture for it moves on such a vast canvas—Rome, Boston and environs, New York (dockside scene only), Georgia, Vienna and back to Rome—with all the richly pictorial ritual of the ordination of a priest, the consecration of a Bishop, later a Cardinal, and the vast public excitement in St Peter's Square for the election of a Pope.

Preminger also selected his cast wisely. Tom Tryon, who has the title role, plays it very well indeed, although there are shadings to the character which do not surface as might be desired. Romy Schneider is captivating as the Viennese girl who cannot disguise her feelings toward Tryon. Carol Lynley is effective as his troubled sister and also in a subsequent role as the latter's illegitimate daughter.

There are, however, two who steal the picture as far as acting goes. They are John Huston and Raf Vallone. Both play the roles of cardinals on distinctive, captivating levels.

1963: NOMINATIONS: Best Director, Supp. Actor (John Huston), Color Cinematography, Color Costume Design, Color Art Direction, Editing

•

CAREER

1959, 105 mins, US b/w

Dir Joseph Anthony ***Prod*** Hal B. Wallis ***Scr*** James Lee ***Ph*** Joseph LaShelle ***Ed*** Warren Low ***Mus*** Franz Waxman ***Art*** Hal Pereira, Walter Tyler

Act Dean Martin, Anthony Franciosa, Shirley MacLaine, Carolyn Jones, Joan Blackman, Robert Middleton (Paramount)

This feature is so limited in production scope as to suggest the possibility that the producer was out to save money the hard way—that is, stinting on the pictorial values. But a closer look is reassuring, for it genuinely appears that Hal Wallis, in placing on the screen James Lee's off-Broadway play of the same name, and director Joseph Anthony were bent on preserving the intimacy of the original.

It's a show business story done in honest-to-goodness fashion. It centers on the ambition-driven but nonetheless agreeable aspiring actor. Whether he's maladjusted husband or insignificant waiter he's where he is because, in his free time, he's out to become a star and his other roles in life are unimportant.

It's a serious theme, to be sure, but somewhere there must have been opportunity to get a little lighthearted. A couple of Lee's story angles hardly seem to fit in, and this is no help in the secondary last-half that follows the attention-getting earlier episodes. Anthony Franciosa's call to the Korean war, with a brief glimpse of same, is not correctly integrated. Neither is the exposure of Dean Martin, as a smalltime director on the way up, as a one-time Communist because, as he puts it, "I was ambitious."

Otherwise, Franciosa and Martin, however sombre their parts, perform convincingly. Shirley MacLaine as a producer's free-wheeling daughter has some misfitting dialog and story situations to cope with but gets across all right, and Carolyn Jones plays it straight as an agent.

1959: NOMINATIONS: Best B&W Cinematography, B&W Costume Design, B&W Art Direction

•

CAREER OPPORTUNITIES
(AKA: ONE WILD NIGHT)

1991, 85 mins, US Ⓥ ⊙ ▭ col

Dir Bryan Gordon ***Prod*** John Hughes ***Scr*** John Hughes ***Ph*** Don McAlpine ***Ed*** Glenn Farr, Peck Prior ***Mus*** Thomas Newman ***Art*** Paul Sylbert

Act Frank Whaley, Jennifer Connelly, Dermot Mulroney, Kieran Mulroney, Barry Corbin, John Candy (Universal/Hughes)

Writer-producer John Hughes's followup to *Home Alone* lacks the spit-polish and magic of the blockbuster but still has plenty of absorbing characters, smart, snappy dialog and delightful stretches of comic foolery.

Like *Home Alone*, story has a young man on his own to defend a fortress against bungling burglars, but in this case he's a 21-year-old trapped in a job he hates (night janitor at a discount store) and pitted against gun-toting hoods out to clean out, not clean up, the store.

Jim (Frank Whaley) is a ne'er-do-well fast talker and nonstop liar bounced from as many deadend jobs as his humble hometown of Munroe, Ill, has to offer. He's been given his last chance to succeed by his blue-collar father—or get kicked out of the house.

That's when he discovers he's not alone. Darkly voluptuous Josie (Jennifer Connelly), princess daughter of the town land baron, is locked in after falling asleep during a shoplifting spree.

Trapped together, the misfits discover each other, and, in the type of scenes Hughes writes best, sort out their differences and common ground from their horrifying high school years. But the guntoting hoods (Dermot and Kieran Mulroney) show up and they must turn their specialties to more immediate escape.

•

CAREFREE

1938, 83 mins, US Ⓥ b/w

Dir Mark Sandrich ***Prod*** Pandro S. Berman ***Scr*** Ernest Pagano, Allan Scott, Dudley Nichols, Hagar Wilde ***Ph*** Robert de Grasse ***Ed*** William Hamilton ***Mus*** Victor Baravalle (dir.) ***Art*** Van Nest Polglase, Carroll Clark

Act Fred Astaire, Ginger Rogers, Ralph Bellamy, Luella Gear, Jack Carson, Clarence Kolb (RKO)

Fred Astaire and Ginger Rogers, with an Irving Berlin set of four good songs, delve into psychoanalysis for their script [from an original story by Marian Ainslee and Guy Endore]. The result may inspire some to wonder if the psyching shouldn't have started in the studio. It's a disappointing story and leaves the viewer bewildered, with Astaire hypnotizing his co-star; Rogers walking to the altar, obsessed with the hypnotic suggestion that Astaire is a cad and Ralph Bellamy a nobleman, etc.

Still, in the dream sequence, as result of a sedative administered by Dr. Astaire, the team does one of its best double numbers ("Color Blind" is the tune), wherein a slow-motion camera truly points up the poetry of their terpsichorean motion.

Astaire's very first specialty, a golf-ball dance, gives it a fast gait, but pretty soon the story asserts its handicaps. Astaire, as part of a flirtation routine, gives out in swingo-highland fling via mouth-organ, thence into a dash of 52nd street hoot-mon, and the topper is that rhythmic routine, driving off a flock of golf balls from the green.

Rogers, while under hypnotic influence, reminds of some of the inhibitions that Paramount's *If I Had a Million* so brightly presented. Here she shatters plate-glass windows, baits policemen, and even broadcasts that her sponsor (she's a radio songstress) puts out the poorest product.

•

CAREFUL HE MIGHT HEAR YOU

1983, 116 mins, Australia Ⓥ ▭ col

Dir Carl Schultz ***Prod*** Jill Robb ***Scr*** Michael Jenkins ***Ph*** John Seale ***Ed*** Richard Francis-Bruce ***Mus*** Ray Cook ***Art*** John Stoddart

Act Wendy Hughes, Robyn Nevin, Nicholas Gledhill, John Hargreaves, Geraldine Turner, Isabelle Anderson (Syme)

A top quality production about the struggle between two sisters for custody of an eight-year-old boy, their nephew, *Careful He Might Hear You* is a completely involving emotional experience.

The Sumner Locke Elliott novel on which Michael Jenkins's excellent screenplay is based was, for many years, a project for Joshua Logan with, at one point, Elizabeth Taylor announced for the role of Vanessa Scott, the lonely frigid spinster whose causes all the trouble, and who is played, commandingly, here by Wendy Hughes.

Story is set in the Depression in Sydney. The boy, nicknamed "PS" by everyone, is homeless after the death of his mother and the departure of his feckless father, Logan, for the goldfields. He's taken in by a loving but impoverished aunt and uncle (Robyn Nevin and Peter Whitford).

Their lives are disrupted, however, by the arrival of Vanessa, another sister, but from the moneyed side of the family. She wants custody of the child.

•

CARETAKER, THE
(US: THE GUEST)

1964, 105 mins, UK b/w

Dir Clive Donner ***Prod*** Michael Birkett ***Scr*** Harold Pinter ***Ph*** Nicolas Roeg ***Ed*** Fergus McDonell ***Mus*** Ron Grainer ***Art*** Reece Pemberton

Act Alan Bates, Donald Pleasence, Robert Shaw (Caretaker)

Harold Pinter adapted his own three-character play for the screen, but made little attempt to broaden the canvas and its stage origins are barely disguised.

This production of *The Caretaker*, was financed by 10 prominent showbiz personalities, each of whom has a $14,000 stake in it, while the author, producer, director and three stars are all on deferment. Among its backers were stars, film producers and legit impresarios, including Elizabeth Taylor, Richard Burton, Peter Sellers, Noel Coward, Harry Saltzman and Peter Bridge.

Instead of using a conventional studio, the unit took over a house in a northeast London suburb, and that provides an ideal, shabby setting for Pinter's offbeat theme. Basically, it's a one-set play, and that made it a tough assignment for director Clive Donner. His fluent treatment, however, makes the most of the macabre verbal exchanges, and overcomes many of the static handicaps of the subject.

The three characters are two brothers and a tramp. One of the brothers, a building worker, owns a house, but it is his brother who lives in it, though just in one room, cluttered with furniture from the remainder of the house. The tramp, homeless and unemployed, is invited to stay the night, and finds himself being tossed around like a shuttlecock, in favor with one brother, and out of favor with the other.

Donald Pleasence's standout performance as the tramp is the acting highlight, but he easily has the choicest role. Robert Shaw gives an intelligent study as the brother who offers the tramp shelter, while Alan Bates completes the stellar trio with another forceful portrayal.

•

CAREY TREATMENT, THE

1972, 101 mins, US Ⓥ ▭ col

Dir Blake Edwards ***Prod*** William Belasco ***Scr*** James P. Bonner ***Ph*** Frank Stanley ***Ed*** Ralph E. Winters ***Mus*** Roy Budd ***Art*** Alfred Sweeney

Act James Coburn, Jennifer O'Neill, Pat Hingle, Skye Aubrey, Elizabeth Allen, Dan O'Herlihy (M-G-M)

The Carey Treatment stars James Coburn as a swinger-type pathologist who single-handedly solves a murder case in order to free a medic colleague from a bum rap. Written, directed, timed, paced and cast like a feature-for-TV, the production is a serviceable release.

Filmed partly in Boston under the title *A Case of Need*, from Jeffery Hudson's novel of that name, screenplay has Coburn arriving from California to join Dan O'Herlihy's medical staff, which includes James Hong, arrested for the alleged abortion-manslaughter of O'Herlihy's daughter (Melissa Torme-March). Coburn gets time off from immediate superior Regis Toomey and wanders through several sequences, played and edited in no particularly meaningful or suspenseful order, until unearthing the real culprits.

•

CARLA'S SONG

1996, 127 mins, UK/Germany/Spain Ⓥ ⦿ col

Dir Ken Loach ***Prod*** Sally Hibbin ***Scr*** Paul Laverty ***Ph*** Barry Ackroyd ***Ed*** Jonathan Morris ***Mus*** George Fenton ***Art*** Martin Johnson

Act Robert Carlyle, Oyanka Cabezas, Scott Glenn, Gary Lewis (Parallax/Channel 4/Road Movies/Tornasol)

Radical Brit filmmaker Ken Loach uses a cross-cultural love story to take a hard look at the New World Order in Central America in *Carla's Song*, set between working-class Glasgow and war-torn Nicaragua. Less exalting and emotionally gratifying than *Land and Freedom*, which saw Loach at his peak, the film still burns with enough spirit.

On a political level, *Carla's Song* takes a stridently anti-American stand, showing how the U.S. government successfully used the CIA to overturn the popular democracy of the Sandinista movement and finance its enemies, the Contra guerrillas.

George (Robert Carlyle) is a plucky Glasgow bus driver on the verge of getting married when he meets Carla (Oyanka Cabezas), a Nicaraguan refugee. In the charming Glasgow scenes, which occupy film's first half, Loach is on the familiar ground of *Riff-Raff*. Film shifts register when George and Carla reach Central America. With the help of a gaunt, prophet-in-the-desert American human rights worker, Bradley (Scott Glen), the two journey across the guerrilla-infested countryside.

Like many Hollywood pictures set amid historical turbulence, politics tends to take a back seat to George's awkward love story. George is merely a sympathetic observer, not a passionate fighter for other people's causes. Distracted viewers who miss a few lines of crucial dialogue may not even know which side the characters are on.

After very different roles in *Riff-Raff* and *Trainspotting*, Carlyle turns in a sensitive humorous portrait of the free-thinking bus driver. Nicaraguan actress and dancer Cabezas has a spirited, down-to-earth beauty but her character is noticeably underwritten.

•

CARLITO'S WAY

1993, 144 mins, US Ⓥ ⦿ ▭ col

Dir Brian De Palma ***Prod*** Martin Bregman, Willi Baer, Michael S. Bregman ***Scr*** David Koepp ***Ph*** Stephen H. Burum ***Ed*** Bill Pankow, Kristina Boden ***Mus*** Patrick Doyle ***Art*** Richard Sylbert

Act Al Pacino, Sean Penn, Penelope Ann Miller, Luis Guzman, John Leguizamo, Viggo Mortensen (Universal/Epic)

The surprise for many upon seeing *Carlito's Way* is that it's a throwback to the kind of ethnic gangster pics of the '30s like *Scarface* with Paul Muni, and not rife with the modern social spin of the later *Scarface* made by *Carlito*'s principals.

On its own terms, the new film is a lively saga of the rise and fall of a Puerto Rican criminal, rich with irony and keen in its attention to detail. Handsomely made, expertly directed and colorfully acted, the saga is bookended by scenes of Carlito (Al Pacino) being rushed to the hospital after he's shot at close range in a subway station.

It's 1975 and, after serving five years, Carlito has had his drug-related sentence reversed. In grand style, he explains how he will not be going back to the street. What we don't know or suspect is that he means it. Additionally, trouble follows him like an obedient lap dog. Eventually he agrees to manage a disco that's a haunt of gangster high rollers.

The great strength of David Koepp's adaptation of two books [*Carlito's Way* and *After Hours*] by Manhattan judge Edwin Torres is a comic strain as unexpected and unpredictable as the hair-trigger personalities of its underworld figures.

Pacino plays the title role with broad strokes. Sean Penn, in his first major screen role since directing 1991's *The Indian Runner*, reminds us of what we've been missing in his performance as Carlito's ambitious, amoral lawyer. Penelope Ann Miller does the most with the underwritten girlfriend role.

•

CARLTON-BROWNE OF THE F.O.
(US: MAN IN A COCKED HAT)

1959, 87 mins, UK Ⓥ b/w

Dir Jeffrey Dell, Roy Boulting ***Prod*** John Boulting ***Scr*** Jeffrey Dell, Roy Boulting ***Ph*** Max Greene ***Ed*** Anthony Harvey ***Mus*** John Addison ***Art*** Albert Witherick

Act Terry-Thomas, Peter Sellers, Luciana Paluzzi, Thorley Walters, Ian Bannen, Raymond Huntley (Boulting)

The F.O. in the title stands for Foreign Office and the film is a crazy peck at the indiscretions of foreign diplomacy. Much of the dialog is brilliantly witty. There are some excellent situations and some first-class prods at dignity. But the comedy tends to get out of hand and, at times, develops merely into a series of not totally relevant sketches.

The pic concerns the mishaps that happen to a Foreign Office junior official when an ex-colony of Britain's—Gaillardia—becomes news. Rich mineral deposits are indicated on the tiny island. Learning that other Great Powers are sniffing around the island, Carlton-Browne (Terry-Thomas) is dispatched to sort things out.

Peter Sellers plays the Gaillardian blackguard of a prime minister with relish. But the Sellers personality tends to throw the part off-balance.

Best of the major performances come from Raymond Huntley, as a pompous Foreign Office minister, and Ian Bannen, who, as the young king suddenly brought to the throne, brings a most engaging charm and humor to his role.

•

CARMEN

1984, 152 mins, France/Italy Ⓥ ⦿ ▭ col

Dir Francesco Rosi ***Prod*** Patrice Ledoux ***Scr*** Francesco Rosi, Tonino Guerra ***Ph*** Pasqualino De Santis ***Ed*** Ruggero Mastroianni, Colette Semprun ***Mus*** Lorin Maazel (dir.) ***Art*** Enrico Job

Act Julia Migenes-Johnson, Placido Domingo, Ruggero Raimondi, Faith Esham, Jean-Philippe Lafont, Gerard Garino (Gaumont/Dassault/Opera Film)

Francesco Rosi, whose best films have been unadorned realistic dramas with socio-political topicality, hasn't even tried to stylize the frilled folklore of Bizet's opera on the screen. Instead we get neo-realistic opera. He might have made a credible straight dramatic picture of Prosper Merimee's source novella, but his filmed opera is a lumbering cultural mammoth, overblown and graceless.

Dramatically the film is feeble. Julia Migenes-Johnson is high-spirited and alluring in the title role, but Rosi finally insists more on her humane qualities than her demoniac sense of fatalism. But she is a plum next to Placido Domingo's Don Jose, which flirts with disaster. A beautiful voice, but a uniformed lump in front of the cameras. Ruggero Raimondi is a chilly Escamillo, but he at least has credible bearing and photogenic line. Faith Esham's Michaela is limpid and touching.

Viewers who dread bullfighting are advised to come five minutes late.

•

CARMEN JONES

1954, 105 mins, US ⦿ ▭ col

Dir Otto Preminger ***Prod*** Otto Preminger ***Scr*** Harry Kleiner ***Ph*** Sam Leavitt ***Ed*** Louis R. Loeffler ***Mus*** Georges Bizet ***Art*** Edward L. Ilou

Act Dorothy Dandridge, Harry Belafonte, Olga James, Pearl Bailey, Diahann Carroll, Roy Glenn (20th Century-Fox)

As a wartime [1943] legit offering *Carmen Jones*—the modernized, all-Negro version of [Georges Bizet's] opera *Carmen*—was a long-run hit both on Broadway and on the road. Otto Preminger has transferred it to the screen with taste and imagination in an opulent production.

The screenplay closely follows the lines of the stage libretto by Oscar Hammerstein II in which Carmen is a pleasure-loving southern gal who works in a Dixie parachute factory, where Joe (Jose) is a member of the army regiment on guard duty. She lures him away from Cindy Lou (Micaela) and he deserts with her. Eventually Carmen tires of him and takes up with Husky Miller (Escamillo) the fighter and Joe kills her when she refuses to return to him.

Preminger directs with a deft touch, blending the comedy and tragedy easily and building his scenes to some suspenseful heights. He gets fine performances from the cast toppers, notably Dorothy Dandridge, a sultry Carmen whose performance maintains the right hedonistic note throughout.

1954: NOMINATIONS: Best Actress (Dorothy Dandridge), Scoring of a Musical Picture

•

CARNAL KNOWLEDGE

1971, 97 mins, US Ⓥ ⦿ ▭ col

Dir Mike Nichols ***Prod*** Mike Nichols ***Scr*** Jules Feiffer ***Ph*** Giuseppe Rotunno ***Ed*** Sam O'Steen ***Art*** Richard Sylbert

Act Jack Nicholson, Art Garfunkel, Candice Bergen, Ann-Margret, Cynthia O'Neal, Rita Moreno (Avco Embassy)

Mike Nichols's *Carnal Knowledge* is a rather superficial and limited probe of American male sexual hypocrisies. Jules Feiffer's episodic story follows for over 20 years the diverse paths of Jack Nicholson and Art Garfunkel as each tries to match their sexual fantasies with an uncooperative reality.

First, Nicholson and Garfunkel are college roommates in the 1940s, where Candice Bergen is the object of attention. Garfunkel, the more sensitive, wins her heart over Nicholson, whose ability to betray close friends is neatly established.

Time jumps ahead about a decade to the late 1950s. Nicholson falls in his own way for Ann-Margret, a sexpot who really would like to get married and have kids. Nicholson still can't cope, and at the same time introduces Garfunkel—now a slightly bored suburban husband—to Cynthia O'Neal.

The final 13 minutes are set in the late 1960s. Garfunkel has gone mod, latching onto Carol Kane, a hippie nymphet, while Nicholson has been reduced to periodic visits to Rita Moreno, a for-hire playmate who helps him play out his fantasies.

The story pussyfoots round some underlying psychological and psychiatric hangups. Nicholson's compulsive stud character is the type that hates women. The film fails by avoiding confrontation with his character.

1971: NOMINATION: Best Supp. Actress (Ann-Margret)

•

CARNEGIE HALL

1947, 136 mins, US b/w

Dir Edgar G. Ulmer ***Prod*** Boris Morros, William LeBaron ***Scr*** Karl Kamb ***Ph*** William Miller ***Ed*** Fred R. Feitshans, Jr. ***Mus*** Sigmund Krumgold (adv.) ***Art*** Max Ree

Act Marsha Hunt, William Prince, Frank McHugh, Martha O'-Driscoll, Hans Yaray, Olin Downes (United Artists/Federal)

The genius of its music and of the artists who present it makes *Carnegie Hall* a quality film. The trite story and direction are completely smothered by the finer points.

On the trite side is the script by Karl Kamb [from Seena Owen's story], loaded with cliche dialog and situations. Edgar G. Ulmer's direction does nothing with this part of the picture but, fortunately, the musical side is a heavy credit balance.

Plot covers an Irish girl who grows up in the service of the Hall and brings her son up to make his debut on its stage. Marsha Hunt surmounts an inane role to make the Irish girl part count.

•

CARNIVAL IN FLANDERS

SEE: LA KERMESSE HEROIQUE

•

CARNIVAL OF SOULS

1962, 80 mins, US Ⓥ b/w

Dir Hark Harvey ***Prod*** Hark Harvey ***Scr*** John Clifford ***Ph*** Maurice Prather ***Ed*** Dan Palmquist, Bill DeJarnette ***Mus*** Gene Moore

Act Candace Hilligoss, Frances Feist, Sidney Berger, Stanley Leavitt, Art Ellison, Herk Harvey (Harcourt)

Occasionally a feature film emerges from the midwest, although this is the first ever out of Lawrence, Kans, where a group of commercial film pros veered off into a try at producing theatrical entertainment.

Carnival of Souls is a creditable can of film considering it was put together for less than $100,000.

The ghost story, on a format more familiar in literature, has Candace Hilligoss, a dressy blonde, and a couple of gal pals, nudged off of a bridge and a watery death in the swirling river. She surprisingly emerges from the river and goes on to an eerie existence as a new organist at a Salt Lake City church.

An old pavilion in a sad state of disintegration peculiarly fascinates her, but pasty faces and fantasies swirl about her, and intermittently head ghost (director Hark Harvey) appears from mirrors and pools to chill her and the audience. In the end the battered car is dragged from the river.

It isn't enough story to prevail, but there is a fair share of suspense and some moments of good comedy. Veteran trouper Frances Feist is standout as the landlady who rents a room to the lithesome haunt, and Hilligoss with a sort of misty quality about her does creditably as the lovely soul without a heart. Sidney Berger, University of Kansas speech instructor, does well with the role of the roomer across the hall who would like to make out with the fascinating phantom.

Most of the technical crew have some affiliation with Centron Studios, commercial film producers at Lawrence, and interiors were shot there.

•

CARNOSAUR

1993, 82 mins, US Ⓥ ⦿ col

Dir Adam Simon ***Prod*** Mike Elliott ***Scr*** Adam Simon ***Ph*** Keith Holland ***Ed*** Richard Gentner ***Mus*** Nigel Holton ***Art*** Aaron Osborne

Act Diane Ladd, Raphael Sbarge, Jennifer Runyon, Harrison Page, Clint Howard (Concorde/New Horizons)

This contemporary dino tale harks back to '50s monster epics in style and sophistication. The ever-vigilant Roger Corman film factory is once again first in the marketplace with an exploitable sensation [two weeks prior to the release of *Jurassic Park*], predictably plotted with bargain-basement effects.

Somewhere in the Nevada desert, genetic scientist Dr. Jane Tiptree (Diane Ladd) has cross-fertilized chicken eggs with T-Rex DNA. The result is a lethal little pecker that dines on the Southwest smorgasbord of truckers and military/industrial support staff.

The unwitting hero is "Doc" Smith (Raphael Sbarge), a plant operations employee who hooks up with Thrush (Jennifer Runyon), a member of a commune of eco-freaks. They eventually wind up in the underground lab, where the full horror is revealed.

Ladd chews up the scenery as the mad doctor; writer-director Adam Simon keeps the action about a step or two ahead of the silliness.

•

CARNY

1980, 105 mins, US Ⓥ col

Dir Robert Kaylor *Prod* Robbie Robertson *Scr* Thomas Baum *Ph* Harry Stradling, Jr. *Ed* Stuart Pappe *Mus* Alex North *Art* William J. Cassidy

Act Gary Busey, Jodie Foster, Robbie Robertson, Elisha Cook, Meg Foster, Kenneth McMillan (United Artists)

Edgy tale [from a story by Phoebe and Robert Kaylor and Robbie Robertson] of three born outsiders living on a tightrope vividly recalls, both in style and content, the doom-laden films noir of the late 1940s.

Gary Busey plays a slightly demented bozo in a cage who mercilessly taunts spectators trying to dump him into water by throwing baseballs. Busey hooks up with runaway Jodie Foster.

As the carny makes its way through the South, Foster is gradually assimilated into the band of outcasts and a three-way relationship develops.

Busey is tremendous. Foster, ostensibly playing her first "adult" role, works wonders with a somewhat underwritten part.

Director Kaylor displays an unerring eye for atmosphere and detail.

•

CAROUSEL

1956, 128 mins, US Ⓥ ⊙ ▭ col

Dir Henry King *Prod* Henry Ephron *Scr* Phoebe Ephron, Henry Ephron *Ph* Charles G. Clarke *Ed* William Reynolds *Mus* Alfred Newman (sup.) *Art* Lyle R. Wheeler, Jack Martin Smith

Act Gordon MacRae, Shirley Jones, Cameron Mitchell, Barbara Ruick, Gene Lockhart, Susan Luckey (20th Century-Fox)

Carousel, presented by the Theatre Guild in April 1945, ran 890 performances at the Majestic Theatre. It here gets the supertreatment in 55mm CinemaScope. There are two production numbers in the picture that are close to classic. Add the staging of the famed "Soliloquy," as sung by Gordon MacRae for strong impact. Musical numbers are all in extremely good taste. Reservations as to some scenes and a certain slowness in pace are minor.

The stars of *Carousel* [based on Ferenc Molnar's *Liliom*, as adapted by Benjamin F. Glazer] remain Rodgers & Hammerstein. The cast is uniformly attractive, from MacRae as the shiftless ne'er-do-well Billy Bigelow, to pretty Shirley Jones as Julie.

Production number that precedes the gay clambake is a tribute to the ingenuity of choreographer Rod Alexander.

If this scene is great, the finale, when Julie's daughter, Louise (danced by Susan Luckey), does a number with handsome Jacques D'Amboise, is even more of a rocking production success [derived from the original stage ballet by Agnes DeMille].

Carousel keeps elements of drama, humor and sentiment but starts out with MacRae already dead and in heaven. His courtship and marriage are then told in flashback.

•

CARPETBAGGERS, THE

1964, 150 mins, US Ⓥ ⊙ ▭ col

Dir Edward Dmytryk *Prod* Joseph E. Levine *Scr* John Michael Hayes *Ph* Joseph MacDonald *Ed* Frank Bracht *Mus* Elmer Bernstein *Art* Hal Pereira, Walter Tyler

Act George Peppard, Alan Ladd, Bob Cummings, Martha Hyer, Elizabeth Ashley, Carroll Baker (Paramount)

Joseph E. Levine's screen version of *The Carpetbaggers* is lusty, vulgar, gusty and, on one notable occasion, painfully brutal.

The story of a ruthless, emotionally unstable chemical-aircraft-film tycoon is told in a vague, often lurching manner in the scenario out of Harold Robbins's tome. The career of the "hero"—a heel in fact—is traced sketchily from the point at which he succeeds his just-deceased father (whom he detests) in business to the phase in which he manages to pull himself together emotionally after an unbroken string of brutally cold-blooded dealings, both business and personal.

George Peppard growls and glowers his way through the pivotal role, wearing one basic expression—a surly, like-it-or-lump-it look—but there is an underlying animal magnetism to this performance. The late Alan Ladd limns with conviction one of the few appealing characters—the cowboy star who ultimately restores Peppard to his senses. Carroll Baker has the flashy role of a Harlowesque sexpot, and makes the most of it.

•

CARQUAKE

SEE: CANNONBALL

•

CARRIE

1952, 118 mins, US Ⓥ ⊙ b/w

Dir William Wyler *Prod* William Wyler *Scr* Ruth Goetz, Augustus Goetz *Ph* Victor Milner *Ed* Robert Swink *Mus* David Raksin *Art* Hal Pereira, Roland Anderson

Act Laurence Olivier, Jennifer Jones, Eddie Albert, Miriam Hopkins, Basil Ruysdael, Ray Teal (Paramount)

Theodore Dreiser's novel of another era, *Sister Carrie*, has been given a literal adaptation for films and the result is a sometimes mawkish, frequently dated drama. As just plain *Carrie*, with such stars as Jennifer Jones and Laurence Olivier, it is somber, low-key entertainment.

Carrie is the turn-of-the-century story of the small-town girl who goes to Chicago to make good. It is the story of her meeting a traveling salesman and of how he becomes her "benefactor." The big love of her life, however, is the manager of a swanky restaurant whom she meets while living with the salesman.

Jones gives one of the bright performances of her career. For Olivier, it is a role that gives him little opportunity for shading or dramatic intensity. Eddie Albert is excellent as the traveling salesman.

1952: NOMINATIONS: Best B&W Costume Design, B&W Art Direction

•

CARRIE

1976, 97 mins, US Ⓥ ⊙ col

Dir Brian De Palma *Prod* Paul Monash *Scr* Lawrence D. Cohen *Ph* Mario Tosi *Ed* Paul Hirsch *Mus* Pino Donaggio *Art* William Kenney, Jack Fisk

Act Sissy Spacek, Piper Laurie, Amy Irving, William Katt, Nancy Allen, John Travolta (United Artists)

Carrie is a modest but effective shock-suspense drama about a pubescent girl, her evangelical mother and cruel schoolmates.

Stephen King's novel, adapted by Lawrence D. Cohen, combines in unusual fashion a lot of offbeat story angles. Sissy Spacek heads cast in title role of an ugly-duckling-type-schoolgirl.

Nancy Allen and other classmates, who normally berate her anyway, really go to town on the girl, until gym teacher Betty Buckley comes to her rescue.

At home, Carrie's mother is a dried-up, abandoned wife-turned-religious freak, played superbly by Piper Laurie, which explains in part the girl's ignorance. At the same time, Carrie discovers that with intense concentration, she can make physical objects move.

1976: NOMINATIONS: Best Actress (Sissy Spacek), Supp. Actress (Piper Laurie)

•

CARRIED AWAY

1996, 107 mins, US Ⓥ col

Dir Bruno Barreto *Prod* Lisa Hansen, Paul Herzberg *Scr* Ed Jones *Ph* Declan Quinn *Ed* Bruce Cannon *Mus* Bruce Broughton *Art* Peter Paul Raubertas

Act Dennis Hopper, Amy Irving, Amy Locane, Julie Harris, Gary Busey, Hal Holbrook (CineTel)

Midlife crisis forms the basis of *Carried Away*, an explicitly told tale culled from a Jim Thompson novel (*Farmer*). Anchored by a powerful performance from Dennis Hopper, it's at turns a sex comedy and a poignant drama, but the two elements never mesh.

Howardsville, the small-town locale, is in an unidentified Midwestern state, and the story apparently occurs in the 1970s. Joseph (Hopper) teaches at the local school, operates the family farm, and tends to his dying mother (Julie Harris). For the past six years he's been engaged to Rosealee (Amy Irving), a fellow teacher and the widow of his former best friend, who was killed in Vietnam.

Joseph is exceptionally good at rationalizing why he's not quite ready to tie the knot. It's at that point that 17-year-old vixen Catherine Wheeler (Amy Locane) arrives for the last semseter. A short time later, she pops up at Joseph's farm with her father (Gary Busey), looking for a stable for her horse.

Director Bruno Barreto appears comfortable deflating sexual and social conventions, but the screen story is otherwise rather mundane. Hopper gets a rare opportunity to remind us that he's a consummate performer. But the two women aren't playing at the level of the picture's star.

•

CARRINGTON

1995, 120 mins, UK/France Ⓥ col

Dir Christopher Hampton *Prod* Ronald Shedlo, John C. McGrath *Scr* Christopher Hampton *Ph* Denis Lenoir *Ed* George Akers *Mus* Michael Nyman *Art* Caroline Amies

Act Emma Thompson, Jonathan Pryce, Steven Waddington, Samuel West, Rufus Sewell, Penelope Wilton (Gramercy/PolyGram)

They should at least have called it *Lytton & Dora*. Despite (and because) of commanding playing by Jonathan Pryce, this between-wars biopic of English painter Dora Carrington and her love for gay Bloomsbury Group scribe Lytton Strachey fails to illuminate either the little-known title character or her life-consuming passion. British scripter-playwright Christopher Hampton's helming debut is a wobbly affair that's too dry by half and isn't helped by a badly miscast Emma Thompson in an already underwritten role.

Hampton first read Michael Holroyd's bio *Lytton Strachey* in the late '60s, and wrote a script for Warner Bros. in the mid-'70s. Project bounced around various companies during the next 10 years and was finally reactivated by producers Ronald Shedlo and John McGrath in the early '90s, with director Mike Newell attached. When financing finally fell into place, Newell was unavailable (following the success of *Four Weddings and a Funeral*), and Hampton took on directing chores at the 11th hour.

It would be easy to attribute much of the film's failure to grab the brass ring to Hampton's behind-the-lens inexperience—from unsuitable choice of music (Michael Nyman) to a lack of any thorough-going camera style. But many of the pic's weaknesses stem from the script, a department in which Hampton (*Dangerous Liaisons*, *Mary Reilly*) has buckets of experience, from legit to TV to features.

The emotional distancing starts with the script's construction—as six chapters of varying length, each titled and dated, stretching from 1915 through 1932. The script's biggest mistake, however, is that it turns its title character into a supporting player. Tossing off waspish remarks with the disdain of a wannabe Oscar Wilde, Pryce simply acts Thompson (and everyone else) off the screen.

•

CARRINGTON V.C.
(US: COURT MARTIAL)

1954, 105 mins, UK Ⓥ b/w

Dir Anthony Asquith *Prod* Teddy Baird *Scr* John Hunter *Ph* Desmond Dickinson *Ed* Ralph Kemplen *Mus* [none] *Art* Wilfrid Shingleton

Act David Niven, Margaret Leighton, Noelle Middleton, Laurence Naismith, Clive Morton, Mark Dignam (Remus)

Carrington V.C., by Dorothy and Campbell Christie, made a definite impact on the West End scene as a subject of dramatic intensity. In its translation to the screen, the drama loses none of the basic qualities.

The plot focuses on the title character, a wartime hero who has the routine job of commanding an artillery battery in peacetime. It's so secret that he is constantly feuding with his regimental commander, is in serious financial difficulties and is harassed by a wife who is desperately clamoring for money.

The army authorities owe him a substantial sum on his expense account, but this cash is not forthcoming. And in a moment of crisis, he helps himself to army funds "to advertise a grievance." His commander orders a court-martial and the main incident of the pic is concerned with this trial.

David Niven gives one of his best performances in recent times as the accused V.C. Some of his courtroom exchanges are dramatic highspots of the plot.

•

CARRY ON AGAIN DOCTOR

1969, 89 mins, UK Ⓥ col

Dir Gerald Thomas *Prod* Peter Rogers *Scr* Talbot Rothwell *Ph* Ernest Steward *Ed* Alfred Roome *Mus* Eric Rogers *Art* John Blezard

Act Sidney James, Kenneth Williams, Charles Hawtrey, Jim Dale, Joan Sims, Barbara Windsor (Rank)

Carry On Again Doctor returns to a well-tilled field, with bedpans, undressed patients, and discussions about symptoms from wind to bowels, being regular dialog fodder. This time the flimsy yarn is mainly geared around the discovery in the Beatific Islands by Jim Dale, an accident-prone young doctor, of a serum which helps girth-control. Jealousy and Machiavellian plots to prevent him from making a fortune out of the discovery leads to double-crossing, female impersonation and a lot of predictable hanky-panky.

In this film much of the patter is flat and vulgar without being over-funny. Some situations (such as when Dale "blows" an electric contraption and turns the hospital into chaos) are very funny. But there aren't enough.

Jim Dale, as the comedy hero, Sid James an an alcoholic steward of a medical mission, Joan Sims, Hattie Jacques, Kenneth Williams and Charles Hawtrey all play the nonsense without tongue in cheek, giving it a lift. Barbara Windsor, a blonde, curvy cutie, is in for pulchritude.

Stock shots cover the arrival of characters at the mythical Beatific Islands. The rest is Pinewood studio. It stands out a mile, but does it matter?

•

CARRY ON CABBY

1963, 91 mins, UK Ⓥ b/w

Dir Gerald Thomas **Prod** Peter Rogers **Scr** Talbot Rothwell **Ph** Alan Hume **Ed** Archie Ludski **Mus** Eric Rogers

Act Sidney James, Hattie Jacques, Kenneth Connor, Charles Hawtrey, Esma Cannon, Liz Fraser (Anglo Amalgamated)

The golden formula of the *Carry On* series is back with a bang with *Carry On Cabby*.

Not at first intended to be one of the series, the film has a rather stronger storyline than usual [from an idea by S. C. Green and R. M. Hills]. Also it has a different screenplay writer, Talbot Rothwell.

Sidney James is the cabby-owner of a prosperous fleet of taxicabs, but his domestic life is edgy because his wife claims he spends too much time with his beloved cabs. She sets up a rival garage called Glamcabs and decks out some shapely young women in revealing uniforms as her drivers. James, still not knowing that his wife is behind the rival firm, sets out to sabotage her business.

Hattie Jacques extracts fun from the role of James's wife. Kenneth Connor, Esma Cannon, Charles Hawtrey as an accident-prone nitwit, and Liz Fraser, as Sally the glamorous waitress–Mata Hari, are old students of the *Carry On* technique, and effortlessly milk the laughter. So, too, are some of the cameo players often used for one gag.

•

CARRY ON CAMPING

1969, 88 mins, UK Ⓥ col

Dir Gerald Thomas **Prod** Peter Rogers **Scr** Talbot Rothwell **Ph** Ernest Steward **Ed** Alfred Roome **Mus** Eric Rogers **Art** Lionel Couch

Act Sidney James, Kenneth Williams, Joan Sims, Charles Hawtrey, Terry Scott, Barbara Windsor (Rank)

While sticking to its well tried, profitable formula, latest *Carry On* suffers somewhat in comparison to some of its predecessors in that it lacks a storyline, however slim.

Sidney James and Bernard Bresslaw (who make a good nonsense team) plan a vacation at a nudist holiday camp at which, they hope, they will be able to break down the prim resistance of their girlfriends (Joan Sims and Dilys Laye). Camp turns out not to be nudie paradise, after all.

Meanwhile, other campers are involved in their own problems, with Terry Scott lumbered with an overhearty wife (Betty Marsden) and Charles Hawtrey as a cuckoo in a nest.

A bunch of schoolgirl teenagers from the St. Chayste Ladies' Seminary (typical of most of the dialogue), chaperoned by prissy Kenneth Williams as the headmaster and Hattie Jacques as the formidable matron, descend on the camp to bring some sexy complications. They're a good-looking bunch, with Barbara Windsor a literal standout as an exuberant sex-mad young trollop.

•

CARRY ON CLEO

1964, 92 mins, US Ⓥ col

Dir Gerald Thomas **Prod** Peter Rogers **Scr** Talbot Rothwell **Ph** Alan Hume **Ed** Archie Ludski **Mus** Eric Rogers **Art** Bert Davey

Act Sidney James, Kenneth Williams, Kenneth Connor, Charles Hawtrey, Joan Sims, Amanda Barrie (Anglo Amalgamated)

Intended as a parody of the expensive *Cleopatra*, this entry from the *Carry On* stables relies on the bludgeon rather than the rapier, so isn't entirely successful in its purpose.

Accent in this frolic is less on situation than on dialog and so there is less action to hold the audience. Talbot Rothwell's dialog is unabashedly corny but this doesn't much matter. But it is also unusually bristling with plodding double entendres. Gags, both verbal and visual, suffer from repetition and few are as neat as Julius Caesar's woeful complaint, "Infamy! Infamy! Everybody's got it in for me!"

The practised cast of Old Regulars are also, mainly, up to form, with Sidney James as Mark Anthony and Kenneth Connor as Hengist the Wheelmaker particularly prominent as they disport among the vestal virgins. Kenneth Williams has a few twittering moments as Caesar but again, irritatingly overplays. Charles Hawtrey's main function is to look incongruous and carry the weight of some of the least-subtle sex patter.

On the femme side, Joan Sims is a hearty gal as Caesar's wife, Sheila Hancock is a shrill one as Hengist's spouse. Best discovery is Amanda Barrie as the poor man's Cleopatra. Her takeoff of the Queen of the Nile gets nearer to the tongue-in-cheek sense of what filmmakers were aiming at than any of her more experienced colleagues.

•

CARRY ON COLUMBUS

1992, 91 mins, UK Ⓥ col

Dir Gerald Thomas **Prod** John Goldstone **Scr** Dave Freeman, John Antrobus **Ph** Alan Hume **Ed** Chris Blunden **Mus** John Du Prez **Art** Harry Pottle

Act Jim Dale, Bernard Cribbins, Maureen Lipman, Peter Richardson, Alexei Sayle, Rik Mayall (Comedy House)

Carry On Columbus resuscitates the bawdy, vaude-like humor of the original low-budget series with nary a nod to changing fashions. *Columbus* is the 30th in the *Carry On* series that started in 1958 with *Sergeant* and halted 20 years later with *Emmanuelle*. Vet director Gerald Thomas returns for behind-the-camera chores.

Current item continues the tradition of grafting on new comic talent but, with the trunk team now dead or absent, company feel is distinctly lacking.

Script starts weakly with the Sultan of Turkey (Rik Mayall, unfunny) sending two spies to spy on Chris Columbus (Jim Dale), a mapmaker with dreams of finding a new sea route to the gold-rich Indies. Financed by the king and queen of Spain (Leslie Phillips, June Whitfield), Columbus sets sail with a motley crew and a map in Hebrew translated by a dumb mariner (Bernard Cribbins). Losing their way, they end up in the Americas, where the natives are street-wise Indians with Brooklyn accents.

Best material is in the final half-hour, with Yank standup comics Larry Miller as a cigar-chewing chieftain and Charles Fleischer (voice of Roger Rabbit) as his sidekick.

Pic's £2.25 million ($3.8 million) budget is all on the screen in handsome costuming and authentically cheesy Pinewood sets.

•

CARRY ON CONSTABLE

1960, 86 mins, UK Ⓥ b/w

Dir Gerald Thomas **Prod** Peter Rogers **Scr** Norman Hudis **Ph** Ted Scaife **Ed** John Shirley **Mus** Bruce Montgomery **Art** Carmen Dillon

Act Sidney James, Kenneth Williams, Hattie Jacques, Eric Barker, Kenneth Connor, Shirley Eaton (Anglo Amalgamated)

This is simply an anthology of police gags and situations. Insofar as there is a storyline [from an idea by Brock Williams], this concerns a flu-stricken police station which is reinforced by four fledgling cops straight from the police school. Of course, in the end the hapless quartet distinguishes itself by rounding up, in improbable fashion, a bunch of crooks.

The producer has brought back most of the team of stalwarts that has been on parade in the three previous *Carry On* films. Kenneth Connor, Kenneth Williams, Charles Hawtrey and Leslie Phillips are the four zany cops; Hattie Jacques and Joan Sims are two policewomen, and Shirley Eaton and Jill Adams provide the glamour and slight touch of romance. Eric Barker is excellent as the inefficient inspector in charge of the station while Sidney James, a newcomer to the team, is in his usual first-class form as the sergeant who is annoyed with the recruits.

•

CARRY ON COWBOY

1966, 94 mins, UK Ⓥ col

Dir Gerald Thomas **Prod** Peter Rogers **Scr** Talbot Rothwell **Ph** Alan Hume **Ed** Rod Keys **Mus** Eric Rogers **Art** Bert Davey

Act Sidney James, Kenneth Williams, Jim Dale, Charles Hawtrey, Joan Sims, Angela Douglas (Anglo Amalgamated)

This Wild West spoof might well be subtitled *How the West Was Lost*. Story, though familiar nonsense, is less a string of irrelevant situations than usual, giving the team more opportunity for comedy thesping.

Stodge City is taken over by The Rumpo Kid (Sidney James), to the horror of Judge Burke (Kenneth Williams), who calls for a marshal to clean up Stodge City. By error a sanitary engineer (Jim Dale) gets sent to the trouble spot, arriving on the same coach as Annie Oakley (Angela Douglas), daughter of the sheriff who has been bumped off by The Rumpo Kid. The sanitary engineer disposes of The Rumpo Kid in a spoof of the *High Noon* long walk along a deserted street, in which the bogus marshal uses his knowledge of drains to good ingenious effect.

Though actually filmed on a common in Surrey the "Wild West locations" are adequately authentic, and Alan Hume's color lensing gives an extra touch of class.

•

CARRY ON CRUISING

1962, 89 mins, UK Ⓥ col

Dir Gerald Thomas **Prod** Peter Rogers **Scr** Norman Hudis **Ph** Alan Hume **Ed** John Shirley **Mus** Bruce Montgomery, Douglas Gamley **Art** Carmen Dillon

Act Sidney James, Kenneth Williams, Kenneth Connor, Liz Fraser, Dilys Laye, Lance Percival (Anglo Amalgamated)

Latest in the *Carry On* string of box-office click comedies. Main difference in this is that it is now launched in color. Maybe Norman Hudis, who has so skillfully scribed this run of comedy hits, should have a sabbatical.

Sidney James is the veteran, highly improbable skipper of a Mediterranean cruising vessel. He is inflicted with five hamheaded substitutes for well-tried key men in his regular complement. They are all overanxious to please and so everything goes disastrously wrong. Jumping, familiarly, through their well-placed circus hoops are Sidney James (he glowers), Kenneth Williams (he plays archly), Kenneth Connor (he dithers), Liz Fraser (she flaunts a shapely figure) and Esma Cannon (she twitters). Lance Percival, as the tyro ship's cook, has some bright moments while Jimmy Thompson, as a suave bartender, copes with little material. Dilys Laye, a comparative newcomer to this frenzied scene, works hard in some brittle comedy campaigns.

Direction by Gerald Thomas is boisterously effective. Major switch in this series is that the original story is by Eric Barker, a comedian who has appeared in a couple of the series.

•

CARRY ON DOCTOR

1968, 95 mins, UK Ⓥ col

Dir Gerald Thomas **Prod** Peter Rogers **Scr** Talbot Rothwell **Ph** Alan Hume **Ed** Alfred Roome **Mus** Eric Rogers **Art** Cedric Dawe

Act Frankie Howerd, Sidney James, Kenneth Williams, Charles Hawtrey, Jim Dale, Barbara Windsor (Rank)

Usual unabashed mixture of double meanings, down-to-earth vulgarity, blue jokes about hypodermic syringes, etc., and slapstick situations. This time the Carry On team returns to hospital life for its farcical goings-on.

Inevitably, the gags and situations waver in comic impact but the general effect is artless yocks in which audience participation is carried to fullest extent, in that part of the fun is anticipating the verbal and physical jokes.

Added zest is given by the inclusion of Frankie Howerd as a quack "mind-over-matter" doctor who becomes a reluctant patient. Howerd's brilliantly droll sense of comedy is given plenty of scope.

Among the grotesque patients are Sidney James, very funny as a cheerful malingerer; Bernard Bresslaw, Charles Hawtrey (more subdued than usual) and Peter Butterworth. The hospital staff is equally energetic and resourceful in providing simple-minded yocks, with Kenneth Williams as a supercilious chief physician.

•

CARRY ON EMMANNUELLE

1978, 88 mins, UK Ⓥ col

Dir Gerald Thomas **Prod** Peter Rogers **Scr** Lance Peters **Ph** Alan Hume **Ed** Peter Boita **Mus** Eric Rogers **Art** Jack Shampan

Act Suzanne Danielle, Kenneth Williams, Kenneth Connor, Jack Douglas, Joan Sims, Peter Butterworth (Cleves/National Film Trustee)

Carry On series now has 30 releases over 20 years. Formula is low budgets, low laughs. Which sums up *Carry On Emmannuelle*.

Emmannuelle, English-style, is wife to the French ambassador. She sleeps with most of London, from key government officials to servants, until an immigrant doctor restores hubby's priapic power and all ends happily in the embassy bedroom.

Rude, rollicking fun, at a breathless pace, was the order of earlier *Carry On* days. This one is rude, certainly, but the relentless phallic innuendo is as labored as makers' determination to show nothing to worry the censor. Leaden comic timing compares poorly with TV sitcoms which pic otherwise resembles in production values.

•

CARRY ON ENGLAND
1976, 89 mins, UK Ⓥ col
Dir Gerald Thomas ***Prod*** Peter Rogers ***Scr*** David Pursall, Jack Seddon ***Ph*** Ernest Steward ***Ed*** Richard Marden ***Mus*** Max Harris ***Art*** Lionel Couch
Act Kenneth Connor, Windsor Davies, Patrick Mower, Judy Geeson, Jack Douglas, Joan Sims (Rank)

Carry On England suffers from a particularly unfortunate hangup. It's not funny! Peter Rogers and Gerald Thomas, the producer/director double act who have canned 28 of these low budgeters, have worked over what must be the dullest script of the series. (Talbot Rothwell, who wrote most of the earlier screenplays, has been dropped.)

Action takes place in a mixed anti-aircraft battery at the start of World War II. There follows 89 minutes of gags, knockabout situations and innuendo which fall as flat as Kenneth Connor, as a bungling captain, is constantly required to do in search of belly laughs.

The cast, especially Connor, Windsor Davies and Jack Douglas, work hard to induce some excitement into the flagging dialog, but labor for a lost cause.

Rogers still manages to bring the pix in for $330,000, a considerable achievement.

•

CARRY ON JACK
(US: CARRY ON VENUS)
1964, 91 mins, UK Ⓥ col
Dir Gerald Thomas ***Prod*** Peter Rogers ***Scr*** Talbot Rothwell ***Ph*** Alan Hume ***Ed*** Archie Ludski ***Mus*** Eric Rogers ***Art*** Jack Shampan
Act Kenneth Williams, Bernard Cribbins, Juliet Mills, Charles Hawtrey, Donald Houston, Cecil Parker (Anglo Amalgamated)

Latest of the *Carry On* gang's shenanigans is an energetic skit on *Mutiny on the Bounty*, even bringing in joshing of certain characters and scenes from the [1962] nautical opus. Only two of the "resident" company—Charles Hawtrey and Kenneth Williams—are on parade. This one, however, has an added credit in its very okay costuming and art work. Mood is set by an opening cameo showing the epic, "Kiss Me, Hardy" incident, played with brief, witty aplomb by Jimmy Thompson and Anton Rodgers. From then on, director Gerald Thomas steers his cast through a maze of mix-ups and misadventure.

The screenplay involves a serving wench taking the place aboard HMS *Venus* of a green midshipman who, with the local nitwit, is press-ganged onto the same ship; a flogging that misfires; an operation at sea; a hilarious walking the plank sequence; a phoney mutiny; and the finale, when the *Venus*, now commanded by the middy, the girl and the birdbrain, puts the Spanish Armada out of action.

Williams, playing the precious Captain Fearless, who hates the sea and violence, is in excellent form while Hawtrey plays his familiar nincompoop with ease. Bernard Cribbins, as the sorely tried middy, Donald Houston, as the bullying second in command, and Percy Herbert, as his aide, bring some virile body to the proceedings. Only sizeable femme role is played by Juliet Mills who doesn't seem very comfortable in the robust male surroundings.

•

CARRY ON LOVING
1970, 90 mins, UK Ⓥ col
Dir Gerald Thomas ***Prod*** Peter Rogers ***Scr*** Talbot Rothwell ***Ph*** Ernest Steward ***Ed*** Alfred Roome ***Mus*** Eric Rogers ***Art*** Lionel Couch
Act Sidney James, Kenneth Williams, Charles Hawtrey, Joan Sims, Hattie Jacques, Terry Scott (Rank)

This time the nondescript "plot" hovers around a phoney matrimonial agency run by the plausible Sidney James and Hattie Jacques, posing as happy man and wife. Their efforts to pair off their unlikely and varied clients lead to riotous misunderstandings, sexy situations, intrigues, double-crossing and a custard-pie finale which is rather too deliberately planned and directed to achieve full comedy effect.

The string of situations, heavily garnished with indigo jokes, are often crazily irrelevant yet somehow manage to fit in with a kind of crazy mad logic.

James (aptly descibed in the film as looking like a dissipated old walnut) gives his usual genial, raffish display. Neat running gag falls to Michael Grady and Valerie Shute as a lovesick young couple who have no dialogue but are seen throughout the film smooching in the most unlikely spots.

•

CARRY ON NURSE
1959, 86 mins, UK Ⓥ b/w
Dir Gerald Thomas ***Prod*** Peter Rogers ***Scr*** Norman Hudis ***Ph*** Reginald Wyer ***Ed*** John Shirley ***Mus*** Bruce Montgomery ***Art*** Alex Vetchinsky
Act Kenneth Connor, Kenneth Williams, Charles Hawtrey, Leslie Phillips, Hattie Jacques, Shirley Eaton (Anglo Amalgamated)

Carry On Nurse does for hospitals what its predecessor [*Carry On Sergeant*] did for military life. The yocks come thick and fast. The humor tends to be repetitious, flirting with sex and dealing with such typical hospital subjects as bedpans, enemas, preparing patients for operations and so on.

There is no story, as such. Scriptwriter Norman Hudis has merely dreamed up an anthology of hospital humor, involving a string of vaude situations and eccentric characters [based on an idea by Patrick Cargill and Jack Beale]. Several of the performers who were in *Carry On Sergeant* crop up again. Others are added, including a number of easy-on-the-eye girls.

In a long cast which involves every type of nurse, a gorgon-like matron and a mixed bag of eccentric patients it is only possible to pick out Hattie Jacques, as the matron; Wilfrid Hyde White, as a suave patient; Ann Firbank, Shirley Eaton, Susan Stephen and Diana Beaumont as pretty, efficient nurses; Joan Sims, as the blunderer; and Kenneth Connor, a pugilist-patient with a broken hand.

Reginald Wyer's photography helps this film, which cost only about $200,000 to make.

•

CARRY ON REGARDLESS
1961, 90 mins, UK Ⓥ b/w
Dir Gerald Thomas ***Prod*** Peter Rogers ***Scr*** Norman Hudis ***Ph*** Alan Hume ***Ed*** John Shirley ***Mus*** Bruce Montgomery
Act Sidney James, Kenneth Connor, Charles Hawtrey, Joan Sims, Kenneth Williams, Liz Fraser (Anglo Amalgamated)

Any serious criticism of *Carry on Regardless* is futile. The story, such as it is, has Sidney James running Helping Hand Ltd., an agency prepared to take on any sort of job any time. On his staff are most of the trained imbeciles of previous films.

Disaster winds up every job. Typical of these are scenes which involve Kenneth Williams in taking a chimp for a walk through London, Kenneth Connor baby-sitting (the baby turns out to be a married woman), and Charles Hawtrey deputizing for a pugilist with this weedy comedian getting the job of a nightclub bouncer. Joan Sims has to demonstrate a bubble bath, Liz Fraser finds herself modeling underwear. The good slapstick climax has the whole gang cleaning out a filthy, antiquated house.

Ingenuity of scriptwriter Norman Hudis is sometimes a bit strained, but he has come up with some sound comedy situations. Film also introduces Stanley Unwin, a TV and radio man who specializes in double-talk.

•

CARRY ON SCREAMING
1966, 97 mins, UK Ⓥ col
Dir Gerald Thomas ***Prod*** Peter Rogers ***Scr*** Talbot Rothwell ***Ph*** Alan Hume ***Ed*** Rod Keys ***Mus*** Eric Rogers
Act Harry H. Corbett, Kenneth Williams, Fenella Fielding, Joan Sims, Charles Hawtrey, Jim Dale (Anglo Amalgamated)

This 12th in the successful *Carry On* series puts the skids under horror pix. Snag is that most horror films themselves teeter on parody and it is rather tough trying to burlesque a parody.

Abduction of a girl by a monster starts a trail of goofy adventures as henpecked Detective Sergeant Bung (Harry H. Corbett) and his bovine assistant (Peter Butterworth) try to unravel this, the latest crime of a series. Investigations lead to an eerie mansion, inhabited by a ghoulish doctor, who is dead but reincarnated, his attractively sexy, evil sister, a sinister butler and a couple of kidnapping monsters. There the brother-and-sister team ply their grisly trade of abducting girls, petrifying them and then selling them as shop dummies.

Gerald Thomas's direction as usual is assured, though some of the gags and situations would be helped by speeding up via more ruthless trimming. Corbett and Fenella Fielding, both debuting with the *Carry On* team, give it added strength. Corbett mugs a great deal but the role demands it and Fielding as the grisly vamp glitters with an overdone seductiveness which is often funny.

•

CARRY ON SERGEANT
1958, 85 mins, UK Ⓥ b/w
Dir Gerald Thomas ***Prod*** Peter Rogers ***Scr*** Norman Hudis, John Antrobus ***Ph*** Peter Hennessy ***Ed*** Peter Boita ***Mus*** Bruce Montgomery ***Art*** Alex Vetchinsky
Act William Hartnell, Bob Monkhouse, Shirley Eaton, Eric Barker, Dora Bryan, Kenneth Connor (Anglo Amalgamated)

Carry On Sergeant is an army farce [from a story by R. F. Delderfield, *The Bull Boys*] exploiting practically every army gag, but while some of the writing is careless and there is no attempt to develop a reasonable story, it is by no means sloppily produced.

William Hartnell is a training sergeant who is about to retire from the service and has one more chance to fulfill his life ambition, which is to train the champion troop of the intake. Moreover, he has a $140 bet on the outcome. He is handed a bunch of rookies which is believable only in farce. The barrack-room attorney, the young man in love, the hypochondriac malingerer, the man always out of step . . . in fact, the repertory company of trainees. There's the sergeant with the bark, the fussy officer.

Kenneth Connor steals most of the honors as the hypochondriac being chased by a love-starved army waitress, played characteristically by Dora Bryan. He has a shade too much to do, but never misses a trick. Bob Monkhouse, called up on his wedding day, Shirley Eaton as his frustrated wife who crops up in camp, Eric Barker as a fussy officer, William Hartnell as the gravelly voiced sergeant and Bill Owen as his faithful corporal add their quota.

•

CARRY ON SPYING
1964, 87 mins, UK b/w
Dir Gerald Thomas ***Prod*** Peter Rogers ***Scr*** Talbot Rothwell, Sid Colin ***Ph*** Alan Hume ***Ed*** Archie Ludski ***Mus*** Eric Rogers ***Art*** Alex Vetchinsky
Act Kenneth Williams, Bernard Cribbins, Charles Hawtrey, Barbara Windsor, Eric Pohlmann, Eric Barker (Anglo Amalgamated)

The Society for Total Extinction of Non-Conforming Humans (STENCH for short) has grabbed a secret formula and the British Operational Security Headquarters (BOSH in brief) tackles the job of getting back Formula X and outwitting its arch enemy, Doctor Crow. Through shortage of personnel, the assignment is handed to Simkins (Kenneth Williams), an agent in charge of training new spies, and three of his pupils.

Best knockabout sequences take place on the Orient Express, in a Viennese restaurant, a murky quarter of the Casbah and in the Automatum Plant where the inept foursome nearly come to a sticky end, but are rescued by good luck and the intervention of a beautiful spy.

Kenneth Williams's brand of camp comedy, while very funny in smallish doses, can pall when he has a lengthy chore as here. But Bernard Cribbins brings some useful virility to his fatuous role, Charles Hawtrey contributes his now familiar performance as the guileless one and Barbara Windsor proves a well-upholstered and perky heroine as the girl spy with a photographic memory.

•

CARRY ON TEACHER
1959, 86 mins, UK Ⓥ b/w
Dir Gerald Thomas ***Prod*** Peter Rogers ***Scr*** Norman Hudis ***Ph*** Reginald Wyer ***Ed*** John Shirley ***Mus*** Bruce Montgomery
Act Ted Ray, Kenneth Connor, Kenneth Williams, Joan Sims, Charles Hawtrey, Hattie Jacques (Anglo Amalgamated)

Third entry in Peter Rogers's sock *Carry On* series combines virtually the same team to use the same yock-raising formula, this time in the scholastic field, and the laughs come readily. This time screenplay writer Norman Hudis has developed a slightly stronger story line and made the characters more credible.

Ted Ray in the acting headmaster of a school who, after 20 years, has set his heart on the headmastership of a new one in the country. Much depends on the report put in to the Ministry of Education by a visiting inspector and a child psychiatrist. Because they don't want the popular master to leave, the students decide to sabotage his chances and start a well-planned campaign of bad behavior to influence the visiting inspectors.

Some of the gags are telegraphed but the cheerful impudence with which they are dropped into the script is completely disarming.

Ray, playing straighter than most of his colleagues, gives a pleasant performance. There's Kenneth Connor giving a fine performance as a nervous science master; Kenneth

Williams and Charles Hawtrey, as a couple of precious masters in charge of literature and music respectively; Hattie Jacques as the formidable mistress who wages war on the saboteurs; and Joan Sims in her usual inimitable form as a games mistress. Leslie Phillips is the psychiatrist and Rosalind Knight is the inspector.

•

CARRY ON UP THE JUNGLE
1970, 90 mins, UK Ⓥ col
Dir Gerald Thomas ***Prod*** Peter Rogers ***Scr*** Talbot Rothwell ***Ph*** Ernest Steward ***Ed*** Alfred Roome ***Mus*** Eric Rogers ***Art*** Alex Vetchinsky
Act Frankie Howerd, Sidney James, Charles Hawtrey, Joan Sims, Terry Scott, Kenneth Connor (Rank)

Brought in at Pinewood for around $440,000 (the jungle foliage which kept melting under the lights was the most expensive item) and with plenty of stock animal shots, this one is a skit on safari in the jungle, with a parody of Tarzan thrown in for good measure.

It involves the characters plunging in and out of the wrong tents mainly in search of sex, a tribe of headhunting cannibals, another tribe of lush dames in search of men to carry on their mating industry, a sex-starved stray gorilla and sundry other Darkest Africa situations and gags.

The usual core of the *Carry On* cast is on parade but notable absentees are the supercilious Kenneth Williams, Hattie Jacques, Peter Butterworth and Jim Dale, and they are missed. Instead, producer Peter Rogers has brought in another notable favorite, Frankie Howerd. Latter, a fine comedian with characteristics of his own, does not jell as well in situation comedy as when he is a stand-up comedian.

Sidney James and Joan Sims, veterans of this series, are towers of strength and, among a bunch of nubile maidens, a comparative newcomer, Jacki Piper, rings a bell.

•

CARRY ON . . . UP THE KHYBER
1968, 87 mins, UK Ⓥ col
Dir Gerald Thomas ***Prod*** Peter Rogers ***Scr*** Talbot Rothwell ***Ph*** Ernest Steward ***Ed*** Alfred Roome ***Mus*** Eric Rogers ***Art*** Alex Vetchinsky
Act Sidney James, Kenneth Williams, Charles Hawtrey, Roy Castle, Joan Sims, Bernard Bresslaw (Adder/Rank)

This one has a slightly stronger storyline than some of its predecessors, but still continues to rely primarily on low-comedy visual and verbal gag situations for its yocks.

Up the Khyber centers on the British occupation of India in Queen Victoria's day and the reputation of the British is rocked when the local rulers suspect that the dreaded Scottish Devils in Skirts, members of the intrepid Third Foot and Mouth Regiment, actually wear drawers under their kilts. Settling of this urgent question causes considerable hoo-hah in the shape of a local uprising engineered by the local Khasi of Kalibar.

There's a small touch of genius in the way the Pass, for instance, can be shot in North Wales to everybody's complete satisfaction. Main highlight in this film is its finale, where the tribal chiefs launch a full-scale attack on the government residence while the governor and his guests with unshaken poise nonchalantly continue dinner amid the turmoil.

Performance of Sidney James as Sir Sidney Ruff-Diamond, the bluff, vulgar British governor, is a gem, impeccably timed, wily and always in character.

•

CARRY ON VENUS
SEE: CARRY ON JACK

•

CARS THAT ATE PARIS, THE
1974, 91 mins, Australia Ⓥ ▭ col
Dir Peter Weir ***Prod*** Jim McElroy, Howard McElroy ***Scr*** Peter Weir, Keith Gow, Piers Daries ***Ph*** John McLean ***Ed*** Wayne LeClos ***Mus*** Bruce Smeaton
Act Terry Camilleri, John Meillon, Melissa Jaffa, Kevin Miles, Max Gillies, Peter Armstrong (Australian Film Development/Royce Smeal)

Paris is a tiny Australian township with a surprising number of car accidents on its outskirts. Involved in one is Arthur, whose brother, is killed while driving a caravan-towing car.

Gradually it becomes evident that the car accidents are planned affairs. As each one occurs the townspeople swoop like vultures on the cars and retrieve any personal effects for themselves, while the doctor carries out strange experiments of his own upon the victims.

Attempting to preserve an air of normality, the mayor orders a scheduled dance to take place, which becomes macabre when the doctor brings his patients along.

Much of the pic is brilliant, although it does not always seem certain of the direction it is taking. At first it seems satirical, then black comedy, degenerating into a thriller.

•

CARVE HER NAME WITH PRIDE
1958, 119 mins, UK Ⓥ b/w
Dir Lewis Gilbert ***Prod*** Daniel M. Angel ***Scr*** Vernon Harris, Lewis Gilbert ***Ph*** John Wilcox ***Ed*** John Shirley ***Mus*** William Alwyn ***Art*** Bernard Robinson
Act Virginia McKenna, Paul Scofield, Jack Warner, Denise Grey, Alain Saury, Maurice Ronet (Keyboard/Rank)

The film pays tribute to the real life exploits of Violette Szabo, a beautiful young woman who became a British cloak-and-dagger agent in France and won a posthumous George Cross after being tortured and executed in Ravensbruck Camp. Part of the pic's attraction is its lack of hysteria. It keeps resolutely to the facts [from a book by R. J. Minney] and refuses to allow the espionage and torture sequences to go past the bounds of credulity.

Virginia McKenna is top-notch. She runs the gamut of humor, charm and toughness. By skillful playing and equally skillful makeup, McKenna's ordeal is expertly revealed. Paul Schofield, as the officer colleague who falls in love with his gallant young comrade, and Alain Saury, as her young husband; Jack Warner and Denise Grey, as her stolid middle-aged parents; Bill Owen, a standout as McKenna's sergeant instructor, all contribute admirably to the thesping.

•

CAR WASH
1976, 97 mins, US Ⓥ col
Dir Michael Schultz ***Prod*** Art Linson, Gary Stromberg ***Scr*** Joe Schumacher ***Ph*** Frank Stanley ***Ed*** Christopher Holmes ***Mus*** Norman Whitfield ***Art*** Robert Clatworthy
Act Franklyn Ajaye, Sully Boyar, Richard Brestoff, George Carlin, Irwin Corey, Ivan Dixon (Universal)

Car Wash uses gritty humor to polish clean the souls of a lot of likeable street people.

The setting is Sully Boyar's downtown car wash, where the colorful ethnic crew contends as much with oddball customers as with themselves. Perhaps the best known of the players is Richard Pryor, shining it on as a fancy-dressed preacher, complete with flashy car and retinue that includes The Pointer Sisters. Pryor's license plate spells out "tithe," a sure evocation of the real-life character he suggests.

Woven into the main proceedings is the lonely sidewalk vigil of a streetwalker, Lauren Jones, which, combined with Bill Duke's equally sensitive portrayal of a frightened black militant, keeps the film in fine balance of humanism.

•

CASABLANCA
1942, 99 mins, US Ⓥ ⊙ b/w
Dir Michael Curtiz ***Prod*** Hal B. Wallis ***Scr*** Julius J. Epstein, Philip G. Epstein, Howard Koch [Casey Robinson] ***Ph*** Arthur Edeson ***Ed*** Owen Marks ***Mus*** Max Steiner ***Art*** Carl Jules Weyl
Act Humphrey Bogart, Ingrid Bergman, Paul Henreid, Claude Rains, Conrad Veidt, Sydney Greenstreet (Warner)

Although the title and Humphrey Bogart's name convey the impression of high adventure rather than romance, there's plenty of the latter. Adventure is there, too, but it's more as exciting background to the Bogart-Ingrid Bergman heart department. Bogart, incidentally, as a tender lover (in addition to being a cold-as-ice nitery operator) is a novel characterization.

Casablanca is pictured as a superficially gay town to which monied refugees flee from Axis terror. There they await visas to Lisbon and then transportation to the United States. The waits are frequently interminable while arrangements for papers are made with corrupt Vichy officials and the wealthy help to allay their impatience with chemin de fer and other games at Rick's. Rick is Bogart, who has opened his fancy joint after being "jilted" by Bergman in Paris.

Bergman turns up one evening with her husband (Paul Henreid) whom she thought was dead during the period of her romance with Bogart. Henreid is leader of the underground in Europe and it is vital that he get to America. Bogart has two visas that will do the trick and the choice is between going with Bergman himself—their torch still aflame—or sending her off with Henreid, who can do so much for the United Nations cause.

Bogart, as might be expected, is more at ease as the bitter and cynical operator of a joint than as a lover, but handles both assignments with superb finesse. Bergman, in a torn-between-love-and-duty role, lives up to her reputation as a fine actress. Henreid is well cast and does an excellent job too.

Superb is the lineup of lesser players. Some of the characterizations are a bit on the overdone side, but each is a memorable addition to the whole [adapted by Aeneas McKenzie and Wally Kline from the then-unproduced play *Everybody Comes to Rick's* by Murray Burnett and Joan Alison].

1943: Best Picture, Director, Screenplay

NOMINATIONS: Best Actor (Humphrey Bogart), Supp. Actor (Claude Rains), B&W Cinematography, Editing, Scoring of a Dramatic Picture

•

CASANOVA
(FELLINI'S CASANOVA)
1976, 166 mins, Italy Ⓥ ⊙ col
Dir Federico Fellini ***Prod*** Alberto Grimaldi ***Scr*** Federico Fellini, Bernardino Zappone ***Ph*** Giuseppe Rotunno ***Ed*** Ruggero Mastroianni ***Mus*** Nino Rota ***Art*** Federico Fellini
Act Donald Sutherland, Tina Aumont, Cicely Browne, Olimpia Carlisi, Adele Angela Lojodice, Marghareth Clementi (PEA)

Casanova is Federico Fellini's demolition of a myth, mounted with studied virtuosity into a rambling but bigger-than-life spectacle divested, by design, of reality and emotion in portraying the legendary Venetian lover as a pathetic victim of his own vanity and virility. Tracing a continuous flux of decline from practically the opening sequence, Fellini relentlessly runs his hero into the ground for 166 minutes.

Shorn of dramatic intensity, detached from the reality of Europe's tremors in the 18th century, *Casanova* depends on the grandscale mechanics of burlesque and circus to reduce the stature of a legend. The pic entered production in July 1975, was interrupted for three months in a dispute between producer and director, and finally completed in mid-April 1976. Budget is variously estimated between $8–10 million.

Donald Sutherland, forced to carry the film, gives the gallant Venetian a measure of dignity and momentarily succeeds in overcoming the mechanics of Fellini's direction. With nothing but flimsy commentary as support, Sutherland is on-screen almost from start to finish as he travels from Venice to Paris, London, Germany, Rome, and Austria hoping to find a niche in the Establishment—a hope triggered principally by the size of his member.

Tina Aumont excels as an urchin of mystery, Enrichetta; Cicely Browne, as a withered blueblood ready to pay for Casanova; and Adele Angela Lojodice, who is remarkable as the lifesized mechanical doll and Casanova's mate in the court of Wurtenberg.

•

CASBAH
1948, 93 mins, US b/w
Dir John Berry ***Prod*** Nat C. Goldstone ***Scr*** Laslo Bush-Fekete, Arnold Manoff ***Ph*** Irving Glassberg ***Ed*** Edward Curtiss ***Mus*** Walter Scharf (arr.) ***Art*** Bernard Herzbrun, John F. DeCuir
Act Yvonne De Carlo, Tony Martin, Peter Lorre, Marta Toren, Hugo Haas, Thomas Gomez (Marston/Universal)

The music is excellent, Tony Martin's singing is sock, and the Pepe Le Moko story has always been good, if familiar, screen fare. That the romantic melodrama doesn't always mesh too well with the musical story [by Erik Charell] makes for a distraction, but on the whole, this Marston production is generally on the credit side.

Martin is good as the dashing thief whose elusive ways are the despair of the police. He makes full use of his s.a. vocalisthenics with the tuneful Leo Robin–Harold Arlen songs.

Story plot hews closely to the original yarn about the thief who hides in the Casbah from the police but is finally lured to his death by a beautiful girl. Suspense and intrigue are forced to a halt by musical portions, making John Berry's direction seem ragged at times, but when film is telling the story the pace is expert.

Yvonne De Carlo is good as the native girl who loves Martin, but major femme interest goes to Swedish newcomer Marta Toren. Peter Lorre clicks strongly as the police inspector who finally gets his man. Hugo Haas sells his tourist guide character well and Douglas Dick scores as the informer.

•

CASINO
1995, 177 mins, US/France Ⓥ ⊙ ▭ col
Dir Martin Scorsese ***Prod*** Barbara De Fina ***Scr*** Nicholas Pileggi ***Ph*** Robert Richardson ***Ed*** Thelma Schoonmaker ***Art*** Dante Ferretti
Act Robert De Niro, Sharon Stone, Joe Pesci, James Woods, Don Rickles, Alan King (Universal/Syalis/Legende)

In fascinating detail and with dazzling finesse, *Casino* lays out how the mob controlled and ultimately lost Las Vegas.

Martin Scorsese's intimate epic about money, sex and brute force is a grandly conceived study of what happens to goodfellas from the mean streets when they outstrip their wildest dreams and achieve the pinnacle of wealth and power.

The film, based on Nicholas Pileggi's contemporaneous book, concentrates on three central figures: Sam "Ace" Rothstein (Robert De Niro), a top gambler installed by the Kansas City mob to run their casino, which he does brilliantly; Nicky Santoro (Joe Pesci), Ace's longtime best friend and impulsively violent enforcer who introduces street thuggery to the Vegas scene; and Ginger McKenna (Sharon Stone), a veteran hustler who marries Ace for his money, falls into Nicky's arms when she becomes unhappy and ends up helping to drag them down and the empire around them.

Pic expands on Scorsese's *Goodfellas* technique of introducing his characters, their milieu and m.o. through a lot of fast-paced narration laid over descriptive, elaborate docu-style evocation of vivid specifics.

As the boom begins to lower on all the characters, there is still an hour to go, and Scorsese moves from the rapid-fire, heavily narrated, music-drenched coverage of the earlier episodes to more protracted, dialogue-dominated dramatic scenes in which Ace, Ginger and Nicky, separately and together, play out their endgames.

Lensed entirely at the Riviera Hotel casino and on other real locations, the film possesses a stylistic boldness and verisimilitude that is virtually matchless.

Stone is simply a revelation here. She lets loose with a corker of a performance as the beautiful, unstable, ultimately pathetic moll with no inner life.

1995: NOMINATION: Best Actress (Sharon Stone)

•

CASINO ROYALE
1967, 131 mins, UK/US Ⓥ ⦿ ▭ col
Dir John Huston, Ken Hughes, Val Guest, Robert Parrish, Joseph McGrath ***Prod*** Charles K. Feldman, Jerry Bresler ***Scr*** Wolf Mankowitz, John Law, Michael Sayers ***Ph*** Jack Hildyard, John Wilcox, Nicolas Roeg ***Ed*** Bill Lenny ***Mus*** Burt Bacharach ***Art*** Michael Stringer
Act Peter Sellers, Ursula Andress, David Niven, Orson Welles, Woody Allen, Joanna Pettet (Famous Artists/Columbia)

Wacky comedy extravaganza, *Casino Royale* is an attempt to spoof the pants off James Bond. The $12 million film is a conglomeration of frenzied situations, "in" gags and special effects, lacking discipline and cohesion. Some of the situations are very funny, but many are too strained.

Based freely on Ian Fleming's novel, the story line defies sane description. Sufficient to say that the original James Bond (David Niven), now knighted and living in eccentric retirement, is persuaded back into the Secret Service to help cope with a disastrous situation.

Niven seems justifiably bewildered by the proceedings, but he has a neat delivery of throwaway lines and enters into the exuberant physical action with pleasant blandness. Peter Sellers has some amusing gags as the gambler, the chance of dressing up in various guises and a neat near-seduction scene with Ursula Andress.

1967: NOMINATION: Best Song ("The Look of Love")

•

CASPER
1995, 100 mins, US Ⓥ ⦿ col
Dir Brad Silberling ***Prod*** Colin Wilson ***Scr*** Sherri Stoner, Deanna Oliver ***Ph*** Dean Cundey ***Ed*** Michael Kahn ***Mus*** James Horner ***Art*** Leslie Dilley
Act Christina Ricci, Bill Pullman, Cathy Moriarty, Eric Idle, Malachi Pearson (voice), Joe Nipote (voice) (Amblin/Universal)

Another demonstration of the hazards involved turning a six-minute animated short into a big budget movie, *Casper* will doubtless spur nostalgic recognition among grown-ups but skews so heavily toward children that it offers little to divert anyone over the age of 8.

Billed as a "live-action fun-house ride" in press notes, *Casper* actually seems to be thinking more along the lines of the next Universal Studios attraction. The complicated nature of the project seems to have overwhelmed 30-year-old director Brad Silberling, making his feature debut after cutting his teeth in episodic TV.

Pic starts with a snarling heiress, Carrigan (Cathy Moriarty), left a haunted mansion by her late father. Determined to gain the treasure rumoured to be within but chased off by the ghostly denizens, she enlists a "ghost therapist," Dr. Harvey (Bill Pullman), to eradicate the problem. Still grieving over his wife's death, Harvey arrives with his teenage daughter, Kat (Christina Ricci), who, like Casper, is lonely and looking for a friend.

After the expected shock wears off, Kat and Casper do form a bond and even Kat's dad warms up to the anti-social ghost trio—Stinkie, Stretch and Fatso—who share the place with Casper.

The movie's biggest asset is of the earthly variety. Ricci is an enchanting young actress who brings to mind a teenage Natalie Wood, and whatever emotional resonance *Casper* can muster is largely to her credit.

•

CASQUE D'OR
1952, 95 mins, France b/w
Dir Jacques Becker ***Scr*** Jacques Becker, Jacques Companeez ***Ph*** Robert Lefebvre ***Ed*** Marguerite Renoir ***Mus*** Georges Van Parys ***Art*** Jean D'Eaubonne
Act Simone Signoret, Serge Reggiani, Claude Dauphin, Raymond Bussieres, Paul Azais, Pierre Gujas (Speva/Paris)

Film is an excellent re-creation of a colorful French period. Brisk in style and full of pictorial interest, it soberly recounts a famous turn-of-the-century love affair. This love, which ends in murder and the guillotine, takes place in the Gallic gangster apache milieu. It has fine atmospheric quality, brilliant thesping and topflight production and technical values.

Based on a true story, it recounts the love of apache moll Marie (Simone Signoret) for the honest, direct and sympathetic Manda (Serge Reggiani). The affair is spiked by the sly, brutal Leca (Claude Dauphin), head of the mob, who wants Marie for himself. Manda, following the apache code, is forced to kill a rival to gain his Marie. Leca has him hauled off to prison on a frame. Manda escapes, and tracks down Leca.

Jacques Becker's direction is perfectly controlled and free of artifice. Signoret gives Marie a cynical, sensual exciting appeal. Reggiani is excellent as the forthright Manda who follows his passion to the guillotine. Dauphin is perfect as the oily Leca who poses as an honest wine merchant while cheerfully masterminding his band of cutthroats. *Casque d'Or* is the gang name for Marie, who wears her golden mane like an old Spanish helmet.

•

CASSANDRA CROSSING, THE
1977, 126 mins, US Ⓥ ▭ col
Dir George Pan Cosmatos ***Prod*** Carlo Ponti ***Scr*** Tom Mankiewicz, Robert Katz ***Ph*** Ennio Guarnieri ***Ed*** Francois Bonnot, Roberto Silvi ***Mus*** Jerry Goldsmith ***Art*** Aurelio Crugnola
Act Sophia Loren, Richard Harris, Ava Gardner, Burt Lancaster, Martin Sheen, Ingrid Thulin (Associated General)

The Cassandra Crossing is a tired, hokey and sometimes unintentionally funny disaster film in which a trainload of disease-exposed passengers lurch to their fate.

One is asked to accept the premise that a terrorist bomber, accidentally exposed to some awesome plague, spreads the disease aboard a European express train. Mismatched leading players, all play directly to the camera, for themselves only, without betraying a hint of belief in their script.

While Richard Harris, cast as a brilliant doctor, is active among those posturing leads on the train, Burt Lancaster and Ingrid Thulin hold down a command post where desperate efforts are made to isolate the train from the rest of civilization.

•

CASS TIMBERLANE
1947, 119 mins, US b/w
Dir George Sidney ***Prod*** Arthur Hornblow, Jr. ***Scr*** Donald Ogden Stewart ***Ph*** Robert Planck ***Ed*** John Dunning ***Mus*** Roy Webb ***Art*** Cedric Gibbons, Daniel B. Cathcart
Act Spencer Tracy, Lana Turner, Zachary Scott, Tom Drake, Mary Astor, Albert Dekker (M-G-M)

Metro has accomplished a highly successful translation to the screen of Sinclair Lewis's bookstore boff [adapted by Donald Ogden Stewart and Sonya Levien]. Lana Turner is the surprise of the picture via her top performance thespically. In a role that allows her the gamut from tomboy to the pangs of childbirth and from being another man's woman to remorseful wife, she seldom fails to acquit herself credibly. Spencer Tracy, as a matter of fact, is made to look wooden by comparison. What fault the picture has is its overlong running time. Director George Sidney is unable to hold the pace for two hours and the film lags in the midsection.

This is a love story all the way. Essentially, it's the tenderness of an older man—41, not too old, of course—for a young girl. Tracy, respected small-town judge, pays tender court to Turner, who's strictly out of his class socially as well as chronologically, until he wins her. She adapts herself to local society and the new life until she thinks she can stand it no more and then is off with the husband's best friend, Zachary Scott. Scott, of course, doesn't want her when he can have her. Tracy's meeting and early courting of the gal is difficult to accept, but once that's passed, the only misgiving is that the yarn telegraphs its punches so far ahead.

•

CAST A GIANT SHADOW
1966, 144 mins, US Ⓥ ▭ col
Dir Melville Shavelson ***Prod*** Melville Shavelson ***Scr*** Melville Shavelson ***Ph*** Aldo Tonti ***Ed*** Bert Bates, Gene Ruggiero ***Mus*** Elmer Bernstein ***Art*** Michael Stringer
Act Kirk Douglas, Senta Berger, Angie Dickinson, Frank Sinatra, Yul Brynner, John Wayne (Mirisch/Llenroc)

Cast a Giant Shadow exemplifies the problems in contemporary film biography, particularly when the subject is less well-known than the events which brought him honor. Some complete fiction and fuzzy composites melodramatize the career of an American Jew who assisted in the fight for the creation of the State of Israel [from the book by Ted Berkman].

Story concerns Col David ("Mickey") Marcus, West Point grad, NY lawyer and cop, and participant in many facets of World War II, who, in the late 1940s, is recruited to volunteer military help in the establishment of Israel, at that time still a dream subject to United Nations equivocation, militant Arab threats and uncertain world support.

Kirk Douglas stars as Marcus in a very good portrayal of a likeable, adventurous soldier-of-fortune who cannot get used to domestic inactivity even when wife Angie Dickinson is sitting by the hearth.

Unfortunately for the overall impact of the film, it is found necessary to go into World War II flashbacks to establish the Marcus character. John Wayne, in one of three featured special appearances, is a composite of every superior officer under whom Marcus served in those days.

•

CASTAWAY
1987, 118 mins, UK Ⓥ ⦿ col
Dir Nicolas Roeg ***Prod*** Rick McCallum ***Scr*** Allan Scott ***Ph*** Harvey Harrison ***Ed*** Tony Lawson ***Mus*** Stanley Myers ***Art*** Andrew Sanders
Act Oliver Reed, Amanda Donohoe, Georgina Hale, Frances Barber (Cannon/United British Artists)

Picture this: London is cold, wet and miserable. What else does a girl do but answer an ad from a man looking for a "wife" to take to a tropical island for a year?

Newcomer Amanda Donohoe spends most of the pic displaying the absence of bikini marks on her body (palm trees always seem to obscure the vital parts of Oliver Reed as Gerald Kingsland), and she copes well with a character whose motives and methods for going to the tiny desert island remain dubious.

Castaway is based on two nonfiction books—Lucy Irvine's version, also called *Castaway*, and Gerald Kingsland's *The Islander*—and tries to tread a path between the two conflicting versions of their sojourn.

Reed gives the performance of his career as a sexually frustrated middle-aged man in search of sun and sex, and is admirably complemented by Amanda Donohoe as the determined, but fickle, object of his lust.

Photography is excellent (especially underwater scenes) but though *Castaway* is a great ad for the tropical Seychelles, it won't be remembered as a Nicolas Roeg classic.

•

CAST AWAY
2000, 143 mins, US Ⓥ ⦿ col
Dir Robert Zemeckis ***Prod*** Steve Sharkey, Tom Hanks, Robert Zemeckis, Jack Rapke ***Scr*** William Broyles Jr. ***Ph*** Don Burgess ***Ed*** Arthur Schmidt ***Mus*** Alan Silvestri ***Art*** Rick Carter
Act Tom Hanks, Helen Hunt, Nick Searcy, Lari White, Michael Forest, Viveka Davis (ImageMovers-Playtone/DreamWorks-20th Century-Fox)

Director Robert Zemeckis and star Tom Hanks take tremendous risks—both dramatic and commercial—and for the most part succeed, in *Cast Away*. In this bold and unique story about a single character stranded on an island, a top-notch Hanks holds the picture on his shoulders with a bravura perf. Meticulous, sumptuous production design and striking visuals compensate for the lack of dramatic momentum in a film that arguably stretches narrative form to its limits.

Hanks plays Chuck, an ambitious FedEx systems engineer. Chuck's fast-paced career takes him to far-flung cities, away from his loving g.f., Kelly (a splendidly understated Helen Hunt). Returning home on a plane, Chuck can't wait to spend New Year's Eve with Kelly. But a mechanical problem causes a terrifying crash, filmed with unprecedented, gritty realism. Chuck is forced to deal with the most basic biological needs. Film plays up well the irony of a career-driven man, used to solving problems, faced with the most urgent problem of all: sheer survival.

Cut to four years later. Tale now finds Chuck trim and muscular, sporting long blond hair and a bushy beard and stripped to a Tarzan-like outfit. Having mastered the four basic needs—food, water, shelter and fire—he begins to deal with his need for companionship. While his memories of Kelly are essential to Chuck's survival, he also establishes an unusual relationship with "Wilson," a volleyball washed ashore. Playing a crucial role, Wilson rescues Chuck from solitude as well as depression. This fellowship also allows Chuck to speak—after an hour's worth of mostly silence.

Pic is replete with ironies and subtle humor. As a FedEx exec, Chuck is dedicated to connecting people all over the world, but the yarn throws him into a situation in which he is disconnected from everything. Moreover, the island's pristine beauty and serenity stand in contrast to Chuck's civilized life. The irony is that for most people the Fiji islands rep tropical paradise, whereas for Chuck they become a prison.

The film revolves around a key question: Once you have learned to survive physically, how do you survive emotionally and spiritually? More problematic is the suggestion that if Chuck hadn't lost everything, he would never have come to understand what's truly important. It's here that the film gets excessively academic and metaphysical. Ultimately, *Cast Away* is about realizing the true meaning of belonging, of finding home, casting away the clutter that complicates life in an effort to rediscover what matters.

Filmed in sequential order, *Cast Away* may be the only pic shot in two parts over 16 months, with a one-year hiatus to allow for Hanks's physical transformation.

•

CASTLE KEEP

1969, 106 mins, US Ⓥ ▭ col

Dir Sydney Pollack ***Prod*** Martin Ransohoff, John Calley ***Scr*** Daniel Taradash, David Rayfiel ***Ph*** Henri Decae ***Ed*** Malcolm Cooke ***Mus*** Michael Legrand ***Art*** Rino Mondellini

Act Burt Lancaster, Patrick O'Neal, Jean-Pierre Aumont, Peter Falk, Scott Wilson, Astrid Heeren (Columbia/Filmways)

Film carries fast and savage action once the actual battle sequences are reached, but it's strictly a conversational war in footage leading up to these moments. Apparent efforts to insert a fresh side of war by concentrating on some of its grim humor act more as a deterrent than a booster to interest. Screenplay is based on William Eastlake's novel *Castle Keep*.

Burt Lancaster is a realistic, one-eyed major who leads a group of eight war-weary infantrymen come to occupy a Belgian castle in 1944 in the Ardennes Forest, which becomes a haven away from war for the men, who get up to all manner of frolics.

Lancaster enacts one of his fast-talking roles with a glib, almost tongue-in-cheek approach, and gets good mileage out of it. Patrick O'Neal as an art-loving captain out to save the treasures of the castle does a good job, as do Jean-Pierre Aumont and Peter Falk.

•

CASTLE OF THE SPIDER'S WEB, THE

SEE: KUMONOSU-JO

•

CASTLE ON THE HUDSON

(UK: YEARS WITHOUT DAYS)

1940, 76 mins, US b/w

Dir Anatole Litvak ***Prod*** Hal B. Wallis (exec.) ***Scr*** Seton I. Miller, Brown Holmes, Courtney Terrett ***Ph*** Arthur Edeson ***Ed*** Thomas Richards ***Mus*** Adolph Deutsch ***Art*** John Hughes

Act John Garfield, Ann Sheridan, Pat O'Brien, Burgess Meredith, Jerome Cowan, Henry O'Neill (Warner)

This is another in the extended series of Warners features based on Warden Lewis E. Lawes's *20,000 Years in Sing Sing*. It's a routine prison melodrama.

John Garfield is a tough, smart-alec gangster who draws a 25–30 year stretch in Sing Sing for knocking over a jewelry store. While he combats the discipline inside the "castle", his loyal girlfriend (Ann Sheridan) tries to effect his release. She is seriously injured in an auto crackup, which gives the parole-minded and humane warden (Pat O'Brien) a chance to let Garfield loose on honor system to see the girl.

Nothing unusual about Anatole Litvak's direction, except that he keeps the yarn moving at a speedy pace. Garfield reads his lines with overemphasis, and is grooved in a routine portrayal. O'Brien is okay as the warden, while Sheridan provides a strong characterization as the gangster's girl. Burgess Meredith is fine in the prison scenes, but is bumped off after piloting a daring break.

•

CASUAL SEX?

1988, 97 mins, US Ⓥ ⊙ col

Dir Genevieve Robert ***Prod*** Ilona Herzberg ***Scr*** Wendy Goldman, Judy Toll ***Ph*** Rolf Kestermann ***Ed*** [uncredited] ***Mus*** Van Dyke Parks ***Art*** Randy Ser

Act Lea Thompson, Victoria Jackson, Stephen Shellen, Jerry Levine, Andrew Dice Clay, Mary Gross (Jascat/Universal)

Scripters have moved the setting of their stage version from the loose environs of a Club Med–type playground to a health and fitness resort—the Oasis [and added a question mark at the end of the title]. Now it's Lea Thompson and Victoria Jackson huffing and puffing through exercises as the excuse to meet an athletic guy who they suppose will have equally healthy attitudes about sex in these precarious times.

They spend a lot of time talking about the joys and disappointments of sex and how much each of them—especially Thompson as the formerly promiscuous Stacy—misses the occasional romp in the sack. With the late 1980s sensibility, their sex conversations are peppered with the girls' finding their own identities in relationships with men outside the sex act. Is it mature? Yes. Is it funny? No.

Andrew Dice Clay stands out as the Italian palooka from Jersey with the thick *New Yawk* accent and equally unsophisticated approach to the opposite sex. Stephen Shellen and Jerry Levine, objects of desire for Thompson and Jackson respectively, are typecast as nice, dumb jocks and Oasis exercise instructors.

All of the inventiveness on this subject comes through when the girls' imaginations take over and director Genevieve Robert makes more of these diversions than any other.

•

CASUALTIES OF WAR

1989, 113 mins, US Ⓥ ⊙ ▭ col

Dir Brian De Palma ***Prod*** Art Linson, Fred Caruso ***Scr*** David Rabe ***Ph*** Stephen H. Burum ***Ed*** Bill Pankow ***Mus*** Ennio Morricone ***Art*** Wolf Kroeger

Act Michael J. Fox, Sean Penn, Don Harvey, John C. Reilly, John Leguizamo, Thuy Thu Le (Columbia)

A powerful metaphor of the national shame that was America's orgy of destruction in Vietnam, Brian De Palma's film deals directly with the harrowing rape and murder of a Vietnamese woman by four GIs.

Journalist Daniel Lang's account of the actual 1966 atrocity first appeared in 1969 as a *New Yorker* article and was later reprinted in book form.

Screen newcomer Thuy Thu Le is the Vietnamese woman kidnapped by a reconnaissance patrol as what the deranged sergeant (Sean Penn) calls "a little portable R&R to break up the boredom, keep up morale." When the men are through using her sexually, they stab and shoot her to death, over the futile objections of the lone holdout, a "cherry" private played by Michael J. Fox.

Casting Fox was a brilliant coup on De Palma's part, since he brings with him an image of all-American boyishness and eager-beaver conservatism. Fox's beautifully acted cowardly passivity in the face of the unthinkable challenges and implicates the viewer to examine his own conscience on the subject of Vietnam.

Wolf Kroeger's production design turns the Thailand locations into a convincing evocation of Vietnam's Central Highlands in 1966.

•

CAT AND THE CANARY, THE

1939, 72 mins, US Ⓥ b/w

Dir Elliott Nugent ***Prod*** Arthur Hornblow, Jr. ***Scr*** Walter De Leon, Lynn Starling ***Ph*** Charles Lang ***Ed*** Archie Marshek ***Mus*** Ernst Toch ***Art*** Hans Dreier, Robert Usher

Act Bob Hope, Paulette Goddard, John Beal, Douglass Montgomery, Gale Sondergaard (Paramount)

In *Canary* Bob Hope carries a straight dramatic characterization, with comedy quips and situations dropping into the plot naturally to accentuate the laughs.

Paulette Goddard gets her first co-star billing, displaying confidence and assurance in her role as the heir to the eccentric millionaire's fortune.

To provide chills and thrills, prospective heirs to the fortune assemble at the bayou home of the deceased 10 years after his death. Will is read, leaving estate to Goddard, when spooky manipulations start from strange sources. There's the low-key lighting, eerie music, and secret passages—all utilized to fullest extent to accentuate the chiller aspect of the piece. After three murders during the night, Hope solves the mystery—but only after Goddard has been placed in constant jeopardy.

Script [from the play by John Willard] is a well-knit and workmanlike job of writing.

•

CAT BALLOU

1965, 97 mins, US Ⓥ col

Dir Elliot Silverstein ***Prod*** Harold Hecht ***Scr*** Walter Newman, Frank R. Pierson ***Ph*** Jack Marta ***Ed*** Charles Nelson ***Mus*** Frank DeVol ***Art*** Malcolm Brown

Act Jane Fonda, Lee Marvin, Michael Callan, Dwayne Hickman, Nat "King" Cole, Stubby Kaye (Columbia)

Cat Ballou spoofs the Old West, whose adherents take their likker neat, and emerges middlingly successful, sparked by an amusing way-out approach and some sparkling performances.

Cat is a girl—Jane Fonda—and she's a young lady (educated to be a schoolteacher) vendetta-minded in Wyoming of 1894 when town baddies murder her father for his ranch. She turns into a rootin', tootin', lovin' gunlady, rounds up a gang of devoted followers and stages a train holdup, getting away with a payroll fortune, and holes up in the old Hole in the Wall outlaw lair.

Script juggles the elements of the Roy Chanslor novel producing a set of characters who fit the mood patly. A novel device has Stubby Kaye and Nat "King" Cole as wandering minstrels of the early west, telling the story of the goings-on via a flock of spirited and tuneful songs composed by Mack David and Jerry Livingston.

Fonda delivers a lively interpretation as Cat. Lee Marvin doubles in brass, playing the gunman who shoots down her father and the legendary Kid Shelleen, a terror with the gun, whom she earlier called in to protect her father. In latter character, Marvin is the standout of the picture.

1965: Best Actor (Lee Marvin)

NOMINATIONS: Best Adapted Screenplay, Editing, Adapted Music Score, Song ("The Ballad of Cat Ballou")

•

CAT CHASER

1989, 88 mins, US Ⓥ col

Dir Abel Ferrara ***Prod*** Peter Davis, William Panzer ***Scr*** James Borrelli, Elmore Leonard, Alan Sharp ***Ph*** Anthony Richmond ***Ed*** Anthony Redman ***Mus*** Chick Corea ***Art*** Dan Leigh

Act Peter Weller, Kelly McGillis, Charles Durning, Frederic Forrest, Tomas Milian, Juan Fernandez (Vestron/Whiskers)

Cat Chaser is another example of how difficult it is to transform a sharp and racy novel into a classy movie. Despite a fine cast and atmospheric direction by Abel Ferrara, the pic [from the novel by Elmore Leonard] doesn't quite make the grade, though it certainly is worth a look.

Peter Weller plays Miami hotel owner George Moran who fought during the American intervention of Santo Domingo. Years later he is drawn back to try and find the woman who taunted him with the name *Cat Chaser*.

He instead is joined by Mary (Kelly McGillis). Ensuing affair convinces Mary that she must end her marriage. Unfortunately she is married to Tomas Milian, former head of the Santo Domingo secret police, who has other thoughts on the matter.

Weller is fine as the intelligent, self-contained hero, but best of all is McGillis, seemingly relishing the part of a sexually charged femme fatale. Charles Durning, as always, gives the pic a dose of class, and manages to make his manipulative killer vaguely charming. Frederic Forrest, however, blusters badly and thankfully comes to a sticky end halfway through.

•

CATCHFIRE

1991, 98 mins, US Ⓥ ⊙ col

Dir Alan Smithee [= Dennis Hopper] ***Prod*** Dick Clark, Dan Paulson ***Scr*** Rachel Kronstadt Mann, Ann Louise Bardach ***Ph*** Ed Lachman ***Ed*** David Rawlins ***Mus*** Curt Sobel ***Art*** Ron Foreman

Act Dennis Hopper, Jodie Foster, Dean Stockwell, Vincent Price, Fred Ward, Joe Pesci (Vestron/Precision)

A quirky comedy-thriller about a hitman who falls for his femme target, scrambled pic [story by Rachel Kronstadt Mann] has an L.A. artiste (Jodie Foster) accidentally witnessing a mob killing when her car breaks down one night. The cops (Fred Ward, Sy Richardson) want her to talk, and the hoods (Joe Pesci, Dean Stockwell, Vincent Price) want her dead. So she dons a blond wig and an alias and goes AWOL.

Meanwhile, Pesci hires a top-league hitman (Dennis Hopper) to do the job his own goons can't, and after months of tracking her around the States finally runs her aground in an ad agency.

Hopper "kidnaps" his quarry, possesses her for himself, and the dynamic duo set of on a weird road-movie-to-nowhere, with the mob and the law in hot pursuit.

Somewhere in here is a dark, sassy picture, but final product is more like a jigsaw with half the pieces. Pic was lensed in L.A., Seattle and Taos, NM, in summer 1988 under Hopper's direction and the title *Backtrack*. After postproduction squabbles (reportedly over Hopper's three-hour cut), he opted for the Director's Guild of America moniker "Alan Smithee."

Apart from Foster, who's strong, shrewd and sexy, thesping is vaudeville all the way. Pesci rants and raves, Stockwell shows a nice line in low-key comedy, Ward looks like he hasn't been shown the whole script, and Hopper has a go at Humphrey Bogart in shades.

●

CATCH ME A SPY
1971, 94 mins, UK/France Ⓥ col
Dir Dick Clement ***Prod*** Steven Pallos, Pierre Braunberger ***Scr*** Dick Clement, Ian La Frenais ***Ph*** Christopher Challis ***Ed*** John Bloom ***Mus*** Claude Bolling ***Art*** Carmen Dillon
Act Kirk Douglas, Marlene Jobert, Trevor Howard, Tom Courtenay, Patrick Mower, Bernadette Lafont (Ludgate/Pleiade/Capitole)

Catch Me a Spy is a straightforward spy thriller. Gimmicks are out but the whole has been put over with tongue-nicely-in-cheek and an impish sense of humor. The cast play their parts for all they are worth.

Kirk Douglas, a smuggler of literary works from Iron Curtain countries, is mistaken for a spy and gets involved in devious situations. Most are provided by Marlene Jobert who resides with a rakish British cabinet minister (Trevor Howard) and is games mistress at a boys' school. Tom Courtenay is the counter-espionage officer who is helplessly inept.

It is all highly improbable and involved but thanks to lively performances and Dick Clement's sharp direction, interest is continually held. The whole is climaxed with an exciting speedboat chase.

●

CATCH-22
1970, 121 mins, US Ⓥ ⊙ ▭ col
Dir Mike Nichols ***Prod*** John Calley, Martin Ransohoff ***Scr*** Buck Henry ***Ph*** David Watkin ***Ed*** Sam O'Steen ***Mus*** [none] ***Art*** Richard Sylbert
Act Alan Arkin, Martin Balsam, Richard Benjamin, Art Garfunkel, Jack Gilford, Buck Henry (Paramount)

Catch-22 stumbles its way through distended burlesque, and contrived stylism to its ultimate root theme: antisocial nihilism.

Alan Arkin heads a large cast of familiar names, playing characters scooped from Joseph Heller's famed novel by adapter Buck Henry. Low, cheap comedy mingles nervously with slick, high-fashion technical polish in a slow-boiling stew of specious philosophy and superficial characterization.

A technical filmmaking brilliance plus a few effective low-comedy gags constitute the pic's assets. Its major liabilities are the script and the directorial concept.

Arkin is Captain Yossarian, the generally reactive character who perceives all the sham and hypocrisy around him; befuddled laundry officer Bob Newhart, elevated to bewildering status as a squadron leader; urbane operations officer Richard Benjamin; simpering medic Jack Gilford; hard-boiled, sex-teasing nurse Paula Prentiss; and Norman Fell, as the good-ole-sarge type.

●

CATCH US IF YOU CAN
(US: HAVING A WILD WEEKEND)
1965, 91 mins, UK/US Ⓥ b/w
Dir John Boorman ***Prod*** David Deutsch ***Scr*** Peter Nichols ***Ph*** Manny Wynn ***Ed*** Gordon Pilkington ***Art*** Tony Woollard
Act Dave Clark, Barbara Ferris, David Lodge, Robin Bailey, Yootha Joyce, David De Keyser (Anglo Amalgamated/Warner)

Apparently producer David Deutsch's idea was to try for the same success formula that made *A Hard Day's Night* more than just a film about a rock 'n' roll group. He hasn't been too successful in trying to turn the Dave Clark Five into actors but has, as cinematic insurance, packed enough action into his "chase" film to keep older members of the audience from squirming.

Dinah (Barbara Ferris), a pretty blond model, is bored with her career and talks Steve (Clark) into escaping with her for a few days. The other members of the quintet, and, shortly thereafter, the rest of the cast, follow in quick pursuit. Her manager (David Lodge) tells the press that she has been kidnapped.

The pair, after losing their car, are picked up by a strange couple (Robin Bailey and Yootha Joyce) with whom the youngsters attend a costume ball before the chase resumes.

The musical five do eight tunes as background music. Cameraman Manny Wynn, who did some beautiful work on *Girl with Green Eyes*, provides some fresh views of the English countryside. Editing and sound recording are poor.

●

CATERED AFFAIR, THE
1956, 92 mins, US Ⓥ b/w
Dir Richard Brooks ***Prod*** Sam Zimbalist ***Scr*** Gore Vidal ***Ph*** John Alton ***Ed*** Gene Ruggiero, Frank Santillo ***Mus*** Andre Previn ***Art*** Cedric Gibbons, Paul Groesse
Act Bette Davis, Ernest Borgnine, Debbie Reynolds, Barry Fitzgerald, Rod Taylor, Robert Simon (M-G-M)

The Bronx bourgeoisie, represented by the Irish Hurley family, is the chief concern of this little comedy-drama originally teleplayed by Paddy Chayefsky, and now put into screen form by Gore Vidal, also from TV for Metro production. The entertainment is mild.

Overall, the performances are good and there are occasionally amusing and touching moments in the otherwise talky, mostly drab, affair under Richard Brooks' direction.

The dramatic to-do set up by the plot whirls around Ma Hurley's decision to give her daughter a catered wedding, overruling the daughter's objections and overwhelming the meager savings of taxi-driving Pa Hurley. Script has a repetitious quality in the spate of pros and cons unloosed.

Dominant emotion aroused is one of feeling sorry for everyone concerned, but principally for the daughter (Debbie Reynolds) and her fiancé (Rod Taylor), both of whom handle their characters very well. As the mother (played on TV by Thelma Ritter), Bette Davis is consistent in performance, if not with her dialect, and proves a strong force on the drama side of the film. Ernest Borgnine's scenes as the father have less force, with the exception of the moment when he tells his side of a weary marriage to his nagging spouse.

●

CAT FROM OUTER SPACE, THE
1978, 103 mins, US Ⓥ col
Dir Norman Tokar ***Prod*** Ron Miller, Norman Tokar ***Scr*** Ted Key ***Ph*** Charles F. Wheeler ***Ed*** Cotton Warburton ***Mus*** Lalo Schifrin ***Art*** John B. Mansridge
Act Ken Berry, Sandy Duncan, Harry Morgan, Roddy McDowall, McLean Stevenson, Jesse White (Walt Disney)

Cartoonist Ted Key turns to noodling over a spaceship commanded by a cat, forced to land on earth for emergency repairs. For help, the cat turns to a likeable physicist, Ken Berry, to help him get $120,000 in gold needed to repair his saucer in time to rendezvous with the space fleet.

Before long, Berry's girlfriend, Sandy Duncan, and buddy McLean Stevenson are in on the problem and planning to parlay the cat's extraterrestrial powers into a series of winning bets with bookie Jesse White. But veterinarian Alan Young mistakenly puts pussy to sleep in the middle of the wagering.

The fun, as usual with Disney pix, comes in the believable sight gags provided along the way. Also as usual, it's a good cast of veterans and nothing to tax them beyond their abilities, all ably kept in pace by director Norman Tokar.

●

CATHERINE THE GREAT
SEE: THE RISE OF CATHERINE THE GREAT

●

CATHY'S CHILD
1979, 89 mins, Australia col
Dir Donald Crombie ***Prod*** Pom Oliver, Errol Sullivan ***Scr*** Ken Quinnell ***Ph*** Gary Hansen ***Ed*** Tim Wellburn ***Art*** Ross Major
Act Michelle Fawdon, Alan Cassell, Bryan Brown, Harry Michael, Anna Hruby, Bob Hughes (CB Films)

Cathy's Child is based on a true story [and the book by Dick Wordley] in which a young Greek mother living in Sydney had her three-year-old daughter abducted by the child's father who returned to Greece with it. The incident was made into a cause célèbre by one of the local afternoon newspapers whose reporters turned the spotlight on bureaucracy's mishandling of the situation.

Michelle Fawdon turns in a super performance as the young migrant mother. To her aid comes battered old pro journalist Wordley (Alan Cassell), who with the help of his tough young city editor forces the story onto the front page. Bryan Brown is a standout as the embittered editor who some years before had been through a similar experience.

Production values are excellent for the budget of less than $800,000, with shooting on location in Greece and in the Sydney area. Pic has an undeniable aura of soap opera; but that is no put-down in this case since director Donald Crombie and the players keep interest up even though it's clear there'll be a happy ending come fade-out.

●

CAT ON A HOT TIN ROOF
1958, 108 mins, US Ⓥ ⊙ col
Dir Richard Brooks ***Prod*** Lawrence Weingarten ***Scr*** Richard Brooks, James Poe ***Ph*** William Daniels ***Ed*** Ferris Webster ***Mus*** [uncredited] ***Art*** William A. Horning, Urie McCleary
Act Elizabeth Taylor, Paul Newman, Burl Ives, Jack Carson, Judith Anderson, Madeleine Sherwood (M-G-M/Avon)

Cat on a Hot Tin Roof is an intense, important motion picture. By no means is this a watered-down version, though "immature dependence" has replaced any hint of homosexuality. Motivations remain psychologically sound.

Cat, per Tennessee Williams, is set in the South, but the land is not as decadent as he has so often pictured it. The earth is fertile, the plantation is large and Big Daddy's wealth now amounts to $10 million.

Burl Ives, playing Big Daddy, is unknowingly dying of cancer, and his first son (Jack Carson) is out for more than his share of the estate. He and his obnoxious wife (Madeleine Sherwood) make capital of the problems besetting Big Daddy's favorite son (Paul Newman) and his wife (Elizabeth Taylor), he being a drunk and she being childless. It's an often gruesome, often amusing, battle.

Taylor has a major credit with her portrayal of Maggie. The frustrations and desires, both as a person and a woman, the warmth and understanding she molds, the loveliness that is more than a well-turned nose—all these are part of a well-accented, perceptive interpretation.

Newman plays cynical underacting against highly developed action. His command of the articulate, sensitive sequences is unmistakable, and the way he mirrors his feelings is basic to every scene. Ives, repeating his legit role, is a vibrant and convincing plantation king.

1958: NOMINATIONS: Best Picture, Director, Actor (Paul Newman), Actress (Elizabeth Taylor), Adapted Screenplay, Color Cinematography

●

CAT PEOPLE
1942, 73 mins, US Ⓥ b/w
Dir Jacques Tourneur ***Prod*** Val Lewton ***Scr*** DeWitt Bodeen ***Ph*** Nicholas Musuraca ***Ed*** Mark Robson ***Mus*** Roy Webb ***Art*** Albert S. D'Agostino, Walter E. Keller
Act Simone Simon, Kent Smith, Tom Conway, Jane Randolph, Jack Holt, Alan Napier (RKO)

This is a weird drama of thrill-chill caliber, with developments of surprises confined to psychology and mental reactions, rather than transformation to grotesque and marauding characters for visual impact on the audiences. Picture is well-made on moderate budget outlay.

Story is one of those it-might-happen dramas, if an old Serbian legend be true. Fable has it that women descendants of a certain tribe, when projected into a jealous rage, change into panthers or other members of the cat family for attack, later reverting to human form.

Script, although hazy for the average audience in several instances, carries sufficient punch in the melodramatic sequences to hold it together in good style. Picture is first feature directed by Jacques Tourneur. He does a fine job with a most difficult assignment.

●

CAT PEOPLE
1982, 118 mins, US Ⓥ ⊙ col
Dir Paul Schrader ***Prod*** Charles Fries ***Scr*** Alan Ormsby ***Ph*** John Bailey ***Ed*** Bud Smith ***Mus*** Giorgio Moroder, David Bowie ***Art*** Edward Richardson
Act Nastassja Kinski, Malcolm McDowell, John Heard, Annette O'Toole, Ruby Dee, Ed Begley, Jr. (RKO-Universal)

Paul Schrader's reworking of the 1942 Val Lewton–Jacques Tourneur *Cat People* is a super-chic erotic horror story of mixed impact.

DeWitt Bodeen's original story held that there is a breed of people descended from ancient coupling of women with big cats, and that when one of their number engages in sex, he or she physically reverts to the animalistic state and must kill before becoming human again. It is therefore "safe" to mate only with relatives.

Reunited in New Orleans with her long-lost brother Malcolm McDowell, Nastassja Kinski meets zoo curator John Heard, takes a job there and soon moves into his home.

At the same time, the Louisiana community is being terrorized by a big black panther. Having repressed her sexuality for a long time, Kinski finally gives in to the genuine love of Heard and condemns herself to repeat the pattern of her brother and ancestors.

Kinski was essential to the film as conceived, and she's endlessly watchable.

•

CAT'S EYE
1985, 93 mins, US Ⓥ ⦿ col
Dir Lewis Teague ***Prod*** Martha J. Schumacher ***Scr*** Stephen King ***Ph*** Jack Cardiff ***Ed*** Scott Conrad ***Mus*** Alan Silvestri ***Art*** Giorgio Postiglione
Act Drew Barrymore, James Woods, Alan King, Kenneth McMillan, Robert Hays, Candy Clark (De Laurentiis)

The idea for this three-parter was hatched during Dino De Laurentiis's production of King's *Firestarter*, which also starred little Drew Barrymore. Asked to do another script for Barrymore, King sketched out an idea about a cat who protects a young girl from a threatening troll in her bedroom wall.

Unfortunately, that idea got tacked onto two other King short stories that De Laurentiis had film rights to, *Quitters, Inc.* and *The Ledge*, lighting the fuse for the ultimate bomb.

The three stories just don't connect and efforts to join them never work. However, an excellent roster of talent does try its best.

•

CAT'S PAW, THE
1934, 101 mins, US b/w
Dir Sam Taylor ***Prod*** Harold Lloyd ***Scr*** Sam Taylor ***Mus*** Alfred Newman
Act Harold Lloyd, Una Merkel, George Barbier, Nat Pendleton, Grace Bradley, Alan Dinehart (Lloyd/Fox)

The Cat's Paw is a big departure for Harold Lloyd in that it is the most adult comedy attempted by him yet.

The story is simply a play on the corrupt politics theme. Lloyd, as a missionary's son, visiting his home town in the U.S. after 20 years in China, is picked for a prize sap by the burg's political czars and nominated for mayor as the 1,000-to-1 shot opponent for their own man. But he surprises everybody, including himself, by winning, and the worm keeps on turning until having cleaned up the city 100 percent.

There are some good, substantial laughs along the way, but the roars are few and far between. Script [from a magazine story by Clarence Buddington Kelland] nurses itself for quite a long stretch to build up to the climax.

There's a girl, too, and no more fortunate choice for the part of this smart-cracking cigar counter femme could have been made. Una Merkel plays it expertly. A gem character performance by George Barbier and some polished gangster and gun moll stuff, respectively, from Alan Dinehart and Grace Brinkley, give Lloyd a lot of help in the support line.

•

CATTLE ANNIE AND LITTLE BRITCHES
1981, 97 mins, US col
Dir Lamont Johnson ***Prod*** Rupert Hitzig, Alan King ***Scr*** David Eyre, Robert Ward ***Ph*** Larry Pizer ***Ed*** Robbe Roberts, William Haugses ***Mus*** Sanh Berti, Tom Slocum ***Art*** Stan Jolley
Act Burt Lancaster, John Savage, Rod Steiger, Scott Glenn, Amanda Plummer, Diane Lane (Hemdale)

Cattle Annie and Little Britches is as cutesy and unmemorable as its title. Primary focus falls upon two teenaged girls, the gutsy and rather reckless Amanda Plummer and the more demure Diane Lane, who aspire to become what might be called outlaw groupies.

They get their chance when the Doolin-Dalton gang, headed up by an aging but still vigorous Burt Lancaster, rides into town, Plummer taking up with dashing John Savage and Lane coming under the fatherly wing of Lancaster himself.

The girls more or less get lost in the shuffle, however, during the central stretch of the film, which has Lancaster and his roaming bank robbers pursued by determined lawman Rod Steiger. Story's only potential resonance rests in the mutual respect-hate relationship between these two veterans of the range.

In fact, whole film [from the novel by Robert Ward] washes over the viewer, with no images or moments sticking in the mind. Effect is partially due to director Lamont Johnson's exceedingly distanced visual style.

•

CATTLE QUEEN OF MONTANA
1954, 88 mins, US Ⓥ col
Dir Allan Dwan ***Prod*** Benedict Bogeaus ***Scr*** Robert Blees, Howard Estabrook ***Ph*** John Alton ***Ed*** James Leicester, Carlo Lodato ***Mus*** Louis Forbes ***Art*** Van Nest Polglase
Act Barbara Stanwyck, Ronald Reagan, Gene Evans, Lance Fuller, Anthony Caruso, Jack Elan (RKO)

There are cowboys and Indians in *Cattle Queen of Montana*, good and bad whites, peaceful and renegade Indians, and colorful Technicolor scenery, but all these ingredients fail to make the Benedict Bogeaus production anything more than a listless and ordinary western.

The screenplay [from an original story by Thomas Blackburn] is short on imagination and long on cliche, and what takes place on screen appears all too familiar. In the picture's favor is an attempt to depict the problems of the Redmen in fighting the encroachment of their land by the white settlers. The Indians are not all evil, scalp-hunting devils.

Barbara Stanwyck is the "Cattle Queen" of the story, a gun-totin' hard-ridin' gal determined to establish a Montana ranch stake after her father is killed by the renegades. Ronald Reagan is an undercover army man charged with the duty of ferreting out the element inciting the Indians.

Lance Fuller is the university-educated Indian chief who wants to bring peace to his tribe while Anthony Caruso is the leader of the rebel Indians.

Allan Dwan's direction is slow-moving, and even the action sequences fail to bring out the necessary excitement.

•

CAT-WOMEN OF THE MOON
1953, 64 mins, US Ⓥ b/w
Dir Arthur Hilton ***Prod*** Al Zimbalist, Jack Rabin ***Scr*** Roy Hamilton ***Ph*** William Whitley ***Ed*** John Bushelman ***Mus*** Elmer Bernstein ***Art*** William Glasgow
Act Sonny Tufts, Victor Jory, Marie Windsor, Carol Brewster, Susan Morrow, Bill Phipps (Zimbalist-Rabin)

This imaginatively conceived and produced science fiction yarn [an original story by producers Zimbalist and Rabin] takes the earth-to-moon premise and embellishes it with a civilization of cat-women on the moon. Femmes, 2 million years ahead of Earth's civilization, very nearly wreck the earthmen's plans to return to their home base, in a scheme to fly the rocketship back to Earth themselves and eventually control this orbit. They use Marie Windsor, navigator on the flight, by making contact with her mentally before the constellation jaunt.

Cast ably portray their respective roles. Sonny Tufts is commander of the expedition, Victor Jory his co-pilot, and Bill Phipps and Doug Fowley are other members of party with Windsor. Carol Brewster is head of the cat-women, an enticing wench, and Susan Morrow also scores as a moon femme.

Arthur Hilton makes his direction count in catching the spirit of the theme, and art direction is far above average for a film of this calibre. William Whitley's 3-D photography provides the proper eerie quality.

•

CAUGHT
1949, 88 mins, US Ⓥ b/w
Dir Max Ophuls ***Prod*** Wolfgang Reinhardt ***Scr*** Arthur Laurents ***Ph*** Lee Garmes ***Ed*** Robert Parrish ***Mus*** Frederick Hollander ***Art*** P. Frank Sylos
Act James Mason, Barbara Bel Geddes, Robert Ryan, Ruth Brady, Curt Bois, Art Smith (Enterprise/M-G-M)

Caught is an out-and-out soap opera on film. The performances are top-notch and consistent. So is the direction and physical production dressing. Where film falls down is in the rather ordinary story [from the novel *Wild Calendar* by Libbie Block] that doesn't take to the twists introduced in an effort to lift it above romantic pulp fiction.

It's the saga of the carhop who aspires to marry a millionaire. She goes to a charm school, becomes a model, and meets and marries her man. A life of riches isn't everything, so she gives it up, goes to work in the office of an East Side medico. They fall in love.

The millionaire is better developed than usual in this type story. He's a tall, dark man of many business interests, odd hours, playboy tendencies and a reluctance to wedlock. Robert Ryan plays him to the hilt.

The shopgirl as played by Barbara Bel Geddes is more rounded and without the empty-headedness such characters usually display. James Mason gives an impressive, underplayed characterization to a not-too-impressive role.

•

CAVALCADE
1933, 110 mins, US b/w
Dir Frank Lloyd ***Prod*** [Winfield Sheehan] ***Scr*** Reginald Berkeley, Sonya Levien ***Ph*** Ernest Palmer ***Ed*** Margaret Clancy ***Mus*** Louis de Francesco (dir.) ***Art*** William S. Darling
Act Diana Wynyard, Clive Brook, Una O'Connor, Herbert Mundin, Beryl Mercer, Irene Browne (Fox)

Noel Coward concocted the original stage pageant the film was made from. In that London production it was all Coward. In the filmization Coward steps somewhat into the background.

Very good performances by almost the entire cast, especially the acting job by Diana Wynyard. But above everything recurs the unison and tenseness created by W. R. Sheehan as producer, and Frank Lloyd as director.

Coward's pageant begins at the birth of the 20th century and the beginning of the Boer War. From that it swells along on through three decades, up and through the World War, and to today. Nothing of world importance is lost sight of, including the sinking of the *Titanic*. And through it all is a strong, wistful story of the growth of a family, and the clinging through years of a loving couple.

The first couple of reels, from an American standpoint, at least, seem slow. The establishment of Jane and Robert Marryot (Wynyard and Clive Brook) as the family who are to be watched through 30 years, is a bit slow of development. The first thrill comes at the sailing of the troop ship for Africa. [War scenes by William Cameron Menzies.]

Then, a half reel or so later, an interior of a London music hall, another big scene as the antiquated show is reproduced and then broken up by the audience and actors going wild with enthusiasm at the announcement the war is over. It's the second big scene in the picture, the biggest scene in the original London play, and so well done in the film that from that point on the audience is completely won.

1932/33: Best Picture, Director, Interior Decoration (William S. Darling)

NOMINATION: Best Actress (Diana Wynyard)

•

CB4
1993, 86 mins, US Ⓥ ⦿ col
Dir Tamra Davis ***Prod*** Nelson George ***Scr*** Chris Rock, Nelson George, Robert LoCash ***Ph*** Karl Walter Lindenlaub ***Ed*** Earl Watson ***Mus*** John Barnes ***Art*** Nelson Coates
Act Chris Rock, Allen Payne, Deezer D, Chris Elliott, Phil Hartman, Charlie Murphy (Universal)

Just as *Wayne's World* cashed in lampooning the addled heavy-metal set, this is a rap spoof attempt by another *Saturday Night Live* performer, Chris Rock.

It starts promisingly enough like a hip-hop version of *This Is Spinal Tap*, with Ice-T and Ice Cube among the well-known rappers turning up in interview-style cameos. That tactic is soon abandoned, however, in favor of a long flashback about how the middle-class trio (Rock, Allen Payne and rapper Deezer D) passed themselves off as badass types (CB stands for "cell block") in order to tap into the rap audience, running afoul of the vicious club owner/drug dealer (Charlie Murphy, a dead ringer for younger brother Eddie) who served as their inspiration.

Tamra Davis, a music video director with the well-received feature debut *Guncrazy* on her resume, might have really had something here had she settled on any one of the many paths the movie starts down. [Screen story by Rock and producer Nelson George.]

•

C.C. AND COMPANY
1970, 94 mins, US Ⓥ col
Dir Seymour Robbie ***Prod*** Allan Carr, Roger Smith ***Scr*** Roger Smith ***Ph*** Charles Wheeler ***Ed*** Fred Chulack ***Mus*** Lenny Stack
Act Joe Namath, Ann-Margret, William Smith, Jennifer Billingsley, Don Chastain, Teda Bracci (Avco Embassy/Rogallan)

Joe Namath frolics with Ann-Margret against a sordid milieu of motorbikes and an uneasy riders' commune in *C.C. and Company*.

Namath and Ann-Margret encounter by chance on the road and he rescues her from a rape attempt by a few of his hippie gang. This leads to sex in the raw between him and her as consenting partners, and then, for Namath, some violent clashes with cult leader William Smith.

It's all put together ineffectually with one exception: Smith is impressive as the motorcyclists' guru; he's a big and handsome young guy who knows how to project. Ann-Margret is cute and Namath is clumsy.

•

CECIL B. DEMENTED
2000, 88 mins, US ⦿ Ⓥ col
Dir John Waters ***Prod*** John Fielder, Joe Caracciolo Jr., Mark Tarlov ***Scr*** John Waters ***Ph*** Robert Stevens ***Ed*** Jeffrey Wolf ***Mus*** Zoe Poledouris, Basil Poledouris ***Art*** Vincent Peranio
Act Melanie Griffith, Stephen Dorff, Alicia Witt, Larry Gilliard Jr., Maggie Gyllenhaal, Eric M. Barry (Polar/Artisan)

What seems like the perfect marriage between director and subject yields inconsistent rewards in John Waters' diverting but uneven satire on guerrilla filmmaking. Film terrorist Cecil B. Demented (Stepen Dorff) and his faithful flock, the Sprocket Holes, have infiltrated the Baltimore theater holding the charity premiere of pampered Hollywood star Honey's (Melanie Griffith) latest picture. Planting an arsenal of bombs and weaponry, they seize the building crying, "Power to the people who punish bad cinema," and kidnap Honey, who shrieks, "Call Jack Valenti!"

Back in the Sprockets' hideout, the captive star is introduced to her fellow cast and crew in Cecil's planned movie, *Raving Beauty*. After being subjected to a trashy makeover, Honey shoots the first scene, playing the vengeful wife of a failed art-film exhibitor, who vows to punish supporters of mainstream cinema. Cecil then reveals his vision of "ultimate reality" and his master plan to shoot the rest of the film with real people and real terror. So far so good. But when the crew hits the streets, the idea starts running out of steam, despite no shortage of entertaining gags, industry references and film homages.

The comedy generally is elementary but enjoyable, with the young thesps playing the Sprockets—all of whom have tattoos illustrating their allegiance to filmmakers like Otto Preminger, Andy Warhol, Sam Peckinpah, Kenneth Anger and Rainer Werner Fassbinder—supplying some amusing turns. These include Jack Noseworthy as a hairdresser ashamed of his heterosexuality and Alicia Witt as porn star Cherish. Her All-Anal Movie Marathon—including *Rear Entry*, in which she co-stars with a gerbil—is one of many moments that represent something of a return to the gleeful bad taste of Water's pre-*Polyester* films.

•

CEILING ZERO

1936, 95 mins, US b/w

Dir Howard Hawks ***Prod*** Harry Joe Brown ***Scr*** Frank Wead ***Ph*** Arthur Edeson ***Ed*** William Holmes ***Mus*** Leo F. Forbstein (dir.) ***Art*** John Hughes

Act James Cagney, Pat O'Brien, June Travis, Stuart Erwin, Barton MacLane, Henry Wadsworth (Cosmopolitan/Warner)

All the punch of the original stage play [by Frank Wead] is intact in *Ceiling Zero*. The Broadway stage version, which Warner bankrolled for a moderate success, depended on its dialog and whatever excitement it could steam up through offstage effects. Picture replaces the effects with visible illustration and the difference is considerable and for the better.

James Cagney reverts to the *Public Enemy* days in that he meets violent death at the finish. Up to then, as a daring and not strictly rational flyer, he has been a devil with the ladies, a pilot who loses his license through irresponsible acts and a man who is indirectly to blame for the death of a close friend.

Perhaps 65 of the picture's 95 minutes unfold in the superintendent's office of a commercial airline. It's here that the exciting drama behind the business of peacetime flying is so graphically and compellingly painted.

Structure of the stage play is faithfully followed.

Stuart Erwin as the ill-fated Clarke turns in a trouping job that always equals Cagney and Pat O'Brien, and now and then even transcends theirs. He approaches his big stuff in a quiet manner, but when he gets there he's in. June Travis is a lovely looking girl for the love interest.

•

CELEBRITY

1998, 113 MINS, US Ⓥ ⊙ b/w

Dir Woody Allen ***Prod*** Jean Doumanian ***Scr*** Woody Allen ***Ph*** Sven Nykvist ***Ed*** Susan E. Morse ***Art*** Santo Loquasto

Act Kenneth Branagh, Melanie Griffith, Judy Davis, Charlize Theron, Famke Janssen, Winona Ryder (Sweetland/Miramax)

The spectacle of Kenneth Branagh and Judy Davis doing over-the-top Woody Allen impersonations creates a neurotic energy meltdown in *Celebrity*, a once-over-lightly rehash of mostly stale Allen themes and motifs.

Shooting in b&w for the first time since *Shadows and Fog* (1992), Allen deals again with such subjects as fame and sexual treachery, but in a much less trenchant and amusing way than in his last picture, *Deconstructing Harry*.

Branagh portrays Lee Simon, a feature writer who is doing a story on screen queen Nicole (Melanie Griffith). Thus begins Lee's mostly desultory series of sexual escapades in the wake of his split from his wife, Robin (Judy Davis), a painfully insecure schoolteacher.

First, in a jaw-droppingly sexy appearance, is Charlize Theron as a supermodel who teases Lee all through a night on the town, only to drop him before they get home. Allen's writing of her wildcat character is dead-on. Lee then becomes serious with the pragmatic Bonnie (Famke Janssen), who is on the verge of moving in with him when he suddenly gets something going with Nola (Winona Ryder).

Paralleling Lee's amorous misadventures is Robin's gradual blossoming under the wing of TV producer Tony Gardella (Joe Mantegna), an Italian-American mensch.

Branagh is simply embarrassing as he flails, stammers and gesticulates in a manner that suggests a direct imitation of Allen himself. Davis simply conveys too much intelligence to convince as a hopeless contemporary woman.

By contrast, some of the huge number of supporting players do nicely. Ryder, as an emotionally volatile aspiring actress, registers forcefully in her few scenes. Leonardo DiCaprio, who turns up at the 55-minute mark playing a spoiled young film star throwing a tantrum in a hotel room, is entirely convincing.

•

CELIA

1989, 102 mins, Australia Ⓥ col

Dir Ann Turner ***Prod*** Timothy White, Gordon Glenn ***Scr*** Ann Turner ***Ph*** Geoffrey Simpson ***Ed*** Ken Sallows ***Mus*** Chris Neal ***Art*** Peta Lawson

Act Rebecca Smart, Nicholas Eadie, Maryanne Fahey, Victoria Longley, William Zappa (Seon)

Celia starts out as a likeable family pic about the traumas of a sensitive 9-year-old girl growing up in a Melbourne suburb in the conservative late 1950s. It winds up as something quite different.

Celia, played by Rebecca Smart, is an only child; when she discovers her grandmother's body, it's the first of several traumas. Troubled by nightmares featuring monsters from a book read to her at school, Celia is delighted when newcomers, with three children, come to live next door; and finds Alice (Victoria Longley) far more sympathetic than her own mother.

Trouble is, Alice and her husband are active members of the Communist Party, and before long Celia is forbidden to see her new friends.

The child's other obsession is her pet rabbit. When a national plague of rabbits results in the Victoria state government calling for the handing over of all domestic bunnies, she blames her uncle, the local policeman, for enforcing the law, and when her beloved rabbit dies in Melbourne Zoo, she takes a surprisingly violent revenge.

Smart, on-screen throughout, is effective as the ultimately scary Celia, but the film's best performance comes from Victoria Longley as the warm-hearted neighbor.

•

CELINE AND JULIE GO BOATING

SEE: CELINE ET JULE VONT EN BATEAU

•

CELINE ET JULIE VONT EN BATEAU
(CELINE AND JULIE GO BOATING)

1974, 190 mins, France Ⓥ col

Dir Jacques Rivette ***Scr*** Eduardo De Gregorio, Juliet Berto, Bulle Ogier, Marie-France Pisier, Jacques Rivette ***Ph*** Jacques Renard ***Ed*** Nicole Lubtchansky

Act Juliet Berto, Dominique Labourier, Bulle Ogier, Marie-France Pisier, Barbet Schroeder (Films du Losange)

Jacques Rivette continues with his improvisatory tactics, allowing lead players to invent quite freely and also collab on the script. He mixes a modernized takeoff on *Alice in Wonderland* and a period tale of Henry James for an over indulged, overlong film that has some gem-like moments but also repetitiveness and preciosity.

Film just does not have the sustaining humor and more irrepressible madcap inventiveness to stave off an arbitrary, intellectual heaviness. One day a girl reading a book of magic in the park, Julie (Dominique Labourier), sees a spindly, overdressed girl scuttle by, dropping things. She follows this comic figure, Celine, played with wit by Juliet Berto, loses her but finds her on her doorstep.

This mythomaniac spins all sorts of tales of adventures and trips she obviously never had. But she touches a chord in Julie with one about a house with a strange triangle of two women and a man, a child and an alcoholic nurse.

Besides Berto and Labourier, who alternate some vivid scenes with lesser-endowed ones, Bulle Ogier, Marie-France Pisier and Barbet Schroeder are effective as the ghost-like family doomed to live out their drama for eternity.

•

CELL, THE

2000, 107 mins, US Ⓥ ⊙ ▭ col

Dir Tarsem Singh ***Prod*** Julio Caro, Eric McLeod ***Scr*** Mark Protosevich ***Ph*** Paul Laufer ***Ed*** Paul Rubell, Robert Duffy ***Mus*** Howard Shore ***Art*** Tom Foden

Act Jennifer Lopez, Vince Vaughn, Vincent D'Onofrio, Jake Weber, Dylan Baker, Marianne Jean-Baptiste (Caro-McLeod/Radical Media/New Line)

Commercials and music videos director Tarsem makes a visually striking feature debut that is, however, flawed by weak narrative in *The Cell*, a sci-fi thriller that tries to differentiate itself from the familiar serial killer genre with an intriguing new premise—and lavishly surreal special effects. Jennifer Lopez plays a psychologist who experiments with a radical therapy that enables her to enter and literally experience the unconscious fantasies in a demented murderer's mind. Unfortunately, the elaborate journeys into the brain, which are breathtaking in their own right, overwhelm a slender story that's not particularly suspenseful or involving, resulting in a schizoid movie that's a feast to the eye but not much for the intellect.

For a while, Mark Protosevich's script is chilling in its mixture of the serial killer's psychology with a Jungian interpretation of dreams. Yarn goes one step beyond *Silence of the Lambs*, delving into a killer's most innermost thoughts.

Problem is that the story is told in the first 40 minutes, after which it's all long sequences of visual effects that occupy at least half of the running time. For all their seamless execution, these journeys don't advance the narrative, and at times arrest its dramatic momentum. Indeed, despite its billing as a suspenser, *The Cell* is more effective as sci-fi in the manner of *Strange Days* or *Blade Runner*, futuristic fever dreams whose power lay not in their linear narrative but in the sensory texture of their imagery.

Lopez is more seductive than persuasive as a compassionate therapist, whose empathy is stripped raw and tested when she's forced to experience what a killer feels. Pic gains an enormous boost from its intelligent co-stars.

•

CELLULOID CLOSET, THE

1995, 102 mins, US Ⓥ col

Dir Rob Epstein, Jeffrey Friedman ***Prod*** Rob Epstein, Jeffrey Friedman ***Scr*** Rob Epstein, Jeffrey Friedman, Sharon Wood, Armistead Maupin ***Ph*** Nancy Schreiber ***Ed*** Jeffrey Friedman, Arnold Glassman ***Mus*** Carter Burwell ***Art*** Scott Chambliss (Telling Pictures/HBO)

In Oscar-winning films such as *The Times of Harvey Milk* and *Common Threads: Stories from the Quilt*, documakers Rob Epstein and Jeffrey Friedman have been instrumental in presenting gay-related issues to a wider audience. Looking at depictions of homosexuality in mainstream American movies in *The Celluloid Closet*, they offer an immensely entertaining, galloping reflection on screen perceptions of lesbians and gay men.

Basis for the film is Vito Russo's landmark 1981 book of the same name. Russo, who died in 1991, was one of the people with AIDS focused on in *Threads*.

Narrator Lily Tomlin's intro points out that in one hundred years of movies, homosexuality has been only rarely acknowledged, mostly as something to get laughs, or inspire fear or pity.

During the moral crackdown of the 1920s, censors set about removing any obvious homosexual elements from the movies, but traces often remained. Screen homosexuals then entered a new phase, becoming evil, predatory villains. Moving into the 1950s, the docu heralds the arrival of tough lesbians behind bars and the sleek socialite model, like Lauren Bacall in *Young Man with a Horn*.

As the film moves systematically through each decade and trend, it shows gay visibility metamorphosing and growing. In the interviews, especially notable contributions come from Gore Vidal, Harvey Fierstein, Tom Hanks, Susan Sarandon, and novelist Armistead Maupin, who wrote the narration. Technically, the operation is pristine.

•

CEMENT GARDEN, THE

1993, 105 mins, Germany/UK/France Ⓥ ⊙ col

Dir Andrew Birkin ***Prod*** Bee Gilbert, Ene Vanaveski ***Scr*** Andrew Birkin ***Ph*** Stephen Blackman ***Ed*** Toby Tremlett ***Mus*** Edward Shearmur ***Art*** Bernd Lepel

Act Andrew Robertson, Charlotte Gainsbourg, Alice Coulthard, Ned Birkin, Sinead Cusack, Hanns Zischler (Neue Constantin/Laurentic/Torii)

Gallic star Charlotte Gainsbourg makes a striking English-lingo debut in *The Cement Garden*, a moody, dramatically uneven drama of sibling incest and teenage alienation from British writer Ian McEwan's 1978 first novel.

The movie is a family affair in more ways that one. Director Andrew Birkin (*Burning Secret*) is Gainsbourg's uncle and his son Ned plays Charlotte's youngest brother in the film.

Pic's setting is a lone house amid a concrete wasteland. When the family's stern father (Hanns Zischler) dies of a heart attack, mom (Sinead Cusack) buckles under the strain of rearing her four children and becomes bedridden. When she, too, dies, the elder kids secretly bury her body in a cement box in the cellar to avoid being taken into care.

Left to their own devices, the children start to give freer vent to their sexual confusion. The eldest, Julie (Gainsbourg), 16, plays with the incestuous infatuation of 15-year-old brother Jack (Andrew Robertson), as well as inviting round an elder boyfriend (Jochen Horst).

The pic lacks the straightforward dramatic smarts of Jack Clayton's 1967 *Our Mother's House*, also about moppets hiding their mom's death. Birkin focuses more on the blurred areas between genders, and the vulnerable world of puberty blues.

•

CENTENNIAL SUMMER

1946, 104 mins, US col

Dir Otto Preminger ***Prod*** Otto Preminger ***Scr*** Michael Kanin ***Ph*** Ernest Palmer ***Ed*** Harry Reynolds ***Mus*** Alfred Newman (dir.) ***Art*** Lyle Wheeler, Lee Fuller

Act Jeanne Crain, Cornel Wilde, Linda Darnell, William Bythe, Walter Brennan, Constance Bennett (20th Century-Fox)

Centennial Summer is pleasant musical filmfare, sparked by a lilting Jerome Kern score. Production dress is lavish to point up the period, and direction adopts a leisurely style in welding together the music and story ingredients. It's not a sock film, but easy to take and will please.

The Kern–Oscar Hammerstein II "All Through the Day" is exploited most often in the score, but workouts are also given to Kern–Leo Robin numbers such as "Love in Vain," "The Right Romance" and "Up with the Lark." Film's weakness is lack of top voices to punch the numbers over, but quality of the cleffing makes them stand out regardless. Speciality spot goes to "Cinderella Sue," with lyrics by E. Y. Harburg and sung by Avon Long.

Script is based on Albert E. Idell's novel of the same title. Background is the Centennial celebration held in Philadelphia during the summer of 1876. Plot spreads itself over several angles, projecting both elderly and younger romantic complications that beset members of a Philadelphia railroading family. Papa (Walter Brennan) makes a mild play for his wife's sophisticated sister, and the two girls (Jeanne Crain, Linda Darnell) of the family both chase the same man (Cornel Wilde).

Side issues are papa's desire to interest the railroad president in a newfangled clock he has invented, a young doctor's efforts to win the heart of one of the daughters, and the sophisticated aunty's (Constance Bennett) maneuvering to make things add up right for the Rogers family.

Producer-director Otto Preminger gets the most from the material and players. Color work isn't up to the usual Technicolor standard.

•

CENTRAL DO BRASIL
(CENTRAL STATION)

1998, 110 mins, Brazil/France Ⓥ ⦿ ⊡ col

Dir Walter Salles ***Prod*** Arthur Cohn, Martine de Clermont-Tonnerre ***Scr*** Joao Emanuel Carneiro, Marcos Bernstein ***Ph*** Walter Carvalho ***Ed*** Isabelle Rathery, Felipe Lacerda ***Mus*** Antonio Pinto, Jaques Morelembaum ***Art*** Cassio Amarante, Carla Caffe

Act Fernanda Montenegro, Marilia Pera, Vinicius de Oliveira, Soia Lira, Othon Bastos, Otavio Augusto (Cohn)

A sensitive art film of the old school, *Central Station* is a melancholy Brazilian road movie shot through with gently stressed cultural commentary. Strongly reminiscent of the work of Vittorio De Sica, with whom producer Arthur Cohn worked several times, this handsomely crafted study of a search for family connections and, in a larger sense, personal and national hope, doesn't quite manage the climactic emotional catharsis at which it aims.

Director Walter Salles's first feature, the 1995 *Foreign Land*, played widely on the fest circuit. A former documaker, helmer here sets an intimate story about the often troubled journey of a young boy (Vinicius de Oliveira) and an aging woman (Fernanda Montenegro) against the backdrop of a country in transition.

While well-judged and credibly played, the film drops dollops of meaning that are, if anything, rather too carefully and gingerly planted, leaving nothing to chance in a work that at least partly means to be open to accident and the randomness of human experience.

All the same, the film is affecting and unsentimental in its portrayal of the often grudging relationship between the gruff, callused Dora and 9-year-old Josue, who only abstractly grasps the importance of the search they've undertaken.

•

CENTRAL STATION
SEE: CENTRAL DO BRASIL

•

CENTURY

1993, 112 mins, UK Ⓥ ⦿ col

Dir Stephen Poliakoff ***Prod*** Therese Pickard ***Scr*** Stephen Poliakoff ***Ph*** Witold Stok ***Ed*** Michael Parkinson ***Mus*** Michael Gibbs ***Art*** Michael Pickwood

Act Charles Dance, Clive Owen, Miranda Richardson, Robert Stephens, Joan Hickson, Neil Stuke (BBC/Beambright)

The dawn of a new era imbues Stephen Poliakoff's provocative *Century*. Centered on a time of great strides in scientific and medical discovery, the film seamlessly incorporates such pertinent issues of turn-of-the-century England as race, religion and sexuality.

The film opens on the eve of 1899 in rural England. Reisner (Robert Stephens), a Romanian Jew by way of Scotland, is a prosperous textile mill owner grudgingly tolerated by the local gentry. Reisner's son Paul (Clive Owen) is a recent medical school grad whose position at a London research hospital proves more commendable than tactical.

Nonetheless, Paul emerges as the star medical researcher and confidant of the operation's chief, Mandry (Charles Dance). He also finds romance with Clara (Miranda Richardson), a lab assistant with a veiled past. The turning point occurs when Paul defies Mandry, who he believes is purposely ignoring vital experiments developed by another doctor.

Woven into the moral tale is an unabashed romanticism. The relationship between the two men, Paul's love for Clara and an affection for a time past combine for a breathtaking emotional experience. Handsomely crafted and cleverly adorned, *Century* gives the sense of an honest perspective on the bygone era.

•

CEREMONIE, LA
(A JUDGEMENT IN STONE)

1995, 109 mins, France/Germany Ⓥ col

Dir Claude Chabrol ***Prod*** Marin Karmitz ***Scr*** Claude Chabrol ***Ph*** Bernard Zitzerman, Michel Thiriet ***Ed*** Monique Fardoulis ***Mus*** Matthieu Chabrol ***Art*** Daniel Mercier

Act Isabelle Huppert, Sandrine Bonnaire, Jacqueline Bisset, Jean-Pierre Cassel, Virginie Ledoyen, Valentin Merlet (MK2/France 3/Prokino/Olga/ZDF)

Underscoring the extent to which good help is hard to find, *A Judgment in Stone* is a character-driven tragicomic treat in which a well-to-do family hires a hardworking but withdrawn young maid to tend their isolated manse, with unforeseen results.

The chic Catherine Lelievre (Jacqueline Bisset) hires Sophie (Sandrine Bonnaire) to be the new live-in housekeeper at the large country estate she shares with her well-heeled husband, Georges (Jean-Pierre Cassel), and their adolescent son. Catherine's 20-year-old step-daughter, Melinda (Virginie Ledoyen), sometimes comes to visit.

Sophie is a disciplined cipher but grows agitated—even ornery—when asked to perform certain basic tasks. Her abrupt behavior eventually leads to her dismissal, but not before she's struck up a liberating friendship with Jeanne (Isabelle Huppert), an insolent live wire who runs the village post office.

A natural busybody, Jeanne is as perky and informal as Sophie is stiff and stern. Each woman harbors at least one dark secret.

From the first frames, Claude Chabrol establishes an expectant atmosphere, with ample payoff in the end, updating Ruth Rendell's mid-1960s novel. Performances are on target across the board, with an intelligently cast ensemble and just the right amount of tension in the master-servant equation.

Shot in the dead of winter near Saint-Malo, pic favors a bleak, pale, washed-out look. Pic's French title stems from the fact that, in olden days, an execution for a capital crime was referred to as "the ceremony."

•

CEREMONY, THE

1963, 106 mins, US b/w

Dir Laurence Harvey ***Prod*** Laurence Harvey ***Scr*** Ben Barzman, Laurence Harvey ***Ph*** Brian West ***Ed*** Ralph Kemplen ***Mus*** Gerard Schurmann

Act Laurence Harvey, Sarah Miles, Robert Walker, John Ireland, Ross Martin, Lee Patterson (United Artists)

Ben Barzman's screenplay relates the dreary tale of a man (Laurence Harvey) about to be executed in a Tangier prison for a crime he did not commit, a murder that actually he tried to prevent but for which he is paying the supreme penalty as a kind of scapegoat. An elaborate escape scheme cooked up by his brother (Robert Walker) succeeds, but Harvey then discovers that little brother has been making time with his girl (Sarah Miles).

Concern is never aroused for any of the characters. The audience is thrust into the heart of the situation and never really allowed to get its bearings. The players are all snowed under by ill-defined, unappealing roles and lack of proper direction. *The Ceremony* is a depressingly dark film.

•

CERTAIN SMILE, A

1958, 105 mins, US ⊡ col

Dir Jean Negulesco ***Prod*** Henry Ephron ***Scr*** Frances Goodrich, Albert Hackett ***Ph*** Milton Krasner ***Ed*** Louis Loeffler ***Mus*** Alfred Newman ***Art*** Lyle R. Wheeler, John F. DeCuir

Act Rossano Brazzi, Joan Fontaine, Bradford Dillman, Christine Carere, Eduard Franz, Kathryn Givney (20th Century-Fox)

In the second of Francoise Sagan's novels to be filmed, once again the principal character is a young and attractive girl, only this time the "shocker" involves her weeklong affair with an older man.

Only the very basic elements in the slim Sagan book have been retained in this glossy, emotional yarn. None of the moody disenchantment of the girl in the book comes through and of course the ending has been totally changed. In Sagan's original the heroine blithely continued her affairs both with regular boyfriend and older lover.

As a film *A Certain Smile* is well made, reasonably well acted and quite magnificently photographed. Having so strenuously toned down the amoral aspects of their story, producer and director apparently decided to go whole hog for the visual aspects. As a result, the film abounds with mouth-watering vistas of the French Riviera, which is photographed from every possible vantage point, providing an idyllic setting for the romantic goings-on between Rossano Brazzi and Christine Carere. Scenes in the Paris streets also come alive temptingly.

Carere is charming and petite, turning in a capable performance that's just a shade too much on the wholesome side. Boyfriend Bradford Dillman, also a newcomer, is good-looking in an unconventional way. He does well in a frustrating role. Brazzi is suavely Continental as the middle-aged Don Juan, and wife Joan Fontaine suffers as required by script.

1958: NOMINATIONS: Best Costume Design, Art Direction, Song ("A Certain Smile")

•

CESAR

1936, 170 mins, France Ⓥ ⦿ b/w

Dir Marcel Pagnol ***Prod*** Marcel Pagnol ***Scr*** Marcel Pagnol ***Ph*** Gricha, Willy, R. Ledru ***Ed*** S. de Troye, J. Ginestet ***Mus*** Vincent Scotto ***Art*** M. Brouquier

Act Raimu, Pierre Fresnay, Orane Demazis, Charpin, Andre Fouche, Alida Rouffe (Pagnol)

This last of Marcel Pagnol's trilogy which started with *Marius* and continued with *Fanny* could be cut by almost half without damaging it to any extent.

Marius bathed in Marseilles sunshine. In *Fanny* the mistakes of impetuous youth are straightened, but not without sufferings and self-sacrifices. With *Cesar* we are faced with grown-ups who bear the scars of the lessons they have learned. Pathos caused by exasperated desires not to be frustrated have replaced the youthful recklessness of *Marius* and the noble self-sacrificing ideals of *Fanny*.

Twenty years after he married Fanny (Orane Demazis) and adopted her love child, after she had been abandoned by Marius (Pierre Fresnay), Panisse (Charpin) dies. Fanny has promised the priest who attended Panisse on his deathbed to tell the entire truth to her son who believes Panisse is his real father.

Young man (Andre Fouche) is at first crushed by the revelation, led to believe that Marius, his father, is nothing but a scoundrel. Marius finally comes to Marseilles. In a stormy family explanation all of the dirty linen is washed clean.

Entire story unrolls in endless dialog, which is rendered with tremendous force and emotion by Raimu as Cesar, the father of Fresnay, Demazis and Fouche. Fouche, although handicapped by the presence of veterans of the stage, shows surprising abilities.

•

C'EST ARRIVE PRES DE CHEZ VOUS
(MAN BITES DOG)

1992, 95 mins, Belgium Ⓥ ⦿ b/w

Dir Remy Belvaux ***Prod*** Remy Belvaux, Andre Bonzel, Benoit Poelvoorde ***Scr*** Remy Belvaux, Andre Bonzel, Benoit Poelvoorde, Vincent Tavier ***Ph*** Andre Bonzel ***Ed*** Eric Dardill, Remy Belvaux ***Mus*** Jean-Marc Chenut

Act Benoit Poelvoorde, Remy Belvaux, Andre Bonzel, Jean-Marc Chenut, Alain Oppexxi, Vincent Tavier (Artistes Anonymes)

Reality programming meets *Henry . . . Portrait of a Serial Killer* in *Man Bites Dog*, an offbeat, darkly hilarious portrait of a freelance hit man whose every move is recorded by a documentary film crew. Well served in black & white verite-style lensing, mordant send-up of questionable news-gathering practices was written, produced, directed by and stars a Franco-Belgian trio whose first feature provides clever patter with its splatter.

A youthful hit man (Benoit Poelvoorde) is both a philosopher and a man of action. When he's not killing people (two dozen graphic murders are committed during the film), he plays chamber music and recites poetry. He scares an old woman into cardiac arrest in order to save bullets, then strips the house of hidden cash. In one great bit, he slaughters a rival team of reporters simply because they are using videotape instead of stock film.

With evolving irony, camera crew is not immune to danger or from the seductive lure of the hit man lifestyle. At first reluctant even to dine with their immoral subject, crew graduates to joining in on the gang rape and disembowelment of a woman in her own home. Not for the righteous or the squeamish, irreverent film follows through to its logical conclusion.

•

CET OBSCUR OBJET DU DESIR
(THAT OBSCURE OBJECT OF DESIRE)
1977, 100 mins, France/Spain Ⓥ ⊙ col
Dir Luis Bunuel ***Prod*** Serge Silberman ***Scr*** Luis Bunuel, Jean-Claude Carriere ***Ph*** Edmond Richard ***Ed*** Helene Plemiannikov ***Mus*** [none] ***Art*** Pierre Guffroy
Act Fernando Rey, Carole Bouquet, Angela Molina, Julien Bertheau, Andre Weber, Milena Vukotic (Greenwich/Galaxie/In Cine)

A gem-like, almost hypnotic, tale of an older man's obsession with a young woman. Loosely based on a 19th century book by Pierre Louys, director Luis Bunuel has updated it and put a good part of the action in Paris. The original was set mainly in Spain.

Filmed in France in 1929 by Jacques De Baroncelli with Conchita Montenegro, and as a talkie by Josef von Sternberg, *The Devil Is a Woman* with Marlene Dietrich, plus a modernized one with Brigitte Bardot, *The Woman and the Puppet* by Julien Duvivier, Bunuel's version uses only the intrinsic theme.

When Maria Schneider had to be replaced near the beginning of shooting, Bunuel decided to go back to an old idea of using two girls to play the sex object. One is willowy, lovely French actress Carole Bouquet, and the other more earthy and sensual, Hispano dancer Angela Molina. They interchange at will.

The tale is told by a rich, middle-aged man to fellow travelers on a train. Fernando Rey, a Bunuel regular, is expert as the sadomasochistic rich man who falls madly for his inept new maid. She makes promises but never gives in. In Spain she flaunts a young lover, though she later says she never did anything.

Rey is dubbed by a lead French actor, Michel Piccoli, which removes any Hispano romantics. Bunuel's Oscar-winning *The Discreet Charm of the Bourgeoisie* was about a group which could never quite sit down to eat.

Here a couple can never consummate sexually. Film shows desire accepting any humiliations.

•

CHAD HANNA
1940, 86 mins, US col
Dir Henry King ***Prod*** Nunnally Johnson ***Scr*** Nunnally Johnson ***Ph*** Ernest Palmer, Ray Rennahan ***Ed*** Barbara McLean ***Mus*** David Buttolph ***Art*** Richard Day
Act Henry Fonda, Dorothy Lamour, Linda Darnell, Guy Kibbee, Jane Darwell, John Carradine (20th Century-Fox)

Chad Hanna is descriptive of early 19th century Americana through the eyes of a roving wagon circus through upper New York State. It's from Walter D. Edmonds's *Saturday Evening Post* serial, *Red Wheels Rolling*.

Chad Hanna (Henry Fonda) is a semi-illiterate stable boy along the Erie Canal in the Mohawk Valley region. Enamored of the gaudily dressed circus rider (Dorothy Lamour), he joins the small one-ringer as a roustabout; and finds Linda Darnell along as a runaway from a whip-wielding father. Chad marries Darnell, who has taken spot of chief equestrienne with the show, and in a brief reunion with Lamour realizes he is really in love with his wife.

Mixed in between in liberal sprinklings are the vicissitudes of the circus in wading through financial, opposition and other battles, including the death of the main attraction, a man-eating lion. Both script and direction handle the yarn in leisurely and rather uneventful tempo.

•

CHAGRIN ET LA PITIE, LE
SEE: THE SORROW AND THE PITY

•

CHAINED HEAT
1983, 95 mins, US/W. Germany Ⓥ ⊙ col
Dir Paul Nicolas ***Prod*** Billy Fine ***Scr*** Vincent Mongol, Paul Nicolas ***Ph*** Mac Ahlberg ***Ed*** Nino Di Marco ***Mus*** Joseph Conlan ***Art*** Bob Ziembicki
Act Linda Blair, John Vernon, Sybil Danning, Tamara Dobson, Stella Stevens, Henry Silva (Heat/TAT/Intercontinental)

Chained Heat is a silly, almost campy follow-up to producer Billy Fine's women's prison hit, *The Concrete Jungle*, that manages to pack in enough sex tease and violent action to satisfy undiscriminating action fans.

Linda Blair headlines as Carol, an innocent young girl serving an 18-month stretch in a California prison run by Warden Backman (John Vernon) and Captain Taylor (Stella Stevens), as corrupt a pair as the scripters can imagine. Real power in stir is shared by statuesque Ericka (Sybil Danning) and Duchess (Tamara Dobson), lording it over the white and black prison populations, respectively.

German director Paul Nicolas displays little feel for the prison genre, emphasizing archaic sex-for-voyeurs scenes.

•

CHAIN OF DESIRE
1993, 107 mins, US Ⓥ ⊙ col
Dir Temistocles Lopez ***Prod*** Brian Cox ***Scr*** Temistocles Lopez ***Ph*** Nancy Schreiber ***Ed*** Suzanne Fenn ***Mus*** Nathan Birnbaum ***Art*** Scott Chambliss
Act Linda Fiorentino, Grace Zabriskie, Assumpta Serna, Patrick Bauchau, Seymour Cassel, Malcolm McDowell (Distant Horizon)

A modern *La Ronde* played out under the shadow of AIDS, *Chain of Desire* is an uneven but alluringly sexy melodrama that gets better as it goes along.

Set in contempo New York, mostly downtown, this version introduces a somewhat jaded, bisexual perspective to the tale, but the characters remain vibrantly alive to life's possibilities, at least where the libido is concerned.

Opening has club chanteuse Linda Fiorentino repairing to the solitude of a church after breaking up with a b.f. She is approached by seductive building restorer Elias Koteas, with whom she begins a torrid affair. Koteas's sexy wife, Angel Aviles, works as a maid for depraved millionaire Patrick Bauchau, who tries to get her into the bondage games in which he indulges with Grace Zabriskie. Latter has seen the passion disappear from her marriage to Malcolm McDowell, a TV commentator.

The situations and incidents become more complex and intense once the pic switches into gay and bi territory. It turns out McDowell prefers boys these days.

Straight and gay viewers of both genders will have plenty to feast their eyes upon here, and thesps deliver with relaxed, humorous, knowing performances.

•

CHAIRMAN, THE
(UK: THE MOST DANGEROUS MAN IN THE WORLD)
1969, 104 mins, U.S. Ⓥ ▭ col
Dir J. Lee Thompson ***Prod*** Mort Abrahams ***Scr*** Ben Maddow ***Ph*** John Wilcox ***Ed*** Richard Best ***Mus*** Jerry Goldsmith ***Art*** Peter Mullins
Act Gregory Peck, Anne Heywood, Arthur Hill, Alan Dobie, Conrad Yama, Zienia Merton (20th Century-Fox)

A quality film, made at Pinewood Studios and on location in the Far East, introducing improbable mission wrapped up in such style it becomes engrossing.

Nobel Prize–winning American scientist Gregory Peck, teaching at the University of London, receives a letter from his former instructor, Professor Soong Li (Keye Luke), telling him it would be impossible for Peck to visit Red China.

Since Peck has no intentions of visiting China, he is further mystified when the president urges him to slip out of London and into the Chinese mainland.

Peck is finally convinced when shown food growing in formerly arid or snow-covered areas inside China.

Task of presenting the film [from a novel by Jay Richard Kennedy] on screen was stupendous, and it has been accomplished with imagination and taste. Peck performs well in a part far more demanding than appears on the surface, while Heywood is totally wasted in what is hardly more than a bit part.

•

CHALK GARDEN, THE
1964, 106 mins, UK Ⓥ col
Dir Ronald Neame ***Prod*** Ross Hunter ***Scr*** John Michael Hayes ***Ph*** Arthur Ibbetson ***Ed*** Jack Harris ***Mus*** Malcolm Arnold ***Art*** Carmen Dillon
Act Deborah Kerr, Hayley Mills, John Mills, Edith Evans, Elizabeth Sellars, Felix Aylmer (Quota Rentals)

The Chalk Garden makes no bones about its legit background. Enid Bagnold's drama had a healthy 17 months' run at the Haymarket in 1956 and producer and director have not done much to disguise the original.

Hayley Mills vigorously plays a 16-year-old girl, in some ways perceptive beyond her years. But audiences will feel that a well-applied hairbrush on her derriere could have swiftly ironed out some of the problems that beset her and the surrounding adults.

The child suffers from the feeling that she is not loved. Her mother has remarried and her grandmother is more obsessed with her arid garden. So the confused, unhappy girl grows up in a world of fantasy and lying. Onto the scene comes a mystery woman as governess. Deborah Kerr's background turns out to be that of a woman straight from prison after a suspended sentence for bumping off her stepsister.

On paper, this sounds like a ripe old piece of Victoriana, but curiously it works, largely because of confident, smooth performances by all concerned.

1964: NOMINATION: Best Supp. Actress (Edith Evans)

•

CHALLENGE, THE
1982, 112 mins, US Ⓥ col
Dir John Frankenheimer ***Prod*** Lyle Poncher, Robert L. Posen, Ron Beckman ***Scr*** Richard Maxwell, John Sayles ***Ph*** Kozo Okazaki ***Ed*** Jack Wheeler ***Mus*** Jerry Goldsmith ***Art*** Yoshiyuki Ishida
Act Scott Glenn, Toshiro Mifune, Kay Lenz, Atsuo Nakamura, Calvin Young, Clyde Kusatsu (CBS Theatrical)

Heads seen being split or cut off in swift but bloody close-ups, along with a lot of aesthetic juxtaposition of ancient Japanese manners and architecture versus modern ditto, are the main attractions of John Frankenheimer's *The Challenge*.

Pitted against each other are two brothers (Toshiro Mifune and Atsuo Nakamura) and two swords of the kind that certain Japanese even today believe to have a soul of their own. The good one wants both weapons back at his own home shrine where the true martial arts are trained daily by a minor Kimono-clad army, while the industrialist's army uses guns and breaks all the rules of gamesmanship.

Into all this is lured a young American boxing bum known only as Rick (Scott Glenn). Later, he is solidly serving on the side of old-fashioneds where he finds his various true loves and a new dignity. When the action gets going, aesthetics are thrown to the side and just as well.

Mifune carries himself with eye-twinkling dignity as the good brother. Glenn, with the long donkey face and occasional grin to match, may well prove to be just the star material Frankenheimer thinks he is.

•

CHAMBER, THE
1996, 11 mins, US Ⓥ ⊙ ▭
Dir James Foley ***Prod*** John Davis, Brian Grazer, Ron Howard ***Scr*** William Goldman, Chris Reese ***Ed*** Mark Warner ***Mus*** Carter Burwell ***Art*** David Brisbin
Act Chris O'Donnell, Gene Hackman, Faye Dunaway, Robert Prosky, Raymond Barry, Bo Jackson (Imagine/Universal)

Fifth screen adaptation of John Grisham's writings in three years, *The Chamber* is an intelligently proficient movie that works more effectively as a family drama than a legal thriller. Pic boasts a brilliant turn from Gene Hackman as a death row inmate and a substantial performance from Chris O'Donnell as the idealistic lawyer who defends him.

O'Donnell plays Adam Hall who, in an effort to confront secrets of his family's dark past, decides to represent his grandfather, Klansman Sam Cayhall (Hackman). After a decade on Mississippi's death row, Sam is only 28 days away from his impending execution in "the chamber." A brief flashback reveals Sam's racist crime in 1967, when a bomb he planted caused the death of two Jewish boys, sons of a civil rights worker.

Sam is at first sneeringly dismissive toward the educated rookie. As the days and hours tick away, Adam uses various legal strategies to win clemency for his grandfather, but loses each of his battles. Still, secret digging into the commission report confirms that Sam was not alone.

What's missing in thrills and suspense is more than made up for by the intimacy of character interaction and superlative acting. Hackman dominates every scene he's in, having shed 30 pounds and sporting a credible Southern drawl. Faye Dunaway delivers a touching perf as Sam's daughter, a tortured belle.

•

CHAMP, THE
1931, 85 mins, US Ⓥ b/w
Dir King Vidor ***Scr*** Frances Marion, Leonard Praskins, Wanda Tuchock ***Ph*** Gordon Avil ***Ed*** Hugh Wynn ***Art*** Cedric Gibbons
Act Wallace Beery, Jackie Cooper, Irene Rich, Roscoe Ates, Edward Brophy, Hale Hamilton (M-G-M)

A good picture, almost entirely by virtue of an inspired performance by a boy, Jackie Cooper. There is none of the usual hammy quality of the average child actor in this kid.

What also makes *The Champ* a good talker is a studied, understanding adult piece of work by the costar, Wallace Beery, who had to step to keep up with Jackie, and a Frances Marion original story that isn't bad for a boxing story.

Beery plays a broken-down ex-heavyweight champ. He's anchored in Tiajuana with his kid and a couple of training camp leeches, and training for a comeback between stews. When not stewing he's gambling and the comeback always seems more distant. He wins enough to buy the kid a racehorse. Then he loses the horse in a crap game.

In the attempts of the Champ's former wife and the boy's mother to regain her son there is some menace, though Irene Rich as the mother and Hale Hamilton as her second husband are painted lily-white by the script.

1931/32: Best Actor (Wallace Beery), Original Story

NOMINATIONS: Best Picture, Director

•

CHAMP, THE
1979, 121 mins, US Ⓥ ⦿ col
Dir Franco Zeffirelli ***Prod*** Dyson Lovell ***Scr*** Walter Newman ***Ph*** Fred J. Koenekamp ***Ed*** Michael J. Sheridan ***Mus*** Dave Grusin ***Art*** Theoni V. Aldredge
Act Jon Voight, Faye Dunaway, Ricky Schroeder, Jack Warden, Strother Martin, Joan Blondell (United Artists/M-G-M)

Walter Newman's script adroitly updates Frances Marion's original scenario, placing down-and-out boxer Jon Voight as a horse handler in Florida, accompanied by sprig Ricky Schroeder. An inveterate gambler and drinker, Voight doesn't hit the comeback trail until ex-wife Faye Dunaway, now a society matron, reappears to threaten his and Schroeder's buddy-buddy relationship.

Even those unfamiliar with the 1931 pic will feel resonances in the current *Champ* and in this edition Schroeder projects a comparable emotional range and depth.

Most debatable, and in some respects unsettling, aspects of the update concern the Voight-Dunaway characters and relationships.

But Voight, under Italian director Franco Zeffirelli, has adopted an accent and outlook that seems at odds with the setting, and seriously weakens the credibility of a relationship between him and the elegant Dunaway.

1979: NOMINATION: Best Original Score

•

CHAMPAGNE FOR CAESAR
1950, 99 mins, US Ⓥ ⦿ b/w
Dir Richard Whorf ***Prod*** George Moskov ***Scr*** Hans Jacoby, Fred Brady ***Ph*** Paul Ivano ***Ed*** Hugh Bennett ***Mus*** Dimitri Tiomkin
Act Ronald Colman, Celeste Holm, Vincent Price, Barbara Britton, Art Linkletter (United Artists)

Champagne for Caesar centers its lampooning on big-time soap companies and the quiz shows that hand out money freely to contestants. Ronald Colman plays an intellectual, a sort of walking encyclopedia who sets out to smash such radio gimmicks and the people who sponsor them.

He gets on Art Linkletter's question-and-answer program after figuring out that show's sponsor is worth about $40 million. Since for each answer the prize is doubled, Colman figures to run it up to the sponsor's value, take over and wipe out the alleged threat to American intellect.

Various styles of comedy range from the quiet statement of the Colman character to the broadly burlesqued soap tycoon portrait drawn by Vincent Price.

•

CHAMPION
1949, 90 mins, US Ⓥ b/w
Dir Mark Robson ***Prod*** Stanley Kramer ***Scr*** Carl Foreman ***Ph*** Franz Planer ***Ed*** Harry Gerstad ***Mus*** Dimitri Tiomkin
Act Kirk Douglas, Marilyn Maxwell, Arthur Kennedy, Paul Stewart, Ruth Roman (Screen Plays)

Adapted from a Ring Lardner short story of the same title, *Champion* is a stark, realistic study of the boxing rackets and the degeneracy of a prizefighter.

Fight scenes, under Franz Planer's camera, have realism and impact. Unrelenting pace is set by the opening sequence.

Cast, under Mark Robson's tight direction, is fine. Kirk Douglas is the boxer and he makes the character live. Second honors go jointly to Arthur Kennedy, the fighter's crippled brother, and Paul Stewart as the knowing manager.

Where the Lardner story made the boxer a no-good from the start, Foreman's screenplay casts him as an appealing Joe in the earlier reels. Already stuck with a persecution complex because of his boyhood poverty, it doesn't take long for him to become a real heel.

1949: Best Editing

NOMINATIONS: Best Actor (Kirk Douglas), Supp. Actor (Arthur Kennedy), Screenplay, B&W Cinematography, Scoring of a Dramatic Picture

•

CHAMPIONS
SEE: THE MIGHTY DUCKS

•

CHANCES ARE
1989, 108 mins, US Ⓥ ⦿ col
Dir Emile Ardolino ***Prod*** Mike Lobell ***Scr*** Perry Howze, Randy Howze ***Ph*** William A. Fraker ***Ed*** Harry Keramidas ***Mus*** Maurice Jarre ***Art*** Dennis Washington
Act Cybill Shepherd, Robert Downey, Jr., Ryan O'Neal, Mary Stuart Masterson, Christopher McDonald, Josef Sommer (Tri-Star)

Here comes *Chances Are* and there goes Mr. Jordan, no doubt in a huff. While this new pic hinges on the same cloud-carpeted conception of heaven as a way station for earthbound souls, the similarity ends there, and a potentially charming premise yields only a handful of chuckles.

The plot hangs on the death of Cybill Shepherd's husband, who flees heaven to be reincarnated before being "inoculated" to prevent a return of past-life memory. He comes back 23 years later as Robert Downey, Jr., and stumbles into the life of Corinne (Shepherd), as well as that of her daughter, Miranda, (Mary Stuart Masterson) and husband's former best friend, Philip (Ryan O'Neal). Philip harbors a long-suffering adoration for Corinne, who has kept him at arm's length.

There's a nice scene when Alex (Downey) first comes to dinner and starts to remember his past life, but from then on the screenplay is patently predictable. Downey sparkles at times simply with his stunned expressions. Beyond that, the rest of the characters are at best absurd: Masterson throws herself at Downey instantaneously.

•

CHANG
1927, 70 mins, US Ⓥ ⦿ ⊗ b/w
Dir Merian C. Cooper, Ernest B. Schoedsack ***Prod*** Merian C. Cooper, Ernest B. Schoedsack ***Ph*** Ernest B. Schoedsack
Act Kru, Chantui, Nah, Ladah, Bimbo (Paramount)

Even before going into details on *Chang* [Thai for "elephant"], mention must be made of the camerawork, primarily the photography, fine under the conditions it must have been taken in and around, and the apparent danger the cameramen seemingly and continuously exposed them to.

Every kind of wild animal is here. Most of them come head-on to the camera, many at close range. With the elephants, a camera or two must have been buried.

As a picture, however, and a wild animal film, the elephant portion is but its biggest incident. Towering above all else as an animal picture is a melodramatic story of native life in the jungle.

Chang is the first animal picture having a scenario and with just an immense jungle for the background. It carries more of a thrill than the other pictures of its sort, for there seems danger frequently and the ferocity of a tiger or leopard here and there is most realistic.

1927/28: NOMINATION: Best Artistic Quality of Production

•

CHANGELING, THE
1980, 107 mins, Canada Ⓥ col
Dir Peter Medak ***Prod*** Joel B. Michaels, Garth H. Drabinsky ***Scr*** William Gray, Diana Maddox ***Ph*** John Coquillon ***Ed*** Lou Lombardo, Lilla Pedersen ***Mus*** Rick Wilkins ***Art*** Trevor Williams
Act George C. Scott, Trish Van Devere, Melvyn Douglas, John Colicos, Jean Marsh, Barry Morse (Michaels-Drabinsky)

The Changeling is a superior haunted house thriller. The story [by Russell Hunter] centers on George C. Scott, a recently widowed music professor, who has moved to Seattle to forget his personal tragedy. His new residence is an old home owned by the local historic society. After moving in, the house begins to do strange things.

It turns out that the noisy spirit is a young, sickly boy who was murdered at the turn of the century. The child's father could not collect an inheritance unless the boy reached the age of 21. After the murder a changeling was put in the boy's place. The changeling is still alive and the dead child wants to wreak his vengeance on him.

Scott and Melvyn Douglas (as a powerful industrialist) register the strongest performances with Trish Van Devere as coming off rather wooden.

•

CHANGE OF SEASONS, A
1980, 102 mins, US Ⓥ col
Dir Richard Lang [Noel Black] ***Prod*** Martin Ransohoff ***Scr*** Erich Segal, Ronni Kern, Fred Segal ***Ph*** Philip Lathrop ***Ed*** Don Zimmerman ***Mus*** Henry Mancini ***Art*** Bill Kenney
Act Shirley MacLaine, Anthony Hopkins, Bo Derek, Mary Beth Hurt, Michael Brandon, Ed Winter (Film Finance/Ransohoff)

It would take the genius of an Ernst Lubitsch to do justice to the incredibly tangled relationships in *A Change of Seasons*, and director Richard Lang is no Lubitsch. The switching of couples seems arbitrary and mechanical, and more sour than amusing.

Shirley MacLaine emerges as the most sympathetic person in the film, the wife of college professor Anthony Hopkins, whose philandering with coed Bo Derek shatters the complacency of their marriage. MacLaine retaliates by taking a young lover (Michael Brandon) and they all head off on a Vermont skiing vacation together in a dubious demonstration of open-mindedness.

Derek and Hopkins romp in slow-motion in a hot tub but that's about all the sexual charge the film carries. Hopkins comes off as a totally self-centered boor who never engages audience sympathy.

•

CHAN IS MISSING
1982, 80 mins, US Ⓥ b/w
Dir Wayne Wang ***Prod*** Wayne Wang ***Scr*** Wayne Wang, Isaac Cronin, Terrel Seltzer ***Ph*** Michael Chin ***Ed*** Wayne Wang ***Mus*** Robert Kikuchi-Yngojo
Act Marc Hayashi, Wood Moy, Laureen Chew, Judy Nihei, Peter Wang (Wang)

Rather roughly lensed in b&w and 16mm tale traces the odyssey of two San Francisco Chinese taxi drivers as they search for an older partner who's vanished with their funds. As in Antonioni's *L'Avventura*, the object of their quest is never found, but suspense in this regard couldn't be further from the point.

Instead, Chan's relatives, local businessmen, politicos and citizens-at-large who are interviewed by the pair constitute a fascinating and often amusing gallery of portraits of contempo Chinese Americans.

Jo, the elder cabbie who serves as narrator, is like a solid working stiff of any race. His youthful cohort, Steve, seems to have fashioned his looks after Burt Reynolds, hiply speaks in a sort of black jive lingo and has little patience for the caution, moderation and discretion widely found in the older generations of Chinese immigrants.

Any filmmaker who can so thoroughly force the viewer to look at the world through his eyes possesses a talent to reckon with.

•

CHANT OF JIMMIE BLACKSMITH, THE
1978, 122 mins, Australia Ⓥ ▭ col
Dir Fred Schepisi ***Prod*** Fred Schepisi ***Scr*** Fred Schepisi ***Ph*** Ian Baker ***Ed*** Brian Kavanaugh
Act Tommy Lewis, Freddy Reynolds, Ray Barrett, Jack Thompson, Peter Carroll, Elizabeth Alexander (Film-house/Australia Party)

Fred Schepisi, for his second film, reveals a sure hand, a dynamic thrust in using a true turn-of-the-century happening [from a book by Thomas Keneally] to delve into the racism of the times against aborigines and the beginnings of governmental federation of its many regions.

The tale of a mulatto aborigine, raised by a Methodist minister, and torn between his people and his Christian teachings, has sweep and interesting insights into the loss of the aboriginal culture and the life of a man who does not belong to either culture anymore.

Tommy Lewis, a non-actor, is well utilized as Jimmie Blacksmith. He works for a white family who allow him to build a hut for his family. When there is no food and no pay, he and his uncle go to the house, where the men are absent. The refusal of food leads to a sudden explosion of all the smoldering resentments and they slaughter the wife, two teenage daughters, a schoolteacher living with them and a young boy. The violence is instinctive, harrowing but not exploited. It is masterfully handled by Schepisi. Jimmie and his brother leave the old uncle and the wife and child and go on the lam as a great manhunt begins.

•

CHAPLIN
1992, 144 mins, US Ⓥ ⊙ col
Dir Richard Attenborough ***Prod*** Richard Attenborough, Mario Kassar ***Scr*** William Boyd, Bryan Forbes, William Goldman [Tom Stoppard, Diana Hawkins] ***Ph*** Sven Nykvist ***Ed*** Anne V. Coates ***Mus*** John Barry ***Art*** Stuart Craig
Act Robert Downey, Jr., Dan Ackroyd, Geraldine Chaplin, Kevin Dunn, Anthony Hopkins, Moira Kelly (Carolco/Canal Plus/RCS Video)

Like a stone skipping across the top of a deep, turbulent sea, *Chaplin* runs through the dramatic highs and lows in the life of the screen's foremost comic genius without stirring the water much.

Telling the entire story of Charles Chaplin's 88 years was probably a hopeless goal for a feature-length film, but Richard Attenborough's latest epic biopic [from Chaplin's *My Autobiography* and David Robinson's *Chaplin: His Life and Art*] does offer the saving grace of an uncanny, truly remarkable central performance by Robert Downey, Jr. and a number of lovely moments along the way.

Attenborough attempts to relate the whole of Chaplin's exceedingly eventful life—his impoverished London East End childhood, early success in vaudeville, quick rise to the top in movies, troubles with wives, young girls and the law, banishment from the U.S., European exile and eventual return to Hollywood in triumph.

As time goes on, the story structure becomes a matter of connecting the historical dots. Douglas Fairbanks (Kevine Kline, perfect) and Mary Pickford are brought on, but not a word is said of United Artists; Chaplin offends J. Edgar Hoover at a dinner party, and the FBI chief hounds him forever after; wives and girls come and go.

In a novel casting stroke, Geraldine Chaplin strongly etches her own grandmother's maternal love and incipient madness. Dan Ackroyd as comedy king Mack Sennett; Moira Kelly as both Chaplin's first love and last, Oona O'Neil; Penelope Ann Miller as his first leading lady, Edna Purviance; Paul Rhys as brother Sydney; John Thaw as music hall impresario Fred Karno—all ring as true as actors can in this sort of enterprise.

NOMINATIONS: Best Actor (Robert Downey, Jr.), Original Score, Art Direction

•

CHAPMAN REPORT, THE
1962, 125 mins, US col
Dir George Cukor ***Prod*** Richard D. Zanuck ***Scr*** Wyatt Cooper, Don M. Mankiewicz ***Ph*** Harold Lipstein ***Ed*** Robert Simpson ***Mus*** Leonard Rosenman ***Art*** Gene Allen
Act Efrem Zimbalist, Jr., Shelley Winters, Jane Fonda, Claire Bloom, Glynis Johns, Ray Danton (Warner)

The Chapman Report is a talky melodramatization of several abnormal patterns in the sexual behaviour of the upper-middle-class American female. The scenario, from an adaptation by Grant Stuart and Gene Allen of Irving Wallace's novel, attempts the feat of dramatically threading the stories of four sexually unstable women together who become voluntary subjects for a scientific sex survey conducted by a noted psychologist and his staff.

One (Claire Bloom) is a hopeless nympho and alcoholic. Another (Jane Fonda) suffers from fears of frigidity. The third (Glynis Johns), a kind of comedy relief figure, is an intellectual who feels there may be more to sex than she has realized in her smugly satisfied marital relationship. The last (Shelley Winters) enters into a clandestine extramarital affair with an irresponsible little theatre director.

Johns does the best acting in the film, rising above the flimsiest of the four episodes with a spirited and infectious performance. Fonda seems miscast and is affected and unappealing in her role. Bloom suffers up a storm. Winters plays with conviction. The men are all two-dimensional pawns.

•

CHAPTER TWO
1979, 124 mins, US Ⓥ ⊙ col
Dir Robert Moore ***Prod*** Ray Stark ***Scr*** Neil Simon ***Ph*** David M. Walsh ***Ed*** Michael A. Stevenson ***Mus*** Marvin Hamlisch ***Art*** Gene Callahan
Act James Caan, Marsha Mason, Joseph Bologna, Valerie Harper, Judy Farrell, Debra Mooney (Columbia)

Chapter Two represents Neil Simon at his big-screen best. Film version of his successful and loosely autobiographical play is tender, compassionate and gently humorous all at once. Marsha Mason's tremendous performance under Robert Moore's sensitive direction gives the pic another boost.

Simon, producer Ray Stark and Moore, in their third film collaboration, have dared to alter the entire focus of the legit version of *Chapter Two*, by subtly but inalterably concentrating on Jennie MacLaine, the actress being wooed by author Schneider, rather than Schneider himself. Result is to downplay the unusual casting of James Caan as Schneider (the choice still pays off richly), and affords Mason the opportunity for her best-realized film work to date.

1979: NOMINATION: Best Actress (Marsha Mason)

•

CHARACTER
SEE: KARAKTER

•

CHARADE
1963, 113 mins, US Ⓥ ⊙ col
Dir Stanley Donen ***Prod*** Stanley Donen ***Scr*** Peter Stone ***Ph*** Charles Lang, Jr. ***Ed*** James Clark ***Mus*** Henry Mancini ***Art*** Jean D'Eaubonne
Act Cary Grant, Audrey Hepburn, Walter Matthau, James Coburn, Ned Glass, George Kennedy (Universal)

Basically a suspenser or chase film, *Charade* has several moments of violence but they are leavened with a generous helping of spoofery. Director Stanley Donen plays the taut tale [by Peter Stone and Marc Behm] against a colorful background of witty dialogue, humorous situations and scenic beauty.

While vacationing at a French Alps ski resort, Audrey Hepburn meets Cary Grant casually. Returning to Paris, she finds herself a widow, her husband having been murdered. Aware that her own life may be in danger, she appeals for help to the U.S. Embassy. There she learns that former World War II associates of her husband, his accomplices in the theft of $250,000 in gold, believe that she knows the money's whereabouts. Walter Matthau, her informant, advises her, for her own safety, to find the money (property of the U.S. government) and turn it over to him.

The two stars carry the film effortlessly, with the only acting competition coming from the versatile Matthau. James Coburn, Ned Glass and George Kennedy make an effective trio of villainous cutthroats. Kennedy's fight with Grant on a slippery rooftop is a real gasper.

Fast-paced from the pretitle shot of a body tossed from a train to the finale under a theatre stage, *Charade* seldom falters (amazing, considering its almost two-hour running time). Repartee between the two stars is sometimes subtle, sometimes suggestive, sometimes satirical but always witty.

1963: NOMINATION: Best Song ("Charade")

•

CHARGE OF THE LIGHT BRIGADE, THE
1936, 116 mins, US Ⓥ ⊙ b/w
Dir Michael Curtiz ***Prod*** [Sam Bischoff] ***Scr*** Michel Jacoby, Rowland Leigh ***Ph*** Sol Polito ***Ed*** George Amy ***Mus*** Max Steiner ***Art*** John Hughes
Act Errol Flynn, Olivia de Havilland, Patric Knowles, Henry Stephenson, Donald Crisp, David Niven (Warner)

Warner has turned out a magnificent production in this story [by Michael Jacoby] based on Tennyson's immortal poem and historical facts. Foreword explains that history was consulted for background, but characters and development are fictionized.

Before the climactic sweeping drive of the cavalry there is the dramatic defense of the Chukoti garrison and the ruthless massacre of soldiers, wives and children after they have surrendered. The major who witnessed the slaughter is depicted as switching an order of the British high command. This results in the 600 cavalrymen riding into "the Valley of Death" in the face of cannon fire and a force four or five times their number.

The tremendous sweep of this surging charge constitutes the feature's highlight. It has been skillfully done by means of close-ups, a traveling camera shot depicting the changing pace of the horses as column after column races towards the enemy, and via some truly extraordinary process shots.

The dual love affair, two brothers seeking the hand of the colonel's daughter, is nicely intertwined with the more adventurous moments of the story.

Errol Flynn lives up to the promise of previous film efforts as the youthful major who sacrifices all to avenge the slaughter of his comrades. Donald Crisp is strong in the character portrayal of the colonel.

1936: Best Assistant Director (Jack Sullivan)

NOMINATIONS: Best Score, Sound

CHARGE OF THE LIGHT BRIGADE, THE
1968, 145 mins, UK Ⓥ ⊙ ▭ col
Dir Tony Richardson ***Prod*** Neil Hartley ***Scr*** Charles Wood ***Ph*** David Watkin ***Ed*** Kevin Brownlow, Hugh Raggett ***Mus*** John Addison ***Art*** Edward Marshall, Julia Trevelyan Oman
Act Trevor Howard, Vanessa Redgrave, John Gielgud, Harry Andrews, Jill Bennett, David Hemmings (United Artists/Woodfall)

Thanks mainly to Lord Tennyson's piece of durable doggerel, millions of people have at least a sketchy idea of the historical incident, though director Tony Richardson's treatment is almost disdainfully indifferent to the actual physical charge.

He is more concerned with analyzing the reasons behind one of the most notorious blunders in military history. He's also intent on attacking by ridicule the class war and bigotry of the British mid-19th-century regime, and the futility of the Crimean War as a whole.

Those fascinated by the class distinction, crass stupidity, muddled thinking and old-school tie snobbishness then prevailing will find richness in the earthy screenplay.

Film starts leisurely, carefully building up to the atmosphere of the times. In fact, despite Richardson's frequently lively direction and the brisk, electric editing, the pace of the film is remarkably easygoing, building up in a vague story line to the crass Charge as a finale which comes almost as an anticlimax.

Apart from some masterly directorial touches, Richardson has made clever use of animated sequences wittily drawn by Richard Williams, living caricatures based on broadsides and cartoons of the mid-Victorian period.

They are not only consistently amusing but also deftly link the action, explain the historical background and compress what would be unwieldy scenes into quick, understandable comment.

•

CHARIOTS OF FIRE
1981, 123 mins, UK Ⓥ ⊙ col
Dir Hugh Hudson ***Prod*** David Puttnam ***Scr*** Colin Welland ***Ph*** David Watkin ***Ed*** Terry Rawlings ***Mus*** Vangelis ***Art*** Roger Hall
Act Ben Cross, Ian Charleson, Nigel Havers, Alice Krige, John Gielgud, Lindsay Anderson (Allied Stars/Enigma)

Chariots of Fire, which weaves the stories of two former British track aces who both won major events at the 1924 Paris Olympics, is about the will to win and why. It's also a winner for director Hugh Hudson in his theatrical bow after an apprenticeship in commercials.

The Colin Welland script has a lot to admire in the engrossing way it counterpoints the progress of its two sporting heroes, each driven by impulse that has little to do with mere fame per se and even less with national honor.

Ian Charleson and Ben Cross are both exemplary as the respective super-runners, Eric Liddell and Harold Abrahams, the first a Christian Scot who believes that by winning can he best honor the Lord; the latter an English Jew with a chip on the shoulder for whom overachieving is his ticket to acceptance in a prejudiced society.

What with two social outsiders hogging the glory for dear old Albion, the snobby establishment doesn't come off to raves.

Hudson's direction gets it all together with admirable assurance and narrative style. No arty tricks, no self-conscious posturing. His use of slow motion and freeze-frames for the various racing sequences turns out to be a valid device for sharpening emotional intensity.

1981: Best Picture, Original Screenplay, Score, Costume Design

NOMINATIONS: Best Director, Supp. Actor (Ian Holm), Editing

•

CHARLEY'S AUNT
1941, 90 mins, US b/w
Dir Archie Mayo ***Prod*** William Perlberg ***Scr*** George Seaton ***Ph*** Peverell Marley ***Ed*** Robert Bischoff ***Mus*** Alfred Newman
Act Jack Benny, Kay Francis, Anne Baxter, Edmund Gwenn, Richard Haydn, James Ellison (20th Century-Fox)

Like Niagara Falls, *Charley's Aunt* stands the test of time. Jack Benny playing with enthusiasm and romping merrily and crazily along the route, takes fullest advantage of laugh opportunities.

Under expert direction of Archie Mayo, there's no letdown in the fast pace maintained for rollicking results. Many situations are double-barrelled for laughs—first when the audience is given advance tipoff on what's going to happen; and a roar when it actually occurs. Only deft timing by both director and comedian can achieve that result, and the Benny–Mayo Team works in perfect synchronization.

Picture closely follows the stage farce [by Brandon Thomas] in unfoldment, carrying Oxford background of 1890. Perennial student Benny is forced to masquerade as Charley's rich aunt from Brazil to provide chaperronage while Charley (Richard Haydn) and James Ellison have their girlfriends for lunch and marriage proposals. The old-fashioned female getup tosses Benny into a series of complications that fall on him in torrents.

•

CHARLEY VARRICK
1973, 111 mins, US Ⓥ col
Dir Don Siegel ***Prod*** Don Siegel ***Scr*** Howard Rodman, Dean Riesner ***Ph*** Michael Butler ***Ed*** Frank Morriss ***Mus*** Lalo Schifrin ***Art*** Fernando Carrere
Act Walter Matthau, Joe Don Baker, Felicia Farr, Andy Robinson, John Vernon, Sheree North (Universal)

Charley Varrick is a sometimes-fuzzy melodrama but so well put together that it emerges a hard-hitting actioner with a sock finale.

Based on the John Reese novel *The Looters* narrative carries the unusual twist of Walter Matthau, a small-time bank robber, trying to return his heist of a small-town New Mexico bank after later discovering his $750,000 take belongs to the Mafia and he wants none of it. He is opposed by a young companion who doesn't see eye-to-eye, and menaced by a Mafia hitman who arrives on the scene.

Director Don Siegel overcomes deficiencies in part by his rugged handling of action and making handsome use of the Nevada landscape where pic was filmed and which provided stuntmen with a field day.

Matthau delivers strongly as a man who wants to limit his heisting to small banks because legal heat isn't so hot. Joe Don Baker scores solidly as Mafia man.

•

CHARLIE BUBBLES
1968, 89 mins, UK col
Dir Albert Finney ***Prod*** Michael Medwin ***Scr*** Shelagh Delaney ***Ph*** Peter Suschitsky ***Ed*** Fergus McDonnell ***Mus*** Misha Donat ***Art*** Edward Marshall
Act Albert Finney, Colin Blakely, Billie Whitelaw, Liza Minnelli, Timothy Garland, Richard Pearson (Memorial)

Albert Finney stars as, and makes his directorial debut in, *Charlie Bubbles*. Comedy-drama concerns a materially successful man, fighting vainly the old ennui. Unfortunately, audiences also are bound to experience the same tedium, via underplaying and limp direction. Finney's boredom is shown in biz relations, brief encounter with secretary Liza Minnelli, and disintegrating ties to his estranged wife (Billie Whitelaw) and alienated child (Timothy Garland).

This type screenplay which, essentially, is little more than exposition of a point made obvious in the first 10 minutes, requires direction which is dynamic both physically and artistically. Finney provides little of the required animation, thereby setting a plodding pace. Among the cast, Whitelaw scores best. Minelli gets a trifle cloying, but is okay. Colin Blakely, Finney's booze companion, has some bright moments, and Alan Lake as a pushy hitchhiker, scores neatly.

•

CHARLIE CHAN AT THE OPERA
1936, 62 mins, US Ⓥ ⊙ b/w
Dir H. Bruce Humberstone ***Prod*** John Stone ***Scr*** Scott Darling, Charles S. Belden ***Ph*** Lucien Andriot ***Ed*** Alex Troffey ***Mus*** Samuel Kaylin (dir.)
Act Warner Oland, Boris Karloff, Keye Luke, Charlotte Henry, Thomas Beck, Gregory Gaye (20th Century-Fox)

Chan's interminable saga gets a shot in the arm which effectively dispels any monotony. It is the creation of a co-feature role, with Boris Karloff to play it.

Being set in an opera house, the action [story by Bess Meredyth, based on the Earl Derr Biggers character] is more complicated than in previous Chan stories and serves as an additional befuddlement for the tyro sleuths in the audience. Backstage nooks and crannies furthermore provide the proper spook atmosphere for Karloff to flit around in. As a cross between a madman and an amnesia victim, Karloff plays a role right down his alley. And 20th doesn't let the audience forget who he is. In one place there's a remark to the effect "Who do you think you are, Frankenstein?"

Supporting cast works well, with Margaret Irving as the diva who gets murdered, Nedda Harrigan as the menace, and William Demarest as a dumb cop, drawing the longest footage. [Film's opera, *Carnival*, was created by Oscar Levant, from a libretto by William Kernell.]

•

CHARLIE CHAN AT TREASURE ISLAND
1939, 72 mins, US b/w
Dir Norman Foster ***Prod*** Sol M. Wurtzel ***Scr*** John Larkin ***Ph*** Virgil Miller ***Ed*** Norman Colbert
Act Sidney Toler, Cesar Romero, Pauline Moore, Sen Yung, Douglas Fowley (20th Century-Fox)

In this one, Charlie Chan bumps into a murder mystery involved with the psychic and astrological rackets, and proceeds to unravel the affair at a performance in a Treasure Island (San Francisco Fair) theatre.

Picture is rather slow in spots, but holds up generally to pace set by [some 25] previous Chan adventures to satisfy whodunit fans.

When fiction writer friend of Chan commits suicide on Clipper plane bound for Frisco, Chan interests himself in uncovering the reasons. Trail leads him to Zodiac, a racketeering mystic, who holds clients in his power through threats of blackmail. Chan is assisted by Cesar Romero, operating illusionist theatre at the fair, and Douglas Fowley, reporter exposing rackets of the mystics and astrologists. Chan's No. 2 son, Sen Yung, does much to confuse things.

•

CHARLIE CHAN CARRIES ON
1931, 69 mins, US b/w
Dir Hamilton MacFadden ***Scr*** Philip Klein, Barry Connors ***Ph*** George Schneidermann ***Ed*** Al DeGaetano ***Art*** Joe Wright
Act Warner Oland, John Garrick, Marguerite Churchill, Warren Hymer, Marjorie White, George Brent (Fox)

This story of the Honolulu detective who solves a murder mystery that baffled Scotland Yard and Europe is well directed and aptly photographed. Cast shows smart selection.

What aids the film more than anything is that the mystery angle is kept paramount to the romance in it. This is between Marguerite Churchill and John Garrick, both personable. She is the granddaughter of the wealthy American found dead in a London hotel. Garrick is the companion of the old man. This romance is kept mild and gets its start only after the dead body is discovered by the police. While the romance ends before the mystery, both follow fast to a happy ending with a wisecrack.

The picture is full of wisecracks: the flippant pieces of philosophy spoken by Chan (Warner Oland) in almost doggerel English and the more funny lingo of Warren Hymer, as the Chicago racketeer.

•

CHARLIE CHAN IN EGYPT
1935, 72 mins, US b/w
Dir Louis King ***Prod*** Edward T. Lowe ***Scr*** Robert Ellis, Helen Logan ***Ph*** Daniel B. Clark
Act Warner Oland, "Pat" Paterson, Thomas Beck, Rita Hayworth, Stepin Fetchit, James Eagles (Fox)

Story framed around Earl Derr Biggers's Chinese crime snooper taking a flyer among the tombs of the Pharaohs and the outcome has all that it takes to satiate the general run of mystery addicts. *Charlie Chan in Egypt* combines a suavely sustained concept of drama and another surehanded interpretation of the central role by Warner Oland.

Chan pops up just outside of Luxor shortly after a noted archaeologist has disappeared. From this mysterious incident stems the plot which, before reaching a denouement, accounts for two slayings and a near murder. Chan, whose mission it is to find out for a French museum why objects taken by the missing explorer have found their way into the open market instead of being shipped to France, uncovers the first murder with the aid of an X-ray machine. The body is located in a sarcophagus which is supposed to contain a mummy.

Obsessed with a dread of impending harm are the dead professor's daughter and son, "Pat" Paterson and James Eagles.

Next to Oland's, the standout performance is that of Eagles, whose superstitious fears drive him to near insanity and are brought to an end by his sudden death by a mysterious source.

•

CHARLIE CHAN IN LONDON
1934, 79 mins, US b/w
Dir Eugene Forde ***Prod*** John Stone ***Scr*** Philip MacDonald ***Ph*** L. William O'Connell ***Mus*** Samuel Kaylin (dir.)
Act Warner Oland, Drue Leyton, Douglas Walton, Alan Mowbray, Mona Barrie, Ray Milland (Fox)

As mystery stories go this is well above average. The most conspicuous item about *London* is that, although it is not by the creator of the Chan series, the tempo is so well imitated by scenarist Philip MacDonald it would pass for an original Earl Derr Biggers composition. For Warner Oland the Chan role is now second nature.

Most of the action takes place on luxurious interior sets of a wealthy country home in England. The story takes advantage of the locale to inject a fox hunt, which adds color without being superfluous. Just who committed the murder is not paid off in any detail until the last reel. While the cast is well chosen its members are so completely subjugated to Chan's importance that they impress collectively rather than as individual players.

•

CHARLIE CHAN IN SHANGHAI
1935, 70 mins, US b/w
Dir James Tinling ***Prod*** John Stone ***Scr*** Edward T. Lowe ***Ph*** Barney McGill
Act Warner Oland, Irene Hervey, Jon Hall, Russell Hicks, Keye Luke, Halliwell Hobbes (Fox)

Charlie Chan is in Shanghai this time. Strange that a film starring the Chinese detective has never been set there before, but that oversight is patched up very nicely in this film. It's right in line with the eight previous Chan pictures.

Warner Oland, the merry Swede who has won himself an international rep as a Chinaman, still handles the Chan assignment with competence and ease. This time he's after a gang of dope smugglers in China. Keye Luke is cast as his son and gets in some nice laughs.

•

CHARLIE CHAN ON BROADWAY
1937, 68 mins, US b/w
Dir Eugene Forde ***Prod*** John Stone ***Scr*** Charles Belden, Jerry Cady ***Ph*** Harry Jackson ***Ed*** Al De Gaetano ***Mus*** Samuel Kaylin (dir.)
Act Warner Oland, Keye Luke, Joan Marsh, J. Edward Bromberg, Douglas Fowley, Harold Huber (20th Century-Fox)

Entry in the Charlie Chan Chinese sleuth series provides an opportunity for the Oriental Sherlock to perform his deductions while a guest of the New York police force. Chan uncovers the killer of two people mixed up in the big city's mob.

Some of the plausible deductions lend more credibility than usual to this typical yarn. Art Arthur, Robert Ellis and Helen Logan combined forces on the original story.

Chan is again faithfully personated by Warner Oland, with just as much interest as ever being shown in his clever portrayal. Keye Luke again is the effervescent son, with the lad even better than before if only because he does more things in his usual enthusiastic style. Joan Marsh makes a pert, candid-camera freelancer among the dailies, though the slight love interest she shows for the columnist is blotted out at the close. Harold Huber's conception of a police inspector is crisp and characteristic if a little too brusque.

•

CHARLIE CHAN'S CHANCE
1932, 73 mins, US b/w
Dir John G. Blystone ***Scr*** Barry Connors, Philip Klein ***Ph*** Joseph August
Act Warner Oland, Alexander Kirkland, H. B. Warner, Marian Nixon, Ralph Morgan, James Kirkwood (Fox)

Earl Derr Biggers's magazine and novel yarns on the subject provide the structure for this chapter, like the others. Biggers also provided the constant philosophical sayings which are delivered through the principal character as a means of sewing the action together and maintaining a regular pace. Chan (Warner Oland) rolls them off his proverbial knife—like "Some heads, like hard nuts, much better if well cracked." In solving the new mystery, Chan has the help of Inspector Fife of Scotland Yard (H. B. Warner) and Inspector Flannery of New York (James Kirkwood). But as far as really helping they're just a couple of stooges.

Another British detective, who gets into the plot as a corpse, is murdered while working on a case in New York. The path to solution is studded with countless false clues and the all-important erroneous arrest of the juve love-interest team (Marian Nixon and Alexander Kirkland). Three people are killed on the way. One is Li Gung (Edward Piel, Sr.), the Chinese accessory to the criminal mastermind. James Todd's too youthful appearance in the heavy role accounts for the picture's chief note of implausibility.

•

CHARLIE'S ANGELS

2000, 98 mins, US Ⓥ ⦿ ⌑ col

Dir Joseph McGinty Nichol ***Prod*** Leonard Goldberg, Drew Barrymore, Nancy Juvonen ***Scr*** Ryan Rowe, Ed Solomon, John August ***Ph*** Russell Carpenter ***Ed*** Wayne Wahrman, Peter Teschner ***Mus*** Edward Shearmur ***Art*** J. Michael Riva

Act Cameron Diaz, Drew Barrymore, Lucy Liu, Bill Murray, Sam Rockwell, Tim Curry (Goldberg-Flower-Tall Trees/Columbia)

"Never send a man to do a woman's job," growls a leather-clad wildcat as she heads off to kick some butt in *Charlie's Angels*, and it's a remark that pretty much sums up the sassy chickpic appeal of this rambunctious, high-octane, latex-thin contempo take on one of the '70s' most popular television series [created by Ivan Goff and Ben Roberts]. Packed with action, attitude, skin-tight costumes and enough dazzling white smiles and slo-mo hair flips for a season's worth of toothpaste and shampoo commercials, this entertaining confection possesses the substance of the TV show, the pacing of a Hong Kong actioner and the production values of a James Bond thriller.

It will be the rare viewer, male and female, who won't enjoy the sheer visual and visceral pleasure of watching Cameron Diaz, Drew Barrymore and Lucy Liu strut, slink, kick, dance and vamp their way through this splashy femme empowerment fantasy. It's the usual potential-end-of-the-world-as-we-know-it action thriller format, this time featuring bad guys brandishing guns and swords being regularly bested by babes blessed with gravity-defying martial-arts skills.

While the spectacle of the three women executing wire-enabled leaps, jumps, flips, kicks and other maneuvers—under the supervision of Cheung-Yan Yuen, the "Master" of *The Matrix* and innumerable Hong Kong actioners' brother—is enjoyable, it's nothing that's not been seen before and has not been shot and, particularly, edited for maximum effectiveness. Script is divided into three half-hour segments, each with its own climax, which gives the picture the feel of three TV episodes played back-to-back, not a bad thing under the circumstances.

Of the three women, Diaz is indisputably the dazzler; with her long limbs, beach-blonde hair, lagoon-blue eyes, mile-wide smile and shimmying booty, she all but pops off the screen as if in 3-D, and rarely has a performer conveyed the impression of being so happy to be in a particular movie. Co-producer Barrymore attractively plays the most sexual of the threesome in a way that's both teasing and demure. Liu's approach is more serious and conventional and therefore makes less of a distinctive impression.

Above all, first-time feature director McGinty Nichol (a commercials and music video whiz kid) supplies the action with endless juice. But he also knows how to frame and move the camera, and the pedal-to-the-metal approach is what's called for given that the material is as substantial as Perrier bubbles.

•

CHARLOTTE'S WEB

1973, 93 mins, US Ⓥ ⦿ col

Dir Charles A. Nichols, Iwao Takamoto ***Prod*** Joseph Barbera, William Hanna ***Scr*** Earl Hamner, Jr. ***Ph*** Roy Wade, Dick Brundell, Ralph Miglioro, Dennis Weaver, George Epperson ***Ed*** Larry Cowan, Pat Foley ***Mus*** Irwin Kostal (sup.) ***Art*** Bob Singer, Ray Aragon, Paul Julian (Hanna-Barbera/Sagittarius)

Charlotte's Web is a saga of a little white porker named Wilbur—petrified with fear he's fated to become a slab of tender bacon—and Charlotte, the benevolent spider, who saves him from this fate through the magic weaving in her web. Based on the E. B. White children's classic, the Hanna-Barbera animated musical [with music by Richard M. and Robert B. Sherman] is heartwarming entertainment.

Described by the author as a tale of "friendship and salvation, a story of miracles—the miracle of birth, the miracle of friendship, the miracle of death," the premise is adroitly and charmingly caught. Debbie Reynolds is heard as the voice of Charlotte, Henry Gibson as Wilbur, Paul Lynde as Templeton, the gluttenous, grouchy rat, and Agnes Moorehead is a stuttering and diligent goose. Rex Allen acts as narrator.

Animation is imaginative and clever and interest is sustained as tale builds to its climax.

•

CHARLY

1968, 103 mins, US Ⓥ ⦿ col

Dir Ralph Nelson ***Prod*** Ralph Nelson ***Scr*** Stirling Silliphant ***Ph*** Arthur Ornitz ***Ed*** Fredric Steinkamp ***Mus*** Ravi Shankar ***Art*** Chas Rosen

Act Cliff Robertson, Claire Bloom, Leon Janney, Lilia Skala, Dick Van Patton, Ed McNally (Selmur)

Charly boasts a most intriguing premise—a variation on the Pygmalion theme in which a mentally retarded adult "grows up" as the result of a brain operation.

Recognizing that this idea [from the short story and novel *Flowers for Algernon* by Daniel Keyes] could be developed along several different lines, producer-director Ralph Nelson and screenwriter Stirling Silliphant try them all, with the result that *Charly* merges a peculiar combination of sentimentalized documentary, romance, science fiction and social drama.

Instead of frittering away time on an unmotivated romance, it would have been interesting if the reasons for this psychologically complicated affair were explored.

Considering the innumerable stumbling blocks, cast does well. Cliff Robertson seems to overdo the external manifestations of retardation, but he is excellent in the post-operative scenes. With more help from the script he could have been a movingly tragic figure.

1968: Best Actor (Cliff Robertson)

•

CHARME DISCRET DE LA BOURGEOISIE, LE
(THE DISCREET CHARM OF THE BOURGEOISIE)

1972, 100 mins, France/Spain/Italy Ⓥ ⦿ col

Dir Luis Bunuel ***Prod*** Serge Silberman ***Scr*** Luis Bunuel, Jean-Claude Carriere ***Ph*** Edmond Richard ***Ed*** Helene Plemiannikov ***Mus*** [none] ***Art*** Pierre Guffroy

Act Fernando Rey, Delphine Seyrig, Stephane Audran, Jean-Pierre Cassel, Paul Frankeur, Bulle Ogier (Greenwich/Jet/Dean)

Luis Bunuel adds another fine film to his solid record with this surrealistically oriented tale of so-called bourgeois types. Film encompasses South American politics, delves into his usual look at Church clerics, the army, and the monied upper-class that is at once timely and timeless.

A haughty ambassador (Fernando Rey), two fairly rich friends and their relatives come for dinner at a rich couple's home but find it is the wrong day. The husband is not there. Going to a restaurant, they cannot eat there as the owner has just died. Pic looks like a reverse twist on Bunuel's *The Exterminating Angel*, where some well-endowed people sit down to eat at a friend's home but then cannot leave the room.

Dinners are interrupted by a group of soldiers on maneuvers, and terrorists breaking in and slaughtering the main characters. Each major male type has a dream that works into the fabric of the pic.

Bunuel again says this is his last film but, hopefully, he will be talked into more. [His last film was *That Obscure Object of Desire*, 1977.] At 72, he is a youthful filmmaker. His handling of a solid cast is impeccable.

1972: Best Foreign Language Film

•

CHARULATA
(THE LONELY WIFE)

1964, 117 mins, India b/w

Dir Satyajit Ray ***Prod*** R. D. Bansai ***Scr*** Satyajit Ray ***Ph*** Subrata Mitra ***Ed*** Dutal Dutta ***Mus*** Satyajit Ray

Act Soumitra Chatterjee, Madhabi Mukherjee, Sailen Mukherjee, Shyamal Ghoshal, Geetali Roy (Bansai)

Possibly more relaxed and leisurely than most Satyajit Ray films, *Charulata* nevertheless has a graciousness and dignity which impart an added sincerity to the simple, yet thoroughly acceptable story.

It is the style that counts as Ray unfolds his story of a successful publisher, whose main interest is interpreting the political scene, while his intelligent wife vegetates by doing embroidery. Eventually, he realizes his responsibility to the woman he sincerely loves but neglects, and invites his brother-in-law and wife as houseguests. Another visitor is a handsome cousin.

Inevitably, the lonely wife and the handsome cousin are drawn to each other, but always maintain an appropriate degree of restraint. The period, after all, is 1879.

The director keeps dialog down to a minimum, allowing the camera to be the main storyteller, and it emerges as a typical example of unhurried filmmaking. The principal performances are universally good, Soumitra Chatterjee making a striking impression as the cousin. Ray's script, based on a novel by Rabindranath Tagore, is literate.

•

CHASE, THE

1946, 86 mins, US Ⓥ b/w

Dir Arthur Ripley ***Prod*** Seymour Nebenzal ***Scr*** Philip Yordan ***Ph*** Franz Planer ***Ed*** Edward Mann ***Mus*** Michel Michelet ***Art*** Robert Usher

Act Robert Cummings, Michele Morgan, Peter Lorre, Steve Cochran (United Artists)

The Chase is a meller that's taut as sprung steel for 75 minutes of its running time then slackens limply into the commonplace. Yarn [from the novel *The Black Path of Fear* by Cornell Woolrich] concerns the attempt of a killer's wife and his chauffeur to make their getaway from his household and henchman.

Through a series of adroit directorial strokes, in the Hitchcock tradition, the pic's momentum is made to mount in a steady, ascending line. Terror stalks the pair in their flight to Havana then explodes with the shocking stillness of a gun with a silencer on it.

Robert Cummings handles himself nicely but, though he tops the cast, is overshadowed by the dominating personality and looks of a newcomer, Steve Cochran, who plays the killer. Cochran is handsome, suave, confident, and menacing in the manner of a Humphrey Bogart. Peter Lorre, in one of his best roles, comes through with a solid assist as the killer's aide-de-camp. Michele Morgan registers nicely, although she isn't given much to do besides modeling a few flashy gowns.

•

CHASE, THE

1966, 138 mins, US Ⓥ ⦿ ⌑ col

Dir Arthur Penn ***Prod*** Sam Spiegel ***Scr*** Lillian Hellman [Horton Foote] ***Ph*** Joseph LaShelle [Robert Surtees] ***Ed*** Gene Milford ***Mus*** John Barry ***Art*** Richard Day

Act Marlon Brando, Jane Fonda, Robert Redford, James Fox, E. G. Marshall, Angie Dickinson (Horizon/Columbia)

Only the framework of Horton Foote's [1956] novel (but little of his [1952] play, which preceded it) has been utilized by Lillian Hellman in her screenplay. The original plot centered on an escaped convict seeking revenge on the sheriff who had sent him up but Hellman makes them only two of the many characters with which she has populated her sociologically sick Texas town.

Through introduction of various other types she manages to provide most of the social grievances which trouble the world today.

Robert Redford, as the escaped convict whose impending return to his hometown gives many of its citizens the jitters, gives the film's best performance. Marlon Brando, in the comparatively small but important role of the sheriff, has obviously given much time and study to the part, but such detailed preparation as a carefully delivered Texas accent means little when other cast members read their lines with a mixture of regional accents.

Jane Fonda, as Redford's wife and the mistress of wealthy oilman James Fox, makes the most of the biggest female role.

•

CHASE, THE

1994, 88 mins, US Ⓥ ⦿ col

Dir Adam Rifkin ***Prod*** Bard Wyman, Cassian Elwes ***Scr*** Adam Rifkin ***Ph*** Alan Jones ***Ed*** Peter Schink ***Mus*** Richard Gibbs ***Art*** Sherman Williams

Act Charlie Sheen, Kristy Swanson, Henry Rollins, Josh Mostel, Wayne Grace, Rocky Carroll (Capitol/20th Century-Fox)

Call this *The Getaway Lite*. Despite considerable energy and occasional laughs, this latest effort from youthful writer-director Adam Rifkin too often feels like it was written by Beavis and Butthead.

Presented virtually in real time, the story shifts into gear immediately, as an escaped convict (Charlie Sheen) kidnaps the heiress to a Donald Trump–type fortune (Kristy Swanson) in a convenience store and takes off for Mexico in her shiny red BMW. Virtually the rest of the action, believe it or not, has them in that car, as the two build a grudging relationship, with the police—as well as local TV stations—in hot pursuit.

Rifkin takes refuge from that claustrophobia sparingly, cutting back and forth to a police car occupied by two officers who are involved in the chase, a *Cops*–style film crew and, most effectively, the various media vultures trying to cash in on the story.

For the most part, however, *The Chase* goes nowhere, wearing out its welcome with music-video techniques and an equally repetitive, percussive score.

While adorable, Swanson doesn't benefit from the whining Valley girl aspects of her role, which could easily be characterized as *Buffy, the Hostage*. On the flip side, Sheen continues to strike the same sullen, Jack Nicholson–wannabe pose he's employed with varying degrees of success. Tech credits are generally subpar.

•

CHASE A CROOKED SHADOW
1958, 92 mins, UK b/w
Dir Michael Anderson ***Prod*** Douglas Fairbanks, Jr. ***Scr*** David D. Osborn, Charles Sinclair ***Ph*** Erwin Hillier ***Ed*** Gordon Pilkington ***Mus*** Matyas Seiber ***Art*** Paul Sheriff
Act Richard Todd, Anne Baxter, Herbert Lom, Alexander Knox, Faith Brook (Associated Dragon/Associated British)

Chase a Crooked Shadow is a glossy, well-directed drama that has its fair quota of absurdities which occasionally strain credulity to the limit. Nevertheless, there are enough twists and artfully planned kicks to keep most audiences guessing.

The yarn concerns Anne Baxter as an heiress who becomes a frightened lady when Richard Todd arrives at her Costa Brava hangout and claims to be her brother, who Baxter knows was killed in a car crash in South Africa a year before. What is the purpose of his visit? Is he a crook? A fortune hunter? Todd builds up so much evidence that even the local chief cop (Herbert Lom) is convinced that his story is true. There begins a nightmare of terror as she believes the plot is to drive her insane and then murder her. Final twist is a sock climax.

Director Michael Anderson carefully builds up the suspense and at one time or other even the most case hardened patron will be wondering about motives and who is really double-crossing who. There are also the advantages of the breathtaking Costa Brava scenery and a rousing racing car sequence. Anderson, an ex-cutter, has edited the film with Gordon Pilkington very ingeniously.

•

CHATO'S LAND
1972, 100 mins, UK Ⓥ col
Dir Michael Winner ***Prod*** Michael Winner ***Scr*** Gerald Wilson ***Ph*** Robert Paynter ***Ed*** Freddie Wilson ***Mus*** Jerry Fielding ***Art*** Manolo Mampaso
Act Charles Bronson, Jack Palance, Richard Basehart, James Whitmore, Simon Oakland, Ralph Waite (Scimitar)

British producer-director Michael Winner in his second western takes a hard look at the early American West and comes up with a violence-drenched meller.

Writer Gerald Wilson, adopting and-then-there-were-none theme, plots an Apache half-breed relentlessly pursued by a ragtag white posse headed by an ex-Confederate officer after the Indian has killed a white sheriff. Charles Bronson portrays the Apache—Chato—and Jack Palance the posse leader.

Action too often slows during an overage of dialog between posse members and an apparent attempt to build characterization defeats its purpose as bickering among posse detracts from the real objective of story.

Narrative is fleshed out when the Indian reverts to a savage vengeful warrior after a few members of posse rape his squaw and the roles of hunter and hunted are reversed.

•

CHATTAHOOCHEE
1989, 103 mins, US Ⓥ ⊙ col
Dir Mick Jackson ***Prod*** Faye Schwab ***Scr*** James Hicks ***Ph*** Andrew Dunn ***Ed*** Don Fairservice ***Mus*** John Keane ***Art*** Patrick Tagliaferro
Act Gary Oldman, Dennis Hopper, Frances McDormand, Pamela Reed, Ned Beatty, M. Emmet Walsh (Hemdale)

Gary Oldman's bravura performance as a victimized patient in a Deep South prison hospital for the criminally insane, circa 1950s, fails to cure the film of its manifold structural and stylistic ills. The tale allegedly is based on a true story of one Chris Calhoun, who could not handle the "expectations" of others when he returned from the Korean War to the Deep South as a "certified hero."

In an opening setup that's frenetically bizarre, Oldman goes berserk one morning, shooting up his small tropical town with a handgun. He is promptly packed off to Chattahoochee, a maximum security hospital for the criminally insane.

The "hospital" is sort of a cross between the Turkish prison barracks of *Midnight Express*, the hard-time joint in *Brubaker* and the good ole' prison farm of *Cool Hand Luke*. Similarities to those three excellent movies end there.

Thoughtless medical bureaucrat Ned Beatty turns aside all complaints of maltreatment. Oldman's bunkmates are maniacs, blithering idiots and worldly wise weirdos like Dennis Hopper and M. Emmet Walsh.

Oldman becomes a jailhouse lawyer, discovers the rule of habeas corpus, and with the help of his steadfast sister (Pamela Reed), eventually gets the governor to investigate.

•

CHE!
1969, 96 mins, US Ⓥ ▭ col
Dir Richard Fleischer ***Prod*** Sy Bartlett ***Scr*** Michael Wilson, Sy Bartlett ***Ph*** Charles Wheeler ***Ed*** Marion Rothman ***Mus*** Lalo Schifrin ***Art*** Jack Martin Smith, Arthur Lonergan
Act Omar Sharif, Jack Palance, Cesare Danova, Robert Loggia, Woody Strode, Barbara Luna (20th Century-Fox)

Producer Sy Bartlett and director Richard Fleischer claimed to have made an "impartial, objective" film [from a screen story by Bartlett and David Kar] about Fidel Castro's Cuban Revolution and of subsequent events in that country. But it's emphatically not true about their viewpoint of Ernesto Che Guevara himself: to them, he was an evil genius who tried to lead Castro down wrong paths, a man whose revolutionary zeal took violent turns which ignored social reality.

As presented, Castro, played smokehouse by Jack Palance, is innocent not only of winning the initial revolution, but also of the deeds afterwards which condemn him in many American eyes. It was Guevara, adequately portrayed by Omar Sharif, who planned the military strategy which resulted in the fall of Havana, who maintained discipline within the rebel forces and who conducted executions after Castro took over.

Pic has been made in a mock-documentary style which comes out poorly. Supposedly, "real" people are being interviewed who are telling Che's story in flashback.

•

CHEAP DETECTIVE, THE
1978, 92 mins, US Ⓥ ⊙ ▭ col
Dir Robert Moore ***Prod*** Ray Stark ***Scr*** Neil Simon ***Ph*** John A. Alonzo ***Ed*** Sidney Levin, Michael A. Stevenson ***Mus*** Patrick Williams ***Art*** Robert Luthardt
Act Peter Falk, Ann-Margret, Eileen Brennan, Sid Caesar, Stockard Channing, James Coco (Columbia)

The Cheap Detective, which might also be called *Son of Casablanca*, is a hilarious and loving takeoff on all 1940s Warner Bros. private eye and foreign intrigue mellers.

The time is 1940, San Francisco, where clumsy gumshoe Peter Falk is accused of murdering his partner, whose wife Marsha Mason (in early Janet Leigh curls) has been Falk's mistress. Detective Vic Tayback and assistants regularly blunder into matters.

Madeline Kahn, with as many smart clothes changes as aliases, appears in Falk's office. She's in league with John Houseman (Sydney Greenstreet to the core), Paul Williams (Elisha Cook Jr was never like this) and Dom DeLuise (a fat Peter Lorre) in search of ancient treasure—a dozen diamond eggs.

Amidst the confusing threads of mystery, Falk is regularly affronted by the overly explicit descriptions of sexual torture inflicted on all the dames. But at fadeout he's got a lot more going for him than Bogart did in the final dissolve.

•

CHECKING OUT
1989, 93 mins, US Ⓥ ⊙ col
Dir David Leland ***Prod*** Ben Myron ***Scr*** Joe Eszterhas ***Ph*** Ian Wilson ***Ed*** Lee Percy ***Mus*** Carter Burwell ***Art*** Barbara Ling
Act Jeff Daniels, Melanie Mayron, Michael Tucker, Kathleen York, Allan Havey (HandMade/Warner)

A dreadfully unfunny one-joke black comedy about hypochondria and mortality, *Checking Out* depends almost entirely for suspense of Jeff Daniels's "Why don't Italians have barbecues?" Sadly, some 90 minutes elapse before he finds out.

In the interim, Daniels, as budget airline executive Ray Macklin, witnesses the death by coronary of his irreverent best buddy, Allan Havey. This trauma triggers the onset of a hysterical, fetishistic hypochondria that propels him through a series of discombobulating misadventures.

Daniels live in a tacky California suburb with wife Melanie Mayron and two kids. The blue-sky normalcy of his middle-class lifestyle is clearly intended to set up a big, soft target for satirical demolition. Potshots also are misfired at American big-business funeral homes, medicine and sexual hypocrisy.

Seeds of a more interesting film are scattered here and there, especially in a dazzingly photographed dream sequence that imagines heaven as a cloyingly hellish redneck cabana club in a desert oasis.

•

CHELSEA GIRLS, THE
1967, 210 mins, US col
Dir Andy Warhol ***Prod*** Andy Warhol
Act Robert Olivio, Ondine, Mary Might, Nico, Ingrid Superstar, Mario Montez (Warhol)

The Chelsea Girls, perhaps the first Underground film to be accorded specifically non-Underground screenings, is a pointless, excruciatingly dull three-and-a-half hours spent in the company of Andy Warhol's friends. Warhol has attempted to counter all conventional methods of filmmaking, and the result is an anti-film or, more accurately, a non-film.

There is no plotline. The single unifying device is that the film takes place in several rooms of a downtown hotel. Typical scenes include a blank-looking blonde trimming and combing her hair, a lesbian bullying her roommates, another lesbian talking endlessly on the phone, a homosexual eating an orange, a middle-aged homosexual and a girl competing for the attentions of a half-nude male, a girl on LSD confessing to a homosexual priest.

•

CHERRY, HARRY & RAQUEL!
1969, 71 mins, US col
Dir Russ Meyer ***Prod*** Russ Meyer ***Scr*** Tom Wolfe, Russ Meyer ***Ph*** Russ Meyer ***Ed*** Russ Meyer, Richard Serly Brummer ***Mus*** William Loose ***Art*** [uncredited]
Act Larissa Ely, Linda Ashton, Charles Napier, Bert Santos, Franklin H. Bolger, Astrid Lillimor (Eve/Panamint)

Film focuses on the narcotics traffic on the Mexican border, where Charles Napier is a sheriff in the pay of the drug operator.

Linda Ashton plays Cherry, his girlfriend, and Larissa Ely portrays Raquel, who takes on all comers. When the two ladies of the title get tired of it all with men, they try some lesbian clinches. Flashes of nudes intersperse the unreeling every minute or so. Maybe they're symbolic; they have no connection with the story.

Meyer inserts plenty of violence in Harry's search for a Yaqui Indian who is leaving the gang for private enterprise. The Yaqui shoots it out with the sheriff in a bloody sequence, and kills a Mexican member of the gang in another bloody encounter after an exciting and suspenseful auto chase. Dialog is on the stag side. Cost was $90,000, up from Meyer's previous $70,000 budgets.

•

CHERRY 2000
1988, 93 mins, US Ⓥ ⊙ col
Dir Steve de Jarnatt ***Prod*** Edward R. Pressman, Caldecot Chubb ***Scr*** Michael Almereyda ***Ph*** Jacques Haitkin ***Ed*** Edward Abroms, Duwayne Dunham ***Mus*** Basil Poledouris ***Art*** John J. Moore
Act Melanie Griffith, David Andrews, Ben Johnson, Tim Thomerson, Harry Carey, Jr., Pamela Gidley (ERP/Orion)

A tongue-in-cheek sci-fi action pic which owes a considerable debt to the *Mad Max* movies, *Cherry 2000*'s greatest asset is top-billed Melanie Griffith, who lifts the material whenever she's on-screen.

Griffith plays E. Johnson, a tracker who lives at the edge of a desert known as the Zone. The year is 2017, and white-collar yuppie Sam Treatwell (David Andrews) seeks Johnson's help in replacing his beloved Cherry 2000 (Pamela Gidley), a robot sex-object who suffered internal meltdown when Treadwell unwisely tried to make love to her in soapsuds. For obscure reasons, replacement Cherry clones are stored far out in the Zone, which is ruled over by the psychotic Lester (Tim Thomerson) and his gang. Bulk of the film [story by executive producer Lloyd Fonvielle] consists of efforts of Johnson and Treadwell to avoid capture by Lester and reach the robot warehouse.

Along the way they meet Ben Johnson as a philosophical old-timer and Harry Carey, Jr., as a treacherous gas-station owner.

Technically, pic is quite lavish and the Nevada locations suitably rugged.

•

CHEYENNE AUTUMN
1964, 161 mins, US Ⓥ ▭ col
Dir John Ford ***Prod*** Bernard Smith ***Scr*** James R. Webb ***Ph*** William Clothier ***Ed*** Otho Lovering ***Mus*** Alex North ***Art*** Richard Day
Act Richard Widmark, Carroll Baker, James Stewart, Edward G. Robinson, Karl Malden, Sal Mineo (Warner)

Cheyenne Autumn is a rambling, episodic account of a reputedly little-known historic Cheyenne Indian migration 1,500 miles through almost unbelievable hardships and dangers to the tribe's home near the Yellowstone in Wyoming. Somewhere in the telling, the original premise of the Mari Sandoz novel is lost sight of in a wholesale insertion of extraneous incidents which bear little or no relation to the subject.

Action follows a small band of Cheyennes attempting to escape from their barren Oklahoma reservation to their own lush Wyoming lands, from which they were transported after having surrendered to the army in 1877. Originally more than 900, their number now has been decimated to 286 through starvation and lack of medical attention.

Richard Widmark in one of his hard-boiled roles is persuasive as a cavalry captain sympathetic to the Indians, detailed to bring them back to the reservation and finally going to Washington to see the Secretary of the Interior in charge of Indian affairs. Gilbert Roland and Ricardo Montalban portray the historic Dull Knife and Little Wolf, leaders of the Cheyennes, and carry off their work with honors. Carroll Baker is somewhat lost as a Quaker schoolteacher who accompanies the Cheyennes because of her love for the children.

James Stewart as Wyatt Earp is in strictly for laughs, not for plot motivation, and Arthur Kennedy also is in briefly as Doc Holliday, neither having much to do. Karl Malden scores as a German captain of U.S. cavalry; Dolores Del Rio plays an Indian woman with conviction; Edward G. Robinson does well by the Interior Secretary part and Patrick Wayne plays a brash young lieutenant with feeling.

1964: NOMINATION: Best Color Cinematography

•

CHEYENNE SOCIAL CLUB, THE

1970, 103 mins, US Ⓥ ⌑ col

Dir Gene Kelly ***Prod*** Gene Kelly ***Scr*** James Lee Barrett ***Ph*** William Clothier ***Ed*** Adrienne Fazan ***Mus*** Walter Scharf ***Art*** Gene Allen

Act James Stewart, Henry Fonda, Shirley Jones, Sue Ane Langdon, Elaine Devry, Jackie Russell (National General)

James Stewart and Henry Fonda are longtime cowpoke buddies, and when the former finds he has inherited from his brother a business in Cheyenne, the latter follows. Turns out the business is the town's pleasure dome, inhabited by Sue Ane Langdon, Elaine Devry, Jackie Russell, Jackie Joseph and Sharon De Bord, under Shirley Jones's supervision. Each girl has her own doorbell signal, so Stewart never can talk to them for long without callers interrupting.

When Stewart learns the truth and plans to shutter the place, the whole male population turns against him, but Fonda works his way through the house, room by room.

The story is a flimsy, one-joke affair, and Gene Kelly's direction is too sluggish to make it perk at the fast pace required to sustain momentum.

•

CHICAGO, CHICAGO

SEE: GAILY, GAILY

•

CHICAGO JOE AND THE SHOWGIRL

1990, 103 mins, UK Ⓥ ⦿ col

Dir Bernard Rose ***Prod*** Tim Bevan ***Scr*** David Yallop ***Ph*** Mike Southon ***Ed*** Dan Rae ***Mus*** Hans Zimmer, Shirley Walker ***Art*** Gemma Jackson

Act Emily Lloyd, Kiefer Sutherland, Patsy Kensit, Keith Allen, Liz Fraser, Alexandra Pigg (PolyGram/Working Title)

Scripter David Yallop was inspired and intrigued by the sensational Hulten/Jones murder case of 1944, which became known as the "Cleft Chin Murder Case" after the disappearance of a London taxi driver. It made household names of American serviceman Karl Hulten and British showgirl Elizabeth Maud Jones, beating war news to the headlines. Shame is Yallop was unable to ignite anything sensational in the finished product.

The trial, which resulted in the hanging of Hulten (the only execution of a Yank by the British) and the reprieve of Jones, is passed up. Yallop instead focuses on duo's six-day London crime spree, beginning with theft of an army truck and a fur, and finishing with murder of the cabbie.

Problem is that Emily Lloyd totally fails to deliver the necessary allurement, and Kiefer Sutherland is weak in playing a weak character. End result is a pair of languid leads fumbling their way through a passionless picture.

Whole pic was shot on sets rather than location, and despite Gemma Jackson's thoughtful designs, the overall look is cheap.

•

CHICKEN RUN

2000, 85 mins, UK/US ⦿ Ⓥ col

Dir Peter Lord, Nick Park ***Prod*** Peter Lord, David Sproxton, Nick Park ***Scr*** Karey Kirkpatrick ***Ph*** David Alex Riddett ***Ed*** Mark Solomon ***Mus*** John Powell, Harry Gregson-Williams ***Art*** Phil Lewis (Aardman/Pathe/DreamWorks)

Chicken Run marks a delightfully clever feature debut by Britain's Aardman team of stop-motion animators that nonetheless doesn't fly quite as high as their justly celebrated shorts or, for that matter, as far as the film's feathered heroes.

In format, *Chicken Run* is like a World War II prison camp thriller in which the inmates plot various rescue attempts before making a spectacular flight for freedom in the end. In this case, however, the cloistered ones are the hens at Tweedy's Egg Farm, who either produce a constant flow of eggs or are served up at dinner.

Chicken Run is always engaging, full of bright humor, marvelous stop-motion work with Plasticine figures, dramatic conflict and wonderfully nuanced characterizations. Latter attribute is particularly notable; it's amazing how expressive of human emotions the filmmakers can make faces composed of such lifeless material. Indeed, the leading characters are given unusually fine shadings for animated creations, which is partly a tribute to the Aardman team's finesse and partly due to the outstanding casting and performances.

Mel Gibson brings his expected energy and an antic, boisterous humour to the cocky Rocky the Flying Rooster, the self-described "lone free-ranger," but the heart of the film is Julia Sawalha's Ginger, a self-sufficient, sometimes officious gal who could probably escape by herself but whose deep concern for her fellow hens compels her to find a way to get everyone out. Jane Horrocks' portly Babs perfectly evokes the complacent, accepting side of chicken life. Miranda Richardson deliciously dishes out Mrs. Tweedy's evil in measured tones, and Benjamin Whitrow, playing an old bird who constantly recalls his glory days with the RAF, represents the film's strongest link to English humor a couple of generations past.

Technical considerations aside, the quasi-historical situation, the mostly subtle quality of the comedy and the tenor of the dialogue in Karey Kirkpatrick's adroit script [from an original story by Peter Lord and Nick Park] give the picture a quaintly '50s feel, which will charm some viewers and no doubt puzzle others. Putting a mild damper on the proceedings is the sometimes dour mood, which plausibly derives from the constant threat hovering over the birds but is also conveyed in dark visuals.

•

CHIENNE, LA

1931, 95 mins, France Ⓥ b/w

Dir Jean Renoir ***Scr*** Jean Renoir ***Ph*** Theodore Sparkuhl, Roger Hubert ***Ed*** Marguerite Renoir ***Art*** Gabriel Scognamillo

Act Michel Simon, Janie Marese, Georges Flamant, Madeleine Berubet, Jean Gehret, Alexandre Rignault (Braunberger/Richebe)

Very cleverly made and beautifully acted. Unseemly title is hardly flavored enough to come up to the story, which was staged from the novel of the same name by Georges de la Fouchardiere at the Renaissance, a legit stand that specializes in sensational plays. The title word is meant to apply to a prostitute who drags down a man, and the story, sordid in itself, is shown in every sordid detail relating to each one of the principals—the prostitute, her man and the sucker.

It opens with the beating of a girl by her boyfriend, who is shown throughout as living on her according to best traditions. This plus the extra inducement of a cashier robbing the till, a bedroom scene, not suggestive, but with the smell the only thing left out, a murder by stabbing done with sufficient delicacy to show the girl's body lying on the bed and her blood staining the pillow, a courtroom scene ending in an innocent sentenced to death and the same innocent later being woken up in the death house to be led to the guillotine, unquestionably constitute a pretty complete index of what is not for family trade.

Technically the film is practically a photograph of the stage version, with hardly any outdoor shots, but direction, photo and sound are good and continuity was planned so as to ensure fast tempo throughout. The three main characters are splendidly acted—the woman by the late Janie Marese, who died in a motor accident on the Riviera. Georges Flamant plays her man with the most true-to-life and realistic naturalness. The middle-class sucker, who, unhappily married, must give vent to his sentimental vein by blinding himself to the fact that the girl he loves is milking him, is done by Michel Simon. Other parts are mere supports and satisfactory.

•

CHILD IS WAITING, A

1963, 104 mins, US Ⓥ b/w

Dir John Cassavetes ***Prod*** Stanley Kramer ***Scr*** Abby Mann ***Ph*** Joseph LaShelle ***Ed*** Gene Fowler ***Mus*** Ernest Gold

Act Burt Lancaster, Judy Garland, Gena Rowlands, Steven Hill, Bruce Ritchey (United Artists)

As in *Judgment at Nuremberg*, producer Stanley Kramer dips into productive source of live television drama and comes up with a poignant, provocative, revealing dramatization. Again it is writer Abby Mann whose original work spawns the effort. This time it is the subject of mentally retarded children.

The film focuses on one profoundly touching case, around which are woven heartrending and often shocking illustrations of behavior and activity in institutions for the mentally retarded as well as academic discussions of the role in society to be played by the afflicted and society's responsibility to them. There is no hokiness in the dramatization.

Burt Lancaster delivers a firm, sincere, persuasive and unaffected performance as the professionally objective but understanding psychologist who heads the institution. Judy Garland gives a sympathetic portrayal of an overly involved teacher who comes to see the error of her obsession with the plight of one child.

That child, a deeply touching "borderline case," is played superbly by young Bruce Ritchey, a professional actor who manages to fit believably into a youthful cast that consists, for the most part, of actual retarded children who are patients of Pacific State Hospital in Pomona. As the lad's two troubled parents, Gena Rowlands (director John Cassavetes's wife) and Steven Hill pitch in with two exceptionally vivid and convincing performances.

•

CHILDREN, THE

1990, 115 mins, UK/W. Germany Ⓥ col

Dir Tony Palmer ***Prod*** Andrew Montgomery, Paul Templeton ***Scr*** Timberlake Wertenbaker ***Ph*** Nic Knowland ***Ed*** Tony Palmer ***Art*** Chris Bradley

Act Ben Kingsley, Kim Novak, Siri Neal, Geraldine Chaplin, Joe Don Baker, Karen Black (Isolde/Arbo/Film Four)

Previously filmed in 1929 by Paramount as *The Marriage Playground*, Edith Wharton's 1928 novel *The Children* comes to the screen as a somewhat dated enterprise. Story of a middle-aged man's infatuation for a teenage girl unfolds at a snail's pace.

Ben Kingsley is Martin Boyne, a middle-aged engineer returning to Europe after years in Brazil. He hopes to marry Rose Sellars (Kim Novak, looking ageless), his lifelong love recently widowed and living in an Alpine village. On the voyage home, he meets a group of seven children, the oldest of which is the budding Judith (Siri Neal).

Martin lingers on in Venice with the children, who seem to fascinate him, but eventually heads for the hills and Rose. The children soon follow. The rest of the film depicts Martin's indecision and his gradual emotional shift away from the demanding Rose to the guileless, appealing Judith, who appears to encourage him.

Kingsley gives one of his most affecting performances as the confused protagonist, and young Siri Neal is a find as the child-woman.

•

CHILDREN OF A LESSER GOD

1986, 110 mins, US Ⓥ ⦿ col

Dir Randa Haines ***Prod*** Burt Sugarman, Patrick Palmer ***Scr*** Hesper Anderson, Mark Medoff ***Ph*** John Seale ***Ed*** Lisa Fruchtman ***Mus*** Michael Convertino ***Art*** Gene Callahan

Act William Hurt, Marlee Matlin, Piper Laurie, Philip Bosco, Alison Gompf, John F. Cleary (Paramount)

Children of a Lesser God is the kind of good-intentioned material that often gets weighed down with sentimentality on the screen. Fortunately, the translation of Mark Medoff's Tony Award–winning [1980] play avoids many of those traps by focusing on a touching and universal love story between a deaf woman and a hearing man.

At the heart of the picture is the attraction between William Hurt and Marlee Matlin. Their need and feeling for each other is so palpable that it is almost impossible not to share the experience and recognize it in one's own life.

It's another seamless performance for Hurt. Matlin, who makes her professional acting debut here and is in real life hearing impaired, as is much of the cast, is simply fresh and alive with fine shadings of expression.

1986: Best Actress (Marlee Matlin)

NOMINATIONS: Best Picture, Actor (William Hurt), Supp. Actress (Piper Laurie), Adapted Screenplay

•

CHILDREN OF PARADISE

SEE: LES ENFANTS DU PARADIS

•

CHILDREN OF THE CORN

1984, 93 mins, US Ⓥ ⦿ col

Dir Fritz Kiersch ***Prod*** Donald P. Porchers, Terrence Kirby ***Scr*** George Goldsmith ***Ph*** Raoul Lomas ***Ed*** Harry Keramidas ***Mus*** Jonathan Elias ***Art*** Craig Stearns

Act Peter Horton, Linda Hamilton, R. G. Armstrong, John Franklin, Courtney Gains, Robby Kiger (Gatlin/Angeles)

Children of the Corn presents a normal couple, played by Peter Horton and Linda Hamilton, thrust into supernatural occurrences while on a cross-country trip. Horton is a newly graduated doctor on his way to start his internship in Seattle. Somewhere in Nebraska the couple happen on the children of the corn, a band of vicious youngsters who have murdered adults and established a religious community worshipping a mysterious deity of the corn fields.

Led by Isaac (John Franklin), an adolescent with an old man's demeanor, the band of outsiders displays a sinister attraction. Shrouded in pseudo-Christian mythology, the children are more appealing than the mundane reality of the adults.

Director Fritz Kiersch and/or author Stephen King seem to play both ends against the middle, neither accepting nor denying the supernatural occurrences.

Children of the Corn does have a few good scare scenes but special effects are surprisingly disappointing.

•

CHILDREN OF THE CORN II: THE FINAL SACRIFICE

1993, 92 mins, US Ⓥ ⦿ col

Dir David F. Price **Prod** Scott A. Stone, David G. Stanley **Scr** A. L. Katz, Gilbert Adler **Ph** Levie Isaacks **Ed** Barry Zetlin **Mus** Daniel Licht **Art** Greg Melton

Act Terence Knox, Paul Scherrer, Ryan Bollman, Christie Clark, Rosalind Allen, Ned Romero (Fifth Avenue)

Coming nine years after the original, this supernatural horror sequel is a competently made but uninspired effort. Gore fans should dig it. Surviving kids are sent to live in a nearby town, including brooding Micah (Ryan Bollman), who's taken in by lovely innkeeper Rosalind Allen. A journalist (Terence Knox) is driving by when he sniffs out an exploitable story. He's traveling with uppity son Paul Scherrer, who has little affection for his old man.

Adults are again murdered in grisly fashion, some by supernatural forces (a few represented by nice visual effects reminiscent of *Wolfen*), some by the deranged kids led by Micah.

Lensing on North Carolina locations (subbing for Nebraska) is well done, with director David Price (son of industry vet Frank Price) keeping the picture chugging along even when the script becomes risible.

•

CHILDREN OF THE DAMNED

1964, 90 mins, UK b b/w

Dir Anton M. Leader **Prod** Lawrence P. Bachmann **Scr** Jack Briley **Ph** Davis Boulton **Ed** Ernest Walter **Mus** Ron Goodwin **Art** Elliot Scott

Act Ian Hendry, Alan Badel, Barbara Ferris, Alfred Burke, Sheila Allen, Clive Powell (M-G-M)

Like most sequels *Children of the Damned* isn't nearly as good as its predecessor—Metro's 1960 *Village of the Damned*. What weakens this sequel is the fact that, unlike the original, it is burdened with a "message."

Jack Briley's screenplay broadens the scope to an international scale of what was originally a taut little sci-fi shocker. This time those strange, handsome parthenogenetic children the genius IQs, destructive dispositions and raygun eyes are not mere invaders from the outer limits bent on occupying earth, but are actually premature samplings of man as he will be in, say, a million years. And they have arrived for a curious purpose—to be destroyed, presumably to enable the silly, warlike contemporary man to learn some sort of lesson.

There are one or two genuinely funny lines in Briley's scenario and they are inherited by the character of a geneticist played engagingly by Alan Badel. A few of Badel's scenes with Ian Hendry, who plays an idealistic psychologist, are the best in the picture. Otherwise it's tedious going, and Anton Leader's lethargic direction doesn't help any.

•

CHILDREN'S HOUR, THE
(UK: THE LOUDEST WHISPER)

1961, 108 mins, US Ⓥ ⦿ b/w

Dir William Wyler **Prod** William Wyler **Scr** John Michael Hayes **Ph** Franz Planer **Ed** Robert Swink **Mus** Alex North **Art** Fernando Carrere

Act Audrey Hepburn, Shirley MacLaine, James Garner, Miriam Hopkins, Fay Bainter, Karen Balkin (Mirisch)

Lillian Hellman's study of the devastating effect of malicious slander and implied guilt comes to the screen for the second time in this crackling production of *The Children's Hour*. William Wyler, who directed the 1936 production (*These Three*), which veered away from the touchier, more sensational aspects of Hellman's Broadway play, this time has chosen to remain faithful to the original source.

Story deals with an irresponsible, neurotic child who spreads a slanderous rumor of a lesbian relationship between the two headmistresses of the private school for girls she attends.

Audrey Hepburn and Shirley MacLaine, in the leading roles, beautifully complement each other. Hepburn's soft sensitivity, marvelous projection and emotional understatement result in a memorable portrayal. MacLaine's enactment is almost equally rich in depth and substance. James Garner is effective as Hepburn's betrothed, and Fay Bainter comes through with an outstanding portrayal of the impressionable grandmother who falls under the evil influence of the wicked child.

1961: NOMINATIONS: Best Supp. Actress, (Fay Bainter), B&W Cinematography, B&W Costume Design, B&W Art Direction

•

CHILD'S PLAY

1972, 100 mins, US col

Dir Sidney Lumet **Prod** David Merrick **Scr** Leon Prochnik **Ph** Gerald Hirschfeld **Ed** Edward Warschilka, Joanne Burke **Mus** Michael Small **Art** Philip Rosenberg

Act James Mason, Robert Preston, Beau Bridges, Ron Weyand, Charles White, David Rounds (Paramount)

Child's Play, a taut and suspenseful drama of a Catholic boys' school, which won critical acclaim on Broadway, repeats in interest as a film production. Unfoldment often carries the aspects of a chiller as mysterious malevolent forces create a reign of terror and build to a powerful climax.

David Merrick gives the same meticulous care to script, written by Leon Prochnik in adapting the Robert Marasco original, and what emerges is compelling.

Situation revolves around deliberate violence as practised by some of the students on others, senseless incidents which cause fear and suspicion.

James Mason delivers a solid performance as a man whose hate of his fellow professor is exceeded, he says, only by Robert Preston's hate of him. Role is deeply dramatic, and Preston, in a different type of characterization, lends equal potency.

•

CHILD'S PLAY

1988, 87 mins, US Ⓥ ⦿ col

Dir Tom Holland **Prod** David Kirschner **Scr** Don Mancini, John Lafia, Tom Holland **Ph** Bill Butler **Ed** Edward Warschilka, Roy E. Peterson **Mus** Joe Renzetti **Art** Daniel A. Lomino

Act Catherine Hicks, Chris Sarandon, Alex Vincent, Brad Dourif, Dinah Manoff, Tommy Swerdlow (United Artists)

Child's Play is a near-miss at providing horrific thrills in a tale [by Don Mancini] of a murderous doll come to life, told with a knowing tongue-in-cheek attitude. Fun withers in stretching the thin material to feature-length.

Director Tom Holland summons impressive technical skill in charting the preposterous story of a nutcase (Brad Dourif) who climaxes a fatal shootout in a Chicago toystore with cop Chris Sarandon by chanting a voodoo incantation and passing his spirit into a cute, redheaded doll.

The next plot device is also hard to swallow as nice mom Catherine Hicks makes a last-minute buy of the doll from a grubby street peddler for her cute son Alex Vincent. The possessed doll, named Chucky, kills Alex's babysitter Dinah Manoff and who else but Sarandon is the detective on the case. Violence and paranoia escalate.

Both Hicks and Sarandon commendably keep straight faces during these outlandish proceedings. Top technical contributions milk the doll gimmick for all it's worth.

•

CHILD'S PLAY 2

1990, 85 mins, US Ⓥ ⦿ col

Dir John Lafia **Prod** David Kirschner **Scr** Don Mancini **Ph** Stefan Czapsky **Ed** Edward Warschilka **Mus** Graeme Revell **Art** Ivo Cristante

Act Alex Vincent, Jenny Agutter, Gerrit Graham, Christine Elize, Brad Dourif, Grace Zabriskie (Universal)

Child's Play 2 is another case of rehashing the few novel elements of an original to the point of utter numbness. The novelty of a smiling doll spouting expletives and crinkling his nose has long since worn off, so the filmmakers simply hammer away at walk-down-the-hallway cliches in an effort to provide the cheapest thrills.

Here, little Andy (Alex Vincent) has been separated from his mother, temporarily institutionalized after the original ordeal. He is placed with two drab parents (Jenny Agutter, Gerrit Graham) and a rebellious teen (Christine Elize), ultimately the only person to believe him. With Chucky (again voiced by Brad Dourif) doing mischief, poor little Andy is blamed for every bad thing that occurs. It's less amusing to note that Andy, this time, is practically the sole focus of Chucky's homicidal rage.

The puppet techniques are finely executed, but it's difficult after a while to take this three-foot-high version of the Terminator seriously. The adults are essentially pincushions, with about as much personality.

•

CHILD'S PLAY 3

1991, 89 mins, US Ⓥ ⦿ col

Dir Jack Bender **Prod** Robert Latham Brown **Scr** Don Mancini **Ph** John R. Leonetti **Ed** Edward Warschilka, Edward A. Warschilka, Jr., Scott Wallace **Mus** Cory Lerios, John D'Andrea **Art** Richard Sawyer

Act Justin Whalin, Perrey Reeves, Jeremy Sylvers, Travis Fine, Dean Jacobson, Brad Dourif (Universal)

Foul-mouthed killer doll Chucky returns in this noisy, mindless sequel. Young protagonist Andy is now a 16-year-old personified by handsome Justin Whalin. First reel prolog is devoted to venal businessman Peter Haskell starting up production on the Good Guy dolls eight years after the factory catastrophe limned in *Child's Play 2*.

First doll off the assembly line is Chucky, possessed by the spirit of dead murderer Brad Dourif (who again ably voices the creature's wisecracks). Chucky tracks Whalin to a military school, has himself mailed there and then becomes obsessed with transferring his spirit to a pint-sized black cadet (Jeremy Sylvers).

Fine doll effects and sporadic gore are par for the genre. Acting is good, with honors going to the original *Dirty Harry* nemesis, Andrew Robinson, amusing as the school's obsessive barber.

•

CHIMES AT MIDNIGHT

1966, 113 mins, Spain/Switzerland Ⓥ ⦿ col

Dir Orson Welles **Prod** Emiliano Piedra, Angel Escolano **Scr** Orson Welles **Ph** Edmond Richard **Ed** Fritz Mueller **Mus** Angelo Francesco Lavagnino **Art** Jose Antonio de la Guerra, Mariano Erdoza

Act Orson Welles, John Gielgud, Jeanne Moreau, Norman Rodway, Keith Baxter, Margaret Rutherford (Internacional Films Espanola/Alpine)

This Swiss–Spanish pic chronicles the story of Shakespeare's Falstaff. Taken from several plays, it details the last days of Falstaff's relationship with the Prince of Wales, the future King Henry V of England. A personal viewpoint, it mixes the grotesque, bawdy, comic and heroic, and does have a melancholy under its carousing and battles. Orson Welles has tried to humanize Falstaff in dwelling on his intimations of old age that make him accept a buffoonish part in the young prince's life. He contrasts this with the sombre reflections of the real father (Henry IV) on whose uneasy head lies the new crown of England. The prince finally has to choose between an indulgent father figure, Falstaff, and the real adult father who means responsibility, dedication and adulthood.

Welles himself is gigantically bloated and full of swagger yet shows glints of lonely pride and fear of rejection under a pompous exterior. John Gielgud, on the other hand, is sombre, suffering and stately as the King Henry IV trying to sort out of the problems of the court and his vassals in order to unite his nobles.

•

CHINA

1943, 78 mins, US b/w

Dir John Farrow **Prod** Richard Blumenthal **Scr** Frank Butler **Ph** Leo Tover **Ed** Eda Warren **Mus** Victor Young

Act Loretta Young, Alan Ladd, William Bendix, Philip Ahn, Iris Wong, Sen Yung (Paramount)

Tale opens in an interior China town, with Jap planes attacking the spot and populace. Among quick evacuees is Alan Ladd, who's been trucking gasoline to the Jap armies out of Shanghai. William Bendix is his sidekick. Along the road, truck is stopped and Ladd is forced to take aboard group of Chinese femme university students in the charge of American instructress Loretta Young. Ladd is arrogant and unconcerned over the Jap atrocities against the Chinese, but wakes up when a Jap plane strafes his truck.

Frank Butler generates authenticity in the dramatic evolvement of his screenplay [from a play by Archibald Forbes], while director John Farrow neatly blends the human and melodramatic elements of the yarn. Interest is hyped in the early reels with pickup of a Chinese baby by Bendix at the bombed town, and gradual breakdown of Ladd's attitude towards the youngster until the point where the latter is murdered by the Jap soldiers and Ladd is transformed into a battler for the Chinese cause.

•

CHINA BLUE
SEE: CRIMES OF PASSION

•

CHINA DOLL
1958, 99 mins, US b/w
Dir Frank Borzage ***Prod*** Frank Borzage ***Scr*** Kitty Buhler ***Ph*** William Clothier ***Ed*** Jack Murray ***Mus*** Henry Vars ***Art*** Howard Richmond
Act Victor Mature, Li Li-hua, Ward Bond, Bob Mathias, Johnny Desmond, Danny Chang (Romina/United Artists)

About average in its war storytelling, *China Doll* has a field day with the warmth and humor of a romance between a burly air corps captain and a fragile oriental beauty.

The script, from a story by James Benson Nablo and Thomas F. Kelly, often is highly interesting, often humorous and sometimes corny. It's a tale of China in 1943, at a time when the Japanese had cut off all supply lines and American airmen took to flying the hump. Smack in the middle is Victor Mature, a lonely leader who has dropped good books and bad women and has taken to the bottle. In one of his most alcoholic states, he unknowingly purchases a young Chinese girl as a housekeeper, and she ends up carrying his child, drawing his love and marrying him, in that order.

Mature displays his share of love, emotion and humor. Highlight of the picture is sumptuous femme Li Li-hua in the title role. Ward Bond is excellent as an understanding man of the cloth, and Danny Chang is fine as the barracks' boy.

•

CHINA GATE
1957, 96 mins, US Ⓥ ▭ b/w
Dir Samuel Fuller ***Prod*** Samuel Fuller ***Scr*** Samuel Fuller ***Ph*** Joseph Biroc ***Ed*** Gene Fowler, Jr., Dean Harrison ***Mus*** Victor Young, Max Steiner ***Art*** John Mansbridge
Act Gene Barry, Angie Dickinson, Nat "King" Cole, Lee Van Cleef, Warren Hsieh, Paul Dubov (Globe/20th Century-Fox)

China Gate is an overlong but sometimes exciting story of the battle between Vietnamese and Red Chinese, told through the efforts of a small band of French Legionnaires to reach and destroy a hidden Communist munitions dump.

Samuel Fuller gives his indie good production values, early use of Oriental war footage clips establishing an interesting story setting. The dominating character is a beautiful Eurasian woman, who leads the Legion demolition patrol to its objective through enemy territory. An added exploitation turn is the casting of Nat "King" Cole in dual assignment of a straight role and warbling title song.

Gene Barry and Angie Dickinson top the cast, former an American in the Legion, in charge of dynamiting operations of the Red ammunition cache; latter the Eurasian who is trusted by the Communists but on the side of the patriots. Romantic conflict is realized through their having once been married.

Dickinson does yeoman service with her colorful role. Barry also handles himself well but part sometimes is negative. Cole as the only other American in Legion patrol shows he can act as well as sing.

•

CHINA GIRL
1942, 98 mins, US b/w
Dir Henry Hathaway ***Prod*** Ben Hecht ***Scr*** Ben Hecht ***Ph*** Lee Garmes ***Ed*** James B. Clark ***Mus*** Hugo Friedhofer
Act Gene Tierney, George Montgomery, Lynn Bari, Victor McLaglen (20th Century-Fox)

Ben Hecht is listed as producer and scripter of this original by Melville Crossman, which is usually Darryl Zanuck's nom de plume when screen-scripting.

Plot has George Montgomery, as an American newsreel cameraman in Mandalay, falling in love with an American-educated Chinese girl (Gene Tierney). There is the usual Jap intrigue and paid spies in persons of Lynn Bari and Victor McLaglen, who try to get Montgomery into their clutches to turn over to the Japs.

Only angle for audience attention is the setting of China under Jap rule and bombing prior to Pearl Harbor, with romance of minor interest due to inadequacies of the script and original yarn. Otherwise, it's regulation stuff that has been retold many times.

•

CHINA GIRL
1987, 88 mins, US Ⓥ ⦿ col
Dir Abel Ferrara ***Prod*** Michael Nozik ***Scr*** Nicholas St. John ***Ph*** Bojan Bazelli ***Ed*** Anthony Redman ***Mus*** Joe Delia ***Art*** Dan Leigh
Act James Russo, Sari Chang, Richard Panebianco, David Caruso, Russell Wong, Joey Chin (Street Lite/Vestron)

China Girl is a masterfully directed, uncompromising drama and romance centering on gang rumbles (imaginary) between the neighboring Chinatown and Little Italy communities in New York City.

Screenplay hypothesizes an outbreak of a gang war when a Chinese restaurant opens in Italian territory. In the midst of the battling, a beautiful Chinese teenager (Sari Chang) falls in love with a pizza parlor gofer (Richard Panebianco). À la *West Side Story*, the adults oppose the relationship and, more to the point, the Mafia dons and Chinese elder gansters are in cahoots to maintain peace in their bordered territory.

Russell Wong (as handsome as a shirt ad model) and sidekick Joey Chin dominate their scenes as the young Chinese gang leaders. Title roler Sari Chang is called upon merely to be an idealized porcelain beauty and she fills the bill.

•

CHINA MOON
1994, 99 mins, US Ⓥ ⦿ ▭ col
Dir John Bailey ***Prod*** Barrie M. Osborne ***Scr*** Roy Carlson ***Ph*** Willy Kurant ***Ed*** Carol Littleton, Jill Savitt ***Mus*** George Fenton ***Art*** Conrad E. Angone
Act Ed Harris, Madeleine Stowe, Benicio Del Toro, Charles Dance, Patricia Healy, Tim Powell (Tig/Orion)

Ed Harris's stellar performance as the fall guy in *China Moon* elevates John Bailey's noir mystery to a cut or two above the usual Hollywood thriller.

Set in small-town Florida, it immediately recalls Lawrence Kasdan's *Body Heat* as well as Victor Nunez's Florida tale of greed and corruption, *A Flash of Green*, which also starred Harris. And the triangle involving Harris, a lonely homicide detective who falls for Madeleine Stowe, a beautifully seductive married woman, bears resemblance to such noir classics as *Double Indemnity* and *The Postman Always Rings Twice*.

Here, however, the appealing, mysterious lady is married to a young and successful banker (Charles Dance). This humanizes Stowe's femme fatale by making her husband physically abusive and engaged in his own adulterous affair. The tension in Roy Carlson's efficient, pared-down narrative derives from the complex relationship between Harris and ambitious rookie detective Benicio Del Toro, once Harris gets drawn into a murder scheme.

Harris brings his customary quiet, focused intensity to a tailor-made role. Stowe is also well cast as a dreamy femme fatale with an active imagination and strong feelings.

•

CHINA 9 LIBERTY 37
1978, 102 mins, Italy Ⓥ ▭ col
Dir Monte Hellman ***Prod*** Gianni Bozzacchi, Valerio De Paolis, Monte Hellman ***Scr*** Jerry Harvey, Douglas Venturelli, Ennio De Concini, Vicente Soriano ***Ph*** Giuseppe Rotunno ***Ed*** Cesare D'Amico ***Mus*** Pino Donaggio ***Art*** Luciano Spadoni
Act Fabio Testi, Warren Oates, Jenny Agutter, Sam Peckinpah, Isabel Mestres, Richard C. Adams (CEA)

An oater made in Spain with Italo backing and American and English thesps in the main roles. Though the director, Monte Hellman, is American, this is a strange Western that eschews Italo pasta violence and camp, Hispano romantics or more robust Yank counterparts.

Fabio Testi is a gunman who runs off after having raped the wife of a gunslinger he was sent by railroad reps to kill. But she follows him and there is love, until railroad men are sent after the gunslinger and the husband reappears with his brothers.

Warren Oates is gruff as the husband, Jenny Agutter pliant as the torn wife who finally ends up again with her husband when the gunman will not kill him.

The Old West looks a bit flat. One cameo scene is done by Sam Peckinpah, a writer selling the legend rather than the reality of the west and who offers his services to the woman in the gunfighters' life but is refused.

•

CHINA SEAS
1935, 87 mins, US Ⓥ b/w
Dir Tay Garnett ***Prod*** Irving G. Thalberg, Albert Lewin ***Scr*** Jules Furthman, James Kevin McGuinness ***Ph*** Ray June ***Ed*** William Levanway ***Mus*** Herbert Stothart
Act Clark Gable, Jean Harlow, Wallace Beery, Rosalind Russell, Lewis Stone, Dudley Digges (M-G-M)

This is a story of love—sordid and otherwise—of piracy and violence and heroism on a passenger boat run from Shanghai to Singapore [from a novel by Crosbie Garstin]. Clark Gable is a valiant sea captain, Wallace Beery a villainous pirate boss, and Jean Harlow a blond trollop who motivates the romance and most of the action. All do their jobs expertly.

Harlow is crossed in love when Gable, who has been her sweatheart in a sort of sparring partner but true-love affair, is tempted to return to English aristocracy. Temptation arrives in the form of the refined Rosalind Russell, a hometown acquaintance. The social gap between Harlow and Rosalind touches off the fireworks.

Spurned by Gable, Harlow seeks to get hunk by slipping Beery the key to the ship's arsenal which makes it a cinch for the raiding pirates. But the raid fails, for Gable refuses to reveal the hiding place of a cargo of gold.

The pirate raid and its unsuccessful termination (for the pirates) is full of shooting, suspense and action. Add a running atmosphere of suspense through the picture, and there's plenty of excitement.

•

CHINA SKY
1945, 78 mins, US Ⓥ ⦿ b/w
Dir Ray Enright ***Prod*** Maurice Geraghty ***Scr*** Brenda Weisberg, Joseph Hoffman ***Ph*** Nicholas Musuraca ***Ed*** Gene Milford ***Mus*** Roy Webb ***Art*** Albert S. D'Agostino, Ralph Berges
Act Randolph Scott, Ruth Warrick, Ellen Drew, Anthony Quinn, Carol Thurston, Philip Ahn (RKO)

Pearl Buck's novel of the tenacity of Chinese guerrillas who harass the Japanese advance, and the American medico who runs the hospital in the key Chinese village, turns out far from the spectacular production it might have been. The guerrilla and fighting angle is played down, while stress is laid on interior sets and romantic conflict. As often happens, this lack of action wears the interest thin.

Scripters and director are so concerned with the triangle between Randolph Scott, as the American doctor, his devoted hospital co-worker (Ruth Warrick), and his wife (Ellen Drew) that they neglect the story's movement. There finally is a bang-up battle at the end between Jap paratroopers and the guerrillas as a wounded Jap officer wangles info out to his forces, but it's too late.

Scott is routine as the hospital head while Warrick is superb, but her role of the doctor's assistant is not sufficient to carry the whole load.

•

CHINA SYNDROME, THE
1979, 122 mins, US Ⓥ ⦿ col
Dir James Bridges ***Prod*** Michael Douglas ***Scr*** Mike Gray, T. S. Cook, James Bridges ***Ph*** James Crabe ***Ed*** David Rawlins ***Mus*** [none] ***Art*** George Jenkins
Act Jane Fonda, Jack Lemmon, Michael Douglas, Scott Brady, James Hampton, Peter Donat (Columbia)

The China Syndrome is a moderately compelling thriller about the potential perils of nuclear energy, whose major fault is an overweening sense of its own self-importance.

Jane Fonda limns a TV anchorwoman stuck in a "happy news" rut, who hires freelance cameraman Michael Douglas for a series on energy that she hopes will break her into the world of hard news.

While filming at a nuclear energy plant, they witness a control room crisis involving supervisor Jack Lemmon, which is surreptitiously lensed by Douglas. The resulting footage becomes a political hot potato, as station manager Peter Donat buckles under pressure from power company exec Richard Herd.

It's not until the final half-hour of *China Syndrome* that its promise catches up to its punch, and the wind-up packs a solid wallop.

1979: NOMINATIONS: Best Actor (Jack Lemmon), Actress (Jane Fonda), Original Screenplay, Art Direction

•

CHINATOWN
1974, 130 mins, US Ⓥ ⦿ ▭ col
Dir Roman Polanski ***Prod*** Robert Evans ***Scr*** Robert Towne ***Ph*** John A. Alonzo ***Ed*** Sam O'Steen ***Mus*** Jerry Goldsmith ***Art*** Richard Sylbert
Act Jack Nicholson, Faye Dunaway, John Huston, Perry Lopez, John Hillerman, Diane Ladd (Long Road/Paramount)

Chinatown is an outstanding picture. Robert Towne's complex but literate and orderly screenplay takes gumshoe Jack Nicholson on a murder manhunt all over the Los Angeles of the late 1930s, where Faye Dunaway is the wife of a dead city official.

Towne, director Roman Polanski and Nicholson have fashioned a sort of low-key Raymond Chandler hero who, with assistants Joe Mantell and Bruce Glover, specializes in matrimonial infidelities. When Diane Ladd, posing as Dunaway, commissions a job on Darrell Zwerling, the city's water commissioner, Nicholson becomes involved in a series of interlocking schemes.

He is in disfavor with the local police, hounded by goons (Roy Jenson and Polanski, in a bit role) in the employ of John Huston, and partially conned by Dunaway despite a romantic vibration between the two.

The many plot angles, including a very discreet development of incest, eventually converge in Chinatown for a climactic shootout which, at fadeout, will likely be papered over as a typical ghetto incident, the kind of event that respectable people never hear about. The phrase "Chinatown" is thus used in a cynical context and has meaning only after the film is over.

1974: Best Original Screenplay

NOMINATIONS: Best Picture, Director, Actor (Jack Nicholson), Actress (Faye Dunaway), Cinematography, Costume Design, Art Direction, Editing, Original Dramatic Score, Sound

•

CHINESE CONNECTION, THE
SEE: JINGWU MEN

•

CHISUM
1970, 110 mins, US Ⓥ ▭ col
Dir Andrew V. McLaglen ***Prod*** Andrew J. Fenady ***Scr*** Andrew J. Fenady ***Ph*** William H. Clothier ***Ed*** Robert Simpson ***Mus*** Dominic Frontiere ***Art*** Carl Anderson
Act John Wayne, Forrest Tucker, Christopher George, Ben Johnson, Glenn Corbett, Andrew Prine (Batjac/Warner)

John Wayne plays a rugged character set down in New Mexico Territory, circa 1878, as King of the Pecos, its greatest landholder and biggest cattle owner. Andrew J. Fenady, who scripted, has taken the events of the bloody Lincoln County cattle war which ended in 1878 to background his story.

Forrest Tucker plays Lawrence Murphy, the ambitious, land-grabbing and power-hungry newcomer who was one of the principals of the infamous cattle war.

Basis of picture is his move in on Chisum, who didn't create his empire through any lack of fighting, and the cattleman's powerful resistance. Wayne clothes his interpretation of the early West figure with vigor and warmth.

•

CHITTY CHITTY BANG BANG
1968, 142 mins, UK Ⓥ ⊙ ▭ col
Dir Ken Hughes ***Prod*** Albert R. Broccoli ***Scr*** Roald Dahl, Ken Hughes, Richard Maibaum ***Ph*** Christopher Challis ***Ed*** John Shirley ***Mus*** Irwin Kostal (sup.) ***Art*** Ken Adam
Act Dick Van Dyke, Sally Ann Howes, Lionel Jeffries, Gert Frobe, Anna Quayle, Benny Hill (Warfield/United Artists)

Chitty derives from (late) Ian Fleming's sole excursion into children's literature, a collection of stories about a fanciful Edwardian motor car. Dick Van Dyke is starred as the widowed, absentminded, unsuccessful inventor whose children convince him to save the pioneer racing auto from destruction. Turned into a spanking and sleek vehicle by Van Dyke, car develops ability to float on water and fly.

Brought into the story by this point are Sally Ann Howes, daughter of a wealthy candy manufacturer (James Robertson Justice), and Lionel Jeffries, Van Dyke's father who likes to imagine that he's still in India fighting the natives.

Gert Frobe, the bullyish, temperamental, childlike prince of a middle European nation, proceeds to kidnap auto and its inventor. He gets wrong car and wrong man, Jeffries, with result that Van Dyke, Howes and the kids fly off to the principality on a rescue mission.

The $10 million film lacks warmth. No real feeling is generated between any two characters. As well as one star performer, from *Mary Poppins* have come all the musical talent—songwriters Richard M. and Robert B. Sherman and the choreographers [Marc Breaux and Dee Dee Wood]. But there has been no desire to reprise the Edwardian music hall tradition, aspects of which so informed *Poppins*.

Howes goes through the romantic motions with Van Dyke and the maternal ones with the kids, but there is no real sentiment between players.

1968: NOMINATION: Best Song ("Chitty Chitty Bang Bang")

•

CHLOE IN THE AFTERNOON
SEE: L'AMOUR, L'APRES-MIDI

•

CHOCOLAT
2000, 121 mins, US Ⓥ ⊙ col
Dir Lasse Hallstrom ***Prod*** David Brown, Kit Golden, Leslie Holleran ***Scr*** Robert Nelson Jacobs ***Ph*** Roger Pratt ***Ed*** Andrew Mondshein ***Mus*** Rachel Portman ***Art*** David Gropman
Act Juliette Binoche, Lena Olin, Johnny Depp, Judi Dench, Alfred Molina, Peter Stormare (Brown/Miramax)

Chocolat is more than a delicious confection; it's a richly textured comic fable that blends Old World wisdom with a winking, timely commentary on the assumed moral superiority of the political right, generously laced with Lasse Hallstrom's trademark observations on the limitless capacity of the human spirit.

Set in France in the late 1950s, story opens in a medieval village unchanged for centuries. And when the blustery north wind blows into town, bringing with it the red-hooded, unwed mother Vianne Rocher (the quietly radiant Juliette Binoche) and her young daughter Anouk (Victoire Thivisol), nothing could be a greater threat to the status quo.

Vianne leases the patisserie during Lent, a plan that the town's mayor and guardian of morality, the Comte de Reynaud (Alfred Molina), insists is nothing short of sacrilege. Not to worry, the rosy-cheeked Vianne informs him cheerily, it's not going to be a pastry shop. It will, in fact, be something much worse: a chocolate shop. Splashed with color and Mayan ceramics, the shop has the decor, sniffs elderly dowager Armande Voizin (Judi Dench), of an "early Mexican brothel." And while she's hardly a madam, Vianne soon exerts a mysterious influence over the townspeople.

But even as some of the townsfolk begin to trust Vianne, others think she is doing the devil's work, prompting the indignant Comte de Reynaud to declare a moral war on Vianne and her chocolate shop. Fed up with the Comte's self-righteousness, Vianne decides to inflame existing tensions by taking up with the roguish Roux (Johnny Depp), an Irish gypsy who arrives in town.

Being a Hallstrom film, however, *Chocolat* tempers the bitter with the sweet. The film, finally, is about having the power to change, to accept others regardless of their differences. Brimming with dualities, it pairs themes of feast with fasting and Christian tradition against pagan rituals. Though Vianne is clearly the heroine, the Comte, who believes he is doing good, is not altogether villainous.

•

CHOICES
1981, 90 mins, US Ⓥ col
Dir Silvio Narizzano ***Prod*** Alicia Rivera Alon, Rami Alon ***Scr*** Rami Alon ***Ph*** Hanania Baer ***Mus*** Sonny Gordon, Paul Carafotes ***Art*** Nancy Auburn
Act Paul Carafotes, Victor French, Lelia Goldoni, Val Avery, Demi Moore (Oaktree)

Director Silvio Narizzano's first U.S. film in 13 years is an engaging feature that confronts its young hero with an unwanted tag of a physical handicap.

Paul Carafotes appears to be an average high schooler whose world consists of football and music. His family attempts to nurture the latter aspect. However, Carafotes is partially deaf and a school medical examiner rules this precludes him from the football team.

Carafotes resents his sudden freak status and his seeming lack of choices. His helplessness manifests itself in his behavior as he adopts an "I don't care" attitude and falls in with a tough gang.

Choices has all its sympathies in the right place and one can't help but warm to its message even if its manipulation often lacks subtlety. At times its moralistic views and approach give the picture the feel of a propaganda piece commissioned by a handicapped rights organization.

Writer-co-producer Rami Alon provides a functional script in his maiden screen effort which has a dash too much preachiness.

•

CHOIRBOYS, THE
1977, 119 mins, US Ⓥ col
Dir Robert Aldrich ***Prod*** Merv Adelson, Lee Rich ***Scr*** Christopher Knopf ***Ph*** Joseph Biroc ***Ed*** Maury Winetrobe, William Martin, Irving Rosenblum ***Mus*** Frank DeVol ***Art*** Bill Kenney
Act Charles Durning, Louis Gossett, Jr., Perry King, Clyde Kusatsu, Stephen Macht, Randy Quaid (Lorimar/Airone)

When Robert Aldrich's filmmaking is good, it's very, very good; and when it's bad it's awful. This cheap-looking ultra-raunchy alleged comedy about policemen leaves no stone unturned in its exploitation of vulgarity.

The story peg apparently is that, underneath the public image of callousness, which many urban police departments today exude, lies the real callousness—bigoted, sexist, unfeeling, alienated, etc.

The leading characters represent a formula cross section of people—old-style cop Charles Durning all the way down through minorities, troubled Vietnam veterans (again!), naive twerps, sexually kinky all-American Boy type, and a special mention of Tim McIntyre who is terrific in portrayal of a person audiences will come to hate.

•

CHOPPER CHICKS IN ZOMBIETOWN
1990, 89 mins, US Ⓥ col
Dir Dan Hoskins ***Prod*** Maria Snyder ***Scr*** Dan Hoskins ***Ph*** Tom Fraser ***Ed*** W. O. Garrett ***Mus*** Daniel May ***Art*** Timothy Baxter
Act Jamie Rose, Catherine Carlen, Kristina Loggia, Lycia Naff, Vicki Frederick, Gretchen Palmer (Chelsea Partners)

Chopper Chicks in Zombietown is a surprisingly funny B-movie spoof with a feminist edge. Writer-director Dan Hoskins has a great deal of fun scrambling genres. It's a classic story of bikers invading a secluded town and rattling the suspicious populace.

At the same time, it's another classic story: the local mad scientist is killing off citizens, reviving them as zombie slaves, and generally making the town a miserable place to live. The bikers are leather-and-chain-wearing women.

Leader of the pack Rox (Catherine Carlen) is a hard-bitten (but not bad-looking) motorcycle mama who proudly proclaims herself "a big, bad bulldyke." Her gang, the Cycle Sluts, includes an ex-homecoming queen (Jamie Rose), an AWOL demolitions expert (Kristina Loggia) and a sex-crazed "nymfomaniac" (Whitney Reis). The mad scientist is played by Don Calfa.

Hoskins isn't able to sustain the level of lunacy and several scenes suggest the Harley-riding actresses have been asked to vamp until a funny line comes along. Still, there is a lot to laugh about, and dialog that moviegoers will quote for days afterward. [Additional scenes directed by Rodney McDonald.]

•

CHORUS LINE, A
1985, 113 mins, US Ⓥ ⊙ ▭ col
Dir Richard Attenborough ***Prod*** Cy Feuer, Ernest Martin ***Scr*** Arnold Schulman ***Ph*** Ronnie Taylor ***Ed*** John Bloom ***Mus*** Marvin Hamlisch ***Art*** Patrizia Von Brandenstein
Act Michael Douglas, Terrence Mann, Alyson Reed, Cameron English, Vicki Frederick, Audrey Landers (Embassy/PolyGram)

Director Richard Attenborough has not solved the problem of bringing the 1975 musical *A Chorus Line* to the screen, but he at least got it there after nearly a decade of diddling around by others.

There's a common wisdom, of course, that a stage show must be "opened up" for the camera, but *Chorus* often seems static and confined, rarely venturing beyond the immediate. Attenborough merely films the stage show as best he could.

Nonetheless, the director and lenser Ronnie Taylor have done an excellent job working within the limitations, using every trick they could think of to keep the picture moving. More importantly, they have a fine cast, good music and a great, popular show to work with. So if all they did was get it on film, that's not so bad.

Michael Douglas is solid as the tough choreographer and Terrence Mann is good as his assistant. Alyson Reed also is sympathetic as Douglas's dancing ex-girlfriend.

Worth special note, too, are Cameron English as the troubled young gay, Vicki Frederick as the older hoofer and Audrey Landers, who romps delightfully through the "T&A" number.

1985: NOMINATIONS: Best Editing, Song ("Surprise, Surprise"), Sound

•

CHORUS OF DISAPPROVAL, A
1989, 100 mins, US Ⓥ col
Dir Michael Winner ***Prod*** Michael Winner ***Scr*** Michael Winner, Alan Ayckbourn ***Ph*** Alan Jones ***Ed*** Chris Barnes ***Mus*** John DuPrez ***Art*** Peter Young
Act Jeremy Irons, Anthony Hopkins, Prunella Scales, Jenny Seagrove, Sylvia Sims, Patsy Kensit (South Gate)

It's tricky trying to convert stage to screen, and this is one play that suffers in translation. As a movie, *A Chorus of Disapproval*, chugs along when Alan Ayckbourn's play raced.

Jeremy Irons shines as Jones, a shy, rather nervous widower who comes to work in the small English seaside town of Scarborough. He is lonely and, to meet people, he joins the local amateur group, which is practicing *A Beggar's Opera*.

The production is directed by Dafydd Llewellyn (Anthony Hopkins), a scruffy solicitor whose only passion is the theatre and who only really comes alive when he is directing a new play.

Jones, without really trying, soon becomes a small Lothario, his actions having hilarious effects on the various members of the drama group. Jones becomes involved with Llewellyn's lonely wife, Hannah (Prunella Scales), but she finds she is not alone in his affections.

Pic is a fine, if uninspired, first screen adaptation of one of Great Britain's favorite playwrights.

•

CHOSEN, THE
SEE: HOLOCAUST 2000

•

CHOSEN, THE
1981, 108 mins, US Ⓥ col
Dir Jeremy Paul Kagan ***Prod*** Edie Landau, Ely Landau ***Scr*** Edwin Gordon ***Ph*** Arthur Ornitz ***Ed*** David Garfield ***Mus*** Elmer Bernstein ***Art*** Stuart Wurtzel
Act Maximilian Schell, Rod Steiger, Robby Benson, Barry Miller (Landau)

The Chosen is a first-rate adaptation of Chaim Potok's novel of friendship between two young Jewish men of widely different religio-cultural upbringings and their individual relationships with strong fathers.

Set in the latter years of World War II, the story has the principles, cultural Jew Barry Miller and orthodox Hassidic Jew Robby Benson, meeting as opponents in a baseball game. To Miller, a typical American kid, Benson's Hassidic upbringing complete with 19th-century attire and long side curls makes him akin to a creature from outer space. Yet the relationship grows and Miller is asked to meet with Benson's legendary father, an orthodox rabbi portrayed by Rod Steiger. In full-bearded Hasidic tradition, Steiger must approve of his son's non-sect friends.

Director Kagan and writer Gordon do wonders with the poignant material. Despite the obvious ethnic slant this is a picture which communicates universally.

Steiger gives an exceptional performance as the somewhat tyranical but loving patriarch whose primary concern is his son's welfare. Maximilian Schell provides an interesting contrast as a Jewish intellectual, reacting to the Holocaust and he instills his son with deep moral values.

•

CHOSES DE LA VIE, LES
(THE THINGS OF LIFE)
1970, 89 mins, France/Italy Ⓥ col
Dir Claude Sautet ***Prod*** Raymond Danon ***Scr*** Jean-Loup Dabadie, Paul Guimard, Claude Sautet ***Ph*** Jean Boffety ***Ed*** Jacqueline Thiedot ***Mus*** Philippe Sarde ***Art*** Andre Piltant
Act Michel Piccoli, Romy Schneider, Lea Massari, Jean Bouise, Boby Lapoint, Gerard Lartigau (Lira/Fida)

Directorial tact and visual solidity, fine, sensitive playing and observant characterization give an engrossing tang to this familiar tale [from the novel by Paul Guimard] of a middle-aged man who has left his wife and grown son for a slightly younger woman. Pic is a private tale of a man at emotional crossroads that builds interest without resort to flashy sentiments or intellectual palaver.

The titles begin with an auto accident—the film is a rethinking of the man's dilemma, with the accident a tragic event that cuts short his attempt to find peace with himself and his choices in life and love. Fragmentation first shows him with his mistress, played with engaging sincerity by Romy Schneider. Michel Piccoli gives a well-regulated limning of the man, a successful architect but somehow a bit ill at ease. He sees his son and promises to spend a summer with him, which angers his mistress. He goes off in a car for a business meeting and on the way decides to break with his mistress, but then changes him mind as the accident occurs.

Claude Sautet has made only two other pix, which were more concerned with low-life characters and delving into their motives sans preaching. Here he shows a fine directorial flair for ordinary people caught up in personal decisions and dramas.

•

CHRISTIAN, THE
1923, 106 mins, US ⊗ b/w
Dir Maurice Tourneur ***Scr*** Paul Bern ***Ph*** Charles Van Enger
Act Richard Dix, Mae Busch, Gareth Hughes, Phyllis Haver, Cyril Chadwick, Claude Gillingwater (Goldwyn)

Here is a real picture with a corking story, a great cast and finely produced.

Hall Caine's novel is a real tale for the screen. It was made about nine or ten years earlier by Vitagraph. Goldwyn secured the American rights.

The cast needs a new adjective to express their work. That goes for everyone, but the performance that stands out as a gem is that by Richard Dix, who, as John Storm, presents a characterization without compare. Next to Dix, Mae Busch is entitled to a full measure. This girl delivers 100 percent as Glory Quayle, and then some, but at the same time Phyllis Haver as Polly Love, on the strength of the death scene alone, is entitled to all that the critics can give her in praise. A great deal of credit is due, especially Cyril Chadwick as the heavy, and Mahlon Hamilton.

In production, nothing is left undone. The company, at least a part of it, was taken to the Isle of Man, England, and the original scenes as described by the author were utilized for the picturization.

•

CHRISTINE
1983, 110 mins, US Ⓥ ⊙ ⊏⊐ col
Dir John Carpenter ***Prod*** Richard Kobritz ***Scr*** Bill Phillips ***Ph*** Donald M. Morgan ***Ed*** Marion Rothman ***Mus*** John Carpenter, Alan Howarth ***Art*** Daniel Lomino
Act Keith Gordon, John Stockwell, Alexandra Paul, Robert Prosky, Harry Dean Stanton, Christine Belford (Columbia/Delphi)

Christine seems like a retread. This time it's a fire-engine red, 1958 Plymouth Fury that's possessed by the Devil, and this déjà vu premise [from the novel by Stephen King] combined with the crazed vehicle format, makes *Christine* appear pretty shop-worn.

Title character's nasty personality is neatly established in an assembly line prologue, which leaves one man dead and another injured. Jump to 1978 and Christine is a broken-down junker. Nevertheless, she's the object of love at first sight for misfit high school student Keith Gordon, who purchases her despite objections from his parents and best friend, and restores her to her 1950s glory.

Gordon also undergoes a transformation, evolving from campus klutz to Mr. Cool and acquiring the foxiest girl in the school (Alexandra Paul) in the process. But when the couple begins making out at a drive-in movie, Christine nearly knocks off Paul in a fit of romantic jealousy. Director John Carpenter's principle challenge was to create a real character of the car, and in this he has succeeded admirably. Flashy auto dominates everything, its jealousy is effectively, and sometimes humorously, conveyed, and some of the best sequences involve incidents in which the car miraculously restores itself to pristine condition after having been banged up and even torched.

Technically, the film is outstanding, and Carpenter's choice of lenses and widescreen work is as astute as ever.

•

CHRISTMAS HOLIDAY
1944, 98 mins, US b/w
Dir Robert Siodmak ***Prod*** Frank Shaw ***Scr*** Herman J. Mankiewicz ***Ph*** Woody Bredell ***Ed*** Ted Kent ***Mus*** Hans J. Salter ***Art*** John B. Goodman, Robert Clatworthy
Act Deanna Durbin, Gene Kelly, Dean Harens, Gale Sondergaard, Richard Whorf (Universal)

The story is Somerset Maugham's tale of a boy who emotionally grew up during a holiday in France (with the locale changed to New Orleans) and the plot switched around. A young army lieutenant, disappointed in love, finds himself stranded in the southern city, and meets up with another heartsick kid in a sad-faced singer at a cheap nightclub. From then on the story is told in flashbacks, as the singer (Deanna Durbin) tells the lieutenant of her brief, happy marriage to a young ne'er-do-well, her husband's arrest for murder, and his imprisonment for life.

As the nitery thrush, Durbin has two incidental songs. "Spring Will Be a Little Late This Year" (Frank Loesser) and the Irving Berlin oldie, "Always." But otherwise the dramatic role is unrelieved except by a few glimpses of a happy, smiling past.

•

CHRISTMAS IN JULY
1940, 67 mins, US Ⓥ ⊙ b/w
Dir Preston Sturges ***Prod*** Paul Jones ***Scr*** Preston Sturges ***Ph*** Victor Milner ***Ed*** Ellsworth Hoagland ***Mus*** Sigmund Krumgold (dir.) ***Art*** Hans Dreier, Earl Hedrick
Act Dick Powell, Ellen Drew, Raymond Walburn, Alexander Carr, William Demarest, Ernest Truex (Paramount)

This is the second combined writer-producer effort of Preston Sturges following his initial dual chore on *Great McGinty*. A mildly diverting programmer, *Christmas in July* lacks both the overall spontaneity and entertainment impress of Sturges's first picture.

Sturges's original script details the adventures of a young romantic pair living on New York's East Side and hoping for the day when fortune will smile broadly enough for them to get hitched. Boy is victim of office joke that advises he won $25,000 in a slogan contest, even though the jury is still fighting over the winner. But he collects the check and proceeds to run up a heavy charge account before cashing the winnings, plays Santa Claus to everyone on the block, including his sweetheart, and then is presented with the payoff that it's a phoney.

Picture has its moments of comedy and interest, but these are interspersed too frequently by obvious and boresome episodes that swing too much to the talkie side. There are flashes of the by-play and incidental intimate touches displayed by Sturges in his first picture, but not enough to bridge over the tedious episodes.

Dick Powell progresses as a straight lead without benefit of vocalizing, providing a dominating performance as the slogan award victim.

•

CHRISTOPHER COLUMBUS
1949, 104 mins, UK ⊙ col
Dir David Macdonald ***Prod*** A. Frank Bundy ***Scr*** Muriel Box, Sydney Box, Cyril Roberts ***Ph*** Stephen Dale ***Ed*** V. Sagovsky ***Mus*** Arthur Bliss ***Art*** Maurice Carter
Act Fredric March, Florence Eldridge, Francis L. Sullivan, Linden Travers, Kathleen Ryan, Derek Bond (Gainsborough/Rank)

Highly dramatized version of discovery of America by Christopher Columbus, with lush Technicolor to enhance opulent settings and colorful backgrounds, turns out to be an uncertain piece of entertainment. Almost half of the footage covers the period before Columbus sets sail on his expedition, dealing with his near-frustrated efforts to get the backing of the Spanish throne. Picture really does not get under way until Columbus sails in the *Santa Maria*. How mutiny is averted and land finally sighted brings in some action.

From then on the picture sketchily traces the closing stages of Columbus's life, including his return to Spain as a shackled prisoner and a deathbed scene is which he has a vision of the New World he has discovered. This ending, designed for American audiences, is omitted from the British version.

In the role of Columbus, Fredric March inevitably dominates the story. Francis L. Sullivan has a made-to-measure part as the Court conspirator and Florence Eldridge is adequately dignified as the Queen of Spain.

•

CHRISTOPHER COLUMBUS: THE DISCOVERY
1992, 120 mins, US Ⓥ ⊙ ⊏⊐ col
Dir John Glen ***Prod*** Ilya Salkind ***Scr*** John Briley, Cary Bates, Mario Puzo ***Ph*** Alec Mills ***Ed*** Matthew Glen ***Mus*** Cliff Eidelman ***Art*** Gil Parrondo
Act Marlon Brando, Tom Selleck, George Corraface, Rachel Ward, Robert Davi, Catherine Zeta Jones (Salkind)

Director John Glen's take on the Genoese explorer adds up to perfectly serviceable commercial entertainment: there are a few moments where Kirk Douglas or Charlton Heston would have felt right at home.

Using his James Bond–honed sense of expediency, Glen tells the story [by Mario Puzo] with broad strokes. Columbus is quickly established as a lusty, playful and self-assured man-with-a-vision whose life, in time-honored biopic tradition, is an uninterrupted series of lively events.

Although script is certainly not devoid of clichés and corniness, good dialogue far outweighs the bad. Leading man George Corraface has the diction and charisma it takes to carry off his role. He is immensely likable—perhaps too much so for authenticity's sake.

Marlon Brando makes a grand Grand Inquisitor. Tom Selleck's wry turn as King Ferdinand is a pleasant surprise, although a wan Rachel Ward as Queen Isabella could use more backbone in her evangelical enthusiasm. Pic concentrates more on Columbus than on the indigenous peoples he conquered, but does boast a better-than-comic-book sensitivity to the initially docile locals, eventually shown to have minds of their own. Production design, especially aboard ship, is convincing.

•

CHU-CHIN-CHOW
1934, 102 mins, UK b/w
Dir Walter Forde ***Prod*** Michael Balcon, Phil Samuel ***Scr*** Edward Knoblock, Sidney Gilliat, L. du Garde Peach ***Ph*** Mutz Greenbaum ***Ed*** Derek Twist ***Mus*** Louis Levy (dir.) ***Art*** Erno Metzner
Act George Robey, Anna May Wong, Fritz Kortner, John Garrick, Pearl Argyle, Francis Sullivan (Gainsborough/Gaumont-British)

This lavish musical from the British studios is a colorful, extravagant costume film that makes its bid for attention purely on an extravaganza platform, and makes the grade. It is, compared to American musicals, slow. But this very slowness happens to fit this type of yarn.

Story of *Chu-Chin-Chow* is the story of Ali Baba from the Arabian tales. George Robey is Ali Baba, the sap who became a millionaire; Anna May Wong is Zahrat, the unfaithful and vengeful slave girl; Fritz Kortner is Abu Hasan, the robber chief. All are excellent choices.

John Garrick is a handsome Nur-al-din, carrying the love interest with Marjanah (Pearl Argyle). Argyle is decorative and Garrick has a splendid singing voice.

Chief honors go to the director, Walter Forde, although there aren't any slipups in casting or other items. Anton Dolin, one of Britain's best name dancers among the modernists, stages the dances very effectively, and Frederic Norton's music from the original show [written by Oscar Asche] is never tiresome.

•

CHUMP AT OXFORD, A

1940, 63 mins, US Ⓥ ⦿ b/w

Dir Alfred Goulding ***Prod*** Hal Roach ***Scr*** Charles Rogers, Felix Adler, Harry Langdon ***Ph*** Art Lloyd ***Ed*** Bert Jordan ***Mus*** Marvin Hatley ***Art*** Charles D. Hall

Act Stan Laurel, Oliver Hardy, James Finlayson, Forrester Harvey, Peter Cushing, Sam Lufkin (Roach/United Artists)

Stan Laurel and Oliver Hardy's farce is mildly comical without offending. Time-worn gags clutter up the earlier footage and only when Laurel and Hardy, as new initiates into Oxford, actually move into the dean's home does the action speed up.

Early episodes have Laurel as a maid and Oliver Hardy as butler in a rich man's home. It looks as though it had been tacked on in order to make up footage. James Finlayson is the wealthy host in this episode but not given any cast credit.

A dinner party brings in all the familiar dress-tearing, pastry-flinging, cork-popping and shot-gun gags. Even that venerable nifty where the cop says "you are liable to blow my brains out" and then exhibits the bullet-marked seat of his trousers is left in.

But once the comedians land in England they fare better. Outside of the lost-in-the-woods stunt and ghost-at-midnight routine, the gagging and all-around material brightens up.

•

CHUNGHING SAMLAM
(CHUNG KING EXPRESS)

1994, 103 mins, Hong Kong Ⓥ ⦿ col

Dir Wong Kar-wai ***Prod*** Chan Yi-kan ***Scr*** Wong Kar-wai ***Ph*** Christopher Doyle, Lau Wai-keung ***Ed*** William Chang, Hai Kit-wai, Kwong Chi-leung ***Mus*** Frankie Chan, Roel A. Garcia ***Art*** William Chang

Act Brigitte Lin, Takeshi Kaneshiro, Tony Leung Chiu-wai, Faye Wong, Valerie Chow (Jet Tone)

Four years after his cult classic *Days of Being Wild*, Hong Kong maverick stylist Wong Kar-wai trampolines back with *Chung King Express*, a quicksilver magical mystery tour through the lives of a bunch of young downtown loners. Hip pic is drenched in neo-'60s nostalgia.

First story (42 minutes), set around the labyrinthine tenement building Chung King Mansions in downtown Kowloon, spins on a romantic young cop (Takeshi Kaneshiro), recently ditched by his g.f. As he mopes around, devouring cans of pineapple and calling up old flames, destiny leads him to cross paths with a cold-hearted drug dealer (Brigitte Lin) in a blond wig and designer shades.

Second, more involving story (61 minutes) centers on another young cop (Tony Leung Chiu-wai), also ditched by his air hostess g.f. (Valerie Chow), who's the unwitting fixation of a dotty worker (Faye Wong) at Midnight Express, a fast-food joint.

Wong made the movie in only three months, between the end of shooting and start of post-production on his mammoth martial arts costumer *Ashes of Time*, already two years in the works. With its plentiful use of handheld camera, fast-cutting, and collage-like approach to storytelling, effect is a little like watching an early Godard movie set in contempo Hong Kong. A richly detailed soundtrack, including classics such as "California Dreamer," accompanies the many dialog-free montage sequences.

•

CHUNG KING EXPRESS
SEE: CHUNGHING SAMLAM

•

CIAO, FEDERICO!

1970, 60 mins, US/Italy col

Dir Gideon Bachmann ***Prod*** Victor Herbert ***Scr*** Gideon Bachmann ***Ph*** Gideon Bachmann, Harvey Felderbaum, Anton Haakma ***Ed*** Regine Heuser (Herbert)

Yank critic-filmmaker Gideon Bachmann, a longtime Rome resident, made this 16mm docu on Italian director Federico Fellini making *Satyricon*.

Pic's glue-like coverage of the sly, wry Fellini, and the latter's charm and interest shows him as a chameleon-like figure. He rages, but with an underlying lack of true anger, and a seeming watching of his own actions. So he rarely reveals himself in words but may do so in actions, even if they appear often calculated.

Pic is as airy, unrevealing but picturesque as Fellini's symbolical, circusy pix and his tender choosing of grotesques and beauty to limn his own fantasy world on film.

•

CIAO MANHATTAN

1973, 90 mins, US Ⓥ ⦿ col

Dir John Palmer, David Weisman ***Prod*** Robert Margouleff, David Weisman ***Scr*** John Palmer, David Weisman ***Ph*** John Palmer, Kjell Rostad ***Ed*** Robert Farren ***Mus*** Gino Piserchio

Act Edie Sedgwick, Wesley Hayes, Isabel Jewell, Paul America, Geoffrey Briggs, Tom Flye (Court)

Ciao Manhattan is Edie Sedgwick's filmed swan song—she died of acute barbituate intoxication in 1971. Monotonous and nearly incomprehensible, *Ciao* consists chiefly of pieced-together short ends from two Sedgwick vehicles, one [in b&w] begun with great fanfare by undergrounder Chuck Wein [from a story by him and Genevieve Charbin] in 1967 when the Andy Warhol "superstar" was at the peak of her celebrity, and the second started three years later in California by John Palmer and David Weisman, who evidently believed they could reconstruct the ruin.

In the last years of her life, says this intendedly anti-dope film, Sedgwick took up residence at the bottom of a tented Santa Barbara pool, narcissistically surrounded by giant blowups of herself. It is here that the film dwells, cruelly exploiting her dope and booze-bloated visage, her siliconed breasts (for at least half the pic she is topless, so proud is she of these new ornaments) and most of the non-plot consists of her drug-zonked recollections of her halcyon days.

•

CIDER HOUSE RULES, THE

1999, 131 mins, US Ⓥ ⦿ ▭ col

Dir Lasse Hallstrom ***Prod*** Richard N. Gladstein ***Scr*** John Irving ***Ph*** Oliver Stapleton ***Ed*** Lisa Zeno Churgin ***Mus*** Rachel Portman ***Art*** David Gropman

Act Tobey Maguire, Charlize Theron, Delroy Lindo, Paul Rudd, Michael Caine, Jane Alexander, Erykah Badu, Kate Nelligan (Film Colony/Miramax)

The Cider House Rules represents one of the most successful attempts yet at filming the work of popular American novelist John Irving, whose colorfully larger-than-life characters and eccentric stories have often proved too page-bound to function onscreen. Dealing in habitual Irving themes of family, love and the search to find a place and purpose in the world, film could have used more dramatic muscle but is nonetheless a touching, old-fashioned charmer that ultimately satisfies.

Adapting this screenplay himself, Irving has successfully whittled down his massive 1985 tome into a workable form. Opening in the 1930s at St. Cloud's orphanage in the Maine countryside, the story outlines how twice-adopted, twice-returned child Homer Wells (Tobey Maguire) was raised with love by bighearted Dr. Wilbur Larch (Michael Caine), who heads the institution. Trained by Larch as a doctor, Homer helps care for abandoned children and deliver unwanted babies. But his moral qualms prevent him from assisting in the illegal abortions Larch performs.

The film feels dramatically undernourished for much of the running time, gaining some thrust only with the arrival of a primary subplot involving both abortion and incest. Maguire, with his hurt vulnerability and fragile, strangely moving voice, is a fine choice for Irving's quiet hero. Caine also scores in an uncharacteristic role and easily the film's most memorable supporting turn, bringing Larch a rich, disarming humanity.

1999: Best Supp. Actor (Michael Caine), Adapted Screenplay

NOMINATIONS: Best Picture, Director, Editing, Original Score, Art Direction

•

CIMARRON

1931, 124 mins, US Ⓥ b/w

Dir Wesley Ruggles ***Prod*** William LeBaron ***Scr*** Howard Estabrook ***Ph*** Edward Cronjager ***Ed*** William Hamilton ***Mus*** Max Steiner ***Art*** Max Ree

Act Richard Dix, Irene Dunne, Estelle Taylor, Nance O'Neil, William Collier, Jr., Roscoe Ates (Radio)

An elegant example of super filmmaking, this spectacular Western [from the novel by Edna Ferber] holds action, sentiment, sympathy, thrills and comedy.

Two outstanders in the playing, Richard Dix and Edna May Oliver, each surprisingly excellent; Dix with his straight character playing of a Westerner and an Oklahoma pioneer who dies before his statue is unveiled in that state, while Oliver is nothing less than exquisite in her eccentric comedy role of a Colonial dame in the wilds.

Perhaps nothing will draw more attention than the skillful aging of the main role players, from 1889 to 1930, a period they pass through of over 40 years on the screen.

Wesley Ruggles's direction misses nothing in the elaborate scenes, as well as in the usual filmmaking procedure.

Big production bits start with the land rush into Oklahoma in 1889, then the gospel meeting in a frontier gambling hall where Dix makes his biggest mark, an attmepted bank robbery and the courtroom trial of Dixie Lee, the harlot.

The land rush starts the action, men on horses and in wagons racing to capture some part of the two million acres released by the government to the first comers after the boom of a cannon at noon.

Estelle Taylor as Dixie Lee somewhat fades Irene Dunne as Dix's young and old wife. Taylor's showings are few but she makes them impressive. Dunne does nicely enough in a role of a loving wife and mother, which does not permit her to be much else. What she later accomplishes in a political way is suggested rather than acted. Roscoe Ates as a stuttering printer lands several laughs.

1930/31: Best Picture, Adaptation, Interior Decoration (Max Ree)

NOMINATIONS: Director, Actor (Richard Dix), Actress (Irene Dunn), Cinematography

•

CIMARRON

1960, 151 mins, US Ⓥ ⦿ ▭ col

Dir Anthony Mann ***Prod*** Edmund Grainger ***Scr*** Arnold Schulman ***Ph*** Robert L. Surtees ***Ed*** John Dunning ***Mus*** Franz Waxman ***Art*** George W. Davis, Addison Hehr

Act Glenn Ford, Maria Schell, Anne Baxter, Arthur O'Connell, Russ Tamblyn, Mercedes McCambridge (M-G-M)

Edna Ferber's novel of the first Oklahoma land rush (1889) shapes up in its second film translation as a good balance between rousing action and the marriage of Glenn Ford and Maria Schell as Yancey and Sabra Cravet. There are many subtle shadings in Schell's performance as she transforms over a period of 25 years from adoring, lovable bride to embittered, abandoned wife, successful newspaper publisher and bigoted mother-in-law when son Cim marries a childhood friend Indian girl. Latter and her mother were taken into the Cravet family by Yancey during the homestead run when the father was lynched by an Indian-hating scoundrel, played in grand bullboy style by Charles McGraw.

Ford emerges a strong and thoroughly likeable adventurer-idealist as the restless rover, Yancey, who is loving and devoted after his own fashion and spurns opportunity to become governor by helping to defraud Indians of their oil rights. Pic pulls no punches in pointing up the greed that discovery of black gold brought out in the rags-to-riches Oklahoma pioneers.

Cimarron starts off with a bang. Spectacle of thousands of land seekers lined up in Conestoga wagons, buckboards and even a surrey with the fringe on top, straining to dash into the new territory at high noon on April 22, 1889, is masterfully handled by director Anthony Mann. This is grand-scale action in spades. Fortunately Arnold Schulman's adaptation doesn't let the performers down after the whirlwind start.

As was the case with *Oklahoma!*, *Cimarron* was photographed on location in Arizona. Producer Edmund Grainger, apparently being more concerned about pictorial composition than actual topography, has permitted mountains to show in backgrounds alien to Oklahoma.

1960: NOMINATIONS: Best Art Direction, Sound

•

CINCINNATI KID, THE

1965, 102 mins, US Ⓥ ⦿ col

Dir Norman Jewison ***Prod*** Martin Ransohoff ***Scr*** Ring Lardner, Jr., Terry Southern ***Ph*** Philip H. Lathrop ***Ed*** Hal Ashby ***Mus*** Lalo Schifrin ***Art*** George W. Davis, Edward Carfagno

Act Steve McQueen, Edward G. Robinson, Ann-Margret, Karl Malden, Tuesday Weld, Joan Blondell (M-G-M)

The Cincinnati Kid is the fast moving story of a burningly ambitious young rambling-gambling man who challenges the king of stud poker to a showdown for the champ title of The Man. Adapted from Richard Jessup's realistically written novel, it emerges a tenseful examination of the gambling fraternity.

Martin Ransohoff has constructed a taut, well-turned-out production. In Steve McQueen he has the near-perfect delineator of the title role. Edward G. Robinson is at his best in some years as the aging, ruthless Lancey Howard, champ of the poker tables for more than 30 years and determined now to defend his title against a cocksure but dangerous opponent. The card duel between the pair is dramatically developed through gruelling action, building in intensity as the final and deciding hand is played.

Ring Lardner, Jr., and Terry Southern have translated the major elements of the book, changing, however, tome's St. Louis locale to a more picturesque New Orleans background. They have added a key situation, too, to point up the game—Karl Malden, in part of Shooter, dealer for the game, is forced by another gambler holding his markers to slip cards to the Kid so he'll cinch his victory. The Kid senses what's going on and eases Malden from his post.

•

CINDERELLA

1950, 74 mins, US Ⓥ ⦿ col

Dir Wilfred Jackson, Hamilton Luske, Clyde Geronimi ***Prod*** Ben Sharpsteen (sup.) ***Scr*** William Peed, Ted Sears, Homer Brightman, Kenneth Anderson, Erdman Penner, Winston Hibler, Harry Reeves, Joe Rinaldi ***Ed*** Donald Halliday ***Mus*** Oliver Wallace, Paul Smith (Walt Disney)

Disney outfit makes entertainment capital out of the animal world with clever drawing-board personifications of a quartet of mice doing battle with an ornery cat. The cartoon, in fact, has far more success in projecting the lower animals than in its central character, Cinderella, who is on the colorless, doll-faced side, as is the Prince Charming.

The menace is supplied by the literally-drawn stepmother, who's a lineal descendant of the flint-hearted, evil-eyed witch in *Snow White*. More inventiveness is used in the characterization of Cinderella's two comically ugly stepsisters, the king, his monocled major domo, and the aunty-like fairy princess.

The musical numbers woven into the fantasy are generally solid, with at least two or three likely hit tunes standing out in the half-dozen songs. Ilene Woods, as Cinderella's voice, uses a sweet soprano on "Cinderella," "So This Is Love," and "A Dream Is a Wish Your Heart Makes," all three being first-rate.

1950: NOMINATIONS: Best Scoring of a Musical Picture, Song ("Bibbidy-Bobbidi-Boo"), Sound

•

CINDERELLA JONES

1946, 90 mins, US b/w

Dir Busby Berkeley ***Prod*** Alex Gottlieb ***Scr*** Charles Hoffman ***Ph*** Sol Polito ***Ed*** George Amy ***Mus*** Frederick Hollander ***Art*** John Hughes

Act Joan Leslie, Robert Alda, S. Z. Sakall, Edward Everett Horton, Elisha Cook, Jr. (Warner)

Cinderella Jones has a musical slant, picture going almost musical comedy on several occasions, but doesn't actually need these touches.

Plot [from a story by Philip Wylie] deals with a girl who wants to inherit $10 million but has to find a husband with a Quiz Kid brain to collect. She figures an exclusively male technology institute is the proper place to find such a husband, and action revolves around her attempts to enroll in the school to find her man.

Around that basis scripter Charles Hoffman has fitted fast dialog and situations that pay off in chuckles. Busby Berkeley's direction generates plenty of speed in the unfolding, maintaining a pace that deftly points the laughs. On the musical side, though, he misses, staging one large production midway that only proves a pace-stopper. Tunes are not particular standouts but make for okay listening. Joan Leslie makes a delightful dumb dame who malaprops all over the place before wising up to the worth of her bandleader, both mentally and as a big hunk of man. Robert Alda gives the baton-waver role plenty of life.

•

CINDERELLA LIBERTY

1973, 117 mins, US Ⓥ ▭ col

Dir Mark Rydell ***Prod*** Mark Rydell ***Scr*** Darryl Ponicsan ***Ph*** Vilmos Zsigmond ***Ed*** Donn Cambera, Patrick Kennedy ***Mus*** John Williams ***Art*** Leon Ericksen

Act James Caan, Marsha Mason, Kirk Calloway, Eli Wallach, Allyn Ann McLerie, Burt Young (20th Century-Fox)

Cinderella Liberty is an earthy but very touching story of a sailor's love for a prostitute. James Caan gives an outstanding performance, and Marsha Mason, in her second picture, is equally superb.

The title comes direct from Navy slang, referring to enlisted men's ashore time cut off at midnight, the one here being Caan's temporary hospitalization and pending transfer to a new ship. In a most realistic bar setting, he meets Mason, who takes him home where the first of many surprises for Caan is the existence of a partially black son (Kirk Calloway). The next surprise is Caan's infatuation, to the extent of busting in on her to eject another trick.

Eli Wallach's strong featured role is that of Caan's long-ago boot camp drill instructor, whose harsh methods provoke a fight years later.

1973: NOMINATIONS: Best Actress (Marsha Mason), Original Score, Song ("Nice to Be Around")

•

CINDERFELLA

1960, 88 mins, US Ⓥ col

Dir Frank Tashlin ***Prod*** Jerry Lewis ***Scr*** Frank Tashlin ***Ph*** Haskell Boggs ***Ed*** Artie Schmidt ***Mus*** Walter Scharf ***Art*** Hal Pereira, Henry Bumstead

Act Jerry Lewis, Ed Wynn, Judith Anderson, Anna Marcia Alberghetti, Henry Silva, Robert Hutton (Paramount)

Jerry Lewis, who produced, stars as the male variation on Cinderella in Frank Tashlin's screenplay, *Cinderfella*. Tashlin also directed the picture and, along with his star-producer, must share the rap for failure of the mirthful to materialize into consistent merriment. There seems to have been a dearth of comic inspiration. Bits of funny business that do show instant promise are milked to extremes. Lewis, in fact, depends almost exclusively on the art of cumulative mugging, but often misjudges the breakoff point The pace engineered by Tashlin is uncomfortably deliberate for a comedy. Breaks for song tend to labor the issue instead of brightening the tempo.

Ed Wynn is whimsical as the fairy godfather, Judith Anderson plays the wicked stepmother, Henry Silva and Robert Hutton the mercenary stepbrothers. They are competent, but the roles are rather choppy, vague and incomplete. Anna Maria Alberghetti is dazzling as the princess.

Walter Scharf's score does a lot toward making the pace seem brighter than it is. There are three songs by Harry Warren and Jack Brooks. None of them comes off very well. The big ball sequence at the climax is enlivened by the driving jazz music of Count Basie's band.

•

CINEMA PARADISO

SEE: NUOVO CINEMA PARADISO

•

CINERAMA HOLIDAY

1955, 119 mins, US ▭ col

Dir Robert Bendick, Philippe de Lacey ***Prod*** Louis de Rochemont ***Scr*** Otis Carney, Louis de Rochemont ***Ph*** Joseph Brun, Harry Squire ***Ed*** Jack Murray, Leo Zochling, Frederick Y. Smith ***Mus*** Morton Gould, Van Cleave (Stanley-Warner Cinerama)

The Fred Waller Cinerama process is seen in its second mounting. Much of the excitement [of the first, *This Is Cinerama*,] remains, although there is some feeling of repeating tried-and-true pictorial effects. Right off, one thing stands out. Here is the greatest trailer for travel ever produced. There is a wisp of continuity in *Holiday*, unlike the predecessor film. Betty and John Marsh of Kansas City and Beatrice and Fred Troller of Zurich do an exchange student type of act, each pair of newlyweds visiting the other's hemisphere.

Since the second part of the show, after a 15-minute intermission, is largely made up of an extended visit to Paris, the impression grows into a conviction that the American couple really went places, did things and met people far beyond the arrangements for the Swiss pair.

•

CIOCIARA, LA

(TWO WOMEN)

1961, 110 mins, Italy/France Ⓥ b/w

Dir Vittorio De Sica ***Prod*** Carlo Ponti ***Scr*** Cesare Zavattini, Vittorio De Sica ***Ph*** Gabor Pogany ***Ed*** Adriana Novelli ***Mus*** Armando Trovajoli ***Art*** Gastone Medin

Act Sophia Loren, Eleonora Brown, Jean-Paul Belmondo, Raf Vallone, Renato Salvatori, Carlo Ninchi (Champion/Marceau-Cocinor/SGC)

Cesare Zavattini's screenplay appears to have transferred Alberto Moravia with scrupulous adherence to the letter of the book, if not quite the spirit—the irony and hope. There is only unremitting horror and soul-trying for the two women—the mother (Sophia Loren) and her 13-year-old daughter (newcomer Eleanora Brown)—as they reel from one wartime adversity to another, cresting with their marathon debauching by a band of Moroccan soldiers. It is the grim life in spades.

Yarn follows the mother and daughter when they leave Rome as bombing attacks increase and journey south to the older woman's girlhood village in the mountains. They join the villagers and other refugees, including Jean-Paul Belmondo as a bespectacled and disillusioned young intellectual. He becomes smitten with the mother but hides the fact till shortly before some German troops requisition him as a guide. Many months later, frustrated by their existence and with Allied forces moving up the Italian boot, the mother decides they should return to Rome and their grocery shop. En route, they are ravished by the Moroccans in a scene set symbolically in a gutted church.

Vittorio De Sica has directed in a way that maximizes the anguish, yet is free of melodrama. Armando Trovajoli's music is a compassionate plus, and other technical aspects are of a polished calibre.

1961: Best Actress (Sophia Loren)

•

CIRCLE OF DANGER

1951, 86 mins, UK b/w

Dir Jacques Tourneur ***Prod*** Joan Harrison ***Scr*** Philip MacDonald ***Ph*** Oswald Morris, Gilbert Taylor ***Ed*** Alan Osbiston ***Mus*** Robert Farnon ***Art*** Duncan Sutherland

Act Ray Milland, Patricia Roc, Marius Goring, Hugh Sinclair, Naunton Wayne, Marjorie Fielding (Coronado)

Despite a novel approach to a melodramatic theme, *Circle of Danger* is too slowly paced to build much suspense. Philip MacDonald's original screenplay takes Ray Milland on a veritable Cook's tour of England and Scotland. Cast as an American, the star is engaged in a relentless hunt to discover the circumstances behind a younger brother's death in a British commando raid during the last war. Search narrows down to a handful of men who took part in the assault with his kin.

Under the calculating direction of Jacques Tourneur, the film minimizes action in favor of a series of character studies of the few commandos remaining from the raid. Plot solution is an odd one, but not totally unexpected.

•

CIRCLE OF FRIENDS

1995, 96 mins, US Ⓥ ⦿ col

Dir Pat O'Connor ***Prod*** Arlene Sellers, Alex Winitsky, Frank Price ***Scr*** Andrew Davis ***Ph*** Ken MacMillan ***Ed*** John Jympson ***Mus*** Michael Kamen ***Art*** Jim Clay

Act Chris O'Donnell, Minnie Driver, Geraldine O'Rawe, Saffron Burrows, Alan Cummings, Colin Firth (Price/Lantana)

Director Pat O'Connor brings his Irish heritage and his expertise to a familiar coming-of-age tale [from Maeve Binchy's novel], set in a small Irish town in 1957. Benny (Minnie Driver) and Eve (Geraldine O'Rawe) eagerly escape the dull confines of hometown Knockglen to attend college in Dublin, where they're reunited with former mate Nan (Saffron Burrows).

Tale focuses on the trio's affairs of the heart—their secrets and dreams, rites of loyalty and betrayal, punishment and redemption.

Pragmatic Nan consciously chases Simon (Colin Firth), a wise guy who's older and richer than the college boys, and Eve becomes infatuated with Aidan (Aidan Gillen). But chief figure is Benny, the "plain Jane" heroine, who begins a passionate romance with Jack (Chris O'Donnell), the handsome star of the university rugby team.

In its good scenes, *Circle of Friends* assumes the nature of a romantic fable with universal meanings. In its worst, however, pic veers off rather sharply into steamed-up melodrama, with shocking revelations, calculated pregnancies, innocent men entrapped as fathers, jaded fools and scheming villains.

Somehow, though, the passion holds and the story's emotions survive, due in large measure to the accomplished acting. The major weight is brilliantly carried off by Driver, who moves the film along while juggling hopes, doubts and anxieties that will ring true to adolescents experiencing first love.

•

CIRCLE OF LOVE

SEE: LA RONDE

•

CIRCUS

1928, 70 mins, US Ⓥ ⊗ b/w

Dir Charles Chaplin ***Prod*** Charles Chaplin ***Scr*** Charles Chaplin ***Ph*** Rollie H. Totheroh

Act Charles Chaplin, Allan Garcia, Merna Kennedy, Harry Crocker, Stanley Sanford, George Davis (United Artists)

In clinging to a tale of logical sequence, without the expected interpolations or detached incidents, Chaplin's *Circus* for speed, gags and laughs has not been equaled on the sheet. But it's very broad, for Chaplin makes no attempt at subtlety in this one.

Pathos to a limited degree is stuck in through Chaplin attempting to protect the bareback riding daughter of the circus owner, the father brutally abusing the girl (Merna Kennedy, the only girl programmed). The tramp falls in love with her, but when the handsome new wire walker arrives the tramp is cold. That is why Chaplin takes to practicing wire walking—to rival his rival.

The finale is real Chaplinesque. Taking the wire walker to the girl the tramp declines to go into their wagon, but returns to the empty lot as the wagon circus starts for the next stand. Seated on the plate left within the ring he watches the circus depart, then trudges in the other direction, again the tramp, permitting his back and wiggly legs only to be seen for the curtain.

•

CIRCUS WORLD
(UK: THE MAGNIFICENT SHOWMAN)
1964, 138 mins, US/Spain Ⓥ ⦿ ▭ col
Dir Henry Hathaway ***Prod*** Samuel Bronston ***Scr*** Ben Hecht, Julian Halevy, James Edward Grant ***Ph*** Jack Hildyard ***Ed*** Dorothy Spencer ***Mus*** Dimitri Tiomkin ***Art*** John F. DeCuir
Act John Wayne, Claudia Cardinale, Rita Hayworth, Lloyd Nolan, Richard Conte, John Smith (Bronston-Midway)

Samuel Bronston's made-in-Spain *Circus World* is a big-screen wedding of spectacle and romance. The pace, as directed by Henry Hathaway, is unslackening.

A major value throughout is the photography of Jack Hildyard, working harmoniously with Hathaway (after Frank Capra, Sr., departed). A second unit directed by Richard Talmadge had Claude Renoir on camera.

Special effects are numerous, perhaps the most memorable being Alex Weldon's capsizing on cue of a 4,000-ton freighter, loaded with the American circus folk, gear and animals, at Barcelona dockside. Barcelona's opera house was planked over to simulate the Hansa Circus Theatre of Hamburg, circa 1910. The plaza at Chinchon, used for the bullfight scene in *Around the World in 80 Days*, may also be recognized. Negative cost was around $8.5 million.

The basic story, by Philip Yordan and Nicholas Ray, is about a runaway aerialist (Rita Hayworth) who returns to watch her daughter (Claudia Cardinale) rehearsing on the lot, like Madame X of long ago, but this time there is a happy reunion of all, the final scene being the performance given hours after a terrible fire in which mother and daughter costar in a two-act.

Hayworth looks very good and acts with warmth and authority. Cardinale, in her fifth English-language film, is ideal for the girl-bursting-into-womanhood. The relationship to foster father John Wayne is developed with a steady sense of the interplay of the stern he-man and the passionate-natured ward.

Wayne is the center-pole, the muscle, the virility and the incarnate courage of this often down-but-never-out circus. The role has been tailored to his talents and personality, a rooting-tooting-shooting figure.

•

CISCO PIKE
1971, 94 mins, US col
Dir B.W.L. Norton ***Prod*** Gerald Ayres ***Scr*** Bill L. Norton ***Ph*** Vilis Lapenieks ***Ed*** Robert C. Jones ***Mus*** Bob Johnston (sup.) ***Art*** Alfred Sweeney
Act Gene Hackman, Karen Black, Kris Kristofferson, Harry Dean Stanton, Viva, Joy Bang (Columbia)

Kris Kristofferson in title role makes an excellent formal acting debut as a faded and drug-busted rock star forced by corrupt cop Gene Hackman into selling marijuana. Well-written and directed by Bill L. Norton, the handsome Gerald Ayres's production sustains a good plot while providing proper amounts of environmental color.

The weakest plot angle is Hackman's motivation: Not until the surprise climax is it made clear that he wants some extra money since police are underpaid. There's a lot more breadth in that angle that writer Norton fails to make viable.

Principal supporting players include Karen Black in another Karen Black role as Pike's amiable but confused girl; the totally delightful Viva; Harry Dean Stanton, excellent as Pike's old partner, pitiably wasted on hard drugs; and Joy Bang, Viva's cruising partner.

Kristofferson's screen presence is very strong. There's a look in his eyes—a combination of resignation, optimism and torture—that sticks in the memory long after the film has ended.

•

CITADEL, THE
1938, 112 mins, UK Ⓥ b/w
Dir King Vidor ***Prod*** Victor Saville ***Scr*** Ian Dalrymple, Frank Wead, Elizabeth Hill ***Ph*** Harry Stradling ***Ed*** Charles Frend ***Mus*** Louis Levy ***Art*** Lazare Meerson, Alfred Junge
Act Robert Donat, Rosalind Russell, Ralph Richardson, Rex Harrison, Emlyn Williams, Penelope Dudley Ward (M-G-M)

The Citadel is Metro's second British-made production. It's an effective drama based on A. J. Cronin's novel which generated quite a controversy in medical circles due to presentation of its subject matter. Major change for picture is a switch to a happy ending.

Story details the adventures of a young physician (Robert Donat) who starts out with high ideals and determination to help humanity. When Welsh miners object to his research to prevent tuberculosis in the community, he goes to London, gets in with a coterie of mulcting doctors who brush aside medical ethics in their chase for money. Snapped out of his new surroundings by a bungling operation on his best friend, the young physician discards the shams of money for his original ideals.

Donat gives a most seasoned performance. Rosalind Russell turns in a sympathetic portrayal of the young wife who struggles through at his side, and gets him back to his ideals after the London experiences.

Picture is studded with many brilliant human and dramatic sequences. Success of Donat in reviving a stillborn baby in a worker's home is a real heart-puller; chiller is episode where entrapped miner's arm is amputated in cave-in; and vivid drama springs forth when Donat stands by while his best friend dies during bungled operation performed by the incompetent, social-climbing surgeon.

1938: NOMINATIONS: Best Picture, Director, Actor (Robert Donat), Screenplay

•

CITE DES ENFANTS PERDUS, LA
(THE CITY OF LOST CHILDREN)
1995, 111 mins, France/Spain/Germany Ⓥ ⦿ ▭ col
Dir Jean-Pierre Jeunet, Marc Caro ***Prod*** Claudie Ossard ***Scr*** Gilles Adrien, Jean-Pierre Jeunet, Marc Caro ***Ph*** Darius Khondji ***Ed*** Herve Schneid ***Mus*** Angelo Badalamenti ***Art*** Jean Rabasse
Act Ron Perlman, Daniel Emilfork, Judith Vittet, Dominique Pinon, Jean-Claude Dreyfus, Genevieve Brunet (Lumiere/Canal Plus/France 3)

A vibrant, bubbling cauldron of breathtaking f/x, gross-out humor and in-your-face imagery, *Delicatessen* duo Jean-Pierre Jeunet and Marc Caro's sophomore outing, *The City of Lost Children*, roller-coasters in as the ne plus ultra of grotesque adult fairy tales. This dark, Dickensian, $14 million-plus pinball machine of a movie hits all the major sensory bumpers but too rarely engages deeper emotions to score much of a bonus. Setting is a multilevel smokestack port littered with industrial detritus, rusty tankers and the biggest collection of weirdos and humans since Tod Browning's *Freaks*. Local heavies are the Cyclops, a Nietzschean sect of one-eyed fanatics who abduct young kids for crazed, aging inventor Krank (Daniel Emilfork), who lives on a castlelike oil rig near a minefield.

The joyless Krank needs the children in order to steal their dreams. The Cyclops's latest kidnap victim is Denree (Joseph Lucien), adopted baby brother of One (Ron Perlman), a former whale harpooner. One teams up with a group of orphan thieves and later bonds with the sassiest of the tykes, 9-year-old Miette (Judith Vittet).

For what is basically an exercise in sustained texture and cartoon-based imagery, Jeunet and Caro (the first again credited with "direction' and the second with "artistic direction") weave a strong enough storyline to sustain the weight of the huge cast of characters, who crisscross and bump into one another like balls on a pool table.

•

CITIZEN KANE
1941, 120 mins, US Ⓥ ⦿ b/w
Dir Orson Welles ***Prod*** Orson Welles ***Scr*** Herman J. Mankiewicz, Orson Welles, [Joseph Cotten, John Houseman] ***Ph*** Gregg Toland ***Ed*** Robert Wise, [Mark Robson] ***Mus*** Bernard Herrmann ***Art*** Van Nest Polglase, Perry Ferguson
Act Orson Welles, Joseph Cotten, Ray Collins, Paul Stewart, Dorothy Comingore, Everett Sloane (RKO/Mercury)

Citizen Kane is a film which distinguishes every daring entertainment venture that is created by a workman who is master of the technique and mechanics of his medium. It is a two-hour show, filled to the last minute with brilliant incident, unreeled in method and effects that sparkle with originality and invention.

In the film's story of a multimillionaire newspaper publisher, political aspirant and wielder of public opinion there are incidents that may be interpreted as uncomplimentary to William Randolph Hearst. Protests against the film's release were made by executives and employees in his organization.

Story is credited jointly to Herman J. Mankiewicz and Welles. The early, rebellious, youthful years of the powerful Kane are described by the family attorney, who neither understood nor had any deep affection for the young man. The thread is picked up by Kane's faithful business manager, then by his second wife, by his only earnest friend and finally by his butler. Pieced together, like a jigsaw puzzle, the parts and incidents omitted by earlier narrators are supplied by others.

When completed the authors' conception of Kane is a man who had every material advantage in life, but who lacked a feeling of human sympathy and tolerance. It is a story of spiritual failure. So intent is the effort to prove Kane a frustrate that no allowance is made to picture him as a human being. On this account he is not wholly real. Neither he nor his associates is blessed with the slightest sense of humor.

Welles portrays the chief character with surprising success, considering that the picture marks his debut as a film actor. His associates are selected from his Mercury Theatre's actors, few of whom had previous screen experience. Whatever else *Citizen Kane* may be, it is a refreshing cinematic novelty, and the general excellence of its acting is not the least of its assets.

1941: Best Original Screenplay

NOMINATIONS: Best Picture, Director, Actor (Orson Welles), B&W Cinematography, B&W Art Direction, Editing, Scoring of a Dramatic Picture, Sound

•

CITIZENS BAND
1977, 98 mins, US Ⓥ col
Dir Jonathan Demme ***Prod*** Freddie Fields ***Scr*** Paul Brickman ***Ph*** Jordan Cronenweth ***Ed*** John F. Link II ***Mus*** Bill Conti ***Art*** Bill Malley
Act Paul Le Mat, Candy Clark, Ann Wedgeworth, Marcia Rodd, Charles Napier, Alex Elias (Fields/Paramount)

Plot peg is the truck accident of philandering husband Charles Napier, who's got Ann Wedgeworth in Dallas and Marcia Rodd in Portland, both with homes and children.

While he is recovering at the hands of Alix Elias (whose charms are mobile), the two suspicious women arrive in a small town where Paul Le Mat and estranged brother Bruce McGill are both courting Candy Clark. Roberts Blossom is the boy's irascible widower-father. Linking all their lives is the CB radio, buzzing away like verbal Muzak.

The CB dialog exemplifies the good-natured horsing around that marks those channels, at the same time the serious emergency traffic that often saves lives.

•

CITY BENEATH THE SEA
(UK: ONE HOUR TO DOOMSDAY)
1953, 87 mins, US col
Dir Budd Boetticher ***Prod*** Albert J. Cohen ***Scr*** Jack Harvey, Ramon Romero ***Ph*** Charles P. Boyle ***Ed*** Edward Curtiss ***Mus*** Joseph Gershenson (dir.) ***Art*** Alexander Golitzen, Emrich Nicholson
Act Robert Ryan, Mala Powers, Anthony Quinn, Suzan Ball, George Mathews, Karel Stepanek (Universal)

High romance of the pulp-fiction variety is niftily shaped in *City Beneath the Sea*. The film stages a thrilling underseas "earthquake" as a capper to the derring-do yarn laid in the West Indies.

A couple of lusty, adventurous deep-sea divers, a sunken treasure, comely femmes and the earthquake are expertly mixed to provide chimerical film entertainment. The direction by Budd Boetticher is slanted to take the most advantage of the action, amatory and thrill situations in the story based on Harry E. Rieseberg's *Port Royal—The Ghost City Beneath the Sea*. Picture is not necessarily logical, but it tells its tale with a robust sense of humor.

The earthquake sequence is a real thriller. Scene is the historic sunken city of Port Royal, Jamaica, which went to the bottom of the Caribbean during a 1692 earthquake. Robert Ryan and Anthony Quinn team excellently as the daring divers, ever ready for the adventures offered by sunken treasure or shapely femmes. They come to Kingston, Jamaica, to dive for $1 million in gold bullion that went down with a freighter, without knowing their employer (Karel Stepanek) doesn't want the treasure found just yet.

Plot tangents boil along while Ryan woos Mala Powers, owner of a small, coastwise ship, and Quinn makes time with Suzan Ball, singer in a waterfront nitery.

•

CITY OF ANGELS

1998, 117 mins, US Ⓥ ⊙ ▭ col

Dir Brad Silberling ***Prod*** Charles Roven, Dawn Steel ***Scr*** Dana Stevens ***Ph*** John Seale ***Ed*** Lynzee Klingman ***Mus*** Gabriel Yared ***Art*** Lilly Kilvert

Act Nicolas Cage, Meg Ryan, Andre Braugher, Dennis Franz, Colm Feore, Robin Bartlett (Atlas/Warner)

Loosely based on Wim Wenders's enchanting 1987 *Wings of Desire*, Brad Silberling's *City of Angels* is a superlatively crafted romantic drama that solidly stands on its own merits. Pic offers a haunting, lyrical meditation on such universal issues as spirit vs. matter, human courage and the true meaning of love and desire.

The endlessly resourceful Nicolas Cage, as a celestial angel, and a terrifically engaging Meg Ryan, as a pragmatic surgeon, create such blissful chemistry that they elevate the drama to a poetic level seldom reached in a mainstream movie.

Pic is a rarity, a big-budget, star-studded studio movie that approximates European art films not only in its thematic concerns but also in tone, style and design. For the most part, the film avoids the pitfalls of schmaltzy Hollywood fare like *Ghost* and *Sleepless in Seattle*.

Seth (Cage) is a restless angel on duty in L.A., and Cassiel (Andre Braugher) is his celestial comrade who's more at ease with himself. Gliding through town on the lookout for human suffering, the two discuss the differences between angels and human beings.

Maggie (Ryan), an accomplished heart surgeon, loses her patient and undergoes a crisis of confidence. Unbeknownst to Maggie, Seth is in the room: watching her misery, he falls hard for her. Narrative gets richer and more complex through the inclusion of secondary characters, such as Messinger (Dennis Franz), Maggie's bright patient, and Anne (Robin Bartlett), a colleague at the hospital.

Departing from the plot of *Wings of Desire*, current pic's angels are more active, and the couple meet in the first reel.

In his sophomore effort, Silberling (*Casper*) makes a huge leap forward, showing his passion for the material with subtle, controlled direction. Tech credits are top-drawer across the board.

•

CITY FOR CONQUEST

1940, 105 mins, US Ⓥ b/w

Dir Anatole Litvak ***Scr*** John Wexley ***Ph*** Sol Polito, James Wong Howe ***Ed*** William Holmes ***Mus*** Max Steiner ***Art*** Robert Haas

Act James Cagney, Ann Sheridan, Frank Craven, Donald Crisp, Arthur Kennedy, Frank McHugh (Warner)

To live in New York you have to have ambition and fortitude against all odds, and battle it through when the going is toughest. That's the basic theme of *City for Conquest*, starring James Cagney and Ann Sheridan, from Aben Kandel's novel. Picture carries plenty of dramatic punch.

Picture is natural for Cagney, who troupes through role of an unwilling prizefighter in vigorous fashion, taking the tough breaks of partial blindness with heroic courage. It's Cagney all the way, but aided considerably by Sheridan for romance, plus two newcomers to films from the stage, Arthur Kennedy and Elia Kazan, who indicate they will stick around Hollywood some time.

Cagney turns down a professional boxing career to become a truck driver, but takes on a fight to help pay the musical tuition of brother Arthur Kennedy. When Sheridan goes into professional dancing with a slick partner (Anthony Quinn) and heads for big time, Cagney takes buildup for welterweight crown and fights champ who deliberately blinds him in a fight with resin gloves.

Idea of Kennedy conducting a Carnegie symphony of his own composition (which consumes around seven minutes near the finish) is reminiscent of the George Gershwin factual event of several years ago (when another East Side boy clicked).

Sheridan is excellent as the girl, displaying dancing abilities in several ballroom numbers with Quinn.

•

CITY GIRL, THE

1984, 85 mins, US Ⓥ ⊙ col

Dir Martha Coolidge ***Prod*** Martha Coolidge ***Scr*** Judith Thompson, Leonard-John Gates ***Ph*** Daniel Hainey ***Ed*** Linda Leeds, Eva Gardos ***Mus*** Scott Wilk, Marc Levinthal ***Art*** Ninkey Dalton

Act Laura Harrington, Joe Mastroianni, Carole McGill, Peter Riegert, Jim Carrington, Lawrence Phillips (Moon)

Martha Coolidge's *The City Girl* reps a hard-nosed, if frequently funny, look at a young woman's attempt to forge a career and self-esteem. It's a predecessor to same director's 1983 indie hit, *Valley Girl*.

Lead character of Anne is a young lady who, in an awfully serious way, is trying to get a foot up as a professional photographer. Joey, her sympathetic but very straight boyfriend, indulges her to a point but would rather have her fill the conventional woman's role, something it's obvious she won't do.

Most bracing aspect of Coolidge's treatment of the relatively plain material is her rigorously objective, unindulgent perspective.

In line with the director's approach, Laura Harrington, who plays Anne, does not sentimentalize her character.

•

CITY HALL

1996, 111 mins, US Ⓥ ⊙ col

Dir Harold Becker ***Prod*** Edward R. Pressman, Ken Lipper, Charles Mulvehill ***Scr*** Ken Lipper, Paul Schrader, Nicholas Pileggi, Bo Goldman ***Ph*** Michael Seresin ***Ed*** Robert C. Jones, David Bretherton ***Mus*** Jerry Goldsmith ***Art*** Jane Musky

Act Al Pacino, John Cusack, Bridget Fonda, Danny Aiello, Martin Landau, Tony Franciosa (Castle Rock/Columbia)

Structured as a whodunit, *City Hall* centers on a credible, colorful rogue's gallery of suspects within a fast-paced thriller framework. At its best, the picture conveys the visceral energy of city politics and problem solving. There are no happy endings, just reelection promises. Kevin Calhoun (John Cusack) believes men in power can make a difference. The transplanted Louisiana boy is the deputy mayor who views Gotham as a place where one should be prepared and willing to be lucky. He reveres his boss, John Pappas (Al Pacino), a passionate and fearless man of the people.

Calhoun's naïveté is put to the test when an off-duty cop winds up in a fatal shootout with a drug dealer that claims the life of a six-year-old black boy. The policeman's breach of conduct reaches into issues far beyond those of race and pension benefits. As the onion skin of the plot is peeled away, the net of implicated parties fans out into the legal system, organized crime and municipal government.

The screenplay derives from a script by producer Ken Lipper, New York deputy mayor under Ed Koch. At the core of this contemporary Greek tragedy is Pacino's Pappas. It's a flamboyant interpretation that reflects the character's self-aware showmanship.

Danny Aiello especially stands out as a councilman with the knack for using power and personality to get what he wants. Bridget Fonda's role as an attorney isn't much more than a plot convenience.

•

CITY HEAT

1984, 97 mins, US Ⓥ ⊙ col

Dir Richard Benjamin ***Prod*** Fritz Manes ***Scr*** Sam O. Brown [= Blake Edwards], Joseph C. Stinson ***Ph*** Nick McLean ***Ed*** Jacqueline Cambas ***Mus*** Lennie Niehaus ***Art*** Edward Carfagno

Act Clint Eastwood, Burt Reynolds, Jane Alexander, Madeline Kahn, Rip Torn, Richard Roundtree (Malpaso/Deliverance/Warner)

City Heat is an amiable but decidedly lukewarm confection geared entirely around the two star turns.

Set in an unnamed city around the end of Prohibition, Clint Eastwood and Burt Reynolds were old pals in their early days as cops, but the former has taken a dim view of the latter's jump over to the private detective business, resulting in a certain tension between them.

Reynolds's partner, Richard Roundtree, gets bumped off in the early going, and Reynolds spends the remainder of the picture attempting to play two mobster kingpins off one another.

Some of the repartee is relatively amusing, and the two stars with tongues firmly in cheek, easily set the prevailing tone of low-keyed facetiousness.

•

CITY LIGHTS

1931, 87 mins, US Ⓥ b/w

Dir Charles Chaplin ***Prod*** Charles Chaplin ***Scr*** Charles Chaplin ***Ph*** Roland Totheroh ***Ed*** Charles Chaplin ***Mus*** Charles Chaplin ***Art*** Charles D. Hall

Act Charles Chaplin, Virginia Cherrill, Harry Myers, Allan Garcia, Hank Mann, Florence Lee (United Artists)

It's not Chaplin's best picture, because the comedian has sacrificed speed to pathos, and plenty of it. This is principally the reason for the picture running some 1,500 or more feet beyond any previous film released by him. But the British comic is still the consummate pantomimist.

All through Chaplin schemes how to procure money for a blind flower girl (Virginia Cherrill).

Script is something of a fable in discovering the comic asleep in the lap of a statue when it is unveiled and then having him in and out of trouble through the means of a millionaire (Harry Myers), whom Chaplin prevents from a drunken suicide, and who thereafter only recognizes the comic when drunk.

It can be imagined how much stuff has been tossed away in getting this picture down to its present length, after spasmodically shooting on it over a period of 18 months or more. As previously, Chaplin mainly paints in broad strokes, with his most subtle maneuvering here being the sly turning of the sympathy away from the girl to himself as the picture draws to a close.

•

CITY LIMITS

1985, 85 mins, US Ⓥ col

Dir Aaron Lipstadt ***Prod*** Rupert Harvey, Barry Opper ***Scr*** Don Opper ***Ph*** Timothy Suhrstedt ***Ed*** Robert Kizer ***Mus*** John Lurie ***Art*** Cyd Smilie

Act Darrell Larson, John Stockwell, Kim Cattrall, Rae Dawn Chong, Robby Benson, James Earl Jones (Sho/Videoform)

Elements of *City Limits* fit it into the category of the post-Holocaust pic, but the historical disaster is a plague which has wiped out an older generation. The young survive in a condition of controlled anarchy and resist attempts to impose a centralized government.

Most successful aspect of the film [based on a story by James Reigle and Aaron Lipstadt] is its depiction of a tribal lifestyle regulated according to rules learned from comic strips. Two gangs of bikers, the Clippers and the DAs, have divided up the city and live under a truce. Infractions of their pact are regulated with competitive jousting or acts of reciprocal revenge. The dead are cremated with their vehicles like Vikings in their boats. The two groups may unite against outside threats.

Less convincing is the portrayal, with allusions to Fritz Lang's classic *Metropolis*, of the totalitarian-inclined Sunya Corp., which attempts to take over the city with the initial cooperation of the DAs.

Film features an ace ensemble cast. Action scenes are well-executed and there's a vibrant score.

•

CITY OF HOPE

1991, 129 mins, US Ⓥ ▭ col

Dir John Sayles ***Prod*** Sarah Green, Maggie Renzi ***Scr*** John Sayles ***Ph*** Robert Richardson ***Ed*** John Sayles ***Mus*** Mason Daring ***Art*** Dan Bishop, Dianna Freas

Act Vincent Spano, Joe Morton, Tony LoBianco, Anthony John Denison, Barbara Williams, John Sayles (Esperanza)

John Sayles's ambitious, wide-ranging study of corruption and community in a small Eastern city has as many parallel plots and characters as *Hill Street Blues*, while at the same time having a richness of theme and specificity of vision more common to serious cinema.

Picture hinges on the oppposite directions of two characters: Nick (Vincent Spano), disillusioned son of a well-connected builder, who has easy access to the system but only wants out of it, and Wynn (Joe Morton), a young black city councilman who's determined to work within the system.

Nick soon gets involved in a robbery to get money to pay off his gambling debts. Meanwhile he's starting a romance with an old high school classmate Angela (Barbara Williams), which draws the wrath of her mad-dog ex-husband and cop (Anthony John Denison). Then a racial crisis erupts when two black kids attack a white college teacher.

For much of the film, the restlessness of focus seems a liability. But when the camera stops long enough to put two characters together one-on-one, dialog and emotional connection emerge.

•

CITY OF JOY

1992, 134 mins, UK/France Ⓥ ⊙ col

Dir Roland Joffe ***Prod*** Jake Eberts ***Scr*** Mark Medoff ***Ph*** Peter Biziou ***Ed*** Gerry Hambling ***Mus*** Ennio Morricone ***Art*** Roy Walker

Act Patrick Swayze, Pauline Collins, Om Puri, Shabana Azmi, Art Malik, Ayesha Dharker (Lightmotive)

A picture divided against itself, *City of Joy* is half American-style gangster melodrama and half inspirational social consciousness.

Impressively produced in Calcutta's teeming poverty-ridden streets and slums, Roland Joffe's noble attempt to portray the tenacity and strength of the human spirit comes off as curiously ineffectual due to predictable plotting and character evolution.

Inspired by selected stories in Dominique Lapierre's 1985 international bestseller, *City of Joy* is a direct descendant of the *Casablanca* school, with a disenchanted, cynical

Yank heading for exotic climes to both alleviate and exult in his ennui, and finally finding something in himself he thought had died or never existed.

Fleeing from the rigors of life as a surgeon in Houston, Patrick Swayze's Dr. Max Lowe arrives in Calcutta with the vague idea of seeking enlightenment. Assaulted and robbed, Max is taken to the City of Joy Self-Help School and Dispensary, presided over by a beleaguered but selflessly saintly British woman (Pauline Collins). Max becomes cheerleader for the dispossessed people of City of Joy in their battle against the local mafia.

An admittedly chancy choice to play a jaded medic, Swayze gives it the old college try, but he doesn't have depth. Appealing as always, Collins has nothing but routine buttons to push as she uses all her wiles to win the doc over to her cause.

•

CITY OF LOST CHILDREN, THE
SEE: LA CITE DES ENFANTS PERDUS

•

CITY ON FIRE
SEE: LUNGFU FUNGWAN

•

CITY SLICKERS
1991, 112 mins, US Ⓥ ⊙ col
Dir Ron Underwood ***Prod*** Irby Smith ***Scr*** Lowell Ganz, Babaloo Mandel ***Ph*** Dean Semler ***Ed*** O. Nicholas Brown ***Mus*** Marc Shaiman, Hummie Mann ***Art*** Lawrence G. Paull
Act Billy Crystal, Daniel Stern, Bruno Kirby, Patricia Wettig, Helen Slater, Jack Palance (Columbia/Castle Rock)

The setup is sheer simplicity, as Billy Crystal, coming to grips with the doldrums of midlife thanks to his 39th birthday, is convinced by his wife (Patricia Wettig) and two best friends (Daniel Stern, Bruno Kirby) to take off for two weeks on a ranch trip driving cattle across the west. The childhood fantasy comes to life in a number of ways, perhaps foremost in the presence of gnarled trail boss Curly (Jack Palance), a figure always seemingly backlit in larger-than-life silhouettes.

The other cowboy wannabes include a father-and-son dentist team (Bill Henderson, Phill Lewis), fraternal ice-cream tycoons (David Paymer, Josh Mostel) and a beautiful woman (Bonnie Rayburn) who braved the trip on her own. A series of increasingly absurd events lead central trio toward an ultimate challenge that turns the vacation into a journey of self-discovery.

Crystal gets plenty of chance to crack wise while he, Stern and Kirby engage in playful and not-so-playful banter—Stern coming off a recently (and publicly) failed marriage while the womanizing Kirby grapples with his own fear of fidelity. Director Ron Underwood (who made his feature debut on *Tremors*) generally keeps the herd moving at a fine pace.

1991: Best Supp. Actor (Jack Palance)

•

CITY SLICKERS II: THE LEGEND OF CURLY'S GOLD
1994, 116 mins, US Ⓥ ⊙ col
Dir Paul Weiland ***Prod*** Billy Crystal ***Scr*** Billy Crystal, Lowell Ganz, Babaloo Mandel ***Ph*** Adrian Biddle ***Ed*** William Anderson ***Mus*** Marc Shaiman ***Art*** Stephen Lineweaver
Act Billy Crystal, Daniel Stern, Jon Lovitz, Jack Palance, Patricia Wettig, Bob Balaban (Castle Rock/Face/Columbia)

The gang that couldn't ride straight is back on the commercial trail in *City Slickers II*. The lively sequel to an original that grossed $123.8 million domestically is a sure-shootin' handsome contempo oater rife with both gags and classic genre lore.

Getting once-bitten urbanite Mitch Robbins (Billy Crystal) back in the saddle proves a bit of a sleight of hand for the scripters. He's running a Manhattan radio station and knee-deep in tsuris because of his big heart. His hire of buddy Phil (Daniel Stern) in sales is pretty much a wash and when his low-life brother Glen (Jon Lovitz) insists on moving in with the family, wife Barbara (Patricia Wettig) envisions divorce court.

Mitch is obsessed by the notion that he just may have buried the grisled cowboy Curly (Jack Palance) a tad prematurely. So, when he stands in the mirror adjusting Curly's Stetson, providence steps in. Tucked into the lining is a map indicating the way to buried gold.

The film comes alive once it heads into sagebrush territory. It hits full stride with the introduction of Duke (Jack Palance), Curly's twin brother. The filmmakers nod appreciately to *The Treasure of the Sierra Madre* and both movies share a fondness for parable and a keen sense of irony.

Crystal's character grounds the yarn in the real and humorous. He also reveals a penchant for clasping hands to face and screaming á la an overaged Macaulay Culkin. He's at the service of the material (which he co-wrote with Lowell Ganz and Babaloo Mandel) and generous to a fault with other performers. Also worth a note is an uncredited turn by Bob Balaban as a radio shrink with a perfect deadpan delivery and attentiveness.

•

CITY STREETS
1931, 83 mins, US b/w
Dir Rouben Mamoulian ***Prod*** E. Lloyd Sheldon ***Scr*** Oliver H. P. Garrett, Max Marcin ***Ph*** Lee Garmes ***Mus*** Sidney Cutner
Act Gary Cooper, Sylvia Sidney, Paul Lukas, William Boyd, Guy Kibbee, Stanley Fields (Paramount)

Probably the first sophisticated treatment of a gangster picture. Story is the usual love-redeeming tale of two kids caught in a gangster vortex.

Picture is lifted from mediocrity through the intelligent acting and appeal of Sylvia Sidney. This legit girl makes her first screen appearance here as co-star with Gary Cooper. From a histrionic standpoint she's the whole works, and that's not detracting from the others who perform ably.

Gang chieftain is shown controlling everything from his henchmen's women to his sidekicks' lives. He doesn't control his own life, though, and a jealous girl sends him low when he tries to shelve her for Babe (Sidney).

Final has Babe and her boyfriend (Cooper) make the heights of dececency when they trick three badmen executioners, trailing them, into a long and speedy ride through the great outdoors.

Camera angles are piled on thick. Most of the time these shots serve to slow up the film and confuse.

•

CITY THAT NEVER SLEEPS
1953, 90 mins, US Ⓥ b/w
Dir John H. Auer ***Prod*** John H. Auer (assoc.) ***Scr*** Steve Fisher ***Ph*** John L. Russell, Jr. ***Ed*** Fred Allen ***Mus*** R. Dale Butts ***Art*** James Sullivan
Act Gig Young, Mala Powers, William Talman, Edward Arnold, Chill Wills, Marie Windsor (Republic)

Production and direction loses itself occasionally in stretching for mood and nuances, whereas a straightline cops-and-robbers action flavor would have been more appropriate. Same flaw is found in the Steve Fisher screen original.

Playing of the four cast toppers, Gig Young, a crazy, mixed-up cop; Mala Powers, a cheap saloon dancer; William Talman, a magician turned hood; and Edward Arnold, suave, crooked attorney, is adequate to script and directorial demands. Chill Wills, principal featured player, walks through the film without any definition, presumably being a character that represents the city of Chicago itself.

One night in life on the Chicago police force finds Young ready to blow his job and wife (Paula Raymond) to run away with Powers. He accepts an assignment from Arnold to take Talman over the state line in order to get money for the flight from reality.

John L. Russell's photography makes okay use of Chicago streets and buildings for the low-key, nightlife effect required to back the melodrama.

•

CIVILIZATION
1916, 121 mins, US Ⓥ ⊗ b/w
Dir Raymond B. West ***Prod*** Thomas H. Ince ***Scr*** C. Gardner Sulivan ***Ph*** Joseph August, Clyde de Vinna, Irvin Willat ***Ed*** Thomas H. Ince ***Mus*** Victor Schertzinger
Act Howard Hickman, Enid Markey, Herschel Mayall, George Fisher, J. Frank Burke (Triangle/KayBee)

Master producer Thomas H. Ince was handicapped here by the limitations of C. Gardner Sulivan's scenario, designed as a strong protest against the horrors of war.

The entertainment opens showing a nation at peace, suddenly plunged headlong into war by its king (Herschel Mayall), due wholly to his selfish desire for conquest. He is dependent for success upon Count Ferdinand (Howard Hickman), who has invented a submarine calculated to destroy the enemy's fleet, thus ensuring victory. The count is in love with Katheryn, "a woman of the people." Katheryn (Enid Markey) belongs to a secret society, which is opposed to war. She takes him to one of the meetings and he becomes a convert.

When the count receives a wireless message to blow up an enemy vessel carrying innocent passengers, he refuses to obey orders and, as his own crew attacks him, sinks his own vessel and deliberately drowns himself and crew. His body is picked up and the king sends for his scientists to restore life in order to secure the secrets of the death-dealing submarine. But it is only the count's body with the soul of Christ who resolves to return to Earth to teach the message of Love not Hate.

There is very little opportunity to criticise Ince's magnificent effort, but Sulivan's captions are altogether too preachy. In his effort to project pathos he slops over into bathos.

•

CLAIRE DOLAN
1998, 95 mins, France/US Ⓥ ⊙ col
Dir Lodge Kerrigan ***Prod*** Ann Ruark ***Scr*** Lodge Kerrigan ***Ph*** Teodoro Maniaci ***Ed*** Kristina Boden ***Mus*** Ahrin Mishan, Simon Fisher Turner ***Art*** Sharon Lomofsky
Act Katrin Cartlidge, Vincent D'Onofrio, Colm Meaney, John Doman, Maryanne Plunkett, Miranda Stuart-Rhyne (MK2/Serene)

A rarified, emotionally distant art film, *Claire Dolan* is a rigorously controlled, occasionally arresting study of a New York prostitute's systematic attempt to take control of her life. Lodge Kerrigan's work represents a slightly disappointing sidestep rather than a significant stride beyond his edgy, genuinely disturbing debut with *Clean, Shaven* in 1993.

Buffs will invoke such names as Bresson and Godard in trying to describe this airless but undeniably impressive picture by a genuinely maverick American director. By imprisoning his characters within walls of mirrors, glass, chrome, plastic and often unadorned surfaces, and by manipulating the sound mix to an unusual degree, Kerrigan skillfully creates an intimidating, claustrophobic world in which his protagonist conducts her determined odyssey toward a new life.

Claire (Katrin Cartlidge) is a Dublin native who devotes nearly all her waking hours to working off a large debt to presumed mobster Roland Cain (Colm Meaney), who has known her since she was a girl. After her mother dies, Claire lets herself be picked up by a good-looking guy in a bar. But she remains intensely bottled up emotionally and physically. Another chance encounter in a bar, with a taxi driver named Elton (Vincent D'Onofrio), shows some promise of changing that.

Very restrained under Kerrigan's tight rein, Cartlidge remains emotionally tamped down; the distance the writer-director creates between character and audience prevents Claire from sharing her inner life.

D'Onofrio is appealing enough if unassertive; one keeps waiting for his character to break through with the pent-up Claire in some significant way that would justify her anointing him as her man of choice. Meaney brings welcome weight and charm to his powerful character.

•

CLAIRE'S KNEEE
SEE: LE GENOU DE CLAIRE

•

CLAN OF THE CAVE BEAR, THE
1986, 98 mins, US Ⓥ ⊙ ▭ col
Dir Michael Chapman ***Prod*** Gerald I. Isenberg ***Scr*** John Sayles ***Ph*** Jan de Bont ***Ed*** Wendy Greene Bricmont ***Mus*** Alan Silvestri ***Art*** Kelly Kimbal
Act Daryl Hannah, Pamela Reed, James Remar, Thomas G. Waites, John Doolittle (PSO/Guber-Peters/Jozak/Decade/Jonesfilm)

The Clan of the Cave Bear is a dull, overly genteel rendition of Jean M. Auel's novel. Handsomely produced on rugged Canadian exteriors, this is the story of pre-history's first feminist.

Although set 35,000 years ago, pic could more or less have been set in any time, as it displays little of the anthropological ambition of *Quest for Fire* and is pitched to appeal to the same sensibilities that responded to *The Blue Lagoon*.

Little imagination is in evidence here. A primitive language has been invented for these early humans to speak (subtitles run throughout), but nothing in their customs, habits or attitudes proves very interesting. Daryl Hannah, at least, is a fetching and sympathetic center of attention, but emoting of the entire cast is limited to expressive grunting.

1986: NOMINATION: Best Makeup

•

CLANSMAN, THE
SEE: THE BIRTH OF A NATION

•

CLARA'S HEART
1988, 108 mins, US Ⓥ ⊙ col
Dir Robert Mulligan ***Prod*** Martin Elfand ***Scr*** Mark Medoff ***Ph*** Freddie Francis ***Ed*** Sidney Levin ***Mus*** Dave Grusin ***Art*** Jeffrey Howard
Act Whoopi Goldberg, Michael Ontkean, Kathleen Quinlan, Neil Patrick Harris, Spalding Gray, Beverly Todd (MTM/Warner)

Buoyed by a beautifully measured star turn by Whoopi Goldberg and a smashing screen debut for young Neil Patrick

Harris, *Clara's Heart* is a powerful, unabashedly sentimental drama. Adaptation of Joseph Olshan's novel pays attention to the values of a well-wrought character study of a noble Jamaican servant (Goldberg) and the young rich kid (Harris) she guides through adolescent rite of passage.

Goldberg enters Harris's spoiled, upper-crust world in a family mansion outside Baltimore in a roundabout fashion: Harris's weepy mom (Kathleen Quinlan) is vacationing in Jamaica with hubbie (Michael Ontkean), tormented by the death of her infant daughter, when the hotel maid Clara (Goldberg) brings her back to life with doses of folk wisdom.

Captured in lush autumnal hues by ace British lenser Freddie Francis, *Clara's Heart* is a beauty to behold, buttressed by a moving, wistful Dave Grusin score. Goldberg's control and strength, including an unwavering Jamaican accent, build cumulatively to deep emotional impact. Support roles are ably filled including the required callousness of Quinlan's and Ontkean's characters.

•

CLASH BY NIGHT

1952, 105 mins, US Ⓥ ⊙ b/w

Dir Fritz Lang ***Prod*** Harriet Parsons ***Scr*** Alfred Hayes, David Dortort ***Ph*** Nicholas Musuraca ***Ed*** George J. Amy ***Mus*** Roy Webb ***Art*** Albert S. D'Agostino, Carroll Clark

Act Barbara Stanwyck, Paul Douglas, Robert Ryan, Marilyn Monroe, J. Carrol Naish, Keith Andes (Wald-Krasna/RKO)

Clifford Odets's *Clash by Night*, presented on Broadway over a decade earlier, reaches the screen in a rather aimless drama of lust and passion.

Clash captures much of the drabness of the seacoast fishing town, background of the pic, but only occasionally does the narrative's suggested intensity seep through. It is the story of a woman, buffeted by life's realities, who returns to her hometown after 10 years, only to find that the escapism she has sought is still beyond her reach. She marries a fisherman for security reasons, ultimately being forced to choose between two men.

Barbara Stanwyck plays the returning itinerant with her customary defiance and sullenness. It is one of her better performances. Robert Ryan plays the other man with grim brutality while Marilyn Monroe is reduced to what is tantamount to a bit role.

•

CLASH OF THE TITANS

1981, 118 mins, UK Ⓥ ⊙ col

Dir Desmond Davis ***Prod*** Charles H. Schneer, Ray Harryhausen ***Scr*** Beverly Cross ***Ph*** Ted Moore ***Ed*** Timothy Gee ***Mus*** Laurence Rosenthal ***Art*** Frank White

Act Laurence Olivier, Harry Hamlin, Claire Bloom, Maggie Smith, Burgess Meredith, Ursula Andress (United Artists/M-G-M)

Clash of the Titans is an unbearable bore that will probably put to sleep the few adults stuck taking the kids to it. This mythical tale of Perseus, son of Zeus, and his quest for the "fair" Andromeda, is mired in a slew of corny dialog and an endless array of flat, outdated special effects.

Watching acclaimed actors like Laurence Olivier, Maggie Smith and Claire Bloom wandering through the clouds in long white gowns as Greek gods is funny enough. But when they start to utter the stylized dialog about what they're going to do to the mortals on the earth below, one wants to look to the Gods for help. But obviously, that's impossible here. Unfortunately, none of the creatures of effects that famed expert Ray Harryhausen (who also coproduced) designed seem anything more than rehashes from B-pictures.

Desmond Davis directs with a tired hand, not helped much by the lackadaisical writing.

•

CLASS

1983, 98 mins, US Ⓥ ⊙ col

Dir Lewis John Carlino ***Prod*** Martin Ransohoff ***Scr*** Jim Kouf, David Greenwalt ***Ph*** Ric Waite ***Ed*** Stuart Pappe, Dennis Dolan ***Mus*** Elmer Bernstein ***Art*** Jack Poplin

Act Rob Lowe, Jacqueline Bisset, Andrew McCarthy, Stuart Margolin, Cliff Robertson, John Cusack (Orion)

Class is anything but classy. About a brainy but virginal prep school student (Andrew McCarthy) who unwittingly begins an affair with his upperclass roommate's sexy mother (Jacqueline Bisset), film seems something like an unofficial remake of one of Bisset's first Hollywood efforts, the 1969 *The First Time*, in which she initiated the nerdy Wes Stern in the pleasures of the flesh. Throw in aspects of *The Graduate*, with the young fellow's best friend, instead of girlfriend, getting mad at the betrayal, and you get the idea.

McCarthy and Rob Lowe (as his roommate) carry most of the picture, and both acquit themselves reasonably well under the circumstances. Lewis John Carlino's direction is frequently awkward, notably in the nudity-less sex scenes.

•

CLASS ACT

1992, 98 mins, US Ⓥ col

Dir Randall Miller ***Prod*** Todd Black, Maynell Thomas ***Scr*** John Semper, Cynthia Friedlob ***Ph*** Francis Kenny ***Ed*** John F. Burnett ***Mus*** Vassal Benford ***Art*** David L. Snyder

Act Christopher Reid, Christopher Martin, Karyn Parsons, Alysia Rogers, Meshach Taylor, Rick Ducommun (Warner)

Mixing elements of *Trading Places* with a Three Stooges short, this latest test for rap duo Kid 'N Play scores low on the SAT spectrum. Infused with some of the energy but not the smarts of pair's debut *House Party*, pic [from a screen story by Michael Swerdlick, Wayne Rice and Richard Brenne] actually has a reasonably engaging premise that gets lost amid the too-broad cartoon elements and emphasis on teen T&A. Two newcomers to a high school—one a certified genius, the other a paroled felon with a nasty reputation—swap identities, giving the nerd the tough guy's rep while replacing his counterpart among the snooty elite. Each is later willing to give up the ruse, except they've both met girls (Alysia Rogers, Karyn Parsons; both very appealing in rather thankless roles) within their new worlds.

Subtlety is a four-letter word to director Randall Miller, a first-time movie helmsman whose TV credits include the series *Parker Lewis Can't Lose*. Action comes to a dead stop near the end so Kid 'N Play can deliver an anti-drug rap number.

Some amusing moments do emerge, thanks largely to the attractive young cast. Kid (Christopher Reid) and Play (Christopher Martin) also reinforce their ability to provide engaging surrogates for the teen set. Comic Pauly Shore also turns up in an insignificant cameo.

•

CLASS ACTION

1991, 109 mins, US Ⓥ ⊙ col

Dir Michael Apted ***Prod*** Ted Field, Scott Kroopf, Robert W. Cort, ***Scr*** Carolyn Shelby, Christopher Ames, Samantha Shad ***Ph*** Conrad Hall ***Ed*** Ian Crafford ***Mus*** James Horner ***Art*** Todd Hallowell

Act Gene Hackman, Mary Elizabeth Mastrantonio, Colin Friels, Joanna Merlin, Larry Fishburne, Donald Moffat (20th Century-Fox/Interscope)

Winning performances by Gene Hackman and Mary Elizabeth Mastrantonio and potent direction by Michael Apted pump life into the sturdy courtroom drama formula once again.

Hackman plays Jed Ward, a veteran civil rights lawyer still dedicated to defending the underdog, though his record, both professional and personal, is not without blotches.

Mastrantonio is his daughter Maggie, a ruthlessly effective corporate advocate and ladder-climber, whose disdain for her father has more to do with his amorous indiscretions than his politics. They wind up on opposite sides of a class action suit filed against an auto company by the maimed survivors of crashes in which the cars exploded on impact.

For the first half, much of the script is by the numbers, as characters deliver plodding dialog to lay out the situation, but things pick up. Viewer sympathy accumulates quickly for Hackman, the charismatic, if flawed, man of the people, but Mastrantonio carves out her own turf and hangs on to it, truly taking on the senior actor.

•

CLASS OF '44

1973, 95 mins, US Ⓥ ▭ col

Dir Paul Bogart ***Prod*** Paul Bogart ***Scr*** Herman Raucher ***Ph*** Andrew Laszlo ***Ed*** Michael A. Hoey ***Mus*** David Shire

Act Gary Grimes, Jerry Houser, Oliver Conant, William Atherton, Sam Bottoms, Deborah Winters (Warner)

Class of '44 is an okay follow-up to *Summer of '42* [1971], taking the three juveniles of the first film through their early college years at the end of World War II. Paul Bogart's production and direction are slightly better than Herman Raucher's script, in which nostalgia pellets fall like hailstones on an essentially programmer plot.

Encoring in the lead roles are Gary Grimes, Jerry Houser and Oliver Conant, all introduced graduating from high school. Conant joins the Marines and virtually disappears from the plot, leaving Houser and Grimes to head for college. Deborah Winters is Grimes's campus sweetheart, and William Atherton is very good as a fraternity president supervising the hazing of pledges.

•

CLASS OF MISS MACMICHAEL, THE

1978, 100 mins, UK/US Ⓥ col

Dir Silvio Narizzano ***Prod*** Judd Bernard ***Scr*** Judd Bernard ***Ph*** Alex Thomason ***Ed*** Max Benedict ***Mus*** Stanley Myers

Act Glenda Jackson, Oliver Reed, Michael Murphy, Rosalind Cash, John Standing, Phil Daniels (Kettledrum/Brut)

This pic [from the book by Sandy Hutson] is about dippy doings at a special school for unruly teenagers whose next steps may be reformatories. Treading the usual characterizations and situations, film adds a more permissive tone in language and freewheeling sex of the students not to forget the harassed teachers and a scheming headmaster.

Though predictable, and the script serviceable for this of-treated theme, with direction average, it has Glenda Jackson adding her presence to the part of a dedicated teacher who eschews a second marriage to stay with her impossible charges.

Jackson's dedicated but world-weary air gives an edge to her character as she is the rare teacher who gets through to her charges. Michael Murphy's nice guy playing, but with hints of stodginess, make his role as Jackson's boyfriend.

Oliver Reed overcharges his role of the martinet, hypocritical, mean principal who uses a false front to visitors and a mailed fist at the school.

•

CLASS OF 1984

1982, 96 mins, Canada Ⓥ ⊙ col

Dir Mark L. Lester ***Prod*** Arthur Kent ***Scr*** Tom Holland, John Saxton, Mark L. Lester ***Ph*** Albert Dank ***Ed*** Howard Kunin ***Mus*** Lalo Schifrin

Act Perry King, Timothy Van Patten, Merrie Lynn Ross, Roddy McDowall, Al Waxman, Michael J. Fox (Guerrilla High)

Class of 1984 is pure exploitation with plenty of action and a manipulative plot [from a story by Tom Holland] designed to have audiences cheering on the blood.

The Canadian production is set at Abraham Lincoln High School in a large American city. Newcomer music teacher Perry King finds his views on education rapidly altered at the school: Students are frisked for weapons, teachers carry guns and the hallways are monitored by guards and cameras.

The chief purveyors of terror are a gang led by Timothy Van Patten. They run a drug and prostitution ring and wield a heavy blow to anyone obstructing their activities.

King refuses to buckle to their strongarm tactics and finds his car first vandalized and later fire-bombed. Walking into a cocaine deal in the school bathroom, King takes Van Patten to the principal, but lack of evidence places the teacher's actions in question.

Performances are generally good with King in fine form as the hard-pressed hero while Van Patten is effectively chilling as Stegman.

•

CLASS OF 1999

1990, 98 mins, US Ⓥ col

Dir Mark L. Lester ***Prod*** Mark L. Lester ***Scr*** C. Courtney Joyner ***Ph*** Mark Irwin ***Ed*** Scott Conrad ***Mus*** Michael Hoenig

Act Bradley Gregg, Traci Lind, Malcolm McDowell, Stacy Keach, Pam Grier, John P. Ryan (Original/Lightning)

A follow-up to the 1982 pic *Class of 1984* this violent exploitation film is too pretentious for its own good. Director Mark L. Lester takes a cynical, fake-hip view of young people's future.

The inconsistent screenplay posits high-schoolers out of control. So-called free-fire zones have been set up in urban areas around the schools as no-man's-land, and are literally under the control of youth gangs.

Hamming it up as an albino megalomaniac, Stacy Keach is carrying out an experiment sending three androids reconverted from army surplus to serve as teachers at Kennedy H.S. in Seattle and whip the students into shape. Simultaneously, hero Bradley Gregg has been let out of jail and returned to class at Kennedy in an experimental furlough program.

John P. Ryan and Pam Grier are loads of fun as the androids, latter mocking her image when not only her breasts but inner works are revealed for the final reel through hokey makeup effects.

•

CLASS OF NUKE 'EM HIGH, PART II: SUBHUMANOID MELTDOWN

1991, 95 mins, US Ⓥ col

Dir Eric Louzil ***Prod*** Michael Herz, Lloyd Kaufman ***Scr*** Lloyd Kaufman, Eric Louzil, Carl Morano, Marcus Roling, Jeffrey W. Sass, Matt Unger, Andrew Osborne ***Ph*** Ron Chapman ***Ed*** Gordon Grinberg ***Mus*** Bob Mithoff ***Art*** [uncredited]

Act Brick Bronsky, Lisa Gaye, Leesa Rowland, Michael Kurtz, Scott Resnick, Shelby Shepard (Troma)

This unwarranted sequel is an incoherent mess that plays more like a trailer than a feature. Director Eric Louzil demonstrates he has no feel for satire or comedy, absolute prerequisites for a Troma pic.

Beefcake star Brick Bronsky narrates a film-long flashback. He's writing for the campus paper at Tromaville Institute of Technology, a combination college/nuclear power plant. Mad scientist Prof. Holt (attractive Lisa Gaye) has created a race of drone subhumanoid workers, including beautiful Victoria (Leesa Rowland). Unfortunately, they are subject to an ailment that causes them to melt into green goo.

An unfunny running gag insists on the subhumanoids having mouths where their belly buttons should be. This is an excuse for plenty of topless footage of starlets, including porn star Trinity Loren.

Lead cast members have trouble reading lines and the sound effects aren't very funny.

•

CLAUDIA AND DAVID
1946, 78 mins, US b/w
Dir Walter Lang *Prod* William Perlberg *Scr* Rose Franken, William Brown Meloney *Ph* Joseph La Shelle *Ed* Robert Simpson *Mus* Cyril J. Mockridge *Art* James Basevi, Alfred Hogsett
Act Dorothy McGuire, Robert Young, Mary Astor, John Sutton, Gail Patrick, Florence Bates (20th Century-Fox)

Strong entertainment for femme theatergoers has been developed from adventures of the Rose Franken magazine characters, Claudia and David. Film is jammed with tears and chuckles, played and directed to realize fully on all values.

Dorothy McGuire makes the scatterbrained Claudia believeable, and Robert Young backs her up with an equally good performance as her longsuffering husband, David.

Plot generally concerns Claudia's susceptibility and strong love for her young son. Trouble starts when a phony mind reader warns her husband he will have an accident if he takes a trip to California. Sudden illness of the son, which Claudia builds into a serious tragedy only to find out it's measles, jealousy of her husband's professional attention to an attractive widow seeking his architectural advice, the attentions paid her by an attractive married man and a serious auto accident in which David is injured are some of the more dramatic moments that are leavened with smart, earthy chuckles.

•

CLAUDINE
1974, 92 mins, US Ⓥ col
Dir John Berry *Prod* Hannah Weinstein *Scr* Tina Pine, Lester Pine *Ph* Gayne Rescher *Ed* Luis San Andres *Mus* Curtis Mayfield *Art* Ted Hawarth
Act Diahann Carroll, James Earl Jones, Lawrence Hinton-Jacobs, Tamu, David Kruger, Yvette Curtis (Third World)

Claudine is an outstanding film. A gritty, hearty, heartful and ruggedly tender story of contemporary urban black family life avoiding blaxploitation genre.

Here we have some too-real problems—Diahann Carroll as a 36-year-old mother of six trying to keep a family together without a man around; James Earl Jones as her garbage collector-boyfriend trapped in the immorality of the welfare system which encourages impropriety and discourages decency.

The affair between Carroll and Jones is further complicated by various real problems with her kids. Eldest son Lawrence Hinton-Jacobs is torn apart by maturing black pride; daughter Tamu is experiencing her first adult female impulses; son David Kruger is on the verge of teenage dropout status.

1974: NOMINATION: Best Actress (Diahnn Carroll)

•

CLEAN AND SOBER
1988, 124 mins, US Ⓥ ⦿ col
Dir Glenn Gordon Caron *Prod* Tony Ganz, Deborah Blum *Scr* Tod Carroll *Ph* Jan Kiesser *Ed* Richard Chew *Mus* Gabriel Yared *Art* Joel Schiller
Act Michael Keaton, Kathy Baker, Morgan Freeman, M. Emmet Walsh, Tate Donovan, Luca Bercovici (Imagine/Warner)

Covering the first 30 days of attempted recovery by middle-class cocaine addict Michael Keaton, *Sober* is sobering indeed, perhaps too grim.

Keaton carries his heavy load well enough, on screen a vast majority of time as a hotshot real estate executive whose cocaine use has gotten him $92,000 into hock on embezzled company money and into bed with a young girl dying of an overdose.

On the run, Keaton decides to hide out in a recovery hospital, attracted more by its policies of strict confidentiality than any desire for rehabilitation. There, he falls under the strict supervision of ex-junkie Morgan Freeman, which will do him good, but also develops a romantic interest in fellow recovering addict Kathy Baker, which won't.

Sober chooses to focus on the couple's shared attraction for each other (and cocaine), and follows them to a predictable end.

•

CLEAN SLATE
1994, 107 mins, US Ⓥ ⦿ col
Dir Mick Jackson *Prod* Richard D. Zanuck, Lili Fini Zanuck *Scr* Robert King *Ph* Andrew Dunn *Ed* Priscilla Nedd-Friendly *Mus* Alan Silvestri *Art* Norman Reynolds
Act Dana Carvey, Valeria Golino, James Earl Jones, Kevin Pollack, Michael Gambon, Michael Murphy (M-G-M)

Any movie stolen by a dog with a depth-perception problem can't be all bad, and *Clean Slate* isn't without a few inspired comic moments. For the most part, however, this convoluted comedy feels like a pale follow-up to *Groundhog Day*.

The clever premise—a guy suffering from a form of amnesia that causes him to forget everything when he goes to sleep—never congeals in the execution. First-time screenwriter Robert King seems to have taken much of his inspiration from '40s film noir in putting together a complex mystery plot with assorted nefarious characters, then dropping his dazed and confused protagonist into the middle.

Dana Carvey plays Pogue, a private detective who's been afflicted with his unique illness after a car explosion. Joined by a mysterious woman (Valeria Golino) who was supposed to have died in the blast, he must try to find a priceless coin while staying alive long enough to testify against the mobster, Cornell (Michael Gambon), who engineered the explosion.

Director Mick Jackson pulls off some amusing sequences, most of them involving Barkley, a Jack Russell terrier who goes through the movie wearing an eye patch and keeps running into things headfirst. Carvey fares reasonably well.

•

CLEAR AND PRESENT DANGER
1994, 141 mins, US Ⓥ ⦿ ▭ col
Dir Phillip Noyce *Prod* Mace Neufeld, Robert Rehme *Scr* Donald Stewart, Steven Zaillian, John Milius *Ph* Donald M. McAlpine *Ed* Neil Travis *Mus* James Horner *Art* Terence Marsh
Act Harrison Ford, Willem Dafoe, Anne Archer, Joaquim de Almeida, Henry Czerny, Harris Yulin (Paramount)

Jack Ryan takes on the Colombian drug cartels and some nefarious members of a duplicitous U.S. government in *Clear and Present Danger*, the third entry in Paramount's Tom Clancy franchise. Narrative complexity and momentum make this a true cinematic equivalent of an absorbing page-turner, even if the excitement only occasionally reaches thrilling levels.

Setting the nasty chain of events in motion is the murder of a prominent U.S. businessman and friend of the president who, it turns out, has been in league with the cartels. Embarrassed and awakened to the ineffectiveness of the country's war on drugs, the prez (Donald Moffat) has Ryan (Harrison Ford), now acting CIA deputy director of intelligence due to the illness of his boss (James Earl Jones), pursue the matter, while secretly setting loose national security adviser James Cutter (Harris Yullin) and CIA hardliner Robert Ritter (Henry Czerny) to send a paramilitary force against the drug lords. To this end, they hire CIA cowboy Clark (Willem Dafoe).

The talents of three top Hollywood screenwriters have been well, if not deeply, used to ensure that the story is coherent and the characters have at least a semblance of plausibility. On an action level, pic is less high-charged than numerous other efforts of its ilk. Final action scene feels a bit flat and anticlimactic, in that it's mainly routine chase and gunplay stuff.

Production values are customarily expensive-looking and professional, with an assortment of Mexican locations attractively standing in for South American settings.

1994: NOMINATIONS: Sound, Sound Effects Editing

•

CLEO DE 5 A 7
(CLEO FROM 5 TO 7)
1961, 90 mins, France Ⓥ col
Dir Agnes Varda *Prod* Georges de Beauregard, Carlo Ponti *Scr* Agnes Varda *Ph* Jean Rabier *Ed* Janine Verneau, Pascale Laverriere *Mus* Michel Legrand *Art* Bernard Evein
Act Corinne Marchand, Antoine Bourseiller, Dominique Davray, Dorothee Blank, Michel Legrand, Jose-Luis de Villalonga (Rome Paris)

The girl is comely and tall. She sings at a session with some zany songwriters, the songs displaying that she is good but not outstanding in this sphere. Then there is a busy businessman lover who never has time for her.

Sometimes invention falters, as in the scene with the songwriters. But Varda then easily picks up the threads and keeps alive interest in the girl and her plight.

She goes to a fortune teller, has a crying jag in public, buys a hat, sees her lover for a while who is loath to admit any sickness she may have, visits a model friend, sees a little film comedy which buoys her up—and finally meets a soldier who helps her face up to getting the test results.

Corinne Marchand is well utilized as the sick girl while others just lend silhouettes to her wanderings, except for Antoine Bourseiller's knowing portrayal of the soldier.

•

CLEO FROM 5 TO 7
SEE: CLEO DE 5 A 7

•

CLEOPATRA
1934, 102 mins, US Ⓥ ⦿ b/w
Dir Cecil B. DeMille *Prod* Cecil B. DeMille *Scr* Bartlett Cormack, Waldemar Young, Vincent Lawrence *Ph* Victor Milner *Ed* Anne Bauchens *Mus* Rudolph Kopp
Act Claudette Colbert, Warren William, Henry Wilcoxon, Gertrude Michael, Joseph Schildkraut, Ian Keith (Paramount)

Splendor and intimacy do not blend any more than the traditional oil and water. Each treads on the other's toes. Cecil B. DeMille adds nothing to his directorial rep in this one other than to again demonstrate his rare skill in the handling of mass action.

Another tribute ought to go to C. Aubrey Smith as a soldier in one of the few sincerely written bits. Claudette Colbert's best moment is the death of Cleo. The rest of the time she's a cross between a lady of the evening and a rough soubrette in a country melodrama. It is not so much her fault as the shortcoming of the scenarists.

In an effort to avoid the blank verse of Shakespeare, from which this story derives, the dialog is made to become colloquial with disastrous results. When Cleopatra stabs a man hiding behind the draperies she explains to Caesar that the eavesdropper was plotting against her life or his. The imperial Julius then strides to the door, throws it open and commands a couple of guards to "take it away," referring to the body. The blankest of blank verse would have been better. The entire dialogue, save for a few moments, is of like calibre.

Warren William, as Caesar, and Henry Wilcoxon, as Antony, play in the drawing-room style, and a not too select drawing room at that. Joseph Schildkraut is a fair Herod.

1934: Best Cinematography

NOMINATIONS: Best Picture, Editing, Sound, Assistant Director

•

CLEOPATRA
1963, 243 mins, US Ⓥ ⦿ ▭ col
Dir Joseph L. Mankiewicz *Prod* Walter Wanger *Scr* Joseph L. Mankiewicz, Ranald MacDougall, Sidney Buchman *Ph* Leon Shamroy *Ed* Dorothy Spencer *Mus* Alex North *Art* John DeCuir
Act Elizabeth Taylor, Richard Burton, Rex Harrison, Roddy McDowall, Martin Landau, Hume Cronyn (20th Century-Fox/MCL-Walwa)

Cleopatra is not only a supercolossal eye-filler (the unprecedented budget shows in the physical opulence throughout), but it is also a remarkably literate cinematic recreation of an historic epoch.

Director and co-author Joseph L. Mankiewicz and producer Walter Wanger's most stunning achievement is that they have managed to tell a story of such scope and complexity in such comparatively brief terms. The film covers the 18 turbulent years leading to the foundation of the Roman Empire, from Cleopatra's first meeting with Julius Caesar until her death in defeat with Mark Antony. The result is a giant panorama, unequalled in the splendor of its spectacle scenes and, at the same time, surprisingly acute in its more personal story.

This is due not only to the quality and focus of the screenplay, but to the talents of the three leading players. In the title role, one of the most difficult ever written, Elizabeth Taylor is a woman of continuous fascination. Though not fully at ease as the child-queen of the film's first part, she grows as the story progresses to become the mature queen who matches the star's own voluptuous assurance.

Rex Harrison is superb as Caesar, shrewd, vain and wise, formed somewhat in the image of the G. B. Shaw conception, but also unexpectedly ruthless and ambitious. His are the film's most brilliant lines, and something is lost with his assassination, which closes the film's first half.

Richard Burton then comes to the fore in the second half. Oddly he does not seem the romantic figure expected and plot-implied, partly perhaps because as a lover he is visibly overweight. The role is of a man of military competence consumed by envy of Caesar's genius and exposed in the end as self-pitying and drunken by the demands of Cleopatra's needs for a man in a larger sense than boudoir. Ironically some of the weakest moments in the film are the love scenes between Liz and Dickie.

Happily, however, the film sweeps along with a very real sense of time and place, building to a climax that is one of inevitable, tragic relief. Responsible to no little extent is the quality of the "big" scenes—Cleopatra's triumphant entry into Rome, a dazzling display of color and sound and ancient pageantry; the grandeur of Cleopatra's barge, sailing into Tarsus; the crucial Battle of Actium, recreated on a scale perhaps unmatched in any spectacle.

The long windup of the story has Cleopatra taking longer to die than Camille. That Fox may still excise more footage is likely, and the second half is the place to do it. [The film was cut by 21 minutes very early in its New York run. No scenes were eliminated in their entirety, but cuts were made to shorten scenes and bridges.]

The real star of *Cleopatra*, however, is Mankiewicz, who brought order out of what had been production chaos. As Caesar observes to Cleopatra, early on: "You have a way of mixing politics and passion." So does Mankiewicz.

1963: Best Color Cinematography, Color Art Direction, Special Effects, Color Costume Design

NOMINATIONS: Best Picture, Actor (Rex Harrison), Editing, Original Music Score

•

CLEOPATRA JONES

1973, 89 mins, US Ⓥ ⊏⊐ col

Dir Jack Starrett ***Prod*** William Tennant, Max Julien ***Scr*** Max Julien, Sheldon Keller ***Ph*** David Walsh ***Ed*** Allan Jacobs ***Mus*** J. J. Johnson, Carl Brandt, Brad Shapiro ***Art*** Peter Wooley

Act Tamara Dobson, Bernie Casey, Brenda Sykes, Antonio Fargas, Bill McKinney, Shelley Winters (Warner)

Cleopatra Jones is a good programmer with the offbeat twist of having a sexy woman detective as the lead character. The script incorporates a slew of action-set pieces, capably directed by Jack Starrett.

Tamara Dobson makes a smart starring debut, after fashion model and teleblurb work, as the title character, a sophisticated undercover agent working to stamp out the world drug trade. But a phony raid on lover Bernie Casey's ghetto halfway house, in which Dobson has a great interest, draws her home to unravel the plot.

Behind Casey's problems, and serving as Dobson's archenemy, is Shelley Winters, in vulgar characterization as a lesbian-type gangleader. The line between offbeat cameo and repulsive casting is wider than a freeway, but Winters crosses it with felicity.

•

CLIENT, THE

1994, 120 mins, US Ⓥ ⦿ ⊏⊐ col

Dir Joel Schumacher ***Prod*** Arnon Milchan, Steven Reuther ***Scr*** Akiva Goldsman, Robert Getchell ***Ph*** Tony Pierce-Roberts ***Ed*** Robert Brown ***Mus*** Howard Shore ***Art*** Bruno Rubeo

Act Susan Sarandon, Tommy Lee Jones, Mary-Louise Parker, Anthony LaPaglia, Anthony Edwards, Ossie Davis (Warner)

The Client is a satisfactory, by-the-numbers child-in-jeopardy thriller [from the John Grisham bestseller] that fills the bill as a very commercial hot-weather popcorn picture. While the tale's hook is powerful and sets up considerable peril for the protagonists and intrigue for the viewer, overriding problem here is the basic lack of suspense.

Opening sequence still stands, two hours later, as the best in the picture. Two little brothers, Mark and Ricky Sway (Brad Renfro, David Speck) witness a big, bearded man park his car in a secluded area, attach a hose to the exhaust pipe and stick it through the window. Mark hears the man's secrets, which involve the whereabouts of the missing body of a U.S. senator who was murdered by the Mob.

Mark becomes the object of relentless attention on the part of the cops, the FBI, the press and, particularly, fierce federal prosecutor Roy Foltrigg (Tommy Lee Jones), who hopes to use the kid's knowledge to further his own political ambitions. Mark finds a lawyer in Reggie Love (Susan Sarandon), a woman who makes up for her limited experience with unflagging tenacity and personal commitment. Action finale has Mark and Reggie moving in on the senator's hidden corpse at the same time the gangsters arrive.

Joel Schumacher's directorial style is strictly presentational, devoted to getting the plot up on the screen in comprehensible fashion with no fuss, no frills, no thrills. Performances are only OK, given the skin-deep characters.

1994: NOMINATION: Best Actress (Susan Sarandon)

•

CLIFFHANGER

1993, 112 mins, US Ⓥ ⦿ ⊏⊐ col

Dir Renny Harlin ***Prod*** Alan Marshall, Renny Harlin ***Scr*** Michael France, Sylvester Stallone ***Ph*** Alex Thomson ***Ed*** Frank J. Urioste ***Mus*** Trevor Jones ***Art*** John Vallone

Act Sylvester Stallone, John Lithgow, Michael Rooker, Janine Turner, Rex Linn, Caroline Goodall (Carolco/Canal Plus/Pioneer)

Cliffhanger lives up to its title as a two-hour roller coaster ride that never stops from first minute to last, a high-octane action suspenser with thrilling vertiginous footage. Director Renny Harlin keeps the adventure in this reputed $65 million production [from a screen story by Michael France, based on a premise by John Long] coming at an astonishing pace.

Nine-minute opening sequence is a heart-stopping stunner. Rocky Mountain Rescue pro Gabe Walker (Sylvester Stallone) has climbed up a needle peak to help rescue the girlfriend of his partner Hal Tucker (Michael Rooker). But the rescue goes awry.

When Gabe returns to Colorado eight months later, he's unable to patch things up with his own g.f., Jessie (Janine Turner), and Hal still blames him for causing the accident.

In the next gasp-quality sequence, a private Treasury Dept. jet is hijacked by turncoat T-Man Travers (Rex Linn) and the nefarious Qualen (John Lithgow). But the three suitcases from the haul containing $100 million fall to the ground and the villains make a crash landing on a mountain. Enter Gabe and Hal, who arrive to rescue the group but are promptly captured and forced to lead them through the snowy, icy terrain to the loot.

What really puts this in a class of its own is the verisimilitude of the action. Despite credits to stunt and climbing doubles and the occasional process shot, there is no doubt that Stallone and other actors were really up on the sides of mountains. Although set in Colorado and partly filmed in Durango, most of the picture was lensed in Italy, both near Cortina D'Ampezzo in the Alps and in Rome. Tech contributions throughout are aces.

1993: NOMINATIONS: Best Sound, Sound Editing, Visual Effects

•

CLINTON AND NADINE

SEE: BLOOD MONEY

•

CLIVE OF INDIA

1935, 90 mins, US b/w

Dir Richard Boleslawski ***Prod*** Darryl F. Zanuck ***Scr*** W. P. Lipscomb, R. J. Minney ***Ph*** Peverell Marley ***Ed*** Barbara McLean ***Mus*** Alfred Newman ***Art*** Richard Day

Act Ronald Colman, Loretta Young, Colin Clive, Francis Lister, C. Aubrey Smith, Cesar Romero (20th Century)

The Black Hole of Calcutta, the battle elephants (with their gargantuan and murderous barbed armor), the famous hindustani monsoons and, of course, the basically courageous warrior, Robert Clive, and his rise from an obscure clerkship with the East India Company—all these elements of fictionalized fact and glorified history are re-created here vividly for the screen.

After the first three-quarters of an hour or so, the film plot veers to the personal romantic troubles besetting Clive and Margaret Maskelyne (later Lady Clive), whom he periodically deserts or ignores whenever trouble in the Far East summons him.

Ronald Colman is an excellent Clive sans his familiar mustache. The powdered wigs of the day do their bit in maintaining romantic illusion. Perhaps Loretta Young's spanning of the years is achieved somewhat too idealistically, but changing of the hairdressing with each period authentically gets across the idea of gracefully growing old.

Performances are consistently fine, notably Mischa Auer as the tyrannical native ruler, and Cesar Romero as the ambitious but friendly to Britain rival maharajah who double-crosses Auer.

•

CLOAK AND DAGGER

1946, 103 mins, US Ⓥ b/w

Dir Fritz Lang ***Prod*** Milton Sperling ***Scr*** Albert Maltz, Ring Lardner, Jr. ***Ph*** Sol Polito ***Ed*** Christian Nyby ***Mus*** Max Steiner ***Art*** Max Parker

Act Gary Cooper, Lilli Palmer, Robert Alda, J. Edward Bromberg, Vladimir Sokoloff, Ludwig Stossel (Warner)

This tale [from a book by Corey Ford and Alastair MacBain] of the OSS and its undercover work during the war is the usual cops-and-robbers story. Fritz Lang's direction manages suspense and several top moments of gripping dramatic conflict, but otherwise fails to rise to sock levels.

Gary Cooper is seen as atomic scientist drafted by OSS to enter first Switzerland and then Italy just prior to close of the war to get a line on Nazi atomic developments. He encounters the usual femme spy in Switzerland, gets out of that episode with whole skin but only after death of Austrian scientist he was contacting, and then moves on to Italy and romance with an Italian partisan who is assigned to aid him contact a Nazi-held scientist.

Cooper fits requirements of his role, turning in his usual top-notch job. A high moment of thrill is his hand-to-hand, silent battle with Marc Lawrence, Nazi agent, in an Italian hallway. It's one of the few top sequences. Film introduces Lilli Palmer as Cooper's romance.

•

CLOCK, THE
(UK: UNDER THE CLOCK)

1945, 90 mins, US Ⓥ b/w

Dir Vincente Minnelli ***Prod*** Arthur Freed ***Scr*** Robert Nathan, Joseph Schrank ***Ph*** George Folsey ***Ed*** George White ***Mus*** George Bassman ***Art*** Cedric Gibbons, William Ferrari

Act Judy Garland, Robert Walker, James Gleason, Keenan Wynn, Marshall Thompson, Lucille Gleason (M-G-M)

Producer Arthur Freed and director Vincente Minnelli, the combination that scored so heavily with the Judy Garland musical, *Meet Me in St. Louis*, show their versatility in this picture which is straight drama sans any music. It's her first straight dramatic role. The entire story takes place in the 48 hours that Cpl. Joe Allen (Walker) is on furlough in New York City.

Minnelli has the knack of getting deep meaning into little footage. For instance, the beanery scene where the jolly inebriate (Keenan Wynn) spouts about life and America. The entire sequence is probably four minutes long, but it is real meat.

Then there's a sequence after the boy and girl get hitched at City Hall. They're sitting in a self-service restaurant, and Garland is weeping because of the unattractiveness of the entire ceremony. The camera keeps concentrated on a lone diner, an unbilled character who just sits there and chews away, staring at the embarrassed couple, but not uttering a word. It is memorable humor.

•

CLOCKERS

1995, 128 mins, US Ⓥ ⦿ col

Dir Spike Lee ***Prod*** Martin Scorsese, Spike Lee, Jon Kilik ***Scr*** Richard Price, Spike Lee ***Ph*** Malik Hassan Sayeed ***Ed*** Sam Pollard ***Mus*** Terence Blanchard ***Art*** Andrew McAlpine

Act Harvey Keitel, John Turturro, Delroy Lindo, Mekhi Phifer, Isaiah Washington, Keith David (40 Acres & a Mule/Universal)

Spike Lee takes up the cudgel against black-on-black violence in *Clockers*, a modern morality play that is gritty and pretentious in roughly equal measure. A study of the urban dope-dealing culture and its toll on everyone who comes in contact with it, the picture has an insider's feel that is constantly undercut by the filmmaker's impulse to editorialize.

Universal originally bought Richard Price's lengthy, heavily researched novel for Martin Scorsese, but when he decided to proceed with *Casino* instead, Lee came aboard as director, with Scorsese taking a producer credit. Lee also rewrote Price's script, shifting the emphasis away from the midlife crisis of one of the white cops and toward the early-life dilemma of a "clocker," or small-time crack dealer.

As a favor to neighborhood drug kingpin Rodney (Delroy Lindo), 19-year-old Strike (Mekhi Phifer) agrees to kill a competitor. Shortly, Strike's hard-working, upstanding brother Victor (Isaiah Washington) turns himself in, to everyone's surprise.

Intense veteran homicide cop Rocco Klein (Harvey Keitel), who works with less obsessed partner Larry Mazilli

(John Turturro), can't buy Victor's confession, and begins to hound Strike. At the same time, Strike takes a lot of heat from some of his neighbors, including black cop Andre (Keith David). Strike resolutely refuses to take responsibility for anything he does, but his own body is informing him of the error of his ways in the form of constant retching.

Keitel gets to be bullying and steamed-up in a shadow of his *Bad Lieutenant* characterization, while Turturro's part has been reduced to nothing. Lanky and shaven-headed, newcomer Phifer brings no psychological depth to the leading role of Strike, but catches the required outer trappings of shiftiness, opportunism, uncertainty and frustration quite well. Taking advantage of the film's showiest part, Lindo oozes command and charisma as the corrupt Rodney.

•

CLOCKWISE
1986, 97 mins, UK Ⓥ ⦿ col
Dir Christopher Morahan ***Prod*** Michael Codron ***Scr*** Michael Frayn ***Ph*** John Coquillon ***Ed*** Peter Boyle ***Mus*** George Fenton ***Art*** Roger Murray-Leach
Act John Cleese, Alison Steadman, Penelope Wilton, Stephen Moore, Joan Hickson, Sharon Maiden (Thorn EMI/Moment)

Clockwise is a somewhat uneven comic road film. John Cleese plays the headmaster of a secondary school whose main trait, obsessive timewatching, turns out to be a strategy to dam up the natural disarray of his personality.

Film's plot is triggered when Stimpson (Cleese) misses the train for a headmaster's conference over which he has been invited to preside. Immediately panic-stricken, he seeks some other way to get to the meeting on time.

The best moments depict his gradually going to pieces as he struggles to complete his journey in the company of an abducted schoolgirl (Sharon Maiden) and former girlfriend (Penelope Wilton).

Clockwise would be a bore were it not for Cleese's comic ability, which derives from broad expressive gesticulations and expressions which mark the simple man still trying to control his world long after he has gone over the edge. Christopher Morahan's direction, in his first feature since the late 1960s, is adequate.

•

CLOCKWORK MICE
1995, 99 mins, UK Ⓥ col
Dir Vadim Jean ***Prod*** Paul Brooks ***Scr*** Rod Woodruff ***Ph*** Gordon Hickie ***Ed*** Liz Webber ***Mus*** John Murphy, David A. Hughes ***Art*** David Munns
Act Ian Hart, Catherine Russell, Ruaidhri Conroy, Art Malik, Claire Skinner, Nigel Planer (Metrodome)

A good old-fashioned heartwarmer about a teacher and a dysfunctional teen, *Clockwork Mice* throws out the kitchen sink to embrace its humanist theme with cinematic verve. Pic is toplined by convinced playing from Ian Hart as the selfless teach, and mounted in infectious feel-good style.

Setting is a fictional school for maladjusted children somewhere in rural England. Idealistic new teacher Steve (Hart) arrives and immediately sets the pulse of colleague Polly (Catherine Russell) racing. Steve's first meeting with problem pupil Conrad (Ruaidhri Conroy) is less successful: the expressionless 14-year-old trashes the classroom when forbidden to play basketball. Finally, they find common ground in cross-country running, and enough other kids join up for Steve to form a club.

There's almost nothing new about Rod Woodruff's script, which glues shavings from *Dead Poet's Society* and *Chariots of Fire* to studies of loners like *Kes* and *The Loneliness of the Long-Distance Runner*. Where director Vadim Jean and producer Paul Brooks score is in gussying up wafer-thin material and giving it a positive spin, rather than settling for a more familiar slice of downbeat British realism.

•

CLOCKWORK ORANGE, A
1971, 137 mins, UK Ⓥ col
Dir Stanley Kubrick ***Prod*** Stanley Kubrick ***Scr*** Stanley Kubrick ***Ph*** John Alcott ***Ed*** Bill Butler ***Mus*** Walter Carlos ***Art*** John Barry
Act Malcolm McDowell, Patrick Magee, Michael Bates, Miriam Carlin, Adrienne Corri, Aubrey Morris (Warner)

A Clockwork Orange is a brilliant nightmare. Stanley Kubrick's film takes the heavy realities of the "do-your-thing" and "law-and-order" syndromes, runs them through a cinematic centrifuge and spews forth the commingled comic horrors of a regulated society. The film employs outrageous vulgarity, stark brutality and some sophisticated comedy to make an opaque argument for the preservation of respect for man's free will—even to do wrong.

Kubrick's screenplay, based on the 1962 Anthony Burgess novel, postulates a society composed of amoral young hedonists, an older generation in retreat behind locked doors, and a political police government no longer accountable to anyone or to any principles except expediency and tenure.

In this world where youthful gangs control the street by night and disperse by dawn, lives anti-hero and narrator Malcolm McDowell and his sidekicks—Warren Clarke, James Marcus and Michael Tarn. They have an Orwellian argot not difficult to grasp. Their escapades include beatings, rape and a bizarre murder.

The resolution is ambiguous to say the least. Is McDowell at last the subdued "Orange" that runs like "Clockwork" or has human nature begun to heal itself?

1971: NOMINATIONS: Best Picture, Director, Adapted Screenplay, Editing

•

CLOSE ENCOUNTERS OF THE THIRD KIND
1977, 135 mins, US Ⓥ ⦿ ▭ col
Dir Steven Spielberg ***Prod*** Julia Phillips, Michael Phillips ***Scr*** Steven Spielberg [Matthew Robbins, Hal Barwood, Paul Schrader, Jerry Belson] ***Ph*** Vilmos Zsigmond, William A. Fraker, Douglas Slocombe, John Alonzo, Laszlo Kovacs ***Ed*** Michael Kahn ***Mus*** John Williams ***Art*** Joe Alves, Dan Lomino
Act Richard Dreyfuss, Francois Truffaut, Teri Garr, Melinda Dillon, Cary Guffey, Bob Balaban (Columbia)

Close Encounters of the Third Kind is a daring film concept which in its special and technical effects has been superbly realized. Steven Spielberg's film climaxes in final 35 minutes with almost ethereal confrontation with life forms from another world; the first 100 minutes, however, are somewhat redundant in exposition and irritating in tone. The near-$20 million production was shot in Wyoming, Alabama, California and India.

Story involves a series of UFO appearances witnessed by Richard Dreyfuss, Indiana power company technician, and Melinda Dillon and her son Cary Guffey. Concurrent with this plot line are the maneuverings of a seemingly international and secret team of military and scientific personnel in which Francois Truffaut is a key member.

The early UFO manifestations vividly depict the strong electromagnetic field exerted on people and objects. Dreyfuss's entire life changes as he gets a fixation on an odd mountain-looking shape that, after overbearing and overdone emphasis, turns out to be Devil's Tower in Wyoming where the UFOs seem to plan an earthly landing. Separately, Dillon's son is kidnapped by a UFO, giving her a fixation.

But there's no denying that the climax is an absolute stunner, literate in plotting, dazzling in execution [special photographic effects by Douglas Trumbull] and almost reverent in tone. At the very least the denouement is light-years ahead of the climactic nonsense of Stanley Kubrick's *2001: A Space Odyssey*.

But there's no big positive rush here; instead a high-tension, nervous, uneasy, often heartless environment in which Dreyfuss and Dillon are helpless flotsam. The uncompromising creative point of view, admirable in a professional sense, is pitched to an above-average level of intelligence.

[In 1980 film was replaced by a 132-minute version, with the central section tightened and extra material showing the inside of the mother ship at end. On posters, but not on prints, this was subtitled *The Special Edition*. In 1998 a 137-min. *Collector's Edition* was issued on home video; this eliminates the inside of the mother ship but restores footage around the hero's nervous breakdown.]

1977: Best Cinematography, Special Achievment Award (sound effects editing)

NOMINATIONS: Best Director, Best Supp. Actress (Melinda Dillon), Art Direction, Editing, Original Score, Sound, Special Visual Effects

•

CLOSELY OBSERVED TRAINS
SEE: OSTRE SLEDOVANE VLAKY

•

CLOSELY WATCHED TRAINS
SEE: OSTRE SLEDOVANE VLAKY

•

CLOSE MY EYES
1991, 105 mins, UK Ⓥ col
Dir Stephen Poliakoff ***Prod*** Therese Pickard ***Scr*** Stephen Poliakoff ***Ph*** Witold Stok ***Ed*** Michael Parkinson ***Mus*** Michael Gibbs ***Art*** Luciana Arrighi
Act Alan Rickman, Clive Owen, Saskia Reeves, Karl Johnson, Lesley Sharp, Kate Gartside (Film Four/Beambright)

Close My Eyes is a powerful British film about incest, with top-flight performances and intense handling of the material by writer-director Stephen Poliakoff.

The early scenes somewhat awkwardly chart the relationship between Natalie (Saskia Reeves) and her younger brother Richard (Clive Owen) over a five-year period. They live in different British cities; one night, Richard stays in his sister's apartment and both sense a new feeling of intimacy between them, though nothing happens.

Five years later, Natalie is married to the wealthy Sinclair (Alan Rickman) and they live in a magnificent house beside the Thames. Natalie visits her brother in his apartment, and the hitherto unspoken passion between them erupts into a sexual encounter.

The central triangular relationship is supported by well-observed and biting scenes involving marginal characters, such as Richard's boss (Karl Johnson), who is quietly dying of AIDS, or the girl (Kate Garside) he picks up to try to get over his passion for Natalie.

Reeves and Owen give brave, strong, unstinting performances. Rickman has his best screen role to date as the pompous but kindly husband.

•

CLOSET LAND
1991, 93 mins, US Ⓥ ⦿ col
Dir Radha Bharadwaj ***Prod*** Janet Meyers ***Scr*** Radha Bharadwaj ***Ph*** Bill Pope ***Ed*** Lisa Churgin ***Mus*** Philip Glass (sup.), Richard Einhorn ***Art*** Eiko Ishioka
Act Madeleine Stowe, Alan Rickman (Imagine)

The highly theatrical *Closet Land*, imaginatively produced on a modest $2.5 million, addresses the horror of political torture. It's a harrowing, focused two-character piece by first-time director Radha Bharadwaj.

Entire thing takes place in a gleaming, stylish, high-tech chamber, with a man (Alan Rickman) trying to break the will of a woman (Madeleine Stowe). Despite the claustrophobic setup, a great deal occurs to hold one's interest.

Rickman as interrogator is no ordinary brute but a complex, highly civilized man who displays a range of emotions and talents, including the ability to voice-act other people to confuse his blindfolded victim. Stowe is a physically captivating victim with a fierce attachment to justice. Given a chance early on to escape, she stays and demands an apology. It's a costly error.

Story has Stowe, an author of children's books, dragged from her bed to face a servant of the government (Rickman) who accuses her of peddling subversive ideas to children in the guise of innocent stories. At issue is her work in progress, *Closet Land*, about a little girl whose mother leaves her locked in a closet.

Rickman deserves a great deal of notice for his powerfully controlled, multifaceted performance. Stowe displays some flash and backbone, but not enough to make this a truly engaging match.

•

CLOSE TO EDEN
SEE: A STRANGER AMONG US

•

CLOUDED YELLOW, THE
1950, 95 mins, UK b/w
Dir Ralph Thomas ***Prod*** Betty E. Box ***Scr*** Janet Green ***Ph*** Geoffrey Unsworth ***Ed*** Gordon Hales
Act Jean Simmons, Trevor Howard, Sonia Dresdel, Kenneth More, Maxwell Reed (Carillon)

Although the plot breaks little new ground, the film grips consistently. Jean Simmons and Trevor Howard make a strong team.

Yarn describes the adventures of an ex-Secret Service agent who helps an innocent girl to escape from a murder charge. On the theory of setting a thief to catch a thief, Scotland Yard puts another secret agent on his tracks. There follows an exciting chase across England into the dockland area of Liverpool, where the hunted pair are hoping to board a ship for Mexico.

The buildup until the manhunt begins is done with a nice mixture of humor, sentiment and drama. But once the chase is on, the suspense is sustained solidly.

•

CZLOWIEK Z MARMARU
SEE: MAN OF MARBLE

•

CLUB, THE
1980, 99 mins, Australia Ⓥ ▭ col
Dir Bruce Beresford ***Prod*** Matt Carroll ***Scr*** David Williamson ***Ph*** Don McAlpine ***Ed*** William Anderson ***Mus*** Mike Brady ***Art*** David Copping

Act Jack Thompson, Graham Kennedy, Frank Wilson, Harold Hopkins, John Howard, Alan Cassell (South Australia Film/New South Wales Film)

Based on his play of the same name, David Williamson's screen adaptation opens out the action, but in doing so somehow manages to close down the characters. The plot has to do with a football club and the behind-the-scenes machinations: ruthless powerplays that make what takes place on the field seem relatively tame.

The game in this case is a local aberration, confined to the State of Victoria mostly, called Australian Rules. Actually the game itself plays a background role and director Bruce Beresford has shrewdly kept the thrust of his film in the hands of his main characters.

Williamson's plays have been described as life at the top of your lungs, and *The Club* is no exception; there are few quiet passages.

•

CLUB PARADISE
1986, 104 mins, US Ⓥ ⊙ col
Dir Harold Ramis *Prod* Michael Shamberg *Scr* Harold Ramis, Brian Doyle-Murray *Ph* Peter Hannan *Ed* Marion Rothman *Mus* David Mansfield *Art* John Graysmark
Act Robin Williams, Peter O'Toole, Rick Moranis, Jimmy Cliff, Twiggy, Adolph Caesar (Warner)

There are enough funny skits in *Club Paradise* to make for a good hour of SCTV, where most of the cast is from, but too few to keep this Club Med satire afloat for 104 minutes.

Screenplay by Harold Ramis (*Ghostbusters*) and Brian Doyle-Murray was originally written with Doyle-Murray's comedian brother, Bill Murray, in mind as the lead.

Murray reportedly was unavailable and Robin Williams was signed to head the cast as a disabled Chicago fireman who uses his insurance settlement to become partners with a reggae musician (Jimmy Cliff) in a seedy Caribbean club they hope to turn into a first-class resort.

Williams can be a terrific actor/comedian, but the spark isn't there. Somehow, Murray might have come up with cleverer ways of getting back at complaining guests (Andrea Martin, Steven Kampmann), nerdy, sex-crazed weaklings (Rick Moranis and Eugene Levy, respectively) and the other expected amalgam of folks.

•

CLUE
1985, 87 mins, US Ⓥ ⊙ col
Dir Jonathan Lynn *Prod* Debra Hill *Scr* Jonathan Lynn *Ph* Victor J. Kemper *Ed* David Bretherton, Richard Haines *Mus* John Morris *Art* John Lloyd
Act Eileen Brennan, Tim Curry, Madeline Kahn, Christopher Lloyd, Lesley Ann Warren, Colleen Camp (Paramount)

Clue is campy, high-styled escapism. In a short 87 minutes that just zip by, the well-known board game's one-dimensional card figures like Professor Plum and others become multidimensional personalities with enough wit, neuroses and motives to intrigue even the most adept whodunnit solver. [Screen story by co-executive producer John Landis and director Jonathan Lynn.] Film is released with three endings.

Tim Curry plays the loquacious organizer of the evening's murder game, which takes place in a Gothic hilltop mansion in New England in 1954 during a storm (of course).

He sends six individuals a letter providing the incentive to attend dinner at the mansion and when each arrives, assigns them a pseudonym—Professor Plum, Mr. Green, Mrs. White and so on.

The unlikely assemblage of characters is mostly portrayed by well-known actors and comedians of which Lesley Ann Warren's Miss Scarlet, Martin Mull's Colonel Mustard and Eileen Brennan's Mrs. Peacock performances stand out.

Terrific performances also are given by relative unknowns: Michael McKean as Mr. Green and Colleen Camp as the French maid, Yvette.

•

CLUELESS
1995, 97 mins, US Ⓥ ⊙ col
Dir Amy Heckerling *Prod* Scott Rudin, Robert Lawrence *Scr* Amy Heckerling *Ph* Bill Pope *Ed* Debra Chiate *Mus* David Kitay *Art* Steven Jordan
Act Alicia Silverstone, Stacey Dash, Brittany Murphy, Paul Judd, Dan Hedaya, Donald Faison (Paramount)

Like an episode of *Beverly Hills, 90210* on helium, *Clueless* is a fresh, disarmingly bright and at times explosively funny comedy well worth a trip to the mall, even if it runs out of gas.

Clueless carries on the traditon of movies like *Fast Times at Ridgemont High* and *Dazed and Confused* in skewering the social strata of teen life, here taking advantage as well of the exaggerated rich-kid setting, where spoiled teens call each other on cellular phones as they parade down the halls.

Taking in her (uncredited) inspiration from Jane Austen's *Emma*, director Amy Heckerling has a dead-on ear for the updated Valley Girl dialogue with a Beverly Hills–Westside twist.

The only child of a widowed corporate lawyer (played with rough charm by Dan Hedaya), Cher (Alicia Silverstone) finds there are few situations she can't talk her way out of, down to manipulating her teachers into a romance in order to mellow them out enough to get better grades.

Cher's big project, however, is Tai (Brittany Murphy), a fashion victim who clearly needs a clue. She begins a wholesale makeover that eventually leads her in a small way to examine her own persona, including her relationship with Josh (Paul Judd), the son of her father's ex-wife by a former marriage.

Though unlikely to win any friends on Capitol Hill, it's somewhat refreshing to see these teens casually drinking, smoking pot and talking about sex, forgoing the by now expected "Just Say No" lectures.

Silverstone is not only adorable but possesses a real comic flair. The rest of the youthful ensemble is stocked with fresh faces. Tech credits are superb.

•

CLUNY BROWN
1946, 100 mins, US b/w
Dir Ernst Lubitsch *Prod* Ernst Lubitsch *Scr* Samuel Hoffenstein, Elizabeth Reinhardt *Ph* Joseph La Shelle *Ed* Dorothy Spencer *Mus* Cyril Mockridge *Art* Lyle R. Wheeler, J. Russell Spencer
Act Jennifer Jones, Charles Boyer, Peter Lawford, Helen Walker, Reginald Gardiner, Reginald Owen (20th Century-Fox)

Apart from its whammo entertainment and box-office aspects *Cluny Brown* can be recorded as glamorizing the first of a clan: a lady plumber. And a looker, no less. The kind for whom stopped-up pipes are a pleasure.

Jennifer Jones is the girl, Charles Boyer her anti-Nazi refugee vis-a-vis, Ernst Lubitsch produced and directed. *Cluny* is in the best Lubitsch tradition of subtle, punchy comedy, and his two stars make the most of it. It is a satire on British manners, with bite and relish. The insipidity of a specific family is the mirror through which is reflected Margery Sharp's novel of British pre-war aristocracy and the middle class. None of it is treated seriously of course.

When Cluny isn't cleaning stopped-up pipes, she's a maid in the home of the aforementioned aristocrats. The family's bowing acquaintance with world events is confined, for example, to the knowledge that an Austrian named Hitler had written a book, or something.

•

COAL MINER'S DAUGHTER
1980, 125 mins, US Ⓥ col
Dir Michael Apted *Prod* Bernard Schwartz *Scr* Tom Rickman *Ph* Ralf D. Bode *Ed* Arthur Schmidt *Mus* Owen Bradley *Art* John W. Corso
Act Sissy Spacek, Tommy Lee Jones, Beverly D'Angelo, Levon Helm, Phyllis Boyens, Ernest Tubb (Universal)

Coal Miner's Daughter is a thoughtful, endearing film charting the life of singer Loretta Lynn from the depths of poverty in rural Kentucky to her eventual rise to the title of "queen of country music." Thanks in large part to superb performances by Sissy Spacek and Tommy Lee Jones, film [based on Lynn's autobiography, with George Vescey] mostly avoids the sudsy atmosphere common to many showbiz tales.

There is seldom a slow moment in the picture, although towards the end short shrift is given to Spacek's bout with drugs, nervous breakdown, marriage troubles and death of her best friend, Beverly D'Angelo, as country singer Patsy Cline.

Both Spacek and D'Angelo deserve a special nod for doing all of their own singing with style and accuracy.

1980: Best Actress (Sissy Spacek)

NOMINATIONS: Best Picture, Adapted Screenplay, Cinematography, Art Direction, Editing, Sound

•

COBB
1994, 128 mins, US Ⓥ ⊙ col
Dir Ron Shelton *Prod* David Lester *Scr* Ron Shelton *Ph* Russell Boyd *Ed* Paul Seydor, Kimberly Ray *Mus* Elliot Goldenthal *Art* Armin Ganz, Scott Ritenour
Act Tommy Lee Jones, Robert Wuhl, Lolita Davidovich, Lou Myers, Stephen Mendillo, William Utay (Regency/Alcor/Warner)

Tyrus Raymond Cobb was the stuff of legend. Baseball's premier hitter, he was a ferocious player on and off the field. He was self-possessed, mean-spirited, a bigot and embodied just about every lowly human quality imaginable. In short, he's an ideal movie subject.

So, the wonder of wonders of *Cobb* is why writer/director Ron Shelton made a movie that more accurately should be titled *Stump*. The film is essentially the chronicle of how sports scribe Al Stump (Robert Wuhl) was summoned to the bedside of the ailing Ty Cobb (Tommy Lee Jones) to write the official bio of Baseball Hall of Fame's first inductee. The two stories aren't complementary, and Shelton's periodic shifts of focus result in an ambivalent, conflicted drama [from Al Stump's book *Cobb: A Biography*].

When Stump arrives at the snowbound Tahoe residence of the great man in 1960, he encounters a pistol-waving, decaying relic. The one-time Detroit Tiger drags him on a drinking and carousing spree through Reno and expects him to be grateful for nonstop stream of abuse.

But if Cobb is secondary, or merely a catalyst, Shelton fumbles just as badly with Stump. His groveling is beneath contempt.

Jones plays Cobb on a Shakespearean scale, with obvious parallels between the Georgia Peach and King Lear. Wuhl is simply no match for his charismatic costar. He's a dedicated second banana, and, when all else fails, he mugs.

•

COBRA
1986, 87 mins, US Ⓥ ⊙ col
Dir George Pan Cosmatos *Prod* Menahem Golan, Yoram Globus *Scr* Sylvester Stallone *Ph* Ric Waite *Ed* Don Zimmerman *Mus* Sylvester Levay *Art* Bill Kenney
Act Sylvester Stallone, Brigitte Nielsen, Reni Santoni, Andrew Robinson, Lee Garlington, John Herzfeld (Cannon)

Cobra is a sleek, extremely violent and exciting police thriller.

Sylvester Stallone is cast as unconventional cop Marion Cobretti, nickname Cobra, who with partner Gonzales (Reni Santoni) works the L.A. zombie squad, doing jobs no other cops will do. They're called in to track down a serial killer who's claimed 16 victims in a month. They protect the one surviving witness, a beautiful model (Brigitte Nielsen) and discover that the killer is actually a neo-fascist army of killers.

Director George Pan Cosmatos tightens the screws for a very fast ride. His low-key personality defined by his funny throwaway lines of dialogue, Stallone's Cobra is a far more ingratiating character than his recent Rocky and Rambo guises.

•

COBRA WOMAN
1944, 70 mins, US col
Dir Robert Siodmak *Prod* George Waggner *Scr* Gene Lewis, Richard Brooks *Ph* George Robinson, W. Howard Greene *Ed* Charles Maynard *Mus* Edward Ward *Art* John B. Goodman, Alexander Golitzen
Act Maria Montez, Jon Hall, Sabu, Lon Chaney (Universal)

Cobra Woman is a super-fantastic melodrama backgrounded on a mythical island that might exist somewhere in the Indian Ocean. Elaborately and colorfully mounted for constant eye-appeal, and with the starring trio of Maria Montez, Jon Hall and Sabu, picture unfolds at fast pace to concentrate on action features of the tale.

Plot combines jungle-island romance with melodramatic complications, temple rituals, chases and fights. Montez is kidnapped on eve of wedding to Hall and carried back to an island where her twin sister rules ruthlessly as high priestess and preys on religious superstitions of the natives to keep latter under control. Hall follows his betrothed to the forbidden island, accompanied by native boy (Sabu) to rescue Montez.

Montez is decidedly shapely as sarong-draped native girl and dazzlingly gowned as the high priestess. She handles the dual assignment very well. Hall and Sabu are typed in regular characterizations.

•

COBWEB, THE
1955, 122 mins, US ⊙ ▭ col
Dir Vincente Minnelli *Prod* John Houseman *Scr* John Paxton, William Gibson *Ph* George Folsey *Ed* Harold F. Kress *Mus* Leonard Rosenman
Act Richard Widmark, Lauren Bacall, Charles Boyer, Gloria Grahame, Lillian Gish, John Kerr (M-G-M)

The neuroses of the staff and patients in a psychiatric clinic serve for drama in this filmization of William Gibson's novel, *The Cobweb*.

The screenplay gives a wordy account of the controversy developed around the hanging of a new set of drapes in the clinic's library, and the reactions of staff and patients sometime make wonder if identities should not be reversed. Gloria Grahame, the neglected wife of Richard Widmark, top doc at the clinic, wants to select the drapes. Lillian Gish, waspish old maid who directs the clinic's business affairs, wants to use cheap muslin to save money. Widmark wants John Kerr, young patient with a suicide complex, to design the drapes.

Screen newcomers Kerr and Susan Strasberg, fellow patient, are responsible for one of the few touching sequences in the film—the simple act of his looking after her on a trip to a film theater has a great deal of heart, an ingredient generally lacking in the footage.

•

COBWEB CASTLE
SEE: KUMONOSU-JO

•

COCA-COLA KID, THE
1985, 94 mins, Australia Ⓥ ⊙ col
Dir Dusan Makavejev ***Prod*** David Roe ***Scr*** Frank Moorhouse ***Ph*** Dean Semler ***Ed*** John Scott ***Mus*** William Motzing ***Art*** Graham "Grace" Walker
Act Eric Roberts, Greta Scacchi, Bill Kerr, Chris Haywood, Kris McQuade, Max Gillies (Cinema Enterprises/Smart Egg)

A decade in preparation and two years in actual production, *The Coca-Cola Kid* emerges with much of the flavor and character of Dusan Makavejev's earlier works such as *WR: Mysteries of the Organism* and *Sweet Movie*. But the mix of earthy symbolism, offbeat eroticism, the picaresque and the rough-and-tumble social, rather unpolitical satire now seems poured from a bottle that has been left uncapped overnight.

The title figure is a young whiz-kid troubleshooter out of Atlanta, sent to Australia by Coca-Cola h.q. to root out whatever trouble might have been overlooked by the local company representative. Georgian Becker, played by Atlanta-raised Eric Roberts with drawl and drool, soon finds the Coca-Cola dry spot on Australia's map in a remote area where land baron (Bill Kerr, playing a Colonel Sanders lookalike), has enforced his own soda pop monopoly on the population.

The ensuing fight between two parties, supposedly juxtaposing American and Australian attitudes, morals, etc., is complicated by a skirmish between Roberts and the local company secretary (Greta Scacchi in her first major film role since *Heat and Dust*).

Behind all its stylistic posturing *The Coca-Cola Kid* has a generally friendly air about it. What is lacking in the brew is true punch.

•

COCKLESHELL HEROES
1955, 97 mins, UK Ⓥ ▭ col
Dir Jose Ferrer ***Prod*** Irving Allen, Albert R. Broccoli ***Scr*** Bryan Forbes, Richard Maibaum ***Ph*** John Wilcox, Ted Moore ***Ed*** Alan Osbiston ***Mus*** John Addison
Act Jose Ferrer, Trevor Howard, Victor Maddern, Anthony Newley, Walter Fitzgerald, Dora Bryan (Warwick/Columbia)

Cockleshell Heroes scores by uncanny accuracy in the feature casting. The subsidiary characters frequently dominate the action and never let the side down. They're aided by a taut script and by having some of the best dialog passages.

Operation Cockleshell was a campaign in miniature against a concentration of German shipping in Bordeaux Harbor, employing only eight men of the Royal Marines who paddled four canoes into enemy waters and stuck limpet mines on the Nazi boats.

Actual assault is the suspense highlight of the yarn, but there's a wealth of admirably exploited incident in the buildup situations showing the volunteers in special training for this hazardous adventure.

Jose Ferrer catches the traditional British touch of understatement in his direction and performance, and completely avoids the pitfall of false heroics.

•

COCKTAIL
1988, 104 mins, US Ⓥ ⊙ col
Dir Roger Donaldson ***Prod*** Ted Field, Robert W. Cort ***Scr*** Heywood Gould ***Ph*** Dean Semler ***Ed*** Neil Travis ***Mus*** J. Peter Robinson ***Art*** Mel Bourne
Act Tom Cruise, Bryan Brown, Elisabeth Shue, Lisa Banes, Laurence Luckinbill, Kelly Lynch (Touchstone/Interscope)

Heywood Gould's script, based upon his book inspired by some years as a New York bartender, contains nary a surprise, as Tom Cruise hits Manhattan after a hitch in the Army and immediately catches on as the hottest thing the uptown girls have seen in a saloon in years.

Under the tutelage of old pro Bryan Brown, Cruise learns every trick in the book, and the pair soon move to the club scene downtown, where Cruise becomes poetaster to the too-hip crowd in addition to taking his pick of trendy ladies.

In Jamaica, Brown goads his buddy into setting his sights on one of the many women with big bucks who patronize the resort, which gets Cruise into trouble with the girl he's becoming sweet on (Elisabeth Shue).

Under Roger Donaldson's impeccably slick direction, film continually plays on Cruise's attractiveness, as women make goo-goo eyes at him throughout as he does his juggling act with liquor bottles, serves up drinks like a disco dancer and charms his way through every situation.

•

COCOANUTS, THE
1929, 90 mins, US Ⓥ b/w
Dir Robert Florey, Joseph Santley ***Prod*** Walter Wanger ***Scr*** Morrie Ryskind ***Ph*** George Folsey ***Ed*** Barney Rogan ***Mus*** Frank Tours (dir)
Act Groucho Marx, Harpo Marx, Chico Marx, Zeppo Marx, Mary Eaton, Oscar Shaw (Paramount)

Here is a musical talker, with the musical background, music, songs and girls, taken from the [1925] Broadway stage success [by George S. Kaufman and Morrie Ryskind] with the Marxes.

Cocoanuts is set in a Florida development hotel barren of guests. Groucho is the fast-thinking and talking boniface. A couple of slickers, girls, bathing beach, etc., some undressing but no s.a.

Groucho is always around and talking as he did in the stage show. Harpo does his work with craftsmanship. Chico has more of the comedy end than usually falls to this foil. Zeppo has to be straight here all of the while.

Only Irving Berlin song of merit is the theme number, "When Our Dreams Come True," good enough musically but as trite in idea as the title suggests.

•

COCOON
1985, 117 mins, US Ⓥ ⊙ col
Dir Ron Howard ***Prod*** Richard D. Zanuck, David Brown, Lili Fini Zanuck ***Scr*** Tom Benedek ***Ph*** Don Peterman ***Ed*** Daniel Hanley, Michael J. Hill ***Mus*** James Horner ***Art*** Jack T. Collis
Act Don Ameche, Wilford Brimley, Hume Cronyn, Brian Dennehy, Jack Gilford, Steve Guttenberg (20th Century-Fox/Zanuck-Brown)

A fountain of youth fable [from a novel by David Saperstein] which imaginatively melds galaxy fantasy with the lives of aging mortals in a Florida retirement home, *Cocoon* weaves a mesmerizing tale.

Film inventively taps a wellspring of universal desire: health and youth, a parable set, in this case, among a pallid group of denizens shuffleboarding their twilight days away until a mysterious quartet of normal-looking visitors shows up on their Floridian shores. They are arrivals from another galaxy, led by friendly Brian Dennehy and attractive Tahnee Welch (Raquel's daughter, in her first U.S. film).

Another nearly silent member of the party is a debuting Tyrone Power, Jr. Dennehy hires a young, out-of-pocket charter boat skipper (engagingly played by Steve Guttenberg) for a plan to scuba dive for what appear to be weird, gigantic oyster shells. Dennehy rents an abandoned estate with a big indoor pool and rests the big pods in the pool's bottom.

Effectively intercut with these scenes is the life of the tight circle of nearby retirees, three of whom, played by Don Ameche, Wilford Brimley and Hume Cronyn, one day discover the cocoon-like shells and after a frolic in the water are soon diving in like 18-year-olds.

The effect of rejuvenation on the gray people, the inevitable mania when the whole retirement hospital wants in on the public bath, and the effect of this on the plans of the visitors from outer space propel the feature toward a suspenseful, ironic conclusion.

1985: Best Supp. Actor (Don Ameche), Visual Effects

•

COCOON: THE RETURN
1988, 116 mins, US Ⓥ ⊙ col
Dir Daniel Petrie ***Prod*** Richard D. Zanuck, David Brown, Lili Fini Zanuck ***Scr*** Stephen McPherson ***Ph*** Tak Fujimoto ***Ed*** Mark Roy Warner ***Mus*** James Horner ***Art*** Lawrence G. Paull
Act Don Ameche, Wilford Brimley, Hume Cronyn, Steve Guttenberg, Maureen Stapleton, Jessica Tandy (Zanuck-Brown/ 20th Century-Fox)

Not altogether charmless, *Cocoon: The Return* still is far less enjoyable a senior folks' fantasy than *Cocoon*. An overdose of bathos weighs down the sprightliness of the characters, resulting in a more maudlin than magic effort.

Quandary begins with the return to St Petersburg, Florida, of the plucky group lead by the twinkle-eyed Don Ameche for a four-day visit from the utopian extraterrestrial world of Antarea. Upon being reunited with family and friends, each questions his own choice for leaving in the first place and, at the end of the picture, the rationale for either returning to space or remaining on terra firma.

Jack Gilford as irascible widower Bernie Lefkowitz and Steve Guttenberg as Jack, the glass-bottom boat tour guide cum shlocky seashell merchandise salesman, keep this overly sappy production afloat.

Ameche, Gwen Verdon and occasionally Hume Cronyn want to play funny and loose but are restrained by Daniel Petrie's direction, which too often is unfocused.

•

CODE OF SILENCE
1985, 101 mins, US Ⓥ ⊙ col
Dir Andrew Davis ***Prod*** Raymond Wagner ***Scr*** Michael Butler, Dennis Shryack, Mike Gray ***Ph*** Frank Tidy ***Ed*** Peter Parasheles, Christopher Holmes ***Mus*** David Frank ***Art*** Maher Ahmed
Act Chuck Norris, Henry Silva, Bert Remsen, Molly Hagan, Joseph Guzaldo, Mike Genovese (Orion)

With 27 stuntmen and Chuck Norris in the credits, *Code of Silence* is a predictability cacophonous cops-and-crooks yarn [by Michael Butler and Dennis Shryack] that is actually quite good for the type.

The best thing about Norris is he never gets involved in all that romance stuff. Granted, there's a pretty girl (Molly Hagan) whose life is at stake, but Norris never does more than hold her hand, lend his brawny chest for her to cry on, and—finally in a fit of passion—kiss her on the forehead.

Norris plays a police sergeant leading a raid on a drug den, who arrives a step behind another gang which gets away with all the dope and money, leaving a bloody mess behind. This sets off a gang war between forces led by properly menacing Henry Silva on one side and less prominent Mike Genovese on the other.

•

COEUR EN HIVER, UN
(A HEART IN WINTER)
1992, 104 mins, France Ⓥ ⊙ col
Dir Claude Sautet ***Prod*** Jean-Louis Livi, Philippe Carcassonne ***Scr*** Claude Sautet, Jacques Fieschi ***Ph*** Yves Angelo ***Ed*** Jacqueline Thiedot ***Mus*** Philippe Sarde ***Art*** Christian Marti
Act Daniel Auteuil, Emmanuelle Beart, Andre Dussolier, Elizabeth Bourgine, Myriam Boyer, Jean-Luc Bideau (Film Par Film/Cinea/Orly/DA/Panavision/FR3)

A Heart in Winter is a cool, elegantly filmed triangular romance in which smiles and glances are used in place of dialogue and conventional action.

Extremely subtle and intensely enjoyable, impressive pic concentrates on Stephane (Daniel Auteuil) and Maxime (Andre Dusolier), partners in a small company that makes and repairs stringed instruments. Maxime is married; Stephane is single, though he has a platonic relationship with Helene (Elizabeth Bourgine).

One day at lunch, Maxime suddenly confesses that he's in love with Camille (Emmanuelle Beart), a beautiful young pianist who's dining with her possessive friend, Regine (Brigitte Catillon), at another table. Though he barely reacts to the news, Stephane is clearly taken aback. His response is to ingratiate himself with the interloper, insinuating himself into her life.

Director Claude Sautet handles this material with great subtlely and is extremely well served by his actors who all give exceptional performances. The picture unfolds against a background of achingly beautiful music (Maurice Ravel, used under the direction of Philippe Sarde), and Beart convincingly acquits herself on the violin.

•

COFFY
1973, 91 mins, US Ⓥ ⊙ col
Dir Jack Hill ***Prod*** Robert A. Papazian ***Scr*** Jack Hill ***Ph*** Paul Lohmann ***Ed*** Charles McClelland ***Mus*** Roy Ayers ***Art*** Perry Ferguson
Act Pam Grier, Booker Bradshaw, Robert DoQui, William Elliott, Allan Arbus, Sid Haig (American International)

Coffy is the story of a black tart, vengeance-minded, who sets out to kill everyone she holds responsible for her 11-year-old sister losing her mind by the dope habit. She blasts her victims, most of them lured into sex, with a shotgun that never misses.

Jack Hill, who wrote and directs with an action-atuned hand, inserts plenty of realism in footage in which Pam Grier in title role ably acquits herself. She takes on her prey, including pushers, crooked cops and politicians, pimps, gangsters et al, with a ferocity which builds into often-suspenseful sequence.

Grier, a statuesque actress with a body she doesn't hesitate to show, is strongly cast. Booker Bradshaw as a city politician and William Elliott as an honest cop score well.

●

COLD HEAVEN
1992, 105 mins, US Ⓥ ⦿ col
Dir Nicolas Roeg ***Prod*** Allan Scott, Jonathan D. Krane ***Scr*** Allan Scott ***Ph*** Francis Kenny ***Ed*** Tony Lawson ***Mus*** Stanley Myers ***Art*** Steven Legler
Act Theresa Russell, Mark Harmon, James Russo, Talia Shire, Will Patton (MCEG)

Infidelity has seldom offered as broad a canvas for torment and religious guilt as in Nicolas Roeg's *Cold Heaven*, a tortured study of love on the rocks that comes off like a jumbled bad dream.

Theresa Russell stars as the restless wife of an unsuspecting surgeon (Mark Harmon). She gets involved with another doctor (James Russo) and plans to break things off with her husband during a Mexican business trip. Before she can do the deed, however, he's killed in a horrifying but oddly convenient boating accident. Or is he? Back home, the distraught wife gets a mysterious note requesting her presence in the cliffside hamlet of Carmel, at the same hotel where her infidelity began.

Intention of Brian Moore's novel on which *Cold Heaven* is based was apparently to make the surgeon's pseudo-death a metaphor for the emotional effect of his wife's betrayal. But the connection is all buried in the film.

Russell, under husband Roeg's direction, does terrific work in her scene with a priest (Will Patton), but she and Harmon have a tough and thankless task in playing out this tormenting psychodrama.

●

COLDITZ STORY, THE
1955, 97 mins, UK Ⓥ b/w
Dir Guy Hamilton ***Prod*** Ivan Foxwell ***Scr*** Guy Hamilton, Ivan Foxwell, William Douglas Home ***Ph*** Gordon Dines ***Ed*** Peter Mayhew ***Mus*** Francis Chagrin ***Art*** Alex Vetchinsky
Act John Mills, Eric Portman, Christopher Rhodes, Lionel Jeffries, Bryan Forbes, Ian Carmichael (Foxwell/British Lion)

Easily one of the best prisoner-of-war yarns to come from any British studio, *The Colditz Story* is a taut real-life meller, based on the personal experiences of the author, Pat Reid.

Colditz Castle, in the heart of Saxony, was the fortress to which the German High Command sent officers who had attempted to escape from conventional prison camps. They regarded it as impregnable although they threatened the death penalty for anyone attempting to break out.

Film is loaded with meaty suspense situations and neatly leavened with good-natured humor to strike an excellent balance between the grim and the natural. The all-male cast keeps the yarn rolling at a lively pace. Eric Portman turns in a distinguished performance as the British colonel.

●

COLD ROOM, THE
1984, 92 mins, UK Ⓥ col
Dir James Dearden ***Prod*** Mark Forstater ***Scr*** James Dearden ***Ph*** Tony Pierce-Roberts ***Ed*** Mick Audley ***Mus*** Michael Nyman ***Art*** Tim Hutchinson
Act George Segal, Amanda Pays, Renee Soutendijk, Warren Clarke, Anthony Higgins, Ursula Howells (Jethro)

The Cold Room, a modestly intriguing psychological thriller, marks the feature debut (after a couple of interesting shorts) of director James Dearden. It's a very confident first feature, intelligently directed and always interesting to look at.

Story centers around an attractive if sulky British teenager (Amanda Pays), who joins her father (George Segal) for a vacation in (of all places) East Berlin.

Spending time in her tiny room in an old-fashioned hotel, she gradually comes under the spell of another girl who lived in the same house during the war.

Segal is relaxed as the baffled father who can't get through to his daughter and fears she may be going insane. Pays is a find as the possessed girl, but Dutch actress Renee Soutendijk has almost nothing to do as Segal's girlfriend.

●

COLD WIND IN AUGUST, A
1961, 79 mins, US b/w
Dir Alexander Singer ***Prod*** Phillip Hazelton ***Scr*** Burton Wohl ***Ph*** Floyd Crosby ***Ed*** Jerry Young ***Mus*** Gerald Fried ***Art*** Gerald McCabe, Jerry Fried
Act Lola Albright, Scott Marlowe, Herschel Bernardi, Joe De Santis, Clark Gordon, Janet Brandt (United Artists/Troy)

No matter how well Vladimir Horowitz might play "Chopsticks," it would still be "Chopsticks." By roughly the same token, all the exceptional ability that went into *A Cold Wind in August* is levelled to the common denominator of its subject—a short course in the seduction, care and feeding of a healthy 17-year-old boy by a nymphomaniacal 28-year-old stripper. This is a hormone opera of considerable quality.

Burton Wohl's screenplay, from his novel, plants the handsome super's son (Scott Marlowe) in the flashy upstairs apartment of a sultry body-goddess (Lola Albright) who is on a kind of annual three-month vacation in respectable anonymity from the questionable life she leads the other nine. Passion matures into love, but the romance goes ker-plop for the lad when he discovers she is not the madonna he naively believed her to be.

Director Alexander Singer has endowed his picture with a blunt and powerful realism. His actors seem perfectly at home in the New York environment.

Another factor in the film's visual impact is the extraordinarily active, inventive camerawork by Floyd Crosby. There is a strip scene (Albright as object) that rivals in sensuality any strip scene ever put on non-stag celluloid—darting images of undulating sections of Albright's partially exposed and admirable epidermis formation.

●

COLLECTOR, THE
1965, 117 mins, US Ⓥ ⦿ col
Dir William Wyler ***Prod*** William Wyler, Jud Kinberg, John Kohn ***Scr*** Stanley Mann, John Kohn ***Ph*** Robert L. Surtees, Robert Krasker ***Ed*** Robert Swink ***Mus*** Maurice Jarre ***Art*** John Stoll
Act Terence Stamp, Samantha Eggar, Maurice Dallimore, Mona Washbourne (Columbia)

William Wyler undertakes a vastly difficult assignment, and carries it off with rare artistry, in bringing to the screen a solid, suspenseful enactment of John Fowles's bestselling novel.

As a character study of two persons—an inferiority-ridden young Englishman with an uncontrollable sex obsession and the young woman he abducts and holds prisoner in the cellar of his secluded farmhouse—the feature is adroitly developed and bears the stamp of class.

Color photography frequently is stunning, always of high quality, picture opening on a visually beautiful note as the leading male character (Terence Stamp) is introduced as a butterfly collector. The screenplay expands on this premise; he broadens his collecting to girls. He falls in love with a young art student, and has an uncontrollable desire to force her to reciprocate his feelings.

Both Stamp and Samantha Eggar turn in remarkably restrained performances under Wyler's guiding dramatic helmsmanship. Stamp makes his character of an insignificant London bank clerk entirely believable and carefully shades his characterization.

1965: NOMINATIONS: Best Director, Actress (Samantha Eggar), Adapted Screenplay

●

COLLEEN
1936, 89 mins, US b/w
Dir Alfred E. Green ***Scr*** Peter Milne, F. Hugh Herbert, Robert Lord ***Ph*** George Barnes ***Ed*** Byron Haskin
Act Dick Powell, Ruby Keeler, Jack Oakie, Joan Blondell, Hugh Herbert, Louise Fazenda (Warner)

An entertaining Dick Powell–Ruby Keeler musical romance which has greater cast than story or production strength. In addition to the top pair, cast includes Jack Oakie and Joan Blondell, working largely as a combination. Hugh Herbert plays a nut role. Louise Fazenda is especially well suited as the hysterical rich aunt of Powell who goes to pieces over scandal and publicity.

Story of *Colleen* is more or less routine, written to fit the characters banded together from the WB musicals factory. It has Herbert, the eccentric, taking over a dress shop and putting Joan Blondell in charge. Along comes Powell, his nephew, who thinks the shop can be made to pay. He puts Keeler in charge.

For Powell and Keeler it's the songs [by Harry Warren and Al Dubin] mostly. Keeler has a bit on the edge of it, since she has Paul Draper, debuting on the screen, as a dance partner. He is a slender, handsome fellow of the Astaire type, very light and agile with the gams. He's from legit and picture houses.

●

COLOR OF MONEY, THE
1986, 119 mins, US Ⓥ ⦿ col
Dir Martin Scorsese ***Prod*** Irving Axelrad, Barbara De Fina ***Scr*** Richard Price ***Ph*** Michael Ballhaus ***Ed*** Thelma Schoonmaker ***Mus*** Robbie Robertson ***Art*** Boris Leven
Act Paul Newman, Tom Cruise, Mary Elizabeth Mastrantonio, Helen Shaver, John Turturro, Bill Cobbs (Touchstone)

The Color of Money is another inside look at society's outsiders from director Martin Scorsese. This time out it's the subculture of professional pool hustlers that consumes the screen with a keenly observed and immaculately crafted vision of the raw side of life. Pic has a distinctive pulse of its own with exceptional performances by Paul Newman and Tom Cruise.

Based on a reworking of Walter Tevis's novel by scripter Richard Price, *The Color of Money* is a continuation of the 1961 film *The Hustler*, 25 years later.

Back as Fast Eddie Felson, Paul Newman is a self-proclaimed "student of human moves"—a hustler. When he happens on Vincent Lauria (Tom Cruise) in a nondescript Midwest pool hall, Eddie's juices start flowing and the endless cycle starts again.

As Vincent's girlfriend Carmen, Mary Elizabeth Mastrantonio is working on her own short fuse and is learning how to use her main talent too—her sexuality. It's a hot and disturbing performance as her actions contradict her choirgirl good looks.

1986: Best Actor (Paul Newman)

NOMINATIONS: Best Supp. Actress (Mary Elizabeth Mastrantonio), Adapted Screenplay, Art Direction

●

COLOR OF NIGHT
1994, 121 mins, US Ⓥ ⦿ col
Dir Richard Rush ***Prod*** Buzz Feitshans, David Matalon ***Scr*** Matthew Chapman, Billy Ray ***Ph*** Dietrich Lohmann ***Ed*** Jack Hofstra ***Mus*** Dominic Frontiere ***Art*** James L. Schoppe
Act Bruce Willis, Jane March, Ruben Blades, Lesley Ann Warren, Scott Bakula, Brad Dourif (Hollywood/Cinergi)

Color of Night is a knuckleheaded thriller [from a screen story by Billy Ray] that means to get a rise out of audiences but will merely make them see red. It's confounding and sad that director Richard Rush waited 14 years to make another film after his striking *The Stunt Man*, only to choose a script as dismal as this.

Pokey script centers upon New York shrink Bill Capa (Bruce Willis), who hies to LA after one of his patients takes a swan dive out of his high-rise window. His best friend, fellow head doctor Bob Moore (Scott Bakula), pulls him into a group therapy session populated by nympho Sondra (Lesley Ann Warren), uptight hypochondriac Clark (Brad Dourif), bereaved widower Buck (Lance Henriksen), twisted artist Casey (Kevin J. O'Connor) and a weird, uncommunicative teenager named Richie.

After Dr. Bob is gruesomely stabbed to death in his office, irreverent detective Martinez (Ruben Blades) comes onto the case. To spice matters up, a lithe young thing named Rose (Jane March) conveniently rear-ends Capa one day, starting a hot affair that, in its original cut, earned the film an NC-17 rating, but now consists of a lot of twisting and turning in a pool, shower and bed.

Motivation behind the murders is obscure at best, and melodramatic climax, with its pathetic echoes of *Vertigo*, is a joke.

●

COLOR PURPLE, THE
1985, 152 mins, US Ⓥ ⦿ col
Dir Steven Spielberg ***Prod*** Steven Spielberg, Kathleen Kennedy, Frank Marshall, ***Scr*** Menno Meyjes ***Ph*** Allen Daviau ***Ed*** Michael Kahn ***Mus*** Quincy Jones ***Art*** J. Michael Riva
Act Danny Glover, Whoopi Goldberg, Margaret Avery, Oprah Winfrey, Willard Pugh, Akosua Busia (Amblin/Warner)

There are some great scenes and great performances in *The Color Purple*, but it is not a great film. Steven Spielberg's turn at "serious" filmmaking is marred in more than one place by overblown production that threatens to drown in its own emotions. But the characters created in Alice Walker's novel are so vivid that even this doesn't kill them off and there is still much to applaud (and cry about) here.

Walker's tale is the story of a black family's growth and flowering over a 40-year period in the south starting around 1909. At the center of everything is Celie, who as a young girl gives birth to two children and is then married into a life of virtual servitude to a man she can refer to only as Mr. (Danny Glover).

Above all *The Color Purple* is a love story between Celie, and her sister, Nettie, from whom she is separated at childhood, and, later in life, the blues singer Shug Avery.

Saving grace of the film are the performances. As the adult Celie, debuting Whoopi Goldberg uses her expressive face and joyous smile to register the character's growth. Equally good is Glover who is a powerful screen presence.

1985: NOMINATIONS: Best Picture, Actress (Whoopi Goldberg), Supp. Actress (Margaret Avery, Oprah Winfrey), Adapted Screenplay, Cinematography, Costume Design, Art Direction, Original Score, Song ("Miss Celie's Blues"), Makeup

•

COLORS

1988, 120 mins, US Ⓥ ⊙ col

Dir Dennis Hopper ***Prod*** Robert H. Solo ***Scr*** Michael Schiffer ***Ph*** Haskell Wexler ***Ed*** Robert Estrin ***Mus*** Herbie Hancock ***Art*** Ron Foreman

Act Sean Penn, Robert Duvall, Maria Conchita Alonso, Randy Brooks, Grand Bush, Don Cheadle (Orion)

Colors is a solidly crafted depiction of some current big-city horrors and succeeds largely because of the Robert Duvall–Sean Penn teaming as frontline cops. They're terrific together as members of the gang crime division of the LAPD.

Filmmakers alert the uninitiated right off that theirs is a tale [story by Michael Schiffer and Richard DiLello] of unequal odds, pointing out that 600 street gangs roam America's second-largest city while local and county police directly assigned to the problem number only 250.

Drawn into this fracas is officer Bob Hodges (Duvall), married, the father of three, who's inexpicably been forced back into the action. He's savvy about his dealings with punks in "bozoland," as Hodges calls the streets, and is unhappy about getting greenhorn Danny McGavin (Penn) as his sidekick.

Latter is a high-strung and cocksure volunteer. He not only busts them with bravado but roughs 'em up out there.

Plot takes Duvall and Penn through investigation of the latest offing of a "Blood" gangmember by the rival "Crips" and shows the police frustrations in working the case against nearly insurmountable obstacles. While nicely avoiding the feel of a docu, film seems to effectively capture the gang "culture."

[In 1989, a 127-min. version was issued on home video.]

•

COLOSSUS OF NEW YORK, THE

1958, 70 mins, US b/w

Dir Eugene Lourie ***Prod*** William Alland ***Scr*** Thelma Schnee ***Ph*** John F. Warren ***Ed*** Floyd Knudtson ***Mus*** Van Cleave ***Art*** Hal Pereira, John Goodman

Act Ross Martin, Mala Powers, Charles Herbert, Otto Kruger, John Baragrey, Ed Wolff (Paramount)

The Willis Goldbeck story, screenplayed by Thelma Schnee, is pretty hokey fare. The pièce de résistance is surgeon Otto Kruger's transplant of a dead man's brain into the body of a mechanical monster.

Brain, incidentally, is that of Kruger's scientist-son Ross Martin who died in an accident. His father felt that Martin's death shouldn't end his services to mankind—hence the transplantation. But lacking a soul, the mechanical man refuses to follow instructions and goes on a rampage until subdued by moppet Charles Herbert who is Martin's son.

The story, direction and performances are just about as mechanical as the monster.

Either economy or perhaps the studio musicians' strike may have accounted for the Van Cleave novel score, played solely by a piano. It proves a lotta mood can be generated by one instrument.

•

COMA

1978, 113 mins, US Ⓥ ⊙ col

Dir Michael Crichton ***Prod*** Martin Erlichman ***Scr*** Michael Crichton ***Ph*** Victor J. Kemper, Gerald Hirschfeld ***Ed*** David Bretherton ***Mus*** Jerry Goldsmith ***Art*** Albert Brenner

Act Genevieve Bujold, Michael Douglas, Elizabeth Ashley, Rip Torn, Richard Widmark, Lois Chiles (M-G-M)

Coma is an extremely entertaining suspense drama in the Hitchcock tradition. Director-adapter Michael Crichton neatly builds mystery and empathy around star Genevieve Bujold, a doctor who grows to suspect her superiors of deliberate surgical error. Michael Douglas also stars as her disbelieving lover.

Robin Cook's novel is adapted by Crichton into a smartly paced tale which combines traditional Hitchcock elements with contemporary personal relationships. Thus Bujold and Douglas wrestle in subplot with separate identity and mutual romantic problems while she becomes the innocent enmeshed in suspicious medical wrongdoing. When lifelong friend Lois Chiles goes into permanent coma during an otherwise routine operation, Bujold begins probing a series of similar incidents.

Arrayed against her are hospital superiors Richard Widmark and Rip Torn, and even Douglas himself. Lance Le Gault is a hired killer whom Bujold outwits to the relief of the entire audience.

Elizabeth Ashley is notable as the head of a dubious medical experimental center where the comatose victims vegetate pending ghoulish, but all-too-plausible disposition.

•

COMANCHEROS, THE

1961, 107 mins, US Ⓥ ⊙ ▭ col

Dir Michael Curtiz ***Prod*** George Sherman ***Scr*** James Edward Grant, Clair Huffaker ***Ph*** William H. Clothier ***Ed*** Louis Loefler ***Mus*** Elmer Bernstein ***Art*** Jack Martin Smith, Alfred Ybarra

Act John Wayne, Stuart Whitman, Ina Balin, Nehemiah Persoff, Lee Marvin, Michael Ansara (20th Century-Fox)

The Comancheros is a big, brash, uninhibited action-western of the old school about as subtle as a right to the jaw.

The screenplay, based on the novel by Paul I. Wellman, is a kind of cloak-and-dagger yarn on horseback. It is set against the Texas of the mid-19th century, a troubled time prior to its statehood when the Comanches were on the warpath and renegade white men, or "Comancheros," were aiding the Indian cause with fighting equipment. The film relates the story of a Texas Ranger (John Wayne) and an itinerant gambler (Stuart Whitman) who team up to detect and destroy the renegade, parasitic society.

Wayne is obviously comfortable in a role tailor-made to the specifications of his easygoing, square-shooting, tight-lipped but watch-out-when-I'm-mad screen personality. Lee Marvin makes a vivid impression in a brief, but colorful, role as a half-scalped, vile-tempered Comanchero agent.

Director Michael Curtiz was fortunate in having aboard some excellent stuntmen whose hard falls, leaps and maneuvers during the raid and battle sequences (directed by Cliff Lyons) are something to see. Cameraman William H. Clothier's sweeping panoramic views of the Moab, Utah, site are something to behold.

•

COMANCHE STATION

1960, 74 mins, US ▭ col

Dir Budd Boetticher ***Prod*** Budd Boetticher ***Scr*** Burt Kennedy ***Ph*** Charles Lawton, Jr. ***Ed*** Edwin Bryant ***Mus*** Mischa Bakaleinikoff ***Art*** Carl Anderson

Act Randolph Scott, Nancy Gates, Claude Akins, Skip Homeier, Richard Rust, Rand Brooks (Ranown/Columbia)

Comanche Station is, by any standard, a good picture. The screenplay by Burt Kennedy is true to western traditions and at the same time there is romance, although not a conventional love story, and criminal elements for suspense, mystery and excitement. Kennedy does not rely on casting for characterization. The dialog is sparse, but colorful, and humor is not neglected.

Randolph Scott plays one of those loners of the old West, who is bringing back to her husband a settler's wife (Nancy Gates) who has been captured by Comanches. Accompanying them are a trio of bad ones, Claude Akins, Skip Homeier and Richard Rust. Jeopardy is compounded from without by Comanches trailing the group.

All of this is resolved with neat, but not pat, solutions. The characters are vivid and Budd Boetticher's direction of his good cast keeps interest high. It is obvious that Gates's Indian captors have, as the saying goes, had their way with her. The issue is not dodged. Scott gives a characteristically stolid but convincing performance. Gates is satisfactory as the story's focal point.

Charles Lawton, Jr.'s camera catches some superb exteriors (there are no interior scenes at all) on the rugged location, and creates some striking personal compositions.

•

COME BACK CHARLESTON BLUE

1972, 100 mins, US Ⓥ col

Dir Mark Warren ***Prod*** Samuel Goldwyn, Jr. ***Scr*** Bontche Schweig, Peggy Elliott ***Ph*** Dick Kratina ***Ed*** Gerald Greenberg, George Bowers ***Mus*** Donny Hathaway ***Art*** Robert Gundlach

Act Godfrey Cambridge, Raymond St. Jacques, Peter De Anda, Percy Rodrigues, Jonelle Allen, Maxwell Glanville (Warner/Goldwyn)

Come Back Charleston Blue is an okay follow-up [from the novel *The Heat's On* by Chester Himes] by producer Samuel Goldwyn, Jr., to his successful 1970 *Cotton Comes to Harlem*, again featuring Godfrey Cambridge and Raymond St. Jacques as offbeat, comedic Harlem gumshoes.

Cambridge and St. Jacques find themselves caught between fading black drug king and mobster Maxwell Glanville, and Peter De Anda, ostensibly a successful photographer out to rid Harlem of drugs, but in reality eyeing the area for himself.

De Anda creates the impression that a series of gangland deaths has been caused by the ghost of Charleston Blue, a Depression-era hood, long dead.

The film lacks punch. The gags just don't quite add up to solid laughs or excitement.

•

COME BACK, LITTLE SHEBA

1952, 95 mins, US Ⓥ ⊙ b/w

Dir Daniel Mann ***Prod*** Hal B. Wallis ***Scr*** Ketti Frings ***Ph*** James Wong Howe ***Ed*** Warren Low ***Mus*** Franz Waxman ***Art*** Hal Pereira, Henry Bumstead

Act Burt Lancaster, Shirley Booth, Terry Moore, Richard Jaeckel, Philip Ober (Paramount)

The Broadway legit success, *Come Back, Little Sheba*, has become a potent piece of screen entertainment. The production is faithful to the William Inge play.

Shirley Booth has the remarkable gift of never appearing to be acting. Opposite her is Burt Lancaster, bringing an unsuspected talent to his role of the middle-aged, alcoholic husband.

The story interest centers on the somewhat dull, middle-aged and middle-class husband and wife portrayed by Lancaster and Booth. She is a frowzy, talkative, earnestly pleasant woman continually living in the past, while he is a man almost beaten by life and a great thirst. Their stoogy, routine existence is brightened one day when a student boarder (Terry Moore) rents a room in their home.

Her cheery, comely presence gives the couple renewed interest, but also brings about the film's climactic punch when Lancaster's fondness for her is jolted by believing the girl is going too far in an affair with another student and amateur romeo (Richard Jaeckel).

1952: Best Actress (Shirley Booth)

NOMINATIONS: Best Supp. Actress (Terry Moore), Editing

•

COME BACK TO THE 5 & DIME, JIMMY DEAN, JIMMY DEAN

1982, 109 mins, US Ⓥ ⊙ col

Dir Robert Altman ***Prod*** Scott Bushnell ***Scr*** Ed Graczyk ***Ph*** Pierre Mignot ***Ed*** Jason Rosenfield ***Art*** David Cropman

Act Sandy Dennis, Cher, Karen Black, Sudie Bond, Marta Heflin, Kathy Bates (Sandcastle 5)

Story is set in a small Texas town in 1975. Five women, who were part of a James Dean fan club, hold a 20th anniversary reunion, in the local Woolworth 5 and Dime. Sandy Dennis and Cher play characters who remained in the town and at the outset are anxious about which of the old crowd will appear.

Robert Altman had previously directed the story on Broadway with the same cast. However, while the location remains the area of the store, the action is far from claustrophobic.

The action occurs on two levels with incidents of the reunion run parallel to events of 20 years earlier. Altman uses a wall-length mirror to effect the time changes.

The women arrive and each offers her memories of the earlier time. The recollections are, at first, comical and innocent but eventually the characters reveal their most painful secrets. The material is told with great emotion and Altman gets wonderful performances from his female ensemble.

•

COME BLOW YOUR HORN

1963, 112 mins, US Ⓥ ▭ col

Dir Bud Yorkin ***Prod*** Norman Lear, Bud Yorkin ***Scr*** Norman Lear ***Ph*** William H. Daniels ***Ed*** Frank P. Keller ***Mus*** Nelson Riddle ***Art*** Hal Pereira, Roland Anderson

Act Frank Sinatra, Lee J. Cobb, Molly Picon, Barbara Rush, Jill St. John, Tony Bill (Paramount)

Art it ain't, fun it is. That about sums up *Come Blow Your Horn*. Like its legit parent, the screen version of Neil Simon's Jewish-oriented family comedy is a superficial but diverting romp.

The simple yarn is concerned with two brothers at opposite extremities of bachelorhood, the older one (Frank Sinatra) ultimately passing into a more mature, responsible phase of life when he sees in his younger brother's (Tony Bill) sensual excesses the reflection of a ferocious personality no longer especially becoming or appealing to him. This is mighty good news to his long-suffering father, a wax fruit manufacturer from Yonkers for whom any unmarried man over 30 is a bum.

Sinatra's role is perfectly suited to his rakish image. It also affords him an opportunity to manifest his most consummate talent—that of singer. He warbles the lilting title tune.

But it's Lee J. Cobb who steals the show (albeit in the juiciest part) with what might be described as a "bum"-bastic portrayal of the explosively irascible old man who is forever appearing at the front door of his son's apartment when more glamorous company is expected.

Tony Bill makes a fairly auspicious screen bow as the younger brother. Barbara Rush is attractive as the girl who eventually gets Sinatra, and Jill St. John is flashy as a guilelessly accommodating sexpot.

1963: NOMINATION: Best Color Art Direction

•

COMEDIANS, THE

1967, 156 mins, US col

Dir Peter Glenville ***Prod*** Peter Glenville ***Scr*** Graham Greene ***Ph*** Henri Decae ***Ed*** Francoise Javet ***Mus*** Laurence Rosenthal ***Art*** Francois De Lamothe

Act Richard Burton, Elizabeth Taylor, Alec Guinness, Peter Ustinov, Paul Ford, Lillian Gish (M-G-M)

The despair of people living under a despot may, indeed, be a sort of living death. Producer-director Peter Glenville's pic, scripted by Graham Greene [from his own novel], is a plodding, low-key and eventually tedious melodrama.

Greene's screenplay rambles on through a seemingly interminable 156 minutes. Not the least of film's flaws is the role played by Elizabeth Taylor (wife of South American ambassador Peter Ustinov), who has a recurring, deteriorating affair with hotel-owner Richard Burton.

The very poorly made story point is that Burton gradually finds something to live for, in his eventual flight to join mountain rebels, pitiably equipped and pitilessly portrayed. Alec Guinness is a society-type arms promoter who fakes a military background. In a climactic scene where he confesses the fraud to Burton, Guinness excels.

•

COMEDY MAN, THE

1964, 92 mins, UK b/w

Dir Alvin Rakoff ***Prod*** Jon Penington ***Scr*** Peter Yeldham ***Ph*** Ken Hodges ***Mus*** Bill McGuffie ***Art*** John Blezard

Act Kenneth More, Cecil Parker, Dennis Price, Billie Whitelaw, Norman Rossington, Angela Douglas (British Lion)

Douglas Hayes's lightweight novel about the struggle of a stock actor who has just passed the dangerous 40s, without making the grade, hardly scratches new ground. But the authenticity and atmosphere are complete and this well made little film recreates that atmosphere splendidly on the screen. A well drawn performance by Kenneth More adds greatly to the entertainment value of the film.

Fired from a stock company in the sticks for being found with the leading lady, who happens to be the producer's wife, More comes to London for one more crack at making good in the big time. In the seedy atmosphere of theatrical digs, promiscuous affairs, doing the agents' rounds he suffers all the humiliations and disappointments. Eventually pride breaks down, he takes a job doing TV commercials as "Mr. Honeybreath," which brings him dough and recognition.

•

COME FILL THE CUP

1951, 112 mins, US b/w

Dir Gordon Douglas ***Prod*** Henry Blanke ***Scr*** Ivan Goff, Ben Roberts ***Ph*** Robert Burks ***Ed*** Alan Crosland, Jr. ***Mus*** Ray Heindorf (dir.) ***Art*** Leo K. Kuter

Act James Cagney, Phyllis Thaxter, Raymond Massey, James Gleason, Gig Young, Selena Royle (Warner)

Warner's has combined a grim study of alcoholism with a typical James Cagney drama.

About the first third of the story [from the novel by Harlan Ware] is taken up with a detailed study of a man with a great thirst which kills his newspaper career, shoves him down the ladder to skid row and into the alcoholic ward of a hospital, where he finds a friend and the will to battle his affliction.

While Cagney scores dramatically in his study of an alcoholic, these phases haven't the commercial appeal of his later character as a reformed drunk who gets back into the newspaper game, rises to city editor, is forced to wet-nurse the publisher's nephew through a bourbon haze, and becomes involved with gangsters.

Gordon Douglas's direction misses few bets. Besides Cagney, two others stand out in performance. They are James Gleason, as the former alcoholic who takes Cagney under his wing after the d.t. siege in the hospital. The other is Gig Young, swell as the publisher's nephew.

•

COME FLY WITH ME

1963, 107 mins, US col

Dir Henry Levin ***Prod*** Anatole de Grunwald ***Scr*** William Roberts ***Ph*** Oswald Morris ***Ed*** Frank Clarke ***Mus*** Lyn Murray ***Art*** William Kellner

Act Dolores Hart, Hugh O'Brian, Karl Boehm, Pamela Tiffin, Karl Malden, Lois Nettleton (M-G-M)

Sometimes one performance can save a picture and in *Come Fly with Me* it's an engaging and infectious one by Pamela Tiffin. The production has other things going for it like an attractive cast, slick pictorial values and smart, stylish direction by Henry Levin, but at the base of all this sheer sheen lies a frail, frivolous and featherweight storyline that, in trying to take itself too seriously, flies into dramatic air pockets and crosscurrents that threaten to send the entire aircraft into a tailspin.

Airline hostesses and their romantic pursuits provide the peg upon which William Roberts has constructed his erratic screenplay from a screen story he concocted out of Bernard Glemser's *Girl on a Wing*. The affairs of three hostesses are described.

One (Dolores Hart) is looking for a wealthy husband and thinks she's found the fellow in a young Continental baron (Karl Boehm). Another (Lois Nettleton) is a nice-girl type who succeeds in winning the heart and hand of yon multimillionaire Texas businessman (Karl Malden). The third (Tiffin), after a series of cockpit falls and hotel ruminations, decides that flying so high with some guy in the sky is her idea of something to do. The "some guy" is first flight officer Hugh O'Brian. Much of the film was shot in Paris and Vienna.

•

COME LIVE WITH ME

1941, 85 mins, US b/w

Dir Clarence Brown ***Prod*** Clarence Brown ***Scr*** Patterson McNutt ***Ph*** George Folsey ***Ed*** Frank E. Hull ***Mus*** Herbert Stothart ***Art*** Cedric Gibbons, Randall Duell

Act James Stewart, Hedy Lamarr, Ian Hunter, Verree Teasdale, Donald Meek, Barton MacLane (M-G-M)

The Metro studio hasn't missed the mark as far as this for a long, long time. It is a silly piece, never believable for a moment, and its romantic and humorous shortcomings are the more conspicuous because of the apparent earnest effort to give the production good settings, fine technical trimmings and polish. Clarence Brown, who is credited both as producer and director, does not frequently muff at the box office.

Story is an original by Virginia Van Upp and concerns itself with the ancient cliché about the beautiful young woman who meets up suddenly with the saddened young man and proposes a fake marriage in order that she may escape deportation. For this convenience she agrees to pay the bridegroom $17.50 a week, which is enough to meet his hall bedroom overhead while he writes his first novel. Then she disappears.

All of this happens in the first reel. The only suspense from this point on is how quickly the first novel, called *Without Love*, is going to be accepted by the publisher, the bridal cash advance refunded and the characters transformed from puppets to people. It takes seven reels, which is too long.

As the young novelist, James Stewart tries his best to create some interest in the boy typist, but there are several passages where even he seems on the verge of giving up. Hedy Lamarr is quite as unhappy in her role, despite fine photographic portraiture and a little pout or two.

•

COMES A HORSEMAN

1978, 118 mins, US col

Dir Alan J. Pakula ***Prod*** Gene Kirkwood, Dan Paulson ***Scr*** Dennis Lynton Clark ***Ph*** Gordon Willis ***Ed*** Marion Rothman ***Mus*** Michael Small ***Art*** George Jenkins

Act James Caan, Jane Fonda, Jason Robards, George Grizzard, Richard Farnsworth, Jim Davis (United Artists/Chartoff-Winkler)

Alan Pakula's *Comes a Horseman* is so lethargic not even Jane Fonda, James Caan and Jason Robards can bring excitement to this artificially dramatic story of a stubborn rancher who won't surrender to the local land baron.

The real star of the film doesn't get billing. It's a stretch of verdant land in Colorado known as the Wet Mountain Valley. Gordon Willis photographs this location with so much love and awe that talk by oil explorers about ripping it up is both moving and repulsive.

Robards's part is the most troublesome. He's the land baron who wants both Fonda and Caan to sell their parcels to complete his empire. Every one of Robards' lines is shaded by a black hat. He is evil in the most convenient way.

Caan, also an independent rancher who recently returned from serving in World War II, teams up with Fonda after his partner is killed (presumably on orders from Robards). When Fonda realizes what an accomplished cowboy Caan is and how much she needs him their relationship warms.

The only really good part in the film is Richard Farnsworth's Dodger, Fonda's aging hand. He's an altogether sympathetic character, close to the land and one of the few who really understands Fonda.

1978: NOMINATION: Best Supp. Actress (Richard Farnsworth)

•

COME SEE THE PARADISE

1990, 138 mins, US col

Dir Alan Parker ***Prod*** Robert F. Colesberry ***Scr*** Alan Parker ***Ph*** Michael Seresin ***Ed*** Gerry Hambling ***Mus*** Randy Edelman ***Art*** Geoffrey Kirkland

Act Dennis Quaid, Tamlyn Tomita, Sab Shimono, Shizuko Hoshi, Stan Egi, Ronald Yamamoto (20th Century-Fox)

In Alan Parker's richly mounted romantic saga of the Second World War relocation camps, the Asian-American cast is exemplary and Dennis Quaid has never been better. Noble if overlong effort depicts the love affair between the Irish-American labor activist and a woman from a well-established Japanese family ripped from its Los Angeles roots.

Quaid plays Jack McGurn, a newcomer to LA in 1936 who gets a job as a projectionist in a Little Tokyo theater and falls in love with the boss' daughter (Tamlyn Tomita). After he's fired and forbidden to see her again, they elope to Seattle, where, unlike in California, it was legal for a Japanese-American and a Caucasian to marry.

In general, Parker avoids most of the complexities behind the internment in favor of a broad, sentimental tale that emphasizes emotions.

Quaid gives a wonderfully open and unaffected performance, putting across romance, charm and integrity without resorting to any of the gimmicks he's used in earlier films. Tomita is a lovely, if under-nuanced, actress, and Egi as her brother is particularly interesting among the large supporting cast.

•

COME SEPTEMBER

1961, 112 mins, US col

Dir Robert Mulligan ***Prod*** Robert Arthur ***Scr*** Stanley Shapiro, Maurice Richlin ***Ph*** William Daniels ***Ed*** Russell F. Schoengarth ***Mus*** Hans J. Salter ***Art*** Henry Bumstead

Act Rock Hudson, Gina Lollobrigida, Sandra Dee, Bobby Darin, Walter Slezak, Brenda de Banzie (Universal)

A rich U.S. businessman (Rock Hudson), who ordinarily spends only one month (September) annually at his Italian villa, abruptly puts in a July appearance to the dismay of his enterprising major domo (Walter Slezak) who has been converting the private abode into a very public hotel for 11 months out of every year.

Even in the film's lesser spans there are occasional kicks and spurts of high good humor, but too often, in manipulating the plot for the purposes of introducing incongruous comedy spectacles (Hudson chasing after La Lollo at the wheel of a battered chicken truck, or the latter, garbed in full wedding gown regalia, chasing after the former in an old jeep), the writers seem inclined to telegraph, repeat and pile it on.

Under director Robert Mulligan's generally keen command, Hudson comes through with an especially jovial performance. Gina Lollobrigida need just stand there to generate sparks, but here she abets her eye-to-eye appeal with plenty of comedy savvy. Slezak is excellent. His scenes with Hudson are the best in the picture.

Sandra Dee has the misfortune to be overshadowed in the glamor department by La Lollo, but the young actress is plenty decorative and capable in her own right. In his first cinematic exposure, Bobby Darin does a workmanlike job.

•

COMFORT AND JOY

1984, 90 mins, UK col

Dir Bill Forsyth ***Prod*** Davina Belling, Clive Parsons ***Scr*** Bill Forsyth ***Ph*** Chris Menges ***Ed*** Michael Ellis ***Mus*** Mark Knopfler ***Art*** Adrienne Atkinson

Act Bill Paterson, Roberto Bernardi, Eleanor David, Clare Grogan, Patrick Malahide, Rikki Fulton (Kings Road)

In *Comfort and Joy* director-scripter Bill Forsyth again sets up a wacko scenario about zany, off-center characters.

But evincing much laughter over an unexpectedly funny couple living together, Forsyth abruptly switches into a more conventional plot. Pic opens with a well-dressed kleptomaniac (Eleanor David) lifting goods at a department store, followed by a man (Bill Paterson). It turns out he's her lover and aware of her stealing. They return home, make love off camera and after a meal she announces she's leaving.

Depressed, he adopts a stiff upper lip attitude and goes to his job as an MOR radio station early morning deejay. He then becomes, innocently at first, a go-between as two warring Mafia families fight for territorial control of selling ice cream by van.

David and Paterson are terrific together and almost every line between them is a joy. From the point she departs with no explanation the pic flashes a sparky moment or two, but it doesn't reach the high spots again.

•

COMFORT OF STRANGERS, THE
1990, 107 mins, Italy/US Ⓥ ⦿ col
Dir Paul Schrader ***Prod*** Angelo Rizzoli ***Scr*** Harold Pinter ***Ph*** Dante Spinotti ***Ed*** Bill Pankow ***Mus*** Angelo Badalamenti ***Art*** Gianni Quaranta
Act Christopher Walken, Rupert Everett, Natasha Richardson, Helen Mirren (Erre/Sovereign)

Neither the beguiling romance of Venice nor the undraped bodies of Natasha Richardson and Rupert Everett can disguise the hollowness of *The Comfort of Strangers*.

Mary (Richardson) and Colin (Everett) are an unmarried, live-apart couple who have returned to Venice in an attempt to rekindle their romance and assess their relationship. While both actors are paradigms of beauty, Harold Pinter's labored scenario [from the novel by Ian McEwan] would have us believe that all of Venice is transfixed by the heart-stopping magnificence of Everett.

Among the many Venetian souls smitten by Everett's Apollonian magnetism is a man in an ice-cream suit, Robert (Christopher Walken), the grave, courtly son of an Italian diplomat. Unbeknownst to the English tourists, Walken has been photographing Everett obsessively since their arrival. The couple are easy prey for Walken's blandishments.

Undermined by the script, the actors are constantly upstaged by the timeless glories of Venice.

•

COMING HOME
1978, 126 mins, US Ⓥ ⦿ col
Dir Hal Ashby ***Prod*** Jerome Hellman ***Scr*** Waldo Salt, Robert C. Jones ***Ph*** Haskall Wexler ***Ed*** Don Zimmerman ***Art*** Mike Haller
Act Jane Fonda, Jon Voight, Bruce Dern, Robert Ginty, Penelope Milford, Robert Carradine (United Artists)

Coming Home is in general an excellent Hal Ashby film which illuminates the conflicting attitudes on the Vietnam debacle from the standpoint of three participants. Jerome Hellman's fine production has Jane Fonda in another memorable and moving performance; Jon Voight, back on the screen much more mature, assured and effective; Bruce Dern, continuing to forge new career dimension.

Nancy Dowd's story was adapted by Waldo Salt and former film editor Robert C. Jones into a homefront drama. Gung-ho Marine officer Dern goes to Vietnam while loyal wife Fonda decides to work in a veterans' hospital where she meets high school classmate Voight, now an embittered cripple from the war. Their lives become completely transformed.

Fonda and Ashby have reined in any tendencies to be smug or pedantic. Instead, she provides a superb characterization. Voight's character evolves as he and Fonda become lovers. A sex scene between the two is a masterpiece of discreet romantic eroticism.

Dern's character is the trigger for certain major events, but there remains enough exposure for him to be convincing as a career soldier disillusioned by Vietnam. Among the large supporting cast are Penelope Milford, excellent as another hospital worker keeping an eye on brother Robert Carradine, very effective as a pitiful, freaked-out and ultimately suicidal case.

1978: Best Actor (Jon Voight), Actress (Jane Fonda), Original Screenplay

NOMINATIONS: Best Picture, Director, Supp. Actor (Bruce Dern), Supp. Actress (Penelope Milford), Editing

•

COMING TO AMERICA
1988, 116 mins, US Ⓥ ⦿ col
Dir John Landis ***Prod*** George Folsey, Jr., Robert D. Wachs ***Scr*** David Sheffield, Barry W. Blaustein ***Ph*** Woody Omens ***Ed*** Malcolm Campbell, George Folsey, Jr. ***Mus*** Nile Rodgers ***Art*** Richard MacDonald
Act Eddie Murphy, Arsenio Hall, John Amos, James Earl Jones, Shari Headley, Eriq LaSalle (Paramount)

Coming to America starts on a bathroom joke, quickly followed by a gag about private parts, then wanders in search of something equally original for Eddie Murphy to do for another couple of hours. It's a true test for loyal fans.

Murphy [credited with the original story] has no difficulty creating a pampered young prince of Zamunda who would like a chance to live a little real life and select his own bride instead of being forced into a royal marriage of convenience. Murphy even makes the prince sympathetic and genuine, complete to his stilted English. He and courtly sidekick Arsenio Hall venture to Queens to find a queen.

Longing for someone to love him for himself, Murphy discovers beautiful Shari Headley and goes to work mopping floors in father John Amos's hamburger emporium to be near her.

She, no surprise, already has a well-to-do, insufferable boyfriend (Eriq LaSalle) that dad is anxious for her to marry. How does a janitor capture the heart of such a maiden?

1988: NOMINATIONS: Best Costume Design, Makeup

•

COMMAND, THE
1954, 94 mins, US col
Dir David Butler ***Prod*** David Weisbart ***Scr*** Russell Hughes ***Ph*** Wilfrid M. Cline ***Ed*** Irene Morra ***Mus*** Dimitri Tiomkin
Act Guy Madison, Joan Weldon, James Whitmore, Carl Benton Reid, Harvey Lembeck, Ray Teal (Warner)

The first feature western under the CinemaScope label, *The Command* has a fundamentally sound cavalry-versus-Indians plot and highly charged action footage.

The picture was actually lensed in what was originally known as Vistarama and later as WarnerScope. With Warner's subsequent tie-up with 20th-Fox for CinemaScope, it was decided to send the film out with the latter label. In *Command*, picture clarity is lacking in many scenes except for center screen, but as attention is centered there the fuzziness around the edges is of little consequence.

Guy Madison turns in a thoroughly able job of the heroics under David Butler's direction. Latter handles the Russell Hughes screenplay [from a *Saturday Evening Post* novel by James Warner Bellah, as adapted by Samuel Fuller] expertly for action, particularly in the latter half when the film takes on more movement.

Madison is an Army medical captain unexpectedly assuming command of a cavalry troop after its regular commander is killed. Story is concerned with how he improvises battle tactics to defeat attacking Indians, wins the respect of his men and saves a wagon train, as well as two companies of infantry.

•

COMMAND DECISION
1948, 111 mins, US Ⓥ b/w
Dir Sam Wood ***Prod*** Sidney Franklin ***Scr*** William R. Laidlaw, George Froeschel ***Ph*** Harold Rosson ***Ed*** Harold F. Kress ***Mus*** Miklos Rozsa ***Art*** Cedric Gibbons, Urie McCleary
Act Clark Gable, Walter Pidgeon, Van Johnson, Brian Donlevy, Charles Bickford, John Hodiak (M-G-M)

Command Decision is a literate war drama, presented with a class touch. It tells of the Second World War from the top level of heavy brass, but with a slant that makes the starwearers human. There's no romance, and none is needed.

In transferring the Broadway legit hit [by William Wister Haines] to the screen, producer Sidney Franklin ["In association with Gottfried Reinhardt"] and director Sam Wood have made it a faithful version. It's still laid, principally, in the GHQ of a bomber command and little attempt is made to broaden that essential locale. Where it gets its added sweep is in the lucid music score (which bows only to the bomber's roar) and in the graphic lensing that gives the story a movement not possible on stage.

Clark Gable walks off with a picture in which everyone of the cast stands out. His is a believable delivery, interpreting the brigadier general who must send his men out to almost certain death with an understanding that bespeaks his sympathy with the soldier—brass or dogface.

Walter Pidgeon is the real big brass—the trafficker with politicos, wheedling and conniving to keep his Air Force supplied with planes and men despite homefront cries against losses.

•

COMMANDO
1985, 88 mins, US Ⓥ ⦿ col
Dir Mark L. Lester ***Prod*** Joel Silver ***Scr*** Steven de Souza ***Ph*** Matthew F. Leonetti ***Ed*** Mark Goldblatt, John F. Link, Glenn Farr ***Mus*** James Horner ***Art*** John Vallone
Act Arnold Schwarzenegger, Rae Dawn Chong, Dan Hedaya, Vernon Wells, David Patrick Kelly, Alyssa Milano (Silver/20th Century-Fox)

In *Commando*, the fetching surprise is the glancing humor between the quixotic and larky Rae Dawn Chong and the straight-faced killing machine of Arnold Schwarzenegger. Chong lights up the film like a firefly; Schwarzenegger delivers a certain light touch of his own and the result is palatable action comics.

Director Mark L. Lester, compelled to deal with an absurd plot [by Joseph Loeb III, Matthew Weisman and Steven de Souza], is blessed by the decision to cast Chong, who enjoys an offbeat sexuality and an insouciance that is irrestible.

Credit Lester with chiseling the quick, subtly romantic byplay between the two stars—unlikely mates thrown together in pursuit of a deadly Latin neo-dictator—and pulling off a terrific series of tracking shots during a riotous chase in a crowded galleria complex.

Heavies are vividly drawn in the cases of the obsessed Vernon Wells, the punk David Patrick Kelly, and sullen, ice-cold Bill Duke.

•

COMMANDOS STRIKE AT DAWN, THE
1942, 100 mins, US Ⓥ b/w
Dir John Farrow ***Prod*** Lester Cowan ***Scr*** Irwin Shaw ***Ph*** William C. Mellor ***Ed*** Anne Bauchens ***Mus*** Louis Gruenberg
Act Paul Muni, Anna Lee, Lillian Gish, Cedric Hardwicke, Robert Coote, Ray Collins (Columbia)

This production has been endowed with all the facilities required to emerge as an exciting tale of the bloodless Nazi subjugation of the people of Norway—and the spirit that prompts a group of Nordics to break the grip of Hitlerian despotism. It is a film [from a story by C. S. Forester] that is frequently slow, sometimes belabored, and occasionally unbelievable in its sentimental dramatics but, withal, one that is a must-see because of its impending—and frequently realized—sense of excitement.

Paul Muni portrays the Nordic fisherman who leads the movement and ultimately the Commando expedition. His is a forthright performance, occasionally underplayed, but always ringing true. Anna Lee is his romantic counterpart, a part acted well, though it's a role that's out of place. Commandos and romance don't strike a favorable note.

•

COMMITMENTS, THE
1991, 116 mins, US/UK Ⓥ ⦿ col
Dir Alan Parker ***Prod*** Roger Randall-Cutler, Lynda Myles ***Scr*** Dick Clement, Ian La Frenais, Roddy Doyle ***Ph*** Gale Tattersall ***Ed*** Gerry Hambling ***Mus*** G. Mark Roswell (sup.), Paul Bushnell (arr.) ***Art*** Brian Morris
Act Robert Arkins, Michael Aherne, Angeline Ball, Maria Doyle, Johnny Murphy, Andrew Strong (Beacon/First Film/Dirty Hands)

Director Alan Parker's story of a band of young Dubliners playing American '60s soul is fresh, well-executed and original.

Set in the working-class north side of contemporary Dublin, where the music scene is rich and teeming, film, based on the novel by Roddy Doyle, tells the story of 21-year-old entrepreneur Jimmy Rabbitte (Robert Arkins), who envisions bringing soul music to Dublin. He pieces together a 10-piece outfit with real musical potential from among his raw or semi-talented contemporaries.

Diverse group includes a messianic 45-year-old trumpeter, Joey (Johnny Murphy) who claims to have toured with the American greats, a stout and vulgar lead singer (played by 16-year-old Andrew Strong) with a voice like a diesel engine, and three scrappy and fetching femme backup singers who blossom into singing leads. Constant friction among players means Jimmy spends much of his energy trying to hold the band together long enough to land at least one paying gig and pay off the rogue from whom he's more or less stolen the equipment.

Parker and the casting directors initially auditioned more than 3,000 Dublin hopefuls. They wound up casting mostly musicians with no acting experience. Ensemble cast, which underwent five weeks of rehearsal, handles itself extremely well, particularly Arkins as Rabbitte and Murphy as the trumpeter.

Pictorially, the film is full of variety and unexpected pleasures, and the complex editing work by Gerry Hambling is marvelously accomplished.

1991: NOMINATION: Best Editing

•

COMO AGUA PARA CHOCOLATE
(LIKE WATER FOR CHOCOLATE)
1992, 114 mins, Mexico Ⓥ ⊙ col
Dir Alfonso Arau ***Prod*** Alfonso Arau ***Scr*** Laura Esquivel ***Ph*** Emmanuel Lubezki, Steve Bernstein ***Ed*** Carlos Bolado ***Mus*** Leo Brower ***Art*** Denise Pizzini, Marco Antonio Arteaga, Leo Brown
Act Lumi Cavazos, Marco Leonardi, Regine Torne John, Mario Ivan Martinez, Ada Carrasco, Claudette Maille (Arau/Imcine/Fonatur/Cinevista)

Strong material has been wasted by inept filmmaking in *Like Water for Chocolate*. Sixth feature by Mexican actor-director Alfonso Arau (known to world audiences for roles in *The Wild Bunch* and *Romancing the Stone*) suffers from an in-your-face approach to direction, with the entire story told mostly in closeup. The film screams to be opened up to northern Mexico's sweeping landscape and the broader notions of story line. Title can more aptly be translated as "boiling mad," since it refers to anger at the boiling point, like water for hot chocolate. Screenplay was penned by Arau's wife, Laura Esquivel, based on her delightful best-seller combining "magic realism" romance and recipe book.

Historical pic opens in the early 1900s on a large estate near the Texas border with the birth of the youngest of three sisters. Unfortunately, Tita (Lumi Cavazos) is part of a family tradition where the youngest daughter is denied matrimony in order to care for her mother in her old age. When Pedro Muzquiz (Marco Leonardi) comes to ask for Tita's hand, he's offered Tita's elder sister Rosaura, and he accepts so that he can be close to Tita, who is the cook at the hacienda.

The film chronicles this sweeping, lifelong romance between an impossible love consummated only through the meals Tita prepares. She pours so much love into her quail with rose petal dish that everyone at the table has an orgasm, and one of her sisters even catches on fire.

Art direction is beautiful, although denied scope, while rich cinematography is misused throughout.

[Version reviewed was director's original 144-min. cut, preemed at the 1992 Guadalajara fest. Pic was subsequently released in Mexico at 114 mins. and in the U.S. at 106 mins.]

•

COMPANY BUSINESS
1991, 98 mins, US Ⓥ ⊙ col
Dir Nicholas Meyer ***Prod*** Charles Jaffe ***Scr*** Nicholas Meyer ***Ph*** Gerry Fisher ***Ed*** Ronald Roose ***Mus*** Michael Kamen ***Art*** Ken Adam
Act Gene Hackman, Mikhail Baryshnikov, Kurtwood Smith, Terry O'Quinn, Daniel Von Bargen, Oleg Rudnick (M-G-M)

This muddled comedic-thriller, which asks what spies do after the Cold War, has a few amusing political references but the indecisive tone scuttles the film.

Gene Hackman plays a former CIA agent wasting his talent in industrial espionage. He's drafted by "the company" to return a former Soviet mole (Mikhail Baryshnikov) to the Soviets—along with $2 million in Colombian drug booty.

The swap goes bad, however, sending the two former spies racing around Europe, with their embarrassed and somewhat bumbling bosses from the CIA (Kurtwood Smith) and KGB (Oleg Rudnick) in lukewarm pursuit.

Writer-director Nicholas Meyer also is all over the map with his direction and script, which begins as a thriller (complete with portentously brooding music by Michael Kamen) then shifts to a sort of screwy comedy.

•

COMPANY OF STRANGERS, THE
1990, 100 mins, Canada Ⓥ col
Dir Cynthia Scott ***Prod*** David Wilson ***Scr*** Gloria Demers, Cynthia Scott, David Wilson, Sally Bochner ***Ph*** David de Volpi ***Ed*** David Wilson ***Mus*** Marie Bernard ***Art*** Christiane Gagnon
Act Alice Diabo, Constance Garneau, Winifred Holden, Cissy Meddings, Mary Meigs, Catherine Roche (NFBC)

The seventh in the National Film Board of Canada series where non-actors play themselves in a fictitious setting, *The Company of Strangers* features seven elderly women marooned in an abandoned country house near an idyllic lake after their bus breaks down. A safe, quiet journey becomes an adventure in survival, and in their quest for food they rediscover the hunger of youth.

These seven perfect strangers and their younger bus driver (a lively Montreal jazz singer, Michelle Sweeney) become fast friends through lengthy conversations, many of which are shot in real time. Pacing is slow and Hollywood-style action nonexistent. Entire story revolves around the women's lives, secrets, fears and joys.

The Mohawk woman (Alice Diabo) teaches them about fishing with pantyhose. A nun (Catherine Roche) in jeans manages to catch a pail full of frogs for dinner and is the self-appointed savior who walks 20 miles for help. Mary Meigs is an artist and lesbian who publishes books. Winnie Holden does great bird imitations. Constance Garneau seems to regret most of her 88 years. Beth Webber is an 80-year-old woman who looks 50 and never stops worrying about looking old. Cissy Meddings steals the show with her sense of humor and indifference to life's perils.

•

COMPANY OF WOLVES, THE
1984, 95 mins, UK Ⓥ ⊙ col
Dir Neil Jordan ***Prod*** Chris Brown, Stephen Woolley ***Scr*** Angela Carter, Neil Jordan ***Ph*** Bryan Loftus ***Ed*** Rodney Holland ***Mus*** George Fenton ***Art*** Anton Furst
Act Angela Lansbury, David Warner, Stephen Rea, Tusse Silberg, Sarah Patterson, Graham Crowden (ITC/Palace)

Admirably attempting an adult approach to traditional fairy tale material, *The Company of Wolves* nevertheless represents an uneasy marriage between old-fashioned story-telling and contemporary screen explicitness.

Virtually the entire film is the dream of the gravely beautiful adolescent Sarah Patterson. Within her dream are other dreams and stories told by others, all of which gives director Neil Jordan, who penned the screenplay with story originator Angela Carter, free imaginative rein, but which also gives the tale a less than propulsive narrative.

Anton Furst's elaborate forest settings, all created within studio-confines, are lovely. Jordan maneuvers well within them, even if Bryan Loftus's lush lensing is sometimes so dark that a claustrophobic feeling sets in.

•

COMPETITION, THE
1980, 129 mins, US Ⓥ ⊙ col
Dir Joel Oliansky ***Prod*** William Sackheim ***Scr*** Joel Oliansky ***Ph*** Richard H. Kline ***Ed*** David Blewitt ***Mus*** Lalo Schifrin ***Art*** Dale Hennesy
Act Richard Dreyfuss, Amy Irving, Lee Remick, Sam Wanamaker, Ty Henderson, James B. Sikking (Columbia/Rastar)

The Competition is a disappointment. Writer-director Joel Oliansky's glibly cynical view of the performing world and his dreary character portraits are matched in clumsiness by his ugly visual style and lack of genuine feeling for music.

The film needed a conductor and composer of background music with a sensitivity to the classical field, but instead it has Lalo Schifrin. Richard Dreyfuss, an aging piano wunderkind, is reunited at a San Francisco music competition with Amy Irving, a less driven but more gifted young woman he had impressed briefly at an earlier festival. She tries to rekindle their attraction, but Dreyfuss is too absorbed in his music at first to respond.

The film is tedious and predictable, curiously portraying music as a grim and joyless profession for these youngsters.

1980: NOMINATIONS: Best Editing, Song ("People Alone")

•

COMPROMISING POSITIONS
1985, 98 mins, US Ⓥ ⊙ col
Dir Frank Perry ***Prod*** Frank Perry ***Scr*** Susan Isaacs ***Ph*** Barry Sonnenfeld ***Ed*** Peter Frank ***Mus*** Brad Fiedel ***Art*** Peter Larkin
Act Susan Sarandon, Raul Julia, Edward Herrmann, Judith Ivey, Mary Beth Hurt, Joe Mantegna (Paramount)

Falling midway between a campy send-up of suburban wives soap operas and a legitimate thriller, *Compromising Positions*, from the 1978 novel by Susan Isaacs, emerges as a silly little whodunnit that's a mild embarrassment to all involved.

Unlikely material, about the murder of a philandering Long Island dentist, the reactions of his many mistresses, and the official and unofficial investigations into it, has hardly been approached with a straight face. The victim is a loathesome gold chain type, and most of his conquests are ladies who lunch with little redeeming social or intellectual value.

Intrigued and naively amazed that nearly everyone she knows has been involved with the late Dr Fleckstein, upper-middle-class housewife Susan Sarandon undertakes some amateur sleuthing with an eye toward reviving her old profession of newspaper reporter.

Action moves along snappily enough. Supporting players such as Judith Ivey and Josh Mostel contribute some tolerably amusing comedy turns, and Sarandon is, as always, highly watchable.

•

COMPULSION
1959, 103 mins, US ▭ b/w
Dir Richard Fleischer ***Prod*** Richard D. Zanuck ***Scr*** Richard Murphy ***Ph*** William C. Mellor ***Ed*** William Reynolds ***Mus*** Lionel Newman
Act Orson Welles, Dean Stockwell, Bradford Dillman, Diane Varsi, E. G. Marshall, Martin Milner (20th Century-Fox)

Compulsion, from Meyer Levin's novel, is almost a literal case study of the notorious Leopold-Loeb murder of Bobby Franks.

The two protagonists, here called Artie and Judd, both have highly neurotic, seething minds bent on destruction as twisted proof of their superiority. That the boys have a homosexual relationship is quite clear, though the subject is not overstressed. Both come from wealthy families that spoiled them.

As Artie Straus, the sneering, arrogant youth who can no longer distinguish between reality and his dreams, but who knows how to hide under the veneer of smooth politeness, Bradford Dillman turns in a superb performance. Opposite him, as Judd Steiner, Dean Stockwell plays an impressionable, sensitive youth, caught up in the spell of his strong-willed companion.

Director Richard Fleischer establishes the characters' from the terrifying opening shot when the two try to run down a drunk on the road, to their appearance in court where lawyer Orson Welles pleads for their life in the same idiom that Clarence Darrow used to save Nathan Leopold, Jr., and Richard Loeb from the Illinois gallows. The lines he speaks become part of the man himself, an almost classic oration against capital punishment.

As the girl who understands more than she knows, and who reaches out for Stockwell, Diane Varsi seems at times awkward. It's not an easy part, and she brings to it a tenseness that doesn't always register.

•

COMPUTER WORE TENNIS SHOES, THE
1970, 90 mins, US Ⓥ col
Dir Robert Butler ***Prod*** Bill Anderson ***Scr*** Joseph L. McEveety ***Ph*** Frank Phillips ***Ed*** Cotton Warburton ***Mus*** Robert F. Brunner ***Art*** John B. Mansbridge
Act Kurt Russell, Cesar Romero, Joe Flynn, William Schallert, Alan Hewitt, Richard Bakalyan (Walt Disney)

The amusing premise of *The Computer Wore Tennis Shoes* is that of a college non-student who, via an electrical accident, becomes brilliant because a computer memory bank has been transferred into his brain. Good-looking production is above average family entertainment, enhanced to great measure by zesty, but never showoff, direction by Robert Butler, in a debut swing to pix from telefilm.

Surrounding Kurt Russell, playing the suddenly smart student, is a most adroitly selected group of superior character actors. Joe Flynn as the college dean, William Schallert as Russell's prof, Alan Hewitt, dean of a competing college who goes after Russell with a recruiting vengence when the kid's fame spreads to a TV show hosted by Pat Harrington.

Also, Cesar Romero, with assistant Richard Bakalyan, provide the major story support: supposedly honest Romero, in reality a computer-oriented crime boss, has given Russell's school his old computer. And in the accident to the youth, Romero's clandestine records are inadvertently revealed.

•

COMRADES: A LANTERNIST'S ACCOUNT OF THE TOLPUDDLE MARTYRS AND WHAT BECAME OF THEM
1987, 160 mins, UK Ⓥ col
Dir Bill Douglas ***Prod*** Simon Relph ***Scr*** Bill Douglas ***Ph*** Gale Tattersall ***Ed*** Mick Audsley ***Mus*** Hans Werner Henze, David Graham ***Art*** Michael Pickwood
Act Robin Soans, William Gaminara, Stephen Bateman, Philip Davis, Jeremy Flynn, Keith Allen (Skreba/NFFC/Curzon/Film Four)

Bill Douglas has an eye for fresh detail, the rituals of rural life, and the dignity of country folk. Rarely before have the poverty, the pains and the pleasures, the oppressiveness of the work routine, even of the weather, been so well conveyed on film.

However, because so much time is spent on building up this rich tapestry of rural England in the 1830s, the focus is lost.

Eventually one pieces together that the Tolpuddle Martyrs, film's subject, were a small group of peasant craftsmen who dared to form a union and ask for higher wages. They were singled out for their subversion by the British authorities and transported to Australia. After a public outcry they were subsequently recalled to England.

Although there is a unique vision at work in *Comrades* it's a pity that more ruthlessness in scripting and editing was not exercised.

•

COMRADE X
1940, 87 mins, US b/w
Dir King Vidor ***Prod*** Gottfried Reinhardt ***Scr*** Ben Hecht, Charles Lederer ***Ph*** Joseph Ruttenberg ***Ed*** Harold F. Kress ***Mus*** Bronislau Kaper ***Art*** Cedric Gibbons, Malcolm Brown
Act Clark Gable, Hedy Lamarr, Oscar Homolka, Felix Bressart, Eve Arden, Natasha Lytess (M-G-M)

As title implies, action is laid in Russia, with Clark Gable, a love-'em-and-leave-'em, elbow-bending American reporter cutting a wide swath as a carefree lothario and outwitter of the censors in coding stories through to the outside. Gable hits a hurdle in maintaining his secret when simpleminded Felix Bressart, hotel porter, threatens exposure of the reporter's true identity unless Gable gets Bressart's daughter out of the country immediately.

Seems the girl, although a rabid Communist, is slated to be liquidated by the Kremlin. Matter-of-fact agreement of the girl to the plan, with ritual of typical Russian marriage ceremony and her quick breakdown under Gable's embraces, sets the stage for a continual series of laugh situations before the pair finally get out of the country.

Picture [from a screen story by Walter Reisch] resembles Garbo's *Ninotchka* only in that it again directs well-aimed shafts of humor at Communist actions and preachments, for plenty of rousing humor.

Gable provides a strong characterization of the ever-resourceful American newspaperman. Hedy Lamarr is handed her strongest role and demonstrates she can be more than decorative by a good display of both deadpan comedy and romantic antics. Natasha Lytess shines as a Russian secretary. Hair-pulling battle between latter and Lamarr over Gable's affections is a honey.

1940: NOMINATION: Best Original Story

•

CON AIR
1997, 115 mins, US Ⓥ ⦿ ▭ col
Dir Simon West ***Prod*** Jerry Bruckheimer ***Scr*** Scott Rosenberg ***Ph*** David Tattersall ***Ed*** Chris Lebenzon, Steve Mirkovich, Glen Scantlebury ***Mus*** Mark Mancina, Trevor Rabin ***Art*** Edward T. McAvoy
Act Nicolas Cage, John Cusack, John Malkovich, Steve Buscemi, Ving Rhames, Colm Meaney (Touchstone)

Apart from not knowing to quit while it's ahead, *Con Air* provides quite an exciting flight prior to its crash and burn. Hiply written and cast, and shrewdly positioned dramatically to exploit both the allure of lawlessness and the appeal of virtue, this first official solo effort by producer Jerry Bruckheimer is as surefire commercial, and just as elaborate, as anything he did with his late partner, Don Simpson.

British commercials and musicvid director Simon West, making his feature bow, in a matter of minutes disposes of the information that army ranger Cameron Poe (Nicolas Cage), unjustly imprisoned for eight years for a killing, is a man of honor, and the plane on which he catches a ride home is a U.S. Marshals Service transport with a passenger list consisting of "every creep and freak in the universe."

Chief among them is Cyrus (The Virus) Grissom (John Malkovich), a certifiably insane but brilliant master criminal commanding enough to lead such other three-time losers as murderous black militant Diamond Dog (Ving Rhames), the violence-prone Bedlam (Nick Chinlund) and fearsome career rapist Johnny 23 (Danny Trejo). Almost at once, the prisoners are able to take over the plane. On the ground, U.S. Marshal Vince Larkin (John Cusack) does his best to keep up with what's going on in the air.

Pic keeps any number of levels of tension going during the flight but one can see the picture deflating right before one's eyes during the utterly overdone and needless climax-upon-a-climax.

Scott Rosenberg's sarcastic, tough-guy dialogue is full of lean-and-mean one-liners, and the superbly cast actors know how to milk them for all they're worth. Unlikely action star Cage, very buff, keeps the audience with him at all times.

1997: NOMINATIONS: Best Original Song ("How Do I Live"), Sound

•

CONAN THE BARBARIAN
1982, 129 mins, US Ⓥ ⦿ ▭ col
Dir John Milius ***Prod*** Buzz Feitshans, Raffaella De Laurentiis ***Scr*** John Milius, Oliver Stone ***Ph*** Duke Callaghan ***Ed*** C. Timothy O'Meara, Fred Stafford ***Mus*** Basil Poledouris ***Art*** Ron Cobb
Act Arnold Schwarzenegger, James Earl Jones, Max von Sydow, Sandahl Bergman, Mako, Gerry Lopez (De Laurentiis)

The opening is promising enough as child Conan witnesses the brutal deaths of his father and mother at the whim of the evil Thulsa Doom (James Earl Jones). Conan, Jr., grows up as a slave who eventually has the good fortune of turning into Arnold Schwarzenegger.

It's the baddies' fatal flaw that they shove Conan into an arena to fight chosen competitors to the death. The guy naturally realizes he's pretty strong and decides to strike out on his own to see how far his muscles can take him.

In those days it was pretty far. On the road he meets up with a fellow drifter (Gerry Lopez), beautiful cohort and eventual lover Sandahl Bergman, needy king Max von Sydow and goofy wizard Mako.

Director John Milius does a nice job of setting up the initial story. There is a real anticipation as Schwarzenegger is unveiled as the barbarian and sets off on the road to independence. But for whatever reasons, the actor has a minimum of dialog and fails to convey much about the character through his actions.

This is compounded by the script by Milius and Oliver Stone, which is nothing more than a series of meaningless adventures and ambiguous references until the final expected confrontation with Jones.

•

CONAN THE DESTROYER
1984, 103 mins, US Ⓥ ⦿ ▭ col
Dir Richard Fleischer ***Prod*** Raffaella De Laurentiis ***Scr*** Stanley Mann ***Ph*** Jack Cardiff ***Ed*** Frank J. Urioste ***Mus*** Basil Poledouris ***Art*** Pier Luigi Basile
Act Arnold Schwarzenegger, Grace Jones, Wilt Chamberlain, Mako, Tracey Walter, Sarah Douglas (De Laurentiis/Pressman)

Conan the Destroyer is the ideal sword and sorcery picture. Plot [by Roy Thomas and Gerry Conway] is appropriately elemental. Conan is recruited by sexy queen Sarah Douglas to accompany teenage princess Olivia D'Abo to a distant castle, wherein lies a gem that will supposedly unleash many secret powers.

Unbeknownst to Conan, Douglas has instructed her henchman Wilt Chamberlain to kill the muscleman once the mission is accomplished, and to deliver D'Abo back home with her virginity intact so that she can be properly sacrificed. Along the way, group also picks up fiery warrioress Grace Jones.

As Conan, Arnold Schwarzenegger seems more animated and much funnier under Fleischer's direction than he did under John Milius's in the original—he even has an amusing drunk scene. Jones just about runs off with the picture. Coming on like a full-fledged star from her very first scene, the singer throws herself into her wild woman role with complete abandon.

•

CONCIERGE, THE
SEE: FOR LOVE OR MONEY

•

CONCORDE, THE—AIRPORT '79
(UK: AIRPORT '80—THE CONCORDE; AKA: AIRPORT—THE CONCORDE)
1979, 123 mins, US Ⓥ ⦿ col
Dir David Lowell Rich ***Prod*** Jennings Lang ***Scr*** Eric Roth ***Ph*** Philip Lathrop ***Ed*** Dorothy Spencer ***Mus*** Lalo Schifrin ***Art*** Henry Bumstead
Act Alain Delon, Susan Blakely, Robert Wagner, Sylvia Kristel, George Kennedy, Eddie Albert (Paramount)

Unintentional comedy still seems the *Airport* series' forte, although excellent special effects work, and some decent dramatics help *Concorde* take off.

This time out [story by Jennings Lang], the title entity is pursued by a dogged electronic missile, avoids an attack by a French fighter jet, barely makes a runway landing with no brakes, suffers a lost cargo door that rips open the bottom of the plane, manages a crash landing in an Alpine snow bank, and explodes just as its chic passengers disembark. That's all just part of a couple of days' work for pilots George Kennedy, Alain Delon and flight engineer David Warner.

Concorde does feature some better-than-average thesping from Delon, who survives the transition to American pix surprisingly well.

•

CONDEMNED OF ALTONA, THE
1963, 112 mins, Italy ▭ b/w
Dir Vittorio De Sica ***Prod*** Carlo Ponti ***Scr*** Abby Mann, Cesare Zavattini ***Ph*** Roberto Gerardi ***Ed*** Adriana Novelli ***Mus*** Nino Rota ***Art*** Elvezio Frigerio
Act Sophia Loren, Maximilian Schell, Fredric March, Robert Wagner, Francoise Prevost (Titanus)

Filmed on location in Hamburg, with interiors in Italy, this tale of postwar Germany, as symbolized by the members of one family, is undoubtedly anti-German. Where Jean-Paul Sartre's play [*Les sequestres d'Altona*] was written from the point of view of a French writer, scripters Abby Mann and Cesare Zavattini have changed these observations to Italian orientation.

The title refers to the Gerlachs, a wealthy Hamburg shipbuilding family, and Altona, the Hamburg suburb in which they live. Director Vittorio De Sica spins the tale as a series of disclosures about the family and the resultant emotional effect on Johanna (Sophia Loren), the actress-wife of the younger son (Robert Wagner).

This throws the major dramatic responsibility on Loren, who creates a shudderingly magnificent protrait of a beautiful, intelligent woman just beginning to recover her dignity and self-respect from the shambles of her country's militaristic past, only to have them threatened by "secrets" of her husband's family.

Striking flames is Maximilian Schell as Franz, the eldest son whose personal war guilt has kept him a self-imposed prisoner in the attic of the Gerlach manor for 15 years until, bordering on insanity, he is roused from his self-delusion by Johanna. Reported as dead by his family, even to Johanna, Franz's self-delusion has been supported by his family, particularly his tycoon father (Fredric March), whose own war guilt has been kept subservient to his indomitable will and industrial genius.

March, whose impending death from cancer brings the family together, creates Gerlach as much through visualization as through dialogue. Wagner makes one weak member of a strong family a memorable character.

•

CONDUCT UNBECOMING
1976, 107 mins, UK Ⓥ col
Dir Michael Anderson ***Prod*** Michael Deeley, Barry Spikings ***Scr*** Robert Enders ***Ph*** Bob Huke ***Ed*** John Glen ***Mus*** Stanley Myers ***Art*** Ted Tester
Act Michael York, Richard Attenborough, Trevor Howard, Stacy Keach, Christopher Plummer, Susannah York (Lion/Crown)

Based on a play by Barry England, this has all the ingredients of good, slightly old-fashioned courtroom drama transposed to 19th-century, British-dominated India to give it an added dimension.

Basically, action centers around a secret trial by his fellow officers of a young lieutenant accused of assaulting an officer's widow in a colonial outpost. In defending the accused, a new arrival slowly uncovers not only the real assaulter, but more especially the hypocrisy which rules and motivates the garrison officers' lives.

Acting is uniformly excellent. Michael York as the defender and James Faulkner as the defendant get top-notch backing. But, perhaps because of his seemingly offbeat casting as a British officer, it's Stacy Keach who surprises and steals acting honors.

•

CONEHEADS
1993, 88 mins, US Ⓥ ⦿ col
Dir Steve Barron ***Prod*** Lorne Michaels ***Scr*** Tom Davis, Dan Aykroyd, Bonnie Turner, Terry Turner ***Ph*** Francis Kenny ***Ed*** Paul Trejo ***Mus*** David Newman ***Art*** Gregg Fonseca
Act Dan Aykroyd, Jane Curtin, Michelle Burke, Michael McKean, Jason Alexander, Lisa Jane Persky (Paramount)

Cones phone home. Those *Saturday Night Live* cranial wonders have arrived on the big screen, and the result is a sweet, funny, anarchic pastiche that transcends the one-joke territory it inhabited on television.

The script begins when the Remulakian scout ship of Beldar (Dan Aykroyd) and Prymaat Conehad (Jane Curtin) runs afoul of USAF fighter planes. Aground in alien territory, the illegals accept fugitive status and employment. Beldar is, briefly, a wizard appliance repairman and a cab driver, changing jobs whenever the INS operatives close in.

After Prymaat reveals that she is with Cone, the two settle into suburban bliss. They buy a bungalow, barbecue with the neighbors, join the country club and confront the typical travails of parents who have teenage daughters. The unexpected strength in this foolishness is the sheer glee in watching other characters relate to the visitors from another universe as if they were the Donna Reed family.

Aykroyd and Curtin have evolved their cartoonish TV-skit characters into figures whose robot-like demeanor just barely hides emotions sparked by human contact. As their daughter Connie, Michelle Burke also proves herself as both a face and brow to watch. Director Steve Barron's light touch, which launched the first *Ninja Turtles*, never falters.

•

CONEY ISLAND
1943, 95 mins, US col
Dir Walter Lang ***Prod*** William Perlberg ***Scr*** George Seaton ***Ph*** Ernest Palmer ***Ed*** Herbert Simpson
Act Betty Grable, George Montgomery, Cesar Romero, Phil Silvers, Charles Winninger (20th Century-Fox)

The true Coney Island, corny, bawdy and brash, evidently wasn't deemed sufficiently colorful for George Seaton, scripter of this film, so he just hung the title on what amounts to a 95-minute audition of Betty Grable's chassis and legs—in color.

Slowness marks the story all the way; also sameness. Both these negative factors were inevitable in view of the fact that Grable is either dancing or singing, or both, in much of the running time. Remainder is taken up by a flash of the Coney Island midway and to sustain an oft-told story about two pals after the same girl.

Only in one musical number is Grable a boff, and that's her brownskin take-off of "Miss Lulu from Louisville," a pictorial review of derriere exercising. Her other Robin-Rainger songs are "Take It from There," "Beautiful Coney Island" and "There's Danger in a Dancer," latter given one of those out-of-this-world-except-in-Hollywood mammoth productions. None of the tunes is distinguished.

•

CONFESSIONAL, THE
SEE: LE CONFESSIONAL

•

CONFESSIONAL, LE
(THE CONFESSIONAL)
1995, 100 mins, Canada/UK/France Ⓥ col
Dir Robert Lepage ***Prod*** Denise Robert, David Puttnam ***Scr*** Robert Lepage ***Ph*** Alain Dostie ***Ed*** Emmanuelle Castro ***Mus*** Sacha Puttnam ***Art*** Francois Laplante
Act Lothaire Bluteau, Patrick Goyette, Jean-Louis Millette, Kristin Scott Thomas, Ron Burrage, Richard Frechette (Cinemaginaire/Enigma/Cinea)

The Confessional, the feature debut from Quebec theater whiz Robert Lepage, is exactly the sort of stunning, eye-popping visual and sonic treat that one would expect from this innovative stage helmer.

Where this engrossing French-lingo pic falters is at the script level: plot lacks full dramatic development and, in the end, falls short of delivering the emotional depth necessary to move audiences. Still, there is no shortage of stylish highs along the way.

Lepage starts with the intriguing idea of setting the story partly in Quebec City in 1952, when Alfred Hitchcock was lensing *I Confess* there. Pic opens with the sleepy, old-fashioned, picturesque city slowly moving into the modern era, thanks to the introduction of television and its first encounter with Hollywood via the Hitchcock production.

Hitchcock (portrayed by Brit look-alike Ron Burrage) is shown at the local preem of *I Confess*, and Lepage's film, which is loosely inspired by the Montgomery Clift starrer, contains several scenes from the Hitchcock original.

Throughout, Lepage keeps viewers on their toes by cutting between events in the early '50s and 1989, when lead character Pierre Lamontagne (Lothaire Bluteau) returns from China to his native Quebec City for his father's funeral. At first, Pierre cannot find his adopted brother, Marc (Patrick Goyette). They finally meet in a beautifully shot, dreamy sequence in a gay sauna.

Pic keeps coming back to the making of *I Confess* as Hitchcock's assistant (Kristin Scott Thomas) negotiates with local church authorities, arranges auditions for the director and generally fails to communicate adequately with the French-speaking locals.

If there's a problem with lack of emotional punch, it's at least partly due to Bluteau, who once again delivers a sullen, doe-eyed performance.

•

CONFESSIONS OF A NAZI SPY
1939, 110 mins, US b/w
Dir Anatole Litvak ***Prod*** Robert Lord ***Scr*** Milton Krims, John Wexley ***Ph*** Sol Polito ***Ed*** Owen Marks ***Mus*** Max Steiner ***Art*** Carl Jules Weyl
Act Edward G. Robinson, Francis Lederer, George Sanders, Paul Lukas, Lya Lys (Warner)

The story itself is told for maximum mass comprehension. Based on articles by Leon G. Turrou, former G-man, it is an adaptation of the spy trials of 1937 which resulted in the conviction of four persons.

Its thesis is that espionage directed from Berlin is tied up with the German-American Bunds, their rallies and summer camps and general parading around in uniforms. The German goal is destruction of democracy.

The cast numbers a fine collection of scar-faced Gestapo agents, guys with crew haircuts and assorted livid sneerers.

Edward G. Robinson comes in very late in the film. Paul Lukas carries through as the Bund leader who finally falls out with the Gestapo. The missing motivation, anti-Semitism, is the one thing not named and ticketed.

•

CONFIDENTIAL AGENT
1945, 113 mins, US b/w
Dir Herman Shumlin ***Prod*** Robert Buckner ***Scr*** Robert Buckner ***Ph*** James Wong Howe ***Ed*** George Amy ***Mus*** Franz Waxman ***Art*** Leo Kuter
Act Charles Boyer, Lauren Bacall, Wanda Hendrix, Peter Lorre, Katina Paxinou, George Coulouris (Warner)

The story attempts to show how in 1937 the success of Franco adherents was to become the prelude to an even greater conflict. The yarn's development is inept, and the link of the romance with the basic story [from a novel by Graham Greene] is too pat, at the expense of the major story line.

Charles Boyer plays a Spanish concert musician who has given up his career to fight the fascists. He's detailed to go to England and outbid the Francoites for British coal. The coal can be the difference between victory and defeat. The plot specifically deals with the obstacles that confront him, including the British fascists, and secondary to this is the romance that evolves between a British coal tycoon's daughter and Boyer.

Boyer, as usual, underplays to gain an effect as adequate as possible under the circumstances. Lauren Bacall suffers from a monotony of voice and an uncertainty of performance. Her s.a., however, is still plenty evident.

•

CONFIDENTIAL REPORT
(US: MR ARKADIN)
1955, 99 mins, France/Spain Ⓥ ⊙ b/w
Dir Orson Welles ***Prod*** Louis Dolivet ***Scr*** Orson Welles ***Ph*** Jean Bourgoin ***Ed*** Renzo Lucidi ***Mus*** Paul Misraki ***Art*** Orson Welles
Act Orson Welles, Michael Redgrave, Patricia Medina, Akim Tamiroff, Robert Arden, Paola Mori (Filmorsa)

Confidential Report is at once a fascinating (inevitably) and dismaying effort, frequently suggestive of self-parody; and indeed, in scenario and technique, it is an echo of *Kane* and that film's bravura style.

Instead of newspaper tycoon Charles Foster Kane, here is Gregory Arkadin, shadow figure, arch-capitalist, graduate of a Polish "white slave" ring, but whose latter-day power and riches are shrouded.

Instead of Kane's Xanadu, Arkadin has a castle in Spain. Instead of inanimate "Rosebud," there is a daughter (Welles's wife, Paola Mori), pretty, vital and overprotected.

The visual trickery in *Report*, albeit often irrelevant, is almost always fascinating just because it's a Welles orchestration, filling the screen with arresting oddment, with delicious detail—with, in short, excitement.

Welles's story is a parable, and verbalized as such by Arkadin at one point. It concerns a scorpion and a frog, and the moral is that character is immutable and thus logical even when seemingly illogical.

Told in flashback, Arkadin is an amnesiac and hires a smalltime Yank smuggler to trace his past. His ulterior purpose is to turn up, and eradicate, old nefarious associates who conceivably might disclose the truth about him to his daughter. The American goes to work, and the murders follow.

Engaging meller it may be, but missing the incisive delineation that marked *Kane*. The melange of darting narrative simply gets the upper hand a case of visual virtuosity overwhelming the Arkadin parable.

•

CONFLICT
1945, 86 mins, US Ⓥ b/w
Dir Curtis Bernhardt ***Prod*** William Jacobs ***Scr*** Arthur T. Horman, Dwight Taylor ***Ph*** Merritt Gerstad ***Ed*** David Weisbart ***Mus*** Frederick Hollander ***Art*** Ted Smith
Act Humphrey Bogart, Alexis Smith, Sydney Greenstreet, Rose Hobart, Charles Drake (Warner)

Conflict is a convincing study of a murderer driven to revealing his crime by psychological trickery. A tight mood is sustained by direction and playing, holding interest in the events despite some obviousness in the eventual outcome of the plot [from a story by Robert Siodmak and Alfred Neumann].

Bogart, married to Rose Hobart, is in love with her younger sister (Alexis Smith). When his wife, aware of misplaced affection, begins to nag, Bogart plots to murder her and nearly accomplishes the perfect crime.

Bogart gives a heavy role convincing reading. Smith also lends interest to the sister role, a girl who is attracted by Bogart's court but holds back due to family loyalty. Sydney Greenstreet is creditably restrained as the psychiatrist and family friend.

•

CONFORMIST, THE
SEE: IL CONFORMISTA

•

CONFORMISTA, IL
(THE CONFORMIST)
1970, 108 mins, Italy/France/W. Germany Ⓥ ⊙ col
Dir Bernardo Bertolucci ***Prod*** Maurizio Lodi-Fe ***Scr*** Bernardo Bertolucci ***Ph*** Vittorio Storaro ***Ed*** Franco Arcalli ***Mus*** Georges Delerve ***Art*** Ferdinando Scarfiotti
Act Jean-Louis Trintignant, Stefania Sandrelli, Dominique Sanda, Enzo Tarascio, Pierre Clementi, Gastone Moschin (Mars/Marianne/Maran)

Bernardo Bertolucci's latest writer-director stint, a free adaptation of Alberto Moravia's book *The Conformist*, is a click from start to finish.

Basically, it's the story of a coward, one of the thousands (millions?) who have, for self-aggrandizement or mere safe-playing self-preservation, "conformed" to the transient ideological dictates of their times.

Marcello (Jean-Louis Trintignant) is such a coward. Just married (also a compromise), he's sent to Paris by the fascist espionage organization he's joined and ordered to murder a leftist political refugee he once studied under in college. But he procrastinates, his mind riddled with doubts and fears, his body attracted by the intended victim's pretty wife who, possibly to save her husband's life, seduces both Marcello and his bride.

Performances are first-rate down to smallest role, with Trintignant reliable as ever in a tailor-made role, Stefania Sandrelli excellent as his wide-eyed middle-class wife, and Dominique Sanda a definite screen presence of considerable promise as the other woman.

Pic is somewhat slow here and there and could stand some trimming to tighten and heighten. Windup is likewise redundant, and the weakest factor in an otherwise very satisfying, powerful film.

•

CONGO
1995, 108 mins, US Ⓥ ⊙ col
Dir Frank Marshall ***Prod*** Kathleen Kennedy, Sam Mercer ***Scr*** John Patrick Shanley ***Ph*** Allen Daviau ***Ed*** Anne V. Coates ***Mus*** Jerry Goldsmith ***Art*** J. Michael Riva
Act Laura Linney, Dylan Walsh, Ernie Hudson, Tim Curry, Grant Heslov, Joe Don Baker (Paramount)

Michael Crichton's bestseller is the only ostensible star in *Congo*, so it's surprising the book doesn't receive better treatment. Dumbed down considerably, the movie is opulent and action-packed but feels like the Cliff Notes version of the novel, and doesn't provide the thrills or suspense those who have read it will doubtless expect.

The story opens with an explorer, Charles Travis (Bruce Campbell), disappearing in the Congo region of Africa while seeking diamonds for the Texas-based conglomerate TraviCom.

Also working on the project is Travis's ex-fiancée, Karen Ross (Laura Linney), who quickly takes off to find him. A former CIA operative, Ross commandeers a safari involving a primatologist (Dylan Walsh) seeking to return his mountain gorilla Amy—who can "speak" using sign language and a verbal translator—to the jungle. Joining them are Herkermer Homolka (Tim Curry), a badly accented fortune-seeker determined to find the diamond-laden lost city of Zinj, and Monroe Kelly (Ernie Hudson), a badly accented mercenary who leads the expedition.

Having decided to proceed without big-name actors, the filmmakers clearly hoped that Amy—wide-eyed and marvelously expressive as realized by Stan Winston (*Jurassic Park*)—emerges as the film's star. The ape is indeed an impressive technical achievement, but in the pell-mell rush to get through the jungle, she provides only a few scenes adorable enough to justify the trip.

The human performers are left to struggle gamely, with Linney appropriately tough and Walsh doing a creditable job playing opposite the gorilla. Curry practically gags on his accent, while Hudson provides most of the pic's best moments.

•

CONGRESS DANCES
SEE: DER KONGRESS TANZT

•

CONNECTICUT YANKEE, A
1931, 93 mins, US Ⓥ b/w
Dir David Butler ***Scr*** William Conselman ***Ph*** Ernest Palmer ***Mus*** Erno Rapee

Act Will Rogers, William Farnum, Myrna Loy, Maureen O'Sullivan, Frank Albertson, Mitchell Harris (Fox)

The [Mark Twain] story was originally turned down by Doug Fairbanks, after which Fox made it with Harry Myers. It was released late in 1920. The staff working on this sound version must have run off the silent print plenty. William Conselman gets the credit for the modern adaptation, but there's no telling how many writers worked on the script. Neither the beginning nor the end is entirely satisfactory, especially the finish. But the main section is a dream, and there are more than sufficient laughs to compensate.

Opening has Will Rogers as a small-town radio store proprietor, called to a mysterious house to install a battery. An armored figure falls over, knocks Rogers out and thence into the dream. The change back to the modern story and finish is decidedly weak.

Rogers's main cast support comes from William Farnum as King Arthur, Mitchell Harris as Merlin, the magician, and Brandon Hurst playing the menace. Myrna Loy does not do much with her femme heavy, while Maureen O'Sullivan has nothing much more than a bit. Frank Albertson, supplying the other half of the love interest, appears to be at a loss in not being able to chatter at his generally furious rate.

•

CONNECTICUT YANKEE IN KING ARTHUR'S COURT, A
(UK: A YANKEE IN KING ARTHUR'S COURT)
1949, 106 mins, US Ⓥ ⊙ col
Dir Tay Garnett **Prod** Robert Fellows **Scr** Edmund Beloin **Ph** Ray Rennahan **Ed** Archie Marshek **Mus** Victor Young **Art** Hans Dreier, Roland Anderson
Act Bing Crosby, Rhonda Fleming, Cedric Hardwicke, William Bendix, Henry Wilcoxon (Paramount)

Bing Crosby, songs and color make pleasant entertainment out of *A Connecticut Yankee in King Arthur's Court*. It's not high comedy and there's little swashbuckling but it is pleasant.

A footnote emphasizes that this latest version of Mark Twain's gentle tale of a Yankee blacksmith who's knocked on the head and awakes in King Arthur's court is adapted strictly from the book as written by the author.

A bit more vigor in the handling would have sharpened the pace. Film also falls down in some of the technical work, which doesn't help to carry out the illusion of the romantic days of 528.

Rhonda Fleming's vocals please and her physical charms as Alisande, King Arthur's niece, are expressive enough to illustrate why the Yankee would develop a yen for her.

•

CONQUEROR, THE
1956, 111 mins, US Ⓥ ▭ col
Dir Dick Powell **Prod** Dick Powell **Scr** Oscar Millard **Ph** Joseph LaShelle, Leo Tover, Harry J. Wild, William Snyder **Ed** Robert Ford, Kennie Marstella **Mus** Victor Young **Art** Albert S. D'Agostino, Carroll Clark
Act John Wayne, Susan Hayward, Pedro Armendariz, Agnes Moorehead, Thomas Gomez, William Conrad (RKO)

Just so there will be no misunderstanding about *The Conqueror*, a foreword baldly states that it is fiction, although with some basis in fact. With that warning out of the way, the viewer can sit back and thoroughly enjoy a huge, brawling, sex-and-sand actioner purporting to show how a 12th Century Mongol leader became known as Genghis Khan. The marquee value of the John Wayne–Susan Hayward teaming more than offsets any incongruity of the casting, which has him as the Mongol leader and she as the Tartar princess he captures and forcibly takes as his mate.

Co-starring with Wayne and Hayward is excellent Mexican actor Pedro Armendariz, who makes believable his role of Wayne's blood-brother and is an important essential in the entertainment.

The s.a. pitch is in a harem dance choreographed by Robert Sidney, in which a covey of lookers give the appearance of being almost completely bare while gyrating to the oriental strains of Victor Young's first-rate music.

•

CONQUEROR WORM, THE
SEE: WITCHFINDER GENERAL

•

CONQUEST
(UK: MARIE WALEWSKA)
1937, 115 mins, US Ⓥ b/w
Dir Clarence Brown **Prod** Bernard H. Hyman **Scr** Samuel Hoffenstein, Salka Viertel, S. N. Behrman **Ph** Karl Freund **Ed** Tom Held **Mus** Herbert Stothart
Act Greta Garbo, Charles Boyer, Reginald Owen, Alan Marshall, Henry Stephenson, Leif Erickson (M-G-M)

Conquest is said to have cost $2.6 million. Visually, it bears the mark of extravagant effort.

With Greta Garbo and Charles Boyer teamed as co-stars, in the characters of Marie Walewska, Polish mistress, and Napoleon Bonaparte, lover and soldier, the film is a romantic mixture of fact and fiction. Intensely emotional in spots, it is a moving and satisfying entertainment [from a book by Waclaw Gasiorowski and dramatization by Helen Jerome].

Major credit goes to Clarence Brown for direction. The Walewska episode in itself is a thrilling romance. Dramatic events led to the meeting of the young Polish countess (she was 18 at the time) and Napoleon, when the latter visited Warsaw at the height of his military successes. He was enraptured by her beauty and wooed her ardently. She joined him during his banishment to Elba.

Walewska role would seem to be a natural for Garbo. Part calls for intense feminine feeling, for coquetry and renunciation. It is not due to any shortcomings on her part, however, that the audience interest is more closely held by Boyer's Napoleon. Boyer plays the love scenes with brusque tenderness, and makes the character understood as a blazing individualist acting under reckless urges for power.

1937: NOMINATIONS: Best Actor (Charles Boyer), Art Direction

•

CONQUEST OF SPACE
1955, 80 mins, US Ⓥ col
Dir Byron Haskin **Prod** George Pal **Scr** James O'Hanlon **Ph** Lionel Lindon **Ed** Everett Douglas **Mus** Van Cleave **Art** Hal Pereira, Joseph MacMillan
Act Walter Brooke, Eric Fleming, Mickey Shaughnessy, Phil Foster, William Redfield, William Hopper (Paramount)

When Byron Haskin's direction has a chance at action and thrills they come over well, but most of the time the pacing is slowed by the talky script fashioned from the adaptation of the Chesley Bonestell–Willy Ley book by Philip Yordan, Barre Lyndon and George Worthington Yates.

Plot time is the future, with the setting divided between a space station wheeling some 1,000 miles above earth and a flight from this floating base to the planet Mars. Best moments deal with a meteor hitting the space station and spilling everything before the wheel is righted, and the near crash of the rocket ship with a meteor on the trip to Mars.

The rocket ship is manned by a stereotype crew. There's Walter Brooke, the commanding officer who loses his screws because he figures God didn't want man jetting off to new planets; Eric Fleming, his son, who didn't want to make the trip anyway; Mickey Shaughnessy, tough old master sergeant, devoted to the c.o.; Phil Foster, a wise-cracking Brooklynite, and Benson Fong and Ross Martin, UN personnel. These and others in the cast are acceptable in undemanding roles. The real stars are the props and lensing.

•

CONQUEST OF THE PLANET OF THE APES
1972, 87 mins, US Ⓥ ▭ col
Dir J. Lee Thompson **Prod** Arthur P. Jacobs **Scr** Paul Dehn **Ph** Bruce Surtees **Ed** Marjorie Fowler, Allan Jaggs **Mus** Tom Scott **Art** Philip Jefferies
Act Roddy McDowall, Don Murray, Ricardo Montalban, Natalie Trundy, Hari Rhodes, Severn Darden (20th Century-Fox/Apjac)

The *Planet of the Apes* series takes an angry turn in the fourth entry, *Conquest of the Planet of the Apes*.

The story begins about 20 years in the future, after a world epidemic has destroyed all dogs. People first had turned to apes as pets, but because of their intelligence the apes have become servants under civil regulation of computer-age overseer Don Murray. Into this milieu comes traveling circus operator Ricardo Montalban who, at the end of the prior film, had concealed the nearly-human offspring of the murdered Roddy McDowall and Kim Hunter. McDowall now has shifted to the role of his son.

In the new world, McDowall has to Uncle-Tom his way through the prevailing slave environment, until Murray's inexorable search for the long-missing ape-human child leads to Montalban's death under torture-grilling by Severn Darden. McDowall then organizes a bloody revolt which occupies the last third of the film.

•

CONRACK
1974, 107 mins, US Ⓥ ▭ col
Dir Martin Ritt **Prod** Martin Ritt, Harriet Frank, Jr. **Scr** Irving Ravetch, Harriet Frank, Jr. **Ph** John Alonzo **Ed** Frank Bracht **Mus** John Williams **Art** Walter Scott Herndon
Act Jon Voight, Paul Winfield, Madge Sinclair, Tina Andrews, Antonio Fargas, Hume Cronyn (20th Century-Fox)

Jon Voight stars as a young Southerner who treks off to an isolated South Carolina island in 1969 for a teaching post, only to find the black children there uniformly illiterate and/or retarded. Through a combination of love and pedagogical razzmatazz, he opens their eyes to the wonders of yoga, Beethoven, Babe Ruth, Ho Chi Minh, and Halloween.

Some may resent the inadvertent white-liberal condescension evident in the initially one-dimensional portrait of the deprived youngsters. Others may be momentarily confused by the lack of explicit data—time, place, personal factors behind the teacher's willingness to submerge obvious intellectual gifts in a backwoods community.

But few will totally resist the surefire appeal of this latest variation on Pygmalion mythology.

•

CONSENTING ADULTS
1992, 100 mins, US Ⓥ ⊙ col
Dir Alan J. Pakula **Prod** Alan J. Pakula, David Permut **Scr** Matthew Chapman **Ph** Stephen Goldblatt **Ed** Sam O'Steen **Mus** Michael Small **Art** Carol Spier
Act Kevin Kline, Mary Elizabeth Mastrantonio, Kevin Spacey, Rebecca Miller, Forest Whitaker, E. G. Marshall (Hollywood Pictures)

Psychotic neighbors are the latest riff on the urban paranoia theme. Most distinctive element here proves to be Kevin Spacey's over-the-top performance as the smarmy newcomer to the block, who ultimately lures his risk-aversive neighbor (Kevin Kline) into a proposed wife-swap that leads to the baseball-bat murder of Spacey's wife (Rebecca Miller) as part of an elaborate insurance scam. Kline's character ends up framed for the murder, forcing him to try to decipher the mystery and win back his own wife (Mary Elizabeth Mastrantonio), who has conveniently and rather inexplicably fled to Spacey.

Pic suffers from an absurdity level that somewhat undermines its chills as well as its few genuiune laughs. Director Alan J. Pakula can't seem to decide whether this is a legitimate drama or conventional thriller—of the cheap scare variety.

Perhaps because of those narrative flaws, neither Kline nor Mastrantonio (reunited after *The January Man*) are particularly distinguished here.

Miller oozes sex appeal, but the real stand-out is Spacey, who established his inordinate skill playing psychopaths with a disarming sense of humor back during TV's *Wiseguy*.

•

CONSPIRACY THEORY
1997, 135 mins, US Ⓥ ⊙ ▭ col
Dir Richard Donner **Prod** Joel Silver, Richard Donner **Scr** Brian Helgeland **Ph** John Schwartzman **Ed** Frank J. Urioste, Kevin Stitt **Mus** Carter Burwell **Art** Paul Sylbert
Act Mel Gibson, Julia Roberts, Patrick Stewart, Cylk Cozart (Silver/Warner)

A below-par vehicle for Mel Gibson and Julia Roberts, *Conspiracy Theory* is a sporadically amusing but listless thriller that wears its humorous, romantic and political components like mismatched articles of clothing.

Pic reps the fifth collaboration of Gibson and director Richard Donner, and the *Lethal Weapon* series is thrust into the viewer's mind by the opening scene, which has wild-eyed New York cabbie Jerry Fletcher (Gibson) amusingly ranting about the diverse conspiracies being perpetrated by everyone in power. Once Jerry is seen voyeuristically lusting for the lovely Alice Sutton (Roberts) via binoculars, then barging into her office at the Justice Dept., it becomes clear the man has at least one foot off the beam.

Jerry puts out a photocopied newsletter forwarding his theories and, in a semi-comic sequence, is torturously interrogated by the deadly serious Dr. Jonas (Patrick Stewart). Jerry manages to get away, setting up the cat-and-mouse pursuit format, with Alice ricocheting between Jerry and the CIA, of the remainder of the overlong film.

This is a film in which all things are treated lightly, even glibly. Having done so many actioners, Donner seems to want to send up some of the genre's more tired elements. Gibson and Roberts sail through the proceedings easily, while Stewart is disappointingly one-note.

•

CONSPIRATOR
1949, 83 mins, UK b/w
Dir Victor Saville **Prod** Arthur Hornblow, Jr. **Scr** Sally Benson **Ph** Skeets Kelly, Bunny Francke **Ed** Frank Clark **Mus** John Wooldridge

Act Robert Taylor, Elizabeth Taylor, Robert Flemyng, Honor Blackman, Thora Hird, Wilfrid Hyde White (M-G-M)

Conspirator is a highly fanciful treatment of an obvious anti-Commie character.

In the unfolding of the major theme the story lacks dramatic intensity, and little effort is made to justify the action of the central character, Maj. Michael Curragh, an officer in the Guards, who passes on highly secret military information to "the Party." The conflict, both emotional and mental, with his newly acquired young wife fails to reach the heights, and throughout the development there is neither powerful drama nor lurid melodrama.

It is effectively mounted; there are some fine settings.

Robert Taylor gets to grips with the starring role but the script doesn't allow wide scope and restricts his performance within a limited frame. Elizabeth Taylor comes out with flying colors.

•

CONSTANCE

1984, 103 mins, New Zealand Ⓥ col

Dir Bruce Morrison **Prod** Larry Parr **Scr** Jonathan Hardy **Ph** Kevin Hayward **Ed** Philip Howe **Mus** John Charles **Art** Ric Kifoed

Act Donogh Rees, Shane Briant, Judie Douglass, Martin Vaughan, Donald MacDonald, Marc Wignall (Mirage)

Constance is a highly stylized film about a beautiful young woman living in Auckland in 1946 who dreams she is a Hollywood superstar.

Constance (Donogh Rees) is given to such contrived charades as dressing as Marlene Dietrich at parties and singing along to a recording of Dietrich's hit, "Falling in Love Again."

Rees's stiffness of manner may be director Bruce Morrison's idea of the artificiality of the concept as a whole.

Imported actor Shane Briant has the right air of handsome, predatory decadence as a visiting Hollywood still-photographer. There is an outburst of sexual violence during a photo session which is given the blurred-lens, freeze-frame, jump-cut treatment, and it makes an effective contrast to the film's otherwise sharply focused sedate pace.

•

CONSTANT HUSBAND, THE

1955, 88 mins, UK col

Dir Sidney Gilliat **Prod** Frank Launder, Sidney Gilliat **Scr** Sidney Gilliat, Val Valentine **Ph** Ted Scaife **Ed** G. Turney-Smith **Mus** Malcolm Arnold **Art** Wilfrid Shingleton

Act Rex Harrison, Margaret Leighton, Kay Kendall, Cecil Parker, Nicole Maurey, George Cole (London/British Lion)

A frothy comedy, *The Constant Husband* is one of the brightest efforts from the Frank Launder and Sidney Gilliat partnership. The screenplay is light and amusing, and none of the sparkle has been lost in the translation to the screen.

The story could not be more slender. Rex Harrison, an amnesia victim, learns, to his horror, that he has seven wives to his credit. A bigamy charge follows, but rather than face seven eager ex-spouses, he pleas in favor of jail.

Harrison is thoroughly diverting as the amnesia victim. Margaret Leighton makes a belated appearance on the screen, but her impact is nonetheless notable. Kay Kendall, as the last of the seven wives, gives a sparkling portrayal. Cecil Parker is typically buoyant and Nicole Maurey is sufficiently alluring as another of the ex-wives.

•

CONSTANT NYMPH, THE

1928, 80 mins, UK ⊗ b/w

Dir Adrian Brunel **Prod** Basil Dean **Scr** Adrian Brunel, Alma Reville, Margaret Kennedy **Ph** Dave Gobbett

Act Mabel Poulton, Ivor Novello, George Heinrich, Dorothy Boyd, Frances Dable (Gainsborough)

That Basil Dean's name is attached to *The Constant Nymph* and Gainsborough is the producing firm cannot alter the facts. The English are so slow in their picture making. No lighting, no camerawork, nothing; just a dull passing through a series of slow scenes.

Story [from the novel by Margaret Kennedy and the play with Basil Dean] is of a hoydenish group, children of a great composer who dies in his studio in the Austrian Tyrol. Later his most hoydenish daughter also dies. In between, the picture dies.

All of the charm of a tale of this kind has been spoiled. No attraction is left. If not the direction, it is the photography, and if neither, then the actors, excepting Ivor Novello. Mabel Poulton as Tessa, the little hoyden, who should look about 15, often looks 25, and again 35. Frances Dable gives an even performance as Florence, but it is wasted in the rabble.

•

CONSTANT NYMPH, THE

1934, 85 mins, UK b/w

Dir Basil Dean **Scr** Dorothy Farnum, Basil Dean, Margaret Kennedy **Ph** Mutz Greenbaum **Mus** Eugene Goosens, John Greenwood **Art** Alfred Junge

Act Brian Aherne, Victoria Hopper, Peggy Blythe, Jane Baxter, Lyn Harding, Mary Clare (Gaumont-British)

Story [by Margaret Kennedy] opens in the Austrian mountains where a slightly mad composer and his daughters, all half-sisters and all hoydens, live a carefree life of idyllic sweetness. There is a younger composer (Brian Aherne), and for him one of the girls (Victoria Hopper) conceives an undying passion.

He marries a respectability minded English cousin (Leonora Corbett) and moves to London. Ultimately he realizes he should have waited for the girl to add a year or two to her age and married her instead of the older woman.

It is a soft, delicate, fragile, meandering yarn, beautifully directed by Basil Dean.

•

CONSTANT NYMPH, THE

1943, 106 mins, US b/w

Dir Edmund Goulding **Prod** Henry Blanke **Scr** Kathryn Scola **Ph** Tony Gaudio **Ed** David Weisbert **Mus** Erich Wolfgang Korngold

Act Charles Boyer, Joan Fontaine, Alexis Smith, Charles Coburn, Peter Lorre, Joyce Reynolds (Warner)

This is the film version of the novel and play of same title [by Margaret Kennedy and Basil Dean]. Devoting plenty of footage to character delineations and incidental episodes, it results in a bumpy screen tale with interlay of both draggy and interesting sequences.

Major portion of excess footage is on the front end, where 40 minutes is consumed in setting up detailed background for the final event, which is a love triangle, with Charles Boyer the focal point for conflict between teenager played by Joan Fontaine and the older Alexis Smith. The stretch hits yawning periods.

This early portion serves to detail movement of Boyer, composer of promise but lacking the necessary fire to write his outstanding composition, from Brussels to home of his friend and mentor (Montagu Love) in Switzerland. Of the four daughters in the house, Fontaine is next to the youngest, with adolescent adoration for Boyer. When Love dies and girls' uncle (Charles Coburn) arrives from England with his own daughter (Smith), Boyer and latter embark on romance culminating in marriage.

Script covers plenty of ground and detail, but general tightening would have helped materially. There's a tang of the stage in the unfolding, which director Edmund Goulding found impossible to overcome with his careful and even-tempoed direction.

1945: NOMINATION: Best Actress (Joan Fontaine)

•

CONTACT

1997, 150 mins, US Ⓥ ⦿ ▭ col

Dir Robert Zemeckis **Prod** Robert Zemeckis, Steve Starkey **Scr** James V. Hart, Michael Goldenberg **Ph** Don Burgess **Ed** Arthur Schmidt **Mus** Alan Silvestri **Art** Ed Verreaux

Act Jodie Foster, Matthew McConaughey, James Woods, John Hurt, Tom Skerritt, William Fichtner (South Side Amusement/Warner)

More down-to-earth and "realistic" than most other Hollywood movies about an encounter with an alien intelligence, Robert Zemeckis's first film since the globe-conquering *Forrest Gump* places at least as much emphasis on science as on fiction, and proves quite an engrossing ride most of the way.

Based upon the 1985 bestseller by Carl Sagan [and story by him and Ann Druyan] and developed with the futurist's active involvement until his death in December 1996, the film explores a plausible case study of how contemporary society might react to the detection of verifiable signals from another world, and how the world might be changed by knowledge of extraterrestrials.

Central focus of the smart but somewhat lumpy scenario is Dr. Ellie Arroway (Jodie Foster), who has government backing for her listening post pulled out from under her by David Drumlin (Tom Skerritt), although not before a brief fling with lapsed seminarian Palmer Joss (Matthew McConaughey). Set up with private backing from a mysterious benefactor, Arroway is still listening away in New Mexico four years later when she tunes into a broadcast emanating from the star Vega that proves to be a diagram for constructing a space capsule.

With astonishing speed and efficiency, the government finances the building of the enormous launch facility. Arroway gets aced out of making the trip by Drumlin. But a weird catastrophe gives the woman another chance at the trip, with results that emphasize the possibility of a convergence between science and religious faith.

When *Contact* is at its best, notably during its strong middle third, it is very good indeed, but it is not as sharp or incisive as it might have been in summarizing its concerns in nonverbal ways. But the picture's style and technical quality are outstanding. Don Burgess's cinematography is particularly noteworthy.

Front and center throughout, Foster is excellent, very credible in her projection of innate intelligence, dedication to career and banishment of any personal life.

1997: NOMINATION: Best Sound

•

CONTE D'ETE (A SUMMER'S TALE)

1996, 113 mins, France Ⓥ col

Dir Eric Rohmer **Prod** Francoise Etchegaray **Scr** Eric Rohmer **Ph** Diane Baratier **Ed** Mary Stephen **Mus** Philippe Eidel, Sebastien Erms

Act Melvil Poupaud, Amanda Langlet, Aurelia Nolin, Gwenaelle Simon (Menegoz/Films du Losange/La Sept)

A Summer's Tale is vintage Eric Rohmer, his most richly satisfying film in a number of outings, precisely and fully playing out the intimate implications of a chaste ménage quatre.

The third in the director's *Tales of the Four Seasons* series is divided into 18 dated chapters recounting events over a nearly three-week period. In a completely relaxed, confident manner, pic intros Gaspard (Melvil Poupaud), a lean, bushy-haired kid, as he arrives in the Brittany resort town of Dinard for a vacation and is quickly chatted up by a perky, bright waitress, Margot (Amanda Langlet).

Gaspard freely confesses his feelings and, in particular, his preoccupation with Lena, a girl who is supposed to arrive soon to see him. But Gaspard begins seeking less of Margot after he spots the sultry Solene (Gwenaelle Simon) in a disco. Solene's interest bolsters Gaspard's ego enormously, until he unexpectedly runs into the long-awaited Lena.

In the telling, *A Summer's Tale* consists mostly of long scenes in which Gaspard and one of the three girls walk along the beach talking of love, attraction, desire, their feelings about life and other familiar Rohmer topics. The thoughts may not be profound, but they are profoundly true to life, and the writer-director's approach to young people's concerns is remarkably universal and timeless. As usual, the young thesps are appealing in their unaffectedness.

•

CONTEMPT

SEE: LE MEPRIS

•

CONTENDER, THE

2000, 126 mins, US Ⓥ ⦿ col

Dir Rod Lurie **Prod** Marc Frydman, Douglas Urbanski, Willi Baer, James Spies **Scr** Rod Lurie **Ph** Denis Maloney **Ed** Michael Jablow **Mus** Larry Groupe **Art** Alexander Hammond

Act Joan Allen, Gary Oldman, Jeff Bridges, Sam Elliott, Christian Slater, William Petersen, Philip Baker Hall (Battleground/DreamWorks)

The Contender is set in the political arena and revolves around the power elite. Joan Allen shines as a vice presidential nominee who decides to take the high moral ground when her candidacy is smeared by a sex scandal from her youth.

When the sitting VP suddenly dies, President Jackson Evans (Jeff Bridges) decides to appoint a woman, Sen. Laine Hanson (Allen). Not surprisingly, his selection meets with opposition not only from his staff members, but also from members of both parties, particularly Shelly Runyon (Gary Oldman), a powerful adversary who will stop at nothing to discredit Jackson's candidate.

Hanson's confirmation hearings set off controversy when it turns out that she is a former Republican who switched parties. A further investigation reveals a shocking incident from Hanson's past, supported by photographs taken during a sexual orgy with two men while she was in college. Hanson doesn't deny the accusations; which threaten both her political future and her personal life, as she's now happily married and the mother of a young boy.

Hanson's courage emerges when she takes the stand and refuses to give in despite coercion from both sides.

Unfortunately, pic is more about debatable principles than real politics, and in the second, excessively schematic half, writer and director Rod Lurie throws into the mix various issues (abortion, women in politics) just in order to expose different points of view. Though serving up the plot, the sudden revelations in the last act are not very convincing.

The large, talented cast elevates the film above the trappings of its loquacious debates, particularly Allen, who uses her trademark intelligence and dignity to give a commanding performance. Playing the film's most cliched role, a president who's more interested in gourmet food than in issues, Bridges is entertaining. The hardly recognizable Oldman (also credited as exec producer) enacts the nasty elements of his part with relish.

•

CONTEST GIRL
SEE: THE BEAUTY JUNGLE

•

CONTEXT, THE
SEE: CADAVERI ECCELLENTI

•

CONTINENTAL DIVIDE
1981, 103 mins, US Ⓥ ⊙ col
Dir Michael Apted ***Prod*** Bob Larson ***Scr*** Lawrence Kasdan ***Ph*** John Bailey ***Ed*** Dennis Virkler ***Mus*** Michael Small ***Art*** Peter Jamison
Act John Belushi, Blair Brown, Allen Garfield, Carlin Glynn, Tony Ganios, Val Avery (Universal/Amblin)

For a picture that you can't really believe for a second, *Continental Divide* still comes off as a reasonably engaging entertainment thanks to some lively performances and a liberal dose of laughs throughout the script.

John Belushi plays a star columnist for the *Chicago Sun Times* who loves dishing the dirt about the latest doings down at city hall. When his stories on a certain corrupt alderman get too hot, Belushi is sent to the Rocky Mountains to track down a crazy bird lady known for her reclusiveness and particular hatred of nosey reporters.

At first, beauteous Blair Brown orders the interloper from her mountaintop retreat but, as his guide won't be back to fetch him for two weeks, they gradually learn to cope and, finally, love together.

The problem is that these two just don't seem made for each other. When Tracy and Hepburn sparred for two hours in films like *Adam's Rib* and *Pat and Mike*, airing every possible reason they shouldn't get, or remain, together, the inevitability of their ultimate match-up was crystal clear.

Lawrence Kasdan displays a keen ability to write sparkling male-female repartee and also creates a believable context for Belushi's beat on the Windy City streets. Michael Apted's direction is solid.

•

CONTRABAND
(US: BLACKOUT)
1940, 91 mins, UK Ⓥ b/w
Dir Michael Powell ***Prod*** John Corfield ***Scr*** Emeric Pressburger, Michael Powell, Brock Williams ***Ph*** Freddie Young ***Ed*** John Seabourne ***Mus*** Richard Addinsell, John Greenwood ***Art*** Alfred Junge
Act Conrad Veidt, Valerie Hobson, Hay Petrie, Joss Ambler, Raymond Lovell, Esmond Knight (British National)

As a dissertation on how to do nothing well, film anent Britain's naval blockade earns a niche all its own. Producers have lavished their brainchild with a wealth of detail that takes care of all except one thing—imagination.

This yarn of the economic war staged by the navy through its control of shipping veers from the sea to take a jaunt on espionage in London.

Conrad Veidt as the Danish seaman is authentic to the point where it's questionable as to his ease as a lover in the smart company of Valerie Hobson. Her role is handled with aplomb. All of the rest reach for the same standard, particular attention going to Hay Petrie for his comedy work in a dual role.

•

CONVERSATION, THE
1974, 113 mins, US Ⓥ ⊙ col
Dir Francis Coppola ***Prod*** Francis Coppola, Fred Roos ***Scr*** Francis Coppola ***Ph*** Bill Butler ***Ed*** Walter Murch, Richard Chew ***Mus*** David Shire ***Art*** Dean Tavoularis
Act Gene Hackman, John Cazale, Allen Garfield, Frederic Forrest, Cindy Williams, Harrison Ford (Paramount)

Francis Coppola's *The Conversation* stars Gene Hackman as a professional surveillance expert whose resurgent conscience involves him in murder and leads to self-destruction.

He is introduced in SF's Union Square at midday, teamed with John Cazale and Michael Higgins in tracking the movements and voices of Frederic Forrest and Cindy Williams. The cleaned-up sound tapes, along with photographs, are to be delivered to a mysterious businessman, played in an unbilled part by Robert Duvall. What appears to be a simple case of marital infidelity suddenly shifts to a possible murder plot.

A major artistic asset to the film—besides script, direction and the top performances—is supervising editor Walter Murch's sound collage and re-recording. Voices come in and out of aural focus in a superb tease.

1974: NOMINATIONS: Best Picture, Original Screenplay, Sound

•

CONVERSATION PIECE
1975, 120 mins, Italy/France Ⓥ col
Dir Luchino Visconti ***Scr*** Luchino Visconti, Suso Cecchi D'Amico ***Ph*** Pasqualino De Santis ***Ed*** Ruggero Mastroianni ***Art*** Mario Garbuglia
Act Burt Lancaster, Silvana Mangano, Helmut Berger, Claudia Marsani, Dominique Sanda, Claudia Cardinale (Rusconi/Gaumont)

Conversation Piece eschews the usually operatic, museum-like pix of Luchino Visconti for a touching tale of the generation gap and the loss of life-contact of an intellectual.

A prof (Burt Lancaster) is addicted to collecting 18th-century British paintings of families called Conversation Pieces. Into this comes a haughty, middle-aged, but still beautiful Italian woman who wants to rent his upstairs apartment.

Lancaster is finally persuaded by her, her cute teenage daughter and her rich fiancé. There is also the mother's lover, a young German (Helmut Berger). The professor gets tangled up with the young people despite himself.

Visconti has kept this talky but rarely verbose pic in the two apartments with only an outside studio view of Rome. The assorted accents are justified and even the peppering of blue lingo Americanisms fit these jet setters. Lancaster is highly effective as the professor.

•

CONVICTED
1950, 91 mins, US b/w
Dir Henry Levin ***Prod*** Jerry Bresler ***Scr*** William Bowers, Fred Niblo, Jr., Seton I. Miller ***Ph*** Burnett Guffey ***Ed*** Al Clark ***Mus*** George Duning
Act Glenn Ford, Broderick Crawford, Millard Mitchell, Dorothy Malone, Ed Begley, Will Geer (Columbia)

Convicted isn't quite as grim a prison film as the title would indicate. It has several offbeat twists to its development, keeping it from being routine.

While plotting is essentially a masculine soap opera, scripting [from a play by Martin Flavin] supplies plenty of polish and good dialog to see it through. Glenn Ford is convicted of manslaughter after a man he has slugged in a barroom brawl dies. Broderick Crawford is the d.a. who obtains the conviction, although sympathetic to Ford and his predicament.

Crawford takes over as warden of the state pen and makes life more bearable for the young con. Just as he is ready for parole, he witnesses the killing of an informer by another convict. His refusal to squeal jeopardizes his parole.

•

CONVOY
1978, 110 mins, US Ⓥ ⊙ ⌴ col
Dir Sam Peckinpah ***Prod*** Robert M. Sherman ***Scr*** B.W.L. Norton ***Ph*** Harry Stradling, Jr. ***Ed*** Graeme Clifford, John Wright, Garth Craven ***Mus*** Chip Davis ***Art*** Fernando Carrere
Act Kris Kristofferson, Ali MacGraw, Ernest Borgnine, Burt Young, Madge Sinclair, Franklyn Ajaye (United Artists)

Sam Peckinpah's *Convoy* starts out as *Smokey and the Bandit*, segues into either *Moby Dick* or *Les Miserables*, and ends in the usual script confusion and disarray, the whole stew peppered with the vulgar excess of random truck crashes and miscellaneous destruction.

Kris Kristofferson stars as a likeable roustabout who accidentally becomes a folk hero, while Ali MacGraw recycles about three formula reactions throughout her nothing part.

B.W.L. Norton gets writing credit using C. W. McCall's c&w pop tune lyric as a basis. No matter. Peckinpah's films display common elements and clumsy analogies, overwhelmed with logistical fireworks and drunken changes of dramatic emphasis.

This time around, Kristofferson (who, miraculously, seems to survive these banalities) is a trucker whose longtime nemesis, speed-trap-blackmailer cop Ernest Borgnine, pursues him with a vengeance through what appears to be three states. Every few minutes there's some new roadblock to run, alternating with pithy comments on The Meaning Of It All. There's a whole lot of nothing going on here.

•

COOGAN'S BLUFF
1968, 93 mins, US Ⓥ ⊙ col
Dir Don Siegel ***Prod*** Don Siegel ***Scr*** Herman Miller, Dean Riesner, Howard Rodman ***Ph*** Bud Thackery ***Ed*** Sam E. Waxman ***Mus*** Lalo Schifrin ***Art*** Alexander Golitzen, Robert C. MacKichan
Act Clint Eastwood, Lee J. Cobb, Susan Clark, Tisha Sterling, Don Stroud, Betty Field (Universal/Malpaso)

Story is of the clash between sophisticated law enforcement and frontier-style simplistics, which is perhaps one of the major internal American problems. Clint Eastwood stars as a laconic, taciturn stranger, this time a deputy sheriff from Arizona in New York City.

Herman Miller's story establishes Eastwood as a cold, selfish desert lawman sent to NY to extradite hippie Don Stroud, whose Arizona offense is never mentioned. Lee J. Cobb, a city detective, tries to explain to Eastwood that things are done differently; latter doesn't listen, contributes to Stroud's escape, but tracks him down for a hastily resolved (or edited) fadeout.

Susan Clark is very good as a probation officer who falls for Eastwood. Tisha Sterling does well as Stroud's hippie girlfriend. Betty Field has an excellent scene as Stroud's mother, impact being second only to Cobb's terrific work.

•

COOKIE
1989, 93 mins, US Ⓥ ⊙ col
Dir Susan Seidelman ***Prod*** Laurence Mark ***Scr*** Nora Ephron, Alice Arlen ***Ph*** Oliver Stapleton ***Ed*** Andrew Mondshein ***Mus*** Thomas Newman ***Art*** Michael Haller
Act Peter Falk, Dianne Wiest, Emily Lloyd, Michael Gazzo, Brenda Vaccaro, Adrian Pasdar (Lorimar/Warner)

Half-baked, bland and flat as a vanilla wafer, *Cookie* rolls out the tired marriage of comedy and organized crime to produce a disorganized mess with little nutritional or comedic value.

The story gets set in motion, such as it is, when mobster Dino Capisco (Peter Falk) is released from prison after 13 years, rejoining his wife (Brenda Vaccaro), mistress (Dianne Wiest) and the headstrong daughter he had with the latter, played by Emily Lloyd.

Sadly, about the only thing Lloyd gets to do here is prove she can affect a New York accent and chew gum at the same time. Thrown together with Falk as his driver, the two fail to build any of the warmth or even grudging admiration they display in the final reel.

The film ultimately turns into an elaborate scheme by which Falk can get even with his treacherous former partner (played by Michael Gazzo), and the payoff is hardly worth the protracted build-up.

Only Wiest emerges in top form with her brassy portrayal of a weepy red-haired gun moll in the Lucille Ball mode.

•

COOKIE'S FORTUNE
1999, 118 mins, US Ⓥ ⊙ col
Dir Robert Altman ***Prod*** Robert Altman, Etchie Stroh ***Scr*** Anne Rapp ***Ph*** Toyomichi Kurita ***Ed*** Abraham Lim ***Mus*** David A. Stewart ***Art*** Stephen Altman
Act Glenn Close, Julianne Moore, Liv Tyler, Chris O'Donnell, Charles S. Dutton, Patricia Neal (Sandcastle 5/Elysian Dreams)

The deceptively modest *Cookie's Fortune* may or may not be Robert Altman's best film in years, but it is certainly his most pleasurable. Distinguished by a generosity of spirit most uncommon in the director's work, as well as by Charles S. Dutton's enormously embraceable performance, this wry melodrama about an eccentric female family in a small Mississippi town becomes more disarming as it proceeds.

Portly, middle-aged black man Willis (Dutton) is caretaker for pipe-smoking old Jewel Mae "Cookie" Orcutt (Patricia Neal), who is still terribly devoted to her late husband, Buck. Also underway this Good Friday night is a rehearsal for a church group production of *Salome*, directed by Jewel

Mae's obsessive niece, Camille (Glenn Close), and starring the latter's seemingly vacant younger sister, Cora (Julianne Moore).

On Saturday, Willis heads for the edge of town to try to convince Cora's "worthless tramp" of a daughter, Emma (Liv Tyler), to move in with Jewel Mae. After half an hour of this genial but hardly compelling activity, Jewel Mae takes one of the pistols the tipsy Willis cleaned the night before and joyfully shoots herself, so that she might be reunited with her beloved Buck.

And so begins a chain of behavior that is at once almost utterly absurd and yet so intensely human that it echoes the immortal line in Jean Renoir's *Rules of the Game* that "Everybody has their reasons."

Altman's storytelling methods are identical to those he's used time and again—intercutting among several characters and parcels of action, but with an ultimate design based on accumulated detail. Neal's Jewel Mae delightfully dominates the first act, but the picture belongs almost entirely to accomplished stage actor Dutton.

•

COOK THE THIEF HIS WIFE & HER LOVER, THE

1989, 126 mins, Netherlands/France Ⓥ ⊙ col

Dir Peter Greenaway ***Prod*** Kees Kasander ***Scr*** Peter Greenaway ***Ph*** Sacha Vierny ***Ed*** John Wilson ***Mus*** Michael Nyman ***Art*** Ben Van Os, Jan Roelfs

Act Richard Bohringer, Michael Gambon, Helen Mirren, Alan Howard, Tim Roth, Liz Smith (Allarts/Erato/Films Inc)

Peter Greenaway's grim sense of humor and cheerful assault on all our sacred cows is evident in this new outing from the iconoclastic filmmaker.

Setting is a smart restaurant, La Hollandaise, where Richard, the chef (Richard Bohringer) prepares a lavish menu every night. Among his regular customers are Albert Spica (Michael Gambon), a loudmouthed, vulgar, violent gangster, who dines with his entourage of seedy yes-men, and his bored, beautiful wife, Georgina (Helen Mirren).

At another table each night sits Michael (Alan Howard), a quiet, diffident man who's always reading books. He and Georgina make eye contact, and soon they're having a series of secret rendezvous. Eventually Albert discovers his wife's infidelity, and takes a typically violent revenge, triggering a more unusual retaliation from her.

Albert is one of the ugliest characters ever brought to the screen. Ignorant, over-bearing and violent, it's a gloriously rich performance by Gambon.

In contrast, Helen Mirren (in a role which was originally to have been played by Vanessa Redgrave) is all calm politeness and mute acceptance until her passion is aroused by the far from handsome Michael.

•

COOLEY HIGH

1975, 107 mins, US Ⓥ ⊙ col

Dir Michael Schultz ***Prod*** Steve Krantz ***Scr*** Eric Monte ***Ph*** Paul vom Brack ***Ed*** Christopher Holmes ***Mus*** Freddie Perren ***Art*** William B. Fosser

Act Glynn Turman, Lawrence Hilton-Jacobs, Garrett Morris, Cynthia Davies (American International)

Cooley High is pitched as a black *American Graffiti*, and the description is apt. Furthermore, you don't have to be black to enjoy it immensely. The Steve Krantz production is a heartening comedy-drama about urban Chicago high school youths, written by Eric Monte.

The story focuses mainly on two frisky students, Glynn Turman and Lawrence Hilton-Jacobs. Girl trouble (principally charming Cynthia Davis), school trouble (with empathetic teacher Garrett Morris), and law trouble (via involvement with toughs Sherman Smith and Norman Gibson) lead the pair through experiences which range from broadly comic to deathly serious. The plot is simply about a lot of believable people and of course that's the way it should be.

•

COOL HAND LUKE

1967, 126 mins, US Ⓥ ⊙ ▭ col

Dir Stuart Rosenberg ***Prod*** Gordon Carroll ***Scr*** Donn Pearce, Frank R. Pierson [Hal Dresner] ***Ph*** Conrad Hall ***Ed*** Sam O'Steen ***Mus*** Lalo Schifrin ***Art*** Cary Odell

Act Paul Newman, George Kennedy, J. D. Cannon, Lou Antonio, Robert Drivas, Jo Van Fleet (Warner)

Paul Newman is *Cool Hand Luke*, a loner role in a film that depicts the social structure of a Dixie chain gang. Versatile and competent cast maintains interest throughout rambling exposition to a downbeat climax.

Luke, obviously supposed to be set in the South, was shot near Stockton, California, where the desired flat land, occasionally broken by gentle rolls, makes for an effective physical backdrop. In this case, it is a chain gang compound, ruled by some patronizing, sadistic guards, to whom Newman will not conform.

Newman gives an excellent performance, assisted by a terrific supporting cast, including George Kennedy, outstanding as the unofficial leader of the cons who yields first place to Newman.

Strother Martin's camp chief is chilling, a first-rate characterization. His goon squad likewise delivers strong performances: Morgan Woodward, Luke Askew, Robert Donner, John McLiam, Charles Tyner. Clifton James, the burly building overseer, is appropriately warmer.

1967: Best Supp. Actor (George Kennedy)

NOMINATIONS: Best Actor (Paul Newman), Adapted Screenplay, Original Music Score

•

COOL RUNNINGS

1993, 97 mins, US Ⓥ ⊙ col

Dir Jon Turteltaub ***Prod*** Dawn Steel ***Scr*** Lynn Siefert, Tommy Swerdlow, Michael Goldberg ***Ph*** Phedon Papamichael ***Ed*** Bruce Green ***Mus*** Hans Zimmer ***Art*** Stephen Marsh

Act Leon, Doug E. Doug, Malik Yoba, Rawle D. Lewis, John Candy, Raymond Barry (Walt Disney)

The travails and triumph of the 1988 Jamaican Olympic bobsled team deliver a highly entertaining combination in *Cool Runnings*. The offbeat, fact-based saga [from a screen story by Lynn Siefert and Michael Ritchie] is enlivened by the perfect balance of humor, emotion and insight. Unlike most sports-based films, this is one tale with universal appeal.

The filmmakers have taken some dramatic liberties, though the essential facts are intact. Derice Bannock (Leon) is, like his Olympian father, a leading runner in the small island republic. When he fails to qualify for the 1988 event, Derice hears a wild tale of an American gold medal bobsledder living in Jamaica. The germ of an idea begins to grow.

The runner recruits his friend Sanka (Doug E. Doug)—a go-cart driver—and they go off to convince Irv Blitzer (John Candy), the former Winter Olympian, to coach a fledgling team. Blitzer whips his athletes into form despite a decided absence of snow.

The idea is preposterous, and were it not for the fact that it actually happened, even cockeyed Hollywood would have taken a pass.

Director Jon Turteltaub has a fresh, uncluttered approach to the story that allows its natural warmth and humor to dominate. Candy gets the opportunity to create a real character and remind us of his facility for pathos—regrettably so rarely employed.

•

COOL WORLD, THE

1963, 125 mins, US Ⓥ col

Dir Shirley Clarke ***Scr*** Shirley Clarke, Carl Lee ***Ph*** Baird Bryant ***Ed*** Shirley Clarke ***Mus*** Mal Waldron

Act Hampton Clayton, Yolanda Rodriguez, Carl Lee (Wiseman)

The Cool World is the world of Harlem. Film deals generally with its physical and human aspects and also comment on the personal feel and outlook of its characters. Both elements are well blended to make this a telling look at Harlem and probably one of the least patronizing films ever made on Negro life in New York.

A sharp, restless, whiplike camera picks up a Black Muslim spouting hate against the white man and claiming supremacy. Then the Harlem streets and the people listening, or letting the fanatic words float by, come to life and out of the crowd is picked a young teenager, Duke, whose one desire seems to be to own a gun that would give him standing in his own gang. Film [from the novel by Warren Miller] alternates Duke's story with general scenes of Harlem life.

The natural thesping is by a mainly non-pro cast. But it is chiefly the virile, well-observed direction of Shirley Clarke that keeps this long film engrossing and revealing most of the way. She creates a tenseness around the familiar characters by a knowing look at Harlem rhythms, gaiety, lurking desperation, boredom tempered with joviality, and the general oppressiveness of bad housing and employment conditions.

Sometimes the characters get a bit lost in the general schematics of the pic, which at times waters down its underlying irony. But, overall, Clarke has a firm hold on her characters and story.

•

COOL WORLD

1992, 102 mins, US Ⓥ ⊙ col

Dir Ralph Bakshi ***Prod*** Frank Mancuso, Jr. ***Scr*** Michael Grais, Mark Victor ***Ph*** John A. Alonzo ***Ed*** Steve Mirkovich, Annamaria Szanto ***Mus*** Mark Isham ***Art*** Michael Corenblith

Act Kim Basinger, Gabriel Byrne, Brad Pitt, Michele Abrams, Deirdre O'Connell, Carrie Hamilton (Paramount)

Style has seldom pummeled substance as severely as in *Cool World*, a combination funhouse ride/acid trip that will prove an ordeal for most visitors in the form of trial by animation. Director Ralph Bakshi has let his imagination run wild with almost brutal vigor, resulting in a guerrilla-like assault virtually unchecked by any traditional rules of storytelling.

Although comparisons have been made to *Who Framed Roger Rabbit* because of the live-action/animation mix, this more closely resembles Joe Dante's *Gremlins* in its reliance on exploding the conventions of Warner Bros. cartoons.

The comic book premise hinges on parallel worlds—the real world and a sphere of animated characters, known as Cool World, which has also been captured by cartoonist Jack Deebs (Gabriel Byrne).

Pulling Deebs into the Cool World is curvaceous fantasy girl Holli Wood, a "doodle" (i.e., cartoon) who dreams of becoming human by coupling with a flesh-and-blood male. The odd-character-out in the story is Frank Harris (Brad Pitt), a human top cop yanked into Cool World in the '40s.

Kim Basinger, who doesn't appear in the flesh until nearly an hour into the film, is one of the few actresses who could convincingly breathe life into Holli, a 36-18-36 bombshell in animated form seemingly pulled straight from the paintings of Frank Frazetta, whose art inspired Bakshi's little-seen fantasy feature *Fire and Ice*.

Because the characters are so undeveloped, *Cool World* is a realm with precious little humor and zero pathos, to be admired only for its brilliant synthesis of live-action and animation, as well as the staggering creation of credible comic book sets around human actors.

•

COP

1988, 110 mins, US Ⓥ ⊙ col

Dir James B. Harris ***Prod*** James B. Harris, James Woods ***Scr*** James B. Harris ***Ph*** Steven Dubin ***Ed*** Anthony M. Spano ***Mus*** Michel Colombier ***Art*** Gene Rudolf

Act James Woods, Lesley Ann Warren, Charles Durning, Charles Haid, Randi Brooks, Raymond J. Barry (Atlantic/Harris-Woods)

Shot under the title *Blood on the Moon*, one of three James Ellroy novels with same central character, *Cop* is a modestly executed, off-target police drama giving actor James Woods another outlet for his compellingly schizophrenic persona. As star vehicles go, this one's good, but the overall package fails to fill the big screen.

Lloyd Hopkins (Woods) is a good LAPD cop who clearly loves his work and his eight-year-old daughter; in that order, harps his ever critical wife (Jan McGill). She's soon out of the picture as Mrs. Hopkins moves out with the child, leaving a note labelling Woods "deeply disturbed."

Domestic pressures and a hard-to-crack serial murder case lead to the detective's lapses in judgement. His affairs with women he meets in the course of his investigation get him into trouble with his superiors (including Charles Durning). One of the implicated is Lesley Ann Warren, a chain-smoking, feminist poet and bookshop-keeper who turns out to play a pivotal role in the murder mystery hounding Woods.

Warren's character and tantalizing performance appear fully 50 minutes into running time, a fact that adds to pic's off-balance feeling.

Technical contributions are routine.

•

COP LAND

1997, 105 mins, US Ⓥ ⊙ col

Dir James Mangold ***Prod*** Cary Woods, Cathy Konrad, Ezra Swerdlow ***Scr*** James Mangold ***Ph*** Eric Edwards ***Ed*** Craig McKay ***Mus*** Howard Shore ***Art*** Lester Cohen

Act Sylvester Stallone, Harvey Keitel, Ray Liotta, Robert De Niro, Peter Berg, Annabella Sciorra (Woods/Miramax)

As police corruption dramas go, this one lacks the complexity and density of such true-life thrillers as *Serpico* and *Prince of the City*. Set mostly in a small New Jersey town just across the Hudson River from Manhattan, writer-director James Mangold's tale has the feel of a classic frontier Western in which the amiable sheriff is forced to wake up to the dastardly doings of the community's most prominent citizens and decide whether to take them on. One guess what he does.

Garrison, NJ, a town whose population of 1,280 is composed largely of New York cops, is understandably virtually crime-free, which gives longtime sheriff Freddy Heflin (Sylvester Stallone) nothing much to do. Freddy still carries a torch for Liz (Annabella Sciorra), but she chose to marry another cop, temperamental macho man Joey (Peter Berg).

Suspecting a coverup [of a recent killing, and the part played by senior cop Ray Donlan (Harvey Keitel)], internal affairs special agent Moe Tilden (Robert De Niro) pays a visit but is unable to rouse Freddy to the smell of the stench around him. Gradually, but with the inevitability of a traditional morality play, Freddy is forced to take a stand. Like such western heroes as Gary Cooper's sheriff in *High Noon*, he must finally take on his enemies alone in the streets.

Having put on quite a bit of weight to play the sluggish Freddy, Stallone shambles along in a way that emphasizes the sadness of the character. Ray Liotta, Keitel, De Niro and Berg register strongly in important supporting parts.

•

COPS AND ROBBERSONS

1994, 93 mins, US Ⓥ ⦿ col

Dir Michael Ritchie ***Prod*** Ned Tanen, Nancy Graham Tanen, Ronald Schwary ***Scr*** Bernie Somers ***Ph*** Gerry Fisher ***Ed*** Stephen Rotter, William Scharf ***Mus*** William Ross ***Art*** Stephen Lineweaver

Act Chevy Chase, Jack Palance, Dianne Wiest, Robert Davi, David Barry Gray, Jason James Richter (Channel/Tri-Star)

There's trouble afoot in Pleasant Valley, and the postcard-perfect suburb is about to burst at the seams in *Cops and Robbersons*. But the mixture of mischief and mayhem served up in the antic affair is never quite in balance. It's a tale long on intriguing ideas and always a millimeter short in its realization.

The complex setup centers on Osborn (Robert Davi), a goon involved in forgery and money laundering. The police know he's about to make a big exchange. Assigned to the case are grizzled vet Jake Stone (Jack Palance) and his *90210*-style partner, Tony Moore (David Barry Gray). They set up their command post in the home of Norman Robberson (Chevy Chase), who lives next door to Osborn and is ready to do his civic duty and get a first-hand lesson in police procedures.

The film's most telling misstep is its focus. While Robberson is the titular lead, it's really Stone who takes center stage. Norman is considerably less interesting. His idea of fun is sitting down to breakfast with the entire family and just talking.

Palance plumbs deep inside his hard-boiled persona and extracts a rich vein of humor and pathos. Chase should get back to more romantic fare a la *Foul Play*. He's simply better playing smart rather than dumb.

•

COPYCAT

1995, 123 mins, US Ⓥ ⦿ ▭ col

Dir Jon Amiel ***Prod*** Arnon Milchan, Mark Tarlov ***Scr*** Ann Biderman, David Madsen ***Ph*** Laszlo Kovacs ***Ed*** Alan Heim, Jim Clark ***Mus*** Christopher Young ***Art*** Jim Clay

Act Sigourney Weaver, Holly Hunter, Dermot Mulroney, William McNamara, Will Patton, Harry Connick, Jr. (Regency/Warner)

Copycat has both the smarts and the tension to rate as a potent entry in the over-worked serial-killer genre. An upscale suspenser by virtue of its classy cast, its extremely bright characters and the chillingly intellectual approach of the murderer, this shrewdly devised pulse-pounder may actually be too refined to click in a big way with mass audiences. Audience suspense is not at all related to whodunnit, but to how the insidiously ingenious villain will be tracked down.

Criminal psychologist Helen Hudson (Sigourney Weaver) delivers a tart lecture in which she points out that 90 percent of all serial killers are white males between 20 and 35 years old. One of them, redneck Daryll Lee Cullum (Harry Connick, Jr.), is in the audience; in a very tense scene, he circumvents security, kills a cop and nearly finishes off Hudson in a bathroom before being caught.

Thirteen months later, Hudson's trauma has made her so agoraphobic she can't bear to leave her apartment or return to her job. But when homicide detective M. J. Monahan (Holly Hunter) is faced with some murders that suggest a new serial killer, she and her partner Ruben (Dermot Mulroney) pay a call on Hudson, whose interest is inevitably piqued by the kinky details of the cases.

As the murders mount, Hudson figures out that the psychopath is imitating some of the most infamous serial killers. This is a murderer with a sense of history, killings as homages to the masters.

Genuine interest is generated in the main characters thanks to better-than-usual writing for this sort of piece and ultra-sharp performances by the lead thesps. Director Jon Amiel delivers the nerve-racking goods in the final showdown between Hudson and her nemesis.

•

CORNERED

1945, 102 mins, US Ⓥ ⦿ b/w

Dir Edward Dmytryk ***Prod*** Adrian Scott ***Scr*** John Paxton ***Ph*** Harry J. Wild ***Ed*** Joseph Noriega ***Mus*** Roy Webb ***Art*** Albert S. D'Agostino, Carroll Clark

Act Dick Powell, Walter Slezak, Nina Vale, Micheline Cheirel, Morris Carnovsky, Luther Adler (RKO)

It's the story [by John Wexley] of the relentless post-war hunt of a Canadian flier for the collaborationist who was responsible for the death of his French bride. Directed and played strictly for suspense and thrills, search gets underway in France, switches to Belgium, Switzerland and then Argentina, where most of the action takes place.

While all evidence points toward the death of the collaborationist, Dick Powell believes the man is still alive. His search reveals hibernation of pro-Nazis in the Argentine, where they are waiting to rise again in the future, and the efforts of good Argentinians to smoke them out.

Cast has many suspects weaving in and out to conceal identity of the mysterious "Marcel Jarnac" whom Powell seeks, and finale has a definite surprise in store for audiences. Edward Dmytryk's direction makes the most of the suspense and concealment, building a mood that never lets down.

•

CORN IS GREEN, THE

1945, 114 mins, US Ⓥ b/w

Dir Irving Rapper ***Prod*** Jack Chertok ***Scr*** Casey Robinson, Frank Cavett ***Ph*** Sol Polito ***Ed*** Frederick Richards ***Mus*** Max Steiner ***Art*** Carl Jules Weyl

Act Bette Davis, Nigel Bruce, John Dall, Joan Lorring, Mildred Dunnock (Warner)

The performances, not only of Bette Davis but of newcomers John Dall and Joan Lorring, together with those of Nigel Bruce and others, capture attention and admiration far and above that of the story itself, which is somewhat slow in the first half. Several sequences could have been edited more sharply. While the exteriors of the Welsh countryside are almost entirely dreary and depressing, they reflect the mood of the Emlyn Williams play and its locale.

Davis, doing the emotional and serious-minded school mistress of the story, whose sociological ideals spur her to untiring efforts in raising the IQ of lowly Welsh mining folk, is cast in the kind of role she does well. Dall, her protégé, is much less an admirable character, though interest stays with him all the way.

The youthful Lorring is also a very intriguing type. As the trollop Bessie Watty, she is particularly socko in the final reel, when returning to the village with the news that she has borne Dall's illegitimate child.

1945: NOMINATIONS: Best Supp. Actor (John Dall), Supp. Actress (Joan Loring)

•

CORRINA, CORRINA

1994, 114 mins, US Ⓥ ⦿ col

Dir Jessie Nelson ***Prod*** Paula Mazur, Steve Tisch, Jessie Nelson ***Scr*** Jessie Nelson ***Ph*** Bruce Surtees ***Ed*** Lee Percy ***Mus*** Rick Cox ***Art*** Jeannine Claudia Oppewall

Act Whoopi Goldberg, Ray Liotta, Tina Majorino, Wendy Crewson, Larry Miller, Erica Yohn (New Line)

Corrina, Corrina, starring Whoopi Goldberg as a perky housekeeper who brings solace and joy to a depressed '50s Jewish household, is a schmaltzy if entertaining comedy-drama. Strong chemistry between Goldberg and Ray Liotta, and a winning performance by child actress Tina Majorino, happily triumph over old-fashioned material and mediocre production values.

Basing her story loosely on personal experience, writer/director Jessie Nelson examines the life of a Jewish family after the mother has suddenly died of cancer. Manny Singer (Liotta) is an ad jingle writer who throws himself into work as a way of dealing with his depression. But his 9-year-old daughter, Molly (Majorino), is so traumatized by the event that she becomes mute.

Tale begins with the desperate Manny interviewing for a maid. Corrina Washington (Goldberg) lands the job. Corrina can't cook, but she possesses a sassy, quirky personality that Manny thinks will be good for the child. After a long silence and enormous efforts by Corrina, Molly utters her first word and grants her first smile.

Novice helmer Nelson shows no instinct for pacing and exhibits little skill at interesting visual presentation or framing. Pic features the final performance of veteran actor Don Ameche, who plays Liotta's dying father.

•

CORSICAN BROTHERS, THE

1941, 111 mins, US Ⓥ b/w

Dir Gregory Ratoff ***Prod*** Edward Small ***Scr*** George Bruce ***Ph*** Harry Stradling ***Ed*** Grant Whytock, William Claxton ***Mus*** Dimitri Tiomkin ***Art*** Nicolai Remisoff

Act Douglas Fairbanks, Jr., Ruth Warrick, Akim Tamiroff, J. Carrol Naish, H. B. Warner, Henry Wilcoxon (Small/United Artists)

Dumas story of the *Corsican Brothers* is widely known. Born Siamese twins of Corsican aristocracy, the babies are separated immediately after birth by a miraculous operation, and saved from a vendetta attack that kills their parents and immediate relatives. One child goes to Paris for upbringing and education, while the other remains to be reared by a former family servant.

Twenty-one years later the twins (both portrayed by Douglas Fairbanks, Jr.) are reunited, introduced, and informed of the enemy of their forebears. Swearing to avenge the family murders, the two boys separate to confuse their enemy with widely separated attacks on his henchmen.

Title foreword warns audiences that this is an incredible tale—and then the picture proceeds on that basis. Script [from a free adaptation by George Bruce and Howard Estabrook] is well set up to display the action qualities, but rather studious on the dialog and story motivation. Gregory Ratoff's direction is okay.

•

COTTON CLUB, THE

1984, 127 mins, US Ⓥ ⦿ col

Dir Francis Coppola ***Prod*** Robert Evans ***Scr*** William Kennedy, Francis Coppola ***Ph*** Stephen Goldblatt ***Ed*** Barry Malkin, Robert Q. Lovett ***Mus*** John Barry, Bob Wilber ***Art*** Richard Sylbert

Act Richard Gere, Gregory Hines, Diane Lane, Lonette McKee, Bob Hoskins, Nicolas Cage (Zoetrope)

The Cotton Club certainly doesn't stint on ambition. Four stories [by William Kennedy, Francis Coppola, Mario Puzo, suggested by James Haskins's pictorial history *The Cotton Club*] thread through and intertwine in the $47 million picture. While the earlier Francis Coppola gangster efforts had a firm hand on the balance between plot elements and characters, *The Cotton Club* emerges as uneven and sometimes unfocused.

Focus is on Dixie Dwyer (Richard Gere), a cornet player in a small Gotham club. As the film opens in 1928, Dixie interrupts a solo to push a patron out of the way of a gunman's bullet. The thankful target turns out to be nightclub owner Dutch Schultz (James Remar).

Another thread involves club tap star Sandman Williams (Gregory Hines), who partners with his brother Clay (Maurice Hines), and has his eyes and heart set on chorus girl Lila Rose Oliver (Lonette McKee).

Dramatically, Coppola and coscreenwriter William Kennedy juggle a lot of balls in the air. The parallel stories of Gere and Hines's professional rise prove more potent, thanks largely to a mixture of romance, music and gangland involvement. Hines and McKee generate real sparks in their relationship and latter adds an interesting dimension as a light-skinned singer trying to hide her racial origins.

1984: NOMINATIONS: Best Art Direction, Editing

•

COTTON COMES TO HARLEM

1970, 97 mins, US col

Dir Ossie Davis ***Prod*** Samuel Goldwyn, Jr. ***Scr*** Arnold Perl, Ossie Davis ***Ph*** Gerald Hirschfeld ***Ed*** John Carter ***Mus*** Galt MacDermot ***Art*** Manuel Gerard

Act Godfrey Cambridge, Raymond St. Jacques, Calvin Lockhart, Judy Pace, Redd Foxx, John Anderson (United Artists)

Actor-director Ossie Davis makes his feature film debut with this slam-bang, all stops out, comedy-action film about expatriate writer Chester Himes's two Harlem detectives, Grave Digger Jones and Coffin Ed Johnson. Godfrey Cambridge and Raymond St. Jacques are Himes's tough, rough, foulmouthed but incorruptible policemen. Cambridge is the buffoon of the pair while St. Jacques (whose performance is easily the best in the film) is the spokesman for the Negro community.

There's occasional evidence of abrupt shortening of explanatory scenes to crowd as much action as possible into the running time. Action there is, from the opening seduction of gullible Harlem "good folks" by con artist-cumpreacher Calvin Lockhart, to the final denouement as to what really happened to that $87,000 stashed away in a bale of cotton.

Strong support is provided by nitery comedian Redd Foxx, John Anderson as the police chief, Emily Yancy as the widow of Lockhart's partner, J. D. Cannon as the white ex-con accomplice of Lockhart, and Equity president Frederick O'Neal as a numbers racket hoodlum.

•

COUCH TRIP, THE
1988, 98 mins, US Ⓥ ⦿ col
Dir Michael Ritchie ***Prod*** Lawrence Gordon ***Scr*** Steven Kampmann, Will Porter, Sean Stein ***Ph*** Donald E. Thorin ***Ed*** Richard A. Harris ***Mus*** Michel Colombier ***Art*** Jimmie Bly
Act Dan Aykroyd, Walter Matthau, Charles Grodin, David Clennon, Donna Dixon, Richard Romanus (Orion)

The Couch Trip is a relatively low-key Dan Aykroyd vehicle that restores some of the comic actor's earlier charm simply by not trying too hard. Relying as much on character as shtick, Aykroyd is a likable everyman here out to right the minor indignities and injustices in the world.

As an obstreperous prisoner biding his time in a Cicero, IL, loony bin, Aykroyd trades places with his attending shrink, Dr. Baird (David Clennon), and moves to L.A. to fill in for radio therapist Dr Maitlin (Charles Grodin), who is having a mental breakdown of his own.

Screenplay [from the novel by Ken Kolb] doesn't break any new ground in suggesting there is a thin line between the certifiably crazy and certifiably sane, but it still manages some gentle jabs at the pretensions of the psychiatric profession.

As a mock priest and another fringe member of society, Walter Matthau is Aykroyd's soulmate, but the connection between the men is too thinly drawn to have much meaning. Donna Dixon, stunningly beautiful though she is, is impossible to swallow as a brilliant psychiatrist, particularly since her duties include signaling commercial breaks on radio and standing around posing.

•

COUNSELLOR-AT-LAW
1933, 80 mins, US b/w
Dir William Wyler ***Prod*** Henry Henigson ***Scr*** Elmer Rice ***Ph*** Norbert Brodine ***Ed*** Daniel Mandell
Act John Barrymore, Bebe Daniels, Doris Kenyon, Onslow Stevens, Isabel Jewell, Melvyn Douglas (Universal)

Elmer Rice's screen adaptation of his own legit play retains enough of its natural dramatic power to rate favorably with the original.

Directed with complete understanding of the subject, expertly cast in its small but important secondary character roles and well produced on the whole, *Counsellor-at-Law* is compelling stuff.

The one flaw is in the casting for the principal role. Elmer Rice's George Simon, an East Side boy who rises to great prominence at the bar, is physically unsuited to John Barrymore, besides being a type of role that he hasn't tackled in pictures before. Barrymore's only means of conquering the role is to reshape George Simon into Barrymore. During the early moments he has a struggle on his hands, but the transformation is slowly completed.

The minor characters whose lives are intertwined with Simon's in this *Grand Hotel* in a lawyer's office were largely responsible for the play's legit success. That fact has not been overlooked in the picture's casting, as is evidenced by the importation of eight of the original stage players by Universal. They know their roles and they don't make any mistakes. These players, all lending valuable aid, are Marvin Kline, Conway Washburn, John Qualen, J. Hammond Dailey, Malka Kornstein, Angela Jacobs, T. H. Manning and Elmer Brown.

Bebe Daniels, like Barrymore, is also out of her own backyard as Simon's secretary whose affection for her troubled boss goes unrequited until the finish, when it's vaguely suggested she'll win her point.

•

COUNTDOWN
1968, 101 mins, US Ⓥ ⦿ ▭ col
Dir Robert Altman ***Prod*** William Conrad (exec.) ***Scr*** Loring Mandel ***Ph*** William W. Spencer ***Ed*** Gene Milford ***Mus*** Leonard Rosenman ***Art*** Jack Poplin
Act James Caan, Joanna Moore, Robert Duvall, Barbara Baxley, Charles Aidman, Steve Ihnat (Warner)

Countdown, a story about a U.S. space shot to the moon, is a literate and generally excellent program. Strong script [based on a novel by Hank Searls], emphasizing human conflict, is well developed and neatly resolved on a note of suspense.

James Caan is a civilian scientist, chosen because of political implications, to replace military officer Robert Duvall as the moon-shot man. Added to this conflict is that between Steve Ihnat, project boss, and Charles Aidman, flight surgeon, who carry on the struggle between safety-of-life considerations and those of beating the Russians.

Although the emphasis is on personal interactions, pic interpolates some stock footage plus speciallyshot technical mock-up scenes.

•

COUNTERPOINT
1967, 105 mins, US ▭ col
Dir Ralph Nelson ***Prod*** Dick Berg ***Scr*** James Lee, Joel Oliansky ***Ph*** Russel Metty ***Ed*** Howard G. Epstein ***Mus*** Bronislau Kaper ***Art*** Alexander Golitzen, Carl Anderson
Act Charlton Heston, Maximilian Schell, Kathryn Hays, Leslie Nielsen, Anton Diffring, Linden Chiles (Universal)

Counterpoint is the story of an American symphony orchestra—on a USO tour in Belgium—taken prisoner by the Germans during the Battle of the Bulge. Some of the incidents are contrived and characterizations of its two leads, as developed in trying to make them strong, are sometimes confusing. But in the main subject has been well handled.

Script, based upon Alan Sillitoe's novel, *The General*, packs suspense as fate of the martinet symph conductor and his 70 musicians at hands of the Germans, under order to execute every prisoner, remains uncertain.

Something new has been added here for a war film; parts of five major musical works, recorded by Los Angeles Philharmonic Orchestra for the action, which should have particular appeal for music lovers.

•

COUNTESS FROM HONG KONG, A
1967, 120 mins, UK col
Dir Charles Chaplin ***Prod*** Jerome Epstein ***Scr*** Charles Chaplin ***Ph*** Arthur Ibbetson ***Ed*** Gordon Hales ***Mus*** Charles Chaplin ***Art*** Bob Cartwright
Act Marlon Brando, Sophia Loren, Sydney Chaplin, Tippi Hedren, Patrick Cargill, Michael Medwin (Universal)

Charles Chaplin says the story was inspired by a trip he made to Shanghai in 1931 but, though the period has been updated, the style of his screenplay and direction are obstinately reminiscent of the 1930s.

Countess is what may be described as a romantic comedy. It has a nebulous plot, slim characterizations and all the trappings of an old-fashioned bedroom farce.

Sophia Loren, who radiates an abundance of charm, plays a Russian emigré countess who, after a night out on the town in Hong Kong with Marlon Brando, stows away in his cabin with the intention of getting to New York. Although the story barely taxes her acting resources, Loren adds a quality to every scene in which she appears. She is stylish, classy and striking. Brando, on the other hand, appears ill-at-ease in what should have been a light comedy role.

Sydney Chaplin as Brando's cruising companion gives a thoroughly reliable performance, while Tippi Hedren, as Brando's wife, is superb in her few scenes at the tail-end of the picture.

•

COUNT OF MONTE CRISTO, THE
1934, 113 mins, US Ⓥ b/w
Dir Rowland V. Lee ***Prod*** Edward Small ***Scr*** Philip Dunne, Dan Totheroh, Rowland V. Lee ***Ph*** Peverell Marley ***Mus*** Alfred Newman
Act Robert Donat, Elissa Landi, Louis Calhern, Sidney Blackmer, Raymond Walburn, O. P. Heggie (Reliance/United Artists)

Monte Cristo is a near-perfect blend of thrilling action and grand dialogue, both of which elements are inherent in Alexandre Dumas's original story.

Robert Donat is a fortunate selection for the lead. His intelligent handling of the many-sided top role hallmarks a sparkling piece of acting. Louis Calhern (De Villefort), Sidney Blackmer (Mondego) and Raymond Walburn (Danglars) are the three principal male supports in the extra large cast, and as the trio upon whom Cristo wreaks his vengeance they fill the order. Elissa Landi as Mercedes looks and acts the part, but the acting in this case isn't as important as the looks, and Landi has had tougher assignments.

•

COUNT OF MONTE CRISTO, THE
1976, 103 mins, UK Ⓥ col
Dir David Greene ***Prod*** Norman Rosemart ***Scr*** Sidney Carroll ***Ph*** Aldo Tonti ***Ed*** Gene Milford ***Mus*** Allyn Ferguson ***Art*** Walter Patriarca
Act Richard Chamberlain, Tony Curtis, Trevor Howard, Louis Jourdan, Donald Pleasence, Kate Nelligan (ITC)

Richard Chamberlain is Edmond Dantes, the romantic young sailor railroaded to prison for 15 years. After his escape, aided by an old fellow prisoner, the story gets down to his obsessive revenge against the four money- and/or power-hungry men who conspired against him.

All this is retold in a most workmanlike fashion. Script and moral values appear respectful of the original text, and the Alexandre Dumas saga is performed with ample conviction and polish. But it's developed with more sincerity than interest or dramatic originality, and with no style of its own.

Chamberlain is appealing and reasonably persuasive as the hero robbed of both his best years and his betrothed, the latter played touchingly in a promising feature bow by British-based Canadian Kate Nelligan.

•

COUNTRY
1984, 109 mins, US Ⓥ ⦿ ▭ col
Dir Richard Pearce ***Prod*** William D. Wittliff, Jessica Lange ***Scr*** William D. Wittliff ***Ph*** David M. Walsh ***Ed*** Bill Yahraus ***Mus*** Charles Gross ***Art*** Ron Hobbs
Act Jessica Lange, Sam Shepard, Wilford Brimley, Matt Clark, Therese Graham, Levi L. Knebel (Touchstone)

Jessica Lange's pet project took a while to get produced, but it winds up firmly on the right track, with its basic theme of the classic struggle of the working man against the forces of government.

Screenplay recalls recent real-life events of how farmers have taken on loans with the government's blessing in order to expand and wind up faced with foreclosure when unable to keep up with the payments.

Lange is the focal point, essaying the mother of the family faced with losing the farm which had been in her lineage for some 100 years. The family, like 40 percent of the farmers in the area, is about to be victimized by get-tough government policies.

Almost overshadowed by Lange is Sam Shepard as the husband, though he gives a quietly effective portrayal of the husband dealt a humiliating blow to his pride when the farm is fingered for liquidation.

1984: NOMINATION: Best Actress (Jessica Lange)

•

COUNTRY DANCE
(US: BROTHERLY LOVE)
1970, 112 mins, UK Ⓥ col
Dir J. Lee Thompson ***Prod*** Robert Emmett Gianna ***Scr*** James Kennaway ***Ph*** Ted Moore ***Ed*** Willy Kemplen ***Mus*** John Addison ***Art*** Maurice Fowler
Act Peter O'Toole, Susannah York, Michael Craig, Harry Andrews, Cyril Cusack, Judy Cornwell (Windward/Keep)

Country Dance is a confusing love triangle film, focusing on a woman and the two men in her life, one her husband and the other her brother. Interiors were lensed at Ardmore Studios, Ireland, and exteriors in Ireland's Wicklow County and in Perthshire, Scotland. The James Kennaway screenplay is based upon both his play, *Country Dance*, and his novel *Household Ghosts*.

Limning the decline and fall of Sir Charles Ferguson (Peter O'Toole), last scion of a noble Scottish family; there is in this descent the distasteful subject of the brother's unhealthy love for his sister (Susannah York), who has left her husband (Michael Craig) to make her home with her brother on their family estate.

O'Toole's enactment of the character who cannot face the reality of either losing his sister or the destruction of his traditional way of life on his dwindling estate is whimsically constructed.

•

COUNTRY GIRL, THE
1954, 104 mins, US Ⓥ b/w
Dir George Seaton ***Prod*** William Perlberg ***Scr*** George Seaton ***Ph*** John F. Warren ***Ed*** Ellsworth Hoagland ***Mus*** Victor Young ***Art*** Hal Pereira, Roland Anderson
Act Bing Crosby, Grace Kelly, William Holden, Anthony Ross, Gene Reynolds, Jacqueline Fontaine (Paramount)

An exceptionally well-performed essay on an alcoholic song man, with Bing Crosby carrying on a bottle romance, *Country Girl* is a show business story that has depth and movement.

Adapted from the 1950 Clifford Odets play of the same title, its key player, a quondam star induced into trying a painful comeback, is a weak, lying, excessive drinker. Grace Kelly is resolute to the hilt, conveying a certain feminine strength and courage that enable her to endure the hardships of being the boozer's wife. William Holden registers in sock style as the legit director determined that Crosby can stand up to the demands of the starring role in a new play.

Crosby pulls a masterly switch, immersing himself in the part with full effect. The film has four songs by Ira Gershwin and Harold Arlen. The bare NY theatre where the show within the show is rehearsed, the Boston house which is the scene of the play's break-in, the squalid tenement apartment where Kelly and Crosby are first found—these are realistically staged. Robert Alton's staging of the musical numbers is adequate.

1954: Best Actress (Grace Kelly), Screenplay

NOMINATIONS: Best Picture, Director, Actor (Bing Crosby), B&W Cinematography, B&W Art Direction

•

COURAGE UNDER FIRE
1996, 115 mins, US Ⓥ ⦿ col
Dir Edward Zwick ***Prod*** John Davis, Joseph M. Singer, David T. Friendly ***Scr*** Patrick Sheane Duncan ***Ph*** Roger Deakins ***Ed*** Steven Rosenblum ***Mus*** James Horner ***Art*** John Graysmark
Act Denzel Washington, Meg Ryan, Lou Diamond Phillips, Michael Moriarty, Matt Damon, Bronson Pinchot (Davis/20th Century-Fox)

A *Rashomon*-like story about the difficulty of establishing the truth about heroism and soldiers' behavior in combat, *Courage Under Fire* is a carefully conceived, dramatically honorable picture that treats its subject with clarity and intelligence, especially by contemporary standards. Notable as the first major studio release to deal with the 1991 Gulf War, Edward Zwick's high-minded new outing offers plenty of old-fashioned movie virtues such as believable action, plausible psychology, fully played-out confrontations and honest emotions.

Lt. Col. Nathaniel Serling (Denzel Washington) is leading an armored tank battalion in nocturnal pursuit of fleeing Iraqis. Suddenly, an empty-looking desert is filled with action, and Serling, in haste and confusion, orders his gunner to fire at a suspicious tank, only to learn shortly that he has killed several of his own men with his "friendly fire." Protected by his superior officer, Gen. Hershberg (Michael Moriarty), the guilt-ridden Serling is shuffled into a routine Pentagon job.

For p.r. purposes, the White House is particularly anxious that Capt. Karen Walden (Meg Ryan) receives a Medal of Honor award posthumously. Serling begins speaking to the survivors of the Medevac chopper accident in which Walden was the pilot, and realizes that what happened among Walden's crewmen was far from clear-cut. Crucially, the testimony of three soldiers varies significantly.

All of Serling's predicaments are palpably and convincingly registered through Washington's probing, reserved and sensitively drawn performance in a role that, in another era, might have been played by the likes of a Montgomery Clift or William Holden. The same can't exactly be said for the other characters, who are boldly etched but exist mainly as expressions of set attitudes rather than three-dimensional people.

Shot in Texas, pic looks impressive.

•

COURT JESTER, THE
1956, 101 mins, US Ⓥ ⦿ col
Dir Norman Panama, Melvin Frank ***Prod*** Norman Panama, Melvin Frank ***Scr*** Norman Panama, Melvin Frank ***Ph*** Ray June ***Ed*** Tom McAdoo ***Mus*** Victor Shoen (dir.) ***Art*** Hal Pereira, Roland Anderson
Act Danny Kaye, Glynis Johns, Basil Rathbone, Angela Lansbury, Cecil Parker, Mildred Natwick (Paramount/Dena)

Costumed swashbucklers undergo a happy spoofing in *The Court Jester* with Danny Kaye heading the fun-poking. Norman Panama and Melvin Frank drag in virtually every time-honored, and timeworn, medieval drama cliche for Kaye and cast to replay for laughs via not-so-subtle treatment.

A major assist comes from the Sylvia Fine–Sammy Cahn songs, of which there are five all tuned to the Kaye talent. There's the quite mad "Maladjusted Jester"; a lullaby, "Loo-Loo-Loo I'll Take You Dreaming"; a ballad, "My Heart Knows a Lovely Song"; the comedic "They'll Never Outfox the Fox," and "Life Could Not Better Be."

Glynis Johns, fetched from England for the hoydenish Maid Jean role opposite Kaye, does exceedingly well. The same is true of Basil Rathbone, a many-seasoned chief heavy; Angela Lansbury, cutting a pretty picture as the Princess Gwendolyn; Cecil Parker, the not-so-bright King Roderick who has ousted the real royal family; and Mildred Natwick, the princess's evil-eyed maid.

•

COURT MARTIAL
SEE: CARRINGTON V.C.

•

COURT-MARTIAL OF BILLY MITCHELL, THE
(UK: ONE MAN MUTINY)
1955, 100 mins, US Ⓥ ⦿ ▭ col
Dir Otto Preminger ***Prod*** Milton Sperling ***Scr*** Milton Sperling, Emmet Lavery ***Ph*** Sam Leavitt ***Ed*** Folmar Blangsted ***Mus*** Dimitri Tiomkin ***Art*** Malcolm Bert
Act Gary Cooper, Charles Bickford, Ralph Bellamy, Rod Steiger, Elizabeth Montgomery, Fred Clark (United States/Warner)

Dealing with real-life events of 1925, the subject matter spotlights something which is always present tense, namely, official rigidity, red tape and intellectual hardening of the arteries in the brains of aging bureaucrats.

The picture is a real kick in the shins for the cult of blind military obedience and the lesson which is laid on the line relates to Pearl Harbor. The picture shows Mitchell predicting the Japanese sneak attack on Pearl Harbor, and describing American vulnerability, all this 16 years before that catastrophic Sunday and in the presence of Douglas MacArthur.

The main trouping is by Gary Cooper, Ralph Bellamy as a congressman counsel with yellow journalistic instincts, Charles Bickford, Fred Clark and Rod Steiger. All are standouts in professionalism though this is a writer's, not an actor's, picture.

1955: NOMINATION: Best Story & Screenplay

•

COURTNEY AFFAIR, THE
SEE: THE COURTNEYS OF CURZON STREET

•

COURTNEYS OF CURZON STREET, THE
(US: THE COURTNEY AFFAIR)
1947, 120 mins, UK Ⓥ b/w
Dir Herbert Wilcox ***Prod*** Herbert Wilcox ***Scr*** Nicholas Phipps ***Ph*** Max Greene ***Ed*** Flora Newton, Vera Campbell ***Mus*** Tony Collins ***Art*** William C. Andrews
Act Anna Neagle, Michael Wilding, Gladys Young, Coral Browne, Michael Medwin, Bernard Lee (British Lion)

Wilcox hasn't worried about any significant theme in this. He tells his four-generation story with smiles and tears, and obviously enjoys seeing two people in love.

Story runs from 1900 to 1945, Michael Wilding plays the soldier son and heir of a baronet. He is in love with his mother's maid (Anna Neagle). Ignoring his mother's warning that he is risking social ostracism, he flouts tradition and marries the girl. Climax to society's persecution comes at a snobbish function with Queen Victoria present to hear first performance of Tchaikovsky's *Symphonie Pathetique*. His wife, nervous, does not behave with conventional stoicism and has to listen to catty remarks about her lowly beginning.

From then on the story tells of the joys and sorrows of the Courtneys, ending in 1945 when their grandson brings home his girl, who hopes her humble family won't object to her marrying into the aristocracy.

•

COURTSHIP OF ANDY HARDY, THE
1942, 94 mins, US b/w
Dir George B. Seitz ***Scr*** Agnes Christine Johnston ***Ph*** Lester White ***Ed*** Elmo Veron
Act Lewis Stone, Mickey Rooney, Donna Reed, William Lundigan (M-G-M)

Picture is studded with laugh lines throughout, and displays general effervescing tempo for maximum reaction. Mickey Rooney—between adolescence and manhood—successfully balances the assignment in excellent style. His is a strong performance with accent on straight acting ability and without recourse to the mugging antics that he called on previously.

Story [from characters created by Aurania Rouverol] opens with Judge Hardy endeavoring to reconcile a couple with an adolescent daughter. He invokes Andy's aid to date the girl and break her of a haughty complex and Andy's campaign is successful in this respect.

Donna Reed is the girl who is turned over to Andy for regeneration, and how he finally succeeds is neatly contrived in the screenplay, with substance in both lines and situations provided by the script.

•

COURTSHIP OF EDDIE'S FATHER, THE
1963, 118 mins, US Ⓥ ⦿ ▭ col
Dir Vincente Minnelli ***Prod*** Joe Pasternak ***Scr*** John Gay ***Ph*** Milton Krasner ***Ed*** Adrienne Fazan ***Mus*** George Stoll ***Art*** George W. Davis, Urie McCleary
Act Glenn Ford, Shirley Jones, Stella Stevens, Dina Merrill, Roberta Sherwood, Jerry Van Dyke (M-G-M/Euterpe-Venice)

The story of a dad and a lad and their divergent views on what constitutes desirable stepmotherhood, the production is richly mounted, wittily written and engagingly played by an expert, spirited and attractive cast.

In adapting the novel by Mark Toby, John Gay has penned an aware, clever and generally well-constructed scenario. Glenn Ford portrays a widower who, in rearing his precocious six-and-a-half-year-old son (Ronny Howard) must, in the course of his romantic pursuits, take into account the future maternal preferences of the boy, whose comic book-eye-view of candidate wives is inclined to judge statistically on the basis of bustlines and eyesockets.

Ford creates a warm, likeable personality and is especially smooth in his reaction takes in scenes with his charge.

Never any question about Shirley Jones's credentials as the kind of woman any red-blooded American type would love to call mommy, bustline notwithstanding. Dina Merrill is an attractive loser. Stella Stevens comes on like gangbusters in her enactment of a brainy but inhibited doll from Montana. It's a sizzling comedy performance of a kook.

Vincente Minnelli's direction tends toward melodramatic heaviness in some of the early "serious" going and some exaggeration in several comic passages, but overall he has managed well enough, coaxing some bright performances from his cast.

•

COUSIN COUSINE
1975, 95 mins, France Ⓥ ⦿ col
Dir Jean-Charles Tacchella ***Prod*** Bertrand Javal ***Scr*** Jean-Charles Tacchella ***Ph*** Georges Lendi ***Ed*** Agnes Guillemot ***Mus*** Gerard Anfasso
Act Marie-Christine Barrault, Victor Lanoux, Marie-France Pisier, Guy Marchand, Ginette Garcin, Sybil Maas (Pomereu/Gaumont)

A gritty comedy of family manners built around the family rituals of marriage, death, etc. A pic that is flippant, observant, with a love story between two new cousins, both married.

Jean-Charles Tacchella did better with his first film, *Trip in Tartarie*, that showed a man roaming about after the violent killing of his wife by a drunk with a gun. Here he shows more content, but there is a predictability and a flat visual treatment that called for more unique angles and more astute, revealing cutting.

Players are acceptable, with Guy Marchand properly callow as the small-time Don Juan who gives up his girls to keep his wife, but finds her attachment to her new cousin has grown so that she finally leaves him and their son to go off. Victor Lanoux and Marie-Christine Barrault are entrancing as the new couple, while Marie-France Pisier is shrewdly perceptive as the neurotic wife of the man.

•

COUSINS, THE
SEE: LES COUSINS

•

COUSINS, LES
(THE COUSINS)
1959, 103 mins, France Ⓥ b/w
Dir Claude Chabrol ***Prod*** Claude Chabrol ***Scr*** Claude Chabrol, Paul Gegauff ***Ph*** Henri Decae ***Ed*** Jacques Gaillard ***Mus*** Paul Misraki ***Art*** Jacques Saulnier, Bernard Evein
Act Gerard Blain, Jean-Claude Brialy, Juliette Mayniel, Claude Cerval, Guy Decomble, Stephane Audran (AJYM)

Tale of a country cousin trying to make it in the big city, and destroyed in the process, gets offbeat treatment from promising new and youthful director Claude Chabrol. It develops into a looksee at a certain restless youth.

The country cousin, Charles (Gerard Blain), comes to stay with his worldly, decadent cousin, Paul (Jean-Claude Brialy). His attempts at love and exams fail while his indolent, debauched cousin gets all.

Chabrol has gone in for a little too much symbolism. The characters sometimes remain murky and literary rather than real form. But concise progression, fine technical aspects, and the look at innocence destroyed by the profane keeps it absorbing, despite the slightly pretentious treatment at times.

•

COUSINS
1989, 110 mins, US Ⓥ ⦿ col
Dir Joel Schumacher ***Prod*** William Allyn ***Scr*** Stephen Metcalfe ***Ph*** Ralf Bode ***Ed*** Robert Brown ***Mus*** Angelo Badalamenti ***Art*** Mark S. Freeborn
Act Ted Danson, Isabella Rossellini, Sean Young, William Petersen, Lloyd Bridges, Norma Aleandro (Paramount)

As derivative as it is, *Cousins* still is a hugely entertaining Americanized version of the French film *Cousin Cousine*, with nearly the same insouciant tone as the Jean-Charles Tacchella comedy of 1975. It's been spiced with a dash of 1980s social commentary and a dollop of Italian ethnic flavoring.

Isabella Rossellini and Ted Danson's sappy, overly sentimental series of rendezvous are well compensated by their relatives' caustic comments, irreverent asides and other antics at the three weddings, one funeral and other functions all attend during the course of the picture. Object of most of the ridicule is William Petersen, the unctuous BMW car salesman and Don Juan pretender who starts everything off in the opening wedding scene drooling at Danson's flamboyantly dressed wife (Sean Young).

It's obvious enough that Rossellini, the martyred Madonna type who knows of her husband's philandering, represents prudishness and purity as much as Young, dressed in outlandish high-fashion ruffles of red and black, represents the opposite.

What's most fun is to get everyone else's thoughts on the matter. There's Rossellini's wealthy mother Edie (Norma Aleandro), cranky old Aunt Sofia (Gina De Angelis) and Danson's son Mitchell (Keith Coogan), who has a penchant for videotaping family gatherings.

Best of all is Lloyd Bridges, Danson's irascible, sporting uncle, who has as much pep in his step and gleam in his eye for Aleandro as the two main couples have combined.

•

COVERED WAGON, THE
1923, 119 mins, US Ⓥ ⦿ ⊗ b/w
Dir James Cruze ***Scr*** Jack Cunningham ***Ph*** Karl Brown ***Ed*** Dorothy Arzner ***Mus*** Hugo Riesenfeld
Act J. Warren Kerrigan, Lois Wilson, Ernest Torrence, Charles Ogle, Alan Hale, Ethel Wales (Paramount)

The Covered Wagon was months in the making with its cost said to have been in the neighborhood of $800,000. It is the biggest thing since Griffith made *The Birth of a Nation*.

Like *Birth* it is based on historical fact. Emerson Hough, who wrote *The Covered Wagon* for the *Saturday Evening Post*, chose for his subject those pioneers who left their farms and safeguarded homes in the territory east of the Ohio and started in prairie schooners for the Pacific Coast in 1847, before the discovery that the California hills contained the glittering metal that was to be a tremendous lure in 1849.

This particular wagon train, which has some 300 vehicles, starts for Oregon. Through it all a very pretty and simple love tale runs, as well as an element of intrigue, which together with the thrills that have been devised makes this production a real picture of pictures.

The big thrills are three: First and foremost is the fording of the Platte by the wagons of the train. Then there is the Indian attack with a corking battle staged, and finally a prairie fire.

•

COVER GIRL
1944, 105 mins, US Ⓥ ⦿ col
Dir Charles Vidor ***Prod*** Arthur Schwartz ***Scr*** Virginia Van Upp ***Ph*** Rudolph Mate, Allen M. Davey ***Ed*** Viola Lawrence ***Mus*** Morris Stoloff (dir.) ***Art*** Lionel Banks, Cary Odell
Act Rita Hayworth, Gene Kelly, Lee Bowman, Phil Silvers, Otto Kruger, Eve Arden (Columbia)

Arthur Schwartz, in his initial film producer spot after years of experience with stage musicals, deftly injects surefire showmanship into the picture, neatly blending the talents of the players with an inspired script by Virginia Van Upp [story by Erwin Gelsey, adaptation by Marion Parsonnet and Paul Gangelin], fine and consistently paced direction by Charles Vidor, and taking full advantage of the technical contributions.

Plot is neatly concocted to get over idea of sudden rise to theatrical fame of Rita Hayworth as result of winning a Cover Girl contest. Gene Kelly, operating the modest Brooklyn nightspot where he stages the floor shows, is in love with Hayworth, a dancer. Latter wins the contest to give the room immediate fame with the upper-crust customers from Manhattan.

Otto Kruger, responsible for Hayworth's prominence, figures she should be lifted out of the lowly nightspot to a Broadway show. Result is break between the girl and Kelly when latter stubbornly blows off steam.

Dance sequences spotlighting the terping abilities of Hayworth and Kelly are expertly staged. Kelly devised his own routines for the picture. Score by Jerome Kern and Ira Gershwin, comprising seven tunes, is of high caliber.

1944: Best Score for a Musical Picture

NOMINATIONS: Best Color Cinematography, Color Art Direction, Song ("Long Ago and Far Away"), Sound

•

COWBOYS, THE
1972, 128 mins, US Ⓥ ▭ col
Dir Mark Rydell ***Prod*** Mark Rydell ***Scr*** Irving Ravetch, Harriet Frank, Jr., William Dale Jennings ***Ph*** Robert Surtees ***Ed*** Robert Swink, Neil Travis ***Mus*** John Williams ***Art*** Philip Jefferies
Act John Wayne, Roscoe Lee Browne, Bruce Dern, Colleen Dewhurst, Slim Pickens, Lonny Chapman (Sanford/Warner)

The Cowboys stars John Wayne as a tough cattleman forced to use some green teenagers to get the beef to market. Handsome, placid and pastoral, the film is a family-type entry, produced and directed by Mark Rydell.

Rustler Bruce Dern fights with Wayne and eventually shoots him dead. This foul deed gives the boys enough courage to plot vengeance under the leadership of Roscoe Lee Browne, an urbane black wagon-train cook who previously had exchanged some pithy comments with Wayne and the kids.

The story [from a novel by William Dale Jennings] is long and episodic, and its gentle treatment makes the length something of a hindrance to maximum enjoyment. Cast includes Colleen Dewhurst in an effective cameo as a traveling bordello madam.

•

COYOTE UGLY
2000, 100 mins, US Ⓥ ⦿ ▭ col
Dir David McNally ***Prod*** Jerry Bruckheimer, Chad Oman ***Scr*** Gina Wendkos ***Ph*** Amir Mokri ***Ed*** William Goldenberg ***Mus*** Trevor Horn ***Art*** Jon Hutman
Act Piper Perabo, Adam Garcia, Maria Bello, John Goodman, Melanie Lynskey, Izabella Miko (Bruckheimer/Touchstone)

If Tony Manero can make it in New York City in *Saturday Night Fever*, then so can Violet Sanford in *Coyote Ugly*, calculated redo on the formulaic fantasy of an innocent conquering Gotham. Tale is an unfettered embrace of Hollywood dream-making in which wet-behind-the-ears Violet (Piper Perabo) succeeds against all odds in her goal of being a songwriter—and falls in love in the bargain.

Catch is that her mode of survival until her big break is mixing drinks and performing for the garrulous, whooping patrons of bar Coyote Ugly, where the staff must hop on the bar and do bumps and grinds and the Texas two-step.

Seeming from the start to be a bit too hip to be the full-on innocent of her character, Perabo is so loving and constantly framed by tyro helmer David McNally's camera that if viewers don't like her, the feature will be like water torture. Actress, though, soon shares screen with engaging Aussie thesp Adam Garcia, who plays a burger flipper named Kevin mistaken by Violet as a club manager. Meeting cute is pushed to nth degree here.

Set pieces in Coyote Ugly are staged with a loose energy that captures the boozy, sexy heat of the place, fortunately paced without the kind of hyperactive cutting typical of Bruckheimer productions.

Pic's major song element is supported by several penned by Diane Warren, whose work is a bit funkier than usual, but they're obviously dubbed by voice other than Perabo's—namely country star LeAnn Rimes, who ultimately makes an appearance herself. Result is rather artificial, in keeping with pic's pre-fab quality.

•

CRACKERS
1984, 92 mins, US Ⓥ ⦿ col
Dir Louis Malle ***Prod*** Edward Lewis, Robert Cortes ***Scr*** Jeffrey Fiskin ***Ph*** Laszlo Kovacs ***Ed*** Susanne Baron ***Mus*** Paul Chihara ***Art*** John J. Lloyd
Act Donald Sutherland, Jack Warden, Sean Penn, Wallace Shawn, Larry Riley, Trinidad Silva (Universal)

A mild little caper comedy with plenty of sociological overtones, *Crackers* comes as a letdown from director Louis Malle. With a flimsy plot that is perhaps rightly treated in a throwaway manner, film basically consists of a wide assortment of character riffs which are offbeat enough to provide moderate moment-to-moment amusement but don't create a great deal of comic impact.

As in dozens of tenement-set plays from *Street Scene* on, virtually all the action takes place within or very near the central setting, in this case a pawnshop owned by shameless profiteer Jack Warden. His buddy, Donald Sutherland, is out of work, and all but a few of the other characters make up a rainbow microcosm of today's unemployed.

•

CRACK IN THE MIRROR
1960, 97 mins, US ▭ b/w
Dir Richard Fleischer ***Prod*** Darryl F. Zanuck ***Scr*** Mark Canfield ***Ph*** William C. Mellor ***Ed*** Roger Dwyre ***Mus*** Maurice Jarre ***Art*** Jean d'Eaubonne
Act Orson Welles, Juliette Greco, Bradford Dillman, Alexander Knox, Catherine Lacy, William Lucas (DFZ/20th Century-Fox)

The screenplay, based on a novel by Marcel Haedrich, tells two parallel stories, both age-old triangle situations in which a not-so-young woman throws over her elderly lover for a much younger man. The first situation involves three working class people and the second, three members of the Paris haute monde. The stories come together when the working class dame and her young paramour are brought to trial for the murder of the older man.

By casting Orson Welles as both the tyrannical old construction worker who is murdered and as the cuckolded lawyer, Juliette Greco as the mistress in both situations and Bradford Dillman as the young laborer and the young lawyer-in-a-hurry, producer and director have obviously intended to make some pertinent statements about guilt and the ironies of justice.

This irony, however, is telegraphed early in the film when the audience first is let in on the fact that the two stories are essentially the same. Another problem is that about halfway through, the film's focal point switches from the working class triangle to the problems of the upper-class trio, with the result that audience interest and emotional involvement are put to a severe test.

Welles is fine as the drunken old slob and close to superb as the elderly lawyer. Dillman is also good as the two young men, both equally opportunistic. However, it's Greco who comes off best—whether it's because of performance or the projection of a unique cinema personality, is hard to say. She's all-girl.

Produced entirely in Paris, picture has a thoroughly French look and sound.

•

CRACK IN THE WORLD
1965, 96 mins, US col
Dir Andrew Marton ***Prod*** Bernard Glasser, Lester A. Sansom ***Scr*** Jon Manchip White, Julian Halevy ***Ph*** Manuel Berenguer ***Ed*** Derek Parsons ***Mus*** John Douglas ***Art*** Eugene Lourie
Act Dana Andrews, Janette Scott, Kieron Moore, Alexander Knox, Peter Damon, Gary Lasdun (Paramount)

Crack in the World, distinguished principally by some startling special effects, imaginatively focuses on an ill-fated experiment to tap the unlimited energy residing within the earth's core which nearly blows up the world.

Produced in Spain for Philip Yordan's Security Pictures, the Paramount release carries a more legitimate premise [story by Jon Manchip White] than the regular science fiction entry, strictly fictional in tone and context. Here is an entirely logical scientific operation, of drilling through the earth's crust to reach the molten mass called magma, which, brought to the surface under controlled conditions, could give the world all the energy it would ever want.

Dana Andrews plays the part of the scientist in charge of the operation, dying with fast cancer, and Kieron Moore his assistant who believes his superior's plan will end in the disaster which eventuates, both handling their roles okay. Janette Scott is Andrews's scientist-wife, actually in love with Moore, a rather thankless role which she sparks as much as possible.

•

CRADLE WILL ROCK
1999, 133 mins, US Ⓥ ⦿ ▭ col
Dir Tim Robbins ***Prod*** John Kilik, Lydia Dean Pilcher, Tim Robbins ***Scr*** Tim Robbins ***Ph*** Jean Yves Escoffier ***Ed*** Geraldine Peroni ***Mus*** David Robbins ***Art*** Richard Hoover
Act Hank Azaria, Ruben Blades, Joan Cusack, John Cusack, Cary Elwes, Philip Baker Hall (Havoc/Touchstone)

A vibrant examination of a rare moment in American history when art and politics were dynamically forged on the same anvil, *Cradle Will Rock* succeeds far more often than not in delivering a credible, kaleidoscopic portrait of creative, and often famous individuals. Erring mainly in its occasional tendency toward caricature, this is Tim Robbins's ambitious $32-million attempt to make his own *Reds*.

Film's title refers to the polemical musical drama *The Cradle Will Rock*, written by Marc Blitzstein in 1936 for the Federal Theater and taken on by a 21-year-old Orson Welles and John Houseman at the height of their celebrated theatrical collaboration in New York. With right-wing politicians on the attack and the theater abruptly shut down by the authorities, the company led the public on a 21-block march to another venue where the actors, forbidden by their union from setting foot onstage, began performing their roles from various spots in the auditorium.

Fashioning his screenplay from scratch, Robbins uses the *Cradle* episode as just one artistic venture to create a larger picture of the dynamic cultural landscape. Contrasting starkly with the rambunctiousness of Welles (Angus Macfadyen) & Co. is the parched world of those who oppose the prevailing sociopolitical currents of the time.

Many perfs are splendid, particularly Cherry Jones (as the Federal Theater leader), John Turturro (an actor in Welles's company), Susan Sarandon (Mussolini's beautiful emissary), Ruben Blades (exiled Mexican painter Diego Rivera), Bill Murray (vaudeville ventriloquist Tommy Crickshaw) and Vanessa Redgrave (arts doyenne Comtesse LaGrange).

•

CRAFT, THE

1996, 100 mins, US Ⓥ col

Dir Andrew Fleming ***Prod*** Douglas Wick ***Scr*** Peter Filardi, Andrew Fleming ***Ph*** Alexander Gruszynski ***Ed*** Jeff Freeman ***Mus*** Graeme Revell ***Art*** Marek Dobrowolski

Act Robin Tunney, Fairuza Balk, Neve Campbell, Rachel True, Skeet Ulrich, Helen Shaver (Columbia)

Four gifted and attractive actresses struggle hard to lend dramatic coherence to *The Craft*, a neatly crafted film that begins most promisingly as a black comedy a la *Heathers* but gradually succumbs to its tricky machinery of special effects.

Story begins with the relocation of Sarah (Robin Tunney) to yet another high school, L.A.'s St. Benedict's Academy, where she's at first completely isolated. Sarah attracts the attention of three outsiders banished to the margins of the school's pecking order—they're described as "the bitches of Eastwick."

The strongest of the bunch is white trash Nancy (Fairuza Balk), whose mother and brutish stepfather endlessly bicker and fight. The other clique members are Bonnie (Neve Campbell), an insecure teenager badly burned and scarred in a fire, and Rochelle (Rachel True), an overachiever who hides her wounds deep inside.

The movie depicts, often quite sharply and humorously, the adventures of tough girls who know they'll never fit in but are nonetheless determined not to let their peers back them into a corner. Early episodes in which the girls probe the dark corners of their minds, as they embark on a journey that takes them from passivity to intoxicating empowerment, are cleverly scripted and sharply acted. The revenge that Sarah and her cohorts take upon obnoxiously insensitive guys like cocky football jock Chris (Skeet Ulrich) are singularly biting.

Unfortunately, pic begins to lose its narrative pull after the first reel, and yarn progressively deteriorates into a series of well-executed special effects, culminating in a power play between Nancy and Sarah that is staged in routine horror-movie style.

•

CRANES ARE FLYING, THE

SEE: LETYAT ZHURAVLI

•

CRASH

1996, 98 mins, Canada Ⓥ ⦿ col

Dir David Cronenberg ***Prod*** David Cronenberg ***Scr*** David Cronenberg ***Ph*** Peter Suschitzky ***Ed*** Ronald Sanders ***Mus*** Howard Shore ***Art*** Carol Spier

Act James Spader, Holly Hunter, Elias Koteas, Deborah Unger, Rosanna Arquette, Peter MacNeil (Alliance)

A forbiddingly frigid piece of esoteric erotica, David Cronenberg's *Crash* goes all the way with a sexual obsession that few people will turn on to. Faithfully adapted from J. G. Ballard's 1973 cult novel and directed with precise control, this attempt to transform a fetish for automobile accidents and bodily injury into a metaphor for human adaptation to the technological age remains an exceedingly intellectual work of cold sensuality.

Cronenberg lays his cards on the table in the opening scene, which has gorgeous blond Catherine Ballard (Deborah Unger) becoming turned on by flesh-to-metal contact before being approached from behind by a man. At the same time, her husband, James (James Spader), has sex with a woman at work. A bad auto accident puts a banged-up James in the hospital with a severely broken leg, and kills the man in the other car. The dead man's wife, Helen Remington (Holly Hunter), suffers only moderate injuries. James and Helen's shared experience leads them into a spontaneous and very hot sexual relationship. A strange scientific researcher from the hospital, Vaughan (Elias Koteas), provides their entry into the netherworld of the automotive turn-on.

Characters lack any meaning or connection with one another except in their pushing of sexual limits. Sex scenes are clear about what's going on, even if below-the-belt nudity is only fleeting. Nothing here is remotely a turn-on from an audience p.o.v.

Set largely at night in Toronto [compared with the original book, set around London], impeccably composed pic is dominated by blues, grays and purples, which accentuate the feeling of utter cool.

•

CRASH DIVE

1943, 105 mins, US col

Dir Archie Mayo ***Prod*** Milton Sperling ***Scr*** Jo Swerling ***Ph*** Leon Shamroy ***Ed*** Walter Thompson, Ray Curtiss ***Mus*** David Buttolph ***Art*** Richard Day, Wiard B. Ihnen

Act Tyrone Power, Anne Baxter, Dana Andrews, James Gleason, May Whitty, Henry Morgan (20th Century-Fox)

Crash Dive is 20th-Fox's salute to the submarine crews of the U.S. Navy. It packs a terrific wallop.

Endowed with a fine cast, headed by Tyrone Power, it has been directed with consummate skill and artistry by Archie Mayo, unfolds a tense, dramatic series of undersea warfare episodes and, visually, through its excellent Technicolor treatment, is at all times highly distinctive.

True, the script concocted by Jo Swerling from an original by W. R. Burnett can hardly lay claim to originality, with the film having a tendency to slip during its maudlin boy-chases-gal sequences in the early chapters. But once the preliminaries have been disposed of and the USS *Corsair* starts hitting the high seas, it's a tense, arresting saga of sub warfare that's as educational as it is entertaining. When the picture deals with the adventures of the sub's crew in maneuvering the ship through narrow channels to elude sub nets and a profusion of mines, with only a matter of inches the difference between life and death, it creates an overwhelming suspense.

1943: Best Special Effects (Fred Sersen, Roger Heman)

•

CRASH OF SILENCE, THE

SEE: MANDY

•

CRAWLING EYE, THE

SEE: THE TROLLENBERG TERROR

•

CRAZY IN ALABAMA

1999, 111 mins, US Ⓥ ⦿ ▭ col

Dir Antonio Banderas ***Prod*** Meir Teper, Linda Goldstein Knowlton, Debra Hill, Diane Sillan Isaacs ***Scr*** Mark Childress ***Ph*** Julio Macat ***Ed*** Maysie Hoy, Robert C. Jones ***Mus*** Mark Snow ***Art*** Cecilia Montiel

Act Melanie Griffith, David Morse, Lucas Black, Cathy Moriarty, Meat Loaf Aday, Rod Steiger (Green Moon/Columbia)

Tackling a dual-tracked story with a blackly comic tone that would rep a tricky challenge even for a seasoned filmmaker, Antonio Banderas pulls off a creditable directorial debut with *Crazy in Alabama*. Novelist-screenwriter Mark Childress's yarn combines an often wacky look at a Southern bombshell, who heads for Hollywood after murdering her husband, and a deadly serious account of racial strife in the South, circa 1965.

Lucille (Melanie Griffith), a 40-ish madcap with a motormouth, leaves seven kids with her mother to pursue the dream she's always put on hold. And, oh yes, she's just killed her husband and is toting his severed head along with her.

Curious events are seen from the p.o.v. of Lucille's insightful 13-year-old nephew Peejoe (Lucas Black), who, along with his brother Wiley (David Speck), temporarily moves into the mortuary where Lucille's brother Dove (David Morse) works. The low-key, wryly humorous events in the small Alabama town contrast oddly with the coarser nature of Lucille's journey. But a lighter and more attentive hand attends the significant developments in the community, where long-standing segregationist norms are about to be tested.

Outfitted in a jet-black wig, Griffith, who pursued the property since its publication six years ago, initially seems a bit long in the tooth as a woman embarking on a Hollywood quest, but the age factor ultimately adds a touch of poignancy to her journey. Black delivers a compellingly sharp-witted teenager, and Morse is appealingly understated as a middle-aged man who comes to the same social awareness as Peejoe.

•

CRAZY MAMA

1975, 82 mins, US Ⓥ col

Dir Jonathan Demme ***Prod*** Julie Corman ***Scr*** Robert Thom ***Ph*** Bruce Logan ***Ed*** Allan Holzman, Lewis Teague ***Mus*** Marshall Lieb (co-ord.) ***Art*** Peter Jamison

Act Cloris Leachman, Stuart Whitman, Ann Sothern, Tisha Sterling, Jim Backus, Donn Most (New World)

Spanning nearly three decades, Cloris Leachman stars as she starts in Jerusalem, Ark, 1932, when lawmen kill papa (Clint Kimbrough), making mother Ann Sothern a widow. They jump the 60-acre farm; next are in Long Beach, CA, circa 1958, where the pair are evicted from their beauty salon for back rent, and Leachman has a pretty, pregnant teenage daughter (Linda Pure) with a boyfriend (Donn Most). The three femmes, upset, steal cars and shoot their way across the U.S.

Next the sextet robs a motorcycle race box office, then does a bank heist, shooting all the way.

This *Bonnie and Clyde*-style, sadistic, sordid unveiling of wasted lives ends in 1959, with Leachman, her daughter and their studs running a Miami Beach snack bar. With good performances from familiar players, *Crazy Mama* appears a waste of top talent in a mindless life of crime.

•

CRAZY PEOPLE

1990, 90 mins, US Ⓥ ⦿ col

Dir Tony Bill ***Prod*** Tom Barad ***Scr*** Mitch Markowitz ***Ph*** Victor J. Kemper ***Ed*** Mia Goldman ***Mus*** Cliff Eidelman ***Art*** John J. Lloyd

Act Dudley Moore, Daryl Hannah, Paul Reiser, Mercedes Ruehl, J. T. Walsh, David Paymer (Paramount)

Crazy People combines a hilarious dissection of advertising with a warm view of so-called insanity. Pic had a rocky production history as two weeks into lensing John Malkovich was replaced by Dudley Moore, and screen-writer Mitch Markowitz ceded his directing chair to Tony Bill. Finished film is a credit to all hands.

Moore toplines as a burnt-out ad man working with fast-talking Paul Reiser (perfect as a type commonplace in business) for a tyranical boss, J. T. Walsh. Under deadline pressure, he turns in campaigns that attempt an honest approach.

This raises more than eyebrows, but when Moore hands in "Most of our passengers get there alive" to promote United Air Lines, the film jump-cuts emphatically to Bennington Sanitarium, his new home.

Director Bill envisions this looney bin as an idyllic retreat, with a natural, warm and beautiful Daryl Hannah as Moore's nutty playmate there. The visual mismatch (she towers over the diminutive star) pays off.

Markowitz's ingenious twists overcome the gag-driven nature of the film. Moore's oddball ads accidentally get printed and create a consumer rush. Walsh hires Moore back and soon the inmates are virtually running the asylum.

•

CRAZY PETE

SEE: PIERROT LE FOU

•

CREATURE FROM THE BLACK LAGOON

1954, 79 mins, US Ⓥ ⦿ b/w

Dir Jack Arnold ***Prod*** William Alland ***Scr*** Harry Essex, Arthur Ross ***Ph*** William E. Snyder ***Ed*** Ted J. Kent ***Mus*** Joseph Gershenson

Act Richard Carlson, Julie Adams, Richard Denning, Antonio Moreno, Nestor Paiva, Whit Bissell (Universal)

This 3-D hackle-raiser reverts to the prehistoric. After the discovery of a web-fingered skeleton hand in the Amazon region, a scientific expedition heads into the steaming tropics to hunt more fossils. In the backwaters of the Amazon they come across a still living Gill Man, half-fish, half-human.

The 3-D lensing adds to the eerie effects of the underwater footage, as well as to the monster's several appearances on land. The below-water scraps between skin divers and the prehistoric thing are thrilling and will pop goose pimples on the susceptible fan, as will the closeup scenes of the scaly, gilled creature. Jack Arnold's direction does a first-rate job of developing chills and suspense, and James C. Havens rates a good credit for his direction of the underwater sequences.

Richard Carlson and Julie Adams co-star in the William Alland production and carry off the thriller very well. As befitting the Amazonian setting, Adams appears mostly in brief shorts or swimsuits.

•

CREEPING UNKNOWN, THE

SEE: THE QUATERMASS EXPERIMENT

•

CREEPSHOW

1982, 129 mins, US Ⓥ ⦿ col

Dir George A. Romero ***Prod*** Richard P. Rubinstein ***Scr*** Stephen King ***Ph*** Michael Gornick ***Ed*** Pasquale Buba, Paul Hirsch, Michael Spolan, George A. Romero ***Mus*** John Harrison ***Art*** Cletus Anderson

Act Hal Holbrook, Adrienne Barbeau, Fritz Weaver, Leslie Nielsen, Carrie Nye, E. G. Marshall (Laurel)

George Romero, collaborating with writer Stephen King, again proves his adeptness at combining thrills with tongue-in-cheek humor. He links five tales with animated bridges in comic book style.

The gimmick is used with reserve and the segments work fine on their own merits. The first, *Father's Day*, is a shaggy-dog tale of a despised patriarch who returns from the grave to collect his holiday cake.

In *The Lonesome Death of Jordy Verrill*, author King takes on the title role. He's a dull hillbilly who sees dollar signs when a meteor falls on his property. However, his fate is to turn into a plant.

In *Something to Tide You Over*, Leslie Nielsen plans a slow watery death for his wife and her lover. This is followed by *The Crate*, about a malevolent creature in a box from an Arctic expedition, and the program finishes off with *They're Creeping Up on You*, in which millionaire E. G. Marshall is literally bugged to death by his phobia of insects.

•

CREEPSHOW 2
1987, 89 mins, US Ⓥ ⊙ col
Dir Michael Gornick ***Prod*** David Ball ***Scr*** George A. Romero ***Ph*** Dick Hart, Tom Hurwitz ***Ed*** Peter Weatherly ***Mus*** Les Reed, Rick Wakemen ***Art*** Bruce Miller
Act Lois Chiles, George Kennedy, Dorothy Lamour, Tom Savini, Domenick John (Laurel)

Tied together with some humdrum animated sequences, the three vignettes on offer obviously were produced on the absolute cheap, and are deficient in imagination and scare quotient.

Whatever interest some might have in seeing George Kennedy and Dorothy Lamour is undercut by their roles as helpless vicims of a small-town robbery and double murder in the first tale, *Old Chief Wood'nhead*, a lifeless and listless yarn about a storefront Indian who comes to life to avenge the crimes.

The Raft concerns four goodtime teens trapped on a platform in the middle of a small lake, then eaten alive by what looks like tarpaulin covered with black goo.

The Hitchhiker is a painfully protracted telling of how rich gal Lois Chiles hits and runs from a hitchhiker on the highway at night and is then haunted by the bloodied but far-from-dead fellow.

•

CRIES AND WHISPERS
SEE: VISKNINGAR OCH ROP

•

CRIME AND PUNISHMENT
1935, 85 mins, US b/w
Dir Josef von Sternberg ***Prod*** B. P. Schulberg ***Scr*** S. K. Lauren, Joseph Anthony ***Ph*** Lucien Ballard ***Mus*** Arthur Honegger ***Art*** Stephen Goosson
Act Edward Arnold, Peter Lorre, Marian Marsh, Tala Birell, Elisabeth Risdon, Douglass Dumbrille (Columbia)

The murder of the miserly pawnbroker (Mrs. Patrick Campbell in a ruthless, unsympathetic characterization) is the premeditated crime by Peter Lorre. Edward Arnold's old-fashioned police methods, combined with psychological auto-suggestion and ultimate self-destruction, is the reincarnation of the punishment. Both contribute capital performances.

Sometimes the situations get out of hand and even Sternberg's directorial and camera genius can't cope with them. Usually it's a script deficiency [from the novel by Dostoyevsky] when that occurs.

One is permitted to become a bit too conscious of the incongruity of a Bible-totin' harlot, an ingenue of a prostie with a Dietrichesque physiognomy and hairstyle. When that realization comes, the audience starts thinking of the past Sternberg and Dietrich pictures. That's when the too pretty Marian Marsh, as the St. Petersburg streetwalker, doesn't assist in the romance chores she's been endowed to sustain.

•

CRIME IN THE STREETS
1956, 91 mins, US b/w
Dir Don Siegel ***Prod*** Vincent M. Fennelly ***Scr*** Reginald Rose ***Ph*** Sam Leavitt ***Ed*** Richard C. Meyer ***Mus*** Franz Waxman ***Art*** Serge Krizman
Act James Whitmore, John Cassavetes, Sal Mineo, Mark Rydell, Virginia Gregg, Peter Votrian (Lindbrook/Allied Artists)

Crime in the Streets, in its jump from a TV origin, sets out to be a gutsy melodrama about slum area delinquents and, within the framework of Reginald Rose's highly contrived story, succeeds in making its shock points under Don Siegel's pat directorial handling.

Plot poses the pitch that the young bums shown here need love and understanding to offset their squalid surroundings. However, as characterized by story and acting, it's likely they would be just as unpleasant and unwholesome in any setting.

John Cassavetes is the bitter, unlovable young tough who leads the street rat pack. When an adult (Malcolm Atterbury) slaps the young bum across the mouth for getting too uppity, the juve hood plots murder.

Only two of the gang (Sal Mineo and Mark Rydell, latter repeating from TV) go along with the scheme to kill Atterbury.

James Whitmore heads the cast as a settlement worker who does little more than observe and offer unheeded counsel.

•

CRIMES AND MISDEMEANORS
1989, 104 mins, US Ⓥ ⊙ col
Dir Woody Allen ***Prod*** Robert Greenhut ***Scr*** Woody Allen ***Ph*** Sven Nykvist ***Ed*** Susan E. Morse ***Art*** Santo Loquasto
Act Martin Landau, Woody Allen, Mia Farrow, Alan Alda, Anjelica Huston, Sam Waterston (Rollins/Joffe)

Woody Allen ambitiously mixes his two favored strains of cinema, melodrama and comedy, with mixed results in *Crimes and Misdemeanors*. Two loosely linked stories here concern eye doctor Martin Landau and documentary director Allen, each facing moral dilemmas. The structural and stylistic conceit is that when Landau is onscreen, the film is dead serious, even solemn, while Allen's own appearance onscreen signals hilarious satire and priceless one-liners.

Landau's problem is simple: his mistress (Anjelica Huston, shrill in an underwritten role) threatens to go to his wife (Claire Bloom) and reveal all, including Landau's previous embezzlement activities. At wit's end, he seeks the assistance of his ne'er-do-well brother (Jerry Orbach), who orders up a hit man from out of town to waste Huston.

Meanwhile, Allen, unhappily married to Joanna Gleason, has fallen in love with TV documentary producer Mia Farrow, whom he meets while directing a TV docu profiling his enemy and brother-in-law, (Alan Alda). Alda is perfect casting as a successful TV comedy producer, whose pompous attitude and easy romantic victories with women (including Farrow) exasperate Allen. Though portrayed as filled with sour grapes and envy, Allen's plight is basically sympathetic.

1989: NOMINATIONS: Best Director, Supp. Actor (Martin Landau), Original Screenplay

•

CRIMES OF DR. MABUSE, THE
SEE: DAS TESTAMENT DES DR. MABUSE

•

CRIMES OF PASSION
(AKA: CHINA BLUE)
1984, 101 mins, US Ⓥ ⊙ col
Dir Ken Russell ***Prod*** Barry Sandler ***Scr*** Barry Sandler ***Ph*** Dick Bush ***Ed*** Brian Tagg ***Mus*** Rick Wakeman ***Art*** Steve Marsh
Act Kathleen Turner, Anthony Perkins, John Laughlin, Annie Potts, Bruce Davison (New World)

The evocative Kathleen Turner thuds into a wall of inanity in this dismally written, Ken Russell-directed seriocomic examination of sexual morality among American savages.

Painfully pretentious screenplay deflects the usual Russell outrageousness and traps the four principals (all other roles are momentary) into the most superficial of characterizations.

Turner leads two lives. By day she is Joanna, a compulsively laboring sportswear designer. She is divorced and, according to her employer, frigid. But by night she is, under a blond-banged wig, China Blue, the hottest $50-a-trick hooker in the local combat zone.

Anthony Perkins's past also goes undetailed. So he has to lean on "psycho"-somatic credentials to portray a glib, sweaty, presumably ministerial, homicidal wacko who would like to be China Blue if only he had the right hormones.

Whatever the intention, and despite the technical efficiency, *Crimes of Passion* falls between the cracks. The fault line here is quite identifiable—it's in the screenplay.

[A 106-minute version was released theatrically in Europe and on video in the U.S.]

•

CRIMES OF THE FUTURE
1970, 63 mins, Canada col
Dir David Cronenberg ***Prod*** David Cronenberg ***Scr*** David Cronenberg ***Ph*** David Cronenberg ***Ed*** David Cronenberg
Act Ronald Mlodzik, Jon Lidolt, Tania Zolty, Paul Mulholland, Jack Messinger, Iain Ewing (Emergent)

Made on a $20,000 budget, David Cronenberg's second feature film, *Crimes of the Future*, bears a strong similarity to his first outing, *Stereo*, produced the year before.

Cronenberg's obsession for such matters as bodily mutation and grotesque growths, aberrant medical experiments, massive plagues and futuristic architecture are all here in a convoluted look at a future gone perverse.

The world's entire female population has evidently been wiped out, and the male population has turned to various, and disappointingly tame, alternative sexual fixations. Prime symptom of the illness is Rouge's Foam, a substance which leaks from bodily orifices and is sexually exciting in its initial stage, but deadly later on.

As he moves through the bleak but architecturally striking settings, the main character, Tripod, begins to take on the dimensions of an Edgar Allan Poe hero, a doomed figure traversing a devastated landscape.

•

CRIMES OF THE HEART
1986, 105 mins, US Ⓥ ⊙ col
Dir Bruce Beresford ***Prod*** Freddie Fields ***Scr*** Beth Henley ***Ph*** Dante Spinotti ***Ed*** Anne Goursaud ***Mus*** Georges Delerue ***Art*** Ken Adam
Act Diane Keaton, Jessica Lange, Sissy Spacek, Sam Shepard, Tess Harper, Hurd Hatfield (Fields/Sugarman/De Laurentiis)

Thoughtfully cast, superbly acted and masterfully written and directed, *Crimes of the Heart* is a winner. Diane Keaton, Jessica Lange and Sissy Spacek are a delight in their roles as southern sisters attempting to come to grips with the world, themselves and the past.

Based on Beth Henley's 1980 play, Lenny (Keaton) is the eldest of three sisters and the only one still living in the large North Carolina home of their youth. It is Lenny's birthday, a day marked by youngest sister Babe's (Spacek) jailing for shooting her husband and the arrival of middle sister Meg (Lange), visiting from L.A. where she pursues a singing career.

Far from being downbeat, the interplay between Keaton's nervously frantic Lenny, Spacek's unpredictable Babe and Lange as the hard-living Meg is as funny as it is riveting.

Bruce Beresford's direction within the house is graceful, effortlessly following the action from room to room. Sam Shepard notches a strong performance in the relatively small part of Doc, and Tess Harper shows her ability as a comic actress in the role of neighbor/relative Chick.

1986: NOMINATIONS: Best Actress (Sissy Spacek), Supp. Actress (Tess Harper), Adapted Screenplay

•

CRIMETIME
1996, 118 mins, UK/Germany Ⓥ ⊙
Dir George Sluizer ***Prod*** David Pupkewitz ***Scr*** Brendan Somers ***Ph*** Jules van den Steenhoven ***Ed*** Fabienne Rawley ***Mus*** Ray Williams (prod.) ***Art*** Bernd Lepel
Act Stephen Baldwin, Pete Postlethwaite, Sadie Frost, Geraldine Chaplin, Karen Black, James Faulkner (Focus/Kinowelt)

Crimetime is a senseless thriller about a futuristic society in which there is no distinction between reality and its representation by the media. Toplined by a seriously miscast Stephen Baldwin and featuring a cop-out ending that's shamelessly lifted from Brian DePalma's *Body Double*, pic is so cynical that it ends up shooting itself in the foot.

Baldwin plays Bobby, an ambitious but unemployed actor catapulted to stardom when he's cast as a serial killer in a TV crime re-enactment program called *Crimetime*. Being a pretentious Method actor, he begins to immerse himself obsessively in the details of the role. Bobby becomes a small-screen idol when Sidney (Pete Postlethwaite), a real psychotic killer, is seduced by the glamorous portrayal of his actions and desperately seeks greater fame.

George Sluizer directs in a glitzy but trivial and impersonal style, continuing a downward slide in a career that includes the genuinely scarey, original Dutch version of *The Vanishing*. As Bobby's g.f., Sadie Frost is so tedious that she makes her role even more unappealing than it is on the page.

•

CRIME WITHOUT PASSION
1934, 70 mins, US b/w
Dir Ben Hecht, Charles MacArthur ***Prod*** Ben Hecht, Charles MacArthur ***Scr*** Ben Hecht, Charles MacArthur ***Ph*** Lee Garmes ***Art*** Albert Johnson
Act Claude Rains, Margo, Whitney Bourne, Stanley Ridges, Paula Trueman, Esther Dale (Paramount)

This is about a great criminal lawyer. Always, up to now, it has been customary to get the mouthpiece into a jam of his own early and then let him wiggle out of it.

But Ben Hecht and Charles MacArthur, who don't like literary rules and regulations and consistently show it in their writing, have taken the great mouthpiece theme and turned it upside down. Their courtroom scene, instead of being the closing clincher, opens the picture, and the story builds up to the lawyer's personal jam in preference to building away from it.

Their lawyer is brilliant in a courtroom, but a combination egomaniac and chump in a boudoir. He's mixed up with a brunette dancer whom he'd like to shake for a blonde, but the brunette has him hooked. His profound egoism in his love-making dictates another procedure for airing a dame, i.e., planting false evidence to throw a suspicion of unfaithfulness upon the lady.

It leads to an accidental shooting and apparent killing of the brunette in a scramble for a gun, and then the picture gets hot.

Claude Rains, an expert actor, plays the lawyer with much intelligence. Leading girl (the brunette) is a young lady named just Margo. In highly dramatic moments, when Margo is expected to scream, by all rules of picture directing, Margo talks softly. Whitney Bourne, another new face, and a good-looking blonde, has much less to do than Margo, and does it satisfactorily.

•

CRIMINAL CODE, THE
1931, 97 mins, US Ⓥ b/w
Dir Howard Hawks ***Prod*** Harry Cohn ***Scr*** Seton I. Miller, Fred Niblo, Jr. ***Ph*** Ted Tetzlaff, James Wong Howe ***Ed*** Edward Curtiss ***Art*** [Edward Jewell]
Act Walter Huston, Phillips Holmes, Constance Cummings, Mary Doran, DeWitt Jennings, Boris Karloff (Columbia)

A prison picture but an excellent interpretation of the play of the same name [by Martin Flavin]. Howard Hawks's direction makes everything count, while Walter Huston here probably turns in his best modern characterization to date as a district attorney with a daughter who becomes warden of a prison. The love theme is taken care of by the girl and a young prisoner whom Huston has previously sent away for manslaughter while knowing a smart defense could have saved him.

The transposition from stage to screen has taken the proverbial liberties in dissolving the tragedy of the play into a happy ending. Plenty of action all the way, in and out of the prison yard, with the performances of Huston. Phillips Holmes, and Boris Karloff always holding it together. Karloff is from the stage cast.

1930/31: NOMINATION: Best Adaptation

•

CRIMINAL LAW
1988, 117 mins, US Ⓥ ⦿ col
Dir Martin Campbell ***Prod*** Robert Maclean, Hilary Heath ***Scr*** Mark Kasdan ***Ph*** Philip Meheux ***Ed*** Christopher Wimble ***Mus*** Jerry Goldsmith ***Art*** Curtis Schnell
Act Gary Oldman, Kevin Bacon, Karen Young, Joe Don Baker, Tess Harper, Elizabeth Sheppard (Hemdale/Northwood)

A very good actor plays a good lawyer in a badly written and directed crime drama and loses the case for suspenseful filmmaking in *Criminal Law*.

Director Martin Campbell (BBC's *Edge of Darkness*) opens his feature with police in Boston (played by Montreal) discovering a mutilated rape victim in a rain-soaked tableau of blackish-blue gloom, a mood/color motif that's recycled throughout the movie. Action then fast-forwards to a courtroom where cocky lawyer Ben Chase, rendered with superb American accent and mannerisms by British Gary Oldman, pulls a sly trick out of his hat to demolish an eyewitness and free his wealthy, self-absorbed client Martin Thiel (Kevin Bacon).

No sooner is Bacon back on the streets, however, than the killer strikes again. Oldman realizes he's unleashed a monster, and is reminded of this constantly by two detectives (Joe Don Baker and Tess Harper). The stage is set for a clumsily plotted psychological cat-and-mouse game between Oldman and Bacon.

Although Bacon is convincing as the icy, deranged killer, his character's menace is undermined by the story's ill-defined pretensions as an essay on the American legal system and a herky-jerky continuity that's fatiguing instead of tingling.

•

CRIMSON KIMONO, THE
1959, 81 mins, US b/w
Dir Samuel Fuller ***Prod*** Samuel Fuller ***Scr*** Samuel Fuller ***Ph*** Sam Leavitt ***Ed*** Jerome Thoms ***Mus*** Harry Sukman ***Art*** William E. Flannery, Robert Boyle
Act Victoria Shaw, Glenn Corbett, James Shigeta, Anna Lee, Paul Dubov, Jaclynne Greene (Globe/Columbia)

In *The Crimson Kimono*, Samuel Fuller tries to wrap up a murder mystery with an interracial romance. The mystery melodrama part of the film gets lost during the complicated romance, and the racial tolerance plea is cheapened by its inclusion in a film of otherwise straight action.

Fuller's story has Glenn Corbett and James Shigeta as officers of the L.A. Homicide Squad, buddies since they were fellow soldiers in the Korean War. When they meet artist Victoria Shaw, they're investigating a murder. Corbett first falls in love with Shaw, then Shigeta succumbs.

The three principals bring credibility to their roles, not too easy during moments when belief is stretched considerably. Anna Lee, Paul Dubov, Jaclynne Green and Neyle Morrow are prominent in the supporting cast.

•

CRIMSON PIRATE, THE
1952, 104 mins, UK/US Ⓥ ⦿ col
Dir Robert Siodmak ***Prod*** [Harold Hecht] ***Scr*** Roland Kibbee ***Ph*** Otto Heller ***Ed*** Jack Harris ***Mus*** William Alwyn ***Art*** Paul Sheriff, Ken Adam
Act Burt Lancaster, Eva Bartok, Nick Cravat, Torin Thatcher, James Hayter, Margot Grahame (Norma/Warner)

Swashbucking sea fables get a good-natured spoofing in *The Crimson Pirate*, with Burt Lancaster providing the muscles and dash for the takeoff.

The screen story is cloaked with a sense of humor as it pictures Lancaster, the famed Crimson Pirate, plying his trade on the high seas.

Opening finds the pirates capturing a 30-gun galleon by trickery and then scheming to sell its cargo of cannon to rebels trying to shake off the shackles of the King of Spain. The buccaneers also plan to then reveal the rebel group's whereabouts to the crown for more gold, but there are a girl and such complications as an awakening to right and wrong.

Lancaster and his deaf-mute pal (Nick Cravat) sock the acrobatics required of hero and partner to a fare-thee-well under Robert Siodmak's direction.

•

CRIMSON TIDE
1995, 115 mins, US Ⓥ ⦿ ⌑ col
Dir Tony Scott ***Prod*** Don Simpson, Jerry Bruckheimer ***Scr*** Michael Schiffer ***Ph*** Dariusz Wolski ***Ed*** Chris Lebenzon ***Mus*** Hans Zimmer ***Art*** Michael White
Act Denzel Washington, Gene Hackman, George Dzundza, Viggo Mortensen, James Gandolfini, Matt Craven (Hollywood)

The torpedoes, missiles and testosterone levels are all on red alert in *Crimson Tide*, the latest exercise in high-tech macho from director Tony Scott and producers Don Simpson and Jerry Bruckheimer. A brink-of-nuclear-disaster thriller [from a screen story by Michael Schiffer and Richard P. Henrick] set aboard a tension-fraught U.S. submarine, this is a boy's movie all the way.

Exposition is handled with terrific dispatch, as a pseudo-CNN news report lays out the state of things in Russia, where some nationalist right-wingers initiate a civil war and grab control of a Pacific Coast nuclear base. The U.S. sends the USS Alabama towards the hot zone.

At the helm is Capt. Frank Ramsey (Gene Hackman). Known for chewing up and spitting out executive officers, he engages for the fateful voyage Lt. Commander Ron Hunter (Denzel Washington), never tested under fire. When an initial message ordering a nuclear attack arrives, the entire crew nervously prepares to launch World War III, even while being pursued by a rogue Russian submarine.

Up to this halfway point, *Crimson Tide* is an exciting, efficient, straight-ahead thriller. But as the inevitable moment of truth arrives, is aborted, arrives again and is once more postponed, and as command of the ship seesaws back and forth, plausibility becomes strained and the story comes to feel waterlogged.

Still, director Scott makes the most of his cramped surroundings, keeping the action and the camera hopping. Washington and Hackman create worthy adversaries.

NOMINATIONS: Film Editing, Best Sound, Best Sound Effects Editing

•

CRISIS
1950, 95 mins, US b/w
Dir Richard Brooks ***Prod*** Arthur Freed ***Scr*** Richard Brooks ***Ph*** Ray June ***Ed*** Robert J. Kern ***Mus*** Miklos Rozsa ***Art*** Cedric Gibbons, Preston Ames
Act Cary Grant, Jose Ferrer, Paula Raymond, Signe Hasso, Ramon Novarro, Gilbert Roland (M-G-M)

Dictatorship versus the right of man to freedom is the theme, and the script [from a story by George Tabori] and direction by Richard Brooks lets it get up on the soapbox too frequently.

Footage kicks off with Cary Grant, a brain surgeon, and his wife (Paula Raymond) vacationing in a revolution-ridden Latin country. The doctor and his wife are kidnapped by the presidente's troops and taken to the besieged capital. There Grant finds the dictator-president suffering from a brain tumor and he is ordered to operate.

Meantime, revolutionaries, led by Gilbert Roland, exert pressure to have the president (Jose Ferrer) die under the knife.

Roland is very good. So is Ramon Novarro, the dictator's colonel.

•

CRISS CROSS
1949, 87 mins, US Ⓥ b/w
Dir Robert Siodmak ***Prod*** Michael Kraike ***Scr*** Daniel Fuchs ***Ph*** Franz Planer ***Ed*** Ted J. Kent ***Mus*** Miklos Rozsa ***Art*** Bernard Herzbrun, Boris Leven
Act Burt Lancaster, Yvonne De Carlo, Dan Duryea, Stephen McNally, Richard Long (Universal)

Utilizing liberal flashbacks, the film [from the novel by Don Tracy] unreels the relentless, unswerving devotion of Burt Lancaster for his divorced wife (Yvonne De Carlo). Basically he's an honest guy in contrast to the shaky character of his ex-spouse, who has become the moll of bigtime crook Dan Duryea.

Caught in a rendezvous with his old flame by Duryea, Lancaster fends off the jealousy of his rival by suggesting the group pull off an armored car holdup. As the driver of the payroll truck, he'll secretly work with the crooks.

Under Robert Siodmak's knowing directiion, the flashbacks blend into a cohesive unit and are never confusing or draggy. His staging of the holdup scene is a masterful job.

Lancaster's role is a made-to-order part of a two-fisted square-shooter who gets fouled up in a jam through no fault of his own.

•

CRISS CROSS
1992, 100 mins, US Ⓥ col
Dir Chris Menges ***Prod*** Anthea Sylbert ***Scr*** Scott Sommer ***Ph*** Ivan Strasburg ***Ed*** Tony Lawson ***Mus*** Trevor Jones ***Art*** Crispian Sallis
Act Goldie Hawn, Arliss Howard, James Gannon, David Arnott, Keith Carradine, J. C. Quinn (M-G-M/Hawn-Sylbert)

Told from the perspective of a 12-year-old boy, this earnest, languid drama [from a novella by Scott Sommer] might have worked if it weren't so painfully obvious and slow.

Set at the time of the 1969 moon landing, *Criss Cross* deals with a boy, Chris (David Arnott), who's lost his moral compass, living with his mom (Goldie Hawn) in a rundown Key West hotel. Hawn's a waitress who turns stripper to pay the rent, while Dad (Keith Carradine, in a brief cameo) split three years earlier.

Almost an hour in, the story finally stumbles into a plot as Chris discovers he's been transporting hidden cocaine from a fisherman to one of the locals. He decides to try and score some cash on his own to help his mother find a respectable job.

Cinematographer-turned-director Chris Menges, who made his directing debut with the 1988 *A World Apart*, has a good eye for trappings of the Key West lifestyle but doesn't bring any life to the story or characters. Pic doesn't display much of Hawn except off-screen sessions with a physical trainer, evident thanks to the skimpy Key West attire and a striptease number.

•

CRITTERS
1986, 86 mins, US Ⓥ ⦿ col
Dir Stephen Herek ***Prod*** Rupert Harvey ***Scr*** Stephen Herek, Domonic Muir, Don Opper ***Ph*** Tom Suhrstedt ***Ed*** Larry Bock ***Mus*** David Newman ***Art*** Gregg Fonseca
Act Dee Wallace, M. Emmet Walsh, Billy Green Bush, Scott Grimes, Nadine Van Der Velde, Terrence Mann (New Line/Sho)

Critters resemble oversize hairballs and roll like tumbleweeds when prodded into action, the perfect menace for this irritatingly insipid and lightweight film which unfolds with plodding predictability and leaves few clichés unturned.

Within minutes of film's start, a small band of voracious Krites (a.k.a., Critters) easily escape from a "maximum security asteroid" and are whizzing toward Kansas with two crack bounty hunters in pursuit.

Establish the sleepy life of farmer (yes) Brown and his wife Helen, as credibly performed by Billy Green Bush and

Dee Wallace as can be expected with such material, rambunctious son Brad and sexually budding daughter April. There's also M. Emmet Walsh as the familiar small-town sheriff.

Co-writers Domonic Muir [who penned the original story] and Stephen Herek, latter doubling as film's director, manage to deflate what little suspense is created by subtitling the Critters's chatter. The final result is neither scary nor humorous.

•

CRITTERS 2: THE MAIN COURSE

1988, 87 mins, US Ⓥ ⦿ col

Dir Mick Garris ***Prod*** Barry Opper ***Scr*** D. T. Twohy, Mick Garris ***Ph*** Russell Carpenter ***Ed*** Charles Bornstein ***Mus*** Nicholas Pike ***Art*** Philip Dean Foreman

Act Scott Grimes, Liane Curtis, Don Opper, Barry Corbin, Tom Hodges (New Line/Sho/Smart Egg)

All concerned are back in small Grover's Bend, where Krites terrorized residents just two years earlier. Tip-off that they've returned is appearance of dozens and dozens of large eggs with colorful patterns on them.

Outer space bounty hunters Ug and Lee (Terrence Mann and Roxanne Kernohan), as well as Charlie (Don Opper), are dispatched to planet Earth to complete their earlier attempt to obliterate the nasty little killers.

Coincidentally, young Brad Brown (Scott Grimes) comes to visit his Nana (Herta Ware) and gets blamed again by some townfolk for arrival of the Critters, which are now hatching and eating at a furious pace.

Film perfectly weaves together the gruesome behaviour of these bloodthirsty creatures and the comic asides that keep things gliding along.

•

"CROCODILE" DUNDEE

1986, 102 mins, Australia Ⓥ ⦿ ▭ col

Dir Peter Faiman ***Prod*** John Cornell ***Scr*** Paul Hogan, Ken Shadie, John Cornell ***Ph*** Russell Boyd ***Ed*** David Stiven ***Mus*** Peter Best ***Art*** Graham Walker

Act Paul Hogan, Linda Kozlowski, John Meillon, Mark Blum, Michael Lombard, David Gulpilil (Rimfire)

As the title character, Paul Hogan limns a laconic if rather dim crocodile hunter who achieves some notoriety after surviving an attack by a giant croc. New York reporter Linda Kozlowski journeys to the Northern Territory to cover the story.

Plot bogs down somewhat as Hogan and Kozlowski trudge through the outback. However, proceedings are intermittently enlivened by John Meillon who is slyly humorous as Dundee's manager and partner in a safari tour business.

Rather implausibly, Kozlowski persuades Hogan to return to Gotham with her. Here he is initiated into the delights of the Big Apple.

Director Peter Faiman, essaying his first theatrical venture after an impressive career in Australian TV, directing Hogan's shows among others, has problems with the pacing and a script [from a story by Hogan] that has its flat, dull spots.

Hogan is comfortable enough playing the wry, irreverent, amiable Aussie that seems close to his own persona, and teams well with Kozlowski, who radiates lots of charm, style and spunk.

[Quotation marks were put around the word *Crocodile* by distributor Paramount on release outside Australia and seven minutes cut from the running time.]

1986: NOMINATION: Best Original Screenplay

•

"CROCODILE" DUNDEE II

1988, 111 mins, US Ⓥ ⦿ ▭ col

Dir John Cornell ***Prod*** John Cornell, Jane Scott ***Scr*** Paul Hogan, Brett Hogan ***Ph*** Russell Boyd ***Ed*** David Stiven ***Mus*** Peter Best ***Art*** Lawrence Eastwood

Act Paul Hogan, Linda Kozlowski, Charles Dutton, Hechter Ubarry, John Meillon, Juan Fernandez (Rimfire/Paramount)

"Crocodile" Dundee II is a disappointing follow-up to the disarmingly charming first feature with Aussie star Paul Hogan. Sequel is too slow to constitute an adventure and has too few laughs to be a comedy.

Story unfolds with Hogan making a passable attempt to find gainful employment at just about the time Linda Kozlowski's ex-lover is killed in Colombia for taking photos of a cocaine king as he shoots one of his runners. The nefarious Rico (Hechter Ubarry is much too cute for this role) learns the photos were sent to Kozlowski and in a flash he sets up an operation in a Long Island fortress with a handful of stereotypical Latino henchmen to get the incriminating evidence back. Hogan has the photos, which means Rico has Kozlowski kidnapped.

Using outback strategy, that is, getting the punks to yelp like a pack of wild dogs, Hogan gains entrance and frees his woman. Kozlowski basically does little but wait at the sidelines as Hogan flies into action.

•

CROMWELL

1970, 139 mins, UK Ⓥ ⦿ ▭ col

Dir Ken Hughes ***Prod*** Irving Allen ***Scr*** Ken Hughes ***Ph*** Geoffrey Unsworth ***Ed*** Bill Lenny ***Mus*** Frank Cordell ***Art*** John Stoll

Act Richard Harris, Alec Guinness, Robert Morley, Dorothy Tutin, Frank Finlay, Timothy Dalton (Allen/Columbia)

The nub of director Ken Hughes's $9 million film (from his own screenplay, with Ronald Harwood as "script consultant") is the confrontation of the two complex leading characters, Oliver Cromwell and King Charles I. Richard Harris and Alec Guinness, respectively, give powerhouse performances.

Harris plays the idealistic, dedicated Cromwell with cold eyes, tortured, rasping voice and an inflexible spirit. He is the man who regarded Jehovah as his main ally and was determined at all costs to rescue the England he loved from the corruption of a weak, greedy court and to set up a Parliament that would be truly democratic—speaking for the people—and not be the puppets of the King.

The battle scenes (shot in Spain and using the Spanish Army) at Nazeby and Edgehill are excitingly drawn.

1970: Best Costume Design

NOMINATION: Best Original Score

•

CROOKLYN

1994, 112 mins, US Ⓥ ⦿ col

Dir Spike Lee ***Prod*** Spike Lee ***Scr*** Joie Susannah Lee, Cinque Lee, Spike Lee ***Ph*** Arthur Jafa ***Ed*** Barry Alexander Brown ***Mus*** Terence Blanchard ***Art*** Wynn Thomas

Act Alfre Woodard, Delroy Lindo, David Patrick Kelly, Zelda Harris, Carlton Williams, Sharif Rashed (40 Acres and a Mule/Universal)

Both annoying and vibrant, casually plotted and deeply personal, Spike Lee's *Crooklyn* ends up being as compelling as it is messy. Fictionalized look at the filmmaker's family life during the early 1970s [from a screen story by Joie Susannah Lee] is loud, grating, disorganized and off-putting for more than half its running time, but eventually jells into an exceedingly vivid portrait of a specific household.

The Carmichaels live in a spacious, eclectically furnished brownstone in Brooklyn. Woody, the patriarch (Delroy Lindo), is a jazz musician at a career standstill. His wife, Carolyn (Alfre Woodard), teaches school to pay the bills, and fights a losing battle trying to control her five children. Family life consists of almost constant hollering and arguing.

Pic takes a turn, both in narrative and style, when, after an hour, the family packs up the Citroen convertible and heads south, where daughter Troy (Zelda Harris) will spend the summer with a middle-class uncle and aunt. Long section devoted to the girl's unhappy stay there is shot so that the images appear squeezed (as if a widescreen film were to be shown in a normal aspect ratio). It's here that the film begins to focus on one character.

More than three dozen period tunes are slapped onto the action, skillfully at times, awkwardly and arbitrarily at others. Performances are mostly high voltage, led by Woodard as the mother understandably about to come apart at the seams.

•

CROSS CREEK

1983, 122 mins, US Ⓥ col

Dir Martin Ritt ***Prod*** Robert B. Radnitz ***Scr*** Dalene Young ***Ph*** John A. Alonzo ***Ed*** Sidney Levin ***Mus*** Leonard Rosenman ***Art*** Walter Scott Herndon

Act Mary Steenburgen, Rip Torn, Peter Coyote, Dana Hill, Alfre Woodard, Joanna Miles (Thorn-EMI)

Cross Creek, based on the memoirs of *The Yearling* author Marjorie Kinnan Rawlings, offers a sanitized vision of her early struggle to publish a novel and the Florida backwoods which inspired her prose.

It's an uncompelling, yet warm, tale which lightly skips over the woman's travails by illustrating a series of vignettes of rural humanity. The overall effect trivializes a life and provides little insight into the artistic process.

Story opens in 1928 with Rawlings (Mary Steenburgen) deciding to leave the security of a marriage to a wealthy New Yorker for the uncertainty of life in a remote region of Florida.

The drama, what little exists in the film, centers on Rawlings's inability to sell her work until she begins writing about the events of the Florida swamp folk.

Remainder of the film focuses on Rawlings's relationship with local hotelier Norton Baskin (Peter Coyote), the recovery of her land and the warm relationship between the author and her young black housekeeper.

1983: NOMINATIONS: Best Supp. Actor (Rip Torn), Supp. Actress (Alfre Woodard), Costume Design, Original Score

•

CROSSED SWORDS

SEE: THE PRINCE AND THE PAUPER (1977)

•

CROSSFIRE

1947, 84 mins, US Ⓥ ⦿ b/w

Dir Edward Dmytryk ***Prod*** Adrian Scott ***Scr*** John Paxton ***Ph*** J. Roy Hunt ***Ed*** Harry Gerstad ***Mus*** Roy Webb ***Art*** Albert S. D'Agostino, Alfred Herman

Act Robert Young, Robert Mitchum, Robert Ryan, Gloria Grahame, Paul Kelly, Sam Levene (RKO)

Crossfire is a frank spotlight on anti-Semitism. Producer Dore Schary, in association with Adrian Scott, has pulled no punches. There is no skirting such relative fol-de-rol as intermarriage or clubs that exclude Jews. Here is a hard-hitting film [based on Richard Brooks's novel, *The Brick Foxhole*] whose whodunit aspects are fundamentally incidental to the overall thesis of bigotry and race prejudice.

There are three Roberts (Young, Mitchum and Ryan) all giving capital performances. Young is unusual as the detective captain; Mitchum is the "right" sort of cynical GI; and Ryan a commanding personality, in this instance the bigoted soldier-killer, whose sneers and leers about Sam Levene and his tribe are all too obvious.

The pic opens with the fatal slugfest in Levene's apartment, when his hospitality is abused and Ryan kills him. Director Edward Dmytryk has drawn gripping portraitures. The flashback technique is effective as it shades and colors the sundry attitudes of the heavy, as seen or recalled by the rest of the cast.

1947: NOMINATIONS: Best Picture, Director, Supp. Actor (Robert Ryan), Supp. Actress (Gloria Grahame), Screenplay

•

CROSSING DELANCEY

1988, 97 mins, US Ⓥ ⦿ col

Dir Joan Micklin Silver ***Prod*** Michael Nozik ***Scr*** Susan Sandler ***Ph*** Theo Van de Sande ***Ed*** Rick Shaine ***Mus*** Paul Chihara ***Art*** Dan Leigh

Act Amy Irving, Reizl Bozyk, Peter Riegert, Jeroen Krabbe, Sylvia Miles, Suzzy Roche (Warner)

In an unexpectedly enjoyable way, *Crossing Delancey* addresses one of the great societal issues of our day—the dilemma of how the 30-ish, attractive, successful, intelligent and unmarried female finds a mate she can be happy with.

Off-off-Broadway fans may remember the title from playwright Susan Sandler's semi-autobiographical 1985 comedy about how her loving, old-worldly and slightly overbearing Lower East Side N.Y. Jewish grandmother engages the services of a matchmaker to find her a suitable marriage partner.

Amy Irving is the dutiful granddaughter who works in a pretentious Manhattan bookstore by day, keeps her own apartment and always finds time to make frequent visits to her precious Bubbie (Yiddish actress Reizl Bozyk).

Matchmaker (Sylvia Miles) brings Irving together with an unlikely candidate, pickle maker Sam Posner (Peter Riegert). The major set-ups focus on Irving's torn affections between the rakish, smooth-talking charm of pulp novelist Anton Maes (Jeroen Krabbe), who gives good readings on rainy days at the bookstore; and the earnest, straightforward, vulnerable Riegert, who unabashedly holds his heart in his hand for her. To the credit of most of the actors, the sentimentality doesn't sink the story.

•

CROSSING GUARD, THE

1995, 114 mins, US Ⓥ ⦿ col

Dir Sean Penn ***Prod*** Sean Penn, David S. Hamburger ***Scr*** Sean Penn ***Ph*** Vilmos Zsigmond ***Ed*** Jay Cassidy ***Mus*** Jack Nitzche ***Art*** Michael Haller

Act Jack Nicholson, David Morse, Anjelica Huston, Robin Wright, Piper Laurie, Richard Bradford (Miramax)

Examining twin journeys of reconcilement—one with grief and one with guilt—Sean Penn's sophomore feature *The Crossing Guard* is a sorrowful account of the aftermath of tragedy. The high-caliber cast frequently generates charged results, and like Penn's 1991 debut, *The Indian Runner*, his roots as an actor are apparent in the film's assiduous focus on performance. But the material too often escapes his grasp as both writer and director.

Jack Nicholson plays Freddy Gale, a jeweler whose life took a seemingly irrevocable downturn following an accident in which drunk driver John Booth (David Morse) ran over and killed his seven-year-old daughter. Story picks up six years later, when Booth is released from prison after having done time for manslaughter, and revenge-obsessed Freddy informs his ex-wife, Mary (Anjelica Huston), of his intention to kill the man. A glitch with his gun leaves Booth unharmed, and a three-day reprieve is negotiated, after which Freddy swears he'll be back.

The deadline hanging over the two men steers them in opposite directions during the interim. Freddy becomes increasingly aggressive, Booth looks to a sensitive painter, JoJo (Robin Wright), to help him over his crippling guilt. The grace period over, Freddy heads back to kill Booth.

Much of the film plays awkwardly, its tone veering undecidedly between volatile drama and contemplative psychological study. Nowhere is this more of a problem than in the final reel, where Penn's skills as director are put to the test.

Nicholson at times is accompanied by a little too much of his own screen persona to completely serve the character. Morse (who top-lined *The Indian Runner*) brings integrity to an unsatisfyingly written part.

•

CROSSING THE LINE
SEE: THE BIG MAN

•

CROSS OF IRON
1977, 130 mins, UK/W. Germany Ⓥ ⊙ col
Dir Sam Peckinpah ***Prod*** Wolf C. Hartwig ***Scr*** Julius J. Epstein, Herbert Asmodi ***Ph*** John Coquillon ***Ed*** Tony Lawson, Mike Ellis, Herbert Taschner ***Mus*** Ernest Gold ***Art*** Ted Haworth, Brian Ackland Snow
Act James Coburn, Maximilian Schell, James Mason, David Warner, Klaus Lowitsch, Roger Fritz (EMI/Rapid/Terra)

Cross of Iron more than anything else affirms director Sam Peckinpah's prowess as an action filmmaker of graphic mayhem.

Told from the German viewpoint as the Wehrmacht's cream were being clobbered on the Russian front circa 1943, the production [from the book by Willi Heinrich] is well but conventionally cast, technically impressive, but ultimately violence-fixated.

The film efficiently employs James Coburn, Maximilian Schell, James Mason and David Warner as frontline Germans. Coburn plays a platoon sergeant of style, ability and soul, contemptuous of the military and sick of the war.

Cross of Iron's overwhelming image is not disillusion, even less war's absurdity, but the war itself.

•

CROSSPLOT
1969, 97 mins, UK col
Dir Alvin Rakoff ***Prod*** Robert S. Blake ***Scr*** Leigh Vance, John Kruse ***Ph*** Brendan J. Stafford ***Ed*** Bert Rule ***Mus*** Stanley Black ***Art*** Ivan King
Act Roger Moore, Martha Hyer, Claudie Lange, Alexis Kanner, Francis Matthews, Bernard Lee (United Artists/Tribune)

A thriller with a few good jokes, red herrings, a few quick genuine thrills, chases, and some mystery. It doesn't jell because the mystery is too cloudy. Motivation of most characters is indecisive and some are badly undeveloped.

Roger Moore plays a debonair ad exec with a flair for his job and a roving eye for the chicks. When a flashy, swinging campaign is okayed by a client, he has little time to find the girl around whom it will center. His only clue is a portrait with her name on it.

His problem sparks off a search for the girl, a mysterious Hungarian, which lands him up to his neck in a bewildering political ploy involving Marchers of Peace members and some anarchists.

Some bright thesps keep the often puzzling events moving deftly and breezily. Moore is not wholly convincing as a man of action.

•

CROSSROADS
1942, 82 mins, US b/w
Dir Jack Conway ***Prod*** Edwin Knopf ***Scr*** Guy Trosper ***Ph*** Joseph Ruttenberg ***Ed*** George Boemler ***Mus*** Bronislau Kaper
Act William Powell, Hedy Lamarr, Claire Trevor, Basil Rathbone, Felix Bressart, H. B. Warner (M-G-M)

This is a Grade A whodunit, with a superlative cast. The novel storyline, which would do credit to an Alfred Hitchcock thriller, has the added potency of Hedy Lamarr and William Powell.

A prominent member of France's Foreign Office, William Powell, is accused of having been a thief prior to a train accident in which he suffered a fractured skull and amnesia. Not remembering anything about his past, and since having married the beauteous Hedy Lamarr, Powell has the blackmailer arrested.

During the trial, he first learns of his alleged criminal activities under another name, but at the last minute Basil Rathbone steps in as a witness and "proves" that it's a case of mistaken identity; that the criminal Powell was supposed to have been actually had died in Africa. Once freed, Powell is then harassed by Rathbone, who says that Powell was, actually, his accomplice in the murder 13 years previously of a bank messenger and the robbery of 2 million francs.

It's good, escapist drama, without a hint of the war despite its Parisian locale, circa 1935, and evidences excellent casting and good direction. The script likewise well turned out, though better pace would have put the film in the smash class. Its only fault is a perceptible slowness at times, although the running time is a reasonable 82 minutes, caused by a plenitude of talk.

•

CROSSROADS
1986, 96 mins, US Ⓥ ⊙ col
Dir Walter Hill ***Prod*** Mark Carliner ***Scr*** John Fusco ***Ph*** John Bailey ***Ed*** Freeman Davies ***Mus*** Ry Cooder ***Art*** Jack T. Collis
Act Ralph Macchio, Joe Seneca, Jami Gertz, Joe Morton, Robert Judd, Steve Vai (Carliner/Columbia-Delphi IV)

Penned partly on the basis of actual experiences he had as a teenager touring the South as a musician, John Fusco's screenplay makes ample use of the legend of the late bluesman Robert Johnson, who left behind a tiny but potent legacy.

Ralph Macchio, a classical guitar student at Juilliard, discovers an old travelling and playing companion of Johnson's in a New York hospital. Hoping to make his reputation by finding and recording Johnson's alleged "unknown 30th song," Macchio springs old Joe Seneca from the facility, and the unlikely pair hit the road for Mississippi Delta country.

Seneca acquits himself very nicely, while director Walter Hill pulls off the expected professional job, but he pushes so hard for pace that he skates right over the opportunities for thought that the subject calls for.

•

CROUCHING TIGER, HIDDEN DRAGON
(WO HU ZANG LONG)
2000, 120 mins, Hong Kong/Taiwan/US Ⓥ ⊙ ▭ col
Dir Ang Lee ***Prod*** Bill Kong, Hsu Li Kong, Ang Lee ***Scr*** James Schamus, Wang Hui Ling, Tsai Kuo Jung ***Ph*** Peter Pau ***Ed*** Tim Squyres ***Mus*** Tan Dun ***Art*** Tim Yip ***Act*** Chow Yun-fat, Michelle Yeoh, Zhang Ziyi, Chang Chen, Lung Sihung, Cheng Pei-pei (Edko/Zoom Hunt)

From the moment 20 minutes into *Crouching Tiger, Hidden Dragon* when two fighting women begin bounding up high walls, using the ground and rooftops as if they were trampolines and treating gravity like a minor annoyance, it's clear that Ang Lee's elaborate and buoyant new production aims to be *The Matrix* of traditional martial arts films. In this, it is wonderfully and sometimes thrillingly successful, as the filmmakers apply intelligence and humor to a cartoonishly melodramatic story of intrigue and revenge and top it off with a series of stupendous combat sequences.

Using a pre-World War II novel (by Wang Du Lu) as his source material but inspired by the martial arts movies of his youth, Taiwanese helmer Lee here returns to Asia after making three English-language pictures over the last five years. This is pulp fiction presented in a grand, knowingly humorous style distinguished by star power, a strong female slant and the latest in stunts and effects. The linchpin to the film's dramatic success is Zhang, who was 19 at the time of the shoot. She has a diamond-hard charisma that the camera absorbs and magnifies, and the sight of this compact young woman holding her own with her larger opponents is a constant delight.

•

CROW, THE
1994, 100 mins, US Ⓥ ⊙ col
Dir Alex Proyas ***Prod*** Edward R. Pressman ***Scr*** David J. Schow, John Shirley ***Ph*** Dariusz Wolski ***Ed*** Dov Hoenig, Scott Smith ***Mus*** Graeme Revell ***Art*** Alex McDowell
Act Brandon Lee, Ernie Hudson, Michael Wincott, David Patrick Kelly, Angel David, Rochelle Davis

The Crow flies high. For a while rumored to be impossible to complete due to the tragic accidental death [March 31, 1993] of star Brandon Lee eight days before lensing was due to wrap, the pic that finally emerges is a seamless, pulsating, dazzlingly visual revenge fantasy that stands as one of the most effective live-actioners derived from a comic book.

Based on James O'Barr's bold comic, which has generated a considerable following since he started drawing it in the early 1980s, *The Crow* centers on a dark angel who literally rises from the dead to settle matters with the gang of thugs who killed him and his fiancée on the eve of their wedding. Tale is more pungent than poignant, however, in that it's set in a generic inner city so hellish it makes Gotham City look like the Emerald City.

Noted Aussie commercials and music video helmer Alex Proyas drenches his debut Yank feature in a claustrophobic, rain-soaked atmosphere that owes more than a little to *Blade Runner*, but pic still generates a distinctive personality.

A rock musician by trade (O'Barr patterned his character design on Iggy Pop and Bauhaus's Peter Murphy, while Lee shed pounds to resemble Black Crowes lead singer Chris Robinson), Eric (Lee) is led, one by one, to his vile assailants by a large crow that flaps above the desolate streets like a mythic bearer of dread tidings.

Pic's main problem is an exceedingly straight, A-B-C-D narrative line with no subplots, twists or turns, which even Proyas's protean direction can't keep comfortably aloft the entire time.

The 28-year-old son of the late Bruce Lee had not had a very distinguished career up until this, but there's no doubt that this role would have made him a performer to reckon with. Film is dedicated to him and his fiancée, Eliza.

•

CROW, THE: CITY OF ANGELS
1996, 84 mins, US Ⓥ ⊙ col
Dir Tim Pope ***Prod*** Edward R. Pressman, Jeff Most ***Scr*** David S. Goyer ***Ph*** Jean-Yves Escoffier ***Ed*** Michael N. Knue, Anthony Redman ***Mus*** Graeme Revell ***Art*** Alex McDowell
Act Vincent Perez, Mia Kirshner, Richard Brooks, Iggy Pop, Thomas Jane, Vincent Castellanos (Pressman/Miramax-Dimension)

European hunk Vincent Perez replaces the late Brandon Lee in the title role as an avenger who returns from the dead to punish those responsible for his murder. Strictly speaking, Perez is playing a different person: Ashe, a motorcycle mechanic who was viciously gunned down, along with his young son, after accidentally witnessing a murder.

In other words, different hero, same m.o. And, for good measure, same makeup and costume. Try to imagine a punk-rock Pierrot, and you'll get the picture.

While the first *Crow* was infused with all the dark, death-obsessed energy of a heavy-metal concert, *City of Angels* is a lumbering and repetitive bore. Worse, a great deal of the movie doesn't make any sense, even on the level of stylized fantasy. Canadian actress Mia Kirshner co-stars as Sarah, a tattoo artist—no kidding!—who, according to the movie's production notes, is supposed to be a grown-up version of the little girl played by Rochelle Davis in *The Crow*. But if director Tim Pope ever filmed a scene in which someone explained this connection, he left it on the cutting-room floor.

Overall, *City of Angels* has the look and feel of a movie that, at some point, was a good deal longer. Not necessarily better, but longer.

•

CROWD, THE
1928, 98 mins, US Ⓥ ⊙ ⊗ b/w
Dir King Vidor ***Scr*** John V. A. Weaver, King Vidor, Harry Behn, Joe Farnham ***Ph*** Henry Sharp ***Ed*** Hugh Wynn ***Art*** Cedric Gibbons, A. Arnold Gillespie
Act Eleanor Boardman, James Murray, Bert Roach, Daniel G. Tomlinson, Dell Henderson, Lucy Beaumont (M-G-M)

A drab, actionless story of ungodly length and apparently telling nothing. The longness of the picture suggests it was designed for a Metro special, but on what, only its authors, John V. A. Weaver and King Vidor, must know. Superficially it reels off as an analytical insight into the life, worries and struggles of two young, ordinary people, who marry and become parents.

The husband is a plodder and dreamer, achieving nothing but two children and an $8 raise of salary in five years. For this he seems in constant reprimand from his wife and her family. Casting aside his permanent desk job through mental strain over the death by a truck of his little daughter, the young husband tries other jobs in vain, until his wife, disgusted, finally slaps him in the face and walks out.

James Murray is the young husband and catches the spirit at times, more in looks than anything else. Both he and Eleanor Boardman have the opportunity for a big scene when seeing their child trampled by a moving truck while walking toward their home. Both actors muff the chance by a mile.

1927/8: NOMINATIONS: Best Director, Artistic Quality of Production

•

CROWD ROARS, THE

1932, 84 mins, US b/w

Dir Howard Hawks *Scr* Howard Hawks, Seton I. Miller, Kubec Glasmon, John Bright *Ph* Sid Hickox *Ed* John Stumar, Thomas Pratt *Mus* Leo Forbstein (dir.) *Art* Jack Okey

Act James Cagney, Joan Blondell, Ann Dvorak, Eric Linden, Guy Kibbee, Frank McHugh (Warner)

All auto-race pictures lead to Indianapolis, and there is no deviation from that schedule here.

Script doesn't unfold unusual acting opportunities for any of the principals. In this instance James Cagney's a front rank pilot who likes his grog and is mixed up with a girl by the time he revisits the old home town after achieving sports-page fame. The kid brother (Eric Linden) has caught the racing bug, too, and this provides the complication which has its source in the feminine angle.

Cagney, having added the brother to his crew, can't reconcile himself to having the kid on too friendly terms with the girl with whom he's been living (Ann Dvorak). To retaliate she sics her girlfriend (Joan Blondell), also of the same stripe, onto the brother, with this latter situation developing into a romance which splits the brothers.

Howard Hawks has received valiant service from his cameramen. The director doesn't seem to have taken his own story too seriously, and the picture is cut so that it just about holds the continuity together, always with the hint that it's anxious to get back to the track.

•

CROWD ROARS, THE

1938, 87 mins, US b/w

Dir Richard Thorpe *Prod* Sam Zimbalist *Scr* Thomas Lennon, George Bruce, George Oppenheimer *Ph* John Seitz *Mus* Edward Ward

Act Robert Taylor, Edward Arnold, Frank Morgan, Maureen O'Sullivan, William Gargan, Lionel Stander (M-G-M)

The manly art of self-defense, otherwise known as the cauliflower industry, alias prizefighting, is a rough-and-tumble racket operated by big time gamblers with small time ethics, according to the film, *The Crowd Roars* in which Robert Taylor leads with his left hand. It's exciting melodrama with plenty of ring action, some plausible romance and several corking good characterizations.

There are moments early in the film when it appears that George Bruce, the author, intends to dwell on the angle of mob psychology. He steers away from any depth in the treatment of his theme, however, and holds to a plot about a choir boy who becomes a contender for the light heavyweight championship.

Frank Morgan creates something interesting out of the role of the pug's father, a drunkard and braggart. Edward Arnold is the conventional bookmaker and fight manager, who works successfully on the theory that the smartest gamblers are the biggest suckers. Heart interest is centred in a love affair between Taylor and Maureen O'Sullivan.

•

CRUCIBLE, THE

1996, 123 mins, US Ⓥ ⊙ col

Dir Nicholas Hytner *Prod* Robert A. Miller, David V. Picker *Scr* Arthur Miller *Ph* Andrew Dunn *Ed* Tariq Anwar *Mus* George Fenton *Art* Lilly Kilvert

Act Daniel Day-Lewis, Winona Ryder, Paul Scofield, Joan Allen, Bruce Davison, Rob Campbell (20th Centruy-Fox)

Never before filmed in English, Arthur Miller's play *The Crucible* doesn't emerge onscreen with its full impact intact. Designed as a class production from top to bottom, this handsomely mounted tale of witch hunts, religious persecution, sexual revenge and social hysteria in 17th-century Salem, Mass, still possesses the power to stir up wrenching emotion, but neither the establishing dramatic linchpin not the final conversion of conscience is terribly convincing.

Proctor (Daniel Day-Lewis), an industrious farmer, had an illicit affair with young Puritan girl Abigail Williams (Winona Ryder) when she worked at his house, but when his wife (Joan Allen) got wind of it, Abigail was tossed out. Abigail attempts to revive the liaison, but John resolutely refuses, rededicating himself to his family. Abigail begins accusing other women [of infidelity], and the hysteria begins. Eminent Judge Danforth (Paul Scofield) arrives to lead the investigation and root out the plague [of Satan] at all costs.

Part of the problem is that, just as in *The Age of Innocence*, there is absolutely no apparent sexual frisson between Day-Lewis and Ryder. Once again not at her best in a period role, Ryder proves just borderline plausible as the sexual avenger who sets the deadly wheels in motion with her reckless accusations. Allen endows the doubly wronged, weathered Elizabeth with an understated power.

Shot on location on Hog Island, Mass, pic has a spare but lived-in quality. Previous film version was the 1957 French-language *Les sorcieres de Salem*, starring Yves Montand and Simone Signoret and directed by Raymond Rouleau.

1996: NOMINATIONS: Best Supp. Actress (Joan Allen), Screenplay Adaptation

•

CRUEL INTENTIONS

1999, 95 mins, US Ⓥ ⊙ col

Dir Roger Kumble *Prod* Neal H. Moritz *Scr* Roger Kumble *Ph* Theo Van de Sande *Ed* Jeff Freeman *Mus* Edward Shearmur *Art* Jon Gary Steele

Act Sarah Michelle Gellar, Ryan Philippe, Reese Witherspoon, Selma Blair, Louise Fletcher, Joshua Jackson

The fourth film and the second modern-dress version to use Choderlos De Laclos's notorious 1782 novel as its inspiration, *Cruel Intentions* is *Dangerous Liaisons* for the teenage crowd. Nasty, profane and wickedly entertaining for the most part, pic is quite a faithful rendition of the scandalous tome.

Changes from the original book reflect demographics as well as trendiness, with a black thesp, Sean Patrick Thomas, playing Cecile's music instructor (Keanu Reeves in the 1988 version) and gay characters (played by Joshua Jackson and Eric Mabius) in major roles.

Set in Manhattan's upper-crust society during summer break, tale revolves around Kathryn Merteuil (Sarah Michelle Gellar) and Sebastian Valmont (Ryan Philippe), two wealthy brats and step-sibs who spend their time conspiring diabolical wagers. With seduction and sexual conquest as chief rewards, the duo select as their new pawns the naive Cecile (Selma Blair in the Uma Thurman part) and the virginal Annette Hargrove (Reese Witherspoon), whose character represents the most drastic deviation from the other film versions.

The first two acts provide the kind of lewd, odious fun seldom encountered in teen films. Unfortunately, in the name of redemption and political correctness, the last chapter is too earnest and obvious in its punitive stance toward some of the characters. Sebastian's role provides Philippe plenty of opportunity to display his considerable skills. In a significant stretch from TV's *Buffy the Vampire Slayer*, Gellar shines as the witty, evil and vulnerable Kathryn. Tech credits are polished across the board, seldom indicating that pic is a first effort.

•

CRUEL SEA, THE

1953, 120 mins, UK Ⓥ b/w

Dir Charles Frend *Prod* Leslie Norman *Scr* Eric Ambler *Ph* Gordon Dines *Ed* Peter Tanner *Mus* Alan Rawsthorne *Art* Jim Morahan

Act Jack Hawkins, Donald Sinden, John Stratton, Denholm Elliott, Stanley Baker, Virginia McKenna (Ealing)

Ealing breaks from its traditional light comedies to offer a serious, authentic reconstruction of the battle of the Atlantic, based on Nicholas Monsarrat's bestseller. Production, despite its overlong running time, emerges as a picture of dramatic intensity.

Much of the original novel's action has been telescoped and quite a few major incidents have been omitted. As the commentator explains, the heroes are the men, the heroines are the ships, and the villain is the cruel sea.

These three elements are put into focus via the activities of a corvette which puts to sea with only one experienced officer—the captain—aboard. The others are the normal wartime recruits from civilian life, including a freelance journalist, lawyer, bank clerk and second-hand car salesman. Their first operational duties land them into a storm, but subsequently they encounter enemy activity and are harassed by U-boats.

Notable thesping comes from Jack Hawkins, who plays the captain with requisite authority. Surrounding cast is well matched, with sterling work contributed by Donald Sinden, John Stratton, Denholm Elliot and Stanley Baker at the head of a handpicked cast. Charles Frend directs with a sure touch.

1953: NOMINATION: Best Screenplay

•

CRUISING

1980, 106 mins, US Ⓥ col

Dir William Friedkin *Prod* Jerry Weintraub *Scr* William Friedkin *Ph* James Contner *Ed* Bud Smith *Mus* Jack Nitzsche *Art* Bruce Weintraub

Act Al Pacino, Paul Sorvino, Karen Allen, Richard Cox, Don Scardino (Lorimar)

In *Cruising*, writer-director William Friedkin explores the S&M life of New York City. Like any approach to the bizarre, it is fascinating for about 15 minutes.

In many respects, *Cruising* [from the novel by Gerald Walker] resembles the worst of the "hippie" films of the 1960s.

Taking away the kissing, caressing and a few bloody killings, Friedkin has no story, though picture pretends to be a murder mystery combined with a study of Al Pacino's psychological degradation.

Pacino is an innocent young cop chosen to go underground in search of a killer. He ultimately zeroes in on the culprit but by now is almost as far around the bend as his prey. But that's not saying much more than the old maxim: "he who lies down with dogs gets up with fleas."

•

CRUSADES, THE

1935, 124 mins, US b/w

Dir Cecil B. DeMille *Prod* Cecil B. DeMille *Scr* Harold Lamb, Dudley Nichols, Waldemar Young *Ph* Victor Milner *Ed* Anne Bauchens *Mus* Rudolph Kopp

Act Loretta Young, Henry Wilcoxon, Ian Keith, C. Aubrey Smith, Katherine DeMille, Joseph Schildkraut (Paramount)

Probably only Cecil B. DeMille could make a picture like *The Crusades*—and get away with it. It's long, and the story is not up to some of his previous films, but the production has sweep and spectacle.

DeMille patently intended his puppets to be subjugated by the generally transcendental theme of this holy war on the infidels. The loose footage at times defeats that. There is no great surge of human sympathy for the ecclesiastic offensive. Only the pious wandering hermit (capably done by C. Aubrey Smith) stands out as the sole symbol of the faith in the invasion of Acre and Jerusalem. Richard-the-Lion-Hearted frankly accepts the call to arms for selfish reasons—the only out he has to sidestep the state marriage to the French king's sister (Loretta Young).

Henry Wilcoxon plays Richard. Full weight of *The Crusades* falls on his performance. For sheer versatility, ranging from horsemanship to boudoir, there are few players who could have done as well.

1935: NOMINATION: Best Cinematography

•

CRY-BABY

1990, 85 mins, US Ⓥ ⊙ col

Dir John Waters *Prod* Rachel Talalay *Scr* John Waters *Ph* David Insley *Ed* Janice Hampton *Mus* Patrick Williams *Art* Vincent Peranio

Act Johnny Depp, Amy Locane, Susan Tyrrell, Polly Bergen, Iggy Pop, Ricki Lake (Imagine)

John Waters's mischievous satire of the teen exploitation genre is entertaining as a rude joyride through another era, full of great clothes and hairdos.

Set on Waters's Baltimore turf, *Cry-Baby* returns to the nascent days of rock 'n' roll when teens were king, where the cleancut "squares" are pitted against the hoodlum "drapes." Cry-Baby (Johnny Depp), a handsome delinquent with a perpetual tear in his eye (in memory of his criminal parents who died in the electric chair), takes the bait from a pony-tailed blonde from the well-bred set (Amy Locane).

Once it's clear the plot is just a raucous rebel without a cause with a handful of inspired elements clipped to a wornout *Romeo and Juliet* storyline, a lot of the foolery begins to wear thin. There's so much commotion in the pic, with its 11 full-fledged dance numbers and elaborate production values, that one can't help but catch on that a story's missing.

Depp is great as the delinquent juve, delivering the melodramatic lines with straight-faced conviction and putting some Elvis-like snap and wiggle into his moves.

•

CRY DANGER

1951, 79 mins, US Ⓥ b/w

Dir Robert Parrish *Prod* Sam Wiesenthal, W. R. Frank *Scr* William Bowers *Ph* Joseph F. Biroc *Ed* Bernard W. Burton *Mus* Emil Newman, Paul Dunlap *Art* Richard Day

Act Dick Powell, Rhonda Fleming, Richard Erdman, William Conrad, Regis Toomey, Jean Porter (Olympic)

All the ingredients for a suspenseful melodrama are contained in *Cry Danger*. Plot [from a story by Jerome Cady] opens with Dick Powell returning after five years in prison, having been pardoned from a life sentence when new evidence turns up that clears him of a robbery rap. Evidence was manufactured by a crippled Marine vet (Richard Erdman) who figures Powell will be grateful enough to cut up some of the $100,000 loot he is supposed to have hidden.

Powell sees the pardon as an opportunity to bring the guilty parties to justice and free a friend still in prison. Scene of all the plot movement is the poorer section of Los Angeles, where Powell and Erdman have holed up in a crummy trailer camp to be near Rhonda Fleming, wife of the friend still in prison.

Robert Parrish, erstwhile film editor, makes a strong directorial bow.

•

CRY FREEDOM

1987, 157 mins, US Ⓥ ⊙ ▭ col

Dir Richard Attenborough ***Prod*** Richard Attenborough ***Scr*** John Briley ***Ph*** Ronnie Taylor ***Ed*** Lesley Walker ***Mus*** George Fenton, Jonas Gwangwa ***Art*** Stuart Craig

Act Kevin Kline, Penelope Wilton, Denzel Washington, Kevin McNally, John Thaw, Timothy West (Marble Arch/Universal)

Cry Freedom personifies the struggle of South Africa's black population against apartheid in the evolving friendship of martyred black activist Stephen Biko and liberal white newspaper editor Donald Woods. It derives its impact less from epic scope than from the wrenching immediacy of its subject matter and the moral heroism of its appealingly played, idealistic protagonists.

John Briley's screenplay is based on two books by Woods, who could publish them only by escaping South Africa (where he was under virtual house arrest as a "banned" person) with his family in harrowing fashion. This produces the singular flaw of *Cry Freedom*—an overemphasis in the film's final hour on the Woods family's escape to exile in England.

Film opens in 1975 with a pitiless dawn raid by bulldozers and armed police on an illegal shantytown of black squatters. Stephen Biko is at first an offscreen presence, revered by blacks as a charismatic advocate of racial self-worth and self-determination, but distrusted by whites—including liberals like Woods—as a dangerous reverse racist whose condemnation of white society carries an implicit threat of violence. Realizing he needs to form an alliance with the liberals he so dislikes, Biko (Denzel Washington) arranges to meet Woods (Kevin Kline), an invitation that dedicated newshound cannot afford to turn down.

Kline's familiar low-key screen presence serves him well in his portrayal of the strong-willed but even-tempered journalist. Washington does a remarkable job of transforming himself into the articulate and mesmerizing black nationalist leader, whose refusal to keep silent led to his death in police custody and a subsequent cover-up.

1987: NOMINATIONS: Best Original Score, Song ("Cry Freedom")

•

CRY "HAVOC"

1943, 96 mins, US b/w

Dir Richard Thorpe ***Prod*** Edwin Knopf ***Scr*** Paul Osborn ***Ph*** Karl Freund ***Ed*** Ralph E. Winters ***Mus*** Daniele Amfitheatrof

Act Margaret Sullavan, Ann Sothern, Joan Blondell, Fay Bainter, Marsha Hunt, Ella Raines (M-G-M)

Plot sets up all-femme cast tossed into a bomb shelter at Bataan, with nine girls rounded up from evacuation of Manila to function as volunteers at an outland field hospital. Each of the nine are from various fields of endeavor, including waitress Ann Sothern, and former burlesque performer Joan Blondell. Girls are assigned auxiliary spots around the camp, but practically all of the footage centers in the bomb shelter for lengthy dialog and mental reactions of the individuals as the going gets tougher.

Best thing about the film is the capable cast tossed in for group of generally fine performances, despite the inadequacies of the plot in both suspense and movement. Sullavan delivers strong portrayal of the army nurse, with Sothern and Blondell clicking solidly in respective roles.

Richard Thorpe is restricted on direction to following too stagey a script [from the play by Allan R. Kenward, first presented at a small Hollywood theatre and then in New York under the new title *Proof thro' the Night*], with no chance of generating more than nominal suspense at points where it should reach peaks.

•

CRYING GAME, THE

1992, 113 mins, UK Ⓥ ⊙ ▭ col

Dir Neil Jordan ***Prod*** Stephen Woolley ***Scr*** Neil Jordan ***Ph*** Ian Wilson ***Ed*** Kant Pan ***Mus*** Anne Dudley ***Art*** Jim Clay

Act Stephen Rea, Miranda Richardson, Forest Whitaker, Jaye Davidson, Adrian Dunbar, Jim Broadbent (Palace/Channel 4)

An astonishingly good and daring film that richly develops several intertwined thematic lines, *The Crying Game* takes giant risks that are stunningly rewarded. Irish director Neil Jordan's seventh film is also his best to date.

The IRA's kidnapping in Northern Ireland of British soldier Jody (Forest Whitaker) serves as the jumping-off point for a fearlessly penetrating examination of politics, race, sexuality and human nature.

First 40-minute act concerns Whitaker's country house incarceration by a small band of terrorists led by Maguire (Adrian Dunbar) and the sexy Jude (Miranda Richardson). They leave him mostly under the guard of Fergus (Jordan stalwart Stephen Rea), who develops an intense rapport with Jody.

Fergus later escapes to London, where he finds Jody's great love, Dil (Jaye Davidson), working in a beauty salon. Dil entices Fergus into a relationship that will test just how far he's willing to go for love.

Acting is uniformly superior. Whitaker's simply terrific, and the Yank thesp has seemingly mastered a very specific British working-class accent. Rea is intriguingly handsome-homely, decisive-passive, gentle-violent. Newcomer Davidson is almost impossibly right as the beautiful, mysterious Dil, while Richardson is equal parts fire and ice as the most resilient IRA member.

1992: Best Original Screenplay

NOMINATIONS: Best Picture, Director, Actor (Stephen Rea), Supp. Actor (Jaye Davidson), Editing

•

CRY IN THE DARK, A
(AUSTRALIA: EVIL ANGELS)

1988, 121 mins, US Ⓥ ⊙ ▭ col

Dir Fred Schepisi ***Prod*** Verity Lambert ***Scr*** Robert Caswell, Fred Schepisi ***Ph*** Ian Baker ***Ed*** Jill Bilcock ***Mus*** Bruce Smeaton ***Art*** Wendy Dickson, George Liddle

Act Meryl Streep, Sam Neill, Bruce Myles, Charles Tingwell, Nick Tate, Lewis Fitz-Gerald (Cannon)

One of the oddest and most illogical murder cases of modern times is recounted in intimate, incredible detail in the classy, disturbing drama *A Cry in the Dark* [from John Bryson's Book *Evil Angels*].

The saga of Lindy Chamberlain's harassment, trial and imprisonment for having allegedly murdered her baby daughter, when there was literally no evidence against her, was the biggest news story in Australia of the 1980s.

In 1980, the Chamberlains visit the monumental Ayers Rock in the outback. With the baby put to sleep in a tent, the family begins enjoying a nighttime barbeque when a cry is heard. Checking the tent, Lindy briefly glimpses a dingo slipping out of it and then, to her horror, finds Azaria missing from her bed.

No trace of the infant is found, and the conclusion appears to be that the dingo made off with her. Astonishingly, however, sentiment begins to grow throughout the country to the effect that Lindy killed her daughter. From there, the press can't let the story die. Lindy is charged with murder and Michael named as accessory after the fact.

If one didn't know who Meryl Streep is, one could easily guess Lindy was played by a fine, unknown Australian actress. Sam Neill, who here looks remarkably like the real Michael Chamberlain, well conveys the tentative strengths and very real weaknesses of a man thrust into an unimaginable situation.

1988: NOMINATION: Best Actress (Meryl Streep)

•

CRY OF THE CITY

1948, 96 mins, US b/w

Dir Robert Siodmak ***Prod*** Sol C. Siegel ***Scr*** Richard Murphy ***Ph*** Lloyd Ahern ***Ed*** Harmon Jones ***Mus*** Alfred Newman ***Art*** Lyle R. Wheeler, Albert Hogsett

Act Victor Mature, Richard Conte, Fred Clark, Shelley Winters, Debra Paget, Hope Emerson (20th Century-Fox)

The hard-hitting suspense of the chase formula is given top-notch presentation in *Cry of the City*. It's an exciting motion picture, credibly put together to wring out every bit of strong action and tension inherent in such a plot. Robert Siodmak's penchant for shaping melodramatic excitement that gets through to an audience is realistically carried out in this one.

The telling screenplay by Richard Murphy, based on a novel, *The Chair for Martin Rome* by Henry Edward Helseth, presents Victor Mature as a police lieutenant in homicide and Richard Conte as a cop-killer—antagonists, although both sprung from New York's Italian sector. Shelley Winters sparks small assignment of a girl who drives the killer through the New York streets while an unlicensed doctor works desperately to patch up his wounds.

•

CRYSTAL BALL, THE

1943, 80 mins, US b/w

Dir Elliott Nugent ***Prod*** Richard Blumenthal ***Scr*** Steven Vass, Virginia Van Upp ***Ph*** Leo Tover ***Ed*** Doane Harrison ***Mus*** Victor Young

Act Paulette Goddard, Ray Milland, Virginia Field, William Bendix, Gladys George, Ernest Truex (United Artists)

A story with a unique plot, a cast of seasoned performers, very capable direction and good comedy relief combine to make this one thoroughly acceptable entertainment.

Though the title may not suggest it, *The Crystal Ball* carries a strong romantic flavor with Ray Milland and Paulette Goddard paired, while Virginia Field is the frustrated fiancée in the triangular setup. Field plays a rich widow, Goddard a stranded gal who goes to work as a shill for a shooting gallery, a job procured for her by a friendly fortune-teller of shady rep.

When the fake medium takes sick, Goddard doubles on the fortune-telling racket and nearly gets Milland into trouble by advising that he take an option on some property that the government is after.

The comic relief is light and refreshing but more could have been done with Ernest Truex and Iris Adrian, a scrapping married couple.

Additional humor is supplied by William Bendix, playing a chauffeur and Sig Arno, a waiter.

•

CRY, THE BELOVED COUNTRY
(US: AFRICAN FURY)

1952, 103 mins, UK Ⓥ b/w

Dir Zoltan Korda ***Prod*** Zoltan Korda ***Scr*** Alan Paton ***Ph*** Robert Krasker ***Ed*** David Eady ***Mus*** R. Gallois-Montbrun ***Art*** Wilfrid Shingleton

Act Canada Lee, Charles Carson, Sidney Poitier, Joyce Carey, Geoffrey Keen, Michael Goodliffe (London/British Lion)

Alan Paton's bestselling novel which was made into a Broadway musical *Lost in the Stars* [1949], has been turned into an absorbing pic. Filmed in its native South African locale, and in London, the pic emerges as a very moving film, full of simplicity and charm.

The picture is a strong social document in its study of the perplexed conditions of a submerged native population ruled by the whites in South Africa.

More particularly, *Cry* is the story of a simple, native Negro country preacher (Canada Lee), who goes to the big city of Johannesburg to seek a missing sister and wayward son, and who finds both in the crime-ridden, slum elements of the city.

Lee's performance, restrained and underplayed, is a rich, heartwarming portrayal, dominating the film. Sidney Poitier is manly and striking as a young Negro preacher.

•

CRY, THE BELOVED COUNTRY

1995, 111 mins, US Ⓥ ⊙ col

Dir Darrell James Roodt ***Prod*** Anant Singh ***Scr*** Ronald Harwood ***Ph*** Paul Gilpin ***Ed*** David Heitner ***Mus*** John Barry ***Art*** David Barkham

Act James Earl Jones, Richard Harris, Vusi Kunene, Leleti Khumalo, Charles S. Dutton, Eric Miyeni (Distant Horizon)

Alan Paton's almost 50-year-old novel of South African racial tension, *Cry, the Beloved Country*, has been dusted off and remade in a markedly different style from its 1952 screen translation. New outing is considerably more majestic in scope, earnest in tone and allegorical in attitude.

Story is spurred by the murder of an upper-crust white man active in native rights, an incident that precipitates a kinship between the dead man's father, James Jarvis (Richard Harris), and Father Stephen Kumalo (James Earl Jones). A letter received by Kumalo—a request that he come to the aid of his sister in the city—is the jumping-off point for a painful odyssey.

Kumalo, who's never strayed far from his village, encounters an alien world of violence, poverty and desperation. He luckily comes under the wing of the knowing Father Msimangu (Vusi Junene).

Jarvis, meanwhile, discovers that his son pitied him, considering him impervious to the plight of his black countrymen. The juncture between these two voyages is that the murdered man was killed by Kumalo's son.

Ronald Harwood's adaptation isn't really interested in the trial or forced theatrics. But the low-key tone eventually works against the material. Both Jones and Harris work hard to convey their characters' innate decency, but they seem unauthentic in their surroundings.

•

CSILLAGOSOK, KATONAK
(THE RED AND THE WHITE)
1967, 92 mins, Hungary/USSR Ⓥ ⊏⊐ b/w
Dir Miklos Jancso ***Scr*** Gyula Hernadi, Georgi Mdivani, Miklos Jancso ***Ph*** Tamas Somlo ***Ed*** Zoltan Farkas ***Mus*** [none] ***Art*** Boris Chebotarev
Act Andras Kozak, Krystyna Mikolajewska, Jacint Juhasz, Tatyana Konyukhova, Mikhail Kozakov, Viktor Avdushko (Mafilm/Mosfilm)

Theme of Miklos Jancso's new pic, the first Hungarian-Soviet coproduction, is an episode in the 1918–22 civil war in Russia.

Somewhere in Russia, two forces fight each other: a unit of the Red Army, which also includes Hungarian Internationalists, and a group of White Guards, mainly former Tsarist officers. It seems that there is only one aim, to liquidate the other side.

Jancso concentrates his message on the philosophical problem of life and death. Unknown and nameless men enter history in a given moment and after some time they step out of the scene with their death.

In a remote hospital, a dozen nurses look after the wounded soldiers, both Whites and Reds. A White Guard unit arrives. They take all the nurses by coaches to a wood. The tension of this scene increases the underlying fear that the nurses will be executed. Instead, the eight nurses, dressed in evening gowns, have to dance to the music of a military orchestra.

Film is as merciless as the necessity which activates history. There is no stirring spectacle in it. The dialogue is limited almost to military commands.

The camera moves without ceasing. This continuous movement, and the continuity of internal cutting, creates a strong tension.

•

CUBA
1979, 122 mins, US Ⓥ col
Dir Richard Lester ***Prod*** Arlene Sellers, Alex Winitsky ***Scr*** Charles Wood ***Ph*** David Watkin ***Ed*** John Victor Smith ***Mus*** Patrick Williams ***Art*** Shirley Russell
Act Sean Connery, Brooke Adams, Jack Weston, Chris Sarandon, Denholm Elliott, Martin Balsam (United Artists)

Cuba is a hollow, pointless non-drama. Cynical and evasive about politics, pic displays uniformly unsympathetic characters enacting a vague plot amidst a splendid re-creation of Havana at the very end of the Batista regime.

Basic *Two Weeks in Another Town* situation has had all conventional melodrama calculatedly drained from it. Revolution is closing in on the upper-crust types who serve as story focus, and Brooke Adams is torn between two men, but treatment deliberately goes against the grain of sentiments normally encountered in such potent dramatic setups.

Given the worthless, motley crew seen to populate Havana—including gross American profiteer Jack Weston and cynical gentleman Denholm Elliott—political outlook would seem to be that things couldn't get much worse, and maybe Castro will be a little bit better.

•

CUJO
1983, 91 mins, US Ⓥ ⦿ col
Dir Lewis Teague ***Prod*** Daniel H. Blatt, Robert Singer ***Scr*** Don Carlos Dunaway, Lauren Currier ***Ph*** Jan De Bont ***Ed*** Neil Travis ***Mus*** Charles Bernstein ***Art*** Guy Comtois
Act Dee Wallace, Danny Pintauro, Daniel Hugh-Kelly, Christopher Stone, Ed Lauter, Kaiulani Lee (Taft/Warner)

Although well-made, this screen adaptation of Stephen King's *Cujo* emerges as a dull, uneventful entry in the horror genre. Novel about a mad dog on the rampage occupies a low place in the King canon, which is understandable if the film's stupefying predictability is an accurate reflection of the book.

Opening sequence has a lovable looking St. Bernard bitten on the nose by a bat, whereupon audience is introduced to the Trentons, a family of young parents and a son which is disintegrating, mostly thanks to Dee Wallace's sideline affair with a local worker. Story basically marks time until, at least halfway through, the dog begins attacking Maine seacoast locals (pic was shot in Northern California).

Except for the appealing kid played by Danny Pintauro, the characters are of little interest.

•

CUL-DE-SAC
1966, 111 mins, UK Ⓥ b/w
Dir Roman Polanski ***Prod*** Gene Gutowski ***Scr*** Roman Polanski, Gerard Brach ***Ph*** Gilbert Taylor ***Ed*** Alastair McIntyre ***Mus*** Krzysztof Komeda ***Art*** Voytek Roman
Act Donald Pleasence, Francoise Dorleac, Lionel Stander, Jack McGowran, William Franklyn, Jacqueline Bisset (Compton)

As a study in kinky insanity, *Cul-de-Sac* creates a tingling atmosphere. This sags riskily at times when the director unturns the screws and does not keep control of his frequently introduced comedy.

Film was shot on location in and around a lonely castle on remote Holy Island off the northeast coast of Britain. Gill Taylor's camera bleakly catches the loneliness and sinister background that sparks the happenings.

Donald Pleasence, with steel-rimmed glasses and head completely shaven, is an obvious neurotic. A retired businessman, he is living like a hermit with his young, bored and flirtatious French wife (Francoise Dorleac), who is blatantly contemptuous of him. Suddenly, two wounded gangsters on the run descend upon them. From then on it's a battle of nerves, a cat-and-mouse psychological tightrope walk, as an uneasy truce develops between Pleasence and Stander, while the latter waits to be rescued by the boss of his gang, who never shows.

Pleasence pours some exaggerated but distinctive thesping into his pathetic role while Lionel Stander, obviously more flamboyant, blends nicely with him, turning in a far more subtle performance of latent brutality, mixed with surface geniality, than the screenplay may have promised.

•

CULPEPPER CATTLE CO., THE
1972, 92 mins, US Ⓥ col
Dir Dick Richards ***Prod*** Paul A. Helmick ***Scr*** Eric Bercovici, Gregory Prentiss ***Ph*** Lawrence Edward Williams, Ralph Woolsey ***Ed*** John F. Burnett ***Mus*** Tom Scott, Jerry Goldsmith ***Art*** Jack Martin Smith, Carl Anderson
Act Gary Grimes, Billy "Green" Bush, Luke Askew, Bo Hopkins, Geoffrey Lewis, Wayne Sutherlin (20th Century-Fox)

The Culpepper Cattle Co. is an unsuccessful attempt to mount a poetic and stylistic ballet of death in the environment of a period western. Gary Grimes is featured as a teenager who matures in the course of a hard, violent and bloody cattle drive.

Director Dick Richards's story has been scripted into a pallid, stilted plot, where the characters mutter and grunt empty aphorisms. Clearly, we have here one of those "important-statement-on-the-human-condition" rationalizations for a gruesome series of blood-lettings.

Billy "Green" Bush plays Culpepper, hard-bitten range boss who takes on Grimes, whose likeable, easy-going and natural manner come across as the only effective performance. Everyone else is saddled with limp dialog and unrestrained posturing. Lots of people are killed.

•

CURLY SUE
1991, 101 mins, US Ⓥ ⦿ col
Dir John Hughes ***Prod*** John Hughes ***Scr*** John Hughes ***Ph*** Jeffrey Kimball ***Ed*** Peck Prior, Harvey Rosenstock ***Mus*** Georges Delerue ***Art*** Doug Kraner
Act James Belushi, Kelly Lynch, Alisan Porter, John Getz, Fred Dalton Thompson, Cameron Thor (Warner)

This predictable crowd-pleaser is at heart a two-hanky affair, a mix of childish gags and shameless melodrama.

Pic clearly aspires to Capraesque sentimentality: a drifting con man (James Belushi) and his adopted nine-year-old daughter (Alisan Porter) scam a corporate attorney (Kelly Lynch) and gradually win her heart, much to the chagrin of her snotty boyfriend (John Getz).

Writer-helmer-producer John Hughes strikes an uneasy balance between slapstick and sappiness, far too frequently relying on Porter's mugging and Georges Delerue's drippingly sentimental score.

Lynch gives an impressive performance that proves to be the film's high point. Belushi is less convincing as the protective dad, while Porter is in the tear-evoking-tots tradition.

•

CURSE OF FRANKENSTEIN, THE
1957, 82 mins, UK Ⓥ col
Dir Terence Fisher ***Prod*** Anthony Hinds ***Scr*** Jimmy Sangster ***Ph*** Jack Asher ***Ed*** James Needs ***Mus*** James Bernard ***Art*** Bernard Robinson
Act Peter Cushing, Christopher Lee, Hazel Court, Robert Urquhart, Valerie Gaunt, Melvyn Hayes (Hammer)

This British version of the [Mary Shelley] classic shocker emphasizes not so much the uncontrollable blood lust of the created monster as the clinical details whereby the crazy scientist accumulates the odd organs with which to assemble the creature.

Story is unfolded to a priest while the infamous Baron Frankenstein is awaiting execution for multiple murders he vainly protests have been committed by his manmade monster (Christopher Lee). In the flashback he is seen as a young boy avid for scientific research and sharing with his tutor his determination to build up a human being through chemical hocus-pocus and graveyard snatchings. When their abominable purpose has been achieved, the tutor breaks off the unholy alliance.

Peter Cushing gets every inch of drama from the leading role, making almost believable the ambitious urge and diabolical accomplishment. Melvyn Hayes as the child skilfully conveys the ruthless self-possession of the embyro man.

•

CURSE OF THE CAT PEOPLE, THE
1944, 70 mins, US Ⓥ ⦿ b/w
Dir Gunther von Fritsch, Robert Wise ***Prod*** Val Lewton ***Scr*** DeWitt Bodeen ***Ph*** Nicholas Musuraca ***Ed*** J. R. Whittredge ***Mus*** Roy Webb ***Art*** Albert S. D'Agostino, Walter E. Keller
Act Simone Simon, Kent Smith, Jane Randolph, Ann Carter, Eve March, Elizabeth Russell (RKO)

Made as sequel to the profitable *Cat People,* this is highly disappointing because it fails to measure up as a horrific opus. Even though having the same principals as in the original chiller, this is an impossible lightweight. Chief trouble seems to be the over-supply of palaver and concern about a cute, but annoying child.

Two directors worked on *Curse of the Cat People,* suggesting production headaches. Pair has turned out a strange cinema stew that is apt to make audiences laugh at the wrong scenes. Many episodes are unbelievably bad, with hardly anything happening in the first three reels.

Plot has the offspring of the first wife of a naval architect (Kent Smith) apparently suffering from the same supernatural beliefs that brought the death of the child's mother. Yarn tries to show the child living in a dream world and imagining she is playing with her mother (Simone Simon). Youngster's visit to a supposedly haunted house where a half-crazed character actress (Julia Dean) lives with her daughter (Elizabeth Russell) builds into the slight horrific angle of film, resulting in the best episodes in the production.

•

CURSE OF THE MUMMY'S TOMB, THE
1964, 80 mins, UK b col
Dir Michael Carreras ***Prod*** Michael Carreras ***Scr*** Henry Younger ***Ph*** Otto Heller ***Ed*** Eric Boyd Perkins ***Mus*** Carlo Martelli ***Art*** Bernard Robinson
Act Terence Morgan, Fred Clark, Ronald Howard, Jeanne Roland, George Pastell, John Paul (Hammer)

It needs a crystal ball to sort out the reasons for some of the contrived goings on in this modest and rather slapdash horror pic. But it doesn't need a soothsayer to guess, early, the identity of the heavy.

Plot hinges around the discovery of an ancient tomb in the Egyptian desert, with a curse on anybody who opens it. Leader of the expedition intends giving the archaeological discoveries to the Egyptian government for its National Museum. But the expedition's smooth backer, a slick talking American showman, sees it as a coast-to-coast peepshow.

Murder and mayhem begins its gory trail and the motivation comes from a plausible stranger (Terence Morgan) who turns out to be a murderous descendant of the ancient Egyptian dynasty.

Morgan performs smoothly enough as the villain but is too patently up to no good from the start. Ronald Howard, Jack Gwillim and George Pastell are among those who provide sound support, but the liveliest performance comes from Fred Clark.

•

CURSE OF THE PINK PANTHER
1983, 109 mins, UK Ⓥ ⊏⊐ col
Dir Blake Edwards ***Prod*** Blake Edwards, Tony Adams ***Scr*** Blake Edwards, Geoffrey Edwards ***Ph*** Dick Bush ***Ed*** Ralph E. Winters, Bob Hathaway, Alan Jones ***Mus*** Henry Mancini ***Art*** Peter Mullins
Act Ted Wass, David Niven, Robert Wagner, Herbert Lom, Capucine, Roger Moore (Titan/Edwards/United Artists)

The eighth in the hit comedy series, *Curse of the Pink Panther* resembles a set of gems mounted in a tarnished setting. Abetted by screen newcomer Ted Wass's flair for physical comedy, filmmaker Blake Edwards has created genuinely funny sight gags but the film's rickety, old-hat story values waste them.

Lensed simultaneously with *Trail of the Pink Panther, Curse* boasts all-new footage but virtually repeats the prior release's story line. Instead of a newshen tracking down the missing Inspector Clouseau, this time Interpol's Huxley 600 computer (an uppity machine named Aldous) is secretly programmed by Clouseau's boss (Herbert Lom) to select the world's worst detective to search for his unwanted employee.

NY cop Clifton Sleigh (Ted Wass) is the bumbling man for the job, simultaneously trying to discover who has stolen (again) the Pink Panther diamond. As with *Trail*, format has him encountering and interviewing characters from earlier films in the series.

Guest stars David Niven (in his final film appearance), Robert Wagner and Capucine have little to do, while pert British blonde Leslie Ash is briefly impressive as a lethally kicking martial arts partner for Wass.

•

CURSE OF THE WEREWOLF, THE

1961, 91 mins, UK Ⓥ col

Dir Terence Fisher ***Prod*** Anthony Hinds ***Scr*** John Elder [= Anthony Hinds] ***Ph*** Arthur Grant ***Ed*** James Needs, Alfred Cox ***Mus*** Benjamin Frankel ***Art*** Bernard Robinson

Act Clifford Evans, Oliver Reed, Yvonne Romain, Catherine Feller, Anthony Dawson, Warren Mitchell (Hammer)

The screenplay, based on the novel *The Werewolf of Paris* by Guy Endore, dwells at extraordinary length, even for a horror picture, on expository background—on the vile heritage responsible for the genesis of the story's monster. But it is a credit to all concerned that this lengthy prolog sustains equal, if not greater, interest than the film's principal story which involves the personal plight of the wolfman himself.

Especially convincing characters are created by Oliver Reed as the compassionate werewolf, Clifford Evans, Anthony Dawson, Richard Wordsworth and Martin Matthews. And there is a restrained portrayal of the budding lycanthrope as a lad by young Justin Walters.

•

CUSTER OF THE WEST

1968, 143 mins, US/Spain ⦿ ▭ col

Dir Robert Siodmak ***Prod*** Louis Dolivet, Philip Yordan ***Scr*** Bernard Gordon, Julian Halevy ***Ph*** Cecilio Paniagua ***Ed*** Maurice Rootes ***Mus*** Bernardo Segall ***Art*** Jean-Pierre D'Eaubonne, Eugene Lourie, Julio Molina

Act Robert Shaw, Mary Ure, Jeffrey Hunter, Ty Hardin, Charles Stanlaker, Robert Hall (Cinerama/Security)

Capable, audience-involving adventure on the visual level which doesn't rise to the epic stature but is content to resume the "facts" about the Seventh Cavalry without taking a coherent attitude to them.

The arid, rock Spanish vistas stand in okay for old Indian territory—especially for those not overly familiar with them.

At the end of the Civil War, Custer is assigned to tame the Cheyenne, whose rights under government treaty are being whittled away by white depredations. He is at first content with his commission, and carries out his orders with zest and zeal. Conscience is represented by one of his junior officers, who looks mighty anxious about the moral probity of this constant onslaught on the Indians.

Robert Shaw gives Custer a simple forthrightness and dash that is effective, despite its naive context. Other thesp support is adequate within its straightforward idiom, with Jeffrey Hunter and Ty Hardin contrasting neatly as the troubled and dedicated junior officers respectively, Mary Ure as Custer's nebulous wife, and Robert Ryan guesting as the deserting gold-hungry soldier with a forceful cameo.

•

CUT ABOVE, A

SEE: GROSS ANATOMY

•

CUTTER AND BONE

SEE: CUTTER'S WAY

•

CUTTER'S WAY

(AKA: *CUTTER AND BONE*)

1981, 105 mins, US Ⓥ ⦿ col

Dir Ivan Passer ***Prod*** Paul R. Gurian ***Scr*** Jeffrey Alan Fiskin ***Ph*** Jordan Cronenweth ***Ed*** Caroline Ferriol ***Mus*** Jack Nitzsche ***Art*** Josan Russo

Act Jeff Bridges, John Heard, Lisa Eichhorn, Ann Dusenberry, Stephen Elliott, Nina Van Pallandt (Gurian)

Cutter's Way [from the novel *Cutter & Bone* by Newton Thornburg] suffers from a terminal case of creative indecision. With any number of intially intriguing plot lines, director Ivan Passer and scripter Jeffrey Alan Fiskin never come close to shedding light on what, if anything, this picture is really about. Jeff Bridges, John Heard and Lisa Eichhorn all deliver exceptionally fine topline performances, but their efforts seem wasted in such a weak vehicle.

Bridges limns a pretty beach boy type taken to supporting himself from the kindness of rich matrons. His best friend is Heard, a wildly bitter yet fiercely adventurous alcoholic who lost his leg in Vietnam. Heard is married to Eichhorn, who's also taken to the bottle but, unlike the other two, is aware that her personal world is crumbling.

Unfortunately, the trio is framed in an obtuse murder mystery concerning Bridges's witnessing an older man with sunglasses dumping the dead body of a teenage girl. Bridges thinks he spots the suspect, a powerful oil corporation head, in a civic parade he attends with Heard. Film then alternately gets mired in attempts to blackmail the oilman, Heard's increasing craziness, Bridges's inability to make a commitment, Eichhorn's love of both men, and a revelation of the unfortunate past of friend Arthur Rosenberg that is supposed to be related to the murder.

•

CUTTHROAT ISLAND

1995, 123 mins, US Ⓥ ⦿ ▭ col

Dir Renny Harlin ***Prod*** Renny Harlin, Joel B. Michaels, Laurence Mark, ***Scr*** Robert King, Marc Norman ***Ph*** Peter Levy ***Ed*** Frank J. Urioste, Ralph E. Winters ***Mus*** John Debney ***Art*** Norman Garwood

Act Geena Davis, Matthew Modine, Frank Langella, Maury Chaykin, Patrick Malahide, Stan Shaw (Carolco/Forge/Studio Canal Plus/TeleCommunications)

Cutthroat Island strenuously but vainly attempts to revive the thrills of old-fashioned pirate pictures. Giving most of the swashbuckling opportunities to star Geena Davis, pic does little with its reversal of gender expectations and features a seriously mismatched romantic duo in Davis and Matthew Modine. This megabudget behemoth is destined to be known as the film that sent Carolco to the bottom once and for all.

Unable to rescue her pirate father from the murderous hand of his blackhearted pirate brother Dawg Brown (Frank Langella), the statuesque Morgan Adams (Davis) ends up with a piece of scalp on which one-third of a map is drawn indicating the location of Cutthroat Island and its purported fortune.

Rousing Dad's crew to the cause, Morgan sallies out to Port Royal, Jamaica, where she buys prisoner William Shaw (Modine) at a slave auction for his knowledge of Latin, in which the map is written. After a breathless escape that entails the destruction of half the city, the eager opportunists set sail for the titular piece of rock, upon which they are dashed by a quite impressively staged storm at sea.

More at home in offbeat contemporary roles, Modine is swimming upstream here. Towering over many of the men and strapping in her feminized pirate gear, Davis nonetheless seems similarly out of her element. In a rare highly physical role, Langella carves out a suitably hissable villain.

Action sequences in general, while vividly staged, have a repetitiveness about them, and lack of proper dramatic ebb and flow is exacerbated by John Debney's self-consciously rousing score.

Pic is a feast for the eyes due to Norman Garwood's lavish production design, Enrico Sabbatini's equally florid costumes and the striking locations in Malta (doubling for 1600s Jamaica) and Thailand.

•

CUTTING EDGE, THE

1992, 101 mins, US Ⓥ col

Dir Paul Michael Glaser ***Prod*** Ted Field, Karen Murphy, Robert W. Cort ***Scr*** Tony Gilroy ***Ph*** Elliot Davis ***Ed*** Michael E. Polakow ***Mus*** Patrick Williams ***Art*** David Gropman

Act D. B. Sweeney, Moira Kelly, Roy Dotrice, Terry O'Quinn, Dwier Brown (M-G-M/Interscope)

The Cutting Edge it isn't, but this neatly formulaic romantic comedy has a sharp enough combination of teen-oriented elements and style. Pic pits frosty-tempered ice queen Kate Mosely (Moira Kelly) against brash, competitive Doug Dorsey (D. B. Sweeney), a former star of the U.S. Olympic hockey team who approaches figure skating with great misgivings.

Doug's rough-hewn relatives view figure skating as a sport for sissies, plus he must contend with Moira's tendency to chew up and spit out would-be partners. But Doug rallies to the challenge, and the pic proceeds with this combustible young pair firing off verbal assaults at each other as they dig in to train, sweat and go for the Olympic gold.

Sport's close physical contact provides some *Dirty Dancing*-style titillation, with interest heightened by the watchable actors. Director Paul Michael Glaser opts for an impressionistic, adrenaline-pumped style in the sporting segs. Filmmakers use a skate-mounted Pogo Cam to get the point of view down where the blades meet the ice and the frost flies.

•

CYNARA

1932, 78 mins, US b/w

Dir King Vidor ***Prod*** Samuel Goldwyn ***Scr*** Frances Marion, Lynn Starling ***Ph*** Ray June ***Ed*** Hugh Bennett ***Art*** Richard Day

Act Ronald Colman, Kay Francis, Phyllis Barry, Henry Stephenson, Viva Tattersall (Goldwyn/United Artists)

Stage play [by H. M. Harwood and Robert Gore-Brown] has been put on the screen with beautiful balance of directness and simplicity. Treatment leans heavily to the British ideal of maintaining a calm and mannered surface that only sharpens the suggestion of emotional tumult beneath.

Ordinarily the device weakens a tale but here the play makes its point in spite of it, largely because it has to do with gallant and likable people—Ronald Colman's very human husband, Kay Francis's glamorous wife, and the eager young London shop girl who stumbled into being the other woman without very well knowing what she was doing, and afterward paying bitterly for her wayward impulse. Story really is a romantic tragedy built out of a minor bit of philandering.

The coroner's inquest sequence is a model of brevity in dialogue, conveying a maximum of dramatic effect with the utmost economy of words and practically no action at all. Tenseness of the passage is strangely conveyed by the very terseness and immobility of the actors.

The family friend is played by Henry Stephenson, who had the same role in the stage play and came within a narrow margin of stealing the honors. Here he is excellent. A newcomer to the screen is Phyllis Barry, an English girl from musical comedy. This story doesn't bring out her best points. For one thing she looks and acts a good deal too refined for the role. Chances are she was cast for the satisfying picture she makes in a bathing suit.

•

CYNTHIA

1947, 97 mins, US b/w

Dir Robert Z. Leonard ***Prod*** Edwin H. Knopf ***Scr*** Harold Buchman, Charles Kaufman ***Ph*** Charles Schoenbaum ***Ed*** Irvine Warburton ***Mus*** Bronislau Kaper, Johnny Green ***Art*** Cedric Gibbons, Edward Carfagno

Act Elizabeth Taylor, George Murphy, S. Z. Sakall, Mary Astor, Spring Byington, Gene Lockhart (M-G-M)

Cynthia [from Vina Delmar's play, *The Rich Full Life*] has a simplicity that projects warmth and feeling, particularly for family audiences familiar with the teenage problems posed by its plot.

Elizabeth Taylor breathes plenty of life into the title role as a sheltered young girl who has never had a date or other fun generally accepted as matter-of-fact by teenagers. Plot builds to her first romance and first high school dance while depicting the myriad details of family life in a small town. Paternal frustration also is a factor in the yarn and is made believable by George Murphy and Mary Astor, the parents who were prevented from carrying out their dreams for the future by Taylor's birth.

Murphy and Astor make an excellent team to carry the adult load. Taylor raises voice in song for school numbers to round out a talent display that registers strongly.

•

CYRANO DE BERGERAC

1950, 112 mins, US Ⓥ ⦿ b/w

Dir Michael Gordon ***Prod*** Stanley Kramer ***Scr*** Carl Foreman ***Ph*** Franz Planer ***Ed*** Harry Gerstad ***Mus*** Dimitri Tiomkin

Act Jose Ferrer, Mala Powers, William Prince, Morris Carnovsky, Lloyd Corrigan (United Artists)

More stage play than motion picture, Carl Foreman's screenplay is wisely concerned with letting the Brian Hooker words speak for themselves.

Interpreting the rhyme and prose of the play is Jose Ferrer. It comes to the screen as an outstanding achievement in histrionics, quick with humor and sadness.

The *Cyrano* plot needs little reprising. A man, made a clown by a great peninsular of a nose, supplies the love words so that another, more handsome of profile, may woo the girl to whom he has lost his heart.

Michael Gordon's direction doesn't always fulfill the

romantic, tragic, comedic and action possibilities, but permits a number of players to account for solid moments in a story that, essentially, belongs to one performer, Ferrer.

1950: Best Actor (Jose Ferrer)

•

CYRANO DE BERGERAC

1990, 138 mins, France Ⓥ ⊙ col

Dir Jean-Paul Rappeneau ***Prod*** Rene Cleitman, Michel Seydoux ***Scr*** Jean-Paul Rappeneau, Jean-Clark Carriere ***Ph*** Pierre Lhomme ***Ed*** Noelle Boisson ***Mus*** Jean-Claude Petit ***Art*** Ezio Frigerio

Act Gerard Depardieu, Anne Brochet, Vincent Perez, Jacques Weber, Roland Bertin, Philippe Morier-Genoud (Hachette Premiere/Camera One/Films A2/DD/UGC)

A winner by more than a nose, *Cyrano de Bergerac* attains a near-perfect balance of verbal and visual flamboyance. Gerard Depardieu's grand performance as the facially disgraced swordsman-poet sets a new standard with which all future *Cyranos* will have to reckon. Jean-Paul Rappeneau's sumptuous ($17 million) screen adaptation of Edmond Rostand's heroic verse play has dash, lyricism, and a superb acting ensemble.

Rappeneau and screenwriter Jean-Claude Carriere have opened up the play conventionally but intelligently. Their basic concern has been to iron out the stagey kinks in Rostand's fanciful plot and provide for a smooth, purely filmic rhythm. Rostand's famous Alexandrine rhyming couplets have been preserved as film dialogue. Carriere invented some 100 new verses of his own for transitions, but only a Rostand scholar would detect the tampering.

The play's 17th-century Paris settings are opulently reimagined by Italian stage designer Ezio Frigerio (who has worked with Giorgio Strehler). Pierre Lhomme's lensing is both subtle and sensational. The charming balcony scene and Cyrano's twilight death scene are both exquisite studies in finely graded light and shadow. There is grandeur in the battle of Arras sequences (shot on location in Hungary).

Roxanne is played with finesse and feeling by Anne Brochet, who captures the romantic immaturity and generosity of soul. Vincent Perez does quite well with the usually dull role of Christian, the young comrade-in-arms in love with and loved by Roxanne. Character's the inverse of Cyrano: a beautiful face, but a shallow inexpressive soul.

•

CZLOWIEK Z MARMURU
(MAN OF MARBLE)

1977, 161 mins, Poland Ⓥ col

Dir Andrzej Wajda ***Prod*** Barbara Pec-Slesicka ***Scr*** Aleksander Scibor-Rylski ***Ph*** Edward Klosinski ***Ed*** Halina Pugarowa, Maria Kalinciska ***Mus*** Andrzej Korzynski ***Art*** Allan Starksi

Act Jerzy Radziwilowicz, Krystyna Janda, Tadeusz Lomnicki, Jacek Lomnicki, Michal Tarkowski, Piotr Cieslak (Group X)

This epic film records two pages of history—the year 1952, when Poland became a People's Republic and the height of the Stalinization period; and the year 1976, when a revealing reassessment of the times takes place through a camera team's investigation into the fate of a former Worker's Hero.

Man of Marble is the story of Mateusz Birkut, a Cracow farmer who comes to the new industrial town of Nowa Huta and becomes overnight a High Performance Worker as a bricklayer. Birkut's gigantic portrait is hung on the main square, a docu pic is made on his life, and our simple, modest worker is raised to the level of a National Hero without quite knowing why.

Pic begins with a 24-year-old femme TV reporter, Agnieszka, working on her diploma pic: She is greedy to tell the full story of what happened to Birkut, who has long since dropped from sight. As in Orson Welles's *Citizen Kane*, she must solve the riddle of this man's life through direct interviews with people and rummaging through museum and film archives. It's her nervous search for "truth" that raises *Man of Marble* to a height of suspense, as in a detective thriller.

Scenes of fast-paced discussion through the corridors of the TV station set the mood and drive of the long-distance pic. The hotter Agnieszka gets on the trail, the less easy it is for her to keep her distance or find support from her TV superior to bring the pic to completion.

Man of Marble stands as a milestone in Polish cinema, another high point and perhaps the climax in Andrzej Wadja's career. All credits are outstanding, but Krystyna Janda as Agnieszka and Jerzy Radziwilowicz as Birkut in the lengthy flashback scenes deserve special praise.

CZLOWIEK Z ZELAZA
(MAN OF IRON)

1981, 140 mins, Poland Ⓥ col

Dir Andrzej Wajda ***Scr*** Aleksander Scibor-Rylski ***Ph*** Edward Klosinski ***Ed*** Halina Prugar ***Mus*** Andrzej Korzynski ***Art*** Allan Starski

Act Jerzy Radziwilowicz, Krystyna Janda, Marian Opania, Irene Byrska, Boguslaw Linda, Wieslawa Kosmalska (Film Unit X/Film Polski)

Man of Iron uses the same screenplay writer, the same key actors, and the exact same thematic approach (an interview technique) employed in *Man of Marble*, which covered the post-war years in Poland from the period of the Personality Cult to the Gdansk riots of 1970 and a little beyond. *Man of Iron* backtracks slightly to take up the main thread of the story from 1968 (the student reform movement) to August 1980 (the historic signing of the strike settlement at the Lenin Shipyards). Pic features the passion and determination of Maciet Tomczyk (Mateusz Birkut's son), one of the "second line" of workers in the Strike Committee headed by Lech Walesa.

It is August 1980. Winkiel (Marian Opania), a radio news reporter from Warsaw, is sent to do a hatchet job on Tomczyk (Jerzy Radziwilowicz) one of the strike leaders at Gdansk whose past record shows that he is a key figure in the movement. Upon arriving in Gdansk, Winkiel also discovers that Tomczyk's wife, Agnieszka (Krystyna Janda), has been arrested by the police in order to investigate her part in aiding the striking workers.

Winkiel can't even get into the shipyards with his Polish press pass. He does, however, meet a young TV technician, Dzidek (Boguslaw Linda), a classmate of Tomczyk's at the university, who invites him to see footage on the August 1970 riots never released. He also tells, in flashbacks, the story of Tomczyk's bitter disappointment when his father did not support the 1968 student movement.

Winkiel then meets three women: Tomczyk's mother, who has come all the way from Zakopane; Anna Hulewicz and her elderly mother, who offer eyewitness information on the death and burial of Birkut (some of the strongest scenes in the film); and Tomczyk's wife, Agnieszka, the student reporter in *Man of Marble*.

Man of Iron records history on the run. Less than eight months were required to make this historical epic, also slated as a five-hour TV series in Poland. The lensing communicates a feeling of restless energy and urgency. The actors, down to the least bit role, perform unaffected before the camera.

DA

1988, 102 mins, US Ⓥ ⊙ col

Dir Matt Clark ***Prod*** Julie Corman ***Scr*** Hugh Leonard ***Ph*** Alar Kivilo ***Ed*** Nancy Nuttal Beyda ***Mus*** Elmer Bernstein ***Art*** Frank Hallinan-Flood

Act Barnard Hughes, Martin Sheen, William Hickey, Karl Hayden, Doreen Hepburn, Hugh O'Connor (Dallas)

This adaptation of Hugh Leonard's autobiographical play and book, *Home Before Night* about an Irish-American playwright's journey of self-discovery from New York to his father's funeral in the Old Sod casts a beguiling spell, thanks to the playful richness of its language and the finely knit acting of Martin Sheen, Barnard Hughes and their supporting cast.

The linchpin of the affecting story is provided by Leonard's dramaturgic sleight of hand in presenting Charlie's (Sheen) dead father, Da (Hughes), and mother (Doreen Hepburn) as living, breathing temporal characters animated by the successful playwright's grief-catalyzed imagination.

Sheen's performance is distinguished by its subtlety, as he's swept up in the conflicting emotions that attend his wry encounters with his stubborn adolescent self (very capably rendered by Karl Hayden), his domineering mother and, most indelibly, the hard-headed, lyrically aphoristic gardener whose failings as an adoptive father the mature playwright must reconcile with his own hard-earned knowledge of human fallibility.

•

DAD

1989, 117 mins, US Ⓥ ⊙ col

Dir Gary David Goldberg ***Prod*** Joseph Stern, Gary David Goldberg ***Scr*** Gary David Goldberg ***Ph*** Jan Kiesser ***Ed*** Eric Sears ***Mus*** James Horner ***Art*** Jack DeGovia

Act Jack Lemmon, Ted Danson, Olympia Dukakis, Kathy Baker, Kevin Spacey, Ethan Hawke (Amblin/Universal)

Pic represents a promising feature directorial debut for TV producer Gary David Goldberg. There's certainly much that's funny, warm and endearing about *Dad*, which, based on William Wharton's novel, deals with the familiar theme of a grown child resolving his sense of duty toward an aging parent.

Unfortunately, prolonged tilling of that emotional terrain and seemingly endless verbalization of feelings diminish most of what's good about the film.

Ted Danson has the pivotal role of Jack Lemmon's somewhat estranged son, who returns from his sheltered world of Wall Street opulence to find his parents failing and infirm. Danson moves in with his parents to ease their final days, in the process finding new meaning in his relationship with his own college-age son (Ethan Hawke).

There's some repartee nicely delivered by the principals, including Kathy Baker and Kevin Spacey as Danson's sister and brother-in-law.

1989: NOMINATION: Best Makeup

•

DADDY LONG LEGS

1931, 80 mins, US b/w

Dir Alfred Santell ***Scr*** Sonya Levien, S. N. Behrman ***Ph*** Lucien Andriot ***Ed*** Ralph Dietrich ***Mus*** Hugo Friedhofer

Act Janet Gaynor, Warner Baxter, Una Merkel, John Arledge, Claude Gillingwater, Sr., Sheila Manners (Fox)

Nearly everybody either knows or imagines the story of *Daddy Long Legs*. Mary Pickford and Marshall Neilan, back in 1919, made a silent hit of it for First National. Fox, in remaking the picture into a talker, has repeated.

Janet Gaynor is the orphanage drudge who suddenly rebels against the harshness of the matron. She is unceremoniously adopted by a bachelor who is also a trustee of the orphanage. She falls in love with this man, who has sent her to college unawares to her.

After the kids depart from sight another funny group come in to keep the humorous end of the story up. These are Una Merkel and John Arledge as brother and sister. He's in love with July Abbott (Gaynor) and his sister is her roommate at college.

Santell's direction is good enough throughout but never better than in the first part where the kids run rampant with precocious talk and action. The orphanage scenes are helped by the presence of Elizabeth Patterson as the dyspeptic matron. Warner Baxter as the millionaire is an appealer here to women on a big scale.

1955: NOMINATIONS: Best Color Art Direction, Scoring of a Musical Picture, Song ("Something's Gotta Give")

•

DADDY LONG LEGS

1955, 126 mins, US Ⓥ ⊙ ▭ col

Dir Jean Negulesco ***Prod*** Samuel G. Engel ***Scr*** Phoebe Ephron, Henry Ephron ***Ph*** Leon Shamroy ***Ed*** William

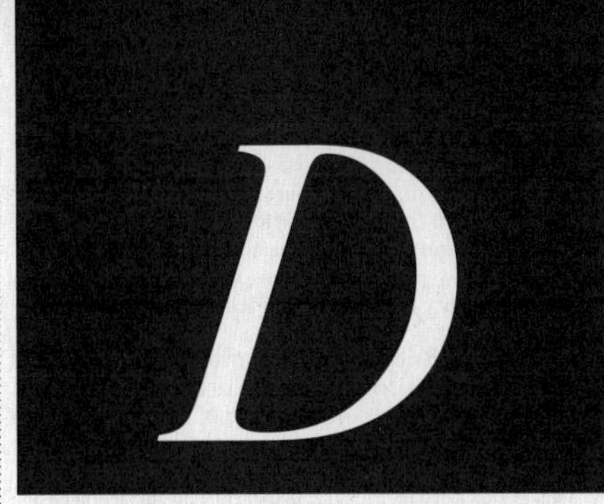

Reynolds ***Mus*** Alfred Newman (sup.) ***Art*** Lyle Wheeler, John DeCuir

Act Fred Astaire, Leslie Caron, Terry Moore, Thelma Ritter, Fred Clark, Charlotte Austin (20th Century-Fox)

Mary Pickford was the American sweetheart of an actress who suffered the orphanage hardships when First National made *Daddy Long Legs* in 1919. With Leslie Caron and Fred Astaire in the leads, the property [Jean Webster's novel] was completely rewritten and fashioned into an appealing musical [words and music by Johnny Mercer; ballet music by Alex North].

Astaire was a good choice and works well as the undisciplined and friendly moneybags who develops a wanna-get-married crush on the girl he sends through college, this despite the acknowledged difference in age. And he's still the agile hoofer, although the choreography he and David Robel blue-printed doesn't require too robust a workout. Caron is beguiling all the way.

Thelma Ritter and Fred Clark, as social and business aides to Astaire, team up for laughs—the Phoebe and Harry Ephron screenplay has some crackling dialogue.

•

DADDY'S DYIN' . . . WHO'S GOT THE WILL?

1990, 95 mins, US Ⓥ ⊙ col

Dir Jack Fisk ***Prod*** Sigurjon Sighvatsson, Steve Golin, Monty Montgomery ***Scr*** Del Shores ***Ph*** Paul Elliott ***Ed*** Edward Warschilka, Jr. ***Mus*** David McHugh ***Art*** Michelle Minch

Act Beau Bridges, Beverly D'Angelo, Tess Harper, Judge Reinhold, Amy Wright, Keith Carradine (Propaganda)

Del Shores's hit play about squabbling Texas siblings is brought to the screen with panache. Shores's script presents a bittersweet family reunion, as three sisters and a brother who don't like each other convene in tiny Loakie, Texas, to find out who got what in the will. Since dotty dad, who hasn't quite slipped away yet, can't remember where he put it, they're stuck together while they ransack the rambling old farmhouse looking for it.

Amy Wright as the pious, mothering sister who became a preacher's wife, Tess Harper as the salty-tongued single gal who wound up taking care of dad, and Molly McClure as righteous Mama Wheelis are all excellent.

Beau Bridges has an uncanny bead on blind, dumb cruelty as Orville, the boorish younger brother, an obstinate redneck garbage collector who keeps his hefty wife Marlene (Patrika Darbo) pinned under his meaty thumb with constant put-downs. Beverly D'Angelo steals scenes as the spoiled, scattered little runaround sister who's brought home a beatific California hippie-musician (Judge Reinhold) as the latest in a long line of consorts.

•

DA HONG DENGLONG GAO GAO GUA
(RAISE THE RED LANTERN)

1991, 122 mins, Hong Kong Ⓥ ⊙ col

Dir Zhang Yimou ***Prod*** Chiu Fu-sheng ***Scr*** Ni Zhen ***Ph*** Zhao Fei ***Ed*** Du Yuan ***Mus*** Zhao Jiping, Naoki Tachikawa ***Art*** Cao Jiuping

Act Gong Li, He Saifei, Ma Jingwu, Cao Cuifeng, Zhou Qi, Kong Lin (Era)

After scoring on the international art circuit with *Red Sorghum* and *Ju Dou*, former cinematographer Zhang Yimou delivers again with *Raise the Red Lantern*.

Pic deals even more pointedly with the oppression of women in China. Set in the 1920s, before the communist revolution, film opens with a beautiful young woman tearfully agreeing to become a concubine for a wealthy master. "Isn't that a woman's fate?" Songlian (Gong Li) asks.

In a lavish compound, Songlian takes her place as the youngest and most attractive of four wives. Insidious intrigue between the women immediately begins. With a slow accretion of insults, one-upmanship and diplomacy, film plays like a chess game.

Pacing is deliberate, but the story [from Su Tong's novella *Wives and Concubines/Qiqie chengqun*] is still gripping and visual textures are extraordinary. Gong's presence gives the film a constant erotic charge.

[Pic was belatedly released in China in 1992.]

•

DAISIES

SEE: SEDMIKRASKY

•

DAISY KENYON

1947, 100 mins, US b/w

Dir Otto Preminger ***Prod*** Otto Preminger ***Scr*** David Hertz ***Ph*** Leon Shamroy ***Ed*** Louis Leoffler ***Mus*** David Raksin ***Art*** Lyle R. Wheeler, George Davis

Act Joan Crawford, Dana Andrews, Henry Fonda, Ruth Warrick, Martha Stewart, Peggy Ann Garner (20th Century-Fox)

Triangle, in which Dana Andrews and Henry Fonda fight it out for the love of Joan Crawford, is basically a shallow lending-library affair [based on the novel by Elizabeth Janeway], but it's made to seem important by the magnetic trio's slick-smart backgrounds—plus, of course, excellent direction, sophisticated dialog, solid supporting cast and other flashy production values.

Crawford, a fashion illustrator living in a glamorized Greenwich Village walkup, plays Andrews's reluctant mistress. He's a wealthy, ruthless attorney who refuses to give up his wife (Ruth Warrick) and two kids (Peggy Ann Garner and Connie Marshall) to make an honest woman of Crawford (in the title role). Fonda, an ex-soldier but somewhat less of a he-man than Andrews, comes along and talks her into marrying him and going to live in a Cape Cod hideaway. But Andrews doesn't give up that easily.

There are some torrid love scenes, a violent sequence in which Crawford musses up Andrews when he tries to break up her marriage, and the several scenes in which the three get together for "civilized discussions" of their affairs. Charles LeMaire's wardrobe for Crawford, Warrick and Martha Stewart, playing Crawford's girlfriend, are knockouts.

Title role is a thesping plum, with the audience never knowing which guy Daisy is going to wind up with, and Crawford really makes the most of it.

•

DAISY MILLER

1974, 90 mins, US Ⓥ col

Dir Peter Bogdanovich ***Prod*** Peter Bogdanovich ***Scr*** Frederic Raphael ***Ph*** Alberto Spagnoli ***Ed*** Verna Fields ***Art*** Ferdinando Scarfiotti

Act Cybill Shepherd, Barry Brown, Cloris Leachman, Mildred Natwick, Eileen Brennan, Duilio Del Prete (Paramount)

Daisy Miller is a dud. Cybill Shepherd is miscast in the title role. Frederic Raphael's adaptation of the Henry James story doesn't play. The period production by Peter Bogdanovich is handsome. But his direction and concept seem uncertain and fumbled. Supporting performances by Mildred Natwick, Eileen Brennan and Cloris Leachman are, respectively, excellent, outstanding, and good.

The story has Shepherd flirting all over Europe, shocking the mannered society there as well as Barry Brown, very good as a captivated young man with a fondness for her. But his aunt (Natwick) quietly disapproves, her mother (Leachman) nervously tolerates it, while a Rome socialite (Brennan) is vocally offended. All form (much of it bad), no substance.

1974: NOMINATION: Best Costume Design

•

DALEKS—INVASION EARTH 2150 A.D.

1966, 84 mins, UK Ⓥ ▭ col

Dir Gordon Flemyng ***Prod*** Milton Subotsky, Max J. Rosenberg ***Scr*** Milton Subotsky, David Whitaker ***Ph*** John Wilcox ***Ed*** Ann Chegwidden ***Mus*** Bill McGuffie, Barry Gray ***Art*** George Provis

Act Peter Cushing, Bernard Cribbins, Ray Brooks, Andrew Keir, Roberta Tovey, Jill Curzon (Aaru)

Dr. Who, in his time and space machine, arrives in London in A.D. 2150 to find it ravaged after a Dalek invasion. The earth's cities have been razed by meteorites and cosmic rays and human beings have been turned into living dead men called Robomen. Prisoners have been taken and forced to work in a secret mine as slaves.

It is all fairly naive stuff [from the BBC TV serial created by Terry Nation] decked out with impressive scientific jargon. Peter Cushing, as the professor; Jill Curzon, as his niece, and Roberta Tovey, as the granddaughter, have learned to play it with the necessary seriousness. Bernard

Cribbins as the policeman provides some amusing light relief.

●

DALLAS
1950, 94 mins, US col
Dir Stuart Heisler ***Prod*** Anthony Veiller ***Scr*** John Twist ***Ph*** Ernest Haller ***Ed*** Clarence Kolster ***Mus*** Max Steiner
Act Gary Cooper, Ruth Roman, Steve Cochran, Raymond Massey, Leif Erickson, Barbara Payton (Warner)

Gary Cooper's return to saddle and six-shooter is to the good, and he makes quite a bit of the heroic and rugged opportunities in the John Twist story. His two co-stars, Ruth Roman and Steve Cochran, also carry off the pretentious aims.

Period is just following the war between the states, and the locale is Texas and the then pioneer town of Dallas. Cooper, a southerner, rides into the territory on the prowl for three brothers, war opportunists who had destroyed his home and family in Georgia. There's a romantic triangle, plus a land grab angle, to pad out the footage.

Direction by Stuart Heisler bogs down several times when story veers away from its main purpose, but the chases, gun battles and other movement come across with good action. Some of the slow spots are due to a lot of script palaver.

●

DAMAGE
1992, 112 mins, UK/France Ⓥ ⊙ col
Dir Louis Malle ***Prod*** Louis Malle ***Scr*** David Hare ***Ph*** Peter Biziou ***Ed*** John Bloom ***Mus*** Zbigniew Preisner ***Art*** Brian Morris
Act Jeremy Irons, Juliette Binoche, Miranda Richardson, Rupert Graves, Ian Bannen, Leslie Caron (Skreba/NEF/Canal Plus)

A complex look at an illicit affair that ends in disaster for all concerned, *Damage* is a cold, brittle film [from the novel by Josephine Hart] about raging, traumatic emotions. Unjustly famous before its release for its hardly extraordinary erotic content, this veddy British-feeling drama from vet French director Louis Malle proves both compelling and borderline risible, wrenching and yet emotionally pinched.

Jeremy Irons plays Stephen Fleming, a graying, very proper figure in the Tory establishment who has married into money and lives a carefully groomed and organized existence. His wife, Ingrid (Miranda Richardson), may be more intelligent than he; and son Martyn (Rupert Graves), has just embarked upon a promising journalism career.

At a boring political cocktail party, Stephen exchanges significant eye contact with his son's striking g.f., Anna Barton (Juliette Binoche), and destiny is written. At their next encounter Stephen is in Anna's pants in record time.

Irons's character becomes more loathsome as he goes along, but thesp's is expertly calibrated performance. Richardson puts frightening force behind her rage when all hell finally breaks loose.

1992: NOMINATION: Best Supp. Actress (Miranda Richardson)

●

DAMA S SOBACHKOY
(THE LADY WITH THE DOG; THE LADY WITH THE LITTLE DOG)
1960, 90 mins, USSR Ⓥ b/w
Dir Yosif Kheifits ***Scr*** Yosif Kheifits ***Ph*** Andrei Moskvin, Dmitri Meskhiev ***Mus*** N. Simonyan ***Art*** B. Manevich, I. Kaplan
Act Aleksei Batalov, Iya Savvina, Ala Chostakova, N. Alisova (Lenfilm)

To commemorate the 100th anni of the birth of the playwright-novelist-story writer Anton Chekhov, the Russians have come up with a perfectly transcribed version of one of his short stories. It concerns the Russia of the 1900s where the upper and middle classes were bored but where propriety stifled any chance of escape.

A married man (Aleksei Batalov) meets a married woman (Iya Savvina) during a stay in Yalta. They have an affair and part. He goes to see her again. She then comes to visit him in his town, but they know there is no way out of their impasse. Subtle direction evokes the inner states of the characters, and shows boredom without being boring.

Lensing is virtually perfect in bringing out the gray, somnolent aspects of the Russia of the times. Director Yosif Kheifits has not tried to impose a personal viewpoint and wisely kept the full feeling of the Chekhov tale. It is a successful pic, but talky and slow.

●

DAM BUSTERS, THE
1955, 125 mins, UK Ⓥ b/w
Dir Michael Anderson ***Prod*** Robert Clark, W. A. Whitaker ***Scr*** R. C. Sherriff ***Ph*** Erwin Hillier ***Ed*** Richard Best ***Mus*** Eric Coates, Leighton Lucas ***Art*** Robert Jones
Act Richard Todd, Michael Redgrave, Ursula Jeans, Derek Farr, Patrick Barr, John Fraser (Associated British)

As a record of a British operational triumph during the last war, *The Dam Busters* [adapted from Paul Brickhill's *Enemy Coast Ahead*] is a small slice of history, told with painstaking attention to detail and overflowing with the British quality of understatement.

This is the story of the successful raid on the Ruhr dams, when a small fleet of British bombers, using a new type of explosive, successfully breached the water supplies, which fed the Ruhr factories and caused desolation and havoc to the German war machine.

For more than 90 minutes, the film is devoted to the planning and preparation, and very absorbing material this proves to be. The reconstruction of the raid and the pounding of the dams is done with graphic realism. The aerial photography is one of the major technical credits.

The production is a personal triumph for Michael Anderson. Michael Redgrave, particularly, gives a vividly human portrayal of Dr. Barnes Wallis, the scientist, while Richard Todd makes a distinguished showing as Guy Gibson, the RAF commander.

1955: NOMINATION: Best Special Effects

●

DAMES
1934, 90 mins, US Ⓥ b/w
Dir Ray Enright, Busby Berkeley ***Scr*** Delmer Daves ***Ph*** Sid Hickox, George Barnes ***Ed*** Harold McLernon ***Art*** Robert Haas, Willy Pogany
Act Joan Blondell, Dick Powell, Ruby Keeler, ZaSu Pitts, Guy Kibbee, Hugh Herbert (Warner)

Heavier on the comedy but lighter on the story than WB's predecessors. There are five song numbers and all amazingly well done. Busby Berkeley pyramids attention in spectacular manner, at times making 'em wide-eyed with his choreographic mating of rhythmic formations with the camera.

Three sets of songwriters fashioned a corking score. Al Dubin and Harry Warren have the cream of the crop with the title song, "I Only Have Eyes for You," and "The Girl at the Ironing Board." Mort Dixon and Allie Wrubel are responsible for "Try and See It My Way," and Irving Kahal and Sammy Fain (latter a personable youth who plays himself in a songwriter's bit) contributed "When You Were a Smile on Your Mother's Lips."

"I Only Have Eyes for You" is one of the two most spectacular numbers with the entire chorus in Benda masks of Ruby Keeler. "Dames" is the spectacular topper-offer with the girls in opera length black tights and white blouses.

Ruby Keeler and Dick Powell again are the romantic interest, and again he is the ambitious songwriter who has just written a surefire musical comedy hit that's only begging for a backer, and again Keeler is the sympathetic and romantic inspiration. Joan Blondell is prominent in a decorously subdued but otherwise flip chorine who perpetrates a mild "shake" on Guy Kibbee.

●

DAMIEN: OMEN II
1978, 109 mins, US Ⓥ ⊙ ▭ col
Dir Don Taylor ***Prod*** Harvey Bernhard ***Scr*** Stanley Mann, Michael Hodges ***Ph*** Bill Butler ***Ed*** Robert Brown, Jr. ***Mus*** Jerry Goldsmith ***Art*** Philip M. Jeffries, Fred Harpman
Act William Holden, Lee Grant, Jonathan Scott-Taylor, Robert Foxworth, Lew Ayres, Sylvia Sidney (20th Century-Fox)

Alas, Little Orphan Damien, lucky enough to be taken in by a rich uncle after bumping off his first pair of foster parents, can't resist killing the second set, too, along with assorted friends of the family. Damien is obviously wearing out his welcome.

Damien is 13 and has a double personality problem, being both an Antichrist and a rather obnoxious teenager. Stoically played by Jonathan Scott-Taylor, Damien has apparently been behaving himself for the past seven years, since his uncle (William Holden) and aunt (Lee Grant) suspect nothing and love him very much as does his cousin (Lucas Donat).

Only cranky old Aunt Marion (Sylvia Sidney) knows something is wrong with the boy, but a raven gets rid of her. Then a pesky reporter (Elizabeth Shepherd) shows up. So the raven pecks her eyes out and she stumbles in front of a truck.

One day, Damien's platoon sergeant at the military school suggests he reads the *Book of Revelations* and find out why he's special. He soon gets the knack of killing people himself, with spectacular touches that top the decapitations of his tender years. [Screen story by Harvey Bernhard, based on characters created by David Seltzer.]

●

DAMNATION ALLEY
1977, 95 mins, US Ⓥ ▭ col
Dir Jack Smight ***Prod*** Jerome M. Zeitman, Paul Maslansky ***Scr*** Alan Sharp, Lukas Heller ***Ph*** Harry Stradling, Jr. ***Ed*** Frank J. Urioste ***Mus*** Jerry Goldsmith ***Art*** Preston Ames
Act Jan-Michael Vincent, George Peppard, Dominique Sanda, Paul Winfield, Jackie Earle Haley, Kip Niven (20th Century-Fox)

Damnation Alley is dull, stirred only occasionally by prods of special effects that only seem exciting compared to the dreariness that proceeded it. What's worse, it's dumb, depending on its stereotyped characters to do the most stupid things under the circumstances in order to keep the story moving.

Jan-Michael Vincent and George Peppard are airforce officers on duty in a desert missile bunker when World War III comes with a lot of stock shots of mushroom explosions.

Skip forward a couple of years through titled explanations that most of the country was destroyed and Earth tilted on its axis. But Vincent and Peppard are still in the desert with the other troops.

●

DAMNED, THE
(US: THESE ARE THE DAMNED)
1963, 87 mins, UK ▭ b/w
Dir Joseph Losey ***Prod*** Anthony Hinds ***Scr*** Evan Jones ***Ph*** Arthur Grant ***Ed*** Reginald Mills, James Needs ***Mus*** James Bernard ***Art*** Bernard Robinson
Act Macdonald Carey, Shirley Anne Field, Viveca Lindfors, Alexander Knox, Oliver Reed, Walter Gotell (Hammer/Swallow)

"What is a director's picture?" This one is. Although the cast is excellent, no one character dominates the action or overshadows the others. Joseph Losey's hand is so apparent that the film's considerable effectiveness must be accredited to him as must its few faults and the fearsome message it conveys.

Much of the film's appeal is visual, although the dialog is a credit to the scripter Evan Jones, [from H. L. Lawrence's novel *The Children of Light*]. The only objection is in its failure to take a stand.

Macdonald Carey, Shirley Anne Field, Alexander Knox (particularly good), Viveca Lindfors and Oliver Reed have principal roles in the quasi-sci fi story which centers on a group of children being exposed to radiation in preparation for the day predicted by Knox when global nuclear warfare will destroy all living things—except these few.

All the principals are excellent, with Reed playing a Teddy boy and brother of Field although his interest in her is strongly incestuous.

●

DAMNED, THE
1969, 163 mins, Italy/W. Germany Ⓥ col
Dir Luchino Visconti ***Prod*** Alfred Levy, Ever Haggiag ***Scr*** Nicola Badalucco, Enrico Medioli, Luchino Visconti ***Ph*** Armando Nannuzzi, Pasquale De Santis ***Mus*** Maurice Jarre ***Art*** Pasquale Romano
Act Dirk Bogarde, Ingrid Thulin, Helmut Berger, Charlotte Rampling, Florinda Bolkan, Rene Kolldehoff (Pegaso/Praesidens)

Luchino Visconti pulls out all stops to detail the progress of Nazism in the 1930s as seen via one upperclass family. This has got to be the most violent family since the Borgias. Screaming, yelling, scheming, and conniving over factory ownership is but part of it: they murder each other with no hesitation to achieve their ends, they have perverse sexual hang-ups, they are dope-fiends, and, in film's most spectacular sequence, a mother amongst them sleeps with her son.

Although obviously based on the Krupp family of steel magnates, the family in *The Damned* could never really exist in quite this way, and it seems clear that Visconti knows that it serves as a microcosm of Germany in the 1930s, a symbol of a country that began a world war.

The acting is so much in an older tradition that it becomes very hard to judge, but Helmut Berger's progress from meek son to matricidal Nazi is clearly a superior job. Ingrid Thulin is able to handle the violent emotions required for her role as Berger's mother, although Dirk Bogarde is sometimes uncomfortable as her lover.

1969: NOMINATIONS: Best Original Story & Screenplay

●

DAMN THE DEFIANT!
SEE: H.M.S. DEFIANT

•

DAMN YANKEES
(UK: WHAT LOLA WANTS)
1958, 110 mins, US Ⓥ ⊙ col
Dir George Abbott, Stanley Donen ***Prod*** George Abbott, Stanley Donen ***Scr*** George Abbott ***Ph*** Harold Lipstein ***Ed*** Frank Bracht ***Mus*** Richard Adler, Jerry Ross ***Art*** William Eckart, Jean Eckart, Stanley Fleischer
Act Tab Hunter, Gwen Verdon, Ray Walston, Russ Brown, Shannon Bolin, Nathaniel Frey (Warner)

The *Damn Yankees* team, which ran the score high for three seasons in Broadway's legit ballpark, was reassembled to go to bat in this sparkling film version. Sole "newcomers" in the trek from Broadway to Burbank are Stanley Donen, who co-produced and co-directed, and Tab Hunter, who stars.

Story, based on the Faust legend and Douglass Wallop's novel, *The Year the Yankees Lost the Pennant,* revolves around a Washington Senator fan who would give his soul for a long-ball hitter and a chance to beat the New York Yankees. Given his chance by the devil himself, the fan is wooshed into a 22-year-old who proceeds to become the national hero of the national pastime in the national capital, thus giving the Senators a pennant and the Yankees a bad name.

Gwen Verdon makes a sprightly 172-year-old witch who has been sumptuously embodied to stalk Tab Hunter. Ray Walston, with exaggerated widow's peak and devilish red accessories, makes a perfect comedy Satan. Hunter [substituting for Broadway's Stephen Douglass] is sympathetic as the young baseball great, confused by all that's happening to him.

Still held in prominence is the Richard Adler–Jerry Ross musical score—a tuneful, storytelling assortment of gag songs and ballads. Top production goes to "Two Lost Souls" (a la "Hernando's Hideaway" from same pair's *Pajama Game*) and "Shoeless Joe from Hannibal, Mo." "You've Gotta Have Heart" remains a standout, with a seductive "Whatever Lola Wants" and a fast-moving "Who's Got the Pain," danced with choreographer Bob Fosse, himself a fine hoofer.

1958: NOMINATION: Best Scoring of a Musical Picture

•

DAMSEL IN DISTRESS, A
1937, 100 mins, US/UK Ⓥ ⊙ b/w
Dir George Stevens ***Prod*** Pandro S. Berman ***Scr*** P. G. Wodehouse, Ernest Pagano, S. K. Lauren ***Ph*** Joseph H. August ***Ed*** Henry Berman ***Mus*** Victor Baravalle (dir.) ***Art*** Van Nest Polglase, Carroll Clark
Act Fred Astaire, George Burns, Gracie Allen, Joan Fontaine, Reginald Gardiner, Constance Collier (RKO)

With Burns & Allen co-starred with the screen's No. 1 tapster, *A Damsel in Distress* holds plenty—dancing, comedy, the usual sumptuous investiture accorded by Pandro Berman and RKO to any Astaire picture. And those Gershwin songs.

It's a gay, frothy book [story by P. G. Wodehouse], in a British background. Astaire is cast as the juvenile who resents the Lothario buildup endowed him by George Burns as his hyper-dynamic p.a. Joan Fontaine is the titular "maiden in distress," an ingenue of nobility which brings the setting to a suburban London estate belonging to Lord Marshmorton (capitally played by Montagu Love).

Astaire and his vet terp aide, Hermes Pan, have devised four corking dance routines which director George Stevens has expertly envisioned and mounted. The finale is a four-minute "drum dance," Astaire's solo. Burns & Allen blend excellently, and their comedy is a standout. Fontaine is passively fair as the ingenue, nicely looking the role but otherwise undistinguished.

Gershwin songs are dandy. "Nice Work If You Can Get It," "A Foggy Day in London Town," "Things Are Looking Up" and "Can't Be Bothered Now" are the titles and all are okay.

1937: Best Dance Direction ("Fun House")

•

DANCE OF THE VAMPIRES: PARDON ME, BUT YOUR TEETH ARE IN MY NECK
(US: THE FEARLESS VAMPIRE KILLERS)
1967, 107 mins, UK Ⓥ ▭ col
Dir Roman Polanski ***Prod*** Gene Gutowski ***Scr*** Gerard Brach, Roman Polanski ***Ph*** Douglas Slocombe ***Ed*** Alastair McIntyre ***Mus*** Christopher Komeda ***Art*** Wilfrid Shingleton
Act Roman Polanski, Jack MacGowran, Alfie Bass, Jessie Robins, Sharon Tate, Ferdy Mayne (M-G-M/Cadre/Filmways)

Dance of the Vampires is a spoof on the Dracula theme. Roman Polanski is on a quadruple assignment. He produced, directed and collaborated on story and screenplay with Gerard Brach and costars. Brach and Polanski wrote script in French and piece then was translated into English by Gillian and John Sutton [version reviewed is 91-minute U.S. one, cut by Martin Ransohoff and disowned by Polanski.]

Plotline (?) deals with an old professor and his assistant who arrive at a Central Europe inn in dead of winter on a crusade to hunt down and destroy the chilling mystery figures of generations of legends, the dreaded vampires who stalk Slovania.

Jack MacGowran [voiced by Warren Mitchell] cavorts as the nimble oldster and Polanski [voiced by David Spenser] plays his somewhat dimwitted assistant, both up to the demands (?) of their roles. Ferdy Mayne is the menacing Dracula, and Sharon Tate, lady in question, looks particularly nice in her bath. Alfie Bass, the innkeeper; Iain Quarrier as the count's effeminate son, who has some fangs all his own; Terry Downes, the toothy hunchback castle handyman (who might be Quasimodo returned), and Jessie Robbins, innkeeper's spouse, lend proper support.

•

DANCER
SEE: BILLY ELLIOT

•

DANCER IN THE DARK
2000, 137 mins, Denmark/Sweden/France Ⓥ ⊙ ▭ col
Dir Lars Von Trier ***Prod*** Vibeke Windelov ***Scr*** Lars Von Trier ***Ph*** Robby Mueller ***Ed*** Molly Malene Stensgaard, Francois Gedigier ***Mus*** Bjork ***Art*** Karl Juliusson
Act Bjork, Catherine Deneuve, David Morse, Peter Stormare, Joel Grey, Vincent Paterson, Cara Seymour, Jean-Marc Barr, Vladica Kostic, Udo Kier, Zeljko Ivanek (Zentropa/Trust Film Svenska/Film i Vast/Liberator)

The legend of Lars Von Trier—part deserved, part self-constructed—comes crashing to the ground with *Dancer in the Dark*, a nearly 2½-hour demo of auteurist self-importance that's artistically bankrupt on almost every level. An attempt to feed off the heritage of the traditional Hollywood musical while reinterpreting it for a young, modern audience through the prism of Von Trier's romantic fatalism, pic shows nary a sign of the bold innovator of *The Kingdom* and *Breaking the Waves* nor the genuine provocateur of *The Idiots*.

Pic has all the feel of a film buff gratuitously deconstructing the genre and lacking any feel for music or movement beyond the most obvious. Typically, Von Trier's inspiration seems to be not so much classic Hollywood/Broadway musicals in their original form but '60s Euro refits (most notably Jacques Demy's *The Young Girls of Rochefort*), sans love or admiration.

Pic's most affecting musical numbers come when Icelandic singer-composer Bjork is left alone to do what she does best, crooning mystically in her cell or, at the very end, pouring out her still-undiminished optimism. Wearing thick, geeky glasses and defiantly unglamorous, Bjork makes an occasionally touching, mostly awkward thesp who's in line with the self-sacrificing heroines of Von Trier's *Waves* and *The Idiots* (to which *Dancer* forms the third of his so-called "Golden Heart" trilogy).

Also dissipating the efforts of the rest of the cast are the yards of feeble, uninteresting dialogue and uninspired, hand-held shooting (with Von Trier himself operating for d.p. Robby Mueller).

Catherine Deneuve, recalling Demy's French musicals simply by her presence, makes little impact in a role originally written for a black American woman.

•

DANCES WITH WOLVES
1990, 183 mins, US/UK Ⓥ ⊙ ▭ col
Dir Kevin Costner ***Prod*** Jim Wilson, Kevin Costner ***Scr*** Michael Blake ***Ph*** Dean Semler ***Ed*** Neil Travis ***Mus*** John Barry ***Art*** Jeffrey Beecroft
Act Kevin Costner, Mary McDonnell, Graham Greene, Rodney A. Grant, Floyd Red Crow Westerman, Tantoo Cardinal (Tig/Majestic)

In his directorial debut, Kevin Costner brings a rare degree of grace and feeling to this elegiac tale of a hero's adventure of discovery among the Sioux Indians on the pristine Dakota plains of the 1860s.

Costner stars as Lt. John Dunbar, a Union officer in the Civil War invited to choose his own post after an act of heroism. Opting for the farthest reaches of the frontier because he wants "to see it before it disappears," he transplants himself from a weary and cynical war culture to the windswept clarity of the Dakota plains.

His only company as he passes the days are his horse, a gangling wolf who keeps a nervous distance, and finally, a Sioux Indian who tries to steal the horse and is frightened off by Dunbar.

He discovers a culture so deeply refreshing to his spirit, compared with the detritus he's left behind, that, by the time the U.S. Army bothers to look for him, he has become a Sioux and his name is Dances With Wolves.

Lensed on location in South Dakota over 17 weeks, pic is infused with the natural grandeur of the plains and sky. Score by John Barry makes a major contribution, varying from the elegiac tone of the main theme to the heart-racing primal rhythms of the buffalo and scalp dances.

From its three-hour length, which amazingly does not become tiresome, to its bold use of subtitled Lakota language (the Sioux tongue) for at least a third of the dialog, it's clear the filmmakers were proceeding without regard for the rules.

Mary McDonnell is impressive as Stands With A Fist, an emotionally traumatized white woman adopted by the Sioux who helps Dunbar communicate with them.

[In December 1991, a 232-min. "extended version" world preemed in the U.K., and was later released on home video.]

1990: Best Picture, Director, Adapted Screenplay, Cinematography, Sound, Original Score, Editing

NOMINATIONS: Best Actor (Kevin Costner), Supp. Actor (Graham Green), Supp. Actress (Mary McDonnell), Art Direction, Costume Design

•

DANCE WITH A STRANGER
1985, 101 mins, UK Ⓥ ⊙ col
Dir Mike Newell ***Prod*** Roger Randall-Cutler ***Scr*** Shelagh Delaney ***Ph*** Peter Hannan ***Ed*** Mick Audsley ***Mus*** Richard Hartley ***Art*** Andrew Mollo
Act Miranda Richardson, Rupert Everett, Ian Holm, Matthew Carroll, Tom Chadbon, Jane Bertish (First Picture/Goldcrest/NFFC)

Dance with a Stranger is a tale of dark passions based on a true story of the London underworld during the 1950s.

Film charts the rocky course of the relationship between Ruth Ellis, a divorcée and prostitute-turned-nightclub manageress, and the upper-class dropout David Blakeley. He's too emotionally immature to care while she's too infatuated to take the commonsense course of ending the affair. Film ends with Ellis entering mythology as the last woman to be hanged under British law, for her shooting of Blakeley.

The script is densely packed with social and psychological nuances. Audiences are left largely to draw their own conclusions as to what drew the seemingly ill-matched couple together.

Miranda Richardson's performance as Ruth Ellis is first rate. With her rolling eyes and impulsive gestures, she captures the delicate nuances of an attractive girl who's both cool and coquettish. Major flaw is Rupert Everett's inability to convey more about David Blakeley than that he's set to fail consistently in work and life.

•

DANCING IN THE DARK
1949, 92 mins, US Ⓥ col
Dir Irving Reis ***Prod*** George Jessel ***Scr*** Mary C. McCall, Jr., Jay Dratler ***Ph*** Harry Jackson ***Ed*** Louis Loeffler ***Mus*** Howard Dietz, Arthur Schwartz
Act William Powell, Mark Stevens, Betsy Drake, Adolphe Menjou, Randy Stuart (20th Century-Fox)

Twist to the backstage yarn places it in Hollywood at the 20th-Fox studio and the settings advantageously capture a showbiz flavor that lends credibility. Old formula of the story could have been trite in less expert hands.

Plot line has William Powell, a has-been, steered into a job at 20th-Fox as talent scout after he has refused help from the Motion Picture Relief Fund. Studio is hot after a Broadway singing star and Powell's friendship with her father is the peg for his job. He goes to New York with studio press rep Mark Stevens to sign her up, but double-crosses the lot by signing unknown Betsy Drake.

Powell's work is a great personal triumph. Drake's performance has warmth and charm and Stevens does well. Adolphe Menjou takes off headman Zanuck to a fare-thee-well.

•

DANCING LADY
1933, 90 mins, US Ⓥ ⊙ b/w
Dir Robert Z. Leonard ***Prod*** David O. Selznick (exec.) ***Scr*** Allen Rivkin, P. J. Wolfson ***Ph*** Oliver T. Marsh ***Ed*** Margaret Booth ***Mus*** Louis Silvers (dir.) ***Art*** Merrill Pye
Act Joan Crawford, Clark Gable, Franchot Tone, May Robson, Winnie Lightner, Fred Astaire (M-G-M)

Joan Crawford's Winter Garden chorine days stand her in good stead in *Dancing Lady,* to demonstrate her versatility as a song-and-dance artist. A formula backstage plot [from a novel by James Warner Bellah] misses nothing, not even the Cinderella rise to stage prominence, the Park Avenue playboy (Franchot Tone) who casually mentions running his yacht down to Tahiti and Cuba, and the taciturn stage producer (Clark Gable) who finally succumbs to the charms of the alumna of the burleycue emporium who hits the limelight in a raid on the theater.

The travail of pre-opening rehearsals, the financial ramifications, the backstage choristers' opinions of the "Duchess" (Crawford), because of Tone's obvious romantic interest, the angling and finally the staging of the big numbers are of generally familiar pattern.

The dance numbers here are all well done by Sammy Lee and Eddie Prinz. Crawford works with Fred Astaire in "Let's Go, Bavarian," both doing their terp stuff with commendable expertness, as a "magic carpet" idea transplants them into a Tyrolean locale amidst a flock of frolicking Bavarians.

Art Jarrett and Nelson Eddy, from radio and the varieties, figure, like Astaire, in lending authenticity to some of the musical stuff. Ditto Bob Benchley, who behaves like a Broadway columnist would.

•

DANCIN' THRU THE DARK

1990, 95 mins, UK Ⓥ col

Dir Mike Ockrent ***Prod*** Andree Molyneux, Annie Russell ***Scr*** Willy Russell ***Ph*** Philip Bonham-Carter ***Ed*** John Stothart ***Mus*** Willy Russell ***Art*** Paul Joel

Act Claire Hackett, Con O'Neill, Angela Clarke, Mark Womack, Julia Deakin, Simon O'Brien (BBC/Formost)

Shirley Valentine writer Willy Russell returns to his native Liverpool with a gritty low-budget comedy.

Pic started life as the play *Stags and Hens* in 1978 and retains many stagebound aspects, especially the male and female toilets where much of the action takes place. Most of the Liverpudlian cast have been in Russell plays before, while tyro helmer Ockrent directed the original West End and U.S. stage versions of Russell's *Educating Rita*.

The strong femme role is Linda (Claire Hackett), who is out on the town with friends on the night before her wedding. Unfortunately her hubbie-to-be and his friends also end up at the same nightspot. Arriving back in Liverpool for a gig is now successful popster Peter (Con O'Neill), Linda's ex-boyfriend. His friends in the band can't believe the seedy side of Liverpool ("Like Beirut without the sun") and the bad news is they're signed to perform at that same nightspot.

Pic is an amusingly accurate look at Liverpool lifestyles amongst the young and aimless, and while the transition from humor to drama is a bit uncomfortable *Dancin' Thru the Dark* is ultimately satisfying and enjoyable.

•

DANDY IN ASPIC, A

1968, 107 mins, UK Ⓥ ⊙ ▭ col

Dir Anthony Mann, [Laurence Harvey] ***Prod*** Anthony Mann ***Scr*** Derek Marlowe ***Ph*** Christopher Challis ***Ed*** Thelma Connell ***Mus*** Quincy Jones, Ernie Sheldon ***Art*** Carmen Dillon, Patrick McLoughlin

Act Laurence Harvey, Tom Courtenay, Mia Farrow, Harry Andrews, Peter Cook, Lionel Stander (Columbia)

A routine, poorly-titled espionage meller loaded with uninteresting, cardboard characters. Laurence Harvey, who finished pic after sudden death in Europe of producer-director Anthony Mann, and Tom Courtenay, both evidently working off pix commitments, are stiff and dull.

All-location lensing, in London and West Berlin, provides some documentary flavor as well as excuse for irrelevant plot setups, interestingly photographed.

Dandy was adapted by Derek Marlowe from his book. Harvey, it seems, is a double agent and everyone in British Intelligence, except Courtenay, knows about it.

All of which leaves an audience wondering what Mia Farrow had to do with the film. Good question. She looks like a combination of Twiggy and the archetypical Hollywood girl-next-door. Farrow's footage is limited and so, unfortunately, is her apparent acting range.

•

DANGER ISLAND
(AKA: MR. MOTO IN DANGER ISLAND)

1939, 70 mins, US b/w

Dir Herbert I. Leeds ***Prod*** John Stone (exec.) ***Scr*** Peter Milne ***Ph*** Lucien Andriot ***Ed*** Harry Reynolds

Act Peter Lorre, Jean Hersholt, Amanda Duff, Warren Hymer, Richard Lane, Leon Ames (20th Century-Fox)

There is a sameness about the Mr. Moto pictures, yet the plot of each new story surrounding the detective's adventures are always intriguing, and the action is usually carried out in such a manner as to be exciting, suspenseful and melodramatic. This one is also well bolstered by comedy relief, with Warren Hymer, a wrestler, becoming a self-appointed assistant to Lorre. His assignment to get laughs has been expertly planned and Hymer carries it out for maximum results.

Locale this time [in the seventh of the series] is Puerto Rico, where unknowns are suspected of engaging in diamond smuggling. Guilt, as usual, points in many directions and, as usual, is too often suggested by various characters who, if natural, wouldn't be arousing so much police concern. The girl is Amanda Duff, a very attractive type, who has comparatively little to do in a romance with a very youngish officer (Robert Lowery).

Lorre is again the suave, calmly calculating Sherlock Holmes, whose size belies his ability to overcome aggressors having twice his apparent stamina. A capable cast of seasoned players surround him, including Jean Hersholt (doing what sounds a bit like a German accent).

•

DANGEROUS

1935, 78 mins, US Ⓥ ⊙ b/w

Dir Alfred E. Green ***Prod*** Harry Joe Brown ***Scr*** Laird Doyle ***Ph*** Ernie Haller ***Ed*** Thomas Richards ***Art*** Hugh Reticker

Act Bette Davis, Franchot Tone, Margaret Lindsay, Alison Skipworth, John Eldredge, Dick Foran (Warner)

Laird Doyle knows his romantic dialog. Better than he knows his plot, but with the former carrying the latter, he has banged out an appealing scenario for the women in *Dangerous*.

The triangle involves a successful young architect, a society girl and an actress. Bette Davis loses the man to the other girl, but she has the closing sequence all to herself, and while the sympathy is distributed equally among all three characters, it's unquestionably Davis's picture at the conclusion.

The actress has been famous but has hit the skids and is soused when the architect first meets her in a cellar joint. There is a series of complications, including the reappearance of an almost forgotten husband and an automobile crash. Society girl hovers in the background after the architect breaks off their engagement upon falling for the actress. The production of a show on his money is also worked in.

Laird's dialog is adult, intelligent and has a rhythmic beat. Davis's performance is fine on the whole, despite a few imperfect moments. When called upon to reach an intense dramatic pitch without hysterics, Davis is capable of turning the trick. Yet there are moments in *Dangerous* when a lighter acting mood would be opportune.

Franchot Tone is splendid as the architect. Margaret Lindsay has a sit-'n'-wait assignment that didn't call for exertion.

•

DANGEROUS GAME
(AKA: SNAKE EYES)

1993, 107 mins, US Ⓥ ⊙ col

Dir Abel Ferrara ***Prod*** Mary Kane ***Scr*** Nicholas St. John ***Ph*** Ken Kelsch ***Ed*** Anthony Redman ***Mus*** Joe Delia ***Art*** Alex Tavoularis

Act Harvey Keitel, Madonna, James Russo, Nancy Ferrara, Reilly Murphy, Victor Argo (Maverick/PentAmerica)

Maverick helmer Abel Ferrara returns to the mood and, to some extent, the theme of his controversial cult item *Bad Lieutenant*, also toplining Harvey Keitel. Perfs, as usually in Ferrara's movies, are powerful but, despite the presence of Madonna, *Dangerous Game* is another abrasive, confrontational downer.

Pic opens in wintry New York, as filmmaker Eddie Israel (Keitel) leaves his wife (Nancy Ferrara, helmer's spouse) and small son to fly to the Coast to work on a new movie, *Mother of Mirrors*, starring actors Sarah Jennings (Madonna) and Francis Burns (James Russo) as a couple whose marriage is disintegrating. Jennings's character, Claire, has found religion and wants to halt a destructive lifestyle of booze, drugs and sexual experimentation. Burns's character, Russell, rejects her change of attitude angrily and with increasing violence.

Regular Ferrara scripter Nicholas St. John has devised a screenplay in which the stresses of filming spill into private lives. As filming nears its close, the director finds his personal traumas intruding more and more into the fictional material.

Dangerous Game is raw, intense material, with an aura of authenticity. But despite extensive four-letter dialogue, pic plays down the sexual content, and Madonna remains clothed almost throughout. Keitel again proves he's one of the finest actors around.

[Pic was world preemed at the 1993 Venice fest under the title *Snake Eyes*. Release title was subsequently changed, for copyright reasons.]

•

DANGEROUS LIAISONS
SEE: LES LIAISONS DANGEREUSES

•

DANGEROUS LIAISONS

1988, 120 mins, US Ⓥ ⊙ col

Dir Stephen Frears ***Prod*** Norma Heyman, Hank Moonjean ***Scr*** Christopher Hampton ***Ph*** Philippe Rousselot ***Ed*** Mick Audsley ***Mus*** George Fenton ***Art*** Stuart Craig

Act Glenn Close, John Malkovich, Michelle Pfeiffer, Swoosie Kurtz, Mildred Natwick, Uma Thurman (Warner)

A scandalous, often-censored literary sensation for two centuries and a highbrow international theatrical hit, *Les Liaisons Dangereuses* has been turned into a good but incompletely realized film.

This incisive study of sex as an arena for manipulative power games takes too long to catch fire and suffers from a deficient central performance.

Choderlos de Laclos's 1782 epistolary novel expertly chronicled the cunning, cold-blooded sexual calculations of the French prerevolutionary upper class as represented by two of its idle, brilliant members, the Marquise de Merteuil and the Vicomte de Valmont. Former lovers, these two ideally matched players hatch schemes of deceit, revenge and debauchery.

The classic rake, Valmont (John Malkovich) at the outset is challenged by Merteuil (Glenn Close) to deflower a 16-year-old virgin, Cecile de Volanges (Uma Thurman), before Merteuil's former lover can go through with his marriage to the exquisite adolescent.

Valmont considers this too easy, however, and instead proposes to seduce Madame de Tourvel (Michelle Pfeiffer), a virtuous, highly moral married woman.

Glenn Close is admirably cast as the proud, malevolent Merteuil while the real problem is Malkovich's Valmont. This sly actor conveys the character's snaky, premeditated Don Juanism. But he lacks the devilish charm and seductiveness one senses Valmont would need to carry off all his conquests.

1988: Best Art Direction, Adapted Screenplay, Costume Design

NOMINATIONS: Best Picture, Actress (Glenn Close), Supp. Actress (Michelle Pfeiffer), Score

•

DANGEROUSLY THEY LIVE

1942, 77 mins, US b/w

Dir Robert Florey ***Prod*** Ben Stoloff ***Scr*** Marion Parsonnet ***Ph*** L. William O'Connell ***Ed*** Harold McLernon

Act John Garfield, Nancy Coleman, Raymond Massey, Lee Patrick, Esther Dale, Moroni Olsen (Warner)

This meller treats with Nazi spies and Bundsmen in the United States. Scripter Marion Parsonnet, although turning in a workmanlike job on the dialogue, is certainly not hep to hospital routine or the methods of neurologists. She makes the treatment of a brain injury resulting in amnesia look so simple as to also look silly.

The story starts excitingly when Nancy Coleman, a British Intelligence operative, is kidnapped by German spies while en route to Grand Central Station in NY with vital shipping information. The phoney cab driver, however, cracks up and she's rushed to a hospital by ambulance-doctor John Garfield.

Garfield looks and acts least impressive when playing a man in white. Later he gets over with his usual expert acting. Coleman is pretty and a fine little actress. She has the most difficult histrionic part and acquits herself all the way.

•

DANGEROUS MINDS

1995, 99 mins, US Ⓥ ⊙ col

Dir John N. Smith ***Prod*** Don Simpson, Jerry Bruckheimer ***Scr*** Ronald Bass ***Ph*** Pierre Letarte ***Ed*** Tom Rolf ***Mus*** Wendy & Lisa ***Art*** Donald Graham

Act Michelle Pfeiffer, George Dzundza, Courtney B. Vance, Robin Bartlett, Bruklin Harris, Renoly Santiago (Hollywood)

Giving the impression that it thinks it's a lot tougher and hard-hitting than it is, *Dangerous Minds* is a kid-gloves treatment of the problems in urban public schools. This earnest, sweet-natured inspirational drama almost seems like something from another, more innocent era.

It's too bad the film feels so fanciful, since it's based on a true-life memoir, *My Posse Don't Do Homework*, of a teacher. A dressed-down Michelle Pfeiffer plays LouAnne Johnson, an ex-Marine who turns up at Parkmont High for a job interview and is immediately thrust into teaching English to some "rejects from hell."

Realizing she needs to grab their attention fast, LouAnne supervises a half-baked karate demonstration, which sets her at odds with the soft-spoken, by-the-book principal (Courtney B. Vance). Most simplistic of all, she constantly relates her teaching to the most clichéd aspects of the students' environments—drugs and violence—in an attempt to get them to relate to it. Also against common practice, LouAnne becomes personally involved in some of her more promising students' lives.

Although shot in Northern California, the picture shows virtually nothing of city life beyond the schoolyard. The kids are given little dimension. The same could be said of LouAnne, who lives alone and has no friends or acquaintances. This can be explained partly by the fact that the character of her boyfriend, played by Andy Garcia, was eliminated from the film after it was shot.

•

DANGEROUS MOONLIGHT
(US: SUICIDE SQUADRON)
1941, 90 mins, UK Ⓥ b/w
Dir Brian Desmond Hurst ***Prod*** William Sistrom ***Scr*** Terence Young ***Ph*** George Perinal ***Ed*** Alan Jaggs ***Mus*** Richard Addinsell ***Art*** John Bryan
Act Anton Walbrook, Sally Gray, Derrick de Marney, Cecil Parker, Percy Parsons, Kenneth Kent (RKO)

Terence Young's screenplay glosses a lot, dialog is okay, but plot is short on action apart from a zingy air battle in last few hundred feet. The same prosaic line is taken by Brian Desmond Hurst in directing tale of a young Polish composer with the hands of a musician and the heart of a flyer. Piloting is slow and methodical, sans highlights.

Fighting a losing air battle when Nazis invade Poland, Stefan Radetzky (Anton Walbrook) is fixed for an escape to Romania since fellow pilots deem his music-making of more use to their country. Prior to winging he meets Carole Peters (Sally Gray), a newsgirl from the U.S. When booked later for a fund-raising concert tour of America, the pair's paths cross again. This time they marry, but Walbrook is unable to repress the pilot urge.

Walbrook enacts with his customary under-playing, this time almost to a point of self-suffocation. Similarly, Gray is screened for glamor that palls after too much of such footage. She's a nifty looker, but over-poses. Effect is something like a series of screen tests.

•

DANGEROUS MOVES
SEE: LA DIAGONALE DU FOU

•

DANGEROUS WHEN WET
1953, 95 mins, US Ⓥ ⊙ col
Dir Charles Walters ***Prod*** George Wells ***Scr*** Dorothy Kingsley ***Ph*** Harold Rosson ***Ed*** John McSweeney, Jr. ***Mus*** Georgie Stoll (dir.) ***Art*** Cedric Gibbons, Jack Martin Smith
Act Esther Williams, Fernando Lamas, Jack Carson, Charlotte Greenwood, Denise Darcel, Donna Corcoran (M-G-M)

A light mixture of tunes, comedy, water ballet and Esther Williams in a bathing suit are offered in *Dangerous When Wet*. Best of the musical stints is an underwater cartoon sequence [by Fred Quimby, William Hanna and Joseph Barbera] involving Williams and Tom and Jerry to a reprise of "In My Wildest Dreams."

Plot deals with a swimming family that falls in with Jack Carson, a salesman of a liquid vitamin, and decides to swim the English Channel en masse, so they can get enough money to buy a prize bull for their Arkansas farm. Romance comes Williams's way in the person of Fernando Lamas, wealthy peddler of French champagne, when he rescues her after she has lost her bearings in a heavy Channel fog while practicing.

Williams becomes the costumes designed by Helen Rose and looks good in her water work. Also, she handles dialogue easily in scenes with Lamas and Carson. Lamas charms his way through a role that, essentially, requires that type of emphasis. Carson is topnotch as the producer, a sort of traveling salesman with an interest in the farmer's daughter that gets nowhere. Instead, he gets Denise Darcel, a French entry in the Channel swim, and she's worth getting.

•

DANGEROUS WOMAN, A
1993, 101 mins, US Ⓥ ⊙ col
Dir Stephen Gyllenhaal ***Prod*** Naomi Foner ***Scr*** Naomi Foner ***Ph*** Robert Elswit ***Ed*** Harvey Rosenstock ***Mus*** Carter Burwell ***Art*** David Brisbin
Act Debra Winger, Barbara Hershey, Gabriel Byrne, David Strathairn, Chloe Webb, John Terry (Amblin/Rollercoast)

Both absorbing and exasperating, *A Dangerous Woman* is such a small-scale character piece that it might have been more at home on the small screen. Film's main attraction is totally change-of-pace lead performance by Debra Winger that some will find heartbreaking and others will consider amusing.

Winger has transformed herself considerably to play Martha, a pudgy, goggle-eyed nerd who dresses like a high school wallflower and has probably never had a date, let alone a boyfriend. Martha works at a small town cleaners, and lives with her aunt Frances (Barbara Hershey), a wealthy California widow rancher. Martha's distinguishing trait is that she cannot lie.

When she rightly accuses white trash employee Getso (David Strathairn) of stealing money, she's canned. Back on the ranch, itinerant handyman Mackey (Gabriel Byrne) has begun hanging around in hopes of some work. With time on her hands, Martha befriends him and, in the first of several off-putting scenes, the two make love. When Mackey gets it on with her sexy aunt, Martha violently takes out her rejection on Getso.

Adapted from Mary McGarry Morris's well-received 1991 novel, the film carries some fundamental contradictions. The mostly leisurely pace established by director Stephen Gyllenhaal is the tradeoff for the accumulation of character detail, but the lurches into outright melodrama feel jarring in this context, particularly in the final reel.

•

DANIEL AND THE DEVIL
SEE: THE DEVIL AND DANIEL WEBSTER

•

DANIEL
1983, 129 mins, US Ⓥ col
Dir Sidney Lumet ***Prod*** Burtt Harris ***Scr*** E. L. Doctorow ***Ph*** Andrzej Bartkowiak ***Ed*** Peter C. Frank ***Art*** Philip Rosenberg
Act Timothy Hutton, Mandy Patinkin, Lindsay Crouse, Ed Asner, Ellen Barkin, Julie Bovasso (World Film Services)

Faithfully adapted by E. L. Doctorow from his own acclaimed novel, *The Book of Daniel* and directed by Sidney Lumet with his customary intensity, *Daniel* is nonetheless a curiously detached filmization of the highly charged book.

It's generally well acted and occasionally evokes the sense of tragedy surrounding the effect of Julius and Ethel Rosenberg's trial and eventual execution as Russian atom spies.

Taking its form from the novel, the film flashes back and forth in time between 1967—as Daniel Isaacson (Timothy Hutton) an aloof, uncommitted grad student is prodded by the near-suicide of his activist sister (Amanda Plummer) into probing the events behind his parents' execution—and the period of his parents' last years from the 1930s to 1953.

Most effective portions of the film are those chronicling the parents (Lindsay Crouse in a staggeringly subtle performance as Daniel's mother, Mandy Patinkin superb as his father).

•

DANTE'S PEAK
1997, 108 mins, US Ⓥ ⊙ ▭ col
Dir Roger Donaldson ***Prod*** Gale Anne Hurd, Joseph M. Singer ***Scr*** Leslie Bohem ***Ph*** Andrzej Bartkowiak ***Ed*** Howard Smith, Conrad Buff ***Mus*** John Frizzell, James Newton Howard ***Art*** Dennis Washington
Act Pierce Brosnan, Linda Hamilton, Charles Hallahan, Grant Heslov, Elizabeth Hoffman, Jamie Renee Smith (Pacific Western/Universal)

The effects go boom but the human story is a bust in *Dante's Peak*. A midlevel entry in the retro disaster cycle, physically impressive production contains elements familiar from *Twister*, but unfortunately resembles the same screenwriter's *Daylight* in its sense of dramatic conviction. Picture at least appears to be less extravagant and, certainly, less expensive than the film it beat to market, *Volcano* [released two months later, in April].

Volcanologist Harry Dalton (Pierce Brosnan) is dispatched to the pristine Pacific Northwest community of Dante's Peak and meets its comely mayor, Rachel Wando (Linda Hamilton). The U.S. Geological Survey has sent Harry in to check out some vague activity in the dormant volcano that towers above the friendly community.

At exactly the one-hour point, the old cone, which hasn't exploded in 7,000 years, blows its top. It's Pompeii all over again, except the victims are cappuccino-chugging tree-huggers rather than wine-slurping debauchers.

The visual effects are an eyeful; the devastation is palpable and realistic. The dramatis personae are as inoffensive as they are bland. Brosnan comes off as a low-key gentleman, while Hamilton is a serviceable good match for him; still, neither character possesses behavioral quirks or psychological layers to provoke sustained interest.

•

DANTON
1983, 136 mins, France/Poland Ⓥ col
Dir Andrzej Wajda ***Prod*** Margaret Menegoz ***Scr*** Jean-Claude Carriere, Andrzej Wajda, Agnieszka Holland, Boleslaw Michalek, Jacek Gasiorowski ***Ph*** Igor Luther ***Ed*** Halina Prugar-Ketling ***Mus*** Jean Prodromides ***Art*** Allan Starski
Act Gerard Depardieu, Wojciech Pszoniak, Patrice Chereau, Roger Planchon, Jacques Villeret, Angela Winkler (Films du Losange/Gaumont/TF1/SFPC/Film Polski)

Danton is the first French-language film by Polish filmmaker Andrzej Wajda, directing, in the wake of recent tragic events in his homeland, a historical film about the French Revolution. Pic is a dull, plodding affair, resembling more a windy, biased history lecture than a dramatic motion picture. Too often it has the characteristic gloss of French costume television drama, in which roles and outfits are filled but not lived in.

The script is based, ironically, on a Polish play of the 1930s [Stanislawa Przybyszewska's *The Danton Affair*], which Wajda (who commutes back and forth from cinema to theatre) has staged several times. Like the play, the film limits itself to the climactic death struggle between the two titans of the Revolution, Georges Danton and Maximilian Robespierre, and attempts to dramatize their emotional, intellectual and political differences.

Action opens in November, 1793, with Danton returning to Paris from his country retreat upon learning that the insidious Committee of Public Safety, under Robespierre's incitement, has begun a massive series of executions, The Terror. Confident in the people's support, Danton locks horns with his former ally, but the calculating Robespierre soon rounds up Danton and his followers, tries them before a revolutionary tribunal and dispatches them to the guillotine.

The acting barely improves matters and Wajda has sometimes cast poorly. Gerard Depardieu is Danton: huff and puff as he may, he still looks uneasy in period costume and powdered wig, and his gestures and mannerisms are resolutely 20th century. Wojciech Pszoniak, a fine Polish actor of commanding presence, looks right as the cold, conniving Robespierre, but the dubbed voice that issues from his mouth saps his performance.

The supporting roles vary from fair to poor, with German actress Angela Winkler (also dubbed) miscast as Lucile Desmoulins, the wife of the Dantonist journalist, Camille Desmoulins (played competently by wunderkind stage director Patrice Chereau).

•

DARK ANGEL, THE
1935, 105 mins, US b/w
Dir Sidney Franklin ***Prod*** Samuel Goldwyn ***Scr*** Lillian Hellman, Mordaunt Shairp ***Ph*** Gregg Toland ***Ed*** Sherman Todd ***Mus*** Alfred Newman (dir.) ***Art*** Richard Day
Act Fredric March, Merle Oberon, Herbert Marshall, Janet Beecher, John Halliday, Henrietta Crosman (Goldwyn)

A sockeroo woman's picture. Has Fredric March, Merle Oberon and Herbert Marshall and a forthright sentimental romance, well directed by Sidney Franklin to sustain almost every element [of the play by Guy Bolton, a.k.a. R. B. Trevelyan, adapted by Claudine West].

Grown up together from childhood, the war throws Kitty Vane (Oberon) to March as her natural romantic choice. Marshall and Oberon later berate themselves in mistaken belief they have sent March to his doom. Instead, after nursing in a German prison camp and later back in his native England, March turns up under a nom de plume, an author of bestsellers for juveniles, but permanently blind and in constant mental dread of becoming a burden to his bride without benefit of clergy.

Oberon is a revelation as a reformed vamp. In simple hairdo and sans any great sartorial display, her emotional opportunities are fully met upon every occasion. Marshall and March are superb as the war-torn, love-torn boyhood chums, mutually in love with Oberon. Both refuse to avail themselves of any opportunities to stretch the emotional tension.

1935: Best Interior Decoration (Richard Day)

NOMINATION: Best Actress (Merle Oberon)

•

DARK AT THE TOP OF THE STAIRS, THE
1960, 123 mins, US col
Dir Delbert Mann ***Prod*** Michael Garrison ***Scr*** Harriet Frank, Jr., Irving Ravetch ***Ph*** Harry Stradling, Sr. ***Ed*** Folmar Blangsted ***Mus*** Max Steiner ***Art*** Leo K. Kuter
Act Robert Preston, Dorothy McGuire, Eve Arden, Angela Lansbury, Shirley Knight, Lee Kinsolving (Warner)

The William Inge play on which the picture is based is a poignant study of an Oklahoma family torn by internal conflicts. Its relationships are barred with perception and penetration, and the problems of the parents, described in frank terms but handled in good taste, center on the bed and the activities which do, or more accurately, do not, take place in it.

The film is well cast and persuasively acted. Its chief cast value lies in Robert Preston, whose newly-won fame via *The Music Man* can be used to spur box office for the WB picture. Easily detectable is the similarity in manner and speech between his Harold Hill of *The Music Man* and Robin Flood of *Dark*. Each is a high-powered salesman—one flamboyant, the other serious. But there's a strength and an independence that's the same.

Dorothy McGuire is tops as the mother caught between devotion to her children and the knowledge she must sever the cord. Eve Arden is convincing and highly effective as the sister, performing with spirit and proving she could have done even more with her big scene if given the chance. Angela Lansbury plays one of her better and more sympathetic roles as the woman who wants Robin, and she fills it well. Shirley Knight is fine as the daughter.

1960: NOMINATION: Best Supp. Actress (Shirley Knight)

•

DARK CITY
1950, 97 mins, US Ⓥ ▭ b/w
Dir William Dieterle ***Prod*** Hal B. Wallis ***Scr*** John Meredyth Lucas, Larry Marcus ***Ph*** Victor Milner ***Ed*** Warren Low ***Mus*** Franz Waxman (dir.) ***Art*** Hans Dreier, Franz Bachelin
Act Charlton Heston, Lizabeth Scott, Viveca Lindfors, Dean Jagger, Dean DeFore, Jack Webb (Paramount)

Picture serves to introduce Charlton Heston, from legit, and his film debut is impressive. The script [from a story by Larry Marcus, adaptation by Ketti Frings] leans towards psychosis to make its character tick.

Heston has turned to gambling. He and two associates trim Don DeFore in a fixed card game. DeFore hangs himself. A crazy older brother starts stalking the gamblers, intent on giving them the same kind of death suffered by DeFore.

Heston takes off to Los Angeles to see DeFore's widow so that he may get a clue to the killer's appearance.

Lizabeth Scott, nitery chirp and in love with Heston, gives a fine portrayal of the character. Viveca Lindfors as the widow has decided worth. Dean Jagger registers strongly as a police captain.

•

DARK CITY
1998, 101 mins, US Ⓥ ⊙ ▭ col
Dir Alex Proyas ***Prod*** Andrew Mason, Alex Proyas ***Scr*** Alex Proyas, Lem Dobbs, David S. Goyer ***Ph*** Dariusz Wolski ***Ed*** Dov Hoenig ***Mus*** Trevor Jones ***Art*** George Liddle, Patrick Tatopolous
Act Rufus Sewell, Kiefer Sutherland, Jennifer Connelly, William Hurt, Richard O'Brien, Ian Richardson (Mystery Clock/New Line)

A fusion of *The Crow* and Kafka, *Dark City* trades in such weighty themes as memory, thought control, human will and the altering of reality, but is engaging mostly in the degree to which it sustains a visually startling alternate universe.

This is essentially an old film noir amnesiac yarn, set in a hostile urban environment defined by late '40s noir. But tale [by Proyas] is shot through with a futuristic element that vastly increases the visual opportunities.

It takes awhile for viewers to get their bearings. The Strangers—lean, bald, vampirelike men in wide-brimmed hats and floor-length black coats and the ability to transform reality to their own purposes—have come to Earth to find a cure for their accursed mortality. Through a process known as Tuning, they can will the world to a complete standstill.

What is less clear is what any of this has to do with John Murdoch (Rufus Sewell), a young man who, after a break with his wife, Emma (Jennifer Connelly), awakens in a hotel room with his memory gone and under suspicion in a series of murders. Murdoch attracts the attention of a clearly demented genius doctor, Schreber (Kiefer Sutherland), as well as a curiously sympathetic inspector, Frank Bumstead (William Hurt).

Structured like a detective mystery, pic quickly comes to resemble Kafka's *The Trial*. Murdoch has been robbed of his memory to help the Strangers try to unlock the key to the human soul. How all this is supposed to happen remains obscure, but by the final third the emphasis is on big set-pieces anyway.

The eponymous metropolis was entirely created in the new Fox Film Studios in Sydney. Performances are solid.

•

DARK CRYSTAL, THE
1983, 94 mins, UK Ⓥ ⊙ col
Dir Jim Henson, Frank Oz ***Prod*** Jim Henson, Gary Kurtz ***Scr*** David Odell ***Ph*** Oswald Morris ***Ed*** Ralph Kemplen ***Mus*** Trevor Jones ***Art*** Brian Froud, Harry Lange (ITC)

The Dark Crystal, besides being a dazzling technological and artistic achievement by a band of talented artists and performers, presents a dark side of *Muppet* creators Jim Henson and Frank Oz that could teach a lesson in morality to youngsters at the same time it is entertaining their parents.

While there is plenty of humor in the film, it is actually an allegory of the triumph of good over evil, of innocence over the wicked. This world is inhabited with monstrously evil Skeksis, who are temporarily in command of the world wherein only a handful of wise and virtuous creatures manage to stay alive.

Until, of course, Jen and Kira, a boy and girl gelfling, set out to defeat the Skeksis by replacing a shard that has been taken from the Dark Crystal, which awaits its return before Doomsday is due.

The creation of a small world of memorable characters is the main contribution of Henson and Oz. The outstanding character is the Aughra, an ancient one-eyed harridan of an oracle who somehow reminds one of a truly blowsy Shelley Winters.

•

DARK HALF, THE
1993, 122 mins, US Ⓥ ⊙ col
Dir George A. Romero ***Prod*** Declan Baldwin ***Scr*** George A. Romero ***Ph*** Tony Pierce-Roberts ***Ed*** Pasquale Buba ***Mus*** Christopher Young ***Art*** Cletus Anderson
Act Timothy Hutton, Amy Madigan, Michael Rooker, Julie Harris, Robert Joy, Chelsea Field (Orion/Dark Half)

The writer's desk intriguingly becomes a gladitorial arena for warring manifestations of the same personality in *The Dark Half*, George A. Romero's adaptation of Stephen King's 1989 bestseller, a classic Jekyll-and-Hyde story.

After a 1968-set prologue establishes Thad Beaumont as a precocious kid writer and a grotesque operation gives physical evidence of a twin in Thad's brain, story proper picks up in the current day, with Thad (Timothy Hutton) married to the solid, resourceful Liz (Amy Madigan). Under the pseudonym George Stark, he's authored four disreputable bestsellers.

When a grungy student discovers Thad's double life and demands money to keep silent, Thad literally buries "George Stark." But Stark begins manifesting his existence in places other than the bestseller list. The killings mount up.

Hutton's George Stark is a terrific contrast, a cowboy greaser in black who's all razor edges, cigarettes and booze. All performers register favorably, including Madigan, Michael Rooker as the cop reluctantly on the writer's case, and Julie Harris as an eccentric academic colleague.

•

DARKMAN
1990, 95 mins, US Ⓥ ⊙ col
Dir Sam Raimi ***Prod*** Robert Tapert ***Scr*** Chuck Pfarrer, Sam Raimi, Ivan Raimi, Daniel Goldin, Joshua Goldin ***Ph*** Bill Pope ***Ed*** Bud Smith, Scott Smith, David Stiven ***Mus*** Danny Elfman, Jonathan Sheffer ***Art*** Randy Ser
Act Liam Neeson, Frances McDormand, Colin Friels, Larry Drake, Nelson Mashita, Jenny Agutter (Universal/Renaissance)

Despite occasional silliness, Sam Raimi's *Darkman* has more wit, pathos and visual flamboyance than is usual in contemporary shockers.

Universal, studio that first brought the Phantom of the Opera to the screen, returns to its hallowed horror-film traditions with this tale of a hideously disfigured scientist (Liam Neeson) seeking revenge on L.A. mobsters.

Raimi's gripping story (unevenly scripted by the director and others) more closely echoes the 1941 Peter Lorre chiller *The Face Behind the Mask* in its nightmarish tale of a man whose burned face makes him a social pariah and brutal criminal.

Neeson, working on a holographic technique to synthetically re-create damaged skin and body parts, is the innocent victim of sadistic thug Larry Drake, who likes to snip people's fingers off with his cigar cutter. He orders his minions to dip Neeson's head into an acid vat before blowing up his lab.

Drake's expertly vicious and campy villain is after an incriminating document left in Neeson's lab by the scientist's lawyer/g.f. (Frances McDormand) who has caught a client, real estate developer Colin Friels, in corrupt practices.

Director Raimi, lenser Bill Pope and production designer Randy Ser conjure up a flamboyantly expressionistic world out of downtown L.A.'s bizarre architectural mix of gleaming skyscrapers and decaying warehouses.

•

DARK MIRROR, THE
1946, 85 mins, US Ⓥ b/w
Dir Robert Siodmak ***Prod*** Nunnally Johnson ***Scr*** Nunnally Johnson ***Ph*** Milton Krasner ***Ed*** Ernest Nims ***Mus*** Dimitri Tiomkin ***Art*** Duncan Cramer
Act Olivia de Havilland, Lew Ayres, Thomas Mitchell, Richard Long, Charles Evans, Gary Owen (Universal/Inter-John)

The Dark Mirror runs the full gamut of themes currently in vogue at the box office—from psychiatry to romance back again to the double identity gimmick and murder mystery. But, despite the individually potent ingredients, somehow the composite doesn't quite come off.

Opening with a promising gait, the pic [from a story by Vladimir Pozner] gets lost in a maze of psychological gadgets and speculation that slow it down. Olivia de Havilland, playing a twin role, carries the central load of the picture. She's cast simultaneously as a sweet, sympathetic girl and her vixenish, latently insane twin sister. A murder is committed, and while one girl has been positively identified as coming out of the man's apartment on the night of the murder, the other establishes a foolproof alibi.

Lew Ayres is cast in his familiar role as a medico—a specialist on identical twins. Slightly older looking and sporting a mustache, Ayres still retains much of his appealing boyish sincerity. But in the romantic clinches, Ayres is stiff and slightly embarrassed looking.

Copping thespic honors, despite a relatively light part, Thomas Mitchell plays the baffled dick with a wry wit and assured bearing that carries belief.

1946: NOMINATION: Best Original Story

•

DARK OBSESSION
SEE: DIAMOND SKULLS

•

DARK OF THE SUN
U.K. THE MERCENARIES
1968, 106 mins, US ▭ col
Dir Jack Cardiff ***Prod*** George Englund ***Scr*** Quentin Werty, Adrian Spies ***Ph*** Ted Scaife ***Ed*** Ernest Walter ***Mus*** Jacques Loussier ***Art*** Elliot Scott
Act Rod Taylor, Yvette Mimieux, Peter Carsten, Jim Brown, Kenneth More, Andre Morell (M-G-M)

Based on the Congo uprising, this is a raw adventure yarn (from a novel by Wilbur Smith) with some glib philosophizing which skates superficially over the points of view of the cynical mercenaries and the patriotic Congolese.

Rod Taylor plays a hardbitten mercenary major who's prepared to sweat through any task, however dirty, providing his fee is okay. He's assigned by Congo's president to take a train through rebel Simba-held country and bring back fugitives and a load of uncut diamonds stashed away in a beleaguered town.

The action is taken care of effectively but the rapport between some of the characters is rarely smooth nor convincing enough. Pic was filmed in Africa and at Metro's British studios.

Acting is mostly of a straightforward nature for the script does not lend itself to a subtlety of characterization. Taylor makes a robust hero while Jim Brown brings some dignity and interest to the role of the Congolese native.

•

DARK PASSAGE
1947, 106 mins, US Ⓥ ⊙ b/w
Dir Delmer Daves ***Prod*** Jerry Wald ***Scr*** Delmer Daves ***Ph*** Sid Hickox ***Ed*** David Weisbart ***Mus*** Franz Waxman ***Art*** Charles H. Clarke
Act Humphrey Bogart, Lauren Bacall, Bruce Bennett, Agnes Moorehead, Tom D'Andrea, Clifton Young (Warner)

The film [from the novel by David Goodis] has a sharp, brutal opening, macabre touches throughout, and a thick, gruesome quality. What starts out as a thriller switches en route into a sagging, psychological drama, but recovers in time to give out with the satisfying gory stuff. Lauren Bacall's charm and Humphrey Bogart's ruggedness count heavily in a strange treatment of a murder story, which if it doesn't withstand scrutiny, does sustain mood and interest.

Scripting is superior and dialog frequently crackles. Direction is smart, with suggestion of the impressionistic approach. What begins as an apparent imitation of the *Lady in the Lake* technique with the central figure speaking but not being visible to the audience, explains itself part way into the film in a clever fashion. Bogart isn't shown at the start because he's supposed to look like someone else. When a doctor has done a plastic surgery job on him to hide him from the police, and he looks the familiar Bogart, the point of his late appearance in the film is evident.

Pic is a story of a man imprisoned on circumstantial evidence for the murder of his wife, his escape from jail, and the efforts of a girl to help him, because her father similarly had suffered unjust imprisonment.

Bacall, in a simple, unglamorous pose at the start, even then has a pleasant appeal, that hypoes intensely as soon as the old, sultry makeup and sexy charm are turned on. Bogart is impressive in something of a lackluster character for him. Agnes Moorehead is sufficiently vicious as the discarded femme who turns killer, giving the film some of its most vivid moments.

•

DARK PAST, THE
1948, 75 mins, US Ⓥ b/w
Dir Rudolph Mate ***Prod*** Buddy Adler ***Scr*** Malvin Wald, Oscar Saul ***Ph*** Joseph Walker ***Ed*** Viola Lawrence ***Mus*** George Duning ***Art*** Cary Odell
Act William Holden, Lee J. Cobb, Nina Foch, Adele Jergens, Stephen Dunne (Columbia)

A crisp melodrama is *The Dark Past* which Columbia remade from its 1939 release, *Blind Alley* [and the play of that title by James Warwick].

Delinquency angle is the peg on which is hung the flashbacked central plot. An example of what psychiatry can do for a criminal is graphically shown by college prof Lee J. Cobb, who brings escaped convict William Holden to bay merely by probing into his mind to discover what impels him to be a murderer. When Holden realizes what has warped his brain he finds he no longer can kill.

Locale for Cobb's psychoanalysis is his own hunting lodge where his family and several guests have been taken prisoner by Holden and his accomplices.

Always self-assured, the pipesmoking Cobb racks up a neat portrayal of the medico. Holden is believable as the high-strung con on the lam. Nina Foch handles her role well as Holden's moll.

•

DARK STAR
1974, 83 mins, US Ⓥ ⊙ col
Dir John Carpenter ***Prod*** John Carpenter ***Scr*** John Carpenter, Dan O'Bannon ***Ph*** Douglas Knapp ***Ed*** Dan O'Bannon ***Mus*** John Carpenter ***Art*** Dan O'Bannon
Act Brian Narelle, Andreijah Pahich, Carl Duniholm, Dan O'Bannon (Carpenter/Harris)

Dark Star is a limp parody of Stanley Kubrick's *2001: A Space Odyssey* that warrants attention only for some remarkably believable special effects achieved with very little money. [Pic began in 1970 as a 45-minute USC Film School short. Final budget was $60,000.]

The screenplay cloisters four astronauts together on a lengthy extraterrestrial jaunt. To pass the time, the men joke, record their diaries on videotape, take sunlamp treatments, reminisce about their past earth lives and play with their alien mascot (an inflated beach ball with claws). Eventually their talking female computer misfires, the spaceship conks out and only one, an ex-surfer, manages to careen back to earth on an improvised board.

The dim comedy consists of sophomoric notations and mistimed one-liners.

•

DARK VICTORY
1939, 105 mins, US Ⓥ ⊙ b/w
Dir Edmund Goulding ***Prod*** Hal B. Wallis (exec.) ***Scr*** Casey Robinson ***Ph*** Ernest Haller ***Ed*** William Holmes ***Mus*** Max Steiner ***Art*** Robert Haas
Act Bette Davis, George Brent, Humphrey Bogart, Geraldine Fitzgerald, Ronald Reagan, Henry Travers (Warner)

Intense drama, with undercurrent of tragedy ever present, *Dark Victory* is a nicely produced offering. It presents Bette Davis in a powerful and impressive role.

In play form [by George Emerson Brewer, Jr. and Bertram Bloch] Tallulah Bankhead was not able to overcome the morbid dramatics of the piece and *Dark Victory* had a brief Broadway run. Film rights were originally purchased by David Selznick, but he shelved production plans some weeks before picture was due to hit the production stages.

Story unfolds the tragic circumstances of Davis, gay heiress, afflicted with a malignant brain tumor. A delicate operation by specialist George Brent is temporarily successful, but when the girl finally accidentally discovers her true condition, she embarks on a wild whirl of parties. In love with Brent, Davis quickly marries the medic for a brief happiness on his Vermont farm.

Important is the uncovering of Geraldine Fitzgerald in her first effort, as Davis's confidential secretary. Seems rather unnecessary to toss away the ability of Humphrey Bogart, himself satisfactory, but role is extraneous.

1939: NOMINATIONS: Best Picture, Actress (Bette Davis)

•

DARK WATERS
1944, 90 mins, US Ⓥ ⊙ b/w
Dir Andre de Toth ***Prod*** Benedict Bogeaus ***Scr*** Joan Harrison, Marian Cockrell ***Ph*** Archie J. Stout, John J. Mescall ***Ed*** James Smith ***Mus*** Miklos Rozsa ***Art*** Charles Odds
Act Merle Oberon, Franchot Tone, Thomas Mitchell, Fay Bainter, Rex Ingram, John Qualen (United Artists)

A strong cast that handles itself superbly throughout aided by the capable direction of Andre de Toth, is responsible for whatever entertainment value this picture might have. Obviously, the film set out to be a study in characterizations, destined to make the story [from a *Saturday Evening Post* serial by Frank and Marian Cockrell] itself secondary to the characters portrayed, thus giving it a lift out of the ordinary. But somewhere along the line this idea was sidetracked.

Merle Oberon gives one of the best portrayals of her career in the role of a young heiress beset by psychological neuroses due to the loss of her parents when a ship on which they were returning from Batavia to America is sunk, she being one of four survivors.

Thomas Mitchell, as the conniver intent on driving the heiress into an asylum and gaining her riches, has some poor lines to toss away before coming through with a meaty performance. Franchot Tone's portrayal of a bayou country doctor who falls for Oberon is forthright, but never too weighty.

•

DARK WIND, THE
1992, 109 mins, US Ⓥ ⊙ col
Dir Errol Morris ***Prod*** Patrick Markey ***Scr*** Eric Bergren, Neal Jimenez, Mark Horowitz ***Ph*** Stefan Czapsky ***Ed*** Freeman Davies ***Mus*** Michel Colombier ***Art*** Ted Bafaloukos
Act Lou Diamond Phillips, Fred Ward, Gary Farmer, John Karlen, Lance Baker, Jane Loranger (Dark Wind/Northfork)

The Dark Wind is a good-looking version of Tony Hillerman's 1982 cult policier that goes for the same slow burn. Lou Diamond Phillips toplines strongly as the Navajo flatfoot.

Corkscrew plot, set on an Arizona reservation divided between Navajo and Hopi, warms up gradually with the discovery of a Navajo corpse with its palms and soles flayed. Then the cop, on tedious night watch by a disputed water-windmill, finds a crashed airplane with two dead coke smugglers on board.

Story fans out as the feds turn up. Phillips is warned off the case by his superior (Fred Ward), and the main smuggler's young widow (Jane Loranger) comes looking for justice. All the locals, including store owner John Karlen, act mighty suspicious.

Despite the fact that most of the action is purely police procedure, the combination of Phillips's mystical voiceovers, Michel Colombier's atmospheric score and Stefan Czapsky's striking lensing of the ruddy mesa landscape keeps the mood taut.

•

DARLING
1965, 128 mins, UK Ⓥ ⊙ b/w
Dir John Schlesinger ***Prod*** Joseph Janni ***Scr*** Frederic Raphael ***Ph*** Ken Higgins ***Ed*** James Clark ***Mus*** John Dankworth ***Art*** Ray Simm
Act Julie Christie, Dirk Bogarde, Laurence Harvey, Roland Curran, Jose Villalonga, Basil Henson (Vic)

In many ways, this Joseph Janni production can be described as a British *Dolce Vita*. Its central character is a lovely, young, irresponsible and completely immoral girl, who can see little wrong in jumping in and out of bed with a complete lack of discrimination, and who goes on a shop-lifting expedition in one of London's more famous stores just for kicks.

While a fair slice of the credit must go to the three stars and to scripter Frederic Raphael, the lion's share is due to John Schlesinger, a documentary-trained director who skillfully uses that technique to give in-depth portraits to three principals.

Everyone calls Diana Scott (Julie Christie) "darling." She's that kind of girl—gay, good-looking, amusing company. She is married to a young, immature man, and once she has met the more sophisticated Robert (Dirk Bogarde) there is little doubt that the marriage will go on the rocks. He, too, is married, but leaves his family to set up house with her. But no sooner has she met Miles (Laurence Harvey) than she hops into bed with him.

Christie almost perfectly captures the character of the immoral Diana, and very rarely misses her target.

1965: Best Actress (Julie Christie), Original Story & Screenplay, B&W Costume Design

NOMINATIONS: Best Picture, Director

•

DARLING LILI
1970, 139 mins, US Ⓥ ▭ col
Dir Blake Edwards ***Prod*** Blake Edwards ***Scr*** Blake Edwards, William Peter Blatty ***Ph*** Russell Harlan ***Ed*** Peter Zinner ***Mus*** Henry Mancini ***Art*** Fernando Carrere
Act Julie Andrews, Rock Hudson, Jeremy Kemp, Lance Percival, Michael Witney, Jacques Marin (Paramount/Geoffrey)

Darling Lili is a conglomerate. In its World War I expanse, the Blake Edwards presentation has comedy, adventure melodrama, aerial dogfights, spectacular production numbers, nostalgia, Julie Andrews and Rock Hudson, lush trappings, lack of a decisive hand, and smash moments. These elements are juggled sometimes with eclat and a flair, on other occasions abruptly and none too successfully.

Andrews is a German spy whose mission is to ferret out war secrets. She latches onto a relationship with Hudson, in role of a dashing American air squadron commander, who knows all.

Andrews's best moments are her singing sequences, in which she does full justice to five numbers cleffed by Johnny Mercer and Henry Mancini.

1970: NOMINATIONS: Best Costume Design, Original Song Score, Song ("Whistling Away the Dark")

•

D'ARTAGNAN'S DAUGHTER
SEE: LA FILLE DE D'ARTAGNAN

•

D.A.R.Y.L.
1985, 99 mins, US Ⓥ ⊙ ▭ col
Dir Simon Wincer ***Prod*** John Heyman ***Scr*** David Ambrose, Allan Scott, Jeffrey Ellis ***Ph*** Frank Watts ***Ed*** Adrian Carr ***Mus*** Marvin Hamlisch ***Art*** Alan Cassie
Act Mary Beth Hurt, Michael McKean, Kathryn Walker, Colleen Camp, Josef Sommer, Barret Oliver (Paramount)

Pic manages to get off to a strong start with a scenic chase through a curving mountain road as a chopper bears down on a racing car. Just before crashing, the driver pushes out a young boy who is rescued and taken into a foster home by the Richardsons (Mary Beth Hurt and Michael McKean). The Richardsons later find that this strange young man is a robot.

After establishing a cozy domestic situation the film takes off in a different direction when his "parents" come to take Daryl (Barret Oliver) home. Home is a top security research facility where scientists Josef Sommer and Kathryn Walker have given birth to D.A.R.Y.L. Acronym stands for Data Analyzing Robot Youth Lifeform and Daryl is described as "an experiment in artificial intelligence."

Second half of the picture is the most far-fetched and also the most fun as the young robot gets to show off some of his powers.

•

DATE WITH A LONELY GIRL, A
SEE: T. R. BASKIN

•

DATE WITH DEATH, A
SEE: THE HIGH BRIGHT SUN

•

DATE WITH JUDY, A
1948, 113 mins, US Ⓥ ⊙ col
Dir Richard Thorpe ***Prod*** Joe Pasternak ***Scr*** Dorothy Cooper, Dorothy Kingsley ***Ph*** Robert Surtees ***Ed*** Harold F. Kress ***Art*** Cedric Gibbons, Paul Groesse
Act Wallace Beery, Jane Powell, Elizabeth Taylor, Carmen Miranda, Robert Stack, Scotty Beckett (M-G-M)

A Date with Judy is loaded with youthful zest, making for gay, light entertainmt, based on the familiar air characters created by Aleen Leslie.

Jane Powell registers appealingly with vocals on five numbers and for her comedy antics as wheelhorse of plot motivation. "It's a Most Unusual Day," by Jimmy McHugh and Harold Adamson, is opening number and also is reprised by Powell for finale. Carmen Miranda gives her customary treatment to "Cooking with Glass" and "Quanto la Gusto," clicking strongly.

Plot concerns teenage love affair between Powell and Scotty Beckett which goes sour when the gal gets a crush on an older man, Robert Stack. It takes on another facet when Powell suspects her father, Wallace Beery, of a romance with Miranda, and the youngsters join forces to balk such a folly.

Beery does an ace job, and with little of his customary mugging, as the father who's taking rhumba lessons so he can surprise his wife, Selena Royle. Elizabeth Taylor, rival for Stack's affections, makes a talented appearance.

•

DAUGHTERS OF DARKNESS
1971, 87 mins, US/France Ⓥ col
Dir Harry Kumel *Prod* Paul Collet, Alain C. Guilleaume *Scr* Pierre Drouot, Harry Kumel *Ph* Edward Van Der Enden *Ed* Gust Verschueren, Denis Bonan *Mus* Francois de Roubiax
Act Delphine Seyrig, Daniele Ouimet, John Karlen, Andrea Rau, Paul Esser, Fons Rademakers (Gemini/Maya)

Delphine Seyrig's silver lamé presence and Harry Kumel's evocative direction make this an above-par vampire tale. Updating the old chestnut about the butch countess who remains forever young by drinking and bathing in the blood of maidens, *Daughters of Darkness* is so intentionally perverse that it often slips into impure camp, but Kumel and Seyrig hold interest by piling twists on every convention of the vampire genre.

Spending their honeymoon at a mammoth but deserted seaside resort hotel in Belgium, newlyweds John Karlen and Daniele Ouimet are marked by the countess (Seyrig) and her lesbian "secretary" (Andrea Rau). Karlen is actually a sadistic mama's boy, but "Mother" (played by Dutch film director Fons Rademakers) is an aging homosexual who's been keeping him in London. When Karlen vents his belt-wielding sexuality on his bride, she seeks refuge with the countess.

Avoiding standard fang-in-the-neck fright, Kumel keeps the gore limited to the two death sequences, but there he goes all out. Both are stunningly directed and edited.

•

DAVE
1993, 110 mins, US Ⓥ ⦿ col
Dir Ivan Reitman *Prod* Lauren Shuler-Donner, Ivan Reitman *Scr* Gary Ross *Ph* Adam Greenberg *Ed* Sheldon Kahn *Mus* James Newton Howard *Art* J. Michael Riva
Act Kevin Kline, Sigourney Weaver, Frank Langella, Kevin Dunn, Ving Rhames, Ben Kingsley (Warner/Northern Lights)

Dave, the story of a run-of-the mill guy asked to stand-in for a major leader who suddenly falls ill, is a delightful, buoyant new take on an old theme, deftly mixing political cynicism with elements of *Mr. Smith Goes to Washington*.

In this case, the office is President of the United States, and Dave (Kevin Kline), a sometime presidential-impersonator, gets drafted by White House chief of staff Bob Alexander (Frank Langella) and his communications director (Kevin Dunn), who want to keep Dave in office long enough to engineer a sort of coup in which Alexander can take over. Just to be safe, they dispatch the Vice President (Ben Kingsley, in a small but effective cameo) on a fool's errand to Africa. Dave also thaws the icy relationship between the President and First Lady (Sigourney Weaver), providing a nifty romantic element.

Kline stands forth as the glue that holds it all together, but he benefits from strong supporting performances all around such as Ving Rhames's stony Secret Service agent, who pulls off the film's most affecting moment.

1993: NOMINATION: Best Original Screenplay

•

DAVID AND BATHSHEBA
1951, 153 mins, US Ⓥ ⦿ col
Dir Henry King *Prod* Darryl F. Zanuck *Scr* Philip Dunne *Ph* Leon Shamroy *Ed* Barbara McLean *Mus* Alfred Newman *Art* Lyle Wheeler, George Davis
Act Gregory Peck, Susan Hayward, Raymond Massey, Kieron Moore, James Robertson Justice, Jayne Meadows (20th Century-Fox)

This is a big picture in every respect. The reign of King David projects the Old Testament in broad sweeps, depicting the obligation of David (Gregory Peck) to his subjects while at the same time spotlighting his frailties, namely his relationship with the beauteous Bathsheba (Susan Hayward). He is shown forsaking his first wife (of his harem) for Bathsheba, and pinpointed is the stoning of an adultress for the same crime—her faithlessness while her husband was off to the wars with the Ammonites.

Expert casting throughout focuses on each characterization. Raymond Massey plays the prophet Nathan, whom Jehovah sends to King David to hold him up to judgment. The parable of David's atonement for his lechery and treachery is capped by the 23rd Psalm which he, in his poetic youth, had conjured along with his other psalms.

Peck is a commanding personality as the youth destined to rule Israel. He shades his character expertly. His emotional reflexes are not as static as the sultry Hayward in the femme lead. Kieron Moore is earnest as the Hittite whom David betrays because he covets his wife, Bathsheba. Massey, as the prophet, is a dominant personality throughout.

1951: NOMINATIONS: Best Story & Screenplay, Color Cinematography, Color Costume Design, Color Art Direction, Scoring of a Dramatic Picture

•

DAVID AND LISA
1963, 85 mins, US Ⓥ ⦿ b/w
Dir Frank Perry *Prod* Paul M. Heller *Scr* Eleanor Perry *Ph* Leonard Hirschfield *Ed* Irving Oshman *Mus* Mark Lawrence *Art* Paul M. Heller
Act Keir Dullea, Janet Margolin, Howard da Silva, Neva Patterson, Clifton James (Continental)

Tact, taste, insight and forthrightness make this one of the most incisive and original films treating mental problems.

A young man is brought to a mental home by his doting mother. He seems intelligent, haughty and sophisticated. But he cannot bear to be touched by anybody.

He is worshipped by a younger boy and becomes interested in the case of a schizophrenic girl called Lisa who talks backwards in rhyme and takes herself for two girls. He manages to get to her and both are aware of each other's weak spots.

Film appears clinically observant and authentic and is refreshingly free of jargon and pseudo-psycho dramatics. It does have a tendency to be too spare and make each scene a point about psychotic behaviour or reactions to it by outsiders.

But there is no forced love affair or cliche suspense aspects. Keir Dullea has the knifelike, frigid presence that is right in his case of bottled up feelings that have made him fear death and any human emotion. And Janet Margolin has the touching disorder and mute need for help required for the part of the girl.

For a first film Frank Perry shows a concise feel for making the telling points in each scene. A tight ordered script by Eleanor Perry also helps. It was taken from a book by a practicing psychiatrist [Theodore Isaac Rubin].

1963: NOMINATIONS: Best Director, Adapted Screenplay

•

DAVID COPPERFIELD
1935, 129 mins, US Ⓥ ⦿ b/w
Dir George Cukor *Prod* David O. Selznick *Scr* Howard Estabrook, Hugh Walpole *Ph* Oliver T. Marsh *Ed* Robert J. Kern *Mus* Herbert Stothart
Act W. C. Fields, Lionel Barrymore, Freddie Bartholomew, Frank Lawton, Edna May Oliver, Roland Young (M-G-M)

Charles Dickens did not write with the idea of being dramatized. The strange charm of his characters is more important than the fidelity of his characterizations. It was almost an adventure to try to bring to the screen the expansively optimistic Micawber, but he lives again in W. C. Fields, who only once yields to his penchant for horseplay. In the main he makes Micawber as real as David. The same may be said for Edna May Oliver, who does low comedy in the high comedy manner and shows flashes of the underlying tenderness of Aunt Betsey.

The adapters have not always been as successful. Now and then they linger too elaborately in a scene and they put the play completely off the track in introducing the mechanically melodramatic shipwreck scene, which might easily have been left undone.

Lionel Barrymore, as Dan Peggotty, proves again that it is possible to wear chin whiskers and still not be a comic, and Herbert Mundin does well by the willing Barkis.

A fine performance is that of Freddie Bartholomew as the child David. He is acceptable in his more quiet moments, but in times of stress he seems to be spurred up to the situation, and with Basil Rathbone, as Mr. Murdstone, he raises the whipping scene to a high point. Rathbone is not as happily cast as the others. Frank Lawton is a believable grown David and Maureen O'Sullivan, Madge Evans and Elizabeth Allan, as the three chief women, all rate bows.

1935: NOMINATIONS: Best Picture, Editing, Assistant Director (Joseph Newman)

•

DAVID COPPERFIELD
1970, 118 mins, UK Ⓥ col
Dir Delbert Mann *Prod* Frederick Brugger *Scr* Jack Pulman *Ph* Ken Hodges *Ed* Peter Boita *Mus* Malcolm Arnold *Art* Alex Vetchinsky
Act Robin Phillips, Susan Hampshire, Edith Evans, Michael Redgrave, Ralph Richardson, Laurence Olivier (Omnibus)

Director Delbert Mann and his scriptwriter, Jack Pulman, elected to tell this version of *David Copperfield* through the eyes of David as a young man. A very woebegone chap he is. Just returned from a self-imposed exile abroad he wanders up and down a deserted beach, pondering over the last few years of his life and what went so despairingly wrong with them.

The story is jerkily and bitterly related, mainly in flashbacks, but the constant return to the brooding, self-pitying Copperfield makes for a melancholy drag.

It also means that through constant flashbacks few of Dickens's wonderful array of characters get much opportunity to develop their roles.

Notably, Laurence Olivier, as the schoolmaster Creakle, and Richard Attenborough, as his cringing, one-legged assistant, Tungay. Their brilliant brief appearances light up the screen in about 60 seconds flat. Then they disappear.

•

DAWN OF THE DEAD
(UK: ZOMBIES)
1979, 125 mins, US Ⓥ ⦿ col
Dir George A. Romero *Prod* Richard Rubinstein *Scr* George A. Romero *Ph* Michael Gornick *Ed* George A. Romero, Kenneth Davidow *Mus* The Goblins, Dario Argento
Act Scott Reiniger, Ken Foree, David Emge, Gaylen Ross, Tom Savini (Laurel/Cuomo-Argento)

Dawn pummels the viewer with a series of ever-more-grisly events—decapitations, shootings, knifings, flesh tearings—that make Romero's special effects man, Tom Savini, the real "star" of the film—the actors are as woodenly uninteresting as the characters they play. Romero's script is banal when not incoherent—those who haven't seen *Night of the Living Dead* may have some difficulty deciphering exactly what's going on at the outset of *Dawn*.

The plot isn't worth detailed description. Enough said those carnivorous corpses that stalked through *Night* return in sufficient numbers to threaten extinction of the entire U.S. population.

Pic was shot for under $1.5 million in the Pittsburgh area, Romero's professional base. Michael Gornick's photography warrants a special nod.

•

DAWN PATROL, THE
1930, 90 mins, US b/w
Dir Howard Hawks *Prod* Robert North *Scr* Dan Totheroh, Seton I. Miller *Ph* Ernest Haller *Ed* Ray Curtiss *Mus* Leo F. Forbstein *Art* Jack Okey
Act Richard Barthelmess, Douglas Fairbanks, Jr., Neil Hamilton, Gardner James, Clyde Cook (First National)

Dawn Patrol finds well-bred English gentlemen running up against the grim realities of war and always remaining true to the best Oxford traditions.

At the start, the air exploits are more talked about than revealed, but as the womanless chronicle unfolds the fighting becomes more visual and less commented upon. Richard Barthelmess and Douglas Fairbanks, Jr., in one sequence raid the home ground of the Germans and spend 10 minutes dropping bombs and ploughing the helpless German air squadron with machine-gun fire.

This little mission of death and destruction is in the nature of a boyish lark because the Germans had taunted them on the quality of their aviatorship. Neil Hamilton, the commanding officer, awaits their return in fury.

Howard Hawks has handled his material intelligently. Camerawork is excellent throughout and the effects are vivid.

•

DAWN PATROL, THE
1938, 103 mins, US Ⓥ b/w
Dir Edmund Goulding *Prod* Hal B. Wallis (exec.) *Scr* Seton I. Miller, Dan Totheroh *Ph* Tony Gaudio *Ed* Ralph Dawson *Mus* Max Steiner *Art* John Hughes
Act Errol Flynn, David Niven, Basil Rathbone, Donald Crisp, Melville Cooper, Barry Fitzgerald (Warner)

Dawn Patrol sparkles because of vigorous performances of the entire cast and Edmund Goulding's sharp direction. Story [by John Monk Saunders] is reminiscent of previous yarns about the flying service at the front during the World War. Yet it is different in that it stresses the unreasonableness of the "brass hats"—the commanders seated miles from the front who dispatched the 59th Squadron to certain death in carrying out combat assignments.

Picture emphasizes the routine of the "dawn patrol," as day after day new replacements, each time consisting of younger men, come up to take the place of those killed in action.

Director Goulding maintains an even pace, alternating the happier, drinking scenes in barracks with the ill-fated takeoffs at dawn and battle gyrations in the sky.

Errol Flynn is Courtney, squadron flight commander. It is a character made to order for him. Even where he deliberately gets his junior officer intoxicated to take his place on a daring single-handed exploit, he makes the action appear lifelike.

David Niven makes the character of Flynn's great friend stand out. Basil Rathbone is superb as the aviator who suffers inwardly the loss of every man while he is forced to remain in command on the ground.

1930/31: Best Original Story

•

DAY AT THE RACES, A

1937, 100 mins, US Ⓥ ⦿ b/w

Dir Sam Wood ***Prod*** Max Siegel ***Scr*** Robert Pirosh, George Seaton, George Oppenheimer ***Ph*** Joseph Ruttenberg ***Ed*** Frank Hull ***Mus*** Bronislau Kaper, Walter Jurmann ***Art*** Cedric Gibbons, Stan Rogers

Act Groucho Marx, Chico Marx, Harpo Marx, Allan Jones, Maureen O'Sullivan, Margaret Dumont (M-G-M)

Surefire film fun and up to the usual parity of the madcap Marxes, even though a bit hectic in striving for jolly moments and bright quips. This is the picture which the late Irving Thalberg started and Max Siegel, Sam Harris's former legit production associate, completed as his initial Hollywood chore at Metro.

Obviously painstaking is the racehorse code-book sequence, a deft switch on the money-changing bit; the long-distance telephoning between the horse doctor (Groucho) and the light-heavy; the midnight rendezvous business between Groucho and Esther Muir, including the paper-handing slapstickery; the orchestra pit hokum, which permits the standard virtuosity by Chico at the Steinway and Harpo at the harp, including a very funny breakaway piano.

Allan Jones and Maureen O'Sullivan sustain the romance and Jones gets his baritone opportunities during a water carnival which is cameraed in light brown sepia. Esther Muir is a good foil, topped only by Margaret Dumont as the moneyed Mrs Upjohn, who is stuck on Groucho and stands for much of his romantic duplicity, even unto paying off the mortgage on the sanatorium owned by O'Sullivan.

1937: NOMINATION: Best Dance Direction ("All God's Children Got Rhythm")

•

DAYBREAK

SEE: LE JOUR SE LEVE

•

DAYBREAK

1931, 73 mins, US b/w

Dir Jacques Feyder ***Scr*** Ruth Cumming, Zelda Sears, Cyril Hume ***Ph*** Merritt B. Gerstad

Act Ramon Novarro, Helen Chandler, Jean Hersholt, C. Aubrey Smith, William Bakewell, Karen Morley (M-G-M)

Lack of action stands against *Daybreak*, that gets its title because the two principals stay out all night the first time they meet. Both of them, Ramon Novarro and Helen Chandler, give a perfectly blah performance. With the locale apparently in Vienna and its Imperial Guard, Novarro speaks with his Latin accent.

In the Imperial Guards you pay your honor debts like an officer and a gentleman, which is in cash or suicide. And when Novarro goes in hock to Jean Hersholt for 14,000 guilders, Navarro has to either pay off or bump off. He is about ready to bump when his uncle comes across with his last 14,000 to save the lad, who thereupon resigns his lieutenancy in the Guards and doubles up with the dame who has become Hersholt's mistress.

The picture dies all the way through the playing. Chandler starts wrong and never rights herself. Novarro tries the light juvenile style as the lieutenant but it flattens at every try.

•

DAY FOR NIGHT

SEE: LA NUIT AMERICAINE

•

DAY IN THE DEATH OF JOE EGG, A

1972, 108 mins, UK Ⓥ col

Dir Peter Medak ***Prod*** David Deutsch ***Scr*** Peter Nichols ***Ph*** Ken Hodges ***Ed*** Ray Lovejoy ***Mus*** Marcus Dods (dir.) ***Art*** Ted Tester

Act Alan Bates, Janet Suzman, Peter Bowles, Sheila Gish, Joan Hickson, Murray Melvin (Domino)

A splendid adaptation by Peter Nichols from his play, simpatico direction by Peter Medak and stellar playing combine to make *A Day in the Death of Joe Egg* a superior black comedy-drama about a young couple trying to cope with a spastic child.

Lachrymal but unsentimentalized, the gut moral issue is euthanasia. The almost surreal narrative unfolds yo-yo style—from bitter or hilarious (or both) humor to emotional wrench and back again, repeatedly. Medak achieves this with seemingly unerring timing and balance.

Alan Bates and Janet Suzman as the couple who play games to survive their nightmare are firstrate in their sardonic despair. *Joe Egg* is less about their defective moppet than the struggle of their own connubial existence, the often foiled appetite for carnal contact, and their very sanity.

•

DAYLIGHT

1996, 115 mins, US Ⓥ ⦿ col

Dir Rob Cohen ***Prod*** John Davis, Joseph M. Singer, David T. Friendly ***Scr*** Leslie Bohem ***Ed*** Peter Amundson ***Mus*** Randy Edelman ***Art*** Benjamin Fernandez

Act Sylvester Stallone, Amy Brenneman, Viggo Mortensen, Dany Hedaya, Jay O. Sanders, Karen Young (Davis-Singer/Universal)

A lower-echelon disaster thriller, in which the best character is knocked off early on and the leading man runs out of ideas with a third of the picture still to go, *Daylight* is a noisy, technically proficient actioner about a group of people trapped in the Holland Tunnel after an explosion.

Sylvester Stallone, in a familiar working-class hero role, is a take-charge guy, former Emergency Medical Services chief Kit Latura, who happens to be in the right place at the right time to attempt a rescue of a carefully selected cross-section of contempo New Yawkers. Unfortunately, these characters, who spend too much of their time alternately whining and arguing, are mostly a drag to be around, making their fates a matter of relative indifference.

There's a neurotic aspiring writer Madelyne (Amy Brenneman); a good-natured cop (Stan Shaw); a dysfunctional family (Jay O. Saunders, Karen Young, Danielle Harris); a dashing, egotistical sporting-goods tycoon (Viggo Mortensen); an upper-class society doyenne (Claire Bloom), and several teenage prisoners in a police van.

Mortensen makes the tycoon the most charismatic figure in the picture, and his demise leaves the party at a loss until Sly arrives. In the film's best sequence, one that should have been truly great but isn't quite, Kit is lowered into the tunnel through a succession of giant vent fans that can be turned off only for seconds at a time. Stallone's stunts and heroics here pale in comparison to his physical feats in his last good action outing, *Cliffhanger* [1993]. Pic features plenty of big explosions and close calls, but nothing that will blow audiences away.

1996: NOMINATION: Best Sound Effects Editing (Richard L. Anderson, David A. Whittaker)

•

DAY OF THE DEAD

1985, 102 mins, US Ⓥ ⦿ col

Dir George A. Romero ***Prod*** Richard P. Rubinstein ***Scr*** George A. Romero ***Ph*** Michael Gornick ***Ed*** Pasquale Buba ***Mus*** John Harrison ***Art*** Cletus Anderson

Act Lori Cardille, Terry Alexander, Joseph Pilato, Jarlath Conroy, Antone DiLeo, Jr., Richard Liberty (Laurel)

Day of the Dead is an unsatisfying part three in George A. Romero's zombie saga.

Set in Florida (but filmed mainly in Pennsylvania plus Fort Myers, FL), *Day* postulates that the living dead have now taken over the world with only a handful of normal humans still alive, outnumbered by about 400,000 to one. In a claustrophobic format reminiscent of early 1950s science fiction films, the human protagonists debate and fight among themselves in an underground missile silo while the common enemy masses topside.

Representing the scientific community are stalwart heroine Sarah (Lori Cardille), who is working on long-range research to find a way to reverse the process whereby dead humans become unreasoning, cannibalistic zombies, and loony Dr. Logan (Richard Liberty), engaged in conditioning experiments on captured zombies to domesticate them.

The acting here is generally unimpressive and in the case of Sarah's romantic partner, Miguel (Antone DiLeo, Jr.), unintentionally risible.

•

DAY OF THE DOLPHIN, THE

1973, 104 mins, US Ⓥ ⦿ ▭ col

Dir Mike Nichols ***Prod*** Robert E. Relyea ***Scr*** Buck Henry ***Ph*** William A. Fraker ***Ed*** Sam O'Steen ***Mus*** Georges Delerue ***Art*** Richard Sylbert

Act George C. Scott, Trish Van Devere, Paul Sorvino, Fritz Wearer, Jon Korkes, Edward Herrmann (Avco Embassy)

Mike Nichols's film of *The Day of the Dolphin* is a rare and regrettably uneven combination of ideas and action. George C. Scott stars as a marine scientist whose work with dolphins faces corruption by his own sponsors. The story climax strains belief, but Nichols is one of a handful of directors who can get away with occasional improbability.

Robert Merle's novel has been adapted into a screenplay which commingles creative obsession, materialism, covert espionage and overt skulduggery. This rich mixture eventually turns to lead, but while it works it is very mind boggling.

Scott and wife Trish Van Devere are conducting advanced research into dolphins, under the sponsorship of a foundation where Fritz Weaver is a senior executive. Paul Sorvino, at first an apparent blackmailing writer, emerges in time as a government agent investigating Weaver's outfit. Scott's scientific breakthrough—communicating verbally with the mammals—becomes the means by which Weaver and associates would blow up the yacht of the U.S. President.

A major asset of the film is the magnificent score by Georges Delerue.

1973: NOMINATIONS: Best Original Score, Sound

•

DAY OF THE JACKAL, THE

1973, 141 mins, UK/France Ⓥ ⦿ col

Dir Fred Zinnemann ***Prod*** John Woolf ***Scr*** Kenneth Ross ***Ph*** Jean Tournier ***Ed*** Ralph Kemplen ***Mus*** Georges Delerue ***Art*** Willy Holt, Ernest Archer

Act Edward Fox, Alan Badel, Tony Britton, Cyril Cusack, Michel Lonsdale, Delphine Seyrig (Universal)

Fred Zinnemann's film of *The Day of the Jackal* is a patient, studied and quasi-documentary translation of Frederick Forsyth's big-selling political suspense novel. Film appeals more to the intellect than the brute senses as it traces the detection of an assassin hired to kill French President Charles de Gaulle.

The recruitment of Edward Fox as the assassin and his planning of the murder is a sort of carrier frequency for the story. Around this is the mobilization of French and other national law enforcement agencies to discover and foil the plot. The final confluence of the plot lines is somewhat brief and anticlimactic.

The major asset of the film is that it succeeds in maintaining interest and suspense despite obvious viewer foreknowledge of the outcome. Fox does very well as the innocent-looking youth who plans his stalk with meticulous care.

1973: NOMINATION: Best Editing

•

DAY OF THE LOCUST, THE

1975, 144 mins, US Ⓥ ⦿ col

Dir John Schlesinger ***Prod*** Jerome Hellman ***Scr*** Waldo Salt ***Ph*** Conrad Hall ***Ed*** Jim Clark ***Mus*** John Barry ***Art*** Richard MacDonald

Act Donald Sutherland, Karen Black, Burgess Meredith, William Atherton, Geraldine Page, Richard A. Dysart (Paramount)

Magnificent production, combined with excellent casting and direction, make *The Day of the Locust* as fine a film (in a professional sense) as the basic material lets it be. Nathanael West's novel about losers on the Hollywood fringe has lost little of its verisimilitude in adaptation.

The Day of the Locust puts its focus on the loser, the never-was and the never-will-be. The story of destined failure features Karen Black in a fine performance as an aspiring, selfish would-be starlet, the daughter of broken down vaudevillian Burgess Meredith (a brilliant characterization). Donald Sutherland, laboring under the most striking burden of fuzzy writing, still evokes a good measure of pity as the hick whose immature love for Black is abused by her.

The principals are surrounded by a truly superb supporting cast: and the physical and technical support is beyond belief.

1975: NOMINATIONS: Best Supp. Actor (Burgess Meredith), Cinematography

•

DAY OF THE TRIFFIDS, THE

1963, 93 mins, UK Ⓥ ⦿ ▭ col

Dir Steve Sekely ***Prod*** George Pitcher ***Scr*** Bernard Gordon ***Ph*** Ted Moore ***Ed*** Spencer Reeve ***Mus*** Ron Goodwin, Johnny Douglas ***Art*** Cedric Dawe

Act Howard Keel, Kieron Moore, Janette Scott, Nicole Maurey, Mervyn Johns, Ewan Roberts (Allied Artists)

Basically, this is a vegetarian's version of *The Birds*, a science-fiction-horror melodrama about a vile people-eater of the plant kingdom with a voracious appetite. Although riddled with script inconsistencies and irregularities, it is a more-than-adequate film of its genre.

John Wyndham's novel served as the source for the screenplay. The proceedings begin with a spectacular display of celestial fireworks, a meteorite shower that leaves the earth's population heir to two maladies: blindness and the sinister company of a fast-multiplying plant aptly called Triffidus Celestus that looks like a Walt Disney nightmare and sounds like a cauldron of broccoli cooking in Margaret Hamilton's witchin' kitchen.

Hero of the piece is Howard Keel as a Yank seaman who, ironically spared the ordeal of blindness by having had his ill optics bandaged during the meteorite invasion, makes his way through a world haplessly engaged in a universal game of blind man's bluff while under mortal threat of the carnivorous chlorophyll. Ultimately a marine biologist (Kieron Moore) stranded in a lighthouse with his wife (Janette Scott) discovers the means to dissolve and destroy the triffids.

The acting is generally capable. Steve Sekely's otherwise able direction has a bothersome flaw in the contradictory manner in which the triffids seem to approach and assault their victims.

•

DAYS OF HEAVEN

1978, 95 mins, US Ⓥ ⊙ col

Dir Terrence Malick **Prod** Bert Schneider, Harold Schneider **Scr** Terrence Malick **Ph** Nestor Almendros, Haskell Wexler **Ed** Billy Weber **Mus** Ennio Morricone, Leo Kottke **Art** Jack Fisk

Act Richard Gere, Brooke Adams, Sam Shepard, Linda Manz, Robert Wilke, Stuart Margolin (OP/Paramount)

Days of Heaven is a dramatically moving and technically breathtaking American art film, one of the great cinematic achievements of the 1970s. Told through the eyes and words of an innocent but wise teenage migrant worker (Linda Manz), it traces a trio of nomads as their lives intersect with a wealthy wheat farmer.

The story opens in Chicago with Richard Gere shoveling coal in a steel mill. After an altercation with a foreman he's fired. He, his sister (Manz) and girlfriend (Brooke Adams), hit the road to find work in the fields, traveling as brother and sisters.

They find employment on a farm owned by a young, wealthy Sam Shepard. Like the other performances, Shepard's is quiet—this isn't from the tour de force school—but it is a marvel nonetheless.

The trio become entangled with Shepard when he falls in love with Adams and marries her. Suddenly the threesome—once so poor they travelled in freight cars like cattle—are rich. And it seems that the days of heaven have arrived. But with wealth, they learn, also comes idleness. And with idleness boredom.

Told in 95 minutes, it is an efficient, meaningful story filled with some offbeat touches, literary references and beautifully developed characters.

1978: Best Cinematography

NOMINATIONS: Best Costume Design, Original Score, Sound

•

DAYS OF THUNDER

1990, 107 mins, US Ⓥ ⊙ ▭ col

Dir Tony Scott **Prod** Don Simpson, Jerry Bruckheimer **Scr** Robert Towne **Ph** Ward Russell **Ed** Billy Weber, Chris Lebenzon **Mus** Hans Zimmer **Art** Benjamin Fernandez, Thomas E. Sanders

Act Tom Cruise, Robert Duvall, Nicole Kidman, Randy Quaid, Michael Rooker, Cary Elwes (Paramount)

This expensive genre film about stock car racing has many of the elements that made the same team's *Top Gun* a blockbuster, but the producers recruited scripter Robert Towne to make more out of the story [by Towne and Tom Cruise] than junk food.

There's the cocky but insecure young challenger (Tom Cruise) breaking into the big time, the hardened champion he's trying to unseat (Michael Rooker), the grizzled manager who dispenses fatherly wisdom (Robert Duvall), the crass promoter (Randy Quaid), and the sexy lady from outside (Nicole Kidman) who questions the point of it all.

Director Tony Scott plunges the viewer into the maelstrom of stock car racing. A highly effective blending of car-mounted camerawork and long lenses imparts documentary credibility and impact.

Days of Thunder zigzags between exploiting Cruise's likable grin and charming vulnerability and portraying him as an emotional loser. It's an uncertain and unsatisfying mix.

The film's real glory is Duvall. His duplicitous, ruthless streak hovers just below the surface, giving a sense of inner danger to the racing scenes in which he coaches the untrusting Cruise by radio from trackside.

1990: NOMINATION: Best Sound

•

DAYS OF WINE AND ROSES

1962, 116 mins, US Ⓥ ⊙ b/w

Dir Blake Edwards **Prod** Martin Manulis **Scr** J. P. Miller **Ph** Philip Lathrop **Ed** Patrick McCormack **Mus** Henry Mancini **Art** Joseph Wright

Act Jack Lemmon, Lee Remick, Charles Bickford, Jack Klugman, Alan Hewitt, Tom Palmer (Warner)

Days of Wine and Roses hails from television's *Playhouse 90* series, and has been faithfully and painstakingly translated to the screen by two of the men responsible for the praised TV version—producer Martin Manulis and writer J. P. Miller.

Miller's gruelling drama illustrates how the unquenchable lure of alcohol can supersede even love, and how marital communication cannot exist in a house divided by one-sided boozing. The wife (Lee Remick), originally a non-drinker with a yen for chocolates that is a tip-off of her vulnerability to the habit pattern, begins to drink when her husband (Jack Lemmon), a p.r. man and two-fisted belter whose career is floundering, is dismayed by a gap in their togetherness. Upshot is the disastrous compatibility of mutual alcoholism.

Lemmon gives a dynamic and chilling performance. Scenes of his collapse, particularly in the violent ward, are brutally realistic and terrifying. Remick, too, is effective, and there is solid featured work from Charles Bickford and Jack Klugman and a number of fine supporting performances.

1962: Best Song ("Days of Wine and Roses")

NOMINATIONS : Best Actor (Jack Lemmon), Actress (Lee Remick), B&W Costume Design, B&W Art Direction

•

DAY THE EARTH CAUGHT FIRE, THE

1961, 99 mins, UK Ⓥ ▭ b/w

Dir Val Guest **Prod** Val Guest **Scr** Wolf Mankowitz, Val Guest **Ph** Harry Waxman **Ed** Bill Lenny **Mus** Stanley Black **Art** Tony Masters

Act Janet Munro, Leo McKern, Edward Judd, Bernard Braden, Michael Goodliffe, Peter Butterworth (British Lion/Pax)

Val Guest's production has a fascinating yarn, some very sound thesping and an authentic Fleet Street (newspaper) background.

By mischance, an American nuclear test at the South Pole is conducted on the same day as a Russian one at the North Pole. It first causes a sinister upheaval in the world's weather and then it is discovered that the globe has been jolted out of orbit and is racing towards the sun and annihilation. It's figured that four giant bombs exploded simultaneously might save the grave situation and the world's powers unite, for once, to help a possibly doomed civilization.

Drama of this situation is played out as a newspaper scoop. Picture was shot largely in the building of the *Daily Express*. Arthur Christiansen, ex-editor of the *Express*, acted as technical advisor as well as playing the editor.

Guest's direction is brisk and makes good use of newsreel sequences and special effects, designed by Les Bowie. Dialogue is racy and slick without being too parochial for the layman.

The acting all round is effective. Edward Judd, making his first star appearance, clicks as the hero, the reporter who brings in the vital facts that make the story take shape. He shows rugged charm in his lightly romantic scenes with Janet Munro, who is pert and pleasant in the only considerable distaff role. Outstanding performance comes from Leo McKern, who is tops as a dependable gruff and understanding science reporter.

•

DAY THE EARTH STOOD STILL, THE

1951, 92 mins, US Ⓥ ⊙ b/w

Dir Robert Wise **Prod** Julian Blaustein **Scr** Edmund H. North **Ph** Leo Tover **Ed** William Reynolds **Mus** Bernard Herrmann **Art** Lyle Wheeler, Addison Hehr

Act Michael Rennie, Patricia Neal, Hugh Marlowe, Sam Jaffe, Billy Gray, Frances Bavier (20th Century-Fox)

Screenplay, based on a story by Harry Bates, tells of an invasion of the earth by a single spaceship from an unidentified planet in outer space. Ship has two occupants, an eight-foot robot, and an earth-like human. They have come to warn the earth's people that all other inhabited planets have banded together into a peaceful organization and that peace is being threatened by the wars of the earth-people. If that happens, the inter-planetary UN is prepared to blast the earth out of the universe.

Spaceship lands in Washington and the man, leaving the robot on guard, leaves to hide among the people, to discover for himself what they are like. His findings of constant bickerings and mistrust aren't too favorable for the earth's humans. Situation naturally creates fear throughout the world and the U.S. brings out army tanks, howitzers, etc., to guard the ship and the robot, while a frantic search goes on for the man.

Cast, although secondary to the story, works well. Michael Rennie is fine as the man from space. Patricia Neal is attractive and competent as the widowed mother of the young boy whom he befriends and who is the first to know his secret.

•

DAZED AND CONFUSED

1993, 94 mins, US Ⓥ ⊙ col

Dir Richard Linklater **Prod** Jim Jacks, Sean Daniel, Richard Linklater **Scr** Richard Linklater **Ph** Lee Daniel **Ed** Sandra Adair **Art** Jenny C. Patrick

Act Jason London, Wiley Wiggins, Sasha Jenson, Rory Cochrane, Milla Jovovich, Marissa Ribisi (Alphaville)

The teenage wasteland, 1976-style, of *Dazed and Confused* is smack-dab between *The Brady Bunch* and *Children of the Damned*, and it's a scary, if sometimes giddily amusing, place to visit. This is Richard Linklater's followup to his no-budget *Slacker*.

All the action takes place within 24 hours, as listless Austin, Texas, teens endure their last day of school, making bongs in shop and cataloguing every episode of *Gilligan's Island* in history, before the summer's serious business of drinking, fighting and generally humiliating each other and themselves.

In this suburban delirium, a few personalities emerge: Pink (Jason London) is a gentle, hunky quarterback unsure about his future in football; his pal Don (Sasha Jenson) is less interested in sports than in developing his gal-getting patter, and O'Bannion (Ben Affleck) takes the ritualistic paddling of new freshmen to psycho-sexual extremes. One victim is the slight, scraggly haired Mitch (Wiley Wiggins), who gets invited to join the older boys in their graduation-night debauchery.

One-liners and dry sight gags still abound, but the ennui-sodden formlessness of *Slacker* doesn't fly as well in this $6 million, smoothly lensed package, which calls for shapelier narrative and resolution.

•

D-DAY: THE SIXTH OF JUNE

1956, 106 mins, US Ⓥ ▭ col

Dir Henry Koster **Prod** Charles Brackett **Scr** Ivan Moffat, Harry Brown **Ph** Lee Garmes **Ed** William Mace **Mus** Lyn Murray **Art** Lyle R. Wheeler, Louis M. Creber

Act Robert Taylor, Richard Todd, Dana Wynter, Edmond O'Brien, John Williams, Jerry Paris (20th Century-Fox)

Along with the account of the significant historical event, the picture spins an extremely moving wartime love story, distinctively done by a finely performing cast. While the atmosphere and threat of war are always present in the top-notch Charles Brackett production, it isn't until near the end that actual fighting is shown in all of its frightening detail.

Footage opens with the sailing of the forerunners of the invasion fleet, then sets its characters and tells its story through the medium of two flashbacks, skillfully handled in the first-rate scripting from the Lionel Shapiro novel, before coming back to the June 6 date and the days immediately following.

There are a number of fine masculine performances by such as Robert Taylor, Richard Todd and Edmond O'Brien, but it remains for the sensitive, tremendously compelling work by Dana Wynter to give the real point to the drama and make the love story a valid thing.

The plot, simply, tells of an English girl (Wynter), virtually committed romantically to a British soldier (Todd), who meets and falls deeply in love with a married American officer (Taylor), and how this triangle is worked out in the overwhelming upset of war. There's a bitterly ironic note to the ending.

O'Brien creates a sock portrayal of a rank-bucking American officer who eventually cracks under the force of his own drive and the strain of war. John Williams is an embittered oldline brigadier who resents being sidetracked in this war.

DEAD, THE
1987, 83 mins, US Ⓥ ⊙ col
Dir John Huston ***Prod*** Wieland Schulz-Keil ***Scr*** Tony Huston ***Ph*** Fred Murphy ***Ed*** Roberto Silvi ***Mus*** Alex North ***Art*** Stephen Grimes
Act Anjelica Huston, Donal McCann, Rachael Dowling, Cathleen Delany, Helena Carroll, Dan O'Herlihy (Vestron Zenith/Liffey)

A well-crafted miniature, this dramatization of the Joyce story directly addresses the theme of how the "shades" from "that other world" can still live in those who still walk the earth.

Opening hour is set exclusively in the warm Dublin town house of two spinster sisters, who every winter holiday season throw a festive party and dinner for their relatives and friends. Time is 1904.

By evening's end, the focus clearly has been placed upon the handsome couple of Gretta and Gabriel (Anjelica Huston and Donal McCann). Back at their hotel, Gabriel attempts some rare intimacy with his distracted wife, who throws him into deep melancholy by telling him a secret of a youthful love. Gabriel sets upon a profound discourse about the living and the dead to the visual accompaniment of snow falling on bleak Irish landscapes.

Brought in for the California shoot, the virtually all-Irish cast brings the story to life completely and believably, with Helena Carroll's big-hearted Aunt Kate and Donal Donnelly's drunken Freddy Malins being special delights. Huston proves fully up to the demands of her emotionally draining monolog, and McCann simply is ideal as the thoughtful husband.

1987: NOMINATIONS: Best Adapted Screenplay, Costume Design

•

DEAD AGAIN
1991, 111 mins, US Ⓥ ⊙ col
Dir Kenneth Branagh ***Prod*** Lindsay Doran, Charles H. Maguire ***Scr*** Scott Frank ***Ph*** Matthew F. Leonetti ***Ed*** Peter E. Berger ***Mus*** Patrick Doyle ***Art*** Tim Harvey
Act Kenneth Branagh, Emma Thompson, Andy Garcia, Derek Jacobi, Robin Williams, Hanna Schygulla (Paramount/Mirage)

Director and star Kenneth Branagh brings the same zest and bravura style to this actors' romp of a mystery-thriller as he did to *Henry V*. Supernatural tale of murder, hypnosis and reincarnation involves a woman (Emma Thompson) wandering around in an amnesiac daze, tormented by memories of someone else's life.

Taken into the care of a cavalier private detective (Branagh) who finds himself mysteriously drawn to her, she reveals to a hypnotist (Derek Jacobi) her shockingly vivid memories of a glamorous life as a 1940s concert pianist married to a celebrated composer who was sentenced to death after he allegedly murdered her with a pair of scissors. Mystery is Thompson's true identity. Is the detective really her ex-husband, come back to life to kill her again?

Branagh illustrates the 1940s segs in giddily stylized black & white, with a tongue-in-cheek Wellesian theatricality, while the present-day action takes place in a pungently humanistic LA rife with bizarre characters.

Engaging film style is buoyed by an infectious sense of fun and punctuated by wild and woolly character turns. Robin Williams plays a psychiatrist who's gone off the deep end, and Andy Garcia is a seedy journalist with an accent seemingly wafting in from various ports.

Branagh and real-life spouse Thompson—each of whom plays dual roles in past and present—are excellent thesps, but they don't make a very seductive screen couple. Jacobi is a pure delight as the eccentric antiques dealer and hypnotist.

•

DEAD CALM
1989, 96 mins, Australia Ⓥ ⊙ ▭ col
Dir Phillip Noyce ***Prod*** Terry Hayes, Doug Mitchell, George Miller ***Scr*** Terry Hayes ***Ph*** Dean Semler ***Ed*** Richard Francis-Bruce ***Mus*** Graeme Revell ***Art*** Graham "Grace" Walker
Act Sam Neill, Nicole Kidman, Billy Zane (Kennedy Miller)

Though not always entirely credible, *Dead Calm* is a nail-biting suspense pic [from the novel by Charles Williams] handsomely produced and inventively directed.

It's basically a three-hander: A happily married couple John and Rae Ingram (Sam Neill and Nichole Kidman), have found peace alone on the Pacific on their well-equipped yacht after the trauma of the death of their baby son in a car accident when they're threatened by a vicious, unstable young killer, Hughie (Billy Zane).

They come to Hughie's aid initially, when he seeks help, but Ingram doesn't believe his story that the passengers and crew on the decrepit yacht he's abandoned all died from food poisoning. Leaving Hughie asleep, Ingram goes across to the delapidated vessel to discover dead bodies in the bilges and a video tape indicating that a deranged Hughie killed them.

While he's away, Hughie awakens, overpowers Rae, and sets sail in the opposite direction, abandoning Ingram. Throughout the film, Kidman is excellent. She gives the character of Rae real tenacity and energy. Neill is good, too, as a husband who spends most of the film unable to contact his wife, and Yank newcomer Zane is suitably manic and evil as the deranged Hughie.

•

DEAD END
1937, 90 mins, US Ⓥ ⊙ b/w
Dir William Wyler ***Prod*** Samuel Goldwyn ***Scr*** Lillian Hellman ***Ph*** Greg Toland ***Ed*** Daniel Mandell ***Mus*** Alfred Newman (dir.) ***Art*** Richard Day
Act Sylvia Sidney, Joel McCrea, Humphrey Bogart, Wendy Barrie, Claire Trevor, Allen Jenkins (Goldwyn/United Artists)

Producer Samuel Goldwyn has made a near-literal film translation of Sidney Kingsley's play *Dead End*, the New York stage success. The Kingsley theme is that tenements breed gangsters, and no one does anything about it. The play whammed the idea across the footlights; the picture says and does everything the play said and did, and stops right there.

All the action is limited merely to a larger background setting of the river front in the East 50s (NY) than the Belasco theatre stage could contain. Only material plot change is to heroize the character of Dave, the student architect (Joel McCrea).

Performances are uniformly fine, topped by the acting of the boy players from the New York production who seem better in the film because they do not crowd their lines so fast.

Sylvia Sidney is excellent. Her sister-and-brother scenes with the wild Tommy (Billy Halop) are tender, moving and tragic. McCrea does a fine bit in a scene with Wendy Barrie, the keptive in the fashionable apartment, when he turns down her proposition. The Barrie role is indefinite in outline, due to censoring.

Humphrey Bogart looks the part of Baby Face Martin and plays with complete understanding of the character. Claire Trevor is Francey, the street walker. In this instance also censorship has stripped the role of the shocking features which made it stand out in the play.

1937: NOMINATIONS: Best Picture, Supp. Actress (Claire Trevor), Cinematography, Art Direction

•

DEADFALL
1968, 120 mins, UK col
Dir Bryan Forbes ***Prod*** Paul Monash ***Scr*** Bryan Forbes ***Ph*** Gerry Turpin ***Ed*** John Jympson ***Mus*** John Barry ***Art*** Ray Simm
Act Michael Caine, Giovanna Ralli, Eric Portman, Nanette Newman, David Buck, Carlos Pierre (Salamander)

An apparent attempt to pull off an Alfred Hitchcock suspenser, with added Freudian schleps, *Deadfall* falls dead as little more than ponderous, tedious trivia. Adapted from Desmond Cory's novel, the talky, convoluted writing is hurt by hyped-up cinematics.

Michael Caine is introduced in a sanitorium as a cured alcoholic; Giovanna Ralli lures him to the home she shares with husband Eric Portman, who plays a homosexual, a point hammered home incessantly by dialog, plus the presence of Carlos Pierre, a pretty-boy-for-hire. The three principals join in a jewel heist, a 23-minute sequence which brings a halting pace to a complete stop. The "real" story is Caine's love for Ralli, complicated by the presence of Portman.

Composer John Barry appears as a symphony conductor in that 23-minute sequence of cross-cuts between guitarist Renata Tarrago, and Caine-Portman at work stealing somebody's loot.

•

DEAD FUNNY
1995, 96 mins, US Ⓥ col
Dir John Feldman ***Prod*** Richard Abramowitz, David Hannay ***Scr*** John Feldman, Cindy Oswin ***Ph*** Todd Crockett ***Ed*** Einar Westerlund ***Mus*** Sheila Silver ***Art*** Mike Shaw
Act Elizabeth Pena, Andrew McCarthy, Paige Turco, Blanche Baker, Allison Janney, Adelle Lutz (Avondale/Movie Screen/Film Four)

Topliner Elizabeth Pena again proves her mettle by carrying this slight, quirky tale of relationship intrigue in the Big Apple. Her oddball chemistry with a hirsute Andrew McCarthy, whose character turns up dead in very first scene (and is revived via flashbacks), helps enliven what could be claustrophobic material.

Trouble starts when Pena's Vivian, a spunky Museum of Modern Art employee, returns to her Manhattan walk-up, only to find immature b.f. Reggie (McCarthy) on the kitchen table, skewered by a Samurai sword. At first, she's convinced that this is yet another one of his elaborate practical jokes, since it's exactly one year since they met (hired to paint her place, he basically never left).

Reality strikes soon enough, but instead of calling the cops, confused Viv asks her pal Louise (funny Paige Turco) to come over. The women try to piece together what happened, downing much anniversary-intended champagne in the process. Baffled and blotto, they're about to give up when Viv's women's group arrives for a forgotten meeting.

Perfs are top-notch, with a special nod to Michael Mantell as a boring rival for Viv's affections.

•

DEAD HEAT ON A MERRY-GO-ROUND
1966, 107 mins, US Ⓥ col
Dir Bernard Girard ***Prod*** Carter DeHaven ***Scr*** Bernard Girard ***Ph*** Lionel Lindon ***Ed*** William Lyon ***Mus*** Stu Phillips ***Art*** Walter M. Simonds
Act James Coburn, Camilla Sparv, Aldo Ray, Nina Wayne, Robert Webber, Rose Marie (Columbia)

The idea and the premise of *Dead Heat on a Merry-Go-Round* is okay but it doesn't jell, and the title, a deliberate attempt to be cute, is meaningless. What leads up to the comedy-melodrama O. Henry finale most likely was very funny in the producers' minds, but much of the action is so fragmentary and episodic that there is not sufficient exposition and the treatment goes overboard in striving for effect.

James Coburn, who charms his way out of a prison into a parole via an affair with a femme psychologist (a nice trick if you know how to do it), has in mind the burglary of a bank at LA International Airport. Date set for the heist coincides with arrival of the Russian premier, when security will engage full attention of all arms of the law.

Coburn plays a rather sardonic character who is capable of meeting every situation successfully and with what is given him comes through with a deft performance. Camilla Sparv, whom he weds and is an innocent accomplice, rivals him in interest, displaying a fresh note which communicates engagingly.

•

DEADLIER THAN THE MALE
1967, 98 mins, UK ▭ col
Dir Ralph Thomas ***Prod*** Betty E. Box ***Scr*** Jimmy Sangster, David Osborn, Liz Charles-Williams ***Ph*** Ernest Steward ***Ed*** Alfred Roome ***Mus*** Malcolm Lockyer ***Art*** Alex Vetchinsky
Act Richard Johnson, Elke Sommer, Sylva Koscina, Nigel Green, Suzanna Leigh, Steve Carlson (Rank)

There is no doubt that *Deadlier than the Male* is loaded with colorful and exciting production values. Opinion thereafter is likely to divide, however, for the film will strike some as okay dual-bill escapism, and others as overly raw and single entendre. Sadism, sex and attempted sophistication mark this Bulldog Drummond pic.

David Osborn, Liz Charles-Williams and Jimmy Sangster scripted the latter's original story, in which Elke Sommer and Sylva Koscina are two cohorts of Nigel Green in his industrial deal-making.

Green's modus operandi is simple: intervene in major deals and promise consummation, then kill off all opposition and collect the promised fee. Scripters had a major task in making explicit murder appear as nonchalant as taking tea, and they rarely achieve the goal.

•

DEADLINE AT DAWN
1946, 83 mins, US Ⓥ b/w
Dir Harold Clurman ***Prod*** Adrian Scott ***Scr*** Clifford Odets ***Ph*** Nicholas Musuraca ***Ed*** Roalnd Gross ***Mus*** Hanns Eisler ***Art*** Albert S. D'Agostino, Jack Okey
Act Susan Hayward, Paul Lukas, Bill Williams, Joseph Calleia, Osa Massen, Lola Lane (RKO)

Combine of playwright Clifford Odets and director Harold Clurman, two onetime NY Group Theatre stalwarts, should have produced a more plausible murder melodrama of Manhattan than this one. Film has an arty approach to an otherwise plain whodunit, and is shot through with phoney bits of story and dialog. Performances are of a mixed quality.

Story [from the novel by Willian Irish] concerns a naive gob (Bill Williams) on leave in New York, who wanders into a cafe to be fleeced in a card game, and who wanders out with a dame to—of all things—fix a radio in her home. A few drinks under his belt, and he remembers nothing—how he came to be one-stepping with a gal in a dime-a-dance joint, how he came to have a huge roll on him, or how the dame whose radio he fixed was murdered. A dancer (Susan Hayward) feels sympathy for him and tries to help him find the murderer.

Rest of film recounts the efforts of the two to track down the clues they find, the meanwhile involving a gangster (Joseph Calleia), a taxi-driver (Paul Lukas), a shoestring theatrical producer, a blind pianist and a couple of two-timing gals.

The romance between gob and gal that develops has a phoney ring. The speech of characters, especially the gullible gob who talks bookish English as if out of Shakespeare, hardly ever rings true.

•

DEADLINE U.S.A.

1952, 87 mins, US Ⓥ b/w

Dir Richard Brooks ***Prod*** Sol C. Siegel ***Scr*** Richard Brooks ***Ph*** Milton Krasner ***Ed*** William B. Murphy ***Mus*** Cyril J. Mockridge ***Art*** Lyle Wheeler, George Patrick

Act Humphrey Bogart, Ethel Barrymore, Kim Hunter, Ed Begley, Warren Stevens, Paul Stewart (20th Century-Fox)

Humphrey Bogart is the traditionally intrepid big-city, big-sheet editor whose responsibility to his job, his corps of 1,500 fellow-workers on *The Day* (as this composite but mythical rag is called), and his moxie in locking horns with the No. 1 mobster, is chiefly sparked when one of his news staff gets beaten up by Martin Gabel's gang.

Complicating this is the projected sale of the paper by the founder-publisher's heirs. In midst of the imminence of job layoffs, Bogart proceeds to break the mob, stall the courts' approval of the sale, on his impassioned, informal plea in the surrogate's court that a newspaper, its functions, and its relation to its 300,000 faithful daily readers, is more than that of just another chattel. Much of the footage was shot in the NY *Daily News* pressrooms.

Bogart gives a convincing performance all the way, from his constantly harassed deadline existence, his personal romantic stalemate, and his guts in avenging the beating given his crime reporter.

•

DEADLY AFFAIR, THE

1967, 107 mins, UK Ⓥ col

Dir Sidney Lumet ***Prod*** Sidney Lumet ***Scr*** Paul Dehn ***Ph*** Freddie Young ***Ed*** Thelma Connell ***Mus*** Quincy Jones ***Art*** John Howell

Act James Mason, Simone Signoret, Maximilian Schell, Harriet Andersson, Lynn Redgrave, Harry Andrews (Columbia/Lumet)

The Deadly Affair is based on *Call for the Dead* by John le Carre. Shrewd and powerful development is given this tale of a British Home Office intelligence officer seeking to unravel the supposed suicide of a high Foreign Office diplomat.

Mason is cast as an unromantic civil servant whose official problems are further complicated by his being wed to a compulsively sexual young woman who has many affairs. His is a thorough acting job as he conducts his investigation in which he delivers one of his best performances.

Harry Andrews, as a retired CIP inspector called in to assist the intelligence officer, gives a rugged portrayal of police methods in dealing with criminals, which in this instance is a buildup to learning the identity of a foreign spy responsible for the death of the diplomat.

•

DEADLY BEES, THE

1967, 123 mins, UK ▭ col

Dir Freddie Francis ***Prod*** Max J. Rosenberg, Milton Subotsky ***Scr*** Robert Bloch, Anthony Marriott ***Ph*** John Wilcox ***Ed*** Oswald Hafenrichter ***Mus*** Wilfred Josephs ***Art*** Bill Constable

Act Suzanna Leigh, Frank Finlay, Guy Doleman, Catherine Finn, John Harvey, Michael Ripper (Paramount/Amicus)

The Deadly Bees is like *The Birds* only on a smaller scale. It boasts of uneven suspense, a plot long in unraveling and some gripping cinematic moments, provided by bees in deadly pursuit.

Suzanna Leigh has a mental breakdown from overwork and is sent to rest on a remote British island. The innkeeper (Guy Doleman) is a beekeeper. Leigh stumbles across the chic cottage of Frank Finlay, who also keeps bees.

A swarm of killer bees soon attack Doleman's wife, and suspense builds in a manner that viewer does not know which of the beekeepers is responsible for these beehavings. Throughout, characters show little emotional involvement, except for Leigh, who has command of all she does.

•

DEADLY COMPANIONS, THE

1961, 90 mins, US Ⓥ ⦿ ▭ col

Dir Sam Peckinpah ***Prod*** Charles B. FitzSimons ***Scr*** A. S. Fleischman ***Ph*** William B. Clothier ***Ed*** Stanley E. Rabjon ***Mus*** Marlin Skiles

Act Maureen O'Hara, Brian Keith, Steve Cochran, Chill Wills, Strother Martin (Pathe-America)

A. S. Fleischman's adaptation of his own novel is the dramatic tale of four characters who encounter their respective moments of truth in a ghost town smack dab in the heart of Apache country. One (Maureen O'Hara) is a dancehall woman heading for the ghost town to bury her son next to her late husband, thus erasing the stigma of her shady reputation. Another is Brian Keith, whose motivation is revenge against Chill Wills, an unstable galoot with whom he has an old score to settle. Fourth member of the odd party is Steve Cochran, a gunslinger with eyes for O'Hara.

Fleischman's screenplay is pretty farfetched and relies heavily on coincidence but, for the most part, it plays. This thanks to superior emoting by the four principals and an auspicious debut as director by Sam Peckinpah, a fine TV helmsman.

Keith plays with customary reserve and masculine authority a character refreshingly different from the usual impregnable western "tall man."

•

DEADLY FRIEND

1986, 99 mins, US Ⓥ ⦿ col

Dir Wes Craven ***Prod*** Robert M. Sherwood ***Scr*** Bruce Joel Rubin ***Ph*** Philip Lathrop ***Ed*** Michael Eliot ***Mus*** Charles Bernstein ***Art*** Daniel Lomino

Act Matthew Laborteaux, Kristy Swanson, Michael Sharrett, Anne Twomey, Anne Ramsey, Richard Marcus (Pan Arts/Layton)

Pic has enough gore, suspense and requisite number of shocks to keep most hearts pounding through to the closing credits.

Paul (Matthew Laborteaux) is a bit accelerated for his age, having built a semi-intelligent robot named BB.

One night, neighbour Richard Marcus goes a bit too far slapping his daughter (Kristy Swanson) around and she ends up having to be hospitalized. Just when the doctors determine she's brain-dead, Laborteaux steals her body and transplants BB's "brain" into her gray matter. That's when the fun begins.

Viewers can just as easily scream as laugh through *Deadly Friend* watching the obviously made-up Swanson come back to life and walk around like a robot, crushing her enemies one by one.

•

DEADLY HERO

1976, 99 mins, US Ⓥ col

Dir Ivan Nagy ***Prod*** Thomas J. McGrath ***Scr*** George Wislocki ***Ph*** Andrzej Bartkowiak ***Ed*** Susan Steinberg ***Mus*** Brad Fiedel, Tommy Mandel ***Art*** Alan Herman

Act Don Murray, Diahn Williams, James Earl Jones, Lilia Skala, George S. Irving, Treat Williams (Avco Embassy)

Deadly Hero is a neat little thriller about a psychotic NY City cop terrorizing a woman who has complained about his violent behaviour in saving her from assault. If it sounds complex, it is, and the characters are drawn with believable shades of gray.

The film, made entirely on NY City locations, expertly captures the nightmarish mood of the metropolitan jungle, buttressing plot credibility through good detail work and character vignettes, without wallowing in violence.

George Wislocki's screenplay keeps up an unrelenting mood of stomach-wrenching anxiety as cellist Diahn Williams is first brutalized by James Earl Jones, then pursued by hothead cop Don Murray.

Jones has the flashiest role, and makes it a frightening portrait of a maniac.

•

DEADLY IS THE FEMALE

SEE: GUN CRAZY

•

DEADLY PURSUIT

SEE: SHOOT TO KILL

DEAD MAN

1995, 134 mins, US Ⓥ ⦿ b/w

Dir Jim Jarmusch ***Prod*** Demetra J. MacBride ***Scr*** Jim Jarmusch ***Ph*** Robby Muller ***Ed*** Jay Rabinowitz ***Mus*** Neil Young ***Art*** Bob Ziembicki

Act Johnny Depp, Gary Farmer, Lance Henriksen, Michael Wincott, Mili Avital, Crispin Glover (Pandora/JVC/Newmarket/L.P.)

Dead Man resembles a pokey stroll through the Old West rather than an exciting ride. Jim Jarmusch's first period outing possesses a piquant humor and eccentric mood that brand it with the mark of one of America's most distinctive indie filmmakers, but pic's unassertiveness and considerable overlength give it a diffused impact.

Like many Westerns before it, notably Robert Benton's debut feature, *Bad Company*, among relatively contemporary pictures, this one charts the progression from "civilized" values to outlawry in the course of a picaresque journey involving many odd, colorful characters. The almost inadvertent transformation of Johnny Depp's William Blake from a mild-mannered Ohio accountant to a notorious gunman has to do with circumstances being able to completely transform a man's life from what he intended it to be.

This happens when Blake finds that the job for which he has traveled from Cleveland to the remote frontier has already been filled by the time he gets there. In short order, Blake runs afoul of ornery factory boss John Dickinson (Robert Mitchum in a relatively colorless cameo), then kills for the first time when Dickinson's son (Gabriel Byrne) shoots his woman upon finding her in bed with Blake, forcing the latter to retaliate.

Three bounty hunters, led by sadistic man-in-black Cole Wilson (Lance Henriksen), are only the first of many who try to track down the fugitive, who takes to the hills. His chaperone and guide on good bits of this trip is a one-of-a-kind Indian named Nobody (Gary Farmer), who speaks PhD-candidate English, takes mind-altering drugs and is well acquainted with the poet William Blake.

As he has before, Depp makes for an eminently watchable, if essentially reactive, hero. Henriksen is the model of a vicious Western killer. Other thesps, unfortunately, are either so heavily hidden behind hair and furry costumes as to be virtually unrecognizable or seen so briefly as to not make any special use of their talents, including Mitchum, John Hurt, Byrne, Alfred Molina and Crispin Glover.

•

DEAD MAN WALKING

1995, 120 mins, US Ⓥ ⦿ col

Dir Tim Robbins ***Prod*** Jon Kilik, Tim Robbins, Rudd Simmons ***Scr*** Tim Robbins ***Ph*** Roger A. Deakins ***Ed*** Lisa Zeno Churgin ***Mus*** David Robbins ***Art*** Richard Hoover

Act Susan Sarandon, Sean Penn, Robert Prosky, Raymond J. Barry, R. Lee Ermey, Celia Weston (Working Title/Havoc/PolyGram)

Following his 1992 feature debut, *Bob Roberts*, Tim Robbins makes a quantum leap forward as writer and director of *Dead Man Walking*, a highly intriguing drama about the complex relationship between a devout nun and a death row convict. An intimate chamber piece for two, superbly acted by Susan Sarandon and Sean Penn, this is a mature, well-crafted movie.

Inspired by true events and figures in Sister Helen Prejean's bestselling 1993 book, pic defies the conventions of both Hollywood crime melodramas and TV movies.

Set in St. Thomas Housing Project and Angola Prison in New Orleans, tale begins with a correspondence between Sister Helen Prejean (Sarandon), a pious but down-to-earth nun, and Matthew Poncelet (Penn), a convicted killer awaiting execution.

During the crucial week that frames the film, the duo undergo emotional journeys that are parallel and complementary.

Robbins shrewdly inserts flashbacks of the rapes and murders with increasing frequency in the last reel—there's genuine suspense as to which specific crimes Poncelet committed the night he and his macho buddy were out partying in the woods, both heavily drugged.

Sans makeup, Sarandon inhabits the nun's role with powerful conviction, expressing the character's valor and vulnerability. Penn's tough yet intricate Poncelet complements Sarandon superbly.

1995: Best Actress (Susan Sarandon)

NOMINATIONS: Actor (Sean Penn), Director, Original Song ("Dead Man Walking")

•

DEAD MEN DON'T WEAR PLAID
1982, 89 mins, US Ⓥ ⦿ b/w
Dir Carl Reiner ***Prod*** David V. Picker, William E. McEwen ***Scr*** Carl Reiner, George Gipe, Steve Martin ***Ph*** Michael Chapman ***Ed*** Bud Molin ***Mus*** Miklos Rozsa ***Art*** John DeCuir
Act Steve Martin, Rachel Ward, Reni Santoni, Carl Reiner, George Gaynes, Frank McCarthy (Universal/Aspen)

Lensed in black-and-white and outfitted with a "straight" mystery score by Miklos Rozsa and authentic 1940s costumes by Edith Head, this spoof of film noir detective yarns sees Steve Martin interacting with 18 Hollywood greats by way of intercutting of clips from some 17 old pictures.

Thus, when sultry Rachel Ward enters his seedy LA office to discuss her father's murder, $10-per-day sleuth Martin is able to call Bogart's Philip Marlowe for assistance on the case. And so it goes with such additional tough guys as Burt Lancaster, Kirk Douglas and Edward Arnold and such dames as Barbara Stanwyck, Ingrid Bergman, Veronica Lake, Bette Davis, Lana Turner and Joan Crawford.

Film is most engaging in its romantic sparring between Martin and his gorgeous client, Ward. Latter looks sensational in period garb and is not above such Martinesque gags as removing bullets from his wounds with her teeth or having her breasts "rearranged" by the hardboiled detective.

Sporting dark hair and facetious confidence, Martin also looks spiffy in trenchcoat and hat. Only other roles of note see Carl Reiner essentially essaying Otto Preminger as a Nazi, and Reni Santoni as a zealous Peruvian offficer.

•

DEAD OF NIGHT
1945, 103 mins, UK Ⓥ ⦿ b/w
Dir Alberto Cavalcanti, Basil Deardén, Robert Hamer, Charles Crichton ***Prod*** Michael Balcon ***Scr*** John V. Baines, Angus MacPhail, T.E.B. Clarke ***Ph*** Jack Parker, H. Julius ***Ed*** Charles Hasse ***Mus*** Georges Auric ***Art*** Michael Relph
Act Googie Withers, Michael Redgrave, Sally Ann Howes, Mervyn Johns, Roland Culver, Frederick Valk (Ealing)

Tightly woven script [from stories by John V. Baines, Angus MacPhail, E. F. Benson and H. G. Wells] tells the story of a man who has foreknowledge of the future through his dreams. Summoned on business to a British estate, he's shocked to find that the place and people have all been in his dreams. When he tells his dream, one of the house-guests, a psychiatrist, scoffs at the story and attempts to find a scientific explanation for it all. Other guests, however, are more sympathetic and each then tells of a strange, similarly psychic situation in which he's been involved.

Producer Michael Balcon turned each individual episode over to a different director and, told via flashback, they're equally good. Best is the one featuring Redgrave as a ventriloquist whose dummy seemed imbued with a human brain and soul. Redgrave turns in a masterful piece of acting as he's driven to "kill" the dummy.

•

DEAD OF WINTER
1987, 100 mins, US Ⓥ ⦿ col
Dir Arthur Penn ***Prod*** John Bloomgarden, Marc Shmuger ***Scr*** Marc Shmuger, Mark Malone ***Ph*** Jan Weincke ***Ed*** Rick Shaine ***Mus*** Richard Einhorn ***Art*** Bill Brodie
Act Mary Steenburgen, Roddy McDowall, Jan Rubes, William Russ, Mark Malone, Ken Pogue (M-G-M)

Mary Steenburgen is first rate as the struggling actress hired by an unusually accommodating casting director (Roddy McDowall) to audition as a double for an actress removed from a film-in-progress because of an alleged nervous breakdown.

She's taken to the isolated country estate of a psychiatrist-turned-producer during a violent snowstorm (hence the title *Dead of Winter*) where she undergoes a complete makeover until she—quite uncannily—resembles the stricken actress.

Little does she know she's become the patsy for a couple of blackmailers who have bumped off the other actress, as revealed in the very first scene of the film.

Suspense is built artfully around her gradual realization that she's trapped with a sly shrink and his obsequious factotum, McDowall, considerably more malevolent than he first appeared.

Steenburgen and McDowall are the adversaries to follow, even though it would seem more likely that the wheelchair bound doctor (Jan Rubes) should be the one to watch. Rubes is simply not sinister enough to be the mastermind behind this scheme.

•

DEAD POETS SOCIETY
1989, 128 mins, US Ⓥ ⦿ col
Dir Peter Weir ***Prod*** Steven Haft, Paul Junger Witt, Tony Thomas ***Scr*** Tom Schulman ***Ph*** John Seale ***Ed*** William Anderson ***Mus*** Maurice Jarre ***Art*** Wendy Stites
Act Robin Williams, Robert Sean Leonard, Ethan Hawke, Josh Charles, Gale Hansen, Dylan Kussman (Touchstone)

Pic is not so much about Robin Williams, as unconventional English teacher John Keating at a hardline New England prep school, as it is about the youths he teaches and how the creative flames within them are kindled and then stamped out.

Director Peter Weir fills the screen with a fresh gang of compelling teenagers, led by Robert Sean Leonard as outgoing Neil Perry and balanced by Ethan Hawke as deeply withdrawn Todd Anderson. Keating enters their rigidly traditional world and has them literally rip out the pages of their hidebound textbooks in favor of his inventive didactics on the spirit of poetry.

Captivated by Keating's spirit, the influential Neil provokes his mates into reviving a secret club, the Dead Poets Society, that Keating led in his prep school days. Meanwhile the gifted, medical-school-bound Neil begins to pursue acting, his true aspiration, against the strenuous objections of his domineering father (Kurtwood Smith).

Story sings whenever Williams is onscreen. Screen belongs just as often to Leonard, who as Neil has a quality of darting confidence mixed with hesitancy. Hawke, as the painfully shy Todd, gives a haunting performance.

1989: Best Original Screenplay

NOMINATIONS: Best Picture, Director, Actor (Robin Williams)

•

DEAD POOL, THE
1988, 91 mins, US Ⓥ ⦿ col
Dir Buddy Van Horn ***Prod*** David Valdes ***Scr*** Steve Sharon ***Ph*** Jack N. Green ***Ed*** Joel Cox, Ron Spang ***Mus*** Lalo Schifrin ***Art*** Edward C. Carfagno
Act Clint Eastwood, Patricia Clarkson, Evan C. Kim, Liam Neeson, David Hunt, Michael Currie (Malpaso/Warner)

Dirty Harry Callahan isn't the best and brightest of cops but you can't kill him with cannon, mace and chain. *The Dead Pool* isn't the best and brightest of the Dirty Harry films, either, but just as invincible. It's possible that Clint Eastwood and crew are just enjoying a bit of self-mockery with this one [the fifth in the series].

From the original on, Harry has always been a fantasy character but his stories have been involving. Here, he remains absurdly separate from reality in an exceedingly lame yarn [by Steve Sharon, Durk Pearson and Sandy Shaw] that lurches from one shootout to the next.

The plot has something to do with a crime lord whom Harry has dispatched to San Quentin and a psychotic film fan out to eliminate local celebrities, which includes the cop and lady friend Samantha Walker (Patricia Clarkson, in the current cliche role of the peppery newscaster). In the background is a low-budget film company boringly run by Peter (Liam Neeson), a suspect who's never remotely suspicious for a moment.

There are chuckles here and there and a wildly preposterous car chase up and down the hills of Frisco. This time, though, it's a teeny little toy car in pursuit of the policemen, intending to overtake them with a bomb.

•

DEAD PRESIDENTS
1995, 119 mins, US Ⓥ ⦿ ▭ col
Dir Allen Hughes, Albert Hughes ***Prod*** Allen Hughes, Albert Hughes ***Scr*** Michael Henry Brown ***Ph*** Lisa Rinzler ***Ed*** Dan Lebental ***Mus*** Danny Elfman ***Art*** David Brisbin
Act Larenz Tate, Keith David, Chris Tucker, N'Bushe Wright, Freddy Rodriguez, Rose Jackson (Underworld/Hollywood)

An extremely ambitious follow-up to their crackling debut, *Menace II Society*, the Hughes brothers' mordant *Dead Presidents* [from a screen story by them and Michael Henry Brown] may eventually box itself into a narrative dead end, but its muscular engagement of weighty themes and explosive situations makes it a powerful drama, a potent social panorama from a black perspective spanning the convulsive transitional years of 1968–74.

In a relatively proper, lower middle-class Bronx neighborhood of 1968, the somewhat naive 18-year-old Anthony (Larenz Tate) is just finishing high school. While he may run numbers for pool hall operator Kirby (Keith David) on the side, and isn't inclined to follow his studious brother Cleon (Bokeem Woodbine) to college, the well-reared Anthony is far from likely criminal material. His best buddies are the somewhat crazy, life-of-the-party Skip (Chris Tucker) and the unpredictable Jose (Freddy Rodriguez).

A half-hour in, action jumps to the war, and for 20 intense minutes, pic chronicles Anthony's coming-of-age under fire. Once back home in 1973, Anthony faces the sad legacy of many Vietnam vets. Ultimately jobless and desperate, Anthony decides to pull off a big heist in cahoots with Kirby, Jose, Skip, Juanita's revolutionary sister Delilah (N'Bushe Wright) and, most unlikely of all, his brother, who's now a neighborhood preacher. This final section, a sort of mini-*Asphalt Jungle*, feels partly like a different movie.

Tate, who appeared in the Hughes' first film, carries this one ably, moving convincingly from youthful cheerfulness to grim anger. Of the large supporting cast, standouts include David as the short-tempered Kirby, the riotous Tucker as the sassy sidekick and the powerful Clifton Powell as hair-triggered pimp.

•

DEAD RECKONING
1947, 100 mins, US Ⓥ ⦿ b/w
Dir John Cromwell ***Prod*** Sidney Biddell ***Scr*** Oliver H. P. Garrett, Steve Fisher ***Ph*** Leo Tover ***Ed*** Gene Havlick ***Mus*** Marlin Skiles ***Art*** Stephen Goosson, Rudolph Sternad
Act Humphrey Bogart, Lizabeth Scott, Morris Carnovsky, William Prince, Charles Cane, Marvin Miller (Columbia)

Humphrey Bogart's typically tense performance raises this average whodunit quite a few notches. Film has good suspense and action, and some smart direction and photography.

Columbia borrowed Bogart from Warners to play the role of a tough ex-paratrooper captain returning home with a pal to be honored by the War Dept. for their achievements. When the pal jumps the DC train, to go home instead, the perplexed captain follows to find himself enmeshed in gangland, murders and romance. His pal, he learns, had enlisted under an alias because he was convicted of a killing. Two days after said pal arrives home, he gets bumped off.

Determined to solve the mystery and avenge his friend, the captain digs into his pal's haunts. Script uses a flashback method for part of the telling, to add variety.

Bogart absorbs one's interest from the start as a tough, quick-thinking ex-skyjumper. Lizabeth Scott stumbles occasionally as a nitery singer, but on the whole gives a persuasive sirenish performance.

•

DEAD RINGERS
1988, 115 mins, Canada Ⓥ ⦿ col
Dir David Cronenberg ***Prod*** David Cronenberg, Marc Boyman ***Scr*** David Cronenberg, Norman Snider ***Ph*** Peter Suschitzky ***Ed*** Ronald Sanders ***Mus*** Howard Shore ***Art*** Carol Spier
Act Jeremy Irons, Genevieve Bujold, Heidi Von Palleske, Barbara Gordon, Shirley Douglas, Stephen Lack (Mantle Clinic II)

Dead Ringers is about identical twin gynecologists, both expertly played by Jeremy Irons, whose intense bond is fatally sliced when they both fall in love with the same internationally known actress (Genevieve Bujold).

The doctors are renowned, interchangeably taking on the same patients and making public appearances, with no one guessing who's who. Yet one is outgoing, a smooth talker and a ladies man, and the other, more dependent and less sociable. Bujold chooses the shy twin, and from that point, disintegration of the twins' bond and their careers sets in.

Director David Cronenberg handles his usual fondness for gore in muted style; a brief scene has the shy twin dreaming of biting apart the skin joining Siamese twins; and the final operation, though bloody, is not lingered over.

•

DEAD ZONE, THE
1983, 102 mins, US Ⓥ ⦿ col
Dir David Cronenberg ***Prod*** Debra Hill ***Scr*** Jeffrey Boam ***Ph*** Mark Irwin ***Ed*** Ronald Sanders ***Mus*** Michael Kamen ***Art*** Carol Spier
Act Christopher Walken, Brooke Adams, Tom Skerritt, Herbert Lom, Anthony Zerbe, Martin Sheen (Dino De Laurentiis)

Joining the half-dozen shock-oriented directors who have filmed novelist Stephen King's horror and suspense yarns, David Cronenberg turns *The Dead Zone* into an accomplished psychological thriller.

Focus is Johnny Smith, a shy schoolteacher who snaps out of a long coma with the questionable gift of second sight. Convincingly played by Christopher Walken, Johnny can see into anybody's past or future merely by grasping the person's hand. The "dead zone" seems to refer to the brain damage that enables him to change the outcome of events he "sees."

His first premonition enables a nurse to save her daughter from a domestic conflagration. The news of the patient's ESP spreads quickly and he experiences some pretty horrible incidents, inside and outside his head.

A lot happens in the 102-minute suspenser. There's the girlfriend (Brooke Adams) Johnny loses to his near-fatal accident and regains for awhile. There's also a sheriff (Tom Skerritt) who desperately needs a psychic solution to crack a murder case, and the wealthy businessman (Anthony Zerbe) who hires Johnny to tutor his problem son (Simon Craig).

•

DEALERS
1989, 89 mins, UK Ⓥ col
Dir Colin Bucksey ***Prod*** William P. Cartlidge ***Scr*** Andrew MacLear ***Ph*** Peter Sinclair ***Ed*** Jon Costelloe ***Mus*** Richard Hartley ***Art*** Peter J. Hampton
Act Paul McGann, Rebecca DeMornay, Derrick O'Connor, John Castle, Paul Guilfoyle, Rosalind Bennett (Euston)

Dealers though well produced, is a less than enthralling pic about a yuppie high-flyer and his glamorous mistress.

Paul McGann is a dollar dealer in a London bank, set for promotion when his superior commits suicide after a botched deal. To his chagrin, McGann's boss brings in an outsider over his head, beautiful Rebecca DeMornay, the latest whiz kid in the banking business (and the boss' mistress to boot). Before long, though, McGann is romancing his rival and taking her home for a nightcap in his seaplane, which he parks near Tower Bridge.

Pic's most interesting character is Derrick O'Connor as a cockney dealer who's pinkslipped from the bank and sinks into a coke-snorting decline.

•

DEAR BRIGITTE
1965, 100 mins, US Ⓥ col
Dir Henry Koster ***Prod*** Henry Koster ***Scr*** Hal Kanter ***Ph*** Lucien Ballard ***Ed*** Marjorie Fowler ***Mus*** George Duning ***Art*** Jack Martin Smith, Malcolm Brown
Act James Stewart, Fabian, Glynis Johns, Cindy Carol, Billy Mumy, Brigitte Bardot (20th Century-Fox)

An entertaining comedy with something for everyone, *Dear Brigitte* shapes up as an excellent family pic.

Hal Kanter's screenplay, based on John Haase's novel *Erasmus with Freckles,* focuses on poet-professor Robert Leaf who's not only pro-humanities but very much anti-science. James Stewart is perfect in characterization of the idealistic voice in academic wilderness, as nuclear labs and computer setups encroach upon his domain of arts and letters at mythical modern university.

Complications arise when eight-year-old son Erasmus turns tone-deaf, then color-blind (hence unsuited for artistic career) but displays mathematical genius which indicates great scientific future. Kanter's yarn is lightweight, but a sufficiently strong fiber to support a string of varied and effective comedy situations, including Erasmus's puppy love for Brigitte Bardot to whom he secretly writes letters from Sausalito riverboat home.

In role of Stewart's wife, Glynis Johns is standout as steadying influence on hubby, son Billy Mumy, teenage daughter Cindy Carol and latter's boyfriend Fabian.

•

DEAREST LOVE
SEE: LE SOUFFLE AU COEUR

•

DEATH AND THE MAIDEN
1994, 103 mins, US/France/UK Ⓥ col
Dir Roman Polanski ***Prod*** Thom Mount, Josh Kramer ***Scr*** Rafael Yglesias, Ariel Dorfman ***Ph*** Tonino Delli Colli ***Ed*** Herve De Luze ***Mus*** Wojciech Kilar ***Art*** Pierre Guffroy
Act Sigourney Weaver, Ben Kingsley, Stuart Wilson (Fine Line/Capitol/Flach/C4)

Three fine actors and a top director give a very good account of Ariel Dorfman's *Death and the Maiden* in this tense, adroit film version of the play. But as vivid and suspenseful as Roman Polanski has made this claustrophobic tale of a torture victim turning the tables on her putative tormentor, one is still left with a film in which each character represents a mouthpiece for an ideology.

Dorfman's play, which was produced on Broadway in 1992 with Glenn Close, Richard Dreyfuss and Gene Hackman (directed by Mike Nichols), was clearly based on the contemporary history of his native Chile, but took the universal route by not identifying its locale or specific events. Similarly, the film is set in "a country in South America . . . after the fall of the dictatorship."

The early scene-setting has Paulina Escobar (Sigourney Weaver) nervously pacing about a remote beach house during a rainstorm. At length, a car pulls up through the darkness and Dr. Roberto Miranda (Ben Kingsley) drops off Paulina's husband, Gerardo (Stuart Wilson), whose car has broken down.

It doesn't take long for Paulina to tell that the stranger's voice belongs to the man who brutalized her long ago. As the men proceed to get drunk, she sneaks outside and pushes Miranda's car over a cliff, then returns to pistol-whip the visitor and bind him to a chair, her panties neatly stuffed in his mouth. Thus is Miranda put on trial, with the audience as jury.

Dorfman, who has expanded but not opened up his play with the help of Rafael Yglesias (*Fearless*), keeps the audience guessing about whether Miranda is the right man up to the very end. Cast is excellent, though having Anglo-American actors portray South Americans will bother some people. Veteran lenser Tonino Delli Colli's work indoors is superlative, as is his night shooting on location.

•

DEATH BECOMES HER
1992, 103 mins, US Ⓥ ⦿ col
Dir Robert Zemeckis ***Prod*** Robert Zemeckis, Steve Starkey ***Scr*** Martin Donovan, David Koepp ***Ph*** Dean Cundey ***Ed*** Arthur Schmidt ***Mus*** Alan Silvestri ***Art*** Rick Carter
Act Meryl Streep, Bruce Willis, Goldie Hawn, Isabella Rossellini, Ian Ogilvy, Adam Storke (Universal)

Mordant, daring and way, way out there, *Death Becomes Her* is a very dark comedy yielding far more strange fascination than outright laughs. Robert Zemeckis's stretch of state-of-the-art special effects within a character-oriented context is a treat for somewhat specialized tastes.

Long-arc script describes the epic competition between vain actress Meryl Streep and troubled author Goldie Hawn, initially for the love of superstar plastic surgeon Bruce Willis, but, more important, for the secret to eternal life and youth. After an amusing prolog, Zemeckis serves up his first amazing scene with the introduction, seven years later, of Hawn as an embittered fat slob. As everywhere else here, effects work is seamless and first rate, with a clearly big-time budget (estimated at $40 million).

Another seven years pass, and Streep, now a washed-up mess, is living in sterile Bev Hills splendor with alcoholic Willis. Streep insists on attending a chic book party for Hawn, but is horrified to discover the 50-year-old writer looks like a health club ad.

Frantic to outdo her bitter enemy, Streep ends up at the fabulous mansion of Isabella Rossellini, a kinky beauty who turns out to be a high priestess of eternal life.

Streep does an acid sendup of aging beauty queens that will be relished by devotees of showbiz and its icons. Hawn plays very well with her co-star but is mostly limited to rabid vengeance. Willis is okay, but lacks the daft quality of Kevin Kline, original choice for the role. An uncredited Sydney Pollack is great fun as a Bev Hills doctor.

1992: Best Visual Effects

•

DEATH IN A FRENCH GARDEN
SEE: PERIL EN LA DEMEURE

•

DEATH IN VENICE
1971, 130 mins, Italy Ⓥ ⦿ ▭ col
Dir Luchino Visconti ***Prod*** Luchino Visconti ***Scr*** Luchino Visconti, Nicola Badalucco ***Ph*** Pasquale de Santis ***Mus*** Gustav Mahler ***Art*** Ferdinand Scarfiotti, Piero Tosi
Act Dirk Bogarde, Bjorn Andresen, Silvana Mangano, Marisa Berenson, Mark Burns (Warner)

Based on Thomas Mann's novella, *Death in Venice* could have been no easy task to translate to the screen. But Visconti and Dirk Bogarde clearly have a rapport and Bogarde gives a subtle and moving performance which fits beautifully into the atmospheric realism of [pre-World War I] Venice.

Bogarde plays a German composer and conductor (made up to look very like Gustav Mahler, whose music is used for the score) who visits Venice on vacation when on the verge of a mental and physical collapse. He is concerned with the violent accusations of his friend (Mark Burns) that he has dodged the issue of emotion until he is now no longer capable of feeling it.

He is fastidious and will not react to the uncouth behavior of the people he meets until, at his hotel, he sees a young boy with his family. The lad looks to Bogarde to be the most beautiful thing he has ever seen. He never seeks to contact the lad but follows him and watches him with a hunger which, thanks to Bogarde's performance, is clearly more intellectual and emotional than homosexual.

The story has its troubles. It attempts to show how innocence can cause problems of corruption and yet there is a pervading air over the film that is far from innocent.

Bogarde is both pathetic and compelling. Bjorn Andresen undoubtedly is a remarkably attractively featured lad and gives a memorable performance. Silvana Mangano plays his mother with a haughty charm.

1971: NOMINATION: Best Costume Design

•

DEATH OF A GUNFIGHTER
1969, 94 mins, US Ⓥ col
Dir Allen Smithee [= Robert Totten, Don Siegel] ***Prod*** Richard E. Lyons ***Scr*** Joseph Calvelli ***Ph*** Andrew Jackson ***Ed*** Robert F. Shugrue ***Mus*** Oliver Nelson ***Art*** Alexander Golitzen, Howard E. Johnson
Act Richard Widmark, Lena Horne, John Saxon, Carroll O'Connor, David Opatoshu, Kent Smith (Universal)

Story concerns an offbeat sort of gunman, a smalltown marshal with 12 killings to his credit. But now he is to be removed by a disgruntled city council. His efforts to remain in post end in a flashy finish.

Richard Widmark punches over title role and gives tone to the character who has always tried to run a clean town. Script from Lewis B. Patten's novel builds suspense as the council plans his departure but doesn't know how, other than to gun him down.

Widmark elicits certain sympathy for his actions in his hardboiled interpretation, and for co-star has Lena Horne, in role of a madam. [Pic is first use on a feature film of official Directors Guild of America pseudonym "Allen Smithee" for directors who want no credit. Don Siegel replaced Robert Totten, who was fired after 25 days.]

•

DEATH OF A SALESMAN
1951, 115 mins, US Ⓥ b/w
Dir Laslo Benedek ***Prod*** Stanley Kramer ***Scr*** Stanley Roberts ***Ph*** Franz P. Planer ***Ed*** William Lyon ***Mus*** Alex North ***Art*** Rudolph Sternad, Cary Odell
Act Fredric March, Mildred Dunnock, Kevin McCarthy, Cameron Mitchell, Howard Smith, Royal Beal (Kramer/Columbia)

The vise-like grip with which *Death of a Salesman* held Broadway theatergoers for almost two years continues undiminished in Stanley Kramer's production of the film version. Arthur Miller's Pulitzer Prize–winner has been closely followed in the screen adaptation.

Salesman starkly reveals how Willy Loman's disillusionments catch up with him, his sons, his wife Linda; of how, after 34 years selling for the same house, he is finally fired, thus bringing about his complete mental collapse. During the period when his mental processes are breaking down, the film images Willy's memories of the past 20 years in illustrating how his desire for importance somehow became enmeshed in his confused dreams.

Fredric March, in the part created on the New York stage by Lee Cobb, gives perhaps the greatest performance of his career. Mildred Dunnock, in her original Broadway part, is superb as Willy's wife Linda. Kevin McCarthy, as Biff, is a film newcomer who entrenches himself strongly in the role performed on Broadway by Arthur Kennedy, Cameron Mitchell is an engaging "Happy" Loman, the other brother, which he played on Broadway.

1951: NOMINATIONS: Best Actor (Fredric March), Supp. Actor (Kevin McCarthy), Supp. Actress (Mildred Dunnock), B&W Cinematography, Scoring of a Dramatic Picture

•

DEATH ON THE NILE
1978, 140 mins, UK Ⓥ ⦿ col
Dir John Guillermin ***Prod*** John Brabourne, Richard Goodwin ***Scr*** Anthony Shaffer ***Ph*** Jack Cardiff ***Ed*** Malcolm Cooke ***Mus*** Nino Rota ***Art*** Peter Murton
Act Peter Ustinov, Jane Birkin, Lois Chiles, Bette Davis, Mia Farrow, Jon Finch (EMI)

Death on the Nile is a clever, witty, well-plotted, beautifully produced and splendidly acted screen version of Agatha Christie's mystery. It's old-fashioned stylized entertainment with a big cast and lush locations.

Peter Ustinov is the fourth actor to play Belgian sleuth Hercule Poirot.

Anthony Shaffer's adaptation doesn't have a hole. When Ustinov reveals the killer in the final drawing room scene it comes as a complete surprise. Every one of the dozen characters floating down the Nile is a suspect. Everyone on board could have and might have murdered Lois Chiles, the arrogant millionairess who has stolen her best friend's fiance.

Shaffer has also created a number of purposely exaggerated characters to complement Ustinov. There's Angela Lansbury's tipsy portrayal of a romantic novelist; Bette Davis as a stuffy and overbearing Washington socialite and

Maggie Smith as her bitter companion; Jack Warden as an hysterical Swiss physician; I. S. Johar in a marvelously offbeat performance as the manager of the ship on which the murders take place; David Niven as Poirot's sidekick, Colonel Race; and Jon Finch as a Marxist spouting rebel.

But the star is Ustinov and the penetrating mind of his character, Hercule Poirot.

1978: Best Costume Design

•

DEATH RACE 2000
1975, 78 mins, US Ⓥ col
Dir Paul Bartel ***Prod*** Roger Corman ***Scr*** Robert Thom, Charles Griffith ***Ph*** Tak Fujimoto ***Ed*** Tina Hersch ***Mus*** Paul Chihara ***Art*** Robinson Royce, B. B. Neel
Act David Carradine, Simone Griffeth, Sylvester Stallone, Mary Woronov, Roberta Collins, Martin Kove (New World)

Roger Corman's quickie production deals with ultra-violent sport in a futuristic society, in this case an annual cross-country road race with drivers scoring points by running down pedestrians.

Script, from an Ib Melchior story, makes its satirical points economically, and director Paul Bartel keeps the film moving quickly. Almost all of the film takes place on the road, with carnage and crashes occurring like clockwork.

David Carradine, clad in a spooky black leather outfit, is the national champion driver, challenged by thug-like Sylvester Stallone and four other drivers, including Amazon-like Mary Woronov. While fending off Stallone's attacks, Carradine also has to deal with radicals trying to sabotage the race.

•

DEATHSPORT
1978, 83 mins, US Ⓥ col
Dir Henry Suso, Allan Arkush ***Prod*** Roger Corman ***Scr*** Henry Suso, Donald Stewart ***Ph*** Gary Graver ***Ed*** Larry Bock ***Mus*** Andrew Stein ***Art*** Sharon Compton
Act David Carradine, Claudia Jennings, Richard Lynch, William Smithers, Will Walker, David McLean (New World)

Deathsport is Roger Corman's futuristic science fiction gladiator picture. And what is a futuristic science fiction gladiator picture? It's a film set 1,000 years into the future, post neutron wars, where the good warriors ride horses and wield see-through sabres fighting bad guys known as Statesmen who drive lethal motorcycles known as "Death Machines."

The good guys, Ranger Guides, are quiet, live by a code, make temporary unions and roam desert wastelands trying to avoid the cannibal mutants and those motorcycles, which are very noisy.

Statesmen have other plans. They have two ways of amusing themselves: beating up Ranger Guides—no easy task since Ranger Guides are superior warriors—and capturing female rangers, who they strip, lock up in a dark room with metal chandeliers and then apply electricity and special effects. Nice guys.

David Carradine is the quiet good guy and the best thing that can be said about his acting and his part is that he doesn't say much. Claudia Jennings is his partner good guy, the one who gets to amuse the bad guy in the dark room. The best thing that can be said about her performance is that she gets to take off her clothes, twice.

•

DEATH TAKES A HOLIDAY
1934, 79 mins, US b/w
Dir Mitchell Leisen ***Scr*** Maxwell Anderson, Gladys Lehman ***Ph*** Charles Lang ***Art*** Hans Dreier, Ernst Fegte
Act Fredric March, Evelyn Venable, Guy Standing, Katherine Alexander, Gail Patrick, Helen Westley (Paramount)

Because it has the word "death" in it, Paramount tested the picture under another title, *Strange Holiday,* in California. Results showed that the original title meant the most at the box office.

Action of picture [from a play by Alberto Casella] is laid in and around a foreign estate, the grandeur of which at times is singularly Hollywoodian. Fredric March is on top, playing Death. Wanting to take a holiday from that role, he wishes himself on a duke and his guests for three days, with death meanwhile stopping throughout the world.

Though highly fantastic, the plot provides many interesting situations as Death in the disguise of a prince moves through a strata of love interests which must end after the three-day furlough.

March turns in a skillful performance, here playing a foreigner in an accent from which there is never a break or slip. He has opposite him for main heart interest Evelyn Venable, who screens well.

•

DEATHTRAP
1982, 115 mins, US Ⓥ col
Dir Sidney Lumet ***Prod*** Burtt Harris ***Scr*** Jay Presson Allen ***Ph*** Andrzej Bartkowiak ***Ed*** John J. Fitzstephens ***Mus*** Johnny Mandel ***Art*** Tony Walton
Act Michael Caine, Christopher Reeve, Dyan Cannon, Irene Worth, Henry Jones, Joe Silver (Warner)

Sidney Lumet is no stranger to stage adaptations. Despite its intermittently amusing dialog, however, *Deathtrap* comes across as a minor entertainment, cleverness of which cannot conceal its essential artificiality when blown up on the big screen.

There are countless twists and turns in the plot of Ira Levin's 1978 play and the dramatic surprises are not necessarily easy to predict. Michael Caine essays a writer who was once the Neil Simon of Broadway mystery writers but has now cranked out a quartet of clinkers. Into his lap falls the manuscript of a perfect suspenser penned by unknown Christopher Reeve. Desperate for a hit, Caine invites Reeve over one evening in the guise of potential collaborator, while in fact he intends to kill him and then present the work as a new effort of his own.

Actors turn in pro jobs in a technical sense, with Reeve skillfully walking the fine line of his pretty boy part. But actors' charm just doesn't balance out the distastefulness of their characters.

•

DEATH WATCH
1980, 128 mins, France/W. Germany Ⓥ ⦿ ▭ col
Dir Bertrand Tavernier ***Prod*** Gabriel Boustani, Janine Rubeiz ***Scr*** Bertrand Tavernier, David Rayfiel ***Ph*** Pierre-William Glenn ***Ed*** Armand Psenny, Michael Ellis ***Mus*** Antoine Duhamel ***Art*** Tony Pratt
Act Romy Schneider, Harvey Keitel, Harry Dean Stanton, Therese Liotard, Max von Sydow, Caroline Langrishe (Selta/Little Bear)

The story, shrewdly crafted by Bertrand Tavernier and American screenwriter David Rayfiel from a novel by David Compton [*The Unsleeping Eye*], is a throat-catcher. In a future society people die of old age, science having almost completely banished disease.

A cunning TV producer, Vincent Ferriman, played with chillingly unctuous serenity by Harry Dean Stanton, hits on the idea of a program that would cover live the last days of an individual who has managed to contract a terminal illness.

Ferriman's proposed subject is Katherine Mortenhoe (finely played by Romy Schneider), whose fierce independence and sensitivity would seem to provide poignant fodder for the camera eye. But Katherine, after signing a contract, flees the city.

Death Watch is a compelling drama centered on the human implications of its fanciful premise, as well as a harsh indictment of the media's role in society.

•

DEATH WISH
1974, 92 mins, US Ⓥ ⦿ ▭ col
Dir Michael Winner ***Prod*** Hal Landers, Bobby Roberts, Michael Winner ***Scr*** Wendell Mayes ***Ph*** Arthur J. Ornitz ***Ed*** Bernard Gribble ***Mus*** Herbie Hancock ***Art*** Robert Gundlach
Act Charles Bronson, Hope Lange, Vincent Gardenia, Steven Keats, William Redfield, Stuart Margolin (Paramount/De Laurentiis)

Poisonous incitement to do-it-yourself law enforcement is the vulgar exploitation hook on which *Death Wish* is awkwardly hung. Charles Bronson stars as a husband-turned-assassin after his wife is killed and daughter raped by muggers.

Adaptation of Brian Garfield's novel is functionally simplistic, which is precisely the intellectual level desired for straightout exploitation treatment. Hope Lange and daughter Kathleen Tolan are victims of assault, after which husband Bronson freaks out in vengeance.

Plot angles are mostly overwhelmed by the easier, conventional cutting to the action, in this case one killing about every 10 minutes.

•

DEATH WISH II
1982, 93 mins, US Ⓥ ⦿ col
Dir Michael Winner ***Prod*** Menahem Golan, Yoram Globus ***Scr*** David Engelbach ***Ph*** Richard H. Kline, Tom Del Ruth ***Ed*** Arnold Crust [= Michael Winner], Julian Semilian ***Mus*** Jimmy Page ***Art*** William Hiney
Act Charles Bronson, Jill Ireland, Vincent Gardenia, J. D. Cannon, Anthony Franciosa, Ben Frank (Cannon/City)

Director Michael Winner, who usually leaves nothing to the imagination (censors permitting), does it again with *Death Wish* revisited. Charles Bronson, as the avenging vigilante Paul Kersey, is turned loose this time on the creeps of Los Angeles and the results are every bit as revolting as in the original 1974 jackpot fantasy.

For openers, Bronson's Spanish cook is gangbanged and killed, and his catatonic daughter (still unrecovered from the first assault in Gotham) is raped yet again before winding up impaled on an iron railing pike as she tries to elude her savage captors.

What little performing style pic offers comes from Vincent Gardenia encoring from the original edition as a NY gumshoe who finally gets knocked off for his trouble coming to the aid of Bronson in an L.A. ravine.

•

DEATH WISH 3
1985, 90 mins, US Ⓥ ⦿ col
Dir Michael Winner ***Prod*** Menahem Golan, Yoram Globus ***Scr*** Michael Edmonds ***Ph*** John Stanier ***Ed*** Arnold Crust [= Michael Winner] ***Mus*** Jimmy Page ***Art*** Peter Mullins
Act Charles Bronson, Deborah Raffin, Ed Lauter, Martin Balsam, Gavan O'Herlihy, Kirk Taylor (Cannon)

Death Wish 3 adds significantly to the body count scored to date in this street-rampant series. Thrills, however, are way down due to script's failure to build motivation for Paul Kersey's latest killing spree.

Set in NY, but lensed mostly in London, pic's release was timed to capitalize on the controversy around subway vigilante Bernhard Goetz.

Attempts to justify the ensuing mass-murder are perfunctory. Film opens with the butchering of an old man who turns out to be an old mate of Kersey, but there's no suggestion that the relationship was intimate. Kersey's response, like Bronson's acting, is automaton-like. Mystery is why he came to New York in the first place without the tools of his brutal trade and has to make regular visits to the post office to accumulate firepower.

Michael Winner directs with customary tongue-in-cheek panache. There are occasional moments of wit as when apartment resident Bennett (Martin Balsam) wields his rusty machine gun.

•

DEATH WISH 4: THE CRACKDOWN
1987, 99 mins, US Ⓥ ⦿ col
Dir J. Lee Thompson ***Prod*** Pancho Kohner ***Scr*** Gail Morgan Hickman ***Ph*** Gideon Porath ***Ed*** Peter Lee Thompson ***Mus*** Paul McCallum, Valentine McCallum, John Bisharat ***Art*** Whitney Brooke Wheeler
Act Charles Bronson, Kay Lenz, John P. Ryan, Perry Lopez, George Dickerson, Soon-Teck Oh (Cannon)

It's a risky business getting close to Charles Bronson. His wife, daughter and friends have been blown away in the first three installments of *Death Wish.* Now the vigilante is back to revenge the death of his girlfriend's daughter.

What raises *Death Wish 4* above the usual blowout is a semi-engaging script and sure pacing by veteran action director J. Lee Thompson. As architect turned crusader, Paul Kersey (Bronson) is a curious blend of soft-spoken family man and detached seeker of justice. When he turns up the heat he does so with a measured, methodical passion as if it were his true calling in life to measure out justice in his corner of the world.

Bronson's treatment of drug trafficking is akin to chopping off the weeds and thinking that they won't grow back. It's a good excuse for him to break out some heavy ammunition in pursuit of the two rival gangs who supposedly supply 90% of the cocaine in Los Angeles.

•

DEATH WISH V: THE FACE OF DEATH
1994, 95 mins, US Ⓥ ⦿ col
Dir Allan A. Goldstein ***Prod*** Damian Lee ***Scr*** Allan A. Goldstein ***Ph*** Curtis Petersen ***Ed*** Patrick Rand ***Mus*** Terry Plumeri ***Art*** Csaba A. Kertesz
Act Charles Bronson, Lesley-Anne Down, Michael Parks, Saul Rubinek, Kenneth Welsh (21st Century)

Twenty years after pacifist-turned-vigilante Paul Kersey blasted his way through the first *Death Wish* melodrama, *Death Wish V* finds both the character and the franchise looking mighty tired. Bronson—still fit and fearsome at 72—could play Kersey in his sleep. Indeed, there are one or two scenes where he appears to be doing just that.

Once again, Bronson is trying to live a reasonably nonviolent life, having promised d.a. Saul Rubinek and police detective Kenneth Walsh that he's hung up his guns for good. Once again, he has found the love of a good woman—in this case, fashion designer Lesley-Anne Down. The only difference this time is, instead of muggers, street gangs or drug dealers, the villains are slightly more upscale creeps. Down is killed by the goons of her ex-husband (Michael Parks), a smooth-talking mobster who's bent on taking over the Manhattan garment district. That's when Bronson gets the old revolver out of the wall safe.

As *Death Wish* pix go, this one—set in New York but filmed mostly in Toronto—has a surprisingly small body count. Canadian filmmaker Allan A. Goldstein provides little that's new in the way of revivifying plot innovations.

●

DECALOGUE, THE
SEE: DEKALOG

●

DECEIVED
1991, 103 mins, US Ⓥ ⊙ col
Dir Damian Harris ***Prod*** Michael Finnell, Wendy Dozoretz, Ellen Collett ***Scr*** Mary Agnes Donoghue, Derek Saunders [= Bruce Joel Rubin] ***Ph*** Jack N. Green ***Ed*** Neil Travis ***Mus*** Thomas Newman ***Art*** Andrew McAlpine
Act Goldie Hawn, John Heard, Robin Bartlett, Ashley Peldon, Tom Irwin, Amy Wright (Touchstone)

Thrills, chills and a convincing perf by Goldie Hawn mark this stylishly absorbing thriller. Farfetched plot doesn't bear much scrutiny, but mesmerizing visual tone, macabre developments and sound entertainment value should sweep audiences along.

Hawn plays a New York art restoration expert who appears to be living a perfect life with her attractive career, cute kid (Ashley Peldon) and attentive, romantic husband (John Heard), who's also in the ancient art biz. But when a forgery's discovered at the museum, fingers are pointed at Heard. Then he's killed in a car accident, and a Social Security worker informs Hawn her husband wasn't whom he said he was—the real guy died years ago.

Pic segues ably into thriller territory as the undead husband (corpse buried was actually a charred hitchhiker) begins haunting his former home to try to recover a stolen Egyptian necklace he left behind. Meanwhile, Hawn has turned sleuth and is closing in on the disheartening truth about the con she married.

Their inevitable encounter packs the requisite scream value, and pic heightens into a chilling game of cat and mouse, climaxed by a horrifically successful pursuit sequence.

Director Damian Harris appears in full control of the medium, weaving in some effective Hitchcockian allusions and a couple of intentional good laughs.

●

DECEIVERS, THE
1988, 112 mins, US Ⓥ ⊙ col
Dir Nicholas Meyer ***Prod*** Ismail Merchant ***Scr*** Michael Hirst ***Ph*** Walter Lassally ***Ed*** Richard Trevor ***Mus*** John Scott ***Art*** Ken Adam
Act Pierce Brosnan, Saeed Jaffrey, Shashi Kapoor, Helena Michell, Keith Michell, David Robb (Merchant Ivory)

Sumptuously produced historical action adventure tale, set in pre-Raj India circa 1825, falls short of fully developing its most interesting theme—the struggle of the rational Western psyche with the supernatural seductions of the East.

Pierce Brosnan is William Savage, a "resident collector" for the British East India Co., which blazed the trail for England's colonizalation of the Indian subcontinent. A company patrol is mysteriously ambushed and murdered in the dead of night. When Brosnan discovers the bodies in a gruesome mass grave, the fearless, straight-arrow officer is outraged. A rising company star who has married the commander's daughter (Helena Michell), he risks his career by setting out to prove the murders are part of a horrifying conspiracy by the Thuggees—a centuries-old, pan-Indian brotherhood of evildoers who worship Kali, the goddess of destruction.

Adapting John Masters's fact-derived novel, director Nicholas Meyer makes the most of an opportunity for homage to Alexander Korda adventure movies. As psychological drama, Meyer's effort to depict Brosnan's spiritual struggle with dark forces unleashed by Kali-worship is undermined by the actor's limited range and an elliptical screenplay which fails to exploit the complex possibilities inherent in the cross-cultural confrontation.

●

DECEPTION
1946, 111 mins, US Ⓥ b/w
Dir Irving Rapper ***Prod*** Henry Blanke ***Scr*** John Collier, Joseph Than ***Ph*** Ernest Haller ***Ed*** Alan Crosland ***Mus*** Erich Wolfgang Korngold ***Art*** Anton Grot
Act Bette Davis, Paul Henreid, Claude Rains, John Abbot, Benson Fong (Warner)

Deception, a story of matrimonial lies that builds to a murder climax, gives Bette Davis a potent vehicle. Plot is backed with lavish production, strong playing of a story loaded with femme interest, and bright direction.

Davis plays to the hilt, using full dramatic talent. It's not all her show, though. Claude Rains as her elderly teacher and sponsor walks off with considerable portion of the picture in a fine display of acting ability. By contrast, Paul Henreid suffers although turning in a smooth performance in a role with not too much color.

Plot [from a play by Louis Verneuil] concerns deception practiced by Davis to prevent husband Henreid from discovering that she had been the mistress of Rains before her marriage. Henreid, refugee cellist, is a jealous man whose temperamental instability is reason for the wife's deception. Pickup to story comes with Rains's entrance and his mad jealousy over his desertion by his mistress. To him falls juicy plums in the form of dialog and situations that carry the story along.

Music importance is emphasized by Erich Wolfgang Korngold's score and staging of orchestral numbers by LeRoy Prinz. Korngold's original music and the Cello Concerto are outstanding highlights.

●

DECEPTION
SEE: RUBY CAIRO

●

DECISION AT SUNDOWN
1957, 77 mins, US col
Dir Budd Boetticher ***Prod*** Harry Joe Brown ***Scr*** Charles Lang, Jr. ***Ph*** Burnett Guffey ***Ed*** Al Clark ***Mus*** Heinz Roemheld ***Art*** Robert Peterson
Act Randolph Scott, John Carroll, Karen Steele, Valerie French, Noah Beery, Andrew Duggan (Columbia/Ranown)

Complex screenplay from Vernon L. Fluherty tale spans a single day in cow town of Sundown. Randolph Scott, a mysterious, revengeful gunman, rides into town. He's after unsavory local wheel John Carroll, who's slated to marry local belle Karen Steele on that day. Scott breaks up the wedding and is besieged with sidekick Noah Beery by Carroll's henchmen. Step by step, it develops that Carroll, in his none-too-scrupulous past, had stolen and later discarded Scott's wife (since dead); and that she hadn't been unwilling, a fact Scott cannot face.

Role is an offbeat one for Scott, but he carries off the gunman's frustrated rage very well. Carroll makes convincingly menacing heavy in the suave tradition. Steele, as his understandably confused fiancée, shows much promise of things to come.

●

DECISION BEFORE DAWN
1951, 119 mins, US b/w
Dir Anatole Litvak ***Prod*** Anatole Litvak, Frank McCarthy ***Scr*** Peter Viertel ***Ph*** Franz Planer ***Ed*** Dorothy Spencer ***Mus*** Franz Waxman
Act Richard Basehart, Gary Merrill, Oskar Werner, Hildegarde Neff, O. E. Hasse, Hans Christian Blech (20th Century-Fox)

Anatole Litvak gives this Second World War spy thriller a strong feeling of reality through a semi-documentary treatment, the use of mostly unknown faces, and by location lensing entirely in Germany, where the scars of the War still fit graphically into the story's 1945 period.

Story [from the novel *Call It Treason* by George Howe] really gets going when Oskar Werner, a sensitive Allied prisoner, volunteers to aid his captors by obtaining information behind the lines in his own country. He believes his actions will help, rather than betray, Germany. Werner's excursion is fraught with danger, and his playing and Litvak's direction milk the situation of drama while drawing a rather clear picture of events within Germany at that stage of the war and of how the people were taking it.

Richard Basehart and Gary Merrill, latter the commander of the intelligence unit using prisoners of war, are excellent. Hildegarde Neff creates a fine portrait of a German woman made a victim of war, and Dominique Blanchar is equally good as a French girl aiding the Allies.

1951: NOMINATIONS: Best Picture, Editing

●

DECKS RAN RED, THE
1958, 97 mins, US b/w
Dir Andrew L. Stone ***Prod*** Andrew L. Stone, Virginia Stone ***Scr*** Andrew L. Stone ***Ph*** Meredith M. Nicholson ***Ed*** Virginia Stone
Act James Mason, Dorothy Dandridge, Broderick Crawford, Stuart Whitman, Katharine Bard (M-G-M)

The Decks Ran Red is a descriptive title for this story, presented as fact, of an attempted mutiny at sea. Before the mutineers have been beaten down, they have spilled enough blood to make the decks sticky, if not running, with gore.

The plot is a plan by Broderick Crawford and Stuart Whitman, crew members of a chartered freighter, to kill off other members of the crew, rig the ship to make it look like an abandoned derelict, and then bring it in as salvage. According to maritime law, it's said, they will get half the ship's value—$1 million—as prize money.

James Mason, who has been first officer on a trim Matson liner, is flown to Australia to take charge of this dingy vessel when its captain mysteriously dies. He quickly discovers he is in for trouble from a lackluster and sullen crew, trouble that is compounded by taking aboard a native Maori cook and his wife, latter being Dorothy Dandridge.

The story is faintly incredible at times and there is a tendency to impose dialogue on a scene when the action has already spoken for itself. But the picture moves swiftly and absorbingly.

●

DECLIN DE L'EMPIRE AMERICAIN, LE
(THE DECLINE OF THE AMERICAN EMPIRE)
1986, 101 mins, Canada Ⓥ col
Dir Denys Arcand ***Prod*** Rene Malo, Roger Frappier ***Scr*** Denys Arcand ***Ph*** Guy Dufaux ***Ed*** Monique Fortier ***Mus*** Francois Dompierre ***Art*** Gaudeline Sauriol
Act Pierre Curzi, Remy Girard, Yves Jacques, Dominique Michel, Louise Portal, Dorothee Berryman (Image M&M/ONFC)

Behind the ironically sweeping title of Denys Arcand's film is a mordant small-scale study of private lives and sexual mores among a group of contemporary Canadian academics. Writer-director Arcand deploys a smart script, fluent technique and a first-rate cast for this deviously sardonic comedy of carnal manners.

Arcand gives his story a theatrical cast, with a distinct two-act structure, two principal settings (a modern gym complex and a lakeside chalet cloaked in snow) and its eight principal characters—four men and four women—at first presented like two separate sexual choruses. They are to gather that evening at the chalet for a casual, friendly dinner. However, it is the menfolk who are in the kitchen while the ladies work out in the gym, with each group engaging in supposedly frank and liberated exchanges of jocular sex talk and reminiscences. But the day's mood of levity and well-being disintegrates around the dinner table.

The smooth ensemble acting throws into trenchant relief the shallowness and hypocrisy of their attitudes. Pierre (Pierre Curzi), a divorcée who clings to his freedom despite his relationship with the much younger Danielle (Genevieve Roux), who pays for her studies with a job in a sexual massage parlor, where the two met; Diane (Louise Portal), a faculty member who is engaged in a kinky affair with a sinister hippie lover (Gabriel Arcand); Claude (Yves Jacques), homosexual prof; and Alan (Daniel Briere), a young faculty assistant who finds himself seduced by Dominique.

●

DECLINE AND FALL
1968, 90 mins, US col
Dir John Krish ***Prod*** Ivan Foxwell ***Scr*** Ivan Foxwell, Alan Hackney, Hugh Whitemore ***Ph*** Desmond Dickinson ***Ed*** Archie Ludski ***Mus*** Ron Goodwin ***Art*** John Barry
Act Robin Phillips, Genevieve Page, Donald Wolfit, Colin Blakely, Patience Collier, Leo McKern (20th Century-Fox)

This humorous and elegantly confectioned adaptation of Evelyn Waugh's first (1928) literary success makes for a witty bundle of entertainment for discriminating audiences in search of tongue-in-cheek entertainment. Writer-producer Ivan Foxwell has opted for a lightweight, spoofy approach to the Waugh story, with the result that everything is played one stop further out than normal. Consequently, some of the story's absurdities become almost acceptable in the context.

Pace is sprightly as we follow Paul Pennyfeather, the schoolboy who becomes teacher, then foil for a dazzling white slaver, then jailbird until his final rebirth as, literally, a different man.

Robin Phillips, in his first pic role, is excellent as the scapegoat predestined to a bitter-sweet fate. Genevieve Page is as elegant and alluring as ever in another tailor-cast role as the source of most of Paul's troubles.

John Krish's direction helps underline the spoofish plot elements.

●

DECLINE OF THE AMERICAN EMPIRE, THE
SEE: LE DECLIN DE L'EMPIRE AMERICAIN

•

DECLINE OF WESTERN CIVILIZATION, THE
1981, 100 mins, US Ⓥ col
Dir Penelope Spheeris ***Prod*** Penelope Spheeris ***Ph*** Steve Conant ***Ed*** Charles Mullin, Peter Wiehl (Spheeris)

A bracing, stimulating and technically superb close-up look at the L.A. punk scene, pic is pitched at a perfect distance to allow for simultaneous engagement in the music and spectacle, and for rueful contemplation of what it all might mean.

Artistic strategy here is to combine provocative performance footage with "at home" interviews with punk group members and talks with club owners, managers, critics and hardcore fans.

Film constitutes a 100-minute total immersion in the indigenous California punk world.

While a few of the rockers come off as artificial poseurs, many more surprise through revealing articulation of whys and wherefores of their lifestyle, and what comes through most strongly is purity of their dedication to their music.

Given top-notch craftsmanship, it's hard to believe effort was made independently for $100,000, and well-nigh impossible to detect that 35mm print is a 16mm blowup.

•

DECONSTRUCTING HARRY
1997, 96 mins, US Ⓥ ⊙ col
Dir Woody Allen ***Prod*** Jean Doumanian ***Scr*** Woody Allen ***Ph*** Carlo Di Palma ***Ed*** Susan E. Morse ***Art*** Santo Loquasto
Act Woody Allen, Billy Crystal, Judy Davis, Demi Moore, Elisabeth Shue, Robin Williams (Doumanian/Fine Line)

Deconstructing Harry is abrasive, lacerating and self-revelatory. It's also very funny, most of the time. A tremendous, stellar cast is mostly confined to minor roles, but all shine under Woody Allen's assured direction.

Harry Block (Allen), though in late middle age, has never really grown up. He has a reputation as novelist and short-story writer, but has already spent the advance for his next book, and is unable to find true inspiration to work on it. He's had three wives and six shrinks (one of whom he married), plus countless lovers along the way.

Picture's core, similar to that of *Wild Strawberries,* by Allen hero Ingmar Bergman, deals with a journey the protagonist must make to a small upstate seat of learning to receive an award. Trouble is, his latest girlfriend, Fay (Elisabeth Shue), has chosen this moment to marry Larry (Billy Crystal), Block's best friend. Meanwhile, Block's former sister-in-law (Judy Davis) is furious that in his last book he described their clandestine relationship.

Gradually, Block's obsessions and demons are revealed. He sees Larry as, literally, the Devil, yet his own treatment of Fay was never on the level. Sprinkled through all of this are vignettes culled from Block's short stories, among them a hilarious episode in which a movie actor (Robin Williams) goes out of focus—literally.

From the beginning, Allen establishes an edgy, disjointed style to illustrate Block's fractured way of life. With an almost constant stream of mostly funny one-liners, Block is a typical Allen protag, yet darker, sadder, more isolated, less mature. Among the higher-profile cast members, Williams isn't seen in focus at all, Crystal is supprisingly subdued, and Demi Moore is dryly amusing as the shrink/wife. There's the expectedly delightful soundtrack of jazz standards.

1997: NOMINATION: Best Original Screenplay

•

DEEP, THE
1977, 124 mins, US Ⓥ ⊙ ▭ col
Dir Peter Yates ***Prod*** Peter Guber ***Scr*** Peter Benchley, Tracy Keenan Wynn ***Ph*** Christopher Challis ***Ed*** Robert L. Wolfe, David Berlatsky ***Mus*** John Barry ***Art*** Tony Masters
Act Robert Shaw, Jacqueline Bisset, Nick Nolte, Louis Gossett, Eli Wallach, Robert Tessier (Columbia-EMI/Casablanca Filmworks)

The Deep is an efficient but rather colorless film based on the Peter Benchley novel about a perilous search for treasure in the waters off Bermuda.

Fully 40 percent of the film takes place underwater, and the actors and crew learned how to dive, playing long scenes without dialog on the ocean floor. Director Peter Yates keeps up the tension in a low-key way—with a few shocker moments thrown in from time to time—and these scenes are more involving than the ones above the surface.

It's possible that inside this slick piece of engineering there is a genuinely mordant satire of human greed struggling to get out, but it never quite gets to the surface.

1977: NOMINATION: Best Sound

•

DEEP BLUE SEA
1999, 105 minus, US Ⓥ ⊙ ▭ col
Dir Renny Harlin ***Prod*** Akiva Goldsman, Tony Ludwig, Alan Riche ***Scr*** Duncan Kennedy, Donna Powers, Wayne Powers ***Ph*** Stephen Windon ***Ed*** Frank J. Urioste, Derek G. Brechin, Dallas S. Puett ***Mus*** Trevor Rabin ***Art*** William Sandell, Joseph Bennett
Act Thomas Jane, Saffron Burrows, Samuel L. Jackson, Jacqueline McKenzie, Michael Rapaport, Stellan Skarsgard (Warner)

Powered by exceptional displays of physical filmmaking, *Deep Blue Sea* is pulled back to shore by the usual suspects—weak plotting and weaker dialogue. The main draw is a trio of 40-foot killer sharks on the loose.

Most troublesome of all is the film's love of technology in its rich display of digital and special effects, even while serving up a *Frankenstein*-like message that science and technology are bad, bad, bad.

One of three test sharks being used by marine biologist Dr. Susan McAlester (Saffron Burrows), in her dubious experiment to wipe out Alzheimer's disease, has somehow compromised her facility's security. Her corporate funder is repped by tycoon Russell Franklin (Samuel L. Jackson), who flies back to Susan's lair—a giant former U.S. Navy sub base off the Baja coast now called Aquatica.

McAlester's aim is to harvest protein from the brains of the test sharks, being fed a steady, rich diet of other sharks. Her cool shark wrangler, Carter (Thomas Jane), barely wrangles one of the sharks and, in a tense sequence, McAlester extracts brain protein. Moments later, all hell breaks loose as the seemingly subdued shark chomps off one of research partner Jim Whitlock's (Stellan Skarsgard) arms.

Digitized sharks are unevenly realized, to sometimes ferocious and sometimes cartoonish effect. And it's easy to suspect that cook Preacher's blend of Bible talk, smack and wit is mainly the product of actor LL Cool J's dialogue insertions. Jane emerges best of all, evincing an ideal blend of brawn and charisma.

•

DEEP COVER
1992, 112 mins, US Ⓥ ⊙ col
Dir Bill Duke ***Prod*** Pierre David, Henry Bean ***Scr*** Michael Tolkin, Henry Bean ***Ph*** Bojan Bazelli ***Ed*** John Carter ***Mus*** Michel Colombier ***Art*** Pam Warner
Act Larry Fishburne, Jeff Goldblum, Victoria Dillard, Charles Martin Smith, Gregory Sierra, Clarence Williams III (David-Bean)

Convoluted and mostly unconvincing as a portrait of the drug underworld, *Deep Cover* [based on a story by Michael Tolkin] still carries some resonance due to its vivid portrait of societal decay and a heavyweight performance by Larry Fishburne.

Tough, straight-arrow cop Fishburne is recruited by government drug-enforcement chief Charles Martin Smith to infiltrate the cartel of dealer Arthur Mendoza, who controls 40 percent of the L.A. cocaine market on behalf of his uncle, a powerful Latin American politician the U.S. government would like to cut down to size.

Taking a grungy downtown room and hitting the streets, Fishburne begins working his way up as a small-time dealer. His network includes suburban attorney dealer Jeff Goldblum, his supplier, vicious Gregory Sierra, and art importer-money launderer Victoria Dillard. Climax gives Fishburne the opportunity to choose which side of the law he wants to live on.

Performances are mostly of the intense, threatening and streetwise variety. Low-budget lensing ace Bojan Bazelli gives numerous sequences a sharp stylized look, but key behind-the-scenes contribution is Michel Colombier's superbly moody, dissonant jazz/rock score.

•

DEEP END
1970, 90 mins, W. Germany/US Ⓥ col
Dir Jerzy Skolimowski ***Prod*** Maran Film-COKG-Kettledrum ***Scr*** Jerzy Skolimowski, Jerzy Gruza, B. Sulik ***Ph*** Charly Steinberger ***Mus*** Cat Ten
Act Jane Asher, John Moulder-Brown, Karl Michael Vogler, Christopher Sandford, Diana Dors (Maran/COKG/Kettledrum)

Though its main locale is a rather seamy London public bath, director Jerzy Skolimowski has avoided tawdriness by a sympathy in, and awareness of, the excessive but essentially pure actions of his love-smitten boy whose good looks make him prey for all types of women who come for their public ablutions.

Film gives the British scene a twist due to Skolimowski's treatment of the tangled desires of a young boy whose need for love goes to a rather vulgar, but enticing fellow worker at the baths.

John Moulder-Brown has the deep voice of the time between puberty and manhood and the childish yet dedicated pursuit of his first deeply troubled reaction to a woman.

Skolimowski keeps the film alive with quirky incidents.

•

DEEP END OF THE OCEAN, THE
1999, 105 mins, US Ⓥ ⊙ col
Dir Ulu Grosbard ***Prod*** Kate Guinzberg, Steve Nicolaides ***Scr*** Stephen Schiff ***Ph*** Stephen Goldblatt ***Ed*** John Bloom ***Mus*** Elmer Bernstein ***Art*** Dan Davis
Act Michelle Pfeiffer, Treat Williams, Whoopi Goldberg, Jonathan Jackson, Ryan Merriman, John Kapelos

The Deep End of the Ocean is an engaging, often heart-wrenching drama that juxtaposes the biological and sociological approaches to family ties. As the young, modern parents who are forced to reexamine their values when their son disappears and, years later, returns, Michelle Pfeiffer and Treat Williams give such magnetic performances that they elevate the film way above its middlebrow sensibility and proclivity for neat resolutions.

Based on Jacquelyn Mitchard's popular 1996 novel, tale begins extremely well by introducing the happily married Cappadoras: Beth (Pfeiffer) and hubby Pat (Williams). First 40 minutes provide a detailed chronicle, day by day, month by month, of the devastating effects of 3-year-old Ben's vanishing on his family, especially Beth. Story then jumps ahead nine years, when, out of the blue, a boy named Sam (Ryan Merriman) knocks on the family's door in Chicago and offers to mow their lawn. Beth immediately recognizes him as her lost son but, in due course, Sam misses his Greek adoptive father and runs away.

Whatever reservations one may have about the narrative, Ulu Grosbard's meticulous direction is impressive. Performances across the board are flawless, particularly Pfeiffer as the imperfect mother. Technical sheen places this outing at the top of Grosbard's oeuvre.

•

DEEP IMPACT
1998, 120 mins, US Ⓥ ⊙ ▭ col
Dir Mimi Leder ***Prod*** Richard D. Zanuck, David Brown ***Scr*** Michael Tolkin, Bruce Joel Rubin ***Ph*** Dietrich Lohmann ***Ed*** David Rosenbloom ***Mus*** James Horner ***Art*** Leslie Dilley
Act Robert Duvall, Tea Leoni, Elijah Wood, Vanessa Redgrave, Morgan Freeman, Maximilian Schell (Zanuck-Brown/DreamWorks/Paramount)

The season's first comet-targets-Earth special-effects extravaganza [released in May, eight weeks before *Armageddon*] is spectacular enough in its cataclysmic scenes but proves far from thrilling in the downtime spent with a largely dull assortment of troubled human beings.

With director Mimi Leder working in the same hyperventilated, would-be realistic style she applied to *The Peacemaker,* the characters all scurry about keeping appointments and fighting deadlines, with all of them facing, of course, the biggest deadline of all.

An unaccountable amount of time, especially in the early going, is given over to Jenny Lerner (Tea Leoni), a rising MSNBC reporter who, while investigating some high-level Washington shenanigans, stumbles onto the traces of a very big story indeed. With impact looming in a year, U.S. President Beck (a solemn Morgan Freeman) announces the news to the world.

The government hasn't been asleep at the wheel, however. A giant spaceship called *Messiah* will blast off in two months' time so that astronauts can plant eight nukes on the comet in the hope of blowing it to smithereens. The mission, which concludes precisely halfway through the picture, proves a dismal failure, succeeding only in splitting the comet into two unequal pieces.

Leoni's Jenny seems so stiff during her broadcasts that she wouldn't last a weekend on the air. The team of astronauts isn't very compelling either. The younger flyers treat Robert Duvall's lead pilot dismissively as a dinosaur, and Duvall makes his character somewhat defensive.

But none of this matters when the first big rock sends the world's biggest tidal wave breaking over the Statue of Liberty and all of Manhattan. The water effects are just the slightest bit phony looking, but they still register dramatically.

•

DEEP THROAT
1972, 73 mins, US col
Dir Jerry Gerard [= Gerard Damiano] ***Prod*** Lou Perry ***Scr*** Jerry Gerard ***Ph*** Harry Flecks ***Ed*** Jerry Gerard ***Art*** Len Camp
Act Linda Lovelace (Vanguard)

While *Deep Throat* doesn't quite live up to its reputation as the *Ben-Hur* of porno pix, it is a superior piece which stands a head above the competition.

Pic takes a tongue-in-cheek approach to conventional hetero hardcore, dishing out enough laughs with the main course to prove sexpo features need as much comic relief as suspenders.

Plot centers on a young lady disappointed because she fails to "hear bells" during her repeated sex bouts with as many as 14 men at a time. Pic's technical quality is above par, including sharp color photography and a satirical musical score which spoofs, among other things, Coca-Cola's "It's the Real Thing" television commercial.

Performances are spirited, especially that of the femme lead, and writer-director-editor Jerry Gerard puts it all together with some style.

•

DEER HUNTER, THE
1978, 183 mins, US Ⓥ ⦿ ▭ col
Dir Michael Cimino ***Prod*** Barry Spikings, Michael Deeley, Michael Cimino, ***Scr*** Deric Washburn ***Ph*** Vilmos Zsigmond ***Ed*** Peter Zinner ***Mus*** Stanley Myers ***Art*** Ron Hobbs, Kim Swados
Act Robert De Niro, John Cazale, John Savage, Meryl Streep, Christopher Walken, George Dzundza (EMI)

Among the considerable achievements of Michael Cimino's *The Deer Hunter* is the fact that the film remains intense, powerful and fascinating for more than three hours.

The picture is a long, sprawling epic-type in many ways more novel than motion picture. It employs literary references stylistically, forecasting events which will happen in the film.

It is a brutal work. Robert De Niro, John Cazale, John Savage and Christopher Walken head cast as friends living in a small Pennsylvania town. They attend a Russian Orthodox wedding at the beginning of the film. Directly afterwards three of them go deer hunting and soon afterwards they are to serve in Vietnam.

While in Southeast Asia, the trio is reunited during a battle scene and later captured by the Vietcong. As POWs they are forced to play a form of Russian roulette.

Throughout the film various ceremonies and cultural rituals are explored, compared and juxtaposed—the wedding, the game and the deer hunt. It is up to the viewer to decide how these rituals fit together and it is a big comprehension demand.

Many will wish that the screenplay by Deric Washburn [from a screen story by Cimino, Washburn, Louis Garfinkle and Quinn K. Redecker] was a bit more straightforward. Still, the film is ambitious and it succeeds on a number of levels and it proves that Cimino is an important director.

1978: Best Picture, Director, Supp. Actor (Christopher Walken), Sound, Editing

NOMINATIONS: Best Actor (Robert De Niro), Supp. Actress (Meryl Streep), Original Screenplay, Cinematography

•

DEFECTOR, THE
1966, 108 mins, W. Germany/France col
Dir Raoul Levy ***Prod*** Raoul Levy ***Scr*** Robert Guenette, Raoul Levy ***Ph*** Raoul Coutard ***Ed*** Albert Jurgenson, Roger Dwyre ***Mus*** Serge Gainsbourg ***Art*** Pierre Guffroy
Act Montgomery Clift, Hardy Kruger, Macha Meril, Roddy McDowall, David Opatoshu, Christine Delaroche (PECF/Rhein-Main)

The last motion picture made by Montgomery Clift prior to his death, *Defector* provides a part that allows him to substitute action of body and mind for the immobility of facial expression that clouded this fine actor's performances during his last years. His taut, troubled face is perfect for the role of a scientist pushed into espionage by his own country and almost erased from it by enemy agents.

Levy and Robert Guenette's collaboration on an adaptation of Paul Thomas's *The Spy* has gone for "suspense" at the sacrifice of logic. Just plain logical loopholes appear that may escape most viewers but will disturb some.

Most of the intellectual byplay is between Clift, as an American scientist, and Hardy Kruger, as the German-born Russian agent given the assignment of getting Clift to defect. The physical action comes from Clift's evasion of the security police and his attempt to escape from East Germany. Kruger makes an excellent contrast, in his cool behavior, to Clift's nervousness.

•

DEFENCE OF THE REALM
1985, 96 mins, UK Ⓥ ⦿ col
Dir David Drury ***Prod*** Robin Douet, Lynda Myles ***Scr*** Martin Stellman ***Ph*** Roger Deakins ***Ed*** Michael Bradsell ***Mus*** Richard Harvey ***Art*** Roger Murray-Leach
Act Gabriel Byrne, Greta Scacchi, Denholm Elliott, Ian Bannen, Fulton MacKay, Bill Paterson (Enigma/NFFC/Rank)

The state of the nation's press and the evil antics of its secret services in the nuclear age are combined in this fast-paced thriller.

Script unravels a relatively uncomplicated story of events following the near crash of a nuclear bomber on an American airforce base in the English countryside. A left-wing MP who gets wind of the event is framed as a Russian spy and forced to resign. His journalist friend is bumped off secretly shortly before publishing details of the incident.

The story centers on a younger hack who enjoys the triumph of cracking the link between parliamentarian Markham and a Russian agent, only to discover after the death of his friend that he has been set up by the secret services.

A female character, Nina Beckman (Greta Scacchi), is strangely marginal. By the time she enters center stage as Mullen's journalistic accomplice, her only function is to tie up a few loose ends.

Gabriel Byrne is somewhat one-dimensional as Mullen. He's a perfect foil, however, to the older journalist caught between friendship, the truth and his career. Denholm Elliott gives an extraordinary performance in that role.

•

DEFENDING YOUR LIFE
1991, 112 mins, US Ⓥ col
Dir Albert Brooks ***Prod*** Michael Grillo ***Scr*** Albert Brooks ***Ph*** Allen Daviau ***Ed*** David Finfer ***Mus*** Michael Gore ***Art*** Ida Random
Act Albert Brooks, Meryl Streep, Rip Torn, Lee Grant, Buck Henry, Shirley MacLaine (Geffen)

Defending Your Life is an inventive and mild bit of whimsy from Albert Brooks. The former standup comedian has a little fun with the *Liliom* idea of being judged in a fanciful afterlife, but he doesn't carry his conceit nearly far enough.

Brooks plays his familiar role of a neurotic, warm-hearted, insecure, bull-headed, upper-middle class mensch who, in the opening reel, dies after crashing his showroom-fresh BMW smack into a bus. The unlucky fellow instantly finds himself being whisked off by tram to Judgment City, a white-bread sort of resort community in which a prosecutor and defender present scenes from the life of the deceased to two judges.

The victim is forced to watch particularly embarrassing moments from his life while listening to a torrent of vilification from the prosecutor (Lee Grant) and just a measure of defense from his cheerleader (Rip Torn). Lending all of this some meaning is Meryl Streep, the dream woman who would be the love his life if only they weren't dead.

•

DEFENSELESS
1991, 104 mins, US Ⓥ ⦿ col
Dir Martin Campbell ***Prod*** Renee Missel, David Bombyk ***Scr*** James Hicks ***Ph*** Phil Meheux ***Ed*** Lou Lombardo, Chris Wimble ***Mus*** Curt Sobel ***Art*** Curtis A. Schnell
Act Barbara Hershey, Sam Shepard, Mary Beth Hurt, J. T. Walsh, Kellie Overbey, Sheree North (New Visions)

A murder mystery with a fine cast and wild and woolly story, *Defenseless* almost continuously wobbles across the line between the deliberately ambiguous and the irritatingly murky. Barbara Hershey portrays T. K. Katwuller, a Los Angeles attorney who, for psychological reasons that remain unexplored, has managed to make a rather spectacular mess of her life.

T. K. is drawn into a web of lies when she discovers that her lover and client, Steven Seldes (the reliably snaky J. T. Walsh), is married to her long-lost college roommate Ellie (Mary Beth Hurt). Steven is later found murdered, and the script asks the audience to swallow the idea that T. K., although she is a material witness to the crime, would become defense attorney for Steven's wife, who has been accused in the case.

James Hicks's screenplay, from a story he wrote with Jeff Burkhart, at least gives the actors some strong, if sometimes goofy, emotions to play with, and they generally make the most of them. As a detective on the case, Sam Shepard quietly but intently gets across multiple motives.

New Zealand–born, British-trained director Martin Campbell pushes things a bit too hard at times but must be given credit for the consistent acting.

•

DEFIANT ONES, THE
1958, 97 mins, US Ⓥ ⦿ b/w
Dir Stanley Kramer ***Prod*** Stanley Kramer ***Scr*** Nathan E. Douglas, Harold Jacob Smith ***Ph*** Sam Leavitt ***Ed*** Frederic Knudtson ***Mus*** Ernest Gold ***Art*** Rudolph Sternad
Act Tony Curtis, Sidney Poitier, Theodore Bikel, Charles McGraw, Cara Williams, Claude Akins (United Artists)

The theme of *The Defiant Ones* is that what keeps men apart is their lack of knowledge of one another. With that knowledge comes respect, and with respect, comradeship and even love. This thesis is exercised in terms of a colored and a white man, both convicts chained together as they make their break for freedom from a Southern prison gang.

The performances by Tony Curtis and Sidney Poitier are virtually flawless. Poitier captures all of the moody violence of the convict, serving time because he assaulted a white man who had insulted him. It is a cunning, totally intelligent portrayal that rings powerfully true.

As "Jocker" Jackson, the arrogant white man chained to a fellow convict whom he hates, Curtis delivers a true surprise performance. He starts off as a sneering, brutal character, willing to fight it out to the death with his equally stubborn companion. When, in the end, he sacrifices a dash for freedom to save Poitier, he has managed the transition with such skill that sympathy is completely with him.

Picture has other surprises, not the least of which is Kramer's sensitive and skilled direction, this being only his third try at calling the scenes. The scenes of Poitier and Curtis groping their way painfully out of a deep clay pit, their perilous journey down the river, as well as their clumsy attempt to break into a store and the subsequent near-lynch scene, become integral parts of the larger chase, for the posse is never far behind.

1958: Best Original Story & Screenplay, B&W Cinematography

NOMINATIONS: Best Picture, Director, Actor (Tony Curtis, Sidney Poitier), Supp. Actor (Theodore Bikel), Supp. Actress (Cara Williams), Editing

•

DEKALOG
(THE DECALOGUE; THE TEN COMMANDMENTS)
1989, 584 mins, Poland/W. Germany Ⓥ col
Dir Krzysztof Kieslowski ***Scr*** Krzysztof Piesiewicz, Krzysztof Kieslowski ***Ph*** Wieslaw Zdort, Edward Klosinski, Piotr Sobocinski, Krzysztof Pakulski, Slawomir Idziak, Witold Adamek, Dariusz Kuc, Andrzej Jarosiewicz, Jacek Blawut ***Ed*** Ewa Smal ***Mus*** Zbigniew Preisner ***Art*** Halina Dobrowolska
Act Henryk Baranowski, Aleksander Bardini, Daniel Olbrychski, Miroslaw Baka, Grazyna Szapolowska, Jerzy Stuhr (Polish TV/Sender Freies Berlin)

The 10 modern moral stories Polish director Krzysztof Kieslowski spins are inspired by the Ten Commandments, but do not refer directly to the Biblical text, nor do they apply theological interpretation to it. This is why Kieslowski insists on using only the number of the commandment as the title for each film, and never mentions the commandment itself in the credits.

All 10 stories are placed in the same gray and depressing block of new concrete buildings in a Warsaw suburb, where university professors and taxi drivers live side by side. Leading characters in one episode emerge again, as passersby or secondary characters, in another episode.

The first episode (55 mins.) is about the trust and affection between a father, his son and their personal computers. In the second one (59 mins.), an old doctor is coerced into predicting the chances of one of his patients to survive. His answer shows how unreliable science is. In the third episode (58 mins.), a man is forced by a former mistress to drive all over town on New Year's Eve. The fourth (58 mins.) explores the dark, incestuous passions of a daughter for her widowed father. In the fifth (60 mins.), best known in its feature-length film version [*A Short Film about Killing*, 85 mins.], he points out the fallacy of justice, which demands an eye for an eye.

The sixth (61 mins.), the most romantic of all, deals with the loss of innocence that prevents an older woman from responding to the advances of a much younger man. [Known as *A Short Film about Love*, 87 mins., in its feature version.] In the seventh episode (57 mins.), a little girl is the object of a ruthless struggle between her mother and her grandmother.

The eighth (56 mins.), the one episode in which ethics are clearly stated as the object of the story, has a professor of ethics faced with her own past and decisions during the Holocaust. The ninth (60 mins.) has an impotent husband struggling helplessly to believe in his wife's fidelity. The 10th (60 mins.), in which black humor abounds, has destitute brothers fall prey to temptation when they inherit their father's stamp collection.

Being a pessimist at heart, Kieslowski, who cowrote all 10 scripts, unfolds a variety of human weaknesses, shows how difficult it is to conform to one commandment, let alone 10, and considers human frailty with sympathy but little hope. All the stories involve two or three characters at the most and proceed in a straightforward, unadorned, linear fashion.

It is difficult to single out performances in the uniformly excellent casts, which feature some of the top talent in Poland. One editor and one art director worked on all 10 films, resulting in a steady, unhurried but inexorable rhythm throughout the series. Kieslowski changed cameramen from film to film, not only to accommodate their schedules, but to give a slightly different look to each film.

•

DELICATESSEN
1991, 96 mins, France Ⓥ ⊙ col
Dir Jean-Pierre Jeunet, Marc Caro ***Prod*** Claudie Ossard ***Scr*** Jean-Pierre Jeunet, Marc Caro, Gilles Adrien ***Ph*** Darius Khondji ***Ed*** Herve Schneid ***Mus*** Carlos D'Alessio ***Art*** Jean-Philippe Carp, Kreka, Aline Bonetto, Jean Rabasse
Act Dominique Pinon, Marie-Laure Dougnac, Jean-Claude Dreyfus, Rufus, Ticky Holgado, Anne-Marie Pisani (Constellation/UGC/Hachette Premiere)

Beautifully textured, cleverly scripted and eerily shot (often with a wideangle lens making characters look even weirder), *Delicatessen* is a zany little film that's a startling and clever debut for co-helmers Jean-Pierre Jeunet and Marc Caro.

In a darkly bizarre, futuristic world where food shortages have led the butcher to serve up human flesh after murdering the locals, a bumbling group of Troglodins, an underground force reminiscent of the government police in *Brazil*, are engaged in a war on cannibal crime.

An excellent cast made up entirely of character actors provides a rich array of eccentrics who live in the building over the deli and the sewers used as tunnels by the Troglodins.

An unsuspecting comedian moves into the flat above the deli and falls in love with neighboring blind girl, who organizes a hilarious tea party for two. Pic then quickly hooks viewers with an outrageous montage of rythmically edited visuals initiated by a sex scene between the butcher and his lover shot from under the bed.

All other wacko characters are well-defined and carefully developed, including the armed postman who holds up people when delivering the mail and the snail eater whose flat is two inches deep in water and escargot shells.

•

DELINQUENTS, THE
1989, 101 mins, Australia Ⓥ ⊙ col
Dir Chris Thomson ***Prod*** Alex Cutler, Michael Wilcox ***Scr*** Clayton Frohman, Mac Gudgeon ***Ph*** Andrew Lesnie ***Ed*** John Scott ***Mus*** Miles Goodman ***Art*** Laurence Eastwood
Act Kylie Minogue, Charlie Schlatter, Angela Punch-McGregor, Bruno Lawrence, Desiree Smith, Todd Boyce (Village-Roadster/Silver Lining)

The story, set in the late 1950s, about the passionate love affair of a couple of teens, is trite stuff. Lola (Kylie Minogue) and Brownie (Charles Schlatter) live in the small town of Bundaberg in Queensland. She's still at school when they become lovers and she gets pregnant. The youngsters plan to elope, but are parted by Lola's alcoholic mother (Angela Punch-McGregor), who forces her daughter to have a backstreet abortion (offscreen).

Brownie goes to sea in despair. However, he happens to walk into a Melbourne bar one night and sees Lola, her hair bleached, sadder but wiser. Love blossoms again but, once more, the lovers are parted by the authorities.

The screenplay [from a novel by Criena Rohan] is repetitive and tame. There's no hint of genuine passion between the young lovers. Far more interesting characters are Mavis (Desiree Smith) and Lyle (Todd Boyce), who befriend Lola and Brownie. Their scenes have a warmth that's lacking in the central relationship.

Technically, pic is good, with great care taken to make the late 1950s setting as authentic as possible.

•

DELIRIOUS
1991, 96 mins, US Ⓥ ⊙ col
Dir Tom Mankiewicz ***Prod*** Lawrence J. Cohen, Fred Freeman, Doug Claybourne ***Scr*** Lawrence J. Cohen, Fred Freeman ***Ph*** Robert Stevens ***Ed*** William Gordean, Tina Hirsch ***Mus*** Cliff Eidelman ***Art*** Angelo Graham
Act John Candy, Mariel Hemingway, Emma Samms, Raymond Burr, Robert Wagner, David Rasche (M-G-M/Star Partners III)

Delirious is a witless comedy about soap operas in which the estimable John Candy mugs uncomfortably through a desperately unfunny script with a plot as tediously convoluted as those it spoofs.

Candy, as the head writer of a show called *Beyond Our Dreams*, has an unrequited crush on the overripe star (Emma Samms), a clone of Joan Collins's Alexis character on *Dynasty*. Mooning over Samms, who plays a treacherous and sluttish character both on and off the set, Candy naturally overlooks the true girl of his dreams, aspiring actress Mariel Hemingway.

A bump on the head sends Candy into a *Twilight Zone*–like reverie in which he finds himself trapped in the fictional small-town setting of his show and inhabiting the character of a Wall Street shark involved with both Samms and Hemingway.

Resemblances to the overly imitated *It's a Wonderful Life* abound in Ashford Falls, a combination of studio backlot and Southern California locations that looks more like the setting for a primetime soap than a daytimer. Lighting, by Robert Stevens, is in the emptily glitzy style of a wine commercial.

•

DELIVERANCE
1972, 109 mins, US Ⓥ ⊙ ▭ col
Dir John Boorman ***Prod*** John Boorman ***Scr*** James Dickey ***Ph*** Vilmos Zsigmond ***Ed*** Tom Priestley ***Art*** Fred Harpman
Act Jon Voight, Burt Reynolds, Ned Beatty, Ronny Cox, Billy McKinney, James Dickey (Warner)

Deliverance can be considered a stark, uncompromising showdown between basic survival instincts against the character pretensions of a mannered and material society. Unfortunately for John Boorman's heavy film of James Dickey's first novel, it can just as easily be argued as a virile, mountain country transposition of nihilistic, specious philosophizing which exploits rather than explores its moments of violent drama.

Against the majestic setting of a river being dammed, Dickey's story takes four city men out for a last weekend trip down the river. Unexpected malevolence forces each to test his personal values in order to survive.

It is, however, in the fleshing out that the script fumbles, and with it the direction and acting. The unofficial group leader of the sailing trip is Burt Reynolds, a volatile, calculating, aggressive and offensive tempter of fate.

Why the best friend Jon Voight would maintain an apparent longstanding relationship with Reynolds's character is an early plot chuck-hole.

What makes for a pervading uneasiness is the implication of the story: the strongest shall survive. The values of Reynolds's character are repulsive; Ronny Cox is a cardboard cutout as an intellectual type; Ned Beatty is the easygoing, middle-class figurehead patronized by both the "doers" and the "thinkers" of the world; leaving Voight apparently as the one to lead them out of travail.

In the depiction of sudden, violent death, there is the rhapsodic wallowing in the deadly beauty of it all: protruding arrows, agonizing expiration, etc. It's the stuff of which slapdash oaters and crime programmers are made but the obvious ambitions of *Deliverance* are supposed to be on a higher plane.

1972: NOMINATIONS: Best Picture, Director, Editing

•

DELTA FORCE, THE
1986, 129 mins, US Ⓥ ⊙ col
Dir Menahem Golan ***Prod*** Menahem Golan, Yoram Globus ***Scr*** James Bruner, Menahem Golan ***Ph*** David Gurfinkel ***Ed*** Alain Jakubowicz ***Mus*** Alan Silvestri ***Art*** Luciano Spadoni
Act Chuck Norris, Lee Marvin, Martin Balsam, Joey Bishop, Robert Forster, Lainie Kazan (Cannon)

Directed with the throttle wide open, pic roots itself firmly in very fresh history, then proceeds to brashly rewrite it, thereby turning itself into an exercise in wish fulfillment for those who favor using force instead of diplomacy.

First hour is mostly devoted to what seems to be a quite accurate rendition of the 1985 TWA Athens hijacking.

From here, film is purest fantasy pitting the noble Yankees against the dirty, low-down Palestinians. In an attempt at "make my day" immortality, Chuck Norris growls at one of them, "Sleep tight, sucker," before blowing him away, and gets a chance to make ample use of his martial arts skills.

•

DELTA FORCE 2: THE COLOMBIAN CONNECTION
(AKA: DELTA FORCE 2 OPERATION STRANGLEHOLD)
1990, 105 mins, US Ⓥ ⊙ col
Dir Aaron Norris ***Prod*** Yoram Globus, Chrisopher Pearce ***Scr*** Lee Reynolds ***Ph*** Joao Fernandes ***Ed*** Michael J. Duthie ***Mus*** Frederic Talgorn
Act Chuck Norris, Billy Drago, Bobby Chavez, John R. Ryan, Richard Jaeckel, Mateo Gomez (Cannon)

Chuck Norris fans have all they could ask for with *Delta Force 2*. Norris and a dozen U.S. marines fly into the South American drug capital San Carlos, destroy half the country's cocaine production, and rub out the land's untouchable drug czar in a carthartic blaze of exploding missiles and flying fists.

(During the filming, five people were killed in a May 15, 1989, helicopter crash in the Philippines: pilot Jo Jo Imperial, stuntmen Geoffrey Brewer, Mike Graham and Gadi Danzig, and gaffer Don Marshall. Three others were injured.)

Production values are high with an endless stream of ammunition and extras. Lensing is pro, and score has a tropical flavor that stays pleasantly in the background.

Norris is a minimalist actor, rightly concentrating on the action. As the sadistic Coda, Billy Drago has a Medusa-like presence that produces shivers just from looking at him.

•

DEMETRIUS AND THE GLADIATORS
1954, 101 mins, US Ⓥ ⊙ ▭ col
Dir Delmer Daves ***Prod*** Frank Ross ***Scr*** Philip Dunne ***Ph*** Milton Krasner ***Ed*** Dorothy Spencer, Robert Fritch ***Mus*** Franz Waxman ***Art*** Lyle Wheeler, George W. Davis
Act Victor Mature, Susan Hayward, Michael Rennie, Debra Paget, Anne Bancroft, Jay Robinson (20th Century-Fox)

Demetrius and the Gladiators is 20th-Fox's answer and followup to its tremendously successful *The Robe*. While Lloyd C. Douglas's fine novel from which 20th-Fox and Frank Ross filmed *The Robe* springboards this follow-up, it is a completely new story.

In the compelling screen story, and under the equally compelling direction by Delmer Daves, *Demetrius* swings from *The Robe*'s mysterious, religious miracle theme of the crucifixion, to a story of the trial of a man's faith by the temptations of an attractive, amoral woman and a pagan Rome.

Victor Mature again scores with the character of the slave. A mighty man is he, battling three huge tigers in the Roman arena to satisfy the mad urges of the crazy Emperor Caligula and the wicked Messalina, dueling to the death with five of Rome's best gladiators, or making love to the same wicked temptress who has temporarily caused him to forget his God. With Mature easily winning top acting honors for his splendidly projected Demetrius, he is pressed by Susan Hayward as the evil Messalina, and Jay Robinson, repeating his mad, effeminate Caligula.

•

DEMI-PARADISE, THE
(US: ADVENTURE FOR TWO)
1943, 115 mins, UK Ⓥ ⊙ b/w
Dir Anthony Asquith ***Prod*** Anatole de Grunwald ***Scr*** Anatole de Grunwald ***Ph*** Bernard Knowles ***Mus*** Nicholas Broadszky
Act Laurence Olivier, Penelope Ward, Marjorie Fielding, Margaret Rutherford, Leslie Henson, Felix Aylmer (Two Cities)

Script consists of a wealth of character drawings with a thin web of a story about a young Russian engineer, the inventor of a new-type propellor for use on icebreakers. He arrives in England some months before the war, with humorous misconceptions of the average native of Britain. He is bewildered by its conventions, smugness and capacity for muddling through. It takes him some time to know the people for what they really are, with their foibles, humors and idiosyncrasies. There is a slight love story with an English girl.

Laurence Olivier, replete with Russian accent, gives a dignified and serious performance full of sincerity and repose. Ablest support comes from Felix Aylmer, veteran stage actor, as a wealthy shipbuilder with a series of eccentricities that would excite risibility in a mummy.

•

DEMOISELLES DE ROCHEFORT, LES
(THE YOUNG GIRLS OF ROCHEFORT)
1967, 125 mins, France Ⓥ ▭ col
Dir Jacques Demy ***Prod*** Mag Bodard ***Scr*** Jacques Demy ***Ph*** Ghislain Cloquet ***Ed*** Jean Hamon ***Mus*** Michel Legrand ***Art*** Bernard Evein

Act Catherine Deneuve, George Chakiris, Francoise Dorleac, Jacques Perrin, Gene Kelly, Danielle Darrieux (Parc/Madeleine)

Jacques Demy, writer-director, and Michel Legrand, composer, who did the successful musical *The Umbrellas of Cherbourg*, reunite for a more ambitious pic that adds dance to a tale of small-town life. It has charm, sustained human observation, mixed with catchy music, dances, and songs to come up as a tuner with grace and dynamism.

Into a sleepy little port town near a naval base comes a carnival used to advertise products. Two of the pitchmen (George Chakiris, Grover Dale) lose their girls to sailors and ask two sisters (Catherine Deneuve, Francoise Dorleac) who give dance lessons and compose music to put on an act for them. Also involved are the sisters' mother (Danielle Darieux), who dreams of a lost love and runs a local cafe, a visiting American composer (Gene Kelly) who falls for one of the girls, and an artist-sailor (Jacques Perrin) who has painted a portrait of his ideal woman who happens to look like one of the girls.

All this evolves mainly in the town square with a cafe in the middle and the girls' apartment and combo dance studio, plus a gleaming white music shop. As in *Cherbourg*, the town has been repainted to look like a colorful, glowing little place.

Deneuve and Dorleac, real sisters, play twins with the right mixture of feminine guile, passiveness and stubborn aggressiveness when it comes to the men they want. Darrieux is fetching as their mother; she is the only one who synched her own songs, at least in the French version.

Kelly is trim, dynamic and both brash and winning, while Chakiris has less to do as one of the carny men who loses out on the girls.

Though a fairly classic musical reminiscent of earlier Yank tuners, it has a Gallic froth, tinged with unobtrusive melancholy and character delineation. Legrand again comes up with sweet but never syrupy music. Norman Maen has contributed simple but deft choreography.

•

DEMOLITION MAN

1993, 114 mins, US Ⓥ ⦿ ▭ col

Dir Marco Brambilla **Prod** Joel Silver, Michael Levy, Howard Kazanjian **Scr** Daniel Waters, Robert Reneau, Peter M. Lenkov **Ph** Alex Thomson **Ed** Stuart Baird **Mus** Elliot Goldenthal **Art** David L. Snyder

Act Sylvester Stallone, Wesley Snipes, Sandra Bullock, Nigel Hawthorne, Benjamin Bratt, Bob Gunton (Silver/Warner)

Demolition Man is a noisy, soulless, self-conscious pastiche that mixes elements of sci-fi, action-adventure and romance, then pours on a layer of comedy replete with Hollywood in-jokes.

The impressive pre-credits sequence, set in L.A. in 1996, gets right to business by contrasting LAPD Sgt. John Spartan (Sylvester Stallone) with his nemesis, Simon Phoenix (Wesley Snipes). Nicknamed "Demolition Man," Spartan is convicted of involuntary manslaughter and sentenced to 70 years of "rehabilitation" as a frozen inmate of CryoPenitentiary.

Story [by Peter M. Lenkov, Robert Reneau] then jumps to 2032, when Phoenix, who has also been imprisoned, is thawed out for a mandatory parole hearing and orchestrates an ingenious escape. He finds himself in San Angeles, a kinder and gentler L.A., now run as "a beacon of order." Life is sterile and devoid of joy—people eat no meat, refrain from smoking, and have no sex.

Feisty, attractive cop Lenina Huxley (Sandra Bullock) is desperate for some action. An expert on the past, she is convinced that only the "barbarian savage" Spartan is a match for Phoenix and arranges to spring him from prison.

First-time helmer Marco Brambilla reveals his TV commercials background in both the positive and negative aspects of the film. The screen is flushed with blue lighting, the pacing is swift, and there is a lot of montage and fast cutting. However, most of the action set pieces are poorly staged: keeping the camera too close to the fights and chases allows viewers no sense of space or where the antagonists stand in relation to each other.

•

DEMON KNIGHT

(AKA: TALES FROM THE CRYPT PRESENTS DEMON KNIGHT)

1995, 92 mins, US Ⓥ ⦿ col

Dir Ernest Dickerson **Prod** Gilbert Adler **Scr** Ethan Reiff, Cyrus Voris, Mark Bishop **Ph** Rick Bota **Ed** Stephen Lovejoy **Mus** Ed Shearmur **Art** Christiaan Wagener

Act Billy Zane, William Sadler, Jada Pinkett, Brenda Bakke, CCH Pounder, Dick Miller (Universal)

Mix *Night of the Living Dead* with Sam Raimi's *Evil Dead* movies, then add a hefty dose of *Beavis and Butt Head*-style silliness, and you have this fang-in-cheek horror thriller that likely will please fans and turn off non-devotees.

Pic marks first attempt by exec producers Richard Donner, David Giler, Walter Hill, Joel Silver, and Robert Zemeckis to transform their popular HBO series (inspired by the notorious EC Comics in the 1950s) into a big screen franchise.

Main story is a familiar but fitfully exciting supernatural tale set in and around a spectacularly seedy desert hotel. Brayker (Willian Sadler), the mysterious new guest, turns out to be the guardian of an ancient key that keeps the forces of darkness from overwhelming mankind. Trouble begins when another stranger, the charismatic Collector (Billy Zane), shows up with two local cops claiming Brayker stole the key from him. The Collector summons skeletal, flesh-eating demons to help him invade the boarding house. Chief among the not-entirely innocent bystanders: Jada Pinkett as a beautiful ex-con who proves to be a dandy demon fighter; CCH Pounder as the gruff, boarding-house manager; Brenda Bakke as a love starved hooker; Thomas Haden Church as a cowardly tough guy who's desperate to save his skin; Charles Fleischer as a nerdy ex-mailman; Gary Farmer as a portly cop; and B-movie favourite Dick Miller as an aging drunk.

Under the lively direction of lenser-turned-helmer Ernest Dickerson, *Demon Knight* basically is an extended cat-and-mouse game, propelled by alternating currents of splatter-pic gore and jet-black humor. But pic is neither funny enough nor scary enough to be fully satisfying as either a shocker or a spoof.

•

DEMON SEED

1977, 94 mins, US Ⓥ ⦿ ▭ col

Dir Donald Cammell **Prod** Herb Jaffe **Scr** Ronald Jaffe, Roger O. Hirson **Ph** Bill Butler **Ed** Francisco Mazzola **Mus** Jerry Fielding **Art** Edward C. Carfagno

Act Julie Christie, Fritz Weaver, Gerrit Graham, Berry Kroeger, Lisa Lu, Larry J. Blake (M-G-M)

Demon Seed tells of the impregnation of a female by a master computer system which seeks to perpetuate itself in human form. Julie Christie stars as the electronic Eve along with Fritz Weaver as her scientist husband.

Excellent performances and direction (Donald Cammell), from a most credible and literate screenplay [from a novel by Dean R. Koontz], make production an intriguing achievement in storytelling.

Christie and Weaver live adjacent to an advanced computer center. Their marriage is crumbling because of his commitment to a new machine, Proteus IV, designed to do almost everything but think.

The burden of the story falls on Christie and she does indeed make the film come off.

•

DENNIS

SEE: DENNIS THE MENACE

•

DENNIS THE MENACE

(UK: DENNIS)

1993, 94 mins, US Ⓥ col

Dir Nick Castle **Prod** John Hughes, Richard Vane **Scr** John Hughes **Ph** Thomas Ackerman **Ed** Alan Heim **Mus** Jerry Goldsmith **Art** James Bissell

Act Walter Matthau, Mason Gamble, Joan Plowright, Christopher Lloyd, Lea Thompson, Robert Stanton (Warner)

Dennis the Menace isn't really appropriate for anyone over the age of 12. Very young children may find the numbskull, by-the-numbers gags here amusing, but teens will consider this kids' stuff and adults will be pained.

Producer-screenwriter John Hughes continues his march down the age-scale from adolescence to babyhood with the antics of five-year-old Dennis Mitchell, for more than 40 years the star of Hank Ketcham's comic strip, for four years star of an early 1960s TV series, and now of a syndicated animated series.

There's no plot per se, just one lame gag after another. Opening scene has little blond Dennis (Mason Gamble) casually torturing next-door neighbor Mr. Wilson (Walter Matthau) in bed. Natch, Dennis' parents (Lea Thompson and Robert Stanton) admonish their sprog to cool it, but soon he's back to his tricks.

In an attempt to introduce some notion of suspense, Hughes drags in a sinister-looking stranger named Switchblade Sam (Christopher Lloyd) who stalks the idyllic town for awhile before kidnapping the little tyke.

The one real pleasure for adults in the film comes from watching Matthau, who has reached deep into his bag of tricks to deliver a huge assortment of slow burns, simmering grimaces, delayed howls and intolerant glances. It's a performance worthy of a real Sunshine boy.

•

DENTELLIERE, LA

(THE LACEMAKER)

1977, 110 mins, France/Switzerland Ⓥ ⦿ col

Dir Claude Goretta **Scr** Pascal Laine, Claude Goretta **Ph** Jean Boffety **Ed** Joelle van Effenterre **Mus** Pierre Jansen

Act Isabelle Huppert, Yves Beneyton, Florence Giorgetti, Anne-Marie Duringer, Michel De Re (Citel/Action/FR3/Janus)

The film is a lacy, gentle probing of an ill-assorted couple. The 19-year-old girl is somewhat too withdrawn and the boy is a reserved student. Film manages to take a literary theme and treat an inarticulate character with feeling.

Isabelle Huppert is extraordinary as the childish girl living with a doting mother and working as an assistant hairdresser. On vacation, she meets a young student and she makes love for the first time. They move in together in Paris but her lack of education, her inability to make contact with him, finally has him driving her out.

Yves Beneyton is helpful as the timid but too demanding student who finally dismisses her rather than trying to adapt, learn from, and live with her.

Not an easy film, due to its measured pacing and playing, it is tastefully produced with good technical qualities.

•

DERNIER METRO, LE

(THE LAST METRO)

1980, 130 mins, France Ⓥ col

Dir Francois Truffaut **Scr** Francois Truffaut, Suzanne Schiffman, Jean-Claude Grumberg **Ph** Nestor Almendros **Ed** Martine Barraque, Marie-Aimee Debril, Jean-Francois Gire **Mus** Georges Delerue **Art** Jean-Pierre Kohut-Svelko

Act Catherine Deneuve, Gerard Depardieu, Jean Poiret, Heinz Bennent, Andrea Ferreol, Paulette Dubost (Films du Carrosse/SEDIF/TF1/SFP)

Francois Truffaut's 19th feature is his richest, most satisfying film in years; adroit dramatic entertainment, gracefully romantic and uplifting. But it is also a fascinating chronicle of Paris life under the German Occupation—its daily terror, material deprivation, opportunism, cowardice, denunciation, as well as its quiet heroism and unexpected moments of laughter.

Pic follows the difficulties of a small Paris theatre struggling to stay open under the constraints of the Nazi occupants. Truffaut has been inspired foremost by the autobiography of Jean Marais. Many of Marais's recollections are deftly woven into the script.

An exiled German Jewish director (Heinz Bennent) has gone into hiding in the cellar of the Paris theatre he had been running prior to the Nazi invasion. His non-Jewish wife (Catherine Deneuve) has taken over management of the troupe, which is rehearsing a Norwegian play. Further emotional complications arise with the arrival of a new actor (Gerard Depardieu), a compulsive womanizer who moonlights as a Resistance fighter.

Truffaut's direction is uncharacteristically restrained, his mise-en-scene almost classical in its invisible camerawork and sober editing. The acting is fine down the line, with Deneuve giving one of her most accomplished performances, particularly in her scenes with Bennent, forlorn and appealing, and Depardieu, who displays vigorous range.

•

DERSU UZALA

1975, 137 mins, USSR/Japan Ⓥ ▭ col

Dir Akira Kurosawa **Prod** Eiti Mattsue **Scr** Akira Kurosawa, Yuri Nagibin **Ph** Asakazu Nakai, Yuri Gantman, Fyodor Dobronravov **Ed** V. Stepanovoi **Mus** Isaak Shvarts **Art** Yuri Raksha

Act Maksim Munzuk, Yuri Solomin (Mosfilm/Toho)

Absent from the screen for two years or more, Akira Kurosawa returns as director of a heartwarming film shot entirely in Eastern Siberia and on interiors in Mosfilm Studios. Contribution of each country to this project (Japan provided only Kurosawa, his cinematographer, and Toho as coproducer) is secondary since the subject matter dwarfs boundaries in its human uplift.

Film [from Vladimir Arsenyev's novel] takes place at the turn of the century in Eastern Siberia where a small army detachment is surveying the unexplored forests and Taiga land. The encounter with a Siberian trapper, Dersu Uzala (Maksim Munzuk), sets the stage for an inseparable friendship between hunter and explorer Vladimir Arsenyev (Yuri Solomin) on three long and difficult survey missions.

The story is told in flashback after explorer Arsenyev returns to the Taiga to search for Uzala's grave, only to find the area lacerated by human progress.

Munzuk, a stage actor in Eastern Russia, emerges as the life-long trapper with plenty of stature. Solomin as the explorer performs with elegant dignity.

1975: Best Foreign Language Film

•

DESERT ATTACK
SEE: ICE COLD IN ALEX

•

DESERT BLOOM
1986, 104 mins, US Ⓥ ⊙ col
Dir Eugene Corr ***Prod*** Michael Hausman ***Scr*** Eugene Corr ***Ph*** Reynaldo Villalobos ***Ed*** David Garfield, John Currin, Cari Coughlin ***Mus*** Brad Fiedel ***Art*** Lawrence Miller
Act Jon Voight, JoBeth Williams, Ellen Barkin, Allen Garfield, Annabeth Gish (Carson)

Desert Bloom emerges a muted, intelligently observed story [by Linda Remy and Eugene Corr] of a girl's growing pains in an emotionally deprived and politically warped environment.

Arid setting in question is Las Vegas, 1950, where Second World War vet Jon Voight runs a gas station and is stepfather to JoBeth Williams's three daughters, the oldest of whom is the 13-year-old Rose, played by Annabeth Gish.

Big events in the household are the arrival of the girls' Aunt Starr (Ellen Barkin), a glamorous showgirl type who will live with the family for the 42 days necessary to obtain a quickie divorce, and the impending atmospheric A-bomb test, for which the entire community is preparing as if it were the second coming.

Due to her good housewife role, Williams can do little but be overshadowed by Barkin, who delivers a wonderfully splashy turn as the unlucky but resilient sexpot. Gish is a find as Rose. Obviously bright and physically reminiscent of another actress of about the same age, Jennifer Connelly, she almost singlehandedly lends the film its intelligent air and makes one root for Rose to survive her squalid upbringing.

•

DESERT FOX, THE
(UK: ROMMEL—DESERT FOX)
1951, 88 mins, US Ⓥ ⊙ b/w
Dir Henry Hathaway ***Prod*** Nunnally Johnson ***Scr*** Nunnally Johnson ***Ph*** Norbert Brodine ***Ed*** James B. Clark ***Mus*** Daniele Amfitheatrof ***Art*** Lyle Wheeler, Maurice Ransford
Act James Mason, Cedric Hardwicke, Jessica Tandy, Luther Adler, Everett Sloane, Leo G. Carroll (20th Century-Fox)

The story of Field Marshal Erwin Rommel, as biographed by Brigadier Desmond Young, comes to the screen as an episodic documentary difficult to follow or understand. A controversial angle is posed by the sympathetic pitch made for Rommel by Young, and the whitewashing given a number of Nazi military leaders previously charged with being war criminals by the British.

Battle action in the film is very good, both that concocted in the studio and that snatched from actual war footage. Picture gets off to an unusually sock opening, depicting the November 1941 raid on Rommel's North African headquarters by British Commandos. This all takes place before the title and credits are flashed but the promise is not borne out for a solid war film after narration and episodic character study take over.

Performances are good, with James Mason's portrait of the Desert Fox extremely able within the shadowy confines of the script. His scenes with Jessica Tandy, playing Frau Rommel, have sound emotional value through the underplaying of both performers. Luther Adler's screaming, hysterical Hitler also is good, although confined to brief footage.

•

DESERT HEARTS
1985, 93 mins, US Ⓥ ⊙ col
Dir Donna Deitch ***Prod*** Donna Deitch ***Scr*** Natalie Cooper ***Ph*** Robert Elswit ***Ed*** Robert Estrin ***Mus*** Robert Estrin (sup.) ***Art*** Jeannine Oppewall
Act Helen Shaver, Patricia Charbonneau, Audra Lindley, Andra Akers, Dean Butler, Katie La Bourdette (Goldwyn/Desert Hearts)

The plot focuses on a guest at a Nevada ranch, Vivian Bell, an English Literature lecturer from New York, frozen stiff by middle class morality and inbred prejudices, and totally confused by the drastic step she is about to take at the age of 35. She is about to get divorced.

To make matters much worse for her, once on the ranch she catches the fancy of the owner's adoptive daughter who starts making advances, first timidly, and then in a pressing fashion, until the prim, respectable East Coast intellectual has to drop her armor and face her own latent homosexuality.

Since the story [from the novel *Desert of the Heart* by Jane Rule] is placed in the 1950s, it is clear that what, by today's standards, would have been an unconventional but by no means exceptional case, becomes an act of defiance against the accepted rules of society.

Helen Shaver, playing the lead, does a most commendable job as a character who starts by being all tied up inside, and ends up by melting and opening up to emotions she couldn't even conceive before.

Patricia Charbonneau, as the avowed lesbian desperate for true affection in female companionship, tends to look too much like the spoiled brat who will have her own way.

•

DESERTO ROSSO, IL
(RED DESERT; THE RED DESERT)
1964, 116 mins, Italy/France Ⓥ ⊙ col
Dir Michelangelo Antonioni ***Prod*** Antonio Cervi ***Scr*** Michelangelo Antonioni, Tonino Guerra ***Ph*** Carlo Di Palma ***Ed*** Eraldo Da Roma ***Mus*** Giovanni Fusco ***Art*** Piero Poletto
Act Monica Vitti, Richard Harris, Carlo Chionetti, Xenia Valderi, Rita Renoir, Aldo Grotti (Federiz/Francoriz)

Red Desert is many things, and symbol-chasers should have a field day for interpretation. Basically, it is on one level an untraditional study of a neurosis, on another a frightening fresco of the destructive dangers and crises implicit in present-day life, with its intensive pace, mechanization, disintegration of established values and traditions.

Pic tells of a woman, Giuliana, (Monica Vitti), who has tried suicide and emerged from the car crash with increased mental injuries. She nevertheless still desperately seeks an escape from the neurotic state of which she is conscious. Her quest for an "oasis" in the desert makes her seek the company of her husband's colleague, Corrado (Richard Harris), who is almost as unprepared and unwilling to assist her as is her husband.

Her crisis has its ups and down, reaching a head after her son fakes a serious illness. She again seeks an escape, first by seducing the friend, later by thinking of sailing away in a ship docked nearby. The pace is slow, objects play as important a role as humans, etc. The novelty here is color (Eastmancolor stock, Technicolor prints), and the director's contribution is masterful—perhaps the first time tint has been used creatively with such effect and power.

•

DESERT PATROL
SEE: SEA OF SAND

•

DESERT RATS, THE
1953, 88 mins, US Ⓥ b/w
Dir Robert Wise ***Prod*** Robert L. Jacks ***Scr*** Richard Murphy ***Ph*** Lucien Ballard ***Ed*** Barbara McLean ***Mus*** Leigh Harline ***Art*** Lyle R. Wheeler, Addison Hehr
Act Richard Burton, Robert Newton, Robert Douglas, James Mason, Torin Thatcher, Chips Rafferty (20th Century-Fox)

Battle of Tobruk is fought in *The Desert Rats* as a followup, but not a sequel, to *The Desert Fox*, the 1951 Field Marshal Rommel feature.

Picture is a rather impersonal account of warfare that lacks the controversial flavor of the Rommel treatment. War scenes are realistically staged under Robert Wise's direction, and a high spot in this action is a commando raid on a Nazi ammunition dump.

James Mason is back to repeat his Rommel characterization, but appears only in a few scenes to tie-in the Tobruk battle with the Nazi plan of conquest that failed in the desert because of the stubbornness of men on the other side who fought back against terrific odds. Mason's work is good, and Richard Burton is excellent as the British captain in charge of the Australian troops that resist attacks on Tobruk. Robert Newton figures as the third star, playing a drunken old schoolteacher of Burton's, whose cowardice poses a problem for the young officer.

1953: NOMINATION: Best Story and Screenplay

•

DESERT SONG, THE
1929, 125 mins, US Ⓥ b/w
Dir Roy Del Ruth ***Scr*** Harvey Gates ***Ph*** Bernard McGill ***Ed*** Ralph Dawson
Act John Boles, Carlotta King, Louise Fazenda, Johnny Arthur, Edward Martindale, Myrna Loy (Warner)

Taking another step forward in the talkie field by doing an operetta, following the story in detail, and getting in the entire musical score and compositions, Warner Brothers has a winner. The only departures are for those scenes narrated in dialog, such as the riding of the Riffs and desert perspectives.

Story starts off rather slowly with the unfolding of the identity of the Red Shadow (John Boles) by himself to his two faithful followers, but straightens itself out after the picture has run for an hour. Through it all there is little of the romantic on the screen as the principal players were chosen more for their voices than for ability to act screen roles.

Boles and Carlotta King do exceptionally well on the screen and, though they may be more convincing on the stage, their conceptions of the film characters are sincere and not flavored of saccharine. Johnny Arthur as Benny Kid is exceptional. Aided by Louise Fazenda, as Susan, he supplies the lighter moments. Picture cost nearly $600,000.

•

DESERT SONG, THE
1944, 90 mins, US col
Dir Robert Florey ***Prod*** Robert Florey ***Scr*** Robert Buckner ***Ph*** Bert Glennon ***Ed*** Frank Magee ***Mus*** Sigmund Romberg ***Art*** Charles Novi
Act Dennis Morgan, Irene Manning, Bruce Cabot, Victor Francen, Lynne Overman (Warner)

In modernizing the story, German agents and plans to construct a new railroad in North Africa for terminus at Dakar provide motivation for Riff uprising and leadership by Dennis Morgan, an American piano player in Morocco nightspot, who's been fighting Franco in Spain prior to moving across the Mediterranean to Africa. Irene Manning is the new singer at the cafe, with mutual romance developing.

Riffs are rounded up by French officers to work on the railroad, with native Victor Francen, a tool of the Nazis, impressing the natives to work. But Morgan, as El Khobar, leader of the Riffs, circumvents the plans by periodic appearances in the desert and Morocco to lead the natives in revolt against the forced labor regulations. From there on it's a series of chases across the desert sands, pitched battles, and wild adventure.

Despite modernization to provide film technique and movement to the operetta, basic entertainment qualities of *Desert Song* are retained to provide a most diverting audience reaction at this time.

Morgan is neatly cast as the Red Rider, delivering both dramatic and vocal assignments in top style. Manning capably handles the girl spot as singer and actress.

1944: NOMINATION: Best Color Art Direction

•

DESERT SONG, THE
1953, 110 mins, US col
Dir H. Bruce Humberstone ***Prod*** Rudi Fehr ***Scr*** Roland Kibbee ***Ph*** Robert Burks ***Ed*** William Ziegler ***Mus*** Ray Heindorf (dir.), Max Steiner (adapt.) ***Art*** Stanley Fleischer
Act Kathryn Grayson, Gordon MacRae, Steve Cochran, Raymond Massey, Dick Wesson, Allyn McLerie (Warner)

After two times around as a film vehicle, once in 1929 and again in 1943, this venerable romantic musical has just about run out of entertainment vitamins. Both story and songs are well-worn [from the 1926 musical play by Otto Harbach, Oscar Hammerstein II, Sigmund Romberg, and Frank Mandel]. Latter wear their age with charm and are nicely delivered by Kathryn Grayson and Gordon MacRae, but aren't of sufficient impact to create much of a stir in this era. Best listening are the title number, "The Riff Song" and "One Alone," as well as added Jack Scholl-Serge Walter cleffing, "Gay Parisienne," which Grayson uses as a special piece.

Making a pretty picture is Grayson, and she serves up her tunes well. MacRae is unbelievable as the mysterious Riff leader, but fares better on the songs. Steve Cochran also has a hard time making anything out of his French legionnaire role, a character who is bothered by both Grayson, the general's flighty daughter, and by the fact that he can't capture the Riff hero who plays Robin Hood to the natives oppressed by Raymond Massey, a cruel sheik who is plotting to overthrow the French.

•

DESIGN FOR LIVING
1933, 90 mins, US ⊙ b/w
Dir Ernst Lubitsch ***Prod*** Ernst Lubitsch ***Scr*** Ben Hecht ***Ph*** Victor Milner ***Ed*** Francis Marsh
Act Fredric March, Gary Cooper, Miriam Hopkins, Edward Everett Horton, Franklin Pangborn, Isabel Jewell (Paramount)

Ben Hecht's screen treatment has transmuted Noel Coward's idea better than Coward's original play. It's a competent job in every respect. What matter it—or perhaps it does—if Hecht threw Coward's manuscript out the window and set about writing a brand new play? The dialog is less lofty, less epigramatic, less artificial. There's more reality.

Coward, of course, has contributed a basic premise that's arresting—a girl and two men, all of whom are very fond of each other. Edward Everett Horton as the patient mentor of the girl (or, as the dialog puts it, "in other words, you never got to first base") is built up here, as much by the script as his own personal histrionic dominance.

Miriam Hopkins's expert handling of the delicate premise which motivates the other three men is a consummate performance in every respect. She glosses over the dirt, but gets the punch through none the less. She confesses quite naively that she is stumped—she likes both Tom and George (Fredric March and Gary Cooper).

Hecht patterns Cooper to a rugged chapeau and March to a more formal top-piece, and Hopkins interprets her reactions in relation to wearing one type of hat or another with the shifting moods.

●

DESIGN FOR SCANDAL

1941, 82 mins, US b/w

Dir Norman Taurog ***Prod*** John W. Considine, Jr. ***Scr*** Lionel Houser ***Ph*** Leonard Smith, William Daniels ***Ed*** Elmo Veron ***Mus*** Franz Waxman ***Art*** Cedric Gibbons, Harry McAfee

Act Rosalind Russell, Walter Pidgeon, Lee Bowman, Jean Rogers, Mary Beth Hughes, Edward Arnold (M-G-M)

Design for Scandal is a lightly concocted romantic farce, with familiar story undercurrent refreshed by expert deliveries in the acting, direction and dialog departments.

When ace reporter Walter Pidgeon is assigned by his alimony-burdened publisher to frame the decision-rendering female judge (Rosalind Russell), it's a cinch that the pair will eventually fall in love and the scandal plan will be tossed into the discard. Despite this obvious conclusion, story unfolds at a consistently amusing clip, held together by deft direction from Norman Taurog, and a group of sterling performances.

Despite exposition of a familiar tale, scripter Lionel Houser injects plenty of sparkling dialog along the line, which clicks continually through excellent piloting by Taurog and delivery by Russell, Pidgeon and supporting cast members. It's fluffy entertainment, holding an amusing tone throughout.

●

DESIGNING WOMAN

1957, 117 mins, US Ⓥ ▭ col

Dir Vincente Minnelli ***Prod*** Dore Schary ***Scr*** George Wells ***Ph*** John Alton ***Ed*** Adrienne Fazan ***Mus*** Andre Previn ***Art*** Cedric Gibbons

Act Gregory Peck, Lauren Bacall, Dolores Gray, Sam Levene, Tom Helmore, Mickey Shaughnessy (M-G-M)

Dore Schary's last personal effort before exiting the Metro lot is a Runyonesque-type romp, based on a "suggestion" by designer Helen Rose and deftly directed by Vincente Minnelli. It cleverly brings together the worlds of haute couture, sports (particularly boxing), show business, and the underworld.

Gregory Peck, a crusading sports writer, marries Lauren Bacall, a prominent fashion designer, and abandons his cluttered Greenwich Village apartment for her elegant East Side abode. Her friends are the chi chi set; his cronies are fellow sports scribes and Stillman Gym characters. The never-the-twain-shall-meet groups get together at their apartment when there's a conflict between his weekly poker game and a reading for a Broadway musical for which she is designing the costumes.

Bacall, turning to comedy, is excellent as the fashion designer confronted by the world of fisticuffs. Peck is fine as the confused sportswriter and Dolores Gray scores solidly as his ex-girlfriend. Top-notch characterizations are also turned in by Sam Levene, as the *Front Page*–type sports editor, Tom Helmore as the producer, Jack Cole as a choreographer, Jesse White as a peddler of information, and Chuck Connors as a mobster.

●

DESIRE

1936, 95 mins, US Ⓥ col

Dir Frank Borzage ***Prod*** Ernst Lubitsch ***Scr*** Edwin Justus Mayer, Waldemar Young, Samuel Hoffenstein ***Ph*** Charles Lang ***Ed*** William Shea ***Mus*** Frederick Hollander ***Art*** Hans Dreier, Robert Usher

Act Marlene Dietrich, Gary Cooper, John Halliday, William Frawley, Ernest Cossart (Paramount)

Desire is the first Marlene Dietrich and Gary Cooper picture since *Morocco* (1930). The two stars work unusually well as a pair.

The direction is subtle and inspired, with many smart little Lubitschian touches adding to the general appeal of the yarn [by Hans Szekely and R. A. Stemmle] and its plot. Dietrich plays a jewel thief who gains possession of a valuable string of pearls. About half the footage is concerned with the efforts of Dietrich and a confederate to retrieve the pearls from Cooper who unknowingly has become their custodian.

The love scenes are excellently handled and written. A very good sequence is framed for the meeting between Cooper and the bogus nobleman, her accomplice, while another occurs later when efforts are made to get the two stars out of their beds one morning. The hand of producer Ernst Lubitsch is apparent here and in many other portions of the smartly-piloted romantic comedy.

●

DESIREE

1954, 110 mins, US Ⓥ ▭ b/w

Dir Henry Koster ***Prod*** Julian Blaustein ***Scr*** Daniel Taradash ***Ph*** Milton Krasner ***Ed*** William Reynolds ***Mus*** Alex North ***Art*** Lyle Wheeler, Leland Fuller

Act Marlon Brando, Jean Simmons, Merle Oberon, Michael Rennie, Cameron Mitchell, Elizabeth Sellars (20th Century-Fox)

There is a theory in Hollywood that nothing bogs down a historical film as easily as the facts of history. It is a maxim which 20th-Fox must have had very much in mind when it CinemaScoped Annemarie Selinko's bestselling novel, *Desiree.*

It tells the story of Desiree, daughter of a Marseilles silk merchant, who meets an impoverished general, Napoleon Bonaparte. They plan to marry. But Napoleon goes to Paris and there meets and weds the rich and influential Josephine. Desiree marries Bernadotte, one of France's most successful generals, who later splits with the emperor and becomes regent—and finally king—of Sweden.

As Napoleon, Brando draws a portrait of a man so sure of the righteousness of his cause that no sacrifice is too great in accomplishing his ends. His Napoleon is arrogant, scheming and temperamental, and yet oddly human in his failings.

Jean Simmons as Desiree is lovely, innocent and naive, as prescribed.

●

DESIRE ME

1947, 90 mins, US b/w

Dir [George Cukor, Mervyn LeRoy, Jack Conway] ***Prod*** Arthur Hornblow, Jr. ***Scr*** Marguerite Roberts, Zoe Akins ***Ph*** Joseph Ruttenberg ***Ed*** Joseph Dervin ***Mus*** Herbert Stothart ***Art*** Cedric Gibbons, Urie McCleary

Act Greer Garson, Robert Mitchum, Richard Hart, George Zucco, Morris Ankrum (M-G-M)

Against the technical excellence of mounting a confused flashback plot [based on the novel, *Karl und Anna*, by Leonhard Frank] is unfolded. Offered is a story of a wife who, after long years of faithful waiting, succumbs to lonesomeness on the eve of her supposedly dead husband's return from war. The husband then kills his rival in a struggle. Locale is a small fishing village on the coast of Normandy and catches interest with colorful settings and seascapes.

Flashbacks within flashbacks make plot hard to follow as the wife talks over her story—and what caused it—with a doctor. There is no director credit, picture having had several during its long camera career, so kudos for some topnotch atmospheric effects, a number of strong, emotional scenes, and occasional suspense go uncredited. George Cukor started it and Mervyn LeRoy finished it, but neither wants the credit apparently. Otherwise pace is slow and interest slack.

Greer Garson's role requires continual emotional stress that makes for a heavy job but she is capable. Robert Mitchum has too little footage as the husband but he makes every scene count. Richard Hart, the betrayer of the faithful wife, is permitted to overstress his designs where underplaying would have aided.

●

DESIRE UNDER THE ELMS

1958, 111 mins, US Ⓥ ⊙ b/w

Dir Delbert Mann ***Prod*** Don Hartman ***Scr*** Irwin Shaw ***Ph*** Daniel L. Fapp ***Ed*** George Boemler ***Mus*** Elmer Bernstein ***Art*** Hal Pereira, J. McMillan Johnson

Act Sophia Loren, Anthony Perkins, Burl Ives, Frank Overton, Pernell Roberts, Rebecca Welles (Paramount)

Despite all the plus factors, *Desire under the Elms* is not satisfactory entertainment. It is painfully slow in getting underway, the characters are never completely understandable or believable, and the ghastly plot climax (of infanticide) plays with disappointingly little force.

Eugene O'Neill's play has been given a reverent translation. But Irwin Shaw, who did the screenplay, has not improved the story. O'Neill wrote a modern version of a Greek tragedy, as raw and chilling as anything in *Oedipus* or *Medea*. He chose the craggy New England of 1840 and its flinty characters with care. The casting of Sophia Loren in the role of the young (third) wife of farmer Burl Ives is a key error because it injects an alien-to-the-scene element that dislocates the drama permanently.

The passion of greed and lust that takes place, in which Anthony Perkins and Loren embark on a semi-incestuous love affair that ends with Loren's having a child that Ives thinks is his, has been handled with discretion. Too much, perhaps.

O'Neill saw it as men fighting the gods and losing. Shaw apparently sees it as men understood through modern psychology, still doomed and damned, but for different reasons.

Despite Loren's unsuitability for the play, she exposes a great variety of emotion and manages the scenes of tenderness with special value. Perkins's character is not as exciting or vivid as it should be. Ives is the best, a bull of a man, cold in emotion and hot in passion.

●

DESPAIR

1978, 119 mins, W. Germany Ⓥ col

Dir Rainer Werner Fassbinder ***Scr*** Tom Stoppard ***Ph*** Michael Ballhaus ***Ed*** Juliane Lorrenz, Franz Walsch ***Mus*** Peer Raben ***Art*** Rolf Zehetbauer

Act Dirk Bogarde, Andrea Ferreol, Volker Spengler, Klaus Lowitsch (Bavaria Atelier/SFP/Geria)

Despite a witty, albeit theatrical, script by Tom Stoppard, prolific German director Rainer Werner Fassbinder does not quite bring off the spirited linguistic innovations, wit, and penetrating insights of Vladimir Nabokov's novel; but it is a good try. This tale of an exiled Russian in Germany in the late 1920s, who is driven to a weird murder, emerges overlong.

Dirk Bogarde, using a generally satisfactory Russo accent, has a pulpy, dim-witted, sensual wife, played in campy period style by Andrea Ferreol. He runs a chocolate factory that is going on the rocks as the the Depression hits the world.

He has strange delusions of seeing a replica of himself watching his carryings-on with his wife or even imagining himself dressed as a budding Nazi going in for macho sadistic sexual actions.

He insures himself and then, on a business trip, meets a down-and-out whom, he thinks, looks just like him. He decides to use this man in a trumped-up action that looks to be a holdup but is aimed at killing the man, passing him off as himself and collecting his insurance.

●

DESPERADO

1995, 103 mins, US Ⓥ col

Dir Robert Rodriguez ***Prod*** Robert Rodriguez, Bill Borden ***Scr*** Robert Rodriguez ***Ph*** Guillermo Navarro ***Ed*** Robert Rodriguez ***Mus*** Karyn Rachtman ***Art*** Cecilia Montiel

Act Antonio Banderas, Salma Hayek, Joaquim de Almeida, Cheech Marin, Steve Buscemi, Quentin Tarantino (Los Hooligans/Columbia)

In *Desperado*, Robert Rodriguez dedicates himself almost exclusively to dreaming up a hundred new ways to blow people away, to ultimately diminishing returns. The young Tex-Mex director's much-anticipated follow-up to his wildly inventive, no-budget 1993 debut, *El Mariachi*, could scarcely be more dazzling on a purely visual level, but it's mortally anaemic in the story, character and thematic departments.

In *Desperado*, the additional influences of John Woo and, especially, Quentin Tarantino also come into play, with latter on hand to personally approve Rodriguez's application to the Club of Cool. Result is both a rehash and extension of *El Mariachi*, with more than a thousandfold upgrade in budget and technical know-how.

Opening stretch is near-brilliant in its audaciousness. A brash gringo (indie fave Steve Buscemi) struts into a Mexican dive, sits at the bar and relates to the assembled lowlifes what he just saw happen at another cantina, where a mysterious stranger wiped everyone out.

The stranger, of course, is El Mariachi, now played by the never-more-handsome Antonio Banderas, a guitar-strummer wandering the country seeking a job and carrying heavy artillery in his guitar case as he seeks revenge for the murder of the woman he loved. El Mariachi eventually walks into bartender Cheech Marin's joint, which is a front for drug dealer Bucho (Joaquim de Almeida).

But there's at least an hour to go and the entire plot consists of El Mariachi trying to nail the well-protected Bucho, while Bucho's men try to ambush him. Along the way, El Mariachi forms an amorous alliance with local beauty Carolina (sexy Salma Hayek) that proves momentarily diverting.

●

DESPERADOES, THE

1943, 85 mins, US col

Dir Charles Vidor ***Prod*** Harry Joe Brown ***Scr*** Robert Carson ***Ph*** George Meehan, Allen M. Davey ***Ed*** Gene Havlick ***Mus*** John Leipold

Act Randolph Scott, Glenn Ford, Claire Trevor, Evelyn Keyes, Edgar Buchanan (Columbia)

In Technicolor mounting, and displaying some excellent exterior photography of the Utah district, *The Desperadoes* dispenses the usual lusty and vigorous melodramatics of the early West. The first color photography venture for Columbia, the tinting lifts the picture from the ordinary western program class to status of topliner.

Nothing new is injected into the story, which has been retold many times before. Randolph Scott is the sheriff of the Utah country in the 1860s, when a bank robbery is staged, and shortly after Glenn Ford wanders into town. He's a former pal of Scott—also boyhood sweetheart of Claire Trevor, who's operating the town's hotel and gambling layout—and is a fugitive with heavy coin riding on his head. But romantic influence of Evelyn Keyes persuades him to go straight.

•

DESPERATE
1947, 73 mins, US Ⓥ b/w
Dir Anthony Mann ***Prod*** Michel Kraike ***Scr*** Harry Essex, Martin Rackin ***Ph*** George E. Diskant ***Ed*** Marston Fay ***Mus*** Paul Sawtell ***Art*** Albert S. D'Agostino, Walter E. Keller
Act Steve Brodie, Audrey Long, Raymond Burr, Douglas Fowley, William Challee, Jason Robards, Sr. (RKO)

Desperate is a ripsnorting gangster meller. Yarn [by Dorothy Atlas and Anthony Mann] is strictly one of those things, and not unfamiliar. Steve Brodie, honest truck driver, becomes involved innocently in a fur warehouse robbery and cop slaying. He's beaten up by the mobsters when they realize he tipped off the police. Brodie flees with his wife, fearing gangster vengeance since the mobster's brother is captured and charged with murder. From then on, picture becomes more or less a continuing flight of Brodie and his wife, Audrey Long, both from the gendarmes and the gangsters.

Surprise ending gives film a lift. Anthony Mann's direction mainly stresses suspense, being done skillfully.

Brodie is okay as the honest truckman who gets into one jam after another. Long, as his wife, shapes up nicely; at times she resembles Ginger Rogers.

•

DESPERATE HOURS, THE
1955, 112 mins, US Ⓥ ⊙ b/w
Dir William Wyler ***Prod*** William Wyler ***Scr*** Joseph Hayes ***Ph*** Lee Garmes ***Ed*** Robert Swink ***Mus*** Gail Kubik ***Art*** Hal Pereira, Joseph MacMillan Johnson
Act Humphrey Bogart, Fredric March, Arthur Kennedy, Martha Scott, Dewey Martin, Gig Young (Paramount)

The Desperate Hours is an expert adaptation by Joseph Hayes of his own novel [and play] about three escaped desperadoes who gunpoint their way to temporary refuge in the suburban Indianapolis home of a respectable middle-class family.

This is a first for VistaVision in black and white. Wise, too, for color might have rendered less effective the strong fact-like appearance of *Hours*.

Wyler worked with major-league performers. This is Humphrey Bogart in the type of role that cues comics to caricature takeoffs. Here he's at his best, a tough gunman capable of murder, snarling delight with the way his captives must abide by his orders, and wise in the ways of self-preservation strategy.

Fredric March is powerful as head of the family, never before cited for bravery but now bent on protecting his family from the three intruders.

•

DESPERATE HOURS
1990, 105 mins, US Ⓥ ⊙ col
Dir Michael Cimino ***Prod*** Dino De Laurentiis, Michael Cimino ***Scr*** Laurence Konner, Mark Rosenthal, Joseph Hayes ***Ph*** Doug Milsome ***Ed*** Peter Hunt ***Mus*** David Mansfield ***Art*** Victoria Paul
Act Mickey Rourke, Anthony Hopkins, Mimi Rogers, Lindsay Crouse, Kelly Lynch, Elias Koteas (De Laurentiis)

Desperate Hours is a coldly mechanical and uninvolving remake of the 1955 Bogart pic *The Desperate Hours*, with Mickey Rourke as the hood terrorizing a suburban family.

Joseph Hayes's plot (first written as a novel, then as a [1955] play) is pure 1950s paranoia about three scruffy guys who invade the sanctity of the home, mocking a family's helplessness until Dad reasserts his control. Despite being minimally updated with intensified blood and brutality on the part of the hoods and the authorities, *Desperate Hours* has no new insights to offer.

The clunky script doesn't permit any vestige of humanity to Rourke, who's portrayed as a simple psycho with a low flashpoint, viciously brutalizing his improbably gorgeous pro-bono lawyer (Kelly Lynch) even as she helps him escape from prison.

Anthony Hopkins, in the Fredric March role of the initially weak-seeming father, brings his formidable skills to the task of involving the audience in the family's terror, but he seems mismatched with his estranged wife Mimi Rogers and implausibly reckless in his defiance of Rourke.

In place of the original film's sheriff (Arthur Kennedy), who made it a priority to avoid endangering the lives of the hostages, the Cimino version has a demented FBI agent (Lindsay Crouse).

Doug Milsome contributes handsome lensing of the autumnal locations of the Colorado wilderness and suburban Salt Lake City (substituting for the Indianapolis setting of the original).

•

DESPERATELY SEEKING SUSAN
1985, 104 mins, US Ⓥ ⊙ col
Dir Susan Seidelman ***Prod*** Sarah Pillsbury, Midge Sanford ***Scr*** Leora Barish ***Ph*** Edward Lachman ***Ed*** Andrew Mondshein ***Mus*** Thomas Newman ***Art*** Santo Loquasto
Act Rosanna Arquette, Madonna, Aidan Quinn, Mark Blum, Robert Joy, Laurie Metcalf (Orion)

Rosanna Arquette does more than her share in the pivotal part of a bored Yuppie housewife who follows the personal ads, wondering about the identities behind a "desperately seeking Susan" item that runs from time to time.

The ads are the way one boyfriend (Robert Joy) communicates with freespirited Madonna between her street-life liaisons with other men, one of whom has been bumped off after stealing a pair of rare Egyptian earrings. Before his demise, Madonna has lifted the jewelry, thinking they are trinkets.

Drawn by curiosity to spy on Madonna, Arquette winds up with a bump on the head and a case of amnesia, complicated by the fact that Joy's pal Aidan Quinn thinks Arquette is Madonna and Arquette doesn't know she isn't.

All of this is cause for consistent smiling and a few outright laughs, without ever building to complete comedy. It's not clear either that director Susan Seidelman and writer Leora Barish ever intend for it to be funnier, so that can't be faulted.

•

DESPERATE TRAIL, THE
1994, 93 mins, US Ⓥ col
Dir P. J. Pesce ***Prod*** Brad Krevoy, Steven Stabler ***Scr*** P. J. Pesce, Tom Abrams ***Ph*** Michael Bonvillain ***Ed*** Bill Johnson ***Mus*** Stephen Endelman ***Art*** Jonathan A. Carlson
Act Sam Elliott, Craig Sheffer, Linda Fiorentino, Frank Whaley (Motion Picture Corp/Turner)

The shadows of spaghetti Western maestros Sergio Leone and Sam Peckinpah loom large over the imagery of *The Desperate Trail*, a new oater with a strong herione played by Linda Fiorentino. Tale's quality and its characters never match helmer P. J. Pesce's technical savvy, speedy pacing, and thrilling shoot-outs.

Fiorentino is felicitously cast as Sarah, a tough, foul-mouthed woman who is being escorted by Marshall Speakes (Sam Elliott) to the nearest town, where he plans to hang her for killing a young man who was sexually abusive. Sharing their stagecoach is a mousy older woman whose bullying hubby gave her a black eye, and Jack (Craig Sheffer), a young man clutching a mysterious box in his lap.

As the story unfolds, it turns out that the man Sarah killed was Speake's son, which means that his obsessive pursuit may be more a matter of personal vendetta than justice restored. Structured as a caper, *Desperate Trail* displays the requisite twists and turns. It's a mouse-and-cat chase in which the roles of captor and captive are often reversed.

What the film has going for it are three or four rousing set-pieces. Displaying a sustained tempo, most of the action flies fast, hurtling the audience along with it.

•

DESTINATION GOBI
1953, 89 mins, US Ⓥ col
Dir Robert Wise ***Prod*** Stanley Rubin ***Scr*** Everett Freeman ***Ph*** Charles G. Clarke ***Ed*** Robert Fritch ***Mus*** Sol Kaplan ***Art*** Lyle R. Wheeler, Lewis Creben
Act Richard Widmark, Don Taylor, Casey Adams, Murvyn Vye, Darryl Hickman, Judy Dann (20th Century-Fox)

Ably directed by Robert Wise, *Destination Gobi* is Edmund G. Love's story (originally titled *Sixty Saddles for Gobi*) of a small U.S. Navy detachment sent to observe weather conditions in the Mongolian desert during World War II. It's a well turned out job.

Screenplay has elements of excitement and choice bits of sharp humor as it focuses on the ordeals and dangers experienced by the group of sailors incongruously trying to win friends among a band of Mongols and fight off Japs in Central Asia. The production captures both the feel and appearance of the vast sandland with its erratic temperatures and driving winds.

Richard Widmark is the hardened navy vet unhappily cast among the observatory gobs far in the parched Asian interior. Commanding officer (Russell Collins) is killed in an early Japanese air attack, and Widmark, as a chief petty officer, takes charge. From there on the pic shares the footage between the efforts to befriend the Mongol natives, headed by Murvyn Vye, and the encounters with the enemy.

•

DESTINATION TOKYO
1943, 133 mins, US Ⓥ b/w
Dir Delmer Daves ***Prod*** Jerry Wald ***Scr*** Delmer Daves, Albert Maltz ***Ph*** Bert Glennon ***Ed*** Chris Nyby ***Mus*** Franz Waxman
Act Cary Grant, John Garfield, Alan Hale, Dane Clark, John Ridgely, Warner Anderson (Warner)

Destination Tokyo runs two hours and 15 minutes, and that's a lot of film. But none of it is wasted. In its unspooling is crammed enough excitement for possibly a couple of pictures.

Here is a film whose hero is the Stars and Stripes; the performers are merely symbols of that heroism. Here is a film of superbly pooled talents.

Destination Tokyo tells of a single mission undertaken by a sub. Its destination is Tokyo. Under sealed orders opened 24 hours after it has sped from San Francisco Harbor, the sub first has a rendezvous with a navy plane near Kiska. There it takes aboard a meteorologist whom the sub is to deposit in Japan to survey conditions as a guide for the attack of the Fortress armada taking off from the aircraft carrier Hornet. Cary Grant has never been better as the sub's skipper, underplaying the role and so setting the pace for the entire pic.

•

DESTINY OF A MAN
SEE: SUDBA CHELOVYEKA

•

DESTRY
1954, 95 mins, US ▭ col
Dir George Marshall ***Prod*** Stanley Rubin ***Scr*** Edmund H. North, D. D. Beauchamp ***Ph*** George Robinson ***Ed*** Ted J. Kent ***Mus*** Joseph Gershenson
Act Audie Murphy, Mari Blanchard, Lyle Bettger, Thomas Mitchell, Edgar Buchanan, Lori Nelson (Universal)

Max Brand's familiar Western hero rides for the third time around under the Universal banner. The soft-spoken, gunless lawman was played by Tom Mix in 1932, and by James Stewart in 1939. This time, Audie Murphy tackles the role, and probably better fits the original Brand conception than his predecessors.

George Marshall, repeating the directorial chore he handled on the 1939 version, runs the deftly plotted script off without a lag. There's humor, hard drama, suspense, romance and sex, the latter more for the grownup than the juvenile oater fan.

Starring with Murphy as the saloon singer bad girl is Mari Blanchard, the same character done to a turn in 1939 by Marlene Dietrich. Blanchard doesn't have to take a back seat in the s.a. department and gives the role a zingy characterization that is most effective.

Murphy does exceptionally well as the quiet hero who is called in to aid Thomas Mitchell, town drunk appointed sheriff in a sardonic joke, and restore law and order to the western town ruled with ruthless hand by Lyle Bettger and Edgar Buchanan.

•

DESTRY RIDES AGAIN
1939, 90 mins, US Ⓥ ⊙ b/w
Dir George Marshall ***Prod*** Joe Pasternak ***Scr*** Felix Jackson, Gertrude Purcell, Henry Myers ***Ph*** Hal Mohr ***Ed*** Milton Carruth ***Mus*** Frank Skinner ***Art*** Jack Otterson, Martin Obzina
Act Marlene Dietrich, James Stewart, Charles Winninger, Mischa Auer, Brian Donlevy, Allen Jenkins (Universal/Realart)

Destry Rides Again is anything but a super-western. It's just plain, good entertainment [from an original story by Felix Jackson suggested by Max Brand's novel], primed with action and laughs and human sentiment. Marlene Dietrich's work as the hardened, ever-scrapping ginmill entertainer serves pretty much as the teeterboard from which this picture flips itself from the level of the ordinary western into a class item.

This gangster fable with an early West background revolves for the most part around the rowdy, gaudy ginmill and dancehall which Brian Donlevy operates in the frontier town of Bottle Neck. With the aid of his No. 1 entertainer (Dietrich), Donlevy cuts a wide swath cheating the townsmen at cards and working a waterhole racket until he makes the mistake of appointing the town rumpot (Charles Winniger) the local sheriff.

•

DETECTIVE, THE
1968, 114 mins, US col
Dir Gordon Douglas *Prod* Aaron Rosenberg *Scr* Abby Mann *Ph* Joseph Biroc *Ed* Robert Simpson *Mus* Jerry Goldsmith *Art* Jack Martin Smith, William Creber
Act Frank Sinatra, Lee Remick, Ralph Meeker, Jacqueline Bisset, Jack Klugman, Horace McMahon (20th Century-Fox)

Although extremely well cast, and fleshed out with some on-target dialog, Abby Mann's script is strictly potboiler material. Homosexuality, police brutality, corruption in high places, and nymphomania are the peas in this literary shell game, which the admirable professional razzle-dazzle of direction, acting and, to an extent, editing, cannot sufficiently legitimize.

Jack Klugman and Frank Sinatra are the only honest cops portrayed. Ralph Meeker is on the take, Robert Duvall likes to bust "queers," and Al Freeman, Jr., decides in time that Nazi-style interrogation produces desired results.

Repeated plot digression—made bearable by the fact that it involves Lee Remick—explores Sinatra's unstable married life.

The promise of erudition in the first reel gives way to programmer superficiality about the two main themes. For one thing, homosexuality is depicted as rampant in either truck stops, or else cheaply elegant salons. Also, the plot is heavily weighted against the police.

•

DETECTIVE
1985, 98 mins, France col
Dir Jean-Luc Godard *Prod* Alain Sarde *Scr* Alain Sarde, Philippe Setbon, Anne-Marie Mieville, Jean-Luc Godard *Ph* Bruno Nuytten *Ed* Jean-Luc Godard
Act Claude Brasseur, Nathalie Baye, Johnny Hallyday, Laurent Terzieff, Jean-Pierre Leaud, Alain Cuny (Sara/JLG)

Detective is a quintessential Godard pic that's more *Grand Hotel* than film noir. The plot, as much as it matters, involves four groups of people, or "families" whose paths intersect in the lobbies, dining rooms, and bedrooms of the Hotel Concorde at Saint Lazare in Paris. There's the hotel detective (Laurent Terzieff) and his manic assistant (Jean-Pierre Leaud), still trying to solve the two-year-old murder of a prince in the hotel. There's an avuncular Mafia boss (Alain Cuny), forever accompanied by a bodyguard, a young man and, incongruously, a small girl. There are also the Chenals (Claude Brasseur, Nathalie Baye) who are trying to get back a large sum of money owed them by a shady boxing promoter (Johnny Hallyday).

All these people, it seems, have business with each other, none of it very clear in the film, but no matter; what counts is Godard's unique style, on display here at its most refined. The pic is chock-full of asides, jokes, and anecdotes.

There are bursts of wonderfully imposing music (the film has a splendid stereo soundtrack), enjoyable, off-center images, clips from other films (Erich Von Stroheim in George Archainbaud's *The Last Squadron* and Jean Marais in Jean Cocteau's *Beauty and the Beast*), eccentric titles, and a splendid last-minute dedication to John Cassavetes, Edgar G. Ulmer and Clint Eastwood!

Technically one of his best films, *Detective* also boasts one of his strongest casts, with everyone excellent, especially singer Hallyday as the boxing impresario.

•

DETECTIVE STORY
1951, 105 mins, US b/w
Dir William Wyler *Prod* William Wyler *Scr* Philip Yordan, Robert Wyler *Ph* Lee Garmes *Ed* Robert Swink *Art* Hal Pereira, Earl Hedrick
Act Kirk Douglas, Eleanor Parker, William Bendix, Lee Grant, Cathy O'Donnell, Joseph Wiseman (Paramount)

William Wyler has polished the legit hit by Pulitzer-prizewinner Sidney Kingsley into a cinematic gem. Scripters have stuck almost to the letter of the original play. Even the location seldom changes from Kingsley's single set, the realistic headquarters room of the detective squad.

Kirk Douglas is the tortured detective determined unswervingly to do his duty as he sees it. Hunting an illicit doctor who has been delivering illegitimate children, Douglas suddenly finds himself being virtually blackmailed by the medico. Douglas's wife, long before she married him, had occasion to use the charlatan's services—and the doctor hadn't forgotten.

Eleanor Parker plays the wife with a dignity and emotional depth that makes a dramatic highlight of the scene in which she is forced to reveal her past. The personal drama is played against a broad and entertaining mosaic of other drama, humor, and young love in the busy squad room. Lee Grant repeats one of the memorable stage roles of recent years as a pathetic, albeit amusing little Brooklynesque femme shoplifter. Another holdover from the legiter, Joseph Wiseman, is tops as a sneering, dope-filled larcenist.

The unfrocked physician was an abortionist in the original. Screen version has him actually delivering the illicit children.

1951: NOMINATIONS: Best Director, Actress (Eleanor Parker), Supp. Actress (Lee Grant), Screenplay

•

DETOUR
1945, 67 mins, US b/w
Dir Edgar G. Ulmer *Prod* Leon Fromkess *Scr* Martin Goldsmith *Ph* Benjamin H. Kline *Ed* George McGuire *Mus* Leo Erdody *Art* Edward C. Jewell
Act Tom Neal, Ann Savage, Claudia Drake, Edmund MacDonald, Tim Ryan, Esther Howard (PRC)

Detour falls short of being a sleeper because of a flat ending and its low-budgeted production mountings. Uniformly good performances and some equally good direction and dialog keep the meller moving, however.

Theme is the buffeting that man gets from the fates. Story revolves around Tom Neal as a down-and-out young pianist hitchhiking his way to the Coast. Director Edgar G. Ulmer achieves some steadily mounting suspense as the pianist becomes implicated in two murders, neither of which he's committed. So he begins hitchhiking his way back east. Story is told by Neal in flashback.

Neal, who's been kicking around for some time in these minor items, does well with a difficult role that rates him a break in something better. Ann Savage is convincing as a tough girl of the roads and gets off some rough lines.

Benjamin H. Kline contributes some outstanding camera work that helps the flashback routine come off well. Leo Erdody's score, revolving around some Chopin themes, aids in backing up the film's grim mood.

•

DETOUR
1993, 89 mins, US col
Dir Wade Williams *Prod* Wade Williams *Scr* Roger Hull, Wade Williams *Ph* Jeff Richardson *Ed* Herbert L. Strock *Mus* Bill Crain
Act Tom Neal, Jr., Lea Lavish, Erin McGrane, Duke Howze, Susanna Foster, Brad Bittiker (Williams)

Fans of Edgar G. Ulmer's noir classic, *Detour*, are in for a disappointment: Wade Williams's low-budget remake features both laughable dialogue and inept acting. And despite vintage cars and flashing neon, the attempt to create a period look is only intermittently successful.

The plot, and even some of the dialogue, is straight out of the hardboiled original. Like the 1945 film, the remake centers on the incredibly bad fortune of Al Roberts (Tom Neal, Jr., whose father played the same part in the first *Detour*).

The film flashes back to a New York club, where he accompanies the singer Sue Harvey (Erin McGrane). Roberts falls in love with her, but she leaves him behind to try her luck in Los Angeles.

The remake's only significant departure from the original is in devoting more time to the singer's character in L.A. Unfortunately, her scenes are among the film's weakest.

•

DEUX ANGLAISES ET LE CONTINENT
(TWO ENGLISH GIRLS; ANNE AND MURIEL)
1971, 130 mins, France col
Dir Francois Truffaut *Prod* Marcel Berbert (exec.) *Scr* Francois Truffaut, Jean Gruault *Ph* Nestor Almendros *Ed* Yann Dedet, Martine Barraque *Mus* Georges Delerue *Art* Michel de Broin
Act Jean-Pierre Leaud, Kika Markham, Stacey Tendeter, Sylvia Marriott, Philippe Leotard, Marie Mansart (Films du Carrosse/Cinetel)

Film is a return to the only other book by Henri Pierre Roche, author of the book Francois Truffaut did as *Jules and Jim*, and reverses the triangle to have two English sisters and a young Frenchmen instead of the two thirtyish friends and an early 20th-century femme libber in *Jules*. It has Truffaut's usual charm and ease but he does not quite imbue it with the poetic flair, elan and life force his previous pic had.

Frenchman Claude Jean-Pierre Leaud goes to visit the sisters in their seaside country home. His mother and theirs, both widows, are old friends. Here, one sister, Anne (Kika Markham), a forthright, tomboyish and liberated type who wants to study art in Paris, pushes him towards her puritanical, intellectual younger sister, Muriel (Stacey Tendeter).

Love blossoms for him but not for her, and then it is decided they should not see each other for a year. Claude becomes the lover of the sister, who comes to study in Paris, and falls out of love with the younger one, who then suddenly feels herself in love with him.

Leaud does not have the elegance for his role of the dilettantish, mother-smothered young man. Markham has grace and charm as the freer sister and Tendeter the red-headed, freckled robustness of the more religious, repressed girl who confesses a childhood lesbo experience and guilty masturbatory activities in her diary.

Others are well cast in minor parts, with fine subdued hues and slow but knowing pacing. Love scenes are tactful though Truffaut dwells on the heavy bloodstains after the deflowering of the 30-year-old virgin, Muriel.

•

DEUXIEME SOUFFLE, LE
1966, 150 mins, France b/w
Dir Jean-Pierre Melville *Scr* Jean-Pierre Melville, Jose Giovanni *Ph* Marcel Combes *Ed* Michel Boheme *Mus* Bernard Gerard *Art* Jean-Jacques Fabre
Act Lino Ventura, Paul Meurisse, Raymond Pellegrin, Daniele Fabrega, Pierre Zimmer, Michel Constantin (Montaigne)

Director Jean-Pierre Melville has built a solid gangster opus influenced by some earlier American types but successfully transferred to the local milieu. It deals with a gangster who finds that there is no longer honor among thieves—or policemen, for that matter.

A middleaged gangster escapes from prison and wants only to get away somewhere. But he finds his sister being blackmailed by some small-time hoods and does them in, and then embarks on a last job to earn enough to retire to some tropical port.

The cool attitudes and flip jargon, used by both police and hoods, are reminiscent of American prototypes but jell well here. Lino Ventura has the right weight and honesty, albeit in a criminal way, and Paul Meurisse is a smooth, competent, and ironically tongued policeman more prone to use torture to extract confessions.

Played with intensity and gusto, with holdups done sharply, it has just that extra feel for milieu and character.

•

DEVIL AND DANIEL WEBSTER, THE
(UK: ALL THAT MONEY CAN BUY; DANIEL AND THE DEVIL)
1941, 100 mins, US b/w
Dir William Dieterle *Prod* William Dieterle *Scr* Dan Totheroh, Stephen Vincent Benet *Ph* Joseph August *Ed* Robert Wise *Mus* Bernard Herrmann *Art* Van Nest Polglase
Act Edward Arnold, Walter Huston, Jane Darwell, Simone Simon, Anne Shirley, John Qualen (RKO)

Material for the screenplay is taken from Stephen Vincent Benet's short story, an O. Henry prizewinner, and the author had a hand in the film version with Dan Totheroh.

The locale is New Hampshire, in 1840, a background of muddy roads, Currier and Ives farm settings, and peopled with struggling American peasantry. The legend is about the rise, fall, and regeneration of a young farmer, Jabez Stone, who is alleged to have sold his soul to the devil for a pittance of gold and seven years of good luck. It's a twist on the Faust theme, but Benet isn't Goethe.

James Craig plays the youth who discovers that crime doesn't pay. He is a quite capable young actor, of pleasing appearance. Anne Shirley is the wife, who gets all the worst of it, and Jane Darwell is the rock-bound New England mother.

Trouble for Dieterle (and the audience) starts when Walter Huston appears on the scene via double-exposure and whispers beguiling temptations into the ear of the young husband-farmer. That's when gold coins appear from strange places and the boy pays off the mortgage. From there to the finish it's mostly symbols and morality play. [Pic was previewed under the title *Here Is a Man*.]

1941: Best Scoring of a Dramatic Picture

NOMINATION: Best Actor (Walter Huston)

•

DEVIL AND MISS JONES, THE
1941, 92 mins, US b/w
Dir Sam Wood *Prod* Frank Ross *Scr* Norman Krasna *Ph* Harry Stradling *Ed* Sherman Todd
Act Jean Arthur, Charles Coburn, Robert Cummings, Edmund Gwenn, S. Z. Sakall, Spring Byington (RKO)

In a foreword, audiences are informed that this is a fanciful and imaginative story, put on the record mainly for amusement purposes. *The Devil and Miss Jones* then unwinds a light and fluffy tale of the richest man in the world who loses his stern front through association with the employees of one of his enterprises—a department store.

Jean Arthur is the Miss Jones, a decidedly personable salesgirl who takes the elderly shoe clerk under her wing to guide him through the intricacies of store routine. Charles Coburn is the richest man who steps into the store job incognito to ferret out the leaders of a union organization.

Coburn's performance as the millionaire who gradually unbends stands out as a fine characterization. Arthur excellently grooves as the salesgirl, but Robert Cummings's characterization is over-sketched in the main as a union organizer. Sam Wood injects deft direction with human byplay to lift the script considerably.

1941: NOMINATIONS: Best Supp. Actor (Charles Coburn), Original Screenplay

•

DEVIL AT 4 O'CLOCK, THE

1961, 125 mins, US Ⓥ ⦿ col

Dir Mervyn LeRoy ***Prod*** Fred Kohlmar ***Scr*** Liam O'Brien ***Ph*** Joseph Biroc ***Ed*** Charles Nelson ***Mus*** George Duning ***Art*** John Beckman

Act Spencer Tracy, Frank Sinatra, Kerwin Mathews, Jean-Pierre Aumont, Gregoire Aslan, Barbara Luna (Columbia)

A small, volcanic, South Seas isle makes a colorful setting for this tale of heroism and sacrifice, but vying with interest in characterizations are the exceptional special effects of an island being blown to pieces.

Based on a novel by Max Catto, plot is off the beaten path for an adventure yarn. Story is of a priest (Spencer Tracy) who, with three convicts (Frank Sinatra, Gregoire Aslan, Bernie Hamilton), saves the lives of the children in a mountain-top leper hospital by leading them through fire and lava flow to the coast and a waiting schooner after the volcano erupts and island is doomed to certain destruction.

Tracy delivers one of his more colorful portrayals in his hard-drinking cleric who has lost faith in his God, walloping over a character which sparks the action of entire film. Sinatra's role, first-class but minor in comparison, is overshadowed in interest by Aslan, one of the convicts in a stealing part who lightens some of the more dramatic action. Third con, Hamilton, also delivers solidly as the strong man who holds up a tottering wooden bridge over a deep gorge while the children and others from hospital cross to safety.

Special effects of Larry Butler and Willis Cook highlight the picture, filmed impressively by Joseph Biroc on the vivid island of Maui in the Hawaiian group.

•

DEVIL-DOLL, THE

1936, 70 mins, US Ⓥ ⦿ b/w

Dir Tod Browning ***Prod*** Edward J. Mannix ***Scr*** Garrett Fort, Guy Endore, Erich von Stroheim ***Ph*** Leonard Smith ***Ed*** Frederick Y. Smith ***Mus*** Franz Waxman

Act Lionel Barrmore, Maureen O'Sullivan, Frank Lawton, Robert Greig, Lucy Beaumont, Henry B. Walthall (M-G-M)

The premise [from the novel *Burn, Witch, Burn* by Abraham Merritt] is a scientist's discovery of a process by which all living things, including humans, can be reduced to one-sixth their normal size. The director, cameraman and art department make the most of it, but the writers' contribution is lacking in originality and seldom is equal to the idea in back of it.

Lionel Barrymore, as a framed convict named Lavond and later in the disguise of old Madam Mandelip, is a scientific Count of Monte Cristo who avenges his false imprisonment. His companion in a prison escape is the inventor of the atom-shrinking process. The inventor dies on the first night of freedom and Barrymore carries on the "great work" with the man's crazy widow.

Two of the big moments derive their power from camerawork, while the third is a remake by Tod Browning of the scene which highlighted his *Unholy Three* (1925). Once again the stolen jewels are concealed in a toy doll and the police inspector has them in his grasp without knowing it. For Barrymore the leading part is a field day. Rafaela Ottiano, with a white streak in her hair and hobbling on a crutch, is convincing as the scientist's wacky widow. Capable ingenue that she is, Maureen O'Sullivan had no trouble as Barrymore's daughter, but Frank Lawton, her opposite in the romantic secondary theme, is much too British and refined for a cab driver assignment.

•

DEVIL IN A BLUE DRESS

1995, 102 mins, US Ⓥ ⦿ col

Dir Carl Franklin ***Prod*** Jesse Beaton, Gary Goetzman ***Scr*** Carl Franklin ***Ph*** Tak Fujimoto ***Ed*** Carole Kravetz ***Mus*** Elmer Bernstein ***Art*** Gary Frutkoff

Act Denzel Washington, Tom Sizemore, Jennifer Beals, Don Cheadle, Maury Chaykin, Terry Kinney (Clinica/Mundy Lane/Tri-Star)

An engrossingly atmospheric dip into the dark waters of postwar urban intrigue, *Devil in a Blue Dress* ushers in the welcome subgenre of black noir. First screen adaptation of a Walter Mosley mystery novel featuring private detective Easy Rawlins, this long-awaited follow-up feature from *One False Move* helmer Carl Franklin navigates a complicated story of blackmail, race, and politics in confident fashion.

It's the United States, 1948, and Easy (Denzel Washington), bounced out of his aircraft-industry job in a dispute, accepts $100 from the shady DeWitt Albright (Tom Sizemore) to find Daphne Monet, a mysterious lady who's been involved with a wealthy mayoral candidate.

Central Avenue, the commercial center of black life at the time, represents the magnet to which the action returns time and again. Vibrantly recreated for the film (virtually nothing remains today of its glory days), it's a pulsating, exciting promenade.

When Easy goes there looking for Daphne, the woman he meets (Lisa Nicole Carson in a spunky turn) mysteriously ends up dead. As the title indicates, the centerpiece is Daphne (Jennifer Beals), a glamorous young lady who straddles the worlds of both L.A.s in ways that may be tragic but aren't all that surprising.

The tone is less edgy and mordant than in *One False Move*, but pic nonetheless has a flavor all its own, thanks variously to its sharply observed cast of characters, astutely re-created setting, adherence to novelistic details and solid p.o.v. Washington's performance is alert and subtle. Unfortunately, nothing about the Daphne character works—from the writing to her costumes and coiffure to Beals' undimensional performance—leaving the picture with something of a soft spot at the center.

•

DEVIL IN MISS JONES, THE

1973, 74 mins, US col

Dir Gerard Damiano ***Prod*** Gerard Damiano ***Scr*** Gerard Damiano ***Ph*** Harry Flecks ***Ed*** Gerard Damiano ***Mus*** Alden Shuman

Act Georgina Spevlin, John Clemens, Harry Reams, Albert Gork [= Gerard Damiano], Rick Livermore, Sue Flaken (Marvin/Damiano)

With *The Devil in Miss Jones*, the hardcore porno feature approaches an "art form." For its genre, the pic is a sensation, marked by a technical polish that pales some Hollywood product and containing some of the most frenzied and erotic sex sequences in porno memory.

Written, directed, and edited by Gerard Damiano, the man who dittoed on *Deep Throat* (under his Jerry Gerard pseudonym), this ambitious meller delivers in spades.

A thirtyish virgin, Justine Jones (Georgina Spevlin), commits suicide and is condemned to eternal damnation. Her suicide has been the only damnable act in a lonely, despairing life, and to make herself "worthy" of the punishment meted out to her, Jones requests a little more time in which to experiment with and to be consumed by lust.

Georgina Spevlin lacks the specific sexpertise of Linda Lovelace and she's no conventional beauty. Male performers are familiar porno vets, with the exception of Damiano himself who appears, under the name of Albert Gork, in pic's hellish finale.

•

DEVIL IS A SISSY, THE

1936, 131 mins, US b/w

Dir W. S. Van Dyke ***Prod*** Frank Davis ***Scr*** John Lee Mahin, Richard Schayer, Rowland Brown ***Ph*** Harold Rosson, George Schneidermann ***Ed*** Tom Held ***Mus*** Herbert Stothart ***Art*** Cedric Gibbons

Act Freddie Bartholomew, Jackie Cooper, Mickey Rooney, Ian Hunter, Peggy Conklin, Katherine Alexander (M-G-M)

This saga of the sidewalks of New York must resurrect thoughts of *Street Scene* (1931) and *Paul Street Boys* (1929), and it'll remind Broadway initiates of the legit hit, *Dead End*; yet it's dissimilar. The almost tragic bravery of "Limey" Freddie Bartholomew to make his roughneck pals, Buck (Jackie Cooper) and Gig (Mickey Rooney), accept him into the fold as a full-fledged little denizen of the Mullberry street sector—overlooking his polished Oxfordian diction and his French and English schooling—one senses is perhaps almost autobiographical in its grim determination.

Freddie takes the rap on sundry escapades without squirming, only to be rebuffed, after having been grudgingly accepted. Unadulterated young mugs, Jackie and Mickey, finally perceive that Claude (alias Limey) has the makin's even though it almost means the English lad's life due to pneumonia.

The three boys are ideal in their assignments. Cooper is quite a young giant, qualifying him as the natural gang-leader. Gene Lockhart as the East Side Babbitt who is still fighting the war for democracy, broadens the role just a shade to put it over. Katherine Alexander is a natural for the wealthy divorcee-mother of Freddie.

•

DEVIL IS A WOMAN, THE

1935, 76 mins, US b/w

Dir Josef von Sternberg ***Scr*** John Dos Passon, Sam Winston ***Ph*** Josef von Sternberg, Lucien Ballard ***Ed*** Sam Winston ***Mus*** Ralph Rainger, Andrea Setaro (arr.) ***Art*** Hans Dreier

Act Marlene Dietrich, Cesar Romero, Lionel Atwill, Edward Everett Horton, Alison Skipworth, Don Alvarado (Paramount)

Josef von Sternberg both directed and photographed *The Devil Is a Woman*, working with a Pierre Louys classic *The Woman and the Puppet* which gives the reader a cross-section of a ruthless courtesan and not much else. While *Devil* is a somewhat monotonous picture, Sternberg has given it clever photography and background. Marlene Dietrich has done the rest in playing the Louys trollop, turning in a fine performance.

Story is told in the background of southern Spain during a fiesta, thus permitting Sternberg some big mob scenes and color, plus music. It opens on la Dietrich of today as a gorgeously desirable woman who has caught the eye of a young visitor. He is about to stage a rendezvous with her when he meets an old friend (Atwill) who tells him of his sad experience with the same woman, most of the story then being told by flashback.

Edward Everett Horton is in on a couple of sequences at opening and near close, he and his political associates raising the only laughs that occur. "Caprice Espagnol," vet classic, and other Spanish music is employed for melodic background in an effective manner.

•

DEVIL MAKES THREE, THE

1952, 89 mins, US b/w

Dir Andrew Marton ***Prod*** Richard Goldstone ***Scr*** Jerry Davis ***Ph*** Vaclav Vich ***Ed*** Ben Lewis ***Mus*** Rudolph G. Kopp (dir.)

Act Gene Kelly, Pier Angeli, Richard Rober, Richard Egan, Claus Clausen, Wilfried Seyferth (M-G-M)

Postwar Germany provides the background for an interesting chase thriller. Snow-covered Munich, Salzburg, Berchtesgaden, and Hitler's bombed-out Adlerhorst are the plot settings.

Lawrence Bachmann's story, *Autobahn*, supplies the basis for the script. Story deals with an underground movement to revive the Nazi Party and how counter-intelligence, with the aid of Gene Kelly's air force captain, and Pier Angeli's German B-girl, put down the aspirations of one would-be fuehrer.

The chase thrills and suspense moments come across expertly under Andrew Marton's direction, but he is inclined to pace the film a bit too slowly in other spots. One of the top thriller sequences is the motorcycle race on a frozen lake during which the villain is revealed.

•

DEVIL NEVER SLEEPS, THE

SEE: SATAN NEVER SLEEPS

•

DEVIL RIDES OUT, THE
(US: THE DEVIL'S BRIDE)

1968, 95 mins, UK col

Dir Terence Fisher ***Prod*** Anthony Nelson-Keys ***Scr*** Richard Matheson ***Ph*** Arthur Grant ***Ed*** James Needs ***Mus*** James Bernard ***Art*** Bernard Robinson

Act Christopher Lee, Charles Gray, Nike Arrighi, Leon Greene, Patrick Mower, Sarah Lawson (Hammer)

Director Terence Fisher has a ball with this slice of black magic, based on the Dennis Wheatley novel. He has built up a suspenseful pic with several tough highlights, and gets major effect by playing the subject dead straight and getting similar serious performances from his capable cast.

Christopher Lee is, for once, on the side of the goodies. As the Duc de Richleau, he and his buddy (Leon Greene) are intent on saving the soul of a young man (Patrick Mower) caught up in black magic and at the mercy of Charles Gray, chief apostle of the evil. Also involved is a mysterious young girl (Nike Arrighi), in the thrall of the black sin. Lee plays the Duc with his usual authority and Gray turns out another of his bland, cold essays in villainy. The weakness lies in the fact that these two rarely confront each other.

Arrighi as a slightly hysterical lass, Mower, and Greene are all adequate.

Fisher's direction makes one of the Satanic orgies a production highspot, aided by some frenzied choreography by David Toguri and apt mood music.

•

DEVILS, THE
1971, 109 mins, UK Ⓥ ▭ col
Dir Ken Russell ***Prod*** Robert H. Solo, Ken Russell ***Scr*** Ken Russell ***Ph*** David Watkin ***Ed*** Michael Bradsell ***Mus*** Peter Maxwell Davies ***Art*** Derek Jarman
Act Vanessa Redgrave, Oliver Reed, Dudley Sutton, Max Adrian, Gemma Jones, Murray Melvin (Warner/Russo)

Working from John Whiting's play of the same title, and Aldous Huxley's book, *The Devils of Loudun*, Ken Russell has taken some historical liberties in fashioning the story of Father Grandier (Oliver Reed), sensually liberated priest in 17th-century France whose ethics brought him into conflict with the political ambitions of Cardinal Richelieu and the Catholic Church, and whose virile presence and backstairs reputation cued the erotic fantasies of a humpbacked nun, Sister Jeanne (Vanessa Redgrave).

When this sister's lustful ravings begin to infect other nuns in her convent, the Church, through its military agent (Dudley Sutton), brings in an exorcist (Michael Gothard) to stage circus-like public purges of the naked, foulmouthed nuns which result in Grandier's conviction on heresy charges, his torture, and burning at the stake.

As if the story alone weren't bizarre enough, Russell has spared nothing in hyping the historic events by stressing the grisly at the expense of dramatic unity.

Given Russell's frantic pacing, performances tend to get lost amid the savagery. Reed carries the film with an admirably restrained portrayal of the doomed priest. Redgrave, on screen only sporadically, is stunning as the salacious sister.

•

DEVIL'S ADVOCATE, THE
1997, 144 mins, US Ⓥ ⦿ ▭ col
Dir Taylor Hackford ***Prod*** Arnold Kopelson, Anne Kopelson, Arnon Milchan ***Scr*** Jonathan Lemkin, Tony Gilroy ***Ph*** Andrzej Bartkowiak ***Ed*** Mark Warner ***Mus*** James Newton Howard ***Art*** Bruno Rubeo
Act Keanu Reeves, Al Pacino, Charlize Theron, Jeffrey Jones, Judith Ivey, Connie Neilsen (Kopelson/Warner)

The Devil's Advocate is a fairly entertaining supernatural potboiler [from Andrew Neiderman's novel] that finally bubbles over with a nearly operatic sense of absurdity and excess.

Kevin Lomax (Keanu Reeves) is a dashing young attorney lured by flattery and a fat paycheck to New York City. Once there, he is impressed by the extravagant offices of the law firm and, most of all, by the big boss, John Milton (Al Pacino). While Kevin is put to work earning his $400-per-hour rate, his gorgeous, adoring wife, Mary Ann (Charlize Theron), is left to come under the dubious influence of good-times neighbor Jackie (Tamara Tunie).

Before long, Kevin believes the only wrong would lie in losing. He is then put to a heavy test by one of the firm's biggest clients, a real estate tycoon (Craig T. Nelson) who is probably guilty of murdering his wife and two others. Left largely alone, Mary Ann begins to go a bit bonkers, paving the way for the ultimate showdown between Kevin and his devious boss.

Although it is not explicitly stated until deep into the picture, the trailer makes no secret that Pacino plays the devil, accentuating all this with occasional wild looks, an insinuating cackle and flicks of his tongue. Reeves does a serious and pleasing job, and more than holds his own with seasoned thesps. Biggest impression among the supporting players is by newcomer Connie Neilsen, who is transfixing as the vixen who turns the young attorney's head.

•

DEVIL'S BRIDE, THE
SEE: THE DEVIL RIDES OUT

•

DEVIL'S BRIGADE, THE
1968, 131 mins, US Ⓥ ⦿ ▭ col
Dir Andrew V. McLaglen ***Prod*** David L. Wolper ***Scr*** William Roberts ***Ph*** William H. Clothier ***Ed*** William Cartwright ***Mus*** Alex North ***Art*** Al Sweeney, Jr.
Act William Holden, Cliff Robertson, Vince Edwards, Andrew Prine, Claude Akins, Richard Jaeckel (United Artists)

The fusion of some U.S. Army roughnecks and Canadian crack troops into a World War II special forces unit known as The Devil's Brigade certainly contained the ingredients for a strong film. But distended and stock scripting, sluggish direction, and limp pacing make an uneven combination of the worst of *The Dirty Dozen* and the best of *What Price Glory*.

Laced with some appropriate salty dialog, William Roberts's adaptation of the book by Robert H. Adelman and Col. George Walton depicts the formation, training, and initial combat of a special forces unit.

Major drawbacks in the film are over-exposition and later dramatic overkill. The formation of the unit occupies 21 minutes; their awkward amalgamation takes another 41 minutes; introduction to actual combat and first battlefield experience runs another half hour; and final, gory incident occupies the last 39 minutes.

In contrast to the exessive underplaying of nearly all officer roles, many enlisted men roles are field days for extroverted playing.

•

DEVIL'S DISCIPLE, THE
1959, 82 mins, US/UK col
Dir Guy Hamilton ***Prod*** Harold Hecht ***Scr*** John Dighton, Roland Kibbee ***Ph*** Jack Hildyard ***Ed*** Alan Osbiston ***Mus*** Richard Rodney Bennett
Act Burt Lancaster, Kirk Douglas, Laurence Olivier, Janette Scott, Eva LeGallienne, Harry Andrews (Bryna/United Artists)

The Devil's Disciple by George Bernard Shaw is better than this film version would indicate to those unfamiliar with the stage original. The final third of the picture is superb Shawmanship, but the major portion preceding it is fumbling and unsatisfactory.

That all is not lost may be credited almost entirely to Laurence Olivier. His character, that of General "Gentleman Johnny" Burgoyne, is a witty, mocking figure and mouthpiece for Shaw's wicked shafts into convention and history, in this case the American Revolution.

The other two stars, Burt Lancaster and Kirk Douglas, fare less well. Lancaster is Anthony Anderson, the peace-spouting person who eventually becomes a fiery rebel. Douglas is Dick Dudgeon, self-proclaimed, a shameless, cowardly scoundrel, who in turn displays the truest Christian attitudes.

Shaw's play is the ironic Irishman's version of how the British, bumbling and fumbling, lost the American colonies. The reason, says Shaw, is that due to the long British weekend, someone at the War Office forgot to notify Lord North to join forces with General Burgoyne and pinch off the colonials.

Directors were changed in mid-filming and there seems in the finished product to be a division of style. Guy Hamilton must bear the blame for the uncertain mood and pace.

•

DEVIL'S DOORWAY
1950, 84 mins, US b/w
Dir Anthony Mann ***Prod*** Nicholas Nayfack ***Scr*** Guy Trosper ***Ph*** John Alton ***Ed*** Conrad A. Nervig ***Mus*** Daniele Amfitheatrof
Act Robert Taylor, Louis Calhern, Paula Raymond, Marshall Thompson, Edgar Buchanan, James Mitchell (M-G-M)

Devil's Doorway is an odd title to hang on this action drama about injustices to the Indians back in the days when the United States was a young nation and spreading its wings westward.

Robert Taylor is the native hero of yarn about the period just after the Civil War when settlers started moving west to take over Indian lands. The whites are made the heavies and the dirty work is keynoted in Louis Calhern's character as a prejudiced, crooked attorney who fosters trouble for the Indians.

Anthony Mann's direction keeps the footage moving. Actionwise, he hits some high spots, particularly Taylor's saloon fight with a gunslinger and in the mass finale clash between whites and Indians. Taylor's assignment as the hero doesn't come off too happily.

•

DEVIL'S ENVOYS, THE
SEE: LES VISITEURS DU SOIR

•

DEVIL'S ISLAND
1939, 62 mins, US b/w
Dir William Clemens ***Scr*** Kenneth Gamet, Don Ryan, Anthony Coldeway, Raymond L. Schrock ***Ph*** George Barnes ***Ed*** Frank Magee ***Art*** Max Parker
Act Boris Karloff, Nedda Harrigan, James Stephenson, Adia Kuznetzoff, Rolla Gourvitch, Robert Warwick (Warner)

This is the picture that brought protest from the French government shortly after it had been placed in release in January 1939, with result that it was withdrawn from circulation throughout the world [but later re-released by Warner in July 1940]. Intrinsically, it is just another meller of the dreaded isle down in the Caribbean.

It traces the experiences of a French doctor convicted of treason who, after arriving at Devil's Island, is called upon to perform a brain operation on the commandant's daughter. The father of the girl fails to keep his promises to release him but the mother, under somewhat dubious circumstances, plots the convict doctor's escape. No love interest figures, however.

Boris Karloff plays the lead convincingly, making himself as pathetic a character as possible. It is rather clearly indicated, however, that he was guilty of breaking the law. James Stephenson, as the colonel in charge of the prison, is a little too British.

•

DEVIL'S OWN, THE
1997, 110 mins, US Ⓥ ⦿ ▭ col
Dir Alan J. Pakula ***Prod*** Lawrence Gordon, Robert F. Colesberry ***Scr*** David Aaron Cohen, Vincent Patrick, Kevin Jarre ***Ph*** Gordon Willis ***Ed*** Tom Rolf, Dennis Virkler ***Mus*** James Horner ***Art*** Jane Musky
Act Harrison Ford, Brad Pitt, Margaret Colin, Ruben Blades, Treat Williams, Natascha McElhone (Columbia)

The Devil's Own is neither the best nor the worst $90–100 million-area picture ever made, but it must be the one in which the cost is least evident on the screen. A reasonably engrossing, well-crafted suspenser that bears no sign of the much-reported on-set difficulties, pic is much more interested in the moral stature and culpability of the main characters than in heavy action and thrills.

"Don't look for a happy ending," Brad Pitt's Irish Republican Army hotshot warns Harrison Ford's standup New York more than once. "It's not an American story, it's an Irish one." By the climax, with its *Key Largo*–esque shootout on board a small boat, the film draws perilously close to conventional American movie melodrama, but for the most part it concentrates on the personalities of the two men who initially bond but must ultimately face each other down in a life-and-death duel.

Frankie McGuire (Pitt) has become the Brits' Public Enemey No. 1, having taken out thirteen soldiers and eleven cops in Ulster. He escapes to New York, where he is welcomed by an IRA-friendly judge (George Hearn) and discreetly placed in the home of a veteran Irish cop, Tom O'Meara (Ford), his wife (Margaret Colin), and three daughters, who know nothing of their guest's true identity. Frankie is in the U.S. to acquire a stock of Stinger missiles.

Whatever contortions the script went through on its way, director Alan J. Pakula has managed to maintain an admirable concentration on the central moral equation, which posits the Irish terrorist's understandable political and emotional motivations for revenge vs. the decent cop's sense of justice and the greater human good. Film decidedly comes down in favor of Tom's religiously reinforced position.

This is very close to Pitt's best work to date. Ford exhibits slight signs of strain in the most emotionally taxing scenes.

•

DEVIL'S PLAYGROUND, THE
1976, 107 mins, Australia Ⓥ col
Dir Fred Schepisi ***Prod*** Fred Schepisi ***Scr*** Fred Schepisi ***Ph*** Ian Baker ***Ed*** Brian Kavanagh ***Mus*** Bruce Smeaton
Act Arthur Dignam, Nick Tate, Simon Burke, Charles McCallum, John Frawley, Jonathan Hardy (Film House)

The Devil's Playground is a Roman Catholic boys' boarding school where the pupils are seen at their everyday work, play, and worship. Stressed are the problems of puberty in such a community, and the evils of succumbing to self-abuse; one boy for instance is chastised for taking off his bathers whilst under a shower.

The more sensitive boys take such things to heart, others merely shrug it off and go their own way. In one quarter it breeds a cell where boys indulge in homosexual, masochistic, and sadistic practices while the teachers react in different ways.

Film, almost like a factual documentary at times, has obviously been made with great sincerity. Lensing is fine with some superb outdoor photography. The direction is always competent, and most of the scenes involving the boys, organized and natural.

•

DEVIL WITHIN HER, THE
SEE: I DON'T WANT TO BE BORN

•

DEVOTION
1946, 108 mins, US b/w
Dir Curtis Bernhardt ***Prod*** Robert Buckner ***Scr*** Keith Winter ***Ph*** Ernest Haller ***Ed*** Rudi Fehr ***Mus*** Erich Wolfgang Korngold ***Art*** Robert M. Haas
Act Ida Lupino, Paul Henreid, Olivia de Havilland, Sydney Greenstreet, Arthur Kennedy, Nancy Coleman (Warner)

Individual performances are expert, with a few standouts, in miming the situations in the script by Keith Winter, but it fails to stir more than a modest response. Script, taken from an original story by Theodore Reeves, is not substantial, and dialog switches confusingly from the modern to the prose of the period.

Plot depicts the Brontes in the village of Haworth, Yorkshire, opening in the period just before they found fame as authors. Shown are the love triangle between Ida Lupino, as Emily; Olivia de Havilland, as Charlotte, and Paul Henreid, as the curate who aids the girls' father in the parish; the brief stay of Emily and Charlotte in Brussels, and the latter's romance with a schoolteacher, Victor Francen.

Lupino and de Havilland are expert as the two older sisters, while Nancy Coleman as the younger Anne Bronte has her moments. Henreid's portrayal is excellent. Greenstreet is good as Thackeray, a role that is almost a bit. Arthur Kennedy's performance as the drunken poet-painter brother of the sisters is a standout.

•

DIABOLIQUE
SEE: LES DIABOLIQUES

•

DIABOLIQUE
1996, 107 mins, US Ⓥ ⊙ col
Dir Jeremiah Chechik ***Prod*** Marvin Worth, James G. Robinson ***Scr*** Don Roos ***Ph*** Peter James ***Ed*** Carol Littleton ***Mus*** Randy Edelman ***Art*** Leslie Dilley
Act Sharon Stone, Isabelle Adjani, Chazz Palminteri, Kathy Bates, Spalding Gray, Shirley Knight (Morgan Creek/Warner)

This *Diabolique* is a thoroughly misguided redressing of the classic 1955 French thriller. Surprisingly dull and suspenseless, given the inherent intrigue of the story, new outing coarsens every aspect of this tale of the wife and mistress of a cruel schoolmaster whose conspiracy to murder him triggers an unexpected aftermath.

The first American remake was John Badham's well-regarded 1974 TV movie *Reflections of Murder*, which featured Tuesday Weld, Joan Hackett and Sam Waterston.

First 20 minutes or so are the worst. To the continuous accompaniment of threatening thunderstorms, Nicole (Sharon Stone) and Mia (Isabelle Adjani), mistress and wife, respectively, of brutal boys' school headmaster Guy Baran (Chazz Palminteri), decide they've each had enough of his domineering and deceitful ways and agree to do him in. Shortly after the women are aghast when the corpse turns up missing after the pool is drained.

Everything has been made cruder and more obvious than necessary. Structurally, Don Roos's script hews fairly closely to the original for about two-thirds of the way, up to and including the introduction of a local detective with time to kill. The famous bathtub scene is present, although in amazingly unscary fashion.

The one element that is underplayed is a suggested sexual relationship between the two women. This is indicated several times through touches and gestures, but the emotional dynamics are too vague.

Director Jeremiah Chechnik, best known for *Benny & Joon*, has only skimmed the surface of his cast's talents. The pic was shot in the Pittsburgh area and tech credits are smooth.

•

DIABOLIQUES, LES
(DIABOLIQUE)
1955, 110 mins, France Ⓥ ⊙ b/w
Dir Henri-Georges Clouzot ***Scr*** Henri-Georges Clouzot, Jerome Geronimi, Rene Masson, Frederic Grendel ***Ph*** Armand Thirard ***Ed*** Madeleine Gug ***Mus*** Georges Van Parys ***Art*** Leon Barsacq
Act Simone Signoret, Vera Clouzot, Paul Meurisse, Charles Vanel, Pierre Larquey, Michel Serrault (Filmsonor)

Although this has a few hallucinatory bits of terror, the film is primarily a creaky-door type of melodrama [from the novel *Celle qui n'etait plus* by Pierre Boileau and Thomas Narcejac]. Its macabre aspects and lack of sympathy for the characters make this a hybrid which flounders between a blasting look at human infamy and an out-and-out contrived whodunit.

A brutal headmaster of a private boy's school tyrannizes his frail, sickly wife, and has a mistress, a teacher at the school, with whom he has just broken off. The women band together and, driven by the steely teacher, plot to kill him, which apparently they do.

Director Henri-Georges Clouzot's interest in terror and human dreariness for its own sake has robbed this of intrinsic honesty. He has gotten a fine, if spotty performance from his real wife, Vera, who plays the frail mate in the pic. It is her second film. Simone Signoret portrays a resoundingly solid competence as the powerful crime investigator. Paul Meurisse is properly despicable as the so-called victim.

•

DIAGONALE DU FOU, LA
(DANGEROUS MOVES)
1985, 100 mins, Switzerland Ⓥ col
Dir Richard Dembo ***Prod*** Arthur Cohn ***Scr*** Richard Dembo ***Ph*** Raoul Coutard ***Ed*** Agnes Guillemot ***Mus*** Gabriel Yared ***Art*** Ivan Maussion
Act Michel Piccoli, Alexandre Arbatt, Leslie Caron, Liv Ullmann, Daniel Olbrychski, Michel Aumont (Cohn)

Dangerous Moves is an absorbing, if not inspired, suspense drama with a great subject, that of a championship chess showdown between a Soviet title-holder and an exiled dissident challenger.

Recalling the famous Karpov-Korchnoi match of some years earlier, script by first-time director Richard Dembo has the aging Russian grand old man of chess (Michel Piccoli) travel to Geneva for a long-anticipated confrontation with a 30-year-old whippersnapper (Alexandre Arbatt) who left his homeland five years before.

Both have two critical people missing from their respective entourages—Piccoli, who is seriously ailing, is denied permission for his doctor, a Jew with family in Israel, to accompany him out of the country, while Arbatt has been forced to live in the West without his wife (Liv Ullmann), who has been detained in the USSR. Both parties come to be used as pawns at crucial stages in the competition.

An opera director and cofounder of the Directors's Fortnight at the Cannes Film Festival, Dembo orchestrates the proceedings with a fair measure of skill and brings in just enough specifics of chess strategy to grab viewer interest in the contest. On the other hand, the roles created for the women in the drama are embarrassingly one-dimensional.

1984: Best Foreign Language Film

•

DIAL M FOR MURDER
1954, 105 mins, US Ⓥ ⊙ col
Dir Alfred Hitchcock ***Prod*** Alfred Hitchcock ***Scr*** Frederick Knott ***Ph*** Robert Burks ***Ed*** Rudi Fehr ***Mus*** Dimitri Tiomkin ***Art*** Edward Carrere
Act Ray Milland, Grace Kelly, Robert Cummings, John Williams, Anthony Dawson, Patrick Allen (Warner)

The melodramatics in Frederick Knott's legit hit, *Dial M for Murder*, have been transferred to the screen virtually intact, but they are not as impressive on film. *Dial M* remains more of a filmed play than a motion picture, unfortunately revealed as a conversation piece about murder which talks up much more suspense than it actually delivers. The 3-D camera's probing eye also discloses that there's very little that's new in the Knott plotting.

Co-starring with Ray Milland are Grace Kelly, his wife and the intended murder victim, and Robert Cummings, her lover, who has a rather fruitless part in the resolution of the melodramatics.

Milland plots his wife's death, figuring on using Anthony Dawson for the actual killing while he has an alibi established elsewhere. The scheme goes awry.

There are a number of basic weaknesses in the setup that keep the picture from being a good suspense show for any but the most gullible. Via the performances and several suspense tricks expected of Hitchcock, the weaknesses are glossed over but not enough to rate the film a cinch winner.

•

DIAMOND HEAD
1962, 107 mins, US Ⓥ ⊙ ▭ col
Dir Guy Green ***Prod*** Jerry Bresler ***Scr*** Marguerite Roberts ***Ph*** Sam Leavitt ***Ed*** William A. Lyon ***Mus*** John Williams ***Art*** Malcolm Brown
Act Charlton Heston, Yvette Mimieux, George Chakiris, France Nuyen, James Darren (Columbia/Bresler)

Improbabilities and inconsistencies galore reside in Marguerite Roberts's heavyhanded screenplay, from Peter Gilman's novel, about a Hawaiian agricultural tycoon, or King Bwana of Pineappleville, hellbent on holding-that-bloodline. When the baron's (Charlton Heston) baby sister (Yvette Mimieux) defiantly announces her engagement to a full-blooded Hawaiian lad (James Darren), the battle lines are drawn.

Heston etches a swaggering portrait of the bullying bigot. Mimieux is spirited as the liberal-minded sister, Chakiris is glum and inexpressive as the half-breed medic who captures the fair sister's heart. He also seems to be the only doctor on the Islands. Nuyen is sweet as Heston's unlikely heartthrob. Darren, despite a rich tan, seems about as 100% Hawaiian as Paul Revere.

Guy Green's direction, at any rate, is high-spirited, and production ingredients are slickly eye-appealing. Sam Leavitt's photography is Eastman colorful and dramatically calculating and alert.

•

DIAMOND HORSESHOE
1945, 104 mins, US col
Dir George Seaton ***Prod*** William Perlberg ***Scr*** George Seaton ***Ph*** Ernest Palmer ***Ed*** Robert Simpson ***Mus*** Alfred Newman (dir.) ***Art*** Lyle R. Wheeler, Joseph C. Wright
Act Betty Grable, Dick Haymes, Phil Silvers, William Gaxton, Margaret Dumont (20th Century-Fox)

You could call the Diamond Horseshoe the Creep Club, and Billy Rose might be Joe Blow for all that matters. True, it lends an authenticity and realism which are undeniable. But more potent are the plot components. It builds a solid heart story in a manner which is enough of a switch on the backstage formula to make it different.

Betty Grable and Dick Haymes are co-starred and this, of course, puts the crooner over solidly as a film juvenile. William Gaxton plays Haymes' father, the lead at the Horseshoe, forever squabbling with Grable, the No. 1 cheesecake. Haymes gives up medicine for a stage career, and while Grable starts out under a cloud she emerges the noble influence to get him back to his M.D. studies, an objective in which Gaxton fails and for which he had blamed his son's romantic vis-a-vis.

Per cinematic custom, some of the so-called cabaret revue numbers could happen only in Madison Square Garden, but this again is accepted Hollywood license. On the other hand, the Diamond Horseshoe decor and policy are sometimes so faithful it's startlingly familiar, even unto a lyrical ad for the joint, such as the line, "Two shows every night (without a cover)."

•

DIAMONDS ARE FOREVER
1971, 119 mins, UK Ⓥ ⊙ ▭ col
Dir Guy Hamilton ***Prod*** Albert R. Broccoli, Harry Saltzman ***Scr*** Richard Maibaum, Tom Mankiewicz ***Ph*** Ted Moore ***Ed*** Bert Bates, John W. Holmes ***Mus*** John Barry ***Art*** Ken Adam
Act Sean Connery, Jill St. John, Charles Gray, Lana Wood, Jimmy Dean, Bruce Cabot (United Artists)

James Bond still packs a lethal wallop in all his cavortings, still manages to surround himself with scantily-clad sexpots. Yet *Diamonds Are Forever* doesn't carry the same quality or flair as its many predecessors.

Sean Connery is back in the role as in five previous Bond entries, and he still has his own way both with broads and deeds. Jill St. John is an agent for a smuggling ring that attempts to smuggle a fortune in diamonds into the U.S., and Charles Gray the head of the organization with all the most advanced stages of nuclear energy at its disposal. Somewhere in the telling, diamonds are forgotten, never to be recalled, while Bond valiantly tries to save the world—one guesses.

The diamond caper takes Bond and his lovely companion to Las Vegas, where one of the funniest sequences in memory focuses on Bond trying to elude the police in downtown Vegas. Up-to-the-minute scientific gadget use is made again when Bond steals a moon machine at a simulated lunar testing-ground in a wild drive across the Nevada desert dunes.

1971: NOMINATION: Best Sound

•

DIAMONDS FOR BREAKFAST
1968, 102 mins, UK col
Dir Christopher Morahan ***Prod*** Carlo Ponti, Pierre Rouve ***Scr*** N. F. Simpson, Pierre Rouve, Ronald Harwood ***Ph*** Gerry Turpin ***Ed*** Peter Tanner ***Mus*** Norman Kaye ***Art*** Reece Pemberton
Act Marcello Mastroianni, Rita Tushingham, Elaine Taylor, Maggie Blye, Francesca Tu, Warren Mitchell (Paramount)

Potentially amusing, light-comedy crime idea is marred via uncertain steering by director Christopher Morahan, making his feature debut, and the clashing styles of the three scripters. Comedy is never fully developed and Marcello Mastroianni, debuting in British pix, lacks his usual elegant confidence.

Mastroianni is a London boutique owner who, happening to be fourth in succession to the Throne of All the Russians, hits on the idea of lifting the Imperial Jewels which he figures belong to him anyway. He rustles up a gang of eyeworthy and skillful young femme crooks, cons the authorities into letting his girls wear the rocks at a charity fashion show, but then runs into trouble as things go wrong.

Mastroianni is clearly not happy with his role in which he's too often the stooge, but the gals around him are good fun.

Femme star Rita Tushingham plays a nutty, Liverpool-Irish safecracker, who eventually gets the hero, but the part's skimpily developed and it's hardly Tushingham's league.

●

DIAMOND SKULLS
(US: DARK OBSESSION)
1990, 87 mins, UK Ⓥ col
Dir Nick Broomfield ***Prod*** Tim Bevan ***Scr*** Tim Rose Price ***Ph*** Michael Coulter ***Ed*** Rodney Holland ***Mus*** Hans Zimmer ***Art*** Jocelyn James
Act Gabriel Byrne, Amanda Donohoe, Michael Hordern, Judy Parfitt, Douglas Hodge, Sadie Frost (Film Four/British Screen)

A stylish melodrama about sex and violence among the British aristocracy, *Diamond Skulls* never quite delivers the punches it promises.

Gabriel Byrne is Sir Hugo, an ex-guards officer now in business. He has a lovely wife (the delectable Amanda Donohoe) of whom he's extremely jealous, suspecting her of having an affair with an Argentine business colleague.

One night, after a drunken dinner with his friends, Hugo is driving someone else's car when he hits a young woman, fatally injuring her. He and his friends leave her to die, though one of them, Jamie (Douglas Hodge), the car owner, wants to report the accident.

Jamie, who's having an affair with Hugo's sister Rebecca (Sadie Frost), threatens to spill the beans, and the friends are forced to silence him.

Donohoe gives another hot performance as the elegant Virginia whose actions belie her name. Veteran Michael Hordern is amusing as Hugo's titled father, though comedy actor Ian Carmichael is totally wasted as the family butler.

●

DIANE
1955, 110 mins, US Ⓥ ▭ col
Dir David Miller ***Prod*** Edwin H. Knopf ***Scr*** Christopher Isherwood ***Ph*** Robert Planck ***Ed*** John McSweeney, Jr. ***Mus*** Miklos Rozsa ***Art*** Cedric Gibbons, Hans Peters
Act Lana Turner, Pedro Armendariz, Roger Moore, Marisa Pavan, Cedric Hardwicke, Taina Elg (M-G-M)

Metro digs back into 16th-century France for this yarn about the countess Diane de Breze who became the most powerful woman at the court of King Henry II. Splendidly caparisonned production-wise, the first half is such old-fashioned costume drama as to draw laughs at unintended places, but picks up in interest during the later phases.

Overlength footage is highlighted by a tournament sequence in which the crossing of lances provides some exciting moments. Pageantry plays a large part in the production, with such well-known historic figures as King Francis I and Catherine de Medici appearing in order to motivate action which revolves around Henry II and his mistress.

John Erksine source story [*Diane de Poitiers*] is given wordy treatment by Christopher Isherwood screenplay, which David Miller's often deft direction finds difficult to bridge into actionful narrative despite romantic implications.

Lana Turner is sympathetic in her role, and Roger Moore delivers a good account of himself as Henry, uncertain first as the callow youth and gaining in stature after he becomes king. As Francis, Pedro Armendariz is strongly romantic and Marisa Pavan impresses as the unhappy Catherine.

●

DIARY OF A CHAMBERMAID
SEE: LE JOURNAL D'UNE FEMME DE CHAMBRE

●

DIARY OF A CHAMBERMAID
1946, 86 mins, US Ⓥ b/w
Dir Jean Renoir ***Prod*** Benedict Bogeaus, Burgess Meredith ***Scr*** Burgess Meredith ***Ph*** Lucien Andriot ***Ed*** James Smith ***Art*** Eugene Lourie
Act Paulette Goddard, Burgess Meredith, Hurd Hatfield, Francis Lederer, Judith Anderson (United Artists)

Diary is interesting from several angles, not the least of which is its adaptation from the original French. The transition is certainly the most important factor in drawing a line on its entertainment values. This is an odd yarn, the type done so well by the French—and so falteringly by almost anyone else. *Diary* in its American form has not nearly the intrigue, nor the color, suggested by the original French version, but it has names and an interest all its own.

It is the yarn of a chambermaid who, tiring of her station in life, vows to achieve wealth whoever the man. The men in her life aren't too sharply defined, nor especially interesting. Nor is the murder of the aging captain by the valet, so he can get money to marry the chambermaid, committed with any degree of climactic excitement.

There is Paulette Goddard, as the chambermaid with a gold glint to her orbs; Burgess Meredith, a psychopathic, aging army captain; Hurd Hatfield, the sensitive consumptive whom the girl loves, and Francis Lederer, the glowering valet-murderer.

●

DIARY OF A COUNTRY PRIEST
SEE: LE JOURNAL D'UN CURE DE CAMPAGNE

●

DIARY OF A HIT MAN
1992, 91 mins, US Ⓥ ⦿ col
Dir Roy London ***Prod*** Amin Q. Chaudhri ***Scr*** Kenneth Pressman ***Ph*** Yuri Sokol ***Ed*** Brian Smedley-Aston ***Mus*** Michel Colombier ***Art*** Stephen Hendrickson
Act Forest Whitaker, Sherilyn Fenn, Sharon Stone, Seymour Cassel, James Belushi, Lois Chiles (Continental/Vision)

An actors' piece invested with remarkable humanity by debuting director Roy London and a gifted cast, the modest $2.5 million *Diary of a Hit Man* transcends an unlikely scenario [expanded by Kenneth Pressman from his 45-minute play *Insider's Price*] to offer moments of cinema well worth savoring.

A hired killer (Forest Whitaker) is losing his taste for his work. He's hired to knock off the wife and child of a born-again commodities broker (Lewis Smith) who claims his wife's a drug addict and the infant is a crack baby and not his. The reluctant killer breaks professional-conduct rules by conversing with the victim (Sherilyn Fenn)—and discovers the broker lied. Long scene that follows is the central conceit of the piece: that a killer and his intended victim could save each other.

Fenn is a revelation in the substance and texture she brings to the role. Whitaker invests his beleaguered hitman with mesmerizing depth and unpolished reality, aided by abundant voiceovers elucidating his thoughts.

London, a writer and acting coach whose pupils include Fenn and Sharon Stone (included in the cast as Fenn's tarty and obnoxious sister), demonstrates firm control of the medium and a knack for engaging flourishes.

●

DIARY OF A MAD HOUSEWIFE
1970, 85 mins, US Ⓥ col
Dir Frank Perry ***Prod*** Frank Perry ***Scr*** Eleanor Perry ***Ph*** Gerald Hirschfeld ***Ed*** Sidney Katz ***Art*** Peter Dohanos
Act Richard Benjamin, Frank Langella, Carrie Snodgress, Lorraine Cullen, Frannie Michel, Lee Addoms (Universal)

An engrossing story of the disintegration of a modern loveless marriage, with Richard Benjamin and Frank Langella effectively portraying the inadequacies of husband and lover, respectively, and Carrie Snodgress as a frustrated, sensitive wife.

Story line [from a novel by Sue Kaufman] has Snodgress reach the breaking point under a marriage to Benjamin that has become sated with his selfish material values. She turns to Langella as an afternoon lover, only to find him just as bad.

Benjamin, who is top-billed, is saddled with the most unsympathetic role as a disenchanted, post-JFK idealist now determined to rise in the middle-class flotsam, he is excellent in maintaining a character so delineated that one wants to throw something at the screen.

1970: NOMINATION: Best Actress (Carrie Snodgress)

●

DIARY OF ANNE FRANK, THE
1959, 170 mins, US Ⓥ ⦿ ▭ b/w
Dir George Stevens ***Prod*** George Stevens ***Scr*** Frances Goodrich, Albert Hackett ***Ph*** William C. Mellor, Jack Cardiff ***Ed*** David Bretherton, Robert Swink, William Mace ***Mus*** Alfred Newman ***Art*** Lyle R. Wheeler, George W. Davis
Act Millie Perkins, Joseph Schildkraut, Shelley Winters, Richard Beymer, Lou Jacobi, Diane Baker (20th Century-Fox)

The Diary of Anne Frank, first published in its original form [as *Anne Frank: The Diary of a Young Girl*], then made into a play by Frances Goodrich and Albert Hackett, is a film of often extraordinary quality. It manages, within the framework of a tense and tragic situation, to convey the beauty of a young and inquiring spirit that soars beyond the cramped confinement of the Frank family's hideout in Nazi-occupied Amsterdam.

And yet, with all its technical perfection, the inspired direction and the sensitivity with which many of the scenes are handled, *Diary* is simply too long. Everything possible is done to keep the action moving within its narrow, cluttered space, and a remarkable balance is achieved between stark terror and comedy relief, yet there are moments when the film lags and the dialog becomes forced. Unlike the play, the picture leaves too little to the imagination.

Millie Perkins plays Anne. It is her first film role and she turns in a charming and captivating performance. Whether Perkins, a model, is absolutely right for the part is open to question. It's certainly difficult to accept her as a 13-year-old, which was Anne's age at the time the Franks went into hiding.

As father Otto Frank, Joseph Schildkraut repeats his marvelous performance on the stage. There is dignity and wisdom in this man, a deep sadness, too, and a love for Anne that makes the scene of his return to the hideout after the war a moment full of pain and compassion.

As the Van Daan couple, Shelley Winters and Lou Jacobi come up with vivid characterizations that score on all levels. As young Peter Van Daan, Richard Beymer is touchingly sincere and perfectly matched with Perkins, a boy who discovers in the girl the depth he has been seeking in himself. Diane Baker's sensitive face is pleasing in the comparatively small role of Margot Frank.

1959: Best Supp. Actress (Shelley Winters), B&W Cinematography, B&W Art Direction

NOMINATIONS: Best Picture, Director, Supp. Actor (Ed Wynn), B&W Costume Design, Scoring of a Dramatic Picture

●

DICK
1999, 95 mins, US Ⓥ ⦿ col
Dir Andrew Fleming ***Prod*** Gale Anne Hurd ***Scr*** Andrew Fleming, Sheryl Longin ***Ph*** Alexander Gruszynski ***Ed*** Mia Goldman ***Mus*** John Debney ***Art*** Barbara Dunphy
Act Kirsten Dunst, Michelle Williams, Jim Breuer, Will Ferrell, Dave Foley, Teri Garr (Pacific Western/Phoenix/Columbia)

This audacious, imaginative political comedy will have Watergate buffs in particular, and baby boomers in general, laughing loud and long. In his fourth feature, director and co-writer Andrew Fleming gleefully throws two teenybopper girls into the vortex of the scandal and extends the possibilities to their most outrageous extremes.

Pic plunks its innocents down in the middle of a legendary historical event much the way *Some Like It Hot* placed its hapless heroes at the scene of the St. Valentine's Day Massacre.

Ditsy teens Betsy Jobs (Kirsten Dunst) and Arlene Lorenzo (Michelle Williams), while sneaking through the garage of the latter's apartment in Washington's Watergate complex one night in 1972 to mail a submission to the "Win a Date with Bobby Sherman" contest, happen upon a certain G. Gordon Liddy (Harry Shearer) and some others up to no good.

When they're on a school tour of the White House, the girls pick up a CREEP hit list that's been stuck to Liddy's shoe. He scowls "they know too much" and has the girls pulled in for interrogation. They then meet Nixon himself (Dan Hedaya), who placates them by giving them the jobs of official White House dog walkers. Thus begins the girls' unlikely access to the upper echelons of power.

If the film is devastating toward the White House crew, it is even more scathing toward Woodward and Bernstein, and this gives the picture a real charge. Only demerits are a tendency to let some sequences play out a tad too long and a depressingly lackluster visual style to the Toronto-lensed production. Cast is solid.

●

DICK TRACY
1945, 61 mins, US Ⓥ ⦿ b/w
Dir William Berke ***Prod*** Herman Schlom ***Scr*** Eric Taylor ***Ph*** Frank Redman ***Ed*** Ernie Leadlay ***Mus*** Roy Webb ***Art*** Albert S. D'Agostino, Ralph Berges
Act Morgan Conway, Anne Jeffreys, Mike Mazurki, Jane Greer, Mickey Kuhn (RKO)

Chester Gould's comic strip lends itself handily to screen melodrama.

Morgan Conway takes on the title role, while Anne Jeffreys is seen as Tess, the detective's girlfriend. Both add plenty of movement to the plot.

Plot has Tracy chasing down a crazy killer tagged Splitface, so called because of a hideous scar running diagonally across his face. Mike Mazurki, as Splitface, is seeking revenge on those who sent him to prison years before, and manages to do in three victims before Tracy calls a halt. Plot is conventional murder melodrama, and is played straight to get over. William Berke's direction keeps the pace fast all the way.

●

DICK TRACY
1990, 103 mins, US Ⓥ ⦿ col
Dir Warren Beatty ***Prod*** Warren Beatty ***Scr*** Jim Cash, Jack Epps, Jr. ***Ph*** Vittorio Storaro ***Ed*** Richard Marks ***Mus*** Danny Elfman ***Art*** Richard Sylbert
Act Warren Beatty, Charlie Korsmo, Glenne Headly, Madonna, Al Pacino, Dustin Hoffman (Touchstone)

Though it looks ravishing, Warren Beatty's longtime pet project is a curiously remote, uninvolving film. Beatty and his collaborators have created a boldly stylized 1930s urban milieu that captures the comic strip's quirky, angled mood, while dazzling the eye with deep primary colors.

Beatty—ultra-stylish in yellow raincoat and snap-brim hat, black suit, red tie and crisp white shirts—is so cool he appears frozen. Torn between Madonna's allure—she's costumed in black & white to look like a steamy, low-rent version of Josef von Sternberg's Marlene Dietrich—and the more low-key beauty and sweetness of Glenne Headly's redhead Tess Trueheart, Beatty simply sits there and mopes, occasionally rousing himself into bursts of action.

A large part of what fun there is in the pic comes from the inventive character makeup by John Caglione, Jr. and Doug Drexler, who mostly succeed in the difficult task of creating live-action cartoon figures. Dustin Hoffman takes an eerie turn as Mumbles, R. G. Armstrong is chilling as Pruneface, Paul Sorvino hilariously disgusting as Lips, William Forsythe spooky as Flattop.

Al Pacino, virtually runs away with the show in a sizable role as Tracy's nemesis, the Richard III-like hunchbacked villain Big Boy Caprice. His manic energy lifts the overall torpor. Equally fine is young street urchin Charlie Korsmo who, together with the lovely Headly, gives the film a necessary counter-balance of normality.

1990: Best Art Direction, Song ("Sooner or Later"), Makeup

NOMINATIONS: Best Supp. Actor (Al Pacino), Cinematography, Costume Design, Sound

•

DICK TRACY'S DILEMMA
1947, 60 mins, US Ⓥ ⦿ b/w
Dir John Rawlins ***Prod*** Herman Schlom ***Scr*** Robert Stephen Brode ***Ph*** Frank Redman ***Ed*** Marvin Coil ***Mus*** Paul Sawtell ***Art*** Albert S. D'Agostino, Lucius O. Croxton
Act Ralph Byrd, Lyle Latell, Kay Christopher, Jack Lambert, Ian Keith, Jimmy Conlin (RKO)

This entry in RKO's Dick Tracy series draws on gruesome character of The Claw as menacing opponent of the pen-and-ink detective. Thrills are backed up with good budget production values.

Ralph Byrd is an okay Tracy, with enough resemblance to the fictional character to carry off the role. Jack Lambert gives expert study to his role as The Claw, grotesque character right out of the Chester Gould strip. Plot moves along under John Rawlins's directorial wing to show how Tracy busts up a fur-stealing racket that's an insurance fraud.

Lyle Latell is the strip Pat. Kay Christopher is Tess and Ian Keith chews scenery as the flamboyant Vitamin Flintheart. Bernadene Hayes shows up well in a brief spot as Longshot Lillie. Jimmy Conlin does an excellent character role as Sightless, pencil-peddler who aids Tracy.

•

DICK TRACY VS. CUEBALL
1946, 62 mins, US Ⓥ ⦿ b/w
Dir Gordon Douglas ***Prod*** Herman Schlom ***Scr*** Dana Lussier, Robert E. Kent ***Ph*** George E. Diskant ***Ed*** Philip Martin ***Mus*** Constantin Bakaleinikoff ***Art*** Albert S. D'Agostino, Lucius O. Croxton
Act Morgan Conway, Anne Jeffreys, Dick Wessel (RKO)

Hot action celluloid that's bang-up and bang-bang from start to finish. RKO, which assumed screen rights to Chester Gould's cartoon after Republic finished using it as basis for a serial, turns out these hour-long features on the "B" corner of its lot, but gives them first-class production dress. Scripting is simply designed, but tightly welded while topnotch direction keeps the accelerator pedal pressed to the floor throughout.

Following the strip closely on essential points, the film is peopled with a rogue's gallery of grotesque cutthroats, degenerates, and slick criminal masterminds who, of course, are outwitted and outslugged by the square-chinned dick.

Story revolves around Dick Tracy's efforts to sniff out a nest of jewel thieves operating through a blind of respectable dealers. Cueball, a brutal looking hombre who's been double-crossed by the gang, knocks off most of them himself with Tracy left only with the job of finishing Cueball.

Portrayal of Tracy by Morgan Conway is straightforward thesping with more emphasis on direct action than any facial expression. Dick Wessell makes an ominous strangler as Cueball while mild romantic interest Tess Truehart, is handled competently by Anne Jeffreys.

•

DICTATOR, THE
1935, 86 mins, UK b/w
Dir Victor Saville, Alfred Santell ***Prod*** Ludovico Toeplitz ***Scr*** Benn W. Levy ***Ph*** Franz Planer ***Ed*** Paul Weatherwax ***Mus*** Karol Rathaus ***Art*** Andre Andrejev
Act Clive Brook, Madeleine Carroll, Emlyn Williams, Alfred Drayton, Nicholas Hannen, Helen Hays (Toeplitz)

This is one of the most lavish costume pictures that has come out of England, supposed to have cost $500,000. Sets and costumes give the impression of tremendous royal wealth; entire film takes place in gorgeous palaces. One banquet scene, with ballet music, is as good as anything ever seen on the screen.

Picture has other fine qualities, too. Clive Brook does an authoriative bit of acting and imposes lots of femme appeal; Madeleine Carroll is attractive; Emlyn Williams is a splendid young debauchee; and Helen Hays (not the American actress) a tough old queen mother. There is humor, particularly in the earlier scenes.

Trouble is with the story [by Ludovico Toeplitz]. It's a love tale of a beautiful queen and an ambitious young man—not developed in such a way as to be really dramatic.

Setting is 18th-century Danish royalty. It opens after the royal wedding, and shows the king (Williams) trying in vain to get into the bedroom of the queen (Carroll), whom he only met the day before. This, like the rest of the first dozen or so sequences, is effective. Then the king beats it to Hamburg to have a good time. Struensee, a Hamburg doctor (Brook), makes an impressive entry. He's called to attend the king, incognito, who has passed out after too much wine and women, and he wins the young man's favor by bringing him back to life unceremoniously. Struensee, taken to Denmark, becomes the power behind the throne. In this he replaces the queen mother, whowith her courtiers, sets out to get him.

•

DIE! DIE! MY DARLING!
SEE: FANATIC

•

DIE HARD
1988, 131 mins, US Ⓥ ⦿ ▭ col
Dir John McTiernan ***Prod*** Lawrence Gordon, Joel Silver ***Scr*** Jeb Stuart, Steven E. de Souza ***Ph*** Jan De Bont ***Ed*** Frank J. Urioste, John F. Link ***Mus*** Michael Kamen ***Art*** Jackson De Govia
Act Bruce Willis, Alan Rickman, Alexander Godunov, Bonnie Bedelia, Reginald VelJohnson, William Atherton (Gordon-Silver/20th Century-Fox)

Die Hard is as high tech, rock hard, and souped up as an action film can be. It's a suspenser [based on the novel *Nothing Lasts Forever* by Roderick Thorp] pitting a lone wolf cop against a group of terrorists that have taken over a high-rise office tower.

Bruce Willis plays John McClane, an overworked New York policeman who flies into Los Angeles at Christmas to visit his two daughters and estranged wife Holly (Bonnie Bedelia).

Planning a rather different holiday agenda are the terrorists led by Hans Gruber (Alan Rickman). The dastardly dozen invade the plush 30th floor offices of Nakatomi Corp. during its Christmas party and hold the employees hostage as a computer whiz cracks a code that will put the mainly German bad boys in possession of $600 million in negotiable bonds.

Slipping out of the party in the nick of time with nothing but his handgun, Willis is the fly in the ointment of the criminals' plans, picking off one, then two more of the scouts sent on pest control missions.

Beefed up considerably for his role, Willis is amiable enough in the opening stretch, but overdoes the grimacing and heavy emoting later on. The cooler and more humorous he is the better. Rickman has a giddy good time but sometimes goes over the top as the henchman.

1988: NOMINATIONS: Best Editing, Sound, Sound Effects Editing, Visual Effects

•

DIE HARD 2
1990, 124 mins, US Ⓥ ⦿ ▭ col
Dir Renny Harlin ***Prod*** Laurence Gordon, Joel Silver, Charles Gordon ***Scr*** Steven E. de Souza, Doug Richardson ***Ph*** Oliver Wood ***Ed*** Stuart Baird ***Mus*** Michael Kamen ***Art*** John Vallone
Act Bruce Willis, Bonnie Bedelia, William Atherton, Franco Nero, William Sadler, Reginald VelJohnson (Gordon-Silver/20th Century-Fox)

Die Hard 2 lacks the inventiveness of the original, but compensates with relentless action. The film [based on the novel *58 Minutes* by Walter Wager] works for the most part as sheer entertainment, a full-color comic book with shootouts, brutal fistfights, and bloodletting aplenty. Minding his own business, John McClane (Bruce Willis) is in D.C.'s Dulles Airport to pick up wife Holly (Bonnie Bedelia) to spend Christmas with her folks. They've reconciled since the events in *Die Hard* and the Gotham cop has joined the LAPD. Unlike most domestic flights, the story takes off immediately, as terrorists seize control of the airport to free a Manuel Noriegaesque foreign dictator (Franco Nero) being transported to the U.S.

Director Renny Harlin does a credible job with such a daunting large-scale assignment. But Harlin lacks *Die Hard* director John McTiernan's vicelike grip on action and strays into areas that derail certain scenes, using slow-motion in early sequences and sapping their energy.

•

DIE HARD WITH A VENGEANCE
1995, 128 mins, US Ⓥ ⦿ ▭ col
Dir John McTiernan ***Prod*** John McTiernan, Michael Tadross ***Scr*** Jonathan Hensleigh ***Ph*** Peter Menzies ***Ed*** John Wright ***Mus*** Michael Kamen ***Art*** Jackson DeGovia
Act Bruce Willis, Jeremy Irons, Samuel L. Jackson, Graham Greene, Colleen Camp, Larry Bryggman (Cinergi/20th Century-Fox)

An over-inflated mishmash that compels the audience to sift through a lot of rubble for the few requisite thrills, this second *Die Hard* sequel leaves a lot of creative wreckage in its wake. Despite the pumped-up volume and budget, this is certainly the least accomplished of the three movies, tracing a scattered plotline that's at times virtually indecipherable.

Even the premise—with Jeremy Irons as as the terrorist brother of the late Hans Gruber, the character played deliciously in the first film by Alan Rickman—doesn't provide much punch. Movie also benefits only sparingly from its *Lethal Weapon*–like rapport between Bruce Willis's John McClane and a Harlem shopkeeper (portrayed by the ubiquitous Samuel L. Jackson) unwillingly drawn into the action, as their bickering eventually grows tiresome.

These shortcomings emerge after a promising start, with Simon (Irons) blowing up a department store, then sending McClane—down on his luck, nearly alcoholic and on suspension—on a series of errands to prevent further explosions.

By happenstance he meets Zeus (Jackson), and the two take a hellbent ride through New York to prevent a subway explosion in perhaps the pic's crowning technical achievement. So far, so good, but then the pic degenerates into an improbable, confusing series of chases and an overly involved heist that takes far too long to set up.

The original script by Jonathan Hensleigh wasn't initially written for the series, and some of the incongruity between the property and the necessities of such a huge action yarn shows. Irons, for example, proves a snide but relatively uninspired villain, and the movie lacks the self-contained simplicity of the earlier films by failing to settle on a venue, instead scampering all over town. Willis doesn't add much to his by now familiar combination of wise-cracking and heroism as McClane.

•

DIFFERENT STORY, A
1978, 106 mins, US Ⓥ col
Dir Paul Aaron ***Prod*** Alan Belkin ***Scr*** Henry Olek ***Ph*** Philip Lathrop ***Ed*** Lynn McCallon ***Mus*** David Frank ***Art*** Lee Poll
Act Perry King, Meg Foster, Valerie Curtin, Peter Donat, Richard Bull, Barbara Collentine (Peterson)

A Different Story certainly is. Stars Perry King and Meg Foster are excellent as a couple whose budding romance has just one problem: they are both gay. This first class production's only—but serious—flaw is a Henry Olek script that begins with brilliant cleverness but dissolves by fade-out into formulaic banality.

The early genius in the script is the casual springing of the basic situation. Real estate agent Stella (Foster) discovers squatter tenant Albert (King), an illegal alien. She takes King home to help him out; he thinks she is straight, only to be as surprised as the audience when date Chris (Lisa James)—and later irate lover Phyllis (Valerie Curtin)—arrive.

The couple evolve a sincere friendship, and Stella marries Albert to prevent deportation. But halfway through the film, the two accidentally wind up having sex; they like it, get serious, have a child, and the rest of the film is not much better than an updated TV sitcom with superficial marital problems and resolutions.

Nevertheless, save for this severe script problem, director and performers have done admirable work.

•

DIGGSTOWN
(UK: MIDNIGHT STING)
1992, 97 mins, US Ⓥ ⊙ col
Dir Michael Ritchie ***Prod*** Robert Schaffel ***Scr*** Steven McKay ***Ph*** Gerry Fisher ***Ed*** Don Zimmerman ***Mus*** James Newton Howard ***Art*** Steve Hendrickson
Act James Woods, Louis Gossett, Jr., Bruce Dern, Oliver Platt, Heather Graham, Randall "Tex" Cobb (M-G-M/Eclectic)

Blending elements of *Rocky* and *The Sting*, this crowd-teaser mixes it up with boxing, revenge, and salty one-liners that should satisfy audiences.

James Woods demonstrates his trademark intensity along with a comic flair as a just-paroled hustler who sets up a big-money boxing match, pitting his ringer "Honey" Roy Palmer (Louis Gossett, Jr.) against any 10 men from the burg of Diggstown.

Like *The Sting*, the target is truly despicable, and few can fit that description more capably than Bruce Dern, whose character stole the town from its citizens and rubs out anyone who crosses him.

All the trademark flourishes are there, including a couple of murders for motivation, a beautiful woman (Heather Graham) of little narrative consequence, a tenuous relationship between Dern and his son (a suddenly quite grown-up Thomas Wilson Brown), and Woods and Gossett's scam-gone-wrong history, leading to ample good-natured bickering.

The boxing sequences are compelling, and Gossett convincingly comes across as an aging brawler with a potent right cross.

•

DILLINGER
1973, 107 mins, US Ⓥ ⊙ col
Dir John Milius ***Prod*** Buzz Feitshans ***Scr*** John Milius ***Ph*** Jules Brenner ***Ed*** Fred R. Feitshans, Jr. ***Mus*** Barry DeVorzon ***Art*** Trevor Williams
Act Warren Oates, Ben Johnson, Michelle Phillips, Cloris Leachman, Harry Dean Stanton, Richard Dreyfuss (American International)

The violent life and death of John Dillinger is graphically portrayed. With Warren Oates in the title role, the screenplay captures the various highlights of the killer's short-lived career as Public Enemy No. 1.

Oates is a good physical choice for role of the bank robber and killer who blazed his way to notoriety during 13 months in 1933 and 1934. Less known to the public was Melvin Purvis, the FBI man responsible for Dillinger's death in a Chicago alley, but as delineated by Ben Johnson he is as forceful a figure.

Actually, the tenor of the film is the FBI hunt of Dillinger; Johnson acts as offscreen commentator as well as acting on screen. Pace is sometimes reduced during events sandwiched inbetween actual gunfire sequences of Dillinger's career, but there can be no criticism of Milius's ability to keep such action sequences at top-heat.

Michelle Phillips, making her film bow after having been a member of *The Mamas and The Papas* singing group, scores heavily as Dillinger's girlfriend.

•

DIMANCHES DE VILLE D'AVRAY, LES
(SUNDAYS AND CYBELE)
1962, 110 mins, France Ⓥ ▭ b/w
Dir Serge Bourguignon ***Scr*** Antoine Tudal, Bernard Eschasseriaux, Serge Bourguignon ***Ph*** Henri Decae ***Ed*** Leonid Azar
Act Hardy Kruger, Nicole Courcel, Patricia Gozzi, Daniel Ivernel, Andre Oumansky (Terra/Fides/Orsay/Trocadero)

A basically dramatic tale [from Bernard Eschasseriaux's novel] of loneliness and mental difficulty is treated in a muted, dreamy style. This makes a slow but pictorially impressive film due to new director Serge Bourguignon's feeling for imagery and style. But it also leads to some preciosity.

An amnesiac pilot, who thinks he killed a little girl during the French-Indonesian War, has blotted it out and is living in a small town with a nurse who has fallen in love with him. One day he sees a little girl being put into a local orphan by a father who runs off. He finds a letter the man has dropped stating he will never be back. Later the pilot wanders into the orphanage and takes the girl for a walk.

They immediately take to each other and she passes him off as her visiting father. Every Sunday their relationship and love grow, but complications lead to tragedy.

Technical qualities are fine. Hardy Kruger is good as the man, while Patricia Gozzi sometimes lacks the spontaneity of childhood. In spite of a tendency to overdo effects, this platonic and spiritual Lolita-like pic marks Bourguignon as a director to be heard from.

1962: Best Foreign Language Film

•

DIM SUM
A LITTLE BIT OF HEART
1985, 85 mins, US Ⓥ ⊙ col
Dir Wayne Wang ***Prod*** Tom Sternberg, Wayne Wang, Danny Yung ***Scr*** Terrel Seltzer ***Ph*** Michael Chin ***Ed*** Ralph Wikke ***Mus*** Todd Boekelheide ***Art*** Danny Yung
Act Laureen Chew, Kim Chew, Victor Wong, Ida F.O. Chung, Cora Miao, John Nishio (CIM)

Dim Sum offers up a few charming observations about cultural differences among assorted generations of Chinese Americans, but the dramatic situations are so underplayed as to be mostly ineffectual.

Taking a cue from countless earlier Asian family pictures that have dwelt upon the subject of family traditions and the responsibilities of children for their aging parents, director Wayne Wang and scripter Terrel Seltzer [working from an idea by them and Laureen Chew] have focused upon the relationship between a traditional Chinese woman in her 60s and her 30-ish daughter who, unlike her brother and sister, is not yet hitched.

A great deal of the sought-after humor stems from the "So when are you gonna get married?" attitudes of family friends.

The authenticity of Wang's depiction of San Francisco's Chinese need not be questioned, but the attitudes expressed are predictable in the extreme and are invested with little sense of dramatic urgency.

•

DINER
1982, 110 mins, US Ⓥ ⊙ col
Dir Barry Levinson ***Prod*** Jerry Weintraub ***Scr*** Barry Levinson ***Ph*** Peter Sova ***Ed*** Stu Linder ***Mus*** Bruce Brody, Ivan Kral ***Art*** Leon Harris
Act Steve Guttenberg, Daniel Stern, Mickey Rourke, Kevin Bacon, Timothy Daly, Ellen Barkin (M-G-M/United Artists)

It's easy to tell that *Diner* was chiefly conceived and executed by a writer. In his directorial debut, Barry Levinson takes great pains to establish characters.

The year is 1959 and the diner is in Baltimore, although the action could take place in any American city. Using the diner as the proverbial street corner hangout, Levinson centers on a close-knit group of guys in their early 20s and how their early adult lives are taking shape. In this case, there's lots to worry about. Among the characters is a young gambler just footsteps ahead of his loanshark; a thinking grad student whose pregnant career-wise girlfriend won't get married; a compulsive husband unhappy with his new wife; a handsome rich kid who gets drunk to escape his cold family; and a closet "virgin" who won't marry his girlfriend until she can pass a football quiz.

Steve Guttenberg, Daniel Stern, Mickey Rourke, Kevin Bacon, Paul Reiser, and Timothy Daly are terrific as the friends as are Ellen Barkin and Kathryn Dowling as the two females involved with different group members.

1982: NOMINATION: Best Original Screenplay

•

DINNER AT EIGHT
1933, 110 mins, US Ⓥ ⊙ b/w
Dir George Cukor ***Prod*** David O. Selznick ***Scr*** Frances Marion, Herman J. Mankiewicz, Donald Ogden Stewart ***Ph*** William Daniels ***Ed*** Ben Lewis ***Mus*** William Axt ***Art*** Hobe Erwin, Fred Hope
Act Marie Dressler, John Barrymore, Wallace Beery, Jean Harlow, Lionel Barrymore, Lee Tracy (M-G-M)

Play [by George S. Kaufman and Edna Ferber] was a fine drama on the stage and has been translated to the screen in workmanlike manner, changes mostly being in the interest of condensation. For this reason, the below stairs action among the servants has been deleted and the finish has been slightly changed to give a gag line to Marie Dressler. The latter being a first-rate device, handing the curtain to the principal two comedy characters—the ancient stage belle and the Jean Harlow role—who have been shrewdly emphasized in the film version.

The story grips from beginning to end with never-relaxing tension, its sombre moments relieved by lighter touches into a fascinating mosaic for nearly two hours. The play is a more searching document than *Grand Hotel* but not quite its equal in dramatic vividness.

Acting honors go to Dressler and Harlow, the latter giving an astonishingly well-balanced treatment of Kitty, the canny little hussy who hooks a hard-bitten and unscrupulous millionaire and then makes him lay down and roll over.

Role of Carlotta doesn't find Dressler in her popular vein; it's a dressed-up part for one thing. But she handles this politer assignment with poise and aplomb.

John Barrymore's playing of the has-been picture star is a stark, uncompromising treatment of a pretty thorough-going blackguard and ingrate. Billie Burke is eminently suited for the role of a fluttering society matron immersed in social trivialities while tragedy stalks unknowing through her home. Wallace Beery is again at home as the millionaire vulgarian, made to order for his type.

•

DINOSAUR
2000, 82 mins, US Ⓥ ⊙ col
Dir Ralph Zondag, Eric Leighton ***Prod*** Pam Marsden, Baker Bloodworth ***Scr*** John Harrison, Robert Nelson Jacobs ***Ph*** Steven Douglas Smith, Dave Hardberger ***Ed*** H. Lee Peterson ***Mus*** James Newton Howard ***Art*** Walter P. Martishius (Walt Disney)

Dinosaur is an eye-popping visual spectacle that serves up a vivid picture of what the planet might have looked like when reptiles ruled the earth. Its almost grotesquely touchy-feely take on prehistoric life will please vegans and compassionate anti-Darwinians more than it will cinematic carnivores looking for some dramatic meat. This technical marvel, at a budget of somewhere between $150 million to $200 million, must qualify as the most expensive film of all time on a cost-per-minute basis.

The startling visions of the first few minutes alone—a ferocious toothsome attack and a flight over huge herds of dinosaurs inhabiting magnificent actual landscapes—are enough to thrill any viewer as well as to serve notice that there's never been anything quite like this before. The visual splendors continue, to be sure, across the pacy 75 minutes of story time (seven minutes of credits follow). But it's also the case that, somewhere around halfway through, you begin to get used to the film's pictorial wondrousness—to take it for granted, even—and start to realize that the characters and story are exceedingly mundane, unsurprising and pre-programmed. Directors Ralph Zondag and Eric Leighton seem afraid to show anything that will be the least bit disturbing or upsetting to anybody.

The various creatures are brilliantly rendered; they interact credibly with one another and are integrated seamlessly into the backdrops. But as realistic and expressive as they are, they don't engage the emotions any more directly than have many more cartoonishly rendered animated characters in the past. Vocalizations of the main characters—D. B. Sweeney as Aladar, Ossie Davis, Alfre Woodard, Max Casella and Hayden Panettiere as the lemur family, Samuel E. Wright as Kron, Julianna Margulies at Neera, Joan Plowright as Baylene, Della Reese as Eeema and Peter Siragusa as Kron's cohort Bruton—are uniformly lively and entertaining.

•

DIP HUT SEUNG HUNG
(THE KILLER)
1989, 110 mins, Hong Kong Ⓥ ⊙ col
Dir John Woo ***Prod*** Tsui Hark (exec.) ***Scr*** John Woo ***Ph*** Wong Wing-hang, Peter Pau ***Ed*** Fan Kung-ming ***Mus*** Lowell Lo ***Art*** Luk Man-wah
Act Chow Yun-fat, Danny Lee, Sally Yeh, Tsang Kong, Chu Kong, Shing Fui-on (Film Workshop/Magnum)

This extremely violent and superbly made actioner demonstrates the tight grasp that director John Woo has on the crime meller genre, and his ability to twist the form into surprisingly satisfying shapes. The picture creeps up on an audience. Melodramatic from the start, it finally goes over the top to deliver a solid emotional punch.

The Killer is a buddy-buddy outing with a vengeance. Male bonding between a maverick hitman (Chow Yun-fat) and a disaffected cop (Danny Lee) is pushed to almost homoerotic extremes.

The plot itself is all too familiar. The cold-blooded assassin is doublecrossed by underworld bosses after knocking off a drug kingpin. The determined cop, on the outs with his superiors, has to catch his man or else.

Chow, a Hong Kong actor of considerable marquee value, is adept at combining pathos and chilling moral callousness. His soft underside is exposed when the plot has him falling for a cabaret singer (Sally Yeh) accidently blinded during a hit. Lee displays appealingly boyish determination and physical grace as the cop.

•

DIPLOMATIC COURIER
1952, 98 mins, US Ⓥ b/w
Dir Henry Hathaway *Prod* Casey Robinson *Scr* Casey Robinson, Liam O'Brien *Ph* Lucien Ballard *Ed* James B. Clark *Mus* Sol Kaplan *Art* Lyle Wheeler, John DeCuir
Act Tyrone Power, Patricia Neal, Hildegarde Neff, Stephen McNally, Karl Malden, James Millican (20th Century-Fox)

A top-notch espionage yarn based on Peter Cheyney's novel, *Sinister Errand*, the script has Tyrone Power playing a diplomatic courier who is used by a counter intelligence division to uncover the whereabouts of a missing Soviet timetable for invasion of Yugoslavia.

Power, the state department's top postman, is sent to Salzburg to pick up vital secret papers from James Millican. At the arranged meeting place in a railway station, Millican refuses contact and is later killed. Aware the Soviets did not get the papers, Power is assigned to trace Hildegarde Neff, a Soviet agent in belief she will have some clue to the mystery. Power is hampered in his work by Patricia Neal, seemingly a slightly nutty American tourist.

•

DIRIGIBLE
1931, 100 mins, US b/w
Dir Frank Capra *Prod* [uncredited] *Scr* Jo Swerling, Dorothy Howell *Ph* Joseph Walker *Ed* Maurice Wright *Mus* [uncredited] *Art* [uncredited]
Act Jack Holt, Ralph Graves, Fay Wray, Hobart Bosworth, Roscoe Karns, Clarence Muse (Columbia)

The big scene is a crack-up of the dirigible in the air; more interesting even than the explosion of the dirigible in *Hell's Angels*. The remainder of *Dirigible* is unconvincing, before or after the crack-up, the latter occurring about midway.

After the crack-up comes the South Pole expedition by plane and dirigible, the latter to rescue the survivors. As Ralph Graves piloting the airplane to the pole is ready to return, the explorer aboard wants to drop an American flag to mark the spot. Graves says no, he will land and let the explorer do it in person. "See that snow," says Graves, "it's perfect for landing," and he lands, right on his neck with the others while the plane burns. After that it's homeward bound, 6,000 miles away and getting there at the rate of seven miles daily. Trudging, starving, dying.

Of the actors, Fay Wray looks the best, earnestly sincere as the wife of Graves' glory-seeking aviator. Graves early in the film is light enough to give the zest the story [by Commander Frank Wilber Wead, USN] needs. Jack Holt is the dirigible's commander and pal of Graves.

•

DIRTY DANCING
1987, 97 mins, US Ⓥ ⊙ col
Dir Emile Ardolino *Prod* Linda Gottlieb *Scr* Eleanor Bergstein *Ph* Jeff Jur *Ed* Peter C. Frank *Mus* John Morris *Art* David Chapman
Act Patrick Swayze, Jennifer Grey, Jerry Orbach, Cynthia Rhodes, Jack Weston, Jane Brucker (Vestron)

It's summer 1963, and college kids carry copies of *The Fountainhead* in their back pockets and condoms in their wallets. It's also a time for *Dirty Dancing* and, in her 17th summer, at a Borscht Belt resort, Baby Houseman (Jennifer Grey) learns how to do it in this skin-deep but inoffensive teen-throb pic designed to titillate teenage girls.

A headstrong girl bucking for a career in Peace Corps, Baby gets an education in life and loses her innocence when she befriends a young dancer (Cynthia Rhodes) in need of an abortion. She also gets involved with the hotel's maverick dance instructor, Johnny Castle (Patrick Swayze).

Good production values, some nice dance sequences, and a likable performance by Grey make the film more than watchable, especially for those acquainted with the Jewish tribal mating rituals that go on in the Catskill Mountain resorts. Swayze's character is played too soft to be convincing.

1987: Best Song ("I've Had the Time of My Life")

•

DIRTY DINGUS MAGEE
1970, 90 mins, US Ⓥ ▭ col
Dir Burt Kennedy *Prod* Burt Kennedy *Scr* Tom and Frank Waldman *Ph* Harry Stradling, Jr. *Ed* William B. Gulick *Mus* Jeff Alexander *Art* George W. Davis
Act Frank Sinatra, George Kennedy, Anne Jackson, Lois Nettleton, Jack Elam, Michele Carey (M-G-M)

Dirty Dingus Magee emerges as a good period western comedy, covering the spectrum from satire through double entendre to low slapstick, starring Frank Sinatra and George Kennedy as double-crossing buddies.

Burt Kennedy produced and directed a script [from the novel *The Ballad of Dingus Magee* by David Markson] which is loaded with effective vignette, and a strong supporting cast.

Sinatra plays an ambiable roustabout, always eager but never quite able to satisfy the unending passions of Indian maiden Michele Carey. When old pal Kennedy shows up en route to California, Sinatra robs him, thus setting up the basic, running, plot line of multiple compound double cross. The gag subplots move along at a good pace.

•

DIRTY DOZEN, THE
1967, 149 mins, US Ⓥ ⊙ ▭ col
Dir Robert Aldrich *Prod* Kenneth Hyman *Scr* Nunnally Johnson, Lukas Heller *Ph* Edward Scaife *Ed* Michael Luciano *Mus* Frank DeVol *Art* W. E. Hutchinson
Act Lee Marvin, Ernest Borgnine, Charles Bronson, Jim Brown, John Cassavetes, George Kennedy (M-G-M)

The Dirty Dozen is an exciting Second World War pre–D-Day drama about 12 condemned soldier-prisoners who are rehabilitated to serve with distinction. Lee Marvin heads a very strong, nearly all-male cast in an excellent performance.

E. M. Nathanson's novel was careful to disclaim any truth to the basic plot for, if ever pressed, the U.S. Army apparently can claim that no records exist on the subject. Still, Nathanson's book, as well as the very good screenplay, has a ring of authenticity to it.

Marvin delivers a top performance probably because he seems at his best in a role as a sardonic authoritarian. Herein, he is a major, handed the task of selecting 12 hardened, stockaded punks, training them for a guerrilla mission with just faintest hope of amnesty. Seeds of official conflict are sewn into plot: Marvin and Robert Ryan do not get along—but later they must.

John Cassavetes is firstrate as the tough Chicago hood who meets his match in Marvin. Charles Bronson stands out as a Polish-American who, once affixing his loyalty, does not shift under even physical brutality.

1967: Best Sound Effects

NOMINATION: Best Supp. Actor (John Cassavetes)

•

DIRTY HARRY
1971, 102 mins, US Ⓥ ⊙ ▭ col
Dir Don Siegel *Prod* Don Siegel *Scr* Harry Julian Fink, R. M. Fink, Dean Riesner [John Milius] *Ph* Bruce Surtees *Ed* Carl Pingitore *Mus* Lalo Schifrin *Art* Dale Hennesy
Act Clint Eastwood, Harry Guardino, Reni Santoni, John Vernon, John Larch, Andy Robinson (Malpaso/Warner)

You could drive a truck through the plotholes in *Dirty Harry*, which wouldn't be so serious were the film not a specious, phony glorification of police and criminal brutality [from a story by Harry Julian Fink and R. M. Fink]. Clint Eastwood, in the title role, is a superhero whose antics become almost satire. Strip away the philosophical garbage and all that's left is a well-made but shallow running-and-jumping meller. Don Siegel produces handsomely and directs routinely.

Andy Robinson plays a mad sniper who attempts to hold up San Francisco for money to stop his random carnage. Mayor John Vernon is willing, police chief John Larch goes along, police lieutenant Harry Guardino unctuously follows the prevailing wind, and the work falls to supercop Eastwood.

Eastwood is dedicated—to his own violence. Perhaps his anger at Robinson is more at the delay in capturing him; after all, between bites on a hot dog, Eastwood foils a bank heist at midday, talks down a suicide jumper, and otherwise expedites assorted "dirty work." The character nearly drools, but Eastwood is far too inert for this bit of business.

There are several chase sequences—before the sadist-with-badge dispatches the sadist-without-badge. Thereupon, Eastwood flings his badge to the wind and walks away. At least Frisco is safe from his protection (but think of the rest of us).

•

DIRTY MARY CRAZY LARRY
1974, 93 mins, US Ⓥ col
Dir John Hough *Prod* Norman T. Herman *Scr* Leigh Chapman, Antonio Santean *Ph* Mike Margulies *Ed* Chris Holmes *Mus* Jimmy Haskell
Act Peter Fonda, Susan George, Adam Roarke, Vic Morrow, Ken Tobey, Roddy McDowall (Academy/20th Century-Fox)

Screenplay is from Richard Unekis novel *The Chase*, but what little narrative or characterization shows up on screen could barely fill an abridged short story. Racing enthusiasts Peter Fonda and Adam Roarke steal $150,000 from a supermarket manager (Roddy McDowall, strangely unbilled) in order to purchase a competition sports car. Joined by sluttish Susan George, they careen around rural California with the law (demonic Vic Morrow) in pursuit.

With more than a third of the footage devoted to spectacular chases and collisions deftly staged by stunt coordinator Al Wyatt, there's little time left to hint at the reasons for Fonda's increasingly unappetizing monomania.

Cast performs ably. Fonda is less wooden than usual.

•

DIRTY ROTTEN SCOUNDRELS
1988, 110 mins, US Ⓥ ⊙ col
Dir Frank Oz *Prod* Bernard Williams *Scr* Dale Launer, Stanley Shapiro, Paul Henning *Ph* Michael Ballhaus *Ed* Stephen A. Rotter, William Scharf *Mus* Miles Goodman *Art* Roy Walker
Act Steve Martin, Michael Caine, Glenne Headly, Anton Rogers, Barbara Harris, Ian McDiarmid (Orion)

Dirty Rotten Scoundrels is a wonderfully crafted, absolutely charming remake of the 1964 film *Bedtime Story*. In this classy version, Steve Martin and Michael Caine play the competing French Riviera conmen trying to outscheme each other in consistently amusing and surprising setups. Martin takes the crass American role played by Marlon Brando, and Caine plays homage to David Niven by sporting a thin mustache, slicked back hair and double-breasted blue blazer in a sort of 1930s British yachtsman look. Nice stands in for the fictional seaside town of Beaumont-sur-Mer.

Caine, ensconced in a seaside mansion, comes upon small-time con artist Martin in a train dining car ordering water instead of a meal while telling some poor, doe-eyed French woman a sob story. Beaumont-sur-Mer, where Martin suddenly turns up, is not big enough for two men to go after the same bait. Caine challenges Martin to a $50,000 wager: the first one to extract that sum from the next unsuspecting fool gets to stay.

Things get very sticky when the femme, a "soap queen" (Glenne Headly) from Cleveland, becomes the object of the bet. Headly doesn't look the part of the innocent abroad, but she plays it well enough.

Director Frank Oz clearly has fun with his subjects, helped out in good part by clever cutting and a great, imitative '30s jazzy score by Miles Goodman.

•

DIRTY WEEKEND
1993, 102 mins, UK Ⓥ col
Dir Michael Winner *Prod* Michael Winner, Robert Earl *Scr* Michael Winner, Helen Zahavi *Ph* Alan Jones *Ed* Arnold Crust [= Michael Winner], Chris Barnes *Mus* David Fanshawe *Art* Crispian Sallis
Act Lia Williams, David McCallum, Ian Richardson, Rufus Sewell, Shaughan Seymour, Sylvia Syms (Scimitar)

Michael Winner aims low and half-misses with *Dirty Weekend*, a jet-black genre-bender of femme vengeance from the 1991 British bestseller by Helen Zahavi. Those expecting a female, Anglo version of Winner's earlier *Death Wish* outings will be disappointed. *Weekend* is more rooted in everyday drama than high-octane thrillers.

Setting is Brighton, where the introverted Bella (Lia Williams) has moved after being dumped by a boyfriend in London. Renting a small basement apartment, she's soon prey to an obscene phone-caller (Rufus Sewell). After an empowering visit to an Iranian fortuneteller (Ian Richardson), she brains the peeper with a hammer in his bed one night. High on the experience, she sets out on a weekend kiilling spree of male porkers. Winner's version (scripted with Zahavi herself) is most successful when sticking closely to the original. The movie's first half-hour largely hangs fire with dreary exposition and lackluster dialogue. Thereafter, pic sticks slavishly to the novel, with whole chunks of dialogue and v.o. by Williams that conjure up much of the book's blackly comic tone and irreverent approach to highly PC, feminist issues.

As the worm who turns, newcomer Williams tent-poles the movie with a fine perf that catches the work's bitter-sardonic tone and pulls off some tricky dialogue.

•

DISCLOSURE
1994, 128 mins, US Ⓥ ⊙ ▭ col
Dir Barry Levinson *Prod* Barry Levinson, Michael Crichton *Scr* Paul Attanasio *Ph* Tony Pierce-Roberts *Ed* Stu Linder *Mus* Ennio Morricone *Art* Neil Spisak
Act Michael Douglas, Demi Moore, Donald Sutherland, Caroline Goodall, Dylan Baker, Roma Maffia (Baltimore/Constant/Warner)

Disclosure is polite pulp fiction, a reasonable rendition of potentially risible material. Fueled by the high-voltage star power of Michael Douglas and Demi Moore, this lavishly appointed screen version of Michael Crichton's page-turner about sexual harassment and corporate power might have been even more commercial had it been more shamelessly trashy.

In this sense, those expecting another *Fatal Attraction* or *Indecent Proposal* might be somewhat disappointed by director Barry Levinson's refusal to emphasize the sleaziest elements of the story and to work the audience up into a primal emotional frenzy.

Cozily ensconced a ferry ride away from Seattle with his lawyer wife (Caroline Goodall) and two kids, Tom (Douglas) is fully expecting a promotion at his high-tech firm, DigiCom. But he's laid low by the news that boss Bob Garvin (Donald Sutherland) instead decides to bring in outsider Meredith Johnson (Moore) for the big job.

In his free-swinging single days, Tom had a hot and heavy thing with Meredith, which she seems intent upon reviving during a wine-enhanced private evening meeting. When he abruptly retreats from fully consummating the act, Meredith, her body fairly popping out of her black lingerie, erupts in full fury. The next day, Meredith claims Tom sexually harassed her at their meeting. Tom instantly engages a smart, feisty woman lawyer (Roma Maffia).

Douglas is very good indeed as the put-upon man forced to play hardball for the first time with the big boys and girls. Moore's dragon lady is strictly a one-dimensional creation but her ripe black-widow looks and malevolent demeanor work perfectly for the intent of the film.

Sutherland and Goodall are good in the primary supporting roles.

•

DISCREET CHARM OF THE BOURGEOISIE, THE

SEE: LE CHARME DISCRET DE LA BOURGEOISIE

•

DISH, THE

2000, 100 mins, Australia Ⓥ ⊙ col

Dir Rob Sitch ***Prod*** Santo Cilauro, Tom Gleisner, Jane Kennedy, Rob Sitch ***Scr*** Santo Cilauro, Tom Gleisner, Jane Kennedy, Rob Sitch ***Ph*** Graeme Wood ***Ed*** Jill Bilcock ***Mus*** Edmund Choi, Jane Kennedy ***Art*** Carrie Kennedy

Act Sam Neill, Kevin Harrington, Tom Long, Patrick Warburton, Genevieve Mooy, Tayler Kane (Dish/Working Dog)

A historical footnote elaborated to fictive mini-epic proportions, *The Dish* is a tale of a far-flung Aussie burg's involvement with the *Apollo II* moon mission. Pic's main course is tart, farcical yet affectionate ribbing of small-townies blinded by the global spotlight.

Down Under in New South Wales, midsized town of Parkes finds itself unexpectedly playing a role in NASA's first man-on-the-moon expedition—or rather the southern hemisphere's largest radio telescope does, a football-field-wide, 1000-ton moveable disc incongruously plunked just outside the city amid sheep paddocks. Device is perfect for NASA use as a backup transmitter.

Sharing even a minor piece of the glory is enough to set Parkes's populace in a tizzy. Genially mate-y Mayor McIntyre (Roy Billing) is a bit overwhelmed by all the fuss, which includes such VIP visitors as the genteel U.S. ambassador (John McMartin) and Australia's own tippling, media-hogging prime minister (Bille Brown). Mayoral spouse May (Genevieve Mooy) orchestrates a series of balls, dinners and cocktail parties that invariably fail to fully muzzle the townies' less-than-refined true nature.

Primary focus is on quartet entrusted with the telescope's crucial performance. The home team is led by senior scientist Cliff (Sam Neill), a pipe-smoking center of calm amid more excitable subordinates: nervous-nelly Keith and brash technician Mitch (Kevin Harrington). The men soon have major crises to deal with. Not only does an oversight temporarily cut the dish adrift from the in-flight *Apollo* spacecraft, but the astronauts are ahead of schedule. This means that the Aussies alone will be able to transmit mankind's first steps on the moon to global TV auds. If, that is, they can: hurriedly re-program their data, regain shuttle contact and reposition the massive dish during unexpected, gale-force winds.

Tone recalls classic Ealing comedies in which woolly eccentrics butted heads against their supposed class/governmental superiors, with no major injuries but much droll chaos the result. Satire here is sharp yet evenhanded, playing local yokels against the brassier yet equally hapless pretentions of opportunistic outsiders.

•

DISHONORED

1931, 91 mins, US Ⓥ b/w

Dir Josef von Sternberg ***Scr*** Daniel N. Rubin ***Ph*** Lee Garmes ***Art*** [Hans Dreier]

Act Marlene Dietrich, Victor McLaglen, Lew Cody, Gustav von Seyffertitz, Warner Oland, Barry Norton (Paramount)

A secret service story [from *X-27* by Josef von Sternberg]. The start of the film, when Gustav von Seyffertitz as the Austrian intelligence chief picks up Dietrich on the street to make her a prize spy, is extremely nice work. But Dietrich rises above her director in this picture, as much as Sternberg smothered her while making *Morocco*. Dietrich is dominant in *Dishonored*. It is she who forces interest.

Her love for the Russian rival spy (Victor McLaglen) is made quite evident at the finish. Barring some silly dialog saddled upon him a couple of times, McLaglen gets through okay. Seyffertitz, always dependable, is more so than usual.

•

DISHONORED LADY

1947, 86 mins, US Ⓥ col

Dir Robert Stevenson ***Prod*** Jack Chertok ***Scr*** Edmund H. North ***Ph*** Lucien Andriot ***Ed*** James E. Newcom, John Foley ***Mus*** Carmen Dragon ***Art*** Nicolai Remisoff

Act Hedy Lamarr, Dennis O'Keefe, John Loder, Morris Carnovsky, William Lundigan, Margaret Hamilton (United Artists)

In this remake of the stage play, [by Edward Sheldon and Margaret Ayer Barnes] Hedy Lamarr character is more psychological than immoral and the film approach lessens interest and clarity. Plot still gets in shadowy implications of character's promiscuous love life, mostly through dialog.

It tells of editor of fashionable femme mag who's not getting the best out of life although apparently enjoying it. Mental desperation drives her to attempted suicide, a visit with a psychiatrist, and renunciation of old way of living. She meets a young doctor, falls in love and becomes involved in a murder.

Male co-stars are Dennis O'Keeefe and John Loder as the young doctor and an old love, respectively. O'Keefe character isn't always even and Loder's role is a bit too smooth. William Lundigan, Morris Carnovsky (psychiatrist), Paul Cavanagh (publisher) and Natalie Schafer are okay among other principals. Margaret Hamilton rates some chuckles in typical rooming housekeeper role.

•

DISNEY'S THE KID

SEE: THE KID

•

DISORDERLY ORDERLY, THE

1964, 89 mins, US Ⓥ col

Dir Frank Tashlin ***Prod*** Paul Jones ***Scr*** Frank Tashlin ***Ph*** W. Wallace Kelley ***Ed*** Arthur P. Schmidt, John Woodcock ***Mus*** Joseph J. Lilley ***Art*** Hal Pereira, Tambi Larsen

Act Jerry Lewis, Glenda Farrell, Everett Sloane, Karen Sharpe, Kathleen Freeman, Susan Oliver (Paramount)

The Disorderly Orderly is fast and madcappish, with Lewis again playing one of his malaprop characters that seem to suit his particular talents. As the orderly, Lewis is himself almost a mental patient as he takes on all the symptoms of the individual patients in the plush sanitarium where he's employed. Ambitious to be a doctor, he flunked out in medical school because of this particular attribute. He's cured through some fancy script-figuring when Susan Oliver, one of the patients, offers him love and he discovers that he's really in love with Karen Sharpe, a nurse. Sandwiched within this premise is Lewis at work, at play, always in trouble.

Star is up to his usual comicking and Frank Tashlin's direction of his own screenplay [from a story by Norm Liebmann and Ed Haas] is fast and vigorous in maintaining a nutty mood. Sharpe is pert and cute, Oliver ably transforms from a would-be suicide to a sexpot, and Glenda Farrell, cast as head of the sanitarium, displays the talent which once made her a star.

•

DISRAELI

1929, 90 mins, US b/w

Dir Alfred E. Green ***Scr*** Julian Josephson ***Ph*** Lee Garmes

Act George Arliss, Joan Bennett, Florence Arliss, Anthony Bushell, David Torrence, Doris Lloyd (Warner)

Acting and characterization are a continuous delight, not to mention a plot that concerns the diplomatic imperative of possessing the Suez Canal.

Disraeli without George Arliss is to shudder. The professional equipment of the central figure carries and dominates both plot and conversation [from the play by Louis N. Parker].

Warner has done it right. Production is unstinted, sedate, and colorful, in the style of 1874. Small bits as well as principal roles are equally meritorious. Florence Arliss, wife of the star, plays his wife in the picture and makes the family circle complete by attaching runner-up honors.

Doris Lloyd as a woman spy is interesting and plausible as she weaves her little net of intrigue. She proves the "menace" to the plan to purchase the big ditch through Egypt.

1929/30: Best Actor (George Arliss)

NOMINATIONS: Best Picture, Writing

•

DISTANT DRUMS

1951, 100 mins, US Ⓥ col

Dir Raoul Walsh ***Prod*** Milton Sperling ***Scr*** Niven Busch, Martin Rackin ***Ph*** Sid Hickox ***Ed*** Folmar Blangsted ***Mus*** Max Steiner ***Art*** Douglas Bacon

Act Gary Cooper, Mari Aldon, Richard Webb, Ray Teal, Arthur Hunnicutt, Robert Barrat (United States/Warner)

This goes back to 1840 and the Seminole War to spin an action-adventure tale grooved along conventional fiction lines. The stock setup was location-lensed in Florida.

Had the screenplay, from a story by Niven Busch, been as realistic as the locales used, *Distant Drums* could have counted as a better-than-average entry in the outdoor, pioneer field. Plot situations are conventional and the dialog banal. However, Raoul Walsh's action-wise direction makes excellent use of the standard framework most of the time to keep the film moving along at an acceptable clip.

The Florida backgrounds lend a lush, fascinating frame for a plot that covers Gary Cooper as an army captain who prefers to live in the swamps with his motherless son. Story is told through the eyes of Richard Webb, naval officer sent to accompany Cooper on a suicidal mission aimed at destroying Seminole munition supplies and thus help shorten the long war.

Performances are just about what might be expected from the formula plotting; adequate and likeable within the story framework. Femme charms are bountifully supplied by Mari Aldon.

•

DISTANT TRUMPET, A

1964, 117 mins, US ▭ col

Dir Raoul Walsh ***Prod*** William H. Wright ***Scr*** John Twist ***Ph*** William Clothier ***Ed*** David Wages ***Mus*** Max Steiner ***Art*** William Campbell

Act Troy Donahue, Suzanne Pleshette, Diane McBain, James Gregory, William Reynolds, Claude Akins (Warner)

The last gasp of the Southwestern tribe of Chiricahua Indians in opposing the encroaching white man is covered by the screenplay from an adaptation by Richard Fielder and Albert Beich of a novel by Paul Horgan. Troy Donahue enacts the role of Lt. Hazard, an idealistic second lieutenant from West Point who arrives at a remote outpost in the middle of the Arizona desert and is thrust into two sizzling circumstances—the battle against War Eagle and the romantic squeeze play between Kitty (Suzanne Pleshette) and Laura (Diane McBain).

The film just seems to mark time in the "middle act" of its 117-minute running (walking) time, but things perk up for the big battle sequence, and the momentum is sustained to the end.

The stunning location terrain of the Red Rocks area of New Mexico and Arizona's Painted Desert gives the production a tremendous pictorial lift. Max Steiner's score is a driving dramatic force but the use of the main theme seems a trifle excessive. The picture would benefit from a lot more pruning by editor David Wages.

Raoul Walsh's direction is generally competent, but the climactic battle strategy is a bit fuzzy. Donahue's range of expression is very slim. Pleshette and McBain's roles hardly tap what histrionic resources may lurk beneath those beautiful facades.

•

DISTANT VOICES, STILL LIVES

1988, 84 mins, UK Ⓥ ⊙ col

Dir Terence Davies ***Prod*** Jennifer Howarth ***Scr*** Terence Davies ***Ph*** William Diver, Patrick Duval ***Ed*** William Diver ***Art*** Miki van Zwanenberg

Act Freda Dowie, Pete Postlethwaithe, Angela Walsh, Dean Williams, Lorraine Ashbourne (BFI/Film Four)

This is the first feature film of Liverpudlian Terence Davies, obviously autobiographical, dealing with a family called Davies and their lives during the 1940s and 1950s.

The film is divided into two parts: *Distant Voices* (45 mins) centers on the wedding of Eileen, eldest of the three Davies children, and the funeral of her father, events which spark memories of the past, including the frightening war years when the city was bombed frequently; *Still Lives* (39 mins) actually was filmed two years after the first part, with the same actors but with a substantially different crew. It's a seamless continuation which climaxes with the wedding of another of the clan, son Tony.

The film is full of singing, as the characters break into familiar songs at family gatherings, or in the local pub. This isn't a film based on nostalgia, though; its very special qualities stem from the beautiful simplicity of direction, writing and playing, and the accuracy of the incidents depicted.

●

DISTINGUISHED GENTLEMAN, THE
1992, 113 mins, US Ⓥ ⦿ col
Dir Jonathan Lynn ***Prod*** Leonard Goldberg, Michael Peyser ***Scr*** Marty Kaplan ***Ph*** Gabriel Beristain ***Ed*** Tony Lombardo, Barry B. Leirer ***Mus*** Randy Edelman ***Art*** Leslie Dilley
Act Eddie Murphy, Lane Smith, Sheryl Lee Ralph, Joe Don Baker, Victoria Rowell, Grant Shaud (Hollywood Pictures)

Mr. Murphy goes to Washington in *The Distinguished Gentleman*, an uneven but occasionally quite funny political satire [from a screen story by Marty Kaplan and Jonathan Reynolds].

The movie starts with a very funny premise but doesn't sustain it once the action shifts to the nation's capital: what if a con man was swept into Washington by using the same name as a recently deceased congressman—playing on the notion most people don't know if their rep is dead or alive anyway.

The twist, of course, is that the biggest scams of all go on legally in Washington. However, Murphy's better nature takes over and prompts him to do the ethical thing.

The screenplay by Marty Kaplan (a former speechwriter for Walter Mondale) certainly has its fun with the depraved ins and outs of politics, even if there are no new wrinkles.

The transformation of Jeff Johnson (Eddie Murphy) into a caring sort is never convincing, other than his understandable desire to woo the niece (Victoria Rowell) of a principled rep (Charles S. Dutton).

Pic is an amalgam of past Murphy roles but most closely resembles *Trading Places*. Director Jonathan Lynn maintains a steady pace but can't avoid arid stretches.

●

DIVA
1981, 123 mins, France Ⓥ ⦿ col
Dir Jean-Jacques Beineix ***Prod*** Irene Silberman ***Scr*** Jean-Jacques Beineix, Jean Van Hamme ***Ph*** Philippe Rousselot ***Ed*** Marie-Josephe Yoyotte, Monique Prim ***Mus*** Vladimir Cosma ***Art*** Hilton McConnico
Act Frederic Andrei, Roland Bertin, Richard Bohringer, Gerard Darmon, Jacques Fabbri, Wilhelmenia Wiggins Fernandez (Films Galaxie/Greenwich)

Diva is an extraordinary thriller and first film from Jean-Jacques Beineix, complex, stylish and fast-moving.

The story [from the novel by Delacorta] involves a young mail courier (Frederic Andrei) with a passion for opera. His idol, Cynthia Hawkins (Wilhelmenia Wiggins Fernandez), has made a career of avoiding the recording studio but the industrious young man manages to covertly make a high-quality tape of her Paris performance. At the same time, a prostitute hides a cassette recording she's made in his delivery motorcycle putting the finger on a drug kingpin before she's killed. His only ally is a mysterious, shadowy character, Gorodish (Richard Bohringer), who lives with a Vietnamese nymphet (Thuy An Luu). Character has been popularized in a series of French novels and provides an element of fun to the picture, popping up to help the hero throughout the story.

The director dots the tale with bizarre types who continually cross each other's paths and wind up doing more harm to each other than to the young postman. A touching novel, bizarre chases and plot twists, breathtaking camerawork by Philippe Rousselot, and tension-filled editing, make *Diva* a superior piece of entertainment.

●

DIVIDING LINE, THE
SEE: THE LAWLESS

●

DIVINE MADNESS
1980, 94 mins, US Ⓥ ⦿ ▭ col
Dir Michael Ritchie ***Prod*** Michael Ritchie ***Scr*** Jerry Blatt, Bette Midler, Bruce Vilanch ***Ph*** William A. Fraker, Bobby Byrne ***Ed*** Glenn Farr ***Mus*** Tony Berg, Randy Kerber (arr.) ***Art*** Albert Brenner
Act Bette Midler, The Harlettes, Irving Sudrow (Ladd)

After years of honing her act in gay baths and on concert stages, Bette Midler in 1980 committed it to film in four days at the Pasadena, Calif, Civic Auditorium. "Because this is the time capsule version of my show," she tells the aud, "I might as well do everything I know." Well, she doesn't quite do everything but she does not stint on energy and showmanship.

The film has a more carefully designed and visually opulent look than most concert pix. Director Michael Ritchie and his supervising cameraman, William A. Fraker, employed a 30-man camera team to shoot more than one million feet of film.

Midler's monologs between songs, largely blue material familiar to devotees of her show, are uproariously funny and she delivers them with infectious physical panache.

As for her voice, Midler is no Streisand, but she has a solid personality to back up her songs, and her versatility is one of her strongest assets.

●

DIVINE WOMAN, THE
1928, 95 mins, US ⊗ b/w
Dir Victor Seastrom ***Scr*** Dorothy Farnum, John Colton ***Ph*** Oliver Marsh ***Ed*** Conrad A. Nervig
Act Greta Garbo, Lars Hanson, Lowell Sherman, Polly Moran, Dorothy Cumming, John Mack Brown (M-G-M)

No denying Greta Garbo. Her beauty is of a simple sort; nothing exotic or hectic—just a super-pretty blonde. And director Victor Seastrom knows just how to handle her.

In this instance [from Gladys Unger's play *Starlight*] she is a peasant girl from Brittany, and here and there the incidents suggest anecdotes of the life of Sarah Bernhardt, though this thread is not consistently followed. She comes to Paris to find fame as an actress. The man who brings her there is her mother's lover, played by Lowell Sherman in his best manner. She falls in love with Lucien, a private soldier, and gets him into all sorts of grief, including arrest as a deserter and prosecution for stealing a dress she admires.

The romance is a rough-and-tumble, cute and juvenile. Greta flirts charmingly, and Lars Hanson, whose features do not indicate Scandinavian origin, takes his love-making quite seriously, which gives a fine effect to her work.

●

DIVORCE AMERICAN STYLE
1967, 109 mins, US Ⓥ col
Dir Bud Yorkin ***Prod*** Norman Lear ***Scr*** Norman Lear ***Ph*** Conrad Hall ***Ed*** Ferris Webster ***Mus*** Dave Grusin ***Art*** Edward Stephenson
Act Dick Van Dyke, Debbie Reynolds, Jason Robards, Jean Simmons, Van Johnson, Joe Flynn (Columbia)

Comedy and satire, not feverish melodrama, are the best weapons with which to harpoon social mores. An outstanding example is *Divorce American Style* [from a story by Robert Kaufman], which pokes incisive, sometimes chilling, fun at U.S. marriage-divorce problems.

Amidst wow comedy situations, the story depicts the break-up after 15 years of the Van Dyke–Debbie Reynolds marriage, followed by the economic tragedies exemplified by Jason Robards and Jean Simmons, caught in a vicious circle of alimony and remarriage problems.

Shelley Berman and Dick Gautier, two chummy lawyers, spotlight the occasional feeling by litigants that their personal problems are secondary to the games attorneys play.

1967: NOMINATION: Best Original Story & Screenplay

●

DIVORCEE, THE
1930, 80 mins, US Ⓥ b/w
Dir Robert Z. Leonard ***Scr*** Nick Grinde, Zelda Sears, John Meehan ***Ph*** Norbert Brodine ***Ed*** Hugh Wynn
Act Norma Shearer, Chester Morris, Conrad Nagel, Robert Montgomery, Florence Eldridge, Helene Millard (M-G-M)

In its adaptation of *Ex-Wife*, the spicy 1929 novel by Ursula Parrott, Metro has taken liberties. Refinement has taken the upper hand here, with only the necessary touch of sauciness to satisfy readers of the novel, which was first published anonymously and later, after thousands of copies were sold, under the author's name.

Metro has even changed the names of the characters as they were in the Parrott story, given it a totally foreign opening, skipped much of the material that made *Ex-Wife* an interesting yarn, missed entirely the spirit with which the heroine accepts the futility of her marriage, suddenly broken off, and for a surprise ending takes the action to Paris and patches everything up.

Norma Shearer is excellent as the ad writer who in the novel finally despairs of ever getting her husband back, but in the picture does and with a very effective, formula-like clinch for the close. Opposite Shearer is Chester Morris, who is actually cast as a newspaper man. You only know that because he says so once. Audiences figuring out things for the finish will probably be fooled to find that Conrad Nagel, the other man, doesn't successfully step in for the final fade, but that's the way it's been done here, the novel notwithstanding.

Besides good performances by Shearer, Morris and Nagel, unusually fine work is contributed by Robert Montgomery, the husband's friend, who helps himself to the wife as he would to an extended cocktail.

1929/30: Best Actress (Norma Shearer)

NOMINATIONS: Best Picture, Director, Writing (John Meehan)

●

DIVORCE—ITALIAN STYLE
SEE: DIVORZIO ALL'ITALIANA

●

DIVORCE OF LADY X, THE
1938, 92 mins, UK Ⓥ col
Dir Tim Whelan ***Prod*** Alexander Korda ***Scr*** Ian Dalrymple, Arthur Wimperis, Lajos Biro ***Ph*** Harry Stradling ***Ed*** L.J.W. Stockviss, William Hornbeck ***Mus*** Miklos Rozsa ***Art*** Lazare Meerson
Act Merle Oberon, Laurence Olivier, Binnie Barnes, Ralph Richardson, Morton Selten, Gus McNaughton (London Films)

Alexander Korda's Technicolored comedy is rich, smart entertainment; a comedy built around several situations and a wrong-identity hoax.

Robert E. Sherwood's deft writing is apparent in the screenplay job he did along with Lajos Biro, author of the play [*Counsel's Opinion*] from which the pic was evolved. Comedy lines have that Sherwood sting.

Merle Oberon attends a costume ball in a London hotel and after the manager can't persuade an annoyed young lawyer (Laurence Olivier) to part with some space in his suite, Oberon maneuvers in and wheedles him out of his bed.

Next day girl vamooses before chap can find out much about her; he's convinced she's married. On arrival at his office, he is plagued by a college classmate to get the latter a divorce. He claims his wife spent the night with an unknown man in the same hotel, after attending the same dance. Girl continues to interest the chap and, when she knows the sort he believes her to be, maintains the ruse.

Oberon impresses. Olivier does his role pretty well, retarded somewhat by an annoying bit of pouting business. Two key performances which sparkle are those of Ralph Richarson and Morton Selten.

●

DIVORZIO ALL'ITALIANA
(DIVORCE—ITALIAN STYLE)
1961, 108 mins, Italy b/w
Dir Pietro Germi ***Prod*** Franco Cristaldi ***Scr*** Pietro Germi, Ennio De Concini, Alfredo Giannetti ***Ph*** Leonida Barboni ***Ed*** Roberto Cinquini ***Mus*** Carlo Rustichelli ***Art*** Carlo Egidi
Act Marcello Mastroianni, Daniela Rocca, Stefania Sandrelli, Leopoldo Trieste, Margherita Girelli, Angela Cardile (Lux/Vides/Galatea)

In its distinctive, tongue-in-cheek way, film suggests a solution to unhappy couples unable to divorce under Catholic Italian law: kill your spouse—but make sure that your deed is recognizably in defense of your and your family's honor. In which case, under article 587 of Italian law, the murderer is penalized only 3 to 7 years in jail; no more, sometimes less.

Plot deals with a fed-up husband (Marceo Mastroianni) who plans several ways to get rid of his nagging wife (Daniela Rocca), finally decides to find a lover for her, spring on the couple and shoot her dead. After several clever plot twists, he does, going on to marry the girl next door while his entire village cheers him as it would a hero. Skillfully written, with a penetrating, almost brutal glimpse of Sicily and its antiquated way of life, it has been directed by Pietro Germi with lagless pace and consistent incisiveness, evoking constant chuckles rather than isolated guffaws.

Mastroianni gives an imaginative performance, Rocca is excellent as his wife, Stefania Sandrelli at times unsure but well cast as his ideal girl, Leopoldo Trieste good as the wife's onetime suitor. A major plus factor is Leonida Barboni's oft-breathtaking camerawork, all on Sicilian locations.

●

DIXIE
1943, 89 mins, US col
Dir A. Edward Sutherland ***Prod*** Paul Jones ***Scr*** Karl Tunberg, Darrell Ware ***Ph*** William C. Mellor, Morgan Padelford, Gordon Jennings ***Ed*** William Flannery ***Mus*** Robert Emmett Dolan (dir.)

Act Bing Crosby, Dorothy Lamour, Billy De Wolfe, Marjorie Reynolds, Raymond Walburn, Eddie Foy, Jr. (Paramount)

Dixie is the saga of pre-Civil War minstrel man and songwriter, Daniel Decatur Emmett (Bing Crosby), who had a song in his soul, and an innate showmanship which inspired what later became the standard blackface minstrel makeup. Born of duress and privation, the vagabond troupers in a New Orleans music hall set a standard which, as the story develops, winds up in the rousing and spirited "I Wish I Were in Dixie," as result of a catastrophic backstage fire.

The story itself is literally a three-fire affair. It seems as if Crosby's careless corncob pipe is always getting him into red-hot trouble. It runs the gamut of burning down his fiancee's father's house (opening), and the backstage finale which, however, caused Crosby to heroically keep singing "Dixie," accelerating it into the spirited tempo with which we now identify the classic American folk song.

As a story it's lightweight. It's also doubtlessly a very free fictionization of Dan Emmett's career, but it's sufficient unto the purpose thereof.

•

D.O.A.

1950, 83 mins, US Ⓥ ⊙ b/w

Dir Rudolph Mate ***Prod*** Leo C. Popkin ***Scr*** Russell Rouse, Clarence Green ***Ph*** Ernest Laszlo ***Ed*** Arthur H. Nadel ***Mus*** Dimitri Tiomkin ***Art*** Duncan Cramer

Act Edmond O'Brien, Pamela Britton, Luther Adler, Beverly Campbell, Lyn Baggett, William Chang (United Artists)

D.O.A. poses the novel twist of having a man looking for his own murderer. That off-beat idea and a strong performance by Edmond O'Brien do a lot to hold it together. But script is difficult to follow and doesn't get into its real meat until about 35 minutes of footage have passed.

O'Brien is seen as a tax counselor who trips to San Francisco for a round of the fleshpots. During a visit of hot spots he is slipped deadly luminous poison in a drink and is told he only has a few days to live. He spends the next few days trying to find his murderer and why he had been made a victim.

Rudolph Mate's direction of the first portion of the story lingers too long over it, spreading the expectancy very thin, but when he does launch his suspense-building it comes over with a solid wallop.

•

D.O.A.

1988, 96 mins, US Ⓥ ⊙ col

Dir Rocky Morton, Annabel Jankel ***Prod*** Ian Sander, Laura Ziskin ***Scr*** Charles Edward Pogue ***Ph*** Yuri Neyman ***Ed*** Michael R. Miller ***Mus*** Chaz Jankel ***Art*** Richard Amend

Act Dennis Quaid, Meg Ryan, Charlotte Rampling, Daniel Stern, Jane Kaczmarek, Christopher Neame (Touchstone)

An excessively morbid and unsubtle second remake of the 1949 film noir classic, *D.O.A.* remains unbelievable and unappealing despite a barnstorming central performance by Dennis Quaid.

Scripter uses two central MacGuffins to get the pot boiling. First Quaid is an English prof who's unwilling to read his precocious student Nick Lang's (played by Rob Knepper) novel. Just as hard-drinking Quaid marks an A on the still unread manuscript, Nick falls to his death past Quaid's window, an apparent suicide.

Second, pic's structure (bookended with black-&-white sequences at the police station) and catalyst are from Russell Rouse and Clarence Green's 1949 screenplay for *D.O.A.* In the third reel Quaid is diagnosed as having ingested a luminous poison, with only one to two days left to live. The protagonist who has given up on life since publishing his last novel four years back now has an obsession to live for: find his own killer.

Convoluted trail of murder and suicide teams Quaid with Meg Ryan, as a pretty coed with a crush on him.

Hailing from music videos and TV's *Max Headroom*, married helmers Rocky Morton and Annabel Jankel overload their maiden feature with visual gimmickry: lots of tilted, or swivelling first-person camerawork plus moire-patterned lighting to create distortion. Acting, particularly by Quaid, Ryan and Knepper, is fine, but Charlotte Rampling is very unflatteringly styled and photographed.

•

DOC

1971, 95 mins, US col

Dir Frank Perry ***Prod*** Frank Perry ***Scr*** Pete Hamill ***Ph*** Gerald Hirschfield ***Ed*** Alan Helm ***Mus*** Jimmy Webb ***Art*** Gene Callahan

Act Stacy Keach, Faye Dunaway, Harris Yulin, Michael Witney, Denver John Collins, Dan Greenburg (United Artists)

Frank Perry in *Doc* attempts to remove the encrustations of myth and fantasy over the rough-hewn facts and persons of Wyatt Earp, Doc Holliday, Kate Elder and Tombstone.

Stacy Keach, Faye Dunaway, and Harris Yulin star in good performances which may shock the naive, outrage the superpatriotic, offend those who prefer the cliches of the American West, but satisfy the well-adjusted. Perry takes care to explore the reality of the situations, to recreate an earthy environment, and then to depict acts and events which, in their own time and morality, made sense. In order to achieve this, the first reel is as delicate as a kick in the groin; once over that pain the rest of the story evolves smoothly.

Earp (Yulin) emerges as a shifty politician of flexible motivation, by today's cynical standards a model pragmatic man of public life. His relationship with Holliday (Keach) has undertones left to the imagination (when little else is). Dunaway shakes her fashion-model fragility to become a believable frontier woman.

•

DOC HOLLYWOOD

1991, 103 mins, US Ⓥ ⊙ col

Dir Michael Caton-Jones ***Prod*** Susan Solt, Deborah D. Johnson ***Scr*** Jeffrey Price, Peter S. Seaman, Daniel Pyne ***Ph*** Michael Chapman ***Ed*** Priscilla Nedd-Friendly ***Mus*** Carter Burwell ***Art*** Lawrence Miller

Act Michael J. Fox, Julie Warner, Barnard Hughes, Woody Harrelson, David Ogden Stiers, Bridget Fonda (Warner)

Doc Hollywood represents an attempt to rekindle the homespun humor and warmth of 1930s and 40s paeans to small-town American life. This heaped serving of recycled Capracorn [from Neil B. Shulman's book *What? . . . Dead Again?* adapted by Laurian Leggett] has no real taste of its own, but, in its mildness and predictability, offers the reassurance of a fast-food or motel chain.

Arrogant young big-city doctor Ben Stone (Michael J. Fox) is, as he puts it, 'waylaid in *Hee-Haw* hell" on his way through the South to L.A. and prospective riches as a plastic surgeon. Detained in Grady, SC, the quaintest li'l ol' town you ever did see, the impatient Ben is forced to perform 32 hours of community service at the local clinic for destroying the judge's white picket fence with his Porsche.

Treating the minor maladies of the charmingly eccentric locals, Ben can't help but become a bit hooked by town happenings and intrigue. But most of all he's taken with the unusually feisty and attractive ambulance driver Lou (Julie Warner), a young woman with a four-year-old daughter. When Ben delivers his first baby, he feels pangs of attachment for the town.

Fox gives an energetic, agreeable, performance. Newcomer Warner is also perfectly pleasant, if not too believable as a young lady from the deep South. Supporting cast is fine down the line, with George Hamilton putting in what amounts to a cameo as the head of a chic cosmetic surgery clinic.

•

DOCK BRIEF, THE
(US: TRIAL AND ERROR)

1962, 88 mins, UK b/w

Dir James Hill ***Prod*** Dimitri De Grunwald ***Scr*** Pierre Rouve ***Ph*** Edward Scaife ***Ed*** Ann Chegwidden ***Mus*** Ron Grainer ***Art*** Ray Simm

Act Peter Sellers, Richard Attenborough, Beryl Reid, David Lodge, Tristram Jellinek (M-G-M)

This offbeat, arty film gets away to a good start with the stellar pull of Peter Sellers and Richard Attenborough. Originally a radio play by John Mortimer, it is a bold attempt to present something different and, on the whole, it's a fair try.

Sellers plays an aging, unsuccessful barrister who gets the chance of a lifetime when briefed to defend Attenborough, a mild, birdseed merchant who has murdered his wife because he wanted peace. He is bored with her because of her raucous sense of humour. It is the last straw when she doesn't elope with their equally raucous and boisterous lodger. Sellers plans his campaign optimistically and is quite undaunted when Attenborough admits the crime and shows the flaws in all Sellers's defense arguments.

The screenplay is a literate job, with a deft mixture of comedy and pathos. Sellers has the opportunity of showing many moods and much of his work is good. Attenborough comes out of the acting duel rather better.

•

DOCKS OF NEW YORK, THE

1928, 80 mins, US Ⓥ ⊗ b/w

Dir Josef von Sternberg ***Scr*** Jules Furthman, Julian Johnson ***Ph*** Harold Rosson ***Art*** Hans Dreier

Act George Bancroft, Betty Compson, Baclanova, Clyde Cook, Mitchell Lewis, Gustav von Seyffertitz (Paramount)

The Docks of New York is not Josef von Sternberg's greatest. But it's a corking program picture, thanks to George Bancroft, a good story and Julian Johnson's titles.

Sternberg's direction is excellent, but it is in the casting that the picture falls short of special classification. Betty Compson as an elliptical-heeled frail, who is punch drunk from life and attempts suicide, only to be rescued by Bancroft, a roughneck stoker, fails to get underneath the characterization. In real life she would probably have four husbands in the rack and be chalking up for the fifth.

Bancroft as Bill Roberts, the husky, hard-drinking, two-fisted stoker, has a role that he can make roll over. Roberts, on his one night ashore, saves the girl, and in a spirit of bravado marries her in a waterfront dive operated by a crimp (Guy Oliver).

Next morning Roberts again is ready for sea. He is on his way to a ship when a crowd and the arrival of the police arouses his curiosity. He returns to find the girl about to be arrested for shooting the third engineer of the crew (Mitchell Lewis), who had entered her room and tried to force his attentions on her.

The scenario is adapted from the John Monk Saunders original, *The Dock Walloper*. Exquisite photography helps a lot. Foggy mystic water shots give the waterfront the same quality of *Street Angel*.

•

DOC SAVAGE: THE MAN OF BRONZE

1975, 100 mins, US Ⓥ col

Dir Michael Anderson ***Prod*** George Pal ***Scr*** George Pal, Joe Morhaim ***Ph*** Fred Koenekamp ***Ed*** Thomas McCarthy ***Mus*** Frank DeVol (adapt.) ***Art*** Fred Harpman

Act Ron Ely, Paul Gleason, Bill Lucking, Michael Miller, Eldon Quick, Darrell Zwerling (Warner)

Execrable acting, dopey action sequences, and clumsy attempts at camp humor mark George Pal's *Doc Savage* as the kind of kiddie film that gives the G rating a bad name. Set in the 1930s and based on the Kenneth Robeson comic strip character, it is below the level of the *Batman* 1960s TV series, which it seems to be emulating.

Ron Ely looks impressive as the blond muscleman superhero, but doesn't do much beyond flexing his muscles and flashing smiles at the group of cronies who join him on an expedition into the South American jungles to avenge his father's murder.

Only thesp who survives the script with any dignity is Pamela Hensley, playing a native girl in love with the stolid hero.

•

DOCTOR, THE

1991, 125 mins, US Ⓥ ⊙ col

Dir Randa Haines ***Prod*** Laura Ziskin ***Scr*** Robert Caswell ***Ph*** John Seale ***Ed*** Bruce Green, Lisa Fruchtman ***Mus*** Michael Convertino ***Art*** Ken Adam

Act William Hurt, Christine Lahti, Elizabeth Perkins, Mandy Patinkin, Adam Arkin, Charlie Korsmo (Touchstone)

The Doctor grapples powerfully with themes of mortality, compassion, social responsibility [from Ed Rosenbaum's book *A Taste of My Own Medicine*]. William Hurt's perf as an emotionally constricted heart and lung surgeon faced with his own medical crisis is all the more moving for its rigor and restraint.

Hurt espouses a philosophy of emotional distance, claiming that empathy interferes with technical demands made on a surgeon. He carries over the approach into his sterile family life in affluent Marin County, keeping wife Christine Lahti and son Charlie Korsmo at arm's length. His life is thrown into turmoil when he is diagnosed with throat cancer.

Director Randa Haines, who previously guided Hurt in *Children of a Lesser God*, first cast Warren Beatty in *The Doctor* before they parted over differences of interpretation. She is fortunate to have an icier actor such as Hurt in the role because it's more of a stretch for him to evolve into a mensch.

Haines's intelligent direction is methodical in the best sense of the word, using documentary-like storytelling techniques with lenser John Seale to take the viewer through the doctor's journey of self-discovery in Ken Adam's chilling silver-blue hospital set.

Hurt's initial self-pity begins to evaporate when he enters the incandescent presence of fellow patient Elizabeth Perkins. Their platonic but intimate relationship becomes the film's emotional crux as Perkins (in a wondrously good performance) teaches Hurt what he failed to learn in med school about unconquerable pain and acceptance of death.

•

DOCTOR AT LARGE

1957, 104 mins, UK Ⓥ col

Dir Ralph Thomas ***Prod*** Betty E. Box ***Scr*** Nicholas Phipps ***Ph*** Ernest Steward ***Ed*** Frederick Wilson ***Mus*** Bruce Montgomery ***Art*** Maurice Carter

Act Dirk Bogarde, Muriel Pavlow, Donald Sinden, James Robertson Justice, Shirley Eaton, Michael Medwin (Rank)

This continues the adventures of the young medico who qualified in *Doctor in the House* and got his first appointment in *Doctor at Sea*. This time round he's on a job hunting spree and the film depicts his experiences and adventures while working for a mean provincial doctor and in a fashionable Park Lane practice.

The yarn develops with a blending of light comedy and a dash of sentiment, with punch comedy lines providing timely shots in the arm. They're welcome when they come, but they're too irregular.

Role of the young doctor again is played by Dirk Bogarde. The story opens at St. Swithin's hospital where Bogarde hopes to achieve his vocational ambitions to practice surgery. But he falls foul of James Robertson Justice, who is the hospital's chief consultant. To gain experience (and pay the rent), he begins his job hunting trail. Bogarde, of course, is the mainstay of the story, but Justice again emerges as the standout character, even though his role is reduced to more modest proportions.

•

DOCTOR AT SEA

1955, 93 mins, UK Ⓥ col

Dir Ralph Thomas *Prod* Betty E. Box *Scr* Nicholas Phipps, Jack Davies *Ph* Ernest Steward *Ed* Frederick Wilson *Mus* Bruce Montgomery *Art* Carmen Dillon

Act Dirk Bogarde, Brigitte Bardot, Brenda de Banzie, James Robertson Justice, Maurice Denham, Michael Medwin (Rank)

As their first British venture in VistaVision, Rank studios plays it safe with a sequel to *Doctor in the House*, but *Doctor at Sea* does not rise to the same laugh-provoking heights as its predecessor.

James Robertson Justice is a gruff ship's captain on whose freighter the young medico has his first appointment at sea. The ship is obliged to take on board the daughter of the chairman of the line and her friend, a pert and attractive cabaret chanteuse.

By far the most dominating performance of the cast is given by Justice. He towers above the others and is the focal point of every scene in which he appears. Dirk Bogarde plays the medico with a pleasing quiet restraint and Brigitte Bardot has an acting talent to match her charm.

•

DOCTOR DOLITTLE

1967, 152 mins, US Ⓥ ▭ col

Dir Richard Fleischer *Prod* Arthur P. Jacobs *Scr* Leslie Bricusse *Ph* Robert Surtees *Ed* Samuel E. Beetley, Marjorie Fowler *Mus* Lionel Newman, Alexander Courage (arr.) *Art* Jack Martin Smith, Ed Graves

Act Rex Harrison, Samantha Eggar, Anthony Newley, Richard Attenborough, Peter Bull, Muriel Landers (20th Century-Fox/Apjac)

Rex Harrison, physically, is not at all the rotund original from Hugh Lofting's stories; but histrionically, he's perfect. Gentle and loving with animals, patient and kind with obtuse and very young friends, he can become a veritable holocaust when confronted with cruel and uncomprehending adults who threaten his animal world.

Leslie Bricusse's adaptation retains the delightful aspects while taking considerable liberty with the plot. His music and lyrics, while containing no smash hits, are admirably suited to the scenario.

Outstanding, considering his brief appearance, is Richard Attenborough as Albert Blossom, the circus owner. He comes on so strong in his one song-and-dance bit that it's nearly a perfect example of why important cameo roles should be turned over to important talents.

Most of the $16 million budget evidently went into the production and it shows.

1967: Best Song ("Talk to the Animals"), Special Visual Effects

NOMINATIONS: Best Picture, Cinematography, Art Direction, Editing, Original Music Score, Adapted Music Score, Sound

•

DOCTOR FAUSTUS

1967, 92 mins, UK Ⓥ col

Dir Richard Burton, Nevill Coghill *Prod* Richard Burton, Richard McWhorter *Scr* Nevill Coghill *Ph* Gabor Pogany *Ed* John Shirley *Mus* Mario Nascimbene *Art* John F. De-Cuir

Act Richard Burton, Elizabeth Taylor, Andreas Teuber, Ian Marter, Elizabeth O'Donovan, David McIntosh (Columbia)

An oddity that may have some archive appeal, for at least it records a performance by Burton [at Oxford University in 1966] that gives an insight into his prowess in classical roles. He is obviously captivated by Christopher Marlowe's 400-year-old verse, and speaks it with sonorous dignity and sense.

The story concerns the medieval doctor's attempt to master all human knowledge by selling his soul to the devil, who dangles before him such delights as nights with Elizabeth Taylor, who flits through the film in various undraped poses as the Helen of Troy siren promising a fate worse than death.

One surprise is the general adequacy of the Oxford amateurs, with a good performance in any terms from Andreas Teuber as Mephistopheles. But the impersonation of the seven deadly sins is hardly likely to send good men off the rail. Production was filmed in Rome.

•

DOCTOR IN THE HOUSE

1954, 92 mins, UK Ⓥ col

Dir Ralph Thomas *Prod* Betty E. Box *Scr* Nicholas Phipps *Ph* Ernest Steward *Ed* Gerald Thomas *Mus* Bruce Montgomery *Art* Carmen Dillon

Act Dirk Bogarde, Muriel Pavlow, Kenneth More, Donald Sinden, Kay Kendall, James Robertson Justice (Rank)

A topdraw British comedy, *Doctor in the House* is bright, diverting entertainment, intelligently scripted [from an adaptation of his own novel by Richard Gordon], and warmly played.

Background to the story is the medical school of a London hospital. Within 92 minutes, the film spans the five years in the life of a student group.

The new recruit to the school is Dirk Bogarde, who is taken under the protective wing of three old-timers who had all failed their preliminary exams. Kenneth More, Donald Sinden, and Donald Houston make up a contrasted quartet who seem to have ideas on most subjects but not how to qualify as a medico.

Much of the comedy incident has been clearly contrived but it is nonetheless effective, particularly in the scenes featuring James Robertson Justice as a distinguished surgeon with More.

•

DOCTOR'S DILEMMA, THE

1959, 98 mins, UK col

Dir Anthony Asquith *Prod* Anatole de Grunwald *Scr* Anatole de Grunwald *Ph* Robert Krasker *Ed* Gordon Hales *Mus* Joseph Kosma *Art* Paul Sheriff

Act Leslie Caron, Dirk Bogarde, Alastair Sim, Robert Morley, Felix Aylmer, Michael Gwynn (M-G-M/Comet)

George Bernard Shaw's stringent wit still shines in this film but, staged in 1903, his comments on Harley Street (London's medical row) and the doctoring profession have lost much of their impact. *Dilemma* remains, relentlessly, an easy-on-the-eye filmed version of an out-of-date play.

It concerns a young woman married to an artist who is a complete bounder—a sponger, a potential blackmailer, and a man who can't resist other women. But she is blinded by hero-worship. He suffers from consumption, she pleads with a doctor to save his life. He thinks that he would do better to use his limited serum on a more worthwhile case.

Dirk Bogarde gives a stimulating performance as the selfish young artist and is particularly convincing in his final, highly theatrical death sequence. Leslie Caron is often moving in her blind belief in her man, but never suggests the strength necessary to fight the cynical doctors. These are played as caricatures.

•

DOCTOR X

1932, 77 mins, US Ⓥ ⊙ col

Dir Michael Curtiz *Scr* Robert Tasker, Earl Baldwin *Ph* [Ray Rennahan,] Richard Towers *Ed* George Amy *Mus* Leo F. Forbstein (dir.) *Art* Anton Grot

Act Lionel Atwill, Fay Wray, Lee Tracy, Preston Foster, John Wray, Harry Beresford (First National)

Nothing has been overlooked on detail in providing a heavy doctor touch, plus sets of an intricate laboratory and surgical apparati, which in itself is sometimes a little gruesome. They have been well done with the color lending much to underscore the tension.

A lot of *Doctor X* is routine, including the love interest and the conventional murder mystery technique and background [from a play by Howard W. Comstock and Allen C. Miller], but it does not become tedious. Lionel Atwill overshadows everyone as the head of a surgical research laboratory, under the roof of which several maniacal murders have been committed.

Atwill's is a much stronger part than that given newspaper reporter Lee Tracy. It's also much better written and carries a great deal more conviction. As the daughter of the surgical lab's boss, Fay Wray quickly becomes involved with the reporter who finally saves her life from the big killer.

The tinting in *Doctor X* is at all times soft rather than strongly defined and, after a time, does not distract attention.

•

DOCTOR ZHIVAGO

1965, 193 mins, US Ⓥ ⊙ ▭ col

Dir David Lean *Prod* Carlo Ponti *Scr* Robert Bolt *Ph* Freddie Young [Nicolas Roeg] *Ed* Norman Savage *Mus* Maurice Jarre *Art* John Box

Act Omar Sharif, Julie Christie, Tom Courtenay, Geraldine Chaplin, Rod Steiger, Alec Guinness (M-G-M)

The sweep and scope of the Russian revolution, as reflected in the personalities of those who either adapted or were crushed, has been captured by David Lean in *Doctor Zhivago*, frequently with soaring dramatic intensity.

Some finely etched performances by an international cast illuminate the diverse characters from the novel for which Boris Pasternak won but did not accept the Nobel Prize. The Pasternak novel turns on an introspective medic-poet who essentially reacts to the people and events before, during, and after the Bolshevik takeover.

At the center of a universe of nine basic characters is Omar Sharif as Zhivago, the sensitive man who strikes different people in different ways. To childhood sweetheart Geraldine Chaplin he is a devoted (if cheating) husband; to Julie Christie, with whom he is thrown together by war, he is a passionate lover; to Tom Courtenay, once an intellectual but later a heartless Red general, he's a symbol of the personal life which revolution has supposedly killed; to lecherous, political log-roller Rod Steiger he's the epitome of "rarefied selfishness", and to halfbrother Alex Guinness, the cold secret police official, he's a man who must be saved from himself.

Sharif, largely through expressions of indignation, compassion and tenderness, makes the character very believable. Christie is outstanding in a sensitive, yet earthy and full-blooded portrayal of a girl who is used and discarded by Steiger, then marries Courtenay only to lose him to his cause.

Lean has devoted as much care to physical values as he has to his players. The bitter cold of winter, the grime of Moscow, the lush countryside, the brutality of war, and the fool's paradise of the declining Czarist era are forcefully conveyed.

1965: Best Adapted Screenplay, Color Cinematography, Color Art Direction, Original Musical Score, Color Costume Design

NOMINATIONS: Best Picture, Director, Supp. Actor (Tom Courtenay), Editing, Sound

•

DODGE CITY

1939, 100 mins, US Ⓥ ⊙ col

Dir Michael Curtiz *Prod* [Robert Lord] *Scr* Robert Buckner *Ph* Sol Polito, Ray Rennahan *Ed* George Amy *Mus* Max Steiner *Art* Ted Smith

Act Errol Flynn, Olivia de Havilland, Ann Sheridan, Bruce Cabot, Frank McHugh, Alan Hale (Warner)

Dodge City is a lusty western, packed with action, including some of the dandiest melee stuff screened.

Falling in the cycle of pioneering and American frontier days, *Dodge City* (Kansas) is essentially a bad man-and-honest-sheriff saga. However Michael Curtiz's forceful direction lifts this into the big league division.

Errol Flynn is a soldier of fortune, which explains his clipped English-Irish brogue as a Texas cattleman, transplanted to this Kansas frontier. Olivia de Havilland is the romance interest, and Ann Sheridan the dancehall girl.

Cabot's gambling saloon effectively typifies all the wickedness of the lawlessness that was Dodge City, as the basic excuse for Flynn's ultimate taking over of the sheriff's post. The street fighting, licentiousness and the skullduggery having to do with cattle trading typify the lusty atmosphere that backgrounds this actioner.

•

DODSWORTH

1936, 90 mins, US Ⓥ ⊙ b/w

Dir William Wyler *Prod* Samuel Goldwyn *Scr* Sidney Howard *Ph* Ruldoph Mate *Ed* Danny Mandell *Mus* Alfred Newman *Art* Richard Day

Act Walter Huston, Ruth Chatterton, Paul Lukas, Mary Astor, David Niven, Gregory Gaye (Goldwyn/United Artists)

Dodsworth is a superb motion picture and a golden borealis over the producer's name.

Sidney Howard transposes his own stage play version of Sinclair Lewis's novel into a picture that uses the camera to open up the vista a little and enrich a basically fertile theme. Picture has a steady flow and an even dramatic wallop from zippy start to satisfying finish. Dodsworth was Walter Huston on the stage and is logically and perfectly the same actor on the screen. This is the kind of a role stars dream about.

It is also obvious that this is Ruth Chatterton's fanciest opportunity on the screen in a long while. Fran Dodsworth is a silly, vain, selfish, shallow kitten and in the playing of Chatterton comes to life with vividness and humanity.

Mary Astor is the sympathetic other woman to whom Dodsworth ultimately turns. Her footage is limited. Her performance is varied and mature.

Three men cross the path of the age-fearing wife on her grand fling. First an Englishman played by David Niven. Then a suave continental played by Paul Lukas. Last a sincere and youthful Austrian played by George Gaye. Each of the lovers is a case of slick casting. Mother of the Austrian who finally strikes home with the pampered American woman is beautifully performed by Maria Ouspenskaya.

1936: Best Interior Decoration (Richard Day)

NOMINATIONS: Best Picture, Director, Actor (Walter Huston), Supp. Actress (Maria Ouspenskaya), Screenplay, Sound

•

DOES, THE
SEE: LES BICHES

•

DOG DAY AFTERNOON
1975, 130 mins, US Ⓥ ⦿ col

Dir Sidney Lumet ***Prod*** Martin Bregman, Martin Elfand ***Scr*** Frank Pierson ***Ph*** Victor J. Kemper ***Ed*** Dede Allen ***Art*** Charles Bailey

Act Al Pacino, John Cazale, Charles Durning, James Broderick, Chris Sarandon, Sully Boyar (Warner)

Dog Day Afternoon is an outstanding film. Based on a real life incident in NY, it stars Al Pacino as the most unlikely bank robber ever to hit the screen.

The holdup was allegedly done for the purpose of financing a sex change operation for the male lover of one of the robbers. That incident is retained in the script, but it is just one of many key elements in a hilarious and moving story.

Pacino and laconic sidekick John Cazale take over the neighborhood bank branch managed by Sully Boyar. The malaprop heist gets the early laughs going, and then the film broadens and deepens as if re-enacting the Battle Of The Bulge.

The introduction of Pacino's lover (Chris Sarandon) is cleverly plotted, and comes as a surprise since Pacino's straight wife (Susan Peretz) has already appeared. The interactions between Pacino and other key characters are magnificently written, acted and directed.

The entire cast is excellent, top to bottom. *Dog Day Afternoon* is, in the whole as well as the parts, filmmaking at its best.

1975: Best Original Screenplay

NOMINATIONS: Best Picture, Director, Actor (Al Pacino), Supp. Actor (Chris Sarandon), Editing

•

DOGFIGHT
1991, 92 mins, US Ⓥ ⦿ col

Dir Nancy Savoca ***Prod*** Peter Newman, Richard Guay ***Scr*** Bob Comfort ***Ph*** Bobby Bukowski ***Ed*** John Tintori ***Mus*** Mason Daring ***Art*** Lester W. Cohen

Act River Phoenix, Lili Taylor, Richard Panebianco, Anthony Clark, Mitchell Whitfield, Holly Near (Warner)

An inherently repellent subject has been given surprisingly benign treatment in *Dogfight*. Title refers to the central event of ex-Marine Bob Comfort's intermittently intriguing screenplay—a party to which a bunch of young servicemen bring the ugliest women they can find.

Full of obnoxious military attitude and macho bravado, Eddie Birdlace and his three buddies hit the streets of San Francisco on the portentous eve of Nov. 21, 1963, and separately scout for a "dog" that might win the prize for most gruesome date. After a little trouble, Eddie (River Phoenix) manages to locate a candidate in young waitress Rose Fenney (Lili Taylor) and drags the unsuspecting young lady along to the nightclub.

The bringing together of a soldier headed for Vietnam and a future hippie on the night before President Kennedy's assassination represents a frightfully schematic screenwriting device. But Savoca underplays the character development to such an extent that the film has a muted, very modest impact. Shot mostly in Seattle, the dark looking film presents a strangely underpopulated San Francisco.

•

DOGS OF WAR, THE
1980, 122 mins, UK Ⓥ ⦿ col

Dir John Irvin ***Prod*** Norman Jewison, Patrick Palmer ***Scr*** Gary DeVore, George Malko ***Ph*** Jack Cardiff ***Ed*** Antony Gibbs ***Mus*** Geoffrey Burgon ***Art*** Peter Mullins

Act Christopher Walken, Tom Berenger, Colin Blakely, Hugh Millais, Paul Freeman, JoBeth Williams (United Artists)

The Dogs of War [from Frederick Forsyth's novel] is an intelligent and occasionally forceful treatment of a provocative but little-examined theme: mercenary warrior involvement in the overthrow of a corrupt black African dictatorship.

Script focuses almost exclusively on Christopher Walken, an "irresponsible" American who is drawn to the mercenary's loner, adventurous life.

Film fails to really get at the heart of the whys and hows of mercenary life, and also rejects the idea of generating any sense of camaraderie among the men.

Details of life in a contempo African dictatorship country, from the bribery and censorship to the military strongarming and oppressive economic conditions, are effectively sketched. Pic displays the political realities without editorializing.

•

DOG SOLDIERS
SEE: WHO'LL STOP THE RAIN

•

DOLCE VITA, LA
1960, 180 mins, Italy/France Ⓥ ⦿ ▭ b/w

Dir Federico Fellini ***Prod*** Giuseppe Amato ***Scr*** Federico Fellini, Tullio Pinelli, Ennio Flaiano, Brunello Rondi ***Ph*** Otello Martelli ***Ed*** Leo Cattozzo ***Mus*** Nino Rota ***Art*** Piero Gherardi

Act Marcello Mastroianni, Yvonne Furneaux, Anouk Aimee, Anita Ekberg, Alain Cuny, Lex Barker (RIAMA/Pathe)

High and low life in modern Rome are seen through the eyes of a reporter, Marcello (Marcello Mastroianni), whose beat brings him into contact with a world-famous film star (Anita Ekberg); with an unhappy and over-rich nymphomanic society girl (Anouk Aimee); with a false miracle "announced" by two lying children and exploited by press and TV; with the suicide of an intellectual (Alain Cuny) whom he's always idolized; with a debauched and tired party in a nobleman's castle peopled by ghosts of past and present; and finally, with an orgy (complete with a striptease performed by the hostess) staged in a futile search for excitement by a grotesque assortment of youths and grownups of all sexes. All the while, the reporter refuses the advances of the only woman (Yvonne Furneaux) who really loves him.

Perhaps many spectators will squirm at the three-hour length of the film or of some of its sequences (though director Federico Fellini cut some 30 minutes from his final print), yet others will never notice they've sat that long.

The performances are uniformly excellent. Mastroianni is perfect in the key role of the basically good and honest boy who succumbs to the sweet life. Ekberg is a revelation as the visiting star, while Furneaux almost runs off with the picture as the reporter's instinctive, possessive mistress.

A fine bit is turned in by Annibale Ninchi as the father, another by Magali Noel as a dancer he befriends, another by Lex Barker as Ekberg's slightly inebriated, slightly separated spouse. Aimee is fine as the society girl who craves company, as is Cuny as Marcello's craggy-faced intellectual friend.

A further nod must go to Otello Martelli's moodful black-and-white lensing, while Nino Rota's musical scoring is another vital plus.

•

$
(UK: THE HEIST)
1971, 120 mins, US Ⓥ ⦿ col

Dir Richard Brooks ***Prod*** M. J. Francovich ***Scr*** Richard Brooks ***Ph*** Petrus Schloemp ***Ed*** George Grenville ***Mus*** Quincy Jones ***Art*** Guy Sheppard

Act Warren Beatty, Goldie Hawn, Gert Frobe, Robert Webber, Scott Brady, Arthur Brauss (Columbia)

Richard Brooks wrote and directed *$* with a sardonic twist to a caper plot. Bank security expert Warren Beatty, aided by friendly hooker Goldie Hawn, steal $1.5 million from three Hamburg safety-deposit boxes used by assorted criminals. An exhausting chase sequence is the ultimate destination of the production which features some good authentic locales.

The key subordinate characters, Las Vegas skimming courier Robert Webber, corrupt U.S. Army black marketeer Scott Brady, and European narcotics dealer Arthur Brauss, are on a dramatic parity with the principals and often overpower them. Hawn's trademark kookiness keeps getting in the way, and Beatty's low-key sensitivity can hardly survive. This film is obviously what is sometimes called "an entertainment." Paradoxically, Brooks maybe is too serious a filmmaker for this sort of thing. He wants his characters to have depth and motivation, but the principle does not work well herein.

•

DOLL'S HOUSE, A
1973, 95 mins, UK Ⓥ col

Dir Patrick Garland ***Prod*** Hillard Elkins ***Scr*** Christopher Hampton ***Ph*** Arthur Ibbetson ***Ed*** John Glen ***Mus*** John Barry ***Art*** Elliott Scott

Act Claire Bloom, Anthony Hopkins, Ralph Richardson, Denholm Elliott, Anna Massey, Edith Evans (Elkins/Freeward)

What is good here is largely what was good in the 1971 Broadway production from which pic directly derives. The latter was produced by Hillard Elkins, toplined his wife Claire Bloom, and was helmed and scripted by Patrick Garland and Christopher Hampton, respectively. All ditto for this film.

Package was assembled as though it were a legit production—two weeks of rehearsals preceded lensing, and scenes were shot in order. Christopher Hampton's interpretation of Henrick Ibsen's text successfully plays down the original's creakier verbal anachronisms but leaves its excellent construction intact. Film, as does play, unfolds grippingly, like a first-rate murder mystery with a cosmic consciousness.

Bloom is topnotch as the childlike and pampered wife of a stuffy bank manager. Bloom's portrayal beautifully captures Nora's initial coquettishness and her emergence as an independent woman of strength and character.

•

DOLL'S HOUSE, A
1973, 108 mins, UK Ⓥ col

Dir Joseph Losey ***Prod*** Joseph Losey ***Scr*** David Mercer ***Ph*** Gerry Fisher ***Ed*** Reginald Beck ***Mus*** Michel Legrand ***Art*** Eileen Diss

Act Jane Fonda, David Warner, Trevor Howard, Delphine Seyrig, Edward Fox, Anna Wing (World)

The second version of the Henrik Ibsen classic to hit the screens in 1973, Joseph Losey's location-filmed (Norway) effort has the director's name plus that of Jane Fonda (playing the woman's lib pre-dating heroine, Nora) and a certain formal elegance to carry it.

Ironically, it is Fonda who appears miscast as the Ibsen heroine who dominates this Nordic drama, lacking as she does the vibrancy, depth, and soul required to convey the transition of a fascinating character. The result, to all but Fonda die-hards, blurs the values of the film as a whole.

This is otherwise a rather striking if academic achievement: physically stunning, diligently acted, told in a linear style by a man who knows his cinema, unexcitingly effective here and there.

•

DOLLY SISTERS, THE
1945, 114 mins, US col

Dir Irving Cummings ***Prod*** George Jessel ***Scr*** John Larkin, Marian Spitzer ***Ph*** Ernest Palmer ***Ed*** Barbara McLean ***Mus*** Alfred Newman (dir.) ***Art*** Lyle R. Wheeler, Leland Fuller

Act Betty Grable, John Payne, June Haver, S. Z. Sakall, Reginald Gardiner (20th Century-Fox)

Regardless of biographical authenticity, this film resurrects a golden era of the theatre and the international set of the early 1900s. The manner in which the benign S. Z. Sakall cons Oscar Hammerstein into giving the pseudo-Budapest pets, Jansci and Rozsicka (Jenny and Rosie) Dolly, a date at the famed Hammerstein's Victoria, and their rise to international stardom thereafter, is a pleasant saga.

But it's dominantly a boy-loses-and-recaptures-girl story with Betty Grable and John Payne as Harry Fox, songwriter and song-and-dance man. Perhaps the major biographical shortcoming is in ascribing "I'm Always Chasing Rainbows" to Fox's (Payne) authorship, considering that Harry Carroll (and Joe McCarthy) long vaude-toured and spotlighted himself as the composer thereof.

•

DOLORES CLAIBORNE
1995, 131 mins, US Ⓥ col

Dir Taylor Hackford ***Prod*** Taylor Hackford, Charles Mulvehill ***Scr*** Tony Gilroy ***Ph*** Gabriel Beristain ***Ed*** Mark Warner ***Mus*** Danny Elfman ***Art*** Bruno Rubeo

Act Kathy Bates, Jennifer Jason Leigh, Judy Parfitt, Christopher Plummer, David Strathairn, Eric Bogosian (Castle Rock/Columbia)

Dark and grim, with a terrific central performance by Kathy Bates, pic offers more to fans of traditional melodrama than to Stephen King devotees. Writer Tony Gilroy has for the most part done a laudable job, taking considerable creative license in turning King's novel—an internal monologue—into a feature detailing the "did she or didn't she" life of Bates's Dolores Claiborne.

Accused of murdering the old woman for whom she's cared the past 22 years, Dolores is forced to confront her estranged daughter Selena (Jennifer Jason Leigh) and the mysterious death two decades earlier of her abusive husband, deemed an accident at the time despite the suspicions of the detective involved (Christopher Plummer).

Selena is a high-strung magazine writer who still blames her mother for the death of her father (David Strathairn) who, through a series of flashbacks, is shown to be a truly despicable character.

Deftly cutting between the past and the present, director Taylor Hackford manages to establish a compelling mood and pace even though the pic lacks a thriller's true "Aha!" moment. The director also exercises welcome restraint in presenting the story's more painful elements—which could easily have been turned into a three-hanky TV movie.

Dolores is a showy role, and Bates plays it to the hilt. Leigh is stuck with a more difficult part as the daughter—a sour, self-absorbed creature fabricated for the movie. British actress Judy Parfitt is a scene-stealer as Dolores's snotty, rich employer.

•

DOMICILE CONJUGAL
(BED AND BOARD)

1970, 104 mins, France/Italy Ⓥ col

Dir Francois Truffaut ***Prod*** Marcel Berbert (exec.) ***Scr*** Francois Truffaut, Claude de Givray, Bernard Revon ***Ph*** Nestor Almendros ***Ed*** Agnes Guillemot ***Mus*** Antoine Duhamel ***Art*** Jean Mandaroux

Act Jean-Pierre Leaud, Claude Jade, Hiroko Berghauer, Barbara Laage, Daniele Girard, Daniel Ceccaldi (Films du Carrosse/Valoria/Fida)

Francois Truffaut carries on the adventures of one Antoine Doinel who saw light in Truffaut's first, *The 400 Blows*, at 13; then in a sketch in *Love at Twenty*; and as a young man of 22 in *Stolen Kisses*. Still played by originator of the role, Jean-Pierre Leaud, Truffaut's alter ego, he is married and pic traces the tribulations of early married life, a brief adulterous fling, a first child and then settling down to married life in earnest.

It is laced with little incidents, quirky characters, incisive insights and quintessentially French national traits of complacency that avoid chauvinism in Truffaut's gentle but never sentimental or indulgent treatment.

His wife, played with the right middle-class gentility and innocence by Claude Jade, bolsters income by teaching the violin. Antoine loses his job and has an affair with a Japanese girl that is found out by his headstrong wife and he leaves home for a while. He has a fling at a local bordello where he meets his father-in-law who Gallicly shrugs it off.

The film's diverse incidents, the offbeat characters, the restrained tenderness and the fine playing down the line welds this into a disarming, charming pic.

•

DOMINO KILLINGS, THE
SEE: THE DOMINO PRINCIPLE

•

DOMINO PRINCIPLE, THE
(UK: THE DOMINO KILLINGS)

1977, 97 mins, US Ⓥ col

Dir Stanley Kramer ***Prod*** Stanley Kramer ***Scr*** Adam Kennedy ***Ph*** Fred Koenekamp, Ernest Laszlo ***Ed*** John F. Burnett ***Mus*** Billy Goldenberg ***Art*** William J. Creber

Act Gene Hackman, Candice Bergen, Richard Widmark, Mickey Rooney, Edward Albert, Eli Wallach (ITC/Associated General)

The Domino Principle is a weak and tedious potboiler starring Gene Hackman as a tool of mysterious international intrigue, and a barely recognizable Candice Bergen in a brief role as his perplexed wife. Stanley Kramer's film contains a lot of physical and logistical nonsense.

Adam Kennedy gets adaptation credit from his own novel. Hackman has been carefully spotted years earlier as an amoral and violent type, just the kind of guy that "they" can use to assassinate selected public figures. We never know who "they" are, but "their" lower-level stooges include Richard Widmark, Eli Wallach, and Edward Albert, each more or less archetypic organizational characters.

•

DONA FLOR AND HER TWO HUSBANDS
SEE: DONA FLOR E SEUS DOIS MARIDOS

•

DONA FLOR E SEUS DOIS MARIDOS
(DONA FLOR AND HER TWO HUSBANDS)

1977, 106 mins, Brazil Ⓥ col

Dir Bruno Barreto ***Prod*** Luis Carlos Barreto, Newton Rique, Cia Serrador ***Scr*** Bruno Barreto ***Ph*** Maurilo Salles ***Ed*** Raimondo Higino ***Mus*** Chico Buarque ***Art*** Anisio Medeiros

Act Sonia Braga, Jose Wilker, Mauro Mendonca, Dinorah Brillanti, Nelson Xavier, Arthur Costa Filho (Barreto-Rique-Serrador)

Reportedly the all-time Brazilian hit which out-paced *Jaws* on its home ground, *Dona Flor* is a simplistic human comedy [from the novel by Jorge Amado] of manners and mores in the colorful Bahia part of Brazil in the 1940s. Pic has a certain raw charm but does not quite achieve the needed cohesion and directorial finesse it calls for.

A lovely mulatto woman, brought up as religious and conventional by her rather hardnosed mother, marries a small-time playboy addicted to bordellos, gambling and carousing. But he awakens the woman, Dona Flor, as proven by some torrid soft love scenes and talk.

One day he dies during a Mardi Gras dance. She marries an exact opposite, a meticulous, unimaginative druggist who makes love twice a week and wants order above all. Her secret yearning for her first husband, despite his faults, has him materializing one night. She fights him off but finally gives in. Nobody but her can see him as he takes his place alongside her in bed.

There is some hothouse local color and fair performances, alongside the expert one by Sonia Braga as the demure but sensual Dona Flor. Direction is uneven but does capture a folksy fable quality.

•

DON IS DEAD, THE

1973, 115 mins, US Ⓥ col

Dir Richard Fleischer ***Prod*** Hal Wallis ***Scr*** Marvin H. Albert ***Ph*** Richard H. Kline ***Ed*** Edward A. Biery ***Mus*** Jerry Goldsmith ***Art*** Preston Ames

Act Anthony Quinn, Frederic Forrest, Robert Forster, Al Lettieri, Angel Tompkins, Charles Cioffi (Universal)

This plodding mafiosi actioner lacks color, verisimilitude and least of all, convincing action. Pic [from Marvin H. Albert's novel, adapted by Christopher Trumbo and Michael Phillip Butler] is contrived concoction about internecine mafia warfare with the young turks (Frederic Forrest and Robert Forster) trying to wrest control from underworld establishment represented by Don Angelo (Anthony Quinn).

The criminal figures here aren't quite out of *The Gang That Couldn't Shoot Straight* [1971], but they could in slightly different circumstances be passed off as incompetent, small-time hoods in, say, mid-Nebraska.

Richard Fleischer's direction doesn't help since nearly each scene appears prolonged far beyond need. Even violent scenes come off as clumsy and antiseptic.

Quinn fares as well as can be expected while Forster overacts as the hotheaded upstart. Best in the cast are Forrest and Louis Zorich as the triumphant young turk and the Don's confidante, respectively.

•

DON JUAN

1926, 100 mins, US Ⓥ ⦿ b/w

Dir Alan Crosland ***Scr*** Bess Meredyth, Walter Anthony, Maude Fulton ***Ph*** Byron Haskin ***Ed*** Harold McCord ***Mus*** William Axt ***Art*** Ben Carre

Act John Barrymore, Mary Astor, Estelle Taylor, Warner Oland, Montagu Love, Myrna Loy (Warner)

Several outstanders in this splendidly written, directed, and produced feature. Not alone does John Barrymore's superb playing become one of them, but his athletics, as well. A chase scene is a bear. It's of Don Juan carrying his Adriana away, followed by about a dozen swordsmen on horses, with Barrymore placing his charge in a tree, to return and knock off all of the riders, one by one or in twos.

The complete surprise is the performance of Estelle Taylor as Lucretia Borgia. Her Lucretia is a fine piece of work. She makes it sardonic in treatment, conveying precisely the woman Lucretia is presumed to have been. The other outstanding performance is that of Mary Astor's Adriana. Astor has but comparatively little action, but fills the part so thoroughly that she is a dominating figure. Warner Oland is Cesare, the savage brother, and he looks the role.

•

DON JUAN DEMARCO

1995, 90 mins, US Ⓥ ⦿ col

Dir Jeremy Leven ***Prod*** Francis Ford Coppola, Fred Fuchs, Patrick Palmer ***Scr*** Jeremy Leven ***Ph*** Ralph Bode ***Ed*** Tony Gibbs ***Mus*** Michael Ramen ***Art*** Sharon Seymour

Act Marlon Brando, Johnny Depp, Faye Dunaway, Geraldine Pailhas, Bob Dishy, Rachel Ticotin (American Zoetrope)

Iconoclastic acting of a high order by three eccentric performers, Marlon Brando, Johnny Depp, and Faye Dunaway, is the most memorable dimension of *Don Juan DeMarco*, a romantic fable whose unique charm outweighs its small-scale, rather slight narrative.

Making his directorial debut, Jeremy Leven (better know as a novelist) works out a modernist variation of the mythic Don Juan. Depp is cast as the world's greatest lover, boasting of the seduction of 1,000 women. But, devastated and distraught by the recent loss of his one true love, and convinced there's no reason for him to go on living, he's determined to take his life.

Fable begins with the young Don Juan DeMarco, masked and cloaked in a cape, standing atop a billboard ready to jump. Certain they're dealing with a lunatic, the police summon veteran psychiatrist Jack Mickler (Brando) who miraculously succeeds in changing the desperado's mind. Mickler is given 10 days to diagnose his patient and recommend proper treatment.

The episodic narrative consists of one-to-one sessions between doctor and patient, with Don Juan recounting in graphic detail his adventurous odyssey and romantic escapades in Mexico. Mickler soon finds himself embracing his delusional patient's romantic world view, and he rekindles the spark long lost in his marriage to Marilyn (Dunaway).

Don Juan DeMarco isn't particularly well directed; the story often drags and the transition from one bizarre tale to another (all of which are narrated and presented in flashback) is at times rough. Happily, the richly textured dialogue sustains interest.

NOMINATION: Original Song ("Have You Ever Really Loved a Woman")

•

DONNIE BRASCO

1997, 126 mins, US Ⓥ ⦿ ▭ col

Dir Mike Newell ***Prod*** Mark Johnson, Barry Levinson, Louis DiGiaimo, Gail Mutrux ***Scr*** Paul Attanasio ***Ph*** Peter Sova ***Ed*** Jon Gregory ***Mus*** Patrick Doyle ***Art*** Donald Graham Burt

Act Al Pacino, Johnny Depp, Michael Madsen, Bruno Kirby, James Russo, Anne Heche (Baltimore/Mandalay/TriStar)

Mob life receives one of its least glamorous screen portraits in *Donnie Brasco*, which concentrates on the human toll of an enormously successful real FBI infiltration of the New York Mafia. The psychological dimensions remain underrealized, but the loaded central premise and intimate focus combine for a very involving and dramatic piece of crime lore.

Al Pacino plays Lefty Ruggiero, a two-bit wiseguy who, as of the tale's start in 1978, has worked as a loyal foot soldier for 30 years. At his barroom hangout, Lefty meets a young man, Donnie Brasco (Johnny Depp), who quickly impresses him with his knowledge of jewels and his tough-guy prowess. Donnie meets Lefty's cohorts, who include the hulking, explosively temperamental Sonny Black (Michael Madsen), the suspicious Paulie (James Russo) and the more voluble Nicky (Bruno Kirby).

What Lefty never knows is that his streetwise willing student is actually FBI agent Joseph Pistone, who is taping hours of revealing talk and accumulates mountains of evidence. Pistone's wife, Maggie (Anne Heche), is forced to endure long months without seeing her husband and the strain on their marriage becomes almost unendurable.

What neither the script [from Pistone and Richard Woodley's book, *Donnie Brasco: My Undercover Life in the Mafia*] nor Depp's performance ever attempt is an investigation into how Donnie/Joe feels about what he's doing. The film does not give him an interior voice, a door into his feelings.

By contrast, Pacino unlooses an unchecked stream of visible thought and emotion. Pacino's fine work is the key to the film succeeding to the extent it does.

1997: NOMINATION: Best Screenplay Adaptation

•

DO NOT DISTURB

1965, 102 mins, US ▭ col

Dir Ralph Levy ***Prod*** Aaron Rosenberg, Martin Melcher ***Scr*** Milt Rosen, Richard Breen ***Ph*** Leon Shamroy ***Ed*** Robert Simpson ***Mus*** Lionel Newman

Act Doris Day, Rod Taylor, Hermione Baddeley, Sergio Fantoni, Reginald Gardiner, Maura McGiveney (20th Century-Fox)

Do Not Disturb is a light, entertaining comedy, set in England but filmed in Hollywood, with Doris Day teamed with a new screen hubby, Rod Taylor.

Milt Rosen and Richard Breen adapted a William Fairchild play, and Day and Taylor star as a Yank couple localed in London, where hubby runs a woolen mill.

Stars play extremely well together, Day as the loving, but slightly wacky wife who grapples with English currency problems, rescues a pursued fox, and never quite gets the home in order, while Taylor is busy getting his factory into the black.

Their lives diverge when Maura McGiveney becomes too much of an assistant to Taylor, and sales chief Reginald Gardiner spells out the key for biz success: getting on the good side of Leon Askin, big wool buyer who throws swinging parties, meaning no wives.

Action cross cuts from Taylor's problem to Day, who becomes innocently entangled with Sergio Fantoni, antique dealer and a prototype Continental charmer.

•

DONOVAN'S REEF

1963, 104 mins, US Ⓥ ⦿ col

Dir John Ford ***Prod*** John Ford ***Scr*** Frank Nugent, James Edward Grant ***Ph*** William H. Clothier ***Ed*** Otho Lovering ***Mus*** Cyril Mockridge ***Art*** Hal Pereira, Eddie Imazu

Act John Wayne, Lee Marvin, Jack Warden, Elizabeth Allen, Cesar Romero, Dorothy Lamour (Paramount/Ford)

Donovan's Reef, for a director of John Ford's stature, is a potboiler. Where Ford aficianados will squirm is during that occasional scene that reminds them this effort-less effort is the handiwork of the men who made *Stagecoach* and *The Informer*.

John Wayne, sailing along like a dreadnaught mothering a convoy of rowboats, conveys an exuberance to match the mayhem, moving from fracas to fracas, facing up to a gang of toughs or a belligerent Boston beauty with equal courage. The only demand made is on his muscles.

Lee Marvin, since their last excursion, has had his reins tightened by Ford. This is only a comic menace where once a malevolent terror smouldered. Jack Warden's role hints at earlier greater prominence, edited down to harmless support and irritating in its omissions. Ford, best when he's faced with an unknown talent, brings out the ability of Elizabeth Allen, a darkling beauty. She's delightful as a Boston ice cube whose melting point is Wayne. Cesar Romero and Dorothy Lamour are the victims of acute scriptitis although Dick Foran is briefly impressive as an Australian naval officer.

The visual beauty of Kauai, in northern Hawaii, is captured by William Clothier's photography. Frank Nugent (an old Ford hand) and James Edward Grant's script [from a story by Edmund Beloin] has more holes in it than Liberty Valance. They've created a paradisical setting, "somewhere in the South Pacific," ruled by a native princess; governed by the French; protected by the Australian navy; "run" by expatriate Americans; and peopled by a league of national types.

•

DON Q, SON OF ZORRO

1925, 110 mins, US Ⓥ ⊗ col

Dir Donald Crisp ***Prod*** Douglas Fairbanks ***Scr*** Jack Cunningham ***Ph*** Henry Sharp ***Ed*** William Nolan ***Art*** Edward M. Langley

Act Douglas Fairbanks, Mary Astor, Jack McDonald, Donald Crisp, Warner Oland, Jean Hersholt (Elton/United Artists)

Don Q gives Fairbanks a chance to play a double role, as the youthful Don Q and as Zorro, the father of the dashing young Californian who is completing his education in Spain. His adventures there form the basis of the picture. He becomes involved with royalty, is accused of the murder of a visiting archduke, feigns suicide, almost loses the girl, but in the end emerges triumphant.

Mary Astor plays opposite the star. She appears to beautiful advantage in the little that she has to do, while Donald Crisp as the heavy scores, although the supporting cast honors of the picture must be divided between Jean Hersholt and Warner Oland. Hersholt gets rather the better of it. His role isn't as strong as the one he had in *Greed*, but it shows him capable of intense characterization that registers heavily.

•

DON'S PARTY

1976, 90 mins, Australia Ⓥ col

Dir Bruce Beresford ***Prod*** Philip Adams ***Scr*** David Williamson ***Ph*** Don McAlpine ***Ed*** Bill Anderson ***Art*** Rhoisin Harrison

Act Ray Barrett, Claire Binney, Pat Bishop, Graeme Blundell, Jeannie Drynan, John Gorton (Double Head)

The eponymous get-together takes place in Australia on Election Night, 1969. The 11 characters are all friends who, save two, have assembled to cheer in a Labor Party victory. The election day atmosphere is added to by a walk-on appearance by John Gorton as the prime minister of the day—which, indeed, he was.

The central characters in David Williamson's play may be grotesque, uncouth, drunken louts, but they do represent a streak in the Australian character that exists. Bringing them together at that particular time and place increases the claustrophobic effect they have on the others. *Don's Party* is a vicious and unrelenting attack on suburbia and a harsh look at these who help populate it. The entire cast turn in superlative performances.

•

DON'T BE A MENACE TO SOUTH CENTRAL WHILE DRINKING YOUR JUICE IN THE HOOD

1996, 88 mins, US Ⓥ col

Dir Paris Barclay ***Prod*** Keenan Ivory Wayans, Eric L. Gold ***Scr*** Shawn Wayans, Marlon Wayans, Phil Beauman ***Ph*** Russ Brandt ***Ed*** William Young, Marshall Harvey ***Mus*** John Barnes ***Art*** Aaron Osborne

Act Shawn Wayans, Marlon Wayans, Tracey Cherelle Jones, Chris Spencer, Suli McCullogh, Darrell Heath (Ivory Way/Island)

This latest product of the prolific Wayans family is much like its marquee-buster of a title: full of very obvious spoofery, and funnier in concept than in execution. Though spirited and hilarious in odd moments, *Don't Be a Menace* hardly expands on *In Living Color* and other Wayans precedents, and compared with a genuinely satiric film like Rusty Cundieff's *Fear of a Black Hat*, it's simple parody, with little in the way of ironic commentary or real invention.

The most frequently lampooned is John Singleton, whose *Boyz N the Hood* provides the prototype for this tale's fond mockery. Ashtray (Shawn Wayans) is a South Central Candide, sent to live with a father who is a model of irresponsibility. Seeking guidance, Ashtray turns to his cousin, Loc Dog (Marlon Wayans), who carries a whole arsenal of Uzis and the like, all color-coordinated with his sneakers, and also keeps a Russian nuclear warhead nearby, just in case.

The cousins' posse includes Preach (Chris Spencer), an Afrocentrist with a yen for white women, and Crazy Legs (Suli McCullough), an aspiring dancer confined to a wheelchair due to a drive-by shooting. Romantically naive, Ashtray soon loses his virginity to the lovely, poetry-writing Dashiki (Tracey Cherelle Jones), whose name supposedly is Swahili for "doggy style."

Pic benefits most from its genial, capable cast. Musicvid-maker Paris Barclay's direction is little more than serviceable.

•

DON'T BOTHER TO KNOCK

1952, 76 mins, US Ⓥ b/w

Dir Roy Ward Baker ***Prod*** Julian Blaustein ***Scr*** Daniel Taradash ***Ph*** Lucien Ballard ***Ed*** George A. Gittens ***Mus*** Lionel Newman (dir.) ***Art*** Lyle Wheeler, Richard Irvine

Act Richard Widmark, Marilyn Monroe, Anne Bancroft, Donna Corcoran, Jeanne Cagney, Elisha Cook, Jr. (20th Century-Fox)

Marilyn Monroe, co-starred with Richard Widmark, gives an excellent account of herself in a strictly dramatic role which commands certain attention, but the story of a psycho baby-sitter lacks interest.

Femme star enters a NY hotel to take on a baby-sitting stint. Actually, she's newly released from a mental institution, sent there when her mind cracked after her fiance crashed in the Pacific and drowned. In Widmark, who glimpses her from his room across the court and comes calling with a bottle, she sees, in her dementia, the man she once loved.

Action progresses at a dull pace, and script by Daniel Taradash [from a novel by Charlotte Armstrong] tries to juggle too many elements.

Monroe's role seems an odd choice, and in this she's anything but glamorous, despite her donning a negligee. Widmark doesn't appear too happy with his role. Anne Bancroft, making her screen bow, scores brightly as a torch singer.

•

DON'T BOTHER TO KNOCK

1961, 88 mins, UK col

Dir Cyril Frankel ***Prod*** Richard Todd ***Scr*** Denis Cannan, Frederick Gotfurt, Frederic Raphael ***Ph*** Geoffrey Unsworth ***Ed*** Anne V. Coates ***Mus*** Elisabeth Lutyens ***Art*** Tony Masters

Act Richard Todd, Nicole Maurey, Elke Sommer, June Thorburn, Judith Anderson, Eleanor Summerfield (Associated British/Haileywood)

Storyline has Richard Todd as an Edinburgh travel agent who goes off on a Continental business trip spree after quarreling with his fiancee (June Thorburn). He falls for a variety of charmers and hands out the key of his apartment to them with abandon. Having patched up his differences with his girlfriend over the phone, he returns to Edinburgh and, of course, all the other feminine complications then arrive and take up residence.

Here is the basis of a spry bedroom farce, but the dialog [from a novel by Clifford Hanley] is heavy handed. And director Cyril Frankel has not been able to induce performances that disguise this sorry fact. Todd spends most of his time looking understandingly bewildered over the naive behavior of the character he is playing. Of the girls, Nicole Maurey is certainly the most attractive, June Thorburn the one who has to work hardest to make any effect, and Elke Sommer the one who proves the biggest disappointment.

•

DON'T LOOK BACK

1967, 96 mins, US Ⓥ ⦿ b/w

Dir D. A. Pennebaker ***Prod*** Albert Grossman, John Court ***Ph*** D. A. Pennebaker ***Ed*** D. A. Pennebaker (Leacock Pennebaker)

Don't Look Back is a cinema verite documentary by D. A. Pennebaker of Bob Dylan's spring 1965 concert tour of Britain. Pennebaker has fashioned a relentlessly honest, brilliantly edited documentary permeated with the troubador-poet's music.

During the month-long tour, Dylan was accompanied by Joan Baez, haunted by the rival reputation of Donovan, and badgered day and night by the press, teenie-boppers and hangers on. Pennebaker shot some 20 hours of film, and edited it chronologically to reveal a portrait that is not always flattering.

There is Dylan, faintly hostile, "putting on" the press. In one classic scene he tells a *Time* magazine reporter exactly where *Time* and its readership are at, and if his outburst lacks tact, it seems to the point.

In one unique sequence Dylan's manager Albert Grossman and agent Tito Burns wheel, deal, and bluff the BBC, playing them against Granada-TV to double the price for a Dylan appearance.

•

DON'T LOOK NOW

1973, 110 mins, UK/Italy Ⓥ ⦿ col

Dir Nicolas Roeg ***Prod*** Peter Katz ***Scr*** Allan Scott, Chris Bryant ***Ph*** Anthony Richmond ***Ed*** Graeme Clifford ***Mus*** Pino Donaggio ***Art*** Giovanni Soccol

Act Julie Christie, Donald Sutherland, Hilary Mason, Clelia Matania, Massimo Serato, Renato Scarpa (Casey/Eldorado)

This British-Italian suspenser, in which the horror gets to one almost subliminally, as in *Rosemary's Baby*, is superior stuff. It can be "read" on two levels: as simply a gripping tale of mysterious goings-on in a wintertime Venice, or dealing with the supernatural and the occult as related to the established patterns of life and society.

Story itself is concocted from a Daphne du Maurier short story about a young British married couple who shortly after the accidental death—or was it?—of their daughter get involved in some strange happenings in a wintry Venice where the man is restoring a church.

A chance meeting in a restaurant with two sisters, one of them blind and suggesting she's "seen" and spoken to the dead child, sets things moving, with puzzling detail following puzzling detail in a mosaic of mystery which crescendos right up to a twist finale.

It's the fillips, visually introduced by director Nicolas Roeg in glimpses and flashes, that make this much more than merely a well-made psycho-horror thriller.

The performances are right on the button; Donald Sutherland is (unusually) at his most subdued, top effectiveness as the materialist who ironically becomes the victim of his refusal to believe in the intangible; Julie Christie does her best work in ages as his wife; while a superbly-chosen cast of British and Italian supporting players etch a number of indelibly vivid portraits.

Editing too, is careful and painstaking (the classically brilliant and erotic love-making scene is merely one of several examples) and plays a vital role in setting the film's mood.

•

DON'T LOSE YOUR HEAD

1967, 90 mins, UK col

Dir Gerald Thomas ***Prod*** Peter Rogers ***Scr*** Talbot Rothwell ***Ph*** Alan Hume ***Ed*** Rod Keys ***Mus*** Eric Rogers ***Art*** Lionel Couch

Act Sidney James, Kenneth Williams, Jim Dale, Charles Hawtrey, Peter Butterworth, Joan Sims (Rank)

Don't Lose Your Head is a wild parody of *Scarlet Pimpernel* adventures in the *Carry On* mould. The film is a crazy debauch of duelling, doublecrossing and disaster. The troupers jump through their well-known hoops with agility.

Sidney James and Jim Dale are the two bored English aristocrats who baffle Robespierre and his chief of police (Citizen Camembert—the Big Cheese) with their audacity. James, posing as "The Black Fingernail," turns up in a variety of disguises, none of which attempts to hide his homely features. He and Dale team up in sharp fashion. Kenneth Williams plays the police chief in his usual shrill style, and Peter Butterworth, Joan Sims, and Charles Hawtrey valiantly cope with the passing nonsense in their usual capable manner.

●

DON'T MAKE WAVES

1967, 100 mins, US ▭ col

Dir Alexander Mackendrick ***Prod*** John Calley, Martin Ransohoff ***Scr*** Ira Wallach, George Kirgo ***Ph*** Philip H. Lathrop ***Ed*** Rita Roland, Thomas Stanford ***Mus*** Vic Mizzy ***Art*** George W. Davis, Edward Carfagno

Act Tony Curtis, Claudia Cardinale, Robert Webber, Joanna Barnes, Sharon Tate, Mort Sahl (M-G-M/Filmways-Reynard)

Don't Make Waves is a mildly amusing film which never gets off the ground in its intended purpose of wacky comedy. Based on Ira Wallach's novel, *Muscle Beach*, film stars Tony Curtis and Claudia Cardinale.

Script has a Southern California setting, mixing romance, infidelity, beach antics, and sky diving with utter confusion as Curtis plays a frantic young man and Cardinale a peppery import with an accent.

Plot(?) gets underway as femme's car causes Curtis's Volkswagen to plunge down a hillside and burn, during which Curtis's pants and all his worldly possessions also go up in flames. Driving home with femme to look at her insurance policy, Curtis finds himself involved in her romance with a swimming pool operator, cheating on his wife.

●

DON'T PLAY US CHEAP

1973, 104 mins, US col

Dir Melvin Van Peebles ***Prod*** Melvin Van Peebles ***Scr*** Melvin Van Peebles ***Ph*** Bob Maxwell ***Ed*** Melvin Van Peebles ***Mus*** Melvin Van Peebles

Act Esther Rolle, Avon Long, Rhetta Hughes, George "Ooppee" McCurn (Yeah)

Melvin Van Peebles's film of his play *Don't Play Us Cheap* offers some terrific musical numbers and an ebullient look at black culture. Utilizing the same cast that he directed on Broadway [in 1972], Van Peebles creates the atmosphere of a house party in Harlem. His fantasy premise of an imp and little devil crashing the party to spoil it out of pure meanness allows the filmmaker's militant themes to be expressed in humor and whimsy.

Fantasy elements climax with black comedy of topliner Esther Rolle smashing the little devil in the form of a cockroach with a rolled up newspaper. Rolle is in great form as the party hostess, ably supported by an ensemble cast.

●

DON'T RAISE THE BRIDGE, LOWER THE RIVER

1968, 99 mins, UK Ⓥ col

Dir Jerry Paris ***Prod*** Walter Shenson ***Scr*** Max Wilk ***Ph*** Otto Heller ***Ed*** Bill Lenny ***Mus*** David Whitaker ***Art*** John Howell

Act Jerry Lewis, Terry-Thomas, Jacqueline Pearce, Bernard Cribbins, Patricia Routledge, Nicholas Parsons (Columbia)

Adapted by Max Wilk from his own novel, *Don't Raise the Bridge, Lower the River*, is a mildly diverting production, filmed at Britain's Shepperton Studios, and starring Jerry Lewis as a perennial dreamer. An initial lack of clarity in plot premise, followed by routine and not very exciting episodic treatment add up to a generally flat result. Weaknesses are apparent at the very beginning: a series of disparate locations, after which it finally is established that Lewis is an eternal dreamer.

Subsequent to this revelation, story plods along in a dramatic monotone, progressing, but never building, toward an inevitable happy ending after 99 slow minutes.

Featured players Terry-Thomas as the typical promoter; Bernard Cribbins as a garage mechanic who doubles as a steward on unscheduled airlines; and Patricia Routledge, a man-hungry Girl Scout leader, are quite excellent in their appearances.

Lewis comes across as uncertain of whether he is supposed to ham it up at times, play it down at others.

●

DON'T TELL MOM THE BABYSITTER'S DEAD

1991, 105 mins, US Ⓥ ⊙ col

Dir Stephen Herek ***Prod*** Robert Newmyer, Brian Reilly, Jeffrey Silver ***Scr*** Neil Landau, Tara Ison ***Ph*** Tim Suhrstedt ***Ed*** Larry Bock ***Mus*** David Newman, Bruce Nazarian ***Art*** Stephen Marsh

Act Christina Applegate, Joanna Cassidy, John Getz, Josh Charles, Keith Coogan, David Duchovny (HBO/Outlaw)

Don't Tell Mom the Babysitter's Dead starts with an enjoyable, if crude, black comedy situation promised by the title, but then it turns into an incredibly dumb teenage girl's fantasy of making it in the business world.

Christina Applegate and her four siblings (Keith Coogan, Robert Hy Gorman, Danielle Harris, Christopher Pettiet) are left by their ditzy vacationing mom (Concetta Tomei) in their suburban L.A. home with a seemingly sweet old lady babysitter (Eda Reiss Merin), who turns out to be a "deranged Mary Poppins."

Following the old lady's death from a heart attack, Applegate has to earn money to support the kids so they won't have to ask mom to come home from Australia. The leaden script turns mind-numbingly silly. Applegate improbably parlays a padded resume into a high-paying job as administrative assistant to glamorous L.A. garment industry exec Joanna Cassidy.

Though she has promise, Applegate is misused in a part making her seem more airheaded than shrewd. Cassidy, whose mature sexiness livens the film for a while, is gradually made to look more and more ridiculous by the pic's clumsy director, Stephen Herek.

●

DOOM GENERATION, THE

1995, 84 mins, US col

Dir Gregg Araki ***Prod*** Andrea Sperling, Gregg Araki ***Scr*** Gregg Araki ***Ph*** Jim Fealy ***Ed*** Gregg Araki ***Art*** Therese Deprez

Act James Duval, Rose McGowan, Johnathon Schaech (UGC/Teen Angst)

With *The Doom Generation*, his fifth and most audacious film to date, L.A. guerrilla filmmaker Gregg Araki proves that, given a reasonable budget (less than $1 million), he can produce a stunning film with superlative production values. A nihilistic comedy about a trio of alienated youngsters, pic is bold not only in its art design, but also in its narrative and tone, a mixture of satire and horror with heavy dosage of steamy sex and macabre violence.

Amy Blue (Rose McGowan), a beautiful, spoiled 17-year-old, her sweet suburban b.f., Jordan White (James Duval), and Xavier Red (Johnathon Schaech), a mysterious drifter, embark on an outlandish trip after Xavier blows off the head of a convenience store clerk. The trio flee into a bizarre world of nightmarish violence and omnipresent danger that gets darker and darker as their odyssey progresses.

Pic's "quieter" moments are provided by stops along the road, in fantastically designed motels, in which the threesome explore their anomie—and sexuality. For a film bluntly described in the opening titles as "heterosexual," story is overripe with homoerotic overtones. Most of the film's violence is played tongue-in-cheek, with hilarious stagings of a severed head or amputated arm flying through the air. In the lead role, the debuting McGowan is incredibly photogenic, commanding the screen with the ease and assuredness of a pro. Duval, who looks and acts like a younger Keanu Reeves, renders a quieter perf, while Schaech projects the kind of eroticism that's both appealing and repellant.

●

DOORS, THE

1991, 141 mins, US Ⓥ ⊙ ▭ col

Dir Oliver Stone ***Prod*** Bill Graham, Sasha Harari, A. Kitman Ho ***Scr*** J. Randal Johnson, Oliver Stone ***Ph*** Robert Richardson ***Ed*** David Brenner, Joe Hutshing ***Art*** Barbara Ling

Act Val Kilmer, Meg Ryan, Kevin Dillon, Kyle MacLachlan, Frank Whaley, Kathleen Quinlan (Carolco/Imagine)

The Doors is another trip into 1960s hell from Oliver Stone. This $40 million look at Jim Morrison's short, wild ride through a rock idol life is everything one expects from the filmmaker—intense, overblown, riveting, humorless, evocative, self-important and impossible to ignore. As rendered with considerable physical accuracy by Val Kilmer, Morrison is drunk and/or stoned practically from beginning to end, providing an acute case study of ruinous excess. The singer's obsession with death and mysticism is rooted, via a sepia-tinged prolog, in a childhood experience in which he views the aftermath of a traffic accident involving some Indians.

Action proper begins in 1965, as Morrison the would-be poet and pretentious UCLA student filmmaker hooks up with flower child Pamela Courson (Meg Ryan) and launches a band in Venice, Cal., with John Densmore, Ray Manzarek and Robby Krieger.

Outside of Morrison's abusive, drug-drenched relationship with Courson, only two of his innumerable sexual trysts are detailed—one with the exotic Velvet Underground star Nico, the other with the demonic Patricia Kenealy (Kathleen Quinlan).

Kilmer is convincing in the lead role, although he never allows the viewer to share any emotions. Morrison's own vocals have been skillfully augmented by Kilmer in some sequences.

The usually engaging Ryan brings little to a vaguely conceived part, whereas Quinlan commands the screen.

●

DO THE RIGHT THING

1989, 120 mins, US Ⓥ ⊙ col

Dir Spike Lee ***Prod*** Spike Lee ***Scr*** Spike Lee ***Ph*** Ernest Dickerson ***Ed*** Barry Alexander Brown ***Mus*** Bill Lee ***Art*** Wynn Thomas

Act Danny Aiello, Ossie Davis, Ruby Dee, Richard Edson, Giancarlo Esposito, Spike Lee (40 Acres & a Mule)

Spike Lee combines a forceful statement on race relations with solid entertainment values in *Do the Right Thing*.

Lee adopts the durable theatrical format of *Street Scene* as his launching point, painstakingly etching an ensemble of neighborhood characters on a Bedford Stuyvesant block in Brooklyn. Centrepiece is Danny Aiello's pizza parlor, which he runs with his sons John Turturro and Richard Edson, with Lee delivering takeout orders.

On the hottest day of the summer, a myriad of contemporary issues covering personal, social, and economic matters are laid on the table in often shrill but sometimes funny confrontations. Ossie Davis is perfect casting as a sort of conciliator, a hobo nicknamed the Mayor who injects folk wisdom into the discussion.

Standing out in a uniformly solid cast are Ruby Dee, the Earth Mother of the microcosmic community; Aiello, Turturro, and Edson as three quite different variations on an ethnic theme; Paul Benjamin, Frankie Faison, and Robin Harris as the funny trio of kibitzers on the block, and Roger Guenveur Smith as he creates an unusual, poetic figure of a stammering simpleton (who sells photos of black leaders) in the midst of such confident figures.

1989: NOMINATIONS: Best Supp. Actor (Danny Aiello), Original Screenplay

DOUBLE DRAGON

1994, 95 mins, US Ⓥ ⊙ col

Dir James Yukich ***Prod*** Sunil R. Shah, Ash R. Shah, Alan Schechter, ***Scr*** Michael Davis, Peter Gould ***Ph*** Gary Kibbe ***Ed*** Florent Retz ***Mus*** Jay Ferguson ***Art*** Mayne Berke

Act Robert Patrick, Mark Dacascos, Scott Wolf, Kristina Malandro Wagner, Julia Nickson, Alyssa Milano (Greenleaf/Imperial/Scanbox)

Even kids won't get much of a kick out this high-energy, low-IQ futuristic slugfest, which plays down to, and, in many ways, below the level of some Saturday-morning cartoons.

Yet another sci-fi story set in earthquake-ravaged Los Angeles (the big joke is that the Hollywood sign is up to its "H" in water), under musicvideo director James Yukich's pacing, *Dragon* never slows down long enough to explain half of what's going on. That would be OK if the dialogue were more palatable, the nonstop action more inventive or the sets and special effects less cheesy.

Mark Dacascos and Scott Wolf play Jimmy and Billy Lee, teenage brothers whose mentor (Julia Nickson) possesses half of a dragon amulet that bestows certain powers on its holder. The other half has been stolen by Koga Shuko, a power-obsessed mogul played so campily by Robert Patrick that even his bad haircut seems appropriate. Shuko spends the entire movie chasing the boys to get their half of the charm, using the gangs who rule New Angeles by night as his minions. The Lees, meanwhile, are befriended by a band of vigilante teens whose leader (Alyssa Milano) has a haircut almost as bad as Koga Shuko's.

Patrick, best known as the evil cyborg in *Terminator 2*, proves a toothless villain here.

●

DOUBLE IMPACT

1991, 108 mins, US Ⓥ ⊙ col

Dir Sheldon Lettich ***Prod*** Ashok Amritraj, Jean-Claude Van Damme ***Scr*** Sheldon Lettich, Jean-Claude Van Damme ***Ph*** Richard Kline ***Ed*** Mark Conte ***Mus*** Arthur Kempel ***Art*** John Jay Moore

Act Jean-Claude Van Damme, Geoffrey Lewis, Alan Scarfe, Alonna Shaw, Philip Chan, Cory Everson (Stone Group)

This double-dose of Jean-Claude Van Damme turns on a typically lame revenge plot while dragging out unimaginatively shot action sequences until no one will give a good Van Damme. The one-time karate champ nicknamed "muscles from Brussels" apparently wanted to stretch his acting hamstring in this dual role as twins separated at six months. Pic [from a story by Van Damme, Sheldon Lettich, Steve Meerson, and Peter Krikes] starts off with the twins' parents being killed by an evil developer (Alan Scarfe). One grows up on the mean streets of Hong Kong, while the other was raised by a family friend (Geoffrey Lewis) and turns up 25 years later as a Los Angeles karate instructor. Lewis's character discovers the other twin is alive and takes his charge back to Hong Kong, reuniting the mismatched pair to reclaim their inheritance.

Van Damme uses two looks—glowering/nasty and friendly/bewildered—to differentiate the characters. It's disturbing that not a single Asian character exhibits any redeeming features. Equal opportunities are provided in the evil henchmen ranks, however, where female bodybuilder Cory Everson joins so-called "Chinese Hercules" Bolo Yeung, a perennial martial arts bad guy who hasn't won a fight in one of these opuses dating back to *Enter the Dragon*.

•

DOUBLE INDEMNITY

1944, 103 mins, US Ⓥ ⊙ b/w

Dir Billy Wilder ***Prod*** Joseph Sistrom ***Scr*** Billy Wilder, Raymond Chandler ***Ph*** John F. Seitz ***Ed*** Doane Harrison ***Mus*** Miklos Rozsa ***Art*** Hans Dreier, Hal Pereira

Act Fred MacMurray, Barbara Stanwyck, Edward G. Robinson, Porter Hall, Jean Heather, Tom Powers (Paramount)

James M. Cain's novel *Double Indemnity*, apparently based on a sensational murder of the 1920s, is an absorbing melodrama in its Paramount adaptation. There are unmistakeable similarities between the pic and the famous Snyder-Gray murder wherein Albert Snyder was sashweighted to death in 1927 in his Queens Village, NY, home by his wife, Ruth, and her lover, Judd Gray. Both the fictional and the real murders were for the slain men's insurance. Both were committed by the murdered men's wives and their amours.

The story's development revolves mainly around the characterizations of Fred MacMurray, Barbara Stanwyck, and Edward G. Robinson, the first two as the lovers and Robinson as an insurance claims agent who balks the pair's "perfect crime" from becoming just what they had intended it to appear—an accidental death from a moving train, for which there would have been a double indemnity.

Stanwyck plays the wife of an oilman, and when MacMurray, an insurance salesman, becomes her paramour, they fraudulently sell to the husband an accidental-death policy. They then kill him and place his body on the railway tracks.

It is a story told in flashback, film opening with MacMurray confessing voluntarily the entire setup into a dictaphone for use by the claims agent, from which the narrative then unfolds.

MacMurray has seldom given a better performance. It is somewhat different from his usually light roles, but is always plausible and played with considerable restraint. Stanwyck is not as attractive as normally with what is seemingly a blonde wig, but it's probably part of a makeup to emphasize the brassiness of the character. Robinson, as the infallible insurance executive quick to determine phoney claims, gives a strong performance, too.

1944: NOMINATIONS: Best Picture, Director, Actress (Barbara Stanwyck), Screenplay, B&W Cinematography, Score of a Dramatic Picture, Sound

•

DOUBLE JEOPARDY

1999, 105 mins, US Ⓥ ⊙ ▭ col

Dir Bruce Beresford ***Prod*** Leonard Goldberg ***Scr*** David Weisberg, Douglas S. Cook ***Ph*** Peter James ***Ed*** Mark Warner ***Mus*** Normand Corbeil ***Art*** Howard Cummings

Act Tommy Lee Jones, Ashley Judd, Bruce Greenwood, Annabeth Gish, Roma Maffia, Davenia McFadden (Paramount)

With a straight-ahead, no-nonsense approach to match its stars, *Double Jeopardy* is single-minded and engaging thriller storytelling without an afterglow. In the first studio project in which she's front and center throughout, Ashley Judd makes her woman scorned an impressive star turn that is equal measures sinewy, determinedly focused and graceful—a yin to Tommy Lee Jones's patented gruff yang as the parole officer tracking her down.

While this marks Judd's second standard-issue thriller in a row after *Kiss the Girls*, current pic is a better example of the genre and offers versatile thesp a far greater challenge. Direction by Bruce Beresford is so unassumingly assured that it barely registers that the thriller is a marked change of pace from his more humanistic, character-driven projects.

Hours after lovemaking with hubby Nick (Bruce Greenwood) on their Whidbey Island, WA, sailboat, Libby (Judd) wakes in a bloodstained bed—but no Nick. On cue, the coast guard appears as Libby holds the knife, and she is convicted of murder.

Libby realizes she's been framed and starts working out like she's in Olympic trials for the Revenge event. In the typically ultra-tidy style of this narrative, Libby gets paroled with no problem after six years. Parole officer Travis (Jones) is all business but this doesn't stop her from going back to Whidbey Island.

It's *Fugitive* time again for Jones and he injects every scene during a lengthy pursuit from the Northwest to New Orleans with a wry, ironic wit. Judd looks and acts pumped for action, just eluding her pursuer every step of the way.

•

DOUBLE LIFE, A

1947, 103 mins, US Ⓥ b/w

Dir George Cukor ***Prod*** Michael Kanin ***Scr*** Ruth Gordon, Garson Kanin ***Ph*** Milton Krasner ***Ed*** Robert Parrish ***Mus*** Miklos Rozsa ***Art*** Harry Horner

Act Ronald Colman, Signe Hasso, Edmond O'Brien, Shelley Winters, Ray Collins, Philip Loeb (Universal/Kanin)

Life is particularly distinguished for the manner in which the characters have been conceived and played. Each character rings true as the story goes into its play-within-a-play about actors and the theatre. There's murder, suspense, psychology, Shakespeare, and romance all wrapped up into one polished package of class screen entertainment.

Plot poses an interesting premise—that an actor takes on some of the characteristics of the role he is playing if the run is long. In this instance Ronald Colman lives his roles without danger until he tackles *Othello*. Gradually, as the play goes into a second year, he is dominated more and more by the character he creates on the stage. It finally leads him to murder a chance acquaintance in the same manner in which Othello snuffs out the life of Desdemona each night on the stage.

Colman realizes on every facet of the demanding part in a performance that is flawless. It's a histrionic gem of unusual versatility. Signe Hasso, his stage co-star and former wife, is a solid click, revealing a talent that has rarely been called upon in her other film roles. Her Desdemona is brilliant and her interpretation of the understanding ex-wife perfect.

1947: Best Actor (Ronald Colman), Score for a Dramatic Picture

NOMINATIONS: Best Director, Original Screenplay

•

DOUBLE LIFE OF VERONIQUE, THE

SEE: LA DOUBLE VIE DE VERONIQUE

•

DOUBLE MAN, THE

1967, 105 mins, UK Ⓥ col

Dir Franklin J. Schaffner ***Prod*** Hal. E. Chester ***Scr*** Frank Tarloff, Alfred Hayes ***Ph*** Denys Coop ***Ed*** Richard Best ***Mus*** Ernie Freeman ***Art*** Arthur Lawson

Act Yul Brynner, Britt Ekland, Clive Revill, Anton Diffring, David Bauer, Lloyd Nolan (Warner-Pathe/Albion)

Frank Tarloff and Alfred Hayes have tailored a solid screenplay from Henry Maxfield's novel, *Legacy of a Spy*, in which intelligence agent Dan Slater (Yul Brynner) is plunged into strange problems when he goes to the Austrian Alps to investigate the death of his son on a ski-slope. The police write it off as an accident. Brynner suspects murder.

The film builds up an intriguing sense of tension with the motives of various people rating suspicion, Brynner being tailed by obvious enemy agents and a big payoff when he is confronted with his double.

Clive Revill, an ex-agent pal of Brynner's, though not fully trusted by him, also turns in an interesting show as an honest but weak, indecisive character who rallies at the critical moment. Anton Diffring is a suave enemy scientist and David Bauer does excellent work as an agent detailed to bring Brynner back to Washington.

•

DOUBLE TROUBLE

1967, 81 mins, US Ⓥ ⊙ ▭ col

Dir Norman Taurog ***Prod*** Judd Bernard, Irwin Winkler ***Scr*** Jo Heims ***Ph*** Daniel L. Fapp ***Ed*** John McSweeney ***Mus*** Jeff Alexander ***Art*** George W. Davis, Merrill Pye

Act Elvis Presley, Annette Day, John Williams, Yvonne Romain, Chips Rafferty, Norman Rossington (M-G-M)

Double Trouble has the sketchiest story-line which leaves spectator wondering what it's all about. Elvis Presley as usual, however, gives a pretty fair account of himself despite what's handed him.

He plays an American singer touring foreign discotheques, and scene shifts from London, where two femmes enter his life, to Bruges and finally Antwerp.

Intertwined in his travels, and femmes chasing him, are a couple of eccentric jewel thieves who have planted a fortune of diamonds in his luggage, mysterious attempts on his life and his arrest for allegedly kidnapping one of the kittens, who happens to be a rich heiress, 17-going-on-18.

•

DOUBLE VIE DE VERONIQUE, LA
(THE DOUBLE LIFE OF VERONIQUE)

1991, 97 mins, France/Poland/Norway Ⓥ ⊙ col

Dir Krzysztof Kieslowski ***Prod*** Leonardo De La Fuente ***Scr*** Krzysztof Kieslowski, Krzysztof Piesiewicz ***Ph*** Slawomir Idziak ***Ed*** Jacques Witta ***Mus*** Zbigniew Preisner ***Art*** Patrice Mercier

Act Irene Jacob, Philippe Volter, Sandrine Dumas, Claude Duneton, Wladyslaw Kowalski, Jerzy Gudejko (Sideral/Canal Plus/Tor/Norsk)

The Double Life of Veronique will have fans of Krzysztof Kieslowski taking sides. Despite pic's many-splendored outbursts of filmic creativity and intense emotion, final result, about the opposite destinies of a Polish girl and a French girl who look alike and have the same name and tics, remains a head-scratching cipher with blurred edges. Pic's first third takes place in Poland in an almost perfect confluence of shots, editing, and dialog that holds the viewer rapt. Weronika (Irene Jacob, dubbed by Anna Gronostaj) is a bubbly, happy girl in love with a young man (Jerzy Gudejko). While she's visiting her aunt in Krakow, her extraordinary voice is discovered by a music teacher.

Her passion shifts from love to singing. She continues despite a dangerous heart condition, and in a scene of overwhelming intensity, dies on stage during a recital.

After the tight, punchy opening, film keeps its momentum for a little while in the French part. Veronique (also a singer) feels an inexplicable urge to quit voice training. She follows her instincts unhesitatingly, later mesmerized by a handsome puppeteer, Alexandre Fabbri (Philippe Volter), a writer of children's books.

Jacob is a sparkling newcomer who imbues both roles with an innocent but powerful magic. Volter attracts as the shadowy puppeteer (a role originally offered to Italo actor-director Nanni Moretti).

•

DOUBLE WEDDING

1937, 87 mins, US Ⓥ b/w

Dir Richard Thorpe ***Prod*** Joseph L. Mankiewicz ***Scr*** Jo Swerling ***Ph*** William Daniels ***Ed*** Frank Sullivan ***Mus*** Edward Ward

Act William Powell, Myrna Loy, Florence Rice, John Beal, Jessie Ralph, Edgar Kennedy (M-G-M)

Those two box-office dynamiters, William Powell and Myrna Loy, are yoked in *Double Wedding*, an outright slapstick comedy which would be funnier if it were shorter.

Powell is a trailer dweller in an auto parking spot in a big city, an artist vagrant with an amusing if somewhat cockeyed philosophy of life which can be summed up by stating that work is for workmen of which he is not one, just as the ocean is for sailors. Jo Swerling wrote the screenplay from a comedy [*Great Love*] by Ferenc Molnar.

Loy is the proprietor of a smart style shop and so engrossed in the problems of moneymaking and the responsibilities of rearing a younger sister that she has no time for play. Sister is screen-struck, dreaming of a Hollywood career. Loy has chosen otherwise and selects a nice boy for her sister to marry. Then the young couple meet Powell in his trailer and Myrna's plans get a rude shuffling. Sister falls for Powell.

•

DOVE, THE

1974, 105 mins, UK Ⓥ ▭ col

Dir Charles Jarrott ***Prod*** Gregory Peck ***Scr*** Peter Beagle, Adam Kennedy ***Ph*** Sven Nykvist ***Ed*** John Jympson ***Mus*** John Barry ***Art*** Peter Lamont

Act Joseph Bottoms, Deborah Raffin, John McLiam, Dabney Coleman, John Anderson, Colby Chester (EMI/Peck)

The Dove is based on the book by round-the-world solo sailor Robin Lee Graham [with Derek Gill]. Though basically a yarn about Graham's five-year solo trip around the world in a small sailboat, an odyssey which provides nautical chills and thrills (as well as breathtaking scenics) aplenty, pic is also a tale of character development as the hero finds himself (and manhood) enroute, plus an unpreachy thesis on ecology.

Pic really takes off when he meets the girl (played with gauche hesitation at first, but then with beauty and considerable charm by Deborah Raffin) who is to provide the driving force behind his trek and on into manhood and maturity. Their yes-no yes-no-yes affair is nicely handled.

Fiji to Australia, South Africa and Madagascar to Panama and the Galapagos Isles, are simply breathtaking.

•

DOWN AND OUT IN BEVERLY HILLS
1986, 97 mins, US Ⓥ ⦿ col
Dir Paul Mazursky ***Prod*** Paul Mazursky ***Scr*** Paul Mazursky, Leon Capetanos ***Ph*** Donald McAlpine ***Ed*** Richard Halsey ***Mus*** Andy Summers ***Art*** Pato Guzman
Act Nick Nolte, Richard Dreyfuss, Bette Midler, Little Richard, Tracy Nelson, Elizabeth Pena (Touchstone)

Down and Out in Beverly Hills continues Paul Mazursky's love-hate relationship with the bourgeoisie and its institutions, especially marriage. It's a loving caricature of the nouveau riche (Beverly Hills variety) and although it is more of a comedy of manners than a well-developed story, there are enough yocks and bright moments to make it a thoroughly enjoyable outing.

Mazursky and co-writer Leon Capetanos have cleverly taken the basic premise of Jean Renoir's 1932 classic *Boudu Saved from Drowning* [from the play by Rene Fauchois] and used it as a looking glass for the foibles of the rich and bored.

Head of the household is the aptly named David Whiteman (Richard Dreyfuss). Bette Midler is the lady of the house with their near anorexic daughter Tracy Nelson and son Evan Richards.

In short it's a household of unhappy people and the fly (perhaps flea is more accurate) in the ointment is Nick Nolte as the bum Jerry Baskin. A disheveled and dirty street person, Jerry is an artist of sorts—a con artist. For the Whitemans he becomes their idealized bum, the family pet.

•

DOWN BY LAW
1986, 106 mins, US Ⓥ b/w
Dir Jim Jarmusch ***Prod*** Jim Jarmusch ***Scr*** Jim Jarmusch ***Ph*** Robby Muller ***Ed*** Franck Kern ***Mus*** John Lurie ***Art*** Roger Knight
Act Tom Waits, John Lurie, Roberto Benigni, Nicoletta Braschi, Ellen Barkin (Black Snake/Grohenberger)

Zack (Tom Waits) is caught driving a car with a body in the trunk and Jack (John Lurie) is found by the cops in a hotel room with an unquestionably underage girl. Both men are framed. They wind up in the slammer, in the same cell. Third cell mate is Roberto (Roberto Benigni), who speaks fractured English but whose naive friendliness proves contagious.

After several funny scenes, the Italian proposes they escape, "just like they do in American movies." And so they do, out into the Louisiana swamps and eventually stumble on an isolated, unlikely diner where, surprise, surprise, the owner chef is a lonely Italian woman (Nicoletta Braschi) who immediately falls for Benigni.

The Jim Jarmusch penchant for off-the-wall characters and odd situations is very much in evidence. The black-and-white photography is a major plus, and so is John Lurie's score, with songs by Tom Waits. Both men are fine in their respective roles, but Benigni steals the film.

•

DOWNHILL RACER
1969, 101 mins, US/UK Ⓥ ⦿ col
Dir Michael Ritchie ***Prod*** Richard Gregson ***Scr*** James Salter ***Ph*** Brian Probyn ***Ed*** Nick Archer, Richard Harris ***Mus*** Kenyon Hopkins ***Art*** Ian Whittaker
Act Robert Redford, Gene Hackman, Camilla Sparv, Karl Michael Vogler, Jim McMullan, Dabney Coleman (Paramount/Wildwood)

Downhill Racer is an intriguing film that balances skiing and the majesty of Alpine scenery with an absorbing story of hero Robert Redford, young American innocent abroad.

The picture was filmed in the Swiss, Austrian and French Alps. Screenplay [based on the novel *The Downhill Racers* by Oakley Hall] plunges into action when Colorado-born Redford, part of an American skiing team coached by tough Gene Hackman, asserts himself both with the personalities surrounding him and on the European slopes.

Redford contributes a sensitive, interesting portrayal. His interpretation is many-faceted and probing. Hackman's characterization is virile and thoroughly human.

Filming of the downhill course, made with camera attached to the skier's helmet, was properly nervewracking. And a heart-in-the-throat Olympic downhill race as a finale tops everything that has gone before.

•

DOWN MEXICO WAY
1941, 72 mins, US Ⓥ b/w
Dir Joseph Santley ***Prod*** Harry Grey ***Scr*** Olive Cooper, Albert Duffy ***Ph*** Jack Marta ***Ed*** Howard O'Neill
Act Gene Autry, Smiley Burnette, Fay McKenzie, Harold Huber (Republic)

After a pair of swindlers work over the small town of Sage City, Gene Autry discovers his townfolk have been bilked out of coin supposedly aimed for picture production. Accompanied by Smiley Burnette and reformed Mexican bad man (Harold Huber), Autry trails the crooks into Mexico, where the swindlers' confederates are repeating activities with a rich Mexican rancher as victim. From there on, it's up to Autry to uncover the machinations of the crooks, which he does with a rousing chase and gunfight for a finale.

Story carries along at a good pace, neatly intermingling action, romance and comedy. Autry carries his assignment as the hero in good style, singing several songs—including a couple of familiar pops—in usual fashion.

Picture carries ambitious production mounting in comparison to previous Autrys in the series; with climactic chase using an auto, horses, and wildly careening motorcycles for variation.

•

DOWN TO EARTH
1947, 100 mins, US Ⓥ ⦿ col
Dir Alexander Hall ***Prod*** Don Hartman ***Scr*** Don Hartman, Edwin Blum ***Ph*** Rudolph Mate ***Ed*** Viola Lawrence ***Mus*** George Duning, Heinz Roemheld, Mario Castelnuovo-Tedesco ***Art*** Stephen Goosson, Rudolph Sternad
Act Rita Hayworth, Larry Parks, Roland Culver, James Gleason, Edward Everett Horton, Marc Platt (Columbia)

Yarn is one of those tricky ideas that look so much better on paper than celluloid. It picks up the characters from Harry Segall's play, *Heaven Can Wait*, filmed by Columbia in 1941 as the tremendously successful *Here Comes Mr. Jordan*, and puts them down in a new setting.

Producer Don Hartman has carried out his cute idea to the extent of using some of the same cast as *Jordan*. James Gleason is back as an agent and Edward Everett Horton is seen once again as the messenger who accompanies the spirit down to earth. Roland Culver subs for Claude Rains in the Jordan role, the guy who runs Heaven.

Rita Hayworth is pictured as Terpsichore, the Greek muse of the theatre. Looking down from Heaven she's unhappy over a Broadway musical about the nine muses, being done in jazz by producer Larry Parks. She makes a request to go down and help him so she can clean the show up. She lands in the star role and there's the usual falling-in-love with the vis-a-vis—in this case Parks.

Explanation necessary to get all this across takes interminable time and constantly slows even the angels to a lazy walk. Making things worse is the fact that all the gags which should give the yarn a bit of pepper fall flat.

Definitely on the credit side are the five tunes provided by Allan Roberts and Doris Fisher. Parks sings one tune. It's definitely a letdown. Hayworth does better in the vocal department and, of course, is fine in the terp routines [staged by Jack Cole].

•

DOWN TO THE SEA IN SHIPS
1949, 120 mins, US Ⓥ b/w
Dir Henry Hathaway ***Prod*** Louis D. Lighton ***Scr*** John Lee Mahin, Sy Bartlett ***Ph*** Joe MacDonald ***Ed*** Dorothy Spencer ***Mus*** Alfred Newman
Act Richard Widmark, Lionel Barrymore, Dean Stockwell, Gene Lockhart, Cecil Kellaway (20th Century-Fox)

Down to the Sea in Ships is a lengthy saga of early whaling ships and the men who commanded them. It is told with emphasis on character study rather than action.

The first half is becalmed in a rather thorough development of the characters. In the last hour, picture really shakes out its sails and goes wing-and-winging before the wind.

The taking of a whale and the rendering of blubber to oil, the dangers of fog and the menace of a wreck on an iceberg is sturdy excitement that serves as a fitting climax to the story of an old whaler captain, his young grandson, and of a young first mate.

Richard Widmark has a chance at a sympathetic role and proves himself versatile. Lionel Barrymore carries off the fat part of whaling captain with fewer of the usual Barrymore tricks. Despite his youth, Dean Stockwell is a skilled thespian who more than holds his own in scenes with the adults.

•

DOWN WENT MCGINTY
SEE: THE GREAT MCGINTY

•

DRACULA
1931, 64 mins, US Ⓥ ⦿ b/w
Dir Tod Browning ***Prod*** Carl Laemmle, Jr. ***Scr*** Garrett Fort, Dudley Murphy ***Ph*** Karl Freund ***Ed*** Milton Carruth ***Art*** Charles D. Hall
Act Bela Lugosi, Helen Chandler, Davis Manners, Dwight Frye, Edward Van Sloan, Herbert Bunston (Universal)

Treatment differs from both the stage version [by Deane and John Balderston] and the original novel [by Bram Stoker]. On the stage it was a thriller carried to such an extreme that it had a comedy punch by its very outre aspect. On the screen it comes out as a sublimated ghost story related with all surface seriousness and above all with a remarkably effective background of creepy atmosphere.

Early in the action is a barren rocky mountain pass, peopled only by a spectral coach driver and shrouded in a miasmic mist. Story proceeds thence into a tomb-like castle. In such surroundings the sinister figure of the human vampire, the living-dead Count Dracula who sustains life by drinking the blood of his victims, seems almost plausible.

It is difficult to think of anybody who could quite match the performance in the vampire part of Bela Lugosi, even to the faint flavor of foreign speech that fits so neatly. Helen Chandler is the blonde type for the clinging-vine heroine, and Herbert Bunston plays the scientist deadly straight, but with a faint suggestion of comedy that dovetails into the whole pattern.

•

DRACULA
(US: HORROR OF DRACULA)
1958, 82 mins, UK Ⓥ col
Dir Terence Fisher ***Prod*** Anthony Hinds ***Scr*** Jimmy Sangster ***Ph*** Jack Asher ***Ed*** James Needs, Bill Lenny ***Mus*** James Bernard ***Art*** Bernard Robinson
Act Peter Cushing, Christopher Lee, Melissa Stribling, Michael Gough, Carol Marsh, Miles Malleson (Hammer)

For those familiar with the original *Dracula* thriller, the screenplay has ably preserved the sanguinary aspects of the Bram Stoker novel. Here again we have Count Dracula sleeping in a coffin by day and plying his nefarious role of a blood-sucking vampire at night. Version has its usual quota of victims before his reign of terror is ended by a fearless doctor.

Both director Terence Fisher as well as the cast have taken a serious approach to the macabre theme that adds up to lotsa tension and suspense. Peter Cushing is impressive as the painstaking scientist-doctor who solves the mystery. Christopher Lee is thoroughly gruesome as Dracula, and Michael Gough is suitably skeptical as a bereaved relative who ultimately is persuaded to assist Cushing.

•

DRACULA
1979, 109 mins, US Ⓥ ⦿ ▭ col
Dir John Badham ***Prod*** Walter Mirisch ***Scr*** W. D. Richter ***Ph*** Gilbert Taylor ***Ed*** John Bloom ***Mus*** John Williams ***Art*** Peter Murton
Act Frank Langella, Laurence Olivier, Donald Pleasence, Kate Nelligan, Trevor Eve, Jan Francis (Universal)

With this lavish retelling of an oft-told tale, *Dracula* puts the male vamp back in vampire. Director John Badham and Frank Langella pull off a handsome, moody rendition, more romantic than menacing [based on a stage play by Hamilton Deane and John L. Balderston, from Bram Stoker's novel].

Langella is the key in coming up with one more interpretation of the vampire out of hundreds previously presented. More humanly seductive, he's terrific with the ladies and the men would like him well-enough if he weren't so good-looking and arrogant.

Film gets under way slowly, bringing the count to England where he's introduced to Donald Pleasence, his daughter Kate Nelligan, her fiance Trevor Eve and visiting friend Jan Francis. Finally, Francis is drained dry and the action starts to pick up.

•

DRACULA
(AKA: BRAM STOKER'S DRACULA)
1992, 123 mins, US Ⓥ ⦿ col
Dir Francis Coppola ***Prod*** Francis Coppola, Fred Fuchs, Charles Mulvehill ***Scr*** James V. Hart ***Ph*** Michael Ballhaus

Ed Nicholas C. Smith, Glen Scantlebury, Anne Gorsaud ***Mus*** Wojciech Kilar ***Art*** Thomas Sanders
Act Gary Oldman, Winona Ryder, Anthony Hopkins, Keanu Reeves, Richard E. Grant, Cary Elwes (Columbia/American Zoetrope/Osiris)

Both the most extravagant screen telling of the oft-filmed story and the one most faithful to its literary scource, this rendition sets grand romantic goals for itself that aren't fulfilled emotionally, and it is gory without being at all scary.

James V. Hart sets epic parameters for his script with a prologue introducing Dracula's historical origins as Vlad the Impaler, a 15th century Romanian king who fought off Turkish invaders. As dramatically sketched here, the ruler's inamorata, Elisabeta, killed herself upon receiving false news of his death in battle, whereupon the monarch furiously renounced God and began his centuries-long devotion to evil. In casting Winona Ryder as both Elisabeta and Mina Murray, the overarching story becomes Dracula's quest for recapturing his great love. Unfortunately, familiar plotting, Coppola's coldly magisterial style and Gary Oldman's plain appearance in the title role combine to prevent this strategy from working in more than theory.

Shot almost entirely on sound-stages, film has the feel of an old-fashioned, 1930s, studio-enclosed production made with the benefit of '90s technology. From the striking, blood-drenched prologue on, viewer is constantly made aware of cinema artifice in its grandest manifestations.

Oldman enacts Dracula with wit, sophistication and proper seriousness. However, the actor lacks the charisma that would put across Coppola's conception of a highly sexualized vampire.

Other performances range from a bit stiff (the young male contingent) to playfully energetic (Anthony Hopkins as Van Helsing) to compelling (Tom Waits as the insect-eating lunatic Renfield). Ryder has just the right combination of intelligence and enticing looks as Mina.

1992: Best Sound Effects Editing, Costume Design, Make-up

NOMINATION: Art Direction

•

DRACULA–PRINCE OF DARKNESS

1966, 90 mins, UK ▭ col
Dir Terence Fisher ***Prod*** Anthony Nelson-Keys ***Scr*** John Sansom, Anthony Hinds ***Ph*** Michael Reed ***Ed*** Chris Barnes, James Needs ***Mus*** James Bernard ***Art*** Bernard Robinson
Act Christopher Lee, Barbara Shelley, Andrew Keir, Francis Matthews, Suzan Farmer, Charles Tingwell (Hammer/Seven Arts)

Four inquistive tourists are lured to Castle Dracula, met by a sinister butler and invited to dinner and to stay the night. The four treat this strange hospitality with incredibly bland acceptance. One of them (Charles Tingwell), wandering the castle at night, is killed and his blood used to reinfuse life into the Dracula ashes. Dracula then plunges his fangs into the neck of the corpse's wife, turning her into a vampire and the two are then arrayed against the other pair in the party.

This simple yarn [from an idea by John Elder (= Anthony Hinds)] is played reasonably straight and the main snag is that the thrills do not arise sufficiently smoothly out of atmosphere. After a slowish start some climate of eeriness is evoked but more shadows, suspense, and suggestion would have helped. Christopher Lee, an old hand at the horror business, makes a latish appearance but dominates the film enough without dialog.

•

DRAG NET, THE

1928, 70 mins, US ⊗ b/w
Dir Josef von Sternberg ***Scr*** Jules Furthman, Charles Furthman, Herman J. Mankiewicz ***Ph*** Harold Rosson ***Art*** Hans Dreier
Act George Bancroft, Evelyn Brent, William Powell, Fred Kohler, Francis MacDonald, Leslie Fenton (Paramount)

The Drag Net, for its swiftness and tenseness, may reflect more credit upon its cutter than the remainder of the technical staff. It's cut with incredible swiftness at times, all-in action and no sequence prolonged. Oliver H. P. Garrett, who wrote the corking story [*Nightstick*], has an interesting tale of cops vs. crooks, the latter in a gang with William Powell their sardonic and cynical leader. Twist is where the gang gets the best of it, through framing George Bancroft, as the captain of detectives, into believing he killed one of his own men, Donovan. That leads Bancroft to resign after he has started a furious drive to clean up Gangville, giving the crooks 24 hours to leave town. Among the crooks is a girlfriend of Powell's. Bancroft falls for her and she for him, the girl walking out on the crook leader after seeing how the chief detective operates with his two-gun stuff.

Bancroft is strong as the bulldog detective. Evelyn Brent is the girl, always doing well in playing but not always looking so well.

•

DRAGNET

1954, 89 mins, US Ⓥ col
Dir Jack Webb ***Prod*** Stanley Meyer ***Scr*** Richard L. Breen ***Ph*** Edward Colman ***Ed*** Robert M. Leeds ***Mus*** Walter Schumann
Act Jack Webb, Ben Alexander, Richard Boone, Ann Robinson, Stacy Harris, Virginia Gregg (Warner/Mark VII)

In making the transition from radio-TV to the big screen and color, this is spotty in entertainment results. As on TV quite a bit is made of the long, tedious toil of thorough police methods. This can be kept in hand in a 30-minute period, but when that time is tripled the pace is often bound to slow to a walk.

Under Jack Webb's direction the film gets off on its melodramatic path with a brutal murder. Thereafter, the homicide and intelligence divisions of the L.A. Police Dept start a widespread hunt for evidence that will pin the killing on some redhot suspects.

Webb's direction of the screenplay is mostly a good job. He stages a four-man fight in which he and his police sidekick (Ben Alexander) are involved rather poorly and it may invoke unwelcome laughs. Otherwise, when sticking to terse handling of facts, or in building honest emotion, such as in the splendidly-done drunk scene by Virginia Gregg, grieving widow of the murdered hood, he brings his show off satisfactorily.

•

DRAGNET

1987, 106 mins, US Ⓥ ⊙ col
Dir Tom Mankiewicz ***Prod*** David Permut, Robert K. Weiss ***Scr*** Dan Aykroyd, Alan Zweibel, Tom Mankiewicz ***Ph*** Matthew F. Leonetti ***Ed*** Richard Halsey, William Gordean ***Mus*** Ira Newborn ***Art*** Robert F. Boyle
Act Dan Aykroyd, Tom Hanks, Christopher Plummer, Harry Morgan, Alexandra Paul, Elizabeth Ashley (Universal/Applied Action)

Dragnet tries very hard to parody its 1950s TV series progenitor but winds up more innocuous than inventive. Dan Aykroyd as Jack Webb as Sgt. Joe Friday gives the role his best, but confines of the ultra-straight cop make humor difficult to sustain. Unfettered by such limits, Tom Hanks becomes the pic's winning wildcard as Friday's zany sidekick, Pep Streebek.

Inevitably, Friday and Streebek must pursue a case. It is here that the pic starts unraveling rapidly—largely due to exaggerated caricatures that recall TV's *Batman* series and the feature film *Superman* outings. Christopher Plummer is the kinkiest of the lot as televangelist Reverend Whirley. He considers L.A. the "current capital of depravity," heads up MAMA (Moral Advanced Movement of America) but secretly leads a cultist outfit called PAGANs (People Against Goodness And Normalcy).

Whirley is somehow allied with Police Commissioner Jane Kirkpatrick (Elizabeth Ashley) and is purportedly at odds with *Bait* sex magazine kingpin Jerry Caesar (Dabney Coleman). Friday and Streebek plunge into the bizarre goings-on by posing undercover as street freaks.

Script doesn't make enough of the opportunities for interplay that used to be a mainstay between Webb and Harry Morgan, who reprises the part here in a nice touch that finds him elevated to captain.

•

DRAGONHEART

1996, 103 mins, US Ⓥ ⊙ ▭ col
Dir Rob Cohen ***Prod*** Raffaella De Laurentiis ***Scr*** Charles Edward Pogue ***Ph*** David Eggby ***Ed*** Peter Amundson ***Mus*** Randy Edelman ***Art*** Benjamin Fernandez
Act Dennis Quaid, David Thewlis, Pete Postlethwaite, Dina Meyer, Julie Christie, Jason Isaacs (Universal)

Freely mixing elements from Arthurian legend, *Robin Hood*, *Siegfried*, *Don Quixote* and assorted other Anglo and Germanic myths, director Rob Cohen has pulled together a simple yarn of an itinerant dragonslayer who decides to team with his prey to rid the land of an evil ruler who has betrayed them both. Tale's poignancy stems from the fact that fire-breathing, armor-plated, high-flying creature is the last of its kind; when he dies, dragons will have entirely passed from the Earth.

The added complication in Charles Edward Pogue's screenplay [from a story by him and Patrick Read Johnson] is that, because the dragon once gave young sovereign Einon (David Thewlis) half its heart so that the monarch could survive a grievous injury, their fates are intertwined; if one dies, the other will expire as well.

Wandering the realm, Bowen (Dennis Quaid), who was once young Einon's tutor in swordsmanship, encounters the Sancho Panza-like monk and poet Gilbert (Pete Postlethwaite) while hunting the few remaining dragons that terrorize the countryside. After roping and cornering a magnificent specimen, Bowen and the beast, which speaks with the inimitable burr and persuasiveness of none other than Sean Connery, come to a cleverly capitalistic business arrangement.

Predictable incidents ensue, including a duel between Bowen and his grown-up former student and, ultimately, the tragic showdown that will spell the joint fates of Einon and Draco.

Everything here has been seen plenty of times before, except for the exceptionally sophisticated, wise, and well-spoken dragon, courtesy of many hands but notably those of Scott Squire's Industrial Light & Magic team, which did *Jurassic Park*. Along with the excellent dragon effects, production's trappings are handsome but economical-looking. Pic was entirely shot in Slovakia.

1996: NOMINATION: Best Visual Effects

•

DRAGON SEED

1944, 145 mins, US Ⓥ b/w
Dir Jack Conway, Harold S. Bucquet ***Prod*** Pandro S. Berman ***Scr*** Marguerite Roberts, Jane Murfin ***Ph*** Sidney Wagner ***Ed*** Harold F. Kress ***Mus*** Herbert Stothart ***Art*** Cedric Gibbons, Lyle R. Wheeler
Act Katharine Hepburn, Walter Huston, Aline MacMahon, Akim Tamiroff, J. Carrol Naish, Agnes Moorehead (M-G-M)

As Katharine Hepburn, Walter Huston, Aline MacMahon, Akim Tamiroff, and all the rest of the very competent cast troupe it, they make *Dragon Seed*, for all its two-and-a-half hours, a compelling saga. Hepburn and MacMahon and Huston are especially effective histrionically, and one soon forgets Tamiroff's vodka accent in the Chinese setting.

It traces the valley of the good earth, with its peaceful inhabitants, to whom the roar of the Japs' cannons is still leagues away. But Jade (Hepburn) learns to read, and eventually Lao Er (Turhan Bey), her husband, is brought from petty marital jealousies into a full realization that their love must carry them beyond their village. They must help Free China remain free, and even the venerable Ling Tan (Huston) and his devoted wife (MacMahon) realize that turning-the-other-cheek is no way to cope with the aggressors.

•

DRAGONSLAYER

1981, 108 mins, UK Ⓥ ⊙ ▭ col
Dir Matthew Robbins ***Prod*** Hal Barwood ***Scr*** Hal Barwood, Matthew Robbins ***Ph*** Derek Vanlint ***Ed*** Tony Lawson ***Mus*** Alex North ***Art*** Elliot Scott
Act Peter MacNicol, Caitlin Clarke, Ralph Richardson, John Hallam, Peter Eyre, Chloe Salaman (Paramount/Walt Disney)

A well intentioned fantasy with some wonderful special effects, *Dragonslayer* falls somewhat short on continuously intriguing adventure. Technically speaking, it is an expertly mounted period piece concerning a boy's attempt to slay a fire-breathing dragon in order to save an entire kingdom. However, the story line is often tedious and the major action sequences appear much too late in the picture.

Ralph Richardson limns the properly mysterious (and too seldom seen) sorcerer that members of a neighbouring kingdom seek as the only person who can slay the terrorizing dragon.

Early on Richardson's powers are put to the test by a representative of the king, who seems to kill the sorcerer. It is then up to his apprentice, newcomer Peter MacNicol, to fight the dragon with the magic at his disposal.

MacNicol has the proper look of innocence to be a little unnatural in his performance. Along the way he is given nice support by Caitlin Clarke as a spunky love interest. The real stars (as expected) of this film are the fabulous special effects. Given the high failure rate, it's especially refreshing to see experts come up with the imaginative and effective devices.

1981: NOMINATION: Best Visual Effects

•

DRAGON: THE BRUCE LEE STORY

1993, 121 mins, US Ⓥ ⊙ ▭ col
Dir Rob Cohen ***Prod*** Raffaella De Laurentiis ***Scr*** Edward Khmara, John Raffo, Rob Cohen ***Ph*** David Eggby ***Ed*** Peter Amundson ***Mus*** Randy Edelman ***Art*** Robert Ziembicki
Act Jason Scott Lee, Lauren Holly, Robert Wagner, Michael Learned, Nancy Kwan, Kay Tong Lim (Universal)

The meteoric, tragic life of martial arts star Bruce Lee forms the basis of *Dragon*, an unlikely pastiche of traditional biography, Hollywood saga, and interracial romance.

The jumping off point of the biopic [from Linda Lee Cadwell's book *Bruce Lee: The Man Only I Knew*] finds the teenage Lee (the not-related Jason Scott Lee) as a young man in Hong Kong. Somewhat awkward socially, he transforms into a confident human dynamo when he's forced to fight. Lee's physical prowess gets him into trouble with the authorities and he's sent to San Francisco for his own safety. Lee holds his own against campus bullies. But the situation propels him into a new career teaching students the art of self-defence. One, Linda Emery (Lauren Holly), becomes the love of his life despite her mother's fierce antipathy. Director Rob Cohen, balancing disparate visual styles, keeps *Dragon* pretty straightforward. Lee's metaphoric demons, visualized as a towering, faceless samurai, avoid cuteness; and the potential hokum ranging from the spontaneous fights to the forays into "inner strength" sidestep the high-toned silliness associated with the kung fu era. Overall it maintains a high technical sheen.

•

DRAGONWYCK

1946, 100 mins, US b/w

Dir Joseph L. Mankiewicz ***Prod*** Darryl F. Zanuck ***Scr*** Joseph L. Mankiewicz ***Ph*** Arthur Miller ***Ed*** Dorothy Spencer ***Mus*** Alfred Newman ***Art*** Lyle R. Wheeler, J. Russell Spencer

Act Gene Tierney, Walter Huston, Vincent Price, Glenn Langan, Anne Revere, Jessica Tandy (20th Century-Fox)

Anya Seton's *Dragonwyck*, the bestseller, has been given a lucid, often-compelling transition to the screen. It's a psychological yarn, its mid-19th century American-feudal background being always brooding with never a break in its flow of morbidity. Yet, it is always interesting if somewhat too pointed at times in its fictional contrivance.

The screenplay concerns the feudal system passed down through the generations by the old-Dutch families on the Hudson. The story specifically concerns one Nicholas Van Ryn who exacts tribute from tenant farmers on his vast estate (the year is 1844). Van Ryn has a wife and daughter whom he dislikes, and his pet anathema is his failure to have a son to carry on the baronial tradition. When a distant relative is invited to be governess to the child, and he falls in love with her, he poisons his wife, thus leaving him free to marry the other girl.

Gene Tierney plays the governess and it is one of her most sympathetical roles. Tierney is photographed attractively, and paced well, too, in the direction, as are all the others.

•

DRAUGHTSMAN'S CONTRACT, THE

1982, 108 mins, UK Ⓥ ⦿ col

Dir Peter Greenaway ***Prod*** David Payne ***Scr*** Peter Greenaway ***Ph*** Curtis Clark ***Ed*** John Wilson ***Mus*** Michael Nyman ***Art*** Bob Ringwood

Act Anthony Higgins, Janet Suzman, Anne Louise Lambert, Hugh Fraser (BFI/Channel 4)

Though seemingly a comedy of manners taking place in the country home of a rich man, Herbert, there is an underlying viciousness of these rich denizens that foreshadows coming upheavals. It is the end of the 17th century.

Film has fine costumes, florid headpieces for men, and lovely surroundings on the big estate. Well-lensed, with a fine limpid narration that switches from observation of this landed class to a sort of foreboding tale of murder.

Herbert is almost estranged from his wife and goes off for two weeks of carousing. His wife beseeches a guest, known draughtsman and landscape painter Neville, to stay and make 12 drawings of the estate to surprise her husband. He refuses but finally says yes if the contract includes daily sexual dalliance with Mrs Herbert. It is accepted.

The daughter, still without a child and oblivious to her husband and his effete ways, also begins to dally with the shrewd, talented Neville. On the day Neville is to leave, Herbert is found dead in the moat. Suspicions are aimed at Neville for it is felt he may have somehow given clues to the murder in his drawings.

•

DR. CYCLOPS

1940, 75 mins, US Ⓥ ⦿ col

Dir Ernest B. Schoedsack ***Prod*** Dale Van Every ***Scr*** Tom Kilpatrick ***Ph*** Henry Sharp, Winton C. Hoch ***Ed*** Ellsworth Hoagland ***Mus*** Ernst Toch, Gerard Carbonara, Albert Hay Malotte ***Art*** Hans Dreier, Earl Hedrick

Act Albert Dekker, Janice Logan, Thomas Coley, Charles Halton, Victor Kilian, Frank Yaconelli (Paramount)

In detailing the discoveries of a madman scientist wherein he is able to reduce the size of men and animals to miniature pygmies, story and direction both fail to catch and hold interest. Achieved through continual use of process and trick photography, idea gets lost in a jumble and pancakes off for a dull effort.

Albert Dekker, researching in the jungles of South America, finds a rich radium deposit from which he can draw concentrated energy for experimental use. He has already used the power to reduce animals to minute size when a pair of mining engineers (Thomas Coley and Victor Kilian) and two biologists (Janice Logan and Charles Halton) arrive and soon discover his secret. Dekker gets the quartet, together with native Frank Yaconelli, into the radium machine room and reduces the group down to beings of a foot tall. From there on, it's an unexciting adventure to escape the madman.

1940: NOMINATION: Best Special Effects

•

DREAM GIRL

1948, 83 mins, US b/w

Dir Mitchell Leisen ***Prod*** P. J. Wolfson ***Scr*** Arthur Sheekman ***Ph*** Daniel L. Fapp ***Ed*** Alma Macrorie ***Mus*** Victor Young ***Art*** Hans Dreier, John Meehan

Act Betty Hutton, Macdonald Carey, Patric Knowles (Paramount)

This film version of Elmer Rice's smash play has strong comedy, with a few moving scenes. It has romantic appeal, lots of color and action, and a satisfying ending.

The screen treatment is naturally, and perhaps properly, broader than the original play. This results primarily from the production and Mitchell Leisen's direction rather than from the Arthur Sheekman adaptation. Thus, the film turns the play's humor into outright comedy and sometimes into slapstick.

This broadening treatment applies to practically every phase of the picture. For instance, the fact that the heroine is a chronic daydreamer isn't left to the yarn's title and the use of fade-into-reverie technique, but is put into explicit words by an off-screen voice, at the very start.

This sledgehammer treatment provides some very funny scenes, as when the heroine daydreams her sister's wedding in terms of school-girl sentimentality, or when she fancies herself a fallen woman committing suicide in a tawdry cabaret.

As the self-preoccupied heroine, Betty Hutton gives one of her most skillful performances to date. Besides her familiar vitality and drive, she underscores the comedy in the part and does reasonably well dramatically.

•

DREAM LOVER

1986, 104 mins, US Ⓥ col

Dir Alan J. Pakula ***Prod*** Alan J. Pakula, Jon Boorstin ***Scr*** Jon Boorstin ***Ph*** Sven Nykvist ***Ed*** Trudy Ship ***Mus*** Michael Small ***Art*** George Jenkins

Act Kristy McNichol, Ben Masters, Paul Shenar, Justin Deas, John McMartin, Gayle Hunnicutt (M-G-M)

With the advice of a Yale University Sleep Laboratory consultant, *Dream Lover* firmly sets itself among some rather fascinating scientific notions. Specifically, some dream doctors believe that, while "asleep," part of the brain reacts to dreams as if they were really happening and sends signals to the muscles to take appropriate action.

Kristy McNichol is an average young lady living alone in a NY apartment. She becomes victim of an intruder (Joseph Culp) whom she stabs in the back.

Was the stabbing really necessary for self-defense or did it leap out of some subconscious fury connected to her domineering father (Paul Shenar) or unfaithful lover (Justin Deas)? Only her brain knows for sure. Limps to a conclusion with no real excitement.

•

DREAM LOVER

1994, 103 mins, US Ⓥ ⦿ col

Dir Nicholas Kazan ***Prod*** Sigurjon Sighvatsson, Wallis Nicita, Lauren Lloyd ***Scr*** Nicholas Kazan ***Ph*** Jean-Yves Escoffier ***Ed*** Susan Crutcher, Jill Savitt ***Mus*** Christopher Young ***Art*** Richard Hoover

Act James Spader, Madchen Amick, Bess Armstrong, Frederic Lehne, Larry Miller, Kathleen York (Propaganda/PFE)

An overly abstract mystery about the difficulty of really knowing another person and the unfathomables of amorous attachment, *Dream Lover* is too rarefied for a popular thriller and too dramatically hokey for an art film. Directorial debut of notable screenwriter Nicholas Kazan displays more of an awareness of film's visual possibilities than a flair for them.

Despite a disastrous first encounter, young divorced LA architect Ray (James Spader) manages to quickly win the favor of fashion model-gorgeous Lena (Madchen Amick). They marry and have kids, but after a while Ray begins to imagine that his wife might not be true to—or truly with—him.

The stakes mount quickly thereafter through accusations and admissions of indiscretions, betrayals, and overt manipulations, all leading up to legal proceedings and a climactic murder in a loony bin.

But without dramatic adornment or terrific surprises, Lena's character striptease, along with Ray's ever-escalating frustration, isn't enough to compel unstinting viewer interest. Lena decidedly falls into the femme fatale category, but Kazan is mostly operating far from neo-noir territory, adopting a bright, modern, highly stylized look.

Spader retreats here to handsome-but-bewildered yuppie territory. Fully looking the part of most men's fantasies, *Twin Peaks* vet Amick does a creditable job.

•

DREAM OF KINGS, A

1969, 109 mins, US Ⓥ col

Dir Daniel Mann ***Prod*** Jules Schermer ***Scr*** Harry Mark Petrakis, Ian Hunter ***Ph*** Richard H. Kline ***Ed*** Walter Hannemann, Ray Daniels ***Mus*** Alex North

Act Anthony Quinn, Irene Papas, Inger Stevens, Sam Levene, Val Avery (Schermer)

The adaptation of Harry Mark Petrakis's book about an epic Greek-American father, philanderer, and gambler whose dubious means of support is dispensing wisdom and wrestling instructions emerges as a warm, upbeat, artistically realized drama. It stars Anthony Quinn portraying super-mensch, the noble ethnic, and it is one of his most powerful and convincing performances.

In the Greek sector of Chicago, Quinn makes his hand-to-mouth living as a small time but honest gambler, since his counseling business in a walk-up dingy tenement building is considerably less than a living. His wife (Irene Papas), two girls, and his fatally ill son (Radames Pera) exist on the widowed mother-in-law's life insurance.

The film captures the gritty visual feel of the Hellenic quarter of a large American city with the winter air redolent with feta and baking Greek bread.

•

DREAM OF PASSION, A

1978, 110 mins, Greece Ⓥ col

Dir Jules Dassin ***Prod*** Jules Dassin ***Scr*** Jules Dassin ***Ph*** George Arvanitis ***Ed*** George Klotz ***Mus*** Iannis Markopoulos ***Art*** Dionysis Fotopoulos

Act Melina Mercouri, Ellen Burstyn, Andreas Voutsinas, Despo Diamantidou, Dimitris Papamichael, Yannis Voglis (Brenfilm/Melina)

Two older women are caught up in a strange parallel. One, Melina Mercouri, is a film star who returns to her native Greece to do *Medea* on stage. The other, Ellen Burstyn, is an American living in Greece who has killed her three children "just as Medea did" due to her husband's flaunting of her love and needs.

A misguided public relations idea, having Burstyn talk to Mercouri after seeing no one for a long time, backfires when photogs and press burst in. While Burstyn screams invectives, Mercouri feels cheapened, guilty and decides to take an interest in the case. She sees Burstyn again and gets her story.

Pic alternates two stories, as Mercouri's life and work are intertwined with her growing interest in Burstyn.

Burstyn is shattering as a religious, partially-educated woman caught up in a foreign land. At the end, Burstyn bursts into hysterical tears, which are intercut with Mercouri's dramatic finale in which she kills Medea's children in the play.

•

DREAMSCAPE

1984, 95 mins, US Ⓥ ⦿ col

Dir Joseph Ruben ***Prod*** Bruce Cohn Curtis ***Scr*** David Loughery, Chuck Russell, Joseph Ruben ***Ph*** Brian Tufano ***Ed*** Richard Halsey ***Mus*** Maurice Jarre

Act Dennis Quaid, Max von Sydow, Christopher Plummer, Eddie Albert, Kate Capshaw, David Patrick Kelly (Zupnick-Curtis)

Film [from a screen story by David Loughery] centers on "dreamlinking," the psychic projection of one person's consciousness into a sleeping person's subconscious, or his dreams. If that sounds far-fetched, it is. Central character is played with gusto by Dennis Quaid as Alex Garland, a reluctant ex-psychic who hooks up with Dr. Paul Novotny (Max von Sydow), who runs a dream research project at the local college that has an elaborate laboratory setup to study the phenomena.

There he meets Dr. Jane de Vriees (Kate Capshaw), Von Sydow's chief assistant who secretly lusts after Quaid, but only until he "eavesdrops" on her erotic dream that involves

Quaid. Enter Christopher Plummer as Bob Blair, a secretive and despicable government type who finances and oversees Von Sydow's research, but covertly plans to use its results for sinister ends.

•

DREAM STREET

1921, 135 mins, US Ⓥ d b/w

Dir D. W. Griffith ***Prod*** D. W. Griffith ***Scr*** Roy Sinclair [= D. W. Griffith] ***Ph*** Hendrik Sartov ***Ed*** James Smith, Rose Smith ***Mus*** Louis Silvers (arr.) ***Art*** Charles M. Kirk

Act Carol Dempster, Ralph Graves, Charles Emmett Mack, Edward Peil, Tyrone Power (Griffith/United Artists)

Director D. W. Griffith has made it his aim to express certain spiritual elements of real life in terms of melodrama. The terms of the story are pehaps theatrical, but its essence is of the spirit.

The theme—from two stories by Thomas Burke, who also wrote the original story from which *Broken Blossoms* was taken—might be set down in its briefest form as this: we are all of us made up of good and bad, and vague but strong forces are at work within and about us to give direction to these raw materials of character. That being the thesis, Griffith makes his meaning plain in the story of two brothers, Billy McFadden, physically weak but spiritually fine, and "Spike" McFadden, a physical giant with a certain arrogance and almost brutal selfishness.

The players are splendid. Carol Dempster as Gypsy seems at first just a suspicion of too hard in her regular beauty, but misted portraits in the closeups correct this.

•

DREAM TEAM, THE

1989, 113 mins, US Ⓥ ⊙ col

Dir Howard Zieff ***Prod*** Christopher W. Knight ***Scr*** Jon Connolly, David Loucka ***Ph*** Adam Holender ***Ed*** C. Timothy O'Meara ***Mus*** David McHugh ***Art*** Todd Hallowell

Act Michael Keaton, Christopher Lloyd, Peter Boyle, Stephen Furst, Dennis Boutsikaris, Lorraine Bracco (Imagine/Universal)

The Dream Team is a hokey comedy that basically reduces mental illness to a grab bag of quirky schtick. Yet with a quartet of gifted comic actors having a field day playing loonies on the loose in Manhattan, much of that schtick is awfully funny.

In an attempt to give his patients a taste of the real world, New Jersey hospital doctor Dennis Boutsikaris decides to treat four of his charges to a day game at Yankee Statium.

Going along for the ride are the certified oddballs: Keaton, who seems to have his wits about him but periodically displays extreme delusions of grandeur, as well as a mean violent streak; Christopher Lloyd, a prissy fuss-budget who enjoys posing as a member of the hospital staff; Peter Boyle, a man with a heavy Jesus complex given to undressing at moments of intense spirituality; and Stephen Furst, an uncommunicative simpleton who speaks mainly in baseball jargon.

As soon as they hit the Big Apple, however, the good doctor is seriously injured after witnessing a killing, and the boys are left to their own devices.

Keaton is at his manic best, Lloyd prompts numerous guffaws with his impersonation of a self-serious tidiness freak, and Furst quietly impresses as the sickest and most helpless of the lot.

•

DREAM WIFE

1953, 99 mins, US b/w

Dir Sidney Sheldon ***Prod*** Dore Schary ***Scr*** Sidney Sheldon, Herbert Baker, Alfred Lewis Levitt ***Ph*** Milton Krasner ***Ed*** George White ***Mus*** Conrad Salinger ***Art*** Cedric Gibbons, Daniel B. Cathcart

Act Cary Grant, Deborah Kerr, Walter Pidgeon, Betta St. John, Eduard Franz, Buddy Baer (M-G-M)

A battle-of-the-sexes theme is used for this fairly entertaining, highly contrived piece of screen nonsense.

Cary Grant, a man who wants a wife in the home, not in business, breaks with Deborah Kerr, state dept. official who is too busy with an oil crisis to have time for matrimony. Remembering a comely princess (Betta St. John) whom he had met on a trip to Bukistan in the Middle East and the fact that she had been raised from birth in the art of pleasing a man, Grant proposes via cable.

Because of the oil situation, the state dept. steps in and assigns Kerr to see that her ex-fiance sticks to protocol in his new courtship. The princess comes to the States, but the feminine craft of Kerr soon has St. John figuring that emancipation is more fun than being a dream wife.

Able performers help to carry the script's silliness through the frenetics, but director Sidney Sheldon lets the action slop over into very broad slapstick too often. This loose handling reflects occasionally in the performances, most notably in Grant's. Dialog and situations have their chuckles, however.

•

DR. EHRLICH'S MAGIC BULLET

1940, 103 mins, US Ⓥ b/w

Dir William Dieterle ***Prod*** Hal B. Wallis (exec.) ***Scr*** John Huston, Heinz Herald, Norman Burnside ***Ph*** James Wong Howe ***Ed*** Warren Low ***Mus*** Max Steiner ***Art*** Carl Jules Weyl

Act Edward G. Robinson, Ruth Gordon, Otto Kruger, Donald Crisp, Maria Ouspenskaya, Montagu Love (Warner)

Here is a splendid production, in which much care and attention to detail has gone into the making. Historical biography [from an idea by Norman Burnside] is based on the life of Dr. Paul Ehrlich, famed bacteriologist, whose most noteworthy contribution to medical science was the search for, and eventual discovery of, 606, which proved to be the positive cure for syphilis.

In tracing the scientist's accomplishments, story follows a span of about 35 years. Edward G. Robinson makes the gradual transition in great style.

Ehrlich is introduced as a young doctor in the Kaiser Wilhelm hospital, Berlin, where he is attempting to find a dye with an affinity for the tubercular germ, to make the latter distinguishable under a microscope. He is finally dismissed, and works at home to discover the necessary dye. Contracting the disease, he goes to Egypt for a year to recuperate, and then discovers the theory of building up immunity to a poison. Returning to Berlin, he plunges into research on a treatment of syphilis, but pauses long enough to cooperate with Dr. Emil Von Behring (Otto Kruger) in concocting a serum for diptheria. Years pass before Ehrlich discovers 606, when the Medical Society asks that he give it to the public immediately.

Ruth Gordon is a most sympathetic and understanding wife of the scientist absorbed in his work; Kruger is excellent as Ehrlich's close friend and colleague; Donald Crisp is the health minister. Ehrlich is a most worthy successor in every respect to *Louis Pasteur*, which Warners produced so intelligently a few years earlier.

•

DREIGROSCHENOPER, DIE
(THE THREEPENNY OPERA)

1931, 112 mins, Germany Ⓥ ⊙ b/w

Dir G. W. Pabst ***Scr*** Leo Lania, Bela Balazs, Ladislas Vajda ***Ph*** Fritz Arno Wagner ***Mus*** Theodore Mackeben (dir.) ***Art*** Andrei Andreyev

Act Rudolph Forster, Carola Neher, Lotte Lenya, Ernst Busch, Valeska Gert, Fritz Rasp, Reinhold Schuenzel (Warner/Tobis/Nero)

The venerable English sardonic *Beggar's Opera* was adapted by Kurt Weill (music) and Berthold Brecht (libretto) into *Three Penny Opera*, a much-produced stage work these last decades. The Nazis suppressed this film version.

Film was seen in New York briefly in 1931, in a cut version [of 97 mins.] and without complete English titles, and created no stir whatsoever. It's a sophisticated, cynically jaunty look at a seamy society. Its only moral: crime does pay—if you're clever enough. As directed by G. W. Pabst, picture is a successful translation of a highly stylized stage work to the realistic screen medium.

Pabst, getting great help from the Weill score and settings by Andrei Andreiev, succeeds in creating a thoroughly believable never-never land, that is, a turn-of-the-century London as imagined by a German who has lived through the post-war chaos of his own land. Within this frame, the Brecht tale of the notorious cut-throat, Mackie Messer ("Mack the Knife") unfolds with complete honesty and a lot of wild, hard-as-nails social satire.

The relationship of Mackie with his one true love, Polly Peachum, and with the prostitute, Jenny, are defined with reality and insight. This is due, not only to the performances of Rudolph Forster as Mackie, Carola Neher as Polly, and Lotte Lenya as Jenny, but, of course, to the Weill music. The 1931 Lenya (Mrs. Weill in private life) is especially appealing with her odd and haunting "Pirate Jenny" number. Camerawork by Fritz Wagner is firstrate.

[Review is of a 1960 restoration, with a re-recorded and equalized soundtrack, shown at the Museum of Modern Art, NY.]

•

DRESSED TO KILL

1980, 105 mins, US Ⓥ ⊙ ▭ col

Dir Brian De Palma ***Prod*** George Litto ***Scr*** Brian De Palma ***Ph*** Ralf Bode ***Ed*** Jerry Greenberg, Bill Pankow ***Mus*** Pino Donaggio ***Art*** Gary Weist

Act Michael Caine, Angie Dickinson, Nancy Allen, Keith Gordon, Dennis Franz, David Margulies (Filmways/Cinema 77)

Brian De Palma goes right for the audience jugular in *Dressed to Kill*, a stylish exercise in ersatz-Hitchcock suspense-terror. Despite some major structural weaknesses, the cannily manipulated combination of mystery, gore, and kinky sex adds up to a slick commercial package.

The film begins with a steamy auto-erotic shower scene and segues to a session between Angie Dickinson and psychiatrist Michael Caine.

Matters begin in earnest when Dickinson enters an elevator and is razor-sliced to death. Enter high-priced hooker Nancy Allen who finds the body and is caught razor-in-hand with no alibi, smack into the arch Hitchcockian position of a circumstantially involved "innocent" forced to clear herself by discovering the real murderer.

Instances of patent manipulation or cheating (and the film's stolen ending from *Carrie*) are generally more annoying in retrospect than while they're happening.

Dickinson, who has an abdominal stand-in for the steamier segments, is used exceptionally well as the sexually torn, quickly disposed-of heroine. Caine, until the film's internal logic breaks down, is excellent as the suave shrink.

•

DRESSER, THE

1983, 118 mins, UK Ⓥ ⊙ col

Dir Peter Yates ***Prod*** Peter Yates ***Scr*** Ronald Harwood ***Ph*** Kelvin Pike ***Ed*** Ray Lovejoy ***Mus*** James Horner ***Art*** Stephen Grimes

Act Albert Finney, Tom Courtenay, Edward Fox, Zena Walker, Eileen Atkins, Michael Gough (Goldcrest/World Film Services)

Adapted by Ronald Harwood from his 1980 London comedy-drama, this is indisputably one of the best films every made about theatre. It's funny, compassionate, compelling, and in its final moments pulls off an uncanny juxtaposition between the emotionally and physically crumbling Albert Finney and the character he's playing on stage for the 227th time, King Lear.

Finney portrays an aging, spoiled, grandiloquent actor-manager of a traditional English touring company whose dedication to his art creates chaos for those around him. The only character who can handle the old actor is his gofer-valet Norman, played with an amazing dexterity and energy by Tom Courtenay.

Director Peter Yates brings to the film, much of it shot at Pinewood, a strong visual sense of the British experience in wartime. And the whiff of greasepaint, particularly notable when aide Courtenay goads Finney into his makeup for Lear, lends the tawdry dressing room world of touring theatre its most physically felt detail.

Harwood is said to have based much of his story on his experiences with flamboyant actor-manager Donald Wolfit (1902–68) and his troupe.

1983: NOMINATIONS: Best Picture, Director, Actor (Albert Finney, Tom Courtenay), Adapted Screenplay

•

DREYFUS

1931, 80 mins, UK b/w

Dir F. W. Kraemer, Milton Rosmer ***Scr*** Reginald Berkeley, Walter Mycroft ***Ph*** W. Winterstein, J. Harvey Wheedon ***Ed*** John Harlow

Act Cedric Hardwicke, Beatrix Thomson, Charles Carson, George Merritt, Sam Livesey, Garry Marsh (British International/Sudfilm)

British International, in making the picture, is understood to have followed closely along the lines of the original film as made by Sudfilm for German consumption. The film has more movement than the average British film.

The Dreyfus case revolved around a framed-up charge against Captain Alfred Dreyfus of the French army for treason. Treason had been committed and Dreyfus was charged, largely because he was the only Jew on the staff. After making the charge, the army had to hold up its case or lose face, so they trumped up the evidence against him.

What made it a world-famous matter, rather than a forgotten incident in French army life, was that Emile Zola, one of the greatest of French writers, took to the Dreyfus case and fought it in the courts. Despite having as counsel Georges Clemenceau, Zola lost, but the story had gotten worldwide attention. After about 15 years Dreyfus was fully vindicated.

The film is not over-acted. If anything it's a little underacted in parts. Cecil Hardwicke as Dreyfus gives a fine performance; George Merritt as Zola is exceptional. Another striking performance is that of Charles Carson as Col. Picquart, who was also degraded because he found proof, after Dreyfus was sent to Devil's Island, pointing to the fact that Major Esterhazy was the criminal and not Dreyfus. Beatrix

Thomson as the wife is only so-so, largely because she's not given much to do.

•

DR. FU MANCHU
1929, 80 mins, US b/w
Dir Rowland V. Lee ***Scr*** Florence Ryerson, Lloyd Corrigan
Act Warner Oland, Jean Arthur, Neil Hamilton, William Austin, Claude King, O. P. Heggie (Paramount)

British legation in Peking is under assault by Boxer hordes. One of the officials, anticipating a massacre, sends his little daughter to the protection of a friendly Chinese noble, Dr. Fu Manchu. In the ensuing attack by English troops, Fu's wife and son are slain. Whereupon the Oriental swears revenge on the white foreign devils.

Years later it is made plain that the same Dr. Fu is on the trail of Sir John, who commanded the English in Peking, having disposed of all the other white commanders by subtle murder. He has brought up the white girl (Jean Arthur) left in his charge and, by putting her in a trance, has her carry out his designs. It all works up to a pip of a melodramatic climax.

Punch of the picture is its speed and sustained suspense. Eerie bits in dives and dim waterfront settings are capitally managed for effect. Picture discloses a fine cast of articulate players, notably Neil Hamilton as the young lead, Claude King as Sir John, and Warner Oland, who seems to be able to make an Oriental heavy believable.

•

DRILLER KILLER, THE
1979, 90 mins, US Ⓥ col
Dir Abel Ferrara ***Prod*** Rochelle Weisberg (exec.) ***Scr*** Nicholas St. John, Louis Mascolo ***Ph*** Ken Kelsch ***Ed*** Orlando Gallini, Bonnie Constant, Michael Constant, Jimmy Laine [= Abel Ferrara] ***Mus*** Joseph Delia ***Art*** Louis Mascolo
Act Jimmy Laine [= Abel Ferrara], Carolyn Marz, Baybi Day, Harry Schultz, Alan Wynroth, Maria Helhoski (Navaron)

This bit of gore was undoubtedly inspired by *The Texas Chain Saw Massacre*. It's hastily shot and technically inept in every department operation.

An artist, living in a tenement near Union Square with two girlfriends who're not reluctant to turn to each other when his attentions are elsewhere, find it increasingly difficult to keep the wolf from the door. Things get worse. A punk rock band moves into the floor below him and the noise pushes him over the edge.

The most stupid thing about the film is why, when he turns into a murderer with an electric drill, he doesn't go downstairs and eliminate the band. No, he picks winos in doorways as his victims before turning to other targets—his girlfriends.

•

DRIVE, HE SAID
1971, 95 mins, US col
Dir Jack Nicholson ***Prod*** Jack Nicholson, Steve Blauner, Bert Schneider ***Scr*** Jack Nicholson, Jeremy Larner ***Ph*** Bill Butler ***Ed*** Pat Somerset, Donn Cambern, Christopher Holmes, Robert L. Wolfe ***Mus*** David Shire ***Art*** Harry Gittes
Act William Tepper, Karen Black, Michael Margotta, Bruce Dern, Robert Towne, Henry Jaglom (BBS)

Director Jack Nicholson seems here to be making a sort of games-people-play charade which takes off on many of the would-be commitments of his characters.

William Tepper, as the central sports star character of the campus convolutions, reflects the changes and protest surrounding his simplistic existence.

His roommate (Michael Margotta), a Che-like student revolutionary, wants to destroy all, for he feels the draft, life around him, the war, will destroy him. Margotta leads a gag raid on a basketball game with guerrilla-clad friends that puts them all in custody, but later they are freed. He beats the draft by playing mad in a raucous induction physical scene, but winds up going mad for real, trying to kill his roommate's woman, who he feels is simply a lech.

Karen Black is the sensual older woman, who sexually grapples with the basketball hero but finally resents being used and tries to claim a personality of her own.

Nicholson deftly illustrates the background cynicism of big time sports against the more obvious cynicism of college life.

•

DRIVER, THE
1978, 91 mins, US Ⓥ col
Dir Walter Hill ***Prod*** Lawrence Gordon ***Scr*** Walter Hill ***Ph*** Philip Lathrop ***Ed*** Tina Hirsch, Robert K. Lambert ***Mus*** Michael Small ***Art*** Harry Horner
Act Ryan O'Neal, Bruce Dern, Isabelle Adjani, Ronee Blakely, Matt Clark, Felice Orlandi (20th Century-Fox)

By the end of *The Driver* you can almost smell rubber burning, there are so many screeching tires. This may be the first film where the star of the show isn't an actor or even a machine but a sound effect.

Ryan O'Neal plays a master getaway driver who does most of his talking with his accelerator toe. Bruce Dern, departing only slightly from his maniac roles, plays an obsessed detective out to nab O'Neal. Isabelle Adjani is another reticent character, a gambler hired as an alibi for O'Neal. Ronee Blakely, in a supporting role, portrays O'Neal's connection; she sets up the jobs.

There's not much more to the plot than that. O'Neal is a great driver and Dern is a detective. They're enemies and one of them is going to win the game.

Director Walter Hill and stunt coordinator Everett Creach have engineered a number of car chases and they are fabulous, if you like car chases.

Because of the quiet and mysterious mood of this picture, it has a pretentious quality to it. Whenever someone does speak, the dialog seems precious, as if the last sentence of each speech were edited out.

•

DRIVING ME CRAZY
SEE: DUTCH

•

DRIVING MISS DAISY
1989, 99 mins, US Ⓥ ⊙ col
Dir Bruce Beresford ***Prod*** Richard D. Zanuck ***Scr*** Alfred Uhry ***Ph*** Peter James ***Ed*** Mark Warner ***Mus*** Hans Zimmer ***Art*** Bruno Rubeo
Act Morgan Freeman, Jessica Tandy, Dan Aykroyd, Patti LuPone, Esther Rolle (Zanuck/Warner)

Driving Miss Daisy is a touching exploration of 25 years of change in Southern race relations (1948–73) as seen through the relationship of an elderly Jewish widow and her stalwart black chauffeur.

Bruce Beresford's sensitive direction complements Alfred Uhry's skillful adapation of his Pulitzer Prize–winning play.

Set in the relatively tolerant city of Atlanta, Daisy effortlessly evokes the changing periods on a limited budget.

Jessica Tandy's Daisy is a captious and lonely old stick, living a bleakly isolated widow's life in her empty old house, and her inability to keep from tyrannizing Morgan Freeman, housekeeper Esther Rolle, and other black helpers gives the film a current of bitter truth, making her gradual friendship with Freeman a hard-won achievement.

Freeman's Hoke is the essence of tact, with a quiet, philosophical acceptance of his role in life and a secret sense of amusement toward whites' behavior.

1989: Best Picture, Actress (Jessica Tandy), Adapted Screenplay, Makeup

NOMINATIONS: Best Actor (Morgan Freeman), Supp. Actor (Dan Aykroyd), Editing, Art Direction, Costume Design

•

DR. JEKYLL AND MR. HYDE
1932, 90 mins, US Ⓥ ⊙ b/w
Dir Rouben Mamoulian ***Prod*** Rouben Mamoulian ***Scr*** Samuel Hoffenstein, Percy Heath ***Ph*** Karl Struss
Act Fredric March, Miriam Hopkins, Rose Hobart, Holmes Herbert, Edgar Norton, Halliwell Hobbes (Paramount)

The fundamental story is that a brilliant scientist turns himself into an ogre who goes upon orgies of lust and murder in peaceful London, all in a misguided frenzy of scientific research, and after murdering a number of other people by extremely horrifying means, destroys himself. That was the length and breadth of the stage play [from the novel by Robert Louis Stevenson], and it served in that form for years.

The picture is infinitely better art—indeed, in many passages it is an astonishing fine bit of interpreting a classic, but as popular fare it loses in vital reaction.

Camera trick of changing a central figure from the handsome Fredric March into the bestial, ape-like monster Hyde, carries a terrific punch, but in each successive use of the device—and it is repeated four times—it weakens in hair-raising effort.

March does an outstanding bit of theatrical acting. His Hyde make-up is a triumph of realized nightmare. Other people in the cast matter little, except that Miriam Hopkins plays Ivy, the London soiled dove, with a capital sense of comedy and coquetry that contributes to the subsequent horror build-up.

Settings and lighting alone are worth seeing as models of atmospheric surroundings.

1931/32: Best Actor (Fredric March)

NOMINATIONS: Best Adaptation, Cinematography

•

DR. JEKYLL AND MR. HYDE
1941, 127 mins, US Ⓥ ⊙ b/w
Dir Victor Fleming ***Prod*** Victor Saville ***Scr*** John Lee Mahin ***Ph*** Joseph Ruttenberg ***Ed*** Harold F. Kress ***Mus*** Franz Waxman ***Art*** Cedric Gibbons, Daniel B. Cathcart
Act Spencer Tracy, Ingrid Bergman, Lana Turner, Ian Hunter, Donald Crisp, C. Aubrey Smith (M-G-M)

In the evident striving to make *Jekyll* a "big" film, by elaborating the theme and introducing new characters and situations, some of the finer psychological points are dulled. John Lee Mahin's screenscript is over-length.

Nevertheless, it has its highly effective moments, and Spencer Tracy plays the dual roles with conviction. His transformations from the young physician, bent on biological and mental research as an escape from his own moral weaknesses, to the demoniac Mr. Hyde are brought about with considerably less alterations in face and stature than audiences might expect.

Ingrid Bergman plays the enslaved victim of Hyde's debauches. In every scene in which the two appear, she is Tracy's equal as a strong screen personality.

The script is meagre on the very important phase of Jekyll's inner struggle to free himself from his deadly alter ego. Millions of Stevenson readers have long found excitement and thrill in the angle that Jekyll's predicament was self-conceived to hide criminal and vicious desires. Mahin emphasizes that misdirected scientific research was the cause of the good doctor's downfall.

1941: NOMINATIONS: Best B&W Cinematography, Editing, Scoring of a Dramatic Picture

•

DR. JEKYLL AND MS. HYDE
1995, 89 mins, US Ⓥ ⊙ col
Dir David Price ***Prod*** Robert Shapiro, Jerry Leider ***Scr*** Tim John, Oliver Butcher, William Davies, William Osborne ***Ph*** Tom Priestley ***Ed*** Tony Lombardo ***Mus*** Mark McKenzie ***Art*** Gregory Melton
Act Sean Young, Tim Daly, Lysette Anthony, Stephen Tobolowsky, Harvey Fierstein, Polly Bergen (Rastar/Savoy)

Dr. Jekyll and Ms. Hyde is a contemporary spin in which the bad side of Jekyll (aka Richard Jacks, played by Tim Daly) is a predatory female (Sean Young) with her sights on climbing the corporate ladder.

Considering the transgressions made against the source material over the years, the new outing is middling successful in attempting to imbue it with modern resonance.

The contempo twists provide one or two surprises; otherwise, plot sticks pretty much to the classic, or at least the best-known film versions. Jacks is a "brilliant" chemist working below potential as chief perfumer, albeit at a top-flight company. When his great-grandfather dies, he gets an odd bequest: his great-granddad's dusty scientific journals, which bear the name Jekyll.

In short order he is physically transformed into Helen Hyde. She seduces key execs, convinces Richard's g.f., Sarah (Lysette Anthony), to leave him, and literally fries a co-worker in order to secure a staff position. She increasingly dominates the shared body, until Richard reckons she will have 100% occupancy unless he can perfect a drug to reverse the process.

Daly's easy charm and Young's full-blooded treachery go a long way to smooth over the picture's rough edges. At least the pic's special and makeup effects have pizazz, and one can say that, in its own unique way, this mixed-sex translation is more worthy of Stevenson than the 1971 *Dr. Jekyll & Sister Hyde*.

•

DR. JEKYLL & SISTER HYDE
1971, 97 mins, UK Ⓥ col
Dir Roy Ward Baker ***Prod*** Albert Fennell, Brian Clemens ***Scr*** Brian Clemens ***Ph*** Norman Warwick ***Ed*** James Needs ***Mus*** David Whitaker ***Art*** Robert Jones
Act Ralph Bates, Martine Beswick, Gerald Sim, Lewis Fiander, Susan Brodrick, Dorothy Alison (Hammer)

Scripter Brian Clemens had the highly imaginative idea of letting Robert Louis Stevenson's 19th-century Dr. Jekyll turn into a homicidal, glamorous Sister Hyde instead of the original hairy monster. He then pinned on him/her the responsibility for the Jack the Ripper murders. Here, Jekyll, played by Ralph Bates, murders to remove organs needed for his experiments to prolong life and then gets his hormones wrong.

Testing the drug he knocks himself out. Coming round he finds he likes himself as a glamour girl in the person of

Martine Beswick and starts to get the best of both sexes when not killing. As male, he attracts the pure young miss living next door and as female fascinates her brother.

Director Roy Ward Baker has set a good pace, built tension nicely and played it straight so that all seems credible. He tops chills and gruesome murders with quite a lot of subtle fun. Bates and Beswick, strong, attractive personalities, bear a strange resemblance to each other making the transitions entirely believable.

•

DR. MABUSE DER SPIELER
(DR. MABUSE, THE GAMBLER; THE FATAL PASSIONS)

1922, 242 mins, Germany Ⓥ ⊗ b/w

Dir Fritz Lang ***Prod*** Erich Pommer ***Scr*** Thea von Harbou ***Ph*** Carl Hoffman ***Art*** Otto Hunte, Stahl-Urach

Act Rudolf Klein-Rogge, Aud Egede Nissen, Gertrude Welcker, Alfred Abel, Bernhard Goetzke, Paul Richter (UCO)

Dr. Mabuse, the Gambler, from the novel by Norbert Jacques, is a good average popular thriller—dime novel stuff in a $100,000 setting—but sufficiently well camouflaged to get by a with a class audience.

The story builds itself about the character of Dr. Mabuse (Rudolf Klein-Rogge), the great gambler, the player with the souls of men and women. He runs an underground counterfeiting establishment, and with this money starts all his enterprises. In the first reel of the film he appears as a stock exchange speculator, stealing an important commercial treaty.

To get money out of a rich young man he sets Carozza (Aud Egede-Nissen), a dancer, on his trail; then hypnotizing him, he wins large sums of money from him at his club. Mabuse meets Countess Told (Gertrude Welcker) and desires her. He fixes the mark of cheating at cards on her husband, and in the ensuing excitement steals her away.

And so it goes on, a bit confusedly but generally with speed and life. The best moments are achieved by the conflict between Mabuse and the attorney, Von Wenk (Bernhard Goetzke), who is trying to uncover him. The first part [*Der Grosse Spieler*, 120 mins.] ends with the stealing of the countess and the second [*Inferno*, 122 mins.] with the finding of Mabuse, insane, in his own counterfeiting cellar, where he has been trapped by Von Wenk.

The film is somewhat hurt by the casting of Klein-Rogge for the title role; he is physically too small and not a clever enough actor to make one forget this. Paul Richter as a millionaire and Goetzke as Von Wenk do very nicely. And the Carozza of Egede-Nissen and the countess of Welcker are fine pieces of film work.

The interiors of Stahl-Urach and Otto Hunte are sumptuous and tasteful, and Carl Hoffmann's photography generally adequate. The direction of Fritz Lang has moments—but Lang somewhat negates his good technical effects by twenty forty-word captions of a ludicrous unconciseness. [Two-part pic was released in the U.S. in 1927 in a single 63-min. version, with florid intertitles in poor English.]

•

DR. MABUSE, THE GAMBLER
SEE: DR. MABUSE DER SPIELER

•

DR. NO

1962, 110 mins, UK Ⓥ ⦿ col

Dir Terence Young ***Prod*** Harry Saltzman, Albert R. Broccoli ***Scr*** Richard Maibaum, Johanna Harwood, Berkely Mather ***Ph*** Ted Moore ***Ed*** Peter Hunt ***Mus*** Monty Norman ***Art*** Ken Adam

Act Sean Connery, Ursula Andress, Joseph Wiseman, Jack Lord, Bernard Lee, Zena Marshall (Eon/United Artists)

First screen adventure of Ian Fleming's hardhitting, fearless, imperturbable, girl-loving Secret Service Agent 007, James Bond, is an entertaining piece of tongue-in-cheek action hokum. Sean Connery excellently puts over a cool, fearless, on-the-ball, fictional Secret Service guy. Terence Young directs with a pace which only occasionally lags.

The hero is exposed to pretty (and sometimes treacherous) gals, a poison tarantula spider, a sinister crook, flame throwers, gunshot, bloodhounds, beating up, near drowning, and plenty of other mayhem and malarkey, and comes through it all with good humour, resourcefulness, and what have you.

Connery is sent to Jamaica to investigate the murder of a British confidential agent and his secretary. Since both murders happen within three or four minutes of the credit titles the pic gets away to an exhilarating start. He becomes involved with the activities of Dr. No, a sinister Chinese scientist (Joseph Wiseman) who from an island called Crab Key is using a nuclear laboratory to divert off course the rockets being propelled from Cape Canaveral.

Among the dames with whom Connery becomes involved are easy-on-the-eye Ursula Andress, who shares his perilous adventures on Crab Key, and spends most of her time in a bikini; Zena Marshall, as an Oriental charmer who nearly decoys him to doom via her boudoir; and Eunice Gayson, whom he picks up in a gambling club in London and who promises to be the biggest menace of the lot.

•

DROP DEAD DARLING

1966, 100 mins, UK col

Dir Ken Hughes ***Prod*** Ken Hughes ***Scr*** Ken Hughes ***Ph*** Denys Coop ***Ed*** John Shirley ***Mus*** Dennis Farnon ***Art*** Seamus Flannery

Act Tony Curtis, Rosanna Schiaffino, Lionel Jeffries, Zsa Zsa Gabor, Nancy Kwan, Fenella Fielding (Seven Arts)

Pic is a silly sex comedy, as amusing at times as it is tasteless, in which Tony Curtis plays a contemporary Bluebeard.

Producer-director Ken Hughes scripted, from a Hughes-Ronald Harwood story, in turn suggested by Richard Deming's *The Careful Man*. Curtis stars as a gold-digging spouse-killer, who meets his match in Rosanna Schiaffino, a femme counterpart.

Story attempts to make likeable a character who arranges the death of his femme guardian, her sailor suitor, later his first two wives and, unsuccessfully, Schiaffino, bride-widow of an a.k. who expires in honeymoon excitement.

Withal, Curtis does a very good job, plotting with Lionel Jeffries to do in Schiaffino. Latter is by no means without acting ability, either. Script abounds in lecherous one-liners, ably put over by Anna Quayle, palpitating in the Marilyn Monroe manner as Curtis's guardian; Zsa Zsa Gabor, the non-stop gabber whom Curtis locks in a space vehicle at blast-off, and Fenella Fielding, the English heiress of robust appetites and bank accounts.

•

DROP DEAD FRED

1991, 98 mins, US/UK Ⓥ ⦿ col

Dir Ate De Jong ***Prod*** Paul Webster ***Scr*** Carlos Davis, Anthony Fingleton ***Ph*** Peter Deming ***Ed*** Marshall Harvey ***Mus*** Randy Edelman ***Art*** Joseph T. Garrity

Act Rik Mayall, Phoebe Cates, Marsha Mason, Tim Matheson, Carrie Fisher, Ron Eldard (PolyGram/Working Title)

Oscillating between long arid stretches, inspired explosions of slapstick and disarming warmth, *Drop Dead Fred* [suggested by a story by Elizabeth Livingston] has an almost irresistible premise—kid's imaginary friend comes back to help the grown woman work out her problems—but it's probably too slow and mushy for kids and too sporadic in its rewards for adults.

Phoebe Cates stars as Elizabeth, a young wife who returns home to her domineering mother (Marsha Mason) after splitting up with her brazenly philandering husband (Tim Matheson). At home she discovers a music box that contains her long-forgotten imaginary friend, Drop Dead Fred (British comic Rik Mayall in a red Beethoven fright wig), who's been released to wreak havoc until she's having fun again.

Elizabeth then sets out to woo back her smarmy hubby [from an uncredited Bridget Fonda], although it's patently obvious she'd be better off with nice if rather boring childhood friend, Mickey (Ron Eldard), who conveniently re-emerges.

Director Ate De Jong has captured the silliness of childhood with the hyperactive title character but too often drills jokes deep into the pavement, until even children will have long stopped laughing.

•

DROP DEAD GORGEOUS

1999, 99 mins, US Ⓥ ⦿ col

Dir Michael Patrick Jann ***Prod*** Gavin Pallone, Judy Hofflund ***Scr*** Lona Williams ***Ph*** Michael Spiller ***Ed*** Janice Hampton, David Codron ***Mus*** Mark Mothersbaugh ***Art*** Ruth Ammon

Act Kirsten Dunst, Ellen Barkin, Allison Janney, Denise Richards, Kirstie Alley, Sam McMurray (Capella/KC Medien/New Line)

Taking bazooka aim at a barn-door-wide target—hinterland beauty contests—*Drop Dead Gorgeous* is a fitfully amusing satire that would have gained a lot of mileage from just a tad more subtlety.

Premise is that a camera crew is hired to document a "typical" small town's participation in the 50th annual Miss American Teen Princess Pageant, as publicity for its corporate sponsor. The burg chosen is Mount Rose, MN, population 5,076.

Early progress introduces each perky teen contestant in turn, from the spaz (Shannon Nelson) to the sexpot (Amy Adams), as well as various pageant organizers and judges. Favored to win are both sweet, Diane Sawyer-worshipping Amber (Kirsten Dunst) and scheming little vixen Becky (Denise Richards). Given that latter is daughter to the town's richest businessman, and that her mother (Kirstie Alley) is a former Teen Princess hell-bent on keeping the crown in-family, no one seriously doubts the outcome.

But someone is very serious about ensuring it. First, one contestant dies in a threshing-machine mishap, then Becky's boyfriend, whose eyes have been straying toward Amber, experiences a fatal "hunting accident."

Pic's worst trait is the way it confuses satire with condescension—everyone here is either stupid, venal or perverse. Pic doesn't have the writing sophistication to render its more questionable jokes (involving anorexia, pedophilia, prosthetic limbs, embalming, mental retardation and pidgin English–speaking Japanese stereotypes) blackly comic.

Nonetheless, fast pacing makes this a relatively pain-free, if brain-free, diversion. The performers do their best to rise above often crude material.

•

DROP ZONE

1994, 101 mins, US Ⓥ ⦿ ▭ col

Dir John Badham ***Prod*** D. J. Caruso, Wallis Nicita, Lauren Lloyd ***Scr*** Peter Barsocchini, John Bishop ***Ph*** Roy H. Wagner ***Ed*** Frank Morriss ***Mus*** Hans Zimmer ***Art*** Joe Alves

Act Wesley Snipes, Gary Busey, Yancy Butler, Michael Jeter, Corin Nemec, Kyle Secor (Paramount)

Pic is little more than a by-the-numbers programmer, reasonably diverting and briskly paced but thinly written [from a screen story by Tony Griffin, Guy Manos, and Peter Barsocchini] and utterly predictable. Wesley Snipes gives a self-assured star performance as Pete Nessip, a U.S. marshal who, with his brother and fellow lawman (Malcolm-Jamal Warner), is assigned guard duty for the transfer of a drug-cartel snitch (Michael Jeter). When their 747 is hijacked by alleged terrorists, Pete's brother is killed and the "terrorists"—along with the snitch—appear to take a fatal free-fall. Pete insists the hijackers and prisoner jumped out of the plane and escaped with parachutes. While on suspension pending an FBI investigation, Peter goes undercover to prove his theory and clear his late brother's name.

Of course, Pete is absolutely right: the hijackers, led by an unusually subdued (by his standards) Gary Busey, are crack skydivers who kidnapped the snitch because of his hacking expertise. As the bad guys prepare to invade the DEA's Washington, DC, headquarters, Pete drafts skydiver Jessie Crossman (Yancy Butler), a beautiful ex-con, to help him gain entry into the skydiving subculture.

Director Badman is an old hand at this kind of full-tilt entertainment, and he brings a straight-shooting professionalism to the enterprise. *Drop Zone* contains no fewer than three midair rescues of people who don't have parachutes by people who do.

Snipes brings a welcome touch of self-effacing humor to his heroics and handles the serious rough stuff with aplomb. Butler holds her own in the action sequences, particularly in a climactic fistfight with the only woman among the bad guys, and she laces her perf with a wise-cracking edge.

•

DROWNING BY NUMBERS

1988, 118 mins, UK/Netherlands Ⓥ ⦿ col

Dir Peter Greenaway ***Prod*** Kees Kasander, Denis Wigman ***Scr*** Peter Greenaway ***Ph*** Sacha Vierny ***Ed*** John Wilson ***Mus*** Michael Nyman ***Art*** Ben Van Os, Jan Roelfs

Act Bernard Hill, Joan Plowright, Juliet Stevenson, Joely Richardson, Jason Edwards, Bryan Pringle (Film Four/Elsevier Vendex/Allarts/VPRO TV Holland)

Drowning by Numbers deals with metaphorical game-playing of sex and death in the best traditions of black humor, all set in an idyllic English summer, and pays tribute to games, landscape, and especially a conspiracy of women.

Pic follows the darkly murderous acts of three women all named Cissie Colpitts (Joan Plowright, Juliet Stevenson, and Joely Richardson) and their friend the local coroner Madgett (Bernard Hill) and his son Smut (Jason Edwards).

Pic opens with Plowright drowning her husband in a tin bath. The families and friends of the three murdered men suspect the three women of the killings and meet under a water tower.

When none of the three Colpitts women submit to Madgett's sexual advances he decides to admit his part in the murders. But his gameplaying instincts take the better of him, and he organizes a game of tug-of-war between the conspirators and the women.

As an aside, Greenaway has placed the numbers 1–100 throughout the film (for example, 1 appears on a tree, 36 is on Joely Richardson's swimsuit)—yet another exercise in game-playing and a challenge for the viewer to spot all the numbers. The acting is uniformly excellent.

●

DROWNING POOL, THE
1975, 108 mins, US Ⓥ ▭ col
Dir Stuart Rosenberg ***Prod*** Lawrence Torman, David Foster ***Scr*** Tracey Keenan Wynn, Lorenzo Semple, Jr., Walter Hill ***Ph*** Gordon Willis ***Ed*** John C. Howard ***Mus*** Michael Small ***Art*** Paul Sylbert
Act Paul Newman, Joanne Woodward, Anthony Franciosa, Murray Hamilton, Gail Strickland, Melanie Griffith (Coleytown/Warner)

Paul Newman again assumes the Lew Harper private eye role he first essayed in *Harper* (1966). *The Drowning Pool* [from Ross MacDonald's novel] is stylish, improbable, entertaining, superficial, well cast, and totally synthetic. Stuart Rosenberg's direction is functional and unexciting.

Newman is summoned by Joanne Woodward to her bayou home because of a blackmail letter to her husband, Richard Derr, alleging infidelity on her part; she's been unfaithful but the current rap is a bummer.

Lots of interesting characters begin appearing. Melanie Griffith, Woodward's sexpot jailbait daughter; Murray Hamilton, very good as an unscrupulous oil baron, and Tony Franciosa, an old Woodward flame, now a police chief.

Title derives from an offbeat and exciting climactic sequence in an abandoned mental asylum hydro-therapy room where Hamilton has imprisoned his wife Gail Strickland and Newman to force disclosure of a black book which will explode lots of swampy intrigue.

●

DR. PHIBES RISES AGAIN
1972, 88 mins, UK Ⓥ ⦿ col
Dir Robert Fuest ***Prod*** Louis M. Heyward ***Scr*** Robert Fuest, Robert Blees ***Ph*** Alex Thomson ***Ed*** Tristan Cones ***Mus*** John Gale ***Art*** Brian Eatwell
Act Vincent Price, Robert Quarry, Valli Kemp, Hugh Griffith, John Thaw, Keith Buckley (American International)

Dr. Phibes, that bizarre evil genius of *The Abominable Dr. Phibes*, is back with all his old diabolic devilry for another excusion into musical camp fantasy.

Dr. Phibes, who went into a state of suspended animation at close of *Abominable*, rises three years later to restore life to his wife who died many years before.

Quest for the necessary elixir hidden in an ancient chamber below a mountain once used by the pharaohs takes him to Egypt, where Robert Quarry is his rival in race for the re-incarnating drug. Phibes starts decimating Quarry's men who would prevent him from bringing his loved one back to life.

Vincent Price, as Phibes, delivers one of his priceless theatric performances, and Quarry is a properly ruthless rival who nearly matches Phibes in knowledge and cunning.

●

DR. SEUSS'S HOW THE GRINCH STOLE CHRISTMAS
SEE: HOW THE GRINCH STOLE CHRISTMAS

●

DR. SOCRATES
1935, 74 mins, US b/w
Dir William Dieterle ***Scr*** Robert Lord ***Ph*** Tony Gaudio ***Ed*** Ralph Dawson ***Mus*** Leo F. Forbstein (dir.) ***Art*** Anton Grot
Act Paul Muni, Ann Dvorak, Barton MacLane, Robert Barrat, John Eldredge, Hobart Cavanaugh (Warner)

Arriving at the tail end of the G-man and gangster cycle, *Dr. Socrates* hasn't the vigor of some of its predecessors, but the constant and basic threat of violence is always present.

Plot [from a story by W. R. Burnett, adaptation by Mary C. McCall, Jr.] departs from what is customary in the gangster school, in that it stars neither the gunman nor the officer of the law, but makes both subservient to a country doctor.

The chief gangster in this case is a Dillinger type of gent who terrorizes a section of the middle west. The young physician is adopted as the gang's medical man, and he takes a chance because he needs the money. But when the gang grabs his girl he goes on the offensive. For Muni, *Socrates* is an easy role, calling for little or no emotional work. For an actor of his calibre the soft-spoken doc seems a minor effort. Ann Dvorak plays a hitchhiking girl who gets innocently tangled with the mobsters and brings romance to the small town sawbones.

●

DR. STRANGELOVE OR: HOW I LEARNED TO STOP WORRYING AND LOVE THE BOMB
1964, 102 mins, UK Ⓥ ⦿ b/w
Dir Stanley Kubrick ***Prod*** Stanley Kubrick ***Scr*** Stanley Kubrick, Terry Southern, Peter George ***Ph*** Gilbert Taylor ***Ed*** Anthony Harvey ***Mus*** Laurie Johnson ***Art*** Ken Adam
Act Peter Sellers, George C. Scott, Sterling Hayden, Keenan Wynn, Slim Pickens, James Earl Jones (Columbia/Hawk)

Nothing would seen to be farther apart than nuclear war and comedy, yet Kubrick's caper eloquently tackles a *Fail Safe* subject with a light touch.

Screenplay based on the book *Red Alert* by Peter George is imaginative and contains many an offbeat touch. Some of the characters have a broad brush in their depiction, but this is the very nature of satire.

It all begins when a Strategic Air Command general on his own initiative orders bomb-carrying planes under his command to attack Russia. From here on it's a hectic, exciting series of events, alternating between the General who has started it all, the planes en route to the USSR, and the Pentagon's war room, where the Chief Executive is trying his best to head off the nuclear war.

It would seem no setting for comedy or satire, but the writers have accomplished this with biting, piercing dialogue, and thorough characterizations. Peter Sellers is excellent, essaying a trio of roles—a British RAF captain assigned to the U.S. base where it all begins, the president and the title character, Dr. Strangelove, a German scientist aiding the U.S. whose Nazi mannerisms overcome him.

George C. Scott as the fiery Pentagon general who seizes on the crisis as a means to argue for total annihilation of Russia offers a top performance, one of the best in the film. Odd as it may seem in this backdrop, he displays a fine comedy touch. Sterling Hayden is grimly realistic as the general who takes it on his own to send our nuclear bomb-carrying planes to attack Russia. He is a man who blames the Communists for fluoridation of water, and just about everything else.

1964: NOMINATIONS: Best Picture, Director, Actor (Peter Sellers), Adapted Screenplay

●

DR. T & THE WOMEN
2000, 121 mins, US Ⓥ ⦿ ▭ col
Dir Robert Altman ***Prod*** Robert Altman, James McLindon ***Scr*** Anne Rapp ***Ph*** Jan Kiesser ***Ed*** Geraldine Peroni ***Mus*** Lyle Lovett ***Art*** Stephen Altman
Act Richard Gere, Helen Hunt, Farrah Fawcett, Laura Dern, Shelley Long, Tara Reid, Kate Hudson, Liv Tyler, Lee Grant (Sandcastle 5)

Robert Altman delivers a gently provocative character study and social portrait in *Dr. T & the Women*. Taking their own sweet time to paint an exceptionally detailed and often quite funny picture of the most rarefied strata of Dallas society, only to detonate some unexpected land mines later on, Altman and his congenially matched screenwriter Anne Rapp wrap some stinging psychological and emotional observations in a beguiling package topped by Richard Gere's most accessible and sympathetic performance in memory.

Gere's handsome high-society gynecologist is, despite his unlimited supply of temptations, a proudly faithful husband who regards women as "saints" who "should be treated as such." Buoyant opening credits sequence deftly establishes the doc's eminence and overbooked daily calendar, as well as the excessively pampered nature of the women in his world. Latter trait extends to Dr. T's immediate family, who include his athletic, well-preserved wife Kate (Farrah Fawcett), college-age daughters Conne (Tara Reid) and Dee Dee (Kate Hudson) and sister-in-law Peggy (Laura Dern).

Although Kate is committed to a psychiatric hospital with a mystery ailment that makes her reject her husband's love, everyone carries on almost unaffectedly with their lives. Dr. T slides into a comfortable friendship with new country club golf pro Bree (Helen Hunt), who slowly but surely nudges things along until the doc, feeling all but abandoned by his wife, succumbs to the lure of a no-strings affair in a beautifully nuanced, mostly silent dinner sequence.

The little visual joke of making all the women blonde suddenly pays off midway through when the jet-black-haired Marilyn (Liv Tyler) arrives to stir things up. As has often been the case with Altman, a certain derisiveness toward some characters occasionally slips in, but prevailing tone is one of sweetness and sympathy.

Gere glides agreeably through the first, less demanding stretch but impressively rises to the occasion of the greater demands of the second half. Gone is the cocky, preening arrogance of his most off-putting performances, and newly evident are a tender vulnerability and concern for others.

●

DR. TERROR'S HOUSE OF HORRORS
1965, 98 mins, UK Ⓥ ▭ col
Dir Freddie Francis ***Prod*** Milton Subotsky, Max J. Rosenberg ***Scr*** Milton Subotsky ***Ph*** Alan Hume ***Ed*** Thelma Connell ***Mus*** Elizabeth Lutyens, Tubby Hayes ***Art*** Bill Constable
Act Peter Cushing, Christopher Lee, Roy Castle, Donald Sutherland, Neil McCallum, Alan Freeman (Amicus)

Five short horror episodes, thinly linked, provide a usefully chilly package deal which will offer audiences several mild shudders and quite a lot of amusement. Even though occasional giggles set in, the cast, headed by experienced horror practitioners such as Peter Cushing, Michael Gough, Christopher Lee, and Max Adrian, sensibly play it straight.

Five young men traveling on a routine train journey, meet up with the sixth passenger. He's a mysterious, bearded stranger (Cushing) who reveals himself as Dr. Schreck. With the aid of a pack of Tarot cards, he foretells the grisly deaths in store for the quintet. The film emerges as a kind of cinemagoers' digest of how to come to a sticky end.

●

DRUGSTORE COWBOY
1989, 100 mins, US Ⓥ ⦿ col
Dir Gus Van Sant ***Prod*** Nick Wechsler, Karen Murphy ***Scr*** Gus Van Sant, Daniel Yost ***Ph*** Robert Yeoman ***Ed*** Curtiss Clayton, Mary Bauer ***Mus*** Elliot Goldenthal ***Art*** David Brisbin
Act Matt Dillon, Kelly Lynch, James Le Gros, Heather Graham, James Remar, William Burroughs (Avenue)

No previous drug-themed film has the honesty or originality of Gus Van Sant's drama *Drugstore Cowboy*. Pic addresses the fact that people take drugs because they *enjoy* them.

Set in Portland, Oregon, in the early 1970s, *Drugstore Cowboy* tells of one self-confessed and completely unrepentant "drug fiend" (his own description), Bob Hughes (Matt Dillon). He robs drugstores, not for money—for drugs. Backed up by a "crew" consisting of his willowy but tough wife Dianne (Kelly Lynch), his dimwitted but true-blue pal Rick (James Le Gros) and Le Gros's weepy, bumbling girlfriend, Nadine (Heather Graham), Dillon revels in his self-described life of crime.

Dillon's world begins to sour when Graham dies of an overdose. The incident so frightens him, he vows to give up drugs entirely. Unfortunately, Lynch refuses to go along with him.

It's a novel conflict. Dillon is kicking the habit for personal reasons—he still likes drugs. He and Lynch still love each other, but for junkies, drugs make every romance a triangle.

Van Sant draws fine performances from his cast, particularly Lynch, who up to now has appeared as the obligatory Sexy Girl. This is her *acting* debut. He also gets one truly great performance from Dillon.

●

DRUM, THE
(US: DRUMS)
1938, 101 mins, UK Ⓥ ⦿ col
Dir Zoltan Korda ***Prod*** Alexander Korda ***Scr*** Lajos Biro, Arthur Wimperis, Patrick Kirwan, Hugh Gray ***Ph*** Georges Perinal, Osmond Borradaile ***Ed*** Henry Cornelius, William Hornbeck ***Mus*** John Greenwood, Miklos Rozsa ***Art*** Vincent Korda, Ferdinand Bellan
Act Sabu, Raymond Massey, Roger Livesey, Valerie Hobson, David Tree, Francis L. Sullivan (London)

Film is based on a story written specially for the screen by A.E.W. Mason. He supplies an excellent machine-made suspensive tale laid in India, with fine dialog.

Entire action is laid in the tribal territory of the northwest frontier of India. An elderly khan is anxious for British protection to ensure his throne for his son, Prince Axim (Sabu). Ruler's brother, Prince Ghul, is fanatically anti-British, kills the old man, and the plot involves the attempt to do away with the young prince.

Sabu, the 14-year-old Indian youth who came to attention in *Elephant Boy* (1937), lives up to the promise given in that film and conducts himself with requisite dignity. He now speaks very good English. Raymond Massey is sufficiently sinister as the throne usurper; Roger Livesey is excellent as the military commander.

●

DRUM
1976, 100 mins, US Ⓥ col
Dir Steve Carver ***Prod*** Ralph Serpe ***Scr*** Norman Wexler ***Ph*** Lucien Ballard ***Ed*** Carl Kress ***Mus*** Charlie Smalls ***Art*** Stan Jolley

Act Warren Oates, Isela Vega, Ken Norton, Pam Grier, Yaphet Kotto, John Colicos (De Laurentiis)

Drum is a grubby followup to *Mandingo* [1975] which invites its own derisive audience laughter. Ham acting like you wouldn't believe, coupled with non-direction by Steve Carver and a correspondence-school script by Norman Wexler, add up to cinematic trash.

There's slave-breeder Warren Oates who buys Ken Norton and Yaphet Kotto from bordello queen Isela Vega, who in reality is Norton's real mother though her lesbian lover-maid Paula Kelly raised the boy; Pam Grier goes along with the deal as Norton's girl and occasional wench to Oates, though Fiona Lewis, her eyes on Oates, has other plans.

Climax of the film is a slave revolt where lots of people get killed, including Royal Dano who manages to keep a straight face as a mean slaver.

•

DRUM BEAT
1954, 107 mins, US Ⓥ ▭ col
Dir Delmer Daves *Scr* Delmer Daves *Ph* J. Peverell Marley *Ed* Clarence Kolster *Mus* Victor Young
Act Alan Ladd, Audrey Dalton, Marisa Pavan, Robert Keith, Rodolfo Acosta, Charles Bronson (Warner/Jaguar)

The Modoc Indian uprising on the California-Oregon border in 1869 is the basis for this Alan Ladd outdoor action starrer.

The scripting is a careful job, in the main holding to fact with some fictionizing for dramatic values.

Alan Ladd is seen as a frontiers-man commissioned by President Grant to negotiate a peace with the rebelling Modocs led by Captain Jack, renegade Indian forcefully played by Charles Bronson. The peace is to be effected without force of arms, which presents two-gun Ladd with quite a problem.

Two femmes star with Ladd. Audrey Dalton does nicely as the eastern girl who comes west and winds up with the hero. Marisa Pavan scores as the Indian Girl who gives her life to save Ladd.

•

DRUMS
SEE: THE DRUM

•

DRUMS ALONG THE MOHAWK
1939, 100 mins, US Ⓥ ⊙ col
Dir John Ford *Prod* Darryl Zanuck *Scr* Lamar Trotti, Sonya Levien *Ph* Bert Glennon, Ray Rennahan *Ed* Robert Simpson *Mus* Alfred Newman *Art* Richard Day, Mark-Lee Kirk
Act Claudette Colbert, Henry Fonda, Edna May Oliver, Arthur Shields, Ward Bond, John Carradine (20th Century-Fox)

Having great sweep and colorful backgrounding, with the photography unusually good, the picture is an outdoor spectacle which highly pleases the eye even if the story [from the novel by Walter D. Edmonds], on occasion, gets a bit slow and some incidents fail to excite.

While the backgrounding is beautiful, as photoged by Bert Glennon, it doesn't always look like the Mohawk Valley (upstate New York) region with wheat fields, evergreens, big birches, etc., as atmosphere.

The story deals with farming pioneers of the Mohawk Valley sector at the time of the Revolutionary War, with Indian terror and English intrigue, plus hardship, testing the stamina of the colonists. Romance of Henry Fonda and Claudette Colbert, who have married and are forging ahead to new frontiers, has pull.

1939: NOMINATION: Best Supp. Actress (Edna May Oliver)

•

DRUNKEN MASTER
SEE: TSUI KUN

•

DRUNK MONKEY IN THE TIGER'S EYES
SEE: TSUI KUN

•

DR. WHO & THE DALEKS
1965, 83 mins, UK Ⓥ ▭ col
Dir Gordon Flemyng *Prod* Milton Subotsky, Max J. Rosenberg *Scr* Milton Subotsky *Ph* John Wilcox *Ed* Oswald Hafenrichter *Mus* Malcolm Lockyer *Art* Bill Constable
Act Peter Cushing, Roy Castle, Jennie Linden, Roberta Tovey, Barrie Ingham, Geoffrey Toone (Aaru)

Absentminded professor Dr. Who (Peter Cushing) has invented Tardis, a Time and Relative Dimension in Space Machine, capable of lugging people to other worlds, in other eras. By accident, the prof, his granddaughters (Jennie Linden and Roberta Tovey), and Linden's boyfriend (Roy Castle) are ejected from the earth and land on a huge, petrified planet at a time many years back.

The planet is ravaged with radiation from a previous war and the quartet finds themselves in a struggle between the Daleks and the Thals. The Daleks, protected from radiation in an all-metal city and wearing mobile metal cones fitted with flame-guns, are determined to wipe out the gentle Thals.

Cushing plays Dr. Who with amiable gravity. Linden is a pretty, routine heroine while Tovey is pleasantly cast as the little girl with scientific knowhow and commonsense. Roy Castle mugs and falls around a little too zestfully as the boyfriend with a fairly good sense of humor.

•

DRY WHITE SEASON, A
1989, 97 mins, US Ⓥ ⊙ col
Dir Euzhan Palcy *Prod* Paula Weinstein *Scr* Colin Welland, Euzhan Palcy *Ph* Kelvin Pike, Pierre-William Glenn *Ed* Sam O'Steen, Glenn Cunningham *Mus* Dave Grusin *Art* John Fenner
Act Donald Sutherland, Winston Ntshona, Zakes Mokae, Jurgen Prochnow, Susan Sarandon, Marlon Brando (M-G-M)

A wrenching picture about South Africa that makes no expedient compromises with feel-good entertainment values, *A Dry White Season* displays riveting performances and visceral style.

Filmmaker Euzhan Palcy—who is black—never tempers her outrage, but the film [from the novel by Andre Brink] drives home the point that the story of South Africa is a story of two races that's unlikely to be resolved by either one alone.

Set in 1976, the film moves quickly to a searing sequence in which a demonstration by black schoolchildren of Soweto is broken up with gratuitous lethal force. Many are brutally beaten and arrested, including the son of Gordon Ngubene (Winston Ntshona), a gardener who works at the comfortable home of naive prep school teacher Ben du Toit (Donald Sutherland).

Du Toit is a basically decent man who cares enough to pay for the missing boy's schooling but not enough to question society's blatantly unjust status quo.

With mounting astonishment this community pillar comes to discover what he's always closed his eyes to: South African "justice and law could be described as distant cousins—not on speaking terms."

Those words are spoken by Ian McKenzie (Marlon Brando), rising with a world-weary magnificence to the role of a prominent human rights attorney whose idealism has been battered into resignation. Sarcasm is his only tactic, the moral high ground his only refuge as McKenzie proves Cpt. Stolz (Jurgen Prochnow) a murderer, but loses his case before a judge who makes no effort to hide his disgraceful bias.

1989: NOMINATION: Best Supp. Actor (Marlon Brando)

•

D3: THE MIGHTY DUCKS
1996, 104 mins, US Ⓥ ⊙ col
Dir Robert Lieberman *Prod* Jordan Kerner, Jon Avnet *Scr* Steven Brill, Jim Burnstein *Ph* David Hemmings *Ed* Patrick Lussier, Colleen Halsey *Mus* J. A. C. Redford *Art* Stephen Storer
Act Emilio Estevez, Jeffrey Nordling, Joshua Jackson, David Selby, Heidi Kling, Joss Ackland (Walt Disney)

Never fear, the teen hockey sensations aren't skating on thin ice in *D3: The Mighty Ducks*. This amazingly resilient film franchise continues to be entertaining in a shamelessly manipulative way. It's chock-full of homilies, youthful hijinx and sound moral observations.

The Ducks' achievement as international junior champs has landed them scholarships to a ritzy private school with East Coast trappings. But coach Gordon Bombay (Emilio Estevez) has passed the baton to Ted Orion (Jeffrey Nordling), a martinet, and Charlie (Joshua Jackson) has been stripped of the position of captain.

It just isn't the sort of fun and games and hot-dogging that took them to two prior championships. When they start losing games and the academy plans to revoke their scholarships, lawyer Bombay takes the case pro bono and reminds the school authorities about what's right and proper. With Estevez in a very supporting role, the film truly rests on Jackson's shoulders, and he graduates with grace from foil to front man.

•

D2: THE MIGHTY DUCKS
1994, 106 mins, US Ⓥ ⊙ col
Dir Sam Weisman *Prod* Jordan Kerner, Jon Avnet *Scr* Steven Brill *Ph* Mark Irwin *Ed* Eric Sears, John F. Link *Mus* J.A.C. Redford *Art* Gary Frutkoff
Act Emilio Estevez, Kathryn Erbe, Michael Tucker, Jan Rubes, Carsten Norgaard, Maria Ellingsen (Walt Disney)

Even disregarding its credibility problems, *D2* is a pretty sorry follow-up to a picture that spawned a National Hockey League franchise and enchanted the box office to the tune of $50 million. While there are plenty of ideas and ideals floating through this youthful action comedy, it's sorely lacking in anything vaguely resembling a script.

With his ongoing attempt to play in the pros again stymied by injury, Gordo (Emilio Estevez) is tipped as the ideal hockeymeister for the upcoming Junior Goodwill Games (winter edition). All he has to do is round up his old Ducks and add some new kids.

But Team U.S.A .isn't really a squad, it's a collection of minorities and social causes. By the final faceoff, these and other problems will be resolved. In truth, it's a wonder these rink rats can outscore the Trinidad team, let alone make the playoffs.

Director Sam Weisman's best shots are on the ice, building the excitement of competition to a fever pitch. But that momentum is DOA every time he has to cut to narrative, complete a plot point, include a product placement shot, or nod to the NHL Ducks's Anaheim arena.

•

DU BARRY WAS A LADY
1943, 96 mins, US Ⓥ col
Dir Roy Del Ruth *Prod* Arthur Freed *Scr* Irving Brecher, Wilkie Mahoney *Ph* Karl Freund *Ed* Blanche Sewell *Mus* Georgie Stoll (dir.), Roger Edens (adapt.) *Art* Cedric Gibbons
Act Red Skelton, Lucille Ball, Gene Kelly, Virginia O'Brien, Zero Mostel, "Rags" Ragland (M-G-M)

In sapolioing the script for celluloid, the studio has taken Red Skelton out of the men's room and put him in the coat room. Otherwise it follows the general outlines of the original 1939 Broadway show by Herbert Fields and B. G. DeSylva [with music and lyrics by Cole Porter]: The club caddy falls for the top warbler at the spot (Lucille Ball).

She pays no attention to him, being enamored of a broke songsmith (Gene Kelly), while she plays Douglas Dumbrille for his chips. Then Skelton wins a Derby pot and some attention from Ball, only to get a Mickey intended for Kelly mixed up with his own drink, which sends him into a dream sequence. He finds himself Louis XV and Ball his Du Barry.

With the weak plot and weaker dialog, Skelton has a tough time living up to his rep as a funnyman. Ball does a bit better, while Kelly, whose forte is terping, suffers from the histrionic and singing demands of his role and lack of opportunity to make with the feet. Virginia O'Brien is disappointing, too, except for the one tune she's given, "Salome Was the Grandma of Them All," in which she literally sparkles.

•

DUCHESS AND THE DIRTWATER FOX, THE
1976, 104 mins, US Ⓥ ▭ col
Dir Melvin Frank *Prod* Melvin Frank *Scr* Melvin Frank, Barry Sandler, Jack Rose *Ph* Joseph Biroc *Ed* Frank Bracht, William Butler *Mus* Charles Fox *Art* Trevor Williams, Robert Emmet Smith
Act George Segal, Goldie Hawn, Roy Jenson, Thayer David, Pat Ast, Sid Gould (20th Century-Fox)

The Duchess and the Dirtwater Fox is a generally pleasant and amiable period western comedy starring George Segal as a fumbling gambler and Goldie Hawn as a singing-dancing frontier chick.

Pair get involved with Roy Jenson's robber gang, Thayer David's group of Mormons, a Jewish wedding, some good gags here, some forced humor there. Barry Sandler's story has been scripted into sketches which tend to a predictably upbeat curtain. The Colorado scenery vies with the interactions of Hawn and Segal; the other players are more or less backdrop.

The stars work well together; Segal's comedy abilities seem in fullest flower when Mel Frank is directing, while Hawn's talents are showcased quite nicely.

•

DUCK SOUP
1933, 70 mins, US Ⓥ ⊙ b/w
Dir Leo McCarey *Prod* [uncredited] *Scr* Bert Kalmar, Harry Ruby, Arthur Sheekman, Nat Perrin *Ph* Henry Sharp *Ed* [LeRoy Stone] *Mus* [Arthur Johnston (adv.)] *Art* [Hans Dreier, Wiard B. Ihnen]
Act Groucho Marx, Chico Marx, Harpo Marx, Zeppo Marx, Margaret Dumont, Louis Calhern (Paramount)

The laughs come often, too often sometimes, which has always been the case with Marx talkers, although in this instance more care appears to have been taken with the timing, since the step-on gags don't occur as frequently as in the past.

In place of the constant punning and dame chasing, *Duck Soup* has the Marxes madcapping through such bits as the old Schwartz Bros. mirror routine, so well done in the hands of Groucho, Harpo, and Chico that it gathers a new and hilarious comedy momentum all over again.

Story is a mythical kingdom burlesque that could easily have been written by a six-year-old with dust in his eyes, but it isn't so much the story as what goes with and on within it. Groucho is the prime minister. For his customary dowager-foil he has the high, wide, and handsome Margaret Dumont, making it perfect for Groucho.

While Groucho soft peddles the verbal clowning for more physical effort this time, the other boys also make a quick change. Chico and Harpo omit their musical specialties, which should make it much easier for the piano and harp numbers the next time, if needed. Zeppo is simply Zeppo. Music and lyrics [by Bert Kalmar and Harry Ruby] through which much of the action is in rhyme and song, serve to carry the story along rather than to stand out on pop song merit on their own. Everything's in keeping with the tempo of the production.

•

DUCK, YOU SUCKER
SEE: A FISTFUL OF DYNAMITE

•

DUDES
1987, 90 mins, US Ⓥ ⦿ col
Dir Penelope Spheeris ***Prod*** Herb Jaffe ***Scr*** J. Randal Johnson ***Ph*** Robert Richardson ***Ed*** Andy Horvvitch ***Art*** Robert Ziembicki
Act Jon Cryer, Daniel Roebuck, Flea, Lee Ving, Catherine Mary Stewart (Vista)

How can a film that brings punk rockers from Queens, cowboys, Indians, and crazed homicidal villains together in Utah be taken seriously? The answer, of course, is that it can't.

Dudes tells the story of three punked-out New Yorkers—Milo, Grant, and Biscuit—who set out for Hollywood in a Volkswagen and get attacked while camping out in Big Sky country. Milo is murdered by Missoula, leader of a wild-eyed gang that roams the west killing Mexicans. Grant and Biscuit vow to avenge Milo's death.

Even if one were inclined to overlook the derivative story line, *Dudes* still manages to throw itself from the saddle so many times it bruises the sensibilities. The humor, when intentional, is slapstick. The dialog is hopelessly adolescent, the music incredibly loud and the plot is dependent on a bizarre sequence of coincidences.

•

DUDLEY DO-RIGHT
1999, 77 mins, US Ⓥ ⦿ col
Dir Hugh Wilson ***Prod*** John Davis, Joseph M. Singer, J. Todd Harris ***Scr*** Hugh Wilson ***Ph*** Donald E. Thorin ***Ed*** Don Brochu ***Mus*** Steve Dorff ***Art*** Bob Ziembicki
Act Brendan Fraser, Sarah Jessica Parker, Alfred Molina, Eric Idle, Robert Prosky, Alex Rocco (David-Singer-Harris/Universal)

Much like the smashingly successful *George of the Jungle*, another comedy based on a Jay Ward–produced animated fave, *Dudley* does right by showcasing Brendan Fraser in the title role. Instead of swinging on vines and crashing into trees, the hunky actor is a dim but dashing Royal Canadian Mountie who always gets his man (usually with the aid of his considerably brighter horse).

Dudley Do-Right is nothing if not dedicated as he keeps the peace in the Canadian Rockies community of Semi-Happy Valley. But he is seriously outmatched in a duel of wits with the wicked Snidely Whiplash (Alfred Molina).

Whiplash is no longer content with robbing banks and foreclosing mortgages. Seeking total control of Semi-Happy Valley, he salts the local streams with stolen bullion, setting off a gold rush and transforms the valley into a garish combination of pioneer boomtown, Disneyesque theme park and Branson, MO.

The locals gladly rename the community Whiplash City. Dudley isn't so easily beguiled, but the effervescent Nell Fenwick (Sarah Jessica Parker), Dudley's childhood sweetheart, warms to Whiplash when she returns to the area after a long absence.

Working from his own witty screenplay, director Hugh Wilson (*Blast from the Past, The First Wives Club*) remains true to the tongue-in-cheek tone of Ward's cartoon shorts, even to the point of using a stentorian narrator (Corey Burton) to provide seriocomic commentary.

Fraser, with his near-beatific smile, again exudes an air of blissfully naive sweetness without seeming cloyingly fey. Molina exuberantly devours the scenery as Whiplash.

•

DUEL
1971, 74 mins, US Ⓥ ⦿ col
Dir Steven Spielberg ***Prod*** George Eckstein ***Scr*** Richard Matheson ***Ph*** Jack A. Marta ***Ed*** Frank Morriss ***Mus*** Billy Goldenberg ***Art*** Robert S. Smith
Act Dennis Weaver, Jacqueline Scott, Eddie Firestone, Lou Frizzell, Gene Dynarski, Lucille Benson (Universal)

In America, a man's car is his castle—a home away from home in which he is master of all he surveys. How well does this freeway monarch behave when his rolling fortress is besieged by an apparently stronger force?

This is the problem the Universal made-for-TV film wrestles with. Dennis Weaver plays a salesman on his way to an appointment. He drives along a narrow highway located in a sparsely settled western locale. Along the way he passes an enormous oil tanker rig, and later he passes it again. From then on the picture is all chase—with the trucker alternately playing dangerous games with Weaver and then actually seeming to want to kill him. A clear case of absolute power corrupting absolutely.

Neither Weaver nor the audience ever gets to see the face of the driver (indeed, he has no credit listing), beyond one view of his lower legs and feet and one of his hands waving Weaver on.

The story is adapted from a short tale [by Richard Matheson] in *Playboy* magazine. But it really plays much more like one of those old dramas in the Golden Age of Radio. For the most part, the production, although clearly not expensively mounted, keeps within the spirit of the teleplay and helps it roll. One intrusive note is the necessity for a good deal of inner dialog voiced over the action to indicate Weaver's feelings. [Version reviewed is the original 74-minute telemovie networked by ABC as "Movie of the Weekend" on November 13, 1971. The 90-minute theatrical version was released in Europe in 1973 and the U.S. in 1983. Jacqueline Scott, as the wife, appears only in that version.]

•

DUEL AT DIABLO
1966, 105 mins, US Ⓥ col
Dir Ralph Nelson ***Prod*** Fred Engel, Ralph Nelson ***Scr*** Marvin Alpert, Michel Grilikhes ***Ph*** Charles F. Wheeler ***Ed*** Fredric Steinkamp ***Mus*** Neal Hefti ***Art*** Alfred Ybarra
Act James Garner, Sidney Poitier, Bibi Andersson, Dennis Weaver, Bill Travers, William Redfield (United Artists)

Duel at Diablo packs enough fast action in its cavalry-Indians narrative to satisfy the most avid follower of this type of entertainment.

Produced with knowhow, and directed with a flourish by Ralph Nelson, the feature is long on exciting and well-staged battle movement and carries a story that, while having little novelty, still stands to good effect. Based on the Marvin Albert novel, *Apache Rising*, screenplay stars James Garner as a scout and Sidney Poitier as a former trooper who now makes his living breaking in horses for the service. Rivalling them in interest and importance, however, is Bill Travers, a cavalry lieutenant who heads the column of raw recruits to a distant fort and is attacked en route by the Apaches.

Garner is properly rugged and acquits himself handsomely, convincing as a plainsman who knows his Indians. Poitier tackles a new type of characterization here, far afield from anything he has essayed in the past. Travers in a strong character part is vigorous and appealing and endears himself with his light and human touch.

•

DUEL IN THE SUN
1946, 134 mins, US Ⓥ ⦿ col
Dir King Vidor ***Prod*** David O. Selznick ***Scr*** David O. Selznick ***Ph*** Lee Garmes, Hal Rosson, Ray Rennahan ***Ed*** Hal C. Kern ***Mus*** Dimitri Tiomkin ***Art*** J. McMillan Johnson
Act Jennifer Jones, Gregory Peck, Joseph Cotten, Lionel Barrymore, Lillian Gish, Walter Huston (Selznick)

The familiar western formula reaches its highest commercialization in *Duel in Sun*. It is raw, sex-laden, western pulp fiction, told in 10-20-30 style. The star lineup is impressive. Vastness of the western locale is splendidly displayed in color by mobile cameras. Footage is overwhelmingly expansive, too much so at times considering its length. Single scenes that stand out include Jennifer Jones's peril in riding bareback on a runaway horse, filmed against the vast scope of the western scene; Gregory Peck's taming of a sex-maddened stallion; the tremendous sweep of hundreds of mounted horsemen riding to do battle with the invading railroad.

King Vidor's direction keeps the playing in step with production aims. He pitches the action to heights in the top moments and generally holds the overall mood desired. Sharing director credit on the mass sequences are Otto Brower and Reaves Eason.

Plot, suggested by a novel by Niven Busch, adapted by Oliver H. P. Garrett, concerns a half-breed girl who goes to the ranch of a Texas cattle baron to live after her father has killed her adulterous mother and lover. The baron's two sons fall for her but the unrestrained younger one captures her emotions. So strong is physical desire that he murders one man who wants to marry her and tries to kill the brother, shown in latter attempts to make the girl a lady.

Jones as the half-breed proves herself extremely capable in quieter sequences but is overly meller in others. Same is true of Peck as the virile younger Texan raised to love 'em and leave 'em. Contrasting is Joseph Cotten as the older son. Role in his hands is believable and never overdrawn.

1946: NOMINATIONS: Best Actress (Jennifer Jones), Supp. Actress (Lillian Gish)

•

DUELLISTS, THE
1977, 95 mins, UK Ⓥ ⦿ col
Dir Ridley Scott ***Prod*** David Puttnam ***Scr*** Gerald Vaughan-Hughes ***Ph*** Frank Tidy ***Ed*** Pamela Power ***Art*** Bryan Graves
Act Keith Carradine, Harvey Keitel, Cristina Raines, Edward Fox, Robert Stephens, Albert Finney (Enigma)

The Napoleonic Wars are behind this stubborn sword-slashing-and-then-pistols of two men whose personalities are caught up in their own personal vendetta within the epic European battles of the times.

Harvey Keitel is an almost obsessed dueller who is asked to appear before the general due to his duels by Keith Carradine who practically volunteers for the job.

Keitel is jaunty and menancing and Carradine more determined and a bit troubled but also caught up in this strange need of one to prove honor and the other slaking a twisted nature.

It does not quite achieve a more lusty visual feel for the times and the strange relations of these two men to themselves and to the women in and out of their lives.

Fine thesps in smaller roles help with even Albert Finney in as the Napoleonic head of the Paris police.

•

DUET FOR ONE
1986, 107 mins, UK Ⓥ col
Dir Andrei Konchalovsky ***Prod*** Menahem Golan, Yoram Globus ***Scr*** Tom Kempinski, Jeremy Lipp, Andrei Konchalovsky ***Ph*** Alex Thomson ***Ed*** Henry Richardson ***Mus*** Michael Linn ***Art*** John Graysmark
Act Julie Andrews, Alan Bates, Max von Sydow, Rupert Everett, Margaret Courtenay, Cathryn Harrison (London Cannon)

The story of a world-class violinist who contracts multiple sclerosis and is forced to abandon her career, as long as *Duet for One* [from the 1980 stage play by Tom Kempinski] stays personal and specific it is a moving portrait of a life in turmoil.

Initially the film is not really about illness but the relationship of an artist to her art. Film is full of lovely musical interludes, both in concert and practice, and Julie Andrews actually looks credible stroking her violin. At the same time Andrews approaches her predicament in a pragmatic, overly rational manner as she plans out her recording schedule and the remaining days of her career.

In addition to the suggestion of a story, first half of the film offers an array of eccentric characters swirling around Andrews's life. As the philandering husband, Bates is a complex and restless soul afraid to face his own failings, whose vulnerability and physical deterioration bring an added and welcome dimension to the film.

•

DUETS
2000, 112 mins, US Ⓥ ⦿ col
Dir Bruce Paltrow ***Prod*** Kevin Jones, Bruce Paltrow, John Byrum ***Scr*** John Byrum ***Ph*** Paul Sarossy ***Ed*** Jerry Greenberg ***Mus*** David Newman ***Art*** Sharon Seymour
Act Maria Bello, Andre Braugher, Paul Giamatti, Huey Lewis, Gwyneth Paltrow, Scott Speedman, Angie Dickinson (Hollywood)

As long as it stays with the music and in a larky, seriocomic vein, *Duets* takes the audience for a jaunty spin. A cross-country road movie about three twosomes headed for a karaoke contest in Omaha, TV vet Bruce Paltrow's big-screen feature displays good reflexes for unpredictable humor and gives several of its actors chances to have fun in ways that are agreeably contagious. Lack of much substance or dramatic payoff makes the whole significantly less than sum of its parts.

Principal figures are slid into the rotation with ease. Ricky Dean (Huey Lewis) is a professional musician who hustles locals at small-time nightspots by pretending to not even know what karaoke is, then knocking the competition dead. Called to Las Vegas to attend the funeral of a long-ago ladyfriend, he for the first time meets the daughter he had with the woman, Liv (Gwyneth Paltrow), a lovely, slinky thing. A real ramblin' man, Ricky wants no part of her, but it's clear that ditching her might not be that easy.

Then there's Todd Woods (Paul Giamatti), a milquetoasty salesman who hits the road to oblivion and somewhere in Utah picks up hitchhiker Reggie Kane (Andre Braugher), a black escaped convict, a philosophically articulate fellow with little to lose himself. On a whim, they team up for a sensational rendition of "Try a Little Tenderness" in a saloon and decide to head for Omaha on a lark.

The third, and by far the least interesting, couple are Suzi Loomis (Maria Bello), a hardbitten waitress with a desperate ambition to make it as a singer, and mild-mannered taxi driver Billy (Scott Speedman), who agrees to take her from the Midwest to California on her provocative promise to "be nice" to him throughout the trip.

Perhaps the film's biggest revelation is that Gwyneth Paltrow has an absolutely fantastic singing voice. By far the most engaging of the duos, however, is Giamatti and Braugher. Latter is solid, as always, but Giamatti all but steals the movie as the meek little pushover who becomes a liberated monster of risk and freedom, a self-declared terrorist against the homogeneity of America as represented by the strip malls and chains that are the film's principal settings.

•

DUFFY

1968, 101 mins, UK col

Dir Robert Parrish ***Prod*** Martin Manulis ***Scr*** Donald Cammell, Harry Joe Brown, Jr. ***Ph*** Otto Heller ***Ed*** Willy Kemplen ***Mus*** Ernie Freeman ***Art*** Phillip Harrison

Act James Coburn, James Mason, James Fox, Susannah York, John Alderton, Guy Deghy (Columbia)

Duffy is the story [by Donald Cammell, Harry Joe Brown, Jr., and Pierre de la Salle] of two alienated sons stealing from their wealthy father. Weak writing and heavy-handed direction by Robert Parrish, eliciting only tepid performances, combine to snuff out much interest before the genuinely perky climax.

James Mason is a cold, calculating industrialist, loathed heartily by his sons, James Fox (who needs dad's money to pay for his hedonistic excesses) and John Alderton (who simply needs someone to rescue him from stupid blunders). Susannah York has some sort of affair going with Fox. Trio recruits drifter James Coburn to help with a money heist, designed to make them independently wealthy and also to embarrass Mason.

Fox's interpretation of his role is so swish (with costumes to match) that one wonders what attractions he holds for York. York in addition looks different in practically every setup. Only Alderton, who plays broadly to the pit, has what seems a definite concept of his part. Coburn tries awfully hard to be a hippie.

•

DUKE WORE JEANS, THE

1958, 90 mins, UK b/w

Dir Gerald Thomas ***Prod*** Peter Rogers ***Scr*** Norman Hudis ***Ph*** Otto Heller ***Ed*** Peter Boita ***Mus*** Bruce Montgomery ***Art*** Harry White

Act Tommy Steele, June Laverick, Michael Medwin, Alan Wheatley, Eric Pohlmann, Noel Hood (Insignia)

With his second film, *The Duke Wore Jeans*, Tommy Steele is lured into doing a certain amount of acting, and though no great shakes as a mummer, he emerges as a likeable personality with acting potentiality. The lissom yarn [by Lionel Bart and Michael Pratt] has Steele playing a dual role. He is a young aristocrat who wants to evade wooing the princess of a wealthy South American oil-monarchy, as desired by his hard-up parents, mainly because he already is secretly married. When he meets a young, brash Cockney who is his exact double, he arranges for him to take his place.

Steele is happier when he takes over for the young peer than in the earlier stages. Opportunities are provided for him to sing several numbers of which "It's All Happening," "Happy Guitar," and "Thanks a Lot" are standouts. Most of the comedy is supplied via a suave performance by Michael Medwin, as a gentleman's gentleman.

•

DUMB & DUMBER

1994, 106 mins, US Ⓥ ⊙ col

Dir Peter Farrelly ***Prod*** Charles B. Wessler, Brad Krevoy, Steve Stabler ***Scr*** Peter Farrelly, Bennett Yellin, Bobby Farrelly ***Ph*** Mark Irwin ***Ed*** Christopher Greenbury ***Mus*** Todd Rundgren ***Art*** Sidney J. Bartholomew, Jr.

Act Jim Carrey, Jeff Daniels, Lauren Holly, Teri Garr, Karen Duffy, Victoria Rowell (New Line)

There's not a lot of brain work involved in *Dumb & Dumber*, a flat-out celebration of stupidity, bodily functions, and pratfalls. Yet the wholeheartedness of this descent into crude and rude humor is so good-natured and precise that it's hard not to partake in the guilty pleasures of the exercise.

Harry Dunne (Jeff Daniels) is a rather inept dog groomer who has transformed his van exterior to resemble a sheep dog. Lloyd Christmas (Jim Carrey), who resembles a latter-day Carl "Alfalfa" Switzer, is a limo driver who's saving to open a worm supply warehouse.

When Mary Swanson (Lauren Holly) enters Lloyd's limo for a ride to the airport, his heart flies out the sun roof. As he pulls away, he notices that his charge has left her briefcase right in the middle of the terminal. Ever gallant, he retrieves it, but not quite in time to get it aboard Mary's flight to Aspen.

It doesn't take a genius to figure where the story is going. The slight variation is that Mary doesn't want the valise; it's filled with $100,000 in ransom money that her husband's kidnappers are supposed to retrieve.

The entire affair escapes the gutter thanks to Daniels, Carrey, Holly, and a string of very good supporting players. Daniel is particularly adroit in his role. Tyro filmmaker Peter Farrelly (who also co-wrote) displays a natural flair for comedy and pacing.

•

DUMBO

1941, 64 mins, US Ⓥ ⊙ col

Dir Ben Sharpsteen ***Prod*** Walt Disney ***Scr*** Joe Grant, Dick Huemer ***Mus*** Oliver Wallace, Frank Churchill ***Art*** Herb Ryman, Ken O'Connor, Terrell Stamp, Don Da Gradi, Al Zinnen, Ernest Nordli, Dick Kelsey, Charles Payzand (Walt Disney)

Walt Disney returns in *Dumbo* to the formula that accounted for his original success—simple animal characterization.

There's a pleasant little story, plenty of pathos mixed with the large doses of humor, a number of appealing new animal characters, lots of good music, and the usual Disney skillfulness in technique.

Defects are some decidedly slow spots and that the film is somewhat episodic in nature.

Story [from a book by Helen Aberson and Harold Pearl] points a nice moral, although not one that gets in the way. Dumbo is a little elephant who is jeered at because of his big ears. But he is shown how to make use of his ears, they enable him to fly, and his handicap thereby becomes his greatest asset.

Yarn is set to a circus background, complete with clowns, the big top, and all the rest. There is also a neatly contrived comedy characterization of gossipy lady elephants, and the even more earthy humor of a typical Disney locomotive being spurred to speed by a goose from the car behind it.

1941: Best Scoring of a Musical Picture

NOMINATION: Best Song ("Baby Mine")

•

DUNE

1984, 140 mins, US Ⓥ ⊙ ▭ col

Dir David Lynch ***Prod*** Raffaella De Laurentiis ***Scr*** David Lynch ***Ph*** Freddie Francis ***Ed*** Antony Gibbs ***Mus*** Toto, Marty Paich, Brian Eno ***Art*** Anthony Masters

Act Francesca Annis, Brad Dourif, Kyle MacLachlan, Sian Phillips, Sting, Max von Sydow (De Laurentiis)

Dune is a huge, hollow, imaginative, and cold sci-fi epic. Visually unique and teeming with incident, David Lynch's film holds the interest due to its abundant surface attractions but won't, of its own accord, create the sort of fanaticism which has made Frank Herbert's 1965 novel one of the all-time favorites in its genre.

Set in the year 10,991, *Dune* is the story of the coming to power of a warrior savior and how he leads the lowly inhabitants of the Dune planet to victory over an evil emperor and his minions.

Lynch's adaptation covers the entire span of the novel, but simply setting up the various worlds, characters, intrigues, and forces at work requires more than a half-hour of expository screen time.

The anointed one, Paul Atreides, travels with his regal mother and father to the desert planet, where an all-powerful "spice" is mined from beneath the sands despite the menace provided by enormous worms which gobble up harvesters in a single gulp.

The horrid Harkonnens conquer the city on Dune, but Paul and his mother escape to the desert. There Paul trains native warriors and achieves his full mystic powers.

Francesca Annis and Jurgen Prochnow make an outstandingly attractive royal couple, Sian Phillips has some mesmerizing moments as a powerful witch, Brad Dourif is effectively loony, and best of all is Kenneth McMillan, whose face is covered with grotesque growths and who floats around like the Blue Meanie come to life.

1984: NOMINATION: Best Sound

•

DUNKIRK

1958, 135 mins, UK b/w

Dir Leslie Norman ***Prod*** Michael Balcon ***Scr*** David Divine, W. P. Lipscomb ***Ph*** Paul Beeson ***Ed*** Gordon Stone ***Mus*** Malcolm Arnold ***Art*** Jim Morahan

Act John Mills, Bernard Lee, Richard Attenborough, Robert Urquhart, Ray Jackson, Maxine Audley (Ealing)

Eighteen years after the event, Ealing Films tackled the mammoth task of committing Dunkirk to the screen. The story of a defeat which, miraculously, blossomed into ultimate victory because it stiffened Britain's resolve and solidarity, offered Michael Balcon and his team many challenging problems. *Dunkirk* is a splendid near-documentary which just fails to reach magnificence.

Director Leslie Norman planned his film [based on a novel by Elleston Trevor and also on a factual account] through the eyes of three men. John Mills, a spry Cockney corporal who, with a few men, becomes detached from his unit and leads them to the beaches without quite knowing what is happening. Bernard Lee, a newspaper correspondent who is suspicious of the red tape of the higher-ups. Richard Attenborough as a civilian having an easy time in a reserved occupation.

The film throughout is deliberately underplayed, with no false heroics and with dialog which has an almost clinical authenticity. On the whole, it is an absorbing rather than an emotion-stirring film.

•

DUNSTON CHECKS IN

1996, 88 mins, US Ⓥ col

Dir Ken Kwapis ***Prod*** Joe Wizan, Todd Black ***Scr*** John Hopkins, Bruce Graham ***Ph*** Peter Collister ***Ed*** Jon Pol ***Mus*** Miles Goodman ***Art*** Rusty Smith

Act Jason Alexander, Faye Dunaway, Eric Lloyd, Rupert Everett, Graham Sack, Paul Reubens (20th Century-Fox)

Dunston Checks In is a first-class, stylish farce with a brisk pace and cool wit.

Robert Grant (Jason Alexander) manages the upscale Majestic Hotel in L.A. A widower, he's raising his two boys (young Eric Lloyd, teenager Graham Sack), who look upon the venerable hostelry as their private playground. They've been warned to cool the hijinx with the impending visit of the capricious, slightly ruthless owner Mrs. Dubrow (Faye Dunaway).

The iron mistress informs Grant that an agent of the prestigious *Le Monde* guide is expected. He'll be traveling incognito, but the Majestic stands to be the first U.S. hotel to earn a six-star rating.

A new guest, Lord Rutledge (Rupert Everett), is mistaken for the discreet inspector when he's spied inspecting the edifice's nooks and crannies. Actually, he's scouting the terrain for security breaches that will allow him to practice his real vocation—thievery. He's abetted by a dexterous simian named Dunston (Sam), who's adept at second-story work.

Director Ken Kwapis displays a deft touch, balancing realistic elements and outsize characterizations. Pic's unflagging pace and the unexpectedly witty script (from a screen story by coscripter John Hopkins) complement the simplicity of this construct.

•

DU RIFIFI CHEZ LES HOMMES *(RIFIFI)*

1955, 120 mins, France ⊙ b/w

Dir Jules Dassin ***Scr*** Jules Dassin, Rene Wheeler ***Ph*** Philippe Agostini ***Ed*** Roger Dwyre ***Mus*** Georgs Auric

Act Jean Servais, Carl Mohner, Robert Manuel, Magali Noel, Janine Darcy, Marie Sabouret (Indus/Prima/Pathe)

It took an experienced U.S. director, Jules Dassin, who has lived in France some years, to give the French gangster pic the proper tension, mounting and treatment. This pic has something intrinsically Gallic without sacrificing the rugged storytelling.

Just out of jail, the hero (Jean Servais) finds his wife living with somebody else and it prompts him to return to his old racket. A big heist of a jewelry store is planned. Then there is one brilliant bit of cinema, 30 minutes of complete silence as the gang cuts its way into the shop and carries out its mission.

Dassin gives this a sharp treatment and does not neglect the Paris streets and atmosphere. Servais has the authority, under a facade of weariness, as Tony, and the remainder of the gang is well etched, with Dassin himself turning in a telling bit as Cesar, whose love for femmes gives the whole thing away. Editing is first-rate as is Philippe Agostini's lensing. This is Dassin's first pic in five years.

●

DUST DEVIL
THE FINAL CUT
1993, 108 mins, UK/US Ⓥ ⊙ col
Dir Richard Stanley ***Prod*** Joanne Sellar ***Scr*** Richard Stanley ***Ph*** Steven Chivers ***Ed*** Derek Trigg, Paul Carlin ***Mus*** Simon Boswell ***Art*** Joseph Bennett
Act Robert Burke, Chelsea Field, Zakes Mokae, John Matshikiza, Rufus Swart, William Hootkins (Palace/Miramax)

Overflowing with ideas, visual invention, and genre references but saddled by a weak, unfocused script, *Dust Devil* is a brilliant mess. Mystical African-set slasher movie is the second feature of pop promo alum Richard Stanley.

The low-budget production was shot in late summer 1991 in Namibia, southern Africa, with Stanley delivering a 125-minute European cut in December. Stanley spent $45,000 of his own coin to reconstruct this version, [a compromise between his original and U.S. coproducer Miramax's much shorter] U.S. cut, American-dubbed and with a new voiceover.

The opening 45 minutes is a tour de force of elaborate cross-cutting and sustained tension as three characters compete for attention. First is a taciturn Yank (Robert Burke) hitching across country, murdering and mutilating strangers and collecting their fingers in a box. Second is black cop Ben (Zakes Mokae), who turns to the witch-doctor owner of a desert drive-in (John Matshikiza) to solve the ghastly murders. Third is Wendy (Chelsea Field), a South African who walks out on her boring hubby (Rufus Swart) and drives north to Namibia on a journey to nowhere.

Story slides into focus halfway through, as the trio's destinies crisscross and it becomes clear Burke is trying to return to the spirit world but is trapped in the present, surviving by claiming human souls. Final impression is of a film that's run amok with too many half-baked ideas, which might have cohered with a stronger script.

●

DUTCH
(UK/AUSTRALIA: DRIVING ME CRAZY)
1991, 105 mins, US Ⓥ ⊙ col
Dir Peter Faiman ***Prod*** John Hughes, Richard Vane ***Scr*** John Hughes ***Ph*** Charles Minsky ***Ed*** Paul Hirsch, Adam Bernardi ***Mus*** Alan Silvestri ***Art*** Stan Jolley
Act Ed O'Neill, Ethan Randall, JoBeth Williams, Christopher McDonald, Ari Meyers, E. G. Daily (20th Century-Fox)

In designing *Dutch*, writer-producer John Hughes lays in some oft-used parts, from the family holiday gathering to the travails of incompatible travelers. In this case, the focus is on Ed O'Neill as Dutch, a salt-of-the-earth guy who's volunteered to pick up his girlfriend's snotty kid, Doyle (Ethan Randall), at an elite boarding school and bring him home for Thanksgiving. Little does Dutch know what he's in for.

Full of rage over his mother's divorce from his callous but absurdly wealthy dad (Christopher McDonald), Doyle wants nothing to do with either his doting mom (JoBeth Williams) or her new boyfriend, and he spews his towering contempt at working-class Dutch.

The kid is so despicable that even Dutch soon loses his taste for the challenge. Therein lies the pic's weakness, as the boy's hateful behavior is so trying that this two-character journey—even with its attendant adventures with fireworks, hookers, tacky motels, and homeless shelters—isn't all that enticing.

O'Neill is well cast as the tough and confident regular guy, but his comic gifts fall short of hilarious, and director Peter Faiman, helming his first project since *Crocodile Dundee*, never really sets a rollicking groove. Filmed in Georgia, Tennessee, rural Illinois, and on L.A. soundstages, film draws texture and comedy from locations.

●

DYING YOUNG
1991, 105 mins, US Ⓥ ⊙ col
Dir Joel Schumacher ***Prod*** Sally Field, Kevin McCormick ***Scr*** Richard Friedenberg ***Ph*** Juan Ruiz Anchia ***Ed*** Robert Brown ***Mus*** James Newton Howard ***Art*** Guy J. Comtois
Act Julia Roberts, Campbell Scott, Vincent D'Onofrio, Colleen Dewhurst, David Selby, Ellen Burstyn (20th Century-Fox/Fogwood)

Julia's hot; *Dying Young* is lukewarm. In this rather thin and maudlin weeper, Julia Roberts does little to extend her range in a performance that seems pieced together from aspects of previous roles.

Campbell Scott (*The Sheltering Sky*) plays Victor Geddes, an immensely wealthy young man who at 28 has been battling leukemia for 10 years. He places an ad for an attractive young lady to nurse him through the bouts of violent illness that accompany chemotherapy.

Enter Roberts as Hilary O'Neil, who in the interest of dramatic contrast is painted as a badly dressed, uneducated street-smart type from bluecollar Oakland. For the lonely, intellectual Victor, she's raw material to be shaped in his image—an irresistible draw.

Director Joel Schumacher (*Flatliners*) apparently doubting an audience will stick around just out of concern for Victor's illness, turns a rather shabbily exploitative camera on Roberts, whose legs seem to play the lead role in the first act. Much of the time pic operates on the level of a teaser sustained by the dangling question of Victor's unconsummated desire.

Roberts displays the usual combo of flintily self-sufficient and winningly vulnerable traits. Her portrayal of a working-class character is not exactly chameleon-like. Scott puts in a beguiling and technically polished turn as the desperately lonely sufferer.

Pic [from Marti Leimbach's novel] plays like a sentiment-soaked escapist fantasy for the bed-and-breakfast set.

●

DYNAMITE
1929, 128 mins, US b/w
Dir Cecil B. DeMille ***Prod*** Cecil B. DeMille ***Scr*** Jeanie Macpherson, John Howard Lawson, Gladys Unger ***Ph*** J. Peverell Marley ***Ed*** Anne Bauchens ***Mus*** Herbert Stothart ***Art*** Cedric Gibbons, Mitchell Leisen
Act Conrad Nagel, Kay Johnson, Charles Bickford, Julia Faye, Muriel McCormac, Tyler Brooke (M-G-M)

Those familiar with Cecil B. DeMille's work will see almost a resume of his entire screen career [to date] in this society picture heavily seasoned with dramatic hoke.

Elaborate boudoir, bath, wild stew party, rakish Mercedes, fantastic sport carnival—they're all here, and always in the background the shadow of the People as expressed, in this instance, by a miner, whom the spoiled society bud has wed in prison on the eve of execution. All to comply with a will, leaving her millions, in order that she may buy another woman's husband.

Story unwinds the gradual urge for each other between the he-man and the spoiled child of wealth, after he has declared that she's worthless and walked out.

It's DeMille's first talker and Kay Johnson's debut in pictures. She butters the screen with a world of class and ability.

EACH DAWN I DIE
1939, 92 mins, US Ⓥ b/w

Dir William Keighley ***Prod*** Hal B. Wallis (exec.) ***Scr*** Norman Reilly Raine, Warren Duff, Charles Perry ***Ph*** Arthur Edeson ***Ed*** Thomas Richards ***Mus*** Max Steiner ***Art*** Max Parker

Act James Cagney, George Raft, Jane Bryan, George Bancroft, Victor Jory, Maxie Rosenbloom (Warner)

Story structure [from the novel by Jerome Odlum] is a bit thin in spots despite the best efforts of director William Keighley, who isn't always able to cover up. The loyalty theme and seeming double-cross motive becomes too involved just when the plot appears heading for a clever climax.

Cagney is kept in typical toughie surroundings, framed by unscrupulous politicians because he has uncovered their crooked work for his newspaper. Embittered by his inability to win a pardon, Cagney is pictured as developing into a hardened prisoner. Then when he helps an underworld big shot (George Raft) go scot free in a daring courtroom break, only to be double-crossed when the big-timer thinks Raft has squealed, the reporter goes haywire.

Cagney fans will be pleasantly surprised at his restrained, skillful performance. Raft is a plausible, gripping underworld big-timer. He rates the co-starring classification.

•

EAGLE, THE
1925, 72 mins, US Ⓥ ⊙ ⊗ b/w

Dir Clarence Brown ***Scr*** Hans Kraly, George Marion, Jr. ***Ph*** George Barnes, Dev Jennings ***Ed*** Hal C. Kern ***Art*** William Cameron Menzies

Act Rudolph Valentino, Vilma Banky, Louise Dresser, Albert Conti, James Marcus (Art Finance/United Artists)

Rudolph Valentino as a Russian Robin Hood of more modern times. In *The Eagle*, he really goes out and does some "he-man" stuff.

Louise Dresser as the Czarina handles herself superbly. She is the old girl of the Russians who liked the boys. Vilma Banky makes a most charming heroine opposite the star, but Louise Dresser is about as much the picture as the star himself.

•

EAGLE AND THE HAWK, THE
1933, 74 mins, US b/w

Dir Stuart Walker, Mitchell Leisen ***Prod*** Bayard Veiller ***Scr*** Bogart Rogers, Seton I. Miller ***Ph*** Harry Fischbeck

Act Fredric March, Cary Grant, Jack Oakie, Carole Lombard, Guy Standing, Forrester Harvey (Paramount)

Strictly a formula story of the Royal Flying Corps by the man who wrote *Wings* [John Monk Saunders] with a laboriously dragged in romantic bit. Nothing much new in the matter of plot, the same old yarn of the man who gets fed up of the uselessness of war.

Basic idea is the hero who is broken by the strain. He has lost observer after observer without serious injury to himself, and it breaks his morale. His last observer is a rather tough-fibered chap and there is bad blood between them. Fredric March is sent back home to regain his poise, there is a brief two-scene interlude with Carole Lombard, and he comes back to the lines still shaken.

Yarn is adroitly told in both dialog and action, Jack Oakie contributing some sorely-needed comedy touches here and there. It is the only relief save for a delightfully played bit between Oakie and Adrienne D'Ambicourt, who makes the most of her single scene. Carole Lombard contributes little in spite of sincere playing. March offers a finely sensitive study, acting with force, but entirely without bombast. Cary Grant is more along the usual lines, but he supplies the complementary action effectively, and Guy Standing as the commander gets a brief chance now and then.

•

EAGLE HAS LANDED, THE
1977, 134 mins, UK Ⓥ ▭ col

Dir John Sturges ***Prod*** Jack Winer, David Niven, Jr. ***Scr*** Tom Mankiewicz ***Ph*** Tony Richmond ***Ed*** Irene Lamb ***Mus*** Lalo Schifrin ***Art*** Peter Murton

Act Michael Caine, Donald Sutherland, Robert Duvall, Jenny Agutter, Donald Pleasence, Anthony Quayle (ITC/Assoc. General)

In November 1943, Winston Churchill is due to spend a weekend at a country house in Norfolk—and the Germans propose to kidnap him there. Under orders from Heinrich Himmler (Donald Pleasence), purportedly coming from Hitler himself, a Nazi colonel (Robert Duvall) organizes the smuggling into Britain of the English-hating Irishman

Donald Sutherland, and the parachuting of a 16-man task force of Germans under the command of another colonel (Michael Caine).

The events take place in the small village of Studley Constable.

Most performances [in this adaptation of the Jack Higgins's novel] are first rate with Sutherland exuding great credibility as the Irishman, and Caine thoroughly convincing as the Nazi commander. Pleasence gives a standout lifelike interpretation of Himmler.

•

EAGLE'S WING
1979, 104 mins, UK Ⓥ ▭ col

Dir Anthony Harvey ***Prod*** Ben Arbeid ***Scr*** John Briley ***Ph*** Billy Williams ***Ed*** Lesley Walker ***Mus*** Marc Wilkinson ***Art*** Herbert Westbrook

Act Martin Sheen, Sam Waterston, Harvey Keitel, Stephane Audran, Caroline Langrishe, John Castle (Rank)

Claiming to evoke "the West, the way it really was, before the myths were born," British director Anthony Harvey's poised, loving linger in the 1830s badlands of New Mexico is primarily an art film—resolutely romantic, high on production values, low on grit.

Ostensibly a tussle for possession of a uniquely fleet white horse (poetically described by the title), the distinctly allegorical plot [from an original story by Michael Syson] pits Martin Sheen as a city-bred, novice trapper against a no-longer-so-young Indian brave, played with remarkable success by Sam Waterston.

Sheen, wild-eyed and vulnerable, is good casting and copes well with the central character's awkward soliloquizing. Harvey Keitel is lowkey but impressive as Sheen's companion and mentor.

•

EARRINGS OF MADAME DE . . . , THE
SEE: MADAME DE . . .

•

EARTH
SEE: ZIMLYA

•

EARTH GIRLS ARE EASY
1988, 100 mins, UK/US Ⓥ ⊙ ▭ col

Dir Julien Temple ***Prod*** Tony Garnett ***Scr*** Julie Brown, Charlie Coffey, Terrence E. McNally ***Ph*** Oliver Stapleton ***Ed*** Richard Halsey ***Mus*** Nile Rodgers, Chaz Jankel, David Storrs ***Art*** Dennis Gassner

Act Geena Davis, Jeff Goldblum, Julie Brown, Jim Carrey, Damon Wayans, Michael McKean (Kestrel/Odyssey)

Earth Girls Are Easy is a dizzy, glitzy fish-out-of-water farce about three horny aliens on the make in L.A.

Julie (Geena Davis), a gorgeous Valley Girl, works as a manicurist in high-tech beauty salon operated by Candy (Julie Brown), a Val-Queen supreme who likes good times and good sex.

Meanwhile in outer space, three aliens who look like tie-dyed werewolves are wandering around our solar system going bonkers with randiness. In keeping with the film's hot-pastel, contempo-trash design motif, their spacecraft looks like the inside of a pinball machine. When it lands in Julie's swimming pool, the broken-hearted girl who's just broken off with her nogoodnik lover takes it for an oversized hair dryer.

Julie brings this gruesome threesome to Candy's beauty parlor for a complete "makeover." They emerge as three hairless hunky dudes: the captain, Jeff Goldblum, and two flaked-out crewmen, Jim Carrey, and Damon Wayans. The two val-gals and their alien "dates" take off for a weekend of L.A. nightlife, where the visitors's smooth adaptation to Coast culture is intended by director Julian Temple and his screenwriters to affectionately skewer Tinseltown lifestyles.

•

EARTHQUAKE
1974, 122 mins, US Ⓥ ⊙ ▭ col

Dir Mark Robson ***Prod*** Mark Robson ***Scr*** George Fox, Mario Puzo ***Ph*** Philip Lathrop ***Ed*** Dorothy Spencer ***Mus*** John Williams ***Art*** Alexander Golitzen, E. Preston Ames

Act Charlton Heston, Ava Gardner, George Kennedy, Lorne Greene, Genevieve Bujold, Richard Roundtree (Universal)

Mark Robson's *Earthquake* is an excellent dramatic exploitation extravaganza, combining brilliant special effects with a multi-character plot line which is surprisingly above average for this type film. Large cast is headed by Charlton Heston, who comes off better than usual because he is not Superman, instead just one of the gang.

Ava Gardner, ravishingly beautiful, plays Heston's jealous wife, who also is the daughter of Lorne Greene, Heston's architect boss. Gardner's fits of pique concern Genevieve Bujold.

The film spends its first 53 minutes establishing most of the key plot situations, but regularly teases the big quake with some foreshocks. When that occurs, the first big special effects sequence provides an excellent, unstinting panorama of destruction.

1974: Best Sound, Special Visual Effects

NOMINATIONS: Best Cinematography, Art Direction, Editing

•

EARTH VS. THE FLYING SAUCERS
1956, 82 mins, US Ⓥ b/w

Dir Fred F. Sears ***Prod*** Charles H. Schneer ***Scr*** George Worthington Yates, Raymond T. Marcus ***Ph*** Fred Jackman ***Ed*** Danny D. Landres ***Mus*** Mischa Bakaleinikoff (dir.) ***Art*** Paul Palmentola

Act Hugh Marlowe, Joan Taylor, Donald Curtis, Morris Ankrum, John Zaremba, Tom Browne Henry (Columbia)

This exploitation programmer does a satisfactory job of entertaining in the science-fiction class. The technical effects created by Ray Harryhausen come off excellently in the Charles H. Schneer production, adding the required out-of-this-world visual touch to the screenplay, taken from a screen story by Curt Siodmak, suggested by Major Donald E. Keyhoe's *Flying Saucers from Outer Space*.

Fred F. Sears's direction mixes the make-believe at a good pace, achieving a neat measure of suspense and thrills as the plot unwinds. Dr. Russell A. Marvin (Hugh Marlowe), space-exploration scientist, interrupts his honeymoon with Carol (Joan Taylor) to find out why the free-flying, artificial satellites he has been launching for the military are being knocked down. Ancient humanoids, manning flying saucers, are the saboteurs and through communication with the hero, advise they intend to take over the earth. Yankee ingenuity comes up with a hastily devised weapon that neutralizes the saucers' magnetic anti-gravity equipment.

•

EASTER PARADE
1948, 102 mins, US Ⓥ ⊙ col

Dir Charles Walters ***Prod*** Arthur Freed ***Scr*** Frances Goodrich, Albert Hackett, Sidney Sheldon ***Ph*** Harry Stradling ***Ed*** Albert Akst ***Mus*** Johnny Green, Roger Edens (dirs.) ***Art*** Cedric Gibbons, Jack Martin Smith

Act Judy Garland, Fred Astaire, Peter Lawford, Ann Miller, Jules Munshin (M-G-M)

Easter Parade is a musical with old and new Irving Berlin tunes and standout dance numbers. The Berlin score includes 17 songs, seven new and 10 from his extensive catalog.

The light story by Frances Goodrich and Albert Hackett, scripted in conjunction with Sidney Sheldon, makes a perfect backing for the Berlin score and playing. Plot opens on Easter 1911 and carries through to Easter 1912. It deals with splitup of Astaire and Miller as partners and recruiting of Garland by the dancer, who is determined to make her outdraw his former hoofer.

Astaire's standout solo is the elaborate production piece "Stepping Out with My Baby," during which he does a slow-motion dance in front of a large chorus terping in regular time.

Highpoint of comedy is reached when Astaire and Garland team for vocals and foot work on "A Couple of Swells."

1948: Best Score for a Musical Picture

•

EAST LYNNE
1931, 102 mins, US b/w

Dir Frank Lloyd ***Scr*** Bradley King, Tom Barry ***Ph*** John Seitz ***Mus*** Richard Fall ***Art*** Joseph Urban

Act Ann Harding, Clive Brook, Conrad Nagel, Cecilia Loftus, Beryl Mercer, O. P. Heggie (Fox)

An excellent piece of work in taking a legendary meller play and transposing it into a screen drama of strength and charm.

The beauty of the cast is that they make the characters believable. All are from the stage, while the dialog is such that it avoids petty pleasantries or overly dramatic orations. It amounts to an outstanding performance by Ann Harding, who is closely allied by Clive Brook and Cecilia Loftus.

Second line of defense is in the able hands of O. P. Heggie and Beryl Mercer. Heggie has somewhat less to do, but impresses as the girl's father.

Joseph Urban's settings are sumptuous and tasteful, evidently having been given a free hand in creating the interior of a big country home. Besides which there is an elaborate Viennese cafe interlude, as also a certain amount of footage given over to the Franco-Prussian war and the bombardment of Paris by the latter forces. It's doubtful if Fox got out with less than $800,000 in production costs.

Frank Lloyd, who directed, has made everything count without lingering unnecessarily over any one episode. His only hint of a false note seems to be in the meeting of Isabel (Harding) and her father in Paris, where she pleads with him to seek permission from her husband to see her child.

1930/31: NOMINATION: Best Picture

•

EAST OF EDEN

1955, 114 mins, US Ⓥ ⊙ ▭ col

Dir Elia Kazan *Prod* Elia Kazan *Scr* Paul Osborn *Ph* Ted McCord *Ed* Owen Marks *Mus* Leonard Rosenman *Art* James Basevi, Malcolm Bert

Act Julie Harris, James Dean, Raymond Massey, Burl Ives, Jo Van Fleet, Albert Dekker (Warner)

Powerfully somber dramatics have been captured from the pages of John Steinbeck's *East of Eden* and put on film by Elia Kazan. It is a tour de force for the director's penchant for hard-hitting forays with life. It is no credit to Kazan that James Dean seems required to play his lead character as though he were straight out of a Marlon Brando mold, although he has a basic appeal that manages to get through to the viewer despite the heavy burden of carboning another's acting style in voice and mannerisms.

Only the latter part of the Steinbeck novel is used in the screenplay, which picks up the principals in this Salinas Valley melodrama at the time the twin sons of a lettuce farmer are graduating in the 1917 class at high school.

Julie Harris gives her particular style to an effective portrayal of the girl.

1955: Best Supp. Actress (Jo Van Fleet)

NOMINATIONS: Best Director, Actor (James Dean), Screenplay

•

EAST SIDE, WEST SIDE

1949, 104 mins, US Ⓥ b/w

Dir Mervyn LeRoy *Prod* Voldemar Vetluguin *Scr* Isobel Lennart *Ph* Charles Rosher *Ed* Harold F. Kress *Mus* Miklos Rozsa

Act Barbara Stanwyck, James Mason, Van Heflin, Ava Gardner, Cyd Charisse, Nancy Davis (M-G-M)

The principal difficulty in Isobel Lennart's screenplay [from Marcia Davenport's bestselling novel] is that there's too much visible planting of threads to be ostentatiously picked up later, and the coincidences are rampant. The opportune ringing of that telephone bell, too, is a device that's overworked.

The yarn itself is one of husbandly infidelity in a New York society setting with all the trimmings. James Mason plays the cad mate who finds other women irresistible in the same way that an alcoholic can't keep from reaching for a bottle. Barbara Stanwyck is the wife done wrong, but who loves him so much she can't give him up despite his widely advertised philandering.

Performances throughout are convincing with Ava Gardner probably grabbing top honors as the willful and attractive vixen. Mervyn LeRoy's direction is, as usual, competent.

•

EASY COME, EASY GO

1967, 95 mins, US Ⓥ col

Dir John Rich *Prod* Hal B. Wallis *Scr* Allan Weiss, Anthony Lawrence *Ph* William Margulies *Ed* Archie Marshek *Mus* Joseph J. Lilley *Art* Hal Pereira, Walter Tyler

Act Elvis Presley, Dodie Marshall, Pat Priest, Pat Harrington, Skip Ward, Sandy Kenyon (Paramount)

Easy Come, Easy Go stars Elvis Presley as an underwater demolitions expert who finds lost treasure. Good balance of script and songs, plus generally amusing performances by a competent, well-directed cast, add up to diverting entertainment.

Partnered with ex-biz partner Pat Harrington (who comes across very well as a bearded beatnik type), Elvis faces surmountable problems in the resistance of Dodie Marshall, whose grandfather owned the sunken ship on which the treasure is discovered.

Elsa Lanchester shines in her bit as the kooky yoga instructor, and Diki Lerner sticks out as an effete artist with a flair for turning automobiles into mobiles.

•

EASY LIVING

1937, 88 mins, US b/w

Dir Mitchell Leisen *Prod* Arthur Hornblow, Jr. *Scr* Preston Sturges *Ph* Ted Tetzlaff *Ed* Doane Harrison *Mus* Boris Morros (dir.) *Art* Hans Dreier, Ernst Fegte

Act Jean Arthur, Edward Arnold, Ray Milland, Luis Alberni, Mary Nash, Franklin Pangborn (Paramount)

Slapstick farce, incredible and without rhyme or reason, is Paramount's contribution to the cycle of goofy pictures which started with *My Man Godfrey* (1936). This one is a poor imitation, lacking spontaneity and cleverness.

Screenplay by Preston Sturges [from a story by Vera Caspary] is a trivia of nonsense. Mitchell Leisen, who directs, tries to overcome the story faults with elaborate settings and Keystone gags.

Opening portrays Edward Arnold as a Wall Street speculative genius whose mad selling and buying has the street agog with his financial didoes. Conflict starts with an altercation between him and his wife over the purchase of a fur coat. Garment is tossed out of the window and strikes a young stenographer (Jean Arthur) on her way to work. In a jealous fit, Arnold insists the young woman retain the coat and whisks her to the milliner to buy a hat to match.

Meanwhile, the news spreads quickly that the big Wall Street man has a mistress, and Arthur, whose resources are measured in nickels, accepts an elaborate suite in the leading hotel. What she wants most is a cup of coffee, and she goes to the automat to get it. There she meets Ray Milland, son of the Wall Street wizard. He is a waiter in the joint. Yarns of this sort are likely to get out of hand by introducing low slapstick comedy. When the food throwing ends there is nothing left for the players to do. All semblance of probability has vanished.

•

EASY RIDER

1969, 94 mins, US Ⓥ ⊙ col

Dir Dennis Hopper *Prod* Peter Fonda *Scr* Peter Fonda, Dennis Hopper, Terry Southern *Ph* Laszlo Kovacs *Ed* Donn Cambern, Henry Jaglom *Art* Jerry Kay

Act Peter Fonda, Dennis Hopper, Jack Nicholson, Robert Walker, Luana Anders, Karen Black (Pando/Raybert)

Film deals with two dropouts on a long trip from Los Angeles to New Orleans's Mardi Gras, a search for freedom thwarted by that streak of ingrained, bigoted violence in the U.S. and their own hangups.

Pic chronicles their trip that ends in tragedy. Their bikes whisk them through the good roads surrounded by all the stretches of land that have housed that mythic American creation of the western.

Script is literate and incisive and Hopper's direction is fluid, observant and catches the pictorial poetics with feeling.

Fonda exudes a groping moral force and Hopper is agitated, touching, and responsive as the sidekick, hoping for that so-called freedom their stake should give them.

Jack Nicholson is excellent as an articulate alcoholic who fills in the smothered needs in a verbal way that the others feel but cannot express.

1969: NOMINATIONS: Best Supp. Actor (Jack Nicholson), Original Story & Screenplay

•

EASY STREET

1917, 29 mins, US d b/w

Dir Charles Chaplin *Scr* Charles Chaplin *Ph* William C. Foster, Rollie Totheroh

Act Charles Chaplin, Edna Purviance, Eric Campbell, Albert Austin (Mutual)

Charlie Chaplin portrays a policeman. He gets the job and is assigned to "Easy Street," a narrow thoroughfare which, from the daily routine, must be the place where all the roughnecks are trained. Leader of them is Eric Campbell, whose burly bulk aptly lends itself to Chaplin's scenario.

Before the new cop's advent, Eric and his mob have cleaned up other policemen by the group. So when Charlie appears with club and shield, it looks like pie to the chief mauler. To awe the new cop, Eric bends a lamp-post in half, but in that endeavor Charlie leaps on his back, shoves Eric's head through the lamp and turns on the gas. Thus is the king of the roughs arrested. But he does not stay long in the station house, simply breaking his handcuffs and starting in search of the new copper.

The roughhouse that results is pretty nearly top class. *Easy Street* certainly has some rough work in it, but it is the kind of stuff that Chaplin fans love.

•

EASY TO LOVE

1953, 96 mins, US Ⓥ col

Dir Charles Walters *Prod* Joe Pasternak *Scr* Laslo Vadnay, William Roberts *Ph* Ray June *Ed* Gene Ruggiero *Mus* Lennie Hayton, George Stoll (dirs.) *Art* Cedric Gibbons, Jack Martin Smith

Act Esther Williams, Van Johnson, Tony Martin, John Bromfield, Edna Skinner, Carroll Baker (M-G-M)

Metro's special knack for turning out big, splashy musicals on a lavish scale that so dazzle the eye that the story becomes negligible is exemplified in *Easy to Love*, produced by the maestro of musical spectacle, Joe Pasternak. The Cypress Gardens, Florida, backgounds, first exploited by Cinerama, contribute some highly scenic footage. Too bad that the story had to be so lightweight, but then, with all the swimming, water skiing, singing and plush mountains maybe there just wasn't room for plot.

Esther Williams, shapely and vivacious as the much sought-after aquatic star whose only aim in life is to "hook" Van Johnson, delivers her usual cheerful performance. Van Johnson is easy-going gent who manages a good comedy line when handed one. Tony Martin does a sock stint and delivers a brace of songs in top-notch fashion. His vocalizing seems quite natural even in situations where musical outbursts would ordinarily be surprising. Call it Metro technique.

Musical numbers, created and directed by Busby Berkeley, move easily and look attractive. There are plenty of lively tunes to help brighten the proceedings. Among them are the ever-lovely Cole Porter song, "Easy to Love," "Didja Ever," "Look Out, I'm Romantic," "That's What a Rainy Day Is For," and "Coquette."

Story has a couple of good laughs in it. Williams loves Van Johnson, who runs Cypress Gardens where she is the star of the show, but his mind is strictly on business. John Bromfield, a performer, has been Esther's steady date, when Van takes her to New York. There she meets Martin, who falls in love with her.

•

EASY TO WED

1946, 109 mins, US col

Dir Edward Buzzell *Prod* Jack Cummings *Scr* Dorothy Kingsley *Ph* Harry Stradling *Ed* Blanche Sewell *Mus* Johnny Green *Art* Cedric Gibbons, Hans Peters

Act Van Johnson, Esther Williams, Lucille Ball, Keenan Wynn, Cecil Kellaway, June Lockhart (M-G-M)

Metro refurbishes the old *Libeled Lady* script with brilliant color, plenty of fun and assured box-office stars. It all adds up to top-notch entertainment. Accent is on comedy with an occasional song in the new treatment.

Eddie Buzzell's direction emphasizes lightness and speed, despite picture's long footage. Plot, briefly, concerns a newspaper faced with a libel suit by a rich playgirl and how the sheet brings in a great lover to compromise the gal so suit can be forgotten.

Van Johnson as the great lover and Esther Williams, the libeled lady, team romantically and acquit themselves effectively in the plot development. Lucille Ball is a standout on the comedy end, particularly her sequence where she indulges in an inebriated flight into fantastic Shakespeare. Keenan Wynn's deft comedy work also presses hard for solid laughs as the newspaper's manager who concocts the schemes designed to save the sheet's bankroll.

•

EAT A BOWL OF TEA

1989, 102 mins, US Ⓥ ⊙ col

Dir Wayne Wang *Prod* Tom Sternberg *Scr* Judith Rascoe *Ph* Amir Mokri *Ed* Richard Candib *Mus* Mark Adler *Art* Bob Ziembicki

Act Cora Miao, Russell Wong, Victor Wong, Lee Sau-kee, Eric Tsang (American Playhouse)

Wayne Wang returns to Chinatown with *Eat a Bowl of Tea*, and recaptures the relaxed humor and deep emotions of his earlier *Dim Sum* in the process.

Pic starts off with Wah Gay (Victor Wong), who runs a New York gambling club, deciding to send his soldier son Ben Loy (Russel Wong) to China to marry the daughter of his best friend. Fortunately, it's love at first sight between

Ben and Mei Oi (Cora Miao), and they marry and return to the States.

Unfortunately, Ben finds the pressures of running a business so severe that his lovelife suffers. Basically, poor Ben is impotent, causing grief to his wife as well as to the couple's fathers, who eagerly want to become grandfathers.

Enter Ah Song (Eric Tsang), a cheerful, rascally gambler who becomes Mei's secret lover, and who succeeds in getting her pregnant. But when words gets out that Ben isn't the father, it's Wah Gay who tries to restore family honor by attacking Ah Song with a meat ax.

Typically, the aforementioned scene is played for laughs, and indeed is the comic high point of a generally charming and amusing film [from a novel by Louis Chu].

EAT DRINK MAN WOMAN
SEE: YINSHI NANNU

EATING
1990, 110 mins, US col

Dir Henry Jaglom ***Prod*** Judith Wolinsky ***Scr*** Henry Jaglom ***Ph*** Hanania Baer
Act Lisa Richards, Mary Crosby, Gwen Welles, Nelly Alard, Frances Bergen, Daphna Kastner (International Rainbow)

The ladies who lunch—and munch, breakfast, binge, dine, diet, starve, and sample—are delicious in *Eating*, but writer-director Henry Jaglom labors over the stove too long, harming a tasty souffle.

Convening a large collection of diverse friends to celebrate a three-tiered birthday party, Lisa Richards is observing her 40th, Mary Crosby her 30th, and Marlena Giovi her 50th. There's plenty of savvy conversation marking each passage, but mainly the birthday girls and their friends reveal how so much of their lives have been dominated by food, either as a substitute for affection or a form of self-destruction.

Richards, Crosby, and Giovi are splendid, as is Frances Bergen as Richards's mother, ultimately shedding her own covers. At the other end of the age scale, Daphna Kastner is also captivating as Giovi's dominated daughter, plumping herself in defense. Gwen Welles stands out as a bitchy, back-biting bulemic.

EATING RAOUL
1982, 83 mins, US Ⓥ col

Dir Paul Bartel ***Prod*** Anne Kimmel ***Scr*** Richard Blackburn, Paul Bartel ***Ph*** Gary Thieltges ***Ed*** Alan Toomayan ***Mus*** Arlon Ober ***Art*** Robert Schulenberg
Act Paul Bartel, Mary Woronov, Robert Beltran, Susan Salger, Ed Begley, Jr., Buck Henry (Bartel)

All poor Paul and Mary Bland want in life is enough money to buy their own restaurant in Valencia, California, and call it Paul and Mary's Country Kitchen. But they have little hope of raising the $20,000 they need to make their dreams come true.

To compound matters, the proper couple, who sleep in separate beds and find sex particularly dirty, live in a tacky Hollywood apartment building chock full of all kinds of crazies. When one of the "low lifes" tries to rape Mary, Paul kills him by a blow to the head with a frying pan.

Alas, the victim had all kinds of money and both Paul and Mary soon realize they have a potential answer to their financial worries. They put an ad in a local sex publication and decide to lure new "perverts" to their home. That way they can get the money for their restaurant and help clean up society in one sweeping stroke.

The appeal of Paul Bartel's tongue-in-cheek approach is that he manages to take his story to such a ridiculous extreme, remain genuinely funny, and successfully tell his perverse story.

ECHO PARK
1985, 92 mins, Austria Ⓥ ⦿ col

Dir Robert Dornhelm ***Prod*** Walter Shenson ***Scr*** Michael Ventura ***Ph*** Karl Hofler ***Ed*** Ingrid Koller ***Mus*** David Ricketts ***Art*** Bernt Capra
Act Susan Dey, Tom Hulce, Michael Bowen, Christopher Walker, Shirley Jo Finney, Timothy Carey (Sascha-Wien)

Although lensed on location in the Echo Park section of Los Angeles, this is another of those quite successful views of the States made by talented European directors.

Wittily scripted and full of oddball twists from start to finish, *Echo Park* features three hapless people looking for the big break as they share an old-style duplex-apartment house in the rundown area of East Los Angeles.

May (Susan Dey) works as a waitress while dreaming of an acting career, but she also has to take care of her eight-year-old son Henry (Christopher Walker). Next door lives August (Michael Bowen), a bodybuilder from Austria who wants to become the second Arnold Schwarzenegger. May needs a tenant in her own flat to meet the payments, and this turns out to be the friendly pizza delivery boy, Jonathan (Tom Hulce), who reads books and writes poetry.

If all of this sounds vaguely like Nathaniel West's *Day of the Locust*, well, no matter. Austrian helmer Robert Dornhelm has a vision of his own. Played by Dey, May is a first-class performance in a role cut snugly to her talent. Ditto for Hulce and Bowen.

ECLIPSE, THE
SEE: L'ECLISSE

ECLISSE, L'
(THE ECLIPSE)
1962, 125 mins, Italy/France Ⓥ ⦿ b/w

Dir Michelangelo Antonioni ***Prod*** Robert Hakim, Raymond Hakim ***Scr*** Michelangelo Antonioni, Tonino Guerra, Elio Bartolini, Ottiero Ottieri ***Ph*** Gianni Di Venanzo ***Ed*** Eraldo Da Roma ***Mus*** Giovanni Fusco ***Art*** Piero Poletto
Act Monica Vitti, Alain Delon, Lilla Brignone, Francisco Rabal, Louis Segnier, Rossana Rory (Interopa/Cineriz/Paris)

As with all this controversial director's films, *The Eclipse* [from a screen story by Michelangelo Antonioni and Tonino Guerra] has the same exasperating pace as well as the same delving at length and in depth into the basic lack of communication between human beings. What results is a series of long silent sequences which are meaningful and powerful to those spectators who, as Antonioni has often said, are both willing and able to "work" for their enjoyment. For those who have seen *L'Avventura* and *La Notte*, *The Eclipse* makes an apt wrapup for a telling trilogy.

Vittoria (Monica Vitti) emerges from an unhappy love affair with an intellectual, Riccardo (Francisco Rabal), and almost by accident accepts the down-to-earth courtship of a young stockbroker (Alain Delon). Both fear involvement, and the melancholy finale signals another split.

Antonioni confirms his mastery of cinema conceived as literature, and there's certainly no one who can match his pregnant silences nor the unity of style and theme as applied to his last three films. On the other hand, it's hard to see how he can go much further in this direction.

Vitti once again proves an ideal performer for Antonioni's thematics in what is probably her best role to date. Delon is excellent as her would-be love. Some trenchant scenes are neatly done by Lilla Brignone, as Vittoria's mother, while Francisco Rabal makes the most of a brief appearance as her previous love.

ECSTASY
SEE: EXTASE

ED
1996, 94 mins, US Ⓥ col

Dir Bill Couturie ***Prod*** Rosalie Swedlin ***Scr*** David Mickey Evans ***Ph*** Alan Caso ***Ed*** Robert K. Lambert ***Mus*** Stephen D. Endelman ***Art*** Curtis A. Schnell
Act Matt LeBlanc, Jayne Brook, Bill Cobbs, Jack Warden, Jay Caputo, Denise Cheshire (Longview/Universal)

Ed serves up a reasonable premise for a comic fantasy kidpic—a chimp good enough to play professional baseball—and has no idea what to do with it. Almost painfuly modest in its ambition and accomplishment, this slow-pitch offering might tolerably amuse the under-10 crowd, but will prove borderline intolerable for everyone else.

This is not exactly the feature debut one would have expected from heavyweight socially conscious documaker Bill Couturie, best known for the likes of *Dear America: Letters Home from Vietnam*. Then again, he did begin his career as an animator for *Sesame Street*.

Nearly half the picture is gone before Ed even takes the field. First 40 minutes are devoted to the tenuous baseball career of Jack Cooper (Matt LeBlanc), whose skill at firing balls through tires down on the farm has never been matched by his ability to get real live batters out for the Santa Rosa Rockets. When the owners bring cute chimp Ed in as a mascot, the manager (Jack Warden) assigns Jack to room with him.

Much of the running time is devoted to tiresome domestic scenes of Ed wreaking havoc while an exasperated Jack looks on. Baseball action is far outweighed by tedious scenes off the diamond, including a tepid romance between Jack and an attractive neighbor (Jayne Brook) that's engineered by her young daughter (Doren Fein), who ends up hanging out with Ed.

Title character is an animatronic creation, inhabited by two actors, that seems pretty credible.

EDTV
1999, 122 mins, US Ⓥ ⦿ col

Dir Ron Howard ***Prod*** Brian Grazer, Ron Howard ***Scr*** Lowell Ganz, Babaloo Mandel ***Ph*** John Schwartzman, Ed Mike Hill, Dan Hanley ***Mus*** Randy Edelman ***Art*** Michael Coernblith
Act Matthew McConaughey, Jenna Elfman, Woody Harrelson, Sally Kirkland, Martin Landau, Ellen DeGeneres

The notion of 15 minutes of fame gets another workout in *EDtv*, a reasonably amusing look at a young man whose life becomes a popular TV show. Ron Howard's film is scruffy, jokey and unassuming where Peter Weir's *The Truman Show* was pristine, bold and thematically ambitious; the main difference is that the hero here is a full-witting accomplice to the television show that documents his every move.

Setup shows how San Fran–based cable docu channel True TV responds to a ratings plunge by initiating its round-the-clock vérité program. Program director Cynthia Topping (Ellen DeGeneres) settles on amiable, good-looking doofus Ed Pekurny (Matthew McConaughey), a 31-year-old vidstore clerk who has yet to get a life. His boisterous older brother, Ray (Woody Harrelson), would sorely like to have been the star.

The one person not into riding the True TV wave is Ed's g.f., Shari (Jenna Elfman), who bails on Ed when 71 percent of the public thinks she's a drag. Management engineers a romance for Ed with British sex bomb Jill (Elizabeth Hurley); their big "date" represents one of the film's rambunctious highlights.

Unfortunately for the picture, the public is right: Shari, as played with a listless cuteisness by Elfman, actually is a drag. But it's McConaughey's picture to carry, and he manages it well; he contributes a natural zaniness that makes Ed an easy-to-take companion on the big screen and a plausible one for the small one.

Based on an obscure 1994 French-Canadian picture, *Louis XIX: King of the Airwaves* [written by Emile Gaudreault and Sylvie Bouchard, directed by Michel Poulette], script cooks up some tasty scenes and savory retorts, particularly for Martin Landau as Ed's hilariously blunt stepfather.

EDDIE
1996, 100 mins, US Ⓥ col

Dir Steve Rash ***Prod*** David Permut, Mark Burg ***Scr*** Jon Connolly/David Loucka, Eric Champnella/Keith Mitchell, Steve Zacharias, Jeff Buhai ***Ph*** Victor Kemper ***Ed*** Richard Halsey ***Mus*** Stanley Clark ***Art*** Dan Davis
Act Whoopi Goldberg, Frank Langella, Dennis Farina, Richard Jenkins, Lisa Ann Walter, John Benjamin Hickey (Hollywood)

Sports comedies are inherently predictable, but this fantasy, about a fan who winds up head coach of an NBA team, seems especially uninspired. Whoopi Goldberg's wholehearted and likable performance, while occasionally funny, is simply not enough to lead this standard-issue programmer to victory.

Goldberg plays the title charcater, a limousine driver and vocal basketball buff who—like all New York sports fans—thinks she knows what's best for her team, in this case the ailing New York Knicks. Enter Wild Bill Burgess, a Texas zillionaire and the team's new owner, played by a woefully miscast Frank Langella. Burgess fires his sourpuss veteran coach (Dennis Farina) and replaces him with, you guessed it, Eddie. From there on, it's strictly by the numbers as Goldberg does her darnedest to light a fire under the aloof, egotistical young millionaires who make up the fictional team.

The cast of real-life players does a decent job of impersonating, well, basketball players, but they—along with everyone else in the film—function strictly as straight men to Goldberg's antics. Worst of all—given the nearly 50 NBA players who appear in the film—there aren't any good basketball scenes to speak of.

EDDIE AND THE CRUISERS
1983, 92 mins, US Ⓥ ⦿ col

Dir Martin Davidson ***Prod*** Joseph Brooks, Robert K. Lifton ***Scr*** Martin Davidson, Arlene Davidson ***Ph*** Fred Murphy ***Ed*** Priscilla Nedd ***Mus*** John Cafferty ***Art*** Gary Weist
Act Tom Berenger, Michael Pare, Joe Pantoliano, Matthew Laurance, Helen Schneider, Ellen Barkin (Aurora)

Eddie and the Cruisers is a mish-mash of a film, combining elements of the ongoing nostalgia for rock music of previous decades with an unworkable and laughable mystery plotline.

Eddie opens in strict *Citizen Kane* fashion as TV news mag reporter Maggie Foley (Ellen Barkin) is using old clips to pitch her investigative story on the early 1960s rock group Eddie and The Cruisers. Unit disbanded in 1964 with the suicide of its leader Eddie Wilson (Michael Pare).

She needs a news hook, and settles on the unlikely gimmick that Eddie (whose body was never found) is still alive and that a search for the missing tapes of his final, unreleased recording session will solve the mystery of his disappearance.

Foley interviews other surviving group members, including the lyricist-keyboard man Frank Ridgeway (Tom Berenger), who is prompted to remember (in frequent flashbacks) those glory days of 1962–63.

Under Martin Davidson's tedious direction (he also co-scripted with his sister Arlene), *Eddie* only comes alive during the flashbacks when John Cafferty's songs provide a showcase for the magnetic screen presences of Pare and Helen Schneider. Real life rock singer Schneider is very sexy on screen, but her contemporary scenes are ruined by unplayable dialog.

•

EDDIE MACON'S RUN
1983, 95 mins, US Ⓥ ⦿ col
Dir Jeff Kanew ***Prod*** Louis A. Stroller ***Scr*** Jeff Kanew ***Ph*** James A. Contner ***Ed*** Jeff Kanew ***Mus*** Norton Buffalo ***Art*** Bill Kenney
Act Kirk Douglas, John Schneider, Lee Purcell, Leah Ayres, Lisa Dunsheath, Tom Noonan (Bregman)

Macon is an involving, enjoyable picture [based on a novel by James McLendon]. Most of the credit for that, however, goes to Kirk Douglas who brings interesting nuances to his part as the policeman in pursuit of John Schneider, and Lee Purcell as a bored but influential rich girl who gets more involved than she wants to in helping Schneider elude Douglas.

Schneider himself is okay and certainly brings more to his role than anything required of him on television. Without reaching towering dramatic heights, he nonetheless ably portrays the anguish of a young husband/father wrongly sent to prison and determined to escape to rejoin his family in Mexico.

With Schneider fleeing on foot for most of the picture, *Macon* has a tendency to drag in spots, especially in the beginning, but writer-director Jeff Kanew wisely keeps cutting back to Douglas in plotting his chase and figuring out the angles.

•

EDDY DUCHIN STORY, THE
1956, 123 mins, US Ⓥ ⦿ ▭ col
Dir George Sidney ***Prod*** Jerry Wald ***Scr*** Samuel Taylor ***Ph*** Harry Stradling ***Ed*** Viola Lawrence, Jack W. Ogilvie ***Mus*** Morris Stoloff
Act Tyrone Power, Kim Novak, Victoria Shaw, James Whitmore, Rex Thompson (Columbia)

Jerry Wald's biopicturing of the career of "10 Magic Fingers" is not all the sorrow and woe that the story of Eddy Duchin might suggest. There's no escaping the fact that the pianist's first wife died shortly after childbirth. And that this was followed 12 years later by Duchin's own death, at the age of 41, as the result of leukemia.

But Samuel Taylor plays up humor and romance as well as the inherent hardship in his script [from a story by Leo Katcher] and George Sidney's direction, sensitive for the most part, sustains a high dramatic tone. Key asset is Tyrone Power in the title role. He's personable and eager as he hits Gotham bent only on tapping out pop and pseudo-classical rhythms on the 88. He looks like he's genuinely thrilled with the splendors of New York and confident that his letter of introduction will land him a job with Leo Reisman's orchestra at the old Central Park Casino.

It's through the intervention of Kim Novak that the position in the band is his. The Novak-Power match builds tenderly.

Newcomer Victoria Shaw, Power's second wife, comes across with particular effectiveness, showing understanding of the role and executing it with proper feeling.

1956: NOMINATIONS: Best Motion Picture Story, Color Cinematography, Scoring of a Musical Picture, Sound

•

EDGE, THE
1997, 117 mins, US Ⓥ ⦿ ▭ col
Dir Lee Tamahori ***Prod*** Art Linson ***Scr*** David Mamet ***Ph*** Donald M. McAlpine ***Ed*** Neil Travis ***Mus*** Jerry Goldsmith ***Art*** Wolf Kroeger
Act Anthony Hopkins, Alec Baldwin, Elle Macpherson, Harold Perrineau, L. Q. Jones (20th Century-Fox)

Although thin character motivation and some far-fetched plotting strain credulity in the late going, for the most part *The Edge* is a tense, pleasurably visceral battle-of-wits thriller played out against a spectacular wilderness background. Screenplay, originally titled *The Bookworm*, is far from vintage David Mamet, but it does contain more than the usual share of wit, cleverness and mordant character shadings.

Charles Morse (Anthony Hopkins), a billionaire of a certain age, accompanies his supermodel trophy wife, Mickey (Elle Macpherson), on a photo shoot in the pristine wilds of Alaska. Entourage's chief members are cocky fashion photographer Robert Green (Alec Baldwin) and his assistant, Stephen (Harold Perrineau).

Robert and Stephen go off on a short private-plane trip to even more remote territory in search of a particular Indian to pose with Mickey, with Charles going along for the ride. The small plane crashes into a lake, and the three men must formulate a strategy for survival. The group manages to survive a bear attack, but Charles has no doubt the bear will track them down.

[New Zealand-born] director Lee Tamahori, after his misstep with *Mulholland Falls*, moves things along at a muscular clip. Everything from the impressive Alberta, Canada, locations (doubling for Alaska) and Jerry Goldsmith's varied score contributes to the film's invigorating dynamic. Hopkins has it over all the other thesps.

•

EDGE OF DARKNESS
1943, 120 mins, US b/w
Dir Lewis Milestone ***Prod*** Henry Blanke ***Scr*** Robert Rossen ***Ph*** Sid Hickox ***Ed*** David Weisbart ***Mus*** Franz Waxman
Act Errol Flynn, Ann Sheridan, Walter Huston, Judith Anderson, Helmut Dantine, Ruth Gordon (Warner)

In *Darkness*, as in *The Moon Is Down*, the story treats with internal conditions and unrest and, more important, the ruthlessness of the Nazis. The populace of Trollness in Norway seethes under the yoke of the Germans and finally erupts into a bloody revolt.

Best feature of this film is its cast. Errol Flynn and Ann Sheridan, as the stars, provide the proper romantic note, plus the necessary dash as the leaders of the Trollness underground. Both turn in some of their best film acting, yet some of the cast's lesser-knowns eclipse them in dramatic power. Notable in this respect are Morris Carnovsky, Ruth Gordon, Judith Anderson, Charles Dingle, and Nancy Coleman.

Carnovsky, as an aged schoolmaster, is outstanding in a throat-catching scene when he pits his culture and kindliness against the brutish thinking of the Nazi commander, played by Helmut Dantine, who is guilty of most of the film's over-acting.

There's one other particularly outstanding scene—the meeting of the underground in the church under the guise of a religious service. Original in concept, it's emotion-gripping in execution.

•

EDGE OF DOOM
1950, 98 mins, US b/w
Dir Mark Robson ***Prod*** Samuel Goldwyn ***Scr*** Philip Yordan ***Ph*** Harry Stradling ***Ed*** Daniel Mandell ***Mus*** Hugo Friedhofer
Act Dana Andrews, Farley Granger, Joan Evans, Robert Keith, Mala Powers, Paul Stewart (RKO/Samuel Goldwyn)

A grim, relentless story, considerably offbeat, gives some distinction to *Edge of Doom*. It is played to the hilt by a good cast and directed with impact by Mark Robson.

The plot [from a novel by Leo Brady] has a single line and pursues it without deviation. It tells the story of a poverty-stricken boy, with a mother fixation after long years of caring for her, who tries to give her the funeral he believes she deserves. He receives unsympathetic treatment from the parish priest and, in a rage, kills the father with a crucifix.

At every turn, the boy is rebuffed in his efforts to set a fine funeral. That, and the weight of a guilty conscience, finally become so oppressive he admits his crime.

•

EDGE OF THE CITY
1957, 85 mins, US b/w
Dir Martin Ritt ***Prod*** David Susskind ***Scr*** Robert Alan Aurthur ***Ph*** Joseph Brun ***Ed*** Sidney Meyers ***Mus*** Leonard Rosenman ***Art*** Richard Sylbert
Act John Cassavetes, Sidney Poitier, Jack Warden, Kathleen Maguire, Ruby Dee, Robert F. Simon (M-G-M)

The first film venture for producer David Susskind, writer Robert Alan Aurthur, and director Martin Ritt is an auspicious bow. Trio, whose roots are in TV and legit, come up with a courageous, thought-provoking and exciting film.

Based on Aurthur's [1955] teleplay, *A Man Is Ten Feet Tall*, it marks a milestone in the screen presentation of an African-American.

The peculiar aspect of *Edge* is that it is not a film dealing with a race problem. The protagonist is a guilt-ridden, psychologically mixed-up white youth, sensitively played by John Cassavetes. Plagued by the memory of his part in the accidental death of his brother and his inability to "belong" either to his family or society, he AWOLs the army. He finds employment in a New York railroad yard where he immediately is befriended by a goodnatured, philosophical lad (Sidney Poitier) and incurs the enmity of a vicious and tough hiring boss.

Filmed on location in New York, the film has a real-life flavor as it roams among New York's railroad yards and upper Manhattan's apartment house district.

•

EDISON, THE MAN
1940, 104 mins, US Ⓥ b/w
Dir Clarence Brown ***Prod*** John W. Considine Jr. ***Scr*** Talbot Jennings, Bradbury Foote ***Ph*** Harold Rosson ***Ed*** Fredrick Y. Smith ***Mus*** Herbert Stothart ***Art*** Cedric Gibbons, John S. Detlie
Act Spencer Tracy, Rita Johnson, Lynne Overman, Charles Coburn, Gene Lockhart, Henry Travers (M-G-M)

Edison, The Man is a sequel to *Young Tom Edison* (Mickey Rooney). The sequel takes up with Edison after he has gone to New York to pursue his vocation as an inventor.

Action opens on the Golden Jubilee of Light banquet held in 1929, at which the now aged Edison is guest of honor. As he is being eulogized for his contributions as an inventor, the story goes back to his early manhood, his heartaches, his ambitions, the romance that came into his life, and the drama as well as lighter moments that figured in an amazing career. After Edison has brought forth the incandescent bulb after heroic struggles, followed by montage shots reviewing the achievements of the Wizard of Menlo Park, the action flashes back to the banquet. Here, Spencer Tracy as an old, but benevolent Edison, makes his speech. It dwells largely on the march that science has made, emphasized by the fact that much that man has created for the benefit of mankind also possesses the ability to turn into monsters.

As a young man, Tracy progresses through the years in a forceful characterization of the noted inventor. Early portions are strong in romantic interest, but after Tracy has married the pretty Rita Johnson, two children being born, his home life is somewhat subjugated to the inventor's work in his laboratory, his financial troubles, the extreme loyalty of his workers, etc., although ostensibly he is a home-loving man.

Though going over his invention of the stock ticker, the phonograph, and other things, the greatest stress [of the story by Hugo Butler and Dore Schary] is laid on the circumstances surrounding Edison's invention of the incandescent lamp. Dramatic interest is drawn largely from the months of toil and discouragement that precede the discovery of the light, topped by Edison's success in getting the franchise to illuminate New York by electricity. Scene when the dynamos go wild, like monsters out of control, is one of the highlights, and well done.

1940: NOMINATION: Best Original Story

•

EDUCATING RITA
1983, 110 mins, UK Ⓥ ⦿ col
Dir Lewis Gilbert ***Prod*** Lewis Gilbert ***Scr*** Willy Russell ***Ph*** Frank Watts ***Ed*** Garth Craven ***Mus*** David Hentschel ***Art*** Maurice Fowler
Act Michael Caine, Julie Walters, Michael Williams, Maureen Lipman, Jeananne Crowley, Malcolm Douglas (Rank/Acorn)

Producer-director Lewis Gilbert has done a marvelous job of bringing the charming British play, *Educating Rita*, to the big screen. Aided greatly by an expert film adaptation by its playwright, Willy Russell, Gilbert has come up with an irresistible story about a lively, lower-class British woman hungering for an education and the rather staid, degenerating English professor who reluctantly provides her with one. Witty, down-to-earth, kind, and loaded with common sense, Rita is the antithesis of the humorless, stuffy, and stagnated academic world she so longs to infiltrate. Julie Walters injects her with just the right mix of comedy and pathos. Michael Caine is the sadly smart, alcoholic teacher who knows the fundamentals of English literature, but long ago lost the ability to enjoy life the way his uneducated pupil does.

The contradictions of the two characters are at the core of the picture, as Walters goes from dependent housewife to intelligent student and Caine begins to learn what it's like to feel again.

1983: NOMINATIONS: Best Actor (Michael Caine), Actress (Julie Walters), Adapted Screenplay

•

EDWARD, MY SON
1949, 112 mins, US/UK b/w
Dir George Cukor ***Prod*** Edwin H. Knopf ***Scr*** Donald Ogden Stewart ***Ph*** Freddie Young ***Ed*** Raymond Poulton ***Mus*** John Wooldridge ***Art*** Alfred Junge
Act Spencer Tracy, Deborah Kerr, Ian Hunter, James Donald, Mervyn Johns, Leueen MacGrath (M-G-M)

Transformation of the stageplay [by Robert Morley and Noel Langley] to the screen has widened the appeal of the original and given it the impetus of movement. There is never any doubt that Edward, son of the Boults, is a spoiled child as his parents rise in the social strata. Arnold Boult is the proud father whose conception of love for his offspring is to anticipate his every wish.

Into the main theme is delicately woven the estrangement between Arnold and Evelyn Boult. When the picture first opens they are seen in modest surroundings and ideally happy. But as Arnold prospers, through shady methods the drift is complete. Although caught in an affair with his secretary, Arnold refuses a divorce, as it may interfere with his ambitious plans.

Skillful direction has brought this play to the screen with full dramatic force. There is no letup in its intensity and it moves surely and swiftly from one dramatic phase to another. Spencer Tracy as Arnold Boult dominates the screen with a forceful portrayal of the ambitious man who allowed nothing to stand in the way of his determination to reach the top rung of the ladder.

Deborah Kerr displays remarkable ability in transforming the character of Evelyn from the demure happy young woman to the embittered, drunken, and miserable wife. Ian Hunter gives a warm, understanding study of the family doctor, who is unable to hide his love for Mrs. Boult.

•

EDWARD SCISSORHANDS
1990, 98 mins, US Ⓥ ⦿ col
Dir Tim Burton ***Prod*** Denise De Novi, Tim Burton ***Scr*** Caroline Thompson ***Ph*** Stefan Czapsky ***Ed*** Richard Halsey ***Mus*** Danny Elfman ***Art*** Bo Welsh
Act Johnny Depp, Winona Ryder, Dianne Wiest, Anthony Michael Hall, Alan Arkin, Kathy Baker (20th Century-Fox)

Director Tim Burton takes a character as wildly unlikely as a boy whose arms end in pruning shears, and makes him the center of a delightful and delicate comic fable.

Johnny Depp plays Edward, who lives in isolation in a gloomy mansion on the hill until a sunny Avon lady (Dianne Wiest) discovers him and takes him into her suburbia home and mothers him like a crippled bird. The creation of an inventor (Vincent Price) who died and left him unfinished, Edward sports an astonishing pair of hands—five-fingered, footlong blades that render him either lethal or extraordinarily skillful.

For the bevy of bored housewives in the pastel-colored nabe, gentle and exotic Edward becomes an instant celeb who amuses them by artistically pruning their hedges, their dogs and their coiffures.

But when he's wrongly accused in a burglary, his star falls and they turn on him. Meanwhile his wistful and impossible attraction to Kim (Winona Ryder), the Avon lady's teenage daughter, adds another level of tension.

Depp, former TV teen idol in his second starring screen role, gives a sensitive reading of Edward. With Ryder kept mostly in the background, Wiest's mother figure shares the screen with Depp, and she's a smash. Also a hoot is Alan Arkin as her unexcitable husband, and Kathy Baker as a sex-starved vixen.

1990: NOMINATION: Best Makeup

•

EDWARD II
1991, 90 mins, UK Ⓥ col
Dir Derek Jarman ***Prod*** Steve Clark-Hall, Antony Root ***Scr*** Derek Jarman, Stephen McBride, Ken Butler ***Ph*** Ian Wilson ***Ed*** George Akers ***Mus*** Simon Fisher Turner ***Art*** Christopher Hobbs
Act Steven Waddington, Andrew Tiernan, Tilda Swinton, Nigel Terry, Kevin Collins, Dudley Sutton (Working Title/BBC/British Screen)

Derek Jarman comes up with a provocative and challenging adaptation of Christopher Marlowe's *Edward II*, a lengthy (about four hours onstage) bio of Britain's only acknowledged gay monarch, whose preference for his lover over his queen sparked conflict with his barons and, eventually, civil war.

Cutting the play to the bone, Jarman fashions the 16th century drama into a radical attack on antigay prejudices in contempo Brit society. Drama is staged in modern dress, with contemporary police/military uniforms for the forces of repression.

Queen Isabella, astringently played by Jarman regular Tilda Swinton, is cruelly treated in the film. Humiliated and rejected by her husband, she tries everything to win him back from his lover. The character finally turns into a raving monster who literally sucks the blood from her victims.

Jarman fails to make the film accessible to heterosexual male audiences. Pic seems to be provoking straight viewers while celebrating the play's homosexual theme.

•

ED WOOD
1994, 124 mins, US Ⓥ ⦿ b/w
Dir Tim Burton ***Prod*** Denise Di Novi, Tim Burton ***Scr*** Scott Alexander, Larry Karaszewski ***Ph*** Stefan Czapsky ***Ed*** Chris Lebenzon ***Mus*** Howard Shore ***Art*** Tom Duffield
Act Johnny Depp, Martin Landau, Sarah Jessica Parker, Patricia Arquette, Jeffrey Jones, Vincent D'Onofrio (Touchstone)

Tim Burton pays elaborate tribute to the maverick creative spirit in *Ed Wood*, a fanciful sweet-tempered biopic [based on Rudolph Grey's book *Nightmare of Ecstasy: The Life and Art of Edward D. Wood, Jr.*] about the man often described as the worst film director of all time. Always engaging to watch and often dazzling in its imagination and technique, picture is also a bit distended, and lacking in weight at its center. Only Burton, who has never had a flop, would have used his clout to make such a personal film about a fringe figure like Wood (to the point of walking from Columbia to Disney in order to make it in black-and-white), and only he could have given such an amiable, sympathetic twist.

Virtually unknown during his lifetime and for some time after his death in 1978, Wood started gaining notoriety as an auteur of the lower depths when his beyond-bad 1950s epics *Glen or Glenda* and *Plan 9 from Outer Space* developed followings in the 1980s. He made several other films with titles such as *Jail Bait*, *Bride of the Monster* and *The Sinister Urge*, all shot in a matter of days on home-movie budgets. Wood's other claim to fame was that he was an avid transvestite, with a particular taste for Angora sweaters.

Wood (Johnny Depp) is able to raise his meager financing by proposing to topline Bela Lugosi (Martin Landau), the old *Dracula* star whom Wood meets by chance in Hollywood. Lugosi is grateful for the work and becomes a friend and sort of spiritual mentor to Wood.

Much of the running time is spent recounting the cockeyed, disrupted shoots of *Bride of the Monster* and *Plan 9*, with Burton and company taking great pains to reproduce the indelibly flat look of the Wood originals. Giving the story its principal weight is the Wood-Lugosi relationship, with Landau's astounding performance as the old Hungarian.

As Wood, Depp is more animated than he has ever been onscreen before. As his first girlfriend Dolores Fuller, Sarah Jessica Parker niftily pulls off some deliberately bad acting, and Patricia Arquette expresses great understanding as the only woman who would put up with Wood's eccentricities.

1994: Best Supp. Actor (Martin Landau), Makeup

•

EFFECT OF GAMMA RAYS ON MAN-IN-THE-MOON MARIGOLDS, THE
1972, 100 mins, US Ⓥ col
Dir Paul Newman ***Prod*** Paul Newman ***Scr*** Alvin Sargent ***Ph*** Adam Holender ***Ed*** Evan Lottman ***Mus*** Maurice Jarre ***Art*** Gene Callahan
Act Joanne Woodward, Nell Potts, Roberta Wallach, Judith Lowry, Richard Venture, Estelle Omens (20th Century-Fox)

Producer-director Paul Newman has made his finest behind-the-camera film to date in the screen version of Paul Zindel's play. As the slovenly, introverted mother of two young girls, Joanne Woodward brilliantly projects the pitiable character.

Alvin Sargent's adaptation provides Woodward with a full complement of the despicable dimensions which make the focal character both a monster and an object of genuine pity.

Roberta Wallach is excellent as the elder daughter, Ruth, an epilepsy-prone, hardening creature almost destined to become her mother. As the younger girl, whose school experiments give the play its title, Nell Potts is equally impressive, with a sensitive screen presence most rare in young actresses.

Newman has gotten it all together here as a director, letting the story and the players unfold with simplicity, restraint and discernment.

•

EGG AND I, THE
1947, 108 mins, US Ⓥ ⦿ b/w
Dir Chester Erskine ***Prod*** Chester Erskine, Fred F. Finklehoffe ***Scr*** Chester Erskine, Fred F. Finklehoffe ***Ph*** Milton Krasner ***Ed*** Russell Schoengarth ***Mus*** Frank Skinner ***Art*** Bernard Herzbrun
Act Claudette Colbert, Fred MacMurray, Marjorie Main, Percy Kilbride, Louise Allbritton, Richard Long (Universal)

In this picturization of Betty MacDonald's bestselling book, Chester Erskine and Fred Finklehoffe tamper very little with the load of amusing situations MacDonald gets herself into when her husband snaps her out of a Boston finishing school and takes her off to the modern-day frontier of the Pacific Northwest to embark on chicken farming.

Shortcoming is in an evenness of treatment—partially in the writing but more importantly in Erskine's direction—that fails to suck the drama out of the situations presented in the book. Even the supposedly big scene where a forest fire licks down at all that the chicken-raising couple have in the world—their home, barn and henhouses—fails to achieve suspense. Claudette Colbert is appealing but not entirely believable as the city gal who accepts so willingly out of wifely love the rugged life husband Fred MacMurray lays out for her. MacMurray runs through his role in his routine, superficial fashion—which is unfortunately accentuated by the impassive manner of the telling of the story itself. Percy Kilbride and Marjorie Main, as the Kettles, the tobacco-roadlike neighbors of Colbert and MacMurray, are literally tops as character players, accounting, by their feeling and understanding of their roles, for high points in the film every time they're on the screen.

1947: NOMINATION: Best Supp. Actress (Marjorie Main)

•

EGYPTIAN, THE
1954, 140 mins, US Ⓥ ⊏⊐ col
Dir Michael Curtiz ***Prod*** Darryl F. Zanuck ***Scr*** Casey Robinson, Philip Dunne ***Ph*** Leon Shamroy ***Ed*** Barbara McLean ***Mus*** Alfred Newman, Bernard Herrmann ***Art*** Lyle Wheeler, George W. Davis
Act Edmund Purdom, Jean Simmons, Victor Mature, Gene Tierney, Michael Wilding, Peter Ustinov (20th Century-Fox)

The decision to bring Mika Waltari's masterly scholarly detailed [novel] *The Egyptian* to the screen must have taken a lot of courage, for this is a long way off the standard spectacle beat. The book tells a strange and unusual story laid against the exotic and yet harshly realistic background of the Egypt of 33 centuries ago, when there was a Pharaoh who believed in one god, and a physician who glimpsed a great truth and tried to live it.

Big coin—around $4.2 million—was splurged on bringing ancient Egypt to life again and the results justify the expense.

A big cast with good marquee appeal goes through its paces with obvious enjoyment. In the title part, Edmund Purdom etches a strong handsome profile. As the truth-seeking doctor who grows from weakness to the maturity of a new conviction, Purdom brings *The Egyptian* to life and makes him a man with whom the audience can easily identify and sympathize. Jean Simmons is lovely and warm as the tavern maid. Victor Mature as the robust Horemheb, the soldier who is to become ruler, is a strong asset to the cast.

1954: Best Color Cinematography

•

EIGER SANCTION, THE
1975, 125 mins, US Ⓥ ⦿ ⊏⊐ col
Dir Clint Eastwood ***Prod*** Robert Daley ***Scr*** Hal Dresner, Warren B. Murphy, Rod Whitaker ***Ph*** Frank Stanley ***Ed*** Ferris Webster ***Mus*** John Williams ***Art*** George Webb, Aurelio Crugnola
Act Clint Eastwood, George Kennedy, Vonetta McGee, Jack Cassidy, Heidi Bruhl, Thayer David (Universal/Malpaso)

The Eiger Sanction, based on the novel by Trevanian, focuses on Clint Eastwood, a retired mountain climber and hired assassin, being recalled from retirement by head of a secret intelligence organization for another lethal assignment.

Pic takes its title from the leader's euphemism for assassination, to be carried out on Switzerland's Eiger Mountain during an international team's climb.

To condition himself for the ascent Eastwood flies to the Arizona ranch of George Kennedy, an old climbing friend, who puts him through his paces in the magnificent reaches of Monument Valley.

Eastwood, who also directs and according to the studio did his own mountain climbing without doubles, manages fine suspense. His direction displays a knowledge that permits rugged action.

•

8½
1963, 140 mins, Italy Ⓥ ⦿ b/w
Dir Federico Fellini ***Prod*** Angelo Rizzoli ***Scr*** Federico Fellini, Tullio Pinelli, Ennio Flaiano, Brunello Rondi ***Ph*** Gianni Di Venanzo ***Ed*** Leo Cattozzo ***Mus*** Nino Rota ***Art*** Piero Gherardi

Act Marcello Mastroianni, Claudia Cardinale, Anouk Aimee, Sandra Milo, Rossella Falk, Barbara Steele (Rizzoli)

With *8½* Federico Fellini tops even his trendsetting *La Dolce Vita* in artistry. Here is the author-director picture par excellence, an exciting, stimulating, monumental creation.

Basically, it is the story [by Fellini and Ennio Flaiano] of a forty-three-year-old director's crucial visit to a health resort to cure an undetermined illness. At the spa, he is confronted with a series of crises of a personal as well as professional nature. He is about to start a major film production, but totally lacks inspiration for it.

At the same time, he is worried about his physical condition, is becoming bored by the voluptuous mistress he has brought along with him, and disappointed by his wife's continued inability to understand him. All the while, he is hounded by production managers, would-be stars, and scriptswriters.

Flashbacks to his youth and flash-forwards in the form of daydreams illustrate the director's inner qualms and worries, resolved at the finale by his realization that, after all: "life is a feast; let's live it together," taking the good with the bad.

8½ defies telling or description. It is a 140-minute séance on the psychiatrist's couch, in which the author turns himself inside out, confessing his innermost thoughts and problems, and finally reaching his apt conclusions.

Once again, Fellini gets top assistance from his large and colorful cast. Marcello Mastroianni is excellent as the middle-aged director, often deliberately bearing an uncanny resemblance to Fellini himself. Sandra Milo and Anouk Aimee fight it out for second honors, respectively as mistress and wife. Claudia Cardinale makes several strikingly effective appearances as Mastroianni's symbol of pure creation. Nino Rota has penned a haunting score for the picture.

1963: Best Foreign Language Film

•

EIGHT MEN OUT

1988, 119 mins, US Ⓥ ⦿ col

Dir John Sayles ***Prod*** Sarah Pillsbury, Midge Sanford ***Scr*** John Sayles ***Ph*** Robert Richardson ***Ed*** John Tintori ***Mus*** Mason Daring ***Art*** Nora Chavooshian

Act John Cusack, Clifton James, David Strathairn, D. B. Sweeney, John Mahoney, Charlie Sheen (Orion)

Perhaps the saddest chapter in the annals of professional American sports is recounted in absorbing fashion in *Eight Men Out.*

Story tells of how the 1919 Chicago White Sox threw the World Series in cahoots with professional gamblers, in what became known as the Black Sox Scandal.

Based on Eliot Asinof's 1963 bestseller, John Sayles's densely packed screenplay lays out how eight players for the White Sox, who were considered shoo-ins to beat the Cincinnati Reds in the World Series, committed an unthinkable betrayal of the national pastime by conspiring to lose the Fall Classic.

The most compelling figures here are pitcher Eddie Cicotte (David Strathairn), a man nearing the end of his career who feels the twin needs to insure a financial future for his family and take revenge on his boss, and Buck Weaver (John Cusack), an innocent enthusiast who took no cash for the fix but, like the others, was forever banned from baseball.

•

8MM

1999, 119 mins, US Ⓥ ⦿ ▭ col

Dir Joel Schumacher ***Prod*** Gavin Polone, Judy Hofflund, Joel Schumacher ***Scr*** Andrew Kevin Walker ***Ph*** Robert Elswit ***Ed*** Mark Stevens ***Mus*** Mychael Danna ***Art*** Gary Wissner

Act Nicolas Cage, Joaquin Phoenix, James Gandolfini, Peter Stormare, Anthony Heald, Chris Bauer (Hofflund-Polone/Columbia)

8MM is a movie that keeps jumping the gate and finally unravels all over the floor. A murky mélange of borrowings from far superior pix like *Se7en, Hardcore* and *The Silence of the Lambs,* this overly dark and often gratuitously nasty film about a PI checking the source of a supposed "snuff movie" raises issues it later junks in favor of mainstream thrills and is toplined by a perf from Nicolas Cage that isn't up to the job.

Buffs expecting another stygian psychothriller from scripter Andrew Kevin Walker (*Se7en*) are going to be massively disappointed. Cage plays Tom Welles, a surveillance specialist who's hired by Mrs. Christian (Myra Carter) to discover the identity of a teenage girl seemingly murdered by a masked man in an 8mm movie she found in her late husband's private safe. The trail leads to L.A., where the girl went in search of fame and fortune in the movies.

Welles makes the acquaintance of porn shop owner Max California (Joaquin Phoenix), whom he hires to guide him through L.A.'s hard-core S&M movie scene. Phoenix's louche, quipping performance brings a welcome touch of humor to the picture. Welles finally gets a major break that leads him to porno moviemaker Eddie Poole (James Gandolfini) and then to New York S&M specialist Dino Velvet (Peter Stormare).

Cage simply doesn't have the range to beef up an underwritten part, which changes from buttoned-down professional to screaming moral avenger in the space of a reel. Phoenix's Max is a severe loss at the two-thirds point from which the picture never recovers.

•

8 MILLION WAYS TO DIE

1986, 115 mins, US Ⓥ ⦿ col

Dir Hal Ashby ***Prod*** Steve Roth ***Scr*** Oliver Stone, David Lee Henry ***Ph*** Stephen H. Burum ***Ed*** Robert Lawrence, Stuart Pappe ***Mus*** James Newton Howard ***Art*** Michael Haller

Act Jeff Bridges, Rosanna Arquette, Alexandra Paul, Randy Brooks, Andy Garcia (PSO)

What could have been a better film delving into complexities of one tough-but-vulnerable alcoholic sheriff out to bust a cocaine ring, instead ends up an oddly paced work that is sometimes a thriller and sometimes a love story, succeeding at neither.

A former L.A. sheriff named Scudder (Jeff Bridges) comes close to death less than a handful of times while trying to dismantle a scummy Latino drug smuggler's empire and at the same time winning his girl (Rosanna Arquette).

Respected director Hal Ashby was reportedly fired from this picture before it was finished, which could explain its unevenness as he wasn't privy to what happened in the editing room.

In isolated scenes, the actors manage to rise above it all to bring some nuances to their fairly stereotypical roles. Arquette is best as the hooker with a heart, coyly playing off main squeeze Angel (Andy Garcia), the ultra-chic cocaine dealer, until she goes over to Scudder's side.

•

84 CHARING CROSS ROAD

1987, 97 mins, US Ⓥ ⦿ col

Dir David Jones ***Prod*** Geoffrey Helman ***Scr*** Hugh Whitemore ***Ph*** Brian West ***Ed*** Chris Wimble ***Mus*** George Fenton ***Art*** Eileen Diss, Edward Pisoni

Act Anne Bancroft, Anthony Hopkins, Judi Dench, Jean De Baer, Maurice Denham, Mercedes Ruehl (Brooksfilms)

An uncommonly and sweetly civilized adult romance between two transatlantic correspondents who never meet, *84 Charing Cross Road* is an appealing film on several counts, one of the most notable being Anne Bancroft's fantastic performance in the leading role.

Helene Hanff's slim volume of letters between herself and a dignified antiquarian bookseller in London [originally adapted for the stage by James Roose-Evans] is the basis of the film. They began in 1949 as formal requests by the New Yorker Hanff for old books and grew over a 20-year period into a warm, loving exchange of missives and gifts between her and much of the staff of the bookshop of Marks & Co.

Built on a basis of mutually held taste, knowledge, interests and consideration, the bond between Hanff (Bancroft) and Frank Doel (Anthony Hopkins) becomes a form of pure love, which is why the film is so touching in spots.

Although well balanced between events on both sides of the pond, story suffers from an imbalance between the active, initiating Hanff, who occasionally addresses the camera directly, and the relatively passive, inexpressive Doel. At the end, the man's humor and high intelligence are described, but these traits are never revealed.

Anne Bancroft brings Helene Hanff alive in all her dimensions, in the process creating one of her most memorable characterizations.

•

80,000 SUSPECTS

1963, 113 mins, UK Ⓑ b/w

Dir Val Guest ***Prod*** Val Guest ***Scr*** Val Guest ***Ph*** Arthur Grant ***Ed*** Bill Lenny ***Mus*** Stanley Black ***Art*** Geoffrey Tozer

Act Claire Bloom, Richard Johnson, Yolande Donlan, Cyril Cusack, Michael Goodliffe, Mervyn Johns (Rank)

Based on the novel [*The Pillars of Midnight*] by Elleston Trevor, the drama concerns a city supposedly gripped by an epidemic of smallpox. Director Val Guest chose the city of Bath and, with complete cooperation from local authorities, the film has a vital authenticity, which gives a fine assist to the production.

The killer epidemic sparks intense activity by local health authorities as they try to trace potential smallpox carriers. It's a painstaking process, carefully reproduced by Guest.

Guest also plays up some human emotional angles. Dedicated doctor (Richard Johnson) is trying to keep together his marriage with an equally dedicated nurse (Claire Bloom). Another medico (Michael Goodliffe) despairs of saving his own marriage to a nympho-dipso who has had an affair with Johnson, and eventually becomes a key figure in the search for the ultimate germ carrier.

The documentary and the fictional elements do not entirely jell. But Guest juggles adroitly enough with the problems to keep interest alert. The thesping is okay.

•

EL
(THIS STRANGE PASSION)

1953, 100 mins, Mexico b/w

Dir Luis Bunuel ***Prod*** Oscar Dancigers ***Scr*** Luis Bunuel, Luis Alcoriza ***Ph*** Gabriel Figueroa ***Ed*** Carlos Savage ***Mus*** Luis Hernandez Breton ***Art*** Edward Fitzgerald

Act Arturo De Cordova, Delia Garces, Luis Beristain, Aurora Walker, Carlos Martinez Baena, Fernando Casanova (National)

Luis Bunuel has fashioned an absorbing melodramatic psycho pic out of *El.* Although the story [from the novel *Pensiamentos* by Mercedes Pinto] borders on the banal, fine direction and acting keep this within bounds, and give a dimension to the harrowing tale of a madman's attempt to love.

Story concerns a middle-aged rich man who sweeps a beautiful young girl off her feet. He seems normal and considerate but in married life turns out to have delusions of persecution and homicidal tendencies. The wife finally escapes in time to avoid the husband's attempts to murder.

Arturo De Cordova is fine in delineating the breakdown of the guilt-ridden hero, while Delia Garces scores as the terrified, cornered wife. Rest of cast is adequate and well-typed. Lensing of Gabriel Figueroa is slick.

•

EL CID

1961, 180 mins, US/Spain/Italy Ⓥ ⦿ ▭ col

Dir Anthony Mann ***Prod*** Samuel Bronston ***Scr*** Fredric M. Frank, Philip Yordan, [Ben Barzman] ***Ph*** Robert Krasker ***Ed*** Robert Lawrence ***Mus*** Miklos Rozsa ***Art*** Veniero Colasanti, John Moore

Act Charlton Heston, Sophia Loren, Raf Vallone, Gary Raymond, John Fraser, Genevieve Page (Bronston/Dear)

El Cid is a fast-action, color-rich, corpse-strewn, battle picture. The Spanish scenery is magnificent, the costumes are vivid, the chain mail and Toledo steel gear impressive. Perhaps the 11th century of art directors Veniero Colasanti and John Moore exceeds reality, but only scholars will complain of that. Action rather than acting characterizes this film.

Yet the film creates respect for its sheer picture-making skills. Director Anthony Mann, with assists from associate producer Michael Waszynski who worked closely with him, battle manager Yakima Canutt, and a vast number of technicians, have labored to create stunning panoramic images.

Of acting there is less to say after acknowledging that Charlton Heston's masculine personality ideally suits the title role. His powerful performance is the central arch of the narrative. Sophia Loren, as first his sweetheart and later his wife, has a relatively passive role.

Two actors in *King of Kings* who remained over in Spain to appear in *El Cid* ended up as bit actors. Hurd Hatfield is the court herald in a couple of scenes, Frank Thring is a most unconvincing Moorish emir with a shaved noggin who lolls about in a harem registering a kind of sulky impatience.

Italy's Raf Vallone is the other man who never has a chance with Chimene. After betraying El Cid he is spared and, at a later period, becomes a follower only to die, tortured, by the invading North African monster, Britain's Herbert Lom.

Most provocative performance among the supporting players is that of Genevieve Page, as the self-willed princess who protects the weakling brother (John Fraser) who becomes king after she, sweet sibling, has the older brother slain.

1961: NOMINATIONS: Best Color Art Direction, Scoring of a Dramatic Picture, Song ("The Falcon and the Dove")

•

EL CONDOR

1996, 101 mins, US Ⓥ col

Dir John Guillermin ***Prod*** Andre De Toth ***Scr*** Larry Cohen, Steven Carabatson ***Ph*** Henri Persin ***Ed*** Jack Slade ***Mus*** Maurice Jarre ***Art*** Julio Molina de Juanes

Act Jim Brown, Lee Van Cleef, Mariana Hill, Patrick O'Neal, Imogen Hassell, Elisha Cook, Jr. (De Toth)

El Condor is Jim Brown and Lee Van Cleef in the wild west of Almeria with an army of Apaches in siege of a mountain fortress of Maximilian's Mexican treasure with enough gun play, explosions, bloodletting, and body count for a Southeast Asian campaign. It is sex and violence, cowboys and Indians, and producer Andre De Toth and director John Guillermin have put it together with blood and guts and gusto.

Brown gets the gold, which turns out to be painted lead, and Mariana Hill who is very much the genuine article. Double-dealing, bushwacking Van Cleef and dastardly Mexican general Patrick O'Neal in turn get theirs from Brown in the end. At the fade-out, Brown stands with his one good arm around Hill amid heaps of gore-smeared bodies of Spanish extras and the smoking ruins of art director Julio Molina de Juanes impressive set of the fortress *El Condor.*

A final duel with O'Neal on horseback and Brown on foot, staged as a parallel to the man-on-horseback bullfighting earlier in the film, is unconvincing in contrast to the other bloody action.

The fact remains that the influence of the made-in-Spain Westerns has undeniably changed the "pure action" format. The Hollywood movie myth of the American West was an extension of the chivalric tales where American Puritanism reigned. The Italian and Spanish have centuries of experience in how men holding guns on other men really act, and that more realistic view frequently, and paradoxically, comes across in the Almeria oaters.

•

EL DORADO

1967, 126 mins, US Ⓥ ⊙ col

Dir Howard Hawks ***Prod*** Howard Hawks ***Scr*** Leigh Brackett ***Ph*** Harold Rosson ***Ed*** John Woodcock ***Mus*** Nelson Riddle ***Art*** Hal Pereira, Carl Anderson

Act John Wayne, Robert Mitchum, James Caan, Charlene Holt, Michele Carey, Ed Asner (Paramount)

Technical and artistic screen fads come and go, but nothing replaces a good story, well told. And Howard Hawks knows how to tell a good story. *El Dorado* [from the novel *The Stars in Their Courses* by Harry Brown] stars John Wayne and Robert Mitchum in an excellent oater drama, laced with adroit comedy and action relief, and set off by strong casting, superior direction, and solid production.

Wayne, a hired gun, is dissuaded from working for landgrabber Ed Asner by Mitchum, a reformed gunslinger now a sharp-looking, disciplined sheriff.

•

ELECTION

1999, 103 mins, US Ⓥ ⊙ ▭ col

Dir Alexander Payne ***Prod*** Albert Berger, Ron Yerxa, David Gale, Keith Samples ***Scr*** Alexander Payne, Jim Taylor ***Ph*** James Glennon ***Ed*** Kevin Tent ***Mus*** Rolfe Kent ***Art*** Jane Ann Stewart

Act Matthew Broderick, Reese Witherspoon, Chris Klein, Jessica Campbell, Mark Harelik, Phil Reeves (MTV)

Election is a dark, insidiously funny satire on the self-involved ways otherwise rational people can allow narrow personal agendas to lead them astray to the point of self-destruction. Shooting once again (he debuted with the mordant social comedy *Citizen Ruth*) in his native Omaha, NE, Alexander Payne has delivered another caustic picture that won't go down too well in Middle America.

Payne knowingly takes on such dicey subjects as teacher-student sex, the uselessness of student government, corrupt administrators, lesbianism at parochial girls' schools and the ruthless cruelty of teenagers, working from the 1998 Tom Perrotta novel inspired by both the three-way 1992 presidential campaign and the true story of how a Southern high school principal invalidated the election of a pregnant girl as prom queen.

We learn about how Novotny (Mark Harelik), a math teacher at Carver High, became involved with the school's overachieving goody-goody, Tracy Flick (Reese Witherspoon), losing his position and family as a result. Novotny was a close friend of history and civics teacher Jim McAllister (Matthew Broderick).

Basically, Jim can't stand Tracy, the school's Little Miss Prim, and when she announces her candidacy for the president of the student body, it's all too much for Jim. He secretly recruits popular jock Paul Metzler (Chris Klein) to join her on the ballot. Unexpectedly, Paul's lesbian sister, Tammy (Jessica Campbell), decides to run as well.

Broderick skillfully offers up a man who is a perfect example of how the path to hell is paved with good intentions. Witherspoon nails Tracy in a nifty performance.

1999: NOMINATION: Best Adapted Screenplay

•

ELECTRA GLIDE IN BLUE

1973, 106 mins, US Ⓥ ⊙ ▭ col

Dir James William Guercio ***Prod*** James William Guercio, Rupert Hitzig ***Scr*** Robert Boris, Michael Butler ***Ph*** Conrad Hall ***Ed*** Jim Benson, John F. Link II, Jerry Greenberg ***Mus*** James William Guercio

Act Robert Blake, Billy "Green" Bush, Mitchell Ryan, Jeannine Riley, Elisha Cook, Royal Dano (United Artists)

Director-producer James William Guercio comes on tall in a first pic about a motorcycle cop in the U.S. West, who is done in by the corruption, change and violence about him.

Guercio at one time played with the rock group of Frank Zappa and brings that ballad-like, terse feel of rock to this extremely well-played and mounted pic.

Robert Blake is effective as a small motorcycle cop in Arizona who has a certain hardheaded dignity, feels he can help people and also wants to graduate to higher police echelons. He is a Vietnam vet without bitterness and expects no condescension from anybody.

Billy "Green" Bush as his slightly violent sidekick, Mitchell Ryan as a flamboyant, sadistic sheriff, Jeannine Riley as a disillusioned starlet all keep up with Blake's fine character composition.

Conrad Hall's extraordinary controlled hues are an asset to this look at the life of a motorized cop.

•

ELECTRIC HORSEMAN, THE

1979, 120 mins, US Ⓥ ⊙ ▭ col

Dir Sydney Pollack ***Prod*** Ray Stark ***Scr*** Robert Garland ***Ph*** Owen Roizman ***Ed*** Sheldon Kahn ***Mus*** Dave Grusin ***Art*** Stephen Grimes

Act Robert Redford, Jane Fonda, Valerie Perrine, John Saxon, Willie Nelson, Allan Arbus (Columbia)

The Electric Horseman is a moderately entertaining film, but no screen magic from Robert Redford and Jane Fonda. The pic is overlong, talky and diffused.

Even though Redford, as an ex-rodeo champ, and Fonda don't create the romantic sparks that might be expected, it's their dramatic professionalism that salvages *Horseman* and makes it a moving and effective film by the time the final credits roll by.

What *Electric Horseman* is peddling is the virtue of "freedom," morally, economically and socially. Redford's attempt to liberate the prizewinning horse of the AMPCO conglomerate from an overabundance of steroids and painkillers is presumably intended as an analogy for the way the American public is force-fed consumerism from today's corporate giants.

1979: NOMINATION: Best Sound

ELECTRIC MAN, THE

SEE: MAN MADE MONSTER

•

ELENI

1985, 117 mins, US Ⓥ ⊙ col

Dir Peter Yates ***Prod*** Nick Vanoff, Mark Pick, Nicholas Gage ***Scr*** Steve Tesich ***Ph*** Billy Williams ***Ed*** Ray Lovejoy ***Mus*** Bruce Smeaton ***Art*** Roy Walker

Act Kate Nelligan, John Malkovich, Linda Hunt, Oliver Cotton, Ronald Pickup, Rosalie Crutchley (CBS)

Adapted from Nicholas Gage's bestselling book about his search for the truth about his mother, who was executed by the communists in Greece in the late 1940s. Pic has the most noble of intentions, but comes off as flat, tedious and crudely biased.

Screenplay cuts back and forth between events separated by 30 years. The Gage figure (John Malkovich) is assigned to the *New York Times* Athens bureau, a base from which he can investigate the events surrounding his mother's death during the civil war. Eleni, Nick's mother (Kate Nelligan), was a peasant woman in the tiny village of Lia. Portrayed as apolitical, she was forced from her home when the communists occupied the area in the fractious period following World War II, then courageously suffered countless other indignities until being convicted as a traitor in a mock trial.

The scenes involving Malkovich's extended search for the evil judge prove more successful than the period stuff, and the climactic scene of their confrontation is undeniably tense, by far the best in the film. It comes as much too little, too late.

Nelligan, Malkovich and Linda Hunt, superior performers all, have strong grips on their characters. Tech credits are fine, with the impoverished Greek village having been suitably re-created in Spain.

•

ELEPHANT BOY

1937, 81 mins, UK Ⓥ b/w

Dir Zoltan Korda, Robert Flaherty ***Prod*** Alexander Korda ***Scr*** John Collier, Akos Tolnay, Marcia De Silva ***Ph*** Osmond Borradaile ***Ed*** Charles Crichton ***Mus*** John Greenwood ***Art*** Vincent Korda

Act Sabu, Walter Hudd, Allan Jeayes, W. E. Holloway, Bruce Gordon, Wilfrid Hyde White (London)

Elephant Boy is a legendary and rather fantastic tale built around the affection that grows up between a native Indian boy and his elephant, an animal that is tops as a hunter. It is a Rudyard Kipling story that reads better than it films, same as the Tarzan yarns, having nothing particularly exciting for the camera, nor any plot to speak of.

Kipling wrote the story under the title of *Toomai of the Elephants*. Toomai is the Indian lad whose great ambition is to be a hunter. Played by a native Indian boy named Sabu, he imparts to it as much charm and naïveté as can be expected. Child has a pronounced native dialect, which doesn't hurt, but many of the other characters are entirely too British to be convincing.

Walter Hudd, with the exception of a couple who appear only in brief scenes, is the only person cast as a white, he being the hunter commissioned by the government to round up much-needed pachyderms.

Aside from the footage used to emphasize the strong affection between the boy and his mammoth pal, the action concerns the routine job of rounding up men and animals for the big hunt, pitching of camp, killing by a tiger of one of the crew and the rather accidental success of little Sabu in leading his trusty elephant to the big herd they're despairing of finding.

•

ELEPHANT MAN, THE

1980, 125 mins, US/UK Ⓥ ⊙ ▭ b/w

Dir David Lynch ***Prod*** Jonathan Sanger ***Scr*** Christopher De-Vore, Eric Bergren, David Lynch ***Ph*** Freddie Francis ***Ed*** Anne V. Coates ***Mus*** John Morris ***Art*** Stuart Craig, Bob Cartwright

Act Anthony Hopkins, John Hurt, Anne Bancroft, John Gielgud, Wendy Hiller, Freddie Jones (Brooksfilms)

Director David Lynch has created an eerily compelling atmosphere in recounting a hideously deformed man's perilous life in Victorian England.

Screenplay was based on two books about the real-life Elephant Man, one [*The Elephant Man and Other Reminiscences*] written by his protector, Sir Frederick Treves, played in the film by Anthony Hopkins [and the other, *The Elephant Man: A Study in Human Dignity* by Ashley Montagu].

Hopkins is splendid in a subtly nuanced portrayal of a man torn between humanitarianism and qualms that his motives in introducing the Elephant Man to society are no better than those of the brutish carny. The centerpiece of the film, however, is the virtuoso performance by the almost unrecognizable John Hurt.

Like Quasimodo in *The Hunchback of Notre Dame*, the Elephant Man gradually reveals suppressed depths of humanity.

Lynch commendably avoids summoning up feelings of disgust.

1980: NOMINATIONS: Best Picture, Director, Actor (John Hurt), Adapted Screenplay, Costume Design, Art Direction, Editing, Original Score

•

ELEPHANT WALK

1954, 102 mins, US Ⓥ col

Dir William Dieterle ***Prod*** Irving Asher ***Scr*** John Lee Mahin ***Ph*** Loyal Griggs ***Ed*** George Tomasini ***Mus*** Franz Waxman

Act Elizabeth Taylor, Dana Andrews, Peter Finch, Abraham Sofaer, Abner Biberman, Noel Drayton (Paramount)

The novelty of the Ceylon backgrounds and pictorial beauty are recommendable points in *Elephant Walk*, an otherwise leisurely-paced romantic drama.

Robert Standish's novel about life among the pekoe-planters rates a sprawling script and direction that lacks attention-holding pace from William Dieterle. Of interest is the fact that in some of the Ceylon-filmed longshots, Vivien Leigh is still seen, although not noticeably so. Illness forced the English star out of the picture after about a month of lensing, with Elizabeth Taylor replacing.

Elephants are the sympathetic heavies in this story of a bride who comes to Ceylon from England and finds her husband, the natives and the tea plantation still under the dominance of a dead man's memory. Added to this tradition worship is the always present threat that the pachyderms may eventually succeed in wrestling back from the white usurpers the trail they had used for centuries in coming down from the wilds to water. The plantation mansion had been built across the trail by the bridegroom's strong-willed late father, who had bowed to nothing, man or beast.

•

ELEVATOR TO THE GALLOWS
SEE: L'ASCENSEUR POUR L'ECHAFAUD

•

11 HARROWHOUSE
1974, 95 mins, UK Ⓥ ▭ col
Dir Aram Avakian ***Prod*** Elliott Kastner ***Scr*** Jeffrey Bloom, Charles Grodin ***Ph*** Arthur Ibbetson ***Ed*** Anne V. Coates ***Mus*** Michael J. Lewis ***Art*** Peter Mullins
Act Charles Grodin, Candice Bergen, John Gielgud, Trevor Howard, James Mason, Helen Cherry (20th Century-Fox)

Charles Grodin stars in, adapted for the screen, and just about ruins *11 Harrowhouse*, a comedy-caper film about a theft of billions in diamonds. Cast as a low-key diamond salesman who wreaks vengeance on the diamond establishment, Grodin messes up the film with ineffective shy-guy acting, and clobbers it with catatonic voiceover that is supposed to be funny.

Gerald A. Browne wrote the novel. The main story, which takes a long time to get going, involves eccentric billionaire Trevor Howard commissioning Grodin and wealthy girlfriend Candice Bergen to rob the diamond vaults presided over by dissatisfied James Mason, who is resentful of his pension treatment at the hands of John Gielgud. Howard and Mason appear close to embarrassed in their roles.

•

EL MARIACHI
1992, 82 mins, US Ⓥ ⊙ col
Dir Robert Rodriguez ***Prod*** Robert Rodriguez, Carlos Gallardo ***Scr*** Robert Rodriguez, Carlos Gallardo ***Ph*** Robert Rodriguez ***Ed*** Robert Rodriguez
Act Carlos Gallardo, Consuelo Gomez, Reinol Martinez, Peter Marquardt, Jaime De Hoyos, Ramiro Gomez (Los Hooligans)

Almost certainly, at $7,000, the cheapest film ever released by a major Hollywood studio, Columbia's pickup *El Mariachi* is a fresh, resourceful first feature by 24-year-old Austin filmmaker Robert Rodriguez. Spanish lingo crime meller has a verve and cheekiness that's partly a smart wedding of such influences as Sergio Leone, George Miller and south-of-the-border noir.

Lensed in two weeks in the Mexican border town of Acuna, the pic can edify and inspire aspiring filmmakers who complain about lack of coin. Even though he shot with a handheld 16mm camera and nonsynch sound, Rodriguez has put a perfectly serviceable picture on the screen (Col paid for the 35mm blowup and Dolby sound add-on).

Simple tale is that of a lone stranger in town who stirs up trouble, although in this case the newcomer is a young, hapless mariachi singer looking for a gig. Also in town is a revenge-crazed drug dealer named Azul at war with his ex-partner, Moco. Like El Mariachi, Azul wears black and carries a guitar case, although one loaded with heavy weaponry rather than a stringed instrument.

Cat-and-mouse plotting sees the earnest El Mariachi chased around town by Moco's henchmen, who themselves are being systematically mowed down by Azul. All El Mariachi wants is a job, which leads him to the cantina of the foxy Domino (Consuelo Gomez).

Given pic's relative levity, amount of carnage at the climax comes as something of a surprise, and fade-out feels uncomfortably close to a setup for a sequel. Carlos Gallardo, who also cowrote and coproduced, makes for an affable Mariachi.

•

ELMER GANTRY
1960, 146 mins, US Ⓥ ⊙ col
Dir Richard Brooks ***Prod*** Bernard Smith ***Scr*** Richard Brooks ***Ph*** John Alton ***Ed*** Marge Fowler ***Mus*** Andre Previn ***Art*** Edward Carrere
Act Burt Lancaster, Jean Simmons, Dean Jagger, Arthur Kennedy, Shirley Jones, Edward Andrews (United Artists)

In filming Sinclair Lewis's contentious 1927 study of a scandalous evangelist, Elmer Gantry, Richard Brooks has framed a big story and bold religioso subject for the old-fashioned rectangular screen (aspect ratio 1.33:1).

Brooks honors the spirit of Lewis's cynical commentary on circus-type primitive exhortation with pictorial imagery that is always pungent. He also has written dialog that is frank and biting.

From the standpoint of technique, this production plays like a symphony, with expertly ordered pianissimo and fortissimo story passages that build to a smashing crescendo in the cremation of Sister Sharon Falconer, an evengelist of questionable sincerity and propriety. The film ends roughly about the halfway mark in Gantry's life, whereas in the book he went on to become an influential Methodist minister, who married and raised a family but continued to indulge in the carnal pleasures he denounced vehemently from the pulpit.

Burt Lancaster pulls out virtually all the stops as Gantry to create a memorable characterization. He acts with such broad and eloquent flourish that a finely balanced, more subdued performance by Jean Simmons as Sister Sharon seems pale by comparison.

1960: Best Actor (Burt Lancaster), Supp. Actress (Shirley Jones), Adapted Screenplay

NOMINATIONS: Best Picture, Scoring of a Dramatic Picture

•

ELUSIVE PIMPERNEL, THE
1950, 109 mins, UK Ⓥ col
Dir Michael Powell, Emeric Pressburger ***Prod*** Michael Powell, Emeric Pressburger ***Scr*** Michael Powell, Emeric Pressburger ***Ph*** Christopher Challis ***Ed*** Reginald Mills ***Mus*** Brian Easdale ***Art*** Hein Heckroth
Act David Niven, Margaret Leighton, Jack Hawkins, Cyril Cusack, Robert Coote, Arlette Marchal (London)

This film version based on the famed Baroness Orczy character almost robs the story of its romance, color and thrills. It is brash, noisy and dull. It does little credit to British film production.

Film takes nearly two hours of screen time to relate, and there is undue padding. Dialog is unusually flat and the flashes of wit expected from the suave Pimpernel are all too rare.

The film shows David Niven, the "Elusive Pimpernel," disguised as an old hag, going through the army cordon with a carriage load of French nobility he has saved from the guillotine. It then goes on to relate his other exploits with members of his league, including the rescue of his wife's brother while his wife is forced to reveal the secret movements of the Scarlet Pimpernel.

There are moments of refreshing beauty in some of the Technicolor shots. Many of the others appear unnecessarily loud and vivid. Niven is smooth, smiling and suave, but all his efforts to lift the picture on to a higher plane are unavailing. Margaret Leighton, as his French-born wife, also falls victim to this uphill fight. Cyril Cusack makes the French ambassador the most obvious of heavies and Jack Hawkins, as the Prince of Wales, indulges in a boisterous romp.

A substantial number of retakes were ordered on the film earlier in the year. Obviously, they have not proved adequate.

•

ELVIRA MADIGAN
1967, 95 mins, Sweden Ⓥ ⊙ col
Dir Bo Widerberg ***Scr*** Bo Widerberg ***Ph*** Jorgen Persson ***Ed*** Bo Widerberg
Act Pia Degermark, Thommy Berggren, Lennart Malmer, Nina Widerberg, Cleo Jensen (Europa)

Based on a true story of a doomed turn-of-the-century love affair, this film opts for the poetic, timeless and lyrical and succeeds right down the line.

Softly hued color and a well-chosen background of Mozart music [from Piano Concerto No. 21] envelop the tale of the love affair of a young Swedish army officer of noble lineage and a young girl from a circus who is a noted tightrope walker. Film begins with them together, and then his desertion and her foregoing the circus and their idyll, until an inability to make any sort of contact with society leads to their suicide pact.

Pia Degermark has the luminous elan and delicacy, underpinned by the strength of her show background, to make her role of the girl always pleasing to the eye and revealing in her feelings. Thommy Berggren is a perfect counterpoint as the man who gives up all for love. Director Bo Widerberg shows a sure hand throughout.

•

EMBRYO
1976, 108 mins, US Ⓥ col
Dir Ralph Nelson ***Prod*** Arnold H. Orgolini, Anita Doohan ***Scr*** Anita Doohan, Jack W. Thomas ***Ph*** Fred Koenekamp ***Ed*** John Martinelli ***Mus*** Gil Melle ***Art*** Joe Alves
Act Rock Hudson, Diane Ladd, Barbara Carrera, Roddy McDowall, Ann Schedeen, John Elerick (Cine Artists)

The story has doctor Rock Hudson grow a beautiful young woman (Barbara Carrera) in his laboratory from fetal beginnings. It's kind of a *Bride of Frankenstein* tale, cast in terms of scientific mumbo-jumbo, an effective blending of old and new plot elements.

Hudson plays with gentleness and restraint, and Carrera's pristine fashion-model beauty is perfect for the role, but there's little feeling of genuine passion or eroticism.

The script [from a story by Jack W. Thomas] is much stronger on plot than it is on character relationships. Suspense built up before Carrera's birth is dissipated in clumsy dramatic confrontations when she and Hudson set out in society.

Diane Ladd is wasted as Hudson's jealous housekeeper.

•

EMERALD FOREST, THE
1985, 113 mins, US Ⓥ ⊙ ▭ col
Dir John Boorman ***Prod*** John Boorman ***Scr*** Rospo Pallenberg ***Ph*** Philippe Rousselot ***Ed*** Ian Crafford ***Mus*** Junior Homrich, Brian Gascoigne ***Art*** Simon Holland
Act Powers Boothe, Meg Foster, Charley Boorman, Dira Pass, Rui Polonah, Claudio Moreno (Embassy)

Based on an uncredited true story about a Peruvian whose son disappeared in the jungles of Brazil, screenplay trades on numerous enduring myths and legends about the return to nature and growing up in the wild.

Powers Boothe, an American engineer and designer assigned to build an enormous dam in Brazil, loses his young son in the wilderness and, against seemingly hopeless odds, sets out to find him.

Ten years later, the two finally meet up under perilous circumstances. By this time, the son, played by the director's own sprog, Charley Boorman, has become well integrated into the ways of a friendly Indian tribe and has little desire to return to the outside world.

Once he has been exposed to the simple virtues of "uncivilized" life, Boothe begins to have serious doubts about the nature of his work in the area.

Despite some lumps in the narrative and characterization and some occasionally awkward tension between the documentary realism enforced by the subject and the heavy stylization of the director's approach, film proves engrossing and visually fascinating.

•

EMMA
1932, 70 mins, US b/w
Dir Clarence Brown ***Scr*** Leonard Praskins, Frances Marion, Zelda Sears ***Ph*** Oliver Marsh ***Ed*** William LeVanway
Act Marie Dressler, Richard Cromwell, Jean Hersholt, Myrna Loy, John Miljan, Barbara Kent (M-G-M)

There are probably 20 actresses who would have fitted the role of the old servant who spent a lifetime with the Smith family, watching the children grow up and then turn against her in her old age. But there is only one Marie Dressler, a trouper with a genius for characters of comic surface but profound pathos.

The whole *Emma* affair is synthetic, in its comedy as well as in its sentiment the purest of hoke, sometimes skillfully wrought, but often far from clever in its manipulation. Dressler's acting alone gives it vitality. There are bits that drag sadly. Such a sequence is the old servant's departure for Niagara Falls on a long deferred vacation.

There is a courtroom scene that is the height of strong arm bathos and some of the passages toward the end are absurd in their determination to pull tears. Nothing but Dressler's astonishing ability to command conviction saves some of these sequences from going flat.

Jean Hersholt delivers a well-paced and nicely restrained performance as an absentminded inventor; Myrna Loy and Barbara Kent help to decorate the picture with grace; and Richard Cromwell gives just the right feeling of a loveable adolescent boy.

1931/32: NOMINATION: Best Actress (Marie Dressler)

•

EMMA
1996, 111 mins, UK Ⓥ ⊙ col
Dir Douglas McGrath ***Prod*** Patrick Cassavetti, Steven Haft ***Scr*** Douglas McGrath ***Ph*** Ian Wilson ***Ed*** Lesley Walker ***Mus*** Rachel Portman ***Art*** Michael Howells
Act Gwyneth Paltrow, Jeremy Northam, Toni Collete, Greta Scacchi, Alan Cumming, Juliet Stevenson (Matchmaker)

Gwyneth Paltrow shines brightly as Jane Austen's most endearing character, the disastrously self-assured matchmaker Emma Woodhouse.

Yet another smart Austen heroine who lives with her doting, dotty father in rural English splendor, Woodhouse is different in that she puts all her creative juices into fixing up everyone *else's* romantic lives. While she doesn't exactly scream "Project!" when Harriet Smith (Toni Collette), a simple young woman of obscure origins, falls into her fold, Emma does become fairly obsessed with finding her a suitable mate. She manages to nudge Harriet into ditching a perfectly eligible farmer by setting her sights on the smarmy Rev. Elton (Alan Cumming). Somehow, Emma hasn't noticed that the less-than-right rev is actually keen on *her*.

These problems are compounded when two other attention-getters come on the scene. Handsome, blond Frank Churchill (Ewan McGregor) never shuts up, and darkly enigmatic Jane Fairfax (Polly Walker) hardly says a word.

No musty Oxford type, first-time helmer and scripter Doug McGrath is a Texas-born humorist best known as a writer for TV's *Saturday Night Live* and for his cowriting of *Bullets over Broadway*. He keeps things moving at a delirious trot without sacrificing period manners or the precision of the original language.

At a reported $7 million, the sunny-looking production stands up to bigger historical sagas, and is definitely funnier than most.

1996: Best Original Score

NOMINATION: Best Costume Design

•

EMMANUELLE
1974, 105 mins, France Ⓥ col
Dir Just Jaeckin ***Scr*** Jean-Louis Richard ***Ph*** Richard Suzuki ***Ed*** Claudine Bouche ***Mus*** Pierre Bachelet, Herve Roy ***Art*** Baptiste Poirot
Act Sylvia Kristel, Alain Cuny, Daniel Sarky, Jeanne Colletin, Marika Green, Christine Boisson (Trinacra/Orphee)

Based on a bestselling book [by "Emmanuelle Arsan"] about the sexual liberation of a young woman, and with some production dress and the exotic locale of Bangkok, this is still softcore. Film is a series of glossy images and appears more a come-on for the civil service than for femme lib.

Emmanuelle (Sylvia Kristel) is a thin, sexy girl who goes to join her husband in Bangkok where he is attached to the French Embassy. Though looking innocent, but enamored of lovemaking, she manages to be seduced by two men on the plane.

In Bangkok she meets a sultry teenager given to masturbation who introduces her to an older man (Alain Cuny), who is to finally reveal the secrets of her true sexual and femme liberation. At the same time, Emmanuelle falls for a lesbian anthropologist, masturbates with the young girl, and is raped in an opium den.

Direction is a bit pompous, but lensing is good. Acting is a bit self-conscious, except for Cuny as the older man who initiates Emmanuelle into the rites of love. Kristel is acceptably ingenuous as the part-innocent, part-sex-obsessed heroine.

•

EMPEROR OF THE NORTH
1973, 118 mins, US Ⓥ col
Dir Robert Aldrich ***Prod*** Stan Hough ***Scr*** Christopher Knopf ***Ph*** Joseph Biroc ***Ed*** Michael Luciano ***Mus*** Frank DeVol ***Art*** Jack Martin Smith
Act Lee Marvin, Ernest Borgnine, Keith Carradine, Charles Tyner, Malcolm Atterbury, Simon Oakland (Inter-Hemisphere/20th Century-Fox)

Premise of a challenge by an easygoing tramp to ride the freight train of a sadistic conductor reputed to kill nonpaying passengers (as his hobo associates and train men lay bets on the outcome) is limited in scope.

The production takes its title from hobos crowning Lee Marvin "Emperor" for riding Ernest Borgnine's train even a mile, something no other hobo has ever accomplished. While there is a wealth of violence under Robert Aldrich's forceful direction, the motivating idea is bogged down frequently with time out while Marvin expounds the philosophy and finer points of hobodom to a brash young kid (Keith Carradine).

Marvin scores again in one of his uncolorful but commanding characterizations. Borgnine's interpretation borders on a caricature of the heavies of the past. [Film was initially released as *The Emperor of the North Pole*.]

•

EMPEROR'S NEW GROOVE, THE
2000, 79 mins, US Ⓥ ⊙ col
Dir Mark Dindal ***Prod*** Randy Fullmer ***Scr*** David Reynolds ***Ed*** Pamela Ziegenhagen-Shefland ***Mus*** John Debney, Sting, David Hartley ***Art*** Paul Felix (Walt Disney)

Disney's new generation of animators has quietly staged a palace revolt. While this long-gestated project retains several classic aspects of the house style from the '40s and '50s, it discards many newer Disney trends and turns to the old competition—namely, the Chuck Jones/Warners look—for considerable inspiration. Light, taut and compact, the zippy adventure [story by Chris Williams and Mark Dindal, based on an original story by Roger Allers and Matthew Jacobs] is sometimes much too hip for the room, and thus over the heads of younger kids.

Only time will tell if the take on the classic fairy tale *The Emperor's New Clothes* (which receives no mention in the credits) sets a trend for a unit that was recently foundering with well-crafted but conservative animation. In some respects, tolerance for pic's humor and contempo attitude will go as far as one can take thesp David Spade, who not only voices the egomaniacal title character but whose trademark smart-assed manner seems to have informed much of the comedic tone.

Pic's opening scenes include brief indications of the project's original Incan theme. Spade's miserable emperor-turned-llama Kuzco recalls, in flashback, when he ruled the roost and could kick plebeians over the palace walls for "throwing off his groove." As Kuzco reaches the pinnacle of his indulgent glory, pic features a Sting-penned song, "Perfect World" (belted out by Tom Jones). (Six songs by the pop star were junked when the serious-minded epic musical transformed into the current comedy.)

Kuzco's prime skill is making enemies, which he does with his evil, conniving adviser, Yzma (Eartha Kitt), and with innocent, salt-of-the-earth shepherd Pacha (John Goodman). A central Disney character as negative as Kuzco is a notable gamble, but it pays off in the friction created with upright Pacha.

The rhythm of the chase and showdown comes as close to Chuck Jones and Tex Avery as any Disney project in memory. An extended riff with an elusive bottle of elixir is milked for every drop, giving the impression of a highly elastic, almost free-form animation style. Perhaps *Groove*'s most successful concept is the modeling of the characters on the thesps voicing them. The effect allows auds to picture the small, spindly Spade playing the narrow-necked llama or the extra-large Goodman as big, lovable Pacha. The sense of energy delivered not by effects but by characters is no better exemplified than in Kitt's unabashedly diva-like performance.

The echoes of Chuck Jones are especially felt in John Debney's frequently punchy underscore, which only rarely drifts into standard sentimental notes. Pic's dominant motif of sharp, simplified line drawings, anatomically fine but not overly precise renderings and less fussy backgrounds is welcome in an animation era when more has become less.

•

EMPEROR'S SHADOW, THE
SEE: QIN SONG

•

EMPEROR WALTZ, THE
1948, 106 mins, US col
Dir Billy Wilder ***Prod*** Charles Brackett ***Scr*** Charles Brackett, Billy Wilder ***Ph*** George Barnes ***Ed*** Doane Harrison ***Mus*** Victor Young ***Art*** Hans Dreier, Franz Bachelin
Act Bing Crosby, Joan Fontaine, Roland Culver, Lucile Watson, Richard Haydn, Sig Ruman (Paramount)

Film is a costumer laid "in the days" (sic) of Emperor Franz Joseph, and is played to the hilt by Crosby, Joan Fontaine and their supporting cast. Picture has a free-and-easy air that perfectly matches the Crosby style of natural comedy. Costar Joan Fontaine, better known for heavy, serious roles, demonstrates adaptability that fits neatly into the lighter demands, and she definitely scores with charm and talent as the Crosby foil.

Multiple functions of Charles Brackett and Billy Wilder on *Waltz* have given film an infectious quality that surmounts the gorgeously apt trappings against which is projected the fable of an American traveling phonograph salesman and his dog who crash the court of the emperor.

There's plenty of pageantry in the staging of the title number, using the colorful swirling of richly costumed dancers in the palace ballroom as eye-filling backdrop. "Friendly Mountains" has backdrop of processed Tyrol crags and valleys (actually Jasper National Park) filled with native yodelers and dancers.

•

EMPIRE DES SENS, L'
(IN THE REALM OF THE SENSES; EMPIRE OF THE SENSES)
1976, 105 mins, France/Japan Ⓥ col
Dir Nagisa Oshima ***Prod*** Anatole Dauman ***Scr*** Nagisa Oshima ***Ph*** Hideo Ito ***Ed*** Keiichi Uraoka, Patrick Sauvion ***Mus*** Minoru Miki ***Art*** Jusho Toda
Act Eiko Matsuda, Tatsuya Fuji, Aoi Nakajima, Yasuko Matsui, Meika Seri, Kanae Kobayashi (Oshima/Shibata/Argos/Oceanic/Oshima

A topflight director working in the porno or erotic belt is still a rarity. This disturbing film, about a love that is so consuming it ultimately leads to sado-masochism and death, is one in the hands of Japanese director Nagisa Oshima.

Oshima made his mark at fests with oblique pics about racism, a family using their son to fake accidents for blackmail, and a probing of Japanese hieratic family structures. This pic's baring of sex as a means and an end, its refusal to soft-pedal either the beauty or its final harrowing results, raises it to an unusual level.

In 1936, the age of rampant Japanese militarism, two lovers meet. She is an ex-prostitute, who works in a restaurant. Insulted by the head waitress, she tries to knife her but is disarmed by the boss. They begin having trysts and make love everywhere.

She insists he no longer sleep with his wife and threatens him with castration. But he continues, as well as with a cleaning woman when she is out. Finally they play strangulation games to reach even higher planes of orgasm.

The extraordinary acting of Eiko Matsuda as the obsessed girl and Tatsuya Fuji as the easygoing male are assets, as are subtle musical score, finely-hued lensing and a directorial blending of theme and visual finesse. [Pic's Japanese title is *Ai no corrida*. All dialogue is in Japanese.]

•

EMPIRE OF THE ANTS
1977, 89 mins, US Ⓥ col
Dir Bert I. Gordon ***Prod*** Bert I. Gordon ***Scr*** Jack Turley ***Ph*** Reginald Morris ***Ed*** Michael Luciano ***Mus*** Dana Kaproff ***Art*** Charles Rosen
Act Joan Collins, Robert Lansing, John David Carson, Albert Salmi, Jacqueline Scott, Pamela Shoop (American International)

The H. G. Wells–inspired exploitationer *Empire of the Ants* is an above-average effort about ants that grow big after munching on radioactive waste, and terrorize a group headed by Joan Collins, Robert Lansing and John David Carson.

Periodic moments of good special effects are separated by reels of dramatic banality as players flounder in flimsy dialog and under sluggish direction.

Collins is a sharpie Florida real estate agent who takes a group of potential suckers on Lansing's boat to remote swampland. There the big ants attack.

•

EMPIRE OF THE SENSES
SEE: L'EMPIRE DES SENS

•

EMPIRE OF THE SUN
1987, 152 mins, US Ⓥ ⊙ col
Dir Steven Spielberg ***Prod*** Steven Spielberg, Kathleen Kennedy, Frank Marshall ***Scr*** Tom Stoppard ***Ph*** Allen Daviau ***Ed*** Michael Kahn ***Mus*** John Williams ***Art*** Norman Reynolds
Act Christian Bale, John Malkovich, Miranda Richardson, Nigel Havers, Joe Pantoliano, Leslie Phillips (Amblin/Warner)

Story of an 11-year-old boy stranded in Japanese-occupied China during World War II is based on J. G. Ballard's autobiographical 1984 novel, which marked the first non-science-fiction book by author. Both it and the film clearly are the work of sci-fi artists channeling their imaginations into a more traditional framework.

Leading the first troupe of Hollywood studio filmmakers ever into Shanghai, Steven Spielberg turns the gray metropolis into a sensational film set as he delineates the edginess and growing chaos leading up to Japan's entry into the city just after Pearl Harbor.

Jim (Christian Bale) is in every way a proper upper-class English lad, but for the fact he has never seen England. Separated from his parents during the spectacularly staged evacuation of Shanghai, Jim hooks up with a pair of American scavengers, with whom in due course, he is rounded up and sent to a prison camp for the rest of the war.

It is there that Jim flourishes, expending his boundless energy on creative projects and pastimes that finally land him a privileged place among the entrepreneurially minded Americans.

John Malkovich's Basie, an opportunistic King Rat type, keeps threatening to become a fully developed character but never does. Other characters are complete blanks, which severely limits the emotional reverberation of the piece. No special use is made of the talents of Miranda Richardson, Nigel Havers, Joe Pantoliano and the others, so it is up to young English thesp Bale to engage the viewer's interest, which he does superbly.

1987: NOMINATIONS: Best Cinematography, Costume Design, Art Direction, Editing, Original Score, Sound

•

EMPIRE STRIKES BACK, THE
1980, 124 mins, US Ⓥ ⦿ ▭ col
Dir Irvin Kershner ***Prod*** Gary Kurtz ***Scr*** Leigh Brackett, Lawrence Kasdan ***Ph*** Peter Suschitzky ***Ed*** Paul Hirsch ***Mus*** John Williams ***Art*** Norman Reynolds
Act Mark Hamill, Harrison Ford, Carrie Fisher, Billy Dee Williams, Frank Oz, Alec Guinness (20th Century-Fox/Lucasfilm)

The Empire Strikes Back is a worthy sequel to *Star Wars*, equal in both technical mastery and characterization, suffering only from the familiarity with the effects generated in the original and imitated too much by others.

From the first burst of John Williams's powerful score and the receding opening title crawl, we are back in pleasant surroundings and anxious for a good time.

This is exec producer George Lucas's world. Though he has turned over the director's chair and his typewriter [apart from providing the original story], there are no recognizable deviations from the path marked by Lucas and producer Gary Kurtz.

They're assisted again by good performances from Mark Hamill, Harrison Ford and Carrie Fisher. And even the ominous Darth Vader (David Prowse [voiced by James Earl Jones]) is fleshed with new—and surprising—motivations.

Among the new characters, Billy Dee Williams gets a good turn as a duplicitous but likeable villain-ally and Frank Oz is fascinating as sort of a guru for the Force.

Vader's admirals now look even more like Japanese admirals of the fleet, intercut with Hamill's scrambling fighter pilots who wouldn't look too out of place on any Marine base today.

1980: Best Sound, Special Achievement Award (visual effects)

NOMINATIONS: Best Art Direction, Original Score

•

ENCHANTED APRIL
1991, 101 mins, UK Ⓥ ⦿ col
Dir Mike Newell ***Prod*** Ann Scott ***Scr*** Peter Barnes ***Ph*** Rex Maidment ***Ed*** Dick Allen ***Mus*** Richard Rodney Bennett ***Art*** Malcolm Thornton
Act Miranda Richardson, Joan Plowright, Josie Lawrence, Polly Walker, Michael Kitchen, Jim Broadbent (BBC)

A slim comedy of manners about Brits discovering their emotions in sunny Italy, *Enchanted April* doesn't spring many surprises. Strong cast's reliable playing is undercut by a script that dawdles over well-trod territory. Pic derives from British pubcaster BBC's Screen Two series.

Story centers on four women who rent a medieval dwelling in San Salvatore, Italy. For two of them (Miranda Richardson, Josie Lawrence), it's an excuse to get away from inattentive hubbies. Also on board are a waspish widow (Joan Plowright) and a society belle (Polly Walker). Lawrence decides to invite her husband (Alfred Molina) over, and Richardson eventually fires off a letter to hers as well. Meanwhile, the house's British owner (Michael Kitchen), who'd already taken a shine to Richardson in Blighty, turns up one day.

Dialog-heavy script [from Elizabeth von Arnim's novel] is well turned but lacking in real conflict or development. All the actors give it their best shot, with Plowright spitting out bons mots with her usual aplomb and Molina brightening things up. Of the younger women, Walker is tops as the cool society vamp. Mike Newell's helming gets everything in the frame but rarely delivers more.

1992: NOMINATIONS: Best Supp. Actress (Joan Plowright), Screenplay Adaptation, Costume Design

•

ENCHANTED COTTAGE, THE
1945, 91 mins, US Ⓥ ⦿ b/w
Dir John Cromwell ***Prod*** Harriet Parsons ***Scr*** DeWitt Bodeen, Herman J. Mankiewicz ***Ph*** Ted Tetzlaff ***Ed*** Joseph Noriega ***Mus*** Roy Webb ***Art*** Albert S. D'Agostino, Carroll Clark
Act Dorothy McGuire, Robert Young, Herbert Marshall, Mildred Natwick, Spring Byington, Hillary Brooke (RKO)

Sensitive love story of a returned war veteran with ugly facial disfigurements and the homely slavey—both self-conscious of their handicaps—is sincerely told both in the script [based on the play by Arthur Wing Pinero] and outstanding direction of John Cromwell.

Brief prolog establishes Robert Young as the flyer who leases a cottage for his honeymoon, but is called to service on eve of his wedding. Two years later he returns to hide his war disfigurements from his family at the cottage, where Dorothy McGuire is hiding from people because of her ugliness. But the girl's tender attention to the flyer results in idyllic love, with each appearing beautiful to the other and pair sincerely believing that the cottage is enchanted and responsible for the transformations.

McGuire turns in an outstanding performance, with Young also sharing the limelight. Herbert Marshall is excellent, while Mildred Natwick scores as the housekeeper.

1945: NOMINATIONS: Best Scoring of a Dramatic Picture

•

ENCINO MAN
(UK: CALIFORNIA MAN)
1992, 89 mins, US Ⓥ ⦿ col
Dir Les Mayfield ***Prod*** George Zaloom ***Scr*** Shawn Schepps ***Ph*** Robert Brinkmann ***Ed*** Eric Sears, Jonathan Siegal ***Mus*** J. Peter Robinson ***Art*** James Allen
Act Sean Astin, Brendan Fraser, Pauly Shore, Megan Ward, Robin Tunney, Michael DeLuise (Hollywood Pictures)

Encino Man is a mindless would-be comedy aimed at the younger set. Low-budget quickie is insulting even within its own no-effort parameters.

Incompetent screenplay [from a screen story by Shawn Schepps and producer George Zaloom] dawdles over the introductions, with well over a reel elapsing before Cro Magnon man Brendan Fraser unfreezes after turning up in a block of ice uncovered by Encino teen Sean Astin while digging a backyard swimming pool.

Pic's sci-fi pretense is immediately abandoned as Astin and buddy Pauly Shore contrive to pass off Fraser as a transfer student to Encino High. Only tension is that he wins the hearts of femmes, including Astin's dream girl Megan Ward.

Debuting feature director Les Mayfield exhibits low aptitude for comedy, resorting to pratfalls and food sloppiness for laughs. Film is nominally a vehicle for MTV comic Shore, who flunks out on screen with his tediously unfunny patter and smaller-than-life personality.

•

ENCORE
1951, 89 mins, UK Ⓥ b/w
Dir Pat Jackson, Anthony Pelissier, Harold French ***Prod*** Antony Darnborough ***Scr*** T.E.B. Clarke, Arthur Macrae, Eric Ambler ***Ph*** Desmond Dickinson ***Ed*** Alfred Roome ***Mus*** Richard Addinsell ***Art*** Maurice Carter
Act Nigel Patrick, Roland Culver, Kay Walsh, Glynis Johns, Ronald Squire, Terence Morgan (Two Cities)

For the third time, a group of Somerset Maugham short stories have been collated to make a quality British film. *Quartet* (1948) was followed by *Trio* (1950). *Encore*, a coproduction between Paramount and Rank, is also based on three of the writer's vignettes.

First of the stories is *The Ant and The Grasshopper* [directed by Pat Jackson, scripted by T.E.B. Clarke], in which Nigel Patrick is a ne'er-do-well who soaks his lawyer brother for cash until he lands a wealthy heiress. Acting of Patrick and Roland Culver, as his brother, sets a high standard.

Winter Cruise [Anthony Pelissier/Arthur Macrae] is another light piece, but of a contrasting type. Kay Walsh plays a middle-aged garrulous spinster who takes a trip by cargo boat to Jamaica, but whose non-stop chattering drives the captain and crew to distraction. Fine acting and a flawless script keeps the fun rolling in this.

The drama and tension of the series is provided by the third subject, *Gigolo and Gigolette* [Harold French/Eric Ambler]. This is a dramatic piece about a young vaudeville artist whose specialty is diving from an eighty-foot platform into a five-foot lake of flames. When the girl begins to feel that her husband is persisting with the act because of the money that goes with it, she loses her nerve. Glynis Johns makes a deep impression as the girl, and Terence Morgan aptly suggests the weak, scheming husband.

•

END, THE
1978, 100 mins, US Ⓥ ⦿ col
Dir Burt Reynolds ***Prod*** Lawrence Gordon ***Scr*** Jerry Belson ***Ph*** Bobby Byrne ***Ed*** Donn Cambern ***Mus*** Paul Williams ***Art*** Jan Scott
Act Burt Reynolds, Dom DeLuise, Sally Field, Strother Martin, David Steinberg, Joanne Woodward (United Artists)

The rather complete failure of Jerry Belson's script makes "The End" of *The End* come none too soon. Star-director Burt Reynolds, as a medically doomed sharpie, exercises and exorcises his fears while milking sympathy from everyone available. Production is a tasteless and overripe comedy that disintegrates very early into hysterical, undisciplined hamming. For a few frames of the film, Reynolds's bearded face suggests that there was some effort to project a different image; to transform his familiar and likable charisma into something different, befitting the last days of a carefree, selfish person who has been informed of fatal illness. There's little more to do than list the featured players: Dom DeLuise, absolutely dreadful; Sally Field, phoning in a kooky-pretty role; David Steinberg, an outtake that crept back into the print; Joanne Woodward, poorly utilized though adroitly cast.

•

ENDLESS LOVE
1981, 115 mins, US Ⓥ ⦿ col
Dir Franco Zeffirelli ***Prod*** Dyson Lovell ***Scr*** Judith Rascoe ***Ph*** David Watkin ***Ed*** Michael J. Sheridan ***Mus*** Jonathan Tunick ***Art*** Ed Wittstein
Act Brooke Shields, Martin Hewitt, Shirley Knight, Don Murray, Richard Kiley, Beatrice Straight (Polygram)

A cotton-candy rendition of Scott Spencer's powerful novel, *Endless Love* is a manipulative tale of a doomed romance that careens repeatedly between the credible and the ridiculous.

With a nod to *Romeo and Juliet*, with which director Franco Zeffirelli enjoyed such success in 1968, plot concerns the scorching love affair between a 17-year-old boy, from a social-activist Chicago family, and a 15-year-old girl. Normally broad-minded, girl's father finally can't take it anymore when the boy more or less moves into his daughter's bedroom, and banishes him from the household for a month.

Since he's center stage most of the time, it's fortunate that newcomer Martin Hewitt registers so strongly. Zeffirelli has dressed and photographed his find almost in the style of some of his mentor, Luchino Visconti's neo-realist heroes, with two-day beard growths and anachronistic Clark Gable undershirts.

Despite top billing, Brooke Shields disappears during entire center section of the film, which reduces extent to which film stands or falls by her work. One can never really tell what her responses to sex are because she's smiling all the time.

1981: NOMINATION: Best Song ("Endless Love")

•

END OF DAYS
1999, 120 mins, US Ⓥ ⦿ ▭ col
Dir Peter Hyams ***Prod*** Armyan Bernstien, Bill Borden ***Scr*** Andrew W. Marlowe ***Ph*** Peter Hyams ***Ed*** Steve Kemper ***Mus*** John Debney ***Art*** Richard Holland
Act Arnold Schwarzenegger, Gabriel Byrne, Kevin Pollak, Robin Tunney, CCH Pounder, Rod Steiger (Beacon/Universal)

A frightfest in which the screen's greatest strongman arm-wrestles Satan over the destiny of the next thousand years, *End of Days* in a middling vehicle that veers repeatedly from the reasonably exciting to the risibly over-the-top. Sporting a trim beard and seemingly a shade leaner than in his pumped-up prime, Schwarzenegger looks great even though he's playing an alcoholic ex-cop, Jericho Cane.

On Dec. 28, 1999, with four days to go before Y2K pandemonium hits, earthquakes and subterranean fires in Manhattan set the stage for Satan's dazzling entrance: The Man (Gabriel Byrne) strides into a restaurant and nonchalantly blows the place to smithereens. As it happens, Jericho has been hired to protect The Man, triggering several action setpieces director Peter Hyams has pulled off with professional skill if not with breathtaking ingenuity.

Rather too conveniently, Jericho figures out that it's Christine York (Robin Tunney) he's meant to protect, a 20-year-old who bears Satan's mark, and is meant to give birth to the Antichrist. For this to happen, Satan must impregnate her in the hour before the new millennium. Fittingly, it all ends in a church where Jericho tosses aside his gun, looks skyward and says, "Please, God, give me strength."

Violence quotient is strong but not too high, while special effects are generally groovy. It's good to see Schwarzenegger doing his thing again after [a more than two-year] sabbatical. The sassy Kevin Pollak proves a good sidekick for the big man, while Byrne takes barely suppressed glee in his role as the ultimate villain.

•

END OF INNOCENCE, THE
1990, 102 mins, US Ⓥ col
Dir Dyan Cannon ***Prod*** Thom Tyson, Vince Cannon ***Scr*** Dyan Cannon ***Ph*** Alex Nepomniaschy ***Ed*** Bruce Cannon ***Mus*** Michael Convertino ***Art*** Paul Eads

Act Dyan Cannon, John Heard, George Coe, Lola Mason, Rebecca Schaeffer, Steve Meadows (Skouras)

A moralistic drama about a woman's struggle for self-determination, *The End of Innocence* is a well-intentioned vehicle for writer-director-star Dyan Cannon.

In its peppy opening, Cannon time-telescopes the childhood, adolescence (played by the late Rebecca Schaeffer) and young womanhood of Stephanie Lewis, a lovely if malleable only child of querulous middle-class Jewish parents.

Predictably enough, selfish, struggling writer Michael (Steve Meadows), turns out to be not much different than the boorish cad who deflowered Stephanie on her prom night long ago.

A caring platonic male friend, lost in the narrative shuffle, tries to warn her off Michael to no avail. Drifting through life with no real career or focus, Stephanie (Cannon) deals with her deep unhappiness with junk food, mood pills and marijuana.

Cannon, looking remarkably good, has a field day dominating the film. But the auteur/star gets too carried away with a sense of mission here.

•

END OF THE AFFAIR, THE
1999, 109 mins, UK/US Ⓥ ⊙ col
Dir Neil Jordan *Prod* Stephen Woolley, Neil Jordan *Scr* Neil Jordan *Ph* Roger Pratt *Ed* Tony Lawson *Mus* Michael Nyman *Art* Anthony Pratt
Act Ralph Fiennes, Julianne Moore, Stephen Rea, Ian Hart, Samuel Bould, Jason Isaacs (Woolley/Columbia)

Fans of British writer Graham Greene's novels will relish Neil Jordan's brilliant version of *The End of the Affair*, Greene's most complex, most autobiographical, and arguably finest novel, previously brought to the screen unsatisfactorily by Edward Dmytryk in 1955. A faithful adaptation that captures the haunting spirit and religious nature of the 1951 novel, this erotic ghost story unfolds as a first-person account of the warped liaison between a selfish novelist and the adulterous wife of a civil servant, splendidly played by Ralph Fiennes, Julianne Moore and Stephen Rea, respectively.

On the surface, the three individuals represent stereotypical characters in a noir melodrama of the '40s, which is the movie's time frame. A passionate woman trapped in a sterile marriage, Sarah Miles (Moore) falls for Maurice Bendrix (Fiennes), a handsome, young novelist, upon meeting him at a party given by her loyal but unexciting civil servant husband, Henry (Rea). Sarah and Bendrix begin an illicit, sexually liberating affair that lasts several years.

What ensues is a subtle, extremely moving chronicle of the end of Bendrix's affair with Sarah, jumping back and forth between the summer of 1939, when they first met, to Sarah's sudden death, seven years later. Haunted by passionate memories of their affair, Bendrix reenters Sarah's life, confronting once more the all-consuming love they had for each other.

Fiennes shines as the disenchanted, skeptical and hate-ridden novelist. Sporting a spot-on English accent, Moore also excels. Jordan regular Rea plays the civil servant in a dignified manner. Remainder of the ensemble is equally good, especially Ian Hart as a private eye.

1999: NOMINATIONS: Best Actress (Julianne Moore), Cinematography

•

ENEMIES
A LOVE STORY
1989, 119 mins, US Ⓥ ⊙ col
Dir Paul Mazursky *Prod* Paul Mazursky *Scr* Roger L. Simon *Ph* Fred Murphy *Ed* Stuart Pappe *Mus* Maurice Jarre *Art* Guzman
Act Ron Silver, Anjelica Huston, Lena Olin, Margaret Sophie Stein, Alan King, Paul Mazursky (Morgan Creek)

Haunting, mordantly amusing, deliciously sexy, *Enemies, a Love Story* is Paul Mazursky's triumphant adapation of the Isaac Bashevis Singer novel about a Holocaust survivor who finds himself married to three women in 1949 New York.

Ron Silver is fascinatingly enigmatic in the lead role of Herman Broder. He's a quietly charming, somewhat withdrawn man whose cushy job as a ghostwriter for a very reformed rabbi (Alan King) gives him plenty of time to attend to his deliriously complicated love life.

The character simultaneously is married to a devoted but cloddish woman (Margaret Sophie Stein), is carrying on a passionate affair with a sultry married woman (Lena Olin) and also finds himself back in the arms of his long-vanished wife (Anjelica Huston), who was thought to be lost in the war.

Like Silver, the audience will find it difficult to prefer one of his three women over the others, since Stein, Olin and Huston are equally captivating. Olin is sensational here as the doomed Masha, for whom lovemaking is the best assertion of life over the inevitability of self-destruction.

1989: NOMINATIONS: Best Supp. Actress (Anjelica Huston, Lena Olin), Adapted Screenplay

•

ENEMIES OF THE PUBLIC
SEE: THE PUBLIC ENEMY

•

ENEMY BELOW, THE
1957, 98 mins, Ⓥ ▭ col
Dir Dick Powell *Prod* Dick Powell *Scr* Wendell Mayes *Ph* Harold Rosson *Ed* Stuart Gilmore *Mus* Leigh Harline *Art* Lyle R. Wheeler, Albert Hogsett
Act Robert Mitchum, Curt Jurgens, Al Hedison, Theodore Bikel, Russell Collins, Kurt Kreuger (20th Century-Fox)

The Enemy Below is an engrossing tale of a chesslike duel of wits between the commanders of an American destroyer escort and a German U-Boat in World War II, locked in single combat and each intent on blowing the other out of this world.

Once in a while, the gallantry gets a bit thick, in the style of World War I aviation films of the '20s and '30s. However, picture is well-made, with solid action and Robert Mitchum and Curt Jurgens. This is Jurgens's first American-made film.

Producer-director Dick Powell has lensed two finishes, but studio publicity is carefully non commital on which will be used in final version. However, since upbeat version was used at press review, it's safe to assume that it's in the lead.

Fast-paced screenplay, from novel by British Comdr. D. A. Rayner, starts with DE's radar contact with the surfaced sub, then follows the pursuit, combat and eventual death of both vessels. Mainly, story concentrates on maneuvers of both captains, as they try for the single mistake on their enemy's part which will end the contest. Finale has two skippers' respectful courtesies on board a rescuing Yank destroyer, after Jurgens's second-in-command Theodore Bikel's burial at sea.

To soft-soap the German side of the fight for American audiences, Jurgens is quickly established as an anti-Nazi, old-line navy man, doing his sworn duty without too much enthusiasm. Mitchum is established as a veteran sub hunter who takes over a new command and has to win his crew's respect, as well as whip them into shape. He does this with fine results, foregoing most of his usual screen mannerisms.

•

ENEMY FROM SPACE
SEE: QUATERMASS 2

•

ENEMY MINE
1985, 108 mins, US Ⓥ ⊙ ▭ col
Dir Wolfgang Petersen *Prod* Stephen Friedman *Scr* Edward Khmara *Ph* Tony Imi *Ed* Hannes Nikel *Mus* Maurice Jarre *Art* Rolf Zehetbauer
Act Dennis Quaid, Louis Gossett, Jr., Brion James, Richard Marcus, Carolyn McCormick, Bumper Robinson (Kings Road/20th Century-Fox)

Enemy Mine is a friendship story [by Barry Longyear] between two disparate personalities carried to extreme lengths. It may be a long way to go to a distant sun system to get to a familiar place, but the $33 million project is largely successful in establishing a satisfying bond.

Story is set up by a kind of videogame battle between the Earth forces and the warring Dracs from the distant planet of Dracon. Space pilot Willis Davidge (Dennis Quaid) goes down with a Drac ship, and is the only survivor on a desolate planet. His initial response to the half human–half-reptilian is inbred hatred, distrust and combativeness, all recognizable human triggers.

Hostility soon gives way to a common goal—survival. Davidge and the Drac (Louis Gossett, Jr.) peel away their outer layers and reveal two similar beings. It's an anthropomorphic view of life but touching nonetheless.

•

ENEMY OF THE PEOPLE, AN
1978, 103 mins, US Ⓥ col
Dir George Schaefer *Prod* George Schaefer *Scr* Alexander Jacobs *Ph* Paul Lohman *Ed* Sheldon Kahn *Mus* Leonard Rosenman *Art* Eugene Lourie
Act Steve McQueen, Charles Durning, Bibi Andersson, Eric Christmas, Michael Cristofer, Richard Dysart (First Artists/Solar)

Transferring stage works to the screen has always been a procedure fraught with peril, and *An Enemy of the People* fails to avoid the obvious pitfalls.

The Henrik Ibsen drama, which was first performed in 1883, concerns a small-town doctor who discovers that his village's new hot springs spa is contaminated by tannery waste. Over the objections of the town leaders (particularly his brother, the mayor), he attempts to publicize the scandal, only to be declared a social outcast, his family and career ruined.

Steve McQueen wanted to do the Ibsen work itself, and that was his undoing. While *An Enemy of the People* has much relevance to current ecological dilemmas, the script, based on an Arthur Miller adaptation, isn't content to simply raise the issues. They are proclaimed in ringing tones, intensifying the preachiness of a work that is already condescending to its audience.

The imbalance wouldn't be so pronounced were Charles Durning not so magnificent in the role of the harshly realistic brother. Without an adequate presence to balance Durning's domination of the proceedings, *Enemy* founders in a sea of verbiage.

•

ENEMY OF THE STATE
1998, 127 MINS, US Ⓥ ⊙ ▭ col
Dir Tony Scott *Prod* Jerry Bruckheimer *Scr* David Marconi *Ph* Dan Mindel *Ed* Chris Lebenzon *Mus* Trevor Rabin *Art* Benjamin Fernandez
Act Will Smith, Gene Hackman, Jon Voight, Lisa Bonet, Regina King, Stuart Wilson (Simpson-Bruckheimer/Touchstone)

Tony Scott's political thriller aspires to the level of the great '70s cycle of conspiracy-paranoia pictures. Reteaming with producer Jerry Bruckheimer for the fifth time and with his *Crimson Tide* actor Gene Hackman, Scott shrewdly uses the very likeable Will Smith in the classic role of an innocent Everyman framed for murder by a corrupt intelligence officer for unwittingly possessing vital information.

In a powerful pre-credits sequence, a congressman (an unbilled Jason Robards) is murdered by Thomas Brian Reynolds (Jon Voight), an ambitious National Security Agency official, in a public park. A nature photographer, Zavitz (Jason Lee), has filmed the incident and now possesses the incriminating video.

In the first of half-a-dozen chase scenes, Zavitz accidentally bumps into old college friend Robert Clayton Dean (Smith), a young hotshot attorney, slips Dean the evidence and embroils him in a cover-up that increasingly grows out of proportion.

It takes precisely an hour for Hackman to show up as Brill, a mysterious underground information broker with a chip on his shoulder. Once Brill steps onto the scene, the whole picture brightens up with much needed tension, and Hackman endows his role, which recalls his characterization in *The Conversation*, with subversive edge and humor. Brill reps Dean's only hope for survival.

Though intended as a cautionary tale about the evils of surveillance, pic doesn't manifest the collective fears generated by the classic paranoia movies for the very reason that the zeitgeist has changed. Scott and scripter David Marconi's strategy for rejuvinating the genre is to stress the techno aspects—and speed up the action. Voight scores big as a ruthless officer, "America's ultimate guardian," who sadly realizes he may never become the agency's head.

Production values are ultra-polished down the line.

•

ENFANT SAUVAGE, L'
(WILD CHILD))
1970, 85 mins, France Ⓥ ⊙ b/w
Dir Francois Truffaut *Prod* Marcel Berbent *Scr* Francois Truffaut, Jean Gruault *Ph* Nestor Almendros *Ed* Agnes Guillemot *Art* Jean Mandroux
Act Jean-Pierre Cargol, Francois Truffaut, Jean Daste, Francoise Seigner, Paul Ville, Claude Miller (Films du Carrosse/Artistes Associes)

This is a lucid, penetrating detailing of a young doctor's attempt to civilize a retarded boy found living in the woods in Southern France in the 18th century. Though based on a true case [Jean Itard's *Memoire et Rapport sur Victor de L'Aveyron*, published in 1806], it eschews didactics and creates a poetic, touching and dignified relationship between the doctor and his savage charge.

Director Francois Truffaut himself plays the young doctor at a deaf-and-dumb school in Paris who takes in the 11- or 12-year-old savage into his personal care to try to turn him into a presentable human being.

The boy is first seen frightening a woman out picking berries and then being captured by a group of peasants. He is naked, caked with dirt and ferocious. Locked up by the police, he is then transferred to the school in Paris. Head there feels the boy may be an idiot but consents to experiment. Main body of the film is the teaching and attempts to break through to the boy's inherent (the doctor believes) humanity.

It progresses slowly but absorbingly. Truffaut underplays but exudes an interior tenderness and dedication. The boy is amazingly and intuitively well played by a tousled gypsy tyke named Jean-Pierre Cargol. Everybody connected with this unusual, off-beat film made in black and white rates kudos.

•

ENFANTS DU PARADIS, LES
(CHILDREN OF PARADISE)
1945, 188 mins, France Ⓥ ⊙ b/w
Dir Marcel Carne ***Prod*** Raymond Borderie ***Scr*** Jacques Prevert ***Ph*** Roger Hubert ***Ed*** Henry Rust ***Mus*** Maurice Thiriet, Joseph Kosma ***Art*** Leon Barsacq, Raymond Gabutti, Alexandre Trauner
Act Arletty, Jean-Louis Barrault, Pierre Brasseur, Marcel Herrand, Pierre Renoir, Maria Casares (Pathe)

This ambitious French film turns out to be a strange mixture of the beautiful, the esoteric and the downright dull. Some startling flashes of inspired mimicry and fresh Gallic humor are wedded to the not un-Hollywoodian concept of the femme fatale who, willy-nilly in this instance, leads men to their ruin in an uneven performance of writing and direction.

Les Enfants du Paradis borrows its title from the denizens (reminiscent of those old silents depicting mobs in French revolution scenes) who frequented the top gallery of a dreary little theater in the Paris of the 1840s. Its poetical concept is to present the world's charade, in which the theater's actors and actresses take part, with the Shakespearian view that life's a stage and those upon it poor players.

Covering a stretch of years in the lives of a players' troupe, the leisurely tale centers on a mimic, Baptiste (Jean-Louis Barrault), and his other-world passion for a demimonde, Garance (Arletty), who moves through the seamy Parisian environs, bestowing her charms on those she likes—but not for coin. Arletty is also pursued by a flamboyant confrere of Barrault's (Pierre Brasseur); by a sinister cutthroat (Marcel Herrand); and an aristocrat (Louis Salou) whose attention is transfixed by Arletty's stage appearance. Hanging on the fringe is Nathalie (Maria Casares), hopelessly in love with Barrault.

Barrault is brilliantly effective as the sensitive, lovelorn mimic. Other lead parts are sharply defined and maintained consistently in a film that is a peak of thespian artistry.

[Version reviewed was a 144-min., inadequately subtitled one released in New York in 1947. Complete version is in two parts: *Le Boulevard du Crime/The Boulevard of Crime* runs 100 mins. and ends with the police questioning Garance; *L'homme Blanc/The Man in White* runs 88 mins.]

•

ENFANTS TERRIBLES, LES
1950, 102 mins, France ⊙ b/w
Dir Jean-Pierre Melville ***Prod*** Jean-Pierre Melville ***Scr*** Jean-Pierre Melville, Jean Cocteau ***Ph*** Henri Decae ***Ed*** Monique Bonnot ***Mus*** Paul Bonneau (dir.) ***Art*** Mathys
Act Nicole Stephane, Edouard Dermithe, Renee Cosima, Jacques Bernard, Roger Gaillard, Melvyn Martin (Melville)

Pic is an avant-garde treatment of an enticing psychological subject. Treatment is unorthodox, full of symbolism and deals with the strange inner world of a strongly attached brother and sister. Jean Cocteau has written the pic and delivers the commentary, which creates a gripping, dreamlike attraction.

A brother and sister live together in a strange littered room. The room is their world and soon takes on a grotesque atmosphere. They rarely venture into the outer world, for they are inbred, selfish, self-dramatizing and inescapably two parts of a single whole. When they do venture out, it leads to some hilarious escapades with their wonder at the world and their complete break with convention. Strange relationship finally leads to tragedy.

Jean-Pierre Melville directs with intelligence, and though working in close quarters, has captured all the suggestiveness and subtleties of the high-powered relationship. Lensing is helpful in sustaining the mood and the editing is effective.

Nicole Stephane, as the sister, is brilliant in the subtelty and neurotic strength she brings to the part. Edouard Dermithe is unsure of himself as the weak-willed brother. American singer Melvyn Martin figures in one scene and gets off a song.

•

ENFORCER, THE
(UK: MURDER, INC.)
1951, 86 mins, US Ⓥ ▭ b/w
Dir Bretaigne Windust, [Raoul Walsh] ***Prod*** Milton Sperling ***Scr*** Martin Rackin ***Ph*** Robert Burks ***Ed*** Fred Allen ***Mus*** David Buttolph ***Art*** Charles H. Clarke
Act Humphrey Bogart, Zero Mostel, Ted De Corsia, Everett Sloane, Roy Roberts, King Donovan (United States/Warner)

The film plays fast and excitingly in dealing with Humphrey Bogart's efforts to bring the head of a gang of killers to justice. The script uses the flashback technique to get the story on film, but it is wisely used so as not to tip the ending and spoil suspense.

Footage kicks off with a brief prolog by Senator Estes Kefauver, crime investigation committee head, explaining necessity of bringing crooks to justice. Story starts with Bogart ready to crack a case on which he has worked four years; he has a witness who can pin a murder rap on the gang head. However, the witness, in fear, escapes and falls to his death. Seeking to find some other tiny clue in the bulk of evidence, Bogart reviews the material gathered over the long years, permitting flashbacks into the past, and finally picks a single twist that gives him his lead and sets up an exciting finale.

Bretaigne Windust's direction is thorough, never missing an opportunity to sharpen suspense values, and the tension builds constantly.

•

ENFORCER, THE
1976, 96 mins, US Ⓥ ⊙ col
Dir James Fargo ***Prod*** Robert Daley ***Scr*** Stirling Silliphant, Dean Reisner ***Ph*** Charles W. Short ***Ed*** Ferris Webster, Joel Cox ***Mus*** Jerry Fielding ***Art*** Allen E. Smith
Act Clint Eastwood, Harry Guardino, Bradford Dillman, John Mitchum, DeVeren Bookwalter, Tyne Daly (Warner)

The bad guys in this third installment from Dirty Harry's life include not only the archly defined criminals (here, DeVeren Bookwalter and a group of post-Vietnam gun crazies), but also his police and political superiors—like Bradford Dillman, captain of detectives, and John Crawford, whose characterization of the mayor is one of the few highlights. Harry Guardino has the role of a weak-kneed detective. Tyne Daly's casting as a femme cop injects some predictable, but enjoyable, male chauvinism sparks in dialog between her and Clint Eastwood.

The spitball script [from a story by Gail Morgan Hickman and S. W. Schurr] lurches along, stopping periodically for the bloodlettings and assorted running and jumping and chasing stuff.

•

ENGLAND MADE ME
1973, 100 mins, UK Ⓥ col
Dir Peter Duffell ***Prod*** Jack Levin ***Scr*** Peter Duffell, Desmond Cory ***Ph*** Ray Parslow ***Ed*** Malcolm Cooke ***Mus*** John Scott ***Art*** Tony Woollard
Act Peter Finch, Michael York, Hildegard Neil, Michael Hordern, Joss Ackland, Tessa Wyatt (Atlantic)

England Made Me is the symbolic title for a tale of moral conflict set in prewar Germany, circa 1935. Based on an early Graham Greene novel, the film is also a well-observed evocation of time, place and mood, directed and coauthored by Peter Duffell with evident intelligence and sensitivity, if not optimum success.

Michael York plays an innocent idealist ultimately snuffed out by the intrigues and ruthlessness that marked Nazi Germany. The title is a reference to his character, his fairness and morality as shaped by a society where they were and are esteemed. Superficially he runs afoul of rascally Peter Finch's great financial empire based in Germany, but his goodness is in wider conflict with the coarsened values of decadence and nihilism.

Finch plays the ruthless financier with competence and physical presence while Hildegard Neil scores well as York's dominating older sister and Finch's mistress.

•

ENGLISHMAN WHO WENT UP A HILL BUT CAME DOWN A MOUNTAIN, THE
1995, 99 mins, UK Ⓥ ▭ col
Dir Christopher Monger ***Prod*** Sarah Curtis ***Scr*** Christopher Monger ***Ph*** Vernon Layton ***Ed*** David Martin ***Mus*** Stephen Endelman ***Art*** Charles Garrad
Act Hugh Grant, Tara Fitzgerald, Colm Meaney, Ian McNeice, Ian Hart, Kenneth Griffith (Parallax)

A flyweight, if well-crafted, load of malarkey with charm to burn, this tale of eccentric country folk confronting slightly stodgy civil servants comes off as an amusing anachronism.

The title character is Reginald Anson (Hugh Grant), a cartographer sent to Wales in 1917 to officially map out the terrain. The villagers take particular pride that the country's "first mountain" looms above them. But when Anson and colleague George Garrad (Ian McNeice) return with news that their mountain, Ffynnon Garw, is in fact a hill, civility becomes unusually strained.

The government has decreed that elevations of more than 1,000 feet will be designated as mountains. According to the pair's measurements, Ffynnon Garw is 984 feet high. So, the only viable solution is to tear up the earth and assist Mother Nature with another 20 feet.

It's obvious that writer-director Christopher Monger loves the lore of his homeland; he gives his film [adapted from his own novel] the quality of a tale told with relish round the campfire. But no amount of gussying-up can disguise its narrative modesty.

Grant, though a gifted farceur, is cast effectively as a callow romantic who goes native. Tara Fitzgerald, as Betty of Cardiff, draws him out for the sake of local pride, but, not surprisingly, something more sincere evolves.

•

ENGLISH PATIENT, THE
1996, 162 mins, US Ⓥ ⊙ col
Dir Anthony Minghella ***Prod*** Saul Zaentz ***Scr*** Anthony Minghella ***Ph*** John Seale ***Ed*** Walter Murch ***Mus*** Gabriel Yared ***Art*** Stuart Craig
Act Ralph Fiennes, Juliette Binoche, Willem Dafoe, Kristin Scott Thomas, Naveen Andrews, Colin Firth (Zaentz)

Long, involving and rather parched emotionally, *The English Patient* is a respectable, intelligent, but less-than-stirring adaptation of Michael Ondaatje's imposingly dense and layered 1992 novel. All the artistic elements have been assembled with great care by producer Saul Zaentz. All the same, film has been nudged in the direction of fairly conventional adulterous melodrama, even as the characters' British reserve keeps the central romance somewhat restrained.

Set against the stunning backdrops of pre-war North Africa and the end of hostilities in Italy, action begins with a spectacular, fiery plane crash in the desert, after which the scorched survivor and title character (Ralph Fiennes) is tended to by Canadian nurse Hana (Juliette Binoche) in the ruins of a Tuscan monastery. In intriguing flashbacks that unfurl slowly like the opening of a scroll, the English patient's strange and ultimately traumatic tale is revealed.

In fact, he is a Hungarian count named Almasy, a dashingly attractive but detached young man based in Cairo in 1938 helping make maps of uncharted desert areas for the British. His aloofness is broken by the arrival of two young Brits, newlyweds Geoffrey and Katharine Clifton (Colin Firth, Kristin Scott Thomas). Resist their mutual attraction as they may, Almasy and Katharine are ultimately stranded together in the desert in a way that makes their affair inevitable.

Fiennes's character remains at a remove, making the film more a clinical study of a complicated life and romance rather than a deeply felt expression of it. As his partner, Scott Thomas gets the chance to be more outgoing, and the actress' customary sharp intelligence and provocatively direct manner are in full working order.

With its exotic, tapestry-like backgrounds, this is a picture of resplendently textured, sensuous surfaces, beginning with the sunbaked Tunisian desert.

1996: Best Picture, Supp. Actress (Juliette Binoche), Director, Cinematography, Editing, Original Dramatic Score, Art Direction, Costume Design (Ann Roth), Sound

NOMINATIONS: Actor (Ralph Fiennes), Actress (Kristin Scott Thomas), Screenplay Adaptation

•

ENIGMA
1983, 101 mins, UK/France Ⓥ ⊙ col
Dir Jeannot Szwarc ***Prod*** Peter Shaw ***Scr*** John Briley ***Ph*** Jean-Louis Picavet ***Ed*** Peter Weatherley ***Mus*** Marc Wilkinson, Douglas Gamley ***Art*** Francois Comtat
Act Martin Sheen, Brigitte Fossey, Sam Neill, Derek Jacobi, Michael Lonsdale, Frank Finlay (Archerwest/SFPC)

Enigma is a well-made but insufficiently exciting spy thriller which rather pleasingly emphasizes the emotional vulnerabilities of the pawns caught up in East–West intrigue.

Martin Sheen ably portrays an East German refugee who, after working as a Radio Free Europe–type broadcaster out of Paris, is recruited by the CIA to return to East Berlin. Assignment: steal a coded microprocessor, or scrambler, from the Russians before the KGB proceeds with the assassination of five Soviet dissidents in the West.

After neatly making his way to his destination, Sheen locates old flame Brigitte Fossey who, while resisting the idea of resuming their romance, sympathizes with his unexplained cause.

John Briley's screenplay [from the novel *Enigma Sacrifice* by Michael Barak] keeps everything coherent, not always easy with this sort of fare, and Jeannot Szwarc's direction is very handsome indeed.

•

ENORMOUS CHANGES AT THE LAST MINUTE
1983, 110 mins, US Ⓥ ⦿ col
Dir Mirra Bank, Ellen Hovde, Muffie Meyer ***Prod*** Mirra Bank ***Scr*** John Sayles, Susan Rice ***Ph*** Tom McDonough ***Ed*** Mirra Bank, Ellen Hovde, Muffie Meyer ***Mus*** Peter Link
Act Ellen Barkin, Kevin Bacon, Maria Tucci, Lynn Milgrim, Sudie Bond, Ron McLarty (Ordinary Lives)

Enormous Changes at the Last Minute is an enormously uneven trilogy of modern urban woman's dilemma in the precarious area of relationships with men [from stories by Grace Paley].

Pic is first fictional feature for the three producer/directors, Mirra Bank, Ellen Hovde and Muffie Meyer, all film editors. First vignette [directed by Hovde and Meyer] pits Virginia (Ellen Barkin) as a housewife with three kids who is newly deserted by her husband. Barkin succumbs to the advances of a former boyfriend (now married with kids), who is also the landlord's son.

In second entry, Faith (Lynn Milgrim) makes a trek to visit her artsy, literary parents in an old-age Jewish residence, to tell her father that she's separated from her husband, Ricardo. This is the weakest and least successful section, failing to capture the potential intimacy and poignancy of the encounter. [Seg, by Bank and Hovde, was shot earliest, in 1978.]

Alexandra (Maria Tucci) is a middle-aged, divorced, social worker who has a ludicrous affair with frenetic cab driver/punk rocker Dennis (Kevin Bacon). When Alexandra becomes pregnant by Dennis she vehemently decides to go it alone and raise it herself. Dennis is hurt and confused by his forced exclusion from the event. [This seg directed by Bank.]

•

ENTER ARSENE LUPIN
1944, 72 mins, US b/w
Dir Ford Beebe ***Prod*** Ford Beebe ***Scr*** Bertram Millhauser ***Ph*** Hal Mohr ***Ed*** Saul A. Goodkind ***Mus*** Milton Rosen ***Art*** John B. Goodman, Abraham Grossman
Act Charles Korvin, Ella Raines, J. Carrol Naish, George Dolenz, Gale Sondergaard (Universal)

Enter Arsene Lupin a Universal cops-and-robbers saga, French style, is a slick enough combination of romance, action and suspense, and offset phony, farfetched plot.

Part of appeal is romantic team of Charles Korvin and Ella Raines in some torrid moments. Korvin isn't much of an actor, but he has the Continental ease of manner and an attractive face to catch the femme trade. Also a draw is the flavorsome caricature of a stupid French detective which J. Carrol Naish, in a change of pace from gangster roles, plays very amusingly, even if he does milk role.

Yarn concerns [Maurice LeBlanc's character] Lupin, renowned suave French thief, who robs a lady of her fabulous emerald on the Paris-Constantinople express. Pic is produced on good scale, with some rich interiors, to help illusion. Raines adds glamour and beauty to role of heiress, and Gale Sondergaard is menacing enough as one of sleek, murderous cousins.

•

ENTERTAINER, THE
1960, 96 mins, UK Ⓥ ⦿ b/w
Dir Tony Richardson ***Prod*** Henry Saltzman ***Scr*** John Osborne, Nigel Kneale ***Ph*** Oswald Morris ***Ed*** Alan Osbiston ***Mus*** John Addison
Act Laurence Olivier, Brenda de Banzie, Joan Plowright, Roger Livesey, Alan Bates, Albert Finney (Woodfall/Bryanston)

There was a bit of a hassle over [the release of] *The Entertainer*, what with arguments with the censor, the film having to be redubbed and cut from 104 to 96 minutes and held over for three months before its West End showing. This version of John Osborne's play is raw, but vital stuff, which you'll either like or loathe.

The yarn is mainly a seedy character study of a broken-down, disillusioned vaude artiste with more optimism than talent, and of the various members of his family and their reactions to his problems. So it depends mainly on the thesping and the direction.

Tony Richardson, the director, makes several mistakes. But he has a sharp perception of camera angles, stimulates some good performances and, particularly, whips up an excellent atmosphere of a smallish British seaside resort.

Mainly, the interest is held by the acting and here there is a lot to praise, if some that may be condemned. The stage sequences in which the third-rate comedian, Archie Rice (Laurence Olivier), has to put over some tatty material in a broken-down show does not come over as effectively as it did on the stage. He is far happier in other sequences. The way he allows his sleazy facade to slip by a twist of the mouth, a throw-away line or a look in the eyes is quite brilliant.

Joan Plowright brings warmth and intelligence to the role of the loyal daughter while Roger Livesey, as Olivier's father, is sympathetic and completely believable. Brenda de Banzie's role, as Olivier's wife, is at times irritating.

1960: NOMINATION: Best Actor (Laurence Olivier)

•

ENTERTAINER, THE
1975, 105 mins, US/Australia Ⓥ col
Dir Donald Wrye ***Prod*** Beryl Vertue, Marvin Hamlisch ***Scr*** Elliott Baker ***Ph*** James Crabe ***Mus*** Marvin Hamlish ***Art*** Bob Mackichan
Act Jack Lemmon, Ray Bolger, Sada Thompson, Tyne Daly, Michael Cristofer, Annette O'Toole (Stigwood/Persky-Bright)

This basically is the John Osborne play in which Laurence Olivier made such an impact. Setting is now America instead of England and period switched from Suez crisis days to 1944.

This time around it's Jack Lemmon as second-rate vaudevillian Archie Rice, desperately trying for laughs from nearly empty houses.

With debt problems, Archie meets Bambi Pasko, a young beauty with little talent but a rich father and starstruck mother. Archie persuades them to back a new show that will feature Bambi, whom he seduces, promising to marry.

Archie's father, Billy, hears of the plan, and he informs the Paskos Archie is already married; they immediately pull out of the new show, and when Billy realizes Archie will face prison, he agrees to return to the stage and saves the day.

Lemmon gives a fine performance as Archie, though is not so awful as he should be on stage.

•

ENTERTAINING MR. SLOANE
1970, 94 mins, UK Ⓥ col
Dir Douglas Hickox ***Prod*** Douglas Kentis ***Scr*** Clive Exton ***Ph*** Wolfgang Suschitzky ***Ed*** John Trumper ***Mus*** Georgie Fame ***Art*** Michael Seymour
Act Beryl Reid, Peter McEnery, Harry Andrews, Alan Webb (Canterbury)

The sacred cow of "good taste" is in for a battering with *Entertaining Mr. Sloane*, based on Joe Orton's play. *Sloane* blends morbid humor, an obsession with sex and an underlying pathos, and result is interest that is always held.

It's no detraction from the rest of the cast to say that it is firmly Beryl Reid's picture. She gives a memorable study of a middle-aged, flabby, arch "nymphette," hazily pining for a lost love.

Her brother (Harry Andrews) also falls for Sloane's superficial charm and makes him his chauffeur, clearly with more furtive and kinky motives.

Director Douglas Hickox, who does an astute job, though sometimes his direction meanders slightly, has opened up the play a little, though not at the expense of the claustrophobic atmosphere.

•

ENTER THE DRAGON
1973, 98 mins, US/Hong Kong Ⓥ ⦿ ⌑ col
Dir Robert Clouse ***Prod*** Fred Weintraub, Paul Heller, Raymond Chow ***Scr*** Michael Allin ***Ph*** Gilbert Hubbs ***Ed*** Kurt Hirschler, George Watters ***Mus*** Lalo Schifrin ***Art*** James Wong Sun
Act Bruce Lee, John Saxon, Jim Kelly, Shih Kien, Bob Wall, Angela Mao (Warner/Concord)

Enter the Dragon marks the final appearance of Bruce Lee, who died suddenly in Hong Kong on July 20, 1973, only a few weeks after he completed the film.

Film is rich in the atmosphere of the Orient, where it was lensed in its entirety, and brims with frequent encounters in the violent arts. Lee plays a James Bond–type of super-secret agent, past-master in Oriental combat, who takes on the assignment of participating in brutal martial arts competition as a cover for investigating the suspected criminal activities of the man staging this annual tournament.

Lee socks over a performance seldom equalled in action. John Saxon, as an American expert drawn to the tournament, is surprisingly adept in his action scenes.

Robert Clouse's realistic direction results in constant fast play by all the principals.

•

ENTER THE NINJA
1982, 99 mins, US Ⓥ col
Dir Menahem Golan ***Prod*** Judd Bernard, Yoram Globus ***Scr*** Dick Desmond ***Ph*** David Gurfinkel ***Ed*** Mark Goldblatt, Michael Duthie ***Mus*** W. Michael Lewis, Laurin Rinder
Act Franco Nero, Susan George, Sho Kosugi, Alex Courtney, Will Hare, Christopher George (Cannon)

Enter the Ninja represents an unusual hybrid action film, an Italian Western–type story filmed as a contemporary Japanese martial arts action film in the Philippines. Results are pleasant though unspectacular.

After a misjudged opening consisting of a series of bloody one-on-one battles later revealed to be just a phony graduation exercise for American ninjitsu student Cole (Franco Nero), pic settles down to a simple landgrabbers story.

Cole arrives to help his old mercenary fighter buddy Landers (Alex Courtney) fight off various nasties out to steal away his plantation to exploit its oil rights. Landers's tough cookie wife (Susan George sporting a very sexy and giggly bra-less look) is on hand to help out.

Well-photographed pic is heavy on the chop-socky stuff, with baddie Venarius (Christopher George) hiring a real Japanese ninja (Sho Kosugi) to neutralize Cole.

•

ENTRAPMENT
1999, 112 mins, US Ⓥ ⦿ ⌑ col
Dir Jon Amiel ***Prod*** Sean Connery, Michael Hertzberg, Rhonda Tollefson ***Scr*** Ron Bass, William Broyles ***Ph*** Phil Meheux ***Ed*** Terry Rawlings ***Mus*** Christopher Young ***Art*** Norman Garwood
Act Sean Connery, Catherine Zeta-Jones, Ving Rhames, Will Patton, Maury Chaykin (Fountainbridge/New Regency/20th Century-Fox)

Designed as a romantic caper for Y2K, *Entrapment* is preposterous whimsy that sort of gets by thanks to its lustrous settings, slick production values and especially, its ultra-attractive stars. A throwback to the lightweight globetrotting thrillers of the '60s, pic concocts a gigantic heist that can take place only on Millennium Eve. It works only as a dollop of make-believe, an opportunity to gaze at Sean Connery and Catherine Zeta-Jones magnetically pretending to enact a wary mating dance.

After a Rembrandt is stolen from a New York high-rise, insurance investigator Gin Baker (Zeta-Jones) convinces her boss, Hector Cruz (Will Patton), that the culprit is legendary art thief Robert "Mac" MacDougal (Connery) and gets the green light to track him down in London. Mac gets the upper hand, whisking her off to his castle in Scotland.

Acknowledging they can't possibly trust each other yet, the two nonetheless plot a job together that takes the picture through its first hour, then hightail it to Malaysia where she unveils her strategy for a stupendous computer heist. Fundamental silliness of the script [from a screen story by Ron Bass and Michael Hertzberg] is that Gin and Mac have precisely one day to prepare for a job that requires them to penetrate the elaborate security of the bank—scenically located in the tallest buildings in the world, the Petronas Twin Towers in Kuala Lumpur.

Idea has something to do with bank transfers that Gin believes she can intercept due to the computer changeovers required by arrival of the year 2000. Action climax makes full use of the ornate tapering towers.

•

EQUINOX
1992, 115 mins, US Ⓥ ⦿ col
Dir Alan Rudolph ***Prod*** David Blocker ***Scr*** Alan Rudolph ***Ph*** Elliot Davis ***Ed*** Michael Ruscio ***Art*** Steven Legler
Act Matthew Modine, Lara Flynn Boyle, Tyra Ferrell, Marisa Tomei, Kevin J. O'Connor, Lori Singer (SC Entertainment)

Equinox is one of Alan Rudolph's patently personal ensemble pieces about criss-crossing destinies. More socially minded in its depiction of a decaying society some of the characters yearn to escape, film is full of ideas and evocative scenes.

Matthew Modine toplines in a double role. Henry is an awkward, nerdy chap who remarks, "My whole life seems to be taking place without me in it," while being induced to reignite a tentative romance with the lovely, painfully shy Beverly (Lara Flynn Boyle). Modine also appears as Freddy, a swaggering, small-time hood who is married to Sharon (Lori Singer), and works his way up in a gang controlled by Paris (Fred Ward).

At the film's heart is a touching little-people romance between Henry and Beverly. Modine and Boyle, both very attractive performers, are effectively dressed down for these roles, and Boyle, in particular, strongly registers the effort it takes for such a thin-skinned character to leap off the deep end into the emotional whirlpool.

•

EQUUS
1977, 137 mins, US Ⓥ ⊙ col
Dir Sidney Lumet ***Prod*** Lester Persky ***Scr*** Peter Shaffer ***Ph*** Oswald Morris ***Ed*** John Victor-Smith ***Mus*** Richard Rodney Bennett ***Art*** Tony Walton
Act Richard Burton, Peter Firth, Colin Blakely, Joan Plowright, Harry Andrews, Eileen Atkins (United Artists)

Equus is an excellent example of film as theater. Peter Shaffer's play, which he adapted for the screen, has become under Sidney Lumet's outstanding direction a moving confrontation between a crudely mystical Peter Firth and the psychiatrist (Richard Burton), who is trying to unravel the boy's mind.

The (screen) story is properly oriented to that of a suspense yarn: why did Firth blind Harry Andrews's horses? Judge Eileen Atkins wants Burton to find out. In the process, Burton discerns the boy's transference of extremely physical religious devotion to Jesus, to the spirit Equus as embodied in horses.

Jenny Agutter is excellent as the young girl whose plausible emotional attitudes trigger the boy's outrage at his personal deity.

1977: NOMINATIONS: Best Actor (Richard Burton), Supp. Actor (Peter Firth), Adapted Screenplay

•

ERASER
1996, 115 mins, US Ⓥ ⊙ ▭ col
Dir Charles Russell ***Prod*** Arnold Kopelson, Anne Kopelson ***Scr*** Tony Puryear, Walon Green ***Ph*** Adam Greenberg ***Ed*** Michael Tronick ***Mus*** Alan Silvestri ***Art*** Bill Kenney
Act Arnold Schwarzenegger, James Caan, Vanessa Williams, James Coburn, Robert Pastorelli, James Cromwell (Warner)

Eraser is midlevel Arnold, a hardware-heavy, high-body-count actioner that tries to compensate for a B-movie script with advanced artillery and high-tech mayhem.

Script by newcomer Tony Puryear and vet Walon Green [from a screen story by them and Michael S. Chernuchin] centers upon Schwarzenegger's John Kruger, a government "eraser" expert at making witnesses disappear for their own safety. His new case isn't so easy: the witness in question, Lee Cullen (Vanessa Williams), has the goods on some turncoats in the defense field who plan to sell a load of top-secret super-guns.

From the beginning, characters are introduced just to serve as cannon fodder—in particular, Cullen's ex-b.f. and a reporter friend. After Kruger stashes Cullen safely in New York's Chinatown, it becomes apparent that she isn't safe after all, indicating a mole in the system and causing a confrontation between the steadfast Kruger and his boss and mentor, Deguerin (James Caan).

Looking leaner than usual, Schwarzenegger strides through the proceedings with his customary unhesitating purposefulness. Williams is similarly all business as the besieged young patriot willing to go the limit to expose government evildoers, while Caan schemes and threatens with evident glee.

Most of the gunplay is pretty standard issue. Special effects are mostly solid without being awe-inspiring or gargantuan.

1996: NOMINATION: Best Sound Effects Editing

•

ERASERHEAD
1977, 100 mins, US Ⓥ ⊙ b/w
Dir David Lynch ***Prod*** David Lynch ***Scr*** David Lynch ***Ph*** Fred Elms ***Ed*** David Lynch ***Mus*** Fats Waller ***Art*** David Lynch
Act Jack Nance, Charlotte Stewart, Jeanne Bates, Allen Josephs, Judith Anna Roberts, Laurel Near (AFI/Lynch)

Eraserhead is a sickening bad-taste exercise made by David Lynch under the auspices of the American Film Institute.

Set, apparently, in some undefined apocalyptic future era, *Eraserhead* consists mostly of a man sitting in a room trying to figure out what to do with his horribly mutated child. Lynch keeps throwing in graphic closeups of the piteous creature, and pulls out all gory stops in the unwatchable climax.

Like a lot of AFI efforts, the pic has good tech values (particularly the inventive sound mixing), but little substance or subtlety. The mind boggles to learn that Lynch labored on this pic for five years.

•

ERIK THE VIKING
1989, 103 mins, UK Ⓥ ⊙ col
Dir Terry Jones ***Prod*** John Goldstone ***Scr*** Terry Jones ***Ph*** Ian Wilson ***Ed*** George Akers ***Mus*** Neil Innes ***Art*** John Beard
Act Tim Robbins, Gary Cady, Mickey Rooney, Eartha Kitt, Terry Jones, John Cleese (Prominent)

The idea of telling the story of a Viking warrior who thought there must be more to life than rape and pillage is an amusing one, and for the most part *Erik the Viking* is an enjoyable film.

Pic opens with Erik (Tim Robbins) falling in love with a girl just as he kills her. Spurred by her death he decides to try and bring the Age of Ragnarok—where men fight and kill—to an end.

He sets off with an unruly band of followers—including the local blacksmith who wants Ragnarok to continue as it helps his sword-making business—and is pursued by Halfdan the Black (John Cleese), the local warlord who quite enjoys Ragnarok and wants it to continue.

American Tim Robbins is fine as the softly spoken and sensitive Erik, and especially seems to enjoy himself in the battle scenes. The film's great strength, though, is the Viking crew, which is full of wonderful characters, such as Tim McInnerny's manic Sven the Berserk, heavily disguised Antony Sher's scheming Loki and best of all Freddie Jones's put-upon missionary.

•

ERIN BROCKOVICH
2000, 131 mins, US Ⓥ ⊙ col
Dir Steven Soderbergh ***Prod*** Danny DeVito, Michael Shamberg, Stacey Sher ***Scr*** Susannah Grant ***Ph*** Ed Lachman ***Ed*** Anne V. Coates ***Mus*** Thomas Newman ***Art*** Phil Messina
Act Julia Roberts, Albert Finney, Aaron Eckhart, Marg Helgenberger, Cherry Jones, Peter Coyote (Jersey/Universal-Columbia)

An exhilarating tale about a woman discovering her full potential and running with it, *Erin Brockovich* is everything that "inspirational" true-life stories should be and rarely are. Vibrant and often quite funny in its account of how an unschooled, twice-divorced mother of three spearheads an investigation that leads to the largest payoff ever made in a direct-action lawsuit, this very satisfying picture takes Julia Roberts into more realistic performance territory than usual. Roberts has never been more winning, bringing the full force of her dazzling personality to bear on a character well on her way to being a total loser but who resolutely refuses to go that route. Some may carp that if you look like Julia Roberts, especially as she's tarted up here with eye-popping, cleavage-enhancing tops and miniskirts, a lot of doors will open that might be closed to others. But the film offers sly proof that the star's showy impersonation isn't a glamorization at all: The real Erin Brockovich, in briefly as a coffee shop waitress, appears to be every bit the knockout that Roberts is.

Based on a case that began developing in 1993, Susannah Grant's lively screenplay has the shape of such previous activist, David-and-Goliath stories as *Norma Rae* and *A Civil Action*, but smartly keeps the focus on its protagonist, stays almost entirely out of the courtroom and mercifully steers clear of easily programmed triumph-of-the-underdog sentimentality. Even when Erin is completely absorbed in her cause, one is constantly aware of the three kids who are resentfully missing their mother, but also of Erin's calculation that the pain and sacrifice might be well worth it.

Story is ultimately about how a downtrodden but determined woman fights to make her innate sense of self-worth stick and be acknowledged by the world. While never letting the film's sharp dramatic focus slacken, director Steven Soderbergh manages to keep things loose and nimble visually.

•

EROICA
1958, 83 mins, Poland b/w
Dir Andrzej Munk ***Scr*** Jerzy Stefan Stawinski ***Ph*** Jerzy Wojcik ***Ed*** Jadwiga Zaicek, Miroslawa Garlicka ***Mus*** Jan Krenz
Act Edward Dziewonski, Barbara Polomska, Leon Niemczyk, Jozef Nowak, Bogumil Kobiela, Tadeusz Lomnicki (Kadr)

Eroica consists of two separate stories [from novellas by Jerzy Stefan Stawinski], unrelated in themselves, but both concerned with an aspect of the disillusionment of Poles in the calamitous days of 1944.

Scherzo alla Polacca, the first vignette, treats this theme in comic form, with the hero cast as a disenchanted volunteer trying to avoid underground training for the Warsaw uprising. His drunkenness, disregard for safety and believable cowardice when sober are stated with humorous effect that often borders on the burlesque, but come out as something sane in a world gone mad. His will to survive finally becomes more acceptable than any desire for heroic death. Edward Dziewonski's portrayal of the cowardly hero is great.

Ostinato Lugubre, more assured as an episode, revolves around the grim joke in which a fictitious escapee from a German POW camp for Polish officers boosts the morale of his fellow prisoners. In point of fact, the "escapee" lies hidden from Germans and comrades alike to maintain the illusion that he did get away.

Technically the film is satisfactory, and music effective. Biggest plus is contained in the visual humor.

•

ERRAND BOY, THE
1961, 92 mins, US Ⓥ b/w
Dir Jerry Lewis ***Prod*** Ernest D. Glucksman ***Scr*** Jerry Lewis, Bill Richmond ***Ph*** W. Wallace Kelley ***Ed*** Stanley E. Johnson ***Mus*** Walter Scharf (arr.) ***Art*** Hal Pereira, Arthur Lonergan
Act Jerry Lewis, Brian Donlevy, Howard McNear, Dick Wesson, Robert Ivers, Pat Dahl (Lewis/Paramount)

The Errand Boy is one of the best and funniest Jerry Lewis pictures to come along. There is an underlying streak of satire that indicates Lewis is maturing as an artist beyond the sphere of the madcap slapstick-and-sentiment. The cream-pies-in-the-kisser are now being flung and licked with more finesse.

Like *The Bellboy* (1960), production is a necklace of related comic situations—some of them cultured pearls of humor, some of them duds. Here Lewis is spoofing something that can stand spoofing—the pretentiousness of certain aspects of filmdom. Often he fails in development of his premises, too often he settles for the antique gag and the obvious or unfulfilled climax, but his film is a success as a whole.

•

ESCAPADE
1935, 93 mins, US b/w
Dir Robert Z. Leonard ***Prod*** Bernard H. Hyman ***Scr*** Walter Reisch, Herman J. Mankiewicz ***Ph*** Ernest Haller ***Ed*** Tom Held ***Mus*** Bronislau Kaper, Walter Jurmann
Act William Powell, Luise Rainer, Virginia Bruce, Frank Morgan, Reginald Owen, Mady Christians (M-G-M)

Escapade, besides being deft and amusing light comedy, is notable as the film introducing Luise Rainer to American audiences. Myrna Loy was originally slated for the part, but walked out. Rainer, the legend goes, had been doing nothing around the studio for quite a spell waiting for the right casting opportunity. It fit her perfectly.

Escapade was made as *Maskerade* in Vienna. Metro bought the print and the script [by Walter Reisch] and had Herman J. Mankiewicz write and Robert Z. Leonard direct an all-new Hollywood version.

Story concerns a sophisticated young rake (William Powell), who tumbles in love with an innocent sprite (Rainer), whose naivete is in marked contrast to the amorous Viennese beauties who have been chasing the debonair gent. Farcical and melodramatic complications concern the accidental publication of a semi-nude drawing for which a willing-to-philander married lady (Virginia Bruce) has posed in violation of the prewar proprieties. Her husband (Frank Morgan) believes that his brother's fiancé (Mady Christians) is the real wayward lassie.

Mady Christians, a star in foreign films and upon the New York legit stage, reveals herself an actress of fine capabilities, and the pert minx of Virginia Bruce is also standout on the performance end.

Nobody, of course, will be making any "discovery" of William Powell, for his professional skill is taken for granted. Rainer acts with her brain. Robert Leonard gives her a swell set of bell-ringing closeups.

•

ESCAPE, THE
1914, 81 mins, US d Ⓥ b/w
Dir D. W. Griffith ***Scr*** D. W. Griffith ***Ph*** Billy Bitzer ***Ed*** James E. Smith, Rose Smith
Act Donald Crisp, Robert Harron, Blanche Sweet, Mae Marsh (Reliance)

Adapted for the sheet from Paul Armstrong's stage play, this isn't a "vice picture," though it does step into the below the line stuff now and then. The tale is hung upon one of those all-wrong families on the East Side where the all-wrongness runs from the father down to the dog, if there is one. In this case the family, real name Joyce, consists of a father, two sisters and a son. The film goes in the tenement house where they live to find misery, and gets nothing else. Even when Owen Moore, as the ambulance surgeon, later a practicing physician, tells May (Blanche Sweet), one of the daughters, he loves her, Owen does it with here's-taking-a-chance look on his face, and May seems to look on the only love affair she has ever known the same as anything else.

It seems foolish to waste the ability and energy of an able director of the Griffith stamp upon a scenario like *The Escape*.

●

ESCAPE
1930, 70 mins, UK/US b/w
Dir Basil Dean ***Prod*** Basil Dean ***Scr*** Basil Dean ***Ph*** Jack Mackenzie ***Ed*** Milner Kitchin
Act Gerald Du Maurier, Edna Best, Mabel Poulton, Madeleine Carroll, Gordon Harker, Austin Trevor (Associated Talking/RKO)

The first of a series of films made in England in conjunction with RKO. As a play John Galsworthy's *Escape* was a hit, but the film suffers by being made mostly with stage players, who do not generally adapt themselves to the screen. This particularly applies to Gerald Du Maurier, who overemphasizes everything.

It tells how a man is sentenced to five years for killing a policeman. The prisoner, perfect English gentleman, doesn't like being treated roughly and escapes.

In approved Galsworthy fashion, the film draws a long simile between a hunted prisoner and foxhunting. As propaganda against bloodsports the picture achieves a certain power.

Cast carries a long list of English stage and screen names, with only Du Maurier having a long role.

Basil Dean's direction is sympathetic no more. Photography scores aces over the lot.

●

ESCAPE
1940, 104 mins, US b/w
Dir Mervyn LeRoy ***Scr*** Arch Oboler, Marguerite Roberts ***Ph*** Robert Planck ***Ed*** George Boemler
Act Norma Shearer, Robert Taylor, Conrad Veidt, Nazimova, Felix Bressart, Albert Basserman (M-G-M)

Authorship of one of 1939's bestselling pieces of fiction, a novel entitled *Escape*, was ascribed to a mysterious Ethel Vance, whose identity was shrouded in mystery under the promotional idea that the revelations of her (his?) plot might inspire Nazi reprisals. *Escape* is laid in Germany, near the Swiss border, and the action takes place soon before the start of World War II when the secret police were terrorizing natives and foreign visitors.

It is excellent, suspenseful material and director Mervyn LeRoy succeeds admirably in sustaining throughout the picture a tense atmosphere of impending danger to the lives and limbs of his actors.

Robert Taylor is the heroic young American who naively brushes against Nazi officialdom while on a search for his mother, lately returned to Germany. She has disappeared after participating in a real estate deal.

Aid is furnished by Norma Shearer, who plays the Countess Von Treck, school mistress and just plain mistress of the cultured Conrad Veidt, a German general, who tempers cruelty with love for Wagnerian music.

The character roles are standouts. Philip Dorn, a young Hollander, makes his initial appearance in an American film in the part of the accomplice, Ritter. Felix Bressart is the old family friend and attendant, and although Albert Basserman has only a brief bit to do, he does it excellently.

●

ESCAPE ARTIST, THE
1982, 93 mins, US Ⓥ col
Dir Caleb Deschanel ***Prod*** Doug Claybourne, Buck Houghton ***Scr*** Melissa Mathison, Stephen Zito ***Ph*** Stephen H. Burum ***Ed*** Arthur Schmidt ***Mus*** Georges Delerue ***Art*** Dean Tavoularis
Act Griffin O'Neal, Raul Julia, Teri Garr, Joan Hackett, Gabriel Dell, Jackie Coogan (Zoetrope)

The Escape Artist is a muted fable [from the novel by David Wagoner] about a gifted child in a never-never-land America. Treatment frequently pushes past the careful to the precious, and the quiet, odd tale never becomes more than mildly intriguing.

After brash but not arrogant youth Griffin O'Neal issues a challenge to the police department that he can break out of their jail in one hour, story flips into an hour-long flashback.

O'Neal imposes himself on his aunt and uncle, small-time vaudevillians, essayed by Joan Hackett and Gabriel Dell, and begins making trouble for himself and the entire Midwestern town by making off with the loot-filled wallet of the corrupt mayor's son, played as a real looney tune by Raul Julia.

It all ends with O'Neal royally turning the tables on Julia and mayor Desiderio (Desi) Arnaz.

In his film debut, O'Neal, who is Ryan's son and Tatum's brother, comes across as spry and able, but seems to come fully alive only in the confrontation scenes with Julia and in a nice flirtation with young waitress Elizabeth Daily.

●

ESCAPE FROM ALCATRAZ
1979, 112 mins, US Ⓥ ⊙ col
Dir Don Siegel ***Prod*** Don Siegel ***Scr*** Richard Tuggle ***Ph*** Bruce Surtees ***Ed*** Ferris Webster ***Mus*** Jerry Fielding ***Art*** Allen Smith
Act Clint Eastwood, Patrick McGoohan, Fred Ward, Roberts Blossom, Bruce M. Fischer, Paul Benjamin (Paramount/Malpaso)

Considering that the escape itself from rock-bound Alcatraz prison consumes only the film's final half hour, screenwriter Richard Tuggle [adapting the book by J. Campbell Bruce] and director Don Siegel provide a model of super-efficient filmmaking. From the moment Clint Eastwood walks onto The Rock to the final title card explaining the three escapees were never heard from again, *Escape from Alcatraz* is relentless in establishing a mood and pace of unrelieved tension. Pic's only fault may be an ambiguous ending, tied, of course, to the historical reality of the 1962 escape, only successful one in Alcatraz's 29-year history as America's most repressive penal institution.

Key counterpoint to Eastwood's character comes from Patrick McGoohan as the megalomaniacal warden.

●

ESCAPE FROM L.A.
(AKA: JOHN CARPENTER'S ESCAPE FROM L.A.)
1996, 101 min, US Ⓥ ⊙ ▭ col
Dir John Carpenter ***Prod*** Debra Hill, Kurt Russell ***Scr*** John Carpenter, Debra Hill, Kurt Russell ***Ph*** Gary B. Kibbe ***Ed*** Edward A. Warschilka ***Mus*** Shirley Walker, John Carpenter ***Art*** Lawrence G. Paull
Act Kurt Russell, Stacy Keach, Steve Buscemi, Valeria Golino, Peter Fonda, Pam Grier (Rysher/Paramount)

A cartoonish, cheesy and surprisingly campy apocalyptic actioner, *Escape from L.A.* is spiked with a number of funny and anarchic ideas, but doesn't begin to pull them together into a coherent whole.

When last seen [in the 1981 *Escape from New York*], Snake Plissken (Kurt Russell) was spiriting the U.S. prez out of a New York City that was an armed fortress controlled by convicts and loonies, circa 1998. Westward migration being what it is, by 2013 all the degenerates are in L.A., part of which has broken off from the mainland courtesy of a 9.8 earthquake in the year 2000.

The nation's undesirables have all been sequestered on L.A. Island as a means of purifying the new "moral" United States, which is lorded over by a Gestapo-like U.S. Police Force and ruled by a right-wing religious hypocrite (Cliff Robertson). But the prexy's goody-goody daughter has suddenly seen through her old man, absconded with his top-secret "black box" and joined forces with gangster revolutionary Cuervo Jones (George Corraface).

Former war hero and full-time bad boy Snake is pulled out of mothballs to retrieve the black box. Snake first meets an old surf bum (Peter Fonda), and is [later] captured and taken to L.A. Coliseum to star in an updated Roman-style life-and-death contest.

Russell hoarse-whispers his way through the picture, knocking off a seemingly limitless supply of bad apples along the way. If not for him, this would be a B movie. Visually, item is much closer to the 1981 *Escape* than to effects-oriented pics being done today.

●

ESCAPE FROM NEW YORK
1981, 99 mins, US Ⓥ ⊙ ▭ col
Dir John Carpenter ***Prod*** Larry Franco, Debra Hill ***Scr*** John Carpenter, Nick Castle ***Ph*** Dean Cundey ***Ed*** Todd Ramsay ***Mus*** John Carpenter, Alan Howarth ***Art*** Joe Alves
Act Kurt Russell, Lee Van Cleef, Ernest Borgnine, Donald Pleasence, Isaac Hayes, Harry Dean Stanton (Avco Embassy/IFI/Goldcrest)

Although execution doesn't quite live up to the fabulous premise, *Escape from New York* is a solidly satisfying actioner. Impressively produced for $7 million, it reps director John Carpenter's biggest budget to date.

In the 1997 New York City neatly turned out (mostly in St Louis) by production designer Joe Alves, Manhattan is a walled, maximum security prison inhabited by millions of felons and loonies. The president of the U.S. has the misfortune of crash landing on the island and being taken hostage by the crazies, who demand their release in exchange for the leader.

Into this cesspool is sent tough criminal Kurt Russell, who is charged with extricating the prexy within 24 hours.

Pic only falls a little short in not taking certain scenes to their dramatic limits. For instance, Russell is finally captured by Isaac Hayes and his cronies and thrown, like a doomed gladiator, into an arena with a hulking behemoth. Instead of milking the confrontation for all it's worth, Carpenter keeps cutting away to parallel events elsewhere. Model and matte work, executed at New World's special effects studio in Venice, is obvious but imaginatively fun enough to get by.

●

ESCAPE FROM THE PLANET OF THE APES
1971, 97 mins, US Ⓥ ⊙ ▭ col
Dir Don Taylor ***Prod*** Arthur P. Jacobs ***Scr*** Paul Dehn ***Ph*** Joseph Biroc ***Ed*** Marion Rothman ***Mus*** Jerry Goldsmith ***Art*** Jack Martin Smith, William Creber
Act Roddy McDowall, Kim Hunter, Bradford Dillman, Natalie Trundy, Eric Braeden, William Windom (20th Century-Fox/Apjac)

Escape from the Planet of the Apes is an excellent film, almost as good as the original *Planet of the Apes*. Arthur Jacobs's production is marked by an outstanding script, using some of the original Pierre Boulle novel characters; excellent direction by Don Taylor; and superior performances from a cast headed by encoring Roddy McDowall and Kim Hunter.

In the previous film one will recall that the world seemed to be ending in nuclear holocaust. Something that trivial never stopped a good writer, so this film opens with Hunter, McDowall and Sal Mineo arriving on earth in a space vehicle.

After about half of the film's literate, suspenseful, delightful and thoughtprovoking 97 minutes, the story emphasis segues from broad comedic antics to a rather horrifying dilemma. Eric Braeden, scientific advisor to U.S. President William Windom, suggests that, if indeed in our future apes would subdue humans, why not remove that distant threat by aborting the life of the child of McDowall and Hunter?

●

ESCAPE ME NEVER
1935, 93 mins, UK b/w
Dir Paul Czinner ***Prod*** Herbert Wilcox, Dallas Bower ***Scr*** Margaret Kennedy, R. J. Cullen ***Ph*** Georges Perinal, Sepp Allgeier ***Ed*** Merrill G. White, David Lean ***Mus*** William Walton ***Art*** Andre Andrejev, Wilfred Arnold
Act Elisabeth Bergner, Hugh Sinclair, Irene Vanbrugh, Griffith Jones, Penelope Dudley-Ward, Lyn Harding (British & Dominions/United Artists)

Escape Me Never, produced as a play [by Margaret Kennedy] in London and New York with the same star, is a well-produced film transcription of a story of moods and morbidity.

Locale includes Venice, where the picture opens, the mountains, and finally London. At the outset Elisabeth Bergner is fashioned as an impish waif of immoral caste, who instantly becomes likable in spite of her character background. Further on, by degrees, she loses a part of this charm and becomes a helpless mother and wife who is figuratively kicked around by her musician husband.

Two brothers figure in the supporting cast, played by Hugh Sinclair and Griffith Jones. Story makes the brothers unreal to some extent, at the same time also stretching logic of actions of Bergner and the other girl (Penelope Dudley-Ward). Latter is unbelievably smitten with one brother, then with the other, and, though appealed to by Bergner, as the latter's wife, stolidly refuses to believe her second choice is married.

Some of the interiors tend to drabness, possibly to lend that touch to a depressing story.

1935: NOMINATION: Best Actress (Elisabeth Bergner)

●

ESCAPE ME NEVER
1947, 101 mins, US Ⓥ b/w
Dir Peter Godfrey ***Prod*** Henry Blanke ***Scr*** Thames Williamson, Lenore Coffee ***Ph*** Sol Polito ***Ed*** Clarence Kolster ***Mus*** Erich Wolfgang Korngold ***Art*** Carl Jules Weyl
Act Errol Flynn, Ida Lupino, Eleanor Parker, Gig Young, Reginald Deny, Isobel Elsom (Warner)

Errol Flynn is given plenty of opportunity to flash the old charm but there's hardly a touch of the usual swashbuckling or boudoir romance activities in his role of a serious composer. Under the capable direction of Peter Godfrey, he turns in one of the best jobs of his career. Ida Lupino, although she's seldom been typed so much as Flynn, has a role here that she can really sink her teeth into and she demonstrates once more her versatility as a serious actress.

Story [from a novel and play by Margaret Kennedy] is cut sharply in half between light romance and heavy drama and therin lies its only fault of note.

Tale is imbued with much of the nostalgic flavor of pre–World War I Europe. It tees off in Venice where Gig

Young, a struggling young composer, wants to marry the wealthy Eleanor Parker. Through a misunderstanding, however, her parents think Young is living with Lupino, a widowed waif with an infant son, and so rush Parker off to a resort in the Alps. Seems, though, that it's been Flynn, Young's happy-go-lucky brother, who took Lupino and child in off the streets. To set things right again, the two brothers, Miss Lupino and the moppet start off on foot through the Alps to find Parker and explain the mistake to her.

Chief production assist is lent by Erich Wolfgang Korngold's score, with both the ballet and theme music standout. Ballet sequences are tastefully staged by LeRoy Prinz and Milada Mladova sparkles in both terping and thesping as the prima ballerina.

•

ESCAPE TO ATHENA
1979, 125 mins, UK Ⓥ ▭ col
Dir George Pan Cosmatos ***Prod*** Jack Wiener ***Scr*** Richard S. Lochte, Edward Anhalt ***Ph*** Gil Taylor ***Ed*** Ralph Kemplen ***Mus*** Lalo Schifrin ***Art*** John Graysmark
Act Roger Moore, Telly Savalas, David Niven, Claudia Cardinale, Richard Roundtree, Stefanie Powers (ITC/Grade)

Escape to Athena not only has the unabashed look of a cynical "package" but also plays like one as well. It's a joke-up wartime action retread, feeble as to both humor and suspense, in which a group of Anglo-American prisoners of the Germans scramble to liberate (a) themselves and (b) some Greek art treasures.

Of those billed above the title, Roger Moore as the Nazi camp commander, Elliott Gould, David Niven, Sonny Bono, Stefanie Powers and Richard Roundtree as POWs (how's that for a motley bunch?), Telly Savalas as a Greek resistance leader, and Claudia Cardinale as a brothel madam, none has much scope to register with any dimension and most are as implausible as the hammy action [based on a story by Richard S. Lochte and George P. Cosmatos].

•

ESCAPE TO HAPPINESS
SEE: INTERMEZZO

•

ESCAPE TO WITCH MOUNTAIN
1975, 97 mins, US Ⓥ ⊙ col
Dir John Hough ***Prod*** Jerome Courtland ***Scr*** Robert Malcolm Young ***Ph*** Frank Phillips ***Ed*** Robert Stafford ***Mus*** Johnny Mandel ***Art*** John B. Mansbridge, Al Roelofs
Act Eddie Albert, Ray Milland, Donald Pleasence, Kim Richards, Ike Eisenmann, Walter Barnes (Walt Disney)

The two leading protagonists are a young orphaned brother and sister who are psychic.

Based on a book by Alexander Key and directed with a light and sure hand by John Hough, script picks up the youngsters as they arrive at a children's home after the loss of their foster parents.

Their unusual powers, displayed early when they warn a man not to enter a car moments before it is demolished by a runaway truck, leads to an eccentric tycoon who craves a gifted clairvoyant who can make him omnipotent, arranging for their transfer to his palatial home where they are held prisoner.

Using their magical talents for an escape, they take up with a cranky old-timer traveling in a motor home. Much of the action focuses on their efforts to elude the millionaire and his men who want the children returned.

Eddie Albert inserts just the proper type of crankiness as the camper-owner who gets entangled with them, and Ray Milland properly hams the multimillionaire. Donald Pleasence scores, too, as Milland's aide.

•

ESPIRITU DE LA COLMENA, EL
(THE SPIRIT OF THE BEEHIVE)
1973, 95 mins, Spain Ⓥ col
Dir Victor Erice ***Prod*** Elias Querejeta ***Scr*** Victor Erice, Angel Fernandez Santos ***Ph*** Luis Cuadrado ***Ed*** Pablo G. del Amo ***Mus*** Luis de Pablo ***Art*** Adolfo Cofino
Act Fernando Fernan Gomez, Teresa Gimpera, Ana Torrent, Isabel Telleria, Laly Soldevilla, Miguel Picazo (Querejeta)

This sensitive, beautifully wrought film about two small girls in a Castilian village in 1940 (just after the end of the Spanish Civil War) couldn't be more authentically Spanish in its evocation of life in the provinces; yet its suggestivity and lyricism transcend local borders.

Two girls are, one night, taken to the village cinema where they see an old Frankenstein film. They only imperfectly understand what is happening on the screen, but are fascinated by the scene where the small girl picks a flower and gives it to the monster. They imagine that the monster is a kind of benevolent spirit who can be invoked by saying certain words.

Rest of pic shows how the two children, especially the younger, Ana (Ana Torrent), search for traces of the spirit in and out of the village and become increasingly obsessed by it: They spin a dream world of their own about the monster. The spirit's existence seems to be somehow further corroborated when an escaped prisoner holes up in a neighboring barn and is discovered and aided by Ana.

Acting is superb, especially by Torrent; also excellent are Fernando Fernan Gomez as the mournful intellectual father who has a small beehive inside the house, and Teresa Gimpera as the mother who pens letters to imaginary correspondents. Much of the film's charm comes from the touching simplicity of scenes.

•

ET DIEU . . . CREA LA FEMME
(. . . AND GOD CREATED WOMAN; AND WOMAN . . . WAS CREATED))
1957, 95 mins, France Ⓥ ⊙ ▭ col
Dir Roger Vadim ***Prod*** Raoul J. Levy ***Scr*** Roger Vadim, Raoul J. Levy ***Ph*** Armand Thirard ***Ed*** Victoria Mercanton ***Mus*** Paul Misraki ***Art*** Jean Andre
Act Brigitte Bardot, Curt Jurgens, Jean-Louis Trintignant, Jeanne Marken, Isabelle Corey, Christian Marquand (IENA/UCIL/Cocinor)

Film even ran into censorship trouble in France via its emphasis on sex, and was shorn of its more intimate sensual aspects. Lagging, familiar storyline is of the passion and drama that a sexy little orphan (Brigitte Bardot) inspires in three men—a worldly casino owner and two worker brothers—in a Riveria port town.

Film unfolds slowly, centering on the questionable attributes of the new star, Bardot. Though a young looker, she lacks the thespian strength to get any depth into her sensual role here. Curt Jurgens acts as a sort of outsider but manages to make his presence felt, while Jean-Louis Trintignant and Christian Marquand are acceptable as the brothers.

Lensing (C'Scope and Eastmancolor) is excellent, and other technical credits good.

•

ETE MEURTRIER, L'
(ONE DEADLY SUMMER)
1983, 130 mins, France Ⓥ col
Dir Jean Becker ***Prod*** Gerard Beytout ***Scr*** Sebastien Japrisot ***Ph*** Etienne Becker ***Ed*** Jacques Witta ***Mus*** Georges Delerue ***Art*** Jean-Claude Gallouin
Act Isabelle Adjani, Alain Souchon, Suzanne Flon, Jenny Cleve, Francois Cluzet, Michel Galabru (SNC)

Sebastien Japrisot's bestselling suspense novel, *One Deadly Summer*, has finally made it to the screen in an adaptation by the author, and Jean Becker (son of the late Jacques Becker) has directed this psychological drama about a dangerously neurotic girl's obsession with a family shame. Often questionable in matters of credibility and wobbly in its dramatic conception, pic is nonetheless fairly engrossing, thanks to Isabelle Adjani, astonishing in the central role.

Story is set in a small southern French town where Adjani, recently arrived with her timid German mother and invalid father (Maria Machado, Michel Galabru), quickly earns the reputation of a local tinsel sexpot, empty-headed, volatile and unattainable.

Traumatized by her knowledge that her mother was raped by three Italian immigrants before she was born, Adjani thinks she's on a trail of vengeance when she's courted by a young garage mechanic (Alain Souchon), whose father, now dead, was an Italian immigrant who owned a mechanical piano, the only clue to the identity of her mother's aggressors.

Japrisot retains in his screenplay the multiple narrative idea: the action is related alternately from the viewpoints of several characters, including Adjani, Souchon and Suzanne Flon, as the humane, partly deaf aunt. In the film this shifting is translated by alternating voiceover commentaries. It becomes something of an obstacle, because Becker fails to differentiate the narratives visually.

•

E.T. THE EXTRA-TERRESTRIAL
1982, 115 mins, US Ⓥ ⊙ col
Dir Steven Spielberg ***Prod*** Steven Spielberg ***Scr*** Melissa Mathison ***Ph*** Allen Davlau ***Ed*** Carol Littleton ***Mus*** John Williams ***Art*** James D. Bissell
Act Dee Wallace, Henry Thomas, Peter Coyote, Robert MacNaughton, Drew Barrymore, K. C. Martel (Universal)

E.T. may be the best Disney film Disney never made. Captivating, endearingly optimistic and magical at times, Steven Spielberg's fantasy is about a stranded alien from outer space protected by three kids until it can arrange for passage home.

E.T. is highly fortunate to be found by young Henry Thomas who, after some understandable initial fright, takes the "goblin" in, first as a sort of pet and then as a friend he must guard against the more preying elements of human society. Over time, Thomas teaches E.T. how to talk and includes his older brother (Robert MacNaughton) and younger sister (Drew Barrymore) in on the secret.

Ultimately, of course, the official representatives of society locate E.T., which seems to occasion a rapid decline in its health until it appears to die.

As superlatively created by Carlo Rambaldi, the creature manages to project both a wondrous childlike quality and a sense of superior powers. It even gets to play a drunk scene, perhaps a first for screen aliens.

All performers fulfill the requirements, and Thomas is perfect in the lead, playing the childhood equivalent of Spielberg's everyman heroes of his previous pics.

1982: Best Sound, Original Score, Sound Effects Editing, Visual Effects

NOMINATIONS: Best Picture, Director, Original Screenplay, Cinematography, Editing

•

EUREKA
1983, 129 mins, UK Ⓥ col
Dir Nicolas Roeg ***Prod*** Jeremy Thomas ***Scr*** Paul Mayersberg ***Ph*** Alex Thomson ***Ed*** Tony Lawson ***Mus*** Stanley Myers ***Art*** Michael Seymour
Act Gene Hackman, Theresa Russell, Rutger Hauer, Jane Lapotaire, Ed Lauter, Mickey Rourke (JF Prods/Recorded Picture)

Even by his own standards, Nicolas Roeg's *Eureka* is an indulgent melodrama [based on a book by Marshall Houts] about the anticlimactic life of a greedy gold prospector after he has struck it rich.

Gene Hackman performs with predictable credit as the man whose jackpot fortune only leaves him bored, surly and suspicious of being ripped off, by one and all, family included. Theresa Russell is the girl-woman daughter who rebelliously marries a putative gigolo (Rutger Hauer) whom paranoid papa psychs as a fortune hunter. Mother Jane Lapotaire, meanwhile, driven to the sauce by an uncaring husband, drifts through life in the tropics with sulky sarcasm. Violent menace permeates pic, radiated by Joe Pesci as a Yiddish-speaking "entrepreneur" who, foiled in his bid to buy a piece of Hackman's island in order to establish a casino, finally sends the hoods after Hackman, leading up to a gruesome prefinale.

•

EUREKA STOCKADE
1949, 103 mins, UK/Australia b/w
Dir Harry Watt ***Prod*** Michael Balcon ***Scr*** Harry Watt, Walter Greenwood ***Ph*** George Heath ***Mus*** John Greenwood
Act Chips Rafferty, Gordon Jackson, Peter Finch, Jane Barrett, Jack Lambert, Peter Illing (Ealing)

Eureka Stockade is staged in the middle of the 19th century when the first gold strike in Australia leads to economic chaos in the colony. There are no men to till the land or sail the ships as they have all gone in search of gold. And there is also a large influx of foreigners, all of whom hope to find their fortune.

In an endeavor to save the nation's finances, vicious taxes are imposed on the diggers, and the men themselves are hounded by the police. The gold seekers seek to impose their will by mob law, but a leader arises. If action alone could make a picture, this one would very nearly take full marks, for the entire emphasis is on movement, and the pitched battle comes as a climax to a series of big-scale scenes.

The main weakness of the production, which contributes in large measure to its failure to grip, is the low standard of acting.

•

EUROPA
(US: (ZENTROPA)
1991, 114 mins, Denmark/France/Germany Ⓥ ⊙ ▭ col
Dir Lars Von Trier ***Prod*** Peter Aalbeck Jensen, Bo Christensen ***Scr*** Lars Von Trier, Niels Vorsel ***Ph*** Henning Bendtsen, Edward Klosinski, Jean-Paul Meurisse ***Ed*** Herve Schneid ***Mus*** Joakim Holbek ***Art*** Henning Bahs
Act Jean-Marc Barr, Barbara Sukowa, Udo Kier, Ernst Hugo, Erik Mork, Eddie Constantine (Nordisk/Obel/Mital)

Bravura film technique doesn't hide an offputting, empty exercise in *Europa*, Lars Von Trier's rumination on war guilt in the form of a low-voltage thriller. Distracting visuals only occasionally support the film's themes while mostly constituting an end in themselves.

In only his third feature, director works on a vast canvas with all manner of special effects to tell the Kafkaesque story of a young American, Leopold (Jean-Marc Barr), working as an apprentice railroad conductor in occupied Germany, 1945. His romance with cold, beautiful Katharina (Barbara Sukowa), daughter of the trainline owner, plays second fiddle to Leopold's surrealistic wanderings through a fantasy landscape.

Contrived plot involves Leopold unwittingly with a gang of "werewolves," namely partisan terrorists who chafe under Allied rule. Film's climax contains many elements of suspense but is drawn out too long and played off against the black humor of Leopold failing a conductor test for visiting inspectors.

Bulk of widescreen footage is in black & white, with the director using front projection for shifting back and forth to muted color. Acting is on the lugubrious side. Joakin Holbek's symphonic score is strong to the point of tongue-in-cheek and includes a credited riff from Bernard Herrmann's Vertigo soundtrack.

•

EUROPEANS, THE

1979, 90 mins, UK Ⓥ col

Dir James Ivory ***Prod*** Ismael Merchant ***Scr*** Ruth Prawer Jhabvala ***Ph*** Larry Pizer ***Ed*** Jeremiah Rusconi ***Mus*** Richard Robbins

Act Lee Remick, Robin Ellis, Wesley Addy, Lisa Eichhorn, Tim Choate, Tim Woodward (Merchant-Ivory)

"The Europeans" are Americans who grew up in Europe in the mid 19th century. They come back to the U.S. to visit rich cousins. Perhaps a bit down on their luck, the arrival leads to a mingling and interaction of cultures, which ends up with the more innocent Yankee outlooks holding their own with the worldly wiles of the European ways.

The European cousins are Lee Remick as a mid-30s baroness now estranged from her Austrian nobleman husband and her younger brother, a free-living portrait painter with bohemian attitudes.

Shot in the U.S., New England is a lovely backdrop with its languid, genteel ways and extraordinary houses that are a mixture of European and local influences.

Director James Ivory handles this roundelay [from the Henry James novel] with subtlety, delivering an engaging drama.

1979: NOMINATION: Best Costume Design

•

EVA

(EVE)

1962, 108 mins, France/Italy b/w

Dir Joseph Losey ***Prod*** Robert Hakim, Raymond Hakim ***Scr*** Hugo Butler, Evan Jones ***Ph*** Gianni Di Venanzo ***Ed*** Reginald Beck, Franca Silvi ***Mus*** Michel Legrand ***Art*** Richard McDonald, Luigi Scaccianoce

Act Jeanne Moreau, Stanley Baker, Virna Lisi, Giorgio Albertazzi, James Villiers, Lisa Gastoni (Paris/Interopa)

Made [from the novel by James Hadley Chase] by an American director in Italy using English, with French producers and French, British and Italian actors, this is a sleek, mannered look at an affair between a cold, almost psychotic, call girl and a writer, who is fraught with overtones of masochism.

A blustering, self-satisfied British writer, who has a best-seller and smash pic under his belt, has also amassed an Italian fiancée and lives in Venice and Rome. His film producer suspects him and, being in love with his fiancée, is having him investigated.

He has to come up with another story, and goes off to a posh secluded house on an isle near Venice. A broken rudder has let a boat in with an enigmatic, hard-looking French girl and an older man. They have broken into the house and she is calmly in the bathtub when the writer comes in. He wants to throw them out until he ogles the femme.

He throws out the older man who had paid off the girl in paintings for a night of love. The writer tries to get next to her but she knocks him cold with an ashtray. Thus starts an obsession.

Picture is reminiscent of prewar Yank femme fatale films. But there is not enough character to give acceptance to the overindulgence in Jeanne Moreau as the cold-hearted harlot. Moreau speaks good English but is hampered by the overdecorated, overstylized vamp she is called on to play. Stanley Baker acquits himself acceptably as the climbing ex-coal miner, and others are adequate.

•

EVE

SEE: EVA

•

EVEN COWGIRLS GET THE BLUES

1994, 96 mins, US Ⓥ ⦿ col

Dir Gus Van Sant ***Prod*** Laurie Parker ***Scr*** Gus Van Sant ***Ph*** John Campbell, Eric Alan Edwards ***Ed*** Curtiss Clayton ***Mus*** k.d. lang, Ben Mink ***Art*** Missy Stewart

Act Uma Thurman, John Hurt, Rain Phoenix, Noriyuki "Pat" Morita, Lorraine Bracco, Keanu Reeves (New Line)

American counterculture and early '70s values come flooding back like a peyote-induced dream in Gus Van Sant's *Even Cowgirls Get the Blues*, a farout, meandering fantasy set on a ranch run by lesbians, from Tom Robbins's 1973 cult novel.

Missing from *Cowgirls* is the poetry of yearning and desperation running through Van Sant's *My Own Private Idaho*. Pic stays on the surface without attempting any exploration of painful depths. Result is at best amusing; at worst, uninvolving, often confusing and sometimes a little boring.

Main character, Sissy (Uma Thurman), is a 29-year-old virgin hippie whose delicate beauty is marred only by giant, phalluslike thumbs. Sissy has a contract with the Countess (John Hurt), a prancing drag queen, to model for feminine hygiene ads.

Leaving behind the flashy New York scene populated by the asthmatic Julian (Keanu Reeves) and his swinging pals, Sissy hitches cross-country to the Countess's Oregon beauty farm, the Rubber Rose Ranch. At the ranch, however, a pack of rebellious, unwashed cowgirls, led by Bonanza Jellybean (Rain Phoenix), foment an uprising against the Countess and his authoritarian hireling (Angie Dickinson).

Thurman's sensual, little-girl presence keeps auds firmly on her side, no matter how absurd the rough-and-tumble situations. The cowgirls (many played by nonpros) have a surreal concreteness, especially brave, grinning Phoenix, playing like a female version of a genre cowboy star. [Review is of 106-min. version world preemed at 1993 Venice fest. Pic was subsequently re-edited to 96 mins. for general release.]

•

EVENING DRESS

SEE: TENUE DE SOIREE

•

EVENSONG

1934, 83 mins, UK b/w

Dir Victor Saville ***Prod*** Michael Balcon ***Scr*** Dorothy Farnum, Edward Knoblock ***Ph*** Mutz Greenbaum ***Ed*** Otto Ludwig ***Mus*** Louis Levy (dir.) ***Art*** Alfred Junge

Act Evelyn Laye, Fritz Kortner, Emlyn Williams, Carl Esmond, Alice Delysia, Conchita Supervia (Gaumont-British)

A highly absorbing and intelligently produced musical, the saga of an opera warbler whose career reaches a tragic end. Evelyn Laye is the singing lead of *Evensong*. By stages she skillfully portrays the professionally successful but tragic life of a prima donna from her teens to the day when inevitably she must learn that her voice is burning out.

The music [composed by Mischa Spoliansky, lyrics by Edward Knoblock] ranges from popular numbers appropriately spotted, as for instance in the soldiers' canteen scene, to heavier opera. *La Traviata* and *La Bohème* numbers figure mostly, together with lighter compositions especially written for the play and picture.

Fritz Kortner tops the support as the diva's manager and romance slaughterer, while Carl Esmond plays moderately well. His accent is foreign rather than English, as with most of the company. Emlyn Williams, first love of the prima donna, dies in the war without having impressed deeply.

•

EVENT HORIZON

1997, 95 mins, US/UK Ⓥ ⦿ ▭ col

Dir Paul Anderson ***Prod*** Lawrence Gordon, Lloyd Levin, Jeremy Bolt ***Scr*** Philip Eisner ***Ph*** Adrian Biddle ***Ed*** Martin Hunter ***Mus*** Michael Kamen ***Art*** Joseph Bennett

Act Laurence Fishburne, Sam Neill, Kathleen Quinlan, Joely Richardson, Richard T. Jones, Jack Noseworthy (Golar/Impact/Paramount)

Despite game efforts from a first-rate cast and acres of impressive production values, *Event Horizon* remains a muddled and curiously uninvolving sci-fi horror show. Initial promise of the offbeat premise—a rescue party finds a derelict spacecraft haunted by supernatural forces—is rapidly dissipated by routine execution and risible dialogue.

Sort of a cross between *Alien* and *The Shining*, screenplay is set in 2047, and begins with the mysterious reappearance of deep-space research vessel *Event Horizon*, which vanished somewhere beyond Neptune. Dr. William Weir (Sam Neill), who worked on the vessel's design, is eager to board the *Lewis & Clark*, a search-and-rescue ship under the demanding command of Capt. Miller (Laurence Fishburne).

Shortly before they reach the *Event Horizon*, Weir spills the beans: the missing ship was testing a new form of "faster than light" propulsion that, in effect, creates "an artificial black hole." Obviously, something went terribly wrong. Just how wrong becomes clear as soon as the team boards.

All of which makes the pic [shot in the U.K.'s Pinewood Studios] sound a lot more interesting than it is. Once the underlying gimmick is announced, the filmmakers do little more than invent messy deaths, unleash special effects—and steadily increase the volume of Michael Kamen's overbearing musical score. The actors—particularly Fishburne, Neill and Kathleen Quinlan—perform far beyond the call of duty, but to little avail.

•

EVE OF ST. MARK, THE

1944, 96 mins, US b/w

Dir John M. Stahl ***Prod*** William Perlberg ***Scr*** George Seaton ***Ph*** Joseph La Shelle ***Ed*** Louis Sackin ***Mus*** Cyril J. Mockridge ***Art*** James Basevi, Russel Spencer

Act Anne Baxter, William Eythe, Michael O'Shea, Vincent Price, Ruth Nelson, Ray Collins (20th Century-Fox)

Maxwell Anderson's stage hit of the 1942–43 season was a subtle flag-waver whose basic purposes were shrouded by the always terse, down-to-earth dialog of American doughboys, pre- and post-Pearl Harbor. Much of this quality the film has retained, though for the screen there was an inevitable elimination of some of the play's salty lines and sex implications. In short, *St. Mark* has become a homey comedy-drama of a farmboy inductee, his family, sweetheart and barracks comrades. It remains almost a Johnny Doughboy documentary.

It is a picture of superlative performances. William Eythe, as the farmboy inductee, has his biggest part to date, and does much with it. He and Anne Baxter share the romance, and she, too, gives a fine characterization, as does, notably, Michael O'Shea, in the same role he created in the Broadway stage version, when he was known as Eddie O'Shea. Vincent Price, as the poetical southerner; Ruth Nelson as the mother; Ray Collins, the father; Stanley Prager and George Mathews are others who stand out in a cast of standouts.

•

EVERGREEN

1934, 92 mins, UK Ⓥ b/w

Dir Victor Saville ***Prod*** Michael Balcon ***Scr*** Emlyn Williams, Marjorie Gaffney ***Ph*** Glen MacWilliams ***Ed*** Ian Dalrymple ***Mus*** Harry Woods ***Art*** Alfred Junge, Peter Pride

Act Jessie Matthews, Sonnie Hale, Betty Balfour, Barry Mackay, Ivor McLaren (Gaumont-British)

Jessie Matthews has the name part, which she created on the stage. The screen adaptation and dialog is, for picture purposes, a better story than the stage version. It is more definite and coherent. Benn Levy and Lorenz Hart wrote the original musical for C. B. Cochran.

In 1909 (this is the plot) Harriet Green is London's pet singing comedienne, making her farewell appearance at the old Tivoli prior to her marriage to a marquis. That night the father of her child, whom she believed to be dead, turns up and demands blackmail. She places the baby girl in the charge of a faithful maid and disappears.

Twenty-five years later the daughter seeks a job in the chorus and is recognized by the mother's old understudy, now the widow of an ancient lord. Daughter is foisted on the public as the original Harriet Green and stars in an elaborate musical. This gives scope for Edwardian and modern costuming and ample advantage is taken of the opportunities. It is the astonishingly competent performances by the principals that is most impressive. They embrace, in addition to Matthews, Sonnie Hale and Ivor McLaren, Betty Balfour and Barry MacKay, all good.

•

EVERLASTING PIECE, AN

2000, 103 mins, US Ⓥ ⦿ col

Dir Barry Levinson ***Prod*** Mark Johnson, Louis DiGiaimo, Jerome O'Connor, Barry Levinson, Paula Weinstein ***Scr*** Barry McEvoy ***Ph*** Seamus Deasy ***Ed*** Stu Linder ***Mus*** Hans Zimmer ***Art*** Nathan Crowley

Act Barry McEvoy, Brian F. O'Byrne, Anna Friel, Colum Convey, Billy Connolly, Pauline McLynn (Bayahibe/DreamWorks-Columbia)

The whimsical, yet politically tinged, double entendre of the title *An Everlasting Piece* serves as a precise reflection of the nature and extent of the humor in this gently eccentric yarn about a Catholic and Protestant team of hairpiece salesmen in '80s Belfast, a diversionary little knockoff for director Barry Levinson amid his usual alternating pattern of big-star vehicles and more personal Baltimore projects.

At its heart there is something quite appealing about the way actor and first-time screenwriter Barry McEvoy makes light of the long-standing religious/political conflict in Northern Ireland by filtering it through faintly absurdist shenanigans. Premise throws together the Catholic Colm (McEvoy) and Protestant George (Brian F. O'Byrne) as barbers at a Belfast hospital. Quickly getting past their religion-based mutual suspicions through their shared love of verse, the young men hatch a business scheme when they find that the only men's hairpiece provider in Northern Ireland is a ferocious fellow named Scalper (Billy Connolly) who's now in for an extended stay at their facility.

Stepping into the void, the young men procure a hairpiece (one of the film's repeated gags hinges upon how this word's Irish pronunciation makes people think the men are offering them herpes) and sell it on partial credit to a disagreeable gent who subsequently refuses to pay the balance. This leads to the picture's big action set piece, a chase triggered when Colm snatches the rug off the man's dome.

More trouble surfaces when another duo, who call themselves Toupee or Not Toupee, start horning in on the action. A big English concern announces that whichever team sells the most hairpieces will become its exclusive distributor for Northern Ireland. Lagging in sales, the Belfast boys struggle to single out a large group of bald people for a big sale, a matter in which Colm's feisty and foxy girlfriend, Bronagh (Anna Friel), proves very helpful.

While there's just enough plot to keep the narrative wheels turning, McEvoy, who got a lot of the material here from his Belfast barber/wig salesman father, devotes most of his writerly attention to inflating anecdotes and small incidents as far as they will bear. A prime example is a long sequence in which Colm and George are accosted by hooded IRA terrorists, who put them through the wringer at gunpoint until the lads turn the confrontation into a sales opportunity.

McEvoy and O'Byrne interact well, with the former embodying a certain brash glibness and the latter conveying a more sensitive, contemplative nature. Friel, who looks smashing in a tartan miniskirt and black tights, adds zip to all her scenes, while supporting players are uniformly responsive to the deadpan drollery of the material.

•

EVERYBODY'S ALL-AMERICAN
(UK: WHEN I FALL IN LOVE)
1988, 127 mins, US Ⓥ ⊙ col
Dir Taylor Hackford ***Prod*** Taylor Hackford, Laura Ziskin, Ian Sander ***Scr*** Tom Rickman ***Ph*** Stephen Goldblatt ***Ed*** Don Zimmerman ***Mus*** James Newton Howard ***Art*** Joe Alves
Act Jessica Lange, Dennis Quaid, Timothy Hutton, John Goodman, Carl Lumbly, Ray Baker (New Visions)

Everybody's All-American [from a book by Frank DeFord] has its moments, and remains watchable due to its two attractive leads, but is too predictable and not nearly incisive enough.

The world of Baton Rouge in the mid 1950s was made for the likes of Gavin and Babs. Dashing, easygoing and likable, Gavin (Dennis Quaid) is the running back who leads his school to triumph in the Sugar Bowl. Gorgeous blond Southern belle Babs (Jessica Lange) represents everyone's dream girl but yearns only to become Mrs. Gavin Grey.

The couple moves comfortably into the expected environs of suburbia, a steady flow of babies, sports-themed restaurant ownership and the like. However, the innocence of youth and the 1950s inevitably yield to the turmoil and doubt of the 1960s. The Greys get wiped out financially and then see Gavin's star fall as his playing career winds down, just as Babs belatedly starts coming into her own.

A viewer could do a lot worse than have to watch Lange and Quaid for two hours, and they definitely get far into their parts here. After just getting by posing as 21-year-olds, both age through the years convincingly.

•

EVERYBODY SING
1938, 80 mins, US Ⓥ b/w
Dir Edwin L. Marin ***Prod*** Harry Rapf ***Scr*** Florence Ryerson, Edgar Allan Woolf, James Gruen ***Ph*** Joseph Ruttenberg ***Ed*** William S. Gray ***Mus*** William Axt (dir.) ***Art*** Cedric Gibbons, Harry McAfee, Edwin B. Willis
Act Allan Jones, Fanny Brice, Judy Garland, Reginald Owen, Billie Burke, Reginald Gardiner (M-G-M)

Everybody sings in this highly successful departure from the stereotyped filmusical. The production is a combination of straight comedy, balanced with some tuneful song interpolations. Fanny Brice scores heavily with her inimitable impersonations. Others profit equally, however, and the diminutive Judy Garland takes a long leap forward to stardom.

Story recounts the weird behavior of a theatrical family headed by Reginald Owen as an exasperated dramatist and Billie Burke, temperamental stage star. The children are Lynne Carver and Garland, who is expelled from boarding school because she insists on singing Mendelssohn to swingtime. Allan Jones is the family chef; Brice, the maid, and Reginald Gardiner is Burke's leading man in a play soon to be produced.

These characters are tossed about in some amusing situations at home, in a night club and backstage of a theater.

•

EVERYBODY WINS
1990, 97 mins, UK/US Ⓥ ⊙ col
Dir Karel Reisz ***Prod*** Jeremy Thomas, Ezra Swerdlow ***Scr*** Arthur Miller ***Ph*** Ian Baker ***Ed*** John Bloom ***Mus*** Mark Isham, Leon Redbone ***Art*** Peter Larkin
Act Debra Winger, Nick Nolte, Will Patton, Judith Ivey, Jack Warden, Kathleen Wilhoite (Recorded Picture)

Everybody Wins is a very disappointing picture. Repping Arthur Miller's first feature film screenplay since *The Misfits* in 1961, the Karel Reisz–helmed film noir is obscure and artificial.

Overladen with pompous and frequently dated dialog, Miller's script (developed from his 1982 pair of one-act plays, *Two-Way Mirror*) is essentially a routine whodunit. Nick Nolte plays an investigator called in by seeming good Samaritan Debra Winger to get young Frank Military out of jail for a murder she claims he did not commit. Nolte doggedly pursues various leads, interviews odd people and discovers a web of corruption engulfing a small Connecticut town.

Winger as a schizo femme fatale copes uneasily with Miller's overblown dialog, which has her alternatively putting on airs to a bewildered Nolte or handing him non sequiturs. Not helping matters is the lack of chemistry between Nolte and Winger in their sex scenes.

•

EVERY DAY'S A HOLIDAY
1937, 80 mins, US b/w
Dir A. Edward Sutherland ***Prod*** Emanuel Cohen ***Scr*** Mae West ***Ph*** Karl Struss ***Ed*** Ray Curtiss ***Mus*** George Stoll (dir.) ***Art*** Wiard Ihnen
Act Mae West, Edmund Lowe, Charles Butterworth, Charles Winninger, Walter Catlett, Lloyd Nolan (Paramount)

By whatever standard posterity judges the acting career of Mae West, it never shall be said that she was dull. *Every Day's a Holiday*, written by herself, is a lively, innocuously bawdy and rowdy entertainment.

West's new characterization is of a Bowery girl named Peaches O'Day, one time actress of the 1890s, a con-girl, with liberal views on the subject of larceny.

Most action of the story takes place in New York on New Year's, 1900. Peaches trims a yokel for $200. Under threat of arrest Peaches takes the boat to Boston, hoping that time will assuage the criminal complaint. Then she disguises as Mlle. Fifi, and returns to Broadway as a French music-hall singer. Her disguise is good, although not good enough to deceive Capt McCarey (Edmund Lowe), chief of detectives.

Through all this, West sways her hips and tosses her plumes in her inimitable manner. She sings a not very naughty song by Sam Coslow.

There is substantial comedy relief supplied by Charles Winninger, as the blustering chairman of the reformers; Charles Butterworth, his butler and political adviser; Walter Catlett, play producer; and Lloyd Nolan, the crooked boss. Louis Armstrong leads his band in a street parade.

•

EVERY GIRL SHOULD BE MARRIED
1948, 85 mins, US Ⓥ ⊙ b/w
Dir Don Hartman ***Prod*** Don Hartman ***Scr*** Don Hartman, Stephen Morehouse Avery ***Ph*** George E. Diskant ***Ed*** Harry Marker ***Mus*** Leigh Harline ***Art*** Albert S. D'Agostino, Caroll Clark
Act Cary Grant, Franchot Tone, Diana Lynn, Betsy Drake, Alan Mowbray, Elisabeth Risdon (RKO)

Every Girl Should Be Married is one of those rare comic delicacies that are always in good season. Out of that venerable theme of the war between the sexes in which the femmes are the guileful aggressors, Don Hartman has fashioned a sparklingly witty comedy of modern manners that will set off a chain reaction of chuckles.

Betsy Drake is the young gal set upon hooking an eligible bachelor. Accidentally bumping into Cary Grant in a drugstore, she maps an elaborate pincer strategy after studiously gathering data on his habits and habitat. When this fails in a series of tactical reversals, she switches to piquing Grant with jealousy, using Franchot Tone, the boss of the department store in which she works, as the foil.

In a long part that keeps her within camera range for the full length of the film, Drake's performance is a tour de force in the romantic comedy vein. She displays a remarkable range of expressiveness, going from pathos to frothiness with firm control.

•

EVERYONE SAYS I LOVE YOU
1996, 101 mins, US Ⓥ ⊙ col
Dir Woody Allen ***Prod*** Robert Greenhut ***Scr*** Woody Allen ***Ph*** Carlo Di Palma ***Ed*** Susan E. Morse ***Mus*** Dick Hyman ***Art*** Santo Loquasto
Act Alan Alda, Woody Allen, Drew Barrymore, Goldie Hawn, Julia Roberts, Tim Roth (Doumanian/Sweetland)

Woody Allen's *Everyone Says I Love You* is the filmmaker's tip of the hat to movie romance, 1930s musicals and modern neurosis. It's a cinematic oxymoron—complex, bold and audacious, and simulataneously simple, guileless and sublime. This is that rare Allen outing that transcends his cozy niche and plays to the masses.

The Manhattan setting is familiar, but when Holden (Edward Norton) looks adoringly into the eyes of Skylar (Drew Barrymore), he isn't prone to spout poetry; rather, he croons the bygone hit "Just You, Just Me." Allen's zeal to provide a modern spin, and his game, engaging cast quickly transform one's initial shock into sheer viewing delight.

The story rather loosely hangs on the young lovers' impending wedding. Skylar's parents—Bob (Alan Alda) and Steffi (Goldie Hawn)—are comfortable, liberal and poster candidates for nuclear family of the year. Steffi used to be married to Joe (Allen), who's trying not to get involved with the wrong woman (Julia Roberts) . . . again. Steffi's latest cause is the rehabilitation of convicted felon Charles (Tim Roth); when he's paroled, naturally he's invited to dinner.

Allen's instinct for the singing prowess of a cast dominated by performers with limited or no experience in the form (Alda and Hawn excepted) is uncanny. Only Barrymore ultimately was dubbed by a professional.

Hawn is just a little brighter and more memorable than the others in the ensemble. Her climactic dance with Allen along the banks of the Seine is truly magical. Another revelation is Norton, particularly in a shopping-spree number set to "My Baby Just Cares for Me."

•

EVERYTHING I HAVE IS YOURS
1952, 91 mins, US col
Dir Robert Z. Leonard ***Prod*** George Wells ***Scr*** George Wells, Ruth Brooks Flippen ***Ph*** William V. Skall ***Ed*** Adrienne Fazan ***Mus*** David Rose (dir.)
Act Marge Champion, Gower Champion, Dennis O'Keefe, Monica Lewis, Dean Miller, Eduard Franz (M-G-M)

The talents of Marge and Gower Champion get a flashy showcasing. The star team is extremely likeable and almost generates enough verve and audience response to carry off even the sagging spots.

Marge Champion, particularly, continues to show promise as an ingenue who can get by even without a dance or song. Gower Champion gives a very pleasing account of himself.

The plot finds the Champions opening to a smash hit on Broadway in an O'Keefe-produced show, only to discover that the gal's dizziness is caused by pregnancy. Forced to retire with only one night in the show, Marge Champion becomes a successful mother for the next few years while Gower Champion continues in show business partnered with Monica Lewis.

•

EVERYTHING YOU ALWAYS WANTED TO KNOW ABOUT SEX (BUT WERE AFRAID TO ASK)
1972, 87 mins, US Ⓥ ⊙ col
Dir Woody Allen ***Prod*** Charles H. Joffe ***Scr*** Woody Allen ***Ph*** David M. Walsh ***Ed*** James T. Heckart, Eric Albertson ***Mus*** Mundell Lowe ***Art*** Dale Hennesy
Act Woody Allen, John Carradine, Anthony Quayle, Tony Randall, Burt Reynolds, Gene Wilder (United Artists)

Borrowing only the title and some typically inane questions from Dr. David Reuben's oft-ingenuous but widely read overview of sexual matters, Woody Allen writes his sixth screenplay, and serves for the third time as his own director.

Pic is divided into seven segments—blackout sketches, really—that presumably are Allen's surrealistic answer to selected questions from the Reuben tome.

One of the episodes is a prolonged piece of nonsense involving a *2001*-inspired mission control center that is engineering a bout of intercourse in a parked car. Idea of Allen as a reluctant sperm may sound funny on paper, but it plays like an adolescent jape.

Allen's gift is in the depiction of a contemporary intellectual shlump who cannot seem to make it with the chicks always tantalizingly out of reach. That persona could well have served him once more as the focus for a good bit of caustic comedy on today's sexual mores.

•

EVERY TIME WE SAY GOODBYE
1986, 95 mins, US Ⓥ ⊙ col
Dir Moshe Mizrahi ***Prod*** Jacob Kotzky, Sharon Harel ***Scr*** Moshe Mizrahi, Rachel Fabien, Leah Appet ***Ph*** Giuseppe Lanci ***Ed*** Mark Burns ***Mus*** Philippe Sarde ***Art*** Micky Zahar
Act Tom Hanks, Cristina Marsillach, Benedict Taylor, Anat Atzmen (Tri-Star)

Every Time We Say Goodbye is a tale of star-crossed lovers played out against a backdrop of Jerusalem in 1942. Tom Hanks is featured as an American pilot recovering from an injury who falls in love with a girl from a traditional Sephardic Jewish family (Cristina Marsillach).

The film is not devoid of humor. Early scenes when Hanks is accepted to dinner by the family as a friend and not yet a suitor are funny and believable. Culturally rich story is aided throughout by the pic's all-Israel shoot, nicely highlighting the different worlds these two lovers come from.

•

EVERY WHICH WAY BUT LOOSE
1978, 119 mins, US Ⓥ ⊙ col
Dir James Fargo ***Prod*** Robert Daley ***Scr*** Jeremy Joe Kronsberg ***Ph*** Rexford Metz ***Ed*** Ferris Webster, Joel Cox ***Mus*** Snuff Garrett (sup.) ***Art*** Elayne Ceder
Act Clint Eastwood, Sondra Locke, Geoffrey Lewis, Beverly D'Angelo, Ruth Gordon (Malpaso/Warner)

Screenplay has Clint Eastwood as a beer-guzzling, country music–loving truck driver who picks up spare change as a barroom brawler. When Sondra Locke, an elusive singer Eastwood meets at The Palomino Club, takes off for Colorado, Eastwood packs his pickup truck in pursuit.

Behind him are a motorcycle gang and an L.A. cop. Both have been victims of Eastwood's fists. They want revenge. Traveling with Eastwood is Geoffrey Lewis and Beverly D'Angelo, whom the two meet on the road. There's also an orangutan. His name is Clyde. Eastwood won him a few years back in a fight. He goes everywhere with Eastwood. He drinks beer, finds a one-night stand at a zoo in New Mexico and cheers on his friend.

For Eastwood fans, the essential elements are there. Lots of people get beat up, Eastwood walks tall and looks nasty, cars are crashed. James Fargo directs limply.

•

EVIL ANGELS
SEE: A CRY IN THE DARK

•

EVIL DEAD, THE
1983, 85 mins, US Ⓥ ⊙ col
Dir Sam Raimi ***Prod*** Robert Tapert ***Scr*** Sam Raimi ***Ph*** Tim Philo ***Ed*** Edna Ruth Paul ***Mus*** Joseph Lo Duca
Act Bruce Campbell, Ellen Sandweiss, Betsy Baker, Hal Delrich, Sarah York (Renaissance)

The Evil Dead emerges as the ne plus ultra of low-budget gore and shock effects.

Story premise has five youngsters (in their 20s) holed up in a remote cabin where they discover a Book of the Dead. Archaeologist's tape recording reveals it having been found among the Khandarian ruins of a Sumerian civilization. Playing the taped incantations unwittingly summons up dormant demons living in the nearby forest, which possess the youngsters in succession until only Ash (Bruce Campbell) is left intact to fight for survival.

While injecting considerable black humor, neophyte Detroit-based writer-director Sam Raimi maintains suspense and a nightmarish mood in between the showy outbursts of special effects gore and graphic violence, which are staples of modern horror pictures. Powerful camerawork suggests the lurking presence of the huge-scale demons in the forest.

Filmed in 1980 on Tennessee and Michigan locations for under $400,000, pic is a grainy blowup from 16mm. Cast is functional.

•

EVIL DEAD II
1987, 85 mins, US Ⓥ ⊙ col
Dir Sam Raimi ***Prod*** Robert Tapert ***Scr*** Sam Raimi, Scott Spiegel ***Ph*** Peter Deming ***Ed*** Kaye Davis ***Mus*** Joseph Lo Duca ***Art*** Philip Duffin, Randy Bennett
Act Bruce Campbell, Sarah Berry, Dan Hicks, Kassie Wesley, Theodore Raimi, Denise Bixler (Renaissance/De Laurentiis)

More an absurdist comedy than a horror film, *Evil Dead II* is a flashy good-natured display of special effects and scare tactics so extreme they can only be taken for laughs.

Action, and there's plenty, is centered around a remote cabin where Ash (Bruce Campbell) and girlfriend Linda (Denise Bixler) run into some unexpected influences. It isn't long before the forces of the Evil Dead have got ahold of Linda and her head winds up in a vise.

It seems Prof Knowby (John Peaks) has unleashed the spirits of the dead and they want to escape limbo by claiming possession of the living. They're a remarkably protean lot and take on all sorts of imaginative and grotesque forms almost instantaneously.

Story here is merely an excuse for director Sam Raimi to explore new ways to shock an audience, and usually he keeps his sense of humor about it.

•

EVIL OF FRANKENSTEIN, THE
1964, 84 mins, UK/US Ⓥ ⊙ col
Dir Freddie Francis ***Prod*** Anthony Hinds ***Scr*** John Elder [Anthony Hinds] ***Ph*** John Wilcox ***Ed*** James Needs ***Mus*** Don Banks ***Art*** Don Mingaye
Act Peter Cushing, Peter Woodthorpe, Duncan Lamont, Sandor Eles, Katy Wild, David Hutcheson (Hammer/Universal)

In this one Peter Cushing plays the baron with his usual seriousness, avoiding tongue-in-the-cheek, and he is the main prop in the proceedings.

This time Cushing returns to the castle that is his scientific playground, and is bent on reviving and coordinating the brain of one of his homemade monsters. Earlier this character had escaped, but is found, conveniently preserved in a glacier. The baron has sundry other problems on his plate, notably a drunken, blackmailing hypnotist, a deaf-and-dumb beggar girl, the local Burgomaster and the police, but keeps a fairly stiff upper lip throughout.

•

EVIL UNDER THE SUN
1982, 102 mins, UK Ⓥ ⊙ col
Dir Guy Hamilton ***Prod*** John Brabourne, Richard Goodwin ***Scr*** Anthony Shaffer ***Ph*** Christopher Challis ***Ed*** Richard Marden ***Mus*** Jack Larchbury (arr.) ***Art*** Elliot Scott
Act Peter Ustinov, Jane Birkin, Colin Blakely, James Mason, Diana Rigg, Maggie Smith (EMI)

Director Guy Hamilton admits to hating Agatha Christie's writing style. He finds it overcrowded with characters and passé in general. Apart from cutting down the number of characters, Hamilton and scripter Anthony Shaffer have also had the audacity to switch things around in the inevitable denouement scene. Poirot points right away at the guilty party, while the true suspense is put into the how's and why's that follow.

But fun it is to follow this cast of English and U.S. characters in their stay at the elegantly old-fashioned resort hotel on a remote Tyrrhenian island (shot in Mallorca, original novel took place in Cornwall), where a famous stage actress gives them all a good motive for doing her in. Through it all, Peter Ustinov's Poirot paddles about, being demanding of staff (beeswax for his shoes) and cuisine and happy about himself.

Next to Ustinov, Maggie Smith shines as the hotel proprietress in love with the murdered woman's husband, played with quiet gusto by Denis Quilley. Diana Rigg as the stage star makes it believable in one short song-and-dance scene that she really is such a star.

•

EVITA
1996, 134 mins, US Ⓥ ⊙ ⊏⊐ col
Dir Alan Parker ***Prod*** Robert Stigwood, Alan Parker, Andrew G. Vajna ***Scr*** Alan Parker, Oliver Stone ***Ph*** Darius Khondji ***Ed*** Gerry Hambling ***Mus*** Andrew Lloyd Webber ***Art*** Brian Morris
Act Madonna, Antonio Banderas, Jonathan Pryce, Jimmy Nail (Cinergi/Stigwood/Dirty Hands/Hollywood)

The long-waited screen version of the celebrated 1978 Andrew Lloyd Webber-Tim Rice musical emerges as a stunningly crafted *object d'art* that evokes serious viewer admiration more than passionate excitement.

Few films can boast such protracted gestation periods as this one. Oliver Stone came closest to doing it, with Meryl Streep in the lead, and enough of his conception evidently remains for him to receive co-screenplay credit with Alan Parker. One can only admire the finesse and resourcefulness with which Parker has visualized *Evita.* As Lloyd Webber's score cascades relentlessly from one number to the next with only the scarcest of spoken dialogue to interrupt them, so do the burnished, indelible images that combine to form a stylized, highly dramatic portrait of the rise and demise of Eva Peron (Madonna), imperious, beloved first lady of fascist Argentina in mid-century.

By the final section, as Evita's strength begins to ebb and Juan Peron's (Jonathan Pryce) grip on power frays a bit, the originality of the film's approach starts fading as well. Along with the score, which sinks into a trough of repetitiveness, the visual coups lose their bloom. One comes to long for a little down time, a few intimate moments.

Madonna gives her all to the title role and pulls it off superbly. As the Everyman observer, Antonio Banderas is ideal, with a vocal conviction that proves highly agreeable. Exteriors in Argentina and Hungary have been integrated seamlessly.

1996: Best Original Song ("You Must Love Me")

NOMINATIONS: Best Cinematography, Editing, Art Direction, Sound

•

EXCALIBUR
1981, 140 mins, US Ⓥ ⊙ col
Dir John Boorman ***Prod*** John Boorman ***Scr*** John Boorman, Rospo Pallenberg ***Ph*** Alex Thomson ***Ed*** John Merritt ***Mus*** Trevor Jones ***Art*** Anthony Pratt
Act Nigel Terry, Nicol Williamson, Nicholas Clay, Helen Mirren, Cherie Lunghi, Corin Redgrave (Orion)

Excalibur is exquisite, a near-perfect blend of action, romance, fantasy and philosophy, finely acted and beautifully filmed by director John Boorman and cinematographer Alex Thomson.

Not surprisingly, *Excalibur* is essentially the legend of King Arthur, embellished a bit by Boorman and coscripter Rospo Pallenberg, working from the Malory classic, *Morte d'Arthur.*

Filmed in timeless Irish locales, the film rests solidly on a feeling that this, indeed, must have been what life was like in the feudal ages, even as it resists being pinned to any historical point and accepts magic and sorcery on faith.

Nicol Williamson stands out early as the wizard Merlin, at times a magician, flim-flam artist and philosopher, always interesting. The tangle of lust and betrayal that leads to Arthur's conception, the planting of Excalibur in the stone and Arthur's rise to Camelot after extracting it, is followed by restlessness and more dark deeds.

If *Excalibur* has a major fault, it's a somewhat extended sequence of the Knights of the Round Table in search of the Grail, seemingly ill-established and overdrawn.

1981: NOMINATION: Best Cinematography

•

EXECUTIONER, THE
1970, 111 mins, UK Ⓥ ⊏⊐ col
Dir Sam Wanamaker ***Prod*** Charles H. Schneer ***Scr*** Jack Pulman ***Ph*** Denys Coop ***Ed*** R. Watts ***Mus*** Ron Goodwin ***Art*** E. Marshall
Act George Peppard, Joan Collins, Judy Geeson, Oscar Homolka, Charles Gray, Nigel Patrick (Schneer/Columbia)

George Peppard is a British undercover agent out to prove that a colleague is really a double agent.

Supposedly a triple-cross suspenser, film [from a story by Gordon McDonell] just lies there so that interest fades fast in the overexposition and redundancy. Peppard is cast as an American-raised Briton whose latest spy caper has been aborted. Nigel Patrick and Charles Gray, Peppard's superiors, don't believe his charges that Keith Michell is a double agent.

Joan Collins appears occasionally as Michell's wife, and sometimes playmate of Peppard and also of George Baker. Judy Geeson appears even less frequently as Peppard's girlfriend who helps him obtain secret information.

•

EXECUTIVE ACTION
1973, 91 mins, US Ⓥ ⊙ col
Dir David Miller ***Prod*** Edward Lewis ***Scr*** Dalton Trumbo ***Ph*** Robert Steadman ***Ed*** George Grenville, Irving Lerner, Melvin Shapiro, Ivan Dryer ***Mus*** Randy Edelman ***Art*** Kirk Axtell
Act Burt Lancaster, Robert Ryan, Will Geer, Gilbert Green, John Anderson, Paul Carr (Lewis/Wakeford-Orloff)

The open lesion known as Watergate revealed a form of governmental-industrial syphilis, which in turn has made more plausible to millions the theory of an assassination conspiracy in 1963 against President John F. Kennedy. *Executive Action*, a part-fiction and documentary style film [from a story by Donald Freed and Mark Lane], dramatized with low-key terror, is an emotional aftershock to the event.

Burt Lancaster, Robert Ryan and Will Geer star as informed men of industry and government service who conclude that JFK must be eliminated. Lancaster is the overall project officer. James MacColl, a remarkable look alike to Lee Harvey Oswald, depicts the alleged Oswald frameup.

Oscar Oncidi plays Jack Ruby, Oswald's own assassin who, per this story, is wired into the plot.

•

EXECUTIVE DECISION

1996, 132 mins, US Ⓥ ⦿ col

Dir Stuart Baird ***Prod*** Joel Silver ***Scr*** Jim Thomas, John Thomas ***Ph*** Alex Thomson, Don Burgess ***Ed*** Dallas Pruitt, Frank J. Urioste, Stuart Baird ***Mus*** Jerry Goldsmith ***Art*** Terence Marsh

Act Kurt Russell, Halle Berry, John Leguizamo, Steven Seagal, Oliver Platt, Joe Morton (Silver/Warner)

This airborne anti-terrorist suspenser is a slick piece of goods with a dark sense of humor, a highly entertaining arsenal of gadgets and a fair share of unexpected developments. Screenplay borrows liberally from a number of film war horses, in particular the James Bond and *Airport* franchises.

At the center is Dr. David Grant (Kurt Russell), the head of a Washington, DC, anti-terrorist think tank. He's enlisted into a daredevil mission when a group of Islamic militants hijack an Athens-DC flight and demand $50 million, the release of their captured leader and their own safe passage.

Grant suspects that the squad is also in possession of a deadly nerve gas. Anti-terrorist commando Travis (Steven Seagal) assembles a crack team, and Grant goes to weapon designer Dennis Cahill (Oliver Platt), who takes his stealth prototype out of mothballs to effect a midair assault.

Russell's credits include a hefty number of he-man roles, but his character in *Executive Decision* relies more on intellect, ingenuity and charm than sheer muscle.

The first feature of acclaimed editor Stuart Baird, *Executive Decision* greatly benefits from a first-class, behind-the-camera team that includes crack production designer Terence Marsh and ace cameraman Alex Thomson. The Thomas brothers' script repeatedly draws us down dead-end alleys only to reverse expectations.

•

EXECUTIVE SUITE

1954, 103 mins, US Ⓥ ⦿ b/w

Dir Robert Wise ***Prod*** John Houseman ***Scr*** Ernest Lehman ***Ph*** George Folsey ***Ed*** Ralph E. Winters ***Mus*** [none]

Act William Holden, June Allyson, Barbara Stanwyck, Fredric March, Walter Pidgeon, Shelley Winters (M-G-M)

This John Houseman production is a real pro job, of a caliber that doesn't come along too often. Cameron Hawley's novel, *Executive Suite*, was good reading, and Ernest Lehman has fashioned it into screen form as a dramatically interesting motion picture humanizing big business and its upper echelon personalities.

Eight scene-stealers vie for the star billing and each is fine, with some standing out over what amounts to standout performances by all concerned in the drama. Certainly Fredric March's characterization of the controller will be remembered among the really sock delineations. So will William Holden's portrayal of the idealistic, but practical, young executive.

Also effective as the other stars are Louis Calhern, cynical stockbroker who tries to turn misfortune to personal gain; Barbara Stanwyck, neurotic heiress; Walter Pidgeon, an executive never able to rise above a number two position; Paul Douglas, the hearty sales executive; June Allyson, Holden's wife; and Shelley Winters, Douglas's secretary and after-hour amour.

The drama is built on the efforts of the several vice presidents to take over the top position, with most of the conflict in the film version centering on March, as he tries to seize power.

1954: NOMINATIONS: Best Supp. Actress (Nina Foch), B&W Cinematography, B&W Costume Design, B&W Art Direction

•

EXISTENZ

1999, 97 mins, Canada/UK Ⓥ ⦿ col

Dir David Cronenberg ***Prod*** Robert Lantos, Andras Hamori, David Cronenberg ***Scr*** David Cronenberg ***Ph*** Peter Suschitzky ***Ed*** Ronald Sanders ***Mus*** Howard Shore ***Art*** Carol Spier

Act Jennifer Jason Leigh, Jude Law, Willem Dafoe, Ian Holm, Don McKellar, Sarah Polley

Fans of Canadian auteur David Cronenberg's more ghoulish productions are likely to be disappointed by *eXistenZ*, in which the director playfully parodies some of his past obsessive horror outings. This is unquestionably Cronenberg Lite, but there is plenty of fun to be had from the absurdities and convoluted plotting.

This is the first time since *Videodrome* in 1982 that Cronenberg has written an original screenplay, and his inspiration was, of all things, the *fatwa* placed by Iranian hard-liners on *Satanic Verses* author Salman Rushdie.

Pic opens with a seminar in which officials of Antenna Research are about to test a new game, eXistenZ, devised by the celebrated Allegra Geller (Jennifer Jason Leigh), the world's No. 1 game programmer. Just as the demonstration is beginning, a member of the audience opens fire, wounding Geller, who escapes with security guard Ted Pikul (Jude Law). Fearful there is a *fatwa* against Geller, the fugitives head for the countryside, and a series of strange encounters as they flee from realism fanatics and agents of Antenna's rival, Cortical Systematics.

Cronenberg parodies [his earlier] films with outrageously sexual jokes and cheerfully sadistic bloodletting, most of it involving strange creatures that seem to be mutant reptiles and amphibians. Jason Leigh, in one of her most attractive recent perfs, enters cheerfully into the spirit of the exercise, as does Law as her unwilling collaborator. Cronenberg keeps the yuks quotient high, although the film gets a little repetitive and predictable in the later stages.

•

EXIT TO EDEN

1994, 113 mins, US Ⓥ col

Dir Garry Marshall ***Prod*** Alex Rose, Garry Marshall ***Scr*** Deborah Amelon, Bob Brunner ***Ph*** Theo Van de Sande ***Ed*** David Finfer ***Mus*** Patrick Doyle ***Art*** Peter Jamison

Act Dana Delany, Paul Mercurio, Rosie O'Donnell, Dan Aykroyd, Hector Elizondo, Stuart Wilson (Savoy)

There's something essentially dishonest in *Exit to Eden* that eats away at the fabric of the picture. The mix of erotic, comic and thriller elements diminishes whatever the original intention might have been for this melange [from Ann Rice's novel].

The thread of the story is the trackdown of Omar (Stuart Wilson), a notorious diamond smuggler, and his accomplice, Nina (Iman). LAPD undercover detectives Sheila Kingston (Rosie O'Donnell) and Fred Lavery (Dan Aykroyd) have been one step away from apprehending them, stymied because no one knows what Omar looks like.

Luck intercedes when it's learned that photographer Elliot Slater (Paul Mercurio), on a hunch, snapped the villain in action. But before the cops can get their hands on his negatives, Slater whisks away for a therapeutic vacation on the sexual fantasy island of Eden. Cops and crooks both don disguises and try to meld into the scenery at the remote retreat in order to nab the visual evidence.

Elliot has come to the spa to confront his "aberrant" sexual inclinations and learn to commit. Somehow he is redeemed through his contact with camp commander Mistress Lisa (Dana Delany). Director Garry Marshall—who truly believes in such pap, as evidenced by *Pretty Woman*—is undone by an inferior script and what would appear to be self-doubt.

Filmed in a slick, bright fashion, the picture is too visually obvious. It has the sophistication of an adolescent bathroom joke indifferently told.

•

EX-MRS. BRADFORD, THE

1936, 80 mins, US Ⓥ ⦿ b/w

Dir Stephen Roberts ***Scr*** Anthony Veiller ***Ph*** J. Roy Hunt ***Ed*** Arthur Roberts ***Mus*** Roy Webb (dir.)

Act William Powell, Jean Arthur, James Gleason, Eric Blore, Robert Armstrong (RKO)

Another sprightly entry for the school of smart comedy, detective mystery yarns, *The Ex-Mrs. Bradford* has a neat combo of names—William Powell and Jean Arthur—backed up by excellent support.

Comparison with *The Thin Man* is natural. But the film is much better than a copy.

Teaming of Powell and Arthur, as doctor and divorced wife, is a happy one. Story [by James Edward Grant] brings the wife right back to the doorstep of the busy physician, where she "moves in" and resumes where she left off annoying him with her interest in writing detective stories.

While the romance between the pair is slowly revived, the whole affair is treated with smart flippancy. Much the same attitude is taken toward the doctor's tumbling efforts to solve a series of killings that has the police baffled, until they attempt to pin them on him. Here, his wife's sharp wit and impertinence help.

•

EXODUS

1960, 212 mins, US Ⓥ ⦿ ▭ col

Dir Otto Preminger ***Prod*** Otto Preminger ***Scr*** Dalton Trumbo ***Ph*** Sam Leavitt ***Ed*** Louis R. Loeffler ***Mus*** Ernest Gold ***Art*** Richard Day, Bill Hutchinson

Act Paul Newman, Eva Marie Saint, Ralph Richardson, Peter Lawford, Lee J. Cobb, Sal Mineo (Carlyle/Alpha/United Artists)

Transposing Leon Uris's hefty novel to the screen was not an easy task. It is to the credit of director Otto Preminger and scenarist Dalton Trumbo that they have done as well as they have. One can, however, wish that they had been blessed with more dramatic incisiveness. (Estimated cost of pic was $3.5–4 million.)

The picture wanders frequently in attempting to bring into focus various political and personal aspirations that existed within the Jewish nationalist movement itself, as well as in regards to Arab opposition to the partitioning of Palestine and the unhappy role that Great Britain played as custodian of the status quo while a young United Nations pondered the fate of a new nation.

One of the overwhelming moments is played aboard a rusty old freighter in which 611 Jews of all ages, from all over the face of Europe and spirited out of an internment camp on Cyprus under the nose of the British, attempt to sail to Palestine. The whole spirit that brought Israel into being is reflected in this particular sequence toward the end of the first part of the film. It's a real dramatic gem.

The romance that develops slowly between young, dedicated Hagana leader Paul Newman and Eva Marie Saint, as a widowed American who contributes her nursing abilities to Jewish refugees on Cyprus and later in Palestine, as Arabs attack the new settlers, is conventional. Technically Newman gives a sound performance, but he fails to give the role warmth. Saint has several good scenes and makes the most of them, as does Ralph Richardson, a sympathetic British general.

Lee J. Cobb gives his customary dependable, thoroughly professionl performance as a conservative elder Hagana community leader, father of Newman and brother of the fanatical violence advocate played by David Opatoshu. The brothers' silent meeting after years of separation through a barred slot in a prison door is great pictorial drama.

Sal Mineo as a loyal Irgun youngster, who has been brutalized by the Nazis, is excellent and John Derek stands out too as an Arab whose friendship for Newman and his family goes back to boyhood.

1960: Best Scoring of a Dramatic Picture

NOMINATIONS: Best Supp. Actor (Sal Mineo), Color Cinematography

•

EXORCIST, THE

1973, 121 mins, US Ⓥ ⦿ col

Dir William Friedkin ***Prod*** William Peter Blatty ***Scr*** William Peter Blatty ***Ph*** Owen Roizman, Billy Williams ***Ed*** Jordan Leondopoulos, Evan Lottman, Norman Gay, Bud Smith ***Mus*** Jack Nitzsche ***Art*** Bill Malley

Act Ellen Burstyn, Max von Sydow, Lee J. Cobb, Kitty Winn, Jack MacGowran, Linda Blair (Hoya/Warner)

William Friedkin's film of William Peter Blatty's novel *The Exorcist* is an expert telling of a supernatural horror story. The well-cast film makes credible in powerful laymen's terms the rare phenomenon of diabolic possession.

Blatty's story is based on a 1949 incident of documented possession, atop which came Friedkin's own investigations. The joint effort is cohesive and compelling, gripping both the senses and the intellect. A compendium of production delays, some of puzzling origin (shooting alone occupied more than 10 months [of the 16-month period]), and rush to completion upped final costs to $8–$10 million.

Jesuit priest Max von Sydow is the leader of an archeological expedition. After unearthing some pagan hex symbol, several near fatal accidents occur. Thence to Georgetown, Maryland.

Ellen Burstyn, a divorced film actress, is on location with daughter, Linda Blair, the latter becoming aware of some apparent inner spiritual friend whom she calls "Captain Howdy," and their rented house now filled with strange sounds and movements. Finally, Jason Miller is a psychiatrist-Jesuit.

The lives of these three gradually converge as Blair's fits become genuinely vicious and destructive, provoking a shocking series of psychiatric tests. At length, Von Sydow, who has exorcised before, is sent to perform the rare rites. The climactic sequences assault the senses and the intellect with pure cinematic terror.

1973: Best Adapted Screenplay, Sound

NOMINATIONS: Best Picture, Director, Actress (Ellen Burstyn), Supp. Actor (Jason Miller), Supp. Actress (Linda Blair), Cinematography, Art Direction, Editing

•

EXORCIST II: THE HERETIC
1977, 117 mins, US Ⓥ col
Dir John Boorman ***Prod*** John Boorman, Richard Lederer ***Scr*** William Goodhart ***Ph*** William A. Fraker ***Ed*** Tom Priestley ***Mus*** Ennio Morricone ***Art*** Richard Macdonald
Act Linda Blair, Richard Burton, Louise Fletcher, Max von Sydow, Kitty Winn, Paul Henreid (Warner)

Since any title containing Roman numerals invites comparison, the answer is: No, *Exorcist II* is not as good as *The Exorcist*. It isn't even close. Gone now is the simple clash between Good and Evil, replaced by some goofy transcendental spiritualism.

Linda Blair is back as Regan, four years older and still suffering the residual effects of her demonic possession. For the most part, however, she's cheerful and good, seemingly no more bothered by her lingering devil than a chronic zit that keeps popping out on prom night.

She is under the kindly care of psychiatrist Louise Fletcher and Kitty Winn, mom's secretary from the old days. Another self-doubting priest (Richard Burton) is assigned to investigate the death of the old exorcist (Max von Sydow).

•

EXORCIST III, THE
1990, 110 mins, US Ⓥ ⊙ col
Dir William Peter Blatty ***Prod*** Carter DeHaven ***Scr*** William Peter Blatty ***Ph*** Gerry Fisher ***Ed*** Todd Ramsay ***Mus*** Barry De-Vorzon ***Art*** Leslie Dilley
Act George C. Scott, Ed Flanders, Brad Dourif, Jason Miller, Nicol Williamson, Scott Wilson (Morgan Creek/20th Century-Fox)

Since *The Exorcist* was one of the most frightening films ever and *Exorcist II* one of the goofiest, chances favored *The Exorcist III* to fall somewhere in between, though not nearly far enough up the scale to rival the original.

The Devil and the Church have clashed in too many other pics since with increasingly ingenious ways to burst bodies, leaving director-writer William Peter Blatty [adapting his own novel, *Legion*] with all mood and no meat. Much too often, he lingers under flickering lights in dark corridors where nothing happens.

It's been 15 years since Father Karras battled the Devil for the little girl and ended up dead at the bottom of the stairway. Now his old policeman friend (George C. Scott) is confronted with a series of sacrilegious murders bearing the trademarks of a killer executed about the same time the priest died.

Anyway, there's a guy in chains over at the nuthouse who sometimes appears to Scott as Karras (Jason Miller) and sometimes as the executed killer (Brad Dourif), and it's all very confusing.

It would be downright incomprehensible, in fact, if Dourif didn't do such a dandy job in explaining things in a couple of long, madman monologs.

•

EXPERIMENT IN TERROR
(UK: THE GRIP OF FEAR)
1962, 123 mins, US Ⓥ ⊙ b/w
Dir Blake Edwards ***Prod*** Blake Edwards ***Scr*** Mildred Gordon, Gordon Gordon ***Ph*** Philip Lathrop ***Ed*** Patrick McCormack ***Mus*** Henry Mancini ***Art*** Robert Peterson
Act Glenn Ford, Lee Remick, Stefanie Powers, Roy Poole, Ned Glass, Anita Loo (Columbia)

Written by Mildred and Gordon Gordon from their book and *Ladies' Home Journal* serial *Operation Terror*. The film treatment embraces a number of unnecessary character bits that merely extend the plot and, despite their striking individual reaction, deter from the suspense buildup. Edwards's particular interest seems to lie in the camera angles. He concentrates on overhead shots and unusual perspective merely for visual effect. Only in the climactic scenes, which take place in San Francisco's Candlestick Park during an actual baseball game of capacity attendance, does the overhead filming become fully valuable.

The "experiment" is a terrifying episode in which a bank teller is forced by a psychopathic killer into embezzling $100,000 under threat of murder. She goes to the FBI.

Glenn Ford and Lee Remick play the FBI agent and bank teller, respectively. For Remick it is a handsome role played with nicely modulated control and a natural feeling that is devoid of the extreme emotional tension often exposed in such characters. Ford has solidarity, but his role is merely that of a staunch agent doing his job well.

Picture was shot extensively in San Francisco, though story could be placed in any area. However, Philip Lathrop's camera took fine advantage of known Bay City landmarks, giving the film a nice visual style.

•

EXPERIMENT PERILOUS
1944, 90 mins, US Ⓥ b/w
Dir Jacques Tourneur ***Prod*** Warren Duff ***Scr*** Warren Duff ***Ph*** Tony Gaudio ***Ed*** Ralph Dawson ***Mus*** Roy Webb ***Art*** Albert S. D'Agostino, Jack Okey
Act Hedy Lamarr, George Brent, Paul Lukas, Albert Dekker, Carl Esmond, Olive Blakeney (RKO)

Plot [from the novel by Margaret Carpenter] centers around Paul Lukas's mansion in the 1903 era. The elderly Lukas has been married to the young and beautiful Hedy Lamarr for about a decade, holding her in close confinement and restraint as he would any other possession. She, in turn, is continually dominated by fear of strange influences that can be felt but not seen.

George Brent, a young doctor, originally is projected into contact with the family through chance meeting with Olive Blakeney, elderly sister of Lukas, who's returning from several years in a midwest sanitarium. She comments on the unseen influences at the family home, and declares against staying there. But she dies on arrival while having tea, and Brent accepts invitation some days later to meet Lamarr and inspect the place that intrigues him.

Picture unfolds in both straightline and flashback techniques. It covers a lot of territory and sets, and depends mainly on dialog to put over its dramatic unfolding. Despite these handicaps, picture carries good pace of suspense.

•

EXPLORERS
1985, 109 mins, US Ⓥ ⊙ col
Dir Joe Dante ***Prod*** Edward S. Feldman, David Bombyk ***Scr*** Eric Luke ***Ph*** John Hora ***Ed*** Tina Hirsch ***Mus*** Jerry Goldsmith ***Art*** Robert F. Boyle
Act Ethan Hawke, River Phoenix, Jason Presson, Amanda Peterson, Dick Miller, Robert Picardo (Paramount/Industrial Light & Magic)

Two young boys, a dreamer (Ethan Hawke) and a nerdy science genius type (River Phoenix), manage, through combining their talents and happening upon an unusual discovery, to fashion a homemade spacecraft.

In league with a lower-class misfit (Jason Presson) who falls in with them, the lads inventively use a leftover Tilt-a-Whirl as their basic chassis and elaborate upon their design with spare parts of all kinds. Along with their extracurricular Advanced Shop work, opening hour is occupied with passable but far from original stuff devoted to bullies vs. nerds, puppy love and schoolroom antics.

Throughout, director Joe Dante and writer Eric Luke load the proceedings with references to sci-fiers of an earlier day, such as *War of the Worlds*, *This Island Earth*, *Journey to the Center of the Earth* and many others, but this is nothing compared to what happens when the trio of youngsters finally take off into outer space and make contact with an alien race.

•

EXPOSED
1983, 100 mins, US Ⓥ col
Dir James Toback ***Prod*** James Toback ***Scr*** James Toback ***Ph*** Henri Decae ***Ed*** Robert Lawrence, Annie Charvein ***Mus*** Georges Delerue ***Art*** Brian Eatwell
Act Nastassja Kinski, Rudolf Nureyev, Harvey Keitel, Ian McShane, Bibi Andersson, Ron Randell (M-G-M/United Artists)

Intelligent and illogical, beautiful and erratic, *Exposed* is a provocative, jet-setter's visit to the worlds of high fashion and international terrorism.

After a prologue in which a foxy blonde is observed blowing up a Paris café, writer-director James Toback himself, as a college English teacher, breaks up romantically with one of his students (Nastassja Kinski).

Kinski returns to her home in Wisconsin and, in one of the film's most striking, and convincing, sequences, is attending an exhibition of photos featuring her when her eye is caught by Rudolf Nureyev.

After a bizarre, cat-and-mouse courtship, the inevitable big love scene arrives. As it happens, Nureyev is also a dedicated terrorist fighter with intensely personal motives, and when Kinski follows him to Paris, she naively becomes involved with the very forces Nureyev is intent upon wiping out. Kinski is delivered into the lair of Carlos-type terrorist Harvey Keitel, a provocateur dedicated to random violence.

Performers seem to have been chosen mostly for their physical attributes, and Kinski and Nureyev lead the way in ably fleshing out characters who are meant to remain mysterious.

•

EXPRESSO BONGO
1959, 111 mins, UK Ⓥ ▭ b/w
Dir Val Guest ***Prod*** Val Guest ***Scr*** Wolf Mankowitz ***Ph*** John Wilcox ***Ed*** Bill Lenny ***Mus*** Robert Farnon (dir.) ***Art*** Tony Masters
Act Laurence Harvey, Sylvia Syms, Yolande Donlan, Cliff Richard, Meier Tzelniker, Ambrosine Phillpotts (British Lion/Britannia)

Soho, with its atmosphere of sleazy stripperies, gaudy coffee bars and frenetic teenagers, is the setting for this amusing satire on how a little talent can be boosted overnight as the result of a successful disk and a click TV appearance. Wolf Mankowitz's story [from the musical comedy by him and Julian More] is slight and not particularly original, but it has pungency, wit and a sharp sense of observation.

Laurence Harvey is a cheap, opportunistic promoter, always on the lookout for an easy buck. In a Soho expresso bar, he picks up an amateur singer and bongo player, signs him up on a dubious contract and boosts him to what is now regarded as stardom.

Harvey gives a brashly amusing, offbeat performance as the small-time operator while Sylvia Syms is cast as a stripper with aspirations toward stardom as a singer. Expresso Bongo is played by Cliff Richard, a wrong piece of casting. The songs are intended to spoof the whole business of pop crooning but they come over, in Richard's larynx, as completely feasible entries into the pop market. Meier Tzelniker plays the part that he did so well on the stage. He's boss of a disk company and here's an excellent characterization—flamboyant, garrulous and only slightly exaggerated.

•

EXTASE
(ECSTASY)
1933, 90 mins, Czechoslovakia Ⓥ b/w
Dir Gustav Machaty ***Scr*** Gustav Machaty ***Ph*** Jan Stallich ***Art*** Bohumil Hes
Act Hedy Lamarr, Andre Nox, Pierre Nay, Rogoz (Elekta)

Extase tells the story [by Viteslav Nezval] of Eva (Hedy Kiesler [later Lamarr]), who on her bridal night finds her husband (Rogoz) unequal to the occasion. She returns to her father (Andre Nox), a breeder of horses, and attempts to forget her chagrin in an active outdoor life. One day, while she is bathing, her mare runs away, carrying off her pajamas on its back. The nude Eva is rushing through the woods after her horse when a young engineer (Pierre Nay) at work nearby on a railroad, meets her and restores both the horse and the pajamas.

Soon the handsome young man awakens in Eva all the pent-up forces of her ardent nature, and that same night she goes to his cabin during a violent storm. Close-ups of the heroine's face shown during her emotional stress are extremely audacious.

The husband returns to reclaim his wife, but finds it is too late. In driving away from Eva's home he is way-laid by the engineer, who asks for a lift. During the course of the journey the engineer-lover displays a string of pearls that are recognized by the husband as his wife's.

There is almost no dialog, though there is music and sound. All the big moments are played silently, to enhance their effect. The camerawork is superb. Every little nuance in the scenic composition and the lighting has a studied and vital meaning. The cast is uniformly good, and Kiesler, young, talented and beautiful in form and face, will certainly bear watching by Hollywood producers.

[Review is from the film's showing in Paris, soon after its Prague premiere. Cuts had already been made for French release; in Germany the pic was banned outright.]

•

EXTERMINATING ANGEL, THE
SEE: EL ANGEL EXTERMINADOR

•

EXTERMINATOR, THE
1980, 101 mins, US Ⓥ ⊙ col
Dir James Glickenhaus ***Prod*** Mark Buntzman ***Scr*** James Glickenhaus ***Ph*** Bob Baldwin ***Ed*** Corky O'Hara ***Mus*** Joe Renzetti
Act Christopher George, Samantha Eggar, Robert Ginty, Steve James, Tony Di Benedetto (Interstar)

For his second pic, writer-director James Glickenhaus commits the major sin of shooting an action film with little action. Contrived script instead opts for grotesque violence in a series of glum, distasteful scenes.

The Exterminator returns to New York City for a listlessly paced tale of Robert Ginty suddenly deciding to avenge his war buddy, paralyzed from an encounter with a youth gang. Absence of proper transition scenes and script's frequent reliance upon coincidence loses credibility for Ginty's actions early on.

Christopher George's walkthrough as a policeman is regrettable, while Samantha Eggar as both the buddy's doctor and George's girlfriend must have calculated that this travesty would never be released.

•

EXTERMINATOR 2

1984, 89 mins, US Ⓥ ⊙ col

Dir Mark Buntzman, William Sachs ***Prod*** Mark Buntzman, William Sachs ***Scr*** Mark Buntzman, William Sachs ***Ph*** Bob Baldwin, Joseph Mangine ***Ed*** Marcus Nanton, George Norris ***Mus*** David Spear ***Art*** Mischa Petrow, Virginia Field

Act Robert Ginty, Mario Van Peebles, Deborah Geffner, Frankie Faison, Scott Randolph, Reggie Rock Bythewood (Cannon)

Exterminator 2 is a silly and tiresome revenge actioner. Mark Buntzman, who produced the original, here wears (and shares with William Sachs) too many hats, ending up with a contradictory mismash.

Reprising his title as Vietman vet Johnny Eastland, an uncomfortable Robert Ginty is supposedly spurred into renewed vigilante action when his flashdancing girlfriend, Caroline (Deborah Geffner), is murdered by all-purpose punks, led by a messianic leader ("I am the streets") X (Mario Van Peebles).

Eastland is teamed with an old mate from Vietnam, Be Gee (Frankie Faison), your friendly neighborhood black garbageman who eagerly endorses Eastland's murderous cleanup policy.

Generally, the sadistic element of the first film (which had Ginty ingeniously feeding bad guys to a meatgrinder, etc.) has been toned down. Geffner gets to show her nude body and dancing ability, while acting honors go to Van Peebles. Why it took such a huge crew (over 300 people are credited with behind-the-camera contributions) to make a B-picture is mighty strange.

•

EXTRAORDINARY SEAMAN, THE

1969, 79 mins, US ▭ col

Dir John Frankenheimer ***Prod*** Edward Lewis, John H. Cushingham ***Scr*** Phillip Rock, Hal Dresner ***Ph*** Lionel Linden ***Ed*** Fredric Steinkamp ***Mus*** Maurice Jarre ***Art*** George W. Davis, Edward Carfagno

Act David Niven, Faye Dunaway, Alan Alda, Mickey Rooney, Jack Carter, Juano Hernandez (M-G-M)

The Extraordinary Seaman is strictly steerage cargo. A tepid story keel, not entirely—but almost—devoid of amusement strength, has been ballasted with padding newsreel footage and other effect to yield an unstable comedy vessel. David Niven, Faye Dunaway, Alan Alda, Mickey Rooney and Jack Carter end up awash in the artistic debris.

Set in the Philippines where three U.S. Navy men, in flight from the Japanese, discover an urbane Niven, as a Royal Navy officer, living in uncanny nattiness aboard a beached ship. Dunaway joins the crew as Niven sets sail for Australia.

To simulate the original environment, pic was shot in Baja, California, but what shows in the final cut could have been shot off Santa Barbara.

•

EXTREME PREJUDICE

1987, 104 mins, US Ⓥ ⊙ col

Dir Walter Hill ***Prod*** Buzz Feitshans ***Scr*** Deric Washburn, Harry Kleiner ***Ph*** Matthew F. Leonetti ***Ed*** Freeman Davis ***Mus*** Jerry Goldsmith ***Art*** Albert Heschong

Act Nick Nolte, Powers Boothe, Michael Ironside, Maria Conchita Alonso, Rip Torn, Clancy Brown (Carolco)

Extreme Prejudice is an amusing concoction that is frequently offbeat and at times compelling. Taut direction and editing prevail despite overstaged hyper-violence that is so gratuitous to be farcical.

Story pivots on the adversarial relationship between small-town Texas Ranger Nick Nolte and drug kingpin Powers Boothe. Originally childhood friends, they are now on opposite sides of the law and the U.S.-Mexican border.

Presented as a severe and humorless straight arrow, Nolte's character is not easy to like but his acting nonetheless intrigues. Free-wheeling and provocative, Boothe is the film's wild card as director Walter Hill signals right off that he's going to have some fun here.

Story proceeds through some interesting twists on the commando front while Nolte and Boothe try to reconcile their friendship and separate paths.

•

EXTREMITIES

1986, 90 mins, US Ⓥ ⊙ col

Dir Robert M. Young ***Prod*** Burt Sugarman ***Scr*** William Mastrosimone ***Ph*** Curtis Clark ***Ed*** Arthur Coburn ***Mus*** J.A.C. Redford ***Art*** Chester Kaczenski

Act Farrah Fawcett, James Russo, Diana Scarwid, Alfre Woodard (Atlantic)

Playwright William Mastrosimone adapted his 1982 off-Broadway work for the screen, but it seems to be director Robert M. Young who is responsible for virtually exploiting cinema's power to propel the viewer into the onscreen action.

Marjorie (Farrah Fawcett) is a museum employee on her way home from work and a workout. A ski-masked assailant imprisons and terrorizes her in her own car.

Marjorie manages to escape but the attacker knows her identity and address. Successive events document the trials of any woman in a similar predicament: essentially unsympathetic police and friends.

Finally, Marjorie's worst nightmare comes true. She is visited at her secluded home by the man who attacked her (James Russo).

Fawcett, who acquainted herself with the role of Marjorie on stage, following Susan Sarandon and Karen Allen, acts with a confidence and control not often seen in her screen work.

•

EYE FOR AN EYE, AN

1981, 106 mins, US Ⓥ col

Dir Steve Carver ***Prod*** Frank Capra, Jr. ***Scr*** William Gray, James Bruner ***Ph*** Roger Shearman ***Ed*** Anthony Redman ***Mus*** William Golstein ***Art*** Vance Lorenzini

Act Chuck Norris, Christopher Lee, Richard Roundtree, Mako, Rosalind Chao, Maggie Cooper (Avco Embassy/Wescom)

An Eye for an Eye is an effective martial arts actioner vehicle for Chuck Norris.

Norris toplines as a San Francisco cop who quits the force and goes after revenge when his partner and partner's girlfriend are killed by drug traffickers. Aided by his former police boss Capt. Stevens (Richard Roundtree), Norris evens the accounts and takes care of the drug ring.

Making solid atmospheric use of S.F. locations, helmer Steve Carver segues from realistic violence and tension to comic strip hokum in the form of a huge oriental villain (Toru Tanaka), whose menacing antics tip the audience that the film is all in fun.

Format has Norris, in traditional Western genre fashion, helped and jeckled by an old pro "master" James Chan (Mako), whose wise-cracks provide comic relief.

•

EYE FOR AN EYE

1995, 111 mins, US Ⓥ ⊙ col

Dir John Schlesinger ***Prod*** Michael I. Levy ***Scr*** Amanda Silver, Rick Jaffa ***Ph*** Amir M. Mokri ***Ed*** Peter Honess ***Mus*** James Newton Howard ***Art*** Stephen Hendrickson

Act Sally Field, Keifer Sutherland, Ed Harris, Beverly D'Angelo, Joe Mantegna, Charlayne Woodard (Paramount)

This muddled revenge melodrama is a B movie that somehow won the lottery and got an A-movie cast and director.

Sally Field toplines to good effect as Karen McCann, the mother of a lovely teenage girl who is viciously raped and murdered in her own living room by a grinning psychopath named Robert Doob (Kiefer Sutherland). Unfortunately, the psycho has a great lawyer.

Mack McCann (Ed Harris), the victim's stepfather, manages to sublimate his rage and frustration, but Karen is neither willing nor able. At first, she follows Doob, maintaining a surveillance like some TV detective. In time, she begins to notice that, in her support group for parents of murdered children, a couple of the members (Philip Baker Hall, Keith David) may be channeling their rage into retribution, prompting her to think that vigilantism may not be such a bad idea.

Vet director John Schlesinger gives *Eye for an Eye* enough tension and immediacy—most of the time, at least—to make this worth a viewer's time. In most other respects, however, the screenplay, taken from a novel by Erika Holzer, is as simplistic as the worst kind of talk-radio diatribe. Doob isn't merely a career criminal or a maladjusted sex offender—he is the Antichrist. Schlesinger even includes a scene where Doob pours hot coffee on a stray dog. No kidding.

When Karen angrily upbraids Joe Denillo, the tough but honorable cop played by Joe Mantegna, for what she sees as his impotence, even bleeding-heart liberals in the audience may be screaming, 'Right on!' To partially appease those liberals, and to keep from unduly ruffling anyone else's feathers, the filmmakers work overtime to cover all their bases. The movie is intended to appeal to the broadest constituency possible.

Sutherland gives a one-note performance in a one-dimensional role, but that note is sustained with impressive efficiency.

•

EYE OF THE CAT

1969, 102 mins, US col

Dir David Lowell Rich ***Prod*** Bernard Schwartz, Phillip Hazelton ***Scr*** Joseph Stefano ***Ph*** Russell Metty, Ellsworth Fredricks ***Ed*** J. Terry Williams ***Mus*** Lalo Schifrin ***Art*** Alexander Golitzen, William D. DeCinces

Act Michael Sarrazin, Gayle Hunnicutt, Eleanor Parker, Tim Henry, Laurence Naismith, Jennifer Leak (Universal)

Pic has a few good jolts, successful buildups, and good-looking people, but stilted dialog and plot shot through with holes keep mystery at a minimum, suspense overdue. Despite San Francisco as backdrop, with North Beach and Sausalito tossed in for spice, film trips over its own cliches and errors.

Beautician Kassia (Gayle Hunnicutt), after witnessing emphysema attack of wealthy San Francisco matron Danny (Eleanor Parker), finds Danny's runaway favorite nephew Wylie (Michael Sarrazin).

Kassia plans to re-establish Wylie in the house and, after Aunt Danny changes her will in his favor, murder her and split the fortune.

David Lowell Rich's direction often misleads, but he does manage to get actors to speak bad lines with straight faces.

•

EYE OF THE DEVIL

1968, 89 mins, UK b/w

Dir J. Lee Thompson ***Prod*** Martin Ransohoff, John Colley ***Scr*** Robin Estridge, Dennis Murphy ***Ph*** Erwin Hillier ***Ed*** Ernest Walter ***Mus*** Gary McFarland ***Art*** Elliot Scott

Act Deborah Kerr, David Niven, Donald Pleasence, Edward Mulhare, Flora Robson, Sharon Tate (M-G-M/Filmways)

Originally titled *13*, film has a production history far more interesting than the final cut. From files, names of Julie Andrews and Kim Novak appear, latter forced out by an accident, after production started, and replaced by Deborah Kerr. Script-wise, *Day of the Arrow*, a Philip Loraine novel, went from Terry Southern (unbilled) to Robin Estridge, who shares screen credit with Dennis Murphy, engaged just before shooting.

The directorial montage includes Sidney J. Furie, Arthur Hiller and Michael Anderson, latter dropping out on medic's orders, with J. Lee Thompson taking over reins.

David Niven, a vineyard manor lord, is called back to his property because of another dry season. Kerr, against his wishes, follows with their children (Suky Appleby and Robert Duncan), latter acting mysteriously at start and finish. At the gloomy ancestral home, characters include Donald Pleasence, the local "priest," butler Donald Bisset, Flora Robson, Niven's aunt who knows (and finally tells) what is going on, and Emlyn Williams, Niven's father.

Sharon Tate and David Hemmings loom as paper threats who speak deadpan dialog about the goings on. Kerr is our only touch with reality, and she tries to carry the pic, to little avail.

•

EYE OF THE NEEDLE

1981, 111 mins, UK Ⓥ ⊙ col

Dir Richard Marquand ***Prod*** Stephen Friedman ***Scr*** Stanley Mann ***Ph*** Alan Hume ***Ed*** Sean Barton ***Mus*** Miklos Rozsa ***Art*** Wilfrid Shingleton

Act Donald Sutherland, Kate Nelligan, Ian Bannen, Christopher Cazenove, Philip Martin Brown (United Artists/Kings Road)

As a study of a ruthless, essentially unsympathetic killer, working for the wrong side, *Eye of the Needle* [from the 1978 bestseller by Ken Follett] perhaps resembles *The Day of the Jackal*. Similarly, this tale of subtle intrigue and skilled maneuvers works rather better in print than on film.

Steely blue-eyed Donald Sutherland is introduced as a low-level British railway functionary in 1940. In prolog, Sutherland is shown murdering his friendly landlady when she discovers him working with a short-wave radio, and newlyweds Kate Nelligan and Christopher Cazenove suffer a horrible auto accident as they speed off on their honeymoon.

Cut to four years later, and Sutherland is soon revealed as perhaps Berlin's most reliable spy still working undetected within Britain. Armed with photos of a phony airbase in Eastern England, Sutherland makes his way to the aptly named Storm Island to rendezvous with a U-boat, waiting there to take him to Germany.

In the meantime, Nelligan and Cazenove have resettled on the bleak outpost of civilization. Formerly a dashing pilot, the latter has become a bitter paraplegic as a result of the accident, so his beauteous wife readily responds to the mysterious stranger when he temporarily lands in their household.

It's a good yarn, reminful of some of Alfred Hitchcock and Fritz Lang's wartime mellers as well as Michael Powell's 1939 tale of a World War I German agent in Scotland, *The Spy in Black.*

●

EYES OF LAURA MARS
1978, 104 mins, US Ⓥ ⦿ col
Dir Irvin Kershner ***Prod*** Jon Peters ***Scr*** John Carpenter, David Zelag Goodman ***Ph*** Victor J. Kemper ***Ed*** Michael Kahn ***Mus*** Artie Kane ***Art*** Gene Callahan
Act Faye Dunaway, Tommy Lee Jones, Brad Dourif, Rene Auberjonois, Raul Julia, Rose Gregorio (Columbia)

Eyes of Laura Mars is a very stylish thriller [from a story by John Carpenter] in search of a better ending.

Faye Dunaway stars as a chic fashion photographer with mysterious and accurate premonitions about a series of murders. All of the victims are either friends or associates. Tommy Lee Jones, in an inspired bit of casting, plays a police lieutenant assigned to the case and an integral element in the mystery. Brad Dourif as Dunaway's driver, Rene Auberjonois as her trendy and obnoxious manager and Raul Julia as her ex-husband, add marvelous supporting performances.

Especially well handled are the screen realizations of Dunaway's premonitions. They look like a blurred videotape, as she explains to Jones at one point, a conception that works well on screen.

The relationships among the characters, Dunaway's portrayal of a chic and haggard photographer-artist and even the choice of Helmut Newton and Rebecca Blake's violent and stark photos as the work of the fictional Dunaway character are satisfying and engaging.

●

EYES WIDE SHUT
1999, 159 mins, UK/US Ⓥ ⦿ col
Dir Stanley Kubrick ***Prod*** Stanley Kubrick ***Scr*** Stanley Kubrick, Frederic Raphael ***Ph*** Larry Smith ***Ed*** Nigel Galt ***Mus*** Jocelyn Pook ***Art*** Les Tomkins, Roy Walker
Act Tom Cruise, Nicole Kidman, Sydney Pollack, Marie Richardson, Rade Sherbedgia, Todd Field (Hobby/Pole Star/Warner)

Less acerbic and more optimistic about the human condition than any of the director's previous films, this intimately focused updating by Stanley Kubrick and Frederic Raphael of Arthur Schnitzler's 1926 novella *Dream Story* remains remarkably faithful to its source while also trading in familiar Kubrick concerns such as paranoia, deception, and the literal and figurative masks people wear.

Film bridges its source's early-20th-century Euro setting with modern New York via a lilting waltz to which the beautiful William and Alice Harford (Tom Cruise, Nicole Kidman) dress in their opulent Central Park West apartment as they prepare for an elegant pre-Christmas party thrown by the wealthy Victor Ziegler (Sydney Pollack). Under the influence of marijuana the next evening, Alice confesses the convulsive physical effect a handsome naval officer had on her during their Cape Cod vacation that summer.

The revelation has a chilling effect on Bill, a medical doctor, who heads out into the night to respond to a call that one of his patients has died. This marks just the beginning of a long, brooding nocturnal journey that sees Bill become the object of a declaration of love by the dead man's distraught daughter (Marie Richardson), go home with a hooker (Vinessa Shaw), and learn of an exclusive costume party from a musician friend (Todd Field).

Kidman is sensational and luminous, reaching a career high-water mark with the remarkable unveiling of her feelings. At face value, Cruise gives a limited, emotionally constrained performance, nor is he entirely convincing as an established favorite doctor to Gotham's elite.

●

EYES WITHOUT A FACE
SEE: LES YEUX SANS VISAGE

●

EYEWITNESS
(US: SUDDEN TERROR)
1970, 95 mins, UK Ⓥ col
Dir John Hough ***Prod*** Irving Allen ***Scr*** Ronald Harwood ***Ph*** Ernest Robinson ***Ed*** Geoffrey Foot ***Mus*** Fairfield Parlor, Van Der Graff Generator
Act Mark Lester, Lionel Jeffries, Susan George, Tony Bonner, Jeremy Kemp, Peter Vaughan (EMI)

Eyewitness has its groundroots in an often-used idea. Angle of a likeable kid with an imagination so vivid that unfeeling adults good-humoredly regard him as a chronic liar. Result is that when a crisis really arises no one fully believes him.

Young victim is Mark Lester and it's the hook on which is hung a fairly conventional crime chase yarn [from a novel by Mark Hebden] set on a Mediterranean island (it was shot in Malta), which has some exciting moments but lacks much of the tension that more astute and experienced directors than John Hough might have given it.

Adventure starts with the assassination of a visiting president. The moppet claims to have seen a policeman pull the fatal trigger. He has to avoid two cops and also convince his relatives that his story's on the level.

●

EYEWITNESS
(UK: THE JANITOR)
1981, 102 mins, US Ⓥ ⦿ col
Dir Peter Yates ***Prod*** Peter Yates ***Scr*** Steve Tesich ***Ph*** Mathew F. Leonetti ***Ed*** Cynthia Scheider ***Mus*** Stanley Silverman ***Art*** Philip Rosenberg
Act William Hurt, Sigourney Weaver, Christopher Plummer, James Woods, Irene Worth, Morgan Freeman (20th Century-Fox)

Once an office-building janitor himself, writer Steve Tesich often wondered in the quiet of the night what evil deeds might be going on behind closed doors. Enter William Hurt on the night-shift discovering the murdered body of a mysterious Chinese businessman.

Tesich's other fantasy concerned a real-life infatuation with a lady reporter on CBS, wondering what she would be like and how far he would go to meet her. Hurt, too, has an obsession for newswoman Sigourney Weaver, so consuming he videotapes her every show to linger over.

When Weaver comes to his building to report on the murder, Hurt pretends to know something secret to prolong this unexpected encounter with his distant sweetheart. That in turn leads him into danger with assorted characters—Christopher Plummer in particular—who really do know something about the murder.

Weaver plays her part very well, but simply can't justify the character's actions, which ripple through the murder plot in several directions. Consequently, the story gets more and more strained before it's resolved.

FABULOUS BAKER BOYS, THE

1989, 113 mins, US Ⓥ ⦿ col

Dir Steve Kloves ***Prod*** Paula Weinstein, Mark Rosenberg ***Scr*** Steve Kloves ***Ph*** Michael Ballhaus ***Ed*** William Steinkamp ***Mus*** Dave Grusin ***Art*** Jeffrey Townsend

Act Jeff Bridges, Michelle Pfeiffer, Beau Bridges, Elie Raab, Jennifer Tilly (Gladden/Mirage)

There's nothing startlingly original about this smoothly made little romantic comedy of two piano-playing brothers who find an attractive young singer to give some much-needed CPR to their dying lounge act. The first look at cynical, seen-it-all Jack Baker (Jeff Bridges) and his bubbling, ever-optimistic brother, Frank (Beau Bridges), tells us all that's necessary to know about them.

When they're joined by sexy-surly singer Susie Diamond (Michelle Pfeiffer), it's obvious exactly where the film is headed. Jack and Susie are on a romantic collision course, with Frank bound to be hurt by the explosion.

The fun part is seeing it all play out, thanks to a standout cast and first-time director Steve Kloves's skill in handling them.

The focus of all eyes is on Pfeiffer. The actress, who does all her own singing, is required to play a character whose vocal abilities are good, but not so good as to make a viewer wonder why she hasn't been signed to a major label. Pfeiffer hits the nail right on the head.

She also hits the spot in the film's certain-to-be-remembered highlight—a version of "Makin' Whoopee" that she sings while crawling all over a piano in a blazing red dress. She's dynamite.

1989: NOMINATIONS: Best Actress (Michelle Pfeiffer), Editing, Original Score

•

FACE BEHIND THE MASK

1941, 69 mins, US b/w

Dir Robert Florey ***Prod*** Wallace McDonald ***Scr*** Allen Vincent, Paul Jarrico ***Ph*** Franz A. Planer ***Ed*** Charles Nelson ***Mus*** Sidney Cutner

Act Peter Lorre, Evelyn Keyes, George E. Stone, Don Beddoe, John Tyrell (Columbia)

This is not so much likely to scare audiences as make them a little sick. Production, acting and story, paradoxically, are all of a fairly high order, but it's all too unpleasant.

Yarn has Peter Lorre an immigrant whose face is badly burned in a rooming-house fire. Seared flesh is bad enough to look at, but it is not helped much by putting Lorre in a rubber mask that's almost equally likely to cause intestinal flip-flops among the more squeamish trade.

Story unfolds at deliberate pace under Robert Florey's direction to emphasize that a sincerely honest man is forced by unfortunate circumstances to turn to crime.

Lorre handles his role ably, hurdling with minimum pain the bits of stilted dialog too frequently handed him by screenwriters Allen Vincent and Paul Jarrico [from a story by Arthur Levinson, based on a radio play by Thomas Edward O'Connell]. Evelyn Keyes, as the blind girl who is the only one he can find to accept his love, does a good job in a role that could easily be hammed up.

•

FACE IN THE CROWD, A

1957, 125 mins, US Ⓥ b/w

Dir Elia Kazan ***Prod*** Elia Kazan ***Scr*** Budd Schulberg ***Ph*** Harry Stradling, Gayne Rescher ***Ed*** Gene Milford ***Mus*** Tom Glazer ***Art*** Richard Sylbert, Paul Sylbert

Act Andy Griffith, Patricia Neal, Anthony Franciosa, Walter Matthau, Lee Remick (Newtown/Warner)

Elia Kazan and Budd Schulberg, who teamed to bring forth *On the Waterfront*, have another provocative and hard-hitting entry, based on Schulberg's short story *The Arkansas Traveler*. It's a devastating commentary on hero-worship and success cults in America.

Its basic story is somewhat similar to that of *The Great Man* in that it exposes a beloved television personality as an unmitigated heel.

Story plucks an ignorant, guitar-playing hillbilly from an Arkansas jail and converts him in a short space of time to America's most popular and beloved television personality. He is in private life an unsavory character, a libertine and an opportunist with loyalty to no one but himself. He enters the political arena, becomes aligned with an "isolationist" senator, and pitches an extreme reactionary philosophy.

Andy Griffith makes his film debut as Lonesome Rhodes, the power-mad hillbilly. As his vis-à-vis, Patricia Neal is the girl who guides Griffith to fame and fortune. Anthony Franciosa plays the unprincipled personal manager, Walter Matthau a cynical writer.

•

FACE OF A STRANGER

SEE: THE PROMISE

•

FACE/OFF

1997, 138 mins, US Ⓥ ⦿ ▭ col

Dir John Woo ***Prod*** David Permut, Barrie M. Osborne, Terence Chang, Christopher Godsick ***Scr*** Mike Werb, Michael Colleary ***Ph*** Oliver Wood ***Ed*** Christian Wagner, Steven Kemper ***Mus*** John Powell ***Art*** Neil Spisak

Act John Travolta, Nicolas Cage, Joan Allen, Alessandro Nivola, Gina Gershon, Dominique Swain (Douglas-Reuther/WCG/Permut/Paramount)

A provocative premise, virtuoso direction and two dazzling lead performances go a long way toward offsetting a lack of dramatic structure and a sense of when to quit in *Face/Off*. Watching John Travolta and Nicolas Cage square off and literally exchange roles partway through brings back the old-fashioned pleasure of astutely judged movie star pairings in a major way, and Hong Kong director John Woo finally gets his chance to shoot the works in a Hollywood picture.

Maniacal criminal Castor Troy (Cage) draws a bead on FBI agent Sam Archer (Travolta) while the latter lovingly cavorts with his son, but accidentally kills the kid instead. Six years later, Archer, the leader of the agency's covert L.A.-based antiterrorism unit, is still obsessed with tracking down his son's murderer. Many killings and considerable breathless excitement later, Archer and Troy have their first of several Mexican standoffs before the latter is apparently blasted to smithereens by a jet engine.

But Archer discovers Troy is still alive, even if comatose, and he and his demented brother, Pollux (Alessandro Nivola), have planted a nerve gas bomb that threatens "to unleash the biblical plague that L.A. deserves." Archer agrees to permit Troy's face, voice and entire physiognomy to be transferred to his own body so he can learn the details of the heinous plot from Pollux.

Gambit gives the actors a delicious opportunity to play two roles, and they make the most of it. Troy is seized by Travolta with great wit and cockiness; the devilish glee this villain takes in assuming the office of an FBI operative, slipping into bed with another man's wife (Joan Allen) and even coming on to his teen daughter (Dominique Swain) is vastly amusing.

While there are some nice twists along the way, the film doesn't build in the swift, sure way it should from this point on. Woo sets up sequence after sequence that appear intended as the climax, only to let Archer and Troy live for yet another confrontation.

1997: NOMINATION: Best Sound Effects Editing

•

FACES

1968, 130 mins, US b/w

Dir John Cassavetes ***Prod*** Maurice McEndree ***Scr*** John Cassavetes ***Ph*** Al Ruban ***Ed*** Maurice McEndree ***Mus*** Jack Ackerman ***Art*** Phedon Papamichael

Act John Marley, Gena Rowlands, Lynn Carlin, Fred Draper, Seymour Cassel (Maurice McEndree)

Faces is a long, long (at least an hour too long) look at a 36-hour splitup in the 14-year marriage of a middle-class couple. At least John Cassavetes, who also wrote the screenplay, describes them as middle-class.

As the result of tensions, inhibitions created by years of trying to adjust and temporary clashes of personality, John Marley and his wife, played frigidly by Lynn Carlin, clash, and Marley leaves the house for the temporary emotional warmth of an attractive prostitute (Gena Rowlands).

Most of the running time of the film is devoted to a melange of observing the husband and wife seeking emotional outlets outside their home; the husband with the prostitute, the wife in a discotheque.

The film uses two homes—that of the couple and that of the prostitute—for most of the action. Rowlands and a few other members of the cast are superior to their material but they're unable to breathe life into an overblown opus.

1968: NOMINATIONS: Best Supp. Actor (Seymour Cassel), Supp. Actress (Lynn Carlin), Original Story & Screenplay

•

FACE TO FACE

1952, 89 mins, US Ⓥ b/w

Dir John Brahm, Bretaigne Windust ***Prod*** Huntington Hartford ***Scr*** Aeneas MacKenzie, James Agee ***Ph*** Karl Struss, George Diskant ***Ed*** Otto Meyer ***Mus*** Hugo Friedhofer

Act James Mason, Gene Lockhart, Michael Pate, Robert Preston, Marjorie Steele, Minor Watson (Theasquare/RKO)

Two short-story classics, Joseph Conrad's *The Secret Sharer* and Stephen Crane's *The Bride Comes to Yellow Sky* have been packaged under the title of *Face to Face*.

The Conrad tale, directed by John Brahm, stars James Mason, and is the story of a young sea captain, taking his first command and aiding a sailor from another ship who is in trouble. Mixed with the measured Conrad pace is suspense and extremely able acting by Mason.

James Agee's treatment of the Crane story, directed by Bretaigne Windust, has not destroyed any of the tale's essential flavor.

Robert Preston is the marshal who has cleaned up the small western town and goes off to get himself a bride while Minor Watson, an unregenerated old gunfighter, goes on a drunken spree and waits for the marshal's return so he can have one last gun battle. The story is well-rounded with incident, mood and excitement while continuing the whimsical note of the original.

•

FACULTY, THE

1998, 102 mins, US Ⓥ ⦿ col

Dir Robert Rodriguez ***Prod*** Elizabeth Avellan ***Scr*** Kevin Williamson ***Ph*** Enrique Chediak ***Ed*** Robert Rodriguez ***Mus*** Marco Beltrami ***Art*** Cary White

Act Jordana Brewster, Elijah Wood, Salma Hayek, Famke Janssen, Piper Laurie, Robert Patrick (Los Hooligans/Dimension)

Movies don't come any more review proof than *The Faculty*, a rip-snorting hunk of giddy, self-aware genre trash. Horror/sci-fi teenpic reps a meeting of minds between two talents, gonzo action director Robert Rodriguez and *Scream*-star scenarist Kevin Williamson [working from a screen story by David Wechter and Bruce Kimmel], who've each made the style-over-substance, movies-referencing-movies equation their personal mantra.

Brainiac Casey (Elijah Wood) discovers a piece of icky tissue on the playing field that does very odd things when moistened in biology class. Then Casey and star jock Stan (Shawn Hatosy) witness something even stranger in the boys' locker room and, a blink of an eye later, Casey and princessy Delilah (Jordana Brewster) narrowly survive more alarming events in the teachers' lounge. By now, punky loner Stokely (Clea DuVall), sardonic Zeke (Josh Harnett) and Southern belle Marybeth (Laura Harris) have joined the nucleus of previously divided youths who believe something very wrong is going on at the school.

Film's pace is frantic yet so well engineered that viewer buys the notion that these students are the only non-"snatched" bodies left about five minutes hence (as a queasy escape from campus makes clear).

With the exception of juve veteran Wood, youthful players are relative unknowns. Adult roles are filled by familiar faces, with Piper Laurie (as a drama teacher), Patrick (football coach) and others joined most memorably on staff by Famke Janssen and Rodriguez regular Salma Hayek. *The Faculty* is crafty and distinctive enough to rate full inclusion in the honor roll of *Invasion of the Body Snatchers* versions to date by Don Siegel, Philip Kaufman and Abel Ferrara.

•

FAHRENHEIT 451

1966, 113 mins, UK Ⓥ ⦿ col

Dir Francois Truffaut ***Prod*** Lewis M. Allen ***Scr*** Francois Truffaut, Jean-Louis Richard ***Ph*** Nicolas Roeg ***Ed*** Thom Nobie ***Mus*** Bernard Herrmann ***Art*** Syd Cain

Act Oskar Werner, Julie Christie, Cyril Cusack, Anton Diffring, Jeremy Spenser, Bee Duffell (Anglo-Enterprise Vineyard/Universal)

With a serious and even terrifying theme, this excursion into science fiction has been thoughtfully directed by Francois Truffaut, and there is adequate evidence of light touches to bring welcome and needed relief to a sombre and scarifying subject.

In author Ray Bradbury's glimpse into the future, books are considered the opium of the people. Their possession is a crime, and the state has a squad of firemen to destroy the illicit literature with flame throwers. Fahrenheit 451, it is explained, is the temperature at which books are reduced to ashes.

The yarn develops just a handful of characters, emphasising the inevitable conflict between state and literate-minded citizens. One of the principals is Montag (Oskar Werner) an obedient and lawful fireman, who does his book-destroying job with efficiency and apparent enthusiasm, while his equally law-abiding wife (Julie Christie) spends her days glued to the mural TV screen.

A young probationary school teacher (also played by Christie) whom Montag meets on the monorail while on the way to the fire station, plants the first seeds of doubt in his mind, and from then on he regularly steals the odd book, which he reads secretly.

Werner, in the difficult role of the once diffident and ambitious fireman, who finally challenges authority, plays the part in low key style that adds to the integrity of the character, and Christie is standout in her dual roles.

Cyril Cusack plays the fire station captain with horrifying dedication, and Anton Diffring is effectively cast as a heavy who has caught Montag in the book-stealing act.

•

FAIL SAFE
1964, 112 mins, US ⦿ b/w
Dir Sidney Lumet ***Prod*** Max E. Youngstein ***Scr*** Walter Bernstein ***Ph*** Gerald Hirschfeld ***Ed*** Ralph Rosenblum ***Mus*** [none] ***Art*** Albert Brenner
Act Henry Fonda, Walter Matthau, Frank Overton, Dan O'Herlihy, Fritz Weaver, Larry Hagman (Columbia)

Fail Safe is a tense and suspenseful piece of filmmaking dealing with the frightening implications of accidental nuclear warfare. It faithfully translates on the screen the power and seething drama of the Eugene Burdick–Harvey Wheeler book, capturing the full menace of the Strategic Air Command's fail-safe device in respect to its possible malfunction, and paints a vivid canvas of an imaginary situation that conceivably could arise.

An earlier Columbia release, *Dr. Strangelove* dealt with precisely the same situation: a U.S. plane loaded with hydrogen bombs is flying toward Moscow and because of technical difficulties barring any communication it is impossible to recall the bomber before it can drop its deadly cargo, which unquestionably will launch a world holocaust.

Identical basic premise and attendant situations between the two story properties led to Columbia and others attached to the production of *Strangelove* to file a Federal Court suit against the authors of *Fail Safe*, the book's publishers and the production company—ECA—which had announced it would film the tome. Charge was made that *Safe* was plagiarized from book on which *Strangelove* was based. Controversy was finally resolved when Columbia took over the financing-distribution of *Safe* and Max E. Youngstein, whose ECA unit had planned its indie production before dissolving, swung over as producer.

Fail Safe is a gripping narrative realistically and almost frighteningly told as the U.S. goes all-out to halt the plane carrying the bombs, even to the extent of trying to shoot it down and advising the Russians of their peril and urging them to destroy the plane. Particularly dramatic are the sequences in which the president—tellingly portrayed by Henry Fonda—talks with the Russian premier over the "hot wire."

Fonda is the only big name in the cast, which uniformly is topflight and socks over respective roles. Frank Overton, as the general in charge of the SAC base in Omaha, home of the fail-safe mechanism that fails to act properly, is a particular standout; Dan O'Herlihy, Edward Binns and Fritz Weaver score as army officers; Walter Matthau as a professor who urges that the U.S. attack the Soviets, and Larry Hagman as the president's interpreter.

•

FAIR GAME
1995, 90 mins, US Ⓥ ⦿ col
Dir Andrew Sipes ***Prod*** Joel Silver ***Scr*** Charles Fletcher ***Ph*** Richard Bowen ***Ed*** David Finfer, Christian Wagner, Steven Kemper ***Mus*** Mark Mancina ***Art*** James Spencer
Act William Baldwin, Cindy Crawford, Steven Berkoff, Christopher McDonald, Salma Hayek, Miguel Sandoval (Silver/Warner)

Destined to linger as a footnote if model Cindy Crawford—who makes her big-screen debut—actually manages to go on to bigger and better things, *Fair Game* is otherwise notable only for its jaw-dropping stupidity, the sort of action yarn that hopes nonstop mayhem will help cloud just how nonsensical it is.

Rarely has so much death and destruction hung on such an absurd plot, with Crawford playing Kate McQuean, a family-law attorney who inexplicably becomes the target of a heavily armed, high-tech KGB assault group.

There to defend her, apparently in no small part because of how good she looks in shorts when they first meet, is Miami cop Max Kirkpatrick (William Baldwin), much to the detriment of his coworkers, relatives, etc., who are graudally killed off as the central duo keeps escaping in what amounts to a mindless Roadrunner cartoon.

There is one impressive highway-chase sequence more than an hour in and one or two funny moments, but for the most part the pic careens along with little rhyme or reason.

Both director Andrew Sipes and writer Charlie Fletcher (working from a novel by Paula Gosling) make their big-screen debuts here. Steven Berkoff is a by-the-numbers villain, with Jenette Goldstein (*Aliens*) striking a blow for femme mercenaries as his chief henchwoman.

•

FAITHLESS
SEE: TROLOSA

•

FALCON AND THE SNOWMAN, THE
1985, 131 mins, US Ⓥ ⦿ col
Dir John Schlesinger ***Prod*** Gabriel Katzka, John Schlesinger ***Scr*** Steven Zaillian ***Ph*** Allen Daviau ***Ed*** Richard Marden ***Mus*** Pat Metheny ***Art*** James D. Bissell
Act Timothy Hutton, Sean Penn, David Suchet, Lori Singer, Pat Hingle, Dorian Harewood (Hemdale)

All the way through *The Falcon and the Snowman* director John Schlesinger and an exemplary cast grapple with a true story so oddly motivated it would be easily dismissed if fictional.

Working backward from a 1977 espionage trial, newspaperman Robert Lindsey wrote a book examining how an idealistic twenty-two-year-old college dropout and a wacked-out drug pusher carried off a successful scheme to sell U.S. secrets to the Soviets. With one working with a mind confused by addled loyalties and the other with a mind confused by chemicals, it remains hard to fathom exactly what they hoped to achieve or how they managed to progress so far toward achieving it.

As the two lads, however, Timothy Hutton and Sean Penn are superb. As the one who comes into unexpected access to state secrets, Hutton has the tougher job in making treason at all sympathetic while Penn is left with the shallower part of the deteriorating druggie, to which he nonetheless adds necessary dimensions.

•

FALLEN ANGEL
1946, 97 mins, US b/w
Dir Otto Preminger ***Prod*** Otto Preminger ***Scr*** Harry Kleiner ***Ph*** Joseph LaShelle ***Ed*** Harry Reynolds ***Mus*** David Raksin ***Art*** Lyle R. Wheeler, Leland Fuller
Act Alice Faye, Dana Andrews, Linda Darnell, Charles Bickford, Anne Revere, Bruce Cabot (20th Century-Fox)

There are lapses in *Angel* from the story viewpoint and character development, but these are few and unlikely to militate against the film's overall entertainment values. Pic deals with a trollop (Linda Darnell) who gets a flock of guys on the string, then gets bumped off. The yarn [from a novel by Marty Holland] revolves around which of her admirers committed the deed.

Linked to the plot is the story's basic romantic tie up between Alice Faye and Dana Andrews, the former as a respectable, wealthy small-town gal who is ripe for the taking, and Andrews is the guy who starts out to do the taking, even marrying her to do it, his idea being to get enough moola so he can cop the other gal.

This is Faye's first straight dramatic part, and she handles herself well, generally, though her one dramatic scene could have gotten better direction. Andrews remains one of the better young dramatic actors in this film though his character is not always too clearly defined in the writing. Darnell looks the trollop part and plays it well.

•

FALLEN IDOL, THE
1948, 94 mins, UK Ⓥ b/w
Dir Carol Reed ***Prod*** Carol Reed ***Scr*** Graham Greene, Lesley Storm, William Templeton ***Ph*** Georges Perinal ***Ed*** Oswald Hafenrichter ***Mus*** William Alwyn ***Art*** Vincent Korda, James Sawyer
Act Ralph Richardson, Michele Morgan, Bobby Henrey, Sonia Dresdel, Jack Hawkins, Dora Bryan (London/20th Century-Fox)

A fine sensitive story, a brilliant child star and a polished cast, headed by Ralph Richardson and Michele Morgan, combine to make *The Fallen Idol* a satisfying piece of intelligent entertainment.

Based on a short story by Graham Greene, the script develops the triangle drama with powerful dramatic force. Briefly, it's a story of the frustrated marriage of a butler, working at a foreign embassy in London, who's in love with an embassy typist. While the lovers are together, the wife, who has pretended to be in the country, comes in and after a hysterical row with her husband, accidentally falls and is killed.

Dominating the entire theme is young Felipe, son of the ambassador, who is left in the servants' care while the parents are away. The butler, Baines, and the boy are great friends, but Mrs. Baines and Felipe are not. When a police investigation suggests that the wife might have been murdered, Felipe lies for all he is worth to defend the butler.

There's hardly a scene in the picture in which the kid, played by Bobby Henrey, doesn't appear, and he comes through like a seasoned trouper. Setting the high standard for the acting is Ralph Richardson, whose masterly portrayal of the butler is a gratifying piece of work.

1943: NOMINATIONS: Best Director, Screenplay

•

FALLING DOWN
1993, 115 mins, US Ⓥ ⦿ ▭ col
Dir Joel Schumacher ***Prod*** Arnold Kopelson, Herschel Weingrod, Timothy Harris ***Scr*** Ebbe Roe Smith ***Ph*** Andrzej Bartkowiak ***Ed*** Paul Hirsch ***Mus*** James Newton Howard ***Art*** Barbara Ling
Act Michael Douglas, Robert Duvall, Barbara Hershey, Rachel Ticotin, Tuesday Weld, Frederic Forrest (Warner)

This at first comes across like a mean-spirited black comedy and then snowballs into a reasonably powerful portrait of social alienation. The tone is unremittingly dour, however.

Seeking to journey "home" to Venice from downtown Los Angeles, Michael Douglas abandons his car in bumper-to-bumper morning traffic and sets off on foot, venting his anger and frustration at all those he encounters.

A laid-off defense worker, estranged from his wife and child, with a borderline propensity for violence, he is a self-obsessed human powderkeg heading to a home no longer his while on the verge of going off.

The film provides Douglas with a real performer's showcase, and he delivers a strong, intense portrayal of a walking time bomb. Robert Duvall, as well, is at his congenial best as a hen-pecked burglary cop in his last day on the job.

The most notable supporting players are Rachel Ticotin as Duvall's former partner and Tuesday Weld in a remarkably unflattering turn as his skittish wife. Barbara Hershey is largely wasted as the protagonist's ex.

•

FALLING IN LOVE
1984, 107 mins, US Ⓥ ⦿ col
Dir Ulu Grosbard ***Prod*** Marvin Worth ***Scr*** Michael Cristofer ***Ph*** Peter Suschitzky ***Ed*** Michael Kahn ***Mus*** Dave Grusin ***Art*** Santo Loquasto
Act Robert De Niro, Meryl Streep, Harvey Keitel, Jane Kaczmarek, George Martin, Dianne Wiest (Paramount)

Falling in Love is a polite little romance, the ambition and appeal of which are modestly slight. Dynamic starring duo of Robert De Niro and Meryl Streep keeps the film afloat most of the time.

Both De Niro, a construction engineer, and Streep, a graphic designer, have marriages which, while not unhappy, have settled into the routine. Meeting in Manhattan and on the commuter train to and from Westchester County, they are compelled to continue seeing one another, but are unsure where it's all headed. More quickly than Streep, De Niro decides he wants to have an affair, but she can't make up her mind.

De Niro is charming and, like Streep, plenty of fun to watch, but he is very contained here compared to his usual work.

•

FALLING IN LOVE AGAIN
1980, 103 mins, US Ⓥ col
Dir Steven Paul ***Prod*** Steven Paul ***Scr*** Steven Paul, Ted Allan, Susannah York ***Ph*** Michael Mileham, Dick Bush, Wolfgang Suschitzky ***Ed*** Bud Smith, Doug Jackson, Jacqueline Cambas ***Mus*** Michel Legrand
Act Elliott Gould, Susannah York, Michelle Pfeiffer, Kaye Ballard, Robert Hackman, Steven Paul (OTA)

Elliott Gould is perfectly cast as Harry Lewis, a New Yorker entering middle age, suffering the usual crisis and recalling the good old days of his youth. On a cross-country trip by car with his family, Gould narrates flashbacks of his romance with Susannah York in the 1940s. Lewis went after and married the beautiful, "unattainable" rich girl. His hopes of career success did not materialize, with duo currently owning a clothing business.

Young actor-turned-director Steven Paul shot *Falling in Love Again* in 1979 at age twenty, but his feel for a past era and emphasis upon old-fashioned (but still effective) picture values bely his youthful status. Pic artfully captures the 1940s look and feel.

Michelle Pfeiffer makes a strong impression as York's younger self.

●

FALL OF BABYLON, THE
1919, 82 mins, US ⊗ b/w
Dir D. W. Griffith ***Prod*** D. W. Griffith ***Scr*** D. W. Griffith ***Ph*** Billy Bitzer
Act Tully Marshall, Constance Talmadge, Elmer Clifton, Alfred Paget, Carl Stockdale, Seena Owen (Griffith)

The public wasn't entirely crazy about D. W. Griffith's massive production *Intolerance* when he presented it [in 1916]. At that time there was too much interest in the greatest drama of the time—the war—so D. W. laid *Intolerance* in mothballs. When he pulled it out of the camphor he decided to take the Babylonian story out of the big feature, shoot a few extra scenes to piece the story out and send it forth as *The Fall of Babylon*.

He opens with a tableau that is part stage and part screen, a special small screen to show New York, the modern Babylon, which, after a dissolve, brings the large screen and the opening scenes of the feature. After the first series of scenes there is a dance on stage by Kyra that outdoes anything that Gertrude Hoffman or Annette Kellerman ever tried. The final scene of the first part is the beginning of the battle before the walls of Babylon.

The second part opens in one of the halls of Babylon and here there are 12 slave girls and Margaret Fritts, a soprano. A number here, entitled "The Mountain Maid," is very pretty and a dance by the girls also helps to fill the picture nicely. The scene is a fitting prelude to the revels that follow on the screen. Finally the fall of Babylon is accomplished and the love story that D. W. threads through the big battle scenes is brought to a fitting close with the lovers in a fond embrace.

The love story is not carried too much in the foreground any time in the feature, Griffith knowing full well that the tremendous scenes of the City of Babylon carry the feature along. Constance Talmadge is always on the job, and one learns to look for her and to like her.

●

FALL OF THE HOUSE OF USHER, THE
SEE: HOUSE OF USHER

●

FALL OF THE ROMAN EMPIRE, THE
1964, 182 mins, US Ⓥ ⦿ ▭ col
Dir Anthony Mann ***Prod*** Samuel Bronston ***Scr*** Ben Barzman, Basilio Franchina, Philip Yordan ***Ph*** Robert Krasker ***Ed*** Robert Lawrence ***Mus*** Dimitri Tiomkin ***Art*** Veniero Colasanti, John Moore
Act Alec Guinness, Sophia Loren, Stephen Boyd, James Mason, Christopher Plummer, Omar Sharif (Bronston)

This made-in-Spain production is a giant-size, three-hour, sweepingly pictorial entertainment. It probably tells all that most film fans will want to know about the glory, grandeur and greed of Rome.

The production reeks of expense—harness and hay for all those horses, arroz con pollo for all those Spanish extras, annuities for all those stars. Attention will focus upon the marblesque replica of downtown Rome in pagan days with temples, squares, forums, statuary, mosaic floors, columned chambers, luxury suites and a plunge for Caesar. If these sets cost a fortune they pay off in stunning camera angles.

The story gets under way speedily. Marcus Aurelius (Alec Guinness) has been compaigning for years in the bleak northern frontiers of Rome. He is dying and knows it, intends to disinherit his undependable son and neglects to do so. Stephen Boyd, a true-blue Tribune, will not claim the succession but instead supports the son, his old wrestling club chum Commodus. The entire subsequent plot swings on the failure of intention of the noble and just emperor to assure the continued peace and prosperity of Rome. In all of which the daughter, played attractively by Sophia Loren, is a desperately unhappy witness and victim.

There is much dialog about the factors which favor, and which oppose, good relations among peoples. The arrogance and cynicism in the Senate is part and parcel of the decline, as much as the vain and cruel Commodus, a man quick with the torch to homes, merciless in the ordering of wholesale crucifixions.

This anti-intellectual sadist is played with smiling malice by Christopher Plummer. He, Guinness and James Mason as a cultivated and honorable Roman minister to Marcus Aurelius pretty much wrap up the acting honors.

1964: NOMINATION: Best Original Music Score

●

FAME
1980, 134 mins, US Ⓥ ⦿ col
Dir Alan Parker ***Prod*** David De Silva, Alan Marshall ***Scr*** Christopher Gore ***Ph*** Michael Seresin ***Ed*** Gerry Hambling ***Mus*** Michael Gore ***Art*** Geoffrey Kirkland
Act Eddie Barth, Irene Cara, Paul McCrane, Laura Dean, Gene Anthony Ray, Anne Meara (M-G-M)

The idea behind Metro's *Fame* is that it is supposed to tell the story, via its actors, of New York's venerable High School of Performing Arts. In truth, the educational institution would have none of the project, so producers had to do with second best—the street outside the school. Alan Parker has come up with an exposure for some of the most talented youngsters seen on screen in years. There isn't a bad performance in the lot.

The great strength of the film is in the school scenes—when it wanders away from the scholastic side as it does with increasing frequency as the overlong feature moves along, it loses dramatic intensity and slows the pace.

With all this talent, there are two individuals who are so outstanding that they dominate every scene they're in. Gene Anthony Ray, plays Leroy—a superb natural dancer, but resentful of anyone trying to help, especially a white. His continuing fight with English teacher Mrs. Sherwood (Anne Meara) is the most believable plotline in the entire film.

1980: Best Song ("Fame"), Original Score

NOMINATIONS: Best Original Screenplay, Editing, Sound, Song ("Out Here on My Own")

●

FAME IS THE SPUR
1947, 116 mins, UK b/w
Dir Roy Boulting ***Prod*** John Boulting ***Scr*** Nigel Balchin ***Ph*** Gunther Krampf ***Ed*** Richard Best ***Mus*** John Woodridge ***Art*** John Howell
Act Michael Redgrave, Rosamund John, Bernard Miles, Carla Lehmann, Hugh Burden, Marjorie Fielding (Two Cities)

Few writers can give poverty such an air of adventure as Howard Spring, and in the Boulting Bros. he found the right producer and director. It was not an easy matter to translate Spring's workmanlike novel of a self-made politician to the screen, but the Boultings have done this with praiseworthy conscientiousness.

Having wisely discarded the flashback, the Boultings begin in 1870 when Hamer Radshaw, a lad in a north country slum, dedicates his life to better the lot of his fellow workers. The sword his grandfather picked up at Peterloo (1819), when soldiers cut down workers crying for "bread and liberty," becomes his talisman and symbol.

Attractive, he becomes a grand rabble-rouser. With his sword he can incite men to their own death, all for the "cause," and as a Labour Member of Parliament he takes the line of least resistance, shedding old friends when necessary, making new ones if they can help, as long as it all leads to glory and power.

Michael Redgrave gives a grand performance as the earnest young idealist who becomes the vain selfish politician. It is a difficult part, but he makes it wholly credible.

●

FAMILY AFFAIR, A
1937, 67 mins, US b/w
Dir George B. Seitz ***Prod*** Lucien Hubbard, Samuel Marx ***Scr*** Kay Van Riper ***Ph*** Lester White ***Mus*** David Snell
Act Lionel Barrymore, Cecilia Parker, Eric Linden, Mickey Rooney, Charley Grapewin, Spring Byington (M-G-M)

A Family Affair is wholesome entertainment, well done by a capable cast and superbly directed.

Picture is a triumph for Lionel Barrymore. As the honest country-town judge, and again as the family-loving father, he is in his element. It is one of those meaty roles that is Barrymore's dish.

Cecilia Parker and Eric Linden are successfully teamed as the youthful romantic interest. As is Mickey Rooney, as the kid, in his puppy-love affair with Margaret Marquis. Young Rooney's interpretation is true boy stuff, and good for the best laughs.

George B. Seitz directs with skill and sincerity, getting the maximum tempo out of a wordy piece [from the play *Skidding* by Aurania Rouveyrol].

●

FAMILY BUSINESS
1989, 115 mins, US Ⓥ ⦿ col
Dir Sidney Lumet ***Prod*** Lawrence Gordon ***Scr*** Vincent Patrick ***Ph*** Andrzej Bartkowiak ***Ed*** Andrew Mondshein ***Mus*** Cy Coleman ***Art*** Robert Guerra
Act Sean Connery, Dustin Hoffman, Matthew Broderick, Rosana DeSoto, Janet Carroll, Victoria Jackson (Regency/Gordon)

Sean Connery steals scenes as well as merchandise in an immensely charismatic turn in *Family Business*, a darkly comic tale about three generations brought together and torn apart by their common attraction to thievery.

Director Sidney Lumet has crafted a film with real pathos while writer Vincent Patrick (adapting his own novel) injects enough bawdy humor to create a delightful mixed bag spiced with almost a European sensibility. The key, however, is Connery, who dives head-first into his part as amoral family patriarch Jessie.

He's an unabashed rogue well into his 60s who, when we meet him, must be bailed out of jail after savaging an off-duty cop in a bar fight.

Connery cuts an irresistible figure to his sheltered Ivy League grandson (Matthew Broderick), who enlists the old man's aid to carry out a high-tech robbery.

Caught in the middle, literally and figuratively, is the boy's father (Dustin Hoffman), who once had the same relationship with his father and ended up doing hard time for it.

●

FAMILY JEWELS, THE
1965, 98 mins, US Ⓥ col
Dir Jerry Lewis ***Prod*** Jerry Lewis ***Scr*** Jerry Lewis, Bill Richmond ***Ph*** W. Wallace Kelley ***Ed*** Arthur P. Schmidt, John Woodcock ***Mus*** Pete King ***Art*** Hal Pereira, Jack Poplin
Act Jerry Lewis, Sebastian Cabot, Donna Butterworth, Neil Hamilton, Jay Adler, Robert Strauss (Lewis/Paramount)

The Family Jewels puts Jerry Lewis in multiple role of contenders for guardianship of moppet and her inherited fortune. Episodic script hits some highs in satire and low comedy. Players and direction are good, but film shapes up as comparatively mild entry.

The script focuses on precocious Donna Butterworth, cute nine-year-old orphan with $30 million in trust to be administered by the uncle whom she picks. Jay Adler and Neil Hamilton make okay lawyers who explain provisions of late pop's will, triggering a visit to each uncle with family chauffeur, Lewis.

Comic's tour de farce effort comes off unevenly. As sympathetic but bumbling chauffeur, he foils a bank-truck holdup, avoids numerous murder attempts and keeps plot thread together in good form. So-so bits include a San Diego ferryboat skipper, also cynical and unpatriotic circus clown quitting the biz for Swiss tax haven.

More successful is his limning of crazy photographer who can't decide on setups. Standout is Lewis as screwy aviator who attempts to haul to Chi a group of five motorcycle-riding biddies. Very good satire on in-flight pix involves Anne Baxter appearing in film clip from *Sustenance*, a gag scene in which banquet guests, silverware and food slide about with aircraft motion.

Sebastian Cabot brightens as foil for Lewis' detective-uncle who gets hung up in zany pool game with Robert Strauss, while gangster-uncle bit is amusing.

●

FAMILY LIFE
1972, 105 mins, UK col
Dir Ken Loach ***Prod*** Tony Garnett ***Scr*** David Mercer ***Ph*** Charles Stewart ***Ed*** Roy Watts ***Mus*** Marc Wilkinson ***Art*** William McCrow
Act Sandy Ratcliff, Bill Dean, Grace Cave, Malcolm Tierney, Alan MacNaughton, Michael Riddall (Kestrel)

Director Ken Loach has succeeded in creating a disturbing and provocative film about a girl sinking into schizophrenia. David Mercer's succinct screenplay [from his TV play *In Two Minds*], Loach's probing direction and the sensitive acting ward off the pitfalls of self-consciousness, didactics and schematics.

The parents, who have made firm middle-class lives for themselves, live on their prejudices and belief in the need for curing any rebelliousness in their children. One daughter has broken away but a younger one is still at home and unable to cut loose. When she gets pregnant there is parental outrage and a carefully planned abortion. But the girl loses job after job and her growing withdrawal from life has her parents seeking psychiatric help.

Sandy Ratcliff is effective as the weak but striving girl who is finally beaten by a system and misunderstanding. Originally a TV film, it has been effectively broadened without losing its intimacy. There are long talky scenes but they're revealing and effective.

•

FAMILY PLOT
1976, 120 mins, US Ⓥ ⊙ col
Dir Alfred Hitchcock ***Prod*** [uncredited] ***Scr*** Ernest Lehman ***Ph*** Leonard J. South ***Ed*** J. Terry Williams ***Mus*** John Williams ***Art*** Henry Bumstead
Act Karen Black, Bruce Dern, Barbara Harris, William Devane, Ed Lauter, Cathleen Nesbitt (Universal)

Family Plot is a dazzling achievement for Alfred Hitchcock masterfully controlling shifts from comedy to drama throughout a highly complex plot. Witty screenplay, transplanting Victor Canning's British novel, *The Rainbird Pattern*, to a California setting, is a model of construction, and the cast is uniformly superb.

Bruce Dern and Barbara Harris are the couple who receive primary attention, a cabbie and a phony psychic trying to find the long-lost heir to the Rainbird fortune.

Dern is a more than slightly absurd figure, oddly appealing; Harris is sensational.

William Devane takes a high place in the roster of Hitchcockian rogues, while Karen Black gives a deep resonance to her relationship with the mercurial Devane.

•

FAMILY VIEWING
1987, 86 mins, Canada col
Dir Atom Egoyan ***Prod*** [uncredited] ***Scr*** Atom Egoyan ***Ph*** Robert Macdonald ***Ed*** Atom Egoyan, Bruce Macdonald ***Mus*** Mychael Danna ***Art*** Linda Del Rosario
Act David Hemblen, Aidan Tierney, Gabrielle Rose, Arsinee Khanjian, Selma Keklikian (Ego)

He's something of a darling to the Canadian new wave cinema, but Atom Egoyan's second feature is particularly exasperating precisely because there are streaks of filmmaking talent visible through the pretentious murk of this disjointed story about a single-minded young man and his emotionally pulverized family life.

Egoyan's film stands shakily upon a glib foundation of familiar themes. These include ruptured familial communication in an impersonal urban society, the displacement of human feelings in an age of instant sensual gratification and the subsuming of modern life to the omnipresent value systems of the video tube.

At the center of all this is college graduate Van (Aidan Tierney), who lives in a high-rise co-op with his slightly kinky father, Stan (David Hemblen) and dad's provocatively flirtatious mistress, Sandra (Gabrielle Rose).

The devices of home movies (in which the family lives on in its happier nuclear past) and the tiresome use of b&w TV static patterns between scenes are clever mostly in the sophomoric sense. By the time Egoyan moves to bring this affair to a hopeful resolution the actors don't seem to care very much and neither should the audience.

•

FAMILY WAY, THE
1967, 114 mins, UK Ⓥ col
Dir Roy Boulting ***Prod*** John Boulting ***Scr*** Bill Naughton ***Ph*** Harry Waxman ***Ed*** Ernest Hosler ***Mus*** Paul McCartney ***Art*** Alan Withy
Act Hayley Mills, Avril Angers, John Comer, Hywel Bennett, John Mills, Wilfred Pickles (British Lion)

Based on Bill Naughton's warmhearted play, *All in Good Time*, and adapted by Roy Boulting and Jeffrey Dell, film is the story of an innocent young couple who marry and are unable to consummate their marriage.

The youngsters (Hayley Mills and Hywel Bennett) marry and because of circumstances have to live with the lad's parents. Even the honeymoon is a disaster since a fly-away travel agent cheats them out of their package deal trip to the Continent.

Hayley Mills gets away from her Disney image as the young bride, even essaying an undressed scene. Bennett is excellent as the sensitive young bridegroom. But it is the older hands who keep the film floating on a wave of fun, sentiment and sympathy.

John Mills is first-class in a character role as the bluff father who cannot understand his son and produces the lower working-class man's vulgarity without overdoing it. Avril Angers as the girl's acid mother and John Comer as her husband are equally effective, but the best performance comes from Marjorie Rhodes as John Mills's astute but understanding wife.

•

FAN, THE
1949, 79 mins, US Ⓥ b/w
Dir Otto Preminger ***Prod*** Otto Preminger ***Scr*** Walter Reisch, Dorothy Parker, Ross Evans ***Ph*** Joseph LaShelle ***Ed*** Louis Loeffler ***Mus*** Daniele Amfitheatrof
Act Jeanne Crain, Madeleine Carroll, George Sanders, Richard Greene, Martita Hunt (20th Century-Fox)

Screen adaptation [from Oscar Wilde's *Lady Windermere's Fan*] is refreshing and neatly uses the flashback technique in telling the 19th-century narrative.

Yarn of the attractive mother who moves in English society so as to be near her married daughter is deftly told. It shows her trying to prevent the daughter from making the same elopement mistake that she herself made only to become one of the most notorious women in Europe.

Madeleine Carroll makes of the young, attractive mother a vivid personality, a woman sought by wealth and nobility in nearly every European capital. Only when pictured as an elderly woman (in postwar London) does she seem a bit unconvincing. George Sanders, as her ardent lover, contributes a believable characterization. Jeanne Crain, as Lady Windermere, achieves further acting laurels.

•

FAN, THE
1981, 95 mins, US Ⓥ ⊙ col
Dir Edward Bianchi ***Prod*** Robert Stigwood ***Scr*** Priscilla Chapman, John Hartwell ***Ph*** Dick Bush ***Ed*** Alan Helm ***Mus*** Pino Donaggio ***Art*** Santo Loquasto
Act Lauren Bacall, James Garner, Maureen Stapleton, Michael Biehn, Hector Elizondo, Anna Maria Horsford (Paramount)

Lauren Bacall makes the film [from a novel by Bob Randall] work with a solid performance as a stage star pursued by a pyschotic fan whose adoration turns to hatred. To be sure, the part doesn't test the broadest range of Bacall's abilities, but she and director Edward Bianchi achieve the essential element: they make the audience care what happens to her.

In his first major feature, TV commercials veteran Michael Biehn contributes solidly toward the picture's believability, gradually transforming his character's fantasies into a deadly delusion. The more his performance is acceptable, the more perilous is Bacall's plight. Maureen Stapleton is also necessarily sympathetic as Bacall's likable secretary who stands between Biehn and what he perceives as true romance, setting herself up as his first victim.

James Garner is given less to do as Bacall's ex-husband, whom she still loves. Mainly, he's limited to standing around for moral support.

•

FAN, THE
1996, 117 mins, US Ⓥ ⊙ ▭ col
Dir Tony Scott ***Prod*** Wendy Finerman ***Scr*** Phoef Sutton ***Ph*** Dariusz Wolski ***Ed*** Christian Wagner, Claire Simpson ***Mus*** Hans Zimmer ***Art*** Ida Ransom
Act Robert De Niro, Wesley Snipes, Ellen Barkin, John Leguizamo, Benicio Del Toro, Patti D'Arbanville (Scott Free/TriStar/Mandalay)

Utterly bankrupt artistically, psychologically and morally, and unconvincing from the overall concept down to the smallest detail, this would-be suspense thriller about an obsessed baseball fan's demented effort to help his favorite team and players represents ground zero from any audience p.o.v.

Utimate hard-core San Francisco Giants fan Gil Renard (Robert De Niro) couldn't be more thrilled when the three-time MVP Bobby Tayburn (Wesley Snipes) signs a $40 million deal to join the team at the start of the new season. When Bobby falls into the worst slump of his career, the finger points at one of the Giants' other sluggers, Juan Primo (Benicio Del Toro), who won't relinquish the number 11 uniform, which Bobby has always worn elsewhere. So it seems perfectly reasonable to Gil to murder Primo for Bobby to regain his number.

Gil remains at large after the killing, and manages to insinuate himself into Bobby's world. But when the star seems ungrateful, Gil, who has a son of his own he's barred from seeing, kidnaps the player's son.

The picture's offenses are nearly innumerable. From a dramatic and character perspective, Phoef Sutton's screenplay [from Peter Abrahams's novel] offers no hook for viewer interest or emotion. De Niro's Gil is clearly an unhinged cretin from the outset, and the actor's been down this road too many times by now. Snipes's Bobby fits one's picture of an arrogant, overpaid contemporary athlete. The principal supporting characters are all one-note creations.

But it's from sports and time-frame angles that the film is most preposterous. The play-by-play that accompanies Bobby's final at-bat is ludicrous. And why would a left-handed actor be engaged to play a former catcher, as left-throwing catchers are as rare as 200-pound jockeys?

•

FANATIC
(US: DIE! DIE! MY DARLING!)
1965, 97 mins, UK Ⓥ col
Dir Silvio Narizzano ***Scr*** Richard Matheson ***Ph*** Arthur Ibbetson ***Ed*** James Needs ***Mus*** Wilfred Josephs
Act Tallulah Bankhead, Stefanie Powers, Peter Vaughan, Maurice Kaufmann, Yootha Joyce, Donald Sutherland (Hammer)

Melodramatic script by Richard Matheson echoes with cliches from other stories set in sinister mansions in English countryside. But it provides Tallulah Bankhead with numerous chances to display virtuosity, from sweet-tongued menace to maniacal bloodlust, as religious-fanatic mother of Stefanie Powers's dead fiancé.

Another standout in small cast is Peter Vaughan, ne'er-do-well major domo of manse, who has roving eye for Powers's trim figure and shapely legs, which are in sharp contrast to drabness of his housekeeper-wife, well-played by Yootha Joyce.

Story line has Powers, modern miss, paying courtesy call to former fiancé's mother, only to be held prisoner while the mother tries to cleanse her soul so she will be fit to meet the son in the hereafter. Escape attempts are violently thwarted by Vaughan, Joyce and Donald Sutherland, who gives vivid portrayal of giant halfwit.

•

FANCY PANTS
1950, 92 mins, US Ⓥ ⊙ col
Dir George Marshall ***Prod*** Robert L. Welch ***Scr*** Edmund Hartmann, Robert O'Brien ***Ph*** Charles B. Lang, Jr. ***Ed*** Archie Marshek ***Mus*** Van Cleave
Act Bob Hope, Lucille Ball, Bruce Cabot, Jack Kirkwood, Eric Blore (Paramount)

Fancy Pants is a bright, bouncy farce with never a serious moment, played in broadest slapstick by Bob Hope, Lucille Ball and a fine cast of comedy characters.

Yarn [from a story by Harry Leon Wilson] basically is a fantastic satire on how New Mexico almost lost its chance for statehood because of a ruse perpetrated on President Theodore Roosevelt. Hope is a hammy American actor masquerading as an English lord among the rough-'n'-tough westerners seeking statehood, and he's forced to continue the impersonation when the president comes a-visiting.

Ball, too, is at her comedic peak in this one, matching Hope gag for gag with her uninhibited zanyisms.

•

FANDANGO
1985, 91 mins, US Ⓥ ⊙ col
Dir Kevin Reynolds ***Prod*** Tim Zinnemann ***Scr*** Kevin Reynolds ***Ph*** Thomas Del Ruth ***Ed*** Arthur Schmidt, Stephen Semel ***Mus*** Alan Silvestri ***Art*** Peter Landsdown Smith
Act Kevin Costner, Judd Nelson, Sam Robards, Chuck Bush, Brian Cesak, Marvin J. McIntyre (Amblin/Warner)

Fandango emerges as a quite promising feature debut by writer-director Kevin Reynolds, with its feet squarely within the overused boys-coming-of-age genre but its heart betraying an appealingly anarchic, iconoclastic bent.

Pic is an elaboration upon *Proof*, a 22-minute picture Reynolds made at the USC Cinema School. Set in 1971, when the Vietnam War and the draft were still looming factors in students' lives, tale describes the final wild fling, or fandango, of five college roommates in Texas before splitting up to face the dreaded realities of the world at large.

Kevin Costner plays the ringleader, a reckless but knowing adventurer who has extended his college stay by three years. Judd Nelson is the outcast of the group by virtue of his involvement in ROTC, Sam Robards has drunkenly called off his wedding to Costner's former flame at the last moment, Chuck Bush is a hulking, silent giant given to reading Jean-Paul Sartre and Kahlil Gibran, while Brian Cesak remains a drunken package just along for the ride.

Despite the mildly rueful tone, pic's highlight is the comic mid-section dominated by hippie pilot and certifiable space cadet Marvin J. McIntyre. Costner, who previously starred in *Stacey's Knights* but was a cutting room floor casualty in both *The Big Chill* and *Frances*, is a dynamic presence at the film's center.

•

FANFAN LA TULIPE
(FAN-FAN THE TULIP; SOLDIER IN LOVE)
1952, 104 mins, France/Italy Ⓥ b/w
Dir Christian-Jaque ***Prod*** Alexandre Mnouchkine ***Scr*** Rene Wheeler, Rene Fallet, Christian-Jaque, Henri Jeanson ***Ph***

Christian Matras *Ed* Jacques Desagneaux *Mus* Maurice Thiriet, Georges Van Parys *Art* Robert Guys
Act Gerard Philipe, Gina Lollobrigida, Marcel Herrand, Olivier Hussenot, Noel Roquevert, Genevieve Page (Filmsonor/Ariane/Amato)

This is a rousing, good-humored costumer on ribald 18th-century France. Done with a fine sense of parody, full of movement, chase and swordplay, Christian-Jaque's tongue-in-cheek, slick pacing animates the antics of Fanfan (Gerard Philipe), a roguish, arrogant ladies' man who joins the king's army to escape a shotgun wedding. A fake gypsy's palm reading convinces him he will some day marry the king's daughter and become one of France's marshals.

His destiny gets a big boost when he comes across a bunch of bandits holding up a stagecoach containing Madame Pompadour (Genevieve Page) and the king's daughter (Sylvie Pelayo). After a fiery one-man sabre bout and mass massacre, he gets an appreciative kiss from the great lady. Then he and his sidekicks manage to win the war single-handed and save the sergeant's daughter, Adeline (Gina Lollobrigida), whom he now loves. Henri Jeanson's dialog peppers the script with a fine cynical humor. Philipe's youth, exuberance and thesp ability obscure his lack of agility and grace and make his Fanfan character a robust and human one. Lollobrigida has beauty, body and acting talent and looks like a Hollywood bet. Noel Roquevert is excellent as the bombastic, martinet sergeant. Production values and trimmings are of the highest order.

•

FAN-FAN THE TULIP
SEE: FANFAN LA TULIPE

•

FANNY
1932, 125 mins, France Ⓥ ⦿ b/w
Dir Marc Allegret *Prod* Marcel Pagnol *Scr* Marcel Pagnol *Ph* Nicolas Toporkoff
Act Raimu, Pierre Fresnay, Orane Demazis, Charpin, Alida Rouffe, Robert Vattier (Pagnol)

Once again, producer-writer Marcel Pagnol plays variations on his favorite theme of the young maid's fall from virtue into pregnancy. The story of *Fanny* [middle seg of the trilogy comprising *Marius* and *Cesar*], however, is secondary to the gallery of superlative portraits drawn by the cast members.

The story revolves around Fanny's (Orane Demazis) plight after she's deserted by her lover, Marius (Pierre Fresnay), who leaves to become a sailor. Under pressure from her outraged mother (Alida Rouffe), Fanny is forced into marrying Panisse (Charpin), who's old enough to be her father.

As Marius's father, Cesar, Raimu delivers one of the best performances of his career. As a barkeep who's broken-hearted over his son's departure, Raimu displays his rich comic vein with a delicacy that never shatters the poignant qualities underlying his role. Charpin also plays superbly. As Fanny, Demazis is slightly short on looks but more than compensates by her sensitivity and fragility. Fresnay, as the impulsive swain, is disappointing in a small part he plays too theatrically.

Chief defects lie in the lensing, which is uneven, and the editing, which causes several choppy transitions.

•

FANNY
1961, 133 mins, US Ⓥ col
Dir Joshua Logan *Prod* Joshua Logan *Scr* Julius J. Epstein *Ph* Jack Cardiff *Ed* William H. Reynolds *Mus* Harold Rome *Art* Rino Mondellini
Act Leslie Caron, Maurice Chevalier, Charles Boyer, Horst Buchholz, Salvatore Baccaloni, Lionel Jeffries (Warner)

Marcel Pagnol's enduring creation has a peculiar history. Center of a trilogy (*Marius, Fanny* and *Cesar*) penned around the early 1930s, it graduated from stage to screen in 1933 French film versions that, sans English titles, died after a week's exhibition in a New York theater. Refurbished with titles and an additional 25 minutes in 1948, it became an unforgettable motion picture and an art house click. Earlier, in 1938, Metro produced a film (a Wallace Beery starrer titled *Port of the Seven Seas*) based on the Pagnol yarn. Then, of course, there was the Broadway musical version in 1956.

Although the deep sentiment in Pagnol's tale constantly threatens to lapse into maudlinity in this film, it never quite does. Pagnol's story, skillfully adapted out of the original Marseilles trilogy and the legit book by S. N. Behrman and Joshua Logan, focuses upon four people: a thrifty waterfront bar operator (Charles Boyer); his son (Horst Buchholz), who has a yen to sail away to the "isles beneath the wind"; a fishmonger's daughter (Leslie Caron) in love with the wanderlustful lad; and an aging, wealthy widower (Maurice Chevalier), whose great wish is to add "& Son" to the sign above his shop.

The contribution of cameraman Jack Cardiff is enormous, ranging from great, sweeping panoramic views of the port of Marseilles and the sea to tight, intimate shots of the faces of the principals. Caron employs that Gallic gamin quality to full advantage again, Buchholz does a nice job as Marius, but a couple of old pros named Boyer and Chevalier walk off with the picture.

1961: NOMINATIONS: Best Picture, Actor (Charles Boyer), Color Cinematography, Editing, Score of a Dramatic Picture

•

FANNY AND ALEXANDER
SEE: FANNY OCH ALEXANDER

•

FANNY BY GASLIGHT
(US: MAN OF EVIL)
1944, 108 mins, UK Ⓥ b/w
Dir Anthony Asquith *Prod* Edward Black *Scr* Doreen Montgomery, Aimee Stuart *Ph* Arthur Crabtree *Ed* R. E. Dearing *Mus* Cedric Mallabey *Art* John Bryan
Act Phyllis Calvert, James Mason, Wilfrid Lawson, Stewart Granger, Jean Kent, Margaretta Scott (Gainsborough)

Unfortunately, Anthony Asquith's direction is hurt by faulty film editing and irritatingly slow tempo. Although the script distorts the original story almost beyond recognition, there is still retained a lot of plot development in the house of ill-fame, which in the book is the main background. For all its being toned down from Michael Sadleir's frank treatment in the novel, the way the curvaceous femmes do their stuff in the underground joint hardly makes for best family trade. As a matter of fact, the film would suffer little if all the bawdy-house sequences were removed. The main theme—the thorny path traveled by the true lovers because the man is "well born" while the girl is an illegitimate child, foster-fathered by the bawdy housekeeper—would be preserved by the mid-Victorian pillorying they both receive.

With so many good performances, it is significant that Phyllis Calvert in the lead more than holds her own. She succeeds in portraying Fanny with girlish wistfulness and appeal.

•

FANNY OCH ALEXANDER
(FANNY AND ALEXANDER)
1982, 188 mins, Sweden/Germany/France Ⓥ ⦿ col
Dir Ingmar Bergman *Prod* Jorn Donner (exec.) *Scr* Ingmar Bergman *Ph* Sven Nykvist *Ed* Sylvia Ingemarsson *Mus* Daniel Bell *Art* Anna Asp
Act Gunn Wallgren, Allan Edwall, Ewa Froling, Bertil Guve, Pernilla Allwin, Jarl Kulle (Swedish Film Institute/STV1/Personafilm/Gaumont

Ingmar Bergman's *Fanny and Alexander* emerges as a sumptuously produced period piece that is also a rich tapestry of childhood memoirs and moods, fear and fancy, employing all the manners and means of the best of cinematic theatrical from high and low comedy to darkest tragedy with detours into the gothic, the ghostly and the gruesome.

Fanny and Alexander just simply has everything to make it the Bergman feature film that could be remembered longest and most fondly by general audiences when his other, more anguished works, are forgotten by all but the initiated. The five-hour TV version, divided into four parts of uneven length, will thrill even larger audiences.

The well-to-do Ekdahl family in the university city of Uppsala has come together in the widow/grandmother Helena's house to celebrate Christmas of 1907. Helena (Gunn Wallgren) is a strong-willed but generous woman. She does worry, however, about her theater manager-actor son Oscar (Allan Edwall) who works too hard and is a pretty bad actor, but a good husband for Emilie (Ewa Froling) and father for their two young children, Fanny and Alexander.

The shadows begin to take over when the actor dies and Emilie marries the Uppsala bishop Edvard Vergerus (Jan Malmsjo) who reveals himself to be a sadistic tyrant under his benign surface. The children are imprisoned in an attic, but smuggled to freedom by old Isak (Erland Josephson), a Jewish antique dealer friend of the Ekdahl family.

Fanny and Alexander combines elegance with intimacy. Its moments of shock are surprisingly subdued (the burning to death of the bishop has a dreamlike quality), and its obvious nostalgia is tempered with the softest irony and the saltiness of home truths.

The playing throughout reflects the mood of the real-life film family reunion that Bergman's homecoming to Sweden has been [after a period of self-exile in Munich, following a row with Sweden's tax authorities in 1976]. The two children perform with quiet authority, totally devoid of any cuteness or lapses into obvious acting. All adult roles are played with a blend of gusto and professionalism.

1982: Best Foreign Language Film

•

FANTASIA
1940, 120 mins, US Ⓥ ⦿ col
Dir Ben Sharpsteen (sup.) *Prod* Walt Disney *Scr* Joe Grant, Dick Huemer *Ed* Stephen Csillag *Mus* Edward H. Plumb (dir.) (Walt Disney)

In *Fantasia* Walt Disney enlists the assistance of Leopold Stokowski, the Philadelphia Symphony Orchestra, and Deems Taylor as screen commentator. The result of mixing all these ingredients, including his own unique approach to things theatrical, is a two-hour, $2 million-plus variety show, which spans the formidable entertainment categories ranging from a Mickey Mouse escapade in the title role of Dukas's *The Sorcerer's Apprentice* to a very lovely musical and visual interpretation of Schubert's *Ave Maria*.

The first offering [directed by Samuel Armstrong] is a flight of sheer fancy on the part of the Disney illustrators. The Bach number, *Toccata and Fugue in D Minor*, is nine minutes of pictorial kaleidoscope, in the course of which various gay and bizarre representations of musical instruments are flashed in grotesque shapes across the screen.

The familiar Tchaikovsky *Nutcracker Suite* [directed by Armstrong] is the second offering, somewhat longer, as it runs 14 minutes. Pictorially, it is a series of charming ballets, the leading and supporting characters of which are flowers, fish and fairies that cavort in whimsical surroundings.

Comes Mickey next as the mischievous apprentice in the Dukas number [directed by James Algar], in the telling of which he becomes highly and humorously involved with a broomstick.

First part closes with Stravinsky's *Rite of Spring* [directed by Bill Roberts and Paul Satterfield], the most ambitious number on the program and a 20-minute gasp for breath. Here is visualized the birth of creation, the heavenly nebulae and the placement of the solar system in the universe.

Reserved for the second part are the Beethoven *Pastoral Symphony* and Ponchielli's *Dance of the Hours*. Former is a mythological allegory, employing Zeus and others on Mt. Olympus. Hamilton Luske, Jim Handley and Ford Beebe supervised the execution that is one of the loveliest tales from the Disney plant. In contrast, the studio tackles the *Dance of the Hours* [directed by T. Hee and Norm Ferguson] in a facetious mood, burlesquing and satirizing the ballet traditions. Among the dancers are elephants, rhinos and ostriches.

Concluding film [directed by Wilfred Jackson] is a combination of Moussorgsky's *Night on Bald Mountain*, a terrifying exposition on evil, and the compensating *Ave Maria*, charmingly sung by Julietta Novis with appropriate decor.

1941: Special Awards (use of sound, creation of a new form of visualized music)

•

FANTASIA/2000
2000, 75 mins, US Ⓥ ⦿ col
Dir Hendel Butoy (sup.) *Prod* Donald W. Ernst *Scr* Don Hahn, Irene Mecchi, David Reynolds *Ph* Tim Suhrstedt *Ed* Jessica Ambinder Rojas, Lois Freeman-Fox *Mus* James Levine (dir.) *Art* Pixote Hunt
Act Steve Martin, Itzhak Perlman, Quincy Jones, Bette Midler, James Earl Jones, Angela Lansbury (Walt Disney)

Fantasia/2000 is the initial full-length film presented in big-screen Imax. If *Fantasia* was too long, formal and somber to sustain the interest of most youngsters, this enjoyable follow-up is simply too breezy and lightweight. As a whole it lacks a knockout punch—one dynamite sequence that will galvanize viewers.

New effort launches into *Beethoven's Fifth Symphony* [directed by Pixote Hunt], accompanied by four minutes of butterfly-like triangles, which mostly move on cue. Effect is passably diverting. Back in the studio, Steve Martin is the first host of the live-action slugs [directed by Don Hahn] that are marked by glib humor and bare-bones info about the piece to come.

Respighi's *Pines of Rome* [directed by Hendel Butoy] unfolds as a 10-minute New Age celebration of whales gliding effortlessly through Antarctic waters. This is basically smooth and silky illustration rather than dramatization.

Gershwin's *Rhapsody in Blue* [directed by Eric Goldberg] is as an attempt at a "Symphony of a City," i.e., New York in the Jazz Age, but also a bit disappointing in its flat comedy and inability to approach the stature of the music in visual terms.

Pic reaches its peak with Shostakovich's *Piano Concerto No. 2, Allegro, Opus 102,* which provides the backdrop to

Hans Christian Andersen's *The Steadfast Tin Soldier*. Brilliantly directed [by Butoy] and animated, this seven-minute story is classically conceived but drawn with a modern edge.

The finale to Saint-Saens's *Carnival of the Animals* [directed by Goldberg] is a two-minute frolic involving some pink flamingos and yo-yos. Penn & Teller comedy team provide the lead-in to the most popular segment from the original, Dukas's *The Sorcerer's Apprentice*, starring Mickey Mouse. Original performance conducted by Leopold Stokowski has been retained, but on the giant Imax screen visual quality is markedly inferior to the rest of the picture.

Elgar's *Pomp and Circumstance* [directed by Francis Glebas] unfolds to the amusing accompaniment of the Noah's Ark story, given the unusual twist of casting Donald Duck as the elderly captain's assistant. Final segment [directed by Gaetan Brizzi and Paul Brizzi], while beautifully designed and set to Stravinsky's powerful *Firebird Suite*, possesses an overreaching ambition of profundity.

•

FANTASTIC VOYAGE
1966, 100 mins, US Ⓥ ⊙ ▭ col
Dir Richard Fleischer ***Prod*** Saul David ***Scr*** Harry Kleiner ***Ph*** Ernest Laszlo ***Ed*** William B. Murphy ***Mus*** Leonard Rosenman ***Art*** Jack Martin Smith, Dale Hennesy
Act Stephen Boyd, Raquel Welch, Edmond O'Brien, Donald Pleasence, Arthur O'Connell, Arthur Kennedy (20th Century-Fox)

Fantastic Voyage is just that. The lavish production, boasting some brilliant special effects and superior creative efforts, is an entertaining, enlightening excursion through inner space—the body of a man.

The original Otto Klement-Jay Lewis Bixby story, adapted by David Duncan, has been updated and fashioned into an intriguing yarn about five people who undergo miniaturization for injection into the bloodstream of a scientist.

Action cross cuts from lifesize medics to the shrunken quintet who encounter, and are endangered by, the miracles of life.

The competent cast is headed by Stephen Boyd, the U.S. agent who has brought scientist Jean Del Val to America, only to have a last-ditch attempt on latter's life cause the blood clot that necessitates the weird journey to come. Boyd is assigned to join the expedition under the command of Donald Pleasence, a medical specialist in circulatory systems, thus qualifying him as navigator for William Redfield's sub. Richard Fleischer's fine direction maintains a zesty pace. Ernest Laszlo's outstanding lensing brings out every lush facet in the superb production values. Over half of the $6.5 million cost went into the special values.

1966: Best Color Art Direction, Special Visual Effects

NOMINATIONS: Best Color Cinematography, Editing, Sound Effects

•

FAR AND AWAY
1992, 140 mins, US Ⓥ ⊙ ▭ col
Dir Ron Howard ***Prod*** Brian Grazer, Ron Howard ***Scr*** Bob Dolman ***Ph*** Mikael Salomon ***Ed*** Michael Hill, Daniel Hanley ***Mus*** John Williams ***Art*** Jack T. Collis, Allan Cameron
Act Tom Cruise, Nicole Kidman, Thomas Gibson, Robert Prosky, Barbara Babcock, Eileen Pollock (Universal/Imagine)

Old-fashioned is the word for *Far and Away*, a time-worn tale [by Bob Dolman and Ron Howard] of 19th-century immigrants making their way in the New World. Handsomely mounted and amiably performed, but leisurely and without much dramatic urgency, Howard's robust epic stars Tom Cruise and Nicole Kidman as class-crossed lovers who take nearly the entire picture to get together.

Pic is notable as the first narrative, noneffects-oriented Hollywood feature in more than two decades to have been shot on 65mm stock (with Panavision's new Super 70 equipment), and released in 70mm.

Cruise is Joseph, a tenant farmer in Western Ireland, circa 1892, who wants to kill his absentee landlord for torching the family home and, in effect, murdering his father.

In fact, just about every character here insists they are oppressed. Landlord's (Robert Prosky) pampered, spirited daughter, Shannon (Kidman), is kept on the tightest of leashes by her mother (Barbara Babcock), and is constantly badgered by her darkly handsome suitor (Thomas Gibson). Joseph makes off with Shannon for the States, arriving in Boston (actually streets of Dublin nicely redressed). However, the land still beckons, and by the next year all the characters find themselves in the epochal Oklahoma land rush.

Cruise's physicality is forcibly in evidence, which will not be unwelcome to his many fans. Stripped down frequently, he is genuinely impressive in the fisticuff action of pic's midsection. Heavily garbed, Kidman has the requisite grit and defiant spirit in her eyes.

•

FAR COUNTRY, THE
1955, 96 mins, US Ⓥ ▭ col
Dir Anthony Mann ***Prod*** Aaron Rosenberg ***Scr*** Borden Chase ***Ph*** William Daniels ***Ed*** Russell Schoengarth ***Mus*** Joseph Gershenson (dir.) ***Art*** Bernard Herzbrun, Alexander Golitzen
Act James Stewart, Ruth Roman, Corinne Calvet, Walter Brennan, John McIntire, Jay C. Flippen (Universal)

Rugged action is featured in *The Far Country* to go with its rugged outdoor scenery, and the results add up to film entertainment. Pic marks the fifth successful combination of James Stewart as star, Aaron Rosenberg as producer, and Anthony Mann as director.

Cast and crew locationed around the Columbia Ice Fields and in Jasper Park to get the chilly atmosphere to go with a story of the far north, set back in the pioneer days [1896] when gold was luring adventurous souls to the snow country. The location areas in Canada provide the film with a good backstop for the Borden Chase outdoor action plot.

Stewart arrives in this setting driving a herd of cattle, which he and his partner (Walter Brennan) figure to unload at fancy prices in the gold-crazy country around Skagway and Dawson. The partners are in trouble almost immediately, because Skagway's self-styled law (John McIntire) tries to commandeer the herd before it can be driven to Dawson.

Stewart and Brennan are completely at home in this type of film and handle their characters with the expected ease. The distaff stars, saloon keeper Ruth Roman and Corinne Calvet, a gold fields girl who gets Stewart at the finale, add quite a bit to the entertainment values.

•

FAREWELL MY CONCUBINE
SEE: BAWANG BIE JI

•

FAREWELL MY LOVELY
SEE: MURDER, MY SWEET

•

FAREWELL, MY LOVELY
1975, 97 mins, US Ⓥ col
Dir Dick Richards ***Prod*** George Pappas, Jerry Bruckheimer ***Scr*** David Zelag Goodman ***Ph*** John A. Alonzo ***Ed*** Walter Thompson, Joel Cox ***Mus*** David Shire ***Art*** Dean Tavoularis
Act Robert Mitchum, Charlotte Rampling, John Ireland, Sylvia Miles, Jack O'Halloran, Anthony Zerbe (EK-ITC)

Farewell, My Lovely is a lethargic, vaguely campy tribute to Hollywood's private eye mellers of the 1940s and to writer Raymond Chandler, whose Phillip Marlowe character has inspired a number of features.

Despite an impressive production and some first-rate performances, this third version fails to generate much suspense or excitement.

The plot has the cynical but humane Marlowe (Robert Mitchum) searching in seedy L.A. for the missing girlfriend of an ex-con. After a number of false leads and predictable murders, Marlowe winds up on a gambling ship for the final confrontation, shootout and body count.

Mitchum, who might appear a natural for the Marlowe role, seems a bit adrift here, underplaying to the point of inertia. Remainder of cast makes effective use of smaller roles.

1975: NOMINATION: Best Supp. Actress (Sylvia Miles)

•

FAREWELL TO ARMS, A
1932, 90 mins, US Ⓥ ⊙ b/w
Dir Frank Borzage ***Prod*** Frank Borzage ***Scr*** Benjamin Glazer, Oliver H. P. Garrett ***Ph*** Charles Lang ***Ed*** [Otho Lovering] ***Art*** [Hans Dreier, Roland Anderson]
Act Gary Cooper, Helen Hayes, Adolphe Menjou, Mary Phillips, Jack La Rue, Henry Armetta (Paramount)

A Farewell to Arms is a corking flicker [from the novel by Ernest Hemingway]. Director Frank Borzage skims over two hyper-delicate situations with deftness and ingenuity. He makes wholly palatable (and highly believable) the premise that a fleeting one hour's meeting behind the front with the resulting seduction (Gary Cooper and Helen Hayes) is the culmination of a love which, in another sphere, would have followed only a long span of courtship and flowers.

Equally acute is the hospital situation where she, as one of the nurses, violates every regulation and remains with the convalescent Cooper in his room.

All this builds up to the finale where Cooper deserts his regiment, to brave frontiers and sentinels to ultimately reach the woman.

Casting Hayes as Catherine Barkley was a natural. Cooper and Adolphe Menjou are aces in the two other major roles. Menjou's suave Italian Major Rinaldi becomes distinguished more through personal histrionics than the script's generosities. Cooper's sincerity as the enlisted American lieut attached to the Italian army, who abjures the dashing Rinaldi's penchant of patronizing joy palaces, once the romance sequences get underway, is consistently impressive in a none too easy assignment.

[At the time, a happy ending, in which Catherine survives, was also made available to exhibitors. Version reviewed is the New York roadshow premiere one, faithful to Hemingway's original novel.]

1932/33: Best Cinematography, Sound Recording

NOMINATIONS: Best Picture, Art Direction

•

FAREWELL TO ARMS, A
1957, 159 mins, US Ⓥ ▭ col
Dir Charles Vidor ***Prod*** David O. Selznick ***Scr*** Ben Hecht ***Ph*** Piero Portalupi, Oswald Morris ***Ed*** James E. Newcom, Gerard J. Wilson, John M. Foley ***Mus*** Mario Nascimbene ***Art*** Alfred Junge
Act Rock Hudson, Jennifer Jones, Vittorio De Sica, Alberto Sordi, Kurt Kasznar, Mercedes McCambridge (20th Century-Fox)

New version of the Ernest Hemingway World War I story conveys some of the Hemingway spirit that speaks of the futility of war and a desperate love that grips two strangers in its midst. But sweep and frankness alone don't make a great picture; and *Farewell* suffers from an overdose of both.

Producer David O. Selznick and director Charles Vidor, shooting all of the film in Italy and a good part of it on location in the Dolomites, have concentrated heavily on nature and war. It's the more unfortunate that Ben Hecht's often mature dialog is also riddled with clichés, and that the relationship between Rock Hudson and Jennifer Jones never takes on real dimensions.

Story, briefly, has American Red Cross ambulance driver Hudson meeting up with nurse Jones and falling violently in love with her. When he's wounded on the front, he's brought back to the hospital, where she joins him. Their protracted affair ends when he's sent back to the front where he's caught up in the disastrous retreat from Caporetto.

Such a tragic story requires great performances to put it across. It gets only a few of them in this picture.

In the supporting roles, Selznick has cast a group of very good actors. Vittorio De Sica plays the cynical Major Rinaldi with dash, and in him the Hemingway spirit comes alive with full force.

1957: NOMINATION: Best Supp. Actor (Vittorio De Sica)

•

FAREWELL TO MY CONCUBINE
SEE: BAWANG BIE JI

•

FAREWELL TO THE KING
1989, 117 mins, US Ⓥ ⊙ col
Dir John Milius ***Prod*** Albert S. Ruddy, Andre Morgan ***Scr*** John Milius ***Ph*** Dean Semler ***Ed*** John W. Wheeler, C. Timothy O'Meara, Anne V. Coates ***Mus*** Basil Poledouris ***Art*** Gil Parrondo
Act Nick Nolte, Nigel Havers, James Fox, Marilyn Tokuda, Frank McRae, Marius Weyers (Vestron)

The cliches are as thick as the foliage in *Farewell to the King*, John Milius's adaptation of a novel [*L'adieu au roi*] by French author-filmmaker Pierre Schoendoerffer. Pic recycles familiar situations and stock characters in an overlong actioner that never builds to a spiritual climax.

Two British army officers (Nigel Havers and Frank McRae) are parachuted into the Borneo jungle to rally the tribes against imminent Japanese invasion in the latter days of World War II. They come across a virile and fulfilled Nick Nolte, playing a freedom-loving white man who's anxious to protect his natives from the barbarities of civilization. Nolte, however, needs no further prompting to fight when the Japanese slaughter his own family. Hitting the Rambo warpath, the ex-Yank sergeant (who deserted after General MacArthur's defeat at Corregidor) performs a ruthless cleanup operation.

Nolte, in a purely exterior performance, never rises to the nobility and tragic majesty the at-first skeptical British officers finally see in him. Havers is a sympathetic presence in an equally empty role. Other performers, including James Fox as Havers's commanding officer, are treated as trite thumbnail portraits.

•

FAR FROM HOME
1989, 86 mins, US Ⓥ ⦿ col
Dir Meiert Avis ***Prod*** Donald P. Borchers ***Scr*** Tommy Lee Wallace ***Ph*** Paul Elliott ***Ed*** Marc Grossman ***Mus*** Jonathan Elias ***Art*** Victoria Paul
Act Matt Frewer, Drew Barrymore, Richard Masur, Karen Austin, Susan Tyrrell, Jennifer Tilly (Lightning/Vestron)

The poorly scripted would-be thriller *Far from Home* is of note only as a transition film to adult roles for child actress Drew Barrymore.

Film is set in remote Banco, NV, where Joleen (Barrymore), just turned 14, is stranded with no gas at a trailer park with her dad (Matt Frewer) on a vacation tour of national parks. A mad killer is offing people in the vicinity. Chief suspect is sinister youngster Jimmy Reed (Andras Jones), who tries to rape Barrymore by the local swimming hole. Loaded with atmosphere, pic [from a story by Ted Gershin] suffers from first-film-itis for director Meiert Avis—a surplus of odd camera angles and poor pacing. It's not as campy as producer Donald Borcher's previous heavy-breather, *Two Moon Junction*, but often as silly with a roster of caricatures.

With a baby face, dreamy eyes and a playboy model's body, Barrymore is sexy but ill-used by a tawdry screenplay that has her volunteering to "go for a swim" no matter how many dead bodies pile up around her.

Interestingly, pic was shot less than six months after her child's role in *See You in the Morning*. Standout in supporting cast is Richard Masur.

•

FAR FROM HOME: THE ADVENTURES OF YELLOW DOG
1995, 80 mins, US Ⓥ ⦿ col
Dir Phillip Borsos ***Prod*** Peter O'Brian ***Scr*** Phillip Borsos ***Ph*** James Gardner ***Ed*** Sidney Wolinsky ***Mus*** John Scott ***Art*** Mark S. Freeborn
Act Mimi Rogers, Bruce Davison, Jesse Bradford, Tom Bower, Joel Palmer, Josh Wannamaker (20th Century-Fox)

There's a preordained dramatic curve to this pic that blunts one's wholehearted enjoyment of the family drama. The yarn of a boy lost in the woods with his faithful canine is familiar territory and, while the craft is superior, the story is emotionally predictable.

Set in the rugged wilderness and shores of British Columbia, the story centers on the McCormick family. Dad (Bruce Davison) runs a hauling company and son Angus (Jesse Bradford) is an industrious, inquisitive lad. Into their world arrives a golden Labrador with innate intelligence. After "Yellow" wins over mom (Mimi Rogers), Angus and his father set out with the dog on a sea-going adventure.

Writer-director Phillip Borsos's work behind the camera is head-and-shoulders above the text. He's a true craftsman, creating a handsome breathing environment for situations and allowing his characters a dignity that keeps the material from sinking to the banal. As in *King of the Hill*, Bradford effortlessly demonstrates an instinct, talent and charisma no other actor of his age can approximate.

•

FAR FROM THE MADDING CROWD
1967, 169 mins, UK Ⓥ ⦿ ▭ col
Dir John Schlesinger ***Prod*** Joseph Janni ***Scr*** Frederic Raphael ***Ph*** Nicolas Roeg ***Ed*** Malcolm Cooke ***Mus*** Richard Rodney Bennett ***Art*** Richard MacDonald
Act Julie Christie, Terence Stamp, Peter Finch, Alan Bates, Prunella Ransome, Fiona Walker (M-G-M)

Literary classics or semiclassics traditionally provide pitfalls in adaptation, and faithfulness can often prove a double-edged sword.

In this case, scripter Frederic Raphael has perhaps hewn too closely to Thomas Hardy's original. Thus he has allowed director John Schlesinger only occasional—and principally mechanical—chances to forge his own film.

It is the story of Bathsheba Everdene's multifaceted love for the three men in her life, Sergeant Troy, Gabriel Oak and Boldwood. Julie Christie, Peter Finch, Terence Stamp and Alan Bates are variedly handsome and have their many effective moments, but there is little they can ultimately and lastingly do to overcome the basic banality of their characters and, to a certain degree, their lines.

Christie has few real opportunities to branch out of her rather muted and pouty lead. Finch struggles manfully against his role as Boldwood, but never really defeats it by convincing one. Stamp is the cocky, sneering Sergeant to the part born, but there's nary a glint of anything more. Nor does Bates have more of a chance as the ever-reliable Oak.

1967: NOMINATION: Best Original Music Score

•

FARGO
1996, 97 mins, US Ⓥ ⦿ col
Dir Joel Coen ***Prod*** Ethan Coen ***Scr*** Ethan Coen, Joel Coen ***Ph*** Toger Deakins ***Ed*** Roderick Jaynes ***Mus*** Carter Burwell ***Art*** Rick Heinrichs
Act Frances McDorman, Steve Buscemi, William H. Macy, Peter Stormare, Harve Presnell, John Carroll Lynch (Working Title)

The slow unraveling of the perfect crime gone awry has long been an almost irresistible movie thriller theme. In the darkly humorous *Fargo*, iconoclastic filmmakers Joel and Ethan Coen manage the precarious balancing act of respecting genre conventions and simultaneously pushing them to an almost surrealistic extreme. Pic, which is based on true events of 1987, is very funny stuff.

Setup involves Jerry Lundegaard (William H. Macy), a financially overextended Minneapolis car salesman. He hires two lumbering ex-cons, Carl Showalter (Steve Buscemi) and Gaear Grimsrud (Peter Stormare), to kidnap his wife. He'll then secure the ransom money from his wealthy father-in-law (Harve Presnell), pay off the goons and get out of debt.

After abducting Jean Lundegaard (Kristin Rudrud), the duo head for a cabin in northern Minnesota. Along the way, they're stopped by a state trooper on a seemingly minor infraction. The following morning, local police chief Marge Gunderson (Frances McDormand) wakes up with a triple homicide on her hands. Despite the unexpected twists in the kidnap scheme, the conspirators proceed to the next stage in their plan—collecting the ransom.

Though McDormand, Macy and Buscemi have few scenes together, they work like an ensemble. The trio and Stormare go for a simple, naturalistic quality right down to the characters' clothing and the amusingly flat accent of the upper Midwestern U.S.

The brothers work hard to convey the essence of direct, documentary-style filmmaking, and they create a masterful illusion. There's not a single conventional angle employed by cinematographer Roger Deakins.

1996: Best Actress (Frances McDormand), Original Screenplay

NOMINATIONS: Best Picture, Director, Supp. Actor (William H. Macy), Cinematography, Editing

•

FARMER'S DAUGHTER, THE
1947, 90 mins, US Ⓥ b/w
Dir H. C. Potter ***Prod*** Dore Schary ***Scr*** Allen Rivkin, Laura Kerr ***Ph*** Milton Krasner ***Ed*** Harry Marker ***Mus*** Leigh Harline ***Art*** Albert S. D'Agostino, Feild Gray
Act Loretta Young, Joseph Cotten, Ethel Barrymore, Charles Bickford, Harry Davenport, Lex Barker (RKO)

The Farmer's Daughter [suggested by a Finnish play by Juhni Tervataa] rolls irresistibly along in a light romantic comedy groove. One of the pic's chief assets is the political tilt given to the story line which, with its rapidly glossed over liberal democratic shibboleths, will give patrons a right-minded feeling in their hearts without disturbing their brain too much.

Loretta Young plays a Swedish country girl, complete with accent and rural garb who, upon coming to the big city, lands a second maid's job in the mansion of Joseph Cotten and his mother, Ethel Barrymore. Latter pair are well-intentioned leaders of the local political machine that is embroiled in a hot fight with the opposition over the election of a congressman.

The country lass, being naive and frank as well as an eyeful for Cotten, openly voices her disapproval of the compromise candidate chosen by her employers and heckles him at the nominating rally.

Although politicking is used only as a once-lightly-over excuse for the romantic bickerings and final clinch, director H. C. Potter slips in a few satirical barbs against the sacrosanct political practice of blarney and buncombe.

Difficulty with the Swedish accent, which occasionally collapses into straight Americanese, is the only flaw in Young's performance.

1947: Best Actress (Loretta Young)

NOMINATION: Best Supp. Actor (Charles Bickford)

•

FARMER TAKES A WIFE, THE
1935, 91 mins, US Ⓥ b/w
Dir Victor Fleming ***Prod*** Winfield R. Sheehan ***Scr*** Edwin Burke ***Ph*** Ernest Palmer ***Ed*** Harold Schuster ***Mus*** Oscar Bradley (dir.) ***Art*** William Darling
Act Janet Gaynor, Henry Fonda, Charles Bickford, Slim Summerville, Andy Devine, Margaret Hamilton (Fox)

Too thin a plot trying to cover entirely too much area is a handicap to this screen adaptation of Walter D. Edmonds's novel *Rome Haul* [and the play by Frank B. Elser and Marc Connelly], of the Erie Canal.

The plot proper is very simple. Molly (Janet Gaynor), cook on a canal boat, and bred in the belief that physical prowess is the only thing that counts and that all farmers are cravens, falls in love with Dan Harrow (Henry Fonda), who is driving a canal team to earn the money for the purchase of a farm.

Gaynor is given a that which permits her to get away from her sometimes too sweet assignments. She's a forthright young woman in this, and she plays the part extremely well. Fonda, as the farmer, is youthfully manly and shows nice personality, but he is made to dress as no New York state farmer or canaler ever did. Charles Bickford, on the other hand, looks like the men who used to string along the Erie and the Champlain Canals. Slim Summerville, out of his usual type of part, plays smoothly and with effect as a driver.

•

FARMER TAKES A WIFE, THE
1953, 80 mins, US Ⓥ col
Dir Henry Levin ***Prod*** Frank P. Rosenberg ***Scr*** Walter Bullock, Sally Benson, Joseph Fields ***Ph*** Arthur E. Arling ***Ed*** Louis Loeffler ***Mus*** Lionel Newman ***Art*** Lyle R. Wheeler, Addison Hehr
Act Betty Grable, Dale Robertson, Thelma Ritter, John Carroll, Eddie Foy Jr (20th Century-Fox)

The Farmer Takes a Wife was first screened in 1935 as a straight drama, the same as it was on the stage, and it doesn't take smoothly to the injection of songs (by Harold Arlen–Dorothy Fields) and dances, probably because the tuning is unimpressive and the terp numbers are lacking in bounce.

The production tells the story of a farm boy who takes a job on the Erie Canal to save money for a farm, meets a barge cook, falls in love, and returns with her to the soil when the railroad puts the canal out of business. Henry Levin's direction hasn't much to work with in the screenplay [from the play by Frank B. Elser and Marc Connelly, based on the novel *Rome Haul* by Walter D. Edmonds], and he fails to add any punch that would keep up interest in the unfoldment.

Grable takes prettily to the Technicolor hues and the period costuming, latter being rather fancy for a canal boat cook. As the farmer-turned-boatman, Robertson is okay, but is out of his element in picture's musical requirements, light as they are. Carroll is asked to do little but bluster through his role of a rival boatman.

•

FAR NORTH
1988, 90 mins, US Ⓥ ⦿ col
Dir Sam Shepard ***Prod*** Carolyn Pfeiffer, Malcolm Harding ***Scr*** Sam Shepard ***Ph*** Robbie Greenberg ***Ed*** Bill Yahraus ***Mus*** The Red Clay Ramblers ***Art*** Peter Jamison
Act Jessica Lange, Charles Durning, Tess Harper, Donald Moffat, Ann Wedgeworth, Patricia Arquette (Alive/Nelson)

In his film-directing debut, Sam Shepard forsakes the fevered elliptical prose flights of his plays, for a straightforward approach of surprising flatness and sentimentality that never gets airborne in this conventional tale of a Minnesota farm family coming to terms with its past and present in a time of accelerating change.

Bertrum (Charles Durning), a veteran of two wars and the railroad, is thrown from a cart by his rebellious runaway horse, and lands in the hospital obsessed with exacting revenge from the nag. His citified, unmarried pregnant daughter Kate (Jessica Lange) flies out from New York to comfort the curmudgeon in his crisis.

In what's meant to be taken as a profound gesture of filial obeisance, Lange reluctantly agrees to assassinate the horse. This mystifies Lange's slightly dotty mom (Ann Wedgeworth) and outrages her fiery farm-bound sister Rita (Tess Harper).

Adding to the emotional fireworks in this world without men is the post-pubescent defiance of Harper's daughter Jilly (Patricia Arquette), who plays fast and loose with the local boys for amusement in this nowhere town.

This loving but fractious little family is intended by Shepard to represent the dislocation of fundamental American values in the socially vertiginous 1980s.

•

FASHIONS OF 1934
1934, 80 mins, US b/w
Dir William Dieterle, Busby Berkeley ***Scr*** F. Hugh Herbert, Carl Erickson ***Ph*** William Rees ***Ed*** Jack Killifer ***Mus*** Leo Forbstein (dir.) ***Art*** Jack Okey, Willy Pogany
Act William Powell, Bette Davis, Frank McHugh, Verree Teasdale, Reginald Owen, Hugh Herbert (First National)

Fashions of 1934 may be a bit farfetched and inconsistent, being predicated on a false premise, but it has color, flash, dash, class, girls and plenty of clothes.

Story [by Harry Collins and Warren Duff] has to do with the bootlegging of exclusive Paris models. Action starts in the U.S. but quickly shifts to the French capital where the slick, racketeering William Powell transfers his ingenuity and buncombe to coincide with the ultra-ateliers of the French fashion founts.

Powell (who is starred) is a wrong guy, despite all his affability, which alone sustains his sympathetic appeal. Just why and how Bette Davis enters the picture never quite rings true. But there she is and she must be accepted.

There's the wow feather scene wherein Busby Berkeley has combined a pageant of ostrich plumes to include a Hall of Human Harps, a Web of Dreams, and Venus and Her Galley Slaves. Berkeley again repeats the prismatic formations, dissolves, overhead shots and other of the now established school of BB cinematerps.

Wisely there isn't an overplus of music. "Broken Melody" [by Sammy Fain and Irving Kahal] is the one big number, reprised for the ostrich feather production, with the blonde lookers camera-angled from every stance.

•

FAST AND LOOSE
1930, 70 mins, US b/w
Dir Fred Newmeyer ***Scr*** Doris Anderson, Jack Kirkland, Preston Sturges ***Ph*** William Steiner
Act Miriam Hopkins, Carole Lombard, Frank Morgan, Charles Starrett, Henry Wadsworth, Winifred Harris (Paramount)

A frothy bit of celluloid [from the play *The Best People* by Avery Hopwood and David Gray]. It is Miriam Hopkins's first picture. The stage artiste plays tick-tack-toe with the camera, sometimes winning, sometimes losing.

Cast principals are almost entirely from the stage, with Charles Starrett opposite Hopkins and Frank Morgan playing the financier father. Carole Lombard is the only name.

Hopkins is engaged to a theatric silly-ass and titled Englishman, while Henry Wadsworth is in love with an on-the-level chorus girl (Lombard). Hopkins seeks an out on her prospective marriage for a title and grasps her chance when accidentally meeting Charles Starrett. Later discovery that he's merely a garage mechanic enhances the romance for her, and it's a grand mixup when the entire family meets in a roadhouse raid. The direction and the players hold the much-used script together.

•

FASTER, PUSSYCAT! KILL! KILL!
1966, 86 mins, US Ⓥ ⊙ b/w
Dir Russ Meyer ***Prod*** Russ Meyer, Eve Meyer ***Scr*** Jack Moran ***Ph*** Walter Schenk ***Ed*** Russ Meyer ***Mus*** Paul Sawtell, Bert Shefter ***Art*** [uncredited]
Act Tura Satana, Haji, Lori Williams, Susan Bernard, Stuart Lancaster, Paul Trinka (Eve)

Faster, Pussycat! Kill! Kill! is a somewhat sordid, quite sexy and very violent murder-kidnap-theft meller, which includes elements of rape, lesbianism and sadism, clothed in faddish leather and boots and equipped with sports cars. Some good performances emerge from a one-note script via very good Russ Meyer direction and his outstanding editing. It was brought in at $44,000 and uses California desert exteriors throughout.

Jack Moran's story concerns a trio of bosomy swingers led by Tura Satana, her female lover Haji, and his ambi-SEXtrous Lori Williams. Out for kicks, Satana does in Ray Barlow via explicit karate, then kidnaps latter's chick, a petite Susan Bernard. Greed takes them to crippled widower Stuart Lancaster's desert diggings, where he dominates his retarded, but muscular son, Dennis Busch, also Paul Trinka, a more sensitive offspring.

It is obvious that Meyer has a directorial talent that belongs in bigger and stronger films. His visual sense is outstanding, also his setups (executed by Walter Schenk's crisp camera). Meyer's editing has a zest and polish which, without being obvious post-production gimmickry, lends proper pace and emphasis. All he needs is stronger scripting and more adept performers.

•

FAST LADY, THE
1963, 95 mins, UK col
Dir Ken Annakin ***Prod*** Julian Wintle, Leslie Parkyn ***Scr*** Jack Davies, Henry Blyth ***Ph*** Reg Wyer ***Ed*** Ralph Sheldon ***Mus*** Norrie Paramor ***Art*** Harry Pottle
Act James Robertson Justice, Stanley Baxter, Leslie Phillips, Kathleen Harrison, Julie Christie, Eric Barker (Rank)

A thin idea is pumped up into a reasonably brisk, amusing situation comedy, which is helped by a cast of experienced farceurs. In dialog, the pic is short on wit but there is enough slapstick fun. Star of the film is an impressive vintage Bentley auto.

Film concerns the efforts of an obstinate, over patriotic and gauche young Scottish civil servant to learn to drive the Bentley sports car and thus ingratiate himself with the tycoon father of a girl for whom he has fallen. Much of the humor is of the prattfall variety but it provides predictable, easy yocks.

Mainly the comedy situations are short and often fairly unrelated. Most hilarious, thanks to a gem of a performance by Eric Barker, is the first driving test taken by the would-be driver (Stanley Baxter).

James Robertson Justice, as the gruff tycoon, who is not as tough as he makes out, has a custom-made part while Baxter, as the shy Scot, and Leslie Phillips, playing a typical role as a wolfish car salesman, are good.

Julie Christie looks cute, but lacks the experience to build up a frail role as the love interest.

•

FAST TIMES AT RIDGEMONT HIGH
1982, 92 mins, US Ⓥ col
Dir Amy Heckerling ***Prod*** Art Linson, Irving Azoff ***Scr*** Cameron Crowe ***Ph*** Matthew R. Leonetti ***Ed*** Eric Jenkins ***Mus*** Joe Walsh ***Art*** Dan Lomino
Act Sean Penn, Jennifer Jason Leigh, Judge Reinhold, Robert Romanus, Phoebe Cates, Ray Walston (Universal)

If anything sets *Fast Times* apart from the average nudie-cutie, it is its literary history. Cameron Crowe, one of the flashy, talented young writers of the hip publications, actually returned to high school after reaching voting age and chronicled his year's adventure there in a well-received book.

Adapting the book now for the screen, Crowe comes up with less. Compressed to fundamentals, the high school characters of the 1980s aren't that different from the 1950s.

There's the virginal girl (Jennifer Jason Leigh) anxious to discover sex but still uncertain. There's the post-virginal girl (Phoebe Cates) who's discovered it time after time but still doesn't understand it. And there are their male counterparts, the nerd (Brian Backer) and his cynical, experienced guide (Robert Romanus).

The nice thing is that Crowe and director Amy Heckerling have provided something pleasant to observe in all of these characters though they really are sadly lacking in anything gripping. All that said, the really good part of *Fast Times* is Sean Penn as a spaced-out, irresponsible surfer. As previously proved in *Taps*, Penn is a joy to watch at work, even when his role has no particular plot importance. Similarly, Judge Reinhold is terrific as a relatively straight kid working his way through various fast-food jobs.

•

FAST-WALKING
1982, 115 mins, US Ⓥ col
Dir James B. Harris ***Prod*** James B. Harris ***Scr*** James B. Harris ***Ph*** King Baggot ***Ed*** Douglas Stewart ***Mus*** Lalo Schifrin ***Art*** Richard Haman
Act James Woods, Tim McIntire, Kay Lenz, Robert Hooks, M. Emmet Walsh, Timothy Carey (Pickman)

A prison drama that focuses on guards rather than prisoners and that reeks of a sort of late 1960s, counter-culture existentialism, pic seems oddly out of time and place. Producer-director-writer James B. Harris, hasn't really pulled it all together into a meaningful finished work.

James Woods plays "Fast-Walking" Miniver, a self-described redneck with little on his mind, who smokes dope even on his job as a prison guard. On the side he drums up business for small-time madam Susan Tyrrell. In due course, Woods becomes involved in two interconnecting plots brewing within the penitentiary walls. First, being engineered by his weird cousin Tim McIntire, involves the assassination of a newly arrived Black militant (Robert Hooks), while the other is a competing scheme to spring Hooks.

He becomes at the same time implicated in McIntire's affairs when he takes up with his g.f. Kay Lenz, and in the blacks' plot by the promise of $50,000 once Hooks escapes. It's a dirty, no-good world, to be sure.

Woods is always interesting to watch, even if his character suffers most from not growing in the course of the drama. In a very strange part, McIntire again proves he's a commanding, offbeat actor, too little seen.

•

FATAL ATTRACTION
1987, 119 mins, US Ⓥ ⊙ col
Dir Adrian Lyne ***Prod*** Stanley R. Jaffe, Sherry Lansing ***Scr*** James Dearden ***Ph*** Howard Atherton ***Ed*** Michael Kahn, Peter E. Berger ***Mus*** Maurice Jarre ***Art*** Mel Bourne
Act Michael Douglas, Glenn Close, Anne Archer, Fred Gwynne, Mike Nussbaum, Stuart Pankin (Paramount)

The screws are tightened expertly in this suspenseful meller about a flipped-out femme who makes life hell for the married man who scorns her.

New York attorney Michael Douglas is happily married to the gorgeous Anne Archer and has a lovely daughter, but succumbs to Glenn Close's provocative flirtations while his wife is out of town.

It appears that these two sophisticated adults are in it just for fun and sport, but when Close slits her wrists in despair over the end of the affair, Douglas knows he's taken on more of a burden than he bargained for.

Douglas, in a family man role, seems warmer and more sympathetic than before, and well conveys the evasiveness and anguish of his cornered character. Close throws herself into the physical abandon of the early reels with surprising relish, and becomes genuinely frightening when it comes clear she is capable of anything.

Unusual credit to James Dearden for his (very good) screenplay "based on his original screenplay" stems from the fact that pic is based on Dearden's 45-minute film *Diversion*, which he wrote and directed in 1979. [Pic's original preview version, in which Close commits suicide using a knife with Douglas's fingerprints on it, played theatrically in Japan and later on French TV, and was released on video in 1992.]

1987: NOMINATIONS: Best Picture, Director, Actress (Glenn Close), Supp. Actress (Anne Archer), Adapted Screenplay, Editing

•

FATAL INSTINCT
1993, 88 mins, US Ⓥ ⊙ col
Dir Carl Reiner ***Prod*** Katie Jacobs, Pierce Gardner ***Scr*** David O'Malley ***Ph*** Gabriel Beristain ***Ed*** Bud Molin, Stephen Myers ***Mus*** Richard Gibbs ***Art*** Sandy Veneziano
Act Armand Assante, Sherilyn Fenn, Kate Nelligan, Sean Young, Christopher McDonald, Tony Randall (M-G-M)

Director Carl Reiner and writer David O'Malley cast their nets too far and wide in this grating sendup, which proves crude without being clever or even remotely funny. The story includes not just passing shots but actual ongoing spoofs of *Basic Instinct*, *Fatal Attraction*, *Body Heat*, *Sleeping with the Enemy* and *Cape Fear*. What's lacking is any wit or subtlety.

Armand Assante gets the thankless job of playing Ned Ravine (if that sounds familiar, William Hurt's moniker in *Body Heat* was Ned Racine), a cop and lawyer who busts bad guys and then defends them in court, while his wife and her lover (Kate Nelligan, Christopher McDonald) plot his death.

O'Malley tries to pack too much into the screenplay, and the few gags of any merit (such as Young's tendency to catch gum, toilet paper and other objects on her high heels, or saxophonist Clarence Clemons's plodding through the background playing the bluesy score) are pounded flat through repetition.

Reiner doesn't seem to have his heart in this effort, and, with the exception of Sean Young, who plays her sex-kitten role to the hilt, neither does the cast. Sherilyn Fenn, a classic femme fatale, is sparingly used.

•

FATAL PASSIONS, THE
SEE: DR. MABUSE DER SPIELER

•

FAT CITY
1972, 100 mins, US Ⓥ col
Dir John Huston ***Prod*** Ray Stark ***Scr*** Leonard Gardner ***Ph*** Conrad Hall ***Ed*** Margaret Booth ***Mus*** Marvin Hamlisch (sup.) ***Art*** Richard Sylbert
Act Stacy Keach, Jeff Bridges, Susan Tyrrell, Candy Clark, Nicholas Colasanto, Art Aragon (Rastar/Columbia)

John Huston has a terse, sharp, downbeat but compassionate look at the underside of small-town American life in the west, actually in central California in the town of Stockton.

It is about boxing, about failures, about part-time agricultural workers, but really about those who, in defeat, still have meaning. The allusion stems from the old American dream of another chance, a reward for trying and for triumph in competition. Huston has been blessed by a brilliantly dialogued script by Leonard Gardner from his own much-praised [1970] novel.

Huston catches the feel of the community with a lean, no-nonsense economy, a hard-boiled but humanly alert feeling that raises the tale from a purely naturalistic low-life depiction of the characters to make a statement on the life style of the drifters and those who accept a moderate place in the small-town hierarchy.

1972: NOMINATION: Best Supp. Actress (Susan Tyrrell)

•

FATE IS THE HUNTER
1964, 106 mins, US b/w
Dir Ralph Nelson ***Prod*** Aaron Rosenberg ***Scr*** Harold Medford ***Ph*** Milton Krasner ***Ed*** Robert Simpson ***Mus*** Jerry Goldsmith ***Art*** Jack Martin Smith, Hilyard Brown
Act Glenn Ford, Nancy Kwan, Rod Taylor, Suzanne Pleshette, Jane Russell, Wally Cox (20th Century-Fox)

Fate Is the Hunter based upon the Ernest K. Gann book, is a realistically produced picture, sparked by good acting right down the line. Its greatest asset is a stirring climax that brings the story line to a satisfactory conclusion, but the buildup, while meeting expository requirements, frequently plods due to lack of significant line and situations.

The production deals with the cause of a spectacular plane crash in which fifty-three people are killed. As the various elements are considered, then discarded, the investigation finally centers on the dead pilot, reported to have been drinking a few hours before the tragedy. With the Civil Aeronautics Board and the FBI already on the case, the airline's director of flight operations and old friend of the pilot pursues his own line of inquiry.

Glenn Ford as the operations director who was a war flyer with the dead pilot (Rod Taylor) underplays his character for good effect. Part isn't as outgoing as Ford generally undertakes, but is dramatically forceful. Taylor's role is more flamboyant and colorful, most of it in flashback sequences as the Harold Medford screenplay limns the character of the man and what made him tick.

Ralph Nelson's taut direction gets the most out of his script, the crash emerging as a thrilling experience and with suspense mounting in Ford's reenactment of the fatality. Under his helming, too, Nancy Kwan, as Taylor's fiancée, and Suzanne Pleshette, the stewardess, register nicely, and Jane Russell makes an appearance as herself playing a World War II army camp.

1964: NOMINATION: Best B&W Cinematography

•

FATHER
SEE: APA

•

FATHER
1990, 100 mins, Australia Ⓥ col
Dir John Power ***Prod*** Damien Parer, Tony Cavanaugh, Graham Hartley ***Scr*** Tony Cavanaugh, Graham Hartley ***Ph*** Dan Burstall ***Ed*** Kerry Regan ***Mus*** Peter Best ***Art*** Phil Peters
Act Max von Sydow, Carol Drinkwater, Julia Blake, Steve Jacobs, Tim Robertson (Barron/Latin Quarter)

Father is strikingly similar to Costa-Gavras's *Music Box*. The story unfolds in Melbourne where German-born Joe Mueller (Max von Sydow) has lived since the war. Since his wife's death, and his retirement, he's lived with his devoted daughter Anne (Carol Drinkwater), son-in-law Bobby (Steve Jacobs) and two granddaughters.

Their peaceful lifestyle is disrupted by a television program in which an old woman, Iya Zetnick (Julia Blake) accuses Mueller of wartime atrocities. Mueller vigorously denies the charges, but winds up in an Australian court.

Writers introduced an extra element into the drama, however: a more general war guilt. Son-in-law is a Vietnam vet and admits that he knows all about making war against civilians. "It's in all of us," he says. Steve Jacobs gives an impressive performance.

Von Sydow is a tower of strength as the accused German who may, or may not, be guilty, while Blake is extremely touching as the accusing survivor of Nazi atrocities.

•

FATHER BROWN
1954, 91 mins, UK Ⓥ b/w
Dir Robert Hamer ***Prod*** Vivian A. Cox ***Scr*** Thelma Schnee, Robert Hamer ***Ph*** Harry Waxman ***Ed*** Gordon Hales ***Mus*** Georges Auric ***Art*** John Hawkesworth
Act Alec Guinness, Joan Greenwood, Peter Finch, Cecil Parker, Bernard Lee, Sidney James (Columbia/Facet)

Father Brown is distinguished mainly by the excellent casting of Alec Guinness in the title role. The G. K. Chesterton stories were adapted by Thelma Schnee, who shares the credit with the director. Between them they've fashioned a warm-hearted narrative based on the exploits of the eccentric priest who sets out to outwit international crooks while the police forces of London and Paris are on his tail.

As the yarn opens Guinness decides that it would not be safe to entrust a priceless cross to Scotland Yard in its journey from London to Rome, and decides to transport it himself. Needless to say he is outsmarted by an international thief with a reputation for stealing rare objets d'art. This is, at all times, a gentle story, leisurely unfolded and always dominated by a masterly performance by Guinness. The nearsighted priest, who learns the secrets of unarmed combat from some of the tougher members of his flock, is admirably brought to life by Guinness. His performance, good though it is, does not overshadow a first-class thesping job by Peter Finch as the international thief who likes to collect the rare treasures he cannot afford.

•

FATHER GOOSE
1964, 115 mins, US Ⓥ col
Dir Ralph Nelson ***Prod*** Robert Arthur ***Scr*** Peter Stone, Frank Tarloff ***Ph*** Charles Lang, Jr. ***Ed*** Ted J. Kent ***Mus*** Cy Coleman ***Art*** Alexander Golitzen, Henry Bumstead
Act Cary Grant, Leslie Caron, Trevor Howard, Jack Good, Sharyl Locke, Pip Sparke (Universal)

Cary Grant comes up with an about-face change of character in this World War II comedy [from a screen story by S. H. Barnett]. As a Japanese plane watcher on a deserted South Sea isle, Grant plays an unshaven bum addicted to tippling and tattered attire, a long way from the suave figure he usually projects but affording him opportunity for nutty characterization. Leslie Caron and Trevor Howard are valuable assists to plottage, which brings in a flock of refugee kids.

Under Ralph Nelson's shrewd helming the screenplay takes amusing form as Grant, who plies the South Seas in his own cruiser at the beginning of the war, is pressed into service by Australian Navy Commander Howard to man a strategic watching station.

Into this harrassed existence comes further harrassment when Grant crosses 40 miles of open sea in an eight-foot dinghy to rescue another watcher, but ends up with Caron and seven young girls, marooned there when a pilot who was transporting them to safety from New Guinea was ordered to pick up survivors of a crashed bomber.

1964: Best Original Story & Screenplay

NOMINATIONS: Best Editing, Sound

•

FATHERLAND
1986, 110 mins, UK/W. Germany Ⓥ col
Dir Ken Loach ***Prod*** Raymond Day ***Scr*** Trevor Griffiths ***Ph*** Chris Menges ***Ed*** Jonathan Morris ***Mus*** Christian Kunert, Gerulf Pannach ***Art*** Martin Johnson
Act Gerulf Pannach, Fabienne Babe, Sigfrit Steiner, Cristine Rose (Film Four/MK2/Clasart/Kestrel II)

Fatherland is a major film from Ken Loach. He has created an ambiguous yet penetrating work about two opposing cultures and the way they both manipulate and control artistic expression, and about the response of two generations to those cultures.

Focus of the drama is Klaus Dritteman, a dissident folk singer first silenced by the East Germans, then allowed to leave quietly. He is greeted in West Berlin with lavish treatment all round, but he is unhappy being treated as a commodity in the West and doesn't know if he can be creative in his new environment.

As usual with Loach, performers are not encouraged to "act" in the expected emotive way, and everyone, notably singer Gerulf Pannach, who plays Klaus, is quietly thoughtful and low-key.

•

FATHER OF THE BRIDE
1950, 92 mins, US Ⓥ ⊙ b/w
Dir Vincente Minnelli ***Prod*** Pandro S. Berman ***Scr*** Frances Goodrich, Albert Hackett ***Ph*** John Alton ***Ed*** Ferris Webster ***Mus*** Adolph Deutsch ***Art*** Cedric Gibbons, Leonid Vasian
Act Spencer Tracy, Joan Bennett, Elizabeth Taylor, Don Taylor, Billie Burke, Russ Tamblyn (M-G-M)

Father of the Bride as a pic smites the risibilities just as hard as it did in book form [by Edward Streeter].

Screenplay provides director Vincente Minnelli with choice situations and dialog, sliced right from life and hoked just enough to bring out the comedy flavor. Opening shot is a daybreak scene among the debris created by a wedding reception. Weary, but relieved, Spencer Tracey recounts the sorry lot of a bride's father, emotionally and financially devastating, and gives a case history of the events leading up to his present state.

On the critical side: Minnelli could have timed many of the scenes so that laughs would not have stepped on dialog tag lines. Also he permits the wedding rehearsal sequence to play too long, lessening the comedic effect.

1950: NOMINATIONS: Best Picture, Actor (Spencer Tracy), Screenplay

•

FATHER OF THE BRIDE
1991, 105 mins, US Ⓥ ⊙ col
Dir Charles Shyer ***Prod*** Nancy Meyers, Carol Baum, Howard Rosenman ***Scr*** Frances Goodrich, Albert Hackett, Nancy Meyers, Charles Shyer ***Ph*** John Lindley ***Ed*** Richard Marks ***Mus*** Alan Silvestri ***Art*** Sandy Veneziano
Act Steve Martin, Diane Keaton, Kimberly Williams, Kieran Culkin, George Newbern, Martin Short (Touchstone)

Remake of the 1950 M-G-M pic with Spencer Tracy and Elizabeth Taylor bears little resemblance to the original. Modernized version [of novel by Edward Streeter] shaped by filmmaking team Charles Shyer and Nancy Meyer (*Baby Boom*, *Private Benjamin*) gets by more on physical shtick than verbal sparkle.

Steve Martin plays the scion of a comfortable San Marino, CA, family that goes a little nuts when he learns that his beloved 22-year-old daughter (Kimberly Williams) is engaged. Beset by separation anxiety, he can't find anything right about her perfectly appealing fiance (George Newbern) or the pricey wedding arrangements. He snoops around the home of the in-laws-to-be and watches *America's Most Wanted* in hopes of getting the goods on them.

Best stuff here comes straight from Martin, such as his frenzied antics in the in-laws' house or his ridiculous Tom Jones imitation in front of a mirror in a too-tight tuxedo. A radiant Diane Keaton gives him first-rate support as the calm, sunny wife charged with the exhausting task of keeping up with him.

•

FATHER OF THE BRIDE PART II
1995, 106 mins, US Ⓥ ⊙ col
Dir Charles Shyer ***Prod*** Nancy Meyers ***Scr*** Nancy Meyers, Charles Shyer ***Ph*** William A. Fraker ***Ed*** Stephen A. Rotter ***Mus*** Alan Silvestri ***Art*** Linda DeScenna
Act Steve Martin, Diane Keaton, Martin Short, Kimberly Williams, George Newbern, Kieran Culkin (Touchstone)

As holiday confections go, this breezy sequel proves pleasant enough, assuming a reasonably high tolerance for sacharine in one's diet. Bearing little resemblance to *Father's Little Dividend*, the whimsical [1951] sequel to the original *Father of the Bride* that starred Spencer Tracy, this latest entry more closely follows the message of the recent Hugh Grant movie *Nine Months*—namely, that having babies solves all of life's little problems.

Steve Martin is again properly irascible as George Banks, who, with his daughter (Kimberly Williams) married and son (Kieran Culkin) heading into middle school, begins looking forward to enjoying his carefree years. George seems to be the only one, in fact, who can't cope with the idea of his daughter becoming pregnant, prompting an amusing midlife crisis sequence leading to an afternoon romp with his wife (Diane Keaton) that—to the shock of everyone—puts her in a family way as well.

Director Charles Shyer and producer Nancy Meyers (who also cowrote the screenplay) deserve a certain amount of credit for diving so unabashedly into this material, moving back and forth between broad comedy and shamelessly tugging at heartstrings.

While Martin's tightly wound antics remain the pic's centerpiece, the filmmakers brighten up the comedy with wacky supporting roles, expanding Martin Short's presence as the foppish Franck nearly to the point of overdoing a good thing, while introducing fellow Second City alumnus Eugene Levy as the gruff buyer of the Banks's home. Keaton and Williams are also both easily charming as the women in George's life.

•

FATHER'S DAY
1997, 98 mins, US Ⓥ ⊙ col
Dir Ivan Reitman ***Prod*** Joel Silver, Ivan Reitman ***Scr*** Lowell Ganz, Babaloo Mandel ***Ph*** Stephen H. Burum ***Ed*** Sheldon Kahn, Wendy Greene Bricmont ***Mus*** James Newton Howard ***Art*** Thomas Sanders
Act Robin Williams, Billy Crystal, Julia Louis-Dreyfus, Nastassja Kinski, Charlie Hofheimer, Bruce Greenwood (Silver/Warner)

Robin Williams and Billy Crystal can each provoke a lot more laughs in a minute of standup than they jointly manage during the entire running time of *Father's Day*. This wan American redo of the 1983 French comedy hit *Les comperes* [directed by Francis Veber, starring Pierre Richard and Gerard Depardieu] mechanically pushes the humor button one moment and the sentiment button the next.

Williams continues to move away from his former antic brilliance, here in the squishy vein of *Jack* and other outings. Crystal strides through it all in the nonchalant manner of Jack Benny or George Burns, with precious little of his customary sass. Combo of styles just doesn't strike the hoped-for sparks.

Situation-heavy plot centers upon a scheme hatched by a long-ago girlfriend (Nastassja Kinski) of both men in which she separately informs each that he is the father of her 16-year-old son (Charlie Hofheimer), who has recently run away. Duly enchanted by the notion of fatherhood, they begin the hunt and decide to team up when they inevitably bump into each other.

•

FATHOM
1967, 99 mins, US ▭ col
Dir Leslie Martinson ***Prod*** John Kohn ***Scr*** Lorenzo Semple Jr ***Ph*** Douglas Slocombe ***Ed*** Max Benedict ***Mus*** John Dankworth ***Art*** Maurice Carter
Act Anthony Franciosa, Raquel Welch, Ronald Fraser, Richard Briers, Greta Chi, Clive Revill (20th Century-Fox)

Fathom, lensed on location in Spain to take full advantage of scenic backdrops, is a melange of melodramatic ingredients personalized by the lush presence of Raquel Welsh. Actress stars with Tony Franciosa in this production, highlighted by some exciting parachute scenes.

Script, based on the Larry Forrester novel, was obviously triggered by the real-life incident of an American H-bomb accidentally lost off the coast of Spain.

Welch's services, as a parachute jumper, are enlised to help recover what is described as an electronic device that will fire the bomb, now in the possession of certain evil forces, and that was not retrieved at the time the bomb itself was salvaged.

•

FAT MAN AND LITTLE BOY
(UK: SHADOW MAKERS)
1989, 126 mins, US Ⓥ ⊙ ▭ col
Dir Roland Joffe ***Prod*** Tony Garnett ***Scr*** Bruce Robinson, Roland Joffe ***Ph*** Vilmos Zsigmond ***Ed*** Francoise Bonnot ***Mus*** Ennio Morricone ***Art*** Gregg Fonseca
Act Paul Newman, Dwight Schultz, Bonnie Bedelia, John Cusack, Laura Dern, Natasha Richardson (Light motive/Paramount)

The problems of this historical drama about the creation of the atom bomb are crystalized in its title. "Fat Man" and "Little Boy" were the nicknames given to the bombs dropped over Hiroshima and Nagasaki. These names aren't mentioned by any of the characters in the film, nor do the bombings figure in the action.

Film concentrates instead on Gen. Groves (Paul Newman), the man assigned to oversee the project, and J. Robert Oppenheimer (Dwight Schultz), the brilliant scientist with far-left-to-all-out-communist connections picked to lead it. This is all well and good, except that few dramatic sparks fly.

Newman has no trouble bringing the tough-talking "can do" general to life. The trouble is the scriptwriters have no interest in exploring the man behind the mission.

This tends to tilt the dramatic balance toward Oppenheimer. The film falls short here, too, partially because of Schultz's lackluster performance, but primarily because the script fails to give a clue to what made this man tick.

•

FBI STORY, THE
1959, 149 mins, US Ⓥ ⊙ col
Dir Mervyn LeRoy ***Prod*** Mervyn LeRoy ***Scr*** Richard L. Breen, John Twist ***Ph*** Joseph Biroc ***Ed*** Philip W. Anderson ***Mus*** Max Steiner
Act James Stewart, Vera Miles, Murray Hamilton, Larry Pennell, Nick Adams, Diane Jergens (Warner)

Mervyn LeRoy takes the factual material of Don Whitehead's bestselling *The FBI Story* and makes of it a tense, exciting film story told in human terms. The method used is to show the work of the FBI through the life of one of its agents (James Stewart), a familiar enough device, but correct and rewarding in this instance.

The fictional story used as a framework sounds conventional enough. Stewart and his wife (Vera Miles), are torn between his dedication to his job with the FBI and the fact that he could give his family a more rewarding life outside the bureau. But Stewart believes what J. Edgar Hoover tells his agents when he takes over the service, that its men must be imbued not only with the service of justice but the love of justice.

The dialog is exemplary, economical in words despite the film's length. Too, the story does not run out of plot. It plunges directly into a revelatory incident before the main titles, and one of the most suspenseful sequences, a fine chase through New York streets, is used for the final crisis.

Stewart gives a restrained performance, wry and intelligent, completely credible as the film covers a span of about twenty-five years to show both the fledgling agent and the older man. Miles, who plays particularly well with Stewart, synchronizes her more direct attack smoothly with his underplaying. Murray Hamilton is memorable as Stewart's fellow agent, felled by gangsters. Larry Pennell and Diane Jergens supply the young love interest believably.

•

FEAR
1996, 96 mins, US Ⓥ ⊙ ▭ col
Dir James Foley ***Prod*** Brian Grazer ***Scr*** Christopher Crowe ***Ph*** Thomas Kloss ***Ed*** David Brenner ***Mus*** Carter Burwell ***Art*** Alex McDowell
Act Mark Wahlberg, Reese Witherspoon, William Peterson, Amy Brenneman, Alyssa Milano, Christopher Gray (Imagine/Universal)

In the mold of the psychological-sexual thrillers of the late '80s and early '90s, James Foley's *Fear* is a gender-reversed *Fatal Attraction*, with a strong measure of *Cape Fear* thrown into the formulaic mix. In his biggest screen role to date, Mark Wahlberg plays the Glenn Close character: a sexy intruder who becomes obsessed with a naive, sexually yearning girl and in due course torments her entire family.

The wonderful Reese Witherspoon plays Nicole Walker, an attractive teenager living with her architect father, Steve (William Petersen); stepmother, Laura (Amy Brenneman); and stepbrother, Toby (Christopher Gray). Her ideal man seems to materialize in the figure of David (Wahlberg), a sexy charmer she meets at a "rave" party she attends with Margo (Alyssa Milano), her thrill-seeking best friend.

It doesn't take long for David to reveal his darker, psychotic side. All along, Nicole's dad senses that something is wrong with David, who's not in school and appears to have no past.

In the first hour, the story perceptively explores tensions that might plague ordinary modern families. But after the initial ground-laying, the film follows the familiar path of its genre, with shrewdly if also predictably planted twists and turns. Foley's stylishly elegant and efficient direction is at least a notch above the material's level.

•

FEAR AND DESIRE
1953, 68 mins, US b/w
Dir Stanley Kubrick ***Prod*** Stanley Kubrick ***Scr*** Howard O. Sackler ***Ph*** Stanley Kubrick ***Ed*** Stanley Kubrick ***Mus*** Gerald Fried ***Art*** Herbert Lebowitz
Act Frank Silvera, Paul Mazursky, Kenneth Harp, Steve Coit, Virginia Leith (Martin Perveler)

Fear and Desire is a literate, unhackneyed war drama, outstanding for its fresh camera treatment and poetic dialog.

Pic is work of Stanley Kubrick, who produced, directed, photographed and edited the film on a $100,000 shoestring budget. Film was written by 23-year-old poet Howard O. Sackler who has confected a blend of violence and philosophy, some of it half-baked, and some of it powerfully moving.

Story deals with four GIs stranded six miles behind enemy lines and what happens to their moral fiber as they try to escape. Kenneth Harp is a glib intellectual, grows weary with his own sophistication. Paul Mazursky, oversensitive to violence, is a weakling who tries to befriend a captured enemy girl, Virginia Leith (a toothsome dish), shoots her, and then goes insane.

Steve Coit is a level-headed Southerner who also winds up confused about his values. Frank Silvera plays the one character who fulfills himself—a tough, brave primitive, who purposely draws the fire of the enemy on himself on a river raft, so that Harp and Coit can shoot an enemy general and escape in a captured plane.

Kubrick shot the entire film in the San Gabriel Mts. and at a river at Bakersfield on the Coast, and he uses mists and tree leaves with telling effect.

Fear and Desire is definitely out of the potboiler class one would expect from a shoestring budget.

•

FEAR AND LOATHING IN LAS VEGAS
1998, 119 MINS, US Ⓥ ⊙ ▭ col
Dir Terry Gilliam ***Prod*** Laila Nabulsi, Patrick Cassavetti, Stephen Nemeth ***Scr*** Terry Gilliam, Tony Grisoni, Tod Davies, Alex Cox ***Ph*** Nicola Pecorini ***Ed*** Lesley Walker ***Mus*** [pop songs] ***Art*** Alex McDowell
Act Johnny Depp, Benicio Del Torro, Craig Bierko, Ellen Barkin, Gary Busey, Cameron Diaz (Rhino/Universal)

Fear and Loathing in Las Vegas is a bad trip. Long-gestating abdaptation of Hunter S. Thompson's hallucinatory 1971 gonzo tome has become an over-elaborate gross-out under Terry Gilliam's direction, a visualization of a flashpoint in the history of trendy phrmaceuticals without a story or detectable point-of-view.

Shot with queasy-making, distorting wide-angle lenses and filled with frenetic activity and a torrent of mostly nonsensical dialog, pic serves up a sensory overload. Film might have worked as a down-and-dirty, on-the-fly lowbudgeter such as [production company] Rhino originally envisioned it with Alex Cox as director.

Some cryptic narration and more than two dozen pop tunes of various vintages provide a fragile frama for the indulgent spree of sportswriter Raoul Duke (Johnny Depp), who drives from L.A. to Vegas with his attorney and partner-in-crime Dr. Gonzo (Benicio Del Toro) ostensibly to cover the off-road Mint 400 motorcycle race but actually to rebel against what they see as the plastic, hypocritical nightmare of Nixon's America by becoming as wasted as possible.

The one semi-sustaining element is Depp's performance, which exerts a certain fascination via the actor's clipped, staccato delivery and unusual body language. Same can't be said for Del Torro, who put on some 40 pounds for the role, all of it seemingly in his belly, but can do nothing to make Dr. Gonzo a coherent character.

Numerous well-known actors make cameo appearances, but only Christina Ricci, as a somnolent teen who paints portraits of Barbra Streisand, and Ellen Barkin, as an abused, vulnerable diner waitress, stick out from the crowd. Technically, film is highly accomplished, but in an overproduced way that proves counterproductive.

•

FEAR CITY
1984, 96 mins, US Ⓥ ⊙ col
Dir Abel Ferrara ***Prod*** Bruce Cohn Curtis, Jerry Tokofsky ***Scr*** Nicholas St. John ***Ph*** James Lemmo ***Ed*** Jack Holmes, Anthony Redman ***Mus*** Dick Halligan ***Art*** Cricket Rowland
Act Tom Berenger, Billy Dee Williams, Jack Scalia, Melanie Griffith, Rossano Brazzi, Rae Dawn Chong (Zupnik/Curtis)

Fear City lives up to its title as a tough, nasty, big-league meller by throwing every element from the exploitation cookbook—gory violence, straight and gay sex, multiple murders, martial arts, raw dialog, mobsters, drugs and gobs of female nudity—into the pot and letting them stew.

Pic is set in the fleshpot of midtown Manhattan and is populated by strippers and the sleazy men who run their lives. Hovering above them are organized crime types on the one side and the cops on the other, and soon a third menace is introduced, that of a roving sicko who launches a systematic genocidal assault on the girls who work at the nude clubs. Teeming plot has B-girl talent agent Tom Berenger trying to get things started again with old flame Melanie Griffith.

•

FEAR EATS THE SOUL
SEE: ANGST ESSEN SEELE AUF

•

FEAR IN THE NIGHT
1947, 71 mins, US Ⓥ b/w
Dir Maxwell Shane ***Prod*** William H. Pine, William C. Thomas ***Scr*** Maxwell Shane ***Ph*** Jack Greenhalgh ***Ed*** Howard Smith ***Mus*** Rudy Schrager ***Art*** F. Paul Sylos
Act Paul Kelly, DeForest Kelley, Ann Doran, Kay Scott, Robert Emmett Keane (Paramount)

Fear in the Night is a good psychological melodrama, unfolded at fast clip and will please the whodunit-and-how fans.

Maxwell Shane, who scripted from a William Irish [= Cornell Woolrich] story, [*Nightmare*], also directed. It's his first directorial chore. He realizes on meller elements for full worth. Plot concerns young man who awakens one morning after dream that he has killed a man. Reality of dream is strengthened when he finds strange button and key in his pocket. He seeks aid from his detective brother-in-law.

Paul Kelly is a believable cop who aids DeForest Kelley solve nightmare riddle.

•

FEAR IS THE KEY
1973, 105 mins, UK Ⓥ ▭ col
Dir Michael Tuchner ***Prod*** Alan Ladd Jr., Jay Kanter ***Scr*** Robert Carrington ***Ph*** Alex Thomson ***Ed*** Ray Lovejoy ***Mus*** Roy Budd ***Art*** Syd Cain, Maurice Carter
Act Barry Newman, Suzy Kendall, John Vernon, Dolph Sweet, Ben Kingsley, Ray McAnally (KLK/ Anglo-EMI)

Sustained interest and suspense mark *Fear Is the Key*, well-made action stuff [from the novel by Alistair MacLean], including the obligatory auto chase routine around the highways and byways of Louisiana where pic was shot.

Barry Newman and Suzy Kendall are top-featured, he as a deepsea salvage expert, she as an oil heiress and kidnap victim. When Newman's wife, brother and child are shot out of the sky while fetching a salvage cargo of priceless gems, he goes undercover in cahoots with the law to avenge the killings. An elaborate charade ensues wherein he feigns the murder of a cop and kidnap of Kendall from a courtroom, all designed to land him in the lair of the villains who are contriving to retrieve the gems from the aircraft on the floor of the Gulf of Mexico.

Michael Tuchner's direction, abetted by tight editing, unravels the yarn at a crisp clip. The auto pursuit sequence is superbly staged by stunt coordinator Carey Loftin and crew.

•

FEARLESS
1993, 121 mins, US Ⓥ ⊙ col
Dir Peter Weir ***Prod*** Paula Weinstein, Mark Rosenberg ***Scr*** Rafael Yglesias ***Ph*** Allen Daviau ***Ed*** William Anderson ***Mus*** Maurice Jarre ***Art*** John Stoddart
Act Jeff Bridges, Isabella Rossellini, Rosie Perez, Tom Hulce, John Turturro, Deirdre O'Connell (Spring Creek/Warner)

Peter Weir's distinctive study of the aftermath of a plane crash [based on Rafael Yglesias's novel] breaks apart thanks to undue symbolism and pretension, as well as a central relationship that doesn't pay off dramatically.

In one of his best performances, Jeff Bridges portrays Max Klein, a man who, after walking away from a plane crash that kills his business partner and many other passengers, enters an exalted state in which he feels that he has "passed through death" and believes that nothing can harm him.

After an odd visit with a childhood friend, he defies expectations by insisting upon flying home to San Francisco, where the architect is written up as a heroic good Samaritan who saved many lives. His new distracted, brutally honest air is disturbing to his ballet teacher wife, Laura (Isabella Rossellini), but things could be far worse.

Three months later, a shrink (John Turturro) brings Max together with Carla (Rosie Perez), a conventionally religious Catholic. Aside from having been on the plane, the two have nothing in common, but Max abruptly announces to his wife that he feels an overwhelming love for Carla.

This is where the film becomes muddled. Symbolism begins intruding when it's evident that Max was injured on his side in the same place as Jesus. Max gets weirder and weirder.

Bridges is transportingly fine, and Rossellini gives by far the best performance of her uneven career. Perez, unfortunately, comes off as grating. Film is beautifully made in all respects.

1993: NOMINATION: Best Supp. Actress (Rosie Perez)

•

FEARLESS FRANK
SEE: FRANK'S GREATEST ADVENTURE

•

FEARLESS VAMPIRE KILLERS, THE
SEE: DANCE OF THE VAMPIRES

•

FEAR NO EVIL
1981, 99 mins, US Ⓥ col
Dir Frank LaLoggia ***Prod*** Frank LaLoggia, Charles LaLoggia ***Scr*** Frank LaLoggia ***Ph*** Fred Goodich ***Ed*** Edna Ruth Paul ***Mus*** Frank LaLoggia, David Spear
Act Elizabeth Hoffman, Kathleen Rowe McAllen, Frank Birney, Stefan Arngrim, Daniel Eden (LaLoggia Productions)

Though the horror genre is sated with maniacs on the menace, *Fear No Evil* stands out. Spooky and surreal, the ultimately hopeful film has its basis in religious morality.

A rotten seed, born to horrified parents, grows into a menacing 17-year-old. He's a hopeless baddie consumed by the power to destroy. At Andrew/Lucifer's wicked island domain, he summons the undead and tangles with Margaret, an old woman with the power of God behind her.

Strong on atmospherics, thanks to slick lensing by Fred Goodich, *Fear No Evil* is a studious chiller that works best in scenes featuring Elizabeth Hoffman, who fairly glows with devotional fervour as Margaret.

At a cost of $1.5 million, *Fear No Evil* is an admirable first feature by writer-director Frank LaLoggia, 27, who also cowrote the lush music. The former U of Miami drama student previously made three award-winning shorts and acted in three television pilots.

•

FEAR STRIKES OUT
1957, 100 mins, US Ⓥ ⊙ b/w
Dir Robert Mulligan ***Prod*** Alan J. Pakula ***Scr*** Ted Berkman, Raphael Blau ***Ph*** Haskell Boggs ***Ed*** Aaron Stell ***Mus*** Elmer Bernstein ***Art*** Hal Pereira, Hilyard Brown
Act Anthony Perkins, Karl Malden, Norma Moore, Adam Williams, Perry Wilson, Peter J. Votrian (Paramount)

Baseball is only a means to an end in this highly effective dramatization of the tragic results that can come from a father pushing his son too hard toward a goal he, himself, was not able to achieve. In trying to be the major leaguer his father had wanted to be, Jim Piersall so filled his life with pressure and tension that he went into a complete mental breakdown right after smashing a home run for the Boston Red Sox. Confined to the Westborough State Hospital under restraint, Piersall gradually started to respond to electro-shock treatments, and was eventually restored. When the 1953 season opened for the Red Sox, Piersall was back in right field.

Anthony Perkins, in the young Piersall role, delivers a remarkably sustained performance of a sensitive young man, pushed too fast to the limits of his ability to cope with life's pressures. Karl Malden is splendid as the father who gets his own ambitions mixed up with love for his son.

•

FEAST OF JULY
1996, 116 mins, UK/US Ⓥ ⊙ ▭ col
Dir Christopher Menaul ***Prod*** Henry Herbert, Christopher Neame ***Scr*** Christopher Neame ***Ph*** Peter Sova ***Ed*** Chris Wimble ***Mus*** Zbigniew Preisner ***Art*** Christopher Robilliard
Act Embeth Davidtz, Ben Chaplin, Tom Bell, Gemma Jones, James Purefoy, Greg Wise (Merchant Ivory/Touchstone)

This Merchant Ivory production is, as expected, visually handsome and decently acted. But it's also a stale trudge through terribly familiar territory, more suited to *Masterpiece Theater* on the tube than to cinema release.

Adapted by producer Christopher Neame (son of director Ronald) from a novel by H. E. Bates and directed by vet British TV helmer Christopher Menaul in his feature bow, this turgid tale deals with a young woman (Embeth Davidtz) who is seduced and abandoned by a philandering man in late 19th-century rural England. When she is taken in by a kindly lamplighter and his wife, tragedy results when the couple's three sons all fall in love with her.

There's smoldering Con (Ben Chaplin, giving the film's best performance), who meets a tragic fate; soldier Jedd (James Purefoy), who tries to win her with his uniform and charm; and shy, artistic Matt (Kenneth Anderson).

On the sidelines is hissable Arch Wilson (Greg Wise), the married man who wronged her in the first place. Tom Bell and Gemma Jones essay the roles of the kindly couple who give Bella shelter, only to see their family destroyed as a result.

Composer Zbigniew Preisner furnishes an attractive score. The title, incidentally, is meaningless.

•

FEDORA
1978, 110 mins, W. Germany/France Ⓥ ⊙ col
Dir Billy Wilder ***Prod*** Billy Wilder ***Scr*** I.A.L. Diamond, Billy Wilder ***Ph*** Gerry Fisher ***Ed*** Stefan Arsten ***Mus*** Miklos Rozsa ***Art*** Alexandre Trauner
Act William Holden, Marthe Keller, Jose Ferrer, Hildegard Knef, Frances Sternhagen, Mario Adorf (Geria/Bavaria)

With *Fedora* based on a tale from Tom Tryon's bestseller, *Crowned Heads*, Billy Wilder goes serenely back to Hollywood treatment of itself as legend, illusion and dreams rather than reality.

In his more successful, acerbic look at an over-the-hill star, *Sunset Blvd.* [1950], the star was a real old-timer, Gloria Swanson. Neither Marthe Keller, as the once great star Fedora, or Hildegard Knef as a crusty Polish countess and the star's keeper, have that ellusive, self absorbed but camera-loving look that stars possessed, though they are good.

William Holden tells most of the tale, as he did in *Boulevard*. But here he is an indie producer down on his luck trying desperately to get a script to the amazingly still youthful star, at 67, Fedora, in a hideaway on a Greek island. It appears she is being held captive by a quack doctor, once famed for keeping personalities youthful, well mimed by Jose Ferrer.

Wilder's directorial flair, the fine production dress, Holden's solid presence, Michael York playing himself as a narcissistic actor and Henry Fonda, also as himself as head of the Academy who delivers a belated Oscar to Fedora, add some flavor to this bittersweet bow to the old star system.

•

FEDS
1988, 91 mins, US Ⓥ ⊙ col
Dir Dan Goldberg ***Prod*** Ilona Herzberg, Len Blum ***Scr*** Len Blum, Dan Goldberg ***Ph*** Timothy Suhrstedt ***Ed*** Donn Cambern ***Mus*** Randy Edelman ***Art*** Randy Ser
Act Rebecca DeMornay, Mary Gross, Ken Marshall, Fred Dalton Thompson, Larry Cedar, Tony Longo (Warner)

Rebecca DeMornay and Mary Gross are FBI academy trainees in a buddy picture that plays more like a biddy picture. There isn't a fresh idea or a new one-liner in all of the script, an anthology of inert retreads from the *Police Academy* series and *Private Benjamin*.

DeMornay as the spunky athletic one and Gross as the uptight, studious one go up against the boys in pizza contests, chin-up exercises and constitutional law classes. They ultimately graduate at the end of the class but not before undergoing considerable humiliation.

Gross trying to stop some bank robbers by making a stick-'em-up gesture with her finger and later garbling her recitation of the Miranda rights to some poor extras cast in this film is groaner material. Dan Goldberg's direction is leaden.

•

FEET FIRST
1930, 93 mins, US b/w
Dir Clyde Bruckman ***Scr*** Felix Adler, Lex Neal, Paul Gerard Smith ***Ph*** Walter Lundin, Henry Kohlen ***Ed*** Bernard W. Burton
Act Harold Lloyd, Robert McWade, Lillianne Leighton, Barbara Kent, Alec B. Francis, Noah Young (Lloyd/Paramount)

Feet First is full of Harold Lloyd gags, stunts and tricks, all in a comedy vein, as always. Dialog is the same way.

That Lloyd was a bit pressed himself for laughs during the lengthy period taken to make *Feet First* may be guessed from the fact that he is again dangling along the front of a skyscraper building. Once more Lloyd gets into all conceivable tangles from the 15th to the 21st stories, doing his acrobatics, escaping death a dozen times, using slapstick besides, and perhaps prolonging this scene too far.

Another stretch of laughs is where Lloyd is on the boat, aboard without baggage or money, from Honolulu to Frisco. He falls for a girl (Barbara Kent) who is on the same boat. She thinks he is a big businessman. Lloyd's endeavor is to prevent her from discovering he is a shoe salesman.

•

FELLINI-SATYRICON
SEE: SATYRICON

•

FELLINI'S CASANOVA
SEE: CASANOVA

•

FELLOW TRAVELLER
1990, 97 mins, UK/US Ⓥ col
Dir Philip Saville ***Prod*** Michael Wearing ***Scr*** Michael Eaton ***Ph*** John Kenway ***Ed*** Greg Miller ***Mus*** Colin Towns ***Art*** Gavin Davies
Act Ron Silver, Hart Bochner, Imogen Stubbs, Daniel J. Travanti, Katherine Borowitz (BFI/BBC/HBO)

Fellow Traveller has the rare distinction of being a British film that actually looks international. Helmer Philip Saville shows a big-screen feel with the story of a blacklisted Hollywood screenwriter during the McCarthy era who is forced to Britain to find work.

Pic goes some way in covering the commie-bashing McCarthy Era 1950s, but eventually becomes rather simplistic when trying to debate the actual politics of the time.

Glossy opening is set beside a luxury swimming pool in Hollywood where film star Clifford Byrne (Hart Bochner) shoots himself. At the same time in London, his friend Asa Kaufman (Ron Silver) is escaping the McCarthyist witch-hunt and—illegally—looking for work.

A series of flashbacks shows that Bochner and Silver were best friends. In England Silver takes a false name, starts writing a TV series *The Adventures of Robin Hood*, and searches for Bochner's English girlfriend (Imogen Stubbs), whom he has a brief affair with; he also mulls over politics with her leftie friends.

Silver is convincing as the cynical writer thrown into a strange English environment, and Hart Bochner looks the handsome leading man, replete with Errol Flynn mustache. Pic is excellent at re-creating the early heady days of independent TV in the U.K.

•

FEMALE PERVERSIONS
1996, 116 mins, US Ⓥ col
Dir Susan Streitfeld ***Prod*** Mindy Affrime ***Scr*** Susan Streitfeld, Julie Herbert ***Ph*** Teresa Medina ***Ed*** Curtiss Clayton, Leo Trombetta ***Mus*** Debbie Wiseman ***Art*** Missy Stewart
Act Tilda Swinton, Amy Madigan, Karen Sillas, Laila Robins, Clancy Brown, Frances Fisher (Trans Atlantic/October/MAP)

The women in *Female Perversions*, a hard-core feminist meditation about gender and sexuality in modern life, are so stunningly beautiful and intriguingly complex that they almost overcome the trappings of a nonlinear, fractured narrative that is often academic and a bit pretentious, inspired by Louise J. Kaplan's Freudian text *Female Perversions: The Temptations of Emma Bovary*.

Tilda Swinton is perfectly cast as Eve, a bright lawyer who has just won a major case. On the brink of an identity crisis, Eve can't seem to control her sexual desires. She recklessly enters into a relationship with Renee (Karen Sillas), a sensitive psychiatrist who has just moved into her building.

Just as Eve is facing the highest point in her life, Madelyn (Amy Madigan), her unstable sister, is experiencing her lowest when she's arrested for shoplifting. Eve goes to rescue Madelyn and finds a Super-8 film that records their mother's humiliating abuse by their father.

Freudian psychiatrists will have a field day observing the sisters' struggle to gain control and power in their lives as a result of their traumatic family experience.

•

FEMALE TROUBLE

1975, 95 mins, US Ⓥ col

Dir John Waters ***Prod*** John Waters ***Scr*** John Waters ***Ph*** John Waters ***Ed*** Charles Roggero

Act Divine, David Lochary, Mary Vivian Pearce, Mink Stole, Edith Massey, Cookie Mueller (Dreamland/New Line)

Female Trouble is the sordid tale of Dawn Davenport, who rises from high school hoyden to mistress of crime before frying in the electric chair. As she climbs the ladder of success, she is raped by a stranger, gives birth to an obnoxious child who later murders the father, marries a beautician whose mother she imprisons in a bird cage before cutting off her hand and opens a nightclub act during which she guns down members of the audience. A true original.

Repeating from *Pink Flamingos* in the stellar role is Divine, a mammoth 300-pound transvestite with a tinsel soul. Though Divine doesn't stoop to devouring dog excrement as at the *Flamingos* fade-out, he does everything else, from cavorting on a trampoline, to playing a rape scene opposite himself, and "giving birth" on camera. Camp is too elegant a word to describe it all.

Sets, lighting, camerawork, editing and sound are all superior to their *Flamingos* counterparts and Waters makes the most of a reported $25,000 budget.

•

FEMININE TOUCH, THE

1941, 96 mins, US b/w

Dir W. S. Van Dyke ***Prod*** Joseph L. Mankiewicz ***Scr*** George Oppenheimer, Edmund L. Hartmann, Ogden Nash ***Ph*** Ray June ***Ed*** Albert Akst ***Mus*** Franz Waxman

Act Rosalind Russell, Don Ameche, Kay Francis, Van Heflin, Donald Meek, Robert Ryan (M-G-M)

The Feminine Touch is important through showcasing Rosalind Russell as one of the top film comediennes. She handles the sophisticated material equally as well as the frequent excursions into slapstick.

Don Ameche, as an absentminded but honest professor, can also pitch comedy. The third star, Kay Francis, likewise shows up well.

The script gives dumb football players a thorough lacing and points up the literary set as a flock of screwball lushes and predatory wolves. Ameche scrams Digby U after refusing to pass an all-American tackle who hasn't the IQ of a six-year-old. With his wife (Russell) he winds up in New York with an academic tome debunking jealousy. Francis, as the assistant to publisher Van Heflin, sees great possibilities in it if Ameche will commercialize it with down-to-earth writing; Heflin sees only Russell.

Russell, who burns every time she fails to make Ameche jealous, is a natural as the small-town girl married to the brilliant if complacent professor. Ameche, with a hefty share of dryly humorous dialog, gets every possible laugh out of the lines.

•

FEMME EST UNE FEMME, UNE

(A WOMAN IS A WOMAN)

1961, 84 mins, France/Italy Ⓥ ▭ col

Dir Jean-Luc Godard ***Prod*** Georges de Beauregard, Carlo Ponti ***Scr*** Jean-Luc Godard ***Ph*** Raoul Coutard ***Ed*** Agnes Guillemot ***Mus*** Michel Legrand ***Art*** Bernard Evein

Act Anna Karina, Jean-Paul Belmondo, Jean-Claude Brialy, Nicole Paquin, Marie Dubois, Jeanne Moreau (Rome-Paris)

Jean-Luc Godard, whose use of unusual cutting, fragmented pacing and cynical jocularity worked in his first film, *Breathless*, has now tried to apply these techniques to a situation comedy [from an idea by Genevieve Cluny]. It does not come off as well, and is only intermittently bright. Too much homage to Yank musicals and comedies point up the lack of polish in this entry.

A stripteaser (Anna Karina), living with a young bookseller (Jean-Claude Brialy), decides she wants a baby. He is against it until they get married. She finally goes to his friend (Jean-Paul Belmondo) so that she can have her child and comes back and tells her beau, who accepts the situation.

There are some good sequences in the strip parlor. Some witty dialog along with visual and sound jokes also are assets. But not enough of the material is effective and too many situation gags fall flat.

Godard has kept wife, Karina, almost continually on screen. She is a fetching featherbrain, but is sometimes lost in the dead spots that call for girlish mugging. Brialy and Belmondo are mainly foils, but acquit themselves well. Color is uneven. At times, however, it aids the story.

•

FEMME INFIDELE, LA

(UNFAITHFUL WIFE)

1969, 97 mins, France/Italy Ⓥ col

Dir Claude Chabrol ***Prod*** Andre Genoves (exec.) ***Scr*** Claude Chabrol ***Ph*** Jean Rabier ***Ed*** Jacques Gaillard ***Mus*** Pierre Jansen ***Art*** Guy Littaye

Act Stephane Audran, Michel Bouquet, Maurice Ronet, Michel Duchaussoy, Guy Marly, Serge Bento (Films La Boetie/Cinegai)

Claude Chabrol has concocted a canny film that subtly looks at a case of adultery sans any false dramatics, moralizing or sexploitation tactics. It is subdued, wise and revealing.

There is a supposedly happy suburban home with loving wife and husband and charming young son. But when he finds she did not go to appointments she told him about, he sets a private detective on her trail, which reveals she has a lover. He sees the man and plays the knowing, liberal husband. But suddenly the husband becomes angry and kills the lover. After the body is disposed of he goes home as if nothing happened. But there is a tension he cannot always control, plus the wife's touchy mood over her lover not appearing at a rendezvous.

Chabrol has fine help from his actors. Stephane Audran is incisive as the wife attached to her family and yet giving in to a romantic need, and Michel Bouquet is brilliantly right as the gentle husband who cannot play the rules of effacement. Maurice Ronet is effective as the dodgy playboy lover who still exudes charm.

A warm color envelope, that counterpoints the drama, and expert technical and production aspects, and, above all, Chabrol's careful direction weld this into a perceptive film.

•

FEMME NIKITA, LA

SEE: NIKITA

•

FEMME PUBLIQUE, LA

1984, 110 mins, France Ⓥ col

Dir Andrzej Zulawski ***Prod*** Rene Cleitman ***Scr*** Andrzej Zulawski, Dominique Garnier ***Ph*** Sacha Vierny ***Ed*** Marie-Sophie Dubus ***Mus*** Alain Wisniak ***Art*** Bohden Paczowski, Christian Siret

Act Francis Huster, Valerie Kaprisky, Lambert Wilson, Diane Delor, Roger Dumas, Patrick Bauchau (Hachette-Fox)

La Femme Publique is just a pulp metaphysical turn by an unusually clever technician, though lovers of the sensational may turn on to it as a potential cult item.

There's plenty of madness but little method or meaning in this tale of an inexperienced actress who lands a role in a film based on Dostoyevsky's *The Possessed*, gets bedded and then bounced out by its rabid pseudo-German director, and winds up playing a real-life role subbing as the dead girlfriend of a Czech immigrant, who is manipulated by the filmmaker into committing a political assassination.

Valerie Kaprisky gives her all as the aspiring thesp without much personality. Her big scenes are a series of lewd, nude convulsive dances for a voyeuristic photographer. Francis Huster is the rabid, pretentious filmmaker, and for once the actor's narcissism finds some effective employ. Lambert Wilson plays the coerced Czech, who has some sexual tangoes with Kaprisky before being set as a decoy to cover the monstrous political plot that never is adequately explained.

Sacha Vierny's lensing is superbly sinister, rendering the Paris locations as uninviting as the Berlin sites in Andrzej Zulawski's last film, *Possession*.

•

FENG YUE

(TEMPTRESS MOON)

1996, 130 mins, Hong Kong Ⓥ ⊙ col

Dir Chen Kaige ***Prod*** Tong Cunlin, Hsu Feng ***Scr*** Shu Kei ***Ph*** Christopher Doyle ***Ed*** Pei Xiaonan ***Mus*** Zhao Jiping ***Art*** Huang Qiagui

Act Leslie Cheung, Gong Li, Kevin Lin, He Saifei, Chang Shih, Xie Tian (Tomson)

Though it reunites two of the leads from his previous film, Chen Kaige's period meller *Temptress Moon* is a very different cup of *cha* from his fresco-esque, history-laden showpiece *Farewell My Concubine*. An emotionally complex look at a young gigolo's obsession with the daughter of a wealthy, decaying family, *Moon* is a visually intoxicating but much darker work.

Pic was conceived as a relatively low-budget affair, entirely set in the household of the extended family; it ended up with a tab of more than $7 million, about double that of *Concubine*. Original femme lead, Taiwanese unknown Wang Ching-ying, was fired halfway through shooting in fall 1994 and production shut down for five months before resuming in April '95, with Gong Li assuming the role.

Opening reels immediately establish the sumptuous-looking, slightly woozy atmosphere that permeates the pic. Flash forward to the '20s, and Zhongliang (Leslie Cheung) is a smooth, blackmailing gigolo in glitzy, decadent Shanghai, not far from the Pang household in Suzhou. Treated almost as a son by his Mafioso boss (Xie Tian), Zhongliang occasionally steals away for secret R&R in the arms of an older woman (Zhou Jie), the only one for whom he feels any warmth.

Meanwhile, at the Pangs's his cousin Ruyi (Gong Li) has effectively taken over as head of the household following the death of the clan elder. Titular management of the household is given to a distant cousin, Duanwu (Kevin Lin), who immediately falls for his beautiful, remote relative. When Zhongliang, at his boss' urging, visits Suzhou, the wheels are set in motion for an obsessive love affair to develop between him and Ruyi. At around the one-hour mark, the picture starts to lose momentum. Gong rarely uncovers the heart of the role, looking a tad too old and composed for the part. Cheung, however, is excellent, moving between his confident gigolo and emotion-wracked lover with ease.

[In the U.S. and U.K., pic showed in a 127-min. fine cut by the director.]

•

FERNGULLY

THE LAST RAINFOREST

1992, 76 mins, US Ⓥ ⊙ col

Dir Bill Kroyer ***Prod*** Wayne Young, Peter Faiman ***Scr*** Jim Cox ***Ed*** Gillian Hutshing ***Mus*** Alan Silvestri ***Art*** Susan Kroyer (FAI)

FernGully is a colorful, lively, extremely "politically correct" animated feature pitting the elfin creatures of the wild against the rapacious monsters who would destroy their habitat. Drawn in brilliantly verdant colors immediately inviting the viewer into a special world, *FernGully* is certainly simple enough for any youngster to understand, yet is sufficiently hip around the edges to contain the sap.

For years, the evil spirit that once destroyed the forest has been locked up, but it is suddenly unleashed by an enormous, omnivorous machine that gobbles up vegetation and leaves waste in its relentless path. A workman on the machine, Zak, gets tossed into the jungle and is shrunk down, permitting a human to see things from the other POV.

Robin Williams asserts his unique personality and wacky humor amazingly well in an animated context as a crazed, brain-fried bat named Batty Koda. Cheech and Chong are reunited, at least vocally, as the raucous Beetle Boys; *Rocky Horror*'s Tim Curry essays the villainous Hexxus, liberated to destroy the forest.

These performers, in addition to such singers as Johnny Clegg, Sheena Easton and Elton John delivering original numbers written by a host of w.k. songsmiths, bring considerable pizzazz and variety to the tightly conceived picture, and provide regular distraction from the more insipid leads.

•

FERRIS BUELLER'S DAY OFF

1986, 103 mins, US Ⓥ ⊙ ▭ col

Dir John Hughes ***Prod*** John Hughes, Tom Jacobson ***Scr*** John Hughes ***Ph*** Tak Fujimoto ***Ed*** Paul Hirsch ***Mus*** Ira Newborn ***Art*** John W. Corso

Act Matthew Broderick, Alan Ruck, Mia Sara, Jeffrey Jones, Jennifer Grey, Cindy Pickett (Paramount)

Ferris Bueller exhibits John Hughes on an off day. Paucity of invention here lays bare the total absence of plot or involving situations.

In a nutshell, the thin premise demonstrates the great lengths to which the irrepressible Ferris Bueller (Matthew Broderick) goes in order to hoodwink his parents and high school principal into thinking he's really sick when, in fact, all he wants to do is play hooky for a day.

Oddly, for a rich kid, Ferris doesn't have his own car, so he shanghais his best friend for the day, appropriates the vintage Ferrari of the buddy's father, spirits his girlfriend out of school and speeds off for downtown Chicago.

Broderick's essential likeability can't replace the loony anarchy of Hughes's previous leading man, Anthony Michael Hall. Alan Ruck can't do much with his underwritten second-banana role, and Mia Sara is fetching as Ferris's g.f.

Picture's one saving grace is the absolutely delicious comic performance of Jeffrey Jones as the high school principal.

•

FEVER PITCH
1985, 96 mins, US Ⓥ col
Dir Richard Brooks ***Prod*** Freddie Fields ***Scr*** Richard Brooks ***Ph*** William A. Fraker ***Ed*** Jeff Jones ***Mus*** Thomas Dolby ***Art*** Raymond G. Storey
Act Ryan O'Neal, Catherine Hicks, Giancarlo Giannini, Bridgette Andersen, Chad Everett, John Saxon (M-G-M)

Weak script, poor acting and miscasting aside, it's the power of the subject that makes this an enjoyable ride. Writer-director Richard Brooks thoroughly researched the territory of the compulsive gambler and captures the obsession with almost a documentary eye.

Unfortunately, plot is a totally unconvincing jumble and Ryan O'Neal as a sports reporter hooked on the gambling game is wooden and unsympathetic. Up to his ears in gambling debts, O'Neal just gets in deeper with loansharks and operators. He's already lost his wife due to gambling.

Most of the action takes place in Las Vegas where O'Neal wins and loses huge sums and gets involved with big-timer Giancarlo Giannini.

Rest of the cast is as stiff as the script. Catherine Hicks as a Vegas cocktail waitress and sometime call girl goes through a few turns that don't quite fit.

•

FEW GOOD MEN, A
1992, 138 mins, US Ⓥ ⦿ ▭ col
Dir Rob Reiner ***Prod*** David Brown, Rob Reiner, Andrew Scheinman ***Scr*** Aaron Sorkin ***Ph*** Robert Richardson ***Ed*** Robert Leighton ***Mus*** Marc Shaiman ***Art*** J. Michael Riva
Act Tom Cruise, Jack Nicholson, Demi Moore, Kevin Bacon, Kiefer Sutherland, Kevin Pollak (Columbia/Castle Rock)

A Few Good Men is a big-time, mainstream Hollywood movie par excellence. Expert story construction and compelling thesping and direction make all the narrative elements pay off in this exposé of peacetime military malfeasance laced with the story of a bright young lawyer's struggle to get out from under the imposing shadow of an illustrious father.

Adapting his own 1989 play, Aaron Sorkin has opened it up just enough to accommodate the requirements of the big screen, and magnified the psychological father–son dilemma of the leading character.

Chosen to defend two young Marines charged with murder is Navy lawyer Lt. Kaffee (Tom Cruise), a hot dog who prefers baseball duds to military uniforms. Briefly alighting in Cuba to interview the base's commanding officer, Col. Nathan Jessep (Jack Nicholson), Kaffee is goaded to press further by the driven special counsel, Lt. Cdr. Joanne Galloway (Demi Moore).

Action ping-pongs back and forth between defense team strategy sessions, interrogations of the two perpetrators, man-to-mans between Kaffee and the friendly but fiercely competitive, skilled prosecuting attorney Capt. Ross (Kevin Bacon), and raging exchanges in which Joanne won't let Kaffee off the hook.

Director Rob Reiner hasn't missed a beat in extracting the most out of the material and his actors. The showiest turn is reserved for Nicholson, and the crafty old pro makes more than the most of it. He's only got three major scenes, but they're all dynamite.

NOMINATIONS: Best Picture, Supp. Actor (Jack Nicholson), Editing, Sound

•

FFOLKES
SEE: NORTH SEA HIJACK

•

F FOR FAKE
1975, 85 mins, France/W. Germany/Iran ⦿ col
Dir Orson Welles, Francois Reichenbach ***Scr*** [Orson Welles, Olga Palinkas] ***Ph*** Christian Odasso, Gary Graver ***Ed*** Marie-Sophie Dubus, Dominique Engerer ***Mus*** Michel Legrand
Act Orson Welles, Oja Kodar [= Olga Palinkas], Joseph Cotten, Francois Reichenbach (SACI/Astrophore/Janus)

Orson Welles has reworked the docu material of Francois Reichenbach on noted art forger Elmyr De Houry, made for TV about 1968, into an intriguing, enjoyable look at illusion in general and his own, Clifford Irving and De Houry's dealing with it in particular.

He has deftly added himself to the affair as he is seen doing some magico stints, and winkingly admitting he is a charlatan.

Welles also brings in his early fakery of becoming an actor in passing himself off as a New York thesp to the Abbey Theater in Ireland at 16 and his Mars radio scare, also a fake, which, unlike Irving, did not lead him to prison but to Hollywood. There, according to Joseph Cotten, interviewed, he was thinking of making a fictional film on Howard Hughes, which finally became *Citizen Kane*, loosely based on W. R. Hearst.

Welles shows his shrewd flair for visuals and montage even if he has shot only a part of the footage. [Earlier title for pic was simply, subtitled *about Fakes*.]

•

FIDDLER ON THE ROOF
1971, 180 mins, US Ⓥ ⦿ ▭ col
Dir Norman Jewison ***Prod*** Norman Jewison ***Scr*** Joseph Stein ***Ph*** Oswald Morris ***Ed*** Antony Gibbs, Robert Lawrence ***Mus*** John Williams (arr.) ***Art*** Robert Boyle
Act Topol, Norma Crane, Leonard Frey, Molly Picon, Paul Mann, Rosalind Harris (Mirisch/Cartier)

Sentimental in a theatrical way, romantic in the old-fashioned way, nostalgic of immigration days, affirmative of human decency, loyalty, bravery and folk humor, here is the screen version of the long-running Hal Prince–produced, Jerome Robbins–directed stage musical smash [with book by Joseph Stein, music by Jerry Bock, lyrics by Sheldon Harnick].

Pictured is the Ukrainian village of pious and tradition-ruled Jews at the point the corrupt Czaristic regime was goading them to move out. A tight-lipped bigot, Vernon Dobtcheff drives into the village in his carriage with an escort of military horsemen and lays down to the reluctant constable (Louis Zorich) the obligatory political line, namely there must be a "distractive" demonstration of the local peasants against "those Christ-killers."

Attention naturally falls on the Tevye. Norman Jewison chose the Israeli actor Topol, who played the role on the London stage. An enormous man with sparkling (not melting) brown eyes, Topol has the necessary combination of bombast and compassion, vitality and doubts. His dialogs with God (and/or the audience) are more cautious and less in the chutzpah style of, say, Zero Mostel. Topol sings passably, but "If I Were a Rich Man" is too serious, losing the fun.

1971: Best Cinematography, Sound, Adapted Score

NOMINATIONS: Best Picture, Director, Actor (Chaim Topol), Supp. Actor (Leonard Frey), Art Direction

•

FIELD, THE
1990, 110 mins, UK Ⓥ ⦿ col
Dir Jim Sheridan ***Prod*** Noel Pearson ***Scr*** Jim Sheridan ***Ph*** Jack Conroy ***Ed*** J. Patrick Duffner ***Mus*** Elmer Bernstein ***Art*** Frank Conway
Act Richard Harris, John Hurt, Tom Berenger, Sean Bean, Frances Tomelty, Brenda Fricker (Granada)

Superb acting and austere visual beauty are offset by a somewhat overheated screenplay in this tragic tale [from the play by John B. Keane] about an indomitable Irish peasant's blood ties to the land. Richard Harris is in the larger-than-life role of a patriarchal Irish tenant farmer with a ferocious temperament and blazing charisma. The time is the 1930s, when the memory of the great famine was fresh and feudal ways held sway in the Irish countryside.

For most of his life, Bull McCabe has farmed a field belonging to a wealthy widow (Frances Tomelty), who one day decides to sell the plot. Bull is outraged.

He holds in thrall his slow-witted son, Tadgh (Sean Bean), and even slower-witted crony, Bird O'Donnell (John Hurt). The suicide of another son during the famine still haunts Bull, and his wife, Maggie (Brenda Fricker), has not spoken to him in the 20 years since.

"Who would insult me by bidding for my field?" he demands at the local pub. No one but an Irish-American from Boston (Tom Berenger), who has returned to his ancestral village with a plan to pave Bull's field for an access road to lucrative limestone deposits.

Harris gives a resonant, domineering performance as the prideful peasant, casting him as a pagan throwback, who views God and nature as one. Incredibly disguised, Hurt is remarkable as the pathetic village idiot who lives for the reflected glory of the most fearsome man in town.

1990: NOMINATION: Best Actor (Richard Harris)

•

FIELD OF DREAMS
1989, 106 mins, US Ⓥ ⦿ col
Dir Phil Alden Robinson ***Prod*** Lawrence Gordon, Charles Gordon ***Scr*** Phil Alden Robinson ***Ph*** John Lindley ***Ed*** Ian Crafford ***Mus*** James Horner ***Art*** Dennis Gassner
Act Kevin Costner, Amy Madigan, Gaby Hoffman, Ray Liotta, James Earl Jones, Burt Lancaster (Gordon/Universal)

Alternately affecting and affected, *Field of Dreams* is a fable about redemption and reconciliation that uses the mythos of baseball as an organizing metaphor.

Kevin Costner plays Ray Kinsella, a new-age farmer who has come to Iowa's cornfields with his college sweetheart (Amy Madigan).

In the fields one day Costner hears a celestial voice that cryptically advises: "If you build it, he will come." Once he convinces himself and his family that he's not going crazy, Costner sets out to sculpt a beautiful baseball diamond from his precious cornfield.

The whole town thinks the outsider has gone bonkers, but one night Costner's faith is rewarded: the spirit of Shoeless Joe Jackson, the most precipitously fallen of the disgraced World Series fixers, the 1919 Chicago White Sox, materializes on his ballfield.

Fully in the grip of supernatural forces, Costner leaves the farm on a cross-country pilgrimage to find the Boston home of America's best-known reclusive writer (James Earl Jones)—a cultural demigod depicted as a cross between J. D. Salinger and Bob Dylan.

Costner, Shoeless Joe, Jones and Burt Lancaster (a failed dead baseballer) are all haunted by regrets over failed relationships, life-shattering mistakes and missed opportunities. All yearn for a collective second chance at inner peace. In spite of a script hobbled with cloying aphorisms and shameless sentimentality, *Field of Dreams* sustains a dreamy mood in which the idea of baseball is distilled to its purest essence: a game that stands for unsullied innocence in a cruel, imperfect world.

1989: NOMINATIONS: Best Picture, Adapted Screenplay, Original Score

•

FIERCE CREATURES
1997, 93 mins, UK/US Ⓥ ⦿ ▭ col
Dir Robert Young, Fred Schepisi ***Prod*** Michael Shamberg, John Cleese ***Scr*** John Cleese, Iain Johnstone ***Ph*** Adrian Biddle, Ian Baker ***Ed*** Robert Gibson ***Mus*** Jerry Goldsmith ***Art*** Roger Murray-Leach
Act John Cleese, Jamie Lee Curtis, Kevin Kline, Michael Palin, Ronnie Corbett, Robert Lindsay (Fish/Jersey)

It takes a stout heart to make a nonsequel sequel, but that's exactly what the makers of *A Fish Called Wanda* have done with *Fierce Creatures*. The ensemble has returned, but the ripping yarn finds them in new roles that are unrelated to the characters in the earlier pic.

The antic mayhem stems from a London zoo recently acquired by Kiwi media mogul Rod McCain (Kevin Kline). Willa Weston (Jamie Lee Curtis), recently hired by McCain's Octopus Inc., arrives for her first day only to discover that her division was sold just hours earlier. Scanning the telephone book of McCain ventures, she decides it would be fun to run the Marwood Zoo.

Meanwhile, befitting the mogul's usual m.o., he's sent in ex–Hong Kong cop Rollo Lee (John Cleese) to turn the operation into a profitable venture. Rollo figures the best way to make it a "sexy" tourist attraction is to eliminate its domesticated animals and have it stocked 100 percent by "fierce creatures."

Far from the usual high-concept gagfest, *Creatures* is an artful combination of high and low comedy that runs like a well-oiled machine. It's winningly character-driven, stretching but not breaking the bounds of credibility.

Briefly known as *Dead Fish 2*, production was unquestionably troubled. Pic was filmed in summer 1995, and Cleese decided to rewrite its third act following test screening. Director Robert Young was unavailable and Fred Schepisi finished new scenes and reshoots. It's a testament to the filmmakers—especially initial cameraman Adrian Biddle and finisher Ian Baker—that the overall picture approaches the consummate stylishness Charles Crichton brought to *Wanda*.

•

FIESTA
1947, 104 mins, US col
Dir Richard Thorpe ***Prod*** Jack Cummings ***Scr*** George Bruce, Lester Cole ***Ph*** Sidney Wagner, Charles Rosher, Wilfrid M. Cline ***Ed*** Blanche Sewell ***Mus*** Johnny Green ***Art*** Cedric Gibbons, William Ferrari
Act Esther Williams, Akim Tamiroff, Ricardo Montalban, John Carroll, Mary Astor, Cyd Charisse (M-G-M)

Fiesta is an eyeful of Esther Williams. It's also pleasant if not socko film fare, "introducing a new personality, Ricardo Montalban."

The new personality is a nice departure in that he's not the Valentino type, but on the other hand neither is he socko in any other direction. As a Mexican juvenile, however, he is a sympathetic vis-a-vis to Williams, who plays his twin sister.

The film plot punches over the fact that "not all Mexicans are bullfighters." Leisurely the story unfolds with the birth of the twins, after the famed matador (well played by Fortunio Bonanova, who does a tip-top interpretation of the role) at first betrays his chagrin that his firstborn is a girl. But when her twin brother arrives 15 minutes later he schools the lad to follow in the bullfighter tradition, even though his penchant is music. Eventually the "Salon Mexico" suite by Aaron Copland (brilliantly orchestrated by Johnny Green) serves as the Mexican Symphony's means to project his virtuosity as a serious composer. Plot projects his doting twin sister (who also has manifested skill in the arena) to masquerade as her brother in order to recapture a distorted loss of family honor.

John Carroll is her romantic vis-a-vis and Cyd Charisse makes a fine impression with her terps and general line-reading as the romantic interest opposite Montalban, with whom she clicks in a couple of intricate native terp routines.

•

5TH AVE. GIRL

1939, 82 mins, US Ⓥ ⊙ b/w

Dir Gregory La Cava ***Prod*** Gregory La Cava ***Scr*** Allan Scott ***Ph*** Robert de Grasse ***Ed*** William Hamilton, Robert Wise ***Mus*** Robert Russell Bennett ***Art*** Van Nest Polglase, Perry Ferguson

Act Ginger Rogers, Walter Connolly, Verree Teasdale, James Ellison, Tim Holt, Kathryn Adams (RKO)

5th Ave. Girl is a cleverly devised comedy drama, expertly guided by Gregory La Cava. Story is basically of Cinderella pattern—always good. Millionaire Walter Connolly, shunned by his family on his birthday, meets Ginger Rogers in Central Park. After a night club celebration, he hires her to pose as a golddigger, and takes her to his Fifth Avenue mansion.

Sock laughs are supplied by situations and surprise dialog. Rogers, bewildered by her sudden catapult into a swank home, carries it all off with a blankness that accentuates her characterization. Connolly deftly handles the assignment of the prosperous manufacturer.

Production is distinctly a La Cava achievement. In motivation, its unfolding lies between the wacky *My Man Godfrey* and the more serious *Stage Door*.

•

FIFTH ELEMENT, THE

1997, 127 mins, France Ⓥ ⊙ ▭ col

Dir Luc Besson ***Prod*** Patrice Ledoux ***Scr*** Luc Besson, Robert Mark Kamen ***Ph*** Thierry Arbogast ***Ed*** Sylvie Landra ***Mus*** Eric Serra ***Art*** Dan Weil

Act Bruce Willis, Gary Oldman, Ian Holm, Milla Jovovich, Chris Tucker, Luke Perry (Gaumont)

A largely misfired attempt to make an American-style sci-fi spectacular, *The Fifth Element* consists of a hodgepodge of elements that don't comfortably coalesce. The splashy and cacophonous $70 million production, which launched the 50th edition of the Cannes Film Festival, stands as by far the most expensive French film project ever undertaken. Sony paid $25 million for the U.S. [distribution] rights.

Director Luc Besson originally conceived the story in his teens, and tale does feel like something that could have been born in a daydream, with little regard to coherent narrative or characterization.

Twelve-minute prologue is not unpromising, with some Western explorers in 1914 Egypt uncovering the meaning of ancient carvings that detail how a malignant force can be conquered by convergence of small totems representing the four elements plus the energy of life. By the year 2259, however, the lessons have been forgotten by all but a sort of high priest (Ian Holm). But it's a good thing somebody remembers, because the Earth finds itself in the path of a huge, fiery planet that conventional weapons only make bigger and stronger.

Possible salvation arrives in the form of a genetically regenerated young woman, Leeloo (Milla Jovovich), a naked, orange-haired acrobat of superhuman strength who escapes from the lab only to land in the flying taxi of New York cabby Korben Dallas (Bruce Willis). While Korben takes Leeloo to see the priest, Zorg (Gary Oldman), overlord of all evil, is equipping some would-be fearsome animal mercenaries for the ultimate battle, which oddly takes place on board an outer-space cruise ship that resembles a Vegas-style tropical casino.

Besson, whose best previous work, such as *Nikita*, had a clean, sharp look, has lost his grip on his sense of style here. The punkish and gender-crossing orientation of many of the characters looks straight out of any trendy contempo nightclub, while the score seems disappointingly stuck in the hip-hop and techno-rock era.

Willis emerges from it all battered but unbowed. Former teen model Jovovich makes a striking impression, but her character disappears for long periods.

1997: NOMINATION: Best Sound Effects Editing

•

55 DAYS AT PEKING

1963, 150 mins, US Ⓥ ▭ ⊙ col

Dir Nicholas Ray, [Andrew Marton, Guy Green] ***Prod*** Samuel Bronston ***Scr*** Philip Yordan, Bernard Gordon, Robert Hamer, [Ben Barzman] ***Ph*** Jack Hildyard ***Ed*** Robert Lawrence ***Mus*** Dimitri Tiomkin ***Art*** Veniero Colasanti, John Moore

Act Charlton Heston, Ava Gardner, David Niven, Flora Robson, John Ireland, Leo Genn (Bronston)

Producer Samuel Bronston shows characteristic lavishness in the pictorial scope, the vivid and realistic sets and extras by the thousands in his reproduction of the capital of Imperial China in 1900. The lensing was in Spain where the company built an entire city. The screenplay presumably adheres to the historical basics in its description of the violent rebellion of the "Boxers" against the major powers of the period—Great Britain, Russia, France, Germany, Italy, Japan, and the United States—because of their commercial exploitation of tradition-bound and unmodern (backward) China. These market-seeking nations have in their Peking outpost gallant fighting men who, although only a few hundred in number, withstand the merciless 55-day siege. While Ray is identified as director, some of the battle scenes actually were directed by Andrew Marton. This came to be in a period when Ray was ill.

David Niven is the British embassy head who stubbornly refuses to surrender, risking the safety of all about him, including his wife and two children. Both he and Charlton Heston perform with conviction, Heston as the American Marine major who commands the defense. Ava Gardner's role is not too well conceived. Hers is the part of the widow of a Russian bigshot who killed himself upon learning of his wife's infidelity with a Chinese official.

Lynne Sue Moon gives a poignant performance as an Oriental twelve-year-old whose American father, an army captain, is killed in battle. Flora Robson appears strikingly authentic as the Dowager Empress Tzu Hsi whose sympathies lie with the outlaws.

Jack Hildyard's photography is excellent, particularly in getting on the big screen the savage attack scenes that take up the major part of the picture. Dimitri Tiomkin provides engaging music.

1963: NOMINATIONS: Best Original Music Score, Song ("So Little Time")

•

52 PICK-UP

1986, 114 mins, US Ⓥ ⊙ col

Dir John Frankenheimer ***Prod*** Menahem Golan, Yoram Globus ***Scr*** Elmore Leonard, John Steppling ***Ph*** Jost Vacano ***Ed*** Robert F. Shugrue ***Mus*** Gary Chang ***Art*** Philip Harrison

Act Roy Scheider, Ann-Margret, Vanity, John Glover, Robert Trebor, Kelly Preston (Cannon)

52 Pick-Up is a thriller without any thrills. Although director John Frankenheimer stuffs as much action as he can into the screen adaptation of Elmore Leonard's novel (previously filmed by Cannon in Israel in 1984 as *The Ambassador*), he can't hide the ridiculous plot and lifeless characters.

Roy Scheider is an all-American hero, married for 23 years to the still attractive Ann-Margret, who has worked his way up by his bootstraps and after many lean years now owns a successful business and a luxurious home in the Hollywood hills.

Caught in a blackmail scheme by an unlikely trio of porno operators who film him in bed with cute young Kelly Preston, Scheider balks at giving up his hard-earned wealth, but even more at being told what to do.

Chemistry between Scheider and Ann-Margret is minimal and undermines the film's foundation. More lively are the three thugs who are fingering Scheider. Ring-leader John Glover gives the role such a decadently sinister turn that he's far more interesting and lively to watch than Scheider.

•

FIGHT CLUB

1999, 139 mins, US Ⓥ ▭ ⊙ col

Dir David Fincher ***Prod*** Art Linson, Cean Chaffin, Ross Grayson Bell ***Scr*** Jim Uhls ***Ph*** Jeff Cronenweth ***Ed*** James Haygood ***Mus*** The Dust Brothers ***Art*** Alex McDowell

Act Brad Pitt, Edward Norton, Helena Bonham Carter, Meat Loaf Aday, Jared Leto (Linson/Fox 2000/Regency)

This bold, inventive, sustained adrenaline rush of a movie about a guru who advocates brutality and mayhem plays mischievously with film conventions, almost winking at the audience to convey the characters' awareness of being part of a movie that deals in hot-button issues.

From *Alien*³ through *Se7en* and *The Game*, David Fincher has always been attracted to dark material. In Chuck Palahniuk's novel of the same name about a cult of men who channel their pent-up physical aggression into increasingly destructive pursuits, the director has found his most disturbing subject matter yet. And in debuting screenwriter Jim Uhls's clever, savagely witty script and the unremitting volley of information it launches, Fincher has found the perfect countermeasures to balance his coldly atmospheric, often distancing style.

Set in an unidentified, semi-stylized city, the story's nameless narrator (Edward Norton), who has troubles with insomnia, meets enigmatic Tyler Durden (Brad Pitt). They get tanked together, after which Tyler amicably picks a fight that seals their bond and marks the beginning of a phenomenon that each week attracts new participants, fighting each Saturday night in a club whose members are sworn to secrecy.

Fight club chapters start springing up across the country, and members take their aggressive behavior into the outside world with acts of violence, vandalism and subversiveness. Tyler's disciples start turning up to enlist in an army for Project Mayhem, the full extent of which is only gradually revealed.

Performances by the leads are uniformly potent, with Norton's character demanding by far the greatest range. Visual aspects are consistently impressive.

1999: NOMINATION: Best Sound Effects Editing

•

FIGHTER SQUADRON

1948, 94 mins, US col

Dir Raoul Walsh ***Prod*** Seton I. Miller ***Scr*** Seton I. Miller ***Ph*** Sid Hickox, Wilfred M. Cline ***Ed*** Christian Nyby ***Mus*** Max Steiner ***Art*** Ted Smith

Act Edmond O'Brien, Robert Stack, John Rodney, Tom D'Andrea, Henry Hull (Warner)

Picture's time of action is the tense days of 1943–44, when the U.S. Air Force was paving the way for D-Day. It centers its story on one English-based squadron of fighter planes and pilots. The film thrives on deadly air action, and the AF combat footage that makes up a substantial part of the picture is a tingling reminder of the Second World War.

It's an all-male picture, except for two brief scenes showing a sergeant, who uses the alias of Kinsey, at work and in trouble. Femmes aren't missed, though. The gal back home and the one in London are constantly talked about by post-bound soldiers. Only Kinsey is able to break bounds, using an ingenious trick with black cats that is good for chuckles.

Cast is very able in portraying the assorted young men who live and die bravely. Edmond O'Brien, squadron leader, stands out, and there are strong assists from Robert Stack and John Rodney as flying mates.

•

FIGHTING KENTUCKIAN, THE

1949, 109 mins, US Ⓥ b/w

Dir George Waggner ***Prod*** John Wayne ***Scr*** George Waggner ***Ph*** Lee Garmes ***Ed*** Richard L. Van Enger ***Mus*** George Antheil

Act John Wayne, Vera Ralston, Philip Dorn, Oliver Hardy, Marie Windsor, Hugo Haas (Republic)

Whether the story of two Kentucky riflemen coming to the aid of French refugees starts a bit incongruous, it all pans out as swift-moving melodrama. Pic also introduces Oliver Hardy, better known as the rotund half of the Laurel-Hardy slapstick team, as a tough albeit corpulent Kentucky backwoods fighter. That he registers speaks well for his natural thespian ability, mugging and all.

A little known bit of American history, that congress granted four townships of land in Alabama to French officers of Napoleon's defeated armies and their families, forms the background for the story. That is until Wayne, one of the Kentucky troopers returning from final battle of the War of 1812, falls in love with Vera Ralston, daughter of French general Hugo Haas.

•

FIGHTING 69TH, THE
1940, 90 mins, US Ⓥ b/w
Dir William Keighley ***Prod*** Louis F. Edelman ***Scr*** Norman Reilly Raine, Fred Niblo, Jr., Dean Franklin ***Ph*** Tony Gaudio ***Ed*** Owen Marks ***Mus*** Adolphe Deutsch ***Art*** Ted Smith
Act James Cagney, Pat O'Brien, George Brent, Jeffrey Lynn, Alan Hale, Frank McHugh (Warner)

Based on the adventures of New York's crack Irish regiment during the First World War, *The Fighting 69th* is a vigorously melodramatic war picture.

Story is a factual presentation of the 69th's war record, from training at Camp Mills through its major engagements at the front, with fictional interpolations for dramatic purposes. It's a vivid display of soldiering under fire—back of the lines, in the front-line trenches and up in No Man's Land.

With an all-male cast, picture carries no semblance of romantic interest. Not only are wives and sweethearts missing from farewells at Camp Mills, but scripters side-stepped the inclusion of French maids to provide diversion for the American doughboys.

Cagney has a definitely unsympathetic role as the smart-alec recruit from Brooklyn whose mental and physical fiber disintegrates under fire. His eventual regeneration through the efforts of Father Duffy (Pat O'Brien) comes too late to evince much audience sympathy for the character.

Despite the handicaps provided by a despicable role, Cagney scores with a highlight performance. O'Brien is effective as the famous Father Duffy, although the script confines his efforts mainly to straightening out the troublesome Cagney. George Brent essays the role of "Wild Bill" Donovan, head of the outfit; Jeffrey Lynn is excellent in too-brief appearances as the poet Joyce Kilmer and Alan Hale is a typical tough top sergeant in the regiment.

•

FIGURES IN A LANDSCAPE
1970, 95 mins, UK ▭ col
Dir Joseph Losey ***Prod*** John Kohn ***Scr*** Robert Shaw ***Ph*** Henri Alekan ***Ed*** Reginald Beck ***Mus*** Richard Rodney Bennett ***Art*** Ted Tester
Act Robert Shaw, Malcolm McDowell, Pamela Brown, Henry Woolf, Christopher Malcolm (Cinema Center)

The plight of two prisoners escaping from a relentless helicopter over "400 miles of hostile terrain" is the armature around which this yarn, which purposely never defines who the prisoners or the forces chasing them are, is spun.

MacConnachie, a 40-year-old "coarse man born to kill" and young Ansell, who supposedly is "propelled by reason and perception" have somewhere joined forces, are scrambling over the wastelands, and are being pursued by an acrobatic helicopter whose job it is to spot them, and whose faceless pilot seems to enjoy swooping down to give them a scare.

It is difficult to get into the characters, who always remain as elusive as the country they are traveling over is supposed to be.

•

FILE ON THELMA JORDON, THE
1950, 100 mins, US b/w
Dir Robert Siodmak ***Prod*** Hal B. Wallis ***Scr*** Ketti Frings ***Ph*** George Barnes ***Ed*** Warren Low ***Mus*** Victor Young ***Art*** Hans Dreier, Earl Hedrick
Act Barbara Stanwyck, Wendell Corey, Paul Kelly, Joan Tetzel, Stanley Ridges, Richard Rober (Paramount)

Thelma Jordon unfolds as an interesting, femme-slanted melodrama, told with a lot of restrained excitement.

Scripting [from a story by Marty Holland] is very forthright, up to the contrived conclusion, and even that is carried off successfully because of the sympathy developed for the misguided and misused character played by Wendell Corey.

Corey is seen as an assistant d.a., a husband and father. One night, after a quarrel with his wife, Joan Tetzel, he is intrigued by the Barbara Stanwyck character. It leads him to further pursuit and a hot amour.

Stanwyck is pretending to be a poor cousin to her rich aunt. When the latter is killed by a house-breaker, Corey attempts to remove evidence that would point toward Stanwyck. Despite this, she is charged with murder.

Robert Siodmak's direction pinpoints many scenes of extreme tension.

•

FILLE DE D'ARTAGNAN, LA
(D'ARTAGNAN'S DAUGHTER)
1994, 125 mins, France Ⓥ ⦿ col
Dir Bertrand Tavernier ***Prod*** Frederic Bourboulon (exec.) ***Scr*** Michel Leviant, Jean Cosmos ***Ph*** Patrick Blossier ***Ed*** Ariane Boeglin ***Mus*** Philippe Sarde ***Art*** Geoffroy Larcher
Act Sophie Marceau, Philippe Noiret, Claude Rich, Sami Frey, Jean-Luc Bideau, Nils Tavernier (CiBy 2000/Little Bear/TF1)

This is a sexy, often very funny sequel to the Alexandre Dumas classic *The Three Musketeers*. Director Bertrand Tavernier has said it is a tribute to the action pix he grew up with, and the film's strength comes from its ability to deliver the thrills 'n' spills of the Errol Flynn–style actioners without being self-consciously nostalgic.

Set in 1650s France, fast-paced story opens with a slave escaping through the woods from the estate of the evil Duke of Crassac (Claude Rich). The Mother Superior of a nearby convent gives refuge to the slave, and is murdered by the Duke's henchman in retaliation.

Eloise (Sophie Marceau), who is studying at the convent, immediately sets off for Paris hoping to enlist her famous dad, D'Artagnan (Philippe Noiret), to help seek revenge. Along the way, she meets up with flaky, romantic poet Quentin (Nils Tavernier, the director's son). She arrives in Paris to find her aging father isn't exactly crazy about jumping back into the musketeer biz.

All-star French thesps are uniformly first-rate. Marceau is captivating and sexy as the spirited female musketeer, and Noiret adds a poignant edge to pic with his portrayal of D'Artagnan as an almost-washed-up hero. Actors look like they're having fun, particularly Rich, who turns in an over-the-top comic turn as the low-IQ bad guy.

Philippe Sarde's wonderfully warm score and Jacqueline Moreau's sumptuous period costumes add to pic's flavor and elegance. [Pic is based on an idea by Riccardo Freda (originally skedded to direct) and Eric Poindron, adapted by Michel Leviant, Tavernier and Jean Cosmos.]

•

FILOFAX
SEE: TAKING CARE OF BUSINESS

•

FINAL ANALYSIS
1992, 124 mins, US Ⓥ ⦿ col
Dir Phil Joanou ***Prod*** Charles Roven, Paul Junger Witt, Tony Thomas ***Scr*** Wesley Strick ***Ph*** Jordan Cronenweth ***Ed*** Thom Noble ***Mus*** George Fenton ***Art*** Dean Tavoularis
Act Richard Gere, Kim Basinger, Uma Thurman, Eric Roberts, Paul Guilfoyle, Keith David (Warner)

Final Analysis is a crackling good psychological melodrama [from a screen story by Robert Berger and Wesley Strick] in which star power and slick surfaces are used to potent advantage. Tantalizing double-crosses mount right up to the eerie final scene.

In the course of treating a patient (Uma Thurman), San Francisco psychiatrist Richard Gere takes the unusual step of meeting the young woman's older sister, who may know more about certain events in Thurman's past than the subject herself.

Sis turns out to be Kim Basinger, who has no trouble overcoming his tenuous sense of professional ethics about bedding a patient's sibling. An aloof workaholic, Gere becomes hopelessly ensnared in his secret affair with Basinger, who in turn promises to find a way out of her marriage. Sympathies ride with her in a murder trial but with the trial's conclusion Basinger assumes the full dimensions of a Warner Bros. bad girl that Joan Crawford would have killed to play.

Greatest hurdle for some viewers may be getting past the idea of Gere as a respected psychiatrist, and the intellectual side of his character is shortchanged. Similarly, Basinger is mostly surface effect, but it's considerable here. Her wardrobe is stunning.

Physical production is one of the film's major stars, as lenser and production designer have conspired to create a darkly shadowed, outrageously attractive world that outdoes even San Francisco's natural beauties.

•

FINAL CONFLICT, THE
1981, 108 mins, US Ⓥ ⦿ ▭ col
Dir Graham Baker ***Prod*** Harvey Bernhard ***Scr*** Andrew Birkin ***Ph*** Robert Paynter, Phil Meheux ***Ed*** Alan Strachan ***Mus*** Jerry Goldsmith ***Art*** Herbert Westbrook
Act Sam Neill, Rossano Brazzi, Don Gordon, Lisa Harrow, Mason Adams (20th Century-Fox)

The Final Conflict is the last chapter in the Omen trilogy, which is too bad because this is the funniest one yet.

This time Sam Neill plays Damien Thorn, all grown up now after killing off two nice families in the previous chapters. Fear of orphanage, of course, never worries Damien because his real father is the Devil, who only wanted him to go to the best schools, get a job and take over the world for evil.

And now he has, or almost. He's running Thorn Industries and will soon be U.S. Ambassador to England when the fellow who has the job sees a bad dog and goes back to the office and blows his head off, the single startling episode in the whole film.

Having memorized the Book of Hebron from The Apocrypha, plus several dopy soliloquies in Andrew Birkin's script, Neill knows the only obstacle to his plan is the baby born when three stars conjoin overhead. There's also the matter of the daggers. If you remember the first two episodes, somebody or other, sometimes mom, sometimes dad, sometimes a stranger, was always trying to stab little Damien to death with the daggers.

This is the first feature for director Graham Baker, a veteran of British TV commercials, and it seems like he doesn't quite know what to do when the daggers don't have a brand-name to hold toward the camera or the dialog stretches beyond two sentences.

•

FINAL COUNTDOWN, THE
1980, 103 mins, US Ⓥ ⦿ ▭ col
Dir Don Taylor ***Prod*** Peter Vincent Douglas ***Scr*** David Ambrose, Gerry Davis, Thomas Hunter, Peter Powell ***Ph*** Victor J. Kemper ***Ed*** Robert K. Lambert ***Mus*** John Scott ***Art*** Fernando Carrere
Act Kirk Douglas, Martin Sheen, Katharine Ross, James Farentino, Ron O'Neal, Charles Durning (Bryna/United Artists)

As a documentary on the USS *Nimitz, The Final Countdown* is wonderful. As entertainment, however, it has the feeling of a telepic that strayed onto the big screen. The magnificent production values provided by setting the film on the world's largest nuclear-powered aircraft carrier can't transcend the predictable cleverness of a plot that will seem overly familiar to viewers raised on *Twilight Zone* reruns.

The liberal sympathies typical of the work of Kirk Douglas are evident in his characterization of the ship's commander as a man whose sense of military honor will not allow him to take the opportunity provided him by a mysterious storm—his ship and crew find themselves transported back in time to 6 December 1941, between Pearl Harbor and the Japanese fleet heading to destroy the American naval base and send the U.S. into World War II.

The philosophical issues raised by the film hardly bear much examination, because the patchwork screenplay by two pairs of writers paints each character in too schematic a fashion. Martin Sheen has much more to work with than Douglas, who seems uncharacteristically subdued.

•

FINAL PROGRAMME, THE
(US: THE LAST DAYS OF MAN ON EARTH)
1973, 89 mins, UK Ⓥ ⦿ col
Dir Robert Fuest ***Prod*** Jon Goldstone, Sandy Lieberson ***Scr*** Robert Fuest ***Ph*** Norman Warwick ***Ed*** Barrie Vince ***Mus*** Paul Beaver, Bernard Krause ***Art*** Robert Fuest, Philip Harrison
Act Jon Finch, Jenny Runacre, Hugh Griffith, Patrick Magee, Stirling Hayden, Julie Ege (Goodtimes/Gladiole)

Pic is a silly, pretentious pot-boiler, done in a jazzed-up style that suggests Ken Russell on an off day. Jon Finch is topcast as a rebellious intellectual in a devastated world seeking a new messiah. Pic alternates high-falutin' allegory with low-brow facetiousness, and the film is a mishmash.

Robert Fuest, who directed, based the story on Michael Moorcock's novel *The Final Programme*. Whatever ideas Fuest is trying to deal with, mostly in the pop cliché fashion of run-of-the-mill sci-fi, are submerged by the relentlessly chic filming style.

The Finch character runs up against some of England's most interesting supportng actors, none of whom has much of a part, and when the forlorn cast is coupled with the junk-strewn landscape, pic could be taken as a sad allegory of the British film industry. Among the talents stranded here are Jenny Runacre, Hugh Griffith, Patrick Magee, Harry Andrews, Graham Crowden and George Coulouris. Sterling Hayden is in for a flash.

•

FINDERS KEEPERS
1966, 94 mins, UK Ⓥ col
Dir Sidney Hayers ***Prod*** George H. Brown ***Scr*** Michael Pertwee ***Ph*** Alan Hume ***Ed*** Tristam Cones ***Mus*** The Shadows ***Art*** Jack Sheripan
Act Cliff Richard, The Shadows, Robert Morley, Peggy Mount, Viviane Ventura, Graham Stark (Interstate/United Artists)

George H. Brown's story line about a minibomb dropped by accident from an American plane over Spain and subsequent attempts by various foreign "spies" to locate it could have had a good astringent and satirical tang. The theme is not only largely frittered away but is hardly suitable for a relaxed, easygoing music-comedy designed to showcase a pop group such as Cliff Richard and The Shadows. Wit gets lost, and incidents are held up, to make room for inevitable song, dance and fiesta.

Richard and The Shadows hitchhike to a hotel in Spain and find it deserted. The dropped bomb has sent everybody scurrying away. The lads, with the help of a local charmer (Viviane Ventura), decide that it's in their interests to find it and hand it over to the U.S. troops, who have moved in on a similar mission.

Michael Pertwee's screenplay does not build up much urgency or suspense but provides opportunity for colorful fiesta, a gentle romance between Richard and Ventura, some verbal dueling between Robert Morley and Graham Stark.

•

FINDERS KEEPERS
1984, 96 mins, US Ⓥ col
Dir Richard Lester ***Prod*** Sandra Marsh, Terence Marsh ***Scr*** Ronny Graham, Terence Marsh, Charles Dennis ***Ph*** Brian West ***Ed*** John Victor Smith ***Mus*** Ken Thorne ***Art*** Terence Marsh
Act Michael O'Keefe, Beverly D'Angelo, Louis Gossett, Jr., Ed Lauter, Pamela Stephenson, Brian Dennehy (CBS)

Director Richard Lester returns to his pell-mell trademark and the result is maddening. Interesting cast is wasted, with bright exception of Beverly D'Angelo.

Producers Sandra and Terence Marsh hang their frenetic tale of stolen money, chases and deceptions on several characters racing up and down a train en route from California to Nebraska.

There's $5 million in a coffin in the baggage car, there's a sexy neurotic (D'Angelo, who steals the movie), a bumbling con man (top-lined Michael O'Keefe), razor sharp con man (Louis Gossett, Jr., on screen only briefly), a sweaty heavy (Ed Lauter) and a gregarious old train conductor (David Wayne). Its parts add up to pieces that artlessly lurch and hurtle around.

•

FINDING FORRESTER
2000, 133 mins, US Ⓥ ⦿ ▭ col
Dir Gus Van Sant ***Prod*** Laurence Mark, Sean Connery, Rhonda Tollefson ***Scr*** Mike Rich ***Ph*** Harris Savides ***Ed*** Valdis Oskarsdottir ***Art*** Jane Musky
Act Sean Connery, Rob Brown, F. Murray Abraham, Anna Paquin, Busta Rhymes, April Grace (Mark/Columbia)

Gus Van Sant's work has always shown a fondness for outsiders, but rather than merely depicting them sympathetically, he places his outcasts in crisis, forcing them to confront their relationship to society and its rules. On the surface, *Finding Forrester* tells a similar story to that of Van Sant's *Good Will Hunting*.

Narrative depicts Forrester (Sean Connery) as a silver-haired eccentric who spends a lot of time at his Bronx apartment window, seemingly observing a bunch of black kids playing ball. Veiled in mystery, the last the world has heard of Forrester was more than 40 years ago, when he was a brilliant Pulitzer-winning novelist. His book, which has since become a cherished classic, is apparently his only literary output.

As the youngsters are aware of Forrester's invisible presence, their curiosity naturally builds. Sneaking into his apartment to get info about the mythical man, 16-year-old Jamal (Rob Brown) accidentally leaves behind a backpack full of his writing. The next day, the bag appears at the window and, to Jamal's surprise, his papers have been read and graded by Forrester. An unlikely relationship begins, marked by all the familiar ups and downs of such bonds. While lines of authority are clearly maintained, the graceful script shows how dependent the mentor becomes on the kid, who evolves from an intrigued fan to a loyal student to a social companion, all the while determined to reignite Forrester's passion for writing.

The text is extremely old-fashioned: A crucial scene at school, in which Jamal is reprimanded for his conduct, functions as the equivalent of a courtroom scene, in which an inflexible teacher (F. Murray Abraham) is contrasted with good ones. A bigger mistake is that the filmmakers signal where the tale will ultimately go about a reel before it gets there.

Forrester is very much a chamber piece for two, with more than half the scenes set in Forrester's cluttered, oversize apartment. Playing the Salinger-like writer of legendary stature, Connery expertly fills the bill as a man who's at once ingratiating and infuriating, a recluse who needs to be rescued from misanthropy. Amazingly, with no previous experience, Brown stands up to Connery, and in some scenes even matches him with his inner strength and stillness.

•

FINE AND DANDY
SEE: THE WEST POINT STORY

•

FINE MADNESS, A
1966, 104 mins, US Ⓥ col
Dir Irvin Kershner ***Prod*** Jerome Hellman ***Scr*** Elliott Baker ***Ph*** Ted McCord ***Ed*** William Ziegler ***Mus*** John Addison ***Art*** Jack Poplin
Act Sean Connery, Joanne Woodward, Jean Seberg, Patrick O'Neal, Colleen Dewhurst, Clive Revill (Pan Arts/Warner)

A Fine Madness is offbeat, and downbeat, in many ways. Too heavyhanded to be comedy, yet too light to be called drama, the well-mounted production depicts a non-conformist poet-stud in an environment of much sex, some violence and modern headshrinking. Fine direction and some good characterizations enhance negative script outlook.

Sean Connery is a virile, headstrong poet, hung up in a dry spell of inspiration. He despises women in general, and to hammer home this point, all femme characters, except second wife, Joanne Woodward, are shrews, battle-axes or shallow broads.

Overdue back alimony cues an outburst, eventually leading Connery to psychiatric care, alternating with a running chase from the fuzz, and climaxed by a curiously ineffective brain lobotomy. A lot of sophisticated throwaway dialogue is dispensed along with sight gags and slapstick.

Director Irvin Kershner has drawn effective performances from Connery, who makes a good comic kook in a switch from the somnambulism of his James Bond roles, and Woodward, almost unrecognizable in face and voice via a good characterization of the loud-mouthed, but loving, wife, done in the Judy Holliday style. Jean Seberg, bored wife of headshrinker Patrick O'Neal, is okay.

•

FINE MESS, A
1986, 88 mins, US Ⓥ ⦿ ▭ col
Dir Blake Edwards ***Prod*** Tony Adams ***Scr*** Blake Edwards ***Ph*** Harry Stradling ***Ed*** John F. Burnett ***Mus*** Henry Mancini ***Art*** Rodger Maus
Act Ted Danson, Howie Mandel, Richard Mulligan, Stuart Margolin, Maria Conchita Alonso, Paul Sorvino (BEE/Columbia-Delphi V)

Blake Edward's obsession with the slapstick comedy genre has produced some all-time comedy classics and some best-forgotten clinkers. *A Fine Mess* belongs in the latter category.

Neither Ted Danson and Howie Mandel nor Richard Mulligan and Stuart Margolin offer audiences much affection, or are likely to receive much. Danson plays a small-time actor who, during location filming at a racing stable, overhears two crooks (Mulligan and Margolin) as they dope a horse on the instructions of their boss (Paul Sorvino). Before long, Danson and his buddy Mandel are being chased all over L.A. by the incompetent villains, cueing in plenty of over-familiar car chases.

A Fine Mess is light on plot and instead concentrates on strenuous, familiar comedy routines. Trouble is, the principal players are all quite charmless.

•

FINE PAIR, A
1969, 88 mins, Italy/US ▭ col
Dir Francesco Maselli ***Prod*** Leo L. Fuchs ***Scr*** Francesco Maselli, Luisa Montagnana, Larry Gelbart, Virgil C. Leone ***Ph*** Alfio Contini ***Ed*** Nicoletta Nardi ***Mus*** Ennio Morricone ***Art*** Luciano Puccino
Act Rock Hudson, Claudia Cardinale, Tomas Milian, Leon Askin, Ellen Corby, Walter Giller (Cinema Center)

A Fine Pair carries a promising original premise but film is so bogged down in contrived and confusing action that its impact is reduced to a minimum. Pic was lensed mostly in Italy. Script never rings true and Rock Hudson is called upon to enact an unconvincing character.

Film opens in NY, where Claudia Cardinale, a sexy 24-year-old who once knew Hudson when he visited her policeman-father in Italy 10 years before, arrives from her native country to enlist his assistance. She claims she's been involved with an international jewel thief, and she wants Hudson's help in returning a fortune in jewels stolen from the winter villa of a rich American family in Austria.

Hudson plays his role in a grim manner and Cardinale is nice to look at even though difficult to understand.

•

FINIAN'S RAINBOW
1968, 145 mins, US Ⓥ ⦿ ▭ col
Dir Francis Coppola ***Prod*** Joseph Landon ***Scr*** E. Y. Harburg, Fred Saidy ***Ph*** Philip Lathrop ***Ed*** Melvin Shapiro ***Mus*** Ray Heindorf, Ken Darby (sups.) ***Art*** Hilyard M. Brown
Act Fred Astaire, Petula Clark, Tommy Steele, Don Francks, Keenan Wynn, Barbara Hancock (Warner)

This translation of the 1947 legituner [music by Burton Lane, lyrics by E. Y. Harburg] is a light, pastoral fantasy with civil rights angles, underscored by comedy values.

Film opens leisurely with Fred Astaire and Petula Clark, his daughter, on a montage tour of the U.S. The stars come to rest in Rainbow Valley, just as the police henchmen of racist judge Keenan Wynn are about to foreclose on property owned by vagabond Don Francks.

Astaire bails out Francks, and latter's romance with Clark develops. Tommy Steele arrives as the leprechaun searching for gold that Astaire has stolen.

Overall, the $4 million film has an ethereal quality: it's a blend of real elements, such as love, greed, compassion, prejudice and other aspects of human nature both noble and otherwise; yet it's also infused with mystical elements of magic, leprechauns, pixies and wishes that come true.

Clark, in her American film debut, has a winsome charm that comes through despite a somewhat reactive role.

1968: NOMINATIONS: Best Adapted Music Score, Sound

•

FIRE AND ICE
1983, 81 mins, US Ⓥ ⦿ col
Dir Ralph Bakshi ***Prod*** Ralph Bakshi, Frank Frazetta ***Scr*** Roy Thomas, Gerry Conway ***Ed*** A. Davis Marshall ***Mus*** William Kraft (PSO)

Ralph Bakshi's newest animation feature is interesting for two special reasons: (1) the production represents a clear design on Bakshi's part to capture a wider and younger audience and (2) the animation marks the film debut of America's leading exponent of heroic fantasy art, Frank Frazetta, who coproduced.

Known for his classic comic book and poster art, Frazetta works some of his famous illustrations into the film, such as his *Death Dealer* painting portraying an axe-wielding figure on horseback. Populating an Armageddon, embellished with subhumans and flying dragonhawks, are a blond hero, Larn; a sensuous-vulnerable dream girl in distress, Teegra; and an icy sorcerer and his willful mother, Lord Nekron and Juliana. Bakshi shot live actors first, to lay the foundation for the animation, in a process called Rotoscope.

•

FIRE BIRDS
(UK: WINGS OF THE APACHE)
1990, 85 mins, US Ⓥ ⦿ col
Dir David Green ***Prod*** William Badalato ***Scr*** Nick Thiel, Paul F. Edwards ***Ph*** Tony Imi ***Ed*** Jon Poll, Norman Buckley, Dennis O'Connor ***Mus*** David Newman ***Art*** Joseph T. Garrity
Act Nicolas Cage, Tommy Lee Jones, Sean Young, Bert Rhine, Bryan Kestner, Dale Dye (Touchstone/Nova)

Originally titled *Wings of the Apache* for the Apache assault helicopters prominently featured, *Fire Birds* resembles a morale booster project leftover from The Reagan era. A paean to Yankee air power, it shows the U.S. army as a take-charge outfit able to kick the butt of those South American drug cartel jerks.

Not surprisingly, given changing times and politics, *Fire Birds* has a tongue-in-cheek aspect. Camaraderie and rat-a-tat-tat dialog may have started out as fun a la Howard Hawks's classic *Only Angels Have Wings* but emerges at times as a satire of the genre.

Formula script, which inevitably recalls *Top Gun*, has Nicolas Cage training to use the army's Apache aircraft while vainly trying to rekindle a romance with old flame Sean Young. Tommy Lee Jones is dead-on as the taskmaster instructor who cornily singles out Cage for rough treatment. Film's main novelty is having Young also sent into combat instead of being the woman sitting on the sidelines.

•

FIRE DOWN BELOW
1957, 116 mins, US Ⓥ ▭ col
Dir Robert Parrish ***Prod*** Irving Allen, Albert R. Broccoli ***Scr*** Irwin Shaw ***Ph*** Desmond Dickinson, Cyril Knowles ***Ed*** Jack Slade ***Mus*** Arthur Benjamin ***Art*** John Box
Act Rita Hayworth, Robert Mitchum, Jack Lemmon, Herbert Lom, Bernard Lee, Anthony Newley (Warwick/Columbia)

Story [from a novel by Max Catto]: bad, bad girl (Rita Hayworth) meets youthful American, and finally agrees to marry him though warning him of her past—that of sort of a Mata Hari in Europe. Robert Mitchum, as Jack Lemmon's pal in a small fishing and smuggling boat operation, is vastly displeased with this development and tips off the Coast Guard on a smuggling trip so that Lemmon abandons the boat rather than be captured as a smuggler.

This lands him on a Greek freighter that crashes into a heavier ship in the fog. Lemmon is pinned down in the hold by a steel girder. Nearly all the second half of the film is centered on efforts to rescue him.

Hayworth is excellent as the comely femme who is always just one step ahead of the law. Lemmon (who takes a bow for composing the harmonica theme) shows plainly that he can handle a dramatic type role while Mitchum, as the tough man of the world, contributes one of his better portrayals.

•

FIREFOX

1982, 137 mins, US Ⓥ ⊙ ▭ col

Dir Clint Eastwood ***Prod*** Clint Eastwood ***Scr*** Alex Lasker, Wendell Wellman ***Ph*** Bruce Surtees ***Ed*** Ferris Webster, Ron Spang ***Mus*** Maurice Jarre ***Art*** John Graysmark, Elayne Ceder

Act Clint Eastwood, Freddie Jones, David Huffman, Warren Clarke, Ronald Lacey, Kenneth Colley (Warner)

Firefox is a burn-out. Lethargic, characterless and at least a half-hour-too-long, Cold War espionage saga [from the novel by Craig Thomas] about an American pilot smuggled into the U.S.S.R. to steal an advanced fighter jet is a disappointment since it possessed the basic elements of a topflight, us *vs* them actioner.

It all sounded good on paper—Clint Eastwood, as a retired ace flyer, infiltrating the Russian Air Force to spirit away the supposedly top-secret Firefox, a plane capable of Mach 5 speed and equipped with a thought-controlled weapons system.

But Eastwood, who generally displays astuteness when controlling his own projects has inexplicably dropped the ball here. Despite the tense mission being depicted, there's no suspense, excitement or thrills to be had, and lackadaisical pacing gives viewer plenty of time to ponder the gaping implausibilities.

•

FIREMAN'S BALL, THE

SEE: HORI, MA PANENKO

•

FIRE OVER ENGLAND

1937, 88 mins, UK Ⓥ b/w

Dir William K. Howard ***Prod*** Erich Pommer ***Scr*** Clemence Dane, Sergei Nolbandov ***Ph*** James Wong Howe ***Ed*** Jack Dennis ***Mus*** Richard Addinsell ***Art*** Lazare Meerson

Act Flora Robson, Raymond Massey, Leslie Banks, Laurence Olivier, Vivien Leigh, Lyn Harding (Pendennis London)

This is a handsomely mounted and forcefully dramatic glorification of Queen Bess. It holds a succession of brilliantly played scenes, a wealth of choice diction, pointed excerpts from English history and a series of impressive tableaux.

It projects Flora Robson in a conception of the British regent, which holds the imagination. Her keen aptitude in dovetailing the strong and frail sides of Elizabeth's nature makes a solid keystone for the production.

Action ranges from cumbersomely dull to sharp, hard-hitting flashes of excitement. Where director William K. Howard seems to get in his most telling dramatic effects are the sequences that build up to Laurence Olivier's undoing as an English spy and his subsequent escape, the queen's confronting of her coterie of exposed betrayers and the burning of the Spanish armada.

Sprightly plied are the romantic passages. It's a two-cornered play for Olivier. First object of his deportment is his childhood sweetheart and lady-in-waiting to the queen, persuasively treated by Vivien Leigh. His other idyllic moments bring him in contact with the daughter of a Spanish nobleman. As the Spanish beauty, Tamara Desni blends a compound of charm and sympathy.

•

FIREPOWER

1979, 104 mins, UK Ⓥ col

Dir Michael Winner ***Prod*** Michael Winner ***Scr*** Gerald Wilson ***Ph*** Robert Paynter, Dick Kratina ***Ed*** Arnold Crust [Michael Winner], Max Benedict ***Mus*** Gato Barbieri ***Art*** John Stoll, John Blezard

Act Sophia Loren, James Coburn, O. J. Simpson, Eli Wallach, Anthony Franciosa, Vincent Gardenia (ITC)

Firepower is one of those international action thrillers designed to combine a top-name cast with lots of shooting and explosions so the story [by Bill Kerby and Michael Winner] can be followed regardless of whether you understand the language.

Though competent with chases and gunfire, producer-director Michael Winner handles the dialogue scenes as if the most significant thing in the world were sunglasses.

Beautiful Sophia Loren believes her chemist husband was murdered at the order of Stegner (George Touliatos), a wealthy, seclusive industrialist. She persuades the Justice Department, who also wants Stegner, to put the pressure on mobster Eli Wallach to entice retired hitman James Coburn to get Stegner.

If the story becomes too tough or tiresome to follow, or the action grows tepid and repetitive, there's always the beautiful scenery of the glamorous Caribbean locales.

•

FIRE SALE

1977, 88 mins, US Ⓥ col

Dir Alan Arkin ***Prod*** Marvin Worth ***Scr*** Robert Klane ***Ph*** Ralph Woolsey ***Ed*** Richard Halsey ***Mus*** Dave Grusin ***Art*** James H. Spencer

Act Alan Arkin, Rob Reiner, Vincent Gardenia, Anjanette Comer, Kay Medford, Barbara Dana (20th Century-Fox)

Fire Sale, Alan Arkin's alleged comedy, is a consummate sophomoric vulgarity. Marvin Worth's production matches in crippled creativity the physical infirmities on which most of the forced and strident humor is based. Arkin and Rob Reiner head the cast as two harried sons of Vincent Gardenia, himself the henpecked husband of Kay Medford.

Gardenia owns a dumpy department store, Reiner his cowed assistant after Arkin years earlier departed the family circle to become a failure as a basketball coach.

Sid Caesar is appropriately offensive as a Veterans' Hospital basket case coaxed by Gardenia into burning the store for insurance, thinking it's a World War II German installation.

•

FIRES ON THE PLAIN

SEE: NOBI

•

FIRESTARTER

1984, 115 mins, US Ⓥ ⊙ ▭ col

Dir Mark L. Lester ***Prod*** Frank Capra, Jr. ***Scr*** Stanley Mann ***Ph*** Giuseppe Ruzzolini ***Ed*** David Rawlins ***Mus*** Tangerine Dream ***Art*** Giorgio Postiglione

Act David Keith, Drew Barrymore, George C. Scott, Martin Sheen, Heather Locklear, Art Carney (De Laurentiis)

Story of a nine-year-old girl who can enflame objects and people by power of her will balances human concern of a pursued and loving father and daughter (David Keith and Drew Barrymore) against a clandestine government agency that wants to use the girl's power for nefarious ends.

Agency is headed by Martin Sheen, with Moses Gunn and George C. Scott as chilly support group.

Film marks the first major picture for director Mark L. Lester. But pic's stars are special effects team Mike Wood and Jeff Jarvis, whose pyrotechnics—flying fireballs, fire trenches, human balls of fire—create the film's impact.

Script by Stanley Mann is quite faithful to the Stephen King novel, but cinematically that loyalty is damaging. Picture's length can't sustain the material.

•

FIRES WITHIN

1991, 86 mins, US Ⓥ ⊙ ▭ col

Dir Gillian Armstrong ***Prod*** Wallis Nicita, Lauren Lloyd ***Scr*** Cynthia Cidre ***Ph*** David Gribble ***Ed*** Lou Lombardo, John Scott ***Mus*** Maurice Jarre ***Art*** Robert Ziembicki

Act Greta Scacchi, Jimmy Smits, Vincent D'Onofrio, Brit Hathaway, Luis Avalos, Bertila Damas (Pathe/M-G-M)

The timely, real-life situation involves an attractive emigre (Greta Scacchi) and her infant daughter (Brit Hathaway), among the "raft people" who continue to flee Cuba via open ocean on makeshift, floating deathtraps—hoping for landfall in the Florida Keys. They're rescued by a seaman (Vincent D'Onofrio), with whom the woman forms a romantic relationship over the next eight years.

She left a husband behind in Cuba, Jimmy Smits as a writer imprisoned for criticizing the Castro regime. His sudden release and subsequent arrival in Miami as a hero creates a classic romantic triangle against the backdrop of Cuban emigre politics.

Director Gillian Armstrong's attempt to cover all the emotional and political ramifications of Cynthia Cidre's thoughtful tale is, for the most part, dramatically respectable. But it is a cold narrative that never lingers on any situation long enough to generate either suspense or romance.

Scacchi's woman-in-the-middle role is confused at worst, detached at best. Smits, as the husband, garners the film's appeal.

•

FIRM, THE

1993, 154 mins, US Ⓥ ⊙ col

Dir Sydney Pollack ***Prod*** Scott Rudin, John Davis, Sydney Pollack ***Scr*** David Rabe, Robert Towne, David Rayfiel ***Ph*** John Seale ***Ed*** William Steinkamp, Frederic Steinkamp ***Mus*** Dave Grusin ***Art*** Richard Macdonald

Act Tom Cruise, Jeanne Tripplehorn, Gene Hackman, Hal Holbrook, Ed Harris, Holly Hunter (Paramount/Mirage)

The Firm is a very smooth adaptation of John Grisham's giant 1991 bestseller. Tom Cruise's hotshot lawyer bent on toppling his corrupt bosses could be a brother to his *A Few Good Men* character. Readers are in for a few extra twists in the final third of the story, as director Sydney Pollack and his trio of screenwriters have added some dramatic and ethical complexity to this yarn.

Cruise portrays Mitch McDeere, a sought-after Harvard grad who shuns offers from big city law offices in favor of a small, lucrative Memphis concern that promotes itself as a family. Mitch's teacher wife, Abby (Jeanne Tripplehorn), smells a rat from the outset, since the firm imposes unusually rigid codes of personal behavior, but Mitch jumps in with the enthusiasm of a puppy, working all hours, currying favor with the boss (Hal Holbrook) and lunching with mentor Avery Tolar (Gene Hackman).

After two of the firm's attorneys die in a mysterious boating accident, Mitch and Avery head to the Cayman Islands to investigate. Later, Mitch begins to suspect that the firm could be responsible for the deaths of four of its employees over the years.

Pollack has done an ultra-pro job in giving spit and polish to this star-driven, sure-fire commercial project. Close attention has been paid to story structure, the narrative is advanced in every sequence, and types of scenes are alternated carefully.

The more than 2 1/2 hour length is a bit indulgent, but pic retains its grip. One couldn't imagine anyone better than Cruise at this sort of star turn, except Robert Redford 25 years ago. Tripplehorn gets to do a bit more than hold down the home front and expresses doubt and fury at Mitch's long hours. Hackman turns in another sterling perf as a top lawyer with unexpected depths of pain and remorse.

1993: NOMINATIONS: Best Supp. Actress (Holly Hunter), Original Score

FIRST A GIRL

1935, 92 mins, UK b/w

Dir Victor Saville ***Prod*** Michael Balcon ***Scr*** Marjorie Gaffney ***Ph*** Glen MacWilliams ***Ed*** A. Barnes ***Mus*** Louis Levy (dir.) ***Art*** Oscar Werndorff

Act Jessie Matthews, Sonnie Hale, Anna Lee, Griffith Jones, Alfred Drayton, Constance Godridge (Gaumont British)

Jessie Matthews's admirers will love to see her rise from her humdrum niche in a dressmaking establishment to the giddy heights of thespian glory.

Though always longing for a stage career, her precipitous plunge comes about accidentally. She pals up with an aspiring Shakespearean actor, in reality a female impersonator. While sheltering her, he gets a wire giving him an unexpected date, which sudden loss of voice makes it impossible for him to accept. He coaches the bewildered girl and insists she take his place.

The variety hall is an awful dump. Billed, and trading, on the doubt concerning her sex, and carefully managed by her new partner, the act is a hit and she quickly makes a name.

The former wealthy customer, a "princess" and her boyfriend become friendly with the couple, but suspect she is really a girl and trick her by stalling on a motor trip to the Riviera, forcing her to share a room at a wayside inn with the two men.

Sonnie Hale plays the impersonator and gives an air of sincerity to a rather dubious situation. The boyfriend (Griffith Jones) has charm and a quiet dignity. The starring role is a natural for Jessie Matthews, where her dancing is unobtrusively displayed.

•

FIRST BLOOD

1982, 94 mins, US Ⓥ ⊙ ▭ col

Dir Ted Kotcheff ***Prod*** Buzz Feitshans ***Scr*** Michael Kozoll, William Sackheim, Sylvester Stallone ***Ph*** Andrew Laszlo ***Ed*** Thom Noble ***Mus*** Jerry Goldsmith ***Art*** Stephane Reichel

Act Sylvester Stallone, Richard Crenna, Brian Dennehy, David Caruso, Jack Starrett, Michael Talbot (Orion)

Sylvester Stallone plays a former Green Beret, a "killing machine" who's so tough if there had been one more of him, the Viet Cong wouldn't have had a chance.

Arriving unshaven at the quiet community of Hope, he's greeted by sheriff Brian Dennehy, who does not invite him to join the local Lion's club. In fact, Dennehy won't even let him linger for a sandwich. This upsets the taciturn Stallone, and he winds up at the slammer. Beating up the whole station house, he escapes into the woods.

Richard Crenna shows up, a Green Beret colonel who trained Stallone. They trap Stallone in a mine and blast the dickens out of it with a rocket. But our boy commandeers an army truck and machine gun and goes back to level Dennehy's quiet little town.

Director Ted Kotcheff has all sorts of trouble with this mess, aside from credibility. Supposedly, the real villain here is society itself, which invented a debacle like Vietnam and must now deal with its lingering tragedies. But *First Blood* cops out completely on that one, not even trying to find a solution to Stallone's problems.

•

FIRST DEADLY SIN, THE
1980, 112 mins, US Ⓥ ⊙ col
Dir Brian G. Hutton ***Prod*** George Pappas, Mark Shanker ***Scr*** Mann Rubin ***Ph*** Jack Priestley ***Ed*** Eric Albertson ***Mus*** Gordon Jenkins ***Art*** Woody Mackintosh
Act Frank Sinatra, Faye Dunaway, Brenda Vaccaro, James Whitmore, David Dukes, Martin Gabel (Kastner/Artanis/Cinema 7)

Otherwise a fairly routine and turgid crime meller, *The First Deadly Sin* commands some interest as Frank Sinatra's first film in 10 years.

Pic presents audience with considerable barriers to involvement from the outset, as first few reels consist predominantly of a bloody operation, a violent murder, dialog conducted over mutilated bodies in an autopsy room and unappetizing hospital scenes.

Plot has Sinatra latching onto an apparent series of arbitrary murders.

Paralleling the crime-and-detection yarn, and slowing down the entire proceedings, are Sinatra's visits to wife, Faye Dunaway, who's not recovering well from a kidney operation.

As for Sinatra, direct and not at all the wise guy, this amounts to a decent performance, even if the role might have called for a more desperate attitude.

•

FIRST GREAT TRAIN ROBBERY, THE
(US: THE GREAT TRAIN ROBBERY)
1979, 110 mins, UK Ⓥ ⊙ col
Dir Michael Crichton ***Prod*** John Foreman ***Scr*** Michael Crichton ***Ph*** Geoffrey Unsworth ***Ed*** David Bretherton ***Mus*** Jerry Goldsmith ***Art*** Maurice Carter
Act Sean Connery, Donald Sutherland, Lesley-Anne Down, Wayne Sleep, Michael Elphick, Alan Webb (United Artists/De Laurentiis)

Based on fact, the story [from the novel by Michael Crichton] concerns the first recorded heist from a moving train. Suave, arch-criminal Sean Connery enlists Donald Sutherland, Wayne Sleep, in a bid to lift a payroll of gold bars destined for the Crimea in 1855. A vital part, or rather series of parts, in the plan is played by Lesley-Anne Down as Connery's versatile yet reliable mistress.

The actual theft is ingenious. The film's highpoint comes when Connery clambers from car roof to car roof as the steam train speeds smokily under low bridges.

Crichton's films drag in dialog bouts, but triumph when action takes over.

Handling of the train sequences by cinematographer Geoffrey Unsworth is a lesson in the superior effectiveness of a well-placed camera over fancy tricks. A final caption dedicates the film to his memory, stating: "His friends miss him." So will his audiences.

•

FIRST KNIGHT
1995, 132 mins, US Ⓥ ⊙ col
Dir Jerry Zucker ***Prod*** Jerry Zucker, Hunt Lowry ***Scr*** William Nicholson ***Ph*** Adam Greenberg ***Ed*** Walter Murch ***Mus*** Jerry Goldsmith ***Art*** John Box
Act Sean Connery, Richard Gere, Julia Ormond, Ben Cross, Liam Cunningham, Christopher Villiers (Columbia)

Aside from casting Richard Gere as Lancelot, *First Knight* marches out as an agreeably intelligent, mature and well-mounted telling of the legendary King Arthur story.

Guinevere (Julia Ormond) is presented as the Lady of Leonesse, the overseer of a peaceful land that is easily sacked by the seethingly villainous Malagant (Ben Cross), a former knight of Arthur's Round Table who now treacherously seeks power for himself. On her way to take King Arthur's hand in a marriage, Guinevere is attacked by Malagant and is saved only through the intercession of Lancelot (Gere).

This Lancelot is not a courtly gentleman of the highest moral standards, but a sort of wandering samurai warrior who goes wherever his sword (or, in this case, his libido) leads him. Within moments of the rescue, Lancelot comes on strong to Guinevere, but, after just one kiss, she makes him promise he'll never do that again and moves on to her pointed rendezvous with Arthur (Sean Connery) in Camelot.

But serene contentment is not to be theirs, as Malagant snatches Guinevere from Camelot and hides her in a horrific dungeon from which Lancelot, miraculously, is able to rescue her. This gives him yet another opportunity to seduce the as-yet-unmarried lady, but, once again, she resists.

Literate, sober-minded and almost rigorously chaste, *First Knight* sweeps the viewer up in the doings of these impressive, larger-than-life characters. The only fly in the ointment is Gere, whose preening air of self-satisfied cockiness clashes hopelessly with the classy style displayed by the other actors. By contrast, Connery is a dream King Arthur, perfect as a man of exceptional character, purpose and righteousness. Ormond is a great match for him as Guinevere, on whom she bestows a becoming level-headedness and rationality.

•

FIRST LOVE
1977, 91 mins, US Ⓥ col
Dir Joan Darling ***Prod*** Lawrence Turman, David Foster ***Scr*** Jane Stanton Hitchcock, David Freeman ***Ph*** Bobby Byrne ***Ed*** Frank Morriss ***Mus*** Joel Sill ***Art*** Robert Luthardt
Act William Katt, Susan Dey, John Heard, Beverly D'Angelo, Robert Loggia, Tom Lacy (Paramount)

First Love is a sensitive and melancholy film about the impact of romance on college student William Katt when he falls for coed Susan Dey.

Harold Brodkey's *New Yorker* story, *Sentimental Education*, has been adapted into a script that takes Katt through the highs and lows of complicated young love.

But an unfortunate element in the story is the never-ending pall of doom that hangs over everything. From frame one the mood is a downer, which dampens the several nice bright moments of exuberance and telegraphs the coming climactic ambiguity.

Katt is excellent. So is Dey, who has an appealing charisma of vivacious sensuality.

•

FIRST MEN IN THE MOON
1964, 102 mins, UK Ⓥ ⊙ ▭ col
Dir Nathan Juran ***Prod*** Charles H. Schneer ***Scr*** Nigel Kneale, Jan Read ***Ph*** Wilkie Cooper ***Ed*** Maurice Rootes ***Mus*** Laurie Johnson ***Art*** John Blezard
Act Edward Judd, Lionel Jeffries, Martha Hyer, Erick Chitty, Betty McDowall, Miles Malleson (BLC/Columbia)

Ray Harryhausen and his special effects men have another high old time in this piece of science-fiction hokum filmed in Dynamation. Picture is based on H. G. Wells's novel and has been neatly updated.

Yarn starts with the arrival on the moon of three United Nations astronauts (Yank, Russian and British) amid world excitement. Pride of the astros receives a jolt when they find a small, faded Union Jack on the moon, together with a yellowed manuscript (a bailiff's receipt) with a scrawl that claims the discovery of the moon on behalf of Queen Victoria—date, 1899.

In a home, an aged man (Edward Judd) is tracked down by U.N. investigators. He tells them the incredible story of how he, his fiancée and an eccentric professor actually did land on the moon. He and the girl escaped. The prof remained to continue his scientific investigations.

The three principals play second fiddle to the special effects and art work, which are impressive in color, construction and animation.

•

FIRST MONDAY ON OCTOBER
1981, 96 mins, US Ⓥ ⊙ ▭ col
Dir Ronald Neame ***Prod*** Paul Heller, Martha Scott ***Scr*** Jerome Lawrence, Robert E. Lee ***Ph*** Fred J. Koenekamp ***Ed*** Peter E. Berger ***Mus*** Ian Fraser ***Art*** Philip M. Jefferies
Act Walter Matthau, Jill Clayburgh, Jan Sterling, Barnard Hughes, James Stephens, Joshua Bryant (Paramount)

Amiable talents of Walter Matthau and Jill Clayburgh make *First Monday in October* a mildly engaging talkfest in which all serious issues serve as window dressing for an almost-romantic comedy.

Rumpled and as likeable as ever, Matthau here portrays the court's "great dissenter," an individualistic civil libertarian à la the late William O. Douglas. In theory he greatly welcomes the appointment of a woman, but his hair stands on end when he learns that America's first female Supreme Court justice is the arch-conservative Clayburgh, "the Mother Superior of Orange County."

Decorum of the widow's installment into the men's club atmosphere of the court provokes smiles, if not big laughs, but it's all a prelude to the civilized sparks that fly when the two tangle over two major cases on the docket.

Scripters, working from their own popular play, have opted for the light treatment, with issues of the day merely providing a means for this odd couple to (sort of) get together.

•

FIRST NAME: CARMEN
SEE: PRENOM CARMEN

•

FIRST OF THE FEW, THE
(US: SPITFIRE)
1942, 118 mins, UK Ⓥ b/w
Dir Leslie Howard ***Prod*** Leslie Howard ***Scr*** Miles Malleson, Anatole de Grunwald, Miles Malleson ***Ph*** Georges Perinal ***Ed*** Douglas Myers ***Mus*** William Walton ***Art*** Paul Sheriff
Act Leslie Howard, David Niven, Rosamund John, Roland Culver, Anne Firth, Tonie Edgar Bruce (British Aviation)

In interpreting the life of R. J. Mitchell, who designed the Spitfire plane, Leslie Howard's work ranks among his finest performances. And it is an epic picture.

Film [from an original story by Henry C. James and Kay Strueby] portrays Mitchell's heartbreaking efforts to get his series of aircraft models accepted. His work was looked upon as too revolutionary, and the reluctance of Whitehall to sponsor anything new was most discouraging.

For big scenes there is the reproduction of a race for the Schneider Cup. For sweet domestic felicity there's Rosamund John as the wife of Mitchell. For a magnificent patriotic gesture there is Toni Edgar Bruce as Lady Houston, who contributed generously to the financing of the inventor. Finally (or should it be firstly?) there's Howard's young airman friend in the person of David Niven, as a lovable philanderer who shares the other's vicissitudes and glories.

•

FIRST TIME, THE
1983, 95 mins, US Ⓥ col
Dir Charlie Loventhal ***Prod*** Sam Irvin ***Scr*** Charlie Loventhal, Susan Weiser-Finley, William Franklin Finley ***Ph*** Steve Fierberg ***Ed*** Stanley Vogel ***Mus*** Lanny Meyers ***Art*** Tom Surgal
Act Tim Choate, Krista Errickson, Marshall Efron, Wendy Fulton, Raymond Patterson, Jane Badler (New Line/Goldmine)

The First Time is a mild but entertaining first feature by writer-director Charlie Loventhal and producer Sam Irvin, former assistants to Brian De Palma. Dealing fictionally with Loventhal's growing-up adventures while a student at formerly all-girls school Sarah Lawrence, the comedy owes much to De Palma's freewheeling satires made in the 1960s.

Charlie (Tim Choate) is an odd-man-out at college: unable to score with the pretty (but believably so) girls there while his black roommate Ronald (Raymond Patterson) shows off and gives him tips.

While pursuing an unattainable dream girl Dana (Krista Errickson), Charlie links up with another lonely soul Wendy (Wendy Fulton), and ultimately loses his virginity with the inevitable older woman Karen (Jane Badler).

Choate is very sympathetic in the lead role, matched by the sex appeal of Errickson, naturalism of Fulton and comedy sex-bomb Wendie Jo Sperber.

•

FIRST WIVES CLUB, THE
1996, 102 mins, US Ⓥ ⊙ col
Dir Hugh Wilson ***Prod*** Scott Rudin ***Scr*** Robert Harling ***Ph*** Donald Thorin ***Ed*** John Bloom ***Mus*** Marc Shaiman ***Art*** Peter Larkin
Act Goldie Hawn, Bette Midler, Diane Keaton, Maggie Smith, Sarah Jessica Parker, Dan Hedaya (Paramount)

Pic's three main characters are grads of Middlebury College's class of '69 reunited by the suicide of a fourth college friend. Each married well, raised a family and has recently been divorced or separated. Their spouses all flew the coop for younger women and, naturally, they're as mad as hell. Their brand of justice provides for a biting social comedy on the order of *The War of the Roses* and *Nine to Five*.

Elise (Goldie Hawn) is an Oscar-winning actress whose age is working against her. Brenda (Bette Midler) set her husband (Dan Hedaya) up in a chain of retail electronics stores. Annie (Diane Keaton) also sacrificed to get her soon-to-be ex (Stephen Collins) established in the ad agency biz.

The sense of anarchy recalls the zaniness of the Marx Brothers. But the filmmakers [adapting a novel by Olivia Goldsmith] relent with a much too tidy, wholesome conclusion that flies in the face of all that preceded it. Still, getting there is almost all the fun.

Midler, Hawn and Keaton are a refreshingly cohesive comedy combo. It's particularly satisfying to see Hawn making sport of her eternally youthful persona and Midler giving vent to her outsize personality. Keaton subtly keeps her co-stars from spinning into the ether.

Director Hugh Wilson wisely gets out of the way of his performers. He and editor John Bloom understand that if one is to play the material big and broad, the story rhythm has to be attuned to the laughter emanating from the back row.

1996: NOMINATION: Best Sound

•

FIRST YEAR, THE
1932, 80 mins, US b/w
Dir William K. Howard ***Scr*** Lynn Starling ***Ph*** Hal Mohr ***Ed*** Jack Murray ***Mus*** Hugo Friedhofer
Act Janet Gaynor, Charles Farrell, Minna Gombell, Leila Bennett, Dudley Digges, Robert McWade (Fox)

Janet Gaynor and Charles Farrell in a story that's as close to perfection for them as any piece of screenwriting could be. Hadn't Frank Craven written and John Golden produced this play for legit in 1922, it could easily be mistaken for a tailor-made job for Gaynor-Farrell in 1932.

Playing house as a couple of kids in their first year of married life may not have been a romp for Gaynor or Farrell but it looks to have been. They were building up to just such a story in all of their previous films. They love each other. Their troubles are typical. They surmount the handicaps and emerge triumphant with love in their hearts and cash in the bank.

Maude Eburne, Robert McWade and Leila Bennett are the comedy relief, the first two as the girl's loving parents. Some of the old man's snappy answers to mother's choice cracks are examples of shrewd comedy writing. Equally well written for comedy effect is Bennett's colored maid role, but the not so convincing makeup makes it tougher for her than anyone else in the cast.

•

FISH CALLED WANDA, A
1988, 108 mins, US Ⓥ ⦿ col
Dir Charles Crichton ***Prod*** Michael Shamberg ***Scr*** John Cleese ***Ph*** Alan Hume ***Ed*** John Jympson ***Mus*** John Du Prez ***Art*** Roger Murray-Leach
Act John Cleese, Jamie Lee Curtis, Kevin Kline, Michael Palin, Tom Georgeson, Maria Aitken (M-G-M/Prominent)

In *A Fish Called Wanda*, Monty Pythoners John Cleese and Michael Palin get caught up in a double-crossing crime caper with a mismatched and hilarious pair of scheming Yanks, Jamie Lee Curtis and Kevin Kline. Though it is less tasteless, irreverent and satirical than the Python pics, film still is wacky and occasionally outrageous in its own, distinctly British way.

John Cleese is Archie Leach (Cary Grant's real name), an uptight, respected barrister who becomes unglued when Wanda (Jamie Lee Curtis), the girlfriend of a crook he's defending, comes on to him for no apparent reason.

Curtis fakes it as an American law student looking to learn about English law when really she just wants to get information out of Cleese about some diamonds she's recently heisted with his client George (Tom Georgeson) and two others—her "brother" Otto (Kevin Kline), who's really no relation, and a stuttering animal rights freak Ken (Michael Palin), the proud owner of a fish tank and a fish named Wanda.

Cleese [scripting from a story by himself and director Charles Crichton] takes an opportunity to poke fun at something ripe for ridicule—this time, the love-hate rivalry between the Brits and the Yanks. It's funny without being mean, since both sides get their due. Curtis steals the show with her keen sense of comic timing and sneaky little grins and asides. Palin has too limited a role.

1988: Best Supp. Actor (Kevin Kline)

NOMINATIONS: Best Director, Original Screenplay

•

FISHER KING, THE
1991, 137 mins, US Ⓥ ⦿ ▭ col
Dir Terry Gilliam ***Prod*** Debra Hill, Lynda Obst ***Scr*** Richard LaGravenese ***Ph*** Roger Pratt ***Ed*** Lesley Walker ***Mus*** George Fenton ***Art*** Mel Bourne
Act Robin Williams, Jeff Bridges, Amanda Plummer, Mercedes Ruehl, Michael Jeter, Harry Shearer (Tri-Star)

The Fisher King has two actors at the top of their form, and a compelling, well-directed and well-produced story. First-time screenwriter Richard LaGravenese's lively, detailed original script deftly delineates the top and bottom rungs of human existence in Manhattan. Jack Lucas (Jeff Bridges) is a callous, egotistical radio shock-jock who falls apart after a caller he has blown off on the air proceeds to blow away seven yuppies in a trendy club. Just as he is about to end it all, Jack is rescued by a goofy gang of derelicts led by a maniac named Parry (Robin Williams).

While recovering from his suicidal state, Jack learns that Parry is obsessed with the Holy Grail, as well as with a gawky young lady Lydia (Amanda Plummer). Jack's earnest attempts to return Parry to normal life and set him up with the elusive Lydia represent his chance at personal redemption.

Film's first two hours zip by quickly and are spiked with memorable scenes such as a flight-of-fancy in which commuters waltz through Grand Central. But the final 20 minutes unspool mechanically and interminably as Jack implausibly follows through on the mythological demands of the story.

Jeff Bridges gives what is undoubtedly his strongest lead performance to date hitting notes he's never tried before in conveying the turmoil inside an arrogant man. Williams is endlessly inventive as usual, Plummer is terrific as the nerdy loner, and Mercedes Ruehl sizzles as Jack's upfront companion, Anne.

1991: Best Supp. Actress (Mercedes Ruehl)

NOMINATIONS: Best Actor (Robin Williams), Original Screenplay, Original Score, Art Direction

•

F.I.S.T.
1978, 145 mins, US Ⓥ ⦿ col
Dir Norman Jewison ***Prod*** Norman Jewison ***Scr*** Joe Eszterhas, Sylvester Stallone ***Ph*** Laszlo Kovacs ***Ed*** Tony Gibbs, Graeme Clifford ***Mus*** Bill Conti ***Art*** Richard MacDonald
Act Sylvester Stallone, Rod Steiger, Peter Boyle, Melinda Dillon, David Huffman, Tony Lo Bianco (United Artists)

In its superb telling of how a humble but idealistic young man escalates to the corrupt heights of unbridled power, *F.I.S.T.* is to the labor movement in the United States what *All the King's Men* was to an era in American politics.

The first hour of the film presents the milieu of unorganized labor circa 1937, a time when the phrase "property rights" was as persistent (and often as shrill) a harangue as "human rights" later became.

Sylvester Stallone and lifelong friend David Huffman are among the workers in Henry Wilcoxon's trucking company. They drift into organizing drivers for local union rep Richard Herd, whose assassination during a brawl triggered by management goons drives Stallone into league with Kevin Conway, a local hood.

The next act depicts the militant labor response of Stallone and Conway, highlighted by a well-staged riot, after which the tentacles of mobsterism—Tony Lo Bianco personifying them well—parallel the growth and power of the truckers' union.

Action then cuts to the late 1950s, when Stallone pushes international union leader Peter Boyle out of office by some private blackmail, only to run head-on into Rod Steiger, crusading U.S. senator.

•

FISTFUL OF DOLLARS
1964, 100 mins, Italy/W. Germany/Spain Ⓥ ⦿ ▭ col
Dir Bob Robertson [= Sergio Leone] ***Prod*** Harry Colombo [= Arrigo Colombo], George Papi [= Giorgio Papi] ***Scr*** Bob Robertson, Duccio Tessari, Mark Lowell ***Ph*** Jack Dalmas [= Massimo Dallamano] ***Ed*** Bob Quintle [= Roberto Cinquini] ***Mus*** Dan Savio [= Ennio Morricone] ***Art*** Charles Simons [= Carlo Simi]
Act Clint Eastwood, Marianne Koch, Johnny Wels [= Gian Maria Volonte], Wolfgang Lukschy, Joe Edger [= Josef Egger], Antonio Prieto (Jolly/Constantin/Ocean)

A cracker-jack western made in Italy and Spain by a group of Italians and an international cast, this is a hard-hitting item, ably directed, splendidly lensed, neatly acted, which has all the ingredients wanted by action fans and then some.

Basically, it's about a loner, Joe (Clint Eastwood), who arrives in a small Southwestern settlement split by the rivalry of two families. For money, he plays both sides against the middle, eventually winning his longstanding battle with the heavy. Tale [by Toni Palombi, based on the 1961 Japanese film *Yojimbo*] is well developed, and though there is plenty of cliché, it's handled with an all-stops-out style, vigorous use of widescreen camera, effective juggling of closeups and long shots. Spanish landscapes pass well for Southwestern areas bordering on Mexico as do costumes and types chosen, be they German, Italian, Spanish or "original" Yanks.

Eastwood handles himself very well as the stranger, shaping a character strong enough to beg a sequel. Further plaudits go to title animation by Luigi Lardani, which sets the style of this film from the start. Also to music, somewhat redundant but effective in the western vein.

[Version reviewed was 100-minute Italian one, with Eastwood dubbed by experienced actor Enrico Maria Salerno. English version was released in U.S. and U.K. in 1967.]

•

FISTFUL OF DYNAMITE, A
(AKA: DUCK, YOU SUCKER)
1972, 157 mins, Italy Ⓥ ⦿ ▭ col
Dir Sergio Leone ***Prod*** Fulvio Morsella ***Scr*** Luciano Vincenzoni, Sergio Donati, Sergio Leone ***Ph*** Giuseppe Ruzzolini ***Ed*** Nino Baragli ***Mus*** Ennio Morricone ***Art*** Andrea Crisanti
Act Rod Steiger, James Coburn, Romolo Valli, Jean Michel Antoine, Vivienne Chandler, David Warbeck (Rafran/Euro International)

Sergio Leone comes up with a tale [copenned with Sergio Donati] of the Mexican revolution. Rod Steiger plays a simple bandit who wants to rob a bank in a Mexican town but instead gets mixed up in a revolution in which he has no interest. He meets Coburn, a veritable storehouse of explosives on his person, and together they become involved in the peasants' revolt.

Leone occasionally inserts a light touch but generally action, which includes firing squads and much shooting. A blown-up bridge, which troops are crossing and a climaxing train collision are realistically portrayed. A paralleling note is offered via flashbacks through Coburn comparing some of his past experiences in the Irish Rebellion to events at hand, but procedure sometimes is clumsy.

[Reviewed above as *Duck, You Sucker*. Film's English-language title was changed soon after to *A Fistful of Dynamite*. In the U.S. pic was released in a 138-min. version.]

•

FIST OF FURY
SEE: JINGWU MEN

•

FISTS IN THE POCKET
SEE: I PUGNI IN TASCA

•

FISTS OF FURY
SEE: TANG SHAN DAXIONG

•

FITZWILLY
1967, 102 mins, US ▭ col
Dir Delbert Mann ***Prod*** Walter Mirisch ***Scr*** Isobel Lennart ***Ph*** Joseph Biroc ***Ed*** Ralph Winters ***Mus*** John Williams ***Art*** Robert F. Boyle
Act Dick Van Dyke, Barbara Feldon, Edith Evans, John McGiver, Harry Townes, John Fiedler (United Artists)

An okay, but sluggish, comedy about a butler who masterminds robberies. Potential in the screenplay, the very good cast and the handsome production is not realized due to generally tame direction by Delbert Mann.

Isobel Lennart adapted Poyntz Tyler's novel *A Garden of Cucumbers*, in which Dick Van Dyke is the devoted butler to Edith Evans, one of those lovable biddies who, in this case, is not at all as wealthy as she thinks. Van Dyke and crew keep planning heists in order to support her fantasies and philanthropies. Arrival of new secretary Barbara Feldon upsets the smooth-running machinery.

Results of the flat direction is a pic that, in the main, draws smiles, not outright laughs, until the department store panic scene, staged in top fashion.

•

FIVE
1951, 93 mins, US b/w
Dir Arch Oboler ***Prod*** Arch Oboler ***Scr*** Arch Oboler ***Ph*** Louis Clyde Stoumen ***Ed*** John Hoffman ***Mus*** Henry Russell ***Art*** Arch Oboler
Act William Phipps, Susan Douglas, James Anderson, Charles Lampkin, Earl Lee (Oboler/Columbia)

Intriguing in theme, but depressing in its assumption. *Five* ranks high in the class of out-of-the-ordinary pix. It is the story of the last five persons on earth, survivors of an atom blast that turns thriving cities into ghost towns.

Writer-producer-director Arch Oboler has injected vivid imagination into the production, but draws a little too much on his radio technique. Principal criticism lies in its dearth of action. However, interest is sustained in suspenseful situations and convincing dialog.

Oboler has selected his characters with care. William Phipps and Susan Douglas are effective as the love interest, with James Anderson doing a commendable job as the heavy. Charles Lampkin is competent as the sole Negro in a minute white world, while Earl Lee makes the most of his role as a bank teller who because of his horror-stricken mind, believes he's on "vacation" from his job.

•

FIVE BRANDED WOMEN
1960, 100 mins, US b/w
Dir Martin Ritt ***Prod*** Dino De Laurentiis ***Scr*** Ivo Perilli ***Ph*** Giuseppe Rotunno ***Ed*** Jerry Webb ***Mus*** Francesco Lavagnino ***Art*** Mario Chiari
Act Silvana Mangano, Vera Miles, Barbara Bel Geddes, Jeanne Moreau, Carla Gravina, Richard Basehart (Paramount/Laurentiis)

Dino De Laurentiis's *Five Branded Women* is a grim account of the Yugoslavian partisans' fight against the invading Nazi army during World War II. The film occasionally plots an overly familiar conflict, but it catches the fervency of the resistance movement.

The film's strength lies in Ritt's direction. If his story bogs down, he is quick to follow with a storm of action, gripping in tone and adventurous in concept. The horrors of war are hammered out with serious intentions by screenwriter Ivo Perilli, who adapted the film from an unpublished novel by Ugo Pirro.

He describes the partisans as savages, willing to execute their own members if necessary, because it is this savagery that ultimately will destroy the Nazis. Scene by scene, the Yugoslavs are depicted as cruel, inhuman fighters who are, in fact, less sympathetic than their German enemy.

The women are Silvana Mangano, Vera Miles, Barbara Bel Geddes, Jeanne Moreau and Carla Gravina. Not all the roles are long, but they are universally rewarding, and the five actresses successfully fashion contrasting personalities.

Van Heflin stars as a partisan leader in one of his better roles. Richard Basehart is excellent as a captured German officer. Steve Forrest is the German soldier whose lovemaking is responsible for the branding of the women, and he scores with an electrifying scene, shouting of his mutilation by the partisans.

•

5 CARD STUD
1968, 101 mins, US Ⓥ col
Dir Henry Hathaway ***Prod*** Hal B. Wallis ***Scr*** Marguerite Roberts ***Ph*** Daniel L. Fapp ***Ed*** Warren Low ***Mus*** Maurice Jarre ***Art*** Walter Tyler
Act Dean Martin, Robert Mitchum, Inger Stevens, Roddy McDowall, Katherine Justice, Yaphet Kotto (Paramount)

Dean Martin is cast as a frontier gambler and Robert Mitchum plays a frontier parson who woos his congregation with a fast six-shooter. Script [from a novel by Ray Gaulden] pits them against one another in the unraveling of whodunit murders, but dramatic buildup suffers thru a premature disclosure of killer's identity and subsequent lessening of what should have been more potent impact.

Action follows the aftermath of a late-night poker game when a stranger is caught cheating and is lynched by five angry players.

Martin injects certain amount of humor into his role and generally acquits himself strongly. Mitchum's character at times seems contrived but he handles himself well nevertheless. Inger Stevens, playing a gold-rush Delilah who mistresses a stable of lady "barbers," lends distaff interest, and Katherine Justice is a nice addition as a ranch girl in love with Martin.

•

FIVE CORNERS
1987, 92 mins, UK Ⓥ ⊙ col
Dir Tony Bill ***Prod*** Forrest Murray, Tony Bill ***Scr*** John Patrick Shanley ***Ph*** Fred Murphy ***Ed*** Andy Blumenthal ***Mus*** James Newton Howard ***Art*** Adrianne Lobel
Act Jodie Foster, Tim Robbins, Todd Graff, John Turturro, Elizabeth Berridge, Rose Gregorio (HandMade)

Five Corners starts out as an affectionate look back at a Bronx neighborhood circa 1964 and then about halfway through takes a darker turn into urban violence.

In his first produced script, Patrick Shanley clearly has drawn from his experience to create the variety of personalities and swirl of influences that make life in the boroughs of New York City so distinctive.

Before would-be freedom fighter in Mississippi Harry (Tim Robbins) goes off to save the world, there is business for him to take care of in the old neighborhood. Local nogoodnik Heinz (John Turturro) is out of jail and looking to renew his old battle with Harry and his old longing for Linda (Jodie Foster).

They are marvelously drawn parts and Robbins as the Irish working-class kid with a social conscience gets into the heart and soul of the character. Turturro is downright scary but also sympathetic as the schoolyard psychotic. Foster is serviceable, but a little out of her element as a tough Catholic kid.

•

FIVE DAYS ONE SUMMER
1982, 108 mins, US Ⓥ col
Dir Fred Zinnemann ***Prod*** Fred Zinnemann ***Scr*** Michael Austin ***Ph*** Giuseppe Rotunno ***Ed*** Stuart Baird ***Mus*** Elmer Bernstein ***Art*** Willy Holt
Act Sean Connery, Betsy Brantley, Lambert Wilson, Jennifer Hilary, Isabel Dean, Anna Massey (Ladd/Warner)

An attempt at an intimate personal drama that just doesn't come off, *Five Days One Summer* is so slow that it seems more like *Five Summers One Day*. A tale of adultery, mountain climbing and death that is as dramatically placid as the Swiss landscape it inhabits, the $15 million production is Fred Zinnemann's first film since *Julia* [1977].

Seeming hale and hearty, Sean Connery plays a Scottish doctor off on an Alpine vacation in 1932 with a twentyish woman he introduces as his wife. He aims to introduce her to his great sport, mountain climbing. Gradually, flashbacks reveal that the girl is not his wife at all, but his niece, that Connery has a wife back home and that young Kate has been not so secretly in love with Connery since she was a child.

Ultimately, it all comes down to whether or not the girl will stay or leave, and if Connery and/or the guide will survive their climb of one of the most difficult mountains in the vicinity.

•

FIVE EASY PIECES
1970, 96 mins, US Ⓥ ⊙ col
Dir Bob Rafelson ***Prod*** Bob Rafelson, Richard Wechsler ***Scr*** Adrien Joyce [= Carolyn Eastman] ***Ph*** Laszlo Kovacs ***Ed*** Christopher Holmes, Gerald Sheppard ***Art*** Toby Rafelson
Act Jack Nicholson, Karen Black, Lois Smith, Susan Anspach, Helena Kallianiotes, Sally Struthers (Columbia/BBS)

Director Bob Rafelson has put together an absorbing, if nerve-wracking, film.

Despite its solid American roots, this pic is reminiscent of nothing so much as the French films of the 1940s and 1950s.

Jack Nicholson is first seen on the job as a Southern California oilrigger sporting a "cracker" accent and consorting with three members of the same breed especially his dumb, sexy girlfriend Rayette (Karen Black).

It's clear from the beginning that he doesn't think he belongs in this environment. But only later, when he quits his job and goes back home to the State of Washington does it become clear that his hard hat and his accent were a masquerade.

The film's nerve-wracking quality is consistent with its content. Nicholson's performance is a remarkably varied and daring exploration of a complex character, equally convincing in its manic and sober aspects.

1970: NOMINATIONS: Best Picture, Actor (Jack Nicholson), Supp. Actress (Karen Black), Story & Screenplay

•

FIVE FINGER EXERCISE
1962, 108 mins, US b/w
Dir Daniel Mann ***Prod*** Frederick Brisson ***Scr*** Frances Goodrich, Albert Hackett ***Ph*** Harry Stradling ***Ed*** William A. Lyon ***Mus*** Jerome Moross ***Art*** Ross Bellah
Act Rosalind Russell, Jack Hawkins, Maximilian Schell, Richard Beymer, Annette Gorman, Lana Wood (Columbia)

Frederick Brisson, who transplanted this 1958 London stage hit to Broadway in 1959, has transplanted it into the more taxing idiom of the screen. It appears that something has been misplaced in the translation, as adapted by Frances Goodrich and Albert Hackett, and directed by Daniel Mann.

For one thing, the trimming to 108 minutes apparently has taken its toll of both characterization and plot. Furthermore, although there are two solid performances by Rosalind Russell and Jack Hawkins, there are three equally weak ones by Maximilian Schell, Richard Beymer and Annette Gorman.

The title refers to the significance of five fingers operating in coordination to create harmonious music, as in a piano study for beginners. The thoroughly uncoordinated "five fingers" in this family melodrama, reset in California from the original England, are an uncultured, intolerant, self-made businessman-father (Hawkins), a culture-obsessed, pseudo-intellectual mother (Russell), a confused, educated, "mama's boy" son (Beymer), an animated, high-spirited daughter (Gorman), and a young German refugee (Schell), who has been employed by the family as tutor, and yearns to become a permanent part of it.

•

5 FINGERS
1952, 107 mins, US Ⓥ b/w
Dir Joseph L. Mankiewicz ***Prod*** Otto Lang ***Scr*** Michael Wilson ***Ph*** Norbert Brodine ***Ed*** James B. Clark ***Mus*** Bernard Herrmann ***Art*** Lyle Wheeler, George W. Davis
Act James Mason, Danielle Darrieux, Michael Rennie, Walter Hampden, Oscar Karlweis, Herbert Berghof (20th Century-Fox)

A good, if somewhat overlong, cloak-and-dagger thriller has been concocted from an actual World War II espionage case. Screenplay is based on the novel *Operation Cicero*, written by L. C. Moyzisch, Nazi agent in the espionage dealings with "Cicero," the fabulous spy.

Mason portrays Ulysses Diello known to the Nazis as Cicero, a valet to the British Ambassador in Turkey. A cold, assured character, he decides to make himself a fortune by selling Allied war plans to the Germans. Cicero's operations are moving forward without a hitch until the British begin to suspect someone within the Embassy and turn Michael Rennie loose on a counter-espionage job.

The script runs to considerable dialog in the first portions. However, pace quickens and becomes sock suspense drama, tight and tingling, when the story gets down to cases. Actual locations in Berlin, Ankara, Turkey, London and Istanbul were used for a documentary background effect.

1952: NOMINATIONS: Best Director, Screenplay

•

FIVE GRAVES TO CAIRO
1943, 96 mins, US Ⓥ b/w
Dir Billy Wilder ***Prod*** Charles Brackett (assoc.) ***Scr*** Charles Brackett, Billy Wilder ***Ph*** John F. Seitz ***Ed*** Doane Harrison ***Mus*** Miklos Rozsa ***Art*** Hans Dreier, Ernst Fegte
Act Franchot Tone, Anne Baxter, Erich von Stroheim, Peter Van Eyck, Akim Tamiroff, Fortunio Bonanova (Paramount)

Idea of making Field Marshal Rommel's campaign into an exciting fable is by Lajos Biro, Hungarian writer, who did so many successful Ernst Lubitsch screen hits. It affords a vivid picture of Rommel, Erich von Stroheim doing a capital job. The characterization is tailor-made for him.

Surprisingly for such a dynamic, moving vehicle, there is a minimum of actual battle stuff. Director Billy Wilder handles the varied story elements, countless suspenseful moments and vivid portrayals in excellent fashion. In some instances the absence of spoken word or muffled sentences have been pointed up through skillful pantomime and action.

Basically *Five Graves* is the story of a British corporal (Franchot Tone) who impersonates a Nazi spy to gain military information from the Germans as they sweep toward Cairo.

Crackling dialog and fine scripting by director Wilder and Charles Brackett enhance the Biro original [play]. Camerawork of John Seitz is outstanding, as is the film editing by Doane Harrison. Use of sound effects, indicating superb recording, especially during the running gun fight, also is topflight.

1943: NOMINATIONS: Best B&W Cinematography, B&W Art Direction, Editing

•

FIVE HEARTBEATS, THE
1991, 122 mins, US Ⓥ ⊙ col
Dir Robert Townsend ***Prod*** Loretha C. Jones ***Scr*** Robert Townsend, Keenen Ivory Wayans ***Ph*** Bill Dill ***Ed*** John Carter ***Mus*** Stanley Clarke ***Art*** Wynn Thomas
Act Robert Townsend, Michael Wright, Leon, Harry J. Lennix, Tico Wells, Diahann Carroll (20th Century-Fox)

Convincing only in its sweet and dazzling musical sequences, this overly sincere effort otherwise misses its mark. Counteracting the negative black stereotyping he lampooned in his directorial debut, *Hollywood Shuffle*, Robert Townsend lays out a parade of positive role models in a clean, upbeat family-oriented entertainment that feels oddly square and unauthentic.

Story begins in 1965 when fictional group the Five Heartbeats begins to emerge among other black pop groups then combining harmonies and slick choreography. Film follows the bouncing ball through the paces of every mediocre music-biz story ever told, from talent contest to record deal to shoestring radio support tour, racism, hit single, media blitz and superstardom.

Script renders characters in the big ensemble cast as little more than types, with a constantly shifting focus and no one to really follow, and Townsend's vision and direction are wildly schizophrenic, veering from tragic depths to manipulative, heart-tugging poignance.

Townsend seems most at home with the music, and there are scenes onstage in which the film really hits its stride.

•

5,000,000 YEARS TO EARTH
SEE: QUATERMASS AND THE PIT

•

FIVE STAR FINAL
1931, 85 mins, US b/w
Dir Mervyn LeRoy ***Scr*** Byron Morgan, Robert Lord ***Ph*** Sol Polito ***Ed*** Frank Ware ***Mus*** Leo Forbstein (dir.) ***Art*** Jack Okey
Act Edward G. Robinson, Marian Marsh, H. B. Warner, Anthony Bushell, George E. Stone, Boris Karloff (First National)

Playwright Louis Weitzenkorn's strong argument against the scandal type of tabloid newspaper makes a strong talker.

Edward G. Robinson means a lot to this entertainment. He represents the margin between Weitzenkorn's story on the stage and on the screen. The picture version had a head start with its unrestricted area foundation, but it needed someone like Robinson as the managing editor.

H. B. Warner and Frances Starr have a suicide scene that could have been botched very easily. But they play it. The experience in back of both stands up and gives its right age in this picture.

A bit of symbolism inserted in the picture is, for once, a help. The editor is given the habit of washing his hands often at the basin in his office. His first washing occurs during his introduction in a speak. Thereafter, as the job gets dirtier, he repeats the soap stunt more often. When Robinson finally washes his hands of the job, he does it with soap and water.

After the yellow tab, for circulation purposes, has caused two suicides by reviving a 20-year-old murder case, the picture starts to move speedily. The daughter of the unfortunate parents goes to the newspaper with a gun in her bag to ask "Why did you kill my mother?"

Marian Marsh is as strong as the rest in the payoff scene. She stands with Georgie Stone, Warner, Starr and Robinson as punch members of the cast.

1931/32: NOMINATION: Best Picture

•

5,000 FINGERS OF DR. T., THE
1953, 89 mins, US Ⓥ ⊙ col
Dir Roy Rowland ***Prod*** Stanley Kramer ***Scr*** Dr Seuss. [= Ted Geisel], Allan Scott ***Ph*** Franz Planer ***Ed*** Al Clark ***Mus*** Frederick Hollander ***Art*** Rudolph Sternad
Act Peter Lind Hayes, Mary Healy, Hans Conried, Tommy Rettig (Columbia)

The mad humor of Dr. Seuss (Ted Geisel) has been captured on film in this odd flight into chimerical fiction. Story and conception were shaped by Dr. Seuss for the Stanley Kramer unit at Columbia, and he also contributed to the screenplay and did lyrics for the songs composed by Frederick Hollander. Results are sometimes fascinating, more often fantastic.

Of all the wild, weird happenings, the film's standout is the fantastically imaginative dungeon ballet—a mad creation.

Tommy Rettig is the kid who would rather be out playing with his baseball and dog than learning the scales under the tutelage of Hans Conried, the Dr. Terwilliker who becomes the villain of the plot. Opening finds the youngster dreaming he is being pursued by strange creatures with butterfly nets in a land full of odd cylinders and mounds, eerie hues and fog.

This new land is a terrifying one, filled with a strong castle in which Dr. T conducts a school of piano for the 500 boys he holds prisoner. In the dungeon, deep below the fortress, is a group of miserable creatures, grown green and moldy with age, who were imprisoned because they dared play instruments other than the piano.

Roy Rowland, an expert in the direction of kids, shows his skill in handling Rettig and does fairly well by most of the fantasy, although the material is such that it's hard to keep the interest from lagging at times.

1953: NOMINATION: Best Scoring of a Musical Picture

•

FIXED BAYONETS!
1951, 92 mins, US Ⓥ b/w
Dir Samuel Fuller ***Prod*** Jules Buck ***Scr*** Samuel Fuller ***Ph*** Lucien Ballard ***Ed*** Nick De Maggio ***Mus*** Roy Webb ***Art*** Lyle Wheeler, George Patrick
Act Richard Basehart, Gene Evans, Michael O'Shea, Richard Hylton, Craig Hill, Skip Homeier (20th Century-Fox)

Story [suggested by a novel by John Brophy] revolves around a platoon left behind temporarily to fight a rear-guard action for a retreating regiment in Korea.

The detail is supposed to be a hand-picked group of veterans. Yet among them is a corporal (Richard Basehart) who cannot bring himself to shoot an enemy soldier. How he shakes off this fixation and ultimately assumes command of the decimated platoon is an underlying theme that pervades the whole yarn.

Writer-director Samuel Fuller's platoon is a typical band of GIs. There's the sergeant (Gene Evans), a bearded vet of the last war who takes to his chores with a skill born of long experience. Sergeant Michael O'Shea is another hard-bitten "20-year man." Privates include men of Italian, Polish and American Indian extraction, among others.

There's a wealth of suspense in the screenplay, for until the closing minutes filmgoers are unaware whether the platoon will succeed in its mission and rejoin the regiment.

•

FIXER, THE
1968, 130 mins, US col
Dir John Frankenheimer ***Prod*** Edward Lewis ***Scr*** Dalton Trumbo ***Ph*** Marcel Grignon ***Ed*** Henry Berman ***Mus*** Maurice Jarre ***Art*** Bela Zeichan
Act Alan Bates, Dirk Bogarde, Georgia Brown, Hugh Griffith, Elizabeth Hartman, Ian Holm (M-G-M)

Much of the unfoldment [of this adaptation of Bernard Malamud's novel] is in the filthy prison cell of its chief protagonist, a Jew accused of the murder of a young boy but never formally charged.

Czarist Russia at the turn of the century is the period and the locality is Kiev, where a handyman is caught up in the wave of anti-Semitism. In his long suffering that follows his refusal to confess to a crime he did not commit, his case becomes known to the world.

Basic character is enacted by Alan Bates in an indefinite delineation frequently baffling to the spectator. Victim of the Russian government's persecution of all Jews and its dedication to his conviction, he is subjected to every form of mental and physical punishment to make him confess.

But reaction to violence is not alone sufficient for a fine sustained performance and overall Bates suffers from the writing.

Dirk Bogarde is fairly persuasive as a government lawyer who tries to help Bates, but his character isn't well developed.

Scoring more satisfactorily, histrionically, is Elizabeth Hartman, as a young woman who tries to seduce Bates.

1968: NOMINATION: Best Actor (Alan Bates)

•

FLAME AND THE ARROW, THE
1950, 89 mins, US Ⓥ ⊙ col
Dir Jacques Tourneur ***Prod*** Frank Ross, Harold Hecht ***Scr*** Waldo Salt ***Ph*** Ernest Haller ***Ed*** Alan Crosland ***Mus*** Max Steiner ***Art*** Edward Carrere
Act Burt Lancaster, Virginia Mayo, Robert Douglas, Nick Cravat, Aline MacMahon, Frank Allenby (Warner/Norma-FR)

The Flame and the Arrow is a romantic costume drama geared to attract action audiences. Setting is medieval Italy with a Robin Hood plot of how injustice is put down under the daring leadership of a heroic mountaineer.

Burt Lancaster does the latter, portraying the Arrow of the title with just the right amount of dash.

Virginia Mayo is the niece of the hated ruler. She figures romantically with Lancaster in the byplay and also gives an assist to the rebellion of the mountain people against Hessian cruelty.

Jacques Tourneur does not overlook the development of any number of interesting characters. Best of these is Cravat, partner of Lancaster during latter's circus-vaude tumbling days before entering films.

1950: NOMINATIONS: Best Color Cinematography, Scoring of a Dramatic Picture

•

FLAME IN THE STREETS
1961, 93 mins, UK col
Dir Roy Ward Baker ***Prod*** Roy Ward Baker ***Scr*** Ted Willis ***Ph*** Christopher Challis ***Ed*** Roger Cherrill ***Mus*** Philip Green ***Art*** Alex Vetchinsky
Act John Mills, Sylvia Syms, Brenda de Banzie, Earl Cameron, Johnny Sekka, Ann Lynn (Rank)

Story, which hasn't much dramatic bounce, concerns the dilemma of a staunch trade unionist who averts a threatened factory strike over a Negro foreman, swaying the staff by urging that the color of a man's skin is unimportant, only to find that his daughter has fallen in love with another colored man. How to reconcile his very different feelings over the two incidents is his problem.

John Mills makes a convincing figure as the father who has neglected his family because of his dedication to union work.

Brenda de Banzie, his wife, bitter and intolerant about colored people, has two telling scenes, one with her husband and one with her daughter. Sylvia Syms, the schoolmistress daughter who outrages her parents by her determination to marry a young Negro schoolteacher, contributes a neat performance in a role that is not developed fully.

Ann Lynn has a couple of neat cameos as a white girl married to the colored foreman, played with dignity and assurance by Earl Cameron. The Negro hero is Johnny Sekka, and he, too, has enough charm, dignity and good breeding to make it appear quite logical that Syms should fall in love with him.

The fact that *Flame in the Streets* is derived from a play *Hot Summer Night* is always obvious. However, by staging the film on Guy Fawkes's Night, the director is able to get his cameras out into well-filled streets for atmosphere. The street riot between the two factions is curiously anticlimactic, mainly because the film's appeal is largely the quietness of its direction and playing.

•

FLAME OF BARBARY COAST
1945, 91 mins, US Ⓥ b/w
Dir Joseph Kane ***Prod*** Joseph Kane ***Scr*** Borden Chase ***Ph*** Robert de Grasse ***Ed*** Richard L. Van Enger ***Mus*** Morton Scott ***Art*** Gano Chittenden
Act John Wayne, Ann Dvorak, Joseph Schildkraut, William Frawley, Virginia Grey, Russell Hicks (Republic)

A Montana cattleman comes to scoff at the pre-earthquake Barbary Coast of San Francisco and stays to like it; a "gentleman" gambler runs the most successful joint in the district until the guy from the tall grass decides to take over; and the gambler's singer-sweetheart is also the toast of the town's haut monde.

Through dialog, songs and music that's distinguished chiefly for the fact that it sounds like 1945 instead of 1906, the story winds a tortuous path until the earthquake breaks things up. But there is never any suspense in the piece, there is no juxtaposition of characters, no inner logic. One is conscious constantly of the dragging proceedings. John Wayne handles himself very well in the role of the man from the plains. Ann Dvorak not only sings well but looks and acts the part of the nitery queen, Joseph Schildkraut as the gambler is socko.

1945: NOMINATIONS: Best Scoring of a Dramatic Picture, Sound

•

FLAME OF NEW ORLEANS, THE
1941, 78 mins, US b/w
Dir Rene Clair ***Prod*** Joe Pasternak ***Scr*** Norman Krasna ***Ph*** Rudolph Mate ***Ed*** Frank Gross ***Mus*** Charles Previn
Act Marlene Dietrich, Bruce Cabot, Roland Young, Anne Revere, Mischa Auer (Universal)

This Marlene Dietrich starrer is a very thin and familiar tale of the romantic interludes of a lady of dubious reputation a century ago. Picture misses its apparent mark of being a smartly sophisticated farce by a considerable margin, winding up as a lightweight entry.

Dietrich arrives in New Orleans after a European tour, determined to grab off a wealthy admirer. Roland Young is an easy victim and proposes marriage, but Bruce Cabot, tough and roving ship captain, holds a strange fascination for her. Plot's a case of how long before she tosses over Young for Cabot.

Picture is Rene Clair's first in America. He works valiantly with the flimsy material, injecting many incidental by-plays that are amusing, but to meagre avail.

Dietrich provides a familiar performance as the questionable lady, shapely in appearance, but sparkles in a role calling for zest. Her attempts at coyness miss badly. Inclusion of a few songs fail to provide a lift to the proceedings.

•

FLAME OVER INDIA
SEE: NORTH WEST FRONTIER

•

FLAMINGO KID, THE
1984, 100 mins, US Ⓥ ⊙ col
Dir Garry Marshall ***Prod*** Michael Phillips ***Scr*** Neal Marshall, Garry Marshall ***Ph*** James A. Contner ***Ed*** Priscilla Nedd ***Art*** Lawrence Miller
Act Matt Dillon, Richard Crenna, Hector Elizondo, Jessica Walter, Molly McCarthy, Janet Jones (ABC/Mercury)

The Flamingo Kid, set in 1963, sports the amusing trappings connected with 18-year-old Matt Dillon working for a summer at the El Flamingo Beach Club in Far Rockaway, NY. At its heart, though, story has to do with the critical choices facing a youth of that age and how they will help determine the rest of one's life.

Taken out of his rundown Brooklyn neighborhood one day to play cards with friends at the club, Dillon ends up getting a job there parking cars. He is soon promoted to cabana boy, and also attracts the attention of blonde UCLA student Janet Jones, with whom he has a skin-deep summer fling, and her uncle Richard Crenna, a sharp-talking sports car dealer.

Dillon does a good job in his fullest, least narcissistic characterization to date.

•

FLAMINGO ROAD
1949, 94 mins, US Ⓥ b/w
Dir Michael Curtiz ***Prod*** Jerry Wald ***Scr*** Robert Wilder, Edmund H. North ***Ph*** Ted McCord ***Ed*** Folmar Blangsted ***Mus*** Max Steiner ***Art*** Leo Kuter
Act Joan Crawford, Zachary Scott, Sydney Greenstreet, David Brian, Gertrude Michael, Gladys George (Warner)

Flamingo Road is a class vehicle for Joan Crawford, loaded with heartbreak, romance and stinging violence. Film is hooped together by a smart, well-meshed screenplay and reinforced by a strong cast and sound direction.

Yarn [from a play by Robert and Sally Wilder] swivels around a deadly antagonism between Crawford and Sydney Greenstreet, a sinister small-town sheriff with a ruthless appetite for power. Film rapidly gathers momentum after Crawford, stranded by a bankrupt sideshow company, falls in love with Zachary Scott, the sheriff's protege.

Crawford imparts convincing personality shadings ranging from strength to tenderness with a continuous and convincing style. As the heavy, Greenstreet delivers a suavely powerful performance that surmounts his overdrawn role.

•

FLAMING STAR
1960, 92 mins, US Ⓥ ▭ col
Dir Don Siegel ***Prod*** David Weisbart ***Scr*** Clair Huffaker, Nunnally Johnson ***Ph*** Charles G. Clarke ***Ed*** Hugh S. Fowler ***Mus*** Cyril J. Mockridge ***Art*** Duncan Cramer, Walter M. Simonds
Act Elvis Presley, Steve Forrest, Barbara Eden, Dolores Del Rio, John McIntire, Richard Jaeckel (20th Century-Fox)

Flaming Star has Indians-on-the-warpath for the youngsters, Elvis Presley for the teenagers and socio-psychological ramifications for adults who prefer a mild dose of sage in their sagebrushers. The plot—half-breed hopelessly involved in war between white man and Red man [from a novel by Clair Huffaker]—is disturbingly familiar and not altogether convincing, but the film is attractively mounted and consistently diverting.

Presley plays the half-breed, pivotal character in the conflict between a group of Texas settlers and the angry Kiowa tribe. Part of a heterogeneous family (full-blooded Indian mother, white father, half brother) resented and tormented by whites, taunted and haunted by Indian ties, Presley is buffeted to and fro between enemy camps by the prevailing winds of prejudice and pride.

The role is a demanding one for Presley. But he lacks the facial and thespic sensitivity and projection so desperately required here. The standouts are the veterans, Dolores Del Rio and John McIntire. Del Rio brings dignity and delicacy to the role of Presley's full-blooded Indian mother. McIntire adds nobility and compassion as the father of the doomed household. Steve Forrest is competent as the brother, Barbara Eden decorative as his girl.

Director Don Siegel has packed plenty of excitement into the picture, notably some realistically staged fistfight, battle and chase passages. But there are a few equally unrealistic-looking scenes.

•

FLASHDANCE
1983, 96 mins, US Ⓥ ⊙ col
Dir Adrian Lyne ***Prod*** Don Simpson, Jerry Bruckheimer ***Scr*** Tom Hedley, Joe Eszterhas ***Ph*** Don Peterman ***Ed*** Bud Smith, Walt Mulconery ***Mus*** Giorgio Moroder ***Art*** Charles Rosen
Act Jennifer Beals, Michael Nouri, Lilia Skala, Sunny Johnson, Kyle T. Heffner, Belinda Bauer (PolyGram/Paramount)

Watching *Flashdance* is pretty much like looking at MTV for 96 minutes. Virtually plotless, exceedingly thin on characterization and sociologically laughable, pic at least lives up to its title by offering an anthology of extraordinarily flashy dance numbers.

Appealing newcomer Jennifer Beals plays an 18-year-old come to Pittsburgh to toil in a steel mill by day and work off steam at night by performing wild, improvised dances in a local bar (much of Beals's dancing was reportedly done by an uncredited double [Marine Jahan]).

What story there is [by Tom Hedley] sees Beals trying to get up the courage to audition for formal dance study and dealing with the advances of her daytime boss Michael Nouri who, to her fury, secretly intervenes to get her admitted to the school.

Female performances all come off as if the sole directorial command was, "All right, girls, let's get physical!" Pic features better bodies and more crotch shots than *Personal Best*, and every effect is of the most vulgar and obvious variety.

1983: Best Original Song ("Flashdance . . . What a Feeling")

NOMINATIONS: Best Cinematography, Editing, Original Song ("Maniac")

•

FLASH GORDON
1980, 110 mins, UK Ⓥ ⊙ ▭ col
Dir Mike Hodges ***Prod*** Dino De Laurentiis ***Scr*** Lorenzo Semple Jr ***Ph*** Gil Taylor ***Ed*** Malcolm Cooke ***Mus*** Howard Blake, Queen ***Art*** Danilo Donati
Act Sam J. Jones, Melody Anderson, Topol, Max von Sydow, Ornella Muti, Brian Blessed (Universal/De Laurentiis)

The expensive new version of *Flash Gordon* is a lot more gaudy, and just as dumb, as the original series starring Buster Crabbe. Sam J. Jones in the title role has even less thespic range than Crabbe, but the badness of his performance is part of the fun of the film.

This film cost around $20 million, a hefty outlay of money for such frivolity. The big differences between this film and the old serial are the lavish sets and costumes, and the colorful lensing by Gil Taylor, who also did *Star Wars*.

Jones, a former *Playgirl* nude centerfold whose only previous film role was the husband of Bo Derek in *10*, lumbers vacantly through the part of Flash Gordon with the naivete, fearlessness, and dopey line readings familiar from the 1930s serials.

Film benefits greatly from the adroit performance of Max von Sydow as Emperor Ming.

•

FLATLINERS
1990, 111 mins, US Ⓥ ⊙ ▭ col
Dir Joel Schumacher ***Prod*** Michael Douglas, Rick Bieber ***Scr*** Peter Filardi ***Ph*** Jan De Bont ***Ed*** Robert Brown ***Mus*** James Newton Howard ***Art*** Eugenio Zanetti
Act Kiefer Sutherland, Julia Roberts, Kevin Bacon, William Baldwin, Oliver Platt, Kimberly Scott (Stonebridge/Columbia)

Death, the ultimate rush, is the target experience for a group of daring young medical students who break on through to the other side—and live to tell about it. A cautionary tale that ends along fairly traditional horror-sci-fi lines, *Flatliners* is a strikingly original, often brilliantly visualized film from director Joel Schumacher and writer Peter Filardi.

Premise is that daring doctor-in-training Nelson (Kiefer Sutherland) decides to make his mark on medicine by stopping his heart and brain ("flatlining," as the lack of vital signs produces a flat line on the EKG and EEG monitors) and then having himself brought back by the gifted medical students he recruits to help him. Initially angry and reluctant, the others end up totally seduced, vying with each other for the chance to go next by offering to flatline the longest.

Problem is, as Nelson discovers, that the curtain of death, once penetrated, doesn't close behind you, and Nelson finds himself haunted by an aggressive demon from another world. Before he can bring himself to admit that his idea wasn't such a good one, all the others but one have gone over.

Sutherland, as always, registers real presence and pulls off a wildly demanding role, but the remarkably gifted Julia Roberts is the film's true grace note as the low-key, private and intensely focused Rachel.

1990: NOMINATION: Best Sound Effects Editing

•

FLAWLESS
1999, 112 mins, US Ⓥ ⊙ col
Dir Joel Schumacher ***Prod*** Joel Schumnacher, Jane Rosenthal ***Scr*** Joel Schumacher ***Ph*** Declan Quinn ***Ed*** Mark Stevens ***Mus*** Bruce Roberts ***Art*** Jan Roelfs
Act Robert De Niro, Philip Seymour Hoffman, Barry Miller, Chris Bauer, Skipp Sudduth, Wilson Jermaine Heredia (Tribeca/M-G-M)

After several disappointing big-budget, star-driven special effects movies (*Batman and Robin*) and a truly trashy thriller (*8MM*), Joel Schumacher takes a step in the right direction with *Flawless*, a small-scale, intimate serio-comedy centering on the unlikely camaraderie that evolves between a macho security guard and a flamboyant transvestite, played by Robert De Niro and Philip Seymour Hoffman.

There is no doubt that *Flawless* is a more personal and meaningful work in Schumacher's output, one that takes him back to his New York roots of the '60s and '70s. Unfortunately, this is also one of the film's main problems—in mores and sexual politics the movie is very much grounded in the zeitgeist of the post-Stonewall era.

Mostly set within a racially diverse apartment complex on the Lower East Side, tale introduces Walt Koontz (De Niro) as a retired security guard, a proud, ultraconservative man who's set in his ways. Walt frequents a tango dance hall where he dances with his beautiful girl, Karen (Wanda De Jesus), who exploits him, and is courted by a younger, more sincere woman, Tia (Daphne Rubin-Vega).

Rusty (Hoffman), Walt's upstairs neighbor, is exactly his opposite: a street-smart drag queen who functions as a mother hen to a whole entourage of cross-dressers. After Walt is injured trying to help his neighbor, he reluctantly agrees to a rehabilitative program that includes singing lessons from Rusty.

De Niro is good at conveying the gradual physical and psychological transformation of a middle-aged man. Hoffman has many marvelous moments but ultimately his performance lacks depth.

•

FLEET'S IN, THE
1942, 93 mins, US b/w
Dir Victor Schertzinger ***Prod*** Paul Jones ***Scr*** Walter DeLeon, Sid Silvers, Ralph Spence ***Ph*** William Mellor ***Ed*** Paul Weatherwax ***Mus*** Victor Schertzinger
Act Dorothy Lamour, William Holden, Eddie Bracken, Betty Hutton, Cass Daley, Leif Erickson (Paramount)

Paul Jones, the producer of this musical version of *Sailor Beware*, has surrounded Dorothy Lamour with a miscellaneous collection of talent, including two first-starters who click strongly; but while he has turned out something that generally pleases, it falls short of being a smash.

Holden handles himself well opposite Lamour as the sailor who falls for her while the battleship crew is on furlough in Frisco.

The quarrel is less with the story itself than the musical side. There are no production numbers but an overdose of vocalists, backed by the Dorsey band.

•

FLESH
1932, 95 mins, US b/w
Dir John Ford ***Scr*** Leonard Praskins, Edgar Allan Woolf, Moss Hart ***Ph*** Arthur Edeson ***Ed*** William S. Gray
Act Wallace Beery, Karen Morley, Ricardo Cortez, Jean Hersholt, John Miljan (M-G-M)

Wallace Beery plays a big-hearted, big-muscled, small-brained guy with lovable qualities, a sort of cross between Emil Jannings of *Variety* (1926) and the same Beery of *The Champ* (1931). Instead of being an acrobat or a punch-drunk fighter, he's a wrestler. He goes chump for a faithless woman, according to pattern, and the finish is sad, only this time there's a suggestion of ultimate happiness to deaden the pain.

As an inside on the honorable profesh of grappling, the original yarn by Edmund Goulding takes huge Polikai (Beery) out of a waiter's suit in a German beer garden to the wrassling championship of that country, and then to America where he has to play ball with the gamblers. He wins the world's title when he's supposed to lose.

Karen Morley is with him all through the climb as the double-crossing lady who loves her man on the side. Latter, and doing a perfect job of an 100% unsympathetic character, is Ricardo Cortez.

•

FLESH
1968, 105 mins, US col
Dir Paul Morrissey ***Prod*** Andy Warhol ***Scr*** Paul Morrissey ***Ph*** Paul Morrissey

Act Joe Dallesandro, Geraldine Smith, John Christian, Maurice Bardell, Candy Darling, Patti D'Arbanville (Warhol)

Blithely, as if it were as natural a romantic yarn as would appear in a popular magazine, the synopsis of Andy Warhol's opus reads: "The story of a young married couple and the efforts of the husband, Joe, to sell himself to earn money for his wife's girl friend's abortion."

Paul Morrissey wrote, directed and lensed this hapless erotica freakout as Warhol was recuperating from gunshot wounds inflicted by Gloria Solanis. Morrisey's efforts, true to the master, are pedestrian in both form and content, but much worse is the technical amateurishness with camera and sound.

Half sentences are abundant. But it probably doesn't matter to any great extent since the wild sound recorded during the action bounces off the walls, rendering most interchanges between characters largely incoherent.

The principal character Joe concerns himself mainly with floating from one homosexual encounter to the next in order to make the required coin, sporting an abundance of frontal nudity. The anticlimax comes when Joe finds his wife in bed with her girlfriend.

●

FLESH + BLOOD
1985, 126 mins, US Ⓥ ⦿ ▭ col
Dir Paul Verhoeven *Prod* Gys Versluys *Scr* Gerard Soeteman, Paul Verhoeven *Ph* Jan de Bont *Ed* Ine Schenkkan *Mus* Basil Poledouris *Art* Felix Murcia
Act Rutger Hauer, Jennifer Jason Leigh, Tom Burlinson, Jack Thompson, Susan Tyrrell, Ronald Lacey (Orion/Riverside)

Flesh + Blood is a vivid and muscular, if less than fully startling, account of lust, savagery, revenge, betrayal and assorted other dark doings in the Middle Ages.

Drama opens with a successful siege on a castle by Lord Arnolfini (Fernando Hillbeck), who has recently been ousted from the premises. After promising them loot, Hillbeck goes back on his word and banishes the mercenaries who have helped him in his conquest.

Before long, warrior leader Martin (Rutger Hauer) and his ragtag band gets theirs back by nearly killing Hillbeck in an ambush and capturing lovely young Agnes (Jennifer Jason Leigh), the intended bride of Hillbeck's studious son Steven (Tom Burlinson).

Director Paul Verhoeven has told his tale in visceral, involving fashion and, for the amount of carnage that piles up, explicit gore is kept to a minimum.

Fine use is made of Belmonte Castle (on view in *El Cid*) and other Spanish locales.

●

FLESH AND BONE
1993, 124 mins, US Ⓥ ⦿ col
Dir Steve Kloves *Prod* Mark Rosenberg, Paula Weinstein *Scr* Steve Kloves *Ph* Philippe Rousselot *Ed* Mia Goldman *Mus* Thomas Newman *Art* Jon Hutman
Act Dennis Quaid, Meg Ryan, James Caan, Gwyneth Paltrow, Scott Wilson, Christopher Rydell (Mirage/Spring Creek/Paramount)

Despite arresting images and moments, writer-director Steve Kloves doesn't quite fill the vast Texas landscapes of *Flesh and Bone* with enough dramatic blood and muscle.

Tautly and quietly, Kloves presents an isolated family insidiously invaded by outsiders, first a seemingly bereft little boy, then his evil father, who proceeds to wipe out nearly the entire clan on a botched robbery. Tale jumps ahead by 25 years or so and begins moseying up on Sam Shepard territory of blood ties, betrayals and dues being paid.

Arlis (Dennis Quaid) is a solitary guy who traverses the endless highways tending to vending machines. Before long, Kay (Meg Ryan) stumbles into his life, and it's only a matter of time until they roll in the hay. An hour in, the evil father, Roy (James Caan), pops up.

Pic had the potential for poetic reverberations concerning futures lost and fates tangled across the generations. But this possibility fades as it becomes clear that Kloves is trying to shoehorn a cute romance of temperamental opposites into an essentially somber, violent format.

Compared with Quaid's impressively self-contained, withdrawn man, Ryan's boisterous little Texas tart comes off as just too much. Caan has the scary, unpredictable side down pat, but comes off as somewhat mannered when he's trying to be ingratiating. Gwyneth Paltrow steals every scene she's in as Caan's bad-girl sometime companion.

●

FLESH AND FANTASY
1943, 92 mins, US b/w
Dir Julien Duvivier *Prod* Charles Boyer, Julien Duvivier *Scr* Ernest Pascal, Samuel Hoffenstein, Ellis St. Joseph *Ph* Paul Ivano, Stanley Cortez *Ed* Arthur Hilton *Mus* Alexandre Tansman
Act Edward G. Robinson, Charles Boyer, Barbara Stanwyck, Betty Field, Robert Cummings, Thomas Mitchell (Universal)

This is a decidedly novel and unusual picture, displaying the impress on individuals of dreams, fortune-telling and other supernatural phenomena. Picture idea was contrived by Charles Boyer and Julien Duvivier and sold to Universal, with pair combining as producers, Duvivier also directing, and Boyer handling a major acting assignment. Clubmen Robert Benchley and David Hoffman discuss dreams, predictions and the supernatural to provide necessary interweave of the three episodes on display.

First delves into romance of Betty Field, who's become calloused, bitter and defeated through ugly features. But on Mardi Gras night she is handed a beautiful face mask and romances with Robert Cummings and finally discovers truth in the moral: faith in yourself is the main thing.

Second episode presents Thomas Mitchell as a palmist at a socialite group, and after attorney Edward G. Robinson scoffs at the predictions, latter nevertheless submits to a reading, and becomes intrigued when he's told he will commit murder.

Boyer shares starring honors with Barbara Stanwyck in the final episode, which has the former upset by dream which predicts disaster to himself while performing as a circus high-wire artist.

●

FLESH AND THE DEVIL
1926, 91 mins, US Ⓥ ⊗ b/w
Dir Clarence Brown *Scr* Benjamin F. Glazer, Marian Ainslee *Ph* William Daniels *Ed* Lloyd Nosler *Art* Cedric Gibbons, Frederic Hope
Act John Gilbert, Greta Garbo, Lars Hanson, Barbara Kent, William Orlamond (M-G-M)

This film [based on *The Undying Past* by Hermann Sudermann] is a battle between John Gilbert, starred, and Greta Garbo, featured, for honors. Gilbert has to keep moving to overshadow her, even though she has a most unsympathetic role.

The story is laid in a small German or Austrian town. Two boys have, as kids, sworn eternal friendship through a blood bond. They are both at military school when the picture opens. Back home there is a ball and Lee (Gilbert), the more sophisticated of the two, sees a girl that he admired at the station. He dances with her, but fails to learn her name. Her husband walks in on the picture and the youngster then knows for the first time that she is married. The husband strikes the boy, and it calls for a duel. The husband is killed. The military authorities "advise" foreign service for five years for the youngster. Before going he asks his bloodbound friend to seek out the widow and console her. After three years away, Leo discovers that she has wed the friend. Then a series of incidents occurs that almost brings on a duel between the friends.

A corking story, exceptionally acted and cleverly directed. A lot of glory to be distributed among all concerned.

●

FLESH FOR FRANKENSTEIN
(US: ANDY WARHOL'S FRANKENSTEIN)
1974, 95 mins, France/Italy Ⓥ ⦿ ▭ col
Dir Paul Morrissey *Prod* Andrew Braunsberg *Scr* Paul Morrissey *Ph* Luigi Kueveillier *Ed* Ted Johnson *Mus* Carlo Gizzi
Act Joe Dallesandro, Udo Kier, Monique Van Vooren, Arno Juerging, Srdjan Zelenovic, Dalila Di Lazzaro (CC-Champion & 1/Ponti/Yanne/Rassam

Paul Morrissey of the Andy Warhol stable made this pic back-to-back with *Blood for Dracula*, with an added gimmick of 3-D and more skillfully directed. Morrissey plays some variations on the old Prometheus myth. He adds plenty of gore, with some dollops of sex.

Morrissey otherwise plays this for neat Gothic atmosphere in Frankenstein's castle where his nympho sister (Monique Van Vooren), also mother of his children, carries on with servants as the kids and Frankenstein (Udo Kier) look on.

Joe Dallesandro is a servant who suspects foul doings, especially when he sees the head of his friend on one of Frankenstein's monsters and breaks up things to find he may be a victim of the Baron's two children as he hangs helplessly by his hands.

●

FLESH GORDON
1974, 78 mins, US Ⓥ col
Dir Howard Ziehm, Michael Benveniste *Prod* Howard Ziehm, Bill Osco *Scr* Michael Benveniste *Ph* Howard Ziehm *Mus* Ralph Ferraro *Art* Donald Harris
Act Jason Williams, Suzanne Fields, Joseph Hudgins, John Hoyt, William Hunt (Graffiti)

Puerile is the word for this soft-core spoof of the sci-fi serials of the 1930s which, for their time, had genuine merit as audience hair-raisers. By attempting to combine sexplicity and low-level camp, pic emerges as an expensive-looking mish-mash of obvious double entendres, idiotic characterizations and dull situations. Only compensation is flash of bawdy humor.

Title character (Jason Williams) heads a group of earthlings out to defeat evil forces on the planet Porno, bent on flooding the universe with chaos-inducing sex rays. Porno is manned by sinister Emperor Wang (William Hunt). Flesh, his girl (Suzanne Fields) and sidekick (Joseph Hudgins) rocket to Porno and encounter various of the emperor's evil minions and a mildly entertaining series of monsters.

●

FLETCH
1985, 96 mins, US Ⓥ ⦿ col
Dir Michael Ritchie *Prod* Alan Greisman, Peter Douglas *Scr* Andrew Bergman *Ph* Fred Schuler *Ed* Richard A. Harris *Mus* Harold Faltermeyer *Art* Boris Leven
Act Chevy Chase, Dana Wheeler-Nicholson, Tim Matheson, Joe Don Baker, Richard Libertini, Geena Davis (Universal)

What propels this contempo L.A. yarn about a dissembling newspaper columnist on the trail of a nefarious con man (Tim Matheson) is the obvious and successful byplay between Chevy Chase's sly, glib persona and the satiric brushstrokes of director Michael Ritchie. Their teamwork turns an otherwise hair-pinned, anecdotal plot into a breezy, peppy frolic and a tour de force for Chase.

Most supporting players have little to do, such as M. Emmet Walsh as an inane M.D. The film is sparked by some hilarious moments, among them Chase as an unwitting surgeon in attendance at an autopsy conducted by a cackling pathologist and, in the script's funniest scene, Chase donning the guise of a legionnaire in a hall full of VFW stalwarts.

●

FLETCH LIVES
1989, 95 mins, US Ⓥ ⦿ col
Dir Michael Ritchie *Prod* Alan Greisman, Peter Douglas *Scr* Leon Capetanos *Ph* John McPherson *Ed* Richard A. Harris *Mus* Harold Faltermeyer *Art* Cameron Birnie, Jimmie Bly, W. Steven Graham, Donald B. Woodruff
Act Chevy Chase, Hal Holbrook, Julianne Phillips, Cleavon Little, R. Lee Ermey, Richard Libertini (Universal)

Chevy Chase is perfectly suited to playing a smirking, wisecracking, multiple-identitied reporter in *Fletch Lives*.

Ridiculous and anecdotal plot that transports Chase from his beloved L.A. base to Louisiana's bayou country to take over his dead aunt's crumbling plantation works for the simple reason that Chase's sly, glib persona is in sync with Michael Ritchie's equally breezy direction.

From Gregory McDonald's popular novel, script works out an excessive and cliché-ridden portrait of a Southern, insular town. Dimwits abound as if inbreeding has been going on since the days of slavery.

The night Chase arrives, he beds the sexy executor/lawyer of his aunt's estate (Patricia Kalember as a convincing belle), who is then murdered while they're slumbering.

Chase tracks the murderer through some inane sequences as only he could do. Film's saving grace is its scathing satirical sketches of fictional televangelist preacher Jimmy Lee Farnsworth.

●

FLIGHT OF THE DOVES
1971, 101 mins, US col
Dir Ralph Nelson *Prod* Ralph Nelson *Scr* Frank Gabrielson, Ralph Nelson *Ph* Harry Waxman *Ed* John Jympson *Mus* Roy Budd *Art* Frank Arrigo
Act Ron Moody, Jack Wild, Dorothy McGuire, Stanley Holloway, William Rushton, Dana (Columbia)

Ralph Nelson's film version of Walter Macken's story, *Flight of the Doves*, is a heartwarming, often funny, often suspenseful story of two runaway children, fleeing from a cruel stepfather (British) to their grandmother (Irish) who lives "somewhere in Ireland."

The screenplay takes some liberties in casting. Dorothy McGuire is a delight as a bright-eyed, most articulate grandmother, standing up to authority, both Irish and British, on behalf of the young runaways, but is much too young looking to make anyone believe that she could have a grandson as large as Jack Wild.

It allows Ron Moody to dominate the film from his first appearance. With almost as many character changes as Alec

Guinness had in *Kind Hearts and Coronets*, Moody is so good at his disguises that the audience starts imagining that each new character who appears might be the irresponsible Moody. Ostensibly the villain, he's so captivating that no one really believes that he won't survive (even after seeing him plunged into a wild Irish sea).

As the uncle of Wild and Helen Raye, he's described as the eventual heir to money left by the children's grandfather should they die before he does.

•

FLIGHT OF THE INTRUDER
1991, 113 mins, US Ⓥ ⊙ ▭ col
Dir John Milius ***Prod*** Mace Neufeld ***Scr*** Robert Dillon, David Shaber, [John Milius] ***Ph*** Fred J. Koenekamp ***Ed*** C. Timothy O'Meara, Steve Mirkovich, Peck Prior ***Mus*** Basil Poledouris ***Art*** Jack T. Collis
Act Danny Glover, Willem Dafoe, Brad Johnson, Rosanna Arquette, Tom Sizemore, J. Kenneth Campbell (Paramount)

Flight of the Intruder is the most boring Vietnam War pic since *The Green Berets* (1968), but lacks the benefit of the latter's political outrageousness to spark a little interest and humor.

Set mostly aboard a giant aircraft carrier, yarn [from the novel by Stephen Coonts] unspools in 1972. Prevented from bombing Hanoi and other strategic spots while the Paris peace talks are in progress, fighter pilots are reduced to assaulting meaningless targets and facing the likelihood that the massive U.S. war effort will have been in vain.

Nonetheless, officers have to keep discipline and morale up, a task that falls to Danny Glover, the tough-talking but humorous squadron leader. Title refers to the A-6, a small, low-altitude bomber designed for quick in-and-out strikes. Acc of the outfit is Brad Johnson, who loses a bombardier in an elaborate credit sequence and is thereafter interested in "payback."

Opportunity presents itself with the arrival of a vet bombardier (Willem Dafoe) not averse to hijinks. Johnson and Dafoe cook up a scheme to devastate People's Resistance Park in downtown Hanoi, a.k.a. SAM City, where captured U.S. artillery is on display.

Glover brings energy and glee to his reams of dialog. Dafoe puts a few cynical spins on his delivery, but his character pales next to his role in *Platoon*. Johnson, again playing a flier, is even more lackluster than in *Always*. Hawaiian locations, when viewed from the air, are too lushly recognizable to be an entirely credible Vietnam.

•

FLIGHT OF THE NAVIGATOR
1986, 90 mins, US Ⓥ ⊙ col
Dir Randal Kleiser ***Prod*** Robby Wald, Dimitri Villard ***Scr*** Michael Burton, Matt MacManus ***Ph*** James Glennon ***Ed*** Jeff Gourson ***Mus*** Alan Silvestri ***Art*** William J. Creber
Act Joey Cramer, Veronica Cartwright, Cliff De Young, Sarah Jessica Parker, Matt Adler, Howard Hesseman (Walt Disney/PSO)

Instead of creating an eye-opening panorama, *Flight of the Navigator* looks through the small end of the telescope. Life on Earth is magnified but without an expansive vision.

Young David Freeman (Joey Cramer) vanishes from his Fort Lauderdale home only to return to the identical spot unchanged eight years later. When a sleek silver flying saucer turns up on the scene, NASA gets into the act and all roads lead to David. It seems his head has been filled with star charts and he's been serving as navigator for an exploratory ship from a distant planet.

Film finally gets on track when 12-year-old David is reunited with the spacecraft for a trip which ultimately will deposit him right back where he started. Along the way the journey is imaginative and fun but earthbound, with a robotic flight commander (voiced by an uncredited Paul Reubens, a.k.a. Pee-wee Herman) who becomes fascinated with American pop culture.

As is often the problem with extraterrestrial adventures, all life forms are anthropomorphized with a selection of cute and cuddly creatures. There are some nifty special effects in the spacecraft sequences. Performances are all workmanlike, with Cramer doing a believable job.

•

FLIGHT OF THE PHOENIX, THE
1965, 149 mins, US Ⓥ ⊙ col
Dir Robert Aldrich ***Prod*** Robert Aldrich ***Scr*** Lukas Heller ***Ph*** Joseph Biroc ***Ed*** Michael Luciano ***Mus*** Frank DeVol ***Art*** William Glasgow
Act James Stewart, Richard Attenborough, Peter Finch, Hardy Kruger, Ernest Borgnine, Ian Bannen (Associates & Aldrich/20th Century-Fox)

The Flight of the Phoenix is a grim, tenseful, realistic tale of a small group of men forced down on the North African desert and their desperate efforts to build a single-engine plane out of the wreckage of the twin job in which they crashed during a sandstorm. Robert Aldrich's filmic translation of the Elleston Trevor book is an often-fascinating and superlative piece of filmmaking highlighted by standout performances and touches that show producer-director at his best.

James Stewart, as the pilot of a desert oil company cargo-passenger plane who flies by the seat of his pants, is strongly cast in role and is strongly backed by entire cast. Each, seemingly hand-picked for the individual parts, is an everyday person who might either be employees of an oil company or business visitors.

A young aircraft designer, who had been visiting his brother at the oil camp, comes up with the extraordinary idea that a makeshift plane might be fashioned to fly the survivors to safety. So work starts, and it is this endeavor in its various phases that makes the story.

1965: NOMINATIONS: Best Supp. Actor (Ian Bannen), Editing

•

FLIM-FLAM MAN, THE
(UK: ONE BORN EVERY MINUTE)
1967, 104 mins, US Ⓥ ▭ col
Dir Irvin Kershner ***Prod*** Lawrence Turman ***Scr*** William Rose ***Ph*** Charles Lang ***Ed*** Robert Swink ***Mus*** Jerry Goldsmith ***Art*** Jack Martin Smith
Act George C. Scott, Sue Lyon, Michael Sarrazin, Harry Morgan, Jack Albertson, Alice Ghostley (20th Century-Fox)

An outstanding comedy starring George C. Scott as a Dixie drifter. Socko comedy-dramatic direction by Irvin Kershner makes the most of a very competent cast and a superior script. Michael Sarrazin, as Scott's fellow traveler, makes an impressive feature film bow.

Guy Owen's novel, *The Ballad of the Flim-Flam Man*, has been adapted into a finely balanced screenplay which exploits inherent comedy situations while understating, appropriately, the loneliness of a rootless man. A series of flim-flams are pulled off only on people who seemingly deserve to be stiffed, thus minimizing any complaint that lawlessness is being made attractive.

•

FLINTSTONES, THE
1994, 92 mins, US Ⓥ ⊙ col
Dir Brian Levant ***Prod*** Bruce Cohen ***Scr*** Tom S. Parker, Jim Jennewein, Steven E. de Souza ***Ph*** Dean Cundey ***Ed*** Kent Beyda ***Mus*** David Newman ***Art*** William Sandell
Act John Goodman, Elizabeth Perkins, Rick Moranis, Rosie O'Donnell, Kyle MacLachlan, Elizabeth Taylor (Hanna-Barbera/Amblin/Universal)

With all manner of friendly beasts, a superenergetic John Goodman and colorful supporting cast inhabiting a Bedrock that resembles a Stone Age version of Steven Spielberg suburbia, this live-action translation of the perennial cartoon favorite is a fine popcorn picture for small fry, and perfectly inoffensive for adults.

Film's use of at least a dozen writers, of whom only three receive final screen credit, was widely reported, and choice of a storyline involving embezzlement is slightly puzzling given the 7-year-old target audience. Fred Flintstone (Goodman) is the happy, rock-solid working man, thick of bicep and skull, who shockingly wins a promotion out of the rock pile and into the executive suites of Slate & Co. when his best friend, Barney Rubble (Rick Moranis), substitutes his own exam answers for Fred's. The boss (Kyle MacLachlan) and his foxy secretary (Halle Berry) easily manipulate the lazy simpleton, setting him up for a big fall as they plot to make off with ill-gotten gains.

Meanwhile, at home, Fred manages to get in hot water with his sprightly wife, Wilma (Elizabeth Perkins), whose mother (Elizabeth Taylor) keeps harping about how Wilma could have done a lot better.

Pic centers squarely on Goodman, and he brings tremendous energy and enthusiasm to the role of Fred. Other performers take a relative back seat but are also well-cast. Taylor looks beauteous in her first screen appearance in some time and amusingly ends up in the mouth of a dinosaur.

One significant point of interest is that the ostensible attitude of this money machine of a movie, which is so loaded with highly calculated marketing and product plugs, is pro-working stiff and anti-big business.

•

FLIPPER
1963, 87 mins, US Ⓥ col
Dir James B. Clark ***Prod*** Ivan Tors ***Scr*** Arthur Weiss ***Ph*** Lamar Bowen, Joseph Brun ***Ed*** Warren Adams ***Mus*** Henry Vars
Act Chuck Connors, Luke Halpin, Connie Scott, Kathleen Maguire, Jane Rose, Joe Higgins (M-G-M)

Boy meets dolphin, boy loses dolphin, boy wins dolphin. Thus substituting gill for gal, producer Ivan Tors has fashioned a serviceable little family picture that to all intents and porpoises, should satisfy aquabrats everywhere.

Actually this little fish story, or Tors opera, amounts to a kind of bubbly variation on *Androcles and the Lion*. Arthur Weiss's screenplay, from a story by Ricou Browning and Jack Cowden, has a boy (Luke Halpin) rescuing an eight-foot dolphin from permanent residence in that big fish tank in the sky by removing a skin diver's spear from its torso and nursing it back to health in his dad's Florida Keys fish pen.

Chuck Connors limns the father firmly but agreeably, and young Halpin, in his screen bow, demonstrates keen acting instincts as the boy on a dolphin.

•

FLIPPER
1996, 96 mins, US Ⓥ ⊙ col
Dir Alan Shapiro ***Prod*** James J. McNamara, Perry Katz ***Scr*** Alan Shapiro ***Ph*** Bill Butler ***Ed*** Peck Prior ***Mus*** Joel McNeely ***Art*** Thomas A. Walsh
Act Elijah Wood, Paul Hogan, Chelsea Field, Isaac Hayes, Jonathan Banks, Jason Fuchs (American/Universal)

The effectively offbeat casting of Paul Hogan and some impressive underwater cinematography do much to enliven *Flipper*, an otherwise unremarkable attempt to revive the franchise that spawned two features and a popular TV series in the mid-1960s.

Writer-director Alan Shapiro has slightly updated the premise of the original Ivan Tors productions. In this version, Sandy, the teen hero played here by Elijah Wood, is an embittered child of divorce. And the ecologically conscious story line has Flipper battling polluters who dump toxic waste into his watery environs

Sandy is sent by his mother to spend the summer with his Uncle Porter (Hogan), an easygoing ex-hippie who lives as a part-time fisherman and full-time beach bum in a coastal community near Key West. Sandy is a quietly horrified witness when some boisterous blowhards try to shoot a pair of frolicking dolphins. Impulsively, Sandy saves one of the dolphins, names the mammal Flipper and adopts him as a pet.

Hogan takes a dry-witted and refreshingly eccentric approach to playing a stereotypical character. Wood manages to be appealing even when his character is borderline tedious. He gets capable support from Jessica Wesson as a cute local girl.

Jaws cinematographer Bill Butler handles the open-ocean lensing with his customary skill. (Pic was shot on location in the Bahamas.)

•

FLIRT
1996, 84 mins, US/Germany/Japan Ⓥ col
Dir Hal Hartley ***Prod*** Ted Hope ***Scr*** Hal Hartley ***Ph*** Michael Spiller ***Ed*** Hal Hartley ***Mus*** Ned Rifle, Jeffrey Taylor ***Art*** Karin Wiesel, Ric Schachtebeck, Tomoyuki Mazuo
Act Bill Sage, Martin Donovan, Dwight Ewell, Geno Lechner, Miho Nikaidoh, Hal Hartley (True Fiction/Pandora/Nippon)

Slight but sleek, *Flirt* is still fun. Hal Hartley's three-legged set of variations on an emotional situation plays like a compressed version of his oeuvre to date, a lighter divertissement after the more portentous *Amateur*.

Pic grew in an unplanned way out of a short (which now forms the first seg) that Hartley shot in early '93. Following screenings at the Toronto and Rotterdam fests, producer Ted Hope raised German and Japanese coin for a feature, which Hartley had decided should be variations on the original rather than an expansion.

Picture gets off to a crowd-pleasing start with the first episode (*New York, February 1993*, 16 mins), the most compressed and wittiest of the three. Lolling on a bed prior to leaving for Paris, Emily (Parker Posey) quizzes an off-screen lover by phone on the depth of his commitment. Bill (Bill Sage) finally promises to get off the dime and make a decision when he picks her up in 90 minutes. In the seg's funniest sequence, Bill verbalizes his confusion in a wash-room, seemingly to himself, only to be advised by a Greek chorus of three bums on the john.

Berlin, October 1994 (30 mins.) is essentially a straightforward reprise on different instruments, opening with two gay men—black Yank Dwight (Dwight Ewell) and his older German lover, Johan (Dominik Bender), an art dealer. Though the seg initially has fun transposing the same dialogue and situations to a homosexual and German setting, the joke isn't pushed past its limits.

For the third episode, *Tokyo, March 1995* (35 mins), Hartley lets place dictate content even more, opening with a rehearsal by a butoh mime ensemble. Out of this oblique opening emerges a similar but looser variation, with one of the dancers, the kooky Miho (Miho Nikaidoh), torn between choreographer Ozu (Toshizo Fujisawa) and departing American filmer Hal (Hartley himself).

As a whole, pic's main problem is its shifts of tone, especially given the fact that it starts out gangbusters in familiar Hartley territory and moves to a gentle, romantic close (clearly with some autobiographical elements). Pacing and editing also get slacker as pic progresses.

•

FLIRTATION WALK
1934, 95 mins, US b/w
Dir Frank Borzage ***Prod*** Frank Borzage ***Scr*** Delmer Daves, Lou Edelman ***Ph*** Sol Polito, George Barnes ***Ed*** William Holmes ***Art*** Jack Okey
Act Dick Powell, Ruby Keeler, Pat O'Brien, Ross Alexander, John Eldredge (First National)

Flirtation Walk is bright and diverting entertainment in which the musical sequences [dance numbers directed by Bobby Connolly, music and lyrics by Allie Wrubel and Mort Dixon] are logically worked in, albeit with the usual Hollywood flair for exaggeration. Background of West Point allows the picture to possess some snappy drill and brass-button stuff. Deft direction of Frank Borzage gives the production the tempo and zing that stamps it swell amusement.

Dick Powell, in his plebe year at the Point, plays the situations for excellent natural comedy. Ruby Keeler does not dance. She has a lot to do and does it with considerable assurance. Ross Alexander as Powell's roommate will be liked, a personable young man with a knack for light comedy and horseplay.

Laughs and drama of the story are derived from the interplay of officer-private class distinctions and military discipline. The quiet competence of John Eldredge's performance as the disappointed suitor rates a few merit stripes.

1934: NOMINATION: Best Picture

•

FLIRTING
1991, 96 mins, Australia Ⓥ ⊙ col
Dir John Duigan ***Prod*** George Miller, Terry Hayes, Doug Mitchell ***Scr*** John Duigan ***Ph*** Geoff Burton ***Ed*** Robert Gibson ***Art*** Roger Ford
Act Noah Taylor, Thandie Newton, Nicole Kidman, Bartholomew Rose, Kiri Paramore, Kym Wilson (Kennedy Miller)

Miles ahead of the average teen film, *Flirting* is a most agreeable sequel to John Duigan's earlier pic *The Year My Voice Broke*. The new film doesn't pack the emotional wallop of the first, but it still charms. This depiction of well-to-do teens in sexually segregated schools also looks obliquely at latent racism at the time of the "white Australia" policy. Events that led to the Vietnam War already were in motion.

Noah Taylor reprises his character of Danny Embling. It's 1965, and Danny's parents have sent him to a boys-only boarding school across the lake from a similar institution for girls. In the girls' school, a young Ugandan student suffers racial slurs. Thandiwe (Thandie Newton) and Danny meet and are attracted to each other.

Duigan handles this material with a great deal of humor and charm, demonstrating a sharp ear for contemporaneous teen dialog. A curiosity is Nicole Kidman's appearance as one of the girls' school students. *Flirting* was shot before she went to the States to appear in *Days of Thunder* [released in summer 1990].

•

FLIRTING WITH DISASTER
1996, 92 mins, US Ⓥ ⊙ col
Dir David O. Russell ***Prod*** Dean Silvers ***Scr*** David O. Russell ***Ph*** Eric Edwards ***Ed*** Christopher Tellefsen ***Mus*** Stephen Endelman ***Art*** Kevin Thompson
Act Patricia Arquette, Ben Stiller, Tea Leoni, Alan Alda, Mary Tyler Moore, George Segal (Miramax)

Although it eventually throws more balls in the air than it can easily juggle, *Flirting with Disaster* is, most of the time, a diabolically clever satire that has its way with any number of contemporary shiboleths.

Expanding upon the insights into dysfunctional families writer-director David O. Russell served up in his promising but uneven first feature, *Spanking the Monkey*, this whacked-out road comedy about a young man's search for his real parents takes any number of unexpected turns, most of them bitingly funny.

Mel Coplin (Ben Stiller) is a young New York dad who decides he can't name his four-month-old son without having met his biological parents. Despite the objections of his loudly overbearing adoptive parents (George Segal, Mary Tyler Moore), Mel, his moody wife Nancy (Patricia Arquette), and infant son fly to San Diego along with adoption agency shrink Tina (Tea Leoni), a hot number tense over her impending divorce. But their stay in California is brief. As the trip progresses, relations between Mel and Nancy go from strained to dire, and everyone's heads are sent spinning when they arrive at the sprawling desert home of Richard and Mary Schlicting (Alan Alda, Lily Tomlin). Troubles mount when Mel's New York folks, thinking he's in trouble, show up as well.

By the final reel or so, a bit of strain is detectable in the film's determined eccentricity. Still, the laughs fly thick and fast through most of this oddball odyssey, in which parents of the last two generations are shown no quarter. Russell has fun puncturing what's left of '60s cultural mores.

Cast is aces across the board.

•

FLOWER DRUM SONG
1961, 133 mins, US Ⓥ ⊙ ▭ col
Dir Henry Koster ***Prod*** Ross Hunter ***Scr*** Joseph Fields ***Ph*** Russell Metty ***Ed*** Milton Carruth ***Mus*** Alfred Newman (sup.) ***Art*** Alexander Golitzen, Joseph Wright
Act Nancy Kwan, James Shigeta, Juanita Hall, Jack Soo, Miyoshi Umeki, Benson Fong (Universal)

Much of the fundamental charm, grace and novelty of Rodgers & Hammerstein's [1958 Broadway hit] *Flower Drum Song* has been overwhelmed by the sheer opulence and glamour with which Ross Hunter has translated it to the screen. As a film, it emerges a curiously unaffecting, unstable and rather undistinguished experience.

The dominant issue in the screenplay, based on the novel [*The Flower Drum Song*] by C. Y. Lee and adapted from the legit book by Joseph Fields and Oscar Hammerstein, is the clash of East-West romantic-marital customs as it affects four young people of Chinese descent living in San Francisco's Chinatown.

The four are Nancy Kwan, a gold-digging, husband-hungry nightclub dancer; Jack Soo, a kind of Chinese Nathan Detroit; James Shigeta, most eligible bachelor in Chinatown—the student prince of Grant Avenue; and Miyoshi Umeki, "picture (or mail-order) bride" fresh (and illegally) off a slowboat from China and ticketed for nuptials with Soo.

As in most R&H enterprises, the meat is in the musical numbers. There are some bright spots in this area but even here the effect isn't overpowering. Music supervisor-conductor Alfred Newman has fashioned some rousing orchestrations, with the assistance of Ken Darby. Dong Kingman's watercolored title paintings are a delight.

1961: NOMINATIONS: Best Color Cinematography, Color Costume Design, Color Art Direction, Scoring of a Musical Picture, Sound

•

FLOWERS IN THE ATTIC
1987, 95 mins, US Ⓥ ⊙ col
Dir Jeffrey Bloom ***Prod*** Sy Levin, Tom Fries ***Scr*** Jeffrey Bloom ***Ph*** Frank Byers, Gil Hubbs ***Ed*** Tom Fries ***Mus*** Christopher Young ***Art*** John Muto
Act Louise Fletcher, Victoria Tennant, Kristy Swanson, Jeb Stuart Adams, Ben Ganger, Lindsay Parker (New World/Fries)

V. C. Andrews's novel of incestuous relationships and confined childhood always has been a superb candidate for a film treatment, but director Jeffrey Bloom has taken this narrative and squeezed the life from it. Performances are as stiff and dreary as the attic these children are imprisoned in. The ridiculous ending (different from the book) was one of several shot.

After her husband's death, Corinne (Victoria Tennant) takes the family—teenagers Chris (Jeb Stuart Adams) and Cathy (Kristy Swanson) and pre-adolescent twins Carrie (Lindsay Parker) and Cory (Ben Ganger)—and becomes gold digger deluxe, moving back to her parents' house, intent on getting reinstated into her father's will.

Kids aren't crazy about the arrangement after meeting their sadistic, Bible-toting, taskmaster grandmother (Louise Fletcher, doing a lot with this one-dimensional role) and getting locked into a guest room, where they are informed they must stay until their grandfather dies, so Tennant can win his affections.

Cathy and Chris's gradual mutual attraction has been excised and is only hinted at here. More problematic is the script, which attributes none of the qualities of teenagers to the teens and portrays the younger children as mindless drones.

•

FLUBBER
1997, 93 mins, US Ⓥ ⊙ col
Dir Les Mayfield ***Prod*** John Hughes, Ricardo Mestres ***Scr*** John Hughes, Bill Walsh ***Ph*** Dean Cundey ***Ed*** Harvey Rosenstock ***Mus*** Danny Elfman ***Art*** Andrew McAlpine
Act Robin Williams, Marcia Gay Harden, Christopher McDonald, Raymond Barry, Clancy Brown, Ted Levine (Great Oaks/Walt Disney)

After a slow, singularly unpromising start, this new version of *The Absent Minded Professor* emerges as funny and frenetic family entertainment.

In the role originally essayed by Fred MacMurray, Robin Williams is unusually subdued as Philip Brainard, an easily distracted college professor. But once he gets into the laboratory to concoct the title substance, Williams hits his stride and never looks back. Quite by accident, Brainard invents Flubber—"flying rubber"—a greenish goo with a mischievous personality all its own.

Unlike the original, the remake has a magical, morphing costar created by Industrial Light & Magic and visual effects supervisor Tom Bertino. At times, the little critter looks like a malleable bean bag. It even has something of a voice, provided by Scott Martin Gershin.

John Hughes did the rewrite of the late Bill Walsh's original screenplay and, predictably, the creator of *Home Alone* emphasizes comic mayhem and physical shtick. But some of the funniest bits are updated and expanded gags from the 1961 comedy.

Except for a few moments of improvisational silliness with Flubber, Williams pretty much remains in character throughout the comedy.

•

FLUKE
1995, 96 mins, US Ⓥ col
Dir Carlo Carlei ***Prod*** Paul Maslansky, Lata Ryan ***Scr*** Carlo Carlei, James Carrington ***Ph*** Raffaele Mertes ***Ed*** Mark Conte ***Mus*** Carlo Siliotto ***Art*** Hilda Stark
Act Matthew Modine, Nancy Travis, Eric Stoltz, Max Pomeranc, Samuel L. Jackson, Ron Perlman (Rocket/M-G-M)

Intended for children as well as their parents, *Fluke*, the dramatic tale of a dog who was once a man, is strange family fare, a non-formulaic pic that tries to blend the expected magic of animal adventures with more serious ideas.

Italian Carlo Carlei makes his U.S. directorial debut with a film that is stylistically excessive, flaunting his facility with the camera at the expense of simpler, more coherent storytelling, as befits children's films.

Tale begins with a disastrous car race between Thomas Johnson (Matthew Modine) and Jeff Newman (Eric Stoltz), close friends and business partners, that ends with a fatal accident, after which Thomas wakes up as a dog.

Pic's first part, which is almost devoid of dialogue, details the travails of Fluke the puppy as he's separated from his family and mistreated in various ways by humans, until he's adopted by a homeless woman. When she dies, Fluke befriends Rumbo (voice provided by Samuel L. Jackson), a street-smart dog who serves as his mentor, teaching him the ropes of the canine world.

Pic changes gears (for the better) once Rumbo is brutally shot and Fluke, still haunted by vague memories of his former life with his attractive wife (Nancy Travis) and sensitive son (Max Pomeranc), decides to find his family and go home. Through brief flashbacks, which might prove too confusing for young kids, saga reconstructs Fluke's conflict with his partner.

•

FLY, THE
1958, 94 mins, US Ⓥ ⊙ ▭ col
Dir Kurt Neumann ***Prod*** Kurt Neumann ***Scr*** James Clavell ***Ph*** Karl Struss ***Ed*** Merrill G. White ***Mus*** Paul Sawtell ***Art*** Lyle R. Wheeler, Theobold Holsopple
Act Al Hedison, Patricia Owens, Vincent Price, Herbert Marshall, Kathleen Freeman, Betty Lou Gerson (20th Century-Fox)

The Fly is a high-budget, beautifully and expensively mounted exploitation picture [derived from a story by George Langelaan]. Al Hedison plays a scientist who has invented a machine that reduces matter to disintegrated atoms and another machine that reassembles the atoms. He explains to his wife (Patricia Owens) that this will enable humans to travel—disintegrated—anywhere in the world at the speed of light. In experimenting on himself, however, a fly gets into the disintegration chamber with him.

When Hedison arrives in the integration chamber, he discovers some of his atoms have been scrambled with the fly's. Hedison has the head and "arm" of a fly; the fly has the head and arm of the man—each, of course, in his own scale of size. The problem is to catch the fly and rescramble. But before this can happen, Hedison finds the predatory instincts of the insect taking over.

One strong factor of the picture is its unusual believability. It is told as a mystery suspense story, so that it has a compelling interest aside from its macabre effects. There is an appealing and poignant romance between Owens and Hedison, which adds to the reality of the story, although the flashback technique purposely robs the picture of any doubt about the outcome.

•

FLY, THE

1986, 100 mins, US Ⓥ ⊙ col

Dir David Cronenberg ***Prod*** Stuart Cornfeld ***Scr*** Charles Edward Pogue, David Cronenberg ***Ph*** Mark Irwin ***Ed*** Ronald Sanders ***Mus*** Howard Shore ***Art*** Carol Spier

Act Jeff Goldblum, Geena Davis, John Getz, Joy Booshel, Les Carlson (Brooksfilms)

David Cronenberg's remake of the 1958 horror classic *The Fly* is not for the squeamish. Casting Jeff Goldblum was a good choice as he brings a quirky, common touch to the spacey scientist role. Cronenberg gives him a nice girl friend (Geena Davis), too.

But there's trouble in paradise. Goldblum's got a set of teleporters that he promises will "change the world as we know it," and indeed, it changes his.

Even though the machinery is not yet perfected, Goldblum, in a moment of drunken jealousy, throws himself in the works. Unbeknownst to him a fly accompanies him on the journey and he starts to metamorphise.

Chris Walas's design for *The Fly* is never less than visually intriguing. Production design by Carol Spier, particularly for Goldblum's warehouse lab, is original and appropriate to the hothouse drama. Cronenberg contains the action well in a limited space with a small cast.

1986: Best Makeup

•

FLY II, THE

1989, 105 mins, US Ⓥ ⊙ col

Dir Chris Walas ***Prod*** Steven-Charles Jaffe ***Scr*** Mick Garris, Jim Wheat, Ken Wheat, Frank Darabont ***Ph*** Robin Vidgeon ***Ed*** Sean Barton ***Mus*** Christopher Young ***Art*** Michael S. Bolton

Act Eric Stoltz, Daphne Zuniga, Lee Richardson, John Getz, Frank Turner, Anne Marie Lee (Brooksfilms)

The Fly II is an expectedly gory and gooey but mostly plodding sequel to the 1986 hit that was a remake of the 1958 sci-fier that itself spawned two sequels.

After a shock opening in which the late man-fly's son is born within a horrible insectlike encasement, slickly produced pic [story by Mick Garris] generates some promise as little Martin Brundle is raised in laboratory conditions provided by scientific tycoon Anton Bartok (Lee Richardson).

Afflicted with a dramatically accelerated lifecycle, Martin quickly demonstrates genius, and by the age of five emerges fully grown in the person of Eric Stoltz. Martin becomes determined to perfect his father's teleportation machine, which Bartok controls, and also takes an interest in researcher Beth Logan (Daphne Zuniga).

Martin gradually becomes aware that Bartok's motives are far from benign, and simultaneously begins mutating into a hideous beast while retaining his human sensibility.

By the climax, the film more closely comes to resemble *Aliens* than the previous *Fly*, as the transformed Martin hides behind walls and in the ceiling before pouncing on Bartok's goons, spitting on them, chewing them up and spitting them out.

•

FLY AWAY HOME

1996, 107 mins, US Ⓥ ⊙ col

Dir Carroll Ballard ***Prod*** John Veitch, Carol Baum ***Scr*** Robert Rodat, Vince McKewin ***Ph*** Caleb Deschanel ***Ed*** Nicholas C. Smith ***Mus*** Mark Isham ***Art*** Seamus Flannery

Act Jeff Daniels, Anna Paquin, Dana Delany, Terry Kinney, Holter Graham, Jeremy Ratchford (Sandollar/Columbia)

An animal, kid and family picture of the first order, *Fly Away Home* marks an impressive return to form for Carroll Ballard, his best work since *The Black Stallion* (1979). [Based on the autobiography of Bill Lishman, pic is] an unexpectedly engrossing tale about an adolescent girl who raises a bunch of orphan goslings to maturity, then leads them on a migratory path by flying a homemade plane.

Much of the airborne footage of the second half is genuinely remarkable, with lots of closeup footage of the big birds flying in formation taken from an accompanying tiny plane.

Although some adults could find them a bit on the treacly side, the scenes of the flightless little birds scurrying around the Canadian farm to follow 13-year-old Amy (Anna Paquin) wherever she goes are mightily disarming. The father-daughter relationship simultaneously gathers strength, as it is her endlessly resourceful dad, Thomas (Jeff Daniels), who proposes the seemingly outrageous solution of how to get the geese to migrate south.

The dynamic between Daniels's vigorous, if self-involved, artist father and Paquin's initially sullen teenager is warmly and believably conveyed. Cinematographer Caleb Deschanel, who burst upon the scene so spectacularly with *The Black Stallion* but had not shot a feature in a number of years, reteams with Balard to outstanding effect.

1996: NOMINATION: Best Cinematography

•

FLY BY NIGHT

1942, 74 mins, US b/w

Dir Robert Siodmak ***Prod*** Sol C. Siegel ***Scr*** Jay Drather, F. Hugh Herbert ***Ph*** John F. Seitz ***Ed*** Arthur Schmidt

Act Nancy Kelly, Richard Carlson, Albert Basserman, Martin Kosleck (Paramount)

This is one of those sinister mellers, photographed in low light tones, with a generally implausible story populated with spies, secret weapons and nice young couples who get innocently mixed up in espionage. It's well done, but the maddeningly impossible plot [from an original story by Ben Roberts and Sidney Sheldon] sets it down as routine.

Nancy Kelly and Richard Carlson, as the innocents who get caught in the meshes of the spy ring, both give surprisingly good performances for roles of this type.

Carlson is a young physician into whose car climbs an inventor who has escaped from a sanitorium, where he has been held by the spies.

Robert Siodmak's direction varies from the slow pace of mystery thrillers to chase sequences, but never achieves full success at either end of the scale. That's largely due, however, to the unreal story.

•

FLYING DEUCES, THE

1939, 67 mins, US Ⓥ ⊙ b/w

Dir A. Edward Sutherland ***Prod*** Boris Morros ***Scr*** Ralph Spence, Alfred Schiller, Charles Rogers, Harry Langdon ***Ph*** Art Lloyd ***Ed*** Jack Dennis ***Mus*** Leo Shuken, John Leipold ***Art*** Boris Leven

Act Stan Laurel, Oliver Hardy, Jean Parker, Reginald Gardiner (RKO)

Comedy is of early Keystone vintage with squirting water and bumps into walls used extensively to create laughs. Overall, it's pretty dull. Laurel and Hardy are Paris sightseers, the latter falling in love with a waitress. She turns him down, and the pair enlist in the Foreign Legion. Breaking all regulations, they are tossed to the laundry, and finally rebel and try to desert.

Not much enthusiasm displayed for the comedy attempted, with exception of two brief episodes. Hardy sings chorus of "Shine On Harvest Moon" while Laurel does some light stepping. Later, Laurel's utilization of bedsprings to play a harp solo is the picture's highlight.

Boris Morros bought the rights to a French picture, *The Two Aces*, but in the remake dropped the picture down to the bottom of the deck with the new title.

•

FLYING DOWN TO RIO

1934, 88 mins, US Ⓥ ⊙ b/w

Dir Thornton Freeland, George Nicholls Jr. ***Prod*** Merian C. Cooper (exec.) ***Scr*** Cyril Hume, H. W. Hanemann, Erwin Gelsey ***Ph*** J. Roy Hunt ***Ed*** Jack Kitchin ***Mus*** Max Steiner (dir.) ***Art*** Van Nest Polglase, Carroll Clark

Act Dolores Del Rio, Gene Raymond, Raul Roulien, Ginger Rogers, Fred Astaire, Blanche Friderici (RKO)

The main point of *Flying Down to Rio* is the screen promise of Fred Astaire. He's distinctly likeable on the screen, the mike is kind to his voice and as a dancer he remains in a class by himself.

This picture makes its bid via numbers staged by Dave Gould to Vincent Youman melodies. But *Rio*'s story [from a play by Anne Caldwell, based on an original story by Louis Brock] lets it down. It's slow and lacks laughs to the point where average business seems its groove. From the time of the opening melody ("Music Makes Me"—and hot) to the next number, "Carioca," almost three reels elapse and anybody can take a walk, come back and be that much ahead.

It takes all that time for Gene Raymond, as a band leader, to be enticed by Dolores Del Rio, as a South American belle, and frame her into a plane ride to Rio de Janeiro. This hop includes a faked, overnight forced landing on a beach, strictly in the platonic manner. When they finally get off the sand and to Rio, Raymond finds his Brazilian pal is engaged to the girl, but the Latin member gives the damsel to him and takes a novel way out via a parachute dive at the finish. Meanwhile, the opening of a new hotel by the girl's father, for which Raymond's band has been engaged, is the premise for continuing the musical portion below the equator.

1934: NOMINATION: Best Song ("Carioca")

•

FLYING LEATHERNECKS

1951, 103 mins, US Ⓥ ⊙ col

Dir Nicholas Ray ***Prod*** Edmund Grainger ***Scr*** James Edward Grant ***Ph*** William E. Snyder ***Ed*** Sherman Todd ***Mus*** Roy Webb ***Art*** Albert S. D'Agostino, James W. Sullivan

Act John Wayne, Robert Ryan, Don Taylor, Janis Carter, Jay C. Flippen, William Harrigan (RKO)

Marquee pull of John Wayne and Robert Ryan in the action market has been teamed with a story of Marine fighter pilots.

Actual color footage of battle action in the Pacific has been smartly blended with studio shots to strike a note of realism.

James Edward Grant scripted the Kenneth Gamet story, which deals with a small squadron of flying leathernecks stationed in the Pacific and the frictions that develop between its commander (Wayne) and its executive officer (Ryan) when they are not busy fighting the war. Ryan is disappointed because he has not been recommended for command of the squadron but works with Wayne until latter's rigid discipline and impartiality build a bitter friction between them.

This purely masculine yarn sidetracks when Wayne goes on leave to the States for time with his wife (Janis Carter) and small son. These scenes are excellently done, both in playing, direction and writing, but do have the effect of ending the action. This starts in again, however, when Wayne is re-assigned to the Pacific.

•

FLYING TIGERS

1942, 96 mins, US Ⓥ ⊙ b/w

Dir David Miller ***Prod*** Edmund Grainger (assoc.) ***Scr*** Kenneth Gamet, Barry Trivers ***Ph*** Jack Marta ***Ed*** Ernest Nims ***Mus*** Victor Young

Act John Wayne, John Carroll, Anna Lee, Paul Kelly, Mae Clarke, Gordon Jones (Republic)

Flying Tigers is based on exploits of American flyers in China who took up the cudgels against the Japs long before Pearl Harbor.

Aside from a foreword written by Generalissimo Chiang Kai-shek, paying tribute to the American Volunteer Group who "have become the symbol of the invincible strength of the forces now upholding the cause of humanity and justice," there is nothing to distinguish this film from other conventional aviation yarns.

Handicapped primarily by a threadbare script, production also suffers from slow pacing while John Wayne, John Carroll, Anna Lee and Paul Kelly are barely adequate in the major acting assignments. Some of the scenes look repetitious, the same Jap flyers apparently being shot down and killed three or four times over.

1942: NOMINATIONS: Best Scoring of a Dramatic Picture, Sound, Special Effects

•

FOG, THE

1980, 91 mins, US Ⓥ ⊙ ▭ col

Dir John Carpenter ***Prod*** Debra Hill ***Scr*** John Carpenter, Debra Hill ***Ph*** Dean Cundey ***Ed*** Tommy Lee Wallace, Charles Bornstein ***Mus*** John Carpenter ***Art*** Tommy Lee Wallace

Act Adrienne Barbeau, Hal Holbrook, Janet Leigh, Jamie Lee Curtis, John Houseman, Tom Atkins (Avco Embassy)

John Carpenter is anything but subtle in his approach to shocker material. Premise is obvious from almost the first frame, as a grizzled John Houseman tells youngsters grouped around a campfire about a foggy curse that surrounds a coastal town where a horrible shipwreck took place 100 years ago.

Story exposition and setting are well-established before the opening titles are over, and *The Fog* proceeds to layer one fright atop another.

Adrienne Barbeau makes her film debut as the husky-voiced deejay of the town's sole radio station, perched atop a lighthouse from which the title phenomenon becomes increasingly apparent.

Thesping is okay in all departments although Janet Leigh isn't given much to do, nor is daughter Jamie Lee Curtis.

•

FOLIES BERGERE DE PARIS

1935, 83 mins, US b/w

Dir Roy Del Ruth ***Prod*** William Goetz, Raymond Griffith ***Scr*** Bess Meredyth, Hal Long ***Ph*** Barney McGill, Peverell Mar-

ley *Ed* Allen McNeil, Sherman Todd *Mus* Alfred Newman (dir.) *Art* Richard Day
Act Maurice Chevalier, Ann Sothern, Merle Oberon, Eric Blore, Ferdinand Munier, Walter Byron (20th Century)

Picture has nothing whatever to do with the Folies Bergere of Paris, except that one of the characters is supposed to be the head comic of the show at the Paris music hall, and that allows for three musical numbers [photographed by Peverell Marley] on the stage thereof. For plot and continuity purposes studio has taken an old continental farce, *The Red Cat* [by Rudolph Lothar and Hans Adler] and switched it about a bit [in an adaptation by Jessie Ernst].

Maurice Chevalier does excellent work. He handles the double assignment of Charlier, the Folies comic, and the Baron Cassini. Baron gets into a financial jam so Charlier is hired to impersonate him while he's off to London to dig up some coin. Baron has been having marital difficulties with his wife, too, and Charlier manages to fix up both the homework and the office work for the baron with happy fadeout all around.

Chevalier shows, perhaps for the first time in films, that he has range as an actor. Ann Sothern as Charlier's wife is pretty and effective. She sings and dances with Chevalier and makes a definite sock impression. Merle Oberon, as the baron's wife, on the other hand, gets a tough break. Dance routines by Dave Gould are nifty.

1935: Best Dance Direction ("Straw Hat")

•

FOLLOW THAT BIRD
(AKA: SESAME STREET PRESENTS FOLLOW THAT BIRD)
1985, 88 mins, US Ⓥ ⊙ col
Dir Ken Kwapis *Prod* Tony Garnett *Scr* Tony Geiss, Judy Freudberg *Ph* Curtis Clark *Ed* Stan Warnow, Evan Landis *Mus* Van Dyke Parks, Lennie Niehaus *Art* Carol Spier
Act Caroll Spinney, Jim Henson, Frank Oz, Paul Bartel, Sandra Bernhard, John Candy (Warner)

Simple premise has the slightly goofy yellow, eight-foot fowl Big Bird taken away from Sesame Street by the officious Miss Finch so he can grow up among his own kind, a bird family named the Dodos, in Oceanview, IL. The Dodos are a bunch of loons, however, so B. B. begins the long trek back to New York on foot, while the Sesame Street gang mobilizes in assorted vehicles to find its dear friend.

En route, B. B. has a pleasant encounter with country singing truck driver Waylon Jennings, but a distinctly nasty one with the Sleaze Brothers (SCTV's Joe Flaherty and Dave Thomas), unscrupulous amusement park operators who abduct B. B. for their own nefarious purposes.

All turns out for the best, of course, and spicing things up along the way are Chevy Chase and Kermit the Frog as TV newscasters, Sandra Bernhard and Paul Bartel as the proprietors of a low-down roadside diner, and John Candy as a motorcycle cop.

•

FOLLOW THAT CAMEL
1967, 95 mins, UK Ⓥ col
Dir Gerald Thomas *Prod* Peter Rogers *Scr* Talbot Rothwell *Ph* Alan Hume *Ed* Alfred Roome *Mus* Eric Rogers *Art* Alex Vetchinsky
Act Phil Silvers, Jim Dale, Peter Butterworth, Charles Hawtrey, Kenneth Williams, Anita Harris (Rank)

Story line provides adequate excuse for a "Carry On" foray into the Foreign Legion territory, with a young hero (Jim Dale), accused of cheating at cricket, enlisting with his manservant to exculpate his disgrace. There he encounters Phil Silvers, as a sergeant who invents acts of heroism and is much decorated, Kenneth Williams as the German commanding officer, Charles Hawtrey, as his deft adjutant, and Joan Sims, as a much-cleavage siren.

They are involved in running skirmishes with an Arab chieftain, serving a master called Mustapha Leak, and the farrago climaxes in a hilarious battle at a desert fort, after a forced march through waterless wastes. It all works with considerable bounce, with elements of parody of *Beau Geste*–style movies for those alert to them. All the regular comics are on first-rate form.

•

FOLLOW THAT DREAM
1962, 109 mins, US Ⓥ ▭ col
Dir Gordon Douglas *Prod* David Weisbart *Scr* Charles Lederer *Ph* Leo Tover *Ed* William B. Murphy *Mus* Hans J. Salter *Art* Mal Bert
Act Elvis Presley, Arthur O'Connell, Anne Helm, Joanna Moore, Jack Kruschen, Simon Oakland (United Artists)

Follow That Dream is a kind of second cinematic cousin to *Tammy* with Elvis Presley as the hinterland's answer to the supposed advantages of formal booklarnin'. Scenarist Charles Lederer has constructed several highly amusing scenes in tailoring Richard Powell's novel, *Pioneer, Go Home*, to fit the specifications of the screen. There are lags and lapses in the picture, to be sure, but, by Presley pix standards, it's above average.

Presley portrays what amounts to a cross between Li'l Abner and male counterpart of Tammy, a sort of number one son in a makeshift, itinerant brood of real McCoy types who plant themselves on a strip of unclaimed Florida beach and proceed to play homesteaders whilst befuddled officials of city and state, welfare workers and thugs haplessly attempt to unsquat them from their profitable perch.

•

FOLLOW THE BOYS
1944, 122 mins, US Ⓥ b/w
Dir A. Edward Sutherland *Prod* Charles K. Feldman *Scr* Lou Breslow, Gertrude Purcell *Ph* David Abel *Ed* Fred R. Feitshans, Jr. *Mus* Leigh Harline *Art* John B. Coodman, Harold H. MacArthur
Act George Raft, Vera Zorina, George Macready, Charles Butterworth, Regis Toomey, Grace McDonald (Universal)

Prime trouble with *Follow the Boys* is its overgenerosity. The running time shows that a good thing can be overdone.

Charles K. Feldman, Hollywood agent and "package" producer, who was prominent in Hollywood Victory Committee and allied USO-Camp Shows activities, conceived the idea of glorifying the professional undertaking with which he was long associated and familiar. The sum total is a highly entertaining film package.

Plot after a spell wears thin. George Raft and Vera Zorina, as the married stars, part because of what seems a rather thin reason. But from this is motivated Raft's preoccupation with organizing the Hollywood Victory Committee, and thus are paraded Jeanette MacDonald, Orson Welles, Dietrich, Dinah Shore, W. C. Fields, Andrews Sisters, Artur Rubinstein, Carmen Amaya, Sophie Tucker, Delta Rhythm Boys, et al.

Everybody does something, the songs running the gamut of the Hit Parade of three decades. Raft even gets in his "Sweet Georgia Brown," and W. C. Fields revives an almost forgotten pool-table scene he did in an earlier *Ziegfeld Follies*.

•

FOLLOW THE BOYS
1963, 96 mins, US ⊙ ▭ col
Dir Richard Thorpe *Prod* Lawrence P. Bachmann *Scr* David T. Chantler, David Osborn *Ph* Ted Scaife *Ed* John Victor Smith *Mus* Ron Goodwin, Alexander Courage *Art* Bill Andrews
Act Connie Francis, Paula Prentiss, Dany Robin, Janis Paige, Russ Tamblyn, Richard Long (M-G-M)

Youth must be served, but the service isn't very good in this lackluster romantic comedy about a group of gobs who find the same girls in every port—their faithfully itinerant wives or fiancees. It is roughly—very roughly—a sequel to *Where the Boys Are*.

Heroines of the story [by producer Laurence P. Bachmann] are a group of girls dubbed "seagulls" because, like their namesake, they are perpetually following ships. The story dwells on four such couples and illustrates, haphazardly, their togetherness difficulties.

Problems of couple number one, a guileless singer (Connie Francis) and a radar man (Roger Perry) practicing to be a good husband by watching a blank radar screen and pretending it's a television set, is the fact they've never consummated their marriage. The marital relationship of couple number two (Janis Paige and Ron Randell) is in jeopardy because he prefers the seafaring life and she wants him on dry land.

Couples number three and four are all mixed up. The two guys (Russ Tamblyn and Richard Long) are wolfish swabbies of the breed who seek a girl in every port and some port in every girl. But the lads get their signals crossed and Tamblyn winds up with the lass (Paula Prentiss) loosely affianced to Long, while Long gets collared by the gal (Dany Robin) intended for Tamblyn.

•

FOLLOW THE FLEET
1936, 110 mins, US Ⓥ b/w
Dir Mark Sandrich *Prod* Pandro S. Berman *Scr* Dwight Taylor, Allan Scott *Ph* David Abel *Ed* Henry Berman *Mus* Max Steiner (dir.) *Art* Van Nest Polglase, Carroll Clark
Act Fred Astaire, Ginger Rogers, Randolph Scott, Harriet Hilliard, Astrid Allwyn, Betty Grable (RKO)

With Ginger Rogers again opposite, and the Irving Berlin music to dance to and sing, Astaire once more legs himself and his picture into the big-time entertainment class.

Imperfections in *Fleet* are confined to story. That's usual with musicals, stage or screen. This is a rather free adaptation of [Hubert Osborne's play] *Shore Leave*, a David Belasco oldie. Yet the story never detracts from the important element—the Astaire-Rogers musical efforts.

There are seven songs which is a bit too much—all by Irving Berlin, with "Face the Music," a cross between "Piccolino" and "Lovely Day," easily the leader. The score on the whole is pleasant but save for "Face the Music," the last number, not particularly distinguished.

Story is a double romance involving the starred duo and Harriet Hilliard-Randolph Scott. Yarn breaks them up and teams them again for the finish.

This is Hilliard's first picture. She's from radio, having sung mostly with the Ozzie Nelson band and chiefly on the Joe Penner programs. A blonde originally, she's in brunette wig in this film, presumably in deference to Rogers.

•

FOLLOW YOUR DREAMS
SEE: INDEPENDENCE DAY

•

FOOL, THE
1991, 135 mins, UK Ⓥ b/w
Dir Christine Edzard *Prod* Richard Goodwin, Christine Edzard *Scr* Christine Edzard, Olivier Stockman *Ph* Robin Vidgeon *Ed* Olivier Stockman *Mus* Michel Sanvoisin
Act Derek Jacobi, Cyril Cusack, Ruth Mitchell, Paul Brooke, Corin Redgrave, John McEnery (Sands/Film Four/British Screen/Tyler

Three years after their marathon, *Little Dorrit*, husband-and-wife producers Richard Goodwin and Christine Edzard tread the same streets to lesser effect in *The Fool*.

In 1857, an obscure theater clerk (Derek Jacobi) engineers a financial scam to show up the monied classes. Problems start when, posing as the carefree Sir John, he's recognized by some theater folk, and he starts taking his alter ego too seriously.

Later scenes, with their *Wall Street* lingo and Jacobi's crisis of conscience, are an obvious allegory of the me-too 1980s. But they're a long time coming, and the thrill of the paper chase is lacking. Without a strong central yarn like Dickens's *Dorrit*, pic becomes a series of one-off routines by w.k. Brit thesps.

Helmer and coscripter Edzard shows off her research and top-notch design with street characters based on interviews by 19th-century social journalist Henry Mayhew. They're fine on their own terms, right down to the dirt under their fingernails, but Edzard needs to make up her mind whether she's building a museum or making a movie.

•

FOOL FOR LOVE
1985, 106 mins, US Ⓥ ▭ col
Dir Robert Altman *Prod* Menahem Golan, Yoram Globus *Scr* Sam Shepard *Ph* Pierre Mignot *Ed* Luce Grunenwaldt *Mus* George Burt *Art* Stephen Altman
Act Sam Shepard, Kim Basinger, Harry Dean Stanton, Randy Quaid, Martha Crawford, Louise Egolf (Cannon)

Robert Altman directs a fine cast with all the authority and finesse a good play deserves, so it's too bad the play fooled them all. Sam Shepard's drama of intense, forbidden love in the modern West is made to seem like specious stuff filled with dramatic ideas left over from the 1950s.

Opening up the play, which was set entirely in a dingy motel room, Shepard and Altman have spread out the action all around a rundown motel complex on the edge of the desert.

Eddie, a rangy, handsome cowboy, returns after a long absence to try to get back with the sexy May, with whom he has a can't-live-with-or-without-her relationship. The two shout, argue, make up, make out, split up, pout, dance around each other and start up all over again, while an old drunk observer takes it all in. Finally, the arrival of another fellow to take May out prompts a nocturnal spilling of the beans about Eddie and May's taboo love affair.

Beginning with the impressive Shepard, cast is handpicked with care. As the saucy May, Kim Basinger alternately conjures up Marilyn Monroe in *The Misfits* and *Bus Stop* and Brigitte Bardot in *And God Created Woman*. Harry Dean Stanton is excellent as the washed-up cause of all the problems.

•

FOOLISH WIVES
1922, 180 mins, US Ⓥ ⊙ ⊗ b/w
Dir Erich von Stroheim *Scr* Erich von Stroheim *Ph* Ben Reynolds, William Daniels *Mus* Sigmund Romberg *Art* E. E. Sheeley, Richard Day
Act Erich von Stroheim, Rudolph Christians, Miss Du Pont, Maude George, Mae Busch, Louis K. Webb (Universal)

According to Universal's press department, the picture cost $1,103,736.38; was 11 months and six days in filming; six months in assembling and editing; consumed 320,000 feet of negative, and employed as many as 15,000 extras for atmosphere.

Foolish Wives shows the cost—in the sets, beautiful backgrounds and massive interiors that carry a complete suggestion of the atmosphere of Monte Carlo, the locale of the story. And the sets, together with a thoroughly capable cast, are about all the picture has for all the heavy dough expended.

Obviously intended to be a sensational sex melodrama, *Foolish Wives* is at the same time frankly salacious.

Erich von Stroheim wrote the script, directed, and is the featured player. He's all over the lot every minute. His character is a Russian Captain of Hussars. The uniform may be Russian, but von Stroheim's general facial and physical appearance clearly suggests the typical Prussian military officer.

The story starts with a flirtation between the Count (Von Stroheim) and the American diplomat's wife, continues along with his obvious attempts to possess her, right under her husband's nose, and with the woman's evident liking for the count's attentions.

•

FOOLS OF FORTUNE

1990, 104 mins, UK Ⓥ ⦿ col

Dir Pat O'Connor ***Prod*** Sarah Radclyffe ***Scr*** Michael Hirst ***Ph*** Jerzy Zielinski ***Ed*** Michael Bradsell ***Mus*** Hans Zimmer ***Art*** Jamie Leonard

Act Mary Elizabeth Mastrantonio, Iain Glen, Julie Christie, Michael Kitchen, Sean T. McClory, Niamii Cusack (Poly-Gram/Working Title)

Fools of Fortune is an historical saga written with lucidity and performed with sensitivity, but tending to melodrama.

The Irish war of independence is the starting point for the story [from the novel by William Trevor] of a family's destruction and the survival of an unlikely love. The Quinton family seem sheltered in their grand rural home until the British-employed soldiers, the Black and Tans, burn down the house. The only survivors of the massacre are Quinton's wife (Julie Christie), her son Willie (first, Sean T. McClory, and then as an adult, Iain Glen), and their maid (Niamii Cusack).

Willie becomes an introspective and withdrawn young man, while his mother becomes a manic depressive and chronic alcoholic, a role which Christie relishes in.

When Christie finally commits suicide, Willie is comforted by childhood playmate Marianne, who's grown into an exquisitely beautiful woman (Mary Elizabeth Mastrantonio). Result of this comfort is a child.

•

FOOTLIGHT PARADE

1933, 102 mins, US Ⓥ ⦿ b/w

Dir Lloyd Bacon, Busby Berkeley ***Scr*** Manuel Seff, James Seymour ***Ph*** George Barnes ***Ed*** George Amy ***Art*** Anton Grot, Jack Okey

Act James Cagney, Joan Blondell, Ruby Keeler, Dick Powell, Guy Kibbee, Ruth Donnelly (Warner)

Footlight Parade is not as good as *42nd Street* and *Gold Diggers* but the three socko numbers here eclipse some of the preceding Busby Berkeley staging for spectacle.

The first hour is a loose, disjointed plot to plant the Fanchon & Marco presentation production stuff. F&M isn't mentioned but that's the setting, with James Cagney as the unit stager who's being rooked by his partners.

As in *Gold Diggers*, where Ned Sparks puts on a Ziegfeld production with a $15,000 budget, similarly no picture house ever saw such tabs as Cagney gives 'em here. But that's cinematic license.

That water ballet, the hokum "Honeymoon Hotel" and "Shanghai Lil" are punchy and undeniable. They more than offset the lethargy of what has preceded and sweeps the spectator away.

Characters are formula. Ruby Keeler is again the mousey type who becomes a swell number, and Dick Powell again is the juve lead. Cagney is the dynamic stager of units and Joan Blondell is his overly efficient secretary who contributes an element of unrequited love while Cagney gets rid of one wife and falls for another phoney dame.

•

FOOTLIGHT SERENADE

1942, 81 mins, US Ⓥ b/w

Dir Gregory Ratoff ***Prod*** William Le Baron ***Scr*** Richard Ellis, Helen Logan, Lynn Starling ***Ph*** Lee Garmes ***Ed*** Robert Simpson ***Mus*** Lee Robin, Ralph Rainger

Act John Payne, Betty Grable, Victor Mature, Jane Wyman, Phil Silvers, James Gleason (20th Century-Fox)

Footlight Serenade is a typical backstage number. New twist of minor importance has been provided for the boy-meets-girl-and-both-get-into-Broadway-show formula. Victor Mature is the champ, with the show built around him by producer James Gleason. His characterization is decidedly reminiscent of a heavyweight champ of the 1930s. Betty Grable gets a chorine job, while her fiancé John Payne is projected into a line of candidates for stumble-bum for the champ in the show.

Although Mature successfully pictures the egoistic and swaggering fight champ for reverse angles, he's painted with lily-white duco for the finish.

Gregory Ratoff carries the direction at a good pace. With the backstage filmusical angles well culled, there was nothing new for the scripters to devise on their own.

•

FOOTLOOSE

1984, 107 mins, US Ⓥ ⦿ col

Dir Herbert Ross ***Prod*** Lewis J. Rachmil, Craig Zadan ***Scr*** Dean Pitchford ***Ph*** Ric Waite ***Ed*** Paul Hirsch ***Mus*** Miles Goodman (adapt.), Becky Shargo (sup.) ***Art*** Ron Hobbs

Act Kevin Bacon, Lori Singer, John Lithgow, Dianne Wiest, Christopher Penn, Sarah Jessica Parker (Paramount)

In addition to his usual directorial skill and considerable choreographic experience, Herb Ross brings to *Footloose* an adult sensibility often lacking in troubled-teen pics.

To be sure, from its toe-tapping titles onward, *Footloose* is mainly a youth-oriented rock picture, complete with big-screen reminders of what's hot today in music video. And there's usually a stereo in sight to explain where the music's coming from, even on the side of tractors. But by writing both the screenplay and contributing lyrics to nine of the film's songs, Dean Pitchford has come up with an integrated story line that works.

Essential to the result is young Kevin Bacon, superb in the lead part. Bacon really just wants to get along in the small town he's been forced to move to from Chicago. Sure to complicate his life, however, is pretty Lori Singer, a sexually and otherwise confused preacher's daughter.

1984: NOMINATIONS: Best Song ("Footloose," "Let's Hear It for the Boy")

•

FOOTSTEPS IN THE DARK

1941, 96 mins, US b/w

Dir Lloyd Bacon ***Scr*** Lester Cole, John Wexley ***Ph*** Ernie Haller ***Ed*** Owen Marks ***Mus*** Frederick Hollander

Act Errol Flynn, Brenda Marshall, Ralph Bellamy, Alan Hale, Lee Patrick, Lucile Watson (Warner/First National)

Errol Flynn becomes a detective book author and amateur Sherlock in *Footsteps in the Dark*, his first comedy in years. Not his best picture, this modest budgeter gives the star a chance to appear in a role different from his usual costume or military films. Lloyd Bacon's direction furnishes the film with plenty of suspense and hokey but socko absurdities.

Flynn is depicted as an investment banker, leading a double life as a writer under the nom de plume of F. X. Pettijohn. His search for story material takes him on nightly prowls which get him into hot water in his own home.

Flynn does well enough as the amateur Sherlock. It's a role that calls for much action, with the plot [from a play by Laslo Fodor] centered about him in almost every scene. His portrayal indicates he could do better in future semicomic roles, especially if given brighter material.

•

FOR A FEW DOLLARS MORE

1966, 130 mins, Italy/Spain/W. Germany Ⓥ ⦿ ▭ col

Dir Sergio Leone ***Prod*** Alberto Grimaldi ***Scr*** Luciano Vincenzoni, Sergio Leone ***Ph*** Massimo Dallamano ***Ed*** Adriana Novelli, Eugenio Alabiso, Giorgio Serralonga ***Mus*** Ennio Morricone ***Art*** Carlo Simi

Act Clint Eastwood, Lee Van Cleef, Gian Maria Volonte, Mara Krup, Luigi Pistilli, Klaus Kinski (PEA/Gonzales/Constantin)

A hard-hitting western with uppercase values out of the busy Italo stable, this is a topnotch action entry.

Story [by director Sergio Leone and Fulvio Morsella] deals with a race between two bounty killers (Clint Eastwood and Lee Van Cleef) for reward money riding on head of a bandit (Gian Maria Volonte). First separately, then via a somewhat shaky and untrusting allegiance, the pair manage to set the stage for the killing of the bandido, El Indio. In the finale, it turns out that Van Cleef's real reason for getting El Indio was not the coin involved.

Script generally manages to avoid the cliché pitfalls traditional to the western, and Luciano Vincenzoni's dialogue is literate and satisfying to the ear. But it's principally thanks to Leone's bigger-than-life style, which combines upfront action and closeup details with a hard-hitting pace, that this acquires its impactful dimension.

Eastwood is fine in a tailor-made role of the squint-eyed opportunist who plays his cards right. Van Cleef etches a neat picture of his partner-rival. Volonte makes a suitably villainous heavy (for an added fillip, script makes him a drug addict to boot).

Spanish countryside and Italo studio interiors combine for realistic southwestern effect. Ennio Morricone's music, without measuring up to his previous efforts in the oater belt, is nevertheless pleasing. Pic is somewhat overlong at 130 minutes. [Version reviewed was Italian-language one. English-dubbed version was released in U.S. in 1967 and U.K. in 1968.]

•

FORBIDDEN GAMES

SEE: LES JEUX INTERDITS

•

FORBIDDEN PLANET

1956, 98 mins, US Ⓥ ⦿ ▭ col

Dir Fred M. Wilcox ***Prod*** Nicholas Nayfack ***Scr*** Cyril Hume ***Ph*** George J. Folsey ***Ed*** Ferris Webster ***Mus*** Louis Barron, Bebe Barron ***Art*** Cedric Gibbons, Arthur Lonergan

Act Walter Pidgeon, Anne Francis, Leslie Nielsen, Warren Stevens, Jack Kelly, Earl Holliman (M-G-M)

Imaginative gadgets galore, plus plenty of suspense and thrills, make the production a top offering in the space travel category. Best of all the gadgets is Robby, the Robot, and he's well-used for some comedy touches.

The conception of space cruisers, space planet terrain, the monstrous self-operating power plant, and of the terribly frightening spectre that threatens the human principals in the story [by Irving Black and Allen Adler] is weird and wonderful.

With all the technical gadgetry on display and carrying the entertainment load, the players are more or less puppets with no great acting demands made. Leslie Nielsen, space cruiser commander, lands on Altair-4 to search for survivors from a previous flight. He finds Walter Pidgeon, super-scientist, and the latter's daughter (Anne Francis) who, with Robby, are the planet's only inhabitants.

Pidgeon, who has gained knowledge beyond usual human limits, wants the rescuers to be gone. Nielsen takes to Francis and she to him, so he determines to seek out the unseen menace.

Credited for the special effects that add the punch to the show are A. Arnold Gillespie, Warren Newcombe, Irving G. Ries and Joshua Meador.

1956: NOMINATION: Best Special Effects

•

FORCE OF ARMS

1951, 98 mins, US b/w

Dir Michael Curtiz ***Prod*** Anthony Veiller ***Scr*** Orin Jannings ***Ph*** Ted McCord ***Ed*** Owen Marks ***Mus*** Max Steiner

Act William Holden, Nancy Olson, Frank Lovejoy, Gene Evans, Dick Wesson, Katherine Warren (Warner)

The Richard Tregaskis story, on which the script is based, uses an Italian battlefront setting as the frame for the compellingly projected romance between William Holden and Nancy Olson, a soldier and a WAC.

Holden, as a sergeant, and others of the company commanded by Frank Lovejoy, are pulled from the San Pietro front for a brief rest period. During the siesta, Holden meets Olson, a WAC lieutenant, and from an antagonistic start they soon are drawn to each other. In his next battle action Holden is wounded.

Script gets them married and, despite Holden being assigned to limited duty, he returns to his company to prove himself.

The story line is filled out with many gripping scenes. The romance rings true and the battle action sequences are dangerously alive under the forthright staging of Michael Curtiz.

Olson and Holden are most effective in the natural reactions to the circumstances in which they are plunged. Lovejoy makes his role of the friendly major a standout.

•

FORCE OF EVIL

1948, 78 mins, US Ⓥ ⦿ b/w

Dir Abraham Polonsky ***Prod*** Bob Roberts ***Scr*** Abraham Polonsky, Ira Wolfert ***Ph*** George Barnes ***Ed*** Art Seid ***Mus*** David Raksin ***Art*** Richard Day

Act John Garfield, Beatrice Pearson, Thomas Gomez, Marie Windsor, Roy Roberts, Howland Chamberlin (M-G-M/Enterprise)

Force of Evil fails to develop the excitement hinted at in the title. Makers apparently couldn't decide on the best way to present an exposé of the numbers racket, winding up with neither fish nor fowl as far as hard-hitting racketeer meller is concerned. A poetic, almost allegorical, interpretation keeps intruding on the tougher elements of the plot. This factor adds no distinction and only makes the going tougher.

Garfield, as to be expected, comes through with a performance that gets everything out of the material furnished. Film also introduces Beatrice Pearson but she garners no great honors for herself.

Plot, based on Ira Wolfert's novel *Tucker's People*, deals with the racketeers who fatten off the little person's nickels and dimes that daily are played on the numbers game. It is not a lucid exposé as filmed.

On the technical side, the production fares better than story-wise. The physical mounting is expertly valued; the New York locale shots give authenticity; and lensing by George Barnes, while a bit on the arty side, displays skilled craftsmanship.

•

FORCE 10 FROM NAVARONE

1978, 118 mins, UK Ⓥ ⦿ ▭ col

Dir Guy Hamilton ***Prod*** Oliver A. Unger ***Scr*** Robin Chapman ***Ph*** Christopher Challis ***Ed*** Raymond Poulton ***Mus*** Ron Goodwin ***Art*** Geoffrey Drake

Act Robert Shaw, Harrison Ford, Edward Fox, Barbara Bach, Franco Nero, Richard Kiel (Navarone)

This is not a sequel to the 1961 hit, *Guns of Navarone*, although *Force 10* opens with the bang-up conclusion of the earlier exercise in World War II commando heroics.

Two survivors of the spiking of the guns, British Major Mallory (now played by Robert Shaw) and demolitions expert Miller (Edward Fox) provide the link that gives some purpose to the title [from the novel by Alistair MacLean; screen story by Carl Foreman].

Director Guy Hamilton manages over the course of almost two hours to keep his audience on edge. For a finale he has a double whammy destruction of a giant Yugoslav dam which sets loose forces of nature that crumble a seemingly indestructible bridge.

This next-to-last film appearance of Robert Shaw is not his glory farewell. He is very good in what he is called upon to do, but the role is not one that makes any particular demand upon an exceptionally talented person.

Harrison Ford does a creditable job as the American Colonel; Fox is excellent as the British demolitions expert; Carl Weathers gives a powerful performance as the unwanted black GI who proves himself in more ways than one. Barbara Bach, lone femme, does fine in a tragic, patriotic role as a Partisan. Franco Nero as a Nazi double agent who fools the Partisans is slickly nefarious.

•

FOREIGN AFFAIR, A

1948, 113 mins, US b/w

Dir Billy Wilder ***Prod*** Charles Brackett ***Scr*** Charles Brackett, Billy Wilder, Richard Breen, Robert Harari ***Ph*** Charles B. Lang Jr. ***Ed*** Doane Harrison ***Mus*** Frederick Hollander ***Art*** Hans Dreier, Walter Tyler

Act Jean Arthur, Marlene Dietrich, John Lund, Millard Mitchell, Peter Von Zerneck, Stanley Prager (Paramount)

A Foreign Affair is a witty satire developed around a Congressional investigation of GI morals in Germany. Much of the action is backgrounded against actual Berlin footage. The humor to which such a theme lends itself has been given a stinging bite, even though presented broadly to tickle the risibilities.

While subject is handled for comedy, Charles Brackett and Billy Wilder have managed to underlay the fun with an exposé of human frailties and, to some extent, indicate a passive bitterness among the conquered in the occupied areas.

Jean Arthur is in a topflight characterization as a spinsterish congresswoman, who furnishes the distaff touch to an elemental girl-meets-boy angle in the story. The boy is John Lund, and Marlene Dietrich personifies the eternal siren as an opportunist German femme who furnishes Lund with off-duty diversion. Also, she gives the Dietrich s.a. treatment to three Frederick Hollander tunes, lyrics of which completely express the cynical undertones of the film.

1948: NOMINATIONS: Best Screenplay, B&W Cinematography

•

FOREIGN BODY

1986, 108 mins, US/UK Ⓥ col

Dir Ronald Neame ***Prod*** Colin M. Brewer ***Scr*** Celine La Freniere ***Ph*** Ronnie Taylor ***Ed*** Andrew Nelson ***Mus*** Ken Howard ***Art*** Roy Stannard

Act Victor Banerjee, Warren Mitchell, Geraldine McEwan, Denis Quilley, Amanda Donohoe, Trevor Howard (Neame/Brewer)

If *Foreign Body* [based on the novel by Roderick Mann] doesn't have quite the comic and narrative richness of Ronald Neame's Ealing Studios classics, this variation on the "great imposter" plot device is still an unalloyed pleasure to watch.

Built solidly upon a fluid, comic virtuoso performance by Victor Banerjee, the picaresque fable of an impoverished refugee from Calcutta faking it as a doctor to London's upper crust [in 1975] makes some jaunty points about racism, gullibility and pluck.

Even though he's a deceiver, sincerity is a bedrock trait of the *Foreign Body* hero, Ram Das, and Banerjee is free to romp with bug-eyed zaniness through the improbable adventures of this Asian naif abroad.

•

FOREIGN CORRESPONDENT

1940, 119 mins, US Ⓥ ⦿ b/w

Dir Alfred Hitchcock ***Prod*** Walter Wanger ***Scr*** Charles Bennett, Joan Harrison, James Hilton, Robert Benchley ***Ph*** Rudolph Mate ***Ed*** Otho Lovering, Dorothy Spencer ***Mus*** Alfred Newman ***Art*** Alexander Golitzen, Richard Irvine

Act Joel McCrea, Laraine Day, Herbert Marshall, George Sanders, Albert Basserman, Edmund Gwenn (Wanger/United Artists)

Story is essentially the old cops-and-robbers. But it has been set in a background of international political intrigue of the largest order. It has a war flavor, the events taking place immediately before and at the start of World War II; yet it can in no sense be called a war picture. Mystery and intrigue march in place.

Add to all this a cast carefully selected by director Alfred Hitchcock to the last, unimportant lackey. Joel McCrea neatly blends the self-confidence and naiveté of the reporter-hero, while Laraine Day, virtually a fledgling in pictures, only in the most difficult sequences misses out as a top-grade dramatic player. Vet Herbert Marshall as the heavy, George Sanders as McCrea's fellow-reporter, 72-year-old refugee Albert Basserman as a Dutch diplomat, Edmund Gwenn as a not-to-be-trusted bodyguard, Eduardo Ciannelli as the usual hissable villain, are all tops. Comic touch is provided by Robert Benchley and Eddie Conrad.

Story uncorks with the editor of a New York paper going nuts because his foreign correspondents cable nothing but rumor and speculation. He hits on the idea of sending one of his police reporters to dig factual material out of the Europe of August 1939. McCrea, who knows nothing of foreign affairs, immediately runs into the tallest story a reporter can imagine—a big-league peace organization, headed by Marshall, which is operating as nothing but a spy ring.

McCrea runs into the double-cross organization when it kidnaps an honest Dutch diplomat (Basserman) and assassinates his imposter to give the impression that he is dead. Assassination sequence in the rain on the broad steps of an Amsterdam building (set is a tremendous and excellent recreation of a whole block in Amsterdam) is virtually a newsreel in its starkness.

1940: NOMINATIONS: Best Picture, Supp. Actor (Albert Basserman), Original Screenplay, B&W Cinematography, B&W Art Direction, Special Effects

•

FOREVER AMBER

1947, 140 mins, US col

Dir Otto Preminger ***Prod*** William Perlberg ***Scr*** Philip Dunne, Ring Lardner, Jr. ***Ph*** Leon Shamroy ***Ed*** Louis Loeffler ***Mus*** David Raksin ***Art*** Lyle R. Wheeler

Act Linda Darnell, Cornel Wilde, Richard Greene, George Sanders, Jessica Tandy, Anne Revere (20th Century-Fox)

Here is a $4 million (and claimed to be more) picture that looks its cost. That goes even for the lost footage through mishap with Peggy Cummins, the original candidate until Linda Darnell replaced. And she does quite well.

The lusty yarn [from the novel by Kathleen Winsor] is treated for what it is. Darnell runs the gamut from romantic opportunist to prison degradation and up again to being the king's favorite and finally a discarded mistress, grateful that the royal equerry invites her to supper after Charles II gives her the brush-off.

In between there's a wealth of derring-do, 17th-century knavery and debauchery, the love of a good woman (Jane Ball), and the rest of a depraved court's atmosphere. It's solid escapology.

Darnell manages her chameleon Amber character very well. Her blonde beauty shows off well in Technicolor, and she is equally convincing when she is thrown in a pauper's gaol.

Cornel Wilde is the No. 1 juve, although Glenn Langan suggests he might have made an excellent choice for that role instead of a secondary swain. Richard Haydn plays his a.k. role well as the arrogant earl who Amber premeditatedly weds in order to gain a title. John Russell is convincing as the highwayman; Anne Revere is sufficiently despicable as a keeper of a thieves' den; Jessica Tandy does all right as Amber's maid; George Sanders turns a neat character.

1947: NOMINATION: Best Scoring of a Dramatic Picture

•

FOREVER AND A DAY

1943, 104 mins, US Ⓥ b/w

Dir Rene Clair, Edmund Goulding, Cedric Hardwicke, Frank Lloyd, Victor Saville, Robert Stevenson, Herbert Wilcox ***Scr*** Charles Bennett, C. S. Forrester, Lawrence Hazard, Michael Hogan, W. P. Lipscomb, Alice Duer Miller, John Van Druten, Alan Campbell, Peter Godfrey, S. M. Herzig, Christopher Isherwood, Gene Lockhart, R. C. Sheriff, Claudine West, Norman Corwin, Jack Hartfield, James Hilton, Emmet Lavery, Frederick Lonsdale, Donald Ogden Stewart, Keith Winter ***Ph*** Robert de Grasse, Lee Garmes, Russell Metty, Nicholas Musuraca ***Ed*** Elmo J. Williams, George Crone ***Mus*** Anthony Collins

Act Merle Oberon, Gladys Cooper, C. Aubrey Smith, Claude Rains, Anna Neagle, Ray Milland (RKO)

Forever and a Day is a sentimental romantic-adventure yarn, encompassing in cavalcade manner Britain's epochal struggles to retain the integrity of an empire and the freedom of its people in face of periodical threats of would-be world conquerors. Interwoven is the quaint history of a picturesque London mansion—its illustrious builder and his descendants—built during the Napoleonic period, that withstands the ravages of time and world-shattering conflict until the days of the Nazi blitz.

In a star-studded cast, including some 45 name players, a number of top-notchers are necessarily limited. However, a large proportion of the subordinate sequences have been handled with telling effect.

Picture, in the making for about a year, rolled up a negative cost of around $500,000 at RKO, which financed the production. This is exclusive of the players, who undertook the assignment on a gratis basis, some 21 writers and the seven accredited directors who also contributed their services.

Yarn revolves around the fusing of two families after a feud dating back to the early part of the 19th century when C. Aubrey Smith, as the robust, swashbuckling British admiral, first built the house. Claude Rains, as the vindictive guardian of Anna Neagle, who runs away to marry one of the Smith tribe, does not impress as the menace.

•

FOREVER IN LOVE

SEE: PRIDE OF THE MARINES

•

FOREVER MINE

1999, 115 mins, UK/US Ⓥ ⦿ ▭ col

Dir Paul Schrader ***Prod*** Damita Nikapota, Kathleen Haase, Amy J. Kaufman ***Scr*** Paul Schrader ***Ph*** John Bailey ***Ed*** Kristina Boden ***Mus*** Angelo Badalamenti ***Art*** Francois Seguin

Act Joseph Fiennes, Ray Liotta, Gretchen Mol, Vincent Laresca (Moonstar/J&M)

After reaching a career high point with his *Affliction*, Paul Schrader hits a low watermark with *Forever Mine*, a strenuously straight-faced film noir wannabe that edges perilously close to self-parody. This glumly unimaginative rumination on transcendent love in a modern criminal context is outfitted with staggeringly routine pulp conventions that have in no way been tweaked, subverted or played with by a normally outstanding writer who certainly knows the territory.

Yarn sports two story strands spanning 14 years. In a jet heading for New York City sits well-heeled Latino Manuel Esquema (Joseph Fiennes), the right side of his face hideously scarred and his right arm outfitted with a prosthetic hand, traveling with his bulked-up buddy, Javier (Vincent Laresca).

Jump back to 1974 and Fiennes materializes as Alan Riply, a lanky towel boy at an ornate Florida resort. When he sees a stunning blonde vision arise from the sea, he knows he must have her, even though Ella (Gretchen Mol) is newly married to businessman and nascent tough guy Mark Brice (Ray Liotta). The penniless Alan manages to seduce the young bride.

Ella confesses her dalliance to a suspicious Mark, who pulls strings to get him jailed, blasts the defenseless young man in the face and leaves him for dead at the film's halfway point—the big mistake that, of course, comes back to haunt him 14 years later.

Fiennes is aggressively sincere and sadly bereft of anything resembling humor or irony. Liotta has trod his thug's ground before in more convincing fashion, while Mol is physically fetching but lacking in any depth or mystery.

●

FOREVER YOUNG

1992, 102 mins, US Ⓥ ⦿ col

Dir Steve Miner ***Prod*** Bruce Davey ***Scr*** Jeffrey Abrams ***Ph*** Russell Boyd ***Ed*** John Poll ***Mus*** Jerry Goldsmith ***Art*** Gregg Fonseca

Act Mel Gibson, Jamie Lee Curtis, Elijah Wood, Isabel Glasser, George Wendt, Joe Morton (Warner/Icon)

Warner Bros. has a big, rousing, old-fashioned romance on its hands, a perfect "women's picture" alternative to action fare and kid-oriented sequels.

The action begins in 1939, as test pilot Daniel (Mel Gibson) can't bring himself to propose to Helen (Isabel Glasser), right up until the moment she walks in front of a speeding truck. Helen ends up in a coma, and the distraught Daniel volunteers for an experiment in which his best friend Harry (George Wendt) is to freeze him for a year in an early test of cryogenics.

Cut to 1992, when Daniel is thawed out by two mischievous 10-year-olds and moves in with one of the boys (Elijah Wood) and his single mom (Jamie Lee Curtis). With the Army in pursuit of their long-forgotten experiment gone awry, the film takes some clever and extremely satisfying turns.

The director manages to toe the line of melodrama without ever slipping over into camp, balancing those elements with humor and suspense to carry *Forever Young* if not over the moon, at least into the clouds.

●

FORGET PARIS

1995, 101 mins, US Ⓥ ⦿ col

Dir Billy Crystal ***Prod*** Billy Crystal ***Scr*** Billy Crystal, Lowell Ganz, Babaloo Mandel ***Ph*** Don Burgess ***Ed*** Kent Beyda ***Mus*** Marc Shaiman ***Art*** Terence Marsh

Act Billy Crystal, Debra Winger, Joe Mantegna, Cynthia Stevenson, Richard Masur, Julie Kavner (Castle Rock/Face/Columbia)

Packed with a potentially unwieldy mix of shtick, bathos, sitcom-friendly slapstick and echoes of Woody Allen's angst-ridden yuppie romances, *Forget Paris* teeters on the edge of disaster, just like the dauntless courtship that serves as the core of this comedic look at midlife love and marriage. But, amazingly, actor/cowriter/director/producer Billy Crystal manages to keep the predictable plotline and discordant elements from stymieing the pic's pull on the tear ducts and prod to the funny bone.

Sportswriter Andy (Joe Mantegna) and his fiancée, Liz (Cynthia Stevenson), a fortyish duo on the verge of nuptials, are sitting in a restaurant. Andy starts regaling Liz with the details of the romantic travails of his friends Mickey (Crystal) and Ellen (Debra Winger). As the story unfolds, other guests arrive, including car salesman Craig (Richard Masur) and his wife, Lucy (Julie Kavner), who add their own details to the Mickey and Ellen legend, which grows darker as the tale unwinds.

Mickey, one of the top referees in the National Basketball Assoc., fell in love with airlines exec Ellen four years earlier while visiting Paris. While the couple's week in Paris was full of laughs, trysts and visits to the Louvre, the marriage that follows is a nightmare of Los Angeles and San Fernando Valley ennui.

Crystal at the top of his game can shotgun one-liners and bon mots while setting up comedic set pieces that deliver howling laughs. Stevenson takes a supporting part that is basically reactive and just about steals the movie. The rest of the cast is sturdy, as is the lensing and Crystal's generally unobtrusive direction.

●

FORGIVEN SINNER, THE

SEE: LEON MORIN, PRETRE

●

FOR HEAVEN'S SAKE

1926, 58 mins, US ⊗ b/w

Dir Sam Taylor ***Prod*** Harold Lloyd ***Scr*** John Grey, Ted Wilde, Clyde Bruckman, Ralph Spence ***Ph*** Walter Lundin ***Ed*** Allen McNeil ***Art*** Liell K. Vedder

Act Harold Lloyd, Jobyna Ralston, Noah Young, James Mason, Paul Weigel (Lloyd/Paramount)

The first Harold Lloyd comedy feature to be made by the comedian's own company for release through Paramount. As a gag picture it is a perfect wow. As to actual story, there is very little in the picture. Just a slender thread of a love tale on which to hang the gags.

Lloyd portrays a young society boy who has more money than he knows what to do with. That's the uptown angle of the picture. The downtown end has Jobyna Ralston as the daughter of a mission worker in the slums. Lloyd and the daughter meet. He falls and pulls a flock of laughs in a chase designed to round up business for the mission.

When Lloyd announces his engagement to wed the little mission worker, his society friends decide that they are going to take a hand in matters and kidnap the groom-to-be, with the reception committee of gangsters going after them to find out what it is all about.

Lloyd, Ralston and Noah Young carry the entire picture and the action is always in Lloyd's hands. The gags are so numerous that they have to be seen to be appreciated.

●

FOR LOVE OF IVY

1968, 101 mins, US Ⓥ col

Dir Daniel Mann ***Prod*** Edgar J. Scherick, Jay Weston ***Scr*** Robert Alan Aurthur ***Ph*** Joseph Coffey ***Ed*** Patricia Jaffe ***Mus*** Quincy Jones ***Art*** Peter Dohanos

Act Sidney Poitier, Abby Lincoln, Beau Bridges, Nan Martin, Lauri Peters, Carroll O'Connor (Palomar)

Ivy is at bottom an innocuous romantic comedy, not unlike those cranked out regularly in the 1940s, without sufficiently high-powered drama, clever humor or moving romance to offer. What little force the pic has stems from Sidney Poitier's clear enjoyment of a role cut from Cary Grant cloth.

Simple story line provided by Poitier is not rich in character motivation. He plays a lovable rogue who runs a (literally) floating crap game in the van of a truck, a gambling ploy that will probably strike even the most inveterate New York gamblers as doubtfully authentic.

Prodded by two teenagers into dating their late-20s maid (Abby Lincoln), who has threatened to abandon their household to the stupefying incompetence of their mother, he gradually falls in love.

Lincoln has a spirited freshness and supporting cast all performs diligently.

1968: NOMINATION: Best Song ("For the Love of Ivy")

●

FOR LOVE OF THE GAME

1999, 137 mins, US Ⓥ ⦿ ▭ col

Dir Sam Raimi ***Prod*** Armyan Bernstein, Amy Robinson ***Scr*** Dana Stevens ***Ph*** John Bailey ***Ed*** Eric L. Beason, Arthur Coburn ***Mus*** Basil Poledouris ***Art*** Neil Spisak

Act Kevin Costner, Kelly Preston, John C. Reilly, Jena Malone, Brian Cox, J. K. Simmons (Beacon/Tig/Mirage/Universal)

As all-American and all-Hollywood as a movie can get in the late '90s, *For Love of the Game* represents a modest personal comeback for star Kevin Costner [after *The Postman* and *Message in a Bottle*], in the best combo of his strengths as a romantic lead and athletic guy since *Tin Cup* (1996). This marks a kind of capper on Costner's baseball trilogy, from the minor leagues of *Bull Durham* to the fantasy of *Field of Dreams* to this highly uneven study of an aging vet in his swan song game in the bigs.

Few genres have consistently landed in the cellar as often as baseball movies, and no picture has captured the absurdly funny nature and characters of the sport. Pic ignores the game's grit and eccentricities in favor of a mood of valedictory romance, both for the game and for its lead characters.

Per many superstar throwers, Billy Chapel (Costner) has his own designated catcher in Gus Sinski (John C. Reilly). Sinski's against manager Frank Perry's (J. K. Simmons) decision to pitch Chapel against the contending New York Yankees in Yankee Stadium—especially since the last-place Detroit Tigers' season is over—but Chapel's life soon gives him motivation.

In a set of contrived plot moves taken faithfully from Michael Shaara's brief, posthumously published novel, Chapel is stood up by his g.f. (Kelly Preston) and informed by Tigers owner Gary Wheeler (Brian Cox) that he's selling the club. Dialogue is as pat as this sounds, but tech credits raise several moments of the pic to majestic heights

●

FOR LOVE OR MONEY

1963, 108 mins, US col

Dir Michael Gordon ***Prod*** Robert Arthur ***Scr*** Larry Markes, Michael Morris ***Ph*** Clifford Stine ***Ed*** Alma Macrorie ***Mus*** Frank DeVol ***Art*** Alexander Golitzen, Malcolm Brown

Act Kirk Douglas, Mitzi Gaynor, Gig Young, Thelma Ritter, Julie Newmar, Leslie Parrish (Universal)

The glib, sharp scenario is seasoned with spicy spoofery of three worthy targets: motivational research, physical fitness and modern art—and the people who practice these fads and/or professions.

The wild plot has to do with a wealthy and eccentric widow's scheme to marry her three daughters off to the candidates of her choice, a goal for which she assigns her attorney the additional duties of matchmaker. All of this is engineered at a bright, effervescent clip by director Michael Gordon.

Kirk Douglas uncorks a flair for zany comedics as the pivotal figure in the proceedings. He plays the attorney-matchmaker who falls for the eldest daughter, a consumer research bug with Madison Avenue phraseology vivaciously played by Mitzi Gaynor. The other daughters are Julie Newmar, a delectable blonde amazon as the health addict, and Leslie Parrish, slightly miscast as the pretty beatnik. Even Thelma Ritter, as the screwball widow, gets the glamor treatment.

Gig Young delivers another of his amiable boozing wolf-playboy characterizations. William Bendix comes through nicely as a good-naturedly hapless Pinkerton.

●

FOR LOVE OR MONEY

(UK: THE CONCIERGE)

1993, 94 mins, US Ⓥ ⦿ col

Dir Barry Sonnenfeld ***Prod*** Brian Grazer ***Scr*** Mark Rosenthal, Lawrence Konner ***Ph*** Oliver Wood ***Ed*** Jim Miller ***Mus*** Bruce Broughton ***Art*** Peter Larkin

Act Michael J. Fox, Gabrielle Anwar, Anthony Higgins, Michael Tucker, Bob Balaban, Udo Kier (Imagine/Universal)

Michael J. Fox has charm to burn in *For Love or Money*. A contemporary spin on bygone romantic comedies, the tale of an ambitious young man and the seemingly elusive woman in his life has a definite emotional pull. It falls short on story, however, and no amount of good humor can deter the thin tale from evaporating before the final clinch.

Doug Ireland (Fox) takes on the role of head concierge at an upscale Manhattan hotel with the zeal of a Sammy Glick. What makes Doug tick is the dream of putting together the financial package for a luxury hotel. Unlike the fictional prototype, Doug wouldn't step over someone to reach his goal. The only trouble can come from his association with charismatic financier Christian Hanover (Anthony Higgins). Hanover just happens to be deep into an extramarital affair with Andy (Gabrielle Anwar), the very woman for whom Doug would actually take time out in his busy schedule. Just how much crow can Doug eat for $5 million? Healthy guy that he is, quite a bit.

Call it screwball, call it zany, call it just a bit too convenient for comfort. Writers Mark Rosenthal and Lawrence Konner lack the deft touch of Preston Sturges or Billy Wilder, and director Barry Sonnenfeld has not quite perfected a modern Lubitsch touch.

●

FOR ME AND MY GAL

1942, 104 mins, US Ⓥ ⦿ b/w

Dir Busby Berkeley ***Prod*** Arthur Freed ***Scr*** Richard Sherman, Fred Finklehoffe, Sid Silvers ***Ph*** William Daniels ***Ed*** Ben Lewis ***Mus*** Georgie Stoll (dir.), Roger Edens (adapt.) ***Art*** Cedric Gibbons, Gabriel Scognamillo

Act Judy Garland, George Murphy, Gene Kelly, Marta Eggerth, Richard Quine, Keenan Wynn (M-G-M)

Story [by Howard Emmett Rogers] of vaudeville troupers before and during the First World War is obvious, naive and sentimental. It's also genuine and affectionate and lively.

Picture's title is taken from one of the song numbers, the oldie, "For Me and My Gal." The tune that brings Judy Garland and Gene Kelly together, first as vaudeville team and ultimately as a romance, it gets a sock presentation in a song-and-dance routine by them.

The picture's early scenes, as the vaudevillians tour the sticks and dream of some day playing the Palace, are colorful and convincing. Interpolated through them and the subsequent war sequences are numerous old faves, from "Beautiful Doll" and "You Wore a Tulip" to the World War I standbys, "Over There," "Long, Long Trail," "Oui, Oui, Marie" and so on.

Garland is a knockout as the warm-hearted young song-and-dance girl, selling a number of the songs persuasively and getting by neatly in the hoofing routines with Kelly. George Murphy is ingratiating as Garland's faithful but mute suitor, while Kelly gives a vividly drawn portrayal of the song-and-dance man and imperfect hero, practically another "Pal Joey" character that he played so well on Broadway in the musical of that name.

●

FORMULA, THE
1980, 117 mins, US Ⓥ ⊙ col
Dir John G. Avildsen ***Prod*** Steve Shagan ***Scr*** Steve Shagan ***Ph*** James Crabe ***Ed*** David Bretherton, John G. Avildsen, John Carter ***Mus*** Bill Conti ***Art*** Herman A. Blumenthal
Act George C. Scott, Marthe Keller, Marlon Brando, John Gielgud, Beatrice Straight, Richard Lynch (M-G-M)

M-G-M refused to let director John Avildsen take his name off this picture. According to Avildsen, it was not his original cut, nor producer-writer Steve Shagan's cut, but sort of a combination of the two, plus a few snips and patches by M-G-M president David Begelman. Given the combined efforts of 14 Oscar nominees and a solid bestseller [by Shagan] to start from, it's truly amazing that *The Formula* is such a clump of sludge, impossible to understand for at least an hour before it grinds to a halt.

Initial sequences solidly establish the closing hours of World War II when a German general (Richard Lynch) is entrusted with top secret documents to take to Switzerland in hopes the Nazis can use them to bargain for amnesty. But Lynch is captured by a U.S. major (Robin Clarke) who recognizes what the secrets will be worth in the postwar world of commerce.

Cut forward 35 years and Clarke is a fresh corpse, murdered in his bed. George C. Scott is called in to investigate the murder of his old friend and before long establishes Clarke had some mysterious dealings with oil supertycoon Marlon Brando.

Appearing grotesquely fat and ridiculous, Brando apparently thinks he's making some visual comment on the nature of his character.

1980: NOMINATION: Best Cinematography

•

FOR PETE'S SAKE
1974, 90 mins, US Ⓥ col
Dir Peter Yates ***Prod*** Martin Erlichman, Stanley Shapiro ***Scr*** Stanley Shapiro, Maurice Richlin ***Ph*** Laszlo Kovacs ***Ed*** Frank Keller ***Art*** Gene Callaghan
Act Barbra Streisand, Michael Sarrazin, Estelle Parsons, William Redfield, Molly Picon, Louis Zorich (Rastar/Columbia)

For Pete's Sake is a flaccid, relentlessly "zany" comedy that in the 1960s might have been offered to Doris Day.

Coscripter and coproducer Stanley Shapiro, who penned those Doris Day–Rock Hudson comedies of yore, has tailor-made this tale of a brash Brooklyn housewife (Barbra Streisand) married to a poor taxi driver (Michael Sarrazin) who yearns to return to school. Sarrazin is given inside info about a pending meat deal between the U.S. and the Soviet Union which promises to zoom the price of pork bellies. (Pic's original title was *July Pork Bellies*.)

To get the $3,000 necessary to invest in pork belly futures on the stock exchange, Streisand secretly goes to a loan shark. When the Soviet deal is delayed and she can't pay up, her "contract" is sold. Each contract sale increases the debt while allowing maximum opportunity for broad comedy shtick.

•

FORREST GUMP
1994, 142 mins, US Ⓥ ⊙ ▭ col
Dir Robert Zemeckis ***Prod*** Wendy Finerman, Steve Tisch, Steve Starkey ***Scr*** Eric Roth ***Ph*** Don Burgess ***Ed*** Arthur Schmidt ***Mus*** Alan Silvestri ***Art*** Rick Carter
Act Tom Hanks, Robin Wright, Gary Sinise, Mykelti Williamson, Sally Field, Michael Humphreys (Paramount)

A picaresque story of a simpleton's charmed odyssey through 30 years of tumultuous American History, *Forrest Gump* is whimsy with a strong cultural spine. Elegantly made and winningly acted by Tom Hanks in his first outing since his Oscar-winning *Philadelphia*, Robert Zemeckis's technically dazzling film will make post-yuppies feel they're seeing their lives passing by onscreen.

Gump narrates his story to a succession of listeners at a Savannah, GA, bus stop. Raised in an old plantation mansion by his abandoned mother (Sally Field), young Forrest (Michael Humphreys) finds his only friend in a beautiful little girl, Jenny (Hanna R. Hall).

It's at the U. of Alabama that the grown-up Forrest has his first date with destiny, as a dopey-looking bystander next to Gov. George Wallace as the first black students are admitted through the school's doors. After another encounter, with JFK, Forrest heads for Vietnam. On the way, he meets Bubba Blue (Mykelti Williamson), who's like Forrest's black brother.

Forrest saves the lives of several men, including his commanding officer, Lt. Dan (Gary Sinise), and receives the Medal of Honor from LBJ. Through it all, Forrest retains his love and idealized image of Jenny (Robin Wright).

Pic is a bit long and excessive at times, but this is more than compensated for by its humor and sharp-witted storytelling [from Winston Groom's novel]. Affecting a Southern drawl and affable sweetness, Hanks manages to keep one intrigued and amused throughout. Sinise and Williamson are excellent. Wright has little to play until the late moments.

1994: Best Picture, Director, Actor (Tom Hanks), Adapted Screenplay, Art Direction, Film Editing, Visual Effects

NOMINATIONS: Best Supp. Actor (Gary Sinise), Cinematography, Sound, Sound Effects Editing, Makeup, Original Score

•

FORSAKING ALL OTHERS
1934, 84 mins, US Ⓥ b/w
Dir W. S. Van Dyke ***Prod*** Bernard H. Hyman ***Scr*** Joseph L. Mankiewicz ***Ph*** Gregg Toland, George Folsey ***Ed*** Tom Held ***Mus*** William Axt
Act Joan Crawford, Clark Gable, Robert Montgomery, Charles Butterworth, Billie Burke, Frances Drake (M-G-M)

The picture alternates between scintillating, gay and sophisticated dialog, and such hoke as a bicycle ride with Joan Crawford on Robert Montgomery's handlebars, and both (dressed in white) catapulting over a fence into a pig-stye.

At other points Crawford falls off a masseuse's table, does a slide in the rain, is tousled in an automobile crash. As for Montgomery, he is, figuratively, just a banana peel migrating from sequence to sequence.

Custard pie or not the picture is excellent diversion, directed and written, apart from the debatable scenes, with fine skill. It was a stage play by Edward Roberts and Frank Cavett during 1933.

Picture gets into gear with a sly siren rendered into convincing felinity by Frances Drake copping Montgomery on the eve of his impending marriage. Crawford is literally left waiting at and in the church. Thereafter her wounded pride, the remorse of Montgomery, the nastiness of the scheming wife (Drake), and "big brother" Clark Gable form the guideposts of the action. On the performance end it is one of Crawford's best. She is believable throughout.

•

FORT APACHE
1948, 127 mins, US Ⓥ ⊙ b/w
Dir John Ford ***Prod*** Merian C. Cooper, John Ford ***Scr*** Frank S. Nugent ***Ph*** Archie Stout ***Ed*** Jack Murray ***Mus*** Richard Hageman ***Art*** James Basevi
Act John Wayne, Henry Fonda, Shirley Temple, John Agar, Pedro Armendariz, Victor McLaglen (Argosy/RKO)

Mass action, humorous byplay in the western cavalry outpost, deadly suspense, and romance are masterfully combined in this production [suggested by the story *Massacre* by James Warner Bellah]. Integrated with the tremendous action is a superb musical score by Richard Hageman. Score uses sound effects as tellingly as the music notes to point up the thrills. In particular, the massacre scene where the deadly drumming of the Indian ponies makes more potent the action that transpires.

Cast is as tremendous as the scope achieved by Ford's direction and, as a consequence, some of the roles are very short but all effective. Henry Fonda is the colonel, embittered because he has been assigned to the remote fort after a brilliant war record.

John Wayne makes a virile cavalry captain, wise in the way of the Indian. Shirley Temple, the colonel's daughter, perks her sequences in romance with John Agar, West Point graduate. Latter impresses. Pedro Armendariz is excellent as a sergeant. Making up a group of tough topkicks that are responsible for the film's humor are Victor McLaglen, Dick Foran and Jack Pennick.

•

FORT APACHE THE BRONX
1981, 123 mins, US Ⓥ ⊙ col
Dir Daniel Petrie ***Prod*** Martin Richards, Tom Fiorello ***Scr*** Heywood Gould ***Ph*** John Alcott ***Ed*** Rita Roland ***Mus*** Jonathan Tunick ***Art*** Ben Edwards
Act Paul Newman, Ed Asner, Ken Wahl, Danny Aiello, Rachel Ticotin, Pam Grier (Time-Life)

Driving relentlessly to make points that are almost pointless, *Fort Apache The Bronx* is a very patchy picture, strong on dialog and acting and exceedingly weak on story.

Even while shooting, *Apache* drew protests from neighborhood factions claiming it would show only the bad about the Bronx and ignore the good. Because of that, the pic starts with a tip-of-the-hat title card to the "law abiding" citizens of the community. But that's the last to be seen of them.

Title is taken from the nickname for a real police station uptown, literally surrounded and often under siege from thieves, murderers, hookers, junkies, dealers.

One of the cops (Danny Aiello) is a murderer himself and even the heroes (Paul Newman and Ken Wahl) aren't all that admirable in their feeble attempts to control crime in the streets, their abject cynicism about life in the station house and vacillation over whether to snitch on Aiello after they watch him kill a kid.

Typical of the problem director Daniel Petrie creates for himself, he introduces Pam Grier right away as a drug-crazed cop killer and brings her back a couple of more times for additional murders, effectively grizzly in detail. But she never says much and there's never an inkling of what motivates her, other than dope.

•

FOR THE BOYS
1991, 145 mins, US Ⓥ ⊙ col
Dir Mark Rydell ***Prod*** Bette Midler, Bonnie Bruckheimer ***Scr*** Marshall Brickman, Neal Jimenez, Lindy Laub ***Ph*** Stephen Goldblatt ***Ed*** Jerry Greenberg, Jere Huggins ***Mus*** Dave Grusin ***Art*** Assheton Gorton
Act Bette Midler, James Caan, George Segal, Patrick O'Neal, Chris Rydell, Arye Gross (20th Century-Fox/All Girl)

Fox's song-driven wartime showbiz meller *For the Boys* is a big, creaky balloon of a movie that lumbers along like a dirigible in a Thanksgiving parade, festooned with patriotic sentiment. Ambitious effort spans the 50-year relationship of two USO entertainers (Bette Midler and James Caan) whose song, dance and innuendo carries them through three wars.

Allegedly a "love story" between two difficult people who are each married to others, pic suffers from the couple's lack of electricity. Story begins in the present day, when a dapper production assistant (Arye Gross) arrives by limo to pick up Dixie for a major awards show. Midler makes a shocker of an entrance; pic then dissolves to 1942, when she was a bubbly young mother called up to join the famous Eddie Sparks in a London wartime revue.

The picture doesn't move, it regroups: from Europe to North Africa, then to Korea, through the bloodbath of McCarthyism and finally to Vietnam. The details of costume and design are convincing, but the main idea isn't.

Midler steams through the outing with sass and charm, eking out laughs on her own merit whenever the script stumbles. But Caan, in a role that recalls his pallid backup to Barbra Streisand in *Funny Lady*, seems pinioned by the script and generally uncomfortable.

1991: NOMINATION: Best Actress (Bette Midler)

•

FOR THE LOVE OF BENJI
1977, 85 mins, US Ⓥ col
Dir Joe Camp ***Prod*** Ben Vaughn ***Scr*** Joe Camp ***Ph*** Don Reddy ***Ed*** Leon Seith ***Mus*** Euel Box, Betty Box ***Art*** Harland Wright
Act Patsy Garrett, Cynthia Smith, Allen Fiuzat, Ed Nelson, Art Vasil, Peter Bowles (Mulberry Square)

Only a heart of steel can resist this pooch. Item finds Benji in Greece embroiled in a tale of international espionage.

Director Joe Camp would have audiences believe that Benji is an unwitting participant in this piece of subterfuge. But this pooch is so smart that chances are he had the plot unraveled 15 minutes after Ed Nelson, as a most unmenacing villain, drugged him and placed the vital info about a scientist with a plan to turn one barrel of oil into 10, on his paw.

The tale itself is slim, and while the plot is a bit contrived, and all of the loose ends tied up a bit too neatly in the film's last five minutes, it should be remembered that *For the Love of Benji* is merely a star vehicle. The idea is to watch the dog act.

•

FORTRESS
1993, 89 mins, Australia/US Ⓥ ⊙ col
Dir Stuart Gordon ***Prod*** John Davis, John Flock ***Scr*** Steve Feinberg, Troy Neighbors, Terry Curtis Fox ***Ph*** David Eggby ***Ed*** Timothy Wellburn ***Mus*** Frederic Talghorn ***Art*** David Copping
Act Christopher Lambert, Kurtwood Smith, Loryn Locklin, Lincoln Kilpatrick, Clifton Gonzales Gonzales, Jeffrey Combs (Village Roadshow/Davis)

Fortress is a grim, sometimes bloody, futuristic prison picture that has been well produced and directed within the limitations of a predictable, uninspired screenplay. Fans of director Stuart Gordon's early schlock efforts (*Re-Animator*, *From Beyond*) will be disappointed to find the helmer working with more conventional material.

Pic was shot with an Australian crew in the Warner Roadshow Movie World Studios in Queensland, and David

Copping's production design of a privately run prison of the future built 30 stories underground is the star of the film.

Pic is set in the U.S. after exploding population and depleted resources have resulted in a law against couples having more than one child. The Brennicks (Christopher Lambert and Loryn Locklin) lost their first baby, and now Locklin is pregnant a second time, a felony.

The couple are nabbed trying to cross into Mexico, and both wind up in the Fortress. Locklin manages to charm all-seeing prison director Kurtwood Smith, and uses every opportunity to plan her husband's escape. Too much of the dialogue sounds as if it were written for Dennis Hopper.

FORT SAGANNE

1984, 180 mins, France Ⓥ ▭ col

Dir Alain Corneau *Prod* Albina du Boisrouvray *Scr* Alain Corneau, Henri du Turenne, Louis Gardel *Ph* Bruno Nuytten *Ed* Thierry Derocles *Mus* Philippe Sarde *Art* Jean-Pierre Kohut-Svelko

Act Gerard Depardieu, Philippe Noiret, Catherine Deneuve, Sophie Marceau, Michel Duchaussoy, Robin Renucci (Albina/Films A2/SFPC)

Fort Saganne, which has checked in as one of France's most expensive films at a cost upwards of $6 million, is something of a throwback to the 1920s and '30s colonial sagas that thrived on local screens. Alain Corneau's film of Louis Gardel's prize-winning 1980 novel about an empire builder in the Sahara in the early years of the century, based on the real-life exploits of the author's grandfather, is often fine in its large-scale reconstruction of a time and place and a mentality, but falters in its attempts to inscribe well-detailed characters in its wide-screen canvas.

Charles Saganne is an aspiring young military officer of peasant stock who achieves quasi legendary glory during the French penetration of the Sahara between 1910 and 1914. Gerard Depardieu, who cuts a smashing figure in desert military garb, perched on a camel, followed by a column of faithful, taciturn Arab warriors, brings all his talent and presence to the role, but the immediacy of the personage is only intermittently felt. Costar Philippe Noiret is full-bloodedly excellent as the ambitious colonel seeking general's stars with his advocacy of aggressive military action in the Sahara.

Film is weakest in describing Depardieu's romantic relationships. His brief but intense affair with special guest star Catherine Deneuve, as a journalist who maneuvers him into bed provocatively, lacks fire and poignancy. And young Sophie Marceau gets insufficient screen time to make any impression as the young bourgeois girl who pines for Depardieu and later becomes his wife, then widow.

Without being an anachronistic apology of France's imperialistic past, or a revisionist chronicle, pic does admirably revive some of the epic sweep and romanticism of the old French sagas.

•

FORTUNE, THE

1975, 88 mins, US ▭ col

Dir Mike Nichols *Prod* Mike Nichols, Don Devlin *Scr* Adrien Joyce [= Carol Eastman] *Ph* John A. Alonzo *Ed* Stu Linder *Mus* David Shire *Art* Richard Sylbert

Act Jack Nicholson, Warren Beatty, Stockard Channing, Florence Stanley, Scatman Crothers (Columbia)

The Fortune is an occasionally enjoyable comedy trifle, starring Jack Nicholson and Warren Beatty as bumbling kidnappers of heiress Stockard Channing, who is excellent in her first major screen role. Very classy 1920s production values often merit more attention than the plot.

Beatty elopes with Channing but, not yet free of a former wife, Nicholson actually marries her. Trio sets up housekeeping in Los Angeles, and after Channing is disinherited, the guys try to kill her. If lugging around a passed-out intoxicated girl in clumsy murder attempts does not offend sensibilities, then the alleged fun may be passable.

David Shire superbly recreates some old Joe Venuti-Eddi Lang jazz band arrangements.

•

FORTUNE COOKIE, THE

(UK: MEET WHIPLASH WILLIE)

1966, 125 mins, US Ⓥ ⊙ ▭ b/w

Dir Billy Wilder *Prod* Billy Wilder *Scr* Billy Wilder, I.A.L. Diamond *Ph* Joseph LaShelle *Ed* Daniel Mandell *Mus* André Previn *Art* Robert Luthardt

Act Jack Lemmon, Walter Matthau, Ron Rich, Cliff Osmond, Judi West, Lurene Tuttle (United Artists/Mirisch)

Producer-director-writer Billy Wilder presents in *The Fortune Cookie* another bittersweet comedy commentary on contemporary U.S. morés.

Generally amusing (often wildly so) but overlong, the pic is pegged on an insurance fraud in which Jack Lemmon and Walter Matthau are the conspirators.

Original screenplay is by Wilder, paired for seventh time with I.A.L. Diamond. Plot turns on the complications following TV cameraman Lemmon's accidental injury at the hands of grid star Ron Rich. Matthau, shyster lawyer and Lemmon's brother-in-law, sees fancy damages in the injury, and ex-wife Judi West smells money in a fake reunion with Lemmon.

Lemmon, confined perforce to sickroom immobility (bandages, wheelchair, etc.) is saddled most of the time with the colorless image of a man vacillating with his conscience over the fraud, and its effect on Rich, whose playing has deteriorated from remorse.

Title derives from a scene where Lemmon breaks a fortune cookie, only to find inside Abraham Lincoln's famous aphorism about fooling all/some people all/some of the time.

1966: Best Supp. Actor (Walter Matthau).

NOMINATION: Best Original Story & Screenplay, B&W Cinematography, B&W Art Direction

•

FORT WORTH

1951, 80 mins, US col

Dir Edwin L. Marin *Prod* Anthony Veiller *Scr* John Twist *Ph* Sid Hickox *Ed* Clarence Kolster *Mus* David Buttolph

Act Randolph Scott, David Brian, Phyllis Thaxter, Helena Carter, Dick Jones, Ray Teal (Warner)

The script mixes up a good balance of action and romance for adult western fans, and the well-rounded characters and plot go through their paces under the able direction of the late Edwin L. Marin.

Story gets underway with Randolph Scott, former gunslinger turned crusading editor, setting up shop in Fort Worth so the power of the press can help build the town and drive out lawless elements. He is influenced in the move by two old friends, his former partner in gunplay episodes (David Brian), and the latter's fiancée (Phyllis Thaxter). Plot twist gradually brings out that Brian is the real heavy of the piece as an ambitious man who has tied up most of Fort Worth property in anticipation that he can bring in the railroad for cattle shipments.

Scott's performance is consistently good and Brian colorfully projects the opposing male star character. Thaxter is a charming western heroine, much more able than the usual prairie femme, thanks both to the writing and her playing.

•

48 HOURS

SEE: WENT THE DAY WELL?

•

48HRS.

1982, 96 mins, US Ⓥ ⊙ col

Dir Walter Hill *Prod* Lawrence Gordon, Joel Silver *Scr* Roger Spottiswoode, Walter Hill, Larry Gross, Steven E. De Souza *Ph* Ric Waite *Ed* Freeman Davies, Mark Warner, Billy Weber *Mus* James Horner *Art* John Vallone

Act Nick Nolte, Eddie Murphy, Annette O'Toole, Frank McRae, James Remar, David Patrick Kelly (Paramount)

48HRS. is a very efficient action entertainment which serves as a showy motion picture debut for Eddie Murphy. Pairing of Nick Nolte as a rough-and-tumble San Francisco cop and Murphy as a small-time criminal sprung for two days to help track down former associates makes for a throwback to the buddy-buddy pics of the 1970s.

It's all pretty predictable stuff, but done with plenty of savvy and professionalism. Director Walter Hill has always worked within traditional action genres, but has generally applied an artier, more philosophical slant to them.

Speaking with a voice sanded by a constant supply of booze and cigarettes, Nolte lays on the gruff Wallace Beery stuff a little thick and is generally willing to play second fiddle to Murphy's more kinetic schtick, but registers strongly withal. For his part, Murphy has a lot to do and gets through it amusingly.

•

FORTY-FIRST, THE

SEE: SOROK PYERVI

•

FORTY GUNS

1957, 76 mins, US ▭ b/w

Dir Samuel Fuller *Prod* Samuel Fuller *Scr* Samuel Fuller *Ph* Joseph Biroc *Ed* Gene Fowler Jr *Mus* Harry Sukman *Art* John Mansbridge

Act Barbara Stanwyck, Barry Sullivan, Dean Jagger, John Ericson, Gene Barry, Eve Brent (20th Century-Fox)

Samuel Fuller in triple capacity of producer-scripter-director has devised a solid piece of entertainment which has femme star Barbara Stanwyck playing a ruthless Arizona ranch owner, the boss of Cochise County. Into her realm rides Barry Sullivan and his two brothers, former an ex-gunslinger now working for the U.S. Attorney General, his fame with a gun preceding him.

He's in Tombstone on official business, which means conflict with femme, who rules her domain, including the sheriff, with an iron hand. Further complications arise between the two, even as a romance develops, over Stanwyck's brother (John Ericson), a brawling, would-be killer.

Stanwyck socks over her role in experienced style and Sullivan is persuasive as the marshal who loses his 10-year record for nonkilling by gunning down Ericson after latter has murdered his brother (Gene Barry).

•

49TH PARALLEL

(US: THE INVADERS)

1941, 123 mins, UK Ⓥ ⊙ b/w

Dir Michael Powell *Prod* Michael Powell *Scr* Emeric Pressburger *Ph* Freddie Young *Ed* David Lean *Mus* Ralph Vaughan Williams *Art* David Rawnsley

Act Leslie Howard, Raymond Massey, Laurence Olivier, Anton Walbrook, Glynis Johns, Eric Portman (Ortus)

This is an important and effective propaganda film. Picture started in April 1940 and took 18 months to complete. The British Government invested over $100,000 in the venture.

The locales depict Canadian life from an Eskimo village to a Hutterite settlement in the Canadian wheat fields. Story is the strongest possible indictment against Nazism. Plot concerns six Nazi U-boat men whose craft is blown up in the Hudson Bay straits. They reach land and commit every sort of crime up to murder in their efforts to reach the neutral territory of the U.S. The script of Emeric Pressburger [from a scenario by him and Rodney Ackland] is direct and forceful.

The stars are Leslie Howard, with his comedy gifts at high tide; Laurence Olivier (a bit, but the best thing he has ever done); Raymond Massey (also a bit, but outstanding); and Anton Walbrook, as a dignified Hitlerite leader. Despite the heartbreaking difficulties encountered, such as the defection of Elizabeth Bergner after the picture was well on its way, Michael Powell, the director, has managed to maintain his stature among the top directors.

1942: Best Original Story

NOMINATIONS: Best Picture, Screenplay

•

FORTY POUNDS OF TROUBLE

1962, 106 mins, US ▭ col

Dir Norman Jewison *Prod* Stan Margulies *Scr* Marion Hargrove *Ph* Joe MacDonald *Ed* Marjorie Fowler *Mus* Mort Lindsey *Art* Alexander Golitzen, Robert Clatworthy

Act Tony Curtis, Phil Silvers, Suzanne Pleshette, Claire Wilcox, Stubby Kaye, Larry Storch (Curtis/Universal)

Marion Hargrove's "original" screenplay actually owes a little something to the Little Miss Marker-Sorrowful Jones school of screen comedy, but it's a precocious and likeable offspring. The troublesome 40-pounder of the title is moppet Claire Wilcox, who makes her screen debut as an orphaned youngster who gradually melts the heart of the businesslike, efficient manager of a Lake Tahoe, Nevada gambling resort (Tony Curtis).

In the course of her conquest, she also aids the cause of husband-hunting nitery canary Suzanne Pleshette, whose romance with Curtis is complicated by the latter's relationship with his ex-wife, to whom he refuses to pay alimony, a stubborn stance that places him in jeopardy every time he leaves his Nevada legal sanctuary and crosses the border to California.

Curtis dispatches his role with comic savvy. Pleshette, whose manner is reminiscent of Joan Bennett's, handles her romantic assignment with finesse. Little Miss Wilcox is an appealing youngster, although director Jewison (in his first screen assignment after TV credits) might have obtained even better results from her by striving for more spontaneous, less practiced, childish reactions.

Phil Silvers has some memorable moments as the owner of the gambling establishment, notably one sequence in which he grandly strides into his domain, gruffly urging his customers to "play, play."

•

42ND STREET

1933, 89 mins, US Ⓥ ⊙ b/w

Dir Lloyd Bacon, Busby Berkeley *Scr* James Seymour, Rian James *Ph* Sol Polito *Ed* Thomas Pratt, Frank Ware *Mus* Leo F. Forbstein (dir.) *Art* Jack Okey

Act Warner Baxter, Bebe Daniels, George Brent, Ruby Keeler, Guy Kibbee, Ginger Rogers (Warner)

Everything about the production rings true. It's as authentic to the initiate as the novitiate.

There are good performances by Warner Baxter, as the neurotic showman who whips *Pretty Lady* into a hit musical comedy, and Bebe Daniels in a not particularly sympathetic assignment as the outmoded musical comedy ingenue whose unrequited association with a sap kiddie car manufacturer angels the production. [Script is based on the novel by Bradford Ropes.] Una Merkel and Ginger Rogers, as a pair of dumb and not-so chorines, are types. George E. Stone, as the dance stager, is likewise a believable reflection of the type. Harry Akst is the piano rehearser, and Al Dubin and Harry Warren, who fashioned the film's song ditties, play themselves.

Ruby Keeler, as the unknown who comes through and registers a hit, is utterly convincing.

Not the least of the total belongs to the direction by Lloyd Bacon, who fashioned some novelties in presentation, with Busby Berkeley an excellent aide on the terp mountings. The same overhead style of camera angles, which Berkeley introduced in the Eddie Cantor pictures and elsewhere, is further advanced.

1932/33: NOMINATIONS: Best Picture, Sound

•

FORTY THOUSAND HORSEMEN

1941, 100 mins, Australia Ⓥ b/w

Dir Charles Chauvel *Prod* Charles Chauvel *Scr* Elsa Chauvel *Ph* George Heath *Ed* Bill Shepherd *Mus* Lindley Evans, Willy Redstone, Alfred Hill *Art* Eric Thompson, J. Alan Kenyon

Act Grant Taylor, Betty Bryant, "Chips" Rafferty, Pat Twohill, Harvey Adams, Eric Reiman (Chauvel)

With *Horsemen* Aussie production drops its diapers. The pic, made in cooperation with the Department of Defense, is a three years' dream of Charles Chauvel come true.

Pic portrays in sheer entertaining fashion the story [by Chauvel and E. V. Timms] of the Australian Light Horse, the famous regiment, in Palestine during World War I. Director Chauvel has with easy grace produced a telling action pic, yet carrying sufficient romance to fully satisfy the femme stubholders.

The acting is top-notch, with the honors going to Betty Bryant and "Chips" Rafferty. The story is slight, telling the love of a French girl for an Aussie soldier. The action, however, is the highlight of the pic, with a corking charge sequence tempoing to a swift close. The camera-work is high-class, editing deft, and the sets are tops.

•

FOR WHOM THE BELL TOLLS

1943, 166 mins, US Ⓥ ⦿ col

Dir Sam Wood *Prod* Sam Wood *Scr* Dudley Nichols *Ph* Ray Rennahan *Ed* Sherman Todd, John F. Link *Mus* Victor Young *Art* William Cameron Menzies

Act Gary Cooper, Ingrid Bergman, Akim Tamiroff, Katina Paxinou, Arturo de Cordova, Vladimir Sokoloff (Paramount)

For Whom the Bell Tolls is one of the important pictures of all time although almost three hours of running time can overdo a good thing. Running sans intermission, the saga of Roberto and Maria (Gary Cooper and Ingrid Bergman) asks for too much concentrated attention on what is basically one dramatic episode, that of blasting a crucial bridge, in order to foil the Nationalists.

On a beautiful Technicolor canvas is projected an equally beautiful romance which, perhaps, lays a little too much emphasis on the amorous phase. It's one thing to punch up boy-meets-girl sequencing, but the nature of Ernest Hemingway's bestseller, of course, was predicated on a political aura resulting in the Spanish civil war.

Histrionically, *Bell Tolls* is a triumph for the four subfeatured players. Katina Paxinou, onetime foremost in her native Greek theatre, dominates everything by a shade. A masculine woman who, however, has known of love and beauty, despite her realistic self-abnegation that she is ugly, is standout in everything she does.

For the record *Bell* cost around $150,000 for the screen rights (Hemingway's book sales determined the overage on top of the basic $100,000 price) and the production cost was officially a few thousands under $3 million.

1943: Best Supp. Actress (Katina Paxinou)

NOMINATIONS: Best Picture, Actor (Gary Cooper), Actress (Ingrid Bergman), Supp. Actor (Akim Tamiroff), Color Cinematography, Color Art Direction, Editing, Scoring of a Dramatic Picture

•

FOR YOUR EYES ONLY

1981, 127 mins, UK Ⓥ ⦿ ▭ col

Dir John Glen *Prod* Albert R. Broccoli *Scr* Richard Maibaum, Michael G. Wilson *Ph* Alan Hume *Ed* John Grover *Mus* Bill Conti *Art* Peter Lamont

Act Roger Moore, Carole Bouquet, Topol, Jill Bennett, Lois Maxwell, Lynn-Holly Johnson (United Artists/Eon)

For Your Eyes Only bears not the slightest resemblance to the Ian Fleming novel of the same title, but emerges as one of the most thoroughly enjoyable of the 12 Bond pix [to date] despite fact that many of the usual ingredients in the successful 007 formula are missing.

The film is probably the best-directed on all levels since *On Her Majesty's Secret Service*, as John Glen, moving into the director's chair after long service as second unit director and editor, displays a fine eye.

Story also benefits from presence of a truly sympathetic heroine, fetchingly portrayed by Carole Bouquet, who exhibits a humanity and emotionalism not frequently found in this sort of pop adventure and who takes a long time (the entire picture, in fact) to jump into the sack with him.

M is gone, due to Bernard Lee's death; Bond doesn't make his first feminine conquest until halfway through the picture; there's no technology introduced by Q which saves the hero in the end; no looming supervillain dominates the drama; Bond bon mots are surprisingly sparse, and the fate of the whole world isn't even hanging in the balance at the climax.

1981: NOMINATION: Best Song ("For Your Eyes Only")

•

FOUL PLAY

1978, 116 mins, US Ⓥ ⦿ col

Dir Colin Higgins *Prod* Thomas L. Miller, Edward K. Milkis *Scr* Colin Higgins *Ph* David M. Walsh *Ed* Pembroke J. Herring *Mus* Charles Fox *Art* Alfred Sweeney

Act Goldie Hawn, Chevy Chase, Burgess Meredith, Rachel Roberts, Eugene Roche, Dudley Moore (Paramount)

Foul Play revives a relatively dormant film genre—the crime-suspense-romantic comedy in which low-key leading players get involved with themselves while also caught up in monumental intrigue. The name missing from the credits is Alfred Hitchcock. Writer Colin Higgins makes a good directorial bow.

If you think you've been through the plot before, you have: Goldie Hawn, likable librarian, picks up undercover agent Bruce Solomon who passes her film evidence of how Rachel Roberts, Eugene Roche and other heavies are going to assassinate visiting Pope Pius XIII (played by SF socialite Cyril Magnin) at a performance of *The Mikado* in the Opera House. Chevy Chase, a detective, eventually believes Hawn's stories about attempts on her life. Car chases and theatre shootout climax the film's 116 minutes.

Entire cast comes off very well. In prominent support are Burgess Meredith as Hawn's landlord; Dudley Moore, a dedicated swinger who turns out to be the opera conductor; Marilyn Sokol, Hawn's girlfriend who carries antirapist tools in her handbag.

1978: NOMINATION: Best Song ("Ready to Take a Chance Again")

•

FOUNTAINHEAD, THE

1949, 112 mins, US Ⓥ b/w

Dir King Vidor *Prod* Henry Blanke *Scr* Ayn Rand *Ph* Robert Burks *Ed* David Weisbart *Mus* Max Steiner *Art* Edward Carrere

Act Gary Cooper, Patricia Neal, Raymond Massey, Kent Smith, Henry Hull, Robert Douglas (Warner)

Because the plot is completely devoted to hammering home the theme that man's personal integrity stands above all law, the picture develops a controversial element.

The garrulous script which Ayn Rand did from her novel calls for a great deal of posturing by the cast and King Vidor's direction permits much overacting where underplaying might have helped develop a better emotional feeling and a truer sense of reality. Gary Cooper has an uneasy time in the miscasting as the plot's hero, an architect who is such an individualist that he dynamites a charity project when the builders alter his plans.

As Cooper's costar, Patricia Neal makes a moody heroine, afraid of love or any other honest feeling. Raymond Massey is allowed to be too flamboyant as the publisher.

•

FOUR DAUGHTERS

1938, 90 mins, US Ⓥ b/w

Dir Michael Curtiz *Prod* Benjamin Glazer *Scr* Julius J. Epstein, Lenore Coffee *Ph* Ernest Haller *Ed* Ralph Dawson *Mus* Max Steiner *Art* John Hughes

Act Claude Rains, May Robson, Priscilla Lane, Lola Lane, Rosemary Lane, John Garfield (Warner)

Score one for Warners on this gentle drama from Fannie Hurst's novel, *Sister Act*. It's a beguiling film which reveals John Garfield as an interesting picture prospect. Formerly Jules Garfield, of Broadway's Group Theatre, the actor turns out to be much more forceful personality on the screen than he was on the stage.

This tale deals with the heartthrobs of the four talented daughters of a professor of music. It's a simple, gay and lovable small-town household. And as the various girls acquire beaux, the old man looks on with a twinkling eye, and kindly Aunt Etta bustles about to make the place homelike.

Michael Curtiz's direction is both affectionate and knowing. Claude Rains is irresistibly persuasive and attractive as the father. Priscilla Lane has the best part as the youngest sister. May Robson plays the aunt in proper mother-hen fashion. As the ill-starred newcomer, Garfield plays with such tight-lipped force that for a time he threatens to throw the picture out of focus by drawing too much interest.

1938: NOMINATIONS: Best Picture, Director, Supp. Actor (John Garfield), Screenplay, Sound

•

FOUR FEATHERS

1929, 80 mins, US ⊗ b/w

Dir Merian C. Cooper, Ernest B. Schoedsack *Prod* Merian C. Cooper, Ernest B. Schoedsack *Scr* Howard Estabrook, Hope Loring *Mus* William Frederick Peters

Act Richard Arlen, Fay Wray, Clive Brook, William Powell, Theodore von Eltz, Noah Beery (Paramount)

Four Feathers is a good picture. Merian C. Cooper and Ernest B. Schoedsack were the producers. They made *Chang*. It is no secret that *Feathers's* treatment was primarily photographic. The dramatics followed. Cooper and Schoedsack must also have been the directors of the story part, for no one else is credited. Nor is a photographer named.

Ever see a herd of hippo slide down a steep bank of a jungle watering place? Ever see a large family of baboons hop from limb to limb to escape a forest fire? Or a huge army of black savages dashing to battle on white camels? These three items are *Four Feathers*.

The white feather is the symbol of cowardice in the British army. The principal character and subsequent hero of A. W. Mason's novel receives four white feathers.

Tale is set late in the last century. *Four Feathers* is highly reminiscent of *Beau Geste*. Pictorially they are much the same.

Richard Arlen's performance is good most of the while, excellent at times. William Powell is next with the most to do and does it like Powell. Clive Brook is not handed his usual weighty part and isn't impressive because of that, while Theodore von Eltz, as the lesser of the four chums, has no opportunity to be more than satisfactory. Fay Wray only has to look good.

•

FOUR FEATHERS, THE

1939, 130 mins, UK Ⓥ ⦿ col

Dir Zoltan Korda *Prod* Alexander Korda *Scr* R. C. Sherriff, Lajos Biro, Arthur Wimperis *Ph* Georges Perinal, Osmond Borradaile *Ed* William Hornbeck, Henry Cornelius *Mus* Miklos Rozsa *Art* Vincent Korda

Act John Clements, Ralph Richardson, C. Aubrey Smith, June Duprez, Allen Jeayes, Jack Allen (London)

The Four Feathers has been filmed before, with the book [by A.E.W. Mason] from which it was adapted having enjoyed big world sales.

A young British officer resigns from his regiment the night before it embarks for an Egyptian campaign. Three of his pals and his fiancée hand him white feathers, indicative of cowardice. The next day he disappears. Alone and unaided in Egypt, he goes through harrowing ordeals to gain his reinstatement in their eyes.

June Duprez, the fiancée, is the only woman in the cast. She postulates prettily and attractively, with little else to do. Rest of the cast is excellent, with C. Aubrey Smith enacting a lovable, elderly bore. John Clements, the hero, is excellent.

Photography is excellent along with the direction by Zoltan Korda.

•

FOUR FOR TEXAS

1963, 124 mins, US Ⓥ ⦿ col

Dir Robert Aldrich *Prod* Robert Aldrich *Scr* Teddi Sherman, Robert Aldrich *Ph* Ernest Laszlo *Ed* Michael Luciano *Mus* Nelson Riddle *Art* William Glasgow

Act Frank Sinatra, Dean Martin, Anita Ekberg, Ursula Andress, Charles Bronson, Victor Buono (Aldrich/Warner)

Four for Texas is a western too preoccupied with sex and romance to enthrall sagebrush-happy moppets and too unwilling to take itself seriously to sustain the attention of an adult. The screenplay [from a story by director-producer Robert Aldrich] is a choppy and haphazard dramatization of a feud between two soldiers of fortune (Frank Sinatra and Dean Martin) who ultimately have to join forces in vanquishing the threat of their mutual enemies, a treacherous banker (Victor Buono) and an irresponsible, incredibly hapless gunslinger (Charles Bronson).

Concern for the characters is never aroused by the screenplay, and the casual manner in which it is executed by the players under Aldrich's direction only compounds the problem.

Sinatra and Martin carry on in their accustomed manner, the latter getting most of what laughs there are. The film is loaded with distracting cleavage, thanks to the presence of Anita Ekberg and Ursula Andress. (Stacked up alongside Ekberg's stupendous proportions, even Mae West might seem anemic.) Buono, as the unappealing, dyspeptic and conniving banker, and Bronson as the gunman, make an impression.

Editing leaves something to be desired. At least one scene has been cut out that is still referred to in the dialog of a subsequent scene.

•

FOUR FRIGHTENED PEOPLE
1934, 95 mins, US b/w

Dir Cecil B. DeMille ***Prod*** Cecil B. DeMille ***Scr*** Bartlett Cormack, Lenore J. Coffee ***Ph*** Karl Struss ***Ed*** [Anne Bauchens] ***Mus*** [Karl Hajos, Milton Roder, H. Rohenheld, John Leipold]

Act Claudette Colbert, Herbert Marshall, Mary Boland, William Gargan, Leo Carrillo, Tetsu Komai (Paramount)

The adventures of the quartet who are lost in the Malayan jungle are episodic and disjointed, running the gamut from stark tragedy to unbelievable farce [from a novel by E. Arnot Robertson].

The four frightened people are thrown together by a bubonic plague outbreak on the Dutch coastal steamer which was carrying them from their respective ports of departure back to civilization. In self-preservation they shanghai a lifeboat and meet a half-caste guide who thinks he can safely trek them through the jungle to the sea.

The bombastic newspaper correspondent (William Gargan) talks like something out of Richard Harding Davis and never coincides with the post-*Front Page* conceptions of newspaperdom. Herbert Marshall is a chemist interested in Dutch plantation rubber, licked by life and a wife, who finds romance with the begoggled geography teacher from Chicago (Claudette Colbert) who likewise asserts herself in the jungle. Mary Boland is the wife of a British official which accounts for her presence.

The DeMilleian bathtub penchant evidences itself even in the jungle when Colbert, sans cheaters and very Eve (when a playful chimpanzee steals her clothes), emerges with plenty of s.a. for both men.

An introductory title heralds that the film was actually shot in South Pacific locations.

•

FOUR HORSEMEN OF THE APOCALYPSE, THE
1921, 130 mins, US ⊙ ⊗ b/w

Dir Rex Ingram ***Scr*** June Mathis ***Ph*** John F. Seitz ***Ed*** Grant Whytock ***Mus*** Louis F. Gottschalk ***Art*** Joseph Calder, Amos Myers

Act Rudolph Valentino, Alice Terry, Alan Hale, Nigel de Brulier, Jean Hersholt, Wallace Beery (Metro)

The magnitude of *The Four Horsemen* is staggering, and it is not hard to believe the statistics relative to the production. It is said to have cost approximately $800,000; director Rex Ingram had 14 assistants, each with a cameraman; more than 12,000 persons were used, and 125,000 tons of masonry and other material employed; $375,000 insurance was carried on the artworks, furniture, etc., used in the picture, which was six months in the making.

Horror stalked grinningly bold through the book of Vicente Blasco Ibanez, the greatest of the World War I romances. Ingram has mercifully cloaked it with distance and delicacy of treatment. This is a characteristic of the director's handling of the entire subject. It is a production of many nuances, shadings so artistic and skillful as to intrigue the mind of the spectator.

•

FOUR HORSEMEN OF THE APOCALYPSE, THE
1962, 153 mins, US Ⓥ ▭ col

Dir Vincente Minnelli ***Prod*** Julian Blaustein ***Scr*** Robert Ardrey, John Gay ***Ph*** Milton Krasner ***Ed*** Adrienne Fazan, Ben Lewis ***Mus*** André Previn ***Art*** George W. Davis, Urie McCleary, Elliot Scott

Act Glenn Ford, Ingrid Thulin, Charles Boyer, Lee J. Cobb, Paul Henreid, Yvette Mimieux (M-G-M)

Although *The Four Horsemen of the Apocalypse* is a screen spectacle of dynamic artistic proportions, it gradually becomes a victim of dramatic anemia—a strapping hulk of cinematic muscle rendered invalid by a weak heart. Lamentably, the romantic nucleus of this tragic chronicle of a family divided and devoured by war fails in the adaptation to achieve a realistic and compassionate relationship between the lovers.

Director Minnelli and leads Glenn Ford and Ingrid Thulin must share responsibility with the writers for this fundamental weakness.

It is quite possible that Ford's characterization was plagued by the ghost of Valentino, whose enactment of the leading role in 1921 was his first screen triumph. There is, for instance, a tight eyeball shot of Ford's orbs reminiscent of Valentinography. At any rate, Ford's performance is without warmth, without passion, without magnetism. Warmth is also missing in the performance of Ingrid Thulin.

However, the film shines in other areas. Frank Santillo's montages contribute touches of art and explanation to a picture that is sometimes wobbly, choppy and incomplete in the area of exposition. The device of veiling black-and-white newsreel photography in a splash of hot, vivid color registers with great emotional effect, notably in passages utilizing the novel technique of quadruple image superimposition.

Another major assist is that of André Previn, who has composed a tearing, soaring, emotionally affecting score to take up some of the slack in the love story.

•

400 BLOWS, THE
SEE: LES QUATRE CENTS COUPS

•

FOUR IN THE MORNING
1966, 94 mins, UK b/w

Dir Anthony Simmons ***Prod*** John Morris ***Scr*** Anthony Simmons ***Ph*** Larry Pizer ***Ed*** Fergus McDonnell ***Mus*** John Barry

Act Ann Lynn, Brian Phelan, Judi Dench, Norman Rodway, Joe Melia (West One)

Writer-director Anthony Simmons shows two couples in crisis, tying them in with a gimmick, which works. There's an unidentified girl found in a river. Simmons gives the scene of the discovery and study of the drowned girl a metallic, sombre documentary flavor.

A seemingly rootless young man picks up a singer he knows after her work. At four in the morning they romp around the Thames's shores, steal a boat, leave it, almost touch each other emotionally but part still uncommitted. Hints of the instability of both are carefully and intelligently suggested.

The other couple is shown as a woman waiting for her husband, out on the town with a bachelor crony. The baby cries and exasperates her. The growing incompatibility of the couple is deftly outlined in bold, dramatic strokes.

Judi Dench has the right checked hysteria for her role of the wife with a disposition towards love that makes her poignant. Ann Lynn and Brian Phelan are also effective as the other couple with Joe Melia a pointed counterpoint to the married couple with his personal problems.

•

FOUR JUST MEN, THE
(US: THE SECRET FOUR)
1939, 85 mins, UK Ⓥ col

Dir Walter Forde ***Prod*** Michael Balcon ***Scr*** Angus MacPhail, Sergei Nolbandov, Roland Pertwee ***Ph*** Ronald Neame ***Mus*** Ernest Irving (dir.) ***Art*** Wilfrid Shingleton

Act Hugh Sinclair, Griffith Jones, Francis L. Sullivan, Frank Lawton, Anna Lee, Alan Napier (Associated British)

A skilled and dramatic filmization of one of Edgar Wallace's best known novels. Murder, sabotage and international troublemaking form the basis of this exploit of the Four Just Men who, incognito, spend their lives breaking up dope rings and foiling plots of foreign agitators.

While incarcerated in a foreign prison, the youngest member of the quartet escapes execution by a few seconds, being rescued by two of the others disguised as higher officials. He has learned the name of an eastern conspirator; also that one of the members of parliament is responsible for a leakage of state secrets.

The casting is superb, Frank Lawton making a wistful and pathetic figure of the youngest patriot. Francis L. Sullivan as a French designer, playing one of his rare nonvillainous roles, is his usual suave self as one of the four.

•

FOUR MUSKETEERS
THE REVENGE OF MILADY, THE
1975, 108 mins, Panama/Spain Ⓥ col

Dir Richard Lester ***Prod*** Alexander Salkind ***Scr*** George MacDonald Fraser ***Ph*** David Watkin ***Ed*** John Victor Smith ***Mus*** Lalo Schifrin ***Art*** Brian Eatwell

Act Oliver Reed, Raquel Welch, Richard Chamberlain, Michael York, Frank Finlay, Christopher Lee (20th Century-Fox)

The Four Musketeers continues the story of Oliver Reed, Richard Chamberlain, Frank Finlay and Michael York as they joust with evil plotter Charlton Heston and evil seductress Faye Dunaway, defend fair lady queen Geraldine Chaplin, bypass imbecile King Jean Pierre Cassel, and eventually triumph over arch fiend Christopher Lee.

The same mixture of teenybopper naughtiness, acne spiciness, contrived tastelessness and derring don't as found in the earlier film (*The Three Musketeers*) is laid on with the same deft trowel herein. Perhaps the film is a triumph of controlled and deliberate mediocrity, but it still closer resembles a clumsy carbon of a bad satire on the original.

1975: NOMINATION: Best Costume Design

•

FOUR POSTER, THE
1953, 103 mins, US b/w

Dir Irving Reis ***Prod*** Stanley Kramer ***Scr*** Allan Scott ***Ph*** Hal Mohr ***Ed*** Henry Batista, Harry Gerstad ***Mus*** Dimitri Tiomkin ***Art*** Rudolph Sternard, Carl Peterson

Act Rex Harrison, Lilli Palmer (Kramer/Columbia)

The Four Poster as a pic is still limited to the same two characters of the play, with nary the suggestion of an interloper. Though the stars' performances are excellent, they are unable to salvage audience interest during the film's lesser moments. In fact, the major fault is the inability of the two characters to cope with the lack of incident.

With the four poster bed in the background as the common denominator of their marital relationship, pic traces the lives of a couple from the day the groom carries his bride across the threshold. From then on are detailed his struggles as a writer, the bride's faith in his ability, his success, their children, the son's death in World War I, the romantic escapades of the husband and wife, and finally their deaths.

Lilli Palmer imparts s.a. and natural beauty to the role of the wife.

1953: NOMINATION: Best B&W Cinematography

•

FOUR ROOMS
1995, 98 mins, US Ⓥ ⊙ col

Dir Allison Anders, Alexandre Rockwell, Robert Rodriguez, Quentin Tarantino ***Prod*** Lawrence Bender ***Scr*** Allison Anders, Alexandre Rockwell, Robert Rodriguez, Quentin Tarantino ***Ph*** Rodrigo Garcia, Guillermo Navarro, Phil Parmet, Andrzej Sekula ***Ed*** Margie Goodspeed, Elena Maganini, Sally Menke, Robert Rodriguez ***Mus*** Combustible Edison, Esquivel ***Art*** Gary Frutkoff

Act Tim Roth, Valeria Golino, Jennifer Beals, Antonio Banderas, Quentin Tarantino, Bruce Willis (A Band Apart/Miramax)

Four of America's hottest indie directors—Allison Anders, Alexandre Rockwell, Robert Rodriguez and Quentin Tarantino—get a one-of-a-kind opportunity to display their idiosyncratic talents—and grand follies—in *Four Rooms*, a disappointing, tedious anthology of four short films, set in separate rooms of a once-grand L.A. hotel.

The four stories are set in the same hotel on New Year's Eve (reportedly Rockwell's idea), with a new bellboy, Ted (Tim Roth), the only character who appears in all the segs, on the job.

In the rather pointless first story, *Strange Brew* [later retitled *The Missing Ingredient*; 16 mins.], a story about feminine mystery and power, Anders aims to spoof and deconstruct female archetypes, with a coven of witches checking into the honeymoon suite to resurrect their goddess, Diana, a 1950s entertainer-stripper. The group includes Athena (Valeria Golino), a gypsylike high priestess; the glamorous Elspeth (Madonna), who arrives with her g.f. (Alicia Witt), a juvenile delinquent on probation; Raven (Lili Taylor), Jezebel (Sammi Davis) and Eva (Ione Skye).

Rockwell's *Two Sides to a Plate* [later retitled *The Wrong Man*; 18 mins.], arguably the weakest segment, begins with Ted innocently entering room 404 to find a man named Sigfried (David Proval) wielding a .357 magnum at his beautiful wife, Angela (Jennifer Beals), who's gagged and tied to a chair.

The movie gets a much-needed energy injection in Rodriguez's sequence, *The Misbehavers* [23 mins.], a story of two kids who end up destroying their hotel room while their gangster dad (Antonio Banderas) and mom (Tamlyn Tomita) are having a night on the town.

In the closing chapter, *The Man from Hollywood* [23 mins.], Tarantino pays homage to Hitchcock. Chester Rush (Tarantino)—the town's newest comedy star—and his buddies Leo (Bruce Willis) and Norman (Paul Calderon) recreate *The Man from Rio* episode of *The Alfred Hitchcock Show*, in which Peter Lorre bets that Steve McQueen can't light his cigarette lighter 10 times in a row.

Helmers prove more adept behind the camera than as writers. In a role that was conceived for—and would have been better played by—Steve Buscemi, Roth does a cheap, inconsistent imitation of Jerry Lewis at his most neurotic.

•

FOUR'S A CROWD
1938, 91 mins, US b/w
Dir Michael Curtiz ***Scr*** Casey Robinson, Sid Herzig ***Ph*** Ernest Haller ***Ed*** Clarence Kolster ***Mus*** Heinz Roemheld, Ray Heindorf ***Art*** Max Parker
Act Errol Flynn, Olivia de Havilland, Rosalind Russell, Patric Knowles, Walter Connolly, Hugh Herbert (Warner)

As a true follower of the dizzy school of comedy, *Four's a Crowd* defies and renounces all relationship to reality. Providing much zest and spice to this dizzy dish [story by Wallace Sullivan] is Walter Connolly's characterization of the eccentric millionaire, whose major interest in life is his miniature electric railway system and a kennel of mastiffs that make tough going for unwanted visitors.

While the film has its arid stretches, there is little letdown in action. Deftly developed is the miniature train race sequence, in which the millionaire's entry meets defeat through the artful placement of a chunk of butter on the tracks.

Other laugh cascades derive from Errol Flynn's attempt to carry on twin phone conversations with a couple of insistent dames, and from a double elopement in paralleling cabs with the situation stepped up in a big way by Hugh Herbert's functioning as the cynical justice of the peace. The marriage service builds to a whirlwind finish.

Complications develop from Flynn's efforts to sell the hardboiled Connolly into whitewashing his public-be-damned past by endowing a few clinical foundations. The wily public relations counsel uses his temporary connection as managing ed of Patric Knowles's newspaper to stir up public sentiment against his proposed client.

•

FOUR SEASONS, THE
1981, 107 mins, US Ⓥ ⊙ col
Dir Alan Alda ***Prod*** Martin Bregman ***Scr*** Alan Alda ***Ph*** Victor J. Kemper ***Ed*** Michael Economou ***Mus*** Antonio Vivaldi ***Art*** Jack Collis
Act Alan Alda, Carol Burnett, Len Cariou, Sandy Dennis, Rita Moreno, Jack Weston (Universal)

If *The Four Seasons* was never a play, it should have been, since it's based on the most stagey, dialog-bound original screenplay in memory. A lightweight, overly contrived examination of the relationship among three couples who vacation together four times over course of story, Alan Alda's feature directorial debut is middle-brow, middle-aged material.

Pic's structure is too strikingly similar to that of *Same Time Next Year* to ignore the fact that Alda starred in screen adaptation of that Broadway hit.

Tale is populated strictly with *Ordinary People*, but Alda's script doesn't begin to scratch the surface to discover what makes them tick and is particularly stingy in giving Carol Burnett and Rita Moreno anything to work with.

New England and Virgin Islands locations are fresh and well chosen, and Vivaldi background score helps lend a tony atmosphere to the proceedings.

•

FOUR SONS
1928, 100 mins, US ⊗ b/w
Dir John Ford ***Prod*** William Fox ***Scr*** Philip Klein ***Mus*** S. L. Rothafel, Erno Rapee
Act Margaret Mann, James Hall, Earle Fox, June Collyer, George Meeker, Wendell Franklin (Fox)

A profoundly moving picture [from a story by I. A. R. Wylie] of family life in Germany during the First World War, giving a sympathetic insight into the effect upon the humble people of rural Bavaria of the great struggle. The production is magnificent in the amazing effectiveness of its fine realism and in its utter simplicity.

The story is the commonplace history of a widow and her four sons. Joseph goes to America before the war, marries and has his own little delicatessen shop, and a baby is born. Then the war comes. The other three brothers go to the front and one by one are killed. There is no "war stuff," the war tragedy is enacted in the homely cottage of the lone mother.

Margaret Mann's playing of the big role is a miracle of unaffected naturalness. Her Frau Bernie lives from the moment the film starts to its finish. Something of the same effortless simplicity has been communicated to the whole cast. The picture is rich in fascinating characters, such as the pompous but kindly old German letter carrier (Albert Gran) whose agonizing task it is to deliver the casualty notices to Frau Bernie; the Burgomeister of the village (August Tollaire), and the innkeeper (Hughie Mack).

•

FOURTEEN HOURS
1951, 92 mins, US b/w
Dir Henry Hathaway ***Prod*** Sol C. Siegel ***Scr*** John Paxton ***Ph*** Joe MacDonald ***Ed*** Dorothy Spencer ***Mus*** Alfred Newman ***Art*** Lyle Wheeler, Leland Fuller
Act Richard Basehart, Paul Douglas, Barbara Bel Geddes, Agnes Moorehead, Robert Keith, Grace Kelly (20th Century-Fox)

Suspense elements in a situation that has a would-be suicide swaying precariously on a high window ledge are fully realized in *Fourteen Hours*. Story [by Joel Sayre] is based on an actual suicide case in New York.

Paul Douglas is the traffic policeman who becomes a hero when his routine duties are interrupted one morning by the sight of Richard Basehart perched on a 14-story-high window ledge.

Tension reaches the screaming point often as Douglas and the others try to talk Basehart back into the building, while the citizens of New York make a Roman holiday of the event.

Douglas wallops his policeman role by sound underplaying. Basehart comes over solidly. Barbara Bel Geddes is his girlfriend, adding worth to the character. Agnes Moorehead scores as the selfish mother, and Robert Keith matches her excellence in his playing of the father.

A romance with a nice fresh touch is born in the chance meeting of Debra Paget and Jeffrey Hunter in the crowd. Grace Kelly, drawing a divorce property settlement in a nearby building, decides to make another try at marriage.

1951: NOMINATION: Best B&W Art Direction

•

1492
CONQUEST OF PARADISE
1992, 150 mins, UK/France/Spain Ⓥ ⊙ ▭ col
Dir Ridley Scott ***Prod*** Ridley Scott, Alain Goldman ***Scr*** Roselyne Bosch ***Ph*** Adrian Biddle ***Ed*** William Anderson, Francoise Bonnot ***Mus*** Vangelis ***Art*** Norris Spencer
Act Gerard Depardieu, Armand Assante, Sigourney Weaver, Michael Wincott, Angela Molina, Fernando Rey (Due West/Legende/Cyrk)

All Ridley Scott's vaunted visuals can't transform *1492* from a lumbering, one-dimensional historical fresco into the complex, ambiguous character study that it strives to be.

French journalist and first-time screenwriter Roselyne Bosch offers up a humanistic pacifist driven by an enigmatic mix of motives to settle a new land. "They are not savages, and neither will we be," Columbus (Gerard Depardieu) announces to his crew.

A man allied with monks but disgusted by the Inquisition, he is able to charm the Spanish queen into sending him into the unknown. After a remarkably uneventful voyage spurred by one little inspirational speech to his nervous crew, Columbus reaches his promised "earthly paradise."

After his triumphant return home, a new, 17-ship expedition is launched. Minds dominated by military ambition, religious fervor and greed inevitably gain the upper hand and turn the lush tropical settlement into a living hell.

Scott takes slightly greater interest in the political dynamics informing the yarn. The Crown's treasurer (Armand Assante) plays out an ambiguous relationship with Columbus throughout all the latter's changing fortunes.

Sigourney Weaver briefly suggests a sexual susceptibility to Columbus behind the queen's approval of his grand scheme. But no one is allowed the opportunity to develop a character.

Depardieu's energy, passion and conviction are ideal for the role, but perhaps it remains beyond him at this point to act in English in depth.

•

FOURTH PROTOCOL, THE
1987, 119 mins, UK Ⓥ ⊙ ▭ col
Dir John Mackenzie ***Prod*** Timothy Burrill ***Scr*** Frederick Forsyth ***Ph*** Phil Meheuy ***Ed*** Graham Walker ***Mus*** Lalo Schifrin ***Art*** Alan Cameron
Act Michael Caine, Pierce Brosnan, Joanna Cassidy, Ned Beatty, Ray McAnally, Ian Richardson (Rank)

The Fourth Protocol is a decidedly contempo thriller, a tale of vying masterspies and a chase to head off a nuclear disaster. Its edge is a fine aura of realism.

Novelist Frederick Forsyth, who also was an executive producer, adapted the pic from his book.

The story is pretty straightforward. A ruthless KGB head plans to detonate a nuclear bomb close to a U.S. airbase in England so the Brits blame the Yanks and the NATO alliance will collapse.

What follows is a good old-fashioned race against time as Caine tracks down his Russian alter ego Major Petrofsky (Pierce Brosnan) and after a hand-to-hand scuffle manages to defuse the bomb.

Michael Caine as a maverick counterespionage expert gives a thorough performance in a part that doesn't really stretch his abilities.

•

FOURTH WAR, THE
1990, 91 mins, US Ⓥ ⊙ col
Dir John Frankenheimer ***Prod*** Wolf Schmidt ***Scr*** Stephen Peters, Kenneth Ross ***Ph*** Gerry Fisher ***Ed*** Robert F. Shugrue ***Mus*** Bill Conti ***Art*** Alan Manzer
Act Roy Scheider, Jurgen Prochnow, Tim Reid, Lara Harris, Harry Dean Stanton, Dale Dye (Kodiak)

The Fourth War is a well-made Cold War thriller about private battling that might escalate out of control. Opening title sets the tale in November 1988 on the border of Czechoslovakia and East Germany.

Roy Scheider is well-cast as a hardline colonel who's caused nothing but trouble in his career and is now stationed at a post near the border by his general, Harry Dean Stanton. Scheider witnesses the murder of a fleeing defector through no-man's-land. He rightly blames the Soviet colonel (Jurgen Prochnow) for this dastardly deed and from this minor act of outrage ensues a man-to-man feud of Laurel and Hardy proportions. Tightly directed by Frankenheimer with an eye for comic relief as well as tension maintenance, *The Fourth War* holds the fascination of eyeball-to-eyeball conflict.

Besides the two stars, Tim Reid is very effective as the man on the spot (his commanding officer is out of control), and Lara Harris is convincing as a duplicitous femme fatale.

•

FOUR WEDDINGS AND A FUNERAL
1994, 116 mins, UK Ⓥ ⊙ col
Dir Mike Newell ***Prod*** Duncan Kenworthy ***Scr*** Richard Curtis ***Ph*** Michael Coulter ***Ed*** Jon Gregory ***Mus*** Richard Rodney Bennett ***Art*** Maggie Gray
Act Hugh Grant, Andie MacDowell, Kristin Scott Thomas, Simon Callow, James Fleet, Corin Redgrave (PFE/Channel 4/Working Title)

Truly beguiling romantic comedy is one of the hardest things for a modern film to pull off, but screenwriter Richard Curtis (*The Tall Guy*) has hit just the right balance with this story, which is original in every sense of the word.

Charles (Hugh Grant) is a charming bumbler who, at an English country wedding, is very willingly seduced by another guest, the gorgeous and exceedingly accommodating American, Carrie (Andie MacDowell). Back in London, Charles blurts out his profound feelings for her even as she's heading to the altar with a wealthy older Scotsman (Corin Redgrave).

A sudden death at the reception precipitates the funeral, at which the heretofore unknown diversity and depth of Charles's inner circle is revealed.

The success of such lighthearted nonsense depends upon the appeal, adeptness and timing of the cast, and it is here that the film really soars. Grant's got just the combination of good looks, rueful self-disparagement, quickness and bespectacled nerdiness to carry off refined, sophisticated screen comedy. MacDowell gives her role everything it needs—allure, warmth, a natural breeziness and a worldliness enhanced by romanticism.

1994: NOMINATIONS: Best Picture, Original Screenplay

•

FOX, THE
1968, 110 mins, US/Canada col
Dir Mark Rydell ***Prod*** Raymond Stross ***Scr*** Lewis John Carlino ***Ph*** William Fraker ***Ed*** Thomas Stanford ***Mus*** Lalo Schifrin ***Art*** Charles Bailey
Act Sandy Dennis, Keir Dullea, Anne Heywood, Glyn Morris (Warner/Seven Arts/Motion Pictures International)

D. H. Lawrence's lesbian-themed novella *The Fox* is turned into a beautifully photographed, dramatically uneven Canadian-made film.

Sandy Dennis and Anne Heywood are cast as lesbian lovers who have exiled themselves to a lonely farm. Arrival of Keir Dullea cues a disintegration of the femme relationship and eventual tragedy.

In early reels, Anne Heywood seems the dominant female. She is inwardly uneasy, perhaps afraid of eventual old age.

Dennis has the greater acting burden, and her performance is uneven. Her daffiness in early reels seems overdone, result of which is that her later remarks may draw unwanted smiles, even chuckles, from audiences.

Dullea plays his part with quiet determination to snare Heywood. Whether or not he suspects or comprehends the lesbian relationship is debatable, from script and actions.

First sexual encounter between him and Heywood is awkward—the gaspings, the clutching of turf, etc. A later romantic scene between the two gals, by contrast, is excellent.

1968: NOMINATION: Best Original Music Score

•

FOXES

1980, 106 mins, US Ⓥ ⊙ col

Dir Adrian Lyne ***Prod*** David Puttnam, Gerald Ayres ***Scr*** Gerald Ayres ***Ph*** Leon Bijou ***Ed*** Jim Coblentz ***Mus*** Giorgio Moroder ***Art*** Michel Levesque

Act Jodie Foster, Scott Baio, Sally Kellerman, Randy Quaid, Marilyn Kagan, Cherie Currie (United Artists/PolyGram)

Foxes is an ambitious attempt to do a film relating to some of the not-so-acceptable realities among teenagers that ends up delivering far less than it is capable of.

Story of four teenage girls and their battles often becomes a depressing, one-sided and melodramatic treatise on American youth. It soon becomes clear this is not the usual gaggle of girls portrayed as typical American teenagers. Cherie Currie is a stoned-out former hooker, Marilyn Kagan is an unhappy, overweight girl longing to shed her parents' protective shell, Kandice Stroh is a lying, confused flirt and Jodie Foster is a level-headed intellect.

Constant switching of action between the girls causes Stroh's character to be lost midway and Foster's identity to never fully be explored despite the fact she's the focal point.

•

FOXES OF HARROW, THE

1947, 115 mins, US b/w

Dir John M. Stahl ***Prod*** William A. Bacher ***Scr*** Wanda Tuchock ***Ph*** Joseph La Shelle ***Ed*** James B. Clark ***Mus*** Alfred Newman ***Art*** Lyle R. Wheeler, Maurice Ransford

Act Rex Harrison, Maureen O'Hara, Richard Haydn, Victor McLaglen, Patricia Medina (20th Century-Fox)

The Foxes of Harrow is an elaborate filmization of Frank Yerby's novel. Invested with the polished direction of John M. Stahl, it builds into a powerful drama of an adventurer's rise to fame and fortune in New Orleans of the 19th century. Exciting story has strong production, vivid developments and helped along with excellent pace most of the time.

Technically, *Foxes* runs too long. It contains passages at the outset and near the end that appear superfluous. But because there are so many meaty scenes, even the more tedious ones overflow with nice performances.

Rex Harrison, the child born out of wedlock, rises to the heights in New Orleans business even though his first money is won gambling. Plot shows Harrison being put off a Mississippi steamboat for cheating at cards but being rescued from a sandbar by Victor McLaglen, captain of a pigboat.

Harrison's audacity both at cards and with women catapults him to riches. His main ambition is to build another Harrow estate like his mother had known in Ireland. He finally persuades Maureen O'Hara, daughter of one of New Orleans's aristocrats, to become his wife.

Harrison is perfect as the suave gambler and O'Hara carries the highly dramatic scenes with surprising skill, but it seems a pity that she is not permitted to smile more often.

1947: NOMINATION: Best B&W Art Direction

•

FOX MOVIETONE FOLLIES OF 1929

1929, 80 mins, US col

Dir David Butler, Marcel Silver ***Ph*** Charles Van Enger

Act Sue Carol, David Rollins, Stepin Fetchit, Sharon Lynn, Warren Hymer (Fox)

Fox Movietone Follies is good entertainment all the way. The numbers, specialties and song-and-dance stuff come through very well. One bit done in Technicolor offers a variant from the black-and-white but achieves little itself.

"The Breakaway" and "Walkin' with Susie" are the big numbers. Wisp of a story. A young Virginian sells his plantation and comes north to marry his sweetie. She is in the chorus of a new show and refuses to quit the theater to settle down as a wife.

Chagrined by her refusal to chuck everything and go to the parson's, young man buys the controlling interest in the show and fires her. She refuses to quit and says he cannot fire her. "Why not?" he demands. "Because Equity won't let you," she retorts. "Who's he?" demands the hick.

Most of the action and the *Follies* part of the picture represents the opening night of the revue. Sue Carol takes first honors but needs dancing lessons. Warren Hymer makes a stage manager pretty rough, tough and nasty.

•

FOXY BROWN

1974, 91 mins, US Ⓥ col

Dir Jack Hill ***Prod*** Buzz Feitshans ***Scr*** Jack Hill ***Ph*** Brick Marquard ***Ed*** Chuck McClelland ***Mus*** Willie Hutch ***Art*** Kirk Axtel

Act Pam Grier, Antonio Vargas, Peter Brown, Terry Carter, Kathryn Loder, Harry Holcombe (American International)

Bosomy black starlet Pam Grier plays a gal whose dope-dealing brother (Antonio Fargas) rats on her undercover-narc boyfriend (Terry Carter), cuing latter's gangland murder on her doorstep. Not one to take romantic disappointment lightly, she sets her vengeful eye on the leaders of the local vice ring (Kathryn Loder and Peter Brown).

Before femme might makes right, Grier and call girl Juanita Brown have a brawl in a lesbian bar, Fargas writhes to his gunned-down death, doxy Sally Ann Stroud has her throat slashed, two degenerate thugs who've raped Grier are burned to death, and Brown is castrated.

Even by the gutter-high standards of the genre, *Foxy Brown* is something of a mess. Jack Hill's screenplay has peculiar narrative gaps.

•

FRAMED

1947, 81 mins, US b/w

Dir Richard Wallace ***Prod*** Jules Schermer ***Scr*** Ben Maddow ***Ph*** Burnett Guffey ***Ed*** Richard Fantl ***Mus*** Marlin Skiles ***Art*** Stephen Goosson, Carl Anderson

Act Glenn Ford, Janis Carter, Barry Sullivan, Edgar Buchanan, Karen Morley (Columbia)

Glenn Ford's name heads cast as out-of-work mining engineer who gets involved with beautiful blonde who's trying to steal $250,000. Script doesn't have too much finesse as written by Ben Maddow from Jack Patrick's story, but there's enough deftness to generate interest in unfoldment.

Ford is good as the young man who is supposed to be a murder victim and Janis Carter, the girl of the piece, does excellently. She is mistress of bank vice president and has plotted scheme to loot bank. Twist has girl falling for Ford, who is slated to be killed and become responsible for the theft.

•

FRANCES

1982, 140 mins, US Ⓥ ⊙ col

Dir Graeme Clifford ***Prod*** Jonathan Sanger ***Scr*** Eric Bergren, Christopher DeVore, Nicholas Kazan ***Ph*** Laszlo Kovacs ***Ed*** John Wright ***Mus*** John Barry ***Art*** Richard Sylbert

Act Jessica Lange, Kim Stanley, Sam Shepard, Bart Burns, Jeffrey DeMunn, Jordan Charney (EMI/Brooksfilms)

Rare to the memory is a film like *Frances* which runs 140 minutes and its star is on the screen 85% of the time in one intense scene after another. It's quite an accomplishment for Jessica Lange and it's too bad a better film didn't come of it.

Though her troubled life made headlines around the world, Frances Farmer is still much a mystery. What is agreed is that Farmer was a rebellious young girl in Seattle who first shocked the 1930s with a high-school essay questioning God, then outraged conservatives again a few years later with a visit to Moscow. The publicity, plus her talent, led to a successful Broadway and Hollywood career, followed by some kind of a breakdown and many years in mental institutions.

Resolving the doubts that haunt Farmer's life, the film presents her basically as a woman to be admired for standing behind her convictions regardless of the consequences.

As a directorial debut by editor Graeme Clifford, however, *Frances* tends to trivialize. It's hard to shake the persistent feeling that she brought a lot of woe on herself.

1982: NOMINATIONS: Best Actress (Jessica Lange), Supp. Actress (Kim Stanley)

•

FRANKENHOOKER

1990, 90 mins, US Ⓥ ⊙ col

Dir Frank Henenlotter ***Prod*** Edgar Ievins ***Scr*** Robert Martin, Frank Henenlotter ***Ph*** Robert M. Baldwin ***Ed*** Kevin Tent ***Mus*** Joe Renzetti

Act James Lorinz, Patty Mullen, Charlotte Helmkamp, Shirley Stoler, Louise Lasser, Joseph Gonzalez (Shapiro Glickenhaus)

Frankenhooker is a grisly, grotesque horror comedy recommended only for the stout of heart and strong of stomach.

James Lorinz plays Jeffrey Franken, a New Jersey Gas & Electric worker who aspires to be a mad scientist. There isn't much left of his pretty girlfriend Elizabeth (Patty Mullen) after her fatal run-in with a remote-control lawn mower. But Franken has preserved her head in his garage laboratory. All he needs is a new body to make the package complete. Jeffrey drives across the river to Times Square to find streetwalkers more than willing to sell (or at least rent) their bodies.

Even by genre standards, *Frankenhooker* often is offensive in its repeated reliance on murdering, dismembering and humiliating women for laughs. Lorinz has some inspired moments of self-absorbed craziness as Jeffrey, and Mullen reveals a fine talent for physical comedy when Elizabeth returns as the lumbering, mind-blown Frankenhooker.

•

FRANKENSTEIN

1931, 71 mins, US Ⓥ ⊙ b/w

Dir James Whale ***Prod*** Carl Laemmle, Jr. ***Scr*** Garrett Fort, Francis Edwards Faragoh ***Ph*** Arthur Edeson ***Ed*** Maurice Pivar, Clarence Kolster ***Mus*** [David Broekman] ***Art*** Charles D. Hall

Act Colin Clive, Mae Clarke, John Boles, Boris Karloff, Edward Van Sloan, Dwight Frye (Universal)

Frankenstein looks like a *Dracula* plus, touching a new peak in horror plays and handled in production with supreme craftsmanship.

Picture [based on the compositon by John L. Balderston, from the play by Peggy Webling, based on the novel by Mary W. Shelley] starts with a wallop. Midnight funeral services are in progress on a blasted moor, with the figure of the scientist and his grotesque dwarf assistant hiding at the edge of the cemetery to steal the newly-buried body. Sequence climaxes with the gravedigger sending down the clumping earth upon newly laid coffin. Shudder No. 1.

Shudder No. 2, hard on its heels is when Frankenstein cuts down his second dead subject from the gallows, presented with plenty of realism. The corpses are to be assembled into a semblance of a human body which Frankenstein seeks to galvanize into life, and to this end the story goes into his laboratory, extemporized in a gruesome mountain setting out of an abandoned mill.

Laboratory sequence detailing the creation of the monster patched up of human odds-and-ends is a smashing bit of theatrical effect, taking place during a violent mountain storm.

Playing is perfectly paced. Colin Clive, the cadaverous hero of *Journey's End* (1930), is a happy choice for the scientist driven by a frenzy for knowledge. He plays it with force, but innocent of ranting. Boris Karloff makes a memorable figure of the bizarre monster with its indescribably terrifying face of demoniacal calm.

•

FRANKENSTEIN
(AKA: *MARY SHELLEY'S FRANKENSTEIN*)

1994, 123 mins, US Ⓥ ⊙ col

Dir Kenneth Branagh ***Prod*** Francis Ford Coppola, James V. Hart, John Veitch ***Scr*** Steph Lady, Frank Darabont ***Ph*** Rogert Pratt ***Ed*** Andrew Marcus ***Mus*** Patrick Doyle ***Art*** Tim Harvey

Act Robert De Niro, Kenneth Branagh, Tom Hulce, Helena Bonham Carter, Aidan Quinn, Ian Holm (American Zoetrope/Tri-Star)

Kenneth Branagh has indeed created a monster, but not the kind he originally envisioned. A major disappointment creatively, and far from the definitive version of the tale, this lavish but overwrought melodrama is in many ways less compelling than even a recent made-for-cable movie [*Frankenstein*, directed by David Wickes, starring Patrick Bergen] and a 1973 miniseries [*Frankenstein: The True Story*] starring Michael Sarrazin that was less faithful to the source material.

Tackling a Gothic epic as director/coproducer/star, Branagh seems to overreach himself, playing every aspect at an almost operative level that's too feverish for its own good. In addition, the director and writers seem to get carried away in playing up the story's romance, at the expense of the horror-action elements.

The beginning proves effective and true to the novel, as a sea captain (Aidan Quinn) exploring the arctic stumbles upon the crazed Victor Frankenstein (Branagh), who recounts his cautionary tale about scientific obsession in detail flashback. The account begins with the death of his mother in childbirth, and Victor's own longings for his adopted sister (Helena Bonham Carter).

It's nearly an hour into the film before the creature emerges from the tank, and despite the overamplified tone, there's still hope for the movie at that juncture. However, when the monster befriends a simple country family, learning how to speak and read before ultimately going after his creator to seek vengeance, the movie begins to spin wildly out of control.

De Niro's creature doesn't even approach the terror factor of his role in *Cape Fear*, while failing to inspire the empathy that even Boris Karloff—bolts and all—engendered. De Niro's makeup doesn't help matters, appearing grotesque but not particularly jarring. Branagh's own performance is appropriately crazed, while Carter as always proves radiant and engaging. Patrick Doyle's relentlessly bombastic score is simply overbearing.

1994: NOMINATION: Best Makeup

•

FRANKENSTEIN CREATED WOMAN
1967, 92 mins, UK Ⓥ col
Dir Terence Fisher ***Prod*** Anthony Nelson Keys ***Scr*** John Elder [= Anthony Hinds] ***Ph*** Arthur Grant ***Ed*** James Needs ***Mus*** James Bernard ***Art*** Don Mingaye
Act Peter Cushing, Susan Denberg, Thorley Walters, Robert Morris, Peter Blythe, Barry Warren (Hammer/Seven Arts)

In *Frankenstein Created Woman* the good doctor, as usual, played by Peter Cushing, doesn't really create woman, he just makes a few important changes in the design. Considering the result is beautiful blonde Susan Denberg, most film fans would like to see the doctor get a grant from the Ford Foundation, or even the CIA.

In this version, Frankenstein dabbles as much in transmigration of souls as actual patchwork surgery, capturing the psyche of an executed young man and instilling it in the body of a drowned young woman (Denberg).

The girl, originally a disfigured, shy maiden, is rejuvenated as a beautiful femme whose touch proves trés fatale when the male soul uses the female body to wreak vengeance on the trio of young wastrels responsible for his execution (Peter Blythe, Barry Warren, Derek Fowlds).

•

FRANKENSTEIN MEETS THE WOLF MAN
1943, 72 mins, US Ⓥ ⊙ b/w
Dir Roy William Neill ***Prod*** George Waggner ***Scr*** Curt Siodmak ***Ph*** George Robinson ***Ed*** Edward Curtiss ***Mus*** Hans J. Salter
Act Lon Chaney, Ilona Massey, Patric Knowles, Lionel Atwill, Bela Lugosi, Maria Ouspenskaya (Universal)

In order to put the Wolf Man and the Monster through further film adventures, scripter Curt Siodmak has to resurrect the former from a tomb, and the Frankenstein creation from the ruins of the castle where he was purportedly killed. But he delivers a good job of fantastic writing to weave the necessary thriller ingredients into the piece, and finally brings the two legendary characters together for a battle climax.

Eerie atmosphere generates right at the start, when Lon Chaney, previously killed off with the werewolf stain on him, is disinterred and returns to life. After one transformation, he winds up in a hospital to gain the sympathetic attention of medico Patric Knowles, then seeks out gypsy Maria Ouspenskaya for relief, and she takes him to the continent and the village where Frankenstein held forth. This allows Chaney to discover and revive the monster, role handled by Bela Lugosi, and from there on it's a creepy affair in grand style.

•

FRANKENSTEIN MUST BE DESTROYED
1969, 97 mins, UK Ⓥ col
Dir Terence Fisher ***Prod*** Anthony Nelson Keys ***Scr*** Bert Batt ***Ph*** Arthur Grant ***Ed*** Gordon Hales ***Mus*** James Bernard ***Art*** Bernard Robinson
Act Peter Cushing, Veronica Carlson, Freddie Jones, Simon Ward, Thorley Walters, Maxine Audley (Hammer)

Frankenstein's (Peter Cushing) diabolical plan is, in the cause of science, to preserve the medical knowledge of a brilliant but insane surgeon. This he'll do by murdering the medico, removing his brain and inserting it in the body of a kidnapped man.

With the help of two young accomplices (a doctor, Simon Ward, and his girlfriend, Veronica Carlson), drawn into the plot because Frankenstein is blackmailing them over a drug robbery offense, the mad scientist is hijacked from an asylum, operated on and the brains switched.

The film is a good-enough example of its low-key type, with artwork rather better than usual (less obvious backcloths, etc.), a minimum of artless dialog, good lensing by Arthur Grant and a solid all-around cast.

•

FRANKENSTEIN UNBOUND
1990, 85 mins, US Ⓥ ⊙ col
Dir Roger Corman ***Prod*** Roger Corman, Thom Mount, Kabi Jaeger ***Scr*** Roger Corman, F. X. Feeney, Ed Neumeir ***Ph*** Armando Nannuzzi, Michael Scott ***Ed*** Jay Cassidy ***Mus*** Carl Davis ***Art*** Enrico Tovaglieri
Act John Hurt, Raul Julia, Bridget Fonda, Nick Brimble, Catherine Rabett, Catherine Corman (Mount)

Roger Corman's *Frankenstein Unbound* is a competent but uninspired riff on the venerable legend. For Corman, it's also a return trip to modern British sci-fi, adapting a Brian W. Aldiss novel.

John Hurt toplines as a mad scientist in New Los Angeles of 2031, trying to develop a laser weapon that causes objects to implode. Unfortunately, his experiments are causing time slips, violent dislocations including one that suddenly transports Hurt to Switzerland in 1817.

Hurt chances upon Dr. Frankenstein in a local pub and he's soon visiting gothic folk Mary Godwin (soon to be Shelley), Lord Byron and Percy Shelley. Out on the rampage is Frankenstein's monster, killing people until his creator fabricates a mate for him.

While warring with Frankenstein and his monster, Hurt ultimately identifies with them, leading to an interesting, somber climax set in icy wastes as in Shelley's original novel.

Though some of the dialog is clutzy, acting is generally good with top honors to Raul Julia as a thoughtful Frankenstein. More single-minded is Hurt's sketchy role.

Bridget Fonda is attractive in the Mary Godwin role, overshadowed by British actress Catherine Rabett, who brings panache to the role of Frankenstein's fiancée, later resurrected as bride for the monster.

•

FRANKIE AND JOHNNY
1966, 87 mins, US Ⓥ ⊙ col
Dir Frederick de Cordova ***Prod*** Edward Small ***Scr*** Alex Gottlieb ***Ph*** Jacques Marquette ***Ed*** Grant Whytock ***Mus*** Fred Karger (dir.) ***Art*** Walter Simonds
Act Elvis Presley, Donna Douglas, Harry Morgan, Sue Ane Langdon, Nancy Kovack, Audrey Christie (Small/F&J)

Frankie and Johnny is Elvis all the way in a story built loosely around the classic folk song, coupled with a dozen or so tunes, pretty girls and Technicolor.

The screenplay from a Nat Perrin story has Elvis and Donna Douglas (in her first major film role) as entertainers on a Mississippi riverboat about 100 years ago. Elvis is Frankie, Donna is Johnny, and, like in the ageless song, they love each other. But Frankie gambles too much, losing all the time, until he finds a lucky redhead—Nellie Bly, natch—played by Nancy Kovack.

Elvis is Elvis. He sings and acts, apparently doing both with only slight effort. Presley does little hip swinging, no doubt in keeping with the period of the story, although he does get a chance to bounce out one number—"Shout It Out"—with Dixieland accompaniment.

•

FRANKIE AND JOHNNY
1991, 118 mins, US Ⓥ ⊙ col
Dir Garry Marshall ***Prod*** Garry Marshall ***Scr*** Terrence McNally ***Ph*** Dante Spinotti ***Ed*** Battle Davis, Jacqueline Cambas ***Mus*** Marvin Hamlisch ***Art*** Albert Brenner
Act Al Pacino, Michelle Pfeiffer, Hector Elizondo, Nathan Lane, Kate Nelligan, Jane Morris (Paramount)

Frankie and Johnny is an all-star, high-gloss, feel-good romantic feature sitcom. Amiably written and performed but fearsomely predictable, this middle-of-the-road adaptation of Terrence McNally's off-Broadway hit [the 1987 *Frankie and Johnny in the Clair de Lune*] invites audiences to indulge in watching beautiful movie stars play lonely little people struggling to find love.

Al Pacino and Michelle Pfeiffer are cast in the roles originated onstage by Kathy Bates and F. Murray Abraham in the Manhattan Theater Club Workshop. *Pretty Woman* director Garry Marshall sprinkles a little of his Cinderella dust on this story of an ex-con who takes a job as a short-order chef in Manhattan and instantly falls for a hardcase waitress.

He is as persistent as she is resistant and, at one point during his efforts to woo Frankie, Johnny breaks down and takes a tumble with a brassy waitress (Kate Nelligan). But he is otherwise singleminded in his pursuit.

Like a warm, slobbering dog who can't leave people alone, Pacino's Johnny comes on real strong, and his pronounced neediness is too much at times. No one's going to believe that Pfeiffer hasn't had a date since Ronald Reagan was president, and no matter how hard she tries to look plain, there is no disguising that she just gets more beautiful all the time. But she gives a performance filled with many moods and numerous affecting moments.

•

FRANKIE STARLIGHT
1995, 100 mins, US Ⓥ col
Dir Michael Lindsay-Hogg ***Prod*** Noel Pearson ***Scr*** Chet Raymo, Ronan O'Leary ***Ph*** Paul Laufer ***Ed*** Ruth Foster ***Mus*** Elmer Bernstein ***Art*** Frank Conway
Act Anne Parillaud, Matt Dillon, Gabriel Byrne, Corban Walker, Rudi Davies, Alan Pentony (Ferndale)

There's a considerable amount of blarney, to be sure, in the Irish-set romantic drama *Frankie Starlight*. The offbeat tale of a young dwarf and his mother has considerable charm on its side but lacks clear focus or intent to carry the material to a satisfying conclusion.

Frank Bois (Corban Walker) is a thirtysomething dwarf who walks into an agent's office with a manuscript under his arm. His novel is the story of his youth in a small Irish village.

The story is related via parallel strands from the past and present. Frank's mother, Bernadette (Anne Parillaud), arrived in Ireland illegally on a U.S. troop ship after the Second World War and later was befriended by Jack Kelly (Gabriel Byrne), an immigration officer. Pregnant by an unknown GI, Bernadette gives birth to Frankie and mother and child are taken in by the Kelly family. Jack imbues the young Frank with a fascination for the stars and other celestial bodies.

In the present day, Frank struggles with his condition. He strives for normality but finds that he's denied many of the physical and emotional niceties of life.

Director Michael Lindsay-Hogg, writers Chet Raymo and Ronan O'Leary, in adapting Raymo's book, *The Dork of Cork*, for the screen, have retained too many literary devices. Seemingly peripheral characters—whose significance becomes clear much later in the narrative—draw us away from the protagonists.

Although the narrative favors the title character, it resonates with the sad plight of his mother. Kelly and Terry (Matt Dillon), a GI who lures mother and son to Texas briefly, are more perfunctory than delineated characters, and Emma (Rudi Davies), Jack's daughter, is a seeming side anecdote who, much later, crystallizes into the force that will change Frank's life.

•

FRANK'S GREATEST ADVENTURE
(AKA: FEARLESS FRANK)
1967, 83 mins, US ⌴ col
Dir Philip Kaufman ***Scr*** Philip Kaufman ***Ph*** Bill Butler ***Ed*** Aram Boyajian, Luke Bennet ***Mus*** Meyer Kupferman
Act Jon Voight, Monique Van Vooren, Joan Darling, Severn Darden, Lou Gilbert, Ben Carruthers (Jericho)

In the guise of a far-out tale of a superman and a man-made monster, gangsters and scientists, this is intended to be a disarming spoof of American myths as embodied in films. Indie pic, made in Chicago [in 1965], also benefits from fine color, scope and technical solidity.

Harmless underworld types, an optimistic hick with charm to overcome the so-called intellectuals and city slickers, women of the world who succumb to his charms, and the panoply of big city life versus the small town—all get a going over in this simple pic.

Philip Kaufman, who was codirector of another Chicago-made comedy *Goldstein* (1964), goes it alone as director. Perhaps he is too slack in the second half, and at times overworks a gag. But, on the whole, he shows a fine grasp of filmic comedy.

Plot has Frank (Jon Voight) awakening as a superman after apparently been slain by gangsters.

Little-known players all etch neat performances, with Monique Van Vooren just right as Plethora, the pulpy moll who has time to warble some songs. Voight has the healthy blond openness that lends itself to the dual characters. Joan Darling is both urchin and then a demanding female as the good doctor's daughter, Lois. Severn Darden etches neat limnings as the two doctors.

Kaufman is a filmmaker with verve and know-how.

•

FRANTIC
SEE: L'ASCENSEUR POUR L'ECHAFAUD

•

FRANTIC
1988, 120 mins, US Ⓥ ⊙ col
Dir Roman Polanski ***Prod*** Thom Mount, Tim Hampton ***Scr*** Roman Polanski, Gerard Brach ***Ph*** Witold Sobocinski ***Ed*** Sam O'Steen ***Mus*** Ennio Morricone ***Art*** Pierre Guffroy

Act Harrison Ford, Emmanuelle Seigner, Betty Buckley, John Mahoney, Jimmie Ray Weeks (Mount/Warner)

Frantic is a thriller without much surprise, suspense or excitement. Drama about an American doctor's desperate search for his kidnapped wife through the demimonde of Paris reveals director Roman Polanski's personality and enthusiasm only in brief humorous moments.

San Francisco medic Harrison Ford arrives in Paris with wife Betty Buckley to deliver a paper at a conference and, incidentally, to revisit the scene of their honeymoon 20 years before. While Ford is showering, Buckley disappears from the hotel room, thus setting off an urgent womanhunt that takes the distraught husband to young Emmanuelle Seigner, a sleek, punky drugette and nightclubber who appears to be the only lead to the kidnappers.

The McGuffin, or object of everyone's pursuit, here is a miniature Statue of Liberty which contains an object that, predictably, could endanger the Free World. Action climax takes place alongside the small-scale replica of France's gift to New York Harbor.

Ford sweats a lot while conveying Polanski's view that anxiety is the natural state of the human condition. His latest discovery, Seigner, certainly is eye-catching and proves servicable in her part.

•

FRATERNITY ROW

1977, 101 mins, US col

Dir Thomas J. Tobin ***Prod*** Charles Gary Allison ***Scr*** Charles Gary Allison ***Ph*** Peter Gibbons ***Ed*** Eugene A. Fournier ***Art*** James Sbardellati

Act Peter Fox, Gregory Harrison, Scott Newman, Nancy Morgan, Wendy Phillips, Robert Emhardt (Paramount)

Fraternity Row is a powerful film about emotional and physical violence at an Eastern college frat house in 1954, produced and scripted by USC grad student Charles Gary Allison.

Debuting director Thomas J. Tobin handles the fresh young cast with sensitivity and avoids the thrill-mongering that mars too many youth-market pix.

This is no happy-go-lucky piece of 1950s nostalgia, but a sobering dissection of the brutality and narrow-mindedness too often spawned by the Greek system in that era, before the hippie revolution hit the campuses and depleted frat ranks.

Peter Fox is the sensitive but compromised frat pledge master who opposes Scott Newman's sadistic attitudes towards the pledges, and Gregory Harrison is the innocent one who suffers most in the hazing process.

•

FRAUDS

1993, 92 mins, Australia/UK Ⓥ ⦿ col

Dir Stephan Elliott ***Prod*** Andrena Finlay, Stuart Quin ***Scr*** Stephan Elliott ***Ph*** Geoff Burton ***Ed*** Frans Vandenburg ***Mus*** Guy Gross ***Art*** Brian Thomson

Act Phil Collins, Hugo Weaving, Josephine Byrnes, Peter Mochrie, Helen O'Connor, Rebel Russell (Live/J&M/Latent Image)

First-time director Stephan Elliott breaks a lot of the rules with his wayward first feature, *Frauds*, cheerfully mixing suspense with comic-strip comedy. Pic boasts a top-flight performance from Phil Collins as a con-man insurance investigator with a childlike sense of humor.

The home of a yuppie couple, Jonathan (Hugo Weaving) and Beth (Josephine Byrnes), who like to play games, is burgled by a masked intruder; Beth shoots the stranger with an antique crossbow only to discover that he was a family friend.

Roland Copping (Collins) discovers that Jonathan was the burglar's accomplice and proceeds to play games with the couple, who are at first amused, then annoyed, and finally terrified by his strange, childish antics.

Elliott flings these disparate elements together with sublime confidence, driving the film along at a brisk pace and creating a strange and deliberately unreal world for his eccentric characters. He's aided by the clever production design of Brian Thomson and by Geoff Burton's sterling lensing.

•

FREAKED

1993, 79 mins, US Ⓥ col

Dir Tom Stern, Alex Winter ***Prod*** Harry Ufland, Mary Jane Ufland ***Scr*** Tim Burns, Tom Stern, Alex Winter ***Ph*** Jamie Thompson ***Ed*** Malcolm Campbell ***Mus*** Kevin Kiner ***Art*** Catherine Hardwicke

Act Alex Winter, Megan Ward, Michael Stoyanov, Randy Quaid, William Sadler, Brooke Shields (20th Century-Fox)

Freaked showcases Ted (or is it Bill?) of the *Excellent Adventure* as star, codirector, coproducer, cowriter and conspirator. An anarchic mix of hip comedy, vague, socially correct eco politics and overstated makeup effects, Alex Winter's pic takes a few shots at societal sacred cows but more often misses the target. The effort comes off much in the prankish manner of a student film.

Former child star Ricky Coogin (Winter) has entered into adulthood as a vain, obnoxious, amoral vulgarian. He succumbs to a multimillion dollar offer to go to a banana republic Santa Flan to squelch rumors about the deadly side effects of an industrial giant's Zygrot-24 chemical.

When he encounters eco radicals, all he can think about is effecting a disguise to romance protestor Julie (Megan Ward). With the assistance of buddy Ernie (Michael Stoyanov), he whisks her away from the throng but soon blows his cover.

The trio's discord deepens when they arrive at the ghoulish theme park Freek Land and encounter its maniacal mastermind, Elijah J. Skuggs (Randy Quaid). Skuggs lures them into his lair and, employing Zygrot, turns Julie and Ernie into Siamese twins while Ricky becomes half-man, half-monster.

Showing exceptionally good judgment, actor Keanu Reeves appears uncredited and visually unidentifiable as the Dog Boy.

•

FREAKS

1932, 61 mins, US Ⓥ ⦿ b/w

Dir Tod Browning ***Prod*** Tod Browning ***Scr*** Willis Goldbeck, Leon Gordon, Edgar Allan Woolf, Al Boasberg ***Ph*** Merritt B. Gerstad ***Ed*** Basil Wrangell ***Art*** Cedric Gibbons

Act Wallace Ford, Leila Hyams, Olga Baclanova, Roscoe Ates, Harry Earles, Daisy Earles (M-G-M)

Freaks is sumptuously produced, admirably directed, and no cost was spared. But Metro failed to realize that even with a different sort of offering the story still is important. Here it is not sufficiently strong to get and hold the interest, partly because interest cannot easily be gained for a too fantastic romance.

The plot outline is the love of a midget in a circus for a robust gymnast, her marriage with the idea of getting his fortune and putting him out of the way through poisoning and effecting a union with the strongman of the show.

The story [from *Spurs* by Tod Robbins] is laid in a European touring circus. It is only a one-ring affair, but it carries three times as many high-class freaks as the Ringling show ever trouped in one season, and the dressing tent is larger than the main top.

No effort is made to show the ring performance, most of the action occurring in the dressing tent and much of it while the show is closed. The midget leads are Harry and Daisy Earles. Earles builds on his fine performance in *The Unholy Three* (1930) but he fails in the stronger scenes, when he seeks to gain sympathy through his despair.

Daisy Earles is less successful as the midget rival to Olga Baclanova. She is a doll-like little woman who reads her lines with extreme care, but seldom succeeds in acting. Baclanova as the rather rowdy gymnast has several fine opportunities but at other times is handicapped by action too obvious and her cheerful effort to poison her tiny spouse carries no suggestion of menace. Harry Victor, as the strongman, is conventional and Wallace Ford and Leila Hyams, heading the cast, have little more than walk-through parts. The one sincere human note is Rose Dione in an unfortunately brief bit.

•

FREAKY FRIDAY

1976, 95 mins, US Ⓥ ⦿ col

Dir Gary Nelson ***Prod*** Ron Miller ***Scr*** Mary Rodgers ***Ph*** Charles F. Wheeler ***Ed*** Cotton Warburton ***Mus*** Johnny Mandel ***Art*** John B. Mansbridge, Jack Senter

Act Barbara Harris, Jodie Foster, John Astin, Patsy Kelly, Dick Van Patten, Ruth Buzzi (Walt Disney)

Freaky Friday is certainly one of the most offbeat films Walt Disney Productions has ever made, but it isn't one of the best. A promising concept—quarreling mother and teenage daughter switch personalities for a day—has been bungled by a talky, repetitive screenplay and overbroad direction. Barbara Harris and Jodie Foster salvage some scenes through sheer behavioral charm.

Mary Rodgers's screenplay, adapted from her 1972 book, touches more directly on modern social morés, particularly on women's lib issues, than is common for the studio. And pic has some eyebrow-raising Freudian undertones of the type which Disney pix usually avoid or suppress.

Foster is a normally unkempt and tomboyish prepubescent teen. She hates her mother (Harris) and worships her father (John Astin), a cardboard go-getter type. Both Harris and Foster reveal desires to escape their situations, and presto, they switch personalities while their bodies go about the usual daily routine.

The film's sexual undertones are mostly hidden beneath the continual barrage of sight gags, but they are there nonetheless. This is Disney's version of *Lolita*. Astin gets turned on when Harris starts calling him "daddy," and Foster gets furiously jealous when she encounters her father's curvaceous secretary. The film is a minefield of double meanings.

•

FREDDIE AS F.R.0.7.

1992, 90 mins, UK Ⓥ ⦿ col

Dir Jon Acevski ***Prod*** Norman Priggen, Jon Acevski ***Scr*** Jon Acevski, David Ashton ***Ph*** Rex Neville ***Ed*** Alex Rayment, Mick Manning ***Mus*** David Dundas, Rick Wentworth ***Art*** Paul Shardlow (Hollywood Road)

A shake 'n' bake mixture of virtually every toon genre going, *Freddie As F.R.0.7.* makes up in energy what it lacks in originality.

Billing itself before the main titles as "an amazing fantasy of a new kind," pic delivers plenty of the former but shortchanges on the latter. Yarn starts out as a Never Never Land fairy tale, segues rapidly to Disney-like anthropomorphism and finally launches into a mix of James Bonderie and *Star Wars*.

Plot kicks off with Freddie (voiced by Ben Kingsley) reminiscing about his origins as young Prince Frederic, turned into a frog by shape-shifting Aunt Messina (Billie Whitelaw) and saved from her cobra alter ego by kindly Nessie (Phyllis Logan), the Loch Ness monster. Growing up underwater, he later relocates to Paris as superagent F.R.0.7.

In place of a properly developed plotline, director Jon Acevski busies the screen with characters and incident, every now and then breaking into pleasant enough musical numbers that don't advance the action a jot.

•

FREDDY'S DEAD THE FINAL NIGHTMARE

1991, 90 mins, US Ⓥ ⦿ col

Dir Rachel Talalay ***Prod*** Robert Shaye, Aron Warner ***Scr*** Michael DeLuca ***Ph*** Declan Quinn ***Ed*** Janice Hampton ***Mus*** Brian May ***Art*** C. J. Strawn

Act Robert Englund, Lisa Zane, Shon Greenblatt, Lezlie Deane, Ricky Dean Logan, Yaphet Kotto (New Line)

Sixth and final edition in the *Nightmare on Elm Street* feature series delivers enough violence, black humor and even a final reel in 3-D to hit paydirt with horror-starved audiences.

Tired nature of the original Wes Craven concept is acknowledged by a new plotline by debutante helmer Rachel Talalay, with vengeful, undead murderer Freddy Krueger (Robert Englund, again in fine form) supposedly having killed off all the local children and teens in a little Ohio town, now set 10 years in the future.

He's using a young amnesiac, John (Shon Greenblatt) to revitalize his powers and ultimately seeking his daughter (Lisa Zane), who works as a counseller in a teen rehab shelter, in an effort to spread his vengeance to Elm Streets worldwide.

Most imaginative sequence deals with hearing impaired teen Carlos (Ricky Dean Logan). Freddy tears out the kid's hearing aid and torments him silently. Less successful is the 15-minute 3-D capper. Projected using the old-fashioned anaglyphic (red and blue lenses) glasses, sequence's color is thereby distorted compared to modern polarized lens efforts.

Guest stars Roseanne Arnold and hubbie Tom Arnold (cast as a childless couple of the future) and Alice Cooper (typecast as Freddy's abusive stepfather) add little to the stew. Johnny Depp, featured in 1984 original, pops up briefly as a teen on TV.

•

FREEBIE AND THE BEAN

1974, 112 mins, US Ⓥ ⦿ ▭ col

Dir Richard Rush ***Prod*** Richard Rush ***Scr*** Robert Kaufman ***Ph*** Laszlo Kovacs ***Ed*** Fredric Steinkamp, Michael McLean ***Mus*** Dominic Frontiere ***Art*** Hilyard Brown

Act Alan Arkin, James Caan, Loretta Swit, Jack Kruschen, Mike Kellin, Valerie Harper (Warner)

Freebie and the Bean stars Alan Arkin and James Caan as two allegedly "funny" lawless lawmen. Richard Rush's tasteless film, from a spitball script by Robert Kaufman, utilized lots of stunt and action crews disturbing the peace all over San Francisco.

The purported "humor" between the two stars largely hinges on Caan's delivery of what are nothing more than repeated racist slurs on Arkin's character's Chicano ancestry. Arkin's performance adds even more concrete nuances to this characterization. What passes for a basic story line is something about their nabbing bigtime gangster Jack Kruschen, and between car chases and mindless destruction of cars and other things, the plot lurches forward.

•

FREEJACK
1992, 108 mins, US Ⓥ ⊙ ▭ col
Dir Geoff Murphy ***Prod*** Ronald Shusett, Stuart Oken ***Scr*** Steven Pressfield, Ronald Shusett, Dan Gilroy ***Ph*** Amir Mokri ***Ed*** Dennis Virkler ***Mus*** Trevor Jones ***Art*** Joe Alves
Act Emilio Estevez, Mick Jagger, Rene Russo, Anthony Hopkins, Jonathan Banks, Amanda Plummer (Morgan Creek)

Employing a nightmarish vision of the year 2009 solely as a backdrop for a banal action yarn [based on Robert Sheckley's novel *Immortality Inc.*], *Freejack* has a curious list of talent (Mick Jagger and Anthony Hopkins). The primary plot—about a racecar driver (Emilio Estevez) who's plucked from a fiery death in 1991 to become a host body for the consciousness of a dying rich man—feels as superfluous as it is strained next to the other depressing evils on display.

Director Geoff Murphy, seen as an up-and-coming talent after his U.S. debut (*Young Guns II*) and two productions in his native New Zealand (*Utu*, *The Quiet Earth*), seems to have been either overwhelmed by the material or bored by it. Effect on the audience is a little of both.

The principal pursuers are equally one-dimensional, with Jagger as a body-snatching bounty hunter, and Jonathan Banks as the smarmy lieutenant of the business tycoon (Hopkins).

The most notable performance is that of Amanda Plummer as an abusive, gun-toting nun, providing a rare comic highlight.

•

FREE WILLY
1993, 111 mins, US Ⓥ ⊙ ▭ col
Dir Simon Wincer ***Prod*** Jennie Lew Tugend, Lauren Shuler-Donner ***Scr*** Keith A. Walker, Corey Blechman ***Ph*** Robbie Greenberg ***Ed*** O. Nicholas Brown ***Mus*** Basil Poledouris ***Art*** Charles Rosen
Act Jason James Richter, Lori Petty, Jayne Atkinson, August Schellenberg, Michael Madsen, Michael Ironside (Le Studio Canal Plus/Regency/Alcor)

Free Willy is an exhilarating drama of boy and nature that unabashedly pulls at the heart strings.

Jesse (Jason James Richter), an abandoned child in his umpteenth foster home, is running with a gang of outsiders who are into petty theft and random vandalism. But on one outing, he's nabbed at a Portland amusement park and winds up doing community service in lieu of juvenile detention. The sullen Jesse soon becomes enthralled by Willy, a killer whale, who's the unwilling and unresponsive main attraction of the resident aquatic show. They are kindred souls.

Jesse may at last be getting to apply himself to something practical but his new home life is by no means a slice of pristine Americana. His new folks (Jayne Atkinson, Michael Madsen) are unresolved about the decision to take him in and the boy's natural aversion to home life does little to make the transition easy.

Willy responds to Jesse's commands after months of ignoring the park animal trainer (Lori Petty) and the knowing native supervisor (August Schellenberg). This attracts the park's evil owner (Michael Ironside), who sees an opportunity for a sell-out attraction. When that venture fails, the management decides the only way out is sabotage. Jesse gets wind of the danger and enlists his friends to do the right thing as the story hurtles to its exciting conclusion.

In director Simon Wincer's hands the process of caring and observation of the orca is handled to perfection. As Jesse, Richter is a welcome antidote to the scrubbed contemporary moppet stars. The adults have less meaty parts but Schellenberg and Madsen bring a dignity to what might have been predictable parts.

•

FREE WILLY 2: THE ADVENTURE HOME
1995, 96 mins, US Ⓥ ⊙ ▭ col
Dir Dwight Little ***Prod*** Lauren Schuler-Donner, Jennie Lew Tugend ***Scr*** Karen Janszen, Corey Blechman, John Mattson ***Ph*** Laszlo Kovacs ***Ed*** Robert Brown, Dallas Puett ***Mus*** Basil Poledouris ***Art*** Paul Sylbert
Act Jason James Richter, August Schellenberg, Michael Madsen, Jayne Atkinson, Mary Kate Schellhardt, Francis Capra (Canal Plus/Regency/Warner)

Initially one senses that *Free Willy 2* is caught rudderless in a dreaded whirlpool and will wind up seeming more mechanical than any of the picture's pod of whales. But once free of clunky plot constraints, the continuing family saga is a swimmingly satisfying emotional yarn.

The enduring strength of this unexpected franchise is its theme of family. Both the young protagonist, Jesse (Jason James Richter), and the title orca are in search of that hallowed unit. In Willy's case, the search is a literal trek obstructed by ecological dangers.

Jesse's quest is more complex. He has an abundance of warm, caring people in his life—his foster parents, Glen (Michael Madsen) and Annie (Jayne Atkinson), who are superhuman paragons of patience; Randolph (August Schellenberg), his former ally at the aquarium; and Randolph's goddaughter, Nadine (Mary Kate Schellhardt).

But he then learns his mother, a drug addict, is dead, and Elvis, the half-brother he didn't know existed, is about to make a visit. He's also distracted by the ache of raging hormones and the proximity of Nadine. Add to all this personal angst an oiler gone aground and bleeding into the whale lanes off Washington state and you have *Free Willy 2* in a tightly packed nutshell. The movie is less a narrative arc than it is a juggling act. Director Dwight Little may be a tad awkward in his form, but he does manage to keep all the balls in the air.

Technical credits are clean and crisp without being cold. The mechanical whales rarely betray their wire-and-mesh origins.

•

FREE WILLY 3
THE RESCUE
1997, 86 mins, US Ⓥ ⊙ col
Dir Sam Pillsbury ***Prod*** Jennie Lew Tugend ***Scr*** John Mattson ***Ph*** Tobias Schliessler ***Ed*** Margie Goodspeed ***Mus*** Cliff Eidelman ***Art*** Brent Thomas
Act Jason James Richter, August Schellenberg, Annie Corley, Vincent Berry, Patrick Kilpatrick, Tasha Simms (Regency/Shuler-Donner/Warner)

Willy's latest adventure pits him and human buddy Jesse (Jason James Richter) against illegal whalers plying the seas of the Pacific Northwest, a decided entertainment improvement over the preceding outing.

Jesse has been hired as a research assistant on a floating marine biology lab, the *Noah*. Also aboard is his mentor, Randolph (August Schellenberg), and scientist Drew (Annie Corley). Their mission is to find whales, rig them with a monitoring device and watch to discover what's depleting their ranks.

Eco concerns aside, the screenplay fashions a compelling, adult human drama. Paralleling the *Noah*'s activities is a tough-minded story about John Wesley (Patrick Kilpatrick), captain of an illegal poaching ship, and his preteen son, Max (Vincent Berry).

Though director Sam Pillsbury has been absent from the bigscreen since 1990, he's in total control of the wide canvas here. The film is beautifully crafted in all departments.

•

FRENCH CONNECTION, THE
1971, 104 mins, US Ⓥ ⊙ col
Dir William Friedkin ***Prod*** Philip D'Antoni ***Scr*** Ernest Tidyman ***Ph*** Owen Roizman ***Ed*** Jerry Greenberg ***Mus*** Don Ellis ***Art*** Ben Kazaskow
Act Gene Hackman, Fernando Rey, Roy Scheider, Tony Lo-Bianco, Marcel Bozzuffi, Frederic De Pasquale (20th Century-Fox/D'Antoni)

So many changes have been made in Robin Moore's taut, factual reprise of one of the biggest narcotics hauls in New York police history that only the skeleton remains, but producer and screenwriter have added enough fictional flesh to provide director William Friedkin and his overall top-notch cast with plenty of material, and they make the most of it.

Gene Hackman and Roy Scheider are very believable as two hard-nosed narcotics officers who stumble onto what turned out to be the biggest narcotics haul to date. As suave and cool as the two cops are overworked, tired and mean, Fernando Rey is the French mastermind of the almost-perfect plan.

Friedkin includes a great elevated train-automobile chase sequence that becomes almost too tense to be enjoyable, especially for New Yorkers who are familiar with such activities.

Shot almost entirely in and around New York, Owen Roizman's fluid color camera explores most of Manhattan and much of Brooklyn without prettifying the backgrounds.

1971: Best Picture, Director, Actor (Gene Hackman), Adapted Screenplay, Editing

NOMINATIONS: Best Supp. Actor (Roy Scheider), Cinematography, Sound

•

FRENCH CONNECTION II
1975, 119 mins, US Ⓥ ⊙ col
Dir John Frankenheimer ***Prod*** Robert L. Rosen ***Scr*** Alexander Jacobs, Robert Dillon, Laurie Dillon ***Ph*** Claude Renoir ***Ed*** Tom Rolf ***Mus*** Don Ellis ***Art*** Jacques Saulnier
Act Gene Hackman, Fernando Rey, Bernard Fresson, Philippe Leotard, Ed Lauter, Cathleen Nesbitt (20th Century-Fox)

John Frankenheimer's *French Connection II* [from a screen story by Robert and Laurie Dillon] is both complementary to, yet distinctly different from, William Friedkin's *The French Connection*.

Gene Hackman as Popeye Doyle goes to Marseilles in search of heroin czar Fernando Rey (also encoring from the first pic). The assignment in reality is a setup (thereby implying that high-level law enforcement corruption still exists), and Hackman is duly kidnapped, drugged and left for dead by Rey.

Hackman's addiction and withdrawal sequences are terrifyingly real and make uncompromisingly clear the personal and social horror of drug abuse.

This plot turn is both intelligent and clever. Bernard Fresson is excellent as the French narc who must cope not only with his country's dope problem, but also Hackman's unruly presence.

Hackman's performance is another career highlight, ranging from cocky narc, Ugly American, helpless addict, humbled ego and relentless avenger.

•

FRENCH DRESSING
1964, 86 mins, UK b/w
Dir Ken Russell ***Prod*** Kenneth Harper ***Scr*** Peter Myers, Ronald Cass, Peter Brett ***Ph*** Ken Higgins ***Ed*** Jack Slade ***Mus*** Georges Delerue ***Art*** Jack Stephens
Act James Booth, Roy Kinnear, Marisa Mell, Alita Naughton, Bryan Pringle, Robert Robinson (Associated British)

It's a pity to see a promising comedy idea go busted through sheer lack of bright wit and irony. *French Dressing* is a light comedy which needed the satirical touch, but instead suffers from a flat, heavy treatment. This squelches many of the lighter, more promising moments.

Gormleigh-on-Sea is one of those British holiday resorts that suffer from acute dull-itis. A bright young deckchair attendant (James Booth) cons the local entertainments manager and the mayor into running a film festival. They persuade an ambitious young French actress to be the star of the proceedings which lead to some inevitable disasters and coy jokes such as a total washout at the opening of a new nudist beach and a riot at a premiere. Only quick thinking by the young American journalist girl friend of James Booth saves the situation.

Too much stodgy joking does not aid predictable slapstick situations. Quick cutting and speeding up of camerawork are not enough to disguise the fact that this is not a soufflé but mainly an indigestible pancake.

•

FRENCH KISS
1995, 111 mins, US Ⓥ ⊙ ▭ col
Dir Lawrence Kasdan ***Prod*** Tim Bevan, Eric Fellner, Meg Ryan, ***Scr*** Adam Brooks ***Ph*** Owen Roizman ***Ed*** Joe Hutshing ***Mus*** James Newton Howard ***Art*** Jon Hutman
Act Meg Ryan, Kevin Kline, Timothy Hutton, Jean Reno, Francois Cluzet, Susan Anbeh (Working Title/20th Century-Fox/PolyGram)

French Kiss is one of those travelogues where flipping through the pictures would be more fun than actually taking the trip.

Meg Ryan (who also coproduced through her Prufrock Pictures) and Kevin Kline generally outshine the material in this wispy and somewhat anachronistic romance, which has Ryan's high-strung Kate overcoming her fear of flying and winging to Paris to recapture her fiancé (Timothy Hutton) after he dumps her for another woman.

Kate hooks up on the plane with Luc (Kline), an oily French thief who plants one of his prized possessions in Kate's purse. When that bag gets stolen, the two are forced into a cross-country journey that's both postcard-pretty and somewhat aimless, with a shortage of laughs between the promising start and predictable finale.

For starters, the script by Adam Brooks waffles between the romantic quadrangle (the last side being Hutton's stunning new flame, played by French actress Susan Anbeh) and Luc's apparent thievery, with a genial cop (Jean Reno) in not-so-hot pursuit.

This is the fifth collaboration between Kasdan and Kline, and the latter clearly has a good time creating this suave if smarmy character. For Ryan, Kate represents merely the latest and probably least appealing in a string of persnickety romantic dreamers, though on the plus side Ryan does provide a few disarmingly funny scenes of broad physical comedy. Hutton has little to do as her wayward beau.

•

FRENCH LIEUTENANT'S WOMAN, THE
1981, 127 mins, UK Ⓥ ⊙ col
Dir Karel Reisz ***Prod*** Leon Clore ***Scr*** Harold Pinter ***Ph*** Freddie Francis ***Ed*** John Bloom ***Mus*** Carl Davis ***Art*** Assheton Gorton
Act Meryl Streep, Jeremy Irons, David Warner, Leo McKern, Charlotte Mitchell, Hilton McRae (United Artists/Junipaer)

Diverse directing talents including Fred Zinnemann, Richard Lester and Mike Nichols all tried and failed to conquer the complicated narrative of John Fowles's epic romantic novel, *The French Lieutenant's Woman*.

Finally, it took director Karel Reisz and playwright Harold Pinter to develop an ingenious method to convey the essence of Fowles's book. The film retells the novel's story, set in 1867, of a strange young woman dishonored by her involvement with a French soldier and the English gentleman who finds her mystery and sadness irresistible.

Simultaneously, a parallel story of the affair between the two actors portraying the central roles in a film within-a-film unfolds on screen.The effect of the two interwoven stories is at times irritating and confusing, but ultimately most affecting. This is due in large part to the strong performances of Meryl Streep as Sarah Woodruff/Anna and Jeremy Irons as Charles Smithson/Mike.

The action flip-flops between the two tales, but favors the historic story. Reisz employs several lightning mixes to bridge the action, but more often abruptly moves from past to present.

The unconventional approach to Fowles's novel takes some getting used to but succeeds in conveying the complexity of the original in the final analysis.

Cameraman Freddie Francis deserves special mention for his painterly skill of recreating 19th-century Dorset and the contrasting sheen of the contemporary segments.

The casting of Meryl Streep as Sarah/Anna could not have been better. Sarah comes complete with unbridled passions and Anna is the cool, detached professional. There is never a false note in the sharply contrasting characters.

1981: NOMINATIONS: Best Actress (Meryl Streep), Adapted Screenplay, Costume Design, Art Direction, Editing

•

FRENCH LINE, THE

1954, 102 mins, US Ⓥ col

Dir Lloyd Bacon ***Prod*** Edmund Grainger ***Scr*** Mary Loos, Richard Sale ***Ph*** Harry J. Wild ***Ed*** Robert Ford ***Mus*** Constantin Bakaleinikoff

Act Jane Russell, Gilbert Roland, Arthur Hunnicutt, Mary McCarty, Joyce MacKenzie, Paula Corday (RKO)

Except for a four-minute, censorably costumed dance by Jane Russell, this is a rather mild, gabby, fashion parade in 3-D.

The plot is the long-worked one about a rich girl who wants to be loved for herself and goes incognito as a working frail to find the right man. It's an okay basis for a musical if ingenuously handled, but there is little of the imaginative displayed in Lloyd Bacon's direction or in the screenplay by Mary Loos and Richard Sale [based on a story by Matty Kemp and Isabel Dawn]. Once in a while a snappy quip breaks through the long passages of verbiage that strain too hard to be smart talk. And in line with the film's principal concern, these snappy quips are bosom-conscious.

Russell is an eye-pleaser, and she can be a good musical comedy actress (*Gentlemen Prefer Blondes*) when given material and direction. Gilbert Roland's suave way with the ladies helps his character of the French lover who pursues oil-rich Russell for herself, not her millions.

•

FRENCHMAN'S CREEK

1945, 113 mins, US col

Dir Mitchell Leisen ***Prod*** Mitchell Leisen ***Scr*** Talbot Jennings ***Ph*** George Barnes ***Ed*** Alma Macrorie ***Mus*** Victor Young ***Art*** Hans Dreier, Ernst Fegte

Act Joan Fontaine, Arturo de Cordova, Basil Rathbone, Nigel Bruce, Cecil Kellaway, Ralph Forbes (Paramount)

Frenchman's Creek is a 17th-century romance about the lady and the pirate, beautifully Technicolored and lavishly mounted. Film reputedly cost over $3 million to produce, Paramount's costliest investment [at the time].

The romantic pirate from France who invades the Cornish coast of England, hiding his frigate in what thus becomes known as Frenchman's Creek, plays his role with all the musical comedy bravado the part calls for.

The romance is supposedly forthright and played straight. Joan Fontaine seeks refuge in the Cornish castle to get away from a stupid husband (Ralph Forbes) and a ducal menace. The scoundrelly servant at the Cornish retreat is actually the pirate chief's hireling, and the romance between the two is but one of a sequence of similar adventures.

The performances are sometimes unconsciously tongue-in-cheek, but withal come off well. Cecil Kellaway is particularly good as the servant.

The scripting [from the novel by Daphne du Maurier] at times borders on the ludicrous, especially when almost all the sympathetic figures wax near hysteria in their scoffing at the dangers which may beset them. Productionally it is ultra. And no minor assist is an excellent Victor Young score.

1945: Best Color Art Decoration

•

FRENCH VAMPIRE IN AMERICA

SEE: INNOCENT BLOOD

•

FRENZY

1972, 116 mins, UK Ⓥ ⦿ col

Dir Alfred Hitchcock ***Prod*** Alfred Hitchcock ***Scr*** Anthony Shaffer ***Ph*** Gil Taylor ***Ed*** John Jympson ***Mus*** Ron Goodwin ***Art*** Syd Cain

Act Jon Finch, Barry Foster, Barbara Leigh-Hunt, Anna Massey, Alec McCowen, Vivien Merchant (Universal)

Armed with a superior script by Anthony Shaffer, an excellent cast, and a top technical crew, Alfred Hitchcock fashions a first-rate melodrama about an innocent man hunted by Scotland Yard for a series of sex-strangulation murders.

Working from Arthur La Bern's novel, *Goodbye Piccadilly, Farewell Leicester Square*, Shaffer develops a finely structured screenplay. Jon Finch heads the cast as something of a loser who becomes trapped by circumstantial evidence in the sordid murders of several women, including his former wife (Barbara Leigh-Hunt), and current girlfriend (Anna Massey). The audience knows early who the real culprit is—in this case, Finch's friend, Barry Foster—so the interest lies in hoping for the rescue of the hero. Hitchcock has used this basic dramatic situation before.

•

FRESA Y CHOCOLATE

(STRAWBERRY AND CHOCOLATE)

1994, 111 mins, Cuba/Mexico/Spain Ⓥ col

Dir Tomas Gutierrez Alea, Juan Carlos Tabeo ***Scr*** Senel Paz, Tomas Gutierrez Alea ***Ph*** Mario Garcia Joya ***Ed*** Miriam Talavera, Osvaldo Donatien ***Mus*** Jose Maria Vitier ***Art*** Fernando O'Reilly

Act Jorge Perugorria, Vladimir Cruz, Mirta Ibarra, Francisco Gattorno, Jorge Angelino, Marilyn Solaya (ICAIC/Imcine/Tabasco/Telemadrid/SGAE)

This comedy from Cuba is a gem. Filled with malicious swipes against the Castro regime, it's a provocative but very humane comedy about sexual opposites.

David (Vladimir Cruz) is a macho but naive and inexperienced youth who believes passionately in communism and the Cuban Revolution. He's an idealist who has accepted the official line on everything, but his knowledge of the world, especially of art, music and literature, is scanty.

Diego (Jorge Perugorria) is an effeminate gay who revels in his gayness. He's instantly attracted to the handsome David when they share a table at an outdoor cafe, and he manages to persuade David to come to his apartment on a pretext. The homophobic David is most uneasy during this first encounter, especially when Diego prattles on about the ills of Cuban society and decides it's his duty to expose this most unrevolutionary Cuban.

Though the film's a bit long, vet director Tomas Gutierrez Alea and his partner Juan Carlos Tabio (director of the hilarious *Plaff*, who was brought in when Alea was taken ill) have come up with a winner here, with much credit going to the two lead actors.

1994: NOMINATION: Best Foreign Language Film

•

FRESH

1994, 112 mins, US/France Ⓥ ⦿ col

Dir Boaz Yakin ***Prod*** Lawrence Bender, Randy Ostrow ***Scr*** Boaz Yakin ***Ph*** Adam Holender ***Ed*** Dorian Harris ***Mus*** Stewart Copeland ***Art*** Dan Leigh

Act Sean Nelson, Giancarlo Esposito, Samuel L. Jackson, N'Bushe Wright, Ron Brice, Jean LaMarre (Lumiere)

Fresh is the story of one young boy's way out of the vicious circle of drug violence that defines the world in which he has grown up.

Skillfully made and involving, French-financed first feature by Boaz Yakin stands to generate considerable controversy.

Living with 11 female cousins in New York under the care of his Aunt Frances, black, 12-year-old Fresh (Sean Nelson) keeps his own counsel as he delivers for local heroin kingpin Esteban (Giancarlo Esposito) and does freelance work for assorted sidewalk and backroom dealers.

Fresh surreptitiously meets his father, Sam (the excellent Samuel L. Jackson), in Washington Square for sessions of speed chess. What chess has to do with the rest of Fresh's life only slowly becomes apparent. In a shocking sequence, a pickup basketball game turns deadly as well-known crack dealer Jake (a very scary Jean LaMarre) shoots dead an opponent. A clear witness to the crimes, the taciturn Fresh can't say anything to authorities if he wants to stay alive, but cleverly begins pitting against each other all his employers, those responsible for the violence and death all around him.

Performances are terrifically intense from top to bottom. Esposito is particularly riveting as the sinewy drug baron, and Ron Brice also scores as a rival dealer. Producing team has made this look like a big, polished film on a no-doubt limited budget.

•

FRESH BAIT

SEE: L'APPAT

•

FRESHMAN, THE

1990, 102 mins, US Ⓥ ⦿ col

Dir Andrew Bergman ***Prod*** Mike Lobell ***Scr*** Andrew Bergman ***Ph*** William A. Fraker ***Ed*** Barry Malkin ***Mus*** David Newman ***Art*** Ken Adam

Act Marlon Brando, Matthew Broderick, Bruno Kirby, Penelope Ann Miller, Paul Benedict, Maximilian Schell (Tri-Star)

Marlon Brando's sublime comedy performance elevates *The Freshman* from screwball comedy to a quirky niche in film history—among films that comment on cult movies.

Mario Puzo and Francis Coppola's *The Godfather* is director Andrew Bergman's starting point. Incoming NYU film student Matthew Broderick is exposed not only to that Paramount film (and its sequel) in pretentious prof Paul Benedict's classroom but meets up with a virtual doppelganger for Don Vito Corleone in the form of mobster Carmine Sabatini (Brando).

The ornate and intentionally screwy plotline has Brando making an irresistible offer to Broderick to work for him part-time as a delivery boy. Broderick's first assignment is transporting a huge (but real) lizard from the airport. Broderick quickly tumbles to the criminality of Brando and his nutty partner Maximilian Schell, but is unable to extricate himself.

Pic's weakest element is the recurring satire of film studies. Although Benedict is droll as an academic poseur, the mocking of film analysis is puerile and obvious.

Broderick is ably abetted by two previous costars: Penelope Anne Miller (*Biloxi Blues*), winning as an offbeat form of mafia princess; and B. D. Wong (who popped up in *Family Business*) as Schell's goofy partner in culinary crime. Tech credits on the mixed New York and Toronto shoot are good, capturing the right amount of Greenwich Village ambience.

•

FREUD

(UK: FREUD—THE SECRET PASSION)

1962, 140 mins, US b/w

Dir John Huston ***Prod*** Wolfgang Reinhardt ***Scr*** Charles Kaufman, Wolfgang Reinhardt ***Ph*** Douglas Slocombe ***Ed*** Ralph Kemplen ***Mus*** Jerry Goldsmith ***Art*** Stephen B. Grimes

Act Montgomery Clift, Susannah York, Larry Parks, Susan Kohner, Eric Portman, David McCallum (Universal)

Intricate scenario by Charles Kaufman and producer Reinhardt, from the former's story, translates into dramatic, not biographical, terms the events of five key years (1885–90) in Freud's life, the years during which he formulated his principal theory—that sexual instinct is the basic one in the human personality—and led him to discover and describe the presence of sexual behavior even in infancy.

The drama revolves around Freud's (Montgomery Clift) treatment of a young patient (Susannah York) who has broken down mentally and physically upon the death of her father. In treating her, and relating her neuroses to his own, he is able not only to cure her, but to formulate the Oedipus Complex theory—the child's fixation on the parent of the opposite sex. This is the dramatic nucleus of the film.

The appropriately bewhiskered Clift delivers an intense, compassionate and convincing personification of Freud. York is vivid and true as his agitated patient, although the character is not always in sharp focus. Larry Parks etches a warm and appealing portrait of Freud's friend, colleague and associate. Susan Kohner is fine as Freud's understanding wife. Among the supporting players, Eric Portman stands out with a crisp, biting enactment of Freud's orthodox superior who reveals the contradictory nature of his inner personality only when he is dying.

1962: NOMINATIONS: Best Original Story & Screenplay, Original Music Score

•

FREUDLOSE GASSE, DIE
(JOYLESS STREET; STREETS OF SORROW; THE STREET OF SORROW)
1925, 96 mins, Germany Ⓥ ⦿ ⊗ b/w
Dir G. W. Pabst ***Scr*** Willi Haas ***Ph*** Guido Seeber, Kurt Oertel ***Art*** Sohnie Erdmann, Otto Erdmann
Act Asta Nielsen, Greta Garbo, Valeska Gert, Werner Krauss, Einar Hanson, Karl Ettlinger (Sofar)

The picture's only commercial value is the presence at the head of the cast of Greta Garbo. The role is a poor one of a rather furtive and bedraggled heroine which does not gain much sympathy.

The picture has minor virtues and major defects. The principal drawback is that it's fearfully long and dull, besides being hard to follow in its complications. The central idea is good. It deals with the middle class enmity in Europe toward the post-war social upstarts, rich war profiteers and dealers in the necessities of life who oppress the poor and become wealthy on hard-wrung profits. Probably the novel [by Hugo Bettauer] dealt more adequately with these materials.

The screen story gets them tangled up with shoddy melodrama in what one takes to be the red-light district of Vienna. The pure girl who is lured into the house of ill-fame doesn't deliver much of a sensation here. Neither does the murder mystery. One solves the mystery immediately and there isn't any suspense.

Some of the character types—the pompous butcher and the two fat, sleek profiteers among others—are excellent in portraiture, and the settings are generally interesting.

Photography is far from high grade. Often the quality is thin and sometimes blurred, the best effects being in the handling of heavy light and shade masses.

[Version reviewed was a toned-down 95-min. version released in the U.S. in 1927.]

•

FREUD—THE SECRET PASSION
SEE: FREUD

•

FRIDAY
1995, 89 mins, US Ⓥ col
Dir F. Gary Gray ***Prod*** Pat Charbonnet ***Scr*** Ice Cube, DJ Pooh ***Ph*** Gerry Lively ***Ed*** John Carter ***Mus*** Frank Fitzpatrick (sup.), Hidden Faces ***Art*** Bruce Bellamy
Act Ice Cube, Chris Tucker, Nia Long, Tiny "Zeus" Lister, Jr., John Witherspoon, Anna Maria Horsford (New Line)

Rather like a cross between *Up in Smoke* and an episode of *The Jeffersons*, *Friday* is a crudely made, sometimes funny bit of porchfront humor from the 'hood.

The South Central L.A. community on view here center on lazybones Craig (Ice Cube) who spends the day hanging out with his fast-talking, bud-smoking buddy Smokey (Chris Tucker). Craig's working-stiff dad (John Witherspoon) takes a dump while admonishing his slacker son to hit the pavement, and Craig's girlfriend, Joi (Paula Jai Parker), is a braying banshee viciously suspicious of any other woman who might come within Craig's range, especially the foxy Debbie (Nia Long).

What laughs there are mostly come from the reefer-puffing comedian Tucker, a lanky, rubber-faced, hyperactive near-hysteric whose character always has an outrageous rationalization for his irresponsible behavior and, in his comic devotion to leafy highs, reps a throwback to the druggy humor of the '70s.

Ice Cube functions—for the most part, literally—as Tucker's straight man, and his slow-on-the-uptake line readings and physical inertness drag things down.

•

FRIDAY FOSTER
1975, 89 mins, US Ⓥ col
Dir Arthur Marks ***Prod*** Arthur Marks ***Scr*** Orville Hampton ***Ph*** Harry May ***Ed*** Stanley Fragen ***Mus*** Luchi De Jesus
Act Pam Grier, Yaphet Kotto, Godfrey Cambridge, Thalmus Rosulala, Eartha Kitt, Jim Backus (American International)

Friday Foster is based on a comic strip of the same name; Pam Grier is a fearless magazine fotog, sort of a female Clark Kent, who stumbles onto a St. Valentine's Day–type massacre involving black millionaire Thalmus Rasulala and lots of political and underworld opponents mixed up on both sides.

There's a truly impressive credit sheet, including Yaphet Kotto as a cop, Godfrey Cambridge as a swishy criminal type, Eartha Kitt as an outrageously camp fashion designer, Scatman Crothers as a dirty-minded minister, Ted Lange as a sardonic pimp, and Jim Backus as the Mr. Big who pulls the strings behind the action.

Grier has some steamy sex scenes and a lot of rugged action, though she isn't totally macho and radiates a lot of traditional feminine charm along the way.

•

FRIDAY THE THIRTEENTH
1933, 65 mins, UK b/w
Dir Victor Saville ***Scr*** Emlyn Williams ***Ph*** Charles Van Enger ***Ed*** R. E. Dearing ***Mus*** Louis Levy (dir.) ***Art*** Alfred Junge, Alex Vetchinsky
Act Sonnie Hale, Jessie Matthews, Edmund Gwenn, Max Miller, Emlyn Williams, Ralph Richardson (Gainsborough/Gaumont-British)

There's a good idea here and the execution is far from bad. It's a combination *Grand Hotel* and bus idea [story by C. H. Moresby-White and Sidney Gilliat] that's pretty well thought out.

Opens with a bus going down a London street in a rainstorm. A crash, two people are killed and several wounded. Then the clock goes back over the day of all the passengers that were in the bus, relating the incidents that got them there at the time. All unrelated, of course. But the bus crash fixes things up all around.

There's the chorus girl who's had a spat with her sweetie and, hurt, is en route to keep a date with the fresh guy who's been trying vainly to make her, up to then. There's the blackmailer who's just taken the last money from a poor boy with the threat of returning for more.

There's the henpecked husband, en route home late, after working overtime and not knowing that when he gets home he'll find his wife has run off with another man. There's a wisecracking and rather sympathetic crook being baited by detectives. So on down the line and none of it boring.

Cast is exceptionally good. Jessie Matthews as the chorine, is best. Frank Lawton and Ursula Jeans don't come out too well, being over-directed and in unfortunate spots. Max Miller impresses nicely in a comedy bit and Ralph Richardson does well by a character bit. Gordon Harker repeats his comedy characterization that brought him attention in *Rome Express* and Edmund Gwenn and Mary Jerrold both do exceptionally well in character bits.

•

FRIDAY THE 13TH
1980, 95 mins, US Ⓥ ⦿ col
Dir Sean S. Cunningham ***Prod*** Sean S. Cunningham ***Scr*** Victor Miller ***Ph*** Barry Abrams ***Ed*** Bill Freda ***Mus*** Harry Manfredini ***Art*** Virginia Field
Act Betsy Palmer, Adrienne King, Harry Crosby, Laurie Bartram, Robbi Morgan (Cunningham)

Low-budget in the worst sense—with no apparent talent or intelligence to offset its technical inadequacies—*Friday the 13th* has nothing to exploit but its title.

Another teenager-in-jeopardy entry, contrived to lure the profitable *Halloween* audience, this one is set at a crumbling New Jersey summer camp, shuttered for 20 years after a history of "accidental" deaths and other spooky stuff, and about to be reopened for the summer.

Six would-be counselors arrive to get the place ready, then are progressively dispatched by knife, hatchet, spear and arrow.

Producer-director Sean S. Cunningham telegraphs the six murders too far ahead to keep anyone in even vague suspense, and without building a modicum of tension in between.

•

FRIDAY THE 13TH, PART II
1981, 87 mins, US Ⓥ ⦿ col
Dir Steve Miner ***Prod*** Steve Miner ***Scr*** Ron Kurz ***Ph*** Peter Stein ***Ed*** Susan E. Cunningham ***Mus*** Harry Manfredini ***Art*** Virginia Field
Act Amy Steel, John Furey, Adrienne King, Kirsten Baker, Stu Charno, Warrington Gillette (Paramount/Georgetown)

Horror fans will probably delight in seeing yet another group of sexy, teen camp counselors gruesomely executed by yet another unknown assailant, but the enthusiasm will dampen once they recognize too many of the same twists and turns used in the original.

When we last left Camp Crystal Lake one nubile counselor (Adrienne King) managed to survive the murderous spree of surprise villain Betsy Palmer who, it might be remembered, was killing all of the counselors as a symbolic revenge for her son drowning in camp years earlier.

Now five years have gone by and a new group of counselors (that seems to be the operating vocation here) have returned next door to the legendary camp. They know about the past violence and are even told of the legend of Palmer's son Jason, who supposedly lives on in the woods.

Producer-director Steve Miner doesn't move in and out of scenes with the flair of original producer-director Sean Cunningham nor is he able to create the same nauseatingly realistic murder situations (perhaps he's better off for the latter).

•

FRIDAY THE 13TH, PART III
1982, 95 mins, US Ⓥ ⦿ ⊏⊐ col
Dir Steve Miner ***Prod*** Frank Mancuso, Jr. ***Scr*** Martin Kitrosser, Carol Watson ***Ph*** Gerald Feil ***Ed*** George Hively ***Mus*** Harry Manfredini ***Art*** Robb Wilson King
Act Dana Kimmell, Richard Brooker, Tracie Savage, Catherine Parks, Paul Kratka, Jeffrey Rogers (Paramount/Jason)

Friday the 13th was dreadful and took in more than $17 million. *Friday the 13th Part 2* was just as bad and took in more than $10 million. *Friday the 13th Part III* is terrible, too.

This time it's Dana Kimmell who leads the gang up to evil Lake Crystal for an outing. Crazy Jason is still there, though played this time by Richard Brooker instead of Warrington Gillette.

Kimmel has had some previous contact with Jason but doesn't quite remember it. All the kids are just about that bright, especially her boyfriend Paul Kratka. The most shocking scene in the film, in fact, is when Kratka gets his brains squeezed out; up until then, you would have sworn he didn't have any brains.

There are some dandy 3-D sequences, however, of a yo-yo going up and down and popcorn popping.

•

FRIDAY THE 13TH: THE FINAL CHAPTER
1984, 91 mins, US Ⓥ ⦿ col
Dir Joseph Zito ***Prod*** Frank Mancuso, Jr. ***Scr*** Barney Cohen ***Ph*** Joao Fernandes ***Ed*** Joel Goodman, Daniel Loewenthal ***Mus*** Harry Manfredini ***Art*** Shelton H. Bishop III
Act Crispin Glover, Kimberly Beck, Barbara Howard,, E. Erich Anderson, Corey Feldman, Alan Hayes (Paramount)

Opening line of film—"I don't want to scare anyone, but Jason is still out there"—is film's only laugh, aside from unintended chuckle in the credit roll for First Aid. Everyone in sight of the lake gets it this time, except for a little boy with a fetish for masks who slaughters the crazed Jason and the boy's older sister (Corey Feldman and Kimberly Beck).

That leaves a dozen others who don't make it. More accurately, most are butchered after making it.

Of course, nobody is expected to take this stuff seriously. [Screen story by Bruce Hidemi Sakow.] Given, however, the consistent pro production value, the evisceration on parade is not campy.

Implausibilities abound as ever, and several *Friday the 13th* veteran players make brief appearances in an opening flashback compilation of old footage [from the three previous pics].

•

FRIDAY THE 13TH , PART V: A NEW BEGINNING
1985, 92 mins, US Ⓥ ⦿ col
Dir Danny Steinmann ***Prod*** Timothy Silver ***Scr*** Martin Kitrosser, David Cohen, Danny Steinmann ***Ph*** Stephen L. Posey ***Ed*** Bruce Green ***Mus*** Harry Manfredini ***Art*** Robert Howland
Act John Shepard, Melanie Kinnaman, Shavar Ross, Richard Young, Marco St. John, Juliette Cummins (Paramount)

The fifth *Friday the 13th* film reiterates a chronicle of butcherings with even less variation than its predecessors. Director Danny Steinmann (who made his theatrical debut with 1984's *Savage Streets*) does a lot with rain in this film and his conclusion is moderately well-orchestrated for maximum effect.

However, the film, which features a new Jason this time (but the same hockey mask), takes too long to set up its litany of eviscerations. For the record, the little boy who helped kill Jason in the last film is now a troubled teenager (John Shepard) hell-bent on a crazed future of his own. [Screen story by Martin Kitrosser and David Cohen.]

•

FRIDAY THE 13TH, PART VI
SEE: JASON LIVES

•

FRIDAY THE 13TH, PART VII: THE NEW BLOOD
1988, 90 mins, US Ⓥ ⦿ col
Dir John Carl Buechler ***Prod*** Iain Paterson ***Scr*** Daryl Haney, Manuel Fidello ***Ph*** Paul Elliott ***Ed*** Barry Zetlin, Maureen O'Connell, Martin Jay Sadoff ***Mus*** Harry Manfredini, Fred Mollin ***Art*** Richard Lawrence

Act Lar Park Lincoln, Kevin Blair, Susan Blu, Terry Kiser, Susan Jennifer Sullivan, Elizabeth Kaitan (Paramount/Friday Four)

After a prolog with scenes from earlier *Fridays*, routine screenplay introduces Tina (Lar Park Lincoln), a pretty young blonde who is under psychiatric care because flashbacks of her father's death won't go away. Her troubled mind's eye also sees tragedies before or just after they happen, and she can move objects without touching them.

On the advice of her less-than-dedicated shrink (Terry Kiser), Tina and her mother (Susan Blu), head up to Crystal Lake for a little on-site therapy. When a guilt-ridden Tina wishes her father back, she accidentally releases Jason from his watery grave. The rest is formula in both content and execution.

The still indestructible Jason (played by stunt coordinator Kane Hodder) has deteriorated so much that parts of his skeleton protrude from flesh and rags. He meets his match with the girl who cooks up her own storm with a willful stare. Although their duel offers original effects-laden thrills and stunts, it's too little and too late.

•

FRIDAY THE 13TH, PART VIII: JASON TAKES MANHATTAN
1989, 100 mins, US Ⓥ ⦿ col
Dir Rob Hedden *Prod* Randolph Cheveldave *Scr* Rob Hedden *Ph* Bryan England *Ed* Steve Mirkovich *Mus* Fred Mollin *Art* David Fischer
Act Jensen Daggett, Scott Reeves, Peter Mark Richman, Barbara Bingham, V. C. Dupree, Kane Hodder (Horror/Paramount)

Paramount's latest cynical excursion into sadistic violence is lifted slightly above its generic mire by the stylish efforts of debuting director Rob Hedden.

The minimal variation this time in Hedden's script is to have most of the action take place on a cruise ship taking the Crystal Lake high school grads to Manhattan, where some humor naturally arises from the locals' indifference to the madman in their midst.

The film devotes its energies to recycling all the tried-and-true methods of dispatching teens by stabbing, strangling, electrocuting, burning, head-smashing, slashing and spearing.

Jensen Daggett is a standout as the troubled young girl on whom Jason is fixated. V. C. Dupree has vibrant energy in his boxing scenes, Sharlene Martin has a fine time with the bitch role, and Martin Cummins is funny as a video freak who compulsively films the proceedings.

•

FRIEDA
1947, 97 mins, UK Ⓥ b/w
Dir Basil Dearden *Prod* Michael Balcon *Scr* Ronald Millar, Angus MacPhail *Ph* Gordon Dines *Ed* Leslie Norman *Mus* John Greenwood *Art* Jim Morahan
Act Mai Zetterling, David Farrar, Glynis Johns, Flora Robson, Albert Lieven, Gladys Henson (Ealing)

The thoughtful play [by Ronald Millar] that scored a fair success on the London stage has been turned into a thoughtful picture.

Story begins in April 1945, in the bombed shell of a Polish Protestant church, when Robert (David Farrar), a British Officer, marries Frieda (Mai Zetterling), a Catholic German nurse who helped him escape. She loves him, but Robert is merely repaying a debt with a British passport and a trip to his home in a small English town.

Frieda gets a cool welcome. Only person to show any warmth is Robert's sister-in-law Judy (Glynis Johns), a war widow who loves Robert. Being the sixth year of the war, and the era of flying bombs, there is natural hostility among the townspeople. Peace comes, and gradually Frieda is accepted.

On the eve of the ceremony to ratify their marriage with the Roman Catholic Church brother Ricky (Albert Lieven) arrives dressed as a Polish soldier. She soon discovers that beneath the uniform is a fanatical Nazi looking forward to the next war.

Political implications constantly intruding on this tragic love story, as they are doubtless intended to do, hinder it from being poignant and moving. To play the name part, Zetterling was imported from Sweden. No pinup girl, and with a liking for the Veronica Lake hair-do, she has a strong personality but she's given a limited opportunuty to reveal her range.

•

FRIED GREEN TOMATOES
(UK: FRIED GREEN TOMATOES AT THE WHISTLE STOP CAFE)
1991, 130 mins, US Ⓥ ⦿ col
Dir Jon Avnet *Prod* Jon Avnet, Jordan Kerner *Scr* Fanny Flagg, Jon Avnet *Ph* Geoffrey Simpson *Ed* Debra Neil *Mus* Thomas Newman *Art* Barbara Ling
Act Kathy Bates, Jessica Tandy, Mary Stuart Masterson, Mary-Louise Parker, Nick Searcy, Cicely Tyson (Universal/Act III)

Celebrating the crucial, sustaining friendships between two sets of modern-day and 1930s Southern femmes, pic [based on Fanny Flagg's novel *Fried Green Tomatoes at the Whistle Stop Cafe*] emerges as absorbing and life-affirming quality fare, but for a story celebrating fearlessness, it's remarkably cautious.

Kathy Bates plays a frumpy middle-aged Southern suburbanite, who finds inspiration in the tales spun by a feisty nursing-home resident (Jessica Tandy). These center on a gambling, brawling but good-hearted rural Alabama girl (Mary Stuart Masterson), and how she almost got fingered for murder.

Seems the girl had developed a deep friendship with a demure, God-fearing young woman (Mary Louise Parker) who later on in life was having trouble with her abusive husband (Nick Searcy). Masterson helped her find the courage to run off with her baby and come to work as the cook at her Whistle Stop Cafe. When Searcy turns up missing Masterson and her "colored man" (Stan Shaw) are arrested on suspicion of murder.

Actual trial is merely a peg for a story that's mostly about the stalwart friendship between the two young femmes, isolated in a world of ham-handed, bigoted menfolk. Since the Masterson character is clearly in love with Parker, it's annoying that pic skates over the question of her sexuality.

Still, Tandy is at her sparkling best as the endearing old storyteller. Bates is also terrif in a funny and sympathetic turn. Director Jon Avnet, in his feature film debut, gets first-rate work from the featured performers.

1991: Best Supp. Actress (Jessica Tandy)

NOMINATION: Best Adapted Screenplay

•

FRIED GREEN TOMATOES AT THE WHISTLE STOP CAFE
SEE: FRIED GREEN TOMATOES

•

FRIENDLY PERSUASION
1956, 137 mins, US Ⓥ ⦿ col
Dir William Wyler *Prod* William Wyler *Scr* [Michael Wilson] *Ph* Ellsworth Fredricks *Ed* Robert Swink, Edward Biery Jr. *Mus* Dimitri Tiomkin *Art* Edward S. Haworth
Act Gary Cooper, Dorothy McGuire, Anthony Perkins, Marjorie Main, Robert Middleton, Richard Eyer (Allied Artists)

While it is the simple story [from a novel by Jessamyn West] of a Quaker family in Indiana back in the 1860s, the footage contains just about everything in the way of comedy and drama, suspense and action. Producer-director William Wyler had the project in mind for eight years and brought the property to Allied Artists from Paramount. Production cost was reportedly over $3 million. Film is without a screenplay credit.

After many warm, beguiling vignettes of family life, story works into its key dramatic point tying onto the Quaker feeling against bearing arms against a fellow man.

Role of the Quaker father, a man touched with gentle humor and inward strength, is glove-fit for Gary Cooper and he carries it off to an immense success. So does Dorothy McGuire in playing the mother of the family. Marjorie Main tops an extremely broad comedy episode involving Cooper's yen for a faster horse so he can beat a friend to church each Sunday, and three out-sized daughters who go on the make for Cooper's unworldly son (Anthony Perkins).

Figuring importantly in the way the picture plays is Dimitri Tiomkin's conducting of his own score.

1956: NOMINATIONS: Best Picture, Director, Supp. Actor (Anthony Perkins), Adapted Screenplay [nominee unnamed, because of blacklist], Song ("Friendly Persuasion (Thee I Love)"), Sound

•

FRIENDS
1993, 109 mins, UK/France Ⓥ col
Dir Elaine Proctor *Prod* Judith Hunt *Scr* Elaine Proctor *Ph* Dominique Chapuis *Ed* Tony Lawson *Mus* Rachel Portman *Art* Carmel Collins
Act Kerry Fox, Dambisa Kente, Michele Burgers, Marius Weyers, Tertius Meintjes, Dolly Rathebe (Friends/Chrysalide/Rio)

The tense, divided realities of life in contemporary South Africa are vividly brought to the screen in *Friends*, a provocative pic from first-time writer-director Elaine Proctor. Despite intriguing characters and good performances, however, the film is saddled with a schematic screenplay that leaves many questions unanswered.

Proctor's screenplay is structured around the three titular friends, representatives of three key factions in the South African tragedy. Kerry Fox is Sophie, who comes from a privileged, white English-speaking family; Michele Burgers is Aninka, a Boer, whose family live in a rural area; and Dambisa Kente is Thoko, a black woman whose mother lives in a township. A major problem is that the audience is asked to take the friendship of the three women entirely on trust.

Sophie is Proctor's principal concern, and the young woman's combative attitude toward apartheid is indicated early on at the wedding of Aninka to a liberal, older man. When a parcel bomb she left at Jan Smuts Airport explodes killing two people, including an elderly black cleaning woman, Sophie is devastated.

The prison scenes in the second half of the film are grueling, but the film raises questions about the use of terrorism as a weapon against apartheid that it never really confronts.

•

FRIENDS OF EDDIE COYLE, THE
1973, 100 mins, US Ⓥ col
Dir Peter Yates *Prod* Paul Monash *Scr* Paul Monash *Ph* Victor J. Kemper *Ed* Patricia Lewis Jaffe *Mus* Dave Grusin *Art* Gene Callahan
Act Robert Mitchum, Peter Boyle, Richard Jordan, Steven Keats, Alex Rocco, Joe Santos (Paramount)

The Friends of Eddie Coyle is a very fine film about real people on the fringes of both crime and law enforcement. Shot in Boston, Paul Monash's top adaptation of a first novel by MA asst. attorney general George V. Higgins, stars Robert Mitchum and Peter Boyle as middle-aged, small-time hoods.

Mitchum is very effective as an aging small-timer, complete with a most believable Boston-area accent (as are all the players), who retails in guns obtained from younger hotshot supplier Steven Keats. Boyle, ostensibly a bartender, is a conduit for murder contracts, criminal contacts, and, for weekly pay, tip-offs to Richard Jordan, terrific in a true "Southie" evocation of a plainsclothes narc. Alex Rocco heads a bank heist gang which also includes Joe Santos.

The plot is electric with the endless, daily trading of favors and betrayals which are necessary for survival in this gray jungle.

•

FRIGHTENED CITY, THE
1961, 97 mins, UK b/w
Dir John Lemont *Prod* John Lemont, Leigh Vance *Scr* Leigh Vance *Ph* Desmond Dickinson *Ed* Bernard Gribble *Mus* Norrie Paramor *Art* Maurice Carter
Act Herbert Lom, John Gregson, Sean Connery, Alfred Marks, Yvonne Romain, Kenneth Griffiths (Anglo-Amalgamated/Zodiac)

The Frightened City is a conventional but brisk gangster yarn. Accent of the film is tough and hard-hitting and concerns intergang warfare plus the clash between the cops and the crooks, the cops, as a spokesman bitterly says, finding themselves hampered by outdated laws. "We're trying to fight 20th-century crime with 19th-century legislation."

Six main gangs are running the protection racket and a bent accountant hits on the idea of organizing the gangs into one all-powerful syndicate. All goes well for awhile but then the boss of the organization makes a successful play for a deal involving a $560,000 block of offices being built. One of the gangsters fights shy of this bigger game, backs out of the organization and re-forms his own gang. This sparks off gang warfare.

Herbert Lom plays the brains of the crooked organization with urbane villainy and equally reliable John Gregson makes a solid, confident job of the dedicated cop. Alfred Marks is cast offbeat as Lom's gangster lieutenant. Marks gives a rich, oily, sinister and yet often amusing portrayal of an ambitious thug who is prepared to turn killer to get his own way. Comparative newcomer, rugged Sean Connery makes a distinct impression as an Irish crook, with an eye for the ladies. Connery combines toughness, charm and Irish blarney.

•

FRIGHT NIGHT
1985, 105 mins, US Ⓥ ⦿ ▭ col
Dir Tom Holland *Prod* Herb Jaffe *Scr* Tom Holland *Ph* Jan Kiesser *Ed* Kent Beyda *Mus* Brad Fiedel *Art* John De Cuir Jr.
Act Chris Sarandon, William Ragsdale, Amanda Bearse, Roddy McDowall, Stephen Geoffreys, Jonathan Stark (Columbia/Vistar)

Director Tom Holland keeps the picture wonderfully simple and entirely believable (once the existence of vampires is accepted, of course). In a quick 105 minutes, the film simply answers the question of what would probably happen if a charming, but deadly sinister, vampire moved in next door to a likable teenager given to watching horror films on the late show—and the only one the kid can turn to for help is a washed-up actor who hosts the show.

Chris Sarandon is terrific as the vampire, quite affable and debonair until his fingernails start to grow and his eyes get that glow. William Ragsdale superbly maintains due sympathy as a fairly typical youngster who can't get anybody to believe him about the odd new neighbor next door.

Roddy McDowall hams it up on the telly as the "fearless vampire killer." Naturally, when Ragsdale comes looking for help, McDowall is more than aware of his humanly limitations, becoming a consistently amusing, unwilling ally in invading Sarandon's lair.

•

FRIGHT NIGHT PART 2

1988, 101 mins, US Ⓥ ⦿ ▭ col

Dir Tommy Lee Wallace ***Prod*** Herb Jaffe, Mort Engelberg ***Scr*** Tim Metcalfe, Miguel Tejada-Flores, Tommy Lee Wallace ***Ph*** Mark Irwin ***Ed*** Jay Lash Cassidy ***Mus*** Brad Fiedel ***Art*** Dean Tschetter

Act Roddy McDowall, William Ragsdale, Traci Lin, Julie Carmen, Russell Clark, Brian Thompson (Vista)

Pic begins with scenes from 1985's original, and continues in the same vein. Though its camp humor and goopy effects are familiar, it's better than the average shlocker.

At the outset young Charley (William Ragsdale) has completed therapy and is cautiously certain he just imagined that vampire neighbor. Before long a quartet of sinister types has come to live in the old apartment where Charley's friend, TV horror host Peter Vincent (Roddy McDowall) resides and the mayhem starts all over again. This time, the vampires are led by a slinky femme fatale (Julie Carmen) and include an androgynous black, a leather-jacketed hood and a musclebound, silent type.

Helmer Tommy Lee Wallace brings freshness to the proceedings via inventive use of the wide screen and a ghoulish sense of humor. Special effects are very good.

•

FRISCO KID

1935, 80 mins, US b/w

Dir Lloyd Bacon ***Prod*** Sam Bischoff ***Scr*** Warren Duff, Seton I. Miller ***Ph*** Sol Polito ***Ed*** Owen Marks ***Mus*** Leo F. Forbstein (dir.) ***Art*** John Hughes

Act James Cagney, Margaret Lindsay, Ricardo Cortez, Lili Damita, Donald Woods, Barton MacLane (Warner)

So similar to *Barbary Coast* as to be almost its twin *Frisco Kid* is, nevertheless, good entertainment. Since an identical locale and period are used in both, outstanding characters have been twice fictionalized and resemblances are great.

Vigilantes, meetings, hangings, burning of the Coast, crusading newspaper and other details are used once again. For its principal character *Frisco Kid* has James Cagney as against *Barbary*'s Miriam Hopkins. That is the only point in which the two films differ to any real extent.

Through Cagney this picture has the benefit of a more vigorous central character. Romantic phase is secondary and, with Cagney to handle the punches, *Frisco* takes in more territory and contains more action.

Story traces the career of Cagney from his arrival as a poor sailor through his rise to power and riches by right of might, his almost hopeless romance with a girl from the other and nicer side of the tracks, and finally his reformation.

•

FRISCO KID, THE

1979, 122 mins, US Ⓥ col

Dir Robert Aldrich ***Prod*** Mace Neufeld ***Scr*** Michael Elias, Frank Shaw ***Ph*** Robert B. Hauser ***Ed*** Maury Winetrobe, Irving Rosenblum, Jack Horger ***Mus*** Frank DeVol ***Art*** Terence Marsh

Act Gene Wilder, Harrison Ford, Ramon Bieri, William Smith (Warner)

Director Robert Aldrich has always adroitly mixed comedic and dramatic aspects in his films, and *Frisco Kid* is no exception. For audiences expecting Mel Brooks belly-laughs amidst the Yiddishisms, however, there's bound to be disappointment.

As Avram Belinsky, Yeshiva flunky packed off to an American rendezvous with a leaderless 1850s San Francisco congregation, Gene Wilder has his best role in years. The manic gleam featured in early Wilder pix has now turned into a mature twinkle.

Excellent counterpoint is provided by Harrison Ford, as the cowboy, who proves the perfect foil for Wilder's gaffes.

Frisco Kid remains a series of set pieces, however, and not a cohesive film. For all his skills, Wilder is given too many solo shots. As is his practice, Aldrich has also inserted some action sequences that are jarring in their sadistic intensity.

•

FRISK

1995, 83 mins, US Ⓥ col

Dir Todd Verow ***Prod*** Marcus Hu, John Gerrans ***Scr*** Jim Dwyer, La Voo, Todd Verow ***Ph*** Greg Watkins ***Ed*** Todd Verow ***Art*** Jennifer Graber

Act Michael Gunther, Craig Chester, Parker Posey, Alexis Arquette, Raoul O'Connell, Jaie Laplante (Industrial Eye)

Director Todd Verow's debut feature, *Frisk*, is an uneven but generally successful attempt to translate the work of novelist Dennis Cooper to the screen. Like the earlier *Swoon*—which also dealt with loaded violent and sexual behavior in a morally ambivalent tone—pic invites general controversy.

Adapting Cooper's 1991 novel, the screenplay adopts a more chronological format while maintaining his complex, somewhat unresolved balance between multiple storytellers. They might be relating actual events or mere fantasies; some aren't sure themselves.

Protagonist Dennis (Michael Gunther) is attracted as an L.A. teen to envelope-pushing sexual images; he later meets a masochist, Henry (Craig Chester), he'd once seen "dead" in apparent snuff photos. A move to San Francisco does little to alter his brutal course. Dennis becomes obsessed with a gay porn actor (Michael Stock), then succumbs to his homicidal urges—first acting alone on a hustler, then "joining forces" with a like-minded couple (James Lyons, Parker Posey).

Pic's obsessive, sealed atmosphere lends Verow's slaying set pieces a real banality-of-evil queasiness. Perfs are variable. The director succeeds less in straight dialogue scenes, which run a tad flat, than in using experimental montages to create a decadent "underground" milieu. Lensing in 16mm deploys some hot-color lighting to good effect.

•

FRITZ THE CAT

1972, 77 mins, US Ⓥ col

Dir Ralph Bakshi ***Prod*** Steve Krantz Scr Ralph Bakshi ***Ed*** Renn Reynolds ***Mus*** Ed Bogas, Ray Shanklin (Krantz/Cinemation)

Fritz the Cat, X-rated cartoon feature based on the characters created by Robert Crumb, is an amusing, diverting, handsomely executed poke at youthful attitudes. Production follows the title character through a series of bawdy and playpen-political encounters. Excellent animation and montage shore up a plot which has a few howls, several chuckles and many smiles.

With an excellent vocal characterization by Skip Hinnant, Fritz lurches his amiable way through group-sex encounters, police chases, black ghettos, motorcycle revolutionaries and assorted devastation of property. Rosetta Le Noire, John McCurry and Judy Engles vocalize the other characters, with as much success as Hinnant.

•

FROGMEN, THE

1951, 96 mins, US Ⓥ b/w

Dir Lloyd Bacon ***Prod*** Samuel G. Engel ***Scr*** John Tucker Battle ***Ph*** Norbert Brodine ***Ed*** William Reynolds ***Mus*** Cyril Mockridge ***Art*** Lyle Wheeler, Albert Hogsett

Act Richard Widmark, Dana Andrews, Gary Merrill, Jeffrey Hunter, Warren Stevens, Robert Wagner (20th Century-Fox)

Stress is on realism in this war action-thriller kudoing the exploits of Underwater Demolition Teams that served so effectively in the last world war. Location use of installations at Norfolk and in the Virgin Islands increase the effect.

In the film, the unit commanded by Richard Widmark realistically goes about such missions as venturing close to Japheld islands to plot against underwater obstacles that would hamper beach landings, then demolishing these barricades.

Storyline is slight and rather commonplace. Widmark is a new commander of the UDT unit depicted, replacing a loved officer who had been lost on a mission. Noncom Dana Andrews and the other men do not understand him, and resentment to his coldly given orders and strict attention to duty causes them to ask for transfer.

Widmark, Andrews and Gary Merrill, who captains the Navy craft that ferrys the UDTs, come over strongly. The various crew members also impress and among them is Jeffrey Hunter.

•

FROGS

1972, 90 mins, US Ⓥ col

Dir George McCowan ***Prod*** George Edwards, Peter Thomas ***Scr*** Robert Hutchison, Robert Blees ***Ph*** Mario Tosi ***Ed*** Fred R. Feitshans ***Mus*** Les Baxter

Act Ray Milland, Sam Elliott, Joan Van Ark, Adam Roarke, Judy Pace, Lynn Borden (American International)

Frogs is a story [from an original by Robert Hutchison] of Nature striking back at man. Snakes, giant lizards, alligators, quicksand, frogs and toads, savage fish, granddad turtles.

Action takes place on a private island in the Deep South where great-grandfather Ray Milland has gathered his family at the ancestral mansion to celebrate his birthday and the Fourth of July. Instead of the usual joyousness a sense of strangeness pervades the air. Growing numbers of large frogs are beginning to appear, large lizards and strange crawling life are converging onto the estate, right up to the windows.

One by one different members of the family meet their tragic fate through violent attack. In each case it is a frightening finish.

Cast is generally first-class and Milland's presence, though comparatively brief, is always commanding.

•

FROKEN JULIE

(MISS JULIE)

1951, 88 mins, Sweden b/w

Dir Alf Sjoberg ***Scr*** Alf Sjoberg ***Ph*** Goran Strindberg ***Ed*** Lennart Wallen

Act Anita Bjork, Ulf Palme, Marta Doff, Anders Henrikson, Lissi Aland, Inger Nordberg (Sandrews)

This is a somber study of heavy passion and conflicting social morés on an estate. Brilliant technical assets and fine stylized megging by Alf Sjoberg, who did *Torment*, make this a good entry.

Film hews close to the August Strindberg play. In the poetic, murky atmosphere, there is a ruthless battle between a high-born girl, Julie (Anita Bjork), taught by her mother to hate men, and a social-climbing valet (Ulf Palme) which ends in tragedy.

Photography by Goran Strindberg is adequately translucent and helps to maintain the mood of frustration and depression. Sjoberg directs with skill. Bjork is a striking actress who brings strength to the role of Julie. Remainder of the cast is fine, with Palme standout.

•

FROM DUSK TILL DAWN

1996, 107 mins, US Ⓥ ⦿ col

Dir Robert Rodriguez ***Prod*** Gianni Nunnari ***Scr*** Quentin Tarantino ***Ph*** Guillermo Navarro ***Ed*** Robert Rodriguez ***Mus*** Graeme Revell ***Art*** Cecilia Montiel

Act Harvey Keitel, George Clooney, Quentin Tarantino, Juliette Lewis, Cheech Marin, Fred Williamson (A Band Apart)

It's easy to imagine *From Dusk Till Dawn* as the all-time favorite film of Christian Slater's film-geek character in *True Romance*. A deliriously trashy, exuberantly vulgar, lavishly appointed exploitation picture, this weird combo of roadkill movie and martial-arts vampire gorefest is made to order for the stimulation of teenage boys.

Written by Quentin Tarantino in 1990, two years before *Reservoir Dogs* made him a major cult figure, *Dusk* is actually two films in one, the longer first section being a brotherly variation on *Natural Born Killers*, the second coming off as a *Night of the Living Dead*-tinged offshoot of John Carpenter's 1976 low-budget classic, *Assault on Precinct 13*—a fact acknowledged by one character's T-shirt.

What demands attention by a wider audience is George Clooney's instant emergence as a full-fledged movie star. What also jumps out from the opening scene is a reminder of Tarantino's indelible touch with dialogue.

Michael Parks, as a Texas Ranger, gives an uproarious reading of some corking redneck speeches before getting blown away by the unstable Gecko brothers (Clooney and Tarantino), who are headed for a safe haven in Mexico after a bloody crime spree. After the more psychotic of the two, Tarantino's Richard, needlessly murders one hostage, the boys find new ones in Jacob Fuller (Harvey Keitel), a preacher who's lost his faith, and his two teenage kids—Kate (Juliette Lewis) and Scott (Ernest Liu). The Geckos commandeer the Fullers's RV for the trip over the border, where they pull up at a joint called the Titty Twister, which qualifies as the raunchiest bar on Earth even before the full nature of its entertainment offerings is revealed.

It's thoroughly juvenile stuff pulled off with lowdown flair and relentless energy by Robert Rodriguez. As the weird kid brother, Tarantino isn't bad, and generates a few laughs with his straight-faced portrait of dementia and lasciviousness. Keitel is a bit miscast as the solemn ex-pastor, Lewis is at her most subdued.

•

FROM HERE TO ETERNITY
1953, 118 mins, US Ⓥ ⊙ b/w
Dir Fred Zinnemann ***Prod*** Buddy Adler ***Scr*** Daniel Taradash ***Ph*** Burnett Guffey ***Ed*** William Lyon ***Mus*** George Duning ***Art*** Cary Odell
Act Burt Lancaster, Montgomery Clift, Deborah Kerr, Donna Reed, Frank Sinatra, Ernest Borgnine (Columbia)

The James Jones bestseller is an outstanding motion picture in this smash, screen adaptation. The bawdy vulgarity and the outhouse vocabulary, the pros and non-pros among its easy ladies, and the slambang indictment of army brass have not been emasculated in the transfer to the screen.

Burt Lancaster wallops the character of Top Sergeant Milton Warden, the professional soldier who wet-nurses a weak, pompous commanding officer and the GIs under him. Montgomery Clift, with a reputation for sensitive, three-dimensional performances, adds another to his growing list as the independent GI who refuses to join the company boxing team, taking instead the "treatment" dished out at the c.o.'s instructions. Frank Sinatra scores a decided hit as Angelo Maggio, a violent, likeable Italo-American GI.

Additional performance surprises are in the work turned in by Deborah Kerr, the nymphomaniac wife of the faithless c.o., and Donna Reed as a hostess (sic) in the New Congress Club, which furnished femme and other entertainment for relaxing soldiers.

The story opens in the summer of 1941 before Pearl Harbor with the setting Schofield Barracks, Honolulu, where much of the footage was taken. It deals with the transfer of Clift to the company under Philip Ober, the pompous, unfaithful husband of Kerr, who is interested only in getting a promotion to major, in his boxing team and extracurricular affairs. When Clift refuses to join the boxing team, he is subjected to all the unpleasantness the idle GI mind can think up.

Eyes will moisten and throats will choke when Clift plays taps on an army bugle for his friend Sinatra after the latter dies from the brutality administered by Ernest Borgnine, the sadist sergeant in charge of the prison stockade.

1953: Best Picture, Director, Supp. Actor (Frank Sinatra), Supp. Actress (Donna Reed), Screenplay, B&W Cinematography, Sound Recording, Editing

NOMINATIONS: Best Actor (Burt Lancaster, Montgomery Clift), Actress (Deborah Kerr), B&W Costume Design, Scoring of a Dramatic Picture

•

FROM NOON TILL THREE
1976, 98 mins, US Ⓥ col
Dir Frank D. Gilroy ***Prod*** Mike Frankovich ***Scr*** Frank D. Gilroy ***Ph*** Lucien Ballard ***Ed*** Maury Winetrobe ***Mus*** Elmer Bernstein ***Art*** Robert Clatworthy
Act Charles Bronson, Jill Ireland, Douglas V. Fowley, Stan Haze, Damon Douglas, Hector Morales (United Artists)

From Noon till Three is an offbeat and amiable, if uneven and structurally awkward, western comedy. Frank D. Gilroy scripted his novel and directed the good-looking production.

Film stars Charles Bronson as an amateur bank robber whose mistaken death supports a worldwide romantic legend, and Jill Ireland, beneficiary of the fantasy.

Bronson is a frontier drifter recruited into the bank robber gang headed by Douglas V. Fowley. En route, Bronson has a dream of a heist, later spoiled by an aware townsfolk. That's enough for him to stay behind at widow Ireland's prairie home when his horse goes lame.

He and the widow evolve from antagonism to the beginning of love, when news arrives that the Fowley gang is caught.

•

FROM RUSSIA WITH LOVE
1963, 110 mins, UK Ⓥ ⊙ col
Dir Terence Young ***Prod*** Harry Saltzman, Albert R. Broccoli ***Scr*** Richard Maibaum, Johanna Harwood ***Ph*** Ted Moore ***Ed*** Peter Hunt ***Mus*** John Barry ***Art*** Syd Cain
Act Sean Connery, Daniela Bianchi, Pedro Armendariz, Lotte Lenya, Robert Shaw, Bernard Lee (Eon)

From Russia with Love is a preposterous, skillful slab of hard-hitting, sexy hokum. After a slowish start, it is directed by Terence Young at zingy pace.

This one has to do with Sean Connery being detailed to go to Istanbul and lift a top secret Russian decoding machine from the embassy. British Intelligence senses that this may be a trap, but getting the machine is important. Connery can pull it off if he will help a young Russian cipher clerk (Daniela Bianchi) to escape to the West. She thinks she is working for her Russian government, but actually she is a pawn of Spectre, an international crime syndicate.

Bond has a glorious slap-up fight to the death with Robert Shaw, the killer detailed to bump him off. He is hounded by a helicopter as he runs across moorland clutching the decoding machine. He beats off his pursuers in a motorboat by setting fire to the sea. He referees a fight between two jealous gypsy girls just before the encampment is invaded by the crime gang.

Connery is well served by some crisp wisecracking dialog by Richard Maibaum [in his script adapted by Johanna Harwood]. Robert Shaw is an impressive, icy, implacable killer and the late Pedro Armendariz weighs in with a formidable, yet lightly played, performance as the man who knows the sinister secrets of Istanbul.

The distaff side is less well served. Newcomer Daniela Bianchi is a good-looking Italian girl with shapely legs and promising smile. Lotte Lenya has been lumbered with a part that doesn't fully come off. Disguised with an Eaton Crop and heavy pebble spectacles, she stands out as somebody up to no good from the first glimpse.

•

FROM THE TERRACE
1960, 144 mins, US Ⓥ ⊙ ▭ col
Dir Mark Robson ***Prod*** Mark Robson ***Scr*** Ernest Lehman ***Ph*** Leo Tover ***Ed*** Dorothy Spencer ***Mus*** Elmer Bernstein ***Art*** Lyle R. Wheeler, Maurice Ransford, Howard Richman
Act Paul Newman, Joanne Woodward, Myrna Loy, Ina Balin, Leon Ames, Felix Aylmer (20th Century-Fox)

It's apparent that scripter Ernest Lehman faced a Herculean task in condensing John O'Hara's fat novel to the exigencies of the screen. On the assumption that Lehman followed the O'Hara story closely, the blame must be placed squarely on the novelist, for *From the Terrace* builds up to one big cliché.

The picture is the study of one man's pursuit of success and money. During his climb up the Wall Street ladder, he neglects his wife, sacrifices his integrity, and unrelentingly pursues his goal. But in keeping with American popular culture, he is overcome at end by the moment of truth.

Mark Robson's old-fashioned approach to the direction is no help. He has his characters speaking in sepulchral tones, particularly in the scenes between Paul Newman and Ina Balin, as if to give their conversations a world-shaking meaning. They seem to be reciting blank verse in a background of soft hearts-and-flowers music.

Woodward is excellent as the wife who married Newman despite the objections of her socially prominent family. There is a strong indication that the marriage is based more on sexual attraction than on deeper love. Balin, a dark-haired beauty, makes a nice contrast to blonde Woodward. However, she plays her role with such a dedicated seriousness that it is difficult to believe.

•

FROM THIS DAY FORWARD
1946, 96 mins, US b/w
Dir John Berry ***Prod*** William L. Pereira ***Scr*** Hugo Butler ***Ph*** George Barnes ***Ed*** Frank Doyle ***Mus*** Leigh Harline ***Art*** Albert S. D'Agostino, Alfred H. Herman
Act Joan Fontaine, Mark Stevens, Rosemary DeCamp, Bobby Driscoll (RKO)

Story unfolds in flashback. This makes it sometimes difficult to follow as a whole, but there can be no quarrel with the merit of presentation and acting of the individual sequences. Plot deals with marriage of a young couple, fear for their security, the draft and the husband's return to establish himself again. Scenes show a soldier's mind as he goes through the red tape of government employment centers for the veteran.

Joan Fontaine and Mark Stevens are the young couple. Under John Berry's direction they make real the courtship, marriage and marital existence of the two young people.

Hugo Butler rates smart credit for his scripting job, working from adaptation by Garson Kanin, based on Thomas Bell's novel, *All Brides Are Beautiful*.

•

FRONT, THE
1976, 94 mins, US Ⓥ ⊙ col
Dir Martin Ritt ***Prod*** Martin Ritt ***Scr*** Walter Bernstein ***Ph*** Michael Chapman ***Ed*** Sidney Levin ***Mus*** Dave Grusin ***Art*** Charles Bailey
Act Woody Allen, Zero Mostel, Herschel Bernardi, Michael Murphy, Andrea Marcovicci, Remak Ramsay (Columbia)

The Front is a disappointing drama about showbiz blacklisting. The offbeat casting of Woody Allen, as a perennial loser who lends his name and person to blacklisted writers, is far more showmanlike than successful.

Michael Murphy, very good as an Allen chum from high-school days, gets Allen to put his name on scripts for live TV producer Herschel Bernardi and story editor Andrea Marcovicci, latter becoming the target of Allen's emotions. Lloyd Gough and David Margulies also feed their scripts through Allen. This attracts the attention of Remak Ramsay, professional "clearance consultant" to the network where Scott McKay is the liaison exec.

The real-life story of the blacklist in NY-based broadcasting is certainly not unfamiliar to several of the filmmakers here.

1976: NOMINATION: Best Original Screenplay

•

FRONT PAGE, THE
1931, 100 mins, US Ⓥ b/w
Dir Lewis Milestone ***Prod*** Howard Hughes ***Scr*** Bartlett Cormack, Charles Lederer ***Ph*** Glen MacWilliams, Hal Mohr, Tony Gaudio ***Ed*** W. Duncan Mansfield ***Art*** Richard Day
Act Adolphe Menjou, Pat O'Brien, Mary Brian, Edward Everett Horton, Walter Catlett, George E. Stone (Caddo/United Artists)

A very entertaining picture. Action is here all of the time, even with and during the dialog. All of it is contained within a single setting, the press room at the courthouse. It's of newspaper men, waiting in the pressroom for a hanging the following morning at 7 A.M. General tenor may be taken from one of the reporters asking the sheriff if he can't advance the hanging to 5 A.M. so the story can make the first edition.

The star reporter for the *Post* is between love and a good story all the while. He has arranged for a wedding in New York, bought the tickets, but is obliged through the breaks and conniving of his managing editor to keep the girl and her mother waiting while he continues to be the reporter.

Lewis Milestone's big idea appears to have been to keep it moving, and he does. It's a panorama of blended action without fireworks.

A standout performance, one of three, is by Adolphe Menjou as the managing editor. He's the cold-blooded story man, knowing only news and believing nothing should ever get in its way. Next is Mae Clarke as Molly, a prostie who is the murderer's only sympathizer. The third is Pat O'Brien as the star reporter, who maintains the same even tempo of liveliness in his work and lovemaking.

Ben Hecht and Charles MacArthur turned out a stage wallop that lasted a long while through George Kaufman's stage direction, but Bartlett Cormack's adaptation for the screen, with Milestone, improves the original.

1930/31: NOMINATIONS: Best Picture, Director, Actor (Adolphe Menjou)

•

FRONT PAGE, THE
1974, 105 mins, US Ⓥ ⊙ col
Dir Billy Wilder ***Prod*** Paul Monash ***Scr*** Billy Wilder, I.A.L. Diamond ***Ph*** Jordan S. Cronenweth ***Ed*** Ralph E. Winters ***Mus*** Billy May (adapt.) ***Art*** Henry Bumstead
Act Jack Lemmon, Walter Matthau, Carol Burnett, Susan Sarandon, Vincent Gardenia, David Wayne (Universal)

The reteaming of Jack Lemmon and Walter Matthau, in a Billy Wilder remake of a famous 1920s period newspaper story, *The Front Page*, with a featured spot by Carol Burnett, sure looks good on paper. But that's about the only place it looks good. The production has the slick, machine-tooled look of certain assembly line automobiles that never quite seem to work smoothly.

The 1928 play by Ben Hecht and Charles MacArthur has, in this third screen version, been "liberated" from old production code restraints. The extent of the liberation appears to be in the tedious use of undeleted expletives.

The basic story takes place in a Chicago police press room on the eve of a politically railroaded execution of a supposed radical who killed a cop in a scuffle.

Matthau and Lemmon again demonstrate their fine screen empathy.

•

FRONT PAGE WOMAN
1935, 80 mins, US b/w
Dir Michael Curtiz ***Prod*** Samuel Bischoff ***Scr*** Laird Doyle, Lillie Hayward, Roy Chanslor ***Ph*** Tony Gaudio ***Ed*** Terry Morse ***Mus*** Leo F. Forbstein (dir.) ***Art*** John Hughes
Act Bette Davis, George Brent, Roscoe Karns, Winifred Shaw, Walter Walker, J. Carrol Naish (Warner)

As the title indicates, this is a newspaper yarn and a completely screwy one. Lacks authenticity and is so far-fetched it'll hand newsscribes around the country a constant run of ripples. But it's light and has some funny lines and situations [from a story by Richard Macauley].

George Brent and Bette Davis are working for opposing papers. They're in love but always trying to outdo each other on stories. They keep topping each other on one story or another for the entire length of the film and then clinch in a truce.

But there are some laughs. And there are grand performances by Davis, Brent, Winifred Shaw and Joseph Crehan. And nice bit work by Roscoe Karns, J. Farrell MacDonald, Addison Richards, Walter Walker, Dorothy Dare, June Martel and Mike Morita.

•

F.T.W.
1994, 100 mins, US Ⓥ col
Dir Michael Karbelnikoff ***Prod*** Tom Mickel ***Scr*** Mari Kornhauser ***Ph*** James L. Carter ***Ed*** Joe D'Augustine ***Mus*** Gary Chang ***Art*** J. K. Reinhart
Act Mickey Rourke, Lori Singer, Brion James, Peter Berg, Rodney A. Grant, Aaron Neville (HKM)

Mickey Rourke does better in the rodeo ring than in the arena of life in *F.T.W.*, a mostly ho-hum cross between a modern cowboy yarn and a lovers-on-the-run crime saga. Quiet, even delicate mood set by Rourke's performance is disrupted by clichéd scripting and the leading characters' predictably self-destructive downward spiral.

All Frank T. Wells (Rourke) wants after 10 years in prison is the usual cowboy dream—ridin' free and havin' a little place of his own. Scarlett Stuart (Lori Singer) is another story altogether, a wildcat involved in a highly abusive, frankly sexual relationship with her intimidating brother, Clem (Peter Berg). After Clem kills four people in a bank robbery, the cops mow him down. Scarlett escapes, only to meet Frank on the road.

Bunking in Frank's trailer, Scarlett realizes that fate might be playing its hand here, in that Frank has the same initials that she has tattooed on her hand—F.T.W., as in what the world can go do with itself. The two inevitably hook up, and remainder of the film parallels his re-emergence as a bronco rider with her misguided attempts to give them financial security by robbing convenience stores and banks.

Rodeo footage is kept to a relative minimum, and Big Sky locations rep a major plus.

•

FUGITIVE, THE
1947, 99 mins, US Ⓥ ⦿ b/w
Dir John Ford ***Prod*** John Ford, Merian C. Cooper ***Scr*** Dudley Nichols ***Ph*** Gabriel Figueroa ***Ed*** Jack Murray ***Mus*** Richard Hageman ***Art*** Alfred Ybarra
Act Henry Fonda, Dolores Del Rio, Pedro Armendariz, J. Carrol Naish, Leo Carrillo, Ward Bond (Argosy/RKO)

Made in Mexico with Hollywood leads and native extras, *The Fugitive* tells how the government of one of the Mexican states, in a ruthless drive to stamp out religion, hunts down the last remaining priest, captures him by a cruel ruse and has him executed by a firing squad. The picture is rich in atmosphere and is sincerely done, but it is slow in spots and uneven in dramatic power.

According to the opening screen narration, *The Fugitive* is a true story, with Biblical overtones and with "topical, timeless and universal" qualities. It is apparently based on the efforts of the Mexican government 20-odd years ago to curtail the power of the Catholic church and control its priests. But it will probably be widely regarded as an attack on Communism.

Parts of the story [from Graham Greene's novel *The Labyrinthine Ways*, also published as *The Power and the Glory*] aren't clear. The government's drive against the church, for instance, isn't fully motivated. In addition, there is a character of an American bandit-murderer (Ward Bond) whose function isn't satisfactorily established, but who risks his life in helping the fleeing priest to reach temporary haven.

The Fugitive is handsomely photographed, with colorful village scenes and impressive landscapes. Henry Fonda is expressive in the subdued and somewhat static role of the priest. Dolores Del Rio is decorative and mutely impassioned as a devout victim of the law.

•

FUGITIVE, THE
1993, 127 mins, US Ⓥ ⦿ col
Dir Andrew Davis ***Prod*** Arnold Kopelson ***Scr*** Jeb Stuart, David Twohy ***Ph*** Michael Chapman ***Ed*** Dennis Virkler, David Finfer, Dean Goodhill, Don Brochu, Richard Nord, Dov Hoenig ***Mus*** James Newton Howard ***Art*** Dennis Washington
Act Harrison Ford, Tommy Lee Jones, Sela Ward, Joe Pantoliano, Jeroen Krabbe, Julianne Moore (Warner)

The Fugitive, inspired by the vintage television series [1963–67, starring David Janssen and Barry Morse], is a giant toy-train entertainment with all stops pulled out. A consummate nail-biter that never lags, it leaves you breathless from the chase yet anxious for the next bit of mayhem or clever plot twist.

This is one film that doesn't stint on thrills and knows how to use them. It has a sympathetic lead, a stunning antagonist, state-of-the-art special effects, top-of-the-line craftsmanship and a taut screenplay that breathes life into familiar territory.

The new screenplay [from a story by David Twohy] retains the essence of Roy Huggins's (who serves as exec. producer) original concept and characters. Once again Kimble (Harrison Ford) returns home to find his wife (Sela Ward) murdered. He struggles with a one-armed man lurking in his house. After a trial built on circumstantial evidence, he's found guilty and sentenced to death.

But fate steps in when prisoners on the bus transporting him to death row stage a daring escape that backfires. Kimble escapes in the course of a show-stopper bus-train wreck that alone is worth the price of admission. Enter Marshal Gerard (Tommy Lee Jones) and his crack investigative team.

Andrew Davis takes us through storm drains, into the midst of Chicago's St. Patrick's Day parade, down hospital wards, on elevated trains and into the county lockup. The guts of the story is the confrontation between wronged man and his tracker. It's another opportunity for Jones to remind us of his acting chops, a man part Mountie, part maniac who loves his job, respects his team and thrives on the hunt. Ford, in contrast, has the non-showy role. The large supporting cast works like a beautifully oiled machine.

1993: Best Supp. Actor (Tommy Lee Jones)

NOMINATIONS: Best Picture, Cinematography, Original Score, Sound, Sound Effects Editing, Editing

•

FUGITIVE KIND, THE
1960, 119 mins, US Ⓥ b/w
Dir Sidney Lumet ***Prod*** Martin Jarow, Richard A. Shepherd ***Scr*** Tennessee Williams, Meade Roberts ***Ph*** Boris Kaufman ***Ed*** Carl Lerner ***Mus*** Kenyon Hopkins
Act Marlon Brando, Anna Magnani, Joanne Woodward, Maureen Stapleton, Victor Jory, R. G. Armstrong (United Artists)

Another helping from Tennessee Williams's seemingly inexhaustible closet of mixed-up Southern skeletons is exposed here with only occasional flashes of cinematic power.

The Fugitive Kind is not basically one of Williams's better works and, as directed by Sidney Lumet, it sputters more often than it sizzles. The combination of Marlon Brando and Anna Magnani fails to generate the electricity hoped for. Joanne Woodward, looking like a battered fugitive from skid row, pops in and out of the story to provide a distasteful and often ludicrous extra dash of degeneracy.

The only fully rounded character is that of Lady Torrance portrayed by Magnani with a faded veneer of lustfulness. At least one can understand her frustration and loneliness, being married to a dying older man she doesn't love, and her bitterness toward fellow townsfolk, her father having died trying to save his wine garden set afire by vigilantes because he sold liquor to Negroes.

Brando's role as a disillusioned guitar-singer, who becomes involved, as hired hand and lover, with Lady in a small Mississippi town while trying to put aside the wild life he experienced in New Orleans hot spots, is less clearly defined. Brando is back to mumbling with marbles in his mouth too often.

Much of the picture was filmed on location in Milton, New York, and at the Gold Medal Studios in the Bronx. Boris Kaufman's photography is good.

•

FUKUSHU SURE WA WARE NI ARI
(VENGEANCE IS MINE)
1979, 128 mins, Japan Ⓥ ⦿ col
Dir Shohei Imamura ***Scr*** Ataru Baba ***Ph*** Shinsaku Himeda ***Ed*** Keiichi Uraoka ***Mus*** Shinichiro Ikebe
Act Ken Ogata, Rentaro Mikuni, Chocho Miyako, Mitsuko Baisho, Mayumi Ogawa, Nijiko Kiyokawa (Imamura/Shochiku)

Unfolding through multiple flashbacks something like a Japanese *In Cold Blood*, Shohei Imamura's *Vengeance Is Mine* is extremely violent, sociologically probing and packed with incident.

Inspired by real-life story of a notorious criminal who murdered small-time money collectors and then led police on a wild goose chase across Japan, pic is a red-hot examination of personal rage and insolence toward society. Killer's rationale is not unearthed as much as his contemptuous attitude is vividly portrayed, with his physical lust and brutal hostility being acted out in equal measures.

After the rough crimes of the opening reel, film starts jumping back in time to show his pathetic youth and increasingly antisocial young manhood. Stuck in prison, he begins to suspect his wife and father of having an affair and later, as a fugitive, enters into a destructive mad love relationship with a prostitute and her mother.

As erotic as it is violent, pic is ravishingly made and momentum never flags over the long running time. Ken Ogata dominates proceedings with a ferocious performance. Script is based on a "non-fiction novel" by Ryuzo Saki.

•

FULL CIRCLE
1977, 98 mins, UK/Canada Ⓥ col
Dir Richard Loncraine ***Prod*** Peter Fetterman, Alfred Pariser ***Scr*** Dave Humphries ***Ph*** Peter Hannan ***Ed*** Ron Wisman ***Mus*** Colin Towns ***Art*** Brian Morris
Act Mia Farrow, Keir Dullea, Tom Conti, Jill Bennett, Robin Gammell, Cathleen Nesbitt (Fester)

Film has a fairly tight script which, in first half at least, builds up scary tensions nicely. There's a performance by Mia Farrow which is somewhat reminiscent of *Rosemary's Baby*, and enough supernatural trappings to please those who are fascinated by the occult.

Yarn uses all the old warhorses of the genre: the creaking stairs, the throbbing eerie music at moments of mounting danger, a gloomy house in rainy Kensington, the mysterious light that is turned on and off, a seance, and the close-up of the heroine climbing the lonely stairs of a deserted house.

Pic gets off to a running start as an American family's daughter suddenly chokes at breakfast on a piece of apple. Though mom (Farrow) tries to save her by cutting open her throat with a kitchen knife, the daughter succumbs to the apple. After a couple of months in a London hospital to get over the shock, mom goes and buys an old Victorian house.

The mysterious events then start happening. The plot thickens and starts to become difficult to follow as Farrow's tinkering British boyfriend is electrocuted in his bathtub.

•

FULL METAL JACKET
1987, 116 mins, US Ⓥ ⦿ col
Dir Stanley Kubrick ***Prod*** Stanley Kubrick ***Scr*** Stanley Kubrick, Michael Herr, Gustav Hasford ***Ph*** Douglas Milsome ***Ed*** Martin Hunter ***Mus*** Abigail Mead [= Vivian Kubrick] ***Art*** Anton Furst
Act Matthew Modine, Adam Baldwin, Vincent D'Onofrio, R. Lee Ermey, Dorian Harewood, Arliss Howard (Warner)

Stanley Kubrick's *Full Metal Jacket* is an intense, schematic, superbly made Vietnam War drama.

Like the source material, Gustav Hasford's ultraviolent novel *The Short-Timers*, Kubrick's picture is strikingly divided into two parts. First 44 minutes are set exclusively in a Marine Corps basic training camp, while remaining 72 minutes embrace events surrounding the 1968 Tet Offensive and skirmishing in the devastated city of Hue.

While it doesn't develop a particularly strong narrative line, script is loaded with vivid, outrageously vulgar military vernacular that contributes heavily to the film's power.

Performances by the all-male cast (save for a couple of Vietnamese hookers) are also exceptional. Surrounded on one side by humorously macho types such as Cowboy and Rafterman, Matthew Modine holds the center effectively by embodying both what it takes to survive in the war and a certain omniscience.

1987: NOMINATION: Best Adapted Screenplay

•

FULL MONTY, THE
1997, 91 mins, UK/US Ⓥ ⦿ col
Dir Peter Cattaneo ***Prod*** Uberto Pasolini ***Scr*** Simon Beaufoy ***Ph*** John De Borman ***Ed*** David Freeman, Nick More ***Mus*** Anne Dudley ***Art*** Max Gottlieb
Act Robert Carlyle, Tom Wilkinson, Mark Addy, Lesley Sharp, Emily Woof, Steve Huison (Redwave/Fox Searchlight)

Bright and sassy, *The Full Monty* is a treat, a small but muscular British pic about a bunch of gawky unemployeds launching a striptease act.

Modernization has led to the South Yorkshire town of Sheffield's steel mills being closed and workers laid off. Among them is easygoing divorcee Gaz (Robert Carlyle) and his bumbling, overweight pal Dave (Mark Addy). They occasionally pop into the local job center that's also frequented by their snooty ex-foreman, Gerald (Tom Wilkinson). All three men's personal lives are in a mess.

Inspired by a visit of the Chippendale dancers, and in need of some quick cash to pay off his alimony arrears, Gaz has the idea of the three of them doing a strip act to raise some coin. They're joined by Guy (Hugo Speer), whose largest qualification is between his legs, Horse (Paul Barber), a middle-age dancer with a hopelessly out-of-date repertoire, and the suicidal Lomper (Steve Huison).

The particular magic of the film is the way in which it draws credible characters in a recognizable setting but elevates them and their story into crowd-pleasing fare without losing sight of the big social picture.

Yet again, the chameleon Carlyle surprises in a role far removed from Begbie in *Trainspotting*. His Gaz is the motor of the movie and the last few minutes of the film, as he leads the lads in a full monty (a complete strip) in front of cheering women, are the stuff of standing ovations.

1997: Best Original Comedy Score

NOMINATIONS: Best Picture, Director, Original Screenplay

•

FUN
1994, 105 mins, US Ⓥ col
Dir Rafal Zielinski ***Prod*** Rafal Zielinski ***Scr*** James Bosley ***Ph*** Jens Sturup ***Ed*** Monika Lightstone ***Mus*** Marc Tschanz ***Art*** Vally Mestroni
Act Alicia Witt, Renee Humphrey, William R. Moses, Leslie Hope, Ania Suli (Neo Modern)

Startlingly good lead performances by two new actresses give some distinction to *Fun*, an absorbing study of crime and absent values among contempo teenagers that nonetheless feels unjelled and schizophrenic.

Rafal Zielinski, Polish-born helmer who has spent most of his career on commercial fodder such as *Screwballs* and *Spellcaster*, tries hard to give an edgy, artistic veneer and succeeds up to a point.

James Bosley's screenplay, which is based on his play, delineates the exceedingly brief criminal careers of Bonnie (Alicia Witt) and Hillary (Renee Humphrey), two girls who meet by chance on a California roadside, start sharing intimacies and secrets that are largely lies, and finally knock off a little old lady just for the hell of it.

This narrative, which is shot in vibrant color, is broken up and set in relief by an equal amount of raw, black-and-white material set in the juvenile detention facility where the girls are being held.

The tale is not sufficiently fleshed out or analyzed to get chillingly under the skin, and the rendering is too schematic to make it emotionally affecting. Still, the performances by Witt and Humphrey go a long way toward giving the film a stinging legitimacy.

•

FUNERAL IN BERLIN
1967, 102 mins, UK Ⓥ ⊙ ▭ col
Dir Guy Hamilton ***Prod*** Charles Kasher ***Scr*** Evan Jones ***Ph*** Otto Heller ***Ed*** John Bloom ***Mus*** Konrad Elfers ***Art*** Ken Adam
Act Michael Caine, Paul Hubschmid, Oscar Homolka, Eva Renzi, Guy Doleman, Rachel Gurney (Paramount/Saltzman)

Funeral in Berlin is the second presentation of the exploits of Harry Palmer, the soft-sell sleuth, this time enmeshed in Berlin counter-espionage. Michael Caine encores in the role that made him a star. Excellent scripting, direction and performances, plus colorful and realistic production, add up to surprise-filled suspense, relieved adroitly by subtle irony. Len Deighton's novel has been adapted by Evan Jones to a taut, economical screenplay, just right for the semi-documentary feel.

Herein, amidst a clutch of running gags which never wear out their appeal, Caine is sent to East Berlin, where Communist spy chief Oscar Homolka is making the motions of trying to defect. Paul Hubschmid is the local British contact for Caine, and Eva Renzi pops up as an undercover agent for Israel, tracking down Nazis before statutes of limitation run out.

This being a well-developed suspenser, few people are as they seem, including prissy-pedantic Hugh Burden, a secret documents clerk in Doleman's British spy group.

•

FUNHOUSE, THE
1981, 96 mins, US Ⓥ ⊙ ▭ col
Dir Tobe Hooper ***Prod*** Derek Power, Steven Bernhardt ***Scr*** Larry Block ***Ph*** Andrew Laszlo ***Ed*** Jack Hofstra ***Mus*** John Beal ***Art*** Morton Rabinowitz
Act Elizabeth Berridge, Cooper Huckabee, Sylvia Miles, Largo Woodruff, William Finley, Kevin Conway (Universal)

The Funhouse is a spitty movie, full of great expectorations. That is, there's more drool on view than blood, which is a new twist for the horror genre.

Set-up is a variation on the old dark house premise, as four pot-smoking teens work up the nerve to spend the night in the spooky funhouse of a traveling carnival. After some hanky panky in the midst of goblins and skeletons, kids witness a carny Frankenstein being serviced by, then strangling, fortune-teller Sylvia Miles, upon which malevolent barker Kevin Conway locks them in for a night of unanticipated chills and thrills.

For all the elegance of photography, pic has nothing in particular up its sleeves, and devotees of director Tobe Hooper's *The Texas Chain Saw Massacre* will be particularly disappointed with the almost total lack of shocks and mayhem.

•

FUN IN ACAPULCO
1963, 100 mins, US Ⓥ col
Dir Richard Thorpe ***Prod*** Hal Wallis ***Scr*** Allan Weiss ***Ph*** Daniel L. Fapp ***Ed*** Stanley E. Johnson ***Mus*** Joseph J. Lilley ***Art*** Hal Pereira, Walter Tyler
Act Elvis Presley, Ursula Andress, Elsa Cardenas, Paul Lukas, Alejandro Rey (Paramount)

Elvis Presley fans won't be disappointed—he sings serviceable songs and wiggles a bit to boot. However, Presley is deserving of better material than has been provided in this screenplay in which he portrays an ex-trapeze catcher who has lost his nerve after a fatal mishap.

Arriving in Acapulco, he hires on as an entertainer-lifeguard at a resort, in hopes the latter job may afford him the opportunity to dive off the high board and erase his fear of heights. A romantic entanglement leads to the moment of truth.

The other three-fourths of the central romantic quartet are Ursula Andress, Elsa Cardenas and Alejandro Rey, fine-looking specimens, all. Others of note in the cast are Paul Lukas as an ex-duke-turned-chef and young Larry Domasin as a business-minded urchin more or less adopted by Presley.

Richard Thorpe's direction keeps the routine story on the move, a strong asset since opportunity for developing characterization is virtually nil.

•

FUNNY ABOUT LOVE
1990, 101 mins, US Ⓥ ⊙ col
Dir Leonard Nimoy ***Prod*** Jon Avnet, Jordan Kerner ***Scr*** Norman Steinberg, David Frankel ***Ph*** Fred Murphy ***Ed*** Peter E. Berger ***Mus*** Miles Goodman ***Art*** Stephen Storer
Act Gene Wilder, Christine Lahti, Mary Stuart Masterson, Robert Prosky, Anne Jackson, Susan Ruttan (Paramount)

Funny About Love is a not-so-funny Gene Wilder vehicle. Tale of the biological clock regarding procreation is told from a male point of view here. However, Wilder's problems as a would-be-daddy aren't interesting or compelling.

Inability to conceive with wife Christine Lahti bogs the film down in almost clinical detail. Funniest bit has Wilder sticking ice cubes in his jockey shorts on doctor's advice to get his sperm temperature down.

Film takes an absurd turn in the third reel when Wilder's child bride of a mother (Anne Jackson) is killed by a falling stove (meant to be black humor). Pic hardly recovers from this failed bit of whimsy.

Costar Mary Stuart Masterson doesn't enter the scene until a full hour has elapsed. Wilder meets her at a convention of beautiful sorority girls where he's guest speaker. Another whirlwind romance ensues, and Masterson is pregnant.

Wilder has his moments in a role that overdoes the crying jags and self-pity. Both Lahti and Masterson remain most appealing actresses in search of challenging roles, not provided here.

•

FUNNY BONES
1995, 126 mins, US Ⓥ ⊙ col
Dir Peter Chelsom ***Prod*** Simon Fields, Peter Chelsom ***Scr*** Peter Chelsom, Peter Flannery ***Ph*** Eduardo Serra ***Ed*** Martin Walsh ***Mus*** John Altman ***Art*** Caroline Hanania
Act Oliver Platt, Lee Evans, Richard Griffith, Leslie Caron, Jerry Lewis, Oliver Reed (Hollywood)

Homage, memory and unabashed zaniness infect *Funny Bones*. It is a tour-de-force for filmmaker Peter Chelsom, who chronicles a complex saga of vaudeville and shtick, pathos and absurdity.

Tommy Fawkes (Oliver Platt) is the belligerent son of comedy icon George Fawkes (Jerry Lewis). He bombs spectacularly in Vegas with his father as a prime witness. So Tommy sets out to reinvent himself and heads out to Blackpool, England, the seaside entertainment resort where he was raised until the age of six and where his father had his first success.

Tommy believes the area is rife with novel entertainment ideas. But the performers he auditions are largely a string of freak-show attractions from a bygone era, with one key exception—the Parker family and, principally, son Jack. The knotty dilemma confronting young Fawkes is that the Parker repertoire is akin to routines that established his father as an original voice. It's obvious to him that the British vaudevillians were robbed. Jack is also his half-brother, the result of a brief liason between George and Katie (Leslie Caron).

As with Chelsom's earlier *Hear My Song*, the relative modesty of the physical production is offset by big emotions that rise to a deafening crescendo in the film's closing section. His keen sense of character paves over narrative bumps and sharp emotional turns. Still, he's occasionally undone by his fascination with the performance pieces.

•

FUNNY FACE
1957, 103 mins, US Ⓥ ⊙ col
Dir Stanley Donen ***Prod*** Roger Edens ***Scr*** Leonard Gershe ***Ph*** Ray June ***Ed*** Frank Bracht ***Mus*** Adolph Deutsch (adapt.) ***Art*** Hal Pereira, George W. Davis
Act Audrey Hepburn, Fred Astaire, Kay Thompson, Michel Auclair, Robert Flemyng, Suzy Parker (Paramount)

While it wears the title and bears several of the songs, *Funny Face*'s relationship to the Broadway musical [of 1927] stops right there. With a different book and new, added tunes, this is a lightly diverting, modish, Parisian-localed tintuner.

Originally slated for production at Metro, film moved to Paramount as a package so Audrey Hepburn could have the femme lead opposite Fred Astaire. This May-November pairing gives the production the benefits of Astaire's debonair style and terp accomplishments, and the sensitive acting talents of Hepburn.

Hepburn plays a bookish introvert who is suddenly swept from her literary existence in a Greenwich Village shop to a heady, high-fashion round of Paris when she's discovered by glamour photog Astaire.

Style runs rampant, with Hubert de Givenchy creating the Paris wardrobe worn by Hepburn as a model, while Edith Head takes care of things elsewhere. Tune-wise, there are six George and Ira Gershwin numbers from the stage musical and five from producer Roger Edens and scripter Leonard Gershe. All are either sung or used as backing for dance numbers, with director Stanley Donen handling the song staging while Astaire and Eugene Loring take care of the choreography.

1957: NOMINATIONS: Best Original Story & Screenplay, Cinematography, Costume Design, Art Direction

•

FUNNY FARM
1988, 101 mins, US Ⓥ col
Dir George Roy Hill ***Prod*** Robert I. Crawford ***Scr*** Jeffrey Boam ***Ph*** Miroslav Ondricek ***Ed*** Alan Heim ***Mus*** Elmer Bernstein ***Art*** Henry Bumstead
Act Chevy Chase, Madolyn Smith, Kevin O'Morrison, Joseph Maher, Jack Gilpin, Brad Sullivan (Warner)

Chevy Chase tones down his goofy shtick, moves to the country with wife Madolyn Smith and has an occasional humorous encounter or two with the locals in *Funny Farm*. As pleasant yuppie comedies go, this is about par. Chase is a sportswriter with ambitions as a novelist. The wife is a schoolteacher with no other apparent ambitions, except initially to make the clapboard home cozy with chintz and antiques from the local shop of nearby Redbud.

Along with the fact that Chase suffers from writer's block and then when he does manage to crank it out, his wife lets him know it's awful, none of the townsfolk are even friendly. This really goads him and he takes to the bottle.

Director George Roy Hill shows little distinction with this material [from Jay Cronley's book], but then again, the material here isn't very distinctive. Some of the setups work better than others, though most are of the sitcom variety.

•

FUNNY GIRL
1968, 145 mins, US Ⓥ ⊙ ▭ col
Dir William Wyler ***Prod*** William Wyler, Ray Stark ***Scr*** Isobel Lennart ***Ph*** Harry Stradling ***Ed*** Robert Swink ***Mus*** Walter Scharf (sup.) ***Art*** Gene Callahan
Act Barbra Streisand, Omar Sharif, Kay Medford, Anne Francis, Walter Pidgeon, Lee Allen (Columbia/Rastar)

Barbra Streisand in her Hollywood debut makes a marked impact. The saga of the tragi-comedienne Fanny Brice of the ungainly mien and manner, charmed by the suave cardsharp Nick Arnstein, is perhaps of familiar pattern, but it is to the credit of all concerned that it plays so convincingly.

Streisand's basic Grecian-profiled personality has not been photographically camouflaged.

The projection of Fanny Brice's rise from the pushcart-laden lower East Side to Ziegfeld stardom and a baronial Long Island estate is achieved in convincing broad strokes.

The durable Jule Styne-Bob Merrill songs, from the [1964] stage score, are given fuller enhancement under the flexibility of the cinematic sweep.

"People," "You Are Woman, I Am Man," "Don't Rain on my Parade," "I'm the Greatest Star" have been enhanced by the original Broadway songsmiths with "Roller Skate Rag" a parody on "The Swan" ballet and a title song, not part of the original score.

1968: Best Actress (Barbra Streisand)

NOMINATIONS: Best Picture, Supp. Actress (Kay Medford), Cinematography, Editing, Scoring of a Musical Picture, Song ("Funny Girl"), Sound

•

FUNNY LADY

1975, 136 mins, US Ⓥ ⊙ ▭ col

Dir Herbert Ross ***Prod*** Ray Stark ***Scr*** Jay Presson Allen, Arnold Schulman ***Ph*** James Wong Howe ***Ed*** Marion Rothman ***Mus*** Peter Matz (arr.) ***Art*** George Jenkins

Act Barbra Streisand, James Caan, Omar Sharif, Roddy McDowall, Ben Vereen, Carole Wells (Rastar/Columbia)

Barbra Streisand was outstanding as the younger Fanny Brice in *Funny Girl*, and in *Funny Lady* she's even better. Ray Stark's extremely handsome period production also stars James Caan in an excellent characterization of Billy Rose, the second major influence in Brice's personal life.

The story [by Arnold Schulman] picks up Brice in 1930, an established Ziegfeld star in a career lull as her mentor has trouble finding depression-era backing. Enter Rose, the brash comer who learns some showmanship savvy from her and marries her, after which the two drift apart as public careers and personal attachments diverge.

The plot is partially fictionalized in its apparent main thrust of showing how Brice finally purged her first love, for gambler Nick Arnstein (Omar Sharif), but in the process lost Rose as well. Thereafter, she was prepared to go it alone, a perfect hook for first-rate dramatic climax.

More than half a dozen older songs, on which Billy Rose's name appears as one of the authors, are used to good advantage. [Music and lyrics of new songs are by John Kander and Fred Ebb.]

The film cost about $8.5 million to which Columbia contributed about $4.9 million and the rest from one of those tax shelter consortia.

1975: NOMINATIONS: Best Cinematography, Costume Design, Adapted Score, Song ("How Lucky Can You Get"), Sound

•

FUNNY THING HAPPENED ON THE WAY TO THE FORUM, A

1966, 99 mins, US Ⓥ ⊙ col

Dir Richard Lester ***Prod*** Melvin Frank ***Scr*** Melvin Frank, Michael Pertwee ***Ph*** Nicolas Roeg ***Ed*** John Victor Smith ***Mus*** Ken Thorne (arr.) ***Art*** Tony Walton

Act Zero Mostel, Phil Silvers, Buster Keaton, Jack Gilford, Michael Crawford, Annette Andre (Quadrangle/United Artists)

A Funny Thing Happened on the Way to the Forum—after the [1962 Stephen Sondheim] stage musicomedy of the same name—will probably stand out as one of the few originals of two repetition-weary genres, the film musical comedy and the toga-cum-sandal "epic." Flip, glib and sophisticated, yet rump-slappingly bawdy and fast-paced, *Forum* is a capricious look at the seamy underside of classical Rome through a 20th-century hipster's shades.

Plot follows the efforts of a glib, con-man slave, Pseudolus (Zero Mostel), to cheat, steal or connive his freedom from a domineering mistress, Domina (Patricia Jessel), and his equally victimized master, the henpecked Senex (Michael Hordern). Unwilling ally, through blackmail, is the timorous toady Hysterium (Jack Gilford), another household slave.

Early instrument of Pseudolus's plot is the callow Hero (Michael Crawford), who, smitten by one of the luscious courtesans peddled by Lycus (Phil Silvers), local flesh supplier, promises Mostel his freedom if he can finagle the "virgin's" purchase. Plot complications multiply like the film's pratfalls, however, and the winsome object of Hero's passion has already been sold to the egomaniacal Miles (Leon Greene), a legion captain of legendary ferocity, who thunders onto the scene to claim the girl.

Interwoven through the plot is the presence of Erronius (Buster Keaton) who, searching for his lost children, unties the knotted situation.

1966: Best Adapted Score

•

FUN WITH DICK AND JANE

1977, 95 mins, US Ⓥ col

Dir Ted Kotcheff ***Prod*** Peter Bart, Max Palevsky ***Scr*** David Giler, Jerry Belson, Mordecai Richler ***Ph*** Fred Koenekamp ***Ed*** Danford B. Greene ***Mus*** Ernest Gold ***Art*** James G. Hulsey

Act George Segal, Jane Fonda, Ed McMahon, Dick Gautier, Allan Miller, Hank Garcia (Columbia)

Fun with Dick and Jane is a great comedy idea [from a story by Gerald Gaiser] largely shot down by various bits of tastelessness, crudity and nastiness. Stars George Segal and Jane Fonda are an upper middle-class family which turns to armed robbery when hubby loses his aerospace job.

Fonda and Segal have all the basic comedy essentials necessary to fulfill the minimum demands of the story, and that seems to be the problem: they seem to have gotten no help from direction and/or writing in getting off the ground.

Ed McMahon is terrific as Segal's employer whose boozy bonhomie conceals the heart of a true Watergater. Making this essentially shallow and hypocritical character into a fascinating figure of corporate logrolling was a major challenge.

•

FURIES, THE

1950, 109 mins, US b/w

Dir Anthony Mann ***Prod*** Hal Wallis ***Scr*** Charles Schnee ***Ph*** Victor Milner ***Ed*** Archie Marshek ***Mus*** Franz Waxman

Act Barbara Stanwyck, Wendell Corey, Walter Huston, Judith Anderson, Gilbert Roland (Paramount)

The Furies is a big-scale western drama, expertly put together by Hal Wallis. Story is the familiar one about cattle barons and sprawling western empires.

Picture was the final assignment for Walter Huston and to his role of cattle baron, ruler of vast ranch acreage and the dwellers thereon, he brought a colorful job that adds a lot of punch.

Story [from the novel by Niven Busch] interest falls chiefly to Barbara Stanwyck, strong-willed daughter of Huston who takes the place of his son in guiding the cattle empire until the father marries a conniving widow, craftily portrayed by Judith Anderson. Stanwyck disfigures her stepmother in a fit of rage. She swears to break the ranch, The Furies, and her father when he spitefully hangs Gilbert Roland, a Mexican friend whose family has dwelt for ages on the ranch.

While the pacing keeps the plot moving at climax-punctuated speed, it is the dialog that has the sock to keep the attention intrigued for adult viewers.

•

FURY

1923, 116 mins, US b/w

Dir Henry King ***Scr*** Edmund Goulding ***Ph*** Roy Overbaugh ***Ed*** Duncan Mansfield ***Art*** Robert M. Haas

Act Richard Barthelmess, Tyrone Power, Pat Hartigan, Barry Macollum, Dorothy Gish (Inspiration/First National)

Fury is a great story as screened, coupling a corking touch of humor here and there through a story that is replete with action and heart interest.

Fury has a little touch of the strength of *Madame X* in it, only in this instance the boy discovers his mother who was lured away and tackles the man who seduced her.

The tale is laid in the Limehouse district of London and the wharves of Glasgow, with the star on board the *Lady Spray*, his father being the master of the craft. The father is embittered at the world due to the fact that his wife deserted him for another man.

Then on shore there is revealed Dorothy Gish. She is her same flip, half humorous, half pathetic self as of yore, with the first mate of the *Lady Spray* and the master's son both trying to win her. The latter is one that she favors and finally she consents to go to Glasgow to meet him there and marry. It is on that trip along the coast that the father dies and places into the hands of his son the task of finding the man responsible for his mother's downfall.

Through it all Richard Barthelmess as the boy carries with him a certain wistfulness bound to appeal, especially with Gish acting as an excellent foil for his work.

•

FURY

1936, 90 mins, US Ⓥ b/w

Dir Fritz Lang ***Prod*** Joseph L. Mankiewicz ***Scr*** Bartlett Cormack, Fritz Lang ***Ph*** Joseph Ruttenberg ***Ed*** Frank Sullivan ***Mus*** Franz Waxman ***Art*** Cedric Gibbons, William Horning, Edwin B. Willis

Act Sylvia Sidney, Spencer Tracy, Walter Abel, Bruce Cabot, Edward Ellis, Walter Brennan (M-G-M)

Punchy story [by Norman Krasna] has been masterfully guided by the skillful direction of the Viennese Fritz Lang. It's his first in America and represents the culmination of a year and a half of waiting, while being carried on the Metro payroll, until finally finding something to his liking. It coincides also with the debut efforts of Joseph L. Mankiewicz as a Metro producer.

Spencer Tracy gives his top performance as the upright young man until he's involved in a kidnapping mess through mistaken identity. Escaping a necktie lynching party, the jailhouse is burned down, despite the meagre protective efforts of the constabulary, and legally he is dead. But somehow he had managed to escape and he is intent on vengeance on the 22 (including one woman who had whirled the igniting torch into the kerosened pyre at the jailhouse door), who are ultimately brought to trial.

Walter Abel, as the state attorney, virtually walks away with the proceedings during the courtroom scene. Sylvia Sidney, whose tender love scenes in the early motivations are relatively passive, rises to the proper heights in the dramatic testimony. Tracy is capital during the somewhat slowly pacing scenes up until the pseudo-lynching; then he becomes the dominating character in the scenes where he hides out and permits the trial to proceed.

1936: NOMINATION: Best Original Story

•

FURY, THE

1978, 117 mins, US Ⓥ ⊙ col

Dir Brian De Palma ***Prod*** Frank Yablans ***Scr*** John Farris ***Ph*** Richard H. Kline ***Ed*** Paul Hirsch ***Mus*** John Williams ***Art*** Bill Malley

Act Kirk Douglas, John Cassavetes, Carrie Snodgress, Charles Durning, Amy Irving, Fiona Lewis (Yablans/20th Century-Fox)

The Fury features Kirk Douglas and John Cassavetes as adversaries in an elaborate game of mind control. Director Brian De Palma is on home ground in moving the plot pieces around effectively.

John Farris adapted his novel for the screen. Most viewers will enjoy the razzle-dazzle of the lengthy pursuit by Douglas of son Andrew Stevens, kidnapped by Cassavetes because of his mystical powers. But apart from a few throwaway references to government agencies and psychic phenomena, there is never, anywhere, a coherent exposition of what all the running and jumping is about.

Strong cast also includes Carrie Snodgress as a staffer in Charles Durning's research institute where Amy Irving (also blessed/cursed with psychic powers) is being readied as a substitute for Stevens. Seems that Stevens is freaking out, despite the attentions and care of Fiona Lewis, and he is targeted for elimination.

•

FUTURE COP

SEE: TRANCERS

•

FUTUREWORLD

1976, 107 mins, US Ⓥ col

Dir Richard T. Heffron ***Prod*** Paul Lazarus III, James T. Aubrey Jr. ***Scr*** Mayo Simon, George Schenck ***Ph*** Howard Schwartz, Gene Polito ***Ed*** James Mitchell ***Mus*** Fred Karlin ***Art*** Trevor Williams

Act Peter Fonda, Blythe Danner, Arthur Hill, Yul Brynner, Jim Antonio, John Ryan (American International)

Futureworld is a strong sequel to *Westworld* in which the rebuilt pleasure dome aims at world conquest by extending the robot technology to duplicating business and political figures.

Peter Fonda and Blythe Danner come across very well in their starring roles as investigative reporters on a junket to help promote the rebuilt and enlarged theme park.

The reporters are hosted by Arthur Hill, repping the theme park owners, and John Ryan, the chief scientist. Fonda and Danner eventually discover the world domination plot with the help of Stuart Margolin, one of the few nonrobot technicians still employed.

Yul Brynner makes a cameo reappearance as the robot gunslinger so prominent in *Westworld*, a good bridging element between the two pix.

•

FUZZ

1972, 92 mins, US Ⓥ col

Dir Richard A. Colla ***Prod*** Jack Farren ***Scr*** Evan Hunter ***Ph*** Jacques Marquette ***Ed*** Robert Kimble ***Mus*** Dave Grusin ***Art*** Hilyard Brown

Act Burt Reynolds, Jack Weston, Tom Skerritt, Yul Brynner, Raquel Welch, James McEachin (Filmways/Javelin)

Fuzz has an excellent screenplay by Evan Hunter, from his 87th Precinct series written under the name Ed McBain. The basic plotline is a search for a mysterious meticulous bomber, played by Yul Brynner, who keeps killing local officials. The search is conducted against a backdrop of an urban neighborhood police station where the cops are as humanized as those under arrest or suspicion.

The assorted people involved innocently or criminally with the police are neither patronized middle-class nor anointed low-life.

There is compassion in the treatment of all characters while at the same time their foibles are milked for both laughs and occasionally chilling reality.

Burt Reynolds is very good, Jack Weston and James McEachin are excellent, and Tom Skerritt is outstanding as the principal quartet of detectives.

•

F/X
(AKA: F/X - MURDER BY ILLUSION)
1986, 106 mins, US Ⓥ ⦿ col
Dir Robert Mandel ***Prod*** Dodi Fayed, Jack Wiener ***Scr*** Robert T. Megginson, Gregory Fleeman ***Ph*** Miroslav Ondricek ***Ed*** Terry Rawlings ***Mus*** Bill Conti ***Art*** Mel Bourne
Act Bryan Brown, Brian Dennehy, Diane Venora, Cliff De Young, Mason Adams, Jerry Orbach (Orion)

As contrived and plot-hole ridden as it is, *F/X* still works quite effectively as a crowd-pleasing popcorn picture. Basic premise here is so strong that it proves well-nigh indestructable, even in the face of numerous implausibilities, some silly dialogue and less-than-great casting in secondary roles.

Crackerjack film special-effects man Bryan Brown is recruited by the Justice Dept. to stage a phony assassination of big-time mobster Jerry Orbach, who is ready to squeal. The authorities want the Mafia to think Orbach is dead. Brown is convinced to act the role of hitman himself, but he finds himself a marked man, the target of both government goons and New York Police.

Last 80 minutes of film constitute a relentless, multifaceted chase, as Brown must rely on his wits and resoursefull talents as an F/X wizard to elude and, ultimately, hunt down the baddies who set him up. Old-style Irish cop Brian Dennehy so flagrantly disobeys the rule book in his pursuit of justice that he gets tossed off the force. But even this doesn't stop him.

Roles are one dimensional, but Brown and Dennehy possess sufficient personality and physical presence to fill them well. Special effects, stunts and special makeup are all they intended to be—top drawer.

•

F/X2
(AKA: FX2—THE DEADLY ART OF ILLUSION)
1991, 109 mins, US Ⓥ ⦿ col
Dir Richard Franklin ***Prod*** Jack Wiener, Dodi Fayed ***Scr*** Bill Condon ***Ph*** Victor J. Kemper ***Ed*** Andrew London, Michael Tronick ***Mus*** Lalo Schifrin, Michael Boddicker ***Art*** John Jay Moore
Act Bryan Brown, Brian Dennehy, Rachel Ticotin, Joanna Gleason, Philip Bosco, Kevin J. O'Connor (Orion)

With all the ingenuity that went into toys and gadgetry in this five-years-removed sequel, it's a shame no one bothered to hook a brain up to the plot. Beyond the engaging leads, there's little here on the level that made 1986's *F/X* so entertaining, as the sequel throttles a stale police-corruption setup loaded with genre clichés.

Because the pic's basic conceit is so simple—a film effects man using his "reel" skills to thwart dense public officials and criminals—the story actually gets off to a rather slow start, as the semiretired Rollie Tyler (Bryan Brown) is talked into participating in a police sting operation by his g.f.'s ex-husband (Tom Mason).

The operation goes haywire, the ex-husband is killed and Tyler starts looking into the intrigue behind it. In over his head, he recruits the help of Leo (Brian Dennehy), the cop he teamed with at the end of the first pic.

The lack of an interesting villain also hurts. Philip Bosco is more a comic foil than anything else, while other bad guys are merely shadowy mob types left on the film's fringe.

Dennehy remains one of the more effortlessly likable actors around, while Brown may be a little too self-assured this time in using his fantasy skills in life-or-death situations.

GABLE AND LOMBARD
1976, 131 mins, US Ⓥ col
Dir Sidney J. Furie ***Prod*** Harry Korshak ***Scr*** Barry Sandler ***Ph*** Jordan S. Cronenweth ***Ed*** Argyle Nelson ***Mus*** Michel Legrand ***Art*** Edward C. Carfagno
Act James Brolin, Jill Clayburgh, Allen Garfield, Red Buttons, Melanie Mayron, Joanne Linville (Universal)

Gable and Lombard is a film with many major assets, not the least of which is the stunning and smashing performance of Jill Clayburgh as Carole Lombard. James Brolin manages excellently to project the necessary Clark Gable attributes while adding his own individuality to the characterization.

Sidney J. Furie's direction of handsome period production supplies zest as well as romance to the tragi-comedy aspects of the two stars' offscreen life together.

Barry Sandler's original screenplay conveys the excitement and fun of an era when everyone seemed to enjoy themselves in the profession of making pictures.

Gable and Lombard is candid without being prurient; delightful without being superficially glossy; heartwarming without being corny.

•

GABRIEL OVER THE WHITE HOUSE
1933, 83 mins, US Ⓥ ⦿ b/w
Dir Gregory La Cava ***Prod*** [Walter Wanger] ***Scr*** Carey Wilson, Bertram Bloch ***Ph*** Bert Glennon ***Ed*** Basil Wrangell ***Mus*** William Axt ***Art*** Cedric Gibbons
Act Walter Huston, Karen Morley, Franchot Tone, Arthur Byron, Dickie Moore, C. Henry Gordon (M-G-M/Cosmopolitan)

A mess of political tripe superlatively hoked up into a picture of strong popular possibilities, Walter Wanger's first Metro production as a supervisor is a cleverly executed commercial release [from the anonymous novel of the same name].

A new President (Walter Huston), up to then a pretty practical politician, is dying after an automobile smash and is miraculously revived. Divine intervention stays the hand of the reaper and brings the President back to lead the nation and the world out of the trials of depression.

The resurrected President goes before Congress in a big scene, asks to be made a dictator to deal with the emergency, and when Congress refuses he declares martial law and takes control. While all these sprightly doings are in process the President's girl secretary (Karen Morley) and his young aide (Franchot Tone) fall in love.

Huston plays the part so persuasively that witnessers will be tricked into accepting its monstrous exaggerations. Tone, young newcomer for whom Metro has high hopes, and Morley, a satisfying player in almost any sort of an assignment, carry what amount to walk-on parts and make them look like leads.

•

GAILY, GAILY
(UK: CHICAGO, CHICAGO)
1969, 100 mins, US col
Dir Norman Jewison ***Prod*** Norman Jewison ***Scr*** Abram S. Ginnes ***Ph*** Richard Kline ***Ed*** Ralph Winters ***Mus*** Henry Mancini ***Art*** Robert Boyle
Act Beau Bridges, Melina Mercouri, Brian Keith, George Kennedy, Hume Cronyn, Margot Kidder (Mirisch-Cartier)

Ben Hecht's pseudo-reminiscences of a cub reporter in 1910 Chicago emerges on the screen as a lushly staged, handsomely produced, largely unfunny comedy.

Director-producer Norman Jewison seemingly works on the comedic theory that nothing succeeds like excess. The very basic decision to play *Gaily, Gaily* broadly as possible, lay it on with a trowel, divorces the film from the realities of 1910 Chicago.

Based on Hecht's book *Gaily, Gaily* the situations and characters are unbelievable, and because they are, they are unfunny. The paradox is that Jewison sets the stage and Richard Kline photographs it with a lover's eye for the richness, earthiness, brawling vitality and raw meat of the era. The sets, costuming and resurrected locations in Chicago and Milwaukee are a glorious period pageant.

1969: NOMINATIONS: Best Costume Design, Art Direction, Sound

•

GALAXY QUEST
1999, 104 mins, US Ⓥ ⦿ ▭ col
Dir Dean Parisot ***Prod*** Mark Johnson, Charles Newirth ***Scr*** David Howard, Robert Gordon ***Ph*** Jerzy Zielinski ***Ed*** Don Zimmerman ***Mus*** David Newman ***Art*** Linda DeScenna
Act Tim Allen, Sigourney Weaver, Alan Rickman, Tony Shalhoub, Sam Rockwell, Daryl Mitchell (DreamWorks)

A mischievously clever and slickly commercial sci-fi comedy with strong cross-generational appeal, pic gets impressive mileage from a one-joke premise—stars of a *Star Trek*–type TV series are drafted into battling real extraterrestrial villains—thanks in large measure to game efforts of a first-rate cast.

Scripters persuasively limn a parallel universe where a cheesy primetime space opera called *Galaxy Quest* continues to inspire a cult following almost 20 years after its cancellation. Jason Nesmith (Tim Allen) is an unreliable egotist who enjoys the adulation he receives at conventions. Since his heyday as Cmdr. Peter Quincy Taggart, in charge of the starship *Protector*, Nesmith's career has been in almost total eclipse.

Nesmith's overshadowed co-stars haven't done much either: Gwen DeMarco (a becomingly blond Sigourney Weaver), who did little more than serve as a bosomy babe; Alexander Dane (Alan Rickman), a cynical Shakespearean actor who played the half-reptilian Dr. Lazarus; Fred Kwan (Tony Shalhoub), a conspicuously non-Asian fellow who played Tech Sgt. Chen; and Tommy Webber (Daryl Mitchell), who played the 10-year-old navigator.

The real fun begins when Nesmith is approached by a group of fans who turn out to be extraterrestrials in human guise. Mathesar (Enrico Colantoni) is leader of the Thermians, who assume the TV programs they've picked up from Earth are documentaries, not dramas. They believe Cmdr. Taggart and his crew are true-blue heroes who can help the Thermians defend themselves against the dreaded Sarris (Robin Sachs).

Allen's quite good at charting Nesmith's evolution from self-absorbed ham to empathetic hero. Weaver demonstrates her talents for graceful pratfalls and spirited self-mockery.

•

GALLIPOLI
1981, 110 mins, Australia Ⓥ ⦿ ▭ col
Dir Peter Weir ***Prod*** Robert Stigwood, Patricia Lovell ***Scr*** David Williamson ***Ph*** Russell Boyd ***Ed*** William Anderson ***Mus*** Brian May ***Art*** Wendy Weir
Act Mel Gibson, Mark Lee, Bill Kerr, Robert Grubb, Bill Hunter, David Argue (Associated R&R)

Against a backdrop broader than his previous outings, Weir has fashioned what is virtually an intimate epic [from his own screen story]. A very big picture by Aussie standards, the film is all the same a finely considered story focusing closely on the relationship that builds between Frank (Mel Gibson) and Archy (Mark Lee), and how it is affected by events on the battlefield of Gallipoli.

Gallipoli is as much an essential part of the Australian ethos as, say The Alamo is to Texas: a military defeat that became rationalized over the years into a moral victory. In April 1915 a combined force of Australian and New Zealand troops numbering about 35,000 joined an Allied attempt to control the Dardanelles waterway by capturing Istanbul. Bungling by the generals allowed the Turks time to dig in and the landings devolved into stalemate, but not before much bitter fighting.

The Australian-New Zealand Army Corps in great part bore the brunt of the bitterest exchanges. Thus Peter Weir's *Gallipoli* tackles a legend in human terms and emerges as a highly entertaining drama on a number of levels, none of them inaccessible to anyone unfamiliar with the actual events.

•

GAMBIT
1966, 107 mins, US Ⓥ ▭ col
Dir Ronald Neame ***Prod*** Leo L. Fuchs ***Scr*** Jack Davies, Alvin Sargent ***Ph*** Clifford Stine ***Ed*** Alma Macrorie ***Mus*** Maurice Jarre ***Art*** Alexander Golitzen, George C. Webb
Act Shirley MacLaine, Michael Caine, Herbert Lom, Roger C. Carmel, Arnold Moss, John Abbott (Universal)

Shirley MacLaine and Michael Caine star in a first-rate suspense comedy, cleverly scripted, expertly directed and handsomely mounted.

Sidney Carroll's original story has been adapted into a zesty laugh-getter as MacLaine becomes Miss Malaprop in Caine's scheme to loot the art treasures of mid-East potentate Herbert Lom. An idealized swindle sequence lasting 27 minutes opens pic, after which the execution of the plan shifts all characterizations and sympathies.

Director Ronald Neame has obtained superior characterizations from all hands. MacLaine, playing a Eurasian gal, displays her deft comedy abilities after the opening segment, in which she is stone-faced and silent. Caine socks over a characterization which is at first tight-lipped and cold, then turning warm with human and romantic frailty. Lom is excellent as the potentate, so assured of his security devices that audience sympathy encourages the machinations of Caine and MacLaine.

1966: NOMINATIONS: Best Color Costume Design, Color Art Direction, Sound

•

GAMBLER, THE
1974, 109 mins, US Ⓥ ⦿ col
Dir Karel Reisz ***Prod*** Irwin Winkler, Robert Chartoff ***Scr*** James Toback ***Ph*** Victor J. Kemper ***Ed*** Roger Spottiswoode ***Mus*** Jerry Fielding ***Art*** Philip Rosenberg
Act James Caan, Paul Sorvlno, Lauren Hutton, Morrls Carnovsky, Jacqueline Brookes, Burt Young (Paramount)

The Gambler is a compelling and effective film. James Caan is excellent and the featured players are superb. However, it is somewhat overlong in early exposition and has one climax too many.

James Toback's script comingles candor and compassion, without hostility or superficial sociology or patronizing.

After getting off to a good start, film slows down in some redundant and/or sluggishly paced exposition, at least understandable considering the calibre of players such as Paul Sorvino, Jacqueline Brookes, Morris Carnovsky (Caan's wealthy grandfather who declines to bail him out), Burt Young (a very cordial yet simultaneously merciless and brutal loan shark collection agent), whose roles provide full dimension and bitter irony to the story. The pace quickens towards the end.

Jerry Fielding's score, based on Mahler's Symphony No. 1, is excellent, making the point that a contemporary urban drama can be underscored to great effect without tinny transistor radio source excerpts or mickey-mouse rock riffs.

•

GAME, THE
1997, 128 mins, US/UK Ⓥ ⦿ ▭ col
Dir David Fincher ***Prod*** Steve Golin, Cean Chaffin ***Scr*** John Brancato, Michael Ferris ***Ph*** Harris Savides ***Ed*** James Haygood ***Mus*** Howard Shore ***Art*** Jeffrey Beecroft
Act Michael Douglas, Sean Penn, Deborah Kara Unger, James Rebhorn, Peter Donat, Carroll Baker (Propaganda/PolyGram)

A high-toned mind game of a movie, crafted with a commanding, aloof precision by David Fincher in his first outing since *Se7en*, this unusual dive into the world of a pastime without apparent rules generates a chilly intellectual intrigue that will arouse buffs.

Michael Douglas plays Nicholas Van Orton, a fabulously wealthy San Francisco investment banker whose forbidding coldness sets the tone for the picture. His jumpy younger brother, Conrad (Sean Penn), turns up after a long absence and offers Nicholas an entree to unusual "entertainment" courtesy of something called Consumer Recreation Services.

"We provide—whatever is lacking," CRS rep Feingold (James Rebhorn) teasingly explains. Primed for an unusual trip, Nicholas is stunned to be informed that CRS has rejected him—merely the first of many increasingly disorienting and ultimately threatening events that turn Nicholas's life upside down and inside out. The Alice in Wonderland aspect is suggested by the use of Jefferson Airplane's "White Rabbit" as the nominal theme song.

The film is limited by the material's nature as a brainy exercise and by its narrow focus; but it is more than just a technical exercise, with the specter of the total loss of privacy always lurking in the background.

Douglas carries the picture well. Penn pops up only intermittently, his quicksilver personality used to contrast the ne'er-do-well brother with his control-freak sibling.

•

GAME IS OVER, THE
1966, 95 mins, France/Italy Ⓥ ▭ col
Dir Roger Vadim ***Scr*** Jean Cau, Roger Vadim, Bernard Frechtman ***Ph*** Claude Renoir ***Ed*** Victoria Mercanton ***Mus*** J.P. Bourtayre, Jean Bouchety ***Art*** Jean Andre

Act Jane Fonda, Peter McEnery, Michel Piccoli, Tina Marquand, Jacques Monod (Marceau/Cocinor/Mega)

This melodrama is sleek and elegant if sometimes short on motivation. Updated version of an Emile Zola 19th-century novel [*La curée*] deals with a rich financier married to a very young woman (Jane Fonda). He also has a 22-year-old son (Peter McEnery). Love blossoms between this son and the young wife.

Director Roger Vadim has a glossy style that shows the aimless life of the bored wife and the drifting son that finally results in love only to be throttled by his weakness which ends in the woman's breakdown. McEnery is effective as the weak son while Michel Piccoli does not have the right sort of role to be able to limn a strong and overpowering father figure to overcome love and desired freedom.

●

GAME OF DEATH, A

1945, 72 mins, US b/w

Dir Robert Wise ***Prod*** Herman Schlom ***Scr*** Norman Houston ***Ph*** J. Roy Hunt ***Ed*** J. R. Whittredge ***Mus*** Paul Sawtell ***Art*** Albert S. D'Agostino, Lucius O. Croxton

Act John Loder, Audrey Long, Edgar Barrier, Russell Wade, Jason Robards Sr, Russell Hicks (RKO)

A Game of Death is a remake of *The Most Dangerous Game*, filmed by RKO in 1932 from Richard Connell's short story. Despite implausibility, it has expert direction and some good acting to make it a juicy horror cantata.

Edgar Barrier portrays a big game hunter who has a maniacal desire to hunt humans instead. He appropriates an island, where he plots shipwrecks to bring in his human quarry.

After putting them up at the menage for several days, he scares them into the rushes, then embarks on a manhunt with his bow and arrow. John Loder, hunter-novelist, is washed in from a wreck and soon penetrates the madman's scheme.

Loder and Barrier carry the picture with excellent portrayals of implausible roles, while Robert Wise directs in a tempo that sustains suspense.

●

GAMES

1967, 100 mins, US col

Dir Curtis Harrington ***Prod*** George Edwards ***Scr*** Gene Kearney ***Ph*** William A. Fraker ***Ed*** Douglas Stewart ***Mus*** Samuel Matlovsky ***Art*** Alexander Golitzen, William D. DeCinces

Act Simone Signoret, James Caan, Katharine Ross, Don Stroud, Kent Smith, Estelle Winwood (Universal)

Games is a low-key suspenser with more appeal to the intellect than to the emotions. Simone Signoret stars in the first major studio effort by ex-indie filmmakers, producer George Edwards and director Curtis Harrington. Colorful production values add a visual hypo to the apparently deliberate, underplaying of a fairish script, leisurely directed.

The Harrington-Edwards story concerns a modern couple, Paul and Jennifer, played by James Caan and Katherine Ross, who supposedly live in a hedonistic atmosphere. Lisa (Signoret), an immigrant reduced to peddling door-to-door cosmetics, becomes a house guest. A series of practical jokes leads to the murder of Norman (Don Stroud, Universal contractee moved to pix from TV work), and Jennifer eventually loses her mind.

Harrington's evident attempt was to create a quiet terror, long on slow-building suspense and short on blatant shock values; the attempt was admirable, the achievement less so. For in the process, audiences have too much time to think.

Despite script, three stars are competent. Visual consultant Morton Haack and art directors Alexander Golitzen and William D. DeCinces went all out in the far-out interior trappings of the house.

●

GAMES, THE

1970, 97 mins, UK Ⓥ col

Dir Michael Winner ***Prod*** Lester Linsk ***Scr*** Erich Segal ***Ph*** Robert Paynter ***Ed*** Bernard Gribble ***Mus*** Francis Lai ***Art*** Albert Witherick, Fred Carter, Roy Stannard

Act Michael Crawford, Ryan O'Neal, Charles Aznavour, Jeremy Kemp, Elaine Taylor, Stanley Baker (20th Century-Fox)

Story turns on four runners from different nations who eventually compete in a climactic 26-mile marathon in the Rome Olympic Games.

Michael Crawford is the ex-milkman driven to prowess by Stanley Baker; Ryan O'Neal is a fun-loving American college kid—as only Hollywood can define and perpetuate this stereotype; Charles Aznavour is a Czech soldier, forced to return to running as a political pawn; and Athol Compton is the down-under Aborigine exploited by Jeremy Kemp.

Filmed in England, Italy, Austria, Czechoslovakia, Australia and Japan, the pic [from a novel by Hugh Atkinson] is long on production values and nothing else.

Technical adviser Gordon Pirie, a retired British track star and Olympics participant, did a creditable job in the exteriors.

Aznavour, Crawford and Jeremy Kemp come off best.

●

GANDHI

1982, 188 mins, UK/US/India Ⓥ ⊙ col

Dir Richard Attenborough ***Prod*** Richard Attenborough, Rani Dube ***Scr*** John Briley ***Ph*** Billy Williams, Ronnie Taylor ***Ed*** John Bloom ***Mus*** Ravi Shankar, George Fenton ***Art*** Stuart Craig

Act Ben Kingsley, Candice Bergen, Edward Fox, John Gielgud, Trevor Howard, John Mills (Columbia/IFI/Goldcrest/NFDC

The canvas upon which the turmoil of India, through its harshly won independence in 1947 from British rule, is, as depicted by Richard Attenborough, bold, sweeping, brutal; tender, loving and inspiring. He has juggled the varied emotional thrusts with generally expert balance.

Attenborough and scenarist John Briley agreed to attempt to capture the "spirit" of the man and his times, and in this they succeed admirably. Ben Kingsley, the British (half-Indian) actor, who portrays the Mahatma from young manhood as a lawyer in South Africa, is a physically striking Gandhi and has captured nuances in speech and movement which make it seem as though he has stepped through black and white newsreels into the present Technicolor reincarnation.

From the time he first experiences apartheid in being unceremoniously booted off a train in South Africa after obtaining his law degree in London, Mohandas Karamchand Gandhi becomes a man with a mission—a peaceful mission to obtain dignity for every man, no matter his color, creed, nationality.

While the focus of the drama is naturally on the person of Kingsley who gives a masterfully balanced and magnetic portrayal of Gandhi, the unusually large cast, some with only walk-through roles, responds nobly. Calling for individual mention are Edward Fox as General Dyer; Candice Bergen as Margaret Bourke-White; Geraldine James as devoted disciple Mirabehn; John Gielgud as Lord Irwin; Trevor Howard as Judge Broomfield; John Mills as The Viceroy; Rohini Hattangady as Mrs. Gandhi; Roshan Seth as Nehru, and Athol Fugard as General Smuts.

1982: Best Picture, Director, Actor (Ben Kingsley), Original Screenplay, Cinematography, Art Direction, Editing, Costume Design

NOMINATIONS: Best Original Score, Sound, Makeup

●

GANG'S ALL HERE, THE

1939, 75 mins, UK b/w

Dir Thornton Freeland ***Prod*** Walter C. Mycroft, Jack Buchanan ***Scr*** Ralph Spence ***Ph*** Claude Friese-Greene ***Ed*** E. B. Jarvis ***Art*** John Mead, Cedric Dawe

Act Jack Buchanan, Googie Withers, Edward Everett Horton, Otto Kruger (Associated British)

Jack Buchanan plays a private detective for a large insurance company, and never takes anything seriously, even murder. He's ably partnered with Edward Everett Horton as his brother in the farcical byplay.

The story and its method of telling have in it innumerable surefire farcical ingredients, is played by a carefully selected cast and is competently produced.

Story opens with a banquet given in honor of John Forrest (Buchanan), who's retiring from his post as chief investigator for the Stamford Assurance Co. He intends to devote himself to the writing of detective novels. When he learns that his former firm's safe has been robbed of more than $1 million in jewels belonging to a foreign prince, he returns to the scent.

●

GANG'S ALL HERE, THE

(UK: THE GIRLS HE LEFT BEHIND)

1943, 102 mins, US Ⓥ ⊙ col

Dir Busby Berkeley ***Prod*** William LeBaron ***Scr*** Walter Bullock ***Ph*** Edward Cronjager ***Ed*** Ray Curtiss ***Mus*** Alfred Newman, Charles Henderson (dir.) ***Art*** James Basevi, Joseph C. Wright

Act Alice Faye, Carmen Miranda, Charlotte Greenwood, Eugene Pallette, Edward Everett Horton, Phil Baker (20th Century-Fox)

A weak script [based on a screen story by Nancy Wintner, George Root Jr., and Tom Bridges] is somewhat relegated by the flock of tuneful musical numbers that frequently punctuate the picture. Alice Faye has never been screened more fetchingly, and she still lilts a ballad for sock results. Carmen Miranda is given her fattest screen part to date, and she's a comedienne who can handle lines as well as put over her South American rhythm tunes. Phil Baker makes the most of invariably drab comedy lines, while Benny Goodman's orch is always prominently focused.

There's a supporting cast, notably Eugene Pallette, Charlotte Greenwood and Edward Everett Horton, that generally backs up the principals niftily in this yarn of a romantic tangle involving Faye, Sheila Ryan and James Ellison. Latter plays a wealthy doughboy who makes a pitch for Faye, a nitery chorine, though engaged to wealthy Ryan.

The Leo Robin-Harry Warren tunes include several potentially exploitable ones, namely "A Journey to a Star," which Miss Faye reprises a couple of times.

Of the cast, Miranda is outstanding, and the way she kicks around the English lingo affords much of the film's comedy. Faye underplays as usual, but always clicko.

1943: NOMINATION: Best Color Art Direction

●

GANG WAR

SEE: ODD MAN OUT

●

GARBO TALKS

1984, 103 mins, US Ⓥ col

Dir Sidney Lumet ***Prod*** Burtt Harris, Elliott Kastner ***Scr*** Larry Grusin ***Ph*** Andrzej Bartkowiak ***Ed*** Andrew Mondshein ***Mus*** Cy Coleman ***Art*** Philip Rosenberg

Act Anne Bancroft, Ron Silver, Carrie Fisher, Catherine Hicks, Steven Hill, Hermione Gingold (United Artists)

Garbo Talks is a sweet and sour film clearly not for all tastes. Packed with New York in-jokes, not everyone will appreciate its aggressive charm. But beneath its cocky exterior, picture has a beat on some very human and universal truths.

Estelle Rolfe (Anne Bancroft) is a certifiable eccentric who has worshipped Garbo from afar since childhood, until the star has become woven into the fabric of her imagination. Her identification with Garbo has become a way for her to glamorize her day-to-day life.

Estelle is no ordinary housewife. Divorced from her husband (Steven Hill), she is continually arrested for defending any and all causes and fighting the everyday indignities of life in N.Y. If not for Bancroft's spirited performance, Estelle would deteriorate into a caricature.

●

GARDEN, THE

1991, 90 mins, UK Ⓥ col

Dir Derek Jarman ***Prod*** James Mackay ***Scr*** Derek Jarman ***Ph*** Christopher Hughes ***Ed*** Peter Cartwright ***Mus*** Simon Fisher Turner ***Art*** Derek Brown, Christopher Hobbs

Act Derek Jarman, Tilda Swinton, Johnny Mills, Kevin Collins, Pete Lee-Wilson, Roger Cook (Basilisk)

Derek Jarman's dense *The Garden* is a graphic look at homosexual discrimination laden with campy gestures, music and religious dream sequences. As in *Caravaggio* and *The Last of England*, Jarman forfeits the standard storyline for a panoply of images.

Michael Gough's gently resonant voiceover laments "My friends went so silently," and the legacy of AIDS is alluded to powerfully. Jarman combines camera images and backdrops to juxtapose contempo England with the Passion of Christ.

A gay male couple are arrested and persecuted, culminating in an ugly tar-and-feathering session. Mary floats in and out. The gay couple wind up on the cross. Jesus walks under power lines near a nuclear plant.

Simon Fisher Turner's score is excellent, but often out of sync with the self-conscious, symbolic action on the screen.

●

GARDEN OF ALLAH, THE

1927, 96 mins, US Ⓥ d b/w

Dir Rex Ingram ***Prod*** Rex Ingram ***Scr*** Willis Goldbeck ***Ph*** Lee Garmes, Monroe Bennett, Marcel Lucian ***Ed*** Arthur Ellis ***Art*** Henri Menessier

Act Alice Terry, Ivan Petrovich, Marcel Vibert (Ingram/ M-G-M)

The story [based on Robert Hichens's novel] has body and share of fame behind it to lift it above the usual screen tale. Religious angle is of the monk leaving the monastery to hide his identity, wed and repent, after telling his wife of his transgression so that he returns to the monastery.

Director Rex Ingram uncovered a screen bet in Ivan Petrovich, who, it is reported, was sponsored for the part by Alice Terry. His work throughout is capable. Terry does little emoting and will refresh the memories of those who have viewed her in other releases. Marcel Vibert lends outstanding support to the main pair, with other cast members contributing as expected.

What faults *The Garden of Allah* has may either be attributed to the making or the cutting. No question that in certain passages the story becomes dull as it pauses.

At odd moments, some of the photography is beautiful as regards desert scenes. Yet the sandstorm, the kick of the play, doesn't impress here as much more than a flurry.

•

GARDEN OF ALLAH

1936, 80 mins, US Ⓥ col

Dir Richard Boleslawski ***Prod*** David O. Selznick ***Scr*** W. P. Lipscomb, Lynn Riggs ***Ph*** W. Howard Greene, Hal Rosson ***Ed*** Hal C. Kern, Anson Stevenson ***Mus*** Max Steiner

Act Marlene Dietrich, Charles Boyer, Basil Rathbone, C. Aubrey Smith, Joseph Schildkraut, John Carradine (Selznick)

Garden of Allah, sumptuously and impressively mounted by David O. Selznick, impresses in color production but is a pretty dull affair. It is optically arresting and betimes emotionally gripping but, after a spell, the ecclesiastic significance of the Trappist monk whose earthly love cannot usurp his prior secular vows [from the book by Robert Hichens] peters out completely.

Marlene Dietrich and Charles Boyer are more than adequately competent in the leads, although sometimes slurring their lines. Basil Rathbone, C. Aubrey Smith, Tilly Losch (making her screen debut in a Baghdad café dancing sequence, and okay in what she does), Joseph Schildkraut (who almost steals the picture with his exaggerated oriental ingratiations) and John Carradine as the sandseer leave nothing wanting.

The color is particularly flattering to Dietrich, who has also taken off a little weight. In the flowing capes to which she is so partial, the color camera has caught her at her photographic best.

1936: Special Award (color cinematography)

NOMINATIONS: Best Score, Assistant Director (Eric G. Stacey)

•

GARDEN OF EVIL

1954, 100 mins, US ▭ col

Dir Henry Hathaway ***Prod*** Charles Brackett ***Scr*** Frank Fenton ***Ph*** Milton Krasner, Jorge Stahl, Jr. ***Ed*** James B. Clarke ***Mus*** Bernard Herrmann

Act Gary Cooper, Susan Hayward, Richard Widmark, Hugh Marlowe, Cameron Mitchell, Rita Moreno (20th Century-Fox)

Henry Hathaway's direction has a lot of mood-setting, brooding characters and attempts at profundity to contend with in the script, from a story by Fred Freiberger and William Tunberg. All of this occasionally makes it difficult to develop the kind of action an outdoor tale of violence and adventure needs. The new CinemaScope lens greatly increases the visual impact of the outdoor scenes and becomes such an important part of the storytelling it almost overpowers the plot drama at times.

The plot has Gary Cooper, Richard Widmark and Cameron Mitchell as three adventurers stranded in a small Mexican port while the ship on which they were passengers is being repaired. They are hired by Leah (Susan Hayward) to ride with her into dangerous Indian Country to free her husband (Hugh Marlowe) who is trapped in a gold mine.

With two exceptions, the technical credits are important assets to the picture. The exceptions are the process work, and the Bernard Herrmann background score. In some sequences the music becomes so busy concentration on the drama is impossible.

•

GARDEN OF THE FINZI-CONTINIS, THE

SEE: IL GIARDINO DEI FINZI-CONTINI

•

GARDEN OF THE MOON

1938, 94 mins, US b/w

Dir Busby Berkeley ***Scr*** Jerry Wald, Richard Macaulay ***Ph*** Tony Gaudio ***Ed*** George Amy ***Mus*** Leo F. Forbstein (dir.)

Act Pat O'Brien, Margaret Lindsay, John Payne, Johnnie Davis, Melville Cooper, Isabel Jeans (Warner)

Garden of the Moon is a bright musical, due principally to the sparkling Harry Warren and Al Dubin and Johnny Mercer tunes, an ebullient script and the exceptionally adept direction of Busby Berkeley.

As usual with musicals, the book [story by H. Bedford-Jones and Barton Browne] is no great shakes. It's merely the familiar yarn about the unknown band hired as a filler-in at a famous nitery and remaining to establish itself as a name outfit. Love interest is supplied by the feme press agent who falls for the bandleader and contrives a hoax publicity stunt that puts the band over.

Although not given top billing, John Payne has the leading part. As the steel-jacketed, ruthless nitery operator, Pat O'Brien gives a workmanlike performance, but there's never any subtlety to his playing. Margaret Lindsay is the not-too-demure press agent who recognizes her pash at the first glance and proceeds to build him up to her size.

•

GARDENS OF STONE

1987, 111 mins, US Ⓥ ⦿ col

Dir Francis Coppola ***Prod*** Michael I. Levy, Francis Coppola ***Scr*** Ronald Bass ***Ph*** Jordan Cronenweth ***Ed*** Barry Malkin ***Mus*** Carmine Coppola ***Art*** Dean Tavoularis

Act James Caan, Anjelica Huston, James Earl Jones, D. B. Sweeney, Dean Stockwell, Mary Stuart Masterson (Tri-Star)

Gardens of Stone, Francis Coppola's muddled meditation on the Vietnam War, seems to take its name not so much from the Arlington Memorial Cemetery, where much of the action takes place, but from the stiffness of the characters it portrays.

Structured around the small details and formal rituals of military life, pic opens and closes with a funeral and in between is supposed to be the emotional stuff that makes an audience care about the death of a soldier. But there is a hollowness at the film's core.

As a two-time combat vet biding his time training young recruits for the Old Guard, the army's ceremonial unit at Fort Myer, VA, Clell Hazard (James Caan) knows the war is wrong but cannot oppose it. Rather than protest, he feels it is his responsibility to prepare the young soldiers as best he can, especially young Private Willow (D. B. Sweeney), the son of an old Korean war buddy.

Script, from Nicholas Proffitt's novel, attempts to create sympathetic soldiers whose first loyalty is to their brothers in arms. Indeed it is a world unto itself as Caan swaps tales of horrors and heroism with his buddy "Goody" Nelson (James Earl Jones).

Most contrived of the relationships is Caan's affair with Anjelica Huston who plays a *Washington Post* reporter vehemently opposed to the war. Basically the supportive woman waiting in the wings, she also has enough stilted dialog to destroy her character.

•

GAS, FOOD LODGING

1992, 100 mins, US Ⓥ ⦿ col

Dir Allison Anders ***Prod*** Daniel Hassid, Seth Willenson, William Ewart ***Scr*** Allison Anders ***Ph*** Dean Lent ***Ed*** Tracy S. Granger ***Mus*** J. Mascis ***Art*** Jane Ann Stewart

Act Brooke Adams, Ione Skye, Fairuza Balk, James Brolin, Robert Knepper, David Landsbury (Cineville)

Gas, Food Lodging is filled with the kind of personal, small-scale rewards indie filmmakers seem best at delivering. Lensed on location in Deming, NM, on a budget of about $1.3 million, Allison Anders's fresh and unfettered pic [from Richard Peck's novel *Don't Look and It Won't Hurt*] emerges distinctively as an example of a new cinema made by women and expressive of their lives.

Focus is on teenage Shade (Fairuza Balk) and her quest to find a man for her waitress mom, Nora (Brooke Adams), while sorting out her own romantic yearnings and dealing with her loose-living, surly tempered older sister Trudi (Ione Skye).

Shade's self-conscious but eager to reach out; Trudi's sexually wounded and haunted by the specter of male abandonment; and Nora's keeping men at a distance while trying to set an example for her daughters that they're too young to appreciate. Rich, multilevel work is full of rueful humor, fresh turns and small, elegant surprises.

•

GASLIGHT

(US: ANGEL STREET)

1940, 80 mins, UK b/w

Dir Thorold Dickinson ***Prod*** John Corfield ***Scr*** A. R. Rawlinson, Bridget Boland ***Ph*** Bernard Knowles ***Ed*** Sidney Cole ***Mus*** Richard Addinsell ***Art*** Duncan Sutherland

Act Anton Walbrook, Diana Wynyard, Frank Pettingell, Cathleen Cordell, Robert Newton, Jimmy Hanley (British National)

Patrick Hamilton's stageplay *Gaslight* had considerable London success as a legit vehicle. Excellent direction by Thorold Dickinson retains all the psychological drama of the original in presenting the tale of a woman being driven steadily mad.

In transferring story to the screen, scripters have embellished the action with an explanatory opening for the motive behind the events, and stretched it with one or two incidents which neither add nor detract. Anton Walbrook's study of the half insane Paul Mallen, driven to further crime in a search of a handful of ruby stones, is an obnoxious type of characterization. He successfully avoids overplaying. Diana Wynyard brings a sympathy and understanding to her portrayal of the woman who, once married to Mallen, unwittingly stumbles on the secret of his early days, and is influenced by him that she is developing insanity.

•

GASLIGHT

(UK: THE MURDER IN THORNTON SQUARE)

1944, 114 mins, US Ⓥ ⦿ b/w

Dir George Cukor ***Prod*** Arthur Hornblow, Jr. ***Scr*** John Van Druten, Walter Reisch, John L. Balderston ***Ph*** Joseph Ruttenberg ***Ed*** Ralph E. Winters ***Mus*** Bronislau Kaper ***Art*** Cedric Gibbons, William Ferrari

Act Charles Boyer, Ingrid Bergman, Joseph Cotten, May Whitty, Angela Lansbury, Barbara Everest (M-G-M)

Patrick Hamilton's London stage melodrama is given an exciting screen treatment by Arthur Hornblow, Jr.'s excellent production starring Charles Boyer, Ingrid Bergman and Joseph Cotten.

It is a faithful adaptation, conspicuously notable for fine performances of the stars and the screenplay by John Van Druten, Walter Reisch and John L. Balderston. There are times when the screen treatment verges on a type of drama that must be linked to the period upon which the title is based, but this factor only serves to hypo the film's dramatic suspense where normally it might be construed as corny theatrics.

Gaslight is the story of a murderer who escaped detection for many years. He kills a famous opera singer for her jewels but is never able to uncover the baubles. Years later he marries the singer's niece so that he can continue his search for the gems in the late singer's home, which has been inherited by her niece and in which the newlyweds make their home.

Director George Cukor keeps the film at an even pace and is responsible for the film lacking the ten-twent-thirt element that was a factor in the stage play.

1944: Best Actress (Ingrid Bergman), B&W Art Decoration

NOMINATIONS: Best Picture, Actor (Charles Boyer), Supp. Actress (Angela Lansbury), Screenplay, B&W Cinematography

•

GAS-S-S-S

(aka: Gas! Or It Became Necessary to Destroy the World in Order to Save It)

1970, 79 mins, US Ⓥ col

Dir Roger Corman ***Prod*** Roger Corman ***Scr*** George Armitage ***Ph*** Ron Dexter ***Ed*** George Van Noy ***Mus*** Country Joe and the Fish, Barry Melton ***Art*** David Nichols

Act Robert Corff, Elaine Giftos, Bud Cort, Talia Shire, Ben Vereen, Cindy Williams (San Jacinto/American International)

Ostensibly about the actions of the under-25s of the world, as displayed by a sample group in Texas, when an experimental gas kills off all those over that age, most of the screenplay is devoted to moving a group of six young people along the highways to a New Mexican commune where they've heard "a brave new world" awaits them.

Obstacles appear in the form of automobile rustlers, headed by a character who calls himself Billy the Kid. After a night of rest, recuperation and rocking at a drive-in theatre, they encounter a gang of football players who try to force them to join the team (whose motto is loot, burn and rape), but they escape.

A brief idyll at the commune is threatened when the fascistic footballers lay siege, but they're converted just in time.

Robert Corff and Elaine Giftos, despite their top billing, devote most of their screen time smiling at and admiring each other's hair, which is almost of equal length.

•

GATHERING OF EAGLES, A

1963, 115 mins, US Ⓥ col

Dir Delbert Mann ***Prod*** Sy Bartlett ***Scr*** Robert Pirosh ***Ph*** Russell Harlan ***Ed*** Russell F. Schoengarth ***Mus*** Jerry Goldsmith ***Art*** Alexander Golitzen, Henry Bumstead

Act Rock Hudson, Rod Taylor, Mary Peach, Barry Sullivan, Kevin McCarthy, Henry Silva (Universal)

Though scenarist Robert Pirosh [working from a story by producer Sy Bartlett] and director Delbert Mann have been hemmed in by formula, within the narrow dramatic horizons of the story design they perform their tasks quite commendably. The familiar postwar air force situations are dramatized about as well as could be expected.

Eagles is a story of the men of the Strategic Air Command, more specifically that of a wing commander (Rock Hudson) whose dedication to the task of shaping up the somewhat negligent outfit to which he is newly assigned forces him, in the course of attempting to analyze and pinpoint what is ailing the unit, to make several unpleasant decisions that almost strain marital relations with his wife (Mary Peach) to the breaking point.

Hudson invests his role with the right blend of authority and warmth. Rod Taylor creates a colorful figure as the undesirably easy going vice commander who shapes up when the chips are down. Peach, a British actress, manages to be appealing. Barry Sullivan capably handles the somewhat obvious role of a veteran base commander whose alcoholic intake gets him the heave-ho from Hudson.

•

GATOR

1976, 115 mins, US Ⓥ ▭ col

Dir Burt Reynolds *Prod* Jules Levy, Arthur Gardner *Scr* William Norton *Ph* William A. Fraker *Ed* Harold F. Kress *Mus* Charles Bernstein *Art* Kirk Axtell

Act Burt Reynolds, Jack Weston, Lauren Hutton, Jerry Reed, Alice Ghostley, Dub Taylor (United Artists)

This follow-up to *White Lightning* never takes itself seriously, veering as it does through many incompatible dramatic and violent moods for nearly two hours.

William Norton's coloring-books script picks up Burt Reynolds's Gator McKlusky character, now on parole from moonshining time. State governor Mike Douglas can't realize political ambitions until a notorious back-water county, run by crime czar Jerry Reed, gets cleaned up.

Enter Jack Weston as Dept. of Justice undercover agent, who (somewhat unclearly) blackmails Reynolds into working against old pal Reed.

Reynolds clearly was shot down as a director by the story structure which also works to defeat much of the time even his screen charisma and credibility.

•

GATTACA

1997, 112 mins, US Ⓥ ⊙ ▭ col

Dir Andrew Niccol *Prod* Danny DeVito, Michael Shamberg *Scr* Andrew Niccol *Ph* Slawomir Idziak *Ed* Lisa Zeno Churgin *Mus* Michael Nyman *Art* Jan Roelfs

Act Ethan Hawke, Uma Thurman, Jude Law, Gore Vidal, Alan Arkin, Loren Dean (Jersey/Columbia)

One of the first major Hollywood movies to deal with the effects of genetic engineering on human civilization, *Gattaca*, New Zealand helmer Andrew Niccol's impressive feature debut, is an intelligent and timely sci-fi thriller.

Tale is set in the not-too-distant future, in a tyrannical, impersonal world in which "designer people," forged in lab tubes, strive for perfection. Conceived by love, Vincent Freeman (Ethan Hawke) is an anomaly, labeled an In-Valid, and prevented from fulfilling his lifelong dream, to become a space navigator at Gattaca Corp.

Vincent enlists the assistance of German (Tony Shalhoub), a DNA broker who sells false identities to the genetically inferior. German sets a bizarre partnership with Jerome Morrow (Jude Law), a superior specimen who, paralyzed in an accident, is willing to sell his genetic materials for cash.

Niccol frames the plot as a suspenseful murder mystery: a week before Vincent's flying mission, the director of the space agency is killed and every member of the program becomes suspect. Not neglecting the romantic angle, pic introduces a beautiful woman, Irene (Uma Thurman), a Valid citizen accepted into the program but who suffers from a heart defect.

Film is superlatively produced, designed and edited.

1997: NOMINATION: Best Art Direction

•

GATTOPARDO, IL
(THE LEOPARD)

1963, 205 mins, Italy/France Ⓥ ▭ col

Dir Luchino Visconti *Prod* Goffredo Lombardo *Scr* Suso Cecchi D'Amico, Pasquale Festa Campanile, Massimo Franciosa, Enrico Medioli, Luchino Visconti *Ph* Giuseppe Rotunno *Ed* Mario Serandrei *Mus* Nino Rota *Art* Mario Garbuglia

Act Burt Lancaster, Alain Delon, Claudia Cardinale, Paolo Stoppa, Rina Morelli, Serge Reggiani (Titanus/SNPC/SGC)

Italy's top bestseller of recent literary history, Giuseppe Tomasi Di Lampedusa's *The Leopard* comes to the screen in a magnificent film, munificently outfitted and splendidly acted by a large cast dominated by Burt Lancaster's standout stint in the title role. It must also be added that, at nearly 3 1/2 hours, the film is way overlong. Several sequences fail to trenchantly move forward the story.

Director Luchino Visconti has faithfully followed the book's main outlines, from Prince Salina's city palazzo to the country estate, the Garibaldi interludes, and Tancredi's gradual involvement with Angelica, the pawn in her father's social ascent, symbolizing the changing times, society structure and manners which form the core of Lampedusa's theme. The film story, however, ends before the Prince's death, culminating instead with the lavish Grand Ball sequence as a symbol of an era coming to its end.

Lancaster's Salina is an outstanding achievement, one which almost alone brings together the film's various threads, giving it body and provoking thought. Claudia Cardinale and Alain Delon appear ideally cast as Angelica and Tancredi. Both make the most of their roles despite a certain lack of warmth. Cardinale also makes a brief (veiled) appearance as her own mother.

Paolo Stoppa is excellent as Don Calogero, another tailor-made part, while Rina Morelli has some fine moments as Maria Stella, the princess, as does Romolo Valli, as Father Pirrone. One role stands out among the many colorful supporting performances: that of Leslie French as Chevally, the north Italian emissary who discusses the country's future with Prince Salina.

Production-wise, *The Leopard* has been spared no expense. Its authentic Sicilian settings show, almost to a fault, plenty of spending. The several intimate passages vital to the story are nearly lost in the shuffle.

[Version reviewed was Italian-language one, in which most actors were dubbed. An English-language version, released by 20th Century-Fox, ran 165 mins.]

•

GAUCHO, THE

1927, 102 mins, US ⊗ col

Dir F. Richard Jones *Prod* Douglas Fairbanks *Scr* Lotta Woods, Elton Thomas [= Douglas Fairbanks] *Ph* Tony Gaudio *Ed* William Nolan *Art* Carl Oscar Borg

Act Douglas Fairbanks, Lupe Velez, Gustav von Seyffertitz, Michael Vavitch, Nigel de Brulier, Mary Pickford (Elton/United Artists)

Doug Fairbanks is at it again. The story of *The Gaucho* is credited on the screen to Elton Thomas, but that person is none other than Doug. In doing so, however, he does not hog the picture, but permits a little Mexican girl, new to films, in on the racket.

This youngster, who got her first shot at screen work on the Roach lot, is Lupe Velez, and is not more than 16 or 17.

Though the first 30 minutes or so seem a little slow, the picture then settles down. Looks as though better than $500,000 has been expended, and the picture shows it.

To please the little mountain girl, the Gaucho has a house moved from its base by 100 horses to the town he has come to take because there is an abundance of gold there. The big punch is a stampede of cattle to save the day for the Gaucho. A tremendous herd sweeps the town, driving everything and everybody before it, with the Gaucho and his mob coming in and taking possession on the dust. A pip of a scene.

•

GAUNTLET, THE

1977, 108 mins, US Ⓥ ⊙ ▭ col

Dir Clint Eastwood *Prod* Robert Daley *Scr* Michael Butler, Dennis Shryack *Ph* Rexford Metz *Ed* Ferris Webster, Joel Cox *Mus* Jerry Fielding *Art* Allen E. Smith

Act Clint Eastwood, Sondra Locke, Pat Hingle, William Prince, Bill McKinney, Michael Cavanaugh (Warner/Malpaso)

In a major role reversal, Clint Eastwood stars in *The Gauntlet* as a person who might be on the receiving end of the violence epitomized in his famed Dirty Harry film series.

Eastwood, a flop cop sent to extradite hooker Sondra Locke, finds they are the targets of both the underworld and law enforcement elements tied to the mob.

William Prince is very good as a police commissioner with mob ties who selects Eastwood to bring Locke from Las Vegas as a key witness in a trial which could embarrass a lot of highly-placed people.

Plot provides a series of narrow escapes in van rides, motorcycle rides, train rides, car rides and climactic bus ride. Chuck Gaspar's special effects crew destroys a house, a helicopter and a cross-country bus as the film unfolds.

•

GAY CABALLERO, THE

1940, 58 mins, US b/w

Dir Otto Brower *Prod* Walter Morosco, Ralph Dietrich *Scr* Albert Duffy, John Larkin, Walter Bullock *Ph* Edward Cronjager *Ed* Harry Reynolds *Mus* Emil Newman *Art* Richard Day, Chester Cord

Act Cesar Romero, Sheila Ryan, Robert Sterling, Chris-Pin Martin, Janet Beecher (20th Century-Fox)

The Cisco Kid [created by William Sydney Porter (O. Henry)] continues his Robin Hoodian adventures along the southwest border in a story that grooves along familiar lines of the series.

As usual, Cisco rides into the district with sidekick Chris-Pin Martin to find a grave marked with his name. Deciding to stick around and find out what's going on, he discovers enough plot to step in to protect a pretty girl and her father from nefarious deeds.

Cesar Romero is in the familiar role of Cisco, never losing his composure in the darkest situations. Chris-Pin Martin continues as his Mexican stooge, while Sheila Ryan is the girl in this instance. Edmund MacDonald is the familiar moustached villain, aided by conniving skullduggery by Janet Beecher.

•

GAY DECEPTION, THE

1935, 75 mins, US b/w

Dir William Wyler *Prod* Jesse L. Lasky *Scr* Stephen Avery, Don Hartman, Arthur Richman *Ph* Joseph Valentine *Ed* Robert L. Simpson *Mus* Louis DeFrancesco (dir.) *Art* Max Parker

Act Francis Lederer, Frances Dee, Benita Hume, Alan Mowbray, Lennox Pawle, Akim Tamiroff (Fox)

Smartness of direction, plus a few comedy situations, turn an ordinary Cinderella theme into pleasing light film diversion. *The Gay Deception* is so named because a prince masquerades as a hotel bellboy and makes Cindy's triumph possible.

If nothing else, *Gay Deception* fits Francis Lederer better than anything he's done. Here he's both a bellboy and a prince. One scene provides him with white tie for contrast. While the story is totally fanciful, and to some extent a travesty, it has a way of going along as a little romantic opera bouffe.

William Wyler directed and is a happy selection for this type of story and cast. Casting has been done with a keen sense of appreciation for humor. Frances Dee is excellent as Mirabel, the small-town girl who cashes $5,000 on a sweepstake ticket and goes to New York to live like a queen. As Sandro, Lederer is afforded every liberty as a light comedian by the story and the direction. Lennox Pawle, as a fawning consul-general, is an unusual type.

Locale of most of the action is clearly meant to be the Waldorf-Astoria, for which the film is something of a plug in spite of its gentle ribbing about service and the like. Film labels the hostelry the Waldorf-Plaza.

•

GAY DESPERADO, THE

1936, 90 mins, US b/w

Dir Rouben Mamoulian *Prod* Mary Pickford, Jesse L. Lasky *Scr* Wallace Smith *Ph* Lucien Andriot *Ed* Margaret Clancey *Mus* Alfred Newman (dir.) *Art* Richard Day

Act Nino Martini, Ida Lupino, Leo Carrillo, Harold Huber, James Blakeley, Stanley Fields (Pickford-Lasky)

This Nino Martini mesquiter is a fairly diverting Mexican western. Leo Birinski's original story is one of those things. Wallace Smith's screen treatment, fortified by Rouben Mamoulian's direction, has achieved a certain tempo of insouciance which does much to offset the plot structure.

Leo Carrillo is the bad Mexican hombre who's been influenced by U.S. gangster pix. But he's a pushover for a top tenor apparently and, despite his bloodthirsty celluloid education, this small time Villa seems to take plenty from the singer (Martini).

Plot is complicated by a snatch—another educational throwback at the door of the Hollywood influence on the mesa mayhemmers—and an attempt by a U.S. hoodlum to hijack a snatch. In this consequence there are exaggerated burlesques of the Edward G. Robinson, Cagney and Raft type of sinisterness, cast as henchman to the head hoodlum.

In between all this, Martini tenors in his topnotch Met-opera style, featuring "The World Is Mine" (a corking thematic ballad by Holt Marvell and George Posford, English songsmiths) and an original Mexican serenade, "Adios Mi Tierra" (by Miguel Sandoval). There are also snatches of the aria from *Aida*, "Cielito Lindo."

Carrillo and Harold Huber, his aide-de-banditry, almost take the picture away from Martini, although his light-mannered, comedy style of trouping, coupled with the telling tenoring, make him highly acceptable. Ida Lupino is the ingenue—just an ingenue.

Photography by Lucien Andriot is eye-arresting in spots, particularly the against-the-sky shots, getting some extraordinary camera portraiture into the action.

This is a better entry for the briefly careered Mary Pickford-Jesse Lasky combo than was its first, *One Rainy Afternoon*. *Desperado* is the second and swan song, so the company exits from the production scene as a unit in high gear.

•

GAY DIVORCE, THE

SEE: THE GAY DIVORCÉE

•

GAY DIVORCÉE, THE

(UK: THE GAY DIVORCE)

1934, 107 mins, US Ⓥ ⦿ b/w

Dir Mark Sandrich ***Prod*** Pandro S. Berman ***Scr*** George Marion Jr., Dorothy Yost, Edward Kaufman ***Ph*** David Abel ***Ed*** William Hamilton ***Mus*** Max Steiner (dir.) ***Art*** Van Nest Polglase, Carroll Clark

Act Fred Astaire, Ginger Rogers, Alice Brady, Edward Everett Horton, Erik Rhodes, Eric Blore (RKO)

All through the picture there's charm, romance, gaiety and éclat. There's a dash of Continental spice in the situation of the professional male corespondent who is to expedite Ginger Rogers's divorce. The manner in which Fred Astaire taps himself into an individual click with "Looking for a Needle in Haystack," a hoofing soliloquy in his London flat, while his man hands him his cravat, boutonniere and walking stick, is something which he alone elevates and socks over on individual artistry.

"The Continental," is the smash song and dance hit. Cole Porter's "Night and Day," from the original [1932] show [*Gay Divorce*, book by Dwight Taylor], is alone retained and worthily so, especially as Astaire interprets it. After having done it for months on New York and London stages it's natural that his celluloid translation must be enhanced by much personable business and lyric mannerisms.

Rogers is also excellent, but the performances don't end there. Alice Brady and Edward Everett Horton, as the subteam, are more than just good foils. Erik Rhodes and Eric Blore, both from legit, also impress in no small manner.

Mark Sandrich rates all sorts of bends on the direction. He's colored the story values with a flock of nifty business. His terp stager, Dave Gould, displays considerable imagination with the dance staging.

1934: Best Song ("Continental")

NOMINATIONS: Best Picture, Art Direction, Score, Sound

•

GAY MRS. TREXEL, THE

SEE: SUSAN AND GOD

•

GAZEBO, THE

1959, 102 mins, US Ⓥ ▭ b/w

Dir George Marshall ***Prod*** Lawrence Weingarten ***Scr*** George Wells ***Ph*** Paul C. Vogel ***Ed*** Adrienne Fazan ***Mus*** Jeff Alexander ***Art*** George W. Davis, Paul Groesse

Act Glenn Ford, Debbie Reynolds, Carl Reiner, John McGiver, Mabel Albertson, Doro Merande (Avon/M-G-M)

Gazebo is based on the Alec Coppel play which starred Walter Slezak and Jayne Meadows on Broadway and Tom Ewell and Jan Sterling on the road. In its transfer to the screen, scripter George Wells has spiced the often far-fetched devices of the play with a number of his own delicacies, including a gregarious pigeon named Herman. Director George Marshall, achieving a frisky blend of suspense and tomfoolery, puts it all together with a bright, well-timed hand.

Glenn Ford plays a television writer who is married to a Broadway star (Debbie Reynolds). Several years earlier, Reynolds posed without proper attire, and now the possessor of said photographs is blackmailing Ford. Murder is his only out, Ford reasons, and he invites the blackmailer to his home and shoots him. He hides the body on the spot where a gazebo (summer house) is about to be positioned the following day.

The film is nearly all Ford, and he's up to every scene, earning both sympathy and laughs as he muddles through his farcical "crime," Reynolds is excellent, but her talents are beyond what her limited role requires. The part on Broadway was very minor and has not changed much. Carl Reiner, as the couple's district attorney friend, is good but also beyond the part.

1959: NOMINATION: B&W Costume Design

•

GEISHA BOY, THE

1958, 95 mins, US Ⓥ col

Dir Frank Tashlin ***Prod*** Jerry Lewis ***Scr*** Frank Tashlin ***Ph*** Haskell Boggs ***Ed*** Alma Macrorie ***Mus*** Walter Scharf ***Art*** Hal Pereira, Tambi Larsen

Act Jerry Lewis, Marie McDonald, Sessue Hayakawa, Barton MacLane, Suzanne Pleshette, Nobu McCarthy (Paramount)

The Geisha Boy is a good Jerry Lewis comedy, one that rips along with never a backward glance at shattered remnants of plot behind it. Frank Tashlin, who wrote and directed, loads in wild sight and sound gags, parodies and takeoffs that relieve Lewis of some comic burden and show him in his best light.

Tashlin's screenplay, from a story by Rudy Makoul, has Lewis as a very low man on the show business totem pole. He is a magician who "can't even get a job on daytime television." He and his rabbit, Harry, join a USO tour of the Orient, because they couldn't get a job anywhere else. Lewis first tangles with the troupe's headliner (Marie McDonald) who serves the picture as a kind of young Margaret Dumont; then with the army brass, represented by Barton MacLane, and finally with the Japanese themselves. There is a romance between Lewis and a Japanese widow (Nobu McCarthy) whose young son (Robert Hirano) "adopts" Lewis as his father.

Lewis is at his best when he eschews some of the stock physical mannerisms that were originally his trademarks. He is more appealing and much funnier when he is playing more or less straight, using his timing and more restrained reactions for fine comedy effect. He is also effective in the few serious moments.

•

GENERAL, THE

1927, 77 mins, US Ⓥ ⦿ ⊗ b/w

Dir Buster Keaton, Clyde Bruckman ***Prod*** Joseph M. Schenck ***Scr*** Buster Keaton, Clyde Bruckman, Al Boasberg, Charles Smith ***Ph*** J. Devereaux Jennings, Bert Haines ***Ed*** Sherman Kell ***Art*** Fred Gabourie

Act Buster Keaton, Marien Mack, Glen Cavender, Jim Farley, Frederick Vroom, Charles Smith (Keaton/United Artists)

The General is far from fussy. Its principal comedy scene is built on that elementary bit, the chase, and you can't continue a fight for almost an hour and expect results. Especially is this so when the action is placed entirely in the hands of the star. It was his story, he directed, and he acted. The result is a flop.

The story is a burlesque of a Civil War meller. Buster Keaton has the role of a youthful engineer on the Watern and Atlantic RR, running through Georgia, when war is declared. He tries to enlist, but is turned down, as it is figured that he would be of greater value to the cause as an engineer. His girl, however, won't believe this, and tells him not to see her again until he is in a uniform.

The girl is on a visit to her dad when 10 Union daredevils steal the train in the middle of Confederate territory and start off with it, intending to burn all bridges behind them, so that the line of communication and supplies for the enemy shall be cut. The girl is on the train, and Keaton, sore because his beloved engine has been stolen, gives chase in another locomotive.

There are some corking gags in the picture, but as they are all a part of the chase they are overshadowed.

•

GENERAL, THE

1998, 123 mins, Ireland Ⓥ ⦿ ▭ b/w

Dir John Boorman ***Prod*** John Boorman ***Scr*** John Boorman ***Ph*** Seamus Deasy ***Ed*** Ron Davis ***Mus*** Richie Buckley ***Art*** Derek Wallace

Act Brendan Gleeson, Adrian Dunbar, Sean McGinley, Maria Doyle Kennedy, Angeline Ball, Jon Voight (Merlin)

Rarely has a veteran filmmaker rejuvenated his career to such startling effect as John Boorman with *The General*, a fresh-off-the-slab biopic maverick Irish crime lord Martin Cahill that both challenges and entertains the audience at a variety of levels, as well as reviving the vitality of the helmer's earliest, mid-'60s pics.

With his first feature in three years, the 65-year-old Boorman has poured all his love of his adopted homeland, Ireland, into a movie that says more about the rebellious Irish psyche than a heap of overtly political pictures.

Boorman's choice of the retro format of b&w and widescreen gives the film a certain distance and stylization. But in its vigor and use of music and songs, *The General* at times reaches back to his first feature, *Catch Us If You Can* (1965), and—in its harder, more violent moments—to his classic, California-set gangster movie, *Point Blank* (1967).

Opening in an upscale Dublin suburb on Aug. 18, 1994, pic establishes a tone of almost dreamlike unreality as Cahill (Brendan Gleeson) is gunned down outside his house. The rest of the movie is a long flashback leading up to his death.

Sans date titles, the film moves easily across the years, sketching his gradual rise from petty villain to local mobster, but still portraying Cahill as a likable rogue, effortlessly making dummies of the local cops. Pic assumes a more serious tone when Cahill plans to rob a jeweler that even the IRA reckons is impregnable.

Part childlike joker, part ruthless gang leader, Gleeson's Cahill is one of the screen's most memorable psychopaths, leavened by the Irish thesp's confident juggling of contrary moods. Script's only major fault is not developing the symbiotic relationship between Cahill and cop Ned Kenny: the latter, relaxedly played by Jon Voight with a passable Irish accent, largely disappears in the middle going, making a later heart-to-heart about each taking on aspects of the other's personality less meaningful than it should have been.

•

GENERAL DIED AT DAWN, THE

1936, 98 mins, US Ⓥ b/w

Dir Lewis Milestone ***Prod*** William LeBaron ***Scr*** Clifford Odets ***Ph*** Victor Milner ***Mus*** Werner Janssen ***Art*** Hans Dreier, Ernest Fegte

Act Gary Cooper, Madeleine Carroll, Akim Tamiroff, Dudley Digges, Porter Hall, William Frawley (Paramount)

In Clifford Odets's first film attempt his hand is distinctly visible throughout. But without Gary Cooper and Madeleine Carroll to top an A-1 cast, all the splendid trouping, all the splendid imagery of direction, photography, music and general production might well have jelled into an artistic flop.

Story supplied by Charles G. Booth's novel is an old-fashioned piece of claptrap. It has to do with intrigue in the Far East, gunrunners, smugglers and spies. Odets has left all that alone but has underlined Gary Cooper as the agent for the ammunition runners by making him engaged in the dangerous work not because of the adventure or money, but because he's trying to help the downtrodden Chinese rid themselves of a money-grubbing, rapacious Chinese war lord, General Yang (Akim Tamiroff).

Cooper, as the daredevil American, is at top form throughout; Madeleine Carroll as his vis-a-vis in a very difficult assignment, impresses. Two comparatively unknowns, Tamiroff and Porter Hall, turn in exceptionally strong performances. Hall, as a sniveling, broken-down villain, handles an unusual job beautifully; John O'Hara, the novelist, does a bit as a newspaperman, looking the part. Allegedly Odets, director Milestone and Sidney Skolsky, Hollywood columnist, are also in for a shot or two, but if so it's their secret which scene it is.

1936: NOMINATIONS: Best Supp. Actor (Akim Tamiroff), Cinematography, Score

•

GENERAL'S DAUGHTER, THE

1999, 116 mins, US Ⓥ ⦿ ▭ col

Dir Simon West ***Prod*** Mace Neufeld ***Scr*** Christopher Bertolini, William Goldman ***Ph*** Peter Menzies, Jr. ***Ed*** Glen Scantlebury ***Mus*** Carter Burwell ***Art*** Dennis Washington

Act John Travolta, Madeleine Stowe, James Cromwell, Timothy Hutton, Leslie Stefanson, James Woods (Paramount)

The General's Daughter is the cinematic equivalent of a disposable airplane read, a hokey, kinky, military thriller [from Nelson DeMille's 1992 novel] that's twisty and compelling enough to hook viewers in the mood for a trashy good time.

Second feature from *Con Air* helmer Simon West carries with it some telltale traces of the [action producer Jerry] Bruckheimer stable—sweaty bods, military posturing—but it also reveals a real bent for tasty confrontations between powerful characters, an enthusiasm for colorful actors and an ability to milk the most out of scenes.

John Travolta's U.S. Army criminal investigator Paul Brenner is enlisted to solve the murder at Fort McCallum of Capt. Elisabeth Campbell (Leslie Stefanson), beautiful daughter of retiring Gen. Campbell (James Cromwell), now being paged into politics. He's teamed by chance with fellow Criminal Investigation Division vet Sarah Sunhill (Madeleine Stowe), with whom, it is soon revealed, Paul long ago had an affair.

Paul is told he's got 36 hours to nail the killer before the FBI moves in and the scandal goes embarrassingly public. His first order of business is to question (in a superbly written and acted scene of delicious one-upmanship), then arrest Elisabeth's commanding officer, the disarmingly insightful and manipulative Col. Moore (James Woods). By this time, Paul and Sarah have discovered some decidedly freaky facts about Elisabeth.

Travolta delivers another strong performance that effectively carries the picture. Struggling to hold her own with such a dynamic partner, Stowe gamely gets off a few shots. Production values are excellent.

•

GENERATION, A
SEE: POKOLENIE

•

GENEVIEVE
1953, 86 mins, UK Ⓥ col
Dir Henry Cornelius ***Prod*** Henry Cornelius ***Scr*** William Rose ***Ph*** Christopher Challis ***Ed*** Clive Donner ***Mus*** Larry Adler ***Art*** Michael Stringer
Act John Gregson, Dinah Sheridan, Kenneth More, Kay Kendall, Geoffrey Keen, Joyce Grenfell (Sirius)

The "Genevieve" of the title is a vintage 1904 car which has been entered for the annual London-to-Brighton rally by its enthusiastic owner (John Gregson). His wife (Dinah Sheridan) hardly shares his enthusiasm but joins him on the run and there is constant good-natured bickering between them and their friendly rival (Kenneth More) and his girlfriend (Kay Kendall). But the rivalry becomes intense on the return journey, ending up with a wager as to which car will be first over Westminster Bridge.

First-rate direction by Henry Cornelius keeps the camera focused almost entirely on the four principals, and rarely has a starring foursome been so consistently good. Sheridan's sophisticated performance is a good contrast to Gregson's more sullen interpretation. More's exuberance is well-matched by Kendall's effervescent portrayal.

1953: NOMINATIONS: Best Story & Screenplay, Scoring of a Dramatic Picture

•

GENGHIS KHAN
1965, 124 mins, US ▭ col
Dir Henry Levin ***Prod*** Irving Allen ***Scr*** Clarke Reynolds, Beverley Cross ***Ph*** Geoffrey Unsworth ***Ed*** Geoffrey Foot ***Mus*** Dusan Radic ***Art*** Maurice Carter
Act Stephen Boyd, Omar Sharif, James Mason, Eli Wallach, Francoise Dorleac, Telly Savalas (Allen/CCC/Avala)

Genghis Khan is an introspective biopic about the Mongol chief Temujin who unified Asia's warring tribes in the Dark Ages. An international cast delivers okay performances in occasionally trite script which emphasizes personal motivation rather than sweeping pageantry.

The screenplay, from story by Berkely Mather, hinges on continuing vendetta between tribal chieftain Stephen Boyd and Omar Sharif, once enslaved by Boyd but escaping to forge an empire that threatened western and eastern civilization some eight centuries back.

Sharif does a near-excellent job in projecting with ease the zeal which propelled Temujin from bondage to a political education in China, and finally to realizing at death his dream of Mongol unity. Boyd is less successful as the brutish thorn in Sharif's side, being overall too restrained for sustained characterization despite flashes of earthiness. Most unusual characterization is essayed by James Mason, playing the neatly contrasting urbane imperial counsellor who mentors political savvy.

•

GENOU DE CLAIRE, LE
(CLAIRE'S KNEE)
1970, 107 mins, France Ⓥ ⊙ col
Dir Eric Rohmer ***Prod*** Pierre Cottrell ***Scr*** Eric Rohmer ***Ph*** Nestor Almendros ***Ed*** Cecile Decugis
Act Jean-Claude Brialy, Aurora Cornu, Beatrice Romand, Laurence de Monaghan, Fabrice Luchini, Gerard Falconetti (Films du Losange)

With his fifth so-called "moral tale," Eric Rohmer again deals in people who discuss, analyze, dissect and worry their actions (in this case around friendship, love and desire), but rarely indulge. And if they do, it is talked about rather than seen.

Jean-Claude Brialy is a rather self-dramatizing, thirtyish young man on the eve of marrying a Swedish girl. In France on a holiday, he meets an old friend, a Rumanian woman (Aurora Cornu), who is a novelist and staying with a divorced woman and her teenage daughter, Laura (Beatrice Romand). The latter gets a crush on the visitor, which is the main hinge of the tale. There is a brief flirtation with the determined, headstrong girl and then into it comes her half-sister, Claire (Laurence de Monaghan), who troubles Brialy with her tawny, youthful sensuality.

It is a personal, private film but yet has the wit, sprightly aphorisms, that are right and never trite. This is a worthy followup to Rohmer's *My Night at Maud's.*

•

GENTLEMAN JIM
1942, 104 mins, US Ⓥ ⊙ b/w
Dir Raoul Walsh ***Prod*** Robert Buckner ***Scr*** Vincent Lawrence, Horace McCoy ***Ph*** Sid Hickox ***Ed*** Jack Killifer ***Mus*** Heinz Roemheld ***Art*** Ted Smith
Act Errol Flynn, Alexis Smith, Jack Carson, Alan Hale, John Loder, Ward Bond (Warner)

Warner Bros. has managed to turn out a good film based on the life of James J. Corbett. In doing so, however, the scenarists have sacrificed a good deal of one of the best reputations the boxing game has ever known.

On celluloid, Corbett is a "wise-guy," brash character oozing with braggadocio. In real life the heavyweight champ was a self-effacing, quiet personality so distinctly apart from the general run of mug fighters of that day that the "gentleman" tag was a natural.

Errol Flynn is the screen Corbett and is a real-life prototype only in the fact that Corbett was a bank clerk in Frisco and that his father was a bluff Irishman who operated a livery stable.

From there on, with the exception of some of Corbett's fights, the film is pure fiction. Corbett is shown as a young bachelor, who, because he got a prominent judge out of an embarrassing jam at an illegal bareknuckle fight, gets favored treatment at the bank where he's employed; meets the beauteous daughter of a millionaire miner and thus gains entrance to Frisco's famed Olympic club. At a party, according to the film, Corbett and his friend, Jack Carson, are tossed out of the Olympic when liquor makes Carson's mouth and feet misbehave.

This is so far removed from fact that it's ludicrous. Corbett was a revered member of the Olympic club to the very end.

All this fiction, plus the scenarists' depiction of Sullivan, after being kayoed by Corbett, calling on the latter to wish him well and present him with his championship belt, take this picture out of the biographical class and into fantasy.

•

GENTLEMAN'S AGREEMENT
1947, 118 mins, US Ⓥ ⊙ b/w
Dir Elia Kazan ***Prod*** Darryl F. Zanuck ***Scr*** Moss Hart ***Ph*** Arthur Miller ***Ed*** Harmon Jones ***Mus*** Alfred Newman ***Art*** Lyle R. Wheeler, Mark-Lee Kirk
Act Gregory Peck, Dorothy McGuire, John Garfield, Celeste Holm, Anne Revere, Dean Stockwell (20th Century-Fox)

Just as Laura Z. Hobson's original novel of the writer (character), who poses as a Jew to write a magazine series on anti-Semitism was a milestone in modern fiction, the picture is vital and stirring.

The basic elements of the Hobson work are not only retained, but in some cases given greater dimension and plausibility. The picture is memorable for numerous vivid, impelling passages. For instance the breakfast scene, when Green tries to explain anti-Semitism to his innocent little son, stamps the picture's urgent theme on the spectator's mind virtually at once.

There are also disappointing or confusing scenes. One is the party given by Kathy's sister which remains as unresolved on the screen as in the book and as lacking in realistic atmosphere. In the same scene, the stupid Connecticut dowagers seem exaggerated. Celeste Holm, with some of the film's most pungent lines, frequently reads them too fast for intelligibility.

As Phil Green, the magazine writer, Gregory Peck gives a fine performance. He is quiet, almost gentle, progressively intense and resolute, with just the right suggestion of inner vitality and turbulence. Dorothy McGuire too, is dramatically and emotionally compelling as Kathy. The range from her somewhat flippant opening scene to the searing final one with John Garfield is impressive. Garfield is a natural in the part of Dave, giving it admirable strength and understated eloquence.

1947: Best Picture, Director, Supp. Actress (Celeste Holm)

NOMINATIONS: Best Actor (Gregory Peck), Actress (Dorothy McGuire), Supp. Actress (Anne Revere), Screenplay, Editing

•

GENTLEMEN PREFER BLONDES
1953, 91 mins, US Ⓥ ⊙ col
Dir Howard Hawks ***Prod*** Sol C. Siegel ***Scr*** Charles Lederer ***Ph*** Harry J. Wild ***Ed*** Hugh S. Fowler ***Mus*** Lionel Newman (dir.) ***Art*** Lyle R. Wheeler, Joseph C. Wright
Act Jane Russell, Marilyn Monroe, Charles Coburn, Elliott Reid, Tommy Noonan, George Winslow (20th Century Fox)

An attractive screen tintuner has been fashioned from the musical stage hit *Gentlemen Prefer Blondes.* The Joseph Fields-Anita Loos [1949] stage original has been modernized but the general theme and principal characters are intact. Only three of the stage tunes by Jule Styne and Leo Robin are used, but two numbers were cleffed by Hoagy Carmichael and Harold Adamson.

Together, the two femmes are the picture's outstanding assets. Jane Russell is a standout and handles the lines and songs with a comedy flair she has previously demonstrated. Marilyn Monroe matches with a newly displayed ability to sex a song as well as point up the eye values of a scene by her presence.

The big production number in the presentation is "Diamonds Are a Girl's Best Friend," flashily presented by Monroe and a male line against a vivid red backdrop.

Monroe, a blonde who likes diamonds, and Russell, a brunette who likes men, sail for Paris and fun when Tommy Noonan, the blonde's lovesick millionaire, is unable to make the trip. Noonan's pop (Taylor Holmes), who would like to bust up the son's attachment, sends Elliott Reid, a private eye, along to keep an eye on the girls.

Charles Coburn is in fine form as the diamond tycoon with an eye for dames. Reid and Noonan carry off the romantic male spots nicely. Little George Winslow's big voice in a little body provides a comedy contrast to Monroe's little girl voice in a big girl's body for his two scenes with her.

•

GENTLE SEX, THE
1943, 92 mins, UK b/w
Dir Leslie Howard ***Prod*** Leslie Howard ***Scr*** Mole Charles ***Ph*** Cyril Knowles, Ray Sturges
Act Joan Gates, Joan Greenwood, Jean Gillie, Rosamund John, Lilli Palmer (Two Cities/Concanen)

Story concerns the personalities of seven girls, drawn from various grades of society, who join the ATS (women's army) and go through the routine of breaking in before being sent to different posts. At crucial moments the girls prove themselves as brave and heroic as the male contingent, and the film ends with a toast to "the women." This is spoken by an unprogrammed commentator. The voice is Leslie Howard's, who also directed and coproduced.

Palpably a propaganda war picture, there is plenty of comedy, which savors a little too much of crosstalk wisecracking. Direction and production are intelligent and artistic, but the basic plot is too one-keyish.

Cast, even to the smallest bit parts, deserves commendation. The two outstanding characterizations are those handled by Lilli Palmer and Rosamund John. Palmer enacts a Czech refugee whose family was manhandled by the Nazist, and John is a Scot with a delicious and easily understood dialect. But it is Palmer, in an emotional role delicately and subtly played, who has the best opportunities.

•

GEORGE WASHINGTON SLEPT HERE
1942, 93 mins, US Ⓥ ⊙ b/w
Dir William Keighley ***Prod*** Jerry Wald ***Scr*** Everett Freeman ***Ph*** Ernest Haller ***Ed*** Ralph Dawson ***Mus*** Adolph Deutsch
Act Jack Benny, Ann Sheridan, Charles Coburn, Percy Kilbride, Hattie McDaniel, Franklin Pangborn (Warner)

The Moss Hart-George S. Kaufman play, a moderate legit hit, becomes a sock comedy on the screen under astute handling and with Jack Benny in the principal laugh role.

For Benny, the part of the city fellow who unwillingly struggles through trying to make a home out of an old abandoned country house, is rich in the sort of thing he does best. With others in the picture as vital cogs, Benny is in there pitching in nearly every scene. He hardly has time to get his breath, since much of the dialog is allocated to him. When he isn't using his voice, he's falling into wells, stumbling against things, rolling downstairs or, in other ways, contributing to the fun.

A lot of the action is modified slapstick, while for relief there are many sequences of a highly amusing domestic character.

•

GEORGE WHITE'S 1935 SCANDALS
1935, 83 mins, US b/w
Dir George White ***Prod*** George White ***Scr*** Jack Yellen, Patterson McNutt ***Ph*** George Schneiderman ***Ed*** [uncredited] ***Mus*** Louis De Francesco (dir.) ***Art*** Gordon Wiles
Act George White, Alice Faye, James Dunn, Ned Sparks, Lyda Roberti, Eleanor Powell (Fox)

Once more George White presents himself in his very own conception of a film *Scandals*, the second of the series. Once more it is dull entertainment. Trouble is largely traceable directly to White.

From only one standpoint is the film worthy top-screen entertainment and that is the songs [by Jack Yellen, Cliff Friend, Joseph Meyer, additional lyrics by Herb Magidson]. There are six, two of them real outstanders from a tune standpoint, but all tops on lyrics. Even these numbers, however, are wasted because of poor staging [by White].

Cast is big and studded with featured players, many of them wasted. Most of the work is left to James Dunn and Alice Faye as the boy and girl. They're in a small town show in Georgia when White catches them. He brings 'em to New York and stars 'em immediately. Then follows the usual backstage filmusical story. Inflated egos, pouting, quarrels, the kids leave the show. Girl's aunt from down Georgia way comes to catch the show, White digs them up; they've learned their lesson; all is well.

•

GEORGE WHITE'S SCANDALS
1934, 79 mins, US b/w
Dir George White, Thornton Freeland, Harry Lachman ***Prod*** Robert Kane ***Scr*** Jack Yellen, George White ***Ph*** Lee Garmes, George Schneiderman ***Ed*** Paul Weatherwax ***Mus*** Louis De Francesco (dir.)
Act George White, Rudy Vallee, Alice Faye, Jimmy Durante, Dixie Dunbar, Adrienne Ames (Fox)

As the first musical talker turned out by an important eastern legit revue producer, this is an unintentional but flattering compliment to Hollywood's own stagers of musicals. George White contributes surprisingly little in the way of technique or ideas. *Scandals* follows the regulation Hollywood pattern. He not only borrows the backstage device, but weighs his production down with a dressing-room yarn that almost nullifies the picture's few meritorious moments.

Alice Faye is pretty much on the spot, and in an important part in her first picture. In looks and performance she is a pleasant surprise. She sings adequately, for that's her business. Rudy Vallee, a decidedly more versatile performer than the Vallee of a couple of years earlier, also enjoys more complimentary photography. The two make a pleasant team of singing leads.

Jimmy Durante, carrying the secondary love match with Dixie Dunbar, suffers from bad material most of the time. When he has something to work with, such as in his blackface number, he shines.

•

GEORGE WHITE'S SCANDALS
1945, 95 mins, US Ⓥ b/w
Dir Felix Feist ***Prod*** George White ***Scr*** Hugh Wedlock, Howard Snyder, Parke Levy, Howard J. Green ***Ph*** Robert de Grasse ***Ed*** Joseph Noriega ***Mus*** Leigh Harline (ballet) ***Art*** Albert S. D'Agostino, Ralph Berges
Act Joan Davis, Jack Haley, Martha Holliday, Philip Terry, Jane Greer (RKO)

The George White "Scandals" legit musicals, Ziegfeld's "Follies" and Earl Carroll's "Vanities" date back to the Prohibition era and the current picture, produced by George White, also dates back in that it is reminiscent of the backstage musicals of the early talker days. Though there are a few moments that hit home, on the whole the picture is a drawn-out affair.

Joan Davis and Jack Haley, starred, yeomanly try to overcome the assignments handed them, as do others, but the net result is still very negative. One of the drawbacks is the padding to 95 minutes and the dreary routine concerned with planning a George White's "Scandals" show, the auditioning, the picking of chorines, costuming, etc.

Story, a weak one, concerns two romances in connection with the staging of "Scandals," Davis and Haley being paired on the one side and specialty dancer Martha Holliday and Philip Terry on the other.

•

GEORGIA
1995, 117 mins, France/US Ⓥ col
Dir Ulu Grosbard ***Prod*** Ulu Grosbard, Barbara Turner, Jennifer Jason Leigh ***Scr*** Barbara Turner ***Ph*** Jan Kiesser ***Ed*** Elizabeth Kling ***Mus*** Steven Soles (prod.) ***Art*** Lester Cohen
Act Jennifer Jason Leigh, Mare Winningham, Ted Levine, Max Perlich, John Doe, John C. Reilly (CiBy 2000)

An intense study of sibling rivalry set in the Seattle music world, *Georgia* excels at the expression of painfully unresolvable family conflicts. Performed to maximum effect by a host of top-flight actors, Ulu Grosbard's strong character study is knit together by a tense subtext that underlies even the calmest moments.

Coproduced by star Jennifer Jason Leigh and her mother, Barbara Turner (who wrote the script for her daughter), and originally developed with Robert Altman as director, drama takes a pointed look at the inevitable strains in the relationship between sisters when one is a very together, happy and successful singer and the younger one is far less talented, emotionally immature and dependent on drugs and booze.

Leigh plays a rock 'n' roll urchin named Sadie, a punkette who returns home to Seattle after a stint with a blues singer (Jimmy Witherspoon). Sadie camps out briefly at the idyllic country farmhouse of her sister, Georgia (Mare Winningmam), a beloved folk-rock icon for whom popular acclaim is secondary to her husband (Ted Levine) and her kids.

Always a disruptive presence at her sister's home, Sadie is somewhat reluctantly taken on as a singer in the working band of ex-b.f. Bobby (John Doe) and shortly has the good fortune to meet an unconditionally adoring fan, delivery boy Axel (Max Perlich), who installs himself as Sadie's valet, maid, lover and one-man support team.

The film undisputably belongs to Leigh and Winningham. Leigh's emotional investment in Sadie obviously is considerable, but she also spares her nothing, laying bare a lost soul. On the surface, Winningham has less to do histrionically, but her characterization emerges just as fully.

•

GEORGY GIRL
1966, 100 mins, UK Ⓥ ⊙ b/w
Dir Silvio Narizzano ***Prod*** Robert A. Goldston, Otto Plaschkes ***Scr*** Margaret Forster, Peter Nichols ***Ph*** Ken Higgins ***Ed*** John Bloom ***Mus*** Alexander Faris ***Art*** Tony Woollard
Act James Mason, Alan Bates, Lynn Redgrave, Charlotte Rampling, Rachel Kempson, Bill Owen (Columbia)

The role of a gawky ungainly plain Jane [in this adaptation of the novel by Margaret Forster] is a natural for Lynn Redgrave's talents, and she frequently overwhelms her costars by sheer force of personality.

She's sharing a slovenly apartment with an attractive, brittle and promiscuous girlfriend (Charlotte Rampling). And whenever a lover is being entertained in the communal bedroom, Redgrave takes herself off to the home of her parents' wealthy employer. Girlfriend becomes pregnant, opts for marriage instead of another abortion, but when mother-to-be is in hospital, husband (Alan Bates) realizes he chose the wrong girl.

James Mason, as the wealthy employer, attempts to adopt a father figure in relations to the girl, but is actually nothing more than a conventional old roué.

Redgrave has a pushover of a part, and never misses a trick to get that extra yock, whether it's her first passionate encounter with Alan Bates or her fielding of Mason's amorous overtures.

1966: NOMINATIONS: Best Actress (Lynn Redgrave), Supp. Actor (James Mason), B&W Cinematography, Song ("Georgy Girl")

•

GERMANIA ANNO ZERO
(GERMANY—YEAR ZERO)
1948, 73 mins, Italy Ⓥ b/w
Dir Roberto Rossellini ***Prod*** Roberto Rossellini ***Scr*** Roberto Rossellini, Max Colpet, Carlo Lizzani ***Ph*** Robert Julliard ***Ed*** Eraldo Da Roma ***Mus*** Renzo Rossellini ***Art*** Piero Filippone
Act Edmund Meschke, Ernst Pittschau, Ingetraud Hintze, Franz Krueger, Erich Guehne, Barbara Hintz (Tevere/Sadfilm)

"Germany has backtracked 1948 years. It's now at naught—as if Christ weren't born, since they wanted to kill Him again. Therefore, don't seek traces of our civilization in this film. They've disappeared."

Film opens with this foreword. Not the slightest sign of comedy lightens the pic. Having resolved to mirror a world which has lost every moral rule, producer-director-writer Roberto Rossellini has done it in an extremely objective, cold manner, turning out more document than documentary.

Film deals with terrifying doings. There are boys in it who kill their parents and then commit suicide. There are girls—but they're prostitutes. There are school teachers—but they're of perverted natures. All this, on the terrifying background of bombed-out Berlin, where phantom-like people are living as they can, one selling black market goods which he immediately steals again, another playing for the Allies' enjoyment the record of one of Hitler's speeches among the ruins of the Chancery.

Pic isn't acted but "lived." Pro and nonpro cast play it with uniform sincerity. Edmund Meschke is the most impressive of the lot, delivering a poignant, believable portrayal as the young disgraced hero.

Photography by Robert Julliard keeps a constant balance between location shootings and studio scenes.

•

GERMANY—YEAR ZERO
SEE: GERMANIA ANNO ZERO

•

GERMINAL
1993, 158 mins, France/Belgium/Italy Ⓥ ▭ col
Dir Claude Berri ***Prod*** Claude Berri ***Scr*** Arlette Langmann, Claude Berri ***Ph*** Yves Angelo ***Ed*** Herve de Luze ***Mus*** Jean-Louis Roques ***Art*** Than At Hoang, Christian Marti
Act Renaud, Gerard Depardieu, Miou-Miou, Jean Carmet, Judith Henry, Jean-Roger Milo (Renn/France 2/DD/Alternative/Nuova Artisti Associati)

Though commendable and ambitious, Claude Berri's reverent $30 million adaptation of the 1885 Emile Zola mining saga *Germinal* is strangely flat and matter-of-fact. This earnest depiction of class struggle will be a struggle for many viewers as well.

Story of the brutal conditions in Gallic coal mines in the 1870s is immediate and accessible, even to those with no prior knowledge of the book, which delineates the strained interdependence between starving miners and their well-fed overlords.

Unemployed mechanic Etienne Lantier (renegade folk singer Renaud in his screen bow) stumbles into the hellish pre-dawn bustle of the Montsou mine complex, in northern France, and is drafted by miner Maheu (Gerard Depardieu) to replace a deceased worker on his crew. Maheu's daughter, Catherine (Judith Henry), shows Etienne kindness but ends up in an abusive relationship with the selfish Chaval (Jean-Roger Milo).

Due to management's time-consuming safety demands, tensions are running high. Etienne spreads the idealistic vision of a Workers' Paradise and, when management lowers the per-bin fee, encourages the men to strike. Result is a chain reaction of tragic events.

Zola's meticulously detailed account of deep-seated inequalities and miserable living conditions has been diluted in its transfer to the widescreen. Pic's major shortcoming is that characters speak of poverty and hunger but their privations are not strongly conveyed at a visual level. Performances are strong down the line. Production design is impressive, and music fitting and unobtrusive.

•

GERONIMO
1962, 101 mins, US ▭ col
Dir Arnold Laven ***Prod*** Arnold Laven ***Scr*** Pat Fielder ***Ph*** Alex Phillips ***Ed*** Marsh Hendry ***Mus*** Hugo Friedhofer ***Art*** Roberto Silva
Act Chuck Connors, Kamala Devi, Ross Martin, Pat Conway, Adam West (United Artists)

Time was when Indians on the warpath were known to claim a few scalps in their pursuits. Although Geronimo's band of idealistic warriors are acknowledged to be scalpers in Pat Fielder's screenplay, from the story she penned with producer Laven, there is no evidence of such menacing behavior in this film. In fact, the Indians of Fielder's scenario are unbelievably henpecked, domesticated and generally wishy-washy—proud and arrogant in their war-making but meek enough to be bossed about by a frail, lone white woman in more intimate business.

The story describes the latter, leaner days of Geronimo's career, during which, denied humanitarian treatment by white supervisors on the reservation, he escaped and fled with some 50 tribesmen to Mexico, where he waged a courageous "war" against the U.S. to focus attention on the principle of the issue—treatment of the Indian as a human being. Chuck Connors gives the film a decided lift with an impressive portrayal in the title role.

The picture was filmed in Mexico, and is a fine physical production.

•

GERONIMO AN AMERICAN LEGEND
1993, 115 mins, US Ⓥ ⦿ ▭ col
Dir Walter Hill *Prod* Walter Hill, Neil Canton *Scr* John Milius, Larry Gross *Ph* Lloyd Ahern *Ed* Freeman Davies, Carmel Davies, Donn Aron *Mus* Ry Cooder *Art* Joe Alves
Act Jason Patric, Gene Hackman, Robert Duvall, Wes Studi, Matt Damon, Rodney A. Grant (Columbia)

Sad, stately and ideologically *au courant*, *Geronimo* relates the final stages of the U.S. government's subjugation of the West's native population in absorbing, detailed fashion. Neatly turning long-standing genre conventions upside down while working squarely within them, director Walter Hill has fashioned a physically impressive, well-acted picture whose slightly stodgy literary quality holds it back from an even greater impact.

This large-scale feature [from a screen story by John Milius] intriguingly concentrates on 1885–86, when the U.S. Army devoted 5,000 men, or one-quarter of its entire troop strength, to the effort to stamp out Indian resistance once and for all.

Pic is framed by the words of a secondary character, Lt. Britton Davis (Matt Damon), a freshly scrubbed lad straight from West Point who arrives in Arizona territory just in time for the Geronimo push. Closer to the center of matters is Lt. Charles Gatewood (Jason Patric), a young Virginian who takes Geronimo into custody and peacefully escorts him to Brig. Gen. Crook (Gene Hackman), a veteran Indian fighter.

Geronimo and some followers escape and head for Mexico. The Army again takes up its pursuit with the aide of grizzled scout Al Sieber (Robert Duvall). Crook is replaced by Brig. Gen. Miles, a martinet who orders Gatewood to bring Geronimo in once and for all.

Wes Studi is a rugged, commanding, admirably defiant Geronimo. Pic's tone is kept in a dour straitjacket that Hackman and Duvall manage somewhat to escape with their irony and seasoned humanity. Rich and majestic production values demand big-screen viewing.

1993: NOMINATION: Best Sound

•

GERTRUD
1965, 120 mins, Denmark b/w
Dir Carl Dreyer *Scr* Carl Dreyer *Ph* Henning Bendtsen *Ed* Edith Schlussle *Mus* Jorgen Jersild *Art* Kai Rasch
Act Nina Pens Rode, Ebbe Rode, Bendt Rothe, Baard Owe, Axel Strobye, Karl Gustav Ahlefeldt (Palladium)

Film is the first in nine years by the noted Danish veteran (at 75) Carl Dreyer. From a turn-of-the-century secondary Swedish play [by Hjalmar Soderberg], Dreyer has woven what looks like a meditation on love.

This eschews trying to reconstruct the 1907 period in which it takes place and tries for a timlessness in presenting a theme that has been in most of Dreyer's work, namely that reconciling true love with ordinary life and religion has always been a problem for those who will not compromise.

The heroine is a thirtyish woman who has been an opera singer. She had broken off a liaison with a poet and then married his friend. An affair with a young musician is also disappointing, since it was deep physical love for her but an adventure for him. Follows a look at her as an old woman who has devoted herself to a fairly solitary life of learning but has felt it was all worth it, since she had loved, even if incompatibly. Theme, with echos of Ibsen, in its social haranguing for female independence, and Strindberg, in its difficulty in male and female understanding, lends itself admirably to Dreyer's dry but penetrating style.

Nina Pens Rode has the right luminous quality for the romantic, uncompromising Gertrud, while the men are acceptable if sometimes overindulgent in their roles.

•

GETAWAY, THE
1972, 122 mins, US Ⓥ ⦿ ▭ col
Dir Sam Peckinpah *Prod* David Foster, Mitchell Brower *Scr* Walter Hill *Ph* Lucien Ballard *Ed* Roger Spottiswoode, Robert Wolfe *Mus* Quincy Jones *Art* Ted Haworth, Angelo Graham
Act Steve McQueen, Ali MacGraw, Ben Johnson, Sally Struthers, Al Lettieri, Slim Pickens (First Artists)

The Getaway has several things going for it: Sam Peckinpah's hard-action direction, this time largely channeled into material destruction, although fast-cut human bloodlettings occur frequently enough, and Steve McQueen and Ali MacGraw as stars.

Peckinpah's particular brand of storytelling comes through in the adaptation of the Jim Thompson novel. McQueen, denied parole despite four years of good behavior, gives in to crooked politico Ben Johnson's bank caper scheme in return for release from prison. MacGraw arranges and participates in the robbery plus the rambling escape which follows.

There is an overwritten secondary plot line involving Al Lettieri, so effective in projecting the greasy sadism of one of the robbery gang that his portion of the film eventually becomes vulgar overexposition.

•

GETAWAY, THE
1994, 115 mins, US Ⓥ ⦿ ▭ col
Dir Roger Donaldson *Prod* David Foster, Lawrence Turman, John Alan Simon *Scr* Walter Hill, Amy Jones *Ph* Peter Menzies, Jr. *Ed* Conrad Buff *Mus* Mark Isham *Art* Joseph Nemec III
Act Alec Baldwin, Kim Basinger, Michael Madsen, James Woods, David Morse, Jennifer Tilly (Largo/Universal)

The Getaway is a pretty good remake of a pretty good action thriller. Although the attributes and drawbacks of this well-outfitted retelling of Jim Thompson's edgy crime meller and Sam Peckinpah's gritty 1972 rendition lie in different places, the net effect of this tale of innumerable deceptions, betrayals and double crosses is more or less the same.

Peckinpah's protracted original credit sequence, with Steve McQueen's Doc McCoy in a prison surrounded by deer, was wonderful, but Donaldson has one-upped him with a startlingly fresh prologue, turning on two criminal betrayals, showing how Doc (Alec Baldwin) landed in jail. Early action also firms the characters of Doc's sharp-shooting wife, Carol (Kim Basinger), and their early partner and eventual nemesis, Rudy (Michael Madsen).

Plot clicks in as Doc is released from a Mexican slammer courtesy of slick crime lord Jack Benyon (James Woods), who recruits the master thief and explosives expert to head a heist of a Phoenix dog track vault.

Doc succeeds in nabbing the cash, but things go awry when a guard is killed. As the McCoys uneasily make their way to El Paso and the Mexican border, *Getaway* '94 becomes increasingly identical to the original, down to specific incidents and lines of dialogue.

Baldwin fills the bill perfectly well as the smart, tenacious criminal ready to hang up his hat, but McQueen came with a magnetism and fascination Baldwin doesn't have. Even Basinger bashers might find themselves rather taken with her gritty turn here. [Outside the U.S., pic was released in a hotter version.]

•

GET BACK
1991, 90 mins, UK Ⓥ col
Dir Richard Lester *Prod* Philip Knatchbull, Henry Thomas *Ph* Robert Paynter, Jordan Cronenweth *Ed* John Victor Smith
Act Paul McCartney (Allied Filmmakers/TDK/Front Page)

A stagebound record of Paul McCartney's 1990 world tour, *Get Back* is heavy on nostalgia and light on visual zap. Sans intro or background, pic kicks off on stage and stays there for 90 minutes. Filming took place in England, Holland, Brazil, Canada, Italy, Japan and the U.S., but individual locales are not identified. Audiences and songs blend into one big stage show.

Pic reunites the former Beatle with director Richard Lester, who helmed *A Hard Day's Night* and *Help!* There's none of those mid-1960s pics' groundbreaking elan here. By MTV standards, this is somewhere in a stone age. Lester mostly lets the powerful songs (half Beatles classics) speak for themselves, crosscutting between fans mouthing the lyrics and Macca & Co. on stage.

•

GET CARTER
1971, 111 mins, UK/US Ⓥ col
Dir Mike Hodges *Prod* Michael Klinger *Scr* Mike Hodges *Ph* Wolfgang Suschitzky *Ed* John Trumper *Mus* Roy Budd *Art* Assheton Gorton
Act Michael Caine, Ian Hendry, Britt Ekland, John Osborne, Tony Beckley, George Sewell (M-G-M)

Get Carter is a superior crime action meller. Michael Caine stars as an English hood seeking vengeance for the murder of his brother. Mike Hodges's top-notch adaptation of a Ted Lewis novel not only maintains interest but conveys with rare artistry, restraint and clarity the many brutal, sordid and gamy plot turns.

Lewis's novel, *Jack's Return Home*, is adapted by Hodges into a fast-moving screenplay in which episodes of compounded criminal doublecrossing build gradually but steadily to a logical if ironic climax.

The curious death of Caine's brother triggers his departure from London, where he is a key torpedo for gangsters Terence Rigby and John Bindon, to his Newcastle home, where John Osborne (the playwright) appears the area crime boss. In tracking down his brother's murderer, Caine encounters the full spectrum of contemporary crime, including pornographic pix (in which his niece Petra Markham has been innocently compromised), drugs, high-stakes gambling, and vicious give-and-take retribution.

•

GET OFF MY BACK
SEE: SYNANON

•

GET ON THE BUS
1996, 120 mins, US Ⓥ ⦿ col
Dir Spike Lee *Prod* Reuben Cannon, Bill Borden, Barry Rosenbush *Scr* Reggie Rock Bythewood *Ph* Elliot Davis *Ed* Leander T. Sales *Mus* Terence Blanchard *Art* Ina Mayhew
Act Richard Belzer, DeAundre Bonds, Andre Braugher, Thomas Jefferson Byrd, Gabriel Casseus, Ossie Davis (15 Black Men/Columbia)

A vital regeneration of a filmmaker's talent as well as a bracing and often very funny dramatization of urgent sociopolitical themes, *Get on the Bus* represents Spike Lee's most satisfying work since *Do the Right Thing*, an attempt at creating a microcosm of the black male community via a cross-country trip by 20-odd Los Angeles men to the Million Man March.

Shot guerrilla style in three weeks, the $2.4 million production was entirely financed by 15 black men identified on the end credit crawl. Among those who threw in between $100,000 and $200,000 apiece were actors Danny Glover, Wesley Snipes, Will Smith and Robert Guillaume.

Filming in Super-16 in a jittery verite style that proves invigorating rather than annoying, Lee plunks the viewer down with a bunch of men preparing to board the bus in South Central L.A. Among them are Jeremiah (Ossie Davis), a religious, thoughtful, fun-loving man; Gary (Roger Guenveur Smith), a light-skinned cop whose policeman father was killed by a black man; Jamal (Gabriel Casseus), a recent convert to Islam, and Xavier (Hill Harper), a camera-wielding film student. There is also an on-the-outs gay couple and an egotistical actor (Andre Braugher).

But the most conspicuous duo consists of longtime absent father Evan Thomas, Sr., (Thomas Jefferson Byrd) and his teenage son, Junior (DeAundre Bonds), whom he has shackled to him by a 72-hour court order.

Early going consists of considerable raucous good humor. When the bus breaks down in the middle of nowhere, they are disgruntled to find that the driver (Richard Belzer) of their replacement vehicle is white. Later, the tone turns more serious, and what finally happens to the men simultaneously approaches theatrical melodrama with its convulsive circumstances and resulting speechifying.

•

GET OUT YOUR HANDKERCHIEFS
SEE: PREPAREZ VOS MOUCHOIRS

•

GET SHORTY
1995, 105 mins, US Ⓥ ⦿ col
Dir Barry Sonnenfeld *Prod* Danny DeVito, Michael Shamberg, Stacey Sher *Scr* Scott Frank *Ph* Don Peterman *Ed* Jim Miller *Mus* John Lurie *Art* Peter Larkin
Act John Travolta, Gene Hackman, Rene Russo, Danny DeVito, Dennis Farina, Delroy Lindo (Jersey/M-G-M)

A drolly offbeat look at Hollywood mores dedicated to the proposition that the best preparation for becoming a film producer is a stint in the criminal underworld, *Get Shorty* is good, sly fun. With John Travolta putting on a dazzling demonstration of what being a movie star is all about, this crafty adaptation of Elmore Leonard's filmland-set [1990] bestseller retains an appealingly quirky literary quality, even if it lacks the dramatic dynamics and tension that would have made it an over-the-top success.

Miami loan shark Chili Palmer (Travolta) arrives on the Coast to collect a $150,000 gambling debt from Harry Zimm (Gene Hackman), a Z-movie producer whose sensibility and wardrobe remain stuck in the '70s. Seeing Zimm as his possible doorman to Hollywood, Chili pitches him an idea, and a new producing team is born.

But Chili has competition in the thug-turned-mogul field, notably in the person of Bo Catlett (Delroy Lindo), to whom Zimm also owes big money. Then there's the matter of Leo Devoe (David Paymer), a small-timer who has absconded with a $300,000 insurance payoff intended for big boss Ray "Bones" Barboni (Dennis Farina).

Plot mechanics play second fiddle to the smart, goofy humor generated by the collision of these oddball characters. Best of all is a visit by Chili and scream queen Karen

Flores (Rene Russo) to latter's ex-husband, screen superstar Martin Weir (Danny DeVito). Ostensibly there to convince him to appear in his picture, nonpro Chili ends up giving the thesp a funny lesson in acting and how to project attitude.

Hackman scores as the fast-talking schlockmeister who bids to turn financial misfortune to his advantage, and Farina and Lindo are just the first among many character actors who get to shine here. Russo is mostly along for the ride. Bette Midler juices things up nicely in something more than a cameo, while the similarly unbilled Harvey Keitel and Penny Marshall pop up briefly.

•

GETTING AWAY WITH MURDER
1996, 92 mins, US Ⓥ col
Dir Harvey Miller ***Prod*** Frank Price, Penny Marshall ***Scr*** Harvey Miller ***Ph*** Frank Tidy ***Ed*** Richard Nord ***Mus*** John Debney ***Art*** John Jay Moore
Act Dan Aykroyd, Lily Tomlin, Jack Lemmon, Bonnie Hunt, Brian Kerwin (Price Entertainment/Parkway)

Getting Away with Murder is a distasteful affair that should embarrass all concerned, a lighthearted comedy about the Holocaust and an accused Nazi war criminal.

Dan Aykroyd toplines as Jack Lambert, a college ethics professor who lives next door to Max Mueller (Jack Lemmon, with a bad German accent). Mueller is accused of being Karl Luger, a death camp commandant nicknamed the Beast of Berkau. Enraged that Mueller is going to be able to flee the country without paying for his crimes, Lambert poisons him. Hilarity supposedly ensues when evidence emerges that Mueller is innocent. Lambert repents by marrying Mueller's daughter (played by a stiff Lily Tomlin). Another twist makes us think Mueller may have been guilty after all. It's not exactly a laugh riot.

Aykroyd's bumbling Lambert looks like he should be in another film, while Lemmon and Tomlin may have hit career lows as the German father and daughter. Of the principals, only Bonnie Hunt, as Aykroyd's cast-off girlfriend, comes off unscathed.

•

GETTING EVEN WITH DAD
1994, 108 mins, US Ⓥ ⊙ col
Dir Howard Deutch ***Prod*** Katie Jacobs, Pierce Gardner ***Scr*** Tom S. Parker, Jim Jennewein ***Ph*** Tim Suhrstedt ***Ed*** Richard Halsey ***Mus*** Miles Goodman ***Art*** Virginia L. Randolph
Act Macaulay Culkin, Ted Danson, Glenne Headly, Saul Rubinek, Hector Alizondo, Kathleen Wilhoite (M-G-M)

This schizophrenic comedy can't decide if it wants to be broadly farcical or fuzzily heartwarming. While it fares better on the latter front, pic doesn't succeed on either level.

Macaulay Culkin plays Timmy, an 11-year-old boy dumped on the doorstep of his dad (Ted Danson), an ex-con whom he hasn't seen in years. Timmy has the bad timing to show up just when Dad is about to undertake a major theft, seeking a big enough score to go straight and buy the bakery where he works. Timmy hides his father's ill-gotten gains, forcing him to squire the kid around town in exchange for finding out where the loot it.

That setup is obviously designed to allow father and son to grudgingly grow to love each other, while milking laughs out of Dad's two partners in crime (Saul Rubinek, Gailard Sartain), who follow Timmy and his father everywhere they go, not wanting to let their share of the booty get away from them.

While that provides the opportunity for *Home Alone*-type skewering of the two bumbling criminals, director Howard Deutch never seems comfortable taking the full plunge into those waters. Deutch does a little better with a cat-and-mouse search for the stash that incorporates the local police, including a femme cop (Glenne Headly) who provides a potential love interest for Dad—the narrative undergoing a real stretch to involve a female character.

•

GETTING GERTIE'S GARTER
1945, 72 mins, US b/w
Dir Allan Dwan ***Prod*** Edward Small ***Scr*** Allan Dwan, Karen De Wolf, Joe Bigelow ***Ph*** Charles Lawton, Jr. ***Ed*** Grant Whytock, Walter Hannemann, Truman K. Wood ***Mus*** Hugo Friedhofer ***Art*** Joseph Sternad
Act Dennis O'Keefe, Marie McDonald, Barry Sullivan, Binnie Barnes, J. Carrol Naish, Sheila Ryan (United Artists)

Plot is no more plausible on the screen than it was on the stage [in the play by Wilson Collison and Avery Hopwood] but the sheer frenzy of the slapstick are certain for chuckles.

O'Keefe is seen as the now-married scientist seeking to recover a jeweled garter which he had given a pre-marriage sweetie. The ex-love, about to marry O'Keefe's best friend, decides she should keep the garter—just in case—and her concealment, plus the scientist's frenzied efforts to recover it without his wife finding out, keeps the young man in continual hot water. Comedy is emphasized by the many compromising situations the search leads to and the misunderstandings that develop.

Marie McDonald matches O'Keefe in the comedy as Gertie. Her work indicates plenty of promise. Sheila Ryan also is seen to advantage as the wife who misunderstands her husband's antics. Barry Sullivan shows well as the fiancé.

•

GETTING IT ON
1983, 96 mins, US Ⓥ ⊙ col
Dir William Olsen ***Prod*** Jan Thompson, William Olsen ***Scr*** William Olsen ***Ph*** Austin McKinney ***Ed*** William Olsen ***Mus*** Ricky Keller ***Art*** James Eric
Act Martin Yost, Heather Kennedy, Jeff Edmond, Kathy Brickmeier, Mark Alan Ferri, Charles King Bibby (Comworld)

This North Carolina-lensed teenage comedy nimbly pumps new life into the overdone high school hijinks genre.

Filmmaker William Olsen targets our consumerist and video-obsessed culture for some ribbing in this story of high school freshman Alex Carson (Martin Yost), with a crush on the girl next door, Sally (Heather Kennedy). Devising a video software business to earn money, Alex borrows his startup capital from his very businesslike dad, and with the help of his cutup classmate Nicholas (Jeff Edmond) uses the video equipment to record hidden camera footage of Heather and other pretty girls.

When Nicholas is kicked out of school by mean principal White (Charles King Bibby), the heroes enlist the services of a friendly prostitute (Kim Saunders) to record footage of White in flagrante delicto.

What makes this material work is a fresh, enthusiastic cast, witty writing, and direction by Olsen that bears no hint of malice.

•

GETTING IT RIGHT
1989, 102 mins, US Ⓥ ⊙ col
Dir Randal Kleiser ***Prod*** Jonathan D. Krane, Randal Kleiser ***Scr*** Elizabeth Jane Howard ***Ph*** Clive Tickner ***Ed*** Chris Kelly ***Mus*** Colin Towns ***Art*** Caroline Amies
Act Jessie Birdsall, Helena Bonham Carter, Peter Cook, Lynn Redgrave, Jane Horrocks, John Gielgud (MCEG)

Sweet love trimphs over hollow class consciousness in *Getting It Right*, a wonderful made-in-Britain sex comedy that celebrates romance in funny, quirky ways.

Maggie Thatcher's England, specifically London, is satirized here. Self-taught hairdresser Jesse Birdsall is a 31-year-old virgin still living at home but doing nothing about it. He suffers in silence, preferring instead to daydream about girls. He gets yanked out one night to a trendy loft party along the Thames hosted by a socialite who dresses like a man in drag (Lynn Redgrave).

What ensues reminds one a bit of Griffin Dunne's predicament in *After Hours* except this is a much more complex adventure. It's filled with a cast of delightful English eccentrics. Redgrave, meanwhile, is determined to relieve the mystified Birdsall of his virginity.

Helena Bonham Carter is a terrific and surprisingly convincing bulimic tramp parading as an aristocrat. Director Randal Kleiser is in touch with his subjects and treats them well. The actors clearly know what they are speaking about and seem to enjoy every word of Elizabeth Jane Howard's clever, textured script [based on her own book].

•

GETTING OF WISDOM, THE
1977, 100 mins, Australia Ⓥ col
Dir Bruce Beresford ***Prod*** Phillip Adams ***Scr*** Eleanor Witcombe ***Ph*** Don McAlpine ***Ed*** William Anderson ***Mus*** [uncredited] ***Art*** John Stoddart
Act Susannah Fowle, Barry Humphries, John Waters, Sheila Helpmann, Pat Kennedy, Julia Blake (Southern Cross)

The Getting of Wisdom was a bold choice as the subject of a feature film. The novel by Henry Handel Richardson [pseudonym of Ethel Richardson] was published in 1910, 13 years after the action depicted and was so shocking at the time that the author's name was stricken from the records of the school in which she set the lightly disguised autobiography.

It is the story of a young girl's trials and adjustment to life in a strict, Victorian boarding school. Laura (Susannah Fowle) is strong-willed and rebellious, which creates conflicts with her peers and her teachers. The only real soul mate she finds is a senior girl (Hilary Ryan), but her possessiveness drives a wedge in the relationship.

The plotline is episodic, charting the development of the lead character over the years between her arrival and her graduation.

•

GETTING STRAIGHT
1970, 126 mins, US Ⓥ col
Dir Richard Rush ***Prod*** Richard Rush ***Scr*** Robert Kaufman ***Ph*** Laszlo Kovacs ***Ed*** Maury Winetrobe ***Mus*** Ronald Stein ***Art*** Sydney Z. Witwack
Act Elliott Gould, Candice Bergen, Robert F. Lyons, Jeff Corey, Max Julien, Cecil Kellaway (Columbia)

Getting Straight is an outstanding film. It is a comprehensive, cynical, sympathetic, flip, touching and hilarious story of the middle generation [of the late 1960s]—those millions a bit too old for protest, a bit too young for repression.

The setting is a college campus where Elliott Gould is nearly through an education course. Bergen is his girl. Both represent the post-JFK/RFK generation, who perceive the tremendous flaws in organized civilization, but scorn the often-puerile methods used in protest.

The episodic story [updated from a novel by Ken Kolb] covers lots of ground as it permits the very large and extremely competent supporting cast to limn the attitudes of an entire population.

While the film is a parade of accurately hewn postures, the root story never strays too far.

•

GETTYSBURG
1993, 254 mins, US Ⓥ ⊙ col
Dir Ronald F. Maxwell ***Prod*** Robert Katz, Moctesuma Esparza ***Scr*** Ronald F. Maxwell ***Ph*** Kees van Oostum ***Ed*** Corky Ehlers ***Mus*** Randy Edelman ***Art*** Cary White
Act Tom Berenger, Martin Sheen, Stephen Lang, Richard Jordan, Jeff Daniels, Sam Elliott (Turner/Neufeld-Rehme)

Ted Turner doesn't do anything in a small way. The premiere entry for his new feature production unit is a 4 1/4-hour epic on the biggest battle of the Civil War, and it will prove a hit with history buffs. *Gettysburg* concentrates on the three days of fighting, with about 45 minutes devoted to the day before.

Gen. Robert E. Lee (Martin Sheen) believes that he can end the war with a decisive victory over Federal troops by taking Gettysburg, then marching on Washington with an offer to President Lincoln of terms for peace. The rebel leader and his men are tired after three years of fighting a war most thought would be over in a month. The Northern troops are in disarray.

Thus, the stage is set for a battle that would see more than 53,000 American soldiers killed, more casualties than there were during the entire Vietnam War. Writer-director Ronald F. Maxwell, adapting the Michael Shaara novel *The Killer Angels* and relying on historical research and documents of the era, tries to reconstruct what happened on both sides during the fateful events of early July 1863.

The first day is seen through the eyes of Brig. Gen. John Buford (Sam Elliott), whose actions prevent the South from gaining an early advantage. On the Northern side, the chief point of reference is provided by Col. Joshua Lawrence Chamberlain (Jeff Daniels), a Maine college professor ill-suited to his role.

Among the rebels, the chief conflict is between Lee, who wants a decisive victory, and Lt. Gen. James Longstreet (Tom Berenger), who argues that the risks are astronomical.

There's the sense of this being as close as an audience can come to seeing what the Battle of Gettysburg was like. The final credit scroll runs 10 minutes. Daniels walks away with the film as the mild scholar who, when tossed into battle, rises to the occasion.

In addition to the theatrical release version, Maxwell cut a 4 1/2-hour edition (six hours with commercials) to run on Turner's TNT cable channel in 1994 as a three-part miniseries, and also prepared a 5 1/2-hour version for homevideo release.

•

GHOST
1990, 127 mins, US Ⓥ ⊙ col
Dir Jerry Zucker ***Prod*** Lisa Weinstein ***Scr*** Bruce Joel Rubin ***Ph*** Adam Greenberg ***Ed*** Walter Murch ***Mus*** Maurice Jarre ***Art*** Jane Musky
Act Patrick Swayze, Demi Moore, Whoopi Goldberg, Tony Goldwyn, Rick Aviles, Vincent Schiavelli (Paramount/Koch)

An unlikely grab bag of styles that teeters, spiritlike, between life and death, this lightweight romantic fantasy delivers the elements a *Dirty Dancing* audience presumably hungers for.

Patrick Swayze and Demi Moore play Sam and Molly, a have-it-all Manhattan couple (he's a banker, she's an artist) who have just happily renovated their new Tribeca loft when he's shot and killed by a street thug. Unknown to her, he's walking around as a ghost, desperate to communicate with her because she's still in danger. He stumbles upon a spirit-world medium (Whoopi Goldberg) and drags her in to help him as a money-laundering and murder plot unfolds around them.

As the first dramatic film directed by Jerry Zucker (who collaborated on *Airplane! Ruthless People* and *The Naked Gun* with David Zucker and Jim Abrahams), *Ghost* is an odd creation—at times nearly smothering in arty somberness, at others veering into good, wacky fun.

Two-hour-plus film really takes its time unfolding, and it's not until Goldberg is brought in that the first laughs occur, but things do get wilder as Swayze explores his ghostly powers. Sporting a boyish haircut and her usual husky voice, Moore mostly has to spout tears and look vulnerable as she mourns Swayze and tries to avoid Goldberg, who she's convinced is a con artist.

1990: Best Supp. Actress (Whoopi Goldberg), Original Screenplay

NOMINATIONS: Best Picture, Editing, Original Score

●

GHOST AND MRS. MUIR, THE

1947, 103 mins, US Ⓥ ⊙ b/w

Dir Joseph L. Mankiewicz ***Prod*** Fred Kohlmar ***Scr*** Philip Dunne ***Ph*** Charles Lang, Jr. ***Ed*** Dorothy Spencer ***Mus*** Bernard Herrmann ***Art*** Richard Day, George Davis

Act Gene Tierney, Rex Harrison, George Sanders, Edna Best, Natalie Wood, Robert Coote (20th Century-Fox)

This is the story of a girl who falls in love with a ghost—but not an ordinary spook. As that girl, Gene Tierney gives, what undoubtedly is her best performance to date. It's warmly human and the out-of-this-world romance pulls audience sympathy with an infectious tug that never slackens. In his role as the lusty, seafaring shade, Rex Harrison commands the strongest attention.

Philip Dunne's script lards the R. A. Dick novel with gusty humor and situations that belie the ghostly theme. Dialog makes full use of salty expressions to point up chuckles.

Plot, briefly, deals with young widow who leaves London at turn of century for a seaside cottage. The place is haunted by the ghost of its former owner, Capt. Daniel Gregg. The salty shade seeks to frighten the widow away but she's stubborn and stays. When her income is wiped out, the shade dictates to her his life story; she sells it as successful novel.

George Sanders is in briefly, and effectively, as a married lothario who makes a play for the widow, much to Capt. Gregg's discomfort. Edna Best shows brightly as the widow's maid-companion. Natalie Wood, as the young daughter, is good, as is Vanessa Brown who becomes the grown-up Anna.

1947: NOMINATION: Best B&W Cinematography

●

GHOST AND THE DARKNESS, THE

1996, 109 mins, US Ⓥ ⊙ ▭ col

Dir Stephen Hopkins ***Prod*** Gale Anne Hurd, Paul Radin, A. Kitman Ho ***Scr*** William Goldman ***Ed*** Robert Brown, Steve Mirkovich ***Mus*** Jerry Goldsmith ***Art*** Stuart Wurtzel

Act Michael Douglas, Val Kilmer, Tom Wilkinson, John Kani, Bernard Hill, Brian McCardie (Constellation/Paramount)

A throwback to bygone historical adventures, *The Ghost and the Darkness* is a classy, high-gloss yarn, a literate and eerie true-life chiller. However, while the picture has some stunning action setpieces, its ruminations on the nature of evil tend to be more cerebral than visceral.

At the turn of the century, Great Britain, France and Germany were in a race to build a Pan-African railway and corner the lucrative ivory trade. The British hired an army engineer, Col. John Patterson (Val Kilmer), to build a bridge over the Tsavo River near the end of the line, in eastern Africa. It was scheduled to take five months.

In the almost slavishly accurate version of events, Patterson arrives on the Dark Continent enthusiastic about realizing a lifelong dream of seeing Africa. But the challenge of erecting a span is considerably more difficult than he imagined. Worst piece of luck is that his arrival coincides with the appearance of a "man-eater" lion. Two months later, the title characters arrive: The Ghost and The Darkness are the names given two marauding lions who have killed more than 130 people. What was presumed to be the work of a single animal was in fact being done by the lethal duo.

Director Stephen Hopkins is adroit at building tension and creating a mood of danger. He appears to favor the character of Remington (Michael Douglas), the flamboyant, garrulous American white hunter who kills only in cases of need. Remington provides Douglas with the kind of role one might ordinarily associate with an actor like, well, Kilmer.

1996: Best Sound Effects Editing (Bruce Stambler)

●

GHOST AT NOON

SEE: LE MEPRIS

●

GHOSTBUSTERS

1984, 107 mins, US Ⓥ ⊙ ▭ col

Dir Ivan Reitman ***Prod*** Ivan Reitman ***Scr*** Dan Aykroyd, Harold Ramis ***Ph*** Laszlo Kovacs ***Ed*** Sheldon Kahn, David Blewitt ***Mus*** Elmer Bernstein ***Art*** John DeCuir

Act Bill Murray, Dan Aykroyd, Sigourney Weaver, Harold Ramis, Rick Moranis, Annie Potts (Columbia/Delphi)

Ghostbusters is a lavishly produced ($32 million) but only intermittently impressive all-star comedy lampoon of supernatural horror films.

Originally conceived as a John Belushi–Dan Aykroyd vehicle called *Ghostsmashers* before Belushi's death in 1982, *Ghostbusters* under producer-director Ivan Reitman makes a fundamental error: featuring a set of top comics but having them often work alone.

A Manhattan apartment building inhabited by beautiful Dana Barrett (Sigourney Weaver) and her nerd neighbor Louis Tully (Rick Moranis) becomes the gateway for demons from another dimension to invade the Earth.

To battle them come the Ghostbusters, a trio of scientists who have been kicked off campus and are now freelance ghost catchers for hire. Aykroyd is the gung-ho scientific type, Bill Murray is faking competency (he's had no higher education in parapsychology) and using the job to meet women, while Harold Ramis is the trio's technical expert.

Within the top-heavy cast, it's Murray's picture, as the popular comedian deadpans, ad libs and does an endearing array of physical shtick.

1984: NOMINATIONS: Best Song ("Ghostbusters"), Visual Effects

●

GHOSTBUSTERS II

1989, 102 mins, US Ⓥ ⊙ ▭ col

Dir Ivan Reitman ***Prod*** Ivan Reitman ***Scr*** Harold Ramis, Dan Aykroyd ***Ph*** Michael Chapman ***Ed*** Sheldon Kahn, Donn Cambern ***Mus*** Randy Edelman ***Art*** Bo Welch

Act Bill Murray, Dan Aykroyd, Sigourney Weaver, Harold Ramis, Rick Moranis, Peter MacNicol (Columbia)

Ghostbusters II is baby-boomer silliness. Kids will find the oozing slime and ghastly, ghostly apparitions to their liking and adults will enjoy the preposterously clever dialog.

In *II*, the foe is slime, a pinkish, oozing substance that has odd, selective powers—all of them (humorously) evil. Its origins have something to do with a bad imitation Rembrandt painting, the lecherous art historian with an indecipherable foreign accent who's restoring it (Peter MacNicol), and all the bad vibes generated by millions of cranky, stressed-out New Yorkers. The worse their attitude, the worse the slime problem, which is very bad indeed.

The Ghostbusters, naturally, are the only guys for the job.

Bill Murray gets the plum central role (or he forced it by seemingly ad-libbing dozens of wisecracks) at the same time his character also manages to skip out on a lot of the dirty ghostbusting work, leaving it to his pals Dan Aykroyd, Harold Ramis and Ernie Hudson.

While they are zapping Slimer, the main nasty creature from the original film, Murray's time is spent wooing back Sigourney Weaver, now a single mother.

It may be a first time, but Weaver gets to play a softie, a nice break for the actress and her admirers (even if shots with her cute imperiled baby are scene-stealers).

●

GHOST CATCHERS

1944, 67 mins, US b/w

Dir Edward F. Cline ***Prod*** Edmund L. Hartmann ***Scr*** Edmund L. Hartmann ***Ph*** Charles Van Enger ***Ed*** Arthur Hilton ***Mus*** Edward Ward (dir) ***Art*** John B. Goodman, Richard H. Riedel

Act Ole Olsen, Chic Johnson, Gloria Jean, Martha O'Driscoll, Andy Devine, Leo Carrillo (Universal)

In the best Olsen and Johnson tradition, *Ghost Catchers* is a tuneful, screwy concoction, brief and zippy. Unlike previous O&J endeavors this film has a plot. The boys, with the aid of numerable stooges, join in aiding a southern family, which bought an old, haunted brownstone house in the city as a showcase for the two daughters who are slated to appear at Carnegie Hall, get rid of a ghost.

O&J prove they are strong laugh-getters, while Leo Carrillo, as owner of the nitery where they are employed, and Andy Devine and Lon Chaney, as two of the men house-haunters, manage to have their innings, brief as they are.

Edmund L. Hartmann's production cuts corners at every turn, the film being showcased in not too expensive but substantial settings. Eddie Cline, an old-time comedian himself, pilots the cast in capable fashion, his direction being responsible for the fast pace.

●

GHOST GOES WEST, THE

1935, 90 mins, UK Ⓥ b/w

Dir Rene Clair ***Prod*** Alexander Korda ***Scr*** Robert E. Sherwood ***Ph*** Harold Rosson ***Ed*** William Hornbeck, Harold Earle-Fischbacher, Henry Cornelius ***Mus*** Mischa Spoliansky ***Art*** Vincent Korda

Act Robert Donat, Jean Parker, Eugene Pallette, Elsa Lanchester, Ralph Bunker (London)

The first film in the English language directed by Rene Clair, ace French director, it shows that Clair still has full rein on his sense of humor and one of the screen's best from an artistic and intelligent standpoint.

Story is a bit different from his past (French) efforts. It has to do with an American who picks up a Scottish manse which has only one fault: it is ancient, it is famous, it has background, it has color—but it also has a ghost. Nevertheless, the American buys the castle and imports it to America stone by stone, ghost and all. In Florida he sets it up again, his daughter, by way of romance, falling for the penniless heir of the castle and ghost.

Robert Sherwood, in working up the story with Clair from a London *Punch* piece [by Eric Keown], has injected a number of hilarious sequences, and some splendid dialog. Robert Donat as the young heir and doubling as the ghost, Jean Parker as the girl, and Eugene Pallette as the father drain every possible bit of good out of their roles.

●

GHOST IN THE MACHINE

1993, 95 mins, US Ⓥ ⊙ col

Dir Rachel Talalay ***Prod*** Paul Schiff ***Scr*** William Davies, William Osborne ***Ph*** Phil Meheux ***Ed*** Janice Hampton, Erica Huggins ***Mus*** Graeme Revell ***Art*** James Spencer

Act Karen Allen, Chris Mulkey, Ted Marcoux, Wil Horneff, Jessica Walter, Rick Ducommun (20th Century-Fox)

The so-called ghost is the soul of a serial killer loose in a mainframe and adept at traveling on electrical current to mete out lethal revenge. It's an effective, if predictable, paranoid fantasy.

The filmmakers stay pretty much with convention, beginning the yarn with some gruesome, unexplained carnage to get things rolling. What finally turns the action is a car wreck on a rainy night. The victim, a computer store employee named Karl Hochman (Ted Marcoux), is rushed to the hospital and put in a brain scanner. When lightning causes a citywide power surge, his body is lost but his spirit escapes into the core of the Datanet Corp. system.

Hochman happens to be the notorious "Address Book" killer. He's been lifting people's personal phone books and murdering those listed within. His latest acquisition belongs to single mom Terry Munroe (Karen Allen) and, though physically disembodied, he has the spirit to continue his killing spree. It takes Munroe, her son and computer wiz Bram Walker (Chris Mulkey) some time to realize the killer can't be identified in a conventional police lineup.

Director Rachel Talalay livens up the screenplay with clever computer-generated visuals that nicely obscure the thinness of plot. The skilled cast has precious little to do other than present fear and confusion.

●

GHOSTS . . . OF THE CIVIL DEAD

1988, 92 mins, Australia Ⓥ col

Dir John Hillcoat ***Prod*** Evan English ***Scr*** Nick Cave, Gene Conkie, Evan English, John Hillcoat ***Ph*** Paul Goldman ***Ed*** Stewart Young ***Mus*** Nick Cave ***Art*** Chris Kennedy

Act Dave Field, Mike Bishop, Chris de Rose, Nick Cave, Vincent Gil, Bogdan Koca (Correctional Services/Outlaw Values)

The problem of overcrowded prisons and the fact that they often serve as breeding grounds for even tougher criminals are the concerns of *Ghosts . . . of the Civil Dead*, an ambitious, confronting first feature from John Hillcoat, with ruggedly explicit language and violence.

Setting is a correctional institution of the near future (exterior of the facility was filmed in Nevada). Film traces the events leading up to a riot and "lockdown." Drama centers around the arrival of newcomer Dave Field, who discovers a nightmare world where drugtaking and gay sex are ignored by guards and where violence is the order of the day.

Cast includes rock performers Nick Cave, Chris de Rose and Dave Mason, a handful of pro actors (Vincent Gil, Bogdan Koca) and a large number of nonpros, some of them actual ex-cons. Production design is striking.

•

GHOSTS OF MISSISSIPPI
1996, 130 mins, US Ⓥ ⊙ ▭ col
Dir Rob Reiner *Prod* Frederick Zollo, Nicholas Paleologos, Andrew Scheinman, Rob Reiner *Scr* Lewis Colick *Ph* John Seale *Ed* Robert Leighton *Mus* Marc Shaiman *Art* Lilly Kilvert
Act Alec Baldwin, Whoopi Goldberg, James Woods, Craig T. Nelson, Susanna Thompson, Lucas Black (Castle Rock/Columbia)

When future generations turn to this era's movies for an account of the struggles for racial justice in America, they'll learn the surprising lesson that such battles were fought and won by square-jawed white guys. *Ghosts of Mississippi* is history à la Hollywood that doesn't manage to be particularly vivid or exciting in recounting the chivalry of its real-life white knight, a prosecutor attempting to bring a racist assassin to justice.

Tale opens with the June 1963 slaying of Jackson, MS, NAACP leader Medgar Evers (James Pickens, Jr.) by Byron De La Beckwith (James Woods), an unapologetic hatemonger who later goes free. A quarter-century later, a movement to reopen the case spurs the involvement of Jackson assistant d.a. Bobby DeLaughter (Alec Baldwin).

This being the Hollywood version, DeLaughter (pronounced "Delawter") is a morally far-seeing hero who takes up the cause out of the noblest of motives, while finding inspiration in the unwavering conviction of Evers's widow, Myrlie (Whoopi Goldberg).

Like other Northerners' clichéd visions of the South, Lewis Colick's screenplay has no use for African-Americans who aren't martyrs or rhetorical pawns. Pic's one unarguable asset is Woods's excellent work as Beckwith. The wily old racist ends up more sympathetic than director Rob Reiner and his collaborators might have wished.

1996: NOMINATIONS: Best Supp. Actor (James Woods), Makeup (Matthew W. Mungle, Deborah La Mia Denaver)

•

GHOST STORY
1981, 110 mins, US Ⓥ ⊙ col
Dir John Irvin *Prod* Burt Weissbourd *Scr* Lawrence D. Cohen *Ph* Jack Cardiff *Ed* Tom Rolf *Mus* Philippe Sarde *Art* Norman Newberry
Act Fred Astaire, Melvyn Douglas, Douglas Fairbanks, Jr., John Houseman, Craig Wasson, Alice Krige (Universal)

Authors like Peter Straub can take an essentially familiar spook story and make it work as a novel because of the solitary hold on the reader and ample time to embroider the details. But it's a real challenge to put the novel on screen where hundreds can share the flaws. Helped by solid casting, writer and director make a valiant effort but come up with isolated and excellent moments separated by artful but ordinary stretches.

Even without reading Straub's novel, it's easy to guess early on that Fred Astaire, Melvyn Douglas, Douglas Fairbanks, Jr., and John Houseman share a dark secret that has prompted the appearance of Alice Krige in both bodily (sometimes very bodily) and ethereal forms. And whatever that secret is, they're going to pay for it.

Unfortunately, it then spins backward to an extremely long re-enactment of the events of long ago. By the time it gets back to the present to deal with the haunting menace, the mood is all wrong and the story riddled with questions that aren't answered.

•

GIANT
1956, 198 mins, US Ⓥ ⊙ col
Dir George Stevens *Prod* George Stevens *Scr* Fred Guiol, Ivan Moffat *Ph* William C. Mellor *Ed* William Hornbeck *Mus* Dimitri Tiomkin *Art* Boris Leven
Act Elizabeth Taylor, Rock Hudson, James Dean, Carroll Baker, Mercedes McCambridge, Sal Mineo (Warner)

Producers George Stevens and Henry Ginsberg spent freely to capture the mood of the Edna Ferber novel and the picture is fairly saturated with the feeling of the vastness and the mental narrowness, the wealth and the poverty, the pride and the prejudice that make up Texas.

Trio of Elizabeth Taylor, Rock Hudson and James Dean turns in excellent portrayals, with each character moulded in a strongly individual vein. Carroll Baker, in her first important part, proves herself a most competent actress.

Story starts when Hudson, as Bick Benedict, comes to Maryland and marries Taylor, a beautiful and strong-willed girl, who is transplanted from the gentle green of her state to the dusty gray of Texas in the early twenties.

Jett, a ranchhand, played by James Dean, antagonistic to Hudson, finds oil on his little plot and realizes an ambition to become rich. At the start of World War II he convinces Hudson to allow oil drilling also on Hudson's ranch and the millions come flowing in. But money only intensifies Dean's bad characteristics.

Giant isn't preachy but it's a powerful indictment of the Texas superiority complex. In fact, the picture makes that point even stronger than it's in the book.

As the shiftless, envious, bitter ranchhand who hates society, Dean delivers an outstanding portrayal. It's a sock performance. Taylor turns in a surprisingly clever performance that registers up and down the line. Hudson achieves real stature.

1956: Best Director

NOMINATIONS: Best Picture, Actor (James Dean, Rock Hudson), Supp. Actress (Mercedes McCambridge), Adapted Screenplay, Color Costume Design, Color Art Direction, Editing, Scoring of a Dramatic Picture

•

GIARDINO DEI FINZI-CONTINI, IL
(THE GARDEN OF THE FINZI-CONTINIS)
1971, 103 mins, Italy/W. Germany Ⓥ ⊙ col
Dir Vittorio De Sica *Prod* Gianni Hecht Lucari, Arthur Cohn *Scr* Cesare Zavattini, Vittorio Bonicelli, Ugo Pirro, [Giorgio Bassani] *Ph* Ennio Guarnieri *Ed* Adriana Novelli *Mus* Manuel De Sica *Art* Giancarlo Bartolini Salimbeni, Maurizio Chiari
Act Dominique Sanda, Lino Capolicchio, Helmut Berger, Fabio Testi, Romolo Valli, Camillo Cesarei (Documento/CCC Filmkunst)

This Vittorio De Sica picture is stamped with the trademark of a master of the cinema. His pauses, as much as his actions; the leeway he gives to Ennio Guarnieri's superb camera; the self-confidence with which he develops a somewhat lazy story; his disdain for such b.o. sureties as violence and nudity, all point to the good taste and sure hand of a very mature director.

The story [from the novel by Giorgio Bassani] is built on several layers of a time-pyramid, with a base in the ominous quiet prior to World War II and the pinnacle in the deportation to the Nazi death camps of all the protagonists by the year 1943.

On top stands a Jewish family, the Finzi-Continis, immensely rich, cultured, aristocratic, in the beautiful and deceptively quiet Italian town, Ferrara. They hope, in vain, that the vulgarity of fascism will not penetrate into their ivory world. A middle-class Jewish family in the same town tries to beat the enemy by joining him.

Close to the top of the pyramid is the love story between Micol (Dominique Sanda), the daughter of the Finzi-Continis, and Giorgio (Lino Capolicchio), son of the bourgeois Jews. Micol chooses—for a purely physical affair—a virile communist, Malnate (Fabio Testi), the antithesis of everything which she was brought up with.

De Sica's son Manuel has written a traditional but powerful musical score and the photography, most of it done in Ferrara, is outstanding. The screenplay is well-motivated, sensitive and slow, the dialog terse and sparse and therefore telling.

1971: Best Foriegn Language Film

•

G.I. BLUES
1960, 115 mins, US Ⓥ col
Dir Norman Taurog *Prod* Hal B. Wallis *Scr* Edmund Beloin, Henry Garson *Ph* Loyal Griggs *Ed* Warren Low *Mus* Joseph J. Lilley (arr.) *Art* Hal Pereira, Walter Tyler
Act Elvis Presley, Juliet Prowse, Robert Ivers, Leticia Roman, James Douglas, Sigrid Maier (Paramount)

About the creakiest "book" in musicomedy annals has been revived by the scenarists as a framework within which Elvis Presley warbles 10 wobbly songs and costar Juliet Prowse steps out in a pair of flashy dances [staged by Charles O'Curran].

Plot casts Presley as an all-American-boy tank-gunner stationed in Germany who woos supposedly icy-hearted Prowse for what starts out as strictly mercenary reasons (if he spends the night with her, he wins a hunk of cash to help set up a nitery in the States). Needless to say, the ice melts and amour develops, only to dissolve when Prowse learns of the heely scheme.

Responsibility for penning the 10 tunes is given no one on Paramount's credit sheet. Considering the quality of these compositions, such anonymity is understandable. Joseph J. Lilley is credited with scoring and conducting music for the film. It is not absolutely clear whether he had a hand in composing the pop selections, but it is doubtful. Presley sings them all as a slightly subdued pelvis.

Prowse is a first-rate dancer and has a pixie charm reminiscent of Leslie Caron. She deserves better roles than this.

•

GIDEON OF SCOTLAND YARD
SEE: GIDEON'S DAY

•

GIDEON'S DAY
(US: GIDEON OF SCOTLAND YARD)
1958, 91 mins, UK col
Dir John Ford *Prod* Michael Killanin *Scr* T. E. B. Clarke *Ph* Frederick A. Young *Ed* Raymond Poulton *Mus* Douglas Gamley *Art* Ken Adam
Act Jack Hawkins, Dianne Foster, Anna Lee, Anna Massey, Cyril Cusack, Laurence Naismith (Columbia)

Screenwriter T. E. B. Clarke first earned applause for his police screenplay, *The Blue Lamp*. With his adaptation of J. J. Marric's novel, Clarke returns successfully to crime, with the spotlight on Scotland Yard.

This merely purports to be one busy day in the life of a CID chief inspector and it turns out to be quite a day. He accuses one of his sergeants of taking bribes. A pay snatch ties up with the killing of the sergeant in a hit-and-run car crash. A murder in Manchester has a maniac killer headed for London, and it all finishes up with a safe robbery which involves another slaying.

Jack Hawkins has played this type of role so often that he could probably do it blindfolded. And it is a tribute to him that he can hold the interest with such a run-of-the-mill character. He is also surrounded by some first-rate thesps who bring a touch of distinction to routine parts.

•

GIDGET
1959, 95 mins, US Ⓥ ⊙ ▭ col
Dir Paul Wendkos *Prod* Lewis J. Rachmil *Scr* Gabrielle Upton *Ph* Burnett Guffey *Ed* William A. Lyon *Mus* Morris Stoloff (sup.) *Art* Ross Bellah
Act Sandra Dee, Cliff Robertson, James Darren, Arthur O'Connell, Mary La Roche, Jo Morrow (Columbia)

Sandra Dee is the "gidget" of the title, being a young woman, so slight in stature she is tagged with a nickname which is a contraction of girl and midget. Dee is in that crucial period of growing up where she doesn't like boys very much but is beginning to realize they are going to play a big part in her life.

The screenplay, based on the novel by Frederick Kohner, is played mostly out-of-doors on the oceanfront west of Los Angeles that constitutes the playgrounds and mating grounds for the young of the area.

The simple plot is a contemporary restatement of the *Student Prince* theme. The surf bum who Dee falls in love with (James Darren), turns out to be the respectable son of a business acquaintance of her father.

Paul Wendkos's direction is ingenious in delineating the youthful characters, not so easy in presenting normal youngsters of no particular depth or variety. Direction could have been more fluid, however, particularly in the musical numbers.

Dee makes a pert and pretty heroine, and Cliff Robertson, as the only adult of the beach group, is acceptable. Darren is especially effective as the young man torn between the carefree life and the problems of growing up.

•

GIDGET GOES HAWAIIAN
1961, 101 mins, US Ⓥ col
Dir Paul Wendkos *Prod* Jerry Bresler *Scr* Ruth Brooks Flippen *Ph* Robert J. Bronner *Ed* William A. Lyon *Mus* George Duning *Art* Walter Holscher
Act James Darren, Michael Callan, Deborah Walley, Carl Reiner, Peggy Cass, Eddie Foy, Jr. (Bresler/Columbia)

Those who may have been surf-bored with the Sandra Dee starrer will find even less to cheer about in this follow-up. Fortunately, it is cast with fresh and promising young people; this, together with slick production, invigorating photography, insertion of a few musical breaks and several witty lines of dialog, should bail it out.

Screenplay takes Gidget (now played by Deborah Walley, whom the picture introduces), severs her from the romantic ties that bind her to boyfriend Jeff (James Darren) in California, and plants her in Hawaii, complete with parents and a gang of lads vying for her affection. Romantic complications ensue when Darren arrives on unscheduled flight, setting up a complicated situation of mix-ups and false accusations, chief antagonist being Abby (Vicki Trickett), a spoiled kind of Trader-vixen jealous of Gidget's instant popularity with the woo-woo brigade. It's all resolved in a rather flat finish.

Walley is cute as a button and displays a versatility not matched by the equally attractive Dee in the original. Her emoting is competent enough for the part. Darren is handsome as they come and a good singer, to boot. There are solid performances by Carl Reiner, New York's own Peggy Cass, Eddie Foy, Jr. and Jeff Donnell, although one wishes they had more elbow room to cut up (the film proves that adults are a lot more fun than kids, especially on a Hawaiian vacash).

•

GIFT, THE

2000, 110 mins, US Ⓥ ⦿ col

Dir Sam Raimi ***Prod*** James Jacks, Tom Rosenberg, Gary Lucchesi ***Scr*** Billy Bob Thornton, Tom Epperson ***Ph*** Jamie Anderson ***Ed*** Arthur Coburn, Bob Murawski ***Mus*** Christopher Young ***Art*** Neil Spisak

Act Cate Blanchett, Giovanni Ribisi, Keanu Reeves, Katie Holmes, Greg Kinnear, Hilary Swank (Lakeshore-Alphaville/Paramount Classics)

The Gift is a good, old-fashioned suspenser about a woman whose psychic powers get her involved in a murder case in the modern Gothic South. Putting his faith in a sturdy script and a fine cast led by the ever-remarkable Cate Blanchett, director Sam Raimi eschews trendy, overemphatic effects in favor of a straightforward approach that makes for a solid tale well told. A basis in credible human issues makes it engaging even if one has a predisposition against stories involving clairvoyance, ESP and the like.

Since her husband died, Annie Wilson (Blanchett) has helped support her three boys by doing psychic readings with cards and dispensing considered advice to townsfolk in her community. Annie runs into trouble when, after telling battered wife Valerie Barksdale (Hilary Swank) to get help, Valerie's violent redneck husband, Donnie (Keanu Reeves), warns Annie to mind her own business. A rare social outing throws Annie into the orbit of well-mannered school principal Wayne Collins (Greg Kinnear) and his hot little fiancée, Jessica King (Katie Holmes). Also in her circle is a mentally disturbed auto mechanic, Buddy Cole (Giovanni Ribisi).

Just as Donnie's threats assume truly menacing dimensions, Jessica goes missing, and the stumped cops are ultimately forced to ask Annie to apply her "hocus pocus" skills to the case. When Annie leads them to the pond on Donnie's land and Jessica's body is dredged up, all suspicions fall upon the local bad boy, who's put on trial for murder.

A great deal of attention has been paid to the emotional lives of nearly everyone with lines to say. Annie's telepathic powers are not invested with eerie dimensions in a cheap genre way, but are presented merely as a trait inherited from her grandmother; accordingly, Annie assumes a tentative and modest attitude toward them. Also helping to downplay standard-issue psychic/horror elements is Annie's realistically presented emotional life. She's a character of complexity and multiple emotional investments that Blanchett enhances with an impeccably subtle and nuanced performance, further proof of her extraordinary range.

Some surprising casting in the supporting roles pays off handsomely, particularly in the case of Reeves, who is terrifically effective as a mean and sexy predator. Swank registers vividly in her few scenes as the battered wife.

•

GIFT FROM HEAVEN, A

1994, 102 mins, US Ⓥ col

Dir Jack Lucarelli ***Prod*** Laurent Hatchwell ***Scr*** David Steen ***Ph*** Steve Yaconelli ***Ed*** Steve Mirkovich ***Mus*** Jean-Noel Chaleat ***Art*** Robert Varney

Act Sharon Farrell, Gigi Rice, David Steen, Sarah Trigger, Gene Lythgow, Mark Ruffalo)

Fine scripting and cohesive playing by a trio of female leads gives quality clout to *A Gift from Heaven*, an affecting, nuanced chamber drama of conflicting passions set in the North Carolina boonies in the '70s.

Story, originally written as a play by former actor David Steen, is almost entirely set in a remote backwoods dwelling that houses a middle-aged single mother (Sharon Farrell), her simple son, Charlie (Steen), from a union at age 12 with her evangelist uncle, and adopted daughter Messy (Gigi Rice). Arrival of pretty, naive Cousin Anna (Sarah Trigger), who's come to stay awhile following the death of her parents, sets off a string of sexual and emotional firecrackers that have smoldered for years.

There's enough emotional scarring and tangled passion here to fuel a couple of Tennessee Williams plays, but, to filmer's credit, the dramatic reins are kept so tightly controlled that character, rather than backwoods Greek tragedy, is the keynote.

Though set in North Carolina, the movie was totally shot in California, with no loss of credibility.

•

GIG, THE

1985, 92 mins, US Ⓥ col

Dir Frank D. Gilroy ***Prod*** Norman I. Cohen ***Scr*** Frank D. Gilroy ***Ph*** Jeri Sopanen ***Ed*** Rick Shaine ***Mus*** Warren Vache

Act Wayne Rogers, Cleavon Little, Andrew Duncan, Jerry Matz, Daniel Nalbach, Warren Vache (The Gig)

The Gig is a winning little film about a group of guys who try to fulfill their dream of being jazz players.

Wayne Rogers toplines as a New York businessman who has played Dixieland Jazz with his five pals for their own amusement once a week since 1970. He arranges a two-week pro engagement and talks the group into taking the step, the convincing argument being when their bass player George (Stan Lachow) drops out, promoting solidarity among the other five. The replacement bassist, veteran player Marshall Wilson (Cleavon Little), causes friction in the group, because of his unfriendly personality and condescending attitude towards the budding amateurs.

Filmmaker Gilroy gets maximum comic mileage out of this contrast, while making good points concerning the snobism and purist stance that pervades many jazz circles.

Aided by a very entertaining portrait of life at a Catskills resort, Rogers and Little make a solid team.

•

GIGI

1958, 116 mins, US Ⓥ ⦿ ▭ col

Dir Vincente Minnelli, [Charles Walters] ***Prod*** Arthur Freed ***Scr*** Alan Jay Lerner ***Ph*** Joseph Ruttenberg ***Ed*** Adrienne Fazan ***Mus*** Andre Previn (dir) ***Art*** Cecil Beaton

Act Leslie Caron, Maurice Chevalier, Louis Jourdan, Hermione Gingold, Eva Gabor, Jacques Bergerac (M-G-M)

Gigi is a naughty but nice romp of the hyper-romantic naughty '90s of Paris-in-the-spring, in the Bois, in Maxim's and in the boudoir. Alan Jay Lerner's libretto is tailor-made for an inspired casting job for all principals, and Fritz Loewe's tunes (to Lerner's lyrics) vie with and suggest their memorable *My Fair Lady* score.

Gigi is a French variation, by novelist Colette, of the *Pygmalion* legend. As the character unfolds it is apparent that the hoydenish Gigi has a greater preoccupation with a wedding ring than casual, albeit supercharged romance.

The sophistication of Maurice Chevalier (who well-nigh steals the picture), Isabel Jeans, Hermione Gingold and Eva Gabor are in contrast to the wholesomeness of the Leslie Caron-Louis Jourdan romance. Caron is completely captivating and convincing in the title role.

Produced in France, *Gigi* is steeped in authentic backgrounds from Maxim's to the Tuileries, from the Bois de Boulogne to the Palais de Glace which sets the scene for Gabor's philandering with Jacques Bergerac, her skating instructor, and establishes the pattern of playing musical boudoirs, which was par for the circa 1890s Paris course.

The performances are well nigh faultless. From Chevalier, as the sophisticated uncle, to John Abbott, his equally suave valet; from Gingold's understanding role as Gigi's grandma to Isabel Jeans, the worldly aunt who could tutor Gigi in the ways of demi-mondaine love; from Jourdan's eligibility as the swain to Bergerac's casual courting of light ladies' loves. Caron's London experience in the stage version of Colette's cocotte (Audrey Hepburn did it in the U.S.) stands her in excellent stead.

1958: Best Picture, Director, Adapted Screenplay, Color Cinematography, Art Direction, Song ("Gigi"), Scoring of a Musical Picture, Editing, Costume Design

•

G.I. JANE

1997, 124 mins, US Ⓥ ⦿ ▭ col

Dir Ridley Scott ***Prod*** Roger Birnbaum, Demi Moore, Suzanne Todd ***Scr*** David Twohy, Danielle Alexandra ***Ph*** Hugh Johnson ***Ed*** Pietro Scalia ***Mus*** Trevor Jones ***Art*** Arthur Max

Act Demi Moore, Viggo Mortensen, Anne Bancroft, Jason Beghe, Scott Wilson, Lucinda Jenney (Scott Free/Moving Pictures/Hollywood)

A bracingly gung-ho film for a nonmilitary-minded time, *G.I. Jane* is a very entertaining get-tough fantasy with political and feminist underpinnings. Far from being *Private Benjamin*, this is more like *Flashdance* in fatigues.

Lt. Jordan O'Neil (Demi Moore), a naval intelligence officer who happens to be in pretty great shape, leaves behind her fellow officer and boyfriend (Jason Beghe) and heads for a Navy SEALs training camp in Florida, where she is quickly plunged into Hell Week, an astonishingly grueling series of physical ordeals. When she realizes she is quietly being cut extra slack in some areas, she demands the same full dose of punishment, even shaving her hair down and moving into the men's barracks.

Clearly interested in doing her no favors is the Command Master Chief (Viggo Mortensen), a tough taskmaster whose job it is to get in everyone's face. Just as O'Neil makes it through Hell Week and is sent off as the leader of a simulated commando mission, things become more complicated when it appears that back in Washington Sen. DeHaven (Anne Bancroft) isn't at all sincere about wanting her handpicked guinea pig to make it through training.

Pic [from a screen story by Danielle Alexandra] is as hard, polished and powerfully functional as a newly cleaned gun. Dialogue scenes are highly compressed, and the emphasis on military jargon makes for some extremely colorful exchanges. O'Neil's rejoinder to the Master Chief upon being told to find a life somewhere else ["Suck my dick!"] is bound to become a classic.

Moore makes the exertion of O'Neil's will, and body, entirely believable, and only the musicvideo-style shots of her feverishly doing one-armed push-ups smack of star ego and trendy body fetishizing. Doing his best to steal the film, however, is Mortensen, terrific as the Master Chief who brings everyone to the brink.

[Pic's original main title, showing O'Neil luge training, was included on 1998 videodisc versions, though not the film's preview ending, in which she is killed in the final scenes.]

•

GILDA

1946, 110 mins, US Ⓥ ⦿ b/w

Dir Charles Vidor ***Prod*** Virginia Van Upp ***Scr*** Marion Parsonnet ***Ph*** Rudolph Mate ***Ed*** Charles Nelson ***Mus*** Morris Stoloff, Marlin Skiles (dir.) ***Art*** Stephen Goosson, Van Nest Polglase

Act Rita Hayworth, Glenn Ford, George Macready, Joseph Calleia, Steven Geray, Joe Sawyer (Columbia)

Practically all the s.a. habiliments of the femme fatale have been mustered for *Gilda*, and when things get trite and frequently far-fetched, somehow, at the drop of a shoulder strap, there is always Rita Hayworth to excite the filmgoer.

The story [by E. A. Ellington, adapted by Jo Eisinger] is a confusion of gambling, international intrigue and a triangle that links two gamblers and the wife of one of them. The setting is Buenos Aires. Sneaking in somehow is the subplot of a tungsten cartel operated by the husband, who also runs a swank gambling casino. A couple of Nazis are thrown in also. Hayworth is photographed most beguilingly. The producers have created nothing subtle in the projection of her s.a., and that's probably been wise. Glenn Ford is the vis-a-vis, in his first picture part in several years.

There are a couple of songs ostensibly sung by Hayworth, and one of them, "Put the Blame on Mame," piques the interest because of its intriguing, low-down quality.

Gilda is obviously an expensive production—and shows it. The direction is static, but that's more the fault of the writers.

•

GILDED LILY, THE

1935, 85 mins, US b/w

Dir Wesley Ruggles ***Prod*** Albert Lewis ***Scr*** Claude Binyon, Melville Baker, Jack Kirkland ***Ph*** Victor Milner ***Ed*** Otho Lovering

Act Claudette Colbert, Fred MacMurray, Ray Milland, C. Aubrey Smith, Luis Alberni, Donald Meek (Paramount)

Breezy romance, with plenty of entertainment. Fred MacMurray and Ray Milland love the girl, the one as a matter-of-fact mug, the other as a semi-cad son of an English duke. Claudette Colbert is idealistic and romantic and falls for the Briton, but rebounds for the clinch into the arms of the unembossed Yankee.

More incredible portions of the story are artfully dressed up with gags and dialog by Claude Binyon and slipped through deftly by director Wesley Ruggles so that no opportunities to notice the fictional liberties develop.

Adaptation is from a yarn by Melville Baker and Jack Kirkland. Its basic theme is of a working miss in the U.S., who is catapulted into international fame as the "no" girl who jilted an English lord.

•

GIMME SHELTER

1970, 90 mins, US Ⓥ col

Dir David Maysles, Albert Maysles, Charlotte Zwerin ***Prod*** Porter Bibb ***Ed*** Ellen Gifford, Robert Farren, Joanne Burke,

Kent McKinney, Mirra Bank, Susan Steinberg, Janet Laurentano (Maysles)

Maysles Brothers' 16mm documentary on 1969 Rolling Stones's U.S. concert tour which culminated in violence and death at the Altamont Speedway in California.

What precedes the satanic finale is a riveting close-up look at the Stones in performance. Contrary to the popular image, lead singer Mick Jagger emerges in off-stage footage as a withdrawn, almost catatonic individual totally involved in his music and virtually immune to events occurring around him.

Onstage it's another matter, and *Gimme Shelter* captures that petulant omnisexuality that made many adults consider Jagger a threat to their daughters, sons and household pets alike. Pouting and bumping through such numbers as "I Can't Get No Satisfaction," he is seldom less than mesmerizing.

●

GINGERBREAD MAN, THE
1998, 115, US Ⓥ ⦿ col
Dir Robert Altman ***Prod*** Jeremy Tannenbaum ***Scr*** Al Hayes ***Ph*** Gu Changwei ***Ed*** Geraldine Peroni ***Mus*** Mark Isham ***Art*** Stephen Altman
Act Kenneth Branagh, Embeth Davidtz, Robert Downey, Jr., Daryl Hannah, Tom Berenger, Famke Janssen (Island/Enchanter/PolyGram)

Pic is an adequate thriller [from an original story by John Grisham] that reveals an adventurous filmmaker working obediently within conventional material. Engaging enough through its first hour, this tale of deceit, manipulation, misguided lust, kidnapping and murder down South goes astray with an excess of melodramatic implausibility as the climax approaches.

Brimming with neurotic, deeply flawed characters, story differs from the usual Grisham scenario in that it does not pivot on a bright, idealistic attorney taking on the establishment.

Savannah lawyer Rick Magruder (Kenneth Branagh) is celebrating a court victory. Crucially present are three beautiful women of past, present and future importance: exwife Leeanne (Famke Janssen), with whom he has two children; Lois (Daryl Hannah), his law partner and close friend; and Mallory Doss (Embeth Davidtz), a fidgety member of the catering staff.

After a drunken one-night stand, Rick learns that Mallory's nut-case father (Robert Duvall) seems to have started threatening her again. He puts the weight of his law firm behind her, has Dixon picked up by police, and subpoenas her belligerent ex-husband (Tom Berenger) to testify against the crazy old coot in court. Dixon is put away, but, escapes from the asylum, whereupon the lives of everyone who conspired against him are put into severe jeopardy.

Grisham's scenario, which was reportedly rewritten sufficiently by Altman to result in the pseudonymous sreenwriting credit "Al Hayes," thrusts the story forward on an increasingly narrow track. There is a trumped-up quality to the action climaxes that is perfunctory, and the final revelation is unsurprising.

Brandishing an OK southern accent, Branagh is convincing. Davidtz has a disturbingly haunted, raw-nerve-endings quality. Robert Downey, Jr., enlivens the proceedings whenever his private dick character turns up.

●

GIRL CAN'T HELP IT, THE
1956, 96 mins, US Ⓥ ▭ col
Dir Frank Tashlin ***Prod*** Frank Tashlin ***Scr*** Frank Tashlin, Herbert Baker ***Ph*** Leon Shamroy ***Ed*** James B. Clark ***Mus*** Lionel Newman (sup.) ***Art*** Lyle R. Wheeler, Leland Fuller
Act Tom Ewell, Jayne Mansfield, Edmond O'Brien, Henry Jones, John Emery, Juanita Moore (20th Century-Fox)

The Girl Can't Help It is an hilarious comedy with a beat. On the surface, it appears that producer-director-scripter Frank Tashlin concentrated on creating fun for the juniors—a chore that he completes to a tee. However, the suspicion lurks that he also poked some fun at the dance beat craze. There are so many sight gags and physical bits of business, including Jayne Mansfield and a couple of milk bottles, that males of any age will get the entertainment message.

Mansfield doesn't disappoint as the sexpot who just wants to be a successful wife and mother, not a glamor queen. She's physically equipped for the role, and also is competent in sparking considerable of the fun. Nature was so much more bountiful with her than with Marilyn Monroe that it seems Mansfield should have left MM with her voice. However, the vocal imitation could have been just another part of the fun-poking indulged in.

Edmond O'Brien, rarely seen in comedy, is completely delightful as the hammy ex-gangster who thinks his position demands that his girl be a star name. Tom Ewell scores mightily as the has-been agent who is haunted by the memory of Julie London, another girl he had pushed to reluctant stardom.

●

GIRL CRAZY
1943, 97 mins, US Ⓥ ⦿ b/w
Dir Norman Taurog, Busby Berkeley ***Prod*** Arthur Freed ***Scr*** Fred Finklehoffe ***Ph*** William Daniels, Robert Plancke ***Ed*** Albert Akst ***Mus*** George Gershwin
Act Mickey Rooney, Judy Garland, June Allyson, Nancy Walker, Gil Stratton, Rags Ragland (M-G-M)

This is the second film treatment of the 1930 stage click *Girl Crazy*, the first being an RKO "B" starring Wheeler and Woolsey, with all of the crack tunes tossed out at that time except "I Got Rhythm."

Judy Garland is in the role originally played by Ginger Rogers on the stage, while Nancy Walker, new to the screen in *Best Foot Forward*, is in a semblance of Ethel Merman's part. But all the double entendre is tossed out with the locale switched from a dude ranch to a western university. It's to the latter that a N.Y. newspaper publisher sends his playboy son (Mickey Rooney). Rooney puts the university on its financial feet and makes it coeducational. The girls he attracts are plenty and pretty.

The story thread is light, but enough to string together the George and Ira Gershwin songs, i.e., "Embraceable You," "Treat Me Rough," "Bidin' My Time," "Could You Use Me" and "Not for Me."

Garland is a nifty saleswoman of the numbers right down to the over-produced "Rhythm" finale which was Busby Berkeley's special chore.

●

GIRLFRIENDS, THE
SEE: LES BICHES

●

GIRLFRIENDS
1978, 86 mins, US Ⓥ col
Dir Claudia Weill ***Prod*** Claudia Weill, Jan Sanders ***Scr*** Vicki Polon ***Ph*** Fred Murphy ***Ed*** Suzanne Pettit ***Mus*** Michael Small ***Art*** Patrizia von Brandenstein
Act Melanie Mayron, Eli Wallach, Anita Skinner, Bob Balaban, Christopher Guest, Viveca Lindfors (Cyclops)

This is a warm, emotional and at times wise picture about friendship. It's documentary film-maker Claudia Weill's first feature, although there's no reason to apologetically pigeonhole this movie as a "promising first feature." It's the work of a technically skilled and assured director.

Melanie Mayron is outstanding as a photographer fresh out of college maturing under the strains of professional insecurity and loneliness. Down the line Weill has extracted first-rate performances. Anita Skinner is Mayron's best friend and until she suddenly marries Christopher Guest, her roommate. Eli Wallach portrays a rabbi and almost paramor for whom Mayron sometimes photographs Bar Mitzvahs and weddings. Bob Balaban is Mayron's slightly off center boyfriend and Viveca Lindfors is Beatrice, owner of a Greenwich Village gallery who believes in Mayron and gives her a big break.

Each performance is a little gem and so are the characters developed by Vicki Polon from a story by her and Weill. They look and act like people, which is a relief. There are no false touches of glamour.

●

GIRL FROM TENTH AVENUE, THE
1935, 69 mins, US b/w
Dir Alfred E. Green ***Prod*** Robert Lord ***Scr*** Charles Kenyon ***Ph*** James Van Trees ***Ed*** Owen Marks
Act Bette Davis, Ian Hunter, Colin Clive, Alison Skipworth, John Eldredge, Philip Reed (First National/Warner)

Bette Davis's first starring venture allows her to go high, wide and handsome on the emotions. She takes 'em all in a stride that saves the yarn from dying by its own befuddlement.

Girl from Tenth Avenue is fashioned from a pattern whose every turn and twist the dullest fan can easily anticipate. A weak sister of the social set is tossed over by his Park Avenue girl friend for a guy with a better social position and more coin. The disappointed swain tries to boil his disappointment in alcohol and the girl from 10th Avenue gets him on the rebound. While both are stewed, a justice of the peace, roused out of his sleep at 4 A.M., turns the trick. In time the Park Avenue Jane realizes her mistake and goes on the make for the old heart ailment.

Complications follow, with a verbal clash between the two dames and a newspaper account of the incident precipitating a break between the 10th Avenue girl and her society spouse.

Narrative is chockful of implausible sequences and the plot [from the play by Hubert Henry Davies] often gets itself into blind alleys. But deft direction plus smooth trouping by Davis make these defects not too noticeable for the average fan.

●

GIRL-GETTERS, THE
SEE: THE SYSTEM

●

GIRL HUNTERS, THE
1963, 103 mins, UK Ⓥ ▭ b/w
Dir Roy Rowland ***Prod*** Robert Fellows ***Scr*** Mickey Spillane, Roy Rowland, Robert Fellows ***Ph*** Ken Talbot ***Ed*** Sidney Stone ***Mus*** Phil Green ***Art*** Tony Inglis
Act Mickey Spillane, Shirley Eaton, Lloyd Nolan, Hy Gardner, Scott Peters (Fellane)

A slick and entertaining adventure meller, *The Girl Hunters* also debuts author Mickey Spillane portraying his rough 'n' tumble hero Mike Hammer for the first time on the screen. He turns in a credible job.

Plot finds the private eye in the gutter from seven years of boozing and fretting because he believes that he sent his secretary and best gal to her doom when he gave her an assignment to do. It develops, however, that she may still be alive and Hammer straightens out and goes in search of her "just like the old days," as one of the characters comments. Along the line, he finds himself in a romantic entanglement with one of his prime info sources, played cooly and with seductive restraint by Shirley Eaton who spends much of her time in the film wearing just a bikini.

Scott Peters is police captain Pat Chambers. The actor puts plenty of bite into the role but sometimes tends to overplay his obvious distaste for his ex-chum.

As a federal agent who's also interested in the case which has the foreign intrigue element of the murder of a U.S. Senator which is linked to an international Commie plot, Lloyd Nolan turns in a pro and reliable job.

Pic was lensed in London but considerable care is taken to preserve Gotham locales where the action takes place. Several fave watering spots around town like Al & Dicks and the Blue Ribbon have been faithfully reproduced by art director Tony Inglis.

●

GIRL IN A SWING, THE
1988, 117 mins, US Ⓥ ⦿ col
Dir Gordon Hessler ***Prod*** Just Betzer ***Scr*** Gordon Hessler ***Ph*** Claus Loof ***Ed*** Robert Gordon ***Mus*** Carl Davis ***Art*** Rob Schilling
Act Meg Tilly, Rupert Frazer, Nicholas Le Prevost, Elspet Gray, Lorna Heilbron, Lynsey Baxter (Panorama)

British writer-director Gordon Hessler has turned Richard Adams's 1980 psycho-chiller novel *The Girl in a Swing* into a smooth, fine-looking piece of romantic-erotic entertainment with many a fine Hitchcockian touch and a rather special star turn by Meg Tilly. In Adams's novel, the story is wordy and obscure. Hessler introduces a direct cause-and-effect explanation of heroine Karin Foster's (Tilly) death wish. This keeps her from finding lasting happiness with Alan (Rupert Frazer), a shy British ceramics teacher.

During their brief Florida honeymoon Karin's feelings of guilt and Alan's premonitions of disaster mount. They seek solace in their joy of sex.

When she succeeds in finding, and buying for next to nothing, a third example of the porcelain rarity "The Girl in the Swing," they are assured of instant wealth, and Karin tries to take Holy Communion from a vicar friend to make a clean break with the past. Instead of absolution, Karin finds fear and guilt taking full possession of her, while Alan indulges her.

The recurring theme of guilt, atonement and punishment is gently explored during the development of suspense. Tilly, in spite of a contrived Teutonic accent, is wholly convincing whether expressing sexual abandon, poetic frailty or fear-striken despair.

●

GIRL IN EVERY PORT, A
1928, 64 mins, US Ⓥ b/w
Dir Howard Hawks ***Prod*** William Fox ***Scr*** Seton I. Miller, Reginald Morris, James K. McGuinness, Howard Hawks, Malcolm Stuart Boylan ***Ph*** William O'Connell, R. J. Berquist ***Ed*** Ralph Dixon ***Art*** William S. Darling
Act Victor McLaglen, Robert Armstrong, Louise Brooks, Maria Casajuana, Sally Rand, Francis MacDonald (Fox)

The plot deals with a Damon and Pythias friendship between two rough and tumble seamen. *A Girl in Every Port* is packed with sex, but has no romance; it has a dozen ingenues and no heroine. Of all the beautiful bimbos encountered by the sailors in their world travels not one is on the up-and-up, and the one (Louise Brooks) who inspires Victor McLaglen to daydream over settling down in a cottage for two is the biggest golddigger of all.

The picture is a series of hoke adventures with dames and gendarmes. It holds a lot of laughs and still maintains a human note on the comrade angle. McLaglen is great as the heavy hitting bozo. His buddy is played by Robert Armstrong, legit actor, newly recruited to the screen.

Malcolm Stuart Boylan's titles seem involved and obscure on several occasions. Howard Hawks makes a good job of directing with the exception of an overdone bit of melodramatic acting by McLaglen upon the discovery of what he supposes to be the perfidy of his buddy.

•

GIRL IN EVERY PORT, A

1951, 86 mins, US Ⓥ ⦿ b/w

Dir Chester Erskine ***Prod*** Irwin Allen ***Scr*** Chester Erskine ***Ph*** Nicholas Musuraca ***Ed*** Ralph Dawson ***Mus*** Roy Webb

Act Groucho Marx, Marie Wilson, William Bendix, Don DeFore, Gene Lockhart, Dee Hartford (RKO)

Mirth sparkers are Groucho Marx, Marie Wilson and William Bendix, and the zany plot is nicely paced to keep it on an okay fun level.

Chester Erskine scripted and directed the story [from *They Sell Sailors Elephants* by Frederick Hazlitt Brennan] about two sailors who, during their 20 years of service, have spent plenty of time in the brig for escapades. As plot opens Marx and Bendix are again in hot water, the latter having taken a small inheritance and purchased a broken-down racehorse. Marx is detailed to return the horse and recoup Bendix's money, but the seller (Don DeFore), has broken up his stable at the behest of his fiancée (Dee Hartford). Wilson, a gorgeous carhop, enters the plot when boys discover she owns the twin of their horse and it is sound of limb.

Some race-rigging and plenty of other shenanigans crowd the footage. Marx's wisecracking dialog and antics help the pace. Wilson, less of the dumb Dora than usual, shows to advantage, and Bendix comes over excellently.

•

GIRL, INTERRUPTED

1999, 127 mins, US Ⓥ ⦿ col

Dir James Mangold ***Prod*** Douglas Wick, Cathy Konrad ***Scr*** James Mangold, Lisa Loomer, Anna Hamilton Phelan ***Ph*** Jack Green ***Ed*** Kevin Tent ***Mus*** Mychael Danna ***Art*** Richard Hoover

Act Winona Ryder, Angelina Jolie, Clea Duvall, Brittany Murphy, Elisabeth Moss, Jared Leto (Red Wagon/Columbia)

Veering from the serious to the trivial and from the clinical to the lurid, James Mangold's *Girl, Interrupted* is a middling film that only partially conveys the spirit of its source material, Susanna Kaysen's memoir of her experience at a mental hospital in the late '60s. Hooks are a solid central performance by Winona Ryder and a captivating wild turn by Angelina Jolie in the yarn's flashiest role.

Confused, insecure and baffled by the rapidly changing mores of American society in 1967–68, Susanna (Ryder) appears to be like many other adolescents. Her doctor diagnoses borderline personality disorder, and recommends institutionalization at Claymoore Hospital. Once Susanna lands at the asylum, the story toes a more conventional path.

The clique of eccentrics includes Lisa (Jolie), a charming sociopath who has spent years in the hospital; Daisy (Brittany Murphy), a pampered Daddy's girl; and the sensitive Polly (Elisabeth Moss), whose scarred face offers a sharp contrast to her sensitive heart.

As expected in such tales, there's a benevolent, nononsense nurse, Valerie (Whoopi Goldberg), who befriends Susanna. Vanessa Redgrave shows up in three scenes as head psychiatrist Dr. Wick, whose sessions with Susanna touch upon some of the film's most fascinating issues. Film doesn't bother to explain its title, which is taken from a Vermeer painting, *Girl Interrupted at Her Music*.

Ryder is credibly cast as the rich, spoiled and confused girl. Stealing every scene she's in, Jolie is excellent as the flamboyant, irresponsible girl who turns out to be far more instrumental than the doctors in Susanna's rehabilitation. Production values are unadorned.

1999: Best Supp. Actress (Angelina Jolie)

•

GIRL IN THE CADILLAC

1995, 89 mins, US Ⓥ col

Dir Lucas Platt ***Prod*** Thomas Baer ***Scr*** John Warren ***Ph*** Nancy Schreiber ***Ed*** Norman Hollyn ***Mus*** Anton Sanko ***Art*** Pamela Marcotte

Act Erika Eleniak, William McNamara, Michael Lerner, Bud Cort, Valerie Perrine, Ed Lauter (Steinhardt Baer)

Two terrifically appealing performers, William McNamara and Erika Eleniak, occupy the center of *The Girl in the Cadillac*, an amiable, if also slight and derivative, variation on the perennial theme of "love on the run." Pic is loosely adapted from a depression era James M. Cain novella [*The Enchanted Isle*].

Mandy Baker (Eleniak) is a 17-year-old free spirit seeking adventure that will liberate her from an unfulfilling life in the suffocating small town of Paint Rock, Texas, where she lives with her mother Tilly (Valerie Perrine). At the bus station, setting out for Corpus Cristi, Mandy meets Rick Davis (McNamara), a handsome if somewhat arrogant cowboy.

In Utopia, Rick introduces Mandy to his "Uncle" Pal (Michael Lerner), a failed crook, and Bud (Bud Cort), his wierd sidekick. It doesn't take long before Mandy is convinced into participating in a bank robbery for a tidy sum of $5,000. When the heist turns into a fiasco, Rick and Mandy manage to escape with all the loot, but Pal and Bud follow in hot pursuit.

Pic's central—and best—episodes are those describing the delirious couple on a shopping spree, checking in at a lush hotel, buying a red convertible Cadillac. Problem is that writer John Warren lacks a clear conception of his characters and, worse, doesn't know how to end his tale.

Though looking older than 17, Eleniak acquits herself with a convincing performance. Ultimately, though the film's revelation is McNamara, who sparkles, keeping the movie afloat even in its weaker moments. McNamara and Eleniak were first paired in 1994's *Chasers*.

•

GIRL IN THE NEWS, THE

1940, 77 mins, UK b/w

Dir Carol Reed ***Prod*** Maurice Ostrer, Edward Black ***Scr*** Sidney Gilliat ***Ph*** Otto Kanturek ***Ed*** R.E. Dearling ***Mus*** Louis Levy

Act Margaret Lockwood, Barry K. Barnes, Emlyn Williams, Roger Livesey, Basil Radford (20th Century-Fox)

The Girl in the News [from a novel by Roy Vickers] contains the same distinctive quality of suspenseful melodramatic action as distinguishes *Night Train* and has the benefit of some of its excellent players, including Margaret Lockwood and Basil Radford. Screenplay is by Sidney Gilliat, who did the scripts also for *Night Train* and *The Lady Vanishes*. There the comparisons end, and *The Girl in the News* veers away from the British secret service and becomes a case of murder mystery for Scotland Yard attention.

It is the clever directorial and script twists which make the film unusually entertaining. Carol Reed has a disarming faculty of employing bits of comedy as a means of revealing important plot incidents. His character actors are carefully chosen and his murder trial scene is conducted with the rigid dignity of a British court.

Emlyn Williams, in a villainous role, gets across the murderous type which he used in the stage version of *Night Must Fall*. Lockwood is a registered nurse who escapes from under an almost perfect net of circumstantial evidence.

•

GIRL NAMED TAMIKO, A

1962, 110 mins, US ▭ col

Dir John Sturges ***Prod*** Hal Wallis ***Scr*** Edward Anhalt ***Ph*** Charles Lang, Jr. ***Ed*** Warren Low ***Mus*** Elmer Bernstein ***Art*** Hal Pereira, Walter Tyler

Act Laurence Harvey, France Nuyen, Martha Hyer, Gary Merrill, Michael Wilding, Miyoshi Umeki (Paramount)

This has its share of shortcomings; there's now and again a bit of fuzziness in character development and plot detail. But these may well be overlooked, for the story of emotional conflicts in modern day Japan is a fairly arresting work.

Laurence Harvey's character is not one immediately easy to accept and this is one of the flaws. As Ivan Kalin, he's a Chinese-Russian photographer and looks, speaks and romances like a British matinee idol. The girl of the title is France Nuyen, thoroughly enchanting as the librarian whose family adheres to the Japanese traditions while she breaks away to engage in the romance with Harvey. Martha Hyer, as an American girl, very much on the loose in flitting from man to man, handles the part fittingly.

Gary Merrill fits in as a brooding business man who cares and yearns for Hyer only to have her walk out on him. Michael Wilding is a British art dealer with a distaste for the devious measures taken by Harvey in order to get his much wanted visa to go to the United States. Miyoshi Umeki is a cutie who does the cohabitat bit with Wilding. These two make for a colorful pair and their East-West mating game is rendered plausibly.

•

GIRL OF THE GOLDEN WEST, THE

1938, 120 mins, US Ⓥ b/w

Dir Robert Z. Leonard ***Prod*** William Anthony McGuire ***Scr*** Isabel Dawn, Boyce DeGaw ***Ph*** Oliver T. Marsh ***Ed*** W. Donn Hayes ***Mus*** Sigmund Romberg ***Art*** Cedric Gibbons

Act Jeanette MacDonald, Nelson Eddy, Walter Pidgeon, Leo Carrillo, Buddy Ebsen, Leonard Penn (M-G-M)

This musical mustanger with Jeanette MacDonald and Nelson Eddy finds the stars not only out of their element, but hemmed in by a two hour melange of the great outdoors, Mexican bandits, early Spanish-Californian atmosphere and musical boredom. It's 45 minutes before the stellar pair meet up for the first time, and half as long before MacDonald makes her first appearance.

The Girl of the Golden West is from an old David Belasco play, authored and produced by him in 1905.

MacDonald is rarely convincing as The Girl who runs the mining town's lone saloon, and Nelson Eddy is a cream-puff Mexican bad man. Walter Pidgeon as the lovesick sheriff is another miss-out.

Sigmund Romberg score allows for but two duets by the stars, "Who Are We to Say?" and "Dance with Me, My Love," a sort of tango ballad. "Mariachie" is the sock production number, quite well done in the governor's Spanish courtyard as part of the annual rancho fiesta.

•

GIRL ON A MOTORCYCLE, THE
(AKA: NAKED UNDER LEATHER)

1968, 91 mins, UK/France Ⓥ col

Dir Jack Cardiff ***Prod*** William Sassoon ***Scr*** Ronald Duncan, Jack Cardiff ***Ph*** Jack Cardiff, Rene Guissart ***Ed*** Peter Musgrave ***Mus*** Les Reed ***Art*** Russell Hagg, Jean D'Eaubonne

Act Alain Delon, Marianne Faithful, Roger Mutton, Marius Goring, Catherine Jourdan, Jean Leduc (Mid Atlantic/Ares)

A pretty young girl in a leather formfitting getup covering her nudity rides a powerful motorcycle towards her lover after creeping out of her young husband's bed. Her ride is studded with flashbacks and even flash forwards and psychedelic inserts of torrid lovemaking. The ride gets a bit long and the film lacks a true erotic flair. But it is well lensed and has a shattering finale.

The motorcycle is a present from her lover and is supposed to be an erotic symbol. But treatment [of the 1963 novel *La Motocyclette* by Andre Pieyre de Mandiargues] can rarely give the fiery dash needed to make this acceptable except in the girl's final mixing of metaphors as she literally makes love to the bike.

Marianne Faithful [whose dialogue is revoiced by an uncredited actress] appears a bit too showy and on the surface as the girl and uses facile facial expressions rather than being able to project the girl's feelings. Alain Delon is a sort of hedonistic young college don who does not believe in love in a romantic sense and is mad about motorcycles.

•

GIRLS ABOUT TOWN

1931, 80 mins, US b/w

Dir George Cukor ***Scr*** Raymond Griffith, Brian Marlow ***Ph*** Ernest Haller

Act Kay Francis, Joel McCrea, Lilyan Tashman, Eugene Pallette, Alan Dinehart, Lucille Gleason (Paramount)

There's an unwitting punch scene in this picture to draw laughter. It's where Kay Francis shows off her figure in undies while explaining she's through with the gold-digger racket and intends going straight because she's found love with a rich rube.

When Francis falls for a young-looking sucker from a hick town the burn is on. She's the dame with a twisted virtue. Only the boy friend would rather marry her than take her unawares even if she's willing.

There's some additional sentiment brought in between the elder of the two chumps, as played ingenuously by Eugene Pallette, and his middle-aged wife, as done by Lucile Gleason. He's a tightwad and practical joker from Lansing. With the help of Lilyan Tashman, who does the gold-digger role as natural as it can seem, the bird's wife works the old boy into a mad spree of jewelry buying.

•

GIRLS! GIRLS! GIRLS!

1962, 101 mins, US Ⓥ col

Dir Norman Taurog ***Prod*** Hal B. Wallis ***Scr*** Edward Anhalt, Allan Weiss ***Ph*** Loyal Griggs ***Ed*** Warren Low, Stanley Johnson ***Mus*** Joseph J. Lilley ***Art*** Hal Pereira, Walter Tyler

Act Elvis Presley, Stella Stevens, Jeremy Slate, Laurel Goodwin, Benson Fong, Robert Strauss (Paramount)

Girls! Girls! Girls! is just that—with Elvis Presley there as the main attraction. Hal Wallis's production puts the entertainer back into the nondramatic, purely escapist, light musical vein. The thin plot, scripted by Edward Anhalt and Allan Weiss from an original story by Weiss, has him the romantic interest of two girls. Hackneyed tale is of poor boy fisherman who meets rich girl who doesn't tell him she is rich but who, naturally, falls in love with him.

Weiss also penned story for the earlier *Blue Hawaii*, which Norman Taurog also directed for Wallis.

Most striking thing about the picture is the introduction of new Paramount pactee Laurel Goodwin, who makes an auspicious film bow. The youngster has the cute, home spun potential of a Doris Day.

Stella Stevens, however, is wasted in a standard role as a sultry torch singer who has given up ever really nailing the guy. She does her best but, aside from singing three songs (her first singing in a film) in a style suitable for the character, there just isn't enough for her to do.

•

GIRLS HE LEFT BEHIND, THE
SEE: THE GANG'S ALL HERE

•

GIRLS IN UNIFORM
SEE: MAEDCHEN IN UNIFORM

•

GIRL 6
1996, 107 mins, US Ⓥ ⊙ col
Dir Spike Lee *Prod* Spike Lee *Scr* Suzan-Lori Parks *Ph* Malik Hassan Sayeed *Ed* Sam Pollard *Mus* Prince *Art* Ina Mayhew
Act Theresa Randle, Isaiah Washington, Spike Lee, Jenifer Lewis, Debi Mazar, Quentin Tarantino (40 Acres & a Mule/20th Century-Fox)

Like the lead character's name, *Girl 6* largely remains a cipher. Despite an intriguing premise and an appealing lead performance by Theresa Randle, Spike Lee's modestly scaled look at a young actress who becomes hooked on her job as a phone sex operator crucially lacks narrative momentum and psychological depth. Pic is Lee's first on which he receives no writing credit.

Interludes detailing her indoctrination into the world of this thriving business, presided over in the comforting manner of a no-nonsense but mother hen–like madam named Lil (the wonderful Jenifer Lewis), and her acceptance by the other women there, exert an undeniable fascination. More significantly, she soon not only becomes awfully good at "phone bone," but actually gets to like it. A lot.

Along the way, Girl 6 is persistently pursued by her ex (Isaiah Washington), a rather shifty shoplifter, and is challenged about her lifestyle by her neighbor, Jimmy (Lee), a baseball card collector. The men are seen in diverse locations in footage that was shot in Hi-Def, giving it a deliberately rougher, more electronic look than the otherwise lushly appointed visuals. But all of these diversions can't disguise the lack of a strong story.

Debi Mazar and Naomi Campbell stand out among the great, mutually supportive ladies. Madonna, done up like an old tart, is in briefly as the head of a more hardcore phone service.

•

GIRLS TOWN
1996, 88 mins, US Ⓥ ⊙ col
Dir Jim McKay *Prod* Lauren Zalaznick *Scr* Jim McKay, Anna Grace, Brucklin Harris, Lili Taylor, Denise Hernandez *Ph* Russell Fine *Ed* Jim McKay, Alex Hall *Art* David Doernberg
Act Lili Taylor, Anna Grace, Brucklin Harris, Aunjanue Ellis, Ramya Pratt, Guillermo Diaz (Zalaznick)

Lili Taylor gives a superlative, gut wrenching performance in *Girls Town*, a powerfully raw, ultra-realistic drama about a trio of abused teenage girls. Jim McKay's striking feature debut reveals a sensitive grasp of the feelings of young, mostly working-class women. A quartet of four high school seniors painfully realize that this might be their last year together before each goes her separate way. A bit older than the rest, Patti (Taylor) is also burdened with being a single mom. Like Patti, Emma (Anna Grace) is a tough, foul-mouthed white girl, though she's more educated and ambitious. The two black females, the sensitive Nikki (Aunjanue Ellis) and strong-willed Angela (Bruklin Harris), live with moms who don't understand them. As the story begins, the girls' world is shattered by Nikki's suicide, throwing each woman into a self-probing crisis.

McKay's camera acutely observes the girls's everyday life, at or around school: cutting classes, arguing about sex and boys, fighting with other girls and so on. It's a tribute to the film's intelligent writing and superb ensemble acting that, while dealing with weighty issues, the tale unfolds in a natural manner, without resorting to melodramatic crises or signaling blatant messages.

Taylor is supported vigorously by Grace and Harris, two first-rate thesps who are so believable they never look or sound like actresses. Blowup from 16mm is OK.

•

GIRL WITH GREEN EYES
1964, 91 mins, UK Ⓥ b/w
Dir Desmond Davis *Prod* Oscar Lewenstein *Scr* Edna O'Brien *Ph* Manny Wynn *Ed* Brian Smedley-Aston *Mus* John Addison *Art* Ted Marshall
Act Peter Finch, Rita Tushingham, Lynn Redgrave, Marie Kean, Julian Glover, T. P. McKenna (Woodfall)

This first film by Desmond Davis, who was a cameraman with Tony Richardson on *Loneliness of the Long Distance Runner* and *Saturday Night, Sunday Morning*, has the smell of success. Davis is imaginative, prepared to take chances and has the sympathy to draw perceptive performances from his cast.

Story [from the novel, *The Lonely Girl*, by Edna O'Brien] is set in Dublin where two shopgirls share a room. One (Rita Tushingham) is a quiet, withdrawn girl in the painful throes of awakening. The other (Lynn Redgrave) is a vivacious, gabby, good-natured colleen with a roving eye for the boys. But when the two girls casually meet a quiet, middle-aged writer (Peter Finch), the friendship that starts up is, naturally, between Tushingham and Finch.

Finch does a standout job as the tolerant writer who, despite occasional lapses into impatience, develops a fine understanding of the problems of the girl. Tushingham is often moving, sometimes spritely and always interesting to watch in her puzzled shyness. Redgrave makes an ebullient wench.

•

GIRLY
SEE: MUMSY, NANNY, SONNY & GIRLY

•

GIRO CITY
(US: AND NOTHING BUT THE TRUTH)
1982, 102 mins, UK Ⓥ col
Dir Karl Francis *Prod* Sophie Balhetchet, David Payne *Scr* Karl Francis *Ph* Curtis Clark *Ed* Neil Thomson *Mus* Alun Francis *Art* Jamie Leonard
Act Glenda Jackson, Jon Finch, Kenneth Colley, James Donnelly, Emrys James, Karen Archer (Silvercalm)

Giro City is a British thriller which examines political corruption and media attitudes to the rot on its doorstep. Story involves a documentary filmmaker and a reporter who work for a successful TV magazine program, and their attempts to cover two controversial news stories.

In breaking new ground, the film (shot on Super-16) has to make up in freshness and conviction for the superficiality with which some of the many issues raised are treated. But a hard hitting and emotional core is provided by the story of a family in South Wales who, alone but for the TV crew, take on the local council in their determination to stay on their land.

Glenda Jackson and Jon Finch as filmmaker and journalist are depicted as people for whom work covers up a hollow emotional core. Their pursuit of the corrupt councillor is determined and thrilling.

•

GIULIETTA DEGLI SPIRITI
(JULIET OF THE SPIRITS)
1965, 148 mins, Italy Ⓥ ⊙ col
Dir Federico Fellini *Prod* Angelo Rizzoli *Scr* Federico Fellini, Tullio Pinelli, Ennio Flaiano, Brunello Rondi *Ph* Gianni Di Venanzo *Ed* Ruggero Mastroianni *Mus* Nino Rota *Art* Piero Gherardi
Act Giulietta Masina, Mario Pisu, Sandra Milo, Valentina Cortese, Sylva Koscina, Caterina Boratto (Federiz)

Within a simple, naively romantic narrative frame concerning a wife's desperation over her husband's philanderings, director Federico Fellini has put together an imperial-sized fantasy of a physical opulence to make the old Vincente Minnelli Metro musicals look like army training films.

In the freedom of its form and in its carnival of images, *Juliet* constantly recalls 8½. However, the film adds up to something less than its individual parts. The physical spectacle, photographed in brilliant Technicolor, may be the film's strength as well as its weakness.

In the title role, Giulietta Masina (Mrs. Fellini) is at first humble and appealing as she slowly drifts into a dream world to escape the hard facts of a crumbling marriage. But as the Fellini fantasies grow increasingly more bizarre, there comes the realization that these are not so much the fantasies of an unhappy woman as they are those of an imaginative film director with a huge budget at his disposal.

It is a nonstop show dominated by the secondary performers, particularly a magnificent specimen by the name of Sandra Milo, a female presence seen here in three roles. In the most spectacular, she is a next door demi-mondaine presiding over a nonstop orgy which Giulietta visits and flees. She also turns up as a rather ominous apparition and as a busty circus lady with whom Juliet's frisky old grandpa (Lou Gilbert) elopes in a flying machine. There are also Sylva Koscina, as Giulietta's scatterbrained sister, and Valentina Cortese, a friend who introduces her to the spirit world.

As he has in the past, Fellini uses the rich, fulsome music of Nino Rota to counterpoint the screen images, usually to very good effect.

•

GIVE A GIRL A BREAK
1953, 81 mins, US Ⓥ col
Dir Stanley Donen *Prod* Jack Cummings *Scr* Albert Hackett, Frances Goodrich *Ph* William Mellor *Ed* Adrienne Fazan *Mus* Andre Previn, Saul Chaplin (dir.) *Art* Cedric Gibbons, Paul Groesse
Act Marge Champion, Gower Champion, Debbie Reynolds, Helen Wood, Bob Fosse, Kurt Kasznar (M-G-M)

The talents of a group of youthful performers are showcased in this routine tintuner, a passably pleasant, although uninspired, piece of entertainment. Five tunes were cleffed by Burton Lane and Ira Gershwin, while the sixth, a straight terp piece, was done by Andre Previn and Saul Chaplin.

In addition to the Champions, the other youthful talent consists of Debbie Reynolds, Helen Wood and Bob Fosse. The quintet works hard at its chores and manages to brighten proceedings in spots, although the material in the screenplay, from a story by Vera Caspary, is too lightweight to give much drive. Stanley Donen's direction falters also contributing to the draggy pace.

Plot twist revolves around Champion, Reynolds and Wood competing for the lead in a show being directed by Gower Champion after its femme star (Donna Martell) walks out. This showbiz background is ample excuse to work in the songs and dances and there is a certain amount of suspense over which girl will land the role.

•

GIVE MY REGARDS TO BROADWAY
1948, 89 mins, US col
Dir Lloyd Bacon *Prod* Walter Morosco *Scr* Samuel Hoffenstein, Elizabeth Reinhardt *Ph* Harry Jackson *Ed* William Reynolds *Art* Lyle R. Wheeler, J. Russell Spencer
Act Dan Dailey, Charles Winninger, Nancy Guild, Fay Bainter, Charles Ruggles, Barbara Lawrence (20th Century-Fox)

Despite the mental images of lush production numbers that might be conjured up by the title, *Broadway* has none of that. Instead, it's a simple story about an old vaude family that lives in the hope that the Palace two-a-day will some time be revived. Film has plenty of showbiz nostalgia. Title song, cleffed by George M. Cohan, runs through the film as its theme.

Although he's backed by a fine supporting cast that might otherwise steal his thunder, Dan Dailey has a personal field day. He gets a full chance to demonstrate his amazing versatility.

In addition to Dailey, who's standout as the son, the cast is excellent under the leisurely directorial touch of Lloyd Bacon. Winninger does one of his neatest characterizations as the oldtimer who refuses to toss in the sponge, and Bainter is fine as his understanding spouse.

•

GIVE US THIS DAY
(US: SALT TO THE DEVIL)
1949, 120 mins, UK b/w
Dir Edward Dmytryk *Prod* Rod Geiger, Nat A. Bronsten *Scr* Ben Barzman *Ph* C. Pennington Richards *Ed* John Guthridge *Mus* Benjamin Frankel
Act Sam Wanamaker, Lea Padovani, Kathleen Ryan, Bonar Colleano (Plantagenet)

The moving simplicity of the Pietro Di Donato novel, *Christ in Concrete*, has been brought to the screen with rare sincerity. It is two hours of genuine human drama, which makes no concession to convention. This is one of the few occasions in which British studios have embarked on a production with a New York setting. The expert hand of Edward Dmytryk's direction ensures faithful atmosphere.

Dmytryk presents the story of Geremio, an Italian bricklayer who works in Brooklyn. It is his wife's ambition to have a home of their own, and carefully they save for the down payment. But the Depression overtakes them. Then comes Geremio's opportunity to work as a foreman on a job which he knows to be unsafe and which culminates in tragedy.

Sam Wanamaker has never been better, investing the part with warmth and emotion.

•

GLADIATOR

1992, 98 mins, US Ⓥ ⦿ col

Dir Rowdy Herrington ***Prod*** Frank Price, Steve Roth ***Scr*** Lyle Kessler, Robert Mark Kamen ***Ph*** Tak Fujimoto ***Ed*** Peter Zinner, Harry B. Miller III ***Mus*** Brad Fiedel ***Art*** Gregg Fonseca

Act Cuba Gooding, Jr., James Marshall, Robert Loggia, Ossie Davis, Brian Dennehy, John Heard (Columbia/Price)

Gladiator is an exercise in audience manipulation, an interracial buddy movie. It's as if the producers called in their writers and said, "Give us a boxing picture with some of that *Barton Fink* feeling." Result is a formulaic attempt at an underdog saga that worked far better in the 1930s and 1940s.

Problem is that the filmmakers's bait-and-switch strategies are transparent. Cuba Gooding, Jr., (*Boyz N the Hood*) receives top billing, but the film is relentlessly centered around his white pal, James Marshall (*Twin Peaks*). Early reels exploit the racial tensions in a Chicago high school en route to a predictable revelation that both sets of youngsters have a common enemy, the white businessman (Brian Dennehy) who stages their illegal boxing matches.

Marshall, cast as the new kid in school, is sullen and far too low key through much of the picture. Director Rowdy Herrington, who poured on the trash in *Road House*, aims for a grittier feel this time, with dull results. Gooding is sympathetic and a convincing pugilist.

•

GLADIATOR

2000, 154 mins, US Ⓥ ⦿ ▭ col

Dir Ridley Scott ***Prod*** Douglas Wick, David Franzoni, Branko Lustig ***Scr*** David Franzoni, John Logan, William Nicholson ***Ph*** John Mathieson ***Ed*** Pietro Scalia ***Mus*** Hans Zimmer, Lisa Gerrard ***Art*** Arthur Max

Act Russell Crowe, Joaquin Phoenix, Connie Nielsen, Oliver Reed, Derek Jacobi, Richard Harris (Wick/DreamWorks)

After a virtual absence of 35 years, the Roman Empire makes a thrilling return to the big screen in *Gladiator*. A muscular and bloody combat picture, a compelling revenge drama and a truly transporting trip back nearly 2,000 years, Ridley Scott's bold epic of imperial intrigue and outsize heroism brings new luster and excitement to a tarnished and often derided genre. At its center is a great hero, a "real man," a fellow of few words who speaks plainly and can handle himself in any situation, especially physically.

Ten-minute opening battle in the forests of Germania is a savage spectacle, as General Maximus (Russell Crowe) commands his troops to "unleash hell" on their overmatched adversaries. The arrogant and unbalanced Commodus (Joaquin Phoenix) arrives at the front, along with his beautiful older sister, Lucilla (Connie Nielsen), just in time to learn that his ailing father (Richard Harris) has named the triumphant Maximus his successor as emperor.

Maximus wants no part of this plan but makes the mistake of spurning Commodus. After killing his father in a fit of jealous spite, the insecure new emperor orders the execution of the popular general. The resourceful Maximus escapes this fate but reaches home to find his wife and son dead, his farm torched. In the poetic manner of Sergio Leone, Scott uses a man of action's bitter and idealized memory of his lost family as a motif and a motive for the single-minded pursuit to which he devotes the remainder of his life.

At the 45-minute mark, action shifts to a distant North African outpost of the empire, where the captive Maximus is taken as slave. Purchased by gladiatorial entrepreneur Proximo (Oliver Reed), he conceals his true identity but, when thrown into the arena, he fights well.

The gladiatorial contests are tense, dynamic and brutal, to be sure. *Gladiator*, with its fast flurries of action and jump cuts, emphasizes the ferocious speed and urgency of every move in the arena, to the slight detriment of spatial unity and action continuity. But film enjoys a solid foundation in the strength of Maximus, the vividness of its evocation of the Roman world and the integrity of the story arc.

Crowe is simply splendid, every inch the warrior with his image of a tranquil domestic life an emblazoned but irretrievable memory. Phoenix makes for a neurotic, internalized Commodus, a coddled youngster literally in love (and lust) with his sister. As the latter, Nielsen has a consummately regal beauty and bearing. Harris is excellent as the philosopher emperor. But the scene stealer, in his last role before his death on location, is Reed, who hadn't brought such relish to a performance in years, and to whom the film is dedicated.

•

GLASS BOTTOM BOAT, THE

1966, 110 mins, US Ⓥ ▭ col

Dir Frank Tashlin ***Prod*** Martin Melcher, Everett Freeman ***Scr*** Everett Freeman ***Ph*** Leon Shamroy ***Ed*** John McSweeney ***Mus*** Frank DeVol ***Art*** George W. Davis, Edward Carfagno

Act Doris Day, Rod Taylor, Arthur Godfrey, John McGiver, Paul Lynde, Edward Andrews (M-G-M/Arwin-Reame)

Doris Day enters the world of rocketry and espionage in *The Glass Bottom Boat*, an expensively mounted production given frequently to sight gags and frenzied comedy performances.

Star plays a conscientious public relations staffer in a space laboratory where Rod Taylor, the engineering genius heading the facility, has invented a device both the U.S. government and the Soviets want. He falls for her and to keep her always by his side, invents the idea of having her write a very definitive biography of him. She becomes a spy suspect because she has a dog named Vladimir, which she's always calling on the telephone so its ringing will give her pet exercise when she isn't there, and because she follows a standing order that every bit of paper should be burned.

Arthur Godfrey scores strongly as her father, operator of a glass bottom sightseeing boat at Catalina. Taylor lends his usual masculine presence effectively, both as the inventor and romantic vis-a-vis.

•

GLASS KEY, THE

1935, 77 mins, US b/w

Dir Frank Tuttle ***Prod*** E. Lloyd Sheldon ***Scr*** Kathryn Scola, Kubec Glasmon, Harry Ruskin ***Ph*** Henry Sharp ***Ed*** Hugh Bennett

Act George Raft, Edward Arnold, Claire Dodd, Ray Milland, Rosalind Keith, Guinn Williams (Paramount)

This is a tale [from the story by Dashiell Hammett] of politics which involves murder, gangsterism and rocky romance. As murder mystery material, the story provides interesting plot situations. Performances by Raft and others are excellent, the direction is skilled and the dialog job leaves little to be desired, but too much has gone into the narrative that is up the alley of inconsistency.

It is a little unreasonable to expect that a daughter would dangerously turn against her father because of accusations that he murdered the man she loved, the son of a senator from whom the father was expecting patronage. It is equally implausible to expect that the politician would dig his own grave by shielding the senator.

Three romances are knitted into the murder mystery, but, in the main, the romantic aspects of the picture don't impress.

Raft gives a fine performance, as does Edward Arnold, playing the aspiring politician. Senator isn't much in the hands of Charles Richman, nor do Claire Dodd, Rosalind Keith or Ray Milland register any too well.

•

GLASS KEY, THE

1942, 85 mins, US Ⓥ b/w

Dir Stuart Heisler ***Prod*** B.G. DeSylva (exec.) ***Scr*** Jonathan Latimer ***Ph*** Theodor Sparkuhl ***Ed*** Archie Marshek ***Mus*** Victor Young ***Art*** Hans Dreier, Haldane Douglas

Act Brian Donlevy, Veronica Lake, Alan Ladd, Bonita Granville, William Bendix, Joseph Calleia (Paramount)

Parading a murder mystery amidst background of politics, gambling czars, romance and lusty action, this revised version of Dashiell Hammett's novel—originally made in 1935—is a good picture of its type.

Brian Donlevy is the political boss, a role similar to that he handled in *Great McGinty*. Alan Ladd is his assistant and confidant. Veronica Lake is the vacillating daughter of the gubernatorial candidate who first makes a play for Donlevy but winds up in the arms of Ladd, while Joseph Calleia has the gambling house concessions around the city. Mixed well, the result is an entertaining whodunit with sufficient political and racketeer angles to make it good entertainment for general audiences.

Donlevy makes the most of his role of the political leader who fought his way up from the other side of the tracks.

•

GLASS MENAGERIE, THE

1950, 106 mins, US b/w

Dir Irving Rapper ***Prod*** Jerry Wald, Charles K. Feldman ***Scr*** Tennessee Williams, Peter Berneis ***Ph*** Robert Burks ***Ed*** David Weisbart ***Mus*** Max Steiner

Act Jane Wyman, Kirk Douglas, Gertrude Lawrence, Arthur Kennedy (Warner)

Spotting Jane Wyman as crippled Laura, Arthur Kennedy as her compassionate brother, Gertrude Lawrence as their frowzy mother and Kirk Douglas as the Gentleman Caller who unwittingly changes their lives, for better or worse, is a casting scoop.

Familiar plot [from Tennessee Williams's play] about the aging southern belle who holds her brood together in a St. Louis tenement, only to lose her son when he decides he can take her nagging no longer, unreels engrossingly. Most remarkable is the subtle restraint employed to register Laura's awakening to the fact that life isn't a bust just because you've got a bum gam.

Kennedy, Wyman and Lawrence fight it out for thesp honors, and it would appear to be a draw.

•

GLASS MENAGERIE, THE

1987, 130 mins, US Ⓥ ⦿ col

Dir Paul Newman ***Prod*** Burtt Harris ***Scr*** [uncredited] ***Ph*** Michael Ballhaus ***Ed*** David Ray ***Mus*** Henry Mancini ***Art*** Tony Walton

Act Joanne Woodward, John Malkovich, Karen Allen, James Naughton (Cineplex Odeon)

Paul Newman's adaptation of *The Glass Menagerie* is a reverent record of Tennessee Williams's 1954 dream play, and one watches with a kind of distant dreaminess rather than an intense emotional involvement. It's a play of stunning language and brilliant performances creating living nightmares well defined by Newman's direction.

In this dreamscape, Amanda (Joanne Woodward) is the center of a universe of her own making and her children are satellites. But she is every overbearing mother more than a specific character, and she and her children are drawn in broad strokes and dark colors that keep them at a distance and contain their emotional impact.

Newman has heightened this impression by framing the action at the beginning and the end with Tom (John Malkovich) returning years later to look back at the wreck of his life. Smack in the middle of Depression America, he, too, is any man who longs to escape the banality of his life and demands of his mother.

But the greater victim in this world is his crippled sister Laura (Karen Allen) who is doomed to live in perpetual waiting for a gentleman caller who will never come, and whose life is worthless because of it.

Woodward is a constantly moving center of nervous neurotic energy with her active hands and darting eyes always seeming to be reaching out for something to grab on to.

•

GLASS MOUNTAIN, THE

1949, 97 mins, UK b/w

Dir Henry Cass ***Prod*** George Minter ***Scr*** Joseph Janni, John Hunter, Henry Case ***Ph*** William McLeod ***Ed*** Lister Laurence ***Mus*** Vivian Lambelet, Nino Rota, Elizabeth Anthony

Act Dulcie Gray, Michael Denison, Valentina Cortese, Tito Gobbi, Sebastian Shaw (Victoria)

The Glass Mountain has a theme inspired by a legend of the mountains in the Dolomites.

The romantic legend of thwarted love captivates an airman who is rescued in the Italian mountain district during the war. But on his return home to his wife, obsessed with writing an operatic piece on the theme, he cannot forget the girl he left behind.

Throughout, the story emphasis is placed on the frankly sentimental, but when the plot breaks away from its narrow limitations and gets out among the snow and the mountains, it becomes alive and moving.

Dulcie Gray and Michael Denison, husband and wife in real life, have little difficulty in interpreting that role convincingly on the screen, but the standout performance comes from Valentina Cortese, who possesses a refreshing charm, and an ability to act.

•

GLASS SHIELD, THE

1995, 108 mins, US/France Ⓥ col

Dir Charles Burnett ***Prod*** Tom Byrnes, Carolyn Schroeder ***Scr*** Charles Burnett ***Ph*** Elliot Davis ***Ed*** Curtiss Clayton ***Mus*** Stephen Taylor ***Art*** Penny Barrett

Act Michael Boatman, Lori Petty, Ice Cube, Michael Ironside, Richard Anderson, Elliott Gould (Byrnes-Schroeder-Walker/CiBy 2000)

Although writer/director Charles Burnett throws more weighty social and political issues on the table than he can possibly dramatize coherently in less than two hours, *The Glass Shield* emerges as a powerful moral drama that tries to deal with the racism at the root of many problems in contempo American society. He frames his corrosive portrait around the story of an enthusiastic black rookie cop whose tragic personal journey sees him move from being part of the solution to part of the problem.

At the outset, the youthful J. J. (Michael Boatman) is not exactly given a warm welcome as the first black recruit at the rough, L.A. inner city Edgemar station. It's dominated by a good old boys' group, four members of which have recently been under investigation for using excessive force on the job. His sole ally initially is another outcast, Deborah (Lori Petty), the only woman at the station and a Jew.

Incident that sets the dense plot in motion is the arrest of Teddy Woods (Ice Cube) at a gas station. Woods is obviously pulled over by one of the Southern Cal surfer-type cops only because he's black, but when it turns out he's got a gun hidden under his car seat, he is booked and accused of murdering the wife of the affluent Mr. Greenwall (Elliott Gould) on the basis of the gun ID. Anxious to fit in and prove himself on the squad, J. J., who was also at the scene, goes along with the lie.

By the second half, the film becomes far too top-heavy with content to retain its dramaturgical balance and artistic grace. Boatman gives a lively, sympathetic perf as the eager cop who does the wrong thing, although his private life is scanted to make room for all the sociological and plot baggage.

•

GLASS SLIPPER, THE

1955, 93 mins, US Ⓥ col

Dir Charles Walters ***Prod*** Edwin H. Knopf ***Scr*** Helen Deutsch ***Ph*** Arthur E. Arling ***Ed*** Ferris Webster ***Mus*** Bronislau Kaper

Act Leslie Caron, Michael Wilding, Keenan Wynn, Estelle Winwood, Elsa Lanchester, Barry Jones (M-G-M)

Without making too strong a comparison with *Lili*, a previous flick turned out by the principals connected with this offering, it is probable the makers figured on approaching the previous film's success. While *Slipper* has charm and a somewhat similar ugly duckling-love triumphant plot, it has neither the tremendous heart impact of *Lili* nor sufficient freshness of theme.

Leslie Caron, as drab and dirty as any scullery maid could have ever been, is the Cinderella who rides to the castle on her dreams, magically whisked into an enchantingly gowned, diademed princess fit for the prince played by Michael Wilding. Wilding does not seem happily cast in his character, nor does it get over to the viewer.

Where *Slipper* makes its best points is in the Bronislau Kaper score and in the ballets.

•

GLASS WEB, THE

1953, 81 mins, US b/w

Dir Jack Arnold ***Prod*** Albert J. Cohen ***Scr*** Robert Blees, Leonard Lee ***Ph*** Maury Gertsman ***Ed*** Ted J. Kent ***Mus*** Joseph Gershenson ***Art*** Bernard Herzbrun, Eric Orbom

Act Edward G. Robinson, John Forsythe, Kathleen Hughes, Marcia Henderson, Richard Denning, Hugh Sanders (Universal)

Albert J. Cohen's production is concerned with a TV crime show. A good cast, headed by Edward G. Robinson, a satisfactory murder-mystery script [based on a novel by Max Simon Ehrlich] and nicely valued direction by Jack Arnold make for an okay unfoldment of the melodramatics.

Robinson, frustrated researcher, and John Forsythe, writer, are responsible for the *Crime of the Week* program being televised each week. Both are being taken for money by Kathleen Hughes, TV actress, who is blackmailing Forsythe because of his summer dalliance with her while his wife was away, and bleeding Robinson on the strength of his infatuation for her.

The blonde blackmailer is killed and her death becomes the subject of a show, with her estranged husband apparently the patsy.

Robinson gives an excellent account of the frustrated researcher who feels his true worth isn't appreciated, and Forsythe comes over well as the writer. Hughes turns on the obvious s.a. for her hardboiled role and brings it off neatly.

•

GLEAMING THE CUBE

1988, 105 mins, US Ⓥ ⊙ col

Dir Graeme Clifford ***Prod*** Lawrence Turman ***Scr*** Michael Tolkin ***Ph*** Reed Smoot ***Ed*** John Wright ***Mus*** Jay Ferguson ***Art*** John Muto

Act Christian Slater, Steven Bauer, Min Luong, Art Chudabala, Le Tuan, Richard Herd (Gladden)

A skateboarding-obsessed suburban kid (Christian Slater) goes about solving—exploitation style—the death of his adopted Vietnamese brother (Art Chudabala), who Slater knows in his heart was too smart to commit suicide.

Slater skateboards all over Little Saigon, going in and out of mini-malls skillfully enough to elude Vietnamese hoods on his trail while conducting some Chuck Norris–inspired sleuthing.

Slater, who sounds as if he is trying to imitate Jack Nicholson, is the only character who has a shading of personality. His skateboarding buddies are funny, considering one needs a glossary to translate their dialog, while the Vietnamese are mostly sleazy cardboard figures. The police are inept and the mastermind villain (Richard Herd) seems to be right out of the Method acting school.

•

GLENGARRY GLEN ROSS

1992, 100 mins, US Ⓥ ⊙ ▭ col

Dir James Foley ***Prod*** Jerry Tokofsky, Stanley R. Zupnick ***Scr*** David Mamet ***Ph*** Juan-Ruiz Anchia ***Ed*** Howard Smith ***Mus*** James Newton Howard ***Art*** Jane Musky

Act Al Pacino, Jack Lemmon, Alec Baldwin, Ed Harris, Alan Arkin, Kevin Spacey (New Line/Zupnick-Curtis)

The theatrical roots show rather clearly in *Glengarry Glen Ross*. A superb cast acts out one of David Mamet's major works but it doesn't quite all come together here as it did onstage.

After runs in London and Chicago, Mamet's savage look at a group of slimy small-time real estate salesmen opened on Broadway in 1984. In adapting his short two-act, two-set, seven-character piece, Mamet has moved the action around a bit but the play's basic contours remain very much in place.

Harsh story examines the underhanded, eventually criminal activities of the salesmen as they compete to outdo each other in hustling dubious properties to phone clients.

Most in danger of getting the axe is the oldest employee, Shelley Leverne (Jack Lemmon). In the high-powered sales world personified by Blake (Alex Baldwin), the terrorist from the head office, there's clearly no place for a dinosaur like Shelley.

Also in jeopardy and strategizing in different ways are George (Alan Arkin) and Dave (Ed Harris). In contrast to all these drones is Ricky Roma (Al Pacino), a hotshot salesman who seems to know every trick in the book and how to play them.

Piece remains gripping in a way, but not in as captivating or edifying a way as it did onstage. Reasons for this have to do with the rhythms of the acting, the camera's magnification of artificial devices and director James Foley's mite fancy approach to stagebound material.

1992: NOMINATION: Best Supp. Actor (Al Pacino)

•

GLENN MILLER STORY, THE

1954, 115 mins, US Ⓥ ⊙ col

Dir Anthony Mann ***Prod*** Aaron Rosenberg ***Scr*** Valentine Davies, Oscar Brodney ***Ph*** William Daniels ***Ed*** Russell Schoengarth ***Mus*** Joseph Gershenson (dir.), Henry Mancini (adapt.) ***Art*** Bernard Herzbrun, Alexander Golitzen

Act James Stewart, June Allyson, Charles Drake, George Tobias, Henry Morgan, Barton MacLane (Universal)

Sentiment and swing feature in this biopic treatment on the life of the late Glenn Miller. The Miller music, heard in some 20 tunes throughout the production, is still driving, rhythmic swing at its best.

The Aaron Rosenberg supervision makes excellent use of the music to counterpoint a tenderly projected love story, feelingly played by James Stewart and June Allyson. The two stars, who clicked previously as a man-wife team in *The Stratton Story*, have an affinity for this type of thing.

The first 70 minutes of the picture is given over to Miller's search for a sound in music arrangement that would be his trademark and live after him. Remaining 45 minutes covers the rocketing Miller fame, his enlistment when World War II starts and the service band's playing for overseas troops.

To match the topflight performances of Stewart and Allyson, the picture has some strong thesping by featured and supporting players, as well as guest star appearances. Henry Morgan stands out as Chummy MacGregor. Charles Drake is good as Don Haynes, the band's manager.

1954: Best Sound Recording

NOMINATIONS: Best Story & Screenplay, Scoring of a Musical Picture

•

GLEN OR GLENDA

1953, 65 mins, US Ⓥ b/w

Dir Edward D. Wood, Jr. ***Prod*** George Weiss ***Scr*** Edward D. Wood, Jr. ***Ph*** William C. Thompson ***Ed*** Bud Schelling ***Mus*** Sandford H. Dickinson (cons.) ***Art*** Jack Miles

Act Bela Lugosi, Daniel Davis [= Edward D. Wood, Jr.], "Tommy" Haynes, Lyle Talbot, Dolores Fuller, Timothy Farrell (Screen Classics)

Glen or Glenda is an exploitation film dealing with transvestism and sex change.

Told mainly in semi-documentary fashion, story unfolds as two case histories related by a psychiatrist. Main story concerns Glen (Daniel Davis), a man who secretly dresses in women's clothes, much to the dismay of his fiancée Barbara (Dolores Fuller). Other story briefly deals with Alan ("Tommy" Haynes), identified as a "pseudohermaphrodite," who is changed into Ann by a sex-change operation (presented tastefully without the explicit shock visuals common to such case study pics).

Though opening credits warn of film's *stark realism*, director Edward Wood's use of stock footage, cheap sets, perfunctory visuals and recited-lecture dialog gives the picture a phony quality. What distinguishes it from other low-budget efforts are the occasional mad flights of fancy.

Most involve a weird scientist, delightfully played by Bela Lugosi in eye-popping fashion. Also out of the ordinary is a suggestive (but far from pornographic) sequence of women writhing in their sexy undies, laden with bondage overtones, as well as a surrealist nightmare scene.

•

GLORIA

1980, 123 mins, US Ⓥ ⊙ col

Dir John Cassavetes ***Prod*** Sam Shaw ***Scr*** John Cassavetes ***Ph*** Fred Schuler ***Ed*** George C. Villasenor ***Mus*** Bill Conti

Act Gena Rowlands, John Adames, Buck Henry, Julie Carmen, Lupe Guarnica (Columbia)

Gloria is a glorious broad perhaps pushing 40. She has been in prison but now has her nestegg and just wants to be let alone with her cat, friends and a fairly economically carefree life. But the way things happen, she has to put her neck out again for a precocious kid, half Puerto Rican, whom she has inadvertently pledged to help.

Director-actor John Cassavetes eases up on his unusually probing, darting camera and closeups studying human problems and disarray. Here instead he stands back and churns out a chase film that pits Gloria and the kid against the powerful Mafia.

Gena Rowlands is excellent as the tired woman who decides to take chances for the boy. The kid is a right blend of understanding and childish tantrums.

1980: NOMINATION: Best Actress (Gena Rowlands)

•

GLORY

1989, 122 mins, US Ⓥ ⊙ col

Dir Edward Zwick ***Prod*** Freddie Fields ***Scr*** Kevin Jarre ***Ph*** Freddie Francis ***Ed*** Steven Rosenblum ***Mus*** James Horner ***Art*** Norman Garwood

Act Matthew Broderick, Denzel Washington, Cary Elwes, Morgan Freeman, Cliff DeYoung, Jane Alexander (Tri-Star)

A stirring and long overdue tribute to the black soldiers who fought for the Union cause in the Civil War, *Glory* has the sweep and magnificence of a Tolstoy battle tale or a John Ford saga of American history.

Glory tells the story of the 54th Regiment of Massachusetts Volunteer Infantry, the first black fighting unit raised in the North during the Civil War. As the war went on, 186,107 blacks fought for the Union and 37,300 of them died.

Matthew Broderick's starring role as Col. Shaw, the callow youth from an abolitionist family who proved his mettle in training and leading his black soldiers, is perfectly judged.

Broderick's boyishness becomes a key element of the drama, as the film shows him confiding his inadequacies in letters home to his mother (the unbilled Jane Alexander) and struggling to assert leadership of his often recalcitrant men.

The rage caused by ill treatment is searingly incarnated in a great performance by Denzel Washington, as an unbroken runaway slave whose combative relationship with Broderick provides the dramatic heart of the film.

1989: Best Supp. Actor (Denzel Washington), Cinematography

NOMINATIONS: Best Editing, Art Direction, Sound

•

GLORY GUYS, THE

1965, 111 mins, US Ⓥ ▭ col

Dir Arnold Laven ***Prod*** Arnold Laven, Arthur Gardner, Jules Levy ***Scr*** Sam Peckinpah ***Ph*** James Wong Howe ***Ed*** Melvin Shapiro, Ernst R. Rolf ***Mus*** Riz Ortolani

Act Tom Tryon, Harve Presnell, Senta Berger, James Caan, Andrew Duggan, Slim Pickens (United Artists)

The Glory Guys is an entertaining U.S. Cavalry–Indian conflict, sparked by an opportunist army general who sacrifices dedicated soldiers to his ambition. Brawling fisticuffs, comedy and a romantic triangle mark a slightly forced plot until an exciting climax.

Adaptation by Sam Peckinpah of Hoffman Birney's novel, *The Dice of God*, finds Andrew Duggan very effective as a general again in responsible command despite prior goofs.

Senta Berger is an adequate but voluptuous frontier woman with an unspecified past, who provides romantic interest as Tryon and Presnell vie for her favors. Jeanne Cooper is good as Duggan's vicious and perfectly-matched wife who never fails to insult Berger.

Although Tryon is somewhat wooden and Presnell too refined for a frontier scout, director Arnold Laven has drawn some fine performances from supporting names. Slim Pickens brings a new life to the gruff humor and paternalism of a cliché role as non-com. James Caan makes a sharp impression as the stubborn recruit in an amusing running battle with shavetail Peter Breck.

•

'G' MEN

1935, 84 mins, US Ⓥ b/w

Dir William Keighley *Prod* Louis F. Edelman *Scr* Seton I. Miller *Ph* Sol Polito *Ed* Jack Killifer *Mus* Louis F. Forbstein (dir.) *Art* John Hughes

Act James Cagney, Margaret Lindsay, Ann Dvorak, Robert Armstrong, Barton MacLane, Lloyd Nolan (Warner)

This is red hot off the front page. But beyond that it has nothing but a weak scenario [from a story by Gregory Rogers] along hackneyed lines. *Little Caesar*, *Scarface* and *Public Enemy* were more than portrayals of gangster tactics: they were biographies of curious mentalities. In the new idea of glorifying the government gunners who wipe out the killers, there is no chance for that kind of character development and build-up.

This time James Cagney is a government man; he's in love with his chief's sister and she's thumbs down on him until the final clinch. And his chief rides him constantly, only to give in at the end.

Sprinkled through and around that is just about every situation from the Dillinger-Baby Face Nelson etcetera saga. The Kansas City depot massacre is paralleled, the Dillinger escape from a Chicago apartment, the Wisconsin resort roundup, the bank holdups throughout Kansas-Missouri, et al.

The acting throughout is A-1, and that helps consistently. Beyond Cagney and Robert Armstrong, both at their best, there is Ann Dvorak, a moll who tips off the cops to the final capture. Margaret Lindsay is Armstrong's sister and Cagney's gal. An easy assignment, and she romps off with it.

[A two-minute modern prologue, introducing the film, was added for a 1949 reissue.]

•

GO

1999, 103 mins, US Ⓥ ⊙ ▭ col

Dir Doug Liman *Prod* Paul Rosenberg, Mickey Liddell, Matt Freeman *Scr* John August *Ph* Doug Liman *Ed* Stephen Mirrione *Mus* BT *Art* Tom Wilkins

Act Desmond Askew, William Fichtner, Jane Krakowski, Sarah Polley, Scott Wolf, Jay Mohr (Banner/Columbia)

Customized to appeal to heat-seeking young audiences by brandishing as many trendy, edgy elements as possible, *Go* is an overly calculated concoction that nonetheless delivers a pretty good rush. Doug Liman's third feature reps a notable advance stylistically over his enjoyable prior outing, *Swingers*.

The film exerts a magnetic pull from the outset, thanks in large measure to the mesmerizing Sarah Polley, an actress who is intriguing even when she is doing nothing. Polley plays Ronna, an overworked L.A. supermarket checkout girl who, over Christmas, agrees to fill in for her jumpy Brit co-worker, Simon (Desmond Askew), so he can holiday in Vegas. Approached by a couple of actors (Scott Wolf, Jay Mohr) interested in scoring drugs, Ronna decides to risk doing business with Simon's dealer, Todd (Timothy Olyphant), but ends up betraying him when she senses she's being set up in a sting run by a strange narc, Burke (William Fichtner).

Todd pursues her and appears on the verge of gunning her down when Ronna is run over by a yellow Miata and left for dead in a ditch. Where can first-time screenwriter John August's story go from here? Back to the beginning, to follow Simon's story to Las Vegas, a visit more eventful than the one in *Swingers*. Action then rewinds one last time to concentrate on the two actors, who are not exactly what they at first seem to be.

What's new from Liman is the electricity that the combination of lively action, responsive performances, raging soundtrack and bold widescreen visuals shoots off the screen.

•

GO-BETWEEN, THE

1971, 118 mins, UK Ⓥ ⊙ col

Dir Joseph Losey *Prod* John Heyman, Norman Priggen *Scr* Harold Pinter *Ph* Gerry Fisher *Ed* Reginald Beck *Mus* Michel Legrand *Art* Carmen Dillon

Act Julie Christie, Alan Bates, Margaret Leighton, Michael Redgrave, Michael Gough, Edward Fox (EMI)

In its glimpse of the manners and mores of the British socialites at the beginning of the century, *The Go-Between* is both fascinating and charming. Joseph Losey's direction sets a pace in which incident and characterization take precedence over action.

The Harold Pinter screenplay, based on the L.P. Hartley novel, is, as one would naturally expect, literate and penetrating, yet there are certain obscurities in the treatment.

It is Michael Redgrave looking back at a definitive event of his boyhood, an experience which undoubtedly was largely responsible for his remaining unmarried. For it is during the long hot summer in the lavish country home that the youngster becomes emotionally involved by acting as the contact (or go-between) between the daughter of the house—with whom he believes himself to be in love—and the tenant farmer, although the girl is already betrothed to a member of the aristocracy. And it is in that period that the boy gets his first inkling of what sex is all about.

Though Julie Christie and Alan Bates starred as the girl and the farmer, it is the boy who has the pivotal role, and Dominic Guard, a screen newcomer, appears to play his part effortlessly, with an absence of precociousness.

1971: NOMINATION: Best Supp. Actress (Margaret Leighton)

•

GODFATHER, THE

1972, 175 mins, US Ⓥ ⊙ col

Dir Francis Coppola *Prod* Albert S. Ruddy *Scr* Mario Puzo, Francis Coppola *Ph* Gordon Willis *Ed* William Reynolds, Peter Zinner *Mus* Nino Rota *Art* Dean Tavoularis

Act Marlon Brando, Al Pacino, James Caan, Richard Conte, Robert Duvall, Sterling Hayden (Paramount)

Paramount's film version of Mario Puzo's sprawling gangland novel has an outstanding performance by Al Pacino and a strong characterization by Marlon Brando in the title role. It also has excellent production values, flashes of excitement, and a well-picked cast.

Puzo and director Francis Coppola are credited with the adaptation which best of all gives some insight into the origins and heritage of that segment of the population known off the screen (but not on it) as the Mafia or Cosa Nostra.

In *The Godfather* we have the New York-New Jersey world, ruled by five "families," one of them headed by Brando. This is a world where emotional ties are strong, loyalties are somewhat more flexible at times, and tempers are short. Brando does an admirable job as the lord of his domain.

It is Pacino who makes the smash impression here. Initially seen as the son whom Brando wanted to go more or less straight, Pacino matures under trauma of an assassination attempt on Brando, his own double murder revenge for that on corrupt cop Sterling Hayden and rival gangster Al Lettieri, the counter-vengeance murder of his Sicilian bride, and a series of other personnel readjustments which at fade-out find him king of his own mob.

Among the notable performances are Robert Duvall as Hagen, the nonItalian number two man, Richard Conte as one of Brando's malevolent rivals and Diane Keaton as Pacino's early sweetheart, later second wife. [In 1977, Coppola issued *The Godfather Saga*, a 450-min. assemblage of *The Godfather* and *The Godfather Part II*, with events in chronological order and material cut from the original films. This was initially shown on TV and later made available on video.]

1972: Best Picture, Actor (Marlon Brando), Adapted Screenplay

NOMINATIONS: Best Director, Supp. Actor (James Caan, Robert Duvall, Al Pacino), Music [later declared ineligible], Costume Design, Editing, Sound

•

GODFATHER PART II, THE

1974, 200 mins, US Ⓥ ⊙ col

Dir Francis Coppola *Prod* Francis Coppola *Scr* Francis Coppola, Mario Puzo *Ph* Gordon Willis *Ed* Peter Zinner, Barry Malkin, Richard Marks *Mus* Nino Rota, Carmine Coppola *Art* Dean Tavoularis

Act Al Pacino, Robert Duvall, Diane Keaton, Robert De Niro, John Cazale, Lee Strasberg (Paramount/Coppola)

The Godfather Part II, far from being a spinoff followup to its 1972 progenitor, is an excellent epochal drama in its own right providing bookends in time to the earlier story. Al Pacino again is outstanding as Michael Corleone, successor to crime family leadership. The $15 million production cost about two-and-a-half times the original.

The film's 200 minutes could be broken down into two acts and 10 scenes. The scenes alternate between Pacino's career in Nevada gambling rackets from about 1958 on and Robert De Niro's early life in Sicily and New York City. A natural break comes after 126 minutes when De Niro, involved with low level thievery, brutally assassinates Gaston Moschin the neighborhood crime boss without a shred of conscience. It's the only shocking brutality in the film.

1974: Best Picture, Director, Supp. Actor (Robert De Niro), Adapted Screenplay, Art Direction, Original Score

NOMINATIONS: Best Actor (Al Pacino), Supp. Actor (Michael V. Gazzo, Lee Strasberg), Supp. Actress (Talia Shire), Costume Design

•

GODFATHER PART III, THE

1990, 161 mins, US Ⓥ ⊙ col

Dir Francis Coppola *Prod* Francis Coppola *Scr* Mario Puzo, Francis Coppola *Ph* Gordon Willis *Ed* Barry Malkin, Lisa Fruchtman *Mus* Carmine Coppola, Nino Rota *Art* Dean Tavoularis

Act Al Pacino, Diane Keaton, Talia Shire, Andy Garcia, Eli Wallach, Joe Mantegna (Zoetrope/Paramount)

The Godfather Part III matches its predecessors in narrative intensity, epic scope, socio-political analysis, physical beauty and deep feeling for its characters and milieu. In addition, the $55 million-plus production is the most personal of the three for the director. Like the original, Part III opens with a lengthy festival celebration punctuated by backroom dealings. It is 1979, and Michael Corleone, having divested himself of his illegal operations, is being honored by the Catholic Church for his abundant charitable activities.

Hopeful of bringing his family closer together, Michael dotes on his daughter Mary (Sofia Coppola), and understandably becomes perturbed by her affair with cousin Vincent (Andy Garcia), hot-headed, violence-prone illegitimate son of Michael's late brother Sonny. Vincent has been unhappily working for slumlord and old-style thug Joey Zasa (Joe Mantegna), who has taken on Michael's less savory holdings.

Bad blood between the ruthless Zasa and the Corleone family mounts just as Michael tries, with $600 million, to buy a controlling interest in the European conglomerate Immobiliare, a move that would cement his business legitimacy and financial future.

After 80 minutes, the action switches to Italy, where it remains for the duration. Pacino and Eli Wallach's old dons can't help begin scheming against one another. In one of the most masterful examples of sustained intercutting in cinema, the performance on opening night of Pacino's son in *Cavalleria Rusticana* serves as the backdrop for several murderous missions.

For the third time out in his career role, Pacino is magnificent. Garcia brings much-needed youth and juice to the ballsy Vincent, heir apparent to the Corleone tradition, much as James Caan sparked the first film and Robert De Niro invigorated the second.

Diane Keaton proves a welcome, if brief, presence in warming the film, and Talia Shire seems pleased with the opportunity to do some dirty work at long last.

Film's main flaw, unavoidably, is Sofia Coppola in the important, but not critical, role of Michael's daughter. Unfortunate casting decision was made after original actress Winona Ryder had to bow out at the start of production.

[In 1991 Paramount released a 170-min. *Final Director's Cut* on homevideo only.]

1990: NOMINATIONS: Best Picture, Director, Supp. Actor (Andy Garcia), Cinematography, Art Direction, Editing, Song ("Promise Me You'll Remember")

•

GOD IS MY CO-PILOT
1945, 83 mins, US b/w
Dir Robert Florey ***Prod*** Robert Buckner ***Scr*** Peter Milne, Abem Finkel ***Ph*** Sid Hickox ***Ed*** Folmer Blangsted ***Mus*** Franz Waxman ***Art*** John Hughes
Act Dennis Morgan, Dane Clark, Raymond Massey, Alan Hale, Andrea King (Warner)

Narrative uses flashback technique to condense life of Col. Robert Lee Scott, Jr., army ace who gained fame with General Chennault's Flying Tigers.

Air fight sequences bear an authentic stamp, although studio made, and the thrills are good drama. Title derives from Scott's realization that a pilot doesn't face danger alone, and several of his real-life brushes with death sustain the belief.

There has been considerable condensation of Scott's story, taken from his best-selling book of same title, and undoubtedly commercial license has pointed up some incidents for better dramatic flavor. It's the story of a boy born to fly and spans his days from the time he first jumped off the barn with an umbrella, through model planes, West Point, flying the mail, instructing and his takeoff on a secret mission to China after Pearl Harbor.

Condensation was evidently more in the hands of the film editor than in the script. Finished picture indicates there was considerable scissoring to hold footage to reasonable length. Robert Florey's direction manages authenticity and obtains excellent performances from the cast headed by Dennis Morgan.

•

GOD'S LITTLE ACRE
1958, 112 mins, US Ⓥ b/w
Dir Anthony Mann ***Prod*** Sidney Harmon ***Scr*** Philip Yordan ***Ph*** Ernest Haller ***Ed*** Richard C. Meyer ***Mus*** Elmer Bernstein ***Art*** John S. Poplin, Jr.
Act Robert Ryan, Aldo Ray, Tina Louise, Buddy Hackett, Jack Lord, Fay Spain (United Artists)

Rousing, rollicking and ribald, *God's Little Acre* is a rustic revel with the kick of a Georgia mule. The production of Erskine Caldwell's novel is adult, sensitive and intelligent.

The direct, bucolic humor is virtually intact, and so is Caldwell's larger scheme, the morality play he told through the artless, sometimes disastrous behavior of his foolish and lovable characters. A changed ending gives a different meaning to the story, but the ending is sound, aesthetically and popularly.

The story remains that of a Georgia farmer (Robert Ryan) who believes he can find gold on his farm. In the book it was a gold mine; in the picture it is buried treasure. Ryan has spent years of his life digging for it, all his energies and those of his two sons (Jack Lord and Vic Morrow) go into the search and the dream it represents. The hunt leads everywhere on their farm except on the one acre Ryan has set aside, in the olden way of tithing, for God.

Ryan dominates the picture, as his character should. Aldo Ray, as his son-in-law, creates a moving characterization as the husband torn between his wife, sensitively played by Helen Westcott, and the voluptuous barnyard Susannah, strikingly projected by newcomer from legit Tina Louise.

•

GODS MUST BE CRAZY, THE
1981, 108 mins, Botswana Ⓥ ⦿ ▭ col
Dir Jamie Uys ***Prod*** Jamie Uys ***Scr*** Jamie Uys ***Ph*** Jamie Uys, Buster Reynolds, Robert Lewis ***Ed*** Jamie Uys ***Mus*** John Boshoff
Act Marius Weyers, Sandra Prinsloo, N!xau, Louw Verwey, Michael Thys, Jamie Uys (CAT)

The Gods Must Be Crazy is a comic fable by one-man-band South African filmmaker Jamie Uys, who shot the picture in Botswana in 1979.

Uys's basic story line has Xi (N!xau), a bushman who lives deep in the Kalahari desert, setting off on a trek to destroy a Coca Cola bottle which fell from a passing airplane and by virtue of its strange usefulness as a utensil (thought to be thrown by the gods from heaven) has caused great dissension within his tribe.

Xi plans to throw the unwanted artifact of modern civilization off the edge of the world and in his trek encounters modern people.

Film's main virtues are its striking, widescreen visuals of unusual locations, and the sheer educational value of its narration.

•

GODS MUST BE CRAZY II, THE
1989, 99 mins, Botswana/US Ⓥ ⦿ col
Dir Jamie Uys ***Prod*** Boet Troskie ***Scr*** Jamie Uys ***Ph*** Buster Reynolds ***Ed*** Renee Engelbrecht, Ivan Hall ***Mus*** Charles Fox
Act N!xau, Lena Farugia, Hans Strydom, Eiros, Nadies, Erick Bowen (Troskie/Weintraub)

Jamie Uys has concocted a genial sequel to his 1981 international sleeper hit *The Gods Must Be Crazy* that is better than its progenitor in most respects.

His tongue-clicking Kalahari Bushman hero, again played by a real McCoy named N!xau, is once more unwittingly embroiled in the lunacies of civilization.

First plotline has N!xau's two adorable offspring getting innocently borne away on the trailer truck of a pair of unsuspecting ivory poachers. N!xau follows the tracks and comes across two other odd couples from the nutty outside world.

There is a New York femme lawyer (Lena Farugia), who is stranded in the middle of the Kalahari with a handsome, phlegmatic game warden (Hans Strydom) when their ultralight plane is downed in a sudden storm.

Then there are two hapless mercenaries, an African and a Cuban, who keep taking one another prisoner in a series of table turning pursuits through the brush.

Uys orchestrates a desert farce of crisscrossing destinies with more assured skill and charming sight gags, marred only by facile penchant for speeded up slapstick motion.

•

GODSPELL
1973, 103 mins, US col
Dir David Greene ***Prod*** Edgar Lansbury ***Scr*** David Greene, John-Michael Tebelak ***Ph*** Richard G. Heimann ***Ed*** Alan Heim ***Mus*** Stephen Schwartz ***Art*** Brian Eatwell
Act Victor Garber, David Haskell, Jerry Sroka, Lynne Thigpen, Katie Hanley, Rubin Lamont (Columbia)

Godspell originated as a workshop production at off-off-Broadway's La Mama for a group of actor-graduates of Carnegie-Mellon Univ. Overall concept—a youth-slanted reworking of the gospel according to St. Matthew—was that of director John-Michael Tebelak as part of a master's thesis.

Film follows original 1971 off-Broadway legit production closely but "opens up" the setting to include footage of virtually every New York City tourist landmark, graffiti and all.

Result is that original production's appealing aspects have remained intact—a strong Stephen Schwartz score and an infectious joie de vivre conveyed by an energetic, no-name cast. So also, unfortunately, have its flaws—a relentlessly simplistic approach to the New Testament interpreted in overbearing children's theatre style mugging.

Story line merely consists of a series of ensemble interpretations of gospel parables as enunciated by a Christ figure (Victor Garber) in a superman sweatshirt and workman's overalls.

•

GOD'S WILL
1989, 100 mins, US Ⓥ col
Dir Julia Cameron ***Prod*** Julia Cameron, Pam Moore ***Scr*** Julia Cameron ***Ph*** William Nusbaum ***Mus*** Christopher (Hambone) Cameron
Act Marge Kotlisky, Daniel Region, Laura Margolis, Domenica Cameron-Scorsese, Linda Edmond (Power & Light)

Veteran Hollywood screen writer Julia Cameron moved home to Chicago to produce and direct her first feature, *God's Will*, and discovered firsthand one of a filmmaker's worst nightmares: the production soundtrack was stolen after shooting wrapped.

As a consequence, the scenes's delicate at best under normal low-budget conditions, simply don't play right.

A plus for the Cameron family is an outstanding debut by pre-teen daughter Domenica Cameron-Scorsese (whose father is director Martin Scorsese).

Cameron's intent, obviously, was to create a lighthearted effort at family fun in which a divorced, self-centred show business couple (Daniel Region and Laura Margolis) meet an untimely demise and wind up in heaven squabbling over what will happen now to their daughter.

The little girl has fallen into the custody of the couple's new spouses (Linda Edmond and Mitchell Canoff). Some ghostly haunting is therefore required to free Domenica into the hands of another couple preferred by the parents and the result is a romp.

•

GODZILLA
1998, 138 mins, US Ⓥ ⦿ col
Dir Roland Emmerich ***Prod*** Dean Devlin ***Scr*** Dean Devlin, Roland Emmerich ***Ph*** Ueli Steiger ***Ed*** Peter Amundson, David J. Siegel ***Mus*** David Arnold ***Art*** Oliver Scholl
Act Matthew Broderick, Jean Reno, Maria Pitillo, Hank Azaria, Kevin Dunn, Michael Lerner (Centropolis/TriStar)

Godzilla is not so much a remake as a reinvention of the 1954 Japanese production [by Toho Co., more widely known in the 1956 Americanized version, *Godzilla, King of the Monsters*, incorporating new footage with Raymond Burr as a reporter/narrator] that spawned scores of sequels, comic books and television commercials.

The big difference [in this screen story by Ted Elliott, Terry Rossio, producer Dean Devlin and director Roland Emmerich] is that this Godzilla is not a regenerated dinosaur. Rather, fall-out from French nuclear blasts in the South Pacific have turned a lizard into a gigantic mutant monster.

Dr. Niko Tatopoulos (Matthew Broderick), a biologist, is studying the effect of radiation leakage on earthworms near Chernobyl. A military team led by Col. Hicks (Kevin Dunn) drops in to whisk Tatopoulos away to help with a much bigger problem.

Right from the start, Broderick conveys a gee-whiz ingenuousness that is distracting at best, insipid at worst. In sharp contrast, Jean Reno offers a crafty mix of foreboding and bemusement as Philippe Roache, a French secret agent who's working undercover as an insurance company representative.

By the time Tatopoulos and company get to Manhattan, the creature is ready to make his American debut at the Fulton Fish Market. From there, he rambles over to wreak havoc in the city's financial district, just in time to interrupt a re-election campaign speech by the excitable Mayor Ebert (Michael Lerner).

Most of the action takes place at night, but when the creature is full visible it resembles nothing more than a hybrid of the mother beast from *Alien* and a T-Rex from *Jurassic Park*.

Godzilla designer and supervisor Patrick Tatopoulos—whose name is commandeered for Broderick's character—does a bang up job of creating a lean, mean monster machine. But there is little that is charismatic about his handiwork. Size does matter, of course, but some things matter more.

•

GO FISH
1994, 85 mins, US Ⓥ ⦿ b/w
Dir Rose Troche ***Prod*** Rose Troche, Guinevere Turner ***Scr*** Guinevere Turner, Rose Troche ***Ph*** Ann T. Rossetti ***Ed*** Rose Troche ***Mus*** Brendan Dolan, Jennifer Sharpe, Scott Aldrich
Act V. S. Brodie, Guinevere Turner, T. Wendy McMillan, Migdalia Melendez, Anastasia Sharp (Can I Watch)

Rose Troche makes an auspicious debut as director, cowriter and editor of *Go Fish*, a fresh, hip comedy about contemporary lifestyles within the lesbian community. The most refreshing dimension of *Go Fish* is that it's not dealing with coming out and is not burdened with the stiff, sanctimonious tone of such lesbian films as *Claire of the Moon*.

The comedy is off to a good start when Kia (T. Wendy McMillan), a mature black professor, is speculating with her students about who might be lesbian in American society. Kia, who is romantically involved with Evy (Migdalia Melendez), a divorcée, would like Max (Guinevere Turner), her younger, energetic roommate, to meet a girl. She decides to set her up with Ely (V. S. Brodie), an ex-student of hers who's in the process of terminating a long-distance relationship.

Through cross-cutting between the Max and Ely households, the well-written comedy conveys the folklore that women share when there are no men around—sort of a current, lesbian version of Gregory La Cava's *Stage Door*.

As director, Troche elicits perfectly natural performances from her mostly non-professional ensemble. The performers's mixture of strong physical presence and light self-mockery helps set the film's quirky, offbeat mood. As the central couple, Turner and Brodie inhabit rather than play their roles by projecting an inner verve and verbal charm.

•

GO FOR BROKE!
1951, 90 mins, US Ⓥ b/w
Dir Robert Pirosh ***Prod*** Dore Schary ***Scr*** Robert Pirosh ***Ph*** Paul C. Vogel ***Ed*** James E. Newcom ***Mus*** Alberto Colombo ***Art*** Cedric Gibbons, Eddie Imazu
Act Van Johnson, Lane Nakano, George Miki, Akira Fukunaga, Ken K. Okamoto, Warner Anderson (M-G-M)

The case of the Japanese-Americans who fought with honor in Italy and France during the Second World War is objectively treated in *Go For Broke!*

Title, derived from a colloquialism meaning "shoot the works," was used as the battle cry of the Nisei members of the 442nd Regimental Combat Team who were out to prove that color or racial origin has nothing to do with good Americanism. The social angle is never overplayed and is effectively socked with a humorous touch.

Robert Pirosh keeps his script and direction on an intimate level, projecting the story through Van Johnson, as a typical native American who draws back from the thought of being assigned as a brand new lieutenant to head a group of "Buddha-Heads," as the Nisei are known. Yarn works in quite a number of chuckles in showing training of the squad, and carries this light touch through the shipment overseas to Italy, the battle action there and on into France.

Johnson does an excellent job of his assignment, and the heroes of the 442nd Regiment Combat Team who co-star with him add to the naturalism of the production.

•

GOING HOME

1971, 97 mins, US ⦿ col

Dir Herbert B. Leonard ***Prod*** Herbert B. Leonard ***Scr*** Lawrence B. Marcus ***Ph*** Fred Jackman ***Ed*** Sigmund Neufeld Jr ***Mus*** Bill Walker ***Art*** Peter Wooley

Act Robert Mitchum, Brenda Vaccaro, Jan-Michael Vincent, Jason Bernard, Sally Kirkland, Josh Mostel (M-G-M)

Going Home is a most unusual and intruiging melodrama about a teenage boy's vengeance against his father for the long ago killing of his mother. Robert Mitchum in an offbeat role gives an excellent performance as the crude but sensitive father. Jan-Michael Vincent is very effective as his son. Brenda Vaccaro, as Mitchum's sweetheart, makes a catalytic role into a memorable experience.

The script takes Vincent on a search from prison, where Mitchum was incarcerated, to the sleazy seashore environment where the paroled father is eking out a living. The boy's love-hate relationship with his father is developed neatly and often to a terrifying degree. Vaccaro, in the literal sense an innocent bystander who gets hurt for her trouble, fills in with human emotions the two men cannot express to each other.

As the undaunted but well worn-down Korean War hero 20 years later, fresh out of stir with a son who hates his guts, with a beer belly and a black future, Mitchum presents a characterization that combines a wide range of acting talents.

•

GOING MY WAY

1944, 126 mins, US Ⓥ ⦿ b/w

Dir Leo McCarey ***Prod*** Leo McCarey ***Scr*** Frank Butler, Frank Cavett ***Ph*** Lionel Lindon ***Ed*** LeRoy Stone ***Mus*** Robert Emmett Dolan (dir) ***Art*** Hans Dreier, William Flannery

Act Bing Crosby, Rise Stevens, Barry Fitzgerald, Gene Lockhart, Frank McHugh, James Brown (Paramount)

Bing Crosby gets a tailor-made role in *Going My Way*, and with major assistance from Barry Fitzgerald and Rise Stevens, clicks solidly to provide topnotch entertainment for wide audience appeal.

Picture is a warm, human drama studded liberally with bright episodes and excellent characterizations accentuated by the fine direction of Leo McCarey [who wrote the original story]. Intimate scenes between Crosby and Fitzgerald dominate throughout, with both providing slick characterizations.

Crosby plays a young priest interested in athletics and music who's assigned as an assistant to crusty Fitzgerald in an Eastside church saddled with burdensome mortgage that might be foreclosed by grasping Gene Lockhart. Progressive youth and staid oldster clash continually, but Crosby gradually bends Fitzgerald to his way.

Major thread of gaiety runs through the proceedings, and McCarey has liberally sprinkled sparkling individual episodes along the way for cinch audience reaction. Rise Stevens comes on for the second half, introduced as a Metropolitan Opera star and old friend of Crosby when both were interested in music.

Crosby's song numbers include three new tunes by Johnny Burke and James Van Heusen—"Going My Way," "Would You Like to Swing On a Star" and "Day after Forever."

1944: Best Picture, Director, Actor (Bing Crosby), Supp. Actor (Barry Fitzgerald), Original Story, Screenplay, Song ("Swinging on a Star")

NOMINATIONS: Best Actor (Barry Fitzgerald), B&W Cinematography, Editing

•

GOING PLACES

SEE: LES VALSEUSES

•

GOIN' SOUTH

1978, 101 mins, US Ⓥ ⦿ col

Dir Jack Nicholson ***Prod*** Harry Gittes, Harold Schneider ***Scr*** John Herman Shaner, Al Ramus, Charles Shyer, Alan Mandel ***Ph*** Nestor Almendros ***Ed*** Richard Chew, John Fitzgerald Beck ***Mus*** Van Dyke Parks, Perry Botkin, Jr. ***Art*** Toby Carr Rafelson

Act Jack Nicholson, Mary Steenburgen, Christopher Lloyd, John Belushi, Veronica Cartwright, Danny DeVito (Paramount)

Jack Nicholson playing Gabby Hayes is interesting, even amusing at times, but Hayes was never a leading man, which *Goin' South* desperately needs.

Picture starts off promisingly enough with Nicholson as a hapless outlaw who makes it across the border but the posse cheats and comes across after him, causing his horse to faint.

On his way to the gallows, Nicholson discovers an unordinary county ordinance that would allow him to go free if picked for marriage by a maiden lady in town. Up to now, *Goin' South* is still going strong but here it stops as lovely young Mary Steenburgen steps out of the crowd and agrees to marry the bearded, dirty horse-thief.

Why she should do this is never satisfactorily established in the script carrying the names of four writers. Ostensibly, it's to get the manpower to help her mine her property for gold before the railroad takes over. But it never jells, as Nicholson continues to sputter and chomp, acting more like her grandfather than a handsome roué out to overcome her virginity.

•

GO INTO YOUR DANCE

1935, 92 mins, US ⦿ b/w

Dir Archie Mayo ***Scr*** Earl Baldwin ***Ph*** Tony Gaudio ***Ed*** Harold McLernon ***Mus*** Ray Heindorf (arr.) ***Art*** John Hughes

Act Al Jolson, Ruby Keeler, Glenda Farrell, Barton MacLane, Patsy Kelly, Akim Tamaroff (First National/Warner)

Go into Your Dance has much to recommend it as a lavishly produced, vigorously directed and agreeably entertaining musical picture [based on a story by Bradford Ropes]. Besides everything else, it has Al Jolson in top form, plus a nifty set of songs [by Al Dubin and Harry Warren].

Along with Jolson and for the first time, his screen partner is the missus, Ruby Keeler. A sensible story setting, in which each is permitted to adhere to type, makes them a nice film couple.

Jolson plays the role of a talented star who has broken up many a hit show by going off on bats. The star is finally barred from the musical stage by the combined votes of Actors Equity and an association of producers.

With the help of his devoted sister and a dancing girl with whom he teams up, the banished star starts his comeback via the nightclub field. The comeback is nearly interrupted by gangster bullets, but they miss the star and hit his girl partner.

Keeler is given plenty of footage for her dancing; perhaps more than any dancer, including Astaire, has been accorded in any one picture thus far. On the hoof she's a girl who can take good care of herself, and in the histrionic moments she's carried along by Jolson's aggressive trouping.

1935: NOMINATION: Best Dance Direction ("Lady from Manhattan")

•

GOLD

1974, 118 mins, UK Ⓥ ▭ col

Dir Peter Hunt ***Prod*** Michael Klinger ***Scr*** Wilbur Smith, Stanley Price ***Ph*** Ousama Rawi ***Ed*** John Glen ***Mus*** Elmer Bernstein ***Art*** Alec Vetchinsky, Syd Cain

Act Roger Moore, Susannah York, Ray Milland, Bradford Dillman, John Gielgud, Simon Sabela (Hemdale/Avton)

Power of a major physical disaster as theme for an exciting motion picture [based on Wilbur Smith's novel *Goldmine*] is evidenced in this British item, lensed entirely in the South Africa locale of its well-developed narrative. Punishing action is tempered by a modern love story.

Roger Moore plays a tough mine foreman unwittingly manipulated by an unscrupulous gang of financiers who want to flood the mine to raise the price of gold on the world market.

Particular attention has been given to the terrifying underground sequences, and tremendous realism is accomplished in an opening tragedy of men caught in the grip of a sudden flood and later in the climactic flooding.

Moore delivers in pat fashion and Susannah York is a love as the wife of the mine operator who is used by her husband in the web of deceit woven by an international syndicate whom he represents.

1974: NOMINATION: Best Song ("Wherever Love Takes Me")

•

GOLD DIGGERS OF 1933

1933, 94 mins, US Ⓥ ⦿ b/w

Dir Mervyn LeRoy, Busby Berkeley ***Prod*** [uncredited] ***Scr*** Erwin Gelsey, James Seymour, David Boehm, Ben Markson ***Ph*** Sol Polito ***Ed*** George Amy ***Mus*** Leo F. Forbstein (dir.) ***Art*** Anton Grot

Act Warren William, Joan Blondell, Aline MacMahon, Ruby Keeler, Dick Powell, Guy Kibbee (Warner)

Gold Diggers makes some sort of screen history in that it's the first of the "second editions" of film musicals. In 1929, WB made *Gold Diggers of Broadway*. But the real feature of *Gold Diggers of 1933* are the numbers staged by Busby Berkeley.

The film's superiority to *42nd Street* lies in the greater romantic interest with a multiplicity of amorous complications wherein Warren William and Joan Blondell, and Guy Kibbee and Aline MacMahon, are paired off as subinterests to the Ruby Keeler-Dick Powell coupling. The subromances become mild menances, for William and Kibbee are the Back Bay bluebloods who seek to quell the kid brother's (Powell) stage romance. Kibbee is the family attorney and William the elder brother. They both fall for show girls as well.

Adaptation from the Avery Hopwood–David Belasco–Ina Claire original is as liberal as the 1929 version. At least, in 1933 they don't have Nick Lucas and Winnie Lightner warble numbers every other minute. Once the numbers get going, nothing else matters. There are five impressive songs by Al Dubin and Harry Warren.

Some good trouping, especially where expert playing is necessary, to bolster the loose assignments, such as the difficult roles given William and Kibbee. Powell also overcomes the trite situation of the society blueblood with stage ambitions. For the rest, however, Keeler, Blondell and MacMahon are more or less faithful to their characters. Ned Sparks and Ginger Rogers also score.

1932/33: NOMINATION: Best Sound

•

GOLD DIGGERS OF 1935

1935, 95 mins, US Ⓥ ⦿ ▭ b/w

Dir Busby Berkeley ***Prod*** [uncredited] ***Scr*** Manuel Seff, Peter Milne ***Ph*** George Barnes ***Ed*** George Amy ***Mus*** Leo F. Forbstein (dir.), Ray Heindorf (arr.) ***Art*** Anton Grot

Act Dick Powell, Gloria Stuart, Adolphe Menjou, Glenda Farrell, Grant Mitchell, Alice Brady (Warner)

As in the previous *Diggers*, it's the spec that counts, and the story deficiencies are a bit more acute. Basically, the story [by Robert Lord and Peter Milne] lags for an hour before the fashionable charity show, which is the excuse for the spec, commences.

Dick Powell is the affable hotel clerk (no longer a songwriter) who falls for the stingy millionairess's daughter (Gloria Stuart). Frank McHugh, the scapegrace son, who's checked off three chorus girl wives at the rate of $100,000 settlement to each, is the vis-a-vis of Dorothy Dare.

Adolphe Menjou does the best job as the irascible, chiseling entrepreneur, with Joe Cawthorn as comedy foil. Alice Brady is equally legit and effective in her skinflint assignment. Hugh Herbert's role of an eccentric snuffbox addict is rather hazy.

The Al Dubin-Harry Warren songs this time miss a bit. "The Words Are In My Heart" is the waltz theme, reprised for the choreography with the baby grands—a highly effective ballet of the Steinways. "Lullaby of Broadway" is the final musical elaboration. Latter number, led by Winifred Shaw, runs overboard in footage.

1935: Best Song ("Lullaby of Broadway")

NOMINATIONS: Best Dance Direction ("Lullaby of Broadway," "The Words Are in My Heart")

•

GOLD DIGGERS OF 1937

1936, 101 mins, US b/w

Dir Lloyd Bacon, Busby Berkeley ***Prod*** [uncredited] ***Scr*** Warren Duff ***Ph*** Arthur Edeson ***Ed*** Thomas Richards ***Mus*** Leo F. Forbstein (dir.) ***Art*** Max Parker

Act Dick Powell, Joan Blondell, Victor Moore, Glenda Farrell, Lee Dixon, Osgood Perkins (Warner)

Where some of the *Gold Digger* annuals from Warner have not been overburdened with heavy story material, the current musical opus gets moving with the advantage of a trim backstage yarn taken from *Mystery of Life*, the Broadway play by Richard Maibaum, Michael Wallach and George Haight.

Cast as a cocksure insurance salesman, Dick Powell breezes through the picture like he had been selling policies all his life. He has four outstanding songs, never overdoes them and breaks through with his ballads at the most opportune times.

Victor Moore enters the picture scene again back at his old trick of show thefting. In the role of the hypochondriac theatrical producer, he is the trouper of old and easily the comedy life of the party. Glenda Farrell, a typical gold-digging chorine in the story, works smoothly and for laughable results opposite the pompous show czar.

Joan Blondell, while not given her customary rowdy role, is effective as the chorine-turned-stenog. This spots her opposite Dick Powell again, with a modern-day romance deftly introduced and never permitted to go overboard.

1936: NOMINATION: Best Dance Direction ("Love and War")

•

GOLD DIGGERS OF BROADWAY
1929, 105 mins, US col
Dir Roy Del Ruth ***Scr*** Robert Lord ***Mus*** Al Dubin, Joe Burke
Act Nancy Welford, Conway Tearle, Winnie Lightner, Ann Pennington, Lilyan Tashman, Nick Lucas (Warner)

Lots of color—Technicolor—lots of comedy, girls, songs, music, dancing, production in *Gold Diggers of Broadway*.

When they got through with [Avery Hopwood's play] *Gold Diggers*, Warners had only the title left. Around that they built another show, on and off stage.

Somebody tossed the picture into Winnie Lightner's lap. Mugging, talking, singing or slapsticking, she can do them all, and does in this picture. Nancy Welford does nicely enough what she has to do.

Next to Lightner in work is her comedy opposite, Albert Gran, as a grey haired heavyweight lawyer, whom Winnie lands. Lilyan Tashman does an upstage show dame rather well. Helen Foster and William Bakewell are the kids in a very slim love thread.

In the rewritten *Gold Diggers* the love thing is only the alibi. The new story is hung onto it, with just enough of the digging to hold up the title. Well worked out, with plenty of speed all of the time, and color all of the while.

•

GOLDEN BOWL, THE
2000, 134 mins, US/France/UK Ⓥ ⦿ ▭ col
Dir James Ivory ***Prod*** Ismail Merchant ***Scr*** Ruth Prawer Jhabvala ***Ph*** Tony Pierce Roberts ***Ed*** John David Allen ***Mus*** Richard Robbins ***Art*** Andrew Sanders
Act Uma Thurman, Jeremy Northam, Kate Beckinsale, Nick Nolte, Anjelica Huston, James Fox (Merchant Ivory/TF1/Miramax)

Vastly uneven, with some wonderful period touches but also more than a few tedious moments, *The Golden Bowl* is Ismail Merchant and James Ivory's third screen adaptation of a Henry James novel, following *The Europeans* (1979) and *The Bostonians* (1984).

The first reel is particularly weak and diffuse: It takes the filmmakers a good half hour to establish the historical milieu and dramatis personae, jumping around from 1903 to 1909 and moving back and forth between England and Italy.

Story proper centers on Amerigo (Jeremy Northam), the descendant of an illustrious but bankrupt line of Roman princes. He's about to marry Maggie (Kate Beckinsale), the loving daughter of America's first billionaire, Adam Verver (Nick Nolte), a retired tycoon who lives in Europe. Before his engagement, Amerigo had a passionate affair with Charlotte (Uma Thurman), an American school friend of Maggie's. Too poor to marry, the couple parted. Charlotte's reappearance just days before his wedding triggers a series of events that ultimately will damage two marriages and send four lives spiraling out of control.

Everything in the film, particularly in the last reel, is spelled out in an explicit, literal manner. Ivory lovingly details the settings, with lavish re-creations of costume balls and inventive glimpses of the industrial revolution in America. But impressive and sumptuous as these reconstructions are, they serve to further weaken the storytelling, making the languid pacing even more damaging to the central action.

Film's most disappointing aspect is the work by the two leads. Thurman is effective at conveying modernist cool, but she is not particularly adept in period pieces. Burdened with an unconvincing Italian accent, Northam lacks authority in portraying the conflicting emotions of a man who loves his wife but is passionately involved with another woman. It's Nolte who provides the pic's most resonant performance.

•

GOLDEN CHILD, THE
1986, 93 mins, US Ⓥ ⦿ col
Dir Michael Ritchie ***Prod*** Edward S. Feldman, Robert D. Wachs ***Scr*** Dennis Feldman ***Ph*** Donald E. Thorin ***Ed*** Richard A. Harris ***Mus*** Michel Colombier ***Art*** J. Michael Riva
Act Eddie Murphy, Charles Dance, Charlotte Lewis, Victor Wong, J. L. Reate, Randall "Tex" Cobb (Feldman/Meeker/Murphy)

A strange hybrid of Far Eastern mysticism, treacly sentimentality, diluted reworkings of Eddie Murphy's patented confrontation scenes across racial and cultural boundaries, and dragged in ILM (Industrial Light & Magic) special effects monsters, the film makes no sense on any level.

Concoction has Murphy as a social worker specializing in tracking down missing children who is recruited to rescue the virtually divine Golden Child. Eponymous character, a so-called perfect child with magical powers of good, has been kidnapped in an overblown opening sequence by an unmitigated villain portrayed by a bearded Charles Dance, who wears a long leather coat like a Sergio Leone baddie.

Much nonsense ensues involving assorted bikers, chop-socky-happy Asians and a serpentine sorceress.

•

GOLDENEYE
1995, 130 mins, US Ⓥ ⦿ ▭ col
Dir Martin Campbell ***Prod*** Michael G. Wilson, Barbara Broccoli ***Scr*** Jeffrey Caine, Bruce Feirstein ***Ph*** Phil Meheux ***Ed*** Terry Rawlings ***Mus*** Eric Serra ***Art*** Peter Lamont
Act Pierce Brosnan, Sean Bean, Izabella Scorupco, Famke Janssen, Joe Don Baker, Judi Dench (Broccoli/United Artists)

James Bond definitely is back in business with *GoldenEye*. Among the better of the 17 Bonds and a dynamic action entry in its own right, this first 007 adventure in six years breathes fresh creative and commercial life into the 33-year-old series. Pierce Brosnan makes a solid debut in the role he almost got eight years earlier, and Ian Fleming's very mid-century secret agent has been shrewdly repositioned in the '90s.

Everything, including the wild conceptualization of the action sequences, the impudence, the sexual pugnaciousness and the willingness to have a little fun at the expense of the hero, is pushed a bit further than it has been recently.

Prologue is set back in the old Soviet Union, where Bond and Agent 006, Alec Trevelyan (Sean Bean), are able to penetrate a massive chemical weapons facility beneath a dam. Alec is killed by Gen. Ourumov (Gottfried John), but 007 manages to get away in one of his most hilariously preposterous escapes ever.

Nine years later, ferocious Russian gangster Xenia Onatopp (Famke Janssen) steals a new Stealth helicopter and flies it off to the motherland. Xenia and Ourumov invade a Space Weapons Control station and wipe out nearly all the staff, leaving comely computer programmer Natalya Simonova (Izabella Scorupco) as the only apparent survivor. Realizing they're up against some errant forces in the now unpredictable new Russia, MI6 realizes this is a job for James Bond. In St. Petersburg, Bond discovers that the shadow figure pulling the evil strings is none other than his old pal Alec, 006.

Just about the only holdover from the old days is Desmond Llewelyn's Q, who again outfits Bond with a few bizarre gadgets that just happen to come in handy.

Pic has a fine adversary in Bean's Alec. The stunning Janssen's deliciously sadistic Xenia instantly assumes an almost unique position in the pantheon as a potential Bond girl gone very bad. As Bond's eventual main squeeze, the fetching Scorupco has a rather more conventional assignment.

•

GOLDEN RENDEZVOUS
1977, 103 mins, US Ⓥ col
Dir Ashley Lazarus ***Prod*** Andre Pieters ***Scr*** Stanley Price ***Ph*** Ken Higgins ***Ed*** Ralph Kemplen
Act Richard Harris, Ann Turkel, David Janssen, Burgess Meredith, John Vernon, Gordon Jackson (Film Trust/Okun/Golden Rendezvous)

Despite an overabundance of plot, deaths, and explosions, there's virtually nothing in this puddle of a mid-ocean thriller that wouldn't make a 12-year-old cringe in embarrassment.

Pic [adapted from an Alistair MacLean novel] tells the tale of the Caribbean Star, a combination cargo ship and floating casino, hijacked by mercenary John Vernon. Following the orders of an unknown mastermind, he and his men, with the aid of an atomic device, plan to exchange the captured passengers and bomb for the golden contents of a U.S. Treasury ship.

And so it goes, albeit not as simply, until First Officer Richard Harris, accompanied by Ann Turkel and Gordon Jackson, step in to save the day.

•

GOLDEN VOYAGE OF SINBAD, THE
1974, 105 mins, UK Ⓥ ⦿ col
Dir Gordon Hessler ***Prod*** Charles H. Schneer, Ray Harryhausen ***Scr*** Brian Clemens ***Ph*** Ted Moore ***Ed*** Roy Watts ***Mus*** Miklos Rozsa ***Art*** John Stoll
Act John Phillip Law, Caroline Munro, Tom Baker, Douglas Wilmer, Martin Shaw, Gregoire Aslan (Columbia)

An Arabian Nightish saga told with some briskness and opulence for the childish eye, yet ultimately falling short of implied promise as an adventure spree.

As with producer Charles H. Schneer's *Jason and the Argonauts*, Ray Harryhausen encores as coproducer and special effects collaborator. Among his creations: an animated ship's figurehead, a grotesque centaur, a many-armed religious idol and swordplay adversary, and a couple of small bat-like creatures performing intelligence duty for the black artsy heavy of the piece. Good enough conjuring tricks to impress the kids.

Neither story nor running time are belabored under Gordon Hessler's capable direction. And the play-acting is up to snuff for this kind of throwback, in which John Phillip Law impersonates Sinbad with appealing understatement.

•

GOLDFINGER
1964, 110 mins, UK Ⓥ ⦿ col
Dir Guy Hamilton ***Prod*** Harry Saltzman, Albert R. Broccoli ***Scr*** Richard Maibaum, Paul Dehn ***Ph*** Ted Moore ***Ed*** Peter Hunt ***Mus*** John Barry ***Art*** Ken Adam
Act Sean Connery, Honor Blackman, Gert Frobe, Shirley Eaton, Tania Mallet, Harold Sakata (Eon/United Artists)

There's not the least sign of staleness in this third sample of the Bond 007 formula. Some liberties have been taken with Ian Fleming's original novel but without diluting its flavor. The mood is set before the credits show up, with Sean Connery making an arrogant pass at a chick and spying a thug creeping up from behind; he's reflected in the femme's eyeballs. So he heaves the heavy into bathful of water and connects the bath deftly to a handy supply of electricity.

Thereafter the plot gets its teeth into the real business, which is the duel between Bond and Goldfinger. The latter plans to plant an atomic bomb in Fort Knox and thus contaminate the U.S. hoard of the yellow stuff so that it can't be touched, and thus increase tenfold the value of his own gold, earned by hard international smuggling.

Connery repeats his suave portrayal of the punch-packing Bond, who can find his way around the wine list as easily as he can negotiate a dame. But, if backroom boys got star billing, it's deserved by Ken Adam, who has designed the production with a wealth of enticing invention. There's a ray gun that cuts through any metal, and threatens to carve Bond down the middle. There's Goldfinger's automobile—cast in solid gold. And his farm is stocked with furniture that moves at the press of a button.

Honor Blackman makes a fine, sexy partner for Bond. As Pussy Galore, Goldfinger's pilot for his private plane, she does not take things lying down—she's a judo expert who throws Bond until the final k.o. when she's tumbled herself.

Gert Frobe, too, is near-perfect casting as the resourceful Goldfinger, an amoral tycoon who treats gold cornering as a business like any other.

1964: Best Sound Effects

•

GOLD OF THE SEVEN SAINTS
1961, 89 mins, US b/w
Dir Gordon Douglas ***Prod*** Leonard Freeman ***Scr*** Leigh Brackett, Leonard Freeman ***Ph*** Joseph Biroc ***Ed*** Folmar Blangsted ***Mus*** Howard Jackson ***Art*** Stanley Fleischer
Act Clint Walker, Roger Moore, Leticia Roman, Robert Middleton, Chill Wills, Gene Evans (Warner)

By gold-and-rod western standards this is no *Treasure of the Sierra Madre* by a long shot, but it's a darned good imitation heir apparent, expertly written and colorfully enacted by a polished cast headed by Clint Walker and Roger Moore.

A strong screenplay is the firm foundation upon which the picture remains erect and engrossing until its disappointingly shaky conclusion. Working with a novel by Steve Frazee, the writers have penned some frisky dialog and constructed several gripping situations. Walker and Moore are cast as trapping partners who strike it rich and are chased persistently over the sprawling desert and through craggy hill country by several marauding parties who have one thing in common—total disdain for the golden rule.

Unlike *Treasure*, this film lays a golden egg through the unconvincing nature and transparent spirit of the climactic laughing jag, for the gold did not corrupt these heroes as it did the gentlemen of *Sierra Madre*.

Utilizing his customary heroically reserved approach, Walker does well by the role of anchor man. Moore, as his faithful but emotionally unsettled Irish mate, gives a most colorfully compelling screen characterization.

•

GOLD RUSH, THE
1925, 120 mins, US Ⓥ ⦿ ⊗ b/w
Dir Charles Chaplin ***Prod*** Charles Chaplin ***Scr*** Charles Chaplin ***Ph*** Rollie H. Totheroh ***Art*** Charles D. Hall

Act Charles Chaplin, Mack Swain, Tom Murray, Georgia Hale (Chaplin)

The Gold Rush is a distinct triumph for Charlie Chaplin from both the artistic and commercial standpoints. Billed as a dramatic comedy, the story carries more of a plot than the rule with the star's former offerings.

Charlie is presented as a tramp prospector in the wilds of Alaska, garbed in his old familiar derby, cane, baggy pants and shoes. He seeks refuge from a raging Arctic storm in the cabin of Black Larson (Tom Murray), hunted outlaw, and is allowed to stay by the latter.

Big Jim McKay (Mack Swain), a husky prospector, discovers a huge vein of gold on his claim, but the storm uproots his tent and blows him to the hut of Larson. The latter objects to McKay's intrusion, and a struggle ensues between the two for possession of a rifle. Chaplin scores here with business in trying to keep out of line with the barrel of the gun. McKay finally subdues Larson and elects to stay till the storm subsides. But the blizzard continues for many days, and provisions give out. The final scenes of Charlie and McKay journeying back to the States as multi-millionaires are unusual in that they show Chaplin out of his familiar attire. He is dressed in the height of fashion with evening dress and all the adornments.

Humor is the dominating force, with Chaplin reaching new heights as a comedian. Chaplin naturally carries practically the entire 10 reels of action and performs this task without difficulty.

•

GOLD RUSH, THE

1942, 71 mins, US Ⓥ b/w

Dir Charles Chaplin **Prod** Charles Chaplin **Scr** Charles Chaplin **Ph** Rollie Totheroh **Ed** Reginald McGahann **Mus** Charles Chaplin, Max Terr

Act Charles Chaplin, Mack Swain, Georgia Hale, Tom Murray (United Artists)

With music and narrative dialog added, Charlie Chaplin's *The Gold Rush* [1925] stands the test of time. Chaplin's inimitable cane, derby, hobble and moustache of early days still retain solid comedy for both the younger generation and older folks.

Chaplin did a remarkable job in the editing, background, music and narrative for the new version of his greatest grosser. Original two hours of running time has been edited down to 71 minutes.

Result is a technical achievement in speeding up action of a silent picture to the requirements of sound, and still not making apparent the increased speed in projection. All the episodes of *Gold Rush* are retained to provide strong comedy reaction of original, like the prospector's cabin marooned in the storm with Chaplin stewing the shoe when food runs out; Chaplin's own narrative is crisply delivered, and he refers to his screen character as "The Little Fellow" throughout.

1942: NOMINATIONS: Best Scoring of a Dramatic Picture, Sound

•

GOLDWYN FOLLIES, THE

1938, 113 mins, US Ⓥ col

Dir George Marshall **Prod** Samuel Goldwyn **Scr** Ben Hecht **Ph** Gregg Toland **Ed** Sherman Todd **Mus** Alfred Newman (dir.) **Art** Richard Day

Act Adolphe Menjou, Ritz Bros, Zorina, Kenny Baker, Andrea Leeds, Ella Logan (Goldwyn/United Artists)

The astute Samuel Goldwyn has assembled top names from grand opera, class terpsichore, music, radio and films. The mixture, in the brilliant hues of Technicolor, turns out to be a lavish production in which certain individual performances and ensembles erase the memory of some dull moments. Four of the musical numbers were composed by the late George Gershwin, with lyrics by Ira Gershwin; Vernon Duke completed the score.

Film musical is reported to have cost $2 million. It doesn't parade such extravagance on the screen, which probably is due to some heavy blue penciling en route. Not withstanding, it is a hefty eyeful.

Start shows Adolphe Menjou much concerned that his productions have lost mass appeal—the common touch. Country girl (Andrea Leeds) tells him what's the matter, takes the job of studio censor and passes on the script and casting of the production in progress.

Meanwhile, Edgar Bergen and "Charlie" wait in the outer office of the casting director and exchange quips on the world as they see it and some of the people in it. The Ritz Bros, owners of a traveling animal circus, drive in the studio gates intent on film careers. Phil Baker dashes from stage to wardrobe in an effort to keep pace with script changes of his part. Jerome Cowan directs the revised version, sequences of which introduce Helen Jepson in scenes from *La Traviata*, and Zorina dances with the American Ballet troupe. That's how all of them, except Kenny Baker, get in front of the camera.

1938: NOMINATION: Best Score

•

GO NAKED IN THE WORLD

1961, 103 mins, US ▭ col

Dir Ranald MacDougall **Prod** Aaron Rosenberg **Scr** Ranald MacDougall **Ph** Milton Krasner **Ed** John McSweeney, Jr. **Mus** Adolph Deutsch **Art** George W. Davis, Edward Carfagno

Act Gina Lollobrigida, Anthony Franciosa, Ernest Borgnine, Luana Patten, Will Kuluva, Philip Ober (M-G-M/Arcola)

The screen's obsession with ladies of ill repute is prolonged in *Go Naked in the World*, a plodding account of a call girl's romantic disaster. There are some magnetic personalities in the cast, some flashy melodramatic scenes and a provocative title.

It is Gina Lollobrigida's turn to play the trollop with the heart of gold and bank account to match. She shares an ill-fated love affair with Anthony Franciosa, rebellious son of a dominant, self-made construction tycoon (Ernest Borgnine).

Screenplay from the book by Tom T. Chamalese adds a novel twist and a new dimension to the now classic story of hooked and hooker in that father, like son, has shared intimate relations with the girl.

The character Lollobrigida is playing lacks depth. She brings to it her exciting sensual beauty but the character never comes into focus. Franciosa gives an earnest, virile performance, but there are moments when his unrelenting intensity begins to grow disconcerting and uncomfortable for the spectator. Emoting honors belong to Borgnine.

•

GONE IN SIXTY SECONDS

2000, 117 mins, US ⦿ Ⓥ ▭ col

Dir Dominic Sena **Prod** Jerry Bruckheimer, Mike Stenson **Scr** Scott Rosenberg **Ph** Paul Cameron **Ed** Tom Muldoon, Chris Lebenzon **Mus** Trevor Rabin **Art** Jeff Mann

Act Nicolas Cage, Angelina Jolie, Giovanni Ribisi, Delroy Lindo, Will Patton, Christopher Eccleston, Robert Duvall (Bruckheimer/Touchstone)

Big scenes at the beginning and end of *Gone in Sixty Seconds* prominently feature an auto compactor, which is exactly what should be used on this lemon. Perfectly dreadful in every respect, this big-budget remake of the late H. B. Halicki's 1974 indie hit doesn't even rate on the most basic level as a good car-chase picture. Pic's raison d'etre is the spectacle of a group of car thieves stealing 50 cars in the course of one night. Motivating the action in screenwriter Scott Rosenberg's construct is a serious case of brotherly love: Legendary auto booster Memphis Raines (Nicolas Cage in blondish mode) is recruited from long retirement by shady old pal Atley (Will Patton) to save the butt of Memphis' derelict younger bro, Kip (Giovanni Ribisi, sporting a horrible heroin-chic look), who will be killed by Brit gangster Raymond Calitri (Christopher Eccleston) unless he fulfills the latter's standing order for 50 cars in 72 hours. Memphis rounds up his loyal crew from the old days, most of whom have since gone straight, including chopshop mentor Otto (Robert Duvall), jovial driving instructor Donny (Chi McBride) and old flame Sway (Angelina Jolie).

The sight of all those cars being stolen one after another isn't that interesting, and director Dominic Sena makes no attempt to build suspense from the thefts and getaways; it's only the spectacle of crunching metal, crashing glass and squealing rubber that interests him. Film flops on every level: Attempt to populate the story with human characters and emotional motivation (utterly absent from the original) is lame and programmatic, Paul Cameron's lensing is muddily sulphurous and the insistently chaotic score mechanically uses the beginning of nearly every scene for a music cue. Cage capably holds focus at pic's center, but he's been down this road before to better effect.

•

GONE TO EARTH

(US: THE WILD HEART)

1950, 110 mins, UK col

Dir Michael Powell, Emeric Pressburger **Prod** David O. Selznick **Scr** Michael Powell, Emeric Pressburger **Ph** Christopher Challis **Ed** Reginald Mills **Mus** Brian Easdale **Art** Hein Heckroth

Act Jennifer Jones, David Farrar, Cyril Cusack, Sybil Thorndike, Edward Chapman, Hugh Griffith (London/Vanguard)

Powell and Pressburger freely adapted the novel by Mary Webb which has English fox hunting as its background.

Principal character, Jennifer Jones, lives with her father in the mountains. A simple girl, steeped in local mysticisms, when asked by her father if she will marry the first man to propose, she agrees. The first proposal is from the local parson, but after the wedding, she is induced to run away with the squire and is brought back home by her husband. Primarily a simple yarn about simple people, it is without finesse, polish or sophistication. Dialog just about emerges from the monosyllabical state.

Jones makes the character of Hazel Woodus a pathetic, winsome creature. It is a genuine and, at times, glowing performance.

•

GONE WITH THE WIND

1939, 217 mins, US Ⓥ ⦿ col

Dir Victor Fleming, [George Cukor, Sam Wood, B. Reeves Eason] **Prod** David O. Selznick **Scr** Sidney Howard, [Ben Hecht] **Ph** Ernest Haller, Ray Rennahan, Wilfrid M. Cline, [Lee Garmes] **Ed** Hal C. Kern, James E. Newcom **Mus** Max Steiner **Art** William Cameron Menzies

Act Clark Gable, Vivien Leigh, Leslie Howard, Olivia de Havilland, Hattie McDaniel, Thomas Mitchell (Selznick)

After nearly a year of actual filming, editing and scoring, David O. Selznick's production of *Gone With the Wind*, from Margaret Mitchell's novel of the Civil War and reconstruction period, is one of the truly great films. The lavishness of its production, the consummate care and skill which went into its making, the assemblage of its fine cast and expert technical staff combine in a theatrical attraction completely justifying the princely investment of $3.9 million.

In the leading roles, the casting of which was the subject of national debate and conjecture for many months, are Clark Gable, as Rhett Butler; Vivien Leigh, who gives a brilliant performance as Scarlett O'Hara; Leslie Howard and Olivia de Havilland, as Ashley and Melanie.

In the desire apparently to leave nothing out, Selznick has left too much in.

As in the book, the most effective portions of the saga of the destroyed South deal with human incident against the background of The War Between the States and the impact of honorable defeat to the Southern forces. Director Victor Fleming has caught a series of memorable views of plantation life and scenes and builds a strong case for a civilization of chivalry.

Among the players, Leigh's Scarlett commands first commendation as a memorable performance, of wide versatility and effective earnestness. Gable's Rhett Butler is as close to Mitchell's conception as might be imagined. He gives a forceful impersonation.

On the heels of these two, Hattie McDaniel, as Mammy, comes closest with a bid for top position as a trouper. It is she who contributes the most moving scene in the film, her plea with Melanie that the latter should persuade Rhett to permit burial of his baby daughter.

Of the other principals, de Havilland does a standout as Melanie, and Howard is convincing as the weak-charactered Ashley.

1939: Best Picture, Director, Actress (Vivien Leigh), Supp. Actress (Hattie McDaniel), Screenplay, Color Cinematography, Art Direction, Editing, Special Awards (use of color design and use of coordinated equipment)

NOMINATIONS: Best Actor (Clark Gable), Supp. Actress (Olivia de Havilland), Original Score, Sound, Special Effects

•

GOODBYE CHARLIE

1964, 117 mins, US ▭ col

Dir Vincente Minnelli **Prod** David Weisbart **Scr** Harry Kurnitz **Ph** Milton Krasner **Ed** John W. Holmes **Mus** Andre Previn **Art** Jack Martin Smith, Richard Day

Act Tony Curtis, Debbie Reynolds, Pat Boone, Joanna Barnes, Ellen Burstyn, Walter Matthau (Venice/20th Century-Fox)

Even by delving into fantasy for its wildly implausible premise this picturization of George Axelrod's not-so-successful 1960 Broadway play doesn't come off as anything but the mildest type of entertainment.

A joint effort of Curtis's indie Venice banner and 20th-Fox, story framework of the David Weisbart production takes form when a hotshot Hollywood writer Lothario named Charlie is thoroughly punctured by a gun-wielding Hungarian producer after catching him vis-a-vis with his wife, and writer is reincarnated as a luscious babe.

Debbie Reynolds takes on the task of creating an offbeat character as the reincarnated late-departed who combines the lecherous mind and mores of her former male self with a sexy exterior and newfound femininity while announcing to the world she is the writer's widow.

Tony Curtis plays another writer, victim's best friend who arrives from his Paris home to deliver the eulogy and finds himself saddled not only with a debt-plagued estate, as executor, but this reborn pal as well, now a blonde who decides to cash in on former affairs with filmdom wives and plays cozy with the producer who shot Charlie. Pat Boone is an over-rich boy with a mother complex who falls for Debbie and wants to marry her, while Walter Matthau puts goulash in the producer role.

•

GOODBYE, COLUMBUS
1969, 104 mins, US Ⓥ ⊙ col
Dir Larry Peerce ***Prod*** Stanley R. Jaffe ***Scr*** Arnold Schulman ***Ph*** Gerald Hirschfeld ***Ed*** Ralph Rosenblum ***Mus*** Charles Fox ***Art*** Manny Gerard
Act Richard Benjamin, Ali MacGraw, Jack Klugman, Nan Martin, Michael Meyers, Lori Shelle (Paramount/Willow Tree)

This adaptation of Philip Roth's National Book Award–winning novella is sometimes a joy in striking a boisterous mood and otherwise handling action.

Castwise the feature excels. Richard Benjamin as the boy, a librarian after serving in the army, and Ali MacGraw, making her screen bow as the daughter of wealthy and socially conscious parents, offer fresh portrayals seasoned with rich humor. Their romance develops swiftly after their meeting at a country-club pool.

As girl's hard-working father, Jack Klugman rates a big hand and there is a dramatic sequence between father and daughter at wedding of the son of the house which is both tender and memorable.

Several outstanding sequences, among them the gaiety of a Jewish wedding, and hilarious dinner-table action as Benjamin first meets the family.

1969. NOMINATION. Best Adapted Screenplay

•

GOODBYE GIRL, THE
1977, 110 mins, US Ⓥ ⊙ col
Dir Herbert Ross ***Prod*** Ray Stark ***Scr*** Neil Simon ***Ph*** David M. Walsh ***Ed*** Margaret Booth ***Mus*** Dave Grusin ***Art*** Albert Brenner
Act Richard Dreyfuss, Marsha Mason, Quinn Cummings, Paul Benedict, Barbara Rhoades, Theresa Merritt (M-G-M/Warner)

Richard Dreyfuss in offbeat romantic lead casting, and vibrant Marsha Mason head the cast as two lovers in spite of themselves.

Story peg finds Mason, once-divorced and now jilted, finding out that her ex-lover has sublet their N.Y. pad to aspiring thesp Dreyfuss. Mason has two other problems: a precocious daughter, Quinn Cummings, and her own thirty-ish age which will prevent a successful resumption of a dancing career necessary to make ends meet.

The Neil Simon script evolves a series of increasingly intimate and sensitive character encounters as the adults progress from mutual hostility to an enduring love.

Performances by Dreyfuss, Mason and Cummings are all great, and the many supporting bits are filled admirably.

1977: Best Actor (Richard Dreyfuss)

NOMINATIONS: Best Picture, Actress (Marsha Mason), Supp. Actress (Quinn Cummings), Original Screenplay

•

GOODBYE, MR. CHIPS
1939, 110 mins, UK Ⓥ ⊙ b/w
Dir Sam Wood ***Prod*** Victor Saville ***Scr*** R.C. Sherriff, Claudine West, Eric Maschwitz ***Ph*** Freddie Young ***Ed*** Charles Frend ***Mus*** Richard Addinsell ***Art*** Alfred Junge
Act Robert Donat, Greer Garson, Terry Kilburn, John Mills, Paul Heinreid, Judith Furse (M-G-M)

A charming, quaintly sophisticated account [from the novel *Goodbye, Mr. Chips!* by James Hilton] of the life of a schoolteacher, highlighted by a remarkably fine performance from Robert Donat.

Donat's range of character carries him from youth when he begins to teach at a boys school, through to his middle 30s, then to around the half-century mark, and finally into the slightly doddering age. The character he etches creates a bloodstream for the picture that keeps it intensely alive.

The romance of the schoolteacher and the girl he meets is adroitly and fascinatingly developed. Greer Garson is Katherine, who becomes Donat's wife, only to die all too soon, leaving the schoolmaster nothing but his desire to go forward, with his work and with the boys he tutors.

1939: Best Actor (Robert Donat)

NOMINATIONS: Best Picture, Director, Actress (Greer Garson), Screenplay, Editing, Sound

•

GOODBYE, MR. CHIPS
1969, 151 mins, UK Ⓥ ⊙ ▭ col
Dir Herbert Ross ***Prod*** Arthur P. Jacobs ***Scr*** Terence Rattigan ***Ph*** Oswald Morris ***Ed*** Ralph Kemplen ***Mus*** John Williams (sup.) ***Art*** Ken Adam
Act Peter O'Toole, Petula Clark, Michael Redgrave, George Baker, Michael Bryant, Sian Phillips (M-G-M/Apjac)

Lightning seldom strikes in the same place twice, and Hollywood's record for remaking its classics is only slightly better. M-G-M's reproduction of *Goodbye, Mr. Chips* as a big-budget musical [music and lyrics by Leslie Bricusse] with Peter O'Toole and Petula Clark is a sumptuous near-miss that trips on its own overproduction.

The film tells the love story of an English public school master for his work and wife. The scholarly, somewhat prissy and martinetish teacher who frets that his students don't like him is a total departure from O'Toole's previous roles. But there is a curious lack of warmth and humor, a middle-aged bachelor crotchetiness in the opening sequences. But as he transitions through his troubled love affair and unspectacular career, O'Toole creates a man of strength and dignity, whose tendency to appear ridiculous at times is endearing.

1969: NOMINATIONS: Best Actor (Peter O'Toole), Adapted Music Score

•

GOODBYE, NORMA JEAN
1976, 95 mins, US/Australia Ⓥ ▭ col
Dir Larry Buchanan ***Prod*** Larry Buchanan ***Scr*** Lynn Hubert, Larry Buchanan ***Ph*** Bob Sherry ***Mus*** Joe Beck
Act Misty Rowe, Terrence Locke, Patch Mackenzie, Preston Hanson, Marty Zagon, Andre Philippe (Austamerican)

This is the story of Norma Jean Baker, who finds her body irresistible to men and uses it to fulfill her ambitions of becoming a movie star, Marilyn Monroe.

Starting in 1941, she is raped by a motorcycle officer in lieu of a speeding ticket, which seemingly leaves her disliking sex. She works in a munitions factory, and wins a beauty contest.

Soon it becomes an endless succession of influential film men.

Eventually a retired and ailing movie mogul, Hal James (Preston Hanson), takes a presumably platonic interest in her and grooms her into the Marilyn Monroe image.

Thesping is mostly sound with Misty Rowe, in the title role, giving a fine and sensitive performance, catching the star's own voice exactly.

•

GOODBYE PEOPLE, THE
1984, 104 mins, US Ⓥ ⊙ col
Dir Herb Gardner ***Prod*** David V. Picker ***Scr*** Herb Gardner ***Ph*** John Lindley ***Ed*** Rick Shaine ***Art*** Tony Walton
Act Judd Hirsch, Martin Balsam, Pamela Reed, Ron Silver, Michael Tucker, Gene Saks (Coney Island)

The Goodbye People marks stage author and director Herb Gardner's first foray into film direction. Based on his late 1960s stage flop of the same name, neither time nor the transferal of media has improved the story of three eccentric losers who band together in hopes of changing their luck.

Basically a one set human comedy, the film centers on Arthur Korman (Judd Hirsch), a man in his 40s trapped in a job he cannot stand. To relieve the tension stemming from his inability to chuck working at a toy firm, he makes a daily early morning excursion to Coney Island to watch the sunrise. It is there he meets Max Silverman (Martin Balsam), the former owner of a boardwalk hot dog stand.

The uneasy alliance between the characters is treated in a glib fashion by Gardner.

•

GOODBYE PORK PIE
1981, 100 mins, New Zealand Ⓥ col
Dir Geoff Murphy ***Prod*** Geoff Murphy, Nigel Hutchinson ***Scr*** Geoff Murphy ***Ph*** Alun Bollinger ***Ed*** Michael Horton ***Mus*** John Charles (dir.) ***Art*** Kai Hawkins
Act Kelly Johnson, Tony Barry, Claire Oberman, Shirley Gruar, Bruno Lawrence, John Beach (Ama)

In *Goodbye Pork Pie*, *Easy Rider* meets the Keystone Kops. Following the classic road formula a car chase covers the length of the country and it is a major plus that the pace, fun and general mayhem are such that the pic does not get upstaged by the spectacular scenery.

In the breathing spells between, characters that might have been ciphers—the young punk on the run, the girl hitch-hiker and others whose paths intersect the speeding car—are given human dimensions.

Near the top of New Zealand's North Island Kelly Johnson steals a rental car and heads south, picking up a couple of passengers before he has gone very far. One is pursuing the wife who has walked out on him, and he persuades Johnson to extend what was to have been a short dash into a 1,000-mile marathon, taking in a car ferry crossing on the way.

Claire Oberman is a liberated blond whose frank confession that she is a virgin, given in the same breath with which she introduces herself, leads to a private $2 bet between the two men that this will be changed.

•

GOOD COMPANIONS, THE
1933, 110 mins, UK b/w
Dir Victor Saville ***Prod*** Angus McPhaill, Louis Levy, Ian Dalrymple, ***Scr*** W. P. Lipscomb ***Ph*** Bernard Knowles ***Ed*** Frederick Y. Smith ***Art*** Alfred Junge
Act Jessie Matthews, Edmund Gwenn, John Gielgud, Mary Glynne, Percy Parsons, A. W. Baskcomb (Gaumont-British)

Picturization of the J. B. Priestley bestseller was difficult, the story texture being complex. Story [with songs by George Posford and Douglas Furber] deals with a concert party that goes from bankruptcy to fame and fortune, helped by the stray people who flit across the canvas, the schoolmaster who writes jazz, the fading damsel who finances the show from a thirst for adventure, the little chorus girl who rises to be a great star, and so on.

In comparison to the book, picture may seem sketchy, but the interest is held. Characterizations are outstanding. Edmund Gwenn, as the carpenter who is really the center of the story, does the best bit of work. Mary Glynne is very good as Miss Trant, suggesting the pathetic side of the character with real skill. Jessie Matthews is not as boisterous as usual as the chorus girl.

Max Miller, the music-hall man, contributes an outstanding sketch as a salesman. Victor Saville's direction is straight but sound.

•

GOOD COMPANIONS, THE
1957, 105 mins, UK ▭ col
Dir J. Lee Thompson ***Prod*** Hamilton G. Inglis, J. Lee Thompson ***Scr*** T. J. Morrison, John Whiting, J. L. Hodson ***Ph*** Gilbert Taylor ***Ed*** Gordon Pilkington ***Mus*** Laurie Johnson ***Art*** Robert Jones
Act Eric Portman, Celia Johnson, Hugh Griffith, Janette Scott, John Fraser, Rachel Roberts (Associated British)

J.B. Priestley's homely and colorful yarn of a third-rate touring company makes a pedestrian musical. Much of the characterization and writing quality of the original is lost in the conventional screenplay.

An old-fashioned story line, without surprise twists, is not aided by the moderate quality of the score.

Opening shows some promise. In three short cameos it depicts the way in which Eric Portman, Celia Johnson and John Fraser throw in their lot with the Dinky Doos concert party, who are out of funds and facing disbandment. Johnson provides the cash to keep them in business and the rest of the film describes their unhappy experiences playing No. 3 dates to empty houses, until Janette Scott, the youthful star of the company, and Fraser get their big West End chance.

Scott makes a refreshing and appealing showing as the concert party star with ambitions. Fraser also turns in a sincere performance as a composer-accompanist, but it's also hard to accept his music as so good the publishers would be competing for it. Joyce Grenfell makes a typical contribution as a wealthy admirer.

•

GOOD DIE YOUNG, THE
1954, 98 mins, UK b/w
Dir Lewis Gilbert ***Prod*** Jack Clayton (assoc.) ***Scr*** Vernon Harris, Lewis Gilbert ***Ph*** Jack Asher ***Ed*** Ralph Kemplen ***Mus*** Georges Auric ***Art*** Bernard Robinson
Act Laurence Harvey, Gloria Grahame, Richard Basehart, Joan Collins, John Ireland, Stanley Baker (Romulus)

There is a major lineup of talent in this independently-made British pic, but fulfillment does not quite come up to expectations. Although there is basically a tense dramatic theme, the scrappy treatment, necessitated by the omnibus type of story, robs the film of some of its suspense and values.

The yarn takes four characters, brought together by force of circumstances, who participate in an armed holdup and come to a sticky end, clearly to satisfy a censor's insistence that crime mustn't pay.

First of the four central figures is Richard Basehart, playing an ex-GI and Korean war vet whose English wife had returned home to visit an ailing mother. The second is Stanley Baker, a professional boxer who has decided to abandon the ring with some money saved up, but an injured hand makes him virtually unemployable.

Then there is John Ireland, an American airman stationed in Britain who, while on a 48-hour pass, finds his wife (Gloria Grahame) knocking around with a British film actor. Finally, there is Laurence Harvey, an aristocratic English gent who has never done a day's work in his life and who conceives the holdup and talks the others into participating. The main strength of the film rests in the quality of the acting. All principal roles are expertly played.

•

GOOD EARTH, THE

1937, 140 mins, US Ⓥ b/w

Dir Sidney Franklin ***Prod*** Albert Lewin ***Scr*** Talbot Jennings, Tess Schlesinger, Claudine West ***Ph*** Karl Freund ***Ed*** Basil Wrangell ***Mus*** Herbert Stothart

Act Paul Muni, Luise Rainer, Walter Connolly, Tillie Losch, Charley Grapewin, Jessie Ralph (M-G-M)

Transfer of the [Pearl S.] Buck novel from page to celluloid, with a stop-off via the stage [play by Owen and Donald Davis], is a tough adaptation job. The characters are 100 percent Chinese. In many scenes such occidentals as Paul Muni and Walter Connolly are mixed with genuine Orientals for direct conversational contact, and no harmful false note is struck. Luise Rainer's Viennese amidst this mumble-jumble of dialects is but slightly noticeable, and then only at the beginning.

The marriage of Wang and O-Lan, their raising of the family and care of their land, the drought, Wang's rise to wealth, his desertion of the farm and his taking of a second wife, his return to the farm and the earth are faithfully transcribed. There are some departures for brevity's sake and some additions, such as the locust plague, which is a helpful contribution rather than a distraction, but the members of the House of Wang are Pearl Buck's original creations without change in this reported $3 million production.

Muni as Wang, with great makeup, is a splendid lead. Rainer has more difficulty, since her features are not so receptive to Oriental makeup. Yet a good actress overcomes these things, and Luise Rainer is an actress. Connolly as the semi-villainous and greedy uncle, takes the few laughts in a picture which is very sparing with its lightness. Tilly Losch, a dancer by profession, does little dancing, but plenty of good playing, as the second wife, and Charley Grapewin is splendid as the father of Wang.

The slightly tinted and brownish sepia hues, shading some of the farm sequences, give a magnificent effect.

1937: Best Actress (Luise Rainer), Cinematography

NOMINATIONS: Best Picture, Director, Editing

•

GOOD FAIRY, THE

1935, 98 mins, US b/w

Dir William Wyler ***Prod*** Henry Henigson ***Scr*** Preston Sturges ***Ph*** Norbert Brodine ***Ed*** Daniel Mandell ***Art*** Charles D. Hall

Act Margaret Sullavan, Herbert Marshall, Frank Morgan, Reginald Owen, Alan Hale, Beulah Bondi (Universal)

Preston Sturges has translated Ferenc Molnar's dainty stage comedy for the screen, and has turned out a somewhat vociferous paraphrase. Slightly idealistic atmosphere of the original is missing, and in its place is substituted a style of comedy closely akin to slapstick.

A little too much time is given to the initial sequence in the asylum, which is not funny nor particularly convincing, serving only to give Alan Hale and Beulah Bondi their one opportunity. From the asylum, action moves to the theatre where Lu (Margaret Sullavan) becomes an usher and her encounter, first with Reginald Owen and almost immediately with Frank Morgan, quickly puts the film into its stride. From there on it works to a farcical finish in which the burly waiter (Owen) removes her from the imagined lascivious attentions of her benefactor (Morgan).

Picture is fairly peppered with closeups which, delaying production, brought U and the director, William Wyler, to the mat. These closeups are so beautiful that they seem worthwhile even if a bit profuse.

Frank Morgan, as the benefactor, plays like an eccentric John Barrymore, but makes his points rapidly and surely. Reginald Owen, as a waiter, is an excellent foil and contributes some telling pantomime. Sullavan is uneasy in the asylum opening as she does not suggest the child. Later she performs more surely.

•

GOODFELLAS

1990, 146 mins, US Ⓥ ⊙ col

Dir Martin Scorsese ***Prod*** Irwin Winkler ***Scr*** Nicholas Pileggi, Martin Scorsese ***Ph*** Michael Ballhaus ***Ed*** Thelma Schoonmaker ***Art*** Kristi Zea

Act Robert De Niro, Ray Liotta, Joe Pesci, Lorraine Bracco, Paul Sorvino, Frank Sivero (Warner)

Simultaneously fascinating and repellent, *Goodfellas* is Martin Scorsese's colorful but dramatically unsatisfying inside look at Mafia life in 1955–80 New York City. Working from the nonfiction book *Wiseguy* by Nicholas Pileggi, Scorsese returns to the subject matter of his 1973 *Mean Streets* but from a more distanced, older, wiser and subtler perspective.

First half of the film, introing Ray Liotta, as an Irish-Italian kid, to the Mafia milieu, is wonderful. Scorsese's perfectly cast friezes of grotesque hoodlum types are caricatures in the best sense of the word. There's a giddy sense of exploring a forbidden world.

The second half, however, doesn't develop the dramatic conflicts between the character and the milieu that are hinted at earlier.

Liotta starts as a gofer for laconic neighborhood godfather Paul Sorvino, gradually coming under the tutelage of Robert De Niro, cast as a middle-aged Irish hood of considerable ruthlessness and repute. The skewed concept of loyalty involved is intertwined with an adolescent obsession with machismo, most memorably captured in Joe Pesci's short-statured, short-fused psycho.

One of the film's major flaws is that De Niro, with his menacing charm, always seems more interesting than Liotta, but he isn't given enough screen time to explore the relationship fully in his supporting role.

1990: Best Supp. Actor (Joe Pesci)

NOMINATIONS: Best Picture, Director, Supp. Actress (Lorraine Bracco), Adapted Screenplay, Editing

•

GOOD GUYS AND THE BAD GUYS, THE

1969, 90 mins, US ▭ col

Dir Burt Kennedy ***Prod*** Ronald M. Cohen, Dennis Shryack ***Scr*** Ronald M. Cohen, Dennis Shryack ***Ph*** Harry Stradling, Jr. ***Ed*** Howard Deane ***Mus*** William Lava ***Art*** Stan Jolley

Act Robert Mitchum, George Kennedy, David Carradine, Martin Balsam, Tina Louise, Lois Nettleton (Warners-Seven Arts)

George Kennedy, who stars with Robert Mitchum, plays the film mostly for comedy, and Mitchum's deadpan performance might be interpreted in same lineage. Laughs overshadow the serious moments.

Story concerns two relics of the Old West, an aging marshal no longer wanted by his townsmen and a similarly aging outlaw far past his prime. Onetime enemies, they now combine to thwart the efforts of a band of young outlaws to rob a train of a large shipment of money.

Yarn takes its motivation from Mitchum, retired against his will with a gold watch and pension, taking action against the raid he knows is coming, but which pompous mayor Martin Balsam brushes aside as impossible.

Both Mitchum and Kennedy imbue their roles with sound values.

•

GOOD MORNING, VIETNAM

1987, 120 mins, US Ⓥ ⊙ col

Dir Barry Levinson ***Prod*** Mark Johnson, Larry Brezner ***Scr*** Mitch Markowitz ***Ph*** Peter Sova ***Ed*** Stu Linder ***Mus*** Alex North ***Art*** Roy Walker

Act Robin Williams, Forest Whitaker, Tung Thanh Tran, Chintara Sukapatana, Bruno Kirby, J.T. Walsh (Touchstone)

After airman Adrian Cronauer (Robin Williams) blows into Saigon to be the morning man on Armed Forces Radio, things are never the same. With a machine-gun delivery of irreverencies and a crazed gleam in his eye, Cronauer turns the staid military protocol on its ear.

On the air he's a rush of energy, perfectly mimicking everyone from Gomer Pyle to Richard Nixon as well as the working grunt in the battlefields, blasting verboten rock-'n'roll over the airwaves while doing James Brown splits in the studio. From the start, the film bowls you over with excitement and for those who can latch on, it's a nonstop ride.

Although the film is set in Vietnam in 1965, the fighting seems to take a backseat to Williams's joking. Instead of the disk jockey being the eyes and ears of the events around him, Williams is a totally self-contained character, and despite numerous topical references, his comedy turns in on itself rather than opening on the scene outside.

Bruno Kirby as Cronauer's uptight immediate superior has a few priceless comic moments of his own as he takes to the airwaves with an array of polka music.

1987: NOMINATION: Best Actor (Robin Williams)

•

GOOD MOTHER, THE

1988, 103 mins, US Ⓥ ⊙ col

Dir Leonard Nimoy ***Prod*** Arnold Glimcher ***Scr*** Michael Bortman ***Ph*** David Watkin ***Ed*** Peter Berger ***Mus*** Elmer Bernstein ***Art*** Stan Jolley

Act Diane Keaton, Liam Neeson, Jason Robards, Ralph Bellamy, Teresa Wright, Asia Vieira (Touchstone)

The traumatic subject matter of a child custody fight is handled with restraint and intelligence in *The Good Mother*. Superbly acted by an imaginatively chosen cast, the adaptation of Sue Miller's 1986 bestseller goes so far to avoid tear-jerking pathos, the result may have come out a little drier than anticiapated.

Well judged script presents Anna Dunlap (Diane Keaton) as the recently divorced mother of Molly, an enthusiastic child of six. Living in the Boston area, working part-time in a lab and teaching piano, Anna is committed to her daughter above all else. Skittish and insecure where men are concerned, she nevertheless allows herself to be seduced by Leo (Liam Neeson), an iconoclastic, thoroughly charming Irish sculptor. Shortly, the boom is lowered. Anna's cold ex-husband Brian (James Naughton), an attorney now remarried, slaps a custody suit on her, announcing that Molly has informed him that Leo in some way molested her sexually.

In the legal crunch, Brian and his attorney (Joe Morton) have the easier job to show, in this conservative era, that Anna's bohemian, live-in lifestyle, casual moral stance and negligent attitude toward her boyfriend's behavior with Molly [briefly allowing the curious child to touch his genitals] represent a clear danger to the child.

Despite the moderate dramatic reserve, which partly stems from director Leonard Nimoy's predominant use of medium-shots, this is compelling stuff, and the performances are uniformly first-rate.

•

GOOD NEIGHBOR SAM

1964, 130 mins, US Ⓥ col

Dir David Swift ***Prod*** David Swift ***Scr*** James Fritzell, Everett Greenbaum, David Swift ***Ph*** Burnett Guffey ***Ed*** Charles Nelson ***Mus*** Frank DeVol ***Art*** Dale Hennesy

Act Jack Lemmon, Romy Schneider, Edward G. Robinson, Dorothy Provine, Michael Connors, Neil Hamilton (Columbia)

Jack Lemmon's farcial flair finds amusing exposure in this situation comedy. Lemmon topbills star lineup in his usual competent and zany fashion but it is the Viennese Romy Schneider, making her first Hollywood-lensed feature, who shines the brighest.

Narrative [based on the novel by Jack Finney] jumps with crazy, mixed-up situations, Lemmon playing low man on the totem pole of a San Francisco advertising agency until he suggests a new approach built around the average man in a campaign for a dissatisfied client about to ankle the agency. Suddenly, he is important business-wise. He also finds himself called upon to play the "husband" to his nextdoor neighbor, who is divorced and must come up with a spouse if she is to meet the provisions of her grandfather's will bequeathing her his $15 million estate.

Edward G. Robinson gets chuckles as the client, who demands a wholesome campaign and a wholesome man to conduct it.

•

GOOD SAM

1948, 114 mins, US Ⓥ b/w

Dir Leo McCarey ***Prod*** Leo McCarey ***Scr*** Ken Englund ***Ph*** George Barnes ***Ed*** James McKay ***Mus*** Robert Emmett Dolan ***Art*** John B. Goodman

Act Gary Cooper, Ann Sheridan, Ray Collins, Edmund Lowe, Joan Lorring, Ruth Roman (RKO/Rainbow)

Good Sam is a comedy whose central character, played by Gary Cooper, often slows the film's pace because of a languidness and too obviously premeditated performance in a pic that in itself is unusually long.

Good Sam starts off promisingly with a number of gagged-up situations that click, however contrived, but with the pic's continuance there is the omniscient thought that here is a story that has bags under its gags.

Sam cosigns bank loans for friends who never pay up; he lends his car to neighbors without knowing actually how he's going to get to work or the children to school. Sam loves everybody. In short, everyone sponges on him. And

Lu, his wife, constantly harasses Sam to get some sense, especially when he loses the down payment on a house she always had set her chapeau for.

Ann Sheridan, as something that might have stepped out of a Christian Dior salon instead of being an ever-lovin' wife and mother, is not always credible in a part that's unusual for her. Domestication is hardly Sheridan's cinematic dish, no matter how authentic looking are her scrambled eggs.

Cooper gives one of his standard performances—there is the wan smile, the gawky naiveté and a sartorial manner that suggests Sam's pants need pressing, too.

•

GOOD SON, THE
1993, 87 mins, US Ⓥ ⊙ col
Dir Joseph Ruben ***Prod*** Mary Anne Page, Joseph Ruben ***Scr*** Ian McEwan ***Ph*** John Lindley ***Ed*** George Bowers ***Mus*** Elmer Bernstein ***Art*** Bill Groom
Act Macauley Culkin, Elijah Wood, Wendy Crewson, David Morse, Daniel Hugh Kelly, Jacqueline Brookes (20th Century-Fox)

The *Home Alone* kid as an amoral, psychotic killer? What next, Barney levelling Tokyo? This rather peculiar thriller doesn't deliver enough jolts to leave the audience screaming.

The action centers around another prominent moppet, Elijah Wood (*Avalon, Forever Young*), playing a young boy with some very bad luck. Not only does Mark (Wood) watch his mother die at an early age, but he then gets shipped off to spend a couple of weeks with his aunt and uncle, only to discover that he's sharing a room with a prepubescent psychopath.

At first, Henry (Culkin) seems only a bit eccentric, but the stunts gradually become more outrageous, until he hints that he did away with his brother and tries to off his baby sister (Quinn Culkin, making her debut as yet another sprig on the Culkin money tree).

Working from a script by novelist Ian McEwan, producer-director Joseph Ruben pulls some of the same hackneyed strings as in his *Sleeping with the Enemy* but runs across the pitfall of mixing suspense with day care. In a nutshell, Culkin's cold, dispassionate performance will evoke too many laughs of the derisive kind, not just the genre's characteristic release of nervous tension.

•

GOOD, THE BAD AND THE UGLY, THE
1966, 161 mins, Italy Ⓥ ⊙ ▭ col
Dir Sergio Leone ***Prod*** Alberto Grimaldi ***Scr*** Luciano Vincenzoni, Sergio Leone, Mickey Knox ***Ph*** Tonino Delli Colli ***Ed*** Nino Baragli, Eugenio Alabiso ***Mus*** Ennio Morricone ***Art*** Carlo Simi
Act Clint Eastwood, Eli Wallach, Lee Van Cleef, Aldo Giuffre, Mario Brega, Luigi Pistilli (PEA)

The third in the Clint Eastwood series of Italo westerns, *The Good, the Bad and the Ugly* is exactly that—a curious amalgam of the visually striking, the dramatically feeble and the offensively sadistic.

Story [by Incrocci Agenore, Furio Scarpelli, Luciano Vincenzoni and director Sergio Leone] concerns search for buried treasure by "Good" Eastwood, "Ugly" Eli Wallach and "Bad" Lee Van Cleef (making his second appearance in an Eastwood western). Along the way they taunt and torture each other and also contribute a total of 20 dead bodies to the western landscape, reasonably well-faked by European exteriors. As befits his star status, Eastwood kills 10 of these; as befits his titular Goodness, his victims all draw first. Unlike the earlier Leone efforts, however, the violence here has little of the balletic, even erotic quality.

Leone's visual sense is as strong as ever, however, and his effective alternation of extreme closeups and long shots renders much of the pic graphically electric. Unfortunately, he allows several excursions into laughably sentimental characterization, and his three actors (especially Wallach) overplay to the point of absurdity.

Much of Tonino Delli Colli's photography is a knockout. Ennio Morricone's insistent music and Carlo Simi's baroque art direction further contribute to the pic's toomuchness.

•

GOOD WIFE, THE
1986, 92 mins, Australia Ⓥ col
Dir Ken Cameron ***Prod*** Jan Sharp ***Scr*** Peter Kenna ***Ph*** James Bartle ***Ed*** John Scott ***Mus*** Cameron Allan ***Art*** Sally Campbell
Act Rachel Ward, Bryan Brown, Sam Neill, Steven Vidler, Jennifer Claire, Bruce Barry (Laughing Kookaburra)

Ken Cameron's third feature, *The Good Wife*, is a classy romantic drama set in the small Australian country town of Corrimandel in 1939. Rachel Ward toplines as the eponymous wife who's bored with her unexciting life in this rural backwater. She's married to a burly, well-intentioned logger (real-life hubby Bryan Brown) and spends her time cooking, cleaning and helping other women in childbirth; part of her problem is that she's childless herself.

Neville Gifford (Sam Neill) arrives in town. Marge becomes more and more obsessed with the handsome stranger, eventually openly chasing after him, bringing scandal and shame on herself and her uncomprehending spouse. Fine performances from Ward, Brown and Neill.

•

GOOD WILL HUNTING
1997, 126 mins, US Ⓥ ⊙ col
Dir Gus Van Sant ***Prod*** Lawrence Bender ***Scr*** Ben Affleck, Matt Damon ***Ph*** Jean-Yves Escoffier ***Ed*** Pietro Scalia ***Mus*** Danny Elfman ***Art*** Melissa Stewart
Act Matt Damon, Robin Williams, Ben Affleck, Minnie Driver, Stellan Skarsgard, Casey Affleck (Miramax)

Gus Van Sant's emotionally involving psychological drama is a notch or two above the mainstream therapeutic sensibility of its story. Centering on a brilliant working-class youngster who's forced to come to terms with his creative genius and true feelings, this beautifully realized tale is always engaging and often quite touching. Cowritten by thesps Matt Damon and Ben Affleck, who have known each other since childhood in Boston, protagonist is Will Hunting (Damon), a 20-year-old lad who works as a janitor at MIT and spends most of his time with his coarse friends at the neighborhood bar. When bigshot professor Lambeau (Stellan Skarsgard) presents a math challenge to his students, Will anonymously solves the formula on a blackboard in the corridor.

Lambeau takes him under his wing but makes two conditions: that Will meets with him once a week for a math session and that he begins therapy. A succession of psychologists tries to reach Will; finally Lambeau summons his old classmate Sean McGuire (Robin Williams), a community college instructor and therapist—and the real drama begins.

Most of the narrative consists of intense, one-on-one sessions between Will and Sean, two equally stubborn, equally wounded men. Endowed with good looks and acting skills to match, Damon gives a charismatic performance in a demanding role. Williams's work here is quieter, subtler and far more satisfying than in *Awakenings*, in which he played a shy doctor. Rest of the cast is uniformly good, with standout work from Minnie Driver as an affluent British student who has a crush on Will.

1997: Best Supp. Actor (Robin Williams), Original Screenplay

NOMINATIONS: Best Picture, Actor (Matt Damon), Supp. Actress (Minnie Driver), Director, Editing, Original Dramatic Score, Original Song ("Miss Misery")

•

GOONIES, THE
1985, 111 mins, US Ⓥ ⊙ ▭ col
Dir Richard Donner ***Prod*** Richard Donner, Harvey Bernhard ***Scr*** Chris Columbus ***Ph*** Nick McLean ***Ed*** Michael Kahn ***Mus*** Dave Grusin ***Art*** J. Michael Riva
Act Sean Astin, Josh Brolin, Jeff Cohen, Corey Feldman, Kerri Green, Martha Plimpton (Amblin)

Territory is typical small town Steven Spielberg; this time set in a coastal community in Oregon. Story is told from the kids' point-of-view and takes a rather long time to be set in motion.

Brothers Mikey (Sean Astin) and Brand (Josh Brolin) are being forced to leave their home because land developers are foreclosing on their house to build a new country club. The boys are joined by compulsive eater Chuck (Jeff Cohen) and mumbling Mouth (Corey Feldman) for one final adventure together.

Searching through the attic holding museum pieces under the care of their curator father, the boys uncover a pirate treasure map. Sidetracked only temporarily by the nefarious Fratelli family (Robert Davi, Joe Pantoliano, Anne Ramsey), the boys begin their fairy tale treasure hunt.

The pirate One-Eyed Willie, it seems, was no one's fool; he left a deadly obstacle course to the treasure.

Linking the kids together is their identification as "Goonies," residents of the boondocks. Handle apparently imbues them with a mystical bond and idealized state of grace.

•

GORGEOUS HUSSY, THE
1936, 103 mins, US Ⓥ b/w
Dir Clarence Brown ***Prod*** Joseph L. Mankiewicz ***Scr*** Ainsworth Morgan, Stephen Morehouse Avery ***Ph*** George Folsey ***Ed*** Blanche Sewell ***Mus*** Herbert Stothart ***Art*** Cedric Gibbons, William A. Horning, Edwin B. Willis
Act Joan Crawford, Robert Taylor, Lionel Barrymore, Franchot Tone, Melvyn Douglas, James Stewart (M-G-M)

Picture is primarily Lionel Barrymore's, and not particularly because the character of Andrew Jackson he portrays calls for it. His tenderness towards his backwoods wife, his rough-and-ready fighting spirit in the campaign for presidency, his opening address to Congress, his sorrow over his wife's death and his bitter encounter with his cabinet—all are portrayed with acting acumen.

Joan Crawford figures in four love affairs, two of which are prominent in the picture and two of which result in marriage. Her first two sweethearts are Robert Taylor and Melvyn Douglas, and later James Stewart is spotted as a suitor. Last in the line is Franchot Tone, the cabinet member she is married to at the finish.

Title [from the novel by Samuel Hopkins Adams] obtains from the fact that the daughter of a tavern keeper (sneeringly called the Gorgeous Hussy) is the childhood friend of Andrew Jackson and his wife. When the latter dies, she promises to remain by Andy's side while he is President.

Crawford makes her debut in a costumer. Role naturally is more subdued and confining than generally associated with her. But she fills the role and the billing.

Douglas, as John Randolph, the state-righter Virginian Senator, clicks strongly. Tone contributes a smooth job as the war secretary who wins Crawford as his bride after her first husband is killed in action. Stewart isn't given many opportunities but makes something of them.

1936: NOMINATIONS: Best Supp. Actress (Beulah Bondi), Cinematography

•

GORILLAS IN THE MIST
THE STORY OF DIAN FOSSEY
1988, 129 mins, US Ⓥ ⊙ col
Dir Michael Apted ***Prod*** Arnold Glimcher, Terence Clegg ***Scr*** Anna Hamilton Phelan ***Ph*** John Seale ***Ed*** Stuart Baird ***Mus*** Maurice Jarre ***Art*** John Graysmark
Act Sigourney Weaver, Bryan Brown, Julie Harris, John Omirah Miluwi, Iain Cuthbertson, Constantin Alexandrov (Universal/Warner)

The life story of the late anthropologist Dian Fossey posed considerable challenges to the filmmakers tackling it, and they have been met in admirable fashion in *Gorillas in the Mist* [from a screen story by Anna Hamilton Phelan and Tab Murphy, based on Fossey's work and an article by Harold T. P. Hayes].

Fossey devoted nearly 20 years to observing, and trying to protect, the gorillas who live in a small area in the Virunga mountain range, which extends into Rwanda, where Fossey established her Karisoke Research Center. Thanks to National Geographic and films made by Bob Campbell, her work became internationally known, but she alienated a number of people, and was murdered in 1985. (Although her research assistant was convicted in absentia, many feel guilt lies elsewhere.)

After a while, just as Fossey began making unprecedented physical contact with these imposing animals, Sigourney Weaver seems to establish an exceptional familiarity and rapport with the jungle inhabitants. The intense bond makes the later scenes relating to the gorilla slaughter by poachers all the more powerful.

Campbell, played by Bryan Brown, turns up unannounced to photograph her activities and, after initial resistance, Fossey not only welcomes his presence but takes the married man as her lover.

Weaver is utterly believable and riveting in the role. Her scenes with the apes are captivating. Brown lends a nice lilt to his sympathetic interloper. Lensed high in the mountains of Rwanda, the production looks impressive.

1988: NOMINATIONS: Best Actress (Sigourney Weaver), Adapted Screenplay, Editing, Original Score, Sound

•

GORKY PARK
1983, 128 mins, US Ⓥ ⊙ col
Dir Michael Apted ***Prod*** Gene Kirkwood, Howard W. Koch, Jr. ***Scr*** Dennis Potter ***Ph*** Ralf D. Bode ***Ed*** Dennis Virkler ***Mus*** James Horner ***Art*** Paul Sylbert
Act William Hurt, Lee Marvin, Brian Dennehy, Ian Bannen, Joanna Pacula, Michael Elphick (Orion)

There's enough menace and romance in *Gorky Park* to appeal to many, especially those helped by the memory of Martin Cruz Smith's successful novel.

At the center, however, William Hurt is superb as a Moscow militia detective caught between his desires to be simply a good cop and the unfathomable motives of the secret Soviet government, all complicated by an unexpected love for Joanna Pacula.

Director Michael Apted sets Hurt up well with the discovery of three mutilated, faceless bodies in the city's Gorky Park, leading Hurt to suspect this is all the affair of the dangerous KGB and much to be avoided by plodding policemen such as himself.

Very quickly, Hurt's investigation brings him into contact with Lee Marvin, a wealthy American who enjoys high privilege in important Soviet circles, obviously not simply because he's a successful trader in sabless.

Apted, cinematographer Ralf D. Bode and production designer Paul Sylbert do an excellent job in making Helsinki stand in for Moscow, where they were denied access for filming.

•

GOSPEL ACCORDING TO ST. MATTHEW, THE
SEE: IL VANGELO SECONDO MATTEO

•

GO TELL THE SPARTANS
1978, 114 mins, US Ⓥ ⊙ col
Dir Ted Post ***Prod*** Allan F. Bodoh, Mitchell Cannold ***Scr*** Wendell Mayes ***Ph*** Harry Stradling, Jr. ***Ed*** Millie Moore ***Mus*** Dick Halligan ***Art*** Jack Senter
Act Burt Lancaster, Craig Wasson, Jonathan Goldsmith, Marc Singer, Joe Unger, Dennis Howard (Mar Vista/Spartan)

A good war film needs heroes. But Vietnam had no heroes in the eyes of most Americans. Even a reasonably well-made and well-acted earnest effort like *Go Tell the Spartans*, set in 1964 when the U.S. involvement was limited to "military advisors," can't overcome that disadvantage. Based on Daniel Ford's novel, *Incident at Muc Wa*, Wendell Mayes's script follows a detachment of Americans and Vietnamese mercenaries as they occupy an outpost abandoned by the French a decade ago. Burt Lancaster is the commander of an advisory group at Penang who must order the raw detachment into the jungle. When the Vietcong move in on the soldiers, Lancaster arranges for their evacuation.

Lancaster leads a mostly untried cast, including Marc Singer as his assistant, Jonathan Goldsmith playing a burned-out veteran, Joe Unger as a naive over-zealous lieutenant on his first mission and Evan Kim as the tough leader of the Vietnam mercenaries. All turn in fine performances.

•

GOTHIC
1986, 90 mins, UK Ⓥ ⊙ col
Dir Ken Russell ***Prod*** Penny Corke ***Scr*** Stephen Volk ***Ph*** Mike Southon ***Ed*** Michael Bradsell ***Mus*** Thomas Dolby ***Art*** Christopher Hobbs
Act Gabriel Byrne, Julian Sands, Natasha Richardson, Myriam Cyr, Timothy Spall, Andreas Wisniewski (Virgin)

Ken Russell's films always have been very much an acquired taste, but with *Gothic* he is back to his theatrically extravagant best.

Set on a stormy June night in 1816 at the Villa Diodati in Switzerland, the drug-induced excesses of the poet Byron (Gabriel Byrne) and his four guests inspire both Mary Shelley to write *Frankenstein* and Dr. Polidori *The Vampyre*, two gothic horror classics.

As the group becomes more drug soaked and terrified, the villa with its darkened passages, spiral staircases, shuttered rooms, and menacing candlelight, becomes a labyrinth of horror.

Ken Russell has made an unrelenting nightmare that is both uncomfortable and compulsive to watch. Gabriel Byrne and Natasha Richardson, as Mary Shelley, are powerful and hold the film together.

•

GO WEST
1925, 69 mins, US ⊗ b/w
Dir Buster Keaton ***Scr*** Buster Keaton, Raymond Cannon ***Ph*** Elgin Lessley, Bert Haines
Act Buster Keaton, Kathleen Myers, Howard Truesdale (Keaton/M-G-M)

This has Buster Keaton slipping over a series of comedy stunts that cause but mild laughter.

Buster manages to hop a freight car on the AT&SF. It is a car loaded with barrels of potatoes and he starts a barrel slide through a little phoney-baloney risley work. That is good for a laugh, as is the scene when Buster flops out of the car into the Arizona desert. Then his troubles begin. He gets a job as a cow hand and makes a pet of Brown Eyes, one of the milk cows in the herd. The ranch owner decides to ship 1,000 head to market and includes the cow, but when the hand tries to save her, he is paid off.

A rival rancher, objecting to the early sale of the live stock because he is holding out for a price on his beeves, tries to wreck the train and cause the shipment to be lost, but it is the comic cowhand that saves the day.

The trouble with the picture is that too much of it is shot in the distance and the audience does not get a chance to watch the action sufficiently close to get the benefit of whatever laughs there might have been in the shots.

•

GO WEST
1940, 79 mins, US Ⓥ b/w
Dir Edward Buzzell ***Prod*** Jack Cummings ***Scr*** Irving Brecher ***Ph*** Leonard Smith ***Ed*** Blanche Sewell ***Mus*** Georgie Stoll (dir.) ***Art*** Cedric Gibbons, Stan Rogers
Act Groucho Marx, Harpo Marx, Chico Marx, John Carroll, Diana Lewis, Walter Woolf King (M-G-M)

The three Marx Bros ride a merry trail of laughs and broad burlesque in a speedy adventure through the sagebrush country. Story is only a slight framework on which to parade the generally nonsensical antics of the trio.

Attracted to the wide open spaces by tales of gold lining the street, Chico, Harpo, and Groucho get involved in ownership of a deed to property wanted by the railroad for its western extension, and the action flashes through typical dance hall, rumbling stagecoach and desert waste episodes—with a wild train ride for a climax to outwit the villains.

Material provided by tightly knit script is topnotch while direction by Edward Buzzell smacks over the gags and comedy situations for maximum laughs. The Marxs secured pre-production audience reaction through tour of key picture houses trying out various sequences, which undoubtedly aided in tightening the action and dialog.

Groucho, Chico and Harpo handle their assignments with zestful enthusiasm. There's a bill-changing routine in Grand Central Station, wild melee and clowning in the rolling stagecoach, a comedy safe-cracking episode, and the train chase for a finish that winds up with the upper car structures dismantled by the silent Harpo to provide fuel for the engine. It's all ridiculous, but tuned for fun.

•

GO WEST, YOUNG MAN
1936, 80 mins, US b/w
Dir Henry Hathaway ***Prod*** Emanuel R. Cohen ***Scr*** Mae West ***Ph*** Karl Struss ***Ed*** Ray Curtis
Act Mae West, Warren William, Randolph Scott, Lyle Talbot, Alice Brady, Isabel Jewell (Major/Paramount)

Go West, Young Man is from the stage comedy hit, *Personal Appearance* [by Lawrence Riley]. Mae West, in her own way, is excellent in the role Gladys George created on the stage.

George was not hindered by the limitations of screen censorship, hence the play's sock tag isn't half as punchy in the film, nor are other lines or situations up to the same potency.

West adapted *Appearance* for herself, changing it in various respects to suit her own ideas. Where George, at every opportunity sought to cover up her hard-boiled nature by acting the sweet, coy heroine of the screen when in company that didn't know her in private life, West makes her a rough-and-ready, very sexy character all the way through.

West's swagger, the hands-on-hips business, and various devilish expressions are in almost constant evidence. In the scene in which West makes a play for Randolph Scott while latter is in the parlor of the boardinghouse trying to do some work, the star forces him into a brief dance bit. When she pats him a bit somewhere below the shoulder blades in a rather coyish, affectionate manner, it's one of the big laughs of the feature.

•

GRACE OF MY HEART
1996, 116 mins, US Ⓥ ⊙
Dir Allison Anders ***Prod*** Ruth Charny, Danbiel Hassid ***Scr*** Allison Anders ***Ph*** Jean-Yves Escoffier ***Ed*** Thelma Schoonmaker, James Kwei, Harvey Rosenstock ***Mus*** Larry Klein ***Art*** Francois Seguin
Act Illeana Douglas, Matt Dillon, Eric Stoltz, Bruce Davison, Patsy Kensit, John Turturro (Cappa)

Part biopic of a singer-songwriter who waits most of her career to be heard, and part paean to a golden decade of American pop music, Allison Anders's *Grace of My Heart* is an ambitious comedy-drama that is energetic and entertaining, even if it loses steam in its disharmonious final act. Covering the late '50s through 1970, the film boasts a terrific song score written in the style of that era and amusing performances by a strong cast.

Illeana Douglas would seem an admirably unconventional choice to play the gifted songwriter and later singer Edna Buxton (reportedly modeled on Carole King) who leaves behind her wealthy Philadelphia family to pursue a music career and endures a string of personal disappointments before finding her voice.

Given that much of the action takes place in NYC's legendary Brill Building, Anders's failure to make more of the setting reps an inexplicable shortcoming. The building's exterior is rarely seen (standing in for the site was the Pacific Electric Building in L.A.), and there is no real sense that this was a hit factory spawning hundreds of careers.

There is much to enjoy from the actors, however. John Turturro gives credibility and a great deal of humor to music-biz manager Joel, who is presented as a work-focused, insensitive hustler. Playing a weak-willed womanizer with delusions of integrity, Eric Stoltz also scores. Matt Dillon's is the most problematically conceived role [as a surf music star whom Edna falls for]. Best of many supporting stints is a brief appearance by Bridget Fonda as a big-haired, bubble-gum pop star (believed to be based on Leslie Gore) with a female lover.

•

GRACE QUIGLEY
SEE: THE ULTIMATE SOLUTION OF GRACE QUIGLEY

•

GRADUATE, THE
1967, 105 mins, US Ⓥ ⊙ ▭ col
Dir Mike Nichols ***Prod*** Lawrence Turman ***Scr*** Calder Willingham, Buck Henry ***Ph*** Robert Surtees ***Ed*** Sam O'Steen ***Mus*** Dave Grusin ***Art*** Richard Sylbert
Act Anne Bancroft, Dustin Hoffman, Katharine Ross, William Daniels, Murray Hamilton, Elizabeth Wilson (Embassy)

The Graduate is a delightful, satirical comedy-drama about a young man's seduction by an older woman, and the measure of maturity which he attains from the experience. Anne Bancroft, Katharine Ross and Dustin Hoffman head a very competent cast. An excellent screenplay, based on the Charles Webb novel, focuses on Hoffman, just out of college and wondering what it's all about. Predatory Bancroft, wife of Murray Hamilton, introduces Hoffman to mechanical sex, reaction to which evolves into true love with Ross, Bancroft's daughter.

In the 70 minutes which elapse from Hoffman's arrival home from school to the realization by Ross that he has had an affair with her mother, pic is loaded with hilarious comedy and, because of this, the intended commentary on materialistic society is most effective.

Only in the final 35 minutes, as Hoffman drives up and down the L.A.-Frisco route in pursuit of Ross, does film falter in pacing, result of which the switched on cinematics become obvious, and therefore tiring.

1967: Best Director

NOMINATIONS: Best Picture, Actor (Dustin Hoffman), Actress (Anne Bancroft), Supp. Actress (Katharine Ross), Adapted Screenplay, Cinematography

•

GRAFFITI BRIDGE
1990, 95 mins, US Ⓥ ⊙ col
Dir Prince ***Prod*** Arnold Stiefel, Randy Phillips ***Scr*** Prince ***Ph*** Bill Butler ***Ed*** Rebecca Ross ***Mus*** Prince ***Art*** Vance Lorenzini
Act Prince, Ingrid Chavez, Morris Day, Jerome Benton, Mavis Staples, George Clinton (Warner/Paisley Park)

Reviving the characters from Prince's 1984 hit *Purple Rain*, including a reunited Morris Day and the Time, *Graffiti Bridge* is a $7.5 million indulgence that amounts to a half-baked retread of tired MTV imagery and childish themes.

Plot revolves around rivalry between the Kid (Prince) and Day for control of a club they co-own. Day wants to play the songs the people want to hear; the Kid wants to focus on the music he's hearing from a higher power. They duel it out in various musical showdowns.

Chief embarrassment is the spotlight on Ingrid Chavez, latest of Prince's femme discoveries, as the cooingly coy love child with a direct line to the Maker.

That Prince wrote and directed this homage to his own creative process is evident. Mostly this amounts to a cinematic sandbox in which the Mascaraed One can play, pose and change costumes, inviting most of his gang to join in.

•

GRAND BLEU, LE
(THE BIG BLUE)
1988, 136 mins, France Ⓥ ⊙ ▭ col
Dir Luc Besson ***Prod*** Patrice Ledoux ***Scr*** Luc Besson, Roger Garland, Marylin Goldin, Jacques Mayol ***Ph*** Carlo Varini ***Ed*** Olivier Mauffroy ***Mus*** Eric Serra ***Art*** Dan Weil
Act Jean-Marc Barr, Jean Reno, Rosanna Arquette, Paul Shenar, Sergio Castellito, Jean Bouise (Gaumont/Films du Loup)

Luc Besson, the French wonder boy who moved into the commercial major leagues with his $3 million Gaumont picture *Subway*, joins the international spendthrifts club with *The Big Blue*, a waterlogged yarn about a couple of rival championship divers. Produced on a disproportionately large scale ($12 million budget, a 9-month shoot on international locations from Greece to Peru), this English-language adventure is indigently plotted and lacking in genuine dramatic and human interest.

Besson was in part inspired by the life and exploits of French champion free diver Jacques Mayol, who served as technical adviser on the film and allowed his name to be retained for the protagonist, played by Jean-Marc Barr.

Barr is a renowned experimental diver based on the French Riviera. During an assignment at a frozen lake high in the Peruvian mountains, he runs into Rosanna Arquette, a flightly New York insurance agent who immediately falls in love with him and trails him to Taormina where he is facing off lifelong competitive friend Jean Reno in a diving contest.

Apart from Arquette's increasingly giddy pursuit of the somewhat absent Barr (more concerned with dolphins he befriends than humans who love him), nothing much happens until a climactic runoff in which latter tries to beat his friend's world free-diving depth.

Besson fatally misjudges the cinematic interest of his theme. The underwater sequences, as splendidly lensed as they are, have little intrinsic suspense and quickly become repetitious. The land scenes are boring because Besson has been unable to give his characters any psychological density.

[In the U.S., pic was released in a 119-min. version with a new score by Bill Conti; in the U.K., the original score was retained. In 1989, a 166-min. *Version Longue* was released in Paris.]

•

GRAND CANYON

1991, 134 mins, US Ⓥ ⦿ ⌓ col

Dir Lawrence Kasdan ***Prod*** Lawrence Kasdan ***Scr*** Lawrence Kasdan, Meg Kasdan ***Ph*** Owen Roizman ***Ed*** Carol Littleton ***Mus*** James Newton Howard ***Art*** Bo Welch

Act Danny Glover, Kevin Kline, Steve Martin, Mary McDonnell, Mary-Louise Parker, Alfre Woodard (20th Century-Fox)

Life in L.A. is the pits, according to scripters Lawrence and Meg Kasdan in *Grand Canyon*, their earnest, often moving but not totally successful film. Via its refreshing concentration on a black-white friendship (rare in non-action Hollywood pics), film explores contemporary racial tension and ambivalence.

Danny Glover (a tow-truck driver) and Kevin Kline (an immigration lawyer) come to a warm, if tentative, connection in their paradise-turned-hellhole, a city that still looks lustrous from the oddly smogless air but, up close, shows its "gone to shit" as the film says of both L.A. and the country at large.

Glover is given a juicy role as the moral voice of a film mourning the loss of civility in a society torn apart by the widening chasm—the Grand Canyon—between rich and poor. Kline, also very good in his more understated way, conveys the edgy uncertainty of a white liberal struggling to cope with life in a city whose police routinely terrorize angry black inhabitants.

Kline's also living on the moral edge by carrying on a half-hearted affair with his secretary, fresh young Mary-Louise Parker, who's driven to distraction by his lack of emotional involvement.

The Steve Martin character, who whines, "Nobody in this town will admit that a producer is an artist," is a wicked caricature of action pic maker Joel Silver. But the Kasdans's script vacillates uneasily between treating the character as a comic relief spouter of buzz words and a voice of genuine wisdom.

1991: NOMINATION: Best Original Screenplay

•

GRAND CHEMIN, LE

(THE GRAND HIGHWAY)

1987, 107 mins, France Ⓥ col

Dir Jean-Loup Hubert ***Prod*** Pascal Hommais, Jean-Francois Lepetit ***Scr*** Jean-Loup Hubert ***Ph*** Claude Lecomte ***Ed*** Raymonde Guyot ***Mus*** Georges Granier ***Art*** Thierry Flamand

Act Anemone, Richard Bohringer, Antoine Hubert, Vanessa Guedj, Christine Pascal, Raoul Billery (Flach/Selena/TF1)

Le Grand chemin is a bittersweet heartwarmer about a city boy's near-traumatic stay in the country with a childless couple. Scripted from personal memories and directed with warm restraint by Jean-Loup Hubert, production offers a good blend of pathos and humor, and excellent performances from adult and child thesps alike.

Hubert cast his own son, Antoine, in the pivotal role of a sensitive nine-year-old Parisian packed off by his pregnant mother (Christine Pascal) to spend the summer with an old girlfriend (Anemone) and her husband (Richard Bohringer) in their isolated village [in the late 1950s].

Disconcerted by the unfamiliar environment, the boy befriends a slightly older local girl who initiates him into the mysteries of rural life. The youngster, troubled by the unexplained separation of his parents, finds himself the object of a tug-of-war between Anemone and Bohringer, who vie for his affections to replace the child they lost at birth years ago.

Hubert's script has conscious echoes of Rene Clement's *Forbidden Games* and other classics about children, but there is freshness and poignancy in his dialog and direction of actors. The kids, both new to acting, are fetching—Vanessa Guedj, 11, is particularly winning as the savvy, precocious little village girl. Real acting honors go to Anemone and Bohringer as the embittered rubes whose conjugal life died with their child.

•

GRANDE ILLUSION, LA

(GRAND ILLUSION)

1937, 94 mins, France Ⓥ ⦿ b/w

Dir Jean Renoir ***Scr*** Charles Spaak, Jean Renoir ***Ph*** Christian Matras ***Ed*** Marguerite Renoir, Marthe Huguet ***Mus*** Joseph Kosma ***Art*** Eugene Lourie

Act Jean Gabin, Pierre Fresnay, Eric von Stroheim, Dalio, Dita Parlo, Gaston Modot (RAC)

An artistically masterful feature, the picture breathes the intimate life of warriors on both sides during the [First] World War. It gives a different slant on the inner mental workings of those caught in the maelstrom of warfare, yet never deviates from the central thesis.

There are only two references to the title but both are pertinent. Once when a French soldier exclaims "what an illusion," when a comrade says that the war will be over before they have time to escape from military prison, and again when he describes the end of all wars as an illusion.

While the plot centers about the superhuman efforts of a group of French officers, captured in battle, to escape from prison camps, the story concerns various members of human society all juggled about by the terrific conflict. Both the authors and director have laid emphasis on this in the isolated Siberia-like prison scene when two military leaders, one a shell of humanity serving as a prison keeper and the other a captured enemy officer, console and display hearty respect for each other.

Jean Renoir displays imaginative direction. He also wrote the original story and helped with the scripting. Novelty of the scripting is that the British, French and German officers are heard speaking their native tongues.

Jean Gabin recalls Victor McLaglen with his rugged personality as Marechal, one of the captured French officers who eventually escapes. He is tremendously effective in a moving love sequence with a blond peasant girl (Dita Parlo).

Pierre Fresnay is the polished aristocratic French officer who sacrifices his life in order to insure the freedom of his two friends in prison camp. Eric von Stroheim, cast as a German army officer, appears in one of his most sympathetic roles.

•

GRAND HIGHWAY, THE

SEE: LE GRAND CHEMIN

•

GRAND HOTEL

1932, 105 mins, US Ⓥ ⦿ b/w

Dir Edmund Goulding ***Prod*** [uncredited] ***Scr*** William A. Drake ***Ph*** William Daniels ***Ed*** Blanche Sewell ***Mus*** [uncredited] ***Art*** Cedric Gibbons

Act Greta Garbo, John Barrymore, Joan Crawford, Wallace Beery, Lionel Barrymore, Jean Hersholt (M-G-M)

Better than just a good transcription of the Vicki Baum stage play. Story is many angled in characters and incidents. There is the romantic grip of the actress-nobleman lovers; there is the triumph of the underdog in the figure of Kringelein, the humble bookkeeper doomed to approaching death and determined to spend his remaining days in a splurge of luxury in the Grand Hotel; and there is the everlasting Cinderella element in the not-so-good stenographer who at last finds a friend and protector in the dying Kringelein.

First honors again go to Lionel Barrymore for an inspired performance as the soon-to-die bookkeeper. Greta Garbo gives the role of the dancer something of artificiality, risking a trace of acting swagger, sometimes stagey. Her clothes are ravishing in the well-known Garbo style. John Barrymore is back where he belongs as the down-at-heel but glamorous baron, going about debonairly in a career of crime but with a heart of gold that will not stoop to small meanness.

There remains the stenographer Miss Flaemmchen, not the most fortunate casting for Joan Crawford, who is rather too capable a type to successfully play an unhappy plaything of fate.

Wallace Beery is at home in the part of the German industrialist, a grandiose but pathetic figure in his struggles with business rivals.

1931/32: Best Picture

•

GRAND ILLUSION

SEE: LA GRANDE ILLUSION

•

GRAND MEAULNES, LE

(THE WANDERER)

1967, 110 mins, France Ⓥ ⌓ col

Dir Jean-Gabriel Albicocco ***Scr*** Isabelle Riviere, Jean-Gabriel Albicocco ***Ph*** Quinto Albicocco ***Ed*** Georges Klotz

Act Brigitte Fossey, Jean Blaise, Alain Libolt, Alain Jean, Marcel Cuvilier, Juliette Villard (Madeleine/AWA)

Alain Fournier's novel *Le Grand Meaulnes* has become a romantic literary classic in France and been reprinted in most parts of the world. It deals with the attachment of a young friend to a more dashing and older fellow student whose lyrical imbroglios seem to take the place of his own lack of adventure as the son of a private school director in turn-of-the-century provincial France.

The director, Jean-Gabriel Albicocco, has been extremely literal, and unfortunately somewhat too literary, in translating it to the screen. Result is a rather glossy, sentimental opus that too often uses prettiness in imagery for its own sake and a mixture of styles.

Meaulnes (Jean Blaise) once met a girl at a ball but he can't find her again. He spends time searching and then gives up and goes to Paris where he meets a girl who was the fiancée of the brother of the mysterious girl. If this sounds involved, it is. And so is what follows—unbelievably so, if one has the patience to try to figure out what is happening.

The film overdoes the use of vaselined lenses or smeared glasses to blur what reality there is. Brigitte Fossey has the right quality as the dream symbol, but the pains of adolescence, idealism and youthful coming-of-age are somewhat lost in the maze of pretty images.

•

GRAND PRIX

1966, 179 mins, US Ⓥ ⦿ ⌓ col

Dir John Frankenheimer ***Prod*** Edward Lewis ***Scr*** Robert Alan Aurthur, [William Hanley] ***Ph*** Lionel Lindon ***Ed*** Fredric Steinkamp, Henry Berman, Stewart Linder, Frank Santillo ***Mus*** Maurice Jarre ***Art*** Richard Sylbert

Act James Garner, Eva Marie Saint, Yves Montand, Toshiro Mifune, Brian Bedford, Jessica Walter (Douglas & Lewis/M-G-M)

The roar and whine of engines sending men and machines hurtling over the 10 top road and track courses of Europe, the U.S. and Mexico—the Grand Prix circuits—are the prime motivating forces of this actioncrammed adventure that director John Frankenheimer and producer Edward Lewis have interlarded with personal drama that is sometimes introspectively revealing, occasionally mundane, but generally a most serviceable framework.

Frankenheimer has shrewdly varied the length and the importance of the races that figure in the film and the overplay of running commentary on the various events, not always distinct above the roar of motors, imparts a documentary vitality. The director, moreover, frequently divides his outsized screen into sectional panels for a sort of montage interplay of reactions of the principals—a stream of consciousness commentary—that adroitly prevents the road running from overwhelming the personal drama.

There is a curious thing, however, about the exposition of the characters in this screenplay. Under cold examination they are stock characters. James Garner, American competitor in a field of Europeans, is somewhat taciturn, unencumbered by marital involvement. Yves Montand has a wife in name and forms a genuine attachment for American fashion writer Eva Marie Saint, a divorcée. Brian Bedford is the emotionally confused Britisher competing against the memory of his champion driver brother and whose compulsion to be a champion almost wrecks his marriage to whilom American actress-model Jessica Walter.

1966: Best Sound, Editing, Sound Effects

•

GRAND THEFT AUTO

1977, 89 mins, US Ⓥ ⦿ col

Dir Ron Howard ***Prod*** Jon Davidson ***Scr*** Ranse Howard, Ron Howard ***Ph*** Gary Graver ***Ed*** Joe Dante ***Mus*** Peter Ivers ***Art*** Keith Michael

Act Ron Howard, Nancy Morgan, Marion Ross, Pete Isacksen, Barry Cahill, Hoke Howell (New World)

Grand Theft Auto is a nonstop orgy of comic destructiveness. Ron Howard has directed with a broad but amiable and well-disciplined touch in this screwball comedy about his elopement with heiress Nancy Morgan from L.A. to Las Vegas, with her father, Barry Cahill, and dozens of others in pursuit.

Howard never tries to hog the screen and lets his costars have plenty of funny moments. Morgan is pretty and charming as his spunky partner, and it's a nice touch that Howard lets her drive the getaway car, a gleaming black-and-tan Rolls-Royce.

Also along for the chase are Marion Ross as the angry mother of Morgan's oafish fiancé, played amusingly straight by Paul Linke, and d.j. Don Steele, who broadcasts a cynical running commentary from a helicopter.

•

GRAPES OF WRATH, THE

1940, 129 mins, US Ⓥ ⊙ b/w

Dir John Ford ***Prod*** Darryl F. Zanuck ***Scr*** Nunnally Johnson ***Ph*** Gregg Toland ***Ed*** Robert Simpson ***Mus*** Alfred Newman (dir.) ***Art*** Richard Day, Mark-Lee Kirk

Act Henry Fonda, Jane Darwell, John Carradine, Charley Grapewin, Dorris Bowdon, John Qualen (20th Century-Fox)

It took courage, a pile of money and John Ford to film the story of The Dust Bowl and the tribulations of its unhappy survivors, who sought refuge in inhospitable California. *The Grapes of Wrath*, adapted by Nunnally Johnson from John Steinbeck's bestseller, is an absorbing, tense melodrama, starkly realistic, and loaded with social and political fireworks. The film interprets the consequences of national disaster in terms of a family group—the Joads—who left their quarter section to the wind and dust and started cross-country in an overladen jalopy to the land of plenty.

It is not a pleasant story, and the pictured plight of the Joads, and hundreds of other dust bowl refugee families, during their frantic search for work in California, is a shocking visualization of a state of affairs demanding generous humanitarian attention. Neither book nor film gives any edge to citizens of California who are working diligently to alleviate suffering and conditions not of their origination. Steinbeck offers no suggestion. In this respect the film ends on a more hopeful note. Someway, somehow, Ma Joad declares "the people" will solve the unemployment riddle.

It is all on the screen—everything except the unpalatable Steinbeck dialog, and such other portions of the book which good taste exclude. The characters are there, and under Ford's direction a group of actors makes them into living people, whose frustration catches at the heart and throat. There is humor, too, but the film as a whole scores as a gripping experience.

Henry Fonda does a swell job as Tom and John Carradine is excellent as Casey, the reformed preacher. Jane Darwell gives the family strength and leadership in the mother part. Charley Grapewin's grandpa is rich in humor and tragedy.

1940: Best Director, Supp. Actress (Jane Darwell)

NOMINATIONS: Best Picture, Actor (Henry Fonda), Screenplay, Editing, Sound

•

GRASS HARP, THE

1995, 107 mins, US Ⓥ col

Dir Charles Matthau ***Prod*** James T. Davis ***Scr*** Stirling Silliphant, Kirk Ellis ***Ph*** John A. Alonzo ***Ed*** Sidney Levin, C. Timothy O'Meara ***Mus*** Patrick Williams ***Art*** Paul Sylbert

Act Piper Laurie, Sissy Spacek, Walter Matthau, Edward Furlong, Nell Carter, Jack Lemmon (Matthau-Tokofsky-Davis)

Helmer Charles Matthau combines a sensitive screenplay adaptation of Truman Capote's autobiographical novel *The Grass Harp* with a wonderful ensemble cast to create a jewel of a film.

Collin Fenwick, Capote's alter ego, loses both his parents at an early age. The young Collin (Grayson Frick) is forced to move in with two of his father's cousins, the Talbo sisters (Piper Laurie, Sissy Spacek). Laurie is the sensitive Dolly, who makes do during the Depression peddling a home remedy created in her kitchen with the help of family cook Catherine (Nell Carter). Dolly's sister Verena (Spacek) is a businesswoman who owns most of the stores in town.

Episodic story focuses on Collin's coming of age, with Edward Furlong taking over as the teenage character. Collin loves Dolly and learns from her about the "grass harp," the ability to hear the voices of departed ones as the wind rustles through the tall grasses.

Walter Matthau (the director's father) approaches hamminess as the town's eccentric retired judge but skillfully avoids crossing the line. Frequent Matthau collaborator Jack Lemmon appears as Morris Ritz, a Chicago sharpie who's romancing Verena.

While no performance is off the mark, the film rises or falls on the Talbo sisters, and Laurie and Spacek are riveting. Laurie's performance brings out the best in everyone, including not only Spacek in a powerful reconciliation scene, but Furlong as the moody Collin and Carter's snappy maid.

•

GRASSHOPPER, THE

1970, 96 mins, US Ⓥ col

Dir Jerry Paris ***Prod*** Jerry Belson, Garry Marshall ***Scr*** Jerry Belson, Garry Marshall ***Ph*** Sam Leavitt ***Ed*** Aaron Stell ***Mus*** Billy Goldenberg ***Art*** Tambi Larsen

Act Jacqueline Bisset, Jim Brown, Joseph Cotten, Corbett Monica, Ramon Bieri, Christopher Stone (National General)

The Grasshopper is the dark side of the Hollywood story, every schoolgirl's American Dream gone sour [from the novel *The Passing of Evil* by Mark McShane]. Jacqueline Bisset is the good-looking, well-built, lively chick, bored with a bankteller's job and the prospects of a middle-class husband, suburban home and kids, who is attracted by the tinsel of Las Vegas.

Attractive and busty enough to make the chorus, but neither talented nor ambitious enough to go beyond, she drifts into a bad marriage, being kept by a rich old man and then into outright hustling, having run the gamut by age 22.

Bisset is on camera for almost the entire film, kept carefully within her dramatic depth by Director Jerry Paris, with unexpected outbreaks of a kooky humor.

•

GRASS IS GREENER, THE

1960, 105 mins, US Ⓥ ▭ col

Dir Stanley Donen ***Prod*** Stanley Donen ***Scr*** Hugh Williams, Margaret Williams ***Ph*** Christopher Challis ***Ed*** James Clark ***Mus*** Douglas Gamley, Len Stevens (arrs.) ***Art*** Paul Sheriff

Act Cary Grant, Deborah Kerr, Robert Mitchum, Jean Simmons, Moray Watson (Universal/Grandon)

Merry old England is the site of this not-always-so-merry comedy about a romantic clash between a British Earl-ionaire and an American oil-ionaire. The Hugh and Margaret Wilson screenplay, adapted from their London stage hit, slowly evolves into a talky and generally tedious romantic exercise, dropping the semi-satirical stance that brightens up the early going.

A romantic triangle develops among the Earl (Cary Grant), his wife (Deborah Kerr), and a "rip-roaring Grade A romantic" American millionaire (Robert Mitchum) who wanders off-limits into milady's drawing room during a tour of the Earl's house and promptly and preposterously falls in love with her, she with him. Balance of the picture is concerned with Grant's efforts to woo his wife back to his side.

The uninspired screenplay has its staunchest ally in Grant, whose stiffest comedy competition comes not from his three costars but from Moray Watson, the butler.

There are some compelling views of the English countryside, and the incorporation of some of Noel Coward's memorable tunes gives matters a lift.

•

GRAY LADY DOWN

1978, 111 mins, US Ⓥ ▭ col

Dir David Greene ***Prod*** Walter Mirisch ***Scr*** James Whittaker, Howard Sackler ***Ph*** Stevan Larner ***Ed*** Robert Swink ***Mus*** Jerry Fielding ***Art*** William Tuntke

Act Charlton Heston, David Carradine, Stacy Keach, Ned Beatty, Stephen McHattie, Ronny Cox (Mirisch/Universal)

Charlton Heston is back in jeopardy. He's 60 miles off the coast of Connecticut stuck with 41 other sailors on the edge of an ocean canyon in a nuclear submarine, waiting for Stacy Keach to organize a rescue mission. If Keach doesn't hurry one of three disasters will soon happen: water pressure will crush the sub's hull, oxygen will run out, or the boat will slip off the ledge.

David Carradine and Ned Beatty enter the scene after Heston and crew suffer a pair of double setbacks. First, their surfacing vessel is rammed by a Norwegian freighter and plunges straight down. Then an earth tremor covers the sub's escape hatch.

Up to this point things are fairly routine [in a story based on the novel *Event 1000* by David Lavallee, adaptation by Frank P. Rosenberg]. Heston looks courageous; Ronny Cox, the second in command, freaks out; some crew members get sick, and a handful die; Heston's onshore wife is informed of her husband's condition and adopts a visage of sadness; Keach, a very formal officer, promises Heston and crew that everything will be all right.

But the second disaster—the escape hatch burial—calls for special action. Enter Carradine, a subdued Navy captain and inventor of an experimental diving vessel known as the Snark, and his assistant, Beatty. They resemble a disaster movie's Laurel and Hardy. They're a nice twist.

•

GREASE

1978, 110 mins, US Ⓥ ⊙ ▭ col

Dir Randal Kleiser ***Prod*** Robert Stigwood, Allan Carr ***Scr*** Bronte Woodard ***Ph*** Bill Butler ***Ed*** John F. Burnett ***Mus*** Bill Oakes (sup.) ***Art*** Phil Jefferies

Act John Travolta, Olivia Newton-John, Stockard Channing, Jeff Conaway, Eve Arden, Joan Blondell (Paramount)

Grease has got it, from the outstanding animated titles of John Wilson all the way through the rousing finale as John Travolta and Olivia Newton-John ride off into teenage happiness.

Allan Carr is credited with adapting the 1950s style legituner of Jim Jacobs and Warren Casey, which Bronte Woodard then fashioned into an excellent screenplay that moves smartly. Director Randal Kleiser and choreographer Patricia Birch stage the sequences with aplomb, providing, as necessary, the hoke, hand or heart appropriate to the specific moment.

Plot tracks the bumpy romantic road of Travolta and Newton-John, whose summer beach idyll sours when he feels he must revert to finger-snapping cool in the atmosphere of the high school they both wind up attending.

Stockard Channing provides a nice contrast to Newton-John in a hard but really nice characterization. Jeff Conaway is very good as the type guy for whom Travolta is a natural leader.

1978: NOMINATION: Best Song ("Hopelessly Devoted to You")

•

GREASE 2

1982, 114 mins, US Ⓥ ⊙ ▭ col

Dir Patricia Birch ***Prod*** Robert Stigwood, Allan Carr ***Scr*** Ken Finkleman ***Ph*** Frank Stanley ***Ed*** John F. Burnett ***Mus*** Louis St Louis (arr.) ***Art*** Gene Callahan

Act Maxwell Caulfield, Michelle Pfeiffer, Adrian Zmed, Eve Arden, Connie Stevens, Tab Hunter (Paramount)

It's 1961 now at Rydell High, a becalmed, upbeat time when JFK's photo has replaced Ike's on the school wall. In fact, hardly anything is happening socially or musically.

It's not even a question of will boy get girl, but how. Gorgeous Michelle Pfeiffer plays the leader of the foxy Pink Ladies, whose members are only supposed to go out with greasers from the T-Birds gang. Maxwell Caulfield, fresh from England and complete with accent, is the new boy in school, and it's made clear to him that Pfeiffer is off limits until he proves himself as a leather-clad biker.

Where this film has a decided edge on its predecessor is in the staging and cutting of the musical sequences. Choreographer and director Patricia Birch has come up with some unusual settings (a bowling alley, a bomb shelter) for some of the scenes, and employs some sharp montage to give most of the songs and dances a fair amount of punch.

Pfeiffer is all anyone could ask for in the looks department, and she fills Olivia Newton-John's shoes and tight pants very well, thank you. Caulfield is a less certain choice.

•

GREASED LIGHTNING

1977, 96 mins, US Ⓥ col

Dir Michael Schultz ***Prod*** Hannah Weinstein ***Scr*** Kenneth Vose, Lawrence DuKore, Melvin Van Peebles, Leon Capetanos ***Ph*** George Bouillet ***Ed*** Bob Wyman, Christopher Holmes, Randy Roberts ***Mus*** Fred Karlin ***Art*** Jack Senter

Act Richard Pryor, Beau Bridges, Pam Grier, Cleavon Little, Vincent Gardenia, Richie Havens (Third World)

Greased Lightning is a pleasant, loose and relaxed comedy starring Richard Pryor in an excellent characterization based on real-life racing driver Wendell Scott.

Beau Bridges plays a redneck driver who befriends Pryor's stolid efforts to break the color barrier in car racing. Pam Grier is smashingly decorous but wasted in a supportive wife role, while Cleavon Little is cast as Pryor's close friend.

Story covers about 25 years, from Pryor's release from Second World War Army service to championship race in

1971. Another virtue of the film is its discreet conveyance of an important theme: In any large society, progress by any minority group is accomplished through particular individuals doing notable things.

•

GREAT AMERICAN BROADCAST, THE
1941, 90 mins, US Ⓥ col
Dir Archie Mayo ***Prod*** Kenneth Macgowan (assoc.) ***Scr*** Don Ettlinger, Edwin Blum, Robert Ellis, Helen Logan ***Ph*** Leon Shamroy, Peverell Marley ***Ed*** Robert Simpson ***Mus*** Alfred Newman (dir.) ***Art*** Richard Day, Albert Hogsett
Act Alice Faye, Jack Oakie, John Payne, Cesar Romero, The Four Ink Spots, James Newill (20th Century-Fox)

The Great American Broadcast is light and breezy, a showmanly admixture of comedy, romance, drama and music woven around the extraordinary progress of radio broadcasting during the 1920s. Scripters fudge a few years in setting the year of the Dempsey-Willard heavyweight battle in Toledo. Original shots of the fight are utilized to accompany the radio account.

Picture has many attributes on the entertainment side despite its thin and sketchy story. Most prominent is the breezy and zestful performance of Jack Oakie, who works energetically throughout and holds audience attention every minute he is on the screen.

Story details the adventures of Oakie, John Payne, Faye and Cesar Romero as early pioneers in radio broadcasting. Oakie tinkers with a crystal set in his room, idea-minded Payne gets enthusiastic over wireless entertainment possibilities, Faye is radio's first singing star, and Romero supplies the early coin. Direction by Archie Mayo carries the pace at good speed, and injects many surefire touches for laugh attention.

•

GREAT BALLS OF FIRE!
1989, 108 mins, US Ⓥ ⦿ col
Dir Jim McBride ***Prod*** Adam Fields ***Scr*** Jack Baran, Jim McBride ***Ph*** Affonso Beato ***Ed*** Lisa Day, Pembroke Herring, Bert Lovitt ***Mus*** Jack Baran, Jim McBride ***Art*** David Nichols
Act Dennis Quaid, Winona Ryder, Alec Baldwin, John Doe, Stephen Tobolowsky, Trey Wilson (Orion)

Rock 'n' roll and its legendary characters have always been a tempting subject for filmmakers, but rare is the non-documentary that adds anything to the music. *Great Balls of Fire!* is no exception. It's a thin, cartoonish treatment of the hellbent, musically energetic young Jerry Lee Lewis.

Full-bore performance by Dennis Quaid as the kinetic piano-pumper stops at surface level, and 108 minutes of his gum-cracking smirks and cock-a-doodle-doo dandyism are hard to take.

Pic focuses on the years 1956-59, when Lewis's career took off with the provocative hit "Whole Lotta Shakin' Goin' On" and was nearly destroyed by his marriage to 13-year-old cousin, Myra Gayle Brown (Winona Ryder), which shocked British fans and cut short his first overseas tour.

Mixed up in the Memphis milieu are the presence of Elvis Presley, who preceded Lewis at Sun Studios; Jimmy Swaggart, Lewis's Bible-thumping cousin; and the heady, devilish allure of the jumpin' black juke joints from which Lewis lifts his best music.

Script is based on a book by Myra Lewis and is by-the-numbers, suffering from a lack of grace or metaphor and relying on cash and flash as character motivations.

•

GREAT CARUSO, THE
1951, 109 mins, US Ⓥ col
Dir Richard Thorpe ***Prod*** Joe Pasternak, Jesse L. Lasky ***Scr*** Sonya Levien, William Ludwig ***Ph*** Joseph Ruttenberg ***Ed*** Gene Ruggiero ***Mus*** Johnny Green (sup.) ***Art*** Cedric Gibbons, Gabriel Scognamillo
Act Mario Lanza, Ann Blyth, Dorothy Kirsten, Jarmila Novotna, Richard Hageman, Carl Benton Reid (M-G-M)

This highly fictionalized, sentimental biog of the late, great Metropolitan Opera tenor, Enrico Caruso, handsomely mounted in Technicolor, has a lot of popular ingredients, including a boy-and-girl-vs-disapproving-parent romance, the draw of Caruso's rep, glamor of the Met, a host of surefire, familiar operatic arias, and the pull of Mario Lanza.

Otherwise, the film is a superficial pic, bearing little relationship to Caruso's actual story, which was a much more dramatic one than emerges here. There are strong omissions and some falsifications.

Story is a casual recital of part of Caruso's career, with a few, brief scenes of him as a young Neapolitan cafe singer; then his quick rise as tenor in Milan, London, and other European music capitals; and his triumphs at the NY Met. The film centers early on Caruso's romance with Dorothy Benjamin, his difficulty with her father and their happy marriage. It shows him in some of his Met successes and touches briefly on his breakdown and death. Lanza is handsome, personable and has a brilliant voice. He's a lyric tenor, like Caruso; has his stocky build, his Italianate quality and some of his flair. Dorothy Kirsten, who plays a Met soprano befriending Caruso, is a good actress as well as a gifted singer.

1951: Best Sound Recording

NOMINATIONS: Best Color Costume Design, Scoring of a Musical Picture

•

GREAT CATHERINE
1968, 98 mins, UK col
Dir Gordon Flemyng ***Prod*** Jules Buck, Peter O'Toole ***Scr*** Hugh Leonard ***Ph*** Oswald Morris ***Ed*** Anne V. Coates ***Mus*** Dimitri Tiomkin ***Art*** John Bryan
Act Peter O'Toole, Zero Mostel, Jeanne Moreau, Jack Hawkins, Akim Tamiroff, Kenneth Griffith (Warner/Seven Arts)

A foreword to this film, based on a George Bernard Shaw play, reads: "Mr. Shaw stated that historical portraiture was not the motive of this story and the producers would like to add that any similarity to any historical event will be nothing short of a miracle."

Atmosphere it has, mammoth and impressive sets, Zero Mostel as a wildman like you've never seen, Peter O'Toole as a stuffy Englishman like you've never imagined, all wrapped around the amorous yearnings of Catherine of Russia.

This is a souped-up version of the Russian Empress's romantics, focused on her going on the make for a slightly imbecilic English Light Dragoons captain. Jeanne Moreau essays Catherine with humor. O'Toole, as the beaddled captain on his way to seek an audience with the Empress, and finding himself tossed on her bed by Mostel, in a mad-Russian character, lends credence through underplaying his role.

•

GREAT DICTATOR, THE
1940, 127 mins, US Ⓥ b/w
Dir Charles Chaplin ***Prod*** Charles Chaplin ***Scr*** Charles Chaplin ***Ph*** Karl Struss, Roland Totheroh ***Ed*** Willard Nico ***Mus*** Meredith Willson (dir.) ***Art*** J. Russell Spencer
Act Charles Chaplin, Paulette Goddard, Jack Oakie, Reginald Gardiner, Henry Daniell, Billy Gilbert (Chaplin/United Artists)

Chaplin makes no bones about his utter contempt for dictators like Hitler and Mussolini in his production of *The Great Dictator*. He takes time out to make fun about it, but the preachment is strong, notably in the six minute speech at the finish.

Chaplin speaks throughout the film, but wherever convenient depends as much as he can on pantomime. His panto has always talked plenty.

Chaplin plays a dual role, that of a meek little Jewish barber in Tomania and the great little dictator of that country, billed as Hynkel. It's when he is playing the dictator that the comedian's voice raises the value of the comedy content of the picture to great heights. He does various bits as a Hitler spouting at the mouth in which he engages in a lot of double talk in what amounts to a pig-Latin version of the German tongue, with grunts thrown in here and there, plus a classical "Democracy shtoonk." On various occasions as Hitler, he also speaks English. In these instances, he talks with force, as contrasted by the mousey, half-scared way he speaks as the poor barber.

Somewhat of a shock is the complete transformation of the barber when he delivers the speech at the finish, a fiery and impassioned plea for freedom and democracy. It is a peculiar and somewhat disappointing climax with the picture ending on a serious rather than a comical note.

The vast majority of the action is built around Hynkel and the Jewish barber. Not so much is devoted to the dictator who is Napaloni (Mussolini). Jack Oakie plays the satirized Duce to the hilt and every minute with him is socko.

In making up the billing, Chaplin has displayed an unusually keen sense of humor. While Hynkel is the dictator of Tomania, Napaloni is the ruler of Bacteria. Tomania higher-ups include Garbitsch (Goebels) and Herring (Goering). These are played effectively by Henry Daniell and Billy Gilbert.

1940: NOMINATIONS: Best Picture, Actor (Charles Chaplin), Supp. Actor (Jack Oakie), Original Screenplay, Original Score

•

GREAT ESCAPE, THE
1963, 171 mins, US Ⓥ ⦿ ▭ col
Dir John Sturges ***Prod*** John Sturges ***Scr*** James Clavell, W. R. Burnett ***Ph*** Daniel Fapp ***Ed*** Ferris Webster ***Mus*** Elmer Bernstein ***Art*** Fernando Carrere
Act Steve McQueen, James Garner, Richard Attenborough, James Donald, Charles Bronson, Donald Pleasence (Mirisch)

From Paul Brickhill's true story of a remarkable mass breakout by Allied POWs during World War II, producer-director John Sturges has fashioned a motion picture that entertains, captivates, thrills and stirs.

The film is an account of the bold, meticulous plotting that led to the escape of 76 prisoners from a Nazi detention camp, and subsequent developments that resulted in the demise of 50, recapture of a dozen. Early scenes depict the formulation of the mass break design. These are played largely for laughs, at the occasional expense of reality, and there are times when authority seems so lenient that the inmates almost appear to be running the asylum.

There are some exceptional performances. The most provocative single impression is made by Steve McQueen as a dauntless Yank pilot whose "pen"-manship record shows 18 blots, or escape attempts. James Garner is the compound's "scrounger," a traditional type in the *Stalag 17* breed of war-prison film. Charles Bronson and James Coburn do solid work, although the latter's character is anything but clearly defined. British thespians weigh in with some of the finest performances in the picture. Richard Attenborough is especially convincing in a stellar role, that of the man who devises the break. A moving portrayal of a prisoner losing his eyesight is given by Donald Pleasence. It is the film's most touching character.

Elmer Bernstein's rich, expressive score is consistently helpful. His martial, Prussianistic theme is particularly stirring and memorable.

1963: NOMINATION: Best Editing

•

GREATEST, THE
1977, 101 mins, US Ⓥ col
Dir Tom Gries ***Prod*** John Marshall ***Scr*** Ring Lardner, Jr. ***Ph*** Harry Stradling, Jr. ***Ed*** Byron Brandt ***Mus*** Michael Masser ***Art*** Bob Smith
Act Muhammad Ali, Ernest Borgnine, John Marley, Lloyd Haynes, Robert Duvall, David Huddleston (Columbia)

Muhammad Ali is a natural performer. More to the point, starring in his own autobiopic, *The Greatest*, he brings to it an authority and a presence that lift John Marshall's production above some of the limitations inherent in any film bio.

The film gets off to a fine start with newcomer Phillip MacAllister playing the young Cassius Clay, Jr., displaying the engaging affrontery of a young talent so sure of himself that discretion in self-description knows no bounds.

Plot follows Ali from his early career through formal discipline, professional conflicts and the controversial refusal to be inducted in the U.S. Army. En route is Ali's deliberate public baiting of Sonny Liston.

Intercut are actual sequences from Ali's major fights.

•

GREATEST SHOW ON EARTH, THE
1952, 151 mins, US Ⓥ ⦿ col
Dir Cecil B. DeMille ***Prod*** Cecil B. DeMille ***Scr*** Fredric M. Frank, Barre Lyndon, Theodore St. John ***Ph*** George Barnes, Peverell Marley, Wallace Kelley ***Ed*** Anne Bauchens ***Mus*** Victor Young ***Art*** Hal Pereira, Walter Tyler
Act Betty Hutton, Cornel Wilde, Charlton Heston, Dorothy Lamour, Gloria Grahame, James Stewart (Paramount)

The Greatest Show on Earth is as apt a handle for Cecil B. DeMille's Technicolored version of the Ringling Bros. and Barnum & Bailey circus as it is for the sawdust extravaganza itself. This is the circus with more entertainment, more thrills, more spangles and as much Big Top atmosphere as RB-B&B itself can offer.

As has come to be expected from DeMille, the story line [by Frederic M. Frank, Theodore St. John and Frank Cavett] is not what could be termed subtle. Betty Hutton is pictured as the "queen flyer" who has a yen for Charlton Heston, the circus manager. Lad has sawdust for blood, however. To strengthen the show and thus enable it to play out a full season, he imports another aerialist, the flamboyant and debonair Sebastian (Cornel Wilde). Latter promptly falls for her and she rifts with Heston. That's quickly exploited by elephant girl, Gloria Grahame, who also finds Heston a pretty attractive guy.

James Stewart is woven into the pic as an extraneous but appealing plot element. He's pictured as a police-sought medico who never removes his clown makeup.

1952: Best Picture, Motion Picture Story

NOMINATIONS: Best Director, Color Costume Design, Editing

•

GREATEST STORY EVER TOLD, THE
1965, 225 mins, US Ⓥ ⦿ ▭ col
Dir George Stevens, [David Lean, Jean Negulesco] ***Prod*** George Stevens ***Scr*** George Stevens, James Lee Barrett ***Ph*** William C. Mellor, Loyal Griggs ***Ed*** Harold F. Kress, Argyle Nelson, Jr., Frank O'Neill ***Mus*** Alfred Newman ***Art*** Richard Day, William Creber
Act Max von Sydow, Dorothy McGuire, Robert Loggia, Claude Rains, Jose Ferrer, Charlton Heston (United Artists)

The prophets should speak with respect of this $20 million Biblical epic. *The Greatest Story Ever Told* is the word made manifest. Producer-director George Stevens has elected to stick to the straight, literal, orthodox, familiar facts of the four gospels. He has scorned plot gimmicks and scanted on characterization quirks. What Stevens puts on view, overall, is panoramic cinema and cannily created backgrounds, especially the stupendous buttes of Utah.

Stevens is not particularly original in his approach to the galaxy of talent, some 60 roles. Hollywood's fad for cameo bits by featured players may suffer some discredit in the light of the triviality of footage and impact by such players as Carroll Baker, Pat Boone, Richard Conte, Ina Balin, Frank De Kova, Victor Buono, Marian Seldes, Paul Stewart. John Wayne is ill-at-ease and a waste of name, many may feel, as the captain of the soldiers who escort the Redeemer to the cross. Claude Rains is standout in the opening sequence [directed by David Lean] as the dying ruler of Judea.

Quite properly Stevens has focused on the birth, ministry, execution and resurrection of the Son of God. In the casting of Jesus there is occasion for compliment. The performance of the Swedish actor, Max von Sydow, and his English diction are ideal.

The Baptist (Charlton Heston) is the only out-and-out fanatic in the picture but this takes the form of roaring demands that Herod "repent." Herod, in the remarkably curbed performance of Jose Ferrer, is no worse than a cynical administrative stooge for the Romans.

1965: NOMINATIONS: Best Color Cinematography, Color Costume Design, Color Art Direction, Original Music Score, Visual Effects

•

GREAT EXPECTATIONS
1946, 110 mins, UK Ⓥ b/w
Dir David Lean ***Prod*** Ronald Neame ***Scr*** David Lean, Ronald Neame, Anthony Havelock-Allan ***Ph*** Guy Green ***Ed*** Jack Harris ***Mus*** Walter Goehr ***Art*** John Bryan
Act John Mills, Valerie Hobson, Francis L. Sullivan, Alec Guinness, Jean Simmons, Martita Hunt (Cineguild)

Only rabid Dickensians will find fault with the present adaptation, and paradoxically only lovers of Dickens will derive maximum pleasure from the film.

This adaptation tells how young Pip befriends an escaped convict, who, recaptured and transported to Australia, leaves Pip a fortune so he may become a gentleman with great expectations. Pip believes the unexpected fortune originated with the eccentric Miss Havisham at whose house he has met Estella, the girl he loves.

To condense the novel into a two-hour picture meant sacrificing many minor characters. The period and people are vividly brought to life but so particular have the producers been to avoid offending any Dickensian that every character is drawn so precise that many of them are puppets. That's the great fault of the film. It is beautiful but lacks heart. It evokes admiration but no feeling.

With the exception of John Mills and Alec Guinness, only the secondary characters are entirely credible. Valerie Hobson, whose beauty is not captured by the camera, fails to bring Estella to life, and young Jean Simmons, who plays the role as a girl, is adequately heartless.

1947: Best B&W Cinematography, B&W Art Direction.

NOMINATIONS: Best Picture, Director, Screenplay

•

GREAT EXPECTATIONS
1998, 111 mins, US Ⓥ ⦿ ▭ col
Dir Alfonso Cuaron ***Prod*** Art Linson ***Scr*** Mitch Glazer ***Ph*** Emmanuel Lubezki ***Ed*** Steven Weisberg ***Mus*** Patrick Doyle ***Art*** Tony Burrough
Act Ethan Hawke, Gwyneth Paltrow, Hank Azaria, Chris Cooper, Anne Bancroft, Robert De Niro (20th Century-Fox)

This *Great Expectations* is something less than a pip. A fanciful and free modern-day adaptation of Charles Dickens's classic, beautifully made production lacks the emotional depth and dramatic tension to command attention beyond the level of a talented curiosity.

Second American effort by the gifted Mexican director Alfonso Cuaron after his splendid *The Little Princess*, [pic centers on] eight-year-old orphan Finn Bell, growing up in a sleepy fishing village along the Florida coast. Finn is accosted by an escaped convict (Robert De Niro) who coerces the boy into helping him. The other highlight of Finn's youth are his visits to Paradiso Perduto, an old Venetian-style mansion where he is periodically paged to play with the lovely Estella, niece of the owner, Dinsmoor (Anne Bancroft).

A half-hour in, action jumps to the '80s. Finn (Ethan Hawke) and Estella (Gwyneth Paltrow) meet once again and experience a highly erotic encounter, but Estella abruptly disappears. For seven years, Finn lives on the margins until a mysterious stranger, a New York art world rep (Josh Mostel), offers Finn a one-man show if he'll come to Manhattan and start painting again. Inevitably, Estella reenters his life.

Hawke exhibits limited range as Finn. Paltrow serves up the requisite flintiness and flightiness for Estella, while also nicely conveying the sense of loss in living as effervescently as she does. Bancroft's turn is colorful but predictable.

•

GREAT GABBO, THE
1929, 91 mins, US Ⓥ col
Dir James Cruze ***Prod*** Henry D. Meyer, Nat Cordish ***Scr*** Ben Hecht, Hugh Herbert
Act Erich von Stroheim, Betty Compson, Don Douglas, Margie Kane (Meyer-Cordish)

The story is simplicity itself. Just a pair of show people—one a lovely, considerate girl and the other a ventriloquist with a hyper-egotist complex. The expected break, followed by a rise from the grinds to the individual success of both. Then the too late realization of love by the dummy manipulator.

Erich von Stroheim, as the eccentric and arrogant performer who reveals a Pagliacci heart through the medium of Otto, the dummy, doubles the enhancement of a dominant screen personality with his lines. It is the voice, frenzied and then modulated to a pianissimo, that is one of the strongest threads, carrying the interest over sequences devoted to color and stage show that would be irrelevant gaps in productions less skillfully directed and enacted.

In part of the colored sequence, the print is grainy and the characters blurred but both of these conditions are too brief to be considered drawbacks.

•

GREAT GARRICK, THE
1937, 82 mins, US b/w
Dir James Whale ***Prod*** James Whale, Mervyn LeRoy ***Scr*** Ernest Vajda ***Ph*** Ernest Haller ***Ed*** Warren Low ***Mus*** Adolph Deutsch ***Art*** Anton Grot
Act Brian Aherne, Olivia de Havilland, Edward Everett Horton, Melville Cooper, Lionel Atwill, Lana Turner (Warner)

Among film's distinctive features are a strictly fictional romantic comedy story around the person of David Garrick, 18th-century English actor, a production of superlative workmanship fabricated from old prints of the period, and acting by a fine cast in the flamboyant manner demanded by the script. Release prints wear a sepia tone which enhances the beauty of the visual presentation.

Ernst Vajda has written of an incident in Garrick's career when the English star (Brian Aherne) was invited by the Comedie Francaise to appear for a guest season at the famous Paris theatre, supported by French players. On his farewell night in London, he announces his intentions, which arouse bitter comment from the pit. To appease their wrath, he facetiously explains that some good acting might teach the French a thing or two. These remarks, when conveyed to the players at the Comedie Francaise, arouse animosity, and a plot is conceived to embarrass the visitor.

French actors take over the management of an inn on the Calais-Paris road. Trumped-up quarrels ending in murder, duels and strange happenings take place to frighten the visitor. He sees through the fraud and enters into the scheme as a willing victim. However, a young woman (Olivia de Havilland), who is a stranger to the French actors, arrives at the inn to stay the night.

Tale is not without some very amusing angles. Fact is, it is a farce, should be played as a farce with speed and increasing hilarity. Such, however, is not the case. Whale's direction is geared to a slow tempo. His romantic passages between Aherne and De Havilland are quite charming, but much too long.

Anton Grot's art direction calls for special comment. Ernest Haller's camera work is a series of pastels.

•

GREAT GATSBY, THE
1949, 91 mins, US Ⓥ b/w
Dir Elliott Nugent ***Prod*** Richard Maibaum ***Scr*** Cyril Hume, Richard Maibaum ***Ph*** John F. Seitz ***Ed*** Ellsworth Hoagland ***Mus*** Robert Emmett Dolan ***Art*** Hans Dreier, Roland Anderson
Act Alan Ladd, Betty Field, Macdonald Carey, Ruth Hussey, Barry Sullivan, Shelley Winters (Paramount)

F. Scott Fitzgerald's story of the roaring '20s is peopled with shallow characters and the script [also from the play by Owen Davis] stresses the love story rather than the hijacking, bootlegging elements.

Gatsby is a fabulous bootlegger who has parlayed his relentless drive into fortune. When the stack of blue chips is large enough, he turns his attention to winning back a girl he lost years ago to a wealthy man. Alan Ladd handles his characterization ably, making it as well-rounded as the yarn permits and fares better than other cast members in trying to make the surface characters come to life.

Elliott Nugent's direction skips along the surface of the era depicted. The script doesn't give him much substance to work with.

•

GREAT GATSBY, THE
1974, 144 mins, US Ⓥ ⦿ col
Dir Jack Clayton ***Prod*** David Merrick ***Scr*** Francis Coppola ***Ph*** Douglas Slocombe ***Ed*** Tom Priestley ***Mus*** Nelson Riddle ***Art*** John Box
Act Robert Redford, Mia Farrow, Bruce Dern, Karen Black, Scott Wilson, Sam Waterston (Paramount)

Paramount's third pass at *The Great Gatsby* is by far the most concerted attempt to probe the peculiar ethos of the Beautiful People of the 1920s. The fascinating physical beauty of the $6 million-plus film complements the utter shallowness of most principal characters from the F. Scott Fitzgerald novel.

Robert Redford is excellent in the title role, the mysterious gentleman of humble origins and bootlegging connections; Mia Farrow is his long-lost love, married unhappily but inextricably to brutish Bruce Dern, who has a side affair going with restive working class wife Karen Black.

The Francis Coppola script and Jack Clayton's direction paint a savagely genteel portrait of an upper class generation that deserved in spades what it got circa 1929 and after.

1974: Best Adapted Scoring, Costume Design

•

GREAT JOHN L., THE
1945, 96 mins, US b/w
Dir Frank Tuttle ***Prod*** Bing Crosby ***Scr*** James Edward Grant ***Ph*** James Van Treen ***Ed*** Theodor Bellinger ***Mus*** Victor Young
Act Greg McClure, Linda Darnell, Barbara Britton, J. M. Kerrigan, Otto Kruger, Wallace Ford (United Artists)

In his first independent production, Bing Crosby comes out with both fists swinging through a dramatization of the life of boxer John L. Sullivan.

The story that takes John L. from his early youth as the Boston strong boy, through his great victories, into the days of drunken disillusionment, and finally, to the mature man who becomes the exponent of clean living.

The real star of the film is a man who has never done anything in pictures except as an extra, Greg McClure. He not only looks the part of the Great John L, he acts the part, and grows with it.

But if it's McClure who carries the greatest burden, the rest of the cast is right there with him at all times. The two women in his life, played by Linda Darnell and Barbara Britton, are done effectively. J. M. Kerrigan does Sullivan's parish priest sensitively and without lush sentimentality.

•

GREAT LIE, THE
1941, 102 mins, US Ⓥ ⦿ b/w
Dir Edmund Goulding ***Prod*** Henry Blanke ***Scr*** Lenore Coffee ***Ph*** Tony Gaudio ***Ed*** Ralph Dawson ***Mus*** Max Steiner
Act Bette Davis, George Brent, Mary Astor, Hattie McDaniel, Grant Mitchell, Jerome Cowan (Warner)

The Great Lie is a sophisticated drama providing Bette Davis with opportunity for continued display of her tragic emotionalisms. Excellent performances by the players, deft direction by Edmund Goulding, and a compact script by Lenore Coffee [from a novel by Polan Banks], provides a well-rounded package of dramatic entertainment.

Story presents the situation confronting the father of a child claimed as her own by his wife, but in reality born by the woman to whom he was illegally married. And the problem reaches its apex when both women attempt to use the youngster to hold the man.

Davis gives a most persuasive portrayal of the wife who faces the tragic events of her romance and marriage. In spots, she gushes tears, and in others, hits a few brief moments of light spontaneity. George Brent delivers a strong performance as the husband while Mary Astor scores notably, as the case-hardened concert artist whose ambitions transcend motherly and wifely attributes of womanhood.

•

GREAT LOVER, THE
1949, 89 mins, US Ⓥ b/w
Dir Alexander Hall ***Prod*** Edmund Beloin ***Scr*** Edmund Beloin, Melville Shavelson, Jack Rose ***Ph*** Charles B. Lang, Jr. ***Ed*** Ellsworth Hoagland ***Mus*** Joseph J. Lilley
Act Bob Hope, Rhonda Fleming, Roland Young, Roland Culver (Paramount)

Bob Hope's name toplining *Lover* tips that there'll be little of the Valentino about its amours. Its venture into comedic, never-never doings is well suited to Hope's brash antics. It never bursts into belly laughs, but keeps satisfied chuckles continuously flowing for a fast 80 minutes.

Script has Hope in charge of group of male adolescents on a European tour. That starts the laughs. Plot then mixes in a gambler who murders his victims, a gorgeous duchess and her card-playing father, places these ingredients aboard ship sailing for the U.S. and then lets nature, and Hope, carry on.

Hope prances through his footage in fine style, first as an unwilling leader of kiddies whose code is to save man from tobacco, drink and women. That complicates his romance with Rhonda Fleming.

•

GREAT MAN, THE
1956, 92 mins, US b/w
Dir Jose Ferrer ***Prod*** Aaron Rosenberg ***Scr*** Al Morgan, Jose Ferrer ***Ph*** Harold Lipstein ***Ed*** Sherman Todd, Al Joseph ***Mus*** Herman Stein
Act Jose Ferrer, Dean Jagger, Keenan Wynn, Julie London, Joanne Gilbert, Ed Wynn (Universal)

Like the novel by Al (NBC) Morgan, the film is a series of flash episodes adding into a character study as a probing reporter researches the background of a nationally known and presumably revered radio figure who has died in an auto accident. The research brings out that, away from the mike, the late lamented was a stinker with no scruples. The "great man" is never seen in person.

Jose Ferrer, who stars as the reporter, collaborated with author Morgan on the screenplay and directed. In each function, he is extremely able, with particular emphasis on his direction which brings out several surprise performances.

Ed Wynn is outstanding as the pious owner of a small New England radio station who gave the "morning man" his start. Julie London socks across the dramatic role of the singer who also must hold herself available as a part-time mistress if the Studio King is minded that way. Dean Jagger is fine as the network head and son Keenan Wynn scores, too, as the executive always looking out for himself.

•

GREAT MAN'S LADY, THE
1942, 90 mins, US b/w
Dir William A. Wellman ***Prod*** William A. Wellman ***Scr*** W. L. River ***Ph*** William C. Mellor ***Ed*** Thomas Scott ***Mus*** Victor Young
Act Barbara Stanwyck, Joel McCrea, Brian Donlevy, Thurston Hall, Lloyd Corrigan (Paramount)

Paramount has given this drama the usual production accoutrements that go with "A" pictures, but the disturbance to the film's continuity through the use of the trite flashback technique, plus a tedious story of the pioneering west, tend to slow the picture to a walk.

It's a conglomerate of the familiar story of a woman's inspiration to a man and his ultimate achievement from a pioneer in the west to a seat in the U.S. Senate. It is a story of intense drama, yet it leaves one strangely unmoved.

Opening of the picture shows Barbara Stanwyck as a centenarian being interviewed by reporters upon the unveiling of a statue of the late Senator Ethan Hoyt.

Brian Donlevy, as a gambler, contributes a steady performance in the triangle, but the writing [from a story by Adela Rogers St. John and Seena Owen, based on a short story by Vina Delmar] generally gives him the worst of it.

•

GREAT MCGINTY, THE
(UK: DOWN WENT MCGINTY)
1940, 81 mins, US Ⓥ ⦿ b/w
Dir Preston Sturges ***Prod*** Paul Jones ***Scr*** Preston Sturges ***Ph*** William C. Mellor ***Ed*** Hugh Bennett ***Mus*** Frederick Hollander ***Art*** Hans Dreier, Earl Hedrick
Act Brian Donlevy, Muriel Angelus, Akim Tamiroff, Allyn Joslyn, William Demarest, Steffi Duna (Paramount)

The Great McGinty initiates Preston Sturges into the directing ranks, after a long stretch as a film scenarist. Piloting an original story and screenplay of his own concoction, Sturges displays plenty of ability in accentuating both the comedy and dramatic elements of his material, withal maintaining a consistent pace in the unreeling.

Sturges's story departs radically from accepted formula. His main character is a tough, rowdy and muscular individual who creates more interest than sympathy in his career as a prototype of many political rascals of the American scene.

Story is unfolded by flashback. Brian Donlevy is introduced as the toughened bartender of a dive in a Central American banana republic. He's a fugitive from justice, the same as the young bank clerk who absconded with funds in a weak moment. Across the bar, Donlevy tells the latter his story—a life of crookedness where the first honest thing he attempted chased him from the country. When he first finds that illegal voting brings coin, he becomes a repeater, gets into favor of political boss (Akim Tamiroff) and gradually rises to positions of alderman, mayor and finally, governor of the state.

Portrayal of Donlevy as the slightly educated political apprentice who learns the ropes fast, and wields his fists at every opportunity, is excellent. Tamiroff clicks as the political boss, while Muriel Angelus provides a charming and warmful personality in the role of the politico's wife. Bill Demarest provides attention as a political stooge.

1940: Best Original Screenplay

•

GREAT MOMENT, THE
1944, 83 mins, US Ⓥ b/w
Dir Preston Sturges ***Prod*** Preston Sturges ***Scr*** Preston Sturges ***Ph*** Victor Milner ***Ed*** Stuart Gilmore ***Mus*** Victor Young ***Art*** Hans Dreier, Ernst Fegte
Act Joel McCrea, Betty Field, Harry Carey, William Demarest, Franklin Pangborn, Grady Sutton (Paramount)

Preston Sturges brings to the screen the compelling biography of Dr. W.T.G. Morton, who in 1844 discovered anaesthesia. The film [from the book by Rene Fulop-Muller] is the story of the romance, the trials and the ultimate victory of a Boston dentist, who experimented until he finally hit upon a painless means of extracting teeth, then passed on his discovery to the world of medicine. Performances of Joel McCrea and Betty Field, as well as a solid supporting cast, are well in keeping with the dignity of the yarn.

McCrea gives an excellent portrayal in the role of the impoverished medical student, forced to forego the study of medicine in lieu of a dental career because of lack of funds. Field, as the wife who sometimes gets on his nerves because of her lack of understanding of what he is endeavoring to accomplish, proves again that she is an actress with loads of talent.

Supporting roles of Harry Carey, the doctor who gives McCrea a chance to prove that anaesthesia is suitable for surgical operations, and William Demarest, as the first patient of McCrea, are expertly handled.

•

GREAT MUPPET CAPER, THE
1981, 95 mins, UK Ⓥ ⦿ ▭ col
Dir Jim Henson ***Prod*** David Lazar ***Scr*** Tom Patchett, Jay Tarses, Jerry Juhl, Jack Rose ***Ph*** Oswald Morris ***Ed*** Ralph Kemplen ***Mus*** Joe Raposo ***Art*** Harry Lange
Act Charles Grodin, Diana Rigg, John Cleese, Robert Morley, Peter Ustinov, Jack Warden (Universal/AFD)

Muppet creator Jim Henson took over the directorial reins this second time out and, buttressed by a $14 million budget and top professionalism down the line in the production department, shows a sure hand in guiding his appealing stars through their paces.

Story hook has hapless reporters Kermit, Fozzie Bear and The Great Gonzo literally plunked down in London Town to follow up on a major jewel robbery involving fashion world magnate Diana Rigg. Once there, Kermit mistakenly takes Miss Piggy for beautiful Lady Holiday and instantly falls in love with the rotund aspiring model.

At the same time, Rigg's sly brother, Charles Grodin, puts the make on Miss Piggy himself while also setting her up for arrest in the jewel robbery case.

As before, much of the dialog neatly walks the line between true wit and silly (and sometimes inside) jokes.

Grodin and Rigg are both fine, and cameo appearances are limited to nice turns by John Cleese, Robert Morley, Peter Ustinov and Jack Warden.

1981: NOMINATION: Best Song ("The First Time It Happens")

•

GREAT NORTHFIELD, MINNESOTA RAID, THE
1972, 91 mins, UK Ⓥ b/w
Dir Philip Kaufman ***Prod*** Jennings Lang ***Scr*** Philip Kaufman ***Ph*** Bruce Surtees ***Ed*** Douglas Stewart ***Mus*** Dave Grusin ***Art*** Alexander Golitzen, George Webb
Act Cliff Robertson, Robert Duvall, Luke Askew, R. G. Armstrong, Dana Elcar, Donald Moffat (Universal/Robertson & Associates)

The Great Northfield, Minnesota Raid—described as shedding "new light" on Cole Younger and Jesse James—may be a valiant attempt but fails to come off.

Primarily, this is due to utter lack of sustained narrative, confused and inept writing, overabundance of characters difficult for ready identification, often apparent indecision whether to make this drama or comedy and a mish-mash of irrelevant sequences.

Plottage bases its premise on the outlaws' decision to go from their native Missouri to Minnesota to rob what a newspaper ad claims to be the biggest bank west of the Mississippi. Cliff Robertson plays Cole and Robert Duvall is Jesse.

Perhaps Philip Kaufman, who directs and provides the screenplay, accurately attains historic accuracy in his recital of events leading up to the raid and afterwards, but his treatment is such that characters throughout are dull fellows indeed, and picture itself is in kind.

•

GREAT O'MALLEY, THE
1937, 71 mins, US Ⓥ b/w
Dir William Dieterle ***Prod*** Harry Joe Brown ***Scr*** Milton Krims, Tom Reed ***Ph*** Ernest Haller ***Ed*** Warren Low ***Art*** Hugh Reticker
Act Pat O'Brien, Sybil Jason, Humphrey Bogart, Frieda Inescort, Ann Sheridan, Donald Crisp (Warner)

One of Hollywood's pat formulas for cop pictures, but with less action than usual. Studio gives Humphrey Bogart his initial star billing with this film, apparently a reward for his work in *Black Legion*. His running mate here is Pat O'Brien. No fault of either that this film shoots wide of its mark. A plot [by Gerald Beaumont] that has been redone much too much is the chief drawback.

It is the tough Hibernian policeman theme, with plenty of brogue, and the eventual softening of the copper when a kid creeps into his heart. In this instance the tot is Sybil Jason, who delivers as a crippled slum-child. It's her father (Bogart), whom O'Brien forces into criminal activities and later tries to befriend, after first getting a famous surgeon to straighten out the kid's leg.

William Dieterle has made a valiant attempt to overcome the screenplay's weaknesses in his direction, but no could do. There's practically no action for the first 40 minutes, and subsequent footage hardly is in the very exciting class. If anything, picture depends almost wholly on the appeal of moppet Jason.

•

GREAT OUTDOORS, THE
1988, 90 mins, US Ⓥ ⦿ col
Dir Howard Deutch ***Prod*** Arne L. Schmidt ***Scr*** John Hughes ***Ph*** Ric Waite ***Ed*** Tom Rolf, William Gordean, Seth Flaum ***Mus*** Thomas Newman ***Art*** John W. Corso
Act Dan Aykroyd, John Candy, Stephanie Faracy, Annette Bening, Chris Young, Lucy Deakins (Universal/Hughes)

John Candy stars as a sweet, slightly dopey family man who wagoneers his happy brood up from Chicago for a bigpines getaway. No sooner do they unpack than obnoxious brother-in-law Dan Aykroyd and his maladjusted family blast in uninvited to spend the week. His pampered wife (Annette Bening) eggs him on, while his spooky kids (twins Hilary and Rebecca Gordon) never say a word.

Writer-executive producer John Hughes conjures up a romance between Candy's teenage son (Chris Young) and a local girl (Lucy Deakins), but that proves the film's biggest letdown. Last third of the film is a real mess, as filmmakers try to whip up a crisis that will unite the family, with the redheaded twins getting lost in a mineshaft during a wild rainstorm.

Despite all this, the Aykroyd-Candy pairing is charmed. Stephanie Faracy is excellent as Candy's sweet, happy wife, and Bening is also savvy in her role. Pic teams director Howard Deutch with Hughes for the third time.

•

GREAT RACE, THE
1965, 153 mins, US Ⓥ ⦿ ▭ col
Dir Blake Edwards ***Prod*** Martin Jurow ***Scr*** Arthur Ross ***Ph*** Russell Harlan ***Ed*** Ralph E. Winters ***Mus*** Henry Mancini ***Art*** Fernando Carrere
Act Jack Lemmon, Tony Curtis, Natalie Wood, Peter Falk, Keenan Wynn, Arthur O'Connell (Warner)

The Great Race is a big, expensive, whopping, comedy extravaganza [from a screen story by Blake Edwards and Arthur Ross], long on slapstick and near-inspired tomfoolery whose tongue-in-cheek treatment liberally sprinkled with corn frequently garners belly laughs.

A certain nostalgic flavor is achieved, both in the 1908 period of an automobile race from New York to Paris and Blake Edwards's broad borrowing from *The Prisoner of Zenda* tale and an earlier Laurel and Hardy comedy for some of his heartiest action. [Pic is dedicated to L&H.]

Characters carry an old-fashioned zest when it was the fashion to hiss the villain and cheer the hero. Slotting into this category, never has there been a villain so dastardly as Jack Lemmon nor a hero so whitely pure as Tony Curtis, rivals in the great race staged by an auto manufacturer to prove his car's worth.

Strongly abetting the two male principals is Natalie Wood as a militant suffragette who wants to be a reporter and sells a NY newspaper publisher on allowing her to enter the race and covering it for his sheet.

To carry on the overall spirit, Curtis always is garbed in snowy white, Lemmon in black, a gent whose every tone is a snarl, and whose laugh would put Woody Woodpecker to shame.

Lemmon plays it dirty throughout and for huge effect. Curtis underplays for equally comic effect. Wood comes through on par with the two male stars.

1965: Best Sound Effects

NOMINATIONS: Best Color Cinematography, Editing, Sound, Song ("The Sweetheart Tree")

•

GREAT ROCK 'N' ROLL SWINDLE, THE
1980, 103 mins, UK Ⓥ col
Dir Julien Temple ***Prod*** Jeremy Thomas, Don Boyd ***Scr*** Julien Temple ***Ph*** A. Barker-Mills ***Ed*** R. Bedford, M.D. Maslin, G. Swire ***Mus*** The Sex Pistols
Act Malcolm McLaren, Johnny Rotten, Sid Vicious, Steve Jones, Paul Cook, Jess Conrad (Kendon/Matrix Best/Virgin)

The Great Rock 'n' Roll Swindle is the *Citizen Kane* of rock 'n' roll pictures. An incredibly sophisticated, stupefyingly multilayered portrait of the 1970s phenomenon known as The Sex Pistols, unstintingly cynical pic casts a jaundiced eye at the entire pop culture scene and, if nothing else, represents the most imaginative use of a rock group in films since The Beatles debuted in *A Hard Day's Night*.

Pic, which stars and is narrated after a fashion by Pistols's manager Malcolm McLaren, begins with the basic premise that the campaign of shock tactics was premeditated.

A bubbling brew of devices and styles somehow mesh under first-time helmer Julien Temple's wizardly direction to amplify McLaren's thesis on how to create a rock sensation in 10 easy lessons. Among his dicta are: Demonstrate To Record Companies The Enormous Potential Of A Band That Can't Play; Make It As Hard As Possible For The Press To See It; Insult Your Audiences As Much As Possible, and Cultivate Hatred.

•

GREAT SANTINI, THE
1980, 115 mins, US Ⓥ col
Dir Lewis John Carlino ***Prod*** Charles A. Pratt ***Scr*** Lewis John Carlino ***Ph*** Ralph Woolsey ***Ed*** Houseley Stevenson ***Mus*** Elmer Bernstein ***Art*** Jack Poplin
Act Robert Duvall, Blythe Danner, Michael O'Keefe, Lisa Jane Persky, Julie Anne Haddock, Stan Shaw (Orion)

Robert Duvall gives an excellent portrayal of a semi-psychotic, softened with a warmer side. But Duvall has to fight for every inch of footage against the overwhelming performances by several others in the cast—and that's the strength of *The Great Santini*.

Title is a nickname Duvall picks up as the finest fighter pilot in the U.S. Marines. But this isn't a war picture. Quite the contrary, it's the compellingly relevant story of a supermacho peacetime warrior with nobody to fight except himself and those who love him.

As the sensitive son who strives to meet all of his father's supermasculine standards, Michael O'Keefe is terrific and emerges as the major star of the picture.

Blythe Danner is also strong as the wife who suffers Duvall's excesses.

1980: NOMINATIONS: Best Actor (Robert Duvall), Supp. Actor (Michael O'Keefe)

•

GREAT SCOUT & CATHOUSE THURSDAY, THE
1976, 102 mins, US Ⓥ col
Dir Don Taylor ***Prod*** Jules Buck, David Korda ***Scr*** Richard Shapiro ***Ph*** Alex Phillips, Jr. ***Ed*** Sheldon Kahn ***Mus*** John Cameron ***Art*** Jack Martin Smith
Act Lee Marvin, Oliver Reed, Robert Culp, Elizabeth Ashley, Strother Martin, Kay Lenz (American International)

Richard Shapiro's up-and-down screenplay uses the plot about former partners in crime (here Lee Marvin and Indian sidekick Oliver Reed) going back to get revenge on the partner who cheated them and went respectable with the loot (Robert Culp).

In the midsection, the May-December romance between Marvin's aging cowpoke and Kay Lenz's young prostie rouses some dramatic interest, coming through the general hokiness like rays of sunshine on a smoggy day. Marvin, to his credit, resists the strong temptation to mug it up, playing with an amusing attempt at dignity, and Lenz is a very appealing and spunky actress.

Reed's role is a hammy embarrassment, Culp seems uncomfortable as a strident politico and Sylvia Miles is wasted as a madam.

•

GREAT SMOKEY ROADBLOCK, THE
SEE: THE LAST OF THE COWBOYS

•

GREAT ST. TRINIAN'S TRAIN ROBBERY, THE
1966, 94 mins, UK Ⓥ col
Dir Frank Launder, Sidney Gilliat ***Prod*** Leslie Gilliat ***Scr*** Frank Launder, Ivor Herbert ***Ph*** Kenneth Hodges ***Ed*** Geoffrey Foot ***Mus*** Malcolm Arnold ***Art*** Albert Witherick
Act Frankie Howerd, Reg Varney, Stratford Johns, Eric Barker, Dora Bryan, George Cole (British Lion)

Ronald Searle's little schoolgirl demons from St. Trinian's are berserk again on the screen in a yarn with a topical twist, the [1963] Great Train Robbery.

Having pulled off a $7 million train robbery, a hapless gang of crooks stash the loot in a deserted country mansion. But when they go back to collect, they find the St. Trinian's school has taken over and they are completely routed by the hockey sticks and rough stuff handed out by the little she-monsters. When the gang returns on parents' day for a second attempt at picking up the loot they run into further trouble and complications and eventually get involved in a great train chase which is quite the funniest part of the film, having a great deal in common with the old silent slapstick technique.

Among the many performances which contribute to the gaiety are those of Frankie Howerd as a crook posing as a French male hairdresser, Raymond Huntley as a Cabinet Minister with amorous eyes on the St. Trinian's headmistress (Dora Bryan), Richard Wattis in one of his typical harassed civil servant roles and Peter Gilmore as his confrère. George Cole crops up again as Flash Harry, the school bookie.

•

GREAT TEXAS DYNAMITE CHASE, THE
1976, 90 mins, US Ⓥ col
Dir Michael Pressman ***Prod*** David Irving ***Scr*** David Kirkpatrick ***Ph*** Jamie Anderson ***Ed*** Millie Moore ***Mus*** Craig Safan ***Art*** Russel Smith
Act Claudia Jennings, Jocelyn Jones, Johnny Crawford, Chris Pennock, Tara Strohmeier, Miles Watkins (Yasny Talking Pictures II)

The Great Texas Dynamite Chase is a well-made exploitation film which works on two levels, providing kicks for the ozoner crowd and tongue-in-cheek humor for the more sophisticated. The film had some initial playdates under the title *Dynamite Women*.

Claudia Jennings and Jocelyn Jones are stylish and attractive as a pair of brazen Texas bankrobbers. They stay firmly in character throughout as a loyal but very divergent criminal pair.

Jennings is a hardened prison escapee, while Jones goes on the road to avoid the boredom of being a smalltown bank teller. They use lots of dynamite along the way, but there's little bloodshed until the last part of the film, when the film's dominant spoof tone turns uncomfortably and unsuccessfully close to reality.

•

GREAT TRAIN ROBBERY, THE
SEE: THE FIRST GREAT TRAIN ROBBERY

•

GREAT WALDO PEPPER, THE
1975, 108 mins, US Ⓥ ⦿ ▭ col
Dir George Roy Hill ***Prod*** George Roy Hill ***Scr*** William Goldman ***Ph*** Robert Surtees ***Ed*** William Reynolds ***Mus*** Henry Mancini ***Art*** Henry Bumstead
Act Robert Redford, Bo Svenson, Bo Brundin, Susan Sarandon, Geoffrey Lewis, Edward Herrman (Universal)

The Great Waldo Pepper is an uneven and unsatisfying story of anachronistic, pitiable, but misplaced heroism. Robert Redford stars as an aerial ace, unable to cope with the segue from pioneer barnstorming to bigtime aviation.

George Roy Hill's original story was scripted by William Goldman into yet another stab at dramatizing the effect of inexorable social change on pioneers. In this case, Redford and Bo Svenson, two World War I airmen, scratch out a living, and feed their egos, via daring stunts in midwest fields. But Geoffrey Lewis has made the transition from cocky pilot to aviation official, and inventor Edward Herrmann unwittingly complements the shift through his technological advances.

The film stumbles towards its fuzzy climax.

•

GREAT WALL, A
(AKA: THE GREAT WALL IS A GREAT WALL)
1986, 97 mins, US Ⓥ ⦿ col
Dir Peter Wang ***Prod*** Shirley Sun ***Scr*** Peter Wang, Shirley Sun ***Ph*** Peter Stein, Robert Primes ***Ed*** Grahame Weinbren ***Mus*** David Liang, Ge Ganru ***Art*** Wing Lee, Feng Yuan, Ming Ming Cheung
Act Peter Wang, Sharon Iwai, Kelvin Han Yee, Li Qinqin, Wang Xiao (W&S/Nanhai)

A charming but unduly lightweight film, *A Great Wall* humorously accentuates the many cultural differences between the two giant nations of the U.S. and China, but goes out of its way to avoid dealing with politics or any other issues of substance.

Peter Wang, who appeared in *Chan Is Missing*, portrays a San Francisco computer executive who takes advantage of the opening up of China to visit relatives there as well as to introduce his American-born wife and son to his native land.

Wang quickly sketches in his key players on both sides of the Pacific and deftly characterizes their differing lifestyles but he simply glosses over too many important issues for the film to be considered a true artistic success.

•

GREAT WALTZ, THE
1938, 107 mins, US Ⓥ b/w
Dir Julien Duvivier ***Prod*** [uncredited] ***Scr*** Samuel Hoffenstein, Walter Reisch ***Ph*** Joseph Ruttenberg ***Ed*** Tom Held ***Mus*** Dimitri Tiomkin (arr.) ***Art*** Cedric Gibbons, Paul Groesse, Edwin B. Willis
Act Luise Rainer, Fernand Gravet, Miliza Korjus, Hugh Herbert, Lionel Atwill, Curt Bois (M-G-M)

The Great Waltz is a field day for music lovers plus elegant entertainment. Producers were nearly two years on this film, but the extra effort shows in the nicety with which its many component parts fit together. It is Luise Rainer who makes the film.

While primarily a fanciful tale of Johann Strauss II's rise in the musical firmament [from an original story by Gottfried Reinhardt], entire plot has been constructed around his outstanding works.

The youthful Strauss (Fernand Gravet) is shown quitting his job in a Vienna banking house to carry on as a musician; first as a director of his own neighborhood orchestra playing his newest compositions; and then as a composer whose waltz tunes are recognized even in official court circles, something unheard of in those days.

Strauss marries the baker's daughter soon after he wins his first success. His part in the short-lived revolution serves to develop romance with the opera singer Carla Donner (Miliza Korjus). It is the sudden decision to fight for her mate, after months of self-sacrifice, that takes Mrs. Strauss (Rainer) storming backstage after the successful premiere of his first opera.

Not cast in a thoroughly sympathetic role, operatic singer Korjus suffers at times from photographic angles and does not arouse as much excitement as obviously was intended [in her first American picture].

Besides Rainer's sterling portrayal of the adoring wife, Gravet does surprisingly well as the younger Strauss. Burden of romantic scenes rest on his shoulders and he comes through with élan. His singing measures up also. [Lyrics by Oscar Hammerstein II.]

1938: Best Cinematography

NOMINATIONS: Best Supp. Actress (Miliza Korjus), Editing

•

GREAT WHITE HOPE, THE
1970, 102 mins, US Ⓥ ▭ col
Dir Martin Ritt ***Prod*** Lawrence Turman ***Scr*** Howard Sackler ***Ph*** Burnett Guffey ***Ed*** William Reynolds ***Mus*** Lionel Newman ***Art*** John DeCuir
Act James Earl Jones, Jane Alexander, Lou Gilbert, Joel Fluellen, Chester Morris, Robert Webber (20th Century-Fox)

In its telling of the quasi-fictionalized public life of famed black heavyweight champ, circa 1910, Jack Johnson, the film's pacing and gritty cynicism resembles the best of the old Warner Bros Depression dramas; but in the distended playout of the fighter's tragic private life via involvement with a white woman, the picture sags.

However, a superior cast, headed by James Earl Jones encoring in his stage role, a colorful and earthy script, plus outstanding production, render film quite palatable.

Jones's re-creation of his stage role is an eye-riveting experience. The towering rages and unrestrained joys of which his character was capable are portrayed larger than life.

1970: NOMINATIONS: Best Actor (James Earl Jones), Actress (Jane Alexander)

•

GREAT WHITE HYPE, THE
1996, 90 mins, US Ⓥ col
Dir Reginald Hudlin ***Prod*** Fred Berner, Joshua Donen ***Scr*** Tony Hendra, Ron Shelton ***Ph*** Ron Garcia ***Ed*** Earl Watson ***Mus*** Marcus Miller ***Art*** Charles Rosen
Act Samuel L. Jackson, Jeff Goldblum, Peter Berg, Jon Lovitz, Corbin Bernsen, Cheech Marin (Altman/Berner/20th Century-Fox)

Appealing performers and sporadic moments of dead-on satiric hilarity only partly compensate for the general tepidness of *The Great White Hype*, which depicts the comic consequences of a boxing promotion aimed at giving white fans one of their own to root for in a heavyweight championship. Uneven scripting and unfocused direction create the impression of a TV sketch stretched to feature length.

Since co-scripter Ron Shelton's screenplays for *Bull Durham*, *White Men Can't Jump* and *Cobb* conveyed a devotee's avid knowledge and love of sports, *The Great White Hype* will surely be noted for lacking the same tone of fascination and respect. Script treats boxing mainly as a pretext for showbiz sharks to make money off of dimwitted gladiators.

Set in Las Vegas, tale centers on the larger-than-life and sartorially excessive Rev. Fred Sultan (Samuel L. Jackson), a high-spirited and gleefully devious boxing impresario who is dismayed at the meager profits brought in by his current champ (Damon Wayans). The obvious remedy is to rustle up a Caucasian contender, Terry Conklin (Peter Berg), now a luggish singer for a heavy metal band

Despite his gruff appearance, Terry turns out to be a sweet-tempered sort who agrees to box only when assured that the fight will be used in the campaign to help the homeless. Convincing the rest of the world that Terry and the match are legit is a trickier task, one that Sultan divvies up among helpers that include his publicist (Jon Lovitz), partner (Corbin Bernsen) and lawyer (Rocky Carroll), as well as Terry's trainer (John Rhys-Davies) and the boxing association's crooked president (Cheech Marin).

While the plot strands come together in predictable fashion, there are fun moments along the way, thanks largely to Jackson, who excludes a droll and charismatic joviality even though his character isn't taken much beyond the one-joke stage. Imported from TV's *Chicago Hope*, Berg likewise contributes a genial presence.

•

GREAT ZIEGFELD, THE
1936, 170 mins, US Ⓥ ⊙ b/w
Dir Robert Z. Leonard ***Prod*** Hunt Stromberg ***Scr*** William Anthony McGuire ***Ph*** Oliver T. Marsh, George Folsey, Ray June, Merritt B. Gerstad, Karl Freund ***Ed*** William S. Gray ***Mus*** Arthur Lange (dir.), Frank Skinner (arr.) ***Art*** Cedric Gibbons, Merrill Pye, John Harkrider, Edwin B. Willis
Act William Powell, Myrna Loy, Luise Rainer, Frank Morgan, Fanny Brice, Virginia Bruce (M-G-M)

The Great Ziegfeld is the last gasp in filmusical entertainment. On its running time (10 minutes short of three hours), it is the record holder to date for length of a picture in the U.S. After two years, and a reported $1.5 million, Metro emerges with a picture whose sole shortcoming is its footage.

The production high mark of the numbers is "Pretty Girl" as the first half finale. This nifty Irving Berlin tune becomes the fulcrum for one of Frank Skinner's best arrangements as Arthur Lange batons the crescendos into a mad, glittering potpourri of Saint-Saens and Gershwin, Strauss and Verdi, beautifully blended against the Berlinesque background.

Among riot of song and dance, Seymour Felix's dances and ensembles stand out for imagination and comprehensive execution.

William Powell's Zieggy is excellent. He endows the impersonation with all the qualities of a great entrepreneur and sentimentalist. Luise Rainer is tops of the femmes with her vivacious Anna Held. Myrna Loy's Billie Burke, perhaps with constant regard for a contemporaneous artist, seems a bit under wraps. Frank Morgan almost pars Powell as the friendly enemy.

Fanny Brice is Fanny Brice; ditto Ray Bolger and Harriet Hoctor playing themselves. Character of Sampson is obviously the late Sam Kingston, long Zieggy's general manager who worried and fretted over the glorifyer's extravagances. Reginald Owen's personation here is capital.

1936: Best Picture, Actress (Luise Rainer), Dance Direction ("A Pretty Girl Is Like a Melody")

NOMINATIONS: Best Director, Original Story, Art Direction, Editing

•

GREED
1924, 114 mins, US Ⓥ ⊙ ⊗ col
Dir Erich von Stroheim ***Prod*** Erich von Stroheim ***Scr*** June Mathis, Erich von Stroheim ***Ph*** Ben F. Reynolds, William H. Daniels ***Ed*** Frank Hull, Joseph W. Farnham ***Art*** Cedric Gibbons, Richard Day
Act Gibson Gowland, ZaSu Pitts, Jean Hersholt, Chester Conklin, Sylvia Ashton, Austin Jewell (Metro-Goldwyn)

Greed, the screen adaptation of the Frank Norris story, *McTeague*, was directed by Erich von Stroheim. He utilized two years and over $700,000 of Goldwyn and possibly some Metro money in its making.

Stroheim shot 130 reels in the two years. He finally cut it to 26 reels and told Metro-Goldwyn executives that was the best he could do. It was then taken into hand and cut to 10 reels.

McTeague, a worker in a gold mine, serves an apprenticeship with an itinerant dentist and in years after, sets up an office in Market street, San Francisco. A chum brings in his cousin as a patient. McTeague falls in love with her, but, before Mac and she are married, the girl wins a $5,000 lottery prize.

Several years afterward, the chum, vengeful because of his failure to share in the spoils, tips off the Dentists Society that Mac is practicing without a license. Mac then drifts from bad to worse. With a few drinks of whiskey under his belt he walks out on the money-grabbing wife. Months later he runs across her. She is working as a scrubwoman. He tries to compel her to give him money, later murdering her to secure it.

After the crime, Mac makes his way to the desert, in the direction of Death Valley. A posse starts after him from a small New Mexico town. In it is the former chum, still actuated by his greed for the $5,000.

The picture brings to light three great character performances by Gibson Gowland as McTeague, Jean Hersholt as the chum, and ZaSu Pitts as the wife. Chester Conklin is another who registers with a performance that is marked, although it is noticeable the part that Stroheim's direction plays in it.

•

GREEDY
1994, 113 mins, US Ⓥ ⊙ col
Dir Jonathan Lynn ***Prod*** Brian Grazer ***Scr*** Lowell Ganz, Babaloo Mandel ***Ph*** Gabriel Beristain ***Ed*** Tony Lombardo ***Mus*** Randy Edelman ***Art*** Victoria Paul
Act Michael J. Fox, Kirk Douglas, Nancy Travis, Olivia d'Abo, Phil Hartman, Ed Begley, Jr. (Imagine/Universal)

There's an ambition to *Greedy* one simply has to admire. The concept—that a small army of potential heirs will stoop lower than a limbo dancer to pick up the pelf of a stinking-rich relative—is both timeless and timely. Yet the idea quickly goes awry as the filmmakers find themselves at sea deciding whether this is a notion to disdain or embrace.

The yarn centers on the McTeague brood (a cinematic reference to the protagonist of von Stroheim's silent masterpiece *Greed*, based upon Frank Norris's novel *McTeague*), who live for the death of wheelchair-bound Uncle Joe (Kirk Douglas), a snarly, reprehensible curmudgeon who made a fortune in scrap metal.

Joe barely veils his contempt for the sycophants. But the big bombshell is the arrival of Molly (Olivia d'Abo), a nubile Brit who graduated from delivering pizza into becoming Joe's so-called nurse. The little ace the warring clan turns up is Daniel McTeague, Jr. (Michael J. Fox), about to give up the pro bowler tour as a result of a developing arthritic wrist. He's susceptible to the lure of money.

Director Jonathan Lynn knows exactly what elements to emphasize when the action moves through breakneck drawing-room comedy. But the script aims higher, embracing pathos even when the results are pure bathos.

•

GREEK TYCOON, THE
1978, 106 mins, US Ⓥ ▭ col
Dir J. Lee Thompson ***Prod*** Allen Klein, Ely Landau ***Scr*** Mort Fine ***Ph*** Tony Richmond ***Ed*** Alan Strachan ***Mus*** Stanley Myers ***Art*** Michael Stringer
Act Anthony Quinn, Jacqueline Bisset, Raf Vallone, Edward Albert, James Franciscus, Camilla Sparv (Abkco)

As a thinly disguised biopic of Aristotle Onassis and Jacqueline Kennedy Onassis—accent on thinly disguised—*The Greek Tycoon* has the conviction of its subject. It's a trashy, opulent, vulgar, racy $6.5 million picture. You've read the headlines, now you can watch the movie. Mort Fine's script begins with Anthony Quinn as Theo Tomasis returning from a business trip. He greets his wife, wades through the guests at his island manor searching for his son and quickly spots Jackie Bisset with her husband Senator James Cassidy.

The story moves quickly onto Quinn's yacht. The Cassidys are persuaded to join the affair and while the senator is immersed in conversation with a former British prime minister, Quinn lays the seeds for his own affair.

Quinn is fabulous as Tomasis, a charming, wealthy, conniving and influential tycoon. Raf Vallone as Quinn's brother, James Franciscus as President Cassidy, Edward Albert as Quinn's son and the always reliable Charles Durning as Quinn's lawyer and later attorney general, all turn in good performances. As Liz Cassidy, Bisset capitalizes on her looks, but her accent seems off for the part and much of the acting is just posing.

•

GREEN BERETS, THE
1968, 141 mins, US Ⓥ ⊙ ▭ col
Dir John Wayne, Ray Kellogg ***Prod*** Michael Wayne ***Scr*** James Lee Barrett ***Ph*** Winston C. Hoch ***Ed*** Otto Lovering ***Mus*** Miklos Rozsa ***Art*** Walter M. Simonds
Act John Wayne, David Janssen, Jim Hutton, Aldo Ray, Raymond St. Jacques (Warner/Seven Arts/Batjac)

The Green Berets, based on Robin Moore's book about U.S. Special Forces, sheds no light on the arguments pro and con U.S. involvement in Vietnam. Cliche-cluttered plot structure and dialog, wooden performances by actors playing soldiers, pedestrian direction and lethargic editing dog this production. James Lee Barrett did the flat script, loaded with corn and cardboard.

John Wayne is a colonel sent to Vietnam, while David Janssen plays a hostile newspaper reporter who, from time-to-time, alters his thinking about the fighting.

Role is a shambles for Janssen, because it was a patent setup from the start, and nobody could buck the thankless, inarticulate development. The interminable length permits about every hack character type to be introduced: Jim Hutton, the goofy kid who steals supplies; Aldo Ray, as "good-old-Sarge" type; Raymond St. Jacques, the sensitive medic; Luke Askew, country boy; Jason Evers, an all-American young officer type, and playing it like a toothpaste commercial; Mike Henry, beefy soldier who takes several enemy soldiers with him as he dies, and dies, and dies.

•

GREEN CARD
1990, 108 mins, Australia/France Ⓥ ⊙ col
Dir Peter Weir ***Prod*** Peter Weir ***Scr*** Peter Weir ***Ph*** Geoffrey Simpson ***Ed*** William Anderson ***Mus*** Hans Zimmer ***Art*** Wendy Stites
Act Gerard Depardieu, Andie MacDowell, Bebe Neuwirth, Gregg Edelman, Robert Prosky, Jessie Keosian (Rio/UGC/DD/Serif/Green Card)

Although a thin premise endangers its credibility at times, *Green Card* is a genial, nicely played romance. Gerard Depardieu is winning in the tailor-made role of a French alien who pairs up with New Yorker Andie MacDowell in a marriage of convenience in order to remain legally in the United States.

An Australian-French co-production shot in Gotham and completed Down Under, modest pic is essentially a two-character piece and looks to have been made on a very low budget. Plot is an inversion of the 1930s screwball comedies in which a divorcing couple spend the entire running time getting back together.

Green Card begins with Depardieu and MacDowell, who have scarcely been introduced, getting married, then charts the tricky weekend the two temperamental opposites spend getting to know each other in a hurry when faced with a government probe of their relationship.

Elements that might look hokey on paper—he's a free-wheeling bohemian, she's an uptight prude; he's a smoker and enthusiastic carnivore, she practically faints upon exposure to a cigarette or a piece of meat—go down easily because the two leads incorporate these attitudes believably into generally well-rounded characters.

1990: NOMINATION: Best Original Screenplay

•

GREEN DOLPHIN STREET
1947, 140 mins, US Ⓥ b/w
Dir Victor Saville ***Prod*** Carey Wilson ***Scr*** Samson Raphaelson ***Ph*** George Folsey ***Ed*** George White ***Mus*** Bronislau Kaper ***Art*** Cedric Gibbons, Malcolm Brown
Act Lana Turner, Van Heflin, Donna Reed, Richard Hart, Edmund Gwenn, Frank Morgan (M-G-M)

Metro throws the full weight of its moneybags into *Green Dolphin Street*. To salvage the $4 million or so that went into this epic [based on the novel by Elizabeth Goudge], it must primarily count on the eminent saleability of earthquakes, tidal waves and native uprisings. Its curiously unreal story offers no help.

Flaws in the novel, which verbiage may have made less perceptible, sore-thumb their way through the pic. There's the weak dramatic dodge, for one instance, of the wrong sister being married because she was mistakenly named by the suitor in a letter of proposal to her parents. And it's nothing but a hokey have-your-cake-and-eat-it device to confer happiness on the other by retiring her to a religious order.

Alternately localed in primitive New Zealand and one of the French channel isles (circa 1840), pic details how Lana Turner, mistaken for her sister, Donna Reed, makes the perilous sea voyage to the Antipodes to marry a deserter from the British navy.

When Victor Saville's direction focuses on nature's vengeance on man's works, the handling is superb. The toppling of giant trees, the shuddering of splitting earth and, the sweep of a river rending everything in its path is simon-pure cinematology. Credit, too, the fetching grandeur of the New Zealand country.

Refusal by M-G-M's studio-ites to recognize the ravages of time and events on the human face hampers Turner in depicting her exacting and pivotal role. As the gentler of the sisters, Reed is bogged by the weight of the yarn. Patly performing in the early reels, she fails to turn the hazardous trick of making her later conversion credible.

1947: Best Special Effects

NOMINATIONS: Best B&W Cinematography, Editing, Sound

•

GREEN FIRE
1954, 99 mins, US ▭ col
Dir Andrew Marton ***Prod*** Armand Deutsch ***Scr*** Ivan Goff, Ben Roberts ***Ph*** Paul Vogel ***Ed*** Harold F. Kress ***Mus*** Miklos Rozsa
Act Stewart Granger, Grace Kelly, Paul Douglas, John Ericson, Murvyn Vye, Jose Torvay (M-G-M)

A good brand of action escapism is offered in *Green Fire*. Its story of emerald mining and romantic adventuring in South America is decorated with the names of Stewart Granger, Grace Kelly and Paul Douglas.

The location filming in Colombia ensured fresh scenic backgrounds against which to play the screen story. The script supplies believable dialog and reasonably credible situations, of which Andrew Marton's good direction, takes full advantage, and the picture spins off at a fast 99 minutes.

The adventure end of the plot is served by the efforts of Granger to find emeralds in an old mountain mine; in the face of halfhearted opposition from his partner, Douglas; the more active interference of Murvyn Vye, a bandit, and the danger of the mining trade itself. Romance is served through the presence of Kelly, whose coffee plantation lies at the foot of the mountain on which Granger is mining, and the attraction that springs up between these two.

•

GREEN FOR DANGER
1946, 91 mins, UK Ⓥ b/w
Dir Sidney Gilliat ***Prod*** Frank Launder, Sidney Gilliat ***Scr*** Sidney Gilliat, Claud Curney ***Ph*** Wilkie Cooper ***Ed*** Thelma Myers ***Mus*** William Alwyn ***Art*** Peter Prond
Act Alastair Sim, Leo Genn, Trevor Howard, Sally Gray, Rosamund John, Judy Campbell (Individual)

This whodunit [from the novel by Christianna Brand] has the unusual setting of an emergency wartime hospital with the operating theatre as the scene of two apparently clueless murders. Wounded by a buzz-bomb, local postman is brought to hospital for a slight emergency operation, but dies under the anesthetic. Six people are present at the death—Leo Genn, Trevor Howard, Judy Campbell, Rosamund John, Sally Gray and Megs Jenkins. Judy Campbell finds evidence that the man was murdered and before she can inform the police she is stabbed to death.

Alastair Sim, unconventional detective from Scotland Yard, appears to enjoy the double murder case and has great fun annoying the suspects. He discovers each one had a motive, until an attempt on the life of Sally Gray reduces the number to four.

Gilliat and Launder, one-time masters of suspense, are losing their touch. The plot is too laboriously constructed, and the reason for the murders appears too incredible.

•

GREENGAGE SUMMER, THE
(US: LOSS OF INNOCENCE)
1961, 100 mins, UK col
Dir Lewis Gilbert ***Prod*** Victor Saville ***Scr*** Howard Koch ***Ph*** Freddie Young ***Ed*** Peter Hunt ***Mus*** Richard Addinsell ***Art*** John Stoll
Act Kenneth More, Danielle Darrieux, Susannah York, Jane Asher, Claude Nollier, Maurice Denham (Columbia)

Here's a stylish, warm romantic drama which gets away to a flying start in that it's set in the leisurely champagne country of France. Pic is always a delight to the eye apart from its other qualities.

The screenplay, based on Rumer Godden's novel, works up to holding emotional pitch. Story concerns four English schoolchildren, the oldest (Susannah York) being just over 16. They are en route to a holiday in France's champagne-and-greengage country when their mother is taken ill and is whisked off to the hospital.

Alone and dispirited, they arrive at the hotel which is run by Danielle Darrieux and managed by Claude Nollier. The children get a frigid reception but Kenneth More, a debonair, charming, mysterious Englishman insists that they stay. He's having an affair with Miss Darrieux and she cannot resist his whims. During the long summer, the atmosphere thickens.

The early part of the film, when the relationship between More and the children is developing, is particularly charming and pleasantly staged. York progresses delightfully from the resentful, gawky schoolgirl to the young woman eager to live. She handles some tricky scenes (as when she gets drunk with champagne and when she is assaulted by an amorous scullery boy) with assurance.

More's scenes with the moppets are great as are his rather more astringent skirmishes with Darrieux. She plays the jealous, fading mistress on rather too much of one note, but with keen insight. And there is a subtly drawn relationship of hinted lesbianism between her and Nollier.

•

GREEN MANSIONS
1959, 104 mins, US Ⓥ ⦿ ▭ col
Dir Mel Ferrer ***Prod*** Edmund Grainger ***Scr*** Dorothy Kingsley ***Ph*** Joseph Ruttenberg ***Ed*** Ferris Webster ***Mus*** Bronislau Kaper, Heitor Villa-Lobos
Act Audrey Hepburn, Anthony Perkins, Lee J. Cobb, Sessue Hayakawa, Henry Silva, Nehemiah Persoff (M-G-M)

Filmization of W.H. Hudson's novel has been approached with reverence and taste but fantastic elements puzzle and annoy. Hudson wrote an allegory of eternal love in his story of Rima, the bird-girl, who is discovered in the Venezuelan jungles by the political refugee Abel. In the screenplay, Rima (Audrey Hepburn), is a real girl, but one with unusual communion with the forest and its wild life.

She is found by Abel (Anthony Perkins) when he hides out with an Indian tribe after fleeing a political uprising in which his father had been killed. Rumors of gold in the neighborhood stir Perkins's imagination because he needs money to avenge his father's assassination.

Director Mel Ferrer and his cameraman have done some good location work in South America. It is skillfully utilized, by process and editing, with backlot work. But Ferrer has been less successful in getting his characters to come alive, or in getting his audience to care about them. Hepburn is pretty as the strange young woman, but with no particular depth. Perkins seems rather frail for his role, despite a trial by ordeal given him by Henry Silva's tribe. Silva, on the other hand, gives an exciting performance, fatally damaging to Perkins, the hero, overshadowing him in their dramatic conflict.

•

GREEN MILE, THE
1999, 187 mins, US Ⓥ ⦿ col
Dir Frank Darabont ***Prod*** David Valdes, Frank Darabont ***Scr*** Frank Darabont ***Ph*** David Tattersall ***Ed*** Richard Francis-Bruce ***Mus*** Thomas Newman ***Art*** Terence Marsh
Act Tom Hanks, David Morse, Bonnie Hunt, Michael Clarke Duncan, James Cromwell, Michael Jeter (Darkwoods/Castle Rock/Warner)

Positioning himself as the unassailable specialist in adapting Stephen King period prison novels for the screen, Frank Darabont emerges from his five-year hiatus after *The Shawshank Redemption* with *The Green Mile*, an intermittently powerful and meticulously crafted drama that falls short of its full potential due to excessive duration and some shopworn, simplistic notions at its center.

Working from the 1996 King bestseller that was published in six serialized paperback installments, Darabont proves very adept and lighting numerous long fuses that burn slowly and finally pay off in some big moments, some more satisfying than others.

Tale is largely set within the modest confines of E block (death row) at Cold Mountain Penitentiary in Louisiana in 1935. Title refers to the shade of the faded linoleum on the floor of the facility.

Head guard Paul Edgecomb (Tom Hanks) is a decent middle-aged man dedicated to maintaining as much calm and dignity as possible. Behind bars are good-hearted Creole Eduard Delacroix (Michael Jeter) and repentant Native American murderer Arlen Bitterbuck (Graham Greene); joining them is John Coffey (Michael Clarke Duncan), a towering, sweet-natured black man convicted of killing two little girls. Once the Indian is gone, another takes his place on death row "Wild Bill" Wharton (Sam Rockwell), a three-time killer and swamp rat.

Between taunts from Wharton, Edgecomb becomes convinced not only of Coffey's innocence but of his otherworldly healing powers, leading him to hatch a plot to have the inmate try to secretly cure the advanced cancer consuming the wife (Patricia Clarkson) of the warden (James Cromwell).

The ensemble acting is of a high order, and pic looks terrific.

1999: NOMINATIONS: Best Picture, Adapted Screenplay, Supp. Actor (Michael Clarke Duncan), Sound

•

GREEN PASTURES, THE
1936, 93 mins, US Ⓥ b/w
Dir Marc Connelly, William Keighley ***Prod*** Henry Blanke ***Scr*** Marc Connelly, Sheridan Gibney ***Ph*** Hal Mohr ***Ed*** George Amy ***Mus*** Erich Wolfgang Korngold ***Art*** Allen Salburg, Stanley Fleischer
Act Rex Ingram, Oscar Polk, Eddie Anderson, Frank Wilson, Abraham Gleaves, Myrtle Anderson (Warner)

The Green Pastures is a simple, enchanting, audience-captivating all-Negro cinematic fable. The show [by Marc Connelly, suggested by Roark Bradford's Southern sketches *Ol' Man Adam an' His Chillun'*] made history by touring the hinterland for three years after two years on Broadway.

Rex Ingram's glowing personality is a thoroughly satisfying and convincing Lawd. Ingram's is a yeoman protean contribution, as he also personates Adam and Hezdrel, his images re-created on earth.

The very essence of *Green Pastures* is the Sabbath school. It's the Harlem version of the Old Testament, as the pastor word-paints the mood of De Lawd from Genesis to Exodus and beyond.

Oscar Polk as Gabriel—whom De Lawd colloquially addresses as Gabe—is a human and humorous archangel who efficiently and matter-of-factly sees that De Lawd's will be done, and without the slightest hitches.

Punctuating all the Biblical background are mundane references to gay fishfries, ten cent seegars, generous fishing and plenty of milk-and-honey for the good folks. Yet it's all in fine taste and with due regard to proportions and standards of all races and creeds.

Marc Connelly and William Keighley—the latter the more remarkable in view of his previous specialization in gangster mellers—rate most of the bends for their distinguished transition of the play to the screen.

Frank Wilson's Moses; George Reed's Mr. Deshee; Edna M. Harris and Al Stokes as Zeba and Cain, a couple of hot potatoes, she a uke-strumming slut and he a fancy man; Ernest Whitman, impressive as the regally arrogant Pharaoh; plus the Hall Johnson choir, are among other stand-outs.

•

GREENWICH VILLAGE
1944, 83 mins, US col
Dir Walter Lang ***Prod*** William LeBaron ***Scr*** Earl Baldwin, Walter Bullock ***Ph*** Leon Shamroy, Harry Jackson ***Ed*** Robert

Simpson *Mus* Emil Newman (dir.) *Art* James Basevi, Joseph C. Wright
Act Carmen Miranda, Don Ameche, William Bendix, Vivian Blaine, Felix Bressart (20th Century-Fox)

Title places the locale. Time is in the early 1920s: i.e., the speakeasy era. William Bendix is the speakeasy prop, Don Ameche the tyro composer from the sticks, Carmen Miranda the joint's combination fortuneteller and entertainer, and Vivian Blaine the songstress top-lining at Bendix's joint.

Thin story is held together by several old songs and three new good tunes by Leo Robin–Nacio Herb Brown, of which "It Goes to Your Toes" and "Give Me a Band and a Bandanna" are the best. But the mainstay is a pop interpolation, "Whispering," which is spoken of as the hero's concerto inspiration, which almost makes Carnegie Hall but winds up as the big number of Bendix's musicomedy production.

•

GREEN YEARS, THE
1946, 127 mins, US b/w
Dir Victor Saville *Prod* Leon Gordon *Scr* Robert Ardrey, Sonya Levien *Ph* George Folsey *Ed* Robert J. Kern *Mus* Herbert Stothart *Art* Cedric Gibbons, Hans Peters
Act Charles Coburn, Tom Drake, Beverly Tyler, Hume Cronyn, Gladys Cooper, Dean Stockwell (M-G-M)

Metro, with the skill it has so often demonstrated in transforming a best selling novel to a best selling picture, turns the trick again with this filmization of A. J. Cronin's *The Green Years*.

Since this is essentially a yarn built on careful development of its various characters, a major contribution is in giving new stature and audience appeal to virtually every player in it. That's true all the way from vet Charles Coburn, who evidences his virtuosity in a new type role for him, to moppet Dean Stockwell and Beverly Tyler, both making their second screen appearances.

Ten-year-old Stockwell is the particularly bright spot in the well-turned cast. He gets real opportunity to demonstrate a sensitivity and true dramatic poignancy that definitely set him off from the usual studio moppets.

Young Stockwell plays an orphan boy in this Scottish-localed story of ambitious youth and amusing old age. The oldster, of course, is Coburn, as Dean's great-grandfather, a man of large heart and large desires for the native brew. While this not-so-venerable, but thoroughly enjoyable, citizen is getting himself into one minor scrape after another, the youth (later played by Tom Drake) goes through the process of growing up, going to school and falling in love.

The two principals are set against a household full of characters. Hume Cronyn wreaks every bit of tightfistedness and little man-meanness out of the role of head of the house that takes the small boy in. Tyler and Drake play the teenage romance.

1946: NOMINATIONS: Best Supp. Actor (Charles Coburn), B&W Cinematography

•

GREGORY'S GIRL
1982, 91 mins, UK Ⓥ ⦿ col
Dir Bill Forsyth *Prod* Davina Belling, Clive Parsons *Scr* Bill Forsyth *Ph* Michael Coulter *Ed* John Gow *Mus* Colin Tully *Art* Adrienne Atkinson
Act John Gordon Sinclair, Dee Hepburn, Jake D'Arcy, Clare Grogan, Robert Buchanan, William Greenlees (Lake/NFFC/Scottish TV)

Filmmaker Bill Forsyth, whose friendly, unmalicious approach recalls that of Rene Clair, is concerned with young students (in particular, a soccer team goalie, Gregory) seeking out the opposite sex. Much of the pic's peculiar fascination comes from tangential scenes, limning each character's odd obsession, be it food, girls, soccer, or just watching the traffic drive by.

Main narrative thread has Gregory becoming infatuated with the cute (and athletic) new girl on his soccer team, Dorothy (Dee Hepburn), while her schoolmates delightfully maneuver him into giving the out-going Susan (Clare Grogan) a tumble.

As Gregory, John Gordon Sinclair is adept at physical comedy. Hepburn is properly enigmatic as the object of his desire, with ensemble approach giving Greg's precocious 10-year-old sister played by Allison Forster a key femme role.

•

GREMLINS
1984, 111 mins, US Ⓥ ⦿ col
Dir Joe Dante *Prod* Michael Finnell *Scr* Chris Columbus *Ph* John Hora *Ed* Tina Hirsch *Mus* Jerry Goldsmith *Art* James H. Spencer
Act Zach Galligan, Hoyt Axton, Frances Lee McCain, Phoebe Cates, Polly Holliday, Judge Reinhold (Amblin/Warner)

In what story there is, amiable Hoyt Axton comes across a mysterious creature in Chinatown and takes it home as a Christmas present for his likable teenage son, Zach Galligan. With the gift, he passes along a warning from the inscrutable Chinese that the creature must never get wet, be allowed into the sunshine or fed after midnight.

For a while, all is extremely precious as the little furry thing goes through an array of facial expressions and heartwarming attitudes.

Without giving away too much, suffice to say the creature spawns a townful of evil, snarling, drooling, maniacal killer-creatures who are bound to cause a lot of woe before their predictable downfall.

The humans are little more than dress-extras for the mechanics.

•

GREMLINS 2: THE NEW BATCH
1990, 105 mins, US Ⓥ ⦿ col
Dir Joe Dante *Prod* Michael Finnell *Scr* Charlie Haas *Ph* John Hora *Ed* Kent Beyda *Mus* Jerry Goldsmith, Alexander Courage, Fred Steiner *Art* James Spencer
Act Zach Galligan, Phoebe Cates, John Glover, Robert Prosky, Robert Picardo, Christopher Lee (Amblin)

Joe Dante & Co. have concocted an hilarious sequel featuring equal parts creature slapstick for the small fry and satirical barbs for adults. Addition of Christopher Lee to the cast as a mad genetics engineering scientist is a perfect touch.

Film opens with a wrecking ball demolishing Keye Luke's old curiosity shop in downtown Manhattan to make way for another development project by megalomaniac Daniel Clamp, played with relish by John Glover. The cuddly Mogwai creature Gizmo (wonderfully voiced by Howie Mandel) escapes but is immediately captured by twins Don & Dan Stanton as a research subject for Lee's science lab Splice of Life, Inc. The lab is located in the new Clamp Center office building and, when Gizmo gets loose and exposed to water, the first of hundreds of horrific gremlins are unleashed to wreak mayhem.

Gremlins 2 is sans starpower, but its creatures more than make up for the lack of marquee lure. As realized by Rick Baker, the innumerable creations are quite an eyeful.

•

GREY FOX, THE
1982, 90 mins, Canada Ⓥ ⦿ col
Dir Phillip Borsos *Prod* Peter O'Brian *Scr* John Hunter *Ph* Frank Tidy *Ed* Ray Hall *Mus* Michael Baker
Act Richard Farnsworth, Jackie Burroughs, Wayne Robson, Ken Pogue, David Petersen, Timothy Webber (Mercury)

A graceful, stunningly photographed bio of Bill Miner, a notorious train robber in Canada and the U.S. at the turn of the century.

Director Phillip Borsos approaches his material—a stagecoach robber goes to jail for 30 years and is released into an unknown world where trains have started carrying the mail—as a kind of neo-western very much in sympathy with the bandit. Veteran Hollywood actor and western stunt man Richard Farnsworth was suggested for the role by Francis Coppola. His performance as the gentleman robber is one of the $3 million pic's strong points.

Until trapped by a Pinkerton detective, Miner lives a quiet life in a frontier town passing himself off as a gold digger. Between train robberies, there is a delicately handled love story with a cultured blue-stocking who makes a living as a photographer in the town.

•

GREYFRIARS BOBBY
1961, 91 mins, US Ⓥ col
Dir Don Chaffey *Prod* Walt Disney *Scr* Robert Westerby *Ph* Paul Beeson *Ed* Peter Tanner *Mus* Francis Chagrin *Art* Michael Stringer
Act Donald Crisp, Laurence Naismith, Alex Mackenzie, Kay Walsh, Andrew Cruickshank, Gordon Jackson (Walt Disney)

Greyfriars Bobby sets out to melt the heart and does it skillfully. Central character is a little Skye terrier, and this engaging little animal is quite irresistible. He's a sort of Pollyanna Pooch. Story is a true one, set in and around Edinburgh some 100 years ago.

It tells of an old shepherd who died of old age, exposure and starvation, and was buried in the little Greyfriars Kirk in Edinburgh. From the day of the funeral Bobby resolutely refused to leave his beloved master. In the end, he won over all the local burghers and was solemnly declared a Freeman of the City, handed a collar by the Lord Provost and adopted by the entire populace of Edinburgh. Yes, a true, if odd story, and there's a statue of Greyfriars Bobby in Edinburgh to prove it.

Patiently and brilliantly trained, Bobby wraps up the stellar honors for himself and the humans, knowing they don't stand a chance, wisely are content to play chorus. Nevertheless, there are some very effective pieces of thesping, largely by Scottish actors. Laurence Naismith gives a strong, likeable performance as the kindly eating-house owner who takes Bobby under his wing but, by standing up for a principle, brings the facts of the dog's case into court.

•

GREYSTOKE
THE LEGEND OF TARZAN LORD OF THE APES
1984, 131 mins, US/UK Ⓥ ⦿ ▭ col
Dir Hugh Hudson *Prod* Hugh Hudson, Stanley S. Canter *Scr* P.H. Vazak [= Robert Towne], Michael Austin *Ph* John Alcott *Ed* Anne V. Coates *Mus* John Scott *Art* Stuart Craig
Act Ralph Richardson, Ian Holm, James Fox, Christopher Lambert, Andie MacDowell, Cheryl Campbell (Warner)

One of the main points of *Greystoke* is that the $33 million pic adheres much more closely to the original Edgar Rice Burroughs story than have the countless previous screen tellings of Tarzan stories.

While a little obligatory vine swinging is on view, this is principally the tale of the education of the seventh Earl of Greystoke, first by the family of apes which raises a stranded white child and eventually accepts him as its protector and leader, then by a Belgian explorer who teaches him language, and finally by the aristocracy of Britain, which attempts to make him one of their own. With the exception of the warm, slightly batty Ralph Richardson, nearly all the Englishmen on view are impossible, offensive snobs.

Christopher Lambert is a different sort of Tarzan. Tall, lean, firm but no muscleman, he moves with great agility and mimics the apes to fine effect.

Ian Holm is helpfully energetic as the enterprising Belgian, James Fox is the personification of stiff propriety, and Andie MacDowell [voiced by actress Glenn Close] smiles her way through as the eternally sympathetic Jane.

On a production level, film is a marvel, as fabulous Cameroon locations have been seamlessly blended with studio recreations of jungle settings. [Pic was released in a 138-min. version in continental Europe. Director's personal cut runs 158 mins.]

1984: NOMINATIONS: Best Supp. Actor (Ralph Richardson), Adapted Screenplay, Makeup

•

GRIEF
1993, 88 mins, US Ⓥ ⦿ col
Dir Richard Glatzer *Prod* Ruth Charny, Yoram Mandel *Scr* Richard Glatzer *Ph* David Dechant *Ed* Bill Williams, Robin Katz *Mus* Tom Judson *Art* Don Diers
Act Craig Chester, Jackie Beat, Illeana Douglas, Alexis Arquette, Carlton Wilborn, Lucy Gutteridge (Grief)

Likely to be pegged as a gay *Soapdish*, writer-director Richard Glatzer's *Grief* actually has a good deal more heart and wit.

The setting is a former prostitutes' hotel now supplying offices for a TV production company. They crank out episodes of *The Love Judge*, a tacky tabloid-style syndicated series. Flashback action takes place during a Monday-Friday work week, framed by head writer Mark's (Craig Chester) suicide contemplation on the first anniversary of his lover's death from AIDS.

The imminent departure of no-nonsense exec producer Jo (Jackie Beat, aka Kent Fuher, in an initially disconcerting casting) sets Mark and serious-minded divorcee Paula (Lucy Gutteridge) against one another as competing successors. Emotionally vulnerable Mark has a crush on writer Bill (Alexis Arquette). Career ambitions of Jo's assistant Leslie (Illeana Douglas) are distracted by romantic attentions from a cute copy machine repairman. Scenario starts out looking rather insular, just another amusing look at behind-the-scenes Hollywood incestuousness. But the familiar satire soon develops no end of healthy wrinkles. Video-shot glimpses from the ersatz *Love Judge* series are hilarious—featuring such L.A. underground staples as Paul Bartel, John Fleck, Mary Woronov and Johanna Went. Central performances are excellent.

•

GRIFTERS, THE
1990, 113 mins, US Ⓥ ⦿ col
Dir Stephen Frears *Prod* Martin Scorsese, Robert A. Harris, Jim Painten *Scr* Donald E. Westlake *Ph* Oliver Stapleton *Ed* Mick Audsley *Mus* Elmer Bernstein *Art* Dennis Gassner
Act John Cusack, Anjelica Huston, Annette Bening, Pat Hingle, J. T. Walsh, Charles Napier (Cineplex Odeon)

Jim Thompson's intriguing novel about the subculture of smalltime hustlers is fashioned into a curiously uneven movie in *The Grifters*.

John Cusack plays Roy Dillon, a Los Angeles con man whose salesman's job is a cover for his real vocation. Roy's mother, Lilly (Anjelica Huston), gave birth at the tender age of 14, then fashioned a lucrative career as a roving racetrack bag lady, putting down bets for the Baltimore mob.

Roy is ministered to by his sexy girlfriend Myra (Annette Bening), who lives by her wits and her tightly wrapped body. Meanwhile, the mob boss travels west to teach Lilly a painful lesson for skimming mob money at the track.

When Roy and Myra take a holiday in La Jolla, she reveals her true colors. Myra, is an expert at the "big con," elaborate swindles geared to netting five- and six-figure scores. Myra correctly suspects Roy's little secret: a large horde of hidden cash accumulated from years of grifting.

Cusack underplays Roy, making him an unbelievable wiseguy, a colorless cipher too akin to the saps he loves to fleece.

1990: NOMINATIONS: Best Director, Actress (Anjelica Huston), Supp. Actress (Annette Bening), Adapted Screenplay

•

GRIP OF FEAR, THE
SEE: EXPERIMENT IN TERROR

•

GRISSOM GANG, THE
1971, 127 mins, US Ⓥ col
Dir Robert Aldrich ***Prod*** Robert Aldrich ***Scr*** Leon Griffiths ***Ph*** Joseph Biroc ***Ed*** Michael Luciano, Frank J. Urioste ***Mus*** Gerald Fried ***Art*** James Dowell Vance
Act Kim Darby, Scott Wilson, Tony Musante, Irene Dailey, Robert Lansing, Connie Stevens (ABC/Associates & Aldrich)

The Grissom Gang offers no sympathy at all for the debased human beings it depicts. Rather, it denies their existence as people, treating them instead as the butts of a cruel joke.

The action takes place in Kansas City in 1931, and concerns the kidnapping of a young heiress by an unbelievably depraved gang presided over by venomous Ma Grissom (Irene Dailey) and her cretinous son (Scott Wilson). It begins in a wash of blood, opening the same vein throughout—and the key to its debasing approach is the laughter this mayhem often provokes.

Provided with a script [from a novel by James Hadley Chase] that offers absolutely no insight into the inner lives of its people, director Robert Aldrich takes matters a step further by directing his actors in performances that strain the bounds of credulity. Wilson and Kim Darby, as the kidnapped girl, make stabs at more than one dimension, but when they indulge in caricatures of feeling, as they often do, they cancel out the rest of their work. Dailey is the most persistent mugger, while Robert Lansing, in one of the few sympathetic roles, comes off best.

•

GROSS ANATOMY
(UK: A CUT ABOVE)
1989, 107 mins, US Ⓥ ⦿ col
Dir Thom Eberhardt ***Prod*** Howard Rosenman, Debra Hill ***Scr*** Ron Nyswaner, Mark Spragg ***Ph*** Steve Yaconelli ***Ed*** Bud Smith, Scott Smith ***Mus*** David Newman ***Art*** William F. Matthews
Act Matthew Modine, Daphne Zuniga, Christine Lahti, Todd Field, John Scott Clough, Alice Carter (Touchstone)

Gross Anatomy, a seriocomic look at the first year of medical school, should be required viewing for anyone with aspirations in that direction, but for all others, film is about as exciting as a pop quiz.

The film, trying to be another *Paper Chase*, follows Matthew Modine, as the 26-year-old son of a fisherman, and other students through their courses, with particular focus on the anatomy lab, in which he's teamed with four classmates to work on a cadaver. Dissecting group includes his too-serious, driven roommate Todd Field; married young mother Alice Carter; Modine's nemesis, the judgmental, ultrapreppy John Scott Clough; and hard-working Daphne Zuniga, who reluctantly provides love interest for Modine.

Gross offers some nice, unexpected details: the anatomy profs, and key figures of authority, just happen to be a woman and a black man, played by Christine Lahti and Zakes Mokae. Another plus is the film's convincing portrayal of med-school life.

However, the writers—working from a story by Mark Spragg, Howard Rosenman, Alan Jay Glueckman and Stanley Isaacs—could come up with nothing more than stick figures and repetitive, one-note problems.

Biggest problem is Modine's character; though there's little on-screen evidence of his intelligence, he frequently is described as being so smart he can get by with minimum study. Lahti hasn't much to do but look stern, but she's good in her Big Scene near the end.

•

GROSSE POINTE BLANK
1997, 107 mins, US Ⓥ ⦿ col
Dir George Armitage ***Prod*** Susan Arnold, Donna Arkoff Roth, Roger Birnbaum ***Scr*** Tom Jankiewicz, D. V. DeVincentis, Steve Pink, John Cusack ***Ph*** Jamie Anderson ***Ed*** Brian Berdan ***Mus*** Joe Strummer ***Art*** Stephen Altman
Act John Cusack, Minnie Driver, Dan Aykroyd, Alan Arkin, Joan Cusack, Jeremy Piven (Hollywood)

An artistic triumph, *Grosse Pointe Blank* is hip without being cute, and absurd in a uniquely satisfying fashion.

Martin Blank (John Cusack) is a young man in crisis who's desperately in need of some breathing space to make sense of his life. For the past decade he's carved out a successful career as an independent assassin—one who works for the government. His chief competitor and the bane of his existence, Mr. Grocer (Dan Aykroyd), wants him to become part of a "union," and Blank is naturally wary about joining forces.

The upcoming weekend also happens to be his 10-year high school reunion in Grosse Pointe, MI, a posh suburb of Detroit where, coincidentally, he's compelled to do a hit. The key to what went wrong with Blank's life rests with Debi (Minnie Driver), the prom date he stood up.

Despite its offbeat trappings, pic is foremost a romantic comedy. Its two central characters are likable, and we want to see them get together in the face of considerable obstacles. Among the rogue's gallery of vivid supporting players, Alan Arkin is a standout as Blank's traumatized shrink, who fears there's no easy way to terminate their meetings.

Giddily directed by George Armitage—who's been absent since the equally idiosyncratic *Miami Blues* in 1990—pic never falters in tone.

•

GROUNDHOG DAY
1993, 103 mins, US Ⓥ ⦿ col
Dir Harold Ramis ***Prod*** Trevor Albert, Harold Ramis ***Scr*** Danny Rubin, Harold Ramis ***Ph*** John Bailey ***Ed*** Pembroke J. Herring ***Mus*** George Fenton ***Art*** David Nichols
Act Bill Murray, Andie MacDowell, Chris Elliott, Stephen Tobolowsky, Brian Doyle-Murray, Marita Geraghty (Columbia)

The premise of the romantic comedy *Groundhog Day* is essentially "if you had to do it over again—and again—what would you do differently?" The film is inconsistent in tone and pace; fortunately the pay-off works, bringing some much needed warmth to the area.

Bill Murray, a cynical TV weatherman, finds himself stuck in a private, repetitious hell: Groundhog Day in Punxsutawney, Pa, where he has come for the annual festivities. The day begins, over and over, at 6 A.M., Sonny & Cher on the clock radio, and moves on almost invariably, as Murray undergoes every conceivable emotional permutation—from confusion to anger to cockiness to despair—finally thawing into a beneficent soul.

The situation [from an original story by Danny Rubin] is ripe with comic potential but script provides more chuckles than belly laughs. Some sequences are crisply paced and comically terse, some ramble and others just plain don't work.

Murray's weatherman is tailor-made for his smug screen persona, perhaps too much so. Of the supporting players, Stephen Tobolowsky is hilarious in a loose-limbed turn as Murray's cloying ex-schoolmate.

•

GROUNDSTAR CONSPIRACY, THE
1972, 95 mins, Canada Ⓥ ▭ col
Dir Lamont Johnson ***Prod*** Trevor Wallace ***Scr*** Matthew Howard ***Ph*** Michael Reed ***Ed*** Edward M. Abroms ***Mus*** Paul Hoffert ***Art*** Cam Porteous
Act George Peppard, Michael Sarrazin, Christine Belford, Cliff Potts, James Olson, Tim O'Connor (Universal/Roach)

George Peppard stars as a government agent trying to break up a spy ring. Spectacular locations around Vancouver, plus some excellent and offbeat music by Paul Hoffert, only partially compensate for a script that is as often routine as it is bewildering. Lamont Johnson's direction is one of his lesser efforts.

Matthew Howard adapted L. P. Davies's [novel] *The Alien* into a diffused whodunit. Michael Sarrazin is, or is not, a traitor who worked in a super-secret lab trying to break a computer code. The lab's destruction launches the story.

Hard by the facility is the summer house owned by Christine Belford who, before disappearing completely from the plot, plays an important role in Peppard's trackdown of Sarrazin. There is a lot of rough action and violence, compounded intrigue, and confusing shifts of focus.

•

GROUP, THE
1966, 150 mins, US Ⓥ col
Dir Sidney Lumet ***Prod*** Sidney Buchman ***Scr*** Sidney Buchman ***Ph*** Boris Kaufman ***Ed*** Ralph Rosenblum ***Mus*** Charles Gross (sup.) ***Art*** Gene Callahan
Act Candice Bergen, Joan Hackett, Elizabeth Hartman, Shirley Knight, Joanna Pettet, Jessica Walter (Famartists/United Artists)

The principal problem Sidney Buchman had to face in adapting Mary McCarthy's very successful college classmates novel was to transfer its colorful characterizations and story-telling without overloading his script with the mass of novelistic detail. His script does not completely solve this.

There's little tampering with the original storyline but the filmscript concentrates on the story of Kay (Joanna Pettet), the first girl to be married and the one meeting the most tragic end. Throughout, she and Larry Hagman, as her philandering playwright husband, have the longest roles. However, if less important, the characters played by Joan Hackett and Jessica Walter, thanks to their performances, register as strongly as does Pettet. Hackett, particularly, is provided with a wide range of emotional changes.

Biggest letdown, and doubly so because her few scenes are so effective and played so well, is the part played by Candice Bergen. As Lakey, the ambisextrous leader of the Group (and the novel's most memorable character), her treatment in Buchman's script will puzzle the audience, as her few scenes at the beginning and at the end don't match with the billing she receives.

•

GRUMPIER OLD MEN
1995, 100 mins, US Ⓥ ⦿ col
Dir Howard Deutch ***Prod*** John Davis, Richard C. Berman ***Scr*** Mark Steven Johnson ***Ph*** Tak Fujimoto ***Ed*** Billy Weber, Seth Flaum, Maryann Brandon ***Mus*** Alan Silvestri ***Art*** Gary Frutkoff
Act Jack Lemmon, Walter Matthau, Ann-Margret, Sophia Loren, Burgess Meredith, Kevin Pollak (Lancaster Gate/Warner)

The success of this new outing isn't just the rock-solid bickering combo. The ensemble cast—all reprising, with the addition of Sophia Loren and Ann Guilbert—play the comedy and romance to perfection, with director Howard Deutch adroitly stepping out of the way to ensure that the simple saga remains entertaining and poignant.

Lifelong buddies John Gustafson (Lemmon) and Max Goldberg (Matthau) continue to snipe and spar—for what other sport is there in rural Minnesota?—and pursue the legendary Catfish Hunter in the Land o' Lakes. They refrain from the game of hurling epithets only to engage in marriage plans for John's single-parent daughter, Melanie (Daryl Hannah), and Max's son Jacob (Kevin Pollak). John himself has recently married Ariel (Ann-Margret).

That harmony is threatened by Maria Ragetti (Loren) and mother Francesca (Guilbert), who have arrived from Italy to transform a cousin's bait shop into a ristorante. Max, on principle, objects to any change. But it's spring in the Northland, and animus turns amorous, with a new lease on love for the pair as well as for Mama and the humorously bawdy Grandpa Gustafson (Burgess Meredith).

Dramatically, there are few surprises in this souffle. But to encounter an American film that has a true connection with characters older than 50 is refreshing. The movie has a relaxed tone that's rare but understandable.

•

GRUMPY OLD MEN
1993, 104 mins, US Ⓥ ⦿ col
Dir Donald Petrie ***Prod*** John Davis, Richard C. Berman ***Scr*** Mark Steven Johnson ***Ph*** Johnny E. Jensen ***Ed*** Bonnie Koehler ***Mus*** Alan Silvestri ***Art*** David Chapman
Act Jack Lemmon, Walter Matthau, Ann-Margret, Burgess Meredith, Daryl Hannah, Kevin Pollak (Warner/Lancaster Gate)

On the Jack Lemmon-Walter Matthau scale, *Grumpy Old Men* comes closer to the languor of *Buddy Buddy* than the inspired lunacy of *The Odd Couple* or *The Fortune Cookie*, saddling the two old pros with so-so material. Still, under Donald Petrie's direction, the pic emerges as light, reasonably pleasant and undoubtedly sappy holiday entertainment.

Looking craggy and dour, Lemmon and Matthau play aging Minnesota neighbors whose decades-old feud is rekindled when they become enamored with a fetching widow, the aptly named Ariel (Ann-Margret), who moves in across the street.

There are subplots, though not so you'd notice. Lemmon's daughter (Daryl Hannah) is estranged from her husband, and Matthau's son (Kevin Pollak) harbors a long-standing crush on her. Lemmon also faces the threat of losing his house because of an irksome IRS agent (Buck Henry) and receives romantic advice from his randy 94-year-old father (Burgess Meredith, a hoot in the film's showiest role).

Petrie, who directed *Mystic Pizza*, oscillates a bit awkwardly between humorous and bittersweet moments during the first two acts, and the film provides few big laughs before rushing to its warm, fuzzy and overly tidy conclusion.

The film doesn't truly shine, in fact, until a fabulous, worth-the-price-of-admission outtake sequence over the closing credits.

•

GUADALCANAL DIARY

1943, 90 mins, US Ⓥ b/w

Dir Lewis Seiler ***Prod*** Bryan Foy ***Scr*** Lamar Trotti ***Ph*** Charles Clarke ***Ed*** Fred Allen ***Mus*** David Buttolph ***Art*** James Basevi, Leland Fuller

Act Preston Foster, Lloyd Nolan, William Bendix, Richard Conte, Anthony Quinn, Richard Jaekel (20th Century-Fox)

To anyone unfamiliar with the Richard Tregaskis book, the picture version may or may not be a faithful adaptation [by Jerry Cady] of the original. But it is without question a painstaking, dignified and, in general, eloquent expression of a heroic theme. It is at times a sobering film and at other times an exalting one. It is also an almost continuously entertaining one.

The diary form of the original book is utilized in the picture. Opening with a quiet scene aboard a transport on a Sunday afternoon, as the Marine Corps task force steams toward an as-yet undisclosed objective, the story is narrated by an off-screen voice, fading in and out of the action sequences.

All this is admirably free from bombast and chauvinistic boasting. Although the deeds of the men are heroic, the men themselves reveal no self-consciousness of heroism.

With minor exceptions, *Guadalcanal Diary* is skillfully produced. A few of the incidents seem synthetic and such scenes as the sinking of the Jap submarine are rather obviously faked, but in general both the action and the manner of its presentation are genuinely believable.

Of the cast, William Bendix stands out in a juicy comedy-straight part as a tough-soft taxi driver from Brooklyn, while Preston Foster and Lloyd Nolan give effective performances in the other principal leads.

•

GUARDIAN, THE

1990, 98 mins, US Ⓥ ⊙ col

Dir William Friedkin ***Prod*** Joe Wizan ***Scr*** Steven Volk, Dan Greenburg, William Friedkin ***Ph*** John A. Alonzo ***Ed*** Seth Flaum ***Mus*** Jack Hues ***Art*** Gregg Fonseca

Act Jenny Seagrove, Dwier Brown, Carey Lowell, Brad Hall, Miguel Ferrer, Natalja Nogulich (Universal)

Who knows what possessed director William Friedkin to straight-facedly tell this absurd "tree bites man" tale, but it's an impulse he should have exorcised.

The scant plot [from Dan Greenburg's story *The Nanny*] involves an attractive yuppie couple (Dwier Brown, Carey Lowell) who hire a live-in nanny to take care of their infant son. The nanny (Jenny Seagrove) turns out to be some sort of evil spirit that sacrifices newborns to this big, anthropomorphic tree, a species apparently indigenous to the canyon areas of metropolitan Los Angeles.

Friedkin's first horror film since *The Exorcist*, *The Guardian* is more likely to make viewers think at best of the wan film adaptation of *Pet Sematary*, at worst of the talking trees in *The Wizard of Oz*. The design is so shoddy one half expects it to start talking and pitching apples.

Seagrove looks properly bewitching but never brings much menace or mystery to her role. Lowell, a former Bond girl, has the least to do as the confused wife.

•

GUARDING TESS

1994, 96 mins, US Ⓥ ⊙ col

Dir Hugh Wilson ***Prod*** Ned Tanen, Nancy Graham Tanen ***Scr*** Hugh Wilson, Peter Torokvei ***Ph*** Brian Reynolds ***Ed*** Sidney Levin ***Mus*** Michael Convertino ***Art*** Peter Larkin

Act Shirley MacLaine, Nicolas Cage, Austin Pendleton, Edward Albert, James Rebhorn, Richard Griffiths (Channel/Tri-Star)

There's a little gem of an idea in *Guarding Tess*. The premise has a young, ambitious Secret Service agent (Nicolas Cage) stuck in the thankless job of protecting the widow (Shirley MacLaine) of a U.S. president. Neither truly likes the situation but they like one another, despite constant bickering and endless infractions of protocol.

Aided and abetted by two charismatic performers and an underlying sweetness, the film is indeed likable. But director Hugh Wilson, who co-wrote the script with Peter Torokvei, just skims the surface of potentially rich territory. Comedy, pathos and thrills alternately collide, creating problems in both pacing and developing a consistent tone.

The battle of wills provides pic with its most amusing moments. MacLaine applies her prickliest persona and Cage embodies the ramrod, by-the-books agent.

The problem is that the story develops in the most uninteresting manner. It's not about power and perception as outlined in *Being There* (and whose echoes are felt with MacLaine's presence), and it barely touches the unsettling nature of what reveals itself as essentially a mother-son relationship. Rather, it wanders into the preposterous, shifting and stripping gears when Tess is kidnapped and Doug and his men have to dig her up or wear the mantle of shame.

•

GUERRE DES BOUTONS, LA

(WAR OF THE BUTTONS)

1962, 95 mins, France b/w

Dir Yves Robert ***Scr*** Francois Boyer, Yves Robert ***Ph*** Andre Bac ***Ed*** Marie-Josephe Yoyotte ***Mus*** Jose Berghmans

Act Jean Richard, Jaques Dufilho, Michel Galabru, Yvette Etievant, Martin Lartigue, Pierre Trabaud (Gueville)

Tale [from Louis Pergaud's novel] of kid warfare between the moppets of two neighboring rural towns looks at kids with the distance of grown-ups, on how cute they are, and rarely gives insight into their actions or makes a point about it all. But it is gentle, fairly refreshing and naturally played by a group of youngsters.

The gangs cut each other's buttons off and one even fights nude one day. A stool pigeon and a runaway make up the dramatic aspests of the pic. Grownups are properly stereotyped but, unfortunately, so are most of the kids.

All this is pleasantly concocted but lags and repeats itself. It is technically good, but a lot of the kiddie patter is badly recorded and almost unintelligible at times.

•

GUERRE EST FINIE, LA

(THE WAR IS OVER)

1966, 120 mins, France/Sweden b/w

Dir Alain Resnais ***Scr*** Jorge Semprun ***Ph*** Sacha Vierny ***Ed*** Eric Pluet ***Mus*** Giovanni Fusco ***Art*** Jacques Saulnier

Act Yves Montand, Ingrid Thulin, Genevieve Bujold, Michel Piccoli, Jean Bouise, Francoise Bertin (Sofracima/Argos/Europa)

Alain Resnais's most mature film to date, this demands some patience and attention from audiences. It is the tale of three days in the life of a refugee revolutionary (Yves Montand). He is Spanish but has been living in France since his childhood. He is part of a leftist group which still tries to control revolutionary forces in Spain.

This is a general tale of any sort of revolutionary in exile, even if written by a noted refugee Hispanic writer. The point is made that any change has to come from within.

Ingrid Thulin has a luminous quality as the woman in Montand's life. Another femme, Genevieve Bujold, shows fetching young beauty and poise.

All the small roles are played with a deftness that keeps them from falling into stereotype.

Film is measured, and sometimes arbitrary in its refusal to allow its personages to relax into more familiar human beings. It is thus more a statement on a theme than a simple human tale. It succeeds on this level.

•

GUESS WHO'S COMING TO DINNER

1967, 108 mins, US Ⓥ ⊙ col

Dir Stanley Kramer ***Prod*** Stanley Kramer ***Scr*** William Rose ***Ph*** Sam Leavitt ***Ed*** Robert C. Jones ***Mus*** Frank DeVol ***Art*** Robert Clatworthy

Act Spencer Tracy, Sidney Poitier, Katharine Hepburn, Katharine Houghton, Cecil Kellaway, Beah Richards (Columbia)

Problem: how to tell an interracial love story in a literate, nonsensational and balanced way. Solution: make it a drama with comedy.

Guess Who's Coming to Dinner is an outstanding Stanley Kramer production, superior in almost every imaginable way, which examines its subject matter with perception, depth, insight, humor and feeling. Spencer Tracy, Sidney Poitier and Katharine Hepburn head a perfect cast. Script is properly motivated at all times; dialog is punchy, adroit and free of preaching; dramatic rhythm is superb.

The story covers 12 hours, from arrival in, and departure from, Frisco of Poitier and Katharine Houghton (Hepburn's niece, in a whammo screen debut). Tracy and Hepburn are her parents, of longtime liberal persuasion, faced with a true test of their beliefs: Do they approve of their daughter marrying a Negro?

Between the lovers and two sets of parents, every possible interaction is explored admidst comedy angles which range from drawingroom sophistication to sight gag, from bitter cynicism to telling irony. Film must be seen to be believed.

Apart from the pic itself, there are several plus angles. This is the ninth teaming of Tracy and Hepburn, and the last, unfortunately; Tracy died shortly after principal photography was complete. Also, for Poitier, film marked a major step forward, not just in his proven acting ability, but in the opening-up of his script character.

1967: Best Actress (Katharine Hepburn), Original Story & Screenplay

NOMINATIONS: Best Picture, Director, Actor (Spencer Tracy), Supp. Actor (Cecil Kellaway), Supp. Actress (Beah Richards), Art Direction, Editing, Adapted Score

•

GUEST, THE

SEE: THE CARETAKER

•

GUEST IN THE HOUSE

1944, 117 mins, US Ⓥ b/w

Dir John Brahm ***Prod*** Hunt Stromberg ***Scr*** Ketti Frings ***Ph*** Lee Garmes ***Ed*** James Newcom, Walter Hanneman ***Mus*** Werner Janssen ***Art*** Nicolai Remisoff

Act Anne Baxter, Ralph Bellamy, Aline MacMahon, Ruth Warrick, Scott McKay, Marie McDonald (United Artists)

Hunt Stromberg's film version of the Hagar Wilde-Dale Eunson play [*Dear Evelyn*] is a bit on the arty side. Transition of a legit piece of this kind, dealing with a peculiar type of neurotic, to celluloid is obviously beset with difficulties. There are moments when the illusion is barely maintained. Yet it is a distinct credit to the direction, scripting and cast that the yarn has been made as believable as it is on the screen.

Production's most valuable asset, apart from its first-rate cast, is the suspense and action which are sustained throughout once the motivation is established.

Story is about girl (Anne Baxter) with bats in the belfry and a cardiac condition besides, who is taken into the home of a happy family at the request of the young doctor (Scott McKay) who has befriended her. The girl becomes infatuated with the medico's older, married brother (Ralph Bellamy) and immediately proceeds to distill psychological poison, alienating one member of the family from another so that she can win the man of her choice.

•

GUIDE FOR THE MARRIED MAN, A

1967, 89 mins, US Ⓥ ▭ col

Dir Gene Kelly ***Prod*** Frank McCarthy ***Scr*** Frank Tarloff ***Ph*** Joe MacDonald ***Ed*** Dorothy Spencer ***Mus*** John Williams ***Art*** Jack Martin Smith, William Glasgow

Act Walter Matthau, Robert Morse, Inger Stevens, Sue Ane Langdon, Claire Kelly, Linda Harrison (20th Century-Fox)

Walter Matthau plays a married innocent, eager to stray under the tutelage of friend and neighbor Robert Morse. But this long-married hubby is so retarded in his Immorality (it takes him 12 years to get the seven-year-itch) that, between his natural reluctance and mentor Morse's suggestions (interlarded with warnings against hastiness), he needs the entire film to have his mind made up.

Guide [based on the book by Frank Tarloff] is packed with action, pulchritude, situations, and considerable (if not quite enough) laughs. Inger Stevens is beautiful as Matthau's wife, and so unbelievably perfect that it makes his reluctance most understandable.

Some of the guest talent have no more than one line (Jeffrey Hunter, Sam Jaffe), some are mimed (Wally Cox, Ben Blue) and others have several lines (Sid Caesar, Phil Silvers, Jack Benny, Hal March).

•

GUILTY AS SIN

1993, 104 mins, US Ⓥ ⊙ col

Dir Sidney Lumet ***Prod*** Martin Ransohoff ***Scr*** Larry Cohen ***Ph*** Andrzej Bartkowiak ***Ed*** Evan Lottman ***Mus*** Howard Shore ***Art*** Philip Rosenberg

Act Rebecca DeMornay, Don Johnson, Stephen Lang, Jack Warden, Dana Ivey, Ron White (Hollywood)

It takes too long for the courtroom thriller *Guilty as Sin* to heat up and engage an audience. Despite some intriguing plot twists and a visceral windup, Sidney Lumet's study of a war of wills is of very limited interest.

Don Johnson is effectively cast as the literal ladykiller, who's just been accused of throwing his rich wife out of a highrise window. Like a stalker, he's become fixated on hotshot criminal lawyer Rebecca DeMornay and uses perverse psychology to get her to take his case.

Soon fearing for her very life when it becomes apparent that Johnson's killing spree is open-ended, DeMornay has detective Jack Warden gather evidence of Johnson's previous unsolved murders.

Johnson's upfront sexism and smug role reversal as a narcissistic gigolo generate comic relief and unintentional risibility in equal measure. DeMornay gets top billing but is saddled with a functional, reactive part.

Andrzej Bartkowiak's compositions and lighting add menace to the urban locations, lensed in Canada as a convincing double for Chicago settings.

•

GUILTY BY SUSPICION

1991, 105 mins, US Ⓥ ⊙ col

Dir Irwin Winkler ***Prod*** Arnon Milchan ***Scr*** Irwin Winkler ***Ph*** Michael Ballhaus ***Ed*** Priscilla Nedd ***Mus*** James Newton Howard ***Art*** Leslie Dilley

Act Robert De Niro, Annette Benning, George Wendt, Patricia Wettig, Sam Wanamaker, Martin Scorsese (Warner)

First writing-directing effort by vet producer Irwin Winkler squarely lays out the professional, ethical and moral dilemmas engendered by the insidious political pressures brought to bear on filmmakers in the early 1950s. Robert De Niro is excellent as a top director brought down by reactionary paranoia. But the drama comes to life only fitfully.

De Niro portrays David Merrill, a director on a roll who lives only for his work. Arriving back in Hollywood in 1951 after a European sojourn, he soon finds the atmosphere changed. Charged by a colleague as having attended a couple of left-wing meetings years before, Merrill is asked by 20th Century-Fox boss Darryl F. Zanuck (Ben Piazza) to cooperate with the House Un-American Activities Committee before proceeding with his next big production.

After a disagreeable meeting with an attorney (Sam Wanamaker) and a HUAC rep, Merrill, refusing to cooperate, finds that the chill sets in almost immediately. He is yanked from the Fox film, listens to his agent demand back a $50,000 advance, looks to lose his house and hears his 10-year-old son doubting him. Worst of all, no one will return his calls.

Looking raffish and trim, De Niro perfectly conveys a charming, quiet confidence at the outset. During the extraordinary appearance before HUAC, he finally blossoms into a man of conviction and passion. The actor pulls off this last-minute transformation beautifully.

•

GUINEVERE

1999, 104 mins, US Ⓥ ⊙ col

Dir Audrey Wells ***Prod*** Jonathan King, Brad Weston ***Scr*** Audrey Wells ***Ph*** Charles Minsky ***Ed*** Dody Dorn ***Mus*** Christophe Beck ***Art*** Stephen McCabe

Act Stephen Rea, Sarah Polley, Jean Smart, Gina Gershon, Paul Dooley, Francis Guinan (Bandeira/Millennium)

Wonderfully acted and slickly made, *Guinevere* is an emotionally sensitive and insightful look at a romance between a 20-year-old girl and a bohemian photographer more than twice her age. Acutely written pic represents a highly confident directorial debut by screenwriter Audrey Wells (*The Truth About Cats and Dogs*).

The film remains winning throughout because it never loses sight of how the relationship is a double-edged sword for both parties. It's an enormously truthful portrait, and often amusing as well.

During her sister's elegant wedding party at the family manse in San Francisco, pretty, blond Harper Sloane (Sarah Polley) avoids her social responsibilities by hanging out with the wedding photographer, Connie Fitzpatrick (Stephen Rea), a shaggily attractive Irishman. Thus begins an affair that one might initially expect will be more important for Harper than for the old roué. But, as she soon learns from one of Connie's former flames, Billie (Gina Gershon), Harper is probably in for a five-year run with Connie, as there have been numerous "Guineveres," as he calls his inamoratas.

The details of give and take, the minute ups and downs of the relationship, are wonderfully observed through Wells's often oblique dialogue, which skillfully conveys the essence of scenes without discussing their content directly.

Polley, who made such an impression in *The Sweet Hereafter*, and Rea are both terrific. Lenser Charles Minsky applies the same sort of high-gloss finish he lavished upon *Pretty Woman*.

•

GULLIVER'S TRAVELS

1939, 75 mins, US Ⓥ ⊙ col

Dir Dave Fleischer ***Prod*** Max Fleischer ***Scr*** Dan Gordon, Ted Pierce, Izzy Sparber, Edmond Seward ***Ph*** Charles Schettler ***Mus*** Victor Young(Paramount)

In 1937 Walt Disney released the first feature-length cartoon, *Snow White and the Seven Dwarfs*. Its novelty, production excellence and entertainment factors rolled up terrific grosses for all. *Gulliver's Travels* is the second cartoon feature to hit the market. Turned out by Max Fleischer, who has been making cartoon shorts for 20 years, it is an excellent job of animation, audience interest and all around showmanship.

Jonathan Swift's amusing tale [adapted by Edmond Seward] introduces the inhabitants of Lilliput, on the verge of war with their neighbors because the two countries cannot agree on songs to be sung at wedding of the prince and princess. Gulliver, the giant, is discovered on the Lilliput beach one night, and the inhabitants proceed to tie him up and transport him in a creaky makeshift vehicle to the town. He remains long enough to settle the pending war.

The busy Lilliputians, organized as an army and busily engaged in tieing down the giant, with miniature cranes ravelling their strong ropes around the sleeping Gulliver, and with firefly torches lighting the proceedings, is a particularly effective episode. Gulliver's finger dance with the Lilliputian king, and his capture of the invading navy to save his little friends from attack are both noteworthy.

The two royal lovers capably interpret the several tuneful songs composed by Ralph Rainger and Leo Robin. Lanny Ross is the singing voice for the prince, while Jessica Dragonette handles similar assignment for the princess. Of the songs, "Faithful Forever" and "It's a Hap-Hap-Happy Day" loom as hit tunes. Score numbers eight songs, all way above par.

Gulliver's Travels was a year and a half in preparation and production, with Fleischer setting negative cost at around $1.5 million.

•

GUMBALL RALLY, THE

1976, 106 mins, US Ⓥ ▭ col

Dir Chuck Bail ***Prod*** Chuck Bail ***Scr*** Leon Capetanos ***Ph*** Richard C. Glouner ***Ed*** Gordon Scott, Stuart H. Pappe, Maury Winetrobe ***Mus*** Dominic Frontiere ***Art*** Walter Simonds

Act Michael Sarrazin, Normann Burton, Gary Busey, John Durren, Susan Flannery, Harvey Jason (First Artists)

The Gumball Rally is a silly, forced, one-note, strident comedy about a cross-country auto race by a bunch of formula-kooky characters. Former stunt coordinator Chuck Bail produced and directed but he didn't have much of a plot.

Bail and Leon Capetanos concocted the story which the latter scripted. Dilettante businessman Michael Sarrazin and lifetime rival Tim McIntire are among a group of auto fanatics who periodically assemble for a cross-country race, sanctioned by nobody and psychotically opposed by policeman Normann Burton.

Latter's attempts to thwart the race are supposed to remind one of Wiley E. Coyote's snares for the Roadrunner; the animated capers remain the more effective.

•

GUMSHOE

1971, 85 mins, UK Ⓥ col

Dir Stephen Frears ***Prod*** Michael Medwin ***Scr*** Neville Smith ***Ph*** Christopher Menges ***Ed*** Charles Rees ***Mus*** Andrew Lloyd Webber

Act Albert Finney, Billie Whitelaw, Frank Finlay, Janice Rule, Carolyn Seymour, Fulton Mackay (Memorial)

Gumshoe is an affectionately nostalgic and amusing tribute to the movie-fiction private-eye genre of yesteryear.

Story's about a smalltime Liverpool nitery emcee and would-be comedian with a buff's passion for Bogie and Dashiell Hammett who gets involved in a gun- and drug-running caper. Though often twistful, the tale's not the thing but its telling, and this, thanks to screenplay and direction, is an almost constantly chucklesome homage to the vintage sleuthing era—as the hero acts out his Mittyish adventure in Bogieland—with more reverence than outright spoof, for a curious and effective amalgam.

Albert Finney is brilliant as the key figure with just the right dose of tightlipped panache or—to bridge a plot gap—soliloquizing by quoting chapter and verse from his favorite authors or, again, tipping his hat to them with a look or a gesture. He's ably backed by Billie Whitelaw, Frank Finlay, Janice Rule and especially Fulton Mackay as Straker, another would-be eye.

•

GUMSHOE KID, THE

1990, 98 mins, US col

Dir Joseph Manduke ***Prod*** Joseph Manduke ***Scr*** Victor Bardack ***Ph*** Harvey Genkins ***Ed*** Richard G. Haines ***Mus*** Peter Matz ***Art*** Batia Grafka

Act Jay Underwood, Tracy Scoggins, Vince Edwards, Arlene Golonka, Pamela Springstein, Gino Conforti (Argus)

The Gumshoe Kid, alternately titled *The Detective Kid*, is a charming little comedy that pays homage to the private eye genre.

Jay Underwood, performing with the self-assurance of a younger Tom Hanks, carries the picture as a guy obsessed with Bogart who gets a job in Vince Edwards's agency through the efforts of his mom, Arlene Golonka. Finally assigned to a field case in surveillance, he's thrown together with femme fatale Tracy Scoggins. The two of them are on the lam for the rest of the film after Scoggins's boyfriend is nabbed by persons unknown.

This is breezy, light entertainment. Helmer Joe Manduke maintains a lighthearted mood, giving both principal players a chance to let their hair down engagingly.

•

GUN CRAZY

(AKA: DEADLY IS THE FEMALE)

1950, 87 mins, US Ⓥ b/w

Dir Joseph H. Lewis ***Prod*** Maurice King, Frank King ***Scr*** MacKinlay Kantor, Millard Kaufman ***Ph*** Russell Harlan ***Ed*** Harry Gerstad ***Mus*** Victor Young ***Art*** Gordon Wiles

Act Peggy Cummins, John Dall, Berry Kroeger, Morris Carnovsky, Anabel Shaw, Russ Tamblyn (Pioneer/United Artists)

MacKinlay Kantor's *Sat Eve Post* story, *Gun Crazy*, is a shoot-'em-up story of desperate love and crime.

After a slow beginning, it generates considerable excitement in telling a story of a young man, fascinated by guns, who turns criminal to keep the love of a girl with no scruples. It's not a pleasant story, nor is the telling, but John Dall builds some sympathy as the male. Opposite him is Peggy Cummins, a sideshow Annie Oakley without morals. She is not too convincing.

Because of so much establishing footage, the picture seems long. Latter half, however, races along under Joseph H. Lewis's direction, being a continual chase broken only by new holdup jobs pulled by Dall and Cummins.

Script points up the physical attraction between Dall and Cummins but, despite the emphasis, it is curiously cold and lacking in genuine emotions. Fault is in the writing and direction, both staying on the surface and never getting underneath the characters.

•

GUNCRAZY

1992, 93 mins, US Ⓥ ⊙ col

Dir Tamra Davis ***Prod*** Zane W. Levitt, Diane Firestone ***Scr*** Matthew Bright ***Ph*** Lisa Rinzler ***Ed*** Kevin Tent ***Mus*** Ed Tomney ***Art*** Kevin Constant

Act Drew Barrymore, James LeGros, Billy Drago, Joe Dallesandro, Michael Ironside, Ione Skye (Zeta)

A shoot-'em-up exploitationer with a few interesting ideas, *Guncrazy* lacks the exhilaration of a first-class lovers-on-the-run crime drama. After a promising beginning, competently made indie effort settles into a surprisingly somber mood.

Original screenplay contains echoes of Joseph H. Lewis's B classic, *Gun Crazy*, but script is not explicitly based on any recognizable antecedents, as characters and situations are thoroughly modern.

Drew Barrymore plays Anita, a ripe, lower-class 16-year-old who will willingly have sex with different boys because it's the only way she can feel liked. She also lets herself be bedded by her absent mother's b.f. (Joe Dallesandro), with whom she shares a miserable trailer.

For a class pen pal project, Anita starts corresponding with an imprisoned man, Howard (James LeGros). Helping spring Howard early by finding him a job, Anita welcomes him with feverish anticipation. Gun lust begins to get the better of them and, almost by accident, they begin killing.

Unfortunately, eliminating the sexual element from the pair's relationship saps the story of the thrill it might have had. Still, music video director Tamra Davis makes a creditable debut in territory mined many times over.

•

GUNFIGHT, A
1971, 89 mins, US Ⓥ col
Dir Lamont Johnson ***Prod*** A. Ronald Lubin, Harold Jack Bloom ***Scr*** Harold Jack Bloom ***Ph*** David M. Walsh ***Ed*** Bill Mosher ***Mus*** Laurence Rosenthal ***Art*** Tambi Larsen
Act Kirk Douglas, Johnny Cash, Jane Alexander, Karen Black, Keith Carradine, Raf Vallone (Paramount)

A Gunfight is an offbeat western drama about two aging gunfighters who manipulate, and are manipulated by the blood lust of supposedly peaceful, average folks. Bankrolled by the Jicarilla Apache Tribe of American Indians, an investment-wealthy group making a first venture into pix, the handsome production stars Kirk Douglas and Johnny Cash. Lamont Johnson's very fine direction of the ruggedly sensitive script adds up to a fine depiction in discreet allegorical form of the darker sides of human nature.

Plot is essentially a three-acter. First the stars meet, fence nervously but with good humor, and at Douglas's suggestion, they decide to turn the town's unofficial speculation on the results of a shoot-out confrontation into personal profit for the survivor.

Next, intercut with the objections of Jane Alexander, excellent as Douglas's wife, and Karen Black, very good as a saloon dame who takes to Cash, the pair plan the carnival duel, aided by Raf Vallone, a shopkeeper whose eyes long have been on Alexander. Finally, the event itself, with the survivor really no better off than the deceased, a fact recognized by the friends of both men.

•

GUNFIGHT AT THE O.K. CORRAL
1957, 122 mins, US Ⓥ ⦿ col
Dir John Sturges ***Prod*** Hal B. Wallis ***Scr*** Leon Uris ***Ph*** Charles B. Lang, Jr. ***Ed*** Warren Low ***Mus*** Dimitri Tiomkin ***Art*** Hal Pereira, Walter Tyler
Act Burt Lancaster, Kirk Douglas, Rhonda Fleming, Jo Van Fleet, John Ireland, Lyle Bettger (Paramount)

Producer Hal Wallis has taken the historic meeting of Wyatt Earp, a celebrated lawman of the West, his brothers and Doc Holliday, with the Clanton gang in the O.K. Corral of Tombstone, Arizona, and fashioned an absorbing yarn [suggested by an article by George Scullin] in action leading up to the gory gunfight.

Burt Lancaster and Kirk Douglas enact the respective roles of Earp and Holliday, story opening in Fort Griffin, Texas, when the gun-handy Dodge City marshal saves the other from a lynch mob. Action moves then to the Kansas town, where Holliday, at first ordered to leave town but permitted to stay, helps Earp in gunning three badmen. When the marshal heeds the plea of one of his brothers, marshal of Tombstone, for aid in handling the dangerous Clanton gang, Holliday accompanies him.

Both stars are excellently cast in their respective characters. Rhonda Fleming is in briefly as a femme gambler whom Lancaster romances, beautifully effective, and Jo Van Fleet, as Holliday's constant travelling companion again demonstrates her ability in dramatic characterization.

1957: NOMINATIONS: Best Editing, Sound

•

GUNFIGHTER, THE
1950, 84 mins, US Ⓥ ⦿ b/w
Dir Henry King ***Prod*** Nunnally Johnson ***Scr*** William Bowers, William Sellers ***Ph*** Arthur Miller ***Ed*** Barbara McLean ***Mus*** Alfred Newman ***Art*** Lyle Wheeler, Richard Irvine
Act Gregory Peck, Helen Westcott, Millard Mitchell, Jean Parker, Karl Malden, Skip Homeier (20th Century-Fox)

The Gunfighter is a sock melodrama of the old west. There's never a sag or off moment in the footage as it goes about depicting a lightning draw artist, the fastest man with a gun in the old west, and what his special ability has done to his life.

Gregory Peck perfectly portrays the title role, a man doomed to live out his span killing to keep from being killed. He gives it great sympathy and a type of rugged individualism that makes it real. Peck is a man saddened by his talent, forced to stay on the run by all the young gunners seeking to make a reputation by shooting down the great man.

Despite all the tight melodrama, the picture [from a story by William Bowers and Andre de Toth] finds time for some leavening laughter.

1950: NOMINATION: Best Motion Picture Story

•

GUNGA DIN
1939, 120 mins, US Ⓥ ⦿ b/w
Dir George Stevens ***Prod*** Pandro S. Berman ***Scr*** Joel Sayre, Fred Guiol ***Ph*** Joseph H. August ***Ed*** Henry Berman, John Lockert ***Mus*** Alfred Newman ***Art*** Van Nest Polglase, Perry Ferguson
Act Cary Grant, Victor McLaglen, Douglas Fairbanks, Jr., Sam Jaffe, Joan Fontaine, Montagu Love (RKO)

Aside from the feature's ability to tell a swiftly paced, exciting yarn about British rule in India in the 1890s, it shows Cary Grant, Victor McLaglen and Douglas Fairbanks, Jr., as a trio of happy-go-lucky British army sergeants who typify the type of hard-bitten non-coms described by Rudyard Kipling in his famed poems *Barrack Room Ballads*.

Basis of Ben Hecht and Charles MacArthur's original story, from the barrack ballad, is the outbreak of the Thugs, cruel religious marauders, who revolted against English troops.

George Stevens employs superb change of pace, going from action to character closeups and then tossing in a romantic touch.

As Gunga Din, native water carrier, Sam Jaffe contributes possibly his best screen portrayal since *Lost Horizon*. Eduardo Ciannelli outdoes himself as ruthless native leader of India's Thugs.

•

GUNG HO!
1943, 88 mins, US Ⓥ ▭ b/w
Dir Ray Enright ***Prod*** Walter Wanger ***Scr*** Lucien Hubbard, Joseph Hoffman ***Ph*** Milton Krasner ***Ed*** Milton Carruth ***Mus*** Frank Skinner
Act Randolph Scott, Grace McDonald, Noah Beery, Jr., J. Carrol Naish, Robert Mitchum, Rod Cameron (Universal)

Randolph Scott has the lead in this story, adapted from what is said to be a factual account written by Lieut W. S. Le Francois, USMC. Pertinently, it's the story of how, out of thousands of trainees, a picked group of Marines is slated for a special mission—the first raid on [the tiny Pacific] Makin Island. It's an at-times loosely written script. The "boot training" preliminaries to the raid are just so much of a wait, but the actual attack has its compensating and exciting moments.

Scott gives one of his usually fine heroic performances, while J. Carrol Naish is a tough lieutenant who, somehow, doesn't look the part. Noah Beery, Jr., and David Bruce play half-brothers in a heat over the same blonde (Grace McDonald). Sam Levene, in a small role as a sergeant, is best of the support.

The direction has geared the pic for pace but some of that dialog is strictly for the younger element. The story has been needlessly glamorized, and it's here that it bogs down. It has a love yarn where one need not necessarily exist.

•

GUNG HO
1986, 111 mins, US Ⓥ ⦿ col
Dir Ron Howard ***Prod*** Tony Ganz, Deborah Blum ***Scr*** Lowell Ganz, Babaloo Mandel ***Ph*** Don Peterman ***Ed*** Daniel Hanley, Michael Hill ***Mus*** Thomas Newman ***Art*** James Schoppe
Act Michael Keaton, Gedde Watanabe, George Wendt, Mimi Rogers, John Turturro, Soh Yamamura (Paramount)

Trying to save his town, auto worker Michael Keaton journeys abroad to plead with Japanese industrialists to reopen the plant in Hanleyville, PA, that's been closed by foreign competition. Soon after, the Japanese invasion begins. From the first morning of calisthenics, it's clear the American workers will not adapt well to Japanese management.

Drawn from real life, the conflict between cultures is good for both a laugh and a sober thought along the way. Director Ron Howard has problems straddling the two, sometimes getting bogged down in the social significance.

Keaton can be funny as he puzzles the Japanese. Gedde Watanabe is excellent as the young Japanese exec whose career is threatened by the lack of output by the Americans.

•

GUN IN BETTY LOU'S HANDBAG, THE
1992, 89 mins, US Ⓥ ⦿ col
Dir Allan Moyle ***Prod*** Scott Kroopf ***Scr*** Grace Cary Bickley ***Ph*** Charles Minsky ***Ed*** Janice Hampton, Erica Huggins ***Mus*** Richard Gibbs ***Art*** Michael Corenblith
Act Penelope Ann Miller, Eric Thal, Alfre Woodard, Julianne Moore, Cathy Moriarty, William Forsythe (Touchstone/Interscope)

The Gun in Betty Lou's Handbag is a clever premise that ends up being as bland as its put-upon title character.

Penelope Ann Miller has the title role as a mousy librarian who seizes on a found gun (used in the motelroom slaying of an FBI informant) to shake up her pristine image and become a femme fatale. Her girl-who-cries-wolf plot has one deadly drawback, however, in the form of the sadistic mobster Beaudeen (William Forsythe), who fears Betty Lou possesses evidence that could convict him.

The one area in which the film does excel is its occasionally sharp dialogue and supporting characters, with amusing moments from Alfre Woodard as a novice attorney, Julianne Moore as Betty Lou's hyperkinetic sister and Cathy Moriarty as a helpful hooker. In limited screen time, the reliable Forsythe also brings an uneasy sense of menace to his cajun-drawling heavy.

•

GUNMEN
1994, 90 mins, US Ⓥ ⦿ ▭ col
Dir Deran Sarafian ***Prod*** Laurence Mark, John Davis, John Flock ***Scr*** Stephen Sommers ***Ph*** Hiro Narita ***Ed*** Bonnie Koehler ***Mus*** John Debney ***Art*** Michael Seymour
Act Christopher Lambert, Mario Van Peebles, Denis Leary, Patrick Stewart, Kadeem Hardison, Sally Kirkland (Dimension)

Gunmen is a routine, vacuous actioner that tries to mix thrills with humor. Scripter Stephen Sommers constructs a formulaic tale of chase and revenge that combines elements of both the action and Western genres.

Cole Parker (Mario Van Peebles), a N.Y. special forces agent working with the Drug Enforcement Agency, is sent to an unnamed South American country to confiscate the illegal gains stolen from a drug dealer who murdered his father. The adventure begins when Parker busts out of jail Dani Servigo (Christopher Lambert), an offbeat outlaw who is supposed to know the site of the huge fortune.

The two men are soon pursued by Armor O'Malley (Denis Leary), a ruthless killer hired by drug lord Peter Loomis (Patrick Stewart) to halt Parker and recover the money.

Director Deran Sarafian gives the picture an erratic, high-strung pace. Van Peebles's considerable acting talents are largely wasted on what's basically a stereotypical, underwritten role. Lambert, usually a bland action hero, lacks the necessary skills to pull off what's intended as light and humorous dialogue.

•

GUNN
1967, 94 mins, US col
Dir Blake Edwards ***Prod*** Owen Crump ***Scr*** Blake Edwards, William Peter Blatty ***Ph*** Philip Lathrop ***Ed*** Peter Zinner ***Mus*** Henry Mancini ***Art*** Fernando Carrere
Act Craig Stevens, Laura Devon, Ed Asner, Albert Paulsen, Sherry Jackson, Helen Traubel (Paramount)

Blake Edwards has transplanted his three-season *Peter Gunn* NBC-TV series (which began in the 1959–60 season) to the screen in *Gunn*, a well-made, but a trifle longish, programmer.

Episodic scripting, as befits a murder suspense comedy, is combined with solid Owen Crump production supervision, Henry Mancini music and a surprise ending.

There's a prolog murder of a top-dog gangster. Albert Paulsen, successor to the gangland throne, is the natural suspect. M. T. (Marion) Marshall, a seagoing madame, hires Craig Stevens to prove Paulsen guilty. Eventually, Paulsen forces Stevens to prove him innocent.

Popping up at intervals are Laura Devon, Gunn's occasional dame; Sherry Jackson, in a standout sexpot part; J. Pat O'Malley, excellent as a boozer informer who plays it like Alfred Hitchcock's old TV show intros; and skid-row topster Regis Toomey.

•

GUNS AT BATASI
1964, 102 mins, UK Ⓥ ▭ b/w
Dir John Guillermin ***Prod*** George H. Brown ***Scr*** Robert Holles ***Ph*** Douglas Slocombe ***Ed*** Max Benedict ***Mus*** John Addison ***Art*** Maurice Carter

Act Richard Attenborough, Jack Hawkins, Flora Robson, John Leyton, Mia Farrow, Cecil Parker (20th Century-Fox)

Soldiering and politics don't mix, according to this well developed screenplay and story by Robert Holles [from his novel *The Siege of Battersea*, adapted by Leo Marks and Marshall Pugh, with additional material by C. M. Pennington-Richards]. Dissects with a piercing personal touch the strict disciplinary attitudes that govern a true British soldier and makes him retain his own individual pride in the face of political forces unappreciative of his principles.

Producer and director come up with a strong and frequently exciting piece of work, the story of a British battalion caught in the midst of the African struggle for independence.

Performances throughout are excellent. Richard Attenborough is tough, crisp and staunch as the sergeant, playing with as much starch as the character implies. Errol John has intense qualities of fanaticism as the lieutenant who seizes the government, and Jack Hawkins, in essentially a cameo spot, plays like the resigned warhorse he is meant to be.

•

GUNS FOR SAN SEBASTIAN

1968, 100 mins, France/Mexico/Italy col

Dir Henri Verneuil *Prod* Jacques Bar *Scr* James R. Webb *Ph* Armand Thirard *Ed* Francoise Bonnot *Mus* Ennio Morricone *Art* Robert Clavel

Act Anthony Quinn, Anjanette Comer, Charles Bronson, Sam Jaffe, Silvia Pinal, Jaime Fernandez (M-G-M)

Anthony Quinn stars as an outcast, assumed to be a priest, in the Mexico of two centuries ago. The production, a plodding mix of religious—themed action and comedy-romance, has some good direction and battle scenes, but the very poor dubbing (in dramatic sense) is hard going.

Filmed entirely in Mexico, pic is a three-way coproduction of Mexican, French and Italian companies. Based on *A Wall for San Sebastian*, by William Barby Faherty, story concerns Quinn's influence on frightened mountain peasants, through which they become a cohesive town, instead of being terrorized by Charles Bronson, in league with Indian chief, Jaime Fernandez.

Anjanette Comer plays a peasant gal, only one in town with slit skirts, by the way.

Sam Jaffe, as a priest who dies early and creates the situation whereby Quinn is assumed to be a cleric, is saddled with dubbed banalities. Of course, part of the fault is in the writing, acting and directing of the dubbing.

•

GUNS IN THE AFTERNOON

SEE: RIDE THE HIGH COUNTRY

•

GUNS OF DARKNESS

1962, 102 mins, UK b/w

Dir Anthony Asquith *Prod* Thomas Clyde *Scr* John Mortimer *Ph* Robert Krasker *Ed* Frederick Wilson *Mus* Benjamin Frankel *Art* John Howell

Act Leslie Caron, David Niven, James Robertson Justice, David Opatoshu, Eleanor Summerfield, Ian Hunter (Cavalcade/Associated British)

Director Anthony Asquith is slightly off form with this one. An advocate of anti-violence, he pursues a theme that he has explored before, that violence is sometimes necessary to achieve peace. But the film does not stand up as a psychological study and as a pure "escape yarn," its moments of tension are only spasmodic.

John Mortimer's screenplay [from Francis Clifford's novel *Act of Mercy*] is not positive enough to enable Asquith to keep a firm grip on the proceedings. There are times when the film plods as laboriously as do the stars in their escape to the frontier. It opens in Tribulacion, capital of a South American republic, during a revolution. The president is deposed in a swift coup and, wounded, has to take off in a hurry.

David Niven, a rather boorish PRO with a British-owned plantation, elects to smuggle him across the border, for reasons which are not even clear to Niven himself. Tagging along is Niven's wife (Leslie Caron) with whom he is having an emotional upheaval.

Niven's charm seeps through his mask of boorishness but he manages skilfully to keep up an illusion of high voltage danger. David Opatoshu gives an excellent show as the disillusioned, yet philosophical president. Caron, however, seems uncomfortable, with her role coming over as curiously colorless.

•

GUNS OF NAVARONE, THE

1961, 157 mins, UK col

Dir J. Lee Thompson *Prod* Carl Foreman *Scr* Carl Foreman *Ph* Oswald Morris, John Wilcox *Ed* Alan Osbiston, Raymond Poulton, John Victor Smith, Oswald Hafenrichter *Mus* Dimitri Tiomkin *Art* Geoffrey Drake

Act Gregory Peck, David Niven, Anthony Quinn, Stanley Baker, Anthony Quayle, James Darren (Columbia/Open Road)

A real heap of coin ($6 million), labor, sweat, patience, tears, faith and enthusiasm went into the making of *The Guns of Navarone*. It faced the problem of a director switch in mid-stream. But with a bunch of weighty stars, terrific special effects and several socko situations, producer Carl Foreman and director J. Lee Thompson sired a winner.

Story, adapted from Alistair MacLean's novel, is set in 1943. The Axis has virtually overrun Greece and its islands, except for Crete and the tiny island of Kheros. The only chance for the worn-out garrison of 2,000 men is evacuation by sea, through a channel which is impregnably guarded by a couple of huge, radar controlled guns on Navarone. A small bunch of saboteurs is detailed to spike these guns.

The saboteur gang consists of Anthony Quayle, Gregory Peck, David Niven, Stanley Baker, Anthony Quinn and James Darren. They all turn in worthwhile jobs. Of this sextet, Baker, playing a dour, war-sick expert with a knife, and Darren, as a baby-faced killer, get rather less opportunity than the others. Two women have been written into the story, Greek partisans played very well by Irene Papas and Gia Scala.

The cliff-scaling sequence, a scene when the saboteurs are rounded up by the enemy, a wonderfully directed and lensed storm segment and the final boffo climax are just a few of the nail-biting highlights.

1961: Best Special Effects

NOMINATIONS: Best Picture, Director, Adapted Screenplay, Editing, Score of a Dramatic Picture, Sound

•

GUNS OF THE MAGNIFICENT SEVEN

1969, 95 mins, US col

Dir Paul Wendkos *Prod* Vincent M. Fennelly *Scr* Herman Hoffman *Ph* Antonio Macasoli *Ed* Walter Hannemann *Mus* Elmer Bernstein *Art* Jose Maria Tapiador

Act George Kennedy, James Whitmore, Monte Markham, Bernie Casey, Joe Don Baker, Fernando Ray (United/Mirisch)

Guns of the Magnificent Seven is a handy follow-up to the 1960 original *Magnificent Seven* and *Return of the Seven*. It rises above a routine story line via rugged treatment and action builds to a blazing gunplay climax.

George Kennedy takes on role played by Yul Brynner in two previous films, the only remaining character of the original seven.

Filmed entirely in Spain, as was *Return*, director Paul Wendkos makes interesting use of backgrounds.

Period is Mexico in the late 1890s, the narrative setting an attempt by Kennedy and his men to rescue a patriot who is attempting to assist helpless and downtrodden peasants. Cast is well-chosen and Kennedy is a good choice for the Brynner role.

•

GURU, THE

1969, 112 mins, UK col

Dir James Ivory *Prod* Ismail Merchant *Scr* Ruth Prawer Jhabvala, James Ivory *Ph* Subrata Mitra *Ed* Prabhakar Supare *Mus* Ustad Vilayat Khan *Art* Bansi Chandragupta, Didi Contractor

Act Michael York, Utpal Dutt, Madhur Jaffrey, Rita Tushingham, Aparna Sen (20th Century-Fox/Arcadia/Merchant Ivory)

The Guru is a hazy study of how people can transfer their own ideas about the value or qualities of another person and, in so doing, miss what the person is all about. Script is never realized in concrete dramatic terms.

Michael York is cast as a young Englishman who comes to India to learn the secret of playing the sitar at the house of a master musician, Utpal Dutt. Dutt gives the film's outstanding performance, with just the right amount of annoying egotism and naive pomposity. He doesn't quite understand his guest and tries, without success, to teach him the "mystic" significance of the complicated instrument and the Indian relationship between student and teacher or "guru."

At the same time that York comes into the musical household a wandering "hippie," played by Rita Tushingham, talks her way into staying and learning from the master.

•

GUY NAMED JOE, A

1944, 120 mins, US b/w

Dir Victor Fleming *Prod* Everett Riskin *Scr* Dalton Trumbo *Ph* George Folsey, Karl Freund *Ed* Frederick Brennan *Mus* Herbert Stothart

Act Spencer Tracy, Irene Dunne, Van Johnson, Ward Bond, Lionel Barrymore, Esther Williams (M-G-M)

In taking a fling at the spirit world, Metro doesn't quite succeed in reaching the nebulous but manages to turn out an entertaining and excellently performed picture. Had the fantasy been interpreted wholly in terms of the sharp wit and dry humor which Spencer Tracy, as a ghostly visitor, only occasionally injects, instead of investing it with spiritual counselling, the film [from an original story by David Boehm and Chandler Sprague] might have attained smash proportions.

As it is, there hovers over too many scenes in the cloudy strata a fogginess that isn't made any more acceptable by the final solution. The latter only changes the mood of the film from one of light cockiness to the realm of metaphysics.

Tracy is cast as a squadron commander at an English base who's in a constant jam because of his foolhardy heroics.

Fulfilling a premonition felt by Dunne, he crashes on his last heroic stunt, proceeding to the land where all dead pilots go. There he meets up with The Boss, and is assigned to guide and instruct the new pilots in the earthly world who are making a bid for their wings. It's at this point that the serious overtones of the picture intrude themselves, with the offering of the matter-of-fact solution that "life must go on for the living" too abruptly thrust into the story's continuity.

1944: NOMINATION: Best Original Story

•

GUYS AND DOLLS

1955, 149 mins, US col

Dir Joseph L. Mankiewicz *Prod* Samuel Goldwyn *Scr* Joseph L. Mankiewicz *Ph* Harry Stradling *Ed* Daniel Mandell *Mus* Jay Blackton (sup.), Cyril J. Mockridge (adapt.) *Art* Oliver Smith

Act Marlon Brando, Jean Simmons, Frank Sinatra, Vivian Blaine, Robert Keith, Stubby Kaye (Goldwyn)

Guys and Dolls is a bangup filmusical in the topdrawer Goldwyn manner, including a resurrection of the Goldwyn Girls.

The casting is good all the way. Much interest will focus, of course, around Marlon Brando in the Robert Alda stage original and Jean Simmons as the Salvation Army sergeant (created by Isabel Bigley), and they deport themselves in inspired manner. They make believable the offbeat romance between the gambler and the spirited servant of the gospel. Vivian Blaine is capital in her original stage role. Frank Sinatra is an effective vis-a-vis in the Sam Levene original of Nathan Detroit and among the four they handle the burden of the score.

The action shifts from the Times Square street scenes to the Havana idyll, where Brando had taken the mission doll ("on a bet").

1955: NOMINATIONS: Best Color Cinematography, Color Costume Design, Color Art Direction, Scoring of a Musical Picture

•

GYPSY

1962, 149 mins, US col

Dir Mervyn LeRoy *Prod* Mervyn LeRoy *Scr* Leonard Spigelgass *Ph* Harry Stradling, Sr. *Ed* Philip W. Anderson *Mus* Frank Perkins (sup.) *Art* John Beckman

Act Rosalind Russell, Natalie Wood, Karl Malden, Paul Wallace, Ann Jilliann, Harvey Korman (Warner)

There is a wonderfully funny sequence involving three nails-hard strippers which comes when *Gypsy* has been unreeling about an hour. The sequence is thoroughly welcome and almost desperately needed to counteract a certain Jane One-Note implicit in the tale of a stage mother whose egotisms become something of a bore despite the canny skills of director-producer Mervyn LeRoy to contrive it otherwise. Rosalind Russell's performance as the smalltime brood-hen deserves commendation. It is cleverly managed all the way, with much help from the camera angles of Harry Stradling, Sr.

Russell is less surprising than Karl Malden, as the mother's incredibly loyal lover who finally screams when he perceives that she cares for nobody and nothing except her own ego compulsions.

About Natalie Wood: it is not easy to credit her as a stripper but it is interesting to watch her, under LeRoy's guidance, go through the motions in a burlesque world that is prettied up in soft-focus and a kind of phony innocence.

Any resemblance of the art of strip, and its setting, to reality is purely fleeting.

There are some beguiling satirical touches in the re-creation of the hokey vaudeville routines starring "Baby June" Havoc, well impersonated by Ann Jilliann, whose flight from the mother turns the latter's attention upon the previously neglected sister, Louise, the Gypsy Rose of later show biz. The film, of course, is based upon the autobiography of Gypsy Rose Lee and the [1959] musical comedy in which Ethel Merman starred.

More chronicle than musical, there are advantages still in some of the music (Jule Styne) and lyrics (Stephen Sondheim) and the choreography (Robert Tucker).

[For general release, pic was cut to 143 mins, with the song "Together Wherever We Go" eliminated.]

1962: NOMINATIONS: Best Color Cinematography, Color Costume Design, Adpted Music Score

•

GYPSY GIRL
SEE: SKY WEST AND CROOKED

•

GYPSY MOTHS, THE

1969, 106 mins, US Ⓥ col

Dir John Frankenheimer ***Prod*** Hal Landers, Bobby Roberts ***Scr*** William Hanley ***Ph*** Philip Lathrop ***Ed*** Henry Berman ***Mus*** Elmer Bernstein ***Art*** George W. Davis, Cary Odell

Act Burt Lancaster, Deborah Kerr, Gene Hackman, Scott Wilson, Sheree North, Bonnie Bedelia (M-G-M)

The Gypsy Moths is the story of three barnstorming sky-divers and subsequent events when they arrive in a small Kansas town to stage their exhibition. Pairing Burt Lancaster and Deborah Kerr, stars sometimes are lost in a narrative [from a novel by James Drought] that strives to be a tale of smouldering inner conflicts and pent-up emotions.

At best, aside from exciting sky-diving episodes, picture is a lacklustre affair insofar as the character relationships are concerned. The stars do not appear particularly happy with their roles. Lancaster seldom speaking, Kerr not particularly well cast.

Lancaster delivers well enough considering what the script requires of him, and Kerr is mostly grim. Hackman and Wilson are forceful, both giving excellent accounts of themselves.

HABIT
1996, 93 mins, US col
Dir Larry Fessenden ***Prod*** Dayton Taylor ***Scr*** Larry Fessenden ***Ph*** Frank DeMarco ***Ed*** Larry Fessenden ***Mus*** Geoffrey Kidde ***Art*** John Arlotto
Act Larry Fessenden, Meredith Snaider, Aaron Beall, Patricia Coleman, Heather Woodbury, Jesse Hartman (Glass Eye)

Another hip vampire drama set in New York's East Village, small budget indie *Habit* manages to impress with plausible scripting, first-rate performances and an unsettling mood of mounting dread.

Larry Fessenden performs as a multi-hyphenate, doing quadruple duties as writer, director, editor and leading man. He is effectively cast as Sam, an alcoholic restaurant manager who starts to suspect that his new lover, a mysterious beauty named Ann (Meredith Snaider), may be a vampire.

As their relationship continues, he notices that she never eats, and refuses to enter his apartment when she smells garlicky food. And then there's the business of her controlling wild wolf dogs in Central Park. *Habit* is wickedly amusing as it focuses on the perverse eroticism that is intrinsic to the vampire myth—Sam obviously is enjoying the best sex he's ever had—but the pic wisely refrains from pushing the humor too far. Unfortunately, *Habit* tries to have it both ways in a finale that fails to resolve the mysteries and lacks sufficient emotional punch.

•

HACKERS
1995, 104 mins, US Ⓥ ⊙ col
Dir Iain Softley ***Prod*** Michael Peyser, Ralph Winter ***Scr*** Rafael Moreu ***Ph*** Andrzej Sekula ***Ed*** Christopher Blunden, Martin Walsh Mus Simon Boswell ***Art*** John Beard
Act Johnny Lee Miller, Angelina Jolie, Jesse Bradford, Matthew Lillard, Laurence Mason, Renoly Santiago (United Artists)

Hackers is a brisk little thriller about high-tech pranksters who inadvertently involve themselves in a complex embezzling plot. Newcomer Rafael Moreu's script is a modestly clever reworking of a formulaic concept, pitting members of a hip teen subculture against corrupt and oppressive adults.

The real villain of the piece is the Plague (Fisher Stevens), a computer security agent who is double-crossing his employer, a multinational corporation, by siphoning off money to a Swiss bank account. When one of the good hackers accidentally obtains evidence of the Plague's scheme while surfing through the corporation's computer system, the bad hacker tries to frame the good hackers by making them appear to be ransom-demanding terrorists.

Hackers operates under the assumption that, for a dedicated hacker, breaking into any computer system is only slightly more difficult than installing Windows 95. Director Iain Softley (*Backbeat*) wisely keeps pic moving faster than the speed of skepticism. There is a great deal more style than substance here.

Pic features a fine mix of attractive young newcomers and familiar character actors. Jonny Lee Miller and Angelina Jolie are appropriately engaging as the romantic leads, though they are frequently upstaged by standouts Renoly Santiago and Matthew Lillard. Stevens is aptly flamboyant as the egomaniacal Plague.

Hackers is the first pic in recent memory that has a teen hero comfort his mother by telling her he's still a virgin.

•

HAIL! HAIL! ROCK 'N' ROLL
1987, 120 mins, US Ⓥ col
Dir Taylor Hackford ***Prod*** Stephan Bennett ***Ph*** Oliver Stapleton ***Ed*** Lisa Day Mus Keith Richards (prod.)
Act Chuck Berry, Eric Clapton, Robert Cray, Etta James, Julian Lennon, Keith Richards (Delilah)

"If you had tried to give rock 'n' roll another name, you might call it Chuck Berry," pronounces John Lennon in an old interview at the outset of Taylor Hackford's glowing two-hour love letter to the kingpin of rock 'n' roll.

Hail! Hail! Rock 'n' Roll is a joyous docu that effortlessly weaves luminary rock interviews with performance footage mostly shot at Berry's 60th birthday bash concert at the Fox Theatre, St. Louis.

Talking heads interviews with such rockers at Phil and Don Everly, Jerry Lee Lewis, Bo Diddley, Little Richard, Keith Richards, Roy Orbison and Bruce Springsteen testify to the fact that Berry's influence is all-pervasive in rock. As a singer songwriter, guitarist, and bop-till-you-drop performer, Berry was real "troubadour."

Berry's ruminations cover everything from his love of cars, to breaking the color code, payola, his 40-year marriage, and how he chose to adapt his lyrics and subjects to cross over to white audiences.

•

HAIL THE CONQUERING HERO
1944, 101 mins, US Ⓥ b/w
Dir Preston Sturges ***Prod*** [uncredited] ***Scr*** Preston Sturges ***Ph*** John F. Seitz ***Ed*** Stuart Gilmore Mus Werner Heymann ***Art*** Hans Dreier, Haldane Douglas
Act Eddie Bracken, Ella Raines, William Demarest, Bill Edwards, Raymond Walburn, Freddie Steele (Paramount)

The deft hand of Preston Sturges molded this film, further proof that he is one of the industry's best writer-directors. The numerous situations that lend themselves readily to comedy lines and business are taken advantage of by a cast that sparkles because of the swift pace they are put through.

Yarn finds Eddie Bracken, medically discharged from the Marines after only one month of service because of hay fever, befriended by six real Guadalcanal heroes. During the course of this friendship, Bracken is clothed in his old marine uniform, bodily taken back to his old home town, where he is welcomed as a hero.

Proof that a capable director can take an actor who is willing to listen and get a better-than-good performance out of him or her is amply displayed here. Sturges has a large cast of veterans supporting Bracken, and a former boxing champion, Freddie Steele, as Bugsy, one of the six marines. The vets all do a good job, but Steele's work is standout.

1944: NOMINATION: Best Original Screenplay

•

HAINE, LA
(HATE)
1995, 97 mins, France b/w
Dir Mathieu Kassovitz ***Prod*** Christophe Rossignon ***Scr*** Mathieu Kassovitz ***Ph*** Pierre Aim, Georges Diane ***Ed*** Mathieu Kassovitz, Scott Stevenson ***Mus*** Vincent Tulli ***Art*** Guiseppe Ponturo
Act Vincent Cassell, Hubert Kounde, Said Taghmaoui, Francois Leventhal, Edouarde Montoute, Karim Belkhadra (Lazennec/Canal Plus/La Sept)

A layered conundrum that builds to a stunning crescendo, Mathieu Kassovitz's *Hate* is an extremely intelligent take on an idiotic reality: the mutual mistrust, contempt and hatred between the police and France's disenfranchised young citizens.

Kassovitz has achieved a mature tone and narrative cohesion only hinted at in his previous feature, *Metisse* (*Cafe au Lait* in the U.S.). The scripter-helmer is a multitalented force to be reckoned with.

Hard-hitting tale covers less than 24 crucial hours in the lives of three male buddies who personify a generation that's been relegated to the no-income housing projects beyond Paris.

As title cards precisely clock the passing day, Kassovitz's edgy, intimate camera follows three ethnically diverse friends. Relatively upbeat, hyper Said (Said Taghmaoui) is of North African heritage. Vinz (Vincent Cassel), his dense lug of a buddy, is a lower-class Jew whose brass knuckles-style ring features carved Hebrew lettering. Their more mature friend Hubert (Hubert Kounde) is a black who conscientiously masters his emotions through boxing.

It's 10:38 A.M. on May 27 and the news on TV concerns a second-generation Arab who remains in critical condition after having been beaten senseless by police during interrogation. That fact had prompted the young residents of the victim's housing development to riot the previous evening.

The trio undergoes a subtle, then drastic change on an evening excursion to Paris, during which Hubert and Said are hauled in and interrogated by the cops. The three pals later get in a rumble with skinheads, which prompts an epiphany of sorts. (Kassovitz cameos here as a sniveling skinhead.) The pals finally return to home turf, where an unforeseen conclusion packs a wallop.

•

HAIR
1979, 118 mins, US Ⓥ ⊙ col
Dir Milos Forman ***Prod*** Lester Persky, Michael Butler ***Scr*** Michael Weller ***Ph*** Miroslav Ondricek ***Ed*** Lynzee Klingman ***Mus*** Galt MacDermot ***Art*** Stuart Wurtzel
Act John Savage, Treat Willilams, Beverly D'Angelo, Nicholas Ray, Annie Golden, Dorsey Wright (United Artists)

The storyline imposed on the original musical's book has large expository gaps. These are accentuated by director Milos Forman's determination to have free-form musical numbers evolve out of the tale of a draftee adopted by a bunch of New York hippies, who tune him into their uninhibited lifestyles.

John Savage plays the inductee, fascinated by the group he stumbles upon at a Central Park be-in, composed of Treat Williams, Annie Golden, Dorsey Wright and Don Dacus. They get him stoned, urge him on in his quest for debutante Beverly D'Angelo, and pursue him to his basic training camp in Nevada and a bittersweet finale.

The spirit and élan that captivated the Vietnam protest era are long gone, and what Forman tries to make up with splash and verve fails to evoke potent nostalgia.

•

HAIRDRESSER'S HUSBAND, THE
(SEE: LE MARI DE LA COIFFEUSE)

•

HAIRSPRAY
1988, 90 mins, US Ⓥ ⊙ col
Dir John Waters ***Prod*** Rachal Talalay, Stanley F. Buchthal, John Waters ***Scr*** John Waters ***Ph*** David Insley ***Ed*** Janice Hampton ***Mus*** Bonnie Greenberg ***Art*** Vincent Peranio
Act Sonny Bono, Ruth Brown, Divine, Colleen Fitzpatrick, Michael St. Gerard, Deborah Harry (Buchthal/New Line Cinema)

John Waters's appreciation for the tacky side of life is in full flower in *Hairspray*, a slight but often highly amusing diversion about integration, big girls' fashions and music-mad teens in 1962 Baltimore.

Ricki Lake, chubette daughter of Divine and Jerry Stiller, overcomes all to become queen of an afternoon teenage dance show, much to the consternation of stuck-up blond Colleen Fitzpatrick, whose parents are Deborah Harry and Sonny Bono.

Divine spits out some choice bon mots while denigrating her daughter's pastime, but finally rejoicing in her success, takes Lake off for a pricelessly funny visit to Hefty Hideaway, where full-figure girls can shop to their hearts' content.

Divine, so big he wears a tent-like garment big enough for three ordinary mortals to sleep in, is in otherwise fine form in a dual role. Harry has little to do but act bitchy and sport increasingly towering wigs, while Pia Zadora is virtually unrecognizable as a beatnik chick.

All the kids in the predominantly teenage cast are tirelessly enthusiastic.

•

HAIRY APE, THE
1944, 90 mins, US Ⓥ b/w
Dir Alfred Santell ***Prod*** Jules Levey ***Scr*** Robert D. Andrews, Decla Dunning ***Ph*** Lucien Andriot ***Ed*** William Ziegler ***Mus*** Michel Michelet ***Art*** James Sullivan
Act William Bendix, Susan Hayward, John Loder, Dorothy Comingore, Alan Napier, Eddie Kane (United Artists)

The Eugene O'Neill play, one of his earliest and one carrying plenty of gutter dialog and epithets, dealt with the futility of brawn over brain, but also severely attacked capitalism and at one point, concerned the old IWW (International Workers of the World). Additionally, it took a poke at high society. Film transcription could not go into that, although the basic character, that of a ship's stoker who felt that his strength was all that belonged in the world, is particularly well portrayed, both so far as the part itself is concerned and in the interpretation by William Bendix. He imparts to it all the ape-like qualities that could exist in a man in line with the O'Neill play.

The script given Levey by Robert D. Andrews and Decla Dunning, a well-turned one containing as much of O'Neill's original dialog as possible and judicious, is of the present to furnish some wartime flavor, and opens in Lisbon, where a freighter is about to sail with a load of refugees. Love interest that ultimately peters out is injected through the central woman character, Susan Hayward, who plays the snobbish, badly spoiled daughter of a steel tycoon (as called for by the O'Neill story), and John Loder, second engineer of the ship. It develops that the girl is merely enticing Loder in order to achieve her selfish aims. Also, it is she who, revolted by the sight of Bendix, labels him a hairy ape.

In the play, the central character was called Yank, whereas in Levey's pic he's Hank. Production rates tops as to settings, background, etc.

Most of the dialects, among stokehole associates of Hank's, as written by O'Neill, are missing in the film version.

•

HALF A SIXPENCE

1967, 148 mins, UK Ⓥ ▭ col

Dir George Sidney ***Prod*** Charles H. Schneer, George Sidney ***Scr*** Beverley Cross ***Ph*** Geoffrey Unsworth ***Ed*** Bill Lewthwaite, Frank Santillo ***Mus*** David Heneker ***Art*** Ted Haworth

Act Tommy Steele, Julia Foster, Cyril Ritchard, Grover Dale, Elaine Taylor, Hilton Edwards (Paramount)

As with all good musicals, the story [from the stage musical adapted from H. G. Wells's novel Kipps] has a simple moral—that money can be a troublesome thing—and it is told in a straightforward narrative, without too much complication of character.

Thus, Kipps is projected as a likable lad, temporarily aberrated by his coming into a fortune, and returning to the true common virtues when he loses it.

The cohesive force is certainly that of Tommy Steele, who takes hold of his part like a terrier and never lets go. His assurance is overwhelming, and he leads the terping with splendid vigor and élan.

Of course, the haunting title song and the ebullient "Flash, Bang, Wallop!" remain the showstoppers, and David Heneker's score is a little short of socko tunes elsewhere.

•

HALF MOON STREET

1987, 90 mins, UK/ US Ⓥ ⦿ col

Dir Bob Swaim ***Prod*** Geoffrey Reeve ***Scr*** Bob Swaim, Edward Behr ***Ph*** Peter Hannan ***Ed*** Richard Marden ***Mus*** Richard Harvey ***Art*** Anthony Curtis

Act Sigourney Weaver, Michael Caine, Patrick Kavanagh, Keith Buckley, Nadim Sawalha, Angus MacInnes (RKO/Pressman/Showtime—Movie Channel)

Half Moon Street is a half-baked excuse for a film that is redeemed not a whit by having Sigourney Weaver and Michael Caine in the starring roles. Script, based on Paul Theroux's thriller *Dr. Slaughter*, has been rendered nonsensical and incoherent by screenwriters.

Weaver plays Dr. Slaughter, a scholar at the Middle East Institute in London who turns to working as an escort to supplement her paltry income. She manages to avoid any emotional attachments with her clients until she arrives one rainy night to be the paid guest of Lord Bulbeck, played competently, if uninvolvingly, by Caine.

Caine is somehow mixed up with Arabs in a convoluted scheme and somehow Weaver becomes inextricably and unwittingly wound up in his dealings.

•

HALLELUJAH

1929, 109 mins, US b/w

Dir King Vidor ***Scr*** Wanda Tuchock, Ransom Rideout ***Ph*** Gordon Avil ***Ed*** Hugh Wynn, Anson Stevenson ***Art*** Cedric Gibbons

Act Daniel L. Haynes, Nina Mae McKinney, William Fountaine, Harry Gray, Fannie Belle DeKnight, Victoria Spivey (M-G-M)

In his herculean attempt to take comedy, romance and tragedy and blend them into a big, gripping, Negro talker, King Vidor has turned out an unusual picture from a theme that is almost as ancient as the sun. Vidor's strict adherence to realism is so effective at times it is stark and uncanny.

The story is a plain one, the characters not too many and no fancy long-drawn-out monickers and thus, the average screen fan can follow its theme without the slightest difficulty. This is all a big feather in Vidor's hat.

Nina Mae McKinney as the dynamic, vivacious girl of the colored underworld, who lives by her wits and enmeshes the males with her personality, sex appeal and dancing feet, never had a day's work before a camera.

Daniel L. Haynes as Zeke, the principal male, is the big, rough, lazylike colored boy, who loves his women and is happiest when he sings. Victoria Spivey is the blues singer who does a pretty naturalistic bit of acting as the girl who loves and waits. William Fountaine becomes a dominant figure as the heavy, and acquits himself creditably. Fannie Belle DeKnight is the mother of the film, and what a mammy!

A characteristic figure is Harry Gray as the white bewhiskered parson and daddy of the Johnson family.

1929/30: NOMINATION: Best Director

•

HALLELUJAH, I'M A BUM!

(UK: HALLELUJAH, I'M A TRAMP!)

1933, 83 mins, US Ⓥ ⦿ b/w

Dir Lewis Milestone ***Prod*** Joseph M. Schenck ***Scr*** S. N. Behrman, Ben Hecht ***Ph*** Lucien Andriot ***Mus*** Alfred Newman (dir.) ***Art*** Richard Day

Act Al Jolson, Madge Evans, Frank Morgan, Harry Langdon, Chester Conklin (United Artists)

Almost Barrie-ish in its whimsy, the ethereal quality of the Ben Hecht–S. N. Behrman script foundation is its primary deficiency. Lorenz Hart, while solely credited for the lyrics to Richard Rodgers's music, probably merits as much authorship credit because his lyrical dialog constitutes the main burden of the proceedings.

The whole thing is an unconvincing mixture of the fictional and factional. Ultra-modern realism with the playboy mayor of the city of New York and his weakness for the Central Park Casino and a pretty femme in particular (Madge Evans), is blended with such unconvincing detail as non-existing Central Park's hobos of which Al Jolson is the unofficial mayor.

The rollicking fun of an uncertain but not too unsteady story structure collapses utterly when Evans, a victim of aphasia or amnesia, later figures as the romance interest opposite Jolson, until recovering her senses for the finale with the mayor (Frank Morgan).

The "rhythmic dialog" and the Lewis Milestonian method of wedding the tempo'd music to the action has its moments. The laity will doubtlessly compare this to the Ernst Lubitsch technique in *Trouble in Paradise*.

This must have been one of the toughest pictures to shoot and undoubtedly the most trying for the rest of the cast who had to talk in rhyme and rhythm rather than their accustomed dramatic prose. Jolson's selling of the title song and "You Are Too Beautifu," the former reprised more often, of course leaves little wanting. "Bum" is a pip of a number with its odd-rhythmed style and tempo. "I'll Do It Again" and "What Do You Want with Money" are other songs.

•

HALLELUJAH, I'M A TRAMP!

SEE: HALLELUJAH, I'M A BUM!

•

HALLELUJAH THE HILLS

1963, 88 mins, US b/w

Dir Adolfas Mekas ***Prod*** David C. Stone ***Scr*** Adolfas Mekas ***Ph Ed*** Emshviller ***Ed*** Adolfas Mekas ***Mus*** Meyer Kupferman

Act Peter H. Beard, Martin Greenbaum, Sheila Finn, Peggy Steffans (Vermont)

Formerly, this offbeat NY filmmaking group mainly made dramas. But this zesty unusual romp twits its subject with knowing insight and also packs in some inside film buff gags and allusions.

There is not much of a story. It is mainly a joyous rush of images by a new director who has assimilated his classics and regular run of films.

Two clean-cut, adventurous young American stalwarts vie for the hand of a beauteous young girl only to have her snapped up by a bearded character. Small town life and the seasons pass in review as the two men camp out and take their turns at wooing the girl or trying to cope with outdoor life in the snow and sun.

Writer-director-editor Adolfas Mekas displays a flair for visual revelation, gags and shenanigans that manage to keep this stimulating throughout. The intimations of noted pix culminates with a bow to D. W. Griffith in showing the great ice floe rescue of Lillian Gish by Richard Barthlemess in *Way Down East*.

Mekas assimilates rather than imitates. The actors are all fresh, and cavort with grace and a lack of self-consciousness. Camerawork is clear with sharp editing and the music a counterpoint help. There are glimpses and incisive satiric shafts against war, courting habits, youthful shyness and self absorption in this madcap, bright pic.

•

HALLELUJAH TRAIL, THE

1965, 152 mins, US Ⓥ ⦿ ▭ col

Dir John Sturges ***Prod*** John Sturges ***Scr*** John Gay ***Ph*** Robert Surtees ***Ed*** Ferris Webster ***Mus*** Elmer Bernstein ***Art*** Cary Odell

Act Burt Lancaster, Lee Remick, Jim Hutton, Pamela Tiffin, Donald Pleasence, Brian Keith (Mirisch/Kappa)

It all begins with the burgeoning city of Denver facing the worst threat of its existence—becoming bone dry in 10 days in the approaching winter of 1867. This awesome situation paves the way for one of the nuttiest cinematic mishmashes you ever saw, in which thirsty miners, a worried U.S. Cavalry, a band of whiskey-mad Sioux, a crusading temperance group and a train of 40 wagons carrying 600 barrels of hard likker become so thoroughly involved that even the off-screen narrator has a hard time trying to keep track of them and their proper logistics.

Producer-director John Sturges has pulled every plug in spoofing practically every western situation known to the scripter, and the whole is beautifully packaged. Screenplay, from Bill Gulick's novel, approaches the situations straight.

The cavalry, coloneled by Burt Lancaster, is constantly threatened with breaching the articles of war and the Constitution itself by the demands of temperance leader Lee Remick. Sioux, leaving their reservation when they get wind of the approaching whiskey, can't be attacked by the cavalry because they carry certain signed government papers.

Performances, like situations, are played straight, and therein lies their beauty. Lancaster does a bangup job as the harassed cavalry colonel plagued with having to offer safe conduct to the whiskey train and to the temperance ladies.

One of the standouts in pic is Martin Landau, as Chief Walks-Stooped-Over, as deadpan as any Injun ever lived but socking over his comedy scenes mostly with his eyes.

•

HALLOWEEN

1978, 93 mins, US Ⓥ ⦿ ▭ col

Dir John Carpenter ***Prod*** Debra Hill ***Scr*** John Carpenter, Debra Hill ***Ph*** Dean Cundey ***Ed*** Tomy Wallace, Charles Burnstein ***Mus*** John Carpenter ***Art*** Tommy Wallace

Act Donald Pleasence, Jamie Lee Curtis, Nancy Loomis, P. J. Soles, Charles Cyphers, Kyle Richards (Falcon)

After a promising opening, *Halloween* becomes just another maniac-on-the-loose suspenser. However, despite the prosaic plot, director John Carpenter has timed the film's gore so that the 93-minute item is packed with enough thrills.

The picture opens 15 years earlier, on Halloween night in a small midwestern town. A young boy spies his sister necking with her boyfriend. As they mount the steps for her bedroom, he slips on his Halloween mask, pulls out a butcher knife and does some cutting.

For the rest of the thriller the Hitchcockian influence remains, but the plot ambles along to a predictable conclusion. It is now the present, also Halloween. Donald Pleasence, a psychiatrist who has been caring for the killer during the years, is on his way to the state hospital to make sure that the maniac is never freed.

Of course, the maniac escapes, returns to the scene of the original crime and searches for suitable victims, in this case a trio of babysitting friends.

•

HALLOWEEN II

1981, 92 mins, US Ⓥ ⦿ ▭ col

Dir Rick Rosenthal ***Prod*** Debra Hill, John Carpenter ***Scr*** John Carpenter, Debra Hill ***Ph*** Dean Cundy ***Ed*** Mark Goldblatt ***Mus*** John Carpenter, Alan Howarth ***Art*** J. Michael Riva

Act Jamie Lee Curtis, Donald Pleasence, Charles Cyphers, Dick Warlock, Lance Guest, Jeffrey Kramer (De Laurentiis)

This uninspired version amounts to lukewarm sloppy seconds in comparison to the original film that made director John Carpenter a hot property.

There are incredibly almost never any really terrific scares in 92 minutes—just multiple shots of violence and gore that are more gruesome than anything else.

Script commences with the finale from the original where concerned doctor Donald Pleasence shoots Jamie Lee Curtis's demented predator six times only to have him walk away and continue his killing spree. Young Curtis is rushed to the hospital for care where a whole set of young, nubile hospital staffers are primed as the next victims.

Meanwhile, the zombie-like masked killer makes his way through the town, wandering in and out of houses slashing unsuspecting residents. So many people wander through the proceedings that it becomes difficult to care who is geting sliced or why.

•

HALLOWEEN III: SEASON OF THE WITCH

1982, 96 mins, US Ⓥ ⦿ ▭ col

Dir Tommy Lee Wallace ***Prod*** John Carpenter, Debra Hill ***Scr*** Tommy Lee Wallace, [Nigel Kneale] ***Ph*** Dean Cundey ***Ed*** Millie Moore ***Mus*** John Carpenter, Alan Howarth ***Art*** Peter Jamison

Act Tom Atkins, Stacey Nelkin, Dan O'Herlihy, Ralph Strait, Michael Currie, Jadeen Barbor (De Laurentiis)

There's not much to say about *Halloween III* that hasn't already been said about either of the other two *Halloween* pics or a slew of imitators.

Interesting to note here is producer Debra Hill's earlier claim that this film would steer clear of gore and blood and instead go for the science fiction paranoia genre of *Invasion of the Body Snatchers*. Apparently, yanking someone's head off their shoulders, shoving fingers down a man's eyeballs or inserting a power drill in a woman's head don't qualify as particularly disgusting.

There is the tired old cliché of a crazed toy manufacturer (in this case he makes Halloween masks), the fearless couple out to figure what's "really" going on, and plot holes big enough to shoot another film through. On the latter note, Nigel Kneale, credited screenwriter all through production, somehow managed to get his name removed from the credits.

●

HALLOWEEN 4: THE RETURN OF MICHAEL MYERS
1988, 88 mins, US Ⓥ ⦿ col
Dir Dwight H. Little *Prod* Paul Freeman *Scr* Alan B. McElroy *Ph* Peter Lyons Collister *Ed* Curtiss Clayton *Mus* Alan Howarth *Art* Roger S. Crandall
Act Donald Pleasence, Ellie Cornell, Danielle Harris, George P. Wilbur, Michael Pataki (Trancas)

Fourth entry in the *Halloween* horror series is a no-frills, workmanlike picture [story by Dhani Lipsius, Larry Rattner, Benjamin Ruffner and Alan B. McElroy].

Designed as a direct sequel to John Carpenter's 1978 hit, with no reference to the events chronicled in parts II and III, pic resurrects monster Michael Myers (previously referred to mainly as "The Shape"), who escapes from a hospital to return home and wreak havoc, with the vague notion of getting to his niece Jamie (Danielle Harris).

His face scarred from an earliier altercation with the monster, Donald Pleasence reprises his role as Dr. Loomis, now hell-bent on destroying the obviously unkillable Myers.

●

HALLOWEEN 5
1989, 96 mins, US Ⓥ ⦿ col
Dir Dominique Othenin-Girard *Prod* Ramsey Thomas *Scr* Michael Jacobs, Dominique Othenin-Girard, Shem Bitterman *Ph* Robert Draper *Ed* Jerry Brady *Mus* Alan Howarth *Art* Steven Lee, Chava Danielson
Act Donald Pleasence, Danielle Harris, Wendy Kaplan, Ellie Cornell, Donald L. Shanks, Jeffrey Landman (Magnum)

In its only novel twist, *Halloween 5* takes the liberty of setting up its sequel (albeit clumsily) at the film's end rather than "killing" that pesky Michael Myers and then figuring out how to revive him after counting b.o. receipts. Otherwise, this is pretty stupid and boring fare.

The thread of a plot has the killer empathetically linked to his nine-year-old niece Jamie (Danielle Harris), who goes into a sort of epileptic seizure when she senses he's about to kill again. Meanwhile, the determined Dr. Loomis (Donald Pleasence, getting a bit long in the tooth for this sort of duty) also seems to sense that Michael Myers is still alive and keeps badgering the little girl to help him end his scourge.

Director Dominique Othenin-Girard doesn't bring much to the action, with the exception of a protracted scene in which one of the dimwits in distress (Wendy Kaplan) harangues the killer in a car, thinking it's her boyfriend in Halloween garb.

Kaplan proves vivacious and fetching as the perky Tina even if the character is flaky. Harris is bright-eyed as the disturbingly beset Jamie.

●

HALLOWEEN: H20 TWENTY YEARS LATER
1998, 85 mins, US Ⓥ ⦿ ▭ col
Dir Steve Miner *Prod* Paul Freeman *Scr* Robert Zappia, Matt Greenberg *Ph* Daryn Okada *Ed* Patrick Lusser *Mus* John Ottman *Art* John Willet
Act Jamie Lee Curtis, Adam Arkin, Josh Hartnett, Michelle Williams, Adam Hann-Byrd, Janet Leigh (Nightfall/Dimension)

While plot mechanics aren't wildly imaginative, pic nonetheless delivers requisite jolts in an above-average package, while providing Jamie Lee Curtis sufficient character meat to justify revisiting her career-making debut role.

Using a different name, Michael Myers's beleaguered sister Laurie Strode (Curtis) is now live-in headmistress as a gated, upscale SoCal boarding school, with teenage son John (Josh Hartnett) duly enrolled. Guess who's coming cross-country to visit.

The majority of staff and students are on a camping trip, leaving the few stay-behinds isolated. Plus, it's Halloween.

Some hide-and-seek games at the school gate get Michael (Chris Durand performs the mute, masked role this time) past security guard Ronny (LL Cool J). Soon "The Shape" is slashing his way through California youth en route to his already-suspicious, then panicked little sis.

Director Steve Miner presses the false-scare button a few too many times early on, and once the nonstop running-screaming-snuffing action takes over after 50 minutes or so, script [from a screen story by coscripter Robert Zappia] doesn't evince any special invention. Still, the scares are there.

Despite the now-required addition of sexy TV-recognizable adolescents, pic belongs to Curtis, and care has been taken to make her character one credible, battle-scarred survivor. (One of script's best ideas is having her constantly experience delusional Michael sightings—so when the real thing shows up, she thinks at first it's just another "episode.")

Tech package in economically paced prod is first-rate, with Miner (who started out directing the second and third *Friday the 13ths*) using shadowy, tracking Panavision images that evoke rather than blatantly imitate the mood in John Carpenter's 1978 original.

●

HALLOWEEN: THE CURSE OF MICHAEL MYERS
1995, 88 mins, US Ⓥ col
Dir Joe Chappelle *Prod* Paul Freeman *Scr* Daniel Ferrands *Ph* Billy Dickson *Ed* Randy Bricker *Mus* Alan Howarth *Art* Bryan Ryman
Act Donald Pleasence, Mitch Ryan, Marianne Hagan, Paul Rudd, Leo Geter, George P. Wilbur (Nightfall)

The sixth entry in the profitable *Halloween* series may be an example of going to the well once too often. Run-of-the-mill horror item is notable only for final appearance of the late Donald Pleasence, to whose memory it is dedicated. The masked Michael Myers (George P. Wilbur) now seems to be driven by some ancient Celtic ritual of sacrificing an entire family. As the bodies pile up, it becomes clear he's trying to track down those relatives he missed in the earlier films.

But the explosion of horror/slasher films in the 17 years since the first entry has made Myers's antics seem mundane. Not even the addition of satanic rituals, farm implements or a Howard Stern-like shock jock (Leo Geter) is enough to paint over the creaky trappings. Pleasence reprises his role as the psychiatrist who recognizes that Myers is pure evil.

The press notes point out that the six films together cost less than $20 million and have already grossed more than $200 million.

●

HALLS OF MONTEZUMA
1950, 113 mins, US Ⓥ col
Dir Lewis Milestone *Prod* Robert Bassler *Scr* Michael Blankfort *Ph* Winton C. Hoch *Ed* William Reynolds *Mus* Sol Kaplan
Act Richard Widmark, Jack Palance, Robert Wagner, Karl Malden, Richard Hylton, Richard Boone (20th Century-Fox)

Halls of Montezuma is an account of Marine heroism during the fierce South Pacific fighting of the Second World War.

Rather than a presentation of mass battle, film deals intimately with a small group of Marines under the command of Richard Widmark and how it fulfills a mission to take Jap prisoners for questioning. Footage is long but there is no feeling of great length.

Opening shots feature flashbacks to acquaint the audience with the Marines as civilians and show their strengths and weaknesses.

Widmark is exceptionally good as an officer who masks his fear and encourages his men. Reginald Gardiner adds lightness as a Marine sergeant who scoffs at regulations. Karl Malden stands out as the pharmacist's mate.

●

HAMBURGER HILL
1987, 110 mins, US Ⓥ ⦿ col
Dir John Irvin *Prod* Marcia Nasatir, Jim Carabatsos, Larry De Waay *Scr* Jim Carabatsos *Ph* Peter MacDonald *Ed* Peter Tanner *Mus* Philip Glass *Art* Austen Spriggs
Act Anthony Barrile, Michael Patrick Boatman, Don Cheadle, Michael Dolan, Don James, Dylan McDermott (RKO/Nasatir-Carabatsos/Interaccess)

Well-produced and directed with an eye to documentary-like realism and authenticity, pic centers upon a military undertaking of familiar futility during the Vietnam War. It follows a squad of 14 recruits from initial R&R through 10 days' worth of hell, as the men make 11 agonizing assaults on a heavily fortified hill.

First 40 minutes attempt to show the developing relationships among the guys, and screenwriter-coproducer Jim Carabatsos has been particularly attentive to delineating the tensions between the blacks and whites in the group.

More than an hour is devoted to the protected effort to scale the indistinguished piece of Vietnamese real estate of the title. As physically impressive as some of it is, the action also proves dispiriting and depressing, as the soldiers slide helplessly down the muddy slopes in the rain and are inevitably picked off by enemy gunfire.

Director John Irvin, who shot a documentary in Vietnam in 1969, the year the action takes place, makes fine use of the Philippines locations and the verisimilitude supplied by the production team.

●

HAMLET
1948, 155 mins, UK Ⓥ ⦿ b/w
Dir Laurence Olivier *Prod* Laurence Olivier *Scr* William Shakespeare *Ph* Desmond Dickinson *Ed* Helga Cranston *Mus* William Walton *Art* Roger Furse
Act Laurence Olivier, Eileen Herlie, Basil Sydney, Jean Simmons, Norman Wooland, Felix Aylmer (Rank/Two Cities)

This is picture-making at its best. At a cost of $2 million, it seems incredibly cheap compared with some of the ephemeral trash that is turned out.

Star-producer-director Laurence Olivier was the driving force behind the whole venture. Minor characters and a good deal of verse have been thrown overboard, and a four-and-a-quarter hour play becomes a two-and-a-half hour film.

Pundits may argue that Rosencrantz, Guildenstern and Fortinbras shouldn't have been sacrificed, and that many familiar gems are missing. They will argue about the bewildering crossing and intercrossing of motives. Scholars may complain that this isn't Hamlet as Shakespeare created him, but one that Olivier has made in his own image.

In his interpretation of *Hamlet*, Olivier thinks of him as nearly a great man, damned, as most people are, by lack of resolution. He announces it in a spoken foreword as "the tragedy of a man who couldn't make up his mind."

Special praise is due Eileen Herlie for her playing of the queen. She has made the character really live. Her love for her son, the consciousness of evildoing, her grief and agony, her death—made by Olivier to appear as sacrificing herself for Hamlet—make her a very memorable, pitiful figure. Jean Simmons as Ophelia brings to the role a sensitive, impressionable innocence, although perhaps too childlike.

Basil Sydney repeats his stage success as the king, of whom ambition and lust have taken possession, and rises to his greatest height in his soliloquy trying to pray and seeing himself accursed like Cain.

1948: Best Picture, Actor (Laurence Olivier), B&W Art Direction, B&W Costume Design

NOMINATIONS: Best Director, Supp. Actress (Jean Simmons), Scoring of a Dramatic Picture

●

HAMLET
1990, 135 mins, US Ⓥ ⦿ col
Dir Franco Zeffirelli *Prod* Dyson Lovell *Scr* Christopher De Vore, Franco Zeffirelli *Ph* David Watkin *Ed* Richard Marden *Mus* Ennio Morricone *Art* Dante Ferretti
Act Mel Gibson, Glenn Close, Alan Bates, Paul Scofield, Ian Holm, Helena Bonham Carter (Warner/Nelson)

Mel Gibson's best moments come in the highly physical duelling scene that climaxes the Shakespeare play. Otherwise, Mel's Hamlet is blond and Franco Zeffirelli's *Hamlet* is bland.

By slicing the text virtually in half, and casting a matinee idol in the lead, the director clearly hoped to engage the masses. Unfortunately, this *Hamlet* seems no more modern or pertinent to contemporary concerns than any other on stage, screen or tube in recent decades. Nor does it possess the rugged freshness of Kenneth Branagh's *Henry V*.

Familiar story unfolds in and around a formidable fortress that is actually a combination of three ancient structures in the British Isles. Deeply aggrieved by the death of his father, Hamlet is commanded by his father to avenge his murder at the hands of his brother Claudius, who has since become king and married Hamlet's mother, Gertrude.

Performances all fall in a middle range between the competent and the lackluster. Gibson gets the dialog and soliloquies out decently, but rolls and bugs his eyes a lot. Best is probably Paul Scofield as the ghost, although Zeffirelli irritatingly cuts or pulls away from him midstream. Alan Bates is a solid Claudius, Glenn Close brings a juicy vigor to Gertrude.

1990: NOMINATIONS: Best Art Direction, Costume Design

•

HAMLET

1996, 242 mins, US Ⓥ ⊙ ▭ col

Dir Kenneth Branagh ***Prod*** David Barron ***Scr*** Kenneth Branagh ***Ph*** Alex Thomson ***Ed*** Neil Farrell ***Mus*** Patrick Doyle ***Art*** Tim Harvey

Act Kenneth Branagh, Julie Christie, Billy Crystal, Gerard Depardieu, Charlton Heston, Derek Jacobi (Castle Rock/Columbia)

Kenneth Branagh has mounted a full-bodied, clear-headed, resplendently staged rendition of *Hamlet* that rewards the time required to experience it. A rare unedited version of the Bard's lengthiest play, the result is the second-longest major U.S. or British feature film of all time, only one minute shorter than the original roadshow cut of *Cleopatra*.

The sixth sound-era adaptation, this yields significant artistic dividends through the revelation of normally excised or underemphasized aspects of the play. Above all, the film strives for maximum clarity, for laying out the political, psychological and emotional dimensions of the complex work as thoughtfully as possible, and for making the language accessible and comprehensible to the widest audience.

Branagh, who has played Hamlet onstage close to 300 times, transplants the tale to an unspecified period of the mid-to-late 19th century, a time well-suited to the issues of shifting European borders and interrelated royalty. The downside of Branagh's style is a literal-mindedness that is most evident when he makes rather forlorn attempts at poetic visual flourishes.

Brangah, as a bleach-blond Hamlet, displays an energy and forcefulness that is contagious to the huge cast. At least a couple of the other actors are brilliant, specifically Derek Jacobi (who directed Branagh's stage Hamlet) as a keenly tactical and shrewd Claudius, and Richard Briers, whose Polonius is a revelation, making him a political man of tragically misguided motives.

Also weighing in impressively are Julie Christie, dazzlingly earthy as the ill-considered queen, Kate Winslet as the doomed Ophelia and even Billy Crystal, who gives some sly and impish twists to his line readings as the gravedigger.

This is the first feature shot on 65mm stock and projected in 70mm since *Far and Away* (1992), and the result is a stunningly handsome production with tremendous visual clarity and depth.

[Pic was subsequently released in a 2+-hour, 35mm version.]

1996: NOMINATIONS: Best Screenplay Adaptation, Original Dramatic Score, Art Direction, Costume Design

•

HAMMERSMITH IS OUT

1972, 108 mins, US Ⓥ col

Dir Peter Ustinov ***Prod*** Alex Lucas ***Scr*** Stanford Whitmore ***Ph*** Richard H. Kline ***Ed*** David Blewitt ***Mus*** Dominic Frontiere ***Art*** Robert Benton

Act Elizabeth Taylor, Richard Burton, Peter Ustinov, Beau Bridges, Leon Ames, George Raft (Crean)

What is, apparently, an exercise in spoofery on the part of Elizabeth Taylor, Richard Burton and the even more energetic Peter Ustinov, starts as a variation on the Faust legend but almost immediately turns into a belabored antic.

The somewhat sketchy screenplay is no more than a line on which the three principals hang their rarely inspired improvisations.

Burton, as the lunatic Hammersmith who flees the asylum with the connivance of male nurse Beau Bridges by promising him unworldly riches, goes through the film with a single bored expression. Bridges is sleazy and repulsive and well deserving of his fate. Ustinov, as the asylum keeper committed to recapturing Hammersmith, would be funnier if his lines, spoken with an unintelligible "mad scientist" accent could be understood.

•

HAMMETT

1982, 94 mins, US Ⓥ col

Dir Wim Wenders ***Prod*** Fred Roos, Ronald Colby, Don Guest ***Scr*** Ross Thomas, Dennis O'Flaherty ***Ph*** Philip Lathrop, Joseph Biroc ***Ed*** Barry Malkin, Marc Laub, Robert Q. Lovett, Randy Roberts ***Mus*** John Barry ***Art*** Dean Tavoularis, Eugene Lee

Act Frederic Forrest, Peter Boyle, Marilu Henner, Roy Kinnear, Sylvia Sidney, Lydia Lei (Zoetrope)

Wim Wenders's problems with this, his first Hollywood film, are many and well known. Reportedly hired by producer Francis Coppola on the strength of his complicated murder opus, *The American Friend* [1977], Wenders's *Hammett* was early on dubbed a rough diamond.

Now, overpolished by too many script rewrites [credited adaptation by Thomas Pope, based on the book by Joe Gores], perhaps emasculated by massive footage scraps and belated re-shoots, project (all shot on interiors) emerges a rather suffocating film taking place in a rickety "Chinatown."

But Chinatown it is not. Film is a sort of homage to Dashiel Hammett. Based on a fiction by Joe Gores, it has Hammett far removed from his old private eye days and suffering from TB, eking out a precarious living with short stories penned for pulp detective magazines.

Frederic Forrest looks like Hammett, talks like Humphrey Bogart and is acceptable. His old boss from the Pinkerton Private Eye Co. is played with force by Peter Boyle.

A Chinese prostitute has disappeared and must be found for she might be dangerous to top monied interests. After several chases, killings and muggings, it emerges that the Chinese girl has some incriminating porn pictures of all the men who really run the town.

•

HANA-BI

1997, 103 mins, Japan Ⓥ ⊙ col

Dir Takeshi Kitano ***Prod*** Masayuki Mori, Yasushi Tsuge, Takio Yoshida ***Scr*** Takeshi Kitano ***Ph*** Hideo Yamamoto ***Ed*** Takeshi Kitano, Yoshinori Ota ***Mus*** Joe Hisaishi ***Art*** Norihiro Isoda

Act Beat Takeshi, Kayoko Kishimoto, Ren Osugi, Susumu Terajima, Tetsu Watanabe, Yuko Daike (Office Kitano/Bandai Visual/Television Tokyo/Tokyo FM)

Hana-bi is a poignant reflection on love, violence, grief and loss. This contemplative drama about a tough ex-cop tying up the loose ends of his life and taking his terminally ill wife on a farewell journey is pure poetry.

Detective Nishi (Kitano, under his acting alias, Beat Takeshi) has lost his infant daughter and is about to lose his wife (Kayoko Kishimoto) to a protracted illness. Absenting himself from a stakeout to visit her in hospital, he receives a double blow when a colleague brings news that his partner, Horibe (Ren Osugi), has been seriously wounded.

Plagued by flashes of the violent deaths of his colleagues, Nishi calmly carries out a plan to right some of the wrongs in his life. Having quit the force, he resprays a stolen taxi to pass for a cop car, robs a bank singlehandedly, then delivers packages of loot to Horibe, a young police widow (Yuko Daike) and yakuza loan sharks, keeping the rest to fund a trip that will give his dying wife one last taste of happiness. It's a lyrical, cleansing journey that builds to a soulful conclusion.

Kitano conveys a great deal with minimal dialogue. While the nonlinear structure and constant time shifts of the opening create initial confusion, Kitano's approach is sufficiently mesmerizing to sustain interest while the plot becomes clear. As in his earlier films *A Scene at the Sea* and *Sonatine*, the director choreographs much of the action in peaceful, open spaces like the seaside or snow fields.

•

HAND, THE

1981, 104 mins, US Ⓥ col

Dir Oliver Stone ***Prod*** Edward R. Pressman ***Scr*** Oliver Stone ***Ph*** King Baggott ***Ed*** Richard Marks ***Mus*** James Horner ***Art*** J. Michael Riva

Act Michael Caine, Andrea Marcovicci, Viveca Lindfors, Bruce McGill, Mara Hobel, Annie McEnroe (Orion)

Director-scripter Oliver Stone takes on a premise—that of an autonomous appendage wreaking havoc on anyone crossing the human it was previously attached to—that has, in some form, been effectively executed in many past pix.

Special visual effects consultant Carlo Rambaldi, who performed wonders on *Alien*, should probably share some of the blame for the ineffectiveness of the aforementioned villain.

There is little relief to be found from the relationships in the script [from the book *The Lizard's Tail*]. Cartoonist Michael Caine evokes some sympathy after he loses his hand, particularly in scenes with daughter Mara Hobel, but spends most of his time sweating and grimacing into the camera lens. It's not a pretty sight.

James Horner has concocted an appropriately haunting score throughout.

•

HANDFUL OF DUST, A

1988, 118 mins, UK Ⓥ col

Dir Charles Sturridge ***Prod*** Derek Granger ***Scr*** Tim Sullivan, Derek Granger, Charles Sturridge ***Ph*** Peter Hannan ***Ed*** Peter Coulson ***Mus*** George Fenton ***Art*** Eileen Diss

Act James Wilby, Kristin Scott Thomas, Rupert Graves, Anjelica Huston, Alec Guinness, Judi Dench (LWT/Stagescreen)

A Handful of Dust is classy stuff based on an Evelyn Waugh novel, with a high production standard but an essentially empty story.

Kristin Scott Thomas as a lovely but fickle aristocrat is excellent, with an appealing fey manner. The virtual cameo appearances of Alec Guinness, Anjelica Huston and Judi Dench go some way to giving *Dust* a pedigree it might otherwise not be able to claim.

Set in Britain of the 1930s, at the beautiful country house Hetton Abbey, James Wilby, Scott Thomas and their young son seem content until the weekend visit of idle socialite Rupert Graves.

Scott Thomas slips into an affair with the penniless Graves while Wilby happily wanders his estate unaware he is being cuckolded. When their son is killed in a freak riding accident, Scott Thomas tells her husband she wants a divorce.

When Wilby finds the divorce settlement would mean selling Hetton, he promptly sets sail for South America in search of a lost Amazonian city with an eccentric explorer.

Technically, *A Handful of Dust* cannot be faulted. Where the film disappoints is the story, which though it ably highlights the vacuous attitudes of the English upper classes, is essentially slight.

1988: NOMINATION: Best Costume Design

•

HANDGUN
(US: DEEP IN THE HEART)

1983, 101 mins, UK Ⓥ col

Dir Tony Garnett ***Prod*** Tony Garnett ***Scr*** Tony Garnett ***Ph*** Charles Stewart ***Ed*** William Shapter ***Mus*** Mike Post ***Art*** Lilly Kilvert

Act Karen Young, Clayton Day, Suzie Humphreys, Helena Humann, Ben Jones (Kestrel)

Handgun takes a subject which is the stuff of exploitation and steers it towards social commentary. The result is an intelligent analysis of the political and sexual values of male society in Texas.

Pic is cast in three chapters that follow the maturing of a pretty young girl who goes to the midwest to teach history after a protected Catholic upbringing in Boston. She's just too soft to counter the approaches of a macho attorney who's obsessed with guns and hunting. It's only when he decides to have his own way with her that she realizes what she's up against.

Karen Young is sharp in her depiction of a nervy girl whose eyes are slowly opened. And Clayton Day plays all the subtleties of a decent chap who, nevertheless, has swallowed whole a value system that debases women and seeks to protect its integrity through violent confrontation.

•

HANDGUN

1994, 90 mins, US Ⓥ ⊙ col

Dir Whitney Ransick ***Prod*** Bob Gosse, Larry Meistritch ***Scr*** Whitney Ransick ***Ph*** Michael Spiller ***Ed*** Tom McCardle ***Mus*** Douglas J. Cuomo ***Art*** Andras Kanegson

Act Treat Williams, Seymour Cassel, Paul Schulze, Toby Huss, Angel Caban, Frank Vincent (Workin' Man)

As a comic spin on the action/heist genre, *Handgun* resembles a cross between Hal Hartley's *Simple Men* and Quentin Tarantino's *Reservoir Dogs*. Whitney Ransick's low-budget feature directorial debut is technically uneven, but has sharp dialogue and superlative performances, particularly by Treat Williams.

Wounded during a robbery that goes awry, Jack McCallister (Seymour Cassel) escapes with half a million in payroll booty, which he stashes in a locker. But as soon as the news gets around, a gallery of dubious characters, headed by McCallister's two sons, set out on a desperate hunt for the stolen cash.

McCallister's elder son, George (Williams), is a violent thief who's as quick with words as he is with his gun. Michael (Paul Schulze), his baby brother, is an elegantly dressed, small-time con artist. Realizing that they each possess indispensable but partial info about the loot's location, the siblings are compelled to work together.

Ransick's deadpan humor mixes idiosyncratic wit with laconic and cryptic dialogue. But he never surrenders to the temptation of making his narrative weird for its own sake. All three lead actors are impressively in tune with Ransick's quirky, offbeat sense of characterization.

•

HANDMAID'S TALE, THE
1990, 109 mins, US/W. Germany Ⓥ ⊙ col
Dir Volker Schlondorff ***Prod*** Daniel Wilson ***Scr*** Harold Pinter ***Ph*** Igor Luther ***Ed*** David Ray ***Mus*** Ryuichi Sakamoto ***Art*** Tom Walsh
Act Natasha Richardson, Robert Duvall, Faye Dunaway, Aidan Quinn, Elizabeth McGovern, Victoria Tennant (Cinecom/Bioskop)

The Handmaid's Tale is a provocative portrait of a future totalitarian theocracy where women have lost all human rights. The adaptation of Margaret Atwood's bestseller belongs to that rare category of science fiction film dealing with dystopias.

Even rarer, *Handmaid's Tale* is sci-fi from a woman's point-of-view. Following a military coup, this future society called Gilead operates under martial law in a perpetual state of warfare (à la 1984), with Old Testament religion the rule. The so-called sins of late 20th-century society, ranging from pollution to such activities as birth control and abortion, are blamed by the authorities as causing God's plague of infertility, requiring drastic measures to preserve the race.

Natasha Richardson portrays a young mother who's rounded up by the authorities to serve as a breeder, or handmaid, assigned to the barren family of state security chief Robert Duvall and his wife, Faye Dunaway. Her travails unfold in Harold Pinter's uncharacteristically staight-forward screenplay rather mechanically.

Though helmer Volker Schlondorff succeeds in painting the bleakness of this extrapolated future, he fails to create a strong and persistent connection with the heroine's plight.

•

HANDS OF ORLAC
SEE: ORLACS HAENDE

•

HANDS OF THE RIPPER
1971, 85 mins, UK Ⓥ col
Dir Peter Sasdy ***Prod*** Aida Young ***Scr*** L. W. Davidson ***Ph*** Kenneth Talbot ***Ed*** Christopher Barnes ***Mus*** Christopher Gunning ***Art*** Roy Stannard
Act Eric Porter, Angharad Rees, Jane Merrow, Keith Bell, Derek Godfrey, Dora Bryan (Hammer)

Hammer breaks away from its vampires and monster formula and gives a highly intriguing twist [from a story by Edward Spencer Shaw] to the Jack the Ripper murders which shook London back in the 1890s and have fascinated writers and filmmakers. Well-directed by Peter Sasdy, the tension is skillfully developed. Murders are particularly gruesome and there are shocks that will have the most hardened filmgoer sitting up.

The suggestion is that Jack the Ripper, who murdered prostitutes, killed his wife to stop her denouncing him in front of their three-year-old daughter, and vanished, returning years later supernaturally to force her to murder most viciously. It is a glossy, well-mounted production, admirably performed by a first-rate cast. Angharad Rees makes the pretty killer entirely credible.

•

HANDSOME SERGE
SEE: LE BEAU SERGE

•

HANDS OVER THE CITY
SEE: LA MANI SULLA CITTA

•

HAND THAT ROCKS THE CRADLE, THE
1992, 110 mins, US Ⓥ ⊙ col
Dir Curtis Hanson ***Prod*** David Madden ***Scr*** Amanda Silver ***Ph*** Robert Elswit ***Ed*** John F. Link ***Mus*** Graeme Revell ***Art*** Edward Pisoni
Act Annabella Sciorra, Rebecca DeMornay, Matt McCoy, Ernie Hudson, Julianne Moore, Madeline Zima (Hollywood/Interscope)

The Hand That Rocks the Cradle is a low-key thriller that will make baby boomers double-check the references of any prospective nanny. First screenplay by Amanda Silver, who is the granddaughter of the late, great screenwriter Sidney Buchman, trades in the same devil woman theme that anchored *Fatal Attraction*, with the sanctity of the traditional family unit as the villain's target.

Pleasant existence of pregnant Seattle housewife Claire Bartel (Annabella Sciorra) is disrupted when her new gynecologist crosses the proper boundaries during an exam. With the encouragement of her husband Michael (Matt McCoy), Claire files charges, upon which the doctor commits suicide.

Medic's demise sends his pregnant wife into hysterics, causing her to lose her baby. Cut to six months later, and this woman (Rebecca DeMornay), who now calls herself Peyton, turns up to offer her services as nanny to the Bartels. They readily take her in, and the viewer knows the screws will soon begin turning.

Helmer has obtained taut, impressive performances, notably from cast women. A totally deglamorized Sciorra becomes unglued subtly and slowly, eliciting sympathy without begging for it. DeMornay, her Miss Congeniality exterior masking evil intent, is an ice queen viewers will enjoy watching get hers in the end.

•

HANG 'EM HIGH
1968, 114 mins, US Ⓥ ⊙ col
Dir Ted Post ***Prod*** Leonard Freeman ***Scr*** Leonard Freeman, Mel Goldberg ***Ph*** Leonard South, Richard Kines ***Mus*** Dominic Frontiere
Act Clint Eastwood, Inger Stevens, ***Ed*** Begley, Pat Hingle, Arlene Golonka, Ben Johnson (United Artists/Malpaso)

Hang 'em High comes across as a poor-made imitation of a poor Italian-made imitation of an American western. It stars Clint Eastwood as a man bent on vengeance and is an episodic, rambling tale which glorifies personal justice and mocks orderly justice.

Eastwood is hanged (but not killed) by do-it-yourself vigilantes, headed by Ed Begley; district judge Pat Hingle recruits Eastwood to be a deputy marshal, and part of the job is to round up those who wronged him. Inger Stevens drifts in and out as a forced romantic interest.

From then on, film drags along through at least a dozen killings and legal hangings, shown in meticulous, morbid detail. Plot makes Hingle practically psychotic in his pursuit of "justice," and in the big hanging scene he fairly drools over the event.

Eastwood projects a likeable image, but the part is only a shade more developed over his Sergio Leone Italoaters. Begley goes way overboard in mugging the climactic shootout and hang-in.

•

HANGFIRE
1991, 89 mins, US Ⓥ col
Dir Peter Maris ***Prod*** Brad Krevoy, Steve Stabler ***Scr*** Brian D. Jeffries ***Ph*** Mark Norris ***Ed*** Peter Maris ***Mus*** Jim Price ***Art*** Stephen Greenberg
Act Brad Davis, Kim Delaney, Jan-Michael Vincent, Ken Foree, George Kennedy, Yaphet Kotto (Krevoy-Stabler)

Hangfire is a tight little action thriller about a prison break that attempts to serve as a metaphor for the 1989–90 Middle East crisis, but strains credibility.

Character actor Lee de Broux, in a bravura performance, plays a serial killer/rapist who leads a prison escape in New Mexico. De Broux and his minions take over the town of Sonora and hold its fifty or so inhabitants prisoner. The National Guard is called in, led by gung-ho Jan-Michael Vincent.

Local sheriff Brad Davis and his Vietnam vet pal Ken Foree (who excels in Maris assignments such as Viper), are the secret weapons who manage to defeat de Broux and rescue Davis's wife (Kim Delaney) while the military proves largely ineffectual.

Rest of the cast, including Lyle Alzado and Lou Ferrigno for comic relief, is effective.

•

HANGING TREE, THE
1959, 106 mins, US col
Dir Delmer Daves ***Prod*** Martin Jurow, Richard Shepherd ***Scr*** Wendell Mayes, Halstead Welles ***Ph*** Ted McCord ***Ed*** Owen Marks ***Mus*** Max Steiner
Act Gary Cooper, Maria Schell, Karl Malden, Ben Piazza, George C. Scott, Karl Swenson (Warner)

Wendell Mayes and Halstead Welles did the screenplay from a long short story by Dorothy M. Johnson, who is a kind of western writers' western writer. Johnson's stories show the West as it was, a hard, cruel, lonely frontier, in which the humans were often stripped of the savagery of the country.

In essence, the story follows western classic form. Gary Cooper is the mysterious stranger, a taciturn and quixotic man who drifts into a Montana gold-mining town. He quickly establishes himself as a man equally handy with a scalpel, a Colt and an inside straight, tender in his professional role as M.D., and a paradoxically tough man when dealing with gamblers and con men.

His first action is to rescue young Ben Piazza from a lynch-minded mob and make him his bond-servant on threat of exposure. His second is to take on the recovery of Maria Schell, a Swiss immigrant, who is ill and blinded from exposure. Stirring in these complicated relationships is the character of Karl Malden, an evil and lascivious gold prospector, who wants Piazza's life, Cooper's money and Schell's body, more or less in that order.

There are fine performances from a good cast, but the main contribution comes from the director. The natural splendor of the Washington location is thoroughly exploited in Technicolor, but Delmer Daves doesn't allow his characters to get lost in the forest or mountains.

1959: NOMINATION: Best Song ("The Hanging Tree")

•

HANGIN' WITH THE HOMEBOYS
1991, 88 mins, US Ⓥ ⊙ col
Dir Joseph P. Vasquez ***Prod*** Richard Brick ***Scr*** Joseph P. Vasquez ***Ph*** Anghel Decca ***Ed*** Michael Schweitzer ***Mus*** Joel Sill, David Chackler ***Art*** Isabel Bau Madden
Act Doug E. Doug, Mario Joyner, John Leguizamo, Nestor Serrano, Kimberly Russell, Mary B. Ward (New Line)

Homeboys is a good example of what independents can bring to the party: a vibrant tale told at minimum cost (under $2 million), a focus on cultural minorities (ghetto blacks and Puerto Ricans) and access to the system for a talented minority director (Joseph P. Vasquez, who did *Street Story* and *The Bronx War*).

Ensemble piece follows the misadventures of four South Bronx youths from mid-morning Friday to Saturday dawn. It looks like it could be their last time together, as reality is bearing down.

Willie (Doug E. Doug) is a welfare sponger whose caseworker has run out of patience. Tom (Mario Joyner) is a would-be actor with a telemarketing gig. Johnny (John Leguizamo), a shy, serious Puerto Rican supermarket stocker, ignores his boss's encouragement to try for a Hispanic college scholarship. Vinnie (Nestor Serrano), a Puerto Rican who pretends to be an Italian stud, sleeps all day and funds his party life by cajoling money from young girlfriends.

With plenty of tensions among themselves, they mostly pick on one another and get high on perpetual motion as they bounce from cruising to party-crashing to bars, cafes, peepshows, a billiards hall and a disco. Film is infused with an aggressive and engaging street energy and plenty of humor.

•

HANGMEN ALSO DIE!
1943, 131 mins, US ⊙ b/w
Dir Fritz Lang ***Prod*** Arnold Pressburger ***Scr*** John Wexley, Bert Brecht, Fritz Lang ***Ph*** James Wong Howe ***Ed*** Gene Fowley, Jr. ***Mus*** Hanns Eisler
Act Brian Donlevy, Walter Brennan, Anna Lee, Gene Lockhart, Dennis O'Keefe (United Artists)

From a directorial standpoint this is a triumph for Fritz Lang, who succeeds with singular success in capturing the spirit of the Czech people in the face of the Nazi reign of terror.

UA sunk plenty of coin into the picture. Cameraman James Wong Howe, in particular, turns in a magnificent job.

The cast, topped by Brian Donlevy and Walter Brennan, is uniformly splendid. The performances of Gene Lockhart, as a cowering Quisling Czech, and Alexander Granach, as a shrewd, calculating and ruthless inspector of the Gestapo, are particularly outstanding. Story continuity is fine and absorbing throughout, but essentially it's the incisive terms of the message propounded that sets *Hangmen* apart and points up the fact that propaganda can be art.

Saga of the courageous spirit of the Czechs starts with the assassination of Heydrich, the hangman, by an appointed member of the underground (Donlevy), but the plans for his escape go awry and, due to the stringent curfew laws, he is forced to spend the night at the home of a professor and his daughter. In order to save her father, who is held as hostage along with several hundred others until the assassin will be given up, she goes to the Gestapo to reveal his identity, but realizes that the spirit of the Czech people has made of him a symbol of freedom and that the underground will protect him at all costs.

Both Donlevy and Brennan, as the professor, are excellent, the latter emerging in the film a figure of heroic proportions.

1943: NOMINATION: Best Scoring of a Dramatic Picture, Sound

•

HANGOVER SQUARE

1945, 77 mins, US b/w

Dir John Brahm ***Prod*** Robert Bassler ***Scr*** Barre Lyndon ***Ph*** Joseph La Shelle ***Ed*** Harry Reynolds ***Mus*** Bernard Herrmann ***Art*** Lyle R. Wheeler, Maurice Ransford

Act Laird Cregar, Linda Darnell, George Sanders, Glenn Langan, Faye Marlowe, Alan Napier (20th Century-Fox)

Hangover Square is eerie murder melodrama of the London gaslight era—typical of Patrick Hamilton yarns, of which this is another. And it doesn't make any pretense at mystery. The madman-murderer is known from the first reel.

It is the story of a distinguished young composer-pianist with a Jekyll-Hyde personality. When he becomes overwrought, he's a madman—and his lustful forages are always accompanied by a loss of memory for the periods during which he is murder-bent.

Laird Cregar as the madman-murderer shows markedly the physical decline, through dieting, said to have been a factor in [the actor's] death.

Linda Darnell and George Sanders are co-stars, the former as the two-timing girl and Sanders as a Scotland Yard psychiatrist who provides the tell-tale clues responsible for the denouement.

Production is grade A, and so is the direction by John Brahm, with particular bows to the music score by Bernard Herrmann.

•

HANKY PANKY

1982, 105 mins, US Ⓥ ⦿ col

Dir Sidney Poitier ***Prod*** Martin Ransohoff ***Scr*** Henry Rosenbaum, David Taylor ***Ph*** Arthur Ornitz ***Ed*** Harry Keller ***Mus*** Tom Scott ***Art*** Ben Edwards

Act Gene Wilder, Gilda Radner, Kathleen Quinlan, Richard Widmark, Robert Prosky, Josef Sommer (Columbia)

Hanky Panky is a limp romantic suspense comedy which manages to be neither romantic, suspenseful nor funny. What with Gene Wilder as a hapless Chicago architect caught up in a string of extraordinary coincidences involving government agents, a secret tape, and a big scene taking place at the Grand Canyon, pic appears to be an attempt to duplicate the classy thrills of *North by Northwest*.

Tale opens moodily with an unexplained suicide and then picks up Wilder, whose short cab ride with frantic Kathleen Quinlan plunges him into a web of intrigue obliging him to endure suspicion by the police for murder, beatings by agent Richard Widmark, and an attempt to kill him by a helicopter out in the desert.

He's an innocent, of course, but once he latches onto Gilda Radner, sister of the guy who hanged himself in the opening scene, he's committed to seeing the escapade through.

Casting of Wilder and Radner strikes no sparks. Quinlan, a serious actress who deserves greater challenges than this, disappears in the early going.

•

HANNAH AND HER SISTERS

1986, 106 mins, US Ⓥ ⦿ col

Dir Woody Allen ***Prod*** Robert Greenhut ***Scr*** Woody Allen ***Ph*** Carlo Di Palma ***Ed*** Susan E. Morse ***Art*** Stuart Wurtzel

Act Woody Allen, Michael Caine, Mia Farrow, Carrie Fisher, Barbara Hershey, Dianne Wiest (Orion)

Hannah and Her Sisters is one of Woody Allen's great films. Indeed, he makes nary a misstep from beginning to end in charting the amorous affiliations of three sisters and their men over a two year period. Its structure is a successful mixture of outright comedy, rueful meditation and sexual complications.

Pic begins at a Thanksgiving dinner, and ends at one two years later, with most of the characters going through mate changes in the interim. Hannah, played by Mia Farrow, was formerly married to TV producer Woody Allen but is now happily wed to agent Michael Caine, who, in turn, secretely lusts for his wife's sexy sister, Barbara Hershey, the live-in mate of tormented painter Max von Sydow.

The third sister (Dianne Wiest) is by far the most neurotic of the bunch and, while waiting for her acting, singing or writing career to take off, runs a catering business with Carrie Fisher.

1986: Best Supp. Actor (Michael Caine), Supp. Actress (Dianne Wiest), Original Screenplay

NOMINATIONS: Best Picture, Director, Art Direction, Editing

•

HANNA'S WAR

1988, 158 mins, US Ⓥ ⦿ ▭ col

Dir Menahem Golan ***Prod*** Menahem Golan, Yoram Globus ***Scr*** Menahem Golan ***Ph*** Elemer Ragalyi ***Ed*** Alain Jakubowicz ***Mus*** Dov Seltzer ***Art*** Tividar Bertaian

Act Ellen Burstyn, Maruschka Detmers, Anthony Andrews, Donald Pleasence, David Warner, Vincenzo Ricotta (Cannon)

Hanna Senesh, a talented poet and a martyr who died in a Hungarian jail in 1944, before her 24th birthday, is a mythical figure in Israel, a symbol of gentle but determined heroism. In Menahem Golan's version, heroes and villains are easily distinguished, characters are respectfully observed and admired, or duly abhorred and discredited, and no time is spent dwelling on psychological niceties.

The straightforward script follows her steps from the point she decides, upon graduating high school, to part with her family and leave antisemitic Hungary to go to Palestine for a new start. While there, she is drafted by the British for a special operation behind German lines in Eastern Europe and after a brief Yugoslav interlude, she crosses the border back into Hungary.

The rest is dedicated to the time she spent in Hungarian jail, the tortures she suffered, and her execution by the Hungarians without a trial. Maruschka Detmers may not radiate the spiritual strength required by her role, but she is dedicated and often moving during the prison sequences.

Donald Pleasence and David Warner each notch another villain to their credit. Topbilled Ellen Burstyn has at most a supporting part as Hanna's mother, and Anthony Andrews is a bit top-heavy as the British instructor who leads the expedition. Lensed in Hungary and Israel.

•

HANNIBAL BROOKS

1969, 101 mins, UK col

Dir Michael Winner ***Prod*** Michael Winner ***Scr*** Dick Clement, Ian La Frenais ***Ph*** Robert Paynter ***Ed*** Peter Austen-Hunt, Lionel Selwyn ***Mus*** Francis Lai ***Art*** John Stoll

Act Oliver Reed, Michael J. Pollard, Karin Baal, Wolfgang Preiss, Helmut Lohner, James Donald (Scimitar)

A pleasant, tame tale [from a screen story by Michael Winner and Tom Wright] about a British prisoner (Oliver Reed), assigned to nursemaid an elephant in a Munich Zoo. From here, it is a short jump into attempted escapes, with the elephant in tow, across some mountain passes (à la Hannibal, hence the title) into Switzerland.

The humorous vein, which was evidently intended to be topmost throughout the film, gets sidetracked by the excursion into action and there isn't a laugh in the second half of the film.

The British actor, playing a kindly, animal-loving and, for most of the film, pacifistic soldier, carries the entire film on his admittedly broad shoulders but can't overcome the confused writing, or the even greater burden of a poor performance by costar Michael J. Pollard. The latter is simply dreadful as a cocky Yank prisoner.

Filmed almost entirely on location in Bavaria, the beautiful countryside is caught perfectly by Robert Paynter's color camera.

•

HANNIE CAULDER

1971, 85 mins, UK/US Ⓥ ⦿ ▭ col

Dir Burt Kennedy ***Prod*** Patrick Curtis ***Scr*** Z. X. Jones, [Burt Kennedy, David Haft] ***Ph*** Edward Scaife ***Ed*** Jim Connock ***Mus*** Ken Thorne ***Art*** Jose Alguero

Act Raquel Welch, Robert Culp, Ernest Borgnine, Strother Martin, Jack Elam, Diana Dors (Tigon/Curtwel)

Raquel Welch plays Hannie Caulder who, having been widowed and raped by the Clemens brothers, determines to avenge these wrongs. [Original story by Peter Cooper, based on characters created by Ian Quicke and Bob Richards.] With the aid of a bounty hunter she is soon showing that ladies shoot first and can be more deadly than the male.

The West may never have boasted so immaculate a markswoman but it seems highly unlikely that anyone is expected to take the film too seriously. Welch, with genteel modesty, makes the character for many rather ingratiating though others undoubtedly will find her plain ludicrous. All she has to wear after her farm has been set ablaze, while being raped by the drunken brothers, is a hastily grabbed poncho. The avoidance of more than quick glimpses of a shapely thigh seems her main concern.

She is admirably supported by Ernest Borgnine as the meanest of the brothers and Robert Culp as the bounty hunter who befriends her. Christopher Lee, after his usual horror roles, makes an unusual appearance as a sympathetic gunsmith.

•

HANOI HILTON

1987, 123 mins, US Ⓥ ⦿ col

Dir Lionel Chetwynd ***Prod*** Menahem Golan, Yoram Globus ***Scr*** Lionel Chetwynd ***Ph*** Mark Irwin ***Ed*** Penelope Shaw ***Mus*** Jimmy Webb ***Art*** R. Clifford Searcy

Act Michael Moriarty, Jeffrey Jones, Paul Le Mat, Stephen Davies, Lawrence Pressman, Aki Aleong (Cannon)

Hanoi Hilton is a lame attempt by writer-director Lionel Chetwynd to tell the story of U.S. prisoners in Hoa Lo Prison, in Hanoi, during the Vietnam War. Pic is a slanted view of traditional prison camp sagas, injecting lots of hindsight and taking right-wing potshots that do a disservice to the very human drama of the subject.

Michael Moriarty heads a curiously bland cast. He's thrust into a position of authority when the ranking officer played by Lawrence Pressman is taken off to be tortured. Episodic structure introduces new prisoners as more pilots are shot down over a roughly 10-year span (including some comic relief, such as one prisoner who says he fell off his ship accidentally and was captured). Pic is desperately lacking side issues or subplots of interest with Chetwynd monotonously hammering away at the main issue of survival in the face of inhuman treatment.

•

HANOVER STREET

1979, 109 mins, US Ⓥ ⦿ ▭ col

Dir Peter Hyams ***Prod*** Paul N. Lazarus III ***Scr*** Peter Hyams ***Ph*** David Watkin ***Ed*** James Mitchell ***Mus*** John Barry ***Art*** Philip Harrison

Act Harrison Ford, Lesley-Anne Down, Christopher Plummer, Alec McCowen, Richard Masur, Patsy Kensit (Columbia)

Hanover Street is reasonably effective as a war film with a love story background. Unfortunately, it's meant to be a love story set against a war background.

Drawing his inspiration from M-G-M's 1940 release, *Waterloo Bridge*, and other pix of that ilk, writer-director Peter Hyams has moved this tale of star-crossed lovers up to World War II England, where American flying ace David Halloran (Harrison Ford) and British hospital nurse Margaret Sellinger (Lesley-Anne Down) meet during an air raid and fall hopelessly in love.

Only when Down takes a back seat, and Ford is thrown together with her cuckolded husband, Paul, a British secret service topper (Christopher Plummer), does *Hanover Street* manifest any vital life signs. The last third of the picture becomes a model of efficient war filmmaking.

Down again distinguishes herself in a role that doesn't seem up to her standards, while Ford back in the pilot's seat again projects an earnest, if dull, presence. Rest of the cast is under-utilized. John Barry has contributed a score that evokes Douglas Sirk's glossy tearjerkers of the 1950s.

•

HANS CHRISTIAN ANDERSEN

1952, 112 mins, US Ⓥ ⦿ col

Dir Charles Vidor ***Prod*** Samuel Goldwyn ***Scr*** Moss Hart ***Ph*** Harry Stradling ***Ed*** Daniel Mandell ***Mus*** Walter Scharf (dir.) ***Art*** Richard Day, Antoni Clare

Act Danny Kaye, Farley Granger, Zizi Jeanmaire, Joey Walsh, Philip Tonge, Roland Petit (Goldwyn/RKO)

Hans Christian Andersen [based on a story by Myles Connolly] is a charming fairy tale about the Danish master of the childhood fantasy, done with the taste expected of a Samuel Goldwyn production.

Danny Kaye does a very fine job of the title role, sympathetically projecting the Andersen spirit and philosophy. No attempt at biography is made so the imaginative production has full rein in bringing in songs and ballet numbers to round out the Andersen fairy tales told by Kaye.

Socko is *The Little Mermaid* ballet, a spectacular display backed by the music of Franz Liszt, using six sets that range from a witch's underwater cave to a prince's castle. Roland Petit, who dances the prince in *Mermaid*, designed all the ballets.

On the song side, the picture has the topnotch talents of Frank Loesser contributing eight songs, all given first-rate vocal treatment by Kaye.

1952: NOMINATIONS: Best Color Cinematography, Color Costume Design, Color Art Direction, Scoring of a Musical Picture, Song ("Thumbelina")

•

HAPPENING, THE

1967, 101 mins, US col

Dir Elliot Silverstein *Prod* Jud Kinberg *Scr* Frank R. Pierson, James D. Buchanan, Ronald Austin *Ph* Philip Lathrop *Ed* Philip W. Anderson *Mus* Frank DeVol *Art* Richard Day

Act Anthony Quinn, George Maharis, Michael Parks, Robert Walker, Martha Hyer, Faye Dunaway (Columbia/Horizon)

Intriguing offbeat item, *The Happening* attempts to blend various elements of kick-happy teeny-boppers, melodrama, pop culture, suburban tragedy, suspense, "in" gags, "black humor," Keystone Kops, "beach party" pix, and alienation in the affluent society in a comedic potpourri, which, between expected laughs, seeks to offer satiric peeks at U.S. life and values.

Well-tempered plotline [by James D. Buchanan and Ronald Austin], with several corkscrew twists, follows the weekend hegira of four ennui-laden but debauched Miami beachbums in search of some potent stimuli. They find it, albeit accidentally, by stumbling into an unlikely kidnapping. What is bothersome about this tragi-farce is why it doesn't succeed, with all of the above and generally capable performers going for it.

George Maharis, playing a bull without horns, is spotty but fine, alternating swagger with weakness in his impersonation of a gigolo, while Michael Parks is less convincing but appropriately faceless as a blank-faced rich kid. Newcomer Faye Dunaway, though stunning to view and essaying her role with elan, is too womanly seductive for a teenybopper role.

•

HAPPIEST DAYS OF YOUR LIFE, THE

1950, 81 mins, UK b/w

Dir Frank Launder *Prod* Frank Launder, Sidney Gilliat *Scr* Frank Launder, John Dighton *Ph* Stan Pavey *Ed* Oswald Hafenrichter *Mus* Mischa Spoliansky *Art* Josef Bato

Act Alastair Sim, Margaret Rutherford, Guy Middleton, Joyce Grenfell, Richard Wattis, Edward Rigby, Muriel Aked (London)

Bright script and brisk direction conceal the stage origin [from the play by John Dighton]. The story is given a wider canvas and isn't wanting in action. In fact, the pace never lets up and one hilarious farcical incident only ends to give place to another.

Setting of the film is a college for boys, to which, as a result of a slip at the Ministry of Education, a girl's school is evacuated. The story builds up to a boisterous climax in which the principals are trying to conceal the real situation from visitors to the college.

There is no shortage of laughs, but the joke is a little too protracted and wears thin before the end. It's an ideal vehicle for Alastair Sim as the harassed headmaster, while Margaret Rutherford admirably suggests the overpowering headmistress.

•

HAPPIEST MILLIONAIRE, THE

1967, 164 mins, US Ⓥ col

Dir Norman Tokar *Prod* Bill Anderson (co-prod.) *Scr* A. J. Carothers *Ph* Edward Colman *Ed* Cotton Warburton *Mus* Jack Elliott (arr.) *Art* Carroll Clark, John B. Mansbridge

Act Fred MacMurray, Tommy Steele, Greer Garson, Geraldine Page, Gladys Cooper, Hermione Baddeley (Walt Disney)

The Happiest Millionaire, last major live-action production of Walt Disney, is a family comedy, blending creative and technical elements, scripting, excellent casting, direction, scoring, choreography and handsome, plush production.

Fred MacMurray heads the cast, which includes Britain's Tommy Steele in his U.S. film debut as an Irish servant in 1916 Philadelphia. [Pic is from the play by Kyle Crichton, suggested by a book by Cordelia Drexel Biddle and Kyle Crichton.]

MacMurray, snug in an excellent characterization, is well teamed with Greer Garson as the Philadelphia parents. Lesley Ann Warren, introduced herein, plays the teenage daughter with charm and radiance.

1967: NOMINATION: Best Costume Design

•

HAPPINESS

1998, 139 mins, US Ⓥ ⊙ col

Dir Todd Solondz *Prod* Ted Hope, Christine Vachon *Scr* Todd Solondz *Ph* Maryse Alberti *Ed* Alan Oxman *Mus* Robbie Kondor *Art* Therese Deprez

Act Jane Adams, Dylan Baker, Lara Flynn Boyle, Ben Gazzara, Philip Seymour Hoffman, Cynthia Stevenson (Good Machine/Killer)

Todd Solondz's *Happiness* is a disturbing black comedy that, at bottom, is about all the trouble sex causes people. Skillfully made but overlong pic sees the writer-director flexing his ambition considerably beyond that of his second feature, *Welcome to the Dollhouse*, and successfully sustaining a tricky tone of low-key morbid humor most of the way. But some of the subject matter, including upfront treatment of prepubescent sexual curiosity and pedophilia, will raise hackles in numerous quarters.

Joy (Jane Adams) is the non-achiever among three middle-class New Jersey sisters. Trish (Cynthia Stevenson)is a perennially perky housewife with three-kids and an ultra-straight husband, Bill (Dylan Baker), a suburban shrink who counts among his patients the overweight, sexually frustrated loner Allen (Philip Seymour Hoffman).

Allen is obsessed with his next-door neighbor, the glamorous, sexually omnivorous, fabulously successful author Helen (Lara Flynn Boyle), the third Jordan sister, who doesn't give him the time of day.

That all is not right with Bill becomes clear when he fantasizes mowing down families in a park with an assault rifle, then masturbates to pictures in a teen magazine. At home, Bill honestly addresses the sexual anxieties of his 11-year-old son, Billy (Rufus Read). Shortly thereafter, Bill develops a genuinely abnormal fascination with one of his son's classmates, Johnny (Evan Silverberg). Backgrounding these lurid shenanigans is the marriage breakdown of the sisters' parents (Ben Gazzara, Louise Lasser) after 40 years.

Despite the warped nature of much of the action, nothing comes close to the hushed and shocking climax, a stunningly frank exchange between Bill and little Billy in which the father reveals the full extent of his deviance.

Pic feels a bit indulgent and overextended. Nonetheless, director's control over his material is inarguable and extends uniformly over to his actors. Maryse Alberti's cinematography maintains a cool elegance.

•

HAPPY

1934, 80 mins, UK b/w

Dir Fred Zelnik *Scr* Austin Melford, Stanley Lupino, Frank Launder, Jaques Bachrach, Alfred Halm, Karl Noti *Ph* Claude Friese-Greene *Ed* A. S. Bates *Mus* Fred Schwarz *Art* Clarence Elder

Act Stanley Lupino, Laddie Cliff, Will Fyffe, Renee Gadd, Dorothy Hyson, Gus McNaughton (British International)

Stanley Lupino, Laddie Cliff and Will Fyffe are a splendid trio of comedians. They provide the comedy for this musical melange, which has neither measurement length nor breadth. It is formless, but who cares, it provides entertainment.

There is the usual Bohemian atmosphere. Lupino and Cliff, two musicians, reside in an attic, with Fyffe as the landlord. Lupino is working on an invention, a device which, if attached to a motorcar which is stolen, will automatically yell for the police.

The millionaire president of an insurance company is gnashing his teeth, owing to numerous car thefts. He has a beautiful daughter who visits a cafe where Lupino is directing the band and Laddie is the pianist. They fall in love. He is too manly to marry a rich girl, but she will marry him anyway.

•

HAPPY BIRTHDAY, WANDA JUNE

1971, 105 mins, US col

Dir Mark Robson *Prod* Lester Goldsmith *Scr* Kurt Vonnegut, Jr. *Ph* Fred Koenekamp *Ed* Dorothy Spencer *Art* Boris Leven

Act Rod Steiger, Susannah York, George Grizzard, Don Murray, William Hickey, Steven Paul (Filmakers/Sourdough/Red Lions)

Imagine Ulysses's long voyage home with nothing on board to read but the collected writings of Ernest Hemingway. That must have been in the mind of novelist turned playwright turned screenwriter Kurt Vonnegut, Jr. when he dreamed up the hero for *Happy Birthday, Wanda June*.

Rod Steiger shines as the self-deceiving ultra-masculine hero, returned from eight years in the Amazon jungle, to find that not only has his loving wife, a former pinheaded carhop (played brilliantly by Susannah York), become a levelheaded intellectual equal but has gone to his extreme opposite in seeking another soul mate.

She's trying to decide between a violin-playing doctor and practicing pacifist (George Grizzard) and a clumsy, eager vacuum-cleaner salesman (Don Murray). Only his son remembers him (resenting the non-observance of his supposedly dead father's birthday as a major catastrophe).

The treatment is too irreverent to be taken seriously for a moment, including Vonnegut's preachments.

•

HAPPY ENDING, THE

1969, 117 mins, US Ⓥ ▭ col

Dir Richard Brooks *Prod* Richard Brooks *Scr* Richard Brooks *Ph* Conrad Hall *Ed* George Grenville *Mus* Michel Legrand

Act Jean Simmons, John Forsythe, Lloyd Bridges, Teresa Wright, Dick Shawn, Nanette Fabray (United Artists/Pax-Films)

The American Dream, the affluent upper middleclass marriage, is a conjugal bed of nails peopled by bored-to-tears alcoholic wives and hard working, but less than faithful hubbies, according to producer-director-writer Richard Brooks. A well developed and acted and potentially significant "woman's movie" unfortunately drowns in Brooks' over indulgences and over-writing.

As Mrs. America, class of '53, Jean Simmons fortifies herself with vodka and tranquilizers for her 16th wedding anniversary with tax lawyer John Forsythe.

As the still attractive but anxiously middle-aged and self-pitying matron who is financially secure but personally bankrupted, Simmons gives a moving, emotionally wringing performance. Forsythe has the patience of Job with his spoiled, high-strung wife. His is a basically dull, one-dimensional role.

1969: NOMINATIONS: Best Actress (Jean Simmons), Song ("What Are You Doing the Rest of Your Life")

•

HAPPY GO LUCKY

1943, 79 mins, US col

Dir Curtis Bernhardt *Prod* Harold Wilson *Scr* Walter DeLeon, Norman Panama *Ph* Karl Struss, Wilfred Kline *Ed* Ellsworth Hoagland *Mus* Frank Leesser, Jimmy McHugh

Act Mary Martin, Dick Powell, Eddie Bracken, Betty Hutton, Rudy Vallee, Mabel Paige (Paramount)

Par locales the film on a nameless Caribbean isle which can be identified as Trinidad, inasmuch as it boasts Calypso singers. Mary Martin, playing an ex-hatcheck gal at the Rainbow Room, NY, arrives on the isle with a small b.r. amassed for the purpose of allowing her to act the wealthy lady and catch a wealthy husband in the process.

Plot [adapted by John Jacoby from a story by Michael Uris] is no heavyweight affair, but provides all that is necessary for a musical of this type. It keeps things moving at a fast pace and offers the chandelier on which the tunes can be hung. Martin capably handles the ballad department, with an occasional assist from Dick Powell, while Betty Hutton, of course, is hot on the jive. They divide up six numbers by Frank Loesser and Jimmy McHugh.

•

HAPPY LAND

1943, 75 mins, US b/w

Dir Irving Pichel *Prod* Kenneth Macgowan *Scr* Kathryn Scola, Julian Josephson *Ph* Joseph La Shelle *Ed* Dorothy Spencer *Mus* Emil Newman

Act Don Ameche, Frances Dee, Harry Carey, Ann Rutherford, Richard Crane, Henry Morgan (20th Century-Fox)

MacKinlay Kantor's novel which appeared in serial form in the *Saturday Evening Post* and *Reader's Digest*, has been turned into a strong tearjerker mainly through the keen production given by Kenneth Macgowan and directorial skill of Irving Pichel. Combined efforts of this pair, plus a trim writing job, set off a string of performances topped by Don Ameche, Frances Dee, Harry Carey and Richard Crane.

Happy Land is the story of a typical Iowa country town and a typical family (the Marshes), their joys, disappointments and sorrows. Plot has drugstore operator Ameche bereaved over the loss of his son, killed in naval action. Return of Gramp, his father, dead for some 25 years, in the form of an apparition, is the device used to unfold the principal story up until Richard Crane is killed in service. Explanation of the visionary appearance is that Gramp has returned to set Ameche right, since the grief-stricken father claims that Crane never really lived—never had a home of his own, had not married, etc. Flashback method then traces the life of the youngster from birth.

•

HAPPY NEW YEAR

1987, 85 mins, US Ⓥ col

Dir John G. Avildsen *Prod* Jerry Weintraub *Scr* Warren Lane [= Nancy Dowd] *Ph* James Crabe *Ed* Jane Kurson *Mus* Bill Conti *Art* William J. Cassidy

Act Peter Falk, Charles Durning, Wendy Hughes, Tom Courtenay, Joan Copeland, Tracy Brooks Swope (Columbia/Delphi IV)

Crime pays off in this unpretentious buddy picture about two middle-aged jewel thieves going for the big score in Palm Beach [based on Claude Lelouch's 1973 film *La bonne année*]. Topliners Peter Falk and Charles Durning team with an easygoing charm.

Film is funniest and most engrossing in the first hour or so when Falk and Durning are casing the Palm Beach branch of Harry Winston, jewelers. This leads to a series of amusing encounters with the fey and smarmy jewelry store manager Edward Sanders (expertly rendered by Tom Courtenay), who from Falk's hardboiled honor-among-thieves perspective is a soulless money-grubber deserving the worst.

Along the way Falk meets and falls for a beautiful, high-toned antiques dealer, Carolyn Benedict (Wendy Hughes), who moves in a circle of insufferably smug and wealthy pseudo-sophisticates.

Although the film sags towards its resolution, director John G. Avildsen handles the story with a light touch, including a gentle soundtrack of pre-rock 'n' roll standards that would be at home in a Woody Allen film, and a cameo by Lelouch, who directed the original French film.

1987: NOMINATION: Best Makeup

•

HARAKIRI
SEE: SEPPUKU

•

HARD CONTRACT
1969, 106 mins, US ▭ col
Dir S. Lee Pogostin ***Prod*** Marvin Schwartz ***Scr*** S. Lee Pogostin ***Ph*** Jack Hildyard ***Ed*** Harry Gerstad ***Mus*** Alex North ***Art*** Ed Graves
Act James Coburn, Lee Remick, Lilli Palmer, Burgess Meredith, Patrick Magee, Sterling Hayden (20th Century-Fox)

The principle of the loner, the individual in the jungle of society, the solitary predator, is emphatically portrayed in this skillfully-mounted film about the killer-for-hire who agrees to a hard contract to eliminate three men in Europe.

James Coburn, as Cunningham, accepts the deal dished out by Burgess Meredith. Leaving the U.S. for Torremelinos, he meets the self-indulgent jet set quartet who bloom in the Spanish sun.

Leader of the group is Lee Remick, who finds herself in love with Coburn but not his profession.

Scenery of Spain and Belgium is in sharp focus, which isn't always true of story. A shift of values has been initiated, but no one has raised a signpost to tell where we're going.

Coburn and Remick, effective in their roles, allow characters to develop naturally.

•

HARDCORE
(UK: THE HARDCORE LIFE)
1979, 105 mins, US Ⓥ ⦿ col
Dir Paul Schrader ***Prod*** Buzz Feitshans ***Scr*** Paul Schrader ***Ph*** Michael Chapman ***Ed*** Tom Rolf ***Mus*** Jack Nitzsche ***Art*** Paul Sylbert
Act George C. Scott, Peter Boyle, Season Hubley, Dick Sargent, Leonard Gaines, David Nichols (Columbia/A-Team)

George C. Scott, gives as fine a performance as he's ever done.

An unventuring Calvinist, Scott lives a contented small-town Michigan life until his daughter, Ilah Davis, disappears on a trip to L.A. He hires seedy private-eye Peter Boyle who eventually finds her on film in a porno movie. Forced to watch, Scott's anguish at the sight bespeaks a clash of values still haunting the country.

For many, this will be the first up-close look at the world including nude-conversation encounters, massage parlors, bondage joints and the lowest degradation—"snuff" films.

The easily shocked may want an exposé, or more of a condemnation. The more sophisticated may grow tired of Scott's morality. But shocked, cynical or dissatisfied, nobody's going to be bored.

•

HARDCORE LIFE, THE
SEE: HARDCORE

•

HARD DAY'S NIGHT, A
1964, 83 mins, UK Ⓥ ⦿ b/w
Dir Richard Lester ***Prod*** Walter Shenson ***Scr*** Alun Owen ***Ph*** Gilbert Taylor ***Ed*** John Jympson ***Mus*** George Martin (dir.) ***Art*** Ray Simm
Act John Lennon, Paul McCartney, George Harrison, Ringo Starr, Wilfrid Brambell, Norman Rossington (United Artists)

A Hard Day's Night is a wacky, offbeat piece of filming, charged with vitality and inventiveness by director Dick Lester, slickly lensed and put over at a fair lick. No attempt has been paid to build the Beatles up as Oliviers; they are at their best when the pic has a misleading air of off-the-cuff spontaneity.

Running at 83 minutes, in black and white, it keeps Beatles within their ability. Alun Owen's screenplay merely attempts to portray an exaggerated 36 hours in the lives of the Beatles. But, though exaggerated, the thin story line gives a shrewd idea of the pressure and difficulties under which they work and live.

Four set off by train to keep a live television date and, before taking off by helicopter for their next stint, they have some rum adventures. A skirmish with the police, mobbing by hysterical fans, then a press conference, riotous moments in a tavern, a jazz cellar, a gambling club and TV rehearsals all work into the crazy tapestry and offer the Beatles a chance to display their sense of humor and approach to life.

To give the almost documentary storyline a boost, scriptwriter Owen has introduced Paul's grandfather, a mischief-making mixer with an eye on the main chance. Played by Wilfrid Brambell with sharp perception, his presence is a great buffer for the boys' throwaway sense of comedy.

[In 1982, pic was reissued with an extra song, "I'll Cry Instead," added at the start, and all other songs remixed in stereo.]

1964: NOMINATIONS: Best Story & Screenplay, Adapted Music Score

•

HARDER THEY FALL, THE
1956, 109 mins, US Ⓥ b/w
Dir Mark Robson ***Prod*** Philip Yordan ***Scr*** Philip Yordan ***Ph*** Burnett Guffey ***Ed*** Jerome Thoms ***Mus*** Hugo Friedhofer ***Art*** William Flannery
Act Humphrey Bogart, Rod Steiger, Jan Sterling, Mike Lane, Max Baer, Edward Andrews (Columbia)

Budd Schulberg's vehement novel about the fight racket is given a strong pictorial going-over in *The Harder They Fall*. It's main-event stuff.

The vicious racket within, the promoters and managers who exploit the pugs, tank divers on the take, the press agent who builds the hoax about the phoney ring sensation—they're under scrutiny.

Story concerns a ruthless manager-gambler who imports a behemoth from South America, discovers he's a pugilistic cream puff, but gives him the buildup via fixed fights across the country. Humphrey Bogart is the newspaper man who goes ethically awry when his paper folds. He's glib and persuasive in promoting the boxer, and finally reveals his courage when he breaks with the racket.

Rod Steiger rates hefty mitting as the crooked dealer in ring flesh. Jersey Joe Walcott is surprisingly effective in acting the part of a warm-hearted trainer. Jan Sterling fits in well as Bogart's wife; Mike Lane works well in striking a sympathetic chord as the musclebound captive of Steiger's who's too dumb to know his opponents are paid to fall.

1956: NOMINATION: Best B&W Cinematography

•

HARD, FAST AND BEAUTIFUL
1951, 76 mins, US b/w
Dir Ida Lupino ***Prod*** Collier Young ***Scr*** Martha Wilkerson ***Ph*** Archie Stout ***Ed*** George O. Shrader, William Ziegler ***Mus*** Roy Webb ***Art*** Albert S. D'Agostino, Jack Okey
Act Claire Trevor, Sally Forrest, Carleton Young, Robert Clarke, Kenneth Patterson, Marcella Cisney (Filmakers)

A product of the indie Filmakers unit headed by Ida Lupino and Collier Young, film is an entertaining study of selfish mother love and amateur tennis.

Exposé of "expense" money and other coin-getting channels available to top amateur racket-wielders is not worked too hard. Emphasis is on "mom-ism" and this story line is well exploited, without being overdone, in the top-notch script and through the authority and punch of Lupino's direction.

Claire Trevor socks over her character as the selfish mother of Sally Forrest. Forrest is strong as a promising tennis player whose mother pushes and shoves her into the championship in order to ride along and soak up some of the fame and glamour that goes with the top tennis brackets.

Tennis court footage is expertly interlaced with the story and, creditably, camera angles on the play are smartly set up and there is a minimum use of shots showing head-swinging spectators.

•

HARD TARGET
1993, 94 mins, US Ⓥ ⦿ col
Dir John Woo ***Prod*** James Jacks, Sean Daniel ***Scr*** Chuck Pfarrer ***Ph*** Russell Carpenter ***Ed*** Bob Murawski ***Mus*** Graeme Revell ***Art*** Phil Dagort
Act Jean-Claude Van Damme, Lance Henriksen, Arnold Vosloo, Yancy Butler, Kasi Lemmons, Wilford Brimley (Alphaville/Renaissance/Universal)

John Woo, cult director of the new Hong Kong Cinema, makes his eagerly awaited American debut with *Hard Target*, a briskly vigorous, occasionally brilliant actioner starring Jean-Claude Van Damme. However, hampered by a B script with flat, standard characters, and subjected to repeated editing of the violent sequences to win an R rating, pic doesn't bear the unique vision on display in Woo's *The Killer* and *Hard-Boiled*.

Chuck Pfarrer, who also co-produced and plays a small role, fashions his script as a variation of *The Most Dangerous Game*. With locale switched from a remote island to urban New Orleans, tale centers on a sadistic band of hunters, headed by amoral chief Fouchon (Lance Henriksen) and his deputy, Van Cleaf (Arnold Vosloo), who operate a profitable "safari game" in which the prey are homeless combat veterans.

Van Damme plays Chance Boudreaux, a down-on-his-luck merchant sailor, who comes to the rescue of Natasha Binder (Yancy Butler), a young woman searching for her missing father, the latest victim.

Ultimately, *Hard Target* is a compromised work, a stylistic hybrid of American and Hong Kong action pics. But Woo's distinctiveness is still in evidence. He is a virtuoso at staging and editing intricate set pieces with precision, visual inventiveness and humor. The pacing, in fact, is so fast that Woo manages to cover Van Damme's usual inexpressiveness.

•

HARD TIMES
(UK: THE STREETFIGHTER)
1975, 92 mins, US Ⓥ ⦿ ▭ col
Dir Walter Hill ***Prod*** Lawrence Gordon ***Scr*** Walter Hill, Bryan Gindorff, Bruce Hentsell ***Ph*** Philip Lathrop ***Ed*** Roger Spottiswoode ***Mus*** Barry De Vorzon ***Art*** Trevor Williams
Act Charles Bronson, James Coburn, Jill Ireland, Strother Martin, Maggie Blye, Michael McGuire (Columbia)

Hard Times stars Charles Bronson as a mysterious stranger whose fists make money for him and small-time gambler James Coburn in illegal slugging matches.

Coburn's character lacks substance; he's a likeable heel one minute, an unlikeable one the next. At fadeout, after Bronson has fought one last fight to save Coburn's hide, Bronson meanders out of the film.

Jill Ireland is excellent in a touching performance as a down-and-out girl who has a brief affair with Bronson. Strother Martin is also excellent as a dope addict and unlicensed medic who works with Coburn.

Michael McGuire is strong as a bigtime gambler.

The production has a very handsome mid-1930s New Orleans period flavour but the cast can't lick the script.

•

HARD TO HANDLE
1933, 71 mins, US b/w
Dir Mervyn LeRoy ***Prod*** Robert Lord ***Scr*** Wilson Mizner, Robert Lord ***Ph*** Barney McGill ***Ed*** William Holmes ***Mus*** Leo Forbstein (dir.) ***Art*** Robert M. Haas
Act James Cagney, Mary Brian, Ruth Donnelly, Allen Jenkins, Claire Dodd, Gavin Gordon (Warner)

Plot [from a story by Houston Branch] trips a light fantastic over a series of gags and the gags account for most of the merit. Between the good ones, the yarn rushes James Cagney through some far-fetched situations.

As a sort of safety net to catch any laughs the star might miss, story includes a comedy mother-in-law, played by Ruth Donnelly. For the first half-hour or so Donnelly runs away with the picture, after which the role is softened up by repetition.

Cagney is a press agent in this one, beginning with a dance marathon, and then starting from scratch all over again when his partner kidnaps the gross. That happens in California. When reaching New York, Cagney high-pressures his way into the money, putting over a college, a reducing cream and Florida grapefruit farmland among other projects. Stage-mother stuff sustains the romance background while Cagney is space grabbing on the side.

While his material isn't up to average, Cagney's playing is as usual and as effective in its way as always.

•

HARD TO KILL

1990, 95 mins, US Ⓥ ⦿ col

Dir Bruce Malmuth ***Prod*** Gary Adelson, Joel Simon, Bill Todmore, Jr. ***Scr*** Steven McKay ***Ph*** Matthew F. Leonetti ***Ed*** John F. Link ***Mus*** David Michael Frank ***Art*** Robb Wilson King

Act Steven Seagal, Kelly Le Brock, Bill Sadler, Frederick Coffin, Bonnie Burroughs, Branscombe Richmond (Warner)

The threadbare screenplay, which went into production as *Seven Year Storm*, uses a Rip van Winkle gimmick. As Mason Storm, cop Steven Seagal is nearly killed in the first reel after shooting surveillance film of corrupt politico Bill Sadler. His wife (Bonnie Burroughs) is murdered by Sadler's minions.

Cop buddy Frederick Coffin recognizes the danger and hides evidence of Seagal's last-minute recovery. Seven years later, under the tutelage of impossibly beautiful nurse (and real-life wife) Kelly Le Brock, Seagal comes out of his coma (sporting a laughable phony beard), uses Oriental methods of recovery and plots his revenge.

Sluggish direction by Bruce Malmuth doesn't help, but whenever Seagal is allowed to whip into action the film is a crowdpleaser. Unlike other loner prototypes, he goes beyond merely ruthless into the realm of sadistic, breaking opponents' limbs just for starters (as in a memorable fight here with latino heavy Branscombe Richmond). It ain't pretty, but it gets the action fans off.

•

HARDWARE

1990, 92 mins, UK/US Ⓥ ⦿ col

Dir Richard Stanley ***Prod*** Joanne Sellar, Paul Trybits ***Scr*** Richard Stanley ***Ph*** Steven Chivers ***Ed*** Derek Trigg ***Mus*** Simon Boswell ***Art*** Joseph Bennett

Act Dylan McDermott, Stacey Travis, John Lynch, William Hootkins, Iggy Pop, Mark Northover (Palace/Millimeter/Wicked)

A cacophonic, nightmarish variation on the postapocalyptic cautionary genre, *Hardware* has the makings of a punk cult film.

After the nuclear holocaust, vast reaches of incinerated North America have been reduced to an infrared desert ravaged by guerrilla warfare and littered with cybernetic scrapheaps. Moses (Dylan McDermott) and Shades (John Lynch) are "zone tripper" soldiers of fortune who scavenge the corpse-strewn, irradiated wasteland for techno-detritus to black market in the big city.

Moses, wasting away from radiation cancer, wants to return to his woman, Julie (Stacey Travis). She's a fiercely cynical techno-alchemist, fond of smoking packaged dope, who keeps a fortress workshop in a blasted downtown apartment block. Reunited in a frenzied sexual collision of pulse-pounding eroticism, the couple ponder their outer-limits relationship of love in the ruins.

Hardware veers loonily out of control and becomes a black comic exercise in *F/X* tour-deforce that's ceaselessly pushing itself over the top.

•

HARD WAY, THE

1991, 111 mins, US Ⓥ ⦿ col

Dir John Badham ***Prod*** William Sackheim, Rob Cohen, Peter R. McIntosh ***Scr*** Daniel Pyne, Lem Dobbs ***Ph*** Don McAlpine, Robert Primes ***Ed*** Frank Morriss, Tony Lombardo ***Mus*** Arthur B. Rubinstein ***Art*** Philip Harrison

Act Michael J. Fox, James Woods, Stephen Lang, Annabella Sciorra, LL Cool J, Penny Marshall (Universal/Badham-Cohen)

Too bad there's more method in the acting than the script, as John Badham's tired action-comedy formula squanders its best moments during the film's first act and wastes the nifty pairing of James Woods and Michael J. Fox.

Fox is a popular star of action fluff, like *Smoking Gunn II*, who yearns for a leading role in a film "without a Roman numeral in it." Determined to play a tough street cop, he decides to research the role by partnering New York cop John Moss (Woods), who's involved in hunting a lunatic serial killer (Stephen Lang).

The film exhausts its best Hollywood in-jokes during the first 20 minutes, with a Penny Marshall cameo as Fox's agent and lots of lines about cappuccino, personal trainers and Mel Gibson.

After the initial meeting of Fox and Woods, however, the pic degenerates into a series of random melees that will bring the buddies together—and introduce a stale subplot that has the actor helping Moss woo his sort-of girlfriend (Annabella Sciorra) as an added bonus.

Woods is appropriately gruff and nasty as the cop, and his trademark intensity makes a broad target for Fox to play off.

•

HAREM

1985, 113 mins, France Ⓥ ⦿ ▭ col

Dir Arthur Joffe ***Prod*** Alain Sarde ***Scr*** Arthur Joffe, Tom Rayfiel, Richard Prieur ***Ph*** Pasqualino De Santis ***Ed*** Francoise Bonnot, Ruggero Mastroianni ***Mus*** Philippe Sarde ***Art*** Alexandre Trauner

Act Nastassja Kinski, Ben Kingsley, Dennis Goldson, Zohra Segal, Michel Robin, Juliette Simpson (Sara)

Harem is an album of gorgeous images, aligned to tell a story, but it's a poor excuse for a dramatic motion picture packaged for the international marketplace.

Despite an investment of $10 million, which afforded stars Ben Kingsley and Nastassja Kinski, producer has skimped on the essential screenwriter. Instead, he has disastrously allowed director Arthur Joffe, obviously not yet at ease with an elaborate full-length narrative, to develop his own original story idea.

Tale concerns a fabulously wealthy Arab prince who kidnaps a beautiful young New York girl and has her brought to his desert palace, where she joins his harem.

As played by Kingsley, the unscrupulous potentate turns out to be a hypersentive aesthete, trapped by tradition to maintain, for appearances' sake at least, a way of life he doesn't believe in. The film is visually ravishing, often happily distracting the viewer from the emptiness of the script and the exasperating indigence of the main characters.

•

HARLAN COUNTY, U.S.A.

1976, 103 mins, US Ⓥ col

Dir Barbara Kopple ***Prod*** Barbara Kopple ***Scr*** Barbara Kopple ***Ph*** Hart Perry, Kevin Keating, Phil Parmet, Flip McCarthy, Tom Hurwitz ***Ed*** Nancy Baker, Mary Lampson, Lora Hays, Mirra Bank ***Mus*** Merle Travis, David Morris, Nimrod Workman, Sarah Gunning, Hazel Dickens, Phyllis Boyens (Cabin Creek)

Harlan County, U.S.A. is in essence a straightforward cinema verite documentary about a coal miners' strike in Kentucky. Director Barbara Kopple began the project in 1972 in Kentucky and was on hand to record the year-plus battle of coal miners at the Brookside Mine in Harlan to join the United Mine Workers.

There is much emphasis on the predictable elements which give the pic the impact of a carefully plotted fiction feature.

Actual strike events are fleshed out with vintage film and stills of mining conditions over the years, of previous labor battles and of current living (and dying) conditions in the industry.

The stars of the film are the men and women of Harlan County, portrayed here not as patronized mountain folks but as human beings.

1976: Best Feature Documentary

•

HARLEM NIGHTS

1989, 118 mins, US Ⓥ ⦿ col

Dir Eddie Murphy ***Prod*** Robert D. Wachs, Mark Lipsky ***Scr*** Eddie Murphy ***Ph*** Woody Omens ***Ed*** George Bowers ***Mus*** Herbie Hancock ***Art*** Lawrence G. Paull

Act Eddie Murphy, Richard Pryor, Redd Foxx, Danny Aiello, Michael Lerner, Della Reese (Murphy)

This blatantly excessive directorial debut for Eddie Murphy is overdone, too rarely funny and, worst of all, boring.

The film features Richard Pryor as the sage Sugar Ray to Murphy's hot-tempered Quick, who risk losing their 1930s Harlem nightclub when a corpulent crime boss (Michael Lerner) sets his sights on it.

The pair hatches up a predictable scheme to turn the tables on the mobster, whose henchmen include a cold-hearted mistress (Jasmine Guy) and a crooked cop (Danny Aiello).

There's an obnoxious cameo by Murphy's chum Arsenio Hall that proves pointless and unnecessary, as well as a mean-spirited recurring gag involving the stuttering heavyweight champ (Stan Shaw).

But the film does have its moments, such as when Murphy dukes it out with Reese's growling club madam or beds the carnivorous Dominque (Guy).

1989: NOMINATION: Best Costume Design

•

HARLEY DAVIDSON AND THE MARLBORO MAN

1991, 93 mins, US Ⓥ ⦿ col

Dir Simon Wincer ***Prod*** Jere Henshaw ***Scr*** Don Michael Paul ***Ph*** David Eggby ***Ed*** Corky Ehlers ***Mus*** Basil Poledouris ***Art*** Paul Peters

Act Mickey Rourke, Don Johnson, Chelsea Field, Daniel Baldwin, Tom Sizemore, Vanessa Williams (M-G-M/Krisjair-Laredo)

A dopey, almost poignantly bad actioner about two legends-in-their-own-minds, who bungle their way through a bank robbery on behalf of a friend, stands out only for big stars Mickey Rourke and Don Johnson.

Set in the wild west of Burbank, Calif, in 1996, when gasoline has gone up to $3.50 a gallon and people are getting high on something called Crystal Drano—er, Crystal Dream—*Harley* has two rebellious drifters (Rourke and Johnson) blowing into town to check on an old friend who's in trouble because a bank wants to foreclose on his business, their old hangout, the Rock 'n' Roll Bar & Grill. The big-hearted boys go into action to rob the bank, but their stunt eventually winds up getting all their buddies killed.

Pic scores mainly in the second unit and stunt department, with hotly staged bike chases and an abundance of breaking glass, falling bodies and shoot-outs. The production design is an asset.

•

HARLOW

1965, 107 mins, US Ⓥ b/w

Dir Alex Segal ***Prod*** Lee Savin ***Scr*** Karl Tunberg ***Ph*** Jim Kilgore ***Mus*** Al Ham, Nelson Riddle ***Art*** Duncan Cramer

Act Carol Lynley, Efrem Zimbalist, Jr., Ginger Rogers, Barry Sullivan, Hurd Hatfield, Celia Lovsky (Sargent)

This first-to-market biopic, lensed in the quick-filming Electronovision process, is peopled with a set of characters not altogether convincing and even the star part making small impression. Carol Lynley, as the tragic, platinum-tressed queen of the 1930s, who was a sex symbol of her time, tries valiantly but the outcome is not altogether a triumph.

The script follows the major points of the Harlow tradition although dramatic licenses are taken. The Paul Bern incident figures prominently, a dramatic hook utilized to mold the entire later character of the star.

Hurd Hatfield in the role of the producer-writer who weds the sexy blonde and then commits suicide when he discovers he's impotent, delivers a sincere performance. Celia Lovsky's is another honestly offered delineation, as Maria Ouspenskaya, the veteran actress to whom Jean goes for dramatic instruction after she temporarily deserts her film career.

Technically, this third Electronovision production—preceded by *Hamlet* and *The TAMI Story*—and first to be shot under controlled conditions on a soundstage, still presents many problems. Photography continues to be a major difficulty, grainy and of general poor quality, and bad lighting heightens the effect of old-fashioned production. Filmed in eight days in the TV-type lensing process, picture very often looks it as action sketches the rise of the star until her untimely death while still a young woman. Alex Segal's direction is as good as the script and fast-filming process will permit.

•

HARLOW

1965, 125 mins, US Ⓥ ▭ col

Dir Gordon Douglas ***Prod*** Joseph E. Levine ***Scr*** John Michael Hayes ***Ph*** Joseph Ruttenberg ***Ed*** Frank Bracht, Archie Marshek ***Mus*** Neal Hefti ***Art*** Hal Pereira, Roland Anderson

Act Carroll Baker, Martin Balsam, Red Buttons, Michael Connors, Angela Lansbury, Peter Lawford (Paramount/Levine)

Second biopic of Jean Harlow is handsomely mounted. As the ill-fated Jean Harlow, Carroll Baker is a fairly reasonable facsimile although she lacks the electric fire of the original.

Script by John Michael Hayes is based on the questionable (at least in Hollywood) biog by Irving Shulman, who wrote tome in collaboration with Arthur Landau, the star's first agent. The part of Landau is fashioned almost on a par with the star character herself in the opening reels, past the needs of the story which essentially focuses on girl's rise to become one of the hottest properties in films of that era.

Several real-life characters are thinly veiled while parts of star's mother and stepfather are importantly projected. Angela Lansbury undertakes role of Mama Jean with quiet conviction, and Raf Vallone in the Marino Bello-stepfather role, also lends a persuasive presence. Martin Balsam, head of Harlow's studio (here called Majestic Pictures) who gives her her chance at stardom, is the thinly-veiled Louis B. Mayer.

•

HAROLD AND MAUDE
1971, 90 mins, US Ⓥ ⦿ col
Dir Hal Ashby ***Prod*** Colin Higgins, Charles B. Mulvehill ***Scr*** Colin Higgins ***Ph*** John A. Alonzo ***Ed*** William A. Sawyer, Edward Warschilka ***Mus*** Cat Stevens ***Art*** Michael Haller
Act Ruth Gordon, Bud Cort, Vivian Pickles, Cyril Cusack, Charles Tyner, Ellen Geer (Paramount)

Harold and Maude has all the fun and gaiety of a burning orphanage. Ruth Gordon heads the cast as an offensive eccentric who becomes a beacon in the life of a self-destructive rich boy, played by Bud Cort. Together they attend funerals and indulge in specious philosophizing.
Director Hal Ashby's second feature is marked by a few good gags, but marred by a greater preponderance of sophomoric, overdone and mocking humor.

Cort does well as the spoiled neurotic whose repeated suicide attempts barely ruffle the feathers of mother Vivian Pickles, whose urbane performance is outstanding. She solicits a computer dating service to provide three potential brides: Shari Summers and Judy Engles are frightened off by Cort's bizarre doings, but Ellen Geer is delightful as one who goes him one better.

One thing that can be said about Ashby—he begins the film in a gross and macabre manner, and never once deviates from the concept. That's style for you.

•

HARPER
(UK: THE MOVING TARGET)
1966, 121 mins, US Ⓥ ⦿ ▭ col
Dir Jack Smight ***Prod*** Jerry Gershwin, Elliott Kastner ***Scr*** William Goldman ***Ph*** Conrad Hall ***Ed*** Stefan Arnsten ***Mus*** Johnny Mandel ***Art*** Alfred Sweeney
Act Paul Newman, Lauren Bacall, Julie Harris, Arthur Hill, Janet Leigh, Pamela Tiffin (Warner)

Harper is a contemporary mystery-comedy with Paul Newman as a sardonic private eye involved in a missing person trackdown. Some excellent directorial touches and solid thesping are evident in the colorful and plush production. Abundance of comedy and sometimes extraneous emphasis on cameo characters make for a relaxed pace and imbalanced concept, resulting in overlength and telegraphing of climax.

Ross MacDonald's novel, *The Moving Target*, has Newman commissioned by Lauren Bacall to find her hubby (never seen until climax), although she has no love for either him or step-daughter Pamela Tiffin.

Complications include the spoiled Tiffin, casual companion of family pilot Robert Wagner, himself hung up on Julie Harris, a piano bar entertainer also a junkie. Shelley Winters is the aging actress failure who has known the missing man, and is married to Robert Webber, brains behind a wetback smuggling ring run by religious nut Strother Martin.

Director Jack Smight has inserted countless touches which illuminate each character to the highest degree. In this he complements William Goldman's sharp and often salty lingo. All principals acquit themselves admirably, including Newman, Bacall, Webber, and particularly Winters, who makes every second count as the once-aspiring film star now on the high-calorie sauce.

•

HARP OF BURMA
SEE: BIRUMA NO TATEGOTO

•

HARRY & SON
1984, 117 mins, US Ⓥ ⦿ col
Dir Paul Newman ***Prod*** Paul Newman, Ronald L. Buck ***Scr*** Ronald L. Buck, Paul Newman ***Ph*** Donald McAlpine ***Ed*** Dede Allen ***Mus*** Henry Mancini ***Art*** Henry Bumstead
Act Paul Newman, Robby Benson, Ellen Barkin, Wilford Brimley, Judith Ivey, Joanne Woodward (Orion)

Fuzzily conceived and indecisively executed, *Harry & Son* represents a deeply disappointing return to the director's chair for Paul Newman. Cowritten and coproduced by the star as well, pic [suggested by the novel *A Lost King* by Raymond DeCapite] never makes up its mind who or what it wants to be about and, to compound the problem, never finds a proper style in which to convey the tragicomic events that transpire.

Opening scenes are perhaps the strongest, as Newman gets fired from his job as a Florida construction worker due to an ailment which momentarily blinds him. He goads his son into expanding his horizons beyond polishing cars and pretending to be a young Hemingway.

As presented, Newman's character is in a position either to give up on life or make a fresh start, and perhaps film's overriding frustration is that he goes nowhere. Structurally, it's a mess.

•

HARRY AND THE HENDERSONS
1987, 110 mins, US Ⓥ ⦿ col
Dir William Dear ***Prod*** Richard Vane, William Dear ***Scr*** William Dear, William E. Martin, Ezra D. Rappaport ***Ph*** Allen Daviau ***Ed*** Donn Cambern ***Mus*** Bruce Broughton ***Art*** James Bissell
Act John Lithgow, Melinda Dillon, Margaret Langrick, Joshua Rudoy, Kevin Peter Hall, David Suchet (Universal/Amblin)

Harry and the Hendersons is proof that the folks at Amblin Entertainment, a.k.a., Steven Spielberg's production company, can't keep using the same *E.T.* formula for every kiddie pic. Here, they've taken Big Foot, put him in Chewbacca's leftover *Star Wars* costume and given him E.T.'s sweet disposition—resulting in a lobotomized hairy animal who is so wimpy, it's painful.

Film could be titled, Big Foot Meets a Happy, Loving Suburban Family in the Woods Camping and Goes Home with Them to Become Docile When Bathed and Fed.

The excitement and suspense of running into Big Foot, later named Harry (Kevin Peter Hall), is wrapped up in the first few minutes of the film when Dad (John Lithgow) runs over the beast in the family stationwagon and takes him home to Seattle.

Theirs is a typical Spielberg house in the 'burbs—decorated in yuppie coziness that's soon turned topsy-turvy when Harry revives and scares the living daylights out of the Hendersons. Mom (Melinda Dillon) is genuinely good-natured, with a bratty son (Joshua Rudoy) and a very obedient teenage daughter (Margaret Langrick) to complement Dad's growing hysteria as Harry is sighted around town.

Screenwriters milk it for all it's worth.

1987: Best Makeup

•

HARRY AND TONTO
1974, 115 mins, US Ⓥ col
Dir Paul Mazursky ***Prod*** Paul Mazursky ***Scr*** Paul Mazursky, Josh Greenfeld ***Ph*** Michael Butler ***Ed*** Richard Halsey ***Mus*** Bill Conti ***Art*** Ted Haworth
Act Art Carney, Ellen Burstyn, Chief Dan George, Geraldine Fitzgerald, Larry Hagman, Arthur Hunnicutt (20th Century-Fox)

Harry and Tonto stars Art Carney and a trained cat, respectively, in a pleasant film about an old man who rejuvenates himself on a cross-country trek. Script is a series of good human comedy vignettes, with the large supporting cast of many familiar names in virtual cameo roles.

Carney is excellent as an old NY widower, evicted by force from a building being torn down. The rupture in his life triggers an odyssey, with pet cat named Tonto, to L.A., with family stopovers at the Jersey home of son Phil Bruns, then to Chicago where Ellen Burstyn remains a warm antagonist, finally to L.A. where Larry Hagman emerges as a failure in life. En route, Carney picks up young hitchhiker Melanie Mayron, eventually paired off with grandson Joshua Mostel.

1974: Best Actor (Art Carney)

NOMINATION: Best Original Screenplay

•

HARRY AND WALTER GO TO NEW YORK
1976, 120 mins, US Ⓥ ▭ col
Dir Mark Rydell ***Prod*** Don Devlin, Harry Gittes ***Scr*** John Byrum, Robert Kaufman ***Ph*** Laszlo Kovacs ***Ed*** Fredric Steinkamp, David Bretherton, Don Guidice ***Mus*** David Shire ***Art*** Harry Horner
Act James Caan, Elliott Gould, Michael Caine, Diane Keaton, Charles Durning, Lesley Ann Warren (Columbia)

Harry and Walter Go to New York is an alleged period comedy [from a story by Don Devlin and John Byrum] about two carnival types who get involved with a bigtime safe-cracker plus the femme leader of a radical movement. James Caan, Elliott Gould, Michael Caine and Diane Keaton are the respective stars in this two-hour embarrassment.

Busted for a carny ripoff, Caan and Gould are sent to prison where high-class, urbane Caine is doing time for bank robbery, but living so well that Keaton, repping an underground paper, interviews Caine for a big exposé.

The principals' paths intertwine through miles and miles of forced comedic footage, a climactic bank heist, plus all manner of running and jumping and screaming and hollering.

•

HARRY, HE'S HERE TO HELP
SEE: HARRY, UN AMI QUI VOUS VEUT DU BIEN

•

HARRY IN YOUR POCKET
1973, 102 mins, US col
Dir Bruce Geller ***Prod*** Bruce Geller ***Scr*** James David Buchanan, Ron Austin ***Ph*** Fred Koenekamp ***Ed*** Arthur L. Hilton ***Mus*** Lalo Schifrin ***Art*** William Bates
Act James Coburn, Michael Sarrazin, Trish Van Devere, Walter Pidgeon, Michael C. Gwynne, Tony Giorgio (United Artists)

Any earnest young man mulling a pickpocket career might pick up some valuable pointers in *Harry in Your Pocket*, story of a gang of slick dips. Producer-director Bruce Geller invades the underworld of cannons (master pick-pockets) with a fast expose of how they operate.

Well-paced and credible script poses the situation of a novice with his girlfriend joining a couple of smooth pros to learn the biz. James Coburn and Walter Pidgeon are the experts—Coburn the cannon and Pidgeon his cocaine-sniffing associate—and Michael Sarrazin and Trish Van Devere the apprentices. Presence of Van Devere leads to romantic complications and an underlying feud between Coburn and Sarrazin.

To assure authenticity, Geller hired Tony Giorgio, sleight-of-hand artist well versed in all the dip tricks, who worked both as technical advisor and appears as a detective.

Coburn delivers convincingly as he instructs his amateurs in the art of lifting wallets.

•

HARRY, UN AMI QUI VOUS VEUT DU BIEN
(HARRY, HE'S HERE TO HELP)
2000, 117 mins, France Ⓥ ⦿ ▭ col
Dir Dominik Moll ***Prod*** Michel Saint-Jean ***Scr*** Dominik Moll, Gilles Marchand ***Ph*** Matthieu Poirot-Delpech ***Ed*** Yannick Kergoat ***Mus*** David Sinclair Whitaker ***Art*** Michel Barthelemy
Act Laurent Lucas, Sergi Lopez, Mathilde Seigner, Sophie Guillemin (Diaphana)

Helmer Dominik Moll gets it right in the very first scene of *Harry, He's Here to Help*, perfectly capturing the mundane angst of family vacations, and this twisted black comedy rarely misses the mark for the next two hours. Pic, centering on an old pal who disrupts his former schoolmate's life, showcases remarkably witty writing and tremendous perfs from all four leads, most notably Sergi Lopez as charming psycho Harry. Moll masterfully weaves together Hitchcockian thriller elements and brainy comedy to create an original film that's never less than surprising.

For Harry, who has lived an easy life thanks to his father's wealth, there are no problems, only solutions. If your car's broken down, you just buy a new one. If someone is interfering with you, well, you just get rid of them like an old car. By the one-hour mark, Harry is off on a murderous rampage, and it's a testament to Moll's skill that he manages to maintain the right tone throughout. Once the blood starts flowing, it would be easy—and not all that interesting—for the pic to become either a sledge-hammer satire or a routine thriller. But Moll segues effortlessly from the violent moments to scenes of morbid humor without missing a beat.

The score from veteran composer David Sinclair Whitaker, who penned music for many classic British vampire pics, moves nicely from fluffy fare to increasingly sinister old-fashioned horror pic numbers.

•

HARVEY
1950, 103 mins, US Ⓥ ⦿ b/w
Dir Henry Koster ***Prod*** John Beck ***Scr*** Mary Chase, Oscar Brodney ***Ph*** William Daniels ***Ed*** Ralph Dawson ***Mus*** Frank Skinner
Act James Stewart, Josephine Hull, Peggy Dow, Charles Drake, Cecil Kellaway, Wallace Ford (Universal)

Harvey, Mary Chase's Pulitzer Prize play, loses little of its whimsical comedy charm in the screen translation.

Three of the principals, James Stewart, Josephine Hull and Jesse White, were seasoned in the wacky characters by playing them on stage.

The exploits of Elwood P. Dowd, a man who successfully escaped from trying reality when his invisible six-foot rabbit pal Harvey came into his life, continually spring chuckles, often hilarity, as the footage unfolds. Stewart would seem the perfect casting for the character so well does he convey the idea that escape from life into a pleasant half-world existence has many points in its favor. Josephine Hull, the slightly balmy aunt who wants to have Elwood committed, is immense, socking the comedy for every bit of its worth.

1950: Best Supp. Actress (Josephine Hull)

NOMINATION: Best Actor (James Stewart)

•

HARVEY GIRLS, THE
1946, 101 mins, US Ⓥ ⦿ col
Dir George Sidney ***Prod*** Arthur Freed ***Scr*** Edmund Beloin, Nathaniel Curtis, Harry Crane, James O'Hanlon, Samson Raphaelson, Kay Van Riper ***Ph*** George Folsey ***Ed*** Albert Akst ***Mus*** Lennie Hayton (dir.) ***Art*** Cedric Gibbons, William Ferrari
Act Judy Garland, John Hodiak, Ray Bolger, Angela Lansbury, Marjorie Main, Cyd Charisse (M-G-M)

The Harvey Girls [based on the novel by Samuel Hopkins Adams and the original story by Eleanore Griffin and William Rankin] is a curious blend of Technicolor wild-westernism, frontier town skullduggery and a troupe of Harvey restaurant waitresses who deport themselves in a manner that's a cross between a sorority and a Follies troupe.

John Hodiak is a curious casting in a musical of this nature. Judy Garland, however, makes much of it believable and most of it acceptable. Angela Lansbury is prominent as the Mae West of the casino, Hodiak's No. 1 flame until Garland, Virginia O'Brien and Cyd Charisse, appear on the scene.

There's the usual fol-de-rol such as hijacking all the good steaks; snakes in the Harvey gals's closets; incendiary tactics and the like.

1946: Best Song ("On the Atchison, Topeka and the Santa Fe").

NOMINATION: Best Scoring of a Musical Picture

•

HAS ANYBODY SEEN MY GAL
1952, 88 mins, US col
Dir Douglas Sirk ***Prod*** Ted Richmond ***Scr*** Joseph Hoffman ***Ph*** Clifford Stine ***Ed*** Russell Schoengarth ***Mus*** Joseph Gershenson (dir.) ***Art*** Bernard Herzbrun, Hilyard Brown
Act Piper Laurie, Rock Hudson, Charles Coburn, Gigi Perreau, Lynn Bari, William Reynolds (Universal)

A rather solid piece of nostalgic entertainment is offered in this comedy-drama of the 1920s "flapper" era [based on a story by Eleanor H. Porter]. While the younger Piper Laurie and Rock Hudson are starred over him, it is really Charles Coburn's vehicle.

He wallops the part of a rich old duffer who plans to leave his fortune to the family of a girl who had spurned his proposal of marriage years before.

Incognito, he travels to the small Vermont town where the family lives to find out what kind of people they are. Coburn arranges for the family to receive $100,000 from an "unnamed" benefactor and sits back to observe the results.

Laurie and Hudson team well as the young lovers. She does things to a sweater that were not done during the time of the story, but otherwise the era is re-created rather faithfully.

•

HASTY HEART, THE
1949, 102 mins, US b/w
Dir Vincent Sherman ***Prod*** [uncredited] ***Scr*** Ranald MacDougall ***Ph*** Wilkie Cooper ***Ed*** E. B. Jarvis ***Mus*** Jack Beaver ***Art*** Terence Verity
Act Ronald Reagan, Patricia Neal, Richard Todd, Anthony Nicholls, Howard Crawford, Ralph Michael (Warner)

The John Patrick play has grown in range of feeling on the screen, although the essentials of the legit staging have not been changed. Its background is the Second World War and the setting is an army hospital in Burma, in a ward where six assorted soldiers sweat out their injuries while awaiting shipment home.

Notable is the performance of Richard Todd in the role of the Scot who must die. Todd comes over with a performance that is star calibre in every facet.

Ronald Reagan plays the Yank with the exact amount of gusto such a character should have in a British outpost hospital. Patricia Neal gives feeling to her role as the nurse.

Vincent Sherman directed the production in England. Ranald MacDougall's scripting is wise to the humaneness that marked the play and the tremendous heart that backgrounds the telling.

1949: NOMINATION: Best Actor (Richard Todd)

•

HATARI!
1962, 159 mins, US Ⓥ ⦿ col
Dir Howard Hawks ***Prod*** Howard Hawks ***Scr*** Leigh Brackett ***Ph*** Russell Harlan ***Ed*** Stuart Gilmore ***Mus*** Henry Mancini ***Art*** Hal Pereira, Carl Anderson
Act John Wayne, Hardy Kruger, Elsa Martinelli, Gerard Blain, Red Buttons, Michele Girardon (Paramount)

Hatari! is an ambitious undertaking. Its cast is an international one, populated by players of many countries. Its wild animals do not come charging out of dusty stock footage studio libraries but have been photographed while beating around the bush of Tanganyika, East Africa. However, in this instance, the strapping physique of the film unhappily emphasizes the anemic condition of the story streaming within.

Leigh Brackett's screenplay, from an original story by Harry Kurnitz, describes at exhaustive length the methods by which a group of game catchers in Tanganyika go about catching wild animals for the zoo when not occupied at catching each other for the woo. Script lacks momentum. It never really advances toward a story goal.

John Wayne heads the colorful cast assembled for this zoological field trip. The vet star plays with his customary effortless (or so it seems) authority a role with which he is identified: the good-natured, but hard drinking, hot tempered, big Irishman who "thinks women are trouble" in a man's world.

Germany's Hardy Kruger and French actor Gerard Blain manage, resourcefully, to pump what vigor they can muster into a pair of undernourished roles. Red Buttons and Elsa Martinelli emerge the histrionic stickouts, Buttons with a jovial portrayal of an ex-cabbie who "just pretends it's rush hour in Brooklyn" as he jockeys his vehicle through a pack of frightened giraffe, Martinelli as a sweet but spirited shutterbug and part time pachydermatologist.

1962: NOMINATION: Best Color Cinematography

•

HATE
SEE: LA HAINE

•

HATFUL OF RAIN, A
1957, 109 mins, US ▭ b/w
Dir Fred Zinnemann ***Prod*** Buddy Adler ***Scr*** Michael Vicente Gazzo, Alfred Hayes ***Ph*** Joe MacDonald ***Ed*** Dorothy Spencer ***Mus*** Bernard Herrmann ***Art*** Lyle R. Wheeler, Leland Fuller
Act Eva Marie Saint, Don Murray, Anthony Franciosa, Lloyd Nolan, Henry Silva, William Hickey (20th Century-Fox)

The first film dealing with dope addiction made with the prior approval of the industry's self-governing Production Code, *A Hatful of Rain* is more than a story of a junkie. It touches knowingly and sensitively on a family relationship. Michael V. Gazzo has converted his Broadway play into a provocative and engrossing film drama.

The people involved in this web of narcotics are basically decent human beings. The story revolves about their reactions when one of them turns out to be a junkie. As the pregnant wife of a narcotics addict, Eva Marie Saint handles the emotional peaks and tender moments with sensitive understanding. Don Murray scores, too, as the likeable junkie who desperately attempts to hide his secret from his wife and his obtusely devoted father.

The role of the brother who shares an apartment in a Lower East Side N.Y. housing project with his dope-addicted relative and his wife is compellingly played by Anthony Franciosa, repeating his original stage assignment. Misunderstood and rejected by his father, Franciosa is moving as "his brother's keeper" and sister-in-law's confidant. As the widowed father who left his sons in an orphanage at an early age, Lloyd Nolan turns in a top-notch portrayal. Henry Silva, also repeating his stage role, is convincingly unctuous and contemptible as the dope peddler.

1957: NOMINATION: Best Actor (Anthony Franciosa)

•

HATTER'S CASTLE
1941, 101 mins, UK b/w
Dir Lance Comfort ***Prod*** I. Goldsmith ***Scr*** Rodney Ackland ***Ph*** Mutz Greenbaum ***Mus*** Horace Shepherd
Act Robert Newton, Deborah Kerr, James Mason, Emlyn Williams (Paramount)

Here is a film, if ever there was one, that is best indicative of one player's superlative performance. The player, Robert Newton, disregards tradition and enacts the featured male role without bombast or any sort of vocal pyrotechnics.

There is little in the picturized version of A. J. Cronin's bestseller that is not already stale and the plot travels along stereotyped lines to an obvious conclusion. It is, however, artistically produced, photographed and acted.

It is the story of a strong, hard Scotsman of Gladstonian days, who rules his household with the proverbial iron rod and turns his daughter out to almost certain death in a storm on learning of her dishonor. His only indication of affection is that for his schoolboy son, for whom he has exalted ambitions. It is a character drawing so strongly ruthless as to be fascinating.

The leading lady is Deborah Kerr, charming and sincere as the daughter; the juvenile lead of Doctor Renwick is restrainedly played by James Mason.

•

HAUNTED
1995, 108 mins, UK/US Ⓥ col
Dir Lewis Gilbert ***Prod*** Lewis Gilbert, Anthony Andrews ***Scr*** Tim Prager, Lewis Gilbert, Bob Kellett ***Ph*** Tony Pierce-Roberts ***Ed*** John Jympson ***Mus*** Debbie Wiseman ***Art*** John Fenner, Brian Ackland-Snow
Act Aidan Quinn, Kate Beckinsale, Anthony Andrews, John Gielgud, Anna Massey, Alex Lowe (Lumiere/Double A/American Zoetrope)

Haunted is a jazzed-up British programmer of the kind that companies like Amicus used to crank out in the '60s. Anchored by solid local talent and toplined by Aidan Quinn as the statutory Yank in rural England, this pic version of James Herbert's bestselling spook yarn is competently helmed by veteran Lewis Gilbert.

A brief prolog, set in 1905, introduces two young siblings, David and Juliet, at play in the grounds of a country house in Sussex, southern England. Juliet accidentally drowns, David feels guilty, and the plot basics are staked out.

Flash forward to 1928, when David (Quinn), who's meanwhile been raised in the States, returns to teach a course on the supernatural at a university. He's a skeptic but can't resist a letter from a dotty old nanny (Anna Massey) inviting him to a stately pile she claims is haunted.

The inhabitants of the mansion are an odd lot: elder brother Robert (Anthony Andrews) spends his time painting nude portraits of his voluptuous sister Christina (Kate Beckinsale), and younger brother Simon (Alex Lowe) is a prankster with several screws loose. Soon after arriving, David starts experiencing visions of his dead sister, mysterious fires, and other unexplained events.

Andrews, who optioned the novel six years earlier and produced alongside Gilbert, is the film's strongest presence, with some acidic delivery of limited dialog. Beckinsale, a rising Brit talent, also holds the screen.

•

HAUNTED HONEYMOON
1986, 82 mins, US Ⓥ ⦿ col
Dir Gene Wilder ***Prod*** Susan Ruskin ***Scr*** Gene Wilder, Terence Marsh ***Ph*** Fred Schuler ***Ed*** Christopher Greenbury ***Mus*** John Morris ***Art*** Terence Marsh
Act Gene Wilder, Gilda Radner, Dom DeLuise, Jonathan Pryce, Paul L. Smith, Peter Vaughan (Orion)

Gene Wilder is back in the rut of sending up old film conventions in *Haunted Honeymoon*, a mild farce. Title is a misnomer, since set-up has radio actor Wilder taking his fiancée Gilda Radner out to his family's gloomy country estate to meet the kinfolk just before tying the knot.

Clan is presided over by the tubby, genial Aunt Kate, played by Dom DeLuise, who maintains that a werewolf is on the loose in the vicinity. In any event, Wilder is obliged to contend with numerous assaults on his health, and much of the blessedly brief running time is devoted to frantic running among different rooms in the mansion for reasons that occasionally prove faintly amusing but are singularly uncompelling. Pic provokes a few chuckles along the way, but no guffaws.

•

HAUNTING, THE
1963, 112 mins, US Ⓥ ⦿ ▭ b/w
Dir Robert Wise ***Prod*** Robert Wise ***Scr*** Nelson Gidding ***Ph*** Davis Boulton ***Ed*** Ernest Walter ***Mus*** Humphrey Searle ***Art*** Elliot Scott
Act Julie Harris, Claire Bloom, Richard Johnson, Russ Tamblyn, Lois Maxwell, Fay Compton (Argyle/M-G-M)

The artful cinematic strokes of director Robert Wise and staff are not quite enough to override the major shortcomings of Nelson Gidding's screenplay from the Shirley Jackson novel [*The Haunting of Hill House*]. Gidding's scenario is opaque in spots, but its cardinal flaw is one of failure to follow through on its thematic motivation. After elaborately setting the audience up in anticipation of drawing some scientific conclusions about the psychic phenomena field, the film completely dodges the issue in settling for a half-hearted melodramatic climax.

The story has to do with the efforts of a small psychic research team led by an anthropology professor (Richard Johnson) to study the supernatural powers that seem to inhabit a 90-year-old New England house with a reputation for evil. The group includes an unhappy spinster (Julie Harris) obsessed with guilt feelings over the recent death of her mother; a young woman (Claire Bloom) of unnatural instincts (she has lesbian tendencies coupled with an extraordinary sense of ESP); and a young man (Russ Tamblyn) who is to inherit the house.

The acting is effective all around. The picture excels in the purely cinematic departments. Davis Boulton has employed his camera with extraordinary dexterity in fashioning a visual excitement that keeps the picture alive with images of impending shock. As photographed by Boulton, the house itself is a monstrous personality, most decidedly the star of the film. The pity is that all this production savvy has been squandered on a screen yarn that cannot support such artistic bulk.

•

HAUNTING, THE
1999, 114 mins, US Ⓥ ⊙ ▭ col
Dir Jan De Bont ***Prod*** Susan Arnold, Donna Arkoff Roth, Colin Wilson ***Scr*** David Self ***Ph*** Karl Walter Lindenlaub ***Ed*** Michael Kahn ***Mus*** Jerry Goldsmith ***Art*** Eugenio Zanetti
Act Liam Neeson, Catherine Zeta-Jones, Owen Wilson, Lili Taylor, Bruce Dern, Marian Seldes (Roth-Arnold/DreamWorks)

Extravagant technical prowess has been channeled to negligible effect in *The Haunting*, a wannabe horror classic that turns deadly dull once the sense of anxious expectation wears off. The fabulous sets and elaborate, occasionally graceful special effects provide the $80 million production with its only distinction.

No expense has been spared in the attempt to rev up the low-key spookiness of Robert Wise's identically titled 1963 M-G-M film version of Shirley Jackson's novel *The Haunting of Hill House*. Updating merely stands as yet another illustration that all the money in Hollywood can't necessarily buy imagination, resourcefulness, wit or, apparently, a decent script.

The ruse used to keep the characters under the house's suspicious roof would have seemed lame even in some of the lesser efforts of horrormeisters Jack Arnold and Sam Arkoff, fathers of Susan Arnold and Donna Arkoff Roth, two of this pic's producers.

Researcher Dr. David Marrow (Liam Neeson) is recruiting several insomniacs to test theories he has about fear and rounds up three volunteers: Nell (Lili Taylor), a withdrawn, impressionable woman; Theo (Catherine Zeta-Jones), a raffish artist and woman of the world; and Luke (Owen Wilson), a man of no particular distinction.

As written by first-time screenwriter David Self, they're bores whose few noticeable personality traits are quite irrelevant to anything that goes on. When Bruce Dern is the caretaker of an abandoned old mansion, you know you're in trouble.

Only indie stalwart Taylor, in her major-studio feature starring debut, has something resembling a real role to play.

•

HAVANA
1990, 145 mins, US Ⓥ ⊙ col
Dir Sydney Pollack ***Prod*** Sydney Pollack ***Scr*** Judith Rascoe, David Rayfiel ***Ph*** Owen Roizman ***Ed*** Fredric Steinkamp, William Steinkamp ***Mus*** Dave Grusin ***Art*** Terence Marsh
Act Robert Redford, Lena Olin, Alan Arkin, Tomas Milian, Raul Julia, Mark Rydell (Mirage/Universal)

Much as the filmmakers would like to get there, *Havana* remains a long way from *Casablanca*. In their seventh outing over a 25-year period, director Sydney Pollack and star Robert Redford have lost their normally dependable quality touch as they slog through a notably uncompelling $45 million-plus tale of a gringo caught up in the Cuban revolution.

In a shipboard prolog, Redford's rogue gambler character, Jack Weil, strikes a few sparks with Lena Olin's mysterious Bobby Duran and agrees to smuggle into Havana a radio that will help Castro spread his word in the capital in the waning days of 1958.

Although the city is astir with rumors concerning the rebel leader's activities in the mountains, it's still business as usual under the Batista dictatorship.

Redford's eye for Olin leads him into dangerous political territory involving her wealthy left-wing husband Arturo (played suavely by an uncredited Raul Julia), a CIA spook posing as a food critic, and various military toughs.

Unfortunately, the tentative romance between the two is never really credible. As usual, Redford is cool, reserved and a bit bemused, while the striking Olin is mercurial and intense. The combination doesn't take.

Judith Rascoe's original script was written in the mid-1970s. As rewritten by David Rayfiel, yarn is a mishmash of old-hat Hollywood conventions, political pussyfooting and loads of bad dialog.

1990: NOMINATION: Best Original Score

•

HAVANA WIDOWS
1933, 68 mins, US b/w
Dir Ray Enright ***Scr*** Stanley Logan, Earl Baldwin ***Ph*** George Barnes ***Ed*** Clarence Kolster
Act Joan Blondell, Glenda Farrell, Guy Kibbee, Lyle Talbot, Allen Jenkins, Frank McHugh (First National)

Tip-top rowdy comedy. Joan Blondell and Glenda Farrell are out on the loose as gold diggers again in the spicy surroundings of Havana, and Allen Jenkins is a low comedy character. Completing the welcome package there are lively tunes, an abundance of undressed girls and just the right amount of slapstick fun to give it climactic vigor.

Blondell and Farrell are a couple of hardworking, underpaid gals in a honkey-tonk chorus, discouraged when they're suspended for small infractions of the rules. Mourning in their furnished room they get word that Havana's the land of promise, knee deep in millionaires. They nick the boyfriend (Jenkins) for the roll to make the venture, Jenkins borrowing the coin from his gangster boss, losing it at the wheel and making it up by a rubber check transaction. All this is packed into the early footage.

In Havana they pick up their victim (Guy Kibbee, of course) and in working out their campaign to take him, acquire an inebriated lawyer in the person of Frank McHugh. Meanwhile Jenkins catches up to the Havana mixup with his gambler-boss in pursuit and the tangled threads of story come together in a whooping finale involving the Cuban army, local police and fire department and most of the populace.

Song numbers are entirely incidental, having to do with Havana cabaret bits which background the action itself.

•

HAVING A WILD WEEKEND
SEE: CATCH US IF YOU CAN

•

HAWAII
1966, 179 mins, US Ⓥ ⊙ ▭ col
Dir George Roy Hill ***Prod*** Walter Mirisch ***Scr*** Dalton Trumbo, Daniel Taradash ***Ph*** Russell Harlan ***Ed*** Stuart Gilmore ***Mus*** Elmer Bernstein ***Art*** Cary Odell
Act Julie Andrews, Max von Sydow, Richard Harris, Gene Hackman, Carroll O'Connor, Jocelyne LaGarde (Mirisch)

Based on James A. Michener's novel, which embraced centuries of history, *Hawaii* focuses on a critical period—1820–41—when the islands began to be commercialized, corrupted and converted to Western ways. Superior production, acting and direction give depth and credibility to a personal tragedy, set against the clash of two civilizations.

Filmed at sea off Norway, also in New England, Hollywood, Hawaii and Tahiti, this vast production reps an outlay of about $15 million, including $600,000 for film rights, and seven years of work. Fred Zinnemann, originally set to produce-direct, worked four and a half years on it, after which Hill took over.

Dalton Trumbo and original adapter, Daniel Taradash, are both credited with the screenplay, which develops Max von Sydow's character from a young and overzealous Protestant missionary, through courtship of Julie Andrews, to their religious work in Hawaii. Richard Harris, an old beau, turns up occasionally at major plot turns.

Von Sydow's outstanding performance makes his character comprehensible, if never totally sympathetic. A less competent actor, with less competent direction and scripting, would have blown the part, and with that, the film. Andrews is excellent in a demanding dramatic role. Hill's direction, solid in the intimate dramatic scenes, is as good in crowd shots which rep the major external events.

1966: NOMINATIONS: Best Supp. Actress (Jocelyn Lagarde), Color Cinematography, Color Costume Design, Color Costume Design, Original Music Score, Song ("My Wishing Doll"), Sound, Visual Effects

•

HAWAIIANS, THE
(UK: MASTER OF THE ISLANDS)
1970, 134 mins, US ▭ col
Dir Tom Gries ***Prod*** Walter Mirisch ***Scr*** James R. Webb ***Ph*** Phil Lathrop, Lucien Ballard ***Ed*** Ralph Winters, Byron Brandt ***Mus*** Henry Mancini ***Art*** Cary Odell
Act Charlton Heston, Geraldine Chaplin, John Phillip Law, Tina Chen, Alec McCowen, Mako (United Artists/Mirisch)

While James A. Michener's monumental novel *Hawaii* contained enough material for half a dozen films, the earlier version in 1966 used up most of the first half. This follow-up film devotes most of its time to the growth of Hawaii in the present century and the huge influx of other Orientals, particularly the Chinese and Japanese, into the islands as cheap labor.

Charlton Heston, as the American descendant of early settlers and the only man with the vision and steadfastness to make the Hawaiian Islands one of the garden spots of the world (he's credited with introducing the pineapple as a commercial crop), is less the larger-than-life hero and more a stereotyped islander.

1970: NOMINATION: Best Costume Design

•

HAWKS
1988, 107 mins, UK Ⓥ col
Dir Robert Ellis Miller ***Prod*** Steve Lanning, Keith Cavele ***Scr*** Roy Clarke ***Ph*** Doug Milsome ***Ed*** Malcolm Cook ***Mus*** Barry Gibb ***Art*** Peter Howitt
Act Timothy Dalton, Anthony Edwards, Janet McTeer, Camille Coduri, Connie Booth (Gibb/English/PRO)

This black comedy about terminal cancer patients escaping for one last fling stares death in the face and laughs, but takes too long to get to the punch line.

From the start, it's clear that director Robert Ellis Miller is using the script about men facing an early death to examine how people deal with their fears and how they try, or fail, to disguise it from others.

In this instance, terminal bone cancer pits lawyer Bancroft (Timothy Dalton) and ex-football pro Decker (Anthony Edwards) together in a team effort to thwart their disease (and the ward nurses) with laughs, grit and a last pilgrimage to a Dutch bordello.

Dalton goes a bit overboard as Bancroft, occasionally stretching believability. Edwards plays it straight as the Yank jock, but brings out the laconic ladies' man in his character despite being nonambulatory much of the time.

•

HAXAN
(WITCHCRAFT THROUGH THE AGES; WITCHCRAFT)
1922, 82 mins, Sweden Ⓥ ⊗ b/w
Dir Benjamin Christensen ***Scr*** Benjamin Christensen ***Ph*** Johan Ankerstjerne ***Art*** Richard Louw
Act Benjamin Christensen, Elisabeth Christensen, Astrid Holm, Karen Winther, Maren Pedersen, Ella La Cour (Svensk Filmindustri)

Swedish and Danish pictures easily hold the palm for morbid realism and in many cases for brilliant acting and production. *Witchcraft*, made by [Danish director] Benjamin Christensen [funded by a Swedish production company], leaves all the others beaten. It is in reality a pictorial history of black magic, of witches, of the Inquisition and the thousand and one inhumanities of the superstition-ridden Middle Ages. Many of its scenes are unadulterated horror.

The story tells how a young man lies sick. A priest passes over his body a ladle full of molten metal. This is then cooled in water, and the shape the cold metal assumes proves the patient is under the spell of a witch. An old woman beggar is accused, and the girl-wife comes under suspicion. All are hauled before the Inquisition, and torture is applied.

In her agony the old beggar confesses and implicates the other woman in the sick man's household. They are condemned to the stake. The priest has conceived a guilty longing for the young wife, and submits to a ghastly flagellation. She is accused of bewitching the priest and forced into a confession. She is executed.

Many of the scenes are remarkable, especially those in which the girl wanders stark naked in a world of imaginative horror. Devils and other horrors rise around her. She awakes to find herself in bed, but nerve-shattered. Hysteria is mistaken for witchery, and she is condemned. [Film was reviewed from a screening in London in August 1923, when it had not yet been taken up for distribution. Reviewer declared that "wonderful though this picture is, it is absolutely unfit for public exhibition."]

•

HE GOT GAME
1998, 134 mins, US Ⓥ ⊙ col
Dir Spike Lee ***Prod*** Jon Kilik, Spike Lee ***Scr*** Spike Lee ***Ph*** Malik Hassan Sayeed ***Ed*** Barry Alexander ***Mus*** Alex Stevermark (sup.) ***Art*** Wynn Thomas
Act Denzel Washington, Ray Allen, Mill Jovovich, Rosario Dawson, Hill Harper, Jim Brown (40 Acres & a Mule/Touchstone)

He Got Game is a contemporary basketball drama with comic overtones, centering on the turbulent relationship between a convict-father and extraordinarily gifted athlete son. Lacking the moral indignation, outrage and militant politics that marked Spike Lee's earlier work, this vibrantly colorful film is a tad too soft at the center, and arguably the director's most mainstream movie.

Toplined by a deglamorized Denzel Washington (in his third teaming with Lee) as the errant father desperate for forgiveness, and the immensely engaging Ray Allen, the Milwaukee Bucks basketball superstar, as his resentful son, Jesus, pic is a broad canvas of family drama, black youth, college life and, above all, the obsession with basketball in American culture.

Though grounded in a particular African-American context—the movie is set in Coney Island—the story is meant to provide a humanistic view of intergenerational strife and the universal need for reconciliation and forgiveness.

Lee shrewdly dissects the exploitation of student athletes in the U.S. and the various dimensions of basketball—popular sport, national myth, multibillion-dollar business. Since Jesus is perceived as a "national asset" worth millions of dollars, everybody around him wants a piece of the pie.

The reliable Washington renders solid work in an uncharacteristic role. But the real revelation here is newcomer Allen, who's perfectly cast as the hurting, good-natured son who needs to make peace with his father.

With the exception of John Turturro in a bravura cameo as a campus coach, all the other coaches are played by real-life personalities.

•

HEAD OVER HEELS
(US: HEAD OVER HEELS IN LOVE)

1936, 84 mins, UK b/w

Dir Sonnie Hale ***Scr*** Marjorie Gaffney, Dwight Taylor ***Ph*** Glen MacWilliams ***Ed*** Al Barnes ***Mus*** Louis Levy (dir.) ***Art*** Alfred Junge

Act Jessie Matthews, Louis Borell, Robert Flemyng, Whitney Bourne, Romney Brent, Paul Leyssac (Gaumont-British)

Head over Heels is a topsy-turvy film affair, emulating its title in more than one respect. Of the hybrid Hollywood and Elstree components there's no disputing that, outside of the star's own yeoman work, the Mack Gordon and Harry Revel songs are the most potent contributory factor. So it's just another film, but those click songs are gonna have their good effect.

Story [from Francois de Croisset's play *Pierre ou Jack*, adapted by Fred Thompson and Dwight Taylor] is one of those things—familiar unto being trite. And the support is no panic, embracing two uncertain juveniles in Robert Flemyng and Louis Borell, the latter as a light-heavy who permits himself to be influenced by the visiting glamour-girl from Hollywood (Whitney Bourne), an American film star looking for a new leading man. In between, Jessie Matthews is effectively shown as a cafe song-and-dancer, later a radio chick, and still later as a cigarette girl when the ire of the Actors' Association (for a temperamental breach) chases her from the limelight.

Locale is Paris, and the French version of Equity is mentioned periodically as some sort of a bogeyman which keeps irascible troupers hewing the line, even though their own Pagliacci complications upset them emotionally.

Buddy Bradley always does well by Matthews in staging the dance routines; and this alumnus of the late Billy Pierce's studios in New York (which coached many of the topnotch ingenues of musical comedy in the past decade) has done right by her again. Although her husband, Sonnie Hale, manages fairly well in directing the proceedings, the material calls for inspired niceties to make it stand up. In some spots the camera work is most unflattering to the star.

•

HEAD OVER HEELS

1979, 97 mins, US Ⓥ col

Dir Joan Micklin Silver ***Prod*** Mark Metcalf ***Scr*** Joan Micklin Silver ***Ph*** Bobby Byrne ***Ed*** Cynthia Schneider ***Mus*** Ken Lauber ***Art*** Peter Jamison

Act John Heard, Mary Beth Hurt, Peter Riegert, Kenneth McMillan, Gloria Grahame, Griffin Dunne (United Artists/Triple Play)

Joan Micklin Silver's third directorial effort possesses moderate charm and shows some of the talent she's exhibited before, but ultimately emerges as somewhat thin and one-dimensional.

Based on Ann Beattie's novel *Chilly Scenes of Winter*, Silver's screenplay has affable John Heard reflecting back on his happy past with Mary Beth Hurt from the wistful present. Thrust of pic has him trying to win her back from the clutches of king-sized jock Mark Metcalf.

Ultimately, however, both characters rather wear out their welcome, Heard becoming almost oppressively absolutist in his feelings and Hurt seeming too confused and selfish to be worth all the trouble. After all the difficulties and anxieties that have preceded it, resolution comes off as a bit pat and conventional.

•

HEAD OVER HEELS IN LOVE
SEE: HEAD OVER HEELS

•

H.E.A.L.T.H.

1980, 102 mins, US ▭ col

Dir Robert Altman ***Prod*** Robert Altman ***Scr*** Frank Barhydt, Paul Dooley, Robert Altman ***Ph*** Edmond Koons ***Ed*** Dennis M. Hill

Act Glenda Jackson, Carol Burnett, James Garner, Lauren Bacall, Dick Cavett, Paul Dooley (Lion's Gate/20th Century-Fox)

Since producer-director Robert Altman completed production [18 months ago, in early 1979] of this arch look at a Florida health foods bash, the pic has gradually been stigmatized in the trade as the best known unreleased, major company film in some time. It's a bad rap: *H.E.A.L.T.H.* is overdrawn and thin in too many spots, but the pic is a genuinely humorous effort that affords its good cast often-seized opportunities for incisively funny performances.

Like *A Wedding* and *Nashville*, the rambling format of *H.E.A.L.T.H.* puts a contingent of dotty characters against a frenzied social backdrop. Altman's clever handling of that backdrop permits the cast to develop broad characterizations that most often work.

The convention is set in a garishly statuesque southern Florida hotel, and Altman (considering his satirical intent) somehow got some 100 health food companies to provide their wares in the pic's highly detailed and immensely clever sets. Lauren Bacall plays a well-preserved 83-year-old health authority who claims she's stayed so remarkably fit by maintaining her virginity.

Bacall's running for the presidency of the health foods org that runs the convention, against a vaguely masculine cigar puffer (Glenda Jackson) with a fondness for Adlai Stevenson and taping her own conversations.

Carol Burnett is the film's real surprise. She's first-rate as a sexually frustrated White House health emissary sent to the convention to gladhand the presidential candidates. James Garner is appropriately droll as Burnett's ex-husband, a political p.r. type hustling Bacall's candidacy. Henry Gibson puts in a very funny bit as a political dirty trickster who resorts to eavesdropping in elevators in drag.

[Pic preemed at the Montreal festival in August 1980 and was finally released in 1981.]

•

HEAR MY SONG

1992, 113 mins, UK Ⓥ ⊙ col

Dir Peter Chelsom ***Prod*** Alison Owen ***Scr*** Peter Chelsom, Adrian Dunbar ***Ph*** Sue Gibson ***Ed*** Martin Walsh ***Mus*** John Altman ***Art*** Caroline Hanania

Act Ned Beatty, Adrian Dunbar, David McCallum, Tara Fitzgerald, Shirley Anne Field, William Hootkins (Limelight)

First feature from Peter Chelsom goes straight for the heart with *Hear My Song*, an unabashedly romantic fantasy about a concert promoter (Adrian Dunbar), a seat-of-his-pants operator who's this close to sealing a relationship with his beautiful g.f. (Tara Fitzgerald). The nightclub he's taken over in an Irish neighborhood of Britain is ever on the verge of collapse because of its unreliable bottom-rung bookings. Desperate for a hit, the promoter books a Josef Locke lookalike (William Hootkins) who's quite mad but seems to fill the billing as "Mr X—Is He or Isn't He?" Legendary Irish tenor Locke fled from public view at the height of his popularity to avoid tax evasion charges.

Ned Beatty does much to stem the tide of sentiment in a tough, grounded portrayal of the real Locke, a man of substance and self-awareness firmly entrenched in another life. But by the final reels, it's become too much. Dunbar carries off the lead role in winning fashion, but the real discovery is likely to be Fitzgerald, whose gamine charm is perfectly introduced in this old-fashioned romance.

•

HEAR NO EVIL

1993, 97 mins, US Ⓥ ⊙ col

Dir Robert Greenwald ***Prod*** David Matalon ***Scr*** R.M. Badat, Kathleen Rowell ***Ph*** Steven Shaw ***Ed*** Eva Gardos ***Mus*** Graeme Revell ***Art*** Bernt Capra

Act Marlee Matlin, D. B. Sweeney, Martin Sheen, John C. McGinley, Christina Carlisi, Greg Elam (Great Movie Ventures/20th Century-Fox)

A terminally dull would-be thriller, *Hear No Evil* has a perfunctory story [by R. M. Badat and Danny Rubin] with the gimmick of a deaf damsel-in-distress grafted on uncertainly. Oscar-winner Marlee Matlin's talents are wasted.

Matlin plays a physical trainer in Portland whose client (John C. McGinley) hides a rare stolen coin in her beeper before being nabbed by the cops.

McGinley's car blows up and corrupt cop Martin Sheen starts harassing Matlin to retrieve the coin. McGinley's pal D. B. Sweeney takes Matlin under his wing and the duo finally bring in the FBI to catch Sheen.

Director Robert Greenwald and his scripters show little flair for suspense, nuance or even elementary thrills. In the final reel Matlin has a cat and mouse sequence trapped in a mountain lodge with the killer, but unlike such effective films as *Wait Until Dark*, her handicap (deafness) is not used as an equalizer but instead merely increases her jeopardy.

•

HEARTACHES

1981, 83 mins, Canada Ⓥ ⊙ col

Dir Donald Shebib ***Prod*** Pieter Kroonenburg, David J. Patterson, Jerry Ralbourn ***Scr*** Terence Heffernan ***Ph*** Vic Sarin ***Ed*** Gerry Hambling, Peter Bolta ***Mus*** Simon Michael Mastin

Act Margot Kidder, Annie Potts, Robert Carradine, Winston Rekert, George Touliatis (Rising Star)

Heartaches is a female buddy picture with actresses Margot Kidder and Annie Potts involved in a series of delightful misadventures in love.

Film, plagued by its own financial heartaches, emerges unscathed from production delays and shut downs.

Potts is the wife of perennial juvenile Robert Carradine who spends most of his time racing cars and getting drunk. She splits rather than face him with the hard fact that he's not the father of the child she's carrying.

On her way to the big city for an abortion Potts reluctantly teams up with Kidder. Kidder, in blond wig, tight pants and outrageous jewelry, looks the part of a kook. Her foul-mouthed, man-hungry character is in sharp contrast to Potts's relative innocence.

Cast is outstanding with Kidder giving full performance. However, it is basically Potts's film as the runaway wife who's tired of her husband's immature attitude.

•

HEARTBEAT

1946, 100 mins, US Ⓥ b/w

Dir Sam Wood ***Prod*** Robert Hakim, Raymond Hakim ***Scr*** Morrie Ryskind ***Ph*** Joseph Valentine ***Ed*** Roland Gross ***Mus*** Paul Misraki ***Art*** Lionel Banks

Act Ginger Rogers, Jean-Pierre Aumont, Adolphe Menjou, Melville Cooper, Basil Rathbone (RKO)

Pygmalion theme [from a pre-war French film] lends itself to Ginger Rogers's talents, and strong performances by others in the cast are on the credit side. These factors do considerable work in glossing over production and story weaknesses.

Continental flavor of Paris locale is maintained by Sam Wood's direction in unfolding story of a girl who becomes an apprentice in a pickpocket school, goes to an embassy ball and finds romance after she learns how to be a lady.

Jean-Pierre Aumont is interesting as the young diplomat who falls for the femme purse-snatcher. New romance gets him out of a lightly established previous affair with Mona Maris, Adolphe Menjou's wife. It is the character performances by others in the cast though that give a lift to proceedings. Menjou is expert; Melville Cooper as a cadgering lush is good for chuckles. Basil Rathbone's professional performance furnishes laughs.

•

HEART BEAT

1979, 109 mins, US Ⓥ col

Dir John Byrum ***Prod*** Alan Greisman, Michael Shamberg ***Scr*** John Byrum ***Ph*** Laszlo Kovacs ***Ed*** Eric Jenkins ***Mus*** Jack Nitzsche ***Art*** Jack Fisk

Act Nick Nolte, Sissy Spacek, John Heard, Ray Sharkey, Ann Dusenberry, Tony Bill (Orion)

Heart Beat never manages to expand its loosely biographical tale of Jack Kerouac, Neal and Carolyn Cassady beyond a very narrow scope.

Nick Nolte and Sissy Spacek, as the Cassadys enmeshed in a love-hate relationship, are standout in a film where performers dominate. Ditto Ray Sharkey, in a manic performance as a disguised Allen Ginsberg character. John Heard struggles manfully with the Kerouac character, but writer-director John Byrum has given him few compass points on which to base a reading.

Heart Beat fails to establish either a coherent storyline, or a definitive treatment of the forces that shaped the literary and social explosion following publication of Kerouac's *On the Road* in 1957.

•

HEARTBREAK KID, THE
1972, 104 mins, US Ⓥ ⦿ col
Dir Elaine May **Prod** Edgar J. Scherick **Scr** Neil Simon **Ph** Owen Roizman **Ed** John Carter **Mus** Garry Sherman **Art** Richard Sylbert
Act Charles Grodin, Cybill Shepherd, Jeannie Berlin, Eddie Albert, Audra Lindley, William Prince (Palomar)

The Heartbreak Kid is the bright, amusing saga of a young N.Y. bridegroom whose bride's maddening idiosyncrasies freak him, and he leaves her at the end of a three-day Miami honeymoon to pursue and wed another doll.

Scripted by Neil Simon from Bruce Jay Friedman's *Esquire* mag story ["A Change of Plan"], film has a sudden shut-off ending with no climax whatsoever.

Elaine May's deft direction catches all the possibilities of young romance and its tribulations in light strokes and cleverly accents characterization of the various principals. Most of the pace is as fast as Charles Grodin's speeding to his Florida honeymoon, and falling for a gorgeous blonde on the beach the first day there.

Grodin is slick and able as the fast-talking bridegroom whose patience is worn thin and he's a natural for the charms of another.

1972: NOMINATIONS: Best Supp. Actor (Eddie Albert), Supp. Actress (Jeannie Berlin)

•

HEARTBREAK KID, THE
1993, 97 mins, Australia Ⓥ col
Dir Michael Jenkins **Prod** Ben Gannon **Scr** Michael Jenkins, Richard Barrett **Ph** Nino Martinetti **Ed** Peter Carrodus **Mus** John Clifford White **Art** Paddy Reardon
Act Claudia Karvan, Alex Dimitriades, Steve Bastoni, Nico Lathouris, William McInnes, Doris Younane (View)

The Heartbreak Kid, which has no connection with Elaine May's homonymous 1972 pic, is a warm-hearted, liberating love story. Set in the ethnically mixed suburbs of Melbourne, pic establishes Claudia Karvan as 22-year-old Christina, a well-educated Greek-Australian with wealthy parents. She's just become engaged to the upwardly mobile Dimitri (Steve Bastoni).

Embarking on a teaching career, Christina has been assigned to work a rowdy high school in a working-class area. Spunky 17-year-old Nick (Alex Dimitriades) makes it clear that he has the hots for his teacher and she, gradually, responds, eventually borrowing her girlfriend's apartment for secret afternoon trysts with her willing pupil. Inevitably, the secret gets out.

Kid started life as a stage play, though you'd never guess it, thanks to the skillful adaptation of playwright Richard Barrett and director Michael Jenkins, aided by fine work from lenser Nino Martinetti.

•

HEARTBREAK RIDGE
1986, 130 mins, US Ⓥ ⦿ col
Dir Clint Eastwood **Prod** Clint Eastwood **Scr** James Carabatsos **Ph** Jack N. Green **Ed** Joel Cox **Mus** Lennie Niehaus **Art** Edward Carfagno
Act Clint Eastwood, Marsha Mason, Everett McGill, Moses Gunn, Eileen Heckart, Bo Svenson (Malpaso/Weston)

Heartbreak Ridge offers another vintage Clint Eastwood performance. There are enough mumbled half-liners in this contemporary war pic to satisfy those die-hards eager to see just how he portrays the consummate marine veteran.

Eastwood is Gunnery Sergeant Tom Highway—a man determined to teach some of today's young leathernecks how to behave like a few good men. Eastwood's stern ways inevitably prevail as his platoon is called up for emergency overseas combat. Guns are blazing as Clint's cadre faces its first real action after hitting the beaches. As film moves towards its jingoistic peak in these sequences, Eastwood's insubordinate bent culminates in a final conflict with a modern major (Everett McGill).

1986: NOMINATION: Best Sound

•

HEARTBURN
1986, 108 mins, US Ⓥ ⦿ col
Dir Mike Nichols **Prod** Mike Nichols, Robert Greenhut **Scr** Nora Ephron **Ph** Nestor Almendros **Ed** Sam O'Steen **Mus** Carly Simon **Art** Tony Walton
Act Meryl Streep, Jack Nicholson, Jeff Daniels, Maureen Stapleton, Stockard Channing, Richard Masur (Paramount)

Heartburn is a beautifully crafted film with flawless performances and many splendid moments, yet the overall effect is a bit disappointing. From the start Meryl Streep and Jack Nicholson are never quite a couple. He's a Washington political columnist and she's a New York food writer. They meet at a wedding and he overpowers her. Soon they're having their own wedding.

Nora Ephron adapted her own novel for the screen, which in turn borrowed heavily from her marriage with Watergate reporter Carl Bernstein.

While the day-to-day details are drawn with a striking clarity, Ephron's script never goes much beyond the mannerisms of middle-class life. Even with the sketchy background information, it's hard to tell what these people are feeling or what they want.

Where the film does excel is in creating the surface and texture of their life. Director Mike Nichols knows the territory well enough to throw in some subtle but biting satire, and Nicholson (who replaced Mandy Patinkin during production) and Streep fill in the canvas.

•

HEART IN WINTER, A
SEE: UN COEUR EN HIVER

•

HEART IS A LONELY HUNTER, THE
1968, 122 mins, US Ⓥ col
Dir Robert Ellis Miller **Prod** Thomas C. Ryan, Marc Merson **Scr** Thomas C. Ryan **Ph** James Wong Howe **Ed** John F. Burnett **Mus** Dave Grusin **Art** LeRoy Deane
Act Alan Arkin, Sondra Locke, Laurinda Barrett, Stacy Keach, Chuck McCann, Cicely Tyson (Warner)

Translating to the screen the delicate if specious tragedy of Carson McCullers's first novel was clearly not an easy matter. Nor an entirely successful one, either. *The Heart Is a Lonely Hunter* emerges as a fragmented episodic melodrama, with uneven dramatic impact and formula pacing.

Alan Arkin's starring performance as a deaf-and-mute loner is erratic and mannered, but supporting cast generally is on target.

Story turns on Arkin and his influence on the lives of others. Pivotal character is little more than a prop, but, as rendered by Arkin, a destructive one.

Arkin's performance is marred by twitching mannerisms. Result is slapstick at times, bathos at others. Suffice it to say that when the focus of attention returns to the main character, the pic has a tendency to fall apart.

The motivations of other characters are defined in better fashion, although the credibility of most is doubtful. Actors have an uphill fight, and to their personal credit they rise above the material.

1968: NOMINATIONS: Best Actor (Alan Arkin), Supp. Actress (Sondra Locke)

•

HEART LIKE A WHEEL
1983, 113 mins, US Ⓥ ⦿ col
Dir Jonathan Kaplan **Prod** Charles Roven **Scr** Ken Friedman **Ph** Tak Fujimoto **Ed** O. Nicholas Brown **Mus** Laurence Rosenthal **Art** James William Newport
Act Bonnie Bedelia, Beau Bridges, Leo Rossi, Hoyt Axton, Bill McKinney, Anthony Edwards (Aurora/20th Century-Fox)

Heart Like A Wheel is a surprisingly fine biopic of Shirley Muldowney, the first professional female race car driver. What could have been a routine good ol' gal success story has been heightened into an emotionally involving, superbly made drama.

Winning prolog has pa Hoyt Axton letting his little daughter take the wheel of his speeding sedan, an indelible experience which prefigures Shirley, by the mid-1950s, winning drag races against the hottest rods in town.

Happily married to her mechanic husband, Jack, and with a young son, Shirley finds her innate ability compelling her, by 1966, to enter her first pro race. Roadblocked at first by astonished, and predictably sexist, officials, Shirley proceeds to set the track record in her qualifying run, and her career is underway.

But her husband ultimately can't take her career-mindedness, and she's forced to set out on her own.

Director Jonathan Kaplan has served a long apprenticeship but nothing he has done before prepares one for his mature, accomplished work here.

•

HEART OF MIDNIGHT
1988, 101 mins, US Ⓥ ⦿
Dir Matthew Chapman **Prod** Andrew Gaty **Scr** Matthew Chapman **Ph** Ray Rivas **Ed** Penelope Shaw **Mus** Yanni **Art** Gene Rudolf
Act Jennifer Jason Leigh, Peter Coyote, Gale Mayron, Sam Schacht, Denise Dummont, Frank Stallone (AG)

Heart of Midnight is a twisted little sadomasochistic outing [from a screen story by Matthew Chapman and Everett De Roche] whose plot centers on Carol Rivers (Jennifer Jason Leigh), a young woman with psychological problems. When her uncle Fletcher (Sam Schacht) dies of AIDS, she inherits property being transformed into the "Midnight" club.

Against the wishes of her mother, Betty (Brenda Vaccaro), Carol moves to the building, only to find a bizarre series of rooms upstairs. They suggest Fletcher was hosting sex parties for people of various persuasions.

Carol is plunged into her own hell as a couple of workmen try to rape her. If the assault wasn't problem enough, signs appear that someone else is on the premises.

Events proceed to particularly sadistic circumstances, in which the reason for Carol's years of torment and her relationship to her late uncle also come to light.

Performances are strong all around, particularly by Leigh and Vaccaro.

•

HEART OF THE MATTER, THE
1953, 105 mins, UK b/w
Dir George More O'Ferrall **Prod** Ian Dalrymple **Scr** Ian Dalrymple **Ph** Jack Hildyard **Ed** Sidney Stone **Mus** Edric Connor (adv.) **Art** Joseph Bato
Act Trevor Howard, Elizabeth Allan, Maria Schell, Denholm Elliott, Peter Finch, Gerard Oury (British Lion/London)

The film is set in Sierra Leone during the last war, where Trevor Howard, the assistant police commissioner, is not getting along too well with his wife (Elizabeth Allan). He is forced to borrow money from an unscrupulous blackmailer and made to send his wife away on a vacation. During her absence, he falls in love with a young widow (Maria Schell), one of the survivors of a ship wrecked by a German U-boat.

The story is told in painstaking and deliberate terms. Subject matter is Graham Greene's favorite topic of Catholicism [from his novel, adapted by Lesley Storm]. Stripped of its deeper significance, the story is little more than the conventional triangle meller, but husband and wife are ardent Catholics, and divorce and remarriage cannot be contemplated.

There is considerable merit in the script and much of the dialog has adult appeal. But the conflict between love and religion never emerges with real conviction. The backgrounds filmed on location have an authentic look.

Howard plays his role with great intensity. The part of his wife is done in two contrasting keys by Allan, almost wildly hysterical and subdued and restrained. The third member of the triangle is etched by Maria Schell with real tenderness.

•

HEARTS OF FIRE
1987, 95 mins, US Ⓥ ⦿ ▭ col
Dir Richard Marquand **Prod** Richard Marquand, Jennifer Miller, Jennifer Alward **Scr** Scott Richardson, Joe Eszterhas **Ph** Alan Hume **Ed** Sean Barton **Mus** John Barry **Art** Roger Murray-Leach
Act Bob Dylan, Rupert Everett, Fiona, Julian Glover, Ian Drury, Richie Havens (Phoenix/Lorimar)

It is unfortunate that the last film of helmer Richard Marquand, who died shortly after completing it, should be *Hearts of Fire*. As an epitaph it leaves something to be desired, failing to fire on all cylinders despite a nimble performance by the enigmatic Bob Dylan, typecast as a reclusive rock star.

Pic opens with would-be rock singer Molly McGuire (exuberantly played by Yank singer Fiona) meeting rock star Billy Parker (Dylan) and agreeing to hop over to England with him.

In Blighty she is spotted by British popster James Colt (Rupert Everett), who takes her under his wing—and into his bed—while a drunken Dylan flies home to the security of his chicken farm.

Fiona and Everett head off on tour together and, while Fiona agonizes about the real price of success and worries about which man she prefers, the inevitable climax of the gig in her hometown fast approaches.

Dylan performs well, though he looks a mite uncomfortable during the musical numbers. He certainly appears fitter than Everett, whose voice is as wet and stilted as his performance.

•

HEARTS OF THE WEST
(UK: HOLLYWOOD COWBOY)
1975, 102 mins, US Ⓥ col
Dir Howard Zieff ***Prod*** Tony Bill ***Scr*** Rob Thompson ***Ph*** Mario Tosi ***Ed*** Edward Wearschilka ***Mus*** Ken Lauber ***Art*** Robert Luthardt
Act Jeff Bridges, Andy Griffith, Donald Pleasence, Blythe Danner, Alan Arkin, Richard B. Schull (M-G-M)

Hearts of the West is a pleasant, amusing period comedy featuring Jeff Bridges in an excellent characterization as a cliché-quoting novice Western pulp writer who discovers that his correspondence school is no more than a remote Nevada mailbox pickup operation, the swindle of Richard B. Shull and Anthony James. Escaping their robbery attempt, Bridges accidentally takes their cash stash into the desert wastes where he is rescued by an oater quickie film location unit.

The casting is very adroit, with all principals complementing in style and charisma. The structure of the film is notable in that it tells its story in the manner of films of the 1930s, while in turn keeping separate the ways in which they were then artistically conceived and executed.

•

HEARTS OF THE WORLD
1918, 117 mins, US/UK Ⓥ ⊗ b/w
Dir D. W. Griffith ***Prod*** D. W. Griffith ***Scr*** Gaston de Tolignac [= D. W. Griffith], *Translated into English by* Capt Victor Marier, [= D. W. Griffith] ***Ph*** Billy Bitzer ***Ed*** James E. Smith, Rose Smith ***Mus*** Carl Henfrit Santor Elinor
Act Lillian Gish, Robert Harron, Dorothy Gish, George Fawcett, Erich von Stroheim, Noel Coward (Griffith/Artcraft)

In *Hearts of the World* D. W. Griffith makes his principal love story a fleshless skeleton upon which to hang a large number of brilliant war scenes, in an effort to show the horrors at close range—its effect upon the combatants and non-combatants alike.

Selected for his principals are the son and daughter, respectively, of two American painters who made their homes in France. They fall in love and are betrothed. When war is declared the youth makes the heroic declaration that a country that is good enough to live in is worth fighting for, and joins the French army.

The picture opens with scenes showing the little French village in time of peace and then goes into a depiction of the struggle with the Germans for its possession.

Another role admirably planted, but which fails to develop to the full strength of its promise, is The Little Disturber. Dorothy Gish is the Disturber and her sister Lillian is the heroine. Both are excellent and wholly equal to the demands of their respective parts.

Robert Harron, as the young American, is the outstanding artist of the picture.

•

HEAT
1972, 100 mins, US Ⓥ col
Dir Paul Morrissey ***Prod*** Andy Warhol ***Scr*** Paul Morrissey, John Hollowell ***Ph*** Paul Morrissey ***Ed*** Lara Idel, Jed Johnson ***Mus*** John Cale
Act Sylvia Miles, Joe Dallesandro (Warhol)

Paul Morrissey, who made *Flesh and Trash* for the Andy Warhol Factory Group, always had a soft spot for the so-called Hollywood film. In fact, he often claimed he was making Hollywood films, albeit impregnated by new permissiveness, plus scenes of drugs, sexual freedom and his own kind of social observation.

This one, main centered in Hollywood, might be a sort of homage to Billy Wilder's *Sunset Blvd.* Sex is more implicit here, if tactful, and it is about an out-of-work young actor and an ex-star with daughter troubles and a turning point in her career.

Morrissey has given more fluidity than his other pix but relies mainly on actors in a series of well-meshed scenes as they play out the drama and comedy of a Hollywood that is sliding away.

•

HEAT
1995, 172 mins, US Ⓥ ⊙ ▭ col
Dir Michael Mann ***Prod*** Michael Mann, Art Linson ***Scr*** Michael Mann ***Ph*** Dante Spinotti ***Ed*** Dov Hoenig, Pasquale Buba, William Goldenberg, Tom Rolf ***Mus*** Elliott Goldenthal ***Art*** Neil Spisak
Act Al Pacino, Robert De Niro, Val Kilmer, Jon Voight, Tom Sizemore, Diane Venora (Forward Pass/Warner)

Stunningly made and incisively acted by a large and terrific cast, Michael Mann's ambitious study of the relativity of good and evil stands apart from other films of its type by virtue of its extraordinarily rich characterizations and its thoughtful, deeply melancholic take on modern life.

Showing signs of increased virtuosity with every picture, Mann orchestrates a sprawling tale of an obsessed, brilliantly intuitive cop (Al Pacino) hunting a superbly disciplined master criminal (Robert De Niro) across a sulphurous Los Angeles landscape. But this classic Western-like structure is just the central focus for a very detailed portrait of seemingly equal forces on both sides of the law.

Initial action set piece is a heist that resembles a military operation, as a gang led by Neil McCauley (De Niro) knocks over an armored truck in downtown L.A. When cop Vincent Hanna (Pacino) finally identifies McCauley as his prey, he amusingly finds a way to force him to have a cup of coffee, resulting in a terrific scene, the first ever between these two great actors.

McCauley and a small group of cohorts pull off a bank robbery that precipitates a chase and a mind-boggling machine-gun shootout on downtown Los Angeles streets. From here, it's the small betrayals and Hanna's sure understanding of his adversary that allow the net to tighten around McCauley and his men.

Mann delivers the final face-off between the two equally matched opposite numbers in a fairly staggering nighttime climax that begins during the evacuation of a hotel and ends beneath planes roaring into LAX.

As Hanna's third wife, Diane Venora deserves special mention among a huge cast of outstanding actors, almost all of whom makes an impression even in small roles. Only Val Kilmer seems overcast in a role as a McCauley cohort that is less interestingly written than some others. Bud Cort pops up unbilled as an unpleasant coffee shop boss.

•

HEAT AND DUST
1983, 133 mins, UK Ⓥ ⊙ col
Dir James Ivory ***Prod*** Ismail Merchant ***Scr*** Ruth Prawer Jhabvala ***Ph*** Walter Lassally ***Ed*** Humphrey Dixon ***Mus*** Richard Robbins ***Art*** Wilfrid Shingleton
Act Julie Christie, Christopher Cazenove, Greta Scacchi, Julian Glover, Susan Fleetwood, Shashi Kapoor (Merchant Ivory)

Scripted from her own novel by Ruth Prawer Jhabvala, *Heat and Dust* intercuts the stories of two women and of India past and present. The device is sometimes irritating in its jumps but ultimately successful in conveying the essential immutability of India's mystic character and ambivalent appeal.

Julie Christie, as a distinctly modern Englishwoman researching and to some extent reliving the Indian past of a late great-aunt, is the top name in a fine and well-matched Anglo-Indian cast. But the principal impact, partly by virtue of role, is supplied by British newcomer Greta Scacchi. Portraying the great-aunt as a young bride of scandalous behavior in colonial India, she creates an impressive study of classic underplayed well-bred English turmoil as her affections oscillate between loyal husband and an Indian potentate.

•

HEATHERS
1989, 102 mins, US Ⓥ ⊙ col
Dir Michael Lehmann ***Prod*** Denise Di Novi ***Scr*** Daniel Waters ***Ph*** Francis Kenny ***Ed*** Norman Hollyn ***Mus*** David Newman ***Art*** Jon Hutman
Act Winona Ryder, Christian Slater, Shannen Doherty, Lisanne Falk, Kim Walker, Penelope Milford (New World)

Heathers is a super-smart black comedy about high school politics and teenage suicide that showcases a host of promising young talents.

Daniel Waters's enormously clever screenplay blazes a trail of originality through the dead wood of the teen-comedy genre by focusing on the Heathers, the four prettiest and most popular girls at Westerburg High [in Ohio], three of whom are named Heather.

Setting the tone for the group is founder and queen bitch Heather No. 1 (Kim Walker), who has a devastating put-down or comeback for every occasion and could freeze even a heat-seeking missile in its tracks with her icy stare.

Heathers No. 2 and 3 (Lisanne Falk, Shannen Doherty) get off their own zingers once in a while, while the fourth nubile beauty, Veronica (Winona Ryder), goes along for the ride but seems to have a mind of her own. She also has eyes for a rebellious-looking school newcomer named Jason Dean (Christian Slater).

Goaded by the seductive J. D., Veronica half-heartedly goes along with an attempt to murder Heather No. 1, who has become irritating beyond endurance.

Ryder is utterly fetching and winning as an intelligent but seriously divided young lady. Oozing an insinuating sarcasm reminiscent of Jack Nicholson, Slater has what it takes to make J. D. both alluring and dangerous. The three Heathers look like they've spent their lives practicing putdowns.

•

HEAT'S ON, THE
1943, 79 mins, US b/w
Dir Gregory Ratoff ***Prod*** Milton Carter ***Scr*** Fitzroy Davis, George S. George, Fred Schiller ***Ph*** Franz E. Planer ***Ed*** Otto Meyer
Act Mae West, Victor Moore, Lloyd Bridges, Mary Roche, Hazel Scott, Lester Allen (Columbia)

Picture opens on *Indiscretions*, a Broadway musical that's having trouble getting along, with Mae West singing "I'm Just a Stranger in Town," done in the typical Westian manner, while for the close she is surrounded by a male chorus in "Hello, Mi Amigo," which rates okay. "There Goes That Guitar," used by the Xavier Cugat band as background for a Latinesque dance double, is also a part of the structure of this musical.

Story of *Heat's On*, with West as the actress-siren, her hips a-swinging in a familiar manner and arms akimbo for added familiar effect, plus the affected hard-boiled Westian diction, concerns the efforts of a legit producer, in love with his star, to wrest her from a rival producer after latter has been hoodwinked into believing she's been blacklisted by a reform society.

West looks well but her technique somehow seems dated. William Gaxton does well as the legit producer who's soft for his glamorous star, while Alan Dinehart does okay as a rival prod.

•

HEATWAVE
1981, 93 mins, Australia Ⓥ col
Dir Phillip Noyce ***Prod*** Hillary Linstead, Ross Matthews ***Scr*** Marc Rosenberg, Phillip Noyce ***Ph*** Vincent Monton ***Ed*** John Scott ***Mus*** Cameron Allan ***Art*** Ross Major
Act Judy Davis, Richard Moir, Chris Haywood, Bill Hunter, John Gregg, Anna Jemison (Preston Crothers/M & L)

In his first feature film since the widely acclaimed *Newsfront* [1978], director Phillip Noyce projects Sydney as a cauldron in which hapless individuals are scalded by big business, organized crime, lawyers, police and journalists, working in an unholy alliance.

Noyce's chief protagonists are Richard Moir as a visionary young architect who has designed a $100 million residential complex, and Judy Davis as a radical activist in the forefront of the residents' resistance to its construction.

In part, pic takes on the trappings of the conventional mystery-thriller, pointing to a conspiracy involving the project's financial backer (Chris Haywood), his oily lawyer (John Gregg), Moir's boss (Bill Hunter), a journalist (John Meillon), and union official (Dennis Miller).

Davis, a formidable actress, wrestles with her ambiguous and enigmatic character, and does not quite jell. Moir, however, is a strong, sustaining force as the arrogant, moody, idealistic architect.

•

HEAVEN
1987, 80 mins, US Ⓥ ⊙ col
Dir Diane Keaton ***Prod*** Joe Kelly ***Ph*** Frederick Elmes, Joe Kelly ***Ed*** Paul Barnes ***Mus*** Howard Shore ***Art*** Barbara Ling
(Perpetual/RVF)

Heaven represents an exercise in frivolous metaphysics, an engagingly light-hearted but ultimately light-headed inquiry into the nature of paradise. Diane Keaton's feature directorial debut is a small-scale, non-narrative work using trendily shot interviews, snazzy optical effects and loads of film clips and songs to illustrate fanciful notions of the hereafter.

Close to 100 individuals, all unknown except for boxing promoter Don King, are quizzed on such matters as, "What is Heaven?" and "How do you get to Heaven?"

Peppering all these speculations are often goofy clips from old films and TV shows. Excerpts, none of which are identified, range from extravagant depictions of the afterlife, Hollywood-style, to the hilarious expostulations of early broadcast ministers and evangelists.

•

HEAVEN & EARTH
1993, 140 mins, US Ⓥ ⊙ ▭ col
Dir Oliver Stone ***Prod*** Oliver Stone, Arnon Milchan, Robert Kline, ***Scr*** Oliver Stone ***Ph*** Robert Richardson ***Ed*** David Brenner, Sally Menke ***Mus*** Kitaro ***Art*** Victor Kempster
Act Tommy Lee Jones, Joan Chen, Haing S. Ngor, Hiep Thi Le, Debbie Reynolds, Vivian Wu (Warner/Ixtlan/New Regency/Todd-AO/TAE)

The U.S. stayed in Vietnam too long, and Oliver Stone has returned to the subject one time too many with *Heaven & Earth*.

Drawing upon two autobiographical works [*When Heaven and Earth Changed Places* and *Child of War, Woman of Peace*] by his central figure, Stone presents nearly 40 years in the life of Le Ly as a succession of events with a melodrama quotient that might have challenged even Joan Crawford or Lana Turner.

The vessel for Stone's latest agitated history lesson is a Vietnamese Buddhist peasant who, in the way she is soiled, dominated, exploited, raped, brutalized, colonized, transformed and torn apart from her family, is no doubt supposed to represent Vietnam itself.

An early-1950s prolog presents the rice-farming community of Ky La, in central Vietnam, as a simple paradise. Per the heroine, "everything changed forever" with the arrival of the Viet Cong in 1963. Le Ly (Hiep Thi Le) sees her two brothers run off to join the Communists. She flees to Saigon at 18, later meeting Yank Sgt. Steve Butler (Tommy Lee Jones). At the 90-minute mark, Butler, Le Ly, their son and her previous son arrive in suburban San Diego, and perhaps the film's most effective moments catalog her experiences seeing American middle-class lifestyles and consumerism for the first time.

In writing this screenplay, foreign to him in more ways than one, Stone has taken no overt political position, and consequently adds very little to either the general discussion of Vietnam or his own. Shot mostly in Thailand, with some background views having been grabbed on location in Vietnam, pic looks impressive.

•

HEAVEN CAN WAIT
1943, 112 mins, US Ⓥ ⊙ col
Dir Ernst Lubitsch ***Prod*** Ernst Lubitsch ***Scr*** Samson Raphaelson ***Ph*** Edward Cronjager ***Ed*** Dorothy Spencer ***Mus*** Alfred Newman ***Art*** James Basevi, Leland Fuller
Act Gene Tierney, Don Ameche, Charles Coburn, Marjorie Main, Laird Cregar, Louis Calhern (20th Century-Fox)

Provided with generous slices of comedy, skillfully handled by producer-director Ernst Lubitsch, this is for most of the 112 minutes a smooth, appealing and highly commercial production. Lubitsch has endowed it with light, amusing sophistication and heart-warming nostalgia. He has handled Don Ameche and Gene Tierney, in (for them) difficult characterizations, dexterously.

The Lazlo Bus-Fekete play [*Birthday*] covers the complete span of a man's life, from precocious infancy to, in this case, the sprightly senility of a 70-year-old playboy. It opens with the deceased (Ameche) asking Satan for a passport to hell, which is not being issued unless the applicant can justify his right to it.

This is followed by a recital of real and fancied misdeeds from the time the sinner discovers that, in order to get girls, a boy must have plenty of beetles, through the smartly fashioned hilarious drunk scene with a French maid at the age of 15, to the thefting of his cousin's fiancée, whom he marries.

Charles Coburn, as the fond grandfather who takes a hand in his favorite grandson's romantic and domestic problems, walks away with the early sequences in a terrific comedy performance.

1943: NOMINATIONS: Best Picture, Director, Color Cinematography

•

HEAVEN CAN WAIT
1978, 100 mins, US Ⓥ ⊙ col
Dir Warren Beatty, Buck Henry ***Prod*** Warren Beatty ***Scr*** Warren Beatty, Elaine May ***Ph*** William A. Fraker ***Ed*** Robert C. Jones, Don Zimmerman ***Mus*** Dave Grusin ***Art*** Paul Sylbert
Act Warren Beatty, Julie Christie, James Mason, Jack Warden, Charles Grodin, Dyan Cannon (Paramount)

Heaven Can Wait is an outstanding film. Harry Segall's fantasy comedy-drama play, made in 1941 by Columbia as *Here Comes Mr Jordan*, returns in an updated, slightly more macabre treatment.

Warren Beatty plays an aging football star, prematurely summoned to judgment after a traffic accident because a celestial messenger (played by co-director Buck Henry) jumped the gun. This embarrasses James Mason into permitting Beatty to inhabit temporarily another body. The only available one is that of a wealthy industrialist whose death is plotted by floozy wife Dyan Cannon and Charles Grodin, the tycoon's nerd secretary.

Julie Christie falls for the rich guy, whose main ambition is to resume his football career, in which coach Jack Warden plays an important part.

Script and direction are very strong, providing a rich mix of visual and verbal humor that is controlled and avoids the extremes of cheap vulgarity and overly esoteric whimsy.

1978: Best Art Direction

NOMINATIONS: Best Picture, Directors (Warren Beatty, Buck Henry), Actor (Warren Beatty), Supp. Actor (Jack Warden), Supp. Actress (Dyan Cannon), Adapted Screenplay, Cinematography, Original Score

•

HEAVEN HELP US
(UK: CATHOLIC BOYS)
1985, 104 mins, US Ⓥ ⊙ col
Dir Michael Dinner ***Prod*** Dan Wigutow, Mark Carliner ***Scr*** Charles Purpura ***Ph*** Miroslav Ondricek ***Ed*** Stephen A. Rotter ***Mus*** James Horner ***Art*** Michael Molly
Act Donald Sutherland, John Heard, Andrew McCarthy, Mary Stuart Masterson, Kevin Dillon, Malcolm Danare (HBO/Silver Screen Partners)

Heaven Help Us focuses upon several Catholic school boys, three in particular, who get into an increasing amount of trouble with the presiding priests. Andrew McCarthy, a new arrival at St. Basil's, instantly latches onto reigning outsider in his class, Malcolm Danare, a chubby egghead who is constantly picked on by school bully Kevin Dillon. It's virtually inconceivable that the intelligent, sensible McCarthy or Danare would have anything to do with the likes of ne'er-do-well Dillon in real life, but Dillon intimidates them into something resembling friendship. Along with a couple of other large, silent boys, they receive their share of corporal punishment for relatively harmless offenses, wreak havoc during confession and communion and ultimately inspire some helpful changes to be made in the school hierarchy.

Very funny in spots and wonderfully evocative of Brooklyn, circa 1965, pic suffers somewhat by dividing its attention between outrageous pranks and realistic sketches of the Catholic school experience.

•

HEAVEN KNOWS, MR. ALLISON
1957, 107 mins, US Ⓥ ⊏⊐ col
Dir John Huston ***Prod*** Buddy Adler, Eugene Frenke ***Scr*** John Lee Mahin, John Huston ***Ph*** Oswald Morris ***Ed*** Russell Lloyd ***Mus*** Georges Auric ***Art*** Stephen Grimes
Act Deborah Kerr, Robert Mitchum (20th Century-Fox)

Behind the misleading title is an intriguing yarn [from the novel by Charles Shaw] about two people on opposite ends of the social ladder, thrown together in a highly unusual situation. It's about a marine, marooned on a small Pacific atoll [Tobago] with a nun. They divide their time dodging Japs and trying to steer clear of their emotions.

The film, directed by John Huston with something less than outstanding imagination, but with a good measure of humor and bravado, holds out an early promise which it doesn't keep. The parallel is drawn between the nun and her vocation and the marine with his, both subject to strong discipline. But—apart from a few remarks—the character and motivations of Deborah Kerr remain shrouded in mystery, and she reveals very little of herself.

The high spots of the film involve Robert Mitchum's exploits—and fantastic ones they are—in the midst of the occupying Japanese force when he raids its supply depot for food. These scenes are staged with noise, gusto and a good deal of suspense.

1957: NOMINATIONS: Best Actress (Deborah Kerr), Adapted Screenplay

•

HEAVENLY CREATURES
1994, 99 mins, New Zealand Ⓥ ⊏⊐ col
Dir Peter Jackson ***Prod*** Jim Booth ***Scr*** Peter Jackson, Frances Walsh ***Ph*** Alun Bollinger ***Ed*** James Selkirk ***Mus*** Peter Dasent ***Art*** Grant Major
Act Melanie Lynsky, Kate Winslet, Sarah Peirse, Diana Kent, Clive Merrison, Simon O'Connor (WingNut/Fontana)

An exhilarating retelling of a 1950s tabloid murder, Peter Jackson's *Heavenly Creatures* combines original vision, a drop-dead command of the medium and a successful marriage between a dazzling, kinetic techno-show and a complex, credible portrait of the out-of-control relationship between the crime's two schoolgirl perpetrators.

Opening with the panicked aftermath of the killing itself, Jackson makes an attention-grabbing leap from a fusty Brit newsreel of sedate downtown Christchurch, replete with cheery commentary, to a frenetic Sam Raimiesque tracking sequence in which the blood-spattered teenage girls emerge hysterical from a secluded wood.

He then backtracks to reveal the somewhat morose and short-on-confidence Pauline (Melanie Lynsky) being snapped out of her shell by the arrival at school of imperious English girl Juliet (Kate Winslet), who briskly provides her with a role model.

The friendship quickly spirals to the level of passionate interdependence, tracking the pair's hyperactive pursuit of pleasure with manic, often menacing vigor, and sweeping the audience along to the rollicking sound of tunes sung by the girls' favorite tenor, Mario Lanza. They soon begin seeing themselves on an intellectually superior plane to everyone around them, creating an Arthurian fantasyland which is home to two lovers and their remorseless, mass-murdering son.

Their bond falls into unclassifiable territory, being neither an innocent, misconstrued friendship, nor an acknowledged lesbian relationship.

Backup from the adult cast is strong with Diana Kent and Clive Merrison on the chill, remote side as Juliet's parents.

1994: NOMINATION: Original Screenplay

•

HEAVEN ONLY KNOWS
1947, 97 mins, US b/w
Dir Albert S. Rogell ***Prod*** Seymour Nebenzal ***Scr*** Art Arthur, Rowland Leigh ***Ph*** Karl Struss ***Ed*** Edward Mann ***Mus*** Heinz Roemhold ***Art*** Martin Obzina
Act Robert Cummings, Brian Donlevy, Marjorie Reynolds, Jorja Curtright (United Artists)

Heaven Only Knows is an amusing fantasy done in an almost straight manner to give it credence. There are no astonishing miracles of heavenly power, no fantastic harps and wings to stretch the imagination too far. It's a tongue-in-cheek treatment that lends a lightness to what, otherwise, could have been rather heavy drama.

Story concerns an angel visiting earth to rectify a heavenly bookkeeping error. He had permitted a man to run loose without a soul because his destiny hadn't been properly entered in the books. On earth, he finds the soulless creature just that. He's a ruthless killer operating a saloon in Montana.

The angel's chore is to bring together the killer and the schoolmarm because, according to heaven's books, they should have been married for two years.

Robert Cummings plays the visiting angel with just the right touch. There's a refreshing naiveness in the angel's conduct in the tough Western mining town; his openly friendly approach to his task and occasional chagrin when he encounters a situation where a miracle would have been a big help. Brian Donlevy, too, sparks his assignment as the man without a soul.

•

HEAVENS ABOVE!
1963, 118 mins, UK Ⓥ b/w
Dir John Boulting ***Prod*** John Boulting, Roy Boulting ***Scr*** Frank Harvey, John Boulting ***Ph*** Max Greene ***Ed*** Teddy Farvas ***Mus*** Richard Rodney Bennett
Act Peter Sellers, Bernard Miles, Eric Sykes, Irene Handl, Miriam Karlin, Isabel Jeans (British Lion/Romulus)

A measure of the merit of *Heavens Above!* is that its theme could have been just as acceptably used as a straight drama. But the Boulting Brothers effectively employ their favorite weapon, the rapier of ridicule. The screenplay is full of choice jokes, but the humor is often uneven.

Story concerns the appointment, by a clerical error, of the Reverend John Smallwood (Peter Sellers) to the parish of Orbiston Parva, a prosperous neighborhood ruled by the Despard Family, makers of Tranquilax, the three-in-one restorative (Sedative! Stimulant! Laxative!). He's a quiet, down-to-earth chap who happens to believe in the scriptures and lives by them.

From the moment he gives his first sermon all hell breaks out, so to speak. He shocks the district by making a Negro trashman his warden and takes a bunch of disreputable evicted gypsies into the vicarage. Soon he makes his first convert, Lady Despard.

Within this framework there are some very amusing verbal and visual jokes, and both are largely aided by some deft acting. Sellers gives a guileful portrayal of genuine simplicity. Bernard Miles, as an acquisitive butler; Eric Sykes, Irene Handl, Miriam Karlin and Roy Kinnear (leader of the gypsies); and Isabel Jeans, a regal Lady Despard, all contribute heftily.

•

HEAVEN'S GATE
1980, 219 mins, US Ⓥ ⊙ ⊏⊐ col
Dir Michael Cimino ***Prod*** Joann Carelli ***Scr*** Michael Cimino ***Ph*** Vilmos Zsigmond ***Ed*** Tom Rolf, William Reynolds, Lisa Fruchtman, Gerald Greenberg ***Mus*** David Mansfield ***Art*** Tambi Larsen
Act Kris Kristofferson, Christopher Walken, Isabelle Huppert, Sam Waterston, John Hurt, Jeff Bridges (United Artists)

The first scenes of *Heaven's Gate* are so energetic and beautiful that anyone who knows the saga of the $35 million epic might begin to think it was going to be worth every penny. Unfortunately the balance of director Michael Cimino's film is so confusing, so overlong at three and a half hours and so ponderous that it fails to work at almost every level.

What structure the film does have is based on the Johnson County wars which took place in the 1890s in Wyoming.

The story deals with a group of established cattlemen headed by Canton (Sam Waterston) who are convinced their herds are being looted by immigrant settlers. With the approval of the state, the operators of the large cattle ranches draw up a death list of 125 poor immigrants in Johnson County who are supposedly doing the "rustling." Kris Kristofferson plays the Federal marshal who turned against his class.

Cimino's attempts to draw a portrait of the plight of the immigrants in the West in that period are so impersonal that none of the victims ever get beyond pat stereotypes.

Cimino, who wrote the script himself, has simply not provided enough details for his story, leaving his audience guessing.

1981: NOMINATION: Best Art Direction

●

HEAVEN'S PRISONERS

1996, 126 mins, US/UK Ⓥ col

Dir Phil Joanou ***Prod*** Albert S. Ruddy, Andre E. Morgan, Leslie Greif ***Scr*** Harley Peyton, Scott Frank ***Ph*** Harris Savides ***Ed*** William Steinkamp ***Mus*** George Fenton ***Art*** John Stoddart

Act Alec Baldwin, Kelly Lynch, Mary Stuart Masterson, Eric Roberts, Teri Hatcher, Vondie Curtis Hall (New Line/Savoy/Rank)

Before sinking into a plotline as thick as jambalaya, Phil Joanou's *Heaven's Prisoners* stirs up enough spice to suggest what drew Alec Baldwin to James Lee Burke's novel in the first place. However rudderless and convoluted this Cajun crime mystery becomes, picture at the very least offers Baldwin one of his juicier roles.

Baldwin plays Dave Robicheaux, a former cop who gave up police work and boozer to live the quiet life of a bait shop owner with loving wife Annie (Kelly Lynch). That life is changed forever when Dave and Annie watch a small plane crash into the Gulf and save a little Salvadoran girl (Samantha Lagpacan).

As he gets thicker and thicker into the city's criminal mire, Dave encounters more than his share of colorful, dangerous characters. Topping the list is Bubba Rocque (Eric Roberts) an old high school buddy and now a mid-level drug lord. Teri Hatcher, television's Lois Lane, keeps pace with Roberts as his femme fatale wife. Mary Stuart Masterson, nearly unrecognizable as a torch-carrying stripper who guides Dave through the criminal underbelly, does better with her cliché role than should be expected.

Heaven's Prisoners has the feel of a re-edited movie, all stops and starts, bursts of activity amid stretches of brooding. Film would have been better served with some streamlining in the script stage. Too many bad guys and blind alleys spoil this Cajun stew. [In the U.K. and some other territories, pic was released in a 132-min. version.]

●

HEAVY METAL

1981, 90 mins, US col

Dir Gerald Potterton ***Prod*** Ivan Reitman ***Scr*** Dan Goldberg, Len Blum ***Ed*** Janice Brown ***Mus*** Elmer Bernstein ***Art*** Michael Gross

(Reitman-Moyer)

This technically first-rate six-segment animated anthology is an amalgam of science fiction, sword and sorcery, hip humor, violence, sex and a smidgen of drugs.

The film, which draws its title and sensibility from the adult fantasy magazine of the same name, tends to front-load its virtues. Initial segments have a boisterous blend of dynamic graphics, intriguing plot premises and sly wit that unfortunately slide gradually downhill. Courtesy of a vastly overlong, relatively unrousing 27-minute end-piece that may be the technical highpoint of the film, but lacks the punch and tightness of the earlier segments, the venture tends to run out of steam. Still, the net effect is an overridingly positive one.

●

HEAVY TRAFFIC

1973, 78 mins, US Ⓥ col

Dir Ralph Bakshi ***Prod*** Steve Krantz ***Scr*** Ralph Bakshi ***Ph*** Ted C. Bemiller, Gregg Heschong ***Ed*** Donald W. Ernst ***Mus*** Ray Shanklin, ***Ed*** Bogas

(Film Creations/Krantz)

After their first X-rated animated feature, *Fritz the Cat*, producer Steve Krantz and writer-director Ralph Bakshi turn to "human" creatures, combining animation and live action, a blatant example of hardcore pornography.

There's something to offend everyone in this mélange of crudely conceived, amateurishly animated stuff. From the one extreme of a crude sexually oriented attack on Christianity, it manages to take a crack at every type—from the Jewish mother to the Mafia.

There are heavyhanded attempts to ridicule Godfather-attuned Italian-Americans, homosexuals, the physically deformed, capitalists and labor, slum dwellers, the Church. Even M-G-M is made a victim by the use of an insertion of scenes from the Jean Harlow–Clark Gable *Red Dust*.

●

HEDDA

1975, 104 mins, UK Ⓥ col

Dir Trevor Nunn ***Prod*** Robert Enders ***Scr*** Trevor Nunn ***Ph*** Douglas Slocombe ***Ed*** Peter Tanner ***Mus*** Laurie Johnson ***Art*** Ted Tester

Act Glenda Jackson, Timothy West, Peter Eyre, Jennie Linden, Patrick Stewart, Constance Chapman (Brut)

Hedda is a gem, taking the Royal Shakespeare production of the Henrik Ibsen classic, complete with a fine cast headed by Glenda Jackson.

It's heady stuff, nearly every line to be relished, as one watches the destructively dominant Hedda torturing her friends and relations with rapier-sharp lines and stiletto-like glances.

So persuasively talented and self-assured a performer as Jackson is not everyone's cup of tea, but few should quibble with one of her best parts.

1975: NOMINATION: Best Actress (Glenda Jackson)

●

HEIRESS, THE

1949, 115 mins, US Ⓥ b/w

Dir William Wyler ***Prod*** William Wyler ***Scr*** Ruth Goetz, Augustus Goetz ***Ph*** Leo Tover ***Ed*** William Hornbeck ***Mus*** Aaron Copland ***Art*** John Meehan, Harry Horner

Act Olivia de Havilland, Montgomery Clift, Ralph Richardson, Miriam Hopkins (Paramount)

The Heiress is a meticulous reproduction of the Victorian scene, so faithful to its mores that it is a museum piece.

William Wyler, in his producer-director role, has seen fit to cling exactly to the period portrayed in the Ruth and Augustus Goetz script, based on their stage play suggested by Henry James's novel *Washington Square*.

Olivia de Havilland, in the title role, is the homely daughter of a wealthy physician. A social shyness that cloaks her quick wit and puckishness has kept her suitorless despite a sizeable wealth that will be augmented when her father passes. Montgomery Clift is the first male to show her attention. The father sees through his courting, tries to break up a quick engagement.

Clift plays the difficult part of an ambiguous character who is more opportunist than crook in his fortune-hunting. Ralph Richardson is grand as the stern, strait-laced father.

1949: Best Actress (Olivia de Havilland), B&W Art Direction, Scoring of a Dramatic Picture, B&W Costume Design

NOMINATIONS: Best Picture, Director, Supp. Actor (Ralph Richardson), B&W Cinematography

●

HEIST, THE

SEE: $

●

HELEN MORGAN STORY, THE

1957, 117 mins, US ⊏⊐ b/w

Dir Michael Curtiz ***Prod*** Martin Rackin ***Scr*** Oscar Saul, Dean Riesner, Stephen Longstreet, Nelson Gidding ***Ph*** Ted McCord ***Ed*** Frank Bracht ***Art*** John Beckman

Act Ann Blyth, Paul Newman, Richard Carlson, Gene Evans, Alan King, Cara Williams (Warner)

Warner's feature is little more than a tuneful soap opera, another in what appears to be a growing series of boozy biopix of showbiz greats. [A *Playhouse 90* version of the same story, starring Polly Bergen, was shown on TV a few months before pic's release.] On the studio schedule for a long time, the production finally emerges as the product of four screenwriters, who have taken some of the legends and some of the realities of the Roaring '20s and loosely attributed all of them to La Morgan.

The storyline sometimes strains credulity and the dialog situations occasionally give the production a cornball flavor. Overall plot of a woman in love with a heel is best exemplified by the fadeout shot on the song "Can't Help Lovin' That Man."

Morgan (Ann Blyth) comes to Chicago to seek a career. She gets her start, both professionally and romantically, with Larry (Paul Newman), a shady operator, and his desertion of her after one night sets the pattern of his domination of her career. When he comes back into her life to prey upon her friendship with attorney Wade (Richard Carlson), she takes to the bottle for solace.

Director Michael Curtiz has done a good job with the material at hand, injecting a pacing and bits of business that help maintain interest, and the production gets added benefit from a series of hit tunes of the era, excellently sung offscreen by Gogi Grant. Blyth turns in a sympathetic but not always convincing performance. Newman is very good as the rackets guy, giving the part authority and credibility.

●

HELEN OF TROY

1955, 118 mins, US Ⓥ ⊙ ⊏⊐ col

Dir Robert Wise ***Prod*** [uncredited] ***Scr*** John Twist, Hugh Gray ***Ph*** Harry Stradling ***Ed*** Thomas Reilly ***Mus*** Max Steiner ***Art*** Edward Carrere

Act Rossana Podesta, Jacques Sernas, Cedric Hardwicke, Stanley Baker, Niall MacGinnis, Nora Swinburne (Warner)

The retelling of the Homeric legend, filmed in its entirety in Italy, makes lavish use of the CinemaScope screen.

WB and director Robert Wise piled on the extras in Greek and Trojan armies. Production values ride over shortcomings in John Twist and Hugh Gray's script and dialog [from an adaptation by Gray and N. Richard Nash]. Like many tales of antiquity, the story is occasionally stilted.

As Helen and Paris, the love-smitten Trojan prince, Warners cast two unknowns—Rossana Podesta, an exquisite Italian beauty, and Jacques Sernas, a brawny and handsome Frenchman. Visually both meet the demands of the roles. Their voices have been dubbed.

The story opens with Paris's journey to Sparta to effect a peace treaty between the Greeks and Troy. He falls in love with Helen not knowing she is the queen of Sparta. His peace mission fails, and in making his escape from Sparta, takes Helen with him. The "abduction" unites the Greeks and sends them off on a war against Troy.

●

HELL AND HIGH WATER

1954, 103 mins, US ⊏⊐ col

Dir Samuel Fuller ***Prod*** Raymond A. Klune ***Scr*** Jesse L. Lasky Jr, Samuel Fuller ***Ph*** Joe MacDonald ***Ed*** James B. Clark ***Mus*** Alfred Newman ***Art*** Lyle R. Wheeler, Leland Fuller

Act Richard Widmark, Bella Darvi, Victor Francen, Cameron Mitchell, Gene Evans, David Wayne (20th Century-Fox)

CinemaScope and rip-roaring adventure mate perfectly in *Hell and High Water*, a highly fanciful, but mighty entertaining action feature [from a story by David Hempstead].

As the male star, Richard Widmark takes easily to the rugged assignment, giving it the wallop needed. It is a further projection of the action-adventure type of hero he does quite often, and well. The picture introduces as a new star Polish-born, French-raised Bella Darvi and she creates an interesting impression in her debut.

Plot has to do with a group of individuals of many nationalities who band together to thwart a scheme to start a new world war with an atomic incident that will be blamed on the United States. These private heroes hire Widmark, a former naval submarine officer, to command an underwater trip to the Arctic, where scientists on the voyage will check reports that a Communist atomic arsenal is being built on an isolated island.

1954: NOMINATION: Best Special Effects

●

HELL BENT

1918, 77 mins, US ⊗ b/w

Dir John Ford ***Scr*** John Ford, Harry Carey ***Ph*** Ben Reynolds

Act Harry Carey, Neva Gerber, Duke Lee, Joseph Harris (Universal)

Hell Bent was rediscovered at the Czech Film Archives. Current print is presently the only one of two complete films surviving from the director's 1917–19 beginning years at Universal Studios.

Hell Bent was Ford's 14th film and his ninth feature. Its leading player, Harry Carey, was Ford's most frequent early star and collaborator. Here, Carey again plays his laconic Cheyenne Harry protagonist.

Harry rides into the town of Rawhide where in a long winded comic turn he strikes up a friendship with Cimarron Bill (Duke Lee) and is then smitten by love for Bess (Neva Gerber), a "good girl" forced by circumstances to work in a dance hall. B-plot mechanics take over as Harry tries to rid town of outlaws but is stymied when he learns Bess's weak-willed brother is member of gang led by Bean Ross (Joseph Harris).

Film is enlivened by some of Ford's special moments. As his relationship with Bess develops, Harry awkwardly carries her home in the rain while in the next shot his abandoned pal wanders through the darkened saloon.

•

HELLBOUND
HELLRAISER II

1988, 96 mins, UK/US Ⓥ ⊙ col

Dir Tony Randel ***Prod*** Christopher Figg ***Scr*** Peter Atkins ***Ph*** Robin Vidgeon ***Mus*** Christopher Young ***Art*** Mike Buchanan

Act Clare Higgins, Ashley Laurence, Kenneth Cranham, Imogen Boorman, Sean Chapman, Doug Bradley (Film Futures)

Hellraiser II is a maggoty carnival of mayhem, mutation and dismemberment, awash in blood and recommended only for those who thrive on such junk.

Helmer Tony Randel returns to the off-the-wall tale of a psychotic psychiatrist's long struggle to get the better of something called the Lament Configuration, a kind of demonic, silver-filigreed Rubik's Cube whose solution opens the transdimensional doors into a parallel world of sinful pleasure and unspeakably hellish pain.

This fiendish shrink takes a special interest in a new patient, Kristy, whose family was massacred in appropriately gruesome fashion by box-sprung flesh-eating ghouls called Cenobites.

As Kristy and the shrink head toward the big showdown in Hades, the movie unfolds with a tableau of can-you-top-this gross-outs.

•

HELL DRIVERS

1957, 108 mins, UK Ⓥ b/w

Dir Cy Endfield ***Prod*** S. Benjamin Fisz ***Scr*** John Kruse, Cy Endfield ***Ph*** Geoffrey Unsworth ***Ed*** John D. Guthridge ***Mus*** Hubert Clifford ***Art*** Ernest Archer

Act Stanley Baker, Herbert Lom, Peggy Cummins, Patrick McGoohan, Jill Ireland, Sean Connery (Aqua/Rank)

Hell Drivers is a slab of unabashed melodrama. The story [from a short story by John Kruse, adaptation by Cy Endfield], said to be based on a real one, has to do with the rivalries of a gang of haulage truck drivers, operating between gravel pits and a construction site.

Stanley Baker is an ex-convict who gets a job as one of these drivers and immediately falls foul of Patrick McGoohan, the firm's ace driver. Baker discovers that McGoohan and William Hartnell, the manager, are running a racket. The drama comes to an uneasy head when Baker's lorry is doctored.

Endfield's direction is straightforward and conventional, but some of the speed sequences provide some tingling thrills. Acting is adequate, but uninspired. Baker gives a forceful performance of restrained strength and Herbert Lom has some neat moments as his Italian buddy. Patrick McGoohan gives an exaggerated study as the villain. Peggy Cummins, as a village vamp, fails to spark a tepid love interest.

•

HELLER IN PINK TIGHTS

1960, 100 mins, US Ⓥ col

Dir George Cukor ***Prod*** Carlo Ponti, Marcello Girosi ***Scr*** Dudley Nichols, Walter Bernstein ***Ph*** Harold Lipstein ***Ed*** Howard Smith ***Mus*** Daniele Amfitheatrof ***Art*** Hal Pereira, Eugene Allen

Act Sophia Loren, Anthony Quinn, Eileen Heckart, Ramon Novarro, Margaret O'Brien, Steve Forrest (Paramount)

With *Heller In Pink Tights*, director George Cukor puts tongue in cheek to turn an ordinary story into a gaudy, old-fashioned Western satire with gleeful touches of melodrama.

Taken from a novel by Louis L'Amour, *Heller* follows The Great Healy Dramatic and Concert Co. in two red wagons through the wilds of Wyoming. The traveling theatre is fighting for its survival, and Sophia Loren and Anthony Quinn put up a strong enough battle to make things interesting and amusing. It's when the film's plotage dissolves into pure Western that it becomes somewhat commonplace.

Loren dons blonde tresses for the role of an actress who has a knack for getting into situations. She looks fine with golden head and turns in a respectable, most believable performance. Quinn, as head of the Healy company, adeptly projects as the he-man, yet properly building a tender, calm characterization.

Eileen Heckart just about steals the whole shootin' match as an actress who has given up a "promising" career for her daughter's chances on stage. It's real comedy, and Heckart carries it off with polish. Steve Forrest makes a lovable villain, evil but never evil enough to lose his attraction. Margaret O'Brien is fine in a role that offers her more chances to be seen than heard; Edmund Lowe is very good as a "Shakespearean" actor; and Ramon Novarro is aptly sinister as a well-heeled banker.

•

HELL IN KOREA

SEE: A HILL IN KOREA

•

HELL IN THE PACIFIC

1968, 103 mins, US Ⓥ ▭ col

Dir John Boorman ***Prod*** Reuben Bercovitch ***Scr*** Alexander Jacobs, Eric Bercovici ***Ph*** Conrad Hall ***Ed*** Thomas Stanford ***Mus*** Lalo Schifrin ***Art*** Anthony D. G. Pratt, Masao Yamazaki

Act Lee Marvin, Toshiro Mifune (Selmur)

Tale of two warriors forced to co-exist. Lee Marvin and Toshiro Mifune comprise the entire cast of this World War II drama, directed with an uncertain hand by John Boorman.

Story [by Reuben Bercovitch] takes off with the discovery by Mifune that he no longer is alone on a desolate Pacific island. Pair stalk each other, then attempt to outwit each other, finally collaborate on survival in the form of a raft.

Mifune's unrestrained grunting and running about create an outdated caricature of an Oriental. Marvin has sardonic lines which resemble wisecracks, intended for on-lookers. The subtle humor which was meant to exist becomes overpowering.

Lalo Schifrin could not have served worse the purposes of the film. Phony suspense bits—snapping twigs, etc.—are punched to death through maladroit composing. Net effect of this is the impression that there have got to be 50 musicians lurking just off-camera.

Marvin's arresting screen presence requires appreciative surrounding characters, none of which are present, or meant to be.

Mifune gets few chances to project three-dimensional characterization.

•

HELL IS A CITY

1960, 98 mins, UK b/w

Dir Val Guest ***Prod*** Michael Carreras ***Scr*** Val Guest ***Ph*** Arthur Grant ***Ed*** John Dunsford ***Mus*** Stanley Black ***Art*** Robert Jones

Act Stanley Baker, John Crawford, Donald Pleasence, Maxine Audley, Billie Whitelaw, Joseph Tomelty (Hammer)

Hell Is a City is an absorbing film of a conventional cops and robbers yarn. Val Guest's taut screenplay [from a novel by Maurice Proctor], allied to his own deft direction, has resulted in a notable film in which the characters are all vividly alive, the action constantly gripping and the background of a provincial city put over with authenticity.

The film was shot largely in Manchester. Arthur Grant's camerawork has arrestingly caught the feel of the big city with its grey, sleazy backstreets, its saloons, the surrounding factory chimneys, the bleakness of the moors and the bustle of the city.

The yarn has Stanley Baker as a detective inspector who, married to a bored, unsympathetic wife (Maxine Audley), spends most of his time on his job. In this instance he is concerned with a dangerous escaped convict who, he suspects, will be returning to Manchester to pick up the stolen jewels that sent him to the cooler. When the girl clerk of the local bookie is attacked while on the way to the bank and then found murdered on the nearby moors, Baker suspects that the crook and a small gang are the criminals. Doggedly he starts to track them down.

From the moment when the killer (John Crawford) makes his sudden surprise entrance and sets the wheels of the robbery in motion, suspense rarely lets up. The robbery itself is briskly pulled off, there is a first-rate scene on the moors when the police raid an illegal gathering of gamblers and some down-to-earth police station sequences, with Baker pulling no punches in his determination to get at the truth. Acting all round is admirable.

•

HELL IS FOR HEROES

1962, 90 mins, US Ⓥ ⊙ b/w

Dir Don Siegel ***Prod*** Henry Blanke ***Scr*** Robert Pirosh, Richard Carr ***Ph*** Harold Lipstein ***Ed*** Howard Smith ***Mus*** Leonard Rosenman ***Art*** Hal Pereira, Howard Richmond

Act Steve McQueen, Bobby Darin, Fess Parker, Harry Guardino, James Coburn, Bob Newhart (Paramount)

Producer Henry Blanke has framed and mounted a gripping, fast-paced, hard-hitting dramatic portrait of an interesting World War II battlefield incident. But there are occasional duds in the film's dramatic arsenal.

Recollections of an actual and tightly classified incident near the dragon's teeth of the Siegfried Line during the dark days of World War II inspired the story by Robert Pirosh, adapted into screenplay form by Richard Carr and Pirosh, creative activator of the film who bowed out as its producer along the way.

Pivotal character of the drama is a surly, rebellious, busted NCO (Steve McQueen) whose front-line courage, leadership and keen sense of improvisation in the course of a grim and seemingly hopeless campaign to hold off a large German force in the face of incredible odds backfires into a potential court martial rap for usurping authority.

McQueen plays the central role with hard-bitten businesslike reserve and an almost animal intensity, permitting just the right degree of humanity to project through a war-weary-and-wise veneer. Bobby Darin has a colorful role of a battlefield hoarder, which he portrays with relish. Harry Guardino is excellent as an uncertain sergeant. James Coburn fine as a practical corporal.

•

HELLO AGAIN

1987, 96 mins, US Ⓥ ⊙ col

Dir Frank Perry ***Prod*** Frank Perry ***Scr*** Susan Isaacs ***Ph*** Jan Weincke ***Ed*** Peter C. Frank, Trudy Ship ***Mus*** William Goldstein ***Art*** Edward Pisoni

Act Shelley Long, Judith Ivey, Gabriel Byrne, Corbin Bernsen, Sela Ward, Austin Pendleton (Touchstone)

Viewers are advised to be wary of any romantic comedy in which the ultimate resolution (and very life of the protagonist) depends on the answer to the question, "Are you really ready for me to bring the rubber bone?" That's where this runaway plotline leads to, though, as Shelley Long wanders through a script she can't carry by herself while heading a cast handled with less than a Midas touch by director Frank Perry, who seems to think he's staging a high school play.

Long plays Lucy Chadman, the dull and thoroughly domesticated housewife of Corbin Bernsen's yup-scale Long Island plastic surgeon Jason Chadman. She chokes to death on a chicken ball while in the occultist boutique of her off-the-wall, down-the-hall sister Zelda (Judith Ivey).

After much hocus-pocus, Zelda brings Lucy back from her grave a year to the day after her death. The most predictable thing that could happen does, and Lucy walks in on her husband with her gold-digging, glory-grabbing girlfriend Kim (played with nice salaciousness by Sela Ward, before the script forces her to go out of her character in stupidity).

Scene in which Lucy discovers the lovers is actually funny, but it should have operated as a starting point for some human comedy. Instead it's a jumping-off point, into an abyss of silly plot developments. While all of this is going on, Long is expected to provide cohesion by drawing a zany, goofball character who is lovable in her imperfection.

•

HELLO, DOLLY!

1969, 129 mins, US Ⓥ ⊙ ▭ col

Dir Gene Kelly ***Prod*** Ernest Lehman ***Scr*** Ernest Lehman ***Ph*** Harry Stradling ***Ed*** William Reynolds ***Mus*** Lennie Hayton, Lionel Newman (arrs.) ***Art*** John DeCuir

Act Barbra Streisand, Walter Matthau, Michael Crawford, Louis Armstrong, Marianne McAndrew, Tommy Tune (20th Century-Fox/Chenault)

Hello, Dolly! is an expensive, expansive, sometimes exaggerated, sentimental, nostalgic, wholesome, pictorially opulent $20 million filmusical [from the 1964 Broadway production, music and lyrics by Jerry Herman] with the charisma of Barbra Streisand in the title role.

Streisand is a unique performer, with that inborn vitality that marks great personalities. She brings her own special kind of authority. There is a certain inconsistency, or even confusion, in the speech pattern.

Walter Matthau is hard to accept at first, his dancing being the step-counting sort and his singing somewhat awkward. Nonetheless his experience cannot be discounted.

The film "opens cute" with a long-held still of the 14th St. replica. Immensely and imaginatively detailed, it intrigues the eye and mind directly. When the still "wipes" into live action, the film is off in a flurry of promise and introducing the times (1890) and the heroine (Dolly) en route to Yonkers.

1969: Best Art Direction, Sound, Adapted Score for a Musical Picture

NOMINATIONS: Best Picture, Cinematography, Costume Design, Editing

•

HELLO FRISCO, HELLO

1943, 90 mins, US col

Dir H. Bruce Humberstone ***Prod*** Milton Sperling ***Scr*** Robert Ellis, Helen Logan, Richard Macauley ***Ph*** Charles Clarke, Allen Davey ***Ed*** Barbara McLean ***Mus*** Charles Henderson, Emil Newman (dirs.) ***Art*** James Basevi, Boris Leven

Act Alice Faye, John Payne, Jack Oakie, Lynn Bari, Laird Cregar, June Havoc (20th Century-Fox)

Per usual the typical musical comedy plot is no great shakes, but nicely studded with laughs, pathos and innumerable musical interludes. Laid in San Francisco at the turn of the century when, as the story has it, men were still prospecting for gold nearby, story spots John Payne as the leader of a foursome that includes Alice Faye, Jack Oakie and June Havoc. It's a typical tavern combo that leans on their warbling to keep a regular job in the metropolis's leading saloon.

Rise of quartet, with Payne as business man and showman, is phenomenal until all four are rolling in coin. The yen of Payne to make the grade in Nob Hill society brings the usual complications.

Alice Faye, who has the task of selling the vast majority of tunes, is a revelation. Payne makes a sufficiently zestful business manager for the quartet, though one wonders why he falls so hopelessly for Lynn Bari, the Nob Hill socialite. Jack Oakie, as the happy-go-lucky hoofer, and his partner, June Havoc, make sufficient contrast as the other half of the foursome. Oakie also cashes in on some tricky tap dances and his usual mugging. All four fit nicely in their song-dance routines.

•

HELLRAISER

1987, 90 mins, UK Ⓥ ⊙ col

Dir Clive Barker ***Prod*** Christopher Figg ***Scr*** Clive Barker ***Ph*** David Worley ***Mus*** Christopher Young ***Art*** Jocelyn James

Act Andrew Robinson, Clare Higgins, Ashley Laurence, Sean Chapman, Oliver Smith, Robert Hines (Film Futures)

Hellraiser is a well-paced sci-fi cum horror fantasy [from Clive Barker's own novel *The Hellbound Heart*].

Film concerns a dissipated adventurer who somewhere in the Orient buys a sort of magic music box which is capable of providing its owner hitherto undreamt-of pains and pleasures, and which ultimately causes him to be torn to shreds in a temple which transforms itself into a torture chamber.

Back home, his brother has just moved into a rickety old house with his new wife or girlfriend; digs had formerly been the dwelling of the ill-fated adventurer. Latter returns, by rising through the floorboards, partly decomposed, seeking human flesh and blood which, when devoured, will enable him to regain his human form. Pic is well made, well acted, and the visual effects are generally handled with skill.

•

HELLRAISER III: HELL ON EARTH

1992, 92 mins, US Ⓥ ⊙ col

Dir Anthony Hickox ***Prod*** Lawrence Mortorff ***Scr*** Peter Atkins ***Ph*** Gerry Lively ***Ed*** Christopher Cibelli, James D. R. Hickox ***Mus*** Randy Miller, Christopher Young ***Art*** Steve Hardie

Act Terry Farrell, Doug Bradley, Paula Marshall, Kevin Bernhardt, Ashley Laurence, Ken Carpenter (Fifth Avenue)

Hellraiser III is a highly commercial horror entry. Well-produced effort is an effective combination of imaginative special effects with the strangeness of author Clive Barker's original conception, on which the characters are based. Screen story is by Peter Atkins and Tony Randel.

The previous two *Hellraisers* were filmed in London; the latest was shot in North Carolina. All three films are set in New York.

Terry Farrell toplines as an attractive TV newswoman summoned by the ghost of British World War I Capt. Elliott Spencer, who's contacted her via her recurring nightmares about her dad, who was killed in Vietnam combat before she was born.

Spencer's experiments with the supernatural had unleashed evil on the world in the race of the Cenobites, led by Pinhead, whose adventures were limned in the prior pics. Pinhead is back, with a strange little box that's key to sending him back to Hell.

Farrell is a strong heroine binding the film together, and British thesp Doug Bradley is a commanding presence as Pinhead, while also doubling as the good guy captain.

•

HELLRAISER: BLOODLINE

1996, 85 mins, US Ⓥ ⊙ col

Dir Alan Smithee [= Kevin Yeager] ***Prod*** Nancy Rae Stone ***Scr*** Peter Atkins ***Ph*** Gary Lively ***Ed*** Rod Dean, Randolph K. Bricker, Jim Prior ***Mus*** Daniel Licht ***Art*** Ivo Cristante

Act Bruce Ramsay, Valentina Vargas, Doug Bradley, Kim Myers, Christine Harnos, Charlotte Chatton (Dimension/Trans Atlantic)

Fourth installment of *Hellraiser* series proves to be so bad that the director on record is Alan Smithee, the name used under Directors Guild rules when the real helmer refuses credit. The director billed in early announcements was special effects whiz Kevin Yeager—who retains credit in that category. Except for the most undiscriminating gorehound, pic is a pointless mess.

Story is framed by a confrontation on a space station in the year 2127. Paul (Bruce Ramsay) summons up spawn of hell Pinhead (Doug Bradley) with the emblematic puzzle box of the series. Paul is then taken into custody and questioned by the station's doctor (Christine Harnos).

In flashback, we get the origin of the puzzle box in 18th-century France, involving an ancestor of Paul's (Ramsay again), and then a story set in 1996 with another ancestor (still Ramsay), which takes up the bulk of the movie. Added to the mix is Angelique (Valentina Vargas) who arrives to seduce some of the ancestors only to be brushed aside by Pinhead.

The chief problem is that the films have become an excuse for grotesqueries and sadism. The focus on leather, chains, hooks and blades makes Pinhead's world a cross between a machine shop and an S&M bar. In contrast, the space effects, credited to Blue Studio, are quite good. The less said about the acting, the better.

•

HELL'S ANGELS

1930, 119 mins, US b/w& col

Dir Howard Hughes ***Scr*** Joseph Moncure March, Howard Estabrook, Harry Behn ***Ph*** Tony Gaudio, Harry Perry, E. B Steene, Harry Zach, Dewey Wrigley, Elmer Dyer, Pliny Goodfriend, Alvin Wyckoff, Sam Landers, William Tuers, Glenn Kerschner, Donald Keyes, Roy Klaffki, Paul Ivano, Charles Boyle, Herman Schopp, L. Guy Wilky, John Silver, Edward Snyder, ***Ed*** Krull, Jack Greenhalgh, Henry Cronjager, Edward Cohen, Frank Breamer, Ernest Laszlo ***Ed*** Frank Lawrence, Douglas Biggs, Perry Hollingsworth ***Mus*** Hugo Riesenfeld ***Art*** J. Boone Fleming, Carroll Clark

Act Ben Lyon, James Hall, Jean Harlow, John Darrow, Lucien Prival, Frank Clarke (Caddo)

Howard Hughes's air film was advertised as costing $4 million, which likely means $3 million—plenty.

It's no sappy, imbecilic tale. One of the brothers (Ben Lyon) is strictly a "good-time Charlie" continuously on the make and humanly afraid to die; the girl (Jean Harlow) is no good in the sense that she has and will try anything with either brother, but only does so with Lyon. This is because Jimmy Hall has ideals, idolizes her and wants to make everything official.

The first half of the film builds up to a Zeppelin raid on London which runs two reels and is given a big screen. Second half's main display is an aerial dog fight in which at least 30, maybe 40, planes simultaneously start diving and zooming at each other.

Story actually opens in Munich with Lyon trying to date every femme in town. Highly seasoned portion of the second half comes with Lyon and Hall on a spree. Hall finds Harlow half soused and entwined with another officer in a barroom booth.

Hughes spent three years working on his pet. The story was remade three times. Originally it was silent, with Greta Nissen as the girl; then it was made once in sound and remade again after that. Air shots were taken silent with the sound dubbed in afterward.

James Whale is programmed as having staged the dialog and does that smartly. The one color sequence [a London ball] runs just about a reel and is not important.

1929/30: NOMINATION: Best Cinematography (Tony Gaudio, Harry Perry)

•

HELL'S HIGHWAY

1932, 62 mins, US b/w

Dir Rowland Brown ***Prod*** David O. Selznick ***Scr*** Samuel Ornitz, Robert Tasker, Rowland Brown ***Ph*** Edward Cronjager ***Art*** Carroll Clark

Act Richard Dix, Tom Brown, Louise Carter, Rochelle Hudson, C. Henry Gordon, Warner Richmond (Radio)

In *Hell's Highway* the entire action, with the exception of one scene, occurs in and around a prison camp in some southern state; the preponderance of the convict labor is Negro. The convicts have been hired to work on a new road. The contractor tells his foreman that he bid 50% under his nearest competitor and to win a profit he must get twice as much work out of the convicts.

To force their efforts recourse is had to the lash and the sweatbox, the latter a structure of corrugated iron barely large enough to contain a man, and placed so that the metal absorbs the full force of the burning sun.

Richard Dix is one of the convicts. His brother (Tom Brown) is sent to the gang for having shot and wounded Dix's betrayer. Dix, who is planning an escape, has to prevent the kid from coming along.

The direction is remarkably good at most points. Some handsome scenic backgrounds are created during the hunt for the convicts. The director is rather less successful in his effort to inject comedy. Once or twice a nance camp laborer is employed, once for a genuine if smutty laugh. Other humor is supposed to arise from the smug mouthings of the Hermit (Charles Middleton), a crazed religionist type.

Dix is wasted as the young convict, with Brown much more effective as the kid. Louise Carter is an almost total loss in her single scene, as is Rochelle Hudson. Clarence Muse, in a very small bit, strikes one of the few really human notes.

•

HELLZAPOPPIN'

1942, 92 mins, US b/w

Dir H.C. Potter ***Prod*** [Jules Levey] ***Scr*** Nat Perrin, Warren Wilson ***Ph*** Woody Bredell ***Ed*** Milton Carruth ***Mus*** Frank Skinner ***Art*** Jack Otterson, Martina Obzina

Act Ole Olsen, Chic Johnson, Martha Raye, Hugh Herbert, Jane Frazee, Robert Paige (Universal/Mayfair)

There's the thinnest thread of a romantic story, but it's incidental to Olsen and Johnson's [1938] stage formula for *Hellzapoppin'*.

The yarn itself can be summed up in a few words: the rich girl in love with the poor boy, who in turn doesn't want to cross his rich pal, favored by the girl's socially conscious parents. The poor boy stages a charity show for the girl, and his stagehand pals (O&J) think they can save him from the girl, by lousing it up.

One of the picture's saving graces is the originality of presentation of screwball comedy. The business of O&J talking from the screen to the comic projectionist (Shemp Howard) is one such detail; ditto the slide bit telling a kid in the audience, "Stinky go home," with Jane Frazee and Robert Paige interrupting a duet until Stinky finally leaves.

Don Raye and Gene De Paul have contributed several nice songs for this film. There are some lavish production numbers [choreographed by Nick Castle and Edward Prinz]. Jules Levey (Mayfair), producer, was obviously unstinting.

1942: NOMINATION: Best Song ("Pig Foote Pete")

•

HELP!

1965, 92 mins, UK Ⓥ ⊙ col

Dir Richard Lester ***Prod*** Walter Shenson ***Scr*** Marc Behm, Charles Wood ***Ph*** David Watkin ***Ed*** John Victor Smith ***Mus*** Ken Thorne (dir.) ***Art*** Ray Simm

Act John Lennon, Paul McCartney, Ringo Starr, George Harrison, Leo McKern, Eleanor Bron (Shenson/Subafilms)

The Beatles' second effort is peppered with bright gags and situations and throwaway nonsense. Richard Lester's direction is expectedly alert and the color lensing is a delight. But there are also some frantically contrived spots and sequences that flag badly. The simple good spirits that pervaded *A Hard Day's Night* are now often smothered as if everybody is desperately trying to outsmart themselves and be ultra-clever-clever. Nevertheless, *Help!* is a good, nimble romp with both giggles and belly-laughs.

Story [by Marc Behm] concerns the efforts of a gang of Eastern thugs, led by Leo McKern, to get hold of a sacrificial ring which has been sent to Ringo by a fan and which he is innocently wearing. Also after the ring is a nutty, power-drunk scientist who sees the ring as a key to world domination. The Beatles are given a heck of a runaround which takes them from London to Stonehenge, the Alps and the Bahamas.

The Beatles prove more relaxed in front of the camera but they have still to prove themselves to be actors; as screen personalities they are good material and have a touch of the Marx Bros. in their similarly irreverent flights of fantasy.

•

HEMINGWAY'S ADVENTURES OF A YOUNG MAN

1962, 145 mins, US col

Dir Martin Ritt ***Prod*** Jerry Wald ***Scr*** A.E. Hotchner ***Ph*** Lee Garmes ***Ed*** Hugh S. Fowler ***Mus*** Franz Waxman ***Art*** Jack Martin Smith, Paul Groesse

Act Richard Beymer, Diane Baker, Paul Newman, Ricardo Montalban, Dan Dailey, Arthur Kennedy (20th Century-Fox)

The formidable task of assembling the bits and pieces of Ernest Hemingway's autobiographical young hero, Nick Adams, and welding them into a single, substantial, flesh-and-blood screen personality has nearly been accomplished in *Adventures of a Young Man*. But, while the film has been executed with concern, integrity and respect for the pen from which it flows, it has a disquieting tendency to oscillate between flashes of artistry and truth and interludes of mechanics and melodramatics.

Hotchner's scenario, gleaned from the prose of 10 of Hemingway's short stories, traces the path to maturity of Nick Adams. It follows him in his restless, searching pursuit of knowledge and worldly experience with which to build his character, advance his potential, shape his identity and prepare him for his destiny in the higher sphere to which he aspires.

There are a host of fine performances, and a few weak ones. Paul Newman, almost unrecognizable behind a masterfully grotesque yet realistic makeup mask by Ben Nye, re-creates the punchdrunk Battler character. It's a colorful and compassionate acting cameo.

Other important standouts are Ricardo Montalban as a perceptive Italian officer, Fred Clark as a slick but sympathetic burlesque promoter, Dan Dailey as a down-and-out advance man, Juano Hernandez as the Battler's devoted watchdog "trainer," and Eli Wallach as a practical but kind Italian Army orderly. Probably the finest performance in the film is Arthur Kennedy's as Nick's peace-loving, recessive father. And Jessica Tandy is excellent as the fanatical, domineering mother who leads Kennedy to his self-destruction.

•

HENNESSY

1975, 104 mins, UK Ⓥ col

Dir Don Sharp ***Prod*** Peter Snell ***Scr*** John Gay ***Ph*** Ernest Steward ***Ed*** Eric Boyd-Perkins ***Mus*** John Scott ***Art*** Ray Simm

Act Rod Steiger, Lee Remick, Richard Johnson, Trevor Howard, Eric Porter, Peter Egan (American International)

Good suspense drama starring Rod Steiger as a man planning to blow up the British Parliament in revenge for his family's accidental death in Belfast.

Richard Johnson, who wrote the intriguing original story, plays a Scotland Yard inspector, well versed (and earlier wounded) in Irish tumult, working under Trevor Howard in the attempt to find Steiger, who has come to London with a plan to substitute himself for MP Hugh Moxey on 5 November and, triggering himself as a human bomb, destroy the British power structure.

Ironically, IRA leader Eric Porter, knowing that event would lead to more British, rather than less, in Northern Ireland, sets out to kill Steiger. Steiger does very well in the title role.

•

HENRY & JUNE

1990, 136 mins, US Ⓥ ⊙ col

Dir Philip Kaufman ***Prod*** Peter Kaufman ***Scr*** Rose Kaufman, Philip Kaufman ***Ph*** Philippe Rousselot ***Ed*** Vivien Hillgrove, William S. Scharf, Dede Allen ***Art*** Guy-Claude Francois

Act Fred Ward, Uma Thurman, Maria de Medeiros, Richard E. Grant, Kevin Spacey, Jean-Philippe Ecoffey (Universal/Walrus)

Henry & June will be considered liberating by some and obscene by others. The lovemaking scenes in his previous film, *The Unbearable Lightness of Being* (1988), proved that director Philip Kaufman was perhaps the best director to handle the story of the long-secret, passionate affair between writers Henry Miller and Anaïs Nin in Paris in 1931–32.

Pic's title, also the title of the Nin book, is actually a misnomer. This is the story of Henry and Anaïs; June, playing a marginal role, is offscreen much of the time.

The film opens with Anaïs and her banker husband, Hugo, establishing themselves in Paris. It quickly becomes clear that, although fond of the rather stuffy Hugo, Anaïs, who keeps a secret diary, isn't telling him everything, and is eager to experience the kind of things she imagines in her erotic dreams. Miller's arrival is the catalyst.

Anaïs is also attracted to Miller's wife, June, who visits occasionally from America, and dreams of erotic experiences in which June assumes the male role.

In its depiction of Depression Paris and sexual candor, *Henry & June* succeeds. The central performances of Fred Ward, as the cynical, life-loving Miller, and Maria de Medeiros, as the beautiful, insatiable Anaïs, splendidly fulfill the director's vision.

Pic is less successful in gaining audience sympathy for these hedonists. Also, the character of June (Uma Thurman) is ill defined.

1990: NOMINATION: Best Cinematography

•

HENRY VIII AND HIS SIX WIVES

1972, 125 mins, UK Ⓥ col

Dir Waris Hussein ***Prod*** Roy Baird ***Scr*** Ian Thorne ***Ph*** Peter Suschitzky ***Ed*** John Bloom ***Mus*** David Munro ***Art*** Roy Stannard

Act Keith Michell, Donald Pleasence, Charlotte Rampling, Jane Asher, Frances Cuka, Lynne Frederick (Anglo-EMI)

A beautifully crafted epic, *Henry VIII* is told in flashback form from the king's deathbed. Pic deals almost exclusively with Henry and his succession of wives, deliberately relegating historic events to backdrops, even though audiences are kept in touch at all times with what else was going on in the realm.

Thanks also to a fine, tight script and sensitive but firm direction, the king acquires many more dimensions than those usually credited him. Keith Michell gives an upper-case performance all the way, through a succession of equally very believable makeup transformations.

Somewhat over-stolid at times, and taking itself too seriously, it perhaps needs more amusing change-of-pace sequences such as the one which finds the king saddled, sight unseen, with the ugly Anne of Cleves.

•

HENRY V

1946, 127 mins, UK Ⓥ ⊙ col

Dir Laurence Olivier ***Prod*** Laurence Olivier ***Scr*** Laurence Olivier, Arthur Dent ***Ph*** Robert Krasker ***Ed*** Reginald Beck ***Mus*** William Walton ***Art*** Paul Sheriff

Act Laurence Olivier, Robert Newton, Renee Asherson, Esmond Knight, Leo Genn, Felix Aylmer (Two Cities)

Production cost ran to about $2 million and every cent of it is evident on the screen. The color, the sets, the expanse and the imaginative quality of the filming are unexcelled. *Henry V* as a picture, however, requires that the spectator takes more with him into the theatre in the way of mental preparedness than mere curiosity.

Story is considerably simpler than the boys from Hollywood turn out. Henry's a British king, hardly more than a moppet, when, with the aid of a couple of clergymen, he cons himself into believing that he ought to muscle his way into France and stake his royal claim there on the basis of ancestry. So he loads some 30,000 men and their horses on the 15th-century version of LSTs and hies across the channel.

There are many interesting scenes and one really exciting one—the battle. With thousands of horses, knights in armor and longbowmen in colorful costumes, it's a Technicolor setup. Strong contrast is made between the overstuffed French warriors in armor so heavy they have to be lowered onto their horses with block and tackle, and the British, who won the battle with the longbow, used by men afoot and unhindered by iron pants.

Memorable for their deft humor and poignancy are both scenes in which Renee Asherson, as Princess Katherine, appears. Even Olivier is put well back into the No. 2 spot in the scene in which he woos her.

Treatment is interesting and adds much to the general effect. Picture opens with the camera panning over London and coming into the Old Globe theatre. Heralds' horns announce the opening of the play as the camera gets to the stage—and the show is on.

Acting, at the beginning, is in the stylized pattern of the 16th century and it doesn't get far away from that even when the camera is given full sweep after the Old Globe has been left behind. Sets throughout also give a feeling that you haven't left the theatre, for while tridimensional close to the camera, they fade into purposely obvious painted scenics in the background.

1946: NOMINATIONS: Best Picture, Actor (Laurence Olivier), Color Art Direction, Scoring of a Dramatic Picture

•

HENRY V

1989, 137 mins, UK Ⓥ ⊙ col

Dir Kenneth Branagh ***Prod*** Bruce Sharman ***Scr*** Kenneth Branagh ***Ph*** Kenneth MacMillan ***Ed*** Michael Bradsell ***Mus*** Patrick Doyle ***Art*** Tim Harvey

Act Kenneth Branagh, Derek Jacobi, Brian Blessed, Ian Holm, Paul Scofield, Emma Thompson (Renaissance)

Henry V is a stirring, gritty and enjoyable pic which offers a plethora of fine performances from some of the U.K.'s brightest talents.

Laurence Olivier's *Henry V* (1944) was designed to rally the English with its glorious battle scenes and patriotic verse. Branagh's version is more realistic and tighter in scale, and is a contempo version of Shakespeare.

Pic opens with Derek Jacobi as the chorus wandering around a film studio setting the scene. Branagh (Henry V, King of England) prepares for an invasion of France to secure his legal claim to the French throne. Paul Scofield (the French king) sadly ponders his country's situation and is urged to enter in bloody battle by Michael Maloney (the Dauphin).

After many battles, Branagh's tired and bedraggled army prepares for the final conflict with the massive French forces. After wandering among his troops in disguise, Branagh makes an impassioned speech and his forces win.

One subplot has Emma Thompson (the French king's daughter Katherine) and her maid (Geraldine McEwan) playing at learning English. Branagh declares his love for Thompson after he has won the French throne.

1989: Best Costume Design

NOMINATIONS: Best Director, Actor (Kenneth Branagh)

•

HENRY FOOL

1998, 141 mins, US Ⓥ ⊙ col

Dir Hal Hartley ***Prod*** Hal Hartley ***Scr*** Hal Hartley ***Ph*** Mike Spiller ***Ed*** Steve Hamilton ***Mus*** Hal Hartley ***Art*** Steve Rosenzweig

Act Thomas Jay Ryan, James Urbaniak, Parker Posey, Maria Porter, James Saito, Kevin Corrigan

Henry Fool is the whole nine yards on Hal Hartley in one movie. Poetic, bawdy, contemplative, often side-wrenchingly funny and finally quite touching, this tale about a nerdy garbage man whose life is changed by an egocentric hobo philosopher is flawed only by its length.

Simon Grim (James Urbaniak) is a terminally shy, tongue-tied garbage man who's the sole breadwinner for his clinically depressed mom (Maria Porter) and waspish, libidinous sister, Fay (Parker Posey). Enter Henry Fool (Thomas Jay Ryan), a mysterious unshaven bum with a gift for words who takes up residence in their grotty basement.

Henry encourages Simon to start putting any thoughts he may have on paper. The words start pouring out—and in perfect iambic pentameters, qualifying him as a poet. Soon student journalists are interviewing Simon. Middle America, however, thinks his work is disgusting and pornographic—at a time when a local pol is running on a back-to-basics ticket for the presidency.

Meanwhile, at home Henry casually seduces Simon's mother rather than the more likely Fay and is revealed as a paroled con originally sent down for having sex with a 13-year-old. More than any of Hartley's previous work, *Henry Fool* is many things at the same time: a sly dig at the conformity of American culture, as well as its new conservatism; a near mini-epic on a New Jersey blue-collar family; a basically upbeat portrait of how the unlikeliest people can reinvent themselves; and, most Hartleyesque of all, an examination of the way in which life deals the most unexpected hands and redefines individuals' relationships to one another.

Most of all, the pic delights in its sheer control, and love of the power of words—from the lush verbiage of Henry to one-line zingers from the hard-assed Fay.

In his first screen role, Canadian-born legit actor Ryan is terrific as Henry Fool, dominating the screen like some kind of battered revivalist preacher. As the initially "simple" Simon, Urbaiak grows with the movie. Posey's Fay is one of the consistet delights of the pic as well as one of its subtlest perfs.

[Pic was first shown at the 1997 Toronto fest but not released until the following year.]

•

HENRY PORTRAIT OF A SERIAL KILLER

1989, 83 mins, US Ⓥ ⊙ col

Dir John McNaughton ***Prod*** John McNaughton, Lisa Dedmond, Steven A. Jones ***Scr*** Richard Fire, John McNaughton ***Ph*** Charlie Lieberman ***Ed*** Elena Maganini ***Mus*** John McNaughton, Ken Hale, Steven A. Jones ***Art*** Rick Paul

Act Michael Rooker, Tom Towles, Tracy Arnold (Maljack)

Hard-driving, riveting pic is an unsentimental look at a sociopath as his bloody trail passes through Chicago. Film was finished in 1987.

From the opening shot of a woman's nude body lying in a ditch to the closing shot of a bloody suitcase, there isn't a wasted moment. Story follows Henry (Michael Rooker) while he rooms with his old prison buddy Otis (Tom Towles) and Otis's sister Becky (Tracy Arnold).

Henry has a philosophy about murder, which he shares with Otis. He constantly changes his methods so as not to leave a pattern for the police to follow. Somewhat nervous at first, Otis quickly joins in. Film uses two strategies to keep audiences off balance. First is the use of violence, which starts off subtly but finally moves to a gory extreme. Early killings are shown in flashback, where we only see bodies as grotesque still lifes. The second tactic is the use of Becky to humanize Henry.

Low-budget pic looks surprisingly good, capturing the gritty feel of the characters' lives. Thesping is solid.

●

HER ALIBI

1989, 94 mins, US Ⓥ ⦿ col

Dir Bruce Beresford ***Prod*** Keith Barish ***Scr*** Charlie Peters ***Ph*** Freddie Francis ***Ed*** Anne Goursaud ***Mus*** Georges Delerue ***Art*** Henry Bumstead

Act Tom Selleck, Paulina Porizkova, William Daniels, James Farentino, Hurd Hatfield, Patrick Wayne (Warner)

He's a mystery writer, she's a mystery; and it's also a mystery how TV fodder like this manages to get the high-gloss, top-talent treatment at studios.

Bestselling writer Phil Blackwood (Tom Selleck), out of stories and under pressure for his next book, decides to rescue drop-dead beautiful Nina (Czech-born model Pauline Porizkova) from court custody as a murder suspect.

He gives her an alibi by telling the canny d. a. (rigorously played by James Farentino) that they're having an affair and were together during the time of the alleged murder.

To maintain the facade, Selleck has to take the aloof Rumanian beauty out to his lush country estate to live while he pecks away at his new novel—about her, naturally, and his feverishly imagined version of their relationship.

Porizkova has the disconcerting habit of hurling kitchen knives at the wall and otherwise inventing Selleck's demise. He soon begins to suspect she is a murderer.

Mix of sexual tension, physical danger and quirky black humour has a certain appealing buoyancy, but ultimately it's deflated by general lack of credibility.

●

HERBIE GOES TO MONTE CARLO

1977, 105 mins, US Ⓥ ⦿ col

Dir Vincent McEveety ***Prod*** Ron Miller ***Scr*** Arthur Alsberg, Don Neson ***Ph*** Leonard J. South ***Ed*** Cotton Warburton ***Mus*** Frank DeVol ***Art*** John B. Mansbridge

Act Dean Jones, Don Knotts, Julie Sommars, Jacques Marin, Roy Kinnear, Bernard Fox (Walt Disney)

Herbie, the spunky little Volks beetle with a mind of his own, gets romantic buildup when he becomes a Romeo on wheels infatuated with a flirty powder-blue Lancia named Giselle, as both participate in the annual Paris to Monte Carlo road rally. Herbie is reunited with his original owner and driver, Dean Jones, a former second-rate racer whom he once adopted and won a flock of races for in the U.S.

Together again, Jones finds once more he is at the mercy of Herbie, who time and again takes matters into his own hands for often slapstick and mirthful effect as they roar toward their destination.

Herbie performs in the qualifying races outside Paris where he falls hood over wheels in love with the smart Lancia, driven by Julie Sommars who takes Jones's eye as well.

●

HERBIE RIDES AGAIN

1974, 88 mins, US Ⓥ ⦿ col

Dir Robert Stevenson ***Prod*** Bill Walsh ***Scr*** Bill Walsh ***Ph*** Frank Phillips ***Ed*** Cotton Warburton ***Mus*** George Bruns ***Art*** John B. Mansbridge, Walter Tyler

Act Helen Hayes, Ken Berry, Stefanie Powers, John McIntire, Keenan Wynn, Huntz Hall (Walt Disney)

Herbie Rides Again is Disney's sequel to *The Love Bug*, and a team encore for producer Bill Walsh and director Robert Stevenson. Walsh also scripted from a Gordon Buford story. It adds up, natch, to another fat plug for the Volkswagen "bug" as the runaway (literally) titular star.

Keenan Wynn is a San Francisco construction tycoon hellbent on putting up the tallest skyscraper yet, but the plan is frustrated and ultimately foiled by sweet little old widow lady Helen Hayes. She owns the ramshackle Victorian firehouse that stands in Wynn's greedy way, and she won't budge.

Ken Berry, as Wynn's hayseed nephew lawyer from the midwest, is enlisted to pull off the trick, but instead succumbs to the charms of widow and miniskirted friend, Stefanie Powers.

●

HERCULES

1983, 98 mins, Italy Ⓥ ⦿ col

Dir Lewis Coates [= Luigi Cozzi] ***Prod*** Menahem Golan, Yoram Globus ***Scr*** Lewis Coates ***Ph*** Alberto Spagnoli ***Ed*** James Beshears ***Mus*** Pino Donaggio ***Art*** M.A. Geleng

Act Lou Ferrigno, Mirella D'Angelo, Sybil Danning, Ingrid Anderson, Brad Harris, Rossana Podesta (Golan-Globus)

Golan and Globus have corralled "The Incredible Lou Ferrigno" to topline in a cheesy epic that could just about be titled "Hercules in Outer Space." Since a lumpy space suit would cover Ferrigno's mighty physique from view, the all-powerful one travels through the universe wearing nothing but his gladiatorial briefs.

A lot of it takes place on the moon, as Zeus and wife and daughter Hera and Athena toy from above with the fate of mortals. It is Hercules's task to try to rescue the Princess Cassiopea from the clutches of her evil kidnappers, and given the changing times, the muscleman doesn't have to battle cardboard monsters, but hi-tech mechanical beasts made of metal, which emit deadly laser blasts from their jaws.

Ferrigno is perfectly affable, and physically (if not physiognomally) he more than lives up to his billing. Sybil Danning, Mirella D'Angelo and Ingrid Anderson comprise a fetching trio of femmes.

●

HERCULES

1997, 92 mins, US Ⓥ ⦿ col

Dir John Musker, Ron Clements ***Prod*** Alice Dewey, John Musker, Ron Clements ***Scr*** Ron Clements, John Musker, Bob Shaw, Donald McEnery, Irene Mecchi ***Ed*** Jeff Jones, John K. Carr (assoc.) ***Mus*** Alan Menken ***Art*** Gerald Scarfe (Walt Disney)

He's the strongest man in the world and a darn nice young fellow to boot. *Hercules* is a winning tall tale, cleverly told and wonderfully voiced.

Drawing liberally from Greek mythology, film relates how Olympian gods Zeus (voiced by Rip Torn) and Hera (Samantha Eggar) begat the ever-so-cute Hercules. Meanwhile, lord of the underworld Hades (James Woods) has been told the only thing that could undo his plans to vanquish the folks on Mt. Olympus is Zeus's spawn.

The legend has been tidied up for general audiences, retaining the era, setting, characters and Herculean strength. And there's considerably more humor and music than one would find in the vintage Steve Reeves or contempo Kevin Sorbo incarnations.

The narrative thrust of the Disneyized version is that Hercules learns as a young man that he's adopted. Zeus tells him he must become a hero to be reinstated with the gods, and sends him to the satyr Philoctetes (Danny DeVito), aka Phil, for grueling Rocky-style training to combat all manner of evil. Here, the source of peril is not human frailty but mythical monsters—and bad girl Megara (Susan Egan), aka Meg, forced to do Hades's bidding.

The song score favors tunes that propel the story rather than focusing on character enhancement. That provides the yarn missing from the more recent, sober-sided anti-features. The music itself, while serviceable, is not at all distinctive.

1997: NOMINATION: Best Original Song ("Go the Distance")

●

HERCULES RETURNS

1993, 80 mins, Australia Ⓥ col

Dir David Parker ***Prod*** Philip Jaroslow ***Scr*** Des Mangan ***Ph*** David Connell ***Ed*** Peter Carrodus ***Mus*** Philip Judd ***Art*** Jon Dowding

Act David Argue, Bruce Spence, Mary Coustas, Michael Carman, Brendon Suhr (Philm)

Hercules Returns follows in the footsteps of Woody Allen's *What's Up Tiger Lily?* by completely revamping and revoicing a bad old foreign film.

Melbourne-based comics Des Mangan and Sally Patience have adapted their live show, *Double Take Meets Hercules*, with assistance from first-time director David Parker, who's better known as a screenwriter and cinematographer working in partnership with his wife, Nadia Tass. Parker has directed about 18 minutes of framing footage, but most of *Hercules Returns* consists of the revoiced film.

The framing material features film buff Brad McBain (David Argue), who refurbishes a rundown picture palace to show his favorite movies. But his manic projectionist, Sprocket (Bruce Spence), discovers at the last moment that the print has arrived in its Italo-language version, sans subtitles. McBain, Sprocket and publicist Lisa (Mary Coustas) frantically improvise a voiceover translation for the blacktie audience, and it's a hit.

The improvisation turns the original clinker [Giorgio Capitani's 1965 *Ercole, Sansone, Maciste e Ursus: gli invincibili*] into a hilarious romp, with Hercules now a frustrated singer sent by Zeus to perform at the Pink Parthenon nightclub where he's offered the hand of the lovely Labia, daughter of the club's owners. She, however, prefers Testiculi and rejects Hercules.

Film has an endearing, slapdash feel to it.

●

HERE COMES MR. JORDAN

1941, 93 mins, US Ⓥ ⦿ b/w

Dir Alexander Hall ***Prod*** Everett Riskin ***Scr*** Sidney Buchman, Seton I. Miller ***Ph*** Joseph Walker ***Ed*** Viola Lawrence ***Mus*** Frederick Hollander

Act Robert Montgomery, Evelyn Keyes, Claude Rains, Rita Johnson, Edward Everett Horton, James Gleason (Columbia)

Story [from Harry Segall's play {*Heaven Can Wait*] humorously poses the theory of reincarnation of a personality and soul that has been snatched from its earthly body 50 years before the cosmic schedule. Robert Montgomery is an aggressive prizefighter, determined to be champ, with an airplane and saxophone as hobbies. Flying from training camp to New York, the plane crashes, and Montgomery is snatched by Heavenly messenger Edward Everett Horton from his earthly body, and taken to Heaven for celestial registration.

When it is found Montgomery's arrival is premature, and his earthly body has already been cremated to prevent replacement, it's up to registrar Claude Rains (Mr. Jordan) to secure another body suitable to Montgomery.

In this body, retaining his own soul, Montgomery falls in love with Evelyn Keyes, daughter of a duped financial agent. After wandering for weeks in search of another landing, under guidance of Rains, Montgomery lands permanently in the body of a contender for the boxing championship.

Montgomery's portrayal is a highlight in a group of excellent performances. Keyes displays plenty of charm. James Gleason scores as the fast-gabbing fight manager, who is bewildered by the proceedings. Direction by Alexander Hall sustains a fast pace throughout.

1941: Best Original Story, Screenplay.

NOMINATIONS: Best Picture, Director, Actor (Robert Montgomery), Supp. Actor (James Gleason), B&W Cinematography

●

HERE COMES THE GROOM

1951, 113 mins, US ⦿ b/w

Dir Frank Capra ***Prod*** Frank Capra ***Scr*** Virginia Van Upp, Liam O'Brien, Myles Connolly ***Ph*** George Barnes ***Ed*** Ellsworth Hoagland ***Mus*** Joseph J. Lilley ***Art*** Hal Pereira, Earl Hedrick

Act Bing Crosby, Jane Wyman, Alexis Smith, Franchot Tone, James Barton, Robert Keith (Paramount)

Paramount has a top-notch piece of comedy diversion in *Here Comes the Groom.* The incredibly swift 113 minutes are jam-packed with the kind of fun that never lets up on the risibilities.

Robert Riskin and Liam O'Brien provided the merry yarn of a carefree newspaperman (Bing Crosby) who must marry within a week to be able to adopt two war orphans he has picked up during a lengthy Paris assignment. He hopes the bride will be Jane Wyman, but arrives back in Boston to find her tired of waiting and about to marry wealthy Franchot Tone. His problem is to break up the impending rebound marriage before the adoption deadline.

Crosby is at his casual best, nonchalantly tossing his quips for the most effect. Wyman is a wow as the girlfriend who makes him really work to win her. The two join on the Hit Parade tune "In the Cool, Cool, Cool of the Evening," by Johnny Mercer and Hoagy Carmichael, in a socko song-and-dance session.

1951: Best Song ("In the Cool, Cool, Cool of the Evening")

NOMINATION: Best Motion Picture Story

●

HERE COMES THE NAVY
1934, 88 mins, US b/w
Dir Lloyd Bacon *Scr* Ben Markson, Earl Baldwin *Ph* Arthur Edeson *Ed* George Amy *Mus* Leo F. Forbstein (dir.) *Art* Esdras Hartley
Act James Cagney, Pat O'Brien, Gloria Stuart, Frank McHugh, Dorothy Tree, Robert Barrat (Warner)

Here Comes the Navy is a saga of the U.S. fleet. It's light on story, and because of that it borders on being an elaborate newsreel, i.e., the inner workings of the gobs at maneuvers and navy life, from enlistment to war formations.

The James Cagney–Pat O'Brien feud throughout the footage reminds of the Quirt–Flagg school of masculine venom. Only here Gloria Stuart is O'Brien's sister and he wants Cagney to stay away from her.

Frank McHugh stooges for Cagney as his lone faithful pal, even after the gobs have given wise-guy Cagney a little dose of coventry, having steered clear of him because they think he's a wrong guy. Cagney is twice catapulted into heroic situations, the double parachute jump for the finale packing something of a kick.

1934: NOMINATION: Best Picture

•

HERE COME THE CO-EDS
1945, 85 mins, US b/w
Dir Jean Yarbrough *Prod* John Grant *Scr* Arthur T. Horman, John Grant *Ph* George Robinson *Ed* Arthur Hilton *Mus* Edgar Fairchild (dir.) *Art* John B. Goodman, Richard H. Riedel
Act Bud Abbott, Lou Costello, Peggy Ryan, Martha O'Driscoll, Lon Chaney, Donald Cook (Universal)

Abbott and Costello are easily up to their high laugh standards in *Here Come the Co-Eds*. Pic is helped considerably by presence of Phil Spitalny's nifty all-girl "Hour of Charm" orchestra and Peggy Ryan, who plays a typical college hepcat.

Co-Eds is smartly gagged, smoothly paced, and even the familiar routines are given new twists. The gags or bits cover the field from the face-slapping episodes, down through a comedy wrestling match, farcical basketball game, a mad scramble in a kitchen, to the payoff chase sequence. Yarn shows a moss-covered, tradition-bound femme college that's stirred out of its lethargy by Abbott and Costello.

John Grant, originally from musical comedy, who's done scripts from the A&C team ever since they began to go places, does well by the comedy duo on the production end. He's also responsible for the screen story along with Arthur T. Horman [from a story by Edmund L. Hartmann]. Jean Yarbrough's direction is aces.

•

HERE COME THE GIRLS
1953, 77 mins, US (V) col
Dir Claude Binyon *Prod* Paul Jones *Scr* Edmund L. Hartmann, Hal Kanter *Ph* Lionel Lindon *Ed* Arthur Schmidt *Mus* Lyn Murray (dir.) *Art* Hal Pereira, Roland Anderson
Act Bob Hope, Tony Martin, Arlene Dahl, Rosemary Clooney, Millard Mitchell, William Demarest (Paramount)

Bob Hope is the spark plug who keeps *Here Come the Girls* alive and kicking. The production lives up to its musical connotations and title by using plenty of comely femmes and production numbers. Nearly every one of the eight songs forms a production piece and all of them are eye-pleasers.

Hope, Tony Martin and Rosemary Clooney are the chief song-singers of the Jay Livingston–Ray Evans numbers. Martin's principal chore is the pashy "Heavenly Days," which he croons to an assortment of girls during a production number. A chorus or two of "Never So Beautiful" to Arlene Dahl is his other song spot. "When You Love Someone" gets the full ballad treatment from Clooney, as does, in more razzle-dazzle style, "Ali Baba."

Dance numbers are flashily staged by Nick Castle and prove effective for eight values, as well as a framework for much of Hope's comedy antics as a chorus boy who is made star of the show. He thinks it's final recognition of his talent, not knowing he's only bait to trap a slasher who carves up any admirer of Dahl's. The laughs come from Hope's inability to do any number right and his colossal conceit in believing he can do no wrong.

There's no real belly-laughs. Lionel Lindon's Technicolor lensing is handsome, as are the art direction, the settings and costumes of the 1900 era background.

•

HER ENLISTED MAN
SEE: RED SALUTE

•

HERE WE GO ROUND THE MULBERRY BUSH
1968, 94 mins, UK col
Dir Clive Donner *Prod* Clive Donner *Scr* Hunter Davies, Larry Kramer *Ph* Alex Thomson *Ed* Fergus McDonell *Mus* Simon Napier-Bell (arr.) *Art* Brian Eatwell
Act Barry Evans, Judy Geeson, Angela Scoular, Sheila White, Adrienne Posta, Denholm Elliott (Giant/United Artists)

A lightfooted look at the teenagers with engaging performances from hitherto largely unknown youngsters, the film was made entirely on location in a new town near London. It has a nimble alertness to juve characteristics and a nice flair for comedy.

Story is based on a successful novel by journalist Hunter Davies. Its strength is the wit of characterization and it's pleasantly salted with lines about young sexual ambitions.

The hero is a final-year student at high school, absorbed with stalking gals but finding the hunt leaves him too often up a cul-de-sac.

Barry Evans wins both sympathy and laughs as the boy. Story is spliced with Mitty-type dream bits, which give additional bite to the gap between ideal and reality.

The girls are well chosen, with Angela Scoular scoring with fine comic precision as the uppercrust girl, Judy Geeson purveying easy charm as the final near-conquest, and Adrienne Posta and Sheila White making the most of their chances.

•

HER HUSBAND'S AFFAIRS
1947, 84 mins, US (V) b/w
Dir S. Sylvan Simon *Scr* Ben Hecht, Charles Lederer *Ph* Charles Lawton Jr *Ed* Al Clark *Mus* George Dunning *Art* Stephen Goossen, Carl Anderson
Act Lucille Ball, Franchot Tone, Edward Everett Horton, Mikhail Rasumny, Gene Lockhart, Jonathan Hale (Columbia)

Her Husband's Affairs is well-premised fun that has a laugh a minute. As a comedy team, Lucille Ball and Franchot Tone excel. Tone is a slightly screwball advertising-slogan genius while Ball is his ever-loving wife who somehow always winds up with the credit for his spectacular stunts.

Director S. Sylvan Simon's pace is perfect and he welds zany situations into socko laughs. Motivation for much of the comedy comes from Tone's sponsorship of a screwball inventor and the products that he develops while searching for the perfect embalming fluid. Gentle fun is poked at advertising agencies and bigshot sponsors and public figures.

Mikhail Rasumny is the crazy inventor and wraps up the role for honors. Edward Everett Horton, Gene Lockhart, a business tycoon, Nana Bryant, his wife, and Jonathan Hale are among others who keep the laughs busy.

•

HER MAJESTY LOVE
1931, 75 mins, US b/w
Dir William Dieterle *Scr* Robert Lord, Arthur Caesar *Ph* Robert Kurrle *Ed* Ralph Dawson *Art* Jack Okey
Act Marilyn Miller, Ben Lyon, W. C. Fields, Ford Sterling, Leon Errol, Chester Conklin (First National)

Scene is laid in Berlin and a discursive opening has some trick shots at a fashionable caberet that must have cost a good deal to get set. For a start it does manage to pump up an effect of gaiety as a background for Marilyn Miller's character of a discreet barmaid who has captivated a rich young man. Scene climaxes with Ben Miller and Ben Lyon doing a tango on the cabaret dance floor, which turns out to be the picture's high point.

From that it goes into buffoonery and interest diminishes through dizzy clowning to a frenzied romantic finish, when the heroine, having just married a rich old baron, announces to the lover who had just discarded her that now she was eligible to become his wife.

Picture [from a play by R. Bernaver and R. Oesterreicher] takes care of nearly all the minor details, settings, lighting, music, but ignores utterly the basic things of ingratiating story and acceptable acting.

W. C. Fields does something with the role of the girl's father, a Micawber-like character which would have counted in better surroundings.

•

HERO
(UK/AUSTRALIA: ACCIDENTAL HERO)
1992, 116 mins, US (V) ⊙ col
Dir Stephen Frears *Prod* Laura Ziskin *Scr* David Webb Peoples *Ph* Oliver Stapleton *Ed* Mick Audsley *Mus* George Fenton *Art* Leslie McDonald
Act Dustin Hoffman, Geena Davis, Andy Garcia, Joan Cusack, Kevin J. O'Connor, Maury Chaykin (Columbia)

Third-act heroics help but can't rescue filmmaker Stephen Frears's most concerted mainstream push. Muddled effort cleverly skewering media and societal fascination with heroes doesn't create compelling characters for its big-name leads.

The story centers on Bernie Laplante (Dustin Hoffman), a shiftless, small-time hood who stumbles on to a plane crash and ends up saving the people aboard. A TV reporter on the plane (Geena Davis) begins a search to find the unknown hero, dubbed "the angel of Flight 104."

Eventually, that title falls to John Bubber (Andy Garcia), a homeless Vietnam veteran with movie-star looks under the dirt, who comes forward to claim the $1 million reward after giving Bernie a lift after the accident. Bubber is hailed as the next coming of Jesus and Gandhi, even as Bernie's fortunes continue to sour.

Written by David Webb Peoples (*Unforgiven*), *Hero* is peppered with occasional gems but has to sift through a lot of wreckage to find them. Lacking focus, pic jumps back and forth between Davis, probably pic's most marketable asset as the career-driven reporter attracted to her pseudo-saviour, and the self-centered Bernie, who's hard pressed to explain his act of selfless heroism.

Unfortunately, action tilts too heavily toward Hoffman, who simply mucks it up, seemingly playing a bad version of Ratso Rizzo had he survived events in *Midnight Cowboy*.

•

HEROES
1977, 113 mins, US (V) col
Dir Jeremy Paul Kagan *Prod* David Foster, Lawrence Turman *Scr* James Carabatsos *Ph* Frank Stanley *Ed* Patrick Kennedy *Mus* Jack Nitzsche, Richard Hazard *Art* Charles Rosen
Act Henry Winkler, Sally Field, Harrison Ford, Val Avery, Olivia Cole, Hector Elias (Universal)

Heroes is a poorly written melodrama about a troubled Vietnam veteran and a girl who helps him work out his problems. The multi-location production stars Henry Winkler, in a good though flawed performance, and Sally Field.

Plot peg is standard—boy and girl, running from separate problems, meet "cute" and fall in love with some ups and downs en route.

Speaking of the writing "cutes," there's a plague in this screenplay, mainly in the Winkler character and the actor's performance. Since the character has a history of mental malaise, the kooky bits are many and just awful. See Winkler confound his doctor, Hector Elias. See him escape from the hospital. See him run and jump and streak and shout.

•

HEROES OF TELEMARK, THE
1965, 131 mins, UK (V) ▭ col
Dir Anthony Mann *Prod* S. Benjamin Fisz *Scr* Ivan Moffat, Ben Barzman, [Harold Pinter] *Ph* Robert Krasker *Ed* Bert Bates *Mus* Malcolm Arnold *Art* Tony Masters
Act Kirk Douglas, Richard Harris, Ulla Jacobsson, Michael Redgrave, Anton Diffring, Eric Porter (Benton/Rank)

Producer Benjamin Fisz and director Anthony Mann have made a $5.6 million motion picture that emerges as hefty, gripping and carefully made entertainment.

It's 1942 in Nazi-occupied Norway. The Germans are ahead of the Allies on atomic fission, as reports from the Norsk Hydro heavy water factory near Telemark reveal. It's the job of a tiny band of nine resistance workers to scotch the Nazi plans.

Kirk Douglas, as the scientist drawn unwillingly into the exploit, and Richard Harris, as the resistance leader, turn in powerhouse performances. They detest each other on sight (never satisfactorily explained) but learn to respect and grudgingly like each other during mutual danger. Ulla Jacobsson, as Douglas's ex-wife, also fighting for the resistance, has a sketchy role but plays it with charm and conviction.

Krasker's work over ice- and snow-girt Norway is a joy. Craftily he used Helge Stoylen, a Norwegian ski coach, to help out on some lensing. Stoylen held a Panavision camera between his legs for some of the graceful and gripping ski shots.

•

HERS TO HOLD
1943, 93 mins, US b/w
Dir Frank Ryan *Prod* Felix Jackson *Scr* John D. Klorer, Lewis R. Foster *Ph* Elwood Bredell *Ed* Ted Kent *Mus* Frank Skinner
Act Deanna Durbin, Joseph Cotten, Charles Winninger, Evelyn Ankers, Gus Schilling (Universal)

In *Hers to Hold* Deanna Durbin successfully and permanently completes transition from cinematic sub-deb to young ladyhood.

Felix Jackson, formerly associated as writer on numerous early Durbin starrers, makes his bow as the star's producer here, and clicks solidly. He gets able assistance from freshness and pace in both script by Lewis Foster and direction by Frank Ryan, together with strong performances by supporting cast, and an excellently mounted production overall.

Story, although lightly contrived, generates audience attention through the deft business generously inserted in the script and carried through via direction. Rich deb Durbin is object of amorous flirtation by Joseph Cotten, trifling love-and-leave-'em adventurer, and what starts out as boy chases girl winds up as girl chases boy. When she coyly falls for his pitches after a fast campaign, he tries to get out from under when he sees that look in her eye, but his brush-off is unsuccessful and she follows him to an aircraft plant to get job to seek him out.

Durbin again demonstrates capabilities in carrying acting responsibilities of lead, with her four song numbers neatly spotted along the way.

•

HER WEDDING NIGHT
1930, 78 mins, US b/w
Dir Frank Tuttle ***Scr*** Henry Myers ***Ph*** Harry Fischbeck ***Ed*** Denis Drought
Act Clara Bow, Ralph Forbes, Charles Ruggles, Skeets Gallagher ((Paramount))

Smart showmanship. Combination of jaunty comedy of the spicy Avery Hopwood type [based on his play, *Little Miss Bluebeard*], generous flavoring of spice in title and action, and a wealth of gay romance in hoke farcical setting.

Whole production is deftly handled. Settings and atmosphere beautifully manage to set off the gay tone of the whole affair. And the cast surrounding the Paramount redhead has been fitted to tailor-made roles with nicety. Clara Bow plays the racy heroine with a vigor that compensates for some of her shortcomings of voice and diction.

Plot doesn't matter except that Larry (Ralph Forbes), composer of sentimental songs, persuades his friend, Bob (Skeets Gallagher), to impersonate him to escape hero-worshipping flappers. Bob goes off on a romantic spree under his pal's name, inadvertently marrying Norma (Bow) before a rural Italian magistrate.

•

HE SAID SHE SAID
1991, 115 mins, US Ⓥ ⊙ ▭ col
Dir Ken Kwapis, Marisa Silver ***Prod*** Frank Mancuso Jr ***Scr*** Brian Hohlfeld ***Ph*** Stephen H. Burum ***Ed*** Sidney Levin, Rick Sparr ***Mus*** Miles Goodman ***Art*** Michael Corenblith
Act Kevin Bacon, Elizabeth Perkins, Nathan Lane, Anthony LaPaglia, Sharon Stone, Stanley Anderson (Paramount)

He Said She Said is two awful films rolled into one. The potentially provocative idea of having a male and female director take separate but interlocking looks at the same love story fizzles here in the hokiest, most contrived telling imaginable. Co-directors Ken Kwapis and Marisa Silver, who got engaged during the production, have turned out segments that differ slightly in tone, pacing and lighting styles, but are equal in banality and obviousness.

Sitcom slickness of the enterprise is established at the outset, as TV news commentator team of Kevin Bacon and Elizabeth Perkins apparently breaks up on the air when she beans him with a coffee cup. Pushed along at a frantic, wearying pace, initial hour is devoted to mirthless jokes about the young hotshot's womanizing, fear of marriage and need to feel professionally superior.

Kwapis's high-gloss garishness and antic staging contrasts with the slower, more subdued approach of Silver, who, in covering the same ground, underlines a sense of romance and optimism in Perkins's character to which the male has been oblivious.

What's shocking is how impersonal and unfelt the film is on both sides. On screen virtually throughout, Bacon and Perkins are unable to escape this collision. Supporting performances are uniformly broad and one-dimensional.

•

HESTER STREET
1975, 90 mins, US Ⓥ b/w
Dir Joan Micklin Silver ***Prod*** Raphael D. Silver ***Scr*** Joan Micklin Silver ***Ph*** Kenneth Van Sickle ***Ed*** Katerine Wenning ***Mus*** William Bolcon
Act Steven Keats, Carol Kane, Mel Howard, Dorrie Kavanaugh (Midwest)

Hester Street deftly delves into Jewish emigration to the U.S. just before the turn of the century. Hester Street is a sort of mobile ghetto as Eastern European Jews pour in and go in for their Americanization before moving on to other New York boroughs or to further west U.S. climes. Adapted from Abraham Cahan's story "Yekl," it concerns Jake, who has gone in for Americanization.
He sends for his wife and son but their arrival first fills him with shame at their old world clodishness. However, the wife cannot keep up with her husband's ways as she goes another way towards becoming an American.

Joan Micklin Silver displays a sure hand for her first pic.

•

HE WALKED BY NIGHT
1948, 79 mins, US Ⓥ b/w
Dir Alfred Werker ***Prod*** Bryan Foy ***Scr*** John C. Higgins, Crane Wilbur, Harry Essex ***Ph*** John Alton ***Ed*** Alfred DeGaetano ***Mus*** Leonid Raab
Act Richard Basehart, Scott Brady, Roy Roberts, Whit Bissell, Jim Cardwell (Eagle Lion)

He Walked by Night is a high-tension crime meller, supercharged with violence but sprung with finesse. Top credit for this film's wallop is shared equally by the several scripters, director Alfred Werker and a small, but superb cast headed by Richard Basehart.

Yarn is a straightforward documentary-style saga of a psychotic but brilliant killer who is tracked down through dogged detective work. Taken allegedly from the files of the Los Angeles police department, film opens with the brutal murder of a cop and follows through in detailing the criminal's career while the dragnet is closing in. There are no romantic angles in this all-male operation to slow matters down. Starting in high gear, the film increases in momentum until the cumulative tension explodes in a powerful crime-doesn't-pay climax.

Striking effects are achieved through counterpoint of the slayer's ingenuity in eluding the cops and the police efficiency in bringing him to book. High spot of the film is the final sequence which takes place in L.A.'s storm drainage tunnel system where the killer tries to make his getaway.

With this role, Basehart establishes himself as one of Hollywood's most talented finds in recent years. He heavily overshadows the rest of the cast, although Scott Brady, Roy Roberts and Jim Cardwell, as the detectives, deliver with high competence. Film is also marked by realistic camerawork and a solid score.

•

HE WAS HER MAN
1934, 70 mins, US b/w
Dir Lloyd Bacon ***Scr*** Robert Lord, Tom Buckingham, Niven Busch ***Ph*** George Barnes ***Ed*** George Amy ***Mus*** Leo F. Forbstein (dir.) ***Art*** Anton Grot
Act James Cagney, Joan Blondell, Victor Jory, Frank Craven, Harold Huber, Russell Hopton (Warner)

With Joan Blondell and James Cagney lending apt cast personalities, director Lloyd Bacon has woven from an original story by Robert Lord a forthright narrative about two pieces of human flotsam.

Most of the action is set against the background of a Portuguese fishing village on the Pacific coast. Both Blondell and Cagney turn in deftly confected performances.

Plot gets its motivation from the efforts of a double-crossing cracksman (Cagney) to escape the penalty of gang law. In his flight from the torpedoes Cagney winds up in San Francisco. There he is spotted by an underworld tipoff (Frank Craven) and the word is passed on to the mob back east. Meanwhile he meets the girl (Blondell), who has just decided to call it quits with the wayfaring life she's been leading and accept a proposal of marriage from a Portuguese fisherman located 100 miles south of Frisco. Cagney elects to join the girl on her trip to the groom.

Cagney settles down in the village and the fisherman, capably played by Victor Jory, goes about making the marriage arrangements. In the interim the girl falls for Cagney and there's talk between them of going away together. Overnight Cagney becomes leery of getting himself entangled and unbeknown to her prepares to scram. From here the action starts building to a tense climax.

•

HE WHO RIDES A TIGER
1966, 103 mins, UK Ⓥ ⊙ b/w
Dir Charles Crichton ***Prod*** David Newman ***Scr*** Trevor Peacock ***Ph*** John Von Kotze ***Ed*** Jack Harris, John S. Smith ***Mus*** Alexander Faris ***Art*** Richard Harrison, Seamus Flannery
Act Tom Bell, Judi Dench, Paul Rogers, Kay Walsh, Ray McAnally, Jeremy Spenser (British Lion)

Legal and financial hassles upset the smooth production of this crime meller, but it does not show on the screen. Story concerns a young, nerveless cat burglar (specialty: rocks from stately homes) with a split personality. Kind to children and animals, suave, good-mannered on the one hand. But this personable young guy is equally prone to violent outbursts of impatience and hot temper. Released from the cooler, he sets out on a string of profitable crimes, with Superintendent Taylor (Paul Rogers) breathing down his neck.

Trevor Peacock's screenplay is crisp, and even in the love scenes and with the kids does not teeter overmuch towards the sentimental. Tom Bell as the anti-hero is one of the crop of young actors who emerged around the Finney, Courtenay, Lynch, O'Toole era. He has an easy style and diamond-hard personality which put him among the leading runners in this field.

Judi Dench, in a somewhat indecisive part, again shows her very bright talent and Rogers is fine as the determined, disgruntled cop.

•

HEXED
1993, 90 mins, US Ⓥ col
Dir Alan Spencer ***Prod*** Marc S. Fischer, Louis G. Friedman ***Scr*** Alan Spencer ***Ph*** James Chressanthis ***Ed*** Debra McDermott ***Mus*** Lance Rubin ***Art*** Brenton Swift
Act Arye Gross, Claudia Christian, Adrienne Shelly, Ray Baker, R. Lee Ermey, Michael Knight (Price)

Some surefire slapstick footage is about all that's funny in the stillborn comedy *Hexed*. Writer-director Alan Spencer's debut pic makes one long for the sophistication of *Police Academy* movies.

Hotel desk clerk Matthew (Arye Gross) is anxious to end his rut and pump some excitement into his life. Enter beautiful French model and cover girl Hexina (Claudia Christian). Gross and Christian have sex in scenes imitating *Fatal Attraction* and *Basic Instinct*, after which he finds out she's really a psychotic killer who's spent six years in a mental institution.

Gross is an able farceur but hard pressed to make any of the increasingly silly plot twists believable. Christian's acting is way over the top, though she's well cast as the beautiful loon. Adrienne Shelly, familiar from Hal Hartley films, is appealing as Gross's co-worker and would-be girlfriend.

•

HICKEY & BOGGS
1972, 111 mins, US Ⓥ col
Dir Robert Culp ***Prod*** Fouad Said ***Scr*** Walter Hill ***Ph*** Wilmer Butler ***Ed*** David Berlatsky ***Mus*** Ted Ashford
Act Bill Cosby, Robert Culp, Rosalind Cash, Carmen, Louis Moreno, Michael Moriarty (Film Guarantors/United Artists)

Title of this Bill Cosby–Robert Culp starrer might indicate comedy, but action pairs former stars of pop *I Spy* teleseries, making their first appearance together since then as down-at-the-heel private eyes operating just outside the law.

Culp makes his directorial bow and Fouad Said, who started in the industry as cameraman on *I Spy* series, debuts as a producer. Latter should have paid more attention to storyline of the Walter Hill screenplay, which suffers through audience never being entirely certain as to the identity of some of the characters.

Dicks are employed to find a missing femme and become innocently involved in search for a $400,000 haul stolen from a Pittsburgh bank. Somehow, the femme is connected with missing loot but audience is never let in on secret.

•

HIDDEN, THE
1987, 96 mins, US Ⓥ ⊙ col
Dir Jack Sholder ***Prod*** Robert Shaye, Gerald T. Olson, Michael Meltzer ***Scr*** Bob Hunt ***Ph*** Jacques Haitkin ***Ed*** Michael Knue ***Mus*** Michael Convertino ***Art*** C.J. Strawn, Mick Strawn
Act Michael Nouri, Kyle MacLachlan, *Ed* O'Ross, Clu Gulager, Claudia Christian, Clarence Felder (New Line/Heron)

The Hidden is a well-constructed thriller, directed with swift assurance by Jack Sholder, brought down by an utterly conventional sci-fi ending.

Just as L.A. homicide detective Tom Beck (Michael Nouri) is prepared to close the books on a businessman who went on a crime spree, he's approached by taciturn FBI agent Lloyd Gallagher (Kyle MacLachlan) from Seattle, who's searching for the same man, Jack DeVries (Chris Mulkey). Gallagher is unsatisfied when Beck informs him DeVries is about to die in an L.A. hospital, and the plot begins to unfold when the dying man forcefeeds a reptilian alien down the throat of a fellow patient. A few minutes later the mild-mannered accountant bolts out of bed, escapes the hospital, murders a record store clerk and heads on another crime spree.

This leads to a series of calamitous, well-shot chase scenes in which Beck and Gallagher are trying to catch up with the possessed human before the alien goes mouth to mouth into another life form.

Nouri finally shakes off his *Flashdance* shadow by turning in the best performance of his career.

HIDDEN AGENDA

1990, 108 mins, UK ⓥ ⦿ col

Dir Ken Loach *Prod* Eric Fellner *Scr* Jim Allen *Ph* Clive Tickner *Ed* Jonathan Morris *Mus* Stewart Copeland *Art* Martin Johnson

Act Frances McDormand, Brian Cox, Brad Dourif, Mai Zetterling, Bernard Archard, Maurice Roeves (Hemdale/Initial)

Hidden Agenda is a hard-hitting attack on allegedly ruthless methods of the British police in Northern Ireland. Pic is set in 1982, and seems inspired by the notorious Stalker case. Stalker was a top-level British police officer sent to Northern Ireland to investigate the Royal Ulster Constabulary. His eventual highly critical report was hushed up, and he resigned and went public.

Brian Cox plays the Stalker-like Kerrigan, brought to Belfast to investigate the killings of an IRA sympathizer and an American lawyer (Brad Dourif in a tiny role). Kerrigan befriends Dourif's bereaved girlfriend (Frances McDormand, good in a Jane Fonda–type role). He quickly discovers the men were killed by members of the Royal Ulster Constabulary, and exposes a high-level coverup.

Jim Allen's provocative screenplay includes references to British secret service and their dirty tricks against the Heath and Wilson governments of the 1970s.

But though it attempts to make an acceptable theatrical entertainment out of a complex political saga, *Hidden Agenda* lacks big-screen impact.

HIDDEN CITY

1988, 107 mins, US ⓥ col

Dir Stephen Poliakoff *Prod* Irving Teitelbaum *Scr* Stephen Poliakoff *Ph* Witold Stok *Ed* Peter Coulson *Mus* Michael Storey *Art* Martin Johnson

Act Charles Dance, Cassie Stuart, Bill Paterson, Richard E. Grant, Alex Horton, Tusse Silberg (Hidden City/Channel 4)

First-time writer-director Stephen Poliakoff, an established legit playwright, tries very hard with *Hidden City*. Unfortunately he tries too hard, and the result is an overlong film with too many storylines and not enough good acting that rambles along with an air of self-importance.

Charles Dance plays a statistician whose well-ordered and smug life is shattered when he gets involved with Cassie Stuart, who is obsessed with finding a mysterious piece of film that appears to have been hidden by the government. The search for fragments of the lost film takes them into a maze of tunnels underneath London packed with official government archive film and discarded classified material, and into brushes with the police. At this point the action loses its way.

Dance is in good form as the sexy statistician, though he looks a bit bemused at some of the situations the storyline pushes him into. Stuart has an appealing waif-like quality, but her acting here amounts to looking intense, running about, and shouting "quick, hurry up" to Dance a great deal.

HIDDEN FORTRESS, THE

SEE: KAKUSHI TORIDE NO SAN AKUNIN

HIDDEN ROOM, THE

SEE: OBSESSION (1949)

HIDE IN PLAIN SIGHT

1980, 92 mins, US ⓥ ▭ col

Dir James Caan *Prod* Robert Christiansen, Rick Rosenberg *Scr* Spencer Eastman *Ph* Paul Lohmann *Ed* Fredric Steinkamp, William Steinkamp *Mus* Leonard Rosenman *Art* Pato Guzman

Act James Caan, Jill Eikenberry, Danny Aiello, Robert Viharo, Joe Grifasi, Barbra Rae (M-G-M)

Hide in Plain Sight has some of the makings of a good, honest film. It tells the true story of a working man's fight against the system, features several poignant moments, and makes a number of political messages in an effective yet unobtrusive manner. But in his directorial debut, James Caan never musters the energy or emotion needed to break the unbearably slow, dismal tone.

Caan is wonderfully accurate as the factory worker who becomes an innocent victim of a new witness relocation program that gives a new identity to any person (and his family) who informs on organized crime. In this case, two-bit mobster Robert Viharo testifies against his cronies and the authorities relocate him, his wife (who happens to be Caan's former spouse), and her two children by Caan to another state.

The frustration of the almost hopeless search Caan attempts could have been excellent fodder for a gripping, human drama. Screenplay, based on a book by Leslie Waller, seems true to its subject but somehow fails to create enough dramatic sparks.

HIDER IN THE HOUSE

1989, 108 mins, US ⓥ ⦿ col

Dir Matthew Patrick *Prod* Edward Teets, Michael Taylor *Scr* Lem Dobbs *Ph* Jeff Jur *Ed* Debra T. Smith *Mus* Christopher Young *Art* Victoria Paul

Act Gary Busey, Mimi Rogers, Michael McKean, Kurt Christopher Kinder, Elizabeth Ruscio, Bruce Glover (Precision)

Despite the stalk-and-slash trappings, *Hider in the House* is an intelligent, gripping and sometimes compelling psychological thriller featuring attractive performances by Mimi Rogers and Gary Busey.

Over the opening credits is an explanation that Busey's character, Tom Sykes, was mistreated as a child by his father, from whom he often chose to hide. He eventually killed his parents by setting fire to the house. As a man, Sykes is released from a state institution. In his search to find a real home, he breaks into a recently renovated house and builds himself a secret space behind a false wall in the attic.

Unfortunately, his dreamhouse also is that of the well-to-do Dryer family (Rogers, Michael McKean, children Kurt Christopher Kinder and Candy Hutson). While they settle into their new home, Sykes taps into the intercom system and starts drawing on their relationships, making the family his own. Sykes at first sees Julie Dryer as a mother figure, but he becomes increasingly obsessed with her.

Busey gives a fine performance as the obsessed murderer and Rogers is excellent as the unknowing object of Busey's attentions. The rest of the cast is strong. Helmer Matthew Patrick directs with a good deal of thought and intelligence and does not rely on violence or shock value. He has constructed an admirable psychological thriller, greatly helped by Jeff Jur's elegant camerawork.

HIGH AND DRY

SEE: THE "MAGGIE"

HIGH AND THE MIGHTY, THE

1954, 147 mins, US ▭ col

Dir William A. Wellman *Scr* Ernest K. Gann *Ph* Archie Stout, William Clothier *Ed* Ralph Dawson *Mus* Dimitri Tiomkin

Act John Wayne, Claire Trevor, Laraine Day, Robert Stack, Jan Sterling, Phil Harris (Warner/Wayne-Fellows)

Ernest K. Gann's gripping bestseller *The High and the Mighty* has been turned into an equally socko piece of screen entertainment. It is a class drama, blended with mass appeal into a well-rounded show.

The plot has to do with human reactions to danger, as a troubled plane, carrying 22 persons, limps through stormy skies en route from Honolulu to San Francisco. Shortly after the takeoff, suspense sets in when the audience is tipped there's trouble, maybe death, aboard. Gradually the crew and then the passengers become aware of danger.

Virtually every member of the large cast delivers a discerning performance but the lineup is too long to give each the individual credit rated. Especially good are John Wayne, the older co-pilot under the younger pilot captain, Robert Stack, Wally Brown and William Campbell, crew members, and Doe Avedon, very fine as the stewardess. The technical departments deliver outstandingly. The same can't be said for the score composed and conducted by Dimitri Tiomkin.

1954: Best Score of a Dramatic Picture

NOMINATIONS: Best Director, Supp. Actress (Jan Sterling, Claire Trevor), Editing, Song ("The High and the Mighty")

HIGH ANXIETY

1977, 94 mins, US ⓥ ⦿ col

Dir Mel Brooks *Prod* Mel Brooks *Scr* Mel Brooks, Ron Clark, Rudy DeLuca, Barry Levinson *Ph* Paul Lohmann *Ed* John C. Howard *Mus* John Morris *Art* Peter Wooley

Act Mel Brooks, Madeline Kahn, Cloris Leachman, Harvey Korman, Ron Carey, Howard Morris (Crossbow/20th Century-Fox)

High Anxiety is a straight Hitchcockian sendup—homage applies as well—with highs and lows ranging from a brilliant restaging of the shower scene in *Psycho* to childish bathroom humor.

Besides playing the role of a Harvard professor and psychiatrist with a fear of heights who takes over the Psycho-Neurotic Institute for the Very, Very Nervous, Mel Brooks dons the producer, director and cowriter caps.

Even more than the games he can play with the Hitchcock story, Brooks seems to enjoy toying with the technical references—the tight closeups, shots of hands and feet, stairway sequences and manipulation of the interaction between music and visuals. Nearly all of these gags, and none of them require the background of a buff, score.

HIGH BRIGHT SUN, THE
(US: MCGUIRE, GO HOME!; AKA: A DATE WITH DEATH)

1965, 114 mins, UK ⓥ col

Dir Ralph Thomas *Prod* Betty E. Box, Ralph Thomas *Scr* Ian Stuart Black *Ph* Ernest Steward *Ed* Alfred Roome *Mus* Angelo Lavagnino

Act Dirk Bogarde, George Chakiris, Susan Strasberg, Denholm Elliott, Gregoire Aslan, Colin Campbell (Rank)

Betty E. Box and Ralph Thomas elected to make this film because they regarded it "as a suspenseful drama which could be played against any background." They certainly played safe. Though set in Cyprus during the 1957 troubles, this sits firmly on a fence and makes virtually no attempt to analyze the troubles, the causes or the attitudes of the cardboard characters.

Film comes out with the British looking at times rather silly and at others very dogged, the Cypriots clearly detesting the British occupation, the Turks shadowy almost to a point of non-existence and America, represented by Susan Strasberg, merely a bewildered intruder.

Strasberg, a dewy-eyed young American archeology student of Cypriot parentage, is visiting Cypriot friends who, unbeknown to her, are mixed up in the local terrorist racket. She gets to know more than is good for her and is torn between loyalty to the Cypriots and to the British, as represented by an intelligence major (Dirk Bogarde) whose job it is to keep alive the unhelpful young dame for whom he has fallen.

Strasberg brings intelligence and charm to a sketchy role while Bogarde has no trouble with a part as the major which scarcely strains his thesping ability.

HIGHER AND HIGHER

1943, 90 mins, US ⓥ ⦿ b/w

Dir Tim Whelan *Prod* Tim Whelan *Scr* Jay Dratler, Ralph Spence, William Bowers, Howard Harris *Ph* Robert De Grasse *Ed* Gene Milford *Mus* Richard Rodgers

Act Michele Morgan, Jack Haley, Frank Sinatra, Leon Errol, Victor Borge, Mel Torme (RKO)

In his first starring role on the screen Frank Sinatra at least gets in no one's way. Though a bit stiff on occasion and not as photogenic as may be desired, he generally handles himself ably in song as well as a few brief dialog scenes.

The song-studded story [based on the 1940 legit musical by Rodgers & Hart] is laid principally in the mansion of Leon Errol, who learns, as it opens, that he has gone bankrupt and will have to vacate unless getting up a hunk of coin in a hurry. His valet (Jack Haley) gets the bright idea of picking one of the servants (Michele Morgan), having her pose as Errol's daughter, and getting her married off. Since none of the long list of servants in Errol's employ has been paid in many months, a corporation is formed in order to include them in the deal.

All the musical numbers have been expertly staged by Ernst Matra, with fast pace and novelty commanding characteristics of Matra's work. This is also particularly true of Whelan's direction, while his production backgrounds are all that may be desired.

HIGHER LEARNING

1995, 127 mins, US ⓥ col

Dir John Singleton *Prod* John Singleton, Paul Hall *Scr* John Singleton *Ph* Peter Lyons Collister *Ed* Bruce Cannon *Mus* Stanley Clarke *Art* Keith Brian Burns

Act Omar Epps, Kristy Swanson, Michael Rapaport, Jennifer Connelly, Ice Cube, Jason Wiles (New Deal)

Higher Learning has a great many things on its mind, which immediately places it in a rather exclusive catagory of American films these days. John Singleton's third feature is concerned with matters such as group think, individuality, the importance of education, political correctness, sexual identity, labels, personal responsibility and racial tension.

Focusing mostly on members of an incoming freshman class at fictitious Colombus University, pic takes a heightened interest in three students: Malik (Omar Epps), a politically unformed black runner on a sports scholarship; Kristen (Kristy Swanson), a naive white girl from Orange County who gets a rude awakening at school; and Remy (Michael Rapaport), a social misfit from Idaho.

Malik's early doubts about his enthusiasm for track are turned around by foxy runner Monet (Regina King). Kristen launches her college career by getting drunk and date-raped. Resulting trauma sees her being consoled by earth-motherly lesbian Taryn (Jennifer Connelly). Loner Remy falls in with a tiny band of white supremacists who read aloud from *Mein Kampf*. As one of many character sketches on a broad canvas, this would have been OK. But in the final act, Singleton narrows his focus almost exclusively to Remy and his black adversaries.

Despite this dramatic derailment, *Higher Learning* still packs a fair amount of power thanks to the force of the ideas being discussed. Cast is solid, with Epps, Swanson and Rapaport ably registering their immature characters without actually plumbing psychological depths.

•

HIGH FIDELITY

2000, 113 mins, US/UK Ⓥ ⊙ col

Dir Stephen Frears ***Prod*** Tim Bevan, Rudd Simmons ***Scr*** D. V. DeVincentis, Steve Pink, John Cusack, Scott Rosenberg ***Ph*** Seamus McGarvey ***Ed*** Mick Audsley ***Mus*** Howard Shore ***Art*** David Chapman, Therese DePrez

Act John Cusack, Iben Hjejle, Todd Louiso, Jack Black, Lisa Bonet, Joan Cusack, Tim Robbins, Bruce Springsteen (Working Title/Dogstar/New Crime)

Top reasons why *High Fidelity* is some kind of wonderful: John Cusack's fresh, fearless and ferociously funny lead performance; a trenchantly witty and acutely insightful script; surprising faithfulness to first-rate source material; and cunningly graceful direction by Stephen Frears, who smoothly maneuvers through mood swings and tempo variegations.

Even though the loose-knit plot has been transposed from the funky London environs of Nick Hornby's novel, the picture is smashingly successful at reconstituting the author's sensibility and sense of humor in and around downtown Chicago. Cusack gets most of the best lines, almost all of which are taken verbatim from the book. And he delivers the dialogue with exceptional panache whenever he's knocking down the fourth wall to directly address the audience.

Cusack plays Rob Gordon, a blithely unambitious thirtysomething who fell into a semicomfortable rut years ago when he opened Championship Vinyl, a retro record store. As *Fidelity* begins, Rob is jolted into taking stock of his aimless existence when his longtime live-in girlfriend, Laura (Iben Hjejle), gets fed up and walks out.

When it comes to self-assessment, Rob remains obsessed with list making, to the point of compiling an all-time Top Five Most Memorable Split-Ups. This cues a series of flashbacks as Rob recalls, among others, a dazzling college co-ed (Catherine Zeta-Jones) who unceremoniously dumped him for someone more exciting, and a brokenhearted manic-depressive (Lili Taylor) who did the same. Throughout *High Fidelity*, Cusack remains scrupulously true to the character Hornby created: an overgrown adolescent who's too narcissistic and self-indulgent to be easily liked, but too willing to admit his more unpleasant qualities to be wholly unsympathetic.

•

HIGH HOPES

1988, 112 mins, UK Ⓥ col

Dir Mike Leigh ***Prod*** Victor Glynn, Simon Channing-Williams ***Scr*** Mike Leigh ***Ph*** Roger Pratt ***Ed*** John Gregory ***Mus*** Andrew Dixon ***Art*** Diana Charnley

Act Philip Davis, Ruth Sheen, Edna Dore, Philip Jackson, Heather Tobias, Lesley Manville (Portman/Film Four/British Screen)

In the working-class London district of King's Cross, yuppies are moving into old houses, restoring them and driving out the locals who've lived there for ages. Old Mrs. Bender, a widow, lives in one house; her neighbors are the fearfully upper-crust Booth-Braines and they treat the old lady with ill-disguised contempt.

Mrs. Bender's two children are an ill-assorted pair. Cyril, with long hair and beard, works as a courier, lives with his down-to-earth girlfriend Shirley, and despises the British establishment.

Daughter Valerie, on the other hand, is a would-be yuppie, married to a crass used-car dealer, and living in a garishly over-decorated home. She's completely self-centered and insensitive to her elderly mother's needs.

Around these characters, Leigh builds a slight story intended to be a microcosm of today's London.

•

HIGHLANDER

1986, 111 mins, US Ⓥ ⊙ col

Dir Russell Mulcahy ***Prod*** Peter S. Davis, William N. Panzer ***Scr*** Gregory Widen, Peter Bellwood, Larry Ferguson ***Ph*** Gerry Fisher ***Ed*** Peter Honess ***Mus*** Michael Kamen ***Art*** Allan Cameron

Act Christopher Lambert, Roxanne Hart, Clancy Brown, Sean Connery, Beatie Edney (20th Century-Fox)

Film starts out with a fantastic sword-fighting scene in the garage of Madison Square Garden and then jumps to a medieval battle between the clans set in 16th-century Scotland.

Adding to the confusion in time, director Russell Mulcahy can't seem to decide from one scene to the next whether he's making a sci-fi, thriller, horror, music video or romance—end result is a mishmash. A visit by Sean Connery, playing a campy Obe Wan Kenobi–type character named Ramirez, teaches Connor MacLeod (Christopher Lambert) how to wield a sword like a warrior and to understand his fate is to be an immortal man who cannot have children, facing instead a life fending off other immortals like the evil Kurgan.

Lambert looks and acts a lot better in a tartan than as a nearly non-verbal antiques dealer. Clancy Brown never seems to frighten whether as the supposedly terrifying Kurgan or as the shaven-headed punker. [In 1996 a 116-min. *Director's Cut* was issued on homevideo. This was the version originally distributed in Europe.]

•

HIGHLANDER II: THE QUICKENING

1991, 96 mins, US Ⓥ ⊙ ⊏⊐ col

Dir Russell Mulcahy ***Prod*** Peter S. Davis, William Panzer ***Scr*** Peter Bellwood ***Ph*** Phil Meheux ***Ed*** Herbert C. de la Boullerie ***Mus*** Stewart Copeland ***Art*** Roger Hall

Act Christopher Lambert, Sean Connery, Virginia Madsen, Michael Ironside, John C. McGinley, Allan Rich (Davis-Panzer/El Khoury-Defait/Lam Bear)

Audiences unfamiliar with the first film will be hard put to follow the action [from a story by Brian Clemens] as it incoherently hops about in time and space.

Original topliners Christopher Lambert and Sean Connery are back (as is Aussie director Russell Mulcahy). Lambert plays immortal Connor MacLeod, who, despite his Scottish ancestry, hails from the planet Zeist. He and partner Ramirez (Connery) were banished to Earth for participating in a failed rebellion.

One storyline involves assassins led by Michael Ironside, and the other concentrates on the disappearing ozone layer. Connor joins with scientists to devise a sun shield projected into space. The shield is controlled by a large, untrustworthy (natch) corporation, which keeps the later renewal of the ozone layer a secret.

Lambert manages to decapitate the villains arrayed against him while teaming up with attractive environmental terrorist Virginia Madsen. Connery, sporting long white hair in a ponytail, occasionally appears wielding a broadsword.

Highlander II comes alive during the action scenes, including an unexplained but nail-biting segment in which deranged Ironside takes over a subway train and drives it at 400 mph, sending its terrified passengers crashing through windows.

Pic was lensed in Argentina on an apparently generous budget. [In 1997 a 109-min. *Renegade Version, The Director's Cut* was issued on homevideo.]

•

HIGHLANDER III: THE SORCERER

1994, 99 mins, Canada/France/UK Ⓥ ⊙ ⊏⊐ col

Dir Andy Morahan ***Prod*** Claude Leger ***Scr*** Paul Ohl ***Ph*** Steven Chivers ***Ed*** Yves Langlois, Brett Sullivan, Mark Alchin, [Dov Hoenig] ***Mus*** J. Peter Robinson ***Art*** Gilles Aird, Ben Morahan

Act Christopher Lambert, Mario Van Peebles, Deborah Unger, Mako, Mark Neufeld, Raoul Trujillo (Transfilm/Lumiere/Falling Cloud)

An unbelievably trashy meltdown of the tartan warrior franchise, *Highlander III* checks in as a breakneck, roller-coaster genre ride that's brainless fodder for undiscriminating auds.

Pic starts with a 15-minute, Conan-like prolog in which evil warrior Kane (Mario Van Peebles) surprises Connor MacLeod (Christopher Lambert) and his teacher Nakano (Mako) at the latter's Japanese lair. After decapitating Nakano, Kane and his two sidekicks are buried under the collapsing mountain, and Nakano's super powers pass instead to Connor. Fast-forward 400 years to 1994, and Kane breaks out and sets off in search of Connor.

Spotting the special effects on the horizon while riding in the Moroccan desert with his adopted son, Connor hightails it to New York to work out what on Earth is going on. An amazingly smart NY cop who remembers similar events "eight years ago" (year of the first pic's release) tracks him down under his modern alias, antiques dealer Russell Nash. Meanwhile, Yank archeologist Alex (Deborah Unger) gives Connor a severe case of the flashbacks, as she reminds him of his second wife, Sarah, circa the French Revolution.

Given there's enough material here for a four-hour miniseries, it's hardly surprising the plot jumps more lights than a runaway ambulance. Lumbered with Lambert's largely incomprehensible accent, British video director Andy Morahan wisely keeps dialogue pared to the bone and lets his five separate units (in Canada, Morocco, Scotland, France and New York) and f/x team get on with the job. Acting is video caliber.

•

HIGH NOON

1952, 84 mins, US Ⓥ ⊙ b/w

Dir Fred Zinnemann ***Prod*** Stanley Kramer ***Scr*** Carl Foreman ***Ph*** Floyd Crosby ***Ed*** Harry Gerstad, Elmo Williams ***Mus*** Dimitri Tiomkin ***Art*** Rudolph Sternad

Act Gary Cooper, Grace Kelly, Thomas Mitchell, Lloyd Bridges, Katy Jurado, Otto Kruger (Kramer/United Artists)

A basic Western formula has been combined with good characterization in *High Noon*, making it more of a Western drama than the usual outdoor action feature.

The production does an excellent job of presenting a picture of a small western town and its people as they wait for a gun duel between the marshal and revenge-seeking killer, an event scheduled for high noon. The mood of the citizens, of Gary Cooper the marshal, and his bride (Grace Kelly), a Quaker who is against all violence, is aptly captured by Fred Zinnemann's direction and the graphic lensing of Floyd Crosby, which perfectly pictures the heat and dust of the sun-baked locale.

Script is based on John W. Cunningham's mag story "The Tin Star" and is rather derisive in what it has to say about citizens who are willing to accept law and order if they do not have to put personal effort into obtaining it.

Cooper does an unusually able job of portraying the marshal, ready to retire with his bride and then, for his own self-respect, called upon to perform one last chore as a lawman even though it is the duty of the town's citizens. Kelly fits the mental picture of a Quaker girl nicely, but the femme assignment that has color and s.a. is carried by Katy Jurado, as an ex-girlfriend of the marshal.

Throughout the film is a hauntingly presented ballad that tells the story of the coming gun duel, and is tellingly sung by Tex Ritter.

1952: Best Actor (Gary Cooper), Song ("High Noon"), Scoring of a Dramatic Picture, Editing

NOMINATIONS: Best Picture, Director, Screenplay

•

HIGH PLAINS DRIFTER

1973, 105 mins, US Ⓥ ⊙ ⊏⊐ col

Dir Clint Eastwood ***Prod*** Robert Daley ***Scr*** Ernest Tidyman ***Ph*** Bruce Surtees ***Ed*** Ferris Webster ***Mus*** Dee Barton ***Art*** Henry Bumstead

Act Clint Eastwood, Verna Bloom, Marianna Hill, Mitchell Ryan, Jack Ging, Stefan Gierasch (Malpaso/Universal)

High Plains Drifter is a nervously humorous, self-conscious near satire on the prototype Clint Eastwood formula of the avenging mysterious stranger. Script has some raw violence for the kinks and some dumb humor for audience relief. Eastwood's second directorial effort is mechanically stylish.

Untidy patchwork script involves one of those towns with a collective guilt streak, having engineered the death-by-whipping of its honest marshal by some hoods who themselves were framed after getting out of hand. Into this setting rides Eastwood, emerging from heat waves (among other obvious evocations of films past) as a sort of archangel of retribution.

After establishing himself as a force to be reckoned with, Eastwood is engaged by the town fathers to help defend them against the former local police who are being released from jail after their frame-up.

•

HIGH PRESSURE

1932, 72 mins, US b/w

Dir Mervyn LeRoy ***Scr*** Joseph Jackson ***Ph*** Robert Kurrle ***Ed*** Ralph Dawson ***Mus*** Leo Forbstein (dir.)

Act William Powell, Evelyn Brent, George Sidney, Guy Kibbee, Evalyn Knapp, John Wray (Warner)

The phoney stock or "wall paper" grift gets a pretty expert exposé in this yarn [by S. J. Peters]. William Powell does a swell job as Gar Evans, a fast-talking and -thinking promoter. He keeps his larceny just within the law, but it's when the racket is nearest the edge that the story becomes most interesting.

Powell is first found in a speak's backroom on the tail end of a five-day bender. He told his girlfriend he was going out to the drug store for a dose of bicarbonate. The girlfriend is interpreted by Evelyn Brent, who is called on to do little else than get mad at and make up with her racketeer sweetheart.

George Sidney teams with Powell in grabbing the picture most of the way, Sidney for laughs and Powell for the action. Rest of the cast very good, with still more excellent casting of salesmen types in the "boiler-room" sequence. Whoever framed this scene must have had experience, for it's perfect.

•

HIGH ROAD TO CHINA

1983, 120 mins, US Ⓥ ⊙ col

Dir Brian G. Hutton ***Prod*** Fred Weintraub ***Scr*** Sandra Weintraub Roland, S. Lee Pogostin ***Ph*** Ronnie Taylor ***Ed*** John Jympson ***Mus*** John Barry ***Art*** Robert Laing

Act Tom Selleck, Bess Armstrong, Jack Weston, Wilford Brimley, Robert Morley, Brian Blessed (Golden Harvest/Warner)

High Road to China is a lot of old-fashioned fun, revived for Tom Selleck after his TV schedule kept him from taking the Harrison Ford role in *Raiders of the Lost Ark*. Ford clearly got the better deal because *China* just isn't as tense and exciting.

But it has the same Saturday-matinee spirit, with director Brian G. Hutton nicely mixing a lot of action with a storyline [from a book by Jon Cleary] that never seems as absurd as it is, allowing the two hours to move by very quickly.

Selleck is perfect as a grizzled, boozing biplane pilot whom 1920s flapper Bess Armstrong is forced to hire to help her find her father before he's declared dead and her inheritance is stolen. Selleck and Armstrong make a cute couple, even though their bantering, slowly developing romance is deliberately predictable throughout.

•

HIGH SEASON

1987, 92 mins, US Ⓥ ⊙ col

Dir Clare Peploe ***Prod*** Clare Downs ***Scr*** Mark Peploe, Clare Peploe ***Ph*** Chris Menges ***Ed*** Gabriella Cristianti ***Mus*** Jason Osborn ***Art*** Andrew McAlpine

Act Jacqueline Bisset, James Fox, Irene Papas, Sebastian Shaw, Kenneth Branagh, Robert Stephens (Hemdale)

Someone should have told helmer Clare Peploe that shots of beautiful scenery do not a boffo film make, and since she cowrote the screenplay (with Mark Peploe), she has to shoulder some of the blame for a weak and generally unfunny script.

High Season has a weaving plot with lead characters meandering in and out, but it pivots around Jacqueline Bisset as a photographer and the folk she meets up with in a tiny village on Rhodes. As well as poking fun at the tourists, also thrown in are subplots about a valuable Grecian urn, an elderly Russian spy—an art-historian friend of Bisset, with overtones of Anthony Blunt—and a rebellious Greek national.

Best of the cast are Kenneth Branagh and Lesley Manville as a seemingly archetypal English tourist couple. Irene Papas seems to enjoy herself overacting madly, while James Fox, as Bisset's estranged hubby, looks unsure about what sort of film he is appearing in.

•

HIGH SIERRA

1941, 100 mins, US Ⓥ ⊙ b/w

Dir Raoul Walsh ***Prod*** Hal B. Wallis (exec.), Mark Hellinger (assoc.) ***Scr*** John Huston, W. R. Burnett ***Ph*** Tony Gaudio ***Ed*** Jack Killifer ***Mus*** Adolph Deutsch ***Art*** Ted Smith

Act Humphrey Bogart, Ida Lupino, Arthur Kennedy, Joan Leslie, Alan Curtis, Henry Hull (Warner)

High Sierra is something of a throwback to the gangster pictures of the prohibition era; purely and simply an action story that's partially salvaged by the fine performances of Humphrey Bogart and Ida Lupino. They actually carry a film that is weighted down by too much extraneous story and production matter.

Throwback nature of the yarn is evident in the semi-glorification of Bogart's gangster character. Story depicts him as a country boy who went wrong with John Dillinger's mob, but still retaining a soft spot for green fields and trees, a crippled girl and a stray dog.

The screenplay [from a novel by W. R. Burnett] brings in too many side issues that clutter up the picture. There's no logical reason why the migrant family of Henry Travers and Elisabeth Risdon, with granddaughter Joan Leslie, was included, except as an effort to pad out the yarn in showing Bogart to be a nice guy at heart.

If anything, the film now suffers from slowness, Raoul Walsh's direction evidently being unable to overcome the screenplay plotting.

•

HIGH SOCIETY

1956, 107 mins, US Ⓥ ⊙ col

Dir Charles Walters ***Prod*** Sol C. Siegel ***Scr*** John Patrick ***Ph*** Paul C. Vogel ***Ed*** Ralph E. Winters ***Mus*** Johnny Green, Saul Chaplin (arr.) ***Art*** Cedric Gibbons, Hans Peters

Act Bing Crosby, Grace Kelly, Frank Sinatra, Celeste Holm, John Lund, Louis Armstrong (M-G-M)

Fortified with a strong Cole Porter score, film is a pleasant romp for cast toppers Bing Crosby, Grace Kelly and Frank Sinatra. Their impact is almost equally consistent. Although Sinatra has the top pop tune opportunities, the Groaner makes his specialties stand up and out on showmanship and delivery, and Kelly impresses as a femme lead.

The original Philip Barry play, *The Philadelphia Story*, holds up in its transmutation from the Main Line to a Newport jazz bash. Casting of Louis Armstrong for the jazz festivities was an inspired booking also. The unfolding of the triangle almost assumes quadrangle proportions when Sinatra (as the *Life*-mag–type feature writer), sent with Celeste Holm, almost moves in as a romantic vis-a-vis to the slightly spoiled and madcap Tracy Lord (Kelly).

Crosby is her first, now ex-husband, a hip character with song-smithing predilections, hence the Armstrong band booking on the local scene. Satchmo is utilized as a sort of pleasant play moderator, opening with "High Society Calypso," which sets the al fresco mood of the picture. Porter has whipped up a solid set of songs with which vocal pros like the male stars and Holm do plenty. Latter and Sinatra have a neat offbeat number with "Who Wants to Be a Millionaire?" Crosby makes "Now You Has Jazz" (aided by Armstrong) as his standout solo, although he is also effective with Kelly on "True Love." Crosby and Sinatra milk "Well, Did You Evah?" in a sophisticated smoking-room sequence.

1956: NOMINATIONS: Best Motion Picture Story [withdrawn from final ballot], Scoring of a Musical Picture, Song ("True Love")

•

HIGH SPIRITS

1988, 97 mins, UK/US Ⓥ ⊙ col

Dir Neil Jordan ***Prod*** Stephen Woolley, David Saunders ***Scr*** Neil Jordan ***Ph*** Alex Thomson ***Ed*** Michael Bradsell ***Mus*** George Fenton ***Art*** Anton Furst

Act Daryl Hannah, Peter O'Toole, Steve Guttenberg, Beverly D'Angelo, Liam Neeson, Ray McAnally (Vision/Palace)

High Spirits is a piece of supernatural Irish whimsy with a few appealing dark underpinnings, but it still rises and falls constantly on the basis of its moment-to-moment inspirations.

Elaborate physical production is set almost entirely at Castle Plunkett, a rundown Irish edifice that proprietor Peter O'Toole opens as a tourist hotel in order to meet the mortgage payments. With the American market in mind, O'Toole bills the place as a haunted castle, to this end having his staff dress up like ghouls of various persuasions.

It comes as little surprise that the castle turns out to be actually haunted. Steve Guttenberg, who is not getting along with wife Beverly D'Angelo, comes to meet ghost Daryl Hannah, who was killed on the premises years ago on her wedding night by Liam Neeson, who takes a fancy to D'Angelo.

•

HIGH TIDE

1987, 104 mins, Australia Ⓥ ⊙ col

Dir Gillian Armstrong ***Prod*** Sandra Levy ***Scr*** Laura Jones ***Ph*** Russell Boyd ***Ed*** Nicholas Beauman ***Mus*** Mark Moffiatt, Ricky Fataar ***Art*** Sally Campbell

Act Judy Davis, Jan Adele, Claudia Karvan, Colin Friels, Frankie J. Holden, Monica Trapaga (FGH/SJL)

A powerful emotional, beautifully made film which will touch the hearts of all but the very cynical.

Setting is the small New South Wales coastal town of Eden where Judy Davis rents a cheap trailer by the sea while she awaits completion of the auto repairs. One night, when hopelessly drunk in the toilet block, she's helped by an adolescent girl (Claudia Karvan) who lives with her grandmother (Jan Adele) in another trailer.

Davis befriends the child; only when she meets the grandmother does she realize Karvan is her own daughter who she'd left years before in the aftermath of her husband's death.

Adele makes the grandmother, who still enjoys a sexual fling even though she has a regular lover, a wonderfully warm character. Karvan sharply etches the pain and insecurity hiding beneath the tough, tomboyish exterior of the child; and Judy Davis, always a consummate actress, provides great depth and subtlety, making her character come vividly alive.

•

HIGH TIME

1960, 102 mins, US ▭ col

Dir Blake Edwards ***Prod*** Charles Brackett ***Scr*** Tom Waldman, Frank Waldman ***Ph*** Ellsworth Fredricks ***Ed*** Robert Simpson ***Mus*** Henry Mancini ***Art*** Duncan Cramer, Herman A. Blumenthal

Act Bing Crosby, Fabian, Tuesday Weld, Nicole Maurey, Richard Beymer, Yvonne Craig (Crosby/20th Century-Fox)

High Time is pretty lightweight fare for a star of Bing Crosby's proportions. Beating on the promising premise of Crosby—51, father of two, a millionaire restaurant chain owner—enrolling in college as a freshman and continuing through four years to graduation, film depends on individual situations and gimmicks rather than on straight storyline. The Groaner only trills twice.

The finished product is good fun at times, some of the situations near the belly-laugh stage. Blake Edwards's direction is light and fluid as he catches the college spirit. The screenplay is based on a story by Garson Kanin.

Crosby handles his role in his usual fashion, perfectly timing his laughs, and delivers a pair of Sammy Cahn–James Van Heusen songs, "The Second Time Around" and "Nobody's Perfect." Co-starring with him are Fabian and Tuesday Weld, students, former singing an old folksong effectively, and Nicole Maurey, as the French teacher whom Crosby romances.

•

HIGH WALL

1947, 98 mins, US b/w

Dir Curtis Bernhardt ***Prod*** Robert Lord ***Scr*** Sydney Boehm, Lester Cole ***Ph*** Paul Vogel ***Ed*** Conrad A. Nervig ***Mus*** Bronislau Kaper ***Art*** Cedric Gibbons, Leonid Vasian

Act Robert Taylor, Audrey Totter, Herbert Marshall, H. B. Warner, Warner Anderson (M-G-M)

High Wall [based on a play by Alan R. Clark and Bradbury Foote] garners a high score as a strong entry in the psychomelodrama cycle. Unfolded credibly and with almost clinical attention for detail, film holds the interest and punches all the way.

Robert Lord has given the melodramatics fine production polish and able handling to spotlight best features in story of a man who believes he has murdered his wife during a mental blackout.

Robert Taylor is seen as a man believed homicidally insane, being treated at mental hospital pending trial for murder of his wife. His case seems hopeless until a femme doctor breaks down his reluctance to try treatment to penetrate details that occurred during the lapse of memory.

Taylor scores in his role, making it believable. Audrey Totter registers strongly as the doctor, displaying a marked degree of talent able to handle most any character. Herbert Marshall is another who clicks as the murderer who cloaks his sin behind the garb of a pious publisher of biblical tracts. H. B. Warner movingly creates a pathetic mental case.

•

HIGH, WIDE AND HANDSOME

1937, 110 mins, US b/w

Dir Rouben Mamoulian ***Prod*** Arthur Hornblow, Jr. ***Scr*** Oscar Hammerstein II ***Ph*** Victor Milner, Theodore Sparkuhl ***Ed*** Archie Marshek ***Mus*** Boris Morros (dir.) ***Art*** Hans Dreier, John Goodman

Act Irene Dunne, Randolph Scott, Dorothy Lamour, Elizabeth Patterson, Raymond Walburn, Charles Bickford (Paramount)

Film shapes up as a $1.9 million Western, although possessed of all the elements to have made it a saga of Pennsylvania oilwell pioneering. Something went wrong on scripting and production from what was, undoubtedly, an intriguing script on paper.

Film's title sounds like a musical or operetta, but it's more of a melodramatic romance, with six songs by Jerome Kern and Oscar Hammerstein II, latter also credited for the original story and the screenplay. Wherein lies the film's principal deficiency. It's a cross-section of Americana tinged with too much Hollywood hokum.

As a result, *High, Wide*, after teeing off vigorously, flounders as it progresses, and winds up in a melodramatic shambles of fisticuffs, villainy and skullduggery which smacks of the serial film school.

Irene Dunne is too coy as the daughter of a medicine-show owner and Randolph Scott too forthright as her romantic vis-a-vis. And the menacing by Charles Bickford, at the helm of his hired plug-uglies, with Alan Hale as the villainous banker, is very tent-twent-thirt. Dorothy Lamour is rather heavy eye-laden for the nitery gal who ultimately repays the Scott-Dunne combo for previous kindnesses.

Rouben Mamoulian's production is heavy-handed. While endowed with an elastic budget, save for the fighting scenes there's little that's spectacular or impressive about the result. The mob scenes are as much to the credit of the camera as to the direction.

•

HIGH WIND IN JAMAICA, A
1965, 104 mins, UK Ⓥ ▭ col
Dir Alexander Mackendrick ***Prod*** John Croydon ***Scr*** Stanley Mann, Ronald Harwood, Dennis Cannan ***Ph*** Douglas Slocombe ***Ed*** Derek York ***Mus*** Larry Adler ***Art*** John Howell, John Hoesli
Act Anthony Quinn, James Coburn, Dennis Price, Lila Kedrova, Gert Frobe, Nigel Davenport (20th Century-Fox)

Anthony Quinn's penchant for grizzled characterization gets a colorful boost in this picturization of Richard Hughes's 1929 bestseller, which projects him as a Caribbean pirate. British production is a curious mixture of high melodrama and light overtones, the latter occasioned by presence of a flock of youngsters aboard a pirate ship.

Most of the action takes place at sea. Filmed on location around Jamaica, Alexander Mackendrick's direction keeps his movement alive within the somewhat limited confines of a schooner where Quinn, the Spanish pirate captain, is confronted with the disturbing question of what to do with seven children who unbeknownst to him have slipped from another ship he attacked and now are found in the hold of his own craft.

Quinn endows his role with a subdued humanness in which there is occasional humor. James Coburn, costarred with Quinn as his English mate, socks over character in which he combines humor with dramatic strength.

•

HILL, THE
1965, 125 mins, UK Ⓥ ⦿ b/w
Dir Sidney Lumet ***Prod*** Kenneth Hyman ***Scr*** Ray Rigby ***Ph*** Oswald Morris ***Ed*** Thelma Connell ***Mus*** [none] ***Art*** Herbert Smith
Act Sean Connery, Harry Andrews, Ian Bannen, Alfred Lynch, Ossie Davis, Michael Redgrave (M-G-M/Seven Arts)

Kenneth Hyman's production of *The Hill* is a tough, uncompromising look at the inside of a British military prison in the Middle East during the last war. It is a harsh, sadistic and brutal entertainment, superbly acted and made without any concessions to officialdom.

The "hill" of the title is a man-made pile of sand up and down which the soldier-prisoners have to run with full kit, often until they are physically exhausted, as part of a punishment designed more to break a man's spirit rather than provide corrective treatment.

The screenplay [from a play by Ray Rigby and R. S. Allen] puts the spotlight on a new bunch of prisoners, one of whom (Sean Connery) is a "busted" sergeant-major, and a natural target for the vindictive and sadistic treatment. Another is a Negro sent down for drinking three bottles of Scotch from the officers' mess.

One of the new intake collapses and dies, and that sparks off a mutiny, which is one of the most powerful and dramatic sequences of the pic.

Connery gives an intelligently restrained study, carefully avoiding forced histrionics. The juiciest role, however, is that of the prison regimental sergeant major, and Harry Andrews does a standout job.

•

HILL IN KOREA, A
(US: HELL IN KOREA)
1956, 81 mins, UK b/w
Dir Julian Amyes ***Prod*** Ian Dalrymple ***Scr*** Ian Dalrymple ***Ph*** Freddie Francis ***Ed*** Peter Hunt ***Mus*** Malcolm Arnold
Act George Baker, Harry Andrews, Stanley Baker, Michael Medwin, Ronald Lewis, Stephen Boyd (Wessex/British Lion)

Story is based on a book [by Max Catto] but records actual events. It is little more than an incident, depicting the adventures of a small patrol sent to find out if a village is inhabited by the enemy.

There are no base camp sets, nor home scenes before the inducted boys join the army. All the action, humor and pathos centres on the mixed bunch from every walk of life, wisecracking, beefing and just plain scared, comprising one rookie officer, three regular soldiers, including one sergeant. The remainder are untried civilians.

With the subdued lighting used throughout most of the shots, owing to night marches, and the indistinguishable drab jungle outfit, anonymity swamps most of the characters. Only the closeups of their sweaty faces and calling each other's names bring individuality to the actors.

All the cast has equal opportunities to score, George Baker as the conscientious officer, Harry Andrews as the tough sergeant and Ronald Lewis as the outsider, disliked by his buddies.

•

HILLS HAVE EYES, THE
1978, 89 mins, US Ⓥ ⦿ col
Dir Wes Craven ***Prod*** Peter Locke ***Scr*** Wes Craven ***Ph*** Eric Sadrinen ***Ed*** Wes Craven ***Mus*** Don Peake ***Art*** Robert Burns
Act Susan Lanier, Robert Houston, Virginia Vincent, Russ Grieve, Dee Wallace, Martin Speer (Blood Relations)

Wes Craven's blood-and-bone frightener about an all-American family at the mercy of cannibal mutants is a satisfying piece of pulp.

Reputedly based on genuine 17th-century Scottish cave-dwellers, these savages terrorize a strip of Californian desert in which the Carters are stranded by a snapped axle. Hollywood Movie-dog tradition is put to use in the forms of Beauty and the Beast, Carters' protective pets, which play their part in final outwitting of the marauders.

But there's plenty of death before then, survivors of the symbolic struggle being the teenagers on both sides, one dog and a baby, on whose future (in the world or in the pot) much of the rival hysterias have centered.

Gratifying aspects are Craven's businesslike plotting and pacy cutting, and a script which takes more trouble over the stock characters than it needs. There are plenty of laughs, in the dialog and in the story's disarming twists.

•

HILLS HAVE EYES PART II, THE
1985, 88 mins, US/UK Ⓥ ⦿ col
Dir Wes Craven ***Prod*** Barry Cahn, Peter Locke ***Scr*** Wes Craven ***Ph*** David Lewis ***Ed*** Richard Bracken ***Mus*** Harry Manfredini
Act Michael Berryman, Tamara Stafford, Kevin Blair, John Bloom, Janus Blythe (Castle Hill/Fancey/New Realm/VTC

The Hills Have Eyes Part II is a lower case followup by Wes Craven to his 1977 cult horror pic.

Film concerns two grownup survivors of the earlier pic. Young Bobby Carter (Robert Houston) is plagued by nightmares of the desert massacre that he survived. He has invented a super formula of gasoline which his local moto-cross club is testing in an upcoming race. Ruby (Janus Blythe), a nice-gal survivor, is taking the bikers to the race, when they foolishly try a shortcut across the desert.

From then on, it's dull, formula terror pic clichés, with one attractive teenager after another picked off by the surviving cannibals.

Acting is on the level of a formula shocker, featuring a winsome Candice Bergen-lookalike, Tamara Stafford, as a blind girl.

•

HILLS OF KENTUCKY
1927, 70 mins, US Ⓥ ⊗ b/w
Dir Howard Bretherton ***Scr*** Edward Clark ***Ph*** Frank Keeson
Act Rin-Tin-Tin, Jason Robards, Dorothy Dwan, Tom Santschi, Rin-Tin-Tin, Jr. (Warner)

One of the best action pictures, with Rin-Tin-Tin as the star, that have been turned out in this series.

It's a story of Kentucky, as the title indicates [adapted from the story "The Untamed Heart" by Dorothy Yost]. A little puppy is turned loose by a little boy because his father commands it. When the story itself starts this pup has grown to be the leader of the pack and is known as the Grey Ghost.

In a part of the hills are two Harley brothers, one inclined to be a bully and other a rather diffident youngster. There comes into the picture at this time a young school teacher with her crippled child brother. Both of the Harley men fall in love with her.

There is a moment when there are three suspense sequences being carried on at once: the two brothers fighting over the girl in the woods, the dog swimming down the stream toward the falls for the youngster's crutch and the little fellow himself trying to fight off the dog pack. This carries a wallop.

•

HIMMEL UEBER BERLIN
(WINGS OF DESIRE)
1987, 130 mins, W. Germany/France Ⓥ ⦿ col
Dir Wim Wenders ***Prod*** Wim Wenders, Anatole Dauman ***Scr*** Wim Wenders, Peter Haendke ***Ph*** Henri Alekan ***Ed*** Peter Przygodda ***Mus*** Juergen Knieper ***Art*** Heidi Ludi
Act Bruno Ganz, Solveig Dommartin, Peter Falk, Otto Sander, Curt Bois (Road Movies/Argo)

Wim Wenders returns to Germany with a sublimely beautiful, deeply romantic film for our times. This tale of angels watching over the citizens of Berlin springs from the great tradition of pics about angels involved in human affairs (*It's a Wonderful Life, Here Comes Mr Jordan*, etc), but is a quintessential Wenders film.

Bruno Ganz and Otto Sander are angels who spend their time watching over the humans of the divided city. First part of the film establishes this mysterious world, with the whispering thoughts of humans filling the soundtrack.

Three humans are singled out. One's an old man, played by veteran Curt Bois, with memories of Berlin's shattered past. Another is Peter Falk, American movie actor in Berlin to make a pic about the Nazi era. The third is a beautiful trapeze artist (Solveig Dommartin). The angel played by Ganz begins to feel mortal when he watches the girl, and the film, which hitherto has been in black & white, has moments of color as humanity begins to encroach on the world of this angel.

Wenders invests this potentially risible material with such serenity and beauty that audiences will go along willingly with the fable. The film is a valentine to the city, with Henri Alekan's camera gliding and prowling around familiar landmarks as well as unknown backstreets.

•

HINDENBURG, THE
1975, 125 mins, US Ⓥ ⦿ ▭ col
Dir Robert Wise ***Prod*** Robert Wise ***Scr*** Nelson Gidding ***Ph*** Robert Surtees ***Ed*** Donn Cambern ***Mus*** David Shire ***Art*** Edward Carfagno
Act George C. Scott, Anne Bancroft, William Atherton, Roy Thinnes, Gig Young, Burgess Meredith (Universal/Filmakers)

Michael M. Mooney's non-fiction compendium of the facts and theories behind the German zeppelin's 1937 air disaster at NAS, Lakehurst, New Jersey, was earlier dramatized for the screen by Richard A. Levinson and William Link, and both receive a screen story credit.

George C. Scott stars as an air ace assigned as special security officer on the fatal Atlantic crossing.

The array of characters is dealt boringly from a well-thumbed deck: Anne Bancroft, eccentric German countess; Roy Thinnes, Scott's nasty partner; Gig Young, mysterious and nervous ad agency exec; Burgess Meredith and Rene Auberjonois, an improbable and dull effort at comic relief as tourist-trapping card cheats; Robert Clary, also bombing in cardboard comic relief, the list goes on. William Atherton emerges as the good-guy crewman saboteur who plans to blow up the ship. A battle of mental wits ensues between Scott, Thinnes and Atherton; it's as exciting as watching butter melt.

1975: Honorary Award (visual and sound effects)

NOMINATIONS: Best Cinematography, Art Direction, Sound

•

HIRED HAND, THE
1971, 90 mins, US Ⓥ col
Dir Peter Fonda ***Prod*** William Hayward ***Scr*** Alan Sharp ***Ph*** Vilmos Zsigmond ***Ed*** Frank Mazzola ***Mus*** Bruce Langhorne ***Art*** Lawrence G. Paull
Act Peter Fonda, Warren Oates, Verna Bloom, Robert Pratt, Severn Darden, Ann Doran (Pando)

The Hired Hand doesn't work very well. An offbeat Western, starring and directed by Peter Fonda, the film has a disjointed story, a largely unsympathetic hero, and an obtrusive amount of cinematic gimmickry which renders inarticulate the confused story subtleties. Warren Oates appears as Fonda's loyal and more mature friend, while Verna Bloom is Fonda's abandoned wife.

The script discovers Fonda en route to California with Oates, a fellow-wanderer in the seven years since Fonda abandoned his wife. Robert Pratt, the pair's younger companion, is brutally murdered by Severn Darden's henchmen in a frame-up; Fonda and Oates exact an appropriate revenge, then Fonda returns home with Oates.

Film evidently is trying to show a truer picture of early western life, as opposed to formula plotting; but when one is trying to buck an entrenched cliché, extreme care and artfulness are required to persuade those few not already convinced.

•

HIRELING, THE
1973, 95 mins, UK Ⓥ col
Dir Alan Bridges ***Prod*** Ben Arbeid ***Scr*** Wolf Mankowitz ***Ph*** Michael Reed ***Ed*** Peter Weatherley ***Mus*** Marc Wilkinson ***Art*** Natasha Kroll
Act Robert Shaw, Sarah Miles, Peter Egan, Elizabeth Sellars, Caroline Mortimer, Patricia Lawrence (World)

Based on a novel by L. P. Hartley set in 1923, this heavily atmospheric, painstakingly accoutred and splendidly acted pic deals with the increasingly close relationship, on a conversational-companionship level at first, of a young widow (Sarah Miles) and the hired chauffeur (Robert Shaw) who drives her home after a spell in a clinic recovering from a nervous depression.

Temporarily, class barriers are down—or so he begins to believe. Shortly, however, as she recovers her equilibrium and social contacts, the barriers and demarcations return.

Item has quality written all over it, and patient viewers will savor its many plusses. Miles is splendid as the confused lady, Shaw fine as her momentarily blinded opposite.

•

HIROSHIMA MON AMOUR
1959, 95 mins, France/Japan [A] b/w
Dir Alain Resnais ***Prod*** Sacha Kamenka, Takeo Shirakawa ***Scr*** Marguerite Duras ***Ph*** Sacha Vierny, Michio Takahashi ***Ed*** Henri Colpi, Jasmine Chasney ***Mus*** Giovanni Fusco, Georges Delerve ***Art*** Esaka, Mayo, Petri
Act Emmanuele Riva, Eiji Okada, Stella Dassas, Bernard Fresson, Pierre Barbaud (Argos/Como/Pathe Overseas/Daiei

A first [feature of] its director, film can be classed as a noble try to make a statement on human love and the Atom Bomb (hardly a lovable thing), but it's too literary in conception and too cerebral in treatment.

A woman (Emmanuele Riva) and a man (Eiji Okada), in a lover's embrace, talk of Hiroshima. Horrors of the Bomb are evoked. Lovers are a French woman, in Japan working on a film calling for world peace, and a Japanese architect. Then follows their realization of the impossibility of their love, since both are married.

Film then welds in her souvenirs of a first love during the war in France with a German soldier, his death, her breakdown and her reacceptance of life. The film plods.

Director Alain Resnais directs with sombre feeling and tact. It makes a plea for love and world humanity but does it without finally making the love a real, palpable thing, and it remains a symbolical trauma tied up with Hiroshima and the Occupation.

•

HIS BROTHER'S WIFE
1936, 91 mins, US b/w
Dir W. S. Van Dyke ***Prod*** Lawrence Weingarten ***Scr*** Leon Gordon, John Meehan ***Ph*** Oliver T. Marsh ***Ed*** Conrad A. Nervig ***Mus*** Franz Waxman
Act Barbara Stanwyck, Robert Taylor, Jean Hersholt, Joseph Calleia, John Eldredge, Samuel S. Hinds (M-G-M)

While the title telegraphs the plot [by George Averbach], W. S. Van Dyke, the director, has cannily paced his proceedings so that the suspense values aren't militated against too much. Perhaps that accounts for the somewhat anti-climactic moments in the unscreening, or maybe it's just that 91-minute running time, because somehow there are lapses in the dramatic tension.

Story is ultra-1936, as modern as a Hollywood diary in spots, although this very sparkle and sophistication of dialog at times takes on a phoney gloss.

John Eldredge is oke as the strait-laced brother Tom who, after splitting Robert Taylor and Barbara Stanwyck, is tricked into a "revenge" marriage (of the unkissed-bride type) with Stanwyck, only later to facilitate a divorce. Joseph Calleia is a restrained but sinister menace and Jean Hersholt, per habit, rings the bell again with one of his kindly medico portrayals.

•

HIS BUTLER'S SISTER
1943, 92 mins, US b/w
Dir Frank Borzage ***Prod*** Felix Jackson ***Scr*** Sam Hoffenstein, Betty Reinhardt ***Ph*** Woody Bredell ***Ed*** Ted Kent ***Mus*** Hans J. Salter
Act Deanna Durbin, Pat O'Brien, Franchot Tone, Akim Tamiroff, Evelyn Ankers, Alan Mowbray (Universal)

Universal swings strictly to the Cinderella formula for plot of Deanna Durbin's 13th starrer, *His Butler's Sister*. Neatly contrived situations, consistently good pace, excellent cast and four songs by Durbin combine to make this a top attraction of the Durbin series.

Familiar plot is embellished with fine performances and entertaining situations. Durbin hits New York from her Indiana town to embark on a singing career through visit to older brother (Pat O'Brien) whom she figures wealthy but who's in reality the butler to composer Franchot Tone. She's inducted as maid in the bachelor penthouse but fired in two days on insistence of O'Brien, afraid of losing his job if she sings to catch Tone's attention. Of course the composer becomes interested in girl.

Despite tale's fragility, picture is brimful of light and amusing situations. Durbin is spotlighted with fine performance as the young and ambitious singer, getting sensitive direction under Frank Borzage.

•

HIS GIRL FRIDAY
1940, 92 mins, US Ⓥ b/w
Dir Howard Hawks ***Prod*** Howard Hawks ***Scr*** Charles Lederer ***Ph*** Joseph Walker ***Ed*** Gene Havlick ***Art*** Lionel Banks
Act Cary Grant, Rosalind Russell, Ralph Bellamy, Gene Lockhart, Helen Mack, John Qualen (Columbia)

No doubt aiming to dodge the stigma of having *His Girl Friday* termed a remake, Columbia blithely skips a pertinent point in the credits by merely stating "From a play by Ben Hecht and Charles MacArthur." It's inescapable, however, that this is the former legit and pic smash *The Front Page*. The trappings are different—even to the extent of making reporter Hildy Johnson a femme—but it is still *Front Page*.

Casting is excellent, with Cary Grant and Rosalind Russell in the top roles. Grant is the sophisticated, hard-boiled, smart-alec managing editor who was portrayed by Adolphe Menjou in the earlier version. A newly injected part, required by the switch in sex of Hildy, is taken by Ralph Bellamy.

Principal action of the story still takes place in a courthouse pressroom. All of the trappings are there, including the crew of newshawks who continue their penny-ante poker through everything and the practice of the sheriff's crew on the gallows for an execution in the morning. With the wider vista given the story, there is, in addition, the newspaper office.

Star-reporter Russell tells managing editor Grant, from whom she has just been divorced, that she is quitting his employ to marry another man. Grant neither wants to see her resign nor marry again, retaining hope of a rehitching. To prevent her escaping, he prevails upon her to cover one more story, that of a deluded radical charged with murder and whom the paper thinks is innocent. Escape of the convicted man, his virtual falling into Russell's lap as she sits alone in the pressroom, and attempts by Grant and Russell to bottle up the story, are w.k., but still exciting.

•

HIS KIND OF WOMAN
1951, 120 mins, US Ⓥ b/w
Dir John Farrow ***Prod*** Robert Sparks ***Scr*** Frank Fenton, Jack Leonard ***Ph*** Harry J. Wild ***Ed*** Eda Warren, Frederic Knudtson ***Mus*** Leigh Harline
Act Robert Mitchum, Jane Russell, Vincent Price, Tim Holt, Charles McGraw, Marjorie Reynolds (RKO)

Robert Mitchum, professional gambler, and Jane Russell, posing as a rich girl so she can land a husband, meet at a remote Mexican resort. Mitchum is there to fulfill a strange bargain which will pay him $50,000, details of which he has not yet been informed. Two strike plenty of sparks in their meetings as each waits out plot development. Story draws an obvious parallel on Lucky Luciano. The script has a deported gangster plotting to get back into the States from Italy by taking the face and identification of an American. Mitchum has been chosen as the one to drop out of sight so Raymond Burr can take on the new identity.

Suspense gets in some real licks when Mitchum learns he's to be killed, not just to go into hiding, and the danger of his situation is brought home fully when Tim Holt, government agent who has warned him, is killed by Burr's men.

Both Mitchum and Russell score strongly. Russell's full charms are fetchingly displayed in smart costumes that offer the minimum of protection. Much is made of Vincent Price's scenery-chewing actor character and much of it supplies relief to the film's otherwise taut development.

•

HIS MAJESTY O'KEEFE
1953, 89 mins, US Ⓥ col
Dir Byron Haskin ***Prod*** [Harold Hecht] ***Scr*** Borden Chase, James Hill ***Ph*** Otto Heller ***Ed*** Manuel Del Campo ***Mus*** Robert Farnon ***Art*** Ted Haworth, W. Simpson Robinson
Act Burt Lancaster, Joan Rice, Andre Morell, Abraham Sofaer, Archie Savage, Benson Fong (Warner)

This swashbuckling South Seas adventure feature is ideally suited to Burt Lancaster's muscular heroics. The Fiji Islands location lensing is a plus factor for interest.

The island of Viti Levu in the South Pacific is the locale used. Lancaster is seen as a daredevil Yankee sea captain, cast overboard off the island by a mutinous crew. Intrigued by the possibilities of making a fortune off the island's copra, he stays on to battle other traders, native idleness and superstition, becoming His Majesty O'Keefe with a beautiful Polynesian (Joan Rice) as queen.

The action emphasis of the screenplay, suggested by a novel by Lawrence Kingman and Gerald Green, provides Byron Haskin's direction innumerable opportunities for movement, so the film's pace is quick-tempoed. Rice is a sweet romantic foil for Lancaster's swashbuckling. Tessa Prendergast, as another island beauty, teases the eyes.

•

HISTOIRE D'ADÈLE H., L'
(THE STORY OF ADELE H.)
1975, 97 mins, France Ⓥ ⊏⊐ col
Dir Francois Truffaut ***Scr*** Francois Truffaut, Jean Gruault, Suzanne Schiffman ***Ph*** Nestor Almendros ***Ed*** Yann Dedet ***Mus*** Maurice Jaubert ***Art*** Jean-Pierre Kohut-Svelko
Act Isabelle Adjani, Bruce Robinson, Sylvia Marriott, Reubin Dorey, Joseph Blatchley, Carl Hathwell (Films du Carrosse/Artistes Associes)

Francois Truffaut has made a romantic period drama about a young woman destroyed by her overwhelming love for a philandering British lieutenant.

She is the daughter of French writer Victor Hugo, the latter in political exile from France after he opposed the new Empire. Film begins with her arriving at a British channel island in 1863. She is looking for the lieutenant who had seduced her and whom she loved but who was looked down on by her family. She finds him but he refuses her and she sinks into madness.

She hounds him, announces their marriage and even follows him to Barbados. She is taken back to Paris where she lives out a long life, to die in obscurity.

Truffaut has gotten an exemplary performance from Isabelle Adjani as the anguished Adele H. The film builds a touching portrait and has a concise feel for the times, plus a needed timelessness in this impasse of reason and desire.

•

HISTOIRE SIMPLE, UNE
(A SIMPLE STORY)
1978, 107 mins, France/W. Germany Ⓥ col
Dir Claude Sautet ***Prod*** Alain Sarde ***Scr*** Claude Sautet, Jean-Loup Dabadie ***Ph*** Jean Boffety ***Ed*** Jacqueline Thiedot ***Mus*** Philippe Sarde ***Art*** Georges Levy
Act Romy Schneider, Bruno Cremer, Claude Brasseur, Roger Pigaut, Arlette Bonnard, Francine Berge (Renn/Sara/FR3/Rialto

Director Claude Sautet seems to like the device of weekend country meetings of friends to lay bare their loves, work problems and human outlooks. Quintessentially French, with its series of petty piques, sudden dramas, macho male shenanigans and gathering femme lib, though latter is more personal than a concerted movement, pic benefits from homogeneous thesping and astute direction.

Main thread of the film is Marie (Romy Schneider). She is an attractive, fortyish woman who has decided to abort a child she is bearing and drop her lover. The affair is over for her. She has a 19-year-old son who lives with her.

Working as a draftsman, all her friends seem drawn mainly from her work. There are little subplots alongside Schneider's march towards freedom of her actions. The odyssey ends with her having an affair with her ex-husband.

There is a friend with two kids who will not take back a husband who left her and admits to sometimes making money as an amateur joy girl, a shrewish woman, an easy-going unmarried girlfriend and a man at the end of his tether who is being fired though once a power in the company. Schneider is radiant and effective as a woman reaching fulfillment and maturity, with Claude Brasseur properly vindictive as her discarded lover and yet appealing, and Bruno Cremer is right as the ex-husband who is more effective in business than in human relations.

•

HISTORIA OFICIAL, LA
(THE OFFICIAL STORY)
1985, 112 mins, Argentina Ⓥ ⦿ ⊏⊐ col
Dir Luis Puenzo ***Prod*** Marcelo Pineyro (exec.) ***Scr*** Luis Puenzo, Aida Bortnik ***Ph*** Felix Monti ***Ed*** Juan Carlos Macias ***Mus*** Atilio Stampone ***Art*** Abel Facello
Act Hector Alterio, Norma Aleandro, Chela Ruiz, Chunchuna Villafane, Hugo Arana, Analia Castro (Historias/Progress)

The Official Story is a thought-provoking, indirect yet resolute approach to the greatest Argentine tragedy of the century: the degeneration into secret genocide of the so-called "dirty war" against terrorism in the mid- and late-'70s.

The story takes place during 1983 in Buenos Aires. It evolves around Alicia (Norma Aleandro) and Roberto (Hector Alterio), a married couple with an adopted child, Gabi (Analia Castro). Aleandro teaches history at a private school adhering to the official textbooks, but eventually she is impressed by the investigative, revisionist spirit of some of her pupils.

Significant details lead Alicia to suspect Gabi could be the offspring of a *desaparecida woman*. She decides to investigate, not only finding out who the parents were and who is the grandmother of her adopted daughter, but also realizing her husband is linked with both the paramilitary and the local and foreign businessmen profiting from the corruption in power circles.

Outstanding performances by Aleandro, Alterio and Chela Ruiz as the grandmother greatly help to inject *Story* with credibility, human warmth and pathos without losing intellectual stature and political meaning in its almost wordless yet uncompromising stance for human rights. Moppet actress Castro is a real find.

Luis Puenzo, an ace in the blurbs field, turns out a topical film of sustained tension.

1985: Best Foreign Language Film

•

HISTORY OF MR. POLLY, THE

1949, 94 mins, UK b/w

Dir Anthony Pelissier ***Prod*** John Mills ***Scr*** Anthony Pelissier ***Ph*** Desmond Dickinson ***Ed*** John Seabourne ***Mus*** William Alwyn

Act John Mills, Sally Ann Howes, Finlay Currie, Betty Ann Davies, Edward Chapman, Megs Jenkins (Two Cities)

Faithful adherence to the original H. G. Wells story is one of the main virtues of *The History of Mr. Polly*, which is noted for its fine characterizations.

The story of Mr. Polly is retold simply from the time of his father's death, his inheritance and marriage, subsequent failure as a shopkeeper and final happiness and freedom as a general handyman in a small country inn. Its success is a personal tribute to the sterling acting of John Mills.

Director Anthony Pelissier has put all the emphasis on the principal characters, and has extracted every ounce of human interest from the classic. Every part, right down to the smallest bit, has been selected with care and there is some notable work from an experienced cast.

•

HISTORY OF THE WORLD—PART I

1981, 92 mins, US Ⓥ ⦿ ▭ col

Dir Mel Brooks ***Prod*** Mel Brooks ***Scr*** Mel Brooks ***Ph*** Woody Omens, Paul Wilson ***Ed*** John Howard ***Mus*** John Morris ***Art*** Harold Michelson, Stuart Craig

Act Mel Brooks, Dom DeLuise, Madeline Kahn, Cloris Leachman, Gregory Hines, Sid Caesar (20th Century-Fox)

Boisterous cinematic vaudeville show is comprised of five distinct sections: the *2001* parody Dawn of Man, The Stone Age, featuring Brooks's acid comment on the role of the art critic, and a brief "Old Testament" bit, which together run 10 minutes; The Roman Empire, the best-sustained and, at 43 minutes, longest episode; The Spanish Inquisition, a splashy nine-minute production number; The French Revolution, a rather feeble 24-minute sketch; and Coming Attractions which, with end credits, runs six minutes and at least punches up the finale with the hilarious Jews in Space inter-galactic musical action number.

Although Monty Python's *Life of Brian* went well beyond Brooks in the blasphemy department, many of the pic's most successful gags poke holes in religious pieties. When Brooks as Moses comes down from the mountain, he's carrying three tablets. Frightened by a lightning blast, he drops one of them and quickly switches to 10 commandments instead of 15.

The one interlude which really brings down the house has Brooks working as a waiter at the Last Supper and asking the assembled group, "Are you all together or is it separate checks?"

As the old ad line said, there's something here to offend everybody, particularly the devout of all persuasions and homosexuals.

•

HIT, THE

1984, 97 mins, UK Ⓥ ⦿ col

Dir Stephen Frears ***Prod*** Jeremy Thomas ***Scr*** Peter Prince ***Ph*** Mike Molloy ***Ed*** Mick Audsley ***Mus*** Paco De Lucia, Eric Clapton ***Art*** Andrew Sanders

Act John Hurt, Tim Roth, Laura del Sol, Terence Stamp, Bill Hunter, Fernando Rey (Central/Recorded Picture)

This astringent, sardonically funny thriller is only the second theatrical feature for director Stephen Frears since *Gumshoe* (1971). Frears and writer Peter Prince have taken a potentially familiar tale of a gangland betrayal and revenge and made something richly inventive and most entertaining.

Pic opens in London in 1972 as Willie Parker (Terence Stamp) fingers his fellow criminals. Ten years later, Parker is living an apparently carefree existence in the Spanish countryside when four toughs kidnap him and hand him over to an experienced hit man, Braddock (John Hurt) and his novice sidekick, Myron (Tim Roth), to deliver him to the boss in Paris. It's a journey on which things keep going wrong.

Most disconcerting for the hit men is that Parker is so relaxed and philosophical about his fate. A stopoff at a secret apartment provides a further problem: the apartment is occupied by an Australian criminal, Harry (Bill Hunter) and his young Spanish mistress, Maggie (Laura del Sol). Maggie is taken along as hostage.

Acting is marvelous. Best of all is Roth as a cocky little hood, a bit puzzled as to what's going on and wanting to assert himself a little.

•

HITCHER, THE

1986, 97 mins, US Ⓥ ⦿ ▭ col

Dir Robert Harmon ***Prod*** David Bombyk, Kip Ohman ***Scr*** Eric Red ***Ph*** John Seale ***Ed*** Frank J. Urioste ***Mus*** Mark Isham ***Art*** Dennis Gassner

Act Rutger Hauer, C. Thomas Howell, Jennifer Jason Leigh, Jeffrey DeMunn (HBO/Silver Screen)

The Hitcher is a highly unimaginative slasher that keeps the tension going with a massacre about every 15 minutes.

Film proves mom's admonition not to pick up hitchhikers, especially if they're anything like John Ryder, a psychotic and diabolical killer played with a serene coldness by Rutger Hauer.

Along comes an innocent young man (C. Thomas Howell), who is falling asleep at the wheel and stops to pick Hauer up in the hopes that having a companion will keep him awake. What ensues for the rest of the film is a cat and mouse game where Hauer eliminates just about everyone Howell comes in contact with.

In addition to working with a script that has many holes, filmmakers didn't allow for one laugh in the entire 97 minutes.

•

HITLER'S CHILDREN

1943, 80 mins, US Ⓥ b/w

Dir Edward Dmytryk ***Prod*** Edward A. Golden ***Scr*** Emmet Lavey ***Ph*** Russell Metty ***Ed*** Joseph Noriega ***Mus*** Roy Webb ***Art*** Albert S. D'Agostino, Carroll Clark

Act Tim Holt, Bonita Granville, Kent Smith, Otto Kruger, H. B. Warner, Lloyd Corrigan (RKO)

The philosophies of Nazism and the manner in which the youth of Germany was moulded to a militaristic order are forcefully brought to the screen in *Hitler's Children* [from the novel *Education for Death* by Gregor Ziemer].

Tim Holt essays the leading role of the German boy who grows up to become a Gestapo officer, but cannot grow away from the childhood love he had for a girl who suffers the tortures of the Nazis.

Holt gives an excellent performance and looks the part he plays. Opposite him, Bonita Granville likewise acquits herself very creditably. An outstanding job is done by H. B. Warner as a bishop, whose church service is broken up by Gestapo agents on the hunt for Granville, who has taken shelter there. The dialog given Warner proves very trenchant.

•

HITLER
THE LAST TEN DAYS

1973, 108 mins, UK/Italy Ⓥ ▭ col

Dir Ennio De Concini ***Prod*** Wolfgang Reinhardt ***Scr*** Ennio De Concini, Maria Pia Fusco, Wolfgang Reinhardt, Ivan Moffat ***Ph*** Ennio Guarnieri ***Ed*** Kevin Connor ***Mus*** Mischa Spoliansky ***Art*** Roy Walker

Act Alec Guinness, Simon Ward, Adolfo Celi, Diane Cilento, Gabriele Ferzetti, Eric Porter (Reinhardt/West)

A major fault of the film is that there's no German feeling to it. The cast, with the exception of German actress Doris Kunstmann as Eva Braun, is made up of British and Italian actors. The film's interiors (and a few exteriors) were shot at Shepperton Studios, England.

What is good about the film is the treatment of Hitler by Alec Guinness, who gives perhaps the best portrayal yet of that bizarre figure. Even he, however, never conveys the fanaticism which Hitler certainly had and which he so powerfully conveyed to millions of susceptible German minds. As the film [from Gerhard Boldt's *The Last Days of the Chancellery*] revolves almost entirely around him, other cast members have to work hard to make even a momentary impression. The talent most lost in the shuffle is Simon Ward.

Most outstanding, considering her brief appearance, is Diane Cilento as a test pilot who gets across the authentic if misguided obsessive devotion to Der Fuehrer of some Germans.

•

HITMAN, THE

1991, 95 mins, US Ⓥ ⦿ col

Dir Aaron Norris ***Prod*** Don Carmody ***Scr*** Robert Geoffrian, Don Carmody ***Ph*** Joao Fernandes ***Ed*** Jacqueline Carmody ***Mus*** Joel Derouin ***Art*** Douglas Higgins

Act Chuck Norris, Michael Parks, Al Waxman, Alberta Watson, Salim Grant, Ken Pogue (Cannon)

Chuck Norris goes to Canada in this dreary, unconvincing action vehicle. *The Hitman* is short on action and adopts a film noir visual style that masks its limited production values. Feature is a comedown from their big-budget *Delta Force 2*.

Prolog has Norris and Michael Parks as cops on a stakeout, with Parks shooting Norris and leaving him for dead. Three years later Norris is in Seattle undercover as unsuspecting Italo gangster Al Waxman's No. 2 in command. Working for agent Ken Pogue, Norris's assignment is to get the two rival mobs, Waxman's and Marcel Sabourin's French heavies in Vancouver, to unite so that both can be nabbed. Fly in the ointment is a group of Iranian thugs led by Frank Ferrucci.

Norris is okay as a pretend heavy, but a very poor script violates many rules of the genre. Best thing about *Hitman* is some good stuntwork.

•

HIT PARADE OF 1943

1943, 90 mins, US b/w

Dir Albert S. Rogell ***Prod*** Albert J. Cohen ***Scr*** Frank Gill, Jr., Frances Hyland ***Ph*** Jack Marta ***Ed*** Thomas Richards ***Mus*** Jule Styne, Harold Adamson

Act John Carroll, Susan Hayward, Gail Patrick, Eve Arden, Dorothy Dandridge (Republic)

Here's a little musical which is "little" only compared to some of the majors' past gargantuan efforts, but which actually blends a fetching set of songs, a wealth of variety talent, mostly colored, to a fair story.

The cast names aren't breathtaking as some of the others stabled in the major league studios, but from Al Cohen's production and Al Rogell's direction to the dance-staging and songsmithing it's a very satisfying confection indeed.

You may get captious with the idea of making a thieving songwriter your hero, which is what John Carroll personates, but thus is Susan Hayward, talented young tunesmith, thrown together with him. In fact, the characterization of Rick Farrell, who even continues to let Hayward ghost his songs, is never wholly palatable, but Carroll's personal charm glorifies the double-crossing, two-timing lothario of Lindy's into a model swain in time for the fadeout.

1943: NOMINATIONS: Best Scoring of a Musical Picture, Song ("Change of Heart")

•

HIT THE DECK

1955, 112 mins, US Ⓥ ⦿ ▭ col

Dir Roy Rowland ***Prod*** Joe Pasternak ***Scr*** Sonya Levien, William Ludwig ***Ph*** George Folsey ***Ed*** John McSweeney, Jr. ***Mus*** Vincent Youmans

Act Jane Powell, Tony Martin, Debbie Reynolds, Walter Pidgeon, Vic Damone, Ann Miller (M-G-M)

The emphasis on youth, in the person of a number of personable young players on the Metro contract list, has been put on this remake of the [1927] legit musical *Hit the Deck*.

There's not much producer Joe Pasternak could do to refurbish the shopworn plot about three sailors on the loose, with three femmes on their mind, and the sundry complications that batter at the steadfast portals of Navy redtape and credibility. With the limitations, he has made it a pretty picture, replete with songs from the old footlight piece, complete with new lyrics and flashy production numbers.

The vintage musical takes on its best semblance to life when Debbie Reynolds and Russ Tamblyn are lending their enthusiasm, either alone or together, to the action.

•

HIT THE DUTCHMAN

1992, 118 mins, US/Russia Ⓥ col

Dir Menahem Golan ***Prod*** Menahem Golan ***Scr*** Joseph Goldman ***Ph*** Nicholas Von Sternberg ***Ed*** Bob Ducsay ***Mus*** Terry Plumeri ***Art*** Clark Hunter

Act Bruce Nozick, Eddie Bowz, Will Kempe, Sally Kirkland, Matt Servitto, Christopher Bradley (Power/Start)

Fast-moving, splendidly trashy mobster yarn dishes up the genre goods with grindhouse glee. Pic is the top-rouble half of two back-to-backers lensed in Russia, with similar casts and crews and overlapping plots. Its sibling is *Mad Dog Coll*.

Bruce Nozick toplines as Arthur Fleggenheimer, a cocky 24-year-old Jewish con who's freed from West Hampton pen and straightaway slips off the straight and narrow. After literally biting the nose of Vince Coll (Christopher Bradley), he's introed to Legs Diamond (Will Kempe) by best friend Joey (Eddie Bowz) and soon starts sniffing around Legs's warbler g.f. Frances Ireland (Jennifer Miller). He also adopts the name Dutch Schultz.

Unlike *Coll*, pic isn't constrained by endless interiors and night scenes. Look is considerably bigger budget (though not enough to forge a convincing New York) and the wealth of characters and incidents easily fills up the running time. The large cast plays the dime novel script at full tilt.

•

HIT THE ICE
1943, 81 mins, US Ⓥ b/w
Dir Charles Lamont *Prod* Alex Gottlieb *Scr* Robert Lee, Frederic Rinaldo, John Grant *Ph* Charles Van Enger *Ed* Frank Gross *Mus* Charles Previn (dir.)
Act Bud Abbott, Lou Costello, Ginny Simms, Patric Knowles (Universal)

Abbott and Costello, street candid cameramen, become mistaken for Detroit gunmen by bank robber Sheldon Leonard, are bystanders at the bank holdup and finally head west to Sun Valley to evade arrest on suspicion. Also going west is Leonard and his two thugs, medico Patric Knowles, nurse Elyse Knox, songstress Ginny Simms and Johnny Long with his orchestra, with Simms and band to launch engagement at the winter resort.

Comedians launch a fast pace at the start, with the bank robbery, visit to the hospital and wild race to a fire providing plenty of opportunity for physical and dialog zaniness. Even train trip west gives the boys something to do, while Costello's adventures as end man on a snap-the-whip routine on the ice rink is a smackeroo laugh highlight. Climactic routine slides the two boys down the mountainside in a standout chase which also includes Leonard and his confederates.

•

H. M. PULHAM, ESQ.
1941, 119 mins, US b/w
Dir King Vidor *Prod* [uncredited] *Scr* Elizabeth Hill, King Vidor *Ph* Ray June *Ed* Harold F. Kress *Mus* Bronislau Kaper *Art* Cedric Gibbons, Malcolm Brown
Act Hedy Lamarr, Robert Young, Ruth Hussey, Charles Coburn, Van Heflin, Fay Holden (M-G-M)

What will please the book-readers—and probably the non-readers as well—is the faithfulness with which King Vidor and Elizabeth Hill have transferred the John P. Marquand novel to the screen.

Major defect in the celluloid version is the casting of Hedy Lamarr in principal femme role. It's Lamarr's Viennese accent that is jarring, although her looks and acting otherwise are tops.

Pulham (Robert Young) is of the wool-dyed Boston Backbay, bred in its Brahmanism from the day he was born, when his father registered him for entrance in St. Swithin's School 12 years hence. Coming back from the war, he succeeds in breaking away from his family to take a job in a New York agency, where he and fellow-copywriter Lamarr fall in love. She carries a torch for him for some 20 years.

But Lamarr is not of Boston and refuses to take to it or give up her career. Pulham, when his father dies, marries a family-approved gal (Ruth Hussey) and they live the conventional Hub humdrum until Pulham is called upon to write a biog of himself for a Harvard reunion and sits down to reminisce.

•

H.M.S. DEFIANT
(US: DAMN THE DEFIANT!)
1962, 101 mins, UK Ⓥ ⊙ ▭ col
Dir Lewis Gilbert *Prod* John Brabourne *Scr* Nigel Kneale, Edmund H. North *Ph* Christopher Challis *Ed* Peter Hunt *Mus* Clifton Parker *Art* Arthur Lawson
Act Alec Guinness, Dirk Bogarde, Anthony Quayle, Tom Bell, Maurice Denham, Victor Maddern (Columbia)

H.M.S. Defiant is a strong naval drama about the days of the Napoleonic wars, enhanced by the strong appeal of Alec Guinness, Dirk Bogarde and Anthony Quayle.

Based on Frank Tilsley's novel *Mutiny*, story is of the time of old press gangs. British navy conditions were appalling and it was the mutiny depicted in this pic which did much to give the British naval men a new deal. Guinness plays the skipper of the *Defiant* which, when it sets out to help tackle the Napoleonic fleet, is ruptured by a tussle for power between Guinness and his first lieutenant (Bogarde).

Guinness is a humane man, though a stern disciplinarian. Bogarde is a sadist, anxious to jockey Guinness out of position.

Below deck the crew, led by Quayle and Tom Bell, is plotting mutiny against the bad food, stinking living conditions and constant floggings ordered by Bogarde.

Guinness's role does not give this actor scope for his fullest ability. Bogarde's is the more showy portrayal. Quayle makes an impressive appearance as the leader of the rebels, determined and tough, but realizing that there is a right and a wrong way to stage a mutiny, like anything else.

•

HOBSON'S CHOICE
1954, 107 mins, UK Ⓥ ⊙ b/w
Dir David Lean *Prod* David Lean *Scr* David Lean, Norman Spencer, Wynyard Browne *Ph* Jack Hildyard *Ed* Peter Taylor *Mus* Malcolm Arnold *Art* Wilfrid Shingleton
Act Charles Laughton, John Mills, Brenda de Banzie, Daphne Anderson, Prunella Scales, Richard Wattis (British Lion/London)

There is a wealth of charm, humor and fine characterization in David Lean's picture [of Harold Brighouse's play] made under the Korda banner. The period comedy, with a Lancashire setting, is essentially British in its makeup. Charles Laughton returned to his native country to star.

Laughton plays the widower Hobson, a shoemaker with three unmarried daughters, one of whom is regarded as being permanently on the shelf. After all, as he is always explaining to his cronies in the saloon, she is past it at 30. But the daughter will have none of it; she railroads one of her father's assistants into marriage.

Although Laughton richly overplays every major scene, his performance remains one of the film's highlights. Mills also makes a major contribution in his interpretation of the illiterate shoemaker's assistant who learns to assert himself. Brenda de Banzie captures top femme honors for her playing of the spirited daughter who triumphs over the ridicule of her father and sisters.

•

HOCUS POCUS
1993, 95 mins, US Ⓥ ⊙ col
Dir Kenny Ortega *Prod* David Kirschner, Steven Haft *Scr* Mick Garris, Neil Cuthbert *Ph* Hiro Narita *Ed* Peter E. Berger *Mus* John Debney *Art* William Sandell
Act Bette Midler, Sarah Jessica Parker, Kathy Najimy, Omri Katz, Thora Birch, Vinessa Shaw (Walt Disney)

With Bette Midler and her on-screen sisters shamelessly hamming things up, it looks as if those involved in making this inoffensive flight of fantasy had more fun than anyone over 12 will have watching it. Still, the blend of witchcraft and comedy should divert kids without driving the patience of their parents to the boiling point.

Tried-and-true storyline [by David Kirschner and Mick Garris] has a teenage boy (Omri Katz) feeling out of place having moved to a new town—in this case venerable Salem, Mass—with his parents and kid sister. Stuck with taking moppet Dani (Thora Birch, one of the pic's major assets) trick-or-treating on Halloween night, he meets up with his dream-girl classmate (Vinessa Shaw) and ends up traveling to a musty old museum where, inadvertently, he conjures up three children-hungry witches from the dead.

They are, in fact, the Sanderson sisters: the cruel Winifred (Midler), the daft Mary (Kathy Najimy of *Sister Act*) and the positively dense, boy-crazy Sarah (Sarah Jessica Parker). The trio must suck the life-force out of children by dawn or risk being scattered forever.

Hocus Pocus suffers from inconsistency, careening aimlessly between a sense of menace and a comedic sort of Three Stooges on broomsticks. Choreographer-turned-director Kenny Ortega, whose own last flight was on the ill-fated Disney musical *Newsies*, can't quite pull off this tap dance, even with the ripe comedic possibilities in the setup.

•

HOFFA
1992, 140 mins, US Ⓥ ⊙ ▭ col
Dir Danny DeVito *Prod* Edward R. Pressman, Danny DeVito, Caldecot Chubb *Scr* David Mamet *Ph* Stephen H. Burum *Ed* Lynzee Klingman, Ronald Roose *Mus* David Newman *Art* Ida Random
Act Jack Nicholson, Danny DeVito, Armand Assante, J. T. Walsh, John C. Reilly, Frank Whaley (20th Century-Fox)

Hoffa presents the controversial labor leader as public icon, a man of iron, granite and cojones who bullies his way across the union and political landscape of the mid-century all for the good of the working man. Unfortunately, this grimly ambitious biopic goes no deeper than that, offering hardly a trace of psychology, motivation or inner life. First section consists almost entirely of Hoffa's harangues and agitations on behalf of the union. Jumping into the truck of fictitious everyman Bobby Ciaro (Danny DeVito) one night, Hoffa (Jack Nicholson) preaches the gospel of the Teamsters, expressing it with almost mathematical logic.

As soon as Hoffa achieves some stature, he is abducted by a few fellows whose native language is Italian. Hoffa continues his rise, mixing it up with company goons when he feels like it, finally ascending to the Teamster presidency. But mixed in with the roots of his success are the seeds of his downfall.

Intercut with the flow of historical action are scenes of the aging Hoffa and Ciaro waiting for unknown associates at a roadside cafe. Matter of Hoffa's fate is neatly wrapped up without being too specific. Mainly because of Nicholson's galvanizing performance and scriptwriter David Mamet's peppery, confrontational dialog, all this is not exactly dull, but it is very dry and uninvolving. DeVito's direction tends toward the over-busy, with plenty of crane shots and imaginative but fussy scene transitions.

1992: NOMINATIONS: Best Cinematography, Makeup

•

HOLCROFT COVENANT, THE
1985, 112 mins, UK Ⓥ ⊙ col
Dir John Frankenheimer *Prod* Edie Landau, Ely Landau *Scr* George Axelrod, Edward Anhalt, John Hopkins *Ph* Gerry Fisher *Ed* Ralph Sheldon *Mus* Stanislas *Art* Peter Mullins
Act Michael Caine, Anthony Andrews, Victoria Tennant, Lilli Palmer, Mario Adorf, Michael Lonsdale (Thorn EMI)

This muddled thriller is seemingly aimed at cinemagoers fearful of a fourth Reich. Various scripters have not created a clear narrative line out of Robert Ludlum's complex potboiler novel. Result is a muddled narrative deficient in thrills and plausiblity.

Film starts with the revelation to Noel Holcroft (Michael Caine) that his father, the financial wizard who kept Hitler's plans afloat, left a bequest valued at over $4 billion with which the son is to make amends for the evils of Hitler's Germany. His mother (Lilli Palmer) suspects that the money is designated for the building of a new Nazi empire. Argument is supported by various deaths that happen around Holcroft. The character doesn't attempt to discover what is going on and his attractive escort Helden von Tiebolt (Victoria Tennant) has to keep on reminding him that their lives are in danger.

Caine, whose reputation was built acting wily Britishers in local thrillers, just doesn't convince as a naive New Yorker. (James Caan was originally to play the role.) Victoria Tennant plays her part of femme fatale as if she doesn't know which side she's on.

•

HOLD BACK THE DAWN
1941, 114 mins, US b/w
Dir Mitchell Leisen *Prod* Arthur Hornblow *Scr* Charles Brackett, Billy Wilder *Ph* Leo Tover *Ed* Doane Harrison *Mus* Victor Young *Art* Hans Dreier, Robert Usher
Act Charles Boyer, Olivia de Havilland, Paulette Goddard, Victor Francen, Walter Abel, Rosemary DeCamp (Paramount)

While *Hold Back the Dawn* is basically another European refugee yarn, scenarists Charles Brackett and Billy Wilder exercised some ingenuity and imagination and Ketty Frings's original emerges as fine celluloidia.

Charles Boyer is cast similarly to his role in Algiers—a rogue of hypnotic charm over women. A gigolo in Europe, he's washed up in Mexico by the war and the quota laws make his entry into the United States a dream at least eight years distant. Caught among numerous other Europeans likewise waiting for the bars to be let down, Boyer is rapidly going to seed in the Mexican town when he meets up with Paulette Goddard, his former partner in crime in Paris, Vienna, etc.

She crashed the U.S. by marrying an American jockey, ditching him later, and, still in love with Boyer, she puts him wise to the simple gimmick for making the immigration authorities relax. This sets the trap for Olivia de Havilland, a romance-hungry school teacher escorting a flock of young boys on an excursion in Mexico over the 4 July holiday.

Mitchell Leisen's only visible mistake is a tendency of the film to drag in spots, but this might be unavoidable due to Boyer's slow delivery.

1941: NOMINATIONS: Best Picture, Actress (Olivia de Havilland), Screenplay, B&W Cinematography, B&W Art Direction, Scoring of a Dramatic Picture

•

HOLE, THE
SEE: ONIBABA

•

HOLE, THE
SEE: LE TROU

•

HOLIDAY
1938, 93 mins, US Ⓥ ⦿ b/w
Dir George Cukor ***Prod*** Everett Riskin ***Scr*** Donald Ogden Stewart, Sidney Buchman ***Ph*** Franz Planer ***Ed*** Otto Meyer, Al Clark ***Mus*** Morris Stoloff (dir.) ***Art*** Stephen Goosson, Lionel Banks
Act Katharine Hepburn, Cary Grant, Doris Nolan, Lew Ayres, Edward Everett Horton, Henry Kolker (Columbia)

Philip Barry's play *Holiday* in film form was a smash hit in the Depression's depth in 1930. Futility of riches is the topic and Donald Ogden Stewart and Sidney Buchman, who wrote this version, have tossed in a few timely shots which bolster the Barry original. Changes and interpolations are few, however.

Katharine Hepburn is in her best form and type of role in *Holiday*. Her acting is delightful and shaded with fine feeling and understanding throughout. Cary Grant plays this one straight.

George Cukor brings out the best from all the players. Lew Ayres is the despondent younger brother in the wealthy family who seeks some relief from the monotony of riches by resorting to strong liquor. Comedy by Edward Everett Horton and Jean Dixon is good, and Henry Kolker's portrait of the father is splendid.

1938: NOMINATION: Best Art Direction

•

HOLIDAY FOR LOVERS
1959, 103 mins, US ▭ col
Dir Henry Levin ***Prod*** David Weisbart ***Scr*** Luther Davis ***Ph*** Charles G. Clarke ***Ed*** Stuart Gilmore ***Mus*** Leigh Harline ***Art*** Lyle R. Wheeler, Herman A. Blumenthal
Act Clifton Webb, Jane Wyman, Jill St. John, Carol Lynley, Paul Henreid, Gary Crosby (20th Century-Fox)

This is a romantic farce travelog that plays smoothly with a good many solid laughs. There are drags in spots, the plotting is not always smooth, not all the situations play off. But David Weisbart's production has a good mixture of young players salted with veterans, and Henry Levin's direction keeps things lively. The point of Luther Davis's screenplay, based on Ronald Alexander's Broadway play, is that daughter, not father, knows best.

Clifton Webb is a Boston psychiatrist confronted with two daughters (Jill St. John, Carol Lynley) who are simultaneously bursting the adolescent cocoon to fall in love. The plot requires Webb and the girls' mother (Jane Wyman) to trek through South America in frustrated chaperonage. All ends happily, in the contemporary American idiom, when dense parents capitulate to siblings' wishes.

The background of the film, chiefly Sao Paulo and Rio de Janeiro, gives a fine opportunity to show a good deal of spectacular South American landscape and skyscrapers.

Webb, with his customary acerbity, takes a line and pins it to the wall, often managing to make humor seem like wit. Wyman has only a few opportunities for laughs. St. John is pretty, but seems confused by some of her dialog. Lynley is a real film find, a cameo beauty who plays beat or sensitive and makes the transition with finesse.

•

HOLIDAY INN
1942, 100 mins, US Ⓥ ⦿ b/w
Dir Mark Sandrich ***Prod*** Mark Sandrich ***Scr*** Claude Binyon ***Ph*** David Abel ***Ed*** Ellsworth Hoagland ***Mus*** Irving Berlin, Robert Emmett Dolan (arr)
Act Bing Crosby, Fred Astaire, Virginia Dale, Marjorie Reynolds, Walter Abel, Louise Beavers (Paramount)

Loaded with a wealth of songs, it's meaty, not too kaleidoscopic and yet closely knit for a compact 100 minutes of tiptop filmusical entertainment. The idea is a natural, and Irving Berlin has fashioned some peach songs to fit the highlight holidays.

Plot is a new slant on a backstage story. Bing Crosby is the crooner, Fred Astaire the hoofer, partnered with brunet and fickle Virginia Dale. Latter jilts Crosby for Astaire (who subsequently becomes No. 2 to a Texan millionaire) which thus leaves the frankly lazy Crosby to carry out his Holiday Inn idea on his own. The crooner has figured out there are some 15 holidays in the year and by operating a Connecticut roadhouse on those festive occasions only he can loaf the rest of the 340 days.

Thus are strung together these songs and ideas: "White Christmas"; "Let's Start the New Year Right"; "Abraham", a modern spiritual for Lincoln's Birthday holiday; "Be Careful, It's My Heart" (St Valentine's Day); "I Gotta Say I Love You, 'Cause I Can't Tell a Lie" (Washington's birthday); "Easter Parade," of course; "I'm Singing a Song of Freedom," wherein Crosby, attired as the Freedom Man (with a snatch of "Any Bonds Today?") introduces himself as an American Troubadour.

Mark Sandrich's production and direction are more than half the success of the picture.

1942: Best Song ("White Christmas")

NOMINATIONS: Best Original Story, Scoring of a Musical Picture

•

HOLLOW MAN
2000, 114 mins, US Ⓥ ⦿ col
Dir Paul Verhoeven ***Prod*** Douglas Wick, Alan Marshall ***Scr*** Andrew W. Marlowe ***Ph*** Jost Vacano ***Ed*** Mark Goldblatt ***Mus*** Jerry Goldsmith ***Art*** Allan Cameron
Act Kevin Bacon, Elisabeth Shue, Josh Brolin, Greg Grunberg, Mary Jo Randle, Steve Altes (Wick/Columbia)

Though faintly connected through theme and subject to H. G. Wells' compact cautionary novella *The Invisible Man*, Paul Verhoeven's sci-fi/horror thriller is an intense, radical departure and closest of all to the director's *Starship Troopers* in its combination of mind-blowing, hyper-extreme special effects and near-comic sensibility.

Even though it's concerned with science's moral implications and dramatizes the tragic degeneration of a brilliant mind, pic is a combo of thrills, juicy one-liners and fine star turns by Kevin Bacon and Elisabeth Shue. Clever, effortless exposition is first hallmark of Andrew Marlowe's script [from his and Gary Scott Thompson's story] which observes frustrated Caine (Bacon) trying to—in lab lingo repeated for comic effect—"crack reversion." Oozing cocky arrogance, Caine's so-called "genius" abilities aren't only foiled by computation of how to deconstruct a body's physical structure (for invisibility) and then reconstruct the body back again into visibility. This guy can't even get a break trying to ogle his beautiful neighbor.

His breakthrough brings his lab team together to test an ape. Effects are jaw-dropping in intensity and even visual poetry, as animal's skin dissolves away, exposing its inner anatomy in meticulous detail. Seldom has cinema better visualized poignancy of an animal under human control, pushing the metaphor of being humiliated and stripped of its identity.

In an unexpected moral moment at pic's 30-minute mark, Caine insists that he inject himself with serum, placing responsibility on himself if something goes wrong. Socko sequence of a whole new—seventh?—degree of Kevin Bacon revs into overdrive, as Caine's outer skin vanishes. (Verhoeven, in a touch most Yank helmers would resist, films Bacon's entire body), followed by near heart attack, and finally, invisibility. Not since *Altered States* has the human form been made so fantastical, yet mortal.

Pic's tongue-in-cheek humor keeps apace of building sense of dread, leading to pic's dramatic core, as scientists realize that they can't bring Caine back. Bacon expresses Caine's bitterness at being imprisoned in this limbo state, but subtly suggests the man's devolution to his worst animal instincts of fear and survival. It's an expressionistic triumph of actor and physical effects putting voice and form to the drama's tragic irony of a brilliant mind undone by his own work.

Special f/x supervisor Scott Anderson proves to be a key collaborator here, employing technology unavailable even a year ago. No less crucial is a lush, complex, near-operatic score by Jerry Goldsmith.

•

HOLLYWOOD
1923, 103 mins, US ⊗ b/w
Dir James Cruze ***Scr*** Tom Geraghty, Frank Condon ***Ph*** Karl Brown
Act Hope Drown, Luke Cosgrave, George K. Arthur, Ruby Lafayette, Eleanor Lawson, King Zany (Paramount)

While the players proper are not well known, for a moment or two in the picture the majority of the better-known stars of filmdom are introduced. The list includes: Cecil B. DeMille, Wm. S. Hart, Walter Hiers, May McAvoy, Charles De Roche, Owen Moore, Baby Peggy, Viola Dana, Anna Q. Nilsson, Thomas Meighan, Betty Compson, Leatrice Joy, Theo. Kosloff, George Fawcett, Bryant Washburn, Hope Hampton, Eileen Percy, Bull Montana, Pola Negri, Jack Holt, Jacqueline Logan, Nita Naldi, Wm. de Mille, Jack Pickford, Lloyd Hamilton, Will Rogers, T. Roy Barnes, Agnes Ayres, Lila Lee, Lois Wilson, Noah Beery, Alf. E. Green, Anita Stewart, Ben Turpin, J. W. Kerrigan, Ford Sterling.

The story is cleverly conceived. It concerns a pretty girl in a small town who thinks that she should be in the movies. Having nothing but beauty in her favor, she cannot get a chance; but her grandfather, being a type, is practically forced into film work. He takes on airs, is an honored guest at the homes of the stars, while the girl who expected to prove a sensation in pictures depends on him for her living. The grandmother and an old maid of the family rush to Hollywood on money the old fellow sent home. They are both nabbed as types and get into pictures. Every one connected with her gets into pictures but she herself.

It is an amusing idea, good comedy and the inside life of Hollywood is shown. The girl meets Mary Pickford, to whom she delivers a dress. Mary calls Doug Fairbanks out that the girl may meet him.

•

HOLLYWOOD BOULEVARD
1976, 83 mins, US Ⓥ col
Dir Joe Dante, Allan Arkush ***Prod*** John Davison ***Scr*** Patrick Hobby ***Ph*** Jamie Anderson ***Ed*** Amy Jones, Allan Arkush, Joe Dante ***Mus*** Andrew Stein ***Art*** Jack DeWolfe
Act Candice Rialson, Mary Woronov, Rita George, Jeffrey Kramer, Dick Miller, Richard Doran (New World)

Roger Corman's New World Pictures does as good a satire job on itself as anyone could in *Hollywood Boulevard*.

Writing credit goes to one Patrick Hobby, also the name of the plot's screenwriter, played by Jeffrey Kramer. Candice Rialson goes to Hollywood where agent Dick Miller sends her to low-budget Miracle Pictures's producer Richard Doran who turns out one a week, as director Paul Bartel combines high aspiration with low achievement.

It seems that Mary Woronov, queen of the B-hive, doesn't like the competition from Rialson, Rita George and Tara Strohmeier. A series of bizarre murders gradually eliminate the challengers. Intercut with the new material is a lot of older Corman footage.

•

HOLLYWOOD CANTEEN
1944, 124 mins, US Ⓥ b/w
Dir Delmer Daves ***Prod*** Alex Gottlieb ***Scr*** Delmer Daves ***Ph*** Bert Glennon ***Ed*** Christian Nyby ***Mus*** Ray Heindorf (adapt.) ***Art*** Leo Kuter
Act Robert Hutton, Joan Leslie, Bette Davis, John Garfield, Sydney Greenstreet, Joan Crawford (Warner)

Author-director Delmer Daves scripted *Stage Door Canteen* for Sol Lesser in early 1943 and he parlayed himself into another smasheroo for Warners with *Hollywood Canteen*.

Robert Hutton and Joan Leslie emerge as the real stars of the filmusical. They carry the story and a human one it is, too. Hutton looks like the ideal GI Joe, back with a Purple Heart from the South Pacific, and his buddy (Dane Clark) looks the perfect Brooklynite.

Story has Hutton winding up not only meeting his dream-girl (Leslie) but is also the lucky winner as the millionth guest of the Hollywood Canteen. That entitles him to an Arabian Nights suite, car, gifts and his choice of actresses for his weekend date. Natch, it's Leslie. What's nice is that real-life Leslie plays herself with charm, poise and ease, and the plot is so glib one accepts the romance wholeheartedly.

1944: NOMINATIONS: Best Scoring of a Musical Picture, Sound, Song ("Sweet Dreams Sweetheart")

•

HOLLYWOOD CAVALCADE
1939, 100 mins, US col
Dir Irving Cummings ***Prod*** Darryl F. Zanuck ***Scr*** Ernest Pascal ***Ph*** Allen M. Davey
Act Alice Faye, Don Ameche, J. Edward Bromberg, Alan Curtis, Stuart Erwin, Buster Keaton (20th Century-Fox)

Hollywood Cavalcade relates an interesting and sentimental story of film producing in California, beginning in the pie-throwing, Keystone era of 1913, and winding up when Al Jolson sang from the screen in *The Jazz Singer*, and the silent picture days were ended. The film is excellently produced and brightened by color.

In addition to a brief personal appearance, Mack Sennett plays an important off-screen role in the film, principal novelty of which is the successful and amusing introduction of oldtime Sennett comedy routines and formula. There is a brief sequence also from *The Jazz Singer*, in which Jolson sings "Kol Nidre." Obviously, this was made especially for the film.

From a story by Hilary Lynn and Brown Holmes, *Hollywood Cavalcade* is a deft piece of workmanship, punctuated with numerous mechanical twists and turns. Scenes from the older films are projected in black and white, sometimes framed in colored borders.

As for the yarn itself, it relates the rise, fall and rise again of an enthusiastic young director, played by Don Ameche. At a New York performance of *The Man Who Came Back* in William A. Brady's Playhouse, he sees a promising understudy (Alice Faye) who is substituting for the leading woman. He persuades her to make the jump to Hollywood and the films. Cummings keeps the running account in a light and humorous vein.

•

HOLLYWOOD CHAINSAW HOOKERS
1988, 74 mins, US Ⓥ col
Dir Fred Olen Ray ***Prod*** Fred Olen Ray ***Scr*** Fred Olen Ray, T.L. Lankford ***Ph*** Scott Ressler ***Ed*** William Shaffer ***Mus*** Michael Perilstein ***Art*** Corey Kaplan
Act Gunnar Hansen, Linnea Quigley, Jay Richardson, Michelle Bauer, Dawn Wildsmith (Savage Cinema)

Hollywood Chainsaw Hookers is a self-styled cult film that is entertaining for its intended fringe audience.

Private dick Jay Richardson is hired to find runaway teenage beauty Linnea Quigley, whose dad had been suspected of child abuse. He finds her stripping in a topless club; she slips him a mickey and he awakes to find himself in the midst of a blood cult ritual presided over by Gunnar Hansen (Leatherface in *The Texas Chain Saw Massacre*).

Spoof goes over the edge when cult is revealed to be worshipping the chainsaw, "the cosmic link by which all things are united." Pic's highpoint is an outrageous sequence when voluptuous Michelle Bauer, posing as a hooker, covers her Elvis wall poster with plastic as she strips to an Elvis soundalike record and then bloodily cuts up her customer with a chainsaw. Pic climaxes with a dueling chainsaws battle between Quigley and Bauer.

Richardson is okay as the private eye given to clutzy voiceover, but Hansen's line readings are flat.

•

HOLLYWOOD COWBOY
SEE: HEARTS OF THE WEST

•

HOLLYWOOD HOTEL
1937, 100 mins, US b/w
Dir Busby Berkeley ***Prod*** [uncredited] ***Scr*** Jerry Wald, Maurice Leo, Richard Macauley ***Ph*** Charles Rosher, George Barnes ***Ed*** George Amy ***Mus*** Ray Heindorf (arr.) ***Art*** Robert Haas
Act Dick Powell, Rosemary Lane, Lola Lane, Ted Healy, Hugh Herbert, Glenda Farrell (Warner)

Hollywood Hotel is a smash musical entertainment, with a lively and amusing story and some popular song numbers. Warners has assembled an excellent cast, not the least interesting of whom is Louella O. Parsons, newspaper columnist, who makes an effective debut as an actress.

Production is elaborate, and Busby Berkeley's direction keeps the players going at top speed. Hollywood film studios and broadcasting are the basis of a farcical story which pokes fun at both the picture-making business and the radio industry. Story is by Jerry Wald and Maurice Leo, who have developed a satire which is original and humorous. Eight musical numbers are by Dick Whiting and Johnny Mercer, best of which are "I'm Like a Fish out of Water" and "Silhoueted in the Moonlight."

Lane sisters, Rosemary and Lola, turn in good performances, and Ted Healy and Hugh Herbert have some very funny material. Dick Powell's song numbers are first rate.

•

HOLLYWOOD HOT TUBS
1984, 102 mins, US Ⓥ col
Dir Chuck Vincent ***Prod*** Marke Borde ***Scr*** Mark Borde, Craig McDonnell ***Ph*** Larry Revene ***Ed*** Michael Hoggan ***Mus*** Joel Goldsmith ***Art*** Loma Lee Brookbank
Act Donna McDaniel, Michael Andrew, Paul Gunning, Katt Shea, Edy Williams, Jewel Shepard (Manson International)

A very good premise simply sinks in the Hollywood hot tub.

To save young Jeff from the slammer, his parents get him a job mixing plumbing with pleasure in the Hollywood hot tubs. Everything that can be done to, with, for, in or around hot water finds its way into a plot that goes from the quick and the dirty to the gothic. Each half-hour delivers a coupling in this not-too-funny comedy full of booze, broads and bubbles. The final party offers lookalikes of Burt Reynolds, Lauren Bacall and Bozo. Only the last is convincing.

The kids, at whom this pic is aimed, witness more sex than they enjoy. The most promising moments come with Jewel Shepard, who takes the Valley girl far beyond its usual dips.

•

HOLLYWOOD HOT TUBS 2: EDUCATING CRYSTAL
1990, 100 mins, US Ⓥ col
Dir Ken Raich ***Prod*** Mark Borde, Ken Raich ***Scr*** Brent V. Friedman ***Ph*** Areni Milo ***Ed*** Michael Hoggan ***Mus*** John Lombardo, Bill Bodine ***Art*** Thomas Cost
Act Jewel Shepard, Patrick Day, David Tiefen, Remy O'Neil, Bart Braverman, J.P. Bumstead (Alimar)

Beneath its come-on title, this sequel to Chuck Vincent's 1984 feature moves out of the exploitation film arena to a well-scripted comic look at West Coast life styles.

The Crystal of the title, Jewel Shepard, encores as the bubbley, jiggly Valley girl who heads for business school to learn how to run her mom Remy O'Neill's hot tubs/health spa establishment. Evil Bart Braverman (convincing with beard as a prince) is conspiring to take over the business, even planning to marry O'Neill to achieve his ends. Film is told from the point of view of handsome hero David Tiefen, who's working as a chauffeur to Braverman while writing a book about Shepard.

Under newcomer Ken Raich's direction, film works due to the quirky touches of Brent Frieman's screenplay. Previously wasted in purely decorative assignments, Shepard comes into her own here in a funny and sympathetic role. It's not quite *Educating Rita*, but the formula of gawky ingenue blossoming is a sure-fire one.

•

HOLLYWOOD OR BUST
1956, 94 mins, US Ⓥ col
Dir Frank Tashlin ***Prod*** Hal Wallis ***Scr*** Erna Lazarus ***Ph*** Daniel Fapp ***Ed*** Howard Smith ***Mus*** Walter Scharf (arr.) ***Art*** Hal Pereira, Henry Bumstead
Act Dean Martin, Jerry Lewis, Anita Ekberg, Pat Crowley, Maxie Rosenbloom (Paramount)

Hollywood's in the label and does make a finale appearance, but most of this comedy caper takes place on a cross-country junket from New York, with way stops en route, including Las Vegas.

Direction by Frank Tashlin scores enough comedy high-spots to keep the pace fairly fast, even with the slow spots that his handling and the team's talent cannot overcome. One of the film's funniest bits comes before the title with Dean Martin introducing Jerry Lewis as different types of movie-watchers. Lewis's encounter with a bull and making like a matador is another fun-filled sequence, as is his champagne binge in Vegas after hexing the gambling devices into a big payoff.

By way of making the latter part of the title legit, Anita Ekberg appears as guest star on whom Lewis has a crush. She doesn't have much more to do than to display what nature has wrought in the fjords of Sweden, so it's still a big part. En route west Martin and Lewis pick up Pat Crowley so that Martin will have someone to sing romantic songs to.

•

HOLLYWOOD REVUE
1929, 113 mins, US ⊙ col
Dir Charles Riesner ***Prod*** Harry Rapf ***Scr*** Al Bonsberg, Robert Hopkins ***Ph*** John Arnold, I. G. Reis, Maximilian Fabian ***Ed*** William Gray ***Mus*** Arthur Lange (arr.) ***Art*** Cedric Gibbons
Act John Gilbert, Norma Shearer, Joan Crawford, Bessie Love, Marion Davies, Buster Keaton (M-G-M)

First shot following the list of credits is the original billboard: 16 girls sitting for raised letters spelling the title and reciting the opening lyric in unison. The opening number is terrific: a formation tap routine by the ensemble in black-and-white costume.

The staging of *"Singin' in the Rain"* is a sweet dance melody delivered by Cliff Edwards and his uke under a side-screen tree as the water pours down into a stage-wide pool.

Individually no one stands out like Marie Dressler. Stage veteran has the one real comedy number of the picture in "For I'm the Queen," and runs away with the femme trio, rounded out by Bessie Love and Polly Moran.

Trick camerawork is confined to Jack Benny taking Bessie Love out of his pocket, not as well done as might be supposed, and Charlie King's sudden diminutiveness after hearing Conrad Nagel sing "You Were Meant for Me" and King's song in "Broadway Melody" to Anita Page.

First of the [two] color sequences is John Gilbert and Norma Shearer's *Romeo and Juliet*, a modern version, with Lionel Barrymore briefly flashed directing. Both principals look great and play well, Gilbert appearing a bit nervous on the straight interpretation, but hopping to the slang phrasing.

Joan Crawford sings "Gotta Feelin' for You," assisted by a male quartet, but doesn't do much with it.

It's a revue from gong to gong [in two acts, eight scenes and 18 numbers]. No semblance of a story, and considering cast nobody is going to care.

1928/29: NOMINATION: Best Picture

•

HOLLYWOOD SHUFFLE
1987, 82 mins, US Ⓥ ⊙ col
Dir Robert Townsend ***Prod*** Robert Townsend ***Scr*** Robert Townsend, Keenen Ivory Wayans ***Ph*** Peter Deming ***Ed*** W.O. Garrett ***Mus*** Patrice Rushen, Udi Harpaz ***Art*** Melba Katzman Farquhar
Act Robert Townsend, Anne-Marie Johnson, Starletta Dupois, Helen Martin, Craigus R. Johnson, Domenick Irrera (Conquering Unicorn)

Brimming with imagination and energy, *Hollywood Shuffle* is the kind of shoestring effort more appealing in theory than execution. Produced, directed and co-written by actor Robert Townsend, pic is a freeform look at the trials and tribulations of black actors trying to make it in today's Hollywood. Scattershot humor misses as much as it hits.

At a cattle call for a blaxploitation pic to be made by a white production company, Townsend starts to feel guilty and questions if what he's doing is right after he gets the part. Scenes in the actor's subconscious are dramatized on screen.

Most amusing of these is a school for black actors, run by whites, of course, where the students are trained to shuffle, jive and generally fit the preconceived notion of what blacks are like. Another brilliantly conceived bit is *Sneakin' into the Movies*, a takeoff of the Siskel & Ebert film reviewing TV show.

Performances of the ensemble cast, many of whom play more than one role, are likeable but without much that sticks to the ribs. Production values are predictably crude given the film's $100,000 budget.

•

HOLOCAUST 2000
(US: THE CHOSEN)
1977, 102 mins, Italy/UK Ⓥ ▭ col
Dir Alberto De Martino ***Prod*** Edmondo Amati ***Scr*** Sergio Donati, Aldo De Martino, Michael Robson ***Ph*** Enrico Menczer ***Ed*** Vincenzo Tomassi ***Mus*** Ennio Morricone ***Art*** Umberto Betacca
Act Kirk Douglas, Agostina Belli, Simon Ward, Anthony Quayle, Virginia McKenna, Alexander Knox (Embassy/Aston)

Take the threat of nuclear disaster, the ecological deterioration of the earth, the terror of an all-powerful Antichrist; mix it with an international cast topped by Kirk Douglas, Agostina Belli and a number of convincing British actors like Simon Ward, Anthony Quayle, Alexander Knox and Virginia McKenna and shake well.

The conflict is between Robert Caine (Douglas), an idealist in the realm of nuclear power plants, and his demon son Angelo (Ward) with tenebrous plans to push dad's project for fission power to wipe out human life.

The supernatural pushes superficial arguments about nuclear power to the side and gives the spectator a sense of human helplessness to contend with such an evil and destructive force as the Antichrist.

As striking a beauty as Belli is catapulted into the conflict with only symbolic story roots in a Biblical-like finale and with a slow, pronounced accent for her lines. The dramatic picture-long father-son duel between Douglas with a mid-American accent and Ward with a British lilt keeps the plot in place right up to the inconclusive finale.

•

HOLY MATRIMONY
1943, 87 mins, US b/w
Dir John M. Stahl ***Prod*** Nunnally Johnson ***Scr*** Nunnally Johnson ***Ph*** Lucien Ballard ***Ed*** James B. Clarke ***Mus*** Cyril Mockridge
Act Monty Woolley, Gracie Fields, Laird Cregar, Una O'Connor, Alan Mowbray, Eric Blore (20th Century-Fox)

Arnold Bennett's early 20th-century novel *Buried Alive* has been resurrected by Nunnally Johnson as a Monty Woolley–Gracie Fields starrer. The production and casting credits are all on the plus side in this comedy-drama themed in England at the turn of the century.

Matrimony is a study of characters, and Johnson's script has defined, and Stahl's direction developed, them excellently. Woolley is dominant throughout as Priam Farll, a painter whose fame for 25 years had mounted in England while he worked in solitude in the South Seas, accompanied only by a valet. When a command appearance is ordered by King Edward so he can be knighted, the trip back to England marks a turn of events that form the crux for the story.

The film's development abounds with a story line that at no times strains credibility. Fields gives the film a highly human touch. She's a perfect mate for Woolley's cantankerous characterization.

•

HOLY MATRIMONY
1994, 93 mins, US Ⓥ ⦿ col
Dir Leonard Nimoy ***Prod*** William Stuart, David Madden, Diane Nabatoff ***Scr*** David Weisberg, Douglas S. Cook ***Ph*** Bobby Bukowski ***Ed*** Peter E. Berger ***Mus*** Bruce Broughton ***Art*** Edward Pisoni
Act Patricia Arquette, Joseph Gordon-Levitt, Armin Mueller-Stahl, Tate Donovan, John Schuck, Lois Smith (Hollywood/Interscope/PFE)

A sort of humorous variation on *Witness*, *Holy Matrimony* is an innocuous but problematic comedy.

Pic begins with bosomy sexpot Havana (Patricia Arquette) on the run with boyfriend Peter (Tate Donovan) after they rob a carnival operator's safe. They cross the border into Canada and hide out at the Hutterite religious colony where Peter grew up.

Naturally, the vivacious, blunt-spoken Havana feels stifled by the restraints of Hutterite life—no TV, makeup, cigarettes or four-letter words—and she's even more unhappy when, after marrying Peter, she must serve him as a meekly submissive spouse. But she still doesn't know where Peter has hidden the stolen money.

After Peter is killed in an auto accident, Havana insists on her right to remain by marrying Peter's younger brother. Trouble is, the younger brother, Zeke (Joseph Gordon-Levitt), is all of 12 years old.

Holy Matrimony plays the second marriage mostly for safe, sitcom-style laughs. Pic steers far away from even implied acknowledgment of what surely will be on the minds of many audience members.

Arquette sparkles as Havana, making a believable transition from amoral Marilyn Monroe wannabe to relatively honest Big Sister figure. Gordon-Levitt (last seen as young Norman in *A River Runs Through It*) is unaffected and engaging as Zeke.

•

HOMAGE
1995, 96 mins, US Ⓥ col
Dir Ross Kagan Marks ***Prod*** Mark Medoff, Elan Sassoon ***Scr*** Mark Medoff ***Ph*** Tom Richmond ***Ed*** Kevin Tent ***Mus*** W.G. Snuffy Walden ***Art*** Amy Anconi
Act Blythe Danner, Frank Whaley, Sheryl Lee, Danny Nucci, Bruce Davison (Skyline)

Homage is a slice of American Gothic set in the desolate Southwest. The psychological thriller focuses on three emotionally crippled people whose interdependence threatens to ignite some unpleasant results.

Based on a Mark Medoff play [*The Homage That Follows*] and adapted by the writer, the film opens with the murder of Lucy (Sheryl Lee), a sitcom actress who's returned to New Mexico to patch up a fractured relationship with Katherine (Blythe Danner), her widowed mother. The perp, Archie (Frank Whaley), is a mathematician working as caretaker and gardener on Katherine's ramshackle farm.

The events leading up to the conclusion are related in flashback as "witnesses" provide key plot points to members of the tabloid press who have descended on the small community.

Director Ross Kagan Marks physically opens up the play and provides a seamless depiction of an arid environment, which serves as a chilling complement to the landscape of essentially unpleasant characters. But the story provides no real rooting interest, and the creepiness of the material tries one's patience.

•

HOMBRE
1967, 119 mins, US Ⓥ ⦿ ▭ col
Dir Martin Ritt ***Prod*** Martin Ritt, Irving Ravetch ***Scr*** Irving Ravetch, Harriet Frank, Jr. ***Ph*** James Wong Howe ***Ed*** Frank Bracht ***Mus*** David Rose ***Art*** Jack Martin Smith, Robert E. Smith
Act Paul Newman, Fredric March, Richard Boone, Diane Cilento, Cameron Mitchell, Martin Balsam (20th Century-Fox)

Hombre develops the theme that socially and morally disparate types are often thrown into uneasy, explosive alliance due to emergencies.

An unhurried, measured look at interacting human natures, caught up only for story purposes in a given situation, the characters speak truisms which, sometimes, are overdone platitudes.

Adapted from Elmore Leonard's novel, it tells the story of an Apache-raised white boy who becomes the natural leader of a group in its survival against a robber band headed by Richard Boone.

Paul Newman is excellent as the scorned (but only supposed) Apache. Fredric March, essaying an Indian agent who has embezzled food appropriations for his charges, also scores in a strong, unsympathetic—but eventually pathetic—role. Richard Boone is very powerful, yet admirably restrained as the heavy.

•

HOME ALONE
1990, 102 mins, US Ⓥ ⦿ col
Dir Chris Columbus ***Prod*** John Hughes ***Scr*** John Hughes ***Ph*** Julio Macat ***Ed*** Raja Gosnell ***Mus*** John Williams ***Art*** John Muto
Act Macaulay Culkin, Joe Pesci, Daniel Stern, Catherine O'Hara, John Heard, John Candy (20th Century-Fox)

The family of poor little dumped-upon Kevin (Macaulay Culkin) has rushed off to catch their holiday plane and accidentally left him behind. Now they're in Paris, frantically trying to reach him, and he's home alone, where a storm has knocked out the telephones, the neighbors are away for the holiday and the houses on the street are being systematically cleaned out by a team of burglars.

Generally perceived by his family as a helpless, hopeless little geek, Kevin is at first delighted to be rid of them, gorging on forbidden pleasures like junk food and violent videos, but when the bandits (Joe Pesci, Daniel Stern) begin circling his house, he realizes he's on his own to defend the place.

Kevin proves he's not such a loser by defending the fort with wits and daring and by the time Mom (Catherine O'Hara) comes rushing back from Europe, everything's in order.

A first-rate production in which every element contributes to the overall smartly realized tone, pic boasts wonderful casting, with Culkin a delight as funny, resilient Kevin, and O'Hara bringing a snappy, zesty energy to the role of mom. Pesci is aces in the role of slippery housebreaker Harry, who does a Two Stooges routine with lanky side-kick Stern.

1990: NOMINATIONS: Best Original Score, Song ("Somewhere in My Memory")

•

HOME ALONE 3
1997, 102 mins, US Ⓥ ⦿ col
Dir Raja Gosnell ***Prod*** John Hughes, Hilton Green ***Scr*** John Hughes ***Ph*** Julio Macat ***Ed*** Bruce Green, Malcolm Campbell, David Rennie ***Mus*** Nick Glennie-Smith ***Art*** Henry Bunstead
Act Alex D. Linz, Olek Krupa, Rya Kihlstedt, Lenny Von Dohlen, David Thornton, Haviland Morris (20th Century-Fox)

Five years after proving he could make box office lightning strike twice with *Home Alone 2*, the law of diminishing returns catches up with John Hughes. *Home Alone 3* is essentially a remake of the first *Home Alone*, with a new young protagonist, some slightly craftier villains—and much more brutal comic mayhem.

Newcomer Alex D. Linz has been brought aboard to play Alex Pruitt, another crafty youngster who defends his suburban Chicago home from unwelcome visitors. The baddies burglarize each home on Alex's street, hoping to find a toy car [in which is hidden a stolen microchip, due to a baggage mixup at an airport] before their North Korean client runs out of patience.

Alex comes down with the chicken pox, allowing him to remain home from school and observe the activities outside his window. Unfortunately, he's accused of making prank 911 phone calls. And that's why, when the spies finally narrow their search to Alex's home, our young hero feels compelled to take matters into his own little hands.

Evidently, Alex has spent a great deal of time studying the previous *Home Alone* movies. Either that, or he's naturally sadistic. While the tone is always frenetically comedic, and the mayhem bloodlessly slapsticky, some scenes are pretty rough.

Raja Gosnell, editor of the previous two entries, makes his debut here as a feature director, although there is little doubt that Hughes, who produced and wrote the by-the-numbers screenplay, is the auteur of the project.

•

HOME ALONE 2
LOST IN NEW YORK
1992, 120 mins, US Ⓥ ⦿ col
Dir Chris Columbus ***Prod*** John Hughes ***Scr*** John Hughes ***Ph*** Julio Macat ***Ed*** Raja Gosnell ***Mus*** John Williams ***Art*** Sandy Veneziano
Act Macaulay Culkin, Joe Pesci, Daniel Stern, Catherine O'Hara, John Heard, Tim Curry (20th Century-Fox)

Some day scholars will devote courses to the monstrous box office allure of the original *Home Alone*, which, at the time, surprised even Fox. For a sequel the studio has simply remade the first movie, but with bigger pratfalls. Pic delivers on that level.

Once again, Kevin (Macaulay Culkin), provoked by his older brother, finds himself in the doghouse just before a family vacation, this time accidentally boarding the wrong plane and ending up in New York while the McCallister brood jets off to Florida. Meanwhile, the inept thieves from the first movie, Harry (Joe Pesci) and Marv (Daniel Stern), have conveniently escaped from prison and caught a truck that arrives in New York about the same time Kevin does.

Using his dad's credit card, Kevin checks into a ritzy hotel, where he finds more adults to outwit, in this case a snooty concierge (Tim Curry) as well as the equally haughty staff. Ultimately, however, it's again Kevin versus the two bad guys, setting up elaborate traps at his uncle's being-remodeled home.

Under Chris Columbus's careful direction, the wide-eyed Culkin again shows his skill at being an Everykid—cutely precocious, yet still vulnerable to childish whims such as running up a whopping room-service tab on chocolate sundaes.

•

HOME AT SEVEN
(US: MURDER ON MONDAY)
1952, 85 mins, UK b/w
Dir Ralph Richardson ***Prod*** Maurice Cowan ***Scr*** Anatole De Grunwald ***Ph*** Jack Hildyard, Edward Scaife ***Ed*** Bert Bates ***Mus*** Malcolm Arnold ***Art*** Vincent Korda, Frederick Pusey
Act Ralph Richardson, Margaret Leighton, Jack Hawkins, Campbell Singer, Michael Shepley, Meriel Forbes (London/British Lion)

When [R. C. Sherriff's] *Home at Seven* was produced on the London stage in 1950, it proved to be one of the major successes of the legit season. Ralph Richardson repeats his starring role.

The production is notable for three "firsts." It was the first independent venture of Maurice Cowan; Richardson's first attempt at direction; and the first picture under the Alexander Korda banner to be produced under the speed-up technique of three weeks shooting schedule after extensive rehearsals.

The principal character, a bank clerk, loses a day in his life, and during the time he was an amnesia victim, the funds of his sports club are stolen and the steward is murdered. When the police starts its inquiries, he gives a false alibi, but that is soon exploded and he is convinced of his own guilt.

Richardson directs the piece with a straightforward competence.

•

HOME BEFORE DARK
1958, 137 mins, US b/w
Dir Mervyn LeRoy ***Prod*** Mervyn LeRoy ***Scr*** Eileen Bassing, Robert Bassing ***Ph*** Joseph F. Biroc ***Ed*** Philip W. Anderson ***Mus*** Franz Waxman ***Art*** John Beckman
Act Jean Simmons, Dan O'Herlihy, Rhonda Fleming, Efrem Zimbalist, Jr., Mabel Albertson, Steve Dunne (Warner)

Home Before Dark should give the Kleenex a vigorous workout. Based on one woman's battle to regain her slipping sanity, it is a romantic melodrama of considerable power and imprint.

The screenplay, based on Eileen Bassing's novel of the same name, sometimes seems rather skimpy in its character motivation. It is also difficult at times to understand the mental tone of the mentally ill heroine (Jean Simmons). But while the tale is unfolding it is made so gripping that factual discrepancies are relatively unimportant.

Simmons is the wife of Dan O'Herlihy, who has ceased to love her before mental breakdown and has not changed his attitude on her recovery. Living in their home, to which she returns on her release from hospitalization, are her stepmother (Mabel Albertson) and her stepsister (Rhonda Fleming). They are masterful females who could drive anyone to the edge of madness.

Her only real ally in the house is a stranger (Efrem Zimbalist, Jr.), who is also an alien in the setting of the inbred New England college community. Zimbalist is the only Jewish member of the faculty, and ostensibly a protégé of O'Herlihy's.

The whole picture is seen from Simmons's viewpoint, which means she is "on" virtually the whole time. Her voice is a vibrant instrument, used with thoughtful articulation and placement, the only vital part of her at times.

Joseph Biroc's photography is suited to the grim New England atmosphere. It is winter, a depressingly gray winter, and the locations in Massachusetts give the picture the authentic feel.

•

HOMEBOY

1988, 112 mins, US Ⓥ ⊙ col

Dir Michael Seresin ***Prod*** Alan Marshall, Elliott Kastner ***Scr*** Eddie Cook ***Ph*** Gale Tattersall ***Ed*** Ray Lovejoy ***Mus*** Eric Clapton, Michael Kamen ***Art*** Brian Morris

Act Mickey Rourke, Christopher Walken, Debra Feuer, Thomas Quinn, Kevin Conway, Anthony Alda (Redbury)

Actor Mickey Rourke's decade-old pet project about a battered, burnt-out smalltime boxer is a sort of *Raging Bull* without horns, wallowing dully in the clichés of movieland gutter romanticism.

Though nominally written by Eddie Cook [from a story by Mickey Rourke] and directed by Alan Parker's habitual lenser Michael Seresin in his helming debut, this in fact is all Rourke's show. He's refused himself nothing—except a good screenplay and direction.

Rourke's tale is a purported homage to a boxer he idolized in his youth when he himself trained to be a fighter. Here called Johnny Walker, Rourke's hero is just another inarticulate All-American lowlife.

Adopting a neo-Neanderthal expression and cowboy duds, Rourke is first seen slouching into an Atlantic coastal town for a fight engagement. His zombie-like condition doesn't prevent him from being befriended by Christopher Walken, who steals the show with a colorful portrayal of a narcissistic two-bit hoodlum. Walken tries to sucker Rourke into taking part in a jewelry shop hold-up he has long been dreaming of. But Rourke decides to go back into the ring for the love of a young fairground operator (Debra Feuer, the ex-Mrs. Rourke), whose business is failing.

•

HOMECOMING

1948, 113 mins, US b/w

Dir Mervyn LeRoy ***Prod*** Sidney Franklin ***Scr*** Paul Osborn ***Ph*** Harold Rosson ***Ed*** John Dunning ***Mus*** Bronislau Kaper ***Art*** Cedric Gibbons, Randall Duell

Act Clark Gable, Lana Turner, Anne Baxter, John Hodiak, Ray Collins, Gladys Cooper (M-G-M)

Performances are of top quality all down the line, with Gable and Turner pacing the playing. Story line makes a direct play for the tear ducts and has heart. These two factors overcome some patness in resolving plot's problems.

Gable portrays a successful surgeon, happily married, who joins the Army. Three years of patching up the wounded in close association with his nurse, Turner, gradually changes the man's character from smug successfulness to an awareness of his obligations to others.

Story, scripted by Paul Osborn from an original by Sidney Kingsley, is told in flashback and draws its title from the surgeon's return home after his great war love. The dialog and the characters are made real by the forceful playing. There is strong sympathy for the love between Gable and Turner, even though the doctor's wife, Anne Baxter, waits at home.

A considerable portion of the footage is devoted to detailing heroic work done by doctors and nurses under fire at the front, but film does not class as a war picture. Combat medical scenes add punch.

•

HOME FOR THE HOLIDAYS

1995, 103 mins, US Ⓥ ⊙ col

Dir Jodie Foster ***Prod*** Peggy Rajski, Jodie Foster ***Scr*** W. D. Richter ***Ph*** Lajos Koltai ***Ed*** Lynzee Klingman ***Mus*** Mark Isham ***Art*** Andrew McAlpine

Act Holly Hunter, Robert Downey, Jr., Anne Bancroft, Charles Durning, Geraldine Chaplin, Cynthia Stevenson (Egg/PolyGram/Paramount)

Jodie Foster's second directorial effort, *Home for the Holidays*, is an affectionately drawn, multigenerational portrait of an eccentric family, less ponderous and, on the surface at least, more likable and entertaining than her 1991 debut, *Little Man Tate*.

Cashing in on the ritualistic meaning of Thanksgiving, tale centers on an extended clan whose members feel an urge—by ways of kinship and obligation—to congregate year after year for the holiday.

Claudia (Holly Hunter) is treated by her loony parents like a little girl. The ceaseless banter of her listmaking, coupon-clipping mom (Anne Bancroft) would drive anyone up the wall. Dad (Charles Durning) too, has his peculiarities, grabbing his wife for a romantic dance while she cooks, and washes the neighbors' cars in the dead of winter.

Small, mostly well-observed scenes establish the many characters, who for 36 intense hours fight and reconcile, showing their simultaneously endearing and exasperating personalities. They include gay brother Tommy (Robert Downey, Jr.), who lives an alternative lifestyle unbeknownst to his folks; humorless married sister Joanne (Cynthia Stevenson); and senile Aunt Glady (Geraldine Chaplin), who has a penchant for dropping outrageous stories at the most unlikely moments.

Scripter W. D. Richter vividly captures the paradoxes of family life, its push and pull forces, the eternally conflicted feelings of dread and excitement that going home for the holidays invokes. Hunter's performance as a lonely woman beset by the headaches of a single mom is sincerely felt and commanding, without being truly captivating. Adding another colorful role to his already striking gallery, Downey shines.

•

HOME FROM THE HILL

1960, 150 mins, US Ⓥ ⊙ B col

Dir Vincente Minnelli ***Prod*** Edmund Grainger ***Scr*** Harriet Frank, Jr., Irving Ravetch ***Ph*** Milton Krasner ***Ed*** Harold F. Kress ***Mus*** Bronislau Kaper ***Art*** George W. Davis, Preston Ames

Act Robert Mitchum, Eleanor Parker, George Peppard, George Hamilton, Everett Sloane, Luana Patten (M-G-M)

A full-blown melodrama, high-octane in situation and characters, *Home from the Hill* is like an overtaxed engine. The production throws a plot rod or two in its final moments, but when it is concluded the spectator is at least aware he has seen something.

Even though the screenplay, from William Humphrey's novel, is florid and complicated in the customary Deep South literary manner, it does not neglect humor and the lighter touches. Vincente Minnelli's direction is rich and satisfying.

Illicit and illegitimate romance in two generations occupy the principals. Setting is Texas, a town of which Robert Mitchum is not only the richest citizen but the busiest stud. The latter characteristic has iced his marriage to Eleanor Parker since the birth of their now-grown son (George Hamilton). Mitchum has another son (George Peppard), born out of wedlock at about the same time as Hamilton. Hamilton has been so marked by his parents' relationship that when he falls in love with Luana Patten he lacks the courage to marry her.

Despite the intricacies, the story plays well, due to a fine cast and Minnelli's sure-handed direction.

Mitchum delivers his strongest performance in years, and Parker handles her end of the conflict well, too, although her role is less interesting. But it is Peppard, from the NY stage, who shines through.

•

HOME MOVIES

1979, 90 mins, US Ⓥ ⊙ col

Dir Brian De Palma ***Prod*** Brian De Palma, Jack Temchin, Gil Adler ***Scr*** Robert Harders, Gloria Norris, Kim Ambler, Dana Edelman, Stephen Le May, Charles Loventhal ***Ph*** James L. Carter ***Ed*** Corky Ohara ***Mus*** Pino Donaggio ***Art*** Tom Surgal

Act Kirk Douglas, Nancy Allen, Keith Gordon, Gerrit Graham, Vincent Gardenia (SLC)

Home Movies resulted from Brian De Palma teaching students at Sarah Lawrence College, New York, how to make films by making one with them.

The story has Kirk Douglas running a cult called Star Therapy. He exhorts each pupil to "put your name above the title" in life. Practicing what he preaches, he has his own life continuously filmed, with himself as director and star. The sessions, filmed with a mask reducing the frame, as if by Douglas's own 16mm camera crew, are recurrently hilarious.

Singling out one pupil as an example of "an extra in his own life," Douglas spurs the boy—engagingly played by Keith Gordon—into an ego-quest which involves a successful pursuit of his elder brother's fiancée and some laughably inept attempts to film himself doing not-so-dramatic things like falling asleep.

•

HOMER AND EDDIE

1989, 99 mins, US Ⓥ ⊙ col

Dir Andrei Konchalovsky ***Prod*** Moritz Borman, James Cady ***Scr*** Patrick Cirillo ***Ph*** Lajos Koltai ***Ed*** Henry Richardson ***Mus*** Edvard Artemyev ***Art*** Michel Levesque

Act James Belushi, Whoopi Goldberg, Karen Black, John Waters, Beah Richards (Kings Road/Borman/Cady)

This road film about a mentally deficient dishwasher and a homicidal escaped cancer patient is a downer from beginning to end.

Homer, a mentally retarded dishwasher in Arizona, decides to hitchhike up to Oregon to see his father, who is dying of cancer. He meets up with wacky vagabond Eddie in an old jalopy, and soon they become pals.

On the road Eddie tries to enlighten Homer to the ways of the world. She takes him to a brothel and gets the money to pay for it by holding up a store. Her criminal activities increase, and she winds up shooting people while robbing their stores. The twosome argue about the existence of God. Meanwhile, Eddie tells Homer that the doctors have only given her a month to live.

It is hard to feel much sympathy for these two mental patients. The image of two underprivileged people in a cruel world is rather too pat to be convincing.

•

HOME SWEET HOME

1914, 90 mins, US Ⓥ ⊗ b/w

Dir D. W. Griffith ***Scr*** D. W. Griffith, H. E. Aitken ***Ph*** Billy Bitzer ***Ed*** James E. Smith, Rose Smith

Act Henry B. Walthall, Lillian Gish, Dorothy Gish, Mae Marsh, Donald Crisp, Blanche Sweet (Reliance)

All the best players under Griffith's command are in this feature at one time or another. In illustrating the effect of the immortal song, together with the early life and death of the author of it, along with an allegory of the great good the lyric has accomplished, the scenario writers delved into love and the Wild West.

The first reels are devoted to John Howard Payne, showing him to have written the song in a foreign land, dying shortly after. The next episode is a western mining camp, to which comes a young easterner, who falls in love. They become engaged; the easterner is called back home; his love for a young woman of his own set is rekindled; he returns to the camp, and leaves without seeing Mary, but on his way back is stopped by an organ grinder playing "Home Sweet Home."

In the third episode, a wife about to become unfaithful to her husband is stopped by the music of a violin above her apartment playing the strain, and she travels thereafter in the dutiful path.

•

HOMEWARD BOUND

1993, 84 mins, US Ⓥ ⊙ col

Dir Duwayne Dunham ***Prod*** Franklin R. Levy, Jeffrey Chernov ***Scr*** Caroline Thompson, Linda Woolverton ***Ph*** Reed Smoot ***Ed*** Jonathan P. Shaw ***Mus*** Bruce Broughton ***Art*** Roger Cain

Act Robert Hays, Kim Greist, Jean Smart, Benj Thall, Veronica Lauren, Kevin Chevalia (Walt Disney)

Leave it to the Disney marketing machine to dust off a venerable nature-adventure film like 1963s *The Incredible Journey* and wed it with *Look Who's Talking*, creating a sprightly little entertainment that applies animation principles to live-action by giving personalities to the movie's wayward dogs and cat through the clever use of the voices of Michael J. Fox, Sally Field and Don Ameche.

Although the story [from Sheila Burnford's book] also gets spruced up with some '90s twists, the plot still centers on three pets, left with a family friend, who try to cross the wilderness and make it back home, encountering menaces from bears to porcupines on the way.

The aging Shadow (a golden retriever voiced with stately dignity by Ameche) leads the way, followed by the upstart mutt Chance (Fox) and snooty feline Sassy (Field). For the most part the writers—Linda Woolverton (of *Beauty and the Beast*) and Caroline Thompson (*Edward Scissorhands*)—have done a splendid job capturing what animals seem to be thinking without making them cognizant of what humans are saying, except for the few words the pets recognize.

Duwayne Dunham, a veteran film editor making his [feature film] directing debut, keeps *Journey*'s pace brisk. Pic is dedicated to producer Franklin R. Levy, who died during production.

•

HOMEWARD BOUND II: LOST IN SAN FRANCISCO

1996, 88 mins, US Ⓥ ⊙ col

Dir David R. Ellis ***Prod*** Barry Jossen ***Scr*** Chris Hauty, Julie Hickson ***Ph*** Jack Conroy ***Ed*** Peter E. Berger, Michael A. Stevenson ***Mus*** Bruce Broughton ***Art*** Michael Bolton

Act Robert Hays, Kim Greist, Veronica Lauren, Kevin Chevalia, Benj Thall, Michael Rispoli (Walt Disney)

Homeward Bound II sticks close to formula that worked so well in the original film.

Michael J. Fox and Sally Field are on board again to provide voices for, respectively, Chance, an exuberant bulldog, and Sassy, a finicky cat. Ralph Waite fills in for the late Don Ameche as the voice of Shadow, the retriever who comes off as equal parts elder statesman and sage mentor. Fox and Field get all the funny lines, and they make the most of them. But Waite provides just the right note of grizzled, avuncular wisdom.

Screenwriters do a reasonably persuasive job of contriving another forced separation between the animals and their human owners. This time, the claustrophobic Chance breaks free of a carrying case just before he's loaded onto the airliner carrying the family to a Canadian holiday. Sassy and Shadow follow him off the runway and onto the highway, for another incredible journey home.

Animal coordinator Gary Gero does an impressive job of running his four-legged thespians through their anthropomorphic paces. And the matching of animals with human voices is inspired.

●

HOMICIDE
1991, 100 mins, US Ⓥ ⦿ col
Dir David Mamet ***Prod*** Michael Hausman, Edward R. Pressman ***Scr*** David Mamet ***Ph*** Roger Deakins ***Ed*** Barbara Tulliver ***Mus*** Aeric Jans ***Art*** Michael Merritt
Act Joe Mantegna, William H. Macy, Natalija Nogulich, Ving Rhames, Rebecca Pidgeon (Pressman/Cinehaus)

David Mamet's first-rate writing and boldly idiosyncratic directing redeem this story of a toughened Jewish cop torn between two worlds. *Homicide* presents an urban hell in which stoic survivor Bobby Gold (Joe Mantegna) must negotiate through rotten politics, unpredictable violence and virulent racial tension just to get through a day of police work. Gold sees a chance to regain his enthusiasm when he becomes a key player in a team effort to bring in a cop killer who's eluded the FBI. But he's callously reassigned to a routine investigation of an elderly Jewish woman shot down in her candy store in a black ghetto.

To the disgust of his cynical Irish partner (William H. Macy), Gold gets caught up in the family's claims that they are targets of a deep-rooted and violent anti-Semitic conspiracy. When his fellow cops need him to help bring down the killer, he's busy with initiation rites into his new sect.

Mamet's direction gives much of the film a bracing, refreshing tone as he works to express the shattering tensions of Gold's work.

Excellent work by Mantegna does much to enlist sympathies and interest. Macy is also strong as the flinty partner.

●

HOMME ET UNE FEMME, UN
(A MAN AND A WOMAN)
1966, 103 mins, France Ⓥ ⦿ col
Dir Claude Lelouch ***Prod*** Claude Lelouch ***Scr*** Claude Lelouch, Pierre Uytterhoeven ***Ph*** Claude Lelouch ***Ed*** Claude Lelouch, Claude Barrois ***Mus*** Francis Lai ***Art*** Robert Luchaire
Act Anouk Aimée, Jean-Louis Trintignant, Pierre Barouh, Valerie Lagrange, Henri Chemin, Yane Barry (Les Films 13)

Claude Lelouch, 29, is the do-it-yourself French filmmaker. He has made several pix as director, writer and cameraman, and even produced via his own company. He now repeats with a little more ambition.

Lelouch has practically no story. He has mock scenes speculating on characters thinking, flash-forwards for hopeful consummation. There are practically non-stop car rides, and the inevitable love scene.

It concerns a widow who meets a race car driver at the school where they board their respective offspring. Love blossoms but is frustrated, since she still seems too taken by the memory of her late husband. Ending implies she will finally forget spouse to live with the man.

Film misses puerility and coyness by Lelouch's seeming unfettered joy in filming his scenes. Through constantly roving camera, and especially two charming actors, he redeems rough spots of repetition, archness and a general preciosity.

Sepia and tinted scenes are mixed with regular color and are sometimes effective enough to give a mood to a scene that does not have it in its progression, talk or observation. Music is much too saccharine and insistent.

Anouk Aimée has a mature beauty and an ability to project an inner quality that helps stave off the obvious banality of her character, and this goes too for the perceptive Jean-Louis Trintignant as the man.

●

HONDO
1953, 84 mins, US col
Dir John Farrow ***Scr*** James Edward Grant ***Ph*** Robert Burks, Archie Stout ***Ed*** Ralph Dawson ***Mus*** Emil Newman, Hugo Friedhofer ***Art*** Alfredo Ybarra
Act John Wayne, Geraldine Page, Ward Bond, Michael Pate, James Arness, Rodolfo Acosta (Warner/Wayne-Fellows)

Hondo is an exciting offbeat Western. The stereoscopic 3-D cameras and WarnerColor successfully capture the vast natural beauty of Camargo, Mexico, where the picture was filmed on location.

Hondo, like *Shane*, gives the Western an aura of maturity. It depicts a conflict of interests rather than an individual battle of good versus evil. Vittorio, the Apache chief, is shown as a just leader, concerned about the problems of his people and bewildered by the white man's violations of treaties.

While the skirmishes and armed battles with the Indians are excitingly presented, the screenplay of Louis L'Amour's *Collier's* magazine story deals considerably with the relationship of individuals. John Wayne, as a civilian scout for the U.S. Cavalry, arrives at the isolated ranch in Indian territory of Geraldine Page and her young son. Practically abandoned by her ne'er-do-well husband, she is forced to do the ranch chores by herself, a task with which Wayne assists.

Wayne accidentally comes across Page's husband and kills him in self-defense. While the romantic attachment between Wayne and Page grows, a conflict arises over the death of her husband.

Wayne scores as the silent-yet-outspoken Indian scout. Page, no glamor girl, gives a sensitive portrayal as the ranch wife.

1953: NOMINATIONS: Best Supp. Actress (Geraldine Page), Motion Picture Story (writer not eligible)

●

HONEY, I BLEW UP THE KID
1992, 89 mins, US Ⓥ ⦿ col
Dir Randal Kleiser ***Prod*** Dawn Steel, Edward S. Feldman ***Scr*** Thom Eberhardt, Peter Elbling, Garry Goodrow ***Ph*** John Hora ***Ed*** Michael A. Stevenson, Harry Hitner, Tina Hirsch ***Mus*** Bruce Broughton ***Art*** Leslie Dilley
Act Rick Moranis, Marcia Strassman, Robert Oliveri, Daniel Shalikar, Joshua Shalikar, Lloyd Bridges (Walt Disney)

Honey, I Blew Up the Kid is a diverting, well-crafted sequel to Disney's '89 hit *Honey I Shrunk the Kids*. Taking its cue from 1950s sci-fi pics and inverting the shrinking gags from the original, the sequel has wacky inventor Rick Moranis accidentally blowing up his two-year-old to huge proportions.

There's nothing genuinely menacing about the baby, though, and even his cartoonish would-be captor John Shea, who wants to make him a guinea pig for government experiments, doesn't unduly darken the mood of this tongue-in-cheek yarn, smartly scripted from a story by Garry Goodrow. Nor does Kid have the creepy feeling of the original. The sequel is a romp, escapism at its breeziest, smoothly engineered by director Randal Kleiser and a top-flight tech staff.

A lousy businessman, Moranis has made the mistake of selling his invention to a sinister company headed by Lloyd Bridges, whose huge warehouse includes such items as the Rosebud sled. Moranis and Shea are supposed to be co-directors of the project to develop a new version of his ray machine to enlarge objects for government use, but Moranis has been frozen out.

Initially growing into a 7-foot housewrecker, Adam soon passes the 50-foot mark and eventually balloons into a blithe 112-foot behemoth stomping down the Las Vegas Strip like The Amazing Colossal Man. Joining Moranis's quest to rescue Adam and bring him back to normal is the kid's babysitter (Keri Russell).

●

HONEY, I SHRUNK THE KIDS
1989, 86 mins, US Ⓥ ⦿ col
Dir Joe Johnston ***Prod*** Penney Finkelman Cox ***Scr Ed*** Naha, Tom Schalman ***Ph*** Hiro Narita ***Ed*** Michael A. Stevenson ***Mus*** James Horner ***Art*** Gregg Fonseca
Act Rick Moranis, Matt Frewer, Marcia Strassman, Kristine Sutherland, Thomas Brown, Jared Rushton (Walt Disney)

Borrowing two good end elements from two 1950's sci-fi pics, *The Incredible Shrinking Man* and *Them!*, scripters pit two sets of unfriendly neighbor kids, mistakenly shrunk to only 1/4-inch high, against what ordinarily would be benign backyard fixtures, both alive and inanimate. Their misfortune was to get caught in the beam of ne'er-do-well inventor Wayne Szalinski's (Rick Moranis) molecule-reducing contraption while he's out giving a lecture to a group of skeptical scientists. He sweeps them into the dustpan along with the other flotsam that goes out with the trash.

Now, they must make it back to the house among towering vegetation, humongous bugs and fierce water showers on a quest that would be nightmarish except that it seems mostly like a lot of fun.

Pic [story by Stuart Gordon, Brian Yuzna and Ed Naha] is in the best tradition of Disney and even better than that because it is not so juvenile that adults won't be thoroughly entertained.

●

HONEYMOON IN VEGAS
1992, 95 mins, US Ⓥ ⦿ col
Dir Andrew Bergman ***Prod*** Mike Lobell ***Scr*** Andrew Bergman ***Ph*** William A. Fraker ***Ed*** Barry Malkin ***Mus*** David Newman ***Art*** William A. Elliott
Act James Caan, Nicolas Cage, Sarah Jessica Parker, Pat Morita, Anne Bancroft, Peter Boyle (Castle Rock)

Writer-director Andrew Bergman has plenty of fun with the premise of *Honeymoon in Vegas*, an adult twist on Damon Runyon's *Little Miss Marker*. Sarah Jessica Parker is the saucy, sympathetic prize in a poker game between her divorce-detective fiancé Nicolas Cage and sharkish Vegas gambler James Caan.

Schoolteacher Parker has coerced N.Y. shamus Cage into marrying her, and they take a honeymoon suite at Bally's Casino Resort during the midst of a convention of Elvis impersonators, whose presence provides hilarious running gags throughout.

In an enjoyably manic, self-kidding performance, Caan plays a thug who for a while shows an unexpectedly gentlemanly streak, putting the hapless Cage to shame. "If I was a medieval knight, I woulda jostled for ya," Caan tells Parker after winning a weekend with her in his poker game with Cage.

Parker's natural, unforced charm and honest, strong-willed personality give the film a scintillating uncertainty after she begins taking Caan seriously. William A. Fraker's lensing is cheesy-looking, but the Hawaiian locations compensate in this airy light entertainment.

●

HONEYMOON KILLERS, THE
1969, 115 mins, US Ⓥ ⦿ b/w
Dir Leonard Kastle ***Prod*** Warren Steibel ***Scr*** Leonard Kastle ***Ph*** Oliver Wood ***Ed*** Stan Warnow
Act Shirley Stoler, Tony LoBianco, Mary Higbee, Kip McArdle, Barbara Cason, Doris Roberts (A.I.P./Roxanne)

Made on a very low budget by a writer-director Leonard Kastle, *The Honeymoon Killers*, based on the Lonely Hearts murder case of the late 1940s, is made with care, authenticity and attention to detail.

The acting throughout the film never falters, each of the lonely heart victims presented as a fully rounded character.

Theme, presented with perhaps a shade too heavy an underlining, is the desperate search for love in the U.S., the idea that no woman is complete without a man beside her.

Fernandez has disappeared from the lives of a score of women, after receiving their "dowries," when he meets Martha, but it is only when she becomes intimately involved in his life, bringing her fantastic jealousy to bear on his new targets, that murder enters the picture. There are a few lapses, but the pic goes towards its harrowing climax without losing step.

●

HONEY POT, THE
1967, 150 mins, UK col
Dir Joseph L. Mankiewicz ***Prod*** Joseph L. Mankiewicz, Charles K. Feldman ***Scr*** Joseph L. Mankiewicz ***Ph*** Gianni Di Venanzo ***Ed*** David Bretherton ***Mus Mus*** John Addison ***Art*** John F. DeCuir
Act Rex Harrison, Susan Hayward, Cliff Robertson, Capucine, Edie Adams, Maggie Smith (United Artists)

An elegant, sophisticated screen vehicle for more demanding tastes, previously billed as *Mr. Fox of Venice* and *Anyone for Venice?* Vaguely drawing its inspiration from Ben Jonson's *Volpone*, film's updated plot centers around the fabulously rich Cecil Fox (Rex Harrison) who with the aid of a sometimes gigolo and secretary, William McFly (Cliff Robertson), plays a joke of sorts on three one-time mistresses by feigning grave illness and gauging their reactions as they come flocking to his bedside.

There is the wisecracking hypochondriac, Mrs. Sheridan (Susan Hayward), who was Fox's first love, accompanied by the attractive nurse, Sarah Watkins (Maggie Smith). There's Princess Dominique, a glacially beautiful jetsetter played by Capucine. And there's the ebullient Merle McGill (Edie Adams), a Hollywood star without a care in the world—except for a massive debt to Uncle Sam.

The dialog is often a delight in its hark-back to the days when the turn of a phrase and the tongue-in-cheek were a staple of better Hollywood product. The playing is all of a superior character.

●

HONEYSUCKLE ROSE
1980, 119 mins, US Ⓥ ⦿ ▭ col
Dir Jerry Schatzberg ***Prod*** Gene Taft ***Scr*** Carol Sobieski, William D. Whitliff, John Binder ***Ph*** Robby Muller ***Ed***

Aram Avakian, Norman Gay, Mark Laub, Evan Lottman **Mus** Willie Nelson, Richard Baskin **Art** Joel Schiller
Act Willie Nelson, Dyan Cannon, Amy Irving, Slim Pickens, Joey Floyd, Charles Levin (Warner)

This is not a picture for anybody who doesn't like Willie Nelson. But the picture adroitly blends his musical performances with a gently dramatic acting job in an old-fashioned love story.

Picture catches Nelson at that point in his career around 1970 when his touring band was wildly popular in Texas and nearby regions, but he had yet to break out with the big hit that would make him nationally famous. Dyan Cannon and Joey Floyd nicely set up Nelson's approaching conflict as the wife and son who wait affectionately at home for him to finish his periodic tours.

Slim Pickens is right on target as the guitar-picking sidekick. Amy Irving is near perfect as the woman who has adored Nelson since girlhood.

1980: NOMINATION: Best Song ("On the Road Again")

•

HONKY TONK

1941, 104 mins, US Ⓥ b/w
Dir Jack Conway **Prod** Pandro S. Berman **Scr** Marguerite Roberts, John Sanford **Ph** Harold Rosson **Ed** Blanche Sewell **Mus** Franz Waxman
Act Clark Gable, Lana Turner, Frank Morgan, Claire Trevor, Albert Dekker, Chill Wills (M-G-M)

The major power in *Honky Tonk* is in the love scenes between Clark Gable and Lana Turner. Gable, "Candy" Johnson, is a western grifter, working the three-card monte game. He and his sidekick (Chill Wills) wind up in a gold-strike town where Gable immediately renews an acquaintanceship with Turner. She's the daughter of Frank Morgan, also a former con guy but now the justice of the peace. Gable gets Morgan under his thumb and then proceeds to take over the town.

Claire Trevor is in a standard part for her. As a gambling room hustler and dealer she's tops and the inflection she puts into calling her ex-sweetheart Gable "Candyman" will get a chuckle. Albert Dekker is a fine actor and able menace; Morgan does very well with his part, the same going for Chill Wills. Marjorie Main is excellent as the hard-bitten rooming housekeeper.

The screenplay, though padded a bit, is excellent for this action picture purpose; Jack Conway's direction is good without overplay of naturally exaggerated characters.

•

HONKY TONK FREEWAY

1981, 107 mins, US Ⓥ col
Dir John Schlesinger **Prod** Don Boyd, Howard W. Koch, Jr. **Scr** Edward Clinton **Ph** John Bailey **Ed** Jim Clark **Mus** George Martin **Art** Edwin O'Donovan
Act Beau Bridges, Hume Cronyn, Beverly D'Angelo, William Devane, Teri Garr, Geraldine Page (Universal/AFD/EMI)

Veteran director John Schlesinger, who was responsible for such screen classics as *Midnight Cowboy* and *Sunday Bloody Sunday*, has concocted a kind of *Nashville on Wheels* here.

The thin storyline of this $26 million film revolves around the residents of a small Florida town, Ticlaw, who are miffed that the new super duper freeway won't have an exit for tourists to stop off and spend their money in the area.

Ticlaw's Mayor William Devane tries to bribe some officials for the exit but is double-crossed early on. Major portion of the picture then switches to the collection of people who travel the freeway and eventually (through no fault of their own) wind up in Ticlaw.

Only Hume Cronyn and Jessica Tandy as an offbeat elderly couple, and Deborah Rush as a discontented nun, brighten up the trip along the road. Rest of the cast falls victim to Edward Clinton's meandering script and dismal sense of humor.

•

HONKYTONK MAN

1982, 122 mins, US Ⓥ ⦿ col
Dir Clint Eastwood **Prod** Clint Eastwood **Scr** Clancy Carlile **Ph** Bruce Surtees **Ed** Ferris Webster, Michael Kelly, Joel Cox **Mus** Steve Dorff **Art** Edward Carfagno
Act Clint Eastwood, Kyle Eastwood, John McIntire, Alexa Kenin, Verna Bloom, Matt Clark (Warner/Malpaso)

Honkytonk Man is one of those well-intentioned efforts that doesn't quite work. It seems that Clint Eastwood took great pains in telling this story of an aging, struggling country singer but he is done in by the predictability of the script [from Clancy Carlile's own novel] and his own limitations as a warbler.

It is initially funny to see a drunk Eastwood drive his spiffy car into the rural, Depression-era farm his sister and her burdened family live in. Though he is a breath of fresh air for them, especially his 14-year-old nephew, it soon becomes clear that he is more accurately an alcoholic on his last legs.

Eastwood does his best, though he never really manages to be fully convincing because of his own vocal limitations. His son, Kyle, who has limited acting experience, doesn't seem to know what to do with his key role of the emerging teenager.

•

HONOR AMONG LOVERS

1931, 76 mins, US Ⓥ b/w
Dir Dorothy Arzner **Scr** Austin Parker, Gertrude Purcell **Ph** George Folsey
Act Claudette Colbert, Fredric March, Monroe Owsley, Charles Ruggles, Ginger Rogers, Avonne Taylor (Paramount)

This comedy-drama is much along the lines of many in the series which Paramount's Long Island studio turns out.

A wealthy, young and freedom-loving businessman is nursing an impulse for one of those super feminine screen secretaries. His offer of an apartment or a long cruise frightens her into marriage with a brokerage attaché, a weakling. The two set a pretty fast social pace for a married couple of their means and the crash comes when the husband embezzles the accounts entrusted to him, among which is that of his wife's former employer.

There are no heavy dramatics at any point, it evidently having been Dorothy Arzner's purpose to achieve results more delicately. In this she has been unusually successful, aided no little by excellent dialog and a brilliant cast.

Behind the triangle is Charles Ruggles, again as the inebriated boyfriend, with Ginger Rogers as his dumb companion. Rogers has little to do but Ruggles makes all his items click.

Claudette Colbert, Fredric March and Monroe Owsley are collectively and individually a smooth working trio.

•

HONORARY CONSUL, THE
(US: BEYOND THE LIMIT)

1984, 103 mins, UK Ⓥ ⦿ col
Dir John Mackenzie **Prod** Norma Heyman **Scr** Christopher Hampton **Ph** Phil Meheux **Ed** Stuart Baird **Mus** Stanley Myers, Richard Harvey **Art** Allan Cameron
Act Michael Caine, Richard Gere, Bob Hoskins, Elpidia Carrillo, Joaquim De Almeida, Geoffrey Palmer (World Film Services)

The Honorary Consul represents a weak attempt to adapt Graham Greene's 1973 novel for the screen. Strong talents on both sides of the camera haven't managed to breathe life into this intricate tale of emotional and political betrayal and result is a steady dose of tedium.

Greene's central character was one Eduardo Plarr, a half-Paraguayan, half-British doctor in provincial Argentina who quietly assists some revolutionaries in their attempt to kidnap the American ambassador and equally casually impregnates the very young native wife of the besotted honorary consul from Britain, Charley Fortnum. The rebels blunderingly capture Fortnum instead of the intended Yank, but detain and threaten to execute him anyway unless some of their comrades are released from prison.

First handicap is the casting of Richard Gere as the dispirited Englishman. Actor's accent only manages to stay on course when his lines consist of five words or less. Acting honors easily fall to Michael Caine as the small-time, dipsomaniacal diplomat. Character in the book was in his 60s, but Caine proves an ideal choice. Bob Hoskins registers strongly as a heartless but engaging South American police chief. Using Mexican locales, director John Mackenzie and lenser Phil Meheux have evoked a good sense of place, but end result is on the dull side.

•

HOODLUM PRIEST, THE

1961, 100 mins, US b/w
Dir Irvin Kershner **Prod** Don Murray, Walter Wood **Scr** Don Deer [= Don Murray], Joseph Landon **Ph** Haskell Wexler **Ed** Maurice Wright **Mus** Richard Markowitz **Art** Jack Poplin
Act Don Murray, Larry Gates, Cindi Wood, Keir Dullea, Logan Ramsey (United Artists)

Biographically based on the offbeat activities of the Rev Charles Dismas Clark, a Jesuit priest in St. Louis noted for his rehabilitation work with ex-cons, the sceenplay pinpoints Clark's problems against the tragedy of a confused, but far from hopeless, youth who pays with his life for crimes of which he is not solely responsible. Along the way, the writers illustrate the necessity of meeting ex-cons on their own terms to urge them away from a life of crime, and even take a swipe at capital punishment, going right into the gas chamber to do so in the film's most powerful scene.

The picture, largely photographed in St. Louis, is burdened with loose motivational ends and has a tendency to skip over key expository details. But it is a case of the whole justifying its parts. The moving parts are erratic, but the machine does its job.

Don Murray gives a vigorous, sincere performance in the title role. But the film's most moving portrayal is delivered by Keir Dullea as the doomed lad.

•

HOODLUM SAINT, THE

1946, 92 mins, US b/w
Dir Norman Taurog **Prod** Cliff Reid **Scr** Frank Wead, James Hill **Ph** Ray June **Ed** Ferris Webster **Mus** Nathaniel Shilkret **Art** Cedric Gibbons, Harry McAfee
Act William Powell, Esther Williams, Angela Lansbury, James Gleason (M-G-M)

The Hoodlum Saint is a drama laid in the period just after World War I up through the 1929 stock market crash and deals with the power of belief in St. Dismas, the good thief, to reform all hoodlums. Film gives Esther Williams a chance in something other than a musical.

Cliff Reid has given it plenty of production dress, and Norman Taurog's direction points up the characterizations, but unfoldment is never exciting. There's no feeling of struggle in the development of the plot, everything coming too easily to the characters—love, riches, poverty and eventual belief in St. Dismas's power for good.

Plot concerns disillusionment of a returning army major (William Powell). He finds ideals rapidly pushing him towards the corner applestand, and determines to garner all the coin possible, no matter how.

Powell is his usual assured self as the opportunist, delivering a top-notch characterization. Williams thoroughly pleases as the girl who loves but spurns Powell until his morals improve. Angela Lansbury puts sex emphasis on her assignment as sideline romance for Powell and also sings several pop standards of the period. James Gleason wallops over his part as an old Powell sidekick who gets religion.

•

HOOK

1991, 144 mins, US Ⓥ ⦿ ▭ col
Dir Steven Spielberg **Prod** Kathleen Kennedy, Frank Marshall, Gerald R. Molen **Scr** Jim V. Hart, Malia Scotch Marmo **Ph** Dean Cundey **Ed** Michael Kahn **Mus** John Williams **Art** Norman Garwood
Act Dustin Hoffman, Robin Williams, Julia Roberts, Bob Hoskins, Maggie Smith, Charlie Korsmo (Tri-Star/Amblin)

Hook feels as much like a massive amusement park ride as it does a film. Spirited, rambunctious, often messy and undisciplined, this determined attempt to recast the Peter Pan story in contempo terms [from a screen story by Jim V. Hart and Nick Castle, from J. M. Barrie's play and books] splashes every bit of its megabudget (between $60 million and $80 million) onto the screen.

Screenplay sends a modern, grown-up Peter, a man who has forgotten his youth, back to Neverland to rescue his children from the clutches of the ever-vengeful Captain Hook.

Setup is deftly done, sweeping the viewer right into the world of the Banning family. Peter (Robin Williams) is a workaholic corporate attorney. But he manages to tear himself away to take his wife Moira (Caroline Goodall) and children Jack (Charlie Korsmo) and Maggie (Amber Scott) to London to visit Granny Wendy (Maggie Smith).

Back in Blighty, Jack and Maggie are spirited away, courtesy of Captain James Hook. Mystified, Peter is visited by Tinkerbell (Julia Roberts) and, 36 minutes into the story, is transported to Neverland, where Hook (Dustin Hoffman) lords over a raucous Pirate Town from the deck of his enormous ship.

Sweet and likable through the first half-hour, pic becomes dominated by a vaudeville tone and in-jokes during the pirate section (Glenn Close turns up in a male disguise as a sailor victimized by Hook).

Despite the cascade of wondrous special effects, massive battles between the kids and pirates and face-offs between Pan and Hook, the film doesn't truly take flight. Jokiness gets the better of both Hoffman and Bob Hoskins, who plays the captain's loyal hand Smee. Williams inhabits the main role splendidly. But the standout supporting turns come from Smith, perfect as the aged Wendy, and Goodall.

1991: NOMINATIONS: Best Art Direction, Costume Design, Song ("When You're Alone"), Makeup, Visual Effects

•

HOOPER
1978, 99 mins, US Ⓥ ⊙ col
Dir Hal Needham ***Prod*** Hank Moonjean ***Scr*** Thomas Rickman, Bill Kerby ***Ph*** Bobby Byrne ***Ed*** Donn Cambern ***Mus*** Bill Justis ***Art*** Hilyard Brown
Act Burt Reynolds, Jan-Michael Vincent, Sally Field, Brian Keith, John Marley, James Best (Warner/Reynolds-Gordon)

Individually, the performances in this story of three generations of Hollywood stuntmen are a delight. And Hal Needham's direction and stunt staging are wonderfully crafted.

But it's the ensemble work of Burt Reynolds, Jan-Michael Vincent, Sally Field and Brian Keith, with an able assist from Robert Klein, that boosts an otherwise pedestrian story [by Walt Green and Walter S. Herndon] with lots of crashes and daredevil antics into a touching and likable piece.

Reynolds, in a further extension of his brash, off-handed wise guy screen persona, plays the world's greatest stuntman. He took over that position 20 years back from Brian Keith. His status is being challenged by newcomer Jan-Michael Vincent.

To cement a place in the stuntman's record books, Reynolds must perform one last stunt, in this case a 325-foot jump in a jet-powered car over a collapsed bridge. All this is to take place in a film, *The Spy Who Laughed At Danger*, some sort of a disaster, James Bond–type picture being directed by the deliciously obnoxious Klein.

Besides the final jump over the bridge, Needham and stunt coordinator Bobby Bass have arranged a smorgasbord of stunts—car crashes, barroom brawls, chariot races, helicopter jumps and motorcycle slides.

1978: NOMINATION: Best Sound

•

HOOSIERS
(UK: BEST SHOT)
1986, 114 mins, US Ⓥ ⊙ col
Dir David Anspaugh ***Prod*** Carter De Haven, Angelo Pizzo ***Scr*** Angelo Pizzo ***Ph*** Fred Murphy ***Ed*** C. Timothy O'Meara ***Mus*** Jerry Goldsmith ***Art*** David Nichols
Act Gene Hackman, Barbara Hershey, Dennis Hopper, Sheb Wooley, Fern Persons, Brad Boyle (Hemdale)

Hoosiers is an involving tale about the unlikely success of a smalltown Indiana high school basketball team that paradoxically proves both rousing and too conventional, centered around a fine performance by Gene Hackman as the coach.

During the opening reels, first-time feature director David Anspaugh paints a richly textured portrait of 1951 rural American life, both visually and through glimpses of the guarded reticence of the people. Dialog rings true, and the characters are neither sentimentalized nor caricatured. Tension is built nicely as the farmboys advance through the playoffs.

Pic belongs to Hackman, but Dennis Hopper gets another opportunity to put in a showy turn as a local misfit.

1986: NOMINATIONS: Best Supp. Actor (Dennis Hopper), Original Score

•

HOPE AND GLORY
1987, 113 mins, UK Ⓥ ⊙ col
Dir John Boorman ***Prod*** John Boorman ***Scr*** John Boorman ***Ph*** Philippe Rousselot ***Ed*** Ian Crafford ***Mus*** Peter Martin ***Art*** Anthony Pratt
Act Sarah Miles, David Hayman, Derrick O'Connor, Susan Wooldridge, Sammi Davis, Ian Bannen (Columbia)

Essentially a collection of sweetly autobiographical anecdotes of English family life during World War II.

Tale is narrated from an adult perspective by Billy, an exquisite-looking nine-year-old who finds great excitement in the details of warfare but also has the air of a detached observer and, therefore, possible future writer.

Best scenes are those with Billy centerstage, and particularly those showing the unthinking callousness kids can display in the face of others' misfortune and tragedy.

Then the Rohan family's home is destroyed, and mom Sarah Miles takes the kids out to grandpa's idyllic home by a river in the country, where the raging conflict becomes an afterthought.

Happily, young Sebastian Rice-Edwards is a marvelous camera subject and holds the center well as Bill. His younger sister, played by Geraldine Muir, is even cuter, as is Sara Langton as the girl whose mother is killed. The adults, however, come off rather less well, with Sarah Miles overdoing things and projecting little inner feeling and no one else making much of an impression.

1987: NOMINATIONS: Best Picture, Director, Original Screenplay, Cinematography, Art Direction

•

HOPSCOTCH
1980, 104 mins, US Ⓥ ⊙ ▭ col
Dir Ronald Neame ***Prod*** Edie Landau, Ely Landau ***Scr*** Brian Garfield, Bryan Forbes ***Ph*** Arthur Ibbetson ***Ed*** Carl Kress ***Mus*** Ian Fraser ***Art*** William Creber
Act Walter Matthau, Glenda Jackson, Ned Beatty, Sam Waterston, Herbert Lom (Avco Embassy)

Hopscotch is a high-spirited caper comedy which, unfortunately, reaches its peak too soon. Grizzled as usual, Walter Matthau plays CIA agent whose independent ways are too much for his finicky, double-dealing boss (Ned Beatty). So Matthau is put in charge of the files.

But he never shows up for the new assignment, deciding instead to hide out and write a book that will embarrass not only the CIA but spies in every country, making himself a target for extinction from several directions.

Hiding out, Matthau takes up with Glenda Jackson. They are old flames and their initial moments together serve up the same good bantering chemistry of *House Calls*.

It's all for laughs as Matthau evades the hunters while dreaming up additional ways to make fools of them.

•

HORI, MA PANENKO
(THE FIREMAN'S BALL; LIKE A HOUSE ON FIRE)
1967, 73 mins, Czechoslovakia/Italy Ⓥ col
Dir Milos Forman ***Scr*** Milos Forman, Jarouslav Papousek, Ivan Passer ***Ph*** Miroslav Ondricek ***Ed*** Miroslav Hajek ***Mus*** Karel Mares ***Art*** Karel Cerny
Act Vaclav Stockel, Josef Svet, Jan Vostrcil, Josef Kolb, Frantisek Debelka, Josef Sebanek (Barrandov/Ponti)

Milos Forman comes up with another funny, human but never sentimental pic after his *Loves of a Blonde*. A group of elderly firemen of a small town are planning to bring off a farewell ball for their retiring director. Filmmaker Forman has cannily used a bevy of non-actors to flesh out a practically plotless vehicle, a lively, brimming comedy on human conduct and smalltown life.

An attempt to pick girls for a Miss Fireman prize leads to heavy searching in the dancing, drinking crowds. A scuffle, when the girls are being rounded up to parade, is interrupted by a real fire. And a house burns down when the fire truck is caught in a snowdrift. Back at the ball, the lottery prizes are found to have been stolen.

The probing camera of Miroslav Ondricek, with his finely honed hues, is a big help, as well as the sprightly music and well-paced editing. Title is actually a Czech folk song about firemen.

•

HORIZONS WEST
1952, 80 mins, US Ⓥ col
Dir Budd Boetticher ***Prod*** Albert J. Cohen ***Scr*** Louis Stevens ***Ph*** Charles P. Boyle ***Ed*** Ted J. Kent ***Mus*** Joseph Gershenson ***Art*** Bernard Herzbrun, Robert Clatworthy
Act Robert Ryan, Julie Adams, Rock Hudson, John McIntire, Raymond Burr, James Arness (Universal)

Plot is laid in the post-War Between States period, opening with three Texans returning to their home state. Rock Hudson and James Arness welcome a resumption of ranching, but Robert Ryan's ambition is for a quick dollar. He turns his attention towards easy money and a desire to build a western empire.

From a rather slow start, it then becomes a session of pretentious, cliché-laden talk that even spurts of hardy action fail to enliven. Ryan does what he can with his character but beyond endowing it with a certain ruthless ruggedness can't make it believable enough to carry the tale.

Hudson turns in a sympathetic performance, and Arness is good as the brothers' soldiering buddy. Julie Adams makes a pretty picture as the widow with an eye for Ryan.

•

HORN BLOWS AT MIDNIGHT, THE
1945, 80 mins, US Ⓥ ⊙ b/w
Dir Raoul Walsh ***Prod*** Mark Hellinger ***Scr*** Sam Hellman, James V. Kern ***Ph*** Sid Hickox ***Ed*** Irene Morra ***Mus*** Franz Waxman ***Art*** Hugh Reticker, Clarence Steensen
Act Jack Benny, Alexis Smith, Guy Kibbee, Margaret Dumont, Dolores Moran, Reginald Gardiner (Warner)

This one is a lightweight comedy that never seems able to make up its mind whether to be fantasy or broad slapstick. There are some good laughs but generally *The Horn Blows at Midnight* is not solid.

Jack Benny works hard for his laughs and some come through with a sock, but generally the chuckles are dragged in and overworked. Biggest howls are the scenes depicting Benny and others dangling from atop a 40-story building.

Benny plays third trumpet in a radio station orch. Falling asleep during reading of commercials, Benny dreams he's an angel in Heaven—and still playing third trumpet. The Big Chief, disgusted with conditions on the planet earth, dispatches Benny to earth to destroy it. The angel is to blow his special horn promptly at midnight, the blast to do away with the earth.

Heaven, as depicted, is certainly not a very soul-satisfying spot. It's portrayed as a satire on government and the many bureaus and sub-bureaus, etc.

•

HORROR CHAMBER OF DR. FAUSTUS, THE
SEE: LES YEUX SANS VISAGE

•

HORROR OF DRACULA
SEE: DRACULA (1958)

•

HORSE FEATHERS
1932, 70 mins, US Ⓥ ⊙ col
Dir Norman Z. McLeod ***Scr*** Bert Kalmar, Harry Ruby, S. J. Perelman, Will B. Johnstone ***Ph*** Ray June
Act Groucho Marx, Chico Marx, Harpo Marx, Zeppo Marx, Thelma Todd, David Landau (Paramount)

The madcap Marxes, in one of their maddest screen frolics. The premise of Groucho Marx as the college prexy and his three aides and abettors putting Huxley College on the gridiron map promises much and delivers more.

Zeppo is his usual straight opposite Thelma Todd as the college widow. She's a luscious eyeful and swell foil for the Marxian boudoir manhandling, which is getting to be a trade-marked comedy routine. On the matter of formula, the harp and piano numbers were repeated against the Marxes' personal wishes but by exhibitor demands to the studio. The piano is oke, but the harp reprise of "Everyone Says I Love You" (by Bert Kalmar and Harry Ruby) substantiates the boys' opinion that it tends to slow up the comedy.

The plot, such as it is, is motivated around gambler David Landau's planting of two pros on the Darwin team which meets Huxley. Groucho visits the speak where the Darwin ringers have been engaged and mistakes dogcatcher Harpo and bootlegging iceman Chico as gridiron material.

•

HORSE WHISPERER, THE
1998, 168 mins, US Ⓥ ⊙ ▭ col
Dir Robert Redford ***Prod*** Robert Redford, Patrick Markey ***Scr*** Eric Roth, Richard LaGravenese ***Ph*** Robert Richardson ***Ed*** Tom Rolf, Freeman Davies, Hank Corwin ***Mus*** Thomas Newman ***Art*** Jon Hutman
Act Robert Redford, Kristin Scott Thomas, Sam Neill, Dianne Wiest, Scarlett Johansson, Chris Cooper (Wildwood/Touchstone)

Robert Redford has made an exquisitely crafted, morally and thematically mature picture out of Nicholas Evans's [bestselling] schematic melodrama about a modern cowboy who brings about the physical and spiritual regeneration of a teenage girl and her horse after they suffer crippling injuries. However, an elimination of the book's sexual element, while artistically justifiable, may perplex and frustrate the novel's fans.

Directing himself for the first time, Redford has lavished his usual meticulous care on popular material that comes alive on the screen in ways that it never could on the page, due to the indelible impressions made by the thesps, horses and spectacular Montana settings.

In the throes of dealing with her daughter Grace's (Scarlett Johansson) calamity, high-powered New York magazine editor Annie MacLean (Kristin Scott Thomas) somehow decides not to have the horse, Pilgrim, put down. Vaguely intuiting that her daughter's recovery might be tied to that of Pilgrim's, Annie learns of a man who reputedly has a special gift with horses. She packs Grace in the car and Pilgrim in a trailer and heads for Montana, where the healer man, Tom Booker (Redford), lives.

From the moment he makes his long-delayed entrance, it is apparent that Redford has no intention of playing into clichéd notions of a dirt-kicking, aw-shucksing, man-of-few-words cowboy. He's a thoughtful, thoroughly modern figure who has had to make compromises and concessions.

It's almost unique in modern films for the central couple in a romance not to bed down at least once; when Annie plaintively asks, "Tom, can we have one last ride?" the hero here takes her and literally saddles up a horse.

Redford steps into the role as into a pair of well-worn boots. Scott Thomas is brittle, alert and increasingly radiant as the woman who slowly opens to Tom's love and wisdom.

•

HORSEMAN ON THE ROOF, THE
SEE: LE HUSSARD SUR LE TOIT

•

HORSEMEN, THE
1971, 108 mins, US [A] col
Dir John Frankenheimer ***Prod*** Edward Lewis ***Scr*** Dalton Trumbo ***Ph*** Claude Renoir ***Ed*** Harold Kress ***Mus*** Georges Delerue ***Art*** Pierre Thevenet
Act Omar Sharif, Leigh Taylor-Young, Jack Palance, David De, Peter Jeffrey, Mohammed Shamsi (Columbia)

The *Horsemen* is a would-be epic stretched thin across Hollywood's "profound peasant" tradition. It's a misfire, despite offbeat Afghanistan locations and some bizarre action sequences.

Omar Sharif, son of rural Afghanistan clan leader Jack Palance, is injured and humiliated (he thinks) in a brutal ritual soccer-type game played with the headless carcass of a calf. Returning home in company of his now treacherous servant (David De) and a wandering "untouchable" out for his money (Leigh Taylor-Young), Sharif's leg is amputated below the knee in a remote mountain village. Back with his clan, Sharif forgives De and Taylor-Young for two attempts they made on his life and then trains hard to reestablish his honor and reputation as the greatest horseman in the area.

Dalton Trumbo's cliché script, based on the novel by Joseph Kessel, opts for the kind of mock-poetic dialog even Hugh Griffith might have trouble mouthing. Sharif, however, maintains his composure.

•

HORSE SOLDIERS, THE
1959, 120 mins, US col
Dir John Ford ***Prod*** John Lee Mahin, Martin Rackin ***Scr*** John Lee Mahin, Martin Rackin ***Ph*** William Clothier ***Mus*** David Buttolph
Act John Wayne, William Holden, Constance Towers, Althea Gibson, Hoot Gibson, Anna Lee (Mirisch)

Give John Ford a company of brawny men, let him train his cameras on the U.S. cavalry and provide a script with plenty of action and he's off on the road to glory. In *The Horse Soldiers*, which involves a little-known incident in the Civil War, all these elements are present.

This is the story [from the novel by Harold Sinclair] of Colonel Benjamin Grierson who, in April of 1863, was ordered by General Grant to take three cavalry regiments and ride 300 miles into the heart of the Confederacy to destroy the rail link between Newton Station and Vicksburg and thus choke off supplies from Southern-held Vicksburg.

But with all of Ford's skill for staging battle scenes, and his superb eye for pictorial composition, the film is extremely uneven. The long shots of men on horses tend to become tedious and they considerably slow up the flow of the story. Also, the dramatic scenes involving John Wayne, William Holden and newcomer Constance Towers don't come off with much conviction.

William Clothier's photography is outstanding. Some of the scenes have the quality of paintings. As in all of the Ford films, the music has a fitting, masculine quality, being sung mostly by a male chorus.

•

HOSPITAL, THE
1971, 103 mins, US col
Dir Arthur Hiller ***Prod*** Howard Gottfried ***Scr*** Paddy Chayefsky ***Ph*** Victor J. Kemper ***Ed*** Eric Albertson ***Mus*** Morris Surdin ***Art*** Gene Rudolf
Act George C. Scott, Diana Rigg, Barnard Hughes, Nancy Marchand, Stephen Elliott, Donald Harron (United Artists)

The Hospital is a civilian mis-*MASH*. George C. Scott stars as a N.Y. medical center chief surgeon whose ruined personal life alternates with a daily routine of apparently inept, callous, bored, overworked and murdered staff members. Diana Rigg is the daughter of a deranged doctor-patient whose unmasking destroys most of author Paddy Chayefsky's basic premise.

In the plot's medico environment stands Scott, at 53 a washout as husband and father and on the verge of suicide. The heavily sprayed-on sociological angle is that hospitals today treat patients like baggage. Rigg turns Scott on to the promise of a peaceful life in the western mountains; she is in the hospital because father Barnard Hughes, a goneberserk Boston doctor, has been treated in bungled fashion by Richard Dysart, a medic whose eye is on the stock market more than his avowed profession.

The film is larded with vignettes strung on a series of mysterious murders: girl-chasing doctor Lenny Baker, internist Robert Anthony and nurse Angie Ortega.

1971: Best Original Story & Screenplay

NOMINATION: Best Actor (George C. Scott)

•

HOSTILE HOSTAGES
SEE: THE REF

•

HOSTSONAT
(AUTUMN SONATA)
1978, 97 mins, W. Germany/UK col
Dir Ingmar Bergman ***Prod*** Lew Grade, Martin Starger (exec.) ***Scr*** Ingmar Bergman ***Ph*** Sven Nykvist ***Ed*** Sylvia Ingemarsson ***Art*** Anna Asp
Act Ingrid Bergman, Liv Ullmann, Lena Nyman, Halvar Bjork, Erland Josephson, Gunnar Bjornstrand (Personafilm/ITC)

The most interesting particular about Ingmar Bergman's *Autumn Sonata* is the fact that this is the first time the Swedish director has directed Swedish actress Ingrid Bergman. It makes one wish that they had teamed up a long time ago. The film, shot in Norway by Bergman's Munich-based company and financed by the British, is a return to the world of complex human relationships which he abandoned briefly for the ill-fated Munich-made *Serpent's Egg*.

Ingrid Bergmann is Charlotte, a famous concert pianist who finds herself emotionally alone when her lover of many years dies. She is invited to visit her daughter, Eva (Liv Ullmann), the wife of a country parson in Norway, whom she has not seen for seven years. The film deals with their reunion and the ultimate disclosure of their feelings for each other. It isn't all love and sunshine, by any means.

One might expect Bergman, the director, to stack the cards a bit in favor of Ullmann but he has made Ingrid the much more colorful and interesting of the ill-matched pair. The camerawork by Sven Nykvist devotes much of its exposure to the close-ups of the two women, and they are a lesson in facial histrionics.

The only principal male role is that of Halvar Bjork as Ullmann's parson husband. Bergman buffs will, however, be able to spot some of his better-known males in silent cameos, including Erland Josephson as Josef, Bergman's husband and Ullmann's father, and Gunnar Bjornstrand as Paul, Bergman's agent. Her conversations with him, on the phone and on a train trip, are in English. Ullmann's (and Ingmar Bergman's) daughter, Linn, plays her mother as a child. She is fetching but not yet an actress.

•

HOTEL
1967, 124 mins, US col
Dir Richard Quine ***Prod*** Wendell Mayes ***Scr*** Wendell Mayes ***Ph*** Charles Lang ***Ed*** Sam O'Steen ***Mus*** Johnny Keating ***Art*** Cary Odell
Act Rod Taylor, Catherine Spaak, Karl Malden, Melvyn Douglas, Merle Oberon, Richard Conte (Warner)

Hotel is a very well made, handsomely produced drama about the guests and management of an old hostelry which must modernize or shutter. Uniformly strong performances, scripting and direction make for good pacing.

In an impressive debut as a film producer, Wendell Mayes has dressed the pic with lush settings and wardrobe, while not neglecting scripting chores in adapting Arthur Hailey's novel.

Merle Oberon, dripping in gems, registers well as the wife of Michael Rennie, whose hit-and-run driving cues a blackmail attempt by house gumshoe Richard Conte. Catherine Spaak, in her U.S. film debut, is charming and sexy as Kevin McCarthy's mistress who drifts to Rod Taylor. Karl Malden has a choice role of a key thief who is frustrated at many turns by double-crossing accomplices.

•

HOTEL BERLIN
1945, 98 mins, US b/w
Dir Peter Godfrey ***Prod*** Louis F. Edelman ***Scr*** Jo Pagano, Alvah Bessie ***Ph*** Carl Guthrie ***Ed*** Frank Magee ***Mus*** Franz Waxman ***Art*** John Hughes
Act Helmut Dantine, Andrea King, Raymond Massey, Faye Emerson, Peter Lorre, Alan Hale (Warner)

Grand Hotel in a 1945 Nazi setting, now known as *Hotel Berlin* [both of them based on novels by Vicki Baum], is socko. The war's already lost—or, at least, there's that defeatist aura about Hotel Berlin—and the Nazi higher-ups are packing their loot for a South American getaway.

Producer Lou Edelman has guided his charges well. Productionally the lavishness is by suggestion rather than in reality. There are the periodic Allied air blitzes which chase everybody into the shelters, but otherwise it's a Grand Hotel in the lobby or on the sundry floors, but particularly in the apartments of a general (Raymond Massey), an informer (Faye Emerson), or a theatre darling (Andrea King).

There are many suspenseful touches right along. The footage is replete with arresting meller. Whether it's Dickie Tyler as the resourceful little bellboy of the underground, or the femme star who apparently first falls for Helmut Dantine (the escaped anti-Nazi) and later would turn him in, the situations are constantly intriguing.

•

HOTEL IMPERIAL
1927, 67 mins, US b/w
Dir Mauritz Stiller ***Prod*** Erich Pommer ***Scr*** Jules Furthman ***Ph*** Bert Glennon
Act Pola Negri, James Hall, George Siegmann (Paramount)

In direction and camerawork the picture [based on a play by Lajos Biro] stands out, but the story isn't one that is going to give anyone a great thrill. Mauritz Stiller and Erich Pommer have done their work well, and they have made Pola Negri look like a gorgeous beauty in some shots, and effectively handled her in others, such as her scenes with the Russian general, but to what avail are good direction and supervision, plus acting, when the story isn't there?

It has to do with the advance of Russian armies into Galicia after their defeat of the Austrians. The Hotel Imperial is located in one of the border towns of Austria-Hungary. Here a fleeing Austrian hussar seeks rest and is caught behind the lines of the enemy when they move into the town.

Negri, as the hotel slavey, shelters him and suggests that he act as the waiter to cover himself. The Russian general makes the hotel his headquarters and falls for the girl. The waiter, in turn, loves her also and she reciprocates his feeling.

A corking leading man is James Hall. He has an air that denotes that he is capable of real things in picture work. George Siegmann, as the Russian general, puts all that there should be into the heavy.

•

HOTEL NEW HAMPSHIRE, THE
1984, 110 mins, US col
Dir Tony Richardson ***Prod*** Neil Hartley ***Scr*** Tony Richardson ***Ph*** David Watkin ***Ed*** Robert K. Lambert ***Mus*** Jacques Offenbach, Raymond Leppard ***Art*** Jocelyn Herbert
Act Jodie Foster, Beau Bridges, Rob Lowe, Nastassja Kinski, Wilford Brimley, Dorsey Wright (Woodfall)

While it is decidedly not to all tastes, *The Hotel New Hampshire* is a fascinating, largely successful adaptation of John Irving's 1981 novel. Writer-director Tony Richardson has pulled off a remarkable stylistic tightrope act, establishing a bizarre tone of morbid whimsicality at the outset and sustaining it throughout.

Tale concerns an eccentric New England family that, spurred on by an ever-searching father, establishes a new hotel in locale after locale and mutates in the process.

Among the unusual family members is Jodie Foster, who must endure a punishing gang rape and a prolonged fascination with the young man who did it; her brother, Rob Lowe, an impossibly good-looking fellow who takes on most of the women in the cast; their "queer" brother Paul McCrane; and their little sister Jennie Dundas.

Also virtually part of the family by association, if not by blood, are black jock Dorsey Wright; voluptuous hotel waitress Anita Morris; and Nastassja Kinski, a girl so insecure that she hides most of the time inside an enormous bear suit.

•

HOTEL PARADISO
1966, 100 mins, UK col
Dir Peter Glenville ***Prod*** Peter Glenville ***Scr*** Peter Glenville, Jean-Claude Carriere ***Ph*** Henri Decae ***Ed*** Anne V. Coates ***Mus*** Laurence Rosen ***Art*** Francois de Lamothe
Act Alec Guinness, Gina Lollobrigida, Robert Morley, Peggy Mount, Akim Tamiroff, Marie Bell (M-G-M)

Film version of Georges Feydeau's turn-of-the-century *L'hotel du libre echange* is a second-generation production of Peter Glenville's legit revival of the French farceur in London.

Plot involves a complicated series of mishaps triggered by the 40-year-old "itch" of M. Boniface, played with weariy glossy perfection by Alec Guinness, for the wife of his next-door neighbor, Henri Cot, assayed with appropriate bluster by Robert Morley. Miffed by her neglectful husband, Mme Cot, adequately acted by Gina Lollobrigida, succumbs to Boniface's suggestion that they rendezvous at the seedy Parisian assignation locale, Hotel Paradiso.

A concatenation of endless coincidences, laboriously contrived for the better part of the film, conspire to relegate the rendezvous to farce. Main problem with the film is a bloodless script. Glenville, in an attempt to infuse theatrical brio into the play, only succeeds in overstylizing it.

•

HOT ENOUGH FOR JUNE
(US: AGENT 8[3Q])
1964, 98 mins, UK col
Dir Ralph Thomas *Prod* Betty E. Box *Scr* Lukas Heller *Ph* Ernest Steward *Ed* Alfred Roome *Mus* Angelo Lavagnino *Art* Syd Cain
Act Dirk Bogarde, Sylva Koscina, Robert Morley, Leo McKern, Roger Delgado, John Le Mesurier (Rank)

A faster pace from director Ralph Thomas and a few more red herrings and surprise situations could have worked wonders in lifting this amiable enough spoof of espionage into a top league comedy-thriller.

June is by no means a skit on the Bond adventures. It is simply a genial leg-pull of some of the situations which, in tougher circumstances, Bond might easily be facing. Dirk Bogarde, who plays the hero with ingratiating efficiency, is an unsuccessful writer, content to live on national assistance. When the Labour Exchange unexpectedly sends him to take up a post as a trainee junior-executive in a glassworks, Bogarde finds the combination of a good salary and useful expenses irresistible. He is assigned to visit a Czech factory and bring back a written message which he guilelessly believes to be a simple commercial job. He does not know that he is now attached to the Espionage Department of the Foreign Office.

Most of the humor comes from witty prods at the expense of the Foreign Office and the Iron Curtain Party system. Robert Morley is superb as the boss of the department, with his old Etonian tie, benign plottings and general appearance of a well-poised walrus.

•

HOT MILLIONS
1968, 106 mins, UK col
Dir Eric Till *Prod* Mildred Freed Alberg *Scr* Ira Wallach, Peter Ustinov *Ph* Ken Higgins *Ed* Richard Marden *Mus* Laurie Johnson *Art* Bill Andrews
Act Peter Ustinov, Maggie Smith, Karl Malden, Bob Newhart, Robert Morley, Cesar Romero (M-G-M)

Very good writing, excellent acting, zesty direction and pacing, and handsome production make this story of computer embezzlement a strong laugh-getter. Peter Ustinov, Maggie Smith and Karl Malden, plus Bob Newhart and cameos by Robert Morley and Cesar Romero, comprise the talented cast.

The screenplay gives motivated development to characters, all of whom hit the target. Ustinov, released from prison, decides that the modern embezzler must be a computer expert. Conning his way into the good graces of Malden, head of the British wing of an American industrial conglomerate, Ustinov eventually programs into the computer three phony companies, to which large checks are sent.

Complicating Ustinov's progress are Newhart, suspicious assistant to Malden, and Smith, who falls for Ustinov. Ustinov makes as good an ensemble player as in his solo moments. Malden is excellent in a well-restrained, broad interpretation.

1968: NOMINATION: Best Original Story & Screenplay

•

HOT ROCK, THE
(UK: HOW TO STEAL A DIAMOND IN FOUR UNEASY LESSONS)
1972, 105 mins, US Ⓥ ▭ col
Dir Peter Yates *Prod* Hal Landers, Bobby Roberts *Scr* William Goldman *Ph* Ed Brown *Ed* Frank P. Keller, Fred W. Berger *Mus* Quincy Jones *Art* John Robert Lloyd
Act Robert Redford, George Segal, Ron Leibman, Paul Sand, Zero Mostel, Moses Gunn (20th Century Fox)

With its mixture of suspense, satire and broad comedy, *The Hot Rock* emerges as an offbeat crime feature. Stars Robert Redford and George Segal head a quartet of thieves who usually miss the objective, here a famous diamond which inspired the title of the piece.

Peter Yates's direction and uniformly good cast partly overcome a William Goldman script [from Donald E. Westlake's novel] that has many exciting and funny bits, but lacks a clear, unifying thrust.

However, the plot involves four separate heists, and, given the deliberate exposition of the human frailty of the hoods, the sequential capers lose a lot of momentum, giving the film as a whole the look of a spliced-together multi-episode TV show.

1972: NOMINATION: Best Editing

•

HOT SHOTS!
1991, 85 mins, US Ⓥ ⊙ col
Dir Jim Abrahams *Prod* Bill Badalato *Scr* Jim Abrahams, Pat Proft *Ph* Bill Butler *Ed* Jane Kurson, Eric Sears *Mus* Sylvester LeVay *Art* William A. Elliot
Act Charlie Sheen, Cary Elwes, Valeria Golino, Lloyd Bridges, Kevin Dunn, Kristy Swanson (20th Century Fox/PAP)

Jim Abrahams tries to tap the zany *Airplane!* vein with this *Top Gun* spoof but bats far too low a percentage with the usual rapid-fire assault of numbingly stupid gags. Pic bogs down in motion picture in-jokes, drawing liberally on *Top Gun* and *An Officer and a Gentleman*, while intercutting homages to scenes from *The Fabulous Baker Boys*, *9 1/2 Weeks* and *Gone With the Wind*.

Charlie Sheen is the maverick pilot competing with self-obsessed Kent (Cary Elwes). One film spoof does provide the biggest belly laugh, quite literally, when Sheen begins erotically feeding Valeria Golino grapes and, in escalating passion, cooks breakfast on her sizzling stomach. Most characters are gratingly cartoonish, especially Lloyd Bridges's way-over-the-top tin-headed admiral.

•

HOT SHOTS 2
SEE: HOT SHOTS! PART DEUX

•

HOT SHOTS! PART DEUX
(AUSTRALIA: HOTS SHOTS 2)
1993, 89 mins, US Ⓥ ⊙ col
Dir Jim Abrahams *Prod* Bill Badalato *Scr* Jim Abrahams, Pat Proft *Ph* John R. Leonetti *Ed* Malcolm Campbell *Mus* Basil Poledouris *Art* William A. Elliott
Act Charlie Sheen, Lloyd Bridges, Valeria Golino, Richard Crenna, Brenda Bakke, Miguel Ferrer (20th Century-Fox)

This much better sequel is a clever spoof of *Rambo* and a dozen other movies that employs the usual scattershot *Airplane!* approach but boasts a higher shooting percentage than its forebear.

The latest raid uses the *Rambo* and *Missing in Action* series to pull the audience along, and finds time to throw in clever skewerings of numerous other films, among them *Apocalypse Now*, *Casablanca*, *Star Wars*, *The Wizard of Oz*, even *Lady and the Tramp*.

Charlie Sheen, with wild locks and a buffed-up physique, returns as Topper Harley, recruited by a former commander (Richard Crenna, a brilliant bit of casting due to his *Rambo role*) and a stunningly limber CIA agent (Brenda Bakke) to try to rescue U.S. servicemen held prisoner after Desert Storm.

Valeria Golino also returns as Sheen's former love interest though Bakke, with her impossibly short dresses, serves as the primary ice-cube–melting surface this time around.

Technically, pic doesn't cut corners just because it's a parody. If you haven't seen *The Crying Game*, don't read the closing credits.

•

HOT SPOT
1941, 81 mins, US Ⓥ b/w
Dir H. Bruce Humberstone *Prod* Milton Sperling *Scr* Dwight Taylor *Ph* Edward Cronjager *Ed* Robert Simpson
Act Betty Grable, Victor Mature, Carole Landis, Laird Cregar, Elisha Cook, Jr. (20th Century-Fox)

Hot Spot may suggest a nightclub background, but such scenes are only incidental. The director, H. Bruce Humberstone, has been equipped with a good script and from his cast has obtained results that are all that may be asked in a murder meller with a romantic strain of more than the ordinary strength.

Betty Grable is enormously appealing here as the sister of the slain girl, played by Carole Landis, who disappears at an early stage of the game. Victor Mature plays in a tougher groove than usual and this seems a desirable switch. This time he's a sports promoter with a bit of a snarl in his voice.

In the story Mature is dogged by a detective who loses his girl when Mature takes her from obscurity and glamourizes her to the point where she wins a film contract. The murder of this girl then provides the premise for the remainder of the yarn.

The book on which this picture is based is called *I Wake Up Screaming*. It sounds like a better title than *Hot Spot*, but the film need not beg forgiveness.

•

HOT SPOT, THE
1990, 120 mins, US Ⓥ ⊙ col
Dir Dennis Hopper *Prod* Paul Lewis, Deborah Capograsso *Scr* Nona Tyson, Charles Williams *Ph* Ueli Steiger *Ed* Wende Pheiffer Mate *Mus* Jack Nitzsche *Art* Cary White
Act Don Johnson, Virginia Madsen, Jennifer Connelly, Charles Martin Smith, William Sadler, Barry Corbin (Orion)

Director Dennis Hopper just won't say no to kinky amorality, and that's all to the good in this twisting, languorous and very sexy thriller [based on Charles Williams's novel *Hell Hath No Fury*].

Hopper elicits a sharp, understated performance from *Miami Vice* star Don Johnson, who's neither a cop nor a good guy here. As the low-key, manipulative drifter Harry Madox, Johnson shakes things up in a godforsaken Texas town, where his job at a used car lot involves him with two restless women yearning to beat the heat.

Gloria Harper (Jennifer Connelly) is the sweetly stunning office girl; Dolly Harshaw (Virginia Madsen) is the irresistibly tempting boss's wife. This is the type of town, says Madsen, where there are "only two things to do," and one of them is watching TV. Johnson charts a sexual collision course with both women. But he has another agenda. Once he's insinuated himself into the town, Johnson aims to con the yokels.

Hopper clearly was impressed by what he learned from working with David Lynch on *Blue Velvet*. *The Hot Spot* seeps with atmosphere, unfolds at a deceptively relaxed pace, steadily accumulates noirish grit, then dizzily plunges into a Lynch-like plumbing of the dark passions and nasty secrets at the heart of Main Street, USA.

•

HOUDINI
1953, 105 mins, US Ⓥ col
Dir George Marshall *Prod* George Pal *Scr* Philip Yordan *Ph* Ernest Laszlo *Ed* George Tomasini *Mus* Roy Webb *Art* Hal Pereira, Al Nozaki
Act Tony Curtis, Janet Leigh, Torin Thatcher, Angela Clarke, Douglas Spencer, Sig Ruman (Paramount)

A typical screen biography, presenting a rather fanciful version of Houdini's life. Production does well by illusions and escapes on which Houdini won his fame, using these tricks to give substance to a plot that uses a backstage formula that follows pat lines. Under George Marshall's direction, story spins along nicely, with occasional emphasis on drama in several of escape sequences to keep interest up.

Performances of two stars are likeable, although neither shows any aging in the time span that covers Houdini from 21 to death.

Screenplay, based on book by Harold Kellock, opens at the turn of the century to find Houdini performing as a "wild man" and magician in Schultz's Dime Museum in New York. To this amusement spot comes a group of school girls, including Janet Leigh, and Houdini (Tony Curtis) is attracted to her. After an extremely brief courtship, they marry, try an act together, before she persuades him to take a job in a lock factory. Later, after winning a prize at a magicians' convention, Houdini and his bride go to Europe and he becomes a success with miracle escapes.

•

HOUND OF THE BASKERVILLES, THE
1939, 78 mins, US Ⓥ ⊙ b/w
Dir Sidney Lanfield *Prod* Gene Markey *Scr* Ernest Pascal *Ph* Peverell Marley *Ed* Robert Simpson *Mus* Cyril J. Mockridge *Art* Richard Day, Hans Peters
Act Richard Greene, Basil Rathbone, Nigel Bruce, Lionel Atwill, John Carradine, Wendy Barrie (20th Century-Fox)

The Hound of the Baskervilles retains all of the suspensefully dramatic ingredients of Conan Doyle's popular adventure of Sherlock Holmes. It's a startling mystery-chiller developed along logical lines without resorting to implausible situations and overtheatrics.

Doyle's tale of mystery surrounding the Baskerville castle is a familiar one. When Lionel Atwill learns that Richard Greene, heir to the estate, is marked for death, he calls in Basil Rathbone.

Rathbone gives a most effective characterization of Sherlock Holmes. Greene, in addition to playing the intended victim of the murderer, is the romantic interest opposite Wendy Barrie.

Chiller mood generated by the characters and story is heightened by effects secured from sequences in the medieval castle and the dreaded fogbound moors. Low-key photography by Peverell Marley adds to suspense.

•

HOUND OF THE BASKERVILLES, THE
1959, 88 mins, UK Ⓥ ⦿ col
Dir Terence Fisher ***Prod*** Anthony Hinds ***Scr*** Peter Bryan ***Ph*** Jack Asher ***Ed*** James Needs ***Mus*** James Bernard ***Art*** Bernard Robinson
Act Peter Cushing, Andre Morell, Christopher Lee, Marla Landi, Miles Malleson, David Oxley (Hammer)

This first Sherlock Holmes pic in color takes place in the desolate setting of Dartmoor. The private eye and his faithful stooge, Doctor Watson, are called in following the mysterious slaying of Sir Charles Baskerville. It's thought that his successor, Sir Henry, may meet the same fate.

It is difficult to fault the performance of Peter Cushing, who looks, talks and behaves in precisely the way approved by the Sherlock Holmes Society. Andre Morell is also a very good Watson—stolid, reliable and not as stupidly bovine as he is sometimes depicted. Christopher Lee has a fairly colorless role as the potential victim of the legendary hound, but he plays it competently. Miles Malleson contributes most of the rare humor with one of his first-class studies, as a bumbling bishop.

Terence Fisher's direction captures the eeriness of the atmosphere. Some of the settings are a shade stagey but Jack Asher's lensing also helps to build up the dank gloom of the Dartmoor area.

•

HOUNDS OF ZAROFF, THE
SEE: THE MOST DANGEROUS GAME

•

HOUR OF GLORY
SEE: THE SMALL BACK ROOM

•

HOUR OF JUDGMENT
SEE: THE HOUR OF THE PIG

•

HOUR OF THE GUN
1967, 101 mins, US Ⓥ ▭ col
Dir John Sturges ***Prod*** John Sturges ***Scr*** Edward Anhalt ***Ph*** Lucien Ballard ***Ed*** Ferris Webster ***Mus*** Jerry Goldsmith ***Art*** Alfred Ybarra
Act James Garner, Jason Robards, Robert Ryan, Albert Salmi, Charles Aidman, Steve Ihnat (United Artists/Mirisch)

Edward Anhalt, using Douglas D. Martin's *Tombstone's Epitaph*, has fashioned a heavily populated script which traces Wyatt Earp's moral decline from a lawman to one bent on personal revenge. Produced under earlier title of *The Law and Tombstone*, it continues the story of Earp after *Gunfight at the O.K. Corral*.

Unfortunately, for any filmmaker, probing too deeply into the character of folk heroes reveals them to be fallible human beings—which they are, of course—but to mass audiences, who create fantasies, such exposition is unsettling. Reality often makes for poor drama.

Jason Robards and James Garner play well together, the former supplying an adroit irony in that he, an admitted gambler as much outside the law as in, becomes more moral as Garner lapses into personal vendetta. Robert Ryan is a perfect heavy.

•

HOUR OF THE PIG, THE
(US: HOUR OF JUDGMENT; THE ADVOCATE)
1994, 115 mins, UK/France Ⓥ ⦿ col
Dir Leslie Megahey ***Prod*** David M. Thompson ***Scr*** Leslie Megahey ***Ph*** John Hooper ***Ed*** Isabelle Dedieu ***Mus*** Alexandre Desplat ***Art*** Bruce Macadie
Act Colin Firth, Ian Holm, Donald Pleasence, Nicol Williamson, Lysette Anthony, Amina Annabi (BBC/CiBy 2000)

Any lawyer who has ever taken his client for swine will have the last laugh watching *The Hour of the Pig*, a droll, deftly acted period piece based on the fact that in medieval France animals were accused of crimes and tried in court with counsel.

An industrious young defense lawyer, Courtois (Colin Firth), has left Paris for the allegedly purer framework of the boondocks. In the village of Abbeville there's a long-established prosecuting attorney (Donald Pleasence). Courtois soon learns that superstition, the Church and the local nobleman (Nicol Williamson) have enormous influence. He strikes up a useful friendship with a hypocritical local clergyman (Ian Holm). When a band of Jewish gypsies enters the town, and their prize pig is arrested and accused of killing a young boy, exotic dark-skinned Samira (Amina Annabi) implores Courtois to get the pig acquitted, offering her womanly charms in exchange.

Clever dialog, laced with frank and bawdy observations, is delivered in ultra-dry style. Holm and Williamson are excellent in their roles, and supports are spirited, particularly Jim Carter as Firth's ironic law clerk and Lysette Anthony as Williamson's goofy daughter.

•

HOUSE
1986, 92 mins, US Ⓥ ⦿ col
Dir Steve Miner ***Prod*** Sean S. Cunningham ***Scr*** Ethan Wiley ***Ph*** Mac Ahlberg ***Ed*** Michael N. Knue ***Mus*** Harry Manfredini ***Art*** Gregg Fonseca
Act William Katt, George Wendt, Richard Moll, Kay Lenz, Mary Stavin, Michael Ensign (New World)

Filmmakers Sean S. Cunningham and Steve Miner scored hits with several simple *Friday the 13th* films but tackle a more complex story here with embarrassing results. Cornball script [from a story by Fred Dekker] posits Roger Cobb (William Katt) as a successful horror novelist who moves into the spooky house where he was raised following the suicide of his aunt, as he writes a book based on his war experience in Vietnam. Cobb immediately experiences odd happenings which play as hallucinations, but which the audience is supposed to believe are real. His estranged TV actress wife Susan (Kay Lenz) shows up, apparently changes into a puffy monster and is killed by Cobb.

Though much of this nonsense is played tongue-in-cheek, an audience can hardly be expected to swallow the screenplay's arbitrary approach to Cobb's character. Compounding such credibility problems is a ludicrous subplot with Cobb's neighbor, a wolf-whistle beauty, Tanya (Mary Stavin).

Cast cannot be faulted, especially lead Katt. The monsters are fake and rubbery, better suited to a comedy than a film in search of scares.

•

HOUSE II: THE SECOND STORY
1987, 85 mins, US Ⓥ ⦿ col
Dir Ethan Wiley ***Prod*** Sean S. Cunningham ***Scr*** Ethan Wiley ***Ph*** Mac Ahlberg ***Ed*** Marty Nicholson ***Mus*** Harry Manfredini ***Art*** Gregg Fonseca
Act Arye Gross, Jonathan Stark, Royal Dano, Bill Maher, John Ratzenberger, Amy Yasbeck (New World)

This house isn't worth a visit. What passes for a plot has Arye Gross move into the house in which his parents were murdered 25 years earlier. He hears about the existence of a skull filled with jewelry, supposedly buried with the body of one of his ancestors, so he and entrepreneur pal Jonathan Stark exhume the 170-year-old corpse, played by Royal Dano, unrecognizable under disfiguring makeup.

The oldtimer wants to have fun now that he's alive again, but an evil spirit wants that skull, and soon the trio are transported through the walls of the house into another world—a primeval jungle—to do battle.

Director Ethan Wiley is determined to be cute rather than scary. He intros some cuddly creatures—a baby pterodactyl, plus a critter who's a cross between a dog and a caterpillar—but they don't add anything to the pic's charm. Action scenes aren't very thrilling or suspenseful.

•

HOUSEBOAT
1958, 112 mins, US Ⓥ ⦿ col
Dir Melville Shavelson ***Prod*** Jack Rose ***Scr*** Melville Shavelson, Jack Rose ***Ph*** Ray June ***Ed*** Frank Bracht ***Mus*** George Duning ***Art*** Hal Pereira, John Goodman
Act Cary Grant, Sophia Loren, Martha Hyer, Harry Guardino, Eduardo Ciannelli, Mimi Gibson (Paramount/Scribe)

The voyage of *Houseboat* is to a nearly extinct era in motion pictures when screens and hearts bubbled over with the warmth of original family humor.

It's a perfect role for Cary Grant, who plays a government lawyer separated from his wife and who, upon her accidental death, is brought into contact with his three children, none of whom are very friendly toward him.

Enter Sophia Loren, a full-blown lass with lovely knees who's been kept in tow by her father, a noted Italian symphony conductor and who takes the first chance to get away from it all. Grant, though he takes her for a tramp, hires her as a maid at seeing her ability to handle his children upon first meeting. Off goes everyone to the country, and through living together they begin to understand and love each other. This, of course, also goes for the two adults (by now, he's noticed her knees).

Grant mixes concern with disconcern and says more with a head tilt than most residents of situation comedy are able to say with an entire script. Loren acts better in irate Italian than in emotional English, but she is believable and sometimes downright warm as the lover of Grant and his children.

Harry Guardino is outstanding as a fiery wolf who will take anything but a wife, and Martha Hyer, as the rich "other" woman, is beautiful and skillfully competent. As one might expect, the moppets steal the show.

1958: NOMINATIONS: Best Original Story & Screenplay, Song ("Almost in Your Army")

•

HOUSE BY THE RIVER
1950, 88 mins, US b/w
Dir Fritz Lang ***Prod*** Howard Welsch ***Scr*** Mel Dinelli ***Ph*** Edward Cronjager ***Ed*** Arthur D. Hilton ***Mus*** George Antheil ***Art*** Boris Leven
Act Louis Hayward, Lee Bowman, Jane Wyatt, Dorothy Patrick, Ann Shoemaker, Jody Gilbert (Republic/Fidelity)

House by the River is a fair mystery that lacks sufficient plot twists and suspense.

As screenplayed from an A. P. Herbert novel, the film departs from the conventional whodunit in that the audience knows the identity of the murderer from the opening reel. Subsequent footage is chiefly a character study of the three principals.

Bulk of the action takes place in a gloomy mansion and a courtroom. Yarn revolves around a hack writer who strangles the maid when she rebuffs his advances. His brother, an accountant, realizes murder has been committed, but somehow lets his kin persuade him to assist in disposing of the body.

Role of the writer represents a meaty part for Louis Hayward, who essays it with such gusto that he frequently overplays.

•

HOUSE CALLS
1978, 98 mins, US Ⓥ ⦿ col
Dir Howard Zieff ***Prod*** Alex Winitsky, Arlene Sellers ***Scr*** Max Shulman, Julius J. Epstein, Alan Mandel, Charles Shyer ***Ph*** David M. Walsh ***Ed*** Edward Warschilka ***Mus*** Henry Mancini ***Art*** Henry Bumstead
Act Walter Matthau, Glenda Jackson, Art Carney, Richard Benjamin, Candice Azzara, Dick O'Neill (Universal)

Despite some horsepower casting, *House Calls* is overall a silly and uneven comedy about doctors which wants to be as macabre as, say, *Hospital*, and at the same time as innocuous as a TV sitcom. It manages to be neither.

Walter Matthau, engaging as a middle-aged lech, is one of four stars in the film, herein a newly widowed medic out to make up for lost infidelity time; Glenda Jackson, divorced from a philanderer, seeks a faithful new mate; Art Carney is a near-senile hospital chief of staff whose mistakes are supposed to be funny but come off as really nasty; Richard Benjamin is a young doctor whose part is essentially to provide plot exposition.

The film is thus a middle-years comedy-romance vehicle [story by Max Shulman and Julius J. Epstein] for Matthau and Jackson, latter in her first made-in-Hollywood project and appearing none too comfortable either; the lightness of her *A Touch of Class* Oscar-winning performance is gone.

Carney also huffs and puffs his way uncomfortably through an unsympathetic part. Benjamin relaxes and Matthau seems mellow enough.

•

HOUSEGUEST
1995, 109 mins, US Ⓥ col
Dir Randall Miller ***Prod*** Joe Roth, Roger Birnbaum ***Scr*** Michael J. Di Gaetano, Lawrence Gay ***Ph*** Jerzy Zielinski ***Ed*** Eric Sears ***Mus*** John Debney ***Art*** Paul Peters
Act Sinbad, Phil Hartman, Jeffrey Jones, Kim Greist, Stan Shaw, Tony Longo (Hollywood)

This Disney release is a lightweight but likable comedy. Stand-up comic and sitcom star Sinbad is thoroughly engaging as Kevin Franklin, a hard-luck dreamer whose get-rich-quick schemes usually explode in his face.

On the run from loan sharks, Franklin runs into Gary Young (Hartman), an affable lawyer who's at the airport to meet a former summer camp buddy he hasn't seen for 25 years. Franklin quickly assumes the buddy's name and accepts the lawyer's hospitality.

Gary brings Kevin to his suburban home for a long weekend with his mildly dysfunctional family: Emily (Kim

Greist), his wife, a yogurt shop entrepreneur; Brooke (Kim Murphy), his death-obsessed daughter; Jason (Chauncey Leopardi), his insecure adolescent son; and Sarah (Talia Seider), his precocious six-year-old and the most well-adjusted person in the family. Not surprisingly, Kevin is a big hit with everyone.

Houseguest is funniest in the early scenes in which Sinbad desperately vamps and improvises his way through Kevin's imposture. Scriptwriters are TV sitcom veterans, and they remain true to their roots in their first credited screenplay.

Director Randall Miller gooses along several scenes with speeded-up cinematography and other tricks but is unable to do much with pic's least-amusing element, the overbearing bigotry of Gary's cantankerous boss (Mason Adams).

•

HOUSEKEEPING
1987, 116 mins, US Ⓥ col
Dir Bill Forsyth ***Prod*** Robert I. Colesberry ***Scr*** Bill Forsyth ***Ph*** Michael Coulter ***Ed*** Michael Ellis ***Mus*** Michael Gibbs ***Art*** Adrienne Atkinson
Act Christine Lahti, Sara Walker, Andrea Burchill, Anne Pitoniak, Bill Smillie (Columbia)

Both enervating and exhilarating, *Housekeeping* is a very composed film about eccentric behavior. It is beautifully observed in many of its details, particularly in its very close examination of the relationship between sisters.

Based upon Marilynne Robinson's well-regarded novel, Forsyth's screenplay is structured around the impulsive arrivals and departures of characters fundamental to the lives of two sisters in Washington State after World War II. Men never enter the picture, as the girls successively live with their mother, grandmother, great-aunts and mother's sister in the splendid isolation of a small mountain town. Six years after their abandonment, when the girls are on the brink of adolescence, into their lives steps their long-lost aunt Sylvie (Christine Lahti). Tale then becomes that of the proverbial crazy ladies in the old house on the edge of town, but played rigorously without sentimentality or cuteness.

Newcomers Sara Walker and Andrea Burchill are splendid as the girls, as they manage to suggest the lifelong and quite particular bond between the sisters as much through body language and looks as through dialog.

•

HOUSE OF BAMBOO
1955, 102 mins, US ⊏⊐ col
Dir Samuel Fuller ***Prod*** Buddy Adler ***Scr*** Harry Kleiner, Samuel Fuller ***Ph*** Joe MacDonald ***Ed*** James B. Clark ***Mus*** Leigh Harline ***Art*** Lyle Wheeler, Addison Hehr
Act Robert Ryan, Robert Stack, Shirley Yamaguchi, Cameron Mitchell, Brad Dexter, Sessue Hayakawa (20th Century-Fox)

House of Bamboo is a regulation gangster story played against a modern-day Tokyo setting.

Novelty of scene and a warm, believable performance by Japanese star Shirley Yamaguchi are two of the better values in the production. Had story treatment and direction been on the same level of excellence, *House* would have been an all-round good show.

Pictorially, the film is beautiful to see; the talk's mostly in the terse, tough idiom of yesteryear mob pix. While plot deals with some mighty tough characters who are trying to organize Tokyo along Chicago gangland lines, the violence introduced seems hardly necessary to the melodramatic points being made.

Robert Stack, required to overplay surliness by the direction, is an undercover agent out to get the murderer of a GI and break up the gang of renegade Yanks.

•

HOUSE OF CARDS
1968, 105 mins, US Ⓥ ⊏⊐ col
Dir John Guillermin ***Prod*** Dick Berg ***Scr*** James P. Bonner ***Ph*** Alberto Pizzi ***Ed*** Terry Williams ***Mus*** Francis Lai ***Art*** Aurelio Crugnola
Act George Peppard, Inger Stevens, Orson Welles, Keith Michell, William Job, Maxine Audley (Universal)

George Peppard is in breezy vigorous form as rescuer of a lady in distress in a thriller that has quite a measure of excitement and style, though the screenplay, based on Stanley Ellin's novel, has plenty of straggly ends. However, there are elements of a Hitchcockian thriller.

Story has Peppard as a Yank drifter in France who falls into the job of tutor to the young son of the widow of a French general killed in the Algerian war. He's installed in the de Villemont mansion and meets the curious and sinister de Villemont family.

Peppard offers a nice combo of exuberant cheek and muscle and Inger Stevens as the young widow keeps the romantic angle dangling tantalizingly. Orson Welles is not overused, but his flamboyance fits the role of a menacing conspirator effectively, and Keith Michell is suavely sinister.

Director John Guillermin makes the most of highspots but often cannot get the conversational and plot-laying bits off the ground.

•

HOUSE OF CARDS
1993, 107 mins, US col
Dir Michael Lessac ***Prod*** Dale Pollock, Lianne Halfon, Wolfgang Glattes ***Scr*** Michael Lessac ***Ph*** Victor Hammer ***Ed*** Walter Murch ***Mus*** James Horner ***Art*** Peter Larkin
Act Kathleen Turner, Tommy Lee Jones, Asha Menina, Shiloh Strong, Esther Rolle, Park Overall (Penta)

Well made but narrowly one-note in its concerns, *House of Cards* plays like a top-of-the-line disease-of-the-week TV movie.

Drama [from a screen story by Michael Lessac and Robert Jay Litz] is triggered by the fatal plunge of an archeologist off a site in Mexico, leaving Ruth Matthews (Kathleen Turner) a widow. Returning to the U.S. with her son and daughter, Ruth soon has to deal with the fact that little Sally (Asha Menina) is not talking anymore.

Instead, Menina emits almost deafening, rhythmic shouts when anything seems amiss to her and begins to do weird things, such as building an extraordinary tower of cards in her room. Child psychiatrist Jake Beerlander (Tommy Lee Jones) wants to get his hands on this mysterious six-year-old, whom he believes exhibits classic autistic symptoms.

Ruth is an incompletely written character, and Turner does little to add to its depth or complexity. Menina makes a striking Sally, impressing with the sense of power and other-worldliness she throws off. Jones quietly underplays the shrink.

•

HOUSE OF DOOM
SEE: THE BLACK CAT

•

HOUSE OF DRACULA
1945, 67 mins, US Ⓥ b/w
Dir Erle C. Kenton ***Prod*** Paul Malvern ***Scr*** Edward T. Lowe ***Ph*** George Robinson, John P. Fulton ***Ed*** Russell Schoengarth ***Mus*** Edgar Fairchild ***Art*** John B. Goodman, Martin Obzina
Act Lon Chaney, John Carradine, Martha O'Driscoll, Lionel Atwill, Glenn Strange, Jane Adams (Universal)

Universal has brought all of its terror figures—Dracula, the Wolf Man and Frankenstein's Monster—together in a nifty thriller for the chiller trade.

Plot twist has two of the monster heavies taking a sympathetic angle. Each comes to a doctor for help in curing their strange afflictions. First to appeal for help from Onslow Stevens is John Carradine, the centuries-old vampire. Next is Lon Chaney, the werewolf, who wants the doctor to relieve his madness. Stevens is successful in his experiments with Chaney but the vampire curing backfires. The good doctor eliminates Dracula by letting the sun's rays fall on his sleeping body but finds he himself has acquired the blood-letting urge. In his newly acquired madness he revives Frankenstein's monster, found in sea caverns near the doctor's castle.

Femme spots go to Martha O'Driscoll and Jane Adams as assistants to the doctor. Lionel Atwill is seen briefly as the village police chief, while Glenn Strange dons the garb of the monster.

•

HOUSE OF FRANKENSTEIN
1944, 70 mins, US Ⓥ b/w
Dir Erle C. Kenton ***Prod*** Paul Malvern ***Scr*** Edward T. Lowe ***Ph*** George Robinson ***Ed*** Philip Cahn ***Mus*** Hans J. Salter ***Art*** John B. Goodman, Martin Obzina
Act Boris Karloff, J. Carrol Naish, Lon Chaney, John Carradine, Lionel Atwill, George Zucco (Universal)

Frankenstein's Monster, Dracula, and the Wolf Man provide three-ply horror display in this chiller-diller meller.

Plot [from a story by Curt Siodmak] takes the usual twists of the suspense-chill series. Boris Karloff is the mad scientist with a penchant for delving into transplanting of brains. He escapes from prison with deformed J. Carrol Naish, takes over a traveling chamber of horror exhibit to release the skeleton of Dracula for brief forays among the populace, and then goes to the ruins of the Frankenstein castle to secure records of former transplanting research.

Karloff is the usual menace in lead role of the scientist, with Naish particularly well cast as the hunchback. Lon Chaney is the Wolf Man, while John Carradine steps into the Dracula assignment.

•

HOUSE OF GAMES
1987, 102 mins, US Ⓥ ⦿ col
Dir David Mamet ***Prod*** Michael Hausman ***Scr*** David Memet ***Ph*** Juan Ruiz Anchia ***Ed*** Trudy Ship ***Mus*** Alaric Jans ***Art*** Michael Merritt
Act Lindsay Crouse, Joe Mantegna, Mike Nussbaum, Lilia Skala, J. T. Walsh (Filmhaus/Orion)

Writer David Mamet's first trip behind the camera as a director is entertaining good fun, an American film noir with Hitchcockian touches and a few dead bodies along the way. The action unfolds at a steady pace.

Any story that pairs a psychiatrist and a con man has possibilities. Here the famous Dr. Margaret Ford (Lindsay Crouse) finds her patients' lives more interesting than her own, and with the unwitting encouragement of her mentor (Lilia Skala), allows herself to be drawn into a nest of confidence sharks.

In the tense atmosphere of a smoky backroom cardtable, the irresistible heel Mike (Joe Mantegna) sets her up for a $6,000 drubbing. The good doctor gets out of that one by comic chance, but drawn to Mike and his dangerous life, she comes back the next night for more.

Mantegna is right on target as one of the screen's most likable baddies. His big con involves an elaborate setup to convince a conventioneer, picked up by partner Mike Nussbaum, to offer "security" for a suitcase full of money found on the street. *House of Games* cleverly selects its cons, explains their workings, then twists them around again, all without boring or losing the viewer.

•

HOUSE OF MIRTH, THE
2000, 143 mins, UK Ⓥ ⦿ ⊏⊐ col
Dir Terence Davies ***Prod*** Olivia Stewart ***Scr*** Terence Davies ***Ph*** Remi Adefarasin ***Ed*** Michael Parker ***Art*** Don Taylor
Act Gillian Anderson, Eric Stoltz, Dan Aykroyd, Eleanor Bron, Terry Kinney, Anthony LaPaglia, Elizabeth McGovern (Three Rivers/Granada)

Visually detailed but emotionally dry, Terence Davies' *The House of Mirth* plays more like *Scenes From Edith Wharton's Novel* than a dramatically involving adaptation that brings its characters and period to life. Story of Lily, an ambitious but cash-strapped young woman looking for a provider in early 20th century Gotham high society, may appeal to those who respond to the Brit director's highly rarefied emotional palette.

Davies' first pic in five years is his most linear movie to date, as well as his first not to be shaped as a reminiscence or from a child's p.o.v. By opting for a slice-at-a-time approach to Wharton's novel, however, helmer has again avoided a purely narrative structure, often leaving the viewer to fill in the gaps and flattening out any dramatic highs and lows.

In her first major screen role outside *The X-Files*, Gillian Anderson offers a poised, vocally disciplined perf, marbled with hints of her character's ruthlessness; she handles the formal dialogue with ease. But within the confines of Davies' rigid direction, thesp cannot turn Lily into a genuinely involving woman brought low by the values of the very society she aspires to join.

•

HOUSE OF ROTHSCHILD, THE
1934, 94 mins, US col
Dir Alfred Werker ***Prod*** Darryl F. Zanuck ***Scr*** Nunnally Johnson ***Ph*** Peverell Marley ***Ed*** Allen McNeil, Barbara McLean ***Mus*** Alfred Newman ***Art*** Richard Day
Act George Arliss, Boris Karloff, Loretta Young, Robert Young, C. Aubrey Smith, Reginald Owen (Twentieth Century)

A fine picture on all counts in the acting, writing, and directing. It handles the delicate subject of anti-semitism with tact and restraint. The Rothschild family, through its intimate financial connection with the Napoleonic wars, affords a meaty story [based on a play by George Hembert Westley].

George Arliss plays the father and founder of the family, Mayer Rothschild, and when the narrative skips 35 years he is also the son, Nathan, head of the London branch of the banking firm. Nathan's daughter is played by Loretta Young, who never looked better. She falls in love with an English gentile officer (Robert Young).

Nathan opposes the marriage, fearing his daughter will suffer indignities because of her race. Ultimately his opposition melts and the pair are last seen in the luxuriant colors of the Technicolor sequence, in which Rothschild is made an English baron at a regal investiture, which brings the picture to an opulent close.

The real Mrs. Arliss plays her husband's make-believe wife. Her performance is very able and she is at all times an attractive matron. There are numerous minor performances of merit, including a sentimentalized Duke of Wellington handled by the astute C. Aubrey Smith.

1934: NOMINATION: Best Picture

•

HOUSE OF STRANGERS
1949, 104 mins, US Ⓥ b/w
Dir Joseph L. Mankiewicz ***Prod*** Sol C. Siegel ***Scr*** Philip Yordan ***Ph*** Milton Krasner ***Ed*** Harmon Jones ***Mus*** Daniele Amfitheatrof ***Art*** Lyle Wheeler, George W. Davis
Act Edward G. Robinson, Susan Hayward, Richard Conte, Luther Adler, Paul Valentine, Efrem Zimbalist, Jr. (20th Century-Fox)

Despite a rather weak title, *House of Strangers* is a strong picture. Edward G. Robinson plays a New York eastside Italian banker who switches from barbering to money-lending when he discovers the high interest obtainable. Yarn [from Jerome Weidman's novel *I'll Never Go There Again*] deals with the hate of three of his sons for their father's unyielding nature and slave-driving tactics. The fourth son (Richard Conte), an attorney with headquarters at the bank, sticks by his father.

Care has been used to faithfully show the homelife of a typical Old World Italian family (in the U.S.), while contrasting it with the younger generation.

Robinson is especially vivid when he realizes that the three sons have turned against him and when he seeks revenge through his fourth son. Conte is excellent, and Susan Hayward chips in with one of her standout performances as a society beaut.

•

HOUSE OF THE SPIRITS, THE
1993, 145 mins, Germany Ⓥ ⦿ ⌷ col
Dir Bille August ***Prod*** Bernd Eichinger ***Scr*** Bille August ***Ph*** Jorgen Persson ***Ed*** Janus Billeskov Jansen ***Mus*** Hans Zimmer ***Art*** Anna Asp
Act Jeremy Irons, Meryl Streep, Glenn Close, Winona Ryder, Antonio Banderas, Maria Conchita Alonso (Neue Constantin)

A stellar cast, lavish production values and an epic storyline combine for blue-blooded suds in *The House of the Spirits*. Bille August's high-toned reduction of Isabel Allende's 1985 worldwide bestseller aims to be a bittersweet historical romance on a grand scale, but the herky-jerky meller mostly bumps from one dramatic highlight to the next.

Pic charts 45 eventful years in the lives of the Trueba family in a South American country very much like Chile. At the outset in 1926, Esteban Trueba (Jeremy Irons) is the struggling young man who promises to become worthy of the beautiful, aristocratic Rosa (Teri Polo).

Estaban becomes the most powerful rancher in the area, and marries 20 years later Rosa's sister, Clara (Meryl Streep). Living with them at the remote hacienda is Estaban's spinster sister Ferula (Glenn Close). Jump ahead to 1963, and their daughter, the lovely 17-year-old Blanca (Winona Ryder) is in love with handsome Pedro (Antonio Banderas), the rebellious son of her father's chief ranch hand.

Just as the characters' motivations are mostly crude rather than complex, and the view of class politics superficial and romantic rather than acute or intelligent, so is the film's treatment of the novel's magical realism on the mundane side. The Danish August's sensibility is clearly in the epic realist camp rather than with the Latin fabulists. Performances by the terrific cast are variable. Portuguese locations stand in very serviceably for South American settings.

[Outside Germany, Switzerland, the Netherlands and Scandinavia, pic was released in a 138-min. fine cut by the director himself. Above review is of that version.]

•

HOUSE OF USHER
(UK: THE FALL OF THE HOUSE OF USHER)
1960, 79 mins, US Ⓥ ⌷ col
Dir Roger Corman ***Prod*** Roger Corman ***Scr*** Richard Matheson ***Ph*** Floyd Crosby ***Ed*** Anthony Carras ***Mus*** Les Baxter ***Art*** Daniel Haller
Act Vincent Price, Mark Damon, Myrna Fahey, Harry Ellerbe (American International/Alta Vista)

It's not precisely the Edgar Allan Poe short story that emerges in *House of Usher*, but it's a reasonably diverting and handsomely mounted variation. In patronizingly romanticizing Poe's venerable prose, scenarist Richard Matheson has managed to preserve enough of the original's haunting flavor and spirit. The elaborations change the personalities of the three central characters, but not recklessly so.

In Poe's tale, the first-person hero is a friend of Roderick Usher, not his enemy and the romantic wooer of his doomed sister, the Lady Madeline. Matheson's version, however, accomplishes this alteration without ruining the impact of the chilling climax, in which Madeline (Myrna Fahey), buried alive by her brother (Vincent Price) while under a cataleptic trance, breaks free from her living tomb.

Price is a fine fit as Usher, and Fahey successfully conveys the transition from helpless daintiness to insane vengeance. Hero Mark Damon has his better moments when the going gets gory and frenzied, but lacks the mature command required for the role. Harry Ellerbe is outstanding as an old family retainer.

The cobweb-ridden, fungus-infected, mist-pervaded atmosphere of cadaverous gloom has been photographed with great skill by Floyd Crosby and enhanced further by Ray Mercer's striking photographic effects and the vivid color, most notably during a woozy dream sequence.

•

HOUSE OF WAX
1953, 90 mins, US Ⓥ ⦿ col
Dir Andre de Toth ***Prod*** Bryan Foy ***Scr*** Crane Wilbur ***Ph*** Bert Glennon, Peverell Marley ***Ed*** Rudi Fehr ***Mus*** David Buttolph ***Art*** Stanley Fleischer
Act Vincent Price, Frank Lovejoy, Phyllis Kirk, Carolyn Jones, Paul Picerini, Charles Bronson (Warner)

This remake of Charles Belden's *Mystery of the Wax Museum* (1933) is given the full 3-D treatment in Crane Wilbur's screenplay [from a story by Charles Belden]. Andre de Toth's direction, while uneven, nonetheless gears it to the medium—chairs flying into the audience, cancan dancers pirouetting full into the camera, the barker's ping-pong ball, as a pitchman's prop, likewise shooting out at the audience, the muscular menace springing as if from the theatre into the action. The stereophonic sound further assists in the illusion.

Warners employs the Gunzburg Bros's NaturalVision technique, first introduced in Arch Oboler's *Bwana Devil*. It achieves maximum results with the eerie chases, ghoulish shenanigans in the N.Y. City morgue, the "14th St. Music Hall" (sic!) interior for the cancan, the police headquarters' flashbacks, and the like.

Casting is competent, Vincent Price is capital as the No. 1 menace. Frank Lovejoy is authoritative as the lieutenant. Phyllis Kirk is purty as the ingenue who looks fairly convincingly scared but not so in the scream department—she needs a good, shrill, piercing shrieker as voice stand-in. Paul Picerni is okay as the juvenile and Carolyn Jones makes her moments count as the flighty kid who gets bumped off. Charles Bronson is the No. 2 menace, as the deaf-mute, and Reggie Rymal, as the barker, is also standout.

•

HOUSE ON CARROLL STREET, THE
1988, 100 mins, US Ⓥ ⦿ col
Dir Peter Yates ***Prod*** Peter Yates, Robert F. Colesberry ***Scr*** Walter Bernstein ***Ph*** Michael Ballhaus ***Ed*** Ray Lovejoy ***Mus*** Georges Delerue ***Art*** Stuart Wurtzel
Act Kelly McGillis, Jeff Daniels, Mandy Patinkin, Christopher Rhode, Jessica Tandy, Trey Wilson (Orion)

In this story of a sleuth trailing improbable characters involved in a ridiculous conspiracy, Kelly McGillis is the idealistic and hardly convincing political activist who, in 1951, refuses to answer questions before a Senate hearing on her involvement in a controversial organization.

She takes a job reading to a crochety old blind lady (Jessica Tandy) whose row house garden is adjacent to another brownstone where there are mysterious goings-on. It just so happens the same senator (Mandy Patinkin) who grilled her about her political leanings is in the house shouting as an interpreter translates into German.

McGillis is intrigued. She collects about three clues and figures out Patinkin is smuggling Nazis in by having them take the names of dead Jews.

Jeff Daniels is Ned to McGillis' Nancy Drew. He is the FBI agent who manages to come in at exactly the right moments to save her from whatever perilous predicament she is in at the time—no matter how preposterous.

•

HOUSE ON HAUNTED HILL
1958, 75 mins, US Ⓥ ⦿ b/w
Dir William Castle ***Prod*** William Castle ***Scr*** Robb White ***Ph*** Carl E. Guthrie ***Ed*** Roy Livingston ***Mus*** Von Dexter ***Art*** David Milton
Act Vincent Price, Carol Ohmart, Richard Long, Alan Marshal, Carolyn Craig, Elisha Cook Jr (Allied Artists)

The screenplay is the one about the group of people who promise to spend the night in a haunted house. In this case, it's for pure monetary gain. Vincent Price, owner of the house, is offering $10,000 to anyone who lasts out the night. There is a gimmick in the plot which explains the screams, ghosts, bubbling vats of lye and perambulating skeletons.

Haunted Hill is expertly put together. There is some good humor in the dialog which not only pays off well against the ghostly elements, but provides a release for laughter so it does not explode in the suspense sequences. The characters are interesting and not outlandish, so there is some basis of reality. Director William Castle keeps things moving at a healthy clip.

Robb White and Castle have a new gimmick called "Emergo." This device is an illuminated skeleton mounted on trolley wires, moving out from the side of the screen over the heads of the audience.

•

HOUSE ON HAUNTED HILL
1999, 96 mins, US Ⓥ ⦿ ⌷ col
Dir William Malone ***Prod*** Robert Zemeckis, Joel Silver, Gilbert Adler ***Scr*** Dick Beebe ***Ph*** Rick Bota ***Ed*** Anthony Adler ***Mus*** Don Davis ***Art*** David F. Klassen
Act Geoffrey Rush, Famke Janssen, Taye Diggs, Peter Gallagher, Chris Kattan, Ali Larter (Dark Castle/Warner)

Given the irredeemable cheesiness of the original 1958 *House on Haunted Hill*, it's not exactly a stunning surprise to find the new horror opus is a slicker and scarier piece of work. Of course, even with a better cast and vastly more elaborate special effects, not to mention a couple of nasty new plot twists, it's still nothing but a gussied-up B movie.

In this version, the suavely sardonic host—known as Frederick Loren back when he was played by Vincent Price—is Stephen Price, the multimillionaire owner-designer of frightfully exciting amusement parks. Even more than the name change, Geoffrey Rush's slyly allusive performance comes off as a wink-wink homage to the original pic's star.

Some grisly footage of a Depression-era insane asylum riot is aired more than six decades later on a true-crime TV series. Among the fascinated viewers: Evelyn Price (Famke Janssen), Stephen's shamelessly decadent (and flagrantly unfaithful) trophy wife. Evelyn demands that her husband rent the monolithic art deco edifice atop a spooky oceanside hill so she can throw a birthday party there. He agrees, but replaces her guest list with his own.

Stephen receives the first of several surprises when he greets the invitees: except for Pritchett (Chris Kattan), the last living descendant of the asylum's original owner, he doesn't know any of these people. Evelyn says she didn't invite them, either.

Rush and Janssen set off some amusing sparks while developing a relationship that is less love-hate than hate-revile.

•

HOUSE ON 92ND STREET, THE
1945, 83 mins, US b/w
Dir Henry Hathaway ***Prod*** Louis de Rochemont ***Scr*** Barre Lyndon, Charles G. Booth, John Monks, Jr ***Ph*** Norbert Brodine ***Ed*** Harmon Jones ***Mus*** David Buttolph ***Art*** Lyle Wheeler, Lewis Creber
Act William Eythe, Lloyd Nolan, Signe Hasso, Gene Lockhart, Leo G. Carroll, Mike Evans (20th Century-Fox)

Twentieth-Fox, employing somewhat the technique of *The March of Time* has parlayed the latter with facilities and files of the FBI in arriving at *The House on 92nd Street*. It doesn't matter much whether it's east or west 92nd—the result is an absorbing documentation that's frequently heavily steeped melodrama.

House is comprised of prewar and wartime footage taken by the FBI, and it ties together revelations of the vast Nazi spy system in the United States. Woven into this factual data, along with what the foreword reveals is a thorough cooperation of the FBI in making the film, are the dramatic elements inserted by Hollywood in general and 20th-Fox in particular.

Lloyd Nolan is the FBI inspector in charge of ferreting out the espionage on a secret formula sought by the Nazis; William Eythe is the young German-American sent to Germany by U.S.-located Nazis (and the FBI) to learn espionage and sabotage; Signe Hasso plays a key link to the Nazi system in this country.

1945: Best Original Story (Charles G. Booth)

•

HOUSE ON TELEGRAPH HILL, THE
1951, 93 mins, US b/w
Dir Robert Wise ***Prod*** Robert Bassler ***Scr*** Elick Moll, Frank Partos ***Ph*** Lucien Ballard ***Ed*** Nick De Maggio ***Mus*** Sol Kaplan ***Art*** Lyle Wheeler, John DeCuir
Act Richard Basehart, Valentina Cortese, William Lundigan, Fay Baker, Steven Geray (20th Century-Fox)

This is a slow but interesting melodrama about a psychopathic killer, with San Francisco's quaint hill residential sections as background.

Yarn [from the novel *The Frightened Child* by Dana Lyon] starts a little unexpectedly in the femme concentration camp at Belsen under the Germans. This section is brief, but it's vivid enough to convey the brutalities sustained by Poles and other refugees under the Nazi terror. One Polish woman (Valentina Cortese) sustains herself with the thought that she must someday come out alive.

She gets to America, on a dead woman's identity papers, to find she's pseudo-mother to a boy, heir to a fortune, whose guardian (Richard Basehart) is scheming to acquire the inheritance. Basehart makes a play for Cortese, gets her to marry him, and then plots her death, as he's been plotting that of the child. Rest of film is taken up with his scheming and Cortese's efforts to escape him after she discovers his designs.

Sinister mood, and heightened tensions, are well sustained, and performances by Basehart and Cortese convey the drama convincingly. William Lundigan is okay as the attorney who befriends the woman.

1951: NOMINATION: Best B&W Art Direction

•

HOUSE PARTY

1990, 100 mins, US Ⓥ ⦿ col

Dir Reginald Hudlin ***Prod*** Warrington Hudlin ***Scr*** Reginald Hudlin ***Ph*** Peter Deming ***Ed*** Earl Watson ***Mus*** Marcus Miller ***Art*** Bryan Jones

Act Christopher Reid, Robin Harris, Christopher Martin, Martin Lawrence, Tisha Campbell, A. J. Johnson (New Line)

House Party captures contemporary black teen culture in a way that's fresh, commercial and very catchy. Filmmaking team of Reggie and Warrington Hudlin make a strikingly assured debut feature blending comedy, hip-hop music and dancing in a pic that moves to a kinetic, nonstop rhythm.

Rap duo Kid 'N' Play (Christopher Reid and Christopher Martin) play colleagues in rhyme, trying to get away with throwing a booming house party the night Play's parents are away and Kid is grounded by his Pop (Robin Harris) for getting in a fight at school.

En route to the party, Kid is pursued by the school thugs (rap trio Full Force), and all of them are pursued by the neighborhood cops. Then unwitting Kid becomes an object of desire for both of the young ladies Play is trying to impress (Tisha Campbell and A. J. Johnson).

Writer-director Reggie Hudlin, who expanded *House Party* from a short he made while a student at Harvard, injects pic with the cartoonish style and captivating rhythm of today's rap scene.

•

HOUSE PARTY 2

1991, 94 mins, US Ⓥ ⦿ col

Dir Doug McHenry, George Jackson ***Prod*** Doug McHenry, George Jackson ***Scr*** Rusty Cundieff, Daryl G. Nickens ***Ph*** Francis Kenny ***Ed*** Joel Goodman ***Mus*** Vassal Benford ***Art*** Michelle Minch

Act Christopher Reid, Christopher Martin, Tisha Campbell, Iman, Martin Lawrence, D. Christopher Judge (New Line)

The crowd's the same, but the atmosphere's different in this disappointing follow-up to low-budget hit *House Party*. Absence of filmmakers Reggie and Warrington Hudlin, who've moved on to other things, is keenly felt in a film lacking the original's smarts and cinematic flair.

Debut directors Doug McHenry and George Jackson (*New Jack City* producers) trace the continuing misadventures of rap team Kid 'N' Play (Christopher Reid, Christopher Martin) as they tackle life after high school.

Kid has lost his father (the late Robin Harris) and plans on going to college, but Play is set on pursuing a record contract dangled by a shady promoter (fashion model Iman).

Unfortunately, pic relies heavily on vulgarities and nobrainer plot twists. Whoopi Goldberg cameos as a nightmarish college disciplinarian in a dream scene.

•

HOUSE PARTY 3

1994, 93 mins, US Ⓥ ⦿ col

Dir Eric Meza ***Prod*** Carl Craig ***Scr*** Takashi Bufford ***Ph*** Anghel Decca ***Ed*** Tom Walls ***Mus*** David Allen Jones ***Art*** Simon Dobbin

Act Christopher Reid, Christopher Martin, David Edwards, Angela Means, Tisha Campbell, Betty Lester (New Line)

Lacking the genially goofy and infectious, good-natured tone that marked the initial 1990 entry (and to a lesser extent the second), and hampered by a disjointed structure, *House Party 3* should appeal only to the most ardent fans of the previous pix and Kid 'N' Play's animated TV series.

New installment [based on a story by David Toney and Takashi Bufford] revolves around the engagement of Kid (Christopher Reid) to beautiful Veda (Angela Means), who replaces ex-girlfriend Sydney (Tisha Campbell). Kid's anxieties and fears of matrimony serve as weak glue to a loosely structured comedy composed of uninspired vignettes about Kid's management company, his lifelong friendship with the now threatened Play (Christopher Martin), meeting his disapproving in-laws, and so on.

Pic comes to life only in the last 15 minutes, when everybody shows up at Kid's bachelor party, orchestrated by Immature's three shrewd kids.

•

HOUSESITTER

1992, 100 mins, US Ⓥ ⦿ col

Dir Frank Oz ***Prod*** Brian Grazer ***Scr*** Mark Stein ***Ph*** John A. Alonzo ***Ed*** John Jympson ***Mus*** Miles Goodman ***Art*** Ida Random

Act Steve Martin, Goldie Hawn, Dana Delany, Julie Harris, Donald Moffat, Peter MacNicol (Universal/Imagine)

HouseSitter, a tediously unfunny screwball comedy, is a career misstep for both Steve Martin and Goldie Hawn. Hawn is grating as the kind of giggly flake she played two decades ago on *Laugh-In*, and Martin is more obnoxious than endearing as the architect whose life she invades.

Martin's in love with wholesome Dana Delany, who lives in the quaint New England village of Dobbs Mill, but she deals him an emotional blow by refusing to marry him and move into the new architectural showcase he's built out in the countryside.

Enter Hawn. After they have a one-night stand, she tracks him to the empty house. She moves in, telling everyone in town that she's his new wife, and they believe her.

Frank Oz proves no wizard with his direction of this nonsense [from a screen story by scripter Mark Stein and producer Brian Grazer]. John A. Alonzo's crisp, sunny lensing is about all that keeps the pic bearable to watch.

•

HOWARD . . . A NEW BREED OF HERO

SEE: HOWARD THE DUCK

•

HOWARDS END

1992, 140 mins, UK Ⓥ ⦿ ▭ col

Dir James Ivory ***Prod*** Ismail Merchant ***Scr*** Ruth Prawer Jhabvala ***Ph*** Tony Pierce-Roberts ***Ed*** Andrew Marcus ***Mus*** Richard Robbins ***Art*** Luciana Arrighi

Act Anthony Hopkins, Vanessa Redgrave, Helena Bonham Carter, Emma Thompson, James Wilby, Sam West (Merchant Ivory)

E. M. Forster's *Howards End* makes a most compelling drama, perhaps the best film made during the 30-year partnership of Ismail Merchant and James Ivory. Longtime Merchant Ivory collaborator Ruth Prawer Jhabvala has distilled the 1910 novel into pungent, concise scenes that grab the viewer and maximize the impact of Forster's themes about class differences and the harm caused by repressing true feelings.

Aristocratic matriarch Ruth Wilcox (Vanessa Redgrave) on her deathbed scrawls a note bequeathing her beloved estate Howards End to a recent acquaintance, Margaret Schlegel (Emma Thompson). Redgrave's aristocratic husband Henry (Anthony Hopkins) and daughter Evie (real-life niece Jemma Redgrave) hardly know Thompson and callously destroy the note to selfishly keep the estate in the family even though they don't live there anymore.

A crucial, initially cryptic, subplot involves insurance company clerk Leonard Bast (Sam West) and his wife Jacky (Nicola Duffett). After chance encounters, Schlegel's high-spirited sister Helen (Helena Bonham Carter) begins to look out for West's welfare, resulting in an impromptu tryst and pregnancy.

Hopkins can do no wrong in the acting department, portraying an upper-crust nasty with chilling understatement. In the film's largest role, Thompson is immensely sympathetic. Bonham Carter proves again that she's the best actress today at embodying the look and spirit of period roles. Vanessa Redgrave uses unusual phrasing to create an eerie presence in her successful casting against type as the matriarch in failing health.

1992: Best Actress (Emma Thompson), Adapted Screenplay, Art Direction

NOMINATIONS: Best Picture, Director, Supp. Actress (Vanessa Redgrave), Cinematography, Original Score, Costume Design

•

HOWARD THE DUCK
(UK: *HOWARD . . . A NEW BREED OF HERO*)

1986, 111 mins, US Ⓥ ⦿ col

Dir Willard Huyck ***Prod*** Gloria Katz ***Scr*** Willard Huyck, Gloria Katz ***Ph*** Richard H. Kline ***Ed*** Michael Chandler, Sidney Wolinsky, ***Ed*** Waarschilka, Charles Bornstein ***Mus*** John Barry, Sylvester Levay ***Art*** Peter Jamison

Act Lea Thompson, Jeffrey Jones, Tim Robbins, ***Ed*** Gale, Chip Zien, Paul Guilfoyle (Lucasfilm)

Scripters have taken the cigar-chompin', beer-drinkin' Marvel Comics character [created by Steve Gerber] and turned him into a wide-eyed, cutesy, midget-sized extraterrestrial accidentally blown to Cleveland from a misdirected laser beam.

Howard encounters rock singer Beverly Switzler (Lea Thompson) after a few harrowing minutes on Earth and they become instant friends after he defends her from a couple of menacing punkers.

Pic then lapses into formulaic predictability with nearly an hour of frenetic chase scenes and technically perfect explosions from Industrial Light & Magic as Thompson and Tim Robbins try to thwart the authorities' attempts to capture the duck before he gets a chance to be beamed.

•

HOW GREEN WAS MY VALLEY

1941, 120 mins, US Ⓥ ⦿ b/w

Dir John Ford ***Prod*** Darryl F. Zanuck ***Scr*** Philip Dunne ***Ph*** Arthur Miller ***Ed*** James B. Clark ***Mus*** Alfred Newman ***Art*** Richard Day, Nathan Juran

Act Walter Pidgeon, Maureen O'Hara, Donald Crisp, Roddy McDowall, Barry Fitzgerald, Anna Lee (20th Century-Fox)

Based on a best-selling novel, this saga of Welsh coal-mining life is replete with much human interest, romance, conflict and almost every other human emotion. It's a warm, human story that Richard Llewellyn wrought basically, and the skillful John Ford camera-painting, from a fine scenario by Philip Dunne, needed only expert casting to round out the job.

Donald Crisp and Sara Allgood, as Pa and Ma Morgan, the heads of the Welsh mining family, are an inspired casting. Walter Pidgeon is excellent as the minister; Maureen O'Hara splendid as the object of his unrequited love, who marries the mineowner's son out of pique. And, above all, there is Roddy McDowall. He's winsome, manly, and histrionically proficient in an upright, two-fisted manner.

The transition from book to screen also utilizes the first person singular narrative form, with graphic delineations of how green, indeed, was young Huw (pronounced Hugh) Morgan's valley as he recounts his life from childhood, unfolding the fullness of the Morgans's honest, God-fearing, industrial life span in the Welsh valley.

1941: Best Picture, Director, Supp. Actor (Donald Crisp), B&W Cinematography, B&W Interior Decoration (Richard Day, Nathan Juran)

NOMINATIONS: Best Supp. Actress (Sara Allgood), Screenplay, Editing, Scoring of a Dramatic Picture, Sound

•

HOW I WON THE WAR

1967, 109 mins, UK Ⓥ ⦿ col

Dir Richard Lester ***Prod*** Richard Lester ***Scr*** Charles Wood ***Ph*** David Watkin ***Ed*** John Victor Smith ***Mus*** Ken Thorne ***Art*** Philip Harrison, John Stoll

Act Michael Crawford, John Lennon, Roy Kinnear, Lee Montague, Jack MacGowran, Michael Hordern (United Artists)

Patrick Ryan's novel has been adapted into a screenplay which, as directed by Richard Lester, substitutes motion for emotion, reeling for feeling, and crude slapstick for telling satire. Film opens at a superficial level of fast comedy, but never develops further.

Michael Crawford is top-featured as a gee-whiz British Army officer whose unthinking ineptitude kills off, one by one, all members of his unit. John Lennon, whose billing far exceeds his part, and contribution, plays one of the crew.

Episodic treatment cross-cuts between plot turns, and actual footage of Second World War battles, latter tinted in different hues.

•

HOWLING, THE

1981, 91 mins, Canada Ⓥ ⦿ col

Dir Joe Dante ***Prod*** Michael Finnell, Jack Conrad ***Scr*** John Sayles, Terence H. Winkless ***Ph*** John Hora ***Ed*** Mark Goldblatt, Joe Dante ***Mus*** Pino Donaggio ***Art*** Robert A. Burns

Act Dee Wallace, Patrick Macnee, Dennis Dugan, Christopher Stone, Belinda Balaski, Kevin McCarthy (International/Avco Embassy)

Director Joe Dante's work reflects Alfred Hitchcock's insistence that terror and suspense work best when counterbalanced by a chuckle or two. There are good one-liners throughout, some delivered straight-faced by Kevin McCarthy as an empty-headed TV news producer and Dick Miller as the colorful expert on werewolves. And in a picture like this, John Carradine and Slim Pickens only have to open their mouths to get a laugh from long-time appreciative fans.

But this is supposed to be a horror film, after all [from the novel by Gary Brandner]. And it definitely is in a good old-fashioned way, complete with a girl venturing out alone with a flashlight to investigate a weird noise. In large part the picture works because of the make-up effects created by Rob Bottin.

Dee Wallace, who was exceptional as the lonely woman at the bar in *10*, turns in another solid performance in a much dumber role. As the anchorlady, she has set herself out as bait for psycho Robert Picardo, meeting him in a porno shop where he winds up shot to death by cops. Back at the TV station, Belinda Balaski and Dennis Dugan are still working on the Picardo story, picking up clues that lead them into a study of werewolves.

If the picture has a major problem, it is that Dante uses up his best effects midway through the picture, leaving him with little for the grand surprise that's supposed to come at the end.

•

HOWLING II
YOUR SISTER IS A WEREWOLF
(UK: HOWLING II: STIRBA—WEREWOLF BITCH)

1985, 90 mins, US Ⓥ ⦿ col

Dir Philippe Mora ***Prod*** Steven Lane ***Scr*** Robert Sarno, Gary Brandner ***Ph*** Geoffrey Stephenson ***Ed*** Charles Bernstein ***Mus*** Steve Parsons ***Art*** Karel Vacer

Act Christopher Lee, Annie McEnroe, Reb Brown, Marsha A. Hunt, Sybil Danning, Ferdy Mayne (Hemdale/Granite)

Customers led to expect a werewolf pic in the tradition of Joe Dante's invigorating *The Howling* are in for a disappointment; this is a generally lackluster horror item [based on the novel *Howling II* by Gary Brandner].

Tale opens with the funeral of a femme newsperson; in attendance is Christopher Lee as an expert on werewolves. He advises that the dead woman was such a creature, and is joined by her brother (Reb Brown) and colleague (Annie McEnroe) on a trip to Transylvania to destroy the werewolf queen (Sybil Danning), who is actually Lee's sister.

Despite fancy editing tricks and a few touches of grim humor, suspense is woefully lacking, as Danning is an unformidable villain (she looks as though she's stepped out of a soft-core sex pic) and the plot development is strictly by-the-numbers. Apart from a few moments shot in L.A., pic was lensed in Czechoslovakia, but relatively little is made of the settings. Lee brings a tired authority to the role.

•

HOW STELLA GOT HER GROOVE BACK

1998, 124 mins, US Ⓥ ⦿ col

Dir Kevin Rodney Sullivan ***Prod*** Deborah Schindler ***Scr*** Terry McMillan, Ron Bass ***Ph*** Jeffrey Jur ***Ed*** George Bowers ***Mus*** Michel Colombier ***Art*** Chester Kaczenski

Act Angela Bassett, Taye Diggs, Regina King, Whoopi Goldberg, Suzzanne Douglas, Michael J. Pagan (20th Century-Fox)

Outrageously glossy and sometimes quite funny, this fantasy-driven romance about a gorgeous woman who rediscovers her sexual self in scenic Jamaica is choppy, poorly structured and unconvincing on any number of levels, but still holds strong appeal for the same audience—black women—that made Fox's previous Terry McMillan adaptation, *Waiting to Exhale*, a surprise hit of 1995.

Stella (Angela Bassett) is a stunning, perfectly fit, high-powered 40-year-old San Francisco stockbroker with a well-behaved 11-year-old son. In other words, she's a totally realized woman—except, natch, for her love life.

Stella allows herself a vacation with Delilah (Whoopi Goldberg), who encourages her friend to let herself go, something hesitant Stella begins considering after she meets a strikingly handsome local man with the unlikely name of Winston Shakespeare (Taye Diggs). The only problem is that Winston is just 20 years old—or young enough to be Stella's son.

Goldberg has no end of sassy, sarcastic one-liners that she socks over to maximum effect. So far, not bad. But when Winston suddenly gets a job that will seriously cut into further sack time, Stella abruptly returns to San Francisco, where she amazingly finds herself squeezed out of her job.

Stella returns to Jamaica to discover that Winston is a rich boy. When she is paged to comfort the critically ill Delilah in New York, remainder of the picture lurches awkwardly about as Winston turns up in Manhattan, then heads for Marin County to see if there's a future with Stella.

First-time feature director Kevin Rodney Sullivan, a former teen actor and proficient TV writer-producer-director, buffs the production with countless layers of polish. The dazzling Bassett is a delight to watch throughout, and obligingly plays second banana to Goldberg whenever the latter turns up to steal any and every scene she wants.

•

HOW THE GRINCH STOLE CHRISTMAS

2000, 105 mins, US Ⓥ ⦿ col

Dir Ron Howard ***Prod*** Brian Glazer, Ron Howard ***Scr*** Jeffrey Price, Peter S. Seaman ***Ph*** Don Peterman ***Ed*** Dan Hanley, Mike Hill ***Mus*** James Horner ***Art*** Michael Corenblith

Act Jim Carrey, Jeffrey Tambor, Christine Baranski, Bill Irwin, Molly Shannon, Clint Howard (Imagine/Universal)

This lavishly appointed production reps a sweet and simple tale gone enormously sour. Dr. Seuss's 1957 fable about a grumpy creature with an undersized heart who tries to ruin Christmas for an entire village quickly took its place alongside Dickens's *A Christmas Carol* as a great story of a Christmas-hater converted at the last minute. The illustrated book is distinguished by, among other things, its breezy rhymes and its brevity, qualities that are both lost in this heavy-feeling venture other than in some agreeable turns of phrase gracing Anthony Hopkins's narration.

What this *Grinch* lacks is a sense of style to put across a slight story that demands it, as well as a point of view on its characters, virtually all of whom come off as disagreeable if not insufferable. The town of Whoville seems like a nightmare vision of consumerism run amok, of mercantilism at its most grotesque. It's impossible to tell if this message was fully intended or not, but it is compounded by the piggish look of the inhabitants, whose manner is variously pompous, fawning and simpleminded.

Buried beneath a fuzzy suit and makeup wizard Rick Baker's remarkably flexible Grinch face, Jim Carrey tries out all sorts of intonations, vocal pitches and delivery styles, his tough guy posturing reminding at times of Cagney and his sibilant *S*'s recalling Bogart. His antic gesturing and face-making hit the mark at times, but at other moments seem arbitrary and scattershot. Furthermore, his free-flowing tirades, full of catch-all allusions and references, are pitched for adult appreciation and look destined to sail over the heads of pre-teens.

From the dark corners of the Grinch's cave to the snow-covered streets of Whoville, pic is exceedingly unattractive to look at, and Ron Howard's prosaic direction possesses no stylization to match the extreme design of the set, costumes and makeup.

•

HOW THE WEST WAS WON

1962, 152 mins, US Ⓥ ⦿ ▭ col

Dir Henry Hathaway, John Ford, George Marshall ***Prod*** Bernard Smith ***Scr*** James R. Webb ***Ph*** William H. Daniels, Milton Krasner, Charles Lang Jr, Joseph LaShelle ***Ed*** Harold F. Kress ***Mus*** Alfred Newman ***Art*** George W. Davis, William Ferrari, Addison Hehr

Act James Stewart, Hendry Fonda, Gregory Peck, Debbie Reynolds, Richard Widmark, John Wayne (M-G-M/Cinerama)

It would be hard to imagine a subject which lends itself more strikingly to the wide-screen process than this yarn of the pioneers who opened the American West. It's a story [suggested by the series *How the West Was Won* in *Life* magazine] which naturally puts the spotlight on action and adventure, and the three directors between them have turned in some memorable sequences.

George Marshall [credited with the final segment, "The Railroad"] has the credit for the buffalo stampede, started by the Indians when the railroad was moving out West. This magnificently directed sequence is as vivid as anything ever put on celluloid. Undoubtedly the highlight of Henry Hathaway's contribution ["The Rivers, the Plains, the Outlaws"] is the chase of outlaws who attempt to hold up a train with a load of bullion. John Ford's directorial stint ["The Civil War"] is limited to the Civil War sequences, and though that part does not contain such standout incident, there is the fullest evidence of his high professional standards.

The storyline is developed around the Prescott family, as they start on their adventurous journey out west. Karl Malden and Agnes Moorehead are the parents, and with them are their two daughters, played by Debbie Reynolds and Carroll Baker. They start their journey out West down the Erie Canal, and when James Stewart, a fur trapper, comes on the scene, it's love at first sight for Baker.

Although they've headed in opposite directions, she eventually gets her man. After her parents lose their lives when their raft capsizes in the rapids—and that's another of the highly vivid sequences directed by Hathaway—Reynolds joins a wagon train to continue her journey and tries, in vain, to resist the charms of Gregory Peck, a professional gambler, who is first attracted to her when she's believed to have inherited a gold mine.

Peck gives a suave and polished gloss to his role of the gambler, and Stewart has some fine, if typical, moments in his scenes.

Richard Widmark makes a vital impression as the head man of the construction team building the railroad. John Wayne has a minor part as General Sherman, but he, too, makes the charactor stand out. Spencer Tracy is heard but not seen as the narrator.

1963: Best Original Story & Screenplay, Sound, Editing

NOMINATIONS: Best Picture, Color Cinematography, Color Costume Design, Color Art Direction, Original Music Score

•

HOW TO BE VERY, VERY POPULAR

1955, 89 mins, US ▭ col

Dir Nunnally Johnson ***Prod*** Nunnally Johnson ***Scr*** Nunnally Johnson ***Ph*** Milton Krasner ***Ed*** Louis Loeffler ***Mus*** Cyril J. Mockridge ***Art*** Lyle Wheeler, John DeCuir

Act Betty Grable, Sheree North, Robert Cummings, Charles Coburn, Tommy Noonan, Fred Clark (20th Century-Fox)

The wild and wacky doings dreamed up by Nunnally Johnson are dressed up considerably in eye appeal by having Betty Grable and Sheree North running through most of the footage in costumes appropriate to their striptease profession.

Bearing only a fleeting resemblance to the 1933 stage play *She Loves Me Not* (and a subsequent screen version), these caperings concern two strippers who can identify the bald-headed man who guns down ecdysiast Noel Toy right in the middle of her act in a San Francisco honkytonk. He promises the two dolls the same treatment if they don't get lost. They do, and after a bus ride along the coast take refuge in a fraternity dorm at a college.

•

HOW TO FILL A WILD BIKINI
SEE: HOW TO STUFF A WILD BIKINI

•

HOW TO GET AHEAD IN ADVERTISING

1989, 95 mins, UK Ⓥ ⦿ col

Dir Bruce Robinson ***Prod*** David Wimbury ***Scr*** Bruce Robinson ***Ph*** Peter Hannan ***Ed*** Alan Strachan ***Mus*** David Dundas, Rick Wentworth ***Art*** Michael Pickwood

Act Richard E. Grant, Rachel Ward, Richard Wilson, Jacqueline Tong, John Shrapnel, Susan Wooldridge (Handmade)

As a hotshot go-getter in the British equivalent of Madison Avenue, Richard E. Grant is having a problem coming up with an original campaign for a pimple cream and the pressure is on from the client and his boss (wonderfully droll Richard Wilson).

As dutiful wives do, Rachel Ward tries to assure him that something in his genius will come forward, but he's floundering.

When a small boil breaks out on his own neck, Grant realizes the stress has become too much and it's time to quit the business. It's too late. The boil begins to grow—and starts to talk, giving form to all that's vile and venal in his nature.

The picture would be genuinely hilarious were the subject matter not so overworked.

•

HOW TO MAKE AN AMERICAN QUILT

1995, 116 mins, US Ⓥ ⦿ col

Dir Jocelyn Moorhouse ***Prod*** Sarah Pillsbury, Midge Sanford ***Scr*** Jane Anderson ***Ph*** Janusz Kaminski ***Ed*** Jill Bilock ***Mus*** Thomas Newman ***Art*** Leslie Dilley

Act Winona Ryder, Anne Bancroft, Ellen Burstyn, Kate Nelligan, Jean Simmons, Alfre Woodard (Amblin/Universal)

The patchwork that is *How to Make an American Quilt* is ambitious, poetic, muddled and softer than the inside of a toasted marshmallow.

Finn Dodd (Winona Ryder) is 26 and confused. She's wrestling with a thesis on handicraft and culture and on the cusp of marriage to her carpenter boyfriend, Sam (Dermot Mulroney). Seeking a bit of breathing space, she retreats to the small Northern California town of her youth and the sanctuary of a quilting circle of family and friends.

Jane Anderson's adaptation of the Whitney Otto novel relies heavily on literary conceits, to its undoing. Director

Jocelyn Moorhouse tries valiantly not to make the mess of characters and incidents too ungainly or too symmetrical. It's a significant challenge, considering the weight given flashbacks and the demands of providing each member of the sizable cast his or her moment.

The real dilemma is that this sweet, sincere tale doesn't have a lot to tell that's novel. The fact that several of the flashbacks are set in the 1940s only serves to bolster that sense of déjà vu.

As an acting vehicle, *Quilt* is also a letdown. At best, cast members have a fleeting opportunity to display a glimmer of their talent. Still, several, including Alfre Woodard and Jean Simmons, manage to make their instants vivid.

●

HOW TO MARRY A MILLIONAIRE
1953, 95 mins, US Ⓥ ⦿ ⌑ col
Dir Jean Negulesco ***Prod*** Nunnally Johnson ***Scr*** Nunnally Johnson ***Ph*** Joe MacDonald ***Ed*** Louis Loeffler ***Mus*** Cyril Mockridge ***Art*** Lyle R. Wheeler, Leland Fuller
Act Betty Grable, Marilyn Monroe, Lauren Bacall, David Wayne, Rory Calhoun, Cameron Mitchell (20th Century-Fox)

The script draws for partial source material on two plays, Zoe Akins's *The Greeks Had a Word for It* and *Loco* by Dale Eunson and Katherine Albert. Nunnally Johnson has blended the legiter ingredients with his own material for snappy comedy effect.

The plot has three girls pooling physical and monetary resources for a millionaire man hunt and as the predatory sex game unfolds the chuckles are constant. Each winds up with a man. One is David Wayne, a fugitive from Uncle Sam's Internal Revenue agents whose apartment the girls have leased as a base for the chase. He gets Marilyn Monroe.

Another is Cameron Mitchell, a young tycoon who dresses like a lowly wage slave. He winds up with Lauren Bacall. Third is Rory Calhoun, a poor but honest forest ranger who gains Betty Grable as a fire-watching companion. None is what the femme trio expected to get when the hunt started.

Certain for audience favor is Monroe's blonde with astigmatism who goes through life bumping into things, including men, because she thinks glasses would detract. Also captivating is Grable's Loco, a friendly, cuddly blonde who turns situations to advantage until the great outdoors overwhelms her. As the brains of the trio, Bacall's Schatze is a wise-cracking, hard-shelled gal who gives up millions for love and gets both.

A real standout among the other players is William Powell as the elderly Texas rancher who woos, wins and then gives up Bacall.

[Pic is prefaced by a $5^1/2$]-min. sequence of Alfred Newman conducting his own composition "Street Scene."]

1953: NOMINATION: Best Color Costume Design

●

HOW TO MURDER YOUR WIFE
1965, 118 mins, US Ⓥ col
Dir Richard Quine ***Prod*** George Axelrod ***Scr*** George Axelrod ***Ph*** Harry Stradling ***Ed*** David Wagner ***Mus*** Neal Hefti ***Art*** Richard Sylbert
Act Jack Lemmon, Virna Lisi, Terry-Thomas, Eddie Mayehoff, Claire Trevor, Sidney Blackmer (Murder/United Artists)

George Axelrod's plot deals with the antics of a bachelor cartoonist, played by Jack Lemmon, who has a policy of acting out the escapades of his newsprint sleuth hero to test their credibility before actually committing them to paper. So it is that, awakening one morning to find himself married to an Italian dish who had popped out of a cake at a party the night before and after trying to make a go of this unwanted wedlock, he simulates the "murder" of said spouse one evening by dumping a dummy likeness of her into a building construction site.

When Lemmon's wife, played by Virna Lisi, spots the cartoonist's sketches of his "crime" on his work table she panics and flees. The strip appears in the papers and, unable to explain his wife's whereabouts, Lemmon is arrested for murder and brought to trial.

All of this has moments of fine comic style but, overall, emerges as prefabricated as Lemmon's comic strip character. The comedian's efforts are considerable and consistent but finesse and desire aren't enough to overcome the fact that Axelrod's script doesn't make the most of its potentially antic situations.

●

HOW TO SAVE A MARRIAGE AND RUIN YOUR LIFE
1968, 102 mins, US ⌑ col
Dir Fielder Cook ***Prod*** Stanley Shapiro ***Scr*** Stanley Shapiro ***Ph*** Lee Garmes ***Ed*** Philip Anderson ***Mus*** Michel Legrand ***Art*** Robert Clatworthy
Act Dean Martin, Stella Stevens, Eli Wallach, Anne Jackson, Betty Field, Jack Albertson (Columbia)

How to Save a Marriage and Ruin Your Life is an amusing Stanley Shapiro comedy about divorce and marital infidelity. Made under the title *Band of Gold*, the lush production stars Dean Martin, Stella Stevens, Eli Wallach and Anne Jackson.

Plot complications derive from Wallach's longtime infidelity with Jackson, Katherine Bard demonstrating in her brief footage that Wallach's home life is nothing. Martin confuses Jackson with Stevens, latter assuming his romantic advances are legit, instead of the ruse which Martin intends.

Gag situations include a fake deceased wife, milked for more than it's worth. The situations play better than they can be described; on the other hand, none is especially hard-core hilarity.

●

HOW TO STEAL A DIAMOND IN FOUR UNEASY LESSONS
SEE: THE HOT ROCK

●

HOW TO STEAL A MILLION
1966, 127 mins, US Ⓥ ⦿ ⌑ col
Dir William Wyler ***Prod*** Fred Kohlmar ***Scr*** Harry Kurnitz ***Ph*** Charles Lang ***Ed*** Robert Swink ***Mus*** John Williams ***Art*** Alexandre Trauner
Act Audrey Hepburn, Peter O'Toole, Eli Wallach, Hugh Griffith, Charles Boyer, Marcel Dalio (World Wide/20th Century-Fox)

How to Steal a Million returns William Wyler to the enchanting province of *Roman Holiday*. Lensed in Paris, advantageous use is made of the actual story locale to give unusual visual interest.

Plot centers on a fraud in the art world via forging "masterpieces." Based on [the short story "Venus Rising"] by George Bradshaw, the script twirls around Audrey Hepburn, daughter of a distinguished French family whose father, Hugh Griffith, is a faker of genius. She has given up trying to reform him, continuing only to hope he won't get into too much trouble. Peter O'Toole is a private detective who specializes in solving crimes in the world of art, but whom femme thinks is a burglar after she discovers him in the family home in the middle of the night apparently trying to make off with a canvas.

Griffith is a particular standout as the elegant Parisian oddball with a compulsion to forge the greatest impressionistic painters.

●

HOW TO STUFF A WILD BIKINI
(UK: HOW TO FILL A WILD BIKINI)
1965, 90 mins, US Ⓥ ⌑ col
Dir William Asher ***Prod*** James H. Nicholson, Samuel Z Arkoff ***Scr*** William Asher, Leo Townsend ***Ph*** Floyd Crosby ***Ed*** Fred Feitshans, Eve Newman ***Mus*** Les Baxter
Act Annette Funicello, Dwayne Hickman, Brian Donlevy, Harvey Lembeck, Buster Keaton, Mickey Rooney (American International)

American International's youth contender carries a catchy—if wayout—title, but is a lightweight affair lacking the breeziness and substance of earlier entries. Whole affair seems to have been given the once-over-lightly treatment.

Script by William Asher—who directs—and Leo Townsend is hit and miss, twirling around a mysterious redhead suddenly appearing to fill a bikini which has been floating in midair. Frankie Avalon, on duty in Tahiti with his Naval Reserve unit, enlists the services of Buster Keaton, a witch doctor, to determine whether his girlfriend back home—Annette Funicello—is being true to him. Then there's Mickey Rooney, a fast-talking press agent, trying to promote a motorcycle race with femme stuffed in the wild bikini.

Funicello, usually with a bulk of the footage in these beach romps, obviously is enceinte here, and aside from a couple of songs she has little to do. Avalon, too, has little more than a bit.

●

HOW TO SUCCEED IN BUSINESS WITHOUT REALLY TRYING
1967, 121 mins, US Ⓥ ⦿ ⌑ col
Dir David Swift ***Prod*** David Swift ***Scr*** David Swift ***Ph*** Burnett Guffey ***Ed*** Ralph E. Winters, Allan Jacobs ***Mus*** Nelson Riddle (sup.) ***Art*** Robert Boyle
Act Robert Morse, Michele Lee, Rudy Vallee, Anthony Teague, Maureen Arthur, Sammy Smith (Mirisch)

An entertaining, straightforward filming of the [1961] legituner, featuring many thesps in their stage roles. David Swift's production is generally fast-moving in tracing the rags-to-riches rise of Robert Morse within Rudy Vallee's biz complex. Colorful production values maintain great eye appeal.

Swift, besides producing-directing (and appearing briefly as an elevator operator), adapted the legit book by Abe Burrows, Jack Weinstock and Willie Gilbert, based on Shepherd Mead's novel.

Most of Frank Loesser's literate melodies have been retained, including "I Believe in You," "The Company Way," "Been a Long Day," and "Brotherhood of Man."

Plot concerns window washer Morse who, by superior instinct for advancement and survival, becomes a top exec in Vallee's company in a matter of days. He becomes so big that former well-wishers plot his downfall.

The pixie-like Morse is excellent, with both voice and facial expressions right on target all the time. Michele Lee shows the same uninhibited freshness and charm that made Doris Day a film star.

●

HUANG TUDI
(YELLOW EARTH)
1984, 89 mins, CHINA Ⓥ col
Dir Chen Kaige ***Scr*** Zhang Ziliang ***Ph*** Zhang Yimou ***Ed*** Pei Shuinan ***Mus*** Zhao Jiping ***Art*** He Qun
Act Xue Bai, Wang Xueqi, Tan Tuo, Liu Qiang (Guangxi)

Yellow Earth is the most impressive film from mainland China unveiled so far in the West. Its simple story is told with considerable depth of feeling, allied to classical direction and impeccably composed images. The year is 1939, and China is at war with Japan. However, in the remote north of Shaanxi Province, where peasant farmers live and work in grinding poverty, the war is unknown and far away. Though bordering the swiftly flowing Yellow River, the terrain is rocky, dusty and arid.

Gu Qing (Wang Xueqi), a Communist soldier, is sent from the Army h.q. at Yan'an (depicted as a place of cheerful celebration) to Shaanbei, partly to collect folk songs of the region, partly to influence the locals in favor of Communism. He stays with a poor family—a widower, his 12-year-old daughter, Cui Qiao (Xue Bai), and 10-year-old son, Hanhan (Liu Qiang). At first they are suspicious of the stranger, but gradually he wins them over.

For 32-year-old director Chen Kaige, working out of the small Guangxi Film Studio, this is a quite remarkable achievement. He tells the story (from an essay by Ke Lan) with great subtlety and delicacy, allowing silences, looks and gestures to convey the feelings of his characters. The compositions of cinematographer Zhang Yimou are outstanding.

●

HUCKLEBERRY FINN
1931, 79 mins, US b/w
Dir Norman Taurog ***Scr*** Grover Jones, William Slavens McNutt ***Ph*** David Abel
Act Jackie Coogan, Mitzi Green, Junior Durkin, Jackie Searl, Clara Blandick, Jane Darwell (Paramount)

It's the second Mark Twain story to be done by Paramount, first being *Tom Sawyer*. Same quartet that did Sawyer reunite in Jackie Coogan, Junior Durkin, Mitzi Green and Jackie Searl. The latter two only appear in a minor way at the beginning. That's after the first 1,000 feet or so when Searl, Green and the others practically disappear, a young adolescent (looking like sweet 16) taking up from there on. She's attractive, soft-voiced Charlotte V. Henry for whom Huck Finn changes his mind about women.

Durkin is excellent throughout, overshadowing Coogan, who in spots is permitted to appear and talk in a too adult manner. His early love scene assignments with Mitzi Green drag in an unnatural touch. But for Durkin's able and natural characterization all the way, this might have meant serious injury to the picture.

Norman Taurog's direction is balanced and smooth.

●

HUCKLEBERRY FINN
1939, 88 mins, US Ⓥ b/w
Dir Richard Thorpe ***Prod*** Joseph L. Mankiewicz ***Scr*** Hugo Butler ***Ph*** John F. Seitz ***Ed*** Frank E. Hull ***Mus*** Jerome Moross ***Art*** Cedric Gibbons, Randall Duell
Act Mickey Rooney, Walter Connolly, William Frawley, Rex Ingram, Lynne Carver (M-G-M)

Picture is a fairly close adaptation of the original Mark Twain work, but has not been able to catch the rare and sparkling humor and general sincerity of the author's original. Furthermore, young Rooney seems too mature for his years.

Huckleberry Finn is naturally the dominating character in the story. Taken under the wings of Elisabeth Risdon and

Clara Blandick for upbringing and an education, Mickey can't stand for school and dressing up. When his father appears to demand money from the sisters, Rooney disappears. Meeting Rex Ingram, an escaping slave, pair start down the river on a raft.

Many opportunities for comedy situations are missed.

Rex Ingram stands out boldly in support. He gives an honest and effective characterization of the runaway slave.

•

HUCKSTERS, THE

1947, 110 mins, US Ⓥ b/w

Dir Jack Conway ***Prod*** Arthur Hornblow Jr. ***Scr*** Luther Davis ***Ph*** Harold Rosson ***Ed*** Frank Sullivan ***Mus*** Lennie Hayton ***Art*** Cedric Gibbons, Urie McCleary

Act Clark Gable, Deborah Kerr, Sydney Greenstreet, Adolphe Menjou, Ava Gardner, Keenan Wynn (M-G-M)

Somehow Clark Gable just doesn't quite take hold of the huckster part [from the novel by Frederic Wakeman] in signal manner. Same goes for Deborah Kerr who is a shade prissy for her volatile romantic role. That's as much scripting shortcoming as her personation.

She's cast as a very proper Sutton Place war hero-general's widow, with two children who go for Gable, as she goes, to the extent of a quickie plane flight to his Bel-Air layout where he's cutting a new radio program for Beautee Soap, tycooned by the irascible and tyrannical Evan Llewellyn Evans.

Sydney Greenstreet's portrayal of the soap despot emerges as the performance of the picture, as does Keenan Wynn as the ham ex-burlesque candy butcher gone radio comic. Ava Gardner is thoroughly believable as the on-the-make songstress; Adolphe Menjou is the harassed head of the radio agency which caters to Evans's whilom ways because it's a $10 million account.

Gable looks trim and fit but somehow a shade too mature for the capricious role of the huckster who talks his way into a $35,000 job (and bonus), is a killer with the femmes, and when he has the soap tycoon in his corner throws him over because he sees himself fast getting typed among the ad agency clichés.

•

HUD

1963, 113 mins, US Ⓥ ⦿ ▭ b/w

Dir Martin Ritt ***Prod*** Martin Ritt, Irving Ravetch ***Scr*** Irving Ravetch, Harriet Frank, Jr. ***Ph*** James Wong Howe ***Ed*** Frank Bracht ***Mus*** Elmer Bernstein ***Art*** Hal Pereira, Tambi Larsen

Act Paul Newman, Melvyn Douglas, Patricia Neal, Brandon de Wilde, Whit Bissell, Crahan Denton (Paramount/Salem/Dover)

Hud is a near miss. Where it falls short of the mark is in its failure to filter its meaning and theme lucidly through its characters and story.

The screenplay, adapted from a novel by Larry McMurtry, tells a tale of the modern American West, of its evolution from the land of pioneer ethics, of simple human gratifications unmotivated by greed, to the rangy real estate of shallow, mercenary creatures who have inherited the rugged individualism of the early settlers, but not their souls, their morals or their principles.

The new westerner is Hud (Paul Newman), noxious son of old Homer Bannon (Melvyn Douglas), pioneer Texas Panhandler who detests his offspring with a passion that persists to his bitter end, after he has just witnessed the liquidation of his entire herd of cattle (hoof and mouth disease) and the attempt of his son to have him declared incompetent to run his ranch.

It is in the relationship of father and son that the film slips. It is never clear exactly why the old man harbors such a deep-rooted, irrevocable grudge against his lad.

But the picture has a number of elements of distinction and reward. The four leading performances are excellent. Newman creates a virile, pernicious figure as that ornery title critter. The characteristics of old age are marvelously captured and employed by Douglas. Another fine performance is by Brandon de Wilde as Newman's nephew. Patricia Neal comes through with a rich and powerful performance as the housekeeper assaulted by Newman.

1963: Best Actress (Patricia Neal), Supp. Actor (Melvyn Douglas), B&W Cinematography

NOMINATIONS: Best Director, Actor (Paul Newman), Adapted Screenplay, B&W Art Direction

•

HUDSON HAWK

1991, 95 mins, US Ⓥ ⦿ col

Dir Michael Lehmann ***Prod*** Joel Silver ***Scr*** Steven E. de Souza, Daniel Waters ***Ph*** Dante Spinotti ***Ed*** Chris Lebenzon, Michael Tronick ***Mus*** Michael Kamen, Robert Kraft ***Art*** Jack DeGovia

Act Bruce Willis, Danny Aiello, Andie MacDowell, James Coburn, Richard E. Grant, Sandra Bernhard (Tri-Star/Silver/Ace Bone)

Ever wondered what a Three Stooges short would look like with a $40 million budget? Then meet *Hudson Hawk*, a relentlessly annoying clay duck that crash-lands in a sea of wretched excess and silliness. Those willing to check their brains at the door may find sparse amusement in pic's frenzied pace.

Bruce Willis plays just-released-from-prison cat burglar Hudson Hawk, who's immediately drawn into a plot to steal a bunch of Leonardo Da Vinci artifacts by, among others, a twisted billionaire couple (Richard E. Grant, Sandra Bernhard), a twisted CIA agent (James Coburn) and an agent for the Vatican (Andie MacDowell). Mostly, though, Hawk hangs with his pal Tommy (Danny Aiello), as the two croon old tunes to time their escapades.

Director Michael Lehmann, who made his feature debut with the deliciously subversive *Heathers*, simply seems overwhelmed by the scale and banality of the screenplay [from a story by Willis and Robert Kraft]. Very few of the scenes actually seem connected.

The film primarily gives Willis a chance to toss off poor man's *Moonlighting* one-liners in the midst of utter chaos. Grant, Bernhard and Coburn do produce a few bursts of scatological humor based on the sheer energy of their over-the-top performances.

•

HUDSUCKER PROXY, THE

1994, 111 mins, US Ⓥ ⦿ col

Dir Joel Coen ***Prod*** Ethan Coen ***Scr*** Ethan Coen, Joel Coen, Sam Raimi ***Ph*** Roger Deakins ***Ed*** Thom Noble ***Mus*** Carter Burwell ***Art*** Dennis Gassner

Act Tim Robbins, Jennifer Jason Leigh, Paul Newman, Charles Durning, John Mahoney, Jim True (Warner/Silver)

The Hudsucker Proxy is no doubt one of the most inspired and technically stunning pastiches of old Hollywood pictures ever to come out of the New Hollywood. But a pastiche this $40 million production remains, with a hole in the middle where some emotion and humanity should be. *Hudsucker* plays like a Frank Capra film with a Preston Sturges hero and dialog direction by Howard Hawks.

Norville Barnes (Tim Robbins), straight off the bus from Muncie, IN, lands a mailroom job at the enormous Hudsucker Industries just as the successful company's founder (Charles Durning) hits the pavement after pirouetting out of the boardroom's 44th-floor window.

Norville is installed as the firm's president by the cigar-chomping Machiavellian executive Sidney J. Mussberger (Paul Newman), who intends to forestall a public takeover by lowering investor confidence. But Norville surprises one and all when, after having baffled everyone with the design of his brainstorm—a simple circle on a piece of paper—he pushes through on his invention "for kids," the Hula-Hoop.

Plotwise, it's all been done before. But for connoisseurs of filmmaking style and technique, *Hudsucker* is a source of constant delight and occasional thrills. Throughout, Thom Noble's montage is on a par with just about any classic examples one could cite.

With his gangly frame and appealing pie face, Robbins calls to mind Gary Cooper and Jimmy Stewart, but there's no authentic sweetness or strength. Partly for this reason, no rooting interest develops in the curious romance between Norville and tough-talking reporter Amy. Jennifer Jason Leigh skillfully plays the latter with a Katharine Hepburn accent, Rosalind Russell's rat-a-tat-tat speed in *His Girl Friday* and Barbara Stanwyck attitude in a lot of things, but the character never seems quite right.

•

HUE AND CRY

1947, 82 mins, UK Ⓥ b/w

Dir Charles Crichton ***Prod*** Michael Balcon ***Scr*** T.E.B. Clarke ***Ph*** Douglas Slocombe ***Ed*** Charles Hasse ***Mus*** Georges Auric ***Art*** Norman Arnold

Act Alastair Sim, Valerie White, Jack Warner, Harry Fowler (Ealing)

Principal actor is ex-news vendor Harry Fowler, who has played various cockney parts on the screen, but who fails to make the main character credible. And everything depends on believing in him.

Story revolves around a gang of crooks who use a serial story in *The Trump*, a kids' weekly, as a means of communication. Joe Kirby, an imaginative youngster, spots this, and in spite of discouragement from his boss and an alleged detective, he perseveres, interests his pals, and brings off a great coup when boys of all ages flock to the bomb-ravaged wastes of dockland for a roundup of the criminals.

Director Charles Crichton has been conscientious, but queer camera angles and shadows can add little thrill when the original material lacks it.

•

HUMAN CARGO

1936, 65 mins, US b/w

Dir Allan Dwan ***Prod*** Sol M. Wurtzel ***Scr*** Jefferson Parker, Doris Malloy ***Ph*** Daniel B. Clark ***Ed*** Louis Loeffler ***Art*** Duncan Cramer

Act Claire Trevor, Brian Donlevy, Alan Dinehart, Ralph Morgan, Helen Troy, Rita Hayworth (20th Century-Fox)

Racket exposed and smashed in this instance is that concerned with smuggling aliens into the United States, and then blackmailing them for the rest of their lives under threat of exposure [from the novel *I Will Be Faithful* by Kathleen Shepard]. Smugglers bring 'em in by boat, and if the cops come too close they dump the suckers overboard and thus dispose of the evidence.

Brian Donlevy is the ace reporter and Claire Trevor the society girl who wants to make her own living as a journalist. They work on rival sheets and they do plenty of scrapping, but all the while the audience knows that they're really in love with each other. It's a case of who scoops who up to the finish.

Donlevy is a competent workman and can play a reporter as well as most any other role, but he looks out of place. Trevor makes a nifty society girl-reporter, and too bad they don't come that nifty in real life.

Rita Hayworth as a dancer who's mixed up with the gangsters is a good-looking brunette and not bad on performance.

•

HUMAN COMEDY, THE

1943, 119 mins, US ▭ b/w

Dir Clarence Brown ***Prod*** Clarence Brown ***Scr*** William Saroyan, Howard Estabrook ***Ph*** Harry Stradling ***Ed*** Conrad A. Nervig ***Mus*** Herbert Stothart

Act Mickey Rooney, Frank Morgan, Fay Bainter, Ray Collins, Van Johnson, Donna Reed (M-G-M)

William Saroyan's initial original screenplay is a brilliant sketch of the basic fundamentals of the American way of life, transferred to the screen with exceptional fidelity by director Clarence Brown and cast headed by Mickey Rooney.

Saroyan, after being promoted by Metro to write an original screenplay, reportedly wrote his script in 18 days. Studio heads acclaimed it a "masterpiece," until advised that yarn would consume nearly four hours of running time, and then chilled on the tale.

Figuring the picture would never be produced by Metro, Saroyan returned to northern California and battled out a novel of the yarn. But Clarence Brown, assured he could obtain Mickey Rooney to handle the lead, as originally intended by the writer, decided to get front office approval to make a film version of the Saroyan tale.

Script is episodic, but this is easily overlooked in the entity of the production. Saroyan's original script was lengthy for current picture requirements, and even when it was in rough-cut form for initial sneak review ran about 170 minutes. Editing required that whole chunks and episodes be lifted out, and this was accomplished without detracting from the entertainment factors remaining.

Rooney is the major breadwinner of his little family following departure of his older brother (Van Johnson) into the army service. Rooney, displaying the strongest performance of his career under the Metro banner, shines brilliantly as the boy of Saroyan's tale.

1943: Best Original Story

NOMINATIONS: Best Picture, Director, Actor (Mickey Rooney), B&W Cinematography

•

HUMAN CONDITION, PART I: NO GREATER LOVE, THE

SEE: NINGEN NO JOKEN I-II

•

HUMAN CONDITION, PART II: THE ROAD TO ETERNITY, THE

SEE: NINGEN NO JOKEN III-IV

•

HUMAN CONDITION, PART III: A SOLDIER'S TALE, THE

SEE: NINGEN NO JOKEN V-VI

•

HUMAN DESIRE
1954, 90 mins, US Ⓥ b/w
Dir Fritz Lang ***Prod*** Lewis J. Rachmil ***Scr*** Alfred Hayes ***Ph*** Burnett Guffey ***Ed*** William A. Lyon ***Mus*** Daniele Amfitheatrof ***Art*** Robert Peterson
Act Glenn Ford, Gloria Grahame, Broderick Crawford, Edgar Buchanan, Kathleen Case, Peggy Maley (Columbia)

The audience meets some wretched characters on the railroad in this adaptation of the Emile Zola novel *The Human Beast*. A French picturization of the work was done earlier with heavy accent on psychological study of an alcohol-crazed killer.

Fritz Lang, director, goes overboard in his effort to create mood. Long focusing on locomotive speeding and twisting on the rails is neither entertaining nor essential to the plot.

At the outset the screenplay provides much conversation about the fact that Glenn Ford, who's back on the job as an engineer, had been fighting the war in Korea. There's not much point to this, considering that Ford's background has little bearing on the yarn.

Broderick Crawford, Gloria Grahame and Ford make a brooding, sordid triangle, hopelessly involved. Crawford is utterly frustrated in his effort to please his wife (Grahame) and stay on an even keel with his heartless boss. Grahame is a miserable character, alternately denying and admitting she has given herself to other men. Ford dates Grahame and toys with the idea of murdering her husband.

•

HUMAN FACTOR, THE
1979, 115 mins, UK Ⓥ col
Dir Otto Preminger ***Prod*** Otto Preminger ***Scr*** Tom Stoppard ***Ph*** Mike Molloy ***Ed*** Richard Trevor ***Mus*** Richard Logan, Gary Logan ***Art*** Ken Ryan
Act Richard Attenborough, John Gielgud, Derek Jacobi, Robert Morley, Ann Todd, Nicol Williamson (M-G-M/Preminger)

Graham Greene's low-keyed, highly absorbing 1978 novel of an aging English double agent finding himself trapped into defecting to Moscow and leaving his family behind may have seemed like ideal material for Otto Preminger's style of dispassionate ambiguity, but helmer doesn't seem up to the occasion, bringing little atmosphere or feeling to the delicate ticks of the story.

Nicol Williamson limns the lead role of a Secret Service desk man who, due not to political commitment but loyalty to a friend from his days in Africa, discreetly passes occasional information to the East.

When a leak in his department is discovered and office partner Derek Jacobi, mistakenly identified as the culprit, is eliminated, Williamson feels the walls closing in on him.

•

HUMAN JUNGLE, THE
1954, 82 mins, US b/w
Dir Joseph M. Newman ***Prod*** Hayes Goetz ***Scr*** William Sackheim, Daniel Fuchs ***Ph*** Ellis Carter ***Ed*** Lester Sansom, Samuel Fields ***Mus*** Hans Salter ***Art*** David Milton
Act Gary Merrill, Jan Sterling, Paula Raymond, Emile Meyer, Regis Toomey, Chuck Connors (Allied Artists)

The Human Jungle is a sock big-city police story packed with sex as well as violence and excitement. The politics of a metropolitan police department backdrop an almost documentary narrative which has been imaginatively directed by Joseph M. Newman with punchy overtones. Feature is marked by standout portrayals of a hand-picked cast who insert forceful realism into natural characterizations. Gary Merrill, a police captain who had passed his bar exams and is about to leave the force, is prevailed upon to head the notorious Heights district of the city, where conditions have reached the point that no one is safe. In his revitalization of his department and attempts to solve a murder he meets with opposition both from some of his own men and those above him, but finally cracks the case and whips the district into shape.

Merrill gives true meaning to his part and Jan Sterling belts over the role of a tough blonde who is used as an alibi by Chuck Connors, excellent in his characterizing of the murderer.

•

HUMANOIDS FROM THE DEEP
1980, 80 mins, US Ⓥ ⊙ col
Dir Barbara Peeters ***Prod*** Martin B. Cohen, Hunt Lowry ***Scr*** Frederick James ***Ph*** Daniele Lacambre ***Ed*** Mark Goldblatt ***Mus*** James Horner ***Art*** Michael Erler
Act Doug McClure, Ann Turkel, Vic Morrow, Cindy Weintraub, Anthony Penya, Denise Galik (New World)

With *Humanoids from the Deep*, Roger Corman comes full circle back to his very first film as a producer, *Monster from the Ocean Floor* [1954]. Despite costing 100 times as much, new pic has similar premise and same raison d'etre, that of pocketing a profit from drive-in dates.

Tried-and-true formula of countless sci-fiers of the 1950s is revived as gruesome, amphibious creatures rise from the ocean to stalk and destroy terrified humans. General pattern here has monsters systematically killing the guys and raping the girls.

Given the nonsensical script and fact that considerable footage was added, editor Mark Goldblatt did a good job in making disparate elements at least hang together and play coherently. James Horner's score makes it seem that more is happening than actually takes place.

•

HUMORESQUE
1946, 123 mins, US Ⓥ ⊙ b/w
Dir Jean Negulesco ***Prod*** Jerry Wald ***Scr*** Clifford Odets, Zachary Gold ***Ph*** Ernest Haller ***Ed*** Rudi Fehr ***Mus*** Franz Waxman (cond.) ***Art*** Hugh Reticker
Act Joan Crawford, John Garfield, Oscar Levant, J. Carrol Naish, Joan Chandler, Tom D'Andrea (Warner)

Humoresque combines classical music and drama into a top quality motion picture. A score of unusual excellence gives freshness to standard classics and plays as important a part as Fannie Hurst's familiar story of a young violinist who rises to concert heights from the lower East Side of New York. Technically a remake (it was first produced in 1920), this version is virtually a new story, stripped of any racial connotations as was the case originally. Footage is long, running more than two hours, but does not drag because of the score potency and performance quality.

Integration of music and drama ties the two together so tightly there is never a separation. Some 23 classical numbers are included, plus a number of pop pieces used as background for cafe sequences.

Principal footage goes to John Garfield as the young violinist who, encouraged by his mother's interest, devotes his life to music. He turns in a distinguished, thoroughly believable performance. Adding to the effectiveness is the nigh-flawless fingering and bowing during the violin shots. Joan Crawford's role is an acting part, rather than a typical femme star assignment, and she makes the most of it.

1946: NOMINATION: Best Scoring of a Dramatic Picture

•

HUNCHBACK OF NOTRE DAME, THE
1923, 135 mins, US Ⓥ ⊙ ⊗ b/w
Dir Wallace Worsley ***Scr*** Edward T. Lowe, Perley Poore Sheehan ***Ph*** Robert Newhard, Tony Kornman ***Art*** E.E. Sheeley, Sydney Ullman, Stephen Goosson
Act Lon Chaney, Ernest Torrence, Patsy Ruth Miller, Norman Kerry, Kate Lester, Brandon Hurst (Universal Super-Jewel)

The programmed statistical recordings say this picture cost U over a million; that it called for tons of materials and hundreds of people, all sounding truthful enough (except the cost) after seeing it and the total achieved seems to have been a huge—mistake. *The Hunchback of Notre Dame* [from the novel by Victor Hugo] is a two-hour nightmare. It's murderous, hideous and repulsive.

Lon Chaney's performance entitles him to starring honors. His misshapen figure, from the hump on his back to the dead-eyed eye on his face, cannot stand off his acting nor his acrobatics, nor his general work of excellence throughout this film. And, when the hunchbank dies, you see Jehan (Brandon Hurst) stab him not once, but twice, and in the back or in the hump.

Knives were plentiful in the reign of Louis XI, 1482, in France. So were the tramps, with Clopin (Ernest Torrence) as King of the Bums making the misery stand out.

Patsy Ruth Miller is Esmeralda, a sweetly pretty girl carrying her troubles nicely enough for the heavy work thrust upon her and with the absence of heavy emoting. Norman Kerry is the gallant Phoebus and a lukewarm lover at times.

•

HUNCHBACK OF NOTRE DAME, THE
1939, 115 mins, US Ⓥ ⊙ b/w
Dir William Dieterle ***Prod*** Pandro S. Berman ***Scr*** Sonya Levien ***Ph*** Joseph H. August ***Ed*** William Hamilton, Robert Wise ***Mus*** Alfred Newman ***Art*** Van Nest Polglase, Al Herman
Act Charles Laughton, Cedric Hardwicke, Maureen O'Hara, Thomas Mitchell, Edmond O'Brien, Alan Marshal (RKO)

Parading vivid and gruesome horror, with background of elaborate medieval pageantry and mob scenes, *The Hunchback of Notre Dame* is a super thriller-chiller.

From a strictly critical viewpoint, picture has its shortcomings. The elaborate sets and wide production sweep overshadow to a great extent the detailed dramatic motivation of the Victor Hugo tale. While the background is impressive and eye-filling, it detracts many times from the story, especially in the first half.

Supporting cast is studded with top-notch performers for each role. Cedric Hardwicke is the villainous King's High Justice; Thomas Mitchell is the king of the beggars; Maureen O'Hara (excellent) is the gypsy girl who befriends the hunchback on the pillory and is saved by him later.

Production displays lavish outlay in costs for elaborate sets and thousands of extras for the mob scenes.

1939: NOMINATIONS: Best Score, Sound

•

HUNCHBACK OF NOTRE DAME, THE
1957, 103 mins, US Ⓥ ⊙ ▭ col
Dir Jean Delannoy ***Prod*** Robert Hakim, Raymond Hakim ***Scr*** Jean Aurenche, Jacques Prevert ***Ph*** Michel Kelber ***Ed*** Henri Taverna ***Mus*** Georges Auric ***Art*** Rene Renoux
Act Gina Lollobrigida, Anthony Quinn, Jean Danet, Alain Cuny, Maurice Sarfati, Danielle Dumont (Allied Artists)

This version of the Victor Hugo classic, although beautifully photographed and extravagantly produced, is ponderous, often dull and far overlength.

Gina Lollobrigida is co-starred with Anthony Quinn, who plays the Quasimodo role previously enacted by Lon Chaney and Charles Laughton. Producers seem more inclined to offer spectacle than concentrate on pointing up story line with any degree of freshness.

Lollobrigida appears to be somewhat miscast as a naive gypsy girl of 15th-century Paris, but occasionally displays flashes of spirit. Quinn, as the hunchbacked bellringer of Notre Dame who saves the gypsy girl from hanging and hides her within the sanctuary of the cathedral, where he becomes her devoted slave, gives a well-etched impression of the difficult role. His makeup is not as extreme as either of the two previous characterizations.

•

HUNCHBACK OF NOTRE DAME, THE
1996, 86 mins, US Ⓥ ⊙ col
Dir Gary Trousdale, Kirk Wise ***Prod*** Don Hahn ***Scr*** Tab Murphy, Irene Mecchi, Bob Tzudiker, Noni White/Jonathan Roberts ***Ed*** Ellen Keneshea ***Mus*** Alan Menken ***Art*** David Goetz (Walt Disney)

It's probably no surprise that the deaf, one-eyed, misshapen monster imagined 165 years ago by Victor Hugo would resurface in the Disney version as a gee-whiz, cuddly creature with the innocence of E. T. and the loyalty of Lassie. On the other hand, it is surprising just how dark and horrific Disney's visually astonishing 34th animated feature, *The Hunchback of Notre Dame*, is for most of its 86 minutes.

With a score by composer Alan Menken and lyricist Stephen Schwartz—the team behind *Pocahontas*—that lacks, on first hearing, any breakout numbers, Hunchback doesn't play or sound like the kind of blockbuster Disney is used to. Nevertheless, the dazzling technical achievements reassert the style set by *Beauty and the Beast*, *The Lion King* and *Pocahontas*, particularly with respect to depth of field.

Purists will have a field day with *Hunchback*, much as they had with *Pocahontas*. Scripters have simplified the novel's sprawling narrative and complex characters; centered the action on the Gypsy-born hunchback Quasimodo (voiced with an attractive, childlike innocence by Tom Hulce), the dashing heroic captain Phoebus (brought to sonorous life by Kevin Kline), and the beautiful Gypsy dancer with whom both men fall in love, the green-eyed Esmeralda (gorgeously voiced by Demi Moore, with Heidi Mollenhauer doing the singing); and given the story a ludicrous ending.

They've also given Quasi, as he's called, the inevitable Disney sidekicks, in this case three wisecracking gargoyles voiced by Jason Alexander, Charles Kimbrough and the late Mary Wickes.

Like *Pocahontas*, the source material has been subordinated to the Disney theme, in this case, tolerance for people who are different. And yet such soft-pedaling can't be said to completely displace the story.

1996: NOMINATION: Best Original Musical Score

•

HUNGER
SEE: SULT

•

HUNGER, THE
1983, 97 mins, US Ⓥ ⊙ ▭ col
Dir Tony Scott ***Prod*** Richard A. Shepherd ***Scr*** Ivan Davis, Michael Thomas ***Ph*** Stephen Goldblatt ***Ed*** Pamela Power ***Mus*** Michel Rubini, Denny Jaeger ***Art*** Brian Morris
Act Catherine Deneuve, David Bowie, Susan Sarandon, Cliff De Young, Beth Ehlers, Dan Hedaya (M-G-M/United Artists)

Like so many other films from British commercials directors, *The Hunger* [from the novel by Whitley Strieber] is all visual and aural flash, although this modern vampire story looks so great, as do its three principal performers, and is so bizarre that it possesses a certain perverse appeal.

Opening sequence provides viewers with a pretty good idea of what's in store. Catherine Deneuve and David Bowie pick up a couple of punky rock 'n' rollers. Deneuve and Bowie commit a double murder in their elegantly appointed New York apartment, and the prevailing motif of sex mixed with bloody death is established.

Although Deneuve and Bowie privately vow to stay with one another forever, Bowie soon notices himself growing rapidly older and visits author-doctor Susan Sarandon, who is preoccupied with the problem of accelerated aging. Shunned by her, Bowie deteriorates quickly and Deneuve buries him in a box in her attic next to her previous lovers.

Distraught over her mistreatment of Bowie, Sarandon begins visiting Deneuve, and a provative highlight is their seduction and lovemaking scene.

In his feature debut, director Tony Scott, brother of Ridley, exhibits the same penchant for eleborate art direction, minimal, humorless dialog and shooting in smoky rooms.

•

HUNG FAN KUI
(RUMBLE IN THE BRONX)

1995, 105 mins, Hong Kong Ⓥ ⊙ ▭ col

Dir Stanley Tong ***Prod*** Leonard K. C. Ho ***Scr*** Edward Tang ***Ph*** Jingle Ma ***Ed*** Peter Cheung ***Mus*** [uncredited] ***Art*** Oliver Wong

Act Jackie Chan, Anita Mui, Bill Tung, Francoise Yip, Bai Cheun-wai, Marc Akerstream (Golden Harvest)

The bod's still in shape, and the looks are still boyish, but 40-something Jackie Chan takes it a tad more gently in *Rumble in the Bronx*, an enjoyable comedy-actioner whose ooh-aah moments are mostly confined to the last few reels. This N.Y.-set update of Bruce Lee's *Return of the Dragon* lacks the sheer oomph of Chan's best pics.

Chan is a H.K. cop, Keung, who comes to N.Y. for the wedding of Uncle Bill (vet Bill Tung), who's selling his business after 20 years. The store is bought by the glamorous Elaine (singer-actress Anita Mui), who can't wait to get rid of it when a gang of local bikers gets heavy after she refuses to pay protection money.

In between the various set-tos and chases between Chan and the gang (including one in which he's a target in a bottle-throwing contest), there's a subplot about some stolen diamonds ending up in the wheelchair of a crippled Chinese kid, Danny, whom Chan befriends.

Pic climaxes with visual showpieces (like the supermarket being demolished and a Hovercraft run amok on the streets) that lack a human dimension, though Chan wins his usual stripes for death-defying stunts (one of which put him temporarily in a wheelchair).

Gothamites will be surprised to see their city surrounded by beautiful mountains and bays that look uncommonly like Vancouver. (Aside from a few establishing shots, whole pic was shot in B.C.) [Film was released in the U.S. in a 91-min. version, re-edited by the U.S. distributor.]

•

HUNTED, THE

1995, 110 mins, US Ⓥ ⊙ col

Dir J.F. Lawton ***Prod*** John Davis, Gary W. Goldstein ***Scr*** J.F. Lawton ***Ph*** Jack Conroy ***Ed*** Robert A. Ferretti, Eric Strand ***Mus*** Motofumi Yamaguchi ***Art*** Phil Dagort

Act Christopher Lambert, John Lone, Joan Chen, Yoshio Harada, Yoko Shimada, Mari Natsuki (Bregman-Baer/Davis)

Despite its English-language trappings, this grisly yet often laughable actioner most closely resembles the low budget martial arts movies that used to air, badly dubbed, on independent TV stations. If nothing else, *The Hunted* seems destined for eventual immortality on *Mystery Science Theatre 3000*, with its pretentious dialogue (by *Under Siege* writer J. F. Lawton, also making his major studio directing debut) and campy performers ripe for such skewering.

Christopher Lambert stars as a New York businessman in Japan who happens to pick up, bed, and then witness the murder of a mysterious woman (Joan Chen) by a ninja assassin, Kinjo (John Lone). Wounded and now the target of the ninja cult, Lambert's character finds a benefactor in a samurai (Yoshio Harada) who, it turns out, wants to use the befuddled Westerner as bait to settle a centuries-old feud.

Life is cheap in *The Hunted*, with the ninjas willing to kill a train-load of passengers, one by one, trying to get at this one guy. Lambert isn't terribly convincing as either businessman or reluctant hero, while Lone hams it up mercilessly as a murderer with a conscience. Only Chen, in a brief yet radiant role, escapes relatively unscathed.

Tech credits are passable, with Vancouver at times standing in for the Japanese locations.

•

HUNTER, THE

1980, 117 mins, US Ⓥ ⊙ col

Dir Buzz Kulik ***Prod*** Mort Engelberg ***Scr*** Ted Leighton, Peter Hyams ***Ph*** Fred J. Koenekamp ***Ed*** Robert Wolfe ***Mus*** Michel Legrand ***Art*** Ron Hobbs

Act Steve McQueen, Eli Wallach, Kathryn Harrold, Ben Johnson (Paramount/Rastar/Mort Engelberg)

Fact that the overlong pic is based on adventures of a modern-day bounty hunter may have hampered filmmakers' imagination, as attempt to render contradictions of real-life Ralph "Papa" Thorson, who's into classical music and astrology as well as hauling in fugitives from justice, has made for an annoyingly unrealized and childish onscreen character.

Steve McQueen may have felt that the time had come to revise his persona a bit, but what's involved here is desecration. Given star's rep since *Bullitt* as a terrific driver, someone thought it might be cute to make him a lousy one here, but seeing him crash stupidly into car after car runs the gag into the ground. *The Hunter* [based on the book by Christopher Keane] is a Western in disguise.

Only sequence which remotely delivers the goods has McQueen chasing a gun-toting maniac in Chicago. Pic's finale, which has star fainting when pregnant g.f. Kathryn Harrold gives birth, merely puts capper on overall misconception.

•

HUNT FOR RED OCTOBER, THE

1990, 137 mins, US Ⓥ ⊙ ▭ col

Dir John McTiernan ***Prod*** Mace Neufeld ***Scr*** Larry Ferguson, Donald Stewart, [John Milius] ***Ph*** Jan De Bont ***Ed*** Dennis Virkler, John Wright ***Mus*** Basil Poledouris ***Art*** Terence Marsh

Act Sean Connery, Alec Baldwin, Scott Glenn, Sam Neill, James Earl Jones, Joss Ackland (Paramount)

The Hunt for Red October is a terrific adventure yarn. Tom Clancy's 1984 Cold War thriller has been thoughtfully adapted to reflect the mellowing in the U.S.-Soviet relationship.

Sean Connery is splendid as the renegade Soviet nuclear sub captain pursued by CIA analyst Alec Baldwin and the fleets of both superpowers as he heads for the coast of Maine. The filmmakers have wisely opted to keep the story set in 1984—"shortly before Gorbachev came to power," as the opening title puts it.

Looking magnificent in his captain's uniform and white beard, Connery scores as the Lithuanian Marko Ramius, a cold-blooded killer and a meditator on Hindu scripture.

Baldwin's intelligent and likable performance makes his Walter Mittyish character come alive. He's combating not only the bulk of the Soviet fleet but also the reflexive anti-Communist mentality of most pursuing on the U.S. side—not including his wise and avuncular CIA superior James Earl Jones.

The Industrial Light & Magic special visual effects unit does yeoman work in staging the action with cliffhanger intensity.

1990: Best Sound Effects Editing

NOMINATIONS: Best Editing, Sound

•

HUNTING PARTY, THE

1971, 108 mins, UK Ⓥ col

Dir Don Medford ***Prod*** Lou Morheim ***Scr*** William Norton, Gilbert Alexander, Lou Morheim ***Ph*** Cecilio Paniagua ***Ed*** Tom Rolf ***Mus*** Riz Ortolani ***Art*** Enrique Alarcon

Act Oliver Reed, Candice Bergen, Gene Hackman, Simon Oakland, Mitchell Ryan, L.Q. Jones (United Artists)

It isn't as hard to believe that excellent actors Oliver Reed and Gene Hackman would accept roles like those they are given in *The Hunting Party* because they were undoubtedly well paid (indeed, overpaid, considering the performances they give). But to find such fine supporting players as Mitchell Ryan, Simon Oakland and Dean Selmier in this minor effort is really surprising.

Basically, Reed (who's illiterate) and his gang, kidnap a teacher (Candice Bergen) who turns out to be the wife of the local cattle baron (Gene Hackman), who is out on a hunting party with some other millionaire friends. When he hears the news, Hackman starts a search for the gang, armed with new high-power rifles capable of killing from 800 yards. One by one the gang is picked off from a safe distance until the eventual showdown with only Hackman trailing Reed and Bergen (by now in love with the outlaw, of course) onto a desert.

Seldom has so much fake blood been splattered for so little reason.

•

HUOZHE
(TO LIVE)

1994, 125 mins, Hong Kong Ⓥ col

Dir Zhang Yimou ***Prod*** Chiu Fu-sheng ***Scr*** Yu Hua, Lu Wei ***Ph*** Lu Yue ***Ed*** Du Yuan ***Mus*** Zhao Jiping ***Art*** Cao Jiuping

Act Ge You, Gong Li, Niu Ben, Guo Tao, Jiang Wu, Liu Tianchi (Era)

A family drama set across 30 years of modern Chinese history, Zhang Yimou's *To Live* is a well-crafted but in no way earth-shaking entry in the helmer's oeuvre, topped by finely judged perfs by Gong Li and Ge You as an average couple tossed like corks in a story by civil war, revolution and political strife.

Story, pruned down from a long novel by new wave writer Yu Hua, opens in the '40s in a small village in northern China. Fugui (Ge), eldest son of a prominent family, is hooked on gambling. Wife Jiazhen (Gong) leaves him when Fugui loses the ancestral home to a local smoothie, but she returns.

In the second of the movie's five segments, Fugui is a soldier in the Nationalist (KMT) army fighting the Communists in the late-'40s civil war alongside his buddy Chunsheng (Guo Tao). Postwar, Fugui returns to his now-communized native village. Next jump is to 1958 and the so-called Great Leap Forward, with the whole population mobilized to supply iron for mass industrialization.

Flash forward to 1966, start of the Cultural Revolution, and town chief (Niu Ben) introduces a prospective hus band to Fugui's grown daughter (Liu Tianchi, strong in a wordless part). After the 90-minute mark, the movie starts to develop true clout with the news that Fugui's buddy Chunsheng has been branded a "capitalist roadster."

By adopting a relatively cool photographic look and distanced shooting style, Zhang rarely develops a head of steam to roll the story over the political and social changes that impinge on the characters. For the first time in a Zhang movie, Gong plays second fiddle to a strong, accomplished actor.

•

HURRICANE

1979, 119 mins, US Ⓥ col

Dir Jan Troell ***Prod*** Dino De Laurentiis ***Scr*** Lorenzo Semple, Jr. ***Ph*** Sven Nykvist ***Ed*** Sam O'Steen ***Mus*** Nino Rota ***Art*** Danilo Donati

Act Jason Robards, Mia Farrow, Max von Sydow, Trevor Howard, Dayton Ka'ne, Timothy Bottoms (Paramount/De Laurentiis)

The storm blows fiercely but the love story doesn't match its power in *Hurricane*. Dino De Laurentiis's epic reportedly delivered with a $22 million negative cost.

Charles Nordhoff and James Norman Hall's novel *The Hurricane* was filmed relatively faithfully in 1937 by John Ford.

The context and conflicts in the new production have been altered significantly. Script sets the tale in Eastern Samoa, circa 1920, with Jason Robards lording it over the natives on behalf of the U.S. navy. The female love interest is now a white woman, with Mia Farrow sailing in from Boston to see her commander father, but gradually becoming involved with the young chieftain of a nearby island (Dayton Ka'ne).

The hurricane itself, which runs 25 minutes and was created entirely on location in Bora Bora by a special effects team led by Glen Robinson, who performed the same function on the 1937 production, Aldo Puccini and Joe Day, is impressive enough.

•

HURRICANE, THE

1937, 110 mins, US Ⓥ ⊙ b/w

Dir John Ford ***Prod*** Samuel Goldwyn ***Scr*** Dudley Nichols ***Ph*** Bert Glennon ***Ed*** Lloyd Nosler ***Mus*** Alfred Newman (dir.) ***Art*** Richard Day, Alexander Golitzen

Act Dorothy Lamour, Jon Hall, Mary Astor, C. Aubrey Smith, Thomas Mitchell, Raymond Massey (Goldwyn)

Turned out on a broad canvas, *The Hurricane* is a scenically pretentious and colorful spectacle which has as its climax a hurricane sequence that is compellingly realistic. The authors of the novel, Charles Nordhoff and James Norman Hall, also wrote the story of *Mutiny on the Bounty*.

The force of the story [adapted by Oliver H. P. Garrett] does not stop with the hurricane triumph nor the brutality of prison officers, pictured as worse than ever accredited to Devil's Island. Neither does it stop with the successful dramatic escape of the romantic lead (Jon

Hall) amidst frightful odds. There is also a highly emotional love story woven around Hall and Dorothy Lamour, latter playing the native girl who marries him as the picture opens.

The big blow is reputed to cost $300,000. That's not unbelievable. It is understood the total cost of the picture ran to $1.75 million. Performances are specially good from Hall down. A finely turned character is that of the governor, another Javert (*Les Miserables*), done capitally and forcefully by Raymond Massey.

1937: Best Sound Recording

NOMINATION: Best Score

•

HURRICANE, THE

1999, 125 mins, US Ⓥ ⦿ col

Dir Norman Jewison ***Prod*** Armyan Bernstein, John Ketcham, Norman Jewison ***Scr*** Armyan Bernstein, Dan Gordon ***Ph*** Roger Deakins ***Ed*** Stephen Rivkin ***Mus*** Christopher Young ***Art*** Philip Rosenberg

Act Denzel Washington, Vicellous Reon Shannon, Deborah Kara Unger, Liev Schreiber, John Hannah, Dan Hedaya (Azoff-Langlais/Beacon/Universal)

It's almost impossible to imagine *The Hurricane*, Norman Jewison's heartfelt political drama, without Denzel Washington in the lead role of Rubin "Hurricane" Carter, the black boxer who was wrongly convicted of triple murder and sent to prison, where he spent 19 years before being exonerated and released in 1985. In his most zealous and fully realized performance since *Malcolm X*, Washington elevates the earnest, occasionally simplistic narrative to the level of a genuinely touching moral exposé.

However, the script [based on the books *The Sixteenth Round* by Rubin Carter and *Lazarus and the Hurricane* by Sam Chaiton and Terry Swinton] skips several crucial chapters in its hero's life and consciously takes some liberties with the facts.

Brief flashbacks re-create the 1966 murder, in which three people are killed by two gunmen in the Lafayette Bar in Patterson, NJ. This murder leads to the arrest of Carter and a young fan, John Artis (Garland Whitt), who just happen to be in the wrong place at the wrong time. Cut to Toronto, seven years later, when a black youth named Lesra (Vicellous Reon Shannon) picks up Carter's autobiography for a quarter and finds direction and purpose for the first time in his life. A product of poor, illiterate parents, Lesra has been "adopted" by three Canadian students, Terry Swinton (John Hannah), Lisa Peters (Deborah Kara Unger) and Sam Chaiton (Liev Schreiber). Convinced of Carter's innocence, Lesra soon enlists his social-activist guardians to mount a full-time campaign for his release.

While the central figure dominates, all the thesps do well in the same emotionally truthful vein.

1999: NOMINATION: Best Actor (Denzel Washington)

•

HURRY SUNDOWN

1967, 146 mins, US ▭ col

Dir Otto Preminger ***Prod*** Otto Preminger ***Scr*** Thomas C. Ryan, Horton Foote ***Ph*** Milton Krasner, Loyal Griggs ***Ed*** Louis Loeffler, James D. Wells ***Mus*** Hugo Montenegro ***Art*** Gene Callahan

Act Michael Caine, Jane Fonda, John Phillip Law, Diahann Carroll, Faye Dunaway, Burgess Meredith (Paramount/Sigma)

In *Hurry Sundown*, based on the novel [by K. B. Gilden], producer-director Otto Preminger has created an outstanding, tasteful but hard-hitting, and handsomely produced film about racial conflict in Georgia circa 1945. Told with a depth and frankness, the story develops its theme in a welcome, straightforward way that is neither propaganda nor mere exploitation material. Cast with many younger players, all of whom deliver fine performances.

Michael Caine leads the stars, and delivers an excellent performance as the white social climber managing the Georgia land holdings of wife Jane Fonda.

Two tracts block Caine's plans, those of distant relative John Phillip Law and Negro Robert Hooks, both just-returned war vets.

•

HUSBANDS
A COMEDY ABOUT LIFE, DEATH & FREEDOM

1970, 154 mins, US col

Dir John Cassavetes ***Prod*** Al Ruban, Sam Shaw ***Scr*** John Cassavetes ***Ph*** Victor Kemper ***Ed*** Peter Tanner

Act Ben Gazzara, Peter Falk, John Cassavetes, Jenny Runacre, Jenny Lee Wright, Noelle Kao (Columbia)

Appalled and horrified by the death of their best friend, three middle-class, not-quite-middle-aged family men explode and ricochet off on a marathon New York-to-London binge.

Director-writer-actor John Cassavetes, Ben Gazzara and Peter Falk are the "husbands," who, in the face of death, revert to drunken, giggling, horseplaying adolescence, and, with a stunningly talented supporting cast, create and improvise a memorably touching, human and very funny film.

Fleeing from the beer foam and grime of a lower New York bar in a sudden panicked flight to London, Cassavetes, Falk and Gazzara are three of the uncoolest married men to ever go on the make.

In a superb cast, Jenny Runacre, a tall lovely blond English girl gives a touching performance as Cassavetes' neurotic pick-up.

•

HUSBANDS AND WIVES

1992, 107 mins, US Ⓥ ⦿ col

Dir Woody Allen ***Prod*** Robert Greenhut ***Scr*** Woody Allen ***Ph*** Carlo Di Palma ***Ed*** Susan E. Morse ***Mus*** [various] ***Art*** Santo Loquasto

Act Woody Allen, Judy Davis, Mia Farrow, Sydney Pollack, Juliette Lewis, Liam Neeson (Tri-Star)

Husbands and Wives is major Woody. This sometimes comic drama stands with *Manhattan* and *Hannah and Her Sisters* as a richly satisfying ensemble piece about N.Y. neurotics falling in and out of love. Jarring opening scene gives a strong indication of things to come.

Arriving to dine with their best friends, Allen and Mia Farrow, married couple Sydney Pollack and Judy Davis announce almost matter-of-factly that they're separating. It quickly becomes apparent Allen and Farrow have their own troubles. They've never agreed upon having a child: She's for it, he's not. College English instructor Allen takes a special interest in a talented and provocative student (Juliette Lewis) but steers clear of sexual involvement.

Pollack takes up with knockout New Age bimbo Lysette Anthony. Infuriated with how quickly Pollack has replaced her, the intense Davis goes out with Irish dreamboat Liam Neeson. When Neeson goes for Davis in a big way, Farrow becomes distraught, realizing the depth of her own feelings for him.

Allen creates a full-bodied gallery of hard-headed urbanites who more often than not operate out of self-destructive impulses. This is definitely his edgiest, rawest work in a good while.

While his subjects have remained much the same, Allen's style has undergone a radical change here. Carlo Di Palma's lensing appears to be almost entirely hand-held, creating a look somewhere between early French New Wave and *cinema verite*. Acting is of a very high caliber across the board, but Davis, in a very meaty part, is incandescent, revealing a whole new side to her onscreen personality.

1992: NOMINATIONS: Best Supp. Actress (Judy Davis), Original Screenplay

•

HUSH . . . HUSH, SWEET CHARLOTTE

1964, 134 mins, US Ⓥ b/w

Dir Robert Aldrich ***Prod*** Robert Aldrich ***Scr*** Henry Farrell, Lukas Heller ***Ph*** Joseph Biroc ***Ed*** Michael Luciano ***Mus*** Frank DeVol ***Art*** William Glasgow

Act Bette Davis, Olivia de Havilland, Joseph Cotten, Agnes Moorehead, Cecil Kellaway, Mary Astor (Associates & Aldrich/20th Century-Fox)

Robert Aldrich's followup (but no relation) to *What Ever Happened to Baby Jane?* is a shocker. Bette Davis again stars, with Olivia de Havilland returning to the screen in the role which Joan Crawford started but due to continued illness had to abandon.

Davis lives in the reflection of a dreadful past, the macabre murder and mutilation of her married lover hanging over her as she frequently confuses the past with the present as her mental balance is threatened. De Havilland, as her cousin, lives very much for the present—and future—as she attempts to soothe and rationalize with the deeply emotional mistress of the house.

Based upon a story by Henry Farrell, who also authored *Baby Jane*, screenplay by Farrell and Lukas Heller (latter scripted Jane) opens in 1927 in the Louisiana plantation house of Davis's father, who warns a neighboring married man to break off all romantic relations with his daughter. The main story swings to the present, again in the mansion where Davis lives alone with her memories, which threaten to destroy her.

Davis's portrayal is reminiscent of Jane in its emotional overtones, in her style of characterization of the near-crazed former Southern belle, aided by haggard makeup and outlandish attire. It is an outgoing performance, and she plays it to the limit. De Havilland, on the other hand, is far more restrained but none the less effective dramatically in her offbeat role.

1964: NOMINATIONS: Best Supp. Actress (Agnes Moorehead), B&W Cinematography, B&W Costume Design, B&W Art Direction, Editing, Original Music Score, Song ("Hush . . . Hush, Sweet Charlotte")

•

HUSSARD SUR LE TOIT, LE
(THE HORSEMAN ON THE ROOF)

1995, 135 mins, France Ⓥ ⦿ ▭ col

Dir Jean-Paul Rappeneau ***Prod*** Rene Cleitman ***Scr*** Jean-Paul Rappeneau, Nina Companeez, Jean-Claude Carriere, Thierry Arbogast ***Ed*** Noelle Boisson ***Mus*** Jean-Claude Petit ***Art*** Jacques Rouxel, Christian Marti

Act Olivier Martinez, Juliette Binoche, Isabelle Carre, Francois Cluzet, Jean Yanne, Gerard Depardieu (Hachette Premiere)

Six years after directing Gerard Depardieu to nosy Gascon glory in *Cyrano de Bergerac*, Jean Paul Rappeneau returns with an oddly paced journey through a cholera-ridden Provence of the early 19th century. The $35 million *Roof*—much ballyhooed by producer Hachette for breaking local budget records—delivers an admirable re-creation of the Romantic era. But the pic, like its many cholera victims, goes from vivacious to lifeless.

The world of *Roof* is that of French literary giant Jean Giono, from whose home in the Provencal town of Manosque the atmospheric 1951 novel emerged to enthrall French readers. Giono's Provence is harsh and wild, almost like the Far West.

Pic begins with a bang as Angelo (Olivier Martinez), an Italian officer and mama's boy-turned-revolutionary against his country's Hapsburg overlords, bolts from his hideout in Aix-en-Provence of 1832. His Austrian would-be assassins in hot pursuit, Angelo gallops inland to warn his fellow Italian exiles of the covert death squad at large. He eventually steals into the closed town of Manosque, where he's fed by a mysterious noblewoman (Juliette Binoche), who keeps the plot moving by stirring curiosity in Angelo's heart.

Remainder of pic follows the two as they effortlessly—much too effortlessly—elude or outwit all comers in their picturesque meanderings. Secondary characters rise and fall by the wayside. Binoche's restrained, decorous perf as a restless noblewoman is utterly convincing. As dressed by costume designer Franca Squarciapino, Binoche looks and moves the part of a Romantic heroine, even if her traveling companion does not live up to his Byronic possibilities. Handsome young Martinez struggles with his unforgiving part throughout the film's two hours and change.

•

HUSTLE

1975, 120 mins, US Ⓥ col

Dir Robert Aldrich ***Prod*** Robert Aldrich ***Scr*** Steve Shagan ***Ph*** Joseph Biroc ***Ed*** Michael Luciano ***Mus*** Frank DeVol ***Art*** Hilyard Brown

Act Burt Reynolds, Catherine Deneuve, Ben Johnson, Paul Winfield, Eileen Brennan, Eddie Albert (Paramount/RoBurt)

Robert Aldrich's sharp-looking film reunites him with Burt Reynolds, starring here as a hardening detective trying to short circuit the solution of a femme teenager's dope suicide because the trail may lead to Eddie Albert, a noted lawyer with many uptown and downtown connections.

Reynolds is torn between his duty and his personal attraction-resistance to mistress Catherine Deneuve.

Ben Johnson and Eileen Brennan are the parents of the dead girl, and Johnson on his own doggedly tracks down clues which explode some darker family secrets while goading Reynolds into frantic coverup action. The film's drawbacks are simply a lack of some restraint, since otherwise all the elements are present for a sensational, hardhitting human story.

•

HUSTLER, THE

1961, 134 mins, US Ⓥ ⦿ ▭ b/w

Dir Robert Rossen ***Prod*** Robert Rossen ***Scr*** Sydney Carroll, Robert Rossen, ***Ph*** Eugene Shufton ***Ed*** Dede Allen ***Mus*** Kenyon Hopkins ***Art*** Harry Horner, Albert Brenner

Act Paul Newman, Jackie Gleason, Piper Laurie, George C. Scott, Myron McCormick, Murray Hamilton (20th Century-Fox)

The Hustler belongs to that school of screen realism that allows impressive performances but defeats the basic goal of pure entertainment.

Film is peopled by a set of unpleasant characters set down against a backdrop of cheap pool halls and otherwise dingy surroundings. Chief protagonist is Paul Newman, a pool shark with a compulsion to be the best of the lot—not in tournament play but in beating Chicago's bigtime player (Jackie Gleason). Unfoldment of the screenplay, based on novel by Walter S. Tevis, is far overlength, and despite the excellence of Newman's portrayal of the boozing pool hustler the sordid aspects of overall picture are strictly downbeat.

Newman is entirely believable in the means he takes to defeat Gleason, and latter socks over a dramatic role which, though comparatively brief, generates potency. In some respects, the quiet strength of his characterization overshadows Newman in their scenes together. Piper Laurie establishes herself solidly as a hard-drinking floosie who lives with Newman, and George C. Scott scores as a gambler who promotes Newman and teaches him the psychology of being a winner.

1961: Best B&W Cinematography, B&W Art Direction

NOMINATIONS: Best Picture, Director, Actor (Paul Newman), Actress (Piper Laurie), Supp. Actor (Jackie Gleason, George C. Scott [latter nom. refused]), Adapted Screenplay

I ACCUSE
1958, 99 mins, US/UK b/w
Dir Jose Ferrer ***Prod*** Sam Zimbalist ***Scr*** Gore Vidal ***Ph*** Freddie Young ***Ed*** Frank Clarke ***Mus*** William Alwyn ***Art*** Elliot Scott
Act Jose Ferrer, Anton Walbrook, Viveca Lindfors, Leo Genn, Emlyn Williams, David Farrar (M-G-M)

This version of the drama of the Dreyfus case, one of the greatest miscarriages of justice in history, makes strong, if plodding, entertainment.

The story concerns the plight of a Jewish staff officer of the French army who is unjustly accused of treason, found guilty through being framed to save the army's face, and condemned to life imprisonment on Devil's Island. Friends fighting to restore his tarnished honor force a re-trial.

Jose Ferrer takes on the heavy task of playing Dreyfus and of directing. His performance is a wily, impeccable one, but it comes from the intellect rather than the heart and rarely causes pity. He makes Dreyfus a staid, almost fanatical patriot. The action is throughout rather static, but the court scenes are pregnant with drama, thanks to a literate screenplay by Gore Vidal [from a book by Nicholas Halasz].

Anton Walbrook, the real culprit, gives a splendid performance—suave, debonair and fascinating. And equally impressive is Donald Wolfit as the army's top guy who claims that the honor of the French army is more important than the fate of one man.

•

I AM A CAMERA
1955, 98 mins, UK b/w
Dir Henry Cornelius ***Prod*** Jack Clayton (assoc.) ***Scr*** John Collier ***Ph*** Guy Green ***Ed*** Clive Donner ***Mus*** Malcolm Arnold ***Art*** William Kellner
Act Julie Harris, Laurence Harvey, Shelley Winters, Ron Randell, Lea Seidl, Anton Diffring (Romulus)

John van Druten's hit play, based on *The Berlin Stories* by Christopher Isherwood, is an episodic affair dealing with a young author who gets himself involved, innocently, with a crackpot girl in pre-World War II Berlin. In transferring the play to the screen, scripter John Collier hewed close to the original in dialog and situations and the effect is always more that of a filmed stage play than a motion picture. The direction by Henry Cornelius follows the stage line, too, and the camera handling by Guy Green does not have the flowing freedom usual to most motion pictures.

While not an altogether satisfactory film offering, *Camera* does have its moments. Most of them will probably be more appreciated by distaff viewers than male stub-holders. The femmes will find more identification in the antics, even though most unconventional, of the wacky character so broadly projected by Julie Harris than the men will have with the Isherwood role played by Laurence Harvey.

Quite amusing is the sequence in which Harris gorges on caviar and champagne to the horror of purse-poor Harvey. Another chuckler is the wild party tossed by Clive (Ron Randell), the American playboy with whom the femme screwball has taken up, and the odd characters that drift in and out as the bacchanalian celebration hits its peak. Randell does a convincing job of the character.

Less frequently involved in the story is Shelley Winters, seen as a subdued German girl who, with her fiancé (Anton Diffring), is beginning to feel the first anti-Jewish pressure of the Hitler regime. The top players, and others, are competent in answering the rather light demands of story and direction.

The filming was done in London and lacks the production polish accomplished on practically all domestic features.

•

I AM A FUGITIVE
SEE: I AM A FUGITIVE FROM A CHAIN GANG

•

I AM A FUGITIVE FROM A CHAIN GANG
(UK: I AM A FUGITIVE)
1932, 93 mins, US b/w
Dir Mervyn LeRoy ***Prod*** [Hal B. Wallis] ***Scr*** Howard J. Green, Brown Holmes ***Ph*** Sol Polito ***Ed*** William Holmes ***Mus*** Leo Forbstein (dir.) ***Art*** Jack Okey
Act Paul Muni, Glenda Farrell, Helen Vinson, Noel Francis, Preston Foster, Allen Jenkins (Warner)

I Am a Fugitive from a Chain Gang is a picture with guts. It grips with its stark realism and packs lots of punch.

It's a sympathetic, unbiased cinematic transposition of the Robert E. Burns autobiography.

Paul Muni breaks away from the chain gang twice. In between he achieves success in his preferred field of engineering until a romantic angle prompts him voluntarily to surrender as the wanted fugitive, on the promise and belief

he will be pardoned in 90 days. The prison board stalls that, despite influential appeals, leading into the second break away from the chain gang. The finale is stark in its realism.

Muni turns in a pip performance. Glenda Farrell and Helen Vinson, the only two femmes of any prominence, are oke in their parts. Hale Hamilton as an overly benign and saccharine rev, the brother of the escaped convict, is an especial click in the characterization.

1932/33: NOMINATIONS: Best Picture, Actor (Paul Muni), Sound

•

I CAN GET IT FOR YOU WHOLESALE
(UK: THIS IS MY AFFAIR)
1951, 91 mins, US b/w
Dir Michael Gordon ***Prod*** Sol C. Siegel ***Scr*** Abraham Polonsky ***Ph*** Milton Krasner ***Ed*** Robert Simpson ***Mus*** Sol Kaplan ***Art*** Lyle Wheeler, John DeCuir
Act Susan Hayward, Dan Dailey, George Sanders, Sam Jaffe, Randy Stuart, Marvin Kaplan (20th Century-Fox)

Background of New York's garment-manufacturing sector provides the setting for this adult drama [adapted by Vera Caspary from Jerome Weidman's novel].

Uniformly excellent trouping is turned in by the three stars, Susan Hayward, Dan Dailey and George Sanders. It's the setup of an ambitious woman who schemes her way to establish her own business, then almost throws over her partners for a love nest arrangement with a merchant prince who can make her a world-renowned costume designer.

Hayward is the ambitious femme. She partners with Dailey, a hot garment salesman, and Sam Jaffe, an experienced production man, and their business grows, but not fast enough to satisfy the girl. She meets and charms Sanders, merchant prince, who offers her fame if she can break with her partners. It's more than business with Dailey, who eyes Hayward romantically. This provides some conflict when she goes for Sanders.

•

ICE CASTLES
1978, 113 mins, US col
Dir Donald Wrye ***Prod*** John Kemeny ***Scr*** Donald Wrye, Gary L. Bain ***Ph*** Bill Butler ***Ed*** Michael Kahn, Maury Winetrobe, Melvin Shapiro ***Mus*** Marvin Hamlisch ***Art*** Joel Schiller
Act Lynn-Holly Johnson, Robby Benson, Colleen Dewhurst, Tom Skerritt, Jennifer Warren, David Huffman (Columbia)

Ice Castles combines a touching love story with the excitement and intense pressure of Olympic competition skating.

Lynn-Holly Johnson portrays a farm girl from upstate Iowa who has the raw talent to be a great skater. Under the training and encouragement of local ice rink operator Colleen Dewhurst, she wins a regional competition, where she is spotted by Olympic coach Jennifer Warren.

Warren propels Johnson to instant stardom as a Cinderella figure who comes out of nowhere to win the hearts of the American people. All is progressing smoothly until Johnson has a freak accident, and is partially blinded. Robby Benson, who plays Johnson's boyfriend, and Tom Skerritt, her father, bring the teenager out of her shell, leading up to the inspiring ending.

Dewhurst, who appears all too infrequently in pix, excels in her role as the hard-bitten ex-skater trying not to live out her failed dreams through Johnson. Skerritt gives another outstanding perf as the overly protective father who also realizes his failings. Johnson shows the potential of being an excellent actress, in addition to a top skater. She is consistently believable, even in the more maudlin moments.

1979: NOMINATION: Best Song ("Through the Eyes of Love")

•

ICE COLD IN ALEX
(US: DESERT ATTACK)
1958, 132 mins, UK b/w
Dir J. Lee Thompson ***Prod*** W. A. Whittaker ***Scr*** T. J. Morrison, Christopher Landon ***Ph*** Gilbert Taylor ***Ed*** Richard Best ***Mus*** Leighton Lucas ***Art*** Robert Jones
Act John Mills, Sylvia Syms, Anthony Quayle, Harry Andrews, Diane Clare, Peter Arne (Associated British)

Based on a slight, real-life anecdote, pic [from Christopher Landon's novel] is the story of a handful of people who drive an ambulance through the mine-ridden, enemy-occupied desert after the collapse of Tobruk in 1942.

There is a nerve-strained officer who has taken to the bottle, his tough, reliable sergeant major, a couple of nurses and a South African officer. Director J. Lee Thompson captures the stark, pitiless atmosphere of the desert superbly. The screenplay skillfully blends excitement, a hint of romance and a fearful sense of danger.

John Mills is the skipper, strained to the limit, who seeks solace in a few swift swigs. This is a credible, edgy performance. Anthony Quayle, as the South African, has a suspect accent but brings a plausible charm to the role. Harry Andrews is first-rate as the sergeant-major. Stripped of any glamor, Sylvia Syms fits snugly into the plot. Diane Clare, a newcomer, plays a frightened nurse who gets bumped off halfway through the film.

•

ICE FOLLIES OF 1939
1939, 81 mins, US col
Dir Reinhold Schunzel ***Prod*** Harry Rapf ***Scr*** Leonard Praskins, Florence Ryerson, Edgar Allan Woolf ***Ph*** Joseph Ruttenberg, Oliver Marsh ***Ed*** W. Donn Hayes ***Mus*** Roger Edens
Act Joan Crawford, James Stewart, Lew Ayres, Lewis Stone, Bess Ehrhardt, Lionel Stander (M-G-M)

Metro sucessfully accomplishes the difficult task of welding two rather extended appearances of the International Ice Follies troupe into this production—withal keeping both story and ice show in separate grooves. Joan Crawford has a clear-cut role. She takes full advantage of opportunities to be sincere and glamorous. But, as the title suggests, it's the ice show and spectacle that count, chockfull of specialities and decidedly eye-appealing.

Story is only a framework. Rather light, it would have had trouble unfolding on its own for seven reels. Crawford marries James Stewart, and when he finds tough sledding in securing skating engagements, former conveniently nabs a film stock contract. Crawford gains to stardom in her first picture and Stewart goes east to generate interest and backing in his Ice Follies idea.

Three songs recorded by Miss Crawford for the picture hit the cutting room floor—with exception of a very short chorus retained in the Cinderella spectacle.

•

ICE STATION ZEBRA
1968, 152 mins, US col
Dir John Sturges ***Prod*** Martin Ransohoff ***Scr*** Douglas Heyes ***Ph*** Daniel L. Fapp ***Ed*** Ferris Webster ***Mus*** Michel Legrand ***Art*** George W. Davis, Addison Hehr
Act Rock Hudson, Ernest Borgnine, Patrick McGoohan, Jim Brown, Tony Bill, Lloyd Nolan (M-G-M/Filmways)

Action adventure film, in which U.S. and Russian forces race to recover some compromising satellite photography from a remote Polar outpost. Alistair MacLean's novel adapted into a screen story [by Harry Julian Fink] is seeded with elements of intrigue, as Rock Hudson takes aboard a British secret agent, Patrick McGoohan; an expatriate, professional anti-Communist Russian, Ernest Borgnine; and an enigmatic Marine Corps captain, Jim Brown.

Action develops slowly, alternating with some excellent submarine interior footage, and good shots—of diving, surfacing and maneuvering under an ice field.

Film's biggest acting asset is McGoohan, who gives his scenes that elusive "star" magnetism. He is a most accomplished actor with a three-dimensional presence all his own.

Hudson comes across quite well as a man of muted strength. Borgnine's characterization is a nicely restrained one. Brown, isolated by script to a suspicious personality, makes the most of it.

1968: NOMINATIONS: Best Cinematography, Visual Effects

•

ICE STORM, THE
1997, 113 mins, US col
Dir Ang Lee ***Prod*** Ted Hope, James Schamus, Ang Lee ***Scr*** James Schamus ***Ed*** Tim Squyres ***Mus*** Mychael Danna ***Art*** Mark Friedberg
Act Kevin Kline, Joan Allen, Sigourney Weaver, Christina Ricci, Jamey Sheridan (Good Machine/Fox Searchlight)

A well-observed and deftly performed examination of upper-middle-class emotional deep freeze, *The Ice Storm* is an intelligent, adult American film. Pic reps another insightful look at family and generational strains by Taiwanese director Ang Lee, this time within a morally unhinging East Coast suburbia of the early seventies.

Based on Rick Moody's well-received 1994 novel film tracks the furtive emotional adventures and transgressions of middle-aged parents and their sexually budding teenage kids at a time culturally dominated by Watergate, mind-altering substances and *Brady Bunch* fashions.

Paul Hood (Tobey Maguire) is returning to the New Canaan, CN, home of his parents, Ben (Kevin Kline) and Elena (Joan Allen). A chill has set in on the marriage, though Ben at least makes an attempt to communicate with Paul and his precocious 14-year-old daughter, Wendy (Christina Ricci). Ben has reason to be a little looser than his wife, since he's carrying on a discreet affair with neighbor Janey Carver (Sigourney Weaver).

The dominoes begin falling when Wendy and Janey's son, Mikey (Elijah Wood), thinking they are alone in the latter's house, begin fooling around, but are caught by uncautious Ben, who is upstairs hanging around after an abortive assignation with Janey.

Script is constructed with studious care, attentiveness to dramatic unities and an eye to cultural detail, though pic's rather dark, flat look could have been more evocative. Kline excels; Weaver, amusingly decked out to look like a post-hippie dragon lady, starkly etches the boldest character of the lot.

I CONFESS

1953, 95 mins, US Ⓥ ⦿ b/w

Dir Alfred Hitchcock ***Prod*** Alfred Hitchcock ***Scr*** George Tabori, William Archibald ***Ph*** Robert Burks ***Ed*** Rudi Fehr ***Mus*** Dimitri Tiomkin ***Art*** Edward S. Haworth

Act Montgomery Clift, Anne Baxter, Karl Malden, Brian Aherne, O. E. Hasse, Roger Dann (Warner)

An interesting plot premise holds out considerable promise for this Alfred Hitchcock production, but *I Confess* is short of the suspense one would expect. Hitchcock used the actual streets and buildings of picturesque Quebec to film the Paul Anthelme play on which the screenplay is based.

Intriguing story idea finds a priest facing trial for a murder he didn't commit, and refusing to clear himself even though the killer had confessed to him in the sanctity of the church. Quite a moral question is posed in the problem of just how sacred is a church confessional, particularly when it leaves a killer to roam free to kill again.

Chief exponents of the melodrama are Montgomery Clift, the priest, and Anne Baxter, a married woman who still believes she is in love with him, even though he ended their youthful romance and entered the church. While Hitchcock short-changes on the expected round of suspense for which he is noted, he does bring out a number of top flight performances and gives the picture an interesting polish that is documentary at times. Clift's ability to project mood with restrained strength is a high spot of the film, and he is believable as the young priest. Physically, he doesn't have as mature an appearance as the role opposite Baxter calls for, but otherwise, his work is flawless.

•

I COULD GO ON SINGING

1963, 99 mins, US Ⓥ ⦿ ▭ col

Dir Ronald Neame ***Prod*** Stuart Millar, Lawrence Turman ***Scr*** Mayo Simon ***Ph*** Arthur Ibbetson ***Ed*** Pamela Davies ***Mus*** Mort Lindsey

Act Judy Garland, Dirk Bogarde, Jack Klugman, Aline MacMahon, Gregory Phillips, Pauline Jameson (United Artists)

I Could Go on Singing is pretty weighty cargo. Although handsomely mounted and endowed with Judy Garland, one of the great stylists of her generation, the production is constructed on a frail and fuzzy story foundation.

Originally titled *The Lonely Stage*, the picture is a blend of two primary elements. Musically, it is a kind of femme *Jolson Story*. Dramatically, it is a switch on the old yarn about the child who one day discovers his parents had adopted him.

Screenplay from a story by Robert Dozier has Garland as Jenny Bowman, a celebrated Yank singer who, after her second divorce, decides while in London to look up the medic with whom years ago she had an affair which culminated in the birth of a son. It had been agreed upon at the time that the doctor (Dirk Bogarde) would raise the son, together with his wife (now rather conveniently deceased), as an adopted child, and that Jenny would butt out of the domestic picture.

She now persuades the doctor to let her see the lad, and it isn't long before the true parental beans are spilled. But for some rather foggy reason (which appears to have ended up on the cutting room floor), the boy elects to play it cool and keep his distance from his newfound mother.

A soulful performance is etched by Garland who gives more than she gets from the script. She also belts over four numbers as only she can belt them, yet the impact of a live Garland stage performance is not duplicated on the screen on this occasion. The camera tends to remain in too tight. Bogarde seems somewhat ill at ease in his role, employing two basic expressions—pain and a kind of confused "what am I doing here?" or "somebody must be kidding."

Garland was rather on the plumpish side when this film was shot, and neither costumes nor hairstyles are very becoming to her.

•

I COVER THE WATERFRONT

1933, 72 mins, US Ⓥ b/w

Dir James Cruze ***Prod*** Edward Small ***Scr*** Wells Root, Jack Jevne ***Ph*** Ray June ***Ed*** Grant Whytock ***Art*** Albert D'Agostino

Act Claudette Colbert, Ben Lyon, Ernest Torrence, Hobart Cavanaugh, Maurice Black (United Artists)

Rather than an adaption of the Max Miller book, this is a homemade studio yarn carrying the original's title.

Around Ernest Torrence's Eli Kirk, a deep-sea skipper and smuggler who has few scruples, except those concerning his daughter, the scenarist has built a fable that manages to keep some of Miller's waterfront-reporting color alive, but much of it accomplished by the exaggeration route. Ben Lyon, as the reporter, is still another legman who calls his editor names on the phone and in the office, but holds his job anyway. For years he's been promising a sensational expose on Kirk's activities and finally he delivers. Kirk is caught while landing Chinamen inside shark skins.

Meanwhile Lyon and Claudette Colbert, Kirk's unsuspecting daughter, carry on a hot love affair, including a night at Lyon's apartment, with the customary breakfast in the a.m. Lyon originally intended to get Kirk through his daughter, but he falls in love, which is a cinch to see in advance, as is the finish.

•

I.D.

1995, 108 mins, UK/Germany Ⓥ col

Dir Philip Davis ***Prod*** Sally Hibbin ***Scr*** Vincent O'Connell ***Ph*** Thomas Mauch ***Ed*** Inge Behrens ***Mus*** Will Gregory ***Art*** Max Gottlieb

Act Reece Dinsdale, Richard Graham, Claire Skinner, Sean Pertwee, Saskia Reeves, Warren Clarke (Parallax/Metropolis)

London bobbies come face-to-face with their own personal hell as they go undercover to root out soccer hooligans in *i.d.*, a raw-steak drama that packs a wallop when it's on form but suffers an intermittent i.d. crisis of its own in the script department when it comes to delivering the psychological goods. Pic reps a promising but flawed feature bow by TV actor-director Philip Davis.

Central character is John (Reece Dinsdale), an ambitious cop in his late 20s who's intro'd grilling a suspect in a police interrogation room. Under the leadership of the quiet, taciturn Trevor (Richard Graham), he and two others (Philip Glenister, Perry Fenwick) are assigned to root out the leaders behind a wave of thuggery that's gripped supporters of (fictional) second-league London team Shadwell Town. Dramatic focus early settles on John and Trevor, who pose as Shadwell supporters. To discover the top boys, they need to start drinking at The Rock, a tough East End pub.

Under the guise of local workmen, the duo get to know the barmaid, Lynda (Saskia Reeves). But as John gets further into this violent, self-contained universe, he finds it harder and harder to shut down during off-hours.

Dinsdale is excellent in his gradual transformation from clean-cut cop to long-haired troglodyte, and the copious scenes of pub drinking and tribalistic rituals of "belonging" carry an almost tangible threat of violence that's right on the money. Reeves, looking and sounding uncommonly like a young Billie Whitelaw, is very good in a rare working class outing.

Pic's violence is shockingly real as much thanks to the excellent verisimilitude of casting as to the (relatively little) blood on display. Several interiors in the German co-production were shot in Hamburg, to no loss of effect.

•

I DANCE ALONE

SEE: STEALING BEAUTY

•

I'D CLIMB THE HIGHEST MOUNTAIN

1951, 87 mins, US col

Dir Henry King ***Prod*** Lamar Trotti ***Scr*** Lamar Trotti ***Ph*** Edward Cronjager ***Ed*** Barbara McLean ***Mus*** Sol Kaplan ***Art*** Lyle Wheeler, Maurice Ransford

Act Susan Hayward, William Lundigan, Rory Calhoun, Barbara Bates, Gene Lockhart, Lynn Bari (20th Century-Fox)

The plot line is strung together with a series of episodes in the life of a minister and his city-bred bride on their first duty for The Church. Location of the assignment is in the red-clay hills of North Georgia, and 20th-Fox sent its cast and cameras to the actual sites, giving the picture authenticity.

Episodes are told through the eyes of Susan Hayward, the bride, thrust into a strange life but with enough courage and ingenuity to win out over adversity. While the Corra Harris novel has a familiar ring, in that pattern is similar to novels of other femmes who have gone into the wilderness as brides, the script, the performances and Henry King's understanding direction keep this account always interesting.

Hayward shines as the bride who encounters a completely strange life during her three years in the hills. William Lundigan scores as the very human minister, young enough to err but with a deep belief in his religion to see him through the shepherding of his mountain flock.

•

IDEAL HUSBAND, AN

1947, 96 mins, UK Ⓥ col

Dir Alexander Korda ***Prod*** Alexander Korda ***Scr*** Lajos Biro ***Ph*** Georges Perinal ***Ed*** Oscar Hafenrichter ***Mus*** Arthur Benjamin ***Art*** Vincent Korda

Act Paulette Goddard, Michael Wilding, Hugh Williams, Diana Wynyard, C. Aubrey Smith, Glynis Johns (British Lion)

This version of the Oscar Wilde 1895 play is given handsome mounting by Alexander Korda. Yet he could do little more than put the play on the screen, stage asides and all.

Story relates how Hugh Williams, under-secretary of the foreign office and marked for a Cabinet post, in his youth profited by selling a Cabinet secret about the Suez Canal, thereby founding his fortune and his political career. Arrival of Paulette Goddard, an adventuress and old school friend of his wife complicates matters. She knows about Williams's misdeed and threatens him with exposure if he doesn't support a phony Argentine canal scheme in parliament.

At first he agrees, but his wife, Diana Wynyard, persuades him to refuse. It looks like the end of his career and marriage, until his best friend, Michael Wilding, takes a hand.

It seems a brave experiment to cast Goddard as the adventuress. But it doesn't quite come off. Not a solitary epigram is thrown off with spontaneity, and her loveliness in gorgeous costumes is inadequate compensation.

•

IDEAL HUSBAND, AN

1999, 96 mins, UK Ⓥ ⦿ col

Dir Oliver Parker ***Prod*** Barnaby Thompson, Uri Fruchtmann, Bruce Davey ***Scr*** Oliver Parker ***Ph*** David Johnson ***Ed*** Guy Bensley ***Mus*** Charlie Mole ***Art*** Michael Howells

Act Rupert Everett, Julianne Moore, Jeremy Northam, Cate Blanchett, Minnie Driver, John Wood (Fragile/Icon/Pathe)

Oscar Wilde's legiter about emotional and political chicanery shines like a freshly minted coin in Oliver Parker's adaptation of *An Ideal Husband*. Smooth-flowing direction, a shrewdly pruned script and a top-flight ensemble cast that visibly relishes both the dialogue and one another's perfs make this a tony item.

This has far more panache and helming style than actor-turned-director Parker's iffy debut, *Othello*. Parker and his thesps go for an accessible, only slightly stylized manner that's far less exaggerated than Alexander Korda's lavish, highly theatrical 1947 version, despite being an equally strongly cast for its time.

Textual purists may decry some of the changes Parker has made to the original, but the truth is that such changes, and the elimination of period refs and jokes, work for the movie. Result is a believable milieu in which Wilde's people emerge as flawed heroes and heroines rather than just witty cynics, though the film still dips in the resolution-heavy last act, with Parker not quite negotiating its changes in tone.

Performances are tip-top down the line, with Rupert Everett immaculately poised as the Wilde alter ego, Lord Arthur Goring; Julianne Moore as the unflappable, scheming Laura Cheveley; Cate Blanchett making a real character out of the adoring but strong Gertrud Chiltern; and Minnie Driver bringing a slightly ditzy charm to the love-struck Mabel. Jeremy Northam may not be everyone's idea of Sir Robert Chiltern, but his softer, more human portrayal fits the movie. Both Aussie Blanchett and Yank Moore's English accents are natural and impeccable.

•

IDIOT'S DELIGHT
1939, 100 mins, US Ⓥ ⦿ b/w
Dir Clarence Brown ***Prod*** Hunt Stromberg ***Scr*** Robert E. Sherwood ***Ph*** William Daniels ***Ed*** Robert J. Kern ***Mus*** Herbert Stothart ***Art*** Herbert Stothart
Act Norma Shearer, Clark Gable, Edward Arnold, Joseph Schildkraut, Burgess Meredith (M-G-M)

Author Robert Sherwood, in preparing his own screenplay, deftly added an entertaining prolog establishing the early meeting and a one-night affair between Clark Gable and Norma Shearer in Omaha as small time vaudeville performers. This provides plenty of entertainment when the pair meet later in an Alpine hotel.

Gable milks his role as the small-time vaude performer, and dominates the picture throughout. His cynical yet breezy manner is a new characterization. Shearer does nobly in a part which calls for two distinct characterizations, first as the vaude trouper and later impersonating a Russian aristocrat.

Anti-war angles of the play are considerably softened and made more palatable for the masses and the amount is not sufficient to offend. Brief appearance of Burgess Meredith as the war declaimer is brilliantly handled.

•

IDOL, THE
1966, 109 mins, UK b/w
Dir Daniel Petrie ***Prod*** Leonard Lightstone ***Scr*** Millard Lampell ***Ph*** Ken Higgins ***Ed*** Jack Slade ***Mus*** John Dankworth ***Art*** George Provis
Act Jennifer Jones, Michael Parks, John Leyton, Jennifer Hilary, Guy Doleman, Natasha Pyne (Embassy)

The screenplay, based on Ugo Liberatore's original story, focuses on an irresponsible American art student in London, a disbeliever in everything except himself and his own talents. He has become friendly with a young man studying to be a doctor, completely under his mother's domination, and an English girl, also an art student. They form a romantic triangle, and later the mother, who at first takes a dislike to the brash young American, finds herself attracted to him.

Leonard Lightstone has given impressive physical backing to his production, capturing the feeling of London, which Ken Higgins limns in his sensitive photography, but characters lack much interest. Daniel Petrie's direction registers as well as script will allow and cast performs satisfactorily.

•

IDOLMAKER, THE
1980, 107 mins, US Ⓥ ⦿ col
Dir Taylor Hackford ***Prod*** Gene Kirkwood, Howard W Koch, Jr. ***Scr*** Edward Di Lorenzo ***Ph*** Adam Holender ***Ed*** Neil Travis ***Mus*** Jeff Barry ***Art*** David L. Snyder
Act Ray Sharkey, Paul Land, Olympia Dukakis, Peter Gallagher, Joe Pantoliano, Tovah Feldshuh (United Artists)

Though it's marred by an overly melodramatic and dubious finale, *The Idolmaker* is an unusally compelling film about the music business in the late 1950s and early 1960s. It shows how teen idols were created, promoted, and discarded by entrepreneurs cynically manipulating the adolescent audience. Ray Sharkey is superb in the title role. Script is a roman à clef of the career of Bob Marcucci who, along with Dick Clark, guided Frankie Avalon to stardom and then created Fabian as Avalon's successor.

Viewers will have no trouble recognizing Paul Land as the Avalon figure or Peter Gallagher as Fabian.

All of the elements are shown in believable detail, though the payola and organized crime elements of the record industry are not indicated on the higher levels, an unfortunate omission.

•

I DON'T WANT TO BE BORN
(US: THE DEVIL WITHIN HER)
1975, 90 mins, UK Ⓥ col
Dir Peter Sasdy ***Prod*** Nato De Angeles (exec.) ***Scr*** Stanley Price ***Ph*** Kenneth Talbot ***Ed*** Keith Palmer ***Mus*** Ron Grainer ***Art*** Roy Stannard
Act Joan Collins, Eileen Atkins, Donald Pleasence, Ralph Bates, Caroline Munro, Hilary Mason (Unicapital/Rank)

This is an exceedingly stylish thriller [from an original story idea by exec producer Nato De Angeles] about a satanically possessed infant, Joan Collins's abnormally strong newborn son, who inflicts scratches on cribside visitors, and wreaks havoc on his room when no one is around. After a succession of bizarre occurrences, including the mysterious death of the baby's nursemaid, a frantic Collins (looking and acting splendidly as the begrieved mother) and her Italian husband, nicely played by horror vet Ralph Bates, turn to doctor Donald Pleasence for the answers, then to Bates's nun sister (Eileen Atkins, in a striking performance).

Director Peter Sasdy, whose pacing is near-flawless, works as much below the surface as above it with great effect. There are plenty of shots of the sweetest baby imaginable, followed with shots of the violence it apparently perpetrated, showing only the terrified victims.

•

I DOOD IT
(UK: BY HOOK OR BY CROOK)
1943, 102 mins, US Ⓥ b/w
Dir Vincente Minnelli ***Prod*** Jack Cummings ***Scr*** Sig Herzig, Fred Saidy ***Ph*** Ray June ***Ed*** Robert J. Kern ***Mus*** George Stoll (dir.)
Act Red Skelton, Eleanor Powell, Lena Horne, Patricia Dane, Richard Ainley, Sam Levene (M-G-M)

Metro has wrapped Red Skelton and Eleanor Powell, among other names, around a popular Skelton radio phrase that's used for the film's title, and the net result is moderate entertainment.

I Dood It is, by Metro's usual standards, not one of its best musicals, but that's due mostly to the screenplay. While the plot of a musical can generally be accepted only as a cue for the song-and-dance, the failing is particularly apparent in *Dood It*. The yarn is too unbelievable, though the absurdities fashioned for Skelton have their compensations in the actual performance.

Story is a retake of an old situation, dealing with the love of a valet aide for a dancing star. Skelton courts Powell from a distance, a fashion plate through borrowing his customers' clothes. Then follows a series of situations that find him mixed up in a "spite" marriage with Powell, followed by his discovery and rout of a spy plot. It's all very hectic and uncertain, but pretends to be nothing more than a vehicle for the comic's folderol.

•

I DREAMED OF AFRICA
2000, 114 mins, US Ⓥ ⦿ ▭ col
Dir Hugh Hudson ***Prod*** Stanley R. Jaffe, Allyn Stewart ***Scr*** Paula Milne, Susan Shilliday ***Ph*** Bernard Lutic ***Ed*** Scott Thomas ***Mus*** Maurice Jarre ***Art*** Andrew Sanders
Act Kim Basinger, Vincent Perez, Liam Aiken, Garrett Strommen, Eva Marie Saint, Daniel Craig (Jaffilms/Columbia)

Visually gratifying but dramatically weak, *I Dreamed of Africa* (based on the book by Kuki Gallmann) falls short of its aspiration to be a sweeping romantic epic à la *Out of Africa*. Storytelling has never been the strongest suit of Brit director Hugh Hudson.

Kim Basinger dominates the proceedings as Kuki, the true-life heroine whose fascination with the magic of Africa led to a journey of self-discovery and commitment to social causes. Her story begins in Italy, when Kuki and friends become victims of a freak accident. Kuki is sent to the hospital, where she's regularly visited by her 7-year-old son, Emanuele (Liam Aiken), and her snobbish mother (Eva Marie Saint). It's disclosed that Kuki is a young divorcée who's devoted to raising her son yet feels that excitement and a sense of fulfillment are missing from her routine existence.

She decides the time is ripe for a change. Joining her in the adventure is Paolo (Vincent Perez), who marries her after a brief courtship. Main story is told against the magnificent backdrop of Africa. Paolo is a loving but not always responsible hubby. He goes on wild hunting trips with his buddies. A whole reel recounts Paolo's departures and returns, their ceaseless bickering and the reconciliations that often end with sex. Playing a role similar to Robert Redford's white hunter in *Out of Africa*, Perez is saddled with an undeveloped character. The part of Kuki's son (played as an adolescent by Garrett Strommen) is similarly lacking in depth.

Pic's second half is all plot machinations, giving the impression of a novel being compressed into a two-hour visual format. Whether intentional or not, Kuki's part echoes Meryl Streep's portrait of Isak Dinesen in *Out of Africa* and Sigourney Weaver's turn as Dian Fossey in *Gorillas in the Mist*. Banal as the film is, it gives Basinger a role of stature and intelligence. Pic registers as a one-woman show, with Basinger, who's in every scene but two, admirably holding together the movie. French star Perez is handsome, but fails to impress dramatically.

•

IERI, OGGI, DOMANI
(YESTERDAY, TODAY AND TOMORROW)
1964, 120 mins, Italy Ⓥ col
Dir Vittorio De Sica ***Prod*** Carlo Ponti ***Scr*** Eduardo De Filippo, Isabella Quarantotti, Cesare Zavattini, Billa Billa ***Ph*** Giuseppe Rotunno ***Ed*** Adriana Novelli ***Mus*** Armando Trovajoli ***Art*** Ezio Frigerio
Act Sophia Loren, Marcello Mastroianni, Aldo Giuffre, Armando Trovajoli, Tina Pica, Giovanni Ridolfi (Ponti)

The wonders of Italy and Sophia Loren are the objects of intimate attention in this breezy, non-cerebral, three-episoder. All three parts, separate entities save for the fact that they are set in Italy and co-star Loren and Marcello Mastroianni, have been directed with cinematic flair and invested with sensual gusto by Vittorio De Sica.

The first episode, "Adelina," illustrates the method by which a Neopolitan black-marketeer evades imprisonment over a seven-year span. The law says pregnant women may not be arrested, so she sees to it. This creates an exhausted, mercy-begging husband.

Episode number two, "Anna," is a brief interlude [from a short story by Alberto Moravia] describing the abrupt dissolution of an affair between a Milanese Rolls-Royceterer and her lover. Third item, "Mara," is the flashiest but hokiest of the three. It explores the adventures in Rome of a lovable prostitute, a fanciful client and a confused young student priest. It amounts to an elaborately contrived excuse to get Loren into a bikini.

Rich production values dress up *Yesterday, Today and Tomorrow* (a meaningless title), a reflection of the astute contributions of such men as photographer Giuseppe Rotunno and composer Armando Trovajoli.

1964: Best Foreign Language Film

•

IF. . . .
1968, 110 mins, UK Ⓥ ⦿ col
Dir Lindsay Anderson ***Prod*** Michael Medwin, Lindsay Anderson ***Scr*** David Sherwin ***Ph*** Miroslav Ondricek ***Ed*** David Gladwell ***Mus*** Marc Wilkinson ***Art*** Jocelyn Herbert
Act Malcolm McDowell, David Wood, Richard Warwick, Christine Noonan, Robert Swann, Peter Jeffrey (Memorial)

Punchy, poetic pic that delves into the epic theme of youthful revolt. *if. . . .* is ostensibly about a rigid tradition-ridden British private boarding school for boys from 11 to 18. The film blocks out a series of incidents that lead to a small group rebelling with mortars, machine guns, gas bombs and pistols. Film is divided into chapter headings as the boys arrive for a new term.

The teachers, nurses, housemasters, etc., are all fairly typed characters but never descend to caricatures, which is true of the many students.

There is a romantic dash during the early part of the film in the growing insistence of three rebel friends that all is not right in this caste-ridden school. But there is never any sentimentality, which makes the film's veering to a bloody revolt acceptable.

Film is a generalized tale of revolt. The violence is symbolical and reflects and comments on it rather than sentimentalizing it or trying to make it realistic.

•

IF I HAD A MILLION
1932, 85 mins, US b/w
Dir Ernst Lubitsch, Norman Taurog, Stephen Roberts, Norman Z. McLeod, James Cruze, William A. Seiter, H. Bruce Humberstone ***Scr*** Claude Binyon, Whitney Bolton, Malcolm Stuart Boylan, John Bright, Sidney Buchman, Lester Cole, Isabel Dawn, Boyce DeGaw, Oliver H. P. Garrett, Harvey Gates, Grover Jones, Ernst Lubitsch, Lawton Mackall, Joseph L. Mankiewicz, William Slavens McNutt, Robert Sparks
Act Gary Cooper, Charles Laughton, W. C. Fields, Charles Ruggles, George Raft, Jack Oakie (Paramount)

The episodes depicting what certain individuals would do if they had $1 million are not without their moments, some, of course, more effective than others. With so many cooks concerned, this cinematic porridge [based on a story by Robert D. Andrews] is naturally replete with a diversity of seasonings. Just who's responsible for which sequence isn't disclosed, although the scene with Charles Laughton giving his boss a lusty Bronx cheer, upon becoming one of the beneficiaries, is said to be 100% Ernst Lubitsch in writing and direction.

George Raft's million is worthless because he is a fourth-time offender for forgery, and none believes his signature on the certified check.

Similarly Gary Cooper, Jack Oakie and Roscoe Karns as the triumvirate of marines look at the million dollar check received by Cooper, and also observe that it's April 1 on the calendar, and that's that.

May Robson converts the old ladies' home in which she's a "guest" into a clubhouse, when her million arrives, and bakes pies for Richard Bennett, who plays the eccentric millionaire who had hit upon the telephone directory potshot idea as a means for distributing his wealth.

Charlie Ruggles's sequence has about the longest footage, while Laughton's Bronx cheerio is the snappiest, and probably most effective.

W. C. Fields and Alison Skipworth man a vanguard of used flivvers as the means to attack the road hogs who endanger the other motorists, by running them up the sidewalks and into wrecks themselves.

•

IF IT'S TUESDAY, THIS MUST BE BELGIUM
1969, 99 mins, US col
Dir Mel Stuart ***Prod*** Stan Margulies ***Scr*** David Shaw ***Ph*** Vilis Lapenieks ***Ed*** David Saxon ***Mus*** Donovan ***Art*** Marc Frederix
Act Suzanne Pleshette, Ian McShane, Mildred Natwick, Murray Hamilton, Sandy Baron, Reva Rose (United Artists)

David Shaw's screenplay manages to cover many of the European tour clichés. There are some script anomalies that briefly puzzle, but not to a degree that they detract from the fun.

Although the touring group is conducted by a British guide (Ian McShane), supposedly versed in all languages and emergencies, they suddenly find themselves with a fluttery femme type (Patricia Routledge). She's unexplained, unorthodox and delightful.

While Shaw's main story line is based on the adventures of a polyglot pack of Yank tourists, trying to keep up with a hectic schedule, it is padded with enough sidebar items to make it a miniature *Grand Hotel* on wheels.

Besides the friction caused by the inconveniences en route, there's personal friction between McShane and femme tourist Suzanne Pleshette.

•

IF I WERE KING
1938, 100 mins, US b/w
Dir Frank Lloyd ***Prod*** Frank Lloyd ***Scr*** Preston Sturges ***Ph*** Theodor Sparkuhl ***Ed*** Hugh Bennett ***Mus*** Richard Hageman ***Art*** Hans Dreier, John Goodman
Act Ronald Colman, Basil Rathbone, Frances Dee, Ellen Drew, C. V. France, Henry Wilcoxon (Paramount)

Paramount made a happy choice in deciding to turn out a new version of the adventures of Francois Villon. Ronald Colman's delineation of the adventurous poet-philosopher is excellent, carrying through it a verve and spontaneity for an outstanding performance. Basil Rathbone brilliantly handles the difficult assignment of the eccentric Louis XI.

Preston Sturges has provided much sparkling dialog [from the play by Justin Huntly McCarthy] to greatly enhance entertainment.

After quickly establishing Villon as the hero and leader of the Paris mobs, events bring him and the king together. Appointed grand constable of France and Brittany by the mischief-conniving Louis, in the palace Villon champions the people against the king and his arrogant advisers—to the amusement of Louis. But the latter soon tires of his amusement with Villon, and is ready to put him on a gibbet.

Newcomer Ellen Drew handles the difficult role of Huguette, girl of the slums, for one of the outstanding performances. Interpretation of Katherine by Frances Dee is delivered with sincerity.

•

IF LOOKS COULD KILL
(UK: TEEN AGENT)
1991, 88 mins, US Ⓥ ⦿ col
Dir William Dear ***Prod*** Craig Zadan, Neil Meron ***Scr*** Darren Star ***Ph*** Doug Milsome ***Ed*** John F. Link ***Mus*** David Foster ***Art*** Guy J. Comtois
Act Richard Grieco, Linda Hunt, Roger Rees, Robin Bartlett, Gabrielle Anwar, Geraldine James (Warner)

Young TV star Richard Grieco barely survives silly first film vehicle *If Looks Could Kill*, which spoofs the James Bond formula in tiresome fashion. One-joke script, based on Fred Dekker's story, runs out of gas before the halfway mark.

Grieco plays a high school student who's headed for France with his French teacher (Robin Bartlett) and class. Coincidentally, a CIA spy with the same name is booked on the same plane, and rest of the film stems from both villains and good guy spooks mistaking young Grieco for a secret agent.

Nominal plot has Roger Rees as the megalomaniacal chairman of the European Economic Community who plans to take over Europe and issue gold coinage bearing his own likeness.

Grieco puts up with the silliness, including being clad only in his underpants during a lengthy segment opposite femme fatale Carole Davis. Linda Hunt has only intermittent success with the comic strip role of Rees's chief enforcer, a bullwhip-wielding heavy named Ilsa Grunt.

Heroine Gabrielle Anwar as the vengeful daughter of Britain's late great top spy (played in a miscast, no-impact cameo by Roger Daltrey) looks too young on screen. Best role goes to Bartlett.

•

I FOUND STELLA PARISH
1935, 83 mins, US b/w
Dir Mervyn LeRoy ***Prod*** Harry Joe Brown ***Scr*** John Monk Saunders, Casey Robinson ***Ph*** Sid Hickox ***Ed*** William Clemens ***Mus*** Leo Forbstein (dir.) ***Art*** Robert M. Haas
Act Kay Francis, Ian Hunter, Paul Lukas, Sybil Jason, Jessie Ralph, Barton MacLane (Warner)

Powerful story of an actress and mother love. Kay Francis plays both a young woman and an aging, bespectacled aunt. As the Stella Parish of the London stage she is always a cameo of film loveliness. When she becomes an aunt to her child so that she may escape detection when suddenly fleeing London and a no-good American husband, who has finally caught up with her, she is shown to be an actress of much ability.

Ian Hunter is the London newspaper correspondent, friend of Stella's legit-producer, who follows her back to America and eventually scoops the world with the story of having found the London star. Hunter gives a fine account of himself, he and the little South African discovery, Sybil Jason, being able support for Francis.

•

IF YOU FEEL LIKE SINGING
SEE: SUMMER STOCK

•

IKIRU
(LIVING; TO LIVE)
1952, 143 mins, JAPAN Ⓥ ⦿ b/w
Dir Akira Kurosawa ***Prod*** Shojiro Motoki ***Scr*** Shinobu Hashimoto, Hideo Oguni, Akira Kurosawa ***Ph*** Asakazu Nakai ***Ed*** Akira Kurosawa ***Mus*** Fumio Hayasaka ***Art*** So Matsuyama
Act Takashi Shimura, Nobuo Kaneko, Kyoko Seki, Miki Odagiri, Makoto Kobori, Yunosuke Ito (Toho)

Director Akira Kurosawa, known for *Rashomon* and *The Seven Samurai*, here unspools a work of compassion.

An ordinary white-collar worker (Takashi Shimura), an aging head of a public works bureau, finds he has cancer and a few months to live. He tells nobody but finds that he is really alone and estranged from his son and daughter-in-law. He suddenly sees that his life has been dull and useless, wasted in an office from which he has not been absent in 30 years.

He draws out his money and goes out into the Tokyo night. He meets a deadbeat poet in whom he confides. They go out on the town.

He goes home where his uncomprehending son (Nobuo Kaneko) reproaches him. Meeting one of his office girls (Miki Odagiri) he finds her new job, that of making toys for children, gives him a sudden goal. He pushes a needed children's playground through all the bureaucratic red tape.

Half of the film is told in the third person and half is his sacrifice as seen through the eyes of guests at his funeral. Kurosawa performs a tour de force in keeping a dramatic thread throughout and avoiding the mawkish. It is technically excellent with a telling Occidental-type musical score.

•

I KNOW WHAT YOU DID LAST SUMMER
1997, 101 mins, US Ⓥ ⦿ ▭ col
Dir Jim Gillespie ***Prod*** Neal H. Moritz, Erik Feig, Stokely Chaffin ***Scr*** Kevin Williamson ***Ph*** Denis Crossan ***Ed*** Steve Mirkovich, William Yeh ***Mus*** John Debney ***Art*** Gary Wissner
Act Jennifer Love Hewitt, Sarah Michelle Gellar, Ryan Phillippe, Freddie Prinze, Jr., Muse Wats, Anne Heche (Mandalay/Columbia)

Combining familiar elements from horror staples and a few novel twists, this is a polished genre piece with superior fright elements.

The setting is a North Carolina fishing community where nothing much appears to happen. During the annual Fourth of July celebrations, Helen (Sarah Michelle Gellar) is crowned in a local beauty pageant and goes off to party with her boyfriend, Barry (Ryan Phillippe), and their friends Julie (Jennifer Love Hewitt) and Ray (Freddie Prinze, Jr.). Driving home, they hit something in the road. Just as they're about to drop the body in the water, it comes to life, and a brief struggle forever cements their culpability in a murderous act.

A year later, a malevolent presence disposes of Max (Johnny Galecki)—a classmate who saw the foursome at the side of the road—and goes on to terrorize Barry. Remainder of the film plays out as a cat-and-mouse game.

As with his script for *Scream*, writer Kevin Williamson [working from the novel by Lois Duncan] demonstrates adroitness at creating vivid young protagonists. Both a horror buff and a chronicler of contemporary mores, he struggles to mesh his two pursuits with fitful success, bowing to the demands of the genre at the expense of texture and resonance.

The leads elevate their prototypes considerably. Hewitt and Prinze are particularly good, and Anne Heche is a standout as the hauntingly eviscerated sister of the hit-and-run victim.

•

I KNOW WHERE I'M GOING!
1945, 91 mins, UK Ⓥ b/w
Dir Michael Powell, Emeric Pressburger ***Prod*** Michael Powell, Emeric Pressburger ***Scr*** Michael Powell, Emeric Pressburger ***Ph*** Erwin Hillier ***Ed*** John Seabourne ***Mus*** Allan Gray ***Art*** Alfred Junge
Act Wendy Hiller, Roger Livesey, Pamela Brown, Petula Clark, Nancy Price, Finlay Currie (Archers)

I Know Where I'm Going! has all the values of a documentary as a foundation for the tale of a girl who is sure she knows where she is going until she gets sidetracked—and likes it.

As the girl, Wendy Hiller, repeats her convincing portrayal of character development, which made *Pygmalion* a personal triumph for her. Hard as nails in the opening sequences, when she tells her father, a bank manager, she is off to the Island of Mull to marry the multimillionaire boss of a great chemical combine, she dismisses his objections to the May-December misalliance by insisting her fiancé is no older than her father— "And you're rather nice, Daddy."

It is only when a gale prevents her from reaching the island and her waiting bridegroom-to-be that she finds heartless ambition to marry money becoming less attractive, the process of disillusionment aided and abetted by her proximity to a young navy officer (Roger Livesey) who begins by telling her what he thinks of gold diggers generally, and winds up by walloping her in the best-approved Cagney fashion.

•

I LIKE IT LIKE THAT
1994, 105 mins, US Ⓥ ⦿ col
Dir Darnell Martin ***Prod*** Ann Carli, Lane Janger ***Scr*** Darnell Martin ***Ph*** Alexander Gruszynski ***Ed*** Peter C. Frank ***Mus*** Sergio George ***Art*** Scott Chambliss
Act Lauren Velez, Jon Seda, Tomas Melly, Lisa Vidal, Griffin Dunne, Rita Moreno (Think Again/Columbia)

A thick veneer of happening music, multiethnicity, tough hood attitude and sexual frankness gives a hip feel to what is actually an old-fashioned and conventional story of a bickering family in *I Like It Like That*. Debut feature by Darnell Martin, reputedly the first black American woman to write and direct a film for a Hollywood major, displays plenty of energy and an adeptness at staging scenes vividly.

Story largely stays put within a block of 167th Street in the Bronx, a racially mixed area where the teeming street life is portrayed as volative and contentious.

Chino (Jon Seda) in the opening scene defines his Latin macho posturing by proudly timing his sexual endurance with his wife, Lisette (Lauren Velez). But sex doesn't provide much of a respite from the couple's chaotic family life, which includes three unruly kids; Lauren's aspiring transsexual brother, Alexis (Jesse Borrego); Chino's critical mother (Rita Moreno), and constant financial problems.

Further complicating matters is the constant threat posed by Magdalena (Lisa Vidal), the local fox who is still hot for Chino and whose little child may be his. Crisis is precipitated by a blackout during which Chino steals a stereo, landing him in the slammer.

With her taste for the mobile camera and overhead shots, as well as the contempo street material, Martin shows an affinity with Spike Lee, although in most other respects her sensibility feels more mainstream and conventional. Mostly unknown thesps throw themselves into their roles.

•

I LIKE MONEY
SEE: MR TOPAZE

•

I LIVE IN GROSVENOR SQUARE
(US: A YANK IN LONDON)
1945, 114 mins, UK b/w
Dir Herbert Wilcox ***Prod*** Herbert Wilcox ***Scr*** Nicholas Phipps, William D. Bayles ***Ph*** Otto Heller ***Ed*** Vera Campbell ***Mus*** Anthony Collins ***Art*** William C. Andrews
Act Anna Neagle, Dean Jagger, Rex Harrison, Robert Morley (Associated British)

Story by British newspaperman Maurice Cowan is based on the real-life events—that of the Air Corps crew sacrificing themselves to save inhabitants of an English village.

Anna Neagle gives a most convincing performance. Dean Jagger's love scenes, though a trifle long, are played with the subtlety one would expect in an American sergeant's diffidence towards a duke's grand-daughter. Rex Harrison as the major looks sure to impress American femmes in the service, even though the heroine jilts him.

Of the other players, Jane Darwell gives a lesson in how to play a bit part so it won't be forgotten. Herbert Wilcox's direction is perfect.

•

I LIVE MY LIFE

1935, 83 mins, US b/w

Dir W.S. Van Dyke ***Prod*** Bernard H. Hyman ***Scr*** Joseph L. Mankiewicz, Gottfried Reinhardt, Ethel Borden ***Ph*** George Folsey ***Ed*** Tom Held ***Mus*** Dimitri Tiomkin

Act Joan Crawford, Brian Aherne, Frank Morgan, Aline MacMahon, Eric Blore, Jessie Ralph (M-G-M)

I Live My Life contains all the ingredients, and to good measure, for a conventional Joan Crawford picture. An amusing romance [from a story by A. Carter Goodloe] is backgrounded by clothes, cocktails and butlers.

The premise, as is customary with Crawford operas, is that the rich are not as good as the poor, only in this instance Crawford is on the coin side and it takes a man to trim her down. The man is an archaeologist who follows the girl from Greece to New York. They get along like a pair of wrasslers, always appearing to be fighting but loving each other down deep just the same.

Cast is studded with sturdy players who know their stuff and the reason for much of the merriment can be found in the supporting troupe. Brian Aherne is aces opposite Crawford. His flamboyant Irishman in this film is vigorous, colorful trouping.

Crawford won't disappoint from a sartorial angle. On performance she's also as usual, but if her eyelashes continue getting any longer her leading men will have to start wearing bumpers.

•

I'LL CRY TOMORROW

1955, 117 mins, US Ⓥ ⦿ b/w

Dir Daniel Mann ***Prod*** Lawrence Weingarten ***Scr*** Helen Deutsch, Jay Richard Kennedy ***Ph*** Arthur E. Arling ***Ed*** Harold F. Kress ***Mus*** Alex North ***Art*** Cedric Gibbons, Malcolm Brown

Act Susan Hayward, Richard Conte, Eddie Albert, Jo Van Fleet, Don Taylor, Margo (M-G-M)

This pulls no punches in showing a rising star's fall into alcoholic degradation that plumbs Skid Row sewers before Alcoholics Anonymous provides the faith and guidance to help her up again. [The biopic is based on Lillian Roth's own book.]

No particular person or circumstance is blamed for Roth's downfall, but the viewers will be able to fasten on any one of several possible causes. The first is the stingingly cruel portrayal of the stage mother, played with great trouping skill by Jo Van Fleet, as she pushes her daughter towards the career she never had. The death of Roth's first love, effectively realized by Ray Danton, is a blow of fate and the start of the crackup.

Susan Hayward, along with the sock of her sustained character creation, reveals pleasant pipes and song-belting ability.

1955: Best B&W Costume Design

NOMINATIONS: Best Actress (Susan Hayward), B&W Cinematography, B&W Art Direction

•

I'LL DO ANYTHING

1994, 115 mins, US Ⓥ ⦿ col

Dir James L. Brooks ***Prod*** James L. Brooks, Polly Platt ***Scr*** James L. Brooks ***Ph*** Michael Ballhaus ***Ed*** Richard Marks ***Mus*** Hans Zimmer ***Art*** Stephen J. Lineweaver

Act Nick Nolte, Whittni Wright, Albert Brooks, Julie Kavner, Joely Richardson, Tracey Ullman (Columbia/Gracie)

Destined to be known forever in industry circles as the musical that wasn't, James L. Brooks's $40 million showbiz comedy hits occasional high notes on the laugh scale but suffers from a choppiness that betrays its history.

Brooks—having raised eyebrows initially by casting such dubious crooners as Nick Nolte and Albert Brooks—finally junked the musical numbers after test audiences voted thumbs down, shooting new material and turning *Anything* back into a multi-tiered romantic comedy.

Nolte plays a rarely employed actor, Matt Hobbs, who's saddled with his 6-year-old daughter (Whittni Wright) after his ex (Tracey Ullman) is shipped off to prison. Matt settles for work chauffeuring around Burke Adler (Albert Brooks)—a self-obsessed, hyperkinetic producer of schlocky blockbusters—in the process becoming entangled with comely, if insecure development executive Cathy (Joely Richardson). Brooks displays his characteristic ear for dialogue, particularly in lines spouted by the other Brooks, who inexplicably becomes involved with a divorced test-marketing researcher, Nan (Julie Kavner). Nolte solidly conveys Matt's acting fervor, but his character, in particular, seems to have suffered from the editing process. Tech credits are top-notch.

•

ILLEGALLY YOURS

1988, 102 mins, US Ⓥ col

Dir Peter Bogdanovich ***Prod*** Peter Bogdanovich ***Scr*** M. A. Stewart, Max Dickens ***Ph*** Dante Spinotti ***Ed*** Richard Fields ***Mus*** Phil Marshall ***Art*** Jane Musky

Act Rob Lowe, Colleen Camp, Kenneth Mars, Harry Carey Jr, Kim Myers (De Laurentiis/Crescent Moon)

Illegally Yours is an embarrassingly unfunny attempt at screwball comedy, marking a career nadir for producer-director Peter Bogdanovich and his miscast star Rob Lowe.

Hectic pre-credits sequence, loaded with telltale, expository voice-over by Lowe, crudely sets up an uninteresting story of a blackmailer's murder, witnessed by young Kim Myers and her friend L. B. Straten, in which innocent Colleen Camp is arrested as the fall guy. An audiotape recording of the murder is the item everyone is trying to get their hands on.

Lowe is cast, with unbecoming glasses throughout, as a college dropout trying to get his life in order back home in St. Augustine, FL. Between endless pratfalls Lowe finds himself on jury duty in Camp's case.

En route to sorting out the boring mystery of what became of the kidnaper's corpse, Lowe is thoroughly out of his element, even adopting a silly voice for a dumb drag scene. Camp is given little to do and no chemistry develops between the mismatched stars.

•

ILL MET BY MOONLIGHT
(US: NIGHT AMBUSH)

1957, 104 mins, UK Ⓥ b/w

Dir Michael Powell, Emeric Pressburger ***Prod*** Michael Powell, Emeric Pressburger ***Scr*** Michael Powell, Emeric Pressburger ***Ph*** Christopher Challis ***Ed*** Arthur Stevens ***Mus*** Mikis Theodorakis ***Art*** Alex Vetchinsky

Act Dirk Bogarde, Marius Goring, David Oxley, Cyril Cusack, Laurence Payne, Michael Gough (Rank/Archers)

Michael Powell and Emeric Pressburger take as their subject an operation in occupied Crete [from the book by W. Stanley Moss]. Two British officers, with the aid of local patriots, are given the job of kidnapping the German commander-in-chief and transporting him to Cairo.

The job of hijacking the general is accomplished with remarkable ease and luck. His car is ambushed and he's driven through endless road blocks to a mountain hideout. Then comes the tricky part. The general has to be led to the beachhead selected by the British navy for transportation to Egypt.

Dirk Bogarde turns in a smooth and satisfying performance as a British major, with David Oxley giving valuable aid as his No. 2 man. Marius Goring, as the general, is smugly confident that he'll be rescued by his own men and gallantly accepts the fact that he's been outwitted by a bunch of amateurs.

•

I'LL NEVER FORGET WHAT'S 'IS NAME

1967, 97 mins, UK col

Dir Michael Winner ***Prod*** Michael Winner ***Scr*** Peter Draper ***Ph*** Otto Heller ***Ed*** Bernard Gribble ***Mus*** Francis Lai ***Art*** Seamus Flannery

Act Orson Welles, Oliver Reed, Carol White, Harry Andrews, Michael Hordern, Wendy Craig (Universal/Scimitar)

Story concerns a successful and resentful whiz kid of the advertising game (Oliver Reed), who opts out to join a pal in running an esoteric literary magazine. Separated from his wife, he is a womanizer of perpetual appetite, taking one off to a lonely and disused railroad station and establishing a flightly relationship with a secretary (Carol White), who is prim at heart and takes it all seriously.

Thus the theme is the aridity of fashionable achievement, and the sour smell of success is hammered home by director Michael Winner with an insistence that destroys its own claims and closes with a final scene of stunning vulgarity.

Oliver Reed looks grim and disenchanted throughout, but hasn't the power to suggest that there's much talent going to waste.

In addition to Orson Welles, White registers as the girl torn between her virginal upbringing and her beckoning by Reed. The role is inconclusive, but she gives it the stamp of charm and unforced sweetness.

•

ILLUSTRATED MAN, THE

1969, 103 mins, US Ⓥ ▭ col

Dir Jack Smight ***Prod*** Howard B. Kreitsek, Ted Mann ***Scr*** Howard B. Kreitsek ***Ph*** Philip Lathrop ***Ed*** Archie Marshek ***Mus*** Jerry Goldsmith ***Art*** Joel Schiller

Act Rod Steiger, Claire Bloom, Robert Drivas, Don Dubbins, Jason Evans (Warner/Seven Arts)

The Illustrated Man has going for it two major aspects: a derivative Ray Bradbury story and an obtuse, time-fragmented, humanistic, allegorical morality play.

Rod Steiger and Claire Bloom star in a story told in flashback and flash-forward, from a rural lakeside camp occupied for an afternoon and a night around Labor Day 1933 by wandering drifter Steiger and neighborhood boy Robert Drivas.

Steiger is gradually revealed to be almost totally covered with tattoos—he prefers the phrase "skin illustrations"—each representing some sort of adventure. Plot selects three of those adventures.

The interpretations of the story are manifold. Steiger's character is apparently an eternal Adam, wandering through the ages and encountering challenges, the marks and memories of which are the tattoos.

•

ILLUSTRIOUS CORPSES

SEE: CADAVERI ECCELLENTI

•

I LOVE A SOLDIER

1944, 106 mins, US b/w

Dir Mark Sandrich ***Prod*** Mark Sandrich ***Scr*** Allan Scott ***Ph*** Charles Lang ***Ed*** Ellsworth Hoagland ***Mus*** Robert Emmett Dolan ***Art*** Hans Dreier, Earl Hedrick

Act Paulette Goddard, Sonny Tufts, Barry Fitzgerald, Mary Ireen, Beulah Bondi (Paramount)

Principal reasons for the film's weaknesses are two-fold. From the start the payoff is never in doubt, with little suspense induced. Secondly, its boy-meets-girl plot has a tedious overabundance of twists and turns.

Story concerns a lady welder (Paulette Goddard) who refuses to go for a war marriage and supplements her war effort chore by evening hostess work, entertaining soldiers just back from overseas or on the verge of going. She does fall, though, for Sonny Tufts, but they split twice, first when she discovers he's married although on brink of divorce, and secondly, after the reconciliation, on the self-sacrifice angle. Idea here is that if he's worried about a wife back home, he's likely to forget to concentrate on the war and get knocked off.

Goddard and Tufts are the leads. She's okay in the lighter moments but not too convincing in the heavier spots. Tufts gives an ingratiating and sincere performance.

•

I LOVE MELVIN

1953, 76 mins, US Ⓥ col

Dir Don Weis ***Prod*** George Wells ***Scr*** George Wells, Ruth Brooks Flippen ***Ph*** Harold Rosson ***Ed*** Adrienne Fazan ***Mus*** George Stoll (dir.) ***Art*** Cedric Gibbons, Jack Martin Smith, Eddie Imazu

Act Donald O'Connor, Debbie Reynolds, Una Merkel, Richard Anderson, Jim Backus, Robert Taylor (M-G-M)

This is a lively, youthful musical comedy with a script, taken from a story by Laslo Vadney, that provides interesting substance to a fluffy affair.

Donald O'Connor and Debbie Reynolds are the youthful sparkplugs and both perform to advantage under Don Weis's direction. Bounciest number they do together is "Where Did You Learn to Dance," an informal affair of charm. O'Connor does some skating terps to "Life Has Its Funny Little Ups and Downs," with little Noreen Corcoran supplying the appealing vocal. The big production number is "Saturday Afternoon before the Game," in which Reynolds plays the football and reveals every curve in a pigskin costume. The songs are by Josef Myrow and Mack Gordon.

Plot finds O'Connor a bulb-carrier for Jim Backus, *Look* photog. He falls in love with Reynolds, a chorus cutie, and gives her the impression he is a photographer. He launches a campaign of picture-taking with her as model and she and her family believe the gal will make the *Look* cover. O'Connor fakes a cover but the stunt backfires.

Una Merkel and Allyn Joslyn are very good as Reynolds's parents, as is little Corcoran as her kid sister. Richard Anderson is delightful as Reynolds's stuffed-shirt suitor, favored by Joslyn. Backus plays his photog role for sure chuckles. Robert Taylor makes a brief guest appearance. Robert Alton staged and directed the dances.

•

I LOVE TROUBLE

1994, 123 mins, US Ⓥ ⦿ col

Dir Charles Shyer ***Prod*** Nancy Meyers ***Scr*** Nancy Meyers, Charles Shyer ***Ph*** John Lindley ***Ed*** Paul Hirsch, Walter

Murch, Adam Bernardi ***Mus*** David Newman ***Art*** Dean Tavoularis
Act Julia Roberts, Nick Nolte, Saul Rubinek, James Rebhorn, Robert Loggia, Olympia Dukakis (Touchstone)

A Cary Grant–Audrey Hepburn vehicle some 30 years too late, this ultra-polished romantic suspenser serves up mild romance, mild suspense and mild humor. Having one's taste in the right place is not a substitute for originality and zest, both of which are in relatively short supply in this luxuriously appointed yarn of a rugged, legendary scribe who meets his match in a beautiful, young cub reporter.

Nick Nolte plays Peter Brackett, a Windy City columnist in the Ben Hecht tradition who's a notorious womanizer, boozer and cynic of the old school. Brackett is temporarily forced back onto the beat as punishment for his laziness and finds himself scooped by competing *Globe* newcomer Sabrina Peterson (Julia Roberts).

Story in question involves the derailment of a passenger train in which several people are killed, but it quickly builds into a case of corporate intrigue and subterfuge. After vying to outdo each other for some time, Brackett and Peterson agree to team up on research while still filing separate stories.

Nothing that happens is very surprising, including the outcome, meaning that the film must rely solely on its moment-to-moment charm to seduce the audience. Roberts and Nolte do their share to supply this, but producer Nancy Meyers and director Charles Shyer, who co-wrote the script, have given them more in the way of ticklish situations to contend with than sharp repartée and fizzy dialogue.

•

I LOVE YOU, ALICE B. TOKLAS!

1968, 92 mins, US Ⓥ col
Dir Hy Averback ***Prod*** Charles Maguire ***Scr*** Paul Mazursky, Larry Tucker ***Ph*** Philip Lathrop ***Ed*** Robert C. Jones ***Mus*** Elmer Bernstein ***Art*** Pato Guzman
Act Peter Sellers, Jo Van Fleet, Leigh Taylor-Young, Joyce Van Patten, David Arkin, Herb Edelman (Warner/Seven Arts)

Film is not heavy-handed in its approach either to hippie life, or to what is considered "normal" modes of behavior. Instead, there is a sympathetic look at the advantages and disadvantages of each.

Pic derives its prime value from an excellent screenplay. Story is relatively simple: Peter Sellers, an LA lawyer, turns on to hippie life as an escape from conformity and hypocrisy. Later, he finds out that human nature is independent of superficial environment, returns briefly to his former life, but winds up running away again.

Film blasts off into orbit via top-notch acting and direction. Sellers's performance—both in scenes which spotlight his character as well as ensemble sequences in which everyone is balanced nicely—is an outstanding blend of warmth, sensitivity, disillusion and optimism. Jo Van Fleet is simply brilliant as Sellers's mother, with Salem Ludwig also on target as his dad. Joyce Van Patten's performance as Sellers's pushy fiancée is delightful.

•

I LOVE YOU TO DEATH

1990, 96 mins, US Ⓥ ⦿ col
Dir Lawrence Kasdan ***Prod*** Jeffrey Lurie, Ron Moler, Patrick Wells, ***Scr*** John Kostmayer ***Ph*** Owen Roisman ***Ed*** Anne V. Coates ***Mus*** James Horner ***Art*** Lilly Kilvert
Act Kevin Kline, Tracey Ullman, Joan Plowright, River Phoenix, William Hurt, Keanu Reeves (Chestnut Hill)

I Love You to Death is a stillborn attempt at black comedy.

Opening credits stress tale is based on a true story, but John Kostmayer's screenplay never makes events remotely interesting. Kevin Kline creates a stereotypical Italian restaurant owner who can't help cheating on his frumpish wife, Tracey Ullman with scores of women.

Awkward script has Ullman discovering Kline in a tryst at a library and, after brief consultation with her Yugoslav mom Joan Plowright, resolving to kill him.

Harold and Maude it ain't. Film founders because the cast is out of control. Chief culprit is Hurt, as a hired space cadet hitman, who pulls faces embarrassingly here as a retarded hippie.

At the other extreme, the three British actresses are models of professionalism. Ullman unfortunately fades into the woodwork by steadfastly adopting a bland speech pattern and looking as homely as possible. Plowright is solid as her mom.

•

IMAGES

1972, 100 mins, UK ⦿ ▭ col
Dir Robert Altman ***Prod*** Tommy Thompson ***Scr*** Robert Altman ***Ph*** Vilmos Zsigmond ***Ed*** Graeme Clifford ***Mus*** John Williams ***Art*** Leon Ericksen
Act Susannah York, Rene Auberjonois, Marcel Bozzuffi, Hugh Millais, Cathryn Harrison (Lion's Gate/Hemdale)

Robert Altman made this interior drama about a woman going through hallucination and nearing madness in Ireland. Delving into effects of permissiveness on a hidebound, repressed nature, it also shows a probing insight into mental disorder.

Susannah York, writing a fairy tale for children about mysterious woods and a unicorn that acts as a counterpoint to her real life losing of touch with reality, imagines phone calls saying her husband is with another woman and when they go to their country house for the weekend two men in her life intrude as imaginary, or, in one case, real.

York has the intensity and innocence marked by strain as well as sensual underpinnings, and brings off the final denouement with restraint and potency.

1972: NOMINATION: Best Original Score

•

IMAGINARY CRIMES

1994, 104 mins, US Ⓥ col
Dir Anthony Drazen ***Prod*** James G. Robinson ***Scr*** Kristine Johnson, Davia Nelson ***Ph*** John J. Campbell ***Ed*** Elizabeth Kling ***Mus*** Stephen Endelman ***Art*** Joseph T. Garrity
Act Harvey Keitel, Fairuza Balk, Kelly Lynch, Vincent D'Onofrio, Diane Baker, Chris Penn (Morgan Creek/Warner)

This teenage girl coming-of-age story boasts some fine performances, but is weakened by an overly familiar plot [from the book by Sheila Ballantyne].

Tale opens with Sonya Weiler (Fairuza Balk) looking back on her senior year of high school in 1962 Portland, OR. Her mother (played by Kelly Lynch in flashback) has succumbed to cancer. Her father, Ray (Harvey Keitel), is a well-meaning ne'er-do-well whose get-rich-quick schemes leave a lot of angry people in their wake.

Keeping a promise to his wife, Ray enrolls Sonya at an exclusive girls' school for her senior year, even though it's questionable whether he will be able to pay for it. There she falls under the tutelage of a well-meaning English teacher (Vincent D'Onofrio) who encourages her writing as well as her ambitions to go to college.

We've seen all this before in countless dramas, right down to the sympathetic teacher—who invariably teaches English rather than math or science. Film's key asset is the acting, particularly the perfs by Balk and Lynch. The most remarkable achievement of Keitel's performance is his accent, scrubbed of every trace of New York and the big city.

•

I'M ALL RIGHT JACK

1959, 105 mins, UK Ⓥ b/w
Dir John Boulting ***Prod*** Roy Boulting ***Scr*** Frank Harvey, John Boulting, Alan Hackney ***Ph*** Max Greene ***Ed*** Anthony Harvey ***Mus*** Ken Hare ***Art*** Bill Andrews
Act Ian Carmichael, Peter Sellers, Terry-Thomas, Richard Attenborough, Dennis Price, Margaret Rutherford (British Lion/Charter)

The Boulting Brothers's target [from the novel by Alan Hackney] is British factory life, trade unionism and the general possibility that everybody is working for one person—himself.

Ian Carmichael plays an ex-university type who wants to get an executive job in industry. Instead, he is given a job as a factory worker by his uncle who wants him in as a stooge for a secret, dirty financial deal. Carmichael becomes the unwitting cause of a factory strike that swells to nationwide proportions. Gradually he begins to realize that he has been taken for a ride.

Carmichael slides smoothly through his performance, but it is Peter Sellers, as the chairman of the factory's union works committee, who makes the film. With a makeup that subtly suggests Hitler, he brings rare humor and an occasional touch of pathos to the role. Sellers's strength is that he does not deliberately play for laughs. He produces them from the situations and sharp dialog.

Dennis Price and Richard Attenborough as shady employers and Terry-Thomas as a bewildered personnel manager also provide rich roles.

•

I MARRIED A COMMUNIST
(UK: THE WOMAN ON PIER 13)

1949, 72 mins, US b/w
Dir Robert Stevenson ***Prod*** Sid Rogell ***Scr*** Charles Grayson, Robert Hardy Andrews ***Ph*** Nicholas Musuraca ***Ed*** Roland Gross ***Mus*** Leigh Harline
Act Laraine Day, Robert Ryan, John Agar, Thomas Gomez, Janis Carter (RKO)

As a straight action fare, *I Married a Communist* generates enough tension to satisfy the average customer. Despite its heavy sounding title, pic hews strictly to tried and true meller formula.

Screenplay uses the simple and slightly naive device of substituting Communist for gangsters in a typical underworld yarn.

Pic is so wary of introducing any political gab that at one point when Commie trade union tactics are touched upon, the soundtrack is dropped. Robert Ryan plays an ex-comrade who turns up in San Francisco as vice-prexy of a shipping company and bigtime labor relations expert. In the midst of waterfront union negotiations, the Commie chieftain (Thomas Gomez) enters to remind Ryan that he can't quit the mob and had better follow the Party's directive to stir up labor trouble.

•

I MARRIED A MONSTER FROM OUTER SPACE

1958, 78 mins, US Ⓥ b/w
Dir Gene Fowler, Jr. ***Prod*** Gene Fowler, Jr. ***Scr*** Louis Vittes ***Ph*** Haskell Boggs ***Ed*** George Tomasini ***Art*** Hal Pereira, Henry Bumstead
Act Tom Tryon, Gloria Talbott, Ken Lynch, John Eldredge, Alan Dexter, Jean Carson (Paramount)

Premise of the screenplay deals with a race of monsters from another galaxy who invade the earth and secretly take over the form of some of the male townspeople. Film opens with Gloria Talbott marrying Tom Tryon, unaware the man she loves is now one of these monsters.

After a year of tension she follows him one night and watches him change into his original form and enter a spaceship. Through her doctor, to whom she goes in her terror, enough normal people are recruited to successfully break up the invasion by an attack on spaceship.

Gene Fowler, Jr.'s direction, while sometimes slow, latches on to mounting suspense as action moves to a climax. He gets the benefit of outstanding special photographic effects from John P. Fulton, which aid in maintaining interest.

•

I MARRIED A WITCH

1942, 82 mins, US Ⓥ ⦿ b/w
Dir Rene Clair ***Prod*** Rene Clair ***Scr*** Robert Pirosh, Marc Connelly ***Ph*** Ted Tetzlaff ***Ed*** Eda Warren ***Mus*** Roy Webb
Act Fredric March, Veronica Lake, Robert Benchley, Susan Hayward, Cecil Kellaway, Elizabeth Patterson (United Artists)

I Married a Witch, which deals with spirits, is a fantastic type of story that carries some interest on the novelty angles, if nothing else, but on the whole is generally tepid.

The story opens in 1690 in New England, where a strait-laced Puritan condemns a sorcerer and his witch daughter who are burned at the stake. As a result, a curse is laid on the Puritan and any of his descendants, the action then jumping to the present when Fredric March, a descendant, is running for election as governor. He is in love with the daughter of a publisher backing him. The romance is upset and it appears that March is going to lose in consequence of the actions taken by two departed spirits.

Neither March nor Veronica Lake impresses very importantly, while Robert Benchley has not been well equipped with material designed to afford comic relief.

1942: NOMINATION: Best Scoring of a Dramatic Picture

•

I'M DANCING AS FAST AS I CAN

1982, 106 mins, US Ⓥ ⦿ col
Dir Jack Hofsiss ***Prod*** Edgar J. Scherick, Scott Rudin ***Scr*** David Rabe ***Ph*** Jan de Bont ***Ed*** Michael Bradsell ***Mus*** Stanley Silverman ***Art*** David Jenkins
Act Jill Clayburgh, Nicol Williamson, Dianne Wiest, Joe Pesci, Geraldine Page, James Sutorius (Paramount)

Crucial inability of a film to get inside a character's head spells big trouble for *I'm Dancing As Fast As I Can.* Result here is that Jill Clayburgh's constantly center-stage character comes off as the "pill-popping dingbat" she's called at one point, rather than as a fascinating lady with a major problem.

Based on Barbara Gordon's popular autobiographical tome, screenplay minutely charts Clayburgh's compulsive reliance on Valium, her disastrous effort to go cold turkey and her subsequent rehabilitation in an institution.

At the outset, Clayburgh is presented as a successful docu filmmaker for television. A little professional crisis presents itself. Pop goes a pill or two. A teeny tiff with b.f. Nicol Williamson. Down with another couple of blue tablets.

Only two members of the large supporting cast, Dianne Wiest and Geraldine Page, have any chance to develop their characters, and both do well.

•

I MET HIM IN PARIS
1937, 85 mins, US b/w
Dir Wesley Ruggles ***Prod*** Wesley Ruggles ***Scr*** Claude Binyon ***Ph*** Leo Tover ***Ed*** Otho Lovering ***Art*** Hans Dreier, Ernst Feyte
Act Claudette Colbert, Melvyn Douglas, Robert Young, Mona Barrie, George Davis, Lee Bowman (Paramount)

Long after audiences will have forgotten what this picture is about, the studio probably will be showing the film as one lesson in what a comedy picture ought to be. It's not the story [by Helen Meinardi]. It's not the acting. It's not the production. It's the many infinitesimal touches stuck into the script and action by the adaptor, Claude Binyon, and the director-producer, Wesley Ruggles.

A very simple little yarn with mighty little happening—but all of it pleasantly. Story has Claudette Colbert going to Paris for a vacation on her own. She meets a couple of friendly enemies (Robert Young and Melvyn Douglas), both of whom make a play for her. Douglas is bitter and supercilious; Young is seemingly genuine and sincere, though liberal in his morals. Douglas knows Young is married and is hanging around to make Young play ball on the square. The trio go to Switzerland and much wrangling between the threesome is interspersed with snow stuff.

In between are a French waiter who thinks he knows how to speak English, a Swiss hotel clerk who gets considerable laugh footage by being superior to his guests, a bartender who is brokenhearted every time his customers order Scotch instead of brandy, and any number of other bits.

Colbert is excellent, while Young and Douglas team well opposite. Script has a sophisticated basis and permits Colbert to wear some smart clothes. Indeed, she has seldom looked better.

•

IMITATION OF LIFE
1934, 116 mins, US b/w
Dir John M. Stahl ***Prod*** Carl Laemmle, Jr. ***Scr*** William Hurlburt ***Ph*** Merritt Gerstad ***Ed*** Philip Cahn, Maurice Wright ***Mus*** Heinz Roemheld (dir.) ***Art*** Charles D. Hall
Act Claudette Colbert, Warren William, Louise Beavers, Fredi Washington, Rochelle Hudson, Alan Hale (Universal)

Imitation of Life is a strong picture with an unusual plot. A young white widow (Claudette Colbert) with a baby girl goes into a business partnership with her colored maid (Louise Beavers) who also has a baby girl. In the passage of years a small business becomes a factory and they are wealthy. But neither the white woman nor the negress derives much joy. And because of their daughters.

Most arresting part of the picture and overshadowing the conventional romance between the late thirtyish white widow and Warren William is the tragedy of Aunt Delilah's girl born to a white skin and Negro blood. This subject is treated on the screen for the first time here. Girl is miserable being unable to adjust herself to the lot of her race and unable to take her place among the whites.

John M. Stahl directs this kind of thing very well. He keeps the Fannie Hurst "success story" brand of snobbishness under control and the film flows with mounting interest, if at moments a trifle slowly.

Picture is stolen by the Negress, Beavers, whose performance is masterly. This lady can troupe. She takes the whole scale of human emotions from joy to anguish and never sounds a false note.

1934: NOMINATIONS: Best Picture, Sound, Assistant Director

•

IMITATION OF LIFE
1959, 125 mins, US Ⓥ col
Dir Douglas Sirk ***Prod*** Ross Hunter ***Scr*** Eleanore Griffin, Allan Scott ***Ph*** Russell Metty ***Ed*** Milton Carruth ***Mus*** Frank Skinner ***Art*** Alexander Golitzen, Richard H. Riedel
Act Lana Turner, John Gavin, Sandra Dee, Dan O'Herlihy, Robert Alda, Susan Kohner (Universal)

Imitation of Life is a remake of Fannie Hurst's novel of the early 1930s. Lana Turner is outstanding in the pivotal role played in Universal's 1934 version by Claudette Colbert. Scripters Eleanore Griffin and Allan Scott have transplanted her from the original pancake-and-flour business to the American stage.

While this device lends more scope, it also results in the overdone busy actress/neglected daughter conflict, and thus the secondary plot of a fair-skinned Negress passing as white becomes the film's primary force. The relationship of the young colored girl and her mother—played memorably by Susan Kohner and Juanita Moore—is sometimes overpowering, while the relationship of Turner and her daughter, Sandra Dee, comes to life only briefly when both are in love with same man, John Gavin.

Turner plays a character of changing moods, and her changes are remarkably effective, as she blends love and understanding, sincerity and ambition. The growth of maturity is reflected neatly in her distinguished portrayal. In smaller roles, both Robert Alda, as an opportunist agent, and Dan O'Herlihy, as a playwright, are excellent.

1959: NOMINATIONS: Best Supp. Actress (Juanita Moore, Susan Kohner)

•

IM LAUF DER ZEIT
(KINGS OF THE ROAD)
1976, 165 mins, W. Germany Ⓥ b/w
Dir Wim Wenders ***Prod*** Wim Wenders ***Scr*** Wim Wenders ***Ph*** Robbie Mueller, Martin Schaefer ***Ed*** Peter Przygodda ***Mus*** Axel Lindstaedt
Act Ruediger Vogeler, Hanns Zischler, Lisa Kreuzer, Rudolf Schuendler, Marquard Boehm, Dieter Traier (Wenders)

Wim Wenders's *Kings of the Road* is a pic about men and adventure. For nearly three hours nothing much happens as two men cross the middle of Germany, from Lueneburg to Hof along the East German border, but it's what they see and hear that captures attention. The charm is in the Newman-Redford types, both funny and tragic, and in the pic's improvisational character.

Bruno travels along the border in a moving van that serves as a household camper; he is a projectionist who dismantles old movie equipment for sale elsewhere. Along the Elbe he meets Robert, a child psychologist running away from his women troubles, who drives his VW sleepy-headed right into the middle of the river. It's the beginning of a journey into the past as well as adjusting to the loneliness of the present.

This is an American "road picture" in its most elemental form. It has the flavor of a Howard Hawks pic in the relationship of the two men to one another in an easy, unquestioning manner, but there are also lines out to Fritz Lang and John Ford in the tone and atmosphere of certain scenes. The landscape of deserted towns and movie houses on the border has a '30s look of the Depression Years.

Pic's only drawback is its length; cut of a good half hour or more could tighten up story line measureably. Lensing is top-notch throughout.

•

IMMACULATE CONCEPTION
1992, 122 mins, UK Ⓥ ⦿ col
Dir Jamil Dehlavi ***Prod*** Jamil Dehlavi ***Scr*** Jamil Dehlavi ***Ph*** Nic Knowland ***Ed*** Chris Barnes ***Mus*** Richard Harvey ***Art*** Mike Porter
Act James Wilby, Melissa Leo, Shabana Azmi, Zia Mohyeddin, James Cossins, Ronny Jhutti (Film Four/Dehlavi)

An ambitious culture-clash drama set in troubled 1988 Pakistan, *Immaculate Conception* tries to cover too many bases to score a solid hit.

James Wilby is Alistair, a wildlife conservationist based in Karachi with Jewish-American spouse Hannah (Melissa Leo), daughter of a powerful U.S. senator. Desperate to conceive a child, the couple visit a eunuch-run shrine reputed to have a cure for infertility. In fact, the eunuchs slip them the local version of a Mickey and get teenager Kamal (Ronny Jhutti) to do the business with a semi-comatose Hannah.

Final turn of the screw is Kamal spilling the beans about what really happened when Hannah's brother (Tim Choate) hotfoots it from the States with instructions from Daddy.

Franco-Pakistani helmer Jamil Dehlavi can't be faulted for ambition or political objectivity (pic is often scathing on Pakistan's faults). But without a stronger central dramatic line, pic perpetually shifts in and out of focus, to overall mild emotional effect. Weak dialogue in several crucial scenes is a further minus.

•

IMMEDIATE FAMILY
1989, 95 mins, US Ⓥ ⦿ col
Dir Jonathan Kaplan ***Prod*** Sarah Pillsbury, Midge Sanford ***Scr*** Barbara Benedek ***Ph*** John W. Lindley ***Ed*** Jane Kurson ***Mus*** Brad Fiedel ***Art*** Mark Freeborn
Act Glenn Close, James Woods, Mary Stuart Masterson, Kevin Dillon, Linda Darlow, Jane Greer (Columbia/Sanford-Pillsbury)

Definitely no comedy, *Immediate Family* nonetheless explodes with bursts of laughter that lighten the heartbreak of a lot of nice people tormented by their own best intentions.

For Solomon and generations of juvenile judges since, there's no tougher case to call than competing claims for a baby. But Solomon's solution wouldn't work for *Immediate Family*, in which Glenn Close and Mary Stuart Masterson are each so deserving.

Granted, the plot requires no elaborate examination: After 11 years of marriage, James Woods and Glenn Close are still achingly childless. After no years of marriage, young Mary Stuart Masterson and boyfriend Kevin Dillon face impending parenthood under circumstances that could wreck their chances for a happier life later.

The solution, so obviously simple in a lawyer's office, is that Woods and Close will adopt Masterson's baby. But first the lawyer thinks everybody should get better acquainted.

Clever as she is, Close keeps her potentially cloying part understated; there's no need to hang a sign on her suffering. Young Masterson is simply superb, managing to first earn the audience's sympathy and then keep hold when some might be tempted to turn away.

•

IMMIGRANT, THE
1917, 30 mins, US ⊗ b/w
Dir Charles Chaplin ***Scr*** Charles Chaplin ***Ph*** William C. Foster, Rollie Totheroh
Act Charles Chaplin, Eric Campbell, Edna Purviance, Henry Bergman, Albert Austin (Mutual)

The two-reeler opens up showing Charlie leaning over the [boat's] rail apparently seasick. It develops that he is fishing and lands a one-pounder in mid-ocean. Then he is seen shooting craps and going through all the gyrations of a baseball pitcher every time he "shoots the bones." The rocking and pitching of the vessel furnish unlimited opportunity for his style of comedy.

There is a little heart-interest story, when he befriends a young girl and her mother who have been robbed of their small hoard. Later—all too soon, however—he is seen in New York, broke. He spies a quarter on the street and enters a restaurant to eat. There he meets the girl he befriended on shipboard. She is also down and out, her mother having died.

The $670,000 a year funnyman is still "there." The extremely limited number of titles speaks volumes for the pantomimic art of the comedian.

•

IMMORTAL BATTALION
SEE: THE WAY AHEAD

•

IMMORTAL BELOVED
1994, 121 mins, US Ⓥ ⦿ ▭ col
Dir Bernard Rose ***Prod*** Bruce Davey ***Scr*** Bernard Rose ***Ph*** Peter Suschitzky ***Ed*** Dan Rae ***Mus*** John Stronach (sup.) ***Art*** Jiri Hlupy
Act Gary Oldman, Jeroen Krabbe, Isabella Rossellini, Johanna Ter Steege, Barry Humphries, Valeria Golino (Icon)

Immortal Beloved attempts to travel the *Citizen Kane* route of using a death's door clue left by a difficult great man to penetrate his secret self. The man in question here is Ludwig van Beethoven, and the result is less than compelling due to the fragmentary telling of the story, off-putting nature of the main character and failure of the filmmakers to make their investigation seem of any particular consequence.

The Rosebud here is a letter from Beethoven found soon after his death addressed to an unnamed Immortal Beloved in which he wrote, among other things, that "I can live only completely with you or not at all." The identity of his beloved has stumped all biographers over the years.

Beginning with the hero's death in 1827, film follows the travels throughout Middle Europe of Anton Schindler (Jeroen Krabbe), Beethoven's loyal factotum, as he pursues all his leads in the mystery. He first visits a hotel in Karlsbad where he knows his boss (Gary Oldman) had an assignation many years before. This lands him an interview with the Countess Giulietta Guicciardi (Valeria Golino), who claims to have been Beethoven's great love.

Director Bernard Rose uses flashback glimpses of this romance to illustrate how, even at an early age, the composer's encroaching deafness made him even more arrogant, rude and impossible to other people than he already was. Also sketched is his destructive relationship with his youngest brother and the latter's peasant wife, Johanna (Johanna Ter Steege). Another line of inquiry takes Schindler to Hungary, where the Countess Anna Marie Erdody (Isabella Rossellini) represents his greatest hope of finding the true Immortal Beloved.

•

IMMORTAL SERGEANT, THE
1943, 90 mins, US Ⓥ b/w
Dir John M. Stahl ***Prod*** Lamar Trotti ***Scr*** Lamar Trotti ***Ph*** Arthur Miller ***Ed*** James B. Clark ***Mus*** David Buttolph

Act Henry Fonda, Maureen O'Hara, Thomas Mitchell, Allyn Joslyn, Reginald Gardiner (20th Century-Fox)

Story is a compact drama, interestingly told, of a lost sunrise patrol on the Libyan desert. It's an intimate study of characters and hardships encountered in the desert.

There's the sergeant (Thomas Mitchell), resourceful tactician of the last war and a most inspiring leader for the unit. It's his influence, after fatal wounding, that drives corporal Henry Fonda on with the remnants of the outfit and transforms Fonda from a self-effacing individual into a determined, confident personality.

Desert warfare is vividly displayed, with the little group facing the rigors of forced marches across the sands with limited supplies; and mixing in several engagements against enemy units encountered along the way, including a climactic blasting of a German camp set up in an oasis. Producer-writer Lamar Trotti provides director John M. Stahl with a neatly-woven script [from a novel by John Brophy], and Stahl directs in deft style.

•

I'M NO ANGEL

1933, 87 mins, US b/w

Dir Wesley Ruggles **Scr** Mae West **Ph** Leo Tover **Mus** Harvey Brooks

Act Mae West, Cary Grant, Edward Arnold, Ralf Harolde, Russell Hopton, Gregory Ratoff (Paramount)

It's fairly obvious that the same plot mechanics and situations [from suggestions by Lowell Brentano and a treatment by Harlan Thompson] without Mae West wouldn't be a motion picture at all. But that's no criticism. It's all West, plus a good directing job by Wesley Ruggles and first-rate studio production quality in all departments.

Laughs are all derived from the West innuendos and the general good-natured bawdiness of the heroine, whose progress from a carnival mugg-taker to a deluxe millionaire-annexer is marked by a succession of gentlemen friends, mostly temporary and usually suckers.

When reaching affluence the carnival gal is serviced by four colored maids in an ultra-penthouse and garbed in the flashy manner of an Oriental potentate's pampered pet.

Every now and again West bursts into a song, generally just a chorus or a strain. They're of the Frankie and Johnny genre, but primarily she plays a lion tamer, not a songstress.

•

I, MOBSTER
(UK: THE MOBSTER)

1958, 80 mins, US Ⓥ ▭ b/w

Dir Roger Corman **Prod** Edward L. Alperson, Roger Corman, Gene Corman **Scr** Steve Fisher **Ph** Floyd Crosby **Ed** William B. Murphy **Mus** Gerald Fried, Edward L. Alperson, Jr. **Art** Daniel Haller

Act Steve Cochran, Lita Milan, Robert Strauss, Celia Lovsky, Lili St. Cyr (20th Century-Fox)

I, Mobster is a well-turned-out melodrama with Steve Cochran in title role delivering a slick characterization of the rise and fall of a mobsman.

Steve Fisher screenplay utilizes the flashback technique, opening with Cochran, who heads the national crime syndicate, invoking the Fifth Amendment as he appears before the Senate Rackets Committee in Washington. Narrative dips back to his youth, when he collected horse race bets for a local hoodlum, Robert Strauss; then spans his whole career in crime as he becomes involved in dope traffic, later his hard-hitting entry into strike-breaking and "protection" of strike-breaking unions.

Under Roger Corman's knowhow direction action unfolds smoothly and swiftly. Through very creditable performances, Corman manages to capture the gangster feeling and in addition to Cochran outstanding portrayals are contributed by Lita Milan, as his sweetheart; Strauss, socking over his henchman role after Cochran rises above him; and Celia Lovsky, as Cochran's sorely tried mother.

•

IMPORTANCE OF BEING EARNEST, THE

1952, 95 mins, UK Ⓥ ⦿ col

Dir Anthony Asquith **Prod** Teddy Baird **Scr** Anthony Asquith **Ph** Desmond Dickinson **Ed** John D. Guthridge **Mus** Benjamin Frankel **Art** Carmen Dillon

Act Michael Redgrave, Edith Evans, Michael Denison, Dorothy Tutin, Margaret Rutherford, Joan Greenwood (Javelin/Two Cities)

All the charm and glossy humor of Oscar Wilde's classic comedy emerges faithfully in this British production. Apart from a few minor cuts, director Anthony Asquith has taken few liberties with the original. His skilful direction extracts all the polish of Wilde's brilliant dialog.

Michael Redgrave brings a wealth of sincerity to the role of the earnest young man, without knowledge of his origin, whose invention of a fictitious brother leads to romantic complications. Michael Denison plays the debonair Algernon Moncrieff in a gay lighthearted style, and makes his characterization the pivot for much of the comedy.

The two romantic femme roles are adroitly played by Joan Greenwood and Dorothy Tutin.

•

IMPOSSIBLE OBJECT
(AKA: STORY OF A LOVE STORY)

1973, 110 mins, France col

Dir John Frankenheimer **Scr** Nicolas Mosley **Ph** Claude Renoir **Ed** Albert Jurgenson **Mus** Michel Legrand **Art** Alexandre Trauner

Act Alan Bates, Dominique Sanda, Evans Evans, Lea Massari, Michel Auclair, Paul Crauchet (Franco-London/Euro International)

John Frankenheimer spent over a year in Paris and then made this film for a local company, albeit mainly in English with passages between French people in French. It is a many-pronged affair in a tale of a writer whose inventions and real life may not always be extricable. It mixes romantic drama, situation comedy and insights into Americans or British abroad.

Alan Bates is a writer, living in a country home in France, outside Paris, with three sons and an American wife. He meets brooding but delicately sensual Dominique Sanda, who is married, in a museum and love blossoms. Film flits lightly over the affair, the writer's embroidery on it and sideline events that reflect on it until sudden swerve to tragedy.

Though pic segues from fantasy to implied realism, pic has an airy grace, fine playing down the line.

•

IMPOSTOR, THE

1944, 93 mins, US b/w

Dir Julien Duvivier **Prod** Julien Duvivier **Scr** Julien Duvivier, Stephen Longstreet, Marc Connelly, Lynn Starling **Ph** Paul Ivano **Ed** Paul Landres **Mus** Dimitri Tiomkin **Art** John B. Goodman, Eugene Lourie

Act Jean Gabin, Richard Whorf, Ellen Drew, Peter Van Eyck (Universal)

Fall of France in 1940, and subsequent formation of Free French units in Africa, forms basis for this adventure drama, which unfolds tale of regeneration of a confirmed criminal through comradeship in arms. Julien Duvivier fails to generate pace fast enough to carry picture along for more than moderate attention.

Story tells of how Jean Gabin is saved from the guillotine, for murder, at Tours by Nazi air bombing, heads south and assumes the identity, papers and uniform of a dead French soldier along the road. Joining a group of refugee soldiers who enlist in the Free French forces, Gabin's army association gradually transforms the criminal; he leads a small unit overland for attack on Italian desert base and is decorated for gallantry, under the name of the dead man whose identity he assumed.

•

IMPROMPTU

1991, 109 mins, US Ⓥ ⦿ col

Dir James Lapine **Prod** Stuart Oken, Daniel A. Sherkow **Scr** Sarah Kernochan **Ph** Bruno De Keyzer **Ed** Michael Ellis **Mus** John Strauss (arr.) **Art** Gerard Daoudal

Act Judy Davis, Hugh Grant, Mandy Patinkin, Bernadette Peters, Julian Sands, Emma Thompson (Sovereign)

Impromptu is a retelling of the oft-filmed George Sand/Chopin story that's an entertaining comedy-drama. First-time director James Lapine, who's had Broadway successes (*Into the Woods*), makes the most of a terrific ensemble. Bright playing, a bit broad at times but fitting the material, is pic's strongest suit.

Aussie thesp Judy Davis plays Sand, the strong-willed author who dresses mannishly, smokes cheroots and gets a maddening crush on composer Chopin (Hugh Grant at his most foppish). Bulk of film is light-hearted, set at the royal mansion of Emma Thompson and Anton Rodgers, where Chopin, Liszt (Julian Sands), artist Delacroix (Ralph Brown) and an uninvited George Sand show up for vacation.

Film's tone turns a bit darker in later reels as the duels and fights of the first half turn more serious. Some abrupt editing and overly contrived resolutions of plot threads keep the finale from carrying much emotional force.

Directed by Lapine with a very long leash, Davis is terrific. Bruno De Keyzer captures lovely French locations in realistic terms, not distracting from the protagonists.

•

IMPROPER CHANNELS

1981, 91 mins, Canada Ⓥ ⦿ col

Dir Eric Till **Prod** Morrie Ruvinsky, Alfred Pariser **Scr** Morrie Ruvinsky, Ian Sutherland, Adam Arkin **Ph** Tony Richmond **Mus** Mickey Erbe, Maribeth Solomon **Art** Minkey Dalton, Charles Dunlop

Act Alan Arkin, Mariette Hartley, Sarah Stevens, Monica Parker, Harry Ditson (Paragon)

Alan Arkin puts his hapless schnook characterization to good use in *Improper Channels*. It's a screwball comedy that starts slowly, shifts into overdrive, peters out a bit halfway through and then gets its second wind for a fast-paced, down-with-the-computer finish.

He's an architect, separated from his writer spouse (Mariette Hartley) and precocious five-year-old daughter (Sarah Stevens). And one thing leads to another; the daughter is injured slightly in his camper and when taken to hospital she is thought to have been beaten by her father.

A domineering social worker (Monica Parker) has a computer expert call up all available information on Arkin and the daughter is bundled off by court order to an orphanage. Arkin and Hartley attempt to get her back.

Eric Till's direction is surefire most of the time, though he's let down by a script that wants to do too much. Pic was shot under the title of *Proper Channels* and was changed for reasons not explained.

•

IMPULSE

1984, 88 mins, US Ⓥ ⦿ col

Dir Graham Baker **Prod** Tim Zinnemann **Scr** Bart Davis, Don Carlos Dunaway **Ph** Thomas Del Ruth **Ed** David Holden **Mus** Paul Chihara **Art** Jack T. Collins

Act Tim Matheson, Meg Tilly, Hume Cronyn, John Karlen, Bill Paxton, Amy Stryker (ABC)

Impulse is an ugly little picture that would play better as a comedy if it wasn't so mean-spirited. Picture preys on the premise that when people are allowed to act according to their impulses, they will become violent, destructive and totally anti-social.

Wholesome young couple Meg Tilly and Tim Matheson are literally called to Tilly's hometown when her mother (Lorinne Vozoff) blows her brains out while talking to her daughter on the phone. The fact that she's still alive is only the first of the implausible happenings in Sutcliffe.

Nothing is quite what it seems in this town. Upon their arrival Matheson and Tilly encounter a seething family feud between her father (John Karlen) and her brother (Bill Paxton). Kids set Tilly's car on fire while her old friend (Amy Stryker) tells her it's not easy having children.

Editing has no internal logic with the time sequence totally jumbled. Performances are adequate given the material, with Matheson more convincing as a doctor than a mad-man. Hume Cronyn as the old town doc who succumbs early to the mass mania is effective though he has little to do. Tilly too is underutilized.

•

IMPULSE

1990, 108 mins, US Ⓥ ⦿ col

Dir Sondra Locke **Prod** Albert S. Ruddy, Andre Morgan **Scr** John De Marco, Leigh Chapman **Ph** Dean Semler **Ed** John W. Wheeler **Mus** Michel Colombier **Art** William A. Elliott

Act Theresa Russell, Jeff Fahey, George Dzundza, Alan Rosenberg, Shawn Elliott, Nicholas Mele (Warner)

Theresa Russell gives a solid performance in Sondre Locke's well-directed film noir [from a screen story by John De Marco]. Russell is a beautiful undercover cop whose life is going nowhere, hence the title: she would like to break out of her rut and act on impulse like one of the prostitute or druggie personas she routinely adopts in her work. Along with her sexist boss George Dzundza, she's assigned to work with young assistant d.a. Jeff Fahey to find missing witness Shawn Elliott in an important gangster case. Elliott has $900,000 stolen in a Colombian drug deal, and there's only three weeks to find him before Fahey begins the trial.

Russell and Fahey have some interesting exchanges that expose their characters. Sharpest writing comes in a scene of Fahey and his partner Alan Rosenberg, talking about women and relationships in terms from real estate.

Director Locke, in her second feature after *Ratboy*, gets high marks for the visceral, swift nature of her violent stagings. She also manages an impressively tactile sex scene that involves Russell and Fahey.

•

INADMISSIBLE EVIDENCE

1968, 94 mins, UK b/w

Dir Anthony Page **Prod** Ronald Kinnoch **Scr** John Osborne **Ph** Kenneth Hodges **Ed** Derek York **Art** Seamus Flannery

Act Nicol Williamson, Eleanor Fazan, Jill Bennett, Peter Sallis, David Valla, Eileen Atkins (Woodfall)

As a play, the best thing about *Inadmissible Evidence* was Nicol Williamson, who brought to life the tormented, mediocre, bullying coward that John Osborne had conceived on paper. Same holds true for the screen version in which same actor appears. There is value and insight to the film. Yet much of it is opaque and confusing.

Evidence remains primarily a play. It is Osborne talking about a certain stage of civilization and various kinds of people it produces.

Williamson, as the lawyer who has achieved a certain measure of material success, is flagrantly promiscuous, professionally mediocre and personally a boor.

Williamson achieves the feat of making a big man look fragile, of gaining sympathy for boorish behavior and pitying insights of a coward and scoundrel.

Picture is in black-and-white and it adds to the bleakness of the portrait being presented. Yet the same effect could have been achieved had film been done in color.

●

IN A LONELY PLACE
1950, 92 mins, US Ⓥ b/w
Dir Nicholas Ray *Prod* Henry S. Kesler (assoc.) *Scr* Andrew Solt *Ph* Burnett Guffey *Ed* Viola Lawrence *Mus* George Antheil *Art* Robert Peterson
Act Humphrey Bogart, Gloria Grahame, Frank Lovejoy, Robert Warwick, Jeff Donnell, Martha Stewart (Columbia/Santana)

In *Lonely Place* Humphrey Bogart has a sympathetic role though cast as one always ready to mix it with his dukes. He favors the underdog; in one instance he virtually has a veteran, brandy-soaking character actor (out of work) on his very limited payroll.

As the screenplay scrivener who detests the potboilers, Bogart finds himself innocently suspected of a girl's slaying. Although continually kept under suspicion, he ignores the police attempt to trap him into a confession, at the same time falling for a gal neighbor.

Director Nicholas Ray maintains nice suspense. Bogart is excellent. Gloria Grahame, as his romance, also rates kudos. [Screenplay is from a story by Dorothy B. Hughes, adapted by Edmund H. North.]

●

IN & OUT
1997, 90 mins, US Ⓥ ⦿ col
Dir Frank Oz *Prod* Scott Rudin *Scr* Paul Rudnick *Ph* Rob Hahn *Ed* Dan Hanley, John Jympson *Mus* Marc Shaiman *Art* Ken Adam
Act Kevin Kline, Joan Cusack, Matt Dillon, Debbie Reynolds, Tom Selleck, Bob Newhart (Paramount)

A very broad mainstream comedy, *In & Out* has more trouble than it should stretching a high-concept premise into ninety minutes of mirth.

Penned by Paul Rudnick, best known for the gay-themed Off-Broadway hit *Jeffrey*, this well-cast picture was triggered by Tom Hanks's Oscar acceptance speech in which he thanked his high school drama teacher. Here, however, the ultra-cool young star Cameron Drake (Matt Dillon) goes a step further by outing his mentor to millions of viewers on the telecast, calling him "a great gay teacher."

The problem is, Howard Brackett (Kevin Kline) is not only not "out," he is not, he claims, even gay. True, he wears a trim little bow tie, has an inordinate fondness for Barbra Streisand and has passed the age of 40 without marrying, but the latter situation, at least, is about to change with fellow schoolteacher Emily (Joan Cusack).

The frenzied media descend upon cozy Greenleaf, ID, to nose out the truth. The most persistent and suspicious reporter is slick Peter Malloy (Tom Selleck), a hack tabloid-style broadcaster who disarmingly describes himself as "show business garbage" and freely admits that he's gay. Peter finally finds a way, in a very funny scene almost exactly halfway through the movie, to determine the truth about Howard.

There are a number of big laughs in *In & Out*, but instead of five or six out-and-out guffaws the material seems ripe enough to have provoked two or three times that many. Still, pic is given a gratifying measure of grace by Kline's effortlessly light and dexterous performance. Aside from Dillon, who brightens every scene he's in with his hipper-than-thou 'tude, the delightful surprise here is Selleck as the dirt-digging broadcaster.

1997: NOMINATION: Best Supp. Actress (Joan Cusack)

●

IN BED WITH MADONNA
SEE: TRUTH OR DARE: IN BED WITH MADONNA

●

INCENDIARY BLONDE
1945, 113 mins, US b/w
Dir George Marshall *Prod* Joseph Sistrom *Scr* Claude Binyon, Frank Butler *Ph* Ray Rennahan *Ed* Archie Marshek *Mus* Robert Emmett Dolan *Art* Hans Dreier, William Flannery
Act Betty Hutton, Arturo de Cordova, Albert Dekker, Barry Fitzgerald (Paramount)

Incendiary Blonde is sound musical drama based on the life of Broadway's Texas Guinan.

Script picks up the Guinan career in Texas in 1909 when she first joins a Wild West show to aid her financially busted father.

Production injects considerable spectacle into the early Wild West show sequences but gives picture a slower start than necessary. Her switch to Broadway musicals to escape an unhappy love affair and then desertion of the Great White Way for Hollywood are spanned more quickly.

When misunderstandings again chill love, she returns to Broadway and launches her night club career. The part racketeering and kindred Prohibition ailments of the nation played in her life are all shown and these give dramatic wallop and tenseness to the concluding portions of the story.

●

INCHON
1981, 140 mins, S. Korea/US col
Dir Terence Young *Prod* Mitsuharu Ishii *Scr* Robin Moore, Laird Koenig *Ph* Bruce Surtees *Mus* Jerry Goldsmith
Act Laurence Olivier, Jacqueline Bisset, Ben Gazzara, Toshiro Mifune, Richard Roundtree (One Way)

A major battle of the Korean war is given a decidedly religious viewpoint via *Inchon*, a $46 million pic from One Way Prods, an org affiliated with the Rev Sun Myung Moon (who gets screen credit as special advisor on Korean matters).

Laurence Olivier plays Gen Douglas MacArthur in this film that was four years in the making and bills 50,000 extras.

Plot involves the general's orchestration of the 1950 landing at the South Korean port of Inchon by United Nations forces, with heavy emphasis on divine guidance. Olivier is convincing in his role throughout most of the saga, the only member of the cast to achieve that status.

Screenplay [from a story by Robin Moore and Paul Savage] generally treats all others as one-dimensional buffoons, giving them lines that are unintentionally laughable. One reason is that all plot digressions are simply window dressing to the film's focus on the brutally invading North Koreans and the big-scale counterattack by the good guys. No speaking roles are given the Communists, for example.

●

INCIDENT, THE
1967, 99 mins, US Ⓥ ⦿ col
Dir Larry Peerce *Prod* Monroe Sachson, Edward Meadow *Scr* Nicholas E. Baehr *Ph* Gerald Hirschfeld *Ed* Armand Lebowitz *Mus* Terry Knight *Art* Manny Gerard
Act Tony Musante, Martin Sheen, Beau Bridges, Bob Bannard, Ed McMahon, Diana Van Der Vlis (20th Century-Fox/Moned)

Strong casting, impressive direction and generally sharp writing (from an old TV script) make *The Incident* a very fine episodic drama about two toughs who intimidate passengers on a NY subway train.

Some overexposition and relaxed editing flag the pace, but, overall, the production is a candid indictment, in situation and in dialog, of alienation.

Baehr's screenplay spotlights Tony Musante and Martin Sheen, out-for-kicks pair, who terrorize 16 train riders. Latter include soldiers Beau Bridges and Bob Bannard, middle-class couple Ed McMahon and Diana Van Der Vlis (with child), elderly marrieds Jack Gilford and Thelma Ritter. The two toughs lay bare the weaknesses in all characters.

●

IN COLD BLOOD
1967, 133 mins, US Ⓥ ⦿ ▭ b/w
Dir Richard Brooks *Prod* Richard Brooks *Scr* Richard Brooks *Ph* Conrad Hall *Ed* Peter Zinner *Mus* Quincy Jones *Art* Robert Boyle
Act Robert Blake, Scott Wilson, John Forsythe, Paul Stewart, Gerald S. O'Loughlin, Jeff Corey (Columbia)

In the skillful hands of adapter-director-producer Richard Brooks, Truman Capote's *In Cold Blood*, the nonfiction novel-like account of two Kansas killers, becomes, on screen, a probing, sensitive, tasteful, balanced and suspenseful documentary-drama.

Film has the look and sound of reality, in part from use of action locales in six states and non-pros as atmosphere players, the rest from Brooks's own filmmaking professionalism. Planned as a $3 million, 124-day pic, it came in for $2.2 million in 80 days.

Heading the competent cast are Robert Blake and Scott Wilson, bearing a striking resemblance to the now-dead Kansas drifters who, in the course of a burglary on November 15, 1959, murdered four of a family. Almost six years later, after an exhausted appeal route, they were hanged. John Forsythe plays the chief investigator who broke the case.

Brooks's screenplay and direction are remarkable, in that pic avoids so many pitfalls: it is not a crime meller, told either from the police or criminal viewpoint; it is not social tract against capital punishment; it is not cheap exploitation material; and it is not amateurish in technical execution, despite its realistic flavor.

1967: NOMINATIONS: Best Director, Adapted Screenplay, Cinematography, Original Music Score

●

IN COUNTRY
1989, 120 mins, US Ⓥ ⦿ col
Dir Norman Jewison *Prod* Norman Jewison, Richard Roth *Scr* Frank Pierson, Cynthia Cidre *Ph* Russell Boyd *Ed* Anthony Gibbs, Lou Lombardo *Mus* James Horner *Art* Jackson DeGovia
Act Bruce Willis, Emily Lloyd, Joan Allen, Kevin Anderson, John Terry, Judith Ivey (Warner)

Norman Jewison usually is a commanding storyteller, but *In Country* is a film with two stories that fail to add up to something greater: a country girl's coming of age, and a troubled Vietnam veteran's coming to terms with his haunting memories of war [from the novel by Bobbie Ann Mason].

Emily Lloyd, in a sparky performance that seizes control of the movie, plays Samantha Hughes, a spirited, just-minted high school graduate from the small town of Hopewell, KY. She lives in a ramshackle house with Bruce Willis, who turns in a likeable but unremarkable interpretation of her moody uncle Emmett, a veteran who has suffered lasting emotional damage from his nightmarish tour of duty in 'Nam.

Lloyd's father, who also served "in country," was killed in combat before she was born. She likes the freedom of living with Willis, who permits Lloyd unsupervised liaisons with her callow basketball star boyfriend (Kevin Anderson). She's not especially close to her mother, Willis's sister, played deftly by Joan Allen.

Willis generates sympathy for his tormented character, but the one-dimensional script and his still limited range conspire to make Emmett a stolid caricature of the spiritually wounded veteran.

●

INCREDIBLE JOURNEY, THE
1963, 86 mins, US Ⓥ col
Dir Fletcher Markle *Prod* James Algar *Scr* James Algar *Ph* Kenneth Peach *Ed* Norman Palmer *Mus* Oliver Wallace
Act Emile Genest, John Drainie, Tommy Tweed, Sandra Scott, Syme Jago, Marion Finlayson (Walt Disney)

Sheila Burnford's book of the same title has been given a vivid translation in *The Incredible Journey*, a live actioner exquisitely photographed in the Canadian outdoors.

A bull terrier, Siamese cat and Labrador retriever comprise the unlikely trio of pals who, farmed out to a friend of their owners, embark on the journey—over 200 miles of treacherous terrain. They encounter crisis after crisis in what is a remarkable, nay incredible, fight to survive all sorts of adversities in their trip all the way home.

Director Fletcher Markle, with the assist of an animal trainer, has gotten an abundance of child-appealing excitement on the screen. And he sees to it that the story is told simply and directly, what with the humans on view exchanging dialog in honest fashion and an offscreen commentary by Rex Allen. The astutely-guided animals steal the show.

●

INCREDIBLE SARAH, THE
1976, 105 mins, UK Ⓥ ⦿ col
Dir Richard Fleischer *Prod* Helen M. Strauss *Scr* Ruth Wolff *Ph* Christopher Challis *Ed* John Jympson *Mus* Elmer Bernstein *Art* Elliot Scott
Act Glenda Jackson, Daniel Massey, Yvonne Mitchell, Douglas Wilmer, David Langton, Simon Williams (Readers Digest)

Ruth Wolff's script, conceded in opening titles to be a "free" interpretation of Sarah Bernhardt's early years, follows the famed actress from her early halting years on the French stage through an initial period of fame, notoriety and finally a youthful comeback of sorts at age 35. Glenda Jackson's versatile performance ranges from backstage, intimate situations to several lengthy excerpts from Bernhardt vehicles.

This is the story of a theatrical personality, not your average housewife. The achievement here is that Jackson makes the character comprehensible and, in a qualified way, admirable, notwithstanding the clear evidence of a totally self-centered nature.

Strong supporting cast includes Daniel Massey as a playwright friend, and Simon Williams as an early lover and father of Bernhardt's son.

1976: NOMINATIONS: Best Costume Design, Art Direction

•

INCREDIBLE SHRINKING MAN, THE
1957, 81 mins, US Ⓥ ⦿ b/w
Dir Jack Arnold ***Prod*** Albert Zugsmith ***Scr*** Richard Matheson ***Ph*** Ellis W. Carter ***Ed*** Al Joseph ***Mus*** Joseph Gershenson (sup.) ***Art*** Alexander Golitzen, Robert Clatworthy
Act Grant Williams, Randy Stuart, April Kent, Paul Langton, Raymond Bailey, William Schallert (Universal)

Richard Matheson scripted from his novel and, while most science-fiction thrillers usually contrive a happy ending, there's no compromise here. Six-footer Grant Williams and his wife (Randy Stuart) run into a fog while boating. She's below, so is untouched, but Williams gets the full force. Soon after, he finds himself shrinking and doctors decide the radioactivity in the fog has reversed his growth processes.

Director Jack Arnold works up the chills for maximum effect by the time Williams is down to two inches and the family cat takes after him. Also harrowing are his adventures in the cellar with, to him, a giant spider, which he manages to kill using a straight pin as a lance.

The technical staff has done an outstanding job of the trick stuff. Optical effects by Roswell A. Hoffman and Everett H. Broussard make the shrinking visually effective.

•

INCREDIBLE SHRINKING WOMAN, THE
1981, 88 mins, US Ⓥ ⦿ col
Dir Joel Schumacher ***Prod*** Hank Moonjean ***Scr*** Jane Wagner ***Ph*** Bruce Logan ***Ed*** Jeff Gourson ***Mus*** Suzanne Ciani ***Art*** Raymond A. Brandt
Act Lily Tomlin, Charles Grodin, Ned Beatty, Henry Gibson, Maria Smith, Mark Blankfield (Universal)

Story of a contemporary housewife whose consistent use of chemically injected brand name foods, soap powders and aerosol-propelled products causes her to shrink to miniscule proportions is often strangely humorous with an underlying note of scathing social satire.

Director Joel Schumacher and writer-exec producer Jane Wagner have done a commendable job of creating a portrait of life in Anywhere, USA, where the tireless wife-mother (Lily Tomlin) must run a household, referee screaming kids and spruce up for her hardworking husband by the time evening rolls around. Unfortunately, even Tomlin's talents begin to wear thin two-thirds into the film when she's kidnapped by baddies who want to use her to formulate a serum that will reduce the size of anyone in their way.

In supporting roles, ad exec hubby Charles Grodin (who perpetuates the very products that brought Tomlin to her unfortunate circumstance) and his boss Ned Beatty are first-rate. Problem is the premise just tires prematurely.

•

INDAGINE SU UN CITTADINO AL DI SOPRA DI OGNI SOSPETTO
(INVESTIGATION OF A CITIZEN ABOVE SUSPICION)
1970, 114 mins, Italy Ⓥ col
Dir Elio Petri ***Prod*** Daniel Senatore, Marina Cicogna ***Scr*** Elio Petri, Ugo Pirro ***Ph*** Luigi Kuveiller ***Ed*** Ruggero Mastroianni ***Mus*** Ennio Morricone ***Art*** Carlo Egidi
Act Gian Maria Volonte, Florinda Bolkan, Salvo Randone, Gianni Santuccio, Orazio Orlando, Sergio Tramonti (Vera)

Pic is dramatically effective in its obvious, stacked assault on petty dictators with a life-and-death grip over human beings. And principally because of Gian Maria Volonte's resounding performance as a homicide chief who commits a murder out of Freudian shortcomings and then deliberately points the finger of guilt at himself to prove that his power position places him above the law.

Crime takes place in opening reel shortly before the chief is promoted and transferred to head up the key desk of political crime investigation. Thereafter the story, via interspersed flashbacks, creates a climate of depraved fantasy to shed light on his relationship with the murdered woman, August (Florinda Balkan), while the film otherwise proceeds with stark realism to focus on the investigating sleuths manipulated at will by their power-conscious superiors.

Balkan probably gives her best performance to date to create a woman tormented by instability, sexual drive and psycho demons—disjointedly portrayed in the script. Secondary characters, except for Salvo Randone as an innocent pawn, all play their roles broadly as manipulated underlings.

Ennio Morricone's score is good but somewhat reminiscent of past Neopolitan pix and a bit repetitious.

1970: Best Foreign Language Film

•

INDECENT PROPOSAL
1993, 117 mins, US Ⓥ ⦿ col
Dir Adrian Lyne ***Prod*** Sherry Lansing ***Scr*** Amy Holden Jones ***Ph*** Howard Atherton ***Ed*** Joe Hutshing ***Mus*** John Barry ***Art*** Mel Bourne
Act Robert Redford, Demi Moore, Woody Harrelson, Oliver Platt, Seymour Cassel, Billy Connolly (Paramount)

This is one of those high-concept pictures [from Jack Engelhard's novel] with a big windup and weak delivery. On paper, a film in which billionaire Robert Redford offers down-on-their-luck married couple Woody Harrelson and Demi Moore a cool million in exchange for one-night stand with Moore sounds surefire. Onscreen, the result has little sex, goes nowhere interesting or believable in the long second hour, and sports an idiotic conclusion that looks like Test Marketing Ending No. 6.

Director Adrian Lyne spends the first reel establishing college sweethearts Harrelson and Moore as really in love and still ripping each other's clothes off. But the recession has dented his architecture career and her real estate sales. Needing $50,000 to keep their house, they head for Vegas. When they hit bottom, fate appears in the guise of Redford.

Dressed impeccably and smiling nearly all the time, Redford glides through the action like a latter-day Gatsby, a man who has it all—except a woman to love. What emotional legitimacy the film does possess stems from Moore's performance, which is lively, heartfelt and believable until the script stops letting it. Tech credits are ultralush.

•

INDEPENDENCE DAY
(AKA: FOLLOW YOUR DREAMS)
1983, 110 mins, US Ⓥ col
Dir Robert Mandel ***Prod*** Daniel H. Blatt, Robert Singer ***Scr*** Alice Hoffman ***Ph*** Chuck Rosher ***Ed*** Dennis Virkler, Tina Hirsch ***Mus*** Charles Bernstein ***Art*** Stewart Campbell
Act Kathleen Quinlan, David Keith, Frances Sternhagen, Cliff DeYoung, Dianne Wiest, Josef Sommer (Warner)

Independence Day is an unpleasant dramatic study of young people in a small southwestern town facing family problems and the perennial career decision: to stay home or trek to the big city. Despite some yeoman acting by a talented cast of character actors, the predictable and contrived storyline proves intractable.

Alice Hoffman's unfocused screenplay centers upon two people in their 20s: Mary Ann Taylor (Kathleen Quinlan), a waitress in her dad's diner in the tiny southwestern town and Jack Parker (David Keith), a gas station mechanic just home after an unsuccessful stay at engineering school.

While the duo's romance blossoms, Parker is coping with his suicidal sister Nancy (Dianne Wiest), her philandering, wife-beating husband Les (Cliff DeYoung) and his own brutish father (Noble Willingham).

Keith reinforces his image as a likable and forceful young performer while Quinlan demonstrates the ambivalence of love vs. a career quite skillfully.

•

INDEPENDENCE DAY
1996, 145 mins, US Ⓥ ⦿ ▭ col
Dir Roland Emmerich ***Prod*** Dean Devlin ***Scr*** Dean Devlin, Roland Emmerich ***Ph*** Karl Walter, Lindenlaub ***Ed*** David Brenner ***Mus*** David Arnold ***Art*** Oliver Scholl, Patrick Tatopoulos
Act Will Smith, Bill Pullman, Jeff Goldblum, Mary McDonnell, Judd Hirsch, Margaret Colin (Centropolis/20th Century-Fox)

Independence Day is the biggest B movie ever made, the mother of all doomsday dramas. A spectacularly scaled mix of '50s-style alien invader science fiction, '70s disaster epics and all-season gung-ho military actioners, this airborne leviathan features a bunch of agreeably cardboard characters saving the human race from mass extermination in a way that proves as unavoidably entertaining as it is hopelessly cornball.

This is, in effect, the anti-*Close Encounters*, a throwback to ominous, paranoid thrillers such as *The War of the Worlds, The Day the Earth Stood Still, When Worlds Collide, Invaders from Mars* and television's *V*, a story in which the visitors from space have absolutely no interest in making nice with the earthlings.

In vintage disaster-pic fashion, a host of characters is sketched in. There is David (Jeff Goldblum), a New York computer genius; Capt. Steven Hiller (Will Smith), a hot-dog fighter pilot; and U.S. President Thomas J. Whitmore (Bill Pullman), a rather green national leader widely regarded as a wimp. When some helicopters are summarily blasted out of the sky by the aliens, it becomes clear that the visitors have come not for a picnic, but for a barbecue.

Air attacks on the alien ships reveal that they are surrounded by protective shields, but Hiller manages to make one alien fighter crash and returns the gruesome-looking pilot to Area 51, a top-secret Nevada base where the president has taken refuge. There, 24 floors underground, the resident loony genius (Brent Spiner) reveals the existence of an alien spaceship captured long ago that just may be in working order, opening the door on a long-shot counterattack that plays out on the third day of the story, July 4.

The never-ending special effects, while massively spectacular, are not always that special, ranging from terrific computer-generated airborne battles to frankly old-fashioned-looking matte shots and model work. It's the difference between a $100 million-plus picture and a $71 million effort, which is what this one reportedly is.

Similarly, the cast is just a cut under all-star, but that shouldn't matter either. Playing the main action hero, Smith pushes the cocky arrogance to Mach 3, and Goldblum does a riff on his offbeat scientist bit from *Jurassic Park*. Pullman, who seems to be barely suppressing a smirk at times, will have people asking if he isn't just a bit young to be president. [In 1998 a 153-min. *Special Edition* was released on homevideo.]

1996: Best Visual Effects

NOMINATION: Best Sound

•

INDIANA JONES AND THE LAST CRUSADE
1989, 127 mins, US Ⓥ ⦿ ▭ col
Dir Steven Spielberg ***Prod*** Robert Watts ***Scr*** Jeffrey Boam ***Ph*** Douglas Slocombe ***Ed*** Michael Kahn ***Mus*** John Williams ***Art*** Elliot Scott
Act Harrison Ford, Sean Connery, Denholm Elliott, Alison Doody, John Rhys-Davies, River Phoenix (Paramount/Lucasfilm)

More cerebral than the first two Indiana Jones films, and less schmaltzy than the second, this literate adventure should entertain and enlighten kids and adults alike.

The Harrison Ford–Sean Connery father-and-son team gives *Last Crusade* unexpected emotional depth, reminding us that real film magic is not in special effects.

Witty and laconic screenplay, based on a story by George Lucas and Menno Meyjes, takes Ford and Connery on a quest for a prize bigger than the Lost Ark of the Covenant—the Holy Grail.

Connery is a medieval lit prof with strong religious convictions who has spent his life assembling clues to the grail's whereabouts. Father and more intrepid archaeologist son piece them together in an around-the-world adventure, leading to a touching and mystical finale. The love between father and son transcends even the quest for the Grail, which is guarded by a spectral 700-year-old knight beautifully played by Robert Eddison.

This film minimizes the formulaic love interest, giving newcomer Alison Doody an effectively sinuous but decidedly secondary role.

1989: Best Sound Effects Editing

NOMINATIONS: Best Original Score, Sound

•

INDIANA JONES AND THE TEMPLE OF DOOM
1984, 118 mins, US Ⓥ ⦿ ▭ col
Dir Steven Spielberg ***Prod*** Robert Watts ***Scr*** Willard Huyck, Gloria Katz ***Ph*** Douglas Slocombe ***Ed*** Michael Kahn ***Mus*** John Williams ***Art*** Elliot Scott
Act Harrison Ford, Kate Capshaw, Ke Huy Quan, Amrish Puri, Roshan Seth, Philip Stone (Lucasfilm)

Steven Spielberg has packed even more thrills and chills into this follow-up than he did into the earlier pic, but to exhausting and numbing effect.

Prequel finds dapper Harrison Ford as Indiana Jones in a Shanghai nightclub in 1935, and title sequence, which features Kate Capshaw chirping Cole Porter's "Anything Goes" looks like something out of Spielberg's *1941*.

Ford escapes from an enormous melée with the chanteuse and Oriental moppet Ke Huy Quan and they head by plane to the mountains of Asia where they are forced to jump out in an inflatable raft coming to rest in an impoverished Indian village.

Community's leader implores the ace archaeologist to retrieve a sacred, magical stone that has been stolen by malevolent neighbors.

Remainder of the yarn is set in labyrinth of horrors lorded over by a prepubescent maharajah, where untold dangers await the heroes.

What with John Williams's incessant score and the library full of sound effects, there isn't a quiet moment in the entire picture.

Ford seems effortlessly to have picked up where he left off when Indiana Jones was last heard from, although Capshaw, who looks fetching in native attire, has unfortunately been asked to react hysterically to everything that happens to her.

1984: Best Visual Effects

NOMINATION: Best Original Score

•

INDIAN FIGHTER, THE

1955, 88 mins, US ▭ col

Dir Andre de Toth ***Prod*** William Schorr ***Scr*** Frank Davis, Ben Hecht ***Ph*** Wilfrid M. Cline ***Ed*** Richard Cahoon ***Mus*** Franz Waxman ***Art*** Wiard Ihnen

Act Kirk Douglas, Elsa Martinelli, Walter Abel, Walter Matthau, Diana Douglas, Eduard Franz (Bryna/United Artists)

This frontier actioner, more derring-do than dramatic, spins off 88 minutes of entertainment that will satisfy the demands of the outdoor fan. Andre de Toth's direction reaches its high points in a refreshingly novel Indian attack on a frontier fort and in the death duel, Sioux-style, between Kirk Douglas and Harry Landers. Otherwise, footage is inclined to get monotonous at times.

Sex in the person of Elsa Martinelli, Italian actress introduced here, and the relationship of her Indian maid character with Douglas is a story factor and ballyhoo point.

Douglas dashes about as a grinning, virile hero in the title role. His job here is to lead a wagon train through Indian country into Oregon but he gets sidetracked from duty in wooing Martinelli long enough for some crooks to stir up trouble over Indian gold.

•

INDIAN IN THE CUPBOARD, THE

1995, 96 mins, US Ⓥ ⊙ col

Dir Frank Oz ***Prod*** Kathleen Kennedy, Frank Marshall, Jane Startz ***Scr*** Melissa Mathison ***Ph*** Russell Carpenter ***Ed*** Ian Crafford ***Mus*** Randy Edelman ***Art*** Leslie McDonald

Act Hal Scardino, Litefoot, Lindsay Crouse, Richard Jenkins, Rishi Bhat, David Keith (Kennedy-Marshall)

Based on a popular children's book [by Lynne Reid Banks], *The Indian in the Cupboard* never comes alive as a movie. Earnest and well-intentioned, the promising concept feels stretched to feature length.

For starters, virtually no groundwork is laid before nine-year-old Omri (Hal Scardino) receives for his birthday what turns out to be a magical cupboard that can bring his action figures to life. Though the cabinet works on more extravagant items, from RoboCop to Darth Vader, he becomes enamored of a three-inch-tall Indian named Little Bear (played by recording artist Litefoot, in his acting debut).

Omri shares the secret only with his friend Patrick (Rishi Bhat), who uses the device to animate his own toy figure, a surly Texas cowboy named Boone (David Keith). At first hostile toward Little Bear (cowboys and Indians, after all), Boone eventually warms to him.

Randy Edelman's soundtrack swells to huge crescendos in even the smallest moments. Clearly, someone was working a bit too hard here to try to compensate for missing magic. Technically, Industrial Light & Magic's effects cleverly capture the little-guy-in-big-room scenario.

•

INDIAN RUNNER, THE

1991, 126 mins, US Ⓥ ⊙ col

Dir Sean Penn ***Prod*** Don Phillips ***Scr*** Sean Penn ***Ph*** Anthony B. Richmond ***Ed*** Jay Cassidy ***Mus*** Jack Nitzsche ***Art*** Michael Haller

Act David Morse, Viggo Mortensen, Valeria Golino, Patricia Arquette, Charles Bronson, Sandy Dennis (Mount)

A tortured examination of the disintegration of a Midwestern family, *The Indian Runner* is very much actors' cinema. Rambling, indulgent and joltingly raw at times, Sean Penn's first outing as a director takes a fair amount of patience to get through but has an integrity that intermittently serves it well.

Inspired by the Bruce Springsteen song "Highway Patrolman," overwrought piece looks at the muted tragedy of two brothers in the late 1960s. Joe (David Morse) is a small-town Nebraska cop who tries to welcome his brother Frank (Viggo Mortensen) back into the fold after the latter returns from a stint in Vietnam, but Frank immediately takes off.

Learning that Frank has been in prison, Joe goes to pick him up but Frank shacks up with a blonde sprite named Dorothy (Patricia Arquette). Along the way, traumas hit the family like clockwork.

All this takes more than two hours to get through because Penn, as writer and director, lets his scenes play out at great length. Actors, notably Morse and Mortensen, come off to decent advantage. Charles Bronson puts in a supporting interp of repressed hysteria as the father, while Sandy Dennis and Dennis Hopper are in briefly as the mother and a local bartender. Valeria Golino and Arquette are vital as the women in the brothers' lives.

•

INDIAN SUMMER

1993, 97 mins, US Ⓥ ⊙ ▭ col

Dir Mike Binder ***Prod*** Jeffrey Silver, Robert Newmyer ***Scr*** Mike Binder ***Ph*** Tom Sigel ***Ed*** Adam Weiss ***Mus*** Miles Goodman ***Art*** Craig Stearns

Act Alan Arkin, Matt Craven, Diane Lane, Bill Paxton, Elizabeth Perkins, Vincent Spano (Touchstone/Outlaw)

Awash in romantic nostalgia for childhoods spent in summer camps, *Indian Summer* is a sentimental, TV sitcom-like film. This *Big Chill* regrouping takes place in gorgeous Camp Tamakwa, the site of their 1972 summer.

The seven returning campers include the single and increasingly desperate Jennifer (Elizabeth Perkins), Matthew and Kelly (Vincent Spano and Julie Warner), whose marriage seems in trouble, insensitive "macho" Jamie (Matt Craven) and his much younger g.f. Gwen (Kimberly Williams). Presiding over the group is Unca Lou (Alan Arkin), a benevolent patriarch who has devoted his entire life to the camp.

Drawing on his personal experience in Canada's Algonquin Provincial Park, where actual lensing was done, Binder has constructed a loose series of vignettes, some funnier than others. Fortunately, the highly accomplished ensemble keeps this confection tasty and enjoyable.

Of the entire cast, the three stand-out performers are Elizabeth Perkins and Bill Paxton in two showy roles and Diane Lane in a subtler and more difficult part.

•

INDISCREET

1931, 93 mins, US Ⓥ b/w

Dir Leo McCarey ***Scr*** DeSylva, Brown and Henderson ***Ph*** Ray June, Gregg Toland ***Ed*** Hal C. Kern ***Art*** Alfred Newman

Act Gloria Swanson, Ben Lyon, Monroe Owsley, Barbara Kent, Arthur Lake, Maude Eburne (United Artists)

An original story of the musical comedy writing trio of DeSylva, Brown and Henderson, it is without music of moment or quantity. The three boys have fashioned a composite of a lot of other stories, giving it all an original slant. Direction, production and playing fit. As a comedy-drama it is more comedy than drama.

Story starts with s.a. and never stops. The menace is ever on the make, becoming engaged to a younger sister after being thrown down by the sister he had lived with.

Gloria Swanson has most of the laughs, through dialog mostly, but Arthur Lake, as a lovesick kid, gets his points over punchily. They are not as plentiful as Swanson's but they are more bangy and longer remembered. Ben Lyon plays the light minded but sincere author who falls for Jerry (Swanson) but won't listen about her past when she gets to the point of should a woman tell.

•

INDISCREET

1958, 100 mins, US Ⓥ col

Dir Stanley Donen ***Prod*** Stanley Donen ***Scr*** Norman Krasna ***Ph*** Frederick A. Young ***Ed*** Jack Harris ***Mus*** Richard Rodney Bennett, Ken Jones ***Art*** Don Ashton

Act Cary Grant, Ingrid Bergman, Cecil Parker, Phyllis Calvert, David Kossoff, Megs Jenkins (Grandon/Warner)

A beguiling love story delicately deranged by the complications of sophisticated comedy, *Indiscreet* is an expert film version of Norman Krasna's 1953 stage play, *Kind Sir*. Though tedious in its opening reels, the production warms up in direct relation to the heat of the love affair and, in the end, manages to fade out in a blaze of playful merriment.

As the successful actress who has yet to find love, Ingrid Bergman is alluring, most affectionate and highly amusing. Cary Grant makes a ripping gadabout, conniving and gracious, his performance sometimes hilarious and always smooth.

Moving from the New York of *Kind Sir*, the locale has been shipped to London where Bergman lives and wants to love. Grant, a rich American who holds a NATO post, lives there too (at least on weekends, commuting as he does from Paris) and he too wants to love. But the difference is he wants nothing of marriage and, to protect all concerned, advises Bergman on first meeting that he is a married man, separated and unable to obtain a divorce. Still she invites him to the ballet.

Cecil Parker, as the brother-in-law, becomes funnier as he becomes more unnerved, and Phyllis Calvert is excellent as the sister. Megs Jenkins turns in a fine performance as the maid, and David Kossoff, as the chauffeur, admirably grabs the high spot of hilarity with his pseudo-lover stroll-on.

•

INDISCRETION

SEE: INDISCRETION OF AN AMERICAN WIFE

•

INDISCRETION OF AN AMERICAN WIFE
(UK: INDISCRETION)

1954, 63 mins, ITALY/US Ⓥ b/w

Dir Vittorio De Sica ***Prod*** Vittorio De Sica ***Scr*** Cesare Zavattini, Luigi Chiarini, Giorgio Prosperi, Truman Capote ***Ph*** G. R. Aldo ***Ed*** Eraldo Da Rema, Jean Barker ***Mus*** Alessandro Cicognini

Act Jennifer Jones, Montgomery Clift, Gino Cervi, Richard Beymer (Columbia)

The plot of *Indiscretion of an American Wife* is told rather precisely in the title. It is an Italian-filmed feature, very consciously arty and foreign, but with the American star names of Jennifer Jones and Montgomery Clift.

The picture was directed by Vittorio De Sica from Cesare Zavattini's story *Terminal Station*. The lensing was done in its entirety in the Stazione Termini in Rome, where the story of an American housewife saying farewell to her holiday lover takes place.

U.S. distribution rights to the picture, held by Selznick Releasing Organization, were turned over to Columbia and the footage edited down considerably from its foreign release length [87 minutes]. In fact the trimming was so drastic Columbia ordered a musical prolog from SRO to pad out the footage, so *Indiscretion* got an eight-minute hitchhiker riding along.

As typical of foreign film pretentions, much use is made of bits and types flowing through the busy railway terminal to color and add movement to the picture. Outside of the agonizing moments of farewells between Jones, Philadelphia housewife returning to her safe hearth, and her younger holiday lover, Clift, the story's dramatic suspense pull is developed around the couple's arrest after being discovered in an extremely compromising embrace in a secluded spot.

The stars give the drama a real pro try and the professional standards of delivery are high, even though the character interpretations will not be liked by all.

1954: NOMINATION: Best B&W Costume Design

•

INDOCHINE

1992, 158 mins, FRANCE Ⓥ ⊙ ▭ col

Dir Regis Wargnier ***Prod*** Eric Heumann, Jean Labadie ***Scr*** Erik Orsenna, Louis Gardel, Catherine Cohen, Regis Wargnier ***Ph*** Francoise Catonne ***Ed*** Genevieve Winding ***Mus*** Patrick Doyle ***Art*** Jacques Bufnoir

Act Catherine Deneuve, Vincent Perez, Linh Dan Pham, Jean Yanne, Dominique Blanc, Henri Marteau (Paradis/Generale d'Images/Bac/Orly/Cine 5

Set during rising communist protests in the 1930s, *Indochine* is a riveting romantic saga, thanks to Catherine Deneuve's classy performance, a sizzling story line and eye-catching locales in Vietnam. Pic sticks close to its three main characters: a Frenchwoman who runs one of the country's biggest rubber plantations, her adopted Indochinese daughter and the dashing French navy officer who loves each woman in quick succession.

Deneuve's Eliane is cool if courteous when she meets handsome naval newcomer (Vincent Perez), but she falls for him despite herself. Teenage daughter Camille (Linh Dan Pham) falls instantly in love when the same officer saves her from a terrorist, and frustrated beau asks for a far-away post in the north.

But stubborn daughter takes off after him on foot, discovering along the way her country's miseries. She's rounded up for peasant labor, kills a French slave auctioneer and flees with the stunned officer. Halfway into pic, its intriguing frame becomes clear: In Geneva, at the close of the Indochinese war, Eliane is telling her grown ward his parent's history, since he's about to meet his mother, a Communist Vietnamese representative, for the first time.

Deneuve's impeccable performance brings to life the best and worst of the French colonialism. Perez, first an uncommitted lover and then a feisty Frenchman on the run, handles his fast-changing role with great sensitivity. Newcomer Pham shines as sheltered daughter and hardened revolutionary. Kudos are deserved all round for technical production.

1993: Best Foreign Language Film

•

I NEVER PROMISED YOU A ROSE GARDEN

1977, 96 mins, US Ⓥ col

Dir Anthony Page ***Prod*** Edgar J. Scherick, Terence F. Deane ***Scr*** Gavin Lambert, Lewis John Carlino ***Ph*** Bruce Logan ***Ed*** Garth Craven ***Mus*** Paul Chihara ***Art*** William Sandell

Act Bibi Andersson, Kathleen Quinlan, Sylvia Sidney, Martine Bartlett, Signe Hasso, Susan Tyrrell (Fadsin/New World)

Good intentions and sensationalism compete for viewer interest in this filmization of Hanna Green's novel about the tentative recovery of a psychotic young woman. Unfortunately, both lose. Good intentions resolve into high-minded tedium.

The pic's central problem is its structure. The girl (Kathleen Quinlan) is presented at the outset as a certifiable nutto teenager, being escorted by her parents (Lorraine Gary and Ben Piazza) to what appears to be a tastefully landscaped institution. An improved mental state is a certainty, otherwise there's no film.

Quinlan is an untypical young actress, who lends freshness and admirable reserve to a role that could have lapsed entirely into histrionic hysterics.

1977: NOMINATION: Best Adapted Screenplay

•

I NEVER SANG FOR MY FATHER

1970, 92 mins, US Ⓥ col

Dir Gilbert Cates ***Prod*** Gilbert Cates ***Scr*** Robert Anderson ***Ph*** Morris Hartzband ***Ed*** Angelo Ross ***Mus*** Al Gorgoni, Barry Mann ***Art*** Hank Aldrich

Act Melvyn Douglas, Gene Hackman, Dorothy Stickney, Estelle Parsons, Elizabeth Hubbard, Lovelady Powell (Columbia/Jamel)

Film version of Robert Anderson's 1968 play is distended and lacking clear point of view. Mostly the story of a middle-aged man still strung up by a family umbilical cord, the film veers awkwardly into problems of the aged. However, the performances of father Melvyn Douglas, mother Dorothy Stickney, son Gene Hackman and daughter Estelle Parsons are superb.

Anderson's basic plot line involves the widower Hackman, still lashed to his parents through the verbal bonds of Douglas's cold-hearted feelings. Parsons as the daughter was luckier: she was banished for marrying a Jew, and was forced to make a new life.

Trouble is, given all this acting talent, the direction, writing and pacing are dreary.

1970: NOMINATIONS: Best Actor (Melvyn Douglas), Supp. Actor (Gene Hackman), Adapted Screenplay

•

INFERNO

1953, 83 mins, US col

Dir Roy Ward Baker ***Prod*** William Bloom ***Scr*** Francis Cockrell ***Ph*** Lucien Ballard ***Ed*** Robert Simpson ***Mus*** Paul Sawtell

Act Robert Ryan, Rhonda Fleming, William Lundigan, Larry Keating, Henry Hall, Carl Betz (20th Century-Fox)

Three-D and Technicolor are used effectively to make this suspense melodrama a fairly entertaining entry. Film, announced as 20th-Fox's first and only 3-D presentation, is a romantic triangle that springboards the plot of how a rich, spoiled man finds himself when left to die on the desert by his wife and her lover.

Playboy Carson (Robert Ryan) is left to die of thirst and a broken leg by Geraldine (Rhonda Fleming) and Duncan (William Lundigan) while on a prospecting trip. Driven by a desire to defeat their murder plot and get revenge, he finds resources within himself to conquer the burning heat, the bitter cold and other dangers of a laborious, painful crawling across sands and up and down canyons.

Major acting assists come from Henry Hull, old prospector; Larry Keating, Ryan's business manager; and Carl Betz and Robert Burton, officers directing the search. Roy Baker's direction accents the forceful drama capably. There are no obvious 3-D tricks in the excellent photography by Lucien Ballard.

•

INFORMER, THE

1935, 91 mins, US Ⓥ ⊙ b/w

Dir John Ford ***Prod*** John Ford ***Scr*** Dudley Nichols ***Ph*** Joseph H. August ***Ed*** George Hively ***Mus*** Max Steiner ***Art*** Van Nest Polglase, Charles Kirk

Act Victor McLaglen, Heather Angel, Preston Foster, Margot Grahame, Wallace Ford, Una O'Connor (RKO)

The Informer is forcefully and intelligently written, directed and acted. Story [by Liam O'Flaherty] deals with the Irish rebellion against British authority prior to 1922, when the Irish Free State's creation finally removed the hated symbols of British domination.

Amidst the rebellion-rife slums of Dublin a huge ox of a peasant, named Gypo Nolan (Victor McLaglen), loves Katie Fox (Margot Grahame) who picks up her room rent on the streets. Gypo reproaches her and is in turn taunted for his miserable poverty and inability to provide money. Stung by the girl's bitterness, Gypo, in fascinated horror at his own wickedness, deliberately turns informer on his best friend to obtain $100 reward. Irony of this deed is that Gypo is really a softie, having been court martialed and expelled from the Republican army for failing to carry out a political assassination.

What makes the picture powerful is the faithful characterization of McLaglen as guided and developed by the direction of John Ford. Gypo is a blundering, pathetic fool who is not basically vicious yet is guilty of a truly foul betrayal.

Wallace Ford, as the boy who is turned in, is smartly cast. Margot Grahame grabs some attention as the harlot. Preston Foster, a good actor, is the head of the Republican underground battalion.

1935: Best Director, Actor (Victor McLaglen), Screenplay, Score

NOMINATIONS: Best Picture, Editing

•

IN GOD WE TRUST OR: GIMME THAT PRIME TIME RELIGION

1980, 97 mins, US Ⓥ col

Dir Marty Feldman ***Prod*** Howard West, George Shapiro ***Scr*** Marty Feldman, Chris Allen ***Ph*** Charles Correll ***Ed*** David Blewitt ***Mus*** John Morris ***Art*** Lawrence G. Paull

Act Marty Feldman, Peter Boyle, Louise Lasser, Wilfrid Hyde White, Richard Pryor, Andy Kaufman (Universal)

In God We Trust is a rare achievement—a comedy with no laughs. This one has totally innocent monk Marty Feldman cast out into the mean and nasty world to raise some quick cash to keep his monastery in business. He ends up on Hollywood Blvd. Object of his search is outrageous TV evangelist Armageddon T. Thunderbird (Andy Kaufman), who puts off the meek man of God before taking him in as a partner, only to later turn against him when Feldman wins the ear of G.O.D. (Richard Pryor). At the same time, Feldman takes a tumble or two with gold-hearted prostie Mary (Louise Lasser).

Beneath all the strained attempts at humor, there's a germ of sweetness in Feldman's innocent led astray, but as a director he's unable to give it any play. Nor does he do any favors for the remainder of the cast. Technically, film is a near-shambles.

•

IN HARM'S WAY

1965, 165 mins, US Ⓥ ▭ b/w

Dir Otto Preminger ***Prod*** Otto Preminger ***Scr*** Wendell Mayes ***Ph*** Loyal Griggs ***Ed*** George Tomasini, Hugh S. Fowler ***Mus*** Jerry Goldsmith ***Art*** Lyle Wheeler

Act John Wayne, Kirk Douglas, Patricia Neal, Tom Tryon, Paula Prentiss, Henry Fonda (Sigma/Paramount)

John Wayne is in every sense the big gun of *In Harm's Way*. Without his commanding presence, chances are director-producer Otto Preminger probably could not have built the head of steam this film generates and sustains for two hours and 45 minutes.

Although the personal drama that unites and divides the lives of navy people caught up in this dramatization of U.S. efforts to strike back within the year after the Pearl Harbor disaster doesn't win any prizes for creativity, Preminger uses it effectively to establish a bond between the characters and the audience. It's a full, lusty slice of life in a time of extreme stress that Wendell Mayes has fashioned from the novel by James Bassett.

Romantic coupling of Wayne and Patricia Neal, as a navy nurse, is the most natural stroke of man and woman casting in many a year. Neal brings to her role a beautifully proportioned, gutsy strength and sensitivity. Through skillful blending of fact and fiction, Preminger provides, in the picture's action stretches, a highly suspenseful and, at times, shatteringly realistic account of an underdog U.S. Navy task force boldly seeking out a Japanese group of ships. The sea battle sequences are filmmaking at its best.

There are some heroics that come out of a traditional mold and fall to Kirk Douglas to carry off as a hard-drinking exec officer, and buddy of Wayne, brooding the loss at Pearl Harbor of his double-timing wife. Henry Fonda, as the four-star boss of this navy show, moves in and out of the story, hitting the mark every time.

1965: NOMINATION: Best B&W Cinematography

•

INHERIT THE WIND

1960, 126 mins, US Ⓥ ⊙ b/w

Dir Stanley Kramer ***Prod*** Stanley Kramer ***Scr*** Nathan E. Douglas, Harold Jacob Smith ***Ph*** Ernest Laszlo ***Ed*** Fredric Knudtson ***Mus*** Ernest Gold ***Art*** Rudolph Sternad

Act Spencer Tracy, Fredric March, Gene Kelly, Florence Eldridge, Harry Morgan, Philip Coolidge (United Artists)

This is a rousing and fascinating motion picture. Producer-director Stanley Kramer has held the action in tight check.

One suspects it needed a strong hand to restrain the forensics of Spencer Tracy and Fredric March as defense and prosecution attorneys in this drama inspired by the 1925 trial in Dayton, TN, of a young high school teacher, John T. Scopes, for daring to teach Darwin's theory of evolution. Roles of Tracy and March equal Clarence Darrow and William Jennings Bryan who collided on evolution.

Tracy and March go at each other on the thespic plane as one might imagine Dempsey and Louis. March actually has the more colorful role as Matthew Harrison Brady (Bryan) because, with the aid of face-changing makeup, he creates a completely different character, whereas Tracy has to rely solely upon his power of illusion, a most persuasive power indeed.

The scenario, which broadens the scope of the play by Jerome Lawrence and Robert E. Lee, is a most commendable job. It is shot through with dialog that it florid, witty, penetrating, compassionate and sardonic. A good measure of the film's surface bite is contributed by Gene Kelly as a cynical Baltimore reporter (patterned after Henry L. Menken) whose paper comes to the aid of the younger teacher played by Dick York. Kelly demonstrates again that even without dancing shoes he knows his way on the screen.

1960: NOMINATIONS: Best Actor (Spencer Tracy), Adapted Screenplay, B&W Cinematography, Editing

•

INJI KAU *(ROUGE)*

1988, 93 mins, Hong Kong Ⓥ ⊙ col

Dir Stanley Kwan ***Prod*** Leonard K.C. Ho ***Scr*** Lilian Lee, Chu Tai An-ping ***Ph*** Bill Wong ***Ed*** Cheung Yu-tsung ***Mus*** Lei Siu-tin ***Art*** Poh Yeuk-muk, Ma Kwong-wing

Act Anita Mui, Leslie Cheung, Alex Man, Emily Chu, Tam Tsin-hung, Chu Sui-tong (Golden Way)

Rouge is a classy, elegant, artistic, believable and enjoyable love story with a ghost framework [from the 1987 novel by Lilian Lee]. The movie is set in colorful 1900 and retells the sad story of a high-class prostitute from an exclusive brothel patronized by rich men.

There is a woman called Flower (Anita Mui, a singer who proves that she's also a dramatic actress), who falls in love with a customer (Leslie Cheung, perfect typecasting) as a spoiled, passive young man controlled by family ties. Love blossoms, but things go awry when they plan to marry and must face the opposition of the young man's family.

Flower dies but the young man survives. They are expected to meet in "hell" and Flower waits for years in the spiritual dimension. When he does not come, she returns to earth to look for her lost lover.

Rouge has the technical gloss of an art movie, detailed cinematography to suit the mood, superb art direction and well-balanced acting, especially by Alex Man. It was first released in Taiwan, was a box-office sensation and won three major Golden Horse awards for best actress, cinematography and art direction.

•

IN-LAWS, THE

1979, 103 mins, US Ⓥ col

Dir Arthur Hiller ***Prod*** Arthur Hiller ***Scr*** Andrew Bergman ***Ph*** David M. Walsh ***Ed*** Robert E. Swink ***Mus*** John Morris ***Art*** Pato Guzman

Act Peter Falk, Alan Arkin, Richard Libertini, Nancy Dussault, Arlene Golonka, Ed Begley Jr (Warner)

Peter Falk and Alan Arkin were the perfect choices to play an addled CIA agent and a Gotham dentist, respectively.

Brought together by the impending marriage of their individual offspring (Michael Lembeck and Penny Peyser), they're quickly at one another's throats, as Falk lures Arkin into a neverending series of improbable adventures.

Script elements include stolen U.S. treasury plates, underworld thugs, and a South American banana republic and its deranged leader.

Under Arthur Hiller's fast-paced and engaging direction, everything keeps moving quickly enough to stymie audience qualms about plotting, character developments and a rapidly-compressed time frame.

•

IN LIKE FLINT
1967, 115 mins, US Ⓥ ⦿ ▭ col
Dir Gordon Douglas ***Prod*** Saul David ***Scr*** Hal Fimberg ***Ph*** William C. Daniels ***Ed*** Hugh S. Fowler ***Mus*** Jerry Goldsmith ***Art*** Jack Martin Smith, Dale Hennesy
Act James Coburn, Lee J. Cobb, Jean Hale, Andrew Duggan, Anna Lee, Yvonne Craig (20th Century-Fox)

Girls, gimmicks, girls, gags, and more girls are the essential parameters of *In Like Flint*. With James Coburn encoring as the urbane master sleuth, also harried boss Lee J. Cobb, this pic turns on a femme plot to take over the world.

As for the story, the tongue is best put way out in the cheek. Anne Lee, ever a charming and gracious screen personality, is part of a triumvirate bent on seizing world power.

Lee's plot in this film comes a cropper when her male allies—corrupt General Steve Ihnat and cohorts, who have substituted an actor, Andrew Duggan, for the real U.S. President, also played by Duggan—move in to snatch the ultimate prize.

While the dialog scenes tend to be a mite sluggish, pace picks up regularly with slam-bang action sequences.

•

IN LOVE AND WAR
1958, 107 mins, US ▭ col
Dir Philip Dunne ***Prod*** Jerry Wald ***Scr*** Edward Anhalt ***Ph*** Leo Tover ***Ed*** William Reynolds ***Mus*** Hugo Friedhofer ***Art*** Lyle R. Wheeler, George W. Davis
Act Robert Wagner, Dana Wynter, Jeffrey Hunter, Hope Lange, Bradford Dillman, Sheree North (20th Century-Fox)

In Love and War is a keen appraisal of the utility of love and the futility of war. Based on Anton Myrer's novel *The Big War*, it is hard-hitting, both in action and dialog. The characterizations are built in San Francisco and the Monterey Peninsula, and the sequences are particularly effective. The Pacific war footage, however, tends to ramble and with little or no forward movement.

Story is of the changing ideals and growing maturity of three marines entrenched in the Second World War. At the start, Jeffrey Hunter is the patriot, Robert Wagner the coward and Bradford Dillman the intellectual who fights because he must. More than one of war, the tale is one of love, Wagner for Sheree North, Hunger for Hope Lange and Dillman, having discarded Dana Wynter, for France Nuyen. High spots are numerous, and the seven stars—plus comic Mort Sahl in his first film role—are excellent. Sahl's Jewish marine role was written especially for him, and, from the sound of it, by him.

•

IN LOVE AND WAR
1996, 115 mins, US Ⓥ ⦿ ▭ col
Dir Richard Attenborough ***Prod*** Dimitri Villard, Richard Attenborough ***Scr*** Allan Scott, Clancy Sigal, Anna Hamilton Phelan ***Ph*** Roger Pratt ***Ed*** Lesley Walker ***Mus*** George Fenton ***Art*** Stuart Craig
Act Sandra Bullock, Chris O'Donnell, Mackenzie Astin, Emilio Bonucci, Ingrid Lacey, Margot Steinberg (New Line)

A pallid telling of the fleeting but indelible romance between Ernest Hemingway and his nurse in Italy during World War I, Richard Attenborough's sixth biographical drama goes through the motions of spinning a passionate love story set against a grand historical background, but doesn't get under the skin of its protagonists.

The 19-year-old Hemingway's affair of the heart with his 26-year-old nurse, Agnes von Kurowsky, was the pivotal amorous event of his early life. Kurowsky remained unknown until after Hemingway's death, and the full extent of her relationship became known only with the publication of *Hemingway in Love and War*, the book [by Henry S. Villard and James Nagel] prompted by the discovery of her private diary and letter, and the basis for the present screenplay [from a story by Allan Scott and producer Dimitri Villard, son of Henry].

Neither the script nor Attenborough's stately direction manages to take the careful, restrained romance to the emotional depths desirable in a sweeping bigscreen love story, and Sandra Bullock and Chris O'Donnell seemingly lack the range and nuance to take this journey into uncharted dramatic territory.

Onscreen for much of the running time, Bullock has no trouble holding viewer interest, but even at the end one remains somewhat unclear about the true nature of her feelings for Hemingway.

•

IN NAME ONLY
1939, 94 mins, US Ⓥ ⦿ b/w
Dir John Cromwell ***Prod*** George Haight ***Scr*** Richard Sherman ***Ph*** J. Roy Hunt ***Ed*** William Hamilton ***Mus*** Roy Webb ***Art*** Van Nest Polglase, Perry Ferguson
Act Carole Lombard, Cary Grant, Kay Francis, Charles Coburn, Helen Vinson, Peggy Ann Garner (RKO)

A novel by Bessie Breuer, *Memory of Love*, forms the basis for this wholly capable production. The story is a romantic drama of a familiar but highly poignant brand, relieved by smart comedy lines and touches.

In the steering of the story director John Cromwell has made every situation as believable as could be accomplished in order to sustain the dramatic undercurrent, strife and the beleaguered romance which has developed.

Cary Grant and Carole Lombard emerge highly impressive. Grant figures in some of the comedy relief but Lombard is almost entirely on the romantic drama side, turning in a fine performance.

As the mercenary wife, Kay Francis does well, shading her role well. She does not photograph as well here, however; may-haps the idea was to make her less glamorous.

•

INNER CIRCLE, THE
1991, 134 mins, US Ⓥ col
Dir Andrei Konchalovsky ***Prod*** Claudio Bonivento ***Scr*** Andrei Konchalovsky, Anatoli Usov ***Ph*** Ennio Guarnieri ***Ed*** Henry Richardson ***Mus*** Eduard Artemiev ***Art*** Ezio Frigerio
Act Tom Hulce, Lolita Davidovich, Bob Hoskins, Alexandre Zbruev, Feodor Chaliapin, Jr., Irina Kupchenko (Columbia)

The first Western film to shoot within the Kremlin and KGB h.q., and Andrei Konchalovsky's first Soviet-based pic in 12 years, this idiosyncratic look at the life of Stalin's personal projectionist has numerous points of interest but is too muddled and misconceived.

Set in Moscow, beginning in 1939 and based on a true story, this odd tale focuses on Ivan Sanshin (Tom Hulce), a groveling, pathetic projectionist for the KGB who has a kind of greatness thrust upon him when he is summarily ordered to screen a film for the supreme leader.

At home on Slaughterhouse Street, Ivan and his bride (Lolita Davidovich) celebrate their honeymoon evening as a Jewish family is evicted from the building. Davidovich maintains an obsessive devotion to the family's orphan daughter. Ivan admits he loves Stalin more than his wife, and has her give herself, on a train one night, to a notoriously brutal KGB head (Bob Hoskins).

Pic excels in glimpses of power at the top. Several scenes take place in Stalin's personal projection room, a salon of plush chairs and ample food and drink, where the air is checked for possible poisoning. Ultimately, however, the story proves unwieldy with Konchlovsky unable to integrate the diverse sides of the tale and give it a proper dramatic arc.

Hulce's performance is typically enthusiastic, but the character is so thick-headed that one tires of him after more than two hours. Hoskins makes a sketchily conceived but utterly convincing thug.

•

INNERSPACE
1987, 120 mins, US Ⓥ ⦿ col
Dir Joe Dante ***Prod*** Michael Finnell ***Scr*** Jeffrey Boam, Chip Proser ***Ph*** Andrew Laszlo ***Ed*** Kent Beyda ***Mus*** Jerry Goldsmith ***Art*** James H. Spencer
Act Dennis Quaid, Martin Short, Meg Ryan, Kevin McCarthy, Fiona Lewis, Henry Gibson (Warner/Amblin)

Hot-dog Air Force flyer Dennis Quaid is prepared at the outset to be shrunken and pilot a tiny craft through the bloodstream of a laboratory rabbit. Evildoers are on to the unprecedented experiment and the syringe bearing the fearless voyager finally implants itself in the behind of Martin Short, a hapless grocery clerk.

Filmmakers' ingenuity [screen story by Chip Proser] quickly begins asserting itself. As Quaid travels through different parts of the unsuspecting shnook's body and speaks to him over his radio, Short believes he's going crazy before finally accepting what's happened to him.

Quaid is engagingly reckless and gung-ho as the pioneer into a new dimension, although he is physically constrained in his little capsule for most of the running time. Short has infinitely more possibilities and makes the most of them, coming into his own as a screen personality as a mild-mannered little guy who rises to an extraordinary situation. Meg Ryan is game as the spirited doll both men hanker for, and supporting cast is filled out with a good assortment of familiar faces.

1987: Best Visual Effects

•

INNOCENCE UNPROTECTED
SEE: NEVINOST BEZ ZASTITE

•

INNOCENT, THE
1993, 107 mins, UK/Germany Ⓥ col
Dir John Schlesinger ***Prod*** Norma Heyman, Chris Sievernich, Wieland Schulz-Keil ***Scr*** Ian McEwan ***Ph*** Dietrich Lohmann ***Ed*** Richard Marden ***Mus*** Gerald Gouriet ***Art*** Luciana Arrighi
Act Isabella Rossellini, Anthony Hopkins, Campbell Scott, Ronald Nitschke, Hart Bochner, James Grant (Lakehart/Sievernich/Babelsberg)

John Schlesinger's *The Innocent* rings hollow, under-utilizing both its top draw talent and some compelling Berlin locations. Despite a close screen translation by Ian McEwan of his own novel of intrigue, espionage, betrayal and love, pic lacks real sense of drama.

A bespectacled Campbell Scott plays the central role of Leonard Markham, a young, naive and virginal British engineer sent to Berlin in 1955, at the height of the Cold War, for reasons he does not know. His commanding officer, Lofting (Jeremy Sinden, in a spunky perf), is warily cooperative with U.S. forces.

Lofting turns Markham over to Bob Glass (Anthony Hopkins), a CIA officer overseeing Operation Gold, a British-West German espionage project to intercept communications between East Germany and the Soviet Union. Glass is a reserved type whose mistrust also extends to Maria (Isabella Rossellini), who picks up Markham in a dance hall and with whom he soon falls in love.

Having set the scene, both McEwan's script and Schlesinger's direction forge ahead to resolve the conflicts established in the first two reels. So intent is the film on its narrative purpose that it fails to build tension or suspense.

Performances in the pic are mostly understated, with Hopkins's Glass muted and one-dimensional. As Markham, Scott carries the film well but gets no chance to fill out his role.

•

INNOCENT BLOOD
(AUSTRALIA: FRENCH VAMPIRE IN AMERICA)
1992, 113 mins, US Ⓥ ⦿ col
Dir John Landis ***Prod*** Lee Rich, Leslie Belzberg ***Scr*** Michael Wolk ***Ph*** Mac Ahlberg ***Ed*** Dale Beldin ***Mus*** Ira Newborn ***Art*** Richard Sawyer
Act Anne Parillaud, Robert Loggia, Anthony LaPaglia, David Proval, Don Rickles, Chazz Palminteri (Warner)

Teens and genre fans should eat up John Landis's latest mix of horror and camp comedy. They will "ooh" at the various gross-out scenes and nifty special effects, "aah" at the film's sensuality and Anne Parillaud's easy nudity, and savor the numerous in-jokes and horror references, from cameos by other goremeister directors to clips from various late-show staples.

Using a set-up (by first-time screenwriter Michael Wolk) that can best be described as *Fright Night* meets Landis's *The Blues Brothers*, the director also benefits from a toothy performance by Robert Loggia as a mob boss who, endowed with vampiric powers by the mysterious Marie (Parillaud), goes on a rampage.

Marie ends up dining on several of Loggia's henchmen as well. She normally kills her "food" after draining it but doesn't get the chance in Loggia's case, forcing her to team up with a cop (Anthony LaPaglia) to stop him.

Making her U.S. film debut, Parillaud (*Nikita*) struggles a bit with enunciation and a quickly abandoned voiceover narration but nonetheless has charisma to spare, oozing sexuality, playfulness and menace all at once. LaPaglia is likable and properly confused as the cop, while much of the rest of the cast provide a convincing gallery of *Godfather* rejects.

Cameos include sci-fi/horror guru Forrest J. Ackerman, directors Frank Oz, Sam Raimi, Tom Savini and Michael Ritchie, plus Don Rickles as the mob boss's lawyer. Tech credits are top-notch.

•

INNOCENT BYSTANDERS
1972, 111 mins, UK col
Dir Peter Collinson ***Prod*** George H. Brown ***Scr*** James Mitchell ***Ph*** Brian Probyn ***Ed*** Alan Pattillo ***Mus*** John Keating ***Art*** Maurice Carter
Act Stanley Baker, Geraldine Chaplin, Donald Pleasence, Dana Andrews, Sue Lloyd, Warren Mitchell (Sagittarius)

Innocent Bystanders is a violence-packed, often-confusing but usually interesting meller of secret agents on the prowl to track down and capture a Russian scientist escaped from a Siberian prison. Scene shifts from London to N.Y., thence to Turkey, where major portion of action unfolds against colorful location backgrounds.

Stanley Baker is chief protagonist, once top agent of Britain's hush-hush spy organization but now regarded as slipped by his chief (Donald Pleasence), who in a final assignment gives him a chance to redeem himself on the scientist caper.

Never exactly explained is the reason for the desperate hunt of the scientist. Script by James Mitchell [from a novel by James Munro] is sufficiently exciting, however, and direction by Peter Collinson so realistic, that interest never lags.

•

INNOCENT LIES

1995, 89 mins, UK/France Ⓥ ▭ col

Dir Patrick Dewolf ***Prod*** Simon Perry, Philippe Guez ***Scr*** Kerry Crabbe, Patrick Dewolf ***Ph*** Patrick Blossier ***Ed*** Chris Wimble, Joelle Hache ***Mus*** Alexandre Desplat ***Art*** Bernd Lepel

Act Stephen Dorff, Gabrielle Anwar, Adrian Dunbar, Sophie Aubry, Joanna Lumley, Melvil Poupaud (Red Umbrella/Septieme/PolyGram)

Style almost triumphs over content in *Innocent Lies*, an arty whodunit-cum-thriller that completely unravels in the third act but has a kind of anything-goes bravura that has to be admired. File this one under "interesting failures."

Inspired by Agatha Christie (per movie's end crawl) but not based on a specific work, film gets off to a pacey start with the death of Britisher Joe Green (Donal McCann, uncredited) near a cliff-top manse "somewhere on the French coast" in September '38. On the next plane from Blighty comes Inspector Cross (Adrian Dunbar), bent on discovering the truth behind his best friend's apparent suicide.

A whole raft of characters are rapidly intro'd, starting with the owner of the avant-garde pile, Lady Helena Graves (Joanna Lumley), a snooty, acid-tongued widow with Nazi connections. Other inhabitants of the house are a shifty bunch with secrets to spare. Lady Helena's daughter, Celia (Gabrielle Anwar), is a pouty sexpot about to marry a bemused American (Alexis Denisof). Her brother Jeremy (Stephen Dorff) labors under the guilt of having accidentally killed his brother when a kid, and is married to a Jewish woman (Marianne Denicourt), whom Mom loathes. Just to complicate matters, Celia and Jeremy appear to have a closer relationship than simply sister and brother.

French helmer/co-scripter Patrick Dewolf, who co-wrote several of Patrice Leconte's successes (*Monsieur Hire, Tandem*) as well as directing the noirish English-lingo *Lapse of Memory* (1991), sets up a simmering atmosphere in the opening reels, but the movie falls uneasily between two stools, convincing neither as a murder mystery nor as a sexually charged meller. Anwar lacks a commanding enough screen presence to carry a movie of this sort.

•

INNOCENT MAN, AN

1989, 113 mins, US Ⓥ ⦿ col

Dir Peter Yates ***Prod*** Ted Field, Robert W. Cort ***Scr*** Larry Brothers ***Ph*** William A. Fraker ***Ed*** Stephen A. Rotter, William S. Scharf ***Mus*** Howard Shore ***Art*** Stuart Wurtzel

Act Tom Selleck, F. Murray Abraham, Laila Robins, David Rasche, Richard Young (Touchstone/Silver Screen Partners IV)

This collection of clichés accomplishes the almost unthinkable by bringing the prison genre to a new low.

Nightmarishly structured, the film takes half-hour before Tom Selleck's everyman, Jimmie Rainwood, gets wrongfully framed by two corrupt vice cops (David Rasche and Richard Young). Then he spends more than an hour in stir before he gets released to seek vengeance on the duo in one of the more absurd finales in memory.

In between, Jimmie gets a lesson in prison survival from the cell-wise Virgil (F. Murray Abraham), learning to do the previously unthinkable to survive the hellish conditions.

•

INNOCENTS, THE

1961, 99 mins, UK ▭ b/w

Dir Jack Clayton ***Prod*** Jack Clayton ***Scr*** William Archibald, Truman Capote ***Ph*** Freddie Francis ***Ed*** James Clark ***Mus*** Georges Auric ***Art*** Wilfrid Shingleton

Act Deborah Kerr, Michael Redgrave, Peter Wyngarde, Megs Jenkins, Martin Stephens, Pamela Franklin (20th Century-Fox)

Based on Henry James's story *Turn of the Screw* this catches an eerie, spine-chilling mood right at the start and never lets up on its grim, evil theme. Director Jack Clayton makes full use of camera angles, sharp cutting, shadows, ghost effects and a sinister soundtrack.

Deborah Kerr has a long, arduous role as a governess in charge of two apparently angelic little children in a huge country house. Gradually she finds that they are not all that they seem on the surface. Her determination to save the two moppets' corrupted souls leads up to a tragic, powerful climax.

Clayton's small but expert cast do full justice to their tasks, Kerr runs a wide gamut of emotions in a difficult role in which she has to start with an uncomplicated portrayal and gradually find herself involved in strange, unnatural goings-on, during which she sometimes doubts her own sanity. Clayton has also coaxed a couple of remarkable pieces of playing from the two youngsters, Martin Stephens and Pamela Franklin, extraordinary blends of innocence and sophistry.

•

INNOCENT SLEEP, THE

1996, 99 mins, UK Ⓥ ▭ col

Dir Scott Michell ***Prod*** Matthew Vaughn, Scott Michell ***Scr*** Ray Villis ***Ph*** Alan Dunlop ***Ed*** Derek Trigg ***Mus*** Mark Ayres ***Art*** Eve Mavrakis

Act Rupert Graves, Annabella Sciorra, Michael Gambon, Franco Nero, Graham Crowden, John Hannah (Timedial)

A solid, old-fashioned thriller that touches on recent news stories about corruption in high places, *The Innocent Sleep* is familiar stuff but receives an extra edge from interesting casting and Scott Michell's classy direction.

When Alan Terry (an effective Rupert Graves), a homeless drunk eking out a precarious existence in an unfriendly London, beds down near Tower Bridge, he's got a box seat when a suave Italian (Franco Nero) oversees the execution of a fellow Italian.

His friend George (a rather hammy Graham Crowden), a fellow derelict, advises him to report the killing, which is officially listed as a suicide; he discovers that the officer in charge of the investigation, Matheson (the chillingly intense Michael Gambon), was one of the killers.

Terry enlists the help of a tough-as-nails Yank investigative reporter, Billie Hayman (a delightful Annabella Sciorra), who works for a London tabloid and is recovering from a murky incident in her recent past. Story builds a fair degree of suspense before the rather disappointing finale. [Version reviewed was a 110-min. one screened in the 1995 Cannes market. Pic was subsequently cut to 99 mins.]

•

INN OF THE SIXTH HAPPINESS, THE

1958, 158 mins, US Ⓥ ⦿ ▭ col

Dir Mark Robson ***Prod*** Buddy Adler ***Scr*** Isobel Lennart ***Ph*** Freddie Young ***Ed*** Ernest Walter ***Mus*** Malcolm Arnold ***Art*** John Box, Geoffrey Drake

Act Ingrid Bergman, Curt Jurgens, Robert Donat, Ronald Squire, Athene Seyler, Peter Chong (20th Century-Fox)

Based on Alan Burgess's novel *The Small Woman* which, in turn, was based on the adventures of a real person, the film has Ingrid Bergman as a rejected missionary in China, who gets there determinedly under her own steam. First met with hostility by the natives, she gradually wins their love and esteem. She falls in love with a Eurasian colonel, converts a powerful mandarin to Christianity and becomes involved in the Chino-Japanese war. Finally she guides 100 children to the safety of a northern mission by leading them on an arduous journey across the rugged mountains and through enemy territory.

The inn in the film is run by Bergman and an elderly missionary (Athene Seyler). Here they dispense hospitality and Bible stories to the muleteers in transit. Bergman's early scenes as she strives to get to China and begins the urgent task of winning the confidence of the Chinese are brilliantly done with humor and a sense of urgent dedication.

A standout performance comes from Robert Donat as an astute yet benign mandarin. It was Donat's swan song before his untimely death and only rarely can signs of his physical collapse be detected.

The film was shot in Wales and in the Elstree studio, converted expertly into a Chinese village. Mark Robson's direction slickly catches both the sweep of the crowd sequences and the more intimate ones.

1958: NOMINATION: Best Director

•

IN OLD ARIZONA

1929, 94 mins, US b/w

Dir Irving Cummings, Raoul Walsh ***Scr*** Tom Barry ***Ph*** Arthur Edeson

Act Warner Baxter, Edmund Lowe, Dorothy Burgess, J. Farrell McDonald, Fred Warren (Fox)

It was said that Fox would never turn loose a full-length talkie until the studio was convinced the picture was right. In *Old Arizona*, that it's right is unquestioned at this time. It's the first outdoor talkie and a Western, with a climax twist to make the story stand out from the usual hill and dale thesis. It's outdoors, it talks and it has a great screen performance by Warner Baxter. That it's long and that it moves slowly is also true, but the exterior sound revives the novelty angle again.

Dorothy Burgess is cast as Tonia, a Mexican vixen who plays the boys across the boards and finally gets into a jam between the Cisco Kid (Baxter) and the army sergeant who is pursuing the bandit.

Raoul Walsh is given screen and program credit for having co-directed this film, as he actually started it and was intent on finishing and playing the Cisco Kid in it. An unfortunate accident made this impossible, hence Irving Cumming's assignment.

1928/29: Best Actor (Warner Baxter)

NOMINATIONS: Best Picture, Director, Writing, Cinematography

•

IN OLD CHICAGO

1938, 110 mins, US Ⓥ b/w

Dir Henry King ***Prod*** Darryl Zanuck ***Scr*** Lamar Trotti, Sonya Levien ***Ph*** Peverell Marley ***Ed*** Barbara McLean ***Mus*** Louis Silvers (dir.) ***Art*** William Darling, Rudolph Sternad

Act Tyrone Power, Alice Faye, Don Ameche, Alice Brady, Andy Devine, Brian Donlevy (20th Century-Fox)

An elaborate and liberally budgeted entertainment, the pictorial climax is the Chicago fire of 1871. This portion envisaging mob panic, desperate efforts to stop the fire by dynamiting, etc, is highly effective.

It is historically cockeyed in the placement of its main characters, and its story [by Niven Busch] is mere rehash of corrupt political mismanagement of a growing American city. But as a film entertainment it is socko.

The O'Leary family plays the most important part in the story, even to the point where one of the sons is projected as mayor of the city at the time of the fire, and another is pictured as the dishonest political boss, saloon keeper and villain.

First portion (80 minutes) carries the characters to the eve of the great fire. Scores of elaborate scenes establish the primitive type of architecture of the frame-built, rambling town with its unpaved, muddy streets. Most of the action is laid in gaudy saloons and beer halls. Chicago is pictured as a dirty and corrupt city, a Sodom on the brink, ready for the torch of annihilation. Second part contains views of the holocaust, and a devastating series of actual and processed shots. Alice Brady and Alice Faye give the outstanding performances. Brady is Mrs O'Leary, an honest, hardworking laundress with a pleasing Irish brogue. Tyrone Power as the film's heavy is good in his romantic scenes with Faye, who appears as a musical hall singer. Latter is especially effective when singing several musical numbers, tuned by Mack Gordon and Harry Revel, of which "In Old Chicago" is the best. Don Ameche is a vehement political reformer and Brian Donlevy plays a dive keeper and crooked politician.

1937: Best Supp. Actress (Alice Brady), Assistant Director (Robert Webb)

NOMINATIONS: Best Picture, Original Story, Score, Sound

•

IN OLD KENTUCKY

1935, 85 mins, US Ⓥ b/w

Dir George Marshall ***Prod*** Edward Butcher ***Scr*** Sam Hellman, Gladys Lehman, Henry Johnson ***Ph*** L. William O'Connell ***Mus*** Arthur Lange

Act Will Rogers, Dorothy Wilson, Russell Hardie, Charles Sellon, Louise Henry, Esther Dale (Fox)

It's no less than fitting that Will Rogers's last picture should be one of his best. *In Old Kentucky* is a delightful comedy.

Although [the play by Charles T. Dazey was] first produced nearly 14 years earlier on Broadway and filmed at least twice since then, the story is far from dated on this trip.

As a foil for Rogers and excellent on his own, Bill Robinson hoofs his way to importance. Despite not being a "picture" dancer, such as Fred Astaire, with his hoofery confined to the feet, Robinson nevertheless commands attention by the artistry of his footwork.

The Robinson stepping also gives Rogers a chance to go on the hoof and this is built into a comedy sequence that makes the picture a honey with or without the rest of the footage. Finale horse race reaches the customary happy conclusion, but a comedy switch strikes a different note in bangtail dramatics, with the crazy "rain-making" machine inventor from the book hanging a hilarious tag on the climax.

•

IN SEARCH OF GREGORY
1970, 90 mins, UK/Italy col
Dir Peter Wood ***Prod*** Joseph Janni, Daniele Senatore ***Scr*** Tonnio Guerra, Lucille Laks ***Ph*** Otto Heller, Giorgio Tonti ***Ed*** John Bloom ***Mus*** Ron Grainer ***Art*** Piero Poletto
Act Julie Christie, Michael Sarrazin, John Hurt, Paola Pitagora, Roland Culver, Tony Selby (Vic/Vera)

A superbly wrought gem about the romantic illusions people, especially would-be lovers, search for in one another, with Julie Christie ideally cast as the seeker and Michael Sarrazin as her fantasy.

Christie, the daughter of an incurably romantic and frequently married Swiss financier, played with charming elan by Adolfo Celi, is living a life of quiet domesticity in Rome when she is invited by papa to attend his latest nuptial.

Her real attraction in Geneva is Celi's calculating description of his house guest from San Francisco, a tall, handsome "likeable maniac." At the airport, she spots a giant poster of Sarrazin, an auto-ball champion, and in her imagination he becomes the physical embodiment of her romantic fantasies about Gregory.

•

IN SEARCH OF THE CASTAWAYS
1962, 100 mins, US Ⓥ ⦿ col
Dir Robert Stevenson ***Prod*** Walt Disney ***Scr*** Lowell S. Hawley ***Ph*** Paul Beeson ***Ed*** Gordon Stone ***Mus*** William Alwyn ***Art*** Michael Stringer
Act Maurice Chevalier, Hayley Mills, George Sanders, Wilfrid Hyde White, Michael Anderson, Jr., Wilfrid Brambell (Walt Disney)

Castaways is a blend of every Disney trick, combining adventure and humor. Jules Verne's yarn concerns a French scientist who finds a bottle containing a note that reveals the whereabouts of Captain Grant, who mysteriously disappeared two years before. The Frenchman and the sea captain's two children persuade a wealthy shipping owner and his son to set off for South America in search of the missing man. The trail eventually leads successfully to Australia and New Zealand.

The party survives giant condors, jaguars, flood, lightning, crocodiles, an avalanche, an earthquake, a huge waterspout, mutiny by Grant's former quartermaster, imprisonment by unfriendly Maoris and an erupting volcano.

Thesping is done throughout with a tongue in cheek exuberance that suggests that Disney and director Robert Stevenson have given the actors the go ahead to have fun. At times it almost looks as if they are making up the situations and dialog as they go along.

•

INSERTS
1975, 117 mins, UK Ⓥ col
Dir John Byrum ***Prod*** Davina Belling, Clive Parsons ***Scr*** John Byrum ***Ph*** Denys Coop ***Ed*** Mike Bradsell ***Mus*** Jessica Harper (consult.) ***Art*** John Clark
Act Richard Dreyfuss, Jessica Harper, Stephen Davies, Veronica Cartwright, Bob Hoskins (Film & General)

Despite its British label, this is a thoroughly Yank pic that dips into nostalgia and Hollywood 1930s themes. Richard Dreyfuss is all coiled disdain as a once-great director reduced to stag pix.

Dreyfuss manages to add some unusual touches to them as the moneyman walks in with a lissome girl he is planning to marry but whom he treats as a child.

The boss leaves the girl with Dreyfuss; the girl wants to be in pictures and finally decides to pose for inserts; they are caught by the boss, who is not sure what happened but takes off with the camera and material.

Jessica Harper scores as the shrewd innocent and Stephen Davies and Bob Hoskins are right as the actor and boss respectively. But it is all somewhat too surface despite allusions to Hollywood 1930s types.

•

INSIDE
1996, 94 mins, US col
Dir Arthur Penn ***Prod*** Hillard Elkins ***Scr*** Bima Stagg ***Ph*** Jan Weincke ***Ed*** Suzanne Pillsburg ***Mus*** Robert Levin ***Art*** Dave Barkham
Act Eric Stoltz, Nigel Hawthorne, Louis Gossett, Jr., Ian Roberts, Ross Prelier, Jerry Mofokeng (Elkins/Lo Go/Showtime)

Vet helmer Arthur Penn and two powerful lead performances lend stark force to parts of *Inside*, though Bima Stagg's somewhat awkwardly structured screenplay stretches credibility at times. Another antiapartheid drama largely focused on a sympathetic white protagonist, pic is a provocative if flawed chamber piece.

At the outset, 30-year-old Afrikaaner Peter Martin Strydom (Eric Stoltz) already has been beaten and tortured, but as yet denies any alleged "conspiracy to commit treason, sabotage and terrorism." Interrogating Col. Krueger (Nigel Hawthorne) deploys a wicked array of tactics to encourage Marty's confession and the naming of any fellow "conspirators." He feeds the prisoner possibly bogus information about his girlfriend, father, and the alleged civilian-death consequences of his accused arms-hiding on behalf of freedom fighters.

Ten years later, the colonel reviews these events—under the unforgiving gaze of his own "Questioner" (Louis Gossett, Jr.) investigating the former regime's human-rights crimes in a new, post-apartheid era. Put in the hot seat himself for a change, the colonel remains a model of cool hypocrisy and denial—to a point.

Penn, lenser Jan Weincke and the production designers do a terrific job exploiting the claustrophobia of the central action, which takes place entirely in the colonel's office and one dank cell block, with p.o.v. shots through prisoners' peepholes particularly effective.

Stoltz vividly portrays his figure's steady mental and physical disintegration. But pic's strongest suit is held by Hawthorne, with his meticulously faked empathy and icy, sarcastic lack of conscience.

•

INSIDE DAISY CLOVER
1965, 128 mins, US Ⓥ ⦿ ▭ col
Dir Robert Mulligan ***Prod*** Alan J. Pakula ***Scr*** Gavin Lambert ***Ph*** Charles Lang ***Ed*** Aaron Stell ***Mus*** Andre Previn ***Art*** Robert Clatworthy
Act Natalie Wood, Christopher Plummer, Robert Redford, Roddy McDowall, Ruth Gordon, Katharine Bard (Park Place/Warner)

There will be those who may claim *Inside Daisy Clover* is based upon the true-life story of an actress who rose to shining blonde stardom. Alan J. Pakula and Robert Mulligan focus their sights upon a teenage beach gamin who becomes a Hollywood star of the 1930s. Covering a two-year period, the outcome is at times disjointed and episodic as the title character played by Natalie Wood emerges more nebulous than definitive. Femme star seems to be eternally searching for the meaning of her role; she is almost inarticulate for long intervals and whoever is in a scene with her generally engages in a monolog since there is seldom dialog between them. The Gavin Lambert screenplay, based on his own novel, hop-skips through a brief romance with a screen idol; her one-day marriage, desertion and divorce; a nervous breakdown after the death of her mother.

Probably the outstanding parts of pic are two novel musical numbers [staged by Herbert Ross], one in which the studio boss introduces his new star in a specially-made film shown at a party and second featuring her after she's reached stardom.

Wood is better than her part. Her co-star is Christopher Plummer, who gives polish and some stiffness to the sadistic studio head bound to build himself a star.

1965: NOMINATIONS: Best Supp. Actress (Ruth Gordon), Color Costume Design, Color Art Direction

•

INSIDE MONKEY ZETTERLAND
1992, 92 mins, US Ⓥ col
Dir Jefery Levy ***Prod*** Chuck Grieve, Tani Cohen ***Scr*** Steven Antin, John Boskovich ***Ph*** Christopher Taylor ***Ed*** Lauren Zuckerman ***Mus*** Rick Cox, Jeff Elmassian ***Art*** Jane Stewart
Act Steven Antin, Katherine Helmond, Patricia Arquette, Tate Donovan, Bo Hopkins, Sandra Bernhard (Coast Entertainment)

A charming comedy about contempo L.A. life, *Inside Monkey Zetterland* is infused with a sophisticated gay sensibility. Although pic is populated by gay and lesbian characters, its broad canvas, humanistic vision, magnetic cast and inspired writing extend its appeal.

At the heart of scripter Steven Antin's poetic, loosely autobiographical comedy is the complex, Oedipal relationship between aspiring writer Monkey Zetterland (Antin) and his domineering Jewish mother (Katherine Helmond), a TV soap star.

Dad Mike (Bo Hopkins) is not around much, but Monkey is close to his brother (Tate Donovan), a handsome hairdresser, and even closer to his lesbian sister (Patricia Arquette), who moves into his house during a strain in her relationship with her lover (Sofia Coppola).

Pic's best sequences depict collective gatherings (Thanksgiving dinner, evenings in front of the TV) in which Monkey's friends behave like one big, extended family, expanding the conventional meaning of family life. In tone, the pic resembles Alan Rudolph's best pics (*Welcome to L.A., Choose Me*), and its ironic view and whimsical absurdity contain light and dark humour in equal measure.

Unfortunately, the film's last half-hour becomes too cute and TV-like in its artificial tempo. Pic also errs in deliberating on its least convincing subplot involving a terrorist act against a homophobic insurance company.

•

INSIDE MOVES: THE GUYS FROM MAX'S BAR
1980, 113 mins, US Ⓥ ⦿ ▭ col
Dir Richard Donner ***Prod*** Mark M. Tanz, R. W. Goodwin ***Scr*** Valerie Curtin, Barry Levinson ***Ph*** Laszlo Kovacs ***Ed*** Frank Morriss ***Mus*** John Barry ***Art*** Charles Rosen
Act John Savage, David Morse, Diana Scarwid, Harold Russell, Amy Wright, Tony Burton (AFD/Goodmark)

Inoffensive and essentially compassionate, *Inside Moves* is also a highly conventional and predictable look at handicapped citizens trying to make it in everyday life.

Director Richard Donner focuses on the intermittently tense relationship between insecure, failed suicide John Savage and volatile David Morse.

Basic plot movement [from the novel by Todd Walton] has Savage, permanently hobbled after jumping off a building, gradually regaining confidence.

Performances can't be faulted, with Savage seeming truly disturbed at the start, only to slowly come to terms with himself. In his feature debut, Morse puts across the called-for ambition and later shallowness, and Diana Scarwid hits the right notes as a "normal" young woman forced to confront her own limitations via the outwardly afflicted.

1980: NOMINATION: Best Supp. Actress (Diana Scarwid)

•

INSIDER, THE
1999, 157 mins, US Ⓥ ⦿ ▭ col
Dir Michael Mann ***Prod*** Michael Mann, Pieter Jan Brugge ***Scr*** Eric Roth, Michael Mann ***Ph*** Dante Spinotti ***Ed*** William Goldenberg, Paul Rubell, David Rosenbloom ***Mus*** Lisa Gerrard, Pieter Bourke, Graeme Revell ***Art*** Brian Morris
Act Al Pacino, Russell Crowe, Christopher Plummer, Diane Venora, Philip Baker Hall, Lindsay Crouse (Forward Pass/Mann-Roth/Touchstone)

The impact of a challenging story boldly tackled is diminished by serious overlength and an overriding air of self-importance in *The Insider*. This detailed analysis of the ferocious power, implacable arrogance and ultimate vulnerability of corporate America results in a borderline pretentious, overinflated picture.

The story [based on the *Vanity Fair* article *The Man Who Knew Too Much* by Marie Brenner] of the unheroic scientific researcher who exposed the tobacco companies' official lies about the unhealthful nature of their product might have found its ideal form as the sort of tight, co-flab corporate thriller at which HBO has come to excel.

History has provided director and cowriter Michael Mann with the opportunity for a dual investigation of corporate duplicity, courtesy of CBS's initial decision not to air its explosive *60 Minutes* interview with the whistleblower. In the wake of CBS's cop-out, producer Lowell Bergman (Al Pacino) must battle with a smear campaign launched against Jeffrey Wigand (Russell Crowe), former R&D head at the third-largest U.S. tobacco company, who goes into a suicidal funk in a hotel room.

Despite the always interesting behind-the-scenes look at the legwork and politics necessary to produce *60 Minutes*, the heart of the story is Wigand, and it is upon him that the film should have more squarely concentrated. Crowe makes him a fascinating figure of complicated motives. Pacino invests Bergman with boundless passion for his job, but it's a one-note character.

In his handful of judiciously chosen and sharply written scenes, Christopher Plummer delivers enormous satisfaction in a portrait of celebrated newsman Mike Wallace.

1999: NOMINATIONS: Best Picture, Director, Actor (Russell Crowe), Adapted Screenplay, Cinematography, Editing, Sound

•

INSIGNIFICANCE
1985, 108 mins, UK Ⓥ ⦿ col
Dir Nicolas Roeg ***Prod*** Jeremy Thomas ***Scr*** Terry Johnson ***Ph*** Peter Hannan ***Ed*** Tony Lawson ***Mus*** Stanley Myers ***Art*** David Brockhurst
Act Gary Busey, Tony Curtis, Michael Emil, Theresa Russell, Will Sampson (Zenith/Recorded Picture)

A comedy set in a New York hotel room over a sweaty night in 1953 might seem an odd assignment for such a serious and innovative director as Nicolas Roeg.

Story concerns four celebrated American figures of the 1950s who, for legal reasons, are not specifically named. That's all to the good, since pic dispenses with biographical detail to focus on the nature of celebrity in Cold War America.

Film was scripted by Terry Johnson from his stage play. Although legit text is not opened out in a traditional way, beautifully lensed views of the N.Y. landscape and flashbacks give the film a sense of scale. When, towards the end of the film, the Elevator Attendant greets the dawn Cherokee-style, the hotel room has become a microcosm of the world outside.

Those on the lookout for philosophical reflections will find plenty to think about in the pic's meditations upon relativity and the coming together of time. *Insignificance* also works on a simpler level as a depiction of four people struggling against despair.

•

IN SOCIETY

1944, 73 mins, US b/w

Dir Jean Yarbrough ***Prod*** Edmund L. Hartmann ***Scr*** John Grant, Edmund L. Hartmann, Hal Fimberg ***Ph*** Jerome Ash ***Ed*** Philip Cahn ***Mus*** Edgar Fairchild (dir.) ***Art*** John B. Goodman, Eugene Lourie

Act Bud Abbott, Lou Costello, Marion Hutton, Kirby Grant, Margaret Irving, Anne Gillis (Universal)

Basic idea of story [by Hugh Wedlock, Jr. and Howard Snyder] spots Abbott and Costello as two struggling, extra-dumb plumbers being accidentally invited to a high society weekend soirée. Their exertions and blundering efforts to adjust themselves to new surroundings furnish the pegs on which many gags are strung. But even before reaching Hollywood's idea of effete society, a bunch of new and old comedy routines are dusted off and whipped across deftly.

Costello works in his old stride, while Abbott is more efficient, smooth-working than ever as straight in the laugh combo. Marion Hutton, a femme taxi driver, provides the slight romantic twist opposite the wealthy Kirby Grant. She's supposed to be Costello's sweetie, but that's strictly for laughs, Hutton being Betty Hutton's sis.

•

INSPECTOR CLOUSEAU

1968, 105 mins, UK Ⓥ ▭ col

Dir Bud Yorkin ***Prod*** Lewis J. Rachmil ***Scr*** Tom Waldman, Frank Waldman ***Ph*** Arthur Ibbetson ***Ed*** John Victor Smith ***Mus*** Ken Thorne ***Art*** Michael Stringer

Act Alan Arkin, Frank Finlay, Delia Boccardo, Patrick Cargill, Beryl Reid, Barry Foster (United Artists/Mirisch)

Inspector Clouseau, the gauche and Gallic gumshoe, gets a healthy revitalization via Alan Arkin, in the title role, and director Bud Yorkin. Film is a lively, entertaining and episodic story of bank robbers. Good scripting, better acting and topnotch direction get the most out of the material.

Clouseau is assigned to Scotland Yard to help solve a major bank heist. Story develops to a simultaneous robbery of about a dozen Swiss banks, by a ring whose members wear face masks patterned after Clouseau.

Story develops in leisurely fashion, which could have worked to overall disadvantage were it not for the excellent work of Arkin and Yorkin which keeps plot adrenalin flowing. Instead, enough momentum is sustained to hold amused interest.

•

INSPECTOR GADGET

1999, 77 mins, US Ⓥ ⦿ col

Dir David Kellogg ***Prod*** Jordan Kerner, Roger Birnbaum, Andy Heyward ***Scr*** Kerry Ehrin, Zak Penn ***Ph*** Adam Greenberg ***Ed*** Thom Noble, Alan Cody ***Mus*** John Debney ***Art*** Michael White, Leslie Dilley

Act Matthew Broderick, Rupert Everett, Joely Fisher, Michelle Trachtenberg, Andy Dick, Cheri Oteri (Disney)

A new standard for wretched excess is established by *Inspector Gadget*, a joyless and charmless disaster in which state-of-the-art special effects are squandered on pain-in-the-backside folly. Loosely based on the '80s TV cartoon series [created by Andy Heyward, Jean Chalopin and Bruno Bianchi] about a bumbling bionic crime-fighter, pic is written [from a screen story by Kerry Ehrin and Dana Olsen], acted and directed in a style broad enough to indicate that the presumptive target audience consists of moppets with extremely short attention spans.

Matthew Broderick stars as John Brown, an idealistic security guard who pursues evil billionaire Sanford Scolex (Rupert Everett) and his flunky (Michael G. Hagerty) when they kill scientist Artemus Bradford (Rene Auberjonois).

There isn't much left of our hero when he's wheeled into the hospital. So Brenda Bradford (Joely Fisher), Artemus's daughter, implants several thousand handy-dandy devices in the dying security guard, giving him a new lease on life as a gizmo-enhanced cyborg and renaming him Inspector Gadget. Assigned to Riverton City police department, Gadget resolves to find the killers of Brenda's father.

Under the frantic direction of first-time feature helmer David Kellogg, the film careens from scene to scene like a Ritalin-deprived problem child. Broderick makes a game effort but overdoes the gee-whiz ingenuousness. Everett is disappointingly pedestrian as the villain.

Even with an interminable closing-credits crawl, pic clocks in as one of this decade's shortest major studio releases.

•

INSPIRATION

1931, 73 mins, US Ⓥ ⦿ b/w

Dir Clarence Brown ***Scr*** Gene Markey ***Ph*** William Daniels ***Ed*** Conrad A. Nervig

Act Greta Garbo, Robert Montgomery, Lewis Stone, Marjorie Rambeau, Judith Vosselli, Beryl Mercer (M-G-M)

Garbo has never looked nor played better than in this suitable assignment. Replete with heavy love stuff, she plays it easily and convincingly, even contributing a sparkling brief bit of light comedy, and often helping long passages of awkward dialog to sound almost real. What happens to the free-wheeling Parisian artist's model and the nice boy from the country in this picture can happen to any other pair similarly situated. This model is introduced rather tritely as the town toast amongst the artistic set. She's the inspiration for the latest successful works of an artist, a sculptor, a composer and a writer, and even that flattery doesn't seem undue. The introduction is at a party in a home that looks like Roseland ballroom.

After the model completes the meeting the nice boy takes her home. They fall in love. Her past then becomes and remains the issue until the finish.

Robert Montgomery is an excellent nice boy. Lewis Stone and Marjorie Rambeau are also outstanding.

•

INTERIORS

1978, 93 mins, US Ⓥ ⦿ col

Dir Woody Allen ***Prod*** Charles H. Joffe ***Scr*** Woody Allen ***Ph*** Gordon Willis ***Ed*** Ralph Rosenblum ***Art*** Mel Bourne

Act Kristin Griffith, Mary Beth Hurt, Richard Jordan, Diane Keaton, E. G. Marshall, Geraldine Page (United Artists)

Watching this picture a question keeps recurring: what would Woody Allen think of all this? Then you remember he wrote and directed it. The film is populated by characters reacting to situations Allen has satirized so brilliantly in other pictures. Diane Keaton is a suffering poet married to Richard Jordan, a novelist overshadowed by Keaton's accomplishments and talents. Keaton has two sisters—Kristin Griffith, a television actress, and Mary Beth Hurt, the most gifted of the three, but the least directed.

What would be called the film's action—like Ingmar Bergman's pictures, the movement is interior, in the mind—revolves around the relationship among the sisters and their parents, E. G. Marshall and Geraldine Page. *Interiors* also looks like a Bergman film. Characters are photographed against blank walls, Keaton's discussions with her analyst appear almost to be a confession into the camera. And the final third of *Interiors* was shot near the ocean in Long Island and looks like the Swedish island on which Bergman has photographed so many of his films.

Keaton's role is the most difficult, but her performance the least believable of the eight principals. Maureen Stapleton as the woman Marshall marries after divorcing Page, is the only character who reacts more from the heart than the head.

1978: NOMINATIONS: Best Director, Actress (Geraldine Page), Supp. Actress (Maureen Stapleton), Original Screenplay, Art Direction

•

INTERLUDE

1968, 113 mins, UK Ⓥ col

Dir Kevin Billington ***Prod*** David Deutsch ***Scr*** Lee Langley, Hugh Leonard ***Ph*** Gerry Fisher ***Ed*** Bert Bates ***Mus*** Georges Delerue ***Art*** Tony Woollard

Act Oskar Werner, Barbara Ferris, Virginia Maskell, Donald Sutherland, Nora Swinburne, John Cleese (Columbia/Domino)

Interlude is not just another *Brief Encounter* type of romantic drama; it is one of the best of its class. Oskar Werner and Barbara Ferris are the star-crossed, and star-billed, lovers in this handsome production, filmed in England.

All the excitement and ecstacy, as well as the bittersweet, foredoomed disenchantment of extra-marital romance are contained in the original screenplay. Strong writing, superior acting and first rate direction make this a powerful, personal drama.

Werner plays a temperamental symphonic conductor who is interviewed by Ferris, a newspaper reporter, the story unfolding in flashback format. A tender, fragile atmosphere is established early, and sustained quite well.

Werner's performance is excellent, despite some wardrobe and makeup, which occasionally fights the credibility of his character. Ferris is outstanding; to her goes the burden of commingling the love-hate, up-down, sweet-sour aspects of the affair, and she carries it superbly. Virginia Maskell's character, unlike the stock "wife," comes to life.

•

INTERMEZZO

1936, 88 mins, Sweden Ⓥ ⦿ b/w

Dir Gustaf Molander ***Scr*** Gustaf Molander, Gosta Stevens ***Ph*** Ake Dahlqvist ***Mus*** Heinz Provost

Act Gosta Ekman, Inga Tidblad, Hans Ekman, Britt Hagman, Erik Berglund, Ingrid Bergman (Svensk Filmindustri)

Intermezzo is poignant, full of pathos, and, above all, shows in Ingrid Bergman, a talented, beautiful actress. Although Bergman's beauty and splendid characterization as Anita Hoffman, the ill-fated third person in the triangle, is outstanding, Gosta Ekman, Sweden's veteran of the screen, is not far behind as the violin master, Holder Brandt.

It is through her teaching of piano to Ann-Marie (Britt Hagman), tiny daughter of Brandt, that Anita and the violin player meet. Their friendship, first a mutual professional admiration, ripens to love. Brandt then forsakes his wife and children, leaving on a concert tour, with Anita as his accompanyist.

Brandt establishes new heights to his concert fame but family ties call to Brandt. Finally, the urge to see his small daughter is too much.

Other convincing performances are given by Inga Tidblad, as the wife; Erik Berglund, as an impresario; and Hans Ekman, as the son.

•

INTERMEZZO: A LOVE STORY
(UK: ESCAPE TO HAPPINESS)

1939, 70 mins, US Ⓥ ⦿ b/w

Dir Gregory Ratoff ***Prod*** David O. Selznick ***Scr*** George O'Neil ***Ph*** Gregg Toland ***Ed*** Hal C. Kern, Francis D. Lyon ***Mus*** Louis Forbes (dir.) ***Art*** Lyle R. Wheeler

Act Leslie Howard, Ingrid Bergman, Edna Best, John Halliday, Cecil Kellaway (Selznick)

Intermezzo is an American remake of a picture turned out three years earlier in Sweden, which Gustav Molander directed, with Ingrid Bergman in the femme lead.

Story structure [based on original by Molander and Gosta Stevens] is a love triangle involving a famed concert violinist and a young girl pianist, but the romance lacks persuasiveness.

Leslie Howard, who functions as star and associate producer, is eclipsed by Bergman. Latter is beautiful, talented and convincing, providing an arresting performance and a warm personality that introduces a new stellar asset to Hollywood. She has charm, sincerity and an infectious vivaciousness.

Picture unwinds at a leisurely pace, without theatrics of too great intensity in the romantic passages.

1939: NOMINATION: Best Score

•

INTERNAL AFFAIRS

1990, 117 mins, US Ⓥ ⦿ col

Dir Mike Figgis ***Prod*** Frank Mancuso, Jr. ***Scr*** Henry Bean ***Ph*** John A. Alonzo ***Ed*** Robert Estrin ***Mus*** Mike Figgis, Anthony Marinelli, Brian Banks ***Art*** Waldemar Kalinowski

Act Richard Gere, Andy Garcia, Nancy Travis, Laurie Metcalf, William Baldwin, Annabella Sciorra (Paramount)

The title is a clever double entendre, as Andy Garcia plays LAPD internal affairs division investigator Raymond Avila, pulled into a psychological game of chicken with quarry Dennis Peck (Richard Gere), a much-honored street cop who manipulates his position as easily as he does the people around him.

Played by Gere with a constant sense of menace, Peck preys on Raymond's insecurities by insinuating that he's bedded his wife (Nancy Travis)—increasingly neglected, ironically, as Raymond thrusts his all into the case.

While hardly new territory, director Mike Figgis wrings every ounce of tension from tyro writer Henry Bean's screenplay and, most impressively, elicits first-rate performances from top to bottom.

The look, too, immeasurably helps in creating a foreboding atmosphere. Figgis never lets the pace slow long enough to expose the story's thinness despite, in retrospect, a moderate amount of action.

•

INTERNATIONAL VELVET
1978, 125 mins, UK Ⓥ col
Dir Bryan Forbes ***Prod*** Bryan Forbes ***Scr*** Bryan Forbes ***Ph*** Tony Imi ***Ed*** Timothy Gee ***Mus*** Francis Lai ***Art*** Keith Wilson
Act Tatum O'Neal, Christopher Plummer, Anthony Hopkins, Nanette Newman, Peter Barkworth, Dinsdale Landen (M-G-M)

International Velvet is an extremely fine film for (in the best sense) family audiences. Bryan Forbes wrote, produced and directed the sequel to *National Velvet* [1944] in such a way as to provide sentiment, excitement and dual-level drama that should ring true with its target audience. Tatum O'Neal heads a strong cast as an orphaned teenager whose attachment to a horse leads to her own adjustment and maturity.

In the new script, the original Velvet Brown is now nearing middle age as a childless divorcée though happy in a relationship with Christopher Plummer, an author who provides her much emotional support. It's Nanette Newman's good fortune to play the role, and she does so excellently.

All this is to the good while O'Neal evolves from a hostile alien orphan to a high degree of adolescent maturity. Anthony Hopkins is excellent as the equestrian team trainer whose dedication to the sport will give contemporary audiences a graceful exposition of what is going on.

•

INTERNS, THE
1962, 130 mins, US Ⓥ ⦿ b/w
Dir David Swift ***Prod*** Robert Cohn ***Scr*** Walter Newman, David Swift ***Ph*** Russell L. Metty ***Ed*** Al Clark, Jerome Thoms ***Mus*** Leith Stevens ***Art*** Don Ament
Act Michael Callan, Cliff Robertson, James MacArthur, Nick Adams, Suzy Parker, Telly Savalas (Columbia)

In its apparent attempt to dramatize candidly and irreverently the process by which school-finished candidate medics manage to turn into regular doctors, the film somehow succeeds in depicting the average intern as some kind of a Hippocratic oaf. At times it comes perilously close to earning the nickname, *Carry On, Intern*.

The separate stories of five interns, four male and one female, are traced alternately in a sort of razzle-dazzle style by the screenplay from Richard Frede's novel. Three of the stories are predictable from the word go and the other two are thoroughly unbelievable.

As these personal stories unfold, a kind of cross-section of hospital life is transpiring in the background. Chief features are a rather gory childbirth sequence, a mercy killing incident and a wild party passage imitative of the one in *Breakfast at Tiffany's*, but hardly as appropriate or amusing. Support characters run to stereotype, i.e., the ugly, prim nurse who removes her specs, lets her hair down, gets stinko and becomes the hit of the party.

•

INTERSECTION
1994, 98 mins, US Ⓥ ⦿ col
Dir Mark Rydell ***Prod*** Bud Yorkin, Mark Rydell ***Scr*** David Rayfiel, Marshall Brickman ***Ph*** Vilmos Zsigmond ***Ed*** Mark Warner ***Mus*** James Newton Howard ***Art*** Harold Michelson
Act Richard Gere, Sharon Stone, Lolita Davidovich, Martin Landau, David Selby, Jenny Morrison (Paramount)

Intersection represents a misguided attempt to retool a French art film as a Hollywood big-star vehicle. This lushly appointed meller about a wealthy man caught between his wife and new girlfriend will severely let down audiences hoping for steamy encounters between Richard Gere and Sharon Stone.

Claude Sautet's 1970 Michel Piccoli–Romy Schneider starrer *Les choses de la vie* [from Paul Guimard's novel], like many French films, was more concerned with character and life's texture than with plot. This very loose adaptation attempts to goose things up here and there, but original's essentially meditative nature is left quite unfulfilled. Set in the bracing, gray locale of a wintry Vancouver, the script has trendy architect Vincent (Gere) enjoying sack time with groovy journalist Olivia (Lolita Davidovich) while working at the firm he founded with his refined wife, Sally (Stone). Not only do the two women still adore Vincent, but so does his 13-year-old daughter (Jenny Morrison).

Vincent remains on the fence until the end, when he finally decides which woman he really wants. But a car wreck, telegraphed by the opening sequence, puts him on an unanticipated detour, leaving it to the women to sort things out.

Pic reportedly had test-marketing screenings that included two hot sex scenes between Gere and Davidovich, but there is not a trace of them left.

•

INTERVIEW WITH THE VAMPIRE THE VAMPIRE CHRONICLES
1994, 122 mins, US Ⓥ ⦿ col
Dir Neil Jordan ***Prod*** David Geffen, Stephen Woolley ***Scr*** Anne Rice ***Ph*** Philippe Rousselot ***Ed*** Mick Audsley, Joke Van Wijk ***Mus*** Elliot Goldenthal ***Art*** Dante Ferretti
Act Tom Cruise, Brad Pitt, Antonio Banderas, Stephen Rea, Christian Slater, Kirsten Dunst (Geffen/Warner)

Mortals will be lured, but propably not smitten, by the handsome bloodsuckers in *Interview with the Vampire*. Finally onscreen after innumerable failed attempts over nearly two decades, Anne Rice's perennially popular novel has been given an intelligent, darkly voluptuous reading but the film also has its turgid, dialogue-heavy stretches.

Director Neil Jordan and his richly talented team set a wonderfully evocative mood from the outset, as the camera swoops over the Bay Bridge and down into nocturnal San Francisco to light upon the exquisite, immaculate Louis (Brad Pitt), who is ready to tell his life story into a tape recorder for an interviewer (Christian Slater) in an empty room on Market Street.

This sends the story back to 1791 Louisiana, where the 24-year-old widower Louis is singled out by the devilishly handsome, courtly Lestat (Tom Cruise). The tortured Louis burns down his grand plantation house and moves to New Orleans with Lestat, where they continue to operate out of a lavishly appointed apartment. But their debauched bachelor existence suddenly changes with the arrival of Claudia (Kirsten Dunst), who becomes their vampire daughter and partner.

Tale's second half takes Louis and Claudia to Europe, where their search for others like them leads them to the sinister Theatre des Vampires in Paris, 1870, led by the magnetic Armand (Antonio Banderas).

Pitt's Louis is handsome and personable, but there is no depth to his melancholy. Also coming up short of ideal is Cruise's Lestat, stripped of much of his meanness, his sarcastic, bullying manner and threatening force. When Banderas strides upon the stage in the second half, one suddenly witnesses the kind of compelling, charismatic presence a master vampire should have.

1994: NOMINATIONS: Art Direction, Original Score

•

IN THE BLEAK MIDWINTER
(US/AUSTRALIA: A MIDWINTER'S TALE)
1995, 98 mins, UK/US Ⓥ b/w
Dir Kenneth Branagh ***Prod*** David Barron ***Scr*** Kenneth Branagh ***Ph*** Roger Lanser ***Ed*** Neil Farrell ***Mus*** Jimmy Yuill ***Art*** Tim Harvey
Act Michael Maloney, Richard Briers, Mark Hadfield, Nick Farrell, Gerard Horan, John Sessions (Midwinter/Castle Rock)

A "let's put on a show!" approach is brought to a provincial church production of *Hamlet* to deleterious effect in *In the Bleak Midwinter*. This small-scale, putatively comic meditation on the anxieties and joys of the theatrical life says nothing fresh about the artistic process and manages to be coy and grating in doing so.

From the outset, it is apparent that the writer-director has decided to adopt a cutesy, antic attitude toward the obviously personal material.

With no money or support system, out-of-work thespian Joe Harper (Michael Maloney) decides his time has come to play the melancholy Dane. He secures the unlikely encouragement of his high-powered agent (Joan Collins). Casting the entire play with six unusual suspects, Joe leads his ragtag troupe off to his native village of Hope, where, in just three weeks, they will debut their production in an abandoned church.

Kenneth Branagh divides the action into acts with titles like *There's No Business Like Show Business* and feels compelled to end his scenes with punch lines. The characters are none too interesting, and the denouement, with a Hollywood producer (preposterously caricatured by Jennifer Saunders) in attendance, is more convoluted than convincing.

Pic's one becoming aspect is its modesty; lensed quickly in black-and-white on a low budget, it doesn't pretend to be anything more than it is.

•

IN THE COMPANY OF MEN
1997, 95 MINS, US Ⓥ ⦿ col
Dir Neil Labute ***Prod*** Mark Archer, Stephen Pevner ***Scr*** Neil Labute ***Ph*** Tony Hettinger ***Ed*** Joel Plotch ***Mus*** Ken Williams ***Art*** Julia Henkel
Act Aaron Eckhart, Stacy Edwards, Matt Malloy, Mark Rector, Jason Dixie, Emily Cline (Atlantis)

Neil Labute's astonishing feature directorial debut is a dark, probing, truly disturbing exploration of yuppie angst and male anxieties in both the work and personal arenas. Pic is insightful—and often entertaining—even when the technical aspects don't match its fluently absorbing dialogue.

Labute centers on the complex psychologies of—and equally complex relationship between—two thirtysomething white-collar executives: handsome, arrogant Chad (Aaron Eckhart) and Howard (Matt Malloy), his friend from college and now his superior at work. The two men share their frustrations in life—the tough corporate culture and the equally tough mating game, which has left both rejected by women.

Chad proposes a plan to restore their bruised, insecure egos. They should find an appealing woman, one who's susceptible enough to be lured and dated by both of them. The scheme is to dash this woman's hopes to such an extent that she would lose control and "suddenly call up her mom and start wearing makeup again" They'll be able to laugh about their adventure for years to come. Chad soon spots Christine (Stacy Edwards), a beautiful typist who turns out to be hearing-impaired, the "ideal" prey.

Pic's greatest achievement is its sharply poignant dialogue which, despite the horrible consequences of the contest it describes, is also darkly amusing. Labute keeps the cynical, often misogynistic banter coming and the scenes punchy, making for a lively, edgy movie in which speech is action. Visual style of what appears to be an extremely low-budget effort is simple.

In a career-making performance, Eckhart, a cross between William Hurt and Michael York, aptly embodies a 1990's yuppie. He is ably supported by Malloy and Edwards.

•

IN THE COOL OF THE DAY
1963, 91 mins, US ▭ col
Dir Robert Stevens ***Prod*** John Houseman ***Scr*** Meade Roberts ***Ph*** Peter Newbrook ***Ed*** Thomas Stanford ***Mus*** Francis Chagrin
Act Peter Finch, Jane Fonda, Angela Lansbury, Constance Cummings, Arthur Hill, Alexander Knox (M-G-M)

John Houseman production was written for the screen from the novel by Susan Ertz. It concerns the romantic encounter that is briefly consummated during a mutual visit to Greece by an English book publisher (Peter Finch) who is taunted and tormented by a grudging, embittered, anti-social wife (Angela Lansbury), and a fragile American girl (Jane Fonda) who has been sheltered and protected to the point of absurdity by her adoring, but overly-finicky husband (Arthur Hill).

Most of this romantic schmaltz is set against some interesting Greek scenery such as the Parthenon and the Acropolis.

Peter Newbrook photographs ruins well, but is less effective with people. For example, he manages to disregard the dancers' legs in the course of a Grecian folk dance scene.

Lansbury gets off the best acting in the film as Finch's sour, scar-faced wife. She stirs up the only fun in the generally sour proceedings.

Fonda, sporting a Cleopatra haircut, is all passion and intensity. When she loves, boy, she really loves. Finch wears one expression. It appears to be boredom, which is understandable.

•

IN THE FRENCH STYLE
1963, 104 mins, France/US b/w
Dir Robert Parrish ***Prod*** Irwin Shaw, Robert Parrish ***Scr*** Irwin Shaw ***Ph*** Michel Kelber ***Ed*** Renee Lichtig ***Mus*** Joseph Kosma ***Art*** Rino Mondellini
Act Jean Seberg, Stanley Baker, Addison Powell, James Leo Herlihy, Philippe Forquet, Jack Hedley (Casanna/Orsay/Columbia)

Irwin Shaw and Robert Parrish have fashioned a sophisticated love story of Paris, of an American girl in love with the life not quite for her, in their indie based upon two of Shaw's stories, *In the French Style* and *A Year to Learn the Language*.

Jean Seberg stars as the 19-year-old Chicago girl, a would-be painter who dreams of conquering the capital of art, naive, ambitious, impressionable, who has her father's financial backing for one year to prove herself. She meets early romantic disillusionment, when she becomes involved with a young French engineering student whom she believes older than she.

Seberg brings life and brilliance to her portrayal, registering strongly both in the more dramatic and lighter moments. In Stanley Baker, the correspondent with whom she has a lingering affair, she has a first-rate costar who makes a good impression. Philippe Forquet, the youth, is brash and talented.

•

IN THE HEAT OF THE NIGHT
1967, 109 mins, US Ⓥ ⊙ col
Dir Norman Jewison ***Prod*** Walter Mirisch ***Scr*** Stirling Silliphant ***Ph*** Haskell Wexler ***Ed*** Hal Ashby ***Mus*** Quincy Jones ***Art*** Paul Groesse
Act Sidney Poitier, Rod Steiger, Warren Oates, Lee Grant, Scott Wilson, Larry Gates (Mirisch/United Artists)

An excellent Sidney Poitier performance, and an outstanding one by Rod Steiger, overcome some noteworthy flaws to make *In the Heat of the Night*, an absorbing contemporary murder drama, set in the deep, red-necked South. Norman Jewison directs, sometimes in pretentious fashion, an uneven script.

Stirling Silliphant's script, adapted from John Ball's novel *Heat*, is erratic, indulging in heavy-handed, sometimes needless plot diversion, uncertain character development, and a rapid-fire denouement.

Intriguing plot basis has Poitier as the detective, accidentally on a visit to his Mississippi hometown where a prominent industrialist is found murdered. Arrested initially on the assumption that a Negro, out late at night, must have done the deed, Poitier later is thrust, by his boss in Philadelphia, his own conscience, and a temporary anti-white emotional outburst, into uneasy collaboration with local sheriff Steiger.

Steiger's transformation from a diehard Dixie bigot to a man who learns to respect Poitier stands out in smooth comparison to the wandering solution of the murder.

1967: Best Picture, Actor (Rod Steiger), Adapted Screenplay, Sound, Editing

NOMINATIONS: Best Director, Sound Effects

•

IN THE LINE OF FIRE
1993, 128 mins, US Ⓥ ⊙ ▭ col
Dir Wolfgang Petersen ***Prod*** Jeff Apple ***Scr*** Jeff Maguire ***Ph*** John Bailey ***Ed*** Anne V. Coates ***Mus*** Ennio Morricone ***Art*** Lilly Kilvert
Act Clint Eastwood, John Malkovich, Rene Russo, Dylan McDermott, Gary Cole, Fred Dalton Thompson (Columbia/Castle Rock)

In the Line of Fire is a proficiently made thriller pitting Clint Eastwood's vet Secret Service agent against John Malkovich's insidious would-be presidential assassin.

Frank Horrigan (Eastwood) has been haunted since Nov. 22, 1963, by the possibility that he could have saved John F. Kennedy's life. As JFK's favorite Secret Service agent, Horrigan was with the president in Dallas, and was closest to him when the shot rang out.

It's this weakness that is manipulated by Mitch Leary (Malkovich), a professional assassin who makes no secret of his intention to kill the current president sometime before the election.

Horrigan wins an assignment to cover the chief of state while he tries to nail Leary, who calls every so often to taunt him, and at the same time must endure the gibes of his colleagues, who consider him a "borderline burnout with questionable social skills" and a "dinosaur." What neophyte scripter Jeff Maguire's plot comes down to is the cat-and-mouse game between Horrigan and Leary, and the craftiness and strategies involved on both sides, while not exactly ingenious, are tantalizing enough to compel interest.

Director Wolfgang Petersen sends the story efficiently down its straight and narrow track, deftly engineering the battle of wills between two desperately committed men.

Eastwood splendidly gives Horrigan humor, grit and imagination. Malkovich provides a delicious villain, a true psychopath so sure of himself that he's willing to give his pursuer half a chance of catching him.

1993: NOMINATIONS: Best Supp. Actor (John Malcovich), Original Screenplay, Film Editing

•

IN THE MOOD FOR LOVE
2000, 97 mins, Hong Kong Ⓥ ⊙ col
Dir Wong Kar-wai ***Prod*** Wong Kar-wai ***Scr*** Wong Kar-wai ***Ph*** Christopher Doyle, Mark Li Ping-bing ***Ed*** William Chang Sukping ***Mus*** Michael Galasso, Umebayashi Shigeru ***Art*** William Chang Sukping
Act Tony Leung Chiu-wai, Maggie Cheung Man-yuk, Lai Chin, Rebecca Pan, Siu Ping-lam (Jet Tone/Block 2)

An exquisitely fashioned melodrama about love and regret, this is a seductive mood piece with more style than substance. Set in the Shanghai community of Hong Kong in 1962, the drama unfolds mainly in the tight corridors and confined spaces of a building in which two young couples rent rooms and become neighbors.

Leggy beauty Li-zhen (Maggie Cheung Man-yuk) is a secretary whose husband's job often keeps him away on business. Across the hall, Chow (Tony Leung Chiu-wai) is a newspaper editor married to a woman who is also frequently out of town. Spending a good deal of time alone, Li-zhen and Chow strike up a timid but cordial friendship. Their respective spouses are never shown in full, either glimpsed from behind or partially obscured by obstacles.

Chow is the first to suspect that his wife's absences may not be entirely legitimate. Chow inquires about a handbag of Li-zhen's, identical to his wife's. Informing him that it was a gift from her husband, Li-zhen then reveals that Chow's tie is the same as one her husband often wears. Neither one has to be a genius to deduce that their partners are an item.

Drawn closer together by their sense of humiliation and abandonment, Li-zhen and Chow say nothing to their spouses. They begin a chaste courtship, trying to imagine the nature of their errant partners' first encounters while determining to behave more decorously. But despite their reserve, feelings of love creep up on both of them.

Wong Kar-wai establishes a dreamy mood and rhythm through fluidly edited scenes showing the unrequited lovers at work or stopping to chat in the corridors at home, and hypnotic sequences trailing Li-zhen as she slinks out to the noodle bar for her solitary supper. Repetitive use of slow motion and of Michael Galasso's lovely string compositions and a Spanish-language Nat "King" Cole vocal give a richly sensual feel to the film, but it fails to conjure the depth or heartbreaking emotional charge of the classic melodramas to which it aspires. Those aspirations are evident in the gorgeous look of the production, which echoes the work of Douglas Sirk.

•

IN THE MOUTH OF MADNESS
1995, 94 mins, US Ⓥ ⊙ ▭ col
Dir John Carpenter ***Prod*** Sandy King ***Scr*** Michael De Luca ***Ph*** Gary B. Kibbe ***Ed*** Edward Warschilka ***Mus*** John Carpenter, Jim Lang ***Art*** Jeff Steven Ginn
Act Sam Neill, Julie Carmen, Jurgen Prochnow, Charlton Heston, David Warner, John Glover (New Line)

The "what if" of *In the Mouth of Madness* posits that a famous spinner of horror novels can incite the populace to strange and hideous acts through his prose. It's a nifty idea, and director John Carpenter keeps the story moving a step ahead of the preposterous, almost to the bitter end.

Crack insurance investigator John Trent (Sam Neill) has lapsed into dementia as the curtain rises. He relates the wild tale that brought him to the padded cell.

Trent's seemingly insane explanation is that the work of bestselling author Sutter Cane (Jurgen Prochnow) is the key to the bloody phenomenon. He stumbled onto the truth when the author's publisher (Charlton Heston) hired him to locate his missing meal ticket. Enlisting the help of editor Linda Styles (Julie Carmen), Trent goes in search of Hobb's End, the fictional setting of the errant scribe's tales of the macabre. When they stumble onto the tiny New England hamlet, they know the terror that lies ahead because it's been foretold between the covers of popular past works.

Script is both homage to and parody of the Stephen King oeuvre. While the pic doesn't really have meaty characters, the presence of Neill, Carmen, Heston and Prochnow lends an air of credibility that heightens the proceedings. The film is also blessed with an arsenal of special effects that work with tinker-toy precision.

•

IN THE NAME OF THE FATHER
1993, 132 mins, Ireland/UK/US Ⓥ ⊙ col
Dir Jim Sheridan ***Prod*** Jim Sheridan ***Scr*** Terry George, Jim Sheridan ***Ph*** Peter Biziou ***Ed*** Gerry Hambling ***Mus*** Trevor Jones ***Art*** Caroline Amies
Act Daniel Day-Lewis, Pete Postlethwaite, Emma Thompson, John Lynch, Corin Redgrave, Beatie Edney (Hell's Kitchen/Universal)

The award-winning *My Left Foot* duo of writer/director Jim Sheridan and star Daniel Day-Lewis have reteamed to tell the real-life story of Gerry Conlon, an Irishman who spent 15 years in a British prison before his wrongful sentence was overturned. It's highly political, inflammatory, partisan, and far from comforting.

Gerry Conlon was arrested for the 1974 IRA bombing of a bar in Guildford that killed five people. On the basis of coerced confessions, Conlon, his friend Paul Hill and two others who came to be known as the Guildford Four were convicted and sentenced to long terms, as were other completely innocent bystanders, including Conlon's own father and aunt, who were charged with conspiracy. It wasn't until 1989 that the convictions were overturned, forced by the revelation that crucial evidence that would have exonerated the defendants had been deliberately withheld by the Crown.

The filmmakers have invigorated and enriched the story [based on Conlon's book *Proved Innocent*] through the use of a thousand details, a strong sense of time and place, outstanding characterizations and a display of energy and cinematic flair that marks an advance on *My Left Foot*.

Pic reaches its actorly heights in the intense, intimate scenes between Day Lewis and Pete Postlethwaite, as the former conveys Gerry's growth in the face of deep despair and frustration while the latter reveals innate qualities previously unsuspected in the father. Both thesps are utterly first-rate.

In a decidedly secondary role, Emma Thompson is the picture of a single-minded crusader, and Corin Redgrave scores as the hissable British heavy who railroads the Irish suspects.

1993: NOMINATIONS: Best Picture, Director, Actor (Daniel Day-Lewis), Supp. Actor (Pete Postlethwaite), Supp. Actress (Emma Thompson), Adapted Screenplay, Editing

•

IN THE NAVY
1941, 85 mins, US Ⓥ ⊙ b/w
Dir Arthur Lubin ***Prod*** Alex Gottlieb (assoc.) ***Scr*** Arthur T. Horman, John Grant ***Ph*** Joseph Valentine ***Ed*** Philip Cahn ***Mus*** Charles Previn (dir.) ***Art*** Jack Otterson, Harold H. MacArthur
Act Bud Abbott, Lou Costello, Dick Powell, Claire Dodd, Andrews Sisters, Dick Foran (Universal)

Abbott and Costello continue their zany and familiar antics in nautical garb ashore and aboard a battlewagon [in a story by Arthur T. Horman].

Dick Powell is a radio crooner fed up by continual pestering of fans. He disappears to join the navy in San Diego, where Abbott and Costello are gobs ashore. Claire Dodd discovers identity of Powell in her ambitions to get a newspaper job, and continually attempts to candid camera Powell for a sensational expose. She even gets aboard the battleship, which suddenly pulls out for Hawaii.

Costello is center of a dream sequence in which he becomes established in the captain's cabin, and gives orders to the bridge, that send the battleship in a wild ride through the harbor and other boats in the fleet.

Induction of Powell in this instance allows for broader use of songs than in *Buck Privates*. Powell delivers two tunes in effective style. Andrews Sisters handle three numbers in their usually capable, rhythmic fashion, all delivered with production backgrounds [musical numbers staged by Nick Castle].

•

IN THE REALM OF THE SENSES
SEE: L'EMPIRE DES SENS

•

IN THE SPIRIT
1990, 93 mins, US Ⓥ col
Dir Sandra Seacat ***Prod*** Julian Schlossberg ***Scr*** Jeannie Berlin, Laurie Jones ***Ph*** Dick Quinlan ***Ed*** Brad Fuller ***Mus*** Patrick Williams ***Art*** Michael C. Smith
Act Elaine May, Marlo Thomas, Jeannie Berlin, Peter Falk, Melanie Griffith, Olympia Dukakis (Running River/Castle Hill)

Elaine May and Marlo Thomas make a memorable screen odd couple in *In the Spirit*. Kooky black comedy is an unusual case of big-name talent gathering with friends to make a low-budget pic freed of mainstream good taste and gloss.

Like Jules Feiffer's *Little Murders* (1971) New York is a nightmare, with May moving back to Gotham from Beverley Hills with her just-fired hubby Peter Falk. She's thrown together with ditzy mystic Thomas after hiring her to redecorate an apartment.

Almost as goofy as Thomas is Jeannie Berlin, a prostie neighbor (and real life daughter of May). Coscripter Berlin writes herself out of the picture after the second reel and *Spirit* spins off in a different direction. Thomas and May flee the city to hole up at Michael Emil's new age retreat in upstate NY, pursued by a murderer.

First-time director Sandra Seacat emphasizes slapstick but also female bonding as the gals on the lam reach beyond their wacky survivalist tactics to address feminist issues.

May is very funny, giving a lesson in rat-a-tat-tat delivery. Thomas proves a perfect foil.

•

IN THIS OUR LIFE
1942, 95 mins, US Ⓥ b/w
Dir John Huston ***Prod*** Hal B. Wallis (exec.) ***Scr*** Howard Koch ***Ph*** Ernest Haller ***Ed*** William Holmes ***Mus*** Max Steiner ***Art*** Robert Haas

Act Bette Davis, Olivia de Havilland, George Brent, Dennis Morgan, Charles Coburn, Hattie McDaniel (Warner)

Story, adapted from the novel by Ellen Glasgow, displays the ruthless and selfish personality of Bette Davis and its impress on other members of her family. She lies, cheats and steals to gain her ends; and, when cornered, schemes her way out. As the yarn opens she woos and steals her sister's husband, eloping with him to Baltimore.

John Huston, in his second directorial assignment, provides deft delineations in the varied characters in the script. Davis is dramatically impressive in the lead but gets major assistance from Olivia de Havilland, George Brent, Dennis Morgan, Billie Burke and Hattie McDaniel.

Script succeeds in presenting the inner thoughts of the scheming girl, and carries along with slick dialog and situations. Strength is added in several dramatic spots by Huston's direction.

•

INTIMATE WITH A STRANGER
1995, 93 mins, UK Ⓥ col
Dir Mel Woods ***Prod*** Roderick Mangin-Turner ***Scr*** Mel Woods, Roderick Mangin-Turner ***Ph*** Nicholas Tebbet ***Ed*** Brian Smedley-Aston ***Mus*** Ledsam & Pugh ***Art*** Graeme Story
Act Roderick Mangin-Turner, Daphne Nayar, Janis Lee, Amy Tolsky, Lorelei King, Ellenor Wilkinson (Independent)

American Gigolo bumps up against *sex, lies, and videotape* in *Intimate with a Stranger*, a generally compelling relationships movie by first-time Brit helmer Mel Woods about a burned-out Santa Monica gigolo and his clients.

Main character is Jack (producer/co-scripter Roderick Mangin-Turner), who looks like a beefy, long-haired biker but is actually a dropped-out college prof who's built a lucrative sack business servicing uptight femmes. In private, however, he's living life out of the bottom of a bottle, still scorched by former g.f. Michelle (Daphne Nayar).

Though Jack is technically the central character, the movie is a showcase for a string of terrific female thumbnails, ranging from a tough career type (Ellenor Wilkinson) who starts by giving Jack a hard time, through a teen virgin (Janis Lee) who wants to kick off her sex life in style, to a Jewish wife (Amy Tolsky) whose marriage is low on mattress activity.

Performances by the women are strong down the line, headed by a wonderfully sad-comic and sexy perf by Tolsky as the bruised wife. Lee is also excellent in the tricky part of the California teen, and Wilkinson aces as the hardened career woman. Nayar brings a quiet sophistication to the part of Michelle. Interiors were all shot at the U.K.'s Shepperton Studios.

•

INTOLERANCE
1916, 209 mins, US Ⓥ ⊙ ⊗ b/w
Dir D. W. Griffith ***Prod*** D. W. Griffith ***Scr*** D. W. Griffith ***Ph*** Billy Bitzer, Karl Brown ***Ed*** James E. Smith, Rose Smith ***Mus*** Joseph Carl Breil
Act Lillian Gish, Mae Marsh, Robert Harron, Miriam Cooper, Walter Long, Tully Marshall (Wark)

Intolerance reflects much credit to the wizard director, for it required no small amount of genuine art to consistently blend actors, horses, monkeys, geese, doves, acrobats and ballets into a composite presentation of a film classic.

It attempts to tell four distinct stories at the same time—more or less successfully accomplished by the aid of flashbacks, fade-outs and fade-ins. The four tales are designed to show that intolerance in various forms existed in all ages.

Three of the exemplifications are based upon historical fact, the fourth visualized by a modern melodrama that hits a powerful blow at the hypocrisy of certain forms of up-to-date philanthropy. The ancient periods depict mediaeval France in the reign of Charles IX, with the horrors of massacre perpetrated by Catherine de Medici; Jersualem at the birth of the Christian era, with one or two historical episodes in the life of Christ, and a shadow suggestion of the Crucifixion.

The martial visualizations confined principally to the Babylonian period (about 500 B.C.), when Belshazzar's army was defeated by the Persians under the military direction of Cyrus. Words cannot do justice to the stupendousness of these battle scenes or feasts.

•

INTO THE NIGHT
1985, 115 mins, US Ⓥ ⊙ col
Dir John Landis ***Prod*** George Folsey, Jr., Ron Koslow ***Scr*** Ron Koslow ***Ph*** Robert Paynter ***Ed*** Malcolm Campbell ***Mus*** Ira Newborn ***Art*** John Lloyd
Act Jeff Goldblum, Michelle Pfeiffer, Richard Farnsworth, Irene Papas, Kathryn Harrold, Paul Mazursky (Universal)

Over in the suburbs dwells quiet aerospace engineer Jeff Goldblum whose job is going nowhere while his wife goes too far with another man. Mulling all this over in the middle of the night, Goldblum ambles aimlessly out to the airport where Michelle Pfeiffer has just arrived with six smuggled emeralds.

Apparently, Pfeiffer has performed this chore for one or more boyfriends and the promise of some cash, but she is hardly prepared for the four killers awaiting her arrival. Fleeing them, she leaps into Goldblum's car and from then on, it's just one misadventure and murder after another.

In pursuit of the jewels are a series of cameo-plus parts handled by Irene Papas, Roger Vadim, David Bowie and a band of Iranian zanies that includes director John Landis himself.

The film itself tries sometimes too hard for laughs and at other times strains for shock. Goldblum is nonetheless enjoyable as he constantly tries to figure out just what he's doing in all of this.

•

INTO THE SUN
1992, 100 mins, US Ⓥ ⊙ col
Dir Fritz Kiersch ***Prod*** Kevin M. Kallberg, Oliver G. Hess ***Scr*** John Brancato, Michael Ferris ***Ph*** Steve Grass ***Ed*** Barry Zetlin ***Mus*** Randy Miller ***Art*** Gary T. New
Act Anthony Michael Hall, Michael Pare, Deborah Maria Moore, Terry Kiser, Brian Haley, Michael St Gerard (Trimark)

Top Gun meets *The Hard Way* in the oddball comedy-adventure *Into the Sun*. This time U.S. pilot Michael Pare is assigned to show an action movie star (Anthony Michael Hall) how to portray the real thing. Pare is solid as the real McCoy and even gets to laugh and unbend a bit, compared to his usually stiff roles, as the twosome become friends.

Pic goes over the top when real-life skirmishes with unspecified Arab enemies in the Middle East break out, and Pare disobeys orders in taking the civilian into combat. Their derring-do, with Hall rising to the occasion, is fun if ridiculous. Pic is an important transition effort for Hall, whose comic timing is excellent.

Roger Moore's daughter Deborah (previously billed in *Bullseye!* as Deborah Barrymore) is pert and attractive but overly reserved as the romantic interest of both heroes. Reliable comedian Terry Kiser earns some big laughs as a fast-talking agent.

•

INTO THE WEST
1992, 102 mins, UK/US Ⓥ ⊙ col
Dir Mike Newell ***Prod*** Jonathan Cavendish, Tim Palmer ***Scr*** Jim Sheridan, David Keating ***Ph*** Tom Sigel ***Ed*** Peter Boyle ***Mus*** Patrick Doyle ***Art*** Jamie Leonard
Act Gabriel Byrne, Ellen Barkin, Ciaran Fitzgerald, Ruaidhri Conroy, David Kelly (Majestic/FFI/Miramax/Newcom/Little Bird

Into the West is a likable but modest pic about two Dublin moppets who take to the hills on a beautiful white stallion. Scripter Jim Sheridan, whose *My Left Foot* and *The Field* showed outsiders coping inspiringly with the real world, works with thinner material [a story by Michael Pearce] this time round.

Gabriel Byrne is Papa Reilly, a modern-day gypsy "traveller" (hobo) who's finally settled in a grim, high-rise nabe of Dublin with his two kids, Tito (Ruaidhri Conroy) and Ossie (Ciaran Fitzgerald). His fanciful old father-in-law (David Kelly) captures the brats' imagination with elaborate fairy tales woven around a white horse he's brought back. When the kids move the equine into their ramshackle apartment, the law moves in and sells it to a rich farmer. The kids promptly steal it back and set out for the "wild" west of Ireland, fired by grandpa's stories and cowboy movies. Byrne, joined by fellow "traveller" Kathleen (Ellen Barkin), sets out in hot pursuit, closely followed by the authorities. A major asset throughout is Patrick Doyle's rich, Gaelic-flavoured scoring that carries the movie's emotional line and fairy tale atmosphere.

Byrne gives a credible, if low-key, rendering of the weak, illiterate father. Barkin downplays her looks and carries off an Irish accent with aplomb. The real stars are the two kids, notably Fitzgerald as the younger bro.

•

INTRUDER, THE
1953, 84 mins, UK b/w
Dir Guy Hamilton ***Prod*** Ivan Foxwell ***Scr*** Robin Maugham, John Hunter, Anthony Squire ***Ph*** Ted Scaife ***Ed*** Alan Osbiston ***Mus*** Francis Chagrin ***Art*** Joseph Bato
Act Jack Hawkins, Hugh Williams, Michael Medwin, George Cole, Dennis Price, Arthur Howard (British Lion)

The film [based on Robin Maugham's novel *Line on Ginger*] attempts to answer the question: what turns a wartime hero into a postwar thief? As the yarn opens, Jack Hawkins, a former colonel of the Tank regiment, returns to his home to find that a burglar has broken in. The intruder (Michael Medwin) turns out to be a former member of his regiment.

Through a misunderstanding, the thief believes that Hawkins has telephoned for the police and makes a dash for it over the garden wall. From there on, Hawkins is involved in a countrywide search, containing other members of the old regiment in the hopes of their leading him on the right track

As each former soldier is contacted, the film switches into a nostalgic flashback. There is the rich comedy scene of George Cole's first night in the officers' mess, with Nicholas Phipps doing some magnificent scene-stealing; there is a reminder, too, of Medwin's own heroism in saving the unit while under heavy fire, and that the suave Dennis Price, for all his peace-time arrogance, was a cowardly captain in action; and finally a highly diverting incident when Arthur Howard, a peace-time schoolmaster, is caught by the general while showing Dora Bryan the inside of a tank.

•

INTRUDER, THE
1962, 84 mins, US Ⓥ b/w
Dir Roger Corman ***Prod*** Roger Corman ***Scr*** Charles Beaumont ***Ph*** Taylor Byars ***Ed*** Ronald Sinclair ***Mus*** Herman Stein
Act William Shatner, Frank Maxwell, Beverley Lunsford, Robert Emhardt, Jeanne Cooper, Leo Gordon (Pathe America/Filmgroup)

Roger and Gene Corman's *The Intruder* comes to grips with a controversial issue—integration, and those who would defy the law of the land—in an adult, intelligent and arresting manner.

Charles Beaumont's screenplay, from his novel, dramatizes the campaign instigated in a Southern U.S. town by a slick, cocky, vain, unstable merchant of hate (from the so-called Patrick Henry Society in Washington) to urge the white residents to strike back against the law of integration. The man's primary incentive is actually personal ambition, but the mobs that at first rally round turn away in disgust when the true motives surface after a series of terrifying, reprehensible incidents.

William Shatner masterfully plays the bigot. Especially sharp, noteworthy support is contributed by Jeanne Cooper and Leo Gordon.

•

INTRUDER IN THE DUST
1949, 87 mins, US Ⓥ b/w
Dir Clarence Brown ***Prod*** Clarence Brown ***Scr*** Ben Maddow ***Ph*** Robert Surtees ***Ed*** Robert J. Kern ***Mus*** Adolph Deutsch ***Art*** Cedric Gibbons, Randall Duell
Act David Brian, Claude Jarman, Jr., Juano Hernandez, Charles Kemper, Will Geer, Porter Hall (M-G-M)

Intruder in the Dust, essentially a murder-mystery melodrama, is threaded with the racial and lynch problems of the south but touches the pros and cons of the subject only lightly.

Producer-director Clarence Brown took his troupe to Oxford, Mississippi, to film the William Faulkner novel. Deep South locale lessens impact of the social issues, but strengthens the storytelling.

Hanging over the story is the threat of mob violence as an old Negro, charged with murdering a white man, awaits his fate in a miserable southern jail. He refuses to speak out in his own defense to the white lawyer who believes it to be a hopeless case.

David Brian tries no southern accent to put over his role of the lawyer. There is a standout job of a proud Negro, just as bigoted in his way as the white folks, by Juano Hernandez.

•

INVADERS, THE
SEE: 49TH PARALLEL

•

INVADERS FROM MARS
1953, 78 mins, US Ⓥ ⊙ col
Dir William Cameron Menzies ***Prod*** Edward L. Alperson, Jr. (assoc.) ***Scr*** Richard Blake ***Ph*** John Seitz ***Ed*** Arthur Roberts ***Mus*** Raoul Kraushaar ***Art*** William Cameron Menzies
Act Helena Carter, Arthur Franz, Jimmy Hunt, Leif Erickson, Hillary Brooke, Morris Ankrum (20th Century-Fox)

Screenplay is pegged around a typical American family that resides in a small California town. Their existence is tranquil until the 12-year-old son (Jimmy Hunt) awakens in a thunderstorm to observe a Martian spaceship land on a nearby sandpit. His scientist-father (Leif Erickson) and mother (Hillary Brooke) investigate the scene, but return with a sinister demeanor that's in abrupt contrast to their usual cheerful attitudes. A city physician (Helena Carter) and astronomer (Arthur Franz) are convinced that an invader has landed and the country is in vital danger.

Imaginative yarn makes full use of astronomical and lab equipment as well as government atomic research installations as backgrounds to heighten the realism.

The cast turns in creditable portrayals under William Cameron Menzies's fine direction. Carter is coolly efficient as the femme doctor; Franz likewise is mentally adroit as the astronomer who alerts the army, while young Hunt impresses as the frightened lad.

•

INVADERS FROM MARS
1986, 100 mins, US Ⓥ ⦿ ▭ col
Dir Tobe Hooper ***Prod*** Menahem Golan, Yoram Globus ***Scr*** Dan O'Bannon, Don Jakoby ***Ph*** Daniel Pearl ***Ed*** Alain Jakubowicz ***Mus*** Christopher Young ***Art*** Leslie Dilley
Act Karen Black, Hunter Carson, Timothy Bottoms, Laraine Newman, James Karen, Louise Fletcher (Cannon)

Tobe Hooper's remake of *Invaders from Mars* is an embarrassing combination of kitsch and boredom. Inferior screenplay [based on the 1953 original] fails to bring in new ideas or provide interesting dialog.

First 45 minutes are interminably dull. Little David Gardner (Hunter Carson) sees a spaceship land one night and soon after his father George (Timothy Bottoms), biology teacher Mrs. McKeltch (Louise Fletcher) and even the police chief who investigates (Jimmy Hunt, who as a child played the lead role in the 1953 original) begin behaving out of normal character. Next day mom (Laraine Newman) is scarred and zombie-like as well.

David finally gets his school nurse Linda (Karen Black) to believe his tall tale and they whip into action to stop the invasion and spread of controlled people. Film finally comes alive when David wanders into Martian subterranean tunnels. [Special visual effects by John Dykstra, invader creatures by Stan Winston.]

Not helping is some subpar acting. Trick casting of Black, who's Carson's real-life mother, not as his fictional mom but rather his only friend, doesn't pay off. Best acting is by James Karen as a stereotyped gung-ho marine.

•

INVASION OF PRIVACY
1996, 94 mins, US Ⓥ col
Dir Anthony Hickox ***Prod*** Hanno Huth, Carsten Lorenz ***Scr*** Larry Cohen ***Ph*** Peter Wunstorff ***Ed*** Dana Congdon ***Mus*** Angelo Badalamenti ***Art*** Jane Anne Stewart
Act Mili Avital, Jonathan Schaech, Naomi Campbell, David Keith, Charlotte Rampling, Tom Wright (Senator)

Invasion of Privacy is a stylishly directed thriller from horror helmer Anthony Hickox that centers on the issues of paternal rights and abortion.

Basically three thrillers in one, the story starts with a whirlwind romance between young florist Theresa (Mili Avital), and Josh (Jonathan Schaech). Theresa discovers she is pregnant, and quickly also learns that Josh is violently unbalanced.

The action then switches to courtroom mode. Josh is aided by a steely lawyer (Charlotte Rampling) who beds her client and shrewdly works all the moral angles in his favor. Soon Josh becomes a national cause célèbre, embraced by antiabortion crusaders, while Theresa emerges as a heartless would-be baby-killer.

The final stretch begins after the birth, as Josh insinuates himself into the picture via the child's nanny, and a cop (David Keith) continues his efforts to prove Josh was responsible for two homicides. Hickox keeps things cooking with lots of horror devices, sudden shocks and first-rate technical backup. Canadian cinematographer Peter Wunstorff's work is handsomely lit and razor-sharp.

•

INVASION OF THE BODY SNATCHERS
1956, 80 mins, US Ⓥ ⦿ ▭ b/w
Dir Don Siegel ***Prod*** Walter Wanger ***Scr*** Daniel Mainwaring ***Ph*** Ellsworth Fredricks ***Ed*** Robert S. Eisen ***Mus*** Carmen Dragon ***Art*** Ted Haworth
Act Kevin McCarthy, Dana Wynter, Larry Gates, King Donovan, Carolyn Jones, Whit Bissell (Allied Artists)

This tense, offbeat piece of science-fiction is occasionally difficult to follow, due to the strangeness of its scientific premise. Action nevertheless is increasingly exciting.

Plotwise, narrative opens on a strange hysteria that is spreading among the populace of a small California town. Townspeople appear as strangers to their relatives and friends, while retaining their outward appearances. Kevin McCarthy, a doctor, is confronted with solving these mysterious happenings, and helping him is Dana Wynter, with whom he's in love.

A weird form of plant life has descended upon the town from the skies. Tiny, this ripens into great pods and opens, from each of which emerges a "blank," the form of each man, woman and child in the town. During their sleep, the blank drains them of all but their impulse to survive.

Adapted from Jack Finney's *Collier's* serial, characterizations and situations are sharp. Don Siegel's taut direction is fast-paced generally, although in his efforts to spark the climax he permits McCarthy to overact in several sequences.

•

INVASION OF THE BODY SNATCHERS
1978, 115 mins, US Ⓥ ⦿ col
Dir Philip Kaufman ***Prod*** Robert H. Solo ***Scr*** W. D. Richter ***Ph*** Michael Chapman ***Ed*** Douglas Stewart ***Mus*** Denny Zeitlin ***Art*** Charles Rosen
Act Donald Sutherland, Brooke Adams, Leonard Nimoy, Veronica Cartwright, Jeff Goldblum, Art Hindle (Solofilm/United Artists)

Invasion of the Body Snatchers validates the entire concept of remakes. This new version of Don Siegel's 1956 cult classic not only matches the original in horrific tone and effect, but exceeds it in both conception and execution.

W. D. Richter has updated and changed the locale of Jack Finney's serial story to contemporary San Francisco, where Donald Sutherland is a public health inspector, assisted by Brooke Adams. Following the blanketing of the city by spidery webs, Adams notices unusual and sudden changes in b.f. Art Hindle, who becomes emotionless and distant.

Similar transformations are happening all over the city, and while at first Sutherland doubts Adams's sanity, he is soon won over to her paranoia. He invokes the help of an est-type of psychiatrist played with wonderful shading by Leonard Nimoy.

Jeff Goldblum and Veronica Cartwright portray a couple who stumble on one of the blank pod bodies before Goldblum succumbs. As the legions of zombies grows, these four remain about the only humans left, and the latter part of *Body Snatchers* details, with methodical ominousness, their pursuit.

Sutherland has his best role since *Klute*. He gets excellent support from Adams, who projects a touching vulnerability.

Film buffs will have a delight in spotting Kevin McCarthy, who starred in the original version, picking up exactly where he left off at the first pic's finale.

•

INVASION U.S.A.
1952, 73 mins, US b/w
Dir Alfred E. Green ***Prod*** Albert Zugsmith, Robert Smith ***Scr*** Robert Smith ***Ph*** John L. Russell ***Ed*** W. Donn Hayes ***Mus*** Albert Glasser
Act Gerald Mohr, Peggie Castle, Dan O'Herlihy, Robert Bice, Tom Kennedy, Wade Crosby (Columbia)

This production imaginatively poses the situation of a foreign power invading the U.S. with atom bombs.

Plot, starting out in a Gotham bar, is picked up when voice of a TV broadcaster reports that Alaska has been invaded and taken over by a huge enemy air task force. Almost in minutes, further forces capture the state of Washington through use of atom bombs. Action then has the enemy blasting eastward, to destroy N.Y. and invade Washington, D.C., where a futile defense is being formulated in the Pentagon.

Human story is worked into this background through Gerald Mohr, a TV reporter, and others who are introduced in the bar. Peggie Castle is a debutante; Robert Bice a Frisco manufacturer whose return to his factory is marked by his murder by the enemy and Erik Blythe, an Arizona rancher.

Startling aspects of the screenplay [from a story by Robert Smith and Franz Spencer] are further parlayed through effective use of war footage secured from the various armed services and the Atomic Energy Commission.

•

INVASION U.S.A.
1985, 107 mins, US Ⓥ ⦿ col
Dir Joseph Zito ***Prod*** Menahem Golan, Yoram Globus ***Scr*** James Bruner, Chuck Norris ***Ph*** Joao Fernandes ***Ed*** Daniel Loewenthal, Scott Vickrey ***Mus*** Jay Chattaway ***Art*** Ladislav Wilheim
Act Chuck Norris, Richard Lynch, Melissa Prophet, Alexander Zale, Dehl Berti, Shane McCamey (Cannon)

A brainless plot would be almost forgiveable were it not for the perverse depiction of innocents butchered in *Invasion U.S.A.* Star Chuck Norris hits his nadir with this vicious-minded commodity [from a screen story by Aaron Norris and James Bruner].

An international hoard of ruthless mercenaries, led by foreign agents with Russian-sounding names like Rostov (Richard Lynch) and Nikko (Alexander Zale), invade the southeast U.S., turn neighbor against neighbor in selective slaughters, and are ultimately throttled by Norris's loner of a hero.

A picture like this needs a terrific crazie and Lynch, with solid classical training, is the only excuse to see the film. Melissa Prophet (associate producer on *The Cotton Club*) plays a callow, strident photojournalist in the year's least credible supporting performance in an exploitation film.

•

INVESTIGATION OF A CITIZEN ABOVE SUSPICION
SEE: INDAGINE SU UN CITTADINO AL DI SOPRA DI OGNI SOSPETTO

•

INVISIBLE MAN, THE
1933, 70 mins, US Ⓥ ⦿ b/w
Dir James Whale ***Prod*** Carl Laemmle, Jr. ***Scr*** R. C. Sherriff ***Ph*** Arthur Edeson ***Ed*** Ted Kent ***Mus*** [uncredited] ***Art*** Charles D. Hall
Act Claude Rains, Gloria Stuart, Henry Travers, William Harrigan, Una O'Connor, Holmes Herbert (Universal)

The strangest character yet created by the screen [from the novel by H. G. Wells] roams through *The Invisible Man*. Sometimes he is seen, dressed and bandaged up into a fantastic, eerie-looking figure, at other times he is moving through the action unseen.

As the invisible madman (Claude Rains) is moving around, the negative reflects the things he does, such as rocking in a chair, smoking a cigarette, carrying something, opening doors, or socking someone in the jaw with the impact felt rather than seen.

First reel evokes considerable comedy in sequences at a small country inn where the invisible one secures lodging and indulges in his first murder. The innkeeper and his wife (Forrester Harvey and Una O'Connor, respectively) are swell comedy types and make the most of the opportunity. O'Connor relies a lot on a very shrill scream.

At the outset it is learned that a young chemist has discovered a terrible formula, including a very dangerous drug, that makes human flesh invisible. His interest had been strictly scientific but the drug had the effect, after use, of turning him into a maniac. At about the time he starts the murders he is looking for the antidote to bring him back to a normal condition.

•

INVISIBLE MAN RETURNS, THE
1940, 81 mins, US Ⓥ b/w
Dir Joe May ***Prod*** Ken Goldsmith ***Scr*** Lester Cole, Curt Siodmak ***Ph*** Milton Krasner ***Ed*** Frank Gross ***Mus*** Hans J. Salter ***Art*** Jack Otterson, Martin Obzina
Act Cedric Hardwicke, Vincent Price, Nan Grey, John Sutton, Cecil Kellaway, Alan Napier (Universal)

Stripped of the horror angles of its forerunner, *The Invisible Man Returns* is a fantastic tale of the impossible—but unfolds in such a manner that it maintains interest throughout despite its basic incredibility. Claude Rains portrayed the title role in the first *Invisible Man*, produced by Universal in 1933, and was killed off at the finish. Vincent Price is the second phantom.

Picture is a high spot in special effects and trick photography. John Fulton and his staff, also responsible for the same work in the first *Invisible Man*, provide some amazing scenes and eerie situations.

When Price is convicted of the murder of his brother and sentenced to be hanged, medico-scientist John Sutton gives him a serum injection which makes him invisible, and allows escape from prison. Sutton's brother concocted the serum, but failed to discover an antidote to prevent eventual attack of madness. While Sutton concentrates on finding a serum before his friend becomes a killing maniac, Price's invisibility allows him to uncover the murderer.

Story and script are workmanlike efforts, with Joe May's direction holding a steady and suspenseful pace with few dull moments.

•

INVITATION TO THE DANCE
1956, 93 mins, US Ⓥ col
Dir Gene Kelly ***Prod*** Arthur Freed ***Scr*** Gene Kelly ***Ph*** Freddie Young, Joseph Ruttenberg ***Ed*** Raymond Poulton, Robert Watts, Adrienne Fazan ***Mus*** Andre Previn, Ibert, Rimsky-Korsakov
Act Gene Kelly, Igor Youskevitch, Claire Sombert, Carol Haney, David Kasday, Tamara Toumanova (M-G-M)

Invitation to the Dance, a full-length dance feature, is a bold and imaginative experiment in film-making. Through the medium of the dance alone, producer Arthur Freed and director-choreographer-performer Gene Kelly tell three separate stories. There is no dialog. Just ballet music, colorful costumes, and skillful photography.

Kelly has assembled a crew of outstanding hoofers, including such experts as Tamara Toumanova, Claire Sombert, Carol Haney, Diana Adams, Igor Youskevitch, and Belita. Standout sequence is the middle entry, *Ring around the Rosy*. Using the children's song and game as the teeoff, the dance story to Andre Previn's music follows the career of a bracelet as it changes hands in the perennial game of love.

The opening number is similar to the Pagliacci theme as the clown (Kelly) is frustrated in his unrequited love for the beautiful ballerina (Sombert).

The final sequence is a combination of live action and animations, the cartoon sequences being provided by Fred Quimby, William Hanna and Joseph Barbera.

•

IN WHICH WE SERVE
1942, 113 mins, UK Ⓥ b/w
Dir Noel Coward, David Lean ***Prod*** Noel Coward ***Scr*** Noel Coward ***Ph*** Ronald Neame ***Mus*** Noel Coward ***Art*** David Rawnsley
Act Noel Coward, John Mills, Bernard Miles, Celia Johnson, Michael Wilding, Richard Attenborough (Two Cities)

No less than half a dozen credits for this film go to Noel Coward. And they're well earned. It is the story of a British destroyer, from its completion to its destruction at sea by the Germans. She is dive-bombed in the Battle of Crete, but the survivors carry on the fight. It is a grim tale sincerely picturized and splendidly acted throughout. Only one important factor calls for criticism. It is that all the details are too prolonged.

The author-producer-scriptwriter-composer and co-director gives a fine performance as the captain of the vessel, but acting honors also go to the entire company.

Stark realism is the keynote of the writing and depiction, with no glossing of the sacrifices constantly being made by the sailors. They are seen clinging to a rubber raft, with cut-ins of several of them thinking of their wives and families at home and then flashing back to them in the water. This effect is impressive—to a degree.

1942: Special Award (outstanding production achievement by Noel Coward)

1943: NOMINATIONS: Best Picture, Original Screenplay

•

I OUGHT TO BE IN PICTURES
1982, 107 mins, US Ⓥ col
Dir Herbert Ross ***Prod*** Herbert Ross, Neil Simon ***Scr*** Neil Simon ***Ph*** David M. Walsh ***Ed*** Sidney Levin ***Mus*** Marvin Hamllisch ***Art*** Albert Brenner
Act Walter Matthau, Ann-Margret, Dinah Manoff, Lance Guest, Lewis Smith, Martin Ferrero (20th Century-Fox)

Neil Simon's *I Ought to Be in Pictures* is a moving family drama, peppered with the author's patented gag lines and notable for sock performances by Dinah Manoff and Walter Matthau.

Nimbly opened-out from the 1980 stage version by helmer Herbert Ross, film concerns a 19-year-old, spunky Brooklyn girl Libby (Dinah Manoff reprising her stage role), who hitchhikes to Los Angeles to break into films as an actress but more importantly see her dad who left her, her brother and mom for good 16 years earlier.

Dad is Herb Tucker (Walter Matthau), a once-successful feature and TV scripter now given over to gambling and drinking. Tucker's loyal g.f. Steffie (Ann-Margret) is supportive but has her own children to take care of.

Key factor in making this work is apt casting, with Manoff outstanding in avoiding direct sentimentality in the showy central role. For his part, Matthau makes a ne'er-do-well character immensely sympathetic in spite of his shortcomings.

•

IPCRESS FILE, THE
1965, 109 mins, UK Ⓥ ▭ col
Dir Sidney J. Furie ***Prod*** Harry Saltzman ***Scr*** Bill Canaway, James Doran ***Ph*** Otto Heller ***Ed*** Peter Hunt ***Mus*** John Barry ***Art*** Ken Adam
Act Michael Caine, Nigel Green, Guy Doleman, Sue Lloyd, Gordon Jackson, Aubrey Richards (Rank)

Harry Saltzman and Albert R. Broccoli, who produce the Bond razamatazz, diversify by bringing to the screen a kind of "anti-Bond" spy in the character of Harry Palmer, based on Len Deighton's novel. The result is probably rather more true to the facts of intelligence life than the Bond world of fantasy.

Intelligence man Harry Palmer (Michael Caine) is an undisciplined sergeant who is seconded to intelligence work and finds that it is more legwork and filling in forms than inspired hunches and glamorous adventure.

Present adventure concerns the steps taken to retrieve a missing boffin and involves the agent being captured by the enemy and subjected to acute brainwashing. Pic does not build up to the type of suspense usually demanded of such thrillers.

Sidney J. Furie's direction, allied with Otto Heller's camera, provides some striking effects. But sometimes he gets carried away into arty-crafty fields with low-angle shots and symbolism adding to the confusion of the screenplay.

Caine skillfully resists any temptation he may have had to pep up the proceedings. In fact, his consistent underplaying adds considerably to the pull of the picture.

•

I.Q.
1994, 95 mins, US Ⓥ ⦿ ▭ col
Dir Fred Schepisi ***Prod*** Caril Baum, Fred Schepisi ***Scr*** Andy Breckman, Michael Leeson ***Ph*** Ian Baker ***Ed*** Jill Bilcock ***Mus*** Jerry Goldsmith ***Art*** Stuart Wurtzel
Act Tim Robbins, Meg Ryan, Walter Matthau, Lou Jacobi, Gene Saks, Joseph Maher (Paramount/Sandollar)

The conceit of this 1950s-set yarn is that the world's most famous scientist, Albert Einstein (Walter Matthau), realizes that his egghead niece is in need of some heart massaging. She has a stuffy tenured beau who bores the pants off Al and his German cadre at Princeton.

The promising spark occurs when the niece, Catherine (Meg Ryan), sputters into a garage and encounters mechanic Ed Walters (Tim Robbins). She absentmindedly leaves her watch, and Ed seizes the opportunity it presents. To win the girl for the young man, the professors create an elaborate ruse that extends to refashioning Ed in tweeds and a meerschaum. They also school him in "cold fusion," which Ike declares a major leap in the space race against the Russkies.

A paean to movies past, *I.Q.* recalls the style and attitude of a bygone era while retaining a contemporary spirit and polish. The material provides Robbins with the kind of likable, charismatic role that gained him early recognition.

•

I REMEMBER MAMA
1948, 137 mins, US Ⓥ ⦿ b/w
Dir George Stevens ***Prod*** Harriet Parsons ***Scr*** DeWitt Bodeen ***Ph*** Nicholas Musuraca ***Ed*** Robert Swink ***Mus*** Roy Webb ***Art*** Albert S. D'Agostino, Carroll Clark
Act Irene Dunne, Barbara Bel Geddes, Oscar Homolka, Philip Dorn, Cedric Hardwicke, Edgar Bergen (RKO)

With *I Remember Mama*, RKO is spreading a layer of warm and deeply moving nostalgia. Based on the John van Druten legiter, [and the novel, *Mama's Bank Account*, by Kathryn Forbes] the film encompasses those same broad, human values that lifted the play into the smash hit class.

DeWitt Bodeen's screenplay is a faithful adaptation of the original, adding only an extra dimension of background depth and story detail. In extending the scope, however, it doesn't blunt the impact of the yarn. This reminiscence of growth in a San Francisco Norwegian family is related in a simple and genuine manner. It's frequently sentimental but never hokey.

Irene Dunne is the central pillar of this production. In holding down the most demanding role of her career, she earns new honors as an actress of outstanding versatility. Her Norwegian dialect sounds queer for the first couple of minutes but soon establishes itself solidly as a natural part of her lingo.

The rest of the cast also do yeoman's service in draping this pic with a flesh-and-blood reality. Oscar Homolka, repeating his stage role of the uncle, contributes a massive and memorable performance. As the youngster who matures into an authoress, Barbara Bel Geddes plays a 15-year-old schoolgirl in a tour de force. Her portrait of adolescence is sensitive, compelling and authentic.

1948: NOMINATIONS: Best Actress (Irene Dunne), Supp. Actor (Oscar Homolka), Supp. Actress (Barbara Bel Geddes), B&W Cinematography

•

IRENE
1940, 104 mins, US Ⓥ col
Dir Herbert Wilcox ***Prod*** Herbert Wilcox ***Scr*** Alice Duer Miller ***Ph*** Russell Metty ***Ed*** Elmo Williams ***Mus*** Harry Tierney, Joseph McCarthy ***Art*** L. P. Williams
Act Anna Neagle, Ray Milland, Roland Young, Alan Marshal, May Robson, Billie Burke (Imperadio/RKO)

Back in 1919–20 a smash musical comedy and then in 1926 a hit First National film starring Colleen Moore, *Irene* emerges this time as dated celluloidia. It's old-fashioned from several angles, further handicapped by familiar story pattern.

Starring combination of Anna Neagle and Ray Milland cannot wholly carry this film over the hurdles. The negative factors are not so much in the acting as they are in Alice Duer Miller's screenplay and Herbert Wilcox's direction, neither of which is ultra-1940. The screenplay, and direction too, closely follow the original film. In the Colleen Moore starrer a 1,000-foot segment of a grand ball was given over to a color sequence, quite revolutionary in those days, but reprised now it just makes the fore and after parts in black and white look all the more ordinary in comparison.

Neagle, as the girl who steps from the tenements to a modeling job and then into society, gives a rather spotty performance. She's too broadly Irish, for one thing, and not flattered by the camera in the first 50 minutes for another. In the color sequences she shows up much better, her red hair being especially noticeable, and is okay in one feathery dance routine, and when singing "Alice Blue Gown." However, she doesn't give the part the comedy content Moore did, which makes the Hibernian dialect all the more unnecessary.

"Castle In Your Dreams," "Gown" and the title song are still very worthy tunes, from the original score.

Roland Young, noted for his dry comedy, is merely dry in this picture as manager of Mme Lucy's. Two other performers wasted are Isabel Jewell and Doris Noland, Neagle's tenement house pals. Marsha Hunt hasn't much to do as the almost-jilted sweetie of Alan Marshal, while May Robson's role as the motherly but strait-laced Irish grandmother is overdone and unbelievable.

1940: NOMINATION: Best Score

•

IRISHMAN, THE
1978, 108 mins, Australia Ⓥ col
Dir Donald Crombie ***Prod*** Anthony Buckley ***Scr*** Donald Crombie ***Ph*** Peter James ***Ed*** Tim Wellburn ***Mus*** Charles Marawood ***Art*** Owen Williams
Act Michael Craig, Simon Burke, Robyn Nevin, Lou Brown, Vincent Ball, Bryan Brown (Forest Home)

The north of Queensland in the 1920s must have been much like west Texas at the turn of the century, if we can believe the movies. A hard land, populated by hard men and women working hard in hard conditions. But times are a-changing, and whenever that happens there's usually a rugged but dogged individual who praises the candle and cries out against the light of progress. One such is Paddy Doolan, the eponymous migrated Celt.

Paddy the teamster, with his team of 20 giant Clydesdale draught horses crossing the great wide river, opens the film and immediately creates awe and admiration. The horses are such superb beasts that it is made that much easier to accept Paddy's stubbornness later, when he refuses to see that his team is being superseded by the internal combustion engine.

His wife is sensible, yet acquiescent; his older son, Will, defiant; the youngest, and most sensitive—and ultimately therefore the most affected—is bewildered, but devotedly and hopelessly goes with Paddy. And his "My father, right or wrong" feelings are inevitably eroded. In any event Paddy's recalcitrance demolishes the family, eventually destroys his self-esteem and, ultimately, Paddy himself.

The film has great moments of emotional triumph, and at times is unabashedly sentimental, but it never descends to mawkishness.

•

IRMA LA DOUCE
1963, 143 mins, US Ⓥ ⦿ ▭ col
Dir Billy Wilder ***Prod*** Billy Wilder ***Scr*** Billy Wilder, I.A.L. Diamond ***Ph*** Joseph LaShelle ***Ed*** Daniel Mandell ***Mus*** Andre Previn ***Art*** Alexander Trauner
Act Jack Lemmon, Shirley MacLaine, Lou Jacobi, Bruce Yarnell, Herschel Bernardi, Hope Holiday (Mirisch/Phalanx)

On the plus side of the *Irma* ledger, there are scintillating performances by Jack Lemmon and Shirley MacLaine, a batch of jovial supporting portrayals, a striking physical production and a number of infectious comedy scenes.

But *Irma* also misses on several important counts, and the fact that it does illustrates the sizable problems inherent in an attempt to convert a legit musical into a tuneless motion picture farce. But what hurts the film the most is its length. Two hours and 23 minutes is an awfully long haul for a frivolous farce.

The hot-and-cold scenario, based on the play by Alexandre Breffort [and musical by Marguerite Monnot], traces the love affair of Irma (MacLaine), a proud and profitable practitioner of the oldest profession, and a young gendarme

(Lemmon) who gets bounced off the force when he makes the mistake of taking his job seriously. Lemmon becomes number one mec, or pimp, on the block when he knocks his predecessor's block off, thereby inheriting Irma and the rights to her estate.

Lemmon plays his juicy role to the hilt, and there are moments when his performance brings to mind some of the great visual comedy of the classic silent film clowns. His portrayal of his British alter ego is a kind of cross between Jose Ferrer's characterization of Toulouse-Lautrec and Richard Haydn's caricature of an Englishman. MacLaine delivers a winning performance in the title role, and has never looked better. There's a whale of a comedy portrayal by Lou Jacobi as the versatile bistro boss-barkeep, Moustache.

1963: Best Adapted Musical Score

NOMINATIONS: Best Actress (Shirley MacLaine), Color Cinematography

•

IRON CURTAIN, THE

1948, 88 mins, US b/w

Dir William A. Wellman ***Prod*** Sol C. Siegel ***Scr*** Milton Krims ***Ph*** Charles G. Clarke ***Ed*** Louis Loeffler ***Art*** Lyle R. Wheeler, Mark-Lee Kirk

Act Dana Andrews, Gene Tierney, June Havoc, Berry Kroeger, Edna Best (20th Century-Fox)

Factually dealing with the Soviet undercover activities in Canada, where atomic bomb secrets were thefted, picture is a corking spy melodrama.

Story is the personal one of Igor Gouzenko, former code clerk in the Soviet Embassy in Ottawa. A devoted Communist when he arrives at his new post, Gouzenko is gradually aware of what it means to live without fear and, to help insure his son's future, exposes the Soviet spy network to the world.

William A. Wellman's direction carries out documentary technique, pointing up factual material and the dramatic values by never permitting a scene to be overplayed. Stress on underplaying and the absence of obvious meller tricks goes a long way in adding to realistic air with which the film is imbued.

Dana Andrews does one of his best jobs as Gouzenko, making the character as real on the screen as it is in real life. Gene Tierney is fine as his wife, who first becomes aware of the dead end that Communism leads to. Wisely, there has been no attempt to have the dialog accented, contributing to reality.

•

IRON EAGLE

1986, 119 mins, US Ⓥ ⊙ col

Dir Sidney J. Furie ***Prod*** Ron Samuels, Joe Wizan ***Scr*** Kevin Elders, Sidney J. Furie ***Ph*** Adam Greenberg ***Ed*** George Grenville ***Mus*** Basil Poledouris ***Art*** Robb Wilson King

Act Louis Gossett, Jr., Jason Gedrick, David Suchet, Tim Thomerson, Larry B. Scott, Caroline Lagerfelt (Tri-Star)

Iron Eagle is a crackerjack fighter-pilot picture focusing on a daring rescue of a hostage in a small Middle East country.

Young Jason Gedrick swings into action when word comes that pilot pop Tim Thomerson, has been shot down for venturing too near the borders of the little nation defended by swarthy David Suchet, who almost twirls his moustache in anticipation of hanging the Yankee intruder.

At first Gedrick is hopeful that the U.S. will respond officially, but the government waffles. Fortunately, dad has often taken Gedrick up in an F-16. Equally fortunate, all his high-school friends are Air Force kids, too. After faking the military computers into assigning two jets for their use, Gedrick persuades veteran combat pilot Louis Gossett, Jr., to lead the mission and off the pair go into the wild blue yonder.

Director Sidney J. Furie fills in the rest with breakneck action and some dandy dogfights. Much of the dialog is simply laughable.

•

IRON EAGLE II

1988, 105 mins, Canada/Israel Ⓥ ⊙ col

Dir Sidney J. Furie ***Prod*** Jacob Kotzky, Sharon Herel, John Kemeny ***Scr*** Kevin Elders, Sidney J. Furie ***Ph*** Alain Dostie ***Ed*** Rit Wallis ***Mus*** Amin Bhatia ***Art*** Ariel Roshko

Act Louis Gossett, Jr., Mark Humphrey, Stuart Margolin, Alan Scarfe, Sharon H. Brandon, Maury Chaykin (Alliance)

Iron Eagle II nervily tries to update the formula [of the 1986 original]. Plot meanders and fails to really fire its engines until deep into the story.

Puppy-faced rock 'n' roll fighter pilots, including Tom Cruise–lookalike Mark Humphrey, accidentally stray into Soviet airspace and one gets shot down. The survivor, Cooper (Humphrey), starts nursing a big grudge against Soviets.

Next thing you know he's recruited for a secret mission led by Louis Gossett, Jr., (reprising his role as Chappy) who's been given a general's star as incentive to lead U.S. and Soviet pilots on a joint mission to destroy a nuclear weapons base in an unnamed Mideast country that is a threat to them both.

The American team members are shown as prejudiced slobs given to pranks, insults and dirty tricks. To make things worse, Vardovsky (Alan Scarfe) was part of the squadron that gunned down Cooper's buddy, and also keeps a jealous eye on an alluring female Soviet pilot, Valeri Zuyeniko (Sharon H. Brandon), whom Cooper wastes no time strutting for.

Pic's chief weakness is that for much of the screentime, the "joint mission" seems like just a weak premise to bring together both sides for lowbrow *Police Academy*–style antics and infighting. On the plus side, the goons slowly and grudgingly develop a bond and understanding that proves to be pic's crowning glory.

•

IRON EAGLE IV

1995, 95 mins, Canada Ⓥ col

Dir Sidney J. Furie ***Prod*** Peter Simpson ***Scr*** Michael Stokes ***Ph*** Curtis Peterson ***Ed*** Jeff Warren ***Mus*** Paul Zaza ***Art*** Michael Parks

Act Louis Gossett, Jr., Al Waxman, Jason Cadieux, Joanne Vannicola, Rachel Blanchard, Ross Hill (Norstar)

The fourth installment of the *Iron Eagle* franchise adds a new twist to the airborne saga by combining the sky-high heroics with a feel-good troubled-teens tale, but the new kids on the *Iron Eagle* block are unable to resuscitate this tired series. This Canadian-made actioner never manages to get off the runway.

Louis Gossett, Jr., returns once again as retired Air Force Gen. Charles "Chappy" Sinclair, who is now reduced to running the Iron Eagle Flight School, a training center that caters exclusively to teens on the wrong side of the law. He finally convinces former fighter pilot Doug Masters (Jason Cadieux) to help him run the school.

Masters and a couple of the adolescent would-be pilots land on an abandoned Air Force strip and spot a bunch of soldiers digging up suspicious-looking canisters. Sinclair immediately tells his Air Force buddy Gen. Brad Kettle (Al Waxman) about the mysterious activities but it turns out that Kettle is the head bad guy, and he's intent on dumping the toxic chemicals on Cuba to test them.

Helmer Sidney J. Furie, who directed the first two *Iron Eagle* pics, is unable to breathe much life into the cliché-ridden script. Some of the high altitude stunts are reasonably entertaining, but the ground-level drama is strictly ho-hum. The young thesps fare better, particularly Joanne Vannicola as the drug-dealing wild girl Wheeler.

•

IRON HAND, THE

SEE: JINGWU MEN

•

IRON HORSE, THE

1924, 130 mins, US ⊗ b/w

Dir John Ford ***Prod*** John Ford ***Scr*** Charles Kenyon, John Russell, Charles Darnton ***Ph*** George Schneiderman ***Ed*** Hettie Gray Baker

Act George O'Brien, Madge Bellamy, Charles Edward Hull, Cyril Chadwick, Fred Kohler, J. Farrell MacDonald (Fox)

The Iron Horse is the story of the winning of the West through the linking of the Atlantic and Pacific coasts by rail. It contains a powerful theme of historical value as the basis, around which a romance has been woven, that ties the leading characters to the history of the building of the first transcontinental railway.

There are comedy, tragedy and a love theme, Indians and soldiers, hordes of construction gangs, camp followers, both men and women, gamblers and dance hall girls, shooting and riding, a tremendous cattle drive, the fording of a river by a herd of beeves.

John Ford, who directs, puts his story over on the screen with a lot of punch. His handling of the trio of ex-soldiers of the Civil War who, as the three musketeers of America, battled through the building of the great Union Pacific railroad is exceedingly clever. They lend a touch of comedy as did Ernest Torrence and Tully Marshall in *The Covered Wagon.* Francis Powers, J. Farrell MacDonald and James Welch enact the roles and Ford touches them with just a bit of pathos in the end that makes them stand out as real humans and not as out-and-out buffoons just created for a laugh.

The love interest is carried on by George O'Brien and Madge Bellamy. O'Brien gives a corking performance as the youthful scout and lover and Bellamy shines as his beloved. Kohler's characterization is a piece of classic work.

•

IRON MASK, THE

1929, 95 mins, US Ⓥ ⊙ b/w

Dir Allan Dwan ***Scr*** Elton Thomas [= Douglas Fairbanks] ***Ph*** Henry Sharp ***Mus*** Hugo Riesenfeld

Act Douglas Fairbanks, Nigel de Brulier, Marguerite De La Motte, Leon Barry, Rolfe Sedan, Lon Poff (United Artists)

Typical romantic Fairbanks picture. His direct vocal address is in the form of minute-and-a-half appendages as prologs to the first and second halves, into which the picture was [originally] divided for the premiere. There is no dialog at any time in the direct action.

This is the sequel to Fairbanks's *Three Musketeers* (1921). It's so much of a sequel that, besides Fairbanks, Nigel de Brulier and Lon Poff are again together as Cardinal Richelieu and his aid, Father Joseph; Marguerite de la Motte revives her Constance, and Leon Barry has been recast as Athos.

Current story provides the twist of D'Artagnan going over to the Cardinal's side. It is to protect the young heir apparent who has a twin brother whom Richelieu whisks into hiding at birth to protect the throne.

Allan Dwan, directing, keeps the story moving. Comedy sidelights slip in and out, but Fairbanks and the romantic friendship of the four men hold the picture together.

The brief verbal passages ask the audience to come back to the days of chivalry.

•

IRONWEED

1987, 144 mins, US Ⓥ ⊙ col

Dir Hector Babenco ***Prod*** Keith Barish, Marcia Nasatir ***Scr*** William Kennedy ***Ph*** Lauro Escorel ***Ed*** Anne Goursaud ***Mus*** John Morris ***Art*** Jeannine Oppewall

Act Jack Nicholson, Meryl Streep, Carroll Baker, Michael O'Keefe, Diane Venora, Fred Gwynne (Taft/Barish/Tri-Star)

Unrelentingly bleak, *Ironweed* is a film without an audience and no reason for being except its own self-importance. It's an event picture without the event. Whatever joy or redemption William Kennedy offered in his Pulitzer prize-winning novel is nowhere to be found, surprising since he wrote the screenplay.

The story of Francis Phelan (Jack Nicholson), who returns to his native Albany in 1938 literally carrying a lifetime of ghosts with him, is loaded with elaborate expository passages trying to account for why an obviously intelligent individual has abandoned his family for a bum's life.

Phelan's movement around Albany is like a passage through the rings of hell, but instead of coming out at paradise, he's still the same old bum at the end.

Nicholson and Meryl Streep have approximately three scenes together and though they clearly have a great deal of affection for each other, they are beyond passion.

1987: NOMINATIONS: Best Actor (Jack Nicholson), Actress (Meryl Streep)

•

IRRECONCILABLE DIFFERENCES

1984, 114 mins, US Ⓥ ⊙ col

Dir Charles Shyer ***Prod*** Alex Winitsky, Arlene Sellers ***Scr*** Nancy Meyers, Charles Shyer ***Ph*** William Fraker ***Ed*** John Burnett ***Mus*** Paul de Senneville ***Art*** Ida Random

Act Ryan O'Neal, Shelley Long, Drew Barrymore, Sam Wanamaker, Allen Garfield, Sharon Stone (Hemdale)

Irreconcilable Differences begins strongly as a human comedy about a nine-year-old who decides to take legal action to divorce her parents. Unfortunately, this premise is soon jettisoned for a rather familiar tale of a marriage turned sour as shown step-by-step. Set in the world of Hollywood writers and filmmakers, the story is also more fun for the cognoscenti than the average filmgoer.

On the witness stand the seeds of her dissatisfaction emerge in the three principals' testimony. It is regrettably an uninspired and improbable device to tell the yarn. Not a great deal of perception emerges.

Ryan O'Neal and Shelley Long spark off a nice romantic chemistry but really need a better vehicle to show off their craft.

•

ISADORA

(US: THE LOVES OF ISADORA)

1969, 141 mins, UK Ⓥ col

Dir Karel Reisz ***Prod*** Robert Hakim, Raymond Hakim ***Scr*** Melvyn Bragg, Clive Exton, Margaret Drabble ***Ph*** Larry Pizer ***Ed*** Tom Priestley ***Mus*** Maurice Jarre ***Art*** Jocelyn Herbert

Act Vanessa Redgrave, John Fraser, James Fox, Jason Robards, Ivan Tchenko, Bessie Love (Universal)

The tragic lifelong odyssey of Isadora Duncan, whose consistent non-conformity brought her as much public success as it did personal failure, is told with a remarkable degree of excellence.

The free-thinking aspects of Duncan's life (unabashed out-of-wedlock affairs and births, hedonism, political idealism, naivete, etc.), are emphasized in this sensitive, lucid, beautifully fashioned, and masterfully executed personal tragedy [based on *My Life* by Duncan and *Isadora Duncan—An Intimate Portrait* by Sewell Stokes].

Story unfolds as Duncan (Vanessa Redgrave) dictates memoirs to her secretary. Redgrave's performance in these scenes, with hollow eyes and a weathered face suggesting the inevitable ends of dissipation, plus her perfect projection of aging flamboyance, demands equality with Gloria Swanson's classic performance in *Sunset Blvd.* Where the film falters is its length and pacing.

1969: NOMINATION: Best Actress (Vanessa Redgrave)

•

I SHALL RETURN
SEE: AN AMERICAN GUERRILLA IN THE PHILIPPINES

•

I SHOT ANDY WARHOL
1996, 106 mins, US Ⓥ col
Dir Mary Harron *Prod* Tom Kalin, Christine Vachon *Scr* Mary Harron, Daniel Minahan *Ph* Ellen Kuras *Ed* Keith Reamer *Mus* John Cale *Art* Therese Deprez
Act Lili Taylor, Jared Harris, Lothaire Bluteau, Martha Plimpton, Stephen Dorff, Anna Thompson (Playhouse Intl./Goldwyn)

I Shot Andy Warhol, the story of the radical feminist and Warhol fringe figure Valerie Solanas, who seriously wounded the artist in 1968, is an exemplary and dynamic work that goes about as far as a narrative film can in both analyzing a complex personality and portraying a cultural scene.

The general view of Solanas, who died destitute in 1988, a year later than Warhol, is of a lunatic lesbian acting in revenge for being spurned by the Factory. There is truth to that explanation, but much more to the story as well.

By 1966, Solanas (Lili Taylor) is living on Manhattan rooftops and writing her defining work, *The SCUM Manifesto*, a revolutionary tract for her one-member Society for Cutting Up Men. Along the same lines, she pens a subversive play, *Up Your Ass*, which she determines only Andy Warhol (Jared Harris) can produce. Butting in on the invitation of her transvestite friend, eventual Warhol superstar Candy Darling (Stephen Dorff), Solanas manages to get a copy to him. But her pushy personality and guerilla attire don't jibe with the drugged and zoned-out Factory crowd and its taste for artifice. Warhol tries to placate her with a screen test and one actual film appearance (in *I, a Man*), but soon has Solanas excommunicated from the Factory.

First-time feature director Mary Harron has said that what takes place in the picture is about "95 percent real," and a tendency toward scrupulous accuracy tinged with critique pertains to the portrait of the Factory. But the main opposition is between Solanas and Warhol, the first abrasive, loud and confrontational, the other wimpy, mild-mannered and masterfully evasive. Without question, the picture rides on Taylor's stupendous lead performance, agitated, vibrant and resourceful. John Cale, a survivor of the Warhol-produced Velvet Underground, contributes an excellent score.

•

I SHOT JESSE JAMES
1949, 81 mins, US Ⓥ b/w
Dir Samuel Fuller *Prod* Charles K. Hittleman *Scr* Samuel Fuller *Ph* Ernest Miller *Ed* Paul Landres *Mus* Albert Glasser
Act Preston Foster, Barbara Britton, John Ireland, Reed Hadley, J. Edward Bromberg (Screen Guild)

I Shot Jesse James is a character study of the man who felled the West's most famous outlaw with a coward's bullet. It's an interesting treatment that doesn't overlook necessary plot and action.

While Preston Foster and Barbara Britton carry star roles, it's John Ireland, as the notorious Bob Ford, who dominates the story.

Spiced in the plot footage are any number of forthright physical clashes, capably staged by Samuel Fuller's direction. Latter is not quite as adept in handling the character study motivation but the players carry off these angles with considerable ability.

Ireland's performance is clearly drawn and even manages a trace of sympathy. Britton fits well into the role of his beloved, who turns to Foster in the end. Foster is good as the prospector who turns marshal.

•

ISHTAR
1987, 107 mins, US Ⓥ ⦿ ⊏⊐ col
Dir Elaine May *Prod* Warren Beatty *Scr* Elaine May *Ph* Vittorio Storaro *Ed* Stephen A. Rotter, William Reynolds, Richard Cirincione, William S. Scharf *Mus* Dave Grusin *Art* Paul Sylbert
Act Warren Beatty, Dustin Hoffman, Isabelle Adjani, Charles Grodin, Jack Weston, Tess Harper (Columbia)

Here's how the story goes: Warren Beatty and Dustin Hoffman are struggling and mightily untalented singer-songwriters in New York. They hook up with talent agent Jack Weston (who delivers a fine character performance), and wind up getting booked into the Chez Casablanca in Morocco. Yes, there's the obvious parallels to the Hope-Crosby *Road* films.

Arrival in Africa finds Beatty-Hoffman stopping in the mythical kingdom of Ishtar, where swirl of events leads them into vortex of Middle East political turmoil, with Isabelle Adjani functioning as a left wing rebel trying to overthrow the U.S.-backed Emir of Ishtar.

Enter Charles Grodin, who upstages all involved via his savagely comical portrayal of a CIA agent. He provides the connecting link as a series of zigzag plot points unfold because of an important map.

Desert sequences provide some of the film's high points as Beatty and Hoffman finally develop some genuine rapport under adverse conditions.

There are also a few hilarious scenes as vultures circle an exhausted Hoffman and later as he's thrust into role as a translator for gunrunners and their Arab buyers.

•

ISLAND, THE
1980, 114 mins, US Ⓥ ⦿ ⊏⊐ col
Dir Michael Ritchie *Prod* Richard D. Zanuck, David Brown *Scr* Peter Benchley *Ph* Henri Decae *Ed* Richard A. Harris *Mus* Ennio Morricone *Art* Dale Hennesy
Act Michael Caine, David Warner, Angela Punch McGregor, Frank Middlemass, Don Henderson, Zakes Mokae (Universal/Zanuck-Brown)

This latest summertime tale from the water-obsessed pen of Peter Benchley gets off to a bristling start as a charter boatload of boozy business types is ambushed by something or someone that leaves hatchets planted in their skulls and severed limbs scattered aboard.

Cut to British journalist Michael Caine, who persuades his editor that his latest Bermuda Triangle–type ship disappearance justifies his personal research.

But once the mystery is banally resolved—the island is inhabited by a tribe of buccaneers who've been inbreeding for 300 years and prey on pleasure ships—the film degenerates to a violent chase melodrama. Michael Ritchie's witty direction is abandoned in the violence, and periodic efforts to revive the built-in comedy fall flat.

•

ISLAND AT THE TOP OF THE WORLD, THE
1974, 95 mins, US Ⓥ col
Dir Robert Stevenson *Prod* Winston Hibler *Scr* John Whedon *Ph* Frank Phillips *Ed* Robert Stafford *Mus* Maurice Jarre *Art* Peter Ellenshaw
Act David Hartman, Donald Sinden, Jacques Marin, Mako, David Gwillim, Agneta Eckemyr (Walt Disney)

Title pretty much describes pic's theme, carrying the story of four Polar explorers discovering a lost land inhabited by Vikings. Based on the novel [*The Lost Ones*] by Ian Cameron, script limns a rich Englishman in 1907 flying into the Arctic wilderness in search of his missing son. Pic occasionally takes on the aspect of old-fashioned adventure, as the explorers find a mysterious valley warmed by volcanic heat in the midst of the Arctic wastes and a settlement of Norsemen who might be the descendants of Eric the Red's second expedition to Greenland in the 10th century.

Donald Sinden portrays the titled Englishman and Jacques Marin plays the French designer and captain of the balloon that figures so prominently in suspenseful action. All deliver realistic performances. An interesting newcomer is Agneta Eckemyr, cast as a Viking maid.

1974: NOMINATION: Best Art Direction

•

ISLAND IN THE SKY
1953, 108 mins, US b/w
Dir William A. Wellman *Prod* Robert Fellows *Scr* Ernest K. Gann *Ph* Archie Stout *Ed* Ralph Dawson *Mus* Emil Newman *Art* James Basevi
Act John Wayne, Lloyd Nolan, Walter Abel, James Arness, Andy Devine (Warner/Wayne-Fellows)

An articulate drama of men and planes has been fashioned from Ernest K. Gann's novel. The Wayne-Fellows production was scripted with care by Gann for aviation aficionado William A. Wellman who gives it sock handling to make it a solid piece of drama revolving around an ATC plane crash in Arctic wastes.

The film moves back and forth very smoothly from the tight action at the crash site to the planning and execution of the search. It's a slick job by all concerned.

John Wayne is the ATC pilot downed with his crew, James Lydon, Hal Baylor, Sean McClory and Wally Cassell, in an uncharted section of Labrador. How he holds them together during five harrowing days, before rescue comes on the sixth, is grippingly told. Each of the players has a chance at a big scene and delivers strongly.

The snow-covered Donner Lake area near Truckee, CA, subbed for the story's Labrador locale and provides a frosty, shivery dressing to the picture. Both the lensing by Archie Stout and the aerial photography by William Clothier are important factors in the drama and thrills. Title derives from the fancy that pilots are men apart, their spirits dwelling on islands in the sky.

•

ISLAND IN THE SUN
1957, 123 mins, US col
Dir Robert Rossen *Prod* Darryl F. Zanuck *Scr* Alfred Hayes *Ph* Freddie Young *Ed* Reginald Beck *Mus* Malcolm Arnold *Art* William C. Andrews
Act James Mason, Joan Fontaine, Dorothy Dandridge, Joan Collins, Michael Rennie, Harry Belafonte (Zanuck/20th Century-Fox)

From an artistic point-of-view, this first Darryl F. Zanuck production for 20th-Fox under his new indie status is a letdown of major proportions.

The script by Alfred Hayes [from the novel by Alec Waugh] is jumbled, the acting leaves a lot to wish for, and Reginald Beck's editing is a case of letting down the story. Result is a picture that is flat and even tedious, that hints of raw sex but stops short of even a kiss for fear it might offend. Picture is peopled by characters who appear theatrical and overdrawn simply because the script offers no motivational explanation for their behavior. Even the dubbing in some scenes is mediocre, notably Belafonte's rendition of "Lead Man Holler."

Story is about Santa Marta, an imaginary island in the British West Indies, a beautiful, colorful place. There is John Justin, the governor's aide, who falls in love with attractive Dorothy Dandridge; then there's Stephen Boyd, the governor's son, who romances Joan Collins of the Fleury clan. Romance almost ends in tragedy (Collins becomes pregnant) when it becomes known that her father (Basil Sydney) has some colored blood in him.

The strongest, and dramatically the weakest, episode involves Belafonte as a rising young Negro labor leader, who greatly attracts Joan Fontaine, who is finally rejected by him in an almost embarrassingly conceived scene. Another dramatic incident involves plantation operator James Mason, his wife Patricia Owens, and Michael Rennie. Mason kills Rennie in a fit of jealousy and is then hounded by his conscience, and police inspector John Williams, to confess.

Belafonte's performance is barely satisfactory and, apart from his good looks, he has little to offer. Same is true of Dandridge. Mason as Maxwell Fleury has some strong moments. Fontaine is badly miscast and seems to sleepwalk through the picture. Only really outstanding performance is delivered by Williams as the police chief.

•

ISLAND OF DR MOREAU, THE
1977, 98 mins, US Ⓥ ⦿ col
Dir Don Taylor *Prod* John Temple-Smith, Skip Steloff *Scr* John Herman Shaner, Al Ramrus *Ph* Gerry Fisher *Ed* Marion Rothman *Mus* Laurence Rosenthal *Art* Philip Jefferies
Act Burt Lancaster, Michael York, Nigel Davenport, Barbara Carrera, Richard Basehart, Nick Cravat (American International)

This $6 million adaptation of the H. G. Wells horror-fantasy tale, previously filmed in 1932 by Paramount as *Island of Lost Souls*, is a handsome, well-acted, and involving piece of cinematic storytelling, made in the Virgin Islands.

Burt Lancaster has the lead role of the renegade scientist who dabbles in forbidden eugenic experiments on a remote Pacific island, where Michael York is washed up in a shipwreck in the early days of the 20th century.

Wells showed an uncanny gift for prophecy in his imaginative tales, and the doctor's experiments on beasts and humans eerily foreshadowed the Nazis' use of humans as guinea pigs.

Lancaster, despite his ungodly ideas, is given some resonance as a man who thinks his demented work is for the betterment of the human race.

York gives one of his best performances, and Barbara Carrera's enigmatic beauty is evocatively treated.

•

ISLAND OF DR. MOREAU, THE
1996, 95 mins, US Ⓥ ⦿ ▭ col
Dir John Frankenheimer ***Prod*** Edward R. Pressman ***Scr*** Richard Stanley, Ron Hutchinson ***Ph*** William A. Fraker ***Ed*** Paul Rubell ***Mus*** Gary Chang ***Art*** Graham (Grace) Walker
Act Marlon Brando, Val Kilmer, David Thewlis, Fairuza Balk, Ron Perlman, Marco Hofschneider (Pressman/New Line)

The Island of Dr. Moreau won't be seen in its full glory until it turns up on *Mystery Science Theater 3000*. An embarrassment for all concerned, this updated third screen version of H. G. Wells's disturbingly prophetic novel, published exactly 100 years ago, makes hash of its source and is wildly unfocused dramatically and tonally. Assiduous followers of director John Frankenheimer's career will be put in mind *Prophecy*, of his beastly 1979 outing.

Douglas (David Thewlis), a British UN peace negotiator stranded in the Java Sea after a plane crash, is plucked from his raft by the shady Montgomery (Val Kilmer) and taken ashore at the latter's destination on the titular tropical isle.

The great man himself remains scarce until a half-hour in, when he is conveyed into the village of the Beast People in a vehicle resembling the Popemobile. Marlon Brando's Moreau is a most peculiar creation, almost as weird as the mongrel beasts whose genes he has fused with human ones in an attempt to scientifically forge an obedient new species.

Failing entirely to construct a narrative spine, scripters Richard Stanley (the pic's original director [fired on the fourth day of shooting]) and Ron Hutchinson have an unappetizing upstart creature named Hyena-Swine kill Moreau off after an hour (thereby leaving Brando with just a half-hour's running time in which to maneuver).

Thewlis [who replaced Rob Morrow] is miscast as the accidental tourist. Kilmer creates no characterization whatsoever in a part that bears evidence of severe cutting. Shot in Queensland, Australia, pic has a proficient look.

•

ISLAND OF LOST SOULS
1933, 72 mins, US b/w
Dir Erle C. Kenton ***Scr*** Waldemar Young, Philip Wylie ***Ph*** Karl Struss
Act Charles Laughton, Bela Lugosi, Richard Arlen, Leila Hyams, Kathleen Burke, Arthur Hohl (Paramount)

With such actors as Charles Laughton, Richard Arlen and Bela Lugosi in the cast, *Souls* is provided with a mainstay.

While the action is not designed to appeal to other than the credulous, there are undoubtedly some horror sequences which are unrivaled. Those studies of a galaxy of Dr. Moreau's 50-50 man and beast creations, as an example, will pique any type of mentality.

The tramp steamer in a fog, its decks laden with crates of wild animals consigned to Moreau's mysterious island, is good picturization.

Romance is essentially light, and with a story of this kind [by H. G. Wells] it should be. The extra billing given Kathleen Burke as Lota, the Panther Woman, is strictly for the marquee. Girl is too much like a girl to even suggest transformation from a beast.

•

ISLANDS IN THE STREAM
1977, 105 mins, US Ⓥ ⦿ ▭ col
Dir Franklin J. Schaffner ***Prod*** Peter Bart, Max Palevsky ***Scr*** Denne Bart Petitclerc ***Ph*** Fred Koenekamp ***Ed*** Robert Swink ***Mus*** Jerry Goldsmith ***Art*** William J. Creber
Act George C. Scott, David Hemmings, Gilbert Roland, Susan Tyrrell, Richard Evans, Claire Bloom (Paramount)

While too introspective a story to be really compelling screen drama, Franklin J. Schaffner's film of *Islands in the Stream* is at least a proper valedictory to the era epitomized by author Ernest Hemingway. Hawaiian locations provide a superb physical backdrop (simulating The Bahamas, circa 1940) for the production.

George C. Scott's semi-Hemingway pivotal character lives on a remote island, to which travel his three sons by broken marriages, as the world moves into the globe-shrinking holocaust of World War II.

One can admire and follow the film without ever really getting enthusiastic about it, because of the way in which it has been written, acted and directed. There's a pervading sensitivity and restrained respect for the moral antiquity that is herein represented.

1977: NOMINATION: Best Cinematography

•

ISLE OF THE DEAD
1945, 72 mins, US Ⓥ ⦿ b/w
Dir Mark Robson ***Prod*** Val Lewton ***Scr*** Ardel Wray, Josef Mischel ***Ph*** Jack Mackenzie ***Ed*** Lyle Boyer ***Mus*** Leigh Harline ***Art*** Albert S. D'Agostino, Walter Keller
Act Boris Karloff, Ellen Drew, Marc Cramer, Alan Napier, Jason Robards (RKO)

Isle of the Dead is a slow conversation piece about plagues and vampires on an eerie Greek island. It's better handled and directed than most, though thriller fans will still find its lack of action a drag. Even Boris Karloff fans will note the tired way he rambles through it all.

Yarn is a psychological drama of an assorted group of people gathered on the island, when a plague breaks out and death takes one of them. A doctor is sure only a south wind can blow away the plague; a superstitious native is as positive that one of the guests is a vampire, carrying the plague's spirit within her. A couple of murders help to decimate the group until only a couple are left when the plague runs its course.

Karloff, as a Greek general trying to keep the plague from reaching his troops, is more paternal than menacing. Ellen Drew lends poignancy as a misunderstood nurse, and she and Marc Cramer present an attractive romantic couple.

•

ISN'T LIFE WONDERFUL
1924, 90 mins, US ⦿ ⊗ b/w
Dir D. W. Griffith ***Prod*** D. W. Griffith ***Scr*** D. W. Griffith ***Ph*** Hendrik Sartov, Hal Sintzenich
Act Carol Dempster, Neil Hamilton, Erville Alderson, Helen Lowell, Frank Puglia, Lupino Lane (Griffith/United Artists)

Isn't Life Wonderful is a picture that has something more behind it than mere entertainment. It gives an insight into the lives of simple German folk and their sufferings as a result of the Great War's aftermath.

This is the picture that Griffith shot partly in Germany. Griffith's handling of the theme is little short of wonderful. His composition in mass scenes as well in those with but few characters is in line with the best he has ever done.

The story is of the privations and struggles of a German family following the war and the collapse of the German exchange. A tale at once gripping and interesting, though heartrending and depressing.

A German professor is impoverished. He and his family have been driven from their home. They are in Berlin. One son is studying and working as a waiter in a night club, the other laboring in the shipyards until his strength, weakened through the war, fails him. The entire family is living in two rooms, eating a potato each a day.

Carol Dempster and Neil Hamilton are the lovers. Dempster does work of which she may well be proud. As for Hamilton, his characterization ranks with anything that he has done in this particular line.

•

IS PARIS BURNING?
1966, 185 mins, US/France Ⓥ ▭ b/w
Dir Rene Clement ***Prod*** Paul Graetz ***Scr*** Gore Vidal, Francis Coppola, Marcel Moussy ***Ph*** Marcel Grignon ***Ed*** Robert Lawrence ***Mus*** Maurice Jarre ***Art*** Willy Holt
Act Jean-Paul Belmondo, Charles Boyer, Gert Frobe, Anthony Perkins, Simone Signoret, Orson Welles (Paramount/Seven Arts)

This French-made, Yank-backed spectacle traces the uprising in Paris leading to the oncoming Allies changing their plans to invade the city rather than bypass it, as intended. Underlying dilemma faces the German commander, General Von Choltitz, who has been ordered to destroy Paris if necessary, or if it could not be held. The title is from Hitler's maniacal telephone demands to know if Paris was burning.

It is built on the premature uprising within the French resistance groups, and then the tensions as Paris is undermined with explosives and Von Choltitz hesitates as he realizes that Hitler is mad and that destruction of Paris will not help the German cause or the now hopeless Nazi war effort.

Gert Frobe has the pivotal part as Von Choltitz who is a career soldier and not above destroying Paris if necessary. He plays it with proper despair and does not overdo the sentimental aspect of the man.

The street fighting is done with fervor and dynamism and little cameos gives an ironic, tender, dramatic, pathetic feel to the overall happening.

1966: NOMINATIONS: Best B&W Cinematography, B&W Art Direction

•

I START COUNTING
1970, 105 mins, UK Ⓥ col
Dir David Greene ***Prod*** David Greene ***Scr*** Richard Harris ***Ph*** Alex Thomson ***Ed*** Kwith Palmer ***Mus*** Basil Kirchin ***Art*** Arnold Chapkis
Act Jenny Agutter, Bryan Marshall, Clare Sutcliffe, Simon Ward, Gregory Phillips, Lana Morris (United Artists)

Jenny Agutter plays a schoolgirl, adopted, who worships her elder "brother" who, unwittingly, has become a father-figure in the household. A series of local sex crimes strikes a sinister note, and from slender clues (neatly produced as red herrings) the girl suspects that her worshipped brother is the perpetrator.

Her friend (Clare Sutcliffe) is an extroverted little chippie, pert, provocative and pathetic in the way that she tries to kid everybody that she's sexually experienced. Agutter, who tries to keep up with the fantasy, is the more believable, but perhaps the less amusing, character. The two kids spend much time in the condemned house in which Agutter used to live. It's bang in the middle of woods which is the danger area operated by the sex-maniac.

•

I STILL KNOW WHAT YOU DID LAST SUMMER
1998, 101 MINS, US Ⓥ ⦿ ▭ col
Dir Danny Cannnon ***Prod*** Neal H. Moritz, Erik Feig, Stokely Chaffin, William S. Beasley ***Scr*** Trey Calloway ***Ph*** Vernon Layton ***Ed*** Peck Prior ***Mus*** John Frizzell ***Art*** Doug Kraner
Act Jennnifer Love Hewitt, Freddie Prinze, Jr., Brandy, Mekhi Phifer, Muse Watson, Matthew Settle (Columbia)

Follow-up to 1997's successful teens-in-jeopardy opus piles on the chills, thrills, and body count. Purists will find the pic's obviousness disappointing, but there's no question that the film delivers a sufficient shock quotient to satisfy its youthful target audience.

The new chapter begins on the first anniversary of the previous encounter. Survivor Julie James (Jennifer Love Hewitt) is attending college, and Ray Bronson (Freddie Prinze, Jr.) is catching fish on his boat in North Carolina. He invites her back for Fourth of July celebrations, but Julie is still haunted by nightmares about the hook-handed, slicker-coated killer Ben Willis (Muse Watson).

Then her roommate, Karla (Brandy), is offered a Bahamas vacation for four. Karla invites her squeeze, Tyrell (Mekhi Phifer), and Julie calls Ray to join the fun. On his way north with a buddy, Ray stumbles upon a stalled car and a body in the road. A turn of the head later, the familiar hook has impaled his friend. Ray barely escapes.

Julie reluctantly agrees to include nice guy Will (Matthew Settle) in her travel plans. A plane and a boat ride later, they arrive in the secluded island paradise of Tower Bay. The rest runs to form. The ending leaves promise for yet another chapter.

Director Danny Cannon tosses off the barbs and social commentary in favor of visceral thrills, a prurient perspective and elaborate setpieces. He's a proficient technician who has studied the genre and liberally steals the best from horror favorites—in particular, *The Shining*'s Outlook Hotel ambience. The music recalls *The Omen* and *Exorcist* pics and the oeuvre of Bernard Herrmann.

Once again the producers have assembled a charismatic young cast, augmented by vets Jeffrey Combs as a surly hotel manager and Bill Cobbs as a hotel staffer with a flair for voodoo defense.

•

IT
1927, 64 mins, US Ⓥ ⦿ ⊗ b/w
Dir Clarence Badger ***Prod*** B. P. Schulberg ***Scr*** Hope Loring, Louis D. Lighton, George Marion, Jr., Elinor Glyn ***Ph*** H. Kinley Martin ***Ed*** E. Lloyd Sheldon
Act Clara Bow, Antonio Moreno, William Austin, Jacqueline Gadsdon, Julia Swayne Gordon, Gary Cooper (Paramount)

It is one of those pretty little Cinderella stories where the poor shop girl marries the wealthy owner of the big department store in which she works. Elinor Glyn makes her debut as a picture actress.

But you can't get away from this Clara Bow girl. She certainly has that certain "It" for which the picture is named, and she just runs away with the film.

Antonio Moreno looks just about old enough to fall for the Bow type of flapper, in fact, just a little too old and ready to fall. William Austin is immense and furnishes the greater part of the laughs.

It starts in a department store, where the father has just turned the business over to the son. His pal comes in to congratulate him and makes a tour of inspection with him. He is all het up over the Glyn story of "It" in a magazine and starts looking for "It" among the shop girls, ending up with being sure that he has found "It" in Betty Lou (Bow).

•

ITALIAN JOB, THE
1969, 100 mins, UK col
Dir Peter Collinson ***Prod*** Michael Deeley ***Scr*** Troy Kennedy Martin ***Ph*** Douglas Slocombe ***Ed*** John Trumper ***Mus*** Quincy Jones ***Art*** Disley Jones
Act Michael Caine, Noel Coward, Benny Hill, Raf Vallone, Tony Beckley, Rossano Brazzi (Paramount/Oakhurst)

Michael Caine plays a minor crook who inherits, from a dead pal (Rossano Brazzi), the idea and key plan of a heist for landing a haul of $4 million in gold ingots from a security van in Turin, Italy. Scheme involves an elaborate way of throwing the Turin traffic into a colossal, chaotic tangle on which the robbery and get away depend.

The crime is bankrolled and masterminded by Noel Coward, a top criminal, from a London jail which he virtually controls with sybaratic authority. Caine's assembled gang of crooks seem a bumbling crowd, unfit to take on the Mafia, which is naturally taking a menacing interest in the scheme.

The cast does its stuff to good effect. Coward, as the highly patriotic, business-like master crook, brings all his imperturbable sense of irony and comedy to his role.

•

IT CAME FROM OUTER SPACE
1953, 80 mins, US b/w
Dir Jack Arnold ***Prod*** William Alland ***Scr*** Harry Essex ***Ph*** Clifford Stine ***Ed*** Paul Weatherwax ***Mus*** Joseph Gershenson (dir.) ***Art*** Bernard Herzbrun, Robert Boyle
Act Richard Carlson, Barbara Rush, Charles Drake, Russell Johnson, Kathleen Hughes, Joseph Sawyer (Universal)

Picture has been smartly fashioned to take advantage of all the tricks of science fiction and 3-D. Stereo process is not used as just an excuse to pelt an audience with flying objects and, with one exception, when missiles come out of the screen they are tied in logically with the story.

Direction by Jack Arnold whips up an air of suspense and there is considerable atmosphere of reality created, which stands up well enough if the logic of it all is not examined too closely. Some of the threat posed by the landing on earth of visitors from space is lessened when it is established the chance visitors intend no harm.

Otherwise, the Ray Bradbury story proves to be good science fiction. Yarn opens with Richard Carlson, a scientist, and Barbara Rush, his schoolteacher fiancée, observing the landing of a fiery object in the Arizona desert. At first believing it is a meteor, Carlson changes his opinion when he ventures into the crater. Strange things begin to happen in the community. Townspeople disappear and their likenesses are taken over by the space visitors.

Carlson is excellent as the scientist, and Rush makes an attractive partner. Charles Drake is good as the sheriff, and there are some excellent supporting performances.

•

IT COULD HAPPEN TO YOU
1994, 101 mins, US col
Dir Andrew Bergman ***Prod*** Mike Lobell ***Scr*** Jane Anderson ***Ph*** Caleb Deschanel ***Ed*** Barry Malkin ***Mus*** Carter Burwell ***Art*** Bill Groom
Act Nicolas Cage, Bridget Fonda, Rosie Perez, Wendell Pierce, Isaac Hayes, Seymour Cassel (Tri-Star)

Presented in fairy tale form—down to its awkward, "once upon a time" narrated introduction—cultivates and actually merits the designation "Capra-esque."

The simple premise (very loosely inspired by a true story) has affable New York cop Charlie (Nicolas Cage), finding himself short of cash and promising hard-luck, recently bankrupted waitress Yvonne (Bridget Fonda) that he'll split anything he wins from the lottery with her in lieu of a tip. The ticket turns out to be a $4 million winner and, much to the chagrin of his avaricious wife, Muriel (Rosie Perez), Charlie decides to honor his pledge.

As Muriel proceeds to ostentatiously spend the loot, the bond between Charlie and Yvonne grows, with the two sharing good deeds that range from doling out free subway tokens to entertaining neighborhood kids.

What really make the film are Bergman's general restraint despite the nature of the material, and the strong central performances. Cage and Fonda are extremely natural as the good-hearted lug and goodbye girl, while the squawking, raging Perez only needs to be fitted for a broomstick. Wendell Pierce also proves particularly likable as Charlie's partner, a cop with an affinity for the Knicks and carbohydrates.

•

IT HAPPENED AT THE WORLD'S FAIR
1963, 105 mins, US col
Dir Norman Taurog ***Prod*** Ted Richmond ***Scr*** Si Rose, Seaman Jacobs ***Ph*** Joseph Ruttenberg ***Ed*** Fredric Steinkamp ***Mus*** Leith Stevens ***Art*** George W. Davis, Preston Ames
Act Elvis Presley, Joan O'Brien, Gary Lockwood, Vicky Tiu, Edith Atwater, Yvonne Craig (M-G-M)

This is apt to be tedious going for all but the most confirmed of Presley's young admirers. The 10—count 'em—10 tunes [staged by Jack Baker] he sings may be cause for rejoicing among his more ardent followers but, stacked up proportionately against the skinny story in between, it seems at least three too many. Admitting the slim scenario, so many warbling interruptions upset the tempo of the yarn and prevent plot and picture from gathering momentum.

Screenplay springs off to a fairly bright start, thrusting "bush pilot" Presley and sidekick Gary Lockwood into several situations, airborne and earthbound, that have a fair humor content. Most of the action takes place at the 1962 Seattle Fair and vicinity, the yarn implicating Elvis with a temporarily abandoned type (Vicky Tiu) and a nifty nurse (Joan O'Brien).

Presley effortlessly executes his customary character—red-blooded wolf on the crust, clean-cut nice guy at the core. Lockwood, as his gambling chum, makes a good impression. O'Brien is easy to look at. Little Miss Tiu is tiu precious for words.

•

IT HAPPENED HERE
1964, 99 mins, UK b/w
Dir Kevin Brownlow, Andrew Mollo ***Prod*** Kevin Brownlow, Andrew Mollo ***Scr*** Kevin Brownlow, Andrew Mollo ***Ph*** Peter Suschitzky, Kevin Brownlow ***Ed*** Kevin Brownlow ***Mus*** Jack Beaver ***Art*** Andrew Mollo
Act Pauline Murray, Sebastian Shaw, Nicolette Bernard, Bart Allison, Stella Kemball, Fiona Leland (Rath)

It Happened Here tells the story of what might have happened had England been occupied by the Germans. The action takes place in 1943. There's also a story line going through. It centres on the experience of an English nurse who, in order to help, joins the Fascist-controlled Immediate Organization. She soon finds out that her uniform alienates those around her. She eventually tries to help a wounded partisan. Her action is discovered and she's punished for associating with "the other side."

The film shows brutality on both sides. Its message is that Nazism leads to violence everywhere. Film poses the question: can Nazism only be wiped out by Nazi methods?

But despite all controversy, film reveals a tremendous task. Compliments galore should go to the two young men who created it: Kevin Brownlow and Andrew Mollo, the former a professional film editor, the latter assistant director to Tony Richardson who, incidentally, contributed the money to complete the film.

It Happened Here is a non-professional feature, which began as an amateur project on 16mm, and remained so until financing was secured six years (!) after production had started. The early material was then "blown-up" and rest of the film was shot on standard 35mm. Most of the cast is non-professional. One is hardly aware of this. Film cost a mere $20,000.

•

IT HAPPENED IN BROOKLYN
1947, 102 mins, US b/w
Dir Richard Whorf ***Prod*** Jack Cummings ***Scr*** Isobel Lennart ***Ph*** Robert Planck ***Ed*** Blanche Sewell ***Mus*** Johnny Green ***Art*** Cedric Gibbons, Leonid Vasian
Act Frank Sinatra, Kathryn Grayson, Peter Lawford, Jimmy Durante, Gloria Grahame, Marcy McGuire (M-G-M)

Much of the lure will result from Frank Sinatra's presence in the cast. Guy's acquired the Bing Crosby knack of nonchalance, throwing away his gag lines with fine aplomb. He kids himself in a couple of hilarious sequences and does a takeoff on Jimmy Durante, with Durante aiding him, that's sockeroo.

Other stars also shine, although Durante has to struggle with some lines that don't do his particular brand of comedy too much good. Kathryn Grayson is beauteous and appealing as the love interest but the sound recording doesn't do her singing any good. Peter Lawford also makes out well and pulls a surprise with a jive rendition of a novelty tune "Whose Baby Are You?"

Isobel Lennart's nicely handled adaptation of an original story by John McGowan has Sinatra as a lonesome GI in London, thirsting for the Flatbush camaraderie. Before heading for home, he meets Lawford, young British nobleman whose longhair inclinations have made him a stuffed shirt, and tries to pull the Britisher out of his rut.

Back in Brooklyn, Sinatra returns to his old high school to check with his draft board and meets Grayson, the music teacher, plus Durante, the school's old-time janitor. Unable to find a room, he moves in with Durante, and begins falling in love with Grayson. Lawford appears on the scene and also immediately falls in love with Grayson.

Interspersed in the story are a group of six new tunes from the able pianos of Sammy Cahn and Jule Styne. Richard Whorf has directed the film with a light touch that gets the most out of the comedy situations. [Piano solos are played by Andre Previn.]

•

IT HAPPENED ONE NIGHT
1934, 105 mins, US b/w
Dir Frank Capra ***Prod*** Frank Capra ***Scr*** Robert Riskin ***Ph*** Joseph Walker ***Ed*** Gene Havlick ***Mus*** Louis Silvers (dir.) ***Art*** Stephen Goosson
Act Clark Gable, Claudette Colbert, Walter Connolly, Roscoe Karns, Jameson Thomas, Alan Hale (Columbia)

The story [by Samuel Hopkins Adams] has that intangible quality of charm that arises from a smooth blending of the various ingredients. It starts off to be another long-distance bus story, but they get out of the bus before it palls.

Plot is a simple one. The headstrong but very charming daughter of a millionaire marries a suitor of whom her father does not approve. She quarrels with her father on the yacht off Miami, and the girl goes over the rail. She seeks to make her way to New York, with the old man raising the hue and cry. Clark Gable who has just been fired from his Florida correspondent's job, is on the same bus.

But the author would have been nowhere without the deft direction of Frank Capra and the spirited and good-humored acting of the stars and practically most of their support. Walter Connolly is the only other player to get much of a show, but there are a dozen with bit parts well played.

Claudette Colbert makes hers a very delightful assignment and Gable swings along at sustained speed. Both play as though they really like their characters, and therein lies much of the charm.

1934: Best Picture, Director, Actor (Clark Gable), Actress (Claudette Colbert), Adaptation

•

IT HAPPENED TOMORROW
1944, 84 mins, US b/w
Dir Rene Clair ***Prod*** Arnold Pressburger ***Scr*** Dudley Nichols, Rene Clair ***Ph*** Archie J. Stout ***Ed*** Fred Pressburger ***Mus*** Robert Stolz ***Art*** Erno Metzner
Act Dick Powell, Linda Darnell, Jack Oakie, Edgar Kennedy, Edward Brophy, George Cleveland (United Artists)

It Happened Tomorrow poses a novel premise on which to spin a comedy-drama—what happens when a cub reporter gets a copy of tomorrow's newspaper. Results provide diverting escapist entertainment, with many sparkling moments and episodes along the line.

Although there are numerous broadly sketched sequences aimed for laugh reaction, picture carries undercurrent of Continental directing technique of Rene Clair. The welding is more than passably successful, but main credit for picture's status can be handed to script by Clair and Dudley Nichols [based on "originals" by Lord Dunsany, Hugh Wedlock and Howard Snyder, and ideas of Lewis R. Foster]; it picks up every chance for a chuckle or laugh in both dialog and situation.

Dick Powell, cub on the sheet, is befriended by the rag's veteran librarian who, after death, hands the youth copies of the next day's paper for three successive days.

Interwoven is his meeting and quick romance with Linda Darnell, medium and niece of mind reader Jack Oakie.

1944: NOMINATIONS: Best Scoring of a Dramatic Picture, Sound

•

I, THE JURY
1953, 87 mins, US b/w
Dir Harry Essex ***Prod*** Victor Saville ***Scr*** Harry Essex ***Ph*** John Alton ***Ed*** Fredrick Y. Smith ***Mus*** Franz Waxman ***Art*** Wiard Ihnen
Act Biff Elliot, Preston Foster, Peggie Castle, Margaret Sheridan, Alan Reed, Elisha Cook, Jr. (Parklane/United Artists)

Harry Essex both directed and wrote from Mickey Spillane's novel of the same title. The suspense element is not too strong, but such ingredients as brutal mob strong boys, effete art collectors with criminal tendencies, sexy femmes with more basic tendencies, and a series of unsolved killings, are mixed together in satisfactory quantities. The raw sex that is a prime feature of Spillane's book characters is less forthright on film.

Hardboiled private eye Mike Hammer traces the killer of a friend, uncovers some unsavory rackets while doing so and then shoots down the killer at the finale. The stereo lensing by John Alton is good, and without obvious 3-D trickery. Depth treatment and the Franz Waxman score are good assists for meller mood.

Picture introduces Biff Elliot as the sadistic Hammer, a character with a big chip on his shoulder. Elliot does okay by the assignment, although seemingly a bit less mature than readers may picture the book private eye. Peggie Castle, a psychiatrist, is the chief sex lure and is excellent. Preston Foster is competent as the police captain. Margaret Sheridan shows up in firstrate style as Hammer's secretary.

•

I, THE JURY
1982, 109 mins, US Ⓥ col
Dir Richard T. Heffron ***Prod*** Robert Solo ***Scr*** Larry Cohen ***Ph*** Andrew Laszlo ***Ed*** Garth Craven ***Mus*** Bill Conti ***Art*** Robert Gundlach
Act Armand Assante, Barbara Carrera, Laurene Landon, Alan King, Geoffrey Lewis, Paul Sorvino (American Cinema/Larco/Solofilm)

Almost 30 years after the first screen edition of Mickey Spillane's first Mike Hammer novel, the update of *I, the Jury* has all the updated violence, nudity, wit and style that was missing from the puritanical 1953 original.

By comparison, the souped up remake is hard as nails, with Armand Assante plausibly macho and ruggedly sexy as the amoral private eye who avenges the murder of his old Vietnam war buddy.

Scripter Larry Cohen's plotting is swift, suitably enigmatic and well stocked with well-stacked and well-exposed babes, of which the prime specimen is Barbara Carrera in an arousingly arranged seduction scene with Assante.

Carrera is just one of numerous villains as the operator of a not-to-be-believed sex therapy clinic. The ultimate heavy in this tangled tale is proficiently portrayed by Barry Snider as a former CIA operative whose computerized exurban fortress is penetrated by Hammer in a penultimate sequence of rousing action.

•

IT HURTS ONLY WHEN I LAUGH
SEE: ONLY WHEN I LAUGH

•

IT LIVES AGAIN
1978, 91 mins, US Ⓥ col
Dir Larry Cohen ***Prod*** Larry Cohen ***Scr*** Larry Cohen ***Ph*** Fenton Hamilton ***Ed*** Curt Burch, Louis Friedman, Carol O'Blath ***Mus*** Bernard Herrmann, Laurie Johnson
Act Frederic Forrest, Kathleen Lloyd, John P. Ryan, John Marley, Andrew Duggan, Eddie Constantine (Warner)

In his sequel to *It's Alive*, Larry Cohen aims squarely at the same audience, which should be attracted back for more of the murderous babies.

As in the original, producer-director-writer Cohen does not show a lot of the demonic infants nor explain what they really are. But whatever got into the blood of the first mom is now rampant through the country and they're aborning everywhere, threatening the survival of humanity. Though this is all so much silliness, Cohen effectively uses a good cast topped by Frederic Forrest and Kathleen Lloyd to build up suspense for the slashing, growling attacks by the terrible tykes.

Since the babies are fairly defenseless, except at close range, Cohen must go to ridiculous lengths to get his well-armed characters into vulnerable positions, wrapping up with a totally absurd police siege. When the kids are about to bite, though, it's good horror-house fun.

•

IT'S A GIFT
1935, 73 mins, US Ⓥ ⊙ b/w
Dir Norman Z. McLeod ***Prod*** William LeBaron ***Scr*** Jack Cunningham, Charles Bogle [= W. C. Fields], J. P. McEvoy ***Ph*** Henry Sharp ***Art*** Hans Dreier, John B. Goodman
Act W. C. Fields, Jean Rouverol, Julian Madison, Kathleen Howard, Tammany Young, Baby LeRoy (Paramount)

Practically a comedy monolog for W. C. Fields, with little help from a number of others. No plot, no suspense; rather coarse-grained in spots, but packing a load of belly laughs for people who like that sort of humor.

The plot is merely that Fields buys a California orange grove and drives the family out in the car. It's a bit of desert in between the other groves, but Fields is tipped off that it's vital to the building of a racetrack, so he gets $40,000 and a real grove.

Fields holds the screen about 80 percent of the time, which is just as well since no one else is given anything. Kathleen Howard acts the bossy wife with main strength.

•

IT'S ALIVE
1974, 90 mins, US Ⓥ col
Dir Larry Cohen ***Prod*** Larry Cohen ***Scr*** Larry Cohen ***Ph*** Fenton Hamilton ***Ed*** Peter Honess ***Mus*** Bernard Herrmann
Act John Ryan, Sharon Farrell, Andrew Duggan, Guy Stockwell, James Dixon, Michael Ansara (Larco)

This stomach-churning little film is a "Son of the Exorcist" horror pic about a monstrous newborn baby who goes on a murder rampage through L.A. before being blown to smithereens in a police ambush.

Bernard Herrmann's score, while not one of his most memorable, is highly effective in creating tension, but one wonders why an artist of his caliber lowered himself into such muck.

Script sidesteps an answer to what caused the aberration in the womb of Sharon Farrell. Hubby John Ryan feels vaguely guilty, and his earlier contemplation of an abortion is thrown back in his face.

The far-fetched rampage by the fleetingly-glimpsed infant gives director Larry Cohen the chance to shoot a few technically interesting scenes.

•

IT'S ALL HAPPENING
1963, 101 mins, UK col
Dir Don Sharp ***Prod*** Norman Williams ***Scr*** Leigh Vance ***Ph*** Ken Higgins ***Ed*** John Jympson ***Mus*** Philip Green ***Art*** Scott MacGregor
Act Tommy Steele, Michael Medwin, Angela Douglas, Jean Harvey, Walter Hudd, Bernard Bresslaw (Magna/British Lion)

The warmly exuberant personality of Tommy Steele, plus some polished, slick performances by guest top pop United Kingdom artists, solidly jacks up a lazy, old-fashioned and flabby screenplay by Leigh Vance.

Director Don Sharp brought the whole thing to screen in under six weeks shooting at a cost of around $430,000, most of which has clearly gone to artists' fees.

Steele plays an a&r man who was brought up in an orphanage, spends every afternoon playing uncle to the kids at the home and eventually mounts a benefit show for them. Other muzzy sidelines, such as a slight romance, get lost. Situation allows a number of guest artists to do their warbling stuff, both in recording studio and on "The Night." The final concert strays into the old never-never land of British pop music pix.

Outstanding contributions are made by Danny Williams, a stylish negro singer with a hint of Harry Belafonte about him, singing "Day without You," Marion Ryan, singing and dancing with Steele, a sharp number called "Maximum Plus," Dick Kalmann and the George Mitchell singers and dancers putting over a production number called "Summertime."

The Norman Newell–Philip Green score is the greatest aid to Steele.

•

IT'S ALL TRUE
1993, 85 mins, France Ⓥ col
Dir Richard Wilson, Myron Meisel, Bill Krohn ***Prod*** Regine Konckier, Richard Wilson, Bill Krohn, ***Scr*** Bill Krohn, Richard Wilson, Myron Meisel, Jean-Luc Ormieres ***Ph*** Gary Graver ***Ed*** Ed Marx ***Mus*** Jorge Arriagada

After 51 years in limbo as one of the most legendary of all "lost" films, Orson Welles's *It's All True* finally emerges in lovingly resurrected partial form within the framework of a documentary about Welles's entire 1942 Latin American misadventure.

French-backed docu is essentially divided into two parts. First half-hour effectively sketches the events surrounding Welles's trip to Brazil to shoot a major documentary as part of the U.S. government's Good Neighbor Policy at the start of World War II. Nearly an hour is then devoted to the presentation of *Four Men on a Raft*, which was to have been the centerpiece of Welles's never-finished, multi-part docu.

The scene is set by Welles himself in excerpts from various interviews, as well as by numerous collaborators, including lenser Joseph Biroc, assistants Shifra Haran and Elizabeth Wilson, and associate producer Richard Wilson, who devoted many years to the current project before his death in 1991.

The boy wonder was just 26, flush with the acclaim and controversy of *Citizen Kane*, when he left for Brazil literally the day after wrapping his second film, *The Magnificent Ambersons*. Welles wanted to trace the origins of the samba. In the midst of a management change, RKO ordered Welles to stop shooting, and cut 45 minutes out of *Ambersons* behind his back.

Offering snippets of colorful Carnival material and an entire sequence from another intended *It's All True* episode, *My Friend Bonito*, which was directed under Welles's supervision by Norman Foster in Mexico, the filmmakers, remarkably, have been able to reconstitute *Four Men on a Raft* virtually intact. Story recounts the astonishing two-month journey of four fishermen on a tiny raft from Fortaleza, on Brazil's northeast coast, 1,650 miles to Rio, where they successfully pleaded for social benefits for all Brazilian fishermen.

•

IT'S ALWAYS FAIR WEATHER
1955, 104 mins, US Ⓥ ⊙ ▭ col
Dir Gene Kelly, Stanley Donen ***Prod*** Arthur Freed ***Scr*** Betty Comden, Adolph Green ***Ph*** Robert Bronner ***Ed*** Adrienne Fazan ***Mus*** Andre Previn ***Art*** Cedric Gibbons, Arthur Lonergan
Act Gene Kelly, Dan Dailey, Cyd Charisse, Dolores Gray, Michael Kidd, David Burns (M-G-M)

As well as spoofing television, *It's Always Fair Weather* takes on advertising agencies and TV commercials, and what emerges is a delightful musical satire.

Betty Comden and Adolph Green, vet scripters of both Broadway and film tuners, present Gene Kelly, Dan Dailey, and Michael Kidd as a trio of former GI buddies who meet 10 years after World War II. Somehow the warm friendship that existed during the war years has deteriorated into a sour reunion as different interests have driven the buddies apart.

Dolores Gray, as the temperamental, syrupy hostess, registers excellently in appearance, emoting and warbling. Kidd, better known as a choreographer, emerges as a seasoned musicomedy performer.

Kelly, Dailey and Kidd score in group routines and Kelly and Dailey have a field day in solo outings. Kelly's roller skating routine and Dailey's drunk act at a chi-chi party are standouts. Cyd Charisse has only one terp routine, but she carries it off to perfection.

1955: NOMINATIONS: Best Story & Screenplay, Scoring of a Musical Picture,

•

IT'S A MAD MAD MAD MAD WORLD
1963, 190 mins, US Ⓥ ⊙ ▭ col
Dir Stanley Kramer ***Prod*** Stanley Kramer ***Scr*** William Rose, Tania Rose ***Ph*** Ernest Laszlo ***Ed*** Frederic Knudtson, Robert C. Jones, Gene Fowler, Jr. ***Mus*** Ernest Gold ***Art*** Rudolph Sternad
Act Spencer Tracy, Milton Berle, Sid Caesar, Mickey Rooney, Ethel Merman, Phil Silvers (United Artists)

It's a mad, mad, mad, mad picture. Being a picture of extravagant proportions, even its few flaws are king-sized, but the plusses outweigh by far the minuses. It is a throwback to the wild, wacky and wondrous time of the silent screen comedy, a kind of Keystone Kop Kaper with modern conveniences.

The plot is disarmingly simple. A group of people are given a clue by a dying man (Jimmy Durante) as to the whereabouts of a huge sum of money he has stolen and buried. Unable to come to a compromise in apportionment of the anticipated loot, each sets out for the roughly specified site of the buried cash, breaking his back to beat the others there. All are unaware that they are under secret surveillance by state police authorities, who are allowing them simply to lead the way to the money.

Nothing is done in moderation in this picture. All the stops are out. Nobody goes around what they can go over, under, through or into. Yet, as noted, the film is not without its flaws and oversights. Too often it tries to throw a wild haymaker where a simple left jab would be more apt to locate the desired target. Certain pratfalls and sequences are unneccessarily overdone to the point where they begin to grow tedious and reduce the impact of the whole.

An array of top-ranking comics has been rounded up by director Stanley Kramer, making this one of the most unorthodox and memorable casts on screen record. The comic competition is so keen that it is impossible to single out any one participant as outstanding.

1963: Best Sound Effects

NOMINATIONS: Best Color Cinematography, Editing, Original Music Score, Song ("It's a Mad Mad Mad Mad World"), Sound

•

IT'S A WONDERFUL LIFE

1946, 120 mins, US Ⓥ ⦿ b/w

Dir Frank Capra ***Prod*** Frank Capra ***Scr*** Frances Goodrich, Albert Hackett, Frank Capra, Jo Swerling ***Ph*** Joseph Walker, Joseph Biroc ***Ed*** William Hornbeck ***Mus*** Dimitri Tiomkin ***Art*** Jack Okey

Act James Stewart, Donna Reed, Lionel Barrymore, Thomas Mitchell, Henry Travers, Gloria Grahame (Liberty)

The tale [based on a story by Philip Van Doren Stern], flashbacked, is essentially simple. At 30, a small-town citizen feels he has reached the end of his rope, mentally, morally, financially. All his plans all his life have gone awry. Through no fault of own he faces disgrace. If the world isn't against him, at least it has averted its face. As he contemplates suicide, Heaven speeds a guardian angel, a pixyish fellow of sly humor, to teach the despondent, most graphically, how worthwhile his life has been and what treasures, largely intangible, he does possess.

The recounting of this life is just about flawless in its tender and natural treatment; only possible thin carping could be that the ending is slightly overlong and a shade too cloying for all tastes.

James Stewart's lead is braced by a full fan-spread of shimmering support. In femme lead, Donna Reed reaches full-fledged stardom. As a Scrooge-like banker, Lionel Barrymore lends a lot of lustre. Thomas Mitchell especially is effective as lead's drunken uncle.

1946: NOMINATIONS: Best Picture, Director, Actor (James Stewart), Editing, Sound

•

IT'S A WONDERFUL WORLD

1939, 84 mins, US b/w

Dir W.S. Van Dyke ***Prod*** Frank Davis ***Scr*** Ben Hecht ***Ph*** Oliver T. Marsh ***Ed*** Harold F. Kress ***Mus*** Edward Ward ***Art*** Cedric Gibbons, Paul Groesse

Act Claudette Colbert, James Stewart, Guy Kibbee, Frances Drake, Nat Pendleton, Edgar Kennedy (M-G-M)

Metro saturates the screwball comedy type of picture with some pretty broad burlesque in *It's a Wonderful World.*

Claudette Colbert is a zany poetess in continual conflict and love with James Stewart. Story [an original by Ben Hecht and Herman J. Mankiewicz] is thinly laid foundation to provide the wacky and slapsticky situations and rapid-fire laugh dialog.

Stewart, a novice private detective, is assigned to watch millionaire Ernest Truex. Latter goes on a bender, and winds up convicted of a murder. Stewart is implicated, and escapes from the train en route to prison determined to solve the murder mystery and save his client. Kidnapping Colbert and requisitioning her car, Stewart runs through series of disguises—a Boy Scout leader, chauffeur, and actor.

W. S. Van Dyke presents the yarn with good humor and a let's-have-fun attitude.

•

IT SHOULD HAPPEN TO YOU

1954, 86 mins, US Ⓥ ⦿ b/w

Dir George Cukor ***Prod*** Fred Kohlmar ***Scr*** Garson Kanin ***Ph*** Charles Lang ***Ed*** Charles Nelson ***Mus*** Frederick Hollander

Act Judy Holliday, Peter Lawford, Jack Lemmon, Michael O'Shea, Vaughn Taylor, Connie Gilchrist (Columbia)

Judy Holliday is reunited with director George Cukor and scripter Garson Kanin, a trio that clicked big with *Born Yesterday*, and the laugh range is from soft titters to loud guffaws as Cukor's smartly timed direction sends the players through hilarious situations. Plot is about a small town girl who comes to the big city to make a name for herself. Fresh angles belt the risibilities while dialog is adult, almost racy at times.

As the Gladys Glover of the plot, Holliday has a romp for herself, and she gets major assists in the comedy from Peter Lawford and Jack Lemmon, making his major screen bow.

Gladys has a different angle to flashing her name in the best places. With her meager savings she rents a signboard on Columbus Circle and has her name emblazoned thereon. This quest for fame sets off a lot of repercussions. She becomes a television celebrity and is pursued romantically by Lawford. Also in the amatory chase is Lemmon, who has a hard time keeping his romance with the new celebrity on even keel.

1954: NOMINATION: Best B&W Costume Design

•

IT SHOULDN'T HAPPEN TO A DOG

1946, 70 mins, US b/w

Dir Herbert I. Leeds ***Prod*** William Girard ***Scr*** Eugene Ling, Frank Gabrielson ***Ph*** Glen MacWilliams ***Ed*** Fred J. Rode ***Mus*** David Buttolph ***Art*** James Basevi, Chester Gore

Act Carole Landis, Allyn Joslyn, Margo Woode, Henry Morgan, Jean Wallace, John Ireland (20th Century-Fox)

This film is a solid package of chuckle material. With Allyn Joslyn on the celluloid for the full running time, film is a fast mix of gay situations and bright gags with no letdown at any point.

Pat story of a newspaperman in dutch with his editor is given a screwball twist by the highly competent scripters who place a dog at the center of the plot. The canine, a Doberman Pinscher, closely heels Joslyn as a laugh-winner.

Joslyn plays a reporter victimized, by an April fool's joke, into scooping his rivals on a robbery that never took place. Stickup was allegedly performed by Carole Landis aided by the Doberman who terrorized a barkeep into forking over his receipts.

Joslyn gives full sway to his talents in this pic showing himself off as a maestro with the gag line. Landis, appearing in only a few sequences, is okay. The dog is great.

•

IT'S LOVE AGAIN

1936, 83 mins, UK Ⓥ b/w

Dir Victor Saville ***Prod*** [uncredited] ***Scr*** Marion Dix, Lesser Samuels, Austin Melford ***Ph*** Glen MacWilliams ***Ed*** Al Barnes ***Mus*** Louis Levy, Bretton Byrd ***Art*** Alfred Junge

Act Jessie Matthews, Robert Young, Sonnie Hale, Ernest Milton, Robb Wilton, Sara Allgood (Gaumont-British)

British-made picture has Jessie Matthews at her best. Matthews is the star, but the story [by Marion Dix] is based on rival columnists who invent people to make exclusive news.

Peter Carlton (Robert Young) invents a "Mrs. Smythe-Smythe," supposedly a tiger hunter from India, pursued by a maharajah. Matthews assumes the role of the nonexistent "Mrs. Smythe-Smythe" to strut her stuff and possibly get an opening on the stage. She does, but gives up the impersonation when Carlton's rival senses her disguise and threatens to expose her unless she gives him the inside track on scoops.

Matthews does a variety of dances [arranged by Buddy Bradley], one a mock Indian number in a striking, if scanty, costume. There is a big production number, less impressive, perhaps, than Hollywood numbers, but as well devised and given an unusual staging. Here the costume is full tights with sequins. There is another pretty dance bit in a park and a near society dance in a restaurant set.

Matthews carries her part well and sings several songs [by Sam Coslow and Harry Woods], a couple of which are not in perfect synchrony. Young is a personable columnist and Sonnie Hale, as his idea man, is handicapped by a drunk assignment.

•

IT'S LOVE I'M AFTER

1937, 90 mins, US b/w

Dir Archie Mayo ***Prod*** [Harry Joe Brown] ***Scr*** Casey Robinson ***Ph*** James Van Trees ***Ed*** Owen Marks ***Mus*** [Heinz Roemheld] ***Art*** Carl Jules Weyl

Act Leslie Howard, Bette Davis, Olivia de Havilland, Patric Knowles, Eric Blore, George Barbier (Warner)

Title is trite, but the picture is fresh, clever, excellently directed and produced; and acted by an ensemble that clicks from start to finish.

Leslie Howard and Bette Davis are Shakespearean stars. At the conclusion of a performance, a debutante (Olivia de Havilland) gushes her infatuated adoration for Howard, who senses the prospects of an adventure. Then the girl's fiancé puts in an appearance, appeals to the more generous side of the star and persuades him to become his weekend guest and cure the girl of her madness by behaving in a boorish manner.

Maurice Hanline wrote the original story. Casey Robinson built it into a scenario that sparkles with witty lines, farcical situations and just enough common sense and serious moments to balance perfectly.

Howard's part is possessed of unlimited chances for satiric points, none of which seem to have been missed. Eric Blore, as the star's alter ego and valet, is capital with his antics. De Havilland plays a straight part, and she does it excellently. Bette Davis is the understanding woman of the world, wise in her true estimates of the fickleness of men. The role is a distinct departure from the heavier type of things which she usually plays, and she reveals a fine sense of comedy.

•

IT'S MY LIFE

SEE: VIVRE SA VIE FILM EN DOUZE TABLEAUX

•

IT'S MY PARTY

1996, 110 mins, US Ⓥ col

Dir Randal Kleiser ***Prod*** Joel Thurm, Randal Kleiser ***Scr*** Randal Kleiser ***Ph*** Bernd Heinl ***Ed*** Ila Von Hasperg ***Mus*** Basil Poledouris ***Art*** Clark Hunter

Act Eric Roberts, Gregory Harrison, Lee Grant, Marlee Matlin, Paul Regina, Margaret Cho (Opala/United Artists)

Mixing comedy and drama, Randal Kleiser's *It's My Party* is an emotionally candid chronicle of a young gay man with AIDS who decides to terminate his life while still in control of his faculties. Pic feels like a highly personal work but is severely flawed because its narrative consists entirely of background detail, with no dramatic core to contain its multiple subplots and characters.

Nick Stark (Eric Roberts) is a successful young architect engaged in a long-term relationship with Brandon (Gregory Harrison), his handsome lover who's equally devoted to his filmmaking career. Nick finds out that he's HIV-positive and has a short time to live. He hosts a two-day farewell party to which he invites all his friends and family members. With its loose-knit screenplay, dozens of characters (some actors play themselves), overlapping dialogue and sound and other devices, *It's My Party* boasts an Altmanesque structure, but without Altman's savvy or wit. Once the core situation is established, the picture has nowhere to go.

One of the yarn's most interesting aspects is the contrast between Nick's biological family and his "real" family, a group of friends that includes Tony (Paul Regina), a former b.f., and Charlene (Margaret Cho).

It may be a tribute to superlative acting that Nick's blood family comes across as a loving, most caring unit, especially Nick's divorced mother, Amalia (Lee Grant), and his sensitive sister, Daphne (Marlee Matlin).

•

IT'S MY TURN

1980, 91 mins, US Ⓥ ⦿ col

Dir Claudia Weill ***Prod*** Martin Elfland ***Scr*** Eleanor Bergstein ***Ph*** Bill Butler ***Ed*** Byron Brandt, Marjorie Fowler, James Coblenz ***Mus*** Patrick Williams ***Art*** Jack Delovia

Act Jill Clayburgh, Michael Douglas, Charles Grodin, Beverly Garland, Steven Hill, Daniel Stern (Columbia/Rastar)

In her second feature, director Claudia Weill has managed to zero in on both the funny and tragic sides of falling in love while keeping the action moving and the story intact. If there is a tendency for the editing to be a bit choppy and the camera shots a tinge forced or unimaginative, Weill is a pro with actors.

Jill Clayburgh limns an offbeat but intellectually overachieving mathematics professor residing with perpetually humorous building developer Charles Grodin in Chicago. She quickly finds herself in the arms of Michael Douglas during a trip to New York.

Probably the most endearing aspect here is the way action so easily moves from screwball to intellectual humour and then on to numerous emotionally touching moments.

•

IT'$ ONLY MONEY

1962, 84 mins, b/w

Dir Frank Tashlin ***Prod*** Paul Jones ***Scr*** John Fenton Murray ***Ph*** W. Wallace Kelley ***Ed*** Arthur P. Schmidt ***Mus*** Walter Scharf (sup.) ***Art*** Hal Pereira, Tambi Larsen

Act Jerry Lewis, Joan O'Brien, Zachary Scott, Jack Weston, Jesse White, Mae Questel (York/Paramount)

Jerry Lewis is a would-be private eye undertaking to locate a missing heir who turns out to be himself in *It'$ Only Money*. Lewis is once again the slapstickler for laughs, as of old, sans imitations of Chaplin and Jolson, and when playing himself he plays best.

Lewis, herein, is television repairman Lester March, who has had an overdose of Mike Hammer paperback and yens to be a shamus, as is his friend Peter Flint (Jesse White). They hear about the quest for the missing scion of an electronics tycoon and set out to locate same. Turns out their quarry is none other than Lewis.

That's about the nub of the screenplay. It makes for a sturdy hook upon which to hang a frolicsome string of cinematic shenanigans ranging from Pearl White cliff-hanging and murderous hayhem as per Peter Lorre to the broadest burlesque on private detectiveness.

Mae Questel is an amusing character, a middle-aged Betty Boop who's looking for her late brother's long-lost son and at the same time awaiting her marriage to the family's attorney. Latter is played villainously in the broadest sense by Zachary Scott.

•

IT STARTED IN NAPLES
1960, 100 mins, US Ⓥ col
Dir Melville Shavelson ***Prod*** Jack Rose ***Scr*** Melville Shavelson, Jack Rose, Suso Cecchi D'Amico ***Ph*** Robert L. Surtees ***Ed*** Frank Bracht ***Mus*** Alessandro Cicognini, Carlo Savina ***Art*** Hal Pereira, Roland Anderson
Act Clark Cable, Sophia Loren, Vittorio De Sica, Marietto, Paolo Carlini, Claudio Ermelli (Paramount)

Within this charming pictorial study weaves a frothy, frank and irreverent comedy that stumbles, sputters and stammers when its stretches its one basic gag—American puritanism vs. Italian moral abandon—too far, but partially restores its equilibrium with a parting shot of irony.

The screenplay, from a story by Michael Pertwee and Jack Davies, deposits Philadelphia lawyer Clark Gable in Naples to settle the estate of his brother, recently deceased via an auto accident. What Gable discovers is that his brother's extra-legal spouse also perished in the mishap, leaving their 10-year-old son (Marietto) in the care of the wife's sister (Sophia Loren). While debating (in and out of court and courtship) the relative merits of a Philadelphia and Neapolitan environment for the child, Gable and Loren fall in love.

Both the script and Melville Shavelson's direction try too hard to make the film uproariously funny and risqué. When the wit flows naturally, it is a delight; when it strains, it pains.

Gable and Loren are a surprisingly effective and compatible comedy pair. The latter, more voluptuous than ever, is naturally at home in her native surroundings and gives a vigorous and amusing performance, even tackling a couple of nightclub song-and-dance routines with gusto. Vittorio De Sica is suave as Gable's roving-eyed, pulchritudinously influenced Italian attorney. Young Marietto, as the orphaned waif who smokes ciggies, guzzles wine and ogles the babes, is occasionally the victim of director's apparent desire to overpower the spectator with overly cute postures and smart quips.

1960: NOMINATION: Best Color Art Direction

•

IT STARTED WITH A KISS
1959, 103 mins, US ▭ col
Dir George Marshall ***Prod*** Aaron Rosenberg ***Scr*** Charles Lederer ***Ph*** Robert Bronner ***Ed*** John McSweeney, Jr. ***Mus*** Jeff Alexander ***Art*** Hans Peters, Urie McCleary
Act Glenn Ford, Debbie Reynolds, Eva Gabor, Gustavo Rojo, Fred Clark, Edgar Buchanan (Arcola/M-G-M)

It Started with a Kiss winds up in bed—a half dozen of them, spread from New York to Madrid, in this highly amusing, sex-motivated study of two physically suited newlyweds getting to know each other.

Glenn Ford plays an air force sergeant, and Debbie Reynolds plays a nightclub dancer who wants to marry a millionaire, which Ford is not. After one kiss, however, she judges he's worth a million dollars and within a few hours, they are man and wife. The next day he's moved out to Spain, and she follows, bringing along the $40,000 automobile he won in a raffle. On misunderstanding after she arrives, she's convinced their marriage is solely for physical reasons, and she demands a 30-day test during which time no bed tactics will be allowed.

Ford and Reynolds make an appealing twosome. As the befuddled sergeant, Ford is somewhere between the boy and the man, and he perfectly establishes his instincts and desires as always deserving of sympathy. Reynolds does much to make the audience despise her gold-digging ways and, at her moment of realization, she has no trouble at all in winning everyone back.

•

IT STARTED WITH EVE
1942, 90 mins, US b/w
Dir Henry Koster ***Prod*** Henry Koster, Joe Pasternak ***Scr*** Norman Krasna, Leo Townsend ***Ph*** Rudolph Mate ***Ed*** Bernard W. Burton ***Mus*** Hans J. Salter
Act Deanna Durbin, Charles Laughton, Robert Cummings, Guy Kibbee (Universal)

Expertly tailored to the combined talents of Deanna Durbin and Charles Laughton. *It Started with Eve* is a neatly devised romantic comedy drama. Story is one of those typical Cinderella tales, developed at a consistently fast pace, with plenty of spontaneous comedy exploding en route.

Laughton, crusty and cantankerous old millionaire, has the presses stopped, ready to toss his obit across the front pages. His son (Robert Cummings) suddenly arrives from a Mexican trip with his fiancée. Dying man insists on seeing the future wife, and when Cummings fails to locate her quickly, grabs a hatcheck girl (Durbin) as substitute. Miraculous recovery results from Durbin's visit, with Cummings getting into deep complications through necessity of continuing the duplicity—at the same time placating his fiancée.

Henry Koster gets the utmost out of Durbin's unsophisticated youthfulness, contrasting this effectively with the character performance of Laughton as the dictatorial tycoon for a slick piloting job.

1942: NOMINATION: Best Scoring of a Musical Picture

•

IT'S WONDERFUL TO BE YOUNG
SEE: THE YOUNG ONES

•

IT TAKES TWO
1995, 101 mins, US Ⓥ col
Dir Andy Tennant ***Prod*** James Orr, Jim Cruickshank ***Scr*** Deborah Dean Davis ***Ph*** Kenneth Zunder ***Ed*** Roger Bondelli ***Mus*** Sherman Foote, Ray Foote ***Art*** Edward Pisoni
Act Kirstie Alley, Steve Guttenberg, Mary-Kate Olsen, Ashley Olsen, Philip Bosco, Jane Sibbett (Rysher/Warner)

Quite simply, *It Takes Two* is just too cute for words. This contemporary spin on Mark Twain's public-domain *The Prince and the Pauper* and the less classic *The Parent Trap* from Disney is a tale of love and friendship and fun tied up in the niftiest little bow. Still, the film's underlying sentiment is conveyed effectively, if obviously. The hoary storyline presents Amanda (Mary Kate Olsen), a tough talking, streetwise nine-year-old orphan, in search of ideal foster parents. Her favored choice for mom is social worker Diane (Kirstie Alley).

Alyssa (Ashley Olsen) is the daughter of cellular phone magnate and widower Roger Callaway (Steve Guttenberg), who announces his engagement to shrill socialite Clarice Kensington (Jane Sibbett). The convenient juxtaposition finds the two young girls being crated off to upstate New York's (actually rural Ontario's) Lake Minocqua—Alyssa to a family estate and Amanda just across the lake at Camp Callaway for deprived kids.

Amanda winds up at the presumably haunted Callaway home on a dare just as Alyssa has run off rather than face the torture of the impending engagement party. Of course each of the twins is mistaken for the other. Neither writer nor director has the panache or skill to elevate this enlarged sitcom into graceful farce. It's really the charm and charisma of Alley and Guttenberg that keeps the film from total descent into cotton-candy sweetness.

•

IT!: THE TERROR FROM BEYOND SPACE
1958, 68 mins, US Ⓥ b/w
Dir Edward L. Cahn ***Prod*** Robert E. Kent ***Scr*** Jerome Bixby ***Ph*** Kenneth Peach, Sr. ***Ed*** Grant Whytock ***Mus*** Paul Sawtell, Bert Shefter ***Art*** William Glasgow
Act Marshall Thompson, Shawn Smith, Kim Spalding, Ann Doran, Richard Benedict, Ray Corrigan (Vogue)

"It" is a Martian by birth, a Frankenstein by instinct, and a copycat. The monster dies hard, brushing aside grenades, bullets, gas and an atomic pile, before snorting its last snort. It's old stuff, with only a slight twist.

Film starts some dozen years in the future [from 1958] with a disabled U.S. rocketship on Mars. Only one of the 10 space travellers has survived, and a second rocketship has landed to drag him back to Earth where he is to face a court-martial. The government is of the opinion the spaceman murdered his companions so he could hoard the food and stay alive until help arrived. But the accused swears the nine deaths came at the hands of a strange "It"-type monster.

Most of the film is spent aboard the second rocketship on its way to Earth, and, to spice up the trip, the monster has stowed away. It kills with a swat of its grisly hand, then sucks all available liquids from its victims.

None of the performances is outstanding. Ray "Crash" Corrigan makes a fetching monster. Technical credits are capable.

•

IVAN GROZNI
(IVAN THE TERRIBLE, PART I)
1944, 96 mins, USSR Ⓥ ⦿ b/w
Dir Sergei Eisenstein ***Scr*** Sergei Eisenstein ***Ph*** Eduard Tisse, Andrei Moskvin ***Ed*** Sergei Eisenstein ***Mus*** Sergei Prokofiev ***Art*** Isaak Shpinel, L. Naumova
Act Nikolai Cherkasov, Lyudmila Tselikovskaya, Serafima Birman, Pavel Kadochnikov, Mikhail Nazvanov, Vsevolod Pudovkin (Central Cinema)

Despite usual good Russian photography, a powerful score, a couple of nice performances and flashes of original direction, *Ivan the Terrible* has so much that is tiresome. It has so little action, and becomes so involved that the average history student hardly will recognize this glorified Ivan. Additionally, it has the ususal quota of Soviet propaganda. These heavy-handed propaganda slugs include bows to the common folks, the merchants and tradesmen, pleas for a strong Russia, united to face the world and halt foreign intrigue.

Yarn makes Ivan virtually a saint, and at least the final saviour of his people. Story hardly depicts him as the man known in history, and seldom as one of action. It never measures up to its initial premise or even its opening colorful coronation scene.

There's an impressive final scene where thousands of Ivan's friends follow him in the snow away from Moscow and his scheming enemies. But that sequence, like the battle scene and several others, never quite rises to its potentialities because of flighty direction or cutting, or a combination of both. Principal fault seems to lie in the fact that the producers fail to make up their minds as to whether it is a spectacle, a historical opus or a character study of Ivan.

On the credit side is a splendid score by Sergei Prokofiev, fairly good if spotty direction by Sergei Eisenstein, fine camerawork, and the superb character portrayal of Ivan by Nikolai Cherkasov.

•

IVAN GROZNI, II
(IVAN THE TERRIBLE, PART II: THE REVOLT OF THE BOYARS)
1958, 87 mins, USSR Ⓥ ⦿ col
Dir Sergei Eisenstein ***Scr*** Sergei Eisenstein ***Ph*** Eduard Tisse, Andrei Moskvin ***Ed*** Sergei Eisenstein ***Mus*** Sergei Prokofiev ***Art*** Isaak Shpinel, L. Naumova
Act Nikolai Cherkasov, Serafima Birman, Pavel Kadochnikov, Mikhail Zharov, Andrei Abrikosov, Aleksandr Mgebrov (Central Cinema)

Long withheld by Soviet officials, *Ivan the Terrible, Part II* is hardly an entertaining film. But it is well worth the time of students of history and the cinema. How Ivan, the first Russian czar, subdued a revolt of the boyars (members of an aristocratic order) is the story peg for this Sergei Eisenstein production.

Originally, Eisenstein planned a trilogy on Ivan but he died in 1948 after completing only two of the films. In the first, released in the U.S. in 1947, Ivan's cruel character was largely whitewashed and he was depicted a saint.

In the second film Eisenstein apparently chose to forget the party line and concentrate upon a searching character study of the czar who even killed his own son. His "indecisive" approach caused him to become the target of an officially inspired critical attack and Part II was banned for 12 years. Eisenstein subsequently "confessed" that he had been "idealogically defective."

Nikolai Cherkasov aptly conveys the tragic struggle from within that Ivan was unable to cope with. Less impressive is Serafima Birman's performance as the czar's aunt who plotted his death. Her wooden interpretation makes it heavy going for audiences. Pavel Kadochnikov is suitably doltish as an unwilling candidate for the czar's throne. Eisenstein as the director shows advantageously in a banquet scene, photographed in color (balance of footage is in black-and-white). Choreography in the sequence is a striking backdrop for the czar's crafty machinations. Throughout the film is a fine score by Sergei Prokofiev. [Pic was completed in 1946 but was first shown in Russia and abroad only in 1958.]

•

IVANHOE
1952, 107 mins, UK Ⓥ col
Dir Richard Thorpe ***Prod*** Pandro S. Berman ***Scr*** Noel Langley, Aeneas MacKenzie ***Ph*** Freddie Young ***Ed*** Frank Clarke ***Mus*** Miklos Rozsa ***Art*** Alfred Junge
Act Robert Taylor, Elizabeth Taylor, Joan Fontaine, George Sanders, Emlyn Williams, Robert Douglas (M-G-M)

Ivanhoe is a great romantic adventure, mounted extravagantly, crammed with action, and emerges as a spectacular feast.

Both the romance and the action are concentrated around Robert Taylor who, as Ivanhoe, is the courageous Saxon leader fighting for the liberation of King Richard from an Austrian prison and his restoration to the throne. Two women play an important part in his life. There is Rowena (Joan Fontaine), his father's ward, with whom he is in love;

and Rebecca (Elizabeth Taylor), daughter of the Jew who raises the ransom money. She is in love with him.

Taylor sets the pace with a virile contribution which is matched by George Sanders as his principal adversary. Fontaine contributes to all the requisite charm and understanding as Rowena.

1952: NOMINATIONS: Best Picture, Color Cinematography, Scoring of a Dramatic Picture

•

IVANOVO DYETSTVO
(MY NAME IS IVAN; IVAN'S CHILDHOOD)
1962, 97 mins, USSR b/w
Dir Andrei Tarkovsky ***Scr*** Vladimir Bogomolov, Mikhail Papava ***Ph*** Vadim Yusov ***Ed*** L. Feyginovoy ***Mus*** Vyacheslav Ovchinnikov
Act Kolya Burlayev, Valentin Zubkov, Nikolai Grinko, Yevgeni Zharikov, S. Krylov, V. Malyavina (Gorky)

This is a lyrical war pic like *Ballad of a Soldier* and *The Cranes are Flying*. Done in a flamboyant manner, it is saved by new director Andrei Tarkovsky's obvious deep feeling for the subject.

A 12-year-old boy (Kolya Burlayev) has seen his mother killed and has stayed behind to help the army by spying on the Germans. He is adopted by a captain who wants to send him off to school, but the boy rebels and comes back. Pic details his happy thoughts of his early life and his mother.

Also depicted is a captain's love for a young femme medical soldier. Heroics are kept down, but this has a rich use of camera editing and war's horror as well as its few acceptable features in making man more aware of himself.

Acting is smooth. The boy avoids any mawkishness, while technical credits are first-rate. It is a measured but moving look at war [from Vladimir Bogomolov's short story *Ivan*] through a marked child's eyes.

•

IVAN'S CHILDHOOD
SEE: IVANOVO DYETSTVO

•

IVAN THE TERRIBLE, PART 1
SEE: IVAN GROZNI

•

IVAN THE TERRIBLE, PART II: THE REVOLT OF THE BOYARS
SEE: IVAN GROZNI, II

•

I'VE HEARD THE MERMAIDS SINGING
1987, 81 mins, Canada Ⓥ ⦿ col
Dir Patricia Rozema ***Prod*** Patricia Rozema, Alexandra Raffe ***Scr*** Patricia Rozema ***Ph*** Douglas Koch ***Ed*** Patricia Rozema ***Mus*** Mark Korven ***Art*** Valanne Ridgeway
Act Sheila McCarthy, Paule Baillargeon, Ann-Marie McDonald, John Evans (Vos)

I've Heard The Mermaids Singing neatly blends film and video and comedy with serious undertones.

Plot centers on a klutzy and innocent temporary secretary (Sheila McCarthy) who is jobbed in at an art gallery run by an older femme, whom it is established quickly on takes a flagged fancy to her without the secretary cottoning on.

Living alone in cramped quarters, the secretary lives a fantasy life via deliberately grainy black-&-white scenes in which she flies through the air, walks on water and actually hears mermaids singing. Those sequences are soaringly portrayed with accompanying classical music [from Delibes's *Lakme*]. In other off-times, she observes daily life by taking photographs.

The secretary later discovers what appears to be the owner's own thrill-making canvases. Taking one of them, cleverly just a blaze of framed white light, the secretary hangs it in the gallery; it's heralded by the press, and the gallery owner attains fame. But the secretary is dejected because of the growing love affair between the two other women and rejection of her photos.

McCarthy, a waif-faced Canadian stage thesp in her first lead film role, gives a dynamic, strongly believable and constantly assured performance. She is ably assisted by Paule Baillargeon (the gallery owner).

•

IVORY HUNTER
SEE: WHERE NO VULTURES FLY

•

IVY
1947, 98 mins, US b/w
Dir Sam Wood ***Prod*** William Cameron Menzies ***Scr*** Charles Bennett ***Ph*** Russell Metty ***Ed*** Ralph Dawson ***Mus*** Daniele Amfitheatrof ***Art*** Richard Riedel
Act Joan Fontaine, Patric Knowles, Herbert Marshall, Cedric Hardwicke (Universal/Interwood)

Ivy is an entry in the murderous ladies cycle. William Cameron Menzies's production has an off-the-beaten path design that helps generate the melodramatic mood desired. Sets are small and players and settings are lensed from close range.

Cast performances are good, but reflect directorial obviousness. Joan Fontaine, in the title role, portrays mercenary femme who doesn't mind murder if it will get her what she wants. Star is gorgeously gowned and period costumers permit plenty of eye-attracting cleavage. Patric Knowles, Ivy's lover; Herbert Marshall, wealthy man for whom she has set her cap; and Richard Ney, her husband whom she poisons, are the top male contingent, all performing up to demands.

Period of the Marie Belloc Lowndes novel, *The Story of Ivy*, has been moved back to the turn of the century in England. Charles Bennett scripted the plot which opens with Ivy getting a hint of coming events from fortuneteller. Saddled with a lover and a husband, Ivy wants to be rid of both to take on a wealthy English gentleman. She poisons and husband and transfers blame to the lover.

•

I WAKE UP SCREAMING
1942, 81 mins, US Ⓥ b/w
Dir H. Bruce Humberstone ***Prod*** Milton Sperling ***Scr*** Dwight Taylor ***Ph*** Edward Cronjager ***Ed*** Robert Simpson ***Mus*** Cyril J. Mockridge (dir.) ***Art*** Richard Day, Nathan Juran
Act Betty Grable, Victor Mature, Carole Landis, Laird Cregar, William Gargan, Alan Mowbray (20th Century-Fox)

Most murder mysteries are B's regardless of budget, but this one is an exception to the rule. The director, H. Bruce Humberstone, has been equipped with a good script [from Steve Fisher's novel] and from his cast has obtained results that are all that may be asked in a murder meller with a romantic strain of more than ordinary strength.

Victor Mature plays in a tougher groove than usual. This time he's a sports promoter who is dogged by a detective who loses his girl (Carole Landis) when Mature takes her from obscurity and glamourizes her to the point where she wins a film contract. The murder of this girl then provides the premise for the remainder of the yarn. Betty Grable is enormously appealing here as the sister of the slain girl.

Dwight Taylor, who did the script, has dotted it with trenchant dialog. There isn't much comedy, but no more than the few laughs included are needed in this instance. Force of the melodramatic and romantic features of the yarn is sufficient.

•

I WALK ALONE
1948, 97 mins, US b/w
Dir Byron Haskin ***Prod*** Hal. B. Wallis ***Scr*** Charles Schnee ***Ph*** Leo Tover ***Ed*** Arthur Schmidt ***Mus*** Victor Young ***Art*** Hans Dreier, Franz Bachelin
Act Burt Lancaster, Lizabeth Scott, Kirk Douglas, Wendell Corey, Kristine Miller, George Rigaud (Paramount)

I Walk Alone is tight, hard-boiled melodrama. A number of unusually tough sequences are spotted. One, in particular, is bloody beating handed out to Burt Lancaster by a trio of bruisers who spare no punches. Another is the dark street stalking and gore-tinged death meted out to Wendell Corey.

There's a Rip Van Winkle angle to the plot, wherein a gangster returns from 14 years in prison to find that his former cronies now wear the garb of respectability and are in such pseudo-legit rackets as used cars, night clubs, etc. Charles Schnee's screenplay, from the play *Beggars Are Coming to Town* by Theodore Reeves, makes much of the basic story's flavor, although letting dialog run away with a few scenes.

Lancaster belts over his assignment as the former jailbird who returns from prison to find the parade has passed him by and that old friends have given him the double-cross. Melodrama develops as Lancaster plots to muscle in on Kirk Douglas's nitery.

Lizabeth Scott holds up her end capably as co-star, making role of nitery singer who falls for Lancaster after a cross from Douglas, believable. Douglas is a standout as the hood turned respectable and fighting a losing battle to hold his kingdom together against Lancaster's assault.

•

I WALKED WITH A ZOMBIE
1943, 69 mins, US Ⓥ ⦿ b/w
Dir Jacques Tourneur ***Prod*** Val Lewton ***Scr*** Curt Siodmak, Ardel Wray ***Ph*** J. Roy Hunt ***Ed*** Mark Robson ***Mus*** Roy Webb ***Art*** Albert S. D'Agostino, Walter E. Keller
Act Tom Conway, Frances Dee, James Ellison, Edith Barrett, Christine Gordon, James Bell (RKO)

I Walked with a Zombie fails to measure up to the horrific title. Film contains some terrifying passages, but is overcrowded with trite dialog and ponderous acting.

Scripters haven't particularly improved the Inez Wallace original [story], which hinges on the premise that West Indies voodoo priests actually can produce a "zombie," a live person unable to speak, hear or feel. Weird yarn has two half-brothers competing for the love of a girl, married to one of the pair, and their mother employing voodooism to send the girl into a robot-like existence.

With few exceptions, cast walks through the picture almost as dazed as the zombies. James Ellison makes a loud but totally ineffective "bad" brother. Frances Dee, as a comely nurse, tries to make sense in the inanimate proceedings. Tom Conway is terrifically British as the righteous brother, but inexcusably dull most of the time.

•

I WALK THE LINE
1970, 96 mins, US Ⓥ ▭ col
Dir John Frankenheimer ***Prod*** Harold D. Cohen ***Scr*** Alvin Sargent ***Ph*** David M. Walsh ***Ed*** Henry Berman ***Mus*** Johnny Cash ***Art*** Albert Brenner
Act Gregory Peck, Tuesday Weld, Estelle Parsons, Ralph Meeker, Lonny Chapman, Charles Durning (Columbia)

Like the Johnny Cash ballads that comprise its background scores and make an intangible emotional commentary on the story, *I Walk the Line* has an authentic, somber and gritty feel of life in the Tennessee back hills. Gregory Peck is the sheriff compromised by Tuesday Weld, moonshiner Ralph Meeker's nubile and sexually precocious daughter, and Estelle Parsons is Peck's desperate wife.

Each create thoroughly believable characters whose passions and individual codes are on a course of inevitable tragedy. Aesthetically, director John Frankenheimer has made an offbeat folk ballad that rings true to its people and setting.

Weld is striking as the moonshiner's daughter, capturing just the right accent and qualities of late teenage sensuality, amorality and dumb innocence to make her a fatal attraction for an older married man.

•

I WANT TO GO HOME
1989, 105 mins, France Ⓥ col
Dir Alain Resnais ***Prod*** Marin Karmitz ***Scr*** Jules Feiffer ***Ph*** Charlie Van Damme ***Ed*** Albert Jurgenson ***Mus*** John Kander ***Art*** Jacques Saulnier
Act Adolph Green, Gerard Depardieu, Linda Lavin, Laura Benson, Micheline Presle, Geraldine Chaplin (MK2/Films A2/La Sept)

Jules Feiffer and Alain Resnais make strange bedfellows—the product of their union is this stillborn satiric comedy about an American cartoonist in Paris.

Central character is a cantankerous American cartoonist, played as a likable kvetch by songwriter and musical comedy veteran Adolph Green. He is making his first trip abroad, accompanied by Linda Lavin, to attend an exhibition of comic strip art in which his work figures.

Green's real reason is to see his neurotic daughter (Laura Benson), who's fled uncivilized Cleveland to enroll as a literature student at the Sorbonne. Mad about Flaubert, she has become starry-eyed before her evasive professor Gerard Depardieu, who happens to be a comic-book fan and one of Green's most ardent admirers.

Depardieu drags the flattered Green and Lavin to the posh country manor of his mother Micheline Presle, who indulges her son's obsessive Yank-collecting.

The performances are broad Broadway. Depardieu, in his first English-speaking part, knows how to charm with blithe timing but the role never grows beyond the cultural stereotype of the philandering Paris intellectual.

•

I WANT TO LIVE!
1958, 120 mins, US Ⓥ b/w
Dir Robert Wise ***Prod*** Walter Wanger ***Scr*** Nelson Gidding, Don M. Mankiewicz ***Ph*** Lionel Lindon ***Ed*** William Hornbeck ***Mus*** Johnny Mandel ***Art*** Edward Haworth
Act Susan Hayward, Simon Oakland, Virginia Vincent, Theodore Bikel, Wesley Lau, Philip Coolidge (United Artists/Figaro)

I Want to Live! is a drama dealing with the last years and the execution of Barbara Graham (Susan Hayward), who was convicted at one time or another of prostitution, perjury, forgery and murder. It is a damning indictment of capital punishment.

There is no attempt to gloss the character of Barbara Graham, only an effort to understand it through some fine irony and pathos. She had no hesitation about indulging in any form of crime or vice that promised excitement on her own, rather mean, terms. The screenplay is based on newspaper and magazine articles by San Francisco reporter Ed Montgomery, and on letters written by the woman herself. Its premise is that she was likely innocent of the vicious murder for which she was executed in the California gas chamber.

The final 30–40 minutes of the film are a purposely understated account of the mechanics involved in the state's legal destruction of life. The execution sequence is almost unbearable, mounting unswervingly in its intensity.

Hayward brings off this complex characterization. Simon Oakland, as Montgomery, who first crucified Barbara Graham in print and then attempted to undo what he had done, underplays his role with assurance.

1958: Best Actress (Susan Hayward)

NOMINATIONS: Best Director, Adapted Screenplay, B&W Cinematography, Editing, Sound

•

I WAS A COMMUNIST FOR THE F.B.I.

1951, 82 mins, US b/w

Dir Gordon Douglas ***Prod*** Bryan Foy ***Scr*** Crane Wilbur ***Ph*** Edwin B. DuPar ***Ed*** Folmar Blangsted ***Art*** Leo K. Kuter

Act Frank Lovejoy, Dorothy Hart, Philip Carey, James Millican, Richard Webb, Konstantin Shayne (Warner)

From the real life experiences of Matt Cvetic [published in the *Saturday Evening Post* as "I Posed as a Communist for the F.B.I"], scripter Crane Wilbur has fashioned an exciting film. Direction of Gordon Douglas plays up suspense and pace strongly, and the cast, headed by Frank Lovejoy in the title role, punches over the exposé of the Communist menace.

Cvetic's story is that of a man who, for nine years, was a member of the Commie party so he could gather information for the FBI. His informer role was made all the harder because his patriotic brothers and young son hated him for the Red taint. Picture picks up the double life as Gerhardt Eisler comes to Pittsburgh to ready the Red cell for strike violence and racial hatred.

Excitement and suspense are set up in the many near-escapes from exposure that Lovejoy goes through before he completes his job by revealing Commies and their activities before the UnAmerican Activities Committee. There's a brief touch of romance, too, in the person of Dorothy Hart, a card-carrying schoolteacher who finally sees the light and is saved from Commie reprisal by Lovejoy.

•

I WAS A MALE WAR BRIDE
(UK: YOU CAN'T SLEEP HERE)

1949, 105 mins, US b/w

Dir Howard Hawks ***Prod*** Sol C. Siegel ***Scr*** Charles Lederer, Leonard Spigelgass, Hagar Wilde ***Ph*** Norbert Brodine, Osmond Borrodaile ***Ed*** James B. Clark ***Mus*** Cyril J. Mockridge

Act Cary Grant, Ann Sheridan, Marion Marshall, Randy Stuart, William Neff, Ken Tobey (20th Century-Fox)

Title describes the story perfectly. Cary Grant is a French army officer who, after the war, marries Ann Sheridan, playing a WAC officer. From then on it's a tale of Grant's attempts to get back to the U.S. with his wife by joining a contingent of war brides.

Picture's chief failing, if it can be called that in view of the frothy components, is that the entire production crew, from scripters to director Howard Hawks and the cast, were apparently so intent on getting the maximum in yocks that they overlooked the necessary characterizations.

Story was filmed for the most part in Germany, until illness of the stars and several of the supporting players forced their return to Hollywood, where the remaining interiors were lensed. Illness, however, did not hamper the cast's cavortings.

•

I WAS A SPY

1933, 90 mins, UK Ⓥ b/w

Dir Victor Saville ***Prod*** Michael Balcon ***Scr*** W. P. Lipscomb, Ian Hay ***Ph*** Charles Van Enger ***Ed*** Frederick Y. Smith ***Art*** Alfred Junge

Act Madeleine Carroll, Conrad Veidt, Edmund Gwenn, Herbert Marshall, Donald Calthrop, Gerald du Maurier (Gaumont-British)

Story is based on the life of Martha Cnockhaert, a Belgian girl who was an Allied spy in the [First] World War. A reproduction of the Belgian village, where most of the action takes place, is most realistic, and the German troops of occupation, headed by Kommandant Conrad Veidt, are fine. Their military equipment is remarkable.

The acting honors go to Madeleine Carroll as the fine-spirited young girl. Veidt as the head of the German troops looks his part; Edmund Gwenn makes a realistic burgomaster; and Herbert Marshall is a first-rate Herbert Marshall.

•

I WAS A TEENAGE WEREWOLF

1957, 76 mins, US Ⓥ b/w

Dir Gene Fowler, Jr. ***Prod*** Herman Cohen ***Scr*** Ralph Thornton ***Ph*** Joseph LaShelle ***Ed*** George Gittens ***Mus*** Paul Dunlap

Act Michael Landon, Yvonne Lime, Whit Bissell, Tony Marshall, Dawn Richard, Barney Phillips (American International)

Only thing new about this combo teenager and science fiction yarn is a psychiatrist's use of a problem teenager who comes to him for help using the youth for an experiment in regression, but it's handled well enough to meet the requirements of this type of film.

There are plenty of story points that are sloughed over in the screenplay, but good performances help overcome deficiencies. Final reels, when the lad turns into a hairy-headed monster with drooling fangs, are inclined to be played too heavily.

Michael Landon delivers a first-class characterization as the high school boy constantly in trouble, and has okay support right down the line. Yvonne Lime is pretty as his girl friend who asks him to go to the psychiatrist, and Whit Bissell handles doctor part capably, although some of his lines are pretty thick.

•

I WAS HAPPY HERE
(US: TIME LOST AND TIME REMEMBERED)

1966, 91 mins, UK b/w

Dir Desmond Davis ***Prod*** Roy Millichip ***Scr*** Edna O'Brien, Desmond Davis ***Ph*** Manny Wynn ***Ed*** Brian Smedley-Aston ***Mus*** John Addison ***Art*** Tony Woollard

Act Sarah Miles, Cyril Cusack, Julian Glover, Sean Caffrey, Marie Kean, Cardew Robinson (Partisan)

Sarah Miles plays a girl who escapes from an Irish village to London, believing that her fisherboy sweetheart will follow her. He doesn't and Miles, lonely and unhappy in the big city, falls into a disastrous marriage with a pompous, boorish young doctor. After a Christmas Eve row, she rushes back to the Irish village, but is disillusioned when she finds that though the village has not changed, she has.

The story is told largely in flashback but Davis has skillfully woven the girl's thoughts and the present happenings by swift switching which, occasionally, is confusing but mostly is sharp and pertinent.

Miles gives a most convincing performance, a slick combo of wistful charm but with the femme guile never far below the surface. But Julian Glover makes heavy weather of his role as the girl's insufferable husband.

Filmed entirely on location in County Clare, Ireland, and London, the contrast between the peaceful, lonely sea-coast village and the less peaceful but equally lonely bustling London is artfully wed.

•

I WAS MONTY'S DOUBLE

1958, 100 mins, UK Ⓥ b/w

Dir John Guillermin ***Prod*** Maxwell Setton ***Scr*** Bryan Forbes ***Ph*** Basil Emmott ***Ed*** Max Benedict ***Mus*** John Addison ***Art*** W. E. Hutchinson

Act John Mills, Cecil Parker, M. E. Clifton James, Michael Hordern, Marius Goring, Vera Day (Associated British)

I Was Monty's Double tells about a great and important wartime hoax, almost incredible in its audacity. Clifton James, a small-time stock actor serving as a junior officer in the Royal Army Pays Corps, bore a startling resemblance to General Montgomery. This was used in a daring scheme devised by Army Intelligence to persuade the Germans that the forthcoming Allies' invasion might well take place on the North African coast.

The deception proved so successful that the enemy moved several divisions to the North African coast, a move which helped the actual invasion tremendously. The film has several moments of real tension. Plenty of news footage has been woven into the pic and it has been done with commendable ingenuity. Bryan Forbes's taut screenplay [based on James's book] is liberally spiced with humor. James plays both himself and Montgomery. Apart from his uncanny resemblance to Monty, James shows himself to be a resourceful actor in his own right.

•

I WILL . . . I WILL . . . FOR NOW

1976, 107 mins, US Ⓥ ▭ col

Dir Norman Panama ***Prod*** George Barrie ***Scr*** Norman Panama, Albert E. Lewin ***Ph*** John A. Alonzo ***Ed*** Robert Lawrence ***Mus*** John Cameron ***Art*** Fernando Carrere

Act Elliott Gould, Diane Keaton, Paul Sorvino, Victoria Principal, Robert Alda, Warren Berlinger (Brut)

I Will . . . I Will . . . For Now is passable fluff. Elliott Gould and Diane Keaton (as unhappy marriage/divorce partners), their less-than-disinterested lawyer Paul Sorvino, and condominium sexpot Victoria Principal, star.

Story finds horny Gould jealous that divorced wife Keaton has a lover, but he doesn't know it's Sorvino. When Keaton's sister Candy Clark has a modern contract-type marriage, pair decide to try life again under that new form, drafted with an eye to self-destruction by Sorvino.

Principal and her distant husband Warren Berlinger supply the formula comedy when couples get rooms mixed up in chic sex clinic run by Robert Alda and Madge Sinclair.

JABBERWOCKY

1977, 100 mins, UK Ⓥ ⊙ col

Dir Terry Gilliam ***Prod*** Sandy Lieberson ***Scr*** Terry Gilliam, Charles Alverson ***Ph*** Terry Bedford ***Ed*** Michael Bradsell ***Mus*** De Wolfe ***Art*** Roy Smith

Act Michael Palin, Harry H. Corbett, John Le Mesurier, Warren Mitchell, Max Wall, Deborah Fallender (Umbrella/White)

A Monty Python splinter faction bears responsibility for *Jabberwocky*, a medieval farce based on a Lewis Carroll poem. Film is long on jabber but short on yocks.

Ex-Pythonite Terry Gilliam directed and coscripted. Michael Palin is well-cast as a bumpkin who threads his way through jousting knights, grubby peasants, "drag" nuns and damsels both fair and plump to become the inadvertent hero who slays the vile monster menacing Max Wall's cartoon kingdom. The monster, who doesn't appear till the final minutes, is a work of inspired dark imagination.

Film goes for gags instead of sustained satire, including several typically English lavatorial jokes and also some repulsively bloody ones.

Some of the slapstick works okay but at a very intermittent pace in a mishmash scenario.

•

JACK

1996, 113 mins, US Ⓥ ⊙ col

Dir Francis Coppola ***Prod*** Ricardo Mestres, Fred Fuchs, Francis Coppola ***Scr*** James DeMonaco, Gary Nadeau ***Ph*** John Toll ***Ed*** Barry Malkin ***Mus*** Michael Kamen ***Art*** Angelo Graham

Act Robin Williams, Diane Lane, Jennifer Lopez, Brian Kerwin, Fran Drescher, Bill Cosby (Zoetrope/Great Oaks/Hollywood)

Surrounded by talent but with very little to do himself, Robin Williams delivers what is probably his first altogether tiresome performance. Something of a companion piece for Coppola to *Peggy Sue Got Married* in the mild, gentle way it deals with a fantastical "what if" situation. This new effort has just one thing to say and says it with no sense of surprise or drama.

Karen Powell (Diane Lane) inexplicably gives birth to a baby boy after just a 10-week pregnancy; ten years later, sprig Jack (Williams) is mentally and emotionally his own age but looks 40. Now that the folks have decided to send him to school, Jack and the real world are going to have to come to some understanding.

It's never explained whether Jack feels adult-like sexual stirrings, but when the big little man is turned down for a date by his teacher (Jennifer Lopez), he suffers some sort of heart seizure. He [later] heads out for a little tea and sympathy from dishy Dolores Durante (Fran Drescher), the very available mother of his best friend.

Pic's highlight by quite a margin is the nightclub scene, sparked by vibrant performances from Drescher and Michael McKean, the latter as a confession-prone stool-sitter. This gives Williams a rare opportunity to stretch emotively, and brings to mind the film that might have been.

•

JACKAL, THE

1997, 124 mins, US Ⓥ ⊙ ▭ col

Dir Michael Caton-Jones ***Prod*** James Jacks, Sean Daniel, Michael Caton-Jones, Kevin Jarre ***Scr*** Chuck Pfarrer ***Ph*** Karl Walter Lindenlaub ***Ed*** Jim Clark ***Mus*** Carter Burwell ***Art*** Michael White

Act Bruce Willis, Richard Gere, Sidney Poitier, Diane Venora, Tess Harper, Mathilda May (Alphaville/Mutual/Universal)

The Jackal scores as an involving high-tech thriller that occasionally hits peaks of pulsating excitement. Proficient without being genuinely inspired, and sometimes farfetched in its plotting, this is an exceedingly lavish updating of a well-known novel and film. [Screen credits mention Kenneth Ross's screenplay for Fred Zinnemann's 1973 *The Day of the Jackal*, but not Frederick Forsyth's novel.]

Current outing opens in the new Moscow, where FBI director Carter Preston (Sidney Poitier) joins with the Russians, led by intelligence officer Valentina Koslova (Diane Venore), in nailing an important Russian Mafia figure. In response, the criminal's brother declares war on the FBI and hires the Jackal (Bruce Willis) to take out a top American. He demands $70 million for his services.

The Jackal's solitary ways, skill with disguises and utter perfectionism make him difficult to identify, much less to track. The only people known to actually have met the Jackal are a former Basque terrorist (Mathilda May) and IRA operative Declan Mulqueen (Richard Gere), serving a prison sentence in the U.S. The Irishman is persuaded to help the American authorities.

The film's above-the-title star power burns brightest when the Jackal and Declan come face-to-face for the first time; Willis's and Gere's stares and body language do virtually all the talking before the guns start blazing.

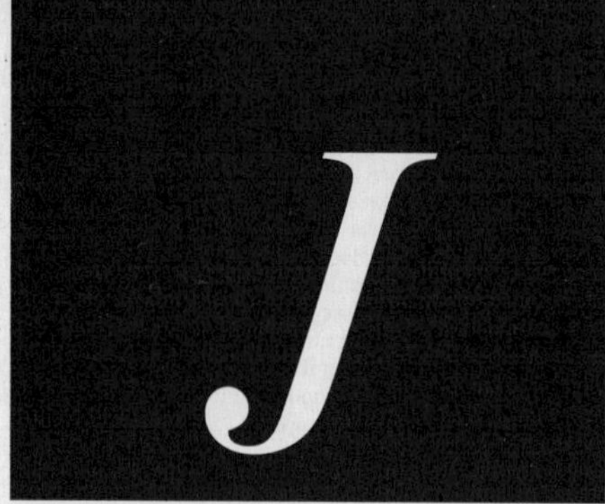

Pic has not one but two action climaxes, one at the very public assassination site and a subsequent chase and shootout in the Washington subway. Director Michael Caton-Jones handles all the physical incident and noose-tightening quite capably.

•

JACK & SARAH

1995, 110 mins, UK/France Ⓥ col

Dir Tim Sullivan ***Prod*** Pippa Cross, Simon Channing-Williams, Janette Day ***Scr*** Tim Sullivan ***Ph*** Jean Yves Escoffier ***Ed*** Lesley Walker ***Mus*** Simon Boswell ***Art*** Christopher J. Bradshaw

Act Richard E. Grant, Samantha Mathis, Judi Dench, Ian McKellen, Eileen Atkins, Cherie Lunghi (Granada/PolyGram/Mainstream)

Sparky playing, a generally sharp script and bright packaging add up to a neat little winner in the romantic comedy *Jack & Sarah*, a kind of *After Nine Months* London style.

Richard E. Grant plays Jack, a highly strung yuppie lawyer whose wife, Sarah (Imogen Stubbs), dies in childbirth. Jack names the sprig after his wife, but finds nappies and notarizing don't mix. His nosy mom (Judi Dench) and mom-in-law (Eileen Atkins) don't help either. Solution? A babysitter.

Enter Amy (Samantha Mathis), a bubbly, slightly klutzy young yank who likes kids but doesn't have any experience as a nanny. She moves in and an edgy friendship develops, with lotsa complications up to fade-out.

Delightful though she is, Mathis faces an uphill struggle establishing a foothold on the pic, which starts to tread water in midsection as the tone gets more serious. Grant is terrific as the obsessive self-centered yuppie. Other casting is flawless down the line.

•

JACK LONDON

1944, 92 mins, US Ⓥ b/w

Dir Alfred Santell ***Prod*** Samuel Bronston ***Scr*** Ernest Pascal ***Ph*** John W. Boyle ***Ed*** William Ziegler ***Mus*** Fred Rich

Act Michael O'Shea, Susan Hayward, Osa Massen, Virginia Mayo (United Artists)

Samuel Bronston has brought to the screen one of the great men of American letters, Jack London, and if ever there was a blood-and-guts subject for Hollywood treatment, London has long seemed a natural. But the play's still the thing. *Jack London*, an adaptation of a book written by the author's wife, Charmian, has much of the writer-adventurer's life crammed into its 92 minutes, but somewhere along the line it has missed fire.

One of the main snags to *London* is the fact that one of the film's two most important characters—Charmian London, the author's wife—fails to appear until the film has consumed half its running time. Susan Hayward is starred in the role, as is Michael O'Shea in the title part, and for a starred performer to be absent for that length of time is dangerous scripting and directing, let alone producing.

O'Shea, comparative newcomer to Hollywood from the Broadway stage, is miscast in the title role. His physique, for one, is not what one might expect of a two-fisted Jack London, and a couple of the scenes in which he delivers kayo blows are too obviously staged. His performance generally is uncertain.

1944: NOMINATION: Best Scoring of a Dramatic Picture

•

JACKNIFE

1989, 102 mins, US Ⓥ ⊙ col

Dir David Jones ***Prod*** Robert Schaffel, Carol Baum ***Scr*** Stephen Metcalfe ***Ph*** Brian West ***Ed*** John Bloom ***Mus*** Bruce Broughton ***Art*** Edward Pisoni

Act Robert De Niro, Ed Harris, Kathy Baker, Charles Dutton, Loudon Wainwright III (Kings Road/Sandollar-Schaffel)

Robert De Niro's tour de force turn as a feisty Vietnam vet fails to save *Jacknife*, a poorly scripted three-hander drama [from Stephen Metcalfe's play *Strange Snow*]. De Niro is Megs (alternately nicknamed Jacknife by his war buddy Bobby, who was killed in action), a burnout working as a Connecticut car repairman. He decides to get another war buddy, Dave (Ed Harris), to break out of his shell by forcing him to have a good time and remember those blocked-out adventures the trio had in 'Nam.

A romance eventually blossoms between Harris's high school teacher sister (Kathy Baker) and De Niro (with Harris opposing the alliance), leading to a prom night where she is the chaperone with De Niro her date; Harris violently disrupts the event.

Besides its romance of "little people," film's central treatment of the Vietnam hangover that hamstrings Harris's return to normal living proves to be flat and uninvolving.

De Niro is spectacular, bringing life to every scene he's in. Unfortunately, helmer David Jones, who had better luck with the Harold Pinter three-hander *Betrayal*, fails to generate much interest in the material.

•

JACKPOT, THE

1950, 85 mins, US Ⓥ b/w

Dir Walter Lang ***Prod*** Sam Engel ***Scr*** Phoebe Ephron, Henry Ephron ***Ph*** Joseph La Shelle ***Ed*** J. Watson Webb ***Mus*** Lionel Newman

Act James Stewart, Barbara Hale, Natalie Wood, James Gleason, Patricia Medina, Alan Mowbray (20th Century-Fox)

One basic gag situation is extended through the entire footage of *The Jackpot* but it doesn't seem overworked.

James Stewart is the pivotal character and handles the spot with amusing bewilderment. His frenzied attempts to sell his prizes won in a radio giveaway show, to meet the internal revenue demands (particularly the situation wherein he's peddling a wristwatch in a bookmaker's betting room when the cops pull a raid), make for clever laugh material. Barbara Hale meets all requirements as Stewart's wife, and there's competent support from all others.

•

JACKSON COUNTY JAIL

1976, 89 mins, US Ⓥ ⊙ col

Dir Michael Miller ***Prod*** Jeff Begun ***Scr*** Donald Stewart ***Ph*** Bruce Logan ***Ed*** Caroline Ferriol ***Mus*** Loren Newkirk ***Art*** Michael McCloskey

Act Yvette Mimieux, Tommy Lee Jones, Robert Carradine, Frederic Cook, Severn Darden, Howard Hesseman (New World)

Pic has a predictable, uncomplicated plot. A fashionable ad woman (Yvette Mimieux) leaves her career and her cheating lover behind in L.A., destination New York. Along the way, she gets beaten up by juvenile hitchhikers (Robert Carradine is one of them) who steal her car, leaving her stranded in some ambiguous western town where she's promptly thrown in jail on phony charges and raped by a psychotic jailkeeper.

She kills the jailkeeper and is forced to go on the lam with a rowdy but caring inmate (Tommy Lee Jones), a radical country boy who steals "because everyone is dishonest."

The after-effects of the rape are handled with more care than usual, and Mimieux turns in a convincing, well-controlled performance.

•

JACK THE BEAR

1993, 98 mins, US Ⓥ ⊙ ▭ col

Dir Marshall Herskovitz ***Prod*** Bruce Gilbert ***Scr*** Steven Zaillian ***Ph*** Fred Murphy ***Ed*** Steven Rosenblum ***Mus*** James Horner ***Art*** Lilly Kilvert

Act Danny DeVito, Robert J. Steinmiller Jr, Miko Hughes, Gary Sinise, Julia Louis-Dreyfus, Reese Witherspoon (American Filmworks/Lucky Dog)

Jack the Bear, a mostly likable first feature from *thirtysomething* co-creator Marshall Herskovitz, concerns a boy who discovers that monsters are to be found not only on television but also in real life. A clever portrayal of eccentric fatherhood by Danny DeVito and a socko performance from young Robert J. Steinmiller, Jr. as the eponymous hero are major assets.

Based on Dan McCall's 1974 tome, and set in suburban Oakland in 1972, film mixes comedy and horror to make its points about latent evil.

Twelve-year-old Jack (Steinmiller) and his younger brother Dylan (Miko Hughes) have moved here with their oddball father, John Leary (DeVito), after the death of their mother (Andrea Marcovicci, glimpsed only in stylized flashbacks). Leary gets a gig as host of a late-night show that recycles old horror movies. But he drinks too much and is often on the brink of losing his job.

The real menace is saved for the final act, when deranged war vet Strick (Gary Sinise) kidnaps Dylan and then, like some monster from a real horror flick, comes after Jack.

•

JACKIE BROWN
1997, 155 mins, US Ⓥ ⊙ col
Dir Quentin Tarantino ***Prod*** Lawrence Bender ***Scr*** Quentin Tarantino ***Ed*** Sally Menke ***Art*** David Wasco
Act Pam Grier, Samuel L. Jackson, Robert Forster, Bridget Fonda, Michael Keaton, Robert De Niro (A Band Apart/Miramax)

Quentin Tarantino treads turf that is both familiar and fresh in *Jackie Brown*. Too long, and lacking the snap and audaciousness of the two pictures that made him the talk of the town, this narratively faithful but conceptually imaginative adaptation of Elmore Leonard's 1995 novel *Rum Punch* nonetheless offers an abundance of pleasures, especially in characterization and atmosphere.

Transferring the action from Leonard's Miami to his own South Bay area of L.A. and changing the leading character from white to black, Tarantino takes his own sweet time setting the gears in motion.

Ordell Robbie (Samuel L. Jackson) is a very smooth and lethal arms dealer operating out of a Hermosa Beach pad he shares with always stoned surfer girl Melanie (Bridget Fonda). Hanging out with his longtime partner, Louis Gara (Robert De Niro), Ordell announces he intends to get out of the business after stashing away another 500 grand down in Mexico.

Trouble lands on Ordell's doorstep when mid-40s stewardess Jackie Brown ('70s blaxploitation icon Pam Grier) is busted at LAX by ATF agent Ray Nicolette (Michael Keaton) and cop Mark Dargus (Michael Bowen) while smuggling money into the country for him.

Middle-aged bail bondsman Max Cherry (Robert Forster) picks Jackie up at jail, falls hard for her, and eventually sets this woman with few options on a path that will see her playing the authorities and Ordell against each other.

Tarantino, in a 20-minute setpiece, stages an intricate money exchange three times from different points of view, each one revealing key aspects of the daredevil maneuver.

Pic suffers not only from overlength, but from a lack of dramatic peaks and valleys. Individually, scenes play wonderfully well but when laid end to end, tend to flatten out. Grier, who has aged beautifully, has tremendous poise. Jackson is superb as the loquacious gunrunner. Forster lends a wonderfully lived-in quality to the bail bondsman who's seen it all. Soundtrack is loaded with soul and funk hits.

1997: NOMINATION: Best Supp. Actor (Robert Forster)

•

JACOB'S LADDER
1990, 113 mins, US Ⓥ ⊙ col
Dir Adrian Lyne ***Prod*** Alan Marshall ***Scr*** Bruce Joel Rubin ***Ph*** Jeffrey L. Kimball ***Ed*** Tom Rolf, Peter Amundsun, B. J. Sears ***Mus*** Maurice Jarre ***Art*** Brian Morris
Act Tim Robbins, Elizabeth Pena, Danny Aiello, Matt Craven, Ving Rhames, Macaulay Culkin (Carolco)

Jacob's Ladder means to be a harrowing thriller about a Vietnam vet (Tim Robbins) bedeviled by strange visions, but the $40 million production is dull, unimaginative and pretentious.

Writer Bruce Joel Rubin (*Ghost*) telegraphs his plot developments and can't resist throwing in supernatural elements that prompt giggles at the most unfortunate moments. Right from the battlefield prolog in Vietnam, where members of Robbins's battalion act strangely and throw fits, it's clear that somebody messed with their brains.

Robbins, whose earnest and touching performance belongs in a better film, spends most of the story struggling to understand the "demons" pursuing him back home in NY.

Director Adrian Lyne adds nothing fresh visually or dramatically to previous film and TV depictions of troubled Viet vets' psyches.

Living in a dim, dingy apartment and working in a dronelike postal service job, Robbins was wrongly told by the army that he was discharged on psychological grounds. His very existence denied by the Veterans Administration, he thinks he's possessed, but eventually pieces together the truth with the help of his battalion buddies.

•

JACQUELINE SUSANN'S ONCE IS NOT ENOUGH
SEE: ONCE IS NOT ENOUGH

•

JADE
1995, 95 mins, US Ⓥ ⊙ col
Dir William Friedkin ***Prod*** Robert Evans, Craig Baumgarten, Gary Adelson ***Scr*** Joe Eszterhas ***Ph*** Andrzej Bartkowiak ***Ed*** Augie Hess ***Mus*** James Horner ***Art*** Alex Tavoularis
Act David Caruso, Linda Fiorentino, Chazz Palminteri, Michael Biehn, Richard Crenna, Donna Murphy (Paramount)

A muddled mix of sex, political corruption and murder, *Jade* is a jigsaw puzzle that never puts all the pieces together.

Director William Friedkin and writer Joe Eszterhas have traveled these streets before, as has Linda Fiorentino in her latest take on a sexy femme fatale and David Caruso in his second so-so feature outing as a leading man after walking away from *NYPD Blue*. This at best adequate entry's best moments tend to merely bring to mind similar scenes from more entertaining films.

Caruso plays David Corelli, a San Francisco prosecutor pulled away from a black-tie ball by word that a local millionaire has been brutally murdered. Gradually, some evidence begins to implicate Trina Gavin (Fiorentino), a clinical psychologist and former lover of Corelli's who happens to be the wife of a high-powered defense attorney (Chazz Palminteri), one of the prosecutor's closest friends.

Photos in the victim's safe show the governor (Richard Crenna) in compromising positions with a prostitute, suggesting Trina may have been involved in kinky sex games with powerful men who, being blackmailed by the millionaire, might possess a motive for murder.

Friedkin's direction focuses more on images than narrative, at times moving aimlessly between action scenes. Along the same lines, the climactic sequence proves so murkily shot there's scant suspense, as it's difficult to keep track of who's doing what to whom, and the ending is cryptic but largely unsatisfying.

•

JAGGED EDGE
1985, 108 mins, US Ⓥ ⊙ col
Dir Richard Marquand ***Prod*** Martin Ransohoff ***Scr*** Joe Eszterhas ***Ph*** Matthew F. Leonetti ***Ed*** Sean Barton, Conrad Buff ***Mus*** John Barry ***Art*** Gene Callahan
Act Jeff Bridges, Glenn Close, Peter Coyote, Robert Loggia, Leigh Taylor-Young, John Dehner (Columbia)

A well-crafted, hard-boiled mystery by Joe Eszterhas, with sharp performances by murder suspect Jeff Bridges and tough-but-smitten defense attorney Glenn Close.

The murder victim was a socialite and heiress. Her husband (Bridges), a very upwardly mobile San Francisco newspaper publisher, now owns his wife's fortune. Embittered by past experiences in criminal law, Close is pressed to defend Bridge, once he convinces her of his innocence. Then she falls in love with him. Triple-Oscar nominees Bridges and Close play a balancing act that is both glossy and psychologically interesting. Courtroom drama, which is becoming increasingly hard to make on the big screen, consumes perhaps 30 percent of this film and, for the most part, the benchmarks are compelling.

Pic, in quick strokes, raises jagged questions about an imperfect justice system. Although the conflicting parameters of mother-lover-professional woman are becoming naggingly repetitive, the Close persona is a fully realized and dimensional one.

1985: NOMINATION: Best Supp. Actor (Robert Loggia)

•

JAILHOUSE ROCK
1957, 96 mins, US Ⓥ ⊙ ▭ b/w
Dir Richard Thorpe ***Prod*** Pandro S. Berman ***Scr*** Guy Trosper ***Ph*** Robert Bronner ***Ed*** Ralph E. Winters ***Mus*** Jeff Alexander (sup.) ***Art*** William A. Horning, Randall Duell
Act Elvis Presley, Judy Tyler, Mickey Shaughnessy, Vaughn Taylor, Jennifer Holden, Dean Jones (M-G-M/Avon)

The production carries a contrived plot but under Richard Thorpe's deft direction unfolds smoothly. Director has been wise enough to allow Elvis Presley (in his third starrer) his own style, and build around him.

Narrative [from a story by Ned Young] intros Presley as a hot-tempered but affable youngster who goes to prison on a manslaughter rap after being involved in a barroom fight. In stir he's cell-mated with Mickey Shaughnessy, who teaches him his dog-eat-dog philosophy, and also some singing tricks. Released, but now embittered and cynical, he claws his way to fame in the music world, riding over friend and foe alike, even Judy Tyler, a music exploitation agent who has helped in his discovery and is partnered with him in their own record company.

Singer is on for six songs, top being the title production number in a prison setting. Star receives good support, Tyler—killed in an auto accident [soon after film completed]—coming through nicely and Shaughnessy hard-hitting as the tough ex-con who becomes Presley's flunky after following youngster in release from prison.

•

JAKE SPEED
1986, 100 mins, US Ⓥ ⊙ col
Dir Andrew Lane ***Prod*** Andrew Lane, Wayne Crawford, William Fay ***Scr*** Wayne Crawford, Andrew Lane ***Ph*** Bryan Loftus ***Ed*** Fred Stafford, Michael Ripps ***Mus*** Mark Snow ***Art*** Norm Baron
Act Wayne Crawford, Dennis Christopher, Karen Kopins, John Hurt, Leon Ames, Donna Pescow (New World)

Jake Speed is fun—a deliberately mindless adventure that keeps tongue firmly in cheek.

A family is worried about their daughter's disappearance in Paris. Pop wanders in, saying they ought to hire Jake Speed, a hero of paperback thrillers to find her. Pop gets sent to bed because he's obviously senile.

But daughter number two gets a note to meet Jake Speed at a seedy bar. She goes, meets Speed and his sidekick author Remo.

After a hilarious false start once in Africa (where the daughter has been sent to), the trio crashes the den of the international white slavers lorded over by a malicious and deliciously evil John Hurt. Speed is well played by a heavy-lidded and laconic Wayne Crawford who talks as an old-fashioned paperback hero would—in clichés.

•

JAMAICA INN
1939, 99 mins, UK Ⓥ ⊙ b/w
Dir Alfred Hitchcock ***Prod*** Erich Pommer, Charles Laughton ***Scr*** Sidney Gilliat, Joan Harrison, J. B. Priestley ***Ph*** Harry Stradling, Bernard Knowles ***Ed*** Robert Hamer ***Mus*** Eric Fenby ***Art*** Tom Morahan
Act Charles Laughton, Maureen O'Hara, Emlyn Williams, Robert Newton, Basil Radford, Mervyn Johns (Mayflower)

Superb direction, excellent casting, expressive playing and fine production offset an uneven screenplay to make *Jamaica Inn* a gripping version of the Daphne du Maurier novel. Since it's frankly a blood-'n'-thunder melodrama, the story makes no pretense at complete plausibility.

Yarn concerns a gang of smugglers and shipwreckers on the Cornish coast in the early 19th century and the district squire who is their undercover brains. Young naval officer joins the band to secure evidence against them and a young girl who comes from Ireland to stay with her aunt saves him from being hanged by the desperadoes.

Balance of the story is a development of the chase technique. Atmosphere of the seacoast and the moors is strikingly recreated and the action scenes have a headlong rush. Withal, there are frequent bits of brilliant camera treatment and injections of salty humor. It's a typical Alfred Hitchcock direction job.

Charles Laughton has a colorful, sinister part in the villainous squire with a strain of insanity. Maureen O'Hara is a looker and plays satisfactorily in the limited confines of the ingenue part.

•

JAMES AND THE GIANT PEACH
1996, 80 mins, US Ⓥ ⊙ col
Dir Henry Selick ***Prod*** Denise Di Novi, Tim Burton ***Scr*** Karey Kirkpatrick, Jonathan Roberts, Steve Bloom ***Ph*** Pete Kozachik, Hiro Narita ***Ed*** Stan Webb ***Mus*** Randy Newman ***Art*** Harley Jessup
Act Joanna Lumley, Miriam Margolyes, Pete Postlethwaite, Paul Terry (Walt Disney)

Combining the mesmerizing stop-motion animation advanced in *The Nightmare Before Christmas* with *Toy Story*–style digital animation as well as live action, *James and the Giant Peach* is a delightfully demented creation that's every bit as surreal and scary as it is touching and, ultimately, uplifting.

The pairing of filmmaker Henry Selick and late fiction weirdmeister Roald Dahl must have seemed inevitable after 1993's offbeat and dazzling *Nightmare*. Add to the mix the anti-Pollyanna vision of children's book illustrator Lane Smith [pic's "conceptual designer"], and the usually dark composer-songwriter Randy Newman in an uncharacteristically sweet mode, and voilà, this *Peach*, a strange, and strangely wonderful, fairy tale.

Yarn opens with a brief, live-action prologue in which young James (Paul Terry), lives a carefree life by the British seashore. When James is orphaned he is remanded to the custody of his hideous aunts, the fat, preening Sponge (Miriam Margolyes) and the skinny, pitiless Spiker (Joanna Lumley).

One day, a mysterious Old Man (Pete Postlethwaite) gives James a bag of glowing green crocodile tongues. The boy drops some of them near a long-dead tree and immediately a peach begins growing. The live-action gives over to animation when the boy, himself now transformed into an animated figure, encounters the six bugs who will become his new family, as the peach eventually rolls down to the sea and they set sail for Gotham.

Audiences will have a great time identifying the bug voices: Simon Callow gives the Grasshopper his gentle reserve; ditto Jane Leeves the prim Ladybug, David Thewlis the Earthworm and Margolyes, who doubles as the sweet Glowworm. But the sure-fire keepers are Richard Dreyfuss, as the cigar-chomping, wise-cracking Centipede, and Susan Sarandon as a Spider so Garbo-like she even gets to say, at one point, "I prefer to be alone."

Both the score and the film reach their pinnacle in "We're Family," a soaring anthem of acceptance and love as the peach sails aloft through space.

1996: NOMINATION: Best Original Music Score

•

JAMES BROTHERS, THE
SEE: THE TRUE STORY OF JESSE JAMES

•

JANE EYRE
1944, 97 mins, US Ⓥ ⊙ b/w
Dir Robert Stevenson ***Prod*** William Goetz (exec.) ***Scr*** Aldous Huxley, Robert Stevenson, John Houseman ***Ph*** George Barnes ***Ed*** Walter Thompson ***Mus*** Bernard Herrmann ***Art*** William Pereira
Act Orson Welles, Joan Fontaine, Margaret O'Brien, Peggy Ann Garner, Agnes Moorehead, Elizabeth Taylor (20th Century-Fox)

Charlotte Brontë's Victorian novel, *Jane Eyre*, reaches the screen in a drama that is as intense on celluloid as it is on the printed page. This picture has taken liberties with the novel that may be chalked up to cinematic expediency, but there is, nonetheless, a certain script articulation that closer heed to the book could possibly not have achieved.

Jane Eyre is the story of a girl who, after a childhood during which she was buffeted about in an orphanage, secures a position as governess to the ward of one Edward Rochester, sire of an English manor house called Thornfield. Jane Eyre eventually falls in love with him, and he with her. When their wedding is interrupted by a man who accuses Rochester of already being married, there is divulged the secret that Rochester has kept for many years.

Joan Fontaine and Orson Welles are excellent, though the latter is frequently inaudible in the slur of his lines. It is a large cast and one that acquits itself well. Notable in the support are Henry Daniell, as Brocklehurst, the cruel overseer of the orphanage; Margaret O'Brien, the ward of Rochester.

•

JANE EYRE
1971, 110 mins, UK Ⓥ col
Dir Delbert Mann ***Prod*** Frederick Brogger ***Scr*** Jack Pulman ***Ph*** Paul Beeson ***Ed*** Peter Boita ***Mus*** John Williams ***Art*** Alex Vetchinsky
Act George C. Scott, Susannah York, Ian Bannen, Jack Hawkins, Nyree Dawn Porter, Rachel Kempson (Omnibus/Sagittarius)

Charlotte Brontë's tearjerker is put over stolidly and fails to touch and move the emotions as fluently as the 1943 version with Joan Fontaine and Orson Welles.

Delbert Mann's direction and Jack Pulman's screenplay both tend to play up incident rather than characters underlining that, despite its fame, Brontë's story is pretty much a novelletish theme.

Casting is by no means right. George C. Scott as Rochester tends to play the role rather like Patton on a well-deserved leave, and fails to bring out the smouldering romanticism, mixed with tyranny and selfishness, which characterized Rochester, though his first scene with Jane has a sharp, sardonic tang. Since Jane Eyre is constantly described as plain, and as Susannah York who plays the heroine, patently isn't plain, credibility is strained. York gives a pleasant but not wholly convincing portrayal.

•

JANE EYRE
1996, 112 mins, Italy/UK/France/US Ⓥ col
Dir Franco Zeffirelli ***Prod*** Dyson Lovell ***Scr*** Hugh Whitemore, Franco Zeffirelli ***Ph*** David Watkin ***Ed*** Richard Marden ***Mus*** Alessio Vlad, Claudio Capponi ***Art*** Roger Hall
Act William Hurt, Charlotte Gainsbourg, Joan Plowright, Anna Paquin, Geraldine Chaplin, Billie Whitelaw (Rochester/Mediaset/RCS/Flach/Majestic/Miramax

Franco Zeffirelli's rendition of Charlotte Brontë's celebrated novel *Jane Eyre* boasts solid craftsmanship and smart thesping from a stellar cast ably led by the vibrant Charlotte Gainsbourg. What's lacking is the spark of inspiration needed to set this costumer, recalling a high-end telefilm, ahead of the pack.

The novel's action transpires in four distinct periods and settings, and the script sensibly condenses the first two, which concern the childhood and early adolescence of young Jane (Anna Paquin). The tale is famous for the romance that emerges in its third section, when the grown Jane (Gainsbourg) takes employment as a governess at the estate of the mysterious Rochester (William Hurt).

Physically and vocally just right, the actress easily suggests the gawky, awkward duckling teetering on the edge of charm and self-confidence. It is her finely shaded delineation of Jane's doubts and vacillations that gives the film its most involving passages.

As Rochester, Hurt contributes another of his quirky, idiosyncratic performances, but one that, in addition to involving a capable Brit accent, productively accents the character's inner damage and heritage of trauma. While David Watkin's muted lensing proves little more than adequate, it's surely also Zeffirelli's doing that pic's visual approach is somewhat staid and conventional, oriented toward the actors rather than aimed at conjuring the inner fires of Brontë's tale.

•

JANITOR, THE
SEE: EYEWITNESS

•

JANUARY MAN, THE
1989, 97 mins, US Ⓥ ⊙ col
Dir Pat O'Connor ***Prod*** Norman Jewison, Ezra Swerdlow ***Scr*** John Patrick Shanley ***Ph*** Jerzy Zielinski ***Ed*** Lou Lombardo ***Mus*** Marvin Hamlisch ***Art*** Philip Rosenberg
Act Kevin Kline, Susan Sarandon, Mary Elizabeth Mastrantonio, Harvey Keitel, Danny Aiello, Rod Steiger (M-G-M)

Kevin Kline as an unorthodox but indispensable detective tracking a serial strangler infuses this improbable Gotham-set romantic policier with personality.

Kline is Nick Starkey, a disgraced cop who can't get along with the establishment but is summoned from exile to crack an unsolvable crime. Kline has been hung out to dry on dubious allegations of graft by his mean-spirited brother, Police Commissioner Frank Starkey (Harvey Keitel), and brutish Mayor Eamon Flynn (Rod Steiger).

Apparently he's also the only investigative genius in the entire NYPD, which Kline agrees to rejoin if he's allowed to cook dinner for Keitel's haughty, social climbing wife Christine (Susan Sarandon). Kline also strikes sexual sparks with the mayor's daughter Bernadette (Mary Elizabeth Mastrantonio), whose friend was murdered by the break-and-enter strangler.

There's a false ending that does little to make up for the picture's dearth of dry-throat suspense. Steiger has some volcanic moments in this comeback turn, while the other supporting actors provide serviceable foils for Kline's quirky cop.

New York is so bereft of grit and character that it could be Toronto—which it often is, with the exception of the Times Square opening and pick-up shots.

•

JAPANESE WAR BRIDE
1952, 91 mins, US b/w
Dir King Vidor ***Prod*** Joseph Bernhard, Anson Hall ***Scr*** Catherine Turney ***Ph*** Lionel Lindon ***Ed*** Terry Morse ***Mus*** Emil Newman, Arthur Lange ***Art*** Danny Hall
Act Shirley Yamaguchi, Don Taylor, Cameron Mitchell, Marie Windsor, James Bell (Bernhard/20th Century-Fox)

Shirley Yamaguchi, Japanese film star, plays the title role and fits naturally into the story. Her restrained personality is ingratiating. Don Taylor is good as the Korean War veteran who marries her and brings her to Salinas, Cal, for a new life in an American farming community where public opinion is prejudiced.

The Catherine Turney script, based on a story by Anson Bond, brings the bride up against such pitfalls as reluctant acceptance by the groom's family, a jealous sister-in-law, anti-Jap feeling among some of the farmers and similar standard dramatic angles that go with plot. Story comes to its head when the sister-in-law spreads rumor that the child born to the couple was actually fathered by a neighboring Japanese farmer.

•

JASON AND THE ARGONAUTS
1963, 104 mins, UK Ⓥ ⊙ col
Dir Don Chaffey ***Prod*** Charles H. Schneer ***Scr*** Jan Read, Beverley Cross ***Ph*** Wilkie Cooper ***Ed*** Maurice Rootes ***Mus*** Bernard Herrmann ***Art*** Geoffrey Drake
Act Todd Armstrong, Nancy Kovack, Gary Raymond, Laurence Naismith, Niall MacGinnis, Douglas Wilmer (Columbia)

Jason and the Argonauts stems from the Greek mythological legend of Jason and his voyage at the helm of the Argo in search of the Golden Fleece. The $3 million film has a workable scenario and has been directed resourcefully and spiritedly by Don Chaffey, under whose leadership a colorful cast performs with zeal.

Among the spectacular mythological landscape and characters brought to life through the ingenuity of illusionist Ray Harryhausen are a remarkably lifelike mobile version of the colossal bronze god, Talos; fluttery personifications of the bat-winged Harpies; a miniature representation of the "crashing rocks" through which Jason's vessel must cruise; a menacing version of the seven-headed Hydra; a batch of some astonishingly active skeletons who materialize out of the teeth of Hydra; and a rare replica of the Argo itself.

Handsome Todd Armstrong does a commendable job as Jason and Nancy Kovak is beautiful as his Medea.

•

JASON GOES TO HELL: THE FINAL FRIDAY
1993, 88 mins, US Ⓥ ⊙ col
Dir Adam Marcus ***Prod*** Sean S. Cunningham ***Scr*** Dean Lorey, Jay Huguely ***Ph*** William Dill ***Ed*** David Handman ***Mus*** Harry Manfredini ***Art*** W. Brooke Wheeler
Act Jon D. LeMay, Kari Keegan, Kane Hodder, Steven Williams, Steven Culp, Erin Gray (New Line)

Jason goes to hell, and not a moment too soon. His descent has been far too long in coming, as the exhausted, witless ninth, allegedly final and supposedly explanatory chapter in the popular *Friday the 13th* series makes clear.

Blame freshman director Adam Marcus [co-writer of the screen story, with Jay Huguely] for the film's complete lack of tension and style, but point a machete or two at a bland, occasionally inept cast and scripters unable to contribute a single innovation to the genre.

Jason attempts to explain Jason—his origins, his secrets for a long, long life and the means by which he can be sent to his just rewards. Aside from some somber mumbo-jumbo about Jason's family tree, the film doesn't even make a stab at explaining the supernatural goings-on.

This time around, Jason Vorhees (Kane Hodder) is after his only living relatives—a sister, a niece and the niece's infant. Enter Creighton Duke (Steven Williams), a bounty hunter specializing in serial killers, who inexplicably knows that Jason can only be killed by blood kin.

Plot, of course, is merely an excuse to see Jason julienne his way through a series of scantily clad teenage campers, stupid cops and, best of all, a sleazy tabloid TV reporter. Tech credits, especially the grainy focus, betray the film's modest budget.

•

JASON LIVES: FRIDAY THE 13TH PART VI
1986, 87 mins, US Ⓥ ⊙ col
Dir Tom McLoughlin ***Prod*** Don Behrns ***Scr*** Tom McLoughlin ***Ph*** Jon Kranhouse ***Ed*** Bruce Green ***Mus*** Harry Manfredini ***Art*** Joseph T. Garrity
Act Thom Mathews, Jennifer Cooke, David Kagen, Renee Jones, Kerry Noonan, Tom Fridley (Paramount/Terror)

Jason lives, but 18 other people die in this sixth entry in *Friday the 13th* series. Body count works out to an average of one corpse every 4.83 minutes.

Vivid and vigorous opening sequence has two dopey kids digging up the grave of the Masked One on a dark and stormy night to make sure he's dead. A bolt of lightning brings the insatiable killer back to life. Believing old Jason croaked for good in *Part V*, the powers-that-be in Crystal Lake refuse to believe Tommy (Thom Mathews) when he insists a new rampage has begun.

But the sheriff's pert teenage daughter (Jennifer Cooke) thinks Tommy's cute, so she gets him out of jail and they head back to the summer camp where it all began to try to head off Jason before he starts playing with all the little kids there.

Writer-director Tom McLoughlin, who made the scare entry *One Dark Night*, puts comic spin on some of the predictable material and turns in a reasonably slick performance under the circumstances.

•

JAWS
1975, 124 mins, US Ⓥ ⊙ ▭ col
Dir Steven Spielberg ***Prod*** Richard D. Zanuck, David Brown ***Scr*** Peter Benchley, Carl Gottlieb, [Matthew Robbins, Hal Barwood, John Milius] ***Ph*** Bill Butler ***Ed*** Verna Fields ***Mus*** John Willliams ***Art*** Joseph Alves, Jr.
Act Roy Scheider, Robert Shaw, Richard Dreyfuss, Lorraine Gary, Murray Hamilton, Carl Gottlieb (Universal)

Jaws, Peter Benchley's bestseller about a killer shark and a tourist beach town, is an $8 million film of consummate suspense, tension and terror. It stars Roy Scheider as the town's police chief torn between civic duty and the mercantile politics of resort tourism; Robert Shaw, absolutely magnificent as a coarse fisherman finally hired to locate the Great White Shark; and Richard Dreyfuss, in another excellent characterization as a likeable young scientist.

The fast-moving film engenders enormous suspense as the shark attacks a succession of people; the creature is not even seen for about 82 minutes, and a subjective camera technique makes his earlier forays excruciatingly terrifying all the more for the invisibility. The final hour of the film shifts from the town to a boat where the three stars track the shark, and vice versa.

The adroit casting extended through the ranks of supporting players, notably Lorraine Gary, very good as Scheider's wife, and Murray Hamilton, excellent as the town mayor.

John Williams's haunting score adds to the mood of impending horror. All other production credits are superior.

1975: Best Sound, Original Score, Editing

NOMINATION: Best Picture

•

JAWS 2

1978, 117 mins, US Ⓥ ⦿ ▭ col

Dir Jeannot Szwarc ***Prod*** Richard D. Zanuck, David Brown ***Scr*** Carl Gottlieb, Howard Sackler ***Ph*** Michael Butler ***Ed*** Neil Travis ***Mus*** John Williams ***Art*** Joe Alves

Act Roy Scheider, Lorraine Gary, Murray Hamilton, Joseph Mascolo, Jeffrey Kramer, Collin Wilcox (Universal)

Despite a notable but effective change in story emphasis, *Jaws 2* is a worthy successor in horror, suspense and terror to its 1975 smash progenitor.

The Peter Benchley characters of offshore island police chief Roy Scheider, loyal spouse Lorraine Gary, temporizing mayor Murray Hamilton and Gee-whiz deputy Jeffrey Kramer are used as the adult pegs for the very good screenplay. The targets of terror, and the principal focus of audience empathy, are scores of happy teenagers.

So strong is the emphasis on adolescent adrenalin that *Jaws 2* might well be described as the most expensive film ($20 million) that American International Pictures never made.

Suffice to say that the story again pits Scheider's concern for safety against the indifference of the town elders as evidence mounts that there's another great white shark out there in the shallow waters. Ever-more complicated teenage jeopardy leads to the climactic showdown with a buried cable.

•

JAWS 3-D

1983, 97 mins, US Ⓥ ⦿ ▭ col

Dir Joe Alves ***Prod*** Robert Hitzig ***Scr*** Richard Matheson, Carl Gottlieb ***Ph*** James A. Contner ***Ed*** Randy Roberts ***Mus*** Alan Parker ***Art*** Woods Mackintosh

Act Dennis Quaid, Bess Armstrong, Simon MacCorkindale, Louis Gossett, Jr., John Putch, Lea Thompson (Universal/Landsburg)

The *Jaws* cycle has reached its nadir with this surprisingly tepid [Arrivision] 3-D version.

Gone are Roy Scheider, the summer resort of Amity, and even the ocean. They have been replaced by Florida's Sea World, a lagoon and an Undersea Kingdom that entraps a 35-foot Great White, and a group of young people who run the tourist sea park.

The picture [from a screen story by Guerdon Trueblood] includes two carry-over characters from the first two *Jaws*, Scheider's now-grown sons, who are played by nominal star Dennis Quaid as the older brother turned machine engineer and kid brother John Putch.

Femme cast is headed by Bess Armstrong as an intrepid marine biologist who lives with Quaid.

Director Joe Alves, who was instrumental in the design of the first *Jaws* shark and was the unsung production hero in both the first two pictures, fails to linger long enough on the Great White.

•

JAWS: THE REVENGE

1987, 100 mins, US Ⓥ ⦿ col

Dir Joseph Sargent ***Prod*** Joseph Sargent ***Scr*** Michael de Guzman ***Ph*** John McPherson ***Ed*** Michael Brown ***Mus*** Michael Small ***Art*** John J. Lloyd

Act Michael Caine, Lorraine Gary, Lance Guest, Mario Van Peebles, Karen Young, Judith Barsi (Universal)

Story for part four picks up after the Roy Scheider character of *Jaws* and *Jaws 2* has died of a heart attack. Lorraine Gary nicely reprises her role as the now-widowed Ellen Brody, living a peaceful life in the New England resort town of Amity. One of her sons, a deputy sheriff, is killed by a shark while out in the channel on a routine complaint.

Ellen heads down to the Bahamas to be with her other son, marine biologist Michael (Lance Guest), and his family (Karen Young makes the most out of the small role of Michael's wife), and tries to convince him to quit his job because she's sure "it" is out to get the family.

Michael Caine is Ellen's delightfully irresponsible suitor, but doesn't get enough screen time to really develop the character. After the shark practically walks up the beach to get a bite out of the third generation Brody (Judith Barsi), Ellen goes after "it" by herself.

Pacing leaves a lot to be desired and the moment-of-attack sequences, full of jagged cuts and a great deal of noise, more closely resemble the view from inside a washing machine.

•

JAZZ ON A SUMMER'S DAY

1959, 78 mins, US Ⓥ col

Dir Bert Stern ***Ph*** Bert Stern, Ray Phelan, Courtney Hafela ***Ed*** Aram Avakian ***Mus*** Hoagy Carmichael, Duke Ellington, Count Basie, Seymour Simons, Gerald Marks, Thelonious Monk, Chuck Berry (Raven)

Outstanding feature-length documentary centered around the Newport Jazz Festival. It's a document of the medium, spanning most of the jazz styles and including a rich selection of top performers and material. It's Americana, and a document of its time as well via observation of audiences and the life surrounding the Newport event, not least the neatly integrated footage concerning the America Cup Yacht Races.

Structure of the film basically follows that of the two-day event around which it centers, with occasional digressions, over the jazz soundtrack, to other nearby scenes such as the cup races, children playing, wave and water effects, reflections, all neatly matched to mood of motif being played. Juxtaposition is sometimes humorous, sometimes ironic, at others merely illustrative, but always deft.

On-the-spot lensing under difficult lighting conditions, both daytime and nighttime, is often incredibly good. Some unprecedented effects are achieved by cameramen Bert Stern, Ray Phelan, and Courtney Hafela (under Stern's imaginative and stylish guidance). Similar plaudits also for an oustanding (magnetic) sound recording job, all part of near-perfect teamwork on pic.

•

JAZZ SINGER, THE

1927, 88 mins, US Ⓥ ⦿ b/w

Dir Alan Crosland ***Scr*** Al Cohn, Jack Jarmuth ***Ph*** Hal Mohr ***Ed*** Harold McCord

Act Al Jolson, May McAvoy, Warner Oland, Eugenie Besserer, William Demarest, Otto Lederer (Warner)

Undoubtedly the best thing Vitaphone has ever put on the screen. The combination of the religious heart interest story [based on the play by Samson Raphaelson] and Jolson's singing "Kol Nidre" in a synagog while his father is dying and two "Mammy" lyrics as his mother stands in the wings of the theatre, and later as she sits in the first row, carries abundant power and appeal.

But *The Jazz Singer* minus Vitaphone [synchronized sound system] is something else again. There's really no love interest in the script, except between mother and son.

Al Jolson, when singing, is Jolson. There are six instances of this, each running from two to three minutes. When he's without that instrumental spur Jolson is camera-conscious. But as soon as he gets under cork the lens picks up that spark of individual personality solely identified with him. That much goes with or without Vitaphone.

The picture is all Jolson, although Alan Crosland, directing, has creditably dodged the hazard of over-emphasizing the star as well as refrained from laying it on too thick in the scenes between the mother and boy. The film dovetails splendidly, which speaks well for those component parts of the technical staff. Cast support stands out in the persons of Eugenie Besserer, as the mother; Otto Lederer, as a friend of the family; and Warner Oland as the father.

1927/28: Special Award (pioneer talking picture)

NOMINATION: Best Adapted Screenplay, Engineering Effects

•

JAZZ SINGER, THE

1952, 106 mins, US col

Dir Michael Curtiz ***Prod*** Louis F. Edelman ***Scr*** Frank Davis, Leonard Stern, Lewis Meltzer ***Ph*** Carl Guthrie ***Ed*** Alan Crosland, Jr. ***Mus*** Ray Heindorf (dir.) ***Art*** Leo K. Kuter

Act Danny Thomas, Peggy Lee, Mildred Dunnock, Eduard Franz, Tom Tully, Allyn Joslyn (Warner)

Warners's remake of Al Jolson's 1927 Vitaphone film hit is still sentimental, sometimes overly so. A drama with songs importantly spotted with beautiful Technicolor cloaking.

Peggy Lee, in her first feature film lead, sparks the song offerings in sock style, and is okay in the acting demands as a musical comedy-record star who loves and promotes the career of a cantor's son (Danny Thomas).

Latter is excellent in a sentimental part, making the most of several genuine tearjerker sequences.

Eduard Franz is the cantor expecting his son to follow in his footsteps, but the updated plot has Thomas returning from two years in Korea with showbiz in mind. He breaks with his father, and goes to New York for a precarious career-launching with the help of Lee, already established.

1952: NOMINATION: Best Scoring of a Musical Picture

•

JAZZ SINGER, THE

1980, 115 mins, US Ⓥ ⦿ col

Dir Richard Fleischer, [Sidney J. Furie] ***Prod*** Jerry Leider ***Scr*** Herbert Baker ***Ph*** Isidore Mankofsky ***Ed*** Frank J. Urioste, Maury Winetrobe ***Mus*** Neil Diamond, Leonard Rosenman ***Art*** Harry Horner

Act Neil Diamond, Laurence Olivier, Lucie Arnaz, Catlin Adams, Paul Nicholas (AFD/Leider)

This third screen version of *The Jazz Singer* asks the same question as the 1927 Al Jolson history maker and the 1952 Danny Thomas update—can a nice cantor's son break with family and tradition to make it as a popular entertainer? No one's going to get sweaty palms waiting for the answer, as Samson Raphaelson's venerable chestnut lacks urgency and plausible incidental detail.

Screenplay, credited to Herbert Baker, with adaptation by Stephen H. Foreman, follows general line of earlier incarnations. However, elimination of the mother character in favor of a traditional wife k.o.'s any attempt at a reprise of "Mammy."

Richard Fleischer took over midway through shooting, and the best that can be said for the direction is that there's no disruption of the by-the-numbers style.

•

JEAN DE FLORETTE

1986, 120 mins, France/Italy Ⓥ ⦿ ▭ col

Dir Claude Berri ***Prod*** Pierre Grunstein ***Scr*** Claude Berri, Gerard Brach ***Ph*** Bruno Nuytten ***Ed*** Arlette Langmann, Herve de Luze, Noelle Boisson ***Mus*** Jean-Claude Petit ***Art*** Bernard Vezat

Act Yves Montand, Daniel Auteuil, Gerard Depardieu, Elisabeth Depardieu, Ernestine Mazurowna, Marcel Champel (Renn/Films A2/RAI-2/DD

This is the first of two related, and simultaneously lensed, films—at a global cost of 120 million francs (about $17 million), the most expensive production in French film history [to date]—that Claude Berri adapted from a two-part novel by Marcel Pagnol, who died in 1974. Pagnol drafted his novel *L'eau des collines* years after making his penultimate feature film, *Manon des sources* in 1952, to which *Jean de Florette* is a prequel. The picture, typically long and talky (four hours in its original release, subsequently cut by distributor Gaumont), supposedly left Pagnol dissatisfied, prompting him to recast and expand his tale in literary form.

Yves Montand and Daniel Auteuil play a proud, self-centered village elder and his rat-faced sub-intelligent nephew who covet a local piece of fertile land, its chief asset being a subterranean spring whose existence is known only to the locals. When the farm's owner kicks off providentially, the greedy pair suddenly find themselves confronted by an heir: a hunchbacked young city slicker (Gerard Depardieu), who has brought his wife (played by Elisabeth Depardieu, the thesp's real life mate) and young daughter, Manon, to settle and live off the land in Rousseauist simplicity.

Depardieu doesn't know about the spring, which Montand and Auteuil have blocked up. Drought, the sirocco winds and the long desperate treks to fetch water from another spring in the mountains wear down Depardieu's optimism. Auteuil befriends him and feeds him hypocritical advice, while Montand watches with patient scorn from the sidelines.

Berri's sympathetic work with his small cast, and his subservience to Pagnol's story and dialog are key factors in the film's robust dramatic appeal. He and co-scripter Gerard Brach have resisted any temptations to revamp or update the story (set in a Provencal village of the 1920s). Berri has directed with tact and feeling, with luminous lensing by Bruno Nuytten.

•

JEANNE D'ARC

SEE: MESSENGER: THE STORY OF JOAN OF ARC, THE

•

JEFFERSON IN PARIS

1995, 136 mins, US Ⓥ ⦿ col

Dir James Ivory ***Prod*** Ismail Merchant ***Scr*** Ruth Prawer Jhabvala ***Ph*** Pierre Lhomme ***Ed*** Andrew Marcus, Isabel Lorente ***Mus*** Richard Robbins ***Art*** Guy-Claude Francois

Act Nick Nolte, Greta Scacchi, Jean-Pierre Aumont, Simon Callow, James Earl Jones, Michael Lonsdale (Touchstone/Merchant Ivory)

The founding fathers have always managed to elude successful capture in films, and while the Merchant Ivory team has done better than some in *Jefferson in Paris*, the baffling track record still holds. The disgruntled team's first effort under the Disney banner, this decorous look at the great man's five years as ambassador to France in the period leading up to the French Revolution touches upon much significant history, incident and emotion but, ironically, lacks the intrigue and drama of great fiction.

Ruth Prawer Jhabvala's original script tacitly pinpoints in Jefferson the root of America's greatness as well as its tragedy. Jefferson authored the Declaration of Independence and was one of the leading visionaries of democracy; but, the film suggests, his inability to extend his principles to cover blacks as well as whites helped foster the fissure in the American dream that persists to this day.

The action proper begins with Jefferson (a full-maned, sternly serious Nick Nolte) being introduced at the French court in 1784. As one of the primary instigators of the successful revolt against the British, Jefferson is also a source of inspiration for the rabblerousers who seek to do to Louis XVI and Marie Antoinette what the Yanks did to the British. Shell-shocked by the loss of his beloved wife three years before, Jefferson is opened up by the beautiful and flirtatious Maria Cosway (Greta Scacchi), the English-Italian wife of foppish British painter Richard Cosway (Simon Callow).

The strong points of James Ivory's approach here are his attentiveness to wonderful detail, including Jefferson's passion for playing violin-piano duets with the women in his life. The downside is that Ivory's reticence makes it additionally tough for an emotionally remote figure like Jefferson to come alive onscreen.

•

JEFFREY

1995, 92 mins, US Ⓥ col

Dir Christopher Ashley ***Prod*** Mark Balsam, Mitchell Maxwell, Victoria Maxwell ***Scr*** Paul Rudnick ***Ph*** Jeffrey Tufano ***Ed*** Cara Silverman ***Mus*** Stephen Endelman ***Art*** Michael Johnston

Act Steven Weber, Michael T. Weiss, Irma St. Paule, Patrick Stewart, Robert Klein, Christine Baranski (Workin' Man/Orion)

The glittering blend of disparate elements that made Paul Rudnick's *Jeffrey* an Off Broadway gem several seasons back doesn't throw off quite the same sparkle on the bigscreen. Onstage, the story of a 30-ish gay New Yorker who has sworn off sex careened from broad (and hilarious) sketch comedy to scissors-sharp camp wit and was underscored by a touch of poignance and humanity. Onscreen, *Jeffrey* doesn't so much careen as amble, a pleasant stroll over flat terrain.

Christopher Ashley, who directed the original stage play and makes his movie debut here, doesn't always seem comfortable with the medium. A more confident directorial hand might have resisted the film-school reliance on title cards, slow-motion glances and action frozen to allow character asides to the audience.

No sooner has he gone on the sexual wagon, than Jeffrey (Steven Weber) meets the man of his dreams, Steve (Michael T. Weiss), an amiable HIV-positive hunk whose initial gym workout with the hapless and horny Jeffrey is none-too-subtly infused with sexual tension. Jeffrey naturally runs scared, and much of the film follows the pursuit-rejection mating dance of the two men.

Along the episodic way, Jeffrey attends a socialite's country-themed Hoedown for AIDS, a New Age revival meeting (with Sigourney Weaver as a Marianne Williamson clone), and New York's gay pride parade, where Jeffrey encounters a supremely tacky New Jersey mother (Olympia Dukakis) marching in pride of her "pre-operative transsexual lesbian son." Nathan Lane appears briefly as a gay, sex-crazed Catholic priest.

Fortunately, the terrific ensemble cast, headed by a charming Weber, sees the picture through its lesser moments, and Rudnick's barbs and one-liners score even when their contexts don't.

•

JENNIFER EIGHT

1992, 124 mins, US Ⓥ ⦿ col

Dir Bruce Robinson ***Prod*** Gary Lucchesi, David Wimbury ***Scr*** Bruce Robinson ***Ph*** Conrad Hall ***Ed*** Conrad Buff ***Mus*** Christopher Young ***Art*** Richard Macdonald

Act Andy Garcia, Uma Thurman, Lance Henriksen, Kathy Baker, Kevin Conway, John Malkovich (Paramount)

Jennifer Eight is an unusually intelligent and unexploitative thriller, notable for avoiding most standard suspense film contrivances.

British writer-director Bruce Robinson's script possesses all the elements for yet another product of the *Fatal Attraction–Basic Instinct* cookie cutter: a burned-out big-city homicide cop getting involved with a mysterious blonde, brutal attacks on women, gruff career cops who resent the probing maverick, an opportunity for female retribution and, in the bargain, a couple of unfortunate plot holes.

Andy Garcia toplines as a wreck of a detective who joins a small-town Northern California police force after crashing and burning in the L.A. fast lane. His sister (Kathy Baker) lives there with cop hubby (Lance Henriksen), and Garcia becomes latter's partner in the search for a woman whose hand is found—in a stunningly shot nocturnal opening sequence—at a dump.

With little evidence to go on, Garcia postulates that the killing is just the latest in a string of murders. Next target could be Uma Thurman, who's blind like the most recent victim and was the last person to "see" her alive.

Lenser Conrad Hall quite possibly surpasses himself here with a virtuoso job highlighted by numerous sequences lit only by flashlights or other single light sources.

Best of all is Thurman, who very touchingly conveys the vulnerability of the blind femme without for a moment begging for audience sympathy.

•

JENNIFER ON MY MIND

1971, 90 mins, US col

Dir Noel Black ***Prod*** Bernard Schwartz ***Scr*** Erich Segal ***Ph*** Andrew Laszlo ***Ed*** Jack Wheeler ***Mus*** Stephen J. Lawrence ***Art*** Ben Edwards

Act Michael Brandon, Tippy Walker, Lou Gilbert, Steve Vinovich, Peter Bonerz, Renee Taylor (United Artists)

Jennifer on My Mind is a black comedy about an aimless wealthy Jewish youth who falls in love with a bored and impulsive upperclass suburban girl whom he meets in Venice. Story unravels through a series of flashbacks narrated by the youth, Marcus, speaking into a tape recorder as he attempts to cope with the fact that he has killed his love, Jennifer, when in response to her painful pleading, he reluctantly injected her with heroin.

Film, written by Erich Segal and directed by Noel Black, is sort of a cross between their respective previous features, *Love Story* and *Pretty Poison* with an added sprinkling of "relevant" social commentary.

The delightfully ridiculous plot, mock-sentimental narration, absurd dialog, infectious syrupy music and intermittent idyllic interludes all parody *Love Story*. And yet, like *Pretty Poison*, this is a potpourri of disarming satire, black comedy and poignancy that creates a strangely haunting aura.

Michael Brandon, as Marcus, is charmingly boyish and natural. Tippy Walker, as Jennifer, comes across with a bitchy ethereal allure.

•

JEOPARDY

1953, 68 mins, US b/w

Dir John Sturges ***Prod*** Sol Baer Fielding ***Scr*** Mel Dinelli ***Ph*** Victor Milner ***Ed*** Newell P. Kimlin ***Mus*** Dimitri Tiomkin ***Art*** Cedric Gibbons, William Ferran

Act Barbara Stanwyck, Barry Sullivan, Ralph Meeker, Lee Aaker (M-G-M)

The misadventures that befall a family of three vacationing at an isolated coast section of Lower California have been put together in an unpretentious, tightly-drawn suspense melodrama.

There's no waste motion or budget dollars in the presentation. Plot has a tendency to play itself out near the finale, but otherwise is expertly shaped in the screenplay from a story by Maurice Zimm.

Barbara Stanwyck, Barry Sullivan and their small son (Lee Asker) are vacationing at a deserted Mexican beach. An accident pins Sullivan's leg under a heavy piling that falls from a rotten jetty. Knowing the rising tide will cover him within four hours Stanwyck takes off in the family car to find either help or a rope strong enough to raise the piling. The mission is sidetracked when she comes across Ralph Meeker, a desperate escaped convict. He takes her prisoner and commandeers the car.

The performances by the four-member cast are very good, being expertly fitted to the change of mood from the happy, carefree start to the danger of the accident and the menace of the criminal. Scenes of Sullivan and young Aaker together bravely facing the peril of the tide while Stanwyck frantically seeks help are movingly done.

•

JEREMIAH JOHNSON

1972, 110 mins, US Ⓥ ⦿ ▭ col

Dir Sydney Pollack ***Prod*** Joe Wizan ***Scr*** John Milius, Edward Anhalt ***Ph*** Duke Callaghan ***Ed*** Thomas Stanford ***Mus*** John Rubinstein, Tim McIntire ***Art*** Ted Haworth

Act Robert Redford, Will Geer, Stefan Gierasch, Delle Bolton, Josh Albee, Joaquin Martinez (Warner)

Jeremiah Johnson, based on Vardis Fisher's novel *Mountain Man* and a story, *Crow Killer*, by Raymond W. Thorp and Robert Bunker, is the sort of man of whom legends or sagas are made. Pic leans towards the latter as it meticulously, sans grandiloquence, lays out the life of a male dropout, circa 1825, who decides to live in the Rocky Mountains as a trapper.

Director Sydney Pollack has given a skilled, observant mounting as he carefully allows the man to grow in experience and knowhow.

Robert Redford, as Johnson, has a solid stamina, a fine feel for the speech of the time, giving an auto-didactic flair as he sometimes comments the actions. He begins to trade with the Indians and wins the esteem of a Crow nation chief to whom he gives a present, to find he must accept the chief's daughter in return.

The film has its own force and beauty and the only carp might lie in its not always clear exegesis of the humanistic spirit and freedom most of its characters are striving for.

•

JERK, THE

1979, 104 mins, US Ⓥ ⦿ col

Dir Carl Reiner ***Prod*** David V. Picker, William E. McEuen ***Scr*** Steve Martin, Carl Gottlieb, Michael Elias ***Ph*** Victor J. Kemper ***Ed*** Bud Molin ***Mus*** Jack Elliott ***Art*** Jack Collis

Act Steve Martin, Bernadette Peters, Catlin Adams, Mabel King, Richard Ward (Universal/Aspen)

Pic is an artless, non-stop barrage of off-the-wall situations, funny and unfunny jokes, generally effective and sometimes hilarious sight gags and bawdy non sequiturs.

The premise of *The Jerk* can be found in one of Steve Martin's more famous routines. Upon receiving the stunning news that he's the adopted, not natural, son of black parents Martin leaves home with his dog to make his way in the world. Opening sequences with the family are among the best.

Martin's odyssey through contemporary America sees him taking odd jobs, such as a gas station attendant for proprietor Jackie Mason and as the driver of an amusement park train, and taking up with women. But lunacy is never strayed from very far, as Martin strikes it rich as the inventor of a ridiculous nose support device for eyeglasses. Hilarity ebbs during his decline and fall.

•

JERKY BOYS, THE

1995, 81 mins, US Ⓥ col

Dir James Melkonian ***Prod*** Joe Roth, Roger Birnbaum ***Scr*** James Melkonian, Rich Wilkes, John G. Brennan, Kamal Ahmed ***Ph*** Veli Steiger ***Ed*** Dennis M. Hill ***Mus*** Ira Newborn ***Art*** Dan Leigh

Act Johnny Brennan, Kamal Ahmed, Alan Arkin, William Hickey, Alan North, Brad Sullivan (Caravan/Touchstone)

The Jerky Boys, a comedy inspired by the antics of prank phone-callers Johnny Brennan and Kamal Ahmed, is a low-brow, high-concept item. Kamal (as he is known professionally) and Brennan more or less play themselves. They are repeatedly described by themselves and others as "a couple of lowlifes from Queens" and do their best to live down to that reputation.

When a former high school classmate (James Lorinz) gets a little too cocky about his low-level job with the local Mafia branch, the Jerky Boys decide to have a little fun. Johnny calls the mob headquarters, passes himself off as a notorious Chicago hood and gets the goodfellas to believe two fugitive hit men will need their hospitality.

Naturally Johnny and Kamal introduce themselves as the hit men. Just as naturally, the mob boss (Alan Arkin) quickly sees through the ruse. Trouble is, a hardboiled cop (Brad Sullivan) isn't nearly so perceptive. He's bent on getting the Jerky Boys to lead him to this criminal mastermind.

Drawing heavily from the cast of characters they introduced on their two top-selling comedy albums, Johnny and

Kamal pretend to be, among other things, a nightclub magician, a hot-headed gangster, a pair of roadies and, while hiding from Mafia hoods, a couple of bathroom-stall Romeos. James Melkonian's direction often seems flat-footed, the tech credits are unremarkable, and the pic on the whole, though just 81 minutes long, seems padded.

●

JERRY MAGUIRE

1996, 138 mins, US Ⓥ ⊙ col

Dir Cameron Crowe ***Prod*** James L. Brooks, Laurence Mark, Richard Sakai, Cameron Crowe ***Scr*** Cameron Crowe ***Ph*** Janusz Kaminski ***Ed*** Joe Hutshing ***Mus*** Nancy Wilson ***Art*** Stephen Lineweaver

Act Tom Cruise, Cuba Gooding Jr., Renee Zellweger, Kelly Preston, Jerry O'Connell, Jay Mohr (Gracie/TriStar)

An exceptionally tasty contempo comedic romance, *Jerry Maguire* runs an unusual pattern on its way to scoring an unexpected number of emotional, social and entertaining points. Smartly written and boasting a sensational cast, Cameron Crowe's shrewdly observed third feature also gives Tom Cruise one of his very best roles.

Ostensibly a tart look at the greed and selfishness rampant in professional sports as seen through the career of a sharp players' agent, the film takes gratifying twists and turns on its way. Although it has its conventional, sitcommy elements and goes on a bit too long, the dialog is so good and the performances so alive to the potential of the characters that the faults remain quite minor.

Jerry Maguire (Cruise) is a slick agent who handles 72 clients for L.A.-based Sports Management Intl. But in a crisis of conscience, Jerry asks himself, "Who had I become? Just another shark in a suit?" and dashes off a long memo to the company staff. Film gets credit for beginning where a more typical Hollyood film would end.

Jerry's ill-advised frankness gets him fired, although agency accountant Dorothy (Renee Zellweger) quits to join him on his Quixotic effort to be true to himself and stay in the game at the same time. Jerry goes to great lengths to represent the top college draft pick, quarterback Frank Cushman (Jerry O'Connell), but when he suddenly begins to look like a loser rather than a winner, his relationship with eyes-on-the-prize fiancée Avery (Kelly Preston) hits the rocks, whereupon he looks at the pretty, vulnerable Dorothy with different eyes.

Cruise shows a self-deprecatory quality and humor that are new and welcome. All the same, there is nothing he can do to prevent the scene-stealing of Cuba Gooding, Jr., as a larger-than-life modern athlete with his strutting ego, show-boating style and frank preference for money over the glory of the game.

1996: Best Supp. Actor (Cuba Gooding, Jr.)

NOMINATIONS: Best Picture, Actor (Tom Cruise), Original Screenplay, Editing.

●

JERSEY GIRL

1992, 95 mins, US Ⓥ ⊙ col

Dir David Burton Morris ***Prod*** David Madden, Nicole Seguin, Staffan Ahrenberg ***Scr*** Gina Wendkos ***Ph*** Ron Fortunato ***Ed*** Norman Hollyn ***Mus*** Misha Segal ***Art*** Lester Cohen

Act Jami Gertz, Dylan McDermott, Sheryl Lee, Joseph Mazzello, Joseph Bologna, Aida Turturro (Electric/Interscope)

Jami Gertz gives a winning perf in *Jersey Girl*, an unoriginal variation on such Italo-Yank romances as *Moonstruck*.

Gertz is the prototypical young woman from New Jersey, living with dad Joseph Bologna (who fears her becoming an old maid) and working in a day care center. She spends much of her time hanging out at the local Bendix Diner with her pals Aida Turturro, Molly Price and Star Jasper. Script's main theme is that old standby: get out of your provincial rut and blossom. Instead of the *Working Girl* approach, Gertz takes a more old-fashioned route, trying to win some young hunk (Dylan McDermott) from Manhattan.

Very attractively lensed by Ron Fortunato, Gertz shows a big talent in her first top-billed film appearance. McDermott certainly looks the part but operates a notch lower. As tough-talking buddy Cookie, Price is a terrific scene-stealer.

●

JESSE JAMES

1939, 103 mins, US Ⓥ ⊙ col

Dir Henry King ***Prod*** Nunnally Johnson (assoc.) ***Scr*** Nunnally Johnson ***Ph*** George Barnes, W. Howard Greene ***Ed*** Barbara McLean ***Mus*** Louis Silvers (dir.) ***Art*** William Darling, George Dudley

Act Tyrone Power, Henry Fonda, Nancy Kelly, Randolph Scott, Brian Donlevy, John Carradine (20th Century-Fox)

Jesse James, notorious train and bank bandit of the late 19th century, and an important figure in the history of the Midwest frontier, gets a drastic bleaching. Script by Nunnally Johnson is an excellent chore, nicely mixing human interest, dramatic suspense, romance and fine characterizations for swell entertainment.

Tyrone Power capably carries the title spot, but is pressed by Henry Fonda as his brother.

Story follows historical fact [assembled by Rosalind Schaeffer and Jo Frances James] close enough with allowance for dramatic license, hitting sidelights of James in his brushes with the law. Initial train holdup is vividly presented, with all other robberies left to imagination. Picture starts with foreword on the ruthless manner in which railroads acquired farms for right-of-way through the Midwest.

●

JESSICA

1962, 105 mins, US/France/Italy ▭ col

Dir Jean Negulesco ***Prod*** Jean Negulesco ***Scr*** Edith Sommer ***Ph*** Pierro Portalupi ***Ed*** Renzo Lucidi ***Mus*** Mario Nascimbene ***Art*** Giulio Bongini

Act Angie Dickinson, Maurice Chevalier, Noel-Noel, Gabriele Ferzetti, Sylva Koscina, Agnes Moorehead (United Artists)

Jean Negulesco's *Jessica* is a trite, frivolous variation on the oft-exploited *Lysistrata* theme. Angie Dickinson enacts the title role of an anatomically streamlined midwife from America who unwittingly tips the Freudian scale in a small Sicilian village just by sheer sex appeal.

As the screenplay from Flora Sandstrom's novel, *The Midwife of Pont Clery*, has it, the misguided senoritas of the community Lysistrategically organize a sex strike. Objective: "no babies, no midwife." As any fool kin plainly see before the pic is a third unspooled, Jessica will fall for yon handsome widower Marquis, and strike will expire of natural causes.

It is no strain on Dickinson's histrionic ability to wiggle through this role. Her proportions are tailored to its specifications, and that's about all that's required.

Maurice Chevalier breezes through the part of village priest with that familiar sunny countenance, and pauses occasionally to narrate or tackle one of several listenable, but undistinguished, ditties by Marguerite Monnet (music) and Dusty Negulesco (lyrics).

●

JESUS CHRIST SUPERSTAR

1973, 107 mins, US Ⓥ ⊙ ▭ col

Dir Norman Jewison ***Prod*** Norman Jewison, Robert Stigwood ***Scr*** Melvyn Bragg, Norman Jewison ***Ph*** Douglas Slocombe ***Ed*** Anthony Gibbs ***Mus*** Andrew Lloyd Webber ***Art*** Richard MacDonald

Act Ted Neeley, Carl Anderson, Yvonne Elliman, Barry Dennen, Bob Bingham, Josh Mostel (Universal)

Norman Jewison's film version of the 1969 legit stage project in a paradoxical way is both very good and very disappointing at the same time. The abstract film concept veers from elegantly simple through forced metaphor to outright synthetic in dramatic impact.

The filming concept is that of a contemporary group of young players performing sequential production numbers in the barren desert, utitlizing sketchy props and costumes. No mob scenes à la DeMille, no heavy production spectaculars, no familiar screen names in cameos. So far, so good. But then something happens as Carl Anderson (outstanding as Judas in the film's best performance) finds himself, in the midst of "Damned for All Time" running away from tanks and ducking modern jet fighters. Suddenly it's *Catch 22*–time, which the very moving "Last Supper" sequence can only counteract instead of contributing to a mounting dramatic impact.

Barry Dennen's Pontius Pilate is intrusively effective far beyond the pragmatic urbanity called for, Joshua Mostel's King Herod is less a dissolute sybarite than a swishy, roly-poly cherub. Finally "Superstar" blares forth with the shallow impact of an inferior imitation of Isaac Hayes.

1973: NOMINATION: Best Adapted Score

●

JET PILOT

1957, 112 mins, US col

Dir Josef von Sternberg ***Prod*** Jules Furthman ***Scr*** Jules Furthman ***Ph*** Winton C. Hoch ***Ed*** Michael R. McAdam, Harry Marker, William M. Moore ***Mus*** Bronislau Kaper ***Art*** Albert S. D'Agostino, Feild Gray

Act John Wayne, Janet Leigh, Jay C. Flippen, Paul Fix, Richard Rober, Roland Winters (RKO)

Jet Pilot was made around 1950 and kept under wraps by indie film-maker Howard Hughes for unstated (but much speculated upon) reasons. Its story has a pretty, young girl as a Russian jet pilot who, on a spy mission, wings into a love match with an American airman in the United States.

Questionable is the casting of Janet Leigh. While John Wayne fits the part of a colonel in the Yank Air Force, the slick chick looks more at home in a bathing suit at Palm Springs than she does jockeying a Soviet MIG, and shooting down her own countrymen, in Russia. The incongruity would appear less glaring if *Pilot* were out to be a takeoff on secret agent stuff. But much of it is played straight.

Film opens at a U.S. airbase in Alaska where Wayne is in charge. Leigh flies in, tells skeptic Wayne that she escaped from Russia, and is taken in tow by the colonel who gets the assignment of seeking information from her. Picture moves to Palmer Field and Palm Springs, love blossoms, marriage follows. Then it's discovered that Leigh is a spy.

●

JEUX INTERDITS, LES (FORBIDDEN GAMES)

1952, 90 mins, France Ⓥ ⊙ b/w

Dir Rene Clement ***Prod*** Robert Dorfman ***Scr*** Francois Boyer, Jean Aurenche, Pierre Bost, Rene Clement ***Ph*** Robert Juillard ***Ed*** Roger Dwyre ***Mus*** Narciso Yepes ***Art*** Paul Bertrand

Act Brigitte Fossey, Georges Poujouly, Lucien Hubert, Suzanne Courtal, Jacques Marin, Laurence Badie (Silver)

Film is moving, poetic idyll of the effect of the [Second World] war on two moppets. It contrasts the world of two youngsters to the ransacked world created by their elders.

Story starts with the French exodus during the war. In the midst of a strafing by the enemy, a little girl's parents and her dog are killed. She is picked up by a little farm boy who takes her home with him. In burying the dog they decide to make a little cemetery for animals. This leads to bloodshed between two feuding farm families.

The relationship of the children is well sustained throughout and though child psychology is strained in spots, it gives a touching counterpoint to the vapid meanderings of the adults. The kids are finally separated when the law claims the little orphan.

Rene Clement's direction is excellent. Moppets Brigitte Fossey and Georges Poujouly are brilliantly handled and give an air of spontaneity to their roles. Lensing is a bit flat but editing is a fine asset. Adult roles are good with Lucien Hubert as the exasperated father a standout.

1952: Best Foreign Language Film

●

JEWEL OF THE NILE, THE

1985, 104 mins, US Ⓥ ⊙ ▭ col

Dir Lewis Teague ***Prod*** Michael Douglas ***Scr*** Mark Rosenthal, Lawrence Konner ***Ph*** Jan De Bont ***Ed*** Michael Ellis, Peter Boita, Edward Abroms ***Mus*** Jack Nitzsche ***Art*** Richard Dawking, Gerry Knight

Act Michael Douglas, Kathleen Turner, Danny DeVito, Spiros Focas, Avner Eisenberg, Paul David Magid (20th Century-Fox)

As a sequel to *Romancing the Stone*, the script of *The Jewel of the Nile* is missing the deft touch of the late Diane Thomas but Lewis Teague's direction matches the energy of the original.

Michael Douglas and Kathleen Turner again play off each other very well, but the story is much thinner. The main problem is the dialog, which retains some of the old spirit but too often relies on the trite.

Story picks up six months after *Stone*'s happy ending and Douglas and Turner have begun to get on each other's nerves. She accepts an invitation from a sinister potentate (Spiros Focas) to accompany him and write a story about his pending ascendency as desert ruler. Left behind, Douglas runs into the excitable Danny DeVito and they become unwilling allies, again in pursuit of a jewel.

●

JEW SUSS

1934, 120 mins, UK b/w

Dir Lothar Mendes ***Prod*** [Michael Balcon] ***Scr*** A. R. Rawlinson ***Ph*** Bernard Knowles ***Ed*** Otto Ludwig ***Mus*** Louis Levy (dir.) ***Art*** Alfred Junge

Act Conrad Veidt, Benita Hume, Gerald du Maurier, Frank Vosper, Cedric Hardwicke, Pamela Ostrer (Gaumont-British)

It's a spectacle of no small proportions, the saga of Jew Josef Suss-Oppenheimer, who ruthlessly achieves the economic power which permits him, a truly sensitive alumnus of the ghetto, to mingle with the Wurttemberg ducal nobility.

In transmuting Lion Feuchtwanger's weighty book to the screen, director Lothar Mendes and his scriptists manifest much ingenuity and skill to paint in celluloid what the German author did in his powerful novel. They just miss in presenting the major story thread. There are too many loose skeins in the plot knitting. (Locale and period is 18th century Duchy of Wurttemberg, Germany.)

Jew Suss is all Conrad Veidt, a consummate screen artist whose histrionic skill pars the best on stage or screen. Frank Vosper as the rapacious duke is excellent. Likewise Cedric Hardwicke and Gerald du Maurier in character assignments, along with Paul Graetz as the homely philosophical Landauer and Pamela Ostrer as Naomi, Suss's daughter.

•

JEZEBEL
1938, 100 mins, US Ⓥ ⦿ b/w
Dir William Wyler ***Prod*** William Wyler ***Scr*** Clements Ripley, Abem Finkel, John Huston ***Ph*** Ernest Haller ***Ed*** Warren Low ***Mus*** Max Steiner ***Art*** Robert Haas
Act Bette Davis, Henry Fonda, George Brent, Margaret Lindsay, Donald Crisp, Fay Bainter (Warner)

This just misses sock proportions. That's due to an anticlimactic development on the one hand, and a somewhat static character study of the Dixie vixen, on the other.

Against an 1852 New Orleans locale, when the dread yellow jack (yellow fever epidemic) broke out, the astute scriveners have fashioned a rather convincing study of the flower of Southern chivalry, honor and hospitality. Detracting is the fact that Bette Davis's "Jezebel" suddenly metamorphoses into a figure of noble sacrifice and complete contriteness.

However, William Wyler's direction draws an engrossing cross-section of old southern manners and hospitality. It's undoubtedly faithful to a degree, and not without its charm. At times it's even completely captivating.

Henry Fonda and George Brent are the two whom Davis viciously pits against each other; and later, Richard Cromwell must likewise challenge the champ dueling Brent. Latter's conception of the southern gentleman who exaggeratedly arranges pistols-for-two, whether in tavern or drawing room, and with equal éclat and Dixie élan, is in keeping with what is the most virile characterization in the picture.

Particularly noteworthy is Max Steiner's expert musical score, which more than merely sets the moods.

1938: Best Actress (Bette Davis), Supp. Actress (Fay Bainter)

NOMINATIONS: Best Picture, Cinematography, Score

•

JFK
1991, 189 mins, US Ⓥ ⦿ ▭ col
Dir Oliver Stone ***Prod*** A. Kitman Ho, Oliver Stone ***Scr*** Oliver Stone, Zachary Sklar ***Ph*** Robert Richardson ***Ed*** Joe Hutshing, Pietro Scalia, Hank Corwin ***Mus*** John Williams ***Art*** Victor Kempster
Act Kevin Costner, Sissy Spacek, Joe Pesci, Tommy Lee Jones, Gary Oldman, Donald Sutherland (Warner/Regency/Canal Plus/Ixtlan)

A rebuke to official history and a challenge to continue investigating the crime of the century, Oliver Stone's *JFK* is electric muckraking filmmaking. This massive, never-boring political thriller, which most closely resembles Costa-Gavras's *Z* in style and impact, lays out just about every shred of evidence yet uncovered for the conspiracy theory surrounding the Nov. 22, 1963 assassination of President John F. Kennedy.

The Warren Report is treated as a cover-up, a myth against which the director, for lack of hard answers that never may be provided, is proposing a myth of his own.

Working in a complex, jumbled style that mixes widescreen, archival footage, TV clips, black & white, slow motion, docu-drama recreations, time jumps, repeated actions from various viewpoints, still photos, the Zapruder film and any other technique at hand [with narration by Martin Sheen], Stone uses the sum of conspiracy theory points made by New Orleans d.a. Jim Garrison and others since to suggest as strongly as possible that Oswald was, as he claimed before he was killed, "a patsy."

[Script is based on the books *On the Trail of the Assassins* by Jim Garrison and *Crossfire: The Plot That Killed Kennedy* by Jim Marrs.]

Garrison (Kevin Costner) begins delving into a mysterious netherworld of right-wing, anti-Castro homosexuals populated by the bewigged David Ferrie (Joe Pesci), suave businessman Clay Shaw (Tommy Lee Jones) and unpredictable hustler Willie O'Keefe (Kevin Bacon). Garrison begins to suspect that the US government's military industrial complex initiated the killing.

Costner may not resemble the real Garrison much, and Stone no doubt slides over many of the attorney's flaws. But the actor, in a low-key but forceful performance, nicely conveys the requisite grit, curiosity and fearlessness. Sissy Spacek is stuck with almost nothing but nagging lines, complaining that his obsessive quest is driving them apart.

1991: Best Cinematography, Editing

NOMINATIONS: Best Picture, Director, Supp. Actor (Tommy Lee Jones), Adapted Screenplay, Original Score, Sound

•

JIMMY HOLLYWOOD
1994, 109 mins, US Ⓥ ⦿ col
Dir Barry Levinson ***Prod*** Mark Johnson, Barry Levinson ***Scr*** Barry Levinson ***Ph*** Peter Sova ***Ed*** Jay Rabinowitz ***Mus*** Robbie Robertson ***Art*** Linda DeScenna
Act Joe Pesci, Christian Slater, Victoria Abril, Jason Beghe, John Cothran, Jr. (Baltimore/Paramount)

At the critical, defining moment in the life of would-be Hollywood actor Jimmy Alto, he comes up firing blanks. The same can be said of Barry Levinson's oddball attempt to mix offbeat comedy with social commentary and fringe-level character study. As a low-budget indie shot on the run and then marketed cleverly, this story of terminal down-and-outers might have made some sense. As a $20 million studio undertaking without major stars, however, it never stood a chance.

Jimmy (Joe Pesci) is no closer to making it now than he was seven years ago when he arrived in L.A. from Jersey. Lucky enough to have a sexy g.f., Lorraine (Spanish star Victoria Abril), Jimmy spends his time hanging out in the company of dimwit grunge puppy William (Christian Slater).

Jimmy then makes an effective tape of himself as Jericho, the fearless leader of S.O.S. (Save Our Streets), a self-appointed "watchdog of Hollywood" vigilante group dedicated to targeting the scum that has made the entertainment capital so dangerous. Exhilarated by the media attention, Jimmy and William don masks and catch any number of bad guys in the act.

In a blond hairpiece almost as awful as his getup in *JFK*, Pesci is more antic than engaging. Slater's thick-headed second-banana role reps the farthest thing from a glamorous star turn as one could imagine, and Abril, in her American film debut, is spirited.

•

JIMMY THE GENT
1934, 66 mins, US b/w
Dir Michael Curtiz ***Scr*** Bertram Milhauser ***Ph*** Ira Morgan ***Ed*** Thomas Richards ***Art*** Esdras Hartley
Act James Cagney, Bette Davis, Alice White, Allen Jenkins, Alan Dinehart, Philip Reed (Warner)

Jimmy the Gent is good fun. James Cagney pops Allen Jenkins, his dumb cluck stooge, every time he gets sore. It's expert, thorough-going, typically Cagney manhandling. And good for plenty of laughs.

Story seems to be the first screen presentation of a plausible racket, namely finding heirs for the fortunes lying around unclaimed in banks. Cagney is crude and primitive in his operations. The girl he is sweet on (Bette Davis) works for a gentlemanly and suave practitioneer of the same racket. Part of the fun is Cagney's trying to make a gent out of himself in emulation of the smoothie (Alan Dinehart).

Plot [from the story *The Heir Chaser* by Laird Doyle and Ray Nazzaro] is extremely ingenious and special plaudits belong with the scenario department. Davis's unusual coiffure and smart deportment helps a lot. Several other slick performances by Dinehart, Arthur Hohl, Jenkins and Alice White rate special bows.

Short running time, just over an hour, keeps *Jimmy the Gent* moving at breakneck speed throughout.

•

JIM THORPE—ALL-AMERICAN
(UK: MAN OF BRONZE)
1951, 107 mins, US Ⓥ ⦿ b/w
Dir Michael Curtiz ***Prod*** Everett Freeman ***Scr*** Douglas Morrow, Everett Freeman ***Ph*** Ernest Haller ***Ed*** Folmar Blangsted ***Mus*** Max Steiner
Act Burt Lancaster, Charles Bickford, Steve Cochran, Phyllis Thaxter, Dick Wesson, Nestor Paiva (Warner)

One of the great stories in American sports history—the real-life yarn of Jim Thorpe, the Indian athlete—is compellingly told in *Jim Thorpe—All-American*. Only a few fictional liberties have been taken in telling of how Thorpe came off an Oklahoma reservation to establish himself as the greatest all-round athlete of modern times.

Pic re-creates a number of events from sports history. There is the sensational 13-13 tie between unbeaten grid-iron Titans—Penn and Carlisle—in the duel in which Ashenbrunner of Penn stacked up against Thorpe of Carlisle. There are re-creations of the 1912 and 1924 Olympics (with an assist from stock shots). There are neatly directed sequences of Thorpe as a professional grid star, of his Herculean mastery of every track event in the book.

All these Burt Lancaster has helped capture in the spirit of the grim-visaged, moody Indian. Charles Bickford plays "Pop" Warner, Thorpe's Carlisle mentor and friend, with restraint and credence. Phyllis Thaxter plays the white girl who became Thorpe's wife, only to divorce him when she could no longer tolerate the sullenness and despair that gripped him following the death of their son and his subsequent athletic decline.

•

JINGLE ALL THE WAY
1996, 88 mins, US Ⓥ ⦿ col
Dir Brian Levant ***Prod*** Chris Columbus, Mark Radcliffe, Michael Barnathan ***Scr*** Randy Kornfield ***Ph*** Victor J. Kemper ***Ed*** Kent Beyda, Wilton Henderson ***Mus*** David Newman ***Art*** Leslie McDonald
Act Arnold Schwarzenegger, Sinbad, Phil Hartman, Rita Wilson, Robert Conrad, James Belushi (1492 Picture/20th Century-Fox)

In this highly formulaic star vehicle, Arnold Schwarzenegger gets to fly like Peter Pan, act like Superman—and fulfill the kind of fantasy many kids imagine for their fathers. Based on an idea similar to *Home Alone*, though not nearly as accomplished or entertaining, and produced by that film's director, Chris Columbus, this family comedy-adventure is decidedly not a vintage Schwarzenegger kidpic on the order of *Kindergarten Cop*.

Jingle reverses the 1990 blockbuster's p.o.v. Instead of focusing on the children, slight tale centers on the desperate efforts of a workaholic father, Howard (Schwarzenegger), to get his son, Jamie (Jake Lloyd), his desired Christmas gift. The action toy Turbo Man is not only the season's hottest gift, but it's been sold out since Thanksgiving.

Attempting to flesh out the extremely slender material, filmmakers have arranged for Howard to fight a corrupt operation, headed by a shady Santa Claus (James Belushi), who dupes Howard into buying a headless, Korean-speaking Turbo Man. Pic credits the efforts of no fewer than 60 stunt people, used in colorful and busy setpieces such as Minneapolis's Mall of America, reportedly the country's biggest.

•

JINGWU MEN
(FIST OF FURY; THE CHINESE CONNECTION; CHINESE CONNECTION; THE IRON HAND)
1972, 105 mins, Hong Kong Ⓥ ⦿ ▭ col
Dir Lo Wei ***Prod*** Raymond Chow ***Scr*** Lo Wei ***Ph*** Chen Chinchu ***Ed*** Peter Cheung ***Mus*** Joseph Koo ***Art*** Chien Hsin
Act Bruce Lee, Nora Miao, Maria Yi, James Tien, Tien Feng, Han Ying-chieh (Golden Harvest)

Bruce Lee is a 32-year-old Chinese-American who has parlayed his skill in kung-fu into a profitable acting career in Hong Kong-produced features. His balletic grace, curled mouth, quivering nostrils, arched eyebrows and clenched fists make his demonstrations of this athletic sport highly entertaining.

Actioner tells of a young kung-fu student who sets out to avenge the murder of his boxing master. Apart from a few tepid romantic interludes, pic focuses on a series of battles in which the fist-wielding Lee defeats anywhere from one to two dozen whimpering opponents in an Oriental paraphrase of Clint Eastwood's Italoaters. Even Joseph Koo's music recalls the Sergio Leone Westerns in its use of choral moans and thumping rhythms.

Lee has a good deal of aggressive boyish charm. However, pic is archaically simple-minded in its storyline and marginally professional in its production. Lo Wei's direction is a juvenile match for his own screenplay.

•

JINXED!
1982, 103 mins, US Ⓥ col
Dir Don Siegel ***Prod*** Herb Jaffe ***Scr*** Bert Blessing, David Newman ***Ph*** Vilmos Zsigmond ***Ed*** Doug Steward ***Mus*** Bruce Roberts, Miles Goodman ***Art*** Ted Haworth
Act Bette Midler, Ken Wahl, Rip Torn, Val Avery, Jack Elam, Benson Fong (M-G-M/United Artists/Jaffe)

They tried and tried to come up with a better title for *Jinxed!*, but somehow they kept returning to the only one that was fitting. The exclamation point emphasizes the totality of the disaster. Director Don Siegel's w.k. disillusionment with the project is fully understandable.

Idea seems to have been a darkly comic version of *The Postman Alway Rings Twice*, with perhaps a touch of *A Place in the Sun*.

Set in Loserville, USA, represented by Reno, tale presents casino dealer Ken Wahl as the hapless victim of seedy gambler Rip Torn. Once Torn sits down at his blackjack table, Wahl knows he'll soon be out of a job, such is the fantastic luck his tormentor enjoys. Torn also gives grief to his smalltime singer g.f. Bette Midler, who is sufficiently taken with Wahl's charms to rope him into a scheme, à la James M. Cain, to bump off her lover.

•

JOANNE D'ARC

SEE: MESSENGER: THE STORY OF JOAN OF ARC, THE

•

JOAN OF ARC

1948, 150 mins, US Ⓥ ⦿ col

Dir Victor Fleming ***Prod*** Walter Wanger ***Scr*** Maxwell Anderson, Andrew Solt ***Ph*** Joseph Valentine ***Ed*** Frank Sullivan ***Mus*** Hugo Friedhofer ***Art*** Richard Day

Act Ingrid Bergman, Jose Ferrer, Ward Bond, Francis L. Sullivan, Cecil Kellaway (RKO/Sierra)

Joan of Arc [from the play, *Joan of Lorraine*, by Maxwell Anderson] is a big picture in every respect. It has size, color, pageantry, a bold, historic bas-relief. It has authority, conviction, an appeal to faith and a dedication to a cause that leaves little wanting. And then, of course, *Joan of Arc* has Ingrid Bergman and a dream supporting cast. Fleming has done an exciting job in blending the symbolism, the medieval warfront heroics, and the basic dramatic elements into a generally well-sustained whole.

There are certain misfires and false keynotes which militate against the desired consistency, such as Jose Ferrer's tiptop impersonation of the Dauphin, later to become the King of France, who makes his characterization so much the complete nitwit that the audience may well wonder at the complete obeisance of Joan to this weakling sovereign, regardless of the fact he is a symbol of the realm. The churchly gradations are also script shortcomings.

The majesty of the earlier sequences is compelling almost all the way. When Joan edicts that "our strength is in our faith", when she leads her army in the Battle of Orleans, when she is betrayed by the Burgundians in calumny with the English, when in the earlier scenes she wins the grudging alliance of the Governor of Vaucouleurs and the courtiers at Chinon, Bergman makes Joan a vivid albeit spiritual personality. The color by Technicolor is magnificent. The production is lavish and looks every bit of its $4 million-plus.

1948: Best Color Cinematography, Color Costume Design

NOMINATIONS: Best Actress (Ingrid Bergman), Supp. Actor (Jose Ferrer), Color Art Direction, Editing, Scoring of a Dramatic Picture

•

JOAN OF PARIS

1942, 93 mins, US Ⓥ b/w

Dir Robert Stevenson ***Prod*** David Hempstead ***Scr*** Charles Bennett, Ellis St. Joseph ***Ph*** Russell Metty ***Ed*** Sherman Todd ***Mus*** Roy Webb ***Art*** Albert S. D'Agostino, Carroll Clark

Act Michele Morgan, Paul Henreid, Thomas Mitchell, Laird Cregar, May Robson, Alan Ladd (RKO)

Most important factors of *Joan of Paris* are the American screen debuts of Michele Morgan and Paul Henreid, RKO importations, with each of the pair getting away to fine start. Story [from an original by Jacques Thery and Georges Kessel] is one of those counter-espionage tales of escaping British flyers, Gestapo shadowing, and French underground.

Although intriguing in first half it gets repetitious in second section to taper off with too mild a climax without the generation of tragic note intended.

Director Robert Stevenson does well to maintain suspense in the first part, but cannot hold up the script deficiencies later. *Joan of Paris* details adventures of five flyers in British bombing forces parachuted in France. The gang scatter and rejoin in a Paris church. Paul Henreid enlists the aid of a priest (Thomas Mitchell), is tailed by Gestapo, and finally makes contact with British Intelligence.

•

JOB, THE

SEE: IL POSTO

•

JOE

1970, 107 mins, US Ⓥ ⦿ col

Dir John G. Avildsen ***Prod*** David Gil ***Scr*** Norman Wexler ***Ph*** John G. Avildsen ***Ed*** George T. Norris

Act Dennis Patrick, Peter Boyle, Susan Sarandon, Patrick McDermott, Audrey Caire, K. Callan (Cannon)

Joe deals with a NY ad agency exec (Dennis Patrick) who murders his daughter's junkie lover after the girl winds up in Bellevue suffering from an overdose of speed. Through a somewhat implausible coincidence, he is found out by a hardhat factory worker, the Joe of the title (Peter Boyle), who applauds his action as a blow struck for God and country. The two begin a class-spanning relationship which brings them nervously together in the realization that the American dream has somehow turned sour for them.

Pretty it's not. By concentrating on the extremist fringes of the various social elements involved, Norman Wexler's script makes audience identification well-nigh impossible and at the same time abstracts the questions in a way that gives the pic real importance.

1970: NOMINATION: Best Original Story & Screenplay

•

JOE GOULD'S SECRET

2000, 104 mins, US Ⓥ ⦿ col

Dir Stanley Tucci ***Prod*** Charles Weinstock, Elizabeth W. Alexander, Stanley Tucci ***Scr*** Howard A. Rodman ***Ph*** Maryse Alberti ***Ed*** Suzy Elmiger ***Mus*** Evan Lurie ***Art*** Andrew Jackness

Act Ian Holm, Stanley Tucci, Patricia Clarkson, Hope Davis, Steve Martin, Susan Sarandon (First Cold Press-Charles Weinstock/USA)

An observant evocation of New York's literary and bohemian world of more than a half-century ago, *Joe Gould's Secret* remains sympathetically engaging even as it sporadically stumbles on its journey through the streets, saloons and salons of Greenwich Village. Pic is marked by a studied directorial style that could be complimented as rigorous when it works and criticized as stiff when it doesn't.

Much of the long-gestating project's intellectual interest stems from its basis in the work of the late Joseph Mitchell, the legendary writer for the *New Yorker* who specialized in profiles of the city's lowlife. Of his subjects, none came to be better known than Gould, a Harvard-educated son of a well-to-do Boston family who dropped out of "respectable" life to pursue a lifelong project, the writing of *The Oral History of Our Time*, a massive tome dedicated to capturing the everyday talk of ordinary folk, with philosophical observations mixed in.

Howard A. Rodman's intelligent, well-judged screenplay is based on Mitchell's two *New Yorker* stories about Gould. While one can read the profiles and never even know that Mitchell was married with kids, script makes good use of his domestic situation as a contrast to Gould's parallel world. A neat, polite and deferential Southerner, Mitchell (helmer Stanley Tucci) lives with his wife, Therese (Hope Davis), a photographer of street subjects, and two young daughters. His work life is similarly well ordered: He writes each day, when he is not out doing field research, in his proper little office at the New Yorker under the tart but tolerant supervision of editor Harold Ross (an excellent Patrick Tovatt).

Having first spied the disheveled, cantankerous Gould in a diner pouring a bottle of ketchup into his bowl of soup, Mitchell learns about his *Oral History* and decides to do a profile of the hobo. Celebrity brings Gould many letters, a roof over his head courtesy of an anonymous donor, his own table at the Minetta Tavern and the attention of a big-time publisher, Charlie Duell (Steve Martin), who's interested in the manuscript, if only Gould would produce it. As for Mitchell, he finds he can't shake the man he's put in the limelight, who turns up at his office anytime he wants.

Convincing at all times as the eccentric who may have been as manipulative as he was nutty, Ian Holm emphasizes Gould's lucidity and chooses to downplay his alcoholism and obnoxious extremes. Tucci remains reined in by a reticence and unassertiveness that keep Mitchell at an emotional remove.

•

JOE KIDD

1972, 87 mins, US Ⓥ ⦿ ▭ col

Dir John Sturges ***Prod*** Sidney Beckerman ***Scr*** Elmore Leonard ***Ph*** Bruce Surtees ***Ed*** Ferris Webster ***Mus*** Lalo Schifrin ***Art*** Alexander Golitzen, Henry Bumstead

Act Clint Eastwood, Robert Duvall, John Saxon, Don Stroud, Stella Garcia, James Wainwright (Malpaso/Universal)

Not enough identity is given Clint Eastwood in a New Mexico land struggle in which no reason is apparent for his involvement, but John Sturges's direction is sufficiently compelling to keep guns popping and bodies falling.

Spectator is never entirely certain of Eastwood's status, apart from his owning a small spread and being hired to lead a party of gunmen to kill a rebellious Spanish-American who heads fight to save original Spanish land grants of his people. Elmore Leonard's script lacks proper motivation as Eastwood throws in with the oldtimers whose land his temporary employer is trying to take over.

Highlight of entire footage is when Eastwood and a few men run a railroad engine through the bar where some of the gunmen are holding forth and mow them down.

•

JOE LOUIS STORY, THE

1953, 88 mins, US Ⓥ b/w

Dir Robert Gordon ***Prod*** Sterling Silliphant ***Scr*** Robert Sylvester ***Ph*** Joseph Brun ***Ed*** David Kummins ***Mus*** George Bassman

Act Coley Wallace, Paul Stewart, Hilda Simms, James Edwards, John Marley, Dots Johnson (United Artists)

The Joe Louis Story is a dramatic recap of the personal and ring history of the respected Negro American fighter. The film, acted out by a predominantly colored cast headed by Coley Wallace (as the champ), rates high on sincerity, is alternately touching, understanding and heartpoundingly exciting.

Coley Wallace is the spitting image of Joe, from his muscular body to the expressionless face that so unexpectedly breaks out into a broad, friendly grin. He carries off the ring scenes and does well against Hilda Simms who plays Mrs. Louis.

Integration of real fight shots, from the early bouts to the pummeling Joe took from Schmeling, the triumphant return match and the tragic attempt in 1951 when the aging Louis came out of retirement to be "murdered" by Rocky Marciano, is excellently handled and accounts for the picture's sock appeal.

Director Robert Gordon deserves kudos for keeping the action tight and dramatic, never losing sight that he is trying to humanize the story of an idol whom most people only knew in the glare of the arena.

Sylvester's intelligent script helps a great deal in making Louis come alive as a slugger and as a colored boy with decent instincts but incompletely equipped to live up to everything that being a "celebrity" implies.

•

JOE MACBETH

1955, 90 mins, UK b/w

Dir Ken Hughes ***Prod*** Mike Frankovich ***Scr*** Philip Yordan ***Ph*** Basil Emmott ***Ed*** Peter Rolfe Johnson ***Mus*** Trevor Duncan ***Art*** Alan Harris

Act Paul Douglas, Ruth Roman, Bonar Colleano, Gregoire Aslan, Sidney James, Harry Green (Columbia)

Joe Macbeth is far removed from the famous Shakespearean character, but there is an analogy between this modern gangster story and the Bard's classic play. Although made in Britain, the film has an American setting. It is expensively mounted, expertly staged and directed with a keen sense of tension.

The plot is basically a battle for supremacy, waged by Paul Douglas, in the title role, and egged on by his determined bride (Ruth Roman).

The lead role makes substantial demands on Douglas, but he emerges with honorable distinction. His characterization changes naturally from the confident henchman to the domineering and frightened bully. Roman has the looks and talent to give a genuine veneer to her performance as his wife.

•

JOE VERSUS THE VOLCANO

1990, 102 mins, US Ⓥ ⦿ ▭ col

Dir John Patrick Shanley ***Prod*** Teri Schwartz ***Scr*** John Patrick Shanley ***Ph*** Stephen Goldblatt ***Ed*** Richard Halsey ***Mus*** Georges Delerue ***Art*** Bo Welch

Act Tom Hanks, Meg Ryan, Lloyd Bridges, Robert Stack, Dan Hedaya, Ossie Davis (Amblin/Warner)

Joe Versus the Volcano is an overproduced, disappointing shaggy dog comedy: A nebbish is bamboozled by unscrupulous types to trade his meaningless existence for a grand adventure that's linked to a suicide pact.

Pic starts promisingly with Tom Hanks going to work in the ad department of the grungy American Panascope surgical supplies factory. Meg Ryan as DeDe (in the first of her three gimmicky roles) sports dark hair in an amusingly ditzy Carol Kane impression as his mousey coworker. As an in-joke, the real Carol Kane pops up also in black wig later in the film, uncredited.

Hanks is a hypochondriac and his doctor, guest star Robert Stack, diagnoses a "brain cloud," giving the hapless guy only six months to live. Coincidentally, eccentric superconductors tycoon Lloyd Bridges pops in to offer Hanks the chance to "live like a king" for 20 days before heading for a remote Polynesian island to "die like a man," i.e., jump into an active volcano to appease the fire god.

Hanks indulges himself in some rather unfunny solo bits. Ryan has fun in her three personas, but they're simply revue sketches.

•

JOHN AND MARY
1969, 92 mins, US col
Dir Peter Yates *Prod* Ben Kadish *Scr* John Mortimer *Ph* Gayne Rescher *Ed* Frank P. Keller *Mus* Quincy Jones *Art* John Robert Lloyd
Act Dustin Hoffman, Mia Farrow, Michael Tolan, Sunny Griffin, Stanley Beck, Tyne Daly (20th Century-Fox/Debrod)

John and Mary is a slight, indeed simple story that begins with sex and ends with love. The two title characters, played by Dustin Hoffman and Mia Farrow, do not even learn each other's name until the final frame.

The skeletal plot [from a novel by Mervyn Jones] has John meet Mary in one of those desperate, swinging singles establishments on New York's upper east side. They return to his apartment, have sex and the film opens with their awakening the next morning.

John is selfish and self-satisfied, but Hoffman projects a screen personality which insists that more is present than is getting through the camera's eye. Mary is much more attractive, feminine and alive. And Farrow enlarges the character sufficiently to make her worth caring about.

The entire charade is smoothly contrived.

•

JOHN CARPENTER'S ESCAPE FROM L.A.
SEE: ESCAPE FROM L.A.

•

JOHN CARPENTER'S VAMPIRES
SEE: VAMPIRES

•

JOHN GRISHAM'S THE RAINMAKER
SEE: THE RAINMAKER

•

JOHNNY ALLEGRO
1949, 80 mins, US b/w
Dir Ted Tetzlaff *Prod* Irving Starr *Scr* Karen DeWolf, Guy Endore *Ph* Joseph Biroc *Ed* Jerome Thomas *Mus* George Duning
Act George Raft, Nina Foch, George Macready, Will Geer, Gloria Henry (Columbia)

Johnny Allegro is a typical George Raft melodrama. Plot rings in a twist or two to dress up the melodrama of an ex-gangster who is trying to go straight and who takes on a dangerous assignment from the government to help prove his good intentions. From the time Raft crosses paths with Nina Foch, wife of a bigtime international agent, his fate is marked with danger.

Foch pleases in her assignment as a gal who is not all bad and only needs Raft to put her on the proper course. George Macready is the villainous husband, working with foreign powers to flood the country with counterfeit and disrupt the national economy.

•

JOHNNY ANGEL
1945, 79 mins, US b/w
Dir Edwin L. Marin *Prod* William L. Pereira *Scr* Steve Fisher *Ph* Harry J. Wild *Ed* Les Millbrook *Mus* Leigh Harline
Act George Raft, Claire Trevor, Signe Hasso, Lowell Gilmore, Hoagy Carmichael, Marvin Miller (RKO)

Johnny Angel is another in the seemingly never-ending series of maritime intrigues involving murder and lust. It is slow and plodding, with poor story development [from a story by Charles Gordon Booth, adaptation by Frank Gruber].

George Raft plays Johnny Angel, a sea captain who becomes involved in the mystery of what happened aboard the ship of his father, also a captain, after the vessel is found adrift, with no one aboard, in the Gulf of Mexico. Involved, too, are the wife of Raft's boss, who is infatuated with Raft; a French girl stowaway who was apparently the only witness as to what actually happened aboard the ship; a whimsical taxi-driver; and the steamship line's owner. They're all seemingly fugitives from a road company of a Jack London sea yarn or perhaps something out of Hemingway.

Raft is his invariably glowering self as a guy who really handles his mitts—and the dames—while Claire Trevor and Signe Hasso are the romantic interests. Rest of the cast is weighted down too much by the story, though of the feature performers, Hoagy Carmichael, the composer, as in the Bogart-Bacall *To Have and Have Not* for Warners, plays the character of whimsy with tongue in cheek.

•

JOHNNY BELINDA
1948, 101 mins, US b/w
Dir Jean Negulesco *Prod* Jerry Wald *Scr* Irmgard von Cube, Allen Vincent *Ph* Ted McCord *Ed* David Weisbart *Mus* Max Steiner *Art* Robert M. Haas
Act Jane Wyman, Lew Ayres, Charles Bickford, Agnes Moorehead, Stephen McNally, Jan Sterling (Warner)

Johnny Belinda is a story that easily could have become a display of scenery-chewing theatrics. It has its theatrics but they spring from a rather earnest development of story fundamentals, tastefully handled. Jean Negulesco's direction never overplays the heart-strings, yet keeps them constantly twanging, and evidences a sympathetic instinct that is reflected in the performance.

[In this adaptation of the stage play by Elmer Harris,] Jane Wyman portrays a mute slattern completely devoid of film glamour. It is a personal success; a socko demonstration that an artist can shape a mood and sway an audience through projected emotions without a spoken word.

Plot essentials cover a deaf-mute girl, dwelling with her father and resentful aunt on a barren farm in Nova Scotia. A village romeo rapes her. She has a baby and events move forward until the deaf-mute kills her ravisher when he tries to take the baby. She is tried for murder. Charles Bickford walks off with the assignment of Belinda's father. His handling of the part of the dour Scot farmer registers strongly, pulling audience interest all the way.

1948: Best Actress (Jane Wyman)

NOMINATIONS: Best Picture, Director, Actor (Lew Ayres), Supp. Actor (Charles Bickford), Supp. Actress (Agnes Moorehead), Screenplay, B&W Cinematogrpahy, B&W Art Direction, Editing, Score of a Dramatic Picture, Sound

•

JOHNNY COME LATELY
1943, 97 mins, US b/w
Dir William K. Howard *Prod* William Cagney *Scr* John Van Druten *Ph* Theodore Sparkuhl *Ed* George Arthur *Mus* Leigh Harline
Act James Cagney, Grace George, Marjorie Main, Hattie McDaniel, Ed McNamara (United Artists)

James Cagney's first independent production via brother Bill Cagney's unit, comes through with a topnotch performance in the story of the crack tramp newspaperman, afflicted with a wanderlust complex, who temporarily halts in his tracks to help an old lady continue publication of her newspaper and battle the crooked politico-financial forces in her town.

Whatever elements of suspense, action and motivation the Louis Bromfield book, *McLeod's Folly*, may have held to attract the Cagney production staff, the screen treatment which has emerged is, for the most part, familiar melodrama. Cagney's performance, however, combined with William K. Howard's direction, offsets scripting flaws.

Action revolves mainly about Cagney's journalistic attacks on the village tycoon (Ed McNamara) after the lady publisher (Grace George) saves him from a stretch in the hoosegow on vagrancy charges.

•

JOHNNY COOL
1963, 103 mins, US b/w
Dir William Asher *Prod* William Asher, Peter Lawford *Scr* Joseph Landon *Ph* Sam Leavitt *Ed* Otto Ludwig *Mus* Billy May
Act Henry Silva, Elizabeth Montgomery, Marc Lawrence, Telly Savalas, Jim Backus, Sammy Davis, Jr. (Chrislaw)

Henry Silva, as a Sicilian-born assassin, is at home as the "delivery boy of death" for deported underworld kingpin Marc Lawrence. While his escapades would probably fall apart if analyzed, he puts such driving force into them that the viewer becomes too involved to dispute his actions.

Elizabeth Montgomery, however, plays the emotionally and morally mixed-up heroine like a high-school drama teacher demonstrating to her class how to play a nymphomaniac—10% sex, 90% self-consciousness.

Joseph Landon's script [from John McPartland's novel *The Kingdom of Johnny Cool*] has more holes in it than a Swiss cheese but he stuffs most of them with action and director William Asher cuts the action in thick slices. Plot centers on Silva doing a job for Lawrence which takes him from Sicily to Rome, then to N.Y., L.A. and Las Vegas before he's finished. When a doll comes into his life and gets worked over by some hoods, he adds revenge to his baser reasons for wiping out his assorted victims.

•

JOHNNY DANGEROUSLY
1984, 90 mins, US col
Dir Amy Heckerling *Prod* Michael Hertzberg *Scr* Norman Steinberg, Bernie Kukoff, Harry Colomby, Jeff Harris *Ph* David M. Walsh *Ed* Pem Herring *Mus* John Morris *Art* Joseph R. Jennings
Act Michael Keaton, Joe Piscopo, Marilu Henner, Maureen Stapleton, Danny DeVito, Griffin Dunne (20th Century-Fox)

Opening with a zip, young Byron Thames gets this 1930s gangster sendup off solidly as the good-hearted, honest lad forced to take up crime to pay for the operations on his multi-ailing mum (Maureen Stapleton).

Stapleton is also well-cast in her clichéd role, as are Peter Boyle as the good mobster Dundee and Joe Piscopo as the bad Vermin. Deliberately overworking the Cagney mannerisms, Michael Keaton is initially good, too, in the title role, as is Griffin Dunne as Johnny's D.A. brother.

As a streetcorner pope extorting Keaton for cash, Dom DeLuise appears for only a few lines, none of them funny. It's Ray Walston's brief contribution that exemplifies the overall content of the film: As a blind news vendor, he gets hit in the head with a bundle of papers, restoring his sight. Then he gets hit again, turning him deaf. Hit a third time, he regains his hearing but loses his memory. Funny stuff.

•

JOHNNY EAGER
1941, 106 mins, US b/w
Dir Mervyn LeRoy *Prod* John W. Considine, Jr. *Scr* John Lee Mahin, James Edward Grant *Ph* Harold Rosson *Ed* Albert Akst *Mus* Bronislau Kaper *Art* Cedric Gibbons, Stan Rogers
Act Robert Taylor, Lana Turner, Edward Arnold, Van Heflin, Robert Sterling, Patricia Dane (M-G-M)

Johnny Eager is an underworld meller with a few new twists to the usual trappings, but by and large it's the familiar tale [by James Edward Grant] of slick gangster vs innocent rich girl.

Robert Taylor, with his hair slightly ruffled to make him a rough-tough guy, drives a taxi for the benefit of the parole board while directing his underworld activities of slot machines, protection and expected opening of a dog track. Debutante Lana Turner meets him at the parole office, and falls in love with the intriguing ex-convict. After discovering his gangster activities, she holds the secret, but is the victim of a phoney murder staged by Taylor so the latter can control the girl's stepfather, the crusading prosecutor, and so open the dog track against injunction.

Taylor effectively handles the pretty-boy (not a reflection on him, personally) characterization, with Turner clicking in the acting line and a most easy subject for the men to look at. Van Heflin, as the perpetually-soused companion of Taylor, is outstanding.

•

JOHNNY GUITAR
1954, 111 mins, US col
Dir Nicholas Ray *Prod* Herbert J. Yates *Scr* Philip Yordan *Ph* Harry Stradling *Ed* Richard L. Van Enger *Mus* Victor Young *Art* James Sullivan
Act Joan Crawford, Sterling Hayden, Mercedes McCambridge, Scott Brady, Ward Bond, Ernest Borgnine (Republic)

Joan Crawford, whose previous western was *Montana Moon* in 1930, has another try at the wide open spaces with *Johnny Guitar*. Like *Moon*, it proves the actress should leave saddles and Levis to someone else and stick to city lights for a background.

The Roy Chanslor novel on which Philip Yordan based the screenplay provides this Republic release with a conventional oater basis. Scripter Yordan and director Nicholas Ray became so involved with character nuances and neuroses, that "Johnny Guitar" never has enough chance to rear up in the saddle and ride at an acceptable outdoor pace.

Crawford plays Vienna, strong-willed owner of a plush gambling saloon standing alone in the wilderness of Arizona. She knows the railroad's coming through and she will build a whole new town and get rich. Opposing her is Mercedes McCambridge, bitter, frustrated leader of a nearby community.

Love, hate and violence, with little sympathy for the characters, is stirred up during the overlong film.

•

JOHNNY HANDSOME
1989, 95 mins, US col
Dir Walter Hill *Prod* Charles Roven *Scr* Ken Friedman *Ph* Matthew F. Leonetti *Ed* Freeman Davies *Mus* Ry Cooder *Art* Gene Rudolf
Act Mickey Rourke, Ellen Barkin, Elizabeth McGovern, Morgan Freeman, Forest Whitaker, Lance Henriksen (Carolco/Guber-Peters)

A promising idea is gunned down by sickening violence and a downbeat ending in *Johnny Handsome*, a Mickey Rourke vehicle [based on *The Three Worlds of Johnny Handsome* by John Godey].

At the outset, John Sedley (Rourke) is anything but handsome. Born with a cleft palate and badly disfigured face, he's struggled through life and wound up a petty criminal.

Johnny is sent to the pen where he comes to the attention of kindly Dr. Resher (Forest Whitaker), a plastic surgeon who, after a series of painful ops, has Johnny looking like Mickey Rourke. Johnny is allowed out of prison each day to work on the docks, where he meets pretty accountant Elizabeth McGovern and a relationship blossoms.

But Johnny isn't content with his new circumstances: he wants revenge. He plots with his old gang members (who don't recognize him) to rob the dockyard payroll, meaning to double-cross them. It all leads to a grim, violent downer of an ending.

Rourke works hard at his character but fails to make Johnny the least bit sympathetic. Ellen Barkin creates one of the ugliest femme characters seen in recent films, while Lance Henriksen is typecast as yet another seedy hood.

•

JOHNNY IN THE CLOUDS
SEE: THE WAY TO THE STARS

•

JOHNNY MNEMONIC
1995, 98 mins, Canada Ⓥ ⦿ col
Dir Robert Longo ***Prod*** Don Carmody ***Scr*** William Gibson ***Ph*** Francois Protat ***Ed*** Ronald Sanders ***Mus*** Brad Fiedel ***Art*** Nilo Rodis Jamero
Act Keanu Reeves, Dolph Lundgren, Takeshi, Ice-T, Dina Meyer, Udo Kier (Alliance)

Johnny Mnemonic is high-tech trash, film as videogame. Scarcely the film Keanu Reeves needed as a follow-up to his commercial breakthrough with *Speed*, this hardware nerd's paradise, with its nondescript look, hodgepodge cast and dialogue that seems dubbed even though it likely isn't, startlingly resembles the polyglot international co-productions of the '70s, notably the late, unlamented Canadian tax-shelter ventures. This will come as a disappointment to fans of cyberpunk writer William Gibson, who penned the adaptation of his short story.

Set in the year 2021, when vast corporations rule the world, pic features one bit of ingenuity, its premise, which sees Johnny (Reeves) outfitted with a computer chip in his head so that he can smuggle the highly classified contents from Asia to North America. The amount of information he has taken on is enough to make his noggin explode unless he gets downloaded in short order.

Chased by yakuza intent on obtaining the info for a giant corporation, Johnny makes his way to the Free City of Newark, a dismal urban ruin, and endures any number of confrontations, assaults and standoffs from those who might profit from the goods carried by the belligerent young man, notably a vicious man of the cloth impersonated by Dolph Lundgren.

The long-awaited razzle-dazzle of Johnny's downloading is an extended visual trip that seems intended as a modern equivalent to the stargate sequence in *2001* but comes off as so much graphic doodling.

Absolutely zero human interest is generated by Reeves, who comes off as gruff, hostile and selfish, all in one dimension.

[Pic premiered in Japan, in 113-min. version containing extra footage of Japanese co-star Takeshi. Version reviewed is North American one.]

•

JOHNNY O'CLOCK
1947, 95 mins, US b/w
Dir Robert Rossen ***Prod*** Edward G. Nealis ***Scr*** Robert Rossen ***Ph*** Burnett Guffey ***Ed*** Warren Low, Al Clark ***Mus*** George Duning ***Art*** Stephen Goosson, Cary Odell
Act Dick Powell, Evelyn Keyes, Lee J. Cobb, Ellen Drew, Nina Foch, Jeff Chandler (Columbia)

This is a smart whodunit, with attention to scripting, casting and camerawork lifting it above the average. Pic has action and suspense, and certain quick touches of humor to add flavor. Ace performances by Dick Powell, as a gambling house overseer, and Lee J. Cobb, as a police inspector, also up the rating.

Plot concerns Powell's operation as a junior partner in Thomas Gomez's gambling joint, and his allure for the ladies, especially Ellen Drew, the boss's wife. A cop tries to cut into the gambling racket and is murdered. The hatcheck girl, sweet on the cop, is also killed. When the checker's dancer sister (Evelyn Keyes) comes to find out what happened to the girl, she steps into a round of mystery centering about Powell.

Although the plot follows a familiar pattern, the characterizations are fresh and the performances good enough to overbalance. Dialog is terse and topical, avoiding the sentimental, phoney touch. Unusual camera angles come along now and then to heighten interest and momentarily arrest the eye. Strong teamplay by Robert Rossen, doubling as director-scripter, and Milton Holmes, original writer and associate producer, also aids in making this a smooth production.

•

JOHNNY SUEDE
1992, 95 mins, US Ⓥ ⦿ col
Dir Tom DiCillo ***Prod*** Yoram Mandel, Ruth Waldburger ***Scr*** Tom DiCillo ***Ph*** Joe DeSalvo ***Ed*** Geraldine Peroni ***Mus*** Jim Farmer, Link Wray ***Art*** Patricia Woodbridge
Act Brad Pitt, Calvin Levels, Alison Moir, Catherine Keener, Tina Louise, Nick Cave (Vega)

Taking place in an imaginary slum that could be on the outskirts of any east coast metropolis (pic was actually shot in New York), Tom DiCillo's gently ironic fantasy focuses on a dreamy young man who rejects reality and, after a pair of suede shoes is literally dropped on his head, adopts the name Johnny Suede and sets out to be a pop star, using the late Ricky Nelson as his model.

Johnny starts a tentative affair with pretty young Alison Moir, who lives nearby with an older, abusive photographer. His dream fades once she decides she prefers rough treatment. On the rebound, he reluctantly picks up a tutor of retarded children (Catherine Keener), and under her guidance he starts on the journey that will land him with both feet on the ground.

One-time cameraman (*Stranger Than Paradise, Variety*), DiCillo exploits pastel colors to advantage in order to flesh out Johnny's fantasy world. Brad Pitt, fresh from stealing scenes in *Thelma & Louise*, gives Johnny the right kind of innocent appeal, and the rest of the cast surround him with loving care.

•

JOHN PAUL JONES
1959, 126 mins, US ▭ col
Dir John Farrow ***Prod*** Samuel Bronston ***Scr*** John Farrow, Jesse Lasky, Jr. ***Ph*** Michel Kelber ***Ed*** Eda Warren ***Mus*** Max Steiner ***Art*** Franz Bachelin
Act Robert Stack, Marisa Pavan, Charles Coburn, Erin O'Brien, Jean-Pierre Aumont, Bette Davis (Warner)

John Paul Jones has some spectacular sea action scenes and achieves some freshness in dealing with the Revolutionary War. But the Samuel Bronston production doesn't get much fire-power into its characters. They end, as they begin, as historical personages rather than human beings.

John Farrow's direction of such scenes as the battle of Jones's *Bon Homme Richard* with the British *Serapis* is fine, colorful and exciting. Perhaps because Jones himself was a man of action, the story gets stiff and awkward when it moves off the quarterdeck and into the drawing room.

The screenplay attempts to give the story contemporary significance by opening and closing with shots of the present U.S. Navy, emphasizing the tradition Jones began almost single-handed. The interim picks up Jones as a Scottish boy who runs away to sea, becomes a sea captain, and winds up in the American colonies as they prepare for the War of Independence.

The historical figures tend to be stiff or unbelievable. Charles Coburn, as Benjamin Franklin, has a fussy charm, and Macdonald Carey, as Patrick Henry, is good. The brief appearance of Bette Davis as Catherine the Great of Russia is the cliché portrait of that vigorous empress, a woman bordering on nymphomania.

Robert Stack in the title role gives a robust portrayal. Marisa Pavan, as a titled Frenchwoman, is sweet but rather lifeless, while Jean-Pierre Aumont, as Louis XVI, seems a stronger monarch than the usual portrait of that doomed king.

•

JOI-UCHI
(REBELLION; SAMURAI REBELLION)
1967, 125 mins, Japan ⦿ ▭ b/w
Dir Masaki Kobayashi ***Prod*** Tomoyuki Tanaka (exec.) ***Scr*** Shinobu Hashimoto ***Ph*** Kazuo Yamada ***Mus*** Toru Takemitsu ***Art*** Yoshiro Muraki
Act Toshiro Mifune, Go Kato, Tatsuya Nakadai, Michiko Otsuka, Yoko Tsukasa, Tatsuo Matsumura (Toho/Mifune)

Written by Shinobu Hashimoto (who also wrote *Rashomon* and *Harakiri*), with music by Toru Takemitsu and directed by the man who created *Harakiri* and *Kwaidan*, this Toho-Mifune production represents all the best in the Japanese period film [from the novel by Yasuhiko Takiguchi].

At the end of the 18th century, a middle-aged court official stationed in the North (Toshiro Mifune), married into the house of a virtuous harridan (Michiko Otsuka), discovers that the local *daimyo* (Tatsuo Matsumura) is demanding back an ex-wife (Yoko Tsukasa), who has since become married to Mifune's elder son (Go Kato).

Mifune questions the authority of, first, his wife's family, then the family council, and finally that of the court secretary (Shigeru Koyama) and the *daimyo* himself.

At first there are various attempts at intimidation and blackmail. When this does not succeed, comes the *daimyo*'s order for Mifune and Kato to kill themselves. Mifune does the unheard of; he refuses. Instead he barricades his house and awaits the worst.

Nothing happens, except talk, for the first hour and 40 minutes, and then screen explodes into the most slashing *chambara* since *Harakiri*. The letting of blood does not purify, nor is it intended to.

•

JOKER IS WILD, THE
(AKA: ALL THE WAY)
1957, 126 mins, US col
Dir Charles Vidor ***Prod*** Samuel J. Briskin ***Scr*** Oscar Saul ***Ph*** Daniel L. Fapp ***Ed*** Everett Douglas ***Mus*** Walter Scharf
Act Frank Sinatra, Mitzi Gaynor, Jeanne Crain, Eddie Albert, Beverly Garland, Jackie Coogan (Paramount)

The Joker Is Wild purports to be the case history of a Prohibition era entertainer who lived through a savage attack by mobsters; loved and lost a pretty, rich girl; married a dancer whom he neglected; often was a self-pitying heel; hit the bottle and gambled all the time; and meanwhile gagged his way to being a heavy favorite in the club-date sweepstakes.

Frank Sinatra was first to carry the ball with this one, having bought Art Cohn's story of Joe E. Lewis in galley proof form and thereafter taking a key part in the packaging. Sinatra obviously couldn't be made to look like Lewis; and Lewis style of delivery is unique. But these are minor reservations in light of the major job Sinatra does—alternately sympathetic and pathetic, funny and sad.

Eddie Albert plays Austin Mack, Lewis's longtime piano accompanist and intimate friend, with considerable feel. Jeanne Crain is touching and fits in fine as the wealthy gal who falls for Lewis (and he for her). The leggy, shapely, cutie-pie-faced Mitzi Gaynor is colorful as a chorus dancer who marries Lewis after Crain takes the powder.

Under Charles Vidor's direction, *Joker* plays out in well-organized and smooth fashion. But it goes overboard on length.

1957: Best Song ("All the Way")

•

JOKERS, THE
1967, 94 mins, UK col
Dir Michael Winner ***Prod*** Maurice Foster, Ben Arbeid ***Scr*** Dick Clement, Ian La Frenais ***Ph*** Kenneth Hodges ***Ed*** Bernard Gribble ***Mus*** Johnny Pearson ***Art*** John Blezard
Act Michael Crawford, Oliver Reed, Harry Andrews, James Donald, Daniel Massey, Michael Hordern (Rank Gildor-Scimitar)

Pic has the supreme virtue of portraying young people as they are, without patronizing or exploiting them: restless, somewhat disenchanted, privately aware of their immaturity, and with a tendency to rush needlessly into action with a later psychological hangover in many cases.

Michael Crawford and Oliver Reed are two brothers, the former just expelled from still another college for a practical joke, the latter the author of that scheme. Together, they plan and execute a national outrage—theft of the Crown Jewels, with no intent to keep them, just to carry off the theft.

Sight gags and underplayed British throwaway gags are interleaved neatly with the growing suspense over whether the guys will succeed.

•

JOLI MAI, LE
1963, 180 mins, France b/w
Dir Chris Marker ***Prod*** Andre Heinrich ***Scr*** Catherine Varlin, Chris Marker ***Ph*** Pierre Lhomme ***Ed*** Eva Zora ***Mus*** Michel Legrand
(Sofracima)

Film details a series of happenings, street and home interviews, plus a general panorama of Paris in May '62. It gives the oo-la-la capital a new look and brings it down out of the frou-frou to reality.

Via intensive editing, people reveal themselves. Pettiness, common sense, posturing, guile, generosity, wit and meanness all come floating out to give a neat look at human foibles. There are shots of riots during the Algerian fracas, an African's attitudes towards the French, stock-market worker outlooks, and many others.

There is also an intensive searching out of the underside of the city, housing problems, displaced persons, a worker priest who has turned leftist, and a fine envelope of well-shot scenes of the city and terse statistics on its overcrowding, arts, etc.

None of the usual Paris clichés are here. It is an absorbing piece of filming and does not seem as long as its three hours. There is already a two-hour version. The commentary is well delivered by Yves Montand. Lensing is also of top quality.

•

JOLSON SINGS AGAIN

1949, 96 mins, US Ⓥ ⊙ col

Dir Henry Levin ***Prod*** Sidney Buchman ***Scr*** Sidney Buchman ***Ph*** William Snyder ***Ed*** William Lyon ***Mus*** George Duning

Act Larry Parks, Barbara Hale, William Demarest, Ludwig Donath, Bill Goodwin (Columbia)

It is only natural that the durability of Al Jolson, as the all-time No. 1 performing personality in show business, would be matched by an equally rich real-life story. *Jolson Sings Again* proves that.

On a broad canvas is projected Jolson's wartime tours under Special Services, singing from the Aleutians to the Caribbean bases until he finally contracts the serious fever which laid him low in North Africa. Barbara Hale reenacts the nurse technician from Little Rock who is now Mrs. Jolson.

Larry Parks, again playing Jolson, remains an uncannily faithful impersonator of the star

1949: NOMINATIONS: Best Story & Screenplay, Color Cinematography, Scoring of a Musical Picture

•

JOLSON STORY, THE

1946, 120 mins, US Ⓥ ⊙ col

Dir Alfred E. Green ***Prod*** Sidney Skolsky ***Scr*** Stephen Longstreet ***Ph*** Joseph Walker ***Ed*** William Lyon ***Mus*** Morris Stoloff (dir.) ***Art*** Stephen Goosson, Walter Holscher

Act Larry Parks, Evelyn Keyes, William Demarest, Bill Goodwin, Ludwig Donath, Tamara Shayne (Columbia)

Jolson's singing proves the big excitement for this Technicolorful film bio of the great mammy-singer's career.

The Jolson Story emerges as an American success story in song. The yearning to sing to give generously of himself, cued by the still famed-in-showbiz catchphrase, "You ain't heard nothin' yet"; the Sunday nights at the Winter Garden, the birth of the runway as Jolson got closer to his audience, the incidental whistling in between vocalizing—all these are recaptured for the screen.

But there's lots more on and off the screen. As Evelyn Keyes plays Ruby Keeler—only she's called Julie Benson—in meticulous manner, she helps carry the boy-girl saga.

But the real star of the production is that Jolson voice and that Jolson medley. It was good showmanship to cast this film with lesser people, particularly Larry Parks as the mammy kid. It's quite apparent how he must have studied the Jolson mannerisms in black-and-white because the vocal synchronization (with a plenitude of closeups) defies detection.

1946: Best Sound Recording, Scoring for a Musical Picture

NOMINATIONS: Best Actor (Larry Parks), Supp. Actor (William Demarest), Color Cinematography, Editing

•

JONATHAN LIVINGSTON SEAGULL

1973, 114 mins, US Ⓥ ▭ col

Dir Hall Bartlett ***Prod*** Hall Bartlett ***Scr*** Richard Bach, Hall Bartlett ***Ph*** Jack Couffer ***Ed*** Frank Keller ***Mus*** Neil Diamond ***Art*** Boris Leven (Paramount)

Before the fact, nobody could have foretold the success of Richard Bach's book, *Jonathan Livingston Seagull*, and Hall Bartlett's $1.5 million film version poses the same question. The pastoral allegory, filmed with live birds and locations while some well-known players essay the vocal chores, is a combination of teenybopper psychedelics, facile moralizing, Pollyanna polemic, and superb nature photography.

Though not credited, per arrangement, the vocal cast draws on many fine players. James Franciscus dubs the title bird, a nonconformist who wants to dive for fish instead of foraging in garbage like gulls always do. A puzzlement to his early girl-friend, essayed by Kelly Harmon, and his parents (Dorothy McGuire and Richard Crenna), Jonathan is banished from the flock by elder Hal Holbrook. After cruising the world, he passes (via saturated color printing) to another level of existence.

Now there's nothing wrong with uplift, except that exhortations customarily are banal. That is, the end is nearly destroyed by the means.

1973: NOMINATIONS: Best Cinematography, Editing

•

JOSEPH ANDREWS

1977, 103 mins, UK Ⓥ col

Dir Tony Richardson ***Prod*** Neil Hartley ***Scr*** Allan Scott, Chris Bryant ***Ph*** David Watkin ***Ed*** Thom Noble ***Mus*** John Addison ***Art*** Michael Annals

Act Ann-Margret, Peter Firth, Michael Hordern, Beryl Reid, Jim Dale, Natalie Ogle (Woodfall)

Joseph Andrews is a tired British period piece about leching and wenching amidst the high- and low-life of Henry Fielding's England. Tony Richardson's film is a ludicrous mix of underplayed bawdiness and sporadic vulgarity.

Large cast of otherwise British players is headed by Ann-Margret, sometimes appearing grotesque in her rendition of Lady Booby, the noblewoman-with-a-past with the hots for servant Peter Firth in title role.

Fielding's story of concealed identities and misplaced birth origins has of course been the inspiration for generations of successively updated farce. Herein, Richardson has attempted to pump up the project via the casting of some famed British thesps—John Gielgud, Peggy Ashcroft, Hugh Griffith among some 14 guest stars in cameos.

•

JOSETTE

1938, 70 mins, US Ⓥ col

Dir Allan Dwan ***Prod*** Gene Markey ***Scr*** James Edward Grant ***Ph*** John Mescall ***Ed*** Robert Simpson ***Mus*** David Buttolph (dir.)

Act Don Ameche, Simone Simon, Robert Young, Joan Davis, Bert Lahr, Paul Hurst (20th Century-Fox)

This is a corking good entertainment. Smartly written, well directed and deftly acted, the piece [from a play by Paul Frank and Georg Fraser, based on a story by Ladislaus Vadnai] has momentum and skips along in a most amusing sort of way. The three principals (Don Ameche, Simone Simon and Robert Young) play it as if they were having a good time, and with no more effort than stepping in out of the rain. When the leads are out of sight, Joan Davis, Bert Lahr and Paul Hurst do their clowning on a slightly broader pattern.

Simon is a cute little trick, pint-size alongside Ameche and Young. These two play brothers who start out with the single thought of separating their philandering father from a cabaret singer named Josette, who is after the sugar. The real Josette fails to appear for her engagement, and Simon, local choir singer, substitutes. Management (Lahr) keeps the original billing, and the brothers, of course, start to put the pressure on the wrong girl.

Brothers fall in love with the girl who takes their attentions big. Ameche and Young get all the laughs obtainable from bright lines. Simon plays coyly, and sings right well two songs written by Mack Gordon and Harry Revel.

•

JOUR DE FETE

1949, 87 mins, France Ⓥ ⊙ b/w

Dir Jacques Tati ***Prod*** Fred Orain ***Scr*** Jacques Tati, Henri Marquet, Rene Wheeler ***Ph*** Jacques Mercanton ***Ed*** Marcel Moreau ***Mus*** Jean Yatove ***Art*** Rene Moulaert

Act Jacques Tati, Guy Decomble, Paul Frankeur, Santa Relli, Maine Vallee, Roger Rafael (Cady)

Borrah Minevitch, an American showman who has been in Paris a couple of years, put together the money, story, star and, above all, the knowhow. Apart from Minevitch, the production setup includes Fred Orain, who is a technician, and Minevitch's comedy discovery, Jacques Tati.

The story, which is of the thinnest, shows a French village on a holiday. There is practically no plot. Supporting cast is of very small importance compared to Tati, who does the village postman. Jean Yatove's music is adequate and direction, technique and tempo are all okay. But the one thing that counts in the picture is Tati's antics, with practically no dialog.

•

JOURNAL D'UN CURE DE CAMPAGNE, LE (*DIARY OF A COUNTRY PRIEST*)

1951, 120 mins, France Ⓥ ⊙ ▭ b/w

Dir Robert Bresson ***Scr*** Robert Bresson ***Ph*** Leonce-Henry Burel ***Ed*** Paulette Robert ***Mus*** Jean-Jacques Grunewald ***Art*** Pierre Charbonnier

Act Claude Laydu, Nicole Maurey, Nicole Ladmirale, Marie-Monique Arkell, Jean Riveyre, Serge Bento (UGC)

A conscientious rendering of a literary study [by Georges Bernanos] of the spiritual anguish of a shy, young priest, this film has ponderous dignity. Made with taste and reverence, pic is slow-moving but impressive.

Film shows the priest's entries in the journal, underlines it with his soliloquies, and then shows it through images. The priest (Claude Laydu) suffers the hostility and misunderstanding of the townspeople. Suffering from a severe stomach ailment, he subsists on bread and wine. The hostile villagers soon take him for a drunkard. All his attempts to win the confidence of his flock lead to failure, except in the eyes of the curate who understands his internal suffering.

Director Robert Bresson has ruthlessly stamped out any incident not in keeping with the mood and feeling of the young priest. The camera dwells on the priest for interminable closeups. All facets of his character and reactions are fully explored.

•

JOURNAL D'UNE FEMME DE CHAMBRE, LE (*DIARY OF A CHAMBERMAID*)

1964, 100 mins, France/Italy Ⓥ ⊙ b/w

Dir Luis Bunuel ***Prod*** Henri Baum (exec.) ***Scr*** Luis Bunuel, Jean-Claude Carriere ***Ph*** Roger Fellous ***Ed*** Louisette Hautecoeur ***Mus*** [none] ***Art*** Georges Wakhevitch

Act Jeanne Moreau, Michel Piccoli, Georges Geret, Francoise Lugagne, Daniel Ivernel, Jean Ozenne (Speva/Cine-Alliance/Filmsonor/Dear

A look at rustic insularity in the 1920s, pic [from the novel by Octave Mirbeau] lays bare human pettiness but does it with a flair and objectivity. This makes the film funny, revealing and, overall, quite engrossing.

A bouncy, zesty, ripe 32-year-old maid (Jeanne Moreau) is on her way to a job with a landed family in the country. And a rugged lot they are. There is the father who is a foot fetishist, his sickly daughter who dreads marital duties with her rakish, skirt-chasing husband, an ominous, racist handyman, and an eccentric old military man next door who insists on throwing rubbish on their land because of an old feud.

The maid is soon chased by the husband and also is asked to try on old-fashioned high-button boots by the father. The latter is found dead one morning, with the boots clutched in his hands. Follows the rape of an eight-year-old girl.

Director Luis Bunuel has embroidered all this richly with revealing characterization, a feel for the period and a refusal to become moralistic or to take sides.

Moreau has the acid self-protection and engaging forthrightness to make her role brim with a bright force. Georges Geret has menace and weight as the violent fascist. Michel Piccoli is rightly contemptible as the marauding husband, while Jean Ozenne's old, perverse landowner is a gem of taste and tact in delineation.

•

JOURNEY, THE

1959, 122 mins, US col

Dir Anatole Litvak ***Prod*** Anatole Litvak ***Scr*** George Tabori ***Ph*** Jack Hildyard ***Ed*** Dorothy Spencer ***Mus*** Georges Auric ***Art*** Werner Schlichting, Isabella Schlichting

Act Yul Brynner, Deborah Kerr, Jason Robards, Robert Morley, E. G. Marshall, Kurt Kasznar (M-G-M/Alby)

The Journey is a relatively short one, geographically speaking. It leads from Budapest to the Austrian frontier, a distance of about 100 miles. A group of passengers, American, British, French, Israeli etc, is trapped at Budapest airport by the 1956 Hungarian uprising. The Red Army grounds the civilian planes, so this particular group has to take a bus to Vienna.

At the last checkpoint on the border the Russian commander is Yul Brynner. He delays the party, ostensibly to verify their passports and exit permits. His reasons are not clear. One seems to be his purely whimsical desire for Western company. Another is his suspicion that one member of the party (Jason Robards) is one of the Hungarian rebel leaders.

What it eventually simmers down to is a political-sexual triangle, with Brynner jealous of Deborah Kerr's attachment to Robards. Litvak finds he can tell his story almost entirely through Kerr (the West) and Brynner (the East), so the subsidiary characters and their subplots suffer. This neglect is justified, however, chiefly by the projection of Brynner's characterization. He is capricious, sentimental, cruel, eager for love and suspicious of attention. Kerr has the difficult assignment of being in love with one man, Robards, and yet unwillingly attracted to another, Brynner, who is the opposite of all she admires and loves. She is brilliant and moving as a woman alone in an unbearable situation. Jason Robards, in his film bow, is excellent.

•

JOURNEY INTO FEAR
1943, 68 mins, US Ⓥ ⦿ b/w
Dir Norman Foster, [Orson Welles] ***Prod*** Orson Welles ***Scr*** Orson Welles, Joseph Cotten ***Ph*** Karl Struss ***Ed*** Mark Robson ***Mus*** Roy Webb ***Art*** Albert S. D'Agostini, Mark-Lee Kirk
Act Joseph Cotten, Dolores Del Rio, Ruth Warrick, Orson Welles, Agnes Moorehead, Everett Sloane (RKO/Mercury)

In *Journey into Fear*, Orson Welles's third release for RKO, he handles only the production reins and takes one of the character leads but leaves direction in the hands of Norman Foster. Picture attempts to catch attention through series of dramatic peaks, but misses that mark by a considerable margin, being too stagey and talky.

Joseph Cotten is the pivotal character—an American naval ordnance engineer returning to the U.S. from Istanbul.

Welles delivers an above-par characterization as the Turkish secret police chief. Cotten is okay in the lead, despite the fact the writers present him as a rather weakling hero throughout.

Direction by Foster is deliberate and slow, pausing too much on unimportant incidentals. Adaptation of Eric Ambler's novel was prepared by Welles and Cotten, and there's nothing new in technique or treatment.

●

JOURNEY OF NATTY GANN, THE
1985, 105 mins, US Ⓥ ⦿ col
Dir Jeremy Paul Kagan ***Prod*** Mike Lobell ***Scr*** Jeanne Rosenberg ***Ph*** Dick Bush ***Ed*** David Holden ***Mus*** James Horner ***Art*** Paul Sylbert
Act Meredith Salenger, John Cusack, Ray Wise, Scatman Crothers, Barry Miller, Lainie Kazan (Walt Disney)

More a period piece of Americana than a rousing adventure, *The Journey of Natty Gann* is a generally diverting variation on a boy and his dog: this time it's a girl and her wolf.

Set in the Depression in Chicago, story has widower Saul Gann desperate to find employment to support himself and daughter Natty. He's offered a job at the lumber camp out in Washington State and reluctantly takes it, promising to send for Natty as soon as he can. He leaves her under the auspices of a floozy hotel manager.

The girl runs away and remainder of pic is her sojourn across America in search of her dad. Along the way she rescues a wolf from its captors, and he becomes her endearing traveling partner.

Director Jeremy Paul Kagan extracts an engaging performance from Meredith Salenger as the heroine. Rest of the cast is fine, with John Cusack as her begrudging but good buddy and Barry Miller as the witty entrepreneurial leader of a hobo brat pack.

1985: NOMINATION: Best Costume Design

●

JOURNEY TOGETHER
1945, 95 mins, UK Ⓥ b/w
Dir [John Boulting] ***Scr*** [Terence Rattigan] ***Ph*** [Stanley Sayer, Harry Waxman] ***Mus*** Gordon Jacob
Act Edward G. Robinson, Richard Attenborough, Jack Watling, David Tomlinson, Ronald Squire, Bessie Love (RAF)

The screen calls it "a story dedicated to the few who trained the many." It's a convincing tribute to the last war aces (Yanks as well as British) and to grounded veterans of the Battle of Britain who took the rawest of raw material and made good airmen out of them.

The production was written, directed, photographed and produced by members of the RAF [all uncredited], some of them vets of the film biz, but all of them honest-to-God fliers. Also the cast, with four exceptions, was recruited from RAF personnel. Ronald Squire and Reginald Beck, in minor roles, and Edward G. Robinson and Bessie Love are the four pros who figure in the cast.

Film covers a wide range of territory, from the cloistered halls of Cambridge University to Falcon Field in Arizona, from the Canadian Navigation School to the blazing inferno of bomb-plastered Berlin. But it is the aerial camerawork in *Journey Together* that sets a new high. Most of final 15 minutes are shot inside a bomber with a degree of great skill.

●

JOURNEY TO THE CENTER OF THE EARTH
1959, 132 mins, US Ⓥ ⦿ ▭ col
Dir Henry Levin ***Prod*** Charles Brackett ***Scr*** Walter Reisch, Charles Brackett ***Ph*** Leo Tover ***Ed*** Stuart Gilmore, Jack W. Holmes ***Mus*** Bernard Herrmann ***Art*** Lyle R. Wheeler, Franz Bachelin, Herman A. Blumenthal
Act Pat Boone, James Mason, Arlene Dahl, Diane Baker, Thayer David, Peter Ronson (20th Century-Fox)

The Charles Brackett production takes a tongue-in-cheek approach to the Jules Verne story, but there are times when it is difficult to determine whether the filmmakers are kidding or playing it straight. The actors neither take themselves nor the picture seriously, which is all on the plus side.

The story concerns an expedition, led by James Mason, who plays a dedicated scientist, to the center of the earth. Among those who descend to the depths with Mason are Pat Boone, one of his students; Arlene Dahl, the widow of a Swedish geologist who steals Mason's information and tries to beat him to the "underworld", and Peter Ronson, an Icelandic guide and jack-of-all-trades.

The descent is a treacherous one, filled with all kinds of dangers—underground floods, unusual winds, excessive heat, devious paths. Before reaching their goal, the intrepid explorers confront prehistoric monsters, a forest of mushrooms, a cavern of quartz crystals and a salt vortex.

Boone is given an opportunity to throw in a couple of songs. Romance is not neglected. Waiting at home in Edinburgh for Boone is Diane Baker, Mason's niece. And it's obvious that Mason and the widow Dahl will end up in a clinch despite their constant bickering during the expedition.

1959: NOMINATIONS: Best Color Art Direction, Sound, Special Effects

●

JOURNEY TO THE FAR SIDE OF THE SUN
SEE: DOPPELGANGER

●

JOUR SE LEVE, LE
(DAYBREAK)
1939, 95 mins, France ⦿ b/w
Dir Marcel Carne ***Prod*** Paul Madeux ***Scr*** Jacques Viot, Jacques Prevert ***Ph*** Curt Courant ***Ed*** Rene Le Henaff ***Mus*** Maurice Jaubert ***Art*** Alexandre Trauner
Act Jean Gabin, Jules Berry, Arletty, Jacqueline Laurent, Mady Berry, Jacques Baumer (Sigma)

Le Jour Se Leve is another of the series of psychological studies in which French directors specialize. An otherwise excellent theme is marred by some basic errors of psychology which a more careful study of the human character would have avoided.

Directed by Marcel Carne and bringing together several of the big names of the French cinema—Jean Gabin, Jules Berry and Arletty—the tale is a cutback pictured in Gabin's mind of Berry. The police come to arrest him, but he locks himself in his apartment determined to resist. They finally close in on him at daybreak. While barricaded in his apartment, Gabin reviews the events leading to his rival's violent death.

The story is excellently conceived and planned. Gabin is an honest, hard-working laborer who commits a crime which is morally acceptable but which might have been avoided if the girl had made a simple explanation. Jacqueline Laurent is miscast as Francoise. A girl with a more sophisticated appearance would have fitted into the role better, as she has something of the coquette beneath the veneer of sentimentality and sweetness.

The action is slow and serves to emphasize Gabin's slow comprehension of the situation. The story is intelligently broken up by returning to the besieged apartment on several occasions.

Arletty and Berry are at their best. As a woman of the world, without illusions and thankful for the interlude in which she was his mistress, Arletty does a realistic piece of acting. Berry gives one of his best performances.

Photography is excellent with numerous angle shots of more than passing interest. The score is appropriate and serves to emphasize the long, tense siege against the police.

●

JOY IN THE MORNING
1965, 101 mins, US col
Dir Alex Segal ***Prod*** Henry T. Weinstein ***Scr*** Sally Benson, Alfred Hayes, Norman Lessing ***Ph*** Ellsworth Fredericks ***Ed*** Tom McCarthy ***Mus*** Bernard Herrmann ***Art*** George W. Davis, Carl Anderson
Act Richard Chamberlain, Yvette Mimieux, Arthur Kennedy, Oscar Homolka, Joan Tetzel, Sidney Blackmer (M-G-M)

Undoubted appeal of the Betty Smith novel fails to come through in any appreciable measure in its filmic translation, at best a lightweight entry.

Story is of a young couple's first year of marriage at a small Midwestern college in late 1920s where groom is working his way through law school. Weakness of picture lies in the treatment. There is an absence of anything unusual happening and nothing is accomplished to overcome this lack through strong buildup of characterization.

Richard Chamberlain seldom appears at ease as the young husband-student who has difficulty in making ends meet as he takes a night watchman job to augment his day jobs, leaving only scarce time for family life and classes. Yvette Mimieux fares a little better, as she baby-sits to help out, then leaves Chamberlain when she finds she's pregnant so he won't have additional worries. Arthur Kennedy as the husband's father brings them together again in a gruff role.

●

JOYLESS STREET
SEE: DIE FREUDLOSE GASSE

●

JOY LUCK CLUB, THE
1993, 138 mins, US Ⓥ ⦿ col
Dir Wayne Wang ***Prod*** Wayne Wang, Amy Tan, Ronald Bass, ***Scr*** Amy Tan, Ronald Bass ***Ph*** Amir Mokri ***Ed*** Maysie Hoy ***Mus*** Rachel Portman ***Art*** Donald Graham Burt
Act Tsai Chin, Kieu Chinh, Lisa Lu, France Nuyen, Rosalind Chao, Tamlyn Tomita (Hollywood)

Wayne Wang's fine adaptation of Amy Tan's *The Joy Luck Club*, the No.1 fiction bestseller of 1989, is a beautifully made and acted dramatic study of trying relationships between Chinese mothers and daughters through the century.

The central occasion of a festive farewell party for June (Ming-na Wen), one of the daughters, on the eve of her departure for China, is skillfully used like the hub of a wheel, with the individual stories its spokes. As flashbacks illustrate the events, June relates how her late mother left two babies behind during her flight from her war-torn country, and adds background about their own estrangement.

Attention then turns to one of June's mahjong-playing "aunties," Lindo (Tsai Chin), who tells of how she was sold into marriage by her mother at 15. Another older woman, Ying Ying (France Nyen), had a son by a playboy husband in China. And young Rose (Rosalind Chao), whose marriage to a white American has come unglued, reveals the devastating saga of her mother An Mei (Lisa Lu).

Tying things together is June's climactic trip to China, and her ultimate reunion with her lost sisters will leave millions teary-eyed at the powerful, if sentimental, fadeout.

After years of ups and downs as an independent filmmaker, Wayne Wang has made a dramatically confident move into the mainstream here, on his own terms. Thesping from the vast cast is top-notch across the boards.

●

JUAREZ
1939, 125 mins, US Ⓥ b/w
Dir William Dieterle ***Prod*** Hal B. Wallis (exec.) ***Scr*** John Huston, Wolfgang Reinhardt, Aeneas Mackenzie ***Ph*** Tony Gaudio ***Ed*** Warren Low ***Mus*** Erich Wolfgang Korngold ***Art*** Anton Grot
Act Paul Muni, Bette Davis, Brian Aherne, Claude Rains, John Garfield, Donald Crisp (Warner)

To the list of distinguished characters whom he has created in films, Paul Muni adds a portrait of Benito Pablo Juarez, Mexican patriot and liberator. With the aid of Bette Davis, costarring in the tragic role of Carlota, and of Brian Aherne giving an excellent performance as the ill-fated Maximilian, Muni again commands attention.

Muni does not dominate in this film [based in part on a play by Franz Werfel and novel *The Phantom Crown* by Bertita Harding]; emphasis constantly is on the figure of Maximilian, the young Austrian prince who was persuaded by Napoleon III of France to proclaim himself and his wife, Carlota, rulers of the Mexican people.

Juarez, native Indian, was the elected head of the republic when the Hapsburg prince took over under sponsorship of French troops. Defeated by foreign invaders Juarez carried on guerilla warfare for several years.

Aherne seldom has appeared to such advantage as in this picture. His desire for fair play, his hopeless plea for Mexican unity and the manner in which he accepts defeat and court martial provide ample reasons for sympathy.

1939: NOMINATION: Best Supp. Actor (Brian Aherne)

●

JUBAL
1956, 100 mins, US Ⓥ ⦿ ▭ col
Dir Delmer Daves ***Prod*** William Fadiman ***Scr*** Delmer Daves, Russell S. Hughes ***Ph*** Charles Lawton Jr. ***Ed*** Al Clark ***Mus*** David Raksin ***Art*** Carl Anderson
Act Glenn Ford, Ernest Borgnine, Rod Steiger, Valerie French, Felicia Farr, Charles Bronson (Columbia)

The strong point of this gripping dramatic story set in pioneer Wyoming is a constantly mounting suspense.

Delmer Daves's direction and the script from Paul I. Wellman's novel carefully build towards the explosion that's certain to come, taking time along the way to make sure that all characters are well-rounded and understandable. Capping all this emotional suspense is the backdrop of the Grand Teton country in Wyoming.

Glenn Ford, a drifting cowpoke, runs into trouble when he takes a job on the cattle ranch operated by Ernest Borgnine. Valerie French, the rancher's amoral wife, makes an open but abortive play for him and Rod Steiger, who doesn't like to see himself replaced in her extramarital activities, plots to get even with his possible rival.

Oddly enough, much of the footage is free of actual physical violence, but the nerves are stretched so taut that it's almost a relief when it does come. Ford is effective in his underplaying of the cowpoke who wants to settle down. Borgnine is excellent as the rough but gentle man. Steiger spews evil venom as the cowhand who wants the ranch and the rancher's wife.

•

JUBILEE
1978, 103 mins, UK Ⓥ col
Dir Derek Jarman ***Prod*** Howard Malin, James Whaley ***Scr*** Derek Jarman ***Ph*** Peter Middleton ***Ed*** Tom Priestley, Nick Barnard ***Mus*** Suzi Pinns, Brian Eno, Adam and the Ants and others ***Art*** Christopher Hobbs
Act Jenny Runacre, Jordan, Little Nell, Linda Spurrier, Toyah Wilcox, Ian Charleson (Megalovision)

Derek Jarman's *Jubilee* is one of the most original, bold, and exciting features to have come out of Britain in the 1970s.

The year is 1578. Queen Elizabeth I is transported by an angel into the future (roughly the present), where she has "the shadow of the time" revealed to her.

Observing a renegade women's collective (a pyromaniac, a punk star, a nympho, a bent historian, etc), Her Majesty watches as the "ladies" and their friends go about their picaresque misadventures—disrupting a cafe, a punk audition, a murder spree.

Through this process of disemboweling the present through the memory of the past and the anticipation of the future, Jarman unravels the nation's social history in a way that other features haven't even attempted.

At times, amidst the story's violence (there are two vicious killings), black humor, and loose, fire-hose energy, the film—like the characters—seems to careen out of control.

Toyah Wilcox, as an over-the-edge firebug, gives the film's finest performance, Jenny Runacre, in a demanding dual role as Elizabeth I and the leader of the collective, is marvelous. And Orlando, as the world-owning impresario Borgia Ginz, steals every scene he's in.

•

JUDE
1996, 123 mins, UK Ⓥ ▭ col
Dir Michael Winterbottom ***Prod*** Andrew Eaton ***Scr*** Hossein Amini ***Ph*** Eduardo Serra ***Ed*** Trevor Waite ***Mus*** Adrian Johnston ***Art*** Joseph Bennett
Act Christopher Eccleston, Kate Winslet, Liam Cunningham, Rachel Griffiths, June Whitfield, Ross Colvin Turnbull (Revolution/PolyGram)

Young English actress Kate Winslet adds luster and energy to *Jude*, a bold and generally successful attempt to adapt Thomas Hardy's final novel, *Jude the Obscure*, to the big screen. Late-19th-century yarn of a country lad's attempts to better himself, and to hook the seemingly unattainable love of his life, has a vigor and freshness that minimizes the downside of Hardy's bleakest novel.

By consciously avoiding British frock-movie clichés, and adopting a fluid, almost Gallic approach to the narrative, young Brit helmer Michael Winterbottom has come up with a movie whose closest parallel in filmmaking style is, in fact, Truffaut's several costume dramas, with their fractured narrative, semi-modern feel and emotional distancing.

The adult Jude (Christopher Eccleston), earnestly studying the classics in his spare time, falls for sexy, come-hither country lass Arabella (Rachel Griffiths). Against the advice of his aunt (June Whitfield), he marries Arabella, who soon ups and leaves him for Australia. Taking control of his life, Jude moves to university town Christminster, where he bumps into Sue (Winslet), a cousin he knows only from photographs. He immediately falls for the feisty, independent-minded young femme.

Scripter Hossein Amini honors the original's structure but boils down the dialogue into a deliberately unliterary, timeless English. Even at two hours, however, the pic moves at a gallop to pack everything in.

Joseph Bennett's clever production design, using locations in Edinburgh (reping Christminster), northeast England and New Zealand (for summery Wessex), allows Eduardo Serra's widescreen camera the freedom to roam rather than rigidly shoot from fixed angles.

•

JUDEX
1963, 95 mins, France/Italy b/w
Dir Georges Franju ***Scr*** Jacques Champreux, Francis Lacassin ***Ph*** Marcel Fradetal ***Ed*** Gilbert Natot ***Mus*** Maurice Jarre ***Art*** Robert Giordani
Act Channing Pollock, Francine Berge, Edith Scob, Michel Vitold, Jacques Jouanneau, Sylva Koscina (CFF/Filmes)

Director Georges Franju has brought off a successful homage to the French film serials of the early, silent days [specifically the 1917 *Judex*, by Arthur Bernede and Louis Feuillade] in this tale of a super crook who rights wrongs and finally gives it all up for a girl. It does not send up this form of pic but rather captures its essential simplicity, adventurousness and innocence.

Judex (Channing Pollock) goes after a nefarious banker who has sent men to prison, swindled, etc. But he does not kill him when his daughter (Edith Scob) intends to give back the ill-gotten gains after the banker's supposed death. A rapacious woman burglar (Francine Berge) complicates things.

Pollock, a Yank magico, has the unruffled deadpan good looks for Judex, while others fit well into their black-and-white figures. A struggle between the black-garbed female heavy (Berge) and a white-clothed circus performer (Sylva Koscina) on a rooftop sum up the film's attitude admirably.

•

JUDGE DREDD
1995, 96 mins, US Ⓥ ⦿ ▭ col
Dir Danny Cannon ***Prod*** Charles M. Lippincott, Beau E. L. Marks ***Scr*** William Wisher, Steven E. de Souza ***Ph*** Adrian Biddle ***Ed*** Alex Mackie, Harry Keramidas ***Mus*** Alan Silvestri ***Art*** Nigel Phelps
Act Sylvester Stallone, Armande Assante, Diane Lane, Rob Schneider, Joan Chen, Max von Sydow (Cinergi/Hollywood)

Crammed with enough special effects for another *Star Wars* trilogy and utterly undeveloped beyond its original comic book origins, the reportedly $75 million *Judge Dredd* is a thunderous, unoriginal futuristic hardware show for teenage boys. Pic [from a screen story by Michael DeLuca and William Wisher] is based on a character [created by John Wagner and Carlos Ezquerra] that first appeared 18 years ago in the British comics magazine *2000 A.D.*

Mega-City One, built on the former New York City, is a sprawling metropolis whose population of 65 million is threatened by teeming criminality at the street level. Combating the anarchy are elite lawmen known as Judges, who mete out instant justice as they patrol the city on their airborne bikes.

The most feared is the infamous Judge Dredd (Sylvester Stallone), an emotionless authoritarian. It's all in a day's work for Dredd until archfiend Rico (Armand Assante) escapes from the high-security Aspen Penal Colony and returns to seek revenge.

Rico gets Dredd convicted of murder and sent up on a life sentence. Dredd manages to escape, along with comic relief Fergie (Rob Schneider), and final half hour charts his assault on the citadel to stop the crazed Rico.

The ruling structure is presented visually as thoroughly totalitarian with Nazi overtones, from the Gianni Versace-designed centurionlike outfits to the German accent of ruling council turncoat Judge Griffin (Jurgen Prochnow).

Young British director Danny Cannon (*The Young Americans*) has his hands full here just getting all the diverse technical elements up on the screen, so any real style is out of the question.

Like James Remar as the lead criminal, Scott Wilson turns up without credit, as the patriarch of a demented religious cult. An uncredited James Earl Jones intones over the opening scroll-up.

•

JUDGEMENT IN STONE, A
SEE: LA CEREMONIE

•

JUDGE PRIEST
1934, 80 mins, US Ⓥ b/w
Dir John Ford ***Prod*** Sol M. Wurtzel ***Scr*** Dudley Nichols, Lamar Trotti ***Ph*** George Schneiderman ***Mus*** Cyril J. Mockridge
Act Will Rogers, Henry B. Walthall, Tom Brown, Anita Louise, Rochelle Hudson, Berton Churchill (Fox)

Difficult, beforehand, to reconcile the idea of Irvin Cobb's *Judge Priest* with Will Rogers. Cobb's long series of stories have suggested another type; portly, slightly pompous on occasion and somewhat lethargic in movement, and that isn't Will Rogers. But Rogers makes the old judge completely his own.

At best the story is thin: the love of his nephew for the girl whose father is not known. The father is in town, and when he slugs a man for jeering at her the victim later gangs up on him with two of his pals. The father cuts his assailant and is put on trial. He refuses to make the explanation which would be his legal out anywhere in the South.

The judge's political rival demands that he surrender the bench, since his nephew is lawyer for the defense. Heartbroken at this aspersion of his integrity, the judge appoints a substitute. But that night the minister talks with him. By a ruse they persuade the pompous old prosecutor to reopen the case.

It's a play of strange reactions. In the court scenes a bit of comedy relief is the effort of one of the jurors to rid himself of the product of his cud chewing. Several of the scenes are punctured with a laugh when the well-aimed shot lands in the cuspidor. Most of the comedy, however, is contributed by Rogers and Stepin Fetchit, a natural foil to the Rogers character. Other efforts at local color through the use of Negroes are less effective.

•

JUDGMENT AT NUREMBERG
1961, 178 mins, US Ⓥ ⦿ b/w
Dir Stanley Kramer ***Prod*** Stanley Kramer ***Scr*** Abby Mann ***Ph*** Ernest Laszlo ***Ed*** Frederic Knudtson ***Mus*** Ernest Gold ***Art*** Rudolph Sternad
Act Spencer Tracy, Burt Lancaster, Richard Widmark, Marlene Dietrich, Maximilian Schell, Judy Garland (United Artists)

Judgment at Nuremberg is twice the size of the concise, stirring and rewarding production on television's *Playhouse 90* early in 1959. A faster tempo by producer-director Stanley Kramer and more trenchant script editing would have punched up picture.

Abby Mann's drama is set in Nuremberg in 1948, the time of the Nazi war crimes trials. It deals not with the trials of the more well-known Nazi leaders, but with members of the German judiciary who served under the Nazi regime.

The intense courtroom drama centers on two men: the presiding judge (Spencer Tracy) who must render a monumental decision, and the principal defendant (Burt Lancaster), at first a silent, brooding figure, but ultimately the one who rises to pinpoint the real issue and admit his guilt.

Where the stars enjoy greater latitude and length of characterization, such as in the cases of Tracy, Maximilian Schell and Richard Widmark (latter two as defense counsel and prosecutor, respectively), the element of personal identity does not interfere. But in the cases of those who are playing brief roles, such as Judy Garland and Montgomery Clift, the spectator has insufficient time to divorce actor from character.

Tracy delivers a performance of great intelligence and intuition. He creates a gentle, but towering, figure, compassionate but realistic, warm but objective. Schell repeats the role he originated, with electric effect, on the TV program, and again he brings to it a fierce vigor, sincerity and nationalistic pride. Widmark is effective as the prosecutor ultimately willing to compromise and soft-pedal his passion for stiff justice when the brass gives the political word.

Lancaster as the elderly, respected German scholar-jurist on trial for his however-unwilling participation in the Nazi legal machine never quite attains the cold, superior intensity that Paul Lukas brought to the part on TV. Marlene Dietrich is persuasive as the aristocratic widow of a German general hanged as a war criminal, but the character is really superfluous to the basic issue.

1961: Best Actor (Maximilian Schell), Adapted Screenplay

NOMINATIONS: Best Picture, Director, Actor (Spencer Tracy), Supp. Actor (Montgomery Clift), Supp. Actress (Judy Garland), B&W Cinematography, B&W Costume Design, B&W Art Direction, Editing

•

JUDGMENT IN BERLIN
1988, 92 mins, US Ⓥ ⦿ col
Dir Leo Penn ***Prod*** Joshua Sinclair, Ingrid Windisch ***Scr*** Joshua Sinclair, Leo Penn ***Ph*** Gabor Pogany ***Ed*** Teddy Darvas ***Mus*** Peter Goldfoot ***Art*** Jan Schlubach, Peter Alteneder
Act Martin Sheen, Sam Wanamaker, Max Gail, Jurgen Heinrich, Harris Yulin, Sean Penn (Bibo/January)

Judgment in Berlin, about an atypical defection that occurred in West Berlin in the late 1970s, is a quality production made on a tight budget but with obvious care and commitment, avoiding didacticism.

An East German couple traveling with a child hijacked a Polish airliner headed for East Berlin, forcing the pilot to land at a West Berlin airport that serves as a U.S. military installation. The big question is who has legal jurisdiction to prosecute the hijackers. It is decided that since they landed in U.S.-occupied territory, a trial conducted by a U.S. judge is the humane solution.

Though the film's action essentially evolves around a courtroom drama, we also get glimpses of the personal lives of the principal characters, including the trial judge (Martin Sheen), and the couple accused of the hijacking, effectively played by Heinz Honig and Jutta Speidel.

There is good work by all concerned, including Leo Penn's deft, understated direction and the serviceable screenplay, adapted from an actual account written by the story's real trial judge, Herbert J. Stern.

Sean Penn (Leo's son) has a plum role as an airline passenger who decided to defect when the opportunity presented itself. His trial testimony provides the film's dramatic center

•

JUDGMENT NIGHT

1993, 109 mins, US Ⓥ ⦿ col

Dir Stephen Hopkins ***Prod*** Gene Levy ***Scr*** Lewis Colick ***Ph*** Peter Levy ***Ed*** Timothy Wellburn ***Mus*** Alan Silvestri ***Art*** Joseph Nemec III

Act Emilio Estevez, Cuba Gooding, Jr., Denis Leary, Stephen Dorff, Jeremy Piven, Peter Greene (Largo/Universal)

The most chilling aspect of the urban thriller *Judgment Night* is truly how infinitely superior its craft is to its art. This is an exceedingly well directed, cleverly filmed and edited, tension-filled affair. It is also a wholly preposterous, muddled, paranoid view of the inner-city nightmare where the slightest misstep is sure to have a fateful result.

The action pivots around a boys' night out in which four young men head from the suburbs to a big boxing match in downtown Chicago. En route they run into gridlock and take an off-ramp into a really bad neighborhood. It doesn't take much to guess what happens next.

Apart from where they live, their age, vocation and attitude provide no linking bond. Frank (Emilio Estevez) is married, has a child and may or may not be out of work. His brother John (Stephen Dorff) is alienated by something that is never defined, and Mike's (Cuba Gooding, Jr.) presence has no other explanation apart from racial diversity.

Script is one long line of falling dominoes defined more by gravity than logic. Amid the rubble, Estevez and Denis Leary, as the chief goon, comport themselves with some dignity and skill.

•

JUDITH

1966, 105 mins, US ⊏⊐ col

Dir Daniel Mann ***Prod*** Kurt Unger ***Scr*** John Michael Hayes ***Ph*** John Wilcox ***Ed*** Peter Taylor ***Mus*** Sol Kaplan ***Art*** Wilfrid Shingleton

Act Sophia Loren, Peter Finch, Jack Hawkins, Hans Verner, Zharira Charifai, Shraga Friedman (Paramount)

Israel in its birth pains backdrops this frequently tenseful adventure tale realistically produced in its actual locale. The production combines a moving story with interesting, unfamiliar characters.

The screenplay, based on an original by Lawrence Durrell, is two-pronged: the story of Sophia Loren, as the Jewish ex-wife of a Nazi war criminal who betrayed her and sent her to Dachau, intent upon finding him and wreaking her own brand of vengeance, and the efforts of the Haganah, Israel's underground army, to capture him.

Under Daniel Mann's forceful direction, the two points are fused as femme finds herself obliged to throw in with the Israelis, who use her to track down the man they know is in the Middle East but do not know how to identify.

Loren is excellent. It is a colorful role for her, particularly in her recollections of the young son she thought murdered until the Nazi, finally captured, tells her he is still alive.

Peter Finch, as a kibbutz leader and one of the Haganah, registers effectively and creates an indelible impression of what Israeli leaders accomplished in setting up their own state. Nicolas Roeg is credited with second unit direction and additional photography.

•

JUDITH OF BETHULIA

1914, 62 mins, US f ⊗ b/w

Dir D. W. Griffith ***Scr*** D. W. Griffith ***Ph*** Billy Bitzer ***Ed*** James E. Smith

Act Blanche Sweet, Henry B. Walthall, Robert Harron, Mae Marsh, Lillian Gish, Lionel Barrymore (Biograph)

Judith of Bethulia is in four-and-a-half reels, founded upon the biblical tale, with the captions probably culled from the poem of Thomas Bailey Aldrich.

In spite of the undoubtedly vast sum expended for architectural and other props to conform to the period in which the story is laid, Lawrence Marsden did not deem it necessary to recruit a cast of star players. He succeeded in utilizing the services of competent ones in the regular Biograph company. For the name part he selected Blanche Sweet; Henry Walthall for Holofernes; Robert Harron for Nathan; J. Jiquel Lanoe for the Chief Eunuch; Harry Carey for the Traitor, and so on.

There are two parts that stand out—Judith far beyond all the others, with Holofernes a safe second. Fine as is the acting of the principals, the chief thing to commend is the totally wonderful handling of the mobs and the seriousness with which each super performs his individual task.

•

JU DOU

SEE: JUDOU

•

JUDOU
(JU DOU)

1990, 95 mins, Japan/China Ⓥ ⊏⊐ col

Dir Zhang Yimou, Yang Fengliang ***Prod*** Zhang Wenze, Hu Jian, Yasuyoshi Tokuma ***Scr*** Liu Heng ***Ph*** Gu Changwei, Lang Lun ***Ed*** Du Yuan ***Mus*** Zhao Jiping ***Art*** Xia Rujin

Act Gong Li, Li Baotian, Li Wei, Zhang Yi, Zheng Jian (Tokuma/Xi'an)

A romantic tragedy set in a mountain village in the '20s, the story centers on the house and factory of dye-maker Yang Jinshan. Yang Tianqing works for his uncle, and becomes fascinated by a pretty young woman, Judou, the old man has bought for a bride.

Tianquing spies on her as she bathes, and she becomes aware of this. One night, the pair become lovers. A son is eventually born. Soon after the old man is crippled from the waist down in an accident. The lovers blatantly display their relationship in front of him, as he lies helpless. But they can never bring themselves to kill him.

The plot [from the novella *Fuxi fuxi* by Liu Heng] has all the elements of a Hollywood melodrama of the '40s (both *The Postman Always Rings Twice* and *Leave Her to Heaven* come to mind), and the picture is, indeed, as deliriously enjoyable as it sounds, but with the added dimension of age-old tradition forcing the characters into roles they don't want to play.

Visually, the picture is extraordinary, with the splendid set of the dye factory impressively used. Lengths of brightly colored cloths hang to dry from poles which extend above the roof. Large tanks of dye cover the floor, and complex wheels and pullies roll the cloth when it's ready to be baled.

Performances are full-blooded. Gong Li (the femme lead in director Zhang Yimou's previous *Red Sorghum*) is superb as the lustful wife, while Li Baotian is dogged as the ardent lover. Li Wei, as the vicious old husband who gets his comeuppance, is also fine.

•

JUGGERNAUT

1974, 109 mins, UK Ⓥ col

Dir Richard Lester ***Prod*** Richard DeKoker ***Scr*** Richard DeKoker, Alan Plater ***Ph*** Gerry Fisher ***Ed*** Tony Gibbs ***Mus*** Ken Thorne ***Art*** Terence Marsh

Act Richard Harris, Omar Sharif, David Hemmings, Anthony Hopkins, Shirley Knight, Ian Holm (United Artists)

Juggernaut stars Richard Harris as an explosives demolition expert aboard Omar Sharif's luxury liner where several bombs have been planted. The action aboard the ship, to which Harris, David Hemmings and other demolition team members have been flown, alternates with land drama, where shipline executive Ian Holm, detective Anthony Hopkins (whose wife Caroline Mortimer and children are aboard the vessel), and others, attempt to locate the phantom bomber who calls himself Juggernaut in a series of telephone calls demanding a huge ransom.

At sea, Shirley Knight wanders in and out of scenes as a romantic interest for Sharif, while Roy Kinnear comes off best of the whole cast as a compulsively cheerful social director.

•

JUGGLER, THE

1953, 84 mins, US b/w

Dir Edward Dmytryk ***Prod*** Stanley Kramer ***Scr*** Michael Blankfort ***Ph*** Roy Hunt ***Ed*** Aaron Stell ***Mus*** George Antheil ***Art*** Rudolph Sternad

Act Kirk Douglas, Milly Vitale, Paul Stewart, Joey Walsh, Alf Kjellin (Kramer/Columbia)

The Juggler deals with a man who has become a neurotic from his long imprisonment in Nazi concentration camps, and how he gradually comes to realize his illness and seek help from new-found friends. The storytelling [from the novel by Michael Blankfort] has one serious flaw. It fails to establish early the nature and cause of Kirk Douglas's illness and, as a result, his acts of violence have an adverse reaction, instead of gaining sympathy.

Once a famous European juggler, Douglas arrives with other DPs for refuge in Israel. While in a temporary camp, his strange actions arouse interest of the camp psychiatrist. Douglas denies any illness and runs away. In his flight across the country, he takes up with Joey Walsh, a young orphan, and together they head north for Nazareth where Douglas hopes to lose himself.

Douglas, under Edward Dmytryk's well-coordinated direction, does an excellent job of selling the erratic character of the juggler. Milly Vitale is very appealing as the girl Douglas meets on a kibbutz.

The camerawork of Roy Hunt flows freely over the Israel countryside, giving an authentic, almost documentary flavor to the story.

•

JUICE

1992, 96 mins, US Ⓥ ⦿ col

Dir Ernest Dickerson ***Prod*** David Heyman, Neal H. Moritz, Peter Frankfurt ***Scr*** Gerard Brown, Ernest Dickerson ***Ph*** Larry Banks ***Ed*** Sam Pollard, Brunilda Torres ***Mus*** Hank Shocklee & the Bomb Squad ***Art*** Lester Cohen

Act Omar Epps, Tupac Shakur, Jermaine Hopkins, Khalil Kain, Cindy Herron, Vincent Laresca (Paramount)

Spike Lee cinematographer Ernest Dickerson starts off the pic promisingly, introducing a well-played quartet of New York ghetto youths and exploring their lives and frustrations in what could almost be viewed as an inner-city *Breaking Away*. After a sudden, tragic robbery attempt, the film takes a peculiar turn into the thriller realm, as one of the teens (Tupac Shakur)—high on the "juice" of having killed the grocery store clerk—begins menacing his one-time friends.

Dickerson and cowriter Gerard Brown exhibit a sharp ear for dialog and have some real finds in their largely unknown cast, particularly Omar Epps as Q, the most introspective and reasoned of the four friends. Shakur, of rap group Digital Underground, is also impressive.

There are several lurches in story logic, from the sudden agreement of the group's leader (Khalil Kain, giving a solid performance) to engage in the robbery, to Q's puzzling relationship with a somewhat older nurse (Cindy Herron).

•

JULES AND JIM

SEE: JULES ET JIM

•

JULES ET JIM
(JULES AND JIM)

1962, 105 mins, France Ⓥ ⦿ ⊏⊐ b/w

Dir Francois Truffaut ***Scr*** Francois Truffaut, Jean Gruault ***Ph*** Raoul Coutard ***Ed*** Claudine Bouche ***Mus*** Georges Delerue

Act Jeanne Moreau, Oskar Werner, Henri Serre, Marie Dubois, Vanna Urbino, Sabine Haudepin (Carrosse/SEDIF)

Francois Truffaut, who made *The 400 Blows*, one of the top New Wave pix, has put together a tender tale [from the novel by Henri-Pierre Roche] that avoids mawkishness and impropriety in treating the lives of two friends who are mixed up with a woman they share. One is a Frenchman, the other an Austrian and the girl is French. Plot covers from 1912 until about 1930.

It depends more on atmosphere, insight into characters and emotions than on story values. Truffaut has shrewdly employed the physiques and characters of his principles sans exploting them. Jeanne Moreau is exceptional as the headstrong girl, Catherine, who never quite finds what she wants. The husband is done in a vein of rumpled honesty and dignity by Oskar Werner.

The three are shown at their first meeting in a frilly 1912 Paris, with Jules (Werner) winning the girl but Jim (Henri Serre) holding aloof, though attracted. The first war comes and goes, and Werner marries the girl and takes her to live in Austria. Serre comes to visit them and finally has a love fling with Moreau, now also a mother. Werner accepts this new situation as he has accepted all of her desires. They then drift apart and back.

Truffaut has a light touch for evoking moods, time, place and desires. Its forthright attempt to grasp life sometimes makes it uneven. But, overall, this is a candid entry. Truffaut uses the scope screen well.

•

JULIA

1977, 116 mins, US Ⓥ ⊙ col

Dir Fred Zinnemann ***Prod*** Richard Roth ***Scr*** Alvin Sargent ***Ph*** Douglas Slocombe ***Ed*** Walter Murch ***Mus*** Georges Delerue ***Art*** Gene Callahan, Willy Holt, Carmen Dillon

Act Jane Fonda, Vanessa Redgrave, Jason Robards, Maximilian Schell, Hal Holbrook, Meryl Streep (20th Century-Fox)

Fred Zinnemann's superbly sensitive film explores the anti-Nazi awakening in the 1930s of writer Lillian Hellman via persecution of a childhood friend, portrayed in excellent characterization by Vanessa Redgrave in title role. Richard Roth's production is handsome and tasteful.

Hellman's book *Pentimento* was the basis for literate screenplay. The warm and innocently intimate childhood relationship between two girls serves as the solid foundation for later contrasting tragedy when their lives diverge.

The period environment, brilliantly recreated in production design, costuming and color processing, complements the top-flight performances and direction.

Jane Fonda and Redgrave, neither one a shrinking violet in real life, are dynamite together on the screen.

1977: Best Supp. Actor (Jason Robards), Supp. Actress (Vanessa Redgrave), Adapted Screenplay

NOMINATIONS: Best Picture, Director, Actress (Jane Fonda), Supp. Actor (Maximilian Schell), Cinematography, Costume Design, Editing, Original Score

•

JULIA HAS TWO LOVERS

1990, 85 mins, US Ⓥ col

Dir Bashar Shbib ***Prod*** Bashar Shbib ***Scr*** Daphna Kastner, Bashar Shbib ***Ph*** Stephen Reizes ***Ed*** Dan Foegelle, Bashar Shbib ***Mus*** Emilio Kauderer

Act Daphna Kastner, David Duchovny, David Charles, Tim Ray, Clare Bancroft, Martin Donovan (Oneira)

While this tale of romance on the telephone has an interesting story concept, the conversation itself drags on for too long, leading to the film's uneven and frequently too-slow pace.

Julia (Daphna Kastner), an attractive but somewhat frustrated woman, has lived with her lover Jack (David Charles) for two years. When he unexpectedly asks her to marry him, she stalls. As Jack leaves for work, Julia answers the phone and encounters an amicable young man, Daniel (capably played by David Duchovny).

Julia soon finds herself drawn to Daniel, who apparently has dialed the wrong number. Neither of them wants to hang up. They spend the morning together following their daily routines, telling each other about themselves. Inevitably (and finally), she invites Daniel over for lunch. At this point (nearly two-thirds into the film), the story begins to take new twists, adding considerably more interest.

Production values are mediocre, with too many blurred images.

•

JULIA MISBEHAVES

1948, 99 mins, US b/w

Dir Jack Conway ***Prod*** Everett Riskin ***Scr*** William Ludwig, Harry Ruskin, Arthur Wimperis ***Ph*** Joseph Ruttenberg ***Ed*** John Dunning ***Mus*** Adolph Deutsch ***Art*** Cedric Gibbons, Daniel B. Cathcart

Act Greer Garson, Walter Pidgeon, Peter Lawford, Elizabeth Taylor, Cesar Romero (M-G-M)

All forms of comedy but the subtle are used to spring the laughs that come from the frenetic antics of a middle-aged couple, long separated but bent on trying romance again. It's gag and situation farcing that's as artful as a slap in the face.

Jack Conway's direction [of this film, based on Margery Sharp's novel, *The Nutmeg Tree*] is fast and vigorous in walloping over the comedy. Laughs are piled on top of each other, making a lot of the dialog unheard and unnecessary.

Garson is punched, doused, muddied and tossed in her unbending process. She wears tights, takes a bubble bath, sings and generally acquits herself like a lady out to prove she can be hoydenish when necessary. The other half of middle-aged team; Walter Pidgeon gives away no honors. He's pitching all the time and skillfully injects just the right amount of underplaying to balance broader delivery of his partner in fun.

The fun starts when Garson, entertainer, receives an invitation to the wedding of her daughter. Not having seen the girl since she was a baby, the mother journeys to France for the wedding.

En route to France, Garson joins an acrobatic act, becomes involved with an elderly wolf, and generally has herself a time. Garson's song, spotlighted during her acro stint, is "When You're Playing with Fire" and is delivered with unharmonious vocals, complete with gestures, for laughs.

•

JULIET OF THE SPIRITS

SEE: GIULIETTA DEGLI SPIRITI

•

JULIUS CAESAR

1953, 121 mins, US Ⓥ b/w

Dir Joseph L. Mankiewicz ***Prod*** John Houseman ***Scr*** Joseph L. Mankiewicz ***Ph*** Joseph Ruttenberg ***Ed*** John Dunning ***Mus*** Miklos Rozsa ***Art*** Cedric Gibbons, Edward Carfagno

Act Marlon Brando, James Mason, John Gielgud, Louis Calhern, Greer Garson, Deborah Kerr (M-G-M)

To those normally allergic to Shakespeare, this will be a surprise—a tense, melodramatic story, clearly presented, and excellently acted by one of the finest casts assembled for a film. Presented in its traditional, classic form, there is no attempt to build up the spectacle or battle scenes to gain sweep.

The black-and-white camera has been used effectively, the stylized settings simulate scope, and the costumes breathe authenticity. Highlight of the film is the thesping. Every performance is a tour de force. Any fears about Marlon Brando appearing in Shakespeare are dispelled by his compelling portrayal as the revengeful Mark Antony. The entire famous funeral speech takes on a new light.

John Gielgud, as the "lean and hungry" Cassius is superb. The English actor portrays the chief conspirator with sympathetic understanding. James Mason, as the noble, honorable Brutus, is equally excellent. As the close friend of Caesar, who joined the conspiracy out of noble motives, Mason is determined though ridden by guilt feelings. His falling out with Cassius at the Battle of Philippi and the scene with his wife, portrayed by Deborah Kerr, make for moving drama.

Louis Calhern's Caesar is another triumph. He plays the soldier-hero with proper restraint and feeling. Edmond O'Brien, though better known for his toughguy roles, is an effective Casca. The picture is so big that the two femme stars, Kerr and Greer Garson, are seen in gloried bits. However, both acquit themselves creditably.

1953: Best B&W Art Direction

NOMINATIONS: Best Picture, Actor (Marlon Brando), B&W Cinematography, Scoring a Dramatic Picture

•

JULIUS CAESAR

1970, 117 mins, UK Ⓥ ⊙ ▭ col

Dir Stuart Burge ***Prod*** Peter Snell ***Scr*** Robert Furnival ***Ph*** Ken Higgins ***Ed*** Eric Boyd Perkins ***Mus*** Michael Lewis ***Art*** Julia Trevelyan Oman

Act Charlton Heston, Jason Robards, John Gielgud, Richard Johnson, Robert Vaughn, Richard Chamberlain (Commonwealth United)

This stab at Shakespeare's *Julius Caesar*, a drama of political intrigue, corruption, ambition, envy, rhetoric and conspiratorial cunning, is disappointing.

Under Stuart Burge's firm direction the high spots are brought out effectively but the backgrounds and crowd sequences are stagey and lack the passion and abandon needed to project the star scenes.

Biggest disappointment is Jason Robards's Brutus. He rarely suggests "the noblest Roman of them all" and his delivery of Shakespeare's verse is flat, uninspired and totally dull.

John Gielgud in the significant but smallish title role, is probably the one that comes nearest to true Shakespearian thesping.

Charlton Heston makes a praiseworthy stab at Mark Antony, giving the role a dominating power.

•

JUMANJI

1995, 104 mins, US Ⓥ ⊙ col

Dir Joe Johnston ***Prod*** Scott Kroopf, William Teitler ***Scr*** Jonathan Hensleigh, Greg Taylor, Jim Strain ***Ph*** Thomas Ackerman ***Ed*** Robert Dalva ***Mus*** James Horner ***Art*** James Bissell

Act Robin Williams, Bonnie Hunt, Kirsten Dunst, Bradley Pierce, Bebe Neuwirth, Jonathan Hyde (Interscope/Teitler/Tri-Star)

Relying on some tried-and-true horror conventions, *Jumanji* is a grim fairy tale about a board game with supernatural powers. The film unleashes an arsenal of special effects that are dazzling to the eye but often a shock to the senses.

Opening in a quiet New England town in 1969, the tale unfolds when young Alan Parrish (Adam Hann-Byrd) discovers a buried game on a construction site. He and a friend begin to play Jumanji, a jungle-themed adventure. After Alan flings the cubes, he disappears, sucked into the vortex of the tiled diversion.

The scene abruptly shifts to the present. Nora (Bebe Neuwirth) has bought the now run-down Parrish estate and moves in with Judy (Kirsten Dunst) and Peter (Bradley Pierce), her orphaned niece and nephew. The two youngsters dust off the seemingly innocent trifle and begin to play. They summon a clutch of giant mosquitoes, a man-eating lion and a jungle wild man who turns out to be the long-absent Alan (Robin Williams).

The trio realize that the only way to undo the havoc is to complete the game. That means tracking down the adult Sarah Whittle (Bonnie Hunt), the girl who went batty with young Alan back in 1969.

What's missing is a soul for this mechanical marvel. The script, based on a kid lit book by Chris Van Allsburg, cozies around the primacy of the family without developing that theme. Director Joe Johnston has an adroit style that well serves the demands of a saga constructed in the fashion of a Rube Goldberg creation.

•

JUMBO
(AKA: *BILLY ROSE'S JUMBO*)

1962, 123 mins, US Ⓥ ⊙ ▭ col

Dir Charles Walters ***Prod*** Joe Pasternak, Martin Melcher ***Scr*** Sidney Sheldon ***Ph*** William H. Daniels ***Ed*** Richard W. Farrell ***Mus*** George Stoll (sup.) ***Art*** George W. Davis, Preston Ames

Act Doris Day, Stephen Boyd, Jimmy Durante, Martha Raye, Dean Jagger, Joseph Waring (M-G-M/Euterpe-Arwin)

One of the final productions ever seen in the old N.Y. Hippodrome, *Jumbo* was a dull, book musical of the 1935 season, with a curious mid-Depression tie-in with Texaco Gas. The showmanship of Metro has turned the combo musical and circus into a great film entertainment.

Much of the Rodgers and Hart score for the 1935 legit version has been retained. "Little Girl Blue," "My Romance," and "Most Beautiful Girl in the World" are given fullscale production. "This Can't Be Love," from Rodgers and Hart's 1938 *Boys from Syracuse* and "Why Can't I?" from their 1929 *Spring Is Here*, have been added.

Jimmy Durante is the circus-owner, with Doris Day as his daughter, and Martha Raye as his 14-year-awaiting fiancée. Durante plays the role as Durante.

Stephen Boyd, handsome, virile, excellent within the limits of his role, has star billing but his part is strictly in support of his leading lady. It's doubtful that singing is his own, but he handles his musical sequences well.

Sidney Sheldon's screenplay (he receives full credit although report has it that several scripters have had a go at it) retains only the basic circus-boy-meets-circus-girl format of Ben Hecht and Charles MacArthur's original book, with the ending the most important switch. Instead of the originally conceived merger of the two circuses then the wedding of the boy and girl, Dean Jagger's villainy drives Boyd into leaving, with Jumbo rejoining Day, Durante and Martha Raye.

1962: NOMINATION: Best Adapted Music Score

•

JUMPING JACKS

1952, 96 mins, US b/w

Dir Norman Taurog ***Prod*** Hal Wallis ***Scr*** Robert Lees, Fred Rinaldo, Herbert Baker ***Ph*** Daniel L. Fapp ***Ed*** Stanley Johnson ***Mus*** Joseph J. Lilley ***Art*** Hal Pereira, Henry Bumstead

Act Dean Martin, Jerry Lewis, Mona Freeman, Don DeFore, Robert Strauss, Richard Erdman (Paramount)

The situation comedy plot is perfectly tailored to show off Jerry Lewis's uninhibited clowning and Dean Martin's pleasant straight man chores and singing. Among the succession of laugh highlights, director Norman Taurog is responsible for the topper sequence that takes place on a train and involves the feeding of a GI hiding under a table.

Martin, a paratrooper, sends for his old vaude partner (Lewis) when a sourpuss general threatens to do away with the camp shows the soldiers are staging unless they are improved. To turn the trick, Lewis has to be passed off as a regular GI, presumably for only the one performance. However, he catches the favor of the general, who orders the group to tour other camps.

•

JUMPIN' JACK FLASH

1986, 100 mins, US Ⓥ ⊙ col

Dir Penny Marshall ***Prod*** Lawrence Gordon, Joel Silver ***Scr*** David H. Franzoni, J. W. Melville, Patricia Irving, Christo-

pher Thompson *Ph* Matthew F. Leonetti *Ed* Mark Goldblatt *Mus* Thomas Newman *Art* Robert Boyle
Act Whoopi Goldberg, Jonathan Pryce, James Belushi, Carol Kane, Annie Potts, Peter Michael Goetz (Gordon/Silver)

Jumpin' Jack Flash is not a gas, it's a bore. A weak idea and muddled plot poorly executed not surprisingly results in a tedious film with only a few brief comic interludes from Whoopi Goldberg to redeem it. Anyone who has been longing for a film in which an office worker talks dirty to a computer terminal should find *Jumpin' Jack Flash* just what they've been waiting for.

Goldberg is Terry Doolittle. Just when her life is looking most bleak along comes Jack (Jonathan Pryce). He's a British spy trapped somewhere behind the Iron Curtain who somehow, someway, taps into Goldberg's terminal and asks for help to escape.

Goldberg is plunged into a web of intrigue involving a sinister repairman (James Belushi) who conveniently disappears, a crippled diplomat (Roscoe Lee Browne) and another spy (Jeroen Krabbe) who winds up floating facedown in the East River.

•

JUNE BRIDE
1948, 96 mins, US b/w
Dir Bretaigne Windust *Prod* Henry Blanke *Scr* Ranald MacDougall *Ph* Ted McCord *Ed* Owen Marks *Mus* David Buttolph *Art* Anton Grot
Act Bette Davis, Robert Montgomery, Fay Bainter, Tom Tully, Barbara Bates, Jerome Cowan (Warner)

June Bride is a sometimes subtle, sometimes wacky, takeoff on home magazines and human nature. It has a starting hurdle as characters are set up, but once on its way never lets itself or the audience down. Bretaigne Windust's direction is always lively and extremely able at milking a line or situation, whether satire or antic, in filming the potent script by Ranald MacDougall [from a play by Eileen Tighe and Graeme Lorimer *Feature for June*].

Bette Davis presents a delightfully slicked up personality as a "through-with-love" home mag editor who does stereotyped articles on before-and-after houses and people. Robert Montgomery costars as a foreign correspondent assigned to aid Davis when news becomes dull in Europe. His glib handling of the assignment sharpens many a scene in the film. Both give socko interpretations.

Basic concern of the plot is the off-again, on-again romance between Davis and Montgomery, but other motivations share the interest.

There's a solid portrayal of youth and budding romance in the characters so ably performed by Betty Lynn and Raymond Roe. They give their roles humor and heart-tug, and make them stand out. Barbara Bates and Ray Montgomery are good as the other young romance team.

•

JUNGFRUKALLAN
(THE VIRGIN SPRING)
1960, 88 mins, Sweden Ⓥ b/w
Dir Ingmar Bergman *Scr* Ulla Isaksson *Ph* Sven Nykvist *Ed* Oscar Rosander *Mus* Erik Nordgren *Art* P. A. Lundgren
Act Max von Sydow, Birgitta Valberg, Birgitta Pettersson, Gunnel Lindblom, Axel Duberg, Tor Isedal (Svensk Filmindustri)

Ingmar Bergman was inspired by a 14th-century ballad [*Tore's Daughter in Wange*] of innocence, rape, murder and revenge for this film. Christianity had moved into Sweden, but the people were still in the grip of heathendom in many ways. Bergman and scriptwriter Ulla Isaksson (a Swedish novelist who also wrote the screenplay for *Brink of Life/So Close to Life*) have made a film rich with details which sometimes are boring.

Karin (Birgitta Pettersson) is to make the virgin's ride to church. A spoiled child, she also persuades her father, Tore (Max von Sydow), to let Ingeri (Gunnel Lindblom), who is bearing an illegitimate child, join her part of the way.

The two girls ride to the edge of the forest, from where Karin rides on alone against Ingeri's protests. Karin encounters herdsmen in the forest, who rape her while their little brother looks on.

Tore seeks revenge, murdering the herdsmen as they sleep. He turns to God, wondering why he allowed the rape and murders.

Spring is loaded with the theme of guilt. And there is no main character. Bergman has carefully mixed Christianity with Odin's raven, a toad, and heathen figures and symbols. Sven Nykvist's photography of the forest is excellent. The acting is superb. This is an extremely powerful film. However, it lacks the human warmth of *Wild Strawberries* and the majesty of *Seventh Seal*.

1960: Best Foreign Language Film

•

JUNGLE BOOK
1942, 108 mins, US Ⓥ ⦿ ⊏⊐ col
Dir Zoltan Korda *Prod* Alexander Korda *Scr* Laurence Stallings *Ph* Lee Garmes, W. Howard Greene *Ed* William Hornbeck *Mus* Miklos Rozsa *Art* Vincent Korda
Act Sabu, Joseph Calleia, John Qualen, Frank Puglia, Rosemary DeCamp, Patricia O'Rourke (Korda)

On the same grand scale of pictorial elaborateness which characterized *Thief of Bagdad*, Alexander Korda brings again to the screen the diminutive East Indian player, Sabu, in a film version of Rudyard Kipling's *Jungle Book*.

Kipling's character, Mowgli, who strayed into the jungle as a child and was brought up by a she-wolf, is most likely to be confused by filmgoers with Tarzan. Laurence Stallings wrote the screenplay and the human interest elements are slighted. Mowgli's return to the native village as a grown-up youth and his subsequent adventures in civilization are handled in neither a humorous nor dramatic manner. The saga of the boy who could converse with animals is related very seriously, whereas the theme might have been better entertainment if treated in a lighter vein.

As directed by Zoltan Korda, the fiction takes secondary place to the highly interesting and sometimes amazing views of jungle animals in the brilliance of colored photography. Some of the vistas, designed by Vincent Korda, give the illusion of deep forest depths, of dank underbrush and forbidden nooks.

Some sign language between the animals and Mowgli might adequately have conveyed all the necessary dramatic values of their intimacy. When Sabu carries on a whispered conversation with his cobras, pythons and some of the wild beasts, it is a little silly.

Korda has neglected any but a slight development of the human equation. Players therefore have unimportant assignments, with the exception of Sabu, who swims and swings his way through the jungle with ease and grace.

1942: NOMINATIONS: Best Color Cinematography, Color Art Direction, Scoring of a Dramatic Picture, Special Effects

•

JUNGLE BOOK, THE
1967, 78 mins, US Ⓥ ⦿ col
Dir Wolfgang Reitherman *Prod* Walt Disney *Scr* Larry Clemmons, Ralph Wright, Ken Anderson, Vance Gerry *Ed* Tom Acosta, Norman Carlisle *Mus* George Bruns (Walt Disney)

The Jungle Book, based on the Mowgli stories by Rudyard Kipling, was the last animated feature under Walt Disney's personal supervision before his death.

It was filmed at a declared cost of $4 million over a 42-month period. Full directorial credit is given to Wolfgang Reitherman, a 35-year Disney vet. Reitherman was one of several *Jungle* hands who worked on Disney's first animated feature, *Snow White and the Seven Dwarfs*.

Friendly panther, vocalized by Sebastian Cabot, discovers a baby boy in the jungle, and deposits him for upbringing with a wolf family, John Abbott and Ben Wright. At age ten, boy, looped by Clint Howard, is seen in need of shift to the human world, because man-hating tiger (George Sanders) has returned to the jungle.

Encounters along the way include a friendship with a devil-may-care bear, expertly cast with the voice of Phil Harris. The standout song goes to Harris, a rhythmic "Bare Necessities" extolling the value of a simple life and credited to Terry Gilkyson.

Robert B. and Richard M. Sherman wrote five other songs, best of which is "Wanna Be Like You," sung in free-wheeling fashion by Louis Prima, vocalizing the king of a monkey tribe.

1967: NOMINATION: Best Song ("Bare Necessities")

•

JUNGLE BOOK, THE
(AKA: RUDYARD KIPLING'S THE JUNGLE BOOK)
1994, 110 mins, US Ⓥ ⦿ col
Dir Stephen Sommers *Prod* Edward S. Feldman, Raju Patel *Scr* Stephen Sommers, Ronald Yanover, Mark D. Geldman *Ph* Juan Ruiz Anchia *Ed* Bob Ducsay *Mus* Basil Poledouris *Art* Allan Cameron
Act Jason Scott Lee, Cary Elwes, Lena Headey, Sam Neill, John Cleese, Jason Flemyng (Walt Disney)

A title people associate with a children's story here comes across as an ambitious hybrid of *Greystoke* and *Indiana Jones and the Temple of Doom*. Unlike the 1942 version starring Sabu, or Disney's animated '60s classic, this *Jungle Book* seeks a more modern tone. One wonders where the movie is going before it dramatically shifts gears into a full-throttled, technically superb adventure—with more bite than most Disney live-action fare—that offers some winning moments but, ultimately, isn't as involving as it needs to be.

For one thing, the narrative [by Ronald Yanover and Mark D. Geldman] keeps changing gears—from nature film to love story to actioner. At the age of five, Mowgli, the son of an Indian guide, gets lost in the jungle and is raised by animals. Soon he becomes a young man (the lithesome Jason Scott Lee), again encountering Kitty (Lena Headey), the young British girl with whom he'd played as a boy.

In section two, Kitty tries to incorporate Mowgli into society, angering Boone (Cary Elwes), a suitor who's also an officer in her father's regiment. Finally, and most effectively, a quest begins to find a lost city filled with treasure, as Mowgli seeks to save his beloved from Boone and her captors.

What ultimately drives the movie is the love story, in true beauty-and-the-beast fashion. Director Stephen Sommers serves up a visual feast of beautiful animals and spectacular vistas (shot largely in Jodhpur, India). Lee is such a striking presence physically that he needn't do much but look happy or baffled, while Headey is at best a passable lure to bring the boy out of the jungle.

•

JUNGLE FEVER
1991, 132 mins, US Ⓥ ⦿ col
Dir Spike Lee *Prod* Spike Lee *Scr* Spike Lee *Ph* Ernest Dickerson *Ed* Sam Pollard *Mus* Stevie Wonder, Terence Clanchard *Art* Wynn Thomas
Act Wesley Snipes, Annabella Sciorra, Spike Lee, Ossie Davis, Ruby Dee, John Turturro (Universal/40 Acres & a Mule)

The jungle is decidedly present but the fever is notably missing in Spike Lee's exploration of racial tensions in urban America. Lee tackles the subject of interracial romance from the unavoidable vantage point that, while things today are more open, they are also considerably more volatile and complex.

Little time is actually spent with the black man and white woman whose relationship is the core of the drama. Steering clear of conventional romantic scenes once the couple gets together, Lee instead uses the affair to detonate dozens of reactive sequences, showing how the blacks and Italians close to the principals deal with the developments.

Given the violent emotions triggered in others, it would have helped to see more of Flipper Purify (Wesley Snipes) and Angie Tucci's (Annabella Sciorra) feelings about each other as the surrounding fireworks go off.

Flipper is unceremoniously kicked out of his Harlem apartment and forced to move back in with his father (Ossie Davis), an ultra-righteous ex-preacher, and kindly mother (Ruby Dee). Angie is brutally beaten by her father and sent packing to a girlfriend's. Performances are all pointed and emotionally edgy. Film feels too long, but it ends powerfully, as the audience exits with the view that both the white and black communities are deeply troubled and have a very long way to go to resolve their differences.

•

JUNGLE FIGHTERS
SEE: THE LONG AND THE SHORT AND THE TALL

•

JUNIOR
1994, 109 mins, US Ⓥ ⦿ col
Dir Ivan Reitman *Prod* Ivan Reitman *Scr* Kevin Wade, Chris Conrad *Ph* Adam Greenberg *Ed* Sheldon Kahn, Wendy Greene Bricmont *Mus* James Newton Howard *Art* Stephen Lineweaver
Act Arnold Schwarzenegger, Danny DeVito, Emma Thompson, Frank Langella, Pamela Reed, Judy Collins (Northern Lights/Universal)

No one can touch Ivan Reitman's record for turning high concepts into popular entertainment—really popular entertainment. His latest, the pregnant-man comedy *Junior*, is no exception. What separates this straightforward chuckler from the pack is its shrewd reliance on character rather than plot, and that human dimension proves surprisingly poignant.

In a cloistered lab on an ivy-shrouded campus, researchers Dr Alex Hesse (Arnold Schwarzenegger) and Dr Larry Arbogast (Danny DeVito) have been working on a "wonder' drug for safer pregnancies. But the FDA concludes that it's not quite ready for the marketplace. So, faster than you can say loss leader, the duo get turfed and top Brit cryogenicist Dr Diana Reddin (Emma Thompson) is ensconced in their former digs.

A Canadian consortium is ready to bankroll Arbogast and the drug dubbed Expectane. What would really cement the deal is data from a human guinea pig. Arbogast fast-talks Hesse into being that test case. All Al has to do is carry the egg through the first trimester.

Junior harks back to *Bringing Up Baby* rather than to past attempts with like material such as *Rabbit Test*. It's intrinsically funny to watch serious, sober scientists involved in totally goofy pursuits.

Reitman delights—as he did in *Twins* and *Kindergarten Cop*—in sending up Mr. Mooscles's persona, and Schwarzenegger's performance is relaxed and assured. The picture also affords Thompson the opportunity to poke fun at her prim, proper image. DeVito and Frank Langella (as the villainous department administrator) nicely round out the cast, albeit in familiar roles.

1994: NOMINATION: Best Original Song ("Look What Love Has Done")

•

JUNIOR BONNER

1972, 100 mins, US Ⓥ ▭ col

Dir Sam Peckinpah ***Prod*** Joe Wizan ***Scr*** Jeb Rosebrook ***Ph*** Lucien Ballard ***Ed*** Robert Wolfe, Frank Santillo ***Mus*** Jerry Fielding ***Art*** Edward S. Haworth

Act Steve McQueen, Robert Preston, Ida Lupino, Ben Johnson, Joe Don Baker, Barbara Leigh (ABC)

The latter-day film genre of misunderstood-rodeo-drifter gets one of its best expositions in *Junior Bonner*. Steve McQueen stars handily in the title role.

Jeb Rosebrook's original screenplay, combined with uniformly adroit casting and sensitive direction, has the virtues of solid construction and economy of dialog. To be sure, the plot is somewhat biased in favor of the restless wanderings of McQueen, in that the alternatives are nearly caricature conformity; but overall there is a good balance.

Filmed in and around Prescott, Arizona, the film depicts the efforts of McQueen to look good in his hometown rodeo. Director Sam Peckinpah's reputation for violence is herein exorcised in the rodeo and brawl sequences. Audiences which consider such rough-and-tumble as innocuous, vicarious ventilation will get their fill, though others may perceive a bit more.

•

JUNO AND THE PAYCOCK

1930, 95 mins, UK Ⓥ ⦿ b/w

Dir Alfred Hitchcock ***Prod*** John Maxwell ***Scr*** Alfred Hitchcock, Alma Reville ***Ph*** Jack Cox ***Ed*** Emile de Ruelle ***Art*** Norman Arnold

Act Sara Allgood, Edward Chapman, Maire O'Neil, Sydney Morgan, Kathleen O'Regan, John Laurie (British International)

Cast consists almost entirely of Irish players. Kathleen O'Regan succeeds only in looking awkward. Edward Chapman is by no means the Paycock of Arthur Sinclair's stage interpretation. He loses a lot of the humor and mugs too much. Sara Allgood is a flat Juno and Maire O'Neil introduces some of the gestures she used on the stage when playing Juno.

Three-quarters of the film is just photographed stage play [by Sean O'Casey]—excellently photographed, but slow in action. The rest moves fast, building up a swift climax of drab tragedy with the seduction of Mary (O'Regan), the shooting of Jerry (John Laurie), and the loss of the money due under the will. The end of the play has been dropped.

Irish atmosphere of the tenement life incidental to the country is well caught, director Alfred Hitchcock having a flair for sniping the real feeling of the submerged tenth.

•

JUPITER'S DARLING

1955, 93 mins, US Ⓥ ⦿ ▭ col

Dir George Sidney ***Prod*** George Wells ***Scr*** Dorothy Kingsley ***Ph*** Paul C. Vogel, Charles Rosher ***Ed*** Ralph E. Winters ***Mus*** David Rose ***Art*** Cedric Gibbons, Urie McCleary

Act Esther Williams, Howard Keel, Marge Champion, Gower Champion, George Sanders, Richard Haydn (M-G-M)

As a takeoff, with satirical treatment, on costume actioners, *Jupiter's Darling* is fairly entertaining, although a hit-and-miss affair. It has Esther Williams in some outstanding swim numbers, and Howard Keel's robust singing.

Robert E. Sherwood's stage play, *Road to Rome*, dealing with Hannibal's invasion of Rome, served as the foundation for Dorothy Kingsley's screenplay.

The two water numbers given Williams stack up with her best. One is an imaginatively staged dream ballet. The other carries an essential part of the story, and its chase theme is developed into taut suspense drama as she flees through vast underwater reaches from pursuing barbarians seeking to recapture her for Keel's conquering Hannibal.

•

JURASSIC PARK

1993, 126 mins, US Ⓥ ⦿ col

Dir Steven Spielberg ***Prod*** Kathleen Kennedy, Gerald R. Molen ***Scr*** Michael Crichton, David Koepp ***Ph*** Dean Cundey ***Ed*** Michael Kahn ***Mus*** John Williams ***Art*** Rick Carter

Act Sam Neill, Laura Dern, Jeff Goldblum, Richard Attenborough, Bob Peck, Martin Ferrero (Universal/Amblin)

Steven Spielberg's scary and horrific thriller may be one-dimensional and even clunky in story and characterization, but definitely delivers where it counts, in excitement, suspense and the stupendous realization of giant reptiles.

The $60 million production (a bargain at the price) follows the general idea if not the letter of coscripter Michael Crichton's 1990 bestseller.

Basis of this hi-tech, scientifically based, up-to-date version lies in the notion that dinosaurs can be biologically engineered using fossilized dino DNA. Having accomplished this in secret on an island off Costa Rica, zillionaire entrepreneur/tycoon John Hammond (Richard Attenborough) brings in a small group of experts to endorse his miracle, which is to be the world's most expensive zoo-cum-amusement park.

Arriving to inspect the menagerie are paleontologists Dr. Alan Grant (Sam Neill) and Ellie Sattler (Laura Dern), as well as oddball mathematician Ian Malcolm (Jeff Goldblum), advocate of the Chaos Theory. Also along are Donald Gennaro (Martin Ferrero), a hard-nosed attorney repping the park's investors, and Hammond's two fresh-faced grandchildren, Lex (Ariana Richards) and Tim (Joseph Mazzello).

Introductory scenes are surprisingly perfunctory and Spielberg lets the dinosaurs out of the bag very early, showing some of them in full view after only 20 minutes. Still, none of these problems ends up mattering once the film clicks into high gear. When a storm strands two carloads of Hammond's guests in the middle of the park at night, a Tyrannosaurus Rex decides it's dinnertime. Events from here on frighteningly verify the mathematician's view of an unpredictable universe.

The monsters are far more convincing than the human characters. Neill's paleontologist comes off rather like a bland Indiana Jones, while Dern considerably overdoes the facial oohs and ahhs. The kids are basically along for the ride, while Jeff Goldblum, attired in all-black, helpfully fires off most of the wisecracks. As for Attenborough, agreeably back on screen for the first time since 1979, his role has been significantly softened from the book.

1993: Best Sound, Sound Editing, Visual Effects

•

JUROR, THE

1996, 116 mins, US Ⓥ ⦿ col

Dir Brian Gibson ***Prod*** Irwin Winkler, Rob Cowan ***Scr*** Ted Tally ***Ph*** Jamie Anderson ***Ed*** Robert Reitano ***Mus*** James Newton Howard ***Art*** Jan Roelfs

Act Demi Moore, Alec Baldwin, Joseph Gordon-Levitt, Anne Heche, James Gandolfini, Lindsay Crouse (Columbia)

The Juror is a somewhat leisurely paced psychological thriller distinguished only by a kinetic, menacing performance by Alec Baldwin. Ted Tally reportedly received $1 million for adapting George Dawes Green's novel after providing similar service on *The Silence of the Lambs*.

Demi Moore plays Annie, a single mother targeted by the mob to swing the jury in a murder trial, with the looming threat that a mysterious hit man (Baldwin) will kill her son (Joseph Gordon-Levitt) if things don't work out as planned.

Oozing charm and malice, Baldwin—known only as the Teacher—terrorizes Moore's character, bugging her house and endangering her child. Eventually, the woman gathers herself, hiding her son with a friend in Latin America before returning to try to turn the tables on her tormentor.

Director Brian Gibson brings welcome restraint to the proceedings, but in the process sacrifices a degree of suspense, and the narrative endures a somewhat languid stretch after the trial before kicking into gear for a climactic segment.

Baldwin does have a role here worthy of his steely-eyed intensity, mixing ruthlessness with seductive charm. Tech credits are sharp, with some pretty shots of Mexico standing in for the jungles of Guatemala.

•

JURY DUTY

1995, 86 mins, US Ⓥ col

Dir John Fortenberry ***Prod*** Yoram Ben-Ami, Peter M. Lenkov ***Scr*** Neil Tolkin, Barbara Williams, Samantha Adams ***Ph*** Avi Karpick ***Ed*** Stephen Semel ***Mus*** David Kitay ***Art*** Deborah Raymond, Dorian Vernaccio

Act Pauly Shore, Tia Carrere, Stanley Tucci, Brian Doyle-Murray, Abe Vigoda, Charles Napier (Tri-Star/Triumph)

While the idea of dropping Pauly Shore into a courtroom setting may have possessed some promise, turning the movie into a half-parody of the O. J. Simpson proceedings is utterly wrong headed, since nothing could equal the amount of media skewering and jokes that attend the trial on a daily basis.

Beyond that, *Jury Duty* comes off like a slapdash effort of almost absurd excess, with no effort whatsoever made to rein in Shore, a nonactor who comes dangerously close here to approaching the ranks of noncomics. You know you're in trouble when the movie's best and most inspired moment involves bombastic ESPN sports announcer Dick Vitale in a cameo as a Court TV–like commentator.

Shore plays Tommy, a sleep-till-noon layabout left suddenly in need of shelter when his mother (Shelley Winters) motors off to Vegas in their trailer. Tommy decides the best solution would be to get empanelled on a long, sequestered trial and winds up on a high-profile case involving a serial killer, who the entire jury assumes to be guilty.

In a *12 Angry Men* riff, Tommy conspires to prolong the deliberations to maintain his posh lifestyle—much to the chagrin of his fellow jurors, including the obligatory babe to be won over (Tia Carrere, looking pretty good even in mousy librarian garb).

Director John Fortenberry, making his feature debut after helming numerous HBO specials, exhibits just how creatively bankrupt the filmmakers are by resorting to several musical montages, apparently just to pad the duration to feature length.

•

JUST A GIGOLO

1978, 105 mins, W. Germany Ⓥ ⦿ col

Dir David Hemmings ***Prod*** Rolf Thiele ***Scr*** Joshua Sinclair, Ennio De Concini ***Ph*** Charly Steinberger ***Ed*** Maxine Julius (release version), Fred Srp, Suzie Jaeger ***Mus*** Gunther Fischer ***Art*** Peter Rothe

Act David Bowie, Sydne Rome, Kim Novak, David Hemmings, Maria Schell, Marlene Dietrich (Leguan)

Handsomely photographed in Berlin and directed with finesse by David Hemmings, David Bowie is a Prussian war vet back from the dead who drifts from one demeaning job to another and finally into employment as a gigolo.

The fascinating casting includes Marlene Dietrich and the return of Kim Novak. Sydne Rome is an appealing revelation.

Dietrich, so long away from the screen, is perforce hypnotic in what amounts to a cameo (she also touchingly croons the evergreen title song), in which she adds Bowie to her gigolo stable. Novak also makes a strong impression.

The film delivers a lot of bittersweet entertainment and is never less than engrossing. Period mood is a great strength, with an effective visual mixture of sepia and soft color tints, and a music track of period ballads and jolly ragtime tunes.

•

JUST ANOTHER GIRL ON THE I.R.T.

1992, 92 mins, US Ⓥ col

Dir Leslie Harris ***Prod*** Erwin Wilson ***Scr*** Leslie Harris ***Ph*** Richard Connors ***Ed*** Jack Haigis ***Mus*** Eric Sadler ***Art*** Michael O'Dell Green

Act Ariyan A. Johnson, Kevin Thigpen, Ebony Jerido, Chequita Jackson, William Badget, Jerard Washington (Truth 24 fps)

Shot independently in New York on a 17-day sked, this debut effort by a young black woman filmmaker is a crude but disturbing exposé of teenage ignorance and denial about the facts of life on the streets and in the bedroom.

In a raw, upfront style, writer-director Leslie Harris lays out a sad, brutal story. Chantel, 17, is an arrogant Brooklyn h.s. student who mouths off to adults, imagines she's far smarter than her classmates, and thinks nothing of dumping her regular b.f. for a hot guy with a Jeep. Determined to escape her community, she intends to finish high school in three years and make a beeline for med school.

Harris seems to be setting Chantel up for a fall, and fall she does, first into the arms of the Jeep man, fast-talking Tyrone, and consequently into unplanned, unwanted teen pregnancy. When Tyrone gives her $500 for an abortion, she shockingly spends it shopping. Finally, it's too late to do anything but have the child, and outcome is appalling and sobering.

Although the film is punched up by some energetic cutting and hip-hop music, many dialog scenes, particularly early on, are badly written and awkwardly staged.

Performances possess vigor but are on the rough side. Ariyan A. Johnson creates a very abrasive character in

Chantel. Kevin Thigpen makes the most favorable impression as Tyrone, a slick operator who becomes gradually more humanized.

•

JUST BEFORE NIGHTFALL
SEE: JUSTE AVANT LA NUIT

•

JUST CAUSE
1995, 102 mins, US Ⓥ ⊙ ⌧ col
Dir Arne Glimcher ***Prod*** Lee Rich, Arne Glimcher, Steve Perry ***Scr*** Jeb Stuart, Peter Stone ***Ph*** Lajos Koltai ***Ed*** William Anderson ***Mus*** James Newton Howard ***Art*** Patrizia von Brandenstein
Act Sean Connery, Laurence Fishburne, Kate Capshaw, Blair Underwood, Ed Harris, Christopher Murray (Warner)

Just Cause ambles along for more than an hour as a perfectly respectable mystery procedural [from John Katzenbach's novel] with Sean Connery's Harvard law professor as a fish out of water in the Florida backwoods gradually trying to set things right for a young man he believes was unjustly sent to death row years before. But then all hell breaks loose, with one unconvincing twist after another being thrown at the audience, to the point where all credibility and suspence are drowned irretrievably in the murk of the Everglades.

Bobby Earl (Blair Underwood) has been convicted of raping and murdering an 11-year-old girl eight years before. Earl claims that his confession was drummed out of him by black cop Tanny Brown (Laurence Fishburne), who is none too welcoming when Armstrong (Connery) tries to resurrect the case. It eventually begins to look like the real murderer was another resident of Florida's death row, maniacal serial killer Blair Sullivan (Ed Harris).

But then the flip-flops, coincidences, surprising disclosures, far-fetched happenings, TV-style chases and illogically protracted confrontations come flying virtually all at once, obliterating the plausible character work and making the film feel like a hundred others.

Second directorial effort, after *Mambo Kings*, by art gallery honcho Arne Glimcher, is professional without being particularly nuanced through the first two-thirds. Thesping is solid as long as the story retains credibility, with Connery effectively anchoring the picture. Fishburne steals most of the scenes he's in as a cop with a nasty streak, while Underwood keeps the audience guessing as to his character's veracity.

•

JUSTE AVANT LA NUIT
(JUST BEFORE NIGHTFALL)
1971, 106 mins, France/Italy Ⓥ col
Dir Claude Chabrol ***Prod*** Andre Genoves (exec.) ***Scr*** Claude Chabrol ***Ph*** Jean Rabier ***Ed*** Jacques Gaillard ***Mus*** Pierre Jansen ***Art*** Guy Littaye
Act Michel Bouquet, Stephane Audran, Francois Perier, Dominique Zardi, Henri Attal, Paul Temps (Films La Boetie/Cinemar)

Michel Bouquet starts with killing the wife of his best friend who had been his mistress. She had egged him on in a depraved, but not serious, manner and finally he does it for keeps.

Then pic [from the novel *The Thin Line* by Edward Atlyah] deals with his living with this deed. In the background are shrewdly concocted visual ideas and events that reflect on his dilemma. His middleaged accountant absconds with funds due a young girl. There is a rat in his ornate house which is finally seen trapped, to counterpoint his own state. He is finally driven by guilt or masochism or twisted moral drive to give himself up, though there is no suspicion of him.

Chabrol is fine with actors and Bouquet has presence and brooding intensity as the killer-despite-himself, while Stephane Audran is effective as the self-effacing but proud wife, and Francois Perier telling as the friend who even accepts a confession of the murder.

Chabrol shows a mixed attitude towards his upper-class types which both condemns and seems to understand their seeming class outlooks, problems and intimations of crack-ups. This might be the best made of all of Chabrol's pix around this subject.

•

JUST FOR YOU
1952, 95 mins, US col
Dir Elliott Nugent ***Prod*** Pat Duggan ***Scr*** Robert Carson ***Ph*** George Barnes ***Ed*** Ellsworth Hoagland ***Mus*** Emil Newman (dir.)
Act Bing Crosby, Jane Wyman, Ethel Barrymore, Robert Arthur, Natalie Wood, Cora Witherspoon (Paramount)

Just For You, a Bing Crosby–Jane Wyman musical, has a rousing, melodic score by Harry Warren and Leo Robin, and a logical story well acted by a fine cast.

Screenplayed from the Stephen Vincent Benet original [*Famous*], the script spins a tale of how a Broadway producer almost loses the affections of his teenage boy and girl because he'd been too intent upon his own career to take note of his motherless children's activities. Woven in as a secondary plot is a story of adolescent love that's solved very handily before the final reel is unspooled.

Crosby and Wyman, turn in bangup performances as the producer and his musicomedy star, respectively. A highly successful composer-impresario, Crosby has romantic leanings toward his shapely leading lady. But complicating the situation is a crush that Crosby's son (Robert Arthur) develops for the actress.

•

JUSTINE
1969, 117 mins, US Ⓥ ⌧ col
Dir George Cukor ***Prod*** Pandro S. Berman ***Scr*** Lawrence B. Marcus ***Ph*** Leon Shamroy ***Ed*** Rita Roland ***Mus*** Jerry Goldsmith ***Art*** Jack Martin Smith, William Creber, Fred Harpman
Act Anouk Aimee, Dirk Bogarde, John Vernon, Anna Karina, Philippe Noiret, Michael York (20th Century-Fox)

Difficulties and hazards involved in compressing four novels into a single film are self-revelatory. Based upon Lawrence Durrell's novel *Justine* and three other volumes comprising author's *Alexandria Quartet*, the plottage is particularly difficult to follow.

While the story rivets on Anouk Aimee as the Egyptian Jewess, a prostitute wed to one of her country's most powerful financiers, there are such a multiplicity of elements and forms of love as to prove overly burdensome for the screen.

As a further hurdle to easy comprehension, Aimee, a French actress, frequently cannot be understood.

Aimee is arresting in her delineation and frequently gives an exciting performance. Michael York, as an Englishman, shares male honors with Dirk Bogarde, playing a British diplomat, and John Vernon, the husband, who heads the Coptics' plans to save their own necks in Egypt.

•

JUST LIKE A WOMAN
1992, 106 mins, UK Ⓥ ⊙ col
Dir Christopher Monger ***Prod*** Nick Evans ***Scr*** Nick Evans ***Ph*** Alan Hume ***Ed*** Nicolas Gaster ***Mus*** Michael Storey ***Art*** John Box
Act Julie Walters, Adrian Pasdar, Paul Freeman, Gordon Kennedy, Ian Redford, Shelley Thompson (Rank/LWT/Zenith)

Except for Edward D. Wood's notorious *Glen or Glenda*, which wasn't intentionally amusing, *Just Like a Woman* is the funniest plea for tolerance of transvestites ever made.

Adrian Pasdar stars as a Yank financial whiz employed by a London investment firm. At first, he seems to have it all: a rewarding job, a wife, two children and all the lacy underwear a cross-dresser could want.

His world comes crashing down when his wife, finding some unfamiliar panties at home, figures her husband is unfaithful and kicks him out. Pasdar moves into a rooming-house operated by the somewhat older (and appreciably wiser) Julie Walters, cast as a divorcée longing for excitement.

Walters offers a tasty mix of sauciness and common sense in her best big-screen turn since *Educating Rita*. Pasdar is sympathetic and engaging in a tricky role, and he certainly looks androgynous enough for the basic gimmick [from Monica Jay's novel *Geraldine*] to work.

•

JUST ONE OF THE GUYS
1985, 100 mins, US Ⓥ ⊙ col
Dir Lisa Gottlieb ***Prod*** Andrew Fogelson ***Scr*** Dennis Feldman, Jeff Franklin ***Ph*** John McPherson ***Ed*** Lou Lombardo ***Mus*** Tom Scott ***Art*** Paul Peters
Act Joyce Hyser, Clayton Rohner, Billy Jacoby, William Zabka, Toni Hudson, Sherilyn Fenn (Summa/Triton)

Popular and tenacious high school girl passing herself off as a boy at a rival campus serves as a deceptive cover for this comedy that's really about what it's like to be an outsider in the rigid teenage caste system.

Joyce Hyser, affecting a lower register, a short haircut, and a subtle swagger, is not totally convincing as a boy because she's too pretty and too chic.

The scenario sets up the motivation for Hyser to act a boy when she becomes convinced that she lost a chance to win a summer intern job on the local daily newspaper because her journalism teacher considered her another pretty face instead of an intelligent writer.

But this feminist point is then abandoned when her new teacher makes it clear she lost the job because her contest entry was boring. You guessed it: she writes about what it's like to be a girl playing a boy in high school locker rooms, etc.

Key male part of quiet outsider whom Hyser brings to life is essayed by another film newcomer, Clayton Rohner, but Rohner looks too old to be a high school kid.

•

J. W. COOP
1971, 112 mins, US col
Dir Cliff Robertson ***Prod*** Cliff Robertson ***Scr*** Cliff Robertson ***Ph*** Frank Stanley ***Ed*** Alex Beaton ***Mus*** Louie Shelton, Don Randi
Act Cliff Robertson, Geraldine Page, Cristina Ferrare, R. G. Armstrong, John Crawford (Columbia)

J. W. Coop is an engaging yarn which follows the reorientation of a rodeo rider, who after spending 10 years in jail for passing a bum check and fighting with a sheriff, is released to discover he is in collision with a totally unexpected present.

Cliff Robertson, who stars, produced, directed and scripted, has fashioned from all angles a strong, believable character study of a professional rider who finds he must not only adjust to radically altered American attitudes, but also to the rodeo circuit, which has taken on a big business air that is alien to him.

There are also startling social changes that Coop must cope with, including adjusting to a free-thinking, on-the-road woman who besides offering him no-strings companionship, attempts to turn him around by educating him to the reality of an altered society, the problems of pollution and humorously trying to turn him on to soybeans and other health foods.

Robertson's sensitive treatment and savvy direction has created a character at once heroic and tragic.

KAFKA
1991, 98 mins, US Ⓥ ⦿ col/b&w
Dir Steven Soderbergh ***Prod*** Stuart Cornfeld, Harry Benn ***Scr*** Lem Dobbs ***Ph*** Walt Lloyd ***Ed*** Steven Soderbergh ***Mus*** Cliff Martinez ***Art*** Gavin Bocquet, Tony Woollard
Act Jeremy Irons, Theresa Russell, Joel Grey, Ian Holm, Jeroen Krabbe, Alec Guinness (Baltimore/Renn-Pricel)

Defiantly not a biopic, Steven Soderbergh's first outing since he burst on the scene with *sex, lies, and videotape* places the literary world's first alienated man in a sinister Prague, c. 1919, echoing author's fictional universe. But the story ultimately feels too conventional, and the portrait of the artist is too shallow to stand as a compelling or convincing evocation of a complex mind.

Penned more than 10 years earlier, Lem Dobbs's script tells of a mild-mannered insurance company clerk who, by night, writes strange stories for little-read magazines. Although somewhat antisocial, Kafka (never Franz) lives a relatively routine, orderly life.

Kafka (Jeremy Irons) is introduced to a group of anarchists by another coworker (Theresa Russell), and although he rejects their overtures to him, Kafka is increasingly drawn into a maze of intrigue through an array of puzzling circumstances. Soon the femme coworker disappears, and Kafka finds himself with a briefcase bomb on a secret mission to the dreaded Castle.

The villain of the piece is not named Dr. Murnau (Ian Holm) for nothing. The old-world setting and exaggerated visual style readily recall German Expressionism. Although shot on the virtually unchanged streets of Prague, and despite some strong staging of individual scenes, *Kafka* is, finally, too normal. Ironically, Soderbergh scores his greatest visual coup when, 74 minutes in, he suddenly switches to color, a la *The Wizard of Oz*, upon Kafka's penetration of the Castle.

Irons acts Kafka's bewilderment expertly but never truly seems like a pawn of society. Nice one-dimensional character turns are put in by the distinguished men in the cast, but Russell, with her untempered U.S. accent and flat readings, sticks out like a sore thumb.

•

KAGEMUSHA
(THE SHADOW WARRIOR)
1980, 179 mins, Japan/US Ⓥ ▭ col
Dir Akira Kurosawa ***Scr*** Akira Kurosawa, Masato Ide ***Ph*** Kazuo Miyagawa, Asakazu Nakai, Takao Saito, Shoji Ueda ***Mus*** Shinichiro Ikebe ***Art*** Yoshiro Muraki
Act Tatsuya Nakadai, Tsutomu Yamazaki, Kenichi Hagiwara, Kota Yui, Hideji Otaki, Hideo Murata (Toho/Kurosawa/20th Century-Fox)

Akira Kurosawa has made this a sweeping epic of the times of clan wars in 16th-century Japan as well as etched particular lives of men involved in the decisions that brought turmoil until a victor emerged to consolidate the country.

It cost $6 million, not much by Hollywood standards but immense in Japan. The money is there on the screen with its meticulous costuming and reconstruction of an era and its battle scenes.

A clan leader, Shingen Takeda, uses doubles to take his place seated on a hill overlooking the battlefields. His younger brother, his usual double, finds a petty thief saved from execution who looks exactly like Takeda. The incredible resemblance pleased Takeda and he is taken on as a new *kagemusha*.

When Takeda dies, the thief is groomed to replace him for three years, per Takeda's last wishes. The double, tutored by the brother, gains dignity and even convinces Takeda's family that he is the real leader.

Tatsuya Nakadai is extraordinary as the leader and his double. The majestic pace, the court intrigues, the ritual and battles give this a tragic and human stature. Kurosawa, at 70, shows himself young indeed in the impressive handling of this historical drama laced with shrewd insights into the almost Shakespearean intrigues of power.

•

KAIDAN
(KWAIDAN)
1964, 164 mins, Japan Ⓥ ⦿ ▭ col
Dir Masaki Kobayashi ***Scr*** Yoko Mizuki ***Ph*** Yoshio Miyajima ***Mus*** Toru Takemitsu ***Art*** Shigemasa Toda
Act Rentaro Mikuni, Michiyo Aratama, Keiko Kishi, Tatsuya Nakadai, Katsuo Nakamura, Ganemon Nakamura (Ninjin Club)

Film is visually and physically stunning but its three tales [from stories by Lafcadio Hearn] of the supernatural are more intellectual than visceral.

First story ["Kurokami"/"The Black Hair"] has a poor samurai leaving his wife to join a ruling clan and to marry again to a rich woman. But his love stays with his first wife and her image haunts him constantly.

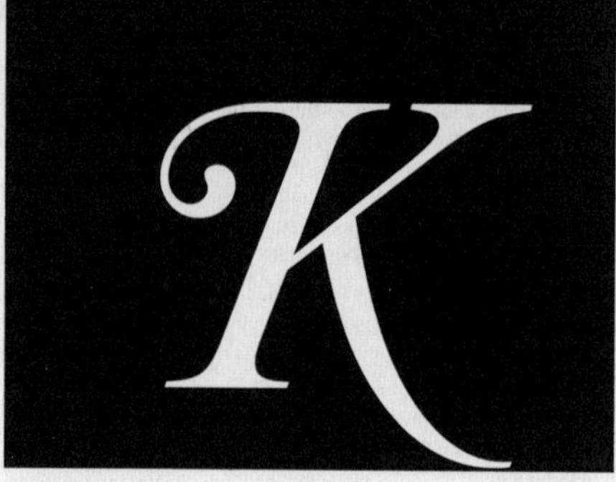

Second tale ["Miminashi Hoichi"/"Hoichi the Earless"] is about a blind monk, taken by a spirit to unfold his story of a famous sea battle to the place where the clan was destroyed. His priest tries to save him by having holy scripture written all over him.

Third ["Chawan no naka"/"In a Cup of Tea"] deals with a man who sees a reflection of someone in a cup of tea and drinks it. He has swallowed the man's soul and is then haunted by him.

Colors are subtle and used for dramatic effect. Production dress is another plus factor, as is the brilliant but sometimes coldly analytical direction of Masaki Kobayashi. Playing has the right stylized flair.

A fourth episode ["Yuki onna"/"Woman of the Snow," positioned second, about a woodcutter and a beautiful woman] was cut for the Cannes festival screening by the director himself on the suggestion pic would be too long. [Version reviewed at Cannes festival ran 125 mins.]

•

KAKUSHI TORIDE NO SAN AKUNIN
(THE HIDDEN FORTRESS)
1958, 137 mins, Japan Ⓥ ⦿ ▭ b/w
Dir Akira Kurosawa ***Prod*** Masumi Fujimoto ***Scr*** Shinobu Hashimoto, Ryuzo Kikushima, Hideo Oguni, Akira Kurosawa ***Ph*** Ichio Yamazaki ***Mus*** Masaru Sato ***Art*** Yoshiro Muraki, Kohei Ezaki
Act Toshiro Mifune, Kamatari Fujiwara, Minoru Chiaki, Eiko Miyoshi, Susumu Fujita, Takashi Shimura (Toho)

A long, interesting, humor-laden picture of medieval Japan, story concerns efforts of a beaten warlord (Toshiro Mifune) to sneak his defeated princess (Misa Uehara) out of enemy territory, where their hidden fortress is situated, into a friendly province with the family's gold. They're aided and distracted, alternately, by two greedy yokels (Minoru Chiaki and Kamatari Fujiwara) who stumble on the gold and their hiding place.

Chiaki and Fujiwara are very funny as the yokels, and Mifune is properly heroic as the warlord. The beautiful Uehara does a nice acting job, too. But the picture is really director Akira Kurosawa's, who takes what could have been a terribly unwieldy subject and makes it believable and highly entertaining. Ichio Yamazaki's camerawork is first-rate.

•

KALEIDOSCOPE
(AKA: THE BANK BREAKERS)
1966, 102 mins, UK/US col
Dir Jack Smight ***Prod*** Elliott Kastner ***Scr*** Robert Carrington, Jane-Howard Carrington ***Ph*** Christopher Challis ***Ed*** John Jympson ***Mus*** Stanley Myers ***Art*** Maurice Carter
Act Warren Beatty, Susannah York, Clive Revill, Eric Porter, Murray Melvin, George Sewell (Winkast/Warner)

Kaleidoscope is an entertaining comedy suspenser about an engaging sharpie who tampers with playing card designs so he can rack up big casino winnings. The production has some eyecatching mod clothing styles, inventive direction and other values which sustain the simple storyline.

The original screenplay turns on the exploits of Warren Beatty as he etches hidden markings on cards, wins big at various Continental casinos and, via an affair with Susannah York, comes under o.o. of her dad, Scotland Yard inspector Clive Revill.

The relaxed progress of the story becomes, under Jack Smight's direction, more dynamic through his use of Christopher Challis's mobile camera. Subsidiary events and characterizations—York's dress shop, her estrangement from Revill, latter's mechanical toy hobby, Eric Porter's deliberate viciousness, climactic card game, chase, etc.—keep the pace moving.

•

KALIFORNIA
1993, 117 mins, US Ⓥ ⦿ ▭ col
Dir Dominic Sena ***Prod*** Steve Golin, Aristides McGarry, Sigurjon Sighvatsson ***Scr*** Tim Metcalfe ***Ph*** Bojan Bazelli ***Ed*** Martin Hunter ***Mus*** Carter Burwell ***Art*** Michael White
Act Brad Pitt, Juliette Lewis, David Duchovny, Michelle Forbes, Sierra Pecheur, Gregory Mars Martin (PFE/Propaganda)

The fascination with the homicidal urge and the inability to recognize it in ourselves and others provides the chilling core of this road movie. Though somewhat overplayed and coy about its destination, the film packs a wallop.

After completing an assignment on a serial killer, magazine writer Brian Kessler (David Duchovny) decides his research on similar psychos would make a nifty coffee-table book. He concocts a cross-country tour of nefarious murder sites to collect info that will be augmented by photos shot by girlfriend Carrie Laughlin (Michelle Forbes). Early Grace (Brad Pitt), meanwhile, happens upon Brian's rideshare ad on a bulletin board at the university where he works as a janitor.

The film [from a screen story by Stephen Levy and Tim Metcalfe] cross-cuts between the relatively mundane lives of the yuppish Pittsburgh couple and scenes of Early with his significant other, the bedraggled, naive Adele Corners (Juliette Lewis), portraying a white-trash trailer-park life in which fragile circumstances tend to erupt into unpleasant consequences.

The charismatic Pitt explores his character with quiet resolve, venting both horror and darkly comic implications. Duchovny is strong in a thankless part, and Forbes is a unique presence in her major-role screen debut. But Lewis steals the show with an affectless performance that registers pity, pathos and pluck.

[A 118-min. unrated version was subsequently issued on a laserdisc.]

•

KAMERADSCHAFT
1931, 87 mins, Germany b/w
Dir G. W. Pabst ***Prod*** Seymour Nebenzal ***Scr*** Laszlo Wajda, Karl Otten, Peter Martin Lampel ***Ph*** Fritz Arno Wagner, Robert Baberske ***Art*** Erno Metzner, Karl Vollbrecht
Act Ernst Busch, Georges Charlia, Alexander Granach, Elizabeth Wendt, Daniel Mendaille, Fritz Kampers (Nero)

A mining catastrophe in the hands of an able director, G. W. Pabst. Story is based upon the disaster at Courrieres, on the German-French border, in which several hundred French miners were imprisoned underground and freed by their German colleagues.

Pabst has made it a powerful recounting and accentuates more the happenings than the men. Breaking mine shafts, giant sheets of flame, the unflagging fight for escape. Panic seizes the whole town.

Photography and architecture are excellent and the sound is clear. Picture sometimes abrupt and there are some superfluous scenes but this is an outstanding film.

•

KANAL
(THEY LOVED LIFE)
1957, 97 mins, Poland Ⓥ b/w
Dir Andrzej Wajda ***Scr*** Jerzy Stefan Stawinski ***Ph*** Jerzy Lipman ***Ed*** Halina Nawrocka ***Mus*** Jan Krenz ***Art*** Roman Mann
Act Wienczyslaw Glinski, Teresa Izewska, Tadeusz Janczar, Emil Karewicz, Wladyslaw Sheybal, Stanislaw Mikulski (Kadr)

Hallucinating pic [from a short story by Jerzy Stefan Stawinski], depicting the last days of the Polish resistance in Warsaw, is not for the squeamish. However, film has a heartfelt reenactment of these days of terror, making a taut penetrating subject.

It takes a company of partisans and deftly blocks out their characters, and then follows them into their nightmarish descent into the sewers to escape the Germans. Here mass heroism and the utter horror of war are made explicit.

Direction, if theatrical at times (but the subject almost calls for this), is dynamic, and acting first-rate, as are technical credits.

•

KANGAROO
1986, 108 mins, Australia Ⓥ ▭ col
Dir Tim Burstall ***Prod*** Ross Dimsey ***Scr*** Evan Jones ***Ph*** Dan Burstall ***Ed*** Edward McQueen-Mason ***Mus*** Nathan Waks ***Art*** Tracy Watt
Act Colin Friels, Judy Davis, John Walton, Julie Nihill, Hugh Keays-Byrne, Peter Hehir (Naked Country)

Kangaroo was written in 1922 by D. H. Lawrence after a brief visit to Australia. The resulting film is a serious, literary pic, handsomely produced and boasting a very strong cast of accomplished players.

Pic opens with a 10-minute prolog set in Cornwall, England, in 1916 and establishing the problems that Lawrence (Colin Friels), called Somers in the book and film, and his

German born wife Harriet (Judy Davis) experienced during the war.

Setting then shifts to Sydney in 1922 as the couple arrive and settle into a suburban house next to Jack and Vicky Calcott. Jack is secretly involved with a society of returned soldiers, The Diggers; under the leadership of the wealthy and charming "Kangeroo," they're training to fight an expected socialist revolution. Somers is courted both by socialist leader Struthers and by the dangerously charming "Kangeroo," a sexually ambivalent fascist.

Given the source material, the film is full of dialog, but it's interesting, well-written dialog. Davis gives another outstanding performance as a very modern woman, abrasive and a bit cynical and world weary, yet passionate. Friels gives a tense, brooding performance, filled with charm.

•

KANSAS CITY
1996, 115 mins, France/US Ⓥ col
Dir Robert Altman ***Prod*** Robert Altman ***Scr*** Robert Altman, Frank Barhydt ***Ph*** Oliver Stapleton ***Ed*** Geraldine Peroni ***Mus*** Hal Willner ***Art*** Stephen Altman
Act Jennifer Jason Leigh, Miranda Richardson, Harry Belafonte, Michael Murphy, Dermot Mulroney, Steve Buscemi (CiBy 2000/Sandcastle 5)

Kansas City is a piece of cold nostalgia, a darkly dreamy tour of Depression-era America that brings together the opposite ends of the class spectrum and emphasizes the most unsavory aspects of the democratic political process. Although it focuses upon two very off-center white female characters, Robert Altman's period-drenched meller basks in the glory of the 1930s black jazz that flourished in his hometown, and the music furnishes a flavorsome distraction even when the narrative riffs onto some weird sidings.

Blondie O'Hara (Jennifer Jason Leigh), has hatched a cockeyed scheme by which she hopes that kidnapping Carolyn Stilton (Miranda Richardson), the socialite wife of Democratic party bigwig Henry Stilton (Michael Murphy), will somehow get her back her husband, two-bit hood Johnny O'Hara (Dermot Mulroney), who's disappeared.

Unfortunately, Johnny has pulled a dimwitted robbery for which he is easily apprehended by Hey-Hey Club owner and underworld kingpin Seldom Seen (Harry Belafonte). Meanwhile Blondie, who likes to think she's Jean Harlow, a Kansas City native, drags the laudanum-addicted Carolyn with her in her meandering search for dense hubby.

The core of the yarn remains the curious odyssey of the two wildly mismatched women. Script by Altman and his *Short Cuts* co-writer, Frank Barhydt, presents more of a situation than a story, and occasional lulls in the roughly 24-hour narrative that indulge character interplay create as much exasperation as insight.

Blondie is played by Leigh at her most eccentric, sketching an ill-educated floozie with plenty of illusions and bad teeth. Richardson plays with great subtlety and finesse, although the script supplies neither much background on her character nor reasons to take a strong interest in her. Belafonte invests his slick gangster with a harsh toughness never before seen from the actor.

The omnipresent jazz score is a constant pleasure.

•

KANSAS CITY BOMBER
1972, 99 mins, US Ⓥ col
Dir Jerrold Freedman ***Prod*** Marty Elfand ***Scr*** Thomas Rickman, Calvin Clements ***Ph*** Fred Koenekamp ***Ed*** David Berlatsky ***Mus*** Don Ellis ***Art*** Joseph R. Jennings
Act Raquel Welch, Kevin McCarthy, Helena Kallianiotes, Norman Alden, Jeanne Cooper, Jodie Foster (M-G-M)

Kansas City Bomber provides a gutsy, sensitive and comprehensive look at the barbaric world of the roller derby. Rugged, brawling action will more than satisfy those who enjoy that type of commercial carnage, while the script explores deftly the cynical manipulation of players and audiences.

Barry Sandler's original story, written for a university thesis, has been scripted into a well-structured screenplay, in which most dialog is appropriate to the environment.

Raquel Welch, who did a lot of her own skating, is most credible as the beauteous but tough star for whom team owner Kevin McCarthy has big plans. A fake grudge fight moves her from K.C. to Portland, where McCarthy is building his team for a profitable sale. At the same time, Welch is torn between her professional life and her two fatherless children.

•

KANSAS CITY CONFIDENTIAL
(UK: THE SECRET FOUR)
1952, 98 mins, US Ⓥ b/w
Dir Phil Karlson ***Prod*** Edward Small ***Scr*** George Bruce, Harry Essex ***Ph*** George Diskant ***Ed*** Buddy Small ***Mus*** Paul Sawtell ***Art*** Edward L. Ilon
Act John Payne, Coleen Gray, Preston Foster, Lee Van Cleef, Neville Brand, Jack Elam (Edward Small/United Artists)

A fast-moving, suspenseful entry for the action market [from a story by Harold R. Greene and Rowland Brown].

Mastermind of a holdup on a Kansas City bank is former police captain Preston Foster. Wearing a mask to conceal his identity, he rounds up three gunmen to pull the job. Heist is executed successfully but police seize ex-con John Payne as a prime suspect.

Cleared later, Payne hunts down the gang whom he suspects of framing him. It's a dangerous mission that leads to Guatemala.

With exception of the denouement, director Phil Karlson reins his cast in a grim atmosphere that develops momentum through succeeding reels.

Payne delivers an impressive portrayal of an unrelenting outsider who cracks the ring.

•

KARAKTER
(CHARACTER)
1997, 120 mins, Netherlands Ⓥ ⊙ col
Dir Mike van Diem ***Prod*** Laurens Geels ***Scr*** Mike van Diem, Laurens Geels, Ruud van Megen ***Ph*** Rogier Stoffers ***Ed*** Jessica de Koning ***Mus*** Het Paleis van Boem ***Art*** Jelier & Schaaf
Act Fedja van Huet, Jan Decleir, Betty Schuurman, Victor Low, Tamar van den Dop, Hans Kesting (First Floor)

A lushly mounted historical drama about a young man's lifelong struggle with his cruel, powerful father, *Character* boasts a rich evocation of '20s Holland, solid thesping and assured, dynamic handling by debuting helmer Mike van Diem.

Tale opens with a bloodied young lawyer named Katadreuffe (Fedja van Huet) being arrested for the murder of an important and feared citizen, bailiff Dreverhaven (Jan Decleir), who also happens to be his father. Flashbacks give the accused's version of events.

Katadreuffe's mother, Joba (Betty Schuurman), was Dreverhaven's maid and gave in to his advances only once before leaving his employ. After the fleeting liaison gave her a son, she refused Dreverhaven's offers of marriage. The boy grew into an adolescent aching to make something of himself. His first step was to take out a business loan that soon turned disastrous, thanks in large part to the influence of his father, who seemed to want to toughen him but also wreak revenge for Joba's rejection of marriage.

Scripted from the celebrated novel by F. Bordewijk, *Character* feels overloaded with incident and shaped by a world view that's more literary than cinematic. Even so, pic has loads to recommend it and its look is extremely impressive for its grand scale and vivid period textures. Shot in Poland, Belgium and Germany as well as several Dutch cities, the film offers an engrossing, expansive evocation of '20s Rotterdam.

1997: Best Foreign Language Film

•

KARATE KID, THE
1984, 126 mins, US Ⓥ ⊙ col
Dir John G. Avildsen ***Prod*** Jerry Weintraub ***Scr*** Robert Mark Kamen ***Ph*** James Crabe ***Ed*** Bud Smith, Walt Mulconery, John G. Avildsen ***Mus*** Bill Conti ***Art*** William J. Cassidy
Act Ralph Macchio, Noriyuki "Pat" Morita, Elisabeth Shue, Martin Kove, Randee Heller, William Zabka (Columbia)

John G. Avildsen is back in the *Rocky* ring with *The Karate Kid*. More precisely, it is a *Rocky* for kids.

Daniel (Ralph Macchio) and his mother (Randee Heller) move from their home in New Jersey to Southern California. Daniel encounters the attacks of his schoolmates and he is well established as an underdog.

Enter Mr. Miyagi (Noriyuki "Pat" Morita), the mysterious maintenance man who takes Daniel under-wing. Daniel wants Miyagi to teach him how to defend himself, but the old man resists until Daniel learns that karate is a discipline of the heart and mind, of the spirit, not of vengeance and revenge.

Morita is simply terrific, bringing the appropriate authority and wisdom to the part.

1984: NOMINATION: Best Supp. Actor (Noriyuki "Pat" Morita)

•

KARATE KID PART II, THE
1986, 113 mins, US Ⓥ ⊙ col
Dir John G. Avildsen ***Prod*** Jerry Weintraub ***Scr*** Robert Mark Kamen ***Ph*** James Crabe ***Ed*** David Garfield, Jane Kurson, John G. Avildson ***Mus*** Bill Conti ***Art*** William J. Cassidy
Act Ralph Macchio, Noriyuki "Pat" Morita, Nobu McCarthy, Danny Kamekona, Yuji Okumoto, Tamlyn Tomita (Columbia)

Film literally picks up where the 1984 one left off, with spunky teen Ralph Macchio winning a karate contest against no-good ruffians. Informed that his father is gravely ill, Noriyuki "Pat" Morita heads back to his native Okinawa, with Macchio in tow. His father, who soon dies, turns out to be the least of Morita's concerns.

Morita loved a young woman on the island but left in deference to her arranged marriage to Sato. Latter, also a karate expert, has never forgiven Morita for backing out of a fight which would have determined who got the girl. In addition, Sato's nephew takes an instant disliking to Macchio.

Script delivers any number of wise old Eastern homilies. Anyone over the age of 18 is liable to start fidgeting when Macchio dominates the action, but then viewers beyond that advanced age are irrelevant with this film.

1986: NOMINATION: Best Song ("Glory of Love")

•

KARATE KID PART III, THE
1989, 111 mins, US Ⓥ ⊙ col
Dir John G. Avildsen ***Prod*** Jerry Weintraub ***Scr*** Robert Mark Kamen ***Ph*** Stephen Yaconelli ***Ed*** John Carter, John G. Avildsen ***Mus*** Bill Conti ***Art*** William F. Matthews
Act Ralph Macchio, Noriyuki "Pat" Morita, Robyn Lively, Thomas Ian Griffith, Martin Kove, Sean Kanan (Columbia)

The makers of *The Karate Kid Part III*—also responsible for its successful predecessors—have either delivered or taken a few too many kicks to the head along the way, resulting in a particularly dimwitted film that will likely spell the death of the series.

The only remarkable things about it are that Ralph Macchio still looks young enough to play a 17-year-old, and that Noriyuki "Pat" Morita can still milk some charm from his character by mumbling sage Miyagi-isms about things like life and tree roots, despite their utter inanity this time around.

Martin Kove reprises his role from the first pic as Kreese, the nasty karate master previously humbled by Miyagi (Morita) and still bitter from the experience.

This time, however, he has a patron—former Vietnam buddy Terry (Thomas Ian Griffith), who apparently has made millions dumping toxic chemicals yet has nothing better to do than devote his time to seeking vengeance against Miyagi and protégé Daniel (Macchio) on Kreese's behalf.

•

KEEP, THE
1983, 96 mins, UK/US Ⓥ ⊙ ▭ col
Dir Michael Mann ***Prod*** Gene Kirkwood, Howard W. Koch, Jr. ***Scr*** Michael Mann ***Ph*** Alex Thomson ***Ed*** Dov Hoenig ***Mus*** Tangerine Dream ***Art*** John Box
Act Scott Glenn, Alberta Watson, Jurgen Prochnow, Robert Prosky, Gabriel Byrne, Ian McKellen (Paramount)

Buried deep within *The Keep*'s mysterious exterior lies that chilling Hollywood question: how do these dogs get made?

After his promising debut with *The Thief*, this is writer-director Michael Mann's second feature [from a novel by F. Paul Wilson], testimony again to the one-step-forward, two-steps-back career theory. Some Germans have arrived at a small Rumanian village, unaware and unafraid that the keep where they will be headquartered has an uneasy history. Their commander (Jurgen Prochnow) is a nice guy despite his job with the Wehrmacht and it's hardly his fault that his troops are gradually being eaten alive and blown apart by an unseen force that moves smokily through the keep.

Professorial Ian McKellen is brought from a concentration camp to help solve the mystery, and brings his imminently assaultable daughter (Alberta Watson). While she's being raped, the monster emerges from his fog and blows those bad guys apart, making a friend of her father.

Somewhere across the dark waters, all this commotion wakes up Scott Glenn, who sets out for the keep to make sure the monster doesn't use the professor to get out.

•

KEEP 'EM FLYING
1941, 86 mins, US Ⓥ ⊙ b/w
Dir Arthur Lubin ***Prod*** Glenn Tryon ***Scr*** True Boardman, Nat Perrin, John Grant ***Ph*** Joseph Valentine, Elmer Dyer ***Ed*** Philip Cahn, Arthur Hilton
Act Bud Abbott, Lou Costello, Martha Raye, Carol Bruce, Dick Foran (Universal)

Abbott and Costello continue their cinematic slaphappy antics in *Keep 'Em Flying*, third in their series of service comedies. Stressing the individualized routines of the duo throughout—with story framework nothing but a lame excuse for this display—picture is easy to laugh at.

Interwoven with the typical A & C byplay are a plentiful supply of physical thrill action and three songs written by

Don Raye and Gene de Paul. It's all thrown together in a loose melange to showcase the two comics.

Opening in a carnival to allow Abbott and Costello to display some knockabout routines, picture swings to a night club and then to the Cal-Aero Academy—prep school for army fliers. The comedy pair are stooges for stunt flier Dick Foran, and when he ditches the carny, pair go along with him to the flying school to become flunkies around the place.

Direction by Arthur Lubin is okay considering loosely woven script. Ralph Ceder, veteran of the Mack Sennett thrill-comedy days, injects plenty of action in the chase and flying sequences in his direction of this portion of the picture.

•

KEEP SMILING

1938, 91 mins, UK b/w

Dir Monty Banks ***Prod*** Robert T. Kane ***Scr*** William Conselman, Val Valentine, Rodney Ackland ***Ph*** Mutz Greenbaum ***Ed*** James B. Clark

Act Gracie Fields, Roger Livesey, Mary Maguire, Peter Coke, Jack Donohue, Hay Petrie (20th Century-Fox)

Keep Smiling was carefully prepared with an eye to establishing the topflight British star Gracie Fields in the U.S. Results are meritorious, mainly due to preparation of the screenplay by William Conselman, Hollywood veteran, and direction by Monty Banks, which injects more of the American type of humor than has been present in earlier Fields starrers.

Film is good entertainment, a fast-moving filmusical with several songs delivered in crackerjack style by Fields. Story concerns show troupe headed by Fields which gets stranded; beds in at farm of girl's grandfather; luckily acquires a bus for a tour; and winds up for a two-year engagement at a pavilion near Brighton.

Fields delivers three comedy numbers, a torch song, one swing tune that has possibilities of popularity with the bands, "Swing Your Way to Happiness," and scores decisively in singing the religious choral, "Jerusalem," in a small church setting.

Mary Maguire is only American player in cast, and is satisfactory as the dancing ingenue who provides the romantic interest. Mr. Skip, the wirehair, is the canine who became rather famous as Asta in *The Thin Man*.

•

KELLY'S HEROES

1970, 148 mins, US Ⓥ ⊙ ▭ col

Dir Brian G. Hutton ***Prod*** Gabriel Katzka, Sidney Beckerman ***Scr*** Troy Kennedy Martin ***Ph*** Gabriel Figueroa ***Ed*** John Jympson ***Mus*** Lalo Schifrin ***Art*** Jonathan Barry

Act Clint Eastwood, Telly Savalas, Don Rickles, Carroll O'Connor, Donald Sutherland, Gavin MacLeod (M-G-M)

Clint Eastwood, Telly Savalas, Don Rickles and Donald Sutherland are among the stars cast as lovable roughnecks who decide to steal $16 million in gold bullion; it belongs to the Germans, so that's okay. Nearly satirical in its overall effect, plot caroms between cliché dogface antics, detailed and gratuitous violence, caper melodramatics and outrageous anachronism.

Eastwood stumbles onto knowledge of the gold stash from captured German officer David Hurst. Savalas, senior non-com in the platoon leisurely commanded by Hal Buckley, comes around to participating in the theft during a dull r&r period.

Eastwood's performance remains in his traditional low-key groove, thereby creating an adrenalin vacuum filled to the brim by the screen-dominating presence of Savalas and Sutherland.

•

KENNEL MURDER CASE, THE

1933, 73 mins, US Ⓥ ⊙ b/w

Dir Michael Curtiz ***Scr*** Robert N. Lee, Peter Milne ***Ph*** William Rees ***Ed*** Harold McLernon ***Art*** Jack Okey

Act William Powell, Mary Astor, Eugene Pallette, Ralph Morgan, Helen Vinson, Etienne Girardot (Warner)

Philo Vance [from the novels of S. S. Van Dyne] comes back to the screen in the hands of William Powell, unravelling a murder mystery in an interesting and entertaining manner. Again Eugene Pallette is with the master detective as the snap-judgment cop, most of the comedy relief issuing via his character.

The title relates to a kennel club on Long Island, various members of which are concerned in the story in addition to the two who are murdered, brothers. Vance himself is a dog fancier as well as master murder unraveler.

Throughout Powell gives a smooth and intelligent performance, aided by dialog and direction with which no serious fault can be found. He in no way figures in the romantic side of the yarn, this secondary element involving Mary Astor and Paul Cavanaugh.

•

KENTUCKIAN, THE

1955, 103 mins, US Ⓥ ⊙ ▭ col

Dir Burt Lancaster ***Prod*** Harold Hecht ***Scr*** A. B. Guthrie, Jr. ***Ph*** Ernest Laszlo ***Ed*** William B. Murphy ***Mus*** Bernard Herrmann

Act Burt Lancaster, Dianne Foster, Diana Lynn, John McIntire, Walter Matthau, John Carradine (United Artists)

The rather simple story of a pioneer father, his son and their dream of new lands is the basis for this adventure-drama. The footage is long and often slow, with the really high spots of action rather scattered.

Burt Lancaster takes on the added chore of director for the production. He does a fairly competent first-job of handling most every one but himself.

Dianne Foster makes a strong impression as Hannah, the bound girl who takes up with Lancaster and his young son (Donald MacDonald) after they use their riverboat passage money to pay off her indentures to a mean tavernkeeper. She, more than anyone else in the cast, adds something other than just a surface response to the story situations.

Diana Lynn is competent and attractive but, unfortunately, her role doesn't count for much in the overall drama. There's too much of ten-twent-thirt flamboyance to Walter Matthau's portrayal of the whip-cracking heavy.

•

KENTUCKY FRIED MOVIE, THE

1977, 90 mins, US Ⓥ col

Dir John Landis ***Prod*** Robert K. Weiss ***Scr*** David Zucker, Jim Abrahams, Jerry Zuker ***Ph*** Stephen M. Katz ***Ed*** George Folsey, Jr. ***Mus*** Igo Kantor ***Art*** Rich Harvel

Act Donald Sutherland, George Lazenby, Henry Gibson, Bill Bixby, Tony Dow (Kentucky Fried Theatre)

The Kentucky Fried Movie boasts excellent production values and some genuine wit, though a few of the sketches are tasteless.

Some of the appeal of this kind of material is purely juvenile—the dubious kick of hearing "TV performers" use foul language and seeing them perform off-color activities—but there is also a more substantial undertone in using satire of TV and films as a means of satirizing American cultural values.

Though each viewer will have his favorites, the standout segs certainly include *Zinc Oxide*, a terrific physical comedy routine spoofing an educational film, and *Cleopatra Schwartz*, parody of a Pam Grier action film, but with a black Amazon woman married to a rabbi.

•

KERMESSE HEROIQUE, LA
(CARNIVAL IN FLANDERS)

1935, 95 mins, France b/w

Dir Jacques Feyder ***Scr*** Bernard Zimmer ***Ph*** Harry Stradling ***Mus*** Louis Beydts ***Art*** Lazare Meerson

Act Francoise Rosay, Jean Murat, Alerme, Louis Jouvet, Lynne Clevers, Micheline Cheirel (Tobis)

This is the biggest French production since talkers began. Cost for two versions (French and German) is reported at $530,000, which puts it in a price class with expensive English pictures. Both versions were made at the Epinay (Paris suburb) lot of the French subsidiary of Dutch-controlled Tobis. It's an attempt to impress the French market with what this outfit can do.

Plot develops with comparative swiftness. It unfolds the Charles Spaak tale of a Flanders village, peopled by rather timid males, visited by a regiment of Spanish soldiers. Recalling the brutal treatment visited on other towns by Spain's military forces in the past, the male gentry decide to play dead.

This is literal in the case of the burgomaster, and it furnishes some of the richest farcical scenes as he feigns death, lying in state. His robust wife rallies the women of the town, prepares a royal welcome for the duke and his men, and showers the Spaniards with such hospitality that the village wins a cancellation of taxes for one whole year, at the duke's order.

What the fundamental structure of this story lacked, Bernard Zimmer, in transferring it to the screen, and Jacques Feyder, in directing, have made up for to a surprising degree. The scintillating performance of vivacious Francoise Rosay and fine fidelity to character of a large part of the cast do the rest. Feyder has had Hollywood directorial training.

Harry Stradling's cameraing presents a fine display of contrasts, first taking in spectacular shots and then grabbing intimate closeups that often bespeak more than the dialog.

•

KES

1970, 112 mins, UK Ⓥ col

Dir Ken Loach ***Prod*** Tony Garnett ***Scr*** Barry Hines, Ken Loach, Tony Garnett ***Ph*** Chris Menges ***Ed*** Roy Watts ***Mus*** John Cameron ***Art*** William McCrow

Act David Bradley, Colin Welland, Freddie Fletcher, Lynne Perrie, Brian Glover, Bob Bowes (Woodfall/Kestrel)

Based on a book [*A Kestrel for a Knave*] by Barry Hines, film tells of a lad brought up in a drab Yorkshire village. He's the product of a downbeat home with a permissive mum and a drunken, bullying brother. He goes to a school where the kids are also bullies and the teaching staff mainly a bunch of aggressive, unsympathetic, impatient robots. Then he finds a baby kestrel (a small falcon) on the moors. He determines to train the kestrel to fly and from then on he's a loner, obsessed by his new interest which gives him his first purpose in life.

Simply, the filmmakers have brought the background of the boy's life vividly into reality. They have surrounded him with local people (only one or two are minor actors) and turned the spotlight on this black side of British education and home life.

The young hero is brilliantly played by David Bradley, particularly in one memorable scene when an understanding master (Colin Welland) persuades him to tell the class about his kestrel and how he trains it.

Filmed entirely on location, *Kes* sometimes seems rough and ready but much of the moorland stuff is superb, and writing, editing and, above all, Ken Loach's direction are all done with dedicated affection.

•

KEY, THE

1934, 82 mins, US b/w

Dir Michael Curtiz ***Scr*** Laird Doyle ***Ph*** Ernest Haller ***Ed*** William Clemens, Thomas Richards ***Art*** Robert Haas

Act William Powell, Edna Best, Colin Clive, Hobart Cavanaugh, Halliwell Hobbes, Henry O'Neill (Warner)

Setting of *The Key*, adapted from the London stage play [by R. Gore-Browne and J. L. Hardy], is the Irish revolution of 1920. Recalled is that chapter of Anglo-Gaelic relations in which the marauding Black-and-Tan troops, the street-sniping patriots and the phantom-moving Michael Collins combined to make a gory, tumultuous time of it.

Only a minor part of the color and dynamic drama that these pages afford has been captured by the picture. But there is enough pulsing sweep to the background episodes to overcome the vapidity of a formula triangle—husband (Colin Clive), wife (Edna Best) and returned lover (William Powell)—to give the film an above-average rating.

Powell is starred, but the acting honors go to Clive. Fault doesn't lie with Powell. It's a role that's as wooden as the central plot itself. When the characterization calls for a debonair, glib fellow with a flair for getting himself out of femme complications, the Powell personality clicks on all cylinders. Later, when the tale gives way to self-sacrificing, Powell becomes a puppet moving this way and that to the tug of the strings.

For Best it's a debut in American films. Hers is also a puppetlike part, giving her little chance to register anything but anguish. Next to Clive the standout bit of acting is delivered by J. M. Kerrigan who, as a noncombatant Irish, does the contacting between the revolutionists and the invading Black-and-Tans.

•

KEY, THE

1958, 134 mins, UK Ⓥ ⊙ ▭ b/w

Dir Carol Reed ***Prod*** Carl Foreman ***Scr*** Carl Foreman ***Ph*** Oswald Morris ***Ed*** Bert Bates ***Mus*** Malcolm Arnold ***Art*** Wilfrid Shingleton

Act William Holden, Sophia Loren, Trevor Howard, Oscar Homolka, Kieron Moore, Bernard Lee (Open Road/Columbia)

Based on Jan De Hartog's novel *Stella*, this is a wartime yarn, with William Holden and Trevor Howard as commanders of tugs engaged on convoy rescue duty in U-Boat Alley—the Western Approaches. This highly hazardous chore provides *The Key* with some standout thrills which alone make the pic great entertainment.

When Holden joins up with his old buddy Howard, he finds him sharing an apartment with a beautiful Swiss refugee, played with dignity and sensitive understanding by Sophia Loren. She identifies both these men with her dead fiancé. When Howard is killed, Holden uses the spare key that Howard has given him to keep the apartment among tug men. Holden and Loren fall in love.

There are some outstanding scenes as, for instance, when Holden takes over command of his ship and indulges in crazy maneuvers to test its seaworthiness; a splendidly played tipsy scene between Howard and Holden; a fierce bombing and fire sequence at sea; and a tender moment when Holden and Loren fall in love.

•

KEY LARGO
1948, 100 mins, US Ⓥ ⊙ b/w
Dir John Huston ***Prod*** Jerry Wald ***Scr*** Richard Brooks, John Huston ***Ph*** Karl Freund ***Ed*** Rudi Fehr ***Mus*** Max Steiner ***Art*** Leo K. Kuter
Act Humphrey Bogart, Edward G. Robinson, Lauren Bacall, Lionel Barrymore, Claire Trevor, Thomas Gomez (Warner)

A tense film thriller has been developed from Maxwell Anderson's play *Key Largo*. Emphasis is on tension in the telling, and effective use of melodramatic mood has been used to point up the suspense.

There are overtones of soapboxing on a better world but this is never permitted to interfere with basic plot. Key West locale is an aid in stressing tension that carries through the plot. Atmosphere of the deadly, still heat of the Keys, the threat of a hurricane and the menace of merciless gangsters make the suspense seem real, and Huston's direction stresses the mood of anticipation.

Humphrey Bogart is seen as a veteran, stopping off at Key Largo to visit the family of a buddy killed in the war. He finds the run-down hotel taken over by a group of gangsters, who are waiting to exchange a load of counterfeit for real cash. Kept prisoners over a long day and night, during which a hurricane strikes, the best and the worst is brought out in the characters.

The excitement generated is quiet, seldom rambunctious or slambang, although there are moments of high action. The performances are of uniform excellence and go a long way towards establishing credibility of the events.

1948: Best Supp. Actress (Claire Trevor)

•

KEYS OF THE KINGDOM, THE
1945, 137 mins, US Ⓥ b/w
Dir John M. Stahl ***Prod*** Joseph L. Mankiewicz ***Scr*** Joseph L. Mankiewicz, Nunnally Johnson ***Ph*** Arthur Miller ***Ed*** James B. Clark ***Mus*** Alfred Newman ***Art*** James Basevi, William Darling
Act Gregory Peck, Thomas Mitchell, Vincent Price, Roddy McDowall, Edmund Gwenn, Cedric Hardwicke (20th Century-Fox)

A cavalcade of a priest's life, played excellently by Gregory Peck, what transcends all the cinemaction is the impact of tolerance, service, faith and godliness.

Where the monsignor (Cedric Hardwicke) comes to oust the aged, limping and poor father (Peck), he departs with humility and a new respect after he reads the good father's journal, first of unrequited love (in youth) and later in unselfish devotion, self-punishing denials and unswerving fealty to his mission as it covers more than a half century. The action (from A. J. Cronin's bestseller) starts in Scotland, shifts to China and thence back to the land of his birth.

There is a spell of prime-of-life accomplishment as he makes some headway in the far province of Chek Kow, even unto saving the life of the wealthy local mandarin's son and heir through emergency lancing of the boy's blood-poisoned arm. But comes civil war, and his mission on the beautiful Hill of the Green Jade happens to fall in direct line of fire between the authoritative army and the Chinese bandits.

1945: NOMINATIONS: Best Actor (Gregory Peck), B&W Cinematography, B&W Art Direction, Scoring of a Dramatic Picture

•

KEY TO THE CITY
1950, 100 mins, US b/w
Dir George Sidney ***Prod*** Z. Wayne Griffin ***Scr*** Robert Riley Crutcher ***Ph*** Harold Rosson ***Ed*** James E. Newcom ***Mus*** Bronislau Kaper
Act Clark Gable, Loretta Young, Marilyn Maxwell, Frank Morgan, Raymond Burr (M-G-M)

Key to the City is a noisy, wise-cracking comedy. Dialog is flip and pseudo-sophisticated, proper for telling the plot of a quickie romance that is bred at a mayors' convention in San Francisco. Clark Gable is the honest mayor of a northern California city. Story brings Loretta Young, the equally honest mayor from New England, into antagonistic contact.

Together they strike sparks despite character opposites, become involved in unwelcome adventures that keep them in and out of jail and find love on the fog-shrouded Telegraph Hill.

George Sidney's direction captures the noisy convention atmosphere and keys the entire movement in that vein. Raucousness was the best method of selling the yarn and keeping the laugh punchy.

•

KHARTOUM
1966, 134 mins, UK Ⓥ ⊙ ▭ col
Dir Basil Dearden ***Prod*** Julian Blaustein ***Scr*** Robert Ardrey ***Ph*** Edward Scaife ***Ed*** Fergus McDonell ***Mus*** Frank Cordell ***Art*** John Howell
Act Charlton Heston, Laurence Olivier, Richard Johnson, Ralph Richardson, Alexander Knox, Johnny Sekka (United Artists)

Khartoum is an action-filled entertainment pic which contrasts personal nobility with political expediency. The colorful production builds in spectacular display, enhanced by Cinerama presentation, while Charlton Heston and Laurence Olivier propel towards inevitable tragedy the drama of two sincere opponents.

Filmed in Egypt and finished at England's Pinewood Studios, the historical drama depicts the events leading up to the savage death of General Charles Gordon, famed British soldier, as he sought to mobilize public opinion against the threat of a religious-political leader who would conquer the Arab world.

Heston delivers an accomplished performance as Gordon, looking like the 50-year-old trim soldier that Gordon was when picked to evacuate Khartoum of its Egyptian inhabitants.

Olivier, playing the Mahdi, is excellent in creating audience terror of a zealot who sincerely believes that a mass slaughter is Divine Will, while projecting respect and compassion for his equally religious adversary.

Basil Dearden directs with a fine hand, while Yakima Canutt, second unit director given prominent screen credit, works simultaneously to create much big-screen razzledazzle action.

1966: NOMINATION: Best Original Story & Screenplay

•

KICKBOXER
1989, 105 mins, US Ⓥ ⊙ col
Dir Mark DiSalle, David Worth ***Prod*** Mark DiSalle ***Scr*** Glenn Bruce ***Ph*** Jon Kranhouse ***Ed*** Wayne Wahram ***Mus*** Paul Hertzog ***Art*** Shay Austin
Act Jean-Claude Van Damme, Denis Alexio, Dennis Chan, Tong Po, Haskell Anderson, Rochelle Ashana (Kings Road)

Combine *Karate Kid* and *Rocky* with a bit more blood and gore, dull direction and a smattering of inept actors and you have *Kickboxer*.

Pic opens with Dennis Alexio (Eric Sloane) being crowned world kickboxing champion, watched by his younger brother Jean-Claude Van Damme. The duo head off to Thailand to take on the originators of kickboxing after being asked some inane questions by a journalist. Alexio fights, and is crippled by top Thai fighter Tong Po, leaving Van Damme to swear revenge. He finds out the only way he can defeat Po is by learning Muay-Thai fighting and sets off to convince eccentric Dennis Chan (Xian Chow) to teach him.

Much of *Kickboxer* is macho nonsense full of cliché characters and risible dialog. There is no denying, though, that the fight scenes—choreographed by Van Damme—are well handled.

•

KID, THE
1921, 80 mins, US Ⓥ ⊗ b/w
Dir Charles Chaplin, Charles Riesner ***Prod*** Charles Chaplin ***Scr*** Charles Chaplin ***Ph*** Rollie Totheroh
Act Charles Chaplin, Jackie Coogan, Edna Purviance, Carl Miller, Tom Wilson, Chuck Reisner (Chaplin/First National)

In this, Chaplin is less of the buffoon and more of the actor. But his comedy is all there and there is not a dull moment once the comedian comes into the picture, which is along about the middle of the first reel.

Introduced as "a picture with a smile—perhaps a tear," it proves itself just that. For while it will move people to uproarious laughter and keep them in a state of uneasing delight, it also will touch their hearts and win sympathy, not only for the star, but for his leading woman, and little Jackie Coogan.

There are characteristic "Chaplin touches." A fine instance of imagination is where he dreams of Heaven. His slum alley is transformed into a bit of Paradise, with everybody—including his Nemesis, the cop and a big bully who had wrecked a brick wall and bent a lamppost swinging at Charlie—turned into angels.

•

KID, THE
2000, 104 mins, US Ⓥ ⊙ col
Dir Jon Turteltaub ***Prod*** Jon Turteltaub, Christina Steinberg, Hunt Lowry ***Scr*** Audrey Wells ***Ph*** Peter Menzies Jr. ***Ed*** Peter Honess, David Rennie ***Mus*** Marc Shaiman ***Art*** Garreth Stover
Act Bruce Willis, Spencer Breslin, Emily Mortimer, Lily Tomlin, Chi McBride, Jean Smart (Junction Entertainment/Disney)

Bruce Willis lands in family-film slop. Script pirouettes on a reasonably intriguing fantasy premise—that a child and adult version of the same person could meet and not like each other. But director Jon Turteltaub's insistence upon hammering every point home with giant closeups and relentless musical underlining makes this insufferably cloying and sickly sweet for anyone with the least intolerance to "find the inner child" saccharinity.

The central notion certainly provides something to work with: Through a magical confluence, successful, arrogant 40-year-old workaholic "image consultant" Russ Duritz (Willis) is annoyingly confronted by his 8-year-old self, Rusty (Spencer Breslin), who over the long run makes Russ realize how far astray he's gone from what he admired and aspired to as a boy. In other words, he's become a mean, insensitive, materialistic bachelor rather than a people-and-animal-loving aviator and dad, and it takes some quality time with the fun-loving Rusty for the man to realize the error of his ways.

This is a theme that could support any number of approaches, nuances and ironies, but this is the Disney version—in the most egregious possible sense. Everything is obvious when it could be subtle, loud when it could be modulated, "cute" when it could be appealing, pat when it could be insightful, contrived when it could be graceful. But so far does the film fall short of any meaningful objective that one might be excused from thinking that there's actually no reason for an 8-year-old to like or understand what he might become three decades hence.

Willis goes with the flow of Turteltaub's strenuous, simplistic approach, broadly laying on Russ' callousness and irritability before turning the key to unlock his softer side. He plays effortlessly with young Breslin, who one might safely say won't grow up to look like Willis but will charm many with his bright assertiveness and staying power opposite the forces of hardened adulthood.

•

KID BROTHER, THE
1927, 83 mins, US ⊗ b/w
Dir Ted Wilde ***Prod*** Harold Lloyd ***Scr*** John Grey, Tom Crizer, Ted Wilde ***Ph*** Walter Lundin
Act Harold Lloyd, Jobyna Ralston, Walter James, Leo Willis, Olin Francis (Lloyd/Paramount)

Harold Lloyd has clicked again with *The Kid Brother*, about as gaggy a gag picture as he has ever done. It is just a series of gags, one following the other, some funny and others funnier.

Lloyd is somewhat different in the picture than he has been heretofore. In this case he is the youngest son of a family of three boys who live with their father, a widower.

His opening scene shows him performing this last task with the aid of a butter churn, an ingenious mechanical arrangement for the wringing out and hanging of the clothes with the aid of a kite which carries the clothes aloft as they come from the wringer.

When dad finds out that a medicine show has made a pitch and that the boy has given them a license, he orders the youngster to go down and close up the show. There are a couple of gags here that get over for howls, especially that of causing the amateur sheriff to disappear and his final hanging up against the back of the stage securely handcuffed.

Jobyna Ralston plays opposite Lloyd as the little medicine show girl and handles herself perfectly. Walter James as the comedian's father acquits himself with honors.

•

KID FOR TWO FARTHINGS, A
1955, 96 mins, UK Ⓥ col
Dir Carol Reed ***Prod*** Carol Reed ***Scr*** Wolf Mankowitz ***Ph*** Ted Scaife ***Ed*** A. S. Bates ***Mus*** Benjamin Frankel ***Art*** Wilfrid Shingleton
Act Celia Johnson, Diana Dors, David Kossoff, Brenda de Banzie, Joe Robinson, Jonathan Ashmore (London)

Carol Reed has extracted a great deal of charm from Wolf Mankowitz's novel. This is not a conventional story, but a series of cameos set in the Jewish quarter of London and around the famed Petticoat Lane. Some of the Petticoat Lane scenes were filmed on location, and the characters mainly are real enough.

Reed's direction is bold and authoritative. He uses color for the first time in his career with telling effect and, within the framework of the setting, has achieved all that could have been expected. David Kossoff gives a performance as the trouser-maker (with an unusual bent towards philosophy) that is a model of sincerity. Diana Dors plays her part as a blonde popsie with complete conviction. Celia Johnson is badly miscast as the boy's mother, and hardly ever comes to grips with the role.

•

KID FROM BROOKLYN, THE

1946, 114 mins, US Ⓥ ⦿ col

Dir Norman Z. McLeod ***Prod*** Samuel Goldwyn ***Scr*** Don Hartman, Melville Shavelson ***Ph*** Gregg Toland ***Ed*** Daniel Mandell ***Mus*** Louis Forbes (sup.), Carmen Dragon (dir.) ***Art*** Perry Ferguson, Stewart Chaney, McClure Capps

Act Danny Kaye, Virginia Mayo, Vera-Ellen, Steve Cochran, Eve Arden, Lionel Stander (Goldwyn)

Based on the old Harold Lloyd starrer, *The Milky Way* (originally legit play by Lynn Root and Harry Clork), the film is aimed straight at the bellylaughs and emerges as a lush mixture of comedy, music and gals, highlighted by beautiful Technicolor and ultra-rich production mountings.

Danny Kaye is spotted in almost three-fourths of the picture's sequences, but the audience will be clamoring for more at the final fadeout. Zany comic clicks with his unique mugging, song stylizing and antics, but still packs in plenty of the wistful appeal.

With a top cast and screenplay to work with, director Norman Z. McLeod gets the most out of each situation. Story [from a screenplay by Grover Jones, Frank Butler and Richard Connell] has Kaye as a mild-mannered milkman who gets involved with a prizefight gang when he accidentally knocks out the current middleweight champ. With the champ's publicity shot to pieces, his manager decides to capitalize on the situation by building Kaye into a contender and then cleaning up on the title bout.

Kaye's supporting cast does uniformly fine work, keeping their sights trained on the comedy throughout. Virginia Mayo, as the love interest, serves as a beautiful foil for Kaye's madcap antics and sings two ballads in acceptable fashion. Vera-Ellen gets in ably on the comedy and does some spectacular terpsichore in two equally spectacular production numbers.

•

KID GALAHAD

1937, 100 mins, US Ⓥ b/w

Dir Michael Curtiz ***Prod*** [uncredited] ***Scr*** Seton I. Miller ***Ph*** Tony Gaudio ***Ed*** George Amy ***Mus*** Leo F. Forbstein (dir.) ***Art*** Carl Jules Weyl

Act Edward G. Robinson, Bette Davis, Humphrey Bogart, Wayne Morris, Jane Bryan, Harry Carey (Warner)

One of the oldest stories in pictures—the grooming of a heavyweight champion—has been done again with good results [from the *Saturday Evening Post* story by Francis Wallace].

The treatment is sophisticated and production deluxe. Also more than the usual amount of romance for a slugfest. This allows room for Bette Davis to moon over the clean kid from the farm, and for the fight manager's convent-bred sister to also fall in love with him.

But essentially it's the story of the kid's manager (Edward G. Robinson) who maneuvers to match the bellhop-pugilist (Wayne Morris) in order to pay off the grudge he holds for a felonious fellow-manager (Humphrey Bogart) whose methods are always on the muscle side.

Davis has two or three nice opportunities and as usual handles herself throughout with plenty of noodle work. She's been photographed for glittering results in a couple of the sequences by Tony Gaudio. Script adroitly avoids any line or allusion that could identify her as the mistress of Robinson, who, however, is constantly walking into her apartment with a proprietary air. Davis also sings one song in a night club sequence, voice seemingly being doubled.

Robinson and Bogart, both grim guys, make their rivalry entirely plausible. Both performers know how.

•

KID GALAHAD

1962, 95 mins, US Ⓥ col

Dir Phil Karlson ***Prod*** David Weisbart ***Scr*** William Fay ***Ph*** Burnett Guffey ***Ed*** Stuart Gilmore ***Mus*** Jeff Alexander ***Art*** Cary Odell

Act Elvis Presley, Gig Young, Lola Albright, Joan Blackman, Charles Bronson, Ned Glass (United Artists)

Two of the screen's most salable staples are united in *Kid Galahad*. One is Elvis Presley. The other is one of the most hackneyed yarns in the annals of cinema fiction—the one about the wholesome, greenhorn kid who wanders into training camp (be it Stillman's Gym or the Catskills), kayoes with one mighty right the hardest belter on the premises, gets an instant nickname and proceeds to score a string of victories en route to the inevitable big fight in which the fix is on.

Presley's acting resources are limited. It is, however, a surprisingly paunchy Presley in this film, and the added avoirdupois, unaided by camera, is not especially becoming. Elvis sings some half a dozen songs. Gig Young labors through the trite, confusing part of the mixed-up proprietor of the upstate boxing stable. Pretty Joan Blackman overacts as Presley's girl. But there are two strong principal performers. One is Lola Albright as Young's unrequited torch-carrier, the other Charles Bronson as an understanding trainer.

Idyllwild, California, does not closely resemble the Catskill Mountain terrain of NY, locale of the story.

•

KID GLOVE KILLER

1942, 76 mins, US b/w

Dir Fred Zinnemann ***Prod*** Jack Chertok ***Scr*** Allen Rivkin, John C. Higgins ***Ph*** Paul Vogel ***Ed*** Ralph Winters ***Mus*** David Snell

Act Van Heflin, Marsha Hunt, Lee Bowman, Samuel S. Hinds (M-G-M)

Kid Glove Killer is one of those moderately budgeted programmers that appear at long intervals to rise far above the level intended. Spotlight shines brightly on Van Heflin in the lead. His skillful timing and delivery of lines holds interest in many sequences that might easily have crumbled in less capable hands.

Story unfolds a compact and interesting drama of political corruption, and the experiences of a scientific criminologist in getting a test-tube solution to the murder of the mayor. Heflin is the expert of the police department, assisted by Marsha Hunt.

In addition to neatly devising entertaining dramatic content, story provides an interesting exposition of the inner workings of a scientific crime detecting laboratory; including functions of spectographs, microscopes, and chemicals.

Newcomer Fred Zinnemann deftly handles the various episodes for fine overall blending.

•

KID MILLIONS

1934, 90 mins, US Ⓥ col

Dir Roy Del Ruth ***Prod*** Samuel Goldwyn ***Scr*** Arthur Sheekman, Nat Perrin, Nunnally Johnson ***Ph*** Ray June ***Ed*** Stuart Heisler ***Mus*** Alfred Newman (dir.) ***Art*** Richard Day

Act Eddie Cantor, Ann Sothern, Ethel Merman, George Murphy, Eve Sully, Jesse Block (Goldwyn)

Another Samuel Goldwyn–Eddie Cantor musical comedy extravaganza and again strong entertainment. Follows more or less the comedy lines of all Cantor pictures. And with Cantor singing the same kind of songs.

For a final sequence an ice cream factory number in Technicolor is one of the finest jobs of tint-work yet turned out by the Kalmus lab, and the joint Seymour Felix–Willy Pogany handling of the colors, mass movements and girls creates a flaming crescendo for the production.

Cantor gives a lot of punch-lines to Eve Sully. Vaudeville comedienne makes a nice impression on her film debut. Jesse Block, her partner, gets plenty of neglect in the script, and so leaves little behind. Ethel Merman tops all her previous screen appearances. Warren Hymer is a strong asset, also.

Story works up to an Egyptian comedy sequence, with harem, mummy, torture chamber and underground wealth as elements.

•

KIDNAPPED

1948, 81 mins, US b/w

Dir William Beaudine ***Prod*** Lindsley Parsons ***Scr*** W. Scott Darling ***Ph*** William Sickner ***Ed*** Leonard W. Herman ***Mus*** Edward J. Kay ***Art*** Dave Milton

Act Roddy McDowall, Sue England, Dan O'Herlihy, Roland Winters, Jeff Corey (Monogram)

Robert Louis Stevenson's swashbuckler of feuding Scots and foul play in the 18th century has lost a lot of its punch in the screen adaptation. *Kidnapped* is only mildly entertaining, telling its story with a too leisurely pace that keeps things at a walk for 81 minutes.

The Stevenson classic concerns a young Scot who comes to claim an inheritance from his uncle. Latter has him kidnapped and shipped off to slavery but lad is saved by a political adventurer.

Roddy McDowall portrays the young Scot and does well enough in the role. (Actor also served as associate producer with Ace Herman on the film.) Dan O'Herlihy is the political adventurer and Sue England the pert young miss who joins the safari across Scotland.

•

KIDNAPPED

1960, 97 mins, US Ⓥ ⦿ col

Dir Robert Stevenson ***Prod*** Hugh Attwooll ***Scr*** Robert Stevenson ***Ph*** Paul Beeson ***Ed*** Gordon Stone ***Mus*** Cedric Thorpe Davie ***Art*** Carmen Dillon

Act Peter Finch, James MacArthur, Bernard Lee, Niall MacGinnis, John Laurie, Peter O'Toole (Walt Disney)

Walt Disney's live-action feature is a faithful recreation of the Robert Louis Stevenson classic. The film itself is sluggish because its storyline is not clear enough and for other reasons does not arouse any great anxiety or excitement in the spectator.

James MacArthur plays the young 18th-century Scottish boy cheated of his inheritance by a conniving uncle. The boy is kidnapped by a cruel shipmaster for sale as an indentured servant in the Carolinas. He escapes through the aid of a dashing fellow Scotsman (Peter Finch).

From a story point of view, the screenplay is weak. It is never clear what the aim of the principals is, so there is not much for the spectator to pull for. Individual scenes play, but there is no mounting or cumulative effect.

Kidnapped was photographed on location in Scotland and at Pinewood, London. The locations pay off richly, with an authentic flavor. Perhaps too richly, with accents as thick as Scotch oatmeal.

Finch as the swashbuckling follower of the exiled Stuart kings is a tremendous aid to the production. MacArthur gives a sturdy performance, handicapped by little opportunity for flexibility of character.

•

KIDNAPPED

1972, 100 mins, UK Ⓥ ▭ col

Dir Delbert Mann ***Prod*** Frederick Brogger ***Scr*** Jack Pulman ***Ph*** Paul Beeson, James Allen ***Ed*** Peter Boita ***Mus*** Roy Budd ***Art*** Alex Vetchinsky

Act Michael Caine, Trevor Howard, Jack Hawkins, Donald Pleasence, Lawrence Douglas, Vivien Heilbron (Omnibus)

Combination of Robert Louis Stevenson's *Kidnapped* and its lesser-known sequel *David Balfour* (titled *Catriona* in England) results in an intriguing adventure piece set against that period in Scottish history when the English were trying to take over that country's rule.

The dying struggle between a few remaining clans who refuse to relinquish their sovereignty, and English King George who sends his redcoats into the Highlands to stamp out rebellion, is graphically depicted through the personalized story of one of the Stuarts. This overshadows the story of David Balfour, hero of *Kidnapped*, the 18th-century Scottish lad cheated of his inheritance by a conniving uncle, but pic loses nothing in the telling.

Michael Caine plays the swashbuckling character of Alan Breck, who embodies the spirit of the bloody but unbowed Highlanders. Delbert Mann's direction catches the proper flavor of the times.

Lawrence Douglas portrays David Balfour, who becomes a follower of Breck, a man with a price on his head, trying to escape to France after the bloodbath of Culloden in 1746.

•

KIDS

1995, 90 mins, US Ⓥ col

Dir Larry Clark ***Prod*** Cary Woods ***Scr*** Harmony Korine ***Ph*** Eric Edwards ***Ed*** Chris Tellefson ***Mus*** Randall Poster (sup.) ***Art*** Kevin Thompson

Act Leo Fitzpatrick, Justin Pierce, Chloe Sevigny, Sarah Henderson, Rosario Dawson, Harold Hunter (Miramax/The Guys Upstairs)

Disturbing precisely because it is so believable, *Kids* goes well beyond any previous American film in frankly describing the lives of at least a certain group of modern teenagers. Celebrated photographer Larry Clark's first feature is bluntly about sex, drugs and irresponsibility, and in an extremely upfront way that viewers will have to admit is convincing, whether they like it or not.

On an aesthetic level, *Kids* is remarkable as a first film by a man in his 50s who indelibly captures the attitudes, speech patterns, rhythms, desires and lack of perspective of his teenage characters.

Covering 24 hours in the lives of a bunch of Manhattan kids on a hot summer day, pic begins with its nominal protagonist deflowering a very young girl, follows with the numbing discovery by another girl that she's HIV-positive thanks to that same boy, and pushes on to document endless sexual bragging, drug-taking, gay-baiting, black-bashing and, ultimately, a debauched party during which another virgin is unknowingly victimized by the thoughtless seducer.

From the opening scene, which unflinchingly observes the cocky Telly (Leo Fitzpatrick) talking a sweet blonde (Sarah Henderson) into surrendering her virginity to him, the film takes a direct, non-judgmental view of what it's presenting. As soon as he accomplishes his morning conquest, an exuberant Telly hits the streets to boast to his buddy Casper (Justin Pierce) about it.

It would seem that Clark and young screenwriter Harmony Korine intend the film as a truthful depiction of urban kids today, with an overlay of a cautionary attitude about the wages of blatant disregard for the need for safe sex. More of a gray area is the extent to which the picture seems voyeuristic and exploitative of its young subjects.

•

KIDS IN THE HALL: BRAIN CANDY
SEE: BRAIN CANDY

•

KIKUJIRO
SEE: KIKUJIRO NO NATSU

•

KIKUJIRO NO NATSU (KIKUJIRO)
1999, 122 mins, Japan Ⓥ ⊙ col
Dir Takeshi Kitano ***Prod*** Masuyuki Mori, Takio Yoshida ***Scr*** Takeshi Kitano ***Ph*** Katsumi Yanagishima ***Ed*** Takeshi Kitano, Yoshinori Ota ***Mus*** Joe Hisaishi ***Art*** Norihiro Isoda
Act Beat Takeshi, Yusuke Sekiguchi, Kayoko Kishimoto, Yuko Daike, Kazuko Yoshiyuki, Beat Kiyoshi (Bandai Visual/Tokyo FM/Nippon Herald/Office Kitano)

A complete departure from the lyrical violence of his gangster films, Japanese actor-director Takeshi Kitano's *Kikujiro* is a disappointment after his international breakthrough film, *Hana-Bi*. Story of a cherubic tyke and a gruff middle-aged tough guy with a soft side who journey together in search of the boy's mother, the film displays many of the inventive visual touches that distinguished Kitano's previous work, but its treacly mix of emotional manipulation and klutzy comedy will make it hard to digest for most audiences.

Set during summer, film centers on lonely 9-year-old Masao (Yusuke Sekiguchi), who lives with his grandmother. Told that his father died in a car accident and that the mother he has never known is forced to stay in a distant town due to her job, Masao sets off with a photo and address to find her. He hooks up with an unlikely traveling companion in Kikujiro (Kitano, using his *nom de thesp* Beat Takeshi), a smart-mouthed goon instructed by his no-nonsense wife (Kayoko Kishimoto) to accompany the boy.

The journey that follows is punctuated by eccentric encounters and by chapter titles and images from Masao's summer-holiday project book. Kitano has traded in sentiment before, most notably in *A Scene at the Sea*, about two deaf-mute teens with a passion for surfing, and in passages of *Kids Return* and *Hana-Bi*.

Kitano plays Kikujiro as an impish, overgrown delinquent, uncovering a more sensitive side as his bond with Masao grows. Film is visually impressive, deftly conjuring the hazy colors and lazy stillness of summer.

•

KILLER, THE
SEE: DIP HUT SEUNG HUNG

•

KILLER
1994, 95 mins, US Ⓥ ⊙ col
Dir Mark Malone ***Prod*** Robert Vince, William Vince ***Scr*** Gordon Melbourne ***Ph*** Tobias Schliessler ***Ed*** Robin Russell ***Mus*** Graeme Coleman ***Art*** Lynne Stopkewich
Act Anthony LaPaglia, Mimi Rogers, Matt Craven, Peter Boyle, Monika Schnarre, Joseph Maher (Keystone)

Equal parts fresh observation and strained contrivance, *Killer*, a film noir with a twist, announces the promising directorial debut of Mark Malone. Pic features a mesmerizing central performance by Anthony LaPaglia as a nihilistic hit man and a solid one by Mimi Rogers as the femme fatale.

Mike (LaPaglia), the tough, cool hero (aka Bulletproof Heart), is the ultimate pro, supplying efficient services for big bucks. Real suspense begins when Mick is assigned a rather unusual duty: killing Fiona (Rogers), a mysterious femme who's not only expecting him but is willing to be murdered.

The unity of the action, which takes place in one night in New York, adds to the film's tightly controlled tension. Most of the scenes are set indoors, which makes the pic appropriately claustrophobic.

Unfortunately, the story [by Malone] falters severely in its mid-section, a long picnic in a cemetery in which Fiona suddenly disappears. But the pic regains its vitality and the tragic closure is satisfyingly coherent.

•

KILLER
A JOURNAL OF MURDER
1996, 90 mins, US Ⓥ col
Dir Tim Metcalfe ***Prod*** Janet Yang, Mark Levinson ***Scr*** Tim Metcalfe ***Ph*** Ken Kelsch ***Ed*** Richard Gentner ***Mus*** Graeme Revell ***Art*** Sherman Williams
Act James Woods, Robert Sean Leonard, Ellen Greene, Cara Buono, Robert John Burke, Steve Forrest (Ixtlan/Spelling)

Based on a true story, this is a disturbing prison drama about the unlikely relationship between a self-proclaimed reprobate, who may have been America's first serial killer, and a conscientious guard seeking the man's redemption. Oliver Stone's production features top-notch performances by James Woods, as the remorseless criminal, and Robert Sean Leonard, as the liberal guard.

Set in 1929 in Leavenworth Prison, story introduces Henry Lesser (Leonard) at the beginning of his career as a guard with lofty dreams and hopes for prison reform. In jail, he meets Carl Panzram (Woods), a vengeful murderer with animalistic instincts who's perceived as unreachable and irredeemable.

Henry finds his value system beginning to collapse, and he starts questioning the validity of the penitentiary system. It soon becomes clear that Henry, an educated, liberal Jew, is fascinated with Carl because he's never met anyone like him before.

The prosaic, earnest nature of some sequences has a TV-movie feel. Still, the acting of the two leads is beyond reproach.

Pic has been given a beautiful production, with a rich, dark, period look enhanced by Ken Kelsch's sharp lensing that mixes black-and-white and color imagery. Production designer Sherman Williams built a gallows modeled on the actual 1930 architect's plans.

•

KILLER ELITE, THE
1975, 122 mins, US Ⓥ ⊙ ⌑ col
Dir Sam Peckinpah ***Prod*** Martin Baum, Arthur Lewis ***Scr*** Marc Norman, Stirling Silliphant ***Ph*** Phil Lathrop ***Ed*** Garth Craven, Tony De Zarraga, Monte Hellman ***Mus*** Jerry Fielding ***Art*** Ted Haworth
Act James Caan, Robert Duvall, Arthur Hill, Bo Hopkins, Mako, Gig Young (Exeter-Persky-Bright/United Artists)

The Killer Elite is an okay Sam Peckinpah actioner starring James Caan and Robert Duvall as two modern mercenaries who wind up stalking each other in a boringly complex double-cross plot [from the novel by Robert Rostand].

The initial Caan-Duvall camaraderie abruptly ends when Duvall switches sides to kill Helmut Dantine and disable Caan. Latter rehabilitates himself, with the help of nurse Katy Heflin (who could cure many a serious illness).

But CIA exec Tom Clancy's subcontract, to protect Asian political leader Mako and family from some other Asian killers who have also hired Duvall, brings Caan back into action. Street shootouts, car chases and a climactic facedown resolve many of the convoluted plot turns.

•

KILLER MCCOY
1947, 103 mins, US b/w
Dir Roy Rowland ***Prod*** Sam Zimbalist ***Scr*** Frederick Hazlitt Brennan ***Ph*** Joseph Ruttenberg ***Ed*** Ralph E. Winters ***Mus*** David Snell ***Art*** Cedric Gibbons, Eddie Imazu
Act Mickey Rooney, Brian Donlevy, Ann Blyth, James Dunn, Tom Tully, Sam Levene (M-G-M)

Metro has concocted a fast action melodrama in *Killer McCoy* [based on the screenplay for their 1938 film *The Crowd Roars*], to introduce Mickey Rooney to adult roles. Sentimental hoke is mixed with prize ring action but never gets too far out of hand.

Rooney makes much of his tailormade assignment in the title role. He's a tough kid who comes up to ring prominence after accidentally killing his friend, the ex-champ, who had started him on the road up. There's nothing that's very original with the story but scripting by Frederick Hazlitt Brennan has given it realistic dialog that pays off.

Plot develops from time Rooney and his sot of a father, James Dunn, become a song-and-dance team to pad out vaude tour being made by a lightweight champion. Through this association Rooney moves into the ring.

Highlights are "Swanee River" soft-shoed by Rooney and Dunn; sweet, sentimental courting of Rooney and Ann Blyth; and the fistic finale that features plenty of rugged action.

Brian Donlevy gives strong touch to the gambler role and Blyth gets the most out of every scene. Dunn hokes up assignment as the drunken actor-father with just the right amount of overplaying to stress "ham" character.

•

KILLERS, THE
1946, 103 mins, US b/w
Dir Robert Siodmak ***Prod*** Mark Hellinger ***Scr*** Anthony Veiller ***Ph*** Woody Bredell ***Ed*** Arthur Hillton ***Mus*** Miklos Rozsa ***Art*** Jack Otterson, Martin Obzina
Act Burt Lancaster, Ava Gardner, Edmond O'Brien, Albert Dekker, Sam Levene, William Conrad (Universal/Hellinger)

Taken from Ernest Hemingway's story of the same title, picture is a hard-hitting example of forthright melodrama in the best Hemingway style.

Performances without exception are top quality. It's a handpicked cast that troupes to the hilt to make it all believable. Film introduces Burt Lancaster from legit. He does a strong job, serving as the central character around whom the plot revolves. Edmond O'Brien, insurance investigator who probes Lancaster's murder, is another pivotal character who adds much to the film's acting polish. Ava Gardner is the bad girl of the piece.

Plot opens with Lancaster's murder in a small town. O'Brien takes it from there, trying to piece together events that will prove the murder of smalltown service station attendant has more significance than appears on the surface. Story has many flashbacks, told when O'Brien interviews characters in Lancaster's past, but it is all pieced together neatly for sustained drive and mood, finishing with exposé of a colossal double-cross. Every character has its moment to shine and does.

Hellinger assured a music score that would heighten mood of this one by using Miklos Rozsa, and the score is an immeasurable aid in furthering suspense.

1946: NOMINATIONS: Best Director, Screenplay, Editing, Scoring of a Dramatic Picture

•

KILLERS, THE
1964, 95 mins, US Ⓥ ⊙ col
Dir Don Siegel ***Prod*** Don Siegel ***Scr*** Gene L. Coon ***Ph*** Richard L. Rawlings ***Ed*** Richard Belding ***Mus*** Johnny Williams ***Art*** Frank Arrigo, George Chan
Act Lee Marvin, Angie Dickinson, John Cassavetes, Ronald Reagan, Clu Gulager, Claude Akins (Universal)

Spawned as the pilot (*Johnny North*) of Revue's projected series of two-hour films for television, but scratched when NBC balked at what was deemed an overdose of sex and brutality, this rehash of *The Killers* was redirected to theatrical exhibition, where it emerges a throwback to the period of crime and violence that monopolized the screen in the late 1930s and early 1940s.

Gene L. Coon's scenario is similar in basic structural respects, but different in character and plot specifics, to Mark Hellinger's 1946 vintage elaboration on Hemingway's concise short story. In this version, the "hero" (John Cassavetes) is a racing car driver, which provides the background for some flashy track scenes. But Coon's screenplay is burdened with affected dialog and contrived plotwork. Virtually nothing of the original Hemingway remains.

Of the actors, Cassevetes and Clu Gulager come off best, the former arousing interest with his customary histrionic drive and intensity, the latter fashioning a colorful study in evil, a portrait of playful sadism. Lee Marvin has some impact as another distorted menace, approaching his role with the cold-blooded demeanor for which he is celebrated. Ronald Reagan fails to crash convincingly through his goodguy image in his portrayal of a ruthless crook.

•

KILLER'S KISS
1955, 67 mins, US Ⓥ b/w
Dir Stanley Kubrick ***Prod*** Stanley Kubrick, Morris Bousel ***Scr*** [Howard O. Sackler, Stanley Kubrick] ***Ph*** Stanley Kubrick ***Ed*** Stanley Kubrick ***Mus*** Gerald Fried ***Art*** [uncredited]
Act Frank Silvera, Jamie Smith, Irene Kane, Jerry Jarret, Mike Dana, Felice Orlands (Minotaur)

Ex-*Look* photographer Stanley Kubrick turned out *Killer's Kiss* on the proverbial shoestring. *Kiss* was more than a warm-up for Kubrick's talents, for not only did he co-produce but he directed, photographed and edited the venture from his own screenplay [originally written by Howard O. Sackler] and original story.

Familiar plot of boy-meets-girl finds smalltime fighter Jamie Smith striking up a romance with taxi dancer Irene Kane [voiced by radio actress Peggy Lobbin].

Kubrick's low-key lensing occasionally catches the flavor of the seamy side of Gotham life. His scenes of tawdry

Broadway, gloomy tenements and grotesque brick-and-stone structures that make up Manhattan's downtown East Side loft district help offset the script's deficiencies.

•

KILLING, THE

1956, 84 mins, US Ⓥ ⊙ b/w

Dir Stanley Kubrick ***Prod*** James B. Harris ***Scr*** Stanley Kubrick, Jim Thompson ***Ph*** Lucien Ballard ***Ed*** Betty Steinberg ***Mus*** Gerald Fried ***Art*** Ruth Sobotka

Act Sterling Hayden, Coleen Gray, Marie Windsor, Elisha Cook, Vince Edwards, Jay C. Flippen (Harris-Kubrick)

This story of a $2 million race track holdup and steps leading up to the robbery, occasionally told in a documentary style which at first tends to be somewhat confusing, soon settles into a tense and suspenseful vein which carries through to an unexpected and ironic windup.

Sterling Hayden, an ex-con, masterminds the plan which includes five men. Stanley Kubrick's direction of his own script [from the novel *Clean Break* by Lionel White, dialog by Jim Thompson] is tight and fast-paced, a quality Lucien Ballard's top photography matches to lend particular fluidity of movement.

Characters involved in the crime include Elisha Cook, a colorless little cashier at the track who is hopelessly in love with his glamorous, trampish wife, Marie Windsor; Ted De Corsia, a racketeering cop; Jay C. Flippen, a reformed drunk; and Joe Sawyer, track bartender.

Hayden socks over a restrained characterization, and Cook is a particular standout. Windsor is particularly good, as she digs the plan out of her husband and reveals it to her boyfriend.

•

KILLING DAD

1989, 93 mins, UK Ⓥ ⊙ col

Dir Michael Austin ***Prod*** Iain Smith ***Scr*** Michael Austin ***Ph*** Gabriel Beristain ***Ed*** Edward Marnier ***Art*** Adrienne Atkinson

Act Denholm Elliott, Julie Walters, Richard E. Grant, Anna Massey, Laura del Sol (Scottish TV/British Screen)

First-time writer-director Michael Austin here proves he can direct; unfortunately his script is not up to par. The black humor he is trying for does not come off and he has to resort to slapstick to get the odd laugh.

Pic opens when Edith Berg (Anna Massey) receives a letter from her long-lost husband Nathy (Denholm Elliott) who left home 23 years ago claiming he was going to buy some cigarettes. He wants to come home, but the news doesn't please his son Alistair Berg (Richard E. Grant) who enjoys a peaceful existence with his mother.

He travels to Southend, on the coast, checks into the same faded hotel as his father with the plan to kill Elliott. What he finds is an unreformed character who gets drunk, lies and "borrows" money and lives with Judith (Julie Walters).

The acting is all first-rate. Elliott has his drunk act down to a fine art, and gives his character an added sly and charming edge. Walters as the faded Judith is excellent, but for her the role is not particularly testing. Grant sports a wacky pudding bowl haircut in an attempt to get laughs, but his performance is gently menacing.

•

KILLING FIELDS, THE

1984, 141 mins, UK Ⓥ ⊙ col

Dir Roland Joffe ***Prod*** David Puttnam ***Scr*** Bruce Robinson ***Ph*** Chris Menges ***Ed*** Jim Clark ***Mus*** Mike Oldfield ***Art*** Roy Walker

Act Sam Waterston, Haing S. Ngor, John Malkovich, Julian Sands, Craig T. Nelson, Bill Patterson (Enigma/Goldcrest/IFI)

A story of perseverance and survival in hell on earth, *The Killing Fields* represents an admirable, if not entirely successful, attempt to bring alive to the world film audience the horror story that is the recent history of Cambodia.

Based on Pulitzer Prize–winning N.Y. *Times* reporter Sydney Schanberg's 1980 article *The Death and Life of Dith Pran*, film is designed as a story of friendship, and it is on this level that it works least well. The intent and outward trappings are all impressively in place, but at its heart there's something missing.

Action begins in 1973, with Schanberg (Sam Waterston) arriving in Cambodia and being assisted in his reporting by Dith Pran (Haing S. Ngor), an educated, exceedingly loyal native.

Through a stupendous effort, and at great risk to his own existence, Dith Pran manages to save the lives of Schanberg and some colleagues after their capture by the victorious Khmer Rouge two years later. Dith Pran is later transferred to a re-education camp in the Cambodian Year Zero. It is during the long camp and escape sequences, which are largely silent, that the film reaches its most gripping heights.

Because of the overall aesthetic, which does not go in for nuances of character, performances are basically functional. Fortunately, nonpro Haing S. Ngor is a naturally sympathetic and camera-receptive man and he effectively carries the weight of the film's most important sequences.

1984: Best Supp. Actor (Haing S. Ngor), Cinematography, Editing

NOMINATIONS: Best Picture, Director, Actor (Sam Waterston), Adapted Screenplay

•

KILLING OF A CHINESE BOOKIE, THE

1976, 135 mins, US col

Dir John Cassavetes ***Prod*** Al Ruban ***Scr*** John Cassavetes ***Ph*** [uncredited] ***Ed*** Tom Cornwell ***Mus*** Bo Harwood ***Art*** Sam Shaw

Act Ben Gazzara, Timothy Çarey, Azizi Johari, Meade Roberts, Seymour Cassel, Alice Friedland (Faces)

True to form, John Cassavetes challenges a Hollywood cliché: that technology is so advanced even the worst films usually look good. With ease, he proves that an awful film can look even worse. As a L.A. strip-show operator, Ben Gazzara gets into hock to the mob, which asks him to erase the debt by knocking off an elderly Chinese bookie (Soto Joe Hugh) who accepts the bullet as if he's glad to get out of the picture.

In the process, Gazzara picks up a stomach wound of his own, which causes great pain initially, but is soon forgotten in the thrill of more aimless improvisation with girls and gangsters.

There's no cinematography credit, which suggests Cassavetes either added that hat to his writer-director wardrobe, or the real culprit left town ahead of the posse.

•

KILLING OF ANGEL STREET, THE

1981, 101 mins, Australia Ⓥ col

Dir Donald Crombie ***Prod*** Anthony Buckley ***Scr*** Evan Jones, Michael Craig, Cecil Holmes ***Ph*** Peter James ***Ed*** Tim Wellburn ***Mus*** Brian May ***Art*** Lindsay Hewson

Act Liz Alexander, John Hargreaves, Alexander Archdale, Reg Lye, Gordon McDougall (Forest Home/AFC)

Director Donald Crombie's fourth feature, like his best-known works, *Caddie* and *Cathy's Child*, boldly tackles an urban problem—rampant redevelopment by unscrupulous corporate manipulators. It is a powerful, hard-hitting and provocative story about corruption permeating the highest levels of society—the more so because it has a strong basis in fact.

The eponymous Angel Street consists of a row of old but charming terrace houses on the shores of Sydney Harbor, almost within spitting-distance of the famed bridge. An outwardly respectable development company, headed by a Knight of the Realm, wants to buy the homes, raze them and erect high-rise apartments. Their methods of persuasion are far from subtle.

Then the crusty leader of the residents' action group, B. C. Simmonds (Alexander Archdale), dies under suspicious circumstances. His daughter, Jessica (Liz Alexander), takes up the cudgels, aided by Communist union official Elliot (John Hargreaves), with whom she has a brief, if improbable romantic interlude. Their opponents are not simply the developers. The film depicts an unholy alliance between big business and government.

•

KILLING OF SISTER GEORGE, THE

1968, 138 mins, US Ⓥ col

Dir Robert Aldrich ***Prod*** Robert Aldrich ***Scr*** Lukas Heller ***Ph*** Joseph Biroc ***Ed*** Michael Luciano ***Mus*** Gerald Fried ***Art*** William Glasgow

Act Beryl Reid, Susannah York, Coral Browne, Ronald Fraser, Patricia Medina, Hugh Paddick (Palomar/Associates & Aldrich)

Frank Marcus's legiter, adapted by Lukas Heller, describes the erosion of a longtime lesbian affair between Beryl Reid—by day, the bleeding-heart heroine of a British TV sudser; by night, gin-guzzling dominant lover—and Susannah York.

Breakup is cued by decision to write Reid out of her key TV role, as executed with relish by Coral Browne, a broadcast exec who catches York's eye.

The basic thrust of the plot is the gradual development of a rapport and sympathy with Reid, in inverse ratio to the loss of respect for York.

Reid, for her part, carries it off superbly, from her pre-title nastiness to the pathetic freeze-frame-out, as she sits alone in a TV studio, contemplating her future career—that of a cartoon voice-over. Browne, with a role pitched at constant level, is excellent.

Director Robert Aldrich has achieved the look and feel of a made-in-Britain pic, although most of it was shot near downtown L.A.

•

KILLING ZOE

1994, 96 mins, US Ⓥ ⊙ col

Dir Roger Avary ***Prod*** Samuel Hadida ***Scr*** Roger Avary ***Ph*** Tom Richmond ***Ed*** Kathryn Himoff ***Mus*** Tomandandy ***Art*** David Wasco

Act Eric Stoltz, Jean-Hugues Anglade, Julie Delpy, Gary Kemp, Bruce Ramsay, Kario Salem (Davis)

If there's a hint of Quentin Tarantino in *Killing Zoe*, it's well deserved, as the tyro talent sherpherded this indie project. However, writer/director Roger Avary is no clone, and *Zoe* is a vivid thriller of a different, more considered tone.

The yarn finds recently released con Zed (Eric Stoltz) arriving in Paris to do a "job" for a friend. His speciality is cracking safes, and Eric (Jean-Hugues Anglade), the mastermind, has selected a particularly difficult one for him at a large bank, in broad daylight. Before getting down to mapping out the details, Zed takes some long overdue r&r with a Parisian professional named Zoe (Julie Delpy).

The bank siege is a botch from the word go. For Zed matters are complicated when he spots Zoe in her day job as a bank teller. Obviously an aficionado of the genre, Avary culls from some classics and twists the material into a new form. The truly chilling aspect of *Killing Zoe* is the correlation Avary makes between the gang's nihilistic attitude and its penchant for violence.

Though set in the French capital, the film was largely filmed on L.A. soundstages to great effect. Stoltz is adept as the slightly naive Zed. Delpy displays dignity in a thankless sketch of a character. But Anglade proves such a dynamo of energy, these and other shortcomings are quickly obscured.

•

KILL ME AGAIN

1989, 96 mins, UK/US Ⓥ ⊙ col

Dir John Dahl ***Prod*** David W. Warfield, Sigurjon Sighvatssen, Steve Golin ***Scr*** John Dahl, David W. Warfield ***Ph*** Jacques Steyn ***Ed*** Frank Jiminez, Jonathan Shaw, Eric Beason ***Mus*** William Olvis ***Art*** Michelle Minch

Act Val Kilmer, Joanne Whalley-Kilmer, Michael Madsen, Jonathan Gries, Michael Greene, Bibi Besch (PolyGram/Propaganda/ITC)

The tale of a down-and-out detective and a seamy femme fatale is a thoroughly professional little entertainment.

Set in contemporary Nevada, pic gets off to a fast start with a small-time con couple (Michael Madsen, Joanne Whalley-Kilmer) scoring big when they cop a suitcase full of cash from a pair of Mafia bagmen. The antiheroine beans her beau with a rock and takes off for a round of fast living in Reno. She asks a seedy detective, Jack (Val Kilmer), to fake her murder.

As he is in hock to a group of ruthless loan sharks, Jack is only too happy to oblige but still smart enough not to trust her. Consequently he's well prepared for the round of murders, double crosses and escapes that make up the film's last half.

Whalley-Kilmer takes to the role of a *really* bad girl with glee, always seeming to be just barely wearing whatever outfit she's shimmied into. Kilmer is somewhat less successful with his part, as it's difficult to tell how smart or stupid he's meant to be. Both Kilmers get fine support from Madsen as a fully functioning psychotic.

•

KILL-OFF, THE

1989, 95 mins, US Ⓥ col

Dir Maggie Greenwald ***Prod*** Lydia Dean Pilcher ***Scr*** Maggie Greenwald ***Ph*** Declan Quinn ***Ed*** James Y. Kwei ***Mus*** Evan Lurie ***Art*** Pamela Woodbridge

Act Loretta Gross, Andrew Lee Barrett, Jackson Sims, Steve Monroe, Cathy Haase, William Russell (Filmworld)

The Kill-Off is a rigorous, well-acted adaptation of a hard-boiled novel by Jim Thompson, with an unrelentingly grim view of human nature.

Loretta Gross gives a strong performance as Luane DeVore, an acid-tongued gossipmonger hated by almost everyone in her little community. She feigns a bedridden, feeble condition so that her husband (Steve Monroe), 20 years her junior, will take care of her hand and foot. Things come to a head when folks decide to get rid of her, including Monroe, a slow-witted fellow whose new girlfriend (Cathy Haase) plots against his wife. Gross's death is followed by some bitter confrontations and a nihilistic finish.

Ensemble acting brings out the bitterness and hopelessness of a ragtag group of trapped characters. It's not a pretty picture, but helmer Maggie Greenwald keeps tight control of mood and tone.

•

KIM

1950, 112 mins, US Ⓥ col

Dir Victor Saville *Prod* Leon Gordon *Scr* Leon Gordon, Helen Deutsch, Richard Schayer *Ph* William Skall *Ed* George Boemler *Mus* Andre Previn *Art* Cedric Gibbons, Hans Peters

Act Errol Flynn, Dean Stockwell, Paul Lukas, Robert Douglas, Thomas Gomez, Cecil Kellaway (M-G-M)

Metro has quite a spectacle, but not much else, in this version of Rudyard Kipling's *Kim*. The story of youthful adventure in India comes to the screen as rambling, overlength, spotty entertainment.

Visual dressing helps somewhat to carry the episodic plotline and story does have its appealing moments, particularly when young Dean Stockwell is on screen—a young orphan who plays at being a native and encounters derring-do adventures while aiding British intelligence ferret out a dastardly Czarist Russian plot to seize India.

Errol Flynn is the star, playing with flamboyant gusto the wily and amorous horse-trader who aids the government and Kim.

The lama sequences, in which Paul Lukas plays the holy man who advises young Kim, are much too long and slow.

•

KINDERGARTEN COP

1990, 110 mins, US Ⓥ ⊙ col

Dir Ivan Reitman *Prod* Ivan Reitman, Brian Grazer *Scr* Murray Salem, Herschel Weingrod, Timothy Harris *Ph* Michael Chapman *Ed* Sheldon Kahn, Wendy Bricmont *Mus* Randy Edelman *Art* Bruno Rubeo

Act Arnold Schwarzenegger, Penelope Ann Miller, Pamela Reed, Linda Hunt, Richard Tyson, Carroll Baker (Universal)

The polished comic vision that gave *Twins*, Arnold Schwarzenegger's comedy breakthrough, a storybook shine completely eludes director Ivan Reitman here. Result is a mish-mash of violence, psycho-drama and lukewarm kiddie comedy [story by Murray Salem].

Schwarzenegger plays a stoic, unfriendly and ultra-dedicated L.A. cop obsessed with putting away a murderous drug dealer (Richard Tyson). He needs the testimony of Tyson's ex-wife, who's supposedly living in Oregon on piles of drug money she stole from Tyson. Plan is for Schwarzenegger's goofy gal-pal partner (Pamela Reed) to infiltrate the kindergarden as a teacher and figure out which kid is Tyson's, but when Reed gets a bad stomach flu Schwarzenegger has to report for the job.

It's supposed to be wildly funny to have this grim, musclebound control freak confronted with five-year-olds he can't intimidate, but it isn't. Schwarzenegger has to carry the pic alone; he never finds his focus. Reed takes a good, feisty stab at holding up her corner of the pic, and Penelope Ann Miller is fittingly sweet and vulnerable as the single mother who romances Schwarzenegger.

•

KIND HEARTS AND CORONETS

1949, 106 mins, UK Ⓥ ⊙ b/w

Dir Robert Hamer *Prod* Michael Balcon *Scr* Robert Hamer, John Dighton *Ph* Douglas Slocombe, Jeff Seaholme *Ed* Peter Tanner *Mus* Ernest Irving (dir.) *Art* William Kellner

Act Dennis Price, Alec Guinness, Valerie Hobson, Joan Greenwood, Miles Malleson, Arthur Lowe (Ealing)

Story of the far-removed heir to the Dukedom of Chalfont who disposes of all the obstacles to his accession to the title and subsequently finds himself tried for a murder of which he is innocent may appear to be somewhat banal. But translation to a screen comedy has been effected with a mature wit.

Opening shot shows the arrival of the executioner at the prison announcing that this is his grand finale. Then the story is told in a constant flashback, recounting the methodical manner in which the one-time draper's boy works his way up to the dukedom. In this role Dennis Price is in top form, giving a quiet, dignified and polished portrayal. Greatest individual acting triumph, however, is scored by Alec Guinness who plays in turn all the members of the ancestral family.

•

KIND LADY

1935, 70 mins, US b/w

Dir George B. Seitz *Prod* Lucien Hubbard *Scr* Bernard Schubert *Ph* George Folsey *Mus* Edward Ward

Act Aline MacMahon, Basil Rathbone, Mary Carlisle, Frank Albertson, Dudley Digges, Doris Lloyd (M-G-M)

Kind Lady, which had a moderate run as a legit show [by Edward Chodorov, from a story by Hugh Walpole] in New York, has been transferred to the screen with Aline MacMahon and Basil Rathbone in prime roles.

Chief flaw is the tedious build-up to a fairly intriguing plot. Requires more than half an hour, much of it comprising irksome English palaver, to reach real thread of yarn—that of blackmail via doping route. Implausible basic idea has been made digestible by skillful direction. Viewers are asked to believe that an English lady, disappointed in her love affairs, would invite a strange man, his wife and baby in as guests of her palatial home while it is rather apparent that he is up to no good.

To adapt herself to the character of an Englishwoman was no mean job, but MacMahon does it with skill. Rathbone makes a suave villain. Dudley Digges adds some lighter moments as his cockney aide.

•

KIND OF LOVING, A

1962, 112 mins, UK Ⓥ b/w

Dir John Schlesinger *Prod* Joseph Janni *Scr* Willis Hall, Keith Waterhouse *Ph* Denys Coop *Ed* Roger Cherrill *Mus* Ron Grainer *Art* Ray Simm

Act Alan Bates, June Ritchie, Thora Hird, James Bolam, Leonard Rossiter, Gwen Nelson (Anglo-Amalgamated)

The screenplay by Keith Waterhouse and Willis Hall [based on the novel by Stan Barstow] is set in a Lancashire industrial town and tells the bittersweet yarn of a young draftsman who is attracted by a typist in the same factory. It is a physical attraction which he cannot resist. She, on the other hand, has a deeper feeling for him.

The fumbling romance proceeds, often hurtfully, often poignantly. The inevitable happens. She becomes pregnant and he grudgingly marries her. It is obvious from the start that the union is purely physical and it is not helped by the nagging of her mother.

Schlesinger handles this film with a sharp documentary eye, but does not forget that he is unfolding a piece of fiction. The tremulous moment when the girl first gives in to the boy's physical craving, an opening wedding sequence, the desolate seashore when they go on honeymoon, the girl discussing birth control hesitantly, a pub crawl, the tender scenes as the young lovers walk in the park. These and many other sequences are all handled with tact, shrewd observation and wit.

June Ritchie makes an appealing debut as the bewildered Lancashire lass. Alan Bates is a likeable hero who will hold most audience's sympathy despite his weaknesses. Photographed in many parts of Lancashire to represent a composite town, lenser Coop has skillfully caught the peculiar grey drabness of the area.

•

KING & COUNTRY

1964, 88 mins, UK b/w

Dir Joseph Losey *Prod* Joseph Losey, Norman Priggen *Scr* Evan Jones *Ph* Denys Coop *Ed* Reginald Mills *Mus* Larry Adler *Art* Richard Macdonald

Act Dirk Bogarde, Tom Courtenay, Leo McKern, Barry Foster, James Villiers, Peter Copley (BHE)

The story of Private Hamp, a deserter from the battle front in World War I, has already been told on radio, television and the stage, but undeterred by this exposure, director Joseph Losey has attacked the subject with confidence and vigor, and the result is a highly sensitive and emotional drama, enlivened by sterling performances and a sincere screenplay.

The action takes place behind the lines at Passchendaele, where Hamp, a volunteer at the outbreak of war, and the sole survivor of his company, decides one day to "go for a walk." In fact, he contemplates walking to his home in London, but after more than 24 hours on the road, he's picked up by the Military Police and sent back to his unit to face court-martial for desertion.

The job of defending the private goes to Dirk Bogarde, a typically arrogant officer who accepts the assignment because it is his duty to do so. But during his preliminary investigation, he responds to Hamp's beguiling simplicity and honesty, coming to the inevitable conclusion that he was not responsible for his actions.

Notwithstanding its technical excellence, the picture [based on a play by John Wilson and a novel by James Lansdale Hodson] is carried by the outstanding performances of its three stars. Tom Courtenay gives a compelling study of a simple-minded soldier, unable to accept the fact that he has committed a heinous crime. Bogarde's portrayal of the defending officer is also distinguished by its sincerity. Completing the stellar trio, Leo McKern's study of the medical officer is faultless, and in his big scene he unerringly stands up to Bogarde's cross-examination.

•

KING AND I, THE

1956, 133 mins, US Ⓥ ⊙ ▭ col

Dir Walter Lang *Prod* Charles Brackett *Scr* Ernest Lehman *Ph* Leon Shamroy *Ed* Robert Simpson *Mus* Alfred Newman (dir.) *Art* Lyle R. Wheeler, John DeCuir

Act Deborah Kerr, Yul Brynner, Rita Moreno, Martin Benson, Terry Saunders, Rex Thompson (20th Century-Fox)

All the ingredients that made Rodgers & Hammerstein's [1951] *The King and I* a memorable stage experience have been faithfully transferred to the screen. The result is a pictorially exquisite, musically exciting and dramatically satisfying motion picture.

With Deborah Kerr in the role originally created by Gertrude Lawrence, and Yul Brynner and Terry Saunders repeating their stage performances, the production has the talent to support the opulence of this truly blockbuster presentation. CinemaScope 55, originally introduced with R&H's *Carousel*, attains its full glory with *The King and I*.

As the Victorian Englishwoman who comes to Siam to teach Western manners and English to the royal household, Kerr gives one of her finest performances. She handles the role of Mrs. Anna with charm and understanding and, when necessary, the right sense of comedy. As the brusque, petulant, awkwardly kind despot confused by the conflicts of Far Eastern and Western cultures, Yul Brynner gives an effective, many-shaded reading.

Although unbilled, the singing voice of Kerr is Marni Nixon. It is ghosted so well that it is hard to believe that it is not Kerr. The film suggests a stronger romantic feeling between Mrs. Anna and the king than was presented in the legituner, but it is done with the utmost delicacy.

[For pic's 1961 reissue in a 70mm blowup, an interval was added after the temple scene, plus music for an overture, entr'acte and playout.]

1956: Best Actor (Yul Brynner), Color Art Direction, Sound Recording, Scoring of a Musical Picture, Color Costume Design

NOMINATIONS: Best Picture, Director, Actress (Deborah Kerr), Color Cinematography, Color Art Direction

•

KING AND THE CHORUS GIRL, THE

1937, 95 mins, US b/w

Dir Mervyn LeRoy *Prod* Mervyn LeRoy *Scr* Norman Krasna, Groucho Marx *Ph* Tony Gaudio *Ed* Thomas Richards *Mus* Leo F. Forbstein (dir.)

Act Fernand Gravet, Joan Blondell, Edward Everett Horton, Alan Mowbray, Jane Wyman, Mary Nash (Warner)

Fernand Gravet, Mervyn LeRoy's Franco-Belgian import, makes an auspicious American debut in pictures. Film is a romantic comedy, silly but funny, inconsequential but swell for Gravet and Joan Blondell. This marks LeRoy's debut as a producer-director.

Towards the end the story goes to pieces, and yet that, too, is in its favor. Becoming broad farce, yarn drops all pretense to reality and finishes with one of the best tags any film has ever had.

Gravet is wholly engaging as the bored ex-monarch, and Joan Blondell is capital as the American chorine in the Folies Bergère. Entire background is Paris. Strong support further enhances. Edward Everett Horton is at his droll best as the king's buffer.

Gravet maintains the farcical proceedings throughout with rare good humor, while Blondell, as his American Cinderella vis-a-vis, supplies a basic boy (king)-meets-girl premise. Blondell has never looked better, and her performance here includes a restraint and softness previously lacking.

•

KING CREOLE

1958, 116 mins, US Ⓥ ⊙ b/w

Dir Michael Curtiz *Prod* Hal B. Wallis *Scr* Michael V. Gazzo, Herbert Baker *Ph* Russell Harlan *Ed* Warren Low *Mus* Walter Scharf (arr.) *Art* Hal Pereira, J. MacMillan Johnson

Act Elvis Presley, Carolyn Jones, Walter Matthau, Dolores Hart, Dean Jagger, Vic Morrow (Paramount)

The picture is based on Harold Robbins's novel, *A Stone for Danny Fisher*, but the locale has been switched to New Orleans, to Bourbon Street and to an indigenous café called the King Creole. Elvis Presley is a high school youth who is prevented from graduation by his attempts to take care of his weakwilled father and the density of his school teachers. He gets involved in a minor theft but thereafter goes straight when given a chance to perform in Paul Stewart's Vieux Carré saloon. His brief fling at crime returns to haunt him when the local crime boss (Walter Matthau) decrees that Presley shall leave Stewart and come sing for him.

Essentially a musical, since Presley sings 13 new songs, including a title number, film runs a little long and the premise that Matthau would launch a minor crime wave just to get one performer for his club is a little shaky.

Presley shows himself to be a surprisingly sympathetic and believable actor on occasion. He also does some very pleasant, soft and melodious, singing. Carolyn Jones contributes a strong and bitter portrait of a good girl gone wrong, moving and pathetic.

•

KING DAVID

1985, 114 mins, US Ⓥ ⊙ ▭ col

Dir Bruce Beresford ***Prod*** Martin Elfand ***Scr*** Andrew Birkin, James Costigan ***Ph*** Donald McAlpine ***Ed*** William Anderson ***Mus*** Carl Davis ***Art*** Ken Adam

Act Richard Gere, Edward Woodward, Denis Quilley, Niall Buggy, Jack Klaff, Cherie Lunghi (Paramount)

King David is an intensely literal telling of familiar portions of the saga of Israel's first two rulers, more historical in approach than religious.

David moves from one monumental event to the next, trying to cover as much of the story as possible. The result is to minimize each step and every complex relationship (and doubtlessly confuse many of those who haven't been to Sunday school for a while).

Though the overall problems may not be of his making, Richard Gere is of little help in the title role. Granted, he could have been truly awful (which he isn't), but he doesn't seem comfortable, either.

Holding back, Gere rarely makes it felt why he loves Absalom so, or lusts after Bathsheba or tolerates Saul's persecution beyond the fact that it says so in the Bible (or in the script).

David really isn't as trifling as quick summary makes it seem. There's a lot of history here, brought to life with good period film work and performances are generally fine.

•

KING IN NEW YORK, A

1957, 105 mins, UK Ⓥ b/w

Dir Charles Chaplin ***Prod*** Charles Chaplin ***Scr*** Charles Chaplin ***Ph*** Georges Perinal ***Ed*** Spencer Reeves ***Mus*** Charles Chaplin ***Art*** Allan Harris

Act Charles Chaplin, Dawn Addams, Oliver Johnston, Maxine Audley, Harry Green, Michael Chaplin (Archway)

Charles Chaplin's first British offering is a tepid disappointment. Tilting against American TV is fair game and while doing this Chaplin contributes some shrewd, funny observations on a vulnerable theme. But when he sets his sights on the problem of Communism and un-American activities, the jester's mask drops. He loses objectivity and stands revealed as an embittered man.

The story has Chaplin as the amiable, dethroned monarch of Estrovia. He survives a revolution and, with his ambassador, seeks New York sanctuary. He arrives to find that his prime minister has decamped with the treasury and the king is financially flat. His matrimonial status is also rocky.

Dawn Addams is a winning telepersonality who charmingly tricks Chaplin into guesting on her show. Overnight, he becomes a TV star. He then befriends a politically minded 10-year-old whose parents are on the mat for not squealing on friends who are suspect by the Un-American Activities Committee. As a result, Chaplin is himself arraigned before this committee.

The way in which Chaplin poses his political problems through the mouth of a child is both queasy and embarrassing. On the funny side, there are such good moments as when Chaplin is being fingerprinted while being enthusiastically interviewed on U.S. as the land of the free. But, largely, the humor is half-hearted and jaded.

•

KING KONG

1933, 100 mins, US Ⓥ ⊙ b/w

Dir Ernest B. Schoedsack, Merian C. Cooper ***Prod*** Ernest B. Schoedsack, Merian C. Cooper ***Scr*** James Creelman, Ruth Rose, [Merian C. Cooper] ***Ph*** Edward Linden, Vernon L. Walker, J. O. Taylor ***Ed*** Ted Cheesman ***Mus*** Max Steiner ***Art*** Carroll Clark, Al Herman

Act Fay Wray, Robert Armstrong, Bruce Cabot, Frank Reicher, Sam Hardy, Noble Johnson (RKO)

Highly imaginative and super-goofy yarn is mostly about a 50-foot ape who goes for a five-foot blonde. According to the billing the story is "from an idea conceived" by Merian C. Cooper and Edgar Wallace. For their "idea" they will have to take a bend in the direction of the late Conan Doyle and his *Lost World*, which is the only picture to which *Kong* can be compared.

Kong is the better picture. It takes a couple of reels for *Kong* to be believed, and until then it doesn't grip. But after the audience becomes used to the machine-like movements and other mechanical flaws in the gigantic animals on view, and become accustomed to the phoney atmosphere, they may commence to feel the power.

Neither the story nor the cast gains more than secondary importance, and not even close. Technical aspects are always on top. The technicians' two big moments arrive in the island jungle, where Kong and other prehistoric creatures reign, and in New York where Kong goes on a bender.

Fay Wray is the blonde who's chased by Kong, grabbed twice, but finally saved. It's a film-long screaming session for her, too much for any actress and any audience. The light hair is a change for Wray. Robert Armstrong, as the explorer, and Bruce Cabot, as the blonde's other boyfriend who doesn't make her scream, are the remaining principal characters and snowed under by the technical end.

A gripping and fitting musical score and some impressive sound effects rate with the scenery and mechanism in providing *Kong* with its technical excellence.

•

KING KONG

1976, 134 mins, US Ⓥ ⊙ ▭ col

Dir John Guillermin ***Prod*** Dino De Laurentiis ***Scr*** Lorenzo Semple, Jr. ***Ph*** Richard H. Kline ***Ed*** Ralph E. Winters ***Mus*** John Barry ***Art*** Mario Chiari, Dale Hennesy

Act Jeff Bridges, Charles Grodin, Jessica Lange, John Rudolph, Rene Auberjonois, Julius Harris (Paramount)

Faithful in substantial degree not only to the letter but also the spirit of the 1933 classic for RKO, this $22 million-plus version neatly balances superb special effects with solid dramatic credibility.

In the original, documentary producer-promoter Robert Armstrong took aspiring actress Fay Wray on an expedition to a lost Pacific island. A gigantic humanoid gorilla was found, then brought back to civilization where he wasted part of N.Y. searching for Wray.

In Lorenzo Semple's literate modernization, Charles Grodin is the promoter, this time a scheming oil company explorer.

Rick Baker is acknowledged for his "special contributions" to the Kong character; this means that Baker did virtually all of the perfectly-matched and expertly sized closeups, in which the beast's range of emotions emerges with telling effect.

1976: Honorary Award (visual effects)

NOMINATIONS: Best Cinematography, Sound

•

KING KONG LIVES

1986, 105 mins, US Ⓥ ⊙ col

Dir John Guillermin ***Prod*** Martha Schumacher ***Scr*** Ronald Shusett, Steven Pressfield ***Ph*** Alec Mills ***Ed*** Malcolm Cooke ***Mus*** John Scott ***Art*** Peter Murton

Act Brian Kerwin, Linda Hamilton, John Ashton, Peter Michael Goetz, Frank Maraden, Jimmy Ray Weeks (De Laurentiis)

Film leads off with the previous [1976] pic's closing footage. Advancing to the present, the giant ape is stunningly revealed to be breathing via life-support systems, with Linda Hamilton heading a surgical team preparing to give him an artificial heart.

Brian Kerwin enters from far-off Borneo, where he has stumbled on a female Kong. He delivers her to the Hamilton group so her blood can be used for the heart transplant operation.

In portraying an Indiana Jones-type figure Kerwin strains for plausibility and film swiftly begins to lose some early credibility. His tough jungle ways are unconvincingly transformed into sensitive concern for both animals [created by Carlo Rambaldi].

Meantime, the proximity of the two Kongs prompts these primates to discover what comes naturally. This would prove to be the moment when director John Guillermin loses all control of the pic. Mindless chase then proceeds pell mell for the rest of the film, with the army in hot pursuit.

•

KING OF COMEDY, THE

1983, 101 mins, US Ⓥ ⊙ col

Dir Martin Scorsese ***Prod*** Arnon Milchan ***Scr*** Paul D. Zimmerman ***Ph*** Fred Schuler ***Ed*** Thelma Schoonmaker ***Mus*** Robbie Robertson ***Art*** Boris Leven

Act Robert De Niro, Jerry Lewis, Diahnne Abbott, Sandra Bernhard, Shelley Hack, Tony Randall (20th Century-Fox)

The King of Comedy is a royal disappointment. To be sure, Robert De Niro turns in another virtuoso performance for Martin Scorsese, just as in their four previous efforts. But once again—and even more so—they come up with a character that it's hard to spend time with. Even worse, the characters—in fact, all the characters—stand for nothing.

De Niro plays a would-be stand-up comic, determined to start at the top by getting a gig on Jerry Lewis's popular talk show. Worse still, he has a sidekick (Sandra Bernhard) who's even nuttier than he is, only slightly more likable because she's slightly more pathetic in her desperate fantasy love for Lewis.

When all else fails, the pair kidnap Lewis to get what they want: He a spot on the show, she a night of amour.

Diahnne Abbott is excellent as a girl embarrassingly drawn into De Niro's fantasy world.

•

KING OF JAZZ, THE

1930, 98 mins, US Ⓥ col

Dir J. Murray Anderson ***Ph*** Hal Mohr, Jerome Ash ***Ed*** Robert Carlisle ***Mus*** Ferde Grofe (dir.) ***Art*** Herman Rosse

Act Paul Whiteman and His Band, John Boles, Laura La Plante, Jeanette Loff (Universal)

The King of Jazz as directed by J. Murray Anderson on his first talker attempt cost Universal $2 million in his inexperienced hands.

The millions who never heard the great Paul Whiteman band play George Gershwin's *Rhapsody in Blue* won't hear it here, either. Anderson sees fit to scramble it up with "production." It's all busted to pieces.

Nothing here counts excepting Whiteman, his band and the finale, "The Melting Pot." This is an elaborately produced number, in the same manner that Anderson or Ziegfeld would have put it on in a stage show.

1929/30: Best Interior Decoration (Herman Rosse)

•

KING OF KINGS, THE

1927, 155 mins, US Ⓥ ⊗ col

Dir Cecil B. DeMille ***Prod*** Cecil B. DeMille ***Scr*** Jeanie Macpherson ***Ph*** Peverell Marley ***Ed*** Anne Bauchens, Harold McLernon ***Art*** Mitchell Leisen, Anton Grot

Act H. B. Warner, Dorothy Cumming, Ernest Torrence, Joseph Schildkraut, James Neill, Jacqueline Logan (DeMille/PDC)

Tremendous is *The King of Kings*—tremendous in its lesson, in the daring of its picturization for a commercial theatre and tremendous in its biggest scene, the Crucifixion of Christ.

Technicolor is employed in two sections of the 14 reels, at its commencement and near the finish.

In scenes such as the Last Supper, the seduction of Judas by the Romans to betray The Christ, the healing miracles, the driving out of the evil spirits from Mary or the carrying of the Cross by Jesus (one of the most excellent in execution after the Crucifixion of the picture), there is a naturalnes that is entrancing.

And the acting is no less. The Schildkrauts (father and son), after H. B. Warner, come first to attention, the father as Caiaphas, the High Priest of Israel, and the younger as Judas, the traitor. And again no less is Ernest Torrence as Peter, Robert Edeson as Matthew, and perhaps others likewise of the Twelve Disciples, whose desertion of Jesus is brought out pathetically, almost, while His reappearance amidst them after the resurrection is an inner thrill.

•

KING OF KINGS

1961, 168 mins, US/Spain Ⓥ ⊙ ▭ col

Dir Nicholas Ray, [Charles Walters] ***Prod*** Samuel Bronston ***Scr*** Philip Yordan, [George Kilpatrick, Ray Bradbury] ***Ph*** Franz F. Planer, Milton Krasner, Manuel Berenguer, [George Folsey] ***Ed*** Harold F. Kress, [Margaret Booth, Renee Lichtig] ***Mus*** Miklos Rozsa ***Art*** Georges Wakhevitch

Act Jeffrey Hunter, Hurd Hatfield, Ron Randell, Harry Guardino, Rip Torn, Frank Thring (M-G-M/Bronston)

King of Kings wisely substitutes characterizations for orgies. Director Nicholas Ray has brooded long and wisely upon the meaning of his meanings, has planted plenty of symbols along the path, yet avoided the banalities of religious calendar art.

The sweep of the story presents a panorama of the conquest of Judea and its persistent rebelliousness, against which the implication of Christ's preachments assume, to pagan Roman overlords, the reek of sedition. All of this is rich in melodrama, action, battle and clash. But author Philip Yordan astutely uses the bloodthirsty Jewish patriots, unable to think except in terms of violence, as telling counterpoint to the Messiah's love-one-another creed.

Jeffrey Hunter's blue orbs and auburn bob (wig, of course) are strikingly pictorial. The handling of the Sermon on the Mount which dominates the climax of the first part before intermission is wonderfully skillful in working masses of people into an alternation of faith and skepticism while cross-cutting personal movement among them of the Saviour and his disciples.

Irish actress Siobhan McKenna as the Virgin Mary infuses a sort of strength-through-passivity, infinitely sad yet never surprised. The 16-year-old Chicago schoolgirl Brigid Bazlen portrays Salomé as a Biblical juvenile delinquent, who bellydances rather than jitterbugs. The brutish, muscle-bound Barabbas of Harry Guardino makes a pretty good case that sedition frequently hurts only itself.

•

KING OF MARVIN GARDENS, THE

1972, 103 mins, US col

Dir Bob Rafelson ***Prod*** Bob Rafelson ***Scr*** Jacob Brackman ***Ph*** Laszlo Kovacs ***Ed*** John F. Link II ***Art*** Toby Carr Rafelson

Act Jack Nicholson, Bruce Dern, Ellen Burstyn, Julia Anne Robinson, Scatman Crothers, Charles Lavine (BBS/Columbia)

Admirers of director Bob Rafelson's previous feature, *Five Easy Pieces*, will be stunned by the tedious pretensions of his newest effort. Chief culprit is undoubtedly former film critic Jacob Brackman, who drafted the screenplay from a story contrived jointly with Rafelson. Tale centers on the relationship between two brothers—the older (Bruce Dern) a self-deceiving wheeler-dealer, flanked by two chippies (Ellen Burstyn and Julia Anne Robinson); the younger (Jack Nicholson) a self-effacing FM-radio monologist who allows himself to be seduced by his brother's bravura lifestyle.

Yet for all the artistic and intellectual shortcomings, there are sufficient moments of demonstrable talent that suggest what Rafelson could have achieved with better material. Both Dern and Burstyn go far toward filling in the many characterizational holes.

•

KING OF NEW YORK

1990, 103 mins, Italy Ⓥ ⊙ col

Dir Abel Ferrara ***Prod*** Mary Kane ***Scr*** Nicholas St John ***Ph*** Bojan Bazelli ***Ed*** Anthony Redman ***Mus*** Joe Delia ***Art*** Alex Tavoularis

Act Christopher Walken, David Caruso, Larry Fishburne, Victor Argo, Wesley Snipes, Janet Julian (Reteitalia/Scena/Caminito)

A violence-drenched fable of Gotham druglords, *King of New York* is unusual in being an all-American production fully financed by European sources (Italy in this case). It's the first bit that's unusual. The screenplay coolly depicts Christopher Walken as a fresh-out-of-prison gangster who vows to take over Gotham's $1 billion-plus drug industry. With his mainly black henchmen he blows away leading Colombian, Italian and Chinese kingpins and soon sets up shop at the Plaza Hotel (protected by two beautiful femme bodyguards) as the King of New York.

Director Abel Ferrara has an ominous view of New York where deadly violence can erupt instantaneously. Also impressive are large-scale setpieces, including a climax shot in Times Square, as well as a balletic orgy of bloodletting (in which Walken's bodyguards are killed). Complementing Walken's bravura turn are equally flamboyant performances by David Caruso as the young Irish cop out to destroy Walken, and Larry Fishburne as Walken's slightly crazy aide-de-camp.

•

KING OF THE HILL

1993, 102 mins, US Ⓥ ▭ col

Dir Steven Soderbergh ***Prod*** Albert Berger, Barbara Maltby, Ron Yerxa ***Scr*** Steven Soderbergh ***Ph*** Elliot Davis ***Ed*** Steven Soderbergh ***Mus*** Cliff Martinez ***Art*** Gary Frutkoff

Act Jesse Bradford, Jeroen Krabbe, Lisa Eichhorn, Karen Allen, Spalding Gray, Elizabeth McGovern (Wildwood/Bona Fide)

King of the Hill has all the rich satisfactions of a fine novel, a marvelous comeback for writer-director Steven Soderbergh after his problematic sophomore effort *Kafka*.

Drawing upon A. E. Hotchner's 1972 book about his St. Louis childhood, Soderbergh creates a vibrant picture of the Middle-American social fabric while maintaining sharp focus on the changing fortunes of 12-year-old Aaron Kurlander (Jesse Bradford), and his disintegrating family, living in the seedy Empire Hotel in a working-class section. While Mr. Kurlander (Jeroen Krabbe) scrapes by, awaiting word of a good job, Aaron excels at school and becomes involved with some of the down-and-outers at the hotel. Ella (Amber Benson) is a nervous, bespectacled, epileptic girl. Mr. Mungo (Spalding Gray) is a formerly wealthy alcoholic who eases his pain with prostie Lydia (Elizabeth McGovern). The grungy bellboy (Joseph Chrest) keeps an eagle eye on everyone.

Down to the smallest roles, all the characters are indelibly drawn, a brilliant gallery of types from all social levels. But the film wouldn't work nearly so well without Bradford. His Aaron is an examplar of the limitless potential that can exist in children before they are damaged, limited or brought down.

•

KING OF THE KHYBER RIFLES

1953, 100 mins, US ▭ col

Dir Henry King ***Prod*** Frank P. Rosenberg ***Scr*** Ivan Goff, Ben Roberts ***Ph*** Leon Shamroy ***Ed*** Barbara McLean ***Mus*** Bernard Herrmann ***Art*** Lyle R. Wheeler, Maurice Ransford

Act Tyrone Power, Terry Moore, Michael Rennie, John Justin, Guy Rolfe (20th Century-Fox)

Picture is laid in the India of 1857 when British colonial troops were having trouble with Afridi tribesmen. The plot opens with Tyrone Power, a half-caste English officer, being assigned to the Khyber Rifles, a native troop at a garrison headed by Michael Rennie, English general. For romance, Rennie has a daughter, Terry Moore, who is instantly attracted to Power despite British snobbery over his mixed blood.

From here on, the footage is taken up with developing the romance while the hero protects the heroine from native dangers and kidnap attempts by Guy Rolfe, leader of the Afridis and a foster brother of Power's. The male heroics are played with a stiff-lipped, stout-fellowish Britishism perfectly appropriate to the characters. Power is a good hero, Moore attractively handles the heroine unabashedly pursuing her man. Rennie is excellent as the commanding general and Rolfe does another of his top-notch villains.

A rousing finale climaxes the story, based on the Talbot Mundy novel, and in between CinemaScope adds sweep and spectacle to the India settings, facsimiled by the terrain around California's Lone Pine area.

•

KING OF THE TURF

1939, 88 mins, US b/w

Dir Alfred E. Green ***Prod*** Edward Small ***Scr*** George Bruce ***Ph*** Robert Planck ***Ed*** Grant Whytock ***Mus*** Frank Tours (dir.) ***Art*** John Du Casse Schulze

Act Adolphe Menjou, Roger Daniel, Dolores Costello, Walter Abel, William Demarest (United Artists)

Alfred E. Green, a director who knows his hosses, has given George Bruce's original plenty of values. Adolphe Menjou is tops as the former horseman turned bum who, through the inspiration of a boy, recovers the position he once held in turfdom as a stable owner.

The lad (Roger Daniel), badly bitten by the racing bug, has run away from home and becomes a stable boy.

The many touching angles of the story and the plot reach a climax when the father turns against him as a means of forcing him to return to his mother. The means are drastic and a bit unbelievable, but make strong drama.

Race in which the jockey is supposed to lose is one of the best ever photographed and is a distinct credit to Robert Planck. It's as thrilling a bangtail contest as seen on the screen.

•

KING, QUEEN, KNAVE

1972, 92 mins, W. Germany/US Ⓥ col

Dir Jerzy Skolimowski ***Prod*** Lutz Hengst ***Scr*** David Seltzer, David Shaw ***Ph*** Charly Steinberger ***Ed*** Mel Shapiro ***Mus*** Stanley Myers ***Art*** Rolf Zehetbauer

Act David Niven, Gina Lollobrigida, John Moulder Brown, Mario Adorf, Carl Fox-Duering, Christopher Sandford (Maran/Wolper)

Polski director Jerzy Skolimowski, working in Germany, brings off an intermittently funny black comedy on first love, avariciousness and underneath, a subversive look at economic booms and human relations in the upper classes.

Based on Vladimir Nabokov's pithy novel, its obvious tricky word play, ironic nostalgia and interplay of love, are hard to duplicate on film. Skolimowski wisely concentrates on making it as visual as possible. It does not work, for the characters are not well blocked out and the humor is oblique, but present enough for some yoks.

A gauche young orphan is invited, by an uncle he has never seen, to Germany. The blundering boy likes his easy-going uncle, David Niven, but is smitten by his sexy aunt Gina Lollobrigida who first decides to seduce the boy and then have him kill her husband to inherit the fortune.

•

KING RALPH

1991, 97 mins, US Ⓥ ⊙ col

Dir David S. Ward ***Prod*** Jack Brodsky ***Scr*** David S. Ward ***Ph*** Kenneth MacMillan ***Ed*** John Jympson ***Mus*** James Newton Howard ***Art*** Simon Holland

Act John Goodman, Peter O'Toole, John Hurt, Camille Coduri, Richard Griffiths, Leslie Phillips (Universal/Mirage/Jbro)

Crowned with John Goodman's lovable loutishness and a regally droll performance by Peter O'Toole, *King Ralph* doesn't carry much weight in the story department, though the wispy premise is handled with a blend of sprightly comedy and sappy romance.

Britain's entire royal family dies in a pre-credit sequence, resulting in a boorish American nightclub entertainer—the product of a dalliance between a prince and the American's paternal grandmother—becoming king.

After that, it's a basic fish-out-of-water tale, with King Ralph (Goodman) adjusting to the perks and constraints of nobility, aided by a group of harried advisers including his mentor Willingham (O'Toole) and officious bureaucratic Phipps (Richard Griffiths).

John Hurt plays a British lord seeking to bring the new king down so his own family can regain the throne. He facilitates a liaison between the king and a buxom lower-class British girl (Camille Coduri) in order to force his resignation.

Lensing was done on U.K. locations and at London's Pinewood Studios.

•

KING RAT

1965, 134 mins, US Ⓥ ▭ b/w

Dir Bryan Forbes ***Prod*** James Woolf ***Scr*** Bryan Forbes ***Ph*** Burnett Guffey ***Ed*** Walter Thompson ***Mus*** John Barry ***Art*** Robert Smith

Act George Segal, Tom Courtenay, James Fox, Patrick O'Neal, Denholm Elliott, John Mills (Coleytown/Columbia)

Filmed near Hollywood but having the feel and casting of an overseas pic, *King Rat* is a grim, downbeat and often raw prison camp drama depicting the character destruction wrought by a smalltime sharpie on fellow inmates of a Japanese POW site in the final days of the Second World War. Pic has some fine characterizations and directions, backed by stark, realistic and therefore solid production values, which offset in part its overlength and some script softness.

George Segal does an excellent job as U.S. Corporal King, the "Rat," a con artist who manipulates the meagre goods and characters of other prisoners, most of whom have higher military rank. Director Bryan Forbes has sharply etched his main character.

Ditto for Tom Courtenay, the young British officer trying to perform provost-marshal duties in the behind-the-wire hierarchy topped by weary, but worldly and practical John Mills, effective in brief footage. James Fox, another young British officer, registers solidly as he comes under Segal's influence and develops an affection for him.

1965: NOMINATIONS: Best B&W Cinematography, B&W Art Direction

•

KING RICHARD AND THE CRUSADERS

1954, 113 mins, US Ⓥ ▭ col

Dir David Butler ***Prod*** Henry Blanke ***Scr*** John Twist ***Ph*** Peverell Marley ***Ed*** Irene Morra ***Mus*** Max Steiner ***Art*** Bertram Tuttle

Act Rex Harrison, Virginia Mayo, George Sanders, Laurence Harvey, Robert Douglas, Michael Pate (Warner)

The Talisman, Walter Scott's classic about the third crusade, gets the full spectacle treatment in this entry.

The Scott classic details the efforts of Christian nations from Europe, marshalled under the leadership of England's King Richard, to gain the Holy Grail from the Mohammedans. In addition to the fighting wiles of the crafty Moslems, King Richard must contend with the sinister ambitions of some of his entourage and these rivalries almost doom the crusade.

David Butler's direction manages to keep a long show nearly always moving at a fast clip. Especially attractive to the action-minded will be the jousting sequences, either those showing training or those in deadly seriousness, and the bold battling is mostly concerned with combat between the forces of good and evil among the crusaders themselves. The script is especially good in its dialog, particularly that handed to Rex Harrison.

•

KINGS GO FORTH

1958, 109 mins, US Ⓥ ⊙ b/w

Dir Delmer Daves ***Prod*** Frank Ross ***Scr*** Merle Miller ***Ph*** Daniel L. Fapp ***Ed*** William Murphy ***Mus*** Elmer Bernstein ***Art*** Fernando Carrere

Act Frank Sinatra, Tony Curtis, Natalie Wood, Leora Dana, Karl Swenson, Ann Codee (United Artists)

Frank Sinatra goes soldiering in this adaptation of Joe David Brown's novel *Kings Go Forth*. It's a simple, rather straightforward action-romance, laid against the attractive background of the French Riviera and the Maritime Alps.

The race angle is played to the hilt. The girl, played by Natalie Wood—an American living in France—is of mixed blood, her mother being white and the (dead) father having been a Negro. This revelation is the key to Wood's romantic entanglements.

It's an odd war that is being fought in this picture. The men fight and die in the mountains during the week. On weekends, there are passes for visits to the Riviera. The year is late 1944, and while Allied armies push into and beyond Paris the American Seventh Army has the job of cleaning out pockets of German resistance in the south.

Among the replacements joining Sinatra's platoon is Curtis, a rich man's son, with charm to spare and an eye for all the angles. Sinatra meets Wood and falls in love with her. She in turn falls in love with Curtis. Sinatra, the rough-tough soldier, creates sympathy by underplaying the role. Wood looks pretty, but that's just all. Curtis has experience acting the heel, and he does a repeat. He's best when acting the charm boy.

•

KINGS OF THE ROAD
SEE: IM LAUF DER ZEIT

•

KINGS OF THE SUN
1963, 108 mins, US ▭ col
Dir J. Lee Thompson *Prod* Lewis J. Rachmil *Scr* Elliott Arnold, James R. Webb *Ph* Joseph MacDonald *Ed* William Reynolds *Mus* Elmer Bernstein *Art* Alfred Ybarra
Act Yul Brynner, George Chakiris, Shirley Anne Field, Richard Basehart, Brad Dexter, Barry Morse (Mirisch)

The screenplay from a story by Elliott Arnold is a kind of southern Western. It describes, in broad, vague, romantic strokes the flight of the Mayan people from their homeland after crushing military defeat, their establishment of a new home and their successful defense of it against their former conquerors thanks to the aid of a friendly resident tribe that has been willing to share the region in which the Mayans have chosen to relocate.

In more intimate terms, it is the story of the young Mayan king (George Chakiris), the leader (Yul Brynner) of the not-so-savage tribe that comes to the ultimate defense of the Mayans and a Mayan maiden (Shirley Anne Field).

Brynner easily steals the show with his sinewy authority, masculinity and cat-like grace. Chakiris is adequate, although he lacks the epic, heroic stature with which the role might have been filled. Field is an attractive pivot for the romantic story. Others of importance include Richard Basehart as a high priest and advisor who gives consistently lousy advice.

Direction by J. Lee Thompson has its lags and lapses, but he has mounted his spectacle handsomely and commandeered the all-important battle sequences with vigor and imagination. The picture was filmed entirely in Mexico: interiors in Mexico City and exteriors in the coastal area of Mazatlan and in Chichen Itza near Yucatan.

•

KING SOLOMON'S MINES
1937, 80 mins, UK Ⓥ b/w
Dir Robert Stevenson *Prod* Geoffrey Barkas *Scr* Michael Hogan, Roland Pertwee, [A. R. Rawlinson, Charles Bennett, Ralph Spence] *Ph* Glen MacWilliams *Ed* Michael Gordon *Mus* Mischa Spoliansky *Art* Alfred Junge
Act Paul Robeson, Cedric Hardwicke, Roland Young, Anna Lee, John Loder, Arthur Sinclair (Gaumont-British)

With all the dramatic moments of H. Rider Haggard's adventure yarn, and production values reaching high and spectacular standards, here is a slab of genuine adventure decked in finely done, realistic African settings [exteriors directed by Geoffrey Barkas, photographed by Cyril J. Knowles] and led off by grand acting from Cedric Hardwicke and Paul Robeson, whose rich voice is not neglected.

Entire action is laid in the African interior, and shifts from the veldt and the desert to a native kraal, where the tale is enlivened by spectacular sequences of native war councils, with a pitched battle between two tribes magnificently and thrillingly staged.

Climax carries the action into the long-lost mines, where untold diamond wealth is hoarded, closing with a terrifying eruption of a volcano.

Robeson is a fine, impressive figure as the native carrier proved to be a king, and puts on a proud dignity that his frequent lapses into rolling song cannot bring down. Hardwicke is excellent as a tough white hunter, and Roland Young puts in his lively vein of comedy to excellent effect. John Loder and Anna Lee are less effective on the romantic side.

•

KING SOLOMON'S MINES
1950, 102 mins, US Ⓥ ⊙ col
Dir Compton Bennett, Andrew Marton *Prod* Sam Zimbalist *Scr* Helen Deutsch *Ph* Robert Surtees *Ed* Ralph E. Winters, Conrad A. Nervig *Mus* [native music] *Art* Cedric Gibbons, Paul Groesse
Act Stewart Granger, Deborah Kerr, Richard Carlson, Hugo Haas, Lowell Gilmore (M-G-M)

King Solomon's Mines has been filmed against an authentic African background, lending an extremely realistic air to the H. Rider Haggard classic novel of a dangerous safari and discovery of a legendary mine full of King Solomon's treasure.

The standout sequence is the animal stampede, minutes long, that roars across the screen to the terrifying noise of panic-driven hoofbeats. It's a boff thriller scene.

Cast-wise, the choice of players is perfect. Stewart Granger scores strongly as the African hunter who takes Deborah Kerr and her brother (Richard Carlson) on the dangerous search for her missing husband. Kerr is an excellent personification of an English lady tossed into the raw jungle life, and Carlson gets across as the third white member of the safari.

1950: Best Color Cinematography, Editing.

NOMINATION: Best Picture

•

KING SOLOMON'S MINES
1985, 100 mins, US Ⓥ ⊙ ▭ col
Dir J. Lee Thompson *Prod* Menahem Golan, Yoram Globus *Scr* Gene Quintano, James R. Silke *Ph* Alex Phillips *Ed* John Shirley *Mus* Jerry Goldsmith *Art* Luciano Spadoni
Act Richard Chamberlain, Sharon Stone, Herbert Lom, John Rhys-Davies, Ken Gampu, June Buthelezi (Cannon)

Cannon's remake of *King Solomon's Mines* treads heavily in the footsteps of that other great modern hero, Indiana Jones—too heavily.

Where Jones was deft and graceful in moving from crisis to crisis, *King Solomon's Mines* is often clumsy with logic, making the action hopelessly cartoonish. Once painted into the corner, scenes don't resolve so much as end before they spill into the next cliff-hanger.

It's an unrelenting pace with no variation that ultimately becomes tedious. Neither the camp humor or the romance between Richard Chamberlain as the African adventurer Allan Quatermain and heroine-in-distress Sharon Stone breaks the monotony of the action.

Script plays something like a child's maze with numerous deadends and detours on the way to the buried treasure.

•

KING'S PIRATE, THE
1967, 100 mins, US col
Dir Don Weis *Prod* Robert Arthur *Scr* Paul Wayne, Aeneas MacKenzie, Joseph Hoffman *Ph* Clifford Stine *Ed* Russell F. Schoengarth *Mus* Ralph Ferraro *Art* Alexander Golitzen, George C. Webb
Act Doug McClure, Jill St. John, Guy Stockwell, Mary Ann Mobley, Kurt Kasznar, Richard Deacon

Madagascar, circa 1700, backdrops the screenplay [from a story by co-scripter Aeneas MacKenzie] which twirls around efforts of the British to halt piracy of the rich trade route to India. Doug McClure, playing a Colonial American, volunteers to silence the guns of the pirate port of Diego Suarez and in regulation style accomplishes his mission. If the plot and dialog creak a bit, ingredients are still there to suffice as an okay buccaneer yarn if the spectator doesn't take it too seriously.

McClure smiles through most of his performance, and Jill St. John dons some beguiling attire sometimes more exciting than the action. Guy Stockwell is the pirate first mate out to get the hero. Mary Ann Mobley as the daughter of the emperor of India and Kurt Kasznar, leader of an acrobatic troup which helps McClure, add their talents to brighten the unfoldment.

Don Weis direction is fast but tighter editing would benefit. Clifford Stine's color photography is handsome.

•

KINGS ROW
1942, 127 mins, US Ⓥ ⊙ b/w
Dir Sam Wood *Prod* Hal B. Wallis (exec.) *Scr* Casey Robinson *Ph* James Wong Howe *Ed* Ralph Dawson *Mus* Erich Wolfgang Korngold *Art* William Cameron Menzies
Act Ann Sheridan, Robert Cummings, Ronald Reagan, Betty Field, Charles Coburn, Claude Rains (Warner)

Kings Row, Henry Bellamann's widely read novel of small-town life at the turn of the century, becomes an impressive and occasionally inspiring, though overlong picture under Sam Wood's eloquent direction. It is an atmospheric story, steadily engrossing and plausible.

In broad outline, it is the story of the town, Kings Row, as well as of several of its people. Yarn is in three distinct parts, opening with the childhood of the five leading characters. Narration then jumps 10 years, picking up the thread as the hero begins studying medicine under the tutelage of the stern, awesome, local physician-recluse.

Concluding portion includes the hero's return from studying in Vienna, his beginnings as a pioneer psychiatrist, his treatment and saving of his boyhood friend, and his romance with a new resident of the town, a beauteous girl from Vienna.

Ann Sheridan seems too casual in the early sequences as the clear-eyed, wholesome girl from the slums. However, she rises admirably to the emotional demands of the later scenes.

Robert Cummings is not entirely able to redeem a slight stuffiness in the character of the hero.

1942: NOMINATIONS: Best Picture, Director, B&W Cinematography

•

KIPPS
1941, 112 mins, UK Ⓥ b/w
Dir Carol Reed *Prod* Edward Black *Scr* Sidney Gilliat *Ph* Arthur Crabtree *Ed* Alfred Roone *Mus* Louis Levy *Art* Alex Vetchinsky
Act Michael Redgrave, Diana Wynyard, Phyllis Calvert, Michael Wilding, Arthur Riscoe, Max Adrian (20th Century-Fox)

Kipps has little of the accepted film style. Paucity of dramatics and action is obvious to point of occasional ennui; yet, withal, there's a certain piquant freshness in the plain tale of an ultra-plain fella—Kipps.

Any effort to give impetus or sharpness to this late Victorian yarn isn't discernible. Sidney Gilliat's screenplay [from H. G. Wells's novel], while in excellent taste and character, remains sprawled writing. Impression sneaks through that Carol Reed wasn't exactly comfortable in the director chore on this type of limp yarn.

Playing throughout is impressive in creating the leeches and well-wishers who descend on Kipps, an illiterate department store clerk, when a fat legacy is dropped in his lap. The sap—and there's no other word for him—undergoes only partial metamorphosis as a gent, eventually sloughing off the new clique for his long-time sweetheart, a servant.

Michael Redgrave is believable as the hick; Phyllis Calvert as the peachy domestic; Diana Wynyard as the tony milady for whom the lower-class Kipps almost sells his heart.

•

KISMET
1944, 100 mins, US col
Dir William Dieterle, [Stanley Donen] *Prod* Everett Riskin *Scr* John Meehan *Ph* Charles Rosher *Ed* Ben Lewis *Mus* Herbert Stothart *Art* Cedric Gibbons, Daniel B. Cathcart
Act Ronald Colman, Marlene Dietrich, James Craig, Edward Arnold, Florence Bates, Joy Ann Page (M-G-M)

The sheer mystic fantasy of Baghdad and its royal pomp and splendor [from Edward Knoblock's play] remain acceptable escapism. The fantasy under lavish Culver City and Natalie Kalmus (Technicolor) production auspices is beautifully investitured. Ronald Colman as the beggar-sometimes-prince, Marlene Dietrich as the dancing girl with the gold-painted gams, Edward Arnold as the double-dealing Grand Vizier, James Craig as the Caliph-sometimes-turned-gardener's son, and Joy Ann Page as Colman's sheltered daughter are a convincing casting.

Colman, the king of beggars, is impressive as the phoney prince. He lends conviction to his role, so dominating the proceedings that he makes Legs Dietrich more or less of a stooge. However, she comes through in the highlight opportunity accorded her when she does her stuff for the Vizier and Colman. Dietrich's terp specialty and getup is out of the dream book, but boffo. Thereafter Kismet (fate) follows the beggar-prince's hopes.

1944: NOMINATIONS: Best Color Cinematography, Color Art Direction, Sound, Scoring of a Dramatic Picture

•

KISMET
1955, 112 mins, US Ⓥ ⊙ ▭ col
Dir Vincente Minnelli, [Stanley Donen] *Prod* Arthur Freed *Scr* Charles Lederer, Luther Davis *Ph* Joseph Ruttenberg *Ed* Adrienne Fazan *Mus* Robert Wright, George Forrest *Art* Cedric Gibbons, Preston Ames
Act Howard Keel, Ann Blyth, Dolores Gray, Vic Damone, Monty Woolley, Sebastian Cabot (M-G-M)

Opulent escapism is what *Kismet* has to sell. Howard Keel is the big entertainment factor and, in somewhat lesser degree, so is Dolores Gray. Without these two there would be very few minutes that could be counted as really good fun. Robust in voice and physique, Keel injects just the right amount of tongue-in-cheek into his role of Baghdad rogue.

The other two stars are Ann Blyth and Vic Damone. Vocally, as Keel's daughter, Blyth does the proper thing with "Baubles, Bangles and Beads," "And This Is My Beloved" and "Stranger in Paradise." So does Damone, as the young caliph who loves the poet's daughter. But otherwise their romantic pairing does not come off.

Founded on Edward Knoblock's *Kismet*, the Baghdad fable tells of how the supposedly magical powers of street poet Keel are commandeered by the scheming wazir to advance his own power.

•

KISS, THE
1929, 62 mins, US Ⓥ ⦿ ⊗ b/w
Dir Jacques Feyder ***Scr*** Hans Kraly ***Ph*** William Daniels ***Ed*** Ben Lewis ***Art*** Cedric Gibbons
Act Greta Garbo, Conrad Nagel, Anders Randolf, Holmes Herbert, Lew Ayres, George Davis (M-G-M)

The Kiss is one of Greta Garbo's best, without stretching the elastic of kindness. Few actresses could weather the series of close-ups required of Garbo in this one.

In several of the sequences, especially the intro when Irene (Garbo) tells Andre (Conrad Nagel) of her love but the impossibility of securing consent for a parting from her husband, Nagel registers the manner of an interpreter.

Pierre, the juvenile admirer of Irene who does not know until the last few story feet of her real interest, is essayed superbly by Lew Ayres.

The title is introduced in the climax when Irene is found in the wild embrace of the lad. Anders Randolf does exceptionally fine playing as the infuriated husband returning unexpectedly.

Action [from a story by George M. Saville] is laid in France. During the trial the tedium of courtroom scenes is minimized by camera moving from short semi-closes on Nagel and the judge to almost a study in black presented by Garbo.

•

KISS, THE
1988, 101 mins, US Ⓥ ⦿ col
Dir Pen Densham ***Prod*** Pen Densham, John Watson ***Scr*** Stephen Volk, Tom Ropelewski ***Ph*** Francois Protat ***Ed*** Stan Cole ***Mus*** J. Peter Robinson ***Art*** Roy Forge Smith
Act Nicholas Kilbertus, Joanna Pacula, Meredith Salenger, Mimi Kuzyk, Priscilla Mouzakiotis (Tri-Star/Astral/Trilogy)

Kernel of a decent story [by Stephen Volk], of an evil woman (Joanna Pacula) who passes on her powers via a kiss, is never fleshed out in the script. If the setups were hokier, they might have been funny.

There's a chilling enough moment when the first devastating kiss is bestowed on the younger version of Pacula (Priscilla Mouzakiotis), but when the action moves back to present-day suburbia in the backyard barbecue of the Hallorans who are celebrating daughter Amy's (Meredith Salenger) confirmation, whatever suspense is foretold dissipates quickly.

There are few connectives to link the elements of the plot. To add to the goulash, there's a shrieking little monster that attacks Pacula's victims, howling winds, mysteriously opened windows and other formula attempts to prop up this weak effort. Of the cast, Mimi Kuzyk is the one saving grace as the Hallorans' neighbor Brenda.

•

KISS BEFORE DYING, A
1956, 94 mins, US ⊏⊐ col
Dir Gerd Oswald ***Prod*** Robert L. Jacks ***Scr*** Lawrence Roman ***Ph*** Lucien Ballard ***Ed*** George Gittens ***Mus*** Lionel Newman
Act Robert Wagner, Jeffrey Hunter, Joanne Woodward, Virginia Leith, Mary Astor, George Macready (Crown/United Artists)

This multiple-murder story is an offbeat sort of film, with Robert Wagner portraying a calculating youth who intends to allow nothing to stand in his way to money. The screenplay is from a novel by Ira Levin. Gerd Oswald's restrained direction suits the mood.

Wagner's troubles start in opening scene, when he learns that his college sweetheart (Joanne Woodward) is expecting a baby, a circumstance that means she'll be disinherited by her wealthy father and his plans to latch onto the family fortune ruined. He pushes her to her death from the top of a building where they've gone to get a wedding license, and since no one knows they've been dating (hard for the spectator to swallow), Wagner is in the clear.

Wagner registers in killer role. Woodward is particularly good as the pregnant girl, and Virginia Leith acceptable as her sister. Jeffrey Hunter is lost as a part-time university professor responsible for the final solution of the crimes. Mary Astor and George Macready are okay as Wagner's mother and the girls' father.

•

KISS BEFORE DYING, A
1991, 95 mins, US Ⓥ ⦿ col
Dir James Dearden ***Prod*** Robert Lawrence ***Scr*** James Dearden ***Ph*** Mike Southon ***Ed*** Michael Bradsell ***Mus*** Howard Shore ***Art*** Jim Clay
Act Matt Dillon, Sean Young, Max von Sydow, James Russo, Diane Ladd, Martha Gehman (Initial)

Played with a satirical edge, this update on the pulpy 1956 thriller about a murderous social climber might have been good for a chill and a hoot, but played straight it's a real clunker.

Based on Ira Levin's novel, director James Dearden's script gives us a brooding, wounded nobody (Matt Dillon) who grew up next to the Pennsylvania railroad tracks, obsessed with the fortunes of the local industrial magnate (Max von Sydow) whose Carlsson Copper cars rumble down the tracks. At college he gets involved with the magnate's daughter, Dory (Sean Young), but throws her over (a ledge, that is) when he learns she is pregnant.

He then moves to New York and gets involved with her twin, social worker Ellen (Young again), passing himself off as her type and eventually marrying her and getting a job as right-hand man to von Sydow. The only problem is Ellen's relentless interest in her sister's unsolved murder.

Young, in a blandly uncommitted pert, connects not at all with Dillon's hunky young beau, and the two of them seem a cardboard couple, going through the paces of a false life. Not even their explicit sex scenes add excitement.

•

KISSIN' COUSINS
1964, 96 mins, US Ⓥ ⊏⊐ col
Dir Gene Nelson ***Prod*** Sam Katzman ***Scr*** Gerald Drayson Adams, Gene Nelson ***Ph*** Ellis W. Carter ***Ed*** Ben Lewis ***Mus*** Fred Karger (sup.) ***Art*** George W. Davis, Eddie Imazu
Act Elvis Presley, Arthur O'Connell, Glenda Farrell, Jack Albertson, Pam Austin, Yvonne Craig (Four Leaf/M-G-M)

This Elvis Presley concoction is a pretty dreary effort. Gerald Drayson Adams came up with a ripe story premise, but he and Gene Nelson appear to have run dry of creative inspiration in trying to develop it. Yarn is concerned with the problem faced by the U.S. government in attempting to establish an ICBM base on land owned by an obstinate hillbilly clan. To solve the problem, the air force sends in a lieutenant (Presley) who is kin to the stubborn critters, among whom is his lookalike cousin (Elvis in a blond wig, no less).

Histrionically, Presley does as well as possible under the circumstances. He also sings eight songs. Arthur O'Connell is excellent as the patriarch of the mountain clan, but what a mountainous waste of talent.

•

KISS ME AGAIN
1925, 67 mins, US ⊗ b/w
Dir Ernst Lubitsch ***Scr*** Hans Kraly ***Ph*** Charles Van Enger
Act Marie Prevost, Monte Blue, John Roche, Clara Bow, Willard Louis (Warner)

One of the virtues of this is that it is enacted by a short cast with the principal trio of players always in the foreground. They are Marie Prevost, Monte Blue and John Roche. Clara Bow triumphs in the role of a lawyer's steno, and Willard Louis manages to exact much from the role of attorney.

The story is decidedly Parisian in its flavor. The Fleurys are married, the husband is a business man, the wife is somewhat fond of music, and Maurice, the musician, is fond of the wife. This brings about a flirtation, and finally the husband decides that he will not stand in the way of his wife's happiness, so he arranges for a divorce with his wife to receive his home and half his fortune.

This naturally delights the musician, who will then marry her and have a made-to-order home and income at his disposal. But the wife in reality loves her husband and wants him back. It is the touch of arranging for the divorce evidence that creates much laughter.

It is well acted, delightfully directed and edited without a wasted foot of film.

•

KISS ME DEADLY
1955, 105 mins, US Ⓥ ⦿ b/w
Dir Robert Aldrich ***Prod*** Robert Aldrich ***Scr*** A. I. Bezzerides ***Ph*** Ernest Laszlo ***Ed*** Michael Luciano ***Mus*** Frank DeVol ***Art*** William Glasgow
Act Ralph Meeker, Albert Dekker, Paul Stewart, Wesley Addy, Maxine Cooper, Cloris Leachman (Parklane)

The ingredients that sell Mickey Spillane's novels about Mike Hammer, the hardboiled private eye, are thoroughly worked over in this presentation built around the rock-and-sock character. Ralph Meeker takes on the Hammer character and as the surly, hit first, ask questions later, shamus turns in a job that is acceptable, even if he seems to go soft in a few sequences.

From the time Hammer picks up a half-naked blonde on a lonely highway he's in for trouble. The girl is killed and he nearly so in an arranged accident. This gets his curiosity aroused and he sets about trying to unravel the puzzle.

The trail leads to a series of amorous dames, murder-minded plug-uglies and dangerous adventures that offer excitement but have little clarity to let the viewer know what's going on.

•

KISS ME GOODBYE
1982, 101 mins, US Ⓥ col
Dir Robert Mulligan ***Prod*** Robert Mulligan ***Scr*** Charlie Peters ***Ph*** Donald Peterman ***Ed*** Sheldon Kahn ***Mus*** Ralph Burns ***Art*** Philip M. Jefferies
Act Sally Field, James Caan, Jeff Bridges, Paul Dooley, Claire Trevor, Mildred Natwick (Boardwalk/Sugarman/Barish/20th Century-Fox

Essentially a mild, de-sexed remake of the 1977 Brazilian art house hit *Dona Flor and Her Two Husbands*, tale begins with Sally Field starting her life up again after the death, three years earlier, of her talented theatrical hubby (James Caan).

Field opens up her old apartment again and, to the bewilderment of her snobbish mother (Claire Trevor), has decided to marry Egyptologist Jeff Bridges. Shortly before the wedding, however, Caan's ghost decides to join Field back in the apartment, making possible all sorts of "zany" scenes such as having Caan talk to his former wife while Bridges tries to make love to her.

Almost all the alleged humor stems from Field relating to Caan, whom no one else can hear or see, while she tries to engage in everyday activities.

Supporting performers are simply called upon to register stock reactions to the same joke, over and over again.

•

KISS ME KATE
1953, 109 mins, US Ⓥ ⦿ col
Dir George Sidney ***Prod*** Jack Cummings ***Scr*** Dorothy Kingsley ***Ph*** Charles Rosher ***Ed*** Ralph E. Winters ***Mus*** Andre Previn, Saul Chaplin (dir.) ***Art*** Cedric Gibbons, Urie McLeary
Act Kathryn Grayson, Howard Keel, Ann Miller, Keenan Wynn, Bobby Van, James Whitmore (M-G-M)

Kiss Me Kate is Shakespeare's *Taming of the Shrew* done over in eminently satisfying fasion via a collaboration of superior song, dance and comedy talents. The pictorial effects achieved with the 3-D lensing mean little in added entertainment.

But the play's the thing, of course, and *Kate* has it. Dorothy Kingsley's screenplay, from the [1948] Samuel and Bella Spewack legiter, was hep handling of a tricky assignment. Under George Sidney's skilled direction, *Kate* unfolds smoothly all the way as it goes back and forth from the backstage story to the play within the play and works in the numerous—and brilliant—Cole Porter tunes.

Howard Keel is a dynamic male lead, in complete command of the acting role and registering superbly with the songs. Kathryn Grayson is fiery and thoroughly engaging as Kate, tamed by Keel in *Shrew* (play within play) and succumbing to his charms backstage after much romantic maneuvering.

Only song not from the play prototype is "From This Moment On" and it's an agreeable newcomer, as delivered by Tommy Rall.

Keenan Wynn and James Whitmore play a couple of hoods bent on collecting an IOU received in a floating crapgame. In a bit of delightful incongruity they segue into a song and dance piece titled "Brush Up Your Shakespeare" that has hilarious effect.

Choreography (Hermes Pan) and musical direction (Andre Previn and Saul Chaplin) round out the list of important credits.

1953: NOMINATION: Best Scoring of a Dramatic Picture

•

KISS ME, STUPID
1964, 126 mins, US Ⓥ ⦿ ▭ b/w
Dir Billy Wilder ***Prod*** Billy Wilder ***Scr*** Billy Wilder, I.A.L. Diamond ***Ph*** Joseph LaShelle ***Ed*** Daniel Mandell ***Mus*** Andre Previn ***Art*** Alexandre Trauner
Act Dean Martin, Kim Novak, Ray Walston, Felicia Farr, Cliff Osmond, Barbara Pepper (Phalanx/Minsch)

Kiss Me, Stupid is not likely to corrupt any sensible audience. But there is a cheapness and more than a fair share of crudeness about the humor of a contrived double adultery situation that a husband-wife combo stumble into. In short, the Billy Wilder–I.A.L. Diamond script—the credits say it was triggered by an Italian play, *L'ora della fantasia* by Anna Bonacci—calls for a generous seasoning of Noel Coward but, unfortunately, it provides a dash of same only now and again.

Wilder, usually a director of considerable flair and inventiveness (if not always impeccable taste), has not been able this time out to rise above a basically vulgar, as well as creatively delinquent, screenplay, and he has got at best only plodding help from two of his principals, Dean Martin and Kim Novak.

The thespic mainstays are Ray Walston and Cliff Osmond, while Felicia Farr registers nicely as the former's attractive and sexually aggressive wife.

Wilder has directed with frontal assault rather than suggestive finesse the means by which Walston and Osmond, a pair of amateur songwriters in a Nevada waystop—called Climax—on the route from Las Vegas to California, contrive to bag girl-crazy star Martin and sell him on their ditties. Idea is to make Martin stay overnight in Walston's house, to get latter's wife out of the way by creating a domestic crisis and substitute as wife for a night of accommodation with the celebrity a floozy (Novak) from a tavern.

The score, which figures rather prominently as story motivation and is orchestrated appropriately under the baton of Andre Previn, carries the unusual credit of songs by Ira and George Gershwin. Introed are three unpublished melodies by the long deceased composer to which brother Ira has provided special lyrics.

•

KISS OF DEATH
1947, 98 mins, US Ⓥ b/w
Dir Henry Hathaway ***Prod*** Fred Kohlmar ***Scr*** Ben Hecht, Charles Lederer ***Ph*** Norbert Brodine ***Ed*** J. Watson Webb Jr. ***Mus*** David Buttolph ***Art*** Lyle R. Wheeler, Leland Fuller
Act Victor Mature, Brian Donlevy, Coleen Gray, Richard Widmark, Karl Malden, Mildred Dunnock (20th Century-Fox)

Kiss of Death [based on a story by Eleazar Lipsky] is given the same semi-documentary treatment that 20th-Fox used in its three fact dramas, *The House on 92nd Street, 13 Rue Madeleine* and *Boomerang!*

Theme is of an ex-convict who sacrifices himself to gangster guns to save his wife and two small daughters. Henry Hathaway's real-life slant on direction brings the picture close to authentic tragedy.

Victor Mature, as the ex-convict, does some of his best work. Brian Donlevy and Coleen Gray also justify their star billing, Donlevy as the assistant district attorney who sends Mature to Sing Sing for a jewelry store robbery, and later makes use of him as a stool pigeon, Gray as the girl Mature marries after being paroled.

The acting sensation of the piece is Richard Widmark, as the dimwit, blood-lusty killer.

Plot hook of the script is the decision of Mature to turn stoolie when he learns that his wife has been driven to suicide by his pals, who had promised to care for her while he was in prison, and that his two children have been put in an orphanage. He fingers Widmark for a murder rap in return for parole, marries Gray and starts a new home for his children, only to live in terror when Widmark is acquitted and set at liberty.

1947: NOMINATIONS: Best Supp. Actor (Richard Widmark), Original Story

•

KISS OF DEATH
1995, 101 mins, US Ⓥ ⦿ col
Dir Barbet Schroeder ***Prod*** Barbet Schroeder, Susan Hoffman ***Scr*** Richard Price ***Ph*** Luciano Tovoli ***Ed*** Lee Percy ***Mus*** Trevor Jones ***Art*** Mel Bourne
Act David Caruso, Samuel L. Jackson, Nicolas Cage, Helen Hunt, Kathryn Erbe, Stanley Tucci (20th Century-Fox)

A very loose and contemporized remake of one of the more celebrated of the '40s film noirs, *Kiss of Death* is a crackling thriller that feels unusually attuned to its lowlife characters. Powered by an ever-tightening plot, muscular New York energy and highly concentrated direction by Barbet Schroeder, pic is most noteworthy for Nicolas Cage's amazing turn as a colossally tough hood.

Ben Hecht and Charles Lederer's densely packed script for Henry Hathaway's 1947 meller detailed the increasing desperation of a small timer (Victor Mature) being squeezed one side by his former shady associates from the neighborhood and from the other by a d.a.'s office hungry for names and evidence against his criminal cohorts.

This basic situation is about all that's left of the original in Richard Price's spiky update, which is based in the pungently sleazy world of the professional car thieves in the shadow of the 7 train in Queens.

Jimmy Kilmartin (David Caruso) is an ex-con rigorously walking the straight and narrow with his wife, Bev (Helen Hunt), and baby daughter. When Jimmy is inadvertently caught up in the wounding of a cop (Samuel L. Jackson), he lands back in the slammer.

Forty minutes in, the film jumps ahead three years. Up for a parole review and anxious to get on with his life, Jimmy agrees to help persistent assistant d.a. Frank Zioli (Stanley Tucci) nail the criminal king, Little Junior (Cage), by taping incriminating conversations while wired with a mike.

Price's script conjures up with extreme verisimilitude the treacherous milieu of chop shops, utterly amoral hoods, sweating informers and wives left on the sidelines.

•

KISS OF THE SPIDER WOMAN
1985, 119 mins, US/Brazil Ⓥ ⦿ col
Dir Hector Babenco ***Prod*** David Weisman ***Scr*** Leonard Schrader ***Ph*** Radolfo Sanchez ***Ed*** Mauro Alice ***Mus*** John Neschling ***Art*** Clovis Bueno
Act William Hurt, Raul Julia, Sonia Braga, Jose Lewgoy, Nuno Leal Maia, Antonio Petrim (SugarLoaf/HB Filmes)

Drama [based on the novel by Manuel Puig] centers upon the relationship between cellmates in a South American prison. Molina, played by William Hurt, is an effeminate gay locked up for having molested a young boy, while Valentin, played by Raul Julia, is a professional journalist in for a long term due to his radical political activities under a fascist regime.

They have literally nothing in common except their societal victimization, but to pass the time Molina periodically entertains Valentin with accounts of old motion pictures.

Puig kicked his book off with a ravishing account of the 1940s horror pic *Cat People*, but director Hector Babenco and scenarist Leonard Schrader have opted to concentrate on two purely imaginary films to intertwine with the narrative.

Individual reactions to the work overall will depend to a great extent on feelings about Hurt's performance. Some will find him mesmerizing, others artificially lowkeyed. By contrast, Julia delivers a very strong, straight and believable performance as an activist who at first has little patience with Hurt's predilection for escapism, but finally meets him halfway.

After the raw street power of *Pixote*, Babenco has employed a slicker, more choreographed style here. Shot entirely in Sao Paulo, film boasts fine lensing.

1985: Best Actor (William Hurt)

NOMINATIONS: Best Picture, Director, Adapted Screenplay

•

KISS THE BLOOD OFF MY HANDS
(UK: BLOOD ON MY HANDS)
1948, 79 mins, US b/w
Dir Norman Foster ***Prod*** Richard Vernon ***Scr*** Leonardo Bercovici, Hugh Gray ***Ph*** Russell Metty ***Ed*** Milton Carruth ***Mus*** Miklos Rozsa ***Art*** Bernard Herzbrun, Nathan Juran
Act Joan Fontaine, Burt Lancaster, Robert Newton, Lewis L. Russell, Aminta Dyne, Jay Novello (Universal)

Kiss the Blood Off My Hands, adapted from Gerald Butler's novel of postwar violence and demoralization [by Ben Maddow and Walter Bernstein], is an intensely moody melodrama.

Concerns an uprooted vet of the Second World War whose life is shattered after he accidentally kills a man in a London pub. Although based on a formula plot, this film is lifted out of the run-of-the-mill class through Norman Foster's superior direction, first-rate thesping and well-integrated production mountings.

Lancaster delivers a convincing and sympathetic portrayal of a tough hombre who can't beat the bad breaks. Fontaine performs with sensitivity and sincerity in a demanding role. As the heavy, Newton is properly oily and detestable.

•

KISS THE BOYS GOODBYE
1941, 83 mins, US b/w
Dir Victor Schertzinger ***Prod*** William LeBaron ***Scr*** Harry Tugend, Dwight Taylor ***Ph*** Ted Tetzlaff ***Ed*** Paul Weatherwax ***Mus*** Victor Schertzinger
Act Mary Martin, Don Ameche, Oscar Levant, Jerome Cowan, Raymond Walburn, Barbara Jo Allen (Paramount)

In converting Clare Boothe's satirical comedy to films, Paramount made some major revisions of the original, substituting a group of tuneful songs for the playwright's satirical barbs, and coming up with a light, humorous and breezy piece of entertainment.

Picture effectively showcases the acting and vocal talents of Mary Martin, who ably carries the full burden of the picture with a top-notch performance.

Boothe's play was a satire on the search for the Scarlett to portray the lead in *Gone With the Wind*. For picture purposes, the lead sought is a southern beauty for a Broadway show to be produced by Jerome Cowan, angeled by Raymond Walburn and staged by Don Ameche. Publicity stunt sends Ameche and composer Oscar Levant on tour of the south.

Schertzinger most ably pilots the compact and laugh-studded script. Songs are deftly spotted, and numerous spontaneous Dixie cracks against the "damn" Yankees catch attention and laughs.

Ameche grooves as the play director and romantic interest in a straight line without much enthusiasm. Levant is Levant—a dour composer without a smile but withal credited with discovering the abilities of Martin about the same time the audience does.

•

KISS THE GIRLS
1997, 120 mins, US Ⓥ ⦿ ▭ col
Dir Gary Fleder ***Prod*** David Brown, Joe Wizan ***Scr*** David Klass ***Ph*** Aaron Schneider ***Ed*** William Steinkamp, Harvey Rosenstock ***Mus*** Mark Isham ***Art*** Nelson Coates
Act Morgan Freeman, Ashley Judd, Cary Elwes, Tony Goldwyn, Jay O. Sanders, Brian Cox (Brown-Wizan/Paramount)

Kiss the Girls is a derivative but fairly effective *Se7en* knockoff, right down to its casting of Morgan Freeman as a shrewd detective pursuing a crafty and kinky serial criminal. Replete with smart, capable characters and crimes so bizarre that they lend the film a suspiciously lurid nature, this tony suspenser [from James Patterson's novel] is hampered by the presence of a villain who is all too obvious from the very beginning.

Freeman plays Dr. Alex Cross, a forensic psychologist on the Washington, DC, police force, as well as a bestselling author, who zips down to Durham, NC, in his Porsche when his niece Naomi goes missing. Naomi is just one of eight women who have recently disappeared; local policemen have found just two bodies, each tied to a tree and sexually ravaged. In both cases, the killer has signed his handiwork, "Casanova."

A lovely local doctor, Kate McTiernan (Ashley Judd), whose favorite sport just happens to be kickboxing, is abducted and strapped down in a dungeon-like cell. Kate makes a run at freedom, which she manages at the cost of some injuries, and is able to confirm the wily Alex's early suspicions: the perpetrator is a "collector," a man dedicated to maintaining a "harem" of strong-willed women who have no choice but to submit to his demands.

Freeman invests this project with more class and dignity than it deserves. Judd, game and looking very fit, plays the polar opposite of a screen wilting lily, and is given a major fight scene at the end when she must fend off the villain one last time, an episode rendered weak only by its groaningly obvious revelation of the bent genius's identity.

•

KISS TOMORROW GOODBYE
1950, 102 mins, US Ⓥ b/w
Dir Gordon Douglas ***Prod*** William Cagney ***Scr*** Harry Brown ***Ph*** Peverell Marley ***Ed*** Truman K. Wood, Walter Hannemann ***Mus*** Carmen Dragon ***Art*** Wiard Ihnen
Act James Cagney, Barbara Payton, Helena Carter, Ward Bond, Luther Adler, Barton MacLane (Warner)

Yarn [from Horace McCoy's story of the same name] opens with the trial of an assorted bunch of heavies and then quickly segues into a flashback to tell how circumstances put them in the courtroom. Flashback kicks off with a jailbreak, and the pace doesn't slow down as it takes James Cagney through a series of murders, robberies and romantic episodes.

Character is tough, but Cagney gives it an occasional light touch. He starts displaying his wanton meanness immediately by ruthlessly killing his jailbreak partner, beating the latter's sister into romantic submission and staging a daring daylight robbery of a market.

Cagney has two femme stars to court. Barbara Payton impresses as the girl who first falls victim to his tough fascination. Helena Carter is very good as a bored rich girl.

•

KITCHEN TOTO, THE
1987, 95 mins, UK Ⓥ ⊙ col
Dir Harry Hook ***Prod*** Ann Skinner ***Scr*** Harry Hook ***Ph*** Roger Deakins ***Ed*** Tom Priestley ***Mus*** John Keane ***Art*** Jamie Leonard
Act Bob Peck, Phyllis Logan, Edwin Mahinda, Kirsten Hughes, Robert Urquhart, Edward Judd (British Screen/Film Four/Skreba)

Pic unfolds in 1950 when the British were facing attacks from a Kikuyu terrorist group known as Mau Mau. Bob Peck plays a regional police officer in charge of a small force of native Africans who lives with his frustrated wife (Phyllis Logan) and son.

When Mau Mau murder a black priest who's condemned them from his pulpit, Peck agrees to take in the dead man's young son (Edwin Mahinda) as his "kitchen toto," or houseboy.

Story unfolds from the perspective of this alert, intelligent youngster who's torn between his tribal feelings on the one hand and the loyalties he has both to his murdered father and to the British who, despite their unthinking and ingrained racism, have been kind to him.

Peck is solid as the cop, Logan suitably tight-lipped as his repressed wife, and young Edwin Mahinda excellent as the troubled, tragic hero, torn between two sides in an ugly conflict.

•

KITTY
1945, 103 mins, US b/w
Dir Mitchell Leisen ***Prod*** Mitchell Leisen ***Scr*** Darrell Ware, Karl Tunberg ***Ph*** Daniel L. Fapp ***Ed*** Alma Macrorie ***Mus*** Victor Young ***Art*** Hans Dreier, Walter Tyler
Act Paulette Goddard, Ray Milland, Patric Knowles, Reginald Owen, Cecil Kellaway (Paramount)

Plot [from a novel by Rosamond Marshall] tells of an 18th-century easy lady who rose from the London slums to high position in court society—a society that was no better than that from which she rose; it only dressed better.

The Kitty depicted in the film is a petty thief and beggar who gets a start towards a cleaner life after becoming a model for Gainsborough's portrait of a lady. The portrait and Kitty attract the attention of several society fops. One, an impoverished nobleman with few scruples, takes her into his home, gives her a fictional background and plots her marriage to a duke.

Paulette Goddard credibly depicts Kitty in the various phases of the slum girl's rise in station. Ray Milland has the more difficult task of keeping the unpleasant, foppish character of Sir Hugh Marcy, Kitty's beloved, consistent and does well by it. Reginald Owen and Cecil Kellaway deliver character gems. The first is the doddering Duke of Malmunster, who strives to keep his faded youth revived with port wine. The other is Gainsborough, the painter who discovers Kitty.

•

KITTY AND THE BAGMAN
1982, 95 mins, Australia Ⓥ ▭ col
Dir Donald Crombie ***Prod*** Anthony Buckley ***Scr*** John Burney, Philip Cornford ***Ph*** Dean Semler ***Mus*** Brian May ***Art*** Owen Williams
Act Liddy Clark, John Stanton, Val Lehman, Gerard Maguire, Collette Mann, Reg Evans (Forest Home)

Donald Crombie, best known for *Caddie* [1976], scores again with a light, frothy bag of entertainment set in Sydney during the naughty 1920s. Pic veers wildly from serious drama to a zany spoofing of the underworld genre.

Yarn revolves around two waterfront crime queens, their pimps and beaus and "bagmen." Latter are not the counterpart of Gotham's bag women, but rather corrupt police gobetweens who hover betwixt the law and the crooks. Kitty, wonderfully and zestfully portrayed by Liddy Clark, rises from an innocent young bride arriving at the end of World War I, to the owner of the "Top Hat," a no-holds-barred niterie.

Story weaves in and out, punctuated by dockside brawls, hair-pulling fights between Kitty and her Irish competitor Big Lil Delaney, shoot-outs in the streets and car chases, most of them handled whimsically.

•

KITTY FOYLE
THE NATURAL HISTORY OF A WOMAN
1940, 105 mins, US Ⓥ ⊙ b/w
Dir Sam Wood ***Prod*** David Hempstead ***Scr*** Dalton Trumbo, Donald Ogden Stewart ***Ph*** Robert de Grasse ***Ed*** Henry Berman ***Mus*** Roy Webb ***Art*** Van Nest Polglase, Mark-Lee Kirk
Act Ginger Rogers, Dennis Morgan, James Craig, Eduardo Ciannelli, Ernest Cossart, Gladys Cooper (RKO)

This is a film translation of Christopher Morley's bestseller expounding the romantic life of a white-collar girl—her happiness and heartbreaks and final decision for lifelong happiness. Picture is unfolded in retrospect from the time the girl is forced to choose between two men—one whom she madly loves, but cannot offer marriage, and the other waiting at church.

This swings the story back to Philadelphia, at time she falls madly in love with scion of rich family on the other side of the tracks. Romance proceeds apace, with girl followed to New York and married. But boy's straitlaced family provides disillusionment, separation and finally divorce, with Kitty suffering double tragedy of her baby's death and remarriage of husband in his own social set.

Despite its episodic, and at times, vaguely defined motivation, picture on whole is a poignant and dramatic portraiture of a typical Cinderella girl's love story. Several good comedy sequences interline the footage, deftly written and directed.

Ginger Rogers provides a strong dramatic portrayal in the title role, aided by competent performances by Dennis Morgan and James Craig.

1940: Best Actress (Ginger Rogers).

NOMINATIONS: Best Picture, Director, Screenplay, Sound

•

KLANSMAN, THE
1974, 112 mins, US Ⓥ col
Dir Terence Young ***Prod*** William Alexander ***Scr*** Millard Kaufman, Samuel Fuller ***Ph*** Lloyd Ahern ***Ed*** Gene Milford ***Mus*** Dale O. Warren, Stu Gardner ***Art*** John S. Poplin
Act Lee Marvin, Richard Burton, Cameron Mitchell, Lola Falana, Luciana Paluzzi, David Huddleston (Paramount)

The Klansman is a perfect example of screen trash that almost invites derision. Terence Young's miserable film stars Lee Marvin, as a Dixie sheriff with lots of unoriginal, cliché racial trouble on his hands, and Richard Burton as an unpopular landowner in a performance as phony as his southern accent. There's not a shred of quality, dignity, relevance or impact in this yahoo-oriented bunk [from a novel by William Bradford Huie].

The small town is a Ku Klux Klan hotbed, headed by mayor David Huddleston. When Linda Evans gets raped, the KKK, including Marvin's deputy (Cameron Mitchell), suspect Spence Wil-Dee, but take out their frustration on a friend of film-debuting O. J. Simpson.

•

KLONDIKE ANNIE
1936, 78 mins, US b/w
Dir Raoul Walsh ***Prod*** William LeBaron ***Scr*** Mae West ***Ph*** George Clemens ***Ed*** Stuart Heisler ***Mus*** Sam Coslow ***Art*** Hans Dreier, Bernard Herzbrun
Act Mae West, Victor McLaglen, Philip Reed, Harold Huber, Lucille Gleason, Helen Jerome Eddy (Paramount)

This one is again Mae West with the usual formula of wisecracks. That is no longer enough. The basic idea of the story [from the play by West, from a story suggested by Marion Morgan and George B. Dowell] is absurd. Scene is the early 1890s, the time of the Klondike rush. West kills her Chinese paramour and flees to Alaska for safety. This projects her into the story as a prostie and a murderess.

West plays it always in the same key, so the Salvation Army mission scenes are merely the peg for some canting hypocrisy and a farcical development. There are a number of songs [by Gene Austin and Jimmie Johnson]. Most have been written to fit the script and lack general appeal.

West is handicapped by having to wear rather dowdy dresses in about half the footage. Victor McLaglen is clearly uncomfortable and under wraps here and Philip Reed is far too much the matinee type to suggest the marshal of a frontier town.

•

KLUTE
1971, 114 mins, US Ⓥ ⊙ ▭ col
Dir Alan J. Pakula ***Prod*** Alan J. Pakula ***Scr*** Andy Lewis, Dave Lewis ***Ph*** Gordon Willis ***Ed*** Carl Lerner ***Mus*** Michael Small ***Art*** George Jenkins
Act Jane Fonda, Donald Sutherland, Charles Cioffi, Roy Scheider, Dorothy Tristan, Rita Gam (Warner)

Despite a host of terminal flaws, *Klute* is notable for presenting Jane Fonda as a much-matured actress in a role that demands that she make interesting an emotionally unstable professional prostitute. Produced handsomely in New York, but directed tediously by Alan J. Pakula, the film is a suspenser without much suspense. Donald Sutherland shares above-title billing in a line-throwing, third-banana trifle of a part.

The script concerns a mysterious disappearance in New York of out-of-towner Robert Milli. Sutherland, a family friend who is also a cop named Klute, tries to discover what happened. The only clue is Fonda, known to the police as a hooker.

It becomes obvious too early that Charles Cioffi, a family friend and business associate of the missing man, has a few kinky sex problems. The film's wanderings through the sordid side of urban life come across more as titillation than logical dramatic exposition.

The only rewarding element is Fonda's performance. At last, and by no means not too late, there is something great coming off the screen.

1971: Best Actress (Jane Fonda)

NOMINATION: Best Original Story & Screenplay

•

KNACK . . . AND HOW TO GET IT, THE
1965, 84 mins, UK Ⓥ ⊙ b/w
Dir Richard Lester ***Prod*** Oscar Lewenstein ***Scr*** Charles Wood ***Ph*** David Watkin ***Ed*** Anthony Gibbs ***Mus*** John Barry ***Art*** Assheton Gorton
Act Rita Tushingham, Ray Brooks, Michael Crawford, Donal Donnelly, John Bluthal, Wensley Pithey (Woodfall)

There is, according to the theory expounded in *The Knack*, quite a knack in the art of making it successfully with girls. And that about sums up the plot [from the play by Ann Jellicoe] of this offbeat production.

The expert exponent of the knack is played by Ray Brooks, and the immediate target is Rita Tushingham, a young girl just up from the country and hopefully setting off in search of the YWCA. The other two characters are both young men being instructed how to acquire the knack from the master. As Michael Crawford plays a schoolteacher, it is a neat trick to cut into schoolroom lessons with the same dialog as that used by Brooks to his two friends.

The four performances are exceptionally good. Tushingham's wide-eyed innocence is just right, and she plays with her familiar charm. Brooks is superbly confident as the glamor boy with the knack, and Crawford and Donal Donnelly both hit the right mixture of eagerness and innocence.

•

KNICKERBOCKER HOLIDAY
1944, 85 mins, US Ⓥ b/w
Dir Harry Joe Brown ***Prod*** Harry Joe Brown ***Scr*** David Boehn, Rowland Leigh, Harold Goldman ***Ph*** Phil Tannura ***Ed*** John F. Link ***Mus*** Kurt Weill ***Art*** Bernard Herzbrun
Act Nelson Eddy, Charles Coburn, Constance Dowling, Shelley Winters, Percy Kilbride, Chester Conklin (United Artists)

Producers Corp of America did not spare the budget in readying this adaptation from the original by Maxwell Anderson and Kurt Weill. Harry Joe Brown, who produced and directed for the screen, has done much to emphasize the film's humor, gaiety and songs in a fast-moving pic.

A comedy set to music, film is laid in old New Amsterdam of Peter Stuyvesant's day. It deals with a gay, singing but fighting newspaper publisher who fights for freedom in the colony and relief for the oppressed from conniving politicians. He crosses the path of the crafty, humorous Governor Stuyvesant in his political and newspaper crusading and also in his desire to wed the daughter of a politician.

Film has nine songs, five more than the [1938] Broadway show. The music ties the production together neatly. Four songs—lyrics by Anderson, music by Weill—carried over from the original. They are "Nowhere to Go but Up," "It Never Was Anywhere You," "Indispensable Man" and "September Song," first two sung by Nelson Eddy, last two by Charles Coburn.

•

KNIFE IN THE WATER
SEE: NOZ W WODZIE

•

KNIGHTRIDERS
1981, 145 mins, US Ⓥ col
Dir George A. Romero ***Prod*** Richard P. Rubinstein ***Scr*** George A. Romero ***Ph*** Michael Gornick ***Ed*** George A. Romero, Pasquale Buba ***Mus*** Donald Rubinstein ***Art*** Cletus Anderson
Act Ed Harris, Gary Lahti, Tom Savini, Amy Ingersoll, Christine Forrest, Brother Blue (Laurel)

A potentially exciting concept—that of modern-day knights jousting on motorcycles—is all that's good with *Knightriders*. Otherwise, George A. Romero's homage to the Arthurian ideal falls flat in all departments.

Premise is that of an itinerant troupe devoted to ancient principles which pays its way staging Renaissance fairs featuring bloodless jousts. Opening reel or so features one such event in agreeable fashion, even as it plants seeds of dissent within the ranks.

But all Romero can come up with in the way of drama over the next two-plus hours is the spectacle of invidious, greedy big-city promoters and agents preying upon the group, with the pure, idealistic King Arthur figure going off to sulk when several of his men are seduced by the notion of becoming media stars.

Both the film's look, with its medieval costumes and bucolic settings, and the long stretches of high-minded talk, most about how pressures to be co-opted into society must be resisted, lend proceedings the air of a stale hippie reverie.

Another liability is the sullen, essentially unsympathetic "King" of Ed Harris, who is never allowed to project the magnetism or romance expected of such a dreamer.

●

KNIGHTS OF THE ROUND TABLE
1953, 115 mins, US/UK Ⓥ ⊙ ▭ col
Dir Richard Thorpe ***Prod*** Pandro S. Berman ***Scr*** Talbot Jennings, Jan Lustig, Noel Langley ***Ph*** Freddie Young, Stephen Dade ***Ed*** Frank Clarke ***Mus*** Miklos Rozsa ***Art*** Alfred Dunge, Hans Peters
Act Ava Gardner, Robert Taylor, Mel Ferrer, Anne Crawford, Stanley Baker, Gabriel Woolf, Felix Aylmer (M-G-M)

Metro's first-time-out via CinemaScope is a dynamic interpretation of Thomas Malory's classic *Morte d'Arthur*. The action is fierce as the gallant Lancelot fights for his king, and armies of lancers are pitted against each other in combat to the death. The story has dramatic movement—it could easily have come off stiltedly under less skillful handling—as the knight's love for his queen nearly causes the death of both.

The carefully developed script plus knowing direction by Richard Thorpe give the legendary tale credibility. It's storybook stuff—and must be accepted as such—but the astute staging results in a walloping package of entertainment for all except, perhaps, the blasé.

Robert Taylor handles the Lancelot part with conviction; apparently he's right at home with derring-do heroics. Not apparently so at home is Ava Gardner. She gets by fair enough but the role of the lovely Guinevere calls for more projected warmth. Mel Ferrer does an excellent job of portraying the sincere and sympathetic King Arthur. Gabriel Woolf, as the knight in search of the Holy Grail, is standout.

1953: NOMINATIONS: Best Color Art Direction, Sound

●

KNIGHT WITHOUT ARMOUR
1937, 108 mins, UK Ⓥ b/w
Dir Jacques Feyder ***Prod*** Alexander Korda ***Scr*** Lajos Biro, Arthur Wimperis ***Ph*** Harry Stradling ***Ed*** William Hornbeck, Francis Lyon ***Mus*** Miklos Rozsa ***Art*** Lazare Meerson
Act Marlene Dietrich, Robert Donat, Irene Vanburgh, Herbert Lomas, Austin Trevor, Basil Gill (London)

A labored effort to keep this picture neutral on the subject of the Russian Revolution finally completely overshadows the simple love story intertwining Marlene Dietrich and Robert Donat.

Film is not a standout because Frances Marion's adaptation, for one thing, has lost a great deal of James Hilton's characterization in the original novel and dispensed almost entirely with the economic and physical-privation angles leading up to the revolution. Result is that only those familiar with the pre-1917 Russia will understand what the shootin's all about.

Story reveals Donat as a young British secret service agent who becomes a Red to achieve his purpose. He's sent to Siberia just before the outbreak of the World War and returns after the revolution as an assistant commissar. He rescues Dietrich's countess from execution.

Performances on the whole are good, though Dietrich restricts herself to just looking glamorous in any setting or costume. Donat handles himself with restraint and capability. There's only one other important cast assignment, John Clements as a hyper-sensitive commissar.

●

K-9
1989, 102 mins, US Ⓥ ⊙ col
Dir Rod Daniel ***Prod*** Lawrence Gordon, Charles Gordon ***Scr*** Steven Siegel, Scott Myers ***Ph*** Dean Semler ***Ed*** Lois Freeman-Fox ***Mus*** Miles Goodman ***Art*** George Costello
Act James Belushi, Mel Harris, Kevin Tighe, Ed O'Neill, Jerry Lee, James Handy (Gordon/Universal)

The mismatched-buddy cop picture has literally and perhaps inevitably gone to the dogs, and the only notable thing about *K-9* is that it managed to dig up the idiotic premise first.

Since the black-white pairing in *48HRS.*, there have been numerous cop film teamings. *K-9* has all the trapping of its predecessors: a flimsy plot dealing with the cop (Belushi) trying to break a drug case, an unwanted partner (Jerry Lee, a gifted German shepherd) being foisted on him and a grudging respect that develops between the two during the course of a series of shootouts, brawls and sight gags.

There are a few amazing moments (the dog's rescue of Belushi in a bar). In between lingers lots of standard action-pic fare, plenty of toothless jokes and some down-right mangy dialog.

●

KNOCK ON ANY DOOR
1949, 98 mins, US Ⓥ ⊙ b/w
Dir Nicholas Ray ***Prod*** Robert Lord ***Scr*** Daniel Taradash, John Monks, Jr. ***Ph*** Burnett Guffey ***Ed*** Viola Lawrence ***Mus*** George Antheil ***Art*** Robert Peterson
Act Humphrey Bogart, John Derek, George Macready (Santana)

An eloquent document on juvenile delinquency, its cause and effect, has been fashioned from *Knock on Any Door*. John Derek is the bad boy of the picture. Story opens when the youth, arrested for the wanton killing of a cop, calls on lawyer Humphrey Bogart to defend him. Bogart, himself a slums product who rose above it, reluctantly takes the case after being convinced Derek, no matter how bad, is innocent.

Nicholas Ray's direction stresses the realism of the script taken from Willard Motley's novel of the same title, and gives the film a hard, taut pace that compels complete attention.

●

KNUTE ROCKNE ALL AMERICAN
1940, 97 mins, US Ⓥ b/w
Dir Lloyd Bacon ***Prod*** Hal B. Wallis (exec.) ***Scr*** Robert Buckner ***Ph*** Tony Gaudio ***Ed*** Ralph Dawson ***Mus*** Ray Heindorf (arr.) ***Art*** Robert Haas
Act Pat O'Brien, Gale Page, Ronald Reagan, Donald Crisp, Albert Basserman, John Qualen (Warner)

Highlights in the colorful life of Knute Rockne, one of the most prominent figures in the world of football, are woven into a biographical film drama [based on private papers of his wife and the University of Notre Dame] that carries both inspirational and dramatic appeal on a wide scale.

Picture is studded with familiar incidents in Rockne's life—the meeting with George Gipp, latter's brief grid glories and death from pneumonia, defeat by Army after a long winning streak and the early morning reception of Rock on his return to South Bend, his decision to accept coaching as a life work in preference to chemical research, and his memorable "go out and win this one for the Gipper" in an Army game.

Through it all runs the theme of Rockne's whole purpose in life—moulding boys under his care to become good Americans who are conscious of their responsibilities and opportunities.

Pat O'Brien delivers a fine characterization of the immortal Rockne, catching the spirit of the role with an understanding of the human qualities of the man. Donald Crisp turns in his usual capable performance as Father John Callahan, head of Notre Dame. Four outstanding grid coaches, friends and contemporaries of Rockne—Howard Jones, Glenn "Pop" Warner, Alonzo Stagg and William Spaulding—are brought in for brief appearances in one sequence.

●

KOLYA
1996, 105 mins, UK/Czech Ⓥ ⊙ col
Dir Jan Sverak ***Prod*** Eric Abraham, Jan Sverak ***Scr*** Zdenek Sverak ***Ph*** Vladimir Smutny ***Ed*** Alois Fisarek ***Mus*** Ondrej Soukup ***Art*** Milos Kohout
Act Zdenek Sverak, Andrej Chalimon, Libuse Safrankova, Ondrez Vetchy, Stella Zazvorkova, Ladislav Smoljak (Portobello/Sverak)

Unfolding during the buildup to the 1989 Velvet Revolution and the end of Communist rule in what was then Czechoslovakia, *Kolya* is a bittersweet comedy-drama about a cherubic Russian tyke and a middle-aged cynic thrown together by circumstance. Fast-rising young Czech director Jan Sverak's fourth feature balances heartwarming sentiment with gentle humor and observations.

Virtuoso cellist Frantisek Louka (director's father and scriptwriter Zdenek Sverak) hits hard times after having slighted a Communist official and agrees to a friend's suggestion to wed Nadezda (Irena Livanova), a young Russian woman seeking Czech citizenship. The cash he earns from the deal allows him to clear his debts and buy a car. Unexpectedly, Nadezda disappears to West Germany, leaving her five-year-old son, Kolya (Andrej Chalimon), with his grandmother. When she is rushed to hospital, Kolya is dumped on Frantisek's doorstep.

The script [based on a story by Pavel Taussig] makes some ironic points on conflicting Czech attitudes towards Russia, most pointedly through Frantisek's mother (Stella Zazvorkova), who becomes hostile on discovering Kolya's origins. But this is textual embroidery on what is essentially a two-handed drama, the components of which are familiar but no less touching for it.

1996: Best Foreign Language Film

●

KONGRESS TANZT, DER
(CONGRESS DANCES)
1931, 95 mins, Germany b/w
Dir Erik Charell ***Prod*** Erich Pommer ***Scr*** Norbert Falk, Robert Liebmann ***Ph*** Carl Hoffmann ***Mus*** Werner R. Heymann (arr.) ***Art*** Walter Roehrig, Robert Herlth
Act Lilian Harvey, Willy Fritsch, Otto Wallburg, Conrad Veidt, Lil Dagover, Alfred Abel (UFA)

A revue more than a story. Erik Charell has directed mass scenes at the UFA studios in Babelsberg instead of staging them at the Grosses Schauspielhaus. He has done it with a seldom-seen luxury, a movement full of dance and life, but also with the disadvantages brought about by unconnected sequences. But Charell offers grace, taste and a light hand.

Plot is rather thin and goes back to the time of the Congress of Vienna, 1814, when all princes, kings and diplomats assembled to confer about the fate of Europe, and Emperor Napoleon. But the Austrian prime minister arranges festivities and dances in order to divert the gentlemen from the actual questions and the political events.

The Russian tsar (Willy Fritsch), especially, seems dangerous to him and he sends two ladies so that he will not trouble about the negotiations. But the tsar is wiser, he has a double take his place at the official festivities. However, he falls in love with one of these women, a Viennese glove maker (Lilian Harvey).

Fritsch has only to look well, which he does, and the charming Harvey, who is on the way to becoming a good actress, is again a dancer and, on orders, pouts her lips. Lil Dagover, as the Countess, only impresses in appearance. Only Otto Wallburg, with his blubbering, breaks the stiff coldness of this revue-play. Carl Hoffmann's photography is not sharp and too indistinct. The sound, however, is excellent.

●

KORHINTA
(MERRY-GO-ROUND)
1956, 100 mins, Hungary b/w
Dir Zoltan Fabri ***Scr*** Imre Sarkadi ***Ph*** Barnabas Hegyi ***Ed*** Mrs Ferenc Szecsenyi ***Mus*** Gyorgy Ranki ***Art*** Zoltan Fabri
Act Bela Barsi, Manyi Kiss, Mari Torocsik, Imre Soos, Adam Szirtes, Antal Farkas (Mafilm)

This is mainly the tale [from Imre Sarkadi's short story "In the Well"] of two lovers separated by social and political conventions who finally assert themselves and their love. It has a human, sentimental quality, never descending to mawkishness. Direction shapes this into an entertaining piece with a fine flair for atmosphere, mood and drama by young director Zoltan Fabri.

Scenes of the lovers first meeting on a fairground swing, a brilliantly mounted dance scene when the young lover makes his desires evident in a long dance with the girl (a masterful piece of cinema) and the treatment of characterization combine to make this a fine pic. Technical credits and playing are excellent.

●

KOTCH
1971, 113 mins, US Ⓥ col
Dir Jack Lemmon ***Prod*** Richard Carter ***Scr*** John Paxton ***Ph*** Richard H. Kline ***Ed*** Ralph E. Winters ***Mus*** Marvin Hamlisch ***Art*** Jock Poplin
Act Walter Matthau, Deborah Winters, Felicia Farr, Charles Aidman, Ellen Geer, Darrell Larson (ABC Pictures)

Kotch is a great film in several ways: Jack Lemmon's outstanding directorial debut; Walter Matthau's terrific performance as an unwanted elderly parent who befriends a pregnant teenager; John Paxton's superior adaptation of Katharine Topkins's novel and a top-notch supporting cast. This heart-warming, human comedy will leave audiences fully nourished, whereas they should be left a bit starved for more.

Paxton's script fully develops many interactions between Matthau and the other players. There's Charles Aidman, smash as his loving son, slightly embarrassed at Dad's apparent dotage; Felicia Farr, Aidman's wife who wants Pop out of the house; and Deborah Winters, as the couple's baby-sitter made pregnant by Darrell Larson, then shipped off in disgrace by her brother.

The film's somewhat too leisurely pace often sacrifices primary plot movement to brilliantly filmed digression-vignette. Basically the story has Matthau and Winters sharing a desert house together. She learns a lot about life from him, and he has the opportunity to act as a loving father and friend.

1971: NOMINATIONS: Best Actor (Walter Matthau), Editing, Song ("Life Is What You Make It"), Sound

•

KOYAANISQATSI

1982, 87 mins, US Ⓥ ⊙ col

Dir Godfrey Reggio ***Prod*** Godfrey Reggio ***Scr*** Ron Fricke, Godfrey Reggio, Michael Hoenig, Alton Walpole ***Ph*** Ron Fricke ***Ed*** Alton Walpole, Ron Fricke ***Mus*** Philip Glass, Michael Hoenig

(IRE)

Koyaanisqatsi is at first awe-inspiring with its sweeping aerial wilderness photography. It becomes depressing when the phone lines, factories and nuke plants spring up. The pic then runs the risk of boring audiences with shot after glossy shot of man's commercial hack job on the land and his resulting misery.

The viewer is relentlessly bombarded with images reminiscent of the title's Hopi Indian meaning, "crazy life," while Philip Glass's tantalizing but dirgelike score drones on.

A lion's share of the pic is a cynical display of decadence intending to edify and anger to action, but instead alienating with its one-sidedness. Simple message in Godfrey Reggio's direction seems to state that Americans are not much more than the cars they assemble and the hot dogs and Twinkies they package.

•

KRAKATOA EAST OF JAVA

1969, 135 mins, US Ⓥ ▭ col

Dir Bernard L. Kowalski ***Prod*** William R. Forman ***Scr*** Clifford Newton Gould, Bernard Gordon ***Ph*** Manuel Berenguer ***Ed*** Maurice Rootes, Warren Low, Walter Hanneman ***Mus*** Frank DeVol ***Art*** Eugene Lourie

Act Maximilian Schell, Diane Baker, Brian Keith, Barbara Werle, Sal Mineo, Rossano Brazzi (ABC/Cinerama)

Krakatoa plods through a search for a sunken treasure on a boat that contains a score of one-dimensional characters.

It is the late 19th century and somewhere in the Far East a boat is loading. An amiable captain, Maximilian Schell, is forced to take on convicts. He has a diver and balloonist to help him, his girl, who is searching for her son, and a mixed crew.

In the background is a rumbling and warning that a big volcano near where they are going, Krakatoa, may erupt again but the captain scoffs that it has been quiet for 200 years.

Director Bernard L. Kowalski, for his first pic, steers for simplicity and gives it a standard action feeling. More inventiveness and perhaps a sympathetic tongue-in-cheek approach could have given this the lift and charm that it lacks.

1969: NOMINATION: Best Visual Effects

•

KRAMER VS. KRAMER

1979, 105 mins, US Ⓥ ⊙ col

Dir Robert Benton ***Prod*** Stanley R. Jaffe ***Scr*** Robert Benton ***Ph*** Nestor Almendros ***Ed*** Jerry Greenberg ***Art*** Paul Sylbert

Act Dustin Hoffman, Meryl Streep, Justin Henry, Jane Alexander, Howard Duff, JoBeth Williams (Columbia)

Kramer vs. Kramer is a perceptive, touching, intelligent film about one of the raw sores of contemporary America, the dissolution of the family unit. In refashioning Avery Corman's novel, director-scripter Robert Benton has used a highly effective technique of short, poignant scenes to bring home the message that no one escapes unscarred from the trauma of separation.

It is in the latter arena that *Kramer* takes place, as Meryl Streep breaks with up-and-coming ad exec Dustin Hoffman and tyke Justin Henry to find her own role in life. Hoffman is thus left with a six-year-old son and begins a process of "parenting" that is both humorous and affecting. Three-quarters into the film, Streep comes to claim her first-born with the traditional mother's prerogative and a nasty court battle ensues.

1979: Best Picture, Director, Actor (Dustin Hoffman), Supp. Actress (Meryl Streep), Adapted Screenplay

NOMINATIONS: Best Supp. Actor (Justin Henry), Supp. Actress (Jane Alexander), Cinematography, Editing

•

KRAYS, THE

1990, 119 mins, UK Ⓥ ⊙ col

Dir Peter Medak ***Prod*** Dominic Anciano, Ray Burdis ***Scr*** Philip Ridley ***Ph*** Alex Thomson ***Ed*** Martin Walsh ***Mus*** Michael Kamen ***Art*** Michael Pickwoad

Act Billie Whitelaw, Tom Bell, Gary Kemp, Martin Kemp, Susan Fleetwood, Kate Hardie (Parkfield/Fugitive)

The Krays is a chilling, if somewhat monotonous, biopic charting the rise and fall of two prominent hoods in 1950–60s London, cockney lads whose psychosexual warping leads them into ultraviolence.

Screenwriter Philip Ridley deftly explores the cynical amorality of the us-vs.-them lower-class milieu, and the destructive effect of smothering mom Billie Whitelaw (in a superb performance) on her sociopathic twins, while virtually ignoring the standard cops-and-robbers dramaturgy of gangster films.

As the Krays, the brothers Kemp, who both had considerable acting experience before beginning their rock careers in Spandau Ballet, are just right in their deadeyed portrayal of what a rival thug calls "a pair of movie gangsters." Indeed, they are among the most repellent gangsters to come along since Richard Widmark pushed an old lady in a wheelchair down the stairs in *Kiss of Death*.

Director Peter Medak, who knew the Krays when he was an a.d., works skilfully to conjure up a cold and eerie atmosphere.

•

KREMLIN LETTER, THE

1970, 118 mins, US ▭ col

Dir John Huston ***Prod*** Carter De Haven, Sam Wiesenthal ***Scr*** John Huston, Gladys Hill ***Ph*** Ted Scaife ***Ed*** Russell Lloyd ***Mus*** Robert Drasnin ***Art*** Ted Haworth

Act Bibi Andersson, Richard Boone, Nigel Green, Dean Jagger, Max von Sydow, Orson Welles (20th Century-Fox)

An American official sends a letter about China to the Kremlin and it must be gotten back because of its explosiveness and lack of authorization. This is the nub of Noel Behn's novel.

The story in cinematic form is a conglomerate of scenes, each of which makes for valuable viewing, but with the piecing together another thing. Thus is this nastiness of the spy business graphically described. It is an engagingly photographed piece of business.

Max von Sydow is a political strong man within the Russian regime. Ex-U.S. Navy officer Patrick O'Neal has the job of salvaging the Kremlin Letter. But Russia, in the person of Richard Boone, also would like to retrieve the document. Participants include George Sanders, as a homo female impersonator in San Francisco. Orson Welles is a key Soviet man who is in New York to address the United Nations; Bibi Andersson is a prostitute married to agent Von Sydow.

•

KRIEMHILD'S REVENGE

SEE: DIE NIBELUNGEN

•

KRONOS

1957, 78 mins, US Ⓥ ⊙ ▭ b/w

Dir Kurt Neumann ***Prod*** Kurt Neumann ***Scr*** Lawrence Louis Goldman ***Ph*** Karl Struss ***Ed*** Jodie Copelan ***Mus*** Paul Sawtell, Bert Shefter ***Art*** Theobold Holsopple

Act Jeff Morrow, Barbara Lawrence, John Emery, George O'Hanlon, Morris Ankrum, Kenneth Alton (Regal)

Kronos is a well-made, moderate budget science-fictioner which boasts quality special effects that would do credit to a much higher-budgeted film.

Script [from a story by Irving Block] tells of the efforts of a people from outer space to capture Earth's energy. To do this, they send an accumulator to Earth, which is directed in its movement by the head of a great American lab, whose brain has been seized by a higher intelligence from space.

Feature takes its title from the accumulator: a huge metal cube-shaped figure 100 feet high, after the mythological god of evil, and which nothing seemingly can destroy.

Jeff Morrow heads cast as a scientist who has charted the course of the asteroid which has transported the accumulator to Earth. John Emery is convincing as the lab head forced by the outer-space intelligence to direct the monster. Barbara Lawrence is in strictly for distaff interest, but pretty.

•

KROTKI FILM O MILOSCI

SEE: DEKALOG

•

KROTKI FILM O ZABIJANIU

SEE: DEKALOG

•

KRULL

1983, 117 mins, US Ⓥ ⊙ ▭ col

Dir Peter Yates ***Prod*** Ron Silverman ***Scr*** Stanford Sherman ***Ph*** Peter Suschitzky ***Ed*** Ray Lovejoy ***Mus*** James Horner ***Art*** Stephen Grimes

Act Ken Marshall, Lysette Anthony, Freddie Jones, Francesca Annis, Alun Armstrong, David Battley (Columbia)

Although inoffensively designed only to please the senses and appeal to one's whimsical sense of adventure, *Krull* nevertheless comes off as a blatantly derivative hodgepodge of *Excalibur* meets *Star Wars*. Lavishly mounted at a reported cost of $27 million, the collection of action set pieces never jells into an absorbing narrative.

Plot is as old as the art of storytelling itself. Young Prince Colwyn (Ken Marshall) falls heir to a besieged kingdom, but must survive a Ulysses-scaled series of tests on the way to rescuing his beautiful bride from the clutches of the Beast, whose army of slayers imperils his journey every step of the way.

Crucial to Colwyn's quest is his recovery of the glaive, a razor-tipped, spinning boomerang which will enable him to combat the Beast. This fancy piece of magical jewelry holds the same importance as the Excalibur sword did for Arthur.

Professionalism of director Peter Yates, the large array of production and technical talents and, particularly, the mainly British actors keep things from becoming genuinely dull or laughable.

•

K2

1991, 111 mins, UK/US Ⓥ ⊙ col

Dir Franc Roddam ***Prod*** Jonathan Taplin, Marilyn Weiner, Tim Van Rellim ***Scr*** Patrick Meyers, Scott Roberts ***Ph*** Gabriel Beristain ***Ed*** Sean Barton ***Mus*** Hans Zimmer ***Art*** Andrew Sanders

Act Michael Biehn, Matt Craven, Raymond J. Barry, Hiroshi Fujioka, Luca Bercovici, Patricia Charbonneau (Trans Pacific)

The buddy movie hits the Himalayas in Franc Roddam's *K2*, an entertaining enough mountain-climbing saga [from the 1983 one-act play by Patrick Meyers]. Script's lack of oxygen is offset by pic's slick packaging plus good onscreen bonding between leads Michael Biehn and Matt Craven.

Story rapidly sets up two main characters: yuppy, womanizing Seattle lawyer Biehn and gentler, married-with-child professor Craven. When a U.S. climbing group funded by millionaire Raymond J. Barry loses two of its members in an Alaskan training session, Biehn and Craven take their places for the big one—an attempt on K2, the world's second-highest peak and a w.k. engorger of climbers.

Both thesps perform far better than the script deserves, with Biehn cocksure but likable, and Craven serious but caring. Barry is solid as the aging sponsor and Luca Bercovici ditto as Biehn's nemesis.

There's no attempt at any mystical relationship between the characters and the mountain. Pic concentrates instead on sheer thrills and spills, with plenty of product placement.

•

KUFFS

1992, 101 mins, US Ⓥ ⊙ col

Dir Bruce A. Evans ***Prod*** Raynold Gideon ***Scr*** Bruce A. Evans, Raynold Gideon ***Ph*** Thomas Del Ruth ***Ed*** Stephen Semel ***Mus*** Harold Faltermeyer ***Art*** Victoria Paul, Armin Ganz

Act Christian Slater, Tony Goldwyn, Milla Jovovich, Bruce Boxleitner, Troy Evans, George De La Pena (De Laurentiis)

Christian Slater's energy fails to carry *Kuffs*, a mishmash cop comedy very reminiscent of several Eddie Murphy films. Film veers from ultraviolence to slapstick comedy in an arbitrary and irritating fashion.

Slater is the fish out of water this time, inheriting his murdered brother's police protection business. Plot hook makes good use of the San Francisco setting, where neighborhoods have relied on these private Patrol Specials since the 1850s.

Gimmick allows ne'er-do-well high school dropout Slater to become an instant cop and prove his mettle under fire. Avenging brother Bruce Boxleitner's death is an utterly conventional quest, but the few laughs along the way are the film's raison d'etre.

As Slater's unwilling partner, Tony Goldwyn demonstrates solid comic talents. Wearing a variety of goofy outfits, Leon Rippy makes a fun killer. Former ballet star George De La Pena is utterly convincing as the slick villain. Less fortunate is lovely Milla Jovovich, too young for the nothing part of Slater's g.f.

•

KUMONOSU-JO
(THRONE OF BLOOD; THE CASTLE OF THE SPIDER'S WEB; COBWEB CASTLE)

1957, 105 mins, Japan Ⓥ ⦿ b/w

Dir Akira Kurosawa ***Prod*** Shojiro Motoki, Akira Kurosawa ***Scr*** Akira Kurosawa, Shinobu Hashimoto, Ryuzo Kikushima, Hideo Oguni ***Ph*** Asakazu Nakai ***Mus*** Masaru Sato ***Art*** Yoshiro Muraki, Kohei Ezaki

Act Toshiro Mifune, Isuzu Yamada, Minoru Chiaki, Takashi Shimura, Akira Kubo, Takamaru Sasaki (Toho)

From a purely cinematic standpoint, this Japanese adaptation of Shakespeare's *Macbeth* is all motion picture, an achievement of mood and photographic invention. Yet, little but the embellished plot skeleton of Shakespeare's masterpiece survives.

Nevertheless, there is no overlooking the masterful direction of Akira Kurosawa, nor the agile, energetic and explosive camerawork of Asakazu Nakai. It is a film of shattering silences and overpowering bursts of action, of moments when the attention is stimulated only by the sinister rustle of silk and others when the screen reverberates with uninhibited sound and fury.

Leading Japanese actor Toshiro Mifune gives a ranting, raving, rooting, tooting performance in the central role. Isuzu Yamada is calm, cool, collected and appropriately despicable as Lady M.

The picture has been filmed in black-and-white. At first this seems odd, but the element of surprise vanishes when one beholds what has been accomplished by these artisans in the two basic shades.

•

KUNDUN

1997, 134 mins, US Ⓥ ⦿ ▭ col

Dir Martin Scorsese ***Prod*** Barbara De Fina ***Scr*** Melissa Mathison ***Ph*** Roger Deakins ***Ed*** Thelma Schoonmaker ***Mus*** Philip Glass ***Art*** Dante Ferretti

Act Tenzin Thuthob Tsarong, Gyurme Tethong, Tulku Jamyang Kunga Tenzin, Tenzin Yeshi Paichang, Tencho Gyalpo, Tsewang Migyur Khangsar (Cappa-De Fina/Touchstone)

Totally disregarding commercial considerations, Martin Scorsese's haunting meditation on the early life of the Dalai Lama is one from the heart, a majestic spectacle of images and sounds. But pic is bogged down by a routine screenplay that fails to provide a fresh perspective on Tibet's culture.

Following a straightforward chronological order, story begins in 1933 with the death of the 13th Dalai Lama and the search for a successor. It's told from the subjective point of view of a child born in a remote rural area and destined to become the new Dalai Lama. Richly detailed, with utmost attention to visual detail and color, first part sets a mysterious, almost surreal tone.

The story gets more somber when it jumps ahead to 1944. At the end of WWII, he is confronted with China's aggressive campaign to convince the world that Tibet belongs to it. Pic's second part begins in 1949, when Gen. Mao Zedong (Robert Lin) ruthlessly enforces communist ideology in his country and tight military control over Tibet. Last section depicts the Chinese massacre of innocent Tibetans and the Dalai Lama's journey into exile.

It's indicative of the script's shortcomings that the film's weakest sequences are those depicting the meetings between the Dalai Lama and Chairman Mao. The Chinese leader comes across as a monstrous caricature, borderline camp.

Kundun (which means "ocean of wisdom") represents an exception in Scorsese's oeuvre, mostly centered on small, male groups of alienated, paranoid individuals. Ultimately, *Kundun* emerges as a movie that's hypnotic without being truly compelling, sensuously stunning but not illuminating.

1997: NOMINATIONS: Best Cinematography, Original Dramatic Score, Art Direction, Costume Design

•

KVARTERET KORPEN
(RAVEN'S END)

1963, 100 mins, Sweden b/w

Dir Bo Widerberg ***Prod*** Gunnar Oldin (assoc.) ***Scr*** Bo Widerberg ***Ph*** Jan Lindestrom ***Ed*** Vic Kjellin ***Art*** Einar Nettelbladt

Act Thommy Berggren, Keve Hjelm, Emy Storm, Ingvar Hirdwall, Christina Framback, Agneta Prytz (Europa)

This is a tender, well-observed pic about the coming of age of a young man in the Sweden of the '30s. However, film is slow and relies on a muted series of scenes to build to its moments of truth.

The well-contrasted lensing brings out the '30s look adequately. The bare little street of the action [set in the southern town of Malmo] is also well notated with its characters and children.

A young writer tries to break out and finally does. That is the essence of it. But in the process, the first rays of worker determination and the need to raise the level of the poverty-stricken sections of the population are well limned.

Anders (Thommy Berggren) has the right élan, divided loyalties and final strength to break with this gray life even if it means leaving a pregnant girl in the lurch. Keve Hjelm is fine as the pathetic father, while Emy Storm gives strength and depth to the mother. The allusions to politics and feel of the times are applicable to most of the countries in depression days.

Film is thus an estimable effort that will still find it hard to make its way out of Sweden. A bit more dramatic edge would have made it more effective. As is, director Bo Widerberg shows himself one of the more gifted among the Swedish newcomers. This is his second film and denotes a deep pro flair.

•

KWAIDAN
SEE: KAIDAN

LA BAMBA
1987, 108 mins, US Ⓥ ⊙ col
Dir Luis Valdez ***Prod*** Taylor Hackford, Bill Borden ***Scr*** Luis Valdez ***Ph*** Adam Greenberg ***Ed*** Sheldon Kahn, Don Brochu ***Mus*** Carlos Santana, Miles Goodman ***Art*** Vince Cresciman
Act Lou Diamond Phillips, Esai Morales, Rosana De Soto, Elizabeth Pena, Danielle von Zerneck, Joe Pantoliano (New Visions)

There haven't been too many people who died at age 17 who have warranted the biopic treatment, but 1950s rock 'n' roller Ritchie Valens proves a worthy exception in *La Bamba*.

Known primarily for his three top-10 tunes, "Come On Let's Go," "Donna," and the title cut, Valens was killed—just eight months after signing his first recording contract—in the 1959 private plane crash that also took the lives of Buddy Holly and The Big Bopper, and thus attained instant legendhood.

For anyone to achieve his dreams by 17 is close to miraculous. It was even more so for Valens who, less than two years before his death, was a Mexican-American fruitpicker named Ricardo Valenzuela living in a tent with his family in Northern California. It wasn't long before small-time gigs, and then ultra-cheap recording sessions were coming his way. Backgrounding this, however, was tremendously emotional turbulence created mostly by Ritchie's half-brother Bob, an ex-con who deals drugs.

La Bamba is engrossing throughout and boasts numerous fine performances. In Lou Diamond Phillips's sympathetic turn, Valens comes across as a very fine young man, caring for those important to him and not overawed by his success. Rosana De Soto scores as his tireless mother, and Elizabeth Pena has numerous dramatic moments as Bob's distraught mate. Most of the fireworks are Bob's, and Esai Morales makes the tormented brother a genuinely complex figure.

•

LA BOHEME
1926, 101 mins, US ⊗ b/w
Dir King Vidor ***Scr*** Ray Doyle, Harry Behn, William Conselman, Ruth Cummings, Fred De Gresac ***Ph*** Hendrik Sartov ***Ed*** Hugh Wynn ***Mus*** William Axt ***Art*** Cedric Gibbons, Arnold Gillespie
Act Lillian Gish, John Gilbert, Renee Adoree, Edward Everett Horton, George Hassell, Roy D'Arcy (M-G-M)

Through the fact that the American representatives of Ricordi, the Milan music publisher who holds the rights to all of the Puccini works, would not permit the utilization of that composer's score as an accompaniment to the picture, William Axt wrote an entirely original accompaniment, taking his theme numbers from the T. B. Harms catalog.

However, as one views the picture, you cannot help but think in the terms of Rodolphe the tenor, Marcel the baritone, Schaunard the basso, Mimi the soprano, and Musette the contralto. And, with that in mind, how could any picturization of an operatic plot be complete without the music that has become all too familiar in connection with the libretto?

The girls are going to go crazy over Jack Gilbert as Rodolphe, the lover, and the boys will like Mimi as played by Lillian Gish, although she gives a rather watered-milk characterization.

•

LABYRINTH
1986, 101 mins, US Ⓥ ⊙ ▭ col
Dir Jim Henson ***Prod*** Eric Rattray ***Scr*** Terry Jones ***Ph*** Alex Thomson ***Ed*** John Grover ***Mus*** Trevor Jones ***Art*** Elliot Scott
Act David Bowie, Jennifer Connelly, Toby Froud, Shelley Thompson, Christopher Malcolm, Natalie Finland (Henson/Lucasfilm)

An array of bizarre creatures and David Bowie can't save *Labyrinth* from being a crashing bore. Characters created by Jim Henson and his team become annoying rather than endearing.

What is even more disappointing is the failure of the film on a story level. Young Sarah (Jennifer Connelly) embarks on an adventure to recover her baby stepbrother from the clutches of the Goblin King (David Bowie) who has taken the child for some unknown reason to his kingdom. Story soon loses its way and never comes close to archetypal myths and fears of great fairy tales. Instead it's an unconvincing coming of age saga.

As the Goblin King, Bowie seems a fish out of water—too serious to be campy, too dumb to be serious.

•

LACEMAKER, THE
SEE: LA DENTELLIERE

•

LACOMBE LUCIEN
1974, 136 mins, France/Italy/W. Germany col
Dir Louis Malle ***Prod*** Claude Nedjar ***Scr*** Louis Malle, Patrick Modiano ***Ph*** Tonino Delli Colli ***Ed*** Suzanne Baron ***Art*** Ghislain Uhry
Act Pierre Blaise, Aurore Clement, Holger Lowenadler, Therese Giehse, Stephane Bouy, Loumi Iacobesco (NEF/UPF/Vides/Hallelujah)

Director Louis Malle's film looks at a young farm boy, 17, who drifts into the French Gestapo by ignorance rather than intent. Pic displays the banality of evil and refrains from didactics or heroics.

Lucien Lacombe, played with a remarkable flair by non-actor Pierre Blaise, works at a hospital. His father is a prisoner of war. He at first wants to join the resistance (it is 1944) but is refused and, when inadvertently out after curfew, is dragged into the local French Gestapo quarters. He is made drunk and gives away the head of the resistance. He takes pride in it, while seemingly unaffected by the torture, decadence and hysteria he sees around him as the Americans approach. Meeting a Jewish family holed up in the town, he is taken by the daughter and a sort of love affair blooms. The father, an ex-Paris tailor, cannot bring himself to hate this young semi-thug who moves in on them.

Pic is expertly directed and acted, with Aurore Clement as the fragile girl and Holger Lowenadler as her father also outstanding, as is the fine lensing that helps capture the period.

•

L.A. CONFIDENTIAL
1997, 136 mins, US Ⓥ ⊙ ▭ col
Dir Curtis Hanson ***Prod*** Arnon Milchan, Curtis Hanson, Michael Nathanson ***Scr*** Brian Helgeland, Curtis Hanson ***Ph*** Dante Spinotti ***Ed*** Peter Honess ***Mus*** Jerry Goldsmith ***Art*** Jeannine Oppewall
Act Kevin Spacey, Russell Crowe, Guy Pearce, James Cromwell, David Strathairn, Kim Basinger (Regency/Warner)

Drenched in the tawdry glamor of Hollywood in the early '50s and up to its ears in the delirious corruption of police and city politics, *L.A. Confidential* is an irresistible treat with enough narrative twists and memorable characters for a half-dozen films. Curtis Hanson's rich and impressively faithful adaptation of James Ellroy's novel will satisfy mystery fans and probably reps the best film of its type since *Chinatown*.

Sgt. Jack Vincennes (Kevin Spacey) made his name busting Robert Mitchum for dope and continues to get plenty of mileage out of arresting celebs in tandem with *Hush-Hush* magazine editor Sid Hudgeons (Danny DeVito) and acting as unofficial adviser on the *Badge of Honor* TV show. Officer Bud White (Russell Crowe) is a rough, quick-tempered cop who refuses to rat on his racist partner, Stensland (Graham Beckel). Ed Exley (Guy Pearce) is a ruthlessly honest, college-educated young officer who won't play along with the code of protecting one another.

Plot proper kicks in with a massacre at the Nite Owl Coffee Shop, a bloodbath that leaves six victims, including Stensland, in its wake. Exley emerges as the hero of the case, and White and Exley are thrown onto a collision course when it appears there may have been more to the Nite Owl case than met the eye—things that bear upon the conduct of the entire LAPD.

The intrigue and tension mount steadily in ways that are complicated but not confusing. No one is beyond suspicion or, for that matter, elimination. Pic serves as an almost overwhelming reminder of the pleasures of deeply involving narrative in the old Hollywood sense.

Aussie actors Crowe and Pearce are dynamite. Spacey is aces as the somewhat older homicide veteran who relishes his status as a "real Hollywood" cop. Kim Basinger's vulnerable whore, a double for Veronica Lake, inspires her best screen work in quite some time. Working deeply within film noir territory, Hanson resists overdoing self-conscious stylistics, telling the story in superbly chosen settings that convey a pungent sense of a virtually vanished L.A.

1997: Best Actress (Kim Basinger), Screenplay Adaptation

NOMINATIONS: Best Picture, Director, Cinematography, Editing, Original Dramatic Score, Art Direction, Sound

•

LADIES' MAN, THE
1961, 106 mins, US Ⓥ ⊙ col
Dir Jerry Lewis ***Prod*** Jerry Lewis ***Scr*** Jerry Lewis, Bill Richmond ***Ph*** W. Wallace Kelley ***Ed*** Stanley Johnson ***Mus*** Walter Scharf ***Art*** Hal Pereira, Ross Bellah
Act Jerry Lewis, Helen Traubel, Kathleen Freeman, Hope Holiday, Lynn Ross, Gretchen Houser (Paramount)

Ladies' Man is a kind of parlay of scraps and ideas apparently left over from Jerry Lewis's last two films, *The Bellboy* and *Cinderfella*. In its episodic nature, it resembles the former. In its lavish production and eye-appeal, it takes after the latter. And the central character is a kind of a combination of the downtrodden *Fella* and the hapless *Bellboy*.

The slight plot concerns a girl-shy goof who becomes the houseboy in a sort of palatial girlatorium. Primarily the plot is little more than a limp excuse for a series of anything-goes slapstick sequences and sight gags punctuated by an occasional song or dance, an occasional romantic interlude and a lethal dose of the star's homely philosophy. Lewis will try anything for a laugh. When he hits, it's a belly laugh. But too often he misses.

The odd characteristic of this picture, and of many of Lewis's pictures, is its close resemblance to the style of an animated cartoon. It can be found in the technique of absurd facial exaggeration, the repetition, the insane body gyrations, the incongruous relationships of sight and sound, the trick effects, the abundance and short duration of scenes, the very fantasy of the thing.

For glamour, he is surrounded by 31 girls and an elaborate set, the exact likes of which has never been seen on the screen. It is a complex three-story multi-roomed, strikingly tinted $350,000 creation that is something to behold. Ditto the $150,000 worth of props and furnishings.

•

LADRI DI BICICLETTE
(THE BICYCLE THIEF; BICYCLE THIEVES)
1948, 90 mins, Italy Ⓥ ⊙ ▭ b/w
Dir Vittorio De Sica ***Scr*** Vittorio De Sica, Cesare Zavattini, Suso Cecchi D'Amico, Oreste Biancoli, Adolfo Franci, Gherardo Gherardi, Garardo Guerrieri ***Ph*** Carlo Montuori ***Ed*** Eraldo Da Roma ***Mus*** Alessandro Cicognini
Act Lamberto Maggiorani, Lianella Carrell, Enzo Staiola, Elena Altieri, Vittorio Antonucci, Gino Saltamerenda (PDS)

Made with a cast of principals who were picked up in Rome's streets and had never before faced a camera, and with a story [from a novel by Luigi Bartolini] incredible in its simplicity as a basis for a 90-minute film, the picture is a pure exercise in directorial virtuosity. The beauty of it, however, is that that is never apparent. There are no obvious tricks and no obvious striving.

On the surface it is nothing more than the theft of a bicycle from one of the army of unemployed in postwar Rome and his efforts to find the thief and recover the vehicle. In the bicycle Antonio sees the security of himself and his family, necessary to his job in a city where jobs are scarce. He sets out with his young son on a Sunday morning to find the bike before nightfall so that he won't be without a job when it comes time for work on Monday morning.

The pair visit Rome's secondhand bicycle mart, get into an evangelical free-lunch mission and even into a brothel, several times see the bike and its thief, finally catch him, and then can't prove he stole it. Antonio, in desperation, is finally driven to stealing one.

As the son Bruno, Enzo Staiola is the star of the film, if it has one. His funny face, serious but urchin-like manner and ability to win laughs with the minor troubles he gets himself into rank him as a top moppet performer, despite lack of any previous experience. Likewise a tyro who turns in a touching performance is Lamberto Maggiorani as Antonio.

Picture moves along at an unaccustomedly good pace, except for one slack spot midway. Fortunately, there are plenty of laughs to balance the more serious drama. Photography throughout is first-rate in a hard documentary manner.

1949: Best Foreign Language Film

•

LADY AND THE TRAMP
1955, 75 mins, US Ⓥ ⊙ ▭ col
Dir Hamilton Luske, Clyde Geronimi, Wilfred Jackson ***Prod*** Walt Disney ***Scr*** Erdman Penner, Joe Rinaldi, Ralph Wright, Don DaGradi ***Ed*** Don Halliday ***Mus*** Oliver Wallace
(Walt Disney)

A delight for the juveniles and lots of fun for adults, *Lady and the Tramp* is the first animated feature in CinemaScope and the wider canvas and extra detail work reportedly meant an additional 30% in negative cost. It was a sound investment.

This time out the producer turned to members of the canine world and each of these hounds of Disneyville reflects astute drawing-board knowhow and richly humorous invention. The songs by Peggy Lee and Sonny Burke figure importantly, too.

Characters of the title are a cutie-pie faced and ultra-ladylike spaniel and the raffish mutt from the other side of the tracks. In "featured" roles are Trusty, the bloodhound who's lost his sense of smell, and Jock, a Scottie with a sense of thrift. Both have a crush on Lady but her on-and-off romance with Tramp finally leads to a mating of the minds, etc., and a litter basket.

•

LADY BE GOOD
1941, 110 mins, US Ⓥ b/w
Dir Norman Z. McLeod ***Prod*** Arthur Freed ***Scr*** Jack McGowan, Kay Van Riper, Jock McClain ***Ph*** George Folsey, Oliver Marsh ***Ed*** Frederick J. Smith ***Mus*** Georgie Stoll (dir.)
Act Eleanor Powell, Ann Sothern, Robert Young, Lionel Barrymore, John Carroll, Red Skelton (M-G-M)

The plot bears no resemblance to the Guy Bolton book of the original 1924 stage musical, which was one of the major springboards for Fred and Adele Astaire. The songs in this picture are likewise no relation to the click Gershwin score.

There are flagrant examples in the film of poor direction, unimaginative storytelling and slipshod photography. The picture looks as though director Norman Z. McLeod was given a time allotment to fill, no matter how, and he did.

While confused, the story pattern is familiar—that of a crack songwriting team splitting up and becoming individually unsuccessful until resuming their partnership. In this instance it's the case of ex-waitress Ann Sothern and composer Robert Young, who click, marry and then get divorced when Young goes high-hat and social. Then they click and marry again—and again she goes into the divorce courts, which gives the audience a double-dose of flashbacks out of the stories told Judge Lionel Barrymore. It's a waste of Barrymore.

1941: Best Song ("The Last Time I Saw Paris")

•

LADYBIRD LADYBIRD
1994, 102 mins, UK Ⓥ ⊙ col
Dir Ken Loach ***Prod*** Sally Hibbin ***Scr*** Rona Munro ***Ph*** Barry Ackroyd ***Ed*** Jonathan Morris ***Mus*** George Fenton, Mauricio Venegas ***Art*** Martin Johnson
Act Crissy Rock, Vladimir Vega, Ray Winstone, Sandie Lavelle, Mauricio Venegas, Clare Perkins (Parallax/Film Four)

Far removed from the boisterous, dryly comic *Raining Stones*, Ken Loach's *Ladybird Ladybird* is a tough, steamrolling, semi-vérité look at a (non-) family life in 1990s Britain through the eyes of a battered but ballsy unmarried mother caught between her own willfulness and an intrusive nanny state.

Pic is propelled by a natural, gutsy performance by newcomer Crissy Rock. In tone and content, Loach hasn't directed anything this emotionally powerful since his earlier work of the 1960s and early 1970s.

Based on a true story, pic has Maggie (Rock), a tough Liverpudlian mother of four, meeting gentle Paraguayan Jorge (Vladimir Vega) in a London bar where she sings. The pair bond fast with flashbacks pasting in Maggie's history, first as a child with an abusive father and later as a battered mother forced to move into a women's refuge. Relationship is cranked into a higher gear by the news that she's expecting another child.

Loach then progressively tightens the screws as the authorities take her baby girl into care, Jorge gets heat from the immigration authorities after his visa expires and the relationship comes under strain as Maggie's insecurities resurface.

A Liverpool standup comedian with no acting experience, Rock exudes a no-nonsense, working-class sensibility, moving easily from acerbic Merseyside wit to sequences of emotional violence that carry a docu charge.

•

LADYBUGS
1992, 90 mins, US Ⓥ ⊙ col
Dir Sidney J. Furie ***Prod*** Albert S. Ruddy, Andre E. Morgan ***Scr*** Curtis Burch ***Ph*** Dan Burstall ***Ed*** John W. Wheeler, Timothy N. Board ***Mus*** Richard Gibbs ***Art*** Robb Wilson King
Act Rodney Dangerfield, Jackee, Jonathan Brandis, Ilene Graff, Vinessa Shaw, Tom Parks (Paramount/Ruddy & Morgan)

A klutzy would-be comedy about a girls' soccer team, *Ladybugs* is sexist, homophobic and woefully unfunny to boot. Paramount apparently thought it was ordering up another *Bad News Bears*, but the garish *Ladybugs* has the look of a third-rate TV movie.

As a salesman for a Colorado tycoon (Tom Parks), Rodney Dangerfield is put in charge of a soccer team. His bright idea for turning them into winners is to have his fiancée's son join the team in drag.

Jonathan Brandis, saddled with a most embarrassing role, is the horny teen who makes minimal attempts to act like a girl but fools everyone anyway. Most of the wisecracks Dangerfield gets here wouldn't go over with a drunken Vegas crowd.

•

LADY CAROLINE LAMB
1972, 122 mins, UK/Italy Ⓥ ▭ col
Dir Robert Bolt ***Prod*** Fernando Ghia ***Scr*** Robert Bolt ***Ph*** Oswald Morris ***Ed*** Norman Savage ***Mus*** Richard Rodney Bennett ***Art*** Carmen Dillon
Act Sarah Miles, Jon Finch, Richard Chamberlain, John Mills, Margaret Leighton, Pamela Brown (Anglo-EMI/Pulsar/Vides)

If it's that relative rarity, a lushly, unabashedly romantic—yet tastefully executed—tale that you relish, then *Lady Caroline Lamb* is your likely cup of tea.

For his first stint behind the camera, Robert Bolt comes up with a period piece which rings a number of contemporary bells, both emotional and intellectual. His tragic heroine, a controversial free thinker of the early British 1800s, has obvious parallels in present-day femme emancipation.

Outlined, her story follows her headlong flight into matrimony with the politically promising Lamb, then into an equally breathless and unpondered but this time scandalous affair with Byron, and on to her final climactic sacrifice on behalf of her husband's career.

Sarah Miles shines in a tailored role. Similarly, Jon Finch, as her husband, lends conviction to the film's most difficult part.

•

LADY CHATTERLEY'S LOVER
1981, 105 mins, France/UK Ⓥ ⊙ col
Dir Just Jaeckin ***Prod*** Andre Djaoui, Christopher Pierce ***Scr*** Just Jaeckin, Christopher Wicking ***Ph*** Robert Fraisse ***Ed*** Eunice Mountjoy ***Mus*** Stanley Myers ***Art*** Anton Furst
Act Sylvia Kristel, Shane Briant, Nicholas Clay, Ann Mitchell, Elizabeth Spriggs (Producteurs Associes/Cannon)

This Franco-British production of *Lady Chatterley's Lover* is a cop-out adaptation of D. H. Lawrence's one time scandalous literary hymn to human sexuality. It's coy and superficial, worth little as erotic fare and not considerably more as sentimental drama.

The sex scenes are all the more unmoving because the surrounding story and characters are inadequately realized. Lady Chatterley (Sylvia Kristel) is the wife of an English aristocrat wounded in World War I and totally paralyzed from the waist down. Starved for carnal affection, she becomes the lover of Chatterley's gamekeeper and meets him daily for long sessions of passionate lovemaking.

The love scenes are commonplace, summary, tritely lyrical, and lacking in sensuality; no more daring than equivalent scenes in any other commercial product with a frank romantic angle.

Kristel is attractive but inexpressive as an actress. Nicholas Clay lacks rawness and definition as her lower-class lover.

•

LADY EVE, THE
1941, 90 mins, US Ⓥ ⊙ b/w
Dir Preston Sturges ***Prod*** Paul Jones ***Scr*** Preston Sturges ***Ph*** Victor Milner ***Ed*** Stuart Gilmore ***Mus*** Sigmund Krumgold (dir.) ***Art*** Hans Dreier, Ernst Fegte
Act Henry Fonda, Barbara Stanwyck, Charles Coburn, Eugene Pallette, William Demarest, Eric Blore (Paramount)

Third writer-director effort of Preston Sturges [from a story by Monckton Hoffe] is laugh entertainment of top proportions with its combo of slick situations, spontaneous dialog and a few slapstick falls tossed in for good measure.

Basically, story is the age-old tale of Eve snagging Adam, but dressed up with continually infectious fun and good humor. Barbara Stanwyck is girl-lure of trio of confidence operators. She's determined, quick-witted, resourceful and personable. Henry Fonda is a serious young millionaire, somewhat sappy, deadpan and slow-thinking, returning from a year's snake-hunting expedition up the Amazon. He's a cinch pushover for girl's advances on the boat—but pair fall in love, while girl flags Charles Coburn's attempts to cold-deck the victim at cards.

Sturges provides numerous sparkling situations in his direction and keeps picture moving at a merry pace. Stanwyck is excellent in the comedienne portrayal, while Fonda carries his assignment in good fashion. Coburn is a finished actor as the con man.

1941: NOMINATION: Best Original Story

•

LADY FOR A DAY
1933, 93 mins, US Ⓥ b/w
Dir Frank Capra ***Prod*** [Frank Capra] ***Scr*** Robert Riskin ***Ph*** Joseph Walker ***Ed*** Gene Havlick ***Mus*** Constantin Bakaleinikoff (dir.) ***Art*** [uncredited]
Act Warren William, May Robson, Guy Kibbee, Glenda Farrell, Ned Sparks, Walter Connolly (Columbia)

Lady for a Day asks the spectator to believe in the improbable. It's Hans Christian Andersen stuff written by a hard-boiled journalist and transferred to the screen by trick-wise Hollywoodites. While not stinting a full measure of credit to director Frank Capra, it seems as if the spotlight of recognition ought to play rather strongly on scriptwriter Robert Riskin [adapting Damon Runyon's story "Madame La Gimp"].

On the performance end, May Robson dominates the first reel but is thereafter rather subordinated as the story gets into the comedy side-plots.

Actually in a well-balanced, smartly directed cast like this it's hard to split the posies. Even in a small role as a nite-club hostess Glenda Farrell looks great. There are half a dozen bits, including a superbly ironic English butler that ought really to get a shoulder pat. Warren William is the superstitious gambler for whom Apple Annie is a good luck omen. It is he who stage manages the gigantic make-believe whereby the shoddy peddler of apples becomes a "lady for a day," to preserve her finely reared daughter's illusions that her mother is a society somebody.

1932/33: NOMINATIONS: Best Picture, Director, Actress (May Robson), Adaptation

•

LADY FROM SHANGHAI, THE
1948, 86 mins, US Ⓥ ⊙ b/w
Dir Orson Welles ***Prod*** Orson Welles ***Scr*** Orson Welles ***Ph*** Charles Lawton, Jr. ***Ed*** Viola Lawrence ***Mus*** Heinz Roemheld ***Art*** Stephen Goosson, Sturges Carne
Act Rita Hayworth, Orson Welles, Everett Sloane, Ted De Corsia, Glenn Anders, Gus Schilling (Columbia)

Script is wordy and full of holes which need the plug of taut storytelling and more forthright action. Rambling style used by Orson Welles has occasional flashes of imagination, particularly in the tricky backgrounds he uses to unfold the yarn, but effects, while good on their own, are distracting to the murder plot. Contributing to the stylized effect stressed by Welles is the photography, which features artful compositions entirely in keeping with the production mood.

Story [from the novel *Before I Die* by Sherwood King] tees off in New York where Welles, as a philosophical Irish seaman, joins the crew of a rich man's luxury yacht. Schooner's cruise and stops along the Mexican coast en route to San Francisco furnish varied and interesting backdrops. Welles's tries for effect reach their peak with the staging of climactic chase sequences in a Chinese theatre where performers are going through an Oriental drama, and in the mirror room of an amusement park's crazy house.

Welles has called on players for stylized performances. He uses an Irish brogue and others depict erratic characters with little reality. Hayworth isn't called on to do much more than look beautiful. Best break for players goes to Everett Sloane, and he gives a credible interpretation of the crippled criminal attorney.

•

LADY GAMBLES, THE
1949, 98 mins, US b/w
Dir Michael Gordon ***Prod*** Michael Kraike ***Scr*** Roy Huggins ***Ph*** Russell Metty ***Ed*** Milton Carruth ***Mus*** Frank Skinner ***Art*** Alexander Golitzen

Act Barbara Stanwyck, Robert Preston, Stephen McNally, Edith Barrett, John Hoyt, Leif Erickson (Universal)

The Lady Gambles is an entry in the psychiatric sweepstakes—this time of a gal who becomes a gambling addict because of a guilt complex. Story [based on one by Lewis Meltzer and Oscar Saul, adaptation by Halsted Welles] meanders too long for top results. Veiled hints are tossed out from time to time on the reasons for the gal's mental instability but, when it is finally revealed at the end, the story twist has lost its punch.

Barbara Stanwyck is the lady who gambles and the role is practically a tour de force for her, giving her numerous opportunities for emotions, ranging from humor to hysterics. She does her usual capable job.

Standout in the film is Stephen McNally, as the professional gambler who takes her under his wing until she snafus even his operations with her excesses, then drops her cold.

•

LADY HAMILTON

SEE: THAT HAMILTON WOMAN

•

LADYHAWKE

1985, 124 mins, US Ⓥ ⦿ ▭ col

Dir Richard Donner **Prod** Richard Donner, Lauren Schuler **Scr** Edward Khmara, Michael Thomas, Tom Mankiewicz **Ph** Vittorio Storaro **Ed** Stuart Baird **Mus** Andrew Powell **Art** Wolf Kroeger

Act Matthew Broderick, Rutger Hauer, Michelle Pfeiffer, Leo McKern, John Wood, Ken Hutchison (Warner/20th Century-Fox)

Ladyhawke is a very likeable, very well-made fairytale that insists on a wish for its lovers to live happily ever after.

Handsome Rutger Hauer is well cast as the dark and moody knight who travels with a hawk by day. Lovely Michelle Pfeiffer is perfect as the enchanting beauty who appears by night, always in the vicinity of a vicious but protective wolf.

As readers of one or more variations of this legend will instantly recognize, Pfeiffer is the hawk and Hauer the wolf, each changing form as the sun rises and sets, former lovers cursed to never humanly share the clock together.

The spell was cast by an evil bishop (John Wood) when Pfeiffer spurned him for Hauer, who is now bent on revenge, with the help of young Matthew Broderick, the only one to ever escape Wood's deadly dungeon. Though simple, the saga moves amidst beautiful surroundings (filmed in Italy), and is worthwhile for its extremely authentic look alone.

•

LADY IN A CAGE

1964, 94 mins, US Ⓥ b/w

Dir Walter Grauman **Prod** Luther Davis **Scr** Luther Davis **Ph** Lee Garmes **Ed** Leon Barsha **Mus** Paul Glass **Art** Hal Pereira, Rudy Sternad

Act Olivia de Havilland, Ann Sothern, Jeff Corey, James Caan, Jennifer Billingsley, Rafael Campos (Paramount)

There's not a single redeeming character or characteristic to producer Luther Davis's sensationalistically vulgar screenplay [based on a novel by Robert Durand]. It is haphazardly constructed, full of holes, sometimes pretentious and in bad taste.

Had the basic premise—of an invalid woman trapped in her private home elevator when the power is cut off—been developed simply, neatly and realistically, gripping dramatic entertainment might have ensued. But Davis has chosen to employ his premise as a means to expose all the negative aspects of the human animal. He has infested the caged woman's house with as scummy an assortment of characters as literary imagination might conceive.

Among those who greedily invade her abode are a delirious wino (Jeff Corey), a plump prostitute (Ann Sothern) and three vicious young hoodlums (James Caan, Jennifer Billingsley and Rafael Campos).

Olivia de Havilland plays the unfortunate woman in the elevator, and gives one of those ranting, raving, wild-eyed performances often thought of as Academy Award oriented. Actually, the role appears to require more emotional stamina than histrionic deftness. Caan, as the sadistic leader of the little ratpack, appears to have been watching too many early Marlon Brando movies.

•

LADY IN CEMENT

1968, 93 mins, US Ⓥ ▭ col

Dir Gordon Douglas **Prod** Aaron Rosenberg **Scr** Marvin H. Albert, Jack Guss **Ph** Joseph Biroc **Ed** Robert Simpson **Mus** Hugo Montenegro **Art** Leroy Deane

Act Frank Sinatra, Raquel Welch, Richard Conte, Martin Gabel, Lainie Kazan, Joe E. Lewis (20th Century-Fox)

Lady in Cement, follow-up to *Tony Rome*, stars Frank Sinatra as a Miami private eye on the trail of people in whom there couldn't be less interest. Raquel Welch adds her limited, but beauteous contribution, and Dan Blocker is excellent as a sympathetic heavy.

Episodic script is from Marvin H. Albert's novel, in which Sinatra, while scuba-diving off his beat, discovers a nude looker anchored in cement on the floor of the bay. Blocker hires Sinatra to find his lost sweetie, who turns out to be the dead gal.

Welch, Martin Gabel and Steve Peck come under suspicion. Richard Conte is a local police detective, and Paul Henry appears as a vice squad officer, one of whose jobs involves working the streets in drag.

•

LADY IN RED, THE

1979, 93 mins, US Ⓥ ⦿ col

Dir Lewis Teague **Prod** Julie Corman **Scr** John Sayles **Ph** Daniel Lacambre **Ed** Larry Bock, Ron Medico, Lewis Teague **Art** Joe McAnelly

Act Pamela Sue Martin, Robert Conrad, Louise Fletcher, Christopher Lloyd, Robert Hogan (New World)

Ostensibly a return to the gangster genre, *The Lady in Red* is in many ways a compendium of variations on the "woman in jeopardy" format. The lady of the title gamely struggles through life as a tyrannized daughter, mistreated lover, ill-paid working girl, prisoner in a women's ward, professional hooker and full-fledged gangster, among other roles.

With her sights vaguely set on Hollywood, farm girl Pamela Sue Martin heads first for Chicago, where one mishap after another lands her in prison, then in the employ of classy madam Louise Fletcher.

Lewis Teague, a former second unit director, guides his large cast reasonably well through John Sayles's craftsmanlike script.

•

LADY IN THE DARK

1944, 100 mins, US col

Dir Mitchell Leisen **Prod** Mitchell Leisen **Scr** Frances Goodrich, Albert Hackett **Ph** Ray Rennahan **Ed** Alma Macrorie **Mus** Robert Emmett Dolan (dir.) **Art** Hans Dreier (sup.), Raoul Pene du Bois

Act Ginger Rogers, Ray Milland, Jon Hall, Warner Baxter, Barry Sullivan, Mischa Auer (Paramount)

Produced on a lavish scale and in very fine taste against backgrounds of a glittering character with costuming that fills the eye, *Lady in the Dark* is at the outset a technically superior piece of craftsmanship. Paramount spent $185,000 on costuming, and total negative nick is reported at $2.8 million. It looks it.

Mitchell Leisen produced and also directed from a sure-fire script based on the [1941] Broadway stage hit by Moss Hart, with music by Kurt Weill and lyrics by Ira Gershwin. An additional song, "Suddenly It's Spring," was written by Johnny Burke and James Van Heusen.

Ginger Rogers plays the editor of a fashion magazine who, realizing she's on the edge of a nervous breakdown, finally places herself in the hands of a psychoanalyst. She resists his ministrations but ultimately goes through with it all and finally finds herself, the wall she had built around herself and her emotions since childhood ultimately being broken down. The dream sessions are reflections of her disturbed mind.

Playing the ad manager for the society mag and the only man in her life who has sought to set himself up as Rogers's superior, irritating her all along the line, Ray Milland gives an excellent performance.

1944: NOMINATIONS: Best Color Cinematography, Color Art Direction, Scoring of a Musical Picture

•

LADY IN THE LAKE

1947, 103 mins, US Ⓥ ⦿ b/w

Dir Robert Montgomery **Prod** George Haight **Scr** Steve Fisher **Ph** Paul C. Vogel **Ed** Gene Ruggiero **Mus** David Snell **Art** Cedric Gibbons, Preston Ames

Act Robert Montgomery, Audrey Totter, Lloyd Nolan, Tom Tully, Leon Ames, Jayne Meadows (M-G-M)

Lady in the Lake institutes a novel method of telling the story, in which the camera itself is the protagonist, playing the lead role from the subjective viewpoint of star Robert Montgomery. Idea comes off excellently, transferring what otherwise would have been a fair whodunit into socko screen fare.

Montgomery starts telling the story in retrospect from a desk in his office, but when the picture dissolves into the action, the camera becomes Montgomery, presenting everything as it would have been seen through the star's eyes. Only time Montgomery is seen thereafter is when he's looking into a mirror or back at his desk for more bridging of the script.

Camera thus gets bashed by the villains, hits back in turn, smokes cigarettes, makes love and, in one of the most suspenseful sequences, drives a car in a hair-raising race that ends in a crash. Paul C. Vogel does a capital job with the lensing throughout, moving the camera to simulate the action of Montgomery's eyes as he walks up a flight of stairs, etc. Because it would be impossible under the circumstances to cut from Montgomery to another actor to whom he's talking, the rest of the cast was forced to learn much longer takes than usual.

Steve Fisher has wrapped up the Chandler novel into a tightly knit and rapidly paced screenplay. Montgomery plays private detective Philip Marlowe, who's dealt into a couple of murders when he tries to sell a story based on his experiences to a horror story mag. Audrey Totter, as the gal responsible for it all, is fine in both her tough-girl lines and as the love interest.

•

LADY IN WHITE

1988, 112 mins, US Ⓥ ⦿ col

Dir Frank LaLoggia **Prod** Andrew G. La Marca, Frank LaLoggia **Scr** Frank LaLoggia **Ph** Russell Carpenter **Ed** Steve Mann **Mus** Frank LaLoggia **Art** Richard K. Hummel

Act Lukas Haas, Len Cariou, Alex Rocco, Katherine Helmond, Jason Presson, Renata Vanni (New Century/Vista)

Lady in White is a superb supernatural horror film from independent filmmaker Frank LaLoggia who, with the help of cousin Charles LaLoggia, raised production money from 4,000 investors—many of whom live in and around the small town of Lyons in upstate New York that doubles for the fictional spooky Willowpoint Falls of the early 1960s.

At the center is big-eyed Lukas Haas, the youngest boy of a loving and earthy Italian family that is headed by his widowed dad, Angelo (Alex Rocco). On Halloween night, his school chums lock him in his classroom cloakroom where he is visited by those who wouldn't ordinarily be there—the ghost of a young girl about his age and a masked man searching for something in the heating grate. As the mystery unravels, it is revealed how they are connected.

LaLoggia manages to direct Haas equally well as a junior sleuth as he does the innocent youngster who fights with his older brother Geno (Jason Presson) and is easily influenced to go places he shouldn't by his bike-riding pals.

Rocco is particularly successful as the concerned father. Equally solid is Haas's brother, a good casting in Jason Presson, who turns out to be much less precocious than his younger sibling. This probably is as good a nightmare as any impressionable boy could have and still be suspenseful enough to get most adults' hearts going.

[A 119-min. *Director's Cut* was released on homevideo in 1997.]

•

LADY IS WILLING, THE

1942, 93 mins, US b/w

Dir Mitchell Leisen **Prod** Charles K. Feldman **Scr** James Edward Grant, Albert McCleery **Ph** Ted Tetzlaff **Ed** Eda Warren **Mus** W. Frank Harling

Act Marlene Dietrich, Fred MacMurray, Aline MacMahon, Arline Judge, Stanley Ridges, Roger Clark (Columbia/Feldman Group)

The Lady Is Willing is a racy and sophisticated marital comedy that carries a good share of amusement for adult audiences.

Picture carries light and breezy tempo in the first portion, with adoration of cute baby as motivating factor in holding interest. An inconclusive finish, with the oldy situation of an emergency operation necessary to save the child's life, and the pendulum-swinging problem of life-and-death crisis, allows the tale to sluff off with elemental formula convenience.

Familiar banter is apparent throughout. Despite this, strong performances by both principals succeed in holding up interest until the tale swings into heart-tug clichés. The baby's crisis is too extended and not handled in manner to hold audience attention on the dramatic elements attempted.

•

LADY JANE

1986, 142 mins, UK/US Ⓥ ⦿ col

Dir Trevor Nunn **Prod** Peter Snell **Scr** David Edgar **Ph** Douglas Slocombe **Ed** Anne V. Coates **Mus** Stephen Oliver **Art** Allan Cameron

Act Helena Bonham Carter, Cary Elwes, John Wood, Michael Hordern, Jill Bennett, Jane Lapotaire (Paramount)

With its emphasis on youthful idealism despoiled by treacherous, manipulative adults, *Lady Jane* emerges as a tragic historical romance tinged with a strong 1960s feeling.

In 1553, six years after the death of King Henry VIII and upon the death of his 16-year-old son, Edward VI, some extraordinary maneuverings brought to the English throne Henry's 15-year-old great-niece, the scholarly but unprepared Lady Jane Grey. She ruled for only nine days, after which she was toppled, imprisoned and finally executed by the Catholic Mary.

Lady Jane's parents and the Duke of Northumberland scheme to force a marriage between Jane and the latter's dissolute 17-year-old son, Guilford Dudley, to keep Britain free of the Pope's influence.

Very much centerstage, however, is the unlikely love story of Jane and Guilford. A grimly serious, exceedingly virginal girl at the outset, Jane is very quickly liberated in body and mind. The pair rhapsodize about a socialist-type utopia where all citizens would have equal rights.

Trevor Nunn has brought little of his tremendous theatrical flair to the screen here. Pic belongs squarely within the traditions of good taste and literate dialog one associates with the British cinema from the 1930s onwards. Performances are all top-drawer, beginning with newcomer Helena Bonham Carter in the title role.

●

LADY KILLER

1933, 67 mins, US Ⓥ ⊙ b/w

Dir Roy Del Ruth ***Prod*** Henry Blanke ***Scr*** Ben Markson, Lillie Hayward ***Ph*** Tony Gaudio ***Ed*** George Amy ***Art*** Robert Haas
Act James Cagney, Mae Clarke, Leslie Fenton, Margaret Lindsay, Henry O'Neill, Willard Robertson (Warner)

This James Cagney picture has the treat-'em-rough star drag his girlfriend by the hair across the room, pitch her emphatically through the door, climaxing with an enthusiastic sample of booting. Whole picture goes on a rampage with the you-be-damned personality that Cagney has so assiduously developed.

Story [*The Finger Man* by Rosalind Keating Shaffer] has other objectionable elements. Cagney plays an underworld crook who by accident crashes a Hollywood studio and earns his way to picture fame.

Crook angle is handled with a cheerful style of humor and there is a certain spirit about the Cagney character, played in his energetic way that carries its own persuasive charm. Comedy is first rate.

Mae Clarke does extremely well as the gang girl with Margaret Lindsay in attractive contrast in the straight role of a real picture actress.

●

LADYKILLERS, THE

1955, 96 mins, UK Ⓥ col

Dir Alexander Mackendrick ***Prod*** Michael Balcon ***Scr*** William Rose ***Ph*** Otto Heller ***Ed*** Jack Harris ***Mus*** Tristram Cary ***Art*** Jim Morahan
Act Alec Guinness, Cecil Parker, Herbert Lom, Peter Sellers, Katie Johnson, Danny Green (Ealing)

This is an amusing piece of hokum, being a parody of American gangsterdom interwoven with whimsy and exaggeration that makes it more of a macabre farce. Alec Guinness sinks his personality almost to the level of anonymity. Basic idea of thieves making a frail old lady an unwitting accomplice in their schemes is carried out in ludicrous and often tense situations.

A bunch of crooks planning a currency haul call on their leader, who has temporarily boarded with a genteel widow near a big London rail terminal. They pass as musicians gathering for rehearsals, but wouldn't deceive a baby.

Guinness tends to overact the sinister leader while Cecil Parker strikes just the right note as a conman posing as an army officer. Herbert Lom broods gloomily as the most ruthless of the plotters, with Peter Sellers contrasting well as the dumb muscle man. Danny Green completes the quintet.

1956: NOMINATION: Best Original Screenplay

●

LADY L

1965, 124 mins, US/Italy ▭ col

Dir Peter Ustinov ***Prod*** Carlo Ponti ***Scr*** Peter Ustinov ***Ph*** Henri Alekan ***Ed*** Roger Dwyre ***Mus*** Jean Francaix
Act Sophia Loren, Paul Newman, David Niven, Claude Dauphin, Philippe Noiret, Michel Piccoli (M-G-M/Ponti)

Experiment of starting and ending this pic with Sophia Loren as an 80-year-old, an alleged aristocrat with a somewhat simpering tedious voice, doesn't come off. Not till the Italian dish reverts to her own radiant, lush self will her followers settle down comfortably. David Niven is immaculately debonair and wittily amusing, but Paul Newman, though turning in a thoroughly competent performance, is not happily cast—his role calling out for the dependable mixture of solidity and lightness.

Film, from Romain Gary's novel, was originally planned as a straight drama, but things misfired. Ustinov was later brought in to do a doctoring job. But, despite the cost, he took on the chore only on the proviso that he could wipe the slate clean and start afresh. His nimble brain and characteristics have since clearly shaped the entire project.

Story, set in Paris and Switzerland at the turn of the century, has Loren as an aging, allegedly aristocratic mystery woman recounting her life story for the benefit of a biographer (Cecil Parker).

Ustinov weighs in with a choice cameo as the doddering Prince Otto.

●

LADY OF BURLESQUE
(UK: STRIPTEASE LADY)

1943, 89 mins, US Ⓥ b/w

Dir William A. Wellman ***Prod*** Hunt Stromberg ***Scr*** James Gunn ***Ph*** Robert de Grasse ***Ed*** James Newcom ***Mus*** Arthur Lange
Act Barbara Stanwyck, Michael O'Shea, J. Edward Bromberg, Iris Adrian, Marion Martin, Pinky Lee (United Artists)

Although *Lady of Burlesque* is based on Gypsy Rose Lee's novel, *G-String Murders*, story plows an obvious straight line in generating the whodunit angles, and two gal burlesque performers are knocked off in succession before the culprit is disclosed. But gallant trouping by Barbara Stanwyck, colorful background provided by Stromberg and speedy direction by William Wellman carry picture through for good entertainment for general audiences.

Story centers around a burlesque stock company established in an old opera house. Stanwyck is the striptease star in process of buildup by manager J. Edward Bromberg, with Michael O'Shea the lowdown comedian who's continually making romantic pitches to the girl.

Picture gets off to zestful start, with stage show background in which Stanwyck socks over "Take Off the E String, Play It On the G String," and Frank Fenton deliberately off-keys "So This Is You." There's a sudden raid and wagon backup; release on bail and then showdown to generate various motives for the coming murders. After swinging into the strange use of a G string for strangulation of the victims, it's just a matter of time before the windup.

1943: NOMINATION: Best Scoring of a Dramatic Picture

●

LADY ON A TRAIN

1945, 96 mins, US b/w

Dir Charles David ***Prod*** Felix Jackson ***Scr*** Edmund Beloin, Robert O'Brien ***Ph*** Woody Bredell ***Ed*** Ted Kent ***Mus*** Miklos Rozsa ***Art*** John B. Goodman, Robert Clatworthy
Act Deanna Durbin, Ralph Bellamy, Edward Everett Horton, Dan Duryea, George Coulouris, Allen Jenkins (Universal)

Lady on a Train is a mystery comedy containing plenty of fun for both whodunnit and laugh fans. Melodramatic elements in the Leslie Charteris original are flippantly treated without minimizing suspense, and the dialog contains a number of choice quips that are good for hefty laughs.

Deanna Durbin sings three tunes as well as handling herself excellently in the comedy role. Songs are all delivered against a background of menace. Actress is seen as a murder mystery addict who witnesses a murder from her train window while arriving in Grand Central station. Police discount her story and she turns to David Bruce, mystery writer, for help. Her pursuit of the writer to enlist his aid is good funning and accounts for some hilarious sequences.

1945: NOMINATION: Best Sound

●

LADY OSCAR

1979, 122 mins, Japan Ⓥ col

Dir Jacques Demy ***Prod*** Mataichiro Yamamoto ***Scr*** Jacques Demy, Patricia Louisiana Knop ***Ph*** Jean Penzer ***Ed*** Paul Davies ***Mus*** Michel Legrand ***Art*** Bernard Evein
Act Catriona Maccoll, Barry Stokes, Christina Bohm, Jonas Bergstrom, Terence Budd, Constance Chapman (Kitty Music)

French filmmaker Jacques Demy has given this international project, delving into French history, an opulent, posey, disarming naivete in keeping with its adaptation from a very popular Japanese comic strip [*Rose of Versailles* by Riyoko Ikeda], also a stage show in Japan.

The film has a historical charm that recalls the innocence of early Hollywood epics. Story takes place in 19th-century France where a girl is brought up like a boy by her noble martinet father fed up with a long line of girls. She becomes the bodyguard of the flighty queen of France, Marie Antoinette, and wears a man's uniform and is known as Oscar. The girl grew up with the family housekeeper's son. The latter loves her but she sees him only as a brother. This is to change as France heads for revolution.

The unknown British cast is acceptable. Catriona Maccoll is wofth further attention for her lovely limning of Oscar, a woman waiting to burst out of a man's clothing.

Film has fine art direction, costuming, music and technical qualities. The actual attack on the Bastille is a bit pithy for the reported $4 million outlay. Shooting on actual location in Versailles is an asset.

●

LADY SINGS THE BLUES

1972, 144 mins, US Ⓥ ⊙ ▭ col

Dir Sidney J. Furie ***Prod*** Jay Weston, James S. White ***Scr*** Terence McCloy, Chris Clark, Suzanne De Passe ***Ph*** John Alonzo ***Ed*** Argyle Nelson ***Mus*** Michel Legrand ***Art*** Carl Anderson
Act Diana Ross, Billy Dee Williams, Richard Pryor, James Callahan, Paul Hampton, Sid Melton (Paramount)

Individual opinions about *Lady Sings the Blues* may vary markedly, depending on a person's age, knowledge of jazz tradition and feeling for it and how one wishes to regard the late Billie Holiday as both a force and a victim of her times. However, the film serves as a very good screen debut vehicle for Diana Ross, supported strongly by excellent casting, handsome 1930s physical values and a script which is far better in dialog than structure.

Basis for the script is Holiday's autobiog *Lady Sings the Blues*, written with William Dufty only three years before her death in 1959 at age 44. Given that the script and production emphasis is on Ross as Holiday (and not on Holiday's life as interpreted by Ross), it still requires a severe gritting of teeth to overlook the truncations, telescoping, and omissions.

Holiday's personal romantic life herein is restricted to Billy Dee Williams as Louis McKay, her third husband. Williams makes an excellent opposite lead, and Richard Pryor registers strongly as her longtime piano-playing friend who eventually is beaten to death in L.A. by hoods who want him to pay for the dope he procured for her.

1972: NOMINATIONS: Best Actress (Diana Ross), Original Story & Screenplay, Costume Design, Art Direction, Adapted Score

●

LADY'S MORALS, A

1930, 86 mins, US b/w

Dir Sidney Franklin ***Scr*** Hans Kraly, Claudine West, John Meehan, Arthur Richman ***Ph*** George Barnes ***Ed*** Margaret Booth ***Art*** Cedric Gibbons
Act Grace Moore, Reginald Denny, Wallace Beery, Gus Shy, Jobyna Howland (Cosmopolitan/M-G-M)

A costume [from a story by Dorothy Farnum] play that rises above traditional handicaps.

The picture is full of brilliant touches and has some fine pictorial backgrounds. It has one serious defect. It suffers from a clumsy finish involving an awkward anti-climax. The romantic story is finished many hundreds of feet before the actual conclusion.

Paul (Reginald Denny), a young composer, is in love with Jenny Lind (Grace Moore) and pursues her from place to place. In a lonely tavern he engages the only room with a stove and tries to make capital out of surrendering it to the diva. He turns up among the spear-bearing supers of an opera troup in another city, at length making an impression on the songstress by his persistency.

Chief of picture's assets is Moore, an actress of indescribable charm. Denny is a revelation in his part, a happy bit of casting in a role that calls for deft handling.

●

LADY VANISHES, THE

1938, 96 mins, UK Ⓥ ⊙ ▭ b/w

Dir Alfred Hitchcock ***Prod*** [Edward Black] ***Scr*** Sidney Gilliat, Frank Launder ***Ph*** Jack Cox ***Ed*** R. E. Dearing ***Mus*** Louis Levy (dir.) ***Art*** Alex Vetchinsky
Act Margaret Lockwood, Michael Redgrave, Paul Lukas, May Whitty, Cecil Parker, Linden Travers (Gainsborough/Gaumont-British)

An elderly English governess, homeward bound, disappears from a transcontinental train, and a young girl, who says she recently received a blow on the head, is confronted by numerous other passengers who say they never saw the governess. This becomes so persistent the girl finally thinks she has gone nuts.

The story [from *The Wheel Spins* by Ethel Lina White] is sometimes eerie and eventually melodramatic, but it's all so well done as to make for intense interest. It flits from one set of characters to another and becomes slightly difficult to follow, but finally all joins up.

This film, minus the deft and artistic handling of the director, Alfred Hitchcock, despite its cast and photography, would not stand up for Grade A candidacy. Margaret Lockwood is the central femme character; Michael Redgrave, as the lead, is a trifle too flippant. Naunton Wayne, Basil Radford, Paul Lukas (as a credibly villainous doctor), May Whitty (as the governess) and Catherine Lacey (a villainess disguised as a nun) are excellent.

•

LADY VANISHES, THE
1979, 99 mins, UK Ⓥ ⊙ col
Dir Anthony Page ***Prod*** Tom Sachs ***Scr*** George Axelrod ***Ph*** Douglas Slocombe ***Ed*** Russell Lloyd ***Mus*** Richard Hartley ***Art*** Wilfrid Shingleton
Act Elliott Gould, Cybill Shepherd, Angela Lansbury, Herbert Lom, Ian Carmichael, Arthur Lowe (Hammer)

The Lady Vanishes is a midatlantic mish-mash with some moderately amusing moments but no cohesive style.

The production has Cybill Shepherd as a madcap Yank heiress and Elliott Gould as a *Life* mag photographer foiling a political conspiracy aboard a train outbound from prewar Germany. Slapstick suspense and mystery elements that will fool almost no one add up to a heavy-handed affair.

The script from an Ethel Lina White novel is best when dwelling on English eccentricity to make the film's most endearing impression. Shepherd and Gould stack up as contrived clichés, characters that jar rather than complement.

Alfred Hitchcock's original version, circa 1938, had pretty much everything the remake doesn't.

•

LADY WINDERMERE'S FAN
1925, 79 mins, US Ⓥ ⊗ b/w
Dir Ernst Lubitsch ***Scr*** Julien Josephson ***Ph*** Charles Van Enger
Act Ronald Colman, Irene Rich, May McAvoy, Bert Lytell, Edward Martindel (Warner)

This is not as good a picture as one might expect from Ernst Lubitsch. The trouble is not with the director, but with those who selected the story for him to direct. The tempo of this Oscar Wilde play is not that which Lubitsch can most effectively handle. Farce is his forte, and here they gave him a comedy-drama which is in reality almost melodrama and expect him to be at his best. He is good, but far from at his best.

Lady Windermere's Fan is an English society drama. Beautifully cast in so far as the five leading players are concerned, well acted by them, and with clever touches of the director's art furnished by Lubitsch. The whole, however, finally evolves into nothing more nor less than a good program picture.

•

LADY WITHOUT PASSPORT, A
1950, 72 mins, US b/w
Dir Joseph H. Lewis ***Prod*** Samuel Marx ***Scr*** Howard Dimsdale ***Ph*** Paul C. Vogel ***Ed*** Fredrick Y. Smith ***Mus*** David Raksin ***Art*** Cedric Gibbons, Edward Carfagno
Act Hedy Lamarr, John Hodiak, James Craig, George Macready, Steven Geray, Bruce Cowling (M-G-M)

Beginning is a bit too cryptic for quick understanding, but when plotline [adapted by Cyril Hume from a suggested story by Lawrence Taylor] does take shape, the story builds and holds attention. Joseph H. Lewis's direction spins it along expertly, neatly pacing the suspenseful sequences.

Hedy Lamarr is the lady of the title. Lingering in Cuba, she is used by an undercover immigration agent to set up a trap for the smuggling ring operated by George Macready. A complication is the romantic development between the lady and the agent.

Footage lensed in Cuba helps to supply an authentic touch. Cuban street scenes and Latin musical strains, an earthy rhumba by cafe dancer Nita Bieber are among the good touches backing the plot runoff.

•

LADY WITH THE DOG, THE
SEE: DAMA S SOBACHKOY

•

LADY WITH THE LAMP, THE
1951, 110 mins, UK b/w
Dir Herbert Wilcox ***Prod*** Herbert Wilcox ***Scr*** Warren Chetham-Strode ***Ph*** Austin Dempster ***Ed*** Bill Lewthwaite ***Mus*** Anthony Collins ***Art*** William C. Andrews
Act Anna Neagle, Michael Wilding, Gladys Young, Felix Aylmer, Sybil Thorndike, Arthur Young (Wilcox-Neagle/British Lion)

In *The Lady with the Lamp*, Anna Neagle adds another portrait to her screen gallery of famous women. Her characterization of Florence Nightingale is a sincerely moving study.

The script, taken from Regginald Berkeley's stage play, focuses attention on the more exciting and colorful aspects of Florence Nightingale's campaign. Main theme is told against a political background which brings in such famous characters as Gladstone, Lord Palmerston and Sidney Herbert.

The story opens shortly before the Crimean war when Florence Nightingale, with a training in nursing, refuses to be a member of the leisure class into which born, but insists on continuing her work. The Minister of War, a steadfast believer in Nightingale's theories, gets her to organize a band of nurses to tend the wounded at Scutari.

Michael Wilding is not too happily cast as Sidney Herbert, War Minister. Within limitations, he makes the best of this part. The strong feature cast includes Felix Aylmer, with an exceptionally good study of Lord Palmerston. Herbert Wilcox, as always, directs in a plain, straightforward manner.

•

LADY WITH THE LITTLE DOG, THE
SEE: DAMA S SOBACHKOY

•

LAIR OF THE WHITE WORM, THE
1989, 93 mins, UK Ⓥ ⊙ col
Dir Ken Russell ***Prod*** Ken Russell ***Scr*** Ken Russell ***Ph*** Dick Bush ***Ed*** Peter Davies ***Mus*** Stanislas Syrewicz ***Art*** Anne Tilby
Act Amanda Donohoe, Hugh Grant, Catherine Oxenberg, Sammi Davis, Peter Capaldi, Stratford Johns (White Lair/Vestron)

Adapted from a tale by Bram Stoker, creator of Dracula, *Lair*, a rollicking, terrifying, post-psychedelic headtrip, features a fangy vampiress of unmatched erotic allure. Lady Sylvia Marsh (Amanda Donohoe) lives in a sprawling mansion not far from the state-of-the-art castle inhabited by Lord James D'Ampton (Hugh Grant).

On the day of a big party, just before nightfall, archaeology student Angus (Peter Capaldi) finds a bizarre, unclassifiable skull. The castle party is celebrating Lord James's inheritance of the estate as well as a family holiday commemorating a legendary ancestor said to have slain a dragon. In the D'Ampton clan mythology, the dragon is represented as an overblown, jawsy white worm.

Soon the duke and the digger divine an eerie connection between the mysteriously burgled skull, the white worm legend and cases of snakebite plus more strange disappearances close by the Lady's mansion. Then things start to get scary.

Donohoe as the vampire seductress projects a beguiling sexuality that should suck the resistance out of all but the most cold-blooded critics. She is also hilarious, a virtue shared by everyone and everything in *The Lair of the White Worm*.

•

LAKE PLACID
1999, 82 mins, US Ⓥ ⊙ ▭ col
Dir Steve Miner ***Prod*** David E. Kelley, Michael Pressman ***Scr*** David E. Kelley ***Ph*** Daryn Okada ***Ed*** Marshall Harvey, Paul Hirsch ***Mus*** John Ottman ***Art*** John Willett
Act Bill Pullman, Bridget Fonda, Oliver Platt, Brendan Gleeson, Betty White, David Lewis (Rocking Chair/Phoenix/Fox 2000)

TV maestro David E. Kelley (*Ally McBeal, Picket Fences*) goes fishing in feature film waters and comes back with nothing for supper. This is a lamer-than-lane attempt at stirring up the summer movie scene with a scary creature-in-the-depths scenario.

The ultra-abbreviated nature of pic suggests major post-production problems; first tip-off is an early, uncredited appearance [as Bridget Fonda's b.f] by Adam Arkin, longtime regular on Kelley's *Chicago Hope* series, who comes and goes so fast as to barely register. More serious is the absence of a genuine third act containing the kind of roller-coaster thrills this genre demands and that would be expected from vet horror helmer Steve Miner.

The mayhem starts promptly on a glassy lake in northern Maine as a diver is chomped in half. Boston paleontologist Kelly Scott (Fonda) goes to study a tooth extracted from the diver's torso and finds it to be "ancient."

Soon, Fish & Game studmuffin Jack Wells (Bill Pullman) must contend not only with Kelly's whining, endlessly unfunny spatting between eccentric millionaire and croc aficionado Hector Cyr (Oliver Platt) and Sheriff Hank Keough (Brendan Gleeson), and a nutty widow who lives by the lake, but with a fresh wave of attacks by the creature, which turns out to be a 30-foot crocodile that has managed to swim all the way from its warm natural habitat in Asia.

Whatever attracted fine actors Pullman, Fonda, Gleeson and Platt to the script is now gone, as they all search desperately for their characters.

•

LA LUNA
1979, 145 mins, Italy col
Dir Bernardo Bertolucci ***Prod*** Giovanni Bertolucci ***Scr*** Giuseppe Bertolucci, Bernardo Bertolucci, Clare Peploe ***Ph*** Vittorio Storaro ***Ed*** Gabriella Cristiani
Act Jill Clayburgh, Matthew Barry, Renato Salvatori, Tomas Milian, Fred Gwynne, Veronica Lazar (20th Century-Fox/Fiction)

La Luna is a spectacle-sized melodrama filled with a variety of themes—plots and subplots that merge asymmetrically into a melodramatic mold. The saga is of Jill Clayburgh as Yank lyric star afflicted with professional neuroses, fading pipes, a son on drugs and a close-to-incest mother-son development.

Sudden death of singer's spouse and decision to resume singing in Italy with son Joe accompanying, moves the scene from Brooklyn Heights to Rome where the mother-son cleft takes over from Verdi appearances. Her battle to break down his detachment and drug habit is the core of the film—with her own career at stake as the voice gives under stress.

Clayburgh is hard pressed to sustain the melodramatics of *Luna*.

•

LAMBADA
1990, 98 mins, US Ⓥ ⊙ ▭ col
Dir Joel Silberg ***Prod*** Peter Shepherd ***Scr*** Joel Silberg, Sheldon Renan ***Ph*** Roberto D'Ettore Piazzoli ***Ed*** Marcus Manton ***Mus*** Greg Manton ***Art*** Bill Cornford
Act J. Eddie Peck, Melora Hardin, Shabba-Doo, Ricky Paull Goldin, Basil Hoffman (Cannon)

Lambada's peripheral dance segs don't add up to $7 worth of lambada. Still, director/cowriter Joel Silberg keeps the story lively on a cartoonish level.

Eddie Peck plays the Beverly Hills teacher by day, East L.A. lambada dancer by night, his sculpted dancer's physique straining the credibility of this most unlikely of teen fantasy scenarios. He forgoes evenings at home with his wife and son to motorbike over to the lambada club where he teaches math in the back room to a gang of East Side dropouts.

His lambada prowess intrigues one of the BH highschoolers, sexually precocious Sandy (Melora Hardin), who stumbles onto the scene and sets out to seduce or blackmail him, unaware of his real, noble reason for leading this double life.

The dancing occupies little screen time compared to the sudsy intrigue Sandy stirs up on the school front, and what lambadaing there is, is photographed mostly in tight titillating shots that lack context.

•

LAMERICA
1994, 125 mins, Italy/France Ⓥ ▭ col
Dir Gianni Amelio ***Prod*** Mario Cecchi Gori, Vittorio Cecchi Gori ***Scr*** Gianni Amelio, Andrea Porporati, Alessandro Sermoneta ***Ph*** Luca Bigazzi ***Ed*** Simona Paggi ***Mus*** Franco Piersanti ***Art*** Giuseppe M. Gaudino
Act Enrico Lo Verso, Michele Placido, Carmelo Di Mazzarelli, Piro Milkani (CGG Tiger/Arena)

Two tough Italian con artists come face to face with the nightmarish despair of post-Communist Albania in *Lamerica*, a hard-hitting, often moving film by top Italo helmer Gianni Amelio. Pic's uncompromising scorn for the two exploiters is matched by its hellish vision of a starving nation desperately searching for an escape hatch.

Enrico Lo Verso, the swarthy young carabineer from Amelio's previous *The Stolen Children*, returns as Gino, an apprentice swindler who comes to Albania with the more experienced Fiore (Michele Placido) to buy a shoe factory they never intend to run. Their get-rich-quick scheme is to cash in on Italian government aid to Albania's devastated post-Communist economy, but first they need to find a local majority partner to play the role of the company's puppet president.

The choice falls on 80-year-old Spiro (non-pro Carmelo Di Mazzarelli), a helpless senior who has been driven mad by 20 years of hard labor in the Communist prisons. The story takes its first turn when Spiro disappears. Gino's angry search for the old man is a frightening descent into the world of no-way-out poverty. His arrogance and cruelty melt away as he is dispossessed of everything he owns.

Despite its grounding in recent history, there's nothing documentary about *Lamerica*'s carefully planned and paced scenes, lensed in chillingly desaturated color and epic widescreen by Luca Bigazzi. Lo Verso is at the height of his powers here, lending intensity to the cocky, despicably self-serving Gino, who gets a comeuppance of biblical proportions.

Title comes from Amelio's metaphoric connection between the Albanians straining to reach the promised land of Italy, and the impoverished generation of Italians who left their country behind to go to America.

•

LANCELOT AND GUINEVERE
(US: SWORD OF LANCELOT)
1963, 116 mins, UK/US Ⓥ ▭ col
Dir Cornel Wilde ***Prod*** Cornel Wilde, Bernard Luber ***Scr*** Richard Schayer, Jefferson Pascal ***Ph*** Harry Waxman ***Ed*** Frederick Wilson ***Mus*** Ron Goodwin ***Art*** Maurice Carter
Act Cornel Wilde, Jean Wallace, Brian Aherne, George Baker, John Longden, Iain Gregory (Emblem/Universal)

This version of the much-told tale of King Arthur and the Knights of the Round Table is an elaborately mounted production that generates fair amounts of interest and excitement when the fighting's going on but barely rises above the routine in storytelling the legend.

It's Cornel Wilde most of the way, he having coproduced, directed and costarred with his wife, Jean Wallace, latter making a beautiful Guinevere.

This outing smacks of modernization in terms of plot situation. But not filmmaking technique. King Arthur eagerly awaits his Guinevere at the altar in his Camelot and she's escorted by the gallant Lancelot (Wilde). The marriage takes place, but despite the affection Lancelot feels for his king, he shares a bed with the lady whose name he reduces in the dialog to just plain Guin.

The outdoor scenes, which were filmed in Yugoslavia with native cavalrymen, are in some measure pictorially effective but at times director Wilde is just focusing on so much confused action. No telling how much footage was left on the plains of Titoland or the cutting-room floor of Pinewood Studios, London, where the interiors were lensed.

An accomplished job is turned in by Brian Aherne, as King Arthur, who's able to give a good reading even when dialog is stilted. Wilde and Wallace are believable, John Longden is properly sinister as Arthur's rival for the crown and Iain Gregory is appealing as a young knight fighting side by side with Lancelot.

•

LAND AND FREEDOM
1995, 106 mins, UK/Spain/Germany Ⓥ col
Dir Ken Loach ***Prod*** Rebecca O'Brien ***Scr*** Jim Allen ***Ph*** Barry Ackroyd ***Ed*** Jonathan Morris ***Mus*** George Fenton ***Art*** llorenc Miquel
Act Ian Hart, Rosana Pastor, Iciar Bollain, Tom Gilroy, Marc Martinez, Frederic Pierrot (Parallax/Messidor/Road Movies)

Brit helmer Ken Loach's most ambitious film to date, *Land and Freedom* follows a Liverpudlian to the Republican trenches and political treachery of the Spanish Civil War. Despite a slight windiness in its political discussions, pic's superb performances, gentle humor, human warmth, action sequences and beautifully teased-out love story should make this one of the must-see art movies of the year.

Script by Jim Allen, who most recently penned *Raining Stones* for Loach, covers much the same historical terrain as George Orwell's celebrated account of the conflict, *Homage to Catalonia*. One crucial difference is that the protagonist here is a salt-of-the-earth Liverpudlian who lacks Orwell's political articulateness, even though he comes to share his indignation. By May 1937, instead of fighting Franco, the Republicans were divided in Barcelona into bitter, rival groups—the militia and anarchists on one side, the Communists on the other.

Young Communist Dave (Ian Hart) decides to go to Spain to fight fascism. He falls in with a French kid and is sent to fight with the militia on the Republican front in Aragon. However, while training some volunteers, Dave's 1896 Mauser blows up in his face. Hospitalized in Barcelona, he enters a delicately portrayed relationship with Blanca (Rosana Pastor), a militia woman from his unit.

Loach and Allen's thesis is that the attempts by Spain's working class to effect a revolution were systematically destroyed by a Stalinist-controlled Republican government, abetted by the Spanish Communist Party, because of Stalin's desire to appease the capitalist West.

Hart and Pastor give outstanding, understated perfs as Dave and Blanca, and other thesps are solid. Though never arid, the film's political gabfests may prove overlong for some. Loach's real triumph, however, is to get the viewer rooting for characters in a conflict that, for most, is as remote as the Trojan War.

•

LAND BEFORE TIME, THE
1988, 66 mins, US Ⓥ ⊙ col
Dir Don Bluth ***Prod*** Don Bluth, Gary Goldman, John Pomeroy ***Scr*** Stu Krieger ***Ph*** Jim Mann ***Ed*** Dan Molina, John K. Carr ***Mus*** James Horner ***Art*** Don Bluth (Sullivan-Bluth/Amblin)

Sure, kids like dinosaurs, but beyond that, premise doesn't find far to go. Story is about Littlefoot (Gabriel Damon), an innocent dinosaur tyke who gets separated from his family and after a perilous journey finds them again in a new land.

In this case it's a journey from a dried-up part of the land to another, known as the Great Valley, where the herds frolic in abundant greenery. After Littlefoot's mother dies, he has to make the journey alone, dodging hazards like earthquakes, volcanoes and a predatory carnivore named Sharptooth. Along the way, he pulls together a band of other little dinosaurs of different species who've been brought up not to associate with each other.

Idea develops that surviving in a changing environment depends on achieving unity among the species.

For the most part, pic is about as engaging as what's found on Saturday morning TV.

•

LANDLORD, THE
1970, 112 mins, US col
Dir Hal Ashby ***Prod*** Norman Jewison ***Scr*** William Gunn ***Ph*** Gordon Willis ***Ed*** William Abbott Sawyer, Edward Warschilka ***Mus*** Al Kooper ***Art*** Robert Boyle
Act Beau Bridges, Lee Grant, Diana Sands, Pearl Bailey, Marki Bey, Louis Gossett (United Artists/Mirisch)

Beau Bridges heads the uniformly excellent cast as a bored rich youth who buys a black ghetto apartment building and learns something about life.

A novel by Kristin Hunter has been scripted into what is essentially a two-part story. First, Bridges and his economically secure family are played off against the black tenants whom he inherits in his ghetto building. Then, Bridges's sexual encounter with married Diana Sands results in a mixed-race baby and a confrontation with some hard facts of life.

The film is most successful when people are interacting with people. Pearl Bailey's performance is a terrific showpiece for her talents. Sands makes a powerful impression as a flirtatious but loving wife to Louis Gossett.

1970: NOMINATION: Best Supp. Actress (Lee Grant)

•

LAND OF THE PHARAOHS
1955, 103 mins, US Ⓥ ⊙ ▭ col
Dir Howard Hawks ***Prod*** Howard Hawks ***Scr*** William Faulkner, Harry Kurnitz, Harold Jack Bloom ***Ph*** Lee Garmes, Russell Harlan ***Ed*** Rudi Fehr, V. Sagovsky ***Mus*** Dimitri Tiomkin ***Art*** Alexandre Trauner
Act Jack Hawkins, Joan Collins, Dewey Martin, Alexis Minotis, James Robertson Justice, Luisa Boni (Continental/Warner)

Egypt of 5,000 years ago comes to life in *Land of the Pharaohs*, a tremendous film spectacle. From the opening shot of a great pharaoh and his thousands of soldiers returning from successful battle laden with vast treasure, an audience is constantly overwhelmed with spectacle, either in the use of cast thousands, tremendously sized settings or the surging background score by Dimitri Tiomkin.

The story tells of a great pharaoh, ably played by Jack Hawkins, who for 30 years drives his people to build a pyramid in which his body and treasure shall rest secure for evermore, and of a woman, portrayed by Joan Collins, a captivating bundle of s.a., who conspires to win his kingdom and riches for herself.

When the viewing senses begin to dull from the tremendous load of spectacle, the script and Hawks's direction wisely switch to sex and intrigue.

Alexis Minotis, Greek actor, lends the picture a fine performance as Hamar, the high priest.

•

LAND THAT TIME FORGOT, THE
1975, 91 mins, UK Ⓥ col
Dir Kevin Connor ***Prod*** John Dark ***Scr*** James Cawthorn, Michael Moorcock ***Ph*** Alan Hume ***Ed*** John Ireland ***Mus*** Douglas Gamley ***Art*** Bert Davey
Act Doug McClure, John McEnery, Susan Penhaligon, Keith Barron, Anthony Ainley, Godfrey James (American International)

Adaptated from Edgar Rice Burroughs's *The Land That Time Forgot*, the "land" in question is an uncharted island, icy on the outside and smoldering within, that's populated with all sorts of big critters.

This island of Caprona is reached by a German submarine which torpedoes an English ship. The survivors, led by Doug McClure, come aboard and capture the sub. But McEnery gets it back. Then McClure takes over again. By this time, it's no wonder the sub is lost in the Antarctic. Luckily, they spot Caprona, easing the sub through an underground tunnel where it's attacked by a mosasaurus.

Somebody identifies the problem immediately. "This can't be. These creatures have been extinct for millions of years."

•

LAND UNKNOWN, THE
1957, 78 mins, US Ⓥ ▭ b/w
Dir Virgil Vogel ***Prod*** William Alland ***Scr*** Laszlo Gorog ***Ph*** Ellis W. Carter ***Ed*** Fred McDowell ***Mus*** Joseph Gershenson ***Art*** Alexander Golitzen, Richard H. Riedel
Act Jock Mahoney, Shawn Smith, William Reynolds, Henry Brandon, Douglas R. Kennedy, Phil Harvey (Universal)

Discovery by Admiral Byrd's 1947 South Pole expedition of a mysterious warm-water area in the center of ice-packed Antarctica serves as a basis for this imaginative science fictioner [from a story by Charles Palmer, adaptation by William N. Robson].

Production recounts adventures of a helicopter party forced down in this strange region which is the objective of a navy expedition. Area is untouched by the Ice Age, going back to the Mesozoic era, a setting which provides thrills as party fights against such creatures as a giant tyrannosaurus rex and a swimming elasmosaurus. Stark realism is afforded through the remarkable smooth and lifelike movement of these creatures, special effected by Fred Knoth, Orien Ernest and Jack Kevan.

Jock Mahoney plays a navy scientist in charge of expedition, Shawn Smith a news hen and William Reynolds the helicopter pilot. Fourth member of the party is a mechanic (Phil Harvey). Cast generally gives a good account of themselves.

•

LASER MAN, THE
1988, 92 mins, US/Hong Kong Ⓥ col
Dir Peter Wang ***Prod*** Peter Wang ***Scr*** Peter Wang ***Ph*** Ernest Dickerson ***Ed*** Grahame Weinbren ***Mus*** Mason Daring ***Art*** Lester Cohen
Act Marc Hayashi, Maryann Urbano, Tony Leung, Peter Wang, Joan Copeland, Sally Yeh (Wang/Film Workshop)

The Laser Man is a quirky, cross-cultural, high-tech comedy about serious matters from Peter Wang, who made an impression with *A Great Wall*. Self-consciously implausible story concerning the manipulation of a laser expert by big business serves as a pegboard on which Wang hangs any number of amusing observations about The Melting Pot, 1988, particularly where Chinese-Americans are concerned.

Laser researcher Arthur Weiss (Marc Hayashi) accidentally kills a colleague in an experiment, and is instantly rendered so unemployable that he is forced to sign on with a suspicious firm involved in space-age weaponry and arms smuggling.

Weiss has a Jewish mother (Joan Copeland) who happens to believe she has a Chinese soul and persists in cooking perfectly dreadful Chinese meals. Joey Chung (Tony Leung), Arthur's best friend, is married to a Jewish woman and reveals that he has never slept with a Chinese, never, that is, until he meets Susu (Sally Yeh), a stunning, newly arrived immigrant who lives and works in a massage parlor and dreams of going to Las Vegas. Last, but certainly not least, there is Janet (Maryann Urbano), a Caucasian woman obsessed with things Oriental, who, to Arthur's distinct frustration, would rather meditate than make love.

Unfortunately, the plotting is not always hospitable to the engagingly flippant tone Wang mostly maintains, especially when one of the major characters becomes the victim of the fancy gun, only to be casually resurrected later on. Scenes with the women are invariably the most human, humorous and resonant in the film.

•

LASKY JEDNE PLAVOVLASKY
(LOVES OF A BLONDE; A BLONDE IN LOVE)
1965, 85 mins, Czechoslovakia Ⓥ ⊙ b/w
Dir Milos Forman ***Scr*** Jaroslav Papousek, Milos Forman, Ivan Passer ***Ph*** Miroslav Ondricek ***Ed*** Miroslav Hajek ***Mus*** Evzen Illin ***Art*** Karel Cerny

Act Hana Brejchova, Vladimir Pucholt, Vladimir Mensik, Antonin Blazejovsky, Jiri Hruby, Milada Jezkova (Barrandov)

This is a lightweight item with plenty of charm to overcome the basic fragility of its plot.

Boy meets girl at a dance organized for factory workers. Couple falls in love and eventually goes to bed where the usual promises are exchanged. The day after, each returns to work, but the gal believes the boy and tracks him down at his surprised parents' home.

Hana Brejchova and Vladimir Pucholt make a charming couple, with the boy especially good in his role. Standout, however, is thesping by an unbilled trio impersonating soldiers on leave who shyly try to contact some girls at a dance.

Milos Forman's direction shows promise, and his handling of a nude scene between boy and girl is tasteful. Humorous observations on the human scene appear to be his forte.

•

LASSIE

1994, 92 mins, US Ⓥ col

Dir Daniel Petrie ***Prod*** Lorne Michaels ***Scr*** Matthew Jacobs, Gary Ross, Elizabeth Anderson ***Ph*** Kenneth MacMillan ***Ed*** Steve Mirkovich ***Mus*** Basil Poledouris ***Art*** Paul Peters

Act Thomas Guiry, Helen Slater, Jon Tenney, Brittany Boyd, Frederic Forrest, Richard Farnsworth (Broadway/Paramount)

New telling is a well-wrought, affecting adventure, thanks to the steady hand of vet helmsman Daniel Petrie and a sensitive, insightful screenplay that focuses on the human drama while providing a long leash to the famed collie's canine charisma, cunning and athletic prowess. This *Lassie* is classy.

Strongest appeal lies in the sharply observed and emotionally rich portrayal of a family confronting challenges together. When contractor Steve Turner (Jon Tenney) decides to move his family from Baltimore to the ancestral country home of his late wife, in the Shenandoah Valley, least thrilled is teen son Matthew (Thomas Guiry), a pint-sized rebel on a skateboard. Little sister Jennifer (Brittany Boyd) is more enthusiastic, and step-mom Laura (Helen Slater) is supportive, if overwhelmed by the prospect of raising the kids and following her man to the boondocks.

On the way to their old Virginia home, a spry four-pawed friend named Lassie leaps into their car and their lives, and helps them face the challenges of living on the land.

One of the strongest elements of this *Lassie* is the authenticity of the Garland clan and their modern farming ethos, which includes spiffy ATVs for the boys, a posh mansion with solar panels, an indoor pool and lots of Santa Fe-chic furnishings. The two sons are particularly well cast and believable as contemporary rural American kids.

•

LASSIE COME HOME

1943, 90 mins, US Ⓥ ⊙ col

Dir Fred M. Wilcox ***Prod*** Samuel Marx ***Scr*** Hugo Butler ***Ph*** Leonard Smith ***Ed*** Ben Lewis ***Mus*** Daniele Amfitheatrof

Act Roddy McDowall, Donald Crisp, May Whitty, Edmund Gwenn, Elsa Lanchester, Elizabeth Taylor (M-G-M)

From the novel of Eric Knight, and with Fred M. Wilcox directing his first feature picture, *Lassie* emerges as nice entertainment enhanced by color photography and good scenic shots.

One of the film's major assets is its cast, good from top to bottom. Lassie, a beautiful collie, is given a great deal of camera attention and is docile, if not extraordinarily trained. The dog is the focal point for a great deal of pathos.

Her Yorkshire owner (Donald Crisp) sells her to the lord of the manor, thus depriving his son (Roddy McDowall) of his bosom companion. The dog escapes a couple of times to rejoin McDowall, then finally makes a trek of hundreds of miles from Scotland to England to get back to the kid. The sentimental angles are something akin to McDowall's *My Friend Flicka* but the kid is a solid trouper. Crisp, as his father, is excellent; ditto Elsa Lanchester, playing McDowall's mother.

Considering this is Wilcox's first effort with a feature film, his work is promising. His characters are believable and that's especially important in a film of this type.

•

LASSITER

1984, 100 mins, US Ⓥ ⊙ col

Dir Roger Young ***Prod*** Albert S. Ruddy ***Scr*** David Taylor ***Ph*** Gil Taylor ***Ed*** Allan Jacobs, Benjamin Weissman ***Mus*** Ken Thorne ***Art*** Peter Mullins

Act Tom Selleck, Jane Seymour, Lauren Hutton, Bob Hoskins, Joe Regalbuto, Ed Lauter (Golden Harvest)

Set in London in 1934, *Lassiter* is part caper picture, part intrigue story. Nick Lassiter (Tom Selleck) is an elegant jewel thief who is blackmailed by a coalition of the FBI and English police to liberate $10 million in Nazi diamonds passing through London. Selleck resists, but really isn't given much choice since the alternative is a stay in a British prison.

The diamonds are to be transported out of London by none other than Lauren Hutton, playing German agent Countess Kari von Fursten.

Hutton is totally unbelievable with her Germanic accent and evil habits. As the girlfriend, Jane Seymour is wasted. Her role is basically to stand by as Selleck races about trying to grab the diamonds and run.

•

LAST ACTION HERO

1993, 130 mins, US Ⓥ ⊙ ▭ col

Dir John McTiernan ***Prod*** Steve Roth, John McTiernan ***Scr*** Shane Black, David Arnott, [William Goldman] ***Ph*** Dean Semler ***Ed*** John Wright ***Mus*** Michael Kamen ***Art*** Eugenio Zanetti

Act Arnold Schwarzenegger, F. Murray Abraham, Art Carney, Charles Dance, Anthony Quinn, Austin O'Brien (Columbia/Oak)

Last Action Hero is a joyless, soulless machine of a movie, an $80 million-plus mishmash of fantasy, industry in-jokes, self-referential parody, film-buff gags and too-big action set-pieces.

Arnold Schwarzenegger plays indestructible screen superhero Jack Slater, whose prophetic signature phrase to his enemies when they try to harm him is, "Big Mistake." That's what he's made here.

The central problem is that the picture is based on a gimmick [from a screen story by Zack Penn and Adam Leff] rather than a story, so the viewer is presented with a succession of arbitrary scenes in which nothing is at stake because, in context, it's almost all "fiction" anyway.

Little 11-year-old Danny Madigan (Austin O'Brien) is invited by projectionist friend Nick (Robert Prosky) to a midnight private screening of Slater's latest picture, simply titled *Jack Slater IV*. Nick presents Danny with a golden magic ticket, a "passport to another world" handed down from Houdini, with which Danny passes into the world onscreen.

Benedict (Charles Dance), sinister triggerman of a mobster (Anthony Quinn), comes into possession of the magic ticket and takes his evil ways into the "real" world of Times Square, followed by Danny and Slater, who is dismayed to discover that violence can actually hurt and that his entire life has been lived in movies.

It's all heavy, empty and exceptionally noisy. On a character level, Arnold is Arnold. Everyone else seems to have checked in for a nice payday. Jabbering incessantly and always badgering his hero, O'Brien, onscreen most of the time, delivers a one-note performance.

•

LAST AMERICAN HERO, THE

1973, 95 mins, US Ⓥ ▭ col

Dir Lamont Johnson ***Prod*** William Roberts, John Cutts ***Scr*** William Roberts ***Ph*** George Silano ***Ed*** Tom Rolf, Robbe Roberts ***Mus*** Charles Fox ***Art*** Lawrence Paull

Act Jeff Bridges, Valerie Perrine, Geraldine Fitzgerald, Ned Beatty, Art Lund, Gary Busey (20th Century-Fox)

After a fumbling start which looks like bad editing for TV, *The Last American Hero* [based on two articles by Tom Wolfe] settles into some good, gritty, family Americana, with Jeff Bridges excellent as a flamboyant auto racer determined to succeed on his own terms and right a wrong to his father, played expertly by Art Lund.

Bridges and Gary Busey are moonshiner Lund's boys, with Geraldine Fitzgerald a concerned wife and mother. Bridges's backroad hot-rodding outrages a revenuer into busting Lund, who gets time for illegal liquor distilling. Bridges takes to the racing circuit to buy Lund some prison privileges.

Between the script, Lamont Johnson's sure direction and the excellent performances, all but the early choppy scenes add up to a well-told story.

•

LAST ANGRY MAN, THE

1959, 100 mins, US Ⓥ col

Dir Daniel Mann ***Prod*** Fred Kohlmar ***Scr*** Gerald Green, Richard Murphy ***Ph*** James Wong Howe ***Ed*** Charles Nelson ***Mus*** George Duning

Act Paul Muni, David Wayne, Betsy Palmer, Luther Adler, Joby Baker, Nancy Pollock (Columbia)

The Last Angry Man is as pungent and indelible as Brooklyn on a hot summer afternoon. It has faults: but it is possible to overlook whatever imperfections stud the production because so much of it is so good and, add, so rare.

The film is taken from Gerald Green's bestselling novel about a Jewish doctor, a character based on Green's own father. Director Daniel Mann had his problems in getting the story on film, shooting much of it on Brooklyn locations, but the finished product is worth the labor.

The conflict in the story arises from the lifetime of selfless service by the doctor (Paul Muni) when placed in conjunction with the commercial demands of contemporary television. Television wants to exploit the Jewish doctor, to associate with him so it can claim some of his virtues. Muni is an immigrant who has absorbed his Americanism from Jefferson, from Emerson and Thoreau, and he believes what they said.

Muni gives a superlative performance. Someone chides him at one point for thinking of himself as an Albert Schweitzer. A Schweitzer he isn't, but in Muni's character delineation it's apparent it's the men like him who keep the world going. David Wayne, as his abrasive agent, is allowed no histrionics, but his conviction must be absolute. Wayne is as persuasive as his narrow lapels and button-down collars.

1959: NOMINATIONS: Best Actor (Paul Muni), B&W Art Direction

•

LAST BOY SCOUT, THE

1991, 105 mins, US Ⓥ ⊙ ▭ col

Dir Tony Scott ***Prod*** Joel Silver, Michael Levy ***Scr*** Shane Black ***Ph*** Ward Russell ***Ed*** Mark Goldblatt, Mark Helfrich ***Mus*** Michael Kamen ***Art*** Brian Morris

Act Bruce Willis, Damon Wayans, Chelsea Field, Noble Willingham, Taylor Negron, Danielle Harris (Geffen/Silver)

Despite the bidding war surrounding Shane Black's script (and its ultimate seven-figure purchase price), there's really nothing special about this entertaining if mindless shoot-'em-up other than an ample supply of amusing juvenile putdowns and elaborate action sequences. Black should know the territory, having penned *Lethal Weapon* and the first draft of its sequel.

Equipped with a persona suited to his gifts, Bruce Willis limns a former Secret Service agent whose devotion to justice (accounting for pic's title) put him out on the street scrounging for work as a sleazy p.i. Willis plays the part as a world-weary Bogart wannabe, grounded in domestic trappings by partial estrangement from his wife and daughter.

The plot [story by Black and Greg Hicks] is a haze of barely connected storylines about political corruption, pro-football, gambling, infidelity, and blackmail—a sort of poor man's *The Big Sleep*, but here all the questions are answered by another car chase, smashing someone in the face or shooting someone in the forehead.

Willis gets yanked into the action when he's asked to protect a stripper (Halle Berry), g.f. of a former pro quarterback (Damon Wayans) banned from the game for gambling. There's not a lot of chemistry between Willis and Wayans, but both can be flat-out funny, and the script provides them plenty of opportunity to zing each other as well as the cartoonish bad guys.

•

LAST COMMAND, THE

1928, 90 mins, US Ⓥ ⊗ b/w

Dir Josef von Sternberg ***Prod*** Joseph Bachman ***Scr*** John F. Goodrich, Herman J. Mankiewicz ***Ph*** Bert Glennon ***Art*** Hans Dreier

Act Emil Jannings, Evelyn Brent, William Powell, Nicholas Soussanin, Michael Visaroff (Paramount)

Russia in the early days of the First World War and the revolution. Emil Jannings is the commander-in-chief of the czar's armies in the field. (The picture's working title was *The General*.) The general, overthrown and overwhelmed by the revolutionists, drifts to Hollywood, to become a $7.50-a-day extra waiting in a rooming house for a call.

It comes when a Russian picture director requiring a movie army recognizes a photo of the general as the same who whipped him in Russia in 1914, when the director then was a starving actor-revolutionist. They make him a general again, at $7.50 daily, with many studio scenes, to lead a movie army of Russians.

Plenty of direction and as much photography. There doesn't appear to be a miss or skip either. Herman Mankiewicz's titles [from an original by Lajos Biro] are no small part of the interest, always perfectly placed and phrased. They hold a couple of laughs, although the subject matter limits that.

1927/28: Best Actor (Emil Jannings)

NOMINATIONS: Best Picture, Original Story

•

LAST DANCE
1996, 103 mins, US Ⓥ col
Dir Bruce Beresford ***Prod*** Steven Haft ***Scr*** Ron Koslow ***Ph*** Peter James ***Ed*** John Bloom ***Mus*** Mark Isham ***Art*** John Stoddart
Act Sharon Stone, Rob Morrow, Randy Quaid, Peter Gallagher, Jack Thompson, Jayne Brook (Touchstone)

Last Dance is *Dead Woman Walking, Lite*. Respectably crafted on most levels and with a central perf by Sharon Stone that will cause her no embarrassment, this pic about an unrepentant death row femme whose case is taken up by a clemency board rookie never resonates at any deep emotional level and completely blows what kudos it's acquired in the final reel.

Pic's center of conscience is young Rick Hayes (Rob Morrow), whose high-flying yuppie brother, John (Peter Gallagher), gets him a job at the Clemency Board in a Southern state where 76% of the voters favor the death penalty. Rick works under the wing of Sam (Randy Quaid), an easygoing type who doesn't rock the boat.

Rick is assigned the case of Cindy Liggett (Stone), who's been on death row for the past 12 years for the murder of a teenage schoolmate and her boyfriend when she was only 19. At their first meeting, Cindy tells Rick that the whole clemency routine is purely for show, as the state's present governor (Jack Thompson) doesn't give pardons. Warned off by John from trying to get Cindy's case retried at the 11th hour, Rick still presses ahead.

One of the film's nicest touches—though it was preempted by Tim Robbins's much-honored pic—is that the audience only learns the full details of Cindy's crime piece by piece in b&w flashbacks as the movie progresses.

With shortish red hair, a tattoo on the back of her hand, a passable Southern accent and blue prison duds, Stone gives her part a decent shot.

•

LAST DAYS OF CHEZ NOUS, THE
1992, 96 mins, Australia Ⓥ ⊙ col
Dir Gillian Armstrong ***Prod*** Jan Chapman ***Scr*** Helen Garner ***Ph*** Geoffrey Simpson ***Ed*** Nicholas Beauman ***Mus*** Paul Grabowsky ***Art*** Janet Patterson
Act Lisa Harrow, Bruno Ganz, Kerry Fox, Miranda Otto, Kiri Paramore, Bill Hunter (Chapman/AFFC)

This post-feminist drama about two sisters involved with the same man is beautifully acted and crafted, despite some script problems.

Fortyish Beth (Lisa Harrow) works hard as a writer, bosses people around, lacks emotion and finds it difficult to "be part of a couple," which is hard on her French husband, J. P. (Bruno Ganz). Beth's daughter by her first marriage, Annie (Miranda Otto), is a gangly teen on the brink of her first love affair.

Despite tension in the household, which also includes a lodger (Kiri Paramore) who romances Annie, everyone gets along until the return from overseas of Vicki (Kerry Fox), Beth's younger sister who's sometimes mistaken for her daughter.

The plotline isn't very original, but the femme characters are observed and played with notable depth.

•

LAST DAYS OF DISCO, THE
1998, 113 mins, US Ⓥ ⊙ col
Dir Whit Stillman ***Prod*** Whit Stillman ***Scr*** Whit Stillman ***Ph*** John Thomas ***Ed*** Andrew Hafitz, Jay Pires ***Mus*** Mark Suozzo ***Art*** Ginger Tougas
Act Chloe Sevigny, Kate Beckinsale, Chris Eigeman, Matt Keeslar, Mackenzie Astin, Matthew Ross (Castle Rock/Westerly)

The good times don't exactly roll in *The Last Days of Disco*, which is as interesting to watch for its serious disjuncture between style and content as for its cute cast and fabulous soundtrack. Whit Stillman's stiff directorial approach ill suits the sensual ambience of the club scene so intently depicted, and the mostly self-conscious, uptight characters seem to have taken a left turn out of *Metropolitan* and walked through the wrong door to turn up in this flamboyant druggie scene.

One September in "the very early 1980s," a bunch of friends converge on the hottest disco in New York, no doubt intended to closely resemble Studio 54. Nervous young ad exec, Jimmy (Mackenzie Astin), is embarrassed that he can't get two dorky clients in, although club assistant manager pal Des (Chris Eigeman) often helps him slip in the back door.

But if you're beautiful, well dressed and female, you have no trouble being ushered into the inner sanctum, and such is the case for Charlotte (Kate Beckinsale) and Alice (Chloe Sevigny). The girls were classmates in college.

While Charlotte and Alice float around the club, the harried Des seems to be in the midst of a sexual identity crisis. Part of the film's dislocation stems from the gay and druggie environment being foregrounded dramatically by sexually constipated preppies who engage in defensive debates as to whether they qualify as yuppies.

While Alice observes everything with a quiet calm that provides the film with its most sypathetic vantage point, Charlotte prattles on, sharing every tiny notion that passes through her head. The young men, for their part, come off as chronically unhip.

Technically, the film is splendidly decked out; Ginger Tougas's production design and Sarah Edwards' costumes effectively capture the era.

•

LAST DAYS OF MAN ON EARTH, THE
SEE: THE FINAL PROGRAMME

•

LAST DAYS OF POMPEII, THE
1935, 96 mins, US Ⓥ b/w
Dir Ernest B. Schoedsack ***Prod*** Merian C. Cooper ***Scr*** Ruth Rose ***Ph*** J. Roy Hunt ***Ed*** Archie Marshek ***Mus*** Roy Webb ***Art*** Van Nest Polglase, Al Herman
Act Preston Foster, Basil Rathbone, David Holt, Alan Hale, Louis Calhern, Dorothy Wilson (RKO)

The Last Days of Pompeii is a spectacle picture, full of action and holds a good tempo throughout.

What is presented is a behind-the-scenes of Roman politics and commerce, both of which are shown as smeared with corruption and intrigue. [An opening caption claims the characters and plot have no relation to those in Edward Bulwer-Lytton's novel of the same name. Original story is credited to James Ashmore Creelman and Melville Baker, adapted by Ruth Rose and Boris Ingster.]

Basil Rathbone comes very close to stealing the picture with his playing of Pontius Pilate. Jesus crosses the path of Marcus (Preston Foster) a one-time gladiator who is in Judea on a little business deal (horse stealing) which he carries out as the silent partner of Pilate.

Foster has the central role. He carries through from the boyish blacksmith of the opening sequence to the rich man who in the end sees his beloved son face probable death in the arena (just before the volcano erupts). On the way he is a gladiator, slave trader, horse-stealer and general tough guy, but more the victim of a fierce semi-barbaric environment than of any personal cruelty trait.

•

LAST DETAIL, THE
1973, 103 mins, US Ⓥ ⊙ col
Dir Hal Ashby ***Prod*** Gerald Ayres ***Scr*** Robert Towne ***Ph*** Michael Chapman ***Ed*** Robert C. Jones ***Mus*** Johnny Mandel ***Art*** Michael Haller
Act Jack Nicholson, Otis Young, Randy Quaid, Clifton James, Michael Moriarty, Carol Kane (Columbia)

The Last Detail is a salty, bawdy, hilarious and very touching story about two career sailors escorting to a naval prison a dumb boot sentenced for petty thievery. Jack Nicholson is outstanding at the head of a superb cast.

Robert Towne's outstanding adaptation of Darryl Ponicsan's novel has caught the flavor of noncombat military life. The dialog vulgarisms are simply part of the eternal environment of men in uniform.

Randy Quaid is cast as a teenage misfit. A bungled ripoff of some charity money has gotten him eight years in Portsmouth. Nicholson and Otis Young, awaiting new assignments at a receiving station, draw escort duty. With several days of transit time allowed, Nicholson decides to set a leisurely pace. The essence of the story is the exchange of compassion between the guards and prisoner, and the latter's effect on his escorts.

1973: NOMINATIONS: Best Actor (Jack Nicholson), Supp. Actor (Randy Quaid), Adapted Screenplay

•

LAST EMBRACE
1979, 103 mins, US Ⓥ ⊙ col
Dir Jonathan Demme ***Prod*** Michael Taylor, Dan Wigutow ***Scr*** David Shaber ***Ph*** Tak Fujimoto ***Ed*** Barry Malkin ***Mus*** Miklos Rozsa ***Art*** Charles Rosen
Act Roy Scheider, Janet Margolin, Christopher Walken, Sam Levene, John Glover, Charles Napier (United Artists)

Director Jonathan Demme proves conclusively that he can handle a strictly commercial assignment, while embellishing it with the creative touches that mark a first-rate filmmaker.

Last Embrace tells of a government agent being phased out after a nervous breakdown, triggered by his wife's murder. Roy Scheider is the paranoid subject of more attention than he'd prefer, especially when it comes from Janet Margolin, a wigged-out grad student. Story is from Murray Teigh Bloom's novel *The 13th Man*. The Hitchcock references are frequent.

Scheider delivers a convincing, nerve-tingling perf that reaffirms he can handle a romantic lead. Margolin is highly appealing as the revenge-minded femme. Christopher Walken is seen briefly in a cameo performance as Scheider's boss.

•

LAST EMPEROR, THE
1987, 160 mins, UK/Italy Ⓥ ⊙ ▭ col
Dir Bernardo Bertolucci ***Prod*** Jeremy Thomas ***Scr*** Mark Peploe, Bernardo Bertolucci ***Ph*** Vittorio Storaro ***Ed*** Gabriella Cristiani ***Mus*** Ryuichi Sakamoto, David Byrne, Cong Su ***Art*** Ferdinando Scarfiotti
Act John Lone, Joan Chen, Peter O'Toole, Ying Ruocheng, Victor Wong, Dennis Dun (Thomas/Columbia)

A film of unique, quite unsurpassed visual splendor, *The Last Emperor* makes for a fascinating trip to another world, but for the most part also proves as remote and untouchable as its subject, the last imperial ruler of China. A prodigious production in every respect, Bernardo Bertolucci's film is an exquisitely painted mural of 20th-century Chinese history as seen from the point of view of a hereditary leader who never knew his people.

In 1908, the three-year-old Pu Yi is installed as Lord of Ten Thousand Years, master of the most populous nation on earth. Shortly, he is forced to abdicate, but is kept on as a symbolic figure, educated by his English tutor and tended to by a court that includes 1,500 eunuchs and countless other manipulative advisers.

Finally booted out by the new government, Pu Yi, by now in his late 20s, moves with his two wives to Tientsin and lives like a Western playboy, wearing tuxedos at elegant dances while gradually coming under the influence of the Japanese, who eventually install him as puppet emperor of Manchuria, home of his ancestors.

After World War II, he is imprisoned for 10 years by the Communists, during which time he writes his memoirs, and ends his life as a gardener and simple citizen in Mao's China.

At every moment, the extraordinary aspects of both the story and the physical realization of it are astonishing to witness. For virtually the first 90 minutes, Bertolucci makes full use of the red-dominated splendor of the Forbidden City, which has never before been opened up for use in a Western film.

John Lone, who plays Pu Yi from age 18 to 62, naturally dominates the picture with his carefully judged, unshowy delineation of a sometimes arrogant, often weak man. Joan Chen is exquisite and sad as his principal wife who almost literally fades away, and Peter O'Toole, as Lone's tutor, doesn't really have that much to do but act intelligently concerned for the emperor's well-being.

[A 219-min. version was issued on laserdisc in Japan.]

1987: Best Picture, Director, Adapted Screenplay, Cinematography, Art Direction, Sound, Original Score, Editing, Costume Design

•

LAST EXIT TO BROOKLYN
1989, 102 mins, W. Germany Ⓥ ⊙ col
Dir Uli Edel ***Prod*** Bernd Eichinger, Herman Weigel ***Scr*** Desmond Nakano ***Ph*** Stefan Czapsky ***Ed*** Peter Przygodda ***Mus*** Mark Knopfler ***Art*** David Chapman
Act Stephen Lang, Jennifer Jason Leigh, Burt Young, Peter Dobson, Jerry Orbach, Alexis Arquette (Neue Constantin/Bavaria/Allied)

Last Exit to Brooklyn is a bleak tour of urban hell, a $16 million Stateside-lensed production of Hubert Selby, Jr.'s, controversial 1964 novel. But it doesn't hold a scalpel to the lacerating torrential prose that made the book so cringingly urgent.

Director Uli Edel, whose international reputation was made on the 1980 teen drug drama *Christiane F.*, proves himself an accomplished professional. What he lacks is that fundamental gift of empathy that would make these damned souls more than just figures under a cinematic microscope.

Action is set in a working-class section of Brooklyn in 1952, close by the navy yards where young Americans are embarking for the Korean War. Many residents are engaged in a bitter six-month strike against a local factory. Film's spectacular centerpiece is a well-staged riot pitting strikers against police when factory management uses scab labour to break the picket lines.

One of the protagonists is Stephen Lang, a venal married shop steward and secretary of the strike office who has been dipping into the union till to subsidize his first homosexual affair. When union boss Jerry Orbach boots him out, Lang is dropped by his mercenary lover. A subhuman band of local goons thrashes Lang to within an inch of his life (and "crucifies" him on a wooden crossbeam).

Other major character is a tawdry, hard-drinking teen hooker named Tralala (Jennifer Jason Leigh), who lures unsuspecting bar-hopping servicemen to a back lot where they are mugged and robbed by the band. One night she gets drunk and defiantly declares herself open for sexual services to the neighbourhood bar's entire clientele.

The resulting gangbang, one of the most horrific passages in Selby, Jr.'s book, is here sanitized and given a hopeful finish.

•

LAST FLIGHT, THE
1931, 80 mins, US b/w
Dir William Dieterle ***Prod*** [uncredited] ***Scr*** John Monk Saunders ***Ph*** Sid Hickox ***Ed*** Al Hall ***Mus*** Leo Forbstein (dir.) ***Art*** Jack Okey
Act Richard Barthelmess, David Manners, John Mack Brown, Helen Chandler, Elliot Nugent, Walter Byron (Warner)

As a novel the story [by John Monk Saunders] was known as *Single Lady*. In *Liberty* weekly, it was known as *Nikki and Her War Birds*. As a sensitively neurotic, sometimes goofy, somtimes dumb but always good-looking Nikki, Helen Chandler can take a bow even though her mutterings in this film may be hard to savvy for the mob. Richard Barthelmess is the consistent performer here, and with the usual wisdom of surrounding himself with a good-looking and able group of young male actors.

It opens with a thrill and a tear to suit the femmes, who see Barthelmess and David Manners coming down in a plane and then in a hospital. Before the picture unwinds much further the two are grown into four, all as handsome, shattered airmen wandering aimlessly against life in sensitive and temperamental progress.

John Mack Brown is killed in the bull ring by a foolish jump in the Mexican arena; Walter Byron manages to cause his own death and the death of two others, Manners and Elliot Nugent, in another sequence. That gives the action a quick finish and good centre action to wind up with a plausible romance between Nikki and Barthelmess.

Direction was successful in keeping the shell-shocked side of the permanently wounded airmen continuously before the audience. The cast acts uniformly good with Barthelmess highlighting and Chandler fitting right in. William Wellman was originally scheduled to direct, but William Dieterle handled. He did German transpositions for WB. This is his first English-speaking picture. His style and work as figuring here point him to a worthy spot in the megaphoning field.

•

LAST GOOD TIME, THE
1994, 90 mins, US Ⓥ col
Dir Bob Balaban ***Prod*** Dean Silvers, Bob Balaban ***Scr*** Bob Balaban, John McLaughlin ***Ph*** Claudia Raschke ***Ed*** Hughes Winborne ***Mus*** Jonathan Tunick ***Art*** Wing Lee
Act Armin Mueller-Stahl, Maureen Stapleton, Lionel Stander, Olivia D'Abo, Adrian Pasdar (Apogee)

Armin Mueller-Stahl delivers a towering performance in *The Last Good Time*, an unusually poignant, finely observed comedy-drama [from Richard Bausch's novel] about an old man whose life changes dramatically as a result of a fateful encounter with a young woman.

Mueller-Stahl plays Joseph Kopple, an elegant 70-year-old widower who still clings to the memories of his beautiful wife. The only grace in his lonely, fastidious life, mostly spent in his walk-up Brooklyn apartment, is nightly violin-playing.

One evening, Joseph witnesses a nasty fight between a young couple upstairs, which ends with Charlotte (Olivia D'Abo) being kicked out of the apartment by boyfriend Eddie (Adrian Pasdar). The freezing Charlotte has no place to go, so Joseph takes her in and gradually they develop a strange friendship.

Director Bob Balaban succeeds in steering away from sentimental melodrama and from imposing obvious turning points on the central relationship. Pic is excellent in chronicling the importance that Joseph attaches to order and routine, particularly his daily visits to a nursing home, where Howard Singer (Lionel Stander), his 89-year-old friend, resides.

As the film's emotional center, Mueller-Stahl renders a splendid lyrical performance. That D'Abo is less impressive may be a result of her less-developed role, as story is told from Joseph's point of view.

•

LAST HARD MEN, THE
1976, 103 mins, US Ⓥ ▭ col
Dir Andrew V. McLaglen ***Prod*** Walter Seltzer, Russell Thacher ***Scr*** Guerdon Trueblood ***Ph*** Duke Callaghan ***Ed*** Fred Chulack ***Mus*** Jerry Goldsmith ***Art*** Edward Carfagno
Act Charlton Heston, James Coburn, Barbara Hershey, Jorge Rivero, Michael Parks, Larry Wilcox (20th Century-Fox)

The Last Hard Men is a fairly good actioner with handsome production values and some thoughtful overtones. Charlton Heston and James Coburn are both fine as a retired lawman and his half-Indian nemesis matching their wits in 1909 Arizona along the way to one last bloody confrontation.

Coburn escapes from a Yuma prison gang to wreak carefully planned revenge on Heston, who killed his wife years ago in a scatter-shot shootout. Recruiting a motley gang, Coburn lures the anxious Heston out of Tucson by kidnapping and molesting his daughter (Barbara Hershey).

The details of life at a crucial transition point in American history are well captured in the script and in the art direction.

•

LAST HURRAH, THE
1958, 121 mins, US Ⓥ ⊙ b/w
Dir John Ford ***Prod*** John Ford ***Scr*** Frank Nugent ***Ph*** Charles Lawton, Jr. ***Ed*** Jack Murray ***Art*** Robert Peterson
Act Spencer Tracy, Jeffrey Hunter, Dianne Foster, Pat O'Brien, Basil Rathbone, James Gleason (Columbia)

Edwin O'Connor's novel has been transmuted to the screen in slick style. Spencer Tracy makes the most of the meaty role of the shrewd politician of the "dominantly Irish-American" metropolis in New England (unmistakably Boston but not Boston).

Tracy's resourcefulness in besting the stuffy bankers who nixed a loan for a much needed low-rent housing development; his foiling of the profiteering undertaker when a constituent is buried (the wake is transformed into a political rally); the passionate loyalty of his political devotees; the rivalry between the "respectable" elements in combating the direct-approach tactics of the Irish-American politicos; the pride in defeat when the "reform" candidate bests Tracy at the polls; and Tracy's own "last hurrah" as he tells off the fatuous banker (Willis Bouchey)—with a parting "like hell I would!"—in reviewing his gaudy career, make for a series of memorable scenes.

Jeffrey Hunter is the shrewd mayor's favored nephew who, despite his ties to the opposition sheet, perceives the old codger's humaneness.

•

LAST MAN STANDING
1996, 100 mins, US Ⓥ ⊙ ▭ col
Dir Walter Hill ***Prod*** Walter Hill, Arthur Sarkissian ***Scr*** Walter Hill ***Ph*** Lloyd Ahern ***Ed*** Freeman Davies ***Mus*** Ry Cooder ***Art*** Gary Wissner
Act Bruce Willis, Christopher Walken, Bruce Dern, Alexandra Powers, David Patrick Kelly, William Sanderson (Lone Wolf/New Line)

Bruce Willis's one-note performance and monotonous plotting doom Walter Hill's combination Western and gangster pic, despite the director's typically virile staging of the numerous gun battles. Screenplay is based on the Akira Kurosawa classic *Yojimbo*, unofficially remade by Sergio Leone in Italy in 1964 as the seminal spaghetti western, *Fistful of Dollars*. Plot also bears a resemblance to the Dashiell Hammett tome, *Red Harvest*.

Hill retains the bones of the original story but updates the action to the dusty one-horse Texas border town of Jericho during Prohibition. The Mifune/Eastwood character has now become John Smith (Willis), a big-city guy en route to Mexico. Jericho has been taken over by rival bootleg gangs who run booze across the border. The local sheriff (Bruce Dern) has given up trying to impose law and order.

The numerous gun battles quickly become boring. Characterization is minimal, making it impossible to identify with anyone, and fine actors like Dern and, especially, Christopher Walken as a sinister, scarred sidekick, are given far too little to do. Ry Cooder's score is serviceable but unexceptional.

•

LAST MARRIED COUPLE IN AMERICA, THE
1980, 103 mins, US Ⓥ col
Dir Gilbert Cates ***Prod*** Edward S. Feldman, John Herman Shaner ***Scr*** John Herman Shaner ***Ph*** Ralph Woolsey ***Ed*** Peter E. Berger ***Mus*** Charles Fox ***Art*** Gene Callahan
Act George Segal, Natalie Wood, Richard Benjamin, Dom DeLuise, Valerie Harper (Universal)

The Last Married Couple in America is basically a 1950s comedy with cursing. John Herman Shaner's script offers not a single new idea about divorce in suburbia and doesn't even develop the clichés well.

Gilbert Cates's direction consists largely of letting his stars reenact favorite roles of the past. So Wood plays the nice pretty lady who wants a happy, faithful marriage to George Segal, who plays the nice, handsome husband befuddled by the world around him.

Richard Benjamin is again the neurotic modern male and Dom DeLuise the likable, nutty fat guy, while Valerie Harper is essentially Rhoda running rampant, tresses turned blonde from the sheer excitement of it all.

•

LAST METRO, THE
SEE: LE DERNIER METRO

•

LAST MOVIE, THE
1971, 110 mins, US Ⓥ col
Dir Dennis Hopper ***Prod*** Paul Lewis ***Scr*** Stewart Stern ***Ph*** Laszlo Kovacs ***Ed*** David Berlatsky ***Art*** Leon Erickson
Act Dennis Hopper, Stella Garcia, Sam Fuller, Peter Fonda, Julie Adams, Kris Kristofferson (Universal)

The narrative fluidity, using of myths for a statement on youth, so effective in Dennis Hopper's *Easy Rider* are here overdone and film suffers from a multiplicity of themes, ideas and its fragmented style with flash-forwards intertwined.

Film begins with Hopper wandering all bloody among Peruvian Indians, playing at filmmaking with cameras, booms, etc., made of rattan. A local priest complains of the violence the film people have left behind among his people whose playing at it leads to a kind of passion play and the hunted and finally crucified figure becomes Hopper.

Then a scene from the film shot there, a gun battle with horses falling and men bloodied. Sam Fuller plays a nononsense director with aplomb in these scenes. Hopper has the canteen, plays stuntman and stays on with a native girl, dreaming of building a resort and using the set for other productions. This does not pan out.

Stella Garcia is effective as the native girl who is not moved by the dead she does not know while Hopper has an American innocence tempered with violent rage when things go beyond his ken.

•

LAST OF ENGLAND, THE
1987, 87 mins, UK/W. Germany Ⓥ col
Dir Derek Jarman ***Prod*** James Mackay, Don Boyd ***Scr*** [uncredited] ***Ph*** Derek Jarman, Christopher Hughes, Cerith Wyn Evans, Richard Heslop ***Ed*** Peter Cartwright, Angus Cook, Sally Yeadon, John Maybury ***Mus*** Simon Turner, Andy Gill, Mayo Thompson, Albert Oehlen, Barry Adamson, El Tito ***Art*** Christopher Hobbs
Act Tilda Swinton, Spencer Leigh, Spring, Gay Gaynor, Matthew Hawkins, Gerard McArthur (British Screen/Film Four/ZDF/Anglo-International)

The Last of England has the rare ability to envelop one in its swirling images and bleak comedy one moment, and send a viewer off to sleep the next.

Following the avant-garde helmer's most accessible film to date, the 1986 *Caravaggio*, he returns with a blatantly personal vision which combines documentary-style footage of ruined streets, home movies and a segment with glimpses of a screen story. All is filmed and linked abstractly, but without the glimmer of plot or narrative line.

The Last of England is a self-indulgent number, opening with an actor (Spring) kicking and abusing a Caravaggio painting, *Profane Love*, and proceeding with a tirade of images of urban destruction and deprived youth. Interspersed are extracts from the Jarman family's home movies, which make an interesting contrast to the abrasive images with their views of colonial and RAF life.

•

LAST OF MRS. CHEYNEY, THE
1937, 95 mins, US Ⓥ b/w
Dir Richard Boleslawski ***Prod*** Lawrence Weingarten ***Scr*** Leon Gordon, Samson Raphaelson, Monckton Hoffe ***Ph*** George Folsey ***Ed*** Frank Sullivan ***Mus*** William Axt
Act Joan Crawford, William Powell, Robert Montgomery, Frank Morgan, Jessie Ralph, Nigel Bruce (M-G-M)

The Last of Mrs. Cheyney is a Metro remake of its own dialog film made in 1929 with Norma Shearer. It's from the [Frederick] Lonsdale play which Ina Claire, Roland Young and A. E. Matthews first did on Broadway in 1925. Present filmization more nearly approximates a picture than the

1929 film which was, then, more a straight transmutation of the play in celluloid form.

This is Richard Boleslawski's post-mortem release. Another director wound up the perfunctory details, but Boleslawski gets, and merits, the sole directorial billing. His hand is evident in a number of fine scenes, pacing this society crook comedy-drama with effective contrasts of suspense and laughs.

Scenes which are outstanding are made so by a rare combination of pace, scripting and direction. The sequence, for example, where the snooty English household is wondering what will happen to the crooks (Joan Crawford and her accomplice, William Powell) is a double-broadside in deft comedy painting.

In similar vein, the weekenders' truth-game less pointedly, but not too subtly, mirrors the foibles of the same group—the two-timing wife who has had 14 "cousins" (male) for constant companionship; her stupid husband; another lady of easy virtue; the engagingly lecherous male (Robert Montgomery), but frankly so; the duchess-hostesss (capably played by Jessie Ralph), who confesses she came into royalty via the London Gayety chorus-line, etc.

●

LAST OF SHEILA, THE

1973, 120 mins, US Ⓥ col

Dir Herbert Ross ***Prod*** Herbert Ross ***Scr*** Stephen Sondheim, Anthony Perkins ***Ph*** Gerry Turpin ***Ed*** Edward Warschilka ***Mus*** Billy Goldenberg ***Art*** Ken Adam

Act Richard Benjamin, Dyan Cannon, James Coburn, Joan Hackett, James Mason, Raquel Welch (Warner)

The Last of Sheila is a major disappointment. Result is far from the bloody *All About Eve* predicted and is simply a confused and cluttered demi *Sleuth*, grossly overwritten and underplayed.

Co-scripters Stephen Sondheim and Anthony Perkins are puzzle game fanatics, and the plot constructed for their first feature is self-indulgent camp at its most deadly.

The *Sheila* of the title is the luxury yacht named after the late wife of a Hollywood producer (James Coburn) killed by a hit-and-run driver shortly after exiting a raucous Beverly Hills party. A year later, Coburn asks six of those party guests for a week's Riviera cruise aboard the *Sheila*. Invitees include a glamorous Hollywood star (Raquel Welch), her business agent husband (Ian McShane), a fading director (James Mason), a struggling scriptwriter (Richard Benjamin), his wife (Joan Hackett) and an aggressive femme talent agent (Dyan Cannon).

On board, Coburn initiates a week-long game in which each guest is given a card indicating a secret which is to be discovered by the others. Since one of the cards reads "I am a hit-and-run driver" the mystery concerns the person responsible for Sheila's demise.

Flashbacks, premature confessions and more murders flesh out the overlong running time. Cast is generally superior to the material with Cannon walking away with the honors as a recognizable femme talent packager with a vulgar, acid tongue.

●

LAST OF THE COWBOYS, THE
(AKA: THE GREAT SMOKEY ROADBLOCK)

1977, 100 mins, US Ⓥ col

Dir John Leone ***Prod*** Allan F. Bodoh ***Scr*** John Leone ***Ph*** Ed Brown, Sr. ***Mus*** Craig Safan

Act Henry Fonda, Eileen Brennan, Robert Englund, Austin Pendelton, Susan Sarandon, Melanie Mayron (Mar Vista/Preminger)

Film shrewdly plays on Henry Fonda's moral force as an aging, ailing truckdriver who has had his big truck taken from him when he got behind in payments due to illness. It seems he is a terminal case. He leaves the hospital, steals the truck and sets out to make one last run across the U.S.

The police begin to close in and he is refused jobs when word gets out. He picks up a young hitchhiker (Robert Englund) whose money he uses for gas. His final haul turns out to be six young prosties working for an old flame of Fonda played with gusto by Eileen Brennan. They also have to leave town and are harbored in the van as they make a run for it.

This touching pic is neatly paced, zesty and manages to pay homage to the oldtime Hollywood films without satirizing them.

●

LAST OF THE FINEST, THE

1990, 106 mins, US Ⓥ ⦿ col

Dir John Mackenzie ***Prod*** John A. Davis ***Scr*** Jere Cunningham, Thomas Lee Wright, George Armitage ***Ph*** Juan Ruiz-Anchia ***Ed*** Graham Walker ***Mus*** Jack Nitzsche, Michael Hoenig ***Art*** Laurence G. Paull

Act Brian Dennehy, Joe Pantoliano, Jeff Fahey, Bill Paxton, Deborra-Lee Furness, Guy Boyd (Davis/Orion)

The Last of the Finest belongs to a rarely attempted brand of pastiche film. The central characters are Brian Dennehy and his band of dedicated cops who tumble upon a bunch of corrupt characters (who parallel the Iran-Contra protagonists) while working on a drug bust.

Despite the deficiencies of a script that unwisely mixes tongue-in-cheek elements with soapbox messages, Scottish director John Mackenzie keeps the pic moving and enjoyable on a strictly thriller level. Its unsubtle references to Iran-Contra are more fun for film historians than action fans.

Dennehy is excellent in delivering a liberal message in the form of a free-thinking independent who's tired of the expediency and greed of a system riddled with phony patriots. Guy Boyd ably leads the group of Machiavellian villains and Aussie thesp Deborra-Lee Furness makes a good impression as Dennehy's wife.

●

LAST OF THE MOHICANS, THE

1936, 91 mins, US Ⓥ b/w

Dir George B. Seitz ***Prod*** Edward Small, Harry M. Goetz ***Scr*** Philip Dunne ***Ph*** Robert Planck ***Ed*** Jack Dennis ***Mus*** Roy Webb ***Art*** John Ducasse Schulze

Act Randolph Scott, Binnie Barnes, Heather Angel, Hugh Buckler, Henry Wilcoxon, Bruce Cabot (United Artists)

The James Fenimore Cooper historical fiction story [adapted by John Balderston, Paul Perez and Daniel Moore] is transferred to the screen with surprising fidelity, though the two love stories are accentuated, quite naturally. Locale is the wide open spaces of eastern America when England and the French were battling all through New York State to see which one was to be boss of this country. Story moves swiftly to that phase in the campaign when the British were rushing to the defense of Fort William Henry on Lake George (upper NY State).

Hawkeye, the colonial scout, is set up as the typical American frontiersman of that day, willing to aid the British, but first interested in defending courageous colonists. Picture is hardly 15 minutes old before the first brush with the cruel Huron Indian tribe.

From then it is a series of carefully conceived and deftly executed climaxes, starting with the siege and surrender of the fort.

Randolph Scott gives a virile interpretation as the scout without going overboard at any time. Henry Wilcoxon, as the snobbish British major, vies for honors on the male side. Binnie Barnes, the English girl in love with Hawkeye, further enhances her reputation as a fascinating actress. Heather Angel has less to do as the sister whose romance with a young Mohican ends tragically.

1936: NOMINATION: Best Assistant Director (Clem Beauchamp)

●

LAST OF THE MOHICANS, THE

1992, 122 mins, US Ⓥ ⦿ ▭ col

Dir Michael Mann ***Prod*** Michael Mann, Hunt Lowry ***Scr*** Michael Mann, Christopher Crowe ***Ph*** Dante Spinotti, Doug Milsome ***Ed*** Dov Hoenig, Arthur Schmidt ***Mus*** Trevor Jones, Randy Edelman, Daniel Lanois ***Art*** Wolf Kroeger

Act Daniel Day-Lewis, Madeleine Stowe, Jodhi May, Russell Means, Eric Schweig, Steven Waddington (20th Century-Fox)

The Last of the Mohicans benefits from rich source material (James Fenimore Cooper's classic [and the screenplay for the 1936 United Artists version]) and good performances. Adventure tale of life in the British colonies in America is a great ode to freedom and self-determination played out against codes of honor and loyalty, c. 1757. Lensed in South Carolina, pic blends pure adventure with a compelling central romance.

Sisters Alice (Jodhi May) and Cora (Madeleine Stowe) Munro are escorted through hostile country to join their colonel dad (Maurice Roeves), British commander of a fort under French siege. Rigid English soldier Duncan Heyward (Steven Waddington) is courting Cora sans success. After an ambush leaves the Munro girls and Heyward unprotected, Hawkeye (Daniel Day-Lewis) and his adopted Mohican father (Russell Means) and brother (Eric Schweig) come to the rescue.

Lean and intense, with a dashing mane of hair, Day-Lewis brings his usual concentration to the role of the courageous woodsman at one with nature. He and Stowe spark a convincing attraction arising from shared ideals and piqued by the excitement of life-and-death ordeals.

Modern lensing techniques allow the camera to run alongside Hawkeye and accompany the trajectory of a bullet or the flight of a spinning tomahawk. Well-staged battle sequences are brutal and bloody.

1992: Best Sound

●

LAST OF THE RED HOT LOVERS

1972, 98 mins, US Ⓥ ⦿ col

Dir Gene Saks ***Prod*** Howard W. Koch ***Scr*** Neil Simon ***Ph*** Victor J. Kemper ***Ed*** Maury Winetrobe ***Mus*** Neal Hefti ***Art*** Ben Edwards

Act Alan Arkin, Sally Kellerman, Paula Prentiss, Renee Taylor (Paramount)

Neil Simon's *Last of the Red Hot Lovers* was a very funny play. It has been made into a funny motion picture.

The wonderful thing about Simon's characters is that they're so self-identifiable. Every husband who ever let his eye wander will empathize with Barney Cashman, happily married for 22 years, trying to make it, "just once," with another gal, and suffer with his repeated failures. Alan Arkin, a very funny man with some personal mannerisms that don't always fit the role, makes good use of all of them here, even those nervous eyes.

Sally Kellerman lacks the brash sexiness of her Hot Lips Hoolihan in *MASH*. Paula Prentiss is missing the swingy verve of *Where the Boys Are* and Renee Taylor, who comes off best of the three, doesn't seem as comfortable as Barney's wife's best friend as she was in *Made for Each Other*.

●

L.A. STORY

1991, 95 mins, US Ⓥ ⦿ col

Dir Mick Jackson ***Prod*** Daniel Melnick, Michael Rachmil ***Scr*** Steve Martin ***Ph*** Andrew Dunn ***Ed*** Richard A. Harris ***Mus*** Peter Melnick ***Art*** Lawrence Miller

Act Steve Martin, Victoria Tennant, Richard E. Grant, Marilu Henner, Sarah Jessica Parker, Susan Forristal (Carolco/Indieprod/LA Films)

Goofy and sweet, *L.A. Story* constitutes Steve Martin's satiric valentine to his hometown and a pretty funny comedy in the bargain. Martin is in typically nutty form as an L.A. TV meteorologist who doesn't hestitate to take the weekends off since the weather isn't bound to change. What he can't predict, however, is the lightning bolt that hits him in the form of Brit journalist Victoria Tennant, who arrives to dish up the latest English assessment of America's new melting pot.

Martin's relationship with his snooty longtime g.f. Marilu Henner is essentially over and, convinced that nothing can ever happen with his dreamgirl, he stumblingly takes up with ditzy shopgirl Sarah Jessica Parker.

Even after Martin and Tennant have gotten together and he has declared the grandest of romantic intentions, the future looks impossible, as she has promised her ex (Richard E. Grant) to attempt a reconciliation.

Despite the frantic style, the feeling behind Martin's view of life and love in L.A. comes through, helped by the seductively adoring treatment of Tennant (actually Martin's wife).

●

LAST PICTURE SHOW, THE

1971, 118 mins, US Ⓥ ⦿ b/w

Dir Peter Bogdanovich ***Prod*** Stephen J. Friedman ***Scr*** Larry McMurty, Peter Bogdanovich ***Ph*** Robert Surtees ***Ed*** Donn Cambern ***Art*** Walter Scott Herndon

Act Timothy Bottoms, Jeff Bridges, Cybill Shepherd, Ben Johnson, Cloris Leachman, Ellen Burstyn (BBS)

Notre Dame professor Edward Fischer has said that "the best films, like the best books, tell how it is to be human under certain circumstances." Larry McMurtry did a beautiful job of this in his small novel (which he transferred to the screen) *The Last Picture Show*.

Timothy Bottoms and Jeff Bridges portray the pair of youths who complement each other's limited potential. Physically, they're much alike—football-playing, lanky, likable products of the Texas plains; mentally, or emotionally, they move on different planes. Bridges is the high school hero, more aggressive; Bottoms is the more sensitive, hence the more lonely, of the pair.

The boys grow a bit, some good people die, a few more secrets are revealed, and another "nothing" decade has passed. Bridges, spurned by his girl, joins the army; Bottoms matures a bit. Not much else happens.

The best, most solid, most moving performances in the film are given by Ben Johnson, that old John Ford regular, as Sam the Lion, the owner of the picture show and pool room where the town boys spend most of their time; and Cloris Leachman as the football coach's wife, who introduces Bottoms to sex.

Peter Bogdanovich elected to shoot the film in black and white, artistically appropriate for the dust-blown, tired little community, but Robert Surtees (who's a master with color) doesn't bring off the tones of gray. There is excellent use of many pop tunes of the period and only introduced in a natural manner—a nickel in a jukebox, a car radio, or an early television set.

1971: Best Supp. Actor (Ben Johnson), Supp. Actress (Cloris Leachman)

NOMINATIONS: Best Picture, Director, Supp. Actor (Jeff Bridges), Supp. Actress (Ellen Burstyn), Adapted Screenplay, Cinematography

•

LAST REMAKE OF BEAU GESTE, THE
1977, 84 mins, US Ⓥ col
Dir Marty Feldman ***Prod*** William S. Gilmore ***Scr*** Marty Feldman ***Ph*** Gerry Fisher ***Ed*** Jim Clark, Arthur Schmidt ***Mus*** John Morris ***Art*** Brian Eatwell
Act Ann-Margret, Marty Feldman, Michael York, Peter Ustinov, James Earl Jones, Trevor Howard (Universal)

Marty Feldman's directorial debut on *The Last Remake of Beau Geste* emerges as an often hilarious, if uneven, spoof of Foreign Legion adventure films. An excellent cast, top to bottom, gets the most out of the stronger scenes, and carries the weaker ones.

Feldman stars [in a story by him and Sam Bobrick] as the ugly duckling brother of Michael York (as Beau Geste), both adopted sons of Trevor Howard, an aging lech whose marriage to swinger Ann-Margret causes York to join the Foreign Legion and Feldman to serve time for alleged theft of a family gem.

Feldman joins York in the desert, where sadistic Peter Ustinov and bumbling Roy Kinnear run the garrison for urbane Henry Gibson, in the character of the Legion general.

•

LAST RITES
1987, 103 mins, US Ⓥ ⊙ col
Dir Donald P. Bellisario ***Prod*** Donald P. Bellisario, Patrick McCormick ***Scr*** Donald P. Bellisario ***Ph*** David Watkin ***Ed*** Pembroke J. Herring ***Mus*** Bruce Broughton ***Art*** Peter Larkin
Act Tom Berenger, Daphne Zuniga, Chick Vennera, Anne Twomey, Dane Clark, Paul Dooley (M-G-M)

Last Rites holds certain interest but also often borders on the ludicrous, accommodating all the ripest themes that can be derived from the dilemma of being an Italo-American Catholic priest and son of a top Mafioso.

Startling opening scene has an elegant woman stride, pistol in hand, into a ritzy hotel suite and gun down a mobster while he is making love to a woman. The woman, a Mexican named Angela (Daphne Zuniga), escapes and eventually comes under the protection of Father Michael Pace (Tom Berenger), a young priest at St. Patrick's Catholic Cathedral in New York.

The rugged holy man finds himself having erotic dreams about the saucy young thing in his bed, and finally spirits her south of the border to shed her pursuers.

Donald P. Bellisario, longtime TV writer and producer who cocreated *Magnum, P.I.*, stages much of the action vividly, but it's just not very convincing. Berenger's casting was an interesting idea but probably a mistake. Zuniga has divided impact as the femme fatale, sporting a highly variable Spanish accent.

•

LAST RUN, THE
1971, 92 mins, US Ⓥ ▭ col
Dir Richard Fleischer ***Prod*** Carter de Haven ***Scr*** Alan Sharp ***Ph*** Sven Nykvist ***Ed*** Russell Lloyd ***Mus*** Jerry Goldsmith ***Art*** Roy Walker, Jose Maria Tapiador
Act George C. Scott, Tony Musante, Trish Van Devere, Colleen Dewhurst (M-G-M)

The Last Run is a suspense melodrama with a set of criminal characters to keep action lively but its story line is so blurred by unexplained elements that it emerges little more than an ordinary actioner. George C. Scott gives certain authority to a hard-hitting role.

Produced in Spain by Carter De Haven and directed by Richard Fleischer, taking over from John Huston, who ankled the assignment, film gains in pictorial interest from constant shrewd use of colorful backgrounds. Original screenplay by Alan Sharp is designed as a saga of a man on the run after his escape from a prison van, and an old hand directing this flight. What comes out on screen militates against ready acceptance of this premise due to haphazard writing.

Scott plays a retired American mobster who once drove for criminals in fast getaways. He returns to activity after nine years to aid an escaped con and whisk him across the Spanish border into France. It's all pretty fuzzy and audience is at a loss to understand the whys and wherefores of the action.

•

LAST SEDUCTION, THE
1994, 109 mins, US Ⓥ ⊙ col
Dir John Dahl ***Prod*** Jonathan Shestack ***Scr*** Steve Barancik ***Ph*** Jeffrey Jur ***Ed*** Eric L. Beason ***Mus*** Joseph Vitarelli ***Art*** Linda Pearl
Act Linda Fiorentino, Peter Berg, Bill Pullman, J. T. Walsh, Bill Nunn, Herb Mitchell (ITC)

This well-paced, cleverly written and quite diabolical thriller is director John Dahl's classy follow-up to *Red Rock West*. Linda Fiorentino toplines as one of the screen's most formidable femmes fatales ever in a sexy and polished performance.

Bridget Gregory (Fiorentino) is an intelligent NY insurance exec who has conned her medic husband, Clay (Bill Pullman), into doing a dangerous but lucrative drug deal. Bridget rewards him by simply ankling with the money, heading for Chicago.

Along the way she stops at a one-horse town for fuel and sexual replenishment. Latter comes from the bruised Mike (Peter Berg), whom she picks up in a bar. When a private eye (Bill Nunn) tracks her down, she's able to dispose of him without too much bother, but realizes Clay must be dealt with permanently. She plots to involve Mike in Clay's murder.

Pacing is on the button, and the film moves inexorably, without any flat moments, toward the suspenseful, if morally indefensible, finale.

Fiorentino is quite wonderful as the diabolical Bridget, who uses her beauty and her body to get what she wants without qualms. Sex scenes are moderately steamy, the more so for being so matter-of-fact.

•

LAST STARFIGHTER, THE
1984, 100 mins, US Ⓥ ▭ col
Dir Nick Castle ***Prod*** Gary Adelson, Edward O. Denault ***Scr*** Jonathan Betuel ***Ph*** King Baggot ***Ed*** C. Timothy O'Meara ***Mus*** Craig Safan ***Art*** Ron Cobb
Act Lance Guest, Robert Preston, Dan O'Herlihy, Catherine Mary Stewart, Barbara Bosson, Norman Snow (Universal/Lorimar)

With *The Last Starfighter*, director Nick Castle and writer Jonathan Betuel have done something so simple it's almost awe-inspiring: They've taken a very human story and accented it with sci-fi special effects, rather than the other way around.

Lance Guest is a teenager with a talent for a lone video game that was somehow dropped off at his mother's rundown, remote trailer park when it should have been delivered to Las Vegas. And when he breaks the record for destroying alien invaders, Guest not only excites the whole trailer park, he attracts a visit from Robert Preston.

There is never a moment when all of this doesn't seem quite possible, accompanied by plenty of building questions about what's going to happen next.

•

LAST SUMMER
1969, 97 mins, US Ⓥ col
Dir Frank Perry ***Prod*** Frank Perry ***Scr*** Eleanor Perry ***Ph*** Gerald Hirschfeld ***Ed*** Sidney Katz ***Mus*** John Simon
Act Barbara Hershey, Richard Thomas, Bruce Davison, Cathy Burns, Ralph Waite, Conrad Bain (Allied Artists/Alsid)

A solid insight into a quartet during a summer that also has fine acting and sensitive direction and writing.

A pretty, vivacious, headstrong girl finds a dying sea gull on the beach. She beseeches two youths to help her. They remove a hook from its throat and the three become friends.

The boys are expertly played by Bruce Davison and Richard Thomas, and Cathy Burns is engaging and touching as the lonely, homely little girl, drawn to those more emancipated friends, but finally appalled by their cowardice and cruelty, only to be the victim of their pent-up inarticulate needs.

Nicely hued, film has a frankness that is not forced and Eleanor Perry's dialog, if sometimes taking precedence over more visual revelations, is just and makes a statement about fairly affluent youth.

1969: NOMINATION: Best Supp. Actress (Cathy Burns)

•

LAST SUMMER IN THE HAMPTONS
1995, 105 mins, US col
Dir Henry Jaglom ***Prod*** Judith Wolinsky ***Scr*** Henry Jaglom, Victoria Foyt ***Ph*** Hanania Baer ***Ed*** Henry Jaglom ***Mus*** Rick Baitz
Act Victoria Foyt, Viveca Lindfors, Jon Robin Baitz, Melissa Leo, Martha Plimpton, Holland Taylor (Jagtoria)

Henry Jaglom's *Last Summer in the Hamptons* is a mildly amusing comedy of manners that evokes the spirit, if not the accomplishment, of Chekhov, Renoir, and, most specifically, Woody Allen. A large, extraordinary cast of mostly eccentric performers almost overcomes the trappings of familiar ideas.

Story is set in a lush East Hampton estate and concerns three generations of a large, narcissistic theatrical family, headed by powerful matriarch Helena (Viveca Lindfors). The group is more a commune than a biological family, as it includes students and friends, all mobilizing their creative energies for the annual summer production.

The usual comic and not-so-comic shenanigans are exacerbated by the arrival of Oona (Victoria Foyt), a young Hollywood star whose unexpected visit wreaks havoc on almost every member of the family. She's presented as a beautiful, rather naive and insecure actress, facing both personal and professional crises.

Most of the film consists of intimate encounters in which the characters bare their hearts and reveal their dreams and frustrations. After 40 minutes or so, pic begins to lose steam and becomes repetitious. Unlike Allen, Jaglom is not adept in alternating the comic with the more serious.

Magnetic acting helps compensate for the lack of insightful originality in the script, cowritten by Jaglom and his wife and leading lady, Foyt.

•

LAST SUPPER, THE
1995, 92 mins, US Ⓥ col
Dir Stacy Title ***Prod*** Mat Cooper, Larry Weinberg ***Scr*** Dan Rosen ***Ph*** Paul Cameron ***Ed*** Luis Colina ***Mus*** Mark Mothersbaugh ***Art*** Linda Burton
Act Cameron Diaz, Ron Eldard, Annabeth Gish, Jonathan Penner, Courtney B. Vance, Jason Alexander (Vault)

The Last Supper, a socially relevant satire that takes as its target the entire political spectrum, heralds the arrival of director Stacy Title as a bright new talent on the American indie scene.

In a brilliant opening sequence, five graduate students engage in a lively discussion with Zac (Bill Paxton), a stranger who gave one of them a ride during a rainstorm. The proceedings heat up when the ultra-patriot right-winger voices his racist views. Zac begins a physical fight, which unexpectedly ends with his own death at the hands of Marc (director's husband Jonathan Penner).

Once the quintet's initial shock and dismay pass, they decide to embark upon a crusade, ridding society of its most deplorable members. More guests lead to more killings—and more backyard burials—all to the benefit of the garden, which begins to blossom with delicious tomatoes.

The Last Supper aims to be at once a black comedy, à la *Arsenic and Old Lace*, and a political critique of the 1990s, but ultimately it's too ambitious for its own good. After the first reel, the narrative becomes progressively schematic—and a bit tiresome. The last sequence, in which the group entertains a conservative TV commentator (Ron Perlman), is stretched way beyond its necessary length.

Considering the budget of just $500,000, tech credits are superb, with particularly impressive contributions from lenser Paul Cameron and composer Mark Mothersbaugh.

•

LAST TANGO IN PARIS
1972, 130 mins, Italy/France Ⓥ ⊙ col
Dir Bernardo Bertolucci ***Prod*** Alberto Grimaldi ***Scr*** Bernardo Bertolucci, Franco Arcalli ***Ph*** Vittorio Storaro ***Ed*** Franco Arcalli, Roberto Perpignani ***Mus*** Gato Barbieri, Oliver Nelson (arr.) ***Art*** Ferdinando Scarfiotti
Act Marlon Brando, Maria Schneider, Maria Michi, Jean-Pierre Leaud, Massimo Girotti, Catherine Allegret (PEA/Artistes Associes)

Bernardo Bertolucci's *Last Tango in Paris* is an uneven, convoluted, certainly dispute-provoking study of sexual passion in which Marlon Brando gives a truly remarkable performance.

Brando plays an aging Lothario trailing the debris of a failed life who has wound up in Paris married to an unfaithful hotelkeeper. Pic opens on the day of his wife's suicide when the distraught Brando meets a young girl (Maria Schneider) while both are inspecting a vacant apartment. After a sudden, almost savage sexual encounter, Brando proposes that they meet in the apartment on a regular basis. Brando insists that no names or personal information be exchanged, that the affair remain purely carnal.

Plot has all the ingredients of a 1940s meller. Bertolucci uses it to explore the psyche of a man at the end of his emotional and sexual tether and at the same time to investigate on the most primitive level the chemistry of romantic love.

Schneider is standout as the girl, a difficult role played semi-tart, but one whose motivations remain cloudy through the murderous finale.

1973: NOMINATIONS: Best Director, Actor (Marlon Brando)

•

LAST TEMPTATION OF CHRIST, THE
1988, 164 mins, US Ⓥ ⊙ col
Dir Martin Scorsese ***Prod*** Barbara De Fina ***Scr*** Paul Schrader ***Ph*** Michael Ballhaus ***Ed*** Thelma Schoonmaker ***Mus*** Peter Gabriel ***Art*** John Beard
Act Willem Dafoe, Harvey Keitel, Barbara Hershey, Harry Dean Stanton, David Bowie, Verna Bloom (Universal/Cineplex Odeon)

A film of challenging ideas, and not salacious provocations, *The Last Temptation of Christ* is a powerful and very modern reinterpretation of Jesus as a man wracked with anguish and doubt concerning his appointed role in life. Pic was lensed on Moroccan locations for a highly restrictive $6.5 million.

As a written prologue simply states, *Last Temptation* aims to be a "fictional exploration of the eternal spiritual conflict," "the battle between the spirit and the flesh," as Nikos Kazantzakis summarized the theme of his novel.

After rescuing Mary Magdalene from the stone-throwers, Jesus tentatively launches his career as religious leader. But only after his return from the desert and his hallucinatory exposure to representations of good and evil, is he transformed into a warrior against Satan, finally convinced he is the son of God.

Blondish and blue-eyed in the Anglo-Saxon tradition, Willem Dafoe offers an utterly compelling reading of his character. Harvey Keitel puts across Judas's fierceness and loyalty, and only occasionally lets a New York accent and mannered modernism detract from total believability.

Barbara Hershey, adorned with tattoos, is an extremely physical, impassioned Mary Magdalene. One could have used more of David Bowie's subdued, rational Pontius Pilate.

1988: NOMINATION: Best Director

•

LAST TIME I SAW PARIS, THE
1954, 116 mins, US Ⓥ col
Dir Richard Brooks ***Prod*** Jack Cummings ***Scr*** Julius J. Epstein, Philip G. Epstein ***Ph*** Joseph Ruttenberg ***Ed*** John Dunning ***Mus*** Conrad Salinger
Act Elizabeth Taylor, Van Johnson, Walter Pidgeon, Donna Reed, Eva Gabor, Kurt Kasznar (M-G-M)

The Last Time I Saw Paris is an engrossing romantic drama that tells a good story with fine performances and an overall honesty of dramatic purpose.

F. Scott Fitzgerald's short story, *Babylon Revisited*, was updated and revised as the basis for the potent screenplay. Elizabeth Taylor's work as the heroine shows a thorough grasp of the character, which she makes warm and real. Richard Brooks's direction also gets a sock response from Van Johnson.

Plot is laid in Paris in the reckless, gay period that followed V-E Day of World War II. There, Johnson meets and marries Taylor and starts a struggling existence as a daytime reporter for a news service and would-be author at night. Even the faith of his wife cannot balance the brand of failure he assumes after too many rejection slips and when some supposedly worthless Texas oil property suddenly gushes into wealth he becomes a playboy himself.

Threading through the footage is the Jerome Kern-Oscar Hammerstein II title song, hauntingly sung by Odette.

•

LAST TRAIL, THE
1927, 53 mins, US ⊗ b/w
Dir Lewis Seiler ***Scr*** John Stone ***Ph*** Dan Clark
Act Tom Mix, Carmelita Geraghty, William Davidson, Robert Brower, Jerry the Giant (Fox)

In this one there is a free-for-all stagecoach race that comes near rivaling the famous chariot race in *Ben-Hur*. It is replete with thrills and spills.

Also, there is something of an added attraction in the fact that Tom Mix has Jerry the Giant, a cute youngster, working with him almost throughout the picture. Carmelita Geraghty, who played a small role in Mix's last picture, *The Canyon of Light*, is his leading woman and she more than makes good.

The Zane Grey story opens with an Indian fight. Mix saves the life of the wife of Joe Pascal and Joe, in return, promises to name his first born in his honor. Ten years later Mix, as Tom Dane, is still riding the West, when he gets a note from his old friend to come and see the youngster that bears his name. Pascal in the meantime is the sheriff at Carson City and the stageline, which is carrying the gold, has been repeatedly robbed until the sheriff decides to drive the stage through to the railroad with a guard.

•

LAST TRAIN FROM GUN HILL
1959, 94 mins, US Ⓥ col
Dir John Sturges ***Prod*** Hal Wallis ***Scr*** James Poe ***Ph*** Charles Lang, Jr. ***Ed*** Warren Low ***Mus*** Dimitri Tiomkin
Act Kirk Douglas, Anthony Quinn, Carolyn Jones, Earl Holliman, Brad Dexter, Brian Hutton (Paramount/Bryna)

Last Train from Gun Hill is a top western. Although there are some psychological undertones, it is a film that plays for almost pure action.

Kirk Douglas's Indian wife is raped and killed by two young brutes (Earl Holliman and Brian Hutton). Douglas, marshal of the town of Pauley, finds a clue that leads him to the neighboring community of Gun Hill. He discovers his fugitive (Holliman) is the son of his old friend (Anthony Quinn). His problem is how to get Holliman away to justice on that "last train," with Quinn and his hired gunhands determined to thwart him.

James Poe's screenplay slips into a few clichés in dialog, but it is remarkable in that it avoids more. It is refreshing in its ability to shut up when action should take over, when a gesture or look completely conveys meaning.

Cameraman Charles Lang also employs an unusual number of very long shots in his sunbaked exteriors, with the human figures barely discernible black miniatures on the raw, yellow landscape.

Douglas and Quinn, by performances in depth, give the film the inevitability of tragedy. Carolyn Jones delivers impressively. Earl Holliman is most effective and sympathetic as the weakling son.

•

LAST TYCOON, THE
1976, 122 mins, US Ⓥ ⊙ col
Dir Elia Kazan ***Prod*** Sam Spiegel ***Scr*** Harold Pinter ***Ph*** Victor Kemper ***Ed*** Richard Marks ***Mus*** Maurice Jarre ***Art*** Gene Callahan
Act Robert De Niro, Tony Curtis, Robert Mitchum, Jeanne Moreau, Jack Nicholson, Donald Pleasence (Paramount)

The Last Tycoon is a handsome and lethargic film, based on F. Scott Fitzgerald's unfinished Hollywood novel of the 1930s, as adapted by Harold Pinter. Producer Sam Spiegel's contribution is admirable, but Elia Kazan's direction of the Pinter plot seems unfocused though craftsmanlike. Robert De Niro's performance as the inscrutable boy-wonder of films is mildly intriguing.

In an apparent attempt to avoid making a nostalgia film, the few choice bits of environmental interest emerge mostly as awkward interruptions in the main plot.

Ingrid Boulting is the elusive charmer who penetrates somewhat into De Niro's interior, but since her own expressions are limited in scope, we don't really know what she finds there. So, too, Theresa Russell, as Robert Mitchum's daughter, tries for De Niro, but at least she emerges as perhaps the only credible principal character in the piece.

1976: NOMINATION: Best Art Direction

•

LAST UNICORN, THE
1982, 84 mins, US Ⓥ col
Dir Arthur Rankin, Jr., Jules Bass ***Prod*** Arthur Rankin, Jr., Jules Bass ***Scr*** Peter S. Beagle ***Ph*** Hiroyasu Omoto ***Ed*** Tomoko Kida ***Mus*** Jimmy Webb ***Art*** Arthur Rankin, Jr. (Rankin-Bass/ ITC)

The Last Unicorn represents a rare example of an animated kids' pic in which the script and vocal performances outshine the visuals.

Quest framework provided by Peter S. Beagle's adaptation of his own novel ideally serves an animated musical film's need to introduce an assortment of colorful characters who can deliver specialty numbers. Continuing thread is the search of the fabled last unicorn, in this case a beautiful white mare, for the rest of her breed, which has reportedly been vanquished by the terrible red bull.

However vapid the unicorn may appear to the eye, Mia Farrow's voice brings an almost moving plaintive quality to the character which sees the entire film through. Alan Arkin also scores as the bumbling magician, as do Christopher Lee as the evil king and, in a show-stopping turn, Paul Frees as a peg-legged, eye-patched cat.

•

LAST VALLEY, THE
1971, 125 mins, UK/US Ⓥ ▭ col
Dir James Clavell ***Prod*** James Clavell ***Scr*** James Clavell ***Ph*** John Wilcox ***Ed*** John Bloom ***Mus*** John Barry ***Art*** Peter Mullins
Act Michael Caine, Omar Sharif, Florinda Bolkan, Nigel Davenport, Per Oscarsson, Arthur O'Connell (ABC/Season)

The Last Valley is a disappointing 17th-century period melodrama about the fluid and violent loyalties attendant on major civil upheaval. Shot handsomely abroad for about $6 million and top-featuring Michael Caine and Omar Sharif in strong performances, James Clavell's film emerges as heavy cinematic grand opera in tab version format, too literal in historical detail to suggest artfully the allegories intended, and, paradoxically, too allegorical to make clear the actual reality of the Thirty Years War.

Clavell adapted a J. B. Pick novel in which Sharif, neither peasant nor nobleman, is fleeing the ravages of war and finds a valley still spared from cross-devastation. Caine, hard-bitten leader of mercenaries, also discovers the locale. At Sharif's urging Caine decides to live in peace for the winter with the residents, headed by Nigel Davenport and an uneasy truce develops.

The fatuous political, religious and social rationalizations of behavior get full exposition. But the whole entity doesn't play well together as Clavell's script often halts for declamations.

•

LAST WAGON, THE
1956, 98 mins, US ▭ col
Dir Delmer Daves ***Prod*** William B. Hawks ***Scr*** James Edward Grant, Delmer Daves, Gwen Bagni Gielgud ***Ph*** Wilfrid Cline ***Ed*** Hugh S. Fowler ***Mus*** Lionel Newman
Act Richard Widmark, Felicia Farr, Susan Kohner, Tommy Rettig, Stephanie Griffin, George Mathews (20th Century-Fox)

The mounting menace of Indian attack as the survivors of a wagon-train massacre make their way through hostile Apache country provides stirring motivation for this excellent production. Its suspenseful plot and rugged characterization by Richard Widmark as a Comanche-reared white man are admirably backdropped by the magnificent Northern Arizona scenery. Under Delmer Daves's shrewd direction, film comes off as an interesting enterprise far off the beaten path of routine westerns. Widmark is seen in a forceful role, a man who killed to avenge the murder of his Comanche wife and two sons, and has none of the refinements of civilization until he meets Felicia Farr, who is one of the survivors.

Farr leads off the lineup of new talent and makes an engaging impression, as does young Rettig in his hero-worship of Widmark. Susan Kohner scores as the half-breed sister of Stephanie Griffin, an interesting newcomer, and Nick Adams and Ray Stricklyn both show promise.

•

LAST WALTZ, THE
1978, 115 mins, US Ⓥ col
Dir Martin Scorsese ***Prod*** Robbie Robertson ***Ph*** Michael Chapman, Laszlo Kovacs, Vilmos Zsigmond, David Myers, Bobby Byrne, Michael Watkins, Hiro Narita ***Ed*** Yeu-Bun Lee, Jan Roblee ***Art*** Boris Leven
Act Bob Dylan, Joni Mitchell, Neil Diamond, Van Morrison, Eric Clapton, The Band (United Artists)

The Last Waltz is an outstanding rock documentary of the last concert by The Band on Thanksgiving 1976 at Winterland in San Francisco.

By itself The Band performs 12 numbers. The group backs up guest artists on another dozen. They include Ronnie Hawkins, Dr. John, Neil Young, the Staples, Neil Diamond, Joni Mitchell, Paul Butterfield, Muddy Waters, Eric Clapton, Emmylou Harris, Van Morrison, Bob Dylan, Ringo Starr and Ron Wood.

Director Martin Scorsese has succeeded on a number of fronts. First, he recognized that this concert deserved cinematic preservation. The Band was an important and intelligent force in rock music on its own and as a backup group for Bob Dylan and Ronnie Hawkins.

This film is a chronicle of one important group very much a part of the music of the late 1960s and 1970s and it's also a commentary on those times. It's 90 percent concert film and 10 percent history. Unlike so many of their colleagues, the members of The Band are competent musicians and spokesmen.

•

LAST WAVE, THE
1977, 106 mins, Australia Ⓥ col
Dir Peter Weir ***Scr*** Tony Morphett, Petru Popescu, Peter Weir ***Ph*** Russell Boyd ***Ed*** Max Lemon ***Mus*** Charles Wain
Act Richard Chamberlain, Olivia Hamnett, David Gulpilil, Frederick Parslow, Nandjiwarra Amagula (Ayer/SAFC/AFC)

Australian director Peter Weir's film about the possibility of a coming tidal wave that may destroy the country or the world. Richard Chamberlain is highly effective as a young lawyer caught up in a case of an aborigine murdered by some others in town.

The lawyer has strange dreams that involve one of the accused men trying to give him some sort of sacred stone. He takes their case and tries to insist it was tribal but the man he has dreamed of, who at first tries to help him, begs off when an old patriarch seems to exert power on him. Film builds, and though it sometimes falters in narrative, picks up again as Chamberlain turns out to be a sort of psychic member of a mysterious people who supposedly came to Australia long ago and disappeared.

•

LAST WILL OF DR. MABUSE, THE
SEE: DAS TESTAMENT DES DR. MABUSE

•

LAST WINTER, THE
1990, 103 mins, Canada col
Dir Aaron Kim Johnston ***Prod*** Jack Clements, Ken Rodeck, Joe MacDonald, ***Scr*** Aaron Kim Johnston ***Ph*** Ian Elkin ***Ed*** Lara Mazur ***Mus*** Victor Davies ***Art*** Perri Gorrare
Act Gerard Parkes, Joshua Murray, David Ferry, Wanda Cannon (Rode/Aaron)

This vivid, imaginative tale of a Manitoba farmboy's coming of age captures a uniquely Canadian heartland experience. Writer-director Aaron Kim Johnston has crafted a tribute to his childhood in a tale seen through the eyes of 10-year-old Will (Joshua Murray) as he resists his family's move to the city.

Beset with growing pains and upset by the prospect of being uprooted, Will creates a fantasy shield between himself and reality, hallucinating a white horse named Winter who charges across the farmland bearing some mysterious message. His closest ties are to his Grampa Jack (Gerard Parkes) and his cousin Kate, whom he's in love with.

The overwhelming presence of the land and weather are captured in Ian Elkin's clean, crisp photography, and the winter storms and snowdrifts painstakingly evoked by the art department. Johnston draws lovely performances from the children, especially Murray. Parkes forges a convincing link with the young actor as his elderly confidant.

•

LAST YEAR AT MARIENBAD
SEE: L'ANNEE DERNIERE A MARIENBAD

•

LATE SHOW, THE
1977, 94 mins, US Ⓥ ⦿ col
Dir Robert Benton ***Prod*** Robert Altman ***Scr*** Robert Benton ***Ph*** Chuck Rosher ***Ed*** Lou Lombardo ***Mus*** Kenn Wannberg ***Art*** Bob Gould
Act Art Carney, Lily Tomlin, Bill Macy, Eugene Roche, Joanna Cassidy, John Considine (Warner)

Art Carney and Lily Tomlin make an arresting screen duo in *The Late Show*, a modest meller and a tribute to the private-eye yarns of the 1940s.

The process has given Carney and Tomlin the freedom to create two extremely sympathetic characters. Both performances are knockout.

Carney plays an aging private detective trying to maintain his dignity while scratching out a living on the sordid underbelly of Los Angeles. When his one-time partner (Howard Duff in an opening cameo) is murdered, Carney, in the best Sam Spade tradition, vows to get the killer.

The trail begins with Tomlin whose stolen cat Duff had been hired to find. Top-heavy plot unwinds with the usual potboiler ingredients—blackmail, murder, philandering wives and double-cross.

1977: NOMINATION: Best Original Screenplay

•

LATIN LOVERS
1953, 104 mins, US col
Dir Mervyn LeRoy ***Prod*** Joe Pasternak ***Scr*** Isobel Lennart ***Ph*** Joseph Ruttenberg ***Ed*** John McSweeney, Jr. ***Mus*** George Stoll (dir.) ***Art*** Cedric Gibbons, Gabriel Scognarillo
Act Lana Turner, Ricardo Montalban, John Lund, Louis Calhern, Jean Hagen, Beulah Bondi (M-G-M)

Plot problem confronting Lana Turner, a girl with $37 million, is to make sure the man she marries is interested in something more than her money. She can't be sure of John Lund, even though he has $48 million, and Ricardo Montalban is well-off, but not in the millionaire class by any means. Playoff of the complications takes place in Brazil, the romantic spot to which she has followed Lund and where she meets Montalban.

Among a number of high spots are the handling of Turner's first meeting with Montalban, what is done with the psychiatrist scenes—with the doc's wife acidly commenting on life and patients—and the red-hot samba, danced by Turner and Montalban to "Come to My Arms" one of several Nicholas Brodszky–Leo Robin tunes that polish the footage.

Featured players contributing to the enjoyment of the offering are Jean Hagen, Turner's secretary; Eduard Franz, the psychiatrist; and Dorothy Neumann, his wife.

•

LAUGHING POLICEMAN, THE
1973, 111 mins, US Ⓥ col
Dir Stuart Rosenberg ***Prod*** Stuart Rosenberg ***Scr*** Thomas Rickman ***Ph*** David Walsh ***Ed*** Robert Wyman ***Mus*** Charles Fox ***Art*** Doug Von Koss
Act Walter Matthau, Bruce Dern, Lou Gossett, Albert Paulsen, Anthony Zerbe, Anthony Costello (20th Century-Fox)

After an extremely overdone prolog of violent mass murder on a bus, *The Laughing Policeman* becomes a handsomely made manhunt actioner, starring Walter Matthau and Bruce Dern in excellent performances as two San Francisco detectives.

The title comes from a book by the Swedish team of Per Wahloo and Maj Sjowall, which has been adapted by Thomas Rickman with a shift from the Stockholm and Malmo environment to SF.

Pre-title action sees Anthony Costello tailing Louis Guss aboard a bus, all of whose passengers are brutally massacred by an unseen rider's shotgun.. Matthau, who was Costello's senior partner, is assigned to the case, along with Dern. Lou Gossett is another detective on the puzzling case, where lack of clear motive, disparity in backgrounds of all the dead people, and absence of clues, sends detective-lieutenant Anthony Zerbe up the wall in frustration. Matthau in time abandons normal procedure to search by instinct.

Matthau's character is developed and played with low key irony. Dern is superbly cast as a callous cop, herein the quintessential Yahoo pig who berates any and all minorities.

•

LAUGHTER
1930, 85 mins, US b/w
Dir Harry D'Arrast ***Scr*** Douglas Doty, Harry D'Arrast, Donald Ogden Stewart ***Ph*** George Folsey ***Ed*** Helene Turner
Act Nancy Carroll, Fredric March, Frank Morgan, Glenn Anders, Diane Ellis, Leonard Carey (Paramount)

Douglas Doty and Harry D' Arrast skeletonize a dandy scenario. Donald Ogden Stewart brightens it up with dialog. Fredric March makes it brilliant with playing. March steals the picture.

Laughter has its drama in a suicide and again in a girl's desire to leave wealth, to gamble with the irresponsible composer she fell in love with in Paris, just before her marriage, to go to gaiety and mingle with laughs. The girl is Nancy Carroll and the composer March.

Hugely enjoyable entertainment with plenty of comedy.

•

LAUGHTER IN PARADISE
1951, 94 mins, UK b/w
Dir Mario Zampi ***Prod*** Mario Zampi ***Scr*** Michael Pertwee, Jack Davies ***Ph*** William McLeod ***Ed*** Giulio Zampi ***Mus*** Stanley Black ***Art*** Ivan King
Act Alastair Sim, Fay Compton, Guy Middleton, George Cole, Beatrice Campbell, Audrey Hepburn (Associated British)

Producer-director Mario Zampi very nearly succeeds in bringing off an outstanding comedy with *Laughter in Paradise*. Plot describes what happens after a practical joker leaves $140,000 to each of four relatives provided they fulfill certain stipulated conditions.

His sister (Fay Compton), who has always been tough on housemaids, has to hold a job as a domestic for 28 days. A cousin (Alastair Sim), who secretly writes trashy thrillers, has to get himself sentenced to 28 days in jail. A distant relative (George Cole), a timid bank clerk, has to hold up his bank manager, while another relation (Guy Middleton), who is something of a philanderer, has to marry the first single girl he meets.

The plum comedy part is undoubtedly Sim's, his endeavors to land in jail being loaded with chuckles.

•

LAUGHTER IN THE DARK
1969, 101 mins, UK/France col
Dir Tony Richardson ***Prod*** Neil Harley ***Scr*** Edward Bond ***Ph*** Dick Bush ***Ed*** Charles Rees ***Art*** Julia Oman
Act Nicol Williamson, Anna Karina, Jean-Claude Drouot, Sheila Burrell, Sian Phillips, Kate O'Toole (Gershwin-Kastner/Marceau/Woodfall)

Fascinating attempt to transpose the Nabokov novel to the screen. Director Tony Richardson is able to capture the novel's profound human insights, and, as in *Lolita*, the compulsions and perversities that for Nabokov are the very stuff of the psyche.

The intricate story centers on a wealthy, titled young art dealer, Edward (Nicol Williamson), who is attracted to usherette Margot (Anna Karina), and continues to return to the theater before finally arranging to meet her.

Richardson's direction ranges from brilliantly evocative to confusing. During some of the most humorous scenes one suspects Richardson is actually serious.

Williamson, who replaced Richard Burton in the lead role, is the perfect physical type and so good as to be almost difficult to watch. Both Karina and Drouot are also excellent.

•

LAURA
1944, 88 mins, US Ⓥ ⦿ b/w
Dir Otto Preminger ***Prod*** Otto Preminger ***Scr*** Jay Dratler, Betty Reinhardt, Samuel Hoffenstein ***Ph*** Joseph LaShelle ***Ed*** Louis Loeffler ***Mus*** David Raksin ***Art*** Lyle R. Wheeler, Leland Fuller
Act Gene Tierney, Dana Andrews, Clifton Webb, Vincent Price, Judith Anderson, Dorothy Adams (20th Century-Fox)

The film's deceptively leisurely pace at the start, and its light, careless air, only heighten the suspense without the audience being conscious of the buildup. What they are aware of as they follow the story [from the novel by Vera Caspary] is the skill in the telling. Situations neatly dovetail and are always credible. Developments, surprising as they come, are logical. The dialog is honest, real and adult.

The yarn concerns an attractive femme art executive who has been brutally murdered in her New York apartment, and the attempts of a police lieutenant to solve the case. Beginning by interviewing the girl's intimates, the sleuth's trail leads him from one friend to another, all becoming suspect in the process.

Clifton Webb makes a debonair critic-columnist. Dana Andrews's intelligent, reticent performance as the lieutenant gives the lie to detectives as caricatures. Gene Tierney makes an appealing figure as the art executive and Vincent Price is convincing as a weak-willed ne'er-do-well.

1944: Best B&W Cinematography

NOMINATIONS: Best Director, Supp. Actor (Clifton Webb), Screenplay, B&W Art Direction

•

LAVENDER HILL MOB, THE
1951, 81 mins, UK Ⓥ ⦿ b/w
Dir Charles Crichton ***Prod*** Michael Balcon, Michael Truman ***Scr*** T.E.B. Clarke ***Ph*** Douglas Slocombe ***Ed*** Seth Holt ***Mus*** Georges Auric ***Art*** William Kellner
Act Alec Guinness, Stanley Holloway, Sidney James, Alfie Bass, Marjorie Fielding, Ronald Adam (Ealing)

With *The Lavender Hill Mob*, Ealing clicks with another comedy winner. Story is notable for allowing Alec Guinness to play another of his w.k. character roles. This time he is the timid escort of bullion from the refineries to the vaults. For 20 years he has been within sight of a fortune, but smuggling gold bars out of the country is a tough proposition. Eventually, with three accomplices, he plans the perfect crime. Bullion worth over £1 million is made into souvenir models of the Eiffel Tower and shipped to France.

One of the comedy highspots of the film is a scene at a police exhibition where Guinness and his principal accomplice (Stanley Holloway) first become suspect. They break out of the cordon, steal a police car, and then radio phony messages through headquarters. This sequence and the other action scenes are handled crisply, and with a light touch.

Guinness as usual shines as the trusted escort, and is at his best as the mastermind plotting the intricate details of the crime. Holloway is an excellent aide, while the two professional crooks in the gang (Sidney James and Alfie Bass) complete the quartet with an abundance of cockney humor.

1952: Best Story & Screenplay

NOMINATION: Best Actor (Alec Guinness)

•

LAW AND DISORDER
1958, 76 mins, UK Ⓥ b/w
Dir Charles Crichton ***Prod*** Paul Soskin ***Scr*** T. E. B. Clarke, Patrick Campbell, Vivienne Knight ***Ph*** Ted Scaife ***Ed*** Oswald Hafenrichter ***Mus*** Humphrey Searle ***Art*** Allan Harris
Act Michael Redgrave, Robert Morley, Ronald Squire, George Coulouris, Joan Hickson, Lionel Jeffries (Hotspur)

Law and Disorder is a highly amusing off-beat comedy [from the novel *Smugglers' Circuit* by Derek Roberts] that notches guffaws and giggles with disarming ease. It has more than a little of the Ealing stamp. There is also a certain amount of confusion due to over-drastic editing. Running at 76 minutes, it lost 15 minutes in the final version and the hacking has left at least a couple scenes in midair.

Michael Redgrave is a con man who does rather well financially in his racket even though Robert Morley, a strict and pompous judge, is constantly sending him to the cooler. Redgrave's only problem is keeping his profession away from his young son, who grows up in the belief that his dad is a missionary away for long stretches in far-off lands. All's well until the boy becomes a barrister and, worse still, marshal to Morley.

So Redgrave retires to a quiet seacoast village. But old habits die hard and he becomes involved with the villagers in an ingenious brandy-smuggling racket.

•

LAWLESS, THE (UK: THE DIVIDING LINE)

1950, 81 mins, US b/w

Dir Joseph Losey ***Prod*** William H. Pine, William C. Thomas ***Scr*** Geoffrey Homes ***Ph*** Roy Hunt ***Ed*** Howard Smith ***Mus*** Mahlon Merrick ***Art*** Lewis H. Creber

Act Macdonald Carey, Gail Russell, Lalo Rios, Maurice Jara, John Sands, Lee Patrick (Paramount)

Racial tolerance gets a working over in *The Lawless*, but the producers don't soapbox the message. Instead, they use it as a peg on which to produce a hard-hitting drama, equipped with action and fast pace.

Joseph Losey has a compact story to tell and he does it in a swift 81 minutes. Performances all stack up as topnotch, with several being standout. Plot concerns itself with so-called "fruit tramps" who make a skimpy living harvesting California's various crops. They are scorned by the Whites and subjected to physical abuse by bullies.

Macdonald Carey strides easily through his assignment as the editor who takes up the cudgels for justice after first trying to steer a middle course. Gail Russell does a fine piece of work. Lalo Rios wallops home his role as the fruit worker.

•

LAWLESS BREED, THE

1952, 83 mins, US col

Dir Raoul Walsh ***Prod*** William Alland ***Scr*** Bernard Gordon ***Ph*** Irving Glassberg ***Ed*** Frank Gross ***Art*** Bernard Herzbrun, Richard H. Riedel

Act Rock Hudson, Julie Adams, Mary Castle, John McIntire, Hugh O'Brian, Dennis Weaver (Universal)

Early-west gunman, John Wesley Hardin, has his life put on film in *The Lawless Breed*. Presumably based on Hardin's actual story of his career, published when he was released from a Texas prison after serving 16 years for killing a lawman, the production has plenty of robust action stirred up by Raoul Walsh's direction.

The plot unfolds episodically and swiftly, telling how Hardin earned his reputation as a killer after getting his first victim in self-defense, goes on the lam from the law and vengeance-seeking kinfolks, is forced into more killings, loses his sweetheart (Mary Castle) to a posse's bullets, and acquires a new one in Julie Adams, the girl who later becomes his wife.

Rock Hudson does a very good job of the main character, and Adams makes much of her femme lead. John McIntire scores in dual roles, one as Hardin's overly righteous preacher father, and the other as the gunman's uncle.

•

LAWMAN

1971, 98 mins, UK Ⓥ ⊙ col

Dir Michael Winner ***Prod*** Michael Winner ***Scr*** Gerald Wilson ***Ph*** Bob Paynter ***Ed*** Freddie Wilson ***Mus*** Jerry Fielding ***Art*** Stan Jolley

Act Burt Lancaster, Robert Ryan, Lee J. Cobb, Sheree North, Joseph Wiseman, Robert Duvall (Scimitar)

Michael Winner, an exuberant British director, led with his chin in deciding to go to the States (Mexico) to make a western—his first.

Burt Lancaster, with cold eyes, strong chin, stiff behavior, minimal talk, and a swift line on the draw, plays a marshal so dedicated to being a lawman that he is inflexible and even arrogant in his interpretation of it. He rides into a nearby town to pick up a bunch of locals who, on a drunken spree, were responsible for the death of an old man. He finds that they all work for the local bossman, played by Lee J. Cobb. Cobb's a guy who enjoys local power but hates violence. Robert Ryan is the town's weak marshal, who in the end is swayed to action with Lancaster.

Point of the story is just how far a man can compromise with his conscience and whether the end justifies the means.

Lancaster as usual is a highly convincing marshal, tough and taciturn. Ryan is also excellent as the faded, weak marshal with only memories. But it's Cobb who quietly steals the film as the local boss who, unlike in many such films, however, is no ruthless villain.

•

LAWNMOWER MAN, THE

1992, 105 mins, US Ⓥ ⊙ col

Dir Brett Leonard ***Prod*** Gimel Everett ***Scr*** Brett Leonard, Gimel Everett ***Ph*** Russell Carpenter ***Ed*** Alan Baumgarten ***Mus*** Dan Wyman ***Art*** Alex McDowell

Act Jeff Fahey, Pierce Brosnan, Jenny Wright, Mark Bringleson, Geoffrey Lewis, Jeremy Slate (Allied Vision/Lane Pringle)

Dazzling computer animation and special effects overcome *The Lawnmower Man*'s mundane story.

Loosely adapted from Stephen King, story has a mentally retarded gardener's assistant (Jeff Fahey) becoming the guinea pig for a scientist (Pierce Brosnan) experimenting with "virtual reality." The concept involves creating a computer simulation that seems real to nearly all the senses and in all directions. As Fahey's intelligence improves, he begins to rebel against those who have been abusing him, and eventually against the relatively benign Brosnan as well.

Tale has various literary influences from Daniel Keyes's *Flowers for Algernon* (*Charly*) to Arthur C. Clarke's *Dial F for Frankenstein*. The melodramatic elements are vintage King, and they are the pic's weakest parts. When Fahey's powers slip over into the extrasensory, he wreaks revenge on his tormentors, and pic comes dangerously close to *Carrie* territory.

The stunning visuals for the "virtual reality" sequences really put *The Lawnmower Man* over. The computer animation doesn't necessarily break new ground, but it marks the first time it has been so well integrated into a live-action story.

The much ballyhooed animated sex sequence is imaginative and surreal, but all too brief, providing barely enough for a subplot.

•

LAWNMOWER MAN 2: BEYOND CYBERSPACE

1996, 93 mins, US Ⓥ ⊙ col

Dir Farhad Mann ***Prod*** Edward Simons, Keith Fox ***Scr*** Farhad Mann ***Ph*** Ward Russell ***Ed*** Peter Berger, Joel Goodman ***Mus*** Robert Folk ***Art*** Ernest M. Roth

Act Patrick Bergin, Matt Frewer, Austin O'Brien, Ely Pouget, Kevin Conway, Camille Cooper (New Line/Allied Entertainments)

Now fully freed from even a nodding acquaintance with the Stephen King short story (King successfully sued to have his name removed from the original film), this serviceable sci-fi actioner can focus on special effects instead of Gothic storyline.

Matt Frewer replaces Jeff Fahey as Jobe, who was transformed into a genius living in a computerized virtual reality in the last film, which is briefly recapped here. Now evil corporate interests (personified by Kevin Conway and Camille Cooper as the maniacal plutocrat and his icy assistant) have brought Jobe back to design a new computer system, to create a global network linking all computers that will be impossible to escape.

Representing the forces of good are a group of kids led by Peter (Austin O'Brien, repeating his role from the first movie) and Dr. Benjamin Trace (Patrick Bergin), the ex-scientist who designed the ultimate computer chip only to see his investors steal it away.

Managing to transcend the formulaic plot are Frewer and Bergin, whose performances make the film work. Frewer, reunited with his *Max Headroom* director, Farhad Mann, veers from the real Jobe to the megalomaniacal virtual Jobe without missing a beat.

The film rises or falls on its special effects, credited to Cinesite. While pic doesn't appear to break new ground in its cyberspace elements, it is handsome throughout, the integration of live actors with the virtual sets seamless. The CD-ROM version was reportedly shot at the same time so that the two versions will closely resemble each other.

•

LAW OF DESIRE, THE

SEE: LA LEY DEL DESEO

•

LAWRENCE OF ARABIA

1962, 222 mins, UK Ⓥ ⊙ ▭ col

Dir David Lean ***Prod*** Sam Spiegel ***Scr*** Robert Bolt, [Michael Wilson] ***Ph*** Freddie Young ***Ed*** Anne V. Coates ***Mus*** Maurice Jarre ***Art*** John Box

Act Peter O'Toole, Alec Guinness, Anthony Quinn, Jack Hawkins, Omar Sharif, Anthony Quayle (Horizon)

Some $15 million, around three years in time, much hardship, and incredible logistics have been poured into this king-size adventure yarn. Made in Technicolor and Super Panavision 70 it is a sweepingly produced, directed, and lensed job. Authentic desert locations, a stellar cast, and an intriguing subject combine to put this into the blockbuster league.

It had best be regarded as an adventure story rather than a biopic, because Robert Bolt's well written screenplay does not tell the audience anything much new about Lawrence of Arabia, nor does it offer any opinion or theory about the character of this man or the motivation for his actions. So he remains a legendary figure and a shadowy one. Another cavil is that clearly so much footage has had to be tossed away that certain scenes are not developed as well as they might have been, particularly the ending.

Story line concerns Lawrence as a young intelligence officer in Cairo in 1916. British Intelligence is watching the Arab revolt against the Turks with interest as a possible buffer between Turkey and her German allies. Lawrence (Peter O'Toole) is grudgingly seconded to observe the revolt at the request of the civilian head of the Arab bureau. Lawrence sets out to find Prince Feisal, top man of the revolt. From then on his incredible adventures begin.

He persuades Feisal to let him lead his troops as guerrilla warriors. He tackles intertribal warfare but still they arduously take the Turkish port of Aqaba. Lawrence is given the task of helping the Arabs to achieve independence and he becomes a kind of desert Scarlet Pimpernel. He reaches Deraa before the British Army is in Jerusalem, he is captured by the Turks, tortured and emerges a shaken, broken, and disillusioned man. Yet still he takes on the job of leading a force to Damascus.

Lean and cameraman F. A. Young have brought out the loneliness and pitiless torment of the desert with an artistic use of color and with almost every frame superbly mounted. Maurice Jarre's musical score is always contributory to the mood of the film.

Peter O'Toole, after three or four smallish, but effective, appearances in films, makes a striking job of the complicated and heavy role of Lawrence. His veiled insolence and contempt of high authority, his keen intelligence and insight, his gradual simpatico with the Arabs and their way of life, his independence, courage, flashy vanity, withdrawn moments, pain, loneliness, fanaticism, idealism, and occasional foolishness.

Jack Hawkins plays General Allenby with confidence and understanding and Arthur Kennedy provides a sharp portrayal of a cynical, tough American newspaperman. The two top support performances come from Alec Guinness as Prince Feisal and Anthony Quayle as a stereotyped, honest, bewildered staff officer. Only Anthony Quinn, as a larger-than-life, proud, intolerant Arab chief seems to obtrude overmuch and tends to turn the performance into something out of the Arabian Nights.

1962: Best Picture, Director, Color Cinematography, Color Art Direction, Sound, Original Music Score, Editing

NOMINATIONS: Best Actor (Peter O'Toole), Supp. Actor (Omar Sharif), Adapted Screenplay

•

LAWYER MAN

1932, 68 mins, US b/w

Dir William Dieterle ***Prod*** Stanley Logan ***Scr*** Rian James, James Seymour ***Ph*** Robert Kurrle ***Ed*** Thomas Pratt

Act William Powell, Joan Blondell, Helen Vinson, Alan Dinehart, Allen Jenkins (Warner)

William Powell is the entire picture as an East Side NY attorney, but in Joan Blondell as his secretary he has the wrong-type opposite. The two don't seem to stack up right together though perhaps Blondell is more the sec type than Kay Francis would have been.

Powell is at his best in the early sequences as a man who is sartorially the equal of a country hick. By degrees he comes out of the hick character into his own.

Quite a number of good laughs permeate the action [from a novel by Max Trell] but there's little in the way of courtroom stuff. Most of what happens in courtrooms is covered by flashes of newspaper headlines entirely out of proportion to what would be given by the conservative New York paper whose masthead is photographed.

David Landau stands out as the political boss who traps the lawyer in a blackmail stunt in order to gain control of him, only to pay for it dearly in the end himself.

William Dieterle, who first came over to the U.S. to make foreign versions, is responsible for a workman-like directorial job.

•

LEAGUE OF GENTLEMEN, THE

1960, 116 mins, UK Ⓥ ⦿ b/w

Dir Basil Dearden ***Prod*** Michael Relph ***Scr*** Bryan Forbes ***Ph*** Arthur Ibbetson ***Ed*** John Guthridge ***Mus*** Philip Green ***Art*** Peter Proud

Act Jack Hawkins, Nigel Patrick, Roger Livesey, Richard Attenborough, Bryan Forbes, Kieron Moore (Allied Film Makers)

The first entry from Allied Film Makers—consisting of actors Jack Hawkins, Richard Attenborough, and Bryan Forbes, producer Michael Relph and director Basil Dearden—is a smooth piece of teamwork.

Hawkins, disgruntled at being axed from the army, which he has faithfully served for many years, decides to have a go at a bank robbery. He picks up the idea from an American thriller and recruits seven broke and shady ex-officers, all experts in their own line in the army. The gang goes into hiding while every phase of the operation is planned down to the last detail. As a military exploit, the entire gang would have earned medals. As it is pulled off they are eventually tripped up by a slight, unforeseen happening.

Forbes has written a strong, witty screenplay from John Boland's novel. It takes time to get under way, but once the gang is formed, the situations pile up to an exciting and funny finale. Dearden's direction is sure and Arthur Ibbetson has turned in some excellent camerawork. The eight members of the gang all give smooth, plausible performances, with Hawkins and Patrick, as his second-in-command, having the meatiest roles.

•

LEAGUE OF THEIR OWN, A

1992, 128 mins, US Ⓥ ⦿ ▭ col

Dir Penny Marshall ***Prod*** Robert Greenhut, Elliot Abbott ***Scr*** Lowell Ganz, Babaloo Mandel ***Ph*** Miroslav Ondricek ***Ed*** George Bowers, Adam Bernardi ***Mus*** Hans Zimmer ***Art*** Bill Groom

Act Tom Hanks, Geena Davis, Madonna, Lori Petty, Jon Lovitz, Garry Marshall (Parkway/Columbia)

Awash in sentimentality and manic energy but only occasionally bubbling over with high humor, *A League of Their Own* hits about .250 with a few RBIs but more than its share of strikeouts.

A comic look at the first season of the women's baseball league in 1943 [based on a story by Kim Wilson and Kelly Candaele], Penny Marshall's gangly fourth film benefits from a fresh, unusual subject—the joy of baseball being played by women having the time of their lives and a wonderful central performance by Geena Davis. Downside includes contrived plotting, obvious comedy and heart-tugging, some hammy thesping and a general hokiness.

Once the teams are picked, most of the obvious plotting possiblities pop up: The attempts of the women to skirt the strict behavior code, the marriage and departure of one of them, the death of another's husband at war, the gradual improvement of their play and resulting growth of popularity and respect, and the inevitable, cornball showdown between rival sisters.

Adding a little testosterone to the recipe is Tom Hanks, a former big-league star who sees life from so deep in the bottle that he virtually sleeps through practice and the initial games.

Of the large cast, Rosie O'Donnell stands out as the brash, smooth-fielding third basewoman, and Megan Cavanagh makes an impression as the dumpy slugger who finds unexpected romance on the road. A brunette Madonna plays a predictably sassy and irreverent type who shows her underwear whenever she can, and Lori Petty is irritatingly petulant as Davis's cry-baby little sister.

Despite the lavish budget, period feel isn't fully realized, as locations are pretty much restricted to ballparks and boardinghouses. An extraordinary effect is created by the appearance of Davis's character as an older woman at the beginning and end. Davis reportedly dubbed the line readings.

•

LEAP OF FAITH

1992, 108 mins, US Ⓥ ⦿ col

Dir Richard Pearce ***Prod*** Michael Manheim, David V. Picker ***Scr*** Janus Cercone ***Ph*** Matthew F. Leonetti ***Ed*** Don Zimmerman, Mark Warner, John F. Burnett ***Mus*** Cliff Eidelman ***Art*** Patrizia Von Brandenstein

Act Steve Martin, Debra Winger, Lolita Davidovich, Liam Neeson, Lukas Haas, Meat Loaf (Paramount)

Steve Martin gives a showy but sober performance as a phony faith healer in *Leap of Faith*, well-made but muddled in its aims.

The foremost problem is that the film waffles as to what it's about, never embarking on a full-scale indictment of charlatans and TV ministries and never unabashedly embracing any higher power, despite its cryptic ending.

The story begins when minister Jonas Nightengale's (Martin) traveling motorcade is forced to make an unscheduled stop-over in a small, depressed Kansas town. The entourage includes Martin's assistant (Debra Winger).

The act starts to unravel, however, as Winger becomes enamored with the local sheriff (Liam Neeson), who isn't fooled by Martin's act, while the ersatz preacher gets entangled with a pretty waitress (Lolita Davidovich) and her crippled brother (Lukas Haas), who were previously victimized by one of his brethren.

First-time writer Janus Cercone's script proves intriguing at first as it goes about debunking the faith-healing mystique. But there's also little insight into Martin and Winger's relationship.

Most other roles are equally underdeveloped, and the budding romance between Winger and Neeson is reduced to scenes that rely more on schmaltzy settings than character.

•

LEARNING TREE, THE

1969, 106 mins, US Ⓥ ▭ col

Dir Gordon Parks ***Prod*** Gordon Parks ***Scr*** Gordon Parks ***Ph*** Burnett Guffey ***Ed*** George R. Rohrs ***Mus*** Gordon Parks ***Art*** Ed Engoron

Act Kyle Johnson, Alex Clarke, Estelle Evans, Dana Elcar, Mira Waters (Warner/Seven Arts)

The Learning Tree is a sentimental, sometimes awkward, but ultimately moving film about a black teenager growing up in rural Kansas during the 1920s. It is apparently the first film financed by a major company to be directed by a Negro.

Film recounts, in short, episodic passages, how a talented and perceptive 15-year-old boy learns about life from a variety of characters, situations, and personal encounters.

The worst moments occur when director Gordon Parks interpolates small sermonettes. Also, the film cannot quite carry the large helping of melodrama that occurs near the end. But on the whole this is an impressive, strong film. His 1963 novel on which it is based is purportedly semi-autobiographical.

•

LEATHER BOYS, THE

1964, 108 mins, UK Ⓥ ▭ b/w

Dir Sidney J. Furie ***Prod*** Raymond Stross ***Scr*** Gillian Freeman ***Ph*** Gerry Gibbs ***Ed*** Reginald Beck ***Mus*** Bill McGuffie ***Art*** Arthur Lawson

Act Rita Tushingham, Colin Campbell, Dudley Sutton, Gladys Henson, Avice Landon, Betty Marsden (British Lion/Garrick)

Main theme is the doomed marriage of a couple immature kids. Reggie (Colin Campbell), who spends a riotous leisure as a motorcyclist, hitches up with Dot (Rita Tushingham), who sees the union as a release from parental control.

The crackup comes when Dot turns out an incompetent wife, chary of making beds and relying on a daily diet of canned beans. This dampens Reggie's sex urge. He departs to live with grandma and takes up with a "buddy" called Peter (Dudley Sutton). Despite Pete's insistent affection, he is reluctant to associate with girls, and has good housekeeping ability. Reggie does not wise up to the fact that Pete's a homosexual. As the audience gets the drift early, this somewhat punctures the plot.

Virtues of the pic lie in Sidney Furie's direction and in the two male performances. Furie has a sharp eye for sleazy detail, and he uses the underprivileged backgrounds with telling visual effect. Gillian Freeman's screenplay, culled from a novel by Eliot George, is also capable in its ear for verbal mannerisms, but it doesn't give coherence to the characters. Little sympathy can be stirred up for any of them.

Dudley Sutton, however, registers strongly as the spry, loyal Pete.

•

LEAVE ALL FAIR

1985, 88 mins, New Zealand col

Dir John Reid ***Prod*** John O'Shea ***Scr*** Stanley Harper, Maurice Pons, Jean Betts, John Reid ***Ph*** Bernard Lutic ***Ed*** Ian John ***Mus*** Stephen McCurdy ***Art*** Joe Bleakley

Act John Gielgud, Jane Birkin, Feodor Atkine, Simon Ward (Pacific/Goldeneye/Challenge)

Lensed entirely in France, this elegiac story about the husband of New Zealand writer Katherine Mansfield, who died in 1922 while returning to places where they'd lived together to oversee the publishing of a book based on her letters to him, is a sober, affecting experience.

John Gielgud, playing another elderly man of letters, returns to France to meet his publisher (Feodor Atkine). The trip brings back memories of his life with Mansfield (Jane Birkin), memories made more painful when he meets Atkine's mistress, Marie (also played by Birkin), who not only resembles his long-dead wife, but is also a New Zealander.

Lushly photographed pic is as gentle and nuanced as Mansfield's own writings, and the scenes between Gielgud and Birkin play with subtlety and insight.

•

LEAVE HER TO HEAVEN

1945, 110 mins, US ⦿ col

Dir John M. Stahl ***Prod*** William A. Bacher ***Scr*** Jo Swerling ***Ph*** Leon Shamroy ***Ed*** James B. Clark ***Mus*** Alfred Newman ***Art*** Lyle R. Wheeler, Maurice Ransford

Act Gene Tierney, Cornel Wilde, Jeanne Crain, Vincent Price, Mary Philips, Ray Collins (20th Century-Fox)

Sumptuous Technicolor mounting and a highly exploitable story lend considerable importance to *Leave Her to Heaven* that it might not have had otherwise. Script based on Ben Ames Williams's bestseller has emotional power in the jealousy theme but it hasn't been as forcefully interpreted by the leads as it could have been in more histrionically capable hands.

Essentially a woman's story it tells of a girl (Gene Tierney) whose possessive jealousy smothered her father and destroyed her husband's infatuation. Story is told in retrospect by Ray Collins, family attorney, and film opens with Cornel Wilde returning to Maine and his waiting love, Jeanne Crain, after serving a prison term for concealing crimes.

Tierney and Wilde use their personalities in interpreting their dramatic assignments. Crain's role of Tierney's foster-sister is more subdued but excellently done. Vincent Price, as the discarded lover, gives a theatrical reading to the courtroom scenes as the district attorney.

1945: Best Color Cinematography

NOMINATIONS: Best Actress (Gene Tierney), Color Art Direction, Sound

•

LEAVING LAS VEGAS

1995, 112 mins, US Ⓥ ⦿ col

Dir Mike Figgis ***Prod*** Lila Cazes, Annie Stewart ***Scr*** Mike Figgis ***Ph*** Declan Quinn ***Ed*** John Smith ***Mus*** Mike Figgis ***Art*** Waldemar Kalinowski

Act Nicolas Cage, Elisabeth Shue, Julian Sands, Richard Lewis, Valeria Golino, Graham Beckel (United Artists/Lumiere)

In *Leaving Las Vegas*, Nicolas Cage assays a character who's on a slide to touch bottom as he sinks deeper into depression and alcoholism. The film pulls no punches, takes no prisoners, and flies in the face of feel-good pictures.

Ben Sanderson (Cage) is a Hollywood talent rep who has dived into the bottle, coming up for air and lucidity from time to time. It's not long before he's shown the door at the agency. He heads for the gambling capital, puts himself on an allowance, and contends that he'll be able to drink himself to death in four to five weeks.

Every conceivable cliché is turned on its head. While focused on Ben, story evolves into a two-character piece in which he's partnered with Sera (Elisabeth Shue), a prostitute whose back story is equally nebulous. She's attracted to his vulnerability, and he agrees to move in with her on condition she never asks him to stop drinking.

The two performers are attractive without pushing it. Cage is in top form as he purposefully stumbles through the movie. Shue is equally skillful. She's neither a hooker with a heart of gold nor an actress dressing down to a role. Rather, one feels her character has fallen into this life while pursuing another path.

Large supporting cast provides many cameos, including director Mike Figgis (as a goon), director Bob Rafelson, and familiar faces Lou Rawls and Valeria Golino. Julian Sands, as Sera's Latvian-born pimp, does a brief, effective turn prior to running afoul of the new Russian mafia. Despite the familiarity of Vegas as a location, Declan Quinn's camera lends a fresh perspective to its outsize urban vistas. Figgis's score is a visceral treat.

1995: Best Actor (Nicolas Cage)

NOMINATIONS: Best Actress (Elisabeth Shue), Director, Screenplay Adaptation

•

LEAVING NORMAL
1992, 110 mins, US Ⓥ ⊙ col
Dir Edward Zwick ***Prod*** Lindsay Doran ***Scr*** Edward Solomon ***Ph*** Ralf D. Bode ***Ed*** Victor Du Bois ***Mus*** W.G. Snuffy Walden ***Art*** Patricia Norris
Act Christine Lahti, Meg Tilly, Patrika Darbo, Lenny Von Dohlen, Maury Chaykin, Eve Gordon (Universal/Mirage)

Cocktail waitress Christine Lahti and battered housewife Meg Tilly meet in a parking lot, immediately bond, and are soon headed from the small western town of Normal to Alaska where Lahti will claim her inherited home and land. First they stop off to visit Tilly's relatives in Portland and get an eyeful of the dreaded "perfect homemaker" existence (nicely caricatured by Eve Gordon as a sister).

After Lahti's GTO breaks down and is ransacked, they get a ride from friendly truckers Maury Chaykin and Lenny Von Dohlen. Lahti's distrust of all men after having been burned too often nips this relationship in the bud, but Tilly is determined to pursue Von Dohlen someday.

Edward Solomon's episodic screenplay has the duo's route and key decisions left to chance. Director Edward Zwick, who previously piloted the quite dissimilar, nearly all-male war pic *Glory*, uses optical effects, matte shots, and other fantasy touches from the outset to avoid realism in depicting the women's fanciful saga.

Though Lahti dominates much of the film as a brassy, tough-as-nails character, the waif-like Tilly gets to blossom in the final reel when she finally finds a home in Alaska and becomes the small town's cheerful mascot.

•

LECTRICE, LA
(THE READER)
1988, 100 mins, France Ⓥ col
Dir Michel Deville ***Prod*** Michel Deville, Rosalinde Deville ***Scr*** Michel Deville, Rosalinde Deville ***Ph*** Dominique Le Rigoleur ***Ed*** Raymonde Guyot ***Art*** Thierry Leproust
Act Miou-Miou, Christian Ruche, Maria Casares, Patrick Chesnais, Marianne Denicourt, Pierre Dux (Elefilm/AAA/TSF/Cine-5)

A stylish frothy "light read" of a film, *La Lectrice* recounts the adventures of a young woman who rents her services as a professional reader to bourgeois clients ill-disposed to doing their own page-turning. Michel Deville has fashioned an elegant entertainment with humor, irony, eroticism [from the books *La Lectrice* and *Un Fontasme de Bella B. et Autre Recits* by Raymod Jean].

Miou-Miou is the engaging heroine, a young woman of Arles who enjoys reading, has an attractive voice and obviously enjoys meeting people. Upon a friend's suggestion she places an ad in a local paper to offer reading services. Naturally, the clientele is varied.

Miou-Miou reads Guy de Maupassant to a young cripple aroused by the view of her casually uncovered thigh, goes through Karl Marx and Tolstoy for the widow of an Eastern European general (Maria Casares), and beleaguers a neurotic inhibited business exec (Patrick Chesnais) with Marguerite Duras while they hop into bed together.

She finally decides to turn the final page on her little metier when an aging local magistrate (Pierre Dux) asks her to read some salacious prose from the Marquis de Sade for a round table of fellow notables. Deville has composed this playful little opus with a deluxe production that makes every scene a pleasure for the eye. Picturesque exteriors of winding streets and alleyways in the old quarter of Arles punctuate the film's glossy look.

•

LEFT HANDED GUN, THE
1958, 105 mins, US Ⓥ b/w
Dir Arthur Penn ***Prod*** Fred Coe ***Scr*** Leslie Stevens ***Ph*** Peverell Marley ***Ed*** Folmar Blangsted ***Mus*** Alexander Courage ***Art*** Art Loel
Act Paul Newman, Lita Milan, Hurd Hatfield, James Congdon, James Best, John Dehner (Warner/Haroll)

The Left Handed Gun is another look at Billy the Kid, probably America's most constantly celebrated juvenile delinquent. In this version he's Billy, the crazy, mixed-up Kid. The picture is a smart and exciting western paced by Paul Newman's intense portrayal.

The screenplay is based on a [1955] teleplay by Gore Vidal called *The Death of Billy the Kid*. The action is concerned with the few events that led up to the slaying of the Brooklyn boy by lawman Pat Garrett.

Scripter Leslie Stevens emphasizes the youthful nature of the desperado by giving him two equally young companions, James Best and James Congdon. The three team after Newman's mentor, cattleman Colin Keith-Johnston, is shot by a crooked officer of the law. Newman is determined to avenge the cattleman's death, and the plot becomes a crazed crusade in which Newman, Best, and Congdon are all killed, the death of a badman and the birth of a legend.

The best parts of the film are the moments of hysterical excitement as the three young desperados rough-house with each other as reckless as any innocent boys and in the next instant turn to deadly killing without flicking a curly eyelash.

In his first picture, director Arthur Penn shows himself in command of the medium. Newman dominates but there are excellent performances from others, including Lita Milan in a dimly seen role as his Mexican girlfriend, John Dehner as the remorseless Pat Garrett, and Hurd Hatfield, a mysterious commentator on events.

•

LEFT HAND OF GOD, THE
1955, 87 mins, US Ⓥ ▭ col
Dir Edward Dmytryk ***Prod*** Buddy Adler ***Scr*** Alfred Hayes ***Ph*** Franz Planer ***Ed*** Dorothy Spencer ***Mus*** Victor Young ***Art*** Lyle Wheeler, Maurice Ransford
Act Humphrey Bogart, Gene Tierney, Lee J. Cobb, Agnes Moorehead, E. G. Marshall, Carl Benton Reid (20th Century-Fox)

Based on the novel by William E. Barrett, the film is somewhat provocative, in that its central character is a man who masquerades as a priest. Carrying on this deception is Yank flier Humphrey Bogart, who believes it to be the sole way he can escape as prisoner of Chinese warlord Lee J. Cobb.

What transpires in a remote Chinese province after Bogart dons the ecclesiastical robes in 1947 largely adds up to character studies of the fake priest and his immediate colleagues at a Catholic mission, where all are stationed. For the drama and suspense aren't to be found in whether the flier escapes from China but in the soul-searching he subjects himself in continuing the masquerade.

Besides Bogart, others who have their own mental conflicts are Gene Tierney, E. G. Marshall, and Agnes Moorehead.

•

LEGACY, THE
1979, 100 mins, US Ⓥ col
Dir Richard Marquand ***Prod*** David Foster ***Scr*** Jimmy Sangster, Patric Tilley, Paul Wheeler ***Ph*** Dick Bush, Alan Hume ***Ed*** Anne V. Coates ***Mus*** Michael J. Lewis ***Art*** Disley Jones
Act Katharine Ross, Sam Elliott, Hildegard Neil, Roger Daltrey, John Standing, Charles Gray (Universal/Turman-Foster)

Using the hoary convention of stranding a young couple in the mansion of a reclusive millionaire whose guests are progressively bumped off in an assortment of gruesome ways, *The Legacy* tries for an added dimension of satanic possession, but winds up a tame, suspenseless victim of its own lack of imagination.

Katharine Ross and Sam Elliott play the Yank couple, a pair of architects mysteriously summoned for an assignment in England. When they're accidentally forced off a country road by a chauffeured Rolls, owner John Standing invites them back for "tea." They find themselves trapped in the house for the weekend.

The film, directed with no tension or suspenseful pacing by former TV director Richard Marquand, takes an eternity to get down to business.

•

LEGAL EAGLES
1986, 114 mins, US Ⓥ ⊙ ▭ col
Dir Ivan Reitman ***Prod*** Ivan Reitman ***Scr*** Jim Cash, Jack Epps, Jr. ***Ph*** Laszlo Kovacs ***Ed*** Sheldon Kahn, Pem Herring, William Gordean ***Mus*** Elmer Bernstein ***Art*** John DeCuir
Act Robert Redford, Debra Winger, Daryl Hannah, Brian Dennehy, Terence Stamp, Steven Hill (Northern Lights)

Loss of intrigue with a scattered plot involving art fraud and murder is made up for by an often witty, albeit lightweight dialog led by the ever-boyish star Robert Redford.

Lavish production opens with charmer Redford as one of the d.a.'s office's winningest attorneys, Tom Logan, assigned to prosecute the daughter of a famous artist for trying to steal one of her dead father's paintings.

He faces the opposing counsel of Laura Kelly (Debra Winger), a court-appointed defense attorney known for daffy courtroom antics to get her clients off.

It's when the burglary charges are suddenly dropped against the unbalanced defendant Chelsea Deardon (Daryl Hannah) that he decides to go over to Winger's side to discover why.

Winger and Redford work well as an attorney team, but in true yuppie form become more friends attracted by each others' professional acumen than by each other's bodies.

•

LEGEND
1986, 94 mins, US Ⓥ ⊙ ▭ col
Dir Ridley Scott ***Prod*** Arnon Milchan ***Scr*** William Hjortsberg ***Ph*** Alex Thomson ***Ed*** Terry Rawlings ***Mus*** Jerry Goldsmith [US version: Tangerine Dream] ***Art*** Assheton Gorton
Act Tom Cruise, Mia Sara, Tim Curry, David Bennent, Alice Playten, Billy Barty (Legend/20th Century-Fox)

Legend is a fairytale produced on a grand scale, set in some timeless world and peopled with fairies, elves, and goblins, plus a spectacularly satisfying Satan. At the same time, the basic premise is alarmingly thin, a compendium of any number of ancient fairytales.

Plot concerns a heroic young peasant, Jack, who takes his sweetheart, Princess Lili, to see the most powerful creatures on earth, the last surviving unicorns. Unknown to the young Lovers, Darkness (i.e., The Devil) is using the innocence of Lili as a bait to trap and emasculate the unicorns.

Kids of all ages should be entranced by the magnificent makeup effects of Rob Bottin and his crew, from the smallest elves to the giant Darkness. The latter is unquestionably the most impressive depiction of Satan ever brought to the screen. Tim Curry plays him majestically with huge horns, cloven feet, red leathery flesh, and yellow eyes, plus a resonantly booming voice.

Also registering strongly is David Bennent as a knowing pixie with large, pointed ears.

Ironically, for a film that celebrates nature, *Legend* was almost entirely lensed on the large Bond set at Pinewood (production was interrupted by a fire that destroyed the set).

1986: NOMINATION: Best Makeup

•

LEGEND OF BAGGER VANCE, THE
2000, 127 mins, US Ⓥ ⊙ col
Dir Robert Redford ***Prod*** Robert Redford, Michael Nozik, Jake Eberts ***Scr*** Jeremy Leven ***Ph*** Michael Ballhaus ***Ed*** Hank Corwin ***Mus*** Rachel Portman ***Art*** Stuart Craig
Act Will Smith, Matt Damon, Charlize Theron, Bruce McGill, Joel Gretsch, Lane Smith (Wildwood-Allied/DreamWorks-20th Century Fox)

A lightweight, modestly engaging yarn sporting reductive mystical and philosophical elements that are both valid and borderline silly, Robert Redford's carefully mounted telling of a fictional '30s golf match between two real-life legends and a local Georgia champion is very much of a piece with his numerous previous films about the "inner game" in athletics, competition and self-realization, such as *Downhill Racer, The Natural, Quiz Show, A River Runs Through It* and *The Horse Whisperer*. But while the picture is involving enough on a moment-to-moment basis, it generates no special excitement or feeling, which is partly attributable to the relaxed nature of golf as well as to the simply defined characters.

Narrated from the vantage point of many decades by an old man (Jack Lemmon), story proper is set in the early stage of the Depression. Adele Invergordon (Charlize Theron), the golden girl of Savannah, faces a mountain of debts left in the wake of the suicide of her once-wealthy father, who also passed along a fabulous new oceanside golf resort. To put Krewe Island on the map, Adele charms the two leading golfers of the day, Atlanta gent Bobby Jones and swaggering Yankee Walter Hagen, into a competition, a stunt that local businessmen will only consent to if one of their own is permitted to play as well.

The only conceivable man for the honor is mid-1910s amateur champ Junuh (Matt Damon), who disappeared for a decade from the still-bitter Adele's life and is now a drunken no-account living outside town. He's persuaded to get a shave and shape up; among the film's best scenes are one in which Junuh tells the idolatrous, 10-year-old narrator-to-be, Hardy Greaves (a captivating J. Michael Moncrief) how alcohol slowly kills different parts of the brain, and another in which Adele comes to seduce Junuh into participating in the match.

As Junuh shoots practice drives one night, a mysterious figure emerges from the darkness and starts giving pointers. Thus does Bagger Vance (Will Smith) become Junuh's caddie and unsolicited spiritual guide. Vance becomes more of a peripheral figure than he was in the book [by Steven Pressfield], indispensable thematically but more obviously a bystander when physicalized as a rather shabbily dressed fellow who mostly hangs around delivering advice while others perform. Role provides Smith with a perfectly sympathetic opportunity for a change of pace, one he handles agreeably while seeming to tax his abilities not in the least. Damon adequately essays one of the many flawed Golden

Boys who populate Redford's pictures but bleaches out somewhat in comparison to Joel Gretsch's utterly dazzling Bobby Jones, the real Golden Boy here. Bruce McGill is a delight as the swaggering Hagen. Pic is physically immaculate in the manner customary with Redford's work.

•

LEGEND OF HELL HOUSE, THE
1973, 94 mins, UK/US Ⓥ ⊙ col
Dir John Hough ***Prod*** Albert Fennell, Norman T. Herman ***Scr*** Richard Matheson ***Ph*** Alan Hume ***Ed*** Geoffrey Foot ***Mus*** Brian Hodgson, Delia Derbyshire ***Art*** Robert Jones
Act Pamela Franklin, Roddy McDowall, Clive Revill, Gayle Hunnicutt, Roland Culver, Peter Bowles (Academy/20th Century-Fox)

Richard Matheson's scripting of his novel *Hell House* builds into an exceptionally realistic and suspenseful tale of psychic phenomena. John Hough's direction maintains this spirit as his cast of characters arrive at the deserted Hell House with an assignment from its present tycoon owner to learn the truth about survival after death, a secret he believes the house with its terrifying history may hold.

Sent on the mission are a physicist, a femme mental medium, and a physical medium. Latter is the only survivor of a similar investigation twenty years before when eight scientists were either killed or driven to insanity. Wife of the physicist is also a member of the party. Shock value is an important element as audience literally feels the unseen power that exists in the house.

Clive Revill, the physicist, who attempts to clear the house of its evil; Pamela Franklin, the mental medium; and Roddy McDowall, the survivor of the previous incursion, are all first-rate.

•

LEGEND OF LYLAH CLARE, THE
1968, 127 mins, US col
Dir Robert Aldrich ***Prod*** Robert Aldrich ***Scr*** Hugo Butler, Jean Rouverol ***Ph*** Joseph Biroc ***Ed*** Michael Luciano ***Mus*** Frank DeVol ***Art*** George W. Davis, William Glasgow
Act Kim Novak, Peter Finch, Ernest Borgnine, Milton Selzer, Rossella Falk, Coral Browne (M-G-M/Associates & Aldrich)

Script spotlights the making of a film about Lylah Clare, a world famous pic star who died some time before under mysterious circumstances.

Her one-time producer-discoverer, who is "fighting the big C" after a visit to the Mayo clinic, wants as his swan song to revive the Clare legend via a biopic, and succeeds in convincing Lewis Zarkan, the director who made her and was briefly in love with her, to coach look-alike Elsa Brinkmann into capturing the departed star's mannerisms.

Pic [from the teleplay by Robert Thom and Edward DeBlasio] is at its best when it spotlights the dilemma of the girl reincarnating the defunct star, especially when Elsa grotesquely switches to Lylah's vulgar German-accented tones and phrases, or when she imagines the scenes of her predecessor's violent death.

Though only intermittently given a challenging scene or two, Kim Novak brings off her dual role as Elsa-Lylah well. Peter Finch is very good as the director who's her doing and undoing, and there's a very amusing and talented performance by Ernest Borgnine as a studio boss.

•

LEGENDS OF THE FALL
1994, 134 mins, US Ⓥ ⊙ col
Dir Edward Zwick ***Prod*** Edward Zwick, Bill Wittliff, Marshall Herskovitz ***Scr*** Susan Shilliday, Bill Wittliff ***Ph*** John Toll ***Ed*** Steven Rosenblum ***Mus*** James Horner ***Art*** Lilly Kilvert
Act Brad Pitt, Anthony Hopkins, Aidan Quinn, Julia Ormond, Henry Thomas, Karina Lombard (Tri-Star/Bedford Falls/Pangaea)

Novelist Jim Harrison's fascination with the primal forces that influence civilized behavior found its apotheosis in his novella *Legends of the Fall*. The sweeping, melodramatic saga is a complex tale with elements both ideal and problematic for the big screen. The Edward Zwick version is intelligent, emotional, and largely succeeds in its transference.

The story, set during the early 20th century, focuses on the three sons of retired cavalry officer William Ludlow (Anthony Hopkins), a renegade with a moral stripe. As the spring thaw of 1913 arrives, the youngest son, Samuel (Henry Thomas), returns from an Eastern school with his fiancée, Susannah Finncannon (Julia Ormond). His older brothers have taken over key areas of the ranch business. Alfred (Aidan Quinn) is a sort of operating manager and Tristan (Brad Pitt) is the barely housebroken head wrangler.

The distant thunder of the first European World War beckons the idealistic Samuel to the call of duty in spite of his father's dissent, and he dies on the battlefield. Reunited in Montana, Tristan and Susannah become lovers.

As densely plotted as *Legends of the Fall* is, it's to the credit of the performers and craftsmen that the film escapes the abyss of melodrama and sentimentality. Zwick imbues the story with an easy, poetic quality that mostly sidesteps the precious. The actors, working as an ensemble, are near perfect in the service of the material.

1994: Best Cinematography

NOMINATIONS: Best Art Direction, Sound

•

LE MANS
1971, 108 mins, US Ⓥ ⊏⊐ col
Dir Lee H. Katzin, [John Sturges] ***Prod*** Jack N. Reddish ***Scr*** Harry Kleiner ***Ph*** Robert B. Hauser, Rene Guissart, Jr. ***Ed*** Donald W. Ernst ***Mus*** Michel Legrand
Act Steve McQueen, Siegfried Rauch, Elga Andersen, Ronald Leigh-Hunt (Solar/Cinema Center)

Marked by some spectacular car-racing footage, *Le Mans* is a successful attempt to escape the pot-boiler of prior films on same subject. The solution was to establish a documentary mood. Steve McQueen stars (and races).

Filmed abroad on actual French locales, the project began under director John Sturges. Creative incompatibilities brought McQueen, his Solar Prods indie, and Cinema Center Films to the mat, and as the dust settled Sturges was out and Lee H. Katzin finished the film and gets solo screen credit.

The spare script finds McQueen returning to compete in the famed car race a year after he has been injured. Elga Andersen, wife of a driver killed in the same accident, also returns, somewhat the worse for emotional wear. Siegfried Rauch is McQueen's continuing rival in racing competition.

The film establishes its mood through some outstanding use of slow motion, multiple-frame printing, freezes, and a most artistic use of sound—including at times no sound. The outstanding racing footage not only enhances the effects, but stands proudly on its own feet in straight continuity.

•

LEMON DROP KID, THE
1951, 91 mins, US Ⓥ ⊙ b/w
Dir Sidney Lanfield ***Prod*** Robert L. Welch ***Scr*** Edmund Hartmann, Robert O'Brien, Frank Tashlin, Irving Elinson ***Ph*** Daniel L. Fapp ***Ed*** Archie Marshek ***Mus*** Victor Young ***Art*** Hal Pereira, Franz Bachelin
Act Bob Hope, Marilyn Maxwell, Lloyd Nolan, Jane Darwell, Andrea King, Fred Clark (Paramount/Hope)

The Lemon Drop Kid is neither true Damon Runyon, from whose short story of the same title it was adapted [story by Edmund Beloin], nor is it very funny Bob Hope.

Although Hope is the principal interest and gets most of the laughs, his comedy style, and particularly his wisecracking lines, are at the root of the picture's failure. It not only destroys the Runyonesque sentimental flavor but actually pulls the props from under the inherent humor of the story.

Marilyn Maxwell is decorative as the sophisticated and therefore un-Runyon love interest, and she teams neatly with the star in the catchy incidental songs [by Jay Livingston and Ray Evans]. Other members of the cast are generally excellent, primarily because they conform to the Runyon requirements. Thus, Lloyd Nolan is passable though a trifle over-suave as a racketeer, while Jane Darwell, Fred Clark, Jay C. Flippen, William Frawley, Harry Bellaver, Sid Melton, and various others are properly intense and therefore genuinely comic as assorted minor hoodlums.

•

LEMON POPSICLE
1978, 100 mins, Israel Ⓥ col
Dir Boaz Davidson ***Prod*** Menahem Golan, Yoram Globus ***Scr*** Boaz Davidson, Eli Tabor ***Ph*** Adam Greenberg ***Ed*** Alain Jakubowicz
Act Yiftach Katzur, Anat Atzmon, Jonathan Segal, Zachi Noy (Noah)

Lemon Popsicle takes place in Tel Aviv in the late 1950s. Three youths—Benz, Momo, and Yudaleh—have only girls on their mind, while the hit-parade on the radio (Elvis Presley) reflects their own emotional engagement in the world.

Benz, a shy, sensitive lad, falls in love with Nili, who prefers his best chum, Momo. Momo gets Nili pregnant, then drops her as the summer vacation starts; Benz stays behind to arrange the necessary abortion. He confesses his love and things appear running his way, when the school term starts and Nili is back again in the arms of Momo.

The schoolboy romance also has a funnier side to it. It's in the search for an initial sexual experience—first with a middle-aged nympho where Benz delivers ice, then with a prostitute who gives them the crabs—both handled with appropriate gags to put the scenes over.

•

LENIN IN OCTOBER
SEE: LYENIN V OKTYABRYE

•

LENNY
1974, 111 mins, US Ⓥ ⊙ b/w
Dir Bob Fosse ***Prod*** Marvin Worth ***Scr*** Julian Barry ***Ph*** Bruce Surtees ***Ed*** Alan Heim ***Mus*** Ralph Burns ***Art*** Joel Schiller
Act Dustin Hoffman, Valerie Perrine, Jan Miner, Stanley Beck, Gary Morton, Rashel Novikoff (United Artists)

Lenny Bruce was one of the precursors of social upheaval, and like most pioneers, he got clobbered for his foresight. Bob Fosse's remarkable film version of Julian Barry's legit play, *Lenny*, stars Dustin Hoffman in an outstanding performance.

Production was photographed in black and white, lending not only a slight period influence but also capturing the grit and the sweat, as well as the private and public tortures of its principal character.

Barry's excellent script takes the form of flashback, but with some partial flashforward scenes. Three key figures in Bruce's life—wife Valerie Perrine in a sensational performance; hardcharger mother Jan Miner in a beautiful characterization; and Stanley Beck in top form as Bruce's agent—are being tape-interviewed after his death by an unseen party, whose motives are never clear.

1974: NOMINATIONS: Best Picture, Director, Actor (Dustin Hoffman), Actress (Valerie Perrine), Adapted Screenplay, Cinematography

•

LEON
(THE PROFESSIONAL)
1994, 106 mins, France Ⓥ ⊙ ⊏⊐ col
Dir Luc Besson ***Prod*** Claude Besson (exec.) ***Scr*** Luc Besson ***Ph*** Thierry Arbogast ***Ed*** Sylvie Landra ***Mus*** Eric Serra ***Art*** Dan Weil
Act Jean Reno, Gary Oldman, Natalie Portman, Danny Aiello, Peter Appel, Ellen Greene (Gaumont/Dauphin)

A dour and illiterate Italian hitman finds redemption in the company of a headstrong, orphaned girl in Luc Besson's *Leon*. Shooting entirely in English for the first time since his runaway local hit *The Big Blue*, Besson delivers a naive fairytale splattered with blood.

Tale dawdles to the half-hour mark when Mathilda (Natalie Portman), a bright but abused 12-year-old truant, returns from the grocery store to find that corrupt cop Stansfield (Gary Oldman) and his trigger-happy crew have used her entire family for target practice. Mathilda is reluctantly taken in by her towering and taciturn neighbor, Leon (Jean Reno), a self-described "cleaner" (Bessonian slang for "hit man"). The ambitious, only mildly bereaved waif thinks that's "cool" and begs 40-ish Leon to teach her his trade. The mismatched couple bonds, and the formerly invincible hitman becomes vulnerable.

Dialog is adequate but lacks a single quotable or memorable line. Fortunately, the visuals—shot on location in Little Italy and Spanish Harlem, with eight weeks of studio interiors in France—put the story across. Wide-screen lensing favors tight close-ups, and multiple shoot-'em-ups are edited with panache.

Newcomer Portman shows an appealing spontaneity although she never registers as a real child. Danny Aiello is good, if familiar, as a restaurateur. Oldman's edgy perf as a drug- and power-crazed turncoat, while not one of his best, is by far the most interesting characterization on display.

[A 132-min. *Version Integrale*, which represented the director's original cut prior to test screenings in the U.S., was released in France in June 1996 and later on laserdisc. This version expands on Mathilda's apprenticeship, and her relationship with Leon.]

•

LEON MORIN, PRETRE
(LEON MORIN, PRIEST; THE FORGIVEN SINNER)
1961, 114 mins, France b/w
Dir Jean-Pierre Melville ***Prod*** Georges de Beauregard ***Scr*** Jean-Pierre Melville ***Ph*** Henri Decae ***Ed*** Jacqueline Meppiel, Nadine Marquand, Marie-Josephe Yoyotte ***Mus*** Martial Solal, Albert Raisner ***Art*** Daniel Gueret
Act Jean-Paul Belmondo, Emmanuele Riva, Irene Tunc, Nicole Mirel, Monique Bertho, Patricia Gozzi (Rome Paris)

Tale [from Beatrix Beck's 1952 novel] of a young agnostic woman's conversion to Catholicism and her physical love for a priest during the Nazi occupation of France is handled with tact and talent.

The woman in question works in an office. One day in a fit of pique she decides to bait a priest but instead meets a young one who seems to be able to cope with her capriciousness. She begins to visit him and finds her true nature. All aspects of religion and attitudes are deftly treated in these well-limned sequences. Then comes the changing times of the war and her finding of religion and, at the same time, a carnal love for the priest.

Jean-Paul Belmondo, the feckless hoodlum of *Breathless*, here displays a reserve and understanding of his role as progressive young priest. Emmanuele Riva, the heroine of *Hiroshima Mon Amour*, gives the role an intensity that is acceptable in spite of some overdone personal tics and mannerisms. Director Jean-Pierre Melville has adroitly underlined the talk with good visual rhythm and an expert recreation of the times.

•

LEON MORIN, PRIEST
SEE: LEON MORIN, PRETRE

•

LEON THE PIG FARMER
1993, 103 mins, UK Ⓥ ⦿ col
Dir Vadim Jean, Gary Sinyor ***Prod*** Gary Sinyor, Vadim Jean ***Scr*** Gary Sinyor, Michael Norman ***Ph*** Gordon Hickie ***Ed*** Ewa J. Lind ***Mus*** John Murphy, David Hughes ***Art*** Simon Hicks
Act Mark Frankel, Janet Suzman, Brian Glover, Connie Booth, David de Keyser, Maryam D'Abo (Leon the Pig Farmer)

A London Jewish kid finds his real dad is in the bacon trade in *Leon the Pig Farmer*, a good-humored riff on Jewish-gentile stereotypes. Billing itself as "the first Jewish comedy feature film to come out of Britain," pic is very different in feel to Yank equivalents. Sitcom elements and British scatological humor keep peeking through the comic fabric. Pacing, too, is milder.

Opening has Leon (Mark Frankel) finding he and his brothers are actually the products of artificial insemination, as Dad has a low sperm count. His real father is gentile pig farmer Chadwick (Brian Glover) up north in the wilds of Yorkshire.

Surprised but delighted, Chadwick and his wife (Connie Booth) go 200% Jewish to make Leon feel at home. Twist comes when Leon, helping out on the farm, accidentally injects a pig with sheep's semen, producing the world's first kosher porker.

Playing of the uneven script is broad all round, with Glover well supported by Booth, dominating all his scenes. Maryam D'Abo livens up the London segs as a horny gentile with the hots for Jewish boys. Franklin is okay as the bemused Leon.

•

LEOPARD, THE
SEE: IL GATTOPARDO

•

LEOPARD MAN, THE
1943, 65 mins, US Ⓥ ⦿ b/w
Dir Jacques Tourneur ***Prod*** Val Lewton ***Scr*** Ardel Wray, Edward Dein ***Ph*** Robert de Grasse ***Ed*** Mark Robson ***Mus*** Roy Webb ***Art*** Albert S. D'Agostini, Walter E. Keller
Act Dennis O'Keefe, Margo, Jean Brooks, Isabel Jewell, James Bell, Margaret Landry (RKO)

Both script [from the novel *Black Alibi* by Cornell Woolrich] and direction noticeably strain to achieve effects of *Cat People* but fall far short of latter standard and follow too many confusing paths. After brief introduction, it's a series of chases and murders, with a tame leopard blamed for the latter until strange happenings are pinned on one of the players. It's all confusion, in fact too much for an audience to follow.

Dennis O'Keefe is press agent for a New Mexican nitery and rents a tame black leopard for a publicity stunt which backfires when the cat escapes and a girl is presumably killed by the fugitive. Yarn then spins through regulation eerie channels with two other strange murders enacted—one being in the time-worn setting of a cemetery and windstorm combined. O'Keefe and Margo stick around long enough to trip the real culprit in time for the fadeout to come along.

•

LEO THE LAST
1970, 103 mins, UK col
Dir John Boorman ***Prod*** Robert Chartoff, Irwin Winkler ***Scr*** William Stair, John Boorman ***Ph*** Peter Suschitzky ***Ed*** Tom Priestley ***Mus*** Fred Myrow ***Art*** Tony Wollard
Act Marcello Mastroianni, Billie Whitelaw, Calvin Lockhart, Glenna Forster-Jones, Vladek Sheybal, Gwen Ffrangcon-Davies (United Artists)

An absurd satire on dethroned European royalty with a neo-realistic view of the London ghetto.

Marcello Mastroianni, the last of his line, lives in exile in a magnificent London townhouse at the end of a cul-de-sac in a black ghetto area. He is a totally ineffectual, sheltered sickly man, whose only human contacts are a flock of parasitic social magpies. Footage on the ghetto comings and goings, as orchestrated by director John Boorman, has a gritty documentary feel.

There is a grotesquely hilarious scene of a mass nude water therapy of Mastroianni's entourage led by society doctor David de Keyser. But the two sequences are all that work in *Leo*. The rest is at best silly, at worst pretentious allegory and unsuccessful social comment.

•

LES GIRLS
1957, 114 mins, US Ⓥ ⦿ ▭ col
Dir George Cukor ***Prod*** Sol C. Siegel ***Scr*** John Patrick ***Ph*** Robert Surtees ***Ed*** Ferris Webster ***Mus*** Cole Porter ***Art*** William A. Horning, Gene Allen
Act Gene Kelly, Mitzi Gaynor, Kay Kendall, Taina Elg, Jacques Bergerac, Leslie Phillips (M-G-M)

Les Girls is an exceptionally tasty musical morsel that is in the best tradition of the Metro studio. It's an original and zestful entry that would have been greeted with critical handsprings if it had been originally presented on the Broadway stage.

The musical is set in London, Paris, and Granada, Spain. It's the story of a song-and-dance team made up of Gene Kelly and Mitzi Gaynor, Kay Kendall and Taina Elg. Known as "Barry Nichols and Les Girls," they are a popular Continental act. Many years after the act has broken up, Kendall, now the wife of an English peer, has written a book of reminiscences that lands her in a London court, the defendant in a libel suit brought by Elg, now married to a French industrialist. The court trial provides the setting for a series of flashbacks. Each gives a different version of what happened.

The excursion into the past provides the setting for a number of Cole Porter tunes and dances brightly staged by Jack Cole as "Les Girls" appear in niteries in France and Spain. Porter created seven new songs for the picture.

Kendall emerges as a delightful comedienne in her first American picture. Elg, a Finnish actress-ballerina who portrays a French girl, has a quality that is exceedingly appealing. Gaynor is the wholesome, uncomplicated member of the troupe.

1957: Best Costume Design

NOMINATIONS: Best Art Direction, Sound

•

LESS THAN ZERO
1987, 98 mins, US Ⓥ ⦿ col
Dir Marek Kanievska ***Prod*** Jon Avnet, Jordan Kerner ***Scr*** Harley Peyton ***Ph*** Edward Lachman ***Ed*** Peter E. Berger, Michael Tronick ***Mus*** Thomas Newman ***Art*** Barbara Ling
Act Andrew McCarthy, Jami Gertz, Robert Downey, Jr., James Spader, Michael Bowen, Tony Bill (20th Century-Fox)

If it's possible, *Less Than Zero* is even more specious and shallow than the Bret Easton Ellis book it is based on. There's a story somewhere tracking the dissipated lifestyles of the super-rich, super-hip kids and their L.A. haunts.

Drugs take over Julian (Robert Downey, Jr.); Clay (Andrew McCarthy) avoids the scene by attending an eastern college; and his g.f. Blair (Jami Gertz) loses her identity, which was never much to begin with. This is where they are at the beginning of the film—and pretty much where they are at the end.

Perhaps this wasn't the best subject matter for British director Marek Kanievska (*Another Country*) to make his American debut. The feel for this distinctly Southern California story escapes him.

Only Downey elicits the kind of sympathy to distinguish this drama from a photojournalist essay of the kind that might run in *Vanity Fair*. Of the secondary roles, James Spader as Downey's pusher is terrifically smarmy. Unfortunately, this sick relationship doesn't become involving until the last third of the film, when Downey really begins to fall apart and is forced into male whoring to pay his drug debts. Visually the picture is a treat.

•

LETHAL WEAPON
1987, 110 mins, US Ⓥ ⦿ col
Dir Richard Donner ***Prod*** Richard Donner, Joel Silver ***Scr*** Shane Black ***Ph*** Stephen Goldblatt ***Ed*** Stuart Baird ***Mus*** Michael Kamen, Eric Clapton ***Art*** J. Michael Riva
Act Mel Gibson, Danny Glover, Gary Busey, Mitchell Ryan, Tom Atkins, Darlene Love (Warner/Silver)

Lethal Weapon is a film teetering on the brink of absurdity when it gets serious, but thanks to its unrelenting energy and insistent drive, it never quite falls.

Danny Glover is a family-man detective who gets an unwanted partner in the possibly psychotic Mel Gibson. Story is on the backburner as the two men square off against each other, more as adversaries than partners.

Gibson is all live wires and still carries Vietnam with him twenty years after the fact. Though he's fifteen years his senior and also a Nam vet, Glover is meant to be a sensitive man of the 1980s. Gibson simmers while Glover worries about his pension.

While the film is trying to establish its emotional underpinnings, a plot slowly unfolds involving a massive drug-smuggling operation headed by the lethal Vietnam vet Joshua (Gary Busey).

Ultimately the common ground for Glover and Gibson is staying alive as the film attempts to shift its buddy story to the battlefields of L.A. Gibson, in one of his better performances, holds the fascination of someone who may truly be dangerous. Glover, too, is likable and so is Darlene Love as his wife, but he and Gibson come from two different worlds the film never really reconciles.

1987: NOMINATION: Best Sound

•

LETHAL WEAPON 4
1998, 127 mins, US Ⓥ ⦿ ▭ col
Dir Richard Donner ***Prod*** Joel Silver, Richard Donner ***Scr*** Channing Gibson ***Ph*** Andrzej Bartkowiak ***Ed*** Frank J. Urioste, Dallas Puett ***Mus*** Michael Kamen, Eric Clapton, David Sanborn ***Art*** J. Michael Riva
Act Mel Gibson, Danny Glover, Joe Pesci, Rene Russo, Chris Rock, Jet Li (Silver/Warner)

The quintessence of the buddy cop pic, *Lethal Weapon 4* is big on action, playful banter and just enough plot to keep our attention from wandering. It matters little that the film is rife with non-sequiturs, nonsense and nihilistic violence, because its heroes are so darn buoyant and charming.

Bare-bones plot [by Jonathan Lemkin, Alfred Gough and Miles Millar] centers on a group of transplanted Chinese triad members in Los Angeles who are smuggling in families from the mainland. Of course, such penny-ante criminal activity is just the tip of the iceberg in a much more nefarious operation. But the film is as concerned with what's going on in the margins as it is with the evil doings of martial arts master and triad leader Wah Sing Ku (Jet Li).

In the six years since Riggs (Mel Gibson) and Murtaugh (Danny Glover) were last on the beat for the LAPD, a lot has happened in their lives. Riggs is about to be a papa as a result of his relationship with Internal Affairs officer Lorna Cole (Rene Russo), and Murtaugh is on the cusp of grandfatherhood, courtesy of his daughter Rianne (Traci Wolfe).

Adding to the humor mix is Leo Getz (Joe Pesci), the mob accountant intro'd in chapter two, who's now a private detective, and Lee Butters (Chris Rock), a cop with an attitude and a staccato riff.

Gibson, Glover, Pesci and Russo have settled into roles that fit their personas as snugly as Italian suits. The addition of Rock enlivens the piece and broadens the appeal of the series. As the chief villain, Li is a mixed bag: his physical prowess is nonpareil, but his limited command of English inadvertently casts him as the sort of Asian devil that borders on caricature.

Series vet director Richard Donner deftly effects a dazzling freeway chase and a well-choreographed duel-to-the-death sequence. Still, the finale is just shy of the balletic quality of John Woo and Tsui Hark's best Hong Kong actioners.

•

LETHAL WEAPON 3
1992, 118 mins, US Ⓥ ⦿ ▭ col
Dir Richard Donner ***Prod*** Joel Silver, Richard Donner ***Scr*** Jeffrey Boam, Robert Mark Kamen ***Ph*** Jan De Bont ***Ed*** Robert Brown, Battle Davis ***Mus*** Michael Kamen, Eric Clapton, David Sanborn ***Art*** James Spencer
Act Mel Gibson, Danny Glover, Joe Pesci, Rene Russo, Stuart Wilson, Steve Kahan (Warner/Silver)

The recipe again works here, producing a pic that's really more about moments—comic or thrilling—than any sort of cohesive whole. The plot [by Jeffrey Boam] hinges on a wispy premise about an ex-cop (Stuart Wilson) providing confiscated guns to gangs.

This time, the emotional focus is on Danny Glover's Roger Murtaugh, who counts down the days to his retirement even as he grapples with whether hanging up his gun will make him an old man. Murtaugh and gonzo partner Martin Riggs (Mel Gibson) stumble onto the gun racket, bringing them into contact with high-kicking investigator Lorna Cole (Rene Russo), a woman who wins Riggs's heart by demonstrating that she can inflict as much damage as he can.

The pic manages to be highly entertaining and sanctions all its violence by making the bad guys so despicable that death seems to be the only solution. The broad scope of the action also brings a requisite make-believe quality to the narrative.

•

LETHAL WEAPON 2

1989, 113 mins, US Ⓥ ⦿ ▭ col

Dir Richard Donner ***Prod*** Richard Donner, Joel Silver ***Scr*** Jeffrey Boam ***Ph*** Stephen Goldblatt ***Ed*** Stuart Baird ***Mus*** Michael Kamen, Eric Clapton, David Sanborn ***Art*** J. Michael Riva

Act Mel Gibson, Danny Glover, Joe Pesci, Joss Ackland, Derrick O'Connor, Patsy Kensit (Warner/Silver)

Loaded with the usual elements, *Lethal Weapon 2* benefits from a consistency of tone that was lacking in the first film. This time, screenwriter Jeffrey Boam [working from a story by Shane Black and Warren Murphy] and director Richard Donner have wisely trained their sights on humor and the considerable charm of Mel Gibson and Danny Glover's on-screen rapport.

They've also dreamed up particularly nasty villains and incorporated enough chases and shootouts to hold the attention of a hyperactive nine-year-old.

Plot sets the duo after South African diplomats using their shield of immunity to smuggle drugs. Tagging along for the ride in a hilarious comic turn is Joe Pesci as an unctuous accountant who laundered the baddies' money and now needs witness protection to stay out of the washing machine himself.

There's also a fleeting entanglement between Riggs (Mel Gibson) and the lead villain's secretary (the sparkling Patsy Kensit) that adds some welcome sex appeal.

•

LET HIM HAVE IT

1991, 115 mins, UK Ⓥ ⦿ col

Dir Peter Medak ***Prod*** Luc Roeg, Robert Warr ***Scr*** Neal Purvis, Robert Wade ***Ph*** Oliver Stapleton ***Ed*** Ray Lovejoy ***Mus*** Michael Kamen ***Art*** Michael Pickwood

Act Chris Eccleston, Paul Reynolds, Tom Courtenay, Tom Bell, Eileen Atkins, Clare Holman (Vivid)

Let Him Have It takes one of the most controversial murder trials in post-war Brit history and comes up with a powerful mix of social conscience and solid entertainment. Pic reconstructs the events leading to the 1952 rooftop shootout in south London between local cops and cocky, gun-crazy Chris Craig. At age 16, Craig was legally too young to be hanged so his 19-year-old partner, Derek Bentley, went to the gallows instead, despite public petitions and last-minute appeals.

Though innocent of any shooting, Bentley was heard to cry "Let him have it" to the rod-wielding Craig. The defense argued the words meant hand over the gun rather than shoot. Craig, released in 1963 and living a reformed life, played no part in the present production, though the filmmakers tried to contact him.

Pic studiously avoids a docu approach. The dramatic focus begins and ends on a tragic figure of Bentley (Chris Eccleston), an epileptic with the mental age of an 11-year-old and a distant relationship with his working-class father (Tom Courtenay) and reticent mother (Eileen Atkins). After a spell in an approved school, he's coaxed out of his shell by older sister (Clare Holman) and comes under the sway of swaggering Craig (Paul Reynolds) and Craig's crooked brother (Mark McGann).

Script is sometimes overladen with exposition, especially in the family scenes and after-trial seg. But it succinctly captures the feel of suburban postwar Britain, and its younger characters' search for thrills through Hollywood movies, flash cars, and pop music. Peter Medak directs fluidly and with an eye for bigscreen values.

•

LET IT BE

1970, 80 mins, UK Ⓥ col

Dir Michael Lindsay-Hogg ***Prod*** Neil Aspinall ***Ph*** Tony Richmond, Les Parrott, Paul Bond ***Ed*** Tony Lenny, Graham Gilding

Act Paul McCartney, John Lennon, George Harrison, Ringo Starr, Yoko Ono (Apple)

As a 16-mm cinema verité of four rock musicians in a studio jamming a bit, trying to get their music together, clowning and rapping a little, and finally doing a brief concert, *Let It Be* is a relatively innocuous, unimaginative piece of film. But the musicians are the Beatles.

Through the studio session, Lennon's wife Yoko Ono is always present—close at hand, silent, not participating, yet somehow distracting Lennon, splitting his attention. The Beatles's past togetherness, the chummy camaraderie, the quickness to seize on a line and build a series of gags, is no longer there.

After the prolonged musical teasing, the film finally settles into a studio concert with "Two of Us" and Paul McCartney's "Let It Be." Then the concert moves onto a London roof with a half-dozen numbers while cameras cut away to the gathering traffic jam in the street below. The outdoor photography, shot with available light under an overcast sky, is muddy, and the long-lens close-up shots from the surrounding roofs are off-focus.

•

LET'S DANCE

1950, 111 mins, US Ⓥ ⦿ col

Dir Norman Z. McLeod ***Prod*** Robert Fellows ***Scr*** Allan Scott, Dane Lussier ***Ph*** George Barnes ***Ed*** Ellsworth Hoagland ***Mus*** Robert Emmett Dolan (dir.)

Act Fred Astaire, Betty Hutton, Roland Young, Lucile Watson, Gregory Moffett (Paramount)

Let's Dance is a light concoction of story, songs and dances, sprinkled with humor that is generally acceptable as escapist filmfare.

Plot [suggested by a story by Maurice Zolotow] kicks off with a prolog showing Betty Hutton and Fred Astaire entertaining troops in England. She reveals to him her marriage to a flyer. Story picks up five years later with Hutton's extrovert character being subdued in the straitlaced environs of a Back Bay Boston mansion, home of her husband, killed in the war. She rebels and steals away in the night with her small son to return to show business.

She meets Astaire again. He gets her a spot; the management and others in the place take to her and the son. In telling this angle the yarn is strung out too long.

•

LET'S DO IT AGAIN

1975, 112 mins, US Ⓥ col

Dir Sidney Poitier ***Prod*** Melville Tucker ***Scr*** Richard Wesley ***Ph*** Donald M. Morgan ***Ed*** Pembroke J. Herring ***Mus*** Curtis Mayfield ***Art*** Alfred Sweeney

Act Sidney Poitier, Bill Cosby, Calvin Lockhart, John Amos, Jimmie Walker, Ossie Davis (Warner)

A Timothy March story has been scripted into a loosely strung series of sketches that amiably advance the story. Sidney Poitier, who has a mysterious hex power, and Bill Cosby, whose versatility herein seems as great as that of Peter Sellers, hie to New Orleans to parlay a bankroll into big winnings for their lodge, presided over by a patriarchal Ossie Davis.

With wives Lee Chamberlin and Denise Nicholas in tow, the pair confound old-time gangster John Amos and new-wave hood Calvin Lockhart. The secret weapon Poitier uses is his hypnotic transformation of puny Jimmie Walker from a "before" gymnasium advertisement into a pugilistic dynamo. The film could have been a nightmare of lethargy, but it's a good mixture of broad comedy.

•

LET'S FACE IT

1943, 76 mins, US b/w

Dir Sidney Lanfield ***Prod*** Fred Kohlmar ***Scr*** Harry Tugend ***Ph*** Lionel Lindon

Act Bob Hope, Betty Hutton, ZaSu Pitts, Eve Arden (Paramount)

Harry Tugend's screenplay closely follows the Herbert and Dorothy Fields-Cole Porter [1941] musical, which in turn had basic similarities to the play *Cradle Snatchers*, with the writers of that, Norma Mitchell and Russell G. Medcraft, included in the screen credits. The yarn is about a wacky soldier, who, with two pals, gets involved with three a.k. dames figuring to get revenge on their philandering husbands by hiring soldiers as consorts.

Tugend, however, has managed to inject many more laughs than were in the Broadway musical click, which was highlighted by Danny Kaye's delivery of "Melody in 4-F," replaced here with a Sammy Cahn–Jule Styne number, "Who Did? I Did, Yes I Did." The laughs, in fact, come so often and so fast as to be stepping on one another, with the audience estimated as missing 25 percent of the gags.

Bob Hope, a master at fast vaudeville timing of comedy material, and Betty Hutton, glamorized to an unprecedented degree for a hoydenish singer, are an okay romantic team. They are given better than average support by Cully Richards and Dave Willock, as Hope's pals; and Eve Arden, who was in the Broadway cast.

•

LET'S GET HARRY

1986, 107 mins, US Ⓥ ⦿ col

Dir Alan Smithee [Stuart Rosenberg] ***Prod*** Daniel H. Blatt, Robert Singer ***Scr*** Charles Robert Carner ***Ph*** James A. Contner ***Ed*** Ralph E. Winters, Rick R. Sparr ***Mus*** Brad Fiedel ***Art*** Mort Rabinowitz, Agustin Ituarte

Act Michael Schoeffling, Tom Wilson, Glenn Frey, Gary Busey, Robert Duvall, Ben Johnson (Tri-Star/Delphi IV & V)

Let's Get Harry is a well made but utterly routine action picture, worth catching for two excellent (as usual) support performances by Robert Duvall and Gary Busey. Director Stuart Rosenberg took his name off the credits, reportedly due to a contretemps during post-production (pic was lensed in Mexico and Illinois in 1985).

Project was planned as a film by Samuel Fuller, writing and directing, in 1981; he is credited with cowriting the story [with Mark Feldberg]. It's the trite concept of a group of young guys, led by Michael Schoeffling, deciding to take matters into their own hands to go to Colombia to rescue Schoeffling's brother Harry (Mark Harmon), kidnaped along with the U.S. ambassador (Bruce Gray) by terrorists.

Picture follows rigidly the clichés of this mini-genre, such as the old hand mercenary (Robert Duvall) who takes the youngsters under his wing. There's even a totally illogical female role written in, played by Elpidia Carrillo, who is cast in virtually every south-of-the-border Hollywood opus.

Film is redeemed somewhat by Duvall, as a gung-ho medal-of-honor winner. Busey is also delightful as a smooth-talking car dealer who agrees to bankroll the mission if he can come along for a "hunting trip."

•

LET'S MAKE IT LEGAL

1951, 77 mins, US Ⓥ b/w

Dir Richard Sale ***Prod*** Robert Bassler ***Scr*** F. Hugh Herbert, I. A. L. Diamond ***Ph*** Lucien Ballard ***Ed*** Robert Fritch ***Mus*** Cyril Mockridge

Act Claudette Colbert, Macdonald Carey, Zachary Scott, Barbara Bates, Robert Wagner, Marilyn Monroe (20th Century-Fox)

Let's Make It Legal is a frothy comedy package about a middle-aged couple's divorce and their eventual reconciliation. Gags and mildly amusing situations abound in the script [from a story by Mortimer Braus], but they're never genuinely effective.

After 20 years of varying bliss, Claudette Colbert and Macdonald Carey call it quits. Just when the final decree becomes effective Zachary Scott comes on the scene. An old beau of Colbert's, he still has the fire of conquest burning in him. Like a blooded racehorse running his last match, Carey rises to meet the competition and manages to throttle it before the last frame is off the spool.

Performances are fairly good. Colbert rolls off her lines easily. Carey, while giving it a valiant try, isn't quite plausible as a man who'd go around spraying roses as well as roues. Scott is well cast as the libertine. Barbara Bates and Robert Wagner are suitably annoying as the young couple who pry into their elders' affairs.

•

LET'S MAKE LOVE

1960, 118 mins, US Ⓥ ▭ col

Dir George Cukor ***Prod*** Jerry Wald ***Scr*** Norman Krasna, Hal Kanter ***Ph*** Daniel L. Fapp ***Ed*** David Bretherton ***Mus*** Lionel Newman (dir.) ***Art*** Lyle R. Wheeler, Gene Allen

Act Marilyn Monroe, Yves Montand, Tony Randall, Frankie Vaughan, Wilfrid Hyde White (20th Century-Fox)

After the film has been underway about 12 minutes, the screen goes suddenly dark (the scene is rehearsal of an off-Broadway show) and a lone spotlight picks up Marilyn Monroe wearing black tights and a sloppy wool sweater. She announces, with appropriate musical orchestration, that her name is Lolita and that she isn't allowed to play (pause) with boys (pause) because her heart belongs to daddy [words and music by Cole Porter].

This not only launches the first of a series of elegantly designed [by Jack Cole] production numbers and marks one of the great star entrances ever made on the screen, but is typical of the entire film—which has taken something not too original (the Cinderella theme) and dressed it up like new.

Monroe, of course, is a sheer delight in the tailor-made role of an off-Broadway actress who wants to better herself intellectually (she is going to night school to study geography), but she also has a uniquely talented costar in Yves

Montand. Latter gives a sock performance, full of both heart and humor, as the richest man in the world who wants to find a woman who'll love him for himself alone.

Whenever the story threatens to intrude with tedium, there's a knockout Cole Porter musical number.

1960: NOMINATION: Best Scoring of a Musical Picture

•

LETTER, THE

1940, 95 mins, US Ⓥ ⦿ b/w

Dir William Wyler ***Prod*** Hal B. Wallis ***Scr*** Howard Koch ***Ph*** Tony Gaudio ***Ed*** George Amy, Warren Low ***Mus*** Max Steiner ***Art*** Carl Jules Weyl

Act Bette Davis, Herbert Marshall, James Stephenson, Gale Sondergaard, Sen Yung (Warner)

The Letter has a history running back to 1927. Twice before it has been seen in legit and once before (1929) in films, each time with a top femme star in the principal role. Yet never has [the W. Somerset Maugham play] been done with greater production values, a better all-around cast or finer direction. Its defect is its grimness. Director William Wyler, however, sets himself a tempo that is in rhythm with the Malay locale.

Story is essentially a mystery. It opens with Bette Davis shooting a man dead as he runs from her plantation house. The question mark from there to the climax is *why*? She explains to her planter-husband (Herbert Marshall) and an attorney friend (James Stephenson) that the murdered man, an old family intimate, had made advances at her and in her angry resentment she picked up a revolver. It's evident from the coolness of her recital that she's not telling the truth.

Stephenson's smart native assistant, excellently played by Sen Yung, brings him word of a letter she has written. It was to the man she killed and was in the hands of his wife, a Malay gal (Gale Sondergaard). Through it, it is revealed that for 10 years the murderess has been having an affair with her victim and the fatal triggerwork resulted when she discovered he had thrown her over for the beauteous native.

Davis's frigidity at times seems to go even beyond the characterization. On the other hand, Marshall never falters. Virtually stealing thesp honors in the pic, however, is Stephenson as the attorney, while Sondergaard is the perfect mask-like threat.

Set is of tremendous proportions and the music by Max Steiner is particularly noteworthy in creating and holding a mood, as well as in pointing up the drama.

1940: NOMINATIONS: Best Picture, Director, Actress (Bette Davis), Supp. Actor (James Stephenson), B&W Cinematography, Editing, Original Score

•

LETTER FROM AN UNKNOWN WOMAN

1948, 84 mins, US Ⓥ ⦿ b/w

Dir Max Ophuls ***Prod*** John Houseman ***Scr*** Howard Koch ***Ph*** Franz Planer ***Ed*** Ted J. Kent ***Mus*** Daniele Amfitheatrof ***Art*** Alexander Goltizen

Act Joan Fontaine, Louis Jourdan, Mady Christians, Marcel Journet, Art Smith, Carol Yorke (Rampart/Universal)

Picture teams Joan Fontaine and Louis Jourdan as costars and they prove to be a solid combination. Both turn in splendid performances in difficult parts that could easily have been overplayed.

Story [based on a novel by Stefan Zweig] follows a familiar pattern, but the taste with which the film has been put together in all departments under John Houseman's production supervision makes it a valid and interest-holding drama. The mounting has an artistic flavor that captures the atmosphere of early-day Vienna [about 1900] and has been beautifully photographed.

Story unfolds in flashback, a device that makes plot a bit difficult to follow at times, but Max Ophuls's direction holds it together. He doesn't rush his direction, adopting a leisurely pace that permits best use of the story. Film is endowed with little touches that give it warmth and heart while the tragic tale is being unfolded.

It concerns a young girl who falls in love with a neighbor, a concert pianist. Years later she again meets her only love but he fails to remember. Story is told as he reads a letter from the girl, written after the second meeting.

•

LETTER TO BREZHNEV

1985, 95 mins, UK Ⓥ ⦿ col

Dir Chris Bernard ***Prod*** Janet Goddard ***Scr*** Frank Clark ***Ph*** Bruce McGowan ***Ed*** Lesley Walker ***Mus*** Alan Gill ***Art*** Lez Brotherston, Nick Englefield, Jonathan Swain

Act Alexandra Pigg, Alfred Molina, Peter Firth, Margi Clarke, Tracy Lea, Ted Wood (Yeardream/Film Four/Palace)

This is a farce, penned with wit and acted with appropriate deadpan honesty by all the principals. Picture a Russian ship docking in Liverpool. Two sailors go ashore for a night on the town, both primed with Beatles folklore and one speaking enough English to get them both by with the lasses in a dancehall.

As for the girls, one works in a chicken factory and does little else than look forward to the weekend conquests. The other is on the dole, but has a romantic view in regard to her bed partners.

Elaine, the Liverpool innocent, meets Peter, the Russian romantic from the Black Sea. They fall in love at first sight. When they part, the naive Elaine finds it unfair that the world's political stage should prove a hindrance to their ever seeing each other again. So she writes a letter to Brezhnev—and gets an answer. To wit: If you really love your Russian sailor, come to the Soviet Union to marry him and settle down as an adopted citizen.

Alexandra Pigg (Elaine) and Margi Clarke (Teresa) are a tickling pair of working girl types right out of that British tradition going back to "Free Cinema" days.

•

LETTER TO THREE WIVES, A

1948, 108 mins, US Ⓥ ⦿ b/w

Dir Joseph L. Mankiewicz ***Prod*** Sol C. Siegel ***Scr*** Joseph L. Mankiewicz ***Ph*** Arthur Miller ***Ed*** J. Watson Webb, Jr. ***Mus*** Alfred Newman ***Art*** Lyle R. Wheeler, J. Russell Spencer

Act Jeanne Crain, Linda Darnell, Ann Sothern, Kirk Douglas, Paul Douglas, Barbara Lawrence (20th Century-Fox)

While the picture is standout in every aspect, there are two factors mainly responsible for its overall quality. One is the unique story, adapted from a John Klempner novel *Vera Caspary* and given a nifty screenplay by Joseph L Mankiewicz.

Idea has three young housewives in Westchester, NY (much of the film was shot on location in the East), all jealous of the same she-wolf who grew up with their husbands. The "other woman" addresses a letter to all three wives explaining that she has run away with one of their spouses but without identifying which one. The audience is then given a chance to figure out which one it is, before a surprise denouement explains all.

Other standout aspect is the fine film debut of legit actor Paul Douglas. His role in *Wives* is that of a big, blustering but slightly dumb tycoon and he really gives it a ride with some neat character shading. He's equally good in the more serious romantic moments with Linda Darnell.

Rest of the cast is equally good. Jeanne Crain, Darnell and Ann Sothern, as the three fraus, each turns in a job as good as anything they've done. Kirk Douglas, playing Sothern's husband, is fine as the serious-minded literature prof who can't take his wife's soap-opera writing.

Story is bridged by the off-screen voice of the she-wolf, who is built into a character resembling every man's dream gal by the dialog. Mankiewicz, wisely, never shows her.

1949: Best Director, Screenplay

NOMINATION: Best Picture

•

LET THE GOOD TIMES ROLL

1973, 99 mins, US ▭ col

Dir Sid Levin, Robert Abel ***Prod*** Gerald I. Isenberg ***Ph*** Robert Thomas, David Myers, Erik Daarstad, Dick Pierce, Steve Larner, Paul Lohmann, Mike Live ***Ed*** Sid Levin, Hyman Kaufman, Bud Friedgen, Yeu-Bun-Yee

Act Chuck Berry, Little Richard, Fats Domino, Chubby Checker, Bo Diddley, The Shirelles (Metromedia)

Let the Good Times Roll is a smash recreation of 1950s rock 'n' roll frenzy, a moving and exciting nostalgia trip.

The production focuses on two rock 'n' roll revival concerts held in Long Island's Nassau Coliseum and Detroit's Cobo Hall, personalizes the thirty-three musical numbers with penetrating backstage views of the performers, and underpins the whole with astutely chosen film and video clips and stills of the decade. The talent lineup resurrected for *Let the Good Times Roll* shames all such previous features save *Woodstock* and reminds one that a lot of performing excitement has not been properly utilized in recent years. In a group consisting of such 1950s giants as Fats Domino, Chubby Checker, the Shirelles, Bill Haley and the Comets, the Five Satins, the Coasters, Danny and the Juniors and the Bobby Comstock Rock & Roll Band, three stand out with especial distinction.

Chuck Berry is clearly wrecked by the audience outpouring that greets him. Bo Diddley also stands out. Best of all, however, is Little Richard, that pompadoured teenage screamer who affects the next best thing to drag for his frenetic workouts with an equally hysteric audience.

•

LETYAT ZHURAVLI
(THE CRANES ARE FLYING)

1957, 90 mins, USSR Ⓥ b/w

Dir Mikhail Kalatozov ***Scr*** Viktor Rosov ***Ph*** Sergei Urusevsky ***Ed*** Ye. Svidetelev ***Mus*** M. Weinberg

Act Tatyana Samoilova, Aleksei Batalov, Vasili Merkuryev, A. Shvorin, S. Kharitonova (Mosfilm)

For the Russians the film is a stride forward, with no propaganda and evoking a moving tale of a tender love affair shattered by the war. Its bravura is sometimes too flashy, but the sensitivity of portrayals lifts this over-contrived plot [from the play by Viktor Rosov] on to a poignant level.

A pair of young lovers are split by the war. He loses touch with her and she is seduced by his brother on a raging, bomb-torn night. They marry but she still keeps her feelings for her absent lover. Story details the life on the homefront, with its heroisms and shirkings, and the warfront. The boy is killed, but the girl finally has the courage to leave her callow husband and embrace life again.

Virile, sometimes overboard direction nonetheless brings out intelligent acting by Tatyana Samoilova and Aleksei Batalov.

•

LEVIATHAN

1989, 98 mins, US Ⓥ ⦿ ▭ col

Dir George Pan Cosmatos ***Prod*** Luigi De Laurentiis, Aurelio De Laurentiis ***Scr*** David Peoples, Jeb Stuart ***Ph*** Alex Thomson ***Ed*** Roberto Silvi, John F. Burnett ***Mus*** Jerry Goldsmith ***Art*** Ron Cobb

Act Peter Weller, Richard Crenna, Amanda Pays, Daniel Stern, Ernie Hudson, Lisa Eilbacher (De Laurentiis/Gordon/M-G-M)

Breed an *Alien* with a *Thing*, marinate in salt water, and you get a *Leviathan*. It's a soggy recycling [story by David Peoples] of gruesome monster attacks unleashed upon a crew of macho men and women confined within a far-flung scientific outpost.

A stock team of six ethnically mixed men and two alluring women is working out of a mining camp 16,000 feet down on the Atlantic floor, and only has a short time to go until heading back to the surface.

In the meantime, one of the crew, the randy Daniel Stern, takes ill after investigating the sunken remains of a Russian ship named *Leviathan*, dies, and begins transforming into a grotesque, eel-like creature. The same fate awaits Lisa Eilbacher, and medic Richard Crenna quickly deduces that some genetic transference is going on. Remainder of the action sees crew members doing fierce battle with the ever-growing creature and being horrifically eliminated one by one.

Shot on elaborate sets in Rome, pic boasts impressive production design by Ron Cobb.

•

LEY DEL DESEO, LA
(THE LAW OF DESIRE)

1987, 101 mins, SPAIN Ⓥ ⦿ col

Dir Pedro Almodovar ***Prod*** Miguel A. Perez Campos ***Scr*** Pedro Almodovar ***Ph*** Angel Luis Fernandez ***Ed*** Jose Salcedo ***Art*** Javier Fernandez

Act Eusebio Poncela, Carmen Maura, Antonio Banderas, Miguel Molina, Manuela Velasco, Bibi Andersen (El Deseo/Laurenfilm)

Spain's master of pop and pastiche, Pedro Almodovar, turns his talents here to a gay love triangle, with extraneous touches of fantasy farce and camp humor. Pic also has a certain outrageous look to it that makes the antics more palatable.

Convoluted story concerns a famous film director, Pablo (Eusebio Poncela), and his way-out sister, Tina (Carmen Maura). Pablo is madly in love with Juan (Miguel Molina), who works in an outdoor bar in Andalucia. The third part of the triangle, Antonio (Antonio Banderas), falls deeply in love with the director, and ultimately decides to get rid of his competitor, Juan, by pushing him off a cliff.

Tina, the sister, turns out to have changed her sex, and lives with her director-brother as well as a 10-year-old girl, who's a model. The model's mother is played by a well-known Spanish transvestite, Bibi Andersen (no relation to the Swedish actress).

Buoying pic are some of Almodovar's clowning touches, such as having a kind of ornate chapel in Pablo's apartment to which Tina and the kid offer mocking prayers, or two mock-heroic detectives investigating Miguel's death. However, some audiences may fail to empathize with the many gay sex sequences, an integral part of the film from the first to the last frame.

•

LIAISONS DANGEREUSES, LES
(DANGEROUS LIAISONS)
1960, 108 mins, France Ⓥ b/w
Dir Roger Vadim ***Prod*** Leopold Schloberg ***Scr*** Roger Vailland, Claude Brule, Roger Vadim ***Ph*** Marcel Grignon ***Ed*** Victoria Mercanton ***Art*** Robert Guisgand
Act Gerard Philipe, Jeanne Moreau, Jeanne Valerie, Annette Vadim, Simone Renant, Jean-Louis Trintignant (Marceau/Cocinor)

Based on an 18th-century classic [novel by Choderlos de Laclos], updated pic is a glossy study of an immoral couple who get their comeuppance.

A young diplomat (Gerard Philipe) and his wife (Jeanne Moreau) have found a perfect harmony. He allows her to have all the affairs she wants and she helps him in his conquests. Both seem content until love comes into this completely immoral household to bring on tragedy.

Film has fine lensing, production dress and mounting, but takes on a literary sheen as tale is spun out via the couple's letters to each other. She sets her husband onto his 17-year-old cousin because the latter has snagged her present lover. But then comes a pure, virtuous young mother (Annette Vadim) and the hero falls for her.

Film is somewhat long and tightening would help. Philipe plays the eternal Don Juan in a pasty way and rarely elicits an understanding of his character and drive. But Moreau is perfect as the cat-like, steely wife who lives mainly off the emotions of others. Annette Vadim lacks the expression to make her role taking.

Though done in a mixture of styles, via satire, comedy of manners, and drama, the film rarely settles on one plane.

•

LIANNA
1983, 110 mins, US Ⓥ col
Dir John Sayles ***Prod*** Jeffrey Nelson ***Scr*** John Sayles ***Ph*** Austin de Besche ***Ed*** John Sayles ***Mus*** Mason Daring ***Art*** Jeanne McDonnell
Act Linda Griffiths, Jane Hallaren, Jon DeVries, Jo Henderson, Jesse Solomon, John Sayles (Winwood)

John Sayles again uses a keen intelligence and finely tuned ear to tackle the nature of friendship and loving in *Lianna*.

Story of a 33-year-old woman (Linda Griffiths), saddled with an arrogant and unsupportive professor-husband (John DeVries) who constricts her life until she finds herself falling in love, for the first time, with a woman teacher (Jane Hallaren).

Particularly well-drawn are her husband's doubly hurt sense of sexual betrayal, the half-formed understandings of her children, who've only just become aware of conventional sexual realities, and the ambivalence of once-close women friends.

Paced by Griffiths's excellent pivotal performance, the film is marked by fine acting overall, particularly Hallaren as the catalytic lover scared off by the intensity of Griffiths's feelings; DeVries as the acerbic, insecure academic mate; Jo Henderson as the retroactively frightened best girlfriend; and Jesse Solomon as the wise-beyond-years pubescent son. Sayles himself appears to good effect as a supportive friend.

•

LIAR LIAR
1997, 87 mins, US Ⓥ ⊙ col
Dir Tom Shadyac ***Prod*** Brian Grazer ***Scr*** Paul Guay, Stephen Mazur ***Ph*** Russell Boyd ***Ed*** Don Zimmerman ***Mus*** John Debney, James Newton Howard ***Art*** Linda DeScenna
Act Jim Carrey, Maura Tierney, Jennifer Tilly, Swoosie Kurtz, Amanda Donohoe, Jason Bernard (Imagine/Universal)

Liar Liar is as surefire a commercial comedy as it gets, awfully funny at times and carefully calculated to hit as many mainstream audience demographics as possible.

Premise, that of a man forced to tell the truth for 24 hours, is nothing new, having served as the basis of the popular 1941 Bob Hope comedy *Nothing But the Truth* (director Tom Shadyac's first job in Hollywood was as a joke writer for Hope).

But it is close to an ideal jumping-off point for Jim Carrey, who spends the better part of an hour grotesquely physicalizing his scummy lawyer's struggle with being obliged to utter cold, hard facts.

Fletcher Reede (Carrey) is a no-scruples attorney who is one big win away from making partner at his downtown L.A. law firm. He's so busy that he can't make it to his son's fifth birthday party, phoning in excuses to ex-wife, Audrey (Maura Tierney), and making further promises to little Max (Justin Cooper) that he will never keep. In response, the sad kid makes the birthday wish that his dad can't tell a lie for 24 hours.

Lo and behold, it comes true, which is a bit inconvenient for Fletcher since he's heading into court on a case in which his whole strategy is based upon flagrant disregard for the truth: a brazen adulteress (Jennifer Tilly) is demanding a huge divorce settlement.

As usual, Carrey is basically the whole show, zinging off innumerable irreverent one-liners and demonstrating his manic clowning, but with relatively legitimate character motivation compared with the first Carrey-Shadyac collaboration, *Ace Ventura, Pet Detective*. Supporting players are all delegated to second-banana status and filmmaking technique is on the rudimentary side.

•

LIBEL
1959, 100 mins, UK ▭ col
Dir Anthony Asquith ***Prod*** Anatole de Grunwald ***Scr*** Anatole de Grunwald, Karl Tunberg ***Ph*** Robert Krasker ***Ed*** Frank Clarke ***Mus*** Benjamin Frankel
Act Dirk Bogarde, Olivia de Havilland, Paul Massie, Robert Morley, Wilfrid Hyde White, Richard Wattis (M-G-M)

Based on a 25-year-old play by Edward Wooll, *Libel* has been turned into a stylish and holding film. The idea is simple enough. Is Sir Mark Loddon (Dirk Bogarde), owner of one of the stately homes of England, really Loddon or an unscrupulous imposter, as alleged by a war-time comrade?

The case is sparked off when a young Canadian airman sees a TV program introducing Loddon. He is convinced that he is really Frank Welney, a small-part actor. The three were in prison camp together and he is confident that Loddon was killed during a prison break. He exposes the alleged phoney in a newspaper and Loddon is persuaded by his wife to sue.

Bogarde carries much of the onus since he plays both Loddon (during the war and at the time of the trial) and Welney. He does a stand-out job, suggesting the difference in the two characters remarkably well with the aid of only a slight difference in hair style. Paul Massie gives a likeable, though somewhat even-key, performance as the young man whose suspicions trigger the drama. Olivia de Havilland, as Bogarde's wife, has two or three very good scenes which she handles well.

Because much of the off-court scenes were actually shot at Woburn Abbey, stately home of the Duke of Bedford, the production is given much budget-value.

1959: NOMINATION: Best Sound

•

LIBELED LADY
1936, 85 mins, US Ⓥ ⊙ b/w
Dir Jack Conway ***Prod*** Lawrence Weingarten ***Scr*** Maurine Watkins, Howard Emmett Rogers, George Oppenheimer ***Ph*** Norbert Brodine ***Ed*** Frederick Y. Smith ***Mus*** William Axt ***Art*** Cedric Gibbons, William A. Horning, Edwin B. Willis
Act Jean Harlow, William Powell, Myrna Loy, Spencer Tracy, Walter Connolly, Charley Grapewin (M-G-M)

Even though *Libeled Lady* goes overboard on plot and its pace snags badly in several spots, Metro has brought in a sockeroo of a comedy. It's broad farce for the most part, and the threesome consisting of William Powell, Spencer Tracy, and Jean Harlow lend themselves perfectly to the task.

Of the starring foursome Myrna Loy's is the only behavior that is kept pretty much on a serious plane. As the much misunderstood poor little rich girl, she projects an effective performance, and with Powell in the later reels, accounts for plenty romantic arias.

Story [by Wallace Sullivan] takes for itself a Park Avenue plus newspaper row theme. Picture seeks to tell of what befalls Powell when, as the troubleshooter for a newspaper, he undertakes to frame a young millionairess and thereby compel her to drop a $5 million libel suit. The expected occurs; he falls in love with her.

Concerned with Powell in the frame are Tracy, managing editor of the sheet, and the latter's fiancée (Harlow). Latter turns out a corking straight for the sophisticated, suave manner of Powell and she frequently steals the picture when the opportunities for cutting loose fall her way.

Tracy has the least juicy assignment, but the characterization is right up his alley. Walter Connolly registers in crack fashion, as usual, in the part of Loy's father.

1936: NOMINATION: Best Picture

•

LIBERATION OF L. B. JONES, THE
1970, 102 mins, US Ⓥ col
Dir William Wyler ***Prod*** Ronald Lubin ***Scr*** Sterling Silliphant, Jesse Hill Ford ***Ph*** Robert Surtees ***Ed*** Robert Swink, Carl Kress ***Mus*** Elmer Bernstein ***Art*** Kenneth A. Reid
Act Lee J. Cobb, Anthony Zerbe, Roscoe Lee Browne, Lola Falana, Lee Majors, Barbara Hershey (Columbia)

This story of a glossed-over Negro's murder by a Dixie policeman is, unfortunately, not much more than an interracial sexploitation film.

Story kicks off as Lee Majors and bride Barbara Hershey come to live with Majors's uncle Lee J. Cobb, while Yaphet Kotto comes home to murder bestial cop Arch Johnson. Roscoe Lee Browne is town's Negro funeral director, the title character who seeks a divorce (the liberation) from unfaithful wife Lola Falana. Her lover is Anthony Zerbe, Johnson's police buddy. The well-structured plot [from the novel *The Liberation of Lord Byron Jones* by Jesse Hill Ford] finds lawyer Cobb trying to avoid an open-court revelation that a white married cop is a Negro woman's lover.

•

LIBERTY HEIGHTS
1999, 127 mins, US Ⓥ ⊙ col
Dir Barry Levinson ***Prod*** Barry Levinson, Paula Weinstein ***Scr*** Barry Levinson ***Ph*** Chris Doyle ***Ed*** Stu Linder ***Mus*** Andrea Morricone ***Art*** Vincent Peranio
Act Adrien Brody, Ben Foster, Orlando Jones, Bebe Neuwirth, Joe Mantegna, Rebekah Johnson (Baltimore/Spring Creek/Warner)

Barry Levinson goes deep with *Liberty Heights*, and the result is a grand slam. Summoning up boyhood memories of the '50s for his fourth "Baltimore picture" and infusing them with mature and pointed observations about race, class and religion in the U.S., this exceptionally successful director seems to be rediscovering his voice as a writer.

Surpassing *Diner, Tin Men* and *Avalon*, the new picture pinpoints a moment when previously partitioned segments of society began gingerly mixing and influencing each other. Pic is rooted in the eponymous neighborhood, a middle-class enclave so ethnically uniform in 1954 that a teenage boy can observe in all sincerity, "The whole world was Jewish."

In the Kurtzman family, the grown-ups live by the motto "If they're not Jewish, they're 'the other kind.' " This attitude is not entirely heeded, however, by the two boys, lanky college student Van (Adrien Brody) and high schooler Ben (Ben Foster). After daring to cross into WASP territory with a couple of buddies to attend a party, Ben falls hard for blond, blue-eyed goddess Dubbie (supermodel Carolyn Murphy).

A quiet rebel, Ben soon pursues an ardent friendship with Sylvia (Rebekah Johnson), the first black student in his class. Story veers perilously close to melodrama when small-time black reefer dealer Little Melvin (Orlando Jones) takes advantage of the opportunity to kidnap Ben, along with Sylvia and two friends. But Levinson reasserts its human grounding in resolutions that are bittersweet, properly scaled and historically prescient.

Performances are outstanding and unshowy across the board. Abundant period details provide ongoing delight.

•

LICENSE TO KILL
1989, 133 mins, UK Ⓥ ⊙ ▭ col
Dir John Glen ***Prod*** Albert R. Broccoli, Michael G. Wilson ***Scr*** Richard Maibaum, Michael G. Wilson ***Ph*** Alec Mills ***Ed*** John Grover ***Mus*** Michael Kamen ***Art*** Peter Lamont
Act Timothy Dalton, Carey Lowell, Robert Davi, Talisa Soto, Anthony Zerbe, Wayne Newton (United Artists/Eon)

The James Bond production team has found its second wind with *License to Kill*, a cocktail of high-octane action, spectacle and drama.

Presence for the second time of Timothy Dalton as the suave British agent has clearly juiced up scripters and director John Glen. Out go the self-parodying witticisms and over-elaborate high-tech gizmos that slowed pre-Dalton pics to a walking pace. Dalton plays 007 with a vigor and physicality that harks back to the earliest Bond pics, letting full-bloodied actions speak louder than words.

The thrills-and-spills chases are superbly orchestrated as pic spins at breakneck speed through its South Florida and Central American locations. Bond survives a series of underwater and mid-air stunt sequences that are above par for the series.

He's also pitted against a crew of sinister baddies (led by Robert Davi and Frank McRae) who give the British agent the chance to use all his wit and wiles. Femme elements in the guise of Carey Lowell and Talisa Soto add gloss but play second fiddle to the action.

•

LIEBELEI
1933, 83 mins, Germany b/w
Dir Max Ophuls ***Scr*** Hans Wilhelm, Curt Alexander ***Ph*** Franz Planer ***Mus*** Theo Mackeben
Act Magda Schneider, Wolfgang Liebeneiner, Luise Ullrich, Gustaf Gruendgens, Willy Eichberger, Olga Tschechowa (Elite)

Arthur Schnitzler's play is the simple little story of two lieutenants picking up two sweet little Vienna girls. With the elder and more experienced couple it's just a gay, harmless love affair; with the other two (not yet out of their teens) it develops into deep love. Although the boy has severed his former connections with a society woman, the husband afterward finds out. A duel ensues. The boy is killed. The girl jumps out of the window.

The film treatment has succeeded in preserving most of the play's flavor, adding a good amount of comedy, music, and background, such as a beautiful sleigh drive up the mountains.

The picture is particularly well cast, even in smallest parts. Magda Schneider shows her first really fine acting. The other youngsters are very good, too. The picture might be almost without flaw, except for a sequence quite unnecessarily melodramatic involving one of the leading characters, just for the sake of introducing an anti-duel argument.

•

LIEBESTRAUM

1991, 102 mins, US Ⓥ ⊙ col

Dir Mike Figgis ***Prod*** Eric Fellner ***Scr*** Mike Figgis ***Ph*** Juan Ruiz Anchia ***Ed*** Mark Hunter ***Mus*** Mike Figgis ***Art*** Waldemar Kalinowski

Act Kevin Anderson, Pamela Gidley, Bill Pullman, Kim Novak, Thomas Kopache, Catherine Hicks (M-G-M/Initial)

Writer-director Mike Figgis returns to the territory of his earlier success, *Stormy Monday*, with plenty of mood but not a lot of plot. Pic is set in a grimy town hoping for an economic turnaround via demolition of a defunct department store and the construction of a shopping mall. The town continues to have repercussions of a murder that took place 30 years earlier (and shown during the opening credits). Figgis gets good use of his Binghamton, NY, locations, including the old building that's the focus of much of the film.

The story properly begins with the arrival of architectural writer Kevin Anderson, summoned to the bedside of his dying mother (Kim Novak), whom he has never known. While in town he runs into old college buddy Bill Pullman, who's in charge of the demolition. He soon meets Pullman's wife (Pamela Gidley), who is suffering in a sexless marriage due to hubby's playing around, and they become involved.

Figgis's problem here is the confused script, which doesn't seem to have a point. Biggest waste is Novak, who spends virtually the entire film bedridden and moaning her few lines. Rest of the thesping is professional, but unmemorable.

[In the UK pic was released in a 113-minute version featuring a sequence in which the local sheriff takes Anderson to a brothel.]

•

LIES MY FATHER TOLD ME

1975, 103 mins, Canada Ⓥ col

Dir Jan Kadar ***Prod*** Anthony Bedrich, Harry Gulkin ***Scr*** Ted Allan ***Ph*** Paul Van Der Linden ***Ed*** Edward Beyer, Richard Marks ***Mus*** Sol Kaplan ***Art*** Francois Barbeau

Act Yossi Yadin, Len Birman, Marilyn Lightstone, Jeffrey Lynas, Ted Allan, Barbara Chilcott (Pentimento/Pentacle VIII)

Set in Montreal in the 1920s, this centers on an emotional relationship between a young boy, portrayed by newcomer Jeffrey Lynas, and his aged, peddler grandfather, played by Israeli actor Yossi Yadin. Threatening this relationship at all times is the boy's hard luck, no-talent father, etched by a ruggedly vigorous Len Birman, and his long-suffering mother, a dramatic leavening force played by Marilyn Lightstone.

The grandfather spins fanciful tales for the boy, and takes him on his peddling rounds, while the father tries to wheedle money from him for various unsuccessful invention schemes.

Czech director Jan Kadar has assembled a topnotch, uniformly handsome cast and his lingering over certain moments is a decided virtue. *Lies My Father Told Me* is an absorbing nostalgic trip for anyone who has ever felt close to a grandparent, and it is a powerful but never pushy statement.

1975: NOMINATION: Best Original Screenplay

•

LIEUTENANT WORE SKIRTS, THE

1956, 98 mins, US ▭ col

Dir Frank Tashlin ***Prod*** Buddy Adler ***Scr*** Albert Beich, Frank Tashlin ***Ph*** Leo Tover ***Ed*** James B. Clark ***Mus*** Cyril J. Mockridge ***Art*** Lyle Wheeler, Leland Fuller

Act Tom Ewell, Sheree North, Rita Moreno, Rick Jason, Les Tremayne, Jean Wiles (20th Century-Fox)

This amusing comedy affair whiles away a pleasant 98 minutes of screen time. Sassy dialog and situations predominate and make for sly fun. Footage occasionally strains into slapstick with the frenetics forcing chuckles, but the plot idea is enough to carry the show along at an amusing pace.

Story pits Tom Ewell against the Air Force, and he wins, with an assist from nature. He's an aging World War II hero now a TV writer, and Sheree North, his wife, is an ex-WAC considerably younger. The comedy of errors tees off when she rejoins the service because he is recalled. However, he's rejected, and then dejected because she likes her uniform. From then on comedy hinges on his efforts to get her discharged.

Ewell makes with the facial expressions for some solid comedy scoring. North mostly acts her role with her legs and hips. It's a performance with which no one should quarrel as she's equipped for such physical thesping. Rita Moreno captures the fancy in a girl-upstairs takeoff from *The Seven Year Itch*.

Beverly Hills and Honolulu serve as backgrounds for the story.

•

LIFE

1999, 108 mins, US Ⓥ ⊙ col

Dir Ted Demme ***Prod*** Brian Grazer, Eddie Murphy ***Scr*** Robert Ramsey, Matthew Stone ***Ph*** Geoffrey Simpson ***Ed*** Jeffrey Wolf ***Mus*** Wyclef Jean ***Art*** Dan Bishop

Act Eddie Murphy, Martin Lawrence, Obba Babatunde, Ned Beatty, Bernie Mac, Miguel A. Nunez, Jr. (Imagine/Universal)

An unexpected tale covering 55 years in the lives of two bickering convicts bonded by a miscarriage of justice and inextinguishable hope, *Life* careens from decade to decade, and from relative dramatic realism to frequent hilarity, in often winning fashion. When in doubt, Ted Demme's tonally unusual film generally opts for impudent and confrontational humor, not a bad idea when your stars are Eddie Murphy and Martin Lawrence, who last teamed in the 1992 *Boomerang*. Idea for the film was Murphy's.

Bookended by a contempo burial scene in which an oldtimer (Obba Babatunde) relates the story of the two lifers, yarn jumps back to 1932 Harlem, where fast-talking hustler Ray Gibson (Murphy) picks the wrong guy, straightlaced but penniless aspiring bank teller Claude Banks (Lawrence), to pickpocket at a swank nightclub.

To pay off a debt to a bootlegger, the New Yorkers drive south to pick up a load of moonshine. When the venal local sheriff then nails them for the murder of a man he himself has killed, the two men are sentenced to life in prison. All along, the two men never give up the idea that they'll somehow get out one day, but their schemes along these lines remain modest and intermittent.

Murphy's rude, live-wire personality is turned on to strong comic effect, but is also channeled so that it stays within bounds of film. Lawrence provides a fine foil, but his increasing anger doesn't go deep enough.

1999: NOMINATION: Best Makeup

•

LIFE AND DEATH OF COLONEL BLIMP, THE

1943, 163 mins, UK Ⓥ ⊙ col

Dir Michael Powell, Emeric Pressburger ***Prod*** Michael Powell, Emeric Pressburger ***Scr*** Michael Powell, Emeric Pressburger ***Ph*** Georges Perinal ***Ed*** John Seabourne ***Mus*** Allan Gray ***Art*** Alfred Junge

Act Roger Livesey, Deborah Kerr, Anton Walbrook, Roland Culver, Albert Lieven, James McKechnie (Archers/Independent)

Here is an excellent film whose basic story could have been told within normal feature limits, but which, instead, is extended close to three hours. Longer or shorter, this panorama of British army life is depicted with a technical skill and artistry that marks it as one of the really fine pix to come out of a British studio.

It's a clear, continuous unreeling of events in the life of an English military man, from the Boer War, through World War I and up to the completion of the training and equipment of England's Home Guard. Story revolves around an officer (Clive Candy) who has spent all his life in the army and still feels the German people as a whole are decent human beings, and that they're only tools of their warlords.

The role of Candy is spasmodically well enacted by Roger Livesey, who looks a little too mature in the scenes of his younger days and a bit too virile at the finish. More generous praise should go to Anton Walbrook as an Uhlan officer. This is an excellent characterization depicted with delicacy and sensitiveness. Deborah Kerr contributes attractively as the feminine lead in three separate characters through the generations, and a score of other artists leave little to criticize from the histrionic side.

Title is based on the symbolic figure of the old-time English officers who have been axed, not only due to age but because of their contempt for present methods of warfare as compared with "the good old days." Cartoonist [David] Low, in the *Evening Standard*, christened them "Colonel Blimps."

•

LIFE AND TIMES OF JUDGE ROY BEAN, THE

1972, 120 mins, US Ⓥ col

Dir John Huston ***Prod*** John Foreman ***Scr*** John Milius ***Ph*** Richard Moore ***Ed*** Hugh S. Fowler ***Mus*** Maurice Jarre ***Art*** Tambi Larsen

Act Paul Newman, Victoria Principal, Anthony Perkins, Ned Beatty, John Huston, Ava Gardner (First Artists)

The Life and Times of Judge Roy Bean has a title card to the effect: "Maybe this isn't the way it was . . . it's the way it should have been." For some, perhaps, that will set up this $4 million freedom freeway spoof.

The two-hour running time is not fleshed out with anything more than scenic vignettes, sometimes attempting to recreate the success of *Butch Cassidy and the Sundance Kid*, with an Alan and Marilyn Bergman-lyricked tune and Maurice Jarre's music sometimes attempting honest spoofing of westerns, and sometimes trying to play the story historically straight. The overkill and the underdone do it in.

Newman (Bean) arrives in Texas badlands, draws a moustache on his wanted poster and announces himself at the saloon. He is promptly beaten, robbed, tied to a horse, and run out over the prairie to die. Mexican towngirl Victoria Principal saves him. He returns to the saloon, massacres everyone there and then sits down to wait to "kill all of your kind."

Newman is good as Bean, injecting charm into the character along with the rough exterior. Principal is impressive in her first major role.

1972: NOMINATION: Best Song ("Marmalade, Molasses and Honey")

•

LIFE AT THE TOP

1965, 118 mins, UK b/w

Dir Ted Kotcheff ***Prod*** James Woolf ***Scr*** Mordecai Richler ***Ph*** Oswald Morris ***Ed*** Derek York ***Mus*** Richard Addinsell ***Art*** Ted Marshall

Act Laurence Harvey, Jean Simmons, Honor Blackman, Michael Craig, Donald Wolfit, Robert Morley (Romulus)

Some of the gloss of *Room at the Top* rubs off on this follow-up, but the film lacks both the motivation and rare subtlety which elevated its predecessor.

Based upon a second novel by John Braine, the sombre, sometimes dreary but usually honest drama picks up its narrative 10 years later. The Mordecai Richler screenplay continues the story of the young, designing opportunist who rose to the top in social and business standing, but at loss of his self-respect, as limned in *Room*. Now, however, after having enjoyed the position he sought for a decade, he is even more aware of the necessity of clinging to his ideals and tries to do something about a life he has found empty.

Laurence Harvey continues in the mood of his character in *Room*, now sales chief of his millionaire father-in-law's woolen mills in a sooty Yorkshire town. Jean Simmons as his wife (replacing Heather Sears in original role) has a rather unsympathetic character that she nonetheless enacts persuasively.

•

LIFE BEGINS

1932, 71 mins, US b/w

Dir James Flood, Elliott Nugent ***Scr*** Earl Baldwin ***Ph*** James Van Trees ***Ed*** George Marks

Act Loretta Young, Eric Linden, Aline MacMahon, Glenda Farrell, Dorothy Petersen, Vivienne Osborne (Warner)

A good picture, a woman's picture, different, and on the serious side. Basis of the theme is childbirth with the entire locale a hospital and the story particularly concerned with a cross-section of probably any maternity ward.

Picture is an adaptation of a play [by Mary M. Axelson] which opened in New York and ran just one week despite a definite degree of favorable word-of-mouth among the women who saw it. Warners paid $6,000 for it. As a film it ignores much of the comedy that it held as a play. It's become a sober screen discourse. There is one cast retention from the play, Glenda Farrell, as a hard-boiled nightclub performer who goes the way of all mothers after insisting she'll have nothing to do with her twins. She sings "Frankie and Johnnie" to one infant, after it arrives, as the closest to a lullaby she can get.

Aline MacMahon, as the ever efficient nurse, and Farrell and Eric Linden comprise the performing highlights. Linden is particularly sincere and believable as the very young and distracted father while MacMahon is outstanding with an impressive performance, which she expertly shades as called upon.

•

LIFE BEGINS IN COLLEGE
1937, 90 mins, US b/w
Dir William A. Seiter ***Prod*** Harold Wilson ***Scr*** Karl Tunberg, Don Ettlinger ***Ph*** Robert Planck ***Ed*** Louis Loeffler ***Mus*** Louis Silvers (dir.)
Act Ritz Bros., Joan Davis, Tony Martin, Gloria Stuart, Fred Stone, Nat Pendleton (20th Century-Fox)

Practically the entire production [from stories by Darrell Ware] depends on the Ritzes. Tony Martin is back again to sing but aside from Gloria Stuart and Fred Stone, who may be recognized, there is not a strong name in support.

The freres Ritz first appear as student tailors with a record of seven years in school and seven on the football bench. Then they're seen in a madcap rhumba specialty; as newly rich undergrads bracing the dean for a favor; as footballers who help the enemy more than their teammates; as an Indian burlesque troupe; and then as hokum Spirit of '76 boys.

Outside of the Ritz Bros., Nat Pendleton's interpretation of the Indian grid star is standout, and Joan Davis, comedienne, serving as his principal foil, especially excellent in that goofy Indian pow-wow song and dance. She's inclined to grimace a bit too much in reaching for laughs at other times. Tony Martin, spotted as band leader, figures only as the singer of one song.

•

LIFEBOAT
1944, 86 mins, US Ⓥ ⦿ b/w
Dir Alfred Hitchcock ***Prod*** Kenneth Macgowan ***Scr*** Jo Swerling ***Ph*** Glen MacWilliams ***Ed*** Dorothy Spencer ***Mus*** Hugo Friedhofer ***Art*** James Basevi, Maurice Ransford
Act Tallulah Bankhead, William Bendix, Walter Slezak, John Hodiak, Hume Cronyn, Canada Lee (20th Century-Fox)

John Steinbeck's devastating indictment of the nature of Nazi bestiality, at times an almost clinical, dissecting room analysis, emerges as powerful adult motion picture fare.

The picture is based on an original idea of director Alfred Hitchcock's. Hitchcock, from accounts, first asked Steinbeck to write the piece for book publication, figuring that if it turned out a big seller the exploitation value for film purposes would be greatly enhanced. The author, however, would not undertake the more ambitious assignment and wrote the story for screen purposes only, with Jo Swerling handling the adaptation.

Patterned along one of the simplest, most elementary forms of dramatic narration, the action opens and closes on a lifeboat. It's a lusty, robust story about a group of survivors from a ship sunk by a U-boat. One by one the survivors find precarious refuge on the lifeboat. Finally they pick up a survivor from the German U-boat. He is first tolerated and then welcomed into their midst. And he repays their trust and confidence with murderous treachery.

Walter Slezak, as the German, comes through with a terrific delineation. Henry Hull as the millionaire; William Bendix as the mariner with a jitterbug complex who loses a leg; John Hodiak as the tough, bitter, Nazi-hater; and Canada Lee as the colored steward, deliver excellent characterizations.

Hitchcock pilots the piece skillfully, ingeniously developing suspense and action. Despite that it's a slow starter, the picture, from the beginning, leaves a strong impact, and before too long develops into the type of suspenseful product with which Hitchcock has always been identified.

1944: NOMINATIONS: Best Director, Original Story, B&W Cinematography

•

LIFEFORCE
1985, 101 mins, US Ⓥ ⦿ ▭ col
Dir Tobe Hooper ***Prod*** Menahem Golan, Yoram Globus ***Scr*** Dan O'Bannon, Don Jakoby ***Ph*** Alan Hume ***Ed*** John Grover ***Mus*** Henry Mancini, Michael Kamen, James Guthrie ***Art*** John Graysmark
Act Steve Railsback, Peter Firth, Frank Finlay, Mathilda May, Patrick Stewart, Michael Gothard (Cannon)

For about the first ten minutes, this $22.5 million pic indicates it could be a scary sci-fier as Yank and British space travelers discover seemingly human remains in the vicinity of Halley's Comet and attempt to bring home three perfectly preserved specimens.

The astronauts don't make it back but the humanoids do, and one of them, Space Girl (Mathilda May), is possessed of such a spectacularly statuesque physique that she could probably have conquered all of mankind even without her special talents, which include a form of electroshock vampirism and the ability to inhabit other bodies.

Pic [from the novel *The Space Vampires* by Colin Wilson] descends into subpar Agatha Christie territory, as fanatical inspector Peter Firth and surviving astronaut Steve Railsback scour the countryside for the deadly Space Girl and make a pit stop at an insane asylum to provide for further hysteria.

Even though she turns millions of Londoners into fruitcakes and threatens the entire world, Railsback just can't get the naked Space Girl out of his mind.

In the meantime, Firth makes his way through scores of zombies in a burning London in hopes of nailing Space Girl.

•

LIFE FOR RUTH
(US: WALK IN THE SHADOW)
1962, 91 mins, UK b/w
Dir Basil Dearden ***Prod*** Michael Relph ***Scr*** Janet Green, John McCormick ***Ph*** Otto Heller ***Ed*** John Guthridge ***Mus*** William Alwyn ***Art*** Alex Vetchinsky
Act Michael Craig, Patrick McGoohan, Janet Munro, Paul Rogers, Megs Jenkins, Frank Finlay (Allied Film Makers)

First problem that confronts an honest working man (Michael Craig) occurs when his eight-year-old daughter and her next-door playmate are involved in a boating accident. His daughter is clinging to the boat and is not in such immediate danger as the drowning boy. Which should he try first to save?

He rescues both, but by then his daughter is gravely ill. Only a blood transfusion can save her. Because of his strict religious principles (he is a member of the Jehovah's Witness sect, though it is not stated in the film) he adamantly refuses, and the child dies. That was his second distressing problem.

The doctor who urged the transfusion is so irate that he gets the father tried for manslaughter. This is good telling stuff for drama and it brings up issues about religion, the law, conscience, marital relationship all posed with intelligence and conviction.

Thesping is crisp all around, with Craig surmounting a gloomy type of role as the dogged religionist, and Janet Munro as his baffled dismayed young wife. Patrick McGoohan is excellent in a tricky role [the doctor], which is not so clearly defined as the other top jobs.

Otto Heller's bleak photography of the North of England setting and William Alwyn's unobtrusive musical score all lend aid to Dearden's adroit direction.

•

LIFEGUARD
1976, 96 mins, US Ⓥ col
Dir Daniel Petrie ***Prod*** Ron Silverman ***Scr*** Ron Koslow ***Ph*** Ralph Woolsey ***Ed*** Argyle Nelson, Jr. ***Mus*** Dale Menten
Act Sam Elliott, Anne Archer, Stephen Young, Parker Stevenson, Kathleen Quinlan, Steve Burns (Paramount)

Lifeguard is an unsatisfying film, of uncertain focus on a 30-ish guy who doesn't yet seem to know what he wants. Script takes Sam Elliott through another Southern California beach summer as a career lifeguard, encountering the usual string of offbeat characters found in the type of made-for-TV feature which this project resembles.

There are, of course, some advantages—like periodic playmate Sharon Weber; Kathleen Quinlan, supposedly underage (but looking far more mature) teenager who has a crush on him; and Anne Archer, long-ago high-school sweetheart now divorced.

Elliott, who has some beefcake value, projects a character who is mostly a passive reactor rather than a person in sure command of his fate.

•

LIFE IS CHEAP . . .
BUT TOILET PAPER IS EXPENSIVE
1990, 85 mins, US Ⓥ col
Dir Wayne Wang, Spencer Nakasako ***Prod*** Winnie Fredriksz ***Scr*** Spencer Nakasako ***Ph*** Amir M. Mokri ***Ed*** Chris Sanderson, Sandy Nervig ***Mus*** Mark Adler ***Art*** Collete Koo
Act Spencer Nakasako, Cora Miao, Victor Wong, John K. Chan, Chan Kim Wan (Far East Stars)

Audaciously stylish and visually mesmerizing, *Life Is Cheap* aims to evoke the uncertain mood of present-day Hong Kong as viewed from the perspective of an Asian-American naif. Director Wayne Wang's tart take on the conundrum of Chinese identity has all the narrative logic of a tilted pinball machine.

Screenwriter-star Spencer Nakasako is a half-Chinese, half-Japanese, all-American stablehand from San Francisco who has agreed to act as a courier for a San Francisco Triad, the Chinese mafia, in return for an all-expenses-paid sojourn in Hong Kong. The black-Stetsoned, cowboy-booted hero wants to see the legendary port before its takeover by China. In the wake of Tiananmen Square, it's a city of "5½ million sitting ducks."

Handcuffed to an attaché case destined for the "Bigé Boss" in Hong Kong, the hero seeks to unlock the enigma of "5,000 years of Chinese culture." Wang skewers the lofty notion of Chinese self-superiority by populating his film with a widely variegated gallery of funny and flawed characters.

•

LIFE IS SWEET
1991, 102 mins, UK Ⓥ ⦿ col
Dir Mike Leigh ***Prod*** Simon Channing-Williams ***Scr*** Mike Leigh ***Ph*** Dick Pope ***Ed*** John Gregory ***Mus*** Rachel Portman ***Art*** Alison Chitty
Act Alison Steadman, Jim Broadbent, Timothy Spall, Claire Skinner, Jane Horrocks, David Thewlis (Thin Man)

Mike Leigh's third pic is a highly sympathetic comedy, embroidered by a superb performance from helmer's wife Alison Steadman.

Steadman is ideally cast as a suburban housewife and mother who sells baby clothes, supports her husband (Jim Broadbent), and attempts to look after her twin teen daughters (one a plumber, the other an anorexic rebel). She still finds time to help a friend (Timothy Spall) open a new restaurant, acting as a waitress on his disastrous opening night. Her husband falls at work, arriving home in plaster. Her rebel daughter veers toward breakdown, and almost everything that could go wrong does. But she is a survivor, who helps others survive too.

As a precise observation of British types and a virtuoso piece of carefully observed ensemble playing, the film would be hard to beat.

•

LIFE LESS ORDINARY, A
1997, 103 mins, UK Ⓥ ⦿ col
Dir Danny Boyle ***Prod*** Andrew Macdonald ***Scr*** John Hodge ***Ph*** Brian Tufano ***Ed*** Masahiro Hirakubo ***Mus*** David Arnold ***Art*** Kave Quinn
Act Ewan McGregor, Cameron Diaz, Holly Hunter, Delroy Lindo, Ian Holm, Stanley Tucci (Figment/PolyGram)

After their accelerated rise with *Shallow Grave* and *Trainspotting*, the Brit trio of helmer Danny Boyle, producer Andrew Macdonald and writer John Hodge hit some major speed bumps. This offbeat comedy-romancer centered on a clumsy kidnapper and his ambitious female victim is a pleasant enough ride in parts, but has too many ideas in the script to satisfy at any emotional level, and fails to make a virtue of its mixed British-American cast.

Part kooky romance, part screwball comedy, part quirky fantasy and part Roadrunner cartoon, this is a movie that has everything except an involving storyline and characters.

In an over-exposed, all-white heaven with an almost '60s feel, Chief Gabriel (Dan Hedaya) dispatches agents O'Reilly (Holly Hunter) and Jackson (Delroy Lindo) to bring together two earthlings, to "unite men and women."

Their targets couldn't be more dissimilar: Celine (Cameron Diaz) is a businessman's pampered daughter, while Robert (Ewan McGregor) works as a janitor in her dad's corporation. When Robert is pinkslipped, and dumped by his girlfriend, he storms into the office of Celine's dad, Naville (Ian Holm), and ends up kidnapping her at gunpoint. The twist is that Celine hates her father and, realizing Robert is no threat, schools the klutzy Scot in bargaining techniques.

There's no shortage of ideas in Hodge's busy script, but less would have translated into more. The humor is basically very British in tone (Hodge originally intended to set the story in the U.K. and France) and often sounds more natural in McGregor's mouth than in Diaz's. Though very cute in her Versace duds, Diaz never unbends sufficiently to make their screen chemistry catch fire.

•

LIFE OF BRIAN
1979, 93 mins, UK Ⓥ ⦿ col
Dir Terry Jones ***Prod*** John Goldstone ***Scr*** Graham Chapman, John Cleese, Terry Gilliam, Eric Idle, Terry Jones, Michael Palin ***Ph*** Peter Biziou ***Ed*** Julian Doyle ***Mus*** Geoffrey Burgon ***Art*** Terry Gilliam
Act Terry Jones, Michael Palin, John Cleese, Eric Idle, Spike Milligan, George Harrison (Warner/Orion)

Monty Python's *Life of Brian*, utterly irreverent tale of a reluctant messiah whose impact proved somewhat less pervasive than that of his contemporary Jesus Christ, is just as wacky and imaginative as their earlier film outings. Film was shot using stunning Tunisian locales.

As an adult in Roman-occupied Palestine, Brian's life parallels that of Jesus, as he becomes involved in the terrorist Peoples Front of Judea, works as a vendor at the Colosseum, paints anti-Roman graffiti on palace walls, unwittingly wins a following as a messiah, and is ultimately condemned to the cross by a foppish Pontius Pilate.

Tone of the film is set by such scenes as a version of the sermon on the mount in which spectators shout out that they can't hear what's being said and start fighting amongst themselves.

•

LIFE OF EMILE ZOLA, THE
1937, 123 mins, US Ⓥ b/w
Dir William Dieterle ***Prod*** Henry Blanke ***Scr*** Heinz Herald, Geza Herczeg, Norman Reilly Raine ***Ph*** Tony Gaudio ***Ed*** Warren Low ***Mus*** Max Steiner ***Art*** Anton Grot
Act Paul Muni, Gloria Holden, Gale Sondergaard, Joseph Schildkraut, Robert Warwick, Robert Barrat (Warner)

The Life of Emile Zola is a vibrant, tense, and emotional story about the man who fought a nation with his pen and successfully championed the cause of the exiled Capt. Alfred Dreyfus. With Paul Muni in the title role, supported by distinguished players, the film is finely made.

The picture is Muni's all the way, even when he is off screen. Covering a period of the last half of the past century, action [from a story by Heinz Herald and Geza Herczeg] is laid in Paris, except for short interludes in England and on Devil's Island, whither Dreyfus was banished by court-martial after conspiracy charges that he betrayed military secrets to Germany. Although the release of Dreyfus is made the principal dramatic incident of the picture, the development of the character and career of Zola remains dominant.

Thus, the audience is informed of the derivation of his earlier novels of *Nana*, in which he stripped the Paris underworld of its glitter and laid it bare, and his other crusading works. In his late years he takes up the fight to free Dreyfus and purge the French army general staff of deceit and conspiracy.

Joseph Schildkraut as Dreyfus, Gale Sondergaard as his wife, and Erin O'Brien-Moore in a lesser role, as the inspiration for the conception of *Nana*, leave deep impressions. Racial theme is lightly touched upon, but impressive notwithstanding.

1937: Best Picture, Supp. Actor (Joseph Schildkraut), Screenplay

NOMINATIONS: Best Director, Actor (Paul Muni), Original Story, Score, Sound, Assistant Director (Russ Saunders)

•

LIFE OF HER OWN, A
1950, 106 mins, US b/w
Dir George Cukor ***Prod*** Voldemar Vetluguin ***Scr*** Isobel Lennart ***Ph*** George Folsey ***Ed*** George White ***Mus*** Bronislau Kaper
Act Lana Turner, Ray Milland, Tom Ewell, Louis Calhern, Jean Hagen (M-G-M)

The soap opera plotting has been polished to considerable extent, the playing by the femme cast members is topnotch, and the direction aids them, but it is still a true confession type of yarn concerned with a big city romance between a married man and a beautiful model.

Script is spotted with feeling and character, and also a lot of conversation that doesn't mean much.

A decided asset is Lana Turner's performance. In appearance, she is believable as the model. Since the entire story is pointed to the distaff side, Ray Milland's role suffers as the man, married to a crippled wife, who goes off the deep end for the model.

•

LIFE STINKS
1991, 95 mins, US Ⓥ ⦿ col
Dir Mel Brooks ***Prod*** Mel Brooks ***Scr*** Mel Brooks, Rudy De Luca, Steve Haberman ***Ph*** Steven Poster ***Ed*** David Rawlins, Anthony Redman, Michael Mulconery ***Mus*** John Morris ***Art*** Peter Larkin
Act Mel Brooks, Lesley Ann Warren, Jeffrey Tambor, Stuart Pankin, Howard Morris, Rudy De Luca (Brooksfilms)

Mel Brooks's *Life Stinks* is a fitfully funny vaudeville caricature about life on skid row. Premise of a rich man who chooses to live among the poor for a spell feels sorely undeveloped, and suffers from the usual gross effects and exaggerations.

Pic gets off to a good start with Brooks's callous billionaire Goddard Bolt informing his circle of yes-men of his plans to build a colossal futuristic development on the site of Los Angeles's worst slums, the plight of its residents be damned.

Tycoon Jeffrey Tambor bets his rival that he can't last a month living out in the neighborhood he intends to buy.

In a series of vignettes that play like black-out routines, Bolt, renamed Pepto by a local denizen, tries various survival tactics, such as dancing for donations. After being robbed of his shoes, he encounters baglady Lesley Ann Warren, a wildly gesticulating man-hater who slowly comes to admit Pepto is the only person she can stand.

Some effective bug-eyed, free-wheeling comedy is scattered throughout, much of it descending to the Three Stooges level of sophistication. But distressingly little is done with the vast possibilities offered by the setting and the characters populating it.

•

LIFE WITH FATHER
1947, 118 mins, US Ⓥ col
Dir Michael Curtiz ***Prod*** Robert Buckner ***Scr*** Donald Ogden Stewart ***Ph*** Peverell Marley, William V. Skall ***Ed*** George Amy ***Mus*** Max Steiner ***Art*** Robert M. Haas
Act Irene Dunne, William Powell, Elizabeth Taylor, Edmund Gwenn, ZaSu Pitts, Jimmy Lydon (Warner)

Irene Dunne and William Powell have captured to a considerable extent the charm of the play by Howard Lindsay and Russel Crouse [based on the book by Clarence Day, Jr.]. The major humor of the story, based on Father's eccentric characteristics and Mother's continual mollifying of his tantrums, is still evident in the pic. The Day children are not as effectively projected as in the play, but this, too, has been shrouded by the lesser intimacy of the pic.

Elizabeth Taylor, as the vis-à-vis for Clarence Day, Jr., is sweetly feminine as the demure visitor to the Day household, while Jimmy Lydon, as young Clarence, is likewise effective as the potential Yale man. Edmund Gwenn, as the minister, and ZaSu Pitts, a constantly visiting relative, head the supporting players who contribute stellar performances.

1947: NOMINATIONS: Best Actor (William Powell), Color Cinematography, Color Art Direction, Scoring of a Dramatic Picture

•

LIFE WITH MIKEY
1993, 91 mins, US Ⓥ ⦿ col
Dir James Lapine ***Prod*** Teri Schwartz, Scott Rudin ***Scr*** Marc Lawrence ***Ph*** Rob Hahn ***Ed*** Robert Leighton ***Mus*** Alan Menken ***Art*** Adrianne Lobel
Act Michael J. Fox, Christina Vidal, Nathan Lane, Cyndi Lauper, David Krumholtz, David Huddleston (Touchstone)

A better version of *Curly Sue*, this Michael J. Fox vehicle screams "cute" from every pore but should play well with kids and won't insult the intelligence of adults.

Michael Chapman (Fox) was once the star of his own sitcom, *Life with Mikey*, making him one of the best-known tykes in America. Unfortunately, he topped out at age 15, and now suffers from a serious case of Peter Pan-itis, while his patient brother (Nathan Lane) runs their business. Then a streetwise 10-year-old (newcomer Christina Vidal) steals Michael's wallet and puts on a Meryl Streep-quality performance when caught. She quickly lands a major commercial gig and moves in with Michael, compelling him to confront some of his own inadequacies.

This is all very stock, predictable stuff, but director James Lapine and writer-coproducer Marc Lawrence bring an easy charm to most of the proceedings. Fox turns in an extremely likable, believable performance sans camp or melodramatics.

•

LIFT, THE
SEE: DE LIFT

•

LIFT, DE
(THE LIFT)
1983, 99 mins, Netherlands Ⓥ col
Dir Dick Maas ***Prod*** Matthijs van Heijningen ***Scr*** Dick Maas ***Ph*** Marc Felperlaan ***Ed*** Hans van Dongen ***Mus*** Dick Maas ***Art*** Harry Ammerlaan
Act Huub Stapel, Willeke van Ammelrooy, Josine van Dalsum (Sigma)

Humor from charcoal gray to pitch black, fine suspense, murders and thrills, and all of it without gratuitous gore combine for a jaunty entertainment in *The Lift*, director Dick Maas's first theatrical test, which he passes handsomely.

Background on young (32) Maas is that up to his feature bow his screen medium was the short, which he often crammed with considerable imagination, and, typically, black humor. He also has numerous TV drama credits.

Hero is an elevator maintenance man, Felix (Huub Stapel). The anti-hero is the elevator itself—an eccentric, malign, office-building conveyance whose passengers either suffocate, are decapitated by the doors, or dumped down the shaft.

With the aid of a femme journalist (Willeke van Ammelrooy) sniffing for a story, the vexed maintenance man (whose life is complicated by a jealous wife) finally gets to the bottom of the mystery. Before he does, thanks to adroit performances and special effects, there are plenty of laughs and thrills.

Maas has a well-developed sense of irony as well as a knack for the unusual sight gag. Film has echoes of Brian De Palma, but at bottom it's no imitation but an original Maas.

•

LIFT TO THE SCAFFOLD
SEE: L'ASCENSEUR POUR L'ECHAFAUD

•

LIGHT AT THE EDGE OF THE WORLD, THE
1971, 120 mins, US Ⓥ ▭ col
Dir Kevin Billington ***Prod*** Kirk Douglas ***Scr*** Tom Rowe, Rachel Billington, Paquita Villanova, Bertha Dominguez ***Ph*** Henri Decae ***Ed*** Bert Bates ***Mus*** Piero Piccioni ***Art*** Enrique Alarcon
Act Kirk Douglas, Yul Brynner, Samantha Eggar, Jean Claude Drouot, Fernando Rey, Renato Salvatori (National General)

Jules Verne's *The Light at the Edge of the World* shapes up as good action-adventure escapism. The stars are Kirk Douglas, who produced on Spanish locations, as the sole survivor on an island captured by pirate Yul Brynner, with Samantha Eggar as a shipwrecked hostage.

Douglas is a bored assistant to lighthouse-keeper Fernando Rey on a rock off the tip of South America in 1865. Massimo Ranieri, a young man rounding out the group, is brutally killed with Rey when Brynner's pirate ship takes over the island. Douglas escapes and ekes out a passive survival. When Brynner's men darken the regular beacon and erect a false light to snare Cape Horn vessels, Douglas rescues Renato Salvatori from slaughter and begins to fight back.

Eggar, saved from the shipwreck, is used by Brynner as a look-alike of Douglas's old secret love. From this point on, it's all downhill until the exciting confrontation between Douglas and Brynner atop the burning lighthouse.

•

LIGHTHORSEMEN, THE
1987, 128 mins, Australia Ⓥ ▭ col
Dir Simon Wincer ***Prod*** Ian Jones, Simon Wincer ***Scr*** Ian Jones ***Ph*** Dean Semler ***Ed*** Adrian Carr ***Mus*** Mario Millo ***Art*** Bernard Hides
Act Jon Blake, Peter Phelps, Tony Bonner, Bill Kerr, John Walton, Anthony Andrews (RKO/Picture Show)

Toward the end of this epic about Aussie cavalry fighting in the Middle East in 1917, there's a tremendously exciting and spectacular 14-minute sequence in which soldiers of the Light Horse charge on German/Turkish-occupied Beersheba. It's a pity writer and coproducer Ian Jones couldn't come up with a more substantial storyline to build around his terrific climax.

Focus of attention is on Dave Mitchell, very well played by Peter Phelps. Opening sequence, which is breathtakingly beautiful, is set in Australia and involves young Dave deciding to enlist in the Light Horse after seeing wild horses being mustered for shipment to the Middle East. Main story involves four friends (Jon Blake, John Walton, Tim McKenzie, Gary Sweet) who are members of the Australian cavalry, chaffing because the British, who have overall command of allied troops in the area, misuse the cavalry time and again, forcing the Australians to dismount before going into battle.

The principal leads are very well played, with Phelps a standout as the most interesting of the young soldiers. Walton scores as the quick-tempered leader of the group, while McKenzie creates a character out of very little material. Top-billed Blake is thoroughly charming as Scotty.

•

LIGHT IN THE DARKNESS
SEE: POKOLENIE

•

LIGHT IN THE PIAZZA
1962, 102 mins, US ▭ col
Dir Guy Green ***Prod*** Arthur Freed ***Scr*** Julius J. Epstein ***Ph*** Otto Heller ***Ed*** Frank Clarke ***Mus*** Mario Nascimbene ***Art*** Frank White
Act Olivia de Havilland, Rossano Brazzi, Yvette Mimieux, George Hamilton, Barry Sullivan (M-G-M)

Discerningly cast and deftly executed under the imaginative guidance of director Guy Green, the Arthur Freed production, filmed in the intoxicatingly visual environments of Rome and Florence, is an interesting touching drama based on a highly unusual romantic circumstance created in prose by Elizabeth Spencer. The film has its flaws, but they are minor kinks in a satisfying whole.

Epstein's concise and graceful screenplay examines with reasonable depth and sensible restraint the odd plight of a beautiful, wealthy 26-year-old American girl (Yvette Mimieux) who, as a result of a severe blow on the head in her youth, has been left with a permanent 10-year-old mentality.

It is, too, the story of her mother's (Olivia de Havilland) dilemma—whether to commit the girl to an institution, as is the wish of her husband (Barry Sullivan), who superficially sees in the measure a solution to his marital instability, or pave the way for the girl's marriage to a well-to-do young Florentine fellow (George Hamilton) by concealing knowledge of the child's retarded intelligence.

It's Mimieux's picture. The role requires an aura of luminous naivete mixed with childish vacancy and a passion for furry things and kind, attractive people. That's precisely what it gets. Hamilton acceptably manages the Italian flavor and displays more animation than he normally has. De Havilland's performance is one of great consistency and subtle projection.

•

LIGHT OF DAY

1987, 107 mins, US Ⓥ ⦿ col

Dir Paul Schrader ***Prod*** Rob Cohen, Keith Barish ***Scr*** Paul Schrader ***Ph*** John Bailey ***Ed*** Jacqueline Cambas ***Mus*** Thomas Newman ***Art*** Jeannine Claudia Oppewall

Act Michael J. Fox, Gena Rowlands, Joan Jett, Michael McKean, Thomas G. Waites, Cherry Jones (Taft/Barish)

At heart, *Light of Day* is a tortured family melodrama with a rock 'n' roll beat. Renegade daughter Patti Rasnick (Joan Jett) and her younger brother Joe (Michael J. Fox) play in the Barbusters, a talented but routine bar band that performs in taverns around Ohio.

Director Paul Schrader, who also wrote the screenplay, has spread enough guilt around this family to fill a book. Jett has a 4-year-old son (Billy Sullivan) but won't tell anyone who the father is. She hates her mother (Gena Rowlands) despite mom's attempts to show her God's way. With the passive father (Jason Miller) and the dutiful son (Fox), this could be anyfamily USA as written by Eugene O'Neill.

Everyone wears their emotions on their sleeve, except Jett, who wears them on her shoulder. Escape hatch from all this backbiting is supposed to be rock 'n' roll but when one talks too much about the saving grace of music, as Jett does, it tends to come out as childish and silly.

Despite the over-the-edge quality of her character, Rowlands makes even the most ludicrous lines seem feasible. Fox is basically miscast as the good-natured brother who idolizes his sister and tries to cover for her. Jett looks the part and even manages to hit the mark from time to time, but for every hit there's a miss.

•

LIGHTSHIP, THE

1985, 89 mins, US Ⓥ col

Dir Jerzy Skolimowski ***Prod*** Bill Benenson, Moritz Borman ***Scr*** William Mai, David Taylor ***Ph*** Charly Steinberger ***Ed*** Barry Vince ***Mus*** Stanley Myers ***Art*** Holger Gross

Act Robert Duvall, Klaus Maria Brandauer, Tom Bower, Robert Costanzo, Badja Djola, William Forsythe (CBS)

Jerzy Skolimowski's *The Lightship* is based on a novella by the highly regarded German writer Siegfried Lenz. It was filmed in West Germany on the island of Sylt with an all English-speaking cast, the story transferred from its North Sea setting to the coastal waters off Norfolk.

The setting is the only seaworthy lightship left, and it's on this precarious wreck that everything takes place. The other major plus is the acting duel between Robert Duvall and Klaus Maria Brandauer, both with thespian styles of their own and in direct contrast to each other. Since the roles of the hijacker Caspary and the Coast Guard captain Miller had to be switched before shooting began, one senses a battle of wits all the way down the line.

Further, Skolimowski is notorious for improvisation himself, so the script reportedly went through three changes—in addition to adding a saving narrative commentary on the editing table.

As a psychological thriller, *The Lightship* has its tense entertainment moments, but the narrative line takes so many detours that the problem is trying to figure out the non sequiturs as they surface out of nowhere.

•

LIGHT SLEEPER

1992, 100 mins, US Ⓥ ⦿ col

Dir Paul Schrader ***Prod*** Linda Reisman ***Scr*** Paul Schrader ***Ph*** Ed Lachman ***Ed*** Kristina Boden ***Mus*** Michael Been ***Art*** Richard Hornung

Act Willem Dafoe, Susan Sarandon, Dana Delaney, David Clennon, Mary Beth Hurt, Victor Garber (Seven Arts)

Paul Schrader has created a pointed companion piece to his earlier portraits of lonely outcasts (*Taxi Driver*, *American Gigolo*). Contemplative and violent by turns, this quasi-thriller about a longtime drug dealer leaving the business has a great deal to recommend it but could have been significantly better had Schrader done some fresh plotting and not relied on his standby gunplay to resolve issues.

A former heavy user himself, LeTour (Willem Dafoe) has long worked as a drug delivery boy for Ann (Susan Sarandon), who sees the handwriting on the wall and gives up the coke trade for cosmetics. With four months to go before Ann packs it in, LeTour continues to drop off packets to characters who look like pathetic 1980s throwbacks.

He runs into the love of his life, Marianne (Dana Delaney), who has gone clean with difficulty and now wants nothing to do with him. When Marianne slips off the wagon to an untimely demise, script becomes more melodramatic.

A superb Dafoe contributes crucially to the degree of success the film achieves. In two bracing and amusing scenes he goes to a psychic (Mary Beth Hurt) to try to see into the future. Sarandon's role is a bit archly written, but she's lively and quick-witted as usual. Delaney is rather bland as the old flame. Better is Jane Adams as her sympathetic sister.

•

LIGHTS OF NEW YORK

1928, 57 mins, US b/w

Dir Bryan Foy ***Scr*** Hugh Herbert, Murray Roth ***Ph*** E. H. Dupar

Act Helene Costello, Cullen Landis, Gladys Brockwell, Mary Carr, Wheeler Oakman, Eugene Pallette (Warner)

This picture got pretty billing in Warners describing it as "The first 100 per cent all-talking picture." Every character speaks, more or less. But it's not an expensively made picture in appearance, either in sets or cast.

This is an open-face story with roll-your-own dialog. It's underworld, starting in a small town and moving to a nite club on the Giddy Wild Way. There are bootleggers and gunmen, cops and muggs, the latter a couple of simps falling for con men back home in a hotel about twice the size of the town—from the looks of the set.

The cast of nearly all vaudeville actors talks the best they may, in lieu of legits or picture actors who can't talk. Gladys Brockwell, as the mistress, runs ahead and far, with Robert Elliott as the detective second. Bryan Foy directed—his first full-length talker. And there's some credit in that for him, considering there's no class to story or picture.

Helene Costello, in the fem lead, is a total loss. For talkers she had better go to school right away. Cullen Landis, opposite, seems to talk with much effort. Wheeler Oakman as the legger gets through fairly, burdened with much of the bad dialog. Mary Carr in a bit as the mother gives an illustration of what may be accomplished from experience. Tom McGuire nicely plays and looks a police chief, with hardly anything to say.

•

LIKE A HOUSE ON FIRE

SEE: HORI, MA PANENKO

•

LIKE WATER FOR CHOCOLATE

SEE: COMO AGUA PARA CHOCOLATE

•

LI'L ABNER

1959, 113 mins, US Ⓥ col

Dir Melvin Frank ***Prod*** Norman Panama, Melvin Frank ***Scr*** Norman Panama, Melvin Frank ***Ph*** Daniel L. Fapp ***Ed*** Arthur P. Schmidt ***Mus*** Nelson Riddle, Joseph L. Lilley (dir.) ***Art*** Hal Pereira, J. McMillan Johnson

Act Peter Palmer, Leslie Parrish, Stubby Kaye, Howard St. John, Julie Newmar, Stella Stevens (Paramount)

The Norman Panama-Melvin Frank filmization of their [1956] Broadway hit is lively, colorful, and tuneful, done with smart showmanship in every department.

Congress plans to use L'il Abner's hometown of Dogpatch for an atom bomb testing ground, it being the most worthless locale in the U.S. Dogpatchers must prove the town has some value so it will be spared. The item found is Mammy Yokum's Yokumberry Tonic, a stimulant to health and wealth and romance. The plot then thickens as private enterprise and the U.S. government compete for the celebrated syrup.

The plimsoll mark on Alvin Colt's costumes for the female members of the cast is notably low throughout, and some of the humor is strongly Chic Sale. The songs, by Gene De Paul and Johnny Mercer, are breezy and amusing.

DeeDee Wood's dances, based on Michael Kidd's stage choreography, move more freely than usual, unconfined by conventional limits, and have considerable dazzle. The vocal numbers tend to get bunched up, as if the missing stage footlights were still imposing their limitations.

Characterizations are as deliberately unreal as the costumes and settings. Because of this, the principals don't have much chance to display anything but the broadest sort of caricature. Peter Palmer, who created the role on Broadway of Li'l Abner, repeats his assignment here. Leslie Parrish, a delectable dish, essays Daisy Mae, and although delectable, the dish could do with a dash of spice. Stubby Kaye, another Gotham original, creates the most fun with a brisk portrayal of Marryin' Sam. Howard St. John, still another of the originals, has the best scene in the film as General Bullmoose. Julie Newmar and Stella Stevens are handsome and amusing as sexy sirens.

1959: NOMINATION: Best Scoring of a Dramatic Picture

•

LILAC TIME

1928, 100 mins, US col

Dir George Fitzmaurice ***Prod*** John McCormick ***Scr*** Carey Wilson, George Marion, Jr. ***Ph*** Sidney Hickox, Alvin Knechtel ***Ed*** Al Hall ***Art*** Horace Jackson

Act Colleen Moore, Gary Cooper, Burr McIntosh, George Cooper, Edward Dillon, Kathryn McGuire (First National)

The story (from the play by Jane Cowl and Jane Murfin, adapted by Willis Goldbeck) has elements recalling *Wings* in the air and *Seventh Heaven* in the closing scenes of the romantic portion. The romance is laid on thick, at times too thick. There is plenty of slack to take up to cut down this picture for the picture house time. It runs in two sections, 60 minutes in the first and 40 in the second.

Worked into the air battle is the Red Ace of Germany, a famous flier of the First World War. He is shown in his machine, brightly red. He gets Capt. Blythe, who falls badly hurt, but a later scene shows the Red Ace also down within the French lines, seemingly gotten in turn by Blythe. It's a picture that, while giving unmeasured opportunity for Colleen Moore, and in which she never misses on the light or heavy side, nevertheless throws too much work on the girl. Her tribulations or those of the fliers and her captain lover never raise a lump.

Gary Cooper readily falls into the role as the captain who also falls for Jeannie (Moore). His physical build helps him to look the part.

•

LILI

1953, 80 mins, US Ⓥ ⦿ col

Dir Charles Walters ***Prod*** Edwin H. Knopf ***Scr*** Helen Deutsch ***Ph*** Robert Planck ***Ed*** Ferris Webster ***Mus*** Bronislau Kaper ***Art*** Cedric Gibbons, Paul Groesse

Act Leslie Caron, Mel Ferrer, Jean-Pierre Aumont, Zsa Zsa Gabor, Kurt Kasznar, Amanda Blake (M-G-M)

Leslie Caron is a young French orphan who turns to a fascinating carnival magician, Jean-Pierre Aumont, for help [in this version of a story by Paul Gallico]. He's a Gallic wolf, but Lili's naive, 16-year-old innocence is too much for him, so he brushes her off with a waitress job with the show. Mel Ferrer, a puppeteer, uses his little friends to woo her from her sorrow.

The impromptu performance is so successful, Ferrer makes it part of the act he does with Kurt Kasznar and four puppets. Gruff and moody in his dealings with the girl, the puppet master actually loves her and is jealous over her continuing infatuation for Aumont. This jealousy leads him to slap her just at the time she is again desperate, after having discovered that Aumont is married to his assistant, Zsa Zsa Gabor. The girl packs her things and leaves.

Caron's metamorphosis from the forlorn little ugly duckling to a pixie-faced, attractive young lady is well-handled. Ferrer goes through most of the film in a pout, both from jealousy and because his dancing career was halted by a war injury. Aumont is delightful as the magician and his act with Gabor, staged almost as a production piece, is a highlight.

1953: Best Scoring of a Dramatic Picture

NOMINATIONS: Best Director, Actress (Leslie Caron), Screenplay, Color Cinematography, Color Art Direction

•

LILIES OF THE FIELD

1963, 94 mins, US Ⓥ b/w

Dir Ralph Nelson ***Prod*** Ralph Nelson ***Scr*** James Poe ***Ph*** Ernest Haller ***Ed*** John McCafferty ***Mus*** Jerry Goldsmith

Act Sidney Poitier, Lilia Skala, Lisa Mann, Stanley Adams, Dan Frazer (Rainbow/United Artists)

Made on a modest budget and filmed entirely on location in Arizona, *Lilies* reveals Sidney Poitier as an actor with a sharp sense of humor. He is a journeyman laborer, touring the countryside in his station wagon, working when the fancy moves him, and traveling on when he feels the need for a change. That is his philosophy until he stops one day at a lonely farm to refill his radiator, but he meets his match in the five women who run the place.

They are all members of a holy order from East Germany, and are working arid land that has been bequeathed them. As the Mother Superior sets eyes on Poitier she is convinced that God has answered her prayers and sent a strong healthy man to fix the roof of their farmhouse.

Many factors combine in the overall success of the film, notably the restrained direction by Ralph Nelson, a thoroughly competent screenplay by James Poe [from a novel by William E. Barrett], and, of course, Poitier's own standout performance. There are a number of diverting scenes that remain in the memory, such as Poitier giving the Sisters an English lesson, with gestures to demonstrate the meaning of the phrases, and later leading them in the singing of "Aymen."

1963: Best Actor (Sidney Poitier)

NOMINATIONS: Best Picture, Supp. Actress (Lilia Skala), Adapted Screenplay, B&W Cinematography

•

LILITH

1964, 110 mins, US Ⓥ b/w

Dir Robert Rossen ***Prod*** Robert Rossen ***Scr*** Robert Rossen ***Ph*** Eugen Shuftan ***Ed*** Aram Avakian ***Mus*** Kenyon Hopkins ***Art*** Richard Sylbert

Act Warren Beatty, Jean Seberg, Peter Fonda, Kim Hunter, Jessica Walter, Gene Hackman (Centaur)

Lilith is the story of a young man who becomes an occupational therapist in a private mental institution where patients share three conditions—schizophrenia, wealth, and uncommon intelligence. Untrained in medicine, he nevertheless takes the job because he feels he can help suffering humanity.

Whatever clarity the narrative has in its early reels is shrouded in mist as his relations with a beautiful young patient begin to develop. Unfoldment is complex and often confusing. Robert Rossen as producer-scripter-director frequently fails to communicate to the spectator. Audience is left in as much of a daze as the hero is throughout most of the film.

Warren Beatty undertakes lead role with a hesitation jarring to the watcher. His dialog generally is restricted to no more than a single, or at most two sentences, and often the audience waits uncomfortably for words that never come while Beatty merely hangs his head or stares into space. As he finds himself falling in love with Jean Seberg, a fragile girl who lives in her own dreamworld and wants love, the change of character from one fairly definitive in the beginning to the gropings of a sexually obsessed mind never carries conviction.

In adapting the J. R. Salamanca novel, Rossen approaches his task with obvious attempt to shock.

•

LIMBO

1972, 111 mins, US col

Dir Mark Robson ***Prod*** Linda Gottlieb ***Scr*** Joan Micklin Silver, James Bridges ***Ph*** Charles F. Wheeler ***Ed*** Dorothy Spencer ***Mus*** Anita Kerr ***Art*** James Sullivan

Act Kate Jackson, Katherine Justice, Stuart Margolin, Hazel Medina, Kathleen Nolan, Russell Wiggins (Filmakers/Omaha-Orange)

Limbo is an excellent melodrama about three wives whose husbands are missing or imprisoned in Vietnam. An outstanding script, terrific performances by a cast of relatively new players, and Robson's finest direction in years add up to solid emotional impact.

The story is by Joan Micklin Silver. Kathleen Nolan is a mid-30s mother of four whose husband has been interned for years; Katherine Justice is a wealthy, sophisticated woman whose husband is technically missing, and she refuses to believe substantial evidence that he was killed; and Kate Jackson, in an outstanding performance, is a young girl, married only two weeks to her missing husband, who falls in love with another man. Framework of the plot is a ride the three principal wives take to an airport where one man is returning.

•

LIMELIGHT

1936, 80 mins, UK b/w

Dir Herbert Wilcox ***Prod*** Herbert Wilcox ***Scr*** Laura Whetter ***Ph*** Henry Harris

Act Anna Neagle, Arthur Tracy, Ellis Jeffreys, Tilly Losch, Alexander Field (Wilcox/GFD)

The high spots of this picture are the graceful dancing in it and Arthur Tracy's fine voice. Anna Neagle is natural in the role of an ambitious chorus girl who dries up so completely when her big moment comes.

There is too much repetition; too much flashing back to the same stage set and recurrence of song scenes. But withal there is an air of sincerity that makes the story pleasing, if not epoch-making.

A chorine hears a down-and-outer singing in the street, and when the star singer of her show loses his voice within a half hour of the first night she drags the boy in and pleads with the management to give him a chance. He becomes a riot, and despite the amorous leanings of a wealthy society girl, remains faithful to the girl who discovered him.

Tilly Losch bestows a few scenes of exotic dancing, with Robinson and Martin responsible for some charming and graceful steps.

•

LIMELIGHT

1952, 135 mins, US Ⓥ b/w

Dir Charles Chaplin ***Prod*** Charles Chaplin ***Scr*** Charles Chaplin ***Ph*** Karl Struss ***Ed*** Joe Inge ***Mus*** Charles Chaplin ***Art*** Eugene Lourie

Act Charles Chaplin, Claire Bloom, Nigel Bruce, Buster Keaton, Sydney Chaplin, Norman Lloyd (Celebrated/United Artists)

Charlie Chaplin's production is probably derivative of his personal career over the years. Its backdrop is the British Stage. Departing from most forms of Hollywood stereotype, the film has a flavor all its own in the sincere quality of the story anent the onetime great vaudemime and his rescue of a femme ballet student from a suicide attempt and subsequently from great mental depression.

Production-wise, *Limelight* is a one-man show since Chaplin does almost everything but grow his own rawstock. The British music hall milieu of 1914 and the third-rate rooming house, where a good deal of the story unfolds, come through as honest reproductions.

While Chaplin is the star, he must surrender some spotlight to Claire Bloom, recruited from the British stage, for the second lead. As the frustrated terper, the delicately beautiful young actress gives a sensitive and memorable performance. Chaplin's real-life son, Sydney, is gentle and shy as the composer in love with Bloom.

1972 [*sic*]: Best Original Score

•

LIMEY, THE

1999, 90 mins, US Ⓥ ⦿ col

Dir Steven Soderbergh ***Prod*** John Hardy, Scott Kramer ***Scr*** Lem Dobbs ***Ph*** Ed Lachman ***Ed*** Sarah Flack ***Mus*** Cliff Martinez ***Art*** Gary Frutkoff

Act Terence Stamp, Peter Fonda, Lesley Ann Warren, Luis Guzman, Barry Newman, Joe Dallessandro (Artisan)

Most interesting element of Steven Soderbergh's crime picture is the positioning of two icons of '60s cinema, the very British Terence Stamp and the very American Peter Fonda, as longtime enemies in what's basically a routine revenge thriller.

Leaving London for the first time, after nine years behind bars, Wilson (Stamp) arrives in L.A. to unravel the death of his daughter. A solitary figure in a lousy motel, he spends his time reading newspaper clippings about Jenny, who died under mysterious circumstances, according to a letter he received from a man called Ed (Luis Guzman).

The only clue Wilson has is that Jenny was involved in a love affair with Valentine (Fonda), an affluent record producer who owns a spectacular house in the Hollywood Hills, where he now carries on an affair with Adhara (Amelie Heinle), a beautiful girl roughly Jenny's age.

Later episodes link Wilson with the graceful Elaine (a splendid Lesley Ann Warren), an aging actress who knew Jenny. A relationship (but no romance) evolves, during which Wilson has to face his irresponsible conduct as a father.

Narrative actually resembles a Western, in which two aging criminals must face the rapidly changing conditions around them and must come to terms with their own identity—and mortality. The film suffers from unfolding as a series of setpieces that don't build much continuity or excitement.

Soderbergh uses extensive footage from Ken Loach's 1967 film *Poor Cow*, in which Stamp played a young thief named, perhaps not so coincidentally, Wilson.

•

LINEUP, THE

1958, 85 mins, US b/w

Dir Don Siegel ***Prod*** Jaime Del Valle ***Scr*** Stirling Silliphant ***Ph*** Hal Mohr ***Ed*** Al Clark ***Mus*** Mischa Bakaleinikoff ***Art*** Ross Bellah

Act Eli Wallach, Robert Keith, Warner Anderson, Richard Jaeckel, Mary LaRoche, William Leslie (Columbia)

The Lineup is based on a popular teleseries [1954–60] and has some of the same characters. But the screenplay is original material. The production is a moderately exciting melodrama based on dope smuggling in San Francisco, but short on action until the final, well-plotted and photographed climax.

The action centers around the attempt by a narcotics gang to retrieve the heroin it has planted abroad in the possession of travelers debarking in San Francisco. Eli Wallach heads the gang's pick-up squad, aided by brains Robert Keith and driver Richard Jaeckel.

The best part of the action is its background, the Mark Hopkins motel, a Nob Hill mansion, Sutro's museum, the Opera House. There is also a good chase sequence at the end on an unfinished freeway. But the early parts of the film waste too much time on police procedure and lingo.

Wallach is wasted in the leading role. He seems an ordinary heavy, competent but not particularly interesting.

•

LINK

1986, 103 mins, UK Ⓥ col

Dir Richard Franklin ***Prod*** Richard Franklin ***Scr*** Everett De-Roche ***Ph*** Mike Molloy ***Ed*** Andrew London ***Mus*** Jerry Goldsmith ***Art*** Norman Garwood

Act Terence Stamp, Elisabeth Shue, Steven Pinner, Richard Garnett (Thorn EMI)

You know right off the film is in trouble when the chimpanzees outperform their human counterparts.

Credit here goes to animal trainer Ray Berwick for getting a full range of expressions out of the primates that director Richard Franklin couldn't get out of the actors.

Film plods along for almost an hour at an isolated English coastal manor house where preeminent primatologist Dr. Steven Phillip (Terence Stamp) conducts rudimentary experiments on a handful of chimps.

The chimps' malevolent ringleader, Link, takes over the lead from the first time he is seen as the tuxedoed butler—even though he never utters a word.

Presumably, it's when we find out that Link is not the dutiful cigar-smoking house servant that things are supposed to get scary.

•

LIONHEART

1987, 104 mins, US Ⓥ ⦿ col

Dir Franklin J. Schaffner ***Prod*** Stanley O'Toole, Talia Shire ***Scr*** Menno Meyjes, Richard Outten ***Ph*** Alec Mills ***Ed*** David Bretherton, Richard Haines ***Mus*** Jerry Goldsmith ***Art*** Gil Parrondo

Act Eric Stoltz, Gabriel Byrne, Nicola Cowper, Dexter Fletcher, Deborah Barrymore, Nicholas Clay (Taliafilm II/Orion)

The Children's Crusade of the 12th century is the subject of Franklin J. Schaffner's *Lionheart*, a flaccid, limp kiddie adventure yarn with little of its intended grand epic sweep realized. Based partly on myth, partly on historical accounts, the story [by Menno Meyjes] concerns bands of medieval tykes who set out to search for the elusive King Richard II on his quest to recapture the Holy Land from the Moslems. Young knight Robert Nerra (Eric Stoltz) rides off disillusioned from his first battle and meets up with mystical Blanche (pretty Nicola Cowper) and her brother Michael (Dexter Fletcher), two teen circus performers who convince him to travel to Paris and join King Richard's crusade. The dark threat of the Black Prince looms overhead in all corners of the misty forest. Gabriel Byrne plays him like an ennui-stricken Darth Vader. His goal is to recruit all the kids and sell them into slavery.

•

LION IN WINTER, THE

1968, 135 mins, UK Ⓥ ⦿ ▭ col

Dir Anthony Harvey ***Prod*** Martin Poll ***Scr*** James Goldman ***Ph*** Douglas Slocombe ***Ed*** John Bloom ***Mus*** John Barry ***Art*** Peter Murton

Act Peter O'Toole, Katharine Hepburn, Jane Merrow, John Castle, Timothy Dalton, Anthony Hopkins (Avco Embassy/Haworth)

The Lion in Winter, based on James Goldman's play (1966) about treachery in the family of England's King Henry II, is an intense, fierce, personal drama put across by outstanding performances of Peter O'Toole and Katharine Hepburn. Director Anthony Harvey has done excellent work with a generally strong cast and a literate adaptation.

Title refers to the late period in the life of Henry II, when a decision on succession is deemed advisable. His exiled, embittered, and imprisoned wife, Eleanor of Aquitaine, and three legitimate male offspring are gathered, along with his mistress and her brother, youthful king Philip of France.

In one day, the seven characters are stripped bare of all inner torments, outward pretensions, and governing personality traits. Goldman has blended in his absorbing screenplay elements of love, hate, frustration, fulfillment, ambition, and greed. O'Toole scores a bull's-eye as the king, while Hepburn's performance is amazing.

1968: Best Actress (Katharine Hepburn), Adapted Screenplay, Original Score

NOMINATIONS: Best Picture, Director, Actor (Peter O'Toole), Costume Design

•

LION IS IN THE STREETS, A

1953, 87 mins, US Ⓥ col

Dir Raoul Walsh ***Prod*** William Cagney ***Scr*** Luther Davis ***Ph*** Harry Stradling ***Ed*** George Amy ***Mus*** Franz Waxman ***Art*** Wiard Ihnen

Act James Cagney, Barbara Hale, Anne Francis, Warner Anderson, John McIntire, Jeanne Cagney (Warner)

The Adrian Locke Langley novel was a long time coming to the screen since first purchased by the Cagneys for filming. Along the way it lost a lot of the shocker quality and emerges as just an average drama of a man's political ambitions.

The production deals with a backwoods politician who nearly forces his ambitions on a cotton-growing state. The novel had him succeeding in doing so for a long time, but the film thwarts his drive for power before he can be elected governor.

The development of the principal character and the story has a sketchy feel, against which Raoul Walsh's direction has its problems.

James Cagney plays the swamp peddler who tries to ride into the governor's mansion by making a crusade of the plight of poor sharecroppers. The portrayal has an occasional strength, but mostly is a stylized performance done with an inconsistent southern dialect that rarely holds through a complete line of dialog.

Barbara Hale is sweet and charming as the schoolteacher who marries him. The fiery Flamingo of the book has been watered down considerably and doesn't give Anne Francis much opportunity.

•

LION KING, THE

1994, 87 mins, US Ⓥ ⦿ col

Dir Roger Allens, Rob Minkoff ***Prod*** Don Hahn ***Scr*** Irene Mecchi, Jonathan Roberts, Linda Woolverton ***Ed*** Tom Finan, John Carnochan ***Mus*** Hans Zimmer ***Art*** Chris Sanders

(Walt Disney)

Set off by some of the richest imagery the studio's animators have produced and held together by a timeless coming-of-age tale, *The Lion King* marks a dazzling—and unexpectedly daring—addition to the Disney canon, abetted by a marvelous cast of star voices and songs by Elton John and Tim Rice tending toward huge, sonorous choral numbers.

A mesmerizing pre-credits opening sets up the story and establishes an epic tone that carries through much of the movie. As the sun rises over the African jungle, the animals gather in teeming flocks and herds and broods—as the anthemic "Circle of Life" builds to a roaring crescendo.

Mufasa (voiced by James Earl Jones), the Lion King, and his Queen, Sarabi (Madge Sinclair), look on approvingly as the mystical baboon Rafiki (Robert Guillaume) presents their cub, Simba (Jonathan Taylor Thomas), as the future Lion King, while Zazu the hornbill (a hilarious Rowan Atkinson) flits about, making sure the King's bidding is attended to.

But there's a shadow on the festivities—Mufasa's brother Scar (Jeremy Irons), who begins his campaign to kill off his competition for the throne, entices Simba and his girlfriend, Nala (Niketa Calame), to venture into forbidden territory, which turns out to be a hyena-packed elephant's graveyard.

While the individual animal characters are represented with typical Disney cleverness, the herds are memorable for their unexpected realism, the zebras in particular. And kudos, too, to an involving screenplay that handles shifts in tone with considerable grace.

1994: Best Original Score, Original Song ("Can You Feel the Love Tonight")

NOMINATIONS: Best Original Song ("Circle of Life," "Hakuna Matata")

•

LION OF THE DESERT

1981, 162 mins, Libya/UK Ⓥ ▭ col

Dir Moustapha Akkad ***Prod*** Moustapha Akkad ***Scr*** H.A.L. Craig ***Ph*** Jack Hildyard ***Ed*** John Shirley ***Mus*** Maurice Jarre ***Art*** Mario Garbuglia

Act Anthony Quinn, Oliver Reed, Rod Steiger, John Gielgud, Irene Papas, Raf Vallone (Falcon International)

Filmed as *Omar Mukhtar* in 1979 at a cost reportedly exceeding $30 million, *Lion of the Desert* is a very well-produced, frequently stirring war film about a Libyan anti-colonial hero.

Functional script by H.A.L. Craig concentrates on the Italians' efforts in 1929–31 to conquer Libya. Mussolini (Rod Steiger in two effective scenes as the strutting fascist leader) sends his general Graziani (Oliver Reed) to put down the Bedouins led by Omar Mukhtar (Anthony Quinn). Quinn is a white-bearded old teacher and freedom fighter who has been battling the Italians for 20 years.

Film's many large-scale battle scenes include two ingenious ambushes where Mukhtar succeeds in beating the better-equipped Italian forces. Producer-director Moustapha Akkad stages such action with laudable scope, but much of the battle footage is impersonal.

While never explicit, the overtones of the Bedouins's desire for international recognition, Mukhtar's insistence that confiscated lands must be returned (with new Italian settlements on them not to be tolerated), and other militant dialog emphasize parallels with today's Palestinians.

Quinn is well cast as Omar Mukhtar and brings warmth and dimension to a stock national hero assignment.

•

LIPSTICK

1976, 89 mins, US Ⓥ ⦿ col

Dir Lamont Johnson ***Prod*** Freddie Fields ***Scr*** David Rayfiel ***Ph*** Bill Butler, William A. Fraker ***Ed*** Marion Rothman ***Mus*** Michel Polnareff, Jimmie Haskell ***Art*** Robert Luthardt

Act Margaux Hemingway, Chris Sarandon, Perry King, Anne Bancroft, Robin Gammell, Mariel Hemingway (Paramount/De Laurentiis)

Lipstick has pretensions of being an intelligent treatment of the tragedy of female rape. But by the time it's over, the film has shown its true colors as just another cynical violence exploitationer.

David Rayfiel's script tells how high-fashion model Margaux Hemingway is brutally assaulted by mild-mannered music teacher Chris Sarandon.

The early-on rape sequence (coming less than 20 minutes into the film) is really the dramatic highlight. Somehow one just knows that society's procedures will degrade the rape victim and that the ending of the film will contrive some opportunity for partially justified violence. Margaux Hemingway's dramatic limitations lend more believability to the role. Sarandon's performance is powerful in its quiet menace.

•

LIQUIDATOR, THE

1966, 104 mins, UK Ⓥ ▭ col

Dir Jack Cardiff ***Prod*** Jon Pennington ***Scr*** Peter Yeldham ***Ph*** Ted Scaife ***Ed*** Ernest Walter ***Mus*** Lalo Schifrin ***Art*** John Blezard

Act Rod Taylor, Trevor Howard, Jill St. John, Wilfrid Hyde White, David Tomlinson, Akim Tamiroff (M-G-M)

This spy yarn features Boysie Oakes, a creation of John Gardner. Peter Yeldham's screenplay and Jack Cardiff's direction combine plenty of action and some crisp wisecracking.

Where Boysie Oakes (Rod Taylor) is different from his [1960s] counterparts is that he is neither a pro undercover agent nor an enthusiastic amateur with a flair. In fact, he is a vulnerable sort of guy who hates killing. An ex-sergeant who accidentally saves Trevor Howard's life, he is conned into joining the service by Howard (Security's No. 2).

He compromises by hiring a professional killer to do the dirty work for him, an angle that has promise as a film plot. But this fairly quickly gets sidetracked when Oakes takes "No. 2's" lush secretary for a dirty weekend on the Riviera.

There are plenty of holes in the plot, but no matter. The vulnerable Oakes is played with plenty of charm and guts by Taylor, though he hardly suggests a character with such fundamental failings and frailties as Boysie.

•

LIQUID SKY

1982, 118 mins, US Ⓥ ⦿ col

Dir Slava Tsukerman ***Prod*** Slava Tsukerman ***Scr*** Slava Tsukerman, Nina Kerova, Anne Carlisle ***Ph*** Yuri Neyman ***Ed*** Sharyn Leslie Ross ***Mus*** Slava Tsukerman, Brenda Hutchinson, Clive Smith ***Art*** Marina Levikova

Act Anne Carlisle, Paula Sheppard, Susan Doukas, Otto Von Wernherr, Bob Brady, Elaine Grove (Z Films)

Liquid Sky is an odd, yet generally pleasing mixture of punk rock, science fiction, and black humor. Story centers on Anne Carlisle, a new wave fashion model who inhabits a world of high-decibel noise, drug addicts (title is slang expression for heroin) and casual sex. Although Carlisle is part of the scene, she doesn't embrace any of its vices. Unbeknownst to the crowd, a pie-plate–sized flying saucer takes up residence in the neighborhood. The creature proceeds to eliminate Carlisle's lovers as they reach orgasm. Carlisle assumes she's developed some strange curse. At first she uses this power for revenge but later attempts to warn her skeptical friends.

Created by Russian emigrees living in New York City, *Liquid Sky* possesses a sophisticated sense of humor. It's view of a changing society is offered up in fiercely black comic tones. Neither the new guard nor the old escapes the filmmakers' barbed observations.

•

LISBON

1956, 90 mins, US Ⓥ ▭ col

Dir Ray Milland ***Prod*** Ray Milland (assoc.) ***Scr*** John Tucker Battle ***Ph*** Jack Marta ***Ed*** Richard L. Van Enger ***Mus*** Nelson Riddle ***Art*** Frank Arrigo

Act Ray Milland, Maureen O'Hara, Claude Rains, Yvonne Furneaux, Francis Lederer, Percy Marmont (Republic)

Lisbon makes a colorful setting for this tale [by Martin Rackin] of nefarious adventure among the international intrigue set. Republic's anamorphic Naturama process and Trucolor go a long way toward visual impressiveness.

Ray Milland stars, produces, and directs. As a smooth, romantically inclined American amusing himself with smuggling operations, his trouping comes off very well. As a production, the picture could have used a little sharper overseeing of story material, particularly the opening sequence in which sadistic Aristides Mavros (Claude Rains), international crook, smashes a songbird with a tennis racket so his hungry cat can have his breakfast.

Maureen O'Hara advantageously plays Sylvia, the young wife of a rich, old man who has been prisoner behind the Iron Curtain for two years. She wants him back, but dead so she can claim his fortune, and Mavros is the big operator who arranges the details, including hiring Evans (Milland) and his boat for the pickup. Yvonne Furneaux plays a very interesting young lady who is one of the beauties Mavros keeps around to satisfy his esthetic tastes. The starring foursome are quite glib and pleasing in the principal roles.

•

LISTEN, DARLING

1938, 72 mins, US Ⓥ b/w

Dir Edwin L. Marin ***Prod*** Jack Cummings ***Scr*** Elaine Ryan, Anne Morrison Chapin ***Ph*** Charles Lawton, Jr. ***Ed*** Blanche Sewell ***Mus*** William Axt, George Stoll

Act Judy Garland, Freddie Bartholomew, Mary Astor, Walter Pidgeon, Alan Hale, Scotty Beckett (M-G-M)

Handicapped by an illogical and unconvincing story [by Katherine Brush], initial effort of Metro to team Judy Garland and Freddie Bartholomew is a lightweight offering that has little aside from three good song numbers handled capably by Garland.

Young Bartholomew is at the age where he is fast sprouting. He is several inches taller than in his previous film appearance [*Lord Jeff*, also 1938] while his voice has dropped down the scale considerably.

When Mary Astor considers marriage to insure security of her two children (Garland and Scotty Beckett), Bartholomew steps in to assist Garland to prevent such a move. Pair abduct the mother and young son in a trailer for a tour, figuring trip may change her mind, and there is always a chance of turning up a more likely candidate for a stepfather. On the road, entourage meets Walter Pidgeon's lawyer, who goes for the wide open spaces in a deluxe trailer. Kids bring Astor and Pidgeon together in a speedy two-day romance to put everything shipshape.

•

LIST OF ADRIAN MESSENGER, THE

1963, 98 mins, US Ⓥ ⦿ b/w

Dir John Huston ***Prod*** Edward Lewis ***Scr*** Anthony Veiller ***Ph*** Joe MacDonald, Ted Scaife ***Ed*** Terry O. Morse ***Mus*** Jerry Goldsmith ***Art*** Alexander Golitzen, Stephen Grimes, George Webb

Act George C. Scott, Dana Wynter, Clive Brook, Gladys Cooper, Herbert Marshall, Jacques Roux (Universal)

Anthony Veiller's screenplay, based on a story by Philip MacDonald, is a kind of straight-laced version of *Kind Hearts and Coronets*. It is the story of a retired British Intelligence officer's efforts to nab a killer who has ingeniously murdered 11 men who represent obstacles to his goal—the acquisition of a huge fortune to which he will become heir as soon as he eliminates the 12th obstacle, the 12-year-old grandson of his aged uncle, the wealthy Marquis of Gleneyre.

The film hums along smoothly and captivatingly until the killer shows up at the estate of the Marquis. Here the story begins to fall apart. Since both Scotland Yard and our principal investigator (George C. Scott) are at this time fully aware of who and where their man is, and what he is up to, it is an incredibly contrived story distortion to suppose that they would let him roam about freely for several days.

An even more damaging miscue is the utilization of stars who are hidden behind facial disguises in fundamentally inconsequential roles. Of the five stars who "guest," Kirk Douglas has the major assignment and carries it off colorfully and credibly. The others are Tony Curtis, Burt Lancaster, Robert Mitchum, and Frank Sinatra. Only Mitchum is easily recognizable beneath the facial stickum.

Huston directs the film with style and flair. Credit is due to makeup man Bud Westmore for his concealment of several of the most familiar faces of the 20th century.

•

LISZTOMANIA

1975, 104 mins, UK Ⓥ ⦿ ▭ col

Dir Ken Russell ***Prod*** Roy Baird, David Puttnam ***Scr*** Ken Russell ***Ph*** Peter Suschitzky ***Ed*** Stuart Baird ***Mus*** Rick Wakeman (arr.) ***Art*** Philip Harrison

Act Roger Daltrey, Sara Kestelman, Paul Nicholas, Fiona Lewis, Veronica Quilligan, Ringo Starr (Goodtimes)

Ken Russell's *Lisztomania* combines his customary zany and bawdy artfulness with a style close to *Tommy*.

Liszt is depicted as somewhat of a self-indulgent professional hustler, outdone only by Wagner, whose added ambition of unifying Germany lends the kind of "meaningful commitment" so often necessary to put over otherwise mediocre pop music. Daltrey and Paul Nicholas handle their parts with flair.

•

LITTLE ANNIE ROONEY

1925, 95 mins, US Ⓥ ⦿ ⊗ b/w

Dir William Beaudine ***Scr*** Katherine Hennessey, Hope Loring, Louis D. Lighton, Tom McNamara ***Ph*** Charles Rosher, Hal Mohr ***Art*** John D. Schulze, Harry Oliver, Paul Youngblood

Act Mary Pickford, William Haines, Walter James, Gordon Griffith, Hugh Fay (Pickford/United Artists)

Mary Pickford is again a smudgy-faced gamin of the streets. She's dirty-hands, dirty-face and all that sort of thing. It is a New York story. A story of that New York that lies south of Fourteenth Street and east of "Thoid avenoo" in the day when the Irish ruled the section.

The story is about the two children of Rooney, the cop. Mary is the daughter, who is about 12, and her brother is around 18 or so. The kids of the neighborhood taunt Mary with "Little Annie Rooney Is My Sweetheart" and she starts a battle, part of the gang being lined up with her and part against her. Abie has to stay home and can't fight 'cause it's a holiday, but when the battle gets too hot you can't keep Abie out and he goes to Annie's aid. It is great kids' stuff and the director makes the most of his chances.

•

LITTLE BIG MAN

1970, 147 mins, US Ⓥ ⦿ ▭ col

Dir Arthur Penn ***Prod*** Stuart Millar ***Scr*** Calder Willingham ***Ph*** Harry Stradling, Jr. ***Ed*** Dede Allen ***Mus*** John Hammond ***Art*** Dean Tavoularis

Act Dustin Hoffman, Faye Dunaway, Martin Balsam, Richard Mulligan, Chief Dan George, Jeff Corey (Hiller-Stockbridge/Cinema Center)

Little Big Man is a sort of vaudeville show, framed in fictional biography, loaded with sketches of varying degrees of serious and burlesque humor, and climaxed by the Indian victory over Gen. George A. Custer at Little Big Horn in 1876.

The story strand [from the novel by Thomas Berger] is Dustin Hoffman's long life (he is over 120 at prolog and epilog brackets), especially his years as an adopted Indian who witnessed Custer's megalomaniacal massacre attempt that backfired.

Might it be a serious attempt to right some irretrievable wrong via gallows humor that avoids the polemics? This seems to be the course taken; the attempt at least can be respected in theory.

Chief Dan George is outstanding as an Indian chief who provides periodic inputs of philosophy. Faye Dunaway is first the preacher's oversexed wife, later a prostitute admired by Wild Bill Hickok, played well by Jeff Corey; and Martin Balsam is a swindling traveling beggar.

1970: NOMINATION: Best Supp. Actor (Chief Dan George)

•

LITTLE BUDDHA

1993, 140 mins, UK/France Ⓥ ⦿ col

Dir Bernardo Bertolucci ***Prod*** Jeremy Thomas ***Scr*** Rudy Wurlitzer, Mark Peploe ***Ph*** Vittorio Storaro ***Ed*** Pietro Scalia ***Mus*** Ryuichi Sakamoto ***Art*** James Acheson

Act Keanu Reeves, Chris Isaak, Bridget Fonda, Alex Wiesendanger, Ying Ruocheng, Jigme Kunsang (Recorded Pictures/CiBy 2000)

Little Buddha is a visually stunning but dramatically underwhelming attempt to forge a bridge between the ancient Eastern religion and modern Western life. Bernardo Bertolucci's second foray into remote Asian territory is considerably less successful than his first, *The Last Emperor*, as the double narrative [by Bertolucci himself] is awkwardly structured and never comes into sharp focus. The lavish $35 million-plus production is like a long art film for kids.

Modern story sees the aged, august Lama Norbu (Ying Ruocheng) traveling from the Himalaya kingdom of Bhutan to Seattle in search of the reincarnation of his order's revered late teacher. Path leads to the home of Dean and Lisa Konrad (Chris Isaak, Bridget Fonda), whose energetic son, Jesse (Alex Wiesendanger), is the suspected enlightened one.

Jesse is told of the life of Siddhartha (a strikingly darkened Keanu Reeves), a handsome prince who abandoned his charmed existence to live in poverty and search for the true path.

Seeking some answers of his own, Dean agrees to Norbu's request to bring Jesse to Bhutan, where the boy will be sized up against two other candidates to determine who is truly the reincarnate.

Isaak is wan and unable to communicate the fruits of introspection. Fonda is OK but overly smiley as his fastidious wife, and Wiesendanger doesn't register much as the son. Reeves makes for a surprisingly watchable and dashing Siddhartha. Ying Ruocheng, who also appeared in *The Last Emperor*, brings a welcome, light gravity to the principal monk. [Pic was cut to two hours for its U.S. release.]

•

LITTLE CAESAR

1931, 77 mins, US Ⓥ ⦿ b/w

Dir Mervyn LeRoy ***Scr*** Francis E. Faragoh, Robert W. Lee ***Ph*** Tony Gaudio ***Ed*** Ray Curtiss ***Mus*** Erno Rapee (dir.) ***Art*** Anton Grot

Act Edward G. Robinson, Douglas Fairbanks, Jr., Glenda Farrell, Sidney Blackmer, Thomas Jackson, Ralph Ince (Warner)

There are enough killings herein to fill the quota for an old time cowboy-Indian thriller. And one tough mugg, in the title part, who is tough all the way from the start, when he's a bum with ambition, to the finish, when he's a bum again, but a dead one.

For a performance as "Little Caesar" no director could ask for more than Edward G. Robinson's contribution. Here, no matter what he has to say, he's entirely convincing.

Young Douglas Fairbanks is splendid as the gunman's friend. Another junior, William Collier, Jr., contributes real trouping to a part that seemed out of his line. There are no off-key performances in the picture.

No new twists to the gunman stuff [from the novel by W. R. Burnett], same formula and all the standard tricks, but Mervyn LeRoy, directing, had a good yarn to start with and gives it plenty of pace besides astute handling.

1930/31: NOMINATION: Best Adaptated Screenplay

•

LITTLE COLONEL, THE

1935, 80 mins, US Ⓥ ⦿ col

Dir David Butler ***Scr*** William Conselman ***Ph*** Arthur Miller, William V. Skall

Act Shirley Temple, Lionel Barrymore, Evelyn Venable, John Lodge, Sidney Blackmer, Alden Chase (Fox)

Cute tots have traditionally been tough subjects to fit with stories. *Little Colonel* is skillful hokum that will please in general, although the sophisticated minority may make a point of being superior to such sentimentality. Widely read book gives the film a head start, too.

A southern colonel (Lionel Barrymore) is embittered when his daughter (Evelyn Venable) elopes with a northerner (John Lodge) and banishes them from the arc of his benevolence. Things go badly with the couple and the wife is forced to return with her small daughter (Shirley Temple) to occupy a cottage near her father's estate.

Of course, the child is the means of patching everything up, finale taking the form of a "pink party" given by the grandfather and photographed in Technicolor [by William V. Skall]. It's a gingerbread fade-out for a film loaded with sweetness and light.

Bill Robinson, vet-colored hoofer from vaudeville, grabs standout attention here. Voice is excellent, he reads lines with the best of 'em, and his hoofing stair dance is ingeniously woven into the yarn. He plays the kindly and aging family butler. A strong point for the film is the youngster doing Robinson's stair dance with him.

Dressed in the bustled costumes of the 1880s, the diminutive miss is a fetching, beautiful, and amiable infant. Her appeal is certain here and her acting range remains surprising.

Barrymore plays the colonel with scarcely one of his usual mannerisms, and with a zippy tempo, in contrast to the sidled-down technique he so often employs. Outside of the principals the other parts are incidental.

•

LITTLE DARLINGS

1980, 92 mins, US Ⓥ ⦿ ▭ col

Dir Ronald F. Maxwell ***Prod*** Stephen J. Friedman ***Scr*** Kimi Peck, Dalene Young ***Ph*** Fred Batka ***Ed*** Pembroke J. Herring ***Mus*** Charles Fox ***Art*** William Hiney

Act Tatum O'Neal, Kristy McNichol, Matt Dillon, Armand Assante, Krista Errickson, Nicholas Coster (Paramount)

Little Darlings makes an honest effort to deal with the sexual stirrings of two teenage girls, but many adults are likely to dismiss the effort as puppy love with appeal to prurient interests.

Tatum O'Neal and Kristy McNichol are both excellent as virgins of widely different social backgrounds who meet at summer camp. O'Neal is a sheltered rich girl and McNichol the poor, streetwise urchin, but their different upbringings do not release their shared hesitancy about making love for the first time.

In his feature debut, director Ronald F. Maxwell isn't perfect. But he gets several fine scenes from his performers, especially when O'Neal deals with her love interest, when NcNichol deals with her love interest, and best of all, when O'Neal and McNichol finally level with each other.

•

LITTLE DORRIT

1987, 360 mins, UK Ⓥ ⦿ col

Dir Christine Edzard ***Prod*** Richard Goodwin, John Brabourne ***Scr*** Christine Edzard ***Ph*** Bruno de Keyzer ***Ed*** Oliver Stockman, Fraser Maclean ***Mus*** Michel Sanvoisin (arr.)

Act Alec Guinness, Derek Jacobi, Cyril Cusack, Sarah Pickering, Joan Greenwood, Max Wall (Sands/Cannon)

Little Dorrit is a remarkable achievement. For writer/director Christine Edzard the epic project [from the novel by Charles Dickens] was obviously a labor of love, and what she has accomplished on a small budget is astounding.

The project is in fact two films, each three hours long [I: *Nobody's Fault*, 177 mins; II: *Little Dorrit's Story*, 183 mins], with the latter being virtually a remake of the former. A large cast of uniformly excellent British actors is topped off by quite brilliant portrayals by Alec Guinness as William Dorrit, and Derek Jacobi as Arthur Clennam.

In the second part you see from a different angle the story of the family's plight, and why they are in prison. Sarah Pickering bestows Amy Dorrit with the gentle firmness to look after her father, brother, and sister, and when Jacobi appears on the scene slowly falls in love with him. The family travels abroad and during a plush dinner in Rome to celebrate the marriage of Fanny Dorrit (Amelda Brown) and Sparkler (Simon Dormandy), Guinness finally goes mad, and delivers a speech as if he were still in the Marshalsea.

Pic then follows Pickering discovering Jacobi is in prison and her efforts to raise the money to free him.

Six hours of viewing obviously allows full characterization and depth of story—though some characters from the novel are still missing—but the style of showing virtually the same story through two people [Clennam and Amy] allows charming reinterpretations of certain scenes, and presents a fully rounded piece as never usually found in the cinema. The pic, which is set in the 1820s, was shot entirely in a studio owned by Sands Films in the middle of Dickens territory, in Rotherhithe close to the Thames, and the painted sets give the film a rich theatrical texture while not deflecting from the story.

1988: NOMINATIONS: Best Supp. Actor (Alec Guinness), Adapted Screenplay

•

LITTLE DRUMMER GIRL, THE
1984, 130 mins, US Ⓥ ⦿ col
Dir George Roy Hill ***Prod*** Robert L. Crawford ***Scr*** Loring Mandel ***Ph*** Wolfgang Treu ***Ed*** William Reynolds ***Mus*** Dave Grusin ***Art*** Henry Bumstead
Act Diane Keaton, Yorgo Voyagis, Klaus Kinski, Sami Frey, Michael Cristofer, David Suchet (Pan Arts)

George Roy Hill has made a disappointingly flat film adaptation of one of John Le Carre's top novels, *The Little Drummer Girl.* Overlong and, for the most part, indifferently staged on a multitude of foreign locales, pic can't help but intrigue due to the intense subject matter, that of complex Israeli and Palestinian espionage and terrorism.

Diane Keaton plays the role of Charlie, in the book a virulently pro-Palestinian British actress generally agreed to have been inspired by Vanessa Redgrave.

No matter, though, for events quickly take Keaton out of the U.K. A team of Israeli operatives, led by the supremely self-confident Klaus Kinski, recruits her in Greece, breaks down her Arab sympathies, and eventually puts her in place as an ideal agent.

Keaton's loud, pushy, erratic showbiz character isn't all that easy to warm up to.

•

LITTLE FAUSS AND BIG HALSY
1970, 98 mins, US Ⓥ ▭ col
Dir Sidney J. Furie ***Prod*** Albert S. Ruddy ***Scr*** Charles Eastman ***Ph*** Ralph Woolsey ***Ed*** Argyle Neson, Jr. ***Mus*** Johnny Cash, Bob Dylan, Carl Perkins ***Art*** Lawrence G. Paul
Act Robert Redford, Michael J. Pollard, Lauren Hutton, Noah Beery, Lucille Benson, Ray Ballard (Paramount)

Little Fauss and Big Halsy is an uneven, sluggish story of two motorcycle racers—Robert Redford playing a callous heel and Michael J. Pollard as a put-upon sidekick who eventually (in modified finale) surpasses his fallen idol.

Hampered by a thin screenplay, film is padded further by often-pretentious direction by Sidney J. Furie against expansive physical values.

What is very disappointing is the lack of strong dramatic development. Redford's character is apparent in his very first scene; it never changes. It is in effect the carrier frequency on which Pollard and others must beat; the end result is erratic.

Pollard is very good in lending depth to his character, though his dialect often obscures his dialog.

•

LITTLE FOXES, THE
1941, 115 mins, US Ⓥ ⦿ b/w
Dir William Wyler ***Prod*** Samuel Goldwyn ***Scr*** Lillian Hellman, Dorothy Parker, Arthur Kober, Alan Campbell ***Ph*** Gregg Toland ***Ed*** Daniel Mandell ***Mus*** Meredith Wilson ***Art*** Stephen Goosson
Act Bette Davis, Herbert Marshall, Teresa Wright, Richard Carlson, Patricia Collinge, Dan Duryea (RKO/Goldwyn)

From starring Bette Davis down the line to the bit roles portrayed by minor Negroes the acting is well nigh flawless. And standing out sharply in Lillian Hellman's searing play about rapacious people are several performers who appeared in the 1939 Broadway stage version, i.e., Patricia Collinge, Carl Benton Reid, Dan Duryea, and Charles Dingle.

In the natural padding out of the story permitted by a screenplay is the injection of romance between Teresa Wright, as Davis's daughter, and Richard Carlson, playing a young newspaperman.

The story is about the Hubbard family of the deep south—as mercenary a foursome as has ever emerged from fact or fiction. In this picture Davis also murders her husband, played by Herbert Marshall, but with the unique weapon of disinterest. When Marshall, in the throes of a heart attack, crashes a bottle of medicine that can save his life, Davis sits by and watches him do a dying swan. That's her way of killing the man who had refused to help finance the get-rich scheme of her brothers. Marshall turns in one of his top performances in the exacting portrayal of a suffering, dying man.

On top of the smooth pace, Wyler has handled every detail with an acutely dramatic touch.

1941: NOMINATIONS: Best Picture, Actress (Bette Davis), Supp. Actress (Patricia Collinge, Teresa Wright), Screenplay, B&W Art Direction, Editing, Scoring of a Dramatic Picture

•

LITTLE GIANTS
1994, 105 mins, US Ⓥ ⦿ col
Dir Duwayne Dunham ***Prod*** Arne L. Schmidt ***Scr*** James Ferguson, Robert Shallcross, Tommy Swerdlow, Michael Goldberg ***Ph*** Janusz Kaminski ***Ed*** Donn Cambern ***Mus*** John Debney ***Art*** Bill Kenney
Act Rick Moranis, Ed O'Neill, John Madden, Shawna Waldron, Mary Ellen Trainor, Matthew McCurley (Amblin/Warner)

Imagine *The Bad News Bears* in Pop Warner football togs, and you'll have a good idea of what to expect from *Little Giants.*

Rick Moranis heads the fine cast as Danny O'Shea, a small-town single father who wants to help his tomboyish daughter Becky (Shawna Waldron)—and maybe upstage Kevin (Ed O'Neill), his cocky older brother—by coaching a team of kids who have been rejected by Kevin for the town's Pop Warner junior team.

No fewer than four screenwriters are credited with cobbling together a scenario [from a screen story by two of them, James Ferguson and Robert Shawcross] that seems cribbed from bits and pieces of other pix about children and their games. Director Duwayne Dunham keeps things moving at an acceptably brisk pace.

In addition to Becky, the well-cast players on Danny's Little Giants team include Rudy (Michael Zwiener), a corpulent youngster whose flatulence is overused as a running gag; Rasheed (Troy Slimmons), an eager-beaver receiver; Nubie (Matthew McCurley), a brainy nerd who uses his computer expertise to plot football plays; Jake (Todd Bosley), whose mother thinks football will improve his self-esteem; and Junior (Devon Sawa), a trigger-armed quarterback who's just hunky enough to make Becky think boys aren't so yucky after all.

Story is pat and predictable, as Danny whips his team into shape for a big practice game against his brother's Cowboys team. On the other hand, pic is never less than engaging, and often manages to be genuinely amusing.

•

LITTLE GIRL WHO LIVES DOWN THE LANE, THE
1977, 91 mins, Canada/France Ⓥ ⦿ ▭ col
Dir Nicholas Gessner ***Prod*** Zev Braun ***Scr*** Laird Koenig ***Ph*** Rene Verzier ***Ed*** Yves Langlois ***Mus*** Christian Gaubert ***Art*** Robert Prevost
Act Jodie Foster, Martin Sheen, Alexis Smith, Mort Shuman, Scott Jacoby, Dorothy Davis (ICL/Filmel)

This film, about a homicidal orphan girl, is farfetched nonsense with precious little to appease shriek freaks. Laird Koenig's screenplay from his novel is riddled with unsuspended disbelief—coincidences, gimmicks.

Jodie Foster plays an all-alone sangfroid little liar of 13 going on 23 who, true to her late daddy's counsel, isn't about to let herself be pushed around or dominated by crummy grownups. Martin Sheen plays a sicko with a thing for little girls who harasses the kid. Alexis Smith is a snoopy big deal in the small local community.

One of the few agreeable angles is the relationship between Foster and Scott Jacoby, wary at first but which ripens into a boudoir romance. As a simpatico lad with a gamy leg from polio, Jacoby's performance has nice verve.

Foster's poise is impressive enough as the cool, calculating adolescent with a passion for Chopin records. But it's a one-note character. Film was shot on locations in Canada.

•

LITTLE HUT, THE
1957, 90 mins, US col
Dir Mark Robson ***Prod*** F. Hugh Herbert, Mark Robson ***Scr*** F. Hugh Herbert ***Ph*** Freddie Young ***Ed*** Ernest Walter ***Mus*** Robert Farnon ***Art*** Elliot Scott
Act Ava Gardner, Stewart Granger, David Niven, Walter Chiari, Finlay Currie, Jean Cadell (Herbson/M-G-M)

Sex is incessantly hinted at in this saucy triangle [from Andre Roussin's play and Nancy Mitford's English stage adaptation], which keeps husband and wife intact for the moral code. It all takes place on a South Pacific island with Ava Gardner down to her lace BVDs and much sly innuendo about her husband's preoccupation with everything else but her gender.

Government business has left Stewart Granger with little time to practice the arts of a husband, so Gardner turns to hubby's best friend (David Niven) for companionship. Transfer this situation to a deserted tropical isle after a shipwreck, feed the principals a stimulating seafood diet, mostly oysters, and something has to give.

As the choice feminine tidbit who fires the masculine libido, Gardner is ideal casting. Equally adept and effective is Granger as Gardner's too-busy-to-love husband. Matching the above two is Niven, in a very amusing takeoff on a proper Englishman who wants to preempt Granger's marital rights with Gardner.

•

LITTLE LORD FAUNTLEROY
1921, 120 mins, US ⊗ b/w
Dir Alfred E. Green, Jack Pickford ***Scr*** Bernard McConville ***Ph*** Charles Rosher ***Mus*** Louis F. Gottschalk
Act Mary Pickford, Claude Gillingwater, Joseph Dowling, James Marcus, Kate Price, Rose Dione (Pickford/United Artists)

Little Lord Fauntleroy is a perfect Pickford picture. It exploits the star in dual roles, one of them one of the immortal and classic boy parts of all times. Mary Pickford shows a range of versatility, between the blue-blooded and sombre mother and the blue-blooded but mischievous kid, that is almost startling. She meets herself many times in double exposures, and she is taller than herself and different from herself, and incredibly true to each.

Only director Jack Pickford could have introduced the whimsical and always amusing touches of raw boyishness in the fighting, grimacing, scheming, lovable kid that Pickford again turns out to be. She jumps off high perches onto other boys' backs, she wrestles and does trick ju-jitsus, she dodges, and climbs, and leans and tumbles, and handstands. While *Fauntleroy* is not sensational, it is a human and appealing story.

•

LITTLE LORD FAUNTLEROY
1936, 98 mins, US Ⓥ b/w
Dir John Cromwell ***Prod*** David O. Selznick ***Scr*** Hugh Walpole ***Ph*** Charles Rosher ***Mus*** Max Steiner ***Art*** Sturges Carne
Act C. Aubrey Smith, Freddie Bartholomew, Dolores Costello Barrymore, Henry Stephenson, Guy Kibbee, Mickey Rooney (Selznick/United Artists)

As his first for Selznick International after leaving Metro, David O. Selznick turns in a fine, sensitive picture in *Little Lord Fauntleroy*, which may well rank with his *David Copperfield* and *A Tale of Two Cities.* It's a transmutation of Frances Hodgson Burnett's mid-Victorian saga. A theme as prissy as *Fauntleroy*, where the earl-to-be calls his mother "Dearest," might have proved quite hazardous in anything but the most expert hands. As Hugh Walpole adapts it, John Cromwell directs it and a sterling cast troups it—all under Selznick's keen aegis—it's very palatable cinematic fare.

Young Freddie Bartholomew is capital in the title role and Dolores Costello Barrymore, marking her film comeback, as "Dearest," his young and widowed mother, are an ideal coupling in the two principal roles.

C. Aubrey Smith as the gruff and grumpy earl who blindly hates his daughter-in-law just because she's American, wellnigh steals the picture in a characterization setup that's a match for this vet thespian. Henry Stephenson as the English barrister is on a par in a role that calls for much restraint.

•

LITTLE MALCOLM AND HIS STRUGGLE AGAINST THE EUNUCHS
1974, 112 mins, UK col
Dir Stuart Cooper ***Prod*** Gavrik Losey ***Scr*** Derek Woodward ***Ph*** John Alcott ***Ed*** Ray Lovejoy ***Mus*** Stanley Myers
Act John Hurt, John McEnery, Raymond Platt, Rosalind Ayres, David Warner (Apple)

Adapted by Derek Woodward from a mid-1960s play by David Halliwell, item emerges as a frequently hilarious, generally thought-provoking and sobering, beautifully acted, but a trifle overlong and repetitious film of uncertain destination.

On one level, story dealing with a carefully plotted sham uprising by a trio of students draws laughs in its Mitty-ish mock evocations of socio-political tirades, while subsurface the conclusions drawn are frightening as evidenced in the climactic scene of useless violence against a girl.

There's a trace of *Clockwork Orange* here and there (and not only because pix share same lenser, John Alcott), and it's grimly amusing in a similar way, but there the resemblance ends. Performances are all tops.

•

LITTLE MAN TATE
1991, 99 mins, US Ⓥ ⦿ col
Dir Jodie Foster ***Prod*** Scott Rudin, Peggy Rajski ***Scr*** Scott Frank ***Ph*** Mike Southon ***Ed*** Lynzee Klingman ***Mus*** Mark Isham ***Art*** Jon Hutman
Act Jodie Foster, Dianne Wiest, Adam Hann-Byrd, Harry Connick, Jr., David Pierce, P. J. Ochlan (Orion)

Jodie Foster makes an appealing, if modest, directorial debut with *Little Man Tate.* Scott Frank (*Dead Again*) penned this nicely observed tale of a year in the life of a seven-year-old genius.

An accomplished painter, poet, and pianist in addition to being a math wizard, Fred Tate (Adam Hann-Byrd) is being raised by his single mother, a mildly tough working-class woman whom he, along with the rest of the world, calls Dede (played with a vulgar accent by Foster).

Before long Fred comes to the attention of wealthy Jane Grierson (Dianne Wiest), a child psychologist and teacher of the gifted. Fred moves in with her when he is invited to attend a summer college course, and strikes up an engaging relationship with a somewhat older, titanically arrogant math genius named Damon (memorably impersonated by P. J. Ochlan).

Most of the film's emotional power lies in the open, alert, eager-to-please face of Hann-Byrd, making his acting debut. Filled with small, telling moments rather than big events, film never really gets inside Fred's head, but it neatly sketches the external aspects of his predicament.

•

LITTLE MERMAID, THE
1989, 82 mins, US Ⓥ ⊙ col
Dir John Musker, Ron Clements ***Prod*** Howard Ashman, John Musker ***Scr*** John Musker, Ron Clements ***Ed*** John Carnochan ***Mus*** Alan Menken ***Art*** Michael A. Peraza, Jr., Donald A. Towns
(Walt Disney)

Borrowing liberally from the studio's classics, *The Little Mermaid* may represent Disney's best animated feature since the underrated *Sleeping Beauty* in 1959. That should come as no surprise to admirers of *The Great Mouse Detective*, writer-director collaborators John Musker and Ron Clements's 1986 animation feature that helped salvage the art form at the studio after it had nearly sunk into *The Black Cauldron*.

The source material is a Hans Christian Andersen tale. The mermaid princess Ariel (voiced by newcomer Jodi Benson) lives in her sea-lord father Triton's (Kenneth Mars) undersea kingdom but yearns for a life above, made all the more haunting to her when she rescues handsome young prince Sebastian (Samuel E. Wright) from the sea. Disobeying her father, she makes a pact with seawitch Ursula (Pat Carroll) enabling her to go ashore and get the prince to fall in love with her—her soul hanging in the balance, her beautiful voice as collateral.

Ursula alone proves a visual feast, a thick-jawed nightmare who swishes about on eight octopus legs in one of the film's more inspired inventions.

The animation proves lush and fluid, augmented by the use of shadow and light as elements like fire, sun, and water illuminate the characters. Key contributions are made by lyricist Howard Ashman (who coproduced with Musker) and composer Alan Menken, whose songs frequently begin slowly but build in cleverness and intensity.

1989: Best Song ("Under the Sea"), Original Score

NOMINATION: Best Song ("Kiss the Girl")

•

LITTLE MISS BROADWAY
1938, 70 mins, US Ⓥ b/w
Dir Irving Cummings ***Prod*** David Hempstead ***Scr*** Harry Tugent, Jack Yellen ***Ph*** Arthur Miller ***Ed*** Walter Thompson ***Mus*** Louis Silvers (dir.)
Act Shirley Temple, George Murphy, Jimmy Durante, Phyllis Brooks, Edna May Oliver, George Barbier (20th Century-Fox)

In *Little Miss Broadway*, Shirley Temple shows an improvement in her tap dancing, her singing, and her ability to turn on at will whatever emotional faucet is demanded by the script.

With Jimmy Durante, George Murphy, Edna Mae Oliver, George Barbier, Donald Meek, and El Brendel in featured roles, something approaching hilarity is expected. The result is far short of the promise. Shirley is a standout, but the others through faulty cutting of the film and undeveloped opportunities in the script never quite get their openings to score.

Shirley is introduced as a ward in an orphan asylum. She is discharged into the care of an uncle (Edward Ellis) who manages a theatrical hotel near Broadway called Variety. Edna May Oliver, who owns the building and lives close by, is annoyed by the constant rehearsing of the acts and decides to close the place by demanding immediate payment of past due rent.

Her nephew (George Murphy) intercedes at the behest of Shirley Temple, but the issue finds its way to court where the acts give a dress rehearsal of a musical revue, which they hope will earn enough money to meet the financial obligation.

Walter Bullock and Harold Spina have written six songs which Shirley sings, some solo, others with chorus.

•

LITTLE MISS MARKER
1980, 103 mins, US Ⓥ col
Dir Walter Bernstein ***Prod*** Jennings Lang ***Scr*** Walter Bernstein ***Ph*** Philip Lathrop ***Ed*** Eve Newman ***Mus*** Henry Mancini ***Art*** Edward C. Carfagno
Act Walter Matthau, Julie Andrews, Tony Curtis, Sara Stimson, Bob Newhart (Universal)

There is something irresistible about the story of a darling little girl left in the care of colorfully kind gamblers, which explains why this is the fourth attempt to bring Damon Runyon's story to the screen. But writer-director Walter Bernstein blows his directorial debut completely.

It's a shame, because seemingly if ever there was an actor who should play "Sorrowful Jones" it's Walter Matthau, and Bob Newhart should have been a wonderful "Regret," while Tony Curtis could have been a respectable antagonist.

But they are all flat in their parts and that has to be Bernstein's fault. Even worse, Julie Andrews is woefully miscast with her British accent and Lee Grant gets no more than a bit part as a judge. The only really decent thing about the picture is little Sara Stimson.

•

LITTLE MURDERS
1971, 110 mins, US Ⓥ col
Dir Alan Arkin ***Prod*** Jack Brodsky, Elliott Gould ***Scr*** Jules Feiffer ***Ph*** Gordon Willis ***Ed*** Howard Kuperman ***Mus*** Fred Kaz
Act Elliott Gould, Marcia Rodd, Vincent Gardenia, Elizabeth Wilson, Donald Sutherland, Alan Arkin (20th Century-Fox)

Alan Arkin, making a most impressive directorial debut, has made a film that is not only funny but devastating in its emotional impact.

Arkin's actors play very broadly, just at the edge of the caricatures they are in Jules Feiffer's screenplay. But they fill in the outlines with such a wealth of human detail that it's impossible not to identify with them. Both comedy and horror, therefore, hit closer to home. Coproducer Elliott Gould plays a photographer who was successful until he began to "lose the people" in his pictures, and found it unnecessary or impossible either to fight or really "feel." Into his life comes Marcia Rodd, a girl who would like to mold him into "a strong, vital, self-assured man, that I can protect and take care of."

Then the world gets in the way, and Feiffer once and for all stops being the amiably satiric cartoonist, and hurtles toward a painful conclusion: that the only way for the "mad" and the "alienated" to get back into the world is to adopt its insanity.

Vincent Gardenia, Elizabeth Wilson, and Jon Korkes are excellent as Rodd's extraordinary family. Juicy "bits" are played by Arkin as a paranoid detective; Lou Jacobi, as a judge who remembers his days on the Lower East Side; and Donald Sutherland, as a hip minister.

•

LITTLE NIGHT MUSIC, A
1977, 124 mins, Austria/US/W. Germany Ⓥ ⊙ col
Dir Hal Prince ***Prod*** Elliott Kastner ***Scr*** Hugh Wheeler ***Ph*** Arthur Ibbetson ***Ed*** John Jumpson ***Mus*** Jonathan Tunick (dir.)
Act Elizabeth Taylor, Diana Rigg, Len Cariou, Hermione Gingold, Lesley-Anne Down, Laurence Guittard (Sascha-Wien/Kastner)

A Little Night Music is based on an earlier film by Ingmar Bergman [*Smiles of a Summer Night*, 1955] that was turned into a [1973] hit Broadway musical with music and lyrics by Stephen Sondheim. In this refilming Hal Prince repeats as director.

All this fuses into an elegant-looking, period-romantic charade. There is one sprightly number as the assorted characters set out for a country dinner that will resolve their complicated love problems. There is a noted promiscuous actress ready to settle down with a steady man and her teenage daughter, a staid lawyer with a young wife of 18 whose marriage has yet to be consummated, plus his son, and a fiery army lieutenant, lover of the actress, and his jealous but submissive wife.

Uneven and sometimes slow, pic has good looks.

1977: Best Adapted Scoring

NOMINATION: Best Costume Design

•

LITTLE NIKITA
(UK: *THE SLEEPERS*)
1988, 98 mins, US Ⓥ ⊙ col
Dir Richard Benjamin ***Prod*** Harry Gittes ***Scr*** John Hill, B. Goldman ***Ph*** Laszlo Kovacs ***Ed*** Jacqueline Cambas ***Mus*** Marvin Hamlisch ***Art*** Gene Callahan
Act Sidney Poitier, River Phoenix, Richard Jenkins, Caroline Kava, Richard Bradford, Loretta Devine (Columbia)

Little Nikita never really materializes as a taut espionage thriller and winds up as an unsatisfying execution of a clever premise—a teen's traumatic discovery that his parents are Soviet spies.

Film opens strongly as parallel storylines unfold and audience is drawn in by the need to decipher the link between the mission of a Soviet agent and an all-American family in the mythical San Diego suburb of Fountain Grove.

Poised at the juncture of these developments is FBI agent Sidney Poitier, whose natural intensity seems just right for the role. Poitier encounters River Phoenix, a youngster who decides to apply for the Air Force Academy, on a routine FBI check. When some peculiar data turns up on Phoenix's parents—convincingly portrayed by Richard Jenkins and Caroline Kava—Poitier begins an investigation that leads to an almost avuncular bonding with Phoenix.

•

LITTLE ODESSA
1994, 98 mins, US Ⓥ ▭ col
Dir James Gray ***Prod*** Paul Webster ***Scr*** James Gray ***Ph*** Tom Richmond ***Ed*** Dorian Harris ***Mus*** Dana Sano (sup.) ***Art*** Kevin Thompson
Act Tim Roth, Edward Furlong, Moira Kelly, Vanessa Redgrave, Maximilian Schell, Paul Guilfoyle (New Line/Addis-Wechsler)

A highly charged, coolly assured directorial bow graced by riveting work from a trio of accomplished leads, *Little Odessa* is a somberly explosive family tragedy set against the brooding backdrop of the Mafia-plagued Russian-Jewish emigre community in Brooklyn's Brighton Beach.

James Gray's mob opera eschews a canvas of aggressively drawn violence and hip dialog constructions to focus more intently on character. Contracted to erase Iranian jeweler, Brooklyn-bred hit man Joshua Shapira (Tim Roth) returns reluctantly to the childhood neighborhood he abandoned years earlier. Despite having no contact with his family, word of his arrival reaches his kid brother Reuben (Edward Furlong), who eagerly tracks him down.

On learning that his mother (Vanessa Redgrave) is slowly dying from a brain tumor, Joshua goes to see her, provoking a violent reaction from his rancorous father (Maximilian Schell). While he lays plans for the hit, he almost indifferently rekindles something approaching romance with hardened neighborhood girl Alla (Moira Kelly).

Roth appears as a man who, in many ways, is already dead, yet he makes the character resonantly sympathetic. Kelly also makes an indelible impression during her brief screen time. But perhaps the most striking is Furlong, whose intense gaze and fragile grace push his character under the audience's skin without artifice. Tom Richmond's arresting widescreen lensing is high on compositional poise and low on fussy camera tricks.

•

LITTLE PRINCE, THE
1974, 88 mins, UK Ⓥ ⊙ col
Dir Stanley Donen ***Prod*** Stanley Donen ***Scr*** Alan Jay Lerner ***Ph*** Christopher Challis ***Ed*** Peter Boita, John Guthridge ***Mus*** Frederick Loewe ***Art*** John Barry
Act Richard Kiley, Steven Warner, Bob Fosse, Gene Wilder, Joss Ackland, Clive Revill (Paramount)

Handsome production plus excellent photography and effects cannot obscure the limited artistic achievement of *The Little Prince*. Alan Jay Lerner's adaptation of the book by Antoine de Saint-Exupery is flat and his lyrics are unmemorable, as are Frederick Loewe's melodies. Richard Kiley is cast as the child-man, and Steven Warner is the man-child, who ruminate on the meaning of a good life. Some okay cameo appearances by Bob Fosse, Gene Wilder, and others lend transient sparkle.

Kiley, who never forgot his youthful fantasies, makes a forced landing in a desert, where Warner, an interspace traveler, comes upon him and his grounded airplane. A series of vignettes, delicate in their import and rendered opaque by the script, supposedly makes Kiley a better man for the experience.

1979: NOMINATIONS: Best Adapted Score, Song ("Little Prince")

•

LITTLE PRINCESS, THE
1939, 95 mins, US Ⓥ ⦿ col
Dir Walter Lang ***Prod*** Gene Markey ***Scr*** Ethel Hill, Walter Ferris ***Ph*** Arthur Miller, William V. Skall ***Ed*** Louis Loeffler ***Mus*** Louis Silvers (dir) ***Art*** Bernard Herzbrun, Hans Peters
Act Shirley Temple, Richard Greene, Anita Louise, Ian Hunter (20th Century-Fox)

Shirley Temple appears in Technicolor for the first time. Transposition of the Frances Hodgson Burnett several-generation favorite, *Sara Crewe*, is accomplished most successfully.

The fairy-tale story is still saccharine to the nth degree, but once the basic premise is established, it rolls along acceptably. And, while the story has been changed for screen purposes, the general line is close enough.

Temple is cast as Sara Crewe. Her father (Ian Hunter) goes off to war with the Boers, and leaves the youngster in Mary Nash's school. Shirley is immediately dubbed "The Little Princess" because of her regal bearing and attitude. When word comes her father has died, Shirley is made a galley slave by Nash, who mistreats her in every way possible.

Solo song and dance sequence, portraying a dream of Shirley's, stands out on its own.

•

LITTLE PRINCESS, A
1995, 97 mins, US Ⓥ ⦿ col
Dir Alfonso Cuaron ***Prod*** Mark Johnson ***Scr*** Richard LaGravenese, Elizabeth Chandler ***Ph*** Emmanuel Lubezki ***Ed*** Steven Weisberg ***Mus*** Patrick Doyle ***Art*** Bo Welch
Act Eleanor Bron, Liam Cunningham, Liesel Matthews, Rusty Schwimmer, Arthur Malet, Vanessa Lee Chester (Baltimore/Warner)

An astonishing work of studio artifice, *A Little Princess* is that rarest of creations, a children's film that plays equally well to kids and adults. A companion piece to Warners's outstanding 1993 *The Secret Garden* by virtue of its origins in a book by the same author, Frances Hodgson Burnett, the new film is even better, an exquisite, perfectly played serious fantasy that movingly stresses the importance of magic and the imagination in the scheme of life.

Who would have expected so much from a kiddie film with a World War I–era Anglo-American backdrop that's a remake of a 1917 Mary Pickford silent and a 1939 Shirley Temple vehicle and that's directed by a virtually unknown young Mexican filmmaker?

But it's clear from the outset that something special is in store. Ten-year-old Sara Crewe (Liesel Matthews) is living the charmed life in India in 1914. The daughter of a loving British Army captain, she is deeply immersed in the exotic, mythical tales of the land. When the war calls Captain Crewe (Liam Cunningham), he enrolls Sara at Miss Minchin's School for Girls, the same tony New York establishment her late mother attended (shifted from the London setting of the novel).

Sara quickly wins over many of the girls by introducing an element of excitement and adventure into their strictly regimented lives. Neither this nor her cheeky attitude toward school rules go over too well with the stern Miss Minchin (Eleanor Bron). When Captain Crewe is reported killed in battle, Miss Minchin strips her of all privileges and possessions and banishes her to the attic, which she must share with black servant girl Becky (Vanessa Lee Chester).

Based on Burnett's novel *Sara Crewe*, which she later adapted into the phenomenally successful play *The Little Princess*, the time-tested story is a riot of cinematic imagination. Alfonso Cuaron, whose exuberant, mildly amusing AIDS-era sex comedy *Love in the Time of Hysteria* made the fest rounds in 1991, has made a Hollywood debut that is never less than dazzling, working entirely in the studio and on a backlot street set.

Performances could scarcely be improved upon. Golden-faced, clear-eyed and utterly self-confident, Matthews is a constant delight as Sara, entirely believable as a born leader among girls.

Faultlessly adopting an Eastern seaboard accent, British actress Bron scores heavily as the repressed and repressive Miss Minchin.

1995: NOMINATIONS: Best Cinematography, Art Direction

•

LITTLE RASCALS, THE
1994, 82 mins, US Ⓥ col
Dir Penelope Spheeris ***Prod*** Michael Kling, Bill Oakes ***Scr*** Paul Guay, Stephen Mazur, Penelope Spheeris ***Ph*** Richard Bowen ***Ed*** Ross Albert ***Mus*** William Ross ***Art*** Larry Fulton
Act Travis Tedford, Bug Hall, Brittany Ashton Holmes, Kevin Jamal Woods, Zachary Mabry, Ross Elliot Bagley (Universal/King World)

Those who grew up watching *The Little Rascals* on murky UHF–TV stations may well be intrigued by the idea of introducing their kids to this full-color, big-screen version. Still, the challenge of stretching those mildly diverting shorts to feature length remains formidable. One has to admire director Penelope Spheeris's perseverance in dealing with revered TV material, having last tackled *The Beverly Hillbillies*, and before that, the neoclassic *Wayne's World*.

Rather conventional plot has love-smitten Alfalfa (Bug Hall) violating the rules of the all-male He-Man Woman-Haters Club by wooing the decidedly feminine Darla (cherubic Brittany Ashton Holmes). This irks his pal, Spanky (Travis Tedford), and inadvertently results in the destruction of their clubhouse. Needing $350 to rebuild, the group embarks on various efforts to raise the money.

It's hard to believe that input from five writers [Spheeris, Robert Wolterstorff, Mike Scott, Paul Guay and Stephen Mazur] was needed to come up with that premise. The quintet struggles at spreading the material over 80 minutes, turning in amusing moments but also some rather arid stretches. Holmes proves a real scene-stealer as Darla, while Kevin Jamal Woods, as Stymie, may be the most natural actor in the bunch.

•

LITTLE ROMANCE, A
1979, 108 mins, US/France Ⓥ ⦿ ▭ col
Dir George Roy Hill ***Prod*** Yves Rousset-Rouard, Robert L. Crawford ***Scr*** Allan Burns ***Ph*** Pierre-William Glenn ***Ed*** William Reynolds ***Mus*** Georges Delerue ***Art*** Henry Bumstead
Act Laurence Olivier, Arthur Hill, Sally Kellerman, Diane Lane, Thelonious Bernard, Broderick Crawford (Orion/Pan Arts/Trinacra)

Scripter Allan Burns has craftily kept the point of view of the youngsters, Diane Lane and Thelonious Bernard, while the adults, with certain exceptions, are seen as suitably grotesque and ridiculous, giving *Romance* a crest of humor on which to ride.

Lane is the offspring of flighty jet-setter Sally Kellerman, who spends the film mooning over auteur director David Dukes, rather than hubby Arthur Hill. The teenagers are drawn to one another, persevere in the face of family pressure, and eventually take off in pursuit of a romantic ideal.

Fulcrum in script is the beneficent boulevardier, limned by Laurence Olivier in a modern refashioning of the old Maurice Chevalier role. The prototypical lovable scoundrel, Olivier, hams it up unmercifully.

1979: Best Original Score

NOMINATION: Best Adapted Screenplay

•

LITTLE SHOP OF HORRORS, THE
1961, 70 mins, US Ⓥ ⦿ b/w
Dir Roger Corman ***Prod*** Roger Corman ***Scr*** Charles B. Griffiths ***Ph*** Archie Dalzell ***Ed*** Marshall Neilan, Jr. ***Mus*** Fred Katz ***Art*** Daniel Haller
Act Jonathan Haze, Jackie Joseph, Mel Welles, Myrtle Vail, Leola Wendorff, Jack Nicholson (FilmGroup)

Reportedly only two shooting days and $22,500 went into the making of this picture, but limited fiscal resources didn't deter Roger Corman and his game, resourceful FilmGroup from whipping up a serviceful parody of a typical screen horror number.

Little Shop of Horrors is kind of one big sick joke, but it's essentially harmless and good-natured. The plot concerns a young, goofy florist's assistant who creates a talking, blood-sucking, man-eating plant, then feeds it several customers from skid row before sacrificing himself to the horticultural gods.

There is a fellow who visits the Skid Row Flower Shop to munch on purchased bouquets ("I like to eat in these little out-of-the-way places"). There is also the Yiddish proprietor, distressed by his botanical attraction ("We not only got a talking plant, we got one dot makes smart cracks"), but content to let it devour as the shop flourishes. And there are assorted quacks, alcoholics, masochists [Jack Nicholson, as a dental patient], sadists, and even a pair of private-eyes who couldn't solve the case of the disappearing fly in a hothouse for Venus flytraps.

The acting is pleasantly preposterous. Mel Welles, as the proprietor, and Jonathan Haze, as the budding Luther Burbank, are particularly capable, and Jackie Joseph is decorative as the latter's girl. Horticulturalists and vegetarians will love it.

•

LITTLE SHOP OF HORRORS
1986, 88 mins, US Ⓥ ⦿ col
Dir Frank Oz ***Prod*** David Geffen ***Scr*** Howard Ashman ***Ph*** Robert Paynter ***Ed*** John Jympson ***Mus*** Miles Goodman ***Art*** Roy Walker
Act Rick Moranis, Ellen Greene, Vincent Gardenia, Steve Martin, James Belushi, John Candy (Warner/Geffen)

Little Shop of Horrors is a fractured, funny production transported rather reluctantly from the stage to the screen. Almost nothing is left besides the setting and story outline from the 1961 Roger Corman film that inspired the 1982 stage musical [book and lyrics by Howard Ashman, music by Alan Menken].

Living a rather mundane life, working in Mushnik's flower shop are Seymour (Rick Moranis) and Audrey (Ellen Greene), that is until lightning strikes and the natural order of things is turned upside down. Through a chain of events just silly enough to be fun, Seymour becomes the proud owner of Audrey II, a rare breed of plant that makes him famous and his boss (Vincent Gardenia) prosperous. Audrey II develops an insatiable appetite for human flesh.

1986: NOMINATIONS: Best Song ("Mean Green Mother from Outer Space"), Visual Effects

•

LITTLEST REBEL, THE
1935, 70 mins, US Ⓥ b/w
Dir David Butler ***Prod*** Darryl F. Zanuck ***Scr*** Edwin Burke ***Ph*** John Seitz ***Ed*** Irene Morra ***Mus*** Cyril Mockridge (arr.) ***Art*** William Darling
Act Shirley Temple, John Boles, Jack Holt, Karen Morley, Bill Robinson, Guinn Williams (20th Century-Fox)

The Littlest Rebel is a good Shirley Temple picture. It happens to be very similar in title, plantation locale, Negro comedy, and in general mechanics to *The Little Colonel* (1935).

Shrewdly playing both sides, as between the North and the South, script [from the play by Edward Peple] throws a lot of dialog to the Confederacy. All bitterness and cruelty has been rigorously cut out and the Civil War emerges as a misunderstanding among kindly gentlemen with eminently happy slaves and a cute little girl who sings and dances through the story.

Picture opens just before war is declared. The tot is giving a party to all the well-mannered children of the Virginia aristocracy. A good deal of sly comedy is slipped in at the table and later when the children skip the minuet with genteel dignity. War brings successive losses culminating in the death of the mother (Karen Morley).

Bill Robinson and the child again dance. Robinson is once more the trusty family butler who guards little missy. John Boles, Jack Holt, and Karen Morley are just routine adults who react to the charm of a little girl.

•

LITTLE WOMEN
1933, 117 mins, US Ⓥ b/w
Dir George Cukor ***Prod*** Kenneth Macgowan (assoc.) ***Scr*** Sarah Y. Mason, Victor Heerman ***Ph*** Henry Gerrard ***Ed*** Jack Kitchin ***Mus*** Max Steiner ***Art*** Van Nest Polglase
Act Katharine Hepburn, Joan Bennett, Paul Lukas, Frances Dee, Jean Parker, Edna May Oliver (RKO)

Little Women is a profoundly moving history of youth and in this celluloid transcription [of the novel by Louisa May Alcott] its deeply spiritual values are revealed with a simple earnestness.

Katharine Hepburn, as Jo, creates a new and stunningly vivid character, strips the Victorian hoyden of her syrupy goody-goodiness, and endows the role with awkwardly engaging youth energy that it makes it the essence of flesh and blood reality.

Story is full of tearfully sentimental passages, but they are managed with beautiful restraint. There is the heavily tearful episode of Beth's sickroom scene, in which the pathetic possibilities are realized to last extreme by the rigid restriction of obvious acting.

A notable company of standard screen names supports the star. Joan Bennett, Frances Dee, and Jean Parker (as Beth) complete the feminine quartet, all playing with a persuasive charm. Paul Lukas contributes a characteristic portrait as Prof. Bhaer and Spring Byington is a conspicuous point of casting strength.

1932/33: Best Adaptation

NOMINATIONS: Best Picture, Director

•

LITTLE WOMEN
1949, 121 mins, US Ⓥ ⦿ col
Dir Mervyn LeRoy ***Prod*** Mervyn LeRoy ***Scr*** Andrew Solt, Sarah Y. Mason, Victor Heerman ***Ph*** Robert Planck,

Charles Schoenbaum ***Ed*** Ralph E. Winters ***Mus*** Adolph Deutsch ***Art*** Cedric Gibbons, Paul Groesse
Act June Allyson, Peter Lawford, Margaret O'Brien, Elizabeth Taylor, Janet Leigh, Rossano Brazzi (M-G-M)

Metro has combined a star constellation for its unstinting remake of Louisa May Alcott's *Little Women*, the old-lace classic of a quartet of daughters and their strivings in Civil War years.

The tender story, with its frank and unashamed assault on the emotions, still has its effective moments at times when the sentiment doesn't grow a little too thick.

Playing Jo, the part which won critical plaudits for Katharine Hepburn in 1933, June Allyson's thesping dominates the film.

As Beth, the youngest of the group, Margaret O'Brien is peculiarly subdued except for one touching scene in which she speaks of her nearing death. In the two other most important parts, Elizabeth Taylor and Janet Leigh neatly counterfoil Allyson's irrepressible cavortings.

1949: Best Color Art Direction

NOMINATION: Best Color Cinematography

•

LITTLE WOMEN
1994, 118 mins, US Ⓥ ⦿ col
Dir Gillian Armstrong ***Prod*** Denise Di Novi ***Scr*** Robin Swicord ***Ph*** Geoffrey Simpson ***Ed*** Nicholas Beauman ***Mus*** Thomas Newman ***Art*** Jan Roelfs
Act Winona Ryder, Gabriel Byrne, Trini Alvarado, Samantha Mathis, Susan Sarandon, Eric Stoltz (Columbia/Di Novi)

This outstanding version of Louisa May Alcott's perennial surpasses even the best previous rendition, George Cukor's 1933 outing starring Katharine Hepburn. Alcott's enduring 1868 novel about the growing up of four sisters in Concord, MA, during and after the Civil War has been filmed four times previously, the first time as a silent in 1918.

One significant hurdle for the filmmakers was to take contemporary audiences over the threshold of vastly different mores and social conventions to a time when earnestness, family solidarity, and sexual reserve were unquestioned standards of behavior. They have been notably successful, thanks to the breezily conversational quality of Robin Swicord's dialog, the warm informality of the young actresses, and the firm concentration on dramatic essentials displayed by director Gillian Armstrong.

The four March "little women," Meg (Trini Alvarado), Jo (Winona Ryder), Beth (Claire Danes), and Amy (initially Kirsten Dunst, then Samantha Mathis), are presided over by their mother, Marmee (Susan Sarandon), while their father is off fighting in the Union Army. The Marches forge a strong friendship with the young man across the way, Laurie (Christian Bale), while the very traditional Meg begins a courtship with stolid tutor John Brooke (Eric Stoltz).

Jo moves to New York City, and at her boarding house she meets a German immigrant philosophy professor, Friedrich Bhaer (Gabriel Byrne), with whom she has an instant accord.

Armstrong paces her scenes at about half the speed that Cukor did, and they are all the better for it in terms of emotional resonance. Performances by the actresses are all at least very good, with Ryder, Alvarado, and Dunst making the strongest impressions. Shot mostly in British Columbia, film has a splendid period look.

Pic is dedicated to kidnap-murder victim Polly Klaas, from Ryder's hometown of Petaluma, CA, and the late agent Judy Fox-Scott.

1994: NOMINATIONS: Best Actress (Winona Ryder), Costume Design, Original Score

•

LIVE AND LET DIE
1973, 121 mins, UK Ⓥ ⦿ ▭ col
Dir Guy Hamilton ***Prod*** Albert R. Broccoli, Harry Saltzman ***Scr*** Tom Mankiewicz ***Ph*** Ted Moore ***Ed*** Bert Bates, Raymond Poulton, John Shirley ***Mus*** George Martin ***Art*** Syd Cain, Bob Laing, Peter Lamont
Act Roger Moore, Yaphet Kotto, Jane Seymour, Clifton James, Julius W. Harris, Geoffrey Holder (United Artists/Eon)

Live and Let Die, the eighth Cubby Broccoli-Harry Saltzman film based on Ian Fleming's James Bond, introduces Roger Moore as an okay replacement for Sean Connery. The script reveals that plot lines have descended further to the level of the old Saturday afternoon serial.

Here Bond's assigned to ferret out mysterious goings-on involving Yaphet Kotto, diplomat from a Caribbean island nation who in disguise also is a big-time criminal. The nefarious scheme in his mind: Give away tons of free heroin to create more American dopers and then he and the telephone company will be the largest monopolies. Jane Seymour, Kotto's tarot-reading forecaster, loses her skill after turning on to Bond-age.

The comic book plot meanders through a series of hardware production numbers. These include some voodoo ceremonies; a hilarious airplane vs. auto pursuit scene; a double-decker bus escape from motorcycles and police cars; and a climactic inland-waterway powerboat chase. Killer sharks, poisonous snakes, and man-eating crocodiles also fail to deter Bond from his mission.

1973: NOMINATION: Best Song ("Live and Let Die")

•

LIVE FOR LIFE
SEE: VIVRE POUR VIVRE

•

LIVE NOW PAY LATER
1962, 104 mins, UK b/w
Dir Jay Lewis ***Prod*** Jack Hanbury ***Scr*** Jack Trevor Story ***Ph*** Jack Hildyard ***Ed*** Roger Cherrill ***Mus*** Ron Grainer ***Art*** Lionel Couch
Act Ian Hendry, June Ritchie, John Gregson, Liz Fraser, Geoffrey Keen, Andrew Cruickshank (Woodlands)

Jack Trevor Story's screenplay [from Jack Lindsay's novel, *All on the Never-Never*] has many amusing moments, but overall it is untidy and does not develop the personalities of some of the main characters sufficiently. Extraneous situations are dragged in without helping the plot development overmuch.

Ian Hendry plays a smart aleck, philandering, double-crossing tallyman who, with two illegitimate babies to his discredit, still finds that the easiest way to bluff his femme patrons into getting hocked up to their eyebrows in installment buying is via the boudoir. The character has a certain brash, breezy assurance, but no charm. And that's the way Hendry plays it, to the point of irritation.

In most of the film he is trying to patch up a row that he has had with his steady girlfriend. For the remainder, he is cheating his employer (John Gregson), a real estate agent, and a string of creditors.

June Ritchie, as the main girl in the case, confirms the promising impression she made in her debut in *A Kind of Loving*, but she can do little in this cardboard role of wronged young mistress.

•

LIVES OF A BENGAL LANCER, THE
1935, 110 mins, US Ⓥ b/w
Dir Henry Hathaway ***Prod*** Louis D. Lighton ***Scr*** Waldemar Young, John L. Balderston, Achmed Abdullah, Grover Jones, W. S. McNutt ***Ph*** Charles Lang, Ernest Schoedsack ***Ed*** Ellsworth Hoagland ***Mus*** Milan Roder ***Art*** Hans Dreier, Roland Anderson
Act Gary Cooper, Franchot Tone, Richard Cromwell, Guy Standing, C. Aubrey Smith, Akim Tamiroff (Paramount)

Work on *Lancer* commenced four years earlier when Ernest Schoedsack went to India for exteriors and atmosphere. Some of the Schoedsack stuff is still in, but in those four years the original plans were kicked around until lost. Included in the scrapping was the Francis Yeats-Brown novel. From the book only the locale and title have been retained. With these slim leads five studio writers went to work on a story, and they turned in a pip. In theme and locale *Lancer* is of the *Beau Geste* school. A sweeping, thrilling military narrative in Britain's desert badlands. There is a stirring emotional conflict between father and son, the former a traditional British commander with whom discipline and loyalty to the service come first, and the boy rebelling at his father's cold-blooded attitude.

Gary Cooper and Franchot Tone, as a pair of experienced officers, are not directly involved in the main theme beyond being actuated by it, but they are the picture's two most important characters and provide the story with its dynamite.

Story concerns their rescue of the colonel's son after the latter's disillusionment over his father's reception of him makes him a setup for capture by a warring native chieftain.

Tone establishes himself as a first-rate light comedian. But in their own way Cooper, Sir Guy Standing, Richard Cromwell, C. Aubrey Smith and Douglas Dumbrille also turn in some first-rate trouping.

1935: Best Assistant Directors (Clem Beauchamp, Paul Wing)

NOMINATIONS: Best Picture, Director, Screenplay, Art Direction, Editing, Sound

•

LIVING
SEE: IKIRU

•

LIVING DAYLIGHTS, THE
1987, 130 mins, UK Ⓥ ⦿ ▭ col
Dir John Glen ***Prod*** Albert R. Broccoli, Michael G. Wilson ***Scr*** Richard Maibaum, Michael G. Wilson ***Ph*** Alec Mills ***Ed*** John Grover, Peter Davies ***Mus*** John Barry ***Art*** Peter Lamont
Act Timothy Dalton, Maryam D'Abo, Jeroen Krabbe, Joe Don Baker, John Rhys-Davies, Art Malik (United Artists/Eon)

Timothy Dalton, the fourth Bond, registers beautifully on all key counts of charm, machismo, sensitivity, and technique. In *The Living Daylights* he's abetted by material that's a healthy cut above the series norm of superhero fantasy.

There's a more mature story of its kind, too, this one about a phony KGB defector involved in gunrunning and a fraternal assassination plot.

There are even some relatively touching moments of romantic contact between Dalton and lead femme Maryam D'Abo as Czech concert cellist.

Belatedly, the Bond characterization has achieved appealing maturity. D'Abo, in a part meant to be something more than that of window-dressed mannequin, handles her chores acceptably. Able support is turned in by Joe Don Baker as a nutcase arms seller, Jeroen Krabbe and John Rhys-Davies as respective KGB bad and good types (a little less arch than the usual types), and Art Malik as an Oxford-educated Afghan freedom fighter.

•

LIVING FREE
1972, 90 mins, UK Ⓥ col
Dir Jack Couffer ***Prod*** Paul Radin ***Scr*** Millard Kaufman ***Ph*** Wolfgang Suschitzky ***Ed*** Don Deacon ***Mus*** Sol Kaplan ***Art*** John Stoll
Act Nigel Davenport, Susan Hampshire, Geoffrey Keen, Edward Judd (Open Road/Highroad)

The same loving care that characterized *Born Free*, based on the true-life experiences of a British couple in Kenya and their pet lioness Elsa, is evident in the sequel.

Sensitive screenplay, based on the Joy Adamson book of her and her game-warden husband's efforts to assure that the cubs, following the death of their mother, shall live free and not be sent to a zoo, often carries a dramatic pitch. Possibly the most remarkable facet of picture is the animal photography of the cubs and other beasts that they encounter.

Some slight confusion exists in opening reels as the past of Elsa is reviewed briefly, but script develops logically as Nigel Davenport and Susan Hampshire, as the couple, are faced with the problem of the cubs' future after they turn to raiding natives' goat herds. Davenport resigns as a warden to devote himself entirely to capturing cubs and transporting them to a game preserve 700 miles distant.

•

LOCAL HERO
1983, 111 mins, UK Ⓥ ⦿ col
Dir Bill Forsyth ***Prod*** David Puttnam ***Scr*** Bill Forsyth ***Ph*** Chris Menges ***Ed*** Michael Bradsell ***Mus*** Mark Knopfler ***Art*** Roger Murray-Leach
Act Burt Lancaster, Peter Riegert, Fulton MacKay, Denis Lawson, Norman Chancer, Peter Capaldi (Enigma/Goldcrest)

While modest in intent and gentle in feel, *Local Hero* is loaded with wry, offbeat humor.

Basic story has Peter Riegert, rising young executive in an enormous Houston oil firm, sent to Scotland to clinch a deal to buy up an entire village, where the company intends to construct a new oil refinery. Far from being resistant to the idea of having their surroundings ruined by rapacious, profit-minded Yankees, local Scots can hardly wait to sign away their town, so strong is the smell of money in the air.

Back in Houston, oil magnate Burt Lancaster keeps up to date on the deal's progress with occasional phone calls to Riegert, but is more concerned with his prodding, sadistic psychiatrist and his obsessive hobby of astronomy, which seems to dictate everything he does.

Riegert's underplaying initially seems a bit inexpressive, but ultimately pays off in a droll performance. As his Scottish buddy, the gangling Peter Capaldi is vastly amusing, and Denis Lawson is very good as the community's chief spokesman.

•

LOCH NESS
1996, 101 mins, UK Ⓥ ⦿ ▭ col
Dir John Henderson ***Prod*** Tim Bevan, Eric Fellner, Stephen Ujlaki ***Scr*** John Fusco ***Ph*** Clive Tickner ***Ed*** Jon Gregory ***Mus*** Trevor Jones ***Art*** Sophie Becher

Act Ted Danson, Joely Richardson, Ian Holm, Kirsty Graham, Harris Yulin, James Frain (Working Title)

Ted Danson goes beastie-hunting in *Loch Ness*, an old-fashioned family pic with feel-good to spare. Okay playing by Danson, an excellent perf by Joely Richardson, and a big-hearted score by Trevor Jones elevate a basically modest picture into medium-size family fare.

Danson plays once-renowned L.A. zoologist Jonathan Dempsey, whose career is one step away from imploding after a series of failed hunts for legendary animals. His boss (Harris Yulin) makes him an offer he can't refuse: disprove once and for all that the Loch Ness monster exists. Unwillingly, Dempsey hightails it to the Highlands.

Finding a room in a small hotel run by feisty single mom Laura MacFeteridge (Richardson), Dempsey sets out scanning the giant loch with local assistant Adrian (James Frain). The Highlanders run the gamut from mystical (Ian Holm's wizened Water Bailiff) to plain hostile (Nick Brimble's Andy, who sees Dempsey as a rival for Laura's affections). The only one to give him time is Laura's young daughter, Isabel (Kirsty Graham), who claims an acquaintance with a "water kelpie."

After its choppily edited opening reels, pic starts to develop its own low-key charm as the Danson and Richardson characters strike up a cautious relationship. The two thesps, and Jones's majestic score, manage to hold one's attention even when nothing much is happening plotwise. In this respect, the 10-year-old script by U.S. writer John Fusco (*Young Guns*, *The Babe*) is more a mismatched love story set in the Scottish Highlands than a monster pic.

•

LOCKET, THE

1947, 83 mins, US b/w

Dir John Brahm **Prod** Bert Granet **Scr** Sheridan Gibney **Ph** Nicholas Musuraca **Ed** J. R. Whittredge **Mus** Roy Webb **Art** Albert S. D'Agostino, Alfred Herman

Act Laraine Day, Brian Aherne, Robert Mitchum, Gene Raymond, Ricardo Cortez, Sharyn Moffet (RKO)

The Locket is a case history of a warped mind and its effect on the lives of those it touches intimately. Vehicle is a strong one for Laraine Day and she does much with the role of Nancy, a girl with an abnormal obsession that wrecks the lives of four men who love her.

Nancy is a young woman, marked in childhood by the cruel misunderstanding of a rich lady in whose home her mother is housekeeper. The misunderstanding, over a missing locket, influences Nancy to strange acts in her adult life.

Story carries the flashback technique to greater lengths than generally employed. The writing by Sheridan Gibney displays an understanding of the subject matter and proves a solid basis for the able performances achieved by John Brahm's direction. Latter gears his scenes for full interest and carefully carries forward the doubt—and audience hope—that Nancy is not the villainess.

•

LOCK UP

1989, 105 mins, US col

Dir John Flynn **Prod** Lawrence Gordon, Charles Gordon **Scr** Richard Smith, Jeb Stuart, Henry Rosenbaum **Ph** Donald E. Thorin **Ed** Michael N. Knue, Donald Brochu **Mus** Bill Conti **Art** Bill Kenney

Act Sylvester Stallone, Donald Sutherland, John Amos, Sonny Landham, Tom Sizemore, Frank McRae (White Eagle/Carolco)

Lock Up is made in the same, simplistic vein as most other Sylvester Stallone pics—putting him, the blue-collar protagonist, against the odds over which he ultimately prevails.

Emotional guy that he is, Stallone couldn't wait for his six-month prison term to be up because in the meantime his foster father may die, so he escapes to see him one last time. It seems his cold-hearted warden (Donald Sutherland) wouldn't allow him a supervised furlough to make the trip.

As revealed through the monosyllabic posturing, Sutherland is the vengeful, sadistic type.

The rest of the film is Stallone trying to survive "hell" that Sutherland, as the Devil, has diabolically allowed to run amok. Short of ordering, "kill, kill," Sutherland allows certain of his uniformed henchmen backed up by lifer prisoner/ringleader Chink (Sonny Landham) to bring Stallone down.

Darlanne Fluegel, as his faithful girlfriend, shows up occasionally to present the soft side of things but her character's only interesting attribute is that she's not a man.

•

LOCK UP YOUR DAUGHTERS!

1969, 102 mins, UK col

Dir Peter Coe **Prod** David Deutsch **Scr** Keith Waterhouse, Willis Hall **Ph** Peter Suschitzky **Mus** Ron Grainer **Art** Tony Woollard

Act Christopher Plummer, Susannah York, Glynis Johns, Ian Bannen, Tom Bell, Elaine Taylor (Columbia/Domino)

Much of the wit and satire in this portrait of the permissive morals and the corruptive decay of the 18th century is blunted, making it a noisy, bawdy, slapstick yarn about three sex-starved sailors on the rampage.

The scrappy storyline, drawn from Henry Fielding's *Rape Upon Rape* and John Vanbrugh's Restoration comedy *The Relapse*, plus the Mermaid Theatre musical written by Bernard Miles, can hardly be defined. It centers around the romantic entanglements of three wenches and their sailors which, after many misfortunes, complications, and misunderstandings, land practically everybody in court.

Christopher Plummer as Lord Foppington hardly does his screen reputation much good. He plays the effete aristocrat in a mannered way but extracts only exaggerated humor from it.

•

LODGER, THE
(US: THE PHANTOM FIEND)

1932, 85 mins, UK b/w

Dir Maurice Elvey **Prod** Julius Hagen **Scr** Ivor Novello, Miles Mander, Paul Rotha, H. Fowler Mear **Ph** Basil Emmott, Sydney Blythe

Act Ivor Novello, Elizabeth Allan, Jack Hawkins, A. W. Baskcomb, Barbara Everest, Peter Gawthorne (Twickenham)

The Lodger, from the novel by Mrs. Belloc Lowndes, was made as a silent some years previously. Despite its subject of Jack the Ripper, this is an eerie, absorbing story without being morbid.

Running parallel with the narration of the frightful murders is a sweet love story, gentle and poetic. Ivor Novello plays a sensitive musician with a sorrow so great he is unable to confide in anyone, not even the girl he loves, and who tells him she would believe anything he told her. Novello has an arresting personality, which photographs romantically.

Love scenes are ably supported by Elizabeth Allan, whose depiction of a working girl carried off her feet by a romantic, soulful musician is a fine piece of acting.

•

LODGER, THE

1944, 84 mins, US b/w

Dir John Brahm **Prod** Robert Bassler **Scr** Barre Lyndon **Ph** Lucien Ballard **Ed** J. Watson Webb **Mus** Hugo Friedhofer **Art** James Basevi, John Ewing

Act Merle Oberon, George Sanders, Laird Cregar, Cedric Hardwicke, Sara Allgood, Aubrey Mather (20th Century-Fox)

With a pat cast, keen direction, and tight scripting, 20th-Fox has an absorbing and, at times, spine-tingling drama concocted from Marie Belloc Lowndes's novel *The Lodger*. It's a super chiller-diller in its picturization of a Scotland Yard manhunt for London's Jack the Ripper. Director John Brahm and scripter Barre Lyndon make it as much a psychological study of the half-crazed "Lodger" (Laird Cregar), as if in a deftly paced horrific whodunit in trying to outline some explanation for the repeated throat slashings of London stage women, neither has even slightly deviated from the swift weaving of events. Aside from preliminary steps, sequence of events mounts in rapid succession with suspense injected time after time with telling effect.

It is Laird Cregar's picture. As "The Ripper" he gives an impressive performance. It is a relentless, at times pathetic, character as he pursues his self-appointed task of avenging his brother. His precise diction and almost studied poise make his characterization all the more impressive.

Merle Oberon is highly effective as Kitty, the dancer, of respectable family whose stardom is nearly abruptly ended. Stage sequences show her a graceful dancer in abbreviated skirt and provide the bright contrast to somber and melodramatic passages. Kept more or less in the background initially, her scene in the dressing room, when she pleads for her life, is the high dramatic spot of the production. George Sanders, cast as a sleuth, is strong.

•

LOGAN'S RUN

1976, 118 mins, US col

Dir Michael Anderson **Prod** Saul David **Scr** David Zelag Goodman **Ph** Ernest Laszlo **Ed** Bob Wyman **Mus** Jerry Goldsmith **Art** Dale Hennesy

Act Michael York, Richard Jordan, Jenny Agutter, Roscoe Lee Browne, Farrah Fawcett, Michael Anderson, Jr. (M-G-M)

Logan's Run is a rewarding futuristic film that appeals both as spectacular-looking escapist adventure as well as intelligent drama. Heading the cast are Michael York and Richard Jordan, two members of a security guard force which supervises the life of a domed-in hedonistic civilization all comprised of persons under the age of 30; after that, the civilization's tribal rules call for a ceremony called "renewal," though nobody's quite sure what that entails.

York, intrigued and abetted by Jenny Agutter, decides to flee with Jordan. Peter Ustinov is featured as a withered old man living alone on the outside, in the ruins of Washington, DC.

The three young principals and Ustinov come off very well.

1976: Honorary Award (visual effects)

NOMINATIONS: Best Cinematography, Art Direction

•

LOLA

1961, 90 mins, France/Italy b/w

Dir Jacques Demy **Prod** Carlo Ponti, Georges de Beauregard **Scr** Jacques Demy **Ph** Raoul Coutard **Ed** Anne-Marie Cotret **Mus** Michel Legrand **Art** Bernard Evein

Act Anouk Aimee, Marc Michel, Elina Labourdette, Alan Scott, Annie Dupereux, Margo Lion (Rome Paris)

Still another first pic with the "new wave" characteristics of on-the-spot lensing, little known names, and an improvised look.

A young man floats through jobs and hopes to leave a stultifying little town. He meets an old flame who dances in a club and has half-hearted affairs with Yank sailors while waiting for her first lover and father of her illegitimate son to come back. The boy falls for her again but up pops her old lover for a wry, happy ending.

A fading middle-class woman and her 14-year-old daughter looking for love are also entwined in the series of sketches that intermingle to give a cross section of life and desires.

But the mixture of melodrama, satire, and poetics does not entirely jell. It is offbeat, with shafts of tender feeling and truth. But trying to touch on too many subjects makes the film uneven.

Anouk Aimee has a pathetic quality as the mythomaniacal dancer who finally finds happiness, while Marc Michel is properly aimless as the boy. Lensing has the proper gray quality for this pleasant, unusual pic.

•

LOLA MONTES

1956, 110 mins, France/W. Germany col

Dir Max Ophuls **Scr** Max Ophuls, Annette Wademant **Ph** Christian Matras **Ed** Madeleine Gug **Mus** Georges Auric **Art** Jean D'Eaubonne

Act Martine Carol, Peter Ustinov, Anton Walbrook, Oskar Werner, Ivan Desny, Henri Guisol (Gamma/Florida/Union)

Max Ophuls brought his three-version film (English, French, and German) in for a whopping negative cost of $2 million. It is a lush color vehicle, relating the life story of a 19th-century courtesan.

Treatment of the lady of easy virtue's life is done via flashbacks while she is being exhibited in a strangely stylized circus somewhere in America. Sketchy method of handling the subject rarely allows sympathy to be built for the much manhandled heroine or to adequately formulate the essentials of the eternal woman the film is striving for. Martine Carol, as Lola Montes, lacks the depth needed. She looks good but never seems to display the temperament required.

Ophuls gives this elegant mounting, and the C'scope has lush and knowing framing. He uses iris-type blacking out of the corners of the screen for more intimate scenes, and even the old fashioned iris-out at times. Some fetching period observation appears from time to time, but life is rarely breathed into this frilly opus. Peter Ustinov has little acting to do but registers as the ringmaster who narrates the round of Lola's life. Anton Walbrook is fine as the king.

•

LOLITA

1962, 152 mins, US b/w

Dir Stanley Kubrick **Prod** James B. Harris **Scr** Vladimir Nabokov **Ph** Oswald Morris **Ed** Anthony Harvey **Mus** Nelson Riddle **Art** Bill Andrews, Syd Cain

Act James Mason, Shelley Winters, Peter Sellers, Sue Lyon, Gary Cockrell, Jerry Stovin (M-G-M)

Vladimir Nabokov's witty, grotesque novel is, in its film version, like a bee from which the stinger has been removed. It still buzzes with a sort of promising irreverence, but it lacks the power to shock, and, eventually, makes very little point either as comedy or satire. The novel has been stripped of its pubescent heroine and most of its lively syntax, graphic honesty, and sharp observations on people and places in a land abundant with clichés.

The result is an occasionally amusing but shapeless film about a middle-aged professor who comes to no good end through his involvement with a well-developed teenager. The fact that the first third of the picture is so good, bristling with Nabokovisms—a gun, for example, referred to as a tragic treasure—underscores the final disappointment. There is much about the film that is excellent. James Mason has never been better than he is as erudite Humbert Humbert, driven by a furious passion for a rather slovenly, perverse "nymphet" (a term, incidentally, which is used only once in the entire film). He is especially good in the early sequences as he pursues Lolita to the point where he even marries her mother, whom Shelley Winters plays to bumptious perfection. Matching these two performances is that of Peter Sellers who, as a preposterously smug American playwright (Mason's rival for Lolita's affections), gets a chance to run through several hilarious changes of character.

Sue Lyon makes an auspicious film debut as the deceitful child-woman who'd just as soon go to a movie as romp in the hay. It's a difficult assignment and if she never quite registers as either wanton or pathetic it may be due as much to the compromises of the script as to her inexperience.

1962: NOMINATION: Best Adapted Screenplay

•

LOLITA

1997, 137 mins, US/France Ⓥ ⦿ col

Dir Adrian Lyne ***Prod*** Mario Kassar, Joel B. Michaels ***Scr*** Stephen Schiff ***Ph*** Howard Atherton ***Ed*** Julie Monroe, David Bremner, F. Paul Benz ***Mus*** Ennio Morricone ***Art*** Jon Hutman

Act Jeremy Irons, Melanie Griffith, Frank Langella, Dominique Swain, Suzanne Shepherd, Keith Reddin (Kassar/Pathe)

The good news about Adrian Lyne's *Lolita* is that it's neither as irredeemable nor as morally shocking as its "untouchable" status would suggest. The bad news is that after an intriguing opening stretch, and despite Jeremy Irons's potent lead performance, the overlong film becomes repetitive, flat and often dull.

The long-finished $62 million film world premiered out of competition at the San Sebastian fest in September 1997, and then opened in Italy, Spain and Germany. [Pic finally opened in the U.S. in mid-1998, just prior to a cable premiere.]

Second screen version of Vladimir Nabokov's scabrous but ironic satire on love depicts Lolita (Dominique Swain) as a knowing manipulator and seductress, and her ardent adult lover as a helpless, frequently pitiable victim.

Having enlisted James Dearden, Harold Pinter and David Mamet to re-adapt the 1955 novel, and keeping elements only from Pinter's draft, Lyne settled on a script by first-time screenwriter Stephen Schiff, best known for his work in *The New Yorker* and *Vanity Fair.* His adaptation generally sticks much closer to the novel than Stanley Kubrick's 1962 one.

The opening section works well. Lyne establishes a light, ironic tone, milking laughs out of Humbert Humbert's dumbstruck surrender to passion. But problems arise when the director succumbs to the urge to make An Adrian Lyne Film, albeit one graced by Nabokov's witty, melodious prose, heard in Irons's voiceovers. In lieu of real dramatic momentum or emotional weight, we get gratuitous art-directional flourishes and aggressive techno-gloss. The crescendo peaks in Humbert's showdown with Quilty (Frank Langella).

Swain takes the role in her stride, but is invariably more bratty than sensual. Sex scenes are fairly chaste, implying more than they show.

•

LOLLY-MADONNA WAR, THE

SEE: LOLLY-MADONNA XXX

•

LOLLY-MADONNA XXX

(UK: THE LOLLY-MADONNA WAR)

1973, 105 mins, US ⌴ col

Dir Richard C. Sarafian ***Prod*** Rodney Carr-Smith ***Scr*** Rodney Carr-Smith, Sue Grafton ***Ph*** Philip Lathrop ***Ed*** Tom Rolf ***Mus*** Fred Myrow ***Art*** Herman Blumenthal

Act Rod Steiger, Robert Ryan, Jeff Bridges, Scott Wilson, Katherine Squire, Tresa Hughes (M-G-M)

Sue Grafton's novel, *The Lolly-Madonna War*, has been handsomely and sensitively filmed. Excellent performances abound by older and younger players in a mountain-country clan feud story that mixes extraordinary human compassion with raw but discreet violence.

It doesn't take much extrapolation effort to lift the story from its down-home setting and transpose it to the level of national and international politics.

Rod Steiger heads one clan, which also includes Katherine Squire in outstanding performance as his wife, plus Scott Wilson, Timothy Scott, Ed Lauter, Randy Quaid, and Jeff Bridges as the sons. The opposition clan is headed by Robert Ryan, with Tresa Hughes also outstanding as his wife.

A land dispute has brought the families to the edge of violence. Trigger for the explosion is a fake postcard sent by Kiel Martin, signed by a nonexistent, apparent bride-to-be named Lolly-Madonna with three X's appended in the childish manner. Wilson and Lauter, having glommed the postcard as Martin knew they would, kidnap Season Hubley, a traveler who arrives at the moment when the fake bride was to have met her husband-to-be.

Steiger and Ryan dominate the film through their children's actions, and director Richard C. Sarafian has endowed the picture with a moody, menacing atmosphere.

•

LONDON BELONGS TO ME

1948, 112 mins, UK b/w

Dir Sidney Gilliat ***Prod*** Frank Launder, Sidney Gilliat ***Scr*** Sidney Gilliat, J. B. Williams ***Ph*** Wilkie Cooper ***Ed*** Thelma Myers ***Mus*** Benjamin Frankel ***Art*** Roy Oxley

Act Richard Attenborough, Alastair Sim, Fay Compton, Stephen Murray, Wylie Watson, Susan Shaw (Individual/Rank)

Adapted from a bestseller by Norman Collins and set in a typical house on a typical street, the plot depicts the struggles and hopes of a group of ordinary people.

They include a benign old couple with their attractive daughter, a widowed mother with her only son, a faded blonde who ekes out a pittance at a nightclub, and the landlady herself, slightly soured but almost falling for a fake spiritualist. All lead a humdrum existence until a young lad in his desire to make some easy money and court the girl downstairs, gets involved in a murder and is sentenced to death.

Until then it has been a vigorous piece of melodrama, tense and exciting, and up to the standard expected from the Launder–Gilliat team. But without warning, and in questionable taste, the tempo changes and the organizing of a petition to save the life of the boy is treated as something meant to be hilariously funny.

With its excellent characterizations, its meaty story, and fine London backgrounds it should have been a first-rate thriller. But it isn't. An exceptionally big cast handles the characterizations with skill, but top honors go to Richard Attenborough, living the part of the flashy youngster who wants to go places the easy way, and Alistair Sim, who just can't miss as the fake medium. [Uncredited opening narration by Leo Genn.]

•

LONDON BY NIGHT

1937, 70 mins, US b/w

Dir William Thiele ***Prod*** Sam Zimbalist ***Scr*** George Oppenheimer ***Ph*** Leonard M. Smith ***Ed*** George Boemler ***Mus*** William Axt

Act George Murphy, Rita Johnson, Virginia Field, Leo G. Carroll, George Zucco (M-G-M)

A workmanlike script [from the play *The Umbrella Man* by Will Scott], the dialog of which is both intelligent and punchy, goes a good distance in making *London by Night* the meritorious melodrama it is. There's no redundance, no sappiness, and no language that would be out of keeping with the characters or the setting.

Entire locale is a certain section of London and much of the action is out-of-doors. Background throughout, in homes, shops, a pub, and elsewhere, also add to the note of authenticity.

Among the virtues of the picture is the skillful manner in which suspense is sustained. Suspicion is pointed in various interesting directions and one of the novelties of the plot is that two murders were of imaginary victims.

Remarkable thing about the picture is that, while its players are not widely known, with minor exceptions the performances are extremely good. In the top spots, George Murphy acquits himself creditably as a romantic lead, while Rita Johnson digs herself deeply into audience favor in a role that calls for less work than allotted Murphy. Eddie Quillan's drunk bit is excellent and his English accent worthy. Another whose work is more than ordinarily competent is George Zucco, who plays a Scotland Yard inspector.

•

LONDON KILLS ME

1991, 107 mins, UK Ⓥ ⦿ col

Dir Hanif Kureishi ***Prod*** Tim Bevan ***Scr*** Hanif Kureishi ***Ph*** Ed Lachman ***Ed*** Jon Gregory ***Mus*** Mark Springer, Sarah Sarhandi ***Art*** Stuart Walker

Act Justin Chadwick, Steven Mackintosh, Emer McCourt, Roshan Seth, Fiona Shaw, Brad Dourif (Polygram/Working Title)

Hanif Kureishi's *London Kills Me*, a flabby slice of London street life among pushers and hustlers, drags itself across the screen for 107 minutes and collapses in a dramatic mess on the sidewalk. First directorial outing by the Anglo-Pakistani scripter of *My Beautiful Laundrette* and *Sammy and Rosie Get Laid* shows the same interest in London's culturally mixed sublife, sans anti-Thatcherism subtext.

Main character is the Candide-like Clint (Justin Chadwick), who hangs out with a group led by small-time dealer Muffdiver (Steven Mackintosh). To raise the cash for a job in a swank local eatery, Clint joins in Muffdiver's plans to go big time and helps himself to latter's hidden stash. He's also got eyes for Muffdiver's heroin-hooked g.f. Sylvie (Emer McCourt).

Loose plot trawls in a host of other characters, including a sex-obsessed liberal (Fiona Shaw), an Indian (Roshan Seth), who runs a Sufi center and Clint's mom (Eleanor David), who lives in the country with a thuggish, middle-aged Elvis freak (Alun Armstrong).

What was obviously meant as an ironic look at lost souls in 1990s London rapidly blurs into a string of undramatic incidents. Pic recalls free-living late 1960s items, but without their buzz and color. Result, under Kureishi's unfocused helming, is drab.

•

LONELINESS OF THE LONG DISTANCE RUNNER, THE

1962, 104 mins, UK Ⓥ ⦿ b/w

Dir Tony Richardson ***Prod*** Tony Richardson ***Scr*** Alan Sillitoe ***Ph*** Walter Lassally ***Ed*** Antony Gibbs ***Mus*** John Addison ***Art*** Ralph Brinton

Act Tom Courtenay, Michael Redgrave, James Bolam, Avis Bunnage, Alec McCowen, Julia Foster (Woodfall)

It is difficult to conjure up much sympathy for the young "hero" who comes out as a disturbed young layabout (he seems thoroughly to deserve his fate of landing in Borstal, the corrective establishment for British juve delinquents). Yet the performance of Tom Courtenay and the imaginative, if sometimes overfussy, direction of Tony Richardson, plus some standout lensing by Walter Lassally makes this a worthwhile pic. Alan Sillitoe has written a sound screenplay for his own short story. Though there are obvious signs of padding, it remains a thoroughly professional job. The flashback technique is used ingeniously, though perhaps overmuch.

Courtenay plays a young man from an unhappy home in the Midlands. Apparently on the ground that the world owes him a living, he seems not interested in work, and inevitably drifts into petty crime and gets sent to Borstal.

He is resentful about "the system" and takes a strange way of getting back at it. A natural born runner ("We had plenty of practice in running away from the police in our family," he says bitterly), he is selected to represent Borstal in a long distance race against a public school team. It is the ambition of the governor (Michael Redgrave) to win the cup for Borstal.

Michael Redgrave as the rather pompous, stuffy governor who, to Courtenay's jaundiced eye, represents the system, brings his polished touch to a role that could have become irritating.

•

LONELY ARE THE BRAVE

1962, 107 mins, US Ⓥ ⦿ ⌴ b/w

Dir David Miller ***Prod*** Edward Lewis ***Scr*** Dalton Trumbo ***Ph*** Philip Lathrop ***Ed*** Leon Barsha ***Mus*** Jerry Goldsmith ***Art*** Alexander Golitzen, Robert E. Smith

Act Kirk Douglas, Gena Rowlands, Walter Matthau, Michael Kane, Carroll O'Connor, George Kennedy (Universal/Joel)

Often touching, and well served by its performances and photography, *Lonely Are the Brave* ultimately blurs its focus on the loner fenced in and bemused by the encroachments and paradoxes of civilization. Its makers have approached the misfit theme with a skittishness not unlike that exhibited by cowboy Kirk Douglas's horse. They have settled for surface instead of substance.

The failure of the Dalton Trumbo screenplay from an Edward Abbey novel [*Brave Cowboy*] is that it does not provide viewers with a sustained probing of the hero's perplexity.

The plot is sparing enough. Douglas, the footloose, arrives back at the New Mexico homestead of old friends Michael Kane and Gena Rowlands. Kane is in the Albuquerque jail on an aid-and-comfort to wetbacks rap, and good guy Douglas contrives to get himself tossed into the same pokey from where he plans to bust out with Kane. The buddy opts to stay, however—his ways are changed, and there is the wife and a son to consider—but Douglas, not one for the year's confinement he faces, makes off and takes to the hills ringing town.

As the loner, Douglas is extremely likable and understands his part within its limitations, as written. Most beguiling performance, however, is turned in by Walter Matthau as the laconic and harassed sheriff, who has never faced his quarry but develops an intuitive sympathy for him.

•

LONELY GUY, THE
1984, 90 mins, US Ⓥ ⊙ col
Dir Arthur Hiller ***Prod*** Arthur Hiller ***Scr*** Ed Weinberger, Stan Daniels ***Ph*** Victor J. Kemper ***Ed*** William Reynolds, Raja Gosnell ***Mus*** Jerry Goldsmith ***Art*** James D. Vance
Act Steve Martin, Charles Grodin, Judith Ivey, Steven Lawrence, Robyn Douglass, Merv Griffin (Universal)

Derived from a comic tome by Bruce Jay Friedman, premise has Steve Martin bounced by sexpot girlfriend Robyn Douglass and thereby banished to the world of Lonely Guys. He meets and commiserates with fellow LG Charles Grodin, who gets Martin to buy a fern with him and throws a party attended only by Martin and a bunch of life-sized cardboard cutouts of celebs like Dolly Parton and Tom Selleck.

Finally, Martin meets cute blonde Judith Ivey, who having been previously married to six Lonely Guys, instantly falls for him. Martin's trademark wacky humor is fitfully in evidence, but seems much more repressed than usual in order to fit into the relatively realistic world of single working people.

•

LONELY HEARTS
1982, 95 mins, Australia Ⓥ ⊙ col
Dir Paul Cox ***Prod*** John B. Murray ***Scr*** Paul Cox, John Clarke ***Ph*** Yuri Sokol ***Ed*** Tim Lewis ***Mus*** Norman Kaye ***Art*** Neil Angwin
Act Wendy Hughes, Norman Kaye, Jon Finlayson, Julia Blake, Jonathan Hardy (Adams-Packer)

A slowly developing romance between a 50-ish bachelor piano tuner and a 30-ish spinsterly bank clerk hardly seems the stuff from which viable motion pictures are made. Director Paul Cox's treatment of his own story is dull, plodding, and uninspiring fare.

Norman Kaye plays Peter, a nervous, vapid character who is so weak he nearly recedes into the woodwork. Wendy Hughes is Patricia, dowdy, sexually repressed, and smothered by her parents. They meet through a dating service after his mother dies, and embark on possibly the world's longest and dreariest courtship.

Both Kaye and Hughes struggle to make their characters interesting or engaging. A few all-too-rare lively moments are provided by Julia Blake as Peter's overbearing sister, Jon Finlayson as a camp theater director, and Ronald Falk as a twee wig salesman.

•

LONELY PASSION OF JUDITH HEARNE, THE
1987, 110 mins, UK Ⓥ col
Dir Jack Clayton ***Prod*** Peter Nelson, Richard Johnson ***Scr*** Peter Nelson ***Ph*** Peter Hannan ***Ed*** Terry Rawlings ***Mus*** Georges Delerue ***Art*** Michael Pickwood
Act Maggie Smith, Bob Hoskins, Wendy Hiller, Marie Kean, Ian McNeice, Prunella Scales (HandMade/United British Artists)

An ensemble of sterling performances highlights *The Lonely Passion of Judith Hearne*, an intelligent, carefully crafted adaptation of Brian Moore's well-regarded first novel. Film's centerpiece is Maggie Smith's exceptionally detailed portrait of the title character, a middle-aged Irish spinster who tragically deludes herself into imagining herself involved in a great romance.

Judith is a fragile bird, a part-time piano teacher in 1950s Dublin who has every reason to be desperate about life but still manages to look on the bright side. Moving into a new boarding house, she takes a liking to her landlady's brother James (Bob Hoskins), a widower recently returned from 30 years in New York, and begins stepping out with him.

Once James takes her to a fancy dinner at the Shelbourne Hotel, Judith is sure his intentions are serious. Unfortunately, she allows a misunderstanding between them to assume traumatic proportions, and her heartbreak and disappointment lead her down a spiraling road of despair, alcoholism, ostracism, and religious rejection. Hoskins, laying a brash New York accent over a hint of the Irish, brings great energy and creative bluster to the irrepressible dreamer who has been instilled with Yankee get-up-and-go.

•

LONELY WOMAN, THE
SEE: VIAGGIO IN ITALIA

•

LONE STAR
1996, 134 mins, US Ⓥ ⊙ ▭ col
Dir John Sayles ***Prod*** Maggie Renzi, Paul Miller ***Scr*** John Sayles ***Ph*** Stuart Dryburgh ***Ed*** John Sayles ***Mus*** Mason Daring ***Art*** Dan Bishop
Act Chris Cooper, Elizabeth Pena, Joe Morton, Ron Canada, Clifton James, Kris Kristofferson (Rio Dulce/Castle Rock)

Lone Star is a richly textured and thoroughly engrossing drama that ranks with indie filmmaker John Sayles's finest work. Bountifully rich in incident and characterization, *Lone Star* recalls the vast canvas of Sayles's *City of Hope*. This time the maverick writer-director focuses on a small Texas bordertown where the sins of fathers continue to haunt sons.

Chris Cooper is first among equals in a strong ensemble cast as Sam Deeds, the taciturn but easygoing sheriff of Frontera. The locals still swap stories about the fateful night 40 years ago when his father, Buddy Deeds (Matthew McConaughey), ran his corrupt predecessor, Charlie Wade (Kris Kristofferson), out of town.

When skeletal remains are uncovered at a long-abandoned Army rifle range near the town, Sam is called in to investigate. Sure enough, the remains are identified as those of Charlie Wade. Sam suspects his father killed the villain, and begins to question Buddy's friends and associates. The more he digs into his father's past, the more he learns about himself. Repeatedly, Sayles emphasizes his central theme: History is merely a collection of highly subjective appraisals. In several scenes, Sayles gracefully glides his camera from a flashback to a contemporary scene, allowing past and present to exist simultaneously in the same tracking shot. Even relatively minor subplots ring true with their persuasive detail.

Kristofferson makes the most of his relatively few scenes, so that his malignant presence hovers over the action even when he's nowhere to be seen. Elizabeth Pena reveals a quiet strength and sad-eyed sensuality in her multifaceted role as wife, mother, and lover.

1996: NOMINATIONS: Best Original Screenplay

•

LONE WOLF MCQUADE
1983, 107 mins, US Ⓥ col
Dir Steve Carver ***Prod*** Yoram Ben-Ami, Steve Carver ***Scr*** B. J. Nelson ***Ph*** Roger Shearman ***Ed*** Anthony Redman ***Mus*** Francesco De Masi ***Art*** Norm Baron
Act Chuck Norris, David Carradine, Barbara Carrera, Leon Isaac Kennedy, Robert Beltran, L. Q. Jones (1818 Production/Orion)

Fans of *Soldier of Fortune* magazine will think they've been ambushed and blown away to heaven by *Lone Wolf McQuade*. Every conceivable type of portable weapon on the world market is tried out by the macho warriors on both sides of the law in this modern western [story by H. Kaye Dyal and B. J. Nelson], which pits Texas Ranger Chuck Norris and his cohorts against multifarious baddies who like to play rough.

Opening sequence, showing the grizzled Norris busting up a gang of Mexican horse rustlers, makes it clear that film's primary source of inspiration is Sergio Leone.

Vile David Carradine is in the business of hijacking U.S. Army weapons shipments and selling them to Central American terrorist groups. Norris and FBI agent Leon Isaac Kennedy finally locate Carradine's secret airstrip, and after a setback there, track him down at a compound loaded with all manner of armaments.

•

LONG AGO TOMORROW
SEE: THE RAGING MOON

•

LONG AND THE SHORT AND THE TALL, THE
(US: JUNGLE FIGHTERS)
1961, 105 mins, UK Ⓥ b/w
Dir Leslie Norman ***Prod*** Michael Balcon ***Scr*** Wolf Mankowitz ***Ph*** Erwin Hillier ***Ed*** Gordon Stone ***Mus*** Stanley Black ***Art*** Terence Verity, Jim Morahan
Act Richard Todd, Laurence Harvey, Richard Harris, Ronald Fraser, David McCallum, John Meillon (Associated British)

Director and scriptwriter have not been able to resist the temptation to take a great deal of Willis Hall's war play into the open air of the jungle. This is a pity. It loses the sense of pent-in suspense that marked the play so effectively and it also shows up the fact that the Elstree "jungle" is rather phoney.

Film depends on characterization rather than on the thinnish plot. It's set in the Far East jungle during the Japanese campaign. A small patrol led by a sergeant (Richard Todd) is cut off. Suddenly "sparks" makes radio contact and jabbering Japanese voices nearby cause them to realize that they're in a spot.

A lone Japanese scout moves into their position and Todd insists that they must get him back to base alive as a source of information. The remainder want to bump him off with the solitary, surprise exception of a loudmouthed and brash private (Laurence Harvey).

Standout performance comes from Harvey. It is dramatic license that enables him to behave in a way that would undoubtedly have had him up on a charge in a real situation.

The bewildered Jap, subtly played by Kenji Takaki, is another very sound performance. In fact there is no weak link in the cast. Todd is a dogged, worried sergeant; Richard Harris shapes very good as his righthand man, and Ronald Fraser is fine as a dour Scot.

•

LONG DAY CLOSES, THE
1992, 83 mins, UK Ⓥ ⊙ col
Dir Terence Davies ***Prod*** Olivia Stewart ***Scr*** Terence Davies ***Ph*** Michael Coulter ***Ed*** William Diver ***Mus*** Bob Last, Robert Lockhart ***Art*** Christopher Hobbs
Act Marjorie Yates, Leigh McCormack, Anthony Watson, Nicholas Lamont, Ayse Owens, Tina Malone (BFI/Film Four)

Terence Davies's *The Long Day Closes* is a technically elaborate, dryly witty moodpiece centered on a shy young daydreamer in mid-1950s working-class Liverpool. Pic builds on the basic elements of Davies's 1988 *Distant Voices, Still Lives*, with a free-form ride down the helmer's memory lane of family, friends, Catholicism, and cinema.

Central character is Bud (movingly limned by 13-year-old newcomer Leigh McCormack), a shy loner who's given a hard time at school, idolizes his mom (Marjorie Yates) and elder sister (Ayse Owens), and finds escape from the grayness of Britain in movie theaters. There's little resolution in conventional terms: Davies simply builds a kaleidoscope out of memory fragments and shakes it every which way in a series of visual vignettes.

Pic's major weakness is its stop-go tempo. Individual segs are stunningly mounted but there is a lack of a longer dramatic line, a reluctance to go with the flow. Davies is still a miniaturist working in a feature-length format.

Nonbuffs could be flummoxed by the soundtrack, a knowing mix of popular melodies, snatches of movie dialog and M-G-M baubles. But strength of Davies's vision is the crux, and holds the line to the final, confident fadeout. Perfs by the no-name cast are all on the money.

•

LONG DAY'S DYING, THE
1968, 93 mins, UK ▭ col
Dir Peter Collinson ***Prod*** Harry Fine, Peter Collinson ***Scr*** Charles Wood ***Ph*** Brian Probyn ***Ed*** John Trumper ***Art*** Disley Jones
Act David Hemmings, Tom Bell, Tony Beckley, Alan Dobie (Paramount)

The Long Day's Dying is a bore. In tracing the steps of three British soldiers and their German captive during a single day of weary trekking through the European countryside, it adds nothing in the way of insight or impact to the dreary platitudes of countless previous anti-war pix. Charles Wood's script is lacking in dramatic momentum and fails to clarify the four protagonists' characters. Even worse, no sympathy or interest is developed for any of the men.

Script's use of interior monologs is clumsy, frequently counterpointing the various men's thoughts in an archly poetic way and never helping to define their inner natures.

Direction by Peter Collinson is lackluster. When not relying on established tricks of documentary filmmaking or more up-to-date visual affectations, he holds on closeups of his "thinking" actors. Fact that all four players register little beyond grim impassivity hardly lightens the pace of this lethargic film.

•

LONG DAY'S JOURNEY INTO NIGHT
1962, 176 mins, US Ⓥ b/w
Dir Sidney Lumet ***Prod*** Ely Landau ***Ph*** Boris Kaufman ***Ed*** Ralph Rosenbaum ***Mus*** Andre Previn ***Art*** Richard Sylbert
Act Katharine Hepburn, Ralph Richardson, Jason Robards, Dean Stockwell, Jeanne Barr (Landau)

This is an excellent film adaption of the late Eugene O'Neill's lengthy stage work. It has power in its characters and their tortured introspective lives. There have been a few cuts but otherwise it is as O'Neill wrote it. And his powerful language manages to overcome the limited sets and dependence on the spoken word.

It takes a family through the probing of themselves, their relations and their relative reasons for acting as they do. It all develops when the mother one day begins to sink back to drug addiction.

Katharine Hepburn's beautifully boned face mirrors her anguish and needs. She makes the role of the mother breathtaking and intensely moving. There is balance, depth, and breadth in her acting. Ralph Richardson brings his authority to the part of the miserly father who had made money as a theatrical matinee idol but can't shake his skinflint habits because of a childhood of poverty. Jason Robards has flair and insight as the tortured older brother while Dean Stockwell is effective as the younger brother.

Made reportedly for $400,000, since the principals took minimum pay because of their desire to do the property.

1962: NOMINATION: Best Actress (Katharine Hepburn)

•

LONG DUEL, THE
1967, 115 mins, UK col
Dir Ken Annakin ***Prod*** Ken Annakin ***Scr*** Peter Yeldham ***Ph*** Jack Hildyard ***Ed*** Bert Bates ***Mus*** John Scott ***Art*** Alex Vetchinsky
Act Yul Brynner, Trevor Howard, Harry Andrews, Andrew Keir, Charlotte Rampling, Virginia North (Rank)

Produced and directed by Ken Annakin at Pinewood and on location in Granada, Spain, this is an ambitious actioner that has plenty of punch. But the yarn, though based on fact, unfolds with little conviction and is repeatedly bogged down by labored dialog and characterization in Peter Yeldham's screenplay [based on a story by Ranveer Singh].

Story is set on the Indian Northwest frontier during the 1920s and basically hinges on the uneasy relationship and lack of understanding between most of the British top brass and the native tribes. Trevor Howard, an idealistic police officer, is very conscious of the need for tact and diplomacy when handling the touchy natives.

When he is ordered to track down the Bhanta tribe leader (Yul Brynner), who is trying to lead his people from the bondage of the British, Howard recognizes Brynner as a fellow idealist and an enemy to respect.

•

LONGEST DAY, THE
1962, 180 mins, US b/w
Dir Ken Annakin, Andrew Marton, Bernhard Wicki ***Prod*** Darryl F. Zanuck ***Scr*** Cornelius Ryan, Romain Gary, James Jones, David Pursall, Jack Seddon ***Ph*** Jean Bourgoin, [Henri Persin], Walter Wottitz ***Ed*** Samuel E. Beetley ***Mus*** Maurice Jarre ***Art*** Ted Haworth, Leon Barsacq, Vincent Korda
Act John Wayne, Robert Mitchum, Henry Fonda, Robert Ryan, Richard Todd, Richard Burton (Zanuck/20th Century-Fox)

Darryl F. Zanuck achieves a solid and stunning war epic. From personal vignettes to big battles, it details the first day of the D-Day Landings by the Allies on June 6, 1944.

The savage fury and sound of war are ably caught on film. It emerges as a sort of grand scale semi-fictionalized documentary concerning the overall logistics needed for this incredible invasion. It carries its three-hour length by the sheer tingle of the masses of manpower in action, peppered with little ironic, sad, silly actions that all add up to war.

The use of over 43 actual star names in bit and pivotal spots helps keep up the aura of fictionalized documentary. But it is the action, time, and place, and the actual machinery of war, that are the things.

The battles [coordinated by associate producer Elmo Williams] ably take their places among some of the best ever put on the screen. A German strafing the beach, Yanks scaling a treacherous cliff only to find that there was no big gun there, British commandos taking a bridge, Yanks blowing up a big bunker, the French taking a town, all are done with massive pungent action. The black and white and CinemaScope screen help keep the focus on surge and movement.

1962: Best B&W Cinematography, Special Effects

NOMINATIONS: Best Picture, B&W Art Direction, Editing

•

LONGEST YARD, THE
(UK: THE MEAN MACHINE)
1974, 121 mins, US col
Dir Robert Aldrich ***Prod*** Albert S. Ruddy ***Scr*** Tracy Keenan Wynn ***Ph*** Joseph Biroc ***Ed*** Michael Luciano ***Mus*** Frank DeVol ***Art*** James S. Vance
Act Burt Reynolds, Eddie Albert, Ed Lauter, Michael Conrad, Jim Hampton, Bernadette Peters (Paramount/Long Road)

The Longest Yard is an outstanding action drama, combining the brutish excitement of football competition with the brutalities of contemporary prison life. Burt Reynolds asserts his genuine star power, here as a former football pro forced to field a team under blackmail of warden Eddie Albert.

In contrast to most hard-action films, this is quality action drama, in which brute force is fully motivated and therefore totally acceptable. At the same time, the metaphysics of football are neatly interwoven with the politics and bestialities of totalitarian authority.

Script, from a story credited to producer Albert S. Ruddy, finds Reynolds arriving at Albert's prison. Ed Lauter, his chief guard, also coaches the guards' clumsy football team. Reynolds is forced to form an inmates team from a ragtag bunch of cons, with a no-win payoff: If he loses, Lauter's guards will rub it in; if he wins, Albert's vengeance is certain.

1974: NOMINATION: Best Editing

•

LONG GOODBYE, THE
1973, 112 mins, US col
Dir Robert Altman ***Prod*** Jerry Bick ***Scr*** Leigh Brackett ***Ph*** Vilmos Zsigmond ***Ed*** Lou Lombardo ***Mus*** John Williams
Act Elliott Gould, Nina Van Pallandt, Sterling Hayden, Henry Gibson, Mark Rydell, Jim Bouton (United Artists)

Robert Altman's film version of Raymond Chandler's novel is an uneven mixture of insider satire on the gumshoe film genre, gratuitous brutality, and sledgehammer whimsy.

Leigh Brackett adapted the Chandler book; she, Jules Furthman, and William Faulkner scripted Chandler's *The Big Sleep* [1946]. Herein, the Philip Marlowe character becomes embroiled in a Malibu murder, stolen money, the apparent death of his best friend, and compounded double-cross.

No longer the sardonic idealist, Marlowe has become part Walter Mitty. Elliott Gould keeps a low dramatic profile throughout as a passive catalyst. Nina Van Pallandt makes an American film bow as the wife of dried-up author Sterling Hayden (Dan Blocker was to have been cast, and his passing is tributed in an end title card "with special remembrance"), whose periodic disappearances include a visit to Henry Gibson's high-priced sanatorium.

Mark Rydell returns to acting after a decade of directing to play a kooky criminal, whose twisted mind runs to bashing in the face of Jo Ann Brody with a soft drink bottle.

•

LONG GOOD FRIDAY, THE
1981, 114 mins, UK col
Dir John Mackenzie ***Prod*** Barry Hanson ***Scr*** Barrie Keeffe ***Ph*** Phil Meheux ***Ed*** Mike Taylor ***Mus*** Francis Monkman ***Art*** Vic Symonds
Act Bob Hoskins, Helen Mirren, Eddie Constantine, Dave King, Brian Hall, Pierce Brosnan (Calendar/Black Lion)

In many respects a conventional thriller set in London's underworld, *The Long Good Friday* is much more densely plotted and intelligently scripted than most such yarns.

Bob Hoskins displays natural, and sizable, big-screen presence, and works out first-rate in the anchor role of a gangland boss faced with a series of seemingly gratuitous reprisals by unknown ill-wishers against his waterfront empire.

He starts as a larger-than-life figure, confidently negotiating American finance for a massive land development project. But Hoskins's overweening exterior crumples as some of his best men are murdered.

When it becomes clear that his adversary is the provisional Irish Republican Army, he pits his Mafia-style muscle against the IRA's professional terrorism.

The narrative is steered competently, but visual style is too stolid to lend due gut-impact.

•

LONG GRAY LINE, THE
1955, 135 mins, US col
Dir John Ford ***Prod*** Robert Arthur ***Scr*** Edward Hope ***Ph*** Charles Lawton, Jr. ***Ed*** William Lyon ***Mus*** George Duning ***Art*** Robert Peterson
Act Tyrone Power, Maureen O'Hara, Robert Francis, Ward Bond, Donald Crisp (Columbia)

The Long Gray Line is a standout drama on West Point. For Tyrone Power the role of Marty Maher, Irishman through whose eyes the story is told, is a memorable one. Maureen O'Hara brings to the role of Maher's wife her Irish beauty and seldom displayed acting ability. Both are very fine.

Robert Arthur's exceptionally well-fashioned production is based on *Bringing Up the Brass*, the autobiography of Maher's 50 years at the Point, which he wrote with Nardi Reeder Campion. A screenplay that is full of wonderfully human touches gives just the right foundation for John Ford to show his love for country (and the Irish) with his direction. Story oscillates between unashamed sniffles and warm chuckles, Ford not being afraid to bring a tear or stick in a laugh.

•

LONG, HOT SUMMER, THE
1958, 115 mins, US col
Dir Martin Ritt ***Prod*** Jerry Wald ***Scr*** Irving Ravetch, Harriet Frank, Jr. ***Ph*** Joseph LaShelle ***Ed*** Louis R. Loeffler ***Mus*** Alex North ***Art*** Lyle R. Wheeler, Maurice Ransford
Act Paul Newman, Joanne Woodward, Anthony Franciosa, Orson Welles, Lee Remick, Angela Lansbury (Wald/20th Century-Fox)

The Long, Hot Summer is a simmering story of life in the Deep South, steamy with sex and laced with violence and bawdy humor. Although the setting is Mississippi, race relations play no part; it is instead a kind of *Peyton Place* with the locale shifted from New England to the warmer climate and—apparently—hotter-blooded citizens. This picture is strikingly directed by Martin Ritt.

The screenplay is based on two stories, *Barn Burning* and *The Spotted Horses* and a part of the novel, *The Hamlet*, all by William Faulkner. It is about a young Mississippi redneck (Paul Newman) who has a reputation for settling his grudges by setting fire to the property of those he opposes.

This notoriety follows him when he drifts into the town owned and operated by Orson Welles, a gargantuan character who has reduced the town to snivelling peonage; his one son (Anthony Franciosa) to the point where he seeks perpetual escape in the love of his pretty wife (Lee Remick); and, by his tactics, frozen his daughter (Joanne Woodward) into a premature old maid. Welles senses immediately in Newman a fellow predator and they set to trying to outdo each other in villainy and connivance.

Scriptwriters have done a phenomenal job of putting together elements of stories that are actually connected only by their core of atmosphere, Faulkner's preoccupation with the rising redneck moneyed class, and their dominance of the former aristocracy. There are still holes in the screenplay but director Martin Ritt slams over them so fast that you are not aware of any vacancies until you are past them. It is melodrama frank and unashamed. It may be preposterous but it is never dull. Most of *Long, Hot Summer* was shot in Louisiana and the locations pay off in the authentic flavor well captured by cameraman Joseph LaShelle. Highlighting the diverse and contrasting moods is the fine score by Alex North.

•

LONG KISS GOODNIGHT, THE
1996, 120 mins, US col
Dir Renny Harlin ***Prod*** Renny Harlin, Stephanie Austin, Shane Black ***Scr*** Shane Black ***Ph*** Guillermo Navarro ***Ed*** William C. Goldenberg ***Mus*** Alan Silvestri ***Art*** Howard Cummings
Act Geena Davis, Samuel L. Jackson, Patrick Malahide, Craig Bierko, Brian Cox, David Morse (Forge/New Line)

A violent and fantastical actioner about the potential for good and evil within the human character, *The Long Kiss Goodnight* has a jokey good time with its outlandish pyrotechnics and offbeat character interplay. Bouncing back from their joint belly flop on *Cutthroat Island*, director Renny Harlin and star Geena Davis supply a rambunctious physicality, wrapped in a breezy attitude.

Shane Black's screenplay, much touted at the time of its record spec-script sale for $4 million, certainly supplies the requisite count of bodies biting the dust—and snow. But the usual numbing feel of such concoctions is partly mitigated by the off-center camaraderie between Davis and co-star Samuel L. Jackson.

Samantha Caine (Davis) is seen as the ideal mom in an ideal New England small town. But this is literally a tale of The Killer Inside Me, as Samantha turns out to have been a highly trained government assassin, Charly, in her previous life—which she can't remember due to an amnesiac block—presumed dead but now feared by her former colleagues for knowing too much.

A tale of double pursuit ensues, as Samantha hooks up with low-rent detective and former jailbird Mitch (Jackson) to seek out the truth, only to be threatened every step of the way by pretty-boy government hit man Timothy (Craig Bierko) and his treacherous intelligence chief, Perkins (Patrick Malahide).

Davis fits the bill of a smart, tough capable femme operative as well as anyone could. Playing a lifelong loser with a lively sense of humor, Jackson lightens the proceedings in a welcome manner.

•

LONG NIGHT, THE
1947, 97 mins, US b/w
Dir Anatole Litvak ***Prod*** Anatole Litvak, Robert Hakim, Raymond Hakim ***Scr*** John Wexley ***Ph*** Sol Polito ***Ed*** Robert Swink ***Mus*** Dimitri Tiomkin ***Art*** Eugene Lourie
Act Henry Fonda, Barbara Bel Geddes, Vincent Price, Ann Dvorak, Elisha Cook, Jr. (RKO)

The Long Night is a sullen brooding film [based on a prewar French film] about vet of World War II who goes on killing spree when his girl takes up with another guy. There's some good, challenging writing that indicts a society in which a guy can kill legally in war and get it in the neck if he does it in peace, but it's cinematic stuff that others may pounce on. Brilliant thesping jobs are turned in by Henry Fonda, Barbara Bel Geddes (making her film bow), Vincent Price, and others, but despite the good cast, picture is too grim.

Film opens with bang-bang as Fonda shoots Price. Squad car arrives and crowd gathers as Fonda resolves to shoot it out with cops. Via flashbacks, Bel Geddes's meeting with Price and subsequent tragic events are revealed. Yarn moves from present to past and back cleverly, winding up where it started.

•

LONG PANTS
1927, 70 mins, US ⊗ b/w
Dir Frank Capra ***Scr*** Arthur Ripley, Robert Eddy ***Ph*** Elgin Lessley, Glen Kirshner
Act Harry Langdon, Gladys Brockwell, Al Roscoe, Alma Bennett, Priscilla Bonner, Frankie Darro (Langdon/First National)

A bit of a let down for Harry Langdon. It hasn't the popular laughing quality of his other full-length productions, principally because the sympathetic element is over-developed at the expense of the gags and the stunts that made *The Strong Man* a riot. By anybody else the picture would be hailed as a great production.

The opening is exceedingly quiet. It is here that the picture seeks to build up a sympathetic background for the Boy, giving a semi-serious twist calculated to heighten its subsequent clowning.

Later on, when they get into rougher material, there are several highly effective comic passages. One of the best is the incident where Langdon, who has unwittingly helped a woman criminal to escape jail in a packing case, sees what he thinks is a policeman sitting on the box. He takes up a position across the street and tries by half a dozen absurd ruses to draw away the cop.

•

LONG RIDERS, THE
1980, 100 mins, US Ⓥ ⦿ col
Dir Walter Hill ***Prod*** Tim Zinnemann ***Scr*** Bill Bryden, Steven Phillip Smith, Stacy Keach, James Keach ***Ph*** Ric Waite ***Ed*** David Holden, Freeman Davies ***Mus*** Ry Cooder ***Art*** Jack T. Collis
Act David Carradine, Keith Carradine, Stacy Keach, James Keach, Dennis Quaid, Randy Quaid (United Artists)

The Long Riders is striking in several ways, not the least of which being the casting of actor brothers as historical outlaw kin, but narrative is episodic in the extreme.

Yarn opens in bang-up fashion with a bank robbery, after which trigger-happy Dennis Quaid is kicked out of the Younger-James-Miller gang for needlessly murdering a man during stick-up. With no time frame provided, pic proceeds by alternating scenes of further crimes, the men at play in whorehouses and courting women, and the law bungling initial attempts to capture the troublemakers.

Director Walter Hill resolutely refuses to investigate the psychology or motivations of his characters, explaining away men's life of banditry as a "habit" acquired in wake of the Civil War.

What's ultimately missing is a definable point of view which would tie together the myriad events on display and fill in the blanks which Hill has imposed on the action by sapping it of emotional or historical meaning.

•

LONG SHIPS, THE
1964, 124 mins, UK/Yugoslavia Ⓥ ▭ col
Dir Jack Cardiff ***Prod*** Irving Allen ***Scr*** Berkely Mather, Beverley Cross ***Ph*** Christopher Challis ***Ed*** Geoff Foot ***Mus*** Dusan Radic ***Art*** John Hoesli
Act Richard Widmark, Sidney Poitier, Russ Tamblyn, Rosanna Schiaffino, Beba Loncar, Oscar Homolka (Columbia/Warwick/Avala)

Any attempt to put this into the epic class falls down because of a hodge-podge of a story line, a mixture of styles and insufficient development of characterization.

The plot, which has obviously suffered in both editing and in censorial slaps, is a conglomeration of battles, double-crossing, seastorms, floggings, unarmed combat with occasional halfhearted peeks at sex. Throughout there's a great deal of noise and the entire experience is a very long drag.

Film [based on the novel by Frans G. Bengtsson] concerns the rivalry of the Vikings and the Moors in search of a legendary Golden Bell, the size of three men and containing "half the gold in the world." Leaders of the rival factors are Richard Widmark, an adventurous Viking con man, who plays strictly tongue-in-cheek, and Sidney Poitier, dignified, ruthless top man of the Moors. In contrast to Widmark, he seeks to take the film seriously. The clash in styles between these two is a minor disaster.

•

LONGTIME COMPANION
1990, 96 mins, US Ⓥ col
Dir Norman Rene ***Prod*** Stan Wlodkowski ***Scr*** Craig Lucas ***Ph*** Tony Jannelli ***Ed*** Katherine Wenning ***Mus*** Greg DeBelles ***Art*** Andrew Jackness
Act Bruce Davison, Campbell Scott, Stephen Caffrey, Mark Lamos, Patrick Cassidy, Mary-Louise Parker (American Playhouse)

The first feature film to tell the story of how AIDS devastated and transformed the gay community, *Longtime Companion* is simply an excellent film, with a graceful, often humorous script and affecting performances.

Story begins during the carefree pre-AIDS party days on Fire Island, where Willy (Campbell Scott) and Fuzzy (Stephen Caffrey) meet and begin a relationship that brings together an extended circle of friends. It's the same day a *New York Times* article announces a rare disease spreading among gay men. A year later, Willy's best friend John (Dermot Mulroney) becomes violently ill and dies. It's only the beginning. One by one, this community of actors, writers, and lawyers is affected.

Among the most piercing events is the deterioration of a TV scripter, Sean (Mark Lamos), who is cared for by his lover, David (Bruce Davison), who owns the beach house where the friends have always gathered. Strength of Craig Lucas's script is the way it weaves emotional and informational material together.

1990: NOMINATION: Best Supp. Actor (Bruce Davison)

•

LONG VOYAGE HOME, THE
1940, 105 mins, US Ⓥ ⦿ b/w
Dir John Ford ***Prod*** Walter Wanger ***Scr*** Dudley Nichols ***Ph*** Gregg Toland ***Ed*** Sherman Todd ***Mus*** Richard Hageman ***Art*** James Basevi
Act John Wayne, Thomas Mitchell, Ian Hunter, Barry Fitzgerald, Wilfrid Lawson, Mildred Natwick (Argosy)

Combining dramatic content of four Eugene O'Neill one-act plays, John Ford pilots adventures of a tramp steamer from the West Indies to an American port, and then across the Atlantic with cargo of high explosives. Picture is typically Fordian, his direction accentuating characterizations and adventures of the voyage.

Story plods along at slow tempo, making onlookers wonder when ship will finally make an English port safely. There's a rather confusing passage in which Ian Hunter, as a deckhand, is pictured as an enemy spy, and although he is finally cleared, nothing explains his actions that lead to original suspicions.

Aside from explosive cargo aboard, little interest is generated in final safety of crew, as yarn points out they are all men of the sea, who will ship out again soon as pay evaporates; all but John Wayne, who wants a nestegg for a farm in Sweden.

Along the voyage there's plenty of dialog and action in the crew's quarters, with Thomas Mitchell the accepted leader of the group. Storm at sea, in which ship's anchor breaks loose, is particularly realistic. Passage through the submarine zone with blackout restrictions is more informative than dramatic. Stuka-bombing and machine-gunning of the ship in sight of land is a dramatic excuse for heroic death of Hunter just before landing.

Mitchell hits a high mark in the seaman's character—two-fisted, domineering, and still kindly and loyal to his pals. Wayne's role is submerged among the sailor characters.

1940: NOMINATIONS: Best Picture, Screenplay, B&W Cinematography, Editing, Original Score

•

LONG WALK HOME, THE
1990, 97 mins, US Ⓥ ⦿ col
Dir Richard Pearce ***Prod*** Howard W. Koch, Jr. ***Scr*** John Cork ***Ph*** Roger Deakins ***Ed*** Bill Yahraus ***Mus*** George Fenton ***Art*** Blake Russell
Act Sissy Spacek, Whoopi Goldberg, Dwight Schultz, Ving Rhames, Dylan Baker, Erika Alexander (New Visions)

Set in Montgomery, Alabama, during the 1955 civil rights bus boycott, *The Long Walk Home* is an effectively mounted drama about the human impact of changing times on two families, with sturdy performances by Sissy Spacek as an uppercrust white housewife and Whoopi Goldberg as her maid.

Spacek's Miriam Thompson is a prim model of upper-middle-class Southern womanhood who cannot run her household without her indispensable maid Odessa.

Racist jokes are commonplace during cocktail parties and family dinners, where Spacek's brother-in-law (Dylan Baker) espouses hard-line segregationist attitudes.

Goldberg's hard-working husband (Ving Rhames) and three well-mannered kids make a loving family, but the household's mood is tense because of external events. Local black leaders call for a bus boycott to end segregated seating. As the black boycott stiffens, so does white resistance, which turns ugly with the bombing of Martin Luther King's house. Afraid of change, the town establishment refuses to compromise. The film resists the temptation to succumb to sentimentality and offers believable characterizations in the context of its time and place.

•

LOOK BACK IN ANGER
1959, 115 mins, UK Ⓥ ⦿ b/w
Dir Tony Richardson ***Prod*** Gordon L. T. Scott ***Scr*** Nigel Kneale, John Osborne ***Ph*** Oswald Morris ***Ed*** Richard Best ***Mus*** John Addison (sup.), Chris Barber and His Band ***Art*** Peter Glazier
Act Richard Burton, Claire Bloom, Mary Ure, Edith Evans, Gary Raymond, Donald Pleasence (Woodfall)

Tony Richardson, who staged the play, *Look Back in Anger*, which helped to hoist John Osborne into the bigtime, tackles the same subject as his first directorial chore. Richardson's is a technical triumph, but somewhere along the line he has lost the heart and the throb that made the play an adventure. The film simultaneously impresses and depresses. In the play, Jimmy Porter was a rebel—but a mixed-up weakling of a rebel. In the film, as played by Richard Burton, he is an arrogant young man who thinks the world owes him something but cannot make up his mind what it is—and certainly doesn't deserve the handout.

Burton glowers sullenly, violently and well as Porter and it is not his fault that the role gives him little opportunity for variety. Mary Ure (repeating her London and Broadway stage role) as the downtrodden, degraded young wife is first-class. Claire Bloom plays the "other woman" with a neat variation of bite and comehitherness. Gary Raymond makes an instant impact as the cosy, kindly friend of the unhappy couple.

•

LOOKER
1981, 94 mins, US Ⓥ ⦿ ▭ col
Dir Michael Crichton ***Prod*** Howard Jeffrey ***Scr*** Michael Crichton ***Ph*** Paul Lohmann ***Ed*** Carl Kress ***Mus*** Barry DeVorzon ***Art*** Dean Edward Mitzner
Act Albert Finney, James Coburn, Susan Dey, Leigh Taylor-Young, Tim Rossovich, Darryl Hickman (Ladd/Warner)

Writer-director Michael Crichton has used interesting material, public manipulation by computer-generated TV commercials, to create *Looker*, a silly and unconvincing contempo sci-fi thriller.

Albert Finney, sporting a neutral American accent, heads the cast as Dr. Larry Roberts, a leading Los Angeles plastic surgeon being set up as the fall guy in a string of murders of beautiful models who happen to be his patients. Bypassing the police detective (Dorian Harewood) on the case, Roberts teams with model Cindy (Susan Dey) to track down the real killers, with Cindy infiltrating a suspicious research institute run by Jennifer Long (Leigh Taylor-Young) as part of the conglomerate Reston Industries headed by John Reston (James Coburn).

Long has been developing the perfect TV commercials, using plastic surgery–augmented beautiful women as models and expanding into computer-generated simulation techniques. Reston has used these experiments to go beyond subliminal advertising to create hypnotic messages that can sell products or even political candidates.

With numerous lapses in credibility, Crichton falls back upon motifs better used in his *Westworld* picture: computer simulations (for robots), TV blurb soundstages (for film backlots), and assorted fancy chases.

●

LOOKING FOR MR. GOODBAR

1977, 135 mins, US Ⓥ ⦿ col

Dir Richard Brooks ***Prod*** Freddie Fields ***Scr*** Richard Brooks ***Ph*** William A. Fraker ***Ed*** George Grenville ***Mus*** Artie Kane ***Art*** Edward Carfagno

Act Diane Keaton, Tuesday Weld, William Atherton, Richard Kiley, Richard Gere, Tom Berenger (Paramount)

In *Looking for Mr. Goodbar*, writer-director Richard Brooks manifests his ability to catch accurately both the tone and subtlety of characters in the most repellant environments—in this case the desperate search for personal identity in the dreary and self-defeating world of compulsive sex and dope. Diane Keaton's performance as the good/bad girl is excellent.

Judith Rossner's novel was the basis for Brooks's fine screenplay about a girl who flees from a depressing home environment into the frantic world of singles bars and one-night physical gropings. The Jekyll-Hyde character caroms from sincere concern for teaching children to night-crawling of the seamiest sort.

At its best, the film, through Tuesday Weld's great performance as Keaton's sister who wanders from trend to trend, suggests dimly some alternatives.

1977: NOMINATIONS: Best Supp. Actress (Tuesday Weld), Cinematography

●

LOOKING FOR RICHARD

1996, 109 mins, US Ⓥ col

Dir Al Pacino ***Prod*** Michael Hadge, Al Pacino ***Scr*** Al Pacino, Frederic Kimball ***Ph*** Robert Leacock, Nina Kedrem, John Kranhouse, Steve Confer ***Ed*** Pasquale Buba, William A. Anderson, Ned Bastille, Andre Betz ***Mus*** Howard Shore ***Art*** Kevin Ritter

Act Al Pacino, Harris Yulin, Penelope Allen, Alec Baldwin, Kevin Spacey, Estelle Parsons (Jam)

High-spirited and infectiously energetic, Al Pacino's *Looking for Richard* is a master class in Shakespeare and acting conducted by an uncommonly passionate and delightful teacher. Ranging from New York's streets to the reconstructed Globe Theater in London, Pacino is the voluble, mercurial center of a film that ingeniously interweaves commentary on Shakespeare with analysis of, rehearsals for, and key segments from a *Richard III* on film.

Pic's initial section registers some of the barriers to general appreciation as Pacino, wearing a backward baseball cap and quizzical expression, samples man-in-the-street opinions as to the off-putting difficulties of Shakespeare's 16th-century lingo. Pic also registers its challenges for American actors who, as John Gielgud notes, often don't grow up experiencing the books and museums that provide the literature's cultural context.

Yet Pacino draws in scholars as well as other actors to elucidate the War of the Roses and other elements of the historical backdrop. Watching topnotch actors grapple with these roles gives both the history and the literature a vivid immediacy.

Key scenes offer a surprisingly complete sense of the drama's trajectory. Richard seduces Lady Anne (Winona Ryder) with his bold lies; Clarence (Alec Baldwin) meets his pathetic end; Richard uses, then abandons, Buckingham (Kevin Spacey); and, finally, Richard faces his own doom in the form of Richmond (Aidan Quinn).

What starts as history lessons and rehearsals has, by its end, left behind all intellectual props and achieved a magnificent emotional force.

●

LOOKING GLASS WAR, THE

1970, 106 mins, UK Ⓥ ▭ col

Dir Frank Pierson ***Prod*** John Box ***Scr*** Frank Pierson ***Ph*** Austin Dempster ***Ed*** Willy Kemplen ***Mus*** Wally Stott ***Art*** Terence Marsh

Act Christopher Jones, Pia Degermark, Ralph Richardson, Paul Rogers, Anthony Hopkins, Susan George (Columbia/Frankovich)

Based on the John Le Carré novel about Cold War espionage, *The Looking Glass War* is most notable as the feature directorial debut of writer Frank Pierson.

Christopher Jones and Pia Degermark head a featured cast that also includes excellent performances by Ralph Richardson and Paul Rogers. Jones, a ship-jumping Polish seaman, is recruited by Richardson and Rogers, two old hands in British espionage, to enter East Germany to verify some missile sites.

Anthony Hopkins, a younger undercover agent, is a key character as he shares many youthful reservations in an atmosphere charged with memories of an earlier, simpler spy game.

Pierson's adaptation has some superior dialog and structuring.

●

LOOKIN' TO GET OUT

1982, 104 mins, US Ⓥ col

Dir Hal Ashby ***Prod*** Robert Schaffel ***Scr*** Al Schwartz, Jon Voight ***Ph*** Haskell Wexler ***Ed*** Robert C. Jones ***Mus*** Johnny Mandel ***Art*** Robert Boyle

Act Jon Voight, Ann-Margret, Burt Young, Bert Remsen, Jude Farese, Allen Keller (Northstar International/Lorimar)

Hal Ashby's *Lookin' to Get Out* is an ill-conceived vehicle for actor (and cowriter) Jon Voight to showcase his character comedy talents in a loose, semi-improvised environment.

Alex (Jon Voight) and Jerry (Burt Young) are the central figures, who flee New York to Las Vegas to escape thugs Harry (Jude Farese) and Joey (Allen Keller) whose $10,000 Alex has dropped in a poker game. In an increasingly contrived and unconvincing series of coincidences and turns of luck, duo set up shop in the *Doctor Zhivago* suite of the M-G-M Grand Hotel and use a false identity to obtain unlimited credit from the casino.

Occasionally amusing, picture often has the feel of being improvised, with director Ashby giving Voight a loose rein to inject physical business and odd dialog into a scene. Interplay between Voight and Young is the film's raison d'etre.

●

LOOKS AND SMILES

1983, 104 mins, UK b/w

Dir Ken Loach ***Prod*** Irving Teitelbaum ***Scr*** Barry Hines ***Ph*** Chris Menges ***Art*** Martin Johnson

Act Graham Green, Carolyn Nicholson, Tony Pitts, Phil Askham, Cilla Mason, Arthur Davies (Black Lion/Kestrel/MK2)

Ken Loach's *Looks and Smiles* is a somber but dramatically right tale of teenagers running into unemployment and broken families in a northern industrial town. The three protagonists are played by non-pros, and very well too.

Mick, played like a young James Cagney by Graham Green, cannot find a mechanical job he covets and spends his time getting into fights. He meets Karen (Carolyn Nicholson) and something develops, but is stymied by his love for soccer, his joblessness, and own problems of divorced parents. Mick's friend, Alan (Tony Pitts), joins the army and gets sent to Ireland and comes home at times with gory tales.

The film certainly has a feel for its characters and place, helped by a sharply dramatic use of b&w lensing, which fits the milieu and theme.

●

LOOK WHO'S TALKING

1989, 90 mins, US Ⓥ ⦿ col

Dir Amy Heckerling ***Prod*** Jonathan D. Krane ***Scr*** Amy Heckerling ***Ph*** Thomas Del Ruth ***Ed*** Debra Chiate ***Mus*** David Kitay ***Art*** Graeme Murray

Act John Travolta, Kirstie Alley, Olympia Dukakis, George Segal, Abe Vigoda, Bruce Willis (Tri-Star/MCEG)

Like a standup comic pouring "flopsweat," this ill-conceived comedy about an infant whose thoughts are given voice by actor Bruce Willis palpitates with desperation. *Look Who's Voice-Overing* would be a far more appropriate moniker, as Willis isn't heard by the film's other characters.

The camera simply hones in on one of the four strikingly dissimilar babies who play the leading role, and Willis lets fly with asides to match their "cute" expressions.

Kirstie Alley does the best she can as the child's mother—an accountant whose married boyfriend (George Segal) gets her pregnant. Convinced he'll leave his wife for her and the child, she spurns the attention of the sweet, earnest cab driver (John Travolta) who helped her at the hospital when she was going into labor.

●

LOOK WHO'S TALKING NOW

1993, 97 mins, US Ⓥ ⦿ col

Dir Tom Ropelewski ***Prod*** Jonathan D. Krane ***Scr*** Tom Ropelewski, Leslie Dixon ***Ph*** Oliver Stapleton ***Ed*** Michael A. Stevenson, Harry Hitner ***Mus*** William Ross ***Art*** Michael Bolton

Act John Travolta, Kirstie Alley, Olympia Dukakis, Lysette Anthony, David Gallagher, Tabitha Lupien (Tri-Star)

Stretching a premise that one might say has gone to the dogs, *Look Who's Talking Now* runs feebly on the calculated steam of its forebears. Once again, pic derives yuks from wisecracking inner monologues of non-talking characters. First, it was the baby boy, then the baby girl. Now, it's the dogs. What's next, the refrigerator? Still, scripters find droll if not witty voices in Danny DeVito's street-smart mutt and Diane Keaton's prissy poodle.

Taxi driver James (John Travolta) and wife Mollie (Kirstie Alley) decide to buy a pooch from the pound for their curious child, Mikey (David Gallagher). Meantime, James's new boss, the sultry, corporate Samantha D'Bonne (Lysette Anthony), dumps her over-coiffed poodle on James's children before making a serious seduction play for him. Somehow, through it all, the dogs save the day.

Reprising their original roles, Travolta and Alley are serviceable. Gallagher and newcomer 5-year-old Tabitha Lupien tap the cute-deviant-lovable formula that Hollywood demands for kids.

●

LOOK WHO'S TALKING TOO

1990, 81 mins, US Ⓥ ⦿ col

Dir Amy Heckerling ***Prod*** Jonathan D. Krane ***Scr*** Amy Heckerling, Neal Israel ***Ph*** Thomas Del Ruth ***Ed*** Debra Chiate ***Mus*** David Kitay, Maureen Crowe ***Art*** Reuben Freed

Act John Travolta, Kirstie Alley, Olympia Dukakis, Elias Koteas, Twink Caplan, Neal Israel (Tri-Star)

This vulgar sequel to 1989's longest-running sleeper hit looks like a rush job. Joined by her husband Neal Israel (who also appears as star Kirstie Alley's mean boss) in the scripting, filmmaker Amy Heckerling overemphasizes toilet humor and expletives to make the film appealing mainly to adolescents rather than an across-the-board family audience. Unwed mom Alley and cabbie John Travolta are married for the sequel, with her cute son Mikey metamorphosed into Lorne Sussman, still voice-overed as precocious by Bruce Willis. First mutual arrival is undeniably cute Megan Milner, unfortunately voiced-over by Roseanne Barr. Comedienne gets a couple of laughs but is generally dull, leaving Willis again to carry the load in the gag department with well-read quips.

Plot line revolves around the bickering of Alley and Travolta whose jobs (accountant and would-be airline pilot) and personalities clash, as well as the rites of passage of the two kids. New characters, notably Alley's obnoxious brother Elias Koteas, are added to ill effect. Mel Brooks is enlisted to voice-over Mr. Toilet Man, a fantasy bathroom bowl come to life, spitting blue water and anxious to bite off Mikey's privates.

●

LOOPHOLE

1981, 105 mins, UK Ⓥ col

Dir John Quested ***Prod*** David Korda, Julian Holloway ***Scr*** Jonathan Hales ***Ph*** Michael Reed ***Ed*** Ralph Sheldon ***Mus*** Lalo Schifrin ***Art*** Syd Cain

Act Albert Finney, Martin Sheen, Susannah York, Colin Blakely, Jonathan Pryce, Robert Morley (Brent Walker)

A clever plan to knock off a rich London bank is about the only thing that works in *Loophole*. The caper, filmed in and around the British capital, squanders some fine talent on a trite, low-voltage script.

Albert Finney as the mastermind of the heist, and Martin Sheen as an honest architect who lends the gang his talents in order to bail himself out of hock to his own bank, perform okay with little room to flex their histrionic skills.

As scripted from a Robert Pollock novel, the plot isn't exactly mint new, with Finney & Co utilizing the rat infested sewer tunnels under mid-town London for access to and getaway from the bank's vault. A downpour almost wreaks its own brand of providential justice in the only sequence with any kind of charge for action or suspense fans.

●

LOOSE CANNONS

1990, 93 mins, US Ⓥ ⦿ col

Dir Bob Clark ***Prod*** Aaron Spelling, Alan Greisman ***Scr*** Richard Christian Matheson, Richard Matheson, Bob Clark ***Ph*** Reginald H. Morris ***Ed*** Stan Cole ***Mus*** Paul Zaza ***Art*** Harry Pottle

Act Gene Hackman, Dan Aykroyd, Dom DeLuise, Ronny Cox, Nancy Travis, Paul Koslo (Tri-Star)

Dan Aykroyd's dexterous multipersonality schtick is the only redeeming feature of this chase-heavy comedy, up on the homevid heap.

Director Bob Clark manages to make his low-brow comedy *Porky's* look like *Amadeus* with this latest salvo into the police-buddy genre, while Gene Hackman continues his befuddling penchant for sprinkling his overflowing resume with shameful losers.

Loose Cannons may be best remembered for its unbelievably convoluted screenplay—a concoction of elements from *Lethal Weapon 2*, *Midnight Run* and *Beverly Hills Cop*, all played at the speed of Warner Bros cartoon. Plot involves gruesome murders, a secret 45-year-old porno film, a candidate for the chancellorship of West Germany and a horde of Uzi-brandishing neo-Nazis. All of that is irrelevant to the main plot, which pairs the gruff Mac (Hackman) with the Sybil-like Ellis (Aykroyd)—recently (and apparently prematurely) reactivated by his police-captain uncle after suffering a nervous breakdown that causes him to lapse into multiple personalities.

•

LOOSE CONNECTIONS

1983, 99 mins, UK Ⓥ col

Dir Richard Eyre ***Prod*** Simon Perry ***Scr*** Maggie Brooks ***Ph*** Clive Tickner ***Ed*** David Martin ***Mus*** Dominic Muldowney, Andy Roberts

Act Stephen Rea, Lindsay Duncan, Jan Niklas, Carole Harrison, Gary Olsen, Frances Low (Umbrella/Greenpoint)

Richard Eyre's second theatrical feature is an exceedingly amiable comic battle of the sexes.

Sally (Lindsay Duncan), together with two girlfriends, has built a jeep in which to drive from London to a feminist conference in Munich, but at the last moment she is left on her own. She takes a newspaper ad for a fellow driver, seeking a female non-smoking vegetarian, who speaks German and knows something about car engines. The only applicant is Harry (Stephen Rea), who claims to fill all the requirements except sex, and furthermore claims he's gay. Needless to say, Harry's a liar. The trip to Munich is one comic disaster after another. But the odd couple are drawn to each other, and the inevitable happens.

Both roles are played to perfection. It's not a film of hearty laughs, but of continual quiet chuckles.

•

LOOT

1970, 101 mins, UK Ⓥ col

Dir Silvio Narizzano ***Prod*** Arthur Lewis ***Scr*** Ray Galton, Alan Simpson ***Ph*** Austin Dempster ***Ed*** Martin Charles ***Mus*** Keith Mansfield, Richard Willing-Denton ***Art*** Anthony Pratt

Act Richard Attenborough, Lee Remick, Hywel Bennett, Roy Holder, Milo O'Shea, Dick Emery (British Lion)

Joe Orton's macabre black comedy has transferred uneasily to the screen, the opening-out in the script having robbed the yarn of much of its comic tension. Nevertheless, it has enough speed, inventiveness, and sharp, acid, irreverent comedy to satisfy many.

Story has Hywel Bennett and Roy Holder as two shiftless chums who, anxious to get rich quick, decide to blow a bank. They pull off the raid and elect to hide the loot in the coffin of Holder's mother, who has conveniently died. But there's no room for the cash and the corpse, so the poor woman's hidden in the lavatory.

The hotel belonging to Holder's father (Milo O'Shea) becomes a bedlam of frenzied rushing around, complicated by the arrival of an eccentric, pompous and venal inspector (Richard Attenborough) and Lee Remick, as a gold-digging sexpot of a private nurse.

Attenborough appears to be trying far too hard to get his effects. O'Shea is amiably amusing and bewildered. Remick is coolly efficient as the femme fatale, and Bennett and Holder keep their body- and loot-snatching roles to a high pitch of energetic activity.

•

LORD JIM

1965, 154 mins, UK/US Ⓥ ▭ col

Dir Richard Brooks ***Prod*** Richard Brooks ***Scr*** Richard Brooks ***Ph*** Freddie Young ***Ed*** Alan Osbiston ***Mus*** Bronislau Kaper ***Art*** Geoffrey Drake

Act Peter O'Toole, James Mason, Curt Jurgens, Jack Hawkins, Eli Wallach, Daliah Lavi (Columbia/Keep)

Many may be disappointed with Richard Brooks's handling of the Joseph Conrad novel. The storyline is often confused, some of the more interesting characters emerge merely as shadowy sketches. Brooks, while capturing the spirit of adventure of the novel, only superficially catches the inner emotional and spiritual conflict of its hero. In this he is not overly helped by Peter O'Toole, whose performance is self-indulgent and lacking in real depth.

The story concerns a young merchant seaman. In a moment of cowardice he deserts his ship during a storm and his life is dogged throughout by remorse and an urge to redeem himself. His search for a second chance takes him to South Asia. There he becomes the conquering hero of natives oppressed by a fanatical warlord.

Brooks has teetered between making it a full-blooded, no-holds-barred adventure yarn and the fascinating psychological study that Conrad wrote. O'Toole, though a fine, handsome figure of a man, goes through the film practically expressionless and the audience sees little of the character's introspection and soul searching.

Of the rest of the cast the two who stand out, mainly because they are provided with the best opportunities, are Eli Wallach and Paul Lukas.

•

LORD LOVE A DUCK

1966, 105 mins, US b/w

Dir George Axelrod ***Prod*** George Axelrod ***Scr*** Larry H. Johnson, George Axelrod ***Ph*** Daniel L. Fapp ***Ed*** William A. Lyon ***Mus*** Neal Hefti ***Art*** Malcolm Brown

Act Roddy McDowall, Tuesday Weld, Lola Albright, Martin West, Ruth Gordon, Harvey Korman (Charleston/United Artists)

Some may call George Axelrod's *Lord Love a Duck* satire, others way-out comedy, still others brilliant, while there may be some who ask, what's it all about?

Whatever the reaction, there is no question that the film [based on Al Hire's novel] is packed with laughs, often of the truest anatomical kind, and there is a veneer of sophistication that keeps showing despite the most outlandish goings-on. Some of the comedy is inspirational, a gagman's dream come true, and there is bite in some of Axelrod's social commentary beneath the wonderful nonsense.

The characters are everything here, each developed brightly along zany lines, topped by Roddy McDowall as a Svengali-type high school student leader who pulls the strings on the destiny of Tuesday Weld, an ingenuish-type sexpot whose philosophy is wrapped up in her words "Everybody's got to love me."

McDowall is in good form as the mastermind of the school, and he has a strong contender for interest in blonde Weld in a characterization warm and appealing. Scoring almost spectacularly is Lola Albright as Weld's mother, a cocktail bar "bunny" who commits suicide when she thinks she's ruined her daughter's chances for marriage.

•

LORD OF ILLUSIONS

1995, 108 mins, US Ⓥ ⊙ col

Dir Clive Barker ***Prod*** JoAnne Sellar, Clive Barker ***Scr*** Clive Barker ***Ph*** Ronn Schmidt ***Ed*** Alan Baumgarten ***Mus*** Simon Boswell ***Art*** Stephen Hardie

Act Scott Bakula, Kevin J. O'Connor, Famke Janssen, Vincent Schiavelli, Barry Del Sherman, Shelie Tousey (Seraphim/United Artists)

Horror novelist and filmmaker Clive Barker offers a potent mix of H. P. Lovecraft and Raymond Chandler in *Lord of Illusions*. Barker has toned down the full-bore gore of his earlier directorial efforts. Even so, there's still enough gruesome stuff here to delight genre fans and unsettle everybody else.

Loosely based on Barker's 1985 short story *The Last Illusion*, *Lord* features Scott Bakula as Harry D'Amour, a New York-based p.i. who has reappeared in several subsequent stories and novels by Barker. Like the original tale, pic introduces D'Amour as a hard-boiled but humane shamus who periodically encounters the supernatural in his work.

While on a routine case in L.A., D'Amour runs across cultists who want to revive their spiritual leader. Prologue reveals how, 13 years earlier, the diabolic Nix (Daniel Von Bargen) was dispatched by Philip Swann (Kevin J. O'Connor), a former acolyte who learned much of Nix's black magic. Dorothea Swann (Famke Janssen) hires D'Amour to look after her husband because she's worried about his safety.

Bakula proves to be an inspired choice to play D'Amour. His virile good looks, low-key humor, and matter-of-fact authority make him an engaging Everyman. Janssen is beautiful and believable as Barker's version of a femme fatale. Vincent Schiavelli is aptly fustian as a rival magician jealous of Swann's success, while Von Bargen is effectively malevolent as Nix. The craftsmen responsible for the grisly makeup and special effects perform far beyond the call of duty.

•

LORD OF THE FLIES

1963, 90 mins, UK Ⓥ b/w

Dir Peter Brook ***Prod*** Lewis Allen, Gerald Feil, Jean-Claude Lubtchansky ***Scr*** Peter Brook ***Ph*** Tom Hollyman ***Ed*** Peter Brook ***Mus*** Raymond Leppard ***Art*** [uncredited]

Act James Aubrey, Tom Chapin, Hugh Emwards, Roger Elwin, Tom Gaman (Two Arts)

The theme of young boys reverting to savagery when marooned on a deserted island has its moments of truth, but this pic rates as a near-miss on many counts.

Titles adequately indicate that evacuation in some future war has a group of youngsters surviving an air crash on a tropical island. They meet, and one boy is elected chief, but with dissent from another. Latter says his group will become hunters and they are soon drawing blood from some wild pigs and evolving tales of a monster on the island. The last-named is a dead paratrooper swaying on a ledge. But soon the hunting group goes completely native and persecutes and even exterminates those of the other group.

Peter Brook has coaxed fairly natural performances from his group of English youths. But he has drawn out his tale on a seemingly too schematic level to emerge more an illustration of the William Golding best-selling book than a film version standing on its own.

Lensing is curiously metallic but the on-the-spot shooting in the Puerto Rican jungles and beaches helps. Pic was made with U.S. and Puerto Rican funds but with a British director and thesps.

•

LORD OF THE FLIES

1990, 90 mins, US Ⓥ ⊙ col

Dir Harry Hook ***Prod*** Ross Milloy, David V. Lester ***Scr*** Sara Schiff ***Ph*** Martin Fuhrer ***Ed*** Tom Priestley ***Mus*** Philippe Sarde ***Art*** Jamie Leonard

Act Balthazar Getty, Chris Furth, Danuel Pipoly, Badgett Dale, Edward Taft, Andrew Taft (Jack's Camp/Signal Hill)

The notion that the story of civilized boys reverting to savagery on a desert isle would be improved by shooting in color and substituting American actors for British child thesps is an odd one indeed.

Peter Brook's black and white version of William Golding's *Lord of the Flies* is no classic, but it stands miles above this thoroughly undistinguished and unnecessary remake. Lewis Allen, one of the producers of the earlier version and exec producer of the remake with Peter Newman, made this film "to protect the first film and to prevent television movie-of-the-week imitations after Golding received the Nobel Prize for literature."

Here, director Harry Hook's literal, unimaginative visual approach makes the tale seem mundane and tedious.

The flat screenplay makes all the boys seem like dullards and does little to help differentiate the cast members, most of whom seem cut from the same mold, of bland cuteness. Nor do these boys seem to be living through the kind of gritty physical experience that would make the allegory spring to life.

•

LORD OF THE RINGS, THE

1978, 131 mins, US Ⓥ col

Dir Ralph Bakshi ***Prod*** Saul Zaentz ***Scr*** Chris Conkling, Peter S. Beagle ***Mus*** Leonard Rosenman

(Fantasy)

Students of animated technique and Tolkien storytelling will find a lot to like in what Ralph Bakshi has done with *Lord of the Rings*. Unquestionably, Bakshi has perfected some outstanding pen-and-ink effects while translating faithfully a portion of J.R.R. Tolkien's trilogy. But in his concentration on craft and duty to the original story—both admirable in themselves—Bakshi overlooks the uninitiated completely.

Quite simply, those who do not know the characters of Middle Earth going in will not know them coming out. The introductory narration explaining the Rings is confusing, making the rest of the quest seem pointless in many places. Boring is an equally good word, especially toward the end of two hours.

•

LORDS OF DISCIPLINE, THE

1983, 102 mins, US Ⓥ ⊙ col

Dir Franc Roddam ***Prod*** Herb Jaffe, Gabriel Katzka ***Scr*** Thomas Pope, Lloyd Fonvielle ***Ph*** Brian Tufano ***Ed*** Michael Ellis ***Mus*** Howard Blake ***Art*** John Graysmark

Act David Keith, Robert Prosky, G. D. Spradlin, Barbara Babcock, Michael Biehn, Rick Rossovich (Paramount)

The Lords of Discipline laces a military school Watergate saga with heavy doses of sadism, racism, and macho bullying. Designed as an exposé of the corruption to be found within the hallowed walls of a venerable American institution, pic wants to have it both ways.

Set around 1964, drama follows cadet David Keith through his senior year at the Carolina Military Institute. Year in question is a notable one for the school because the first black cadet in its history has been enrolled.

As far as the new recruits are concerned, the poop hits the fan on "hell night," which is just as bad as it sounds. With the full sanction of the faculty, upper classmen are permitted, even encouraged, to turn strong young men into oatmeal, running them through an evening of physical horrors under the guise of building character. One boy dies as a result, which leads outsider type Keith onto the existence of The Ten, a secret society to ferret out undesirables.

British director Franc Roddam had to wait over three years to make his American directorial debut and, ironically, ended up doing most of this film in Britain when no U.S. school would allow lensing on its grounds.

•

LORD'S OF FLATBUSH, THE
1974, 86 mins, US Ⓥ ⦿ col
Dir Stephen Verona, Martin Davidson ***Prod*** Stephen Verona ***Scr*** Stephen Verona, Gayle Gleckler, Martin Davidson ***Ph*** Joseph Mangine, Edward Lachman ***Ed*** Stan Siegel, Muffie Meyer ***Mus*** Joe Brooks ***Art*** Glenda Miller
Act Perry King, Sylvester Stallone, Henry Winkler, Paul Mace, Susan Blakely, Maria Smith (Columbia)

Life among the leather-jacket high school set of Flatbush is the subject of this indie filmed in Brooklyn, NY, locale. Pic is episodic in narrative, particularly in first few reels burdened mostly by irrelevant action, but when actual story line is reached focuses on two of the members of a social club called Lord's of Flatbush.

Perry King and Sylvester Stallone play a couple of would-be toughies who occasionally leave their pals for some dating. Stallone's romancing leads to getting his pal (Maria Smith) pregnant, and King to getting the final brushoff from femme (Susan Blakely) he pursues. Not too much finesse distinguishes the script, which carries neither warmth nor particular interest for the various characters.

Both actors do well enough by their roles.

•

LORENZO'S OIL
1992, 135 mins, US Ⓥ ⦿ col
Dir George Miller ***Prod*** Doug Mitchell, George Miller ***Scr*** George Miller, Nick Enright ***Ph*** John Seale ***Ed*** Richard Francis-Bruce, Marcus D'Arcy, Lee Smith ***Mus*** Christine Woodruff (sup.) ***Art*** Kristi Zea
Act Nick Nolte, Susan Sarandon, Peter Ustinov, Kathleen Wilhoite, Gerry Bamman, Zack O'Malley Greenburg (Universal)

Lorenzo's Oil is as grueling a medical case study as any audience would ever want to sit through. A true-life story brought to the screen intelligently and with passionate motivation by George Miller, pic details in a very precise way how a couple raced time to save the life of their young son after he contracted a rare, always fatal disease. A practicing physician himself before forging his filmmaking career with the *Mad Max* actioners, Miller has, from all accounts, scrupulously adhered to the facts in relating the harrowing but inspiring tale of Augusto and Michaela Odone.

In 1984, their five-year-old son Lorenzo was diagnosed with adrenoleukodystrophy (ALD), a condition occurring only in boys that leads to seizures, paralysis, and, within two years, certain death. The Odones took it upon themselves to research the subject from scratch and try to find a cure for Lorenzo.

First section, which details the discovery of Lorenzo's ailment, is the most effective and visually striking. As the film progresses, however, its single-mindedness is such one is not surprised to see an 800 number for ALD info on the end credits, and some other elements have gotten out of hand or lost in the shuffle.

Among the irritants is an acting style that is generally cranked up to full throttle or beyond. As Augusto, Nick Nolte sports an accent unrecognizable until being identified as Italian. As Michaela, Susan Sarandon fares better, as she convincingly conveys a fierceness and tenacity that is almost frightening. The character never lets up, and neither does the film.

1992: NOMINATION: Best Actress (Susan Sarandon), Original Screenplay

•

LORNA
1965, 78 mins, US b/w
Dir Russ Meyer ***Prod*** Russ Meyer ***Scr*** James Griffith ***Ph*** Russ Meyer ***Ed*** Russ Meyer ***Mus*** Hal Hooper, James Griffith
Act Lorna Maitland, Mark Bradley, James Rucker, Hal Hooper, Doc Scortt, James Griffith (Eve)

A sort of sex morality play, *Lorna* is Russ Meyer's first serious effort after six nudie pix.

Myer's story concerns Lorna Maitland as the buxom wife of James Rucker, a handsome young clod who each day joins Hal Hopper and Doc Scortt in commuting to work at a salt mine. (Latter is not the first Biblical overtone, since Griffith portrays a firebrand preacher-Greek chorus who greets audience via clever subjective camera intro with ominous foreboding of sin and payment therefore.)

Mark Bradley, escaped con and vicious killer, encounters Maitland in the fields with predictable results, after which she takes him home for encores.

Maitland has a sensual voice although vocal projection is her least asset. Bradley has rugged looks, a voice to match, and a bigger future in films. His role requires expressions of fear, boredom, tenderness, and amoral viciousness, and he is up to them all. Griffith is a two-time loser, having overacted a trite part that he himself wrote.

•

LORNA DOONE
1934, 100 mins, UK b/w
Dir Basil Dean ***Prod*** [uncredited] ***Scr*** Dorothy Farnum, Gordon Wellesley ***Ph*** Robert G. Martin ***Ed*** Jack Kitchin ***Mus*** C. Armstrong Gibbs ***Art*** Edward Carrick
Act Victoria Hopper, John Loder, Mary Clare, Frank Cellier, Roy Emerton, George Curzon (Associated Talking)

Not a bad effort to make an artistic picture out of a book that is generally rated among the British fiction classics. At the same time, the attempt fails, and it fails because the producer, with all his soft focus photography and his studied use of excellent exterior backgrounds, failed to start off with a really first-class continuity, or else wandered away from it during production. The film has polish. But it lacks drama and grip.

Story on which the film is based tells how a famous family of rebels, the Doones, live in a Somerset valley, the terror of surrounding farms and settlements.

A boy, John Ridd, sees his father killed by the outlaws, and he grows up seeking vengeance, only to fall in love with the Doone daughter, Lorna. He takes her out of the valley and brings her back to his farmhouse. The Doones try and raid her back again. Just when it looks as though he has her for keeps, somebody trots in from the court at St. James, says she isn't a Doone at all.

Victoria Hopper is adequate as Lorna Doone, although she hardly satisfies the mental picture of the violet-eyed heroine.

•

LORNA DOONE
1951, 82 mins, US col
Dir Phil Karlson ***Prod*** Edward Small ***Scr*** Jesse L. Lasky, Jr., Richard Schayer ***Ph*** Charles Van Enger ***Ed*** Al Clark ***Mus*** George Duning
Act Barbara Hale, Richard Greene, Carl Benton Reid, William Bishop, Ron Randell, Sean McClory (Columbia)

This freely adapted [by George Bruce] film version of Richard D. Blackmore's classic is acceptable entertainment for the general market. Familiar plot is a mixture of action and romance against the outdoor beauties of rural England (as location filmed in Yosemite) back in the days of Charles II. It depicts the uprising of poor villagers and farmers, under the leadership of John Ridd (Richard Greene), against the oppression of an arrogant, titled family that ruthlessly rules its lands.

Ridd, who as a boy had lost his father to Doone cruelty, knows of a back entrance through a waterfall to the well-guarded castle high on a mountain overlooking the oppressed valley. Despite a number of slips and treachery, he is successful in leading his men into the castle, and the Doones are put down, leaving him free to marry Lorna (Barbara Hale) after it is proved she is not a Doone.

Hale and Green take to the period garb and settings neatly, and there is a good lineup of featured and supporting players to help bring the film off. Dialog is sometimes stilted, but general framework does a satisfactory job in setting up the heroics. Phil Karlson's direction spots a number of excellent chase and fight scenes to furnish a semblance of movement.

•

LOSERS, THE
1970, 95 mins, US Ⓥ col
Dir Jack Starrett ***Prod*** Joe Solomon ***Scr*** Alan Caillou ***Ph*** Nonong Rasca ***Ed*** James Moore ***Mus*** Stu Phillips
Act William Smith, Bernie Hamilton, Adam Roarke, Daniel Kemp, Houston Savage, Gene Cornelius (Fanfare)

Director Jack Starrett took his motley crew of actors to the Philippines, which is supposed to pass on the screen as Vietnam. The viewer is asked to believe that a contingent of motorcycle bums would be hired by the U.S. to rescue a CIA agent, held prisoner in Cambodia by the North Vietnamese or Red Chinese, but it's never really made clear.

The script is so inane, with not even a feeble attempt at logic, that what are intended as serious moments come off as funny.

Some of the acting is excellent—Bernie Hamilton makes his army captain a human being; Adam Roarke's Duke is better than the part deserves; Paul Koslo, as one of the cycle riders who falls for a native girl (Ana Korita) he meets in a brothel is very effective.

•

LOSING ISAIAH
1995, 106 mins, US Ⓥ col
Dir Stephen Gyllenhaal ***Prod*** Howard W. Koch, Jr., Naomi Foner ***Scr*** Naomi Foner ***Ph*** Andrzej Bartkowiak ***Ed*** Harvey Rosenstock ***Mus*** Mark Isham ***Art*** Jeannine C. Oppewall
Act Jessica Lange, Halle Berry, David Strathairn, Cuba Gooding, Jr., Daisy Eagan, Samuel L. Jackson (Paramount)

The material is emotionally wrenching, but the actors play sociopolitical totems more than flesh-and-blood characters in *Losing Isaiah*, a grimly serious, issue-oriented drama of custody battles between birth and adoptive parents.

With director Stephen Gyllenhaal almost hysterically overusing the camera crane and other visual hypos, the tragic scenario [from Seth Margolis's novel] is played out of Chicago ghetto fringe dweller Khaila Richards (Halle Berry) leaving her little boy in a trash heap in her haste to score another hit of crack. The tot is brought to health by medics and taken home by social worker Margaret Lewin (Jessica Lange), who lives in comfortable digs with hubby Charles (David Strathairn) and awkward-age daughter Hannah (Daisy Eagan).

By the time he's a toddler, little Isaiah (4-year-old Marc John Jefferies) has been officially adopted, as well as having become unbearably adorable despite his periodic, drug-related screaming fits.

Khaila, meanwhile, has gone through rehab, quickly tracks down the Lewins and makes brief contact with Isaiah. A lawyer, Kadar Lewis (Samuel L. Jackson), who specializes in making capital of race issues, tells Khaila she has a good case for asserting her maternal rights, and the battle is on.

Despite its problem-picture format and lack of character depth, film manages to pack a punch due to its subject and many intense scenes of emotional anguish. Lange's part basically calls upon her to be a confident and capable professional mom in the first part and a distraught basket case in the second.

Berry brings vibrancy, wariness, and determination to Khaila, making her credible, if not terribly sympathetic. By contrast, the adult male roles are poorly drawn. Behind-the-scenes contributions are top-drawer.

•

LOSIN' IT
1983, 104 mins, US Ⓥ ⦿ col
Dir Curtis Hanson ***Prod*** Bryan Gindoff, Hannah Hempstead ***Scr*** B.W.L. Norton ***Ph*** Gil Taylor ***Ed*** Richard Halsey ***Mus*** Ken Wannberg ***Art*** Robb Wilson King
Act Tom Cruise, Jackie Earle Haley, John Stockwell, Shelley Long, John P. Navin, Jr., Hector Elias (Embassy)

As often noted, the problem with porno is that there are only so many ways to show people having sex; the problem with films like *Losin'* is that there are only so many ways to show teenagers not having sex. But director Curtis Hanson makes a commendable effort with a rather obvious story about three teenage boys who head for a wild weekend in Tijuana, hoping to trade hard cash for manly experience.

Though none is really very experienced, each is sophisticated to a stereotyped degree. There's the high-school hunk (John Stockwell), who's actually had a girl; the blustering faker (Jackie Earle Haley), whose experience is limited to his own imagination; and the sensitive innocent (Tom Cruise), who isn't sure he wants it, but is destined for the best time to be had by all.

Naturally, they are accompanied by wimpy John P. Navin, Jr., brought along only because he has the necessary cash to make the trip possible. And along the way they pick up crazy—but nice—Shelley Long, on the lam from her husband.

This doesn't sound like much and it isn't, but the picture is a solid credit for all involved.

•

LOSS OF INNOCENCE
SEE: THE GREENGAGE SUMMER

•

LOST ANGEL
1944, 91 mins, US b/w
Dir Roy Rowland ***Prod*** Robert Sisk ***Scr*** Isobel Lennart ***Ph*** Robert Surtees ***Ed*** Frank Hull ***Mus*** Daniele Amfitheatrof ***Art*** Cedric Gibbons, Lynden Sparhawk
Act Margaret O'Brien, James Craig, Marsha Hunt, Keenan Wynn (M-G-M)

Lost Angel reveals Margaret O'Brien as a foundling picked up by a group of scientists as the subject for experiment in human behaviour. A genius at the age of six, the human element, however, has been overlooked. But then a police reporter (James Craig) is assigned to check on the prodigy, and the rest chiefly concerns a rehabilitation to her innate child consciousness with Craig as her tutor. There's a gangster angle brought in but only incidentally.

Roy Rowland intelligently directs the moppet, and his ability to keep the more implausible moments down to a minimum is worthy of note. Isobel Lennart's scripting [from an idea by Angna Enters] also fits nicely into the child characterization.

Craig is satisfying as the reporter. Marsha Hunt helps supply the slight love interest (with Craig) in nice fashion. Keenan Wynn, as a mobster, chips in with a neat characterization.

•

LOST ANGELS
(AKA: THE ROAD HOME)
1989, 116 mins, US Ⓥ ⦿ ▭ col
Dir Hugh Hudson ***Prod*** Howard Rosenman, Thomas Baer ***Scr*** Michael Weller ***Ph*** Juan Ruiz-Anchia ***Ed*** David Gladwell ***Mus*** Philippe Sarde ***Art*** Assheton Gorton
Act Donald Sutherland, Adam Horovitz, Amy Locane, Don Bloomfield, Celia Weston (Orion)

Lost Angels suffers from some of the communication problems that bedevil its young, inarticulate hero. Hugh Hudson's wannabe *Rebel Without a Cause* update tries to be a serious exploration of throwaway middle-class teens in the San Fernando Valley, but despite some gripping moments it's often clichéd and incoherent.

Adam Horovitz of the Beastie Boys rap band has a sympathetic presence but not enough to do as the troubled lead.

It's another of those films about mental illness that tries to have it both ways, perhaps for fear of turning off the audience by presenting a lead who is truly disturbed.

The film powerfully conveys the latent violence just below the brooding surface of Horovitz's quiet demeanor. Whether it's the prelude to a freakout as he learns he's being locked up, or a fistfight with shrink Donald Sutherland, or a nightmarish violence-seeking trip to a Latino area, Horovitz has the ability to impersonate a stick of dynamite. Sutherland brings subtlety to his occasional scenes as a scruffy shrink who has enough emotional problems to be empathetic.

•

LOST BOYS, THE
1987, 92 mins, US Ⓥ ⦿ ▭ col
Dir Joel Schumacher ***Prod*** Harvey Bernhard ***Scr*** Janice Fischer, James Jeremias, Jeffrey Boam ***Ph*** Michael Chapman ***Ed*** Robert Brown ***Mus*** Thomas Newman ***Art*** Bo Welch
Act Jason Patric, Corey Haim, Dianne Wiest, Barnard Hughes, Kiefer Sutherland, Jami Gertz (Warner)

The Lost Boys is a horrifically dreadful vampire teensploitation entry [story by Janice Fischer and James Jeremias] that daringly advances the theory that all those missing children pictured on garbage bags and milk cartons are actually the victims of bloodsucking bikers.

Arriving in a Santa Cruz–like community that is dominated by a huge amusement park, Dianne Wiest and her sons check in at grandpa's creepy house, and the boys quickly fall in with the wrong crowd.

Latter includes some unhealthy looking punks, led by Kiefer Sutherland, who take older brother Jason Patric back to their lair and through the foxy but wasted Jami Gertz, tempt him into the ways of the undead. Getting wind of the vampire problem, little brother Corey Haim teams up with two pint-sized Rambos to combat the plague on their houses, and it all ends in a colossal battle with bats, punks, froth, spears, and blood flying through the air in a frenzy of nonsensical action.

•

LOST COMMAND
1966, 129 mins, US Ⓥ ▭ col
Dir Mark Robson ***Prod*** Mark Robson ***Scr*** Nelson Gidding ***Ph*** Robert Surtees ***Ed*** Dorothy Spencer ***Mus*** Franz Waxman ***Art*** John Stoll
Act Anthony Quinn, Alain Delon, George Segal, Michele Morgan, Maurice Ronet, Claudia Cardinale (Columbia)

Lost Command is a good contemporary action-melodrama about some French paratroopers who survive France's humiliation and defeat in Southeast Asia, only to be sent to rebellious Algeria. Filmed in Spain, the Mark Robson production [based on a novel by Jean Larteguy] has enough pace, action, and exterior eye appeal to overcome a sometimes routine script. Anthony Quinn heads the players as the gruff, low-born soldier who has risen to field grade rank because of the attrition of Indo-Chinese guerrilla warfare, which decimated the ranks of the French army.

Providing a two-way contrast, and exemplifying the extremes to which the Quinn character never extends, are Alain Delon and Maurice Ronet. Delon is the sensitive, quiet but effective assistant who, at fadeout, leaves military service, since fighting in itself has become meaningless. Ronet is brutal, sadistic, and callous, yet with enough fighting effectiveness to be needed in battle.

This very meaty and pathetic plot irony will strike some as underdeveloped, in that Quinn and Segal never effect a personal confrontation until latter is needlessly killed by Ronet, but by then it is too late.

•

LOST HIGHWAY
1997, 135 mins, France/US Ⓥ ⦿ ▭ col
Dir David Lynch ***Prod*** Deepak Nayar, Tom Sternberg ***Scr*** David Lynch, Barry Gifford ***Ph*** Peter Deming ***Ed*** Mary Sweeney ***Mus*** Angelo Badalamenti, Barry Adamson ***Art*** Patricia Norris
Act Bill Pullman, Patricia Arquette, Balthazar Getty, Robert Blake, Natasha Gregson Wagner, Richard Pryor (CiBy 2000/Asymetrical)

Lost Highway is a mysterious, ultra-Lynchian exercise in Designer Noir. The cult filmmaker's first feature in more than four years [since *Twin Peaks: Fire Walk with Me*, 1992] sees him traversing familiar roads involving weird crimes, bizarre sex, sometimes freakish characters, societal unease and fully warranted paranoia with panache and daring. But there remains a nagging sense of a work not quite completely achieved.

In a city resembling Los Angeles but never specified as such, tenor sax player Fred (Bill Pullman) and his wife, Renee (Patricia Arquette), see their life destroyed through a disturbing series of events. Fred is convicted of first-degree murder and sentenced to die in the electric chair.

In the film's great jump into the unexplainable, a young man named Pete (Balthazar Getty) is suddenly occupying Fred's cell, only to emerge and take up his work as a garage mechanic in the employ of a wheelchair-bound boss, Arnie (Richard Pryor). The film's two story strands [eventually come] full circle, after a fashion.

The narrative strategies of Lynch and coscreenwriter Barry Gifford, who penned the novel *Wild at Heart*, create intentional mysteries for which there are no answers, making this a dream-film that will leave its partisans attempting to puzzle out its mysteries and non-fans out in the cold. In the Lynch canon, it stands squarely in the middle. Dramatically, film verges on the lethargic at times. Performances tend toward the low-key.

•

LOST HORIZON
1937, 125 mins, US Ⓥ ⦿ b/w
Dir Frank Capra ***Prod*** Frank Capra ***Scr*** Robert Riskin ***Ph*** Joseph Walker ***Ed*** Gene Havlick, Gene Milford ***Mus*** Dimitri Tiomkin ***Art*** Stephen Goosson
Act Ronald Colman, Edward Everett Horton, H. B. Warner, Jane Wyatt, Sam Jaffe, Margo (Columbia)

So canny are the ingredients that where credulity perhaps rears its practical head, audiences will be carried away by the histrionic illusion, skill, and general Hollywood legerdemain that so effectively capture the best elements in this $2.5 million saga of Shangri-La. Ronald Colman, with fine restraint, conveys the metamorphosis of the foreign diplomat falling in with the Arcadian idyll that he beholds in the Valley of the Blue Moon.

Sam Jaffe is capital as the ancient Belgian priest who first founded Shangri-La some 300 years ago—a Methuselah who is still alive, thanks to the Utopian philosophy of the community he has nurtured.

As H. B. Warner (the venerable Chang and oldest disciple of the High Lama) expounds it, the peaceful valley's philosophy of moderation in work, food, drink, pleasure, acquisition, and all other earthly wants, is cannily scripted for audience appeal. Whether it's James Hilton's original novel or Robert Riskin's celluloid transmutation, the scripting contribution is one of the picture's strongest assets.

It opens vigorously in Bakul, showing the English community evacuating under the onslaught of Chinese bandits. The last plane out throws Colman together with the fussbudget archaeologist (Edward Everett Horton), the Ponzi plumber (Thomas Mitchell), the ailing waif of the world (Isabel Jewell), and Colman's screen brother (well played by John Howard). It's in Shangri-La that Jane Wyatt so vigorously establishes herself as Colman's vis-à-vis, looking decidedly comely and handling her romance opportunities with definite understanding.

1937: Best Interior Decoration (Stephen Goosson), Editing

NOMINATIONS: Best Picture, Supp. Actor (H. B. Warner), Score, Sound, Assistant Director (C. C. Coleman, Jr.)

•

LOST HORIZON
1973, 150 mins, US ⦿ ▭ col
Dir Charles Jarrott ***Prod*** Ross Hunter ***Scr*** Larry Kramer ***Ph*** Robert Surtees ***Ed*** Maury Winetrobe ***Mus*** Burt Bacharach ***Art*** Preston Ames
Act Peter Finch, Liv Ullmann, Sally Kellerman, George Kennedy, Michael York, Olivia Hussey (Columbia)

Some 36 years after Frank Capra's filmization of James Hilton's *Lost Horizon* novel premiered comes producer Ross Hunter's lavish updated and musical adaptation. The form is that of filmed operetta in three acts, superbly mounted, and cast with an eye to international markets.

The script structure parallels that of the Capra film—opening after the majestic main title landscape of snowy mountains with the tumultous escape from rioting Asians in a kidnapped plane; the crash in the uncharted Himalayas rescued by an inscrutable major domo who takes the disparate survivors to the nestled Utopia of Shangri-La, where the outsiders resolve their personal destinies.

Peter Finch heads the cast as Conway, an international statesman selected by High Lama Charles Boyer to succeed to rule of Shangri-La, where the world's wisdom is being preserved against the foreseen Apocalypse. Sir John Gielgud is the high lama's chief aide who reveals the mystery of the place to Finch.

Only Michael York, in a dramatically crippled supporting banana role, and Olivia Hussey, an awkwardly exotic soubrette, fail to get off the ground.

•

LOST IN A HAREM
1944, 88 mins, US Ⓥ ⦿ b/w
Dir Charles Riesner ***Prod*** George Haight ***Scr*** Harry Ruskin, John Grant, Harry Crane ***Ph*** Lester White ***Ed*** George Hively ***Mus*** Johnny Green (sup.) ***Art*** Cedric Gibbons, Daniel B. Cathcart
Act Bud Abbott, Lou Costello, Marilyn Maxwell, John Conte (M-G-M)

Lost in a Harem is good standard fare for Abbott and Costello fans. The boys are in the groove, knocking themselves out for laughs in a slapstick bit of nonsense that is plenty corny at times, but is still funny.

The film has some neat production numbers built around appearances of Jimmy Dorsey and his orchestra. This also adds to the fun, gaudy Oriental costumes on the musicians adding to the incongruity of a modern jazz band in an exotic Baghdad kingdom. Photography in handling the Dorsey music numbers is also fresh and original, for attractive intro of the music into the story.

Story has to do with a mystical eastern land where an American troupe has been stranded. Land is ruled by a sheik who has defrauded his nephew of the throne. Nephew (John Conte), knowing his uncle's weakness for blondes, hires Marilyn Maxwell, troupe's prima donna, and Abbott and Costello, troupe's magic act, to regain his kingdom by stealing some magic rings his uncle wears.

•

LOST IN AMERICA
1985, 91 mins, US Ⓥ col
Dir Albert Brooks ***Prod*** Marty Katz ***Scr*** Albert Brooks, Monica Johnson ***Ph*** Eric Saarinen ***Ed*** David Finfer ***Mus*** Arthur B. Rubinstein ***Art*** Richard Sawyer
Act Albert Brooks, Julie Hagerty, Garry Marshall, Art Frankel, Michael Greene, Tom Tarpey (Geffen)

Film opens on Albert Brooks and wife Julie Hagerty in bed on eve of their move to a $450,000 house and also what Brooks presumes will be his promotion to a senior exec slot in a big ad agency. Brooks is a nervous mess, made worse when vaguely bored Hagerty tells him their life has become "too responsible, too controlled."

Her suppressed wish for a more dashing life comes startlingly true the next day when a confident Brooks glides into his boss's L.A. office only to hear that his expected senior v. p. stripes are going to someone else and he's being transferred to New York.

Brooks quits his job and convinces his wife to quit her personnel job. The pair will liquidate their assets, buy a Winnebago, and head across America.

Brooks, who directed and cowrote with Monica Johnson, is irrepressible but always very human.

•

LOST IN SPACE
1998, 131 mins, US Ⓥ ⦿ ▭ col
Dir Stephen Hopkins ***Prod*** Mark W. Koch, Stephen Hopkins, Akiva Goldsman, Carla Fry ***Scr*** Akiva Goldsman ***Ph*** Peter

Levy *Ed* Ray Lovejoy *Mus* Bruce Broughton *Art* Norman Garwood
Act William Hurt, Mimi Rogers, Heather Graham, Lacey Chabert, Jack Johnson, Gary Oldman (Prelude/New Line)

One of the most endearingly dumb baby-boomer tube faves finally makes it to the bigscreen with the $90 mil *Lost in Space*, New Line's most commercially ambitious, and costly, production to date. Pic provides one hour's decent, eye-filling ride, then crashes and burns amid some of the worst writing since . . . well, since scenarist/producer Akiva Goldsman's last effort, *Batman & Robin*.

The original series started on CBS in 1965 as an earnest, if not particularly bright, b&w primetime space adventure. When the run ended three years later, the show had long since gone color—and very self-consciously campy. The simple premise updated *Swiss Family Robinson*, placing a traditional, all-American nuclear family—plus one romantic-interest hunk for the eldest daughter, a duplicitous stowaway and one loyal robot—on a spaceship that is lost, ensuring a new interplanetary peril each week.

Goldsman and director Stephen Hopkins don't overtly parody the material. But the writer just can't stop forcing his characters to parrot the lamest possible "wisecracks," and an effort to inject contemporary "relevance" by making the Space Family Robinsons a stock dysfunctional unit in need of some quality time together plays even worse than it sounds.

It's 2058 and life on this planet is running out of time. The United Global Space Force sends Prof. John Robinson (William Hurt) and his immediate family to a faraway colony as a partial publicity stunt, one that may help prepare mankind for its "offshore" future. Meanwhile, bad guys hire veteran spy Dr. Smith (Gary Oldman) to sabotage the mission, but then strand him on the vessel whose destruction he's already programmed.

Hopkins (*Blown Away*, *The Ghost and the Darkness*) again delivers satisfying spectacle on a moment-to-moment basis, but no sense of overall structure or pacing. While Hurt lends welcome gravity, Mimi Rogers as his wife is stuck doing the basic honey-be-careful act.

•

LOST IN YONKERS
1993, 112 mins, US Ⓥ ⊙ col
Dir Martha Coolidge *Prod* Ray Stark *Scr* Neil Simon *Ph* Johnny E. Jensen *Ed* Steven Cohen *Mus* Elmer Bernstein *Art* David Chapman
Act Richard Dreyfuss, Mercedes Ruehl, Irene Worth, Brad Stoll, Mike Damus, David Strathairn (Columbia/Rastar)

Lost in Yonkers is a carefully rendered, ultimately unexciting screen version of Neil Simon's 1991 Pulitzer Prize–winning play.

Story of a domineering old woman's tyranny over two generations of offspring is set in the summer of '42. Tale begins as Eddie Krunitz (Jack Laufer) attempts to deposit his two sons with his mother, who lives above her Yonkers candy store and soda fountain. She is sufficiently tended to by her somewhat backward 36-year-old daughter Bella (Mercedes Ruehl), but she finally has little choice.

The two boys, 15-year-old Jay and Arty, two years younger, are bright, presentable, well-behaved kids, and much of the pleasure of the film lies in watching the alert, bright-eyed perfomances of Brad Stoll and Mike Damus. Still, they are susceptible to the brash appeal of their uncle Louie (Richard Dreyfuss), a small-time hood.

Simon has gently opened up the pic by adding a number of characters who didn't appear in the play, and setting quite a few scenes outside the apartment and store. Despite this, the film still seems bound by its theatrical origins in the way everything is stated and spelled out. Performances by the leads could have been brought down a notch or two.

•

LOST PATROL, THE
1934, 74 mins, US Ⓥ b/w
Dir John Ford *Prod* Cliff Reid (assoc.) *Scr* Dudley Nichols, Garrett Fort *Ph* Harold Wenstrom *Ed* Paul Weatherwax *Mus* Max Steiner *Art* Van Nest Polglase, Sidney Ullman
Act Victor McLaglen, Boris Karloff, Wallace Ford, Reginald Denny, J. M. Kerrigan, Alan Hale (RKO)

Not a woman in the cast and substantially little as to story, but under the weight of suspense, dialog, and competency of direction *Lost Patrol* tips the scales favorably as entertainment.

All of the action [from the story *Patrol* by Philip MacDonald] takes place in the Mesopotamian desert during the campaign of the English against militant Arabs in 1917. Outside of the bleak desert, the only other change of scene throughout the picture's length is the oasis which a patrol, lost after the commanding officer has been killed, discovers. It is here where one by one the men either die or are bumped off by Arabs, until Victor McLaglen is the last.

McLaglen, the sergeant who inherits command of the patrol, turns in a good job in the kind of a part that's particularly suited to this actor. As a Bible nut, Boris Karloff is on a somewhat different assignment. He gives a fine account of himself.

1934: NOMINATION: Best Score

•

LOST SQUADRON, THE
1932, 80 mins, US Ⓥ ⊙ b/w
Dir George Archainbaud *Scr* Wallace Smith, Herman J. Mankiewicz, Robert S. Presnell *Ph* Leo Tover, Edward Cronjager *Ed* William Hamilton *Mus* [uncredited] *Art* Max Ree
Act Richard Dix, Mary Astor, Erich von Stroheim, Dorothy Jordan, Joel McCrea, Robert Armstrong (RKO)

Squadron glorifies the cinematic stunt flyer. [From the *Liberty* magazine story] by Dick Grace, the most illustrious of the Hollywood aerial daredevils, it is not without authority, even though the dramatics are a bit strained.

The "behind the scenes" of an aerial film production is the best appeal *Squadron* has. It's a story-within-a-story. Although the basic premise might be regarded as trite and familiar, the detail of the skullduggery of a jealous husband-director, along with his fanatical zeal in injecting realism into the aerial crash stuff, is 100% new for the screen.

Erich von Stroheim plays the director (alias Arnold von Furst in the picture) to the hilt, i.e., the role of a domineering, militaristic Prussian film director who is a martinet on location, callous to all else but the box-office effect of his celluloid production.

Action takes Richard Dix, Joel McCrea, Robert Armstrong, and Hugh Herbert from an aviation corps right after the war to Hollywood, where Armstrong has preceded them and won some standing as an aerial stuntist.

With the quartet reunited as Hollywoodian stunt flyers (Dick Grace, Art Gobel, Leo Nomis, and Frank Clark get the billing for the actual aerial stunting), Stroheim as the jealous director motivates the action toward a realistic crack-up by putting acid on the control wires of the ship, which Dix, as screen antagonist, was supposed to have piloted.

Mary Astor is unhappily cast as an ambitious actress who first throws over Dix while he's on the other side for a sinecure under a masculine protector, and who later marries von Furst to further her career on the screen.

•

LOST WEEKEND, THE
1945, 104 mins, US Ⓥ ⊙ b/w
Dir Billy Wilder *Prod* Charles Brackett *Scr* Charles Brackett, Billy Wilder *Ph* John F. Seitz *Ed* Doane Harrison *Mus* Miklos Rozsa *Art* Hans Dreier, Earl Hedrick
Act Ray Milland, Jane Wyman, Howard da Silva, Philip Terry, Doris Dowling, Frank Faylen (Paramount)

The filming by Paramount of *The Lost Weekend* marks a particularly outstanding achievement in the Hollywood setting. The psychiatric study of an alcoholic, it is an unusual picture. It is intense, morbid—and thrilling.

Weekend is the specific story [from the novel by Charles R. Jackson] of a quondam writer who has yet to put down his first novel on paper. He talks about it continuously but something always seems to send him awry just when he has a mind to work. Booze. Two quarts at a time. He goes on drunks for days. And his typewriter invariably winds up in the pawnshop. Ray Milland has certainly given no better performance in his career.

Drunks may frequently excite laughter, but at no time can there be even a suggestion of levity to the part Milland plays. Only at the film's end is the character out of focus, but that is the fault of the script. The suggestion of rehabilitation should have been more carefully developed. Jane Wyman is the girl, Philip Terry the brother. They help make the story overshadow the characters. The entire cast, in fact, contributes notably. And that goes especially for Howard da Silva as the bartender. Billy Wilder's direction is always certain, always conscious that the characters were never to overstate the situations.

1945: Best Picture, Director, Actor (Ray Milland), Screenplay

NOMINATIONS: Best B&W Cinematography, Editing, Scoring of a Dramatic Picture

•

LOST WORLD, THE
1960, 97 mins, US Ⓥ ▭ col
Dir Irwin Allen *Prod* Irwin Allen *Scr* Charles Bennett, Irwin Allen *Ph* Winton Hoch *Ed* Hugh S. Fowler *Mus* Paul Sawtell, Bert Shefter *Art* Duncan Cramer, Walter M. Simonds
Act Michael Rennie, Jill St. John, David Hedison, Claude Rains, Fernando Lamas, Richard Haydn (Saratoga/20th Century-Fox)

Watching *The Lost World* is tantamount to taking a trip through a Coney Island fun house. The picture's chief attraction is its production gusto. Emphasis on physical and pictorial values makes up, to some extent, for its lack of finesse in the literary and thespic departments. In translating the Arthur Conan Doyle story to the screen for the second time (after a lapse of 36 years since the first, silent version), Irwin Allen and Charles Bennett have constructed a choppy, topheavy, deliberately paced screenplay that labors too long with exposition and leaves several loose ends dangling. Allen's direction is not only sluggish but has somehow gotten more personality into his dinosaurs than into his people.

Among the curious individuals who venture into this treacherous hidden area at the headwaters of the Amazon are Claude Rains, overly affected as Professor George Edward Challenger; Michael Rennie, a bit wooden as a titled playboy with a notorious reputation; Jill St. John, ill-at-ease as an adventuress who chooses tight pink capri pants as suitable garb for an Amazonian exploration; David Hedison, bland as a newsman-photog; and Fernando Lamas, unconvincing as a Latin guitar player and helicopter operator.

With the exception of one or two mighty ineffectual prehistoric spiders and a general absence of genuine shock or tension, the production is something to behold. The dinosaurs are exceptionally lifelike (although they resemble horned toads and alligators more than dinosaurs), as are the violent volcanic scenery (like hot, bubbling chili sauce) and lush vegetation form backdrops that are more interesting and impressive than the action taking place in front of them.

•

LOST WORLD, THE
JURASSIC PARK
1997, 134 mins, US Ⓥ ⊙ col
Dir Steven Spielberg *Prod* Gerald Molen, Colin Wilson *Scr* David Koepp *Ph* Janusz Kaminski *Ed* Michael Kahn *Mus* John Williams *Art* Rick Carter
Act Jeff Goldblum, Julianne Moore, Pete Postlethwaite, Arliss Howard, Richard Attenborough, Vince Vaughn (Amblin/Universal)

Following up the highest grossing film of all time was bound to be a daunting task. The good news is that the dinosaur creations are even better, credible, breathtaking and frightening. As for the rest, every department pales by comparison.

The premise [from the novel by Michael Crichton] is that 80 miles from the original Jurassic Park, there was Site B, the island locale where the prehistoric animals were engineered and shipped off to the failed theme park. As the amusement park was being undone by man, the scientific base was destroyed by a hurricane. Though it was presumed the dinos died for want of a life-giving chemical, they found the element in nature and have been thriving unmonitored ever since.

The idea is to send in a small expedition to chronicle the progress. The quartet is composed of documentarian Nick Van Owen (Vince Vaughn), operations specialist Eddie Carr (Richard Schiff), paleontologist Sarah Harding (Julianne Moore) and reluctant returnee Ian Malcolm (Jeff Goldblum). Then a second, much larger, team descends from the skies for less honorable pursuits. Led by Hammond (Richard Attenborough) nephew and corporate chief Peter Ludlow (Arliss Howard), this crew of mercenaries is to capture a selection of bygone species for a San Diego park.

Underneath the technical virtuosity is a standard chase film, and director Steven Spielberg does little to elevate it dramatically. The cast mostly founders with sketchily written parts. Janusz Kaminski's photography seems rather self-consciously arty for genre, rife with back-lighting to accentuate the eeriness of night and fog. Otherwise, the film moves at a breathless clip that almost makes one forget the thinness of the plot.

1997: NOMINATION: Best Visual Effects

•

LOUDEST WHISPER, THE
SEE: THE CHILDREN'S HOUR

•

LOUISIANA PURCHASE
1941, 95 mins, US col
Dir Irving Cummings *Prod* Harold Wilson *Scr* Jerome Chodorov, Joseph Fields *Ph* Harry Hallenberger, Ray Rennahan *Mus* Irving Berlin
Act Bob Hope, Vera Zorina, Victor Moore, Irene Bordoni, Dona Drake (Paramount)

Paramount production head B. G. DeSylva, who produced the stage version [by Irving Berlin and Morrie Ryskind], evidently was confident that the usual film variations, modifications, and interpolations would only clutter up the action. So *Louisiana Purchase* comes to the screen an almost literal translation from the stage.

Such procedure leads the audience to enjoy Victor Moore in one of the best comedy roles of his career. His Senator Loganberry, who single-handedly invaded the political bayous of graft-besmirched Louisiana, is the high spot of comedy throughout the film, due in considerable measure to the teamwork of his support, including the irrepressible Bob Hope. Latter plays it straight when the script demands.

With a greater portion of the action, including some of the musical numbers, confined to the farcical story, the occasional breakaway into elaborate, many-peopled and multicolored scenes is most effectively presented. Irving Cummings does a smart job of directing throughout. Costuming and floats for the Mardi Gras are brilliant.

•

LOUISIANA STORY
1948, 77 mins, US Ⓥ b/w
Dir Robert Flaherty ***Prod*** Robert Flaherty ***Scr*** Robert Flaherty, Frances Flaherty ***Ph*** Richard Leacock ***Ed*** Helen Van Dongen ***Mus*** Virgil Thomson
Act Joseph Boudreaux, Lionel Le Blanc, Mrs. E. Bienvenu, Frank Hardy, C. T. Guedry (Lopert Films)

Louisiana Story is a documentary-type story told almost purely in camera terms. It has a slender, appealing story, moments of agonizing suspense, vivid atmosphere, and superlative photography.

Filmed entirely in the bayou country of Louisiana, the picture tells of the Cajun (Acadian) boy and his parents, who live by hunting and fishing in the alligator-infested swamps and streams, and of the oil-drilling crew that brings its huge derrick to sink a well.

There probably aren't more than 100 lines of dialog in the entire picture—long sequences being told by the camera, with eloquent sound effects and Virgil Thomson's expressive music as background. There are no real heroes or villains (unless the terrifying alligators could be considered the latter). The simple Cajun family is friendly, and the oil-drilling crew is pleasant and likable.

Standard Oil of NJ contributed the necessary $200,000 production coin to Flaherty.

1948: NOMINATION: Best Motion Picture Story

•

LOUIS PASTEUR
1936, 85 mins, US b/w
Dir William Dieterle ***Scr*** Sheridan Gibney, Pierre Collings ***Ph*** Tony Gaudio
Act Paul Muni, Josephine Hutchinson, Anita Louise, Donald Woods, Fritz Leiber, Henry O'Neill (Warner)

Most audiences won't understand a great deal of the scientific background or import, and a great portion won't care. Try as hard as the producers could, they haven't avoided some dull stretches of scientific discourse certain to baffle average audiences. Expert casting and splendid production are the points in the film's favor, primarily. Paul Muni in the title role is at his very top form.

Film starts out with Louis Pasteur (Muni) already somewhat established, skipping his early life and struggles. His wine and beer discoveries have already been accepted and he's propagandizing for sterilization of doctors and doctors' instruments in childbirth. Doesn't get him very far because of general medical opposition, and he turns to treatment of anthrax in sheep and cattle.

Gets that over and is admitted in to the French Academy, although still scoffed at by the majority of his confreres. Works on a cure for rabies and hydrophobia for the rest of the picture. His reward finally is general acclaim.

Josephine Hutchinson as Pasteur's wife is splendid and believable. Anita Louise as his daughter and Donald Woods as her fincaé are expected to handle the romance and almost do it. Fritz Leiber as Dr. Charbonnet, Pasteur's strongest enemy, turns in an outstanding performance.

•

LOULOU
1980, 110 mins, France Ⓥ col
Dir Maurice Pialat ***Scr*** Arlette Langmann, Maurice Pialat ***Ph*** Pierre-William Glenn, Jacques Loiseleux ***Ed*** Yann Dedet, Sophie Coussein
Act Isabelle Huppert, Gerard Depardieu, Guy Marchand, Humbert Balsan, Bernard Tronczyk, Christian Boucher (Gaumont/Action)

With *Loulou*, director Maurice Pialat deals with a couple formed of a fringe semi-delinquent colossus (Gerard Depardieu), the *Loulou* of the title, and a frail but headstrong middle-class girl (Isabelle Huppert). They make an engaging couple who love and fight and may eventually make it together and even grow old together.

Huppert sometimes slips back to her former lover, who is also her boss in an ad agency. Guy Marchand is effective as a self-indulgent type who cannot see what she can possibly see in Depardieu. Depardieu leads her in the looting of a warehouse of electronic goods, he gets stabbed in a bar fight over a girl and she gets pregnant.

There is a luminous quality about this film. There is humor that springs from situations and character. Pialat may be giving a modern continuance of the French pre-war poetic, naturalistic dramas with worker and sub-proletariat types. But he has eschewed the romanticism and added sharp modern language and an acceptance of conditions with perhaps a possibility of changing them.

•

LOVE
SEE: SZERELEM

•

LOVE
1927, 84 mins, US Ⓥ ⊙ ⊗ b/w
Dir Edmund Goulding ***Prod*** Edmund Goulding ***Scr*** Frances Marion, Marian Ainslee, Ruth Cummings, Lorna Moon ***Ph*** William Daniels ***Ed*** Hugh Wynn ***Mus*** Ernst Luz ***Art*** Cedric Gibbons, Alexander Toluboff
Act Greta Garbo, John Gilbert, George Fawcett, Emily Fitzroy, Brandon Hurst, Philippe De Lacy (M-G-M)

What is there to tell about the Tolstoy story *Anna Karenina*? Its locale is Russia in the time of the Czars. Anna (Greta Garbo) has a husband and a young son; Vronsky (John Gilbert), a military hertiage and a desire for Anna. For screen purposes it's enough that both are of the aristocracy, which permits Garbo long, stately gowns and Gilbert a series of uniforms that would make a buck private out of the student prince.

There are rich interiors, appropriate exteriors and an excellent officers' steeplechase to get the action figuratively off of a couch for a while. Besides which Garbo and Gilbert supposedly care for each other in the script.

Anyway, director Edmund Goulding hasn't let the title run away with his sense of discretion. Possibly has leaned over backward to the extent of keeping this picture from becoming a rave. When all is said and done, *Love* is a cinch because it has Gilbert and Garbo.

•

LOVE AFFAIR
1939, 87 mins, US Ⓥ b/w
Dir Leo McCarey ***Prod*** Leo McCarey ***Scr*** Delmer Daves, Donald Ogden Stewart ***Ph*** Rudolph Mate ***Ed*** Edward Dmytryk, George Hiveley ***Art*** Jack Otterson, Martin Obzina
Act Irene Dunne, Charles Boyer, Maria Ouspenskaya, Lee Bowman, Astrid Allwyn, Maurice Moscovich (RKO)

Leo McCarey's initial production for RKO as a producer-director offers an entirely new approach to accepted technique. Basically, it's the regulation formula of boy-meets-girl [story by McCarey and Mildred Cram]. But first half is best described as romantic comedy, while second portion switches to drama with comedy.

Aboard boat sailing from Naples to New York, Charles Boyer starts a flirtation with Irene Dunne. He is engaged to heiress Astrid Allwyn, and she to Lee Bowman. They separate on docking with pact to meet six months later atop the Empire State building.

Dunne slips to Philadelphia to sing in a night club, while Boyer applies himself to painting. While on her way to keep tryst on appointed day, Dunne is injured in a traffic accident. Faced with life of a cripple, girl refuses to contact Boyer to explain.

Dunne is excellent in a role that requires both comedy and dramatic ability. Boyer is particularly effective as the modern Casanova. Maria Ouspenskaya provides a warmly sympathetic portrayal as Boyer's grandmother in Madeira.

1939: NOMINATIONS: Best Picture, Actress (Irene Dunne), Supp. Actress (Maria Ouspenskaya), Original Story, Art Direction

•

LOVE AFFAIR
1994, 108 mins, US Ⓥ ⊙ col
Dir Glenn Gordon Caron ***Prod*** Warren Beatty ***Scr*** Robert Towne, Warren Beatty ***Ph*** Conrad L. Hall ***Ed*** Robert C. Jones ***Mus*** Ennio Morricone ***Art*** Ferdinando Scarfiotti
Act Warren Beatty, Annette Bening, Katharine Hepburn, Garry Shandling, Chloe Webb, Pierce Brosnan (Mulholland/Warner)

The appeal of this *Love Affair* is only skin deep. A film of gorgeous surfaces and negligible emotional resonance, this third rendition of a perennial sentimental favorite is easy on the eyes and has its share of beguiling moments in the early going, but crucially lacks a compelling climax and any sense of urgency in its storytelling.

Leo McCarey's two versions of this star-crossed romance, *Love Affair*, starring Charles Boyer and Irene Dunne in 1939, and *An Affair to Remember*, top-lining Cary Grant and Deborah Kerr in 1957, were favorites to their respective generations. Contempo audiences will recall that *Sleepless in Seattle* paid extended homage to the latter.

Main hook of this telling is the matchup of Warren Beatty and Annette Bening as jet-setters who, already engaged to others, become irresistably attracted to each other, and after an intense tryst, resolve to meet at the top of the Empire State Building in three months if they are serious about each other. Beyond that, there is the curiosity of seeing Katharine Hepburn on the big screen in a major film for the first time in 13 years.

Setup is jauntily and briskly done, with Beatty plausibly cast as a former L.A. football star-turned-broadcaster engaged to a talk-show doyenne (Kate Capshaw), and glamorous Bening as Terry, the fiancée of a high-finance magnate (Pierce Brosnan). Pair meet on a flight to Sydney. An emergency landing on a tiny South Pacific island fatefully pits the characters together for longer than anticipated, as the travelers board a Russian cruise ship for a brief drunken voyage to Tahiti. It's only upon a visit to Mike's aunt (Katharine Hepburn) at her splendid home in the hills of Bora Bora that the possibility of something meaningful between the two sparring partners becomes apparent.

Beatty has fun with his own image here, but in a mild and innocuous way. Bening is enchantingly vivacious and sparkling, a fine match in looks, wit, and sophistication to her leading man. Capshaw and Brosnan are given short shrift as the cast-off prospective mates.

•

LOVE AND BULLETS
1979, 95 mins, UK Ⓥ ⊏⊐ col
Dir Stuart Rosenberg ***Prod*** Pancho Kohner ***Scr*** Wendell Mayes, John Melson ***Ph*** Fred Koenekamp, Anthony Richmond ***Ed*** Michael Anderson ***Mus*** Lalo Schifrin ***Art*** John DeCuir
Act Charles Bronson, Rod Steiger, Jill Ireland, Strother Martin, Bradford Dillman, Michael Gazzo (ITC/Grade)

Slowly and predictably, script plots Charles Bronson's mission, on behalf of the FBI, to pick up a mobster's moll (Jill Ireland) who's gotten separated from her paramour and is presumed to be a mine of incriminating information.

Bronson's personal obsession with bringing down the gang-land king is accentuated when he discovers the girl knows nothing after all, and then falls for her. When the mob, equally convinced she'll shop them, have her killed, he takes private revenge.

Rod Steiger's performance as the effete Mafia boss is tantalizing. So too is the emergent love affair between Bronson and Ireland, her comic talent largely starved for lack of material.

Director Stuart Rosenberg could have glossed over the plot's less believable twists with a brisker style and a lot more attack.

•

LOVE AND DEATH
1975, 85 mins, US Ⓥ ⊙ col
Dir Woody Allen ***Prod*** Charles H. Joffe ***Scr*** Woody Allen ***Ph*** Ghislain Cloquet ***Ed*** Ralph Rosenblum ***Mus*** Felix Giglio (sup.) ***Art*** Willy Holt
Act Woody Allen, Diane Keaton (United Artists)

Woody Allen and Diane Keaton invade the land and spirit of Anton Chekhov. *Love and Death* is another mile-a-minute visual-verbal whirl by the two comedy talents, this time through Czarist Russia in the days of the Napoleonic Wars.

Allen's script traces his bumbling adventures with distant cousin Keaton, latter outstanding as a prim lady of both philosophical and sexual bent. Between malaprop battlefield heroics and metaphysical deliberations, Allen eventually combines with Keaton in an assassination attempt on Napoleon himself. It is impossible to catalog the comedic blueprint; suffice to say it is another zany product of the terrific synergism of the two stars.

About 54 supporting players have roles that range from a few feet to a few frames. Joffe's location production was shot in France and Germany, where some gorgeous physical values serve as a backdrop to the kooky antics.

•

LOVE AND HUMAN REMAINS
1993, 98 mins, Canada Ⓥ ⊙ col
Dir Denys Arcand ***Prod*** Roger Frappier ***Scr*** Brad Fraser ***Ph*** Paul Sarossy ***Ed*** Alain Baril ***Mus*** John McCarthy ***Art*** Francois Seguin

Act Thomas Gibson, Ruth Marshall, Cameron Bancroft, Mia Kirshner, Joanne Vannicola, Matthew Ferguson (Max/Atlantis)

Denys Arcand's *Love and Human Remains* is a bawdy and spirited comedy about a group of mostly 30ish urbanites trying to get a grip on their sexuality and place in the world. Based on the hit play *Unidentified Human Remains and the True Nature of Love*, by Canadian playwright Brad Fraser, pic instantly grabs viewer attention because the subject is Sex with a capital "S," and in many of its alternative forms.

Lead character is David (Thomas Gibson), a charismatic, devilishly good-looking young Lothario who's made an art form of the casual relationship. David lives with Candy (Ruth Marshall), a former g.f. whose disenchantment with men makes her susceptible to the avid attentions of cute lesbian Jerri (Joanne Vannicola). Overlapping this tryst is a flirtation with bartender Robert (Rick Roberts).

David hangs out some with old friend Bernie (Cameron Bancroft), a raging misogynist, but spends more time with admiring 17-year-old busboy Kane (Matthew Ferguson). Another friend is Benita (Mia Kirshner), a young S&M specialist who, in one extreme and hilarious case, calls upon David to help her out.

Weighing too heavily on the story is a backdrop of serial murders of young women that may or may not be the work of one of the principal characters. Resolution of this framing device proves overly melodramatic and angst-ridden.

•

LOVE AND MONEY

1982, 90 mins, US col

Dir James Toback ***Prod*** James Toback ***Scr*** James Toback ***Ph*** Fred Schuler ***Ed*** Dennis Hill ***Mus*** Aaron Copland ***Art*** Lee Fischer

Act Ray Sharkey, Ornella Muti, Klaus Kinski, Armand Assante, King Vidor, Susan Heldfond (Lorimar/Paramount)

Love and Money is an arresting romantic suspense film which, in spite of several good performances and well-crafted individual scenes, fails to ignite.

Ray Sharkey top-lines as Byron Levin, a case of arrested development who works in an L.A. bank and lives with his senile grandpa (King Vidor) and librarian girlfriend Vicky (Susan Heldfond). He comes out of his robot-like shell upon meeting the beautiful Catherine (Ornella Muti), young wife of multinational business magnate Stockheinz (Klaus Kinski).

Following an intense romance with Catherine, Levin becomes involved in an international plot masterminded by Stockheinz to help him deal with Latin American dictator Lorenzo Prado (Armand Assante), not coincidentally Levin's former college roommate.

Muti makes a strong U.S. picture debut, augmenting her famous exotic beauty with some powerful thesping.

•

LOVE AND OTHER CATASTROPHES

1996, 76 mins, Australia Ⓥ col

Dir Emma-Kate Croghan ***Prod*** Stavros Adonis Efthymiou ***Scr*** Yael Bergman, Helen Bandis, Emma-Kate Croghan ***Ph*** Justin Brickle ***Ed*** Ken Sallows ***Mus*** Oleh Witer

Act Matt Day, Matthew Dyktynski, Alice Garner, Frances O'Connor, Radha Mitchell, Suzi Dougherty (Screwball Five/Beyond)

A tremendously engaging low-budget first feature by 23-year-old Emma-Kate Croghan, *Love and Other Catastrophes* is a fast, funny excursion into the world of college students in the mid-'90s, boosted by a terrific ensemble of five engaging young thesps.

Croghan, a former film school student, is keenly aware of the ups and downs of contempo life on a college campus, and is totally unself-conscious in her depiction of her often confused and lovesick characters. Visually, pic is rough at the edges and looks as though it was made on the run, but it makes up in sheer likability what it lacks in production values.

Alice (Alice Garner) and Mia (Frances O'Connor) are film school students who have just moved into a new apartment. Mia's girlfriend, Danni (Radha Mitchell), is a bit miffed that the independent-minded Mia doesn't want her to move into the pad. Meanwhile, sensitive, straight Michael (Matt Day), a med student, is frantically trying to find a new place to stay. Alice is the romantic type. She has her eye on spunky Ari (Matthew Dyktynski), a classics student who earns money on the side by servicing rich, bored women. Mia, meanwhile, wants to switch to a trendier course run by real-life Melbourne critic Adrian Martin. To add to Mia's woes, the offended Danni has taken up with another woman, the seriously uncommunicative Savita (Suzi Dougherty).

These events unfold in a tight, 24-hour time frame, culminating in a house-warming party at the girls' new apartment.

Pic is punctuated with quotes from such disparate sources as Jane Austen, Lewis Carroll, Alfred Hitchcock, Doris Day, and the Bee Gees. Acknowledgment is also made of the influence Quentin Tarantino has over the students.

•

LOVE AND PAIN AND THE WHOLE DAMN THING

1973, 110 mins, US col

Dir Alan J. Pakula ***Prod*** Alan J. Pakula ***Scr*** Alvin Sargent ***Ph*** Geoffrey Unsworth ***Ed*** Russell Lloyd ***Mus*** Michael Small ***Art*** Enrique Alarcon

Act Maggie Smith, Timothy Bottoms, Jaime de Mora y Aragon, Emiliano Redondo, Charles Baxter, Margaret Modlin (Columbia)

For almost three-quarters of its overlong running time, *Love and Pain . . .* etc. works as a modest, affecting romantic comedy about two mismatched neurotics stumbling into love during a Spanish tour. But pic succumbs to a fatal attack of *Love Story*itis, and goes down for the count.

Timothy Bottoms plays the shy, asthmatic son of a professor packed off to Spain for the summer. Bottoms joins a tourist bus where he is seated next to Maggie Smith, a jumpy lady of middle age who frequently bumps into her own shadow. For most of the film they trip over each other, explore the countryside and gradually accept a warmth and companionship that leads to a believable affair. Then Smith reveals she's dying. Smith, as ever, is luminous, and Bottoms tackles a difficult role with ease. One only wishes the scripter had left well enough alone.

•

LOVE AT FIRST BITE

1979, 96 mins, US Ⓥ ⦿ col

Dir Stan Dragoti ***Prod*** Joel Freeman ***Scr*** Robert Kaufman ***Ph*** Edward Rosson ***Ed*** Mort Fallick, Allan Jacobs ***Mus*** Charles Bernstein ***Art*** Serge Krizman

Act George Hamilton, Susan Saint James, Richard Benjamin, Dick Shawn, Arte Johnson, Sherman Hemsley (American International)

"What would happen if" Dracula was victimized by life in modern New York City?

It's a fun notion and George Hamilton makes it work. In the first place, he's funny just to watch. Veteran makeup artist William Tuttle, who created Lugosi's Dracula look in 1934, retains the gray, drained visage while adding a nutty quality that Hamilton accents with the arch of an eyebrow.

Story evicts Dracula from his Transylvania castle and takes him in pursuit of Susan Saint James, a fashion model he loves from an old photo. In the care of his bumbling manservant, slightly overplayed by Arte Johnson, Hamilton's coffin is naturally misrouted by the airline, winding up in a black funeral home.

Director Stan Dragoti keeps the chuckles coming, spaced by a few good guffaws.

•

LOVE AT LARGE

1990, 97 mins, US Ⓥ ⦿ col

Dir Alan Rudolph ***Prod*** David Blocker ***Scr*** Alan Rudolph ***Ph*** Elliot Davis ***Ed*** Lisa Churgin ***Mus*** Mark Isham ***Art*** Steven Legler

Act Tom Berenger, Elizabeth Perkins, Anne Archer, Ted Levine, Annette O'Toole, Kate Capshaw (Orion)

Alan Rudolph's film is a tongue-in-cheek take on the gumshoe genre that mostly seeks to explore the perplexing possibilities of love.

Wealthy and idle Dolan (Anne Archer) hires rumpled cheap detective Harry Dobbs (Tom Berenger) to trail a lover she underdescribes. Berenger picks the wrong guy and ends up pursuing a quarry far more interesting than the intended—this one's not only married, he's got two separate families. Meanwhile, he's being followed by novice detective Stella (Elizabeth Perkins), who's been hired by his unreasonably jealous, crockery-throwing girlfriend, Doris (Ann Magnuson).

It's the endless round of illogical but irresistible liaisons and the characters' own unfathomable peculiarities that form the basis of this dizzy send-up of romance. Berenger, with his squashed hat and growling delivery, is slyly amusing as Dobbs, while Perkins exudes a flinty, provocative chemistry.

•

LOVE BEFORE BREAKFAST

1936, 65 mins, US b/w

Dir Walter Lang ***Prod*** Edmund Grainger ***Scr*** Herbert Fields ***Ph*** Ted Tetzlaff ***Ed*** Maurice Wright ***Mus*** Franz Waxman ***Art*** Albert D'Agostino

Act Carole Lombard, Preston Foster, Janet Beecher, Cesar Romero, Betty Lawford (Universal)

Boy meets girl, boy loses girl, boy gets girl, and vice versa. *Love Before Breakfast* is the old plot malarkey [from the Faith Baldwin novel *Spinster Dinner*] wrapped up in some pretty fancy trimmings and handled capably by all departments to rate as fairly good entertainment.

A society girl (Carole Lombard) loves a boy, and is in turn loved by a wealthy big businessman. Latter gives the boy a job in Japan to get him out of the way so he can go to town with the lady, lavish her with gifts and win her over. He does, after 65 minutes. In fact, he wins her sooner than that, only the lady won't admit it, and the last half concerns her spectacular exhibition of the correct way to hold out.

Lombard wears some stunning clothes and conducts herself competently. Janet Beecher plays her broad-minded mother for all that the part's worth, and a lot more. Betty Lawford is a good-looking femme semi-menace. In the male contingent are Preston Foster, the b.b. man, in a much lighter role than he's usually holding; Cesar Romero is the unsympathetic other-man role.

•

LOVE BUG, THE

1969, 108 mins, US Ⓥ ⦿ col

Dir Robert Stevenson ***Prod*** Bill Walsh ***Scr*** Bill Walsh, Don DaGradi ***Ph*** Edward Colman ***Ed*** Cotton Warburton ***Mus*** George Bruns ***Art*** Carroll Clark, John B. Mansbridge

Act Dean Jones, Michele Lee, David Tomlinson, Buddy Hackett, Joe Flynn (Walt Disney)

This is a cutie, the story of a little foreign car whose philosophy is "be nice to me and I'll be nice to you." Because Dean Jones, a second-rate racing driver, objects to David Tomlinson, a wealthy, but stuffy, racer, kicking it—the little car, a Volkswagen—adopts Jones and wins a flock of races for him.

For sheer inventiveness of situation and the charm that such an idea projects, *The Love Bug* rates as one of the better entries of the Disney organization.

Treatment is light and imaginative, and Herbie gradually takes on all the attributes of a human. Herbie is all heart, while having a will of iron, muscles of steel, the strength of 10 and a stubborn streak.

Direction by Robert Stevenson, who also helmed the classic *Mary Poppins*, is fast and fanciful, warmly attuned to the demands of the premise and getting the most from his cast.

Jones delivers well as the driver who thinks it's his driving that wins him all those races.

•

LOVE CHILD

1982, 97 mins, US Ⓥ col

Dir Larry Peerce ***Prod*** Paul Maslansky ***Scr*** Anne Gerard, Katherine Specktor ***Ph*** James Pergola ***Ed*** Bob Wyman ***Mus*** Charles Fox ***Art*** Don Ivey

Act Amy Madigan, Beau Bridges, Mackenzie Phillips, Albert Salmi, Joanna Merlin, Margaret Whitton (Ladd/Warner)

Love Child, subtitled "A True Story," is a tasteful and sincere filmization of young Ohioan Terry Jean Moore's battle to have and keep her baby (fathered by a guard) while serving a 20-year robbery term in Broward Correctional Institution in Florida.

In a strong screen debut, freckled Amy Madigan toplines as Moore, who while hitchhiking with her wild cousin Jesse (Lewis Smith), takes the rap when Jesse robs their driver of $5, while trying to steal the car.

Possessing a wild temper and perennial chip on her shoulder, Moore looks headed for doom in stir. Befriended by a personable guard, Jack Hansen (Beau Bridges), and a sympathetic young lesbian, J. J. (Mackenzie Phillips), she adjusts and even seems en route to legal freedom. Targeting the picture squarely at a femme audience, script [from a story by Anne Gerard] emphasizes Moore's self-reform as catalyzed by her awareness of the baby growing inside her and the new responsibility it represents. Madigan is excellent in the physically demanding central role.

•

LOVE CRAZY

1941, 97 mins, US Ⓥ b/w

Dir Jack Conway ***Prod*** Pandro S. Berman ***Scr*** William Ludwig, Charles Lederer, David Hertz ***Ph*** Ray June ***Ed*** Ben Lewis ***Mus*** David Snell ***Art*** Cedric Gibbons, Paul Groesse

Act William Powell, Myrna Loy, Gail Patrick, Jack Carson, Florence Bates, Sidney Blackmer (M-G-M)

William Powell and Myrna Loy romp merrily through another marital comedy loaded with solid comedy, compactly set up and tempoed at a zippy pace. *Love Crazy* is a standout laugh hit of top proportions, a happy successor to previous Powell-Loy teamings.

Under most expert piloting of Jack Conway, pair takes advantage of every opportunity to create maximum of laughs from every situation offered and even dip into broad slapstick and Sennettized chase.

Story [by David Hertz and William Ludwig] is light. It's the happily married pair's fourth anniversary, and they plan to repeat happenings of their wedding night, but mother-in-law arrives to send plans awry. Meeting of Powell with a former flame (Gail Patrick) prompts jealousy, separation, and plans for a divorce.

To gain time, in endeavor to reconcile with his wife, Powell simulates insanity, and lands in a private sanatorium. Escaping, he returns home to masquerade as his sister.

There's a wealth of comedy material in the script for director Jack Conway to capably transform to the screen.

•

LOVE CRIMES

1992, 85 mins, US Ⓥ col

Dir Lizzie Borden ***Prod*** Rudy Langlais, Lizzie Borden ***Scr*** Allan Moyle, Laurie Frank ***Ph*** Jack N. Green ***Ed*** Nicholas C. Smith, Mike Jackson ***Mus*** Graeme Revell, Roger Mason ***Art*** Armin Ganz

Act Sean Young, Patrick Bergin, Arnetia Walker, James Read, Ron Orbach, Wayne Shorter (Sovereign)

Love Crimes is a poorly constructed thriller suffering from a bad lead performance by Sean Young, as a mannishly styled Atlanta assistant district attorney who disobeys her superior's orders and accompanies cops on their stakeouts and arrests.

She becomes obsessed with women's charges against a con man (Patrick Bergin) posing as a famous fashion photographer. He picks up plain-looking women, snaps seminude Polaroids, sexually dominates them, and then robs them. Young travels to Savannah to capture Bergin herself. Screenplay (from Allan Moyle's story based on a real-life 1970s case involving a Richard Avedon impersonator) initially dangles an intriguing issue: Many of the women in retrospect seem to enjoy Bergin's treatment. But director Lizzie Borden stacks the deck, showing Bergin mistreating the women but giving the actresses (other than Young) limited screen time in which to develop their characters.

Bergin delivers a near-duplicate of his villainous role in *Sleeping with the Enemy*. Young is ice-cold as the assistant d.a. Unusual teaming of black femme cop Arnetia Walker, as Young's best friend, and Jewish cop Ron Orbach is pic's best thing.

•

LOVED ONE, THE

1965, 119 mins, US Ⓥ b/w

Dir Tony Richardson ***Prod*** Martin Ransohoff, John Calley, Haskell Wexler ***Scr*** Christopher Isherwood, Terry Southern ***Ph*** Haskell Wexler ***Ed*** Antony Gibbs, Hal Ashby, Brian Smedley-Aston ***Mus*** John Addison ***Art*** Rouben Ter-Arutunian

Act Robert Morse, Anjanette Comer, Jonathan Winters, Rod Steiger, James Coburn, John Gielgud (M-G-M)

Poor taste is prominent in the Terry Southern-Christopher Isherwood script, based on Evelyn Waugh's scathing 1948 satire of the mortuary business in California.

Most of the subtlety of Waugh's approach is lost in an episodic screenplay bearing only a wavering story line and given often to sight gags.

Story centers around the pomp and ceremony attendant upon the daily operation of a posh mortuary and a climaxing idea (not in the book) by a sanctimonious owner of a Southern California cemetery of orbiting cadavers into space so he can convert to a senior citizens' paradise for additional profit.

Robert Morse as the poet who falls in love with the lady cosmetician (later promoted to embalmer), while making arrangements for his uncle's interment, plays it light and airy, like a soul apart. Anjanette Comer, whose life is dedicated to her work and Whispering Glades Memorial Park, gives almost ethereal portraiture to her embalmer character.

Jonathan Winters appears in a dual role, shining both as the owner of Whispering Glades and his twin brother, who operates the nearby pet graveyard and is patron of a 13-year-old scientific whiz who invents a rocket capable of projecting bodies into orbit.

•

LOVE FIELD

1992, 104 mins, US Ⓥ ⦿ col

Dir Jonathan Kaplan ***Prod*** Sarah Pillsbury, Midge Sanford ***Scr*** Don Roos ***Ph*** Ralf Bode ***Ed*** Jane Kurson ***Mus*** Jerry Goldsmith ***Art*** Mark Freeborn

Act Michelle Pfeiffer, Dennis Haysbert, Stephanie McFadden, Brian Kerwin, Louise Latham, Peggy Rea (Orion)

Love Field is a sincere, not fully realized 1960s drama that is yet another variation on the "where were you when you heard JFK was shot" theme.

Story introduces Lurene Hallett (Michelle Pfeiffer), a rather dim Dallas hairdresser with a 100-watt platinum coif who imagines a kinship with Jacqueline Kennedy, since both lost infant children.

Against her husband's (Brian Kerwin) wishes, Lurene hops a Greyhound north to attend the state funeral. On board she meets and gradually befriends a "Negro" man, Paul (Dennis Haysbert), with something to hide. With Paul is his traumatized young daughter, Jonell (Stephanie McFadden). The three are thrown together and must fend for themselves in the all-too-predictable American South.

Pfeiffer notches yet another memorable characterization, although her attempt at defining a not terribly bright woman skirts condescension. Haysbert, in a role that Denzel Washington relinquished over "creative differences," is solid and likable, but the part needed more gradation. The real find is six-year-old McFadden, in her acting debut.

1992: NOMINATION: Best Actress (Michelle Pfeiffer)

•

LOVE HAPPY

1949, 91 mins, US Ⓥ ⦿ b/w

Dir David Miller ***Prod*** Lester Cowan ***Scr*** Frank Tashlin, Mac Benoff ***Ph*** William C. Mellor ***Ed*** Basil Wrangell, Al Joseph ***Mus*** Ann Ronell ***Art*** Gabriel Scognamillo

Act Groucho Marx, Harpo Marx, Chico Marx, Ilona Massey, Vera-Ellen, Raymond Burr (United Artists)

The story [based on one by Harpo Marx], such as it is, deals with a chase for a priceless necklace. Involved are a private eye (Groucho Marx), a blond continental who would stop at nothing to get the gems (Ilona Massey), a mute klepto (Harpo), plus varied others, including a shoestring musicomedy troupe whom Harpo feeds from his daily excursions to a nearby grocer.

The major portion of the film is centered around Harpo and there are a number of his pantomimic scenes that are typically in the Harpo idiom. And some of it too is obviously contrived but plenty laugh-provoking. There is a Times Square chase involving Harpo and Groucho, in which Harpo is pursued along rooftops, through blinking electric-light advertising signs, that gets its share of laughs. It's in situations like this that the Marx Bros. can get away with almost anything.

•

LOVE HAS MANY FACES

1965, 104 mins, US Ⓥ col

Dir Alexander Singer ***Prod*** Jerry Bresler ***Scr*** Marguerite Roberts ***Ph*** Joseph Ruttenberg ***Ed*** Alma Macrorie ***Mus*** David Raksin ***Art*** Alfred Sweeney

Act Lana Turner, Cliff Robertson, Hugh O'Brian, Ruth Roman, Stefanie Powers, Virginia Grey (Bresler/Columbia)

High life among American beach bums in Acapulco is lavishly dramatized in this Jerry Bresler production starring Lana Turner, Cliff Robertson, and Hugh O'Brian. Turner portrays a millionairess surrounded by moochers—including her husband, Robertson—and desperately striving for unfound happiness in her own particular brandy-swilling world. Narrative concerns the love affairs—the many faces of love—at the glamorous resort.

Alexander Singer's direction gets the utmost in values from his story and cast, although none of latter is particularly sympathetic. O'Brian is an expert in the art of sharing his company for money and as a sideline indulges in friendly blackmail, in this case Ruth Roman, a wealthy divorcée.

Turner lends conviction in a demanding part and Robertson is forceful as her husband who married her for her money but finds his life distasteful. O'Brian turns in a good job as a beach parasite who sells his wares to avid young touristas.

•

LOVE IN LAS VEGAS

SEE: VIVA LAS VEGAS

•

LOVE IN THE AFTERNOON

SEE: L'AMOUR, L'APRES-MIDI

•

LOVE IN THE AFTERNOON

1957, 126 mins, US Ⓥ b/w

Dir Billy Wilder ***Prod*** Billy Wilder ***Scr*** Billy Wilder, I.A.L. Diamond ***Ph*** William Mellor ***Ed*** Leonid Azar ***Mus*** Franz Waxman (adapt.) ***Art*** Alexandre Trauner

Act Gary Cooper, Audrey Hepburn, Maurice Chevalier, John McGiver, Van Doude, Lise Bourdin (Allied Artists)

Title-wise, *Love in the Afternoon* is fitting, being far more communicative of the film's content than the original [Claude Anet novel] *Ariane*. It is all about romance before nightfall in Paris, with Audrey Hepburn and Gary Cooper as the participants. Under Billy Wilder's alternately sensitive, mirthful, and loving-care direction, and with Maurice Chevalier turning in a captivating performance as a private detective specializing in cases of amour, the production holds enchantment and delight in substantial quantity.

Love in the Afternoon, though, is long and the casting of Cooper as the eager beaver Romeo is curious. Consider this wealthy American businessman (Cooper) constantly as the woo merchant in his lavish Parisian hotel suite, first with Madame X and then Ariane (Hepburn). Several scenes spill out before Cooper comes on camera, and then on it's love in the afternoon.

It's in Chevalier's files that his daughter, the lovely, wistful Hepburn, as a cello student, comes upon knowledge of Cooper's international conquests, runs to him with the warning that his current passion (Madame X) has a husband (Mr. X) bent on murder, and finds herself soon to become a candidate for one of her own father's file cards.

Mr. X is John McGiver, suitably frenzied as the husband suspecting his mate has taken to play with another. It's a floating-in-air kind of story. And being innocent of earthiness there is no offensiveness in the content.

•

LOVE IS A BALL

1963, 113 mins, US ▭ col

Dir David Swift ***Prod*** Martin H. Poll ***Scr*** David Swift, Tom Waldman, Frank Waldman ***Ph*** Edmond Sechan ***Ed*** Tom McAdoo, Cathy Kelber ***Mus*** Michel Legrand ***Art*** Jean D'Eaubonne

Act Glenn Ford, Hope Lange, Charles Boyer, Ricardo Montalban, Telly Savalas, Ulla Jacobson (Oxford Gold Medal/United Artists)

Love Is a Ball is an airy fairy tale [set on the French Riviera] thrust into cinematicomedic orbit by the devious new campaign of a mercenary cupid, or matri-moneymaker, who designs for fun and profit, with an emphasis on the latter, carefully tailored affairs between his prefabricated "clients" and the most eligible heiresses of the world. As promoter and agent, he is then entitled to his cut when the desired wedlock materializes.

But heiress Hope Lange is a shoo-in to fall not for Ricardo Montalban, who is the scrubbed, polished, though not quite grooma-cum-laude graduate of fearless Eros Charles Boyer's male-order school for candidate instant millionaire husbands, but for Glenn Ford, who has been planted by Boyer as chauffeur in Hope's household, the better to drive her swiftly into the clutches of his prized pupil.

The engaging screenplay is from Lindsay Hardy's novel, *The Grand Duke and Mr. Pimm*, which was to have been the title of the picture. The scenario misfires in many places, particularly in the latter stages when all semblance of credulity abruptly crumbles, but on the whole it plays to advantage, and David Swift as director has made the most of it. The actors bat it out expertly. Ford does what comes naturally. Lange strikes most of the right notes and postures as a sexy all-American kook with 40 million clams in the kitty. Telly Savalas just about steals the show as Lange's gourmet-uncle.

•

LOVE IS A MANY-SPLENDORED THING

1955, 102 mins, US Ⓥ ⦿ ▭ col

Dir Henry King ***Prod*** Buddy Adler ***Scr*** John Patrick ***Ph*** Leon Shamroy ***Ed*** William Reynolds ***Mus*** Alfred Newman ***Art*** Lyle R. Wheeler, George W. Davis

Act William Holden, Jennifer Jones, Torin Thatcher, Isobel Elsom, Virginia Gregg, Richard Loo (20th Century-Fox)

Love, as portrayed and dramatized in this fine and sensitive Buddy Adler production based on the Han Suyin bestseller, is indeed a many-splendored thing. It's an unusual picture shot against authentic Hong Kong backgrounds and offbeat in its treatment, yet as simple and moving a love story as has come along in many a moon.

William Holden as the American correspondent, and Jennifer Jones as the Eurasian doctor, make a romantic team of great appeal. This is something of an emotional tear-jerker, to be sure, but an awfully well-made one. Han [in her autobiographical book *A Many Splendored Thing*] was less concerned with drama than with tracing the mating of two kindred souls in a world strange to both.

Up to the middle of the film, things go rather slowly. Both director Henry King and screenwriter John Patrick apparently thought the romantic theme should be enough. Since

Elliott (Holden) is married and his wife won't give him a divorce, marriage is impossible. Although compromised, and without a job at the end, Han (Jones) holds fast to her love.

King and lenser Leon Shamroy do a magnificent job in utilizing the Hong Kong backgrounds, whether in the opening shots panning down on the teeming city or in the charming little scene where Han returns to her Chungking home and is followed there by Elliott.

Holden is restrained and completely believable. Jones is pure delight in a very difficult part. In her, the spirit of the book is caught completely. Supporting cast is fine, with Isobel Elsom properly superficial as the British matron who resents Jones. Kam Tong, as the Commie doctor who urges Jones to return to Red China and "her people," is sinister, yet wisely refrains from playing the heavy.

1955: Best Color Costume Design, Song ("Love Is a Many-Splendored Thing"), Scoring of a Dramatic Picture

NOMINATIONS: Best Picture, Actress (Jennifer Jones), Color Cinematography, Color Art Direction, Sound

•

LOVE IS A RACKET
1932, 74 mins, US b/w

Dir William A. Wellman ***Scr*** Courtney Terrett ***Ph*** Sid Hickox ***Ed*** William Holmes

Act Douglas Fairbanks, Jr., Ann Dvorak, Frances Dee, Lee Tracy, Lyle Talbot, Andre Luguet (Warner)

A shrewdly wrought comedy-drama [from the novel by Brooklyn newspaperman Rian James] blending the newspaper locale and gangland. Douglas Fairbanks does a nice job in his role of a quiet, but sophisticated, go-getting newspaper columnist who's smart but not smart-aleck, plays the love game with his eyes and his heart both open, and battles or takes it with agreeable grace and jauntiness.

Ann Dvorak makes a light part stand out by the neatly paced playing of a quiet role, and Lee Tracy as a genially humorous reporter is a tower of strength on the comedy side.

•

LOVE LAUGHS AT ANDY HARDY
1946, 93 mins, US Ⓥ b/w

Dir Willis Goldbeck ***Prod*** Robert Sisk ***Scr*** Harry Ruskin, William Ludwig ***Ph*** Robert Planck ***Ed*** Irvine Warburton ***Mus*** David Snell ***Art*** Cedric Gibbons, Harry McAfee

Act Mickey Rooney, Lewis Stone, Bonita Granville, Fay Holden (M-G-M)

This pic doesn't vary much from the basic formula used in the numerous predecessors in the Hardy family saga, but why should it?

Mickey Rooney is a couple of years older but doesn't look it, and certainly doesn't act it. A diminutive dynamo, Rooney bounces through his paces with his usual zest, capering, mugging, and energetically stealing every scene he's in—and he's in practically every one.

Always a pillar of strength, Lewis Stone is back at his old stand as Judge Hardy, still playing the grave, distinguished, and ideally understanding dad. Other cast regulars in the series include Fay Holden, who does a convincing job as Andy's anxious mother, and Sara Haden, in a walk-on part as Aunt Milly. Filling in as Andy's heartthrob is Bonita Granville, who registers nicely as the campus siren but who had better watch her waist and chin line for the future.

Bowing to the fact that Rooney is growing older, if no larger, story line pushes him to the brink of a marital plunge. Back from the wars, Andy picks up his academic career as a college freshman and falls badly for Granville, who trips him up by marrying someone else. Heartbroken, Andy is set to pack up for exile in South America until he's diverted back to normal by the chilly wiles of Lina Romay, a south-of-the-border chick who happens to be visiting the town of Carvel.

•

LOVE LETTERS
1945, 101 mins, US b/w

Dir William Dieterle ***Prod*** Hal Wallis ***Scr*** Ayn Rand ***Ph*** Lee Garmes ***Ed*** Anne Bauchens ***Mus*** Victor Young ***Art*** Hans Dreier, Roland Anderson

Act Jennifer Jones, Joseph Cotten, Ann Richards, Gladys Cooper, Anita Louise, Robert Sully (Paramount)

Let the tears fall where they may—*Love Letters* is that type of story: warm and appealing, sentimental and emotional.

It's the yarn of two British army officers on the Italian front, one of whom writes beautiful love letters for his friend to the latter's fiancée in England. The friend is a shallow egocentric, but in England the girl falls in love with the letters, and in turn with the man whom she thinks has written them. On a furlough in England the friend marries the girl, and she soon learns it wasn't he who wrote the letters but the fellow officer whom she's never met. And she becomes disillusioned by her husband's manner, which is utterly unlike that suggested by his letters.

Jennifer Jones gives to the part of the girl an elfin quality that at times reaches sheer brilliance. Joseph Cotten, as the writer of the letters, gives a fine, quietly restrained characterization, while Robert Sully is the officer-scoundrel she marries, a more-or-less bit part that he handles satisfactorily.

•

LOVE LETTERS
1983, 98 mins, US Ⓥ ⊙ col

Dir Amy Jones ***Prod*** Roger Corman ***Scr*** Amy Jones ***Ph*** Alec Hirschfeld ***Ed*** Wendy Greene ***Mus*** Ralph Jones ***Art*** Jeannine Oppewall

Act Jamie Lee Curtis, James Keach, Amy Madigan, Bud Cort, Matt Clark, Bonnie Bartlett (New World)

Love Letters is a fine intimate drama from writer-director (and former editor) Amy Jones. Although overly schematic and lacking a certain humor that might have been welcome, film is much closer to the tradition of personal European filmmaking.

Although in no way intended to seem typical, Jamie Lee Curtis is seen living a life that is certainly shared by many young contempo women. Suddenly, barely past age 40, Curtis's mother dies, and the daughter discovers a collection of old letters that reveal the secret love of her mother's life, a love that can stand as a pure ideal to Curtis. While poring over the missives, Curtis meets prosperous photographer James Keach, a 40-ish married man with two kids.

Also believable are the intense and sweaty sex scenes, into which Curtis throws herself with increasing abandon, and the exchanges with her best friend (Amy Madigan) who delivers conventional put-downs of modern men by way of rationalizing a vow of celibacy.

•

LOVELY TO LOOK AT
1952, 101 mins, US Ⓥ ⊙ col

Dir Mervyn LeRoy ***Prod*** Jack Cummings ***Scr*** George Wells, Harry Ruby, Andrew Solt ***Ph*** George J. Folsey ***Ed*** John McSweeney, Jr. ***Mus*** Jerome Kern ***Art*** Cedric Gibbons, Gabriel Scognamillo

Act Kathryn Grayson, Howard Keel, Red Skelton, Marge Champion, Gower Champion, Ann Miller (M-G-M)

A pleasant round of light musical comedy entertainment is contained in this remake of *Roberta* [originally produced on Broadway in 1933].

Kathryn Grayson and Howard Keel for songs; Red Skelton for comedy; Marge and Gower Champion and Ann Miller for terps top the talent offerings. All deliver expertly. Score has 10 tunes cleffed by Jerome Kern, including the standard "Smoke Gets in Your Eyes," for which Otto A. Harbach did the lyrics. It also backs the stand-out dance number of the show, terped by the Champions.

Modernization finds Skelton as the comic who inherits half of a Parisian dress shop and he goes to Paris to claim the inheritance so he and his pals (Keel and Champion) can put on a Broadway show.

•

LOVELY WAY TO DIE, A
(UK: A LOVELY WAY TO GO)
1968, 103 mins, US col

Dir David Lowell Rich ***Prod*** Richard Lewis ***Scr*** A. J. Russell ***Ph*** Morris Hartzband ***Ed*** Sidney Katz, Gene Palmer ***Mus*** Kenyon Hopkins ***Art*** Alexander Golitzen, Willard Levitas

Act Kirk Douglas, Sylva Koscina, Eli Wallach, Kenneth Haigh, Martyn Green, Sharon Farrell (Universal)

This is the kind of hard-hitting polished murder-mystery meller that Kirk Douglas can play in his sleep. Cast with the cool, aloof Sylva Koscina and Eli Wallach, the screenplay is crisp and tangy, though the plotline wavers at a few spots.

Douglas is a cop whose belief is that hands are made for shooting, punching, holding drinks, and caressing dames. As a protest at the mollycoddling of hoods by the police he turns in his badge, to be hired by Wallach, a shrewd homespun attorney, to protect Koscina, being defended by Wallach on a rap of murdering her husband.

As a male bodyguard Douglas is intrigued by the girl. As an ex-cop he's intrigued by the murder mystery.

Douglas plays the confident, flip, resourceful he man with a suave winning way with the femmes, in his customary easy-going fashion, and Koscina's hot-and-cold attitude to his boudoir advances are both amusing and helpful to the atmosphere of the mystery yarn.

•

LOVELY WAY TO GO, A
SEE: A LOVELY WAY TO DIE

•

LOVE ME OR LEAVE ME
1955, 122 mins, US Ⓥ ⊙ ⌴ col

Dir Charles Vidor ***Prod*** Joe Pasternak ***Scr*** Daniel Fuchs, Isobel Lennart ***Ph*** Arthur E. Arling ***Ed*** Ralph E. Winters ***Mus*** George Stoll (sup.), Percy Faith (arr.) ***Art*** Cedric Gibbons, Urie McCleary

Act Doris Day, James Cagney, Cameron Mitchell, Robert Keith, Tom Tully, Harry Bellaver (M-G-M)

Metro's concept of the Ruth Etting story [from a screen story by Daniel Fuchs] embodies one of the two basic Hollywood filmusical formulae: and-then-I-wrote or and-then-I-sang. While it's not the usual songsmith cavalcade (Etting was and is depicted essentially as a song delineator), it does blend so rich a medley of some of the more popular standards of the 1920s that it's virtually a salute to ASCAP.

The off-beat aspects of the strange real-life relationship of Etting and "Col." Moe (here called Martin) Snyder has been caught with an honesty and realism that borders on creating mixed emotions. In short, Doris Day as Etting, is so consumed by ambition as to blot out the nefarious antecedents of "The Gimp," so ably played by James Cagney. His personation of the clubfooted Chicago hoodlum and muscleman is the Cagney of the Warner Bros. gangster pictures of the early 1930s—hard-bitten, cruel, sadistic, and unrelenting.

It becomes difficult betimes to know for whom to root. Their "marriage" is a strange thing. Her recourse to the bottle; her dull-eyed acceptance of the somewhat unholy nuptial alliance; her consuming ambition to scale the heights; her careful decorum vis-à-vis pianist-arranger Johnny Alderman (well played by Cameron Mitchell); the patience of the agent (Robert Keith, another good job); the dogged faithfulness of Harry Bellaver as the dimwit stooge-bodyguard; and the rest of it, make for an arresting chunk of celluloid.

Musically there's almost too much but Day does uncork a flock of socko standards, and two good new ones, "I'll Never Stop Loving You" (Brodzky-Cahn) and "Never Look Back" (by Chilton Price).

Under Metro filming, in CinemaScope and color, it's a rich canvas of the Roaring '20s with gutsy and excellent performances.

•

LOVE ME TENDER
1956, 94 mins, US Ⓥ ⌴ b/w

Dir Robert D. Webb ***Prod*** David Weisbart ***Scr*** Robert Buckner ***Ph*** Leo Tover ***Mus*** Lionel Newman ***Art*** Lyle R. Wheeler, Maurice Ransford

Act Richard Egan, Debra Paget, Elvis Presley, Robert Middleton, William Campbell, Neville Brand (20th Century-Fox)

Appraising Presley as an actor, he ain't. Not that it makes much difference. There are four songs, and lotsa Presley wriggles thrown in for good measure.

Screenplay from a story by Maurice Geraghty is synthetic. Story line centers on Presley, the youngest of four brothers, who stayed on their Texas farm while the older three are away fighting the Yankees. The older brother (Richard Egan) left a gal (Debra Paget), and when word comes that he's been killed in battle, she weds Presley. When the three boys come home to resume their civvy ways, it's hard to keep Egan down on the farm because he's still in love with Paget, now his brother's wife.

Egan is properly stoic as the older brother while Paget does nothing more than look pretty and wistful throughout. Mildred Dunnock gets sincerity into the part of mother of the brood, an achievement. Nobody, however, seems to be having as much fun as Presley especially when he's singing the title song, "Poor Boy," "We're Gonna Move," and "Let Me." Tunes were written by Presley and Vera Matson.

•

LOVE ME TONIGHT
1932, 90 mins, US b/w

Dir Rouben Mamoulian ***Scr*** Samuel Hoffenstein, Waldemar Young, George Marion, Jr. ***Ph*** Victor Milner

Act Maurice Chevalier, Jeanette MacDonald, Charles Ruggles, Charles Butterworth, Myrna Loy, C. Aubrey Smith (Paramount)

Treatment takes on the color of a musical comedy frolic, whimsical in its aim and deliciously carried out in its pattern, in its playing, and in its direction. Effect is altogether delightful. Gives Jeanette MacDonald an excellent opportunity for quiet comedy playing, which she rises charmingly to meet.

Story has to do with Maurice Chevalier, a Paris tailor, going to a great French castle to collect a bill run up by a scapegrace scion of the family, and being introduced as

Baron Courtelin and held as an honored guest to keep his mission secret. Fun of the situation arises from the presence of the lively young Parisian commoner among a crowd of fossilized old nobles of both sexes.

The comedy [from a French play by Leopold Marchant and Paul Armont] is exquisitely amusing, particularly in all too brief sequences involving Charlie Ruggles and Charles Butterworth. Adapters also have given the dialog a number of swift and spicy sallies that count for solid laughs. And the production throughout has stunning pictorial beauty. Here is seen the fine hand of director Rouben Mamoulian.

Musical numbers [by Richard Rodgers and Lorenz Hart] are as amusing for once in their lyrics as they are attractive in their melodies, and are blended in smoothly with the action.

•

LOVE ON THE DOLE

1941, 99 mins, UK Ⓥ col

Dir John Baxter ***Prod*** John Baxter ***Scr*** Walter Greenwood, Barbara Emery, Rollo Gamble ***Ph*** James Wilson ***Mus*** Richard Addinsell

Act Deborah Kerr, Clifford Evans, Geoffrey Hibbert (British National)

The camera's facility in pin-pointing the tenets of tragedy has been harnessed in *Love on the Dole*. The Walter Greenwood novel screens as powerful dramatics. Closely followed play and original book's mean subject matter, moral outlook, and frequently the dialog of the characters in the drab tale of near-matrimony under the Depression are served without softening. North Country town and its poverty are authentically caught in atmosphere and sets.

Sepia tintage heightens the gloom of film's representation of a North of England community. John Baxter's direction skillfully builds episode upon episode as he drives for that final decision of the wench, Sally, to trek self and family out of the relief mire via the primrose path. Direction, plus the tight scripting, makes the tragic journey vital and real. Deborah Kerr is satisfactorily hard as Sally; Clifford Evans's Larry shows understanding of the role of the labor crusader out for a better deal in life. Top honors go to young Geoffrey Hibbert, as the girl's kid brother.

•

LOVE ON THE RUN

1936, 70 mins, US b/w

Dir W. S. Van Dyke ***Prod*** Joseph L. Mankiewicz ***Scr*** John Lee Martin, Manuel Seff, Gladys Hurlbut ***Ph*** Oliver T. Marsh ***Ed*** Frank Sullivan ***Mus*** Franz Waxman ***Art*** Cedric Gibbons

Act Joan Crawford, Clark Gable, Franchot Tone, Reginald Owen, Mona Barrie, Donald Meek (M-G-M)

Crowded with ludicrous situations, considerable action, and popular gagging, the film is lightweight and synthetic. In the hands of less capable studio people, many of the more absurd proceedings might have been pretty hard to stomach.

Story [by Alan Green and Julian Brodie] early pits Franchot Tone and Clark Gable as rival scribes working in England for American newspapers. Gable, as usual outwitting the slower-moving Tone, promises to fill the void in the life of Joan Crawford, the abused heiress, who has deserted a titled fortune-seeker at the altar. The newspaperman sees the makings of a great series of articles depicting the rich femme's reactions to real romance.

Reginald Owen is sufficiently ingratiating as the suave spy chief while Mona Barrie contributes a nice job as wife and principal assistant. Donald Meek strains hard to make a nitwit caretaker part humorous.

•

LOVE PARADE, THE

1929, 107 mins, US ⊙ b/w

Dir Ernst Lubitsch ***Scr*** Guy Bolton, Ernst Vajda ***Ph*** Victor Milner ***Mus*** Victor Schertzinger ***Art*** Hans Dreier

Act Maurice Chevalier, Jeanette MacDonald, Lupino Lane, Lillian Roth, Eugene Pallette, Edgar Norton (Paramount)

In *The Love Parade*, second starring talker for Maurice Chevalier, Paramount has its first original screen operetta production whose story is more than made up in magnificence of sets and costumes, tuneful music, subtlety of direction, comedy, and general appeal. It's a fine, near-grand entertainment.

At the outset the Chevalier personality is put to the fore in the manner the Parisian music-hall star knows best. In Jeanette MacDonald, ingenue prima donna from Broadway, Chevalier has an actress opposite who all but steals the picture.

The story says that the philandering Parisian, brought back to Sylvania, ruled by MacDonald, because of his scandalous affairs as a military attache in France's capital, must, in accepting marriage to the queen, keep his fingers out of all matters of state and be subject to her own commands.

The wedding is an extravaganza, with one of the largest sets ever built, but musically lacks the punch of other scenes.

Guy Bolton wrote the libretto for *Love Parade* [from the play *The Prince Consort* by Leon Xanrof and Jules Chancel]. It can be said that this is the first true screen musical.

1929/30: NOMINATIONS: Best Picture, Director, Actor (Maurice Chevalier), Cinematography, Art Direction, Sound

•

LOVER, THE

1992, 110 mins, France/UK Ⓥ ⊙ col

Dir Jean-Jacques Annaud ***Prod*** Claude Berri ***Scr*** Gerard Brach, Jean-Jacques Annaud ***Ph*** Robert Fraisse ***Ed*** Noelle Boisson ***Mus*** Gabriel Yared ***Art*** Thanh At Hoang

Act Jane March, Tony Leung, Frederique Meininger, Arnaud Giovaninetti, Melvil Poupaud, Lisa Faulkner (Renn/Films AZ/Burrill)

The Lover, a sophisticated adaptation of Marguerite Duras's bestselling memoir about her love affair as a 15-year-old with a rich, older Chinese man, lacks the distinctive voice and ambiance of the book, but the abundant sex—soft-core and tasteful—and the splendid sets make up for the film's banal style.

No expense has been spared—the film cost $22 million—in Jean-Jacques Annaud's evocation of the pungent atmosphere of the story's 1920s Vietnam setting.

Part of the fault lies with Jane March, a pretty 17-year-old English actress who plays the young Duras. She pouts to perfection but does not convey the jaded spirit of the girl. Tony Leung is excellent as the shiftless scion whose love for the girl makes him emotionally naked and vulnerable.

In the film's well-handled subplot, Frederique Meininger is superb as the girl's exhausted schoolteacher mother. Most powerful scene deals with the mother's farewell to her son (Arnaud Giovaninetti), who is being sent back to France.

1992: NOMINATION: Best Cinematography

•

LOVER COME BACK

1961, 107 mins, US Ⓥ col

Dir Delbert Mann ***Prod*** Stanley Shapiro, Martin Melcher ***Scr*** Stanley Shapiro, Paul Henning ***Ph*** Arthur E. Arling ***Ed*** Marjorie Fowler ***Mus*** Frank DeVol ***Art*** Alexander Golitzen, Robert Clatworthy

Act Rock Hudson, Doris Day, Tony Randall, Edie Adams, Jack Oakie, Jack Kruschen (Universal)

This is a funny, most-of-the-time engaging, smartly produced show. Farce has Rock Hudson as would-be conqueror of Doris Day, who as the victim of a who's-who deception plays brinkmanship with surrender. There's a bed scene but this is all right because the two, while not remembering the Maryland ceremony (due to being stoned under preposterous circumstances), were legally hitched.

Hudson and Day are rival Madison Avenue ad account people. He deceives her into thinking he's a scientist working on an actually nonexistent product called VIP. She undertakes to wrest the VIP account from the masquerading Hudson. Meanwhile he is trying to maneuver her into romantic conquest.

Tony Randall draws yucks consistently as head of an agency he inherited but doesn't really helm because he can't make decisions. Jack Oakie plays broadly and humorously the part of a floor-wax maker who goes to the agency offering him the best girls and bourbon. Edie Adams clicks as a chorus girl trying to get ahead, and Jack Kruschen, as a partly screwball scientist, also wins laughs.

1961: NOMINATION: Best Original Story & Screenplay

•

LOVERS, THE

SEE: LES AMANTS

•

LOVERS AND OTHER STRANGERS

1970, 104 mins, US Ⓥ col

Dir Cy Howard ***Prod*** David Susskind ***Scr*** Renee Taylor, Joseph Bologna, David Zelag ***Ph*** Andy Laszlo ***Ed*** David Bretherton, Sidney Katz ***Mus*** Fred Karlin ***Art*** Ben Edwards

Act Bea Arthur, Bonnie Bedelia, Michael Brandon, Richard Castellano, Robert Dishy, Harry Guardino (ABC)

Lovers and Other Strangers tells in a delightful way of the marriage of a young couple who have been making it on the sly for over a year. Comedy vignettes reveal in amusing and compassionate fashion the assorted marital foibles of members of both families.

Bonnie Bedelia and Michael Brandon, the couple in question, have their own lifestyle which rubs against but does not destroy relations with their respective parents. Gig Young and Cloris Leachman are her folks, while Richard Castellano and Bea Arthur are his.

Screenplay [from the play by Joseph Bologna and Renee Taylor] is essentially a string of intercut vignettes about the young couple's relatives. On the girl's side of things, Young has been having a side affair with Anne Jackson for some years; she is perfect.

1970: Best Song ("For All We Know")

NOMINATIONS: Best Supp. Actor (Richard Castellano), Adapted Screenplay

•

LOVE SERENADE

1996, 101 mins, Australia Ⓥ ▭ col

Dir Shirley Barrett ***Prod*** Jan Chapman ***Scr*** Shirley Barrett ***Ph*** Mandy Walker ***Ed*** Denise Haratzis ***Mus*** Christine Woodruff ***Art*** Steven Jones-Evans

Act Miranda Otto, Rebecca Frith, George Shevtsov, John Alansu, Jessica Napier (Chapman)

Shirley Barrett's debut, *Love Serenade* is an oblique vision of love and sex in an isolated Australian town. A shade overlong, pic is nonetheless full of delights.

Vicki-Ann and Dimity Hurley, sisters in their 20s, live in a small house in a dusty, seemingly underpopulated town of Sunray. Vicki-Ann (Rebecca Frith) runs a Unisex hair salon called Hairport, reads cheap romantic fiction and wears various shades of pink. Her kid sister, 20-year-old Dimity (Miranda Otto), spends her days aimlessly riding around the dusty streets on her bicycle; in the evening, she works as a waitress at the town's Chinese restaurant.

And so life goes on until Ken Sherry (George Shevtsov) drives into town to take over the local, one-man radio station. A child of the hippie era now well into middle age, Sherry is a jaded hedonist who's dropped out. Inevitably, he seduces both sisters.

The filmmaker has a wry, offbeat sense of humor, and a delight in the foibles and eccentricities of her characters.

Otto (daughter of actor Barry Otto) is touching as the sensitive and vulnerable yet unexpectedly tenacious Dimity. Newcomer Frith has the trickiest role as the rather crass Vicki-Ann, but succeeds in not tipping the sometimes irritating older sister into caricature. Mandy Walker's wide-screen cinematography beautifully captures the details of this one-horse town, and Steven Jones-Evans's production design is remarkable for its witty detail.

•

LOVESICK

1983, 95 mins, US Ⓥ ⊙ col

Dir Marshall Brickman ***Prod*** Charles Okun ***Scr*** Marshall Brickman ***Ph*** Gerry Fisher ***Ed*** Nina Feinberg ***Mus*** Philippe Sarde ***Art*** Philip Rosenberg

Act Dudley Moore, Elizabeth McGovern, Alec Guinness, John Huston, William Shawn, Alan King (Ladd/Warner)

An engaging idea—Dudley Moore as a successful, married shrink who becomes obsessed with a beautiful patient (Elizabeth McGovern)—is rendered inoperable by Marshall Brickman's witless script and uninspired direction.

Perhaps most descriptive of the script's desperation is the gimmicky inclusion of Sigmund Freud, who mystically materializes in the person of Alec Guinness whenever Moore seeks professional help. Guinness properly plays it straight and slightly aloof, telling Moore that his obsession with McGovern "reminds us what we really are—animals—take it or leave it." Pure Freud.

Ron Silver is fine as an arrogant actor but Gene Sacks as a suicidal patient, John Huston and Alan King as stuffy doctors, and Renee Taylor, as a patient, are all embarrassing.

•

LOVE'S LABOUR'S LOST

2000, 93 mins, UK Ⓥ ⊙ ▭ col

Dir Kenneth Branagh ***Prod*** David Barron, Kenneth Branagh ***Scr*** Kenneth Branagh ***Ph*** Alex Thomson ***Ed*** Neil Farrell, Dan Farrell ***Mus*** Patrick Doyle ***Art*** Tim Harvey

Act Alessandro Nivola, Alicia Silverstone, Natascha McElhone, Kenneth Branagh, Carmen Ejogo, Matthew Lillard (Shakespeare/Miramax)

Love's Labour's Lost [from the play by William Shakespeare] is a luscious labor of love. As if to prove the two extremes of his affection for the Bard, Kenneth Branagh has followed his four-hour, belt-and-braces version of *Hamlet* with one of the most audacious adaptations of Will's works, hacked down into a faux, old-style Hollywood tuner and given the handle "A Romantic Musical Comedy." Anyone with an open mind and a hankering for the simple pleasures of Tinseltown's Golden Age will be rewarded with 90-odd minutes of often silly, frequently charming and always honest entertainment.

The original text has been hacked back to almost nothing, and the plot massively simplified; the 10 musical numbers come fast and frequent; and the whole thing is packed as upbeat, widescreen entertainment that doesn't have an ounce of spare flesh in its trim 93 minutes. Where Branagh takes his biggest risk is in retaining rather than modernizing what's left of the original dialogue, which still takes considerable concentration to follow, in between highly hummable classics by Gershwin, Kern, Porter and Berlin.

Plot is pure frippery. The King of Navarre (Alessandro Nivola) has retired to the country with his three friends (Branagh, Mathew Lillard, Adrian Lester) to pursue the intellectual life away from the distractions of beautiful women. But their resolve is soon put to the test when the Princess of France (Alicia Silverstone) and *her* three companions (Natascha McElhone, Carmen Ejogo, Emily Mortimer) pay the King a visit. Branagh sets the whole thing in September 1939, as war clouds gather over Europe and a privileged gentry enjoys an aimless existence. Interspersed through the action, and conveniently summarizing huge chunks of plot, are B&W, fake-scratchy newsreels, with a plummy English voice (Branagh again) putting a jocular gloss on outside events.

Branagh clearly knows his musicals and abides by the well-tested rules that made the classics classics. Sets are relatively few and evoke similar ones from past tuners; most dance numbers employ long takes, with the full length of the dancer's body visible; and segues from dialogue into songs are musically seamless and psychologically apt. All numbers are kept short and brief, never taking over the picture. The overall effect is knowing and joyful at the same time, aided by perfs from the whole cast that are free of pretentiousness and have a superior stock-company glee. Stuart Hopps' choreography artfully disguises the fact that only Lester can really dance; and vocal weaknesses by some of the cast (Ejogo, Silverstone, Branagh) are fleeting.

•

LOVES OF A BLONDE
SEE: LASKY JEDNE PLAVOVLASKY

•

LOVES OF ISADORA, THE
SEE: ISADORA

•

LOVES OF JOANNA GODDEN, THE
1947, 91 mins, UK b/w
Dir Charles Frend *Prod* Michael Balcon *Scr* H. E. Bates *Ph* Douglas Slocombe *Ed* Michael Truman *Mus* Ralph Vaughan Williams *Art* Duncan Sutherland
Act Googie Withers, Jean Kent, John McCallum, Derek Bond, Chips Rafferty (Ealing)

As a record of sheep farming in a corner of England in 1905, this picture [based on *Joanna Godden* by Sheila Kaye-Smith, adapted by Angus MacPhail] may have its points. But as a story of a high-spirited, lovely young woman who inherits a farm and is expected to marry and let her husband do the job, the picture falls short of its intentions.

Set against the background of the Romney Marshes in Kent, Joanna (Googie Withers), impetuous and self-willed, is bequeathed one of the leading farms on the Marsh. A codicil in her father's will expresses the hope that she will marry neighbor-farmer Arthur Alce (John McCallum). Determined to defy the conventions of the time, she outrages the countryside by running the farm herself and by her experiments in cross-breeding and ploughing. Stinting herself and luxury, she sends her young sister, Ellen (Jean Kent), to a finishing school, from which the girl returns an accomplished gold digger.

Joanna has a mild affair with Collard (Chips Rafferty), the man engaged to look after her sheep, before she falls for a local aristocrat, Martin Trevor (Derek Bond). The banns are put up, but Martin is drowned. Meanwhile Ellen has bewitched Arthur Alce, Joanna's "old faithful," marries him and deserts him for an old man with money.

Withers looks as attractive as she has ever done, but her characterization of the name part has a soporific monotony.

The men fare somewhat better, although McCallum is given little to lighten his dourness. Bond gives a natural and pleasant performance as Martin, and Rafferty disappears far too early.

•

LOVE STORY
1970, 99 mins, US Ⓥ ⦿ col
Dir Arthur Hiller *Prod* Howard G. Minsky *Scr* Erich Segal *Ph* Dick Kratina *Ed* Robert C. Jones *Mus* Francis Lai *Art* Robert Gundlach
Act Ali MacGraw, Ryan O'Neal, John Marley, Ray Milland, Russell Nype, Katherine Balfour (Paramount)

Love Story is an excellent film. Made for about $2.2 million the Paramount release is generally successful on all artistic levels, propelled by the bestselling Erich Segal novel written from the original screenplay.

Ali MacGraw is a girl of poor origins who has worked her way to high academic status; Ryan O'Neal, restive in his identity, but at the outset just another rich man's athletic-oriented son at the old family college, develops true manliness from his love for her, through their marriage and the severe challenge of her terminal illness.

John Marley is excellent as MacGraw's father and Ray Milland is outstanding as O'Neal's cold father. Both men go way beyond the superficial trappings of their roles and make the characters vital. It's O'Neal's picture by a good margin.

1970: Best Original Score

NOMINATIONS: Best Picture, Director, Actor (Ryan O'Neal), Actress (Ali MacGraw), Supp. Actor (John Marley), Original Story & Screenplay

•

LOVE STREAMS
1984, 136 mins, US Ⓥ col
Dir John Cassavetes *Prod* Menahem Golan, Yoram Globus *Scr* John Cassavetes, Ted Allan *Ph* Al Ruban *Ed* George Villasenor *Mus* Bo Harwood
Act Gena Rowlands, John Cassavetes, Diahnne Abbott, Seymour Cassel, Margaret Abbott, Jakob Shaw (Cannon)

John Cassavetes's *Love Streams* shapes up as one of the filmmaker's best, both artistically and commercially, in some times emotionally potent, technically assured and often brilliantly insightful.

Reflecting the title, the plot begins with two separate flows. Robert Harmon (Cassavetes) is a successful writer from the Gay Talese school currently researching the subject of love for sale on a firsthand basis. Intercut is Sarah Lawson's (Gena Rowlands) story—an emotionally erratic woman proceeding through a divorce and custody case.

One can nitpick about the picture's length and use of repetition but these are minor points in the overall strength of the production. The dramatic roller-coaster ride of frightening and funny moments leave little room for indifference.

•

LOVE THAT BRUTE
1950, 85 mins, US b/w
Dir Alexander Hall *Prod* Fred Kohlmar *Scr* Karl Tunberg, Darrell Ware, John Lee Mahin *Ph* Lloyd Ahern *Ed* Nick De Maggio *Mus* Cyril J. Mockridge
Act Paul Douglas, Jean Peters, Cesar Romero, Keenan Wynn, Joan Davis, Jay C. Flippen (20th Century-Fox)

Yarn is a parody of the Chicago gangster era, circa 1928. Without stopping for plausibility, it races through a series of screwball situations.

Pic revolves around Paul Douglas, in a tailor-made role of a not-too-bright but big-hearted gangster. He falls for a country gal (Jean Peters) and, in order to give her a governess job inside his house, he pretends to be a widower with a couple of kids. Douglas's auditioning of a juve hoodlum (Peter Price) to play his son is one of the pic's high spots.

Douglas's fine performance is matched by Peters, who registers impressively as a prim governess and a sultry nitery singer, scoring with the Rodgers and Hart oldie, "You Took Advantage of Me." Comedy impact is supplied expertly by Keenan Wynn and Joan Davis.

•

LOVE WALTZ, THE
1930, 70 mins, Germany b/w
Dir Wilhelm Thiele *Prod* Erich Pommer *Scr* Hans Muller, Robert Liebmann *Ph* Werner Brandes, Konstantin Tschet *Mus* Werner Heymann
Act Lilian Harvey, John Batten, Georg Alexander (UFA)

The all-English dialog version of this UFA talker is a presentable piece of work, even allowing for blemishes. Film errs somewhat in starting off as snappy comedy and ending up as the usual Ruritanian romance, being much more entertaining in the first half than in the final reels. Production is a mixture of imitation American slickness and Germanic artistry, with the result much of the footage is very easy to the eye.

Story is the usual sugary mixture expected of the species, telling how a bored youngster rivets himself on an equally bored archduke, who is due to get engaged to an even more bored princess.

Usual Erich Pommer touches are noticeable. Lilian Harvey isn't photographed to the best advantage and John Batten hasn't much difficulty in getting honors among the leads, although Georg Alexander's work as the duke is a smooth job, nicely rounded off.

The English version was done under the supervision of Carl Winston, who went to Berlin. Harvey, being of English extraction, plays her role in both versions, and young Englishman Batten handles the Willi Fritsch character.

•

LOVE WITH THE PROPER STRANGER
1963, 102 mins, US Ⓥ ⦿ b/w
Dir Robert Mulligan *Prod* Alan J. Pakula *Scr* Arnold Schulman *Ph* Milton Krasner *Ed* Aaron Stell *Mus* Elmer Bernstein *Art* Hal Pereira, Roland Anderson
Act Natalie Wood, Steve McQueen, Edie Adams, Herschel Bernardi, Tom Bosley (Paramount)

Proper Stranger is a somewhat unstable picture, fluctuating between scenes of a substantial, lifelike disposition and others where reality is suspended in favor of deliberately exaggerated hokum. Fortunately the film survives these shortcomings through its sheer breezy good nature and the animal magnetism of its two stars.

Arnold Schulman's scenario describes the curious love affair that evolves between two young, New York Italians—a freedom-loving freelance musician (Steve McQueen) and a sheltered girl (Natalie Wood)—when she becomes pregnant following their one-night stand at a summer resort.

Wood plays her role with a convincing mixture of feminine sweetness and emotional turbulence. McQueen displays an especially keen sense of timing. Although he's probably the most unlikely Italian around (the character could and should obviously have been altered to Irish Catholic), he is an appealing figure nevertheless.

Fine supporting work is contributed by Edie Adams as an accommodating stripper, Herschel Bernardi as Wood's overly protective older brother and Tom Bosley as a jittery suitor.

Robert Mulligan's direction runs hot and cold, like the screenplay and the film itself.

1963: NOMINATIONS: Best Actress (Natalie Wood), Original Story & Screenplay, B&W Cinematography, B&W Costume Design, B&W Art Direction

•

LOVING
1970, 89 mins, US Ⓥ col
Dir Irvin Kershner *Prod* Don Devlin, Raymond Wagner *Scr* Don Devlin *Ph* Gordon Willis *Ed* Robert Lawrence *Mus* Bernardo Segall *Art* Walter Scott Herndon
Act George Segal, Eva Marie Saint, Sterling Hayden, Keenan Wynn, Nancie Phillips, Janis Young (Columbia)

A good story about marriage crackups among the fortyish set in suburbia.

A novel by J. M. Ryan was basis for the script, which is handicapped by a protagonist who, while not supposed to be sympathetic, isn't even interesting in his selfishness and immaturity.

George Segal is the character, an aging commercial artist who would seem in reality to have been long-since crushed by the forces against which he continually rails. Eva Marie Saint is quite outstanding as the slightly nagging but steadfast wife. Her character is also hampered by some incredulity of premise, but she more than overcomes the liability. Within script limitations, cast delivers well, Saint in the extreme, Segal however never quite believable.

•

LOVING COUPLES
1980, 97 mins, US Ⓥ col
Dir Jack Smight *Prod* Renee Valente *Scr* Martin Donovan *Ph* Philip Lathrop *Ed* Grey Fox, Frank Urioste *Mus* Fred Karlin *Art* Jan Scott
Act Shirley MacLaine, James Coburn, Susan Sarandon, Sally Kellerman, Stephen Collins (20th Century-Fox)

Loving Couples opens with a snappy, cute meet. Shirley MacLaine is riding a horse and Stephen Collins, driving along in a sports car, stares at her, misses a turn in the road and crashes. She rides over to the prone Collins and rips open his pants. Well, she's a doctor.

Young stud Collins tries to put the make on her. Not too long after he gets it. She's not getting much attention from her work-obsessed doctor husband (James Coburn) who learns of her affair from Collins's live-in friend (Susan Sarandon). And they, in turn, fall into a motel bed.

It's all fun and sexual games. Direction by Jack Smight is assured and never lags. MacLaine is in top form, sassy and sweet in turn. Coburn delivers a casually effective light comedy performance. Sarandon is top-notch.

•

LOVING YOU
1957, 101 mins, US Ⓥ ⦿ col
Dir Hal Kanter ***Prod*** Hal B. Wallis ***Scr*** Herbert Baker, Hal Kanter ***Ph*** Charles Lang ***Ed*** Howard Smith ***Mus*** Walter Scharf (arr.) ***Art*** Hal Pereira, Albert Nozaki
Act Elvis Presley, Lizabeth Scott, Wendell Corey, Dolores Hart, James Gleason (Paramount)

Elvis Presley's second screen appearance is a simple story, in which he can be believed, which has romantic overtones and exposes the singer to the kind of thing he does best, i.e., shout out his rhythms, bang away at his guitar and perform the strange, knee-bending, hip-swinging contortions that are his trademark.

Apart from this, Presley shows improvement as an actor. It's not a demanding part and, being surrounded by a capable crew of performers, he comes across as a simple but pleasant sort. Film introes Dolores Hart in an undemanding role as Presley's girl.

Story has Presley picked up by Lizabeth Scott, a publicity girl touring with a hillbilly band on a whistlestop tour. She gets Wendell Corey, the leader of the outfit, to take on Presley, and they stunt him into a rock 'n' roll personality. Of course, there are complications and Presley takes himself off just as he's supposed to go on a national TV show.

•

LOVIN' MOLLY
1974, 98 mins, US col
Dir Sidney Lumet ***Prod*** Stephen Friedman ***Scr*** Stephen Friedman ***Ph*** Edward Brown ***Ed*** Joanne Burke ***Mus*** Fred Hellerman ***Art*** Gene Coffin
Act Anthony Perkins, Beau Bridges, Blythe Danner, Edward Binns, Susan Sarandon, Conrad Fowkes (Columbia)

The film version of Larry McMurtry's novel, *Leaving Cheyenne*, emerges as a misguided, heavy-handed attempt to span 40 years in the lives of three Texas rustics and their bizarre but homey menage a trois.

Divided into three main sections, *Lovin' Molly* opens in 1925 and sets up the situation in which two farmboy friends (Anthony Perkins, Beau Bridges) wage amicable war for the affections of a liberated earth mother (Blythe Danner) who loves them both in her fashion. Jumping to 1945 with a voice-over bridge, Danner has been married and widowed to a third young man (Conrad Fowkes) while continuing her sidebar relationships and bearing two children by a married Perkins and still-bachelor Bridges.

Pic's final section takes place in 1964 as the three find their time running out. Perkins dies of a heart attack and the ever-ready Bridges beds down with the accommodating Danner for what must be the 4,160th time.

•

L-SHAPED ROOM, THE
1962, 142 mins, UK Ⓥ b/w
Dir Bryan Forbes ***Prod*** James Woolf, Richard Attenborough ***Scr*** Bryan Forbes ***Ph*** Douglas Slocombe ***Ed*** Anthony Harvey ***Mus*** John Barry ***Art*** Ray Simm
Act Leslie Caron, Tom Bell, Brock Peters, Cicely Courtneidge, Avis Bunnage, Bernard Lee (Romulus)

Lynne Reid Banks's bestseller novel seemed, on the surface, to be unlikely material for a film. Largely set in the restricted area of a faded lodging house the novel had little enough glamour or strength of plot to recommended it, excellently written though it was. But Bryan Forbes's screenplay and his tactful, sensitive direction create a tender study in loneliness and frustrated love.

Yarn concerns a girl (Leslie Caron) with a background of provincial France who, in London, has a brief affair resulting in pregnancy. Rejecting the idea of an abortion she decides to live it out on her own. And, in the loneliness of her L-shaped room in a seedy tenement, she finds a new hope and purpose in life through meeting others who, in various ways, suffer their own loneliness and frustration.

This brief outline gives no credit to the film's many subtle undertones. Not a great deal happens but it is a thoroughly holding and intelligent film having the quality of a film like *Marty*.

Caron and Tom Bell make a strong team. Though they, plus Brock Peters, as Negro lad, bear the brunt of such action as there is, the trio are well supported by a number of others.

Vet Cicely Courtneidge makes a sharp comeback as a retired vaude artist, living with her cat and her faded press clippings. Other notable jobs are done by Avis Bunnage (a landlady who prides herself on the respectability of her house, despite two of her lodgers being prosties) and Bernard Lee, as her boozy, hearty gentleman friend.

1963: NOMINATION: Best Actress (Leslie Caron)

•

L.627
1992, 145 mins, France Ⓥ col
Dir Bertrand Tavernier ***Prod*** Alain Sarde, Frederic Bourboulon ***Scr*** Michel Alexandre, Bertrand Tavernier ***Ph*** Alain Choquart ***Ed*** Ariane Boeglin ***Mus*** Philippe Sarde ***Art*** Guy-Claude Francois
Act Didier Bezace, Jean-Paul Comart, Charlotte Kady, Jean-Roger Milo, Nils Tavernier, Philippe Torreton (Little Bear/Sarde)

With extraordinary documentary realism, Bertand Tavernier takes an impassioned look inside the day-to-day activities of a small, ill-equipped branch of the Paris drug squad. Tavernier has said his interest stems from his son Nils's brief involvement in drugs. With the script collaboration of a 15-year veteran of the Paris police, Michel Alexandre, Tavernier takes a probing look at drug unit operations while avoiding cop film cliches.

His protagonist is Lulu (Didier Bezace), a dedicated cop posted to a drug squad run by Dodo (Jean-Claude Comart), a racist with a sick sense of humor, and the attractive Marie (Charlotte Kady), who copes amazingly well with her difficult job. They are underequipped, underpaid, overworked—and they make a lot of mistakes.

Yet there's a camaraderie here, and many, like Lulu, are determined against all odds to get the drug dealers off the streets. Aside from his work, Lulu is involved with two women, his ex-wife (Cecile Garcia-Fogel) and a young prostitute/drug addict (Lara Guirao), who is HIV positive.

Spectacularly well shot by Alain Choquart on backstreets, metro platforms and in rundown apartments, pic makes an impassioned plea for public support for the police, society's only defense against the drug scourge. Precision pacing keeps the film's length from seeming excessive.

Standouts in a generally fine cast are Bezace, Kady and Nils Tavernier, to whom the film is dedicated. Title is that of a French drug law.

•

LUCK OF GINGER COFFEY, THE
1964, 100 mins, US/Canada b/w
Dir Irvin Kershner ***Prod*** Leon Roth ***Scr*** Brian Moore ***Ph*** Manny Wynn ***Ed*** Anthony Gibbs ***Mus*** Bernardo Segall ***Art*** Harry Horner
Act Robert Shaw, Mary Ure, Liam Redmond, Tom Harvey, Libby McClintock, Leo Leyden (Roth)

The Luck of Ginger Coffey is a well-turned-out drama based on a Brian Moore novel.

Robert Shaw and Mary Ure are a married couple who have found the going in Montreal rough since they arrived from Dublin six months before to make their new home in Canada. The husband, who cannot keep a job, has spent the passage money on which the wife was depending to return them to Ireland should they not make the grade. A marital crisis therefore arises, since the wife believes that with her husband's superior attitude he will always be unable to hold a job in Canada.

Shaw plays his brash Irishman with sincerity and Ure lends credence to the wife, both scoring strongly.

•

LUCKY JIM
1957, 95 mins, UK Ⓥ b/w
Dir John Boulting ***Prod*** Roy Boulting ***Scr*** Patrick Campbell, Jeffrey Dell ***Ph*** Max Greene ***Ed*** Max Benedict ***Mus*** John Addison ***Art*** Elliott Scott
Act Ian Carmichael, Terry-Thomas, Hugh Griffith, Sharon Acker, Clive Morton, Kenneth Griffith (Charter/British Lion)

Kingsley Amis's novel has been built up into a farcical comedy which, though slim enough in idea, provides plenty of opportunity for smiles, giggles and belly laughs. John Boulting directs with a lively tempo and even though the comedy situations loom up with inevitable precision, they are still irresistible.

The lightweight story spotlights Ian Carmichael as a junior history lecturer at a British university in the sticks who becomes disastrously involved in such serious college goings-on as a ceremonial lecture on "Merrie England" and a procession to honor the new university chancellor. There are also some minor shenanigans such as a riotous car chase, a slaphappy fistfight, a tipsy entry into a wrong bedroom containing a girl he is trying to shake off and a number of other happy-go-lucky situations.

The screenplay veers from facetiousness to downright slapstick but never lets up on its irresistible attack on the funnybone. Carmichael is a deft light-comedy performer who proves that he also can take hold of a character and make him believable.

•

LUCKY LADY
1975, 177 mins, US col
Dir Stanley Donen ***Prod*** Michael Gruskoff ***Scr*** Willard Huyck, Gloria Katz ***Ph*** Geoffrey Unsworth ***Ed*** Peter Boita, George Hively, Tom Rolf ***Mus*** Ralph Burns ***Art*** John Barry
Act Gene Hackman, Liza Minnelli, Burt Reynolds, Geoffrey Lewis, John Hillerman, Robby Benson (20th Century-Fox)

What appears to have been conceived as a madcap Prohibition-era action comedy, combined with an amusing romantic menage, emerges as forced hokum.

Successive vignettes take the stars through a series of expansive smuggling routines. Burt Reynolds, a gringo on the lam in Mexico, figures he can assume the dual role of major smuggler and lover of Liza Minnelli when her husband dies. Gene Hackman, also on the run, assumes a leadership role and the trio begin running hooch.

They encounter the likes of Michael Hordern, an urbane ship captain; John Hillerman, a feisty hood and Geoffrey Lewis, trigger-happy Coast Guard.

Some smart-looking production work survives the plot (admitted budget was $12.6 million).

•

LUCKY LUCIANO
1973, 113 mins, Italy/France Ⓥ col
Dir Francesco Rosi ***Prod*** Franco Cristaldi ***Scr*** Francesco Rosi, Lino Jannuzzi, Tonino Guerra ***Ph*** Pasqualino De Santis ***Ed*** Ruggero Mastroianni ***Mus*** Piero Piccioni ***Art*** Andrea Crisanti
Act Gian Maria Volonte, Rod Steiger, Charles Siragusa, Edmond O'Brien, Vincent Gardenia, Charles Cioffi (Vides/La Boetie)

Most films by Francesco Rosi probe well under the surface of people and events to establish a constant link between the legal and illegal exercise of power. In *Lucky Luciano* the search is expanded to embrace an interdependent crime empire operating in America and Italy, with roots in many other points on the map. But Rosi takes crime kingpin Lucky Luciano as his main clinical study, objective enough throughout to question his own facts, legendary accusations and hearsay.

Crime action is condensed in first few reels in sharply paced scenes and montage escalating Luciano to the Mafia throne, his arrest and conviction in the mid-1930s, with his deportation to Italy after serving nine years of a 30- to 50-year prison term.

•

LUCKY ME
1954, 99 mins, US Ⓥ ⦿ ▭ col
Dir Jack Donohue ***Prod*** Henry Blanke ***Scr*** James O'Hanlon, Robert O'Brien, Irving Elinson ***Ph*** Wilfrid M. Cline ***Ed*** Owen Marks ***Mus*** Ray Heindorf (dir.)
Act Doris Day, Robert Cummings, Phil Silvers, Eddie Foy, Jr., Nancy Walker, Martha Hyer (Warner)

A round of routine musical ingredients are featured in *Lucky Me*. The screenplay [from a story by coscripter James O'Hanlon] is a tissue of tired, often tiresome gags and situations without redeeming imagination or originality. The songs by Sammy Fain and Paul Francis Webster are only so-so listening.

Miami Beach is the story setting and its beauties take neatly to the squeeze-lensing. A tab show headed by Hap (Phil Silvers) is stranded in the resort city and through a series of remarkable circumstances, Hap, Candy (Doris Day), Duke (Eddie Foy, Jr.) and Flo (Nancy Walker) are working out their debts in the kitchen of a swank hotel. Stopping at the hotel is Dick (Robert Cummings), successful songsmith who is about to stage his own musical if Lorraine's (Martha Hyer) oil-rich Texan dad (Bill Goodwin) turns angel.

While the settings take well to the CinemaScope treatment, the players do not, many of the scenes showing the principles in an unflattering manner.

•

LUDWIG
1973, 186 mins, Italy/France/W. Germany ⦿ ▭ col
Dir Luchino Visconti ***Prod*** Ugo Santalucia ***Scr*** Luchino Visconti, Enrico Medioli, Suso Cecchi D'Amico ***Ph*** Armando Nannuzzi ***Ed*** Ruggero Mastroianni ***Mus*** Franco Mannino (sup.) ***Art*** Mario Chiari, Mario Scisci
Act Helmut Berger, Romy Schneider, Trevor Howard, Silvana Mangano, Gert Frobe, Helmut Griem (Mega/Cinetel/Divina)

As his 12th feature film, and third project based on German history and personages, Luchino Visconti chose King Ludwig II (Helmut Berger), the so-called "mad" monarch of Bavaria. *Ludwig* bears the Visconti stamp of dazzling, tasteful opulence and an operatic style. However, story construction is at first confusing.

To its credit the English version [translated by William Weaver] is literate, free of arch transliteration, and dotted with occasional brilliant aphorism. But it barely helps the limitations of the overall structure. Major phases of Ludwig's life include his patronage of composer Richard Wagner, portrayed effectively by Trevor Howard; the spendthrift erection of castles; the introverted indifference to his responsibilities as king; a long platonic love affair with Empress Elisabeth of Austria, played with great compassion by the spectacularly beautiful Romy Schneider; and a pervading atmosphere of latent, then overt homosexuality.

The score utilizes themes of Wagner, Schumann and Offenbach, with piano solos and orchestra conducting by Franco Mannino. Wagner's last original piano composition is performed publicly for first time herein.

1973: NOMINATION: Best Costume Design

•

LULLABY OF BROADWAY

1951, 91 mins, US Ⓥ ⦿ col

Dir David Butler ***Prod*** William Jacobs ***Scr*** Earl Baldwin ***Ph*** Wilfrid M. Cline ***Ed*** Irene Morra ***Mus*** Ray Heindorf (dir.) ***Art*** Douglas Bacon

Act Doris Day, Gene Nelson, S. Z. Sakall, Billy De Wolfe, Gladys George, Florence Bates (Warner)

Mounted in gorgeous Technicolor, and displaying the song-and-dance talents of costars Doris Day and Gene Nelson, *Lullaby of Broadway* has a solid comedy story line, deft direction and a capable cast.

Film gets away from the regular practice of injecting too many elaborate production numbers. Most of the tunes are hits of the previous two decades. Day scores with her solo song-and-dance routines, including "Just One of Those Things" and "You're Getting to Be a Habit with Me." She teams with Nelson for tune-and-terping of "Somebody Loves Me," "I Love the Way You Say Goodnight" and "Lullaby of Broadway."

Story has Day returning from several years in England to meet her mother (Gladys George), a former stage headliner who hit the skids due to drink. Girl arrives at supposed mansion of her mother, and is taken in tow by Billy De Wolfe and Anne Triola, two at-liberty vaudevillians working as butler and maid. Sakall, elderly owner of the house, takes an interest in the girl and gets involved in ensuing complications when his wife suspects an affair.

•

LUNE DANS LE CANIVEAU, LA
(THE MOON IN THE GUTTER)

1983, 137 mins, France/Italy Ⓥ ⊏⊐ col

Dir Jean-Jacques Beineix ***Prod*** Lise Fayolle (exec.) ***Scr*** Jean-Jacques Beineix ***Ph*** Philippe Rousselot ***Ed*** Monique Prim, Yves Deschamps ***Mus*** Gabriel Yared ***Art*** Hilton McConnico

Act Gerard Depardieu, Nastassja Kinski, Victoria Abril, Vittorio Mezzogiorno, Dominique Pinon, Milena Vukotic (Gaumont/TF1/Opera)

Moon is a FF25 million love-cum-whodunit comedy featuring frames to hang worthily in any museum of photography, some good acting, some stagey acting, plus a plot and dialog that together constitute a catalog of all the favorite corny twists and mouthings of yesterday's popular films and novels. None of this works even as tongue-in-cheek satire. Superficial value is all this film has.

Jean-Jacques Beineix, a confessed conoisseur of trashy novels, has based his script on a murder novel by David Goodis. He has a big, solid longshoreman, Gerard (played with muted strength by Gerard Depardieu), continuing a restless search for the rapist who caused his adult kid sister to borrow his razor and commit suicide with it leaving blood for the moon of the title to be reflected in.

Gerard lives with his kid brother and father, both layabouts and alcoholics, in a derelict house near the city port. The house also serves as a cheap bar and a brothel, where his regular girlfriend Bella works (a vivacious performance by Victoria Abril). A modicum of rough order is maintained by the father's black wife (Bertice Reading, screaming her dialog in an amusing way).

To this place comes one night a rich young man, Newton Channing (Vittorio Mezzogiorno), who stays on with the obvious intent of drinking himself to death. His sister turns up to bring him home. She is Loretta, and she is played with sly, warm smiles by Nastassja Kinski, appearing ready to burst into sexual maturity any minute now. Bernard and Loretta are drawn towards each other.

Film goes on to have a couple of endings, or new beginnings maybe. But most audiences will by then have ceased to care long ago.

•

LUNGFU FUNGWAN
(CITY ON FIRE)

1987, 104 mins, Hong Kong Ⓥ ⦿ col

Dir Ringo Lam ***Prod*** Karl Maka (exec.), Ringo Lam (assoc.) ***Scr*** Tommy Sham ***Ph*** Andrew Lau ***Ed*** Wong Ming-lam ***Mus*** Teddy Robin ***Art*** Luk Tze-fung

Act Chow Yun-Fat, Sun Yueh, Danny Lee, Carrie Ng, Roy Cheung, Lau Kong (Cinema City)

The bloody death of an undercover policeman gets the Royal Hong Kong Police in a complex situation. Inspector Lau (Sun Yueh), now past his prime, is in charge of the case. Besides the politics of being replaced by a younger officer, Lau must find someone immediately to take the place of the deceased.

The man he has in mind is Chow (Chow Yun-Fat with a new haircut is perfect for the serio-comic role) and is recruited for the mission of penetrating the gangsters. He poses as a sly wheeler-dealer of guns for hire. Chow is introduced to Fu (Danny Lee), sort of lieutenant of the syndicate.

Fu is a cautious man and puts Chow to various character tests to assure that security is maintained. In the process, a male bonding is developed between the two supposedly gutter-type characters.

A jewel robbery is set up and implemented with disastrous results, both from the gangsters who panic and the police force who can be faulted for lack of coordination. The tragic finale gives the film more dramatic power.

City on Fire is Cinema City's answer to *The French Connection*. It is highly animated, fast-moving entertainment. The street photography is highly realistic while the dramatic conflicts are well-controlled to avoid the usual soap opera ingredients. The offbeat Canto–jazz/soul musical score complements the well-balanced acting.

•

LUST FOR LIFE

1956, 122 mins, US Ⓥ ⦿ ⊏⊐ col

Dir Vincente Minnelli ***Prod*** John Houseman ***Scr*** Norman Corwin ***Ph*** Freddie Young, Russell Harlan ***Ed*** Adrienne Fazan ***Mus*** Miklos Rozsa ***Art*** Cedric Gibbons, Hans Peters, Preston Ames

Act Kirk Douglas, Anthony Quinn, James Donald, Pamela Brown, Everett Sloane, Niall MacGinnis (M-G-M)

This is a slow-moving picture whose only action is in the dialog itself. Basically a faithful portrait of Van Gogh, *Lust for Life* is nonetheless unexciting. It misses out in conveying the color and entertainment of the original Irving Stone novel. It's a tragic recap that Stone penned, but still there was no absence of amusing incidents. Lensed in Holland and France, *Lust for Life* is largely conversation plus expert tint photography, and both on a high level.

Kirk Douglas plays the title role with undeniable understanding of the artist. He's a competent performer all the way, conveying the frustrations which beset Van Gogh in his quest for knowledge of life and the approach to putting this on canvas.

But somehow the measure of sympathy that should be engendered for the genius who was to turn insane is not realized. To draw a comparison, Jose Ferrer in *Moulin Rouge* made Toulouse-Lautrec "closer" to the audience.

1956: Best Supp. Actor (Anthony Quinn)

NOMINATIONS: Best Actor (Kirk Douglas), Adapted Screenplay, Color Art Direction

•

LUST IN THE DUST

1984, 87 mins, US Ⓥ ⦿ col

Dir Paul Bartel ***Prod*** Allan Glaser, Tab Hunter ***Scr*** Philip Taylor ***Ph*** Paul Lohmann ***Ed*** Alan Toomayan ***Mus*** Peter Matz, Karen Hart ***Art*** Walter Pickette

Act Tab Hunter, Divine, Lainie Kazan, Geoffrey Lewis, Henry Silva, Cesar Romero (Fox Run)

Lust in the Dust is a saucy, irreverent, quite funny send-up of the Western. Film takes some of the old-time conventions—the silent stranger, the saloon singer with a past, the motley crew of crazed gunslingers, the missing stash of gold—and stands them on their head with outrageous comedy and imaginative casting.

Prevailing attitude is established immediately via some florid narration and the sight of the outsized Divine making his way across the desert in full drag on a donkey. Upon meeting Tab Hunter, the epitome of the straight-arrow hero of few words, Divine's character, Rosie, explains to him, in flashback, she's just been gang-raped by Geoffrey Lewis's bunch of Third World outlaws (and outlasted them all).

Duo arrives in the squalid little town of Chili Verde, where the entire populace seems to hang out at the cantina of Lainie Kazan.

Outrageous tale is handled with fine high humor by director Paul Bartel. Picture is Divine's for the taking, and take it he does with a vibrant, inventive comic performance.

•

LUSTY MEN, THE

1952, 112 mins, US Ⓥ ⦿ b/w

Dir Nicholas Ray ***Prod*** Jerry Wald ***Scr*** Horace McCoy, David Dortort ***Ph*** Lee Garmes ***Ed*** Ralph Dawson ***Mus*** Roy Webb ***Art*** Albert S. D'Agostino, Alfred Herman

Act Susan Hayward, Robert Mitchum, Arthur Kennedy, Arthur Hunnicutt, Frank Faylen, Walter Coy (Wald-Krasna/RKO)

Robert Mitchum is a faded rodeo champion who has fallen on bad days after an accident. Returning broke to the tumbledown ranch where he spent his boyhood, he finds the property desired by Arthur Kennedy, poor cowpoke, and his wife (Susan Hayward). Tales of Mitchum's past glory light a fire under Kennedy, who sees a chance at quick realization of his ranch-owning yen via rodeoing prizes.

As the days pass, Kennedy wins money and develops a taste for the glory that goes with success but Mitchum has a growing interest in Hayward. A lot of actual rodeo footage is used to backstop the story [suggested by one by Claude Stanush]. A somewhat slow starter, once underway it is kept playing with growing interest under Nicholas Ray's firm direction.

•

LUV

1967, 93 mins, US Ⓥ ⦿ ⊏⊐ col

Dir Clive Donner ***Prod*** Martin Manulis ***Scr*** Elliott Baker ***Ph*** Ernest Laszlo ***Ed*** Harold F. Kress ***Mus*** Gerry Mulligan ***Art*** Al Brenner

Act Jack Lemmon, Peter Falk, Elaine May, Nina Wayne, Eddie Mayehoff, Paul Hartman (Columbia)

As a play, Murray Schisgal's *Luv* was a hit comedy which ran more than two years on Broadway. Many of the beguiling qualities are lost in its transference to the screen. Where the legiter was wildly absurd and deliciously outlandish, much of the humor of the picture is forced, proving that a sophisticated stage comedy isn't always ideal fare for the screen.

Opening on Manhattan Bridge, where Jack Lemmon, a self-proclaimed failure, is about to commit suicide, story takes form as Peter Falk, a self-proclaimed success, comes along and saves him. Falk recognizes in Lemmon an old school friend and takes him home to meet his wife, whom he immediately tries to palm off on Lemmon so he can get a divorce and marry the girl of his dreams, a gymnasium instructor named Linda.

Clive Donner's direction fits the frantic overtones of unfoldment, but in this buildup occasionally goes overboard for effect. Lemmon appears to over-characterize his role, a difficult one for exact shading. Falk as a bright-eyed schemer scores decisively in a restrained comedy enactment for what may be regarded as pic's top performance.

•

LYDIA

1941, 103 mins, US Ⓥ b/w

Dir Julien Duvivier ***Prod*** Alexander Korda ***Scr*** Ben Hecht, Samuel Hoffenstein ***Ph*** Lee Garmes ***Ed*** William Hornbeck ***Mus*** Miklos Rozsa ***Art*** Vincent Korda

Act Merle Oberon, Edna May Oliver, Alan Marshal, Joseph Cotten, Hans Yaray, Sara Allgood (Korda)

A man loves 'em and leaves 'em but a woman carries the torch for an early romance down through the years. Proceeding on this premise *Lydia* displays the life span of a woman from 20 to 60, and her torching for a lover whose promises and memories are forgotten 35 years later.

Original story, by Julien Duvivier and Ladislas Bush-Fekete, carries on romantic frustration in a minor key. It's strictly a character study of a gal pursued and loved by three men of various standings—football hero, famous doctor, and blind musical genius—but who holds in her heart through the years the brief, but hot, romance with a seafarer-lover.

Dialog and narrative, with frequent use of cutbacks for the story telling, do not add to the speed of the unreeling under the leisurely direction by Duvivier.

Merle Oberon takes full advantage of her prominent role to turn in an excellent performance. Makeup for the span of years is particularly excellent.

1941: NOMINATION: Best Scoring of a Dramatic Picture

•

LYDIA BAILEY

1952, 89 mins, US col

Dir Jean Negulesco ***Prod*** Jules Schermer ***Scr*** Michael Blankfort, Philip Dunne ***Ph*** Harry Jackson ***Ed*** Dorothy Spencer ***Mus*** Hugo Friedhofer ***Art*** Lyle Wheeler, J. Russell Spencer

Act Dale Robertson, Anne Francis, Charles Korvin, William Marshall, Luis Van Rooten, Adeline de Walt Reynolds (20th Century-Fox)

Lydia Bailey, Kenneth Roberts's bestselling novel, is a lush tale of period adventure, action and romance.

With Napoleon attempting to wrest Haiti back from its native government in 1802, the West Indian island is an armed camp swarming with plotters and counter-plotters. Into this atmosphere comes Dale Robertson, a young American attorney whose mission is to secure the signature of Lydia Bailey (Anne Francis) to settle an estate.

It's a tough task to find Francis, who is the fiancée of a wealthy plantation owner (Charles Korvin). But with the help of William Marshall, a burly leader of the Negro Republicans, Robertson survives the trek through the hostile jungle.

Robertson cuts a dashing figure as the intrepid attorney and neatly meets the demands of the role.

•

LYENIN V OKTYABRYE
(LENIN IN OCTOBER)

1937, 92 mins, USSR b/w

Dir Mikhail Romm, Dmitri Vasiliev ***Scr*** Aleksey Kapler ***Ph*** Boris Volchok ***Mus*** Anatoli Aleksandrov ***Art*** Boris Dubrovsky-Eshke

Act Boris Shchukin, Nikolai Okhlopkov, Vasili Vanin, I. Golshtab, N. Svobodin, V. Vladislavsky (Mosfilm)

Lenin in October could be Lenin at any other time and still be a highly interesting production. Ranks with *Gulliver* and other Red films as one of the finest productions to emanate from the Soviet film factories. Treatment belies the impression that Moscow produces naught but soapboxes, film being an accurate historical chronology. Could well be listed among action-romances but for labeled origin. It's a good super-artie.

Pic deals out reams of comedy, suspense, drama and assorted histrionics. Boris Shchukin's characterization of Lenin is an excellent performance.

M

1931, 114 mins, Germany Ⓥ ⊙ b/w

Dir Fritz Lang ***Prod*** Seymour Nebenzal ***Scr*** Thea von Harbou ***Ph*** Fritz Arno Wagner, Gustav Rathje, Karl Vash ***Art*** Karl Vollbrecht, Emil Hasler

Act Peter Lorre, Ellen Widmann, Inge Landgut, Gustav Gruendgens, Fritz Gnass, Fritz Odemar (Nero)

An extraordinary, good, impressive and strong talker. Again fine work by Fritz Lang, and his wife and helper, Thea von Harbou. All the more astonishing as it is Lang's first talker.

M is the sign of recognition of a child's murderer who is sought by the police and an underworld organtization. It is the story of the world-known murderer, Peter Kuerten of Dusseldorf. Amazing thing about this is that von Harbou wrote this manuscript [based on a newspaper report by Egon Jacobson] before Peter Kuerten was ever arrested.

After a thrilling chase the murderer is caught by the gangster organizations. The work of the police, of the criminal department, the raids and police patrols, the spy work of the gangsters, all this is splendidly worked out and realistic. There are a few repetitions and a few draggy scenes.

Peter Lorre does unusually well as the murderer, changing from human despair to bestial lust. It is most gripping when he pleads for human treatment and understanding for his pathological tendencies.

Otto Wernicke, as the chief of the criminal department, achieves such perfect work one is reminded of Lon Chaney's figures. Theodor Loos and Gerhard Bienert are also splendid as criminal policemen. In between are two fine actresses: Rosa Valetti and Margarete Melzer.

•

M

1951, 88 mins, US Ⓥ ⊙ b/w

Dir Joseph Losey ***Prod*** Seymour Nebenzal ***Scr*** Leo Katcher, Norman Reilly Raine, Waldo Salt ***Ph*** Ernest Laszlo ***Ed*** Edward Mann ***Mus*** Michel Michelet ***Art*** Martin Obzina

Act David Wayne, Luther Adler, Howard da Silva, Martin Gabel, Raymond Burr, Glenn Anders (Columbia)

M is a remake of picture produced in Germany by Seymour Nebenzal in 1933. Principal change is its shift in locale, presumably to California. David Wayne, as the killer of small children, is effective and convincing. Luther Adler, as a drunken lawyer member of a gangster mob, turns in an outstanding performance, as do Martin Gabel, the gang-leader, and Howard da Silva and Steve Brodie as police officials.

Story is that of a killer (Wayne), whose only victims are children. The city is up in arms over failure of the police to nab the murderer. A series of raids by police is hampering the activities of a crime syndicate headed by Gabel. Mob knows it cannot continue with its floating dice games, bookie joints and other enterprises until the killer is caught. To protect his rackets, Gabel orders his gang to catch the killer.

Joseph Losey's direction has captured the gruesome theme skilfully.

•

MAC

1992, 117 mins, US Ⓥ col

Dir John Turturro ***Prod*** Nancy Tenenbaum, Brenda Goodman ***Scr*** John Turturro, Brandon Cole ***Ph*** Ron Fortunato ***Ed*** Michael Berenbaum ***Mus*** Richard Termini, Vin Tese ***Art*** Robin Standefer

Act John Turturro, Michael Badalucco, Carl Capotorto, Katherine Borowitz, Ellen Barkin, John Amos (Macfilms)

John Turturro's intense, offbeat personality as an actor comes through equally clearly in his directorial debut, *Mac*. A tribute to the notion of craftsmen loving their work, as well as an expression of quirky humor among three Italian-American brothers, pic is appealing in an idiosyncratic way.

Dedicated to Turturro's father, and inspired by his career as a carpenter, film is centered on the title character, the oldest of three brothers who live in Queens during the 1950s. In the wake of their father's death, the temperamental Mac leaves his construction job to start his own business.

In its eccentric character humor and passionate eruptions of emotion, *Mac* follows in the vein of American cinema arguably started by John Cassavetes and taken up, most prominently, by Martin Scorsese.

Performances are sharp, led by Turturro's own as the headstrong leader of the clan. Michael Badalucco and Carl Capotorto are both distinctive and entirely complementary as the brothers, and Katherine Borowitz, as Turturro's wife, and Ellen Barkin, as a suburban beatnik, are vibrant as the main women on hand.

•

MACAO

1952, 81 mins, US Ⓥ ⊙ b/w

Dir Josef von Sternberg, [Nicholas Ray] ***Prod*** Alex Gottlieb ***Scr*** Bernard C. Schoenfeld, Stanley Rubin ***Ph*** Harry J. Wild

Ed Samuel E. Beetley, Robert Golden ***Mus*** Anthony Collins ***Art*** Albert S. D'Agostino, Ralph Berger

Act Robert Mitchum, Jane Russell, William Bendix, Thomas Gomez, Gloria Grahame, Brad Dexter (RKO)

Macao pairs Jane Russell and Robert Mitchum; contains the cliché elements of adventure, romance and intrigue; and is set in the mysterious Orient.

Story [by Bob Williams] is set in the Portuguese colony south of Hong Kong. It opens with the arrival of three Americans—Russell, a cynical, wisecracking chirper; Mitchum, an ex-GI running away from a minor shooting scrape; and William Bendix, disguised as a salesman but in reality a New York detective entrusted with the job of bringing back to the States Brad Dexter, local gambling kingpin.

Dexter engages Russell to sing at his club and makes a play for her, to the displeasure of his girlfriend (Gloria Grahame). Believing Mitchum to be the New York cop, Dexter fails in an attempt to bribe him to leave the island and resorts to more drastic means.

•

MACARONI

1985, 104 mins, Italy Ⓥ ⊙ col

Dir Ettore Scola ***Prod*** Luigo De Laurentiis, Aurelio De Laurentiis, Franco Committeri ***Scr*** Ruggero Maccari, Furio Scarpelli, Ettore Scola ***Ph*** Claudio Ragona ***Ed*** Carla Simoncelli ***Mus*** Armando Trovaioli ***Art*** Luciano Ricceri

Act Jack Lemmon, Marcello Mastroianni, Daria Nicolodi, Isa Danieli, Maria Luisa Santella, Patrizia Sacchi (Filmauro/Massfilm)

Macaroni is a mild comedy drama teaming the formidable talents of Jack Lemmon and Marcello Mastroianni. Lemmon toplines as Bob Traven, a v.p. visiting Naples as a consultant to Aeritalia. It's his first time back since 1946 when, as a GI, he was stationed there.

An acquaintance from that period, Antonio Jasiello (Marcello Mastroianni) looks Traven up and takes the at-first unwilling (too busy) American around town to meet the family and friends.

Jasiello has been surreptitiously writing letters using Traven's name over the years to his own sister Maria, who had a brief romance in 1946 with the American. She's long since been married and now has adult grandchildren.

Relying too heavily on its two stars, at first abrasive adverseries but later best of friends as Lemmon unbends to Mastroianni's exuberant *joie de vivre*, *Macaroni* rarely achieves the comedic heights of director Ettore Scola's previous work. There simply isn't an abundance of funny situations or witty dialog here.

English language film is hampered by the dialog, with merely okay readings by Mastroianni, artificial dubbing of Isa Danieli as his emphatic wife and rote, direct-sound speeches by Daria Nicolodi as Aeritalia's p.r. officer.

•

MACARTHUR

1977, 128 mins, US Ⓥ ⊙ col

Dir Joseph Sargent ***Prod*** Frank McCarthy ***Scr*** Hal Barwood, Matthew Robbins ***Ph*** Mario Tosi ***Ed*** George Jay Nicholson ***Mus*** Jerry Goldsmith ***Art*** John J. Lloyd

Act Gregory Peck, Ed Flanders, Dan O'Herlihy, Marj Dusay, Sandy Kenyon, Nicolas Coster (Universal/Zanuck-Brown)

MacArthur is as good a film as could be made, considering the truly appalling egomania of its subject. Film stars Gregory Peck in an excellent and remarkable characterization.

Screenplay depicts the public aspects of Douglas MacArthur's life from Corregidor in 1942 to dismissal a decade later in the midst of the Korean War, all framed between segments of his farewell address to West Point cadets.

Unlike *Patton*, which was loaded with emotional and physical action highlights, *MacArthur* is a far more introspective and introverted story. There are moments when, despite all evidence to the contrary, one actually can believe that MacArthur thought he possessed the only true vision of battle strategy; yet a second later, the vibrations of a brass-bound poseur come across all too clearly.

•

MACBETH

1948, 106 mins, US Ⓥ ⊙ b/w

Dir Orson Welles ***Prod*** Richard Wilson (assoc.) ***Scr*** Orson Welles ***Ph*** John L. Russell ***Ed*** Louis Lindsay ***Mus*** Jacques Ibert ***Art*** Fred Ritter

Act Orson Welles, Jeanette Nolan, Dan O'Herlihy, Roddy McDowall, Edgar Barrier, Alan Napier (Republic/Mercury)

Welles's idea of Shakespeare is such a personalized version. Production was comparatively inexpensive and looks it. Mood is as dour as the Scottish moors and crags that background the plot. Film is crammed with scenery-chewing theatrics in the best Shakespearean manner with Welles dominating practically every bit of footage.

Only a few of the Bard's best lines are audible. The rest are lost in strained, dialectic gibbering that is only sound, not prose. At best, Shakespeare dialog requires close attention; but even intense concentration can't make intelligible the reading by Welles and others in the cast [who adopt Scottish accents].

Macbeth, the play, devotes considerable time to depicting femme influence on the male to needle his vanity and ambition into murder for a kingdom. *Macbeth*, the film, devotes that footage to the male's reaction to the femme needling. Several Shakespeare characters have been turned into a Welles-introduced one, a Holy Father.

Welles introduces Jeanette Nolan as Lady Macbeth. Her reading is best in the "out, damned spot" scene. Dan O'Herlihy fares best as Macduff, his reading having the clearest enunciation.

•

MACBETH

1972, 140 mins, UK Ⓥ ⊙ ▭ col

Dir Roman Polanski ***Prod*** Andrew Braunsberg ***Scr*** Roman Polanski, Kenneth Tynan ***Ph*** Gil Taylor ***Ed*** Alastair McIntyre ***Mus*** The Third Ear Band ***Art*** Wilfrid Shingleton

Act Jon Finch, Francesca Annis, Martin Shaw, Nicholas Selby, John Stride, Stephan Chase (Playboy)

Macbeth receives a most handsome treatment by Roman Polanski and artistic adviser Kenneth Tynan, both of whom adapted this production for the entry of Playboy Enterprises into feature filming. Rugged in its telling, raw in its motivated violence, and rich in its appropriate physical trappings, this is the 16th known film version of the story. The players are very good, though Jon Finch's Macbeth is a serious weakness.

Does Polanski's *Macbeth* work? Not especially, but it was an admirable try. The film is traditional in the sense that there are no forced sociological overtones, no Freudianisms, and no pop-art formula-epic "production numbers." Atmospherically it is a heavy trip through a time machine.

The prominent surrounding characters have been cast and directed with the same care. In such heady surroundings Francesca Annis as Lady Macbeth often pales in impact, and Finch as Macbeth completely fades in effectiveness. Both seem almost to be of another time and place: she is closer to Sherwood Forest and pampered gentility; he, almost a 20th-century drawing room psychotic.

•

MACHINE GUN KELLY

1958, 84 mins, US Ⓥ ▭ b/w

Dir Roger Corman ***Prod*** Roger Corman ***Scr*** R. Wright Campbell ***Ph*** Floyd Crosby ***Ed*** Ronald Sinclair ***Mus*** Gerald Fried ***Art*** Daniel Haller

Act Charles Bronson, Susan Cabot, Morey Amsterdam, Jack Lambert, Connie Gilchrist (American-International)

Machine Gun Kelly beats out a tattoo of the 1930s in its account of the criminal career of one of that decade's most notorious outlaws. Roger Corman has taken a good screenplay and made a first-rate little picture out of the depressing but intriguing account of a badman's downfall.

Charles Bronson plays Kelly, shown as an undersized sadist who grows an extra foot or so as soon as he gets a submachine gun tucked under his arm. His exploits, proceeding from penny ante robbery to big-time kidnapping, are adroitly and swiftly shown.

Bronson gives a brooding, taut performance. Susan Cabot is good as the woman behind his deeds, and Morey Amsterdam contributes an offbeat portrayal of a squealer who has the final revenge of turning Kelly in. Gerald Fried, using piano and taps for an unusual and striking combination, has done a fine progressive jazz score.

•

MACKENNA'S GOLD

1969, 128 mins, US Ⓥ ⊙ ▭ col

Dir J. Lee Thompson ***Prod*** Carl Foreman, Dimitri Tiomkin ***Scr*** Carl Foreman ***Ph*** Joseph MacDonald ***Ed*** Bill Lenny ***Mus*** Quincy Jones ***Art*** Geoffrey Drake

Act Gregory Peck, Omar Sharif, Telly Savalas, Julie Newmar, Camilla Sparv, Keenan Wynn (Highroad/Columbia)

Mackenna's Gold is a standard western. The plot [from Will Henry's novel *McKenna's Gold*] is good, the acting adequate. But it's the scenery, the vastness of the West, the use of cameras, and of horses, and the special effects which keep the viewer involved and entertained.

There are a few plot twists, but for the most part the story is predictable. Mackenna (Gregory Peck) has memorized a map, now destroyed, which will lead to a canyon of gold. The gold belongs to the Apaches, and it has been decreed by the Apache gods that the gold remain untouched.

But now the young Apache warriors want the gold to support them in their fight against the white men. The Mexican bandit Colorado (Omar Sharif) wants the gold so he can emigrate to Paris and become a gentleman. Sharif captures Peck and forces him to lead them to the gold.

•

MACKINTOSH MAN, THE

1973, 98 mins, UK Ⓥ col

Dir John Huston ***Prod*** John Foreman ***Scr*** Walter Hill ***Ph*** Oswald Morris ***Ed*** Russell Lloyd ***Mus*** Maurice Jarre ***Art*** Terry Marsh

Act Paul Newman, Dominique Sanda, James Mason, Harry Andrews, Ian Bannen, Michael Hordern (Warner)

The Mackintosh Man is a tame tale of British espionage and counterespionage, starring Paul Newman as a planted assassin, James Mason as a cynical right-wing politician in reality a spy and Dominique Sanda as a combo semiromantic interest and foreign-market star bait.

Walter Hill has adapted Desmond Bagley's novel, *The Freedom Trap*, into a serviceable meller form. Harry Andrews, a British secret agent, recruits Newman to pull a jewel heist by mail, in order to establish his criminal credentials, so that he may escape with Ian Bannen, a state secrets betrayor, and thereby ferret out Mason, who has carried on a 25-year career as a politician but has been a foreign agent.

There's a whole lot of nothing going on here.

•

MACOMBER AFFAIR, THE

1947, 89 mins, US b/w

Dir Zoltan Korda ***Prod*** Benedict Bogeaus ***Scr*** Casey Robinson, Seymour Bennett ***Ph*** Karl Struss ***Ed*** George Feld, Jack Wheeler ***Mus*** Miklos Rozsa ***Art*** Erno Metzner

Act Gregory Peck, Robert Preston, Joan Bennett, Reginald Denny, Carl Hardboard (United Artists)

The Macomber Affair, with an African hunt background, isn't particularly pleasant in content, even though action often is exciting and elements of suspense frequently hop up the spectator. Certain artificialities of presentation, too, and unreal dialog are further strikes against picture [based on a short story by Ernest Hemingway], although portion of footage filmed in Africa is interesting.

Robert Preston enacts role of Francis Macomber, a rich American with an unhappy wife (Joan Bennett), who arrives at Nairobi and hires Gregory Peck, a white hunter, to take him lion hunting. On the safari, this time in cars, Macomber can't stand up under a lion charge and his wife sees him turn coward. The white hunter kills the lion. Thereafter, Macomber broods over his shame and his wife falls for the hunter.

African footage is cut into the story with showmanship effect, and these sequences build up suspense satisfactorily. There are closeups of lions and other denizens of the veldt, and scenes in which lion and water buffalo charge, caught with telescopic lenses by camera crew sent to Africa from England, will stir any audience. These focal points of the story out-interest the human drama as developed in scripters' enmeshing trio of stars.

•

MAD ABOUT MUSIC

1938, 98 mins, US b/w

Dir Norman Taurog ***Prod*** Joe Pasternak ***Scr*** Bruce Manning, Felix Jackson ***Ph*** Joseph Valentine ***Ed*** Philip Kahn

Act Deanna Durbin, Herbert Marshall, Arthur Treacher, Gail Patrick, William Frawley, Jackie Moran (Universal)

Mad About Music has a genuine and enthralling, if somewhat obvious story [by Marcella Burke and Frederick Kohner]. Idea is a simple one. So as not to risk her popularity as a glamour girl, a beauteous widowed film star unwillingly hides her 14-year-old daughter away in a Swiss boarding school. Although the youngster is inordinately proud of her illustrious mother, she must cherish her affection in secret.

When the other girls talk about their parents, the youngster takes refuge in telling of the fabulous exploits of her imaginary father, whom she describes as an explorer and big-game hunter. When circumstances force her to make good the yarns, she imposes on a vacationing British composer to pretend to be her legendary father.

As evidence that Deanna Durbin is growing up, in this film she is given a beau for the first time. It's still purely in the puppy-love status. She has acquired more varied technique before the camera, without losing her ingenuous charm nor her luminous screen personality.

As the adopted-by-surprise father, Herbert Marshall plays with unaccustomed warmth. Although her part is important to the story, Gail Patrick gets comparatively little footage as the actress-mother.

1938: NOMINATIONS: Best Original Story, Cinematography, Art Direction, Score

•

MADAME BOVARY

1949, 114 mins, US Ⓥ ⊙ b/w

Dir Vincente Minnelli ***Prod*** Pandro S. Berman ***Scr*** Robert Ardrey ***Ph*** Robert Planck ***Ed*** Ferris Webster ***Mus*** Miklos Rozsa ***Art*** Cedric Gibbons, Jack Martin Smith

Act Jennifer Jones, James Mason, Van Heflin, Louis Jourdan, Christopher Kent, Gene Lockhart (M-G-M)

As a character study, *Madame Bovary* is interesting to watch, but hard to feel. It is a curiously unemotional account of some rather basic emotions. However, the surface treatment of Vincente Minnelli's direction is slick and attractively presented.

Jennifer Jones is the daring Madame Bovary. The character is short on sympathy, being a greedy woman so anxious to better her position in life that sin and crime do not shock her moral values. Jones answers to every demand of direction and script.

Van Heflin portrays her doctor husband, an essentially weak man whose evident flaws in abiding with a greedy wife are not too satisfactorily explained away by his love for her.

The Bovary quest for something better than she has is brought to light at the trial of Gustave Flaubert, author of the realistically treated novel that brought about his arrest. James Mason is excellent as the author.

1949: NOMINATION: Best B&W Art Direction

•

MADAME CURIE

1943, 125 mins, US Ⓥ b/w

Dir Mervyn LeRoy ***Prod*** Sidney Franklin ***Scr*** Paul Osborn, Paul Rameau ***Ph*** Joseph Ruttenberg ***Ed*** Harold F. Kress ***Mus*** Herbert Stothart ***Art*** Cedric Gibbons, Paul Groesse

Act Greer Garson, Walter Pidgeon, Robert Walker, Van Johnson, Margaret O'Brien, Henry Travers (M-G-M)

Every inch a great picture. *Madame Curie* absorbingly tells of the struggle and heartaches that ultimately resulted in the discovery of radium.

Sidney Franklin, producer, and Mervyn LeRoy, director, have instilled into the story of Madame Curie and her scientist-husband a particularly high degree of entertainment value where in less-skilled hands the romance of radium and its discovery may have struck out.

While the events leading up to the discovery of radium and the fame it brought Madame Curie are of the greatest underlying importance to the picture as entertainment, it's the love story that dominates all the way. Thus, this is not just the saga of a great scientist nor just a story of test tubes and laboratories.

Film is based on the book *Madame Curie*, written by Eve Curie, daughter of the Polish teacher-scientist who quite by accident came upon the source of the element. It is adapted with great skill by Paul Osborn and Paul H. Rameau, with a few stretches of narration by James Hilton. It throws Greer Garson and Walter Pidgeon together immediately after the opening and, as the romance between them ripens, it gathers terrific momentum.

1943: NOMINATIONS: Best Picture, Actor (Walter Pidgeon), Actress (Greer Garson), B&W Cinematography, B&W Art Direction, Scoring of a Dramatic Picture, Sound

•

MADAME DE . . .
(THE EARRINGS OF MADAME DE . . .)

1953, 105 mins, France Ⓥ ⊙ b/w

Dir Max Ophuls ***Scr*** Marcel Achard, Annette Wademant, Max Ophuls ***Ph*** Christian Matras ***Ed*** Borys Lewin

Act Charles Boyer, Danielle Darrieux, Vittorio De Sica, Jean Debucourt, Lea De Leo, Mareille Pierrey (Franco-London)

Max Ophuls has created a delicate, half-toned study of turn-of-century manners and love.

Slight story concerns a general's wife who sells a pair of earrings when she needs the money. The earrings become the motif to keep the plot moving as the general buys them back from the jeweler and gives them to his mistress. The girl loses them, and they are picked up by a diplomat who becomes enamored of the general's wife.

Ophuls gives this a neat photographic framing as he delicately embraces his characters. Main drawback of the film is its outmoded feelings, and the rather lifeless agonizings of its puppetlike characters in a fading era when protocol, and saving of face, was more important than reality.

Danielle Darrieux is fine as the lovely, shallow lady whose indiscretions lead to a tragedy. Charles Boyer and Vittorio De Sica are the rivals, and underplay their roles to fit in with the general style of the piece.

•

MADAME DUBARRY

1934, 75 mins, US b/w

Dir William Dieterle ***Scr*** Edward Chodorov ***Ph*** Sol Polito

Act Dolores Del Rio, Reginald Owen, Victor Jory, Osgood Perkins, Verree Teasdale, Anita Louise (Warner)

Madame Dubarry is a Hollywood idea of Versailles. Under William Dieterle's directorial aegis, the decadent court of Louis XV becomes even more so in its broad well-nigh travesty version of the comtesse's influence on the doddering Louie.

Script is a chameleon affair. It emphasizes the stupid extravagances of a former street waif who wants to go sleighing in the midst of summer; and in another moment seeks to suggest that perhaps some of her devious ways achieved some good. Such as when the English ambassador opines that getting rid of the French prime minister (caught in Dubarry's boudoir) has achieved something which his Britannic majesty and other diplomats in the French court long tried but heretofore couldn't accomplish.

Dolores Del Rio's Dubarry is rarely believable. It's a theatrical conception eclipsed by the performances of Reginald Owen, who is capital as the senile Louie, and Victor Jory as d'Aiguillon. Osgood Perkins's Richelieu doesn't register.

Dubarry as a production is very Busby Berkeley. In its tinsel, costuming, and general pretentiousness it's more musical comedy than history.

•

MADAME ROSA

SEE: LA VIE DEVANT SOI

•

MADAME SOUSATZKA

1988, 122 mins, UK/US Ⓥ ⊙ col

Dir John Schlesinger ***Prod*** Robin Dalton ***Scr*** Ruth Prawer Jhabvala ***Ph*** Nat Crosby ***Ed*** Peter Honess ***Mus*** Gerald Gouriet ***Art*** Luciana Arrighi

Act Shirley MacLaine, Navin Chowdhry, Peggy Ashcroft, Twiggy, Shabana Azmi, Leigh Lawson (Sousatzka/Cineplex Odeon)

Although essentially a rather old-fashioned British pic, *Madame Sousatzka* is filled with pleasures, not the least of them being Shirley MacLaine's effervescent performance.

Setting is London where middle-aged Mme. Sousatzka, of Russian parentage but raised in New York, teaches piano to only the most gifted students. She insists her pupils not only learn to play, but also to live the kind of traditional cultured lifestyle which she herself does.

Her latest protege is a 15-year-old Indian youth, Manek (Navin Chowdhry) whose mother (Shabana Azmi) left Calcutta years before to get away from her husband.

Sousatzka lives in a crumbling house owned by old Lady Emily (Peggy Ashcroft). Besides Sousatzka, her tenants include a model and would-be pop singer (delightfully played by Twiggy) who looks much younger than she is; and a middle-aged gay osteopath (Geoffrey Bayldon).

Crucial, though, is the central relationship between MacLaine, who's seldom been better than she is here, and the youngster, warmly played by Chowdry. All their scenes have great charm, with the piano playing effectively handled.

•

MADAME X

1929, 95 mins, US b/w

Dir Lionel Barrymore ***Scr*** Willard Mack ***Ph*** Arthur Reed ***Art*** Cedric Gibbons

Act Ruth Chatterton, Lewis Stone, Raymond Hackett, John P. Edington, Ullric Haupt, Sidney Toler (M-G-M)

This is Lionel Barrymore's first full-length directorial effort on a talker. Taking *X* as an actor-proof meller and conceding its author, the Frenchman Alexandre Bisson, knew emotion well enough to make it do somersaults in this tale, Barrymore had no difficult job with the story and cast.

But Barrymore excels in the minor bits and roles: the above-par park scene; the immensely human bit in the hotel's corridor with the landlord wanting his room rent from the besotted Jacqueline (Ruth Chatterton); or the superb scene wholly dominated by the doctor (John P. Edington).

The two big moments are Jacqueline killing her small-time blackmailing companion to prevent her son discovering what a horror his mother has become; the other the famous trial scene, the grand finale which made *Madame X* on the stage.

Chatterton has not a flaw in her performance or makeup. Next to Chatterton and Edington comes Raymond Hackett as the son.

1928/29: NOMINATIONS: Best Director, Actress (Ruth Chatterton)

•

MADAME X

1937, 75 mins, US b/w

Dir Sam Wood ***Prod*** James Kevin McGuinness ***Scr*** John Meehan ***Ph*** John Seitz ***Ed*** Frank E. Hull ***Mus*** David Snell ***Art*** Cedric Gibbons, Urie McCleary, Edwin B. Willis

Act Gladys George, John Beal, Warren William, Reginald Owen, William Henry, Henry Daniell (M-G-M)

This is a reverent handling of the Alexandre Bisson play, chosen by M-G-M as a vehicle to demonstrate the dramatic and emotional talent of Gladys George. It's a quiet, comforting sniffle.

Script follows with devotion the familiar developments, and the dialog is as modern as the action permits. Sam Wood's direction is conventionally sound and the production is of the best.

George's performance is effective, and her characterization of the tipsy, defeated and maudlin old woman is faithful and moving. Warren William plays the hard-hearted husband who refuses to forgive his wife's indiscretions; Reginald Owen is the friend, Douvel; Henry Daniell is the villain, Lerocle.

John Beal has the prize spot of Raymond, youthful public defender of his mother, whose identity is unknown to him. His address to the court is recited with conviction and emotion.

•

MADAME X

1966, 99 mins, US Ⓥ col

Dir David Lowell Rich ***Prod*** Ross Hunter ***Scr*** Jean Holloway ***Ph*** Russell Metty ***Ed*** Milton Carruth ***Mus*** Frank Skinner ***Art*** Alexander Golitzen, George Webb

Act Lana Turner, John Forsythe, Ricardo Montalban, Burgess Meredith, Constance Bennett, Keir Dullea (Universal/Hunter)

Latest time out for Alexandre Bisson's now-classic 1909 drama of mother love is an emotional, sometimes exhausting and occasionally corny picture. Lana Turner takes on the difficult assignment of the frustrated mother, turning in what many will regard as her most rewarding portrayal. Producer Ross Hunter draws generally on the original plot but has changed the locale from Paris to the U.S. for pic's opening and climax.

Screenplay now has femme star very much in love with her husband, instead of running away from her spouse, as in the original, to join her lover. However, following an affair with a rich playboy, who is accidentally killed while she is in his apartment, she is talked by her mother-in-law into disappearing in a phony drowning episode to save her politically minded husband and young son from scandal.

John Forsythe excels as the husband, whose political career forces him to absent himself from home for long periods of time and thus lays the ground for his lonely wife's indiscretion. Ricardo Montalban is persuasive as the playboy who falls to his death, and Constance Bennett—in her last film appearance before her death—endows the mother-in-law role with quiet dignity and strength.

•

MAD AT THE MOON

1992, 97 mins, US Ⓥ col

Dir Martin Donovan ***Prod*** Michael Kastenbaum, Cassian Elwes, Matt Devlen ***Scr*** Martin Donovan, Richard Pelusi ***Ph*** Ronn Schmidt ***Ed*** Penelope Shaw ***Mus*** Gerald Gouriet ***Art*** Stephen Greenberg

Act Mary Stuart Masterson, Hart Bochner, Fionnula Flanagan, Cec Verrell, Stephen Blake, Daphne Zuniga (Jaffe/Spectacor)

Miscasting and klutzy plot development take the shine out of *Mad at the Moon*, a Wild West amour fou movie that sprouts hairs halfway and turns into a werewolf pic. The second picture by Argentinian-born Martin Donovan, who staked a cult film claim with the quirky *Apartment Zero*, shows the same glee in blending genres and going for broke. The main problems here are accepting topliner Mary Stuart Masterson as a 25-year-old virgin and figuring out a storyline that takes a left turn 50 minutes in.

Pretty but repressed Jenny (Masterson) has a backstreets rendezvous with charismatic bum Miller Brown (Hart Bochner), whom she's had the hots for since childhood. Despite her secret desires, she bows to the wishes of her mom (Fionnula Flanagan) and marries local milquetoast James Miller (Stephen Blake), the bum's half-brother.

Things begin to go awry (with the pic, too) as soon as the couple settle in James's remote farmhouse. The marriage is unconsummated, Miller haunts the plains outside and Jenny experiences hubby's "moonsickness," during which he starts howling and turns partly vulpine.

Still, Donovan shows he has talent to spare as a pure technician. Pic works best when no one's talking and Donovan can stoke up the atmosphere via sound, music and images alone.

•

MAD DOG AND GLORY

1993, 96 mins, US Ⓥ ⊙ col

Dir John McNaughton ***Prod*** Barbara De Fina, Martin Scorsese ***Scr*** Richard Price ***Ph*** Robby Muller ***Ed*** Craig McKay, Elena Maganini ***Mus*** Elmer Bernstein ***Art*** David Chapman

Act Robert De Niro, Uma Thurman, Bill Murray, David Caruso, Mike Starr, Kathy Baker (Universal)

A pleasurably offbeat picture that manages the rare trick of being both charming and edgy, *Mad Dog and Glory* represents a refreshing, unexpected change of pace for all the major talents concerned.

Amusing premise—a poor schmoe saves a gangster's life and is given a beautiful woman for a week as thanks—ends up taking on unexpected dramatic and romantic dimensions, and leads are played to the hilt by its stellar trio.

Bill Murray plays Frank Milo, a dapper hoodlum in the modern mode. Robert De Niro's Wayne Dobie, ironically nicknamed "Mad Dog," is a retiring middle-aged loner who photographs crime scenes at night for the Chicago Police Dept.

Wayne has greatness thrust upon him when he interrupts an armed robbery in a convenience store and saves Milo from almost certain death. Club bartender Glory (Uma Thurman) turns up at his apartment and announces that she's staying for a week, courtesy of Milo. What follows could easily have been cute, contrived, exploitative, crude or any combination of same. Instead, scriptwriter Richard Price deepens his characters and, with the aid of the exceptional actors, the story takes on a resonance and emotional urgency that aren't initially indicated. The key to the film lies in the intimate scenes involving Wayne and Glory.

•

MADE FOR EACH OTHER

1939, 90 mins, US Ⓥ b/w

Dir John Cromwell ***Prod*** David O. Selznick ***Scr*** Jo Swerling ***Ph*** Leon Shamroy ***Ed*** Hal C. Kern, James E. Newcom ***Mus*** Lou Forbes ***Art*** William Cameron Menzies

Act Carole Lombard, James Stewart, Charles Coburn, Lucile Watson, Eddie Quillan (United Artists)

This is an exquisitely played, deeply moving comedy-drama. It is a happy combination of young love, sharp clean-cut humor and tearjerker. David O. Selznick's production leaves no sagging at the seams.

Picture is noteworthy in that it provides Carole Lombard with virtually her first straight dramatic role. She makes the newlywed Jane Mason a sincere young wife who struggles valiantly through all obstacles to save her newborn baby and make her husband amount to something.

James Stewart as the struggling lawyer who passes up his boss' daughter for a love match dominates the droll moments, but displays further development in the more dramatic sequences.

Story of idyllic young love and sudden marriage, with familiar burdens and in-laws, is not new but the human and ingenious way it is projected makes it appear entirely different.

•

MADE IN AMERICA

1993, 110 mins, US Ⓥ ⊙ col

Dir Richard Benjamin ***Prod*** Arnon Milchan, Michael Douglas, Rick Bieber ***Scr*** Holly Goldberg Sloan ***Ph*** Ralf Bode ***Ed*** Jacqueline Cambas ***Mus*** Mark Isham ***Art*** Evelyn Sakash

Act Whoopi Goldberg, Ted Danson, Will Smith, Nia Long, Paul Rodriguez, Jennifer Tilly (Stonebridge/Kalola/Milchan)

Made in America has the distinction of being better than the last movie involving a sperm bank, *Frozen Assets*, though at times the humor—overplayed to nearly shrill levels—seems to come from the same test tube.

The plot has Zora (Nia Long), a high-school honors student, discovering her mother Sarah (Whoopi Goldberg) conceived her after her father's death using a donor from a sperm bank. Zora finds the name of Hal Jackson (Ted Danson)—a Cal Worthington–like car salesman who cavorts on-air with elephants, bears and chimps and turns out to be white. Hostile toward each other at first, an unlikely relationship develops between Hal and Sarah.

In an effort to bring Sarah and Hal's relationship to a crisis point, the action [from a screen story by Marcia Brandwynne, Nadine Schiff and scripter Holly Goldberg Sloan] suddenly veers into a heavy-handed, semi-serious mode that doesn't mesh with the screwball opening. If there's chemistry between Danson and Goldberg, it's certainly not allowed to unfold adequately or with any sense of pacing in the script. The race issue, for example, quickly dissipates.

It's the supporting players who end up stealing much of the film, particularly rapper Will Smith as Zora's nerdy friend and a golden-locked Jennifer Tilly as Hal's airheaded aerobics instructor girlfriend.

•

MADE IN HEAVEN

1987, 103 mins, US Ⓥ ⊙ col

Dir Alan Rudolph ***Prod*** Raynold Gideon, Bruce A. Evans, David Blocker ***Scr*** Bruce A. Evans, Raynold Gideon ***Ph*** Jan Kiesser ***Ed*** Tom Walls ***Mus*** Mark Isham ***Art*** Paul Peters

Act Timothy Hutton, Kelly McGillis, Maureen Stapleton, Don Murray, Ellen Barkin, Debra Winger (Lorimar)

A gentle comedy which could have been integrated in the romantic fantasy genre along with classics such as *Angel on My Shoulder* and *Here Comes Mr. Jordan*, the script obviously held material that was too abundant for one single feature film.

Mike Shea (Timothy Hutton) is a nice small-town boy who dies and goes to heaven. There he is introduced to eternal life by his long deceased aunt Lisa (Maureen Stapleton), he meets the solicitous Annie (Kelly McGillis), a beautiful guide with whom he falls in love, and finally encounters Emmett (Debra Winger), the strange person who is not God but is in charge of seeing that everything proceeds smoothly, as ordained. Before Mike and Annie can establish a valid union, she is sent to do her stint on Earth. He begs Emmett to let him go back as well and is granted 30 years to find his love again down below.

The nature of the story invites obviously all sorts of religious and philosophical speculations, which are pretty much ignored here, even on the narrative level.

If Hutton and McGillis are likeable, it is mostly through their own personalities that this quality comes out.

Ellen Barkin plays a hellcat who almost deprives Hutton's character of his pure innocence, but she refused a credit. Winger, Hutton's spouse, assumed the part of Emmett on condition that it be kept a secret.

•

MADE IN PARIS

1966, 103 mins, US ▭ col

Dir Boris Sagal ***Prod*** Joe Pasternak ***Scr*** Stanley Roberts ***Ph*** Milton Krasner ***Ed*** William McMillin ***Mus*** George Stoll ***Art*** George W. Davis, Preston Ames

Act Ann-Margret, Louis Jourdan, Richard Crenna, Edie Adams, Chad Everett, John McGiver (Euterpe/M-G-M)

A Parisian setting and some snazzy femme costumes provide the major props for this otherwise weak and formula comedy programmer. Sexy plot overtones are too protracted in scripting, and become boring via heavy-handed direction. Ann-Margret and Louis Jourdan top the list of adequate players.

Stanley Roberts's dull script, strongly reminiscent of yesteryear Doris Day-Rock Hudson-Cary Grant plots (but less effective), finds fashion buyer Ann-Margret rushed to Paris from the lecherous arms of her employer's son (Chad Everett). Jourdan is the French designer, who, it appears, has had what is usually called an adult arrangement with Edie Adams, whom Ann-Margret has replaced. Richard Crenna is a foreign correspondent who bobs from time to time.

Plotting permits Ann-Margret to essay some wild terpery, which David Winters choreographed to the desired effect. Mongo Santamaria and band provide a solid beat for the bumps.

•

MADEMOISELLE

1967, 100 mins, UK/France b/w

Dir Tony Richardson ***Prod*** Oscar Lewenstein ***Scr*** Jean Genet ***Ph*** David Watkin ***Ed*** Anthony Gibbs ***Art*** Jacques Saulnier

Act Jeanne Moreau, Ettore Manni, Keith Skinner, Jeanne Beretta, Mony Rey (United Artists/Woodfall/Procinex)

French-British coproduction mixes Tony Richardson's free-wheeling style and the script of the controversial French writer-playwright Jean Genet. It has two versions, one English and one French, since French star Jeanne Moreau is bilingual.

A small French farming town is the locale. Story is about an arsonist who is terrorizing the people. A poisoned drinking well, and opened irrigation ditches which flood the farms, finally lead the populace to form a lynching mob.

The ingrained suspicion regarding a foreigner makes an Italian (Ettore Manni), living in the town, the scapegoat. Moreau's presence manages to make her schoolmarm character quite plausible in revealing her lurking lusts. But the remainder is somewhat sketchy, even though Manni has the virility to bring on hatreds from the other men and finally his own demise. The script seemingly needed more depth and background to the characters. Either that or almost surrealistic playing and treatment.

●

MAD GAME, THE

1933, 73 mins, US b/w

Dir Irving Cummings ***Prod*** Sol Wurtzel ***Scr*** William Conselman, Henry Johnson ***Ph*** Arthur Miller ***Mus*** Samuel Kaylin (dir.)

Act Spencer Tracy, Claire Trevor, Ralph Morgan, J. Carrol Naish, John Miljan (Fox)

Entertaining film and first of the gangster pictures to deal with the snatch racket, kidnapping.

While in prison, for having evaded income tax, Spencer Tracy turns reformer. His principal purpose for the change is revenge. His indirect purpose is to help the authorities clean up the snatchers. Picture intends to project that the old liquor mobs are the present kidnappers. It amounts to a gangster, turned stool pigeon, winding up as the hero.

Film would be better if it didn't take so long to reach the plot. That's where Tracy, in prison, convinces the warden he can serve society and the government better as a detective than as a prisoner behind the bars. Perhaps far-fetched, but the picture unrolls fast from that point.

Story soon indicates that the friendship between Tracy and a newspaper girl (Claire Trevor) may be more than just a formal acquaintanceship. Trevor impels an exciting interest. About the best portrayal of a newspaper gal which the studios have submitted. Hers is a fine performance, and Tracy gives his usual portrayal, okay throughout.

●

MADIGAN

1968, 101 mins, US Ⓥ ▭ col

Dir Don Siegel ***Prod*** Frank P. Rosenberg ***Scr*** Henri Simoun, Abraham Polonsky ***Ph*** Russell Metty ***Ed*** Milton Shifman ***Mus*** Don Costa ***Art*** Alexander Golitzen, George C. Webb

Act Richard Widmark, Henry Fonda, Inger Stevens, Harry Guardino, James Whitmore, Susan Clark (Universal)

Abraham Polonsky's screenplay adaptation of Richard Dougherty's novel *The Commissioner* is tough and to the point, bringing out the side issue problems but without dallying with them overmuch.

Pic gets away to a flying start, with Richard Widmark as a dedicated cop who isn't above using his badge for some fringe benefits, and sidekick Harry Guardino bursting into a sleazy bedroom to pick up a wanted killer for questioning.

Momentarily distracted by the nude broad in the room Widmark and Guardino are taken off guard and the psychopathic killer, played with menacing hysteria by Steve Ihnat, goes on the lam. Cops are given 72 hours to pick him up.

This is a good solid big-city adventure yarn with Widmark at his best. Guardino tags along satisfactorily as his buddy. Henry Fonda plays the commissioner with the cool austerity and deceptive slowness that he made peculiarly his own and James Whitmore is a tower of strength as the chief inspector.

●

MAD LOVE

1935, 67 mins, US Ⓥ ⦿ b/w

Dir Karl Freund ***Prod*** John W. Considine, Jr. ***Scr*** Guy Endore, P. J. Wolfson, John L. Balderston ***Ph*** Chester Lyons, Gregg Toland ***Ed*** Hugh Wynn ***Mus*** Dimitri Tiomkin

Act Peter Lorre, Frances Drake, Colin Clive, Ted Healy, Sarah Padden (M-G-M)

This is not a new or original story for the screen, but it is ideal starring material for Peter Lorre, making his first appearance in a Hollywood-milled product. Ideal as this French-written novel [*Hands of Orlac* by Maurice Renard] may be for Lorre, however, the results are disappointing.

Settings are strikingly effective and the camerawork far above average, director Karl Freund being a former cameraman and one of the best. Lorre's fine performance does the rest.

Hands of Orlac, under that title, was made in 1928 as a silent by Aywon, an independent company. Main character, in the hands of Lorre, is that of a surgeon-scientist with sadistic tendencies. Among other things, he never misses a guillotining.

Lorre buys a statue of an actress and idolizes it, refusing to recognize that she is in love with her husband, a distinguished pianist (Orlac). When the latter is injured in a train wreck and his hands have to be amputated, the doctor grafts on the mitts of a murderer who choked his victim and who has just been guillotined. Thus the pianist husband finally kills his stepfather.

The girl is Frances Drake, and the husband is played acceptably by Colin Clive.

●

MAD LOVE

1995, 95 mins, US Ⓥ col

Dir Antonia Bird ***Prod*** David Manson ***Scr*** Paula Milne ***Ph*** Fred Tammes ***Ed*** Jeff Freeman ***Mus*** Andy Roberts ***Art*** David Brisbin

Act Chris O'Donnell, Drew Barrymore, Matthew Lillard, Richard Chaim, Robert Nadir, Joan Allen (Touchstone)

Whatever else is wrong with *Mad Love*, yet another variation on *amour fou* and love on the run, the sensual acting of its charismatic leads, Chris O'Donnell and Drew Barrymore, is beyond reproach.

Set in Seattle, story begins as Matt (O'Donnell) observes in his telescope the eccentric behavior of Casey (Barrymore) who lives with her rigid yuppie parents on the other side of the lake. On the verge of adulthood, Matt lives a quiet life with his single dad and twin siblings, but he's never recovered from his mom's desertion of the family when he was 9. Matt is a serious young man, preparing for a college career. It's clear that he's never been in love—and is still a virgin.

Indeed, as soon as he lays his eyes on the beautiful Casey, a free, uninhibited spirit who's precisely his opposite, Matt becomes captivatingly absorbed, willing to abandon everything he's worked for to pursue a liaison.

The movie gains momentum in its second part, effectively capturing the spontaneous, combustible intensity of Matt and Casey's love. Theirs is a heat that consumes everything in its path, most of all reason and common sense. The middle section, when the two hit the road to Mexico, is exciting and believable, thanks to the strong chemistry generated by O'Donnell and Barrymore. Antonia Bird is extremely successful with her actors.

●

MAD MAX

1979, 90 mins, Australia Ⓥ ⦿ ▭ col

Dir George Miller ***Prod*** Byron Kennedy ***Scr*** George Miller, James McCausland ***Ph*** David Eggby ***Ed*** Tony Paterson, Cliff Hayes ***Mus*** Brian May ***Art*** Jon Dowding

Act Mel Gibson, Joanne Samuel, Hugh Keays-Byrne, Steve Bisley, Roger Ward, Tim Burns (Roadshow)

Mad Max is an all-stops-out, fast-moving exploitation pic in the tradition of New World/American International productions. The plot [from an original story by George Miller and Byron Kennedy] is extremely simple. A few years from now (opening title), the Australian countryside is terrorized by marauders who create mayhem on the roads. A crack police force opposes the villains.

Mad Max is one of the fastest and most ruthless of these cops of the future. Max quits the force to take a vacation with his wife and baby. But when The Toecutter's gang kills his wife and child, he dons his leather uniform again to hunt them down.

Stunts themselves would be nothing without a filmmaker behind the camera and George Miller, a doctor and film buff making his first feature, shows he knows what cinema is all about.

The film belongs to the director, cameraman and stunt artists: it's not an actor's piece, though the leads are all effective.

●

MAD MAX 2

(US: THE ROAD WARRIOR)

1981, 94 mins, Australia Ⓥ ⦿ ▭ col

Dir George Miller ***Prod*** Byron Kennedy ***Scr*** Terry Hayes, George Miller, Brian Hannant ***Ph*** Dean Semler ***Ed*** David Stiven, Tim Wellburn, Michael Balson ***Mus*** Brian May ***Art*** Graham "Grace" Walker

Act Mel Gibson, Bruce Spence, Mike Preston, Emil Minty, Max Phipps, Vernon Wells (Kennedy Miller)

Uncomplicated plot has Max (Mel Gibson), a futuristic version of the western gunslinger, reluctantly throwing in his lot with a communal group whose life-support system is a rudimentary refinery in the desert (he needs the gas).

Western parallel continues as the compound is under continual attack from a bunch of marauders led by the gravel-voiced, metal-visored villain Humungus (Kjell Nilsson).

Ever-the-loner, Max decides to strike out on his own again, and is saved by his friend the Gyro Captain (Bruce Spence) who swoops down from the clouds, and takes him back to the safety of the compound.

The climactic chase has Max at the wheel of a super-tanker in a desperate flight to Paradise 2,000 miles away (the promised land is the tourist resort on the Queensland Gold Coast, an unexpected touch of black humour). It's a dazzling demolition derby, as men and machines collide and disintegrate, featuring very fine stunt work and special effects.

Director Miller keeps the pic moving with cyclonic force, photography by Dean Semler is first class, editing is supertight, and Brian May's music is stirring.

●

MAD MAX BEYOND THUNDERDOME

1985, 106 mins, Australia Ⓥ ⦿ ▭ col

Dir George Miller, George Ogilvie ***Prod*** George Miller ***Scr*** Terry Hayes, George Miller ***Ph*** Dean Semler ***Ed*** Richard Francis-Bruce ***Mus*** Maurice Jarre ***Art*** Graham "Grace" Walker

Act Mel Gibson, Tina Turner, Angelo Rossitto, Helen Buday, Bruce Spence, Frank Thring (Kennedy Miller)

The third in the series opens strong with Mel Gibson being dislodged from his camel train by low-flying Bruce Spence in an airborne jalopy (providing as much fun here as he did as the Gyro Captain in the earlier *Max* films, this time accompanied by Adam Cockburn as his daredevil son). To retrieve his possessions, Gibson has to confront Tina Turner, the improbably named Aunty, mistress of Bartertown, a bizarre bazaar where anything—up to and including human lives—is traded as the only form of commerce in the postapocalyptic world.

Turner throws him a challenge: engage in a fight to the death with a giant known as The Blaster (Paul Larsson) in the Thunderdome, a geometric arena which serves as a kind of futuristic Roman Colosseum for the delectation of the locals.

Gibson impressively fleshes out Max, Tina Turner is striking in her role as Aunty (as well as contributing two top-notch songs, which open and close the picture) and the juves are uniformly good.

●

MADNESS OF KING GEORGE, THE

1994, 107 mins, US Ⓥ ⦿ col

Dir Nicholas Hytner ***Prod*** Stephen Evans, David Parfitt ***Scr*** Alan Bennett ***Ph*** Andrew Dunn ***Ed*** Tariq Anwar ***Mus*** George Fenton (arr.) ***Art*** Ken Adam

Act Nigel Hawthorne, Helen Mirren, Ian Holm, Rupert Everett, Rupert Graves, Amanda Donohoe (Samuel Goldwyn/Close Call)

Nicholas Hytner, the Tony Award–winning director who dazzled Broadway with his production of *Miss Saigon* and brilliant revival of *Carousel*, makes a stunning screen directorial debut in *The Madness of King George*, Alan Bennett's comic-tragic drama of the tormented king who almost lost his mind. The effective strategy of Bennett, who adapted his 1991 play for the screen, is to demythologize the members of the royal family without trivializing their lives.

The tale begins in 1788, with King George III (Nigel Hawthorne) a vibrant, robust leader, almost thirty years into his reign. He's happily married to his devoted Queen Charlotte (Helen Mirren), who has borne him 15 children, including the Prince of Wales (Rupert Everett) and the Duke of York (Julian Rhind-Tutt).

The king's veneer of respectability is shattered in a series of brief scenes that disclose his "darker side," as he spews obscenities at the queen or sexually assaults her attractive Mistress of the Robes, Lady Pembroke (Amanda Donohoe). Through his increasingly irrational conduct, it soon becomes evident that the king is ill, though the specific nature of his ailment is unclear.

With the exception of a few excessively theatrical scenes, Bennett's script doesn't betray its stage origins. Helmer Hytner moves the action smoothly from tightly controlled indoor settings to gloriously staged outdoor scenes, such as one showing the hyperactive king rampaging through the fields of Windsor at sunrise with his hysterical staff behind him. Reprising the role he created at the National Theatre, Hawthorne brings to his complex part a strong screen presence, light self-mockery and pathos that set divergent moods throughout the film.

1994: Best Art Direction

NOMINATIONS: Best Actor (Nigel Hawthorne), Supp. Actress (Helen Mirren), Adapted Screenplay

•

MAD ROOM, THE

1969, 93 mins, US col

Dir Bernard Girard ***Prod*** Norman Maurer ***Scr*** Bernard Girard, A. Z. Martin ***Ph*** Harry Stradling, Jr. ***Ed*** Pat Somerset ***Mus*** Dave Grusin ***Art*** Sidney Litwack

Act Shelley Winters, Stella Stevens, Barbara Sammeth, Michael Burns, Skip Ward (Columbia)

Weak story which pretends to be a psycho-suspense yarn. Screenplay is based on the 1940 play, *Ladies in Retirement*, filmed in 1941 by Columbia, with Ida Lupino, Elsa Lanchester, Edith Barrett.

Shelley Winters, surrounded by an able cast, thin plot, good color and some magnificent scenery on and near Vancouver Island, is the better part of the pic.

Barbara Sammeth and Michael Burns, playing brother and sister recently released from a mental institution, are the focus of the story which is long on melodramatics. Script has a patent mystery plot in which the real murderer isn't exposed until the film's end but any astute filmgoer will perceive the twist long before it comes on the screen.

Winters plays a wealthy widow living with young companion Stella Stevens. The young brother and sister of Stevens have been released from a mental institution where they were confined, supposedly for the murder of their parents.

•

MADWOMAN OF CHAILLOT, THE

1969, 142 mins, US Ⓥ ⦿ col

Dir Bryan Forbes ***Prod*** Ely Landau ***Scr*** Edward Anhalt ***Ph*** Claude Renoir, Burnett Guffey ***Ed*** Roger Dwyre ***Mus*** Michael J. Lewis ***Art*** Georges Petitot

Act Katharine Hepburn, Richard Chamberlain, Yul Brynner, Margaret Leighton, John Gavin, Giulietta Masina (Warner/Seven Arts)

Story of struggle between good and evil becomes audience's struggle against tedium. Margaret Leighton with her imaginary dog and Giulietta Masina with her imaginary amours ricochet around the Chaillot district of Paris sharing a phantom world of the past with Katharine Hepburn.

Hepburn, as equally disturbed Countess Aurelia, the madwoman of Chaillot, measures life somewhere between a lover lost years ago and a missing feathered boa. Richard Chamberlain, an active pacifist, and Danny Kaye, a local ragpicker, rattle the countess into the present with the news that there's a plot afoot—or underfoot—to destroy Paris.

Film doesn't come off. Hepburn fails to capture the fantasy-spirit of the countess. Her performance suffers because of indecision.

•

MAEDCHEN IN UNIFORM
(GIRLS IN UNIFORM)

1931, 90 mins, Germany Ⓥ b/w

Dir Leontine Sagan ***Prod*** Carl Froelich ***Scr*** Christa Winsloe, F. D. Andam ***Ph*** Reimar Kuntze, Franz Weihmayr

Act Emilia Unda, Dorothea Wieck, Hedwig Schlichter, Hertha Thiele, Ellen Schwanneke (Deutsche)

A whispering campaign managed to get started to the effect that the picture has to do with the subject of mannish femmes. The film [from Christa Winsloe's novel *The Child Manuela*] really has to do with no such subject, it's merely an overlong and sometimes dull psychological study of a schoolgirl's crush on her teacher. The picture is very arty and dry.

From a strictly artistic standpoint the film is a splendid accomplishment. It is laid in a Prussian military school for girls, a hard, restricted, colorless life with the teachers unbending and the principal (Emilia Unda) a veritable demon for hardness. Into this comes Manuela (Hertha Thiele), a sensitive, lonely child who finds sympathy and kindness only from one teacher, Fraulein von Bernburg (Dorothea Wieck), with the natural result that she idolizes this teacher.

It's poignant and clearly outlined, with the last reel actually exciting. But so slow, so painstaking. Acting is almost perfect, despite almost entirely by people new to films.

•

"MAGGIE", THE
(US: HIGH AND DRY)

1954, 93 mins, UK Ⓥ b/w

Dir Alexander Mackendrick ***Prod*** Michael Truman ***Scr*** William Rose ***Ph*** Gordon Dines ***Ed*** Peter Tanner ***Mus*** John Addison ***Art*** Jim Morahan

Act Paul Douglas, Alex Mackenzie, James Copeland, Abe Barker, Tommy Kearins, Hubert Gregg (Ealing)

One of the small coastal colliers which ply in Scottish waters provides the main setting for this Ealing comedy. The story [by director Alexander Mackendrick] of a hustling American businessman who gets involved with a leisurely minded but crafty skipper gives the film an Anglo-U.S. flavor.

The yarn has been subtly written as a piece of gentle and casual humor. The pace is always leisurely, and the background of Scottish lakes and mountains provides an appropriate backcloth to the story.

The skipper of the *Maggie* is a crafty old sailor, short of cash to make his little coaster seaworthy. By a little smart practice he gets a contract to transport a valuable cargo but when a hustling American executive realizes what has happened, he planes from London to Scotland to get his goods transferred to another vessel.

There is virtually an all-male cast with only minor bits for a few femme players. Paul Douglas, playing the American executive, provides the perfect contrast between the old world and the new. His is a reliable performance which avoids the pitfall of overacting.

•

MAGIC

1978, 106 mins, US Ⓥ ⦿ col

Dir Richard Attenborough ***Prod*** Joseph E. Levine, Richard P. Levine ***Scr*** William Goldman ***Ph*** Victor J. Kemper ***Ed*** John Bloom ***Mus*** Jerry Goldsmith ***Art*** Terence Marsh

Act Anthony Hopkins, Ann-Margret, Burgess Meredith, Ed Lauter, E. J. Andre, Jerry Houser (20th Century-Fox)

The premise is that of a dummy slowly taking over the personality of its ventriloquist-master. In adapting his own bestseller, William Goldman has opted for an atmospheric thriller, a mood director Richard Attenborough fleshes out to its fullest.

The dilemma of *Magic* is that the results never live up to the standards established in the film's opening half-hour. Through flashbacks and claustrophic editing, the relationship between Anthony Hopkins and his eerily realistic dummy, Fats, is well-documented. So is the introduction of Burgess Meredith, well cast as a Swifty Lazar-type of superagent.

When Hopkins declines a lucrative TV contract because of insecurity, and flees to his boyhood Catskills home, where a high-school girl on whom he had a crush (Ann-Margret) is enmeshed in a disastrous marriage to redneck Ed Lauter, *Magic* becomes disappointingly transparent. Goldman has Hopkins becoming involved in the standard love triangle that inevitably leads to disaster for all parties concerned.

The ventriloquism and magic stunts are expertly done by Hopkins, with the aid of tech advisor Dennis Alwood.

But as the Meredith character notes early on, "Magic is misdirection." That sentiment applies equally to the film.

•

MAGIC BOX, THE

1951, 118 mins, UK col

Dir John Boulting ***Prod*** Ronald Neame ***Scr*** Eric Ambler ***Ph*** Jack Cardiff ***Ed*** Richard Best ***Mus*** William Alwyn ***Art*** T. Hopewell Ash

Act Robert Donat, Margaret Johnston, Maria Schell, Robert Beatty, James Kenney, Bernard Miles (Festival/ British Lion)

The Magic Box is a picture of great sincerity and integrity, superbly acted and intelligently directed. Biopic of William Friese-Greene, the British motion picture pioneer, is charged with real-life drama.

Eric Ambler's screenplay is taken from Ray Allister's biography, *Friese-Greene: Close-Up of an Inventor*. The script pinpoints all the major triumphs and tragedies in the life of this pioneer, from his youthful beginnings as a photographer's assistant, to his death in 1921 at a film industry meeting with only the price of a cinema ticket in his pocket.

The selection of Robert Donat as Friese-Greene is an excellent one. Always a polished performer, he brings a new depth of sincerity and understanding to the role. His two wives are portrayed with infinite charm by Maria Schell and Margaret Johnston. Schell, as the ailing girl from Switzerland, shares the inventor's first and greatest triumph. Johnston shares only his failures.

Many front-ranking stars have little more than walk-on bits, and quite a few just make a brief appearance without even dialogue. Mention must be made of a fine cameo from Laurence Olivier as a policeman who is the first to see the inventor's moving picture.

•

MAGIC CHRISTIAN, THE

1969, 95 mins, UK Ⓥ ⦿ col

Dir Joseph McGrath ***Prod*** Denis O'Dell ***Scr*** Terry Southern, Joseph McGrath, Peter Sellers ***Ph*** Geoffrey Unsworth ***Ed*** Kevin O'Connor ***Mus*** Ken Thorne ***Art*** Assheton Gorton

Act Peter Sellers, Ringo Starr, Richard Attenborough, Christopher Lee, Raquel Welch, Laurence Harvey (Commonwealth United/Grand)

A spotty, uneven satire (from the novel by Terry Southern) with a number of good yocks, but insufficient sustained wit or related action.

As Peter Sellers & Co. swipe at the Establishment, authority, blimpishness and sacred cows, there's a great dismal feeling of self-indulgence as of a pic created merely to please an assorted bunch of chums. Much of it is too "clever" by half.

Sellers gives a very bright and stylish performance as the posh Sir Guy Grand, richest man in the world, who adopts a young fallout hobo (Ringo Starr) and then sets out to prove to him man's venality.

Though Sellers gives one of his brightest and best-observed appearances, Ringo Starr's effort to project himself as a non-Beatle actor is a distinct nonevent.

•

MAGIC TOWN

1947, 103 mins, US Ⓥ b/w

Dir William A. Wellman ***Prod*** Robert Riskin ***Scr*** Robert Riskin ***Ph*** Joseph F. Biroc ***Ed*** Sherman Todd, Richard G. Wray ***Mus*** Roy Webb ***Art*** Lionel Banks

Act James Stewart, Jane Wyman, Kent Smith, Ned Sparks, Wallace Ford, Regis Toomey (RKO)

The story [by Robert Riskin and Joseph Krumgold] is a little complicated in starting out to be a yarn about an opinion-polling outfit and winding up as the life, death and rebirth of an average American town.

James Stewart plays an enterprising researcher who plans to get rich quickly with what he calls his "mathematical miracle" method—finding one small town that thinks as the nation does, and by polling it constantly on various issues have a cross section of American opinion at very small cost. He finds the town in Grandview. Posing as an insurance salesman planning to settle there, Stewart and his two cronies (Ned Sparks and Donald Meek) poke their noses into the affairs of the town, and upset plans a young newspaper editor (Jane Wyman) has for improving the place with a new civic center.

•

MAGNIFICENT AMBERSONS, THE

1942, 88 mins, US Ⓥ ⦿ b/w

Dir Orson Welles ***Prod*** Orson Welles ***Scr*** Orson Welles ***Ph*** Stanley Cortez ***Ed*** Robert Wise, [Mark Robson] ***Mus*** [Bernard Herrmann, Roy Webb] ***Art*** Mark-Lee Kirk

Act Joseph Cotten, Dolores Costello, Anne Baxter, Tim Holt, Agnes Moorehead, Ray Collins (RKO/Mercury)

In *The Magnificent Ambersons*, Orson Welles devotes 9,000 feet of film to a spoiled brat who grows up as a spoiled, spiteful young man. This film hasn't a single moment of contrast; it piles on and on a tale of woe, but without once striking at least a true chord of sentimentality. [Novel by Booth Tarkington.]

The central character is Tim Holt, who is portrayed first as the spoiled, curly-haired darling of the town's richest family, and then for the major portion as a conceited, power-conscious, insufferable youth.

Welles comes up with a few more tricks in the direction of the dialogue. He plays heavily on the dramatic impact of a whisper, and on the threatened or actual hysterics of a frustrated woman as played by Agnes Moorehead.

1942: NOMINATIONS: Best Picture, Supp. Actress (Agnes Moorehead), B&W Cinematography, B&W Art Direction

•

MAGNIFICENT DOLL

1946, 93 mins, US b/w

Dir Frank Borzage ***Scr*** Irving Stone ***Ph*** Joseph Valentine ***Ed*** Ted J. Kent ***Mus*** H. J. Salter ***Art*** Alexander Golitzen

Act Ginger Rogers, David Niven, Burgess Meredith, Stephen McNally, Peggy Wood (Universal/Hallmark)

Dolly Madison has always been considered one of the most colorful figures in this country's early history and her true life story would probably have been a natural for films. It's difficult to understand, therefore, why Irving Stone, who's credited with both the original story and screenplay, went out of his way to slough off facts in favor of fiction. Incident in which Dolly salvaged important government documents from under the noses of the British in the War of 1812, for example, is given a quick brushoff. In its place, Stone has substituted such obvious fiction as having Aaron Burr, with a crush on Dolly, give up his claims to the presidency just because Dolly talked him out of it.

Picture's chief graces result from the fine work of the cast under Frank Borzage's competent direction. Ginger

Rogers gives expert handling to the title role, making the transition from one emotion to another in good fashion.

David Niven plays the scoundrelly Burr, sneering when he has to and being tender in his love scenes with Rogers. He hams up several sequences but he couldn't do otherwise with the script. Burgess Meredith shines as James Madison, making the idealistic president convincing enough.

Story is told by Dolly in retrospect, with her monolog bridging the gaps. It picks her up as a young girl on her father's plantation in Virginia, carries through her first unhappy marriage, then her love affair with Burr and eventual marriage to Madison.

•

MAGNIFICENT OBSESSION
1935, 110 mins, US b/w
Dir John M. Stahl ***Prod*** John M. Stahl ***Scr*** George O'Neil, Sarah Y. Mason, Victor Heerman ***Ph*** John Mescall ***Ed*** Milton Carruth ***Mus*** Franz Waxman
Act Irene Dunne, Robert Taylor, Charles Butterworth, Betty Furness, Sara Haden, Ralph Morgan (Universal)

If its 110 minutes' running time makes it appear a bit sluggish, the sensitive and intelligent development (from the novel by Lloyd C. Douglas) ultimately makes the initial-lethargic progression appear justified. With its metaphysical theme of godliness and faith, the spiritual background of *Magnificent* is magnificent.

It's patent that Irene Dunne and Robert Taylor, costarred, must clinch for the finale, even though it was a drunken mishap by the wastrel (Taylor) which had something to do with the death of the venerable Dr. Hudson. Dunne is the widow of Dr. Hudson, and Taylor's ultimate reformation is achieved because of the romantic attachment for her.

That he becomes a Nobel Prize–winner and a surgical marvel in six or seven years, finally achieving the restoration of her sight (after a high-powered battery of medical savants had previously failed to accomplish anything) is rather deftly skirted, for all the theatricalism of the basic elements.

Besides the stellar pair, Charles Butterworth and Betty Furness in secondary prominence scintillate.

•

MAGNIFICENT OBSESSION
1954, 107 mins, US Ⓥ ▭ col
Dir Douglas Sirk ***Prod*** Ross Hunter ***Scr*** Robert Blees ***Ph*** Russell Metty ***Ed*** Milton Carruth ***Mus*** Frank Skinner ***Art*** Bernard Herzbrun, Emrich Nicholson
Act Jane Wyman, Rock Hudson, Barbara Rush, Agnes Moorehead, Otto Kruger, Gregg Palmer (Universal)

The same inspirational appeal which marked the 1935 making of Lloyd C. Douglas's bestseller is again caught in this version of *Magnificent Obsession*, with Jane Wyman and Rock Hudson undertaking the roles previously enacted by Irene Dunne and Robert Taylor. It is a sensitive treatment of faith told in terms of moving, human drama which packs emotional impact.

As megged by Douglas Sirk from Robert Blees's moving and understanding screenplay [adaptation by Wells Root, based on the 1935 screenplay], the Ross Hunter production, impressively mounted, commands dramatic attention. Characters become alive and vital and infuse spiritual theme with a rare sort of beauty.

Hudson is the rich playboy responsible for Wyman's blindness who renounces his past existence to devote himself to study and work, hoping as a surgeon to cure her.

Film takes its title from the "magnificent obsession" which possessed a doctor for whose death Hudson is indirectly responsible.

1954: NOMINATION: Best Actress (Jane Wyman)

•

MAGNIFICENT SEVEN, THE
SEE: SHICHININ NO SAMURAI

•

MAGNIFICENT SEVEN
1960, 128 mins, US Ⓥ ⊙ ▭ col
Dir John Sturges ***Prod*** John Sturges ***Scr*** William Roberts ***Ph*** Charles Lang, Jr. ***Ed*** Ferris Webster ***Mus*** Elmer Bernstein ***Art*** Edward FitzGerald
Act Yul Brynner, Eli Wallach, Steve McQueen, Horst Buchholz, Charles Bronson, Robert Vaughan, Brad Dexter, James Coburn (United Artists)

Until the women and children arrive on the scene about two-thirds of the way through, *The Magnificent Seven* is a rip-roaring rootin' tootin' Western with lots of bite and tang and old-fashioned abandon. The last third is downhill, a long and cluttered anticlimax in which "The Magnificent Seven" grow slightly too magnificent for comfort.

Odd foundation for the able screenplay is the Japanese film, *Seven Samurai*. The plot, as adapted, is simple and compelling. A Mexican village is at the mercy of a bandit (Eli Wallach), whose recurrent "visits" with his huge band of outlaws strip the meek peasant people of the fruits of their labors. Finally, in desperation, they hire seven American gunslingers for the obvious purpose.

There is a heap of fine acting and some crackling good direction by John Sturges mostly in the early stages, during formation of the central septet. Wallach creates an extremely colorful and arresting figure as the chief antagonist. Of the big "Seven," Charles Bronson, James Coburn and Steve McQueen share top thespic honors, although the others don't lag by much, notably Horst Buchholz and Brad Dexter. Bronson fashions the most sympathetic character of the group. Coburn, particularly in an introductory sequence during which he reluctantly pits his prowess with a knife against a fast gun in an electrifying showdown, is a powerful study in commanding concentration.

Elmer Bernstein's lively pulsating score, emphasizing conscious percussion, strongly resembles the work of Jerome Moross for *The Big Country*.

1960: NOMINATION: Best Scoring of a Dramatic Picture

•

MAGNIFICENT SHOWMAN, THE
SEE: CIRCUS WORLD

•

MAGNIFICENT YANKEE, THE
1950, 89 mins, US b/w
Dir John Sturges ***Prod*** Armand Deutsch ***Scr*** Emmet Lavery ***Ph*** Joseph Ruttenberg ***Ed*** Ferris Webster ***Mus*** David Raksin
Act Louis Calhern, Ann Harding, Philip Ober, Ian Wolfe, Eduard Franz, Jimmy Lydon (M-G-M)

Magnificent Yankee is a fine translation to the screen of Emmet Lavery's Broadway play based on the life of Justice Oliver Wendell Holmes.

Louis Calhern makes of the Supreme Court judge a robust, living character, scoring in all departments.

Lavery, in depicting Holmes's life from Theodore Roosevelt through the inauguration in 1933 of Franklin D. Roosevelt, skirts but also mirrors the history of the U.S. through that era. Holmes, with his lifelong friend and associate justice, Louis D. Brandeis (Eduard Franz), at his side, battles his way through many of the legal cases that won him the tag of "The Great Dissenter" and revealed the two of them as the most progressive judges on the High Court bench during that time.

•

MAGNOLIA
1999, 188 mins, US Ⓥ ⊙ ▭ col
Dir Paul Thomas Anderson ***Prod*** Joanne Sellar ***Scr*** Paul Thomas Anderson ***Ph*** Robert Elswit ***Ed*** Dylan Tichenor ***Mus*** John Brion ***Art*** William Arnold, Mark Bridges
Act Jason Robards, Julianne Moore, Tom Cruise, Philip Seymour Hoffman, John C. Reilly, Melora Walters (Sellar-Ghoulardi/New Line)

In its ambitious scope and grand operatic style, *Magnolia*, Paul Thomas Anderson's follow-up to *Boogie Nights*, confirms his status as one of the most audacious filmmakers in Hollywood today. A superlative ensemble headed by Tom Cruise (in his best dramatic turn to date), Jason Robards, Melora Walters and Julianne Moore gives this meditation on urban alienation the aura of a major work highly in tune with the zeitgeist.

At the center of the elaborate maze, set in the San Fernando Valley area of L.A., is patriarch Earl Partridge (Robards), a dying man who's forced to come to terms with cheating on his first wife and walking out on her, leaving their only son, Frank Mackey (Cruise), to care for her when she's sick with cancer.

Earl is married to the much younger Linda (Moore), who can't deal with his impending death. The burdensome routines of his care are carried out by Phil (Philip Seymour Hoffman), a devoted nurse who's unable to separate his professional duties from his emotional involvement with Earl.

The most emotionally engaging—and splendidly acted—story centers on the travails of a religious cop, Jim Kurring (John C. Reilly), who's prone to babbling about the importance of "doing good and helping others." During one of his routine calls, Jim drops in on Claudia (Melora Walters), a high-strung woman who's addicted to drugs and loud music. Eventually she consents to go out on a date, and a tentative courtship follows.

1999: NOMINATIONS: Best Supp. Actor (Tom Cruise), Original Screenplay, Original Song

•

MAGNUM FORCE
1973, 122 mins, US Ⓥ ⊙ ▭ col
Dir Ted Post ***Prod*** Robert Daley ***Scr*** John Milius, Michael Cimino ***Ph*** Frank Stanley ***Ed*** Ferris Webster ***Mus*** Lalo Schifrin ***Art*** Jack Collis
Act Clint Eastwood, Hal Holbrook, Mitchell Ryan, Felton Perry, David Soul, Robert Urich (Malpaso/Warner)

Magnum Force is an intriguing follow-up to *Dirty Harry* [1971] in that nonconformist Frisco detective Clint Eastwood is faced with tracking down a band of vigilante cops headed by Hal Holbrook, his nominal superior and career nemesis. The story contains the usual surfeit of human massacre for the yahoo trade, as well as a few actual thoughts.

In *Harry* there was a script loaded in favor of the end justifying the means by those pledged to law enforcement. The interesting twist in *Magnum Force* is that Eastwood stumbles on a group of bandit cop avengers. The plot [based on a story by John Milius] thus forces Eastwood to render a judgement in favor of the present system.

Eastwood and new partner Felton Perry are helping investigate a number of bloody murders of local crime leaders, but the evidence finally begins to point at four rookie cops—David Soul, Tim Matheson, Robert Urich and Kip Niven—who eventually tip their hand to Eastwood.

•

MAGUS, THE
1969, 117 mins, UK/US ▭ col
Dir Guy Green ***Prod*** Jud Kinberg, John Kohn ***Scr*** John Fowles ***Ph*** Billy Williams ***Ed*** Max Benedict ***Mus*** John Dankworth ***Art*** Don Ashton
Act Michael Caine, Anthony Quinn, Candice Bergen, Anna Karina, Paul Stassino, Julian Glover (Blazer/20th Century-Fox)

The Magus is an esoteric, talky, slowly developing, sensitively executed, and somewhat dull film. Adapted by John Fowles from his novel, the production, filmed largely on Majorca (although setting is Greece), is a black fantasy-drama of self-realization. Michael Caine stars, in one of his better performances, along with Anthony Quinn, Candice Bergen and Anna Karina.

This near-miss is not without many notable virtues. Fowles's script sustains interest in its convolutions; direction is resourceful and sensitive; Caine is far more dynamic than usual and Quinn and the two femme stars register strongly.

Caine is an English teacher dispatched to a Greek island as replacement for a suicide. On the island, he meets Quinn, who is a mystic, or a wealthy spiritual hedonist playing God, or a film producer, or a recluse.

Those eager to shift intellectual planes for sheer enjoyment may find the pacing too expository and pedantic: those willing enough to be drawn along might crave more optical effects.

•

MAHLER
1974, 115 mins, UK Ⓥ ⊙ col
Dir Ken Russell ***Prod*** Roy Baird ***Scr*** Ken Russell ***Ph*** Dick Bush ***Ed*** Michael Bradsell ***Mus*** John Forsythe (coord.) ***Art*** Ian Whittaker
Act Robert Powell, Georgina Hale, Richard Morant, Lee Montague, Rosalie Crutchley, Antonia Ellis (Goodtimes)

Mahler is another maddening meeting of Russellian extremes, brilliant and irritating, inventive and banal, tasteful and tasteless, exciting and disappointing.

Flashbacks during composer Gustav Mahler's 1911 train ride to a Vienna deathbed give us glimpses of oppressed youth, childhood memories mirrored in his work, early frustrations as he is forced to conduct so that he can buy time in which to compose, a love-hate relationship with his young wife, a conversion from Judaism to ease his nomination to an important musical post, his constant obsession with death, and so on.

At its frequent best, it mirrors admirably, movingly and even excitingly, the moments of (musical) creation and inspiration, and the torment and basic loneliness of the artist.

•

MAIN EVENT, THE
1979, 112 mins, US Ⓥ col
Dir Howard Zieff ***Prod*** Jon Peters ***Scr*** Gail Parent, Andrew Smith ***Ph*** Mario Tosi ***Ed*** Edward Warschika ***Mus*** Gary Le Mel ***Art*** Charles Rosen
Act Barbra Streisand, Ryan O'Neal, Paul Sand, Patti D'Arbanville, Rory Calhoun, Ernie Hudson (Warner/First Artists/Barwood)

Instead of a comic knockout, this is more of a cream puff.

Situation of a bankrupt perfume queen left with a sore-handed fighter as her only asset has comic potential, but producers Barbra Streisand and Jon Peters, and director Howard Zieff, pad the story unmercifully.

Streisand is the garrulous yenta, after the passive and resistant Ryan O'Neal to resume his championship form and win her back the $60,000 she unknowingly wasted on him in her plush days.

Zieff has chosen to emphasize sexual innuendo and result is a low-blow effort that evokes more titters than guffaws. Romantic aspects, which should be chief draw of *Main Event*, are also blunted, until a final seduction scene instigated by Streisand that gives the pic its only resonance.

•

MAJOR AND THE MINOR, THE

1942, 100 mins, US b/w

Dir Billy Wilder ***Prod*** Arthur Hornblow, Jr. ***Scr*** Charles Brackett, Billy Wilder ***Ph*** Leo Tover ***Ed*** Doane Harrison ***Mus*** Robert Emmett Dolan ***Art*** Roland Anderson, Hans Dreier
Act Ginger Rogers, Ray Milland, Diana Lynn, Robert Benchley, Rita Johnson, Norma Varden (Paramount)

The Major and the Minor is a sparkling and effervescing piece of farce-comedy. Story [suggested by the play *Connie Goes Home* by Edward Childs Carpenter and the story *Sunny Goes Home* by Fannie Kilbourne] is light, fluffy, and frolicsome.

Ginger Rogers, disillusioned by New York, decides to head back home to Iowa. Her savings are not sufficient for a ticket, she dolls up as a youngster under 12 to ride on half rate. But complications arise that throw her into compartment of Ray Milland, major at a boys' military academy, and into the school for a three-day layover.

During the interim, there's a Cinderella-esque romance developed while Rogers, in the moppet getup, is pursued by the adolescent cadet officers for some rousing laugh episodes.

Both script and direction swing the yarn along at a consistent pace, with the laughs developing naturally and without strain.

•

MAJOR BARBARA

1941, 113 mins, UK Ⓥ b/w

Dir Gabriel Pascal, [Harold French, David Lean] ***Prod*** Gabriel Pascal ***Scr*** George Bernard Shaw ***Ph*** Ronald Neame, [Freddie Young] ***Ed*** Charles Frend, David Lean ***Mus*** William Walton ***Art*** Vincent Korda
Act Wendy Hiller, Rex Harrison, Robert Morley, Robert Newton, Emlyn Williams, Deborah Kerr (Pascal)

Major Barbara is the second film from the partnership of George Bernard Shaw and Gabriel Pascal. Adapted from an old Shaw play, circa 1905, it still carries the lightning thrusts of Shavian caustic satire at any and all levels of society.

The script, prepared by Shaw, closely follows his original. Wendy Hiller, daughter of a multimillionaire sincerely works to save souls as the Salvation Army major in the Limehouse slums. Pecunious Rex Harrison, Greek scholar, falls in love at first sight.

Hiller is suddenly disillusioned in the Army soul-saving when heavy financial aid is gladly accepted from her munitions-making father and a rich distiller. It's then that the father takes his odd family and stranger menage through his factories, demonstrating he is doing more to improve conditions of his workers than could be accomplished in Limehouse.

Hiller, lead in *Pygmalion*, delivers an excellent and personable performance throughout, and does much to carry the story along through some rather dull and weighty passages. Harrison does well as the Greek scholar but secondary acting honors are shared by Robert Morley, as the father, and Robert Newton, a tough limey whose soul is finally saved.

•

MAJOR DUNDEE

1965, 134 mins, US Ⓥ ⦿ ⊏⊐ col

Dir Sam Peckinpah ***Prod*** Jerry Bresler ***Scr*** Harry Julian Fink, Oscar Saul, Sam Peckinpah ***Ph*** Sam Leavitt ***Ed*** William A. Lyon, Don Starling, Howard Kunin ***Mus*** Daniele Amfitheatrof ***Art*** Al Ybarra
Act Charlton Heston, Richard Harris, Jim Hutton, James Coburn, Michael Anderson, Jr., Senta Berger (Bresler/Columbia)

Somewhere in the development of this Jerry Bresler production the central premise was sidetracked and a maze of little-meaning action substituted. What started out as a straight storyline (or at least, idea), about a troop of U.S. Cavalry chasing a murderous Apache and his band into Mexico to rescue three kidnapped white children and avenge an Indian massacre, devolves into a series of subplots and tedious, poorly edited footage in which much of the continuity is lost.

Sam Peckinpah's direction of individual scenes is mostly vigorous but he cannot overcome the weakness of screenplay of whose responsibility he bears a share with Harry Julian Fink [author of the screen story] and Oscar Saul. Use of offscreen narration, ostensibly from the diary of one of the troopers on the march, reduces impact and is a further deterrent to fast unfoldment.

Charlton Heston delivers one of his regulation hefty portrayals and gets solid backing from a cast headed by Richard Harris as the rebel captain, who presents a dashing figure. Jim Hutton as an energetic young lieutenant and James Coburn an Indian scout likewise stand out.

•

MAJORITY OF ONE, A

1961, 156 mins, US col

Dir Mervyn LeRoy ***Prod*** Mervyn LeRoy ***Scr*** Leonard Spigelgass ***Ph*** Harry Stradling, Sr. ***Ed*** Philip W. Anderson ***Mus*** Max Steiner ***Art*** John Beckman
Act Rosalind Russell, Alec Guinness, Ray Danton, Madlyn Rhue, Mae Questel, Marc Marno (Warner)

Leonard Spigelgass's brew of schmaltz and sukiyaki is an outstanding film. Rosalind Russell and Alec Guinness play the parts created on Broadway by Gertrude Berg and Cedric Hardwicke. Russell's Yiddish hex-cent, though at times it sounds like what it is—a Christian imitating a Jew—is close enough to the genuine article. Guinness becomes Japanese through physical suggestion and masterful elocution.

Madlyn Rhue and Ray Danton play Russell's daughter and son-in-law, latter the diplomat whose assignment to Japan paves the way for the unusual romance between middle-class Brooklyn widow and wealthy, influential Tokyo widower. The characters limned by Rhue and Danton are somewhat devoid of vigor, but the performances are sound.

•

MAJOR LEAGUE

1989, 107 mins, US Ⓥ ⦿ col

Dir David S. Ward ***Prod*** Chris Chesser, Irby Smith ***Scr*** David S. Ward ***Ph*** Reynaldo Villalobos ***Ed*** Dennis M. Hill ***Mus*** James Newton Howard ***Art*** Jeffrey Howard
Act Tom Berenger, Charlie Sheen, Corbin Bernsen, Margaret Whitton, James Gammon, Rene Russo (Morgan Creek/Mirage)

Major League lacks the subtlety of *Bull Durham* or the drama of *Eight Men Out*, but for sheer crowd-pleasing fun it belts one high into the left-field bleachers. Writer-director David S. Ward creates an adult version of *The Bad News Bears* in this R-rated baseball comedy about a squad of misfits who rally together to bring the pennant back to Cleveland.

Though the plot turns are mostly predictable, they are executed with wit and style. There's a lot of rooting interest for the audience in the sad sacks cynically assembled by new Indians owner Margaret Whitton with the secret hope that they'll draw so poorly that she'll be able to break the stadium lease and head for Miami.

Naturally, when the guys get wind of this maneuver, they recover their lost pride and bring off the pennant miracle. The cast is a fine ensemble, leading off with Tom Berenger as the battered, world-weary catcher and Charlie Sheen as the juve delinquent pitcher with punk hair-do who fully merits his nickname of "Wild Thing."

As long as it sticks to the field and the clubhouse, the script doesn't falter, but there's time to go out for popcorn during the clichéd love scenes of Berenger trying to jump-start his broken-down romance with yuppie librarian Rene Russo.

Milwaukee County Stadium fills in for the much larger (and contrastingly circular) Cleveland ballpark, which is unconvincingly used for establishing shots.

•

MAJOR LEAGUE II

1994, 104 mins, US Ⓥ ⦿ col

Dir David S. Ward ***Prod*** James G. Robinson, David S. Ward ***Scr*** R. J. Stewart ***Ph*** Victor Hammer ***Ed*** Paul Seydor, Donn Cambern ***Mus*** Michel Colombier ***Art*** Stephen Hendrickson
Act Charlie Sheen, Tom Berenger, Corbin Bernsen, Dennis Haysbert, James Gammon, Omar Epps (Morgan Creek/Warner)

It's a fast trip back to the minors for *Major League II*, a singularly unfunny, dramatically tepid follow-up to 1989's $50 million theatrical success. Time has not been kind to the franchise, with the second season imposing a straitjacket structure that's in direct opposition to the inspired chaos of the original. Apart from an emotional ninth-inning surge, this is one yarn that unravels into a heap of plot strands all too quickly.

Story dives directly into the next season of the fictional Cleveland Indians. Rick "Wild Thing" Vaughn (Charlie Sheen) has gone so legit that he's now a sought-after spokesman for chichi products. Knee injuries send Jake Taylor (Tom Berenger) to the coaching ranks, and Roger Dorn (Corbin Bernsen) has stepped off the field to buy the club from former owner Rachel Phelps (Margaret Whitton). Meanwhile, Willie Mays Hayes (Omar Epps) did an action film, and Pedro Cerrano has switched from voodoo to Buddhism.

The thread running through R. J. Stewart's screenplay [from a screen story by Stewart, Tom S. Parker and Jim Jennewein] is that old, feel-good saw about being yourself. The predictable device robs the film of a lot of momentum. Devoid of pace, much of the humor comes across as forced and insipid. While the original was a true ensemble piece, *Major League II* places its dominant emphasis on Sheen's character.

•

MAJOR PAYNE

1995, 97 mins, US Ⓥ ⦿ col

Dir Nick Castle ***Prod*** Eric L. Gold, Michael Rachmil ***Scr*** Dean Lorey, Damon Wayans, Gary Rosen ***Ph*** Richard Bowen ***Ed*** Patrick Kennedy ***Mus*** Craig Safan ***Art*** Peter Larkin
Act Damon Wayans, Karyn Parsons, Bill Hickey, Michael Ironside, Albert Hall, Steven Martini (Wife 'n' Kids/Universal)

The private war of Maj. Benson Payne (Damon Wayans) is that he's a modern-day military anachronism. A natural born killing machine, his pleasure in an era bereft of enemies is a pain to the Marine Corps. *Major Payne*, the movie, is also a bit of a throwback. It's what is sometimes called a "warmedy," a cuddly comedy in which a crotchety hero sees the light by rubbing shoulders with humanity.

Unlike its movie inspiration—1955-vintage *The Private War of Major Benson*, with Charlton Heston—the new outing presents Payne as a naif, seemingly unaware of a world that includes children, ROTC or virtually anything unrelated to mortal combat. The clash of hard-nosed Marine training and youthful antics are the grist of the film's comedy.

Wayans remains an odd choice for family-film stardom. His rude brand of humour is largely muted here, and when he slyly reveals it, the effect is jarring. Also grating is his choice to sport several gold teeth and assume an awkward pose that strains at the credulity of his romance with a school doctor (Karyn Parsons).

•

MAKE MINE MINK

1960, 101 mins, UK Ⓥ b/w

Dir Robert Asher ***Prod*** Hugh Stewart ***Scr*** Michael Pertwee, Peter Blackmore ***Ph*** Reginald Wyer ***Ed*** Roger Cherrill ***Mus*** Philip Green ***Art*** Carmen Dillon
Act Terry-Thomas, Athene Seyler, Hattie Jacques, Billie Whitelaw, Elspeth Duxbury, Jack Hedley (Rank)

Based on Peter Coke's West-End comedy *Breath of Spring*, plot concerns the blundering excursions into crime of a bunch of pinheaded amateurs, who specialize in lifting valuable furs and devoting the loot to charity.

Dame Beatrice Appleby (Athene Seyler) takes in lodgers to help out her income and also to provide money for her charitable work. The idea of crimes comes to her when she is able safely to return a fur which has been given to her as a present by her devoted maid Lily (Billie Whitelaw), a reformed thief who is now going steady with a policeman.

Her "gang" consists of Albert (Terry-Thomas), a retired officer who plans the raids along strictly military lines, a daffy spinster (Elspeth Duxbury), and Nanette (Hattie Jacques), a heavyweight teacher of deportment. This unlikely quartet carry off several daring raids.

The humor is episodic, but Robert Asher has directed the lively screenplay briskly enough, and the camerawork is okay. The four members of the gang do their chores admirably, with Seyler outstanding.

•

MAKE MINE MUSIC

1946, 75 mins, US col

Dir Jack Kinney, Clyde Geronimi, Hamilton Luske, Bob Cormack, Josh Meador ***Prod*** Joe Grant ***Scr*** Homer Brightman, Dick Kelsey, Roy Williams, Jesse Marsh, Duck Huemer, Jim Bodrero, Cap Palmer, ***Mus*** Charles Wolcott (dir.) (RKO/Disney)

Make Mine Music is a 75-minute Walt Disney treat. You can call it a big short which, technically, is just what it is—10 items pieced together in one "musical fantasy" as it is billed—but it entertains all the way.

Pic tees off with an interesting cinematurgical treatment of "The Martins and the Coys," chirped off-screen (as is everything done by the live talent with the exception of the ballet team) by the King's Men.

This gives way to a clever visualization of Sergei Prokofiev's "Peter and the Wolf" in rich hues with some fine new Disney characters, notably Peter, Sonia the Duck, Ivan the Cat and Sasha the Bird. The Wolf himself is an austere and forbidding menace. Sterling Holloway is capital as the narrator, warmly and dramatically interpreting each musical nuance.

And the finale, "The Whale Who Wanted to Sing at the Met," is as imaginative a conceit as Disney ever essayed. Willie the Whale, fished out of the briny, runs the gamut of familiar operatic excerpts. Audiences are set on their ears as Willie (yclept Nelson Eddy, who sings all three voices, tenor, baritone and bass; and, through scientific alchemy, is made to sing a trio with himself) truly wows the musical world.

•

MAKE WAY FOR TOMORROW

1937, 91 mins, US b/w

Dir Leo McCarey ***Prod*** Leo McCarey ***Scr*** Vina Delmar ***Ph*** William Mellor ***Ed*** LeRoy Stone ***Mus*** Boris Morros (dir.) ***Art*** Hans Dreier, Bernard Herzbrun

Act Victor Moore, Beulah Bondi, Fay Bainter, Thomas Mitchell, Ray Mayer, Barbara Read (Paramount)

Rugged simplicity marks this Leo McCarey production [from a novel by Josephine Laurence and a play by Helen and Noah Leary]. It is a tearjerker, obviously grooved for femme fans.

McCarey, who also directed, has firmly etched the dilemma in which an elderly married couple find themselves when they lose their old dwelling place and their five grown-up children are nonreceptive. He keeps audience interest focused on old Lucy Cooper and Pa Cooper as they are separated, each finding themselves in the way and not fitting in with the two households (one with a son and the other with a daughter).

Victor Moore essays a serious role as Pa Cooper without firmly establishing himself in the new field. He continues to be more Victor Moore than an old grandfather, and he makes the biggest impression in the lighter, more whimsical moments. Beulah Bondi as the aged Lucy is standout from the viewpoint of clever character work and makeup. She has some of the meaty scenes and makes them real.

Fay Bainter does splendidly as the wife of George Cooper, one of the sons to whose house the mother goes to live. Maurice Moscovitch, as the ardent listener to the old man's woes and who understands him better than his own children, contributes a neat portrayal.

•

MAKING IT

SEE: LES VALSEUSES

•

MAKING LOVE

1982, 111 mins, US Ⓥ col

Dir Arthur Hiller ***Prod*** Allen Adler, Daniel Melnick ***Scr*** Barry Sandler ***Ph*** David M. Walsh ***Ed*** William H. Reynolds ***Mus*** Leonard Rosenman ***Art*** James D. Vance

Act Michael Ontkean, Kate Jackson, Harry Hamlin, Wendy Hiller, Arthur Hill, Nancy Olson (20th Century-Fox/Indie)

This homosexual-themed domestic drama of a married man's "coming out" stands up well on all counts, emerging as an absorbing tale.

First half-hour presents Michael Ontkean and Kate Jackson as a successful young L.A. couple, he a medic and she a fast-rising TV exec. Then Ontkean meets Harry Hamlin, a gay writer whose good looks provide him with enough easy one-night stands to do without any emotional commitment. Ontkean takes the plunge with Hamlin and finds he likes it, so much so that he quickly knows his marriage is finished.

Working from a story by A. Scott Berg, Barry Sandler has penned a fine, aware screenplay.

Director Arthur Hiller has elicited strong performances from his three principals, and he also carries off the device of having the trio directly address the audience with their thoughts from time to time.

•

MAKING MR. RIGHT

1987, 95 mins, US Ⓥ ⊙ col

Dir Susan Seidelman ***Prod*** Mike Wise, Joel Tuber ***Scr*** Floyd Byars, Laurie Frank ***Ph*** Edward Lachman ***Ed*** Andrew Mondshein ***Mus*** Chaz Jankel ***Art*** Barbara Ling

Act John Malkovich, Ann Magnuson, Glenne Headly, Ben Masters, Laurie Metcalf, Hart Bochner (Orion/Barry & Enright)

Susan Seidelman has taken nearly every wrong turn in *Making Mr. Right*, a desperately unfunny romance between an android and a New Wave "image consultant." The actors nearly suffocate delivering stiff dialog, with jokes that are bad or vulgar (or both) in scenes that reek of contrivance.

Sharing in the blame should be scripters Floyd Byars and Laurie Frank, who have taken Frankenstein and turned him into Frankie Stone (Ann Magnuson). Her world is Melrose Avenue, Miami style, where she's a very unlikely whiz-bang publicist with a punk 'do and very ordinary sensibilities who practically moves in with an android and his creator (John Malkovich in both roles) to get the best handle on how to sell the invention to the American public before he's launched into space. She's supposed to be teaching the android, Ulysses, social graces, but he ends up learning emotions instead.

Malkovich takes to his role of Ulysses very earnestly, considering he has to utter such gooey lines as "Why do people fall in love?" and suffer mutterings from Magnuson and her horny girlfriend (Glenne Headly) whether he's anatomically correct.

•

MAKIOKA SISTERS, THE

SEE: SASAME YUKI

•

MALAYA

1949, 95 mins, US b/w

Dir Richard Thorpe ***Prod*** Edwin H. Knopf ***Scr*** Frank Fenton ***Ph*** George Folsey ***Ed*** Ben Lewis ***Mus*** Bronislau Kaper

Act Spencer Tracy, James Stewart, Valentina Cortese, Sydney Greenstreet, John Hodiak, Lionel Barrymore (M-G-M)

Malaya is a pulp-fiction, wartime adventure yarn, based on a factual incident early in the fighting, that takes the customer for a pretty fancy chimerical flight.

Kickoff for the story is tied to a letter from President Roosevelt to Manchester Boddy, L.A. newspaper publisher, concerning the government's need to obtain rubber during the war.

James Stewart plays a roaming newspaper reporter who promises to steal rubber for his government, which supplies him with ships for transporting and gold for bribing. He effects the release from prison of Spencer Tracy to aid in the daring adventure.

Tracy and Stewart are at home in their toughie roles. Valentina Cortese appears very well as a jungle torch singer in the Malayan saloon. Sydney Greenstreet's character of a sharp operator, wise in the ways of man, comes over excellently.

•

MALCOLM X

1992, 201 mins, US Ⓥ ⊙ col

Dir Spike Lee ***Prod*** Marvin Worth, Spike Lee ***Scr*** Arnold Perl, Spike Lee ***Ph*** Ernest Dickerson ***Ed*** Barry Alexander Brown ***Mus*** Terence Blanchard ***Art*** Wynn Thomas

Act Denzel Washington, Angela Bassett, Albert Hall, Al Freeman, Jr., Delroy Lindo, Spike Lee (Warner/40 Acres & a Mule)

Spike Lee has made a disappointingly conventional and sluggish film in *Malcolm X*. The pic comes up short in several departments, notably in pacing and in giving a strong sense of why this man became a legend. This is one long sit.

Despite Denzel Washington's forceful, magnetic, multilayered lead performance, the film only clicks sporadically.

The screenplay [based on *The Autobiography of Malcolm X* as told to Alex Haley] by the late Arnold Perl and Lee (James Baldwin's name, often invoked during production, is nowhere mentioned) tellingly begins during "the war years." The initial hour chronicles Malcolm's misadventures in clubs and bars, his affair with a white woman, numbers running, involvement in drugs, and the burglary ring that eventually lands him in the pen.

The subsequent 25 minutes detail Malcolm's prison introduction to Islam and the beliefs of Elijah Muhammad. The next hour presents Malcolm as the rising star of the Nation of Islam.

Malcolm's gradual break with Elijah Muhammad is handled in rather a muddled fashion, and the final, short act of Malcolm's life isn't given the dramatic substance it deserves, despite the time lavished upon it.

Various periods from the 1940s through the mid-1960s have been elaborately evoked by production designer Wynn Thomas, cinematographer Ernest Dickerson, costume designer Ruth Carter and the multitude of behind-the-scenes craftspeople (the end credits last nine minutes).

1992: NOMINATIONS: Best Actor (Denzel Washington), Costume Design

•

MALE AND FEMALE

1919, 107 mins, US ⊙ ⊗ b/w

Dir Cecil B. DeMille ***Prod*** Jesse L. Lasky ***Scr*** Jeanie MacPherson ***Ph*** Alvin Wyckoff ***Art*** Wilfrey Buckland

Act Thomas Meighan, Gloria Swanson, Lila Lee, Bebe Daniels, Theodore Roberts, Raymond Hatton (Paramount)

Cecil B. DeMille's picturization of J. M. Barrie's play, *The Admirable Crichton*, is impressive. The production places DeMille on a par with D. W. Griffith as a far as Babylonian stuff is concerned, and there are several scenes where DeMille steps a little beyond the great Grif. The result on the screen shows that there was no stinting on money. The cast is a pippin and Thomas Meighan does good work. Gloria Swanson and Lila Lee divide the women honors of the piece.

Swanson plays the role of Lady Mary, while Lee is the little slavey, Tweeny. The former appears to advantage in both the London and the desert island scenes, looking beautiful at all times, and especially so as she slips into the sunken bath, while little Lee displays an artistry that is far greater than she showed in any of her previous productions. Bebe Daniels is also in the cast for a small bit in one of the Babylonian scenes, and certainly is good to look upon.

•

MALICE

1993, 107 mins, US Ⓥ ⊙ col

Dir Harold Becker ***Prod*** Rachel Pfeffer, Charles Mulvehill, Harold Becker ***Scr*** Aaron Sorkin, Scott Frank, [William Goldman] ***Ph*** Gordon Willis ***Ed*** David Bretherton ***Mus*** Jerry Goldsmith ***Art*** Philip Harrison

Act Alec Baldwin, Nicole Kidman, Bill Pullman, Bebe Neuwirth, Anne Bancroft, George C. Scott (Columbia/Castle Rock)

The immaculately crafted *Malice* is a virtual scrapbook of elements borrowed from other suspense pics, but no less enjoyable for being so familiar.

The film starts slowly, with college dean Andy (Bill Pullman) concerned over the mysterious rapist who's attacked several students in the sleepy New England college town, and worrying about the mysterious abdominal pains plaguing his wife Tracy (Nicole Kidman). Enter polished, self-assured surgeon Jed (Alec Baldwin), who is new to the area and moves into the third floor of the house Pullman and Kidman are restoring.

After about 40 minutes, the pic shifts into high gear when Baldwin performs emergency surgery on Kidman, which kicks off a series of revelations, plot reversals and character twists.

Script, from a story by Aaron Sorkin and Jonas McCord, touches on big topics like fear of doctors, but doesn't explore them, choosing instead to simply give the audience a piece of escapism. Though a thriller, there's not one big scream in the whole movie.

All the thesps, including George C. Scott and Anne Bancroft in brief cameos, are fine, with Baldwin and Kidman the standouts.

•

MALLRATS

1995, 95 mins, US Ⓥ col

Dir Kevin Smith ***Prod*** James Jacks, Sean Daniel, Scott Mosier ***Scr*** Kevin Smith ***Ph*** David Klein ***Ed*** Paul Dixon ***Mus*** Ira Newborn ***Art*** Dina Lipton

Act Shannen Doherty, Jeremy London, Jason Lee, Claire Forlani, Michael Rooker, Priscilla Barnes (Alphaville)

After a savage, satiric assault on convenience store culture in *Clerks*, writer-director Kevin Smith takes aim at hangin' at the shopping arcade in *Mallrats*. While admittedly ragged and ribald, it's a picture with an innate charm and honesty.

Peeling away the contempo trappings, it's still basically an old-fashioned boy-loses-girl saga and how he proceeds to get her back. In fact, it's two boys who are best friends losing girlfriends on the same day.

T. S. (Jeremy London) is all set to head off to Florida with Brandi (Claire Forlani) when she informs him about the freak death of a friend who was set to appear on her father's game-show pilot. When she tells him she has stepped in, he goes ballistic.

Across town, video addict Brodie (Jason Lee) is camping out in his room engrossed in a game. He just barely registers that Rene (Shannon Doherty) is fed up with his inattentiveness.

Angry and depressed, the young men seek refuge in the security of the spiffy Eden Prairie Mall. But the TV pilot is to film at that locale and the girlfriends, as well as their entire peer group, are much in evidence in the confined environs.

Smith has obvious affection for his *Mallrats*, who, as one nasty character comments, "have no shopping motivation." The ensemble cast is uniformly excellent, including such usually overdrawn youth movie miscreants as adults and heavies.

•

MALTA STORY

1953, 103 mins, UK Ⓥ b/w

Dir Brian Desmond Hurst ***Prod*** Peter de Sarigny ***Scr*** William Fairchild, Nigel Balchin ***Ph*** Robert Krasker ***Ed*** Michael Gordon ***Mus*** William Alwyn ***Art*** John Howell

Act Alec Guinness, Jack Hawkins, Anthony Steel, Muriel Pavlow, Flora Robson, Renee Asherson (Rank)

This is an epic story of the courage and endurance of the people and defenders of the island of Malta. It is handled in grimly realistic but not over-dramatic style. Camerawork is excellent, and some vivid war scenes of attacks on convoys are genuine newsreel shots.

Alec Guinness plays a camera reconnaissance pilot en-route to Egypt. His plane is blown up, leaving him stranded in Malta. He is roped in to continue his activities during the siege of 1942 since his pictures disclose freight trains in Italy packed with gliders obviously intended for an invasion of the island. Jack Hawkins is the air officer in command who stands helplessly by while his airfields are blasted night and day.

A dual love interest impinges rather apologetically upon this war scarred scene, with Muriel Pavlow giving an endearing performance as a Maltese girl in love with her chief, played in a forthright manner by Anthony Steel. Flora Robson gives a distinguished characterization of a steadfast, sorrowing Maltese mother stoically facing the prospect of her son's execution for treason.

Bulk of the acting laurels go to Guinness, who here forsakes his chameleonlike whimsicality for the shy diffident charm of an inexperienced lover.

•

MALTESE FALCON, THE
1931, 80 mins, US Ⓥ b/w
Dir Roy Del Ruth ***Scr*** Maude Fulton, Lucien Hubbard, Brown Holmes ***Ph*** William Rees
Act Bebe Daniels, Ricardo Cortez, Dudley Digges, Una Merkel, Robert Elliot, Thelma Todd (Warner)

Bringing *The Maltese Falcon* to the screen as Warners have done was no easy job. But director Roy Del Ruth lets things take their course and, with a naturally nonchalant although extremely odd private detective in Ricardo Cortez, takes his audience out of the screen story rut for a series of surprise incidents and a totally different finis.

Although four men are murdered and two corpses revealed to the audience, the story treatment [from Dashiell Hammett's novel] and the Cortez smile are such that a quick thrill is permitted, a laugh, and then, through the first 75 percent of the footage, additional interest to well-sustained curiosity.

It can't be called naughty, even though Bebe Daniels as Ruth Wonderly spends the second night in the elaborate apartment of this unusual private detective.

The mystery element is so flung about that not until the last reel or so does the most studious follower know who did any of the killings. Meantime a number of clever gags happen through Sam Spade in disarming people, then apologizing; taking money and then having it taken from him; making love one minute and turning the girl over to the police the next.

•

MALTESE FALCON, THE
1941, 100 mins, US Ⓥ ⦿ b/w
Dir John Huston ***Prod*** Hal B. Wallis (exec.) ***Scr*** John Huston ***Ph*** Arthur Edeson ***Ed*** Thomas Richards ***Mus*** Adolph Deutsch ***Art*** Robert Haas
Act Humphrey Bogart, Mary Astor, Peter Lorre, Sydney Greenstreet, Barton MacLane, Gladys George (Warner)

This is one of the best examples of actionful and suspenseful melodramatic storytelling in cinematic form. Unfolding a most intriguing and entertaining murder mystery, picture displays outstanding excellence in writing, direction, acting and editing.

John Huston makes his debut as a film director. He also wrote the script solo, endowing it with well-rounded episodes of suspense and surprise and carrying along with consistently pithy dialog.

Humphrey Bogart gives an attention-arresting portrayal that not only dominates the proceedings throughout but is the major motivation in all but a few minor scenes. Mary Astor skillfully etches the role of an adventuress. Sydney Greenstreet, prominent member of the Lunt-Fontaine stage troupe, scores heavily in his first screen appearance.

Story in Dashiell Hammett's best style details the experiences of private detective Bogart when called in to handle a case for Astor—shortly finding himself in the middle of double-crossing intrigue and several murders perpetrated by strange characters bent on obtaining possession of the famed bejeweled Maltese Falcon. Keeping just within bounds of the law, and utilizing sparkling ingenuity in gathering up the loose ends and finally piecing them together, Bogart is able to solve the series of crimes for the benefit of the police.

1941: NOMINATIONS: Best Picture, Supp. Actor (Sydney Greenstreet), Screenplay

•

MAMBO
1954, 94 mins, Italy/US Ⓥ b/w
Dir Robert Rossen ***Prod*** Carlo Ponti, Dino De Laurentiis ***Scr*** Robert Rossen, Guido Piovene, Ivo Perilli, Ennio De Concini ***Ph*** Harold Rosson ***Ed*** Adriana Novelli ***Mus*** Bernardo Noriega, Dave Gilbert
Act Silvana Mangano, Michael Rennie, Vittorio Gassman, Shelley Winters, Katherine Dunham, Eduardo Ciannelli (Ponti-De Laurentiis/Paramount)

Story is near soap opera, and involves the trials of a girl who wants to be a dancer. She is torn between the pure love for a dying prince and the passionate embraces of an adventurer. For a while Giovanna (Silvana Mangano) is happy with the dance group led by Tony (Shelley Winters), and soon becomes star of the show. But despite her success on returning to her home town of Venice, she falls once more under the adventurer's (Vittorio Gassman) spell while turning down a marriage proposal by the prince (Michael Rennie).

Like the story, the film is not for the discriminating. Reportedly, it was recut several times and is said to bear little resemblance to the original.

Performances are generally good, with Rennie copping honors in a smooth, sympathetic effort as the doomed prince. Winters contributes ably despite a vaguely drawn character, while Gassman effectively overacts his villain role in keeping with the picture's spirit. Katherine Dunham and Eduardo Cianelli liven up some minor roles, with the former also contributing the pic's choreography.

•

MAMBO KINGS, THE
1992, 101 mins, US Ⓥ ⦿ col
Dir Arne Glimcher ***Prod*** Arnon Milchan, Arne Glimcher ***Scr*** Cynthia Cidre ***Ph*** Michael Ballhaus ***Ed*** Claire Simpson ***Mus*** Robert Kraft ***Art*** Stuart Wurtzel
Act Armand Assante, Antonio Banderas, Cathy Moriarty, Maruschka Detmers, Desi Arnaz, Jr., Roscoe Lee Browne (Warner)

The Mambo Kings is an ambitious, old-fashioned Hollywood film that lovingly recreates the Latino ambience of its Pulitzer Prize–winning source material. With impeccable period sets and costumes and striking cinematography, pic beautifully evokes 1950's New York. Arne Glimcher, an art gallery owner and producer, makes a strong directing debut.

Oscar Hijuelos's novel [*The Mambo Kings Play Songs of Love*] proved a challenge to adapt, and Glimcher and screenwriter Cynthia Cidre pared down the 407-page book to its essential story about the rise and fall of two Cuban immigrant musicians. Most striking sequences take place in smoky, crowded clubs, from the opening in Havana to final image of Cesar Castillo (Armand Assante) singing in a New York club.

Assante makes a likable skirt chaser and later conveys Cesar's downward spiral with great economy. But he occasionally slips into a New York accent and never sounds anything like brother Antonio Banderas, a Spanish actor in Pedro Almodovar's films. As the tormented Nestor, Banderas gives a sensitive performance.

Final scenes pass too quickly, with the sexual tension between Banderas's wife Maruschka Detmers and Assante left unexplored despite one steamy scene.

1992: NOMINATION: Best Song ("Beautiful Maria of My Soul")

•

MAME
1974, 132 mins, US Ⓥ ⦿ ⌑ col
Dir Gene Saks ***Prod*** Robert Fryer, James Cresson ***Scr*** Paul Zindel ***Ph*** Philip Lathrop ***Ed*** Maury Winetrobe ***Mus*** Jerry Herman
Act Lucille Ball, Robert Preston, Beatrice Arthur, Kirby Furlong, Bruce Davison, Joyce Van Patten (Warner/ABC)

The Lucille Ball version, or reincarnation, of *Mame*, lavishly costumed by Theadora van Runkle, with Jerry Herman's [1966] musical numbers smartly choreographed by Onna White is a fantasy of the good old days of prohibition, the depression and the world travel folders.

The narrative pretty much follows the familiar sequence of events. Mame is first discovered in the midst of prohibition, the Charleston and progressive education. She goes down with the market in 1929, tackles show business, then clerking, is rescued by the romantic Beauregard and spends the rest of her life travelling.

A comedy with songs, not a musical comedy, per se, this *Mame* climaxes with its foxhunting number in Georgia.

•

MAMMY
1930, 83 mins, US ⦿ col
Dir Michael Curtiz ***Scr*** L. G. Rigby, Joseph Jackson ***Ph*** Barney McGill ***Mus*** Irving Berlin
Act Al Jolson, Lois Moran, Louise Dresser, Lowell Sherman, Hobart Bosworth, Mitchell Lewis (Warner)

A lively picture [from the musical *Mr. Bones*], with Al Jolson singing new and old songs, including among the Irving Berlin new numbers a couple of melodious hits.

Here is a minstrel show on the stage and on the street—the parade, the blacking up in the dressing room, and the semicircle with its white face interlocutor, songs by the quartet, jokes by the end men, and dancing. The one section where Technicolor is employed is on the extended semicircle minstrel scene.

Jolson is one of the ends and Mitchell Lewis the other. Lowell Sherman is the interlocutor, William West. It's Sherman who starts and bawls up the works. The show owner's daughter (Lois Moran) is in love with him, but he's just fooling around. Sherman does not resent it even when Jolson makes a jealous play to help along Moran, leaving the impression he wants the girl himself.

[When Sherman is accidentally shot during a performance,] Jolson runs away, going home to see mammy. When mammy tells her boy to always hold his head up, he rides the next freight back.

•

MAN, THE
1972, 93 mins, US col
Dir Joseph Sargent ***Prod*** Lee Rich ***Scr*** Rod Serling ***Ph*** Edward C. Rosson ***Ed*** George Nicholson ***Mus*** Jerry Goldsmith ***Art*** James G. Hulsey
Act James Earl Jones, Martin Balsam, Burgess Meredith, Lew Ayres, William Windom, Barbara Rush (ABC Circle)

The Man is a compelling and sometimes explosive adaptation of the Irving Wallace bestseller. James Earl Jones portrays the black man who ascends so unexpectedly and without precedent to the presidency of the United States.

He gains his top position through the rules of succession. As president pro tem of the Senate, he automatically is elevated when the president and speaker of the House are killed in the collapse of a building in Germany, and the vice president, incapacitated by a stroke, announces he cannot take over the office of president.

Jones delivers an honest, forceful characterization of the president who accepts his fate with humility but discovers his own strength as a man through learning his own powers to cope.

•

MAN ALONE, A
1955, 95 mins, US Ⓥ col
Dir Ray Milland ***Prod*** Herbert J. Yates ***Scr*** John Tucker Battle ***Ph*** Lionel Lindon ***Ed*** Richard L. Van Enger ***Mus*** Victor Young ***Art*** Walter Keller
Act Ray Milland, Mary Murphy, Ward Bond, Raymond Burr, Lee Van Cleef, Alan Hale (Republic)

Western suspense, combined with action and drama, shape *A Man Alone* as an okay offering.

Ray Milland turns director with *Man* and acquits himself fairly well in the new chore. He's a mite too deliberate with his pacing, particularly in handling the character he plays, but shows plenty of promise in his guidance of the other players and in an ability to develop dramatics [from a story by Mort Briskin] beyond the level of the usual outdoor feature.

Quarantined in her Arizona desert town home where her father, the sheriff (Ward Bond), is ill with yellow fever, Nadine Corrigan (Mary Murphy) suddenly finds the house has become sanctuary for notorious gunman Wes Steele (Milland), who is being hunted by a lynch mob for several brutal murders. In this isolation, a drama of love and regeneration is developed, leading eventually to the exposure of the guilty parties.

Production rounds up a good array of sight values to backstop for the action and drama, with Lionel Lindon's TruColor photography doing its share.

•

MAN AND A WOMAN, A
SEE: UN HOMME ET UNE FEMME

•

MAN AND HIS MATE
SEE: ONE MILLION B.C.

•

MAN BETWEEN, THE
1953, 101 mins, UK b/w
Dir Carol Reed ***Scr*** Harry Kurnitz ***Ph*** Desmond Dickinson ***Ed*** A. S. Bates ***Mus*** John Addison ***Art*** Andre Andrejew
Act James Mason, Claire Bloom, Hildegarde Neff, Geoffrey Toone, Dieter Krause (London)

Carol Reed picks war-torn Berlin for a story of political intrigue, capitalizing on the obvious potentialities of the divided capital.

From an original story by Walter Ebert, Harry Kurnitz fashions a script crammed with lively suspense values. Atmosphere is created almost from the opening shot although it takes some time for the plot of sinister intrigue to emerge clearly.

It is virtually a battle of wits between east and west, with the Red Zone police striving to end the trafficking of human bodies into the Western Zone. The plot is woven around Claire Bloom, an English girl, who comes to spend a holiday with her brother, an army major, and her sister-in-law, a German girl, and James Mason, an East Berliner who rescues her after she is mistakenly picked up by Red police.

Best suspense derives from the plot by Mason to get the girl back to her brother. The familiar screen chase is heightened by the contrasting locales.

•

MAN BITES DOG
SEE: C'EST ARRIVE PRES DE CHEZ VOUS

•

MAN CALLED HORSE, A
1970, 114 mins, US Ⓥ ▭ col
Dir Elliot Silverstein ***Prod*** Sandy Howard ***Scr*** Jack De Witt ***Ph*** Robert Hauser ***Ed*** Philip Anderson ***Mus*** Leonard Rosenman ***Art*** Dennis Lynton Clark
Act Richard Harris, Judith Anderson, Jean Gascon, Manu Tupou, Corinna Tsopei, Dub Taylor (Cinema Center)

A Man Called Horse is said to be an authentic depiction of American Indian life in the Dakota territory of about 1820. Authentic it may be, but an absorbing film drama it is not. Sandy Howard's Durango-lensed production stars Richard Harris as an English nobleman captured by the Sioux. Captivity segues to understanding and finally to tribal membership.

Jack DeWitt's spare-dialog adaptation of a 1950 Dorothy M. Johnson story, features a lot of nonsubtitled Sioux lingo, broken up by Harris's expository passages with half-breed Jean Gascon.

Performances are generally good, especially that of Gascon, while Judith Anderson lends both pathos and broad comedy in her rendition. Harris is unevenly stiff.

•

MANCHURIAN CANDIDATE, THE
1962, 126 mins, US Ⓥ ⊙ b/w
Dir John Frankenheimer ***Prod*** George Axelrod, John Frankenheimer ***Scr*** George Axelrod ***Ph*** Lionel Lindon ***Ed*** Ferris Webster ***Mus*** David Amram ***Art*** Richard Sylbert
Act Frank Sinatra, Laurence Harvey, Janet Leigh, Angela Lansbury, Henry Silva, Leslie Parrish (United Artists)

George Axelrod and John Frankenheimer's jazzy, hip screen translation of Richard Condon's bestselling novel works in all departments.

Its story of the tracking down of a brainwashed Korean war "hero" being used as the key figure in an elaborate Communist plot to take over the U.S. government is, on the surface, one of the wildest fabrications any author has ever tried to palm off on a gullible public. But the fascinating thing is that, from uncertain premise to shattering conclusion, one does not question plausibility—the events being rooted in their own cinematic reality.

Manchurian Candidate gets off to an early start (before the credits) as a dilemma wrapped in an enigma: A small American patrol in Korea is captured by the Chinese Communists. Shortly thereafter, the sergeant of the group, Laurence Harvey, is seen being welcomed home in Washington as a Congressional Medal of Honor winner, having been recommended for that award by his captain, Frank Sinatra, who led the ill-fated patrol.

But something is obviously wrong. Harvey himself admits to being the least likely of heroes, and Sinatra, though he testifies that the sergeant is "the bravest, most honorable, most loyal" man he knows, realizes this is completely untrue. But why?

The captain's subsequent pursuit of the truth comprises the bizarre plot which ranges from the halls of Congress, New York publishing circles and an extremely unlikely Communist hideout in mid-Manhattan, to a literally stunning climax at a Madison Square Garden political convention.

1962: NOMINATIONS: Best Supp. Actress (Angela Lansbury), Editing

•

MANDALAY
1934, 65 mins, US b/w
Dir Michael Curtiz ***Prod*** Robert Presnell ***Scr*** Austin Parker, Charles Kenyon ***Ph*** Tony Gaudio ***Ed*** Thomas Pratt ***Art*** Anton Grot
Act Kay Francis, Lyle Talbot, Ricardo Cortez, Warner Oland, Lucien Littlefield, Ruth Donnelly (Warner)

Kay Francis is a girl of doubtful past, present and future who eventually casts her lot with an outcast doctor in what an extra reel may have developed as possible reformation for both.

Picture trips along at a nice pace and except for one spot, toward the end, invites no adverse reaction. This is in connection with the faked suicide of Ricardo Cortez, a gunrunner who leaves an empty poison bottle and an open window in his ship's cabin as evidence of his act. The audience is let in on the phony suicide, whereas it would have been more effective to spring the surprise and the explanation on the audience the same as on people in the cast, notably Francis.

Much of the action [from a story by Paul Hervey Fox] occurs on a boat bound from Rangoon for Mandalay. Earlier sequences are in the former seaport, where the heroine has been forced into a life of doubtful purity when her gunrunner boyfriend takes a run-out powder. This portion of the story isn't as convincing as it might be. Manner in which Warner Oland browbeats her into working for his joint is anything but convincing, either.

•

MANDINGO
1975, 126 mins, US Ⓥ ⊙ col
Dir Richard Fleischer ***Prod*** Dino De Laurentiis ***Scr*** Norman Wexler ***Ph*** Richard H. Kline ***Ed*** Frank Bracht ***Mus*** Maurice Jarre ***Art*** Boris Leven
Act James Mason, Susan George, Percy King, Richard Ward, Brenda Sykes, Ken Norton (Paramount)

Based on Kyle Onstott's novel of sexploitation sociology, *Mandingo* is an embarrassing and crude film which wallows in every cliché of the slave-based white society in the pre–Civil War South.

The cornball adaptation is exceeded in banality only by the performances of James Mason, slave-breeder father of son Percy King, who in turn develops what passes for genuine affection for Brenda Sykes, while wife Susan George descends into revenge with Ken Norton, stud slave whom King also has befriended for purposes of pugilistic gambling. Lots of cardboard tragedy ensues.

•

MANDY
(US: THE CRASH OF SILENCE)
1952, 92 mins, UK b/w
Dir Alexander Mackendrick ***Prod*** Leslie Norman ***Scr*** Nigel Balchin, Jack Whittingham ***Ph*** Douglas Slocombe ***Ed*** Seth Holt ***Mus*** William Alwyn ***Art*** Jim Morahan
Act Phyllis Calvert, Jack Hawkins, Terence Morgan, Mandy Miller, Godfrey Tearle, Marjorie Fielding (Ealing)

This story of a deaf-and-dumb child has obvious tearjerking angles which have been freely exploited.

Central character in the yarn, which is based on a novel by Hilda Lewis, *The Day Is Ours*, is a young child who was born deaf and is, inevitably, dumb. Against a background of parental disagreement, the plot traces the methods used in teaching youngsters the art of lipreading and expression.

The dominating performance comes from little Mandy Miller in the title role. The best adult performance comes from Jack Hawkins who makes the headmaster a vital and sincere character. Godfrey Tearle and Marjorie Fielding as the child's grandparents top a sound supporting cast.

•

MAN FOR ALL SEASONS, A
1966, 120 mins, UK Ⓥ ⊙ col
Dir Fred Zinnemann ***Prod*** Fred Zinnemann ***Scr*** Robert Bolt ***Ph*** Ted Moore ***Ed*** Ralph Kemplen ***Mus*** Georges Delerue ***Art*** John Box
Act Paul Scofield, Wendy Hiller, Leo McKern, Robert Shaw, Orson Welles, Susannah York (Highland/Columbia)

Producer-director Fred Zinnemann has blended all filmmaking elements into an excellent, handsome and stirring film version of *A Man for All Seasons*. Robert Bolt adapted his 1960 play, a timeless, personal conflict based on the 16th century politico-religious situation between adulterous King Henry VIII and Catholic Sir Thomas More.

Basic dramatic situation is that of a minister of the crown and his conscience being challenged by the imperious point of view which maintains that the lack of explicit support to an erring king is equivalent to disloyalty. This is the usual human dilemma whenever expediency confronts integrity.

Paul Scofield delivers an excellent performance as More, respected barrister, judge and chancellor who combined an urbane polish with inner mysticism. Faced with mounting pressure to endorse publicly the royal marriage of Henry VIII to Anne Boleyn, but armed with legalistic knowhow, More outfoxed his adversaries until "perjury" was used to justify a sentence of death.

Robert Shaw is also excellent as the king, giving full exposition in limited footage to the character: volatile, educated, virile, arrogant, yet sensitive (and sensible) enough to put the squeeze on More via subordinates, mainly Thomas Cromwell, played by Leo McKern.

Orson Welles in five minutes (here an early confrontation, as Cardinal Wolsey, with More) achieves outstanding economy of expression.

1966: Best Picture, Director, Actor (Paul Scofield), Adapted Screenplay, Color Cinematography, Color Costume Design

NOMINATIONS: Best Supp. Actor (Robert Shaw), Supp. Actress (Wendy Hiller)

•

MAN FRIDAY
1975, 115 mins, UK Ⓥ ▭ col
Dir Jack Gold ***Prod*** David Korda ***Scr*** Adrian Mitchell ***Ph*** Alex Phillips ***Ed*** Anne V. Coates ***Mus*** Carl Davis ***Art*** Peter Murton
Act Peter O'Toole, Richard Roundtree, Peter Cellier, Christopher Cabot, Joel Fluellen, Sam Sebroke (Keep/ABC/ITC)

Another variation of Daniel Defoe's classic has Crusoe (Peter O'Toole) discovering his Friday (Richard Roundtree) after the shipwrecked mariner has brutally shot and killed the black's companions, washed up on "his" island after a storm.

O'Toole's Crusoe proceeds to subdue and then teach and indoctrinate the "savage," with missionary zeal, into the manners and mores of Western society, not forgetting the master-slave relationship.

Slowly, however, Friday begins to question him, his theories and teachings, soon in effect himself becoming the teacher of newer, freer, more open-minded ideas and ideals.

O'Toole speaks his lighter lines with panache and humor, but becoming very moving indeed when seized by loneliness and despair.

•

MAN FROM HONG KONG, THE
1975, 99 mins, Hong Kong/Australia Ⓥ ▭ col
Dir Brian Trenchard-Smith ***Prod*** Raymond Chow, John Fraser ***Scr*** Brian Trenchard-Smith ***Ph*** Russell Boyd ***Ed*** Ron Williams ***Mus*** Noel Quinlan ***Art*** David Copping, Chien Sun
Act Jimmy Wang Yu, George Lazenby, Ros Spiers, Hugh Keays-Byrne, Roger Ward, Rebecca Gilling (Golden Harvest/Movie)

A Hong Kong policeman (Wang Yu) is sent to Australia to extradite a Chinese courier who works for an international drug syndicate. He gets involved with the syndicate, and, as per usual wipes it out in a final battle that ends with Wang escaping from a towering inferno.

Wang, though lacking the charisma of the late Bruce Lee, does have an aura of realism about him. George Lazenby does little for his image as an actor by appearing as a heavy Mr. Big, called Wilton.

The Hong Kong-Australian James Bond hybrid, the first coproduction of its kind, comes off well for a kung-fu pic. There are the usual chases around Sydney, with an unusual kite chase sequence. There is also some excellent aerial photography of both Hong Kong and Sydney.

•

MAN FROM LARAMIE, THE
1955, 102 mins, US Ⓥ ▭ col
Dir Anthony Mann ***Prod*** William Goetz ***Scr*** Philip Yordan, Frank Burt ***Ph*** Charles Lang ***Ed*** William Lyon ***Mus*** George Duning ***Art*** Cary Odell
Act James Stewart, Arthur Kennedy, Donald Crisp, Cathy O'Donnell, Alex Nichol, Aline MacMahon (Columbia)

Basically, the plot concerns the search by James Stewart, army captain on home from leave, for the man guilty of selling repeating rifles to an Apache tribe. The rifles had been used to wipe out a small cavalry patrol to which Stewart's younger brother had been attached so there is a motive of personal vengeance.

Violence gets into the act early and repeats with regularity as Stewart's trail crosses with a number of warped sadistic characters. Stewart goes about his characterization with an easy assurance. Arthur Kennedy, Donald Crisp and Alex Nicol are first-rate in their delineations of the twisted people on the ranch. Distaff characters are done by Cathy O'-Donnell, good as the girl who wants to escape the influence of the ranch, and Aline MacMahon, who gives a socko portrayal of a tough old rancher.

•

MAN FROM PLANET X, THE
1951, 70 mins, US b/w
Dir Edgar G. Ulmer *Prod* Aubrey Wisberg, Jack Pollexfen *Scr* Aubrey Wisberg, Jack Pollexfen *Ph* John L. Russell *Ed* Fred F. Feitshans, Jr. *Mus* Charles Koff *Art* Angelo Scibetti
Act Robert Clarke, Margaret Field, Raymond Bond, William Schallert, Roy Engel, Charles Davis (Mid-Century)

Story is laid on a small Scottish island, cut off from the mainland. Principals are two scientists, the daughter of one, and a newspaperman, there to observe the effect of a strange planet that is swinging close to the earth. No thought of a planetary invasion is in the minds of the observers until the girl accidentally sees a weird creature from out of space.

They take the superior being in, try to communicate with him, but one of the scientists, seeing a chance to control the world, upsets the plans. Edgar Ulmer's direction builds a strong mood and the suspense is sustained. Cast is mostly excellent in putting over thriller aims. Robert Clarke is the reporter and does a good job. Margaret Field is acceptable as the girl, and Raymond Bond does well by his scientist character.

•

MAN FROM SNOWY RIVER, THE
1982, 102 mins, Australia Ⓥ ⊙ col
Dir George Miller *Prod* Geoff Burrowes *Scr* John Dixon, Fred Cul Cullen *Ph* Keith Wagstaff *Ed* Adrian Carr *Mus* Bruce Rowland *Art* Leslie Binns
Act Kirk Douglas, Jack Thompson, Tom Burlinson, Sigrid Thornton, Lorraine Bayly, Chris Haywood (Edgley/Cambridge)

Here is a rattling good adventure story, inspired by a legendary poem [by A. B. "Banjo" Paterson] which nearly every Australian had drummed into him as a child, filmed in spectacularly rugged terrain in the Great Dividing Ranges in Victoria.

Kirk Douglas plays two brothers who have had a terrible falling-out for reasons explained late in the narrative. While one brother, the wealthy autocratic landowner Harrison fits him like a glove, the actor is less believable as Spur, a gruff, grizzled, out-of-luck prospector.

Apparently, Douglas wrote or rewrote some of the dialog; hopefully not some of Spur's groaners like "It's a hard country, made for hard men."

Tom Burlinson shines in his first feature film role as Jim, well matched by Sigrid Thornton as Harrison's high-spirited daughter. Jack Thompson shares top billing with Douglas as Clancy, the crack horseman who becomes Jim's mentor.

•

MAN FROM THE ALAMO, THE
1953, 79 mins, US Ⓥ col
Dir Budd Boetticher *Prod* Aaron Rosenberg *Scr* Steve Fisher, D. D. Beauchamp *Ph* Russell Metty *Ed* Virgil Vogel *Mus* Frank Skinner *Art* Alexander Golitzen, Emrich Nicholson
Act Glenn Ford, Julie Adams, Chill Wills, Hugh O'Brian, Victor Jory, Jeanne Cooper (Universal)

This basic outdoor feature has a rousing climax, good performances and beautifully photographed outdoor values. Glenn Ford and Victor Jory are particularly good in the rugged scenes and the former's performance helps to carry things during some midway story slowness.

Plot is hung on the supposed escape of one man (Ford) from the Alamo before its valiant defenders fell to Santa Ana's forces. He finds his own and the other families wiped out by renegades posing as Mexican soldiers, is branded a coward for deserting the fort, and spends the rest of the footage proving himself and getting revenge on Jory for his assault against the families of the Alamo heroes.

High spot of the footage is the climactic battle between good and evil, with Ford protecting a wagon train against Jory's gang of renegades. It's a sequence that Budd Boetticher's direction fills with violent, but believeable, action. Plotting in the script is generally good and was based on a story by Niven Busch and Oliver Crawford.

Julie Adams is gracious as a girl who helps Ford. Chill Wills is a one-armed pioneer editor stubborn about accepting the hero, as is Hugh O'Brian, army lieutenant.

•

MANHANDLED
1924, 77 mins, US ⊗ b/w
Dir Allan Dwan *Prod* William Le Baron *Scr* Frank V. Tuttle, Julian Johnson, Arthur Stringer *Ph* Hal Rosson *Ed* Julian Johnson
Act Gloria Swanson, Tom Moore, Frank Morgan, Lilyan Tashman, Ian Keith, Arthur Houseman (Paramount)

Manhandled is a story which originated in the brain of S. R. Kent, general sales manager of Paramount. It was first conceived as a picture story, turned over to Arthur Stringer to write, and when completed sold to *The Saturday Evening Post*. By the time it appeared, however, the picture was almost completed.

It is of a typical hick salesgirl in the basement of a department store, one of those tough, gum-chewing slang slingers. She manages to climb out of the cellar into the Bohemian set through the fact that an author who wishes to make an experiment pulls her out of the place and introduces her to artists, sculptors and a gown creator. Each warns her against the other, and all three are trying personally.

Gloria Swanson reveals unsuspected qualities as an actress. Tom Moore plays the young mechanic hero and handles it very well. Director Allan Dwan has shown some clever work. His subway rush-hour scene is true to life and one of the funniest that have been screened of the underground. The studio parties also have touches of comedy here and there that are enjoyable.

•

MANHATTAN
1979, 96 mins, US Ⓥ ⊙ ▭ b/w
Dir Woody Allen *Prod* Charles H. Joffe *Scr* Woody Allen, Marshall Brickman *Ph* Gordon Willis *Ed* Susan E. Morse *Mus* Tom Pierson (arr.) *Art* Mel Bourne
Act Woody Allen, Diane Keaton, Michael Murphy, Mariel Hemingway, Meryl Streep, Anne Byrne (United Artists)

Woody Allen uses New York City as a backdrop for the familiar story of the successful but neurotic urban overachievers whose relationships always seem to end prematurely. The film is just as much about how wonderful a place the city is to live in as it is about the elusive search for love.

Allen has, in black and white, captured the inner beauty that lurks behind the outer layer of dirt and grime in Manhattan.

The core of the story revolves around Allen as Isaac Davis, an unfulfilled television writer and his best friends, Yale and Emily, an upper-middle class, educated Manhattan couple. Isaac has lately taken up with Tracy (Mariel Hemingway), a gorgeous 17-year-old, but the age difference is becoming too much of an obstacle for him.

That's especially the case when he meets Yale's girlfriend, Mary, a fast-talking, pseudo-intellectual, expertly played by Diane Keaton, to whom Isaac is instantly attracted.

1979: NOMINATIONS: Best Supp. Actress (Mariel Hemingway), Original Screenplay

•

MANHATTAN MELODRAMA
1934, 93 mins, US Ⓥ ⊙ b/w
Dir W. S. Van Dyke *Prod* David O. Selznick *Scr* Oliver H. P. Garrett, Joseph L. Mankiewicz *Ph* James Wong Howe *Ed* Ben Lewis *Mus* William Axt *Art* Cedric Gibbons, Joseph Wright, Edwin B. Willis
Act Clark Gable, William Powell, Myrna Loy, Leo Carrillo, Nat Pendleton, Mickey Rooney (Cosmopolitan/M-G-M)

Apart from the Clark Gable-William Powell stellar duo and Myrna Loy, who does an excellent job as the principal femme, the Arthur Caesar story is replete with punchy popularly appealing ingredients. The fast, crisp, intelligent dialog further enhances it.

True there is much to *Manhattan Melodrama* that's very ten-twent-thirt. There are a couple of spots where perhaps Gable as the too-suave hoodlum is glorified a bit, but there are also many offsetting speeches by Powell as the DA as he charges the jury to remember that there's no longer public sympathy with bootleggers.

There are also a couple of somewhat banal spots such as Papa Rosen (George Sidney) adopting the two tough mick kids (Gable and Powell) because his own Morris was drowned in the Slocum disaster. Or, for example, where Papa Rosen is the first to deride the Russian red agitator (and gets trampled to death by the riot squad for his patriotism).

The captiousness embraces such incidents as the governor's wife (Loy) visiting the prisoner (Gable) in the Tombs. Or the inevitable *Last Mile* business in the death house with the colored convict, the surcharged atmosphere of bravado, etc. But in toto *Manhattan Melodrama* will never bore, and please generally.

Mickey Rooney and Jimmy Butler in the juve portions are tiptop. Shirley Ross is the colored warbler who handles the lone Rodgers-Hart song in the picture (which means little) in the Cotton Club setting.

1934: Best Original Story

•

MANHATTAN MURDER MYSTERY
1993, 105 mins, US Ⓥ ⊙ col
Dir Woody Allen *Prod* Robert Greenhut *Scr* Woody Allen, Marshall Brickman *Ph* Carlo Di Palma *Ed* Susan E. Morse *Art* Santo Loquasto
Act Alan Alda, Woody Allen, Anjelica Huston, Diane Keaton, Jerry Adler, Joy Behar (Tri-Star)

Woody Allen once described himself as "thin but fun," and the same could be said for *Manhattan Murder Mystery*. Light, insubstantial and utterly devoid of the heavier themes Allen has grappled with in most of his recent outings, this confection keeps the chuckles coming.

Aside from his *Oedipus Wrecks* episode from *New York Stories*, this represents Allen's first flat-out comedy in nearly a decade. In its feather-weight frivolity and disconnection from any recognizable reality, it resembles nothing so much as the goofy backstage murder mellers of the 1930s, complete with vanishing corpses, high society settings, bickering leads and self-consciously theatrical denouement.

Allen and Diane Keaton play Larry and Carol Lipton, a long-married pair whose next-door neighbors are the chatty middle-aged couple Paul and Lillian House (Jerry Adler, Lynn Cohen). Suddenly, Lillian drops dead of a heart attack, but Carol is suspicious of how cheerful Paul seems afterward and, having just seen *Double Indemnity*, becomes obsessed with the idea that he actually murdered his wife. It is up to fiction writer Marcia Fox (Anjelica Huston) to explain it all to the audience.

Manhattan Murder Mystery is as neurotic a farce as can be imagined, and Allen and cowriter Marshall Brickman, together for the first time since the great duo of *Annie Hall* and *Manhattan*, have amusingly festooned the plot with an array of topical and psychological concerns. Allen's typical phobias are on display as prominently as ever.

Keaton nicely handles her sometimes buffoonish central comedic role, but few strenuous demands are placed on the rest of the agreeable cast.

•

MANHATTAN PROJECT, THE
1986, 117 mins, US Ⓥ ⊙ col
Dir Marshall Brickman *Prod* Jennifer Ogden, Marshall Brickman *Scr* Marshall Brickman, Thomas Baum *Ph* Billy Williams *Ed* Nina Feinborg *Mus* Philippe Sarde *Art* Philip Rosenberg
Act John Lithgow, Christopher Collet, Cynthia Nixon, Jill Eikenberry, John Mahoney, Sully Boyar (Gladden)

Marshall Brickman's *The Manhattan Project* is a warm, comedy-laced doomsday story.

Premise has sixteen-year-old student Paul Stevens (Christopher Collet) tumbling to the fact that the new scientist in town, Dr. Mathewson (John Lithgow), is working with plutonium in what fronts as a pharmaceutical research installation. While Mathewson is romancing Stevens's mom (Jilly Eikenberry), the genius kid is plotting with his helpful girlfriend Jenny (Cynthia Nixon) to steal a canister of plutonium and build an atomic bomb. Their goal: to expose the danger of the secret nuclear plant placed in their community.

Using clever one-liners and many humorous situations, Brickman manages successfully to sugarcoat the story's serious message.

•

MAN HUNT
1941, 100 mins, US b/w
Dir Fritz Lang *Prod* Kenneth Macgowan (assoc.) *Scr* Dudley Nichols *Ph* Arthur Miller *Ed* Allen McNeil *Mus* Alfred Newman *Art* Richard Day, Wiard B. Ihnen
Act Walter Pidgeon, Joan Bennett, George Sanders, John Carradine, Roddy McDowall, Ludwig Stossel (20th Century-Fox)

Extended operations of the Gestapo are displayed in this film version of Geoffrey Household's novel, *Rogue Male*.

Household's tale of an English big-game hunter and adventurer who invades the closely guarded precincts of Berchtesgaden to draw a bead on Hitler with an unloaded rifle, his capture and torture by the Gestapo; escape and return to England and further hounding by German agents; and final dropping back into Germany with a rifle for a future crack at Hitler, fails to sustain adventurous excitement on screen.

Walter Pidgeon is the Englishman hounded by the Gestapo. He does a good job of the assignment throughout. Joan Bennett is the Limey girl who befriends him, but her attempts at affected cockney accents are always synthetic. George Sanders is generally menacing as the Gestapo chief. Fritz Lang's direction maintains excellent suspense in the first half, but yarn hits the skids for the second section to wind up with a series of overdrawn and inconclusive sequences.

•

MANHUNTER
1986, 119 mins, US Ⓥ ⊙ ▭ col
Dir Michael Mann *Prod* Richard Roth *Scr* Michael Mann *Ph* Dante Spinotti *Ed* Dov Hoenig *Mus* The Reds, Michel Rubini *Art* Mel Bourne

Act William Petersen, Kim Greist, Joan Allen, Brian Cox, Dennis Farina, Tom Noonan (De Laurentiis/Roth)

Manhunter is an unpleasantly gripping thriller that rubs one's nose in a sick criminal mentality for two hours.

Pic is based upon Thomas Harris's well-received novel *Red Dragon* and deals with a southern former FBI agent (William Petersen) who is summoned from retirement to work on a particularly perplexing case, that of a mass murderer who appears to stalk and select his victims with particular care.

Petersen's excellent deductive talents are due, in large measure, to his tendency to deeply enter the minds of killers, to begin thinking like them.

This trick takes the film into interesting Hitchcockian guilt transference territory and Mann's grip on his material is tight and sure. Director is at all times preoccupied by visual chic.

Tom Noonan cuts a massive swath as the killer, who late in the game is surprisingly humanized by a blind girl, played in enormously touching fashion by Joan Allen.

•

MANIAC COP

1988, 85 mins, US Ⓥ col

Dir William Lustig **Prod** Larry Cohen **Scr** Larry Cohen **Ph** Vincent J. Rabe **Ed** David Kern **Mus** Jay Chattaway **Art** Jonathon Hodges

Act Tom Atkins, Bruce Campbell, Laurene Landon, Richard Roundtree, William Smith, Sheree North (Shapiro Glickenhaus)

Maniac Cop is a disappointing thriller that wastes an oddball premise and offbeat point of view. Writer-producer Larry Cohen's gimmicky approach has the novelty of all leading characters (male and female) working for the police force. A maniac dressed in police blues is terrorizing New Yorkers and the investigator on the case, Lt. McCrae (nononsense Tom Atkins), is convinced the killer is really a cop.

A fellow cop with marital problems, Jack Forrest (Bruce Campbell of the *Evil Dead* films), is framed by the killer, but after McCrae is murdered, Forrest takes over the investigation to try to clear himself, aided by his girlfriend, undercover vice cop Theresa (Laurene Landon).

Director William Lustig, who helmed the violent horror thriller *Maniac* in 1980, keeps the killer's face offscreen or bathed in shadows, but it's the massively built, angular featured actor Robert Z'Dar who's on the rampage, avenging his being bounced from the force and sent to Sing Sing 20 years ago.

Acting is deadpan and straight ahead. Sheree North has an interesting character role as a hobbling, crippled girlfriend to the maniac, combining bitterness and pathos.

•

MANIAC COP 2

1990, 88 mins, US Ⓥ col

Dir William Lustig **Prod** Larry Cohen **Scr** Larry Cohen **Ph** James Lemmo **Ed** David Kern **Mus** Jay Chattaway **Art** Gene Abel, Charles LaGola

Act Robert Davi, Claudia Christian, Michael Lerner, Bruce Campbell, Laurene Landon, Leo Rossi (Movie House Sales/Fadd)

Maniac Cop 2 is a thinking man's exploitation film, improving on the 1988 original. This time the title character Cordell (Robert Z'Dar), a framed cop killed in prison three years ago, is resurrected as a disfigured supernatural character stalking the streets of Manhattan.

With director William Lustig creating a brooding, morbid atmosphere akin to classical film noir, pic benefits from producer-writer Larry Cohen's extremely dark humor. Time and again the cop-monster shows up at a crime scene and violently aids the criminal rather than the victim.

Most outlandish conceit mocks the genre's most overused subject matter: a serial killer (Leo Rossi) of strippers in the Times Square district is about to be apprehended when the maniac cop comes in and rescues him. The two killers become friends, and guest star Rossi, almost unrecognisable with long hair and bushy beard, is terrific as the nut with the gift of gab.

Hero Robert Davi in slouch hat as the sympathetic but unyielding detective on the case is most persuasive. Claudia Christian also impresses as the no-nonsense police psychologist treating Davi, cop Bruce Campbell and frightened policewoman Laurene Landon.

•

MAN I KILLED, THE

1932, 77 mins, US b/w

Dir Ernst Lubitsch **Prod** Ernst Lubitsch **Scr** Ernest Vajda, Samson Raphaelson, Reginald Berkeley **Ph** Victor Milner

Act Lionel Barrymore, Nancy Carroll, Phillips Holmes, Lucien Littlefield, ZaSu Pitts, Tom Douglas (Paramount)

This is a hard and sombre theme to digest. One which will become tedious to many because of its lack of animation. In telling of the young Frenchman whose conscience drives him to the home of the German boy he killed in the war, producer-director Ernst Lubitsch has made a rigid unravelling [of the French play by Maurice Rostand].

The picture is particularly noteworthy for a superb performance by Lionel Barrymore as the bereaved German father. Barrymore plays a doctor and the head of a small family, consisting of his wife and the departed son's fiancée, who are almost fanatical in their grief over the lost boy a year after the Armistice. The gradual lightening of the burden comes through the Frenchman who, seeking peace of mind through confession to his victim's parents, finds himself incapable of revealing the truth and then explains his presence by saying he was a friend of the son.

Meanwhile, there is the resentment of the men of the village to the presence of the Frenchman stirred up by a rejected suitor of the girl, and the gossiping of the women over the evident attachment between Elsa (Nancy Carroll) and Paul (Phillips Holmes). Lubitsch's direction doesn't permit this animosity to boil over into a demonstration although it does lead to the film's dramatic high point when Barrymore rises from a luncheon table to flay his cronies for a venomous attitude which can only lead to further wars.

Holmes, wearing a mustache to add the years to his appearance, is not a happy choice for the mentally tortured soldier. Yet, his performance is not without its good points.

Carroll, as the girl who is devoting her life to the parents and memory of her fiancée, handles herself capably in a role of little opportunity.

•

MAN I MARRIED, THE

1940, 76 mins, US b/w

Dir Irving Pichel **Prod** Raymond Griffith **Scr** Oliver H. P. Garrett **Ph** Peverell Marley **Ed** Robert Simpson **Mus** David Buttolph

Act Joan Bennett, Francis Lederer, Lloyd Nolan, Anna Sten, Otto Kruger, Maria Ouspenskaya (20th Century-Fox)

This one is a film presentation of the 1939 *Liberty* magazine serial, *I Married a Nazi*, a powerful indictment of the Hitlerized regimentation of the German people. The film version is a powerful dramatic presentation of the Nazi regime in Germany in 1938.

Story sends American-born Joan Bennett to Europe with her husband (Francis Lederer) on a vacation trip. He immediately comes under the influence of the Nazi party, and through an amorous affair with Anna Sten, remains in Germany to become a follower of Hitler. Hypnotized to a fanatical stage, Lederer declares he will divorce his wife in Germany under party decrees, and their son must remain with him. Then his aged father steps in to tell Lederer his mother was a Jewess and the child must be allowed to return to America and freedom.

Strongly contrasted with the winning over of Lederer to the Nazi cause, is the opposite effect on his wife who gradually awakens to the suffering imposed on opponents of Hitler's regimentation, and the elimination of individual liberties.

Bennett is excellent as the educated American wife who sees through the schemes of Nazism, and provides much strength to a difficult assignment. Lederer's transition from a happy being to a stern Nazi is capably handled. Lloyd Nolan clicks as the breezy American newspaper correspondent who knows all the political inside of the Nazi machine.

•

MAN IN A COCKED HAT

SEE: CARLTON-BROWNE OF THE F. O.

•

MAN IN THE GRAY FLANNEL SUIT, THE

1956, 152 mins, US Ⓥ ⌑ col

Dir Nunnally Johnson **Prod** Darryl F. Zanuck **Scr** Nunnally Johnson **Ph** Charles G. Clarke **Ed** Dorothy Spencer **Mus** Bernard Hermann

Act Gregory Peck, Jennifer Jones, Fredric March, Marisa Pavan, Lee J. Cobb, Ann Harding (20th Century-Fox)

This is the story of a young American suburbanite who gets a chance to become a big shot and turns it down because he realizes that he's a nine-to-five man to whom family means more than success.

It's also the story of a man with a conscience, who had a love affair in Rome which resulted in a child. When he tells his wife about it, their marriage almost breaks up.

As the "Man in the Gray Flannel Suit," Gregory Peck is handsome and appealing, if not always convincing. It is only really in the romantic sequences with Marisa Pavan, who plays his Italian love, that he takes on warmth and becomes believable. Pavan is human and delightful.

Playing opposite Peck as his wife is Jennifer Jones, and her concept of the role is faulty to a serious degree. Jones allows almost no feeling of any real relationship between her and Peck. They never come alive as people.

As the broadcasting tycoon, Fredric March is excellent, and the scenes between him and Peck lift the picture high above the ordinary.

•

MAN IN THE IRON MASK, THE

1939, 110 mins, US Ⓥ b/w

Dir James Whale **Prod** Edward Small **Scr** George Bruce **Ph** Robert Planck **Ed** Grant Whytock **Mus** Lucien Moraweck **Art** John DuCasse Schulze

Act Louis Hayward, Joan Bennett, Joseph Schildkraut, Alan Hale, Warren William (United Artists/Small)

Alexander Dumas's classic, presented for the first time in film form, is a highly entertaining adventure melodrama. Story has a verve in its tale of dual heirship to the throne of France, used by Dumas as basis of his novel. D'Artagnan and the Three Musketeers reappear as stalwart supporters of Philippe, twin brother of Louis XIV, who is tossed into the Bastille with a fiendishly designed locked iron mask.

Louis Hayward, carrying the dual role of the arrogant Louis XIV and the vigorously self-assured Philippe, gives one of the finest dual characterizations of the screen. He vividly contrasts the king's personality, with its slight swish, with the manly and romantic attitude of twin brother Philippe.

Joan Bennett is capably romantic. Warren William is carefree and colorful.

1939: NOMINATION: Best Original Score

•

MAN IN THE IRON MASK, THE

1998, 132 mins, US Ⓥ ⦿ col

Dir Randall Wallace **Prod** Randall Wallace, Russell Smith **Scr** Randall Wallace **Ph** Peter Suschitzky **Ed** William Hoy **Mus** Nick Glennie-Smith **Art** Anthony Pratt

Act Leonardo DiCaprio, Jeremy Irons, John Malkovich, Gerard Depardieu, Gabriel Byrne, Anne Parillaud (United Artists/M-G-M)

Leonardo DiCaprio delivers a wonderful double star turn in *The Man in the Iron Mask*. An unusually sober and serious-minded telling of Alexandre Dumas's classic tale, this handsome costumer is routinely made and comes up rather short in boisterous excitement.

Present telling of the story centers on a barbarous king of France, his noble twin brother and the aging musketeers, which reps the directorial debut of *Braveheart* scenarist Randall Wallace. Tone remains uncertain for the first reel or two, and the unmeshed, all-over-the-map accents of the American, English, Irish and French thesps help pic to dig itself further into a little hole.

But once DiCaprio, resplendent in his regal finery, almost single-handedly hoists the film above ground, these concerns fall by the wayside as the pull of high-level intrigue and melodrama take hold.

Wallace's essential seriousness adds some unexpected weight to some of the work's central themes, notably the special nature of father-son bonds; the effects of advancing years on one's abilities and priorities, and the comparative worth of oaths and loyalty to God, state, ideals, family and friends.

Most of all, however, the actors make the film a pleasure to watch. DiCaprio is a splendid vision as the ruthless libertine king; by contrast, his Philippe is kind, sensitive and touchingly unformed. Jeremy Irons displays more energy as Aramis than he's shown onscreen in a while, John Malkovich delivers a well-focused change-of-pace perf in the sympathetic role of Athos, Gerard Depardieu has no trouble enacting Porthos, the buffoon of the group, while Gabriel Byrne brings welcome gravity to his emotionally and morally conflicted D'Artagnan.

Making the most of its French locations and, especially, its many scenes lensed at the Chateau de Fontainebleau, pic has been decked out in fine fashion.

•

MAN IN THE MOON, THE

1991, 99 mins, US Ⓥ ⌑ col

Dir Robert Mulligan **Prod** Mark Rydell **Scr** Jenny Wingfield **Ph** Freddie Francis **Ed** Trudy Ship **Mus** James Newton Howard **Art** Gene Callahan

Act Sam Waterston, Tess Harper, Gail Strickland, Reese Witherspoon, Jason London, Emily Warfield (M-G-M)

A bucolic coming-of-age story set in 1957 Louisiana, *The Man in the Moon* follows Reese Witherspoon, the 14-year-old daughter of Sam Waterston and Tess Harper. She's envious of her college-bound sister (Emily Warfield) and moons over pictures of Elvis Presley. All that changes with the arrival of Jason London.

London, the man of the house since his father's death, becomes friendly with Witherspoon against his better judgment. Inevitable conflict arises when London meets the older sister, and he quickly relegates Witherspoon to the status of kid sister.

Unfortunately, vet director Robert Mulligan and tyro screenwriter Jenny Wingfield could not come up with a dramatic resolution to this triangle, and resort to a melodramatic device that at once brings the conflict between the two sisters to a head while removing the source of it.

The performances are all on the money, but two are outstanding. Newcomer Witherspoon manages to strike exactly the right note as the tomboy on the verge of womanhood while Waterston works on several levels at once. Shot on location in Natchitoches, LA, film is aided by cinematography of Freddie Francis, who catches the summer light and warmth important to the story.

•

MAN IN THE WHITE SUIT, THE
1951, 97 mins, UK Ⓥ ⦿ b/w
Dir Alexander Mackendrick ***Prod*** Michael Balcon, Sidney Cole ***Scr*** Roger MacDougall, John Dighton, Alexander Mackendrick ***Ph*** Douglas Slocombe ***Ed*** Bernard Gribble ***Mus*** Benjamin Frankel ***Art*** Jim Morahan
Act Alec Guinness, Joan Greenwood, Cecil Parker, Michael Gough, Ernest Thesiger, Vida Hope (Ealing)

The plot is a variation of an old theme, but it comes out with a nice fresh coat of paint. A young research scientist invents a cloth that is everlasting and dirt resisting. The textile industry sees the danger signal and tries to buy him out, but he outwits them.

Particular tribute must be paid to the sound effects department. The bubbly sound of liquids passing through specially prepared contraptions in the lab is one of the most effective running gags seen in a British film.

Alec Guinness, as usual, turns in a polished performance. His interpretation of the little research worker is warm, understanding and always sympathetic. Joan Greenwood is nicely provocative as the mill-owner's daughter who encourages him with his work, while Cecil Parker contributes another effective character study as her father. Michael Gough and Ernest Thesiger represent the textile bosses who see disaster. Vida Hope makes a fine showing as one of the strike leaders who fears unemployment returning to the mills.

1952: NOMINATION: Best Screenplay

•

MANI SULLA CITTA, LE
(HANDS OVER THE CITY)
1963, 105 mins, Italy b/w
Dir Francesco Rosi ***Scr*** Francesco Rosi, Raffaele La Capria, Enzo Provenzale, Enzo Forcella ***Ph*** Gianni di Venanzo ***Ed*** Mario Serandrei ***Mus*** Piero Piccioni
Act Rod Steiger, Guido Alberti, Salvo Randone, Marcello Cannavale, Alberto Conocchia, Terenzio Cordova (Galatea)

Rod Steiger, as city councilman Nottola, is out for a 5,000 percent profit on a remote suburban area which he's just bought. Pic shows how he and his party colleagues maneuver the deal by secret alliances and other crooked methods, against the opposition of left-wing elements in the city council.

Film contains a very direct criticism of Italian government laissez-faire in real-life scandals of a similar nature, and there's more than a hint that left-wing, but especially Communist, leaders offer the only hope of saving the people and city (or nation) from such shenanigans.

Francesco Rosi's screenplay is as linear as is his direction in relentlessly pursuing his objectives. His characters have little human depth, but are almost purely symbolic pawns repping various political tendencies.

Steiger gives a powerful performance as the real-estate czar, but neither he nor others dominate picture. Salvo Randone is good as the wavering politician who helps in the deal, and Guido Alberti gives a neat picture of another top local politico. A special bow to Gianni di Venanzo's location lensing (in Naples).

•

MANITOU, THE
1978, 104 mins, US Ⓥ ⦿ ▭ col
Dir William Girdler ***Prod*** William Girdler ***Scr*** William Girdler, Jon Cedar, Tom Pope ***Ph*** Michel Hugo ***Ed*** Bub Asman ***Mus*** Lalo Schifrin ***Art*** Walter Scott Herndon
Act Tony Curtis, Michael Ansara, Susan Strasberg, Stella Stevens, Jon Cedar, Burgess Meredith (Avco Embassy/Weist-Simon)

This bout between good and Satan includes some scares, camp and better than average credits.

This time the demon is a 400-year-old American Indian medicine man. He's a little devil in the literal sense, thanks to overexposure to X rays which has shriveled him into a three-foot-tall redskin monster. Until he makes a rather dramatic entrance onto the floor of a hospital bedroom, he can be found—growing as a fetus—on Susan Strasberg's upper back. Michael Ansara, a modern-day medicine man, is imported from South Dakota to deliver the evil spirit and return him to the place where 400-year-old medicine men hibernate.

Tony Curtis plays a charlatan of the supernatural, reading tarot cards for rich old ladies. He's romantically involved with Strasberg and does most of the coordinating for the exorcism: booking the medicine man, arranging for cooperation from the hospital, etc.

His character is a nice twist—bogus genie in a situation where the unseen powers really are controlling things. But in general Curtis is too serious about it all. Only Burgess Meredith as a befuddled professor of anthropology has any fun with his part.

•

MAN MADE MONSTER
(UK: THE ELECTRIC MAN)
1941, 89 mins, US b/w
Dir George Waggner ***Prod*** Jack Bernhard ***Scr*** Joseph West ***Ph*** Elwood Brendell ***Mus*** Charles Previn
Act Lionel Atwill, Lon Chaney, Jr., Anne Nagel, Frank Albertson, Samuel S. Hinds, Ben Taggart (Universal)

Man Made Monster is a shocker that's in the groove for the horror fans. It makes no pretense of being anything but a freakish chiller, going directly to the point and proving mighty successful.

Weird events resulting from a mad scientist's lab experiments in transforming a normal human being into a monster controlled by electrical impulses could have been made mawkish. Sincere portrayals plus alert direction and deft photography span several implausible pitfalls. Near-climax when the electric man survives an electrocution for murder and goes on a rampage is a bit incredible for average consumption.

Lon Chaney, Jr.'s, excellent work as "Dynamo" Dan McCormick, carnival electrical wizard, who's turned into a monster, is backed up by Lionel Atwill in one of his better characterizations as the crazed Dr. Rigas, who believes electricity can control anything.

•

MANNEQUIN
1938, 92 mins, US Ⓥ b/w
Dir Frank Borzage ***Prod*** Joseph L. Mankiewicz ***Scr*** Lawrence Hazard ***Ph*** George Folsey ***Ed*** Fredrick Y. Smith ***Mus*** Edward Ward ***Art*** Cedric Gibbons, Paul Groesse, Edwin B. Willis
Act Joan Crawford, Spencer Tracy, Alan Curtis, Ralph Morgan, Mary Phillips, Oscar O'Shea (M-G-M)

Mannequin is a down-to-earth story, interestingly related, excellently directed by Frank Borzage, and splendidly acted by Joan Crawford, Spencer Tracy, and a hand-picked cast. Alan Curtis, heretofore a small bit actor, has his big chance and makes the most of it.

There is nothing wrong and everything right about *Mannequin.* It is based on a sound story by Katharine Brush. The story is the old standby plot of the girl of the tenements who forces herself from her environment and climbs in the world.

Curtis is the ne'er-do-well and gives a properly villainous performance, best feature of which is a gradual insight of the despicable side of his nature. Tracy, as a self-made tugboat capitalist, has his serious moments. But the film is primarily director Frank Borzage's. Without the atmosphere he creates and the movement of his characters through believable situations, *Mannequin* would be routine entertainment.

1938: NOMINATION: Best Song ("Always and Always")

•

MANNEQUIN
1987, 89 mins, US Ⓥ ⦿ col
Dir Michael Gottlieb ***Prod*** Art Levinson ***Scr*** Michael Gottlieb, Edward Rugoff ***Ph*** Timothy Suhrstedt ***Ed*** Richard Halsey ***Mus*** Sylvester Levay ***Art*** Josan Russo
Act Andrew McCarthy, Kim Cattrall, Estelle Getty, G. W. Bailey, James Spader, Meshach Taylor (Gladden)

Mannequin is as stiff and spiritless as its title suggests. A mannequin (Kim Cattrall) is the latest reincarnation of an Egyptian princess who has known Christopher Columbus and Michelangelo in her journey through time. He's an aspiring artist working as a model maker (Andrew McCarthy) and creator of a mannequin which has the likeness of a woman he could easily love—if only she were real.

Night work makes strange bedfellows of McCarthy and Hollywood (Meshach Taylor), the flamboyant near-transvestite who dresses the store windows, and of McCarthy and Emmy (Cattrall), his mannequin. She comes alive when they're alone together, but reverts back to her cold self if anyone else appears.

McCarthy and Cattrall certainly are an attractive couple—when she's alive—but they don't get to do much more than kiss and dance around the store after hours. Comic development is given over to the secondary characters (Taylor, James Spader and the night watchman, G. W. Bailey).

1987: NOMINATION: Best Song ("Nothing's Gonna Stop Us Now")

•

MANNEQUIN TWO: ON THE MOVE
1991, 95 mins, US Ⓥ ⦿ col
Dir Stewart Raffill ***Prod*** Edward Rugoff ***Scr*** Edward Rugoff, David Isaacs, Ken Levine, Betsy Israel ***Ph*** Larry Pizer ***Ed*** John Rosenberg, Joan Chapman ***Mus*** David McHugh ***Art*** William J. Creber
Act Kristy Swanson, William Ragsdale, Terry Kiser, Stuart Pankin, Cynthia Harris, Meshach Taylor (Gladden)

It took four writers to struggle with another idea of why a mannequin would come to life in a department store and what would happen if she did. Their solution: the dummy (Kristy Swanson) is actually a Bavarian peasant girl hexed 1,000 years ago to prevent her marriage to the prince.

As part of a promotion, the legendary statue is displayed at a Philadelphia store under the care of William Ragsdale, who's the spitting image of the prince, and the jealous eye of count Terry Kiser, a spit-on descendant of the sorcerer who bewitched her. The hex is in the necklace and when Ragsdale accidentally removes it, he suddenly has a date for the night with a wide-eyed blonde in a micro-miniskirt who still loves him after all this time. Since this is her first date in a thousand years, Ragsdale doesn't rush things.

The only real movement is offered by Meshach Taylor, a prancing decorator who returns from the original *Mannequin* for more stereotyped fun.

•

MAN OF AFRICA
1954, 73 mins, UK col
Dir Cyril Frankel ***Prod*** John Grierson ***Scr*** Montagu Slater ***Ph*** Denny Densham ***Ed*** Alvin Bailey ***Mus*** Malcolm Arnold
Act Violet Mukabureza, Frederick Bijurenda, Mattayo Bukwirwa, Butensa, Seperiera Mpambara, Blaseo Mbalinda (Group Three)

Struggle for existence insofar as a native tribe is concerned is leisurely told in *Man of Africa,* a semidocumentary filmed in the more remote parts of Uganda. To the picture's credit it eschews the hoky aspects found in most films lensed in "darkest Africa," but this British import is often languorous to the point of becoming dull.

Producer of the Group Three picture was noted documentarian John Grierson. It's an interesting phase of African life that he chose to focus upon. But one suspects that a sketchy story contributed by director Cyril Frankel detracts more than adds to the realism.

For, in depicting the migration of a tribe to virgin country after the fertility of their homeland has been exhausted, Grierson has seen fit to include a romance between a clerk-turned-farmer and a native belle.

On the brighter side of the ledger are scenes which show the basic kindness of pygmies who are native to the Kigezi territory. They aid an injured settler and later save his child when malaria strikes the pioneers. If anything this unassuming import shows that even among African natives prejudice thrives upon misunderstanding.

Dialog of the players is in English. Cast is headed by Violet Mukabureza and Frederick Bijurenda who do as best they can in portraying the romantic couple.

•

MAN OF ARAN
1934, 75 mins, UK Ⓥ b/w
Dir Robert Flaherty ***Prod*** Michael Balcon ***Scr*** Robert Flaherty, Frances Flaherty, John Goldman ***Ph*** Robert Flaherty ***Ed*** John Goldman ***Mus*** John Greenwood
Act Colman "Tiger" King, Maggie Dirrane, Michael Dillane, Pat Mullen (Gainsborough/Gaumont-British)

Colman King, Maggie Dirrane, and Michael Dillane are the central characters. They are not actors, but natives of the barren, sea-beaten islands off the western coast of Ireland, where this picture takes place. They play themselves. The sea is the villain and the quest for food the plot of this peasants-among-peasants picture, which rates high artistically.

Naturally the big item in such a picture is the camerawork. This is splendid. With only drab grays and speckled whites to deal with, the lens has done right by the cause of sheer beauty and rugged grandeur. The Aran natives are pictured as brave and indomitable, unembittered by the rigors of their lot.

Said to have been two years in the making, the film bespeaks a canny technique and an inspirational sympathy on the part of Flaherty and his coworkers. There is practically no dialog except short sentences of warning, advice, comment on the hazards of shark-hunting.

•

MAN OF A THOUSAND FACES
1957, 122 mins, US b/w
Dir Joseph Pevney ***Prod*** Robert Arthur ***Scr*** R. Wright Campbell, Ivan Goff, Ben Roberts ***Ph*** Russell Metty ***Ed*** Ted J. Kent ***Mus*** Frank Skinner ***Art*** Alexander Golitzen, Eric Orbom
Act James Cagney, Dorothy Malone, Jane Greer, Jim Backus, Robert J. Evans, Marjorie Rambeau (Universal)

The title stems from the billing given the late Universal, later Metro, star, Lon Chaney by an alert publicity man. The screenplay, based on a story by Ralph Wheelwright, is mainly concerned with Chaney's complicated domestic problems. His achievements as a consummate artist, while woven into the story, are secondary to his mixed-up private life.

The story, in swift sequences, takes Chaney from his early boyhood to his death of throat cancer. Born of deaf and dumb parents, this is an important emotional factor in Chaney's motivations. Screenplay ranges song-and-dance vaudeville days, two marriages, the birth of his son, early struggles as a Hollywood extra, eventual rise to stardom, and tragic death.

As Chaney, James Cagney has immersed himself so completely in the role that it is difficult to spot any Cagney mannerisms. Jane Greer, as his second wife, is particularly appealing in her devotion to her "difficult" spouse. Dorothy Malone is fine as the wife who deems her career as a singer more important than raising children. A real heart-tug is provided by Celia Lovsky as Chaney's deaf and dumb mother. Bud Westmore deserves special mention for the excellent makeup jobs on the various characters portrayed by Chaney.

1957: NOMINATION: Best Original Story & Screenplay

•

MAN OF BRONZE
SEE: JIM THORPE—ALL-AMERICAN

•

MAN OF EVIL
SEE: FANNY BY GASLIGHT

•

MAN OF FLOWERS
1983, 93 mins, Australia Ⓥ ⦿ col
Dir Paul Cox ***Prod*** Jane Ballantyne, Paul Cox ***Scr*** Paul Cox, Bob Ellis ***Ph*** Yuri Sokol ***Ed*** Tim Lewis ***Art*** Asher Bilu
Act Norman Kaye, Alyson Best, Chris Haywood, Sarah Walker, Julia Blake, Bob Ellis (Flowers)

Paul Cox's film, flickering between realism and fantasy, follows the progress of Bremer, a rich naive eccentric (Norman Kaye), whose inherited wealth both protects him from the coldness of the outside world and isolates him from its warmth. He is cocooned in a childlike innocence, dwelling on the sexual exploration of his boyhood.

Man of Flowers opens with an astonishingly erotic strip by Lisa, the model. She strips, nothing more, nothing less. Is her stated affection for him genuine, or is she attracted by his money? Cox keeps the bond teasingly ambiguous.

At times *Man of Flowers* creates Hitchcock-like tension, but when the suspense becomes uncomfortable Cox lets his audience off the hook with a little wry humor. The expected black climax is never quite allowed to occur.

Kaye delivers a wonderful, understated performance as Bremer and Alyson Best is a delightfully enigmatic Lisa.

•

MAN OF IRON
SEE: CZLOWIEKZ ZELAZA

•

MAN OF LA MANCHA
1972, 129 mins, US Ⓥ ⦿ col
Dir Arthur Hiller ***Prod*** Arthur Hiller ***Scr*** Dale Wasserman ***Ph*** Giuseppe Rotunno ***Ed*** Robert C. Jones ***Mus*** Laurence Rosenthal (adapt.) ***Art*** Luciano Damiani
Act Peter O'Toole, Sophia Loren, James Coco, Harry Andrews, John Castle, Brian Blessed (United Artists/PEA)

Man of La Mancha, produced in the style of the [1965 Mitch Leigh-Joe Darion-Dale Wasserman] musical play from which it was adapted, is the fanciful tale of Don Quixote, that fictional Middle Ages lunatic living in a personal world of chivalry long-since past. The Arthur Hiller production of Dale Wasserman's book is more a vehicle for music than the narrative.

Peter O'Toole enacts the dual role of Miguel de Cervantes and his classic character, a difficult assignment which the actor undertakes with heroic overtones. Sophia Loren appears in the dual Dulcinea-Aldonza role, and James Coco is Sancho Panza, the ever-faithful squire.

O'Toole persuasively brings to life the demented would-be knight. Loren, no songbird she, does her own warbling, as does Coco, but O'Toole's numbers actually are sung by Simon Gilbert, a London actor-singer of fine voice.

1972: NOMINATION: Best Adapted Score

•

MAN OF MARBLE
SEE: CZLOWIEK Z MARMURU

•

MAN OF NO IMPORTANCE, A
1995, 98 mins, UK Ⓥ col
Dir Suri Krishnamma ***Prod*** Jonathan Cavendish ***Scr*** Barry Devlin ***Ph*** Ashley Rowe ***Ed*** David Freeman ***Mus*** Julian Nott ***Art*** Jamie Leonard
Act Albert Finney, Brenda Fricker, Michael Gambon, Tara Fitzgerald, Rufus Sewell, Patrick Fitzgerald (Little Bird/Majestic/Newcomm/BBC)

Deception is the key element in the early-1960s, Dublin-set *A Man of No Importance*. While it initially reveals itself as a larkish, romantic ode to a bygone time, it evolves darker tones and comes perilously close to full-bore tragedy by fade-out.

Unquestionably, the emotional roller-coaster ride is kept under control by another full-blooded performance by Albert Finney. He's Alfie Byrne, a fiftysomething bus conductor with a glint of the poet. He's been toying with the idea of staging Oscar Wilde's *Salome* when Adele Rice (Tara Fitzgerald) climbs aboard—his idealized vision of the temptress.

Barry Devlin's screenplay recreates Dublin as a small, provincial town where everyone has their nose in their neighbor's business and the church is the cornerstone of social life. Alfie's sister (Brenda Fricker) finds his immersion in books and "art" unhealthy. Carney (Michael Gambon), the local butcher and King Herod of the piece, is shocked that words such as "virgin" appear in the play, and that Alfie, the director, has his attention focused on Adele.

Finney plays the role like a finely tuned fiddle. The support cast is superlative. Still, director Suri Krishnamma can't quite accommodate the abrupt shifts in tone that infuse the narrative.

•

MAN OF THE HOUSE
1995, 96 mins, US Ⓥ ⦿ col
Dir James Orr ***Prod*** Bonnie Bruckheimer, Marty Katz ***Scr*** James Orr, Jim Cruickshank ***Ph*** Jamie Anderson ***Ed*** Harry Keramidas ***Mus*** Mark Mancina ***Art*** Lawrence G. Paull
Act Chevy Chase, Farrah Fawcett, Jonathan Taylor Thomas, George Wendt, David Shiner, Art LaFleur (Walt Disney/All Girls)

Chevy Chase may get top billing but the movie's one-sheet—with Jonathan Taylor Thomas dangling a puppet-size Chase on strings—is more indicative of its real focus and appeal.

Unfortunately, Thomas (from TV's *Home Improvement* and also the voice of young Simba in *The Lion King*) is stuck playing a character so bratty at first that adults may wonder why someone hasn't throttled the kid, his wry one-liners notwithstanding.

Produced through Bette Midler's company and that of James Orr and Jim Cruickshank, with Orr also directing, the simple premise has Jack Sturges (Chase), a district attorney, trying to win over Ben (Thomas), the young son of the woman he plans to marry (Farrah Fawcett). Abandoned by his real dad and therefore wary of potential suitors, Ben schemes to get Jack out of the picture. The subplot, limited at best, involves a mobster (Richard Portnow) plotting a somewhat more dire revenge against Jack.

The gags concocted by Cruickshank and Orr (their previous collaborations include *Sister Act 2* and *3 Men and a Baby*) at best approach the level of a standard sitcom. Chase is less manic than in some previous incarnations despite a few moments of physical comedy, while Fawcett has little to do but look radiant and occasionally stern.

Tech credits are generally sound, with Vancouver standing in for neighboring Seattle.

•

MANON OF THE SPRING
SEE: MANON DES SOURCES

•

MAN OF THE WEST
1958, 100 mins, US Ⓥ col
Dir Anthony Mann ***Prod*** Walter M. Mirisch ***Scr*** Reginald Rose ***Ph*** Ernest Haller ***Ed*** Richard Heermance ***Mus*** Leigh Harline ***Art*** Hilyard Brown
Act Gary Cooper, Julie London, Lee J. Cobb, Arthur O'Connell, Jack Lord, Royal Dano (United Artists/Mirisch)

The screenplay, from a novel by Will C. Brown, has Gary Cooper as a reformed gunman, now a respected citizen entrusted with the savings of his community. He is on a mission to get the town a schoolteacher when he is robbed of the money by members of his old gang. It is also somewhat by accident that he, and two other victims (Julie London and Arthur O'Connell), wind up taking refuge in the bandits' hideout, which had once been Cooper's, too.

Superficially, the story is simply the account of Cooper's efforts to free himself, London and O'Connell of the outlaws. It is given dimension by the fact that to do this he must revert to the savagery he has forsworn.

Cooper gives a characteristically virile performance, his dominance of the outlaws quietly believable, while London achieves some touching and convincing moments in a difficult role. Lee J. Cobb, a frontier Fagan of demoniac violence and destruction, and Arthur O'Connell, with whimsical grace and gaiety, add considerably to the picture's interest.

•

MAN ON A TIGHTROPE
1953, 105 mins, US b/w
Dir Elia Kazan ***Prod*** Robert L. Jacks ***Scr*** Robert E. Sherwood ***Ph*** Georg Krause ***Ed*** Dorothy Spencer ***Mus*** Franz Waxman ***Art*** Hans H. Kuhnert, Theo Zwirsky
Act Fredric March, Terry Moore, Gloria Grahame, Cameron Mitchell, Adolphe Menjou, Richard Boone (20th Century-Fox)

Man on a Tightrope is a taut "chase" [based on a story, *International Incident* by Neil Paterson]. The chase, in this instance, is an entire circus, a shabby enough troupe but, nonetheless, a burdensome commodity to sneak across any Iron Curtain frontier. But Fredric March does achieve this as he maneuvers his one-ring circus from Czechslovakia into freedom.

Director Elia Kazan limns his characters with proper mood and shade, as the red tape of the Reds becomes mountingly obstructive. He projects beaucoup romance against the general background, including a willful daughter (Terry Moore) and a flirtatious second wife (Gloria Grahame).

Moore is equally volatile in her affections for Cameron Mitchell, an itinerant deckhand whom March suspects as the spy for the Czech secret police. There is effective suspense in Adolphe Menjou's interrogation, as an officious propaganda ministry attache. Robert Beatty is a rival circus owner.

The bold manner in which the circus, in full calliope style, parades right by the auxiliary frontier guards and plans its diversion tactics for escape into the American zone is plausibly staged by Kazan. Much of this footage was shot in Austria and Germany.

MANON DES SOURCES
1953, 222 mins, France b/w
Dir Marcel Pagnol ***Prod*** Marcel Pagnol ***Scr*** Marcel Pagnol ***Ph*** Willy Faktorovitch ***Ed*** Raymonde, Jacques Bianchi ***Mus*** Raymond Legrand ***Art*** Eugene Delfau
Act Jacqueline Pagnol, Raymond Pellegrin, Rellys, Henri Poupon, Robert Vattier, Fernand Sardou (Pagnol)

The Marcel Pagnol novel that inspired Claude Berri's 1986 twin features, *Jean de Florette* and *Manon des Sources*, was itself a literary reworking of Pagnol's penultimate theatrical feature in 1953. Gaumont released the original only after getting Pagnol to make cuts in the nearly 4-hour rural opus.

Action of the 1953 film corresponds roughly to that of the Berri *Manon*, with much of the past history of *Jean de Florette* retraced in Pagnol's favorite medium—dialog. Unlike Berri, who had to cram the story into two hours, Pagnol leisurely unfolds his tale, taking the time to sketch a gallery of colorful types familiar from many of the writer-director's earlier classics (e.g., *The Baker's Wife*).

Manon contains the best and worst of Pagnol. On the debit side notably is the mediocre technical quality, the indifference to classical notions of direction, and a major miscasting, that of Manon, the wild solitary shepherdess who cuts off a village's water supply as vengeance for her father's death. She is played by Jacqueline Pagnol, the filmmaker's lovely wife, whose artificial manner and diction never suggest an orphan who's grown up in the Provencal hills.

Yet the film is buoyed by its other vivid characterizations and the nonstop verve of Pagnol's dialog. Though story is plotted in mostly static sequences, there's an enchanting quality in many scenes that is simply not reproducible on a stage.

[Pic was reviewed at the first showing of the uncut version, in October 1988.]

●

MANON DES SOURCES
(MANON OF THE SPRING)
1986, 113 mins, France/Italy Ⓥ ⦿ ▭ col
Dir Claude Berri ***Prod*** Pierre Grunstein ***Scr*** Claude Berri, Gerard Brach ***Ph*** Bruno Nuytten ***Ed*** Genevieve Louveau, Herve de Luze ***Mus*** Jean-Claude Lepetit ***Art*** Bernard Vezat
Act Yves Montand, Daniel Auteuil, Emmanuelle Beart, Hippolyte Girardot, Elisabeth Depardieu, Margarita Lozano (Renn/Films A2/DD/RAI-2

Manon des Sources is the poignant, but more dramatically wobbly, followup to *Jean de Florette*, producer-director Claude Berri's risky two-film adaptation of a novel by Marcel Pagnol, who, unsatisfied with his own next-to-last feature in 1952, expanded it as a two-part novel. When Pagnol filmed his own *Manon des Sources*, he came up with a picture running just under four hours. Berri had the obligation of squeezing this more diffuse material into a conventional feature length span—hence the feeling of haste and cut corners.

Manon takes place some 10 years after the action of *Jean de Florette*. Manon, the hunchback's daughter, grown into a beautiful young woman who now lives in the hills as a reclusive shepherdess, learns the treachery that brought about her father's death and exacts vengeance on Yves Montand, Daniel Auteuil and the village by blocking up the subterranean spring that provides water to the area. The resulting crisis brings about a public reckoning and the open accusation of Montand and Auteuil, plus a final revelation.

Auteuil is again superb as the ratty unmalicious nephew, Ugolin, and triumphs over the sometimes cramped dramaturgy, notably in his declaration of love to Manon in the hills. Berri is unable to overcome the inherent feebleness of the Manon character, here played ineffectually by the lovely and talented Emmanuelle Beart. As with *Florette*, tech credits are smart.

●

MAN ON FIRE
1957, 95 mins, US b/w
Dir Ranald MacDougall ***Prod*** Sol C. Siegel ***Scr*** Ranald MacDougall ***Ph*** Joseph Ruttenberg ***Ed*** Ralph E. Winters ***Mus*** David Raksin ***Art*** William A. Horning, Hans Peter
Act Bing Crosby, Inger Stevens, Mary Fickett, E. G. Marshall, Malcolm Brodrick, Anne Seymour (M-G-M)

As a doting father embroiled in a harsh custody battle with his ex-wife, Bing Crosby gives an appealing and sensitive performance. Character of Earl Carleton, a successful businessman embittered by a broken marriage is understandable and sympathetic.

The screenplay, based on a story by Malvin Wald and Jack Jacobs, resembles the fiction in better women's magazines. The story tackles the question of divorce and its effect on children. Crosby is stubbornly determined to maintain the custody of his young son at any cost. Not only is he motivated by a sincere love for his child, but his actions, including an effort to "kidnap" his son in the face of a court order, are based on his own hurt feelings and bitterness over the fact that his wife left him to marry another man.

Mary Fickett, from the Broadway stage, is excellent as Crosby's ex-wife. Inger Stevens, as a femme lawyer, is particularly appealing as she nurses Crosby through his vicious and embittered moods.

●

MAN ON THE MOON
1999, 118 mins, US Ⓥ ⦿ ▭ col
Dir Milos Forman ***Prod*** Danny DeVito, Michael Shamberg, Stacey Sher ***Scr*** Scott Alexander, Larry Karaszewski ***Ph*** Anastas Michos ***Ed*** Christopher Tellefsen, Lynzee Klingman ***Mus*** REM ***Art*** Patrizia von Brandenstein
Act Jim Carrey, Danny DeVito, Courtney Love, Paul Giamatti, Vincent Schiavelli, Peter Bonerz (Jersey/Cinehaus/Mutual/Universal)

Given their idiosyncratic treatments of the lives of Ed Wood and Larry Flynt, there was reason to hope that screenwriters Scott Alexander and Larry Karaszewski would give dimension even to the unlikely figure of Andy Kaufman, who made a name for himself in the TV series *Taxi* and died in 1984 of cancer at the age of 35. All the audience is left with is the impression of a hopeless neurotic of little discernible talent other than for making the lives of those around him miserable.

Hollywood agent George Shapiro (Danny DeVito) takes him on and gets him a *Saturday Night Live* gig. This quickly leads to the offer to join *Taxi*, which Shapiro has to goad Kaufman into because the latter professes to hate sitcoms. Kaufman is seen as a highly disruptive prima donna, especially in his insistence upon special guest appearances by his gross and vulgar Las Vegas character, Tony Clifton, which he concocted with friend and writer Bob Zmuda (Paul Giamatti). *Taxi* co-stars Marilu Henner and Judd Hirsch appear as themselves, and Peter Bonerz plays the show's director.

Kaufman seems bereft of true personal connections, and certainly of a romantic life, until he meets Lynne Margulies (Courtney Love), who eventually moves in with him. But even this relationship has a shaky foundation.

Carrey's virtuoso turn unerringly captures the behavioral quirkiness and disquieting vacantness of the man he's portraying; on the other, there is only so far the performance can go, since true psychological penetration is essentially impossible in Kaufman's case.

●

MANPOWER
1941, 100 mins, US b/w
Dir Raoul Walsh ***Prod*** Mark Hellinger ***Scr*** Richard Macauley, Jerry Wald ***Ph*** Ernest Haller ***Ed*** Ralph Dawson ***Mus*** Adolph Deutsch
Act Edward G. Robinson, Marlene Dietrich, George Raft, Alan Hale, Frank McHugh, Eve Arden (Warner)

There's plenty of rough and rowdy action and dialog in this melodrama, premised on the triangle formula.

Zestful direction of Raoul Walsh cannot be discounted here. He keeps things moving at a fast clip and displays the individual talents of Edward G. Robinson, Marlene Dietrich and George Raft to utmost advantage.

Story tells of the adventures of a construction and maintenance crew for power lines. Raft and Robinson are buddies in the outfit, and when Robinson is burned by a high tension wire he's made foreman of the gang. Dietrich is the daughter of crew-member Egon Brecher, getting parole from a year's stretch in prison. She works in a clip joint, and enacts the role to perfection. Raft tabs her immediately, but Robinson falls in love with her for quick marriage.

First third of the picture displays racy action and spicy dialog for maximum attention, and then drifts into formula triangle dramatics. Robinson delivers a vivid portrayal as the foreman-lineman who manhandles the gals too fast until he meets Dietrich. Latter provides a stereotyped performance as the clip-joint inmate, and sings one song chorus throatily.

●

MAN-PROOF
1937, 80 mins, US b/w
Dir Richard Thorpe ***Prod*** Louis D. Lighton ***Scr*** Vincent Lawrence, Waldemar Young, George Oppenheimer ***Ph*** Karl Freund ***Ed*** George Boemler ***Mus*** Frank Waxman
Act Myrna Loy, Franchot Tone, Rosalind Russell, Walter Pidgeon, Rita Johnson, Ruth Hussey (M-G-M)

Man-Proof is a smartly produced, well-directed and excellently acted society comedy-drama [from a story by Fanny Heaslip Lea]. Action takes place in exclusive country homes, the art department of a New York daily, and some gay Manhattan nightclubs.

Myrna Loy plays a young woman who has just received a rude jolt from the man she loves (Walter Pidgeon) when she is handed a message that he is to marry one of her rich girlfriends (Rosalind Russell) and the couple invite her to be a bridesmaid. It's a shock, but she is a thoroughbred and she hides her disappointment and resentment. Thereafter the story recounts, more or less interestingly, the thoughts and actions of a girl on the rebound from a thwarted love affair.

Loy registers the serious aspects of the character effectively. It's her comedy bits, however, which score. With very little to do, Russell does it very well. As most of the talk is about the husband, played by Pidgeon, something more is expected of the character than is conceived by the writers. Franchot Tone is an irresponsible newspaperman with a rather bitter and cynical viewpoint on life, love and women.

●

MAN'S CASTLE
1933, 75 mins, US b/w
Dir Frank Borzage ***Prod*** [uncredited] ***Scr*** Jo Swerling ***Ph*** Joseph August ***Ed*** Viola Lawrence ***Mus*** Frank Harling ***Art*** [uncredited]
Act Spencer Tracy, Loretta Young, Marjorie Rambeau, Glenda Farrell, Walter Connolly, Arthur Hohl (Columbia)

Spencer Tracy is cast in his most distasteful role. It's a story [from the play by Lawrence Hazard] of a worthless mug who rudely picks up a homeless girl and transports her to a shanty town, where he and other no-goods reside in one fashion or another. The story attempts to justify it all by reformation of the calloused, smart-cracking hero via marriage to the girl when she is about to become a mother.

Some of the wisecracks Tracy is called upon to read are of the roughest, most inconsiderate kind. Such things as "Shut up or I'll pour that stew down your back" could hardly be accepted as ever leading to true affection.

It's that way for Tracy throughout. Loretta Young does a noble job as the little girl who stands nearly everything.

Locale is almost entirely in a shanty village, where little more than sheets of tin and some garbage was necessary. The few miniatures employed look phoney.

●

MAN'S FAVORITE SPORT?
1964, 120 mins, US Ⓥ col
Dir Howard Hawks ***Prod*** Howard Hawks ***Scr*** John Fenton Murray, Steve McNeil ***Ph*** Russell Harlan ***Ed*** Stuart Gilmore ***Mus*** Henry Mancini ***Art*** Alexander Golitzen, Tambi Larsen
Act Rock Hudson, Paula Prentiss, Maria Perschy, John McGiver, Charlene Holt, Roscoe Karns (Universal)

The comically ripe premise from the story *The Girl Who Almost Got Away* by Pat Frank, is what happens when a celebrated but fraudulent piscatorial authority and fishing equipment salesman for Abercrombie & Fitch who doesn't know how to fish is suddenly ordered by his unaware boss to compete in a fishing tournament?

For a while, the adventures of this angler (Rock Hudson) romp along with a kind of breezy *Field & Stream* charm, bolstered by some inventive slapstick ideas, cleverly devised characters and occasionally sharp dialog. But then, poof, the fish story begins to sag under the weight of its bulky romantic midsection and lumbers along tediously and repetitiously to a long overdue conclusion.

Matters are helped along somewhat by an attractive and spirited cast, but not enough to keep the film consistently amusing.

Hawks purportedly utilized unorthodox directorial techniques, such as filming in sequence a day at a time in order to capture an air of comic spontaneity. Since some of the sight gag passages are uproarious, there is a lot to be said for this technique. But it appears that the main trouble with Hawks's day-at-a-time approach to comedy is that there were too many days or not enough comedy or a combination of both.

●

MANSFIELD PARK
1999, 110 mins, UK/US Ⓥ ⦿ col
Dir Patricia Rozema ***Prod*** Sarah Curtis ***Scr*** Patricia Rozema ***Ph*** Michael Coulter ***Ed*** Martin Walsh ***Mus*** Lesley Barber ***Art*** Christopher Hobbs
Act Embeth Davidtz, Jonny Lee Miller, Alessandro Nivola, Frances O'Connor, Harold Pinter, Lindsay Duncan (Miramax HAL/BBC)

If ever a picture deserved a possessory credit, it's this one, which should have been called *Patricia Rozema's Mansfield Park*. It certainly isn't Jane Austen's. Janeites are likely to raise more than eyebrows at this often radical reworking of Austen's third published novel; pic reinterprets the central character, Fanny Price, as a cross between Austen herself and a tomboyish proto-feminist, throws in some magical realism and gratuitous lesbian *frissons* to spice up the plot, and too often steps out of its era to adopt a knowing, politically correct, late–20th-century attitude to the society portrayed.

Opening reel starts promisingly as 10-year-old Fanny (Hannah Taylor Gordon) is sent by her impoverished parents to live with her mother's sisters (Lindsay Duncan, Sheila Gish) at the sprawling country mansion Mansfield Park. After rapidly intro'ing the large cast of characters and establishing a sprightly, sardonic tone that's close to the novel, pic neatly dissolves into the story of the grown-up Fanny (Frances O'Connor), who's now a passionate and prolific amateur writer, experienced horsewoman and wearer of tomboyish garb.

Film tries to have it both ways, sometimes giving the viewer pure Austen, and at others belaboring audiences with observations on the evils of slave trading and a nudge-nudge contempo attitude that undermines the story's delicate emotional texture.

Aussie actress O'Connor is excellent and, despite being fourth billed, carries the movie. As her fumbling vis-à-vis, Edmund, Jonny Lee Miller is variable, with the dialogue not always sitting easily in his modern mouth. Supports are all good, with Harold Pinter grave and sonorous as Edmund's father.

•

MANSLAUGHTER

1930, 82 mins, US b/w

Dir George Abbott ***Scr*** George Abbott ***Ph*** Archie J. Stout ***Art*** Otto Lovering

Act Claudette Colbert, Fredric March, Emma Dunn, Natalie Moorhead, Richard Tucker (Paramount Publix)

This is a remake of a 1922 silent with Thomas Meighan doing the d.a. role which Fredric March now has. Leatrice Joy in the silent version of the Alice Duer Miller *SatEve-Post* story gives way to Claudette Colbert.

George Abbott, in adapting and directing, has endeavored to overcome some of the banalities which, in 1922, were standard. Instead of following the original hoke situation of the candidate-for-governor-hero previously reencountering, on a breadline, the girl he sent to prison, March is shown doing a mild stooge bum, but coming back into private law practice without the old hokum bucket trimmings.

The aftermath of maid and mistress meeting on equal terms in jail is retained and rather convincingly carried through, but in between there's much that's baloney.

Colbert follows through the original idea of a snobbish characterization, remade by her prison experience, although it's still a grand excuse for a fashion parade.

•

MANTRAP

1926, 68 mins, US ⊗ b/w

Dir Victor Fleming ***Prod*** B. P. Schulberg, Hector Turnbull ***Scr*** Adelaide Heilbron, Ethel Doherty, George Marion, Jr. ***Ph*** James [Wong] Howe

Act Ernest Torrence, Clara Bow, Percy Marmont, Eugene Pallette (Paramount)

Clara Bow just walks away with the picture from the moment she steps into camera range. Every minute that she is in it she steals it from such a couple of corking troupers as Ernest Torrence and Percy Marmont. In this particular role, that of a fast-working, slang-slinging manicurist from a swell barber shop in Minneapolis, who marries the big hick from the Canadian wilds, she is fitted just like a glove. The picture itself is a wow for laughs, action and corking titles.

The story [from the novel by Sinclair Lewis] deals with a lawyer who is a divorce specialist, sick and tired of vamping females who come to his office with their troubles. To be rid of them he decides to go up into the Canadian wilds.

The contrast to the lawyer character is the owner of a trading store in the lonely country, who is woman-hungry and who goes to Minneapolis, wins himself the flip little manicure girl and takes her back to the wilds.

•

MAN TROUBLE

1992, 100 mins, US Ⓥ ⦿ col

Dir Bob Rafelson ***Prod*** Bruce Gilbert, Carole Eastman ***Scr*** Carole Eastman ***Ph*** Stephen H. Burum ***Ed*** William Steinkamp ***Mus*** Georges Delerue ***Art*** Mel Bourne

Act Jack Nicholson, Ellen Barkin, Harry Dean Stanton, Beverly D'Angelo, Michael McKean, Saul Rubinek (Penta/American Filmworks/Budding Grove)

Jack Nicholson fans should feel cheated by *Man Trouble*, an insultingly trivial star vehicle.

Nicholson portrays a dog trainer who meets opera singer Ellen Barkin when she needs a guard dog after a break-in and other harassment. In a screenplay resembling stage farce rather than a movie, scripter Carole Eastman drags in several pointless subplots. Main one concerns Beverly D'Angelo, who's penned a tell-all book about her relationship with reclusive billionaire Harry Dean Stanton. Barkin is getting divorced from her conductor/husband David Clennon and has been threatened by some homicidal thug who may be the notorious local slasher.

None of this adds up to entertainment or even momentarily involving escapism, as the romantic comedy/thriller genre, typified by *Charade* or *Foul Play*, seems beyond the filmmakers' combined grasp. Instead there's strenuously overacted comic set pieces, most of which fail.

Barkin is saddled with completely unnatural dialogue as well as some overdone physical shtick that seems left over from her last comedy, *Switch*. D'Angelo steals a couple of scenes as Barkin's sister.

•

MA NUIT CHEZ MAUD
(My Night at Maud's) Ⓥ ⦿

1969, 110 mins, France Ⓥ ⦿ b/w

Dir Eric Rohmer ***Prod*** Barbet Schroeder, Pierre Cottrell ***Scr*** Eric Rohmer ***Ph*** Nestor Almendros ***Ed*** Cecile Decugis ***Mus*** [none] ***Art*** Nicole Rachline

Act Jean-Louis Trintignant, Francoise Fabian, Marie-Christine Barrault, Antoine Vitez, Anne Dubot, Marie Becker (Losange/FFP/Simar/Carrosse/Gueville/Renn/Pleiade/Deux-Mondes)

Eric Rohmer's third pic after *Le signe du lion*, which treated a down-and-out American in Paris and the moral indifference of his friends, and *La Collectionneuse*, about a femme who collected lovers and her tilt with an intellectual, looks at a 34-year-old engineer (Jean-Louis Trintignant) living in a small French town. He runs into an old friend, a schoolteacher, who invites him to dinner at the home of his mistress, Maud (Francoise Fabian), a divorcee.

The friend gets drunk and leaves them alone. Maud is a sensuous woman, but the engineer fends off her verbal and physical advances. A confirmed Catholic, he can no longer make love for its own sake.

He meets her again, but is more talk than action. Years later he, his wife and child meet Maud at a beach. She says she has remarried but seems to know his wife.

This moralistic fable is up-to-date in delving into the sexual attitudes of intellectuals, those that gab and rarely grab. It is refined, knowing and has a rich mixture of wit and revealing content.

Trintignant has the correct priggish, self-indulgent but unselfconscious awareness of what he wants. Fabian has middle-aged good looks and limns her role of Maud well. Christine Barrault is right as the Catholic girl.

•

MAN WHO CAME BACK, THE

SEE: SWAMP WATER

•

MAN WHO CAME TO DINNER, THE

1942, 112 mins, US Ⓥ b/w

Dir William Keighley ***Prod*** Jack Saper, Jerry Wald ***Scr*** Julius J. Epstein, Philip G. Epstein ***Ph*** Tony Gaudin ***Ed*** Jack Killifer ***Mus*** Frederick Hollander

Act Bette Davis, Ann Sheridan, Monty Woolley, Jimmy Durante, Richard Travis (Warner)

Only detracting angle in the entire film is slowness of the first quarter. Portion in which the characters are being built up, before the complications of the story actually begin, is overlong.

Superb casting and nifty work by every member of the company rates plenty of breveting. Monty Woolley is even better than he was in the Broadway edition [of the play by George S. Kaufman and Moss Hart] as the bearded lecturer-writer-radio commentator who is inveigled to dinner at a home in a small Ohio town where he happens to be lecturing and slips on the front steps, injuring his hip. He's confined to a wheelchair there for three weeks and with his witty insults, domineering talk and meddling in the affairs of his secretary and of the unfortunate family with whom he is staying, brings havoc upon all.

Bette Davis is in the secondary part of Woolley's secretary. Role has been strengthened slightly from the legit version to add to the slim romance department.

•

MAN WHO FELL TO EARTH, THE

1976, 140 mins, UK Ⓥ ⦿ ▭ col

Dir Nicolas Roeg ***Prod*** Michael Deeley, Barry Spikings ***Scr*** Paul Mayersberg ***Ph*** Anthony Richmond ***Ed*** Graeme Clifford ***Mus*** John Phillips (dir.) ***Art*** Brian Eatwell

Act David Bowie, Candy Clark, Rip Torn, Buck Henry, Bernie Casey, Jackson D. Kane (British Lion)

Basic plot has David Bowie descend to Earth from another planet to secure water supply for the folks at home. To help achieve this end, he soon uses his superior intelligence to accumulate vast earthbound wealth and power.

It's a story that must be seen and not told, so rich is it in subplots mirroring the "pure" spaceman's reaction to a corrupt environment. In fact, pic is perhaps too rich a morsel, too cluttered with themes. Visually and aurally, it's stunning stuff throughout, and Bowie's choice as the ethereal visitor is inspired.

Candy Clark, as his naive but loving mate, performs well in intimate scenes with Bowie, especially the introductory ones, which are among pic's highlights.

•

MAN WHO HAD POWER OVER WOMEN, THE

1970, 89 mins, UK Ⓥ col

Dir John Krish ***Prod*** Judd Bernard ***Scr*** Andrew Meredith ***Ph*** Gerry Turpin ***Ed*** Thom Noble ***Mus*** John Mandel ***Art*** Colin Grimes

Act Rod Taylor, Carol White, James Booth, Penelope Horner, Charles Korvin, Alexandra Stewart (Kettledrum)

Fundamentally, this is a sex comedy done in lively enough fashion. Then it strays into a more serious territory trying to show up the hollowness behind the tinselly pop world.

Rod Taylor plays a successful talent exec in an agency, disenchanted, because he figures that the job makes him a parasite. He's also an inveterate lecher and a heavy drinker.

After a particularly hefty binge his chilly wife (Penelope Horner) walks out and Taylor moves in temporarily with his best friend and colleague, perkily played by James Booth, and latter's wife (Carol White), in whose arms Taylor finds solace.

Meanwhile he's getting tired of nursemaiding a preening pop-singing idol (played with horrible veracity by Clive Francis).

•

MAN WHO HAUNTED HIMSELF, THE

1970, 94 mins, UK Ⓥ col

Dir Basil Dearden ***Prod*** Michael Relph ***Scr*** Basil Dearden, Michael Relph ***Ph*** Tony Spratling ***Ed*** Teddy Darvas ***Mus*** Michael J. Lewis ***Art*** Albert Witherick

Act Roger Moore, Hildegard Neil, Alastair Mackenzie, Hugh Mackenzie, Kevork Malikyan, Thorley Walters (Associated British)

Roger Moore plays a conservative, ambitious City business man who is involved in a car smash in which he was guilty of reckless, out-of-character driving. From the moment of his recovery strange things begin to happen. He is apparently in two places at once. He apparently indulges in sharp business practice. He is apparently having an affair with a girl who he has only once met, and casually.

The uncanny situation begins to prey on Moore's mind. Has he an unscrupulous double? Or is it all a figment of his imagination? These are the headaches that prey on Moore and add up to a tense riddle. Hildegard Neil as Moore's wife has only a cardboard role, but handles the disintegration of her marriage competently.

•

MAN WHO KNEW TOO MUCH, THE

1935, 74 mins, UK Ⓥ ⦿ b/w

Dir Alfred Hitchcock ***Prod*** Michael Balcon ***Scr*** A. R. Rawlinson, Edwin Greenwood, Charles Bennett, D. B. Wyndham-Lewis, Emlyn Williams ***Ph*** Curt Courant ***Ed*** H. St. C. Stewart ***Mus*** Arthur Benjamin ***Art*** Alfred Junge, Peter Proud

Act Leslie Banks, Edna Best, Peter Lorre, Frank Vosper, Hugh Wakefield, Nova Pilbeam (Gaumont-British)

An unusually fine dramatic story handled excellently from a production standpoint. Built along gangster lines, but from an international crook standpoint, with a lot of melodramatic suspense added.

Starts at a party in St Moritz. A man is shot during a dance. He whispers to a friend that there's a message in a brush in his bathroom. Friend realizes the dying man was in the secret service and gets the message. Before he can communicate with the police he is handed a note saying his daughter has been kidnapped and will be killed if he talks.

Back to London and the cops can't make the man or his wife say anything. Finally the man locates the gang's meeting place. He discovers that an attempt will be made to kill a famous international statesman at the Albert Hall that night and manages to communicate that news to his wife, although he is held prisoner.

Scene at Albert Hall is highly exciting and beautifully handled. Acting is splendid most all of the way. Leslie Banks is a fine actor, although the assignment is a bit heavy for him. Edna Best looks well but is not convincing in some of the toughest passages. Peter Lorre's work stands out again. He's the gang chief.

•

MAN WHO KNEW TOO MUCH, THE

1956, 119 mins, US Ⓥ ⦿ col

Dir Alfred Hitchcock ***Prod*** Alfred Hitchcock ***Scr*** John Michael Hayes ***Ph*** Robert Burks ***Ed*** George Tomasini ***Mus*** Bernard Herrmann ***Art*** Hal Pereira, Henry Bumstead

Act James Stewart, Doris Day, Brenda de Banzie, Bernard Miles, Daniel Gelin, Ralph Truman (Paramount)

With Alfred Hitchcock pulling the suspense strings, *The Man Who Knew Too Much* is a good thriller. Hitchcock backstops his mystery in the colorful locales of Marrakesh in French Morocco and in London. While drawing the footage out a bit long, he still keeps suspense working at all times and gets strong performances from the two stars and other cast members. Hitchcock did the same pic under the same title for Gaumont-British back in 1935.

James Stewart ably carries out his title duties—he is a doctor vacationing in Marrakesh with his wife and young son. When he witnesses a murder and learns of an assassination scheduled to take place in London, the boy is kidnapped by the plotters to keep the medico's mouth shut.

Stewart's characterization is matched by the dramatic work contributed by Doris Day as his wife. Both draw vivid portraits of tortured parents when their son is kidnapped. Additionally, Day has two Jay Livingston–Ray Evans tunes to sing: "Whatever Will Be" and "We'll Love Again," which are used storywise and not just dropped into the plot. Young Christopher Olsen plays the son naturally and appealingly.

1956: Best Song ("Whatever Will Be, Will Be")

•

MAN WHO LOVED CAT DANCING, THE

1973, 114 mins, US Ⓥ ⊏⊐ col

Dir Richard C. Sarafian ***Prod*** Martin Poll, Eleanor Perry ***Scr*** Eleanor Perry ***Ph*** Harry Stradling, Jr. ***Ed*** Tom Rolf ***Mus*** John Williams ***Art*** Edward C. Carfagno

Act Burt Reynolds, Sarah Miles, Lee J. Cobb, Jack Warden, George Hamilton, Bo Hopkins (M-G-M)

The Man Who Loved Cat Dancing, supposedly a period western told from a woman's viewpoint, emerges as a steamy, turgid meller, uneven in dramatic focus and development. Crucial flaw is the adaptation by Eleanor Perry.

Marilyn Durham's novel, which gets its offbeat title from fact that "Cat Dancing" is the name of Burt Reynolds's dead Indian wife, tells how Sarah Miles, fleeing from husband George Hamilton, accidentally witnesses a train robbery and is virtually kidnapped by the gang. Reynolds has his hands full, for about two-thirds of the film, keeping brutish Jack Warden and Bo Hopkins (the latter outstanding) from raping Miles; for the last third, his hands are full of her.

The femme lead role calls less for acting ability than a willingness to be dragged, beaten, stomped on and abused in a variety of ways. Lee J. Cobb is the stoic Wells Fargo detective who, with Hamilton in tow, tracks down the surviving bandits to an Indian village.

•

MAN WHO LOVED WOMEN, THE

1983, 110 mins, US Ⓥ col

Dir Blake Edwards ***Prod*** Blake Edwards, Tony Adams ***Scr*** Blake Edwards, Milton Wexler, Geoffrey Edwards ***Ph*** Haskell Wexler ***Ed*** Ralph E. Winters ***Mus*** Henry Mancini ***Art*** Roger Maus

Act Burt Reynolds, Julie Andrews, Kim Basinger, Marilu Henner, Barry Corbin, Cynthia Sikes (Columbia)

The Man Who Loved Women is truly woeful, reeking of production-line, big-star filmmaking and nothing else.

Once again, Burt Reynolds appears as the irresistible, yet sensitive, modern man in search of something fulfilling in his life. This time, Reynolds's angst is examined in flashback from his funeral in the words of his psychiatrist (Julie Andrews). And they are terrible words, to be sure. From the start, the psychobabble she spouts is so stilted and stupid that it raises false hopes that *Women* must surely be a satire, and perhaps a promising one.

Had not director Blake Edwards been fooling around with an "American extension" of Francois Truffaut's 1977 film of the same title, there probably was a better picture contained here in Reynolds's one really amusing sojourn into a bemused, adulterous affair with Kim Basinger. She's great as Houston millionaire Barry Corbin's kinky wife, given to stopwatch dalliances in dangerous places.

•

MAN WHO NEVER WAS, THE

1956, 103 mins, UK Ⓥ ⊏⊐ col

Dir Ronald Neame ***Prod*** Andre Hakim ***Scr*** Nigel Balchin ***Ph*** Oswald Morris ***Mus*** Alan Rawsthorne

Act Clifton Webb, Gloria Grahame, Robert Flemyng, Josephine Griffin, Stephen Boyd, Andre Morell (20th Century-Fox)

Of all the fantastic stories to come out of World War II the use by British Naval Intelligence of a corpse to deceive the Germans about the planned invasion of Sicily undoubtedly out-fictions fiction. The role of Montagu, the "master planner," is distinctly offbeat for Clifton Webb and, on the whole, he handles it competently.

The star of this show is the corpse which, dressed up as a British marine major, is allowed to float ashore on the coast of Spain. It carries confidential letters with references to the forthcoming invasion of Greece, a ruse which actually fooled the Germans and saved many Allied lives.

Wisely realizing that this painstaking process, however unusual, lacks action and is bound to become tedious after a while, scripter Nigel Balchin (adapting the novel by Ewen Montagu) has introduced the figure of a young Irishman sent to London by the Germans to check on the identity of Major Martin. Gloria Grahame, assigned to be the girlfriend of "Major Martin," seems an unhappy choice for the part, and she overplays it badly. By contrast, Josephine Griffin, a British newcomer, is completely believable.

•

MAN WHO SHOT LIBERTY VALANCE, THE

1962, 123 mins, US Ⓥ ⦿ b/w

Dir John Ford ***Prod*** Willis Goldbeck ***Scr*** James Warner Bellah, Willis Goldbeck ***Ph*** William H. Clothier ***Ed*** Otho Lovering ***Mus*** Cyril J. Mockridge ***Art*** Hal Pereira, Eddie Imazu

Act John Wayne, James Stewart, Vera Miles, Lee Marvin, Edmond O'Brien, Andy Devine (Paramount)

The Man Who Shot Liberty Valance is an entertaining and emotionally involving western. Yet, while it is an enjoyable film it falls distinctly shy of its innate story potential.

Director John Ford and the writers have somewhat overplayed their hands. They have taken a disarmingly simple and affecting premise, developed it with craft and skill to a natural point of conclusion, and then have proceeded to run it into the ground, destroying the simplicity and intimacy for which they have striven. The long screenplay from a short story by Dorothy M. Johnson has Stewart as a dude, eastern attorney forging idealistically into lawless western territory, where he is promptly greeted by the sadistic, though sponsored, brutality of Valance (Lee Marvin), a killer who owes his allegiance to the vested interests of wealthy cattlemen opposed to statehood, law and order.

The audience instantly senses that Stewart did not fire the fatal shot that gives him his reputation and destines him for political fame.

Because the audience knows that: (1) Stewart can't hit a paint can at 15 paces, (2) Stewart has won the heart of the sweetheart of John Wayne, best shot in the territory and a man of few words but heroically alert and forthright. Had the body of the film (it is told in flashback) ended at this maximum point, it would have been a taut, cumulative study of the irony of heroic destiny.

Stewart and Wayne do what comes naturally in an engagingly effortless manner. Vera Miles is consistently effective. Marvin is evil as they come. There is a portrayal of great strength and dignity by Woody Strode. But the most memorable characterization in the film is that of Edmond O'Brien as a tippling newspaper editor deeply proud of his profession.

1962: NOMINATION: Best B&W Costume Design

•

MAN WHO WATCHED TRAINS GO BY, THE

(US: THE PARIS EXPRESS)

1952, 80 mins, UK Ⓥ col

Dir Harold French ***Prod*** Raymond Stross ***Scr*** Harold French ***Ph*** Otto Heller ***Ed*** Vera Campbell ***Mus*** Benjamin Frankel ***Art*** Paul Sherrif

Act Claude Rains, Marta Toren, Marius Goring, Anouk Aimee, Herbert Lom, Ferdy Mayne (Stross/Shaftel)

While it varies from the original Georges Simenon novel, this keeps to essentially the same main character about whom the entire plot revolves.

Main figure is Claude Rains, loyal chief clerk to a firm of Dutch merchants, whose world of honesty and integrity is shattered when he discovers that his boss has been misappropriating the company's money to keep a French woman in luxury. But this meek, dutiful servant, who all his life has watched the trains go by to alluring capitals like Brussels and Paris, turns when he discovers his boss is running off with the firm's money. He takes the cash himself and goes to Paris, where he is involved in a series of implausible but exciting adventures with the girl who was at the root of the trouble.

Rains plays the main role of the chief clerk with quiet, dignified restraint. Toren, as the unscrupulous woman, fills the part with a vivid and believable characterization. Marius Goring gives a polished performance as the French detective while Anouk Aimee has a bit as a Paris streetwalker.

•

MAN WHO WOULD BE KING, THE

1975, 129 mins, US Ⓥ ⦿ ⊏⊐ col

Dir John Huston ***Prod*** John Foreman ***Scr*** John Huston, Gladys Hill ***Ph*** Oswald Morris ***Ed*** Russell Lloyd ***Mus*** Maurice Jarre ***Art*** Alexander Trauner

Act Sean Connery, Michael Caine, Christopher Plummer, Saeed Jaffrey, Shakira Caine (Columbia/Allied Artists)

Whether it was the intention of John Huston or not, the tale of action and adventure is a too-broad comedy, mostly due to the poor performance of Michael Caine.

As Peachy Carnehan, a loudmouth braggart and former soldier in the Indian army, Caine joins forces with another veteran, Daniel Dravot (Sean Connery), to make their fortunes in a mountain land beyond Afghanistan. Connery, in the title role, gives a generally credible, but not very sympathetic, portrayal of the man thrust into potential greatness.

The most redeeming aspect of the film is the performance of Christopher Plummer as Rudyard Kipling, from whose classic story pic is a variation. Despite the small amount of footage he well deserves his star billing.

1975: NOMINATIONS: Best Adapted Screenplay, Costume Design, Art Direction, Editing

•

MAN WITH A MILLION

SEE: THE MILLION POUND NOTE

•

MAN WITH BOGART'S FACE, THE

1980, 106 mins, US Ⓥ col

Dir Robert Day ***Prod*** Andrew J. Fenady ***Scr*** Andrew J. Fenady ***Ph*** Richard C. Glouner ***Ed*** Eddie Saeta ***Mus*** George Duning ***Art*** Richard McKenzie

Act Robert Sacchi, Franco Nero, Michelle Phillips, Olivia Hussey, Herbert Lom, Misty Rowe (20th Century-Fox)

Clearly and intentionally the picture is a gimmick. Bogart look-alike Robert Sacchi plays Bogart as Bogart himself might have portrayed private eye Sam Marlow, always relating incidents and personalities to stars and films of yesteryear. Producer Andrew J. Fenady, whose script is based on his own novel, has sprinkled his involved plot with a continuous flow of laugh lines. It adds up to a lot of fun.

As the film opens, the star has just undergone facial surgery, and immediately sets up shop as a private eye, hiring Misty Rowe as his luscious but scatterbrained secretary.

The action—and there is plenty of it—is played against some handsome backgrounds, including expensive yachts and the palacelike home of Turkish magnate Franco Nero, with his bevy of belly dancers.

•

MAN WITHIN, THE

(US: THE SMUGGLERS)

1947, 86 mins, UK col

Dir Bernard Knowles ***Prod*** Sydney Box ***Scr*** Muriel Box, Sydney Box ***Ph*** Geoffrey Unsworth ***Ed*** Alfred Roome ***Mus*** Clifton Parker ***Art*** Andrew Mazzei

Act Michael Redgrave, Jean Kent, Joan Greenwood, Richard Attenborough, Francis L. Sullivan, Ronald Shiner (Gainsborough)

This adaptation of Graham Greene's novel has much to commend it. Most glaring fault is amount of talk used.

Story is told in flashback while Richard Attenborough is undergoing torture in prison. He relates how, as an orphan, he becomes the ward of Michael Redgrave, goes to sea with him and his crew of smugglers and is sharply disciplined because he is a poor sailor. He loathes the life and when he is flogged for an offense he did not commit, his love and admiration for his guardian turn to hate. He takes vengeance by giving him away to the customs men. In the ensuing fight one of the customs men is killed and several smugglers are arrested.

Attenborough flees, taking refuge in a lonely cottage the boy meets the stepdaughter of the murdered man who approves his treachery and incites him to give evidence against his former shipmates.

Most mature performance comes from Redgrave who plays the gentleman-smuggler with a sure touch. Attenborough, as the coward who finds courage, has his moments, but Joan Greenwood is somewhat handicapped by a slow genuine Sussex dialect as Attenborough's real love. Jean Kent is alarmingly modern as an 1820 vamp.

•

MAN WITHOUT A FACE, THE

1993, 114 mins, US Ⓥ ⦿ ⊏⊐ col

Dir Mel Gibson ***Prod*** Bruce Davey ***Scr*** Malcolm MacRury ***Ph*** Donald M. McAlpine ***Ed*** Tony Gibbs ***Mus*** James Horner ***Art*** Barbara Dunphy

Act Mel Gibson, Nick Stahl, Margaret Whitton, Fay Masterson, Gaby Hoffmann, Geoffrey Lewis (Icon/Warner)

Mel Gibson's directing debut reinforces his status as a genuinely fine actor, a fact often lost amid the explosions and car crashes in the *Lethal Weapon* and *Mad Max* trilogies. This simple, sappy film lacks those flashy trappings but compensates with ample heart.

The action begins with a *Cinderella*-type setup: 12-year-old Chuck (fine newcomer Nick Stahl) lives in a Maine coastal village with his uninterested, often-married mother (Margaret Whitton) and two difficult half-sisters. Chuck dreams of getting into his late father's old military academy but has already failed the entrace exam. Needing a tutor, he enlists the aid of Mr. McLeod (Gibson), a gruff, mysterious recluse whose teaching career was ended by an accident that scarred him and took the life of one of his students. Script [from the novel by Isabelle Holland] comes off a bit sitcomish in the early going. Still, the words become more compelling as the action moves along, with Chuck finding a mentor and father figure while McLeod rekindles his contact with the outside world. In addition to the charm of the two main characters, the movie manages to glorify education without being heavy-handed and provides a wry take on the more "groovy" aspects of the late 1960s, when the action takes place.

•

MAN WITHOUT A STAR
1955, 89 mins, US Ⓥ ▭ col
Dir King Vidor ***Prod*** Aaron Rosenberg ***Scr*** Borden Chase, D. D. Beauchamp ***Ph*** Russell Metty ***Ed*** Virgil Vogel ***Mus*** Joseph Gershenson ***Art*** Alexander Golitzen, Richard H. Riedel
Act Kirk Douglas, Jeanne Crain, William Campbell, Claire Trevor, Richard Boone, Jay C. Flippen (Universal)

Kirk Douglas, in the title role, takes easily to the saddle as a tumbleweed cowpoke who has a way with a six-gun or the ladies. William Campbell scores as the young greenhorn who learns his cowboying from Douglas and about the wrong kind of women from Jeanne Crain.

The latter is technically skilled in her delineation of a ruthless owner of a big ranch, not above using sex in her determination to keep the range unfenced, but is not quite believable as a sexpot. Claire Trevor is in a character she does well, playing what is, by implication, the town madam with a heart of gold, and with a soft spot in it for the wandering Douglas.

The plot is basic western in this setup of open versus fenced land, but writing variations keep it fresh and the action high as things move towards the climax.

•

MAN WITH THE DEADLY LENS, THE
SEE: WRONG IS RIGHT

•

MAN WITH THE GOLDEN ARM, THE
1955, 119 mins, US Ⓥ b/w
Dir Otto Preminger ***Prod*** Otto Preminger ***Scr*** Walter Newman, Lewis Meltzer ***Ph*** Sam Leavitt ***Ed*** Louis Loeffler ***Mus*** Elmer Bernstein ***Art*** Joseph Wright
Act Frank Sinatra, Eleanor Parker, Kim Novak, Arnold Stang, Darren McGavin, Robert Strauss (Carlyle/United Artists)

Otto Preminger's *The Man with the Golden Arm* is a feature that focuses on addiction to narcotics. Clinical in its probing of the agonies, this is a gripping, fascinating film, expertly produced and directed and performed with marked conviction by Frank Sinatra as the drug slave. Sinatra returns to squalid Chicago haunts after six months in hospital where he was "cured" of his addiction. Thwarted in his attempt to land a job as a musician, he resumes as the dealer in a smalltime professional poker game.

Eleanor Parker is a pathetic figure as his wife, pretending to be chair-ridden for the sole purpose of making Sinatra stay by her side. A downstairs neighbor is Kim Novak, and the s.a. angles are not overlooked by the camera. Arnold Stang is Sparrow, Sinatra's subservient sidekick with the larcenous inclinations.

It's the story that counts most, however. Screenplay from the Nelson Algren novel, analyzes the drug addict with strong conviction. What goes on looks for real.

Novel titles are by Saul Bass, and the music by Elmer Bernstein deftly sets the mood.

1955: NOMINATIONS: Best Actor (Frank Sinatra), B&W Art Direction, Scoring of a Dramatic Picture

•

MAN WITH THE GOLDEN GUN, THE
1974, 123 mins, UK Ⓥ ⊙ ▭ col
Dir Guy Hamilton ***Prod*** Albert R. Broccoli, Harry Saltzman ***Scr*** Richard Maibaum, Tom Mankiewicz ***Ph*** Ted Moore, Oswald Morris ***Ed*** John Shirley, Raymond Poulton ***Mus*** John Barry ***Art*** Peter Murton
Act Roger Moore, Christopher Lee, Britt Ekland, Maud Adams, Herve Villechaize, Clifton James (United Artists/Eon)

Screenwriters' mission this ninth time around was to give the James Bond character more maturity, fewer gadgetry gimmicks, and more humor. On the last item [*Live and Let Die*, 1973] they fumbled badly; and the comparatively spare arrays of mechanical devices seem more a cost-cutting factor.

Story diverts Bond from tracking down a missing solar energy scientist towards the mission of locating mysterious international hit man (Christopher Lee) who uses tailor-made gold bullets on his contract victims. To nobody's surprise, Lee has the solar energy apparatus installed on his Hong Kong area island hideaway. Bond naturally conquers all obstacles, and finds some fadeout sack time for Britt Ekland, the local British intelligence charmer.

•

MAN WITH THE GREEN CARNATION, THE
SEE: THE TRIALS OF OSCAR WILDE

•

MAN WITH THE X-RAY EYES, THE
SEE: X

•

MAN WITH TWO BRAINS, THE
1983, 93 mins, US Ⓥ ⊙ col
Dir Carl Reiner ***Prod*** David V. Picker, William E. McEuen ***Scr*** Carl Reiner, Steve Martin, George Gipe ***Ph*** Michael Chapman ***Ed*** Bud Molin ***Mus*** Joel Goldsmith ***Art*** Polly Platt
Act Steven Martin, Kathleen Turner, David Warner, Paul Benedict, Richard Brestoff, James Cromwell (Aspen/Warner)

The Man with Two Brains is a fitfully amusing return by Steve Martin to the broad brand of lunacy that made his first feature, *The Jerk* [1979], so successful.

Plot is a frayed crazy quilt barely held together as if by clothespins. Ace neurosurgeon Martin almost kills beauteous Kathleen Turner in an auto accident, only to save her via his patented screwtop brain surgery technique. Turner proves to be a master at withholding her sexual favors from her frustrated husband, who decides to take her on a honeymoon to Vienna in an attempt to thaw her out.

While there, Martin visits the lab of colleague David Warner and meets the love of his life, a charming woman and marvelous conversationalist [voiced by Sissy Spacek] who also happens to be a disembodied brain suspended in a jar, her body having been the victim of a crazed elevator killer.

Much humor, of course, stems from the befuddled Martin groveling at the feet of the knockout Turner he comes to call a "scum queen," but too much of the film seems devoted to frantic overkill to compensate for general lack of belly laughs and top-notch inspiration.

Martin delivers all that's expected of him as a performer, and Turner is a sizzling foil for his comic and pent-up sexual energy.

•

MAN, WOMAN AND CHILD
1983, 99 mins, US Ⓥ col
Dir Dick Richards ***Prod*** Elmo Williams, Elliott Kastner ***Scr*** Erich Segal, David Z. Goodman ***Ph*** Richard H. Kline ***Ed*** David Bretherton ***Mus*** Georges Delerue ***Art*** Dean-Edward Mitzner
Act Martin Sheen, Blythe Danner, Sebastian Dungan, Arlene McIntyre, Missy Francis, David Hemmings (Paramount)

Man, Woman and Child is a sweetly dramatic picture which, unfortunately, reaches so hard for sobs at the end that all logic is suspended.

Despite the problems in the screenplay adaptation of Erich Segal's novel by Segal and David Z. Goodman, there are still some fine performances here, tautly directed.

Martin Sheen is superb as a happily married husband of Blythe Danner and father of Arlene McIntyre and Missy Francis. But trouble arrives with news that a brief fling of the past in France (seen in flashback with Nathalie Nell) has caused a problem for the present.

Nell has been killed in an accident, leaving a son by Sheen that he never knew about. For Sheen, the only decent thing to do is confess all to Danner and invite the boy to the U.S. for a get-acquainted visit.

Danner is also excellent in her hurt reaction, torn between love for her husband and resentment of the young intruder. Young Sebastian Dungan is a real discovery.

But *Man, Woman* concludes with one of those annoying film situations where the characters have several choices of what to do and select the one that makes the least sense.

•

MANXMAN, THE
1929, 98 mins, UK Ⓥ ⊗ b/w
Dir Alfred Hitchcock ***Prod*** John Maxwell ***Scr*** Eliot Stannard ***Ph*** Jack Cox ***Ed*** Emile de Ruelle ***Art*** C. Wilfred Arnold
Act Carl Brisson, Malcolm Keen, Anny Ondra, Randle Ayrton, Clare Greet (British International)

The Hall Caine novel from which this film was adapted is a weak one, but the director has done his best with it. All there is to the story is Pete, a fisherman, having Philip, an attorney, for a buddy; Pete being in love with Kate; getting the cold mitt from her father because he is poor, and going abroad to make money, leaving Kate in care of Philip. Inevitable results—or there would be no story at all—and Pete is said to be dead. Then he turns up and Philip persuades Kate her duty is to marry Pete.

More is actually got out of it by direction and sharply defined characterization than there is in the story. A fair amount of suspense is got into scenes between Pete and Kate arising out of the concealed parentage of the baby and the final revelation.

Minor parts are well cast. Acting comes best from Malcolm Keen, who makes Philip credible but vivid. Carl Brisson (Pete) falls down on dramatic moments. Anny Ondra (Kate) shows she has looks and trouping ability, a small blonde with plenty of s.a.

•

MAP OF THE HUMAN HEART
1993, 106 mins, UK/Australia/France/Canada Ⓥ ⊙ ▭ col
Dir Vincent Ward ***Prod*** Tim Bevan ***Scr*** Louis Nowra ***Ph*** Eduardo Serra ***Ed*** John Scott, George Akers ***Mus*** Gabriel Yared ***Art*** John Beard
Act Jason Scott Lee, Robert Joamie, Anne Parillaud, Patrick Bergin, John Cusack, Jeanne Moreau (Working Title/Ward/Ariane/Sunrise)

New Zealander Vincent Ward's third film is an immensely ambitious and audacious love story spanning 30 years and two continents. Much of it is set and filmed above the Arctic Circle in northern Canada, providing breathtaking icescapes for Eduardo Serra's camera.

The story unfolds in flashback, starting in 1965 as an old Innuit Eskimo tells a Yank mapmaker (a small role for John Cusack) his life story. Back in 1931, a vintage aircraft lands on the ice near the Innuit village, bringing with it dashing Brit, Walter Russell (Patrick Bergin), who intends to chart the area. He befriends Avik (Robert Joamie), a cheerful young Innuit, who later forms a close friendship with a half-French Canadian, half-Indian girl, Albertine (Annie Galipeau).

Ten years later, in 1941, Russell returns to the Arctic on a mission to track down a German U-boat and meets Avik (Jason Scott Lee) again. Hearing that Albertine (Anne Parillaud) is in Europe, Avik enlists in the Canadian air force. Subsequently, he takes part in the notorious bombing of Dresden. Pic's last act, set in the 1960s, records Avik's encounter with the daughter he never knew he had.

Ward [who wrote the story] and celebrated Australian playwright Louis Nowra evidently aimed to create one of those sweeping romantic sagas that are from time to time popular screen fare. They almost succeed, but more romantic passion would have helped.

[Version reviewed was 126-minute "work in progress" shown in a non-competing slot at Cannes in May 1992. Final 106-minute version featured new scenes in the middle of the pic—a romantic triangle played by Bergin, Lee and Parillaud—and a reshaped ending.]

•

MARATHON MAN
1976, 125 mins, US Ⓥ ⊙ col
Dir John Schlesinger ***Prod*** Robert Evans, Sidney Beckerman ***Scr*** William Goldman ***Ph*** Conrad Hall ***Ed*** Jim Clark ***Mus*** Michael Small ***Art*** Richard MacDonald
Act Dustin Hoffman, Laurence Olivier, Roy Scheider, William Devane, Marthe Keller, Fritz Weaver (Paramount)

Film spends literally half of its length getting some basic plot pieces [from the novel by William Goldman] fitted and moving. By which time it's asking a lot if anybody still cares why Dustin Hoffman's brother Roy Scheider is a mysterious globetrotter; why Laurence Olivier as an ex-Nazi disguises his appearance to leave a jungle hideaway to go to NY; why U.S. secret agent William Devane seems in league with Olivier and his goons, Richard Bright and Marc Lawrence; why Marthe Keller throws herself at Hoffman; why the memory of Hoffman's dishonored professor-father, a victim of the McCarthy era, relates to anything.

Hoffman, you see, is stuck in the role of a bewildered man-in-the-middle about whom bodies fall like flies; eventually he gets into the swing of things and kills a few on his own.

1976: NOMINATION: Best Supp. Actor (Laurence Olivier)

•

MARAT/SADE
SEE: THE PERSECUTION AND ASSASSINATION OF JEAN-PAUL MARAT AS PERFORMED BY THE INMATES OF THE ASYLUM OF CHARENTON UNDER THE DIRECTION OF THE MARQUIS DE SADE

•

MARCH OR DIE
1977, 106 mins, US Ⓥ col
Dir Dick Richards ***Prod*** Dick Richards, Jerry Bruckheimer ***Scr*** David Zelag Goodman ***Ph*** John Alcott ***Ed*** John C. Howard, Stanford C. Allen ***Mus*** Maurice Jarre ***Art*** Gil Parrondo
Act Gene Hackman, Terence Hill [= Mario Girotti], Max von Sydow, Catherine Deneuve, Ian Holm, Jack O'Halloran (ITC-Associated General)

This Foreign Legion adventure caper [from a screen story by David Zelag Goodman and Dick Richards], replete with international cast and crew, has lots of actionful battle scenes, a few squeamish torture scenes, and beautiful photography on actual locations.

Terence Hill, the Italian actor with the Yankee name, shows a tongue-in-cheek approach to his role that allows him to dominate every scene he's in. Also first rate is Britisher Ian Holm, as El Krim, the fanatic Arab chieftain.

Biggest disappointment is the "acting" of Gene Hackman who walks listlessly through the major role of a washed-out West Pointer who has given 16 years of his life to the Legion.

This is the film in which Hackman suffered a back injury but there's no indication of it. The most physical activity he undergoes is riding a horse.

•

MARE NOSTRUM
1926, 113 mins, US b/w
Dir Rex Ingram ***Prod*** Rex Ingram ***Scr*** Willis Goldbeck ***Ph*** John F. Seitz ***Ed*** Grant Whytock ***Art*** Ben Carre
Act Alice Terry, Antonio Moreno, Alex Nova (M-G-M)

Mare Nostrum (*Our Sea*) is a war picture. It's war stuff from a naval angle and not too potent in the telling.

Mare Nostrum was a book (by Blasco Ibanez); but those viewing it with no memories and an open mind are liable to find in the story many uninteresting passages plus the handicap of not a single principal character either demanding or holding sympathy. Thus almost immediately the "love interest" is debatable, inasmuch as the woman in the case, Freya (Alice Terry) is a German spy, and the man, Ulysses (Antonio Moreno), a Spanish sea captain who deserts his home for her.

Ingram remained abroad a long time to make this one, and few will deny that he has turned out a picturesque gem. Barcelona, Pompeii, Naples, Marseilles—they're all there "in the flesh," and it's pretty work. But landscapes can't and don't make a picture which runs about five minutes short of two hours.

•

MARGARET'S MUSEUM
1995, 114 mins, Canada/UK Ⓥ col
Dir Mort Ransen ***Prod*** Mort Ransen, Christopher Zimmer, Claudio Luca ***Scr*** Mort Ransen, Gerald Wexler ***Ph*** Vic Sarin ***Ed*** Rita Roy ***Mus*** Milan Kymlicka ***Art*** William Fleming
Act Helena Bonham Carter, Clive Russell, Craig Olejnik, Kate Nelligan, Kenneth Welsh, Andrea Morris (Ranfilm/Imagex/TeleAction/Skyline)

Featuring a remarkable performance from Helena Bonham Carter, *Margaret's Museum* is an emotionally charged story about one woman's fight against the tyranny of the coal mine in her tiny Nova Scotia community.

The script [from a short story by Sheldon Currie] takes a witheringly tough stance on the deadly toll exacted by life—and death—in the coal mines. The title refers to the shrine that Margaret MacNeil (Bonham Carter) builds to commemorate her dead family members, and this bizarre, ghoulish museum features various body parts preserved in all their gore. Story opens with Margaret's first encounter with her future husband, Neil Currie (Clive Russell). Margaret isn't swept off her feet by this unkempt fellow, but she is curious enough to bring him home to her mother (Kate Nelligan). Despite her mother's protests, Neil and Margaret marry after a steamy courtship. Everything is going fine until economic reality rears its ugly head and Neil announces he has to once again don the miner's helmet.

This is Bonham Carter's film from start to finish, and she delivers a stunning performance that's chock-full of emotion, sensuality and rage. Scottish thesp Russell is also first-rate. The only weak link is Nelligan as Margaret's mother in a one-dimensional performance.

•

MARIA'S LOVERS
1984, 100 mins, US Ⓥ ⊙ col
Dir Andrei Konchalovsky ***Prod*** Bosko Djordjevic, Lawrence Taylor-Mortorff ***Scr*** Gerard Brach, Andrei Konchalovsky, Paul Zindel, Marjorie David ***Ph*** Juan Ruiz-Anchia ***Ed*** Humphrey Dixon ***Mus*** Gary S. Remal ***Art*** Jeannine Oppewall
Act Nastassja Kinski, John Savage, Robert Mitchum, Keith Carradine, Anita Morris, Bud Cort (Cannon)

The first American feature film by Russian director Andrei Konchalovsky, *Maria's Lovers* is a turbulent, quite particularized period romance about the sometime lack of synchronization of love and sex.

Opening sequence makes use of excerpts from John Huston's great postwar U.S. Army documentary *Let There Be Light* to introduce the phenomenon of returning soldiers with psychological disabilities. Climaxing this is a mock verite interview with vet John Savage, who survived a Japanese prison camp and is terribly glad to be home in small-town Pennsylvania. His grizzled father Robert Mitchum gives Savage an understated welcome, and latter then has the misfortune of dropping by the home of his great love, Nastassja Kinski, just as she turns up in the grasp of another soldier, Vincent Spano.

Spano finally backs off, leaving the childhood sweethearts free to marry in a Russian Orthodox service.

Konchalovsky's storytelling proceeds at a smooth pace and contains certain interesting wrinkles, such as Mitchum's discouraging his son from pursuing Kinski because he himself is secretly interested in her.

•

MARI DE LA COIFFEUSE, LE
(THE HAIRDRESSER'S HUSBAND)
1990, 80 mins, France Ⓥ ⊙ ⌑ col
Dir Patrice Leconte ***Prod*** Thierry de Ganay ***Scr*** Patrice Leconte, Claude Kotz ***Ph*** Eduardo Serra ***Ed*** Joelle Hache ***Mus*** Michael Nyman ***Art*** Yvan Maussion
Act Jean Rochefort, Anna Galiena, Roland Bertin, Maurice Chevit, Philippe Clevenot, Jacques Mathou (Lambart/TF1)

The Hairdresser's Husband is another of director Patrice Leconte's original, hypnotic efforts about sexual longing and romantic obsession. Delicate and stylish, it's the story of a man who fulfills his childhood dream of marrying a lady hairdresser.

Intercut childhood scenes depict a 12-year-old with an aching crush on a plump hairdresser whose breast he spies through her clothes. Days later he finds her dead on the shop floor from a barbituate overdose. At age 50, still transfixed by her and by wildly dancing to Arabic music, he wanders into a barbershop and immediately proposes to its lovely owner, who accepts as quickly.

Both are loners. They live above the shop, which he, apparently jobless, inhabits all day while she works. In a madcap scene they get drunk on cologne and shaving lotion. Passionately in love, the lady barber frequently questions how long love will last.

Jean Rochefort is outstanding as the man obsessed. Anna Galiena, who has a beautiful model-type presence, is a dream come true as his lovely wife whose past never gets revealed. Excellent script leaves many details unexplained, such as Rochefort's adult background. But in this case, that just heightens the pic's dramatic punch.

•

MARIE
1985, 112 mins, US Ⓥ ⌑ col
Dir Roger Donaldson ***Prod*** Frank Capra, Jr. ***Scr*** John Briley ***Ph*** Chris Menges ***Ed*** Neil Travis, Tony Lawson ***Mus*** Francis Lai ***Art*** Ron Foreman
Act Sissy Spacek, Jeff Daniels, Keith Szarabajka, Morgan Freeman, Fred Thompson, Lisa Banes (De Laurentiis)

Marie is a powerfully made political melodrama, the many strengths of which are vitiated only by the relative familiarity of the expose, little person-vs.-the establishment framework. Sissy Spacek adds another excellent characterization to her credits.

Based on a book [*Marie: A True Story*] by Peter Maas, tale opens in 1968 with a rough scene in which Spacek and her small kids leave home after she is brutalized by her husband. Five years later, after educating herself further, she gets a job as extradition director and, before long, is appointed chairman of the parole board for the State of Tennessee.

Helping guide her up the twisting stairway of the political system is ostensible friend Jeff Daniels, a close aide of Governor Blanton who frequently comes to Spacek with overt suggestions that she speed through the parole of certain individuals.

John Briley has set the story down in cogent fashion, and director Donaldson has brought tremendous freshness to its telling.

Spacek is right at home with her role while Jeff Daniels is outstanding as her duplicitous associate.

•

MARIE ANTOINETTE
1938, 160 mins, US Ⓥ ⊙ b/w
Dir W. S. Van Dyke ***Prod*** Hunt Stromberg ***Scr*** Claudine West, Donald Ogden Stewart, Ernest Vajda ***Ph*** William Daniels ***Ed*** Robert J. Kern ***Mus*** Herbert Stothart ***Art*** Cedric Gibbons, William A. Horning, Edwin B. Willis
Act Norma Shearer, Tyrone Power, John Barrymore, Robert Morley, Anita Louise, Joseph Schildkraut (M-G-M)

Produced on a scale of incomparable splendor and extravagance, *Marie Antoinette* approaches real greatness as cinematic historical literature.

What is related on the screen is a brilliant, historic tragedy—the crushing of the French monarchy by revolution and terror. Stefan Zweig's biography of Marie Antoinette is the source from which the screenwriters have drawn most of their material.

First part is concerned with the vicious intrigues of the Versailles court and the power exerted by Mme. du Barry and the traitorous Orleans. The ensembles, arranged by Albertina Rasch, suggest beautiful paintings. Second portion opens with the expose of the fraudulent sale of a diamond necklace, which precipitated the enmity of the nobility. With an aroused nation and the queen as the point of attack, the action moves swiftly to the pillage of the castle, the royal arrest, the unsuccessful escape to the border, the trials and execution of the rulers.

Norma Shearer's performance is lifted by skillful portrayal of physical and mental transitions through the period of a score of years. Her moments of ardor with Ferson (Tyrone Power) are tender and believable. Outstanding in the acting, however, is Robert Morley, who plays the vacillating King Louis XVI. He creates sympathy and understanding for the kingly character, a dullard and human misfit.

John Barrymore as the aged Louis XV leaves a deep impress. Joseph Schildkraut is the conniving Duc d'Orleans and scores as a fastidious and scheming menace. Gladys George makes much from a few opportunities as Mme. du Barry.

When illness prevented Sidney Franklin from assuming the direction of the film after arduous preparation, W. S. Van Dyke was assigned the task.

1938: NOMINATIONS: Best Actress (Norma Shearer), Supp. Actor (Robert Morley), Art Direction, Original Score

•

MARIE WALEWSKA
SEE: CONQUEST

•

MARIUS
1931, 127 mins, France Ⓥ b/w
Dir Alexander Korda ***Prod*** Marcel Pagnol ***Scr*** Marcel Pagnol ***Ph*** Ted Pahle ***Ed*** R. Spiri-Mercanton ***Mus*** Francis Gromon ***Art*** Alfred Junge, Zoltan Korda
Act Raimu, Pierre Fresnay, Orane Demazis, Charpin, Alida Rouffe, Robert Vattier (Paramount-Joinville)

Made from a popular legit hit [by Marcel Pagnol], and acted by the same cast, the screen version is even better than the stage presentation. It shows the call of the sea acting on the son, Marius (Pierre Fresnay), of an innkeeper, Cesar (Raimu), whose sweetheart, Fanny (Orane Demazis), aids him to satisfy his craving for travel, despite that he has seduced her. It's a very clever mixture of gags peculiar to the Marseilles locale, and of pathos created by the girl's self-sacrifice.

Direction deliberately omits technical tricks. Continuity and dialog are both excellent, with camerawork excellent and sound fair.

Due to the fact that the cast has done the show several hundred times, the acting is unique in French pictures for naturalness, and without exception is of the highest order. Raimu, veteran stage actor, is better on the screen, and so is Fresnay. Demazis, whose personal beauty is not the main asset, is entirely different on the screen, having tremendous personality and charm. She is the outstanding personality of the picture.

Cost of this picture is said to be about $80,000.

[Pic was followed by *Fanny* and *Cesar*, to form a trilogy.]

•

MARJORIE MORNINGSTAR
1958, 125 mins, US Ⓥ col
Dir Irving Rapper ***Prod*** Milton Sperling ***Scr*** Everett Freeman ***Ph*** Harry Stradling ***Ed*** Folmar Blangsted ***Mus*** Max Steiner ***Art*** Malcolm Bert
Act Gene Kelly, Natalie Wood, Claire Trevor, Everett Sloane, Martin Milner, Ed Wynn (Warner/Beachwold)

There was in the original bestseller of Herman Wouk an attempt to isolate and examine a particular segment of American life, the upper-middle-class Jewish stratum of Manhattan. Producer Milton Sperling has kept some aspects of the original idea, the characters are still part of their racial and religious background, but the Jewish flavor has been watered down.

Natalie Wood gives a glowing and touching performance as the title heroine. Gene Kelly is moving as her romantic vis-a-vis, Claire Trevor and Everett Sloane are strong in support and Martin Milner is an important younger leading man. Ed Wynn is the standout as Marjorie's Uncle Samson.

The title is the clue to the story. When Marjorie changes her name from Morgenstern to Morningstar, she unwittingly cuts herself off from her Jewish background and plunges without support into a world of no visible connections and even less stability. She falls in love with Kelly, one of those fascinating men of small talent who flourish in the theatrical fringe of Broadway. He has changed his name, too, and the resulting rootlessness has left him uneasy and unsatisfied, although he never truly understands why. Marjorie caroms from his rejection to a doctor (Martin Balsam). Always standing by is hardworking playwright Milner.

1958: NOMINATION: Best Song ("A Very Precious Love")

•

MARKED FOR DEATH

1990, 94 mins, US Ⓥ ⊙ col

Dir Dwight H. Little ***Prod*** Michael Grais, Mark Victor, Steven Seagal ***Scr*** Michael Grais, Mark Victor ***Ph*** Ric Waite ***Ed*** O. Nicholas Brown ***Mus*** James Newton Howard ***Art*** Robb Wilson King

Act Steven Seagal, Basil Wallace, Keith David, Tom Wright, Joanna Pacula, Elizabeth Gracen (Victor & Grais)

This dim-witted revenge yarn is the simplest of showcases for Steven Seagal—an extremely compelling action presence with his brutal martial arts fighting style, imposing size and nasty demeanor.

It would be hard to imagine a more straightforward plot: former Drug Enforcement Agency troubleshooter Hatcher (Seagal) quits his job and goes home to visit his family. At the local tavern, he crosses a group of Jamaican drug dealers who mark him and his family for death. Naturally, he has to kill the leader to protect his loved ones. The leader of the drug "posse," Screwface (Basil Wallace), practices voodoo and sports braids.

The twist in Seagal's pics is that there's usually some sort of liberal bent—here Hatcher's statement that the drug war has been for naught—in contrast to the right-wing leanings of many other films in the genre. He also has a penchant for black sidekicks, here a former Army buddy (Keith David).

Seagal fans aren't likely to be disappointed, since director Dwight H. Little keeps the pedal to the metal. Beyond the incumbent violence there's a fair amount of nudity in the film.

•

MARKED WOMAN

1937, 96 mins, US Ⓥ ⊙ b/w

Dir Lloyd Bacon ***Prod*** Louis F. Edelman ***Scr*** Robert Rosson, Abem Finkel ***Ph*** George Barnes ***Ed*** Jack Killifer ***Mus*** David Raksin ***Art*** Max Parker

Act Bette Davis, Humphrey Bogart, Isabel Jewell, Eduardo Ciannelli, Lola Lane, Jane Bryan (Warner)

Marked Woman has no romance to sell. This is a hard-hitting yarn of five girls working for a vice king.

Bette Davis's performance is rife with subtleties of expression and gesture. Davis occasionally walks around in unbecoming guise, plus a hospital sequence where she is viewed after having been beaten up by one of the vice king's hirelings. There is nothing pretty about these shots but there also can be no question that they belong.

The five girls are hostesses in an elaborate clip-joint with Davis the only one with any intention of eventually breaking away. Meanwhile, she's reconciled to playing her chips until she can accumulate enough dough to get out. Entanglement, and the death, of her kid sister at the hands of Vanning, the boss, arouses her and the four other girls to become witnesses in the trial which washes him up.

Humphrey Bogart is the prosecuting attorney and again capable. His solicitude for the ringleader of the girls, whom he wants to see get a break after the trial, is the closest the yarn comes to love interest

•

MARK OF ZORRO, THE

1940, 93 mins, US ▭ b/w

Dir Rouben Mamoulian ***Prod*** [Raymond Griffith] ***Scr*** John Taintor Foote ***Ph*** Arthur Miller ***Ed*** Robert Bischoff ***Mus*** Alfred Newman ***Art*** Richard Day, Joseph C. Wright

Act Tyrone Power, Linda Darnell, Basil Rathbone, Gale Sondergaard, Eugene Pallette, J. Edward Bromberg (20th Century-Fox)

In the 1920s Douglas Fairbanks started his series of historical super-spectacles with *The Mark of Zorro*, a tale of early California under Spanish rule, adapted from Johnston McCulley's story, *The Curse of Capistrano*. In the remake [adapted by Garrett Fort and Bess Meredyth] 20th-Fox inducts Tyrone Power into the lead spot.

The colorful background, detailing Los Angeles as little more than a pueblo settlement under the Spanish flag, is utilized for some thrilling melodramatics. In the early portion picture drags considerably, but once it gets up steam, it rolls along with plenty of action and, despite its obvious formula of hooded Robin Hood who terrorizes the tax-biting officials of the district to finally triumph for the peons and caballeros, picture holds plenty of entertainment.

Power is not Fairbanks (the original screen Hood) but, fortunately, neither the script nor direction forces him to any close comparison. He's plenty heroic and sincere in his mission.

After an extensive education in the Spanish army in Madrid, Power returns to California to find his father displaced as Alcalde of Los Angeles by thieving J. Edward Bromberg. Latter, with aid of post captain Basil Rathbone and his command, terrorizes the district and piles on burdensome taxes. Power embarks on a one-man Robin Hoodian campaign of wild riding and rapier-wielding to clean up the situation and restore his father to his rightful position. And there's a sweet romance with Linda Darnell, niece of Bromberg, who is unsympathetic to his policies. Sword duel between Power and Rathbone, running about two minutes, is a dramatic highlight.

1940: NOMINATION: Best Original Score

•

MARLOWE

1969, 95 mins, US Ⓥ col

Dir Paul Bogart ***Prod*** Gabriel Katzka, Sidney Beckerman ***Scr*** Stirling Silliphant ***Ph*** William H. Daniels ***Ed*** Gene Ruggiero ***Mus*** Peter Matz ***Art*** George W. Davis, Addison Hehr

Act James Garner, Gayle Hunnicutt, Carroll O'Connor, Rita Moreno, Sharon Farrell, Bruce Lee (Cherokee/M-G-M)

Raymond Chandler's private eye character, Philip Marlowe, is in need of better handling if he is to survive as a screen hero. *Marlowe*, is a plodding, unsure piece of so-called sleuthing in which James Garner can never make up his mind whether to play it for comedy or hardboil. Stirling Silliphant's adaptation of *The Little Sister* comes out on the confused side, with too much unexplained action. Garner as the private eye is hired by a girl from Kansas to find her missing brother, then finds himself involved in a maze in which he's as mystified as the spectator.

Garner walks through the picture mostly with knotted brow, but Gayle Hunnicutt as the actress is nice to look at toward the end. Rita Moreno as a strip dancer delivers soundly, but a peeler does not a picture make.

•

MARNIE

1964, 130 mins, US Ⓥ ⊙ col

Dir Alfred Hitchcock ***Prod*** Alfred Hitchcock ***Scr*** Jay Presson Allen ***Ph*** Robert Burks ***Ed*** George Tomasini ***Mus*** Bernard Herrmann ***Art*** Robert Boyle

Act Tippi Hedren, Sean Connery, Diane Baker, Martin Gabel, Louise Latham, Bruce Dern (Universal)

Marnie is the character study of a thief and a liar, but what makes her tick remains clouded even after a climax reckoned to be shocking but somewhat missing its point.

Tippi Hedren, whom Hitchcock intro'd in *The Birds*, returns in a particularly demanding role and Sean Connery makes his American film bow, as the two principal protagonists in this adaptation of Winston Graham's bestseller. Complicated story line offers Hedren as a sexy femme who takes office jobs, then absconds with as much cash as she can find in the safe, changing color of her tresses and obtaining new employment for similar purposes. Plot becomes objective when she is recognized by her new employer, book publisher Connery, as the girl who stole $10,000 from a business associate, and rather than turn her in marries her.

That's merely the beginning, and balance of unfoldment dwells on husband's efforts to ferret mystery on why she recoils from the touch of any man—himself included—and why other terrors seem to overcome her. Hedren, undertaking role originally offered Grace Kelly for a resumption of her screen career, lends credence to a part never sympathetic. It's a difficult assignment which she fulfills satisfactorily, although Hitchcock seldom permits her a change of pace which would have made her character more interesting. Connery handles himself convincingly, but here, again, greater interest would have resulted from greater facets of character as he attempts to explore femme's unexplained past.

•

MAROONED

1969, 134 mins, US Ⓥ ▭ col

Dir John Sturges ***Prod*** Mike Frankovich ***Scr*** Mayo Simon ***Ph*** Daniel Fapp ***Ed*** Walter Thompson ***Mus*** [none] ***Art*** R. Wheeler

Act Gregory Peck, Richard Crenna, David Janssen, James Franciscus, Gene Hackman, Lee Grant (Columbia)

What happens when a lunar rocket fails to fire for reentry to earth's gravity? The men on such a capsule become lost in space. Such is the situation presented in the gripping drama, *Marooned*, a film [based on a novel by Martin Cardin] which is part documentary, part science fiction. The film is superbly crafted, taut and a technological cliff-hanger.

The production's major flaw is a hokey, old-fashioned Hollywood Renfrew-to-the-rescue climax that is dramatically, logically and technologically unconvincing.

For the first four-fifths of his mission, director John Sturges fashions spectacular documentary footage of launchings, on location work at Cape Kennedy, special effects, studio set-ups and scenes on close-circuit TV into an edge-of-the-seat drama in which personalities and human conflicts are never subordinated to the hardware.

1969: Best Special Visual Effects

NOMINATIONS: Best Cinematography, Sound

•

MARRIAGE-GO-ROUND, THE

1960, 98 mins, US ▭ col

Dir Walter Lang ***Prod*** Leslie Stevens ***Scr*** Leslie Stevens ***Ph*** Leo Tover ***Ed*** Jack W. Holmes ***Mus*** Dominic Frontiere ***Art*** Duncan Cramer, Maurice Ransford

Act Susan Hayward, James Mason, Julie Newmar, Robert Paige, June Clayworth (20th Century-Fox)

Something appears to have gone wrong somewhere between Broadway, where *The Marriage-Go-Round* sustained itself as a hit play from October 1958 to February 1960, and Hollywood, where it is just a rather tame and tedious film. There isn't a great deal of novelty or merriment in the Leslie production, which Stevens adapted from his own play.

It rotates laboriously around one joke—the idea that an amorous Amazonian doll from Sweden would match endowments, gene for gene, with a brilliant cultural anthropology professor from the U.S. Since the prof is a happily married monogamist, Miss Sweden's forward pass is intercepted right in the shadow of the goal (of bed) posts.

In the role of the professor, James Mason is competent, managing to stay reasonably appealing in a perpetual state of mild flabbergastedness. Susan Hayward does exceptionally well in the role of the wife. Julie Newmar, who won the Antoinette Perry Award as best supporting actress for her Broadway performance as the gregarious glamorpuss from Scandinavia, appears to have misplaced her award-winning attributes. The intimacy of larger-than-life celluloid reveals a queen-sized heap of overacting from the blonde bombshell.

•

MARRIAGE OF A YOUNG STOCKBROKER, THE

1971, 95 mins, US Ⓥ col

Dir Lawrence Turman ***Prod*** Lawrence Turman ***Scr*** Lorenzo Semple, Jr. ***Ph*** Laszlo Kovacs ***Ed*** Fredric Steinkamp ***Mus*** Fred Karlin ***Art*** Pato Guzman

Act Richard Benjamin, Joanna Shimkus, Elizabeth Ashley, Adam West, Patricia Barry, Tiffany Bolling (20th Century-Fox)

Based on a Charles Webb novel, the Lorenzo Semple, Jr., adaptation features Richard Benjamin as a dull husband given to casual voyeurism, and Joanna Shimkus as his equally confused wife. The bittersweet emotional drama unfolds in parallel with some superb high and low comedy.

Benjamin and Shimkus have an all-too-true marital blandness, disrupted by his predilection for eyeing girls. The hang-up is nowhere near criminal; in fact it's rather innocent. But Shimkus has had it, and packs off to Pasadena where barracuda sister Elizabeth Ashley, who already has emasculated hubby Adam West, begins stage-managing a divorce.

Semple's script is well structured and the dialog is superb. The varying elements of farce and satire are neatly interwoven on the genuine marital tragedy in progress. No element overpowers another nor the overall feel. Lawrence Turman's direction is incisive.

•

MARRIED TO IT

1992, 110 mins, US Ⓥ ⊙ col

Dir Arthur Hiller ***Prod*** Thomas Baer ***Scr*** Janet Kovalcik ***Ph*** Victor Kemper ***Ed*** Robert C. Jones ***Mus*** Henry Mancini ***Art*** Robert Gundlach

Act Beau Bridges, Stockard Channing, Robert Sean Leonard, Mary Stuart Masterson, Cybill Shepherd, Ron Silver (Orion/Three Pair)

Auds seeking the wit and polish or an Alan Alda on Neil Simon adult ensemble comedy dealing with the ups and downs of marriage will do best to move on. This Arthur Hiller-directed version unfolds with an unaccountable clumsiness.

Story brings together three couples who gain perspective on their relationships through the course of their friendship. Problem here is one can never figure out why they're friends.

Mary Stuart Masterson and Robert Sean Leonard are the baby yuppies on the move. Born in 1966, these well-heeled "new traditionalists" actually have been a couple since they were eight years old. Stockard Channing and Beau Bridges also were born in the 1960s—ideologically. Today he's still a welfare caseworker, and she's a homemaker for their teenage sons. Ron Silver and Cybill Shepherd are more of a crowd than a couple, given that his 13-year-old daughter and angry ex-wife are pretty much running their relationship—into the ground.

Pic's most effective scenes are the knockdown fights about emotional issues, which finally give the actors something to get their teeth into. Hiller's direction is often slapdash, particularly in the final reel. Film was lensed in Toronto and New York, where former mayor Ed Koch pops up in a party scene cameo.

●

MARRIED TO THE MOB

1988, 103 mins, US Ⓥ ⊙ col

Dir Jonathan Demme **Prod** Kenneth Utt, Edward Saxon **Scr** Barry Strugatz, Mark R. Burns **Ph** Tak Fujimoto **Ed** Craig McKay **Mus** David Byrne **Art** Kristi Zea

Act Michelle Pfeiffer, Matthew Modine, Dean Stockwell, Mercedes Ruehl, Alec Baldwin, Joan Cusack (Mysterious Arts/Orion)

Fresh, colorful and inventive, *Married to the Mob* is another offbeat entertainment from director Jonathan Demme.

Story line's basic trajectory has unhappy suburban housewife Michelle Pfeiffer taking the opportunity presented by the sudden death of her husband, who happens to have been a middle-level gangster, to escape the limitations of her past and forge a new life for herself and her son in New York City.

Opening with a hit on a commuter train and following with some murderous bedroom shenanigans, film establishes itself as a suburban gangster comedy. Demme and his enthusiastic collection of actors take evident delight in sending up the gauche excesses of these particular nouveau riches, as the men strut about in their pinstripes and polyester and the women spend their time at the salon getting their hair teased.

The enormous cast is a total delight, starting with Pfeiffer, with hair dyed dark, a New York accent and a continuously nervous edge. Matthew Modine proves winning as the seemingly inept FBI functionary who grows into his job, and Dean Stockwell is a hoot as the unflappable gangland boss, slime under silk and a fedora.

1988: NOMINATION: Best Supp. Actor (Dean Stockwell)

●

MARRYING KIND, THE

1952, 92 mins, US b/w

Dir George Cukor **Prod** Bert Granet **Scr** Ruth Gordon, Garson Kanin **Ph** Joseph Walker **Ed** Charles Nelson **Mus** Hugo Friedhofer **Art** John Meehan

Act Judy Holliday, Aldo Ray, Madge Kennedy, Sheila Bond, John Alexander, Mickey Shaughnessy (Columbia)

Judy Holliday's first film vehicle since *Born Yesterday* is a melange of marital errors. It introduces Aldo Ray, previously in *Saturday's Hero*, as Holliday's partner. He is equipped with a trick voice of the same raspy tonal quality as the actress's.

The plot gets underway in a divorce court with a kindly judge, played by Madge Kennedy, former silent-screen name, trying to effect a reconciliation between Holliday and Ray, through talking out their troubles and misunderstandings. Footage then becomes a series of dialog-laden flashbacks, taking the couple back.

●

MARRYING MAN, THE

(UK/AUSTRALIA: TOO HOT TO HANDLE)

1991, 115 mins, US Ⓥ ⊙ col

Dir Jerry Rees **Prod** David Permut **Scr** Neil Simon **Ph** Donald E. Thorin **Ed** Michael Jablow **Mus** David Newman **Art** William F. Matthews

Act Kim Basinger, Alec Baldwin, Robert Loggia, Elisabeth Shue, Armand Assante, Paul Reiser (Hollywood/Silver Screen Partners IV)

The Marrying Man is a stillborn romantic comedy of staggering ineptitude. Author Neil Simon reportedly disowned this film. An awkward flashback structure tells of egotistical toothpaste heir Alec Baldwin falling in love with chanteuse Kim Basinger on an outing in 1948 with his buddies to Las Vegas.

Instead of marrying his beautiful g.f. back in LA (Elisabeth Shue), Baldwin is forced into a shotgun wedding with Basinger by Armand Assante as Bugsy Siegel, Basinger's main man. Key plot point is that this is Bugsy's "revenge" for catching Baldwin in the sack with his g.f. Also unbelievable are the duo's several breakups and remarriages.

Lack of chemistry between the two principals is only the first problem with *Marrying Man.* Obvious reshoots result in an unwieldy package that has the film climaxing with perhaps thirty minutes to go, making it play like an original and a sequel spliced together.

●

MARS ATTACKS!

1996, 103 mins, US Ⓥ ⊙ ▭

Dir Tim Burton **Prod** Tim Burton, Larry Franco **Scr** Jonathan Gems **Ph** Peter Suschitzky **Ed** Chris Lebenzon **Mus** Danny Elfman **Art** Wynn Thomas

Act Jack Nicholson, Glenn Close, Annette Bening, Pierce Brosnan, Danny DeVito, Martin Short (Warner)

A goofy cultural artifact, Tim Burton's *Mars Attacks!* is a cult sci-fi comedy miscast as an elaborate, all-star studio extravaganza. Continually inventive, parodistic sendup of alien invasion movies, based on some rare Topps trading cards of the early '60s, owes its style to genre classics of the '50s and possesses a quirky, somewhat facetious insider tone that will appeal to specialized student-age audiences and older SF fans.

During the initial half-hour, as the world awaits the Martians' landing, an assortment of characters in three distinct locations present themselves. In Kansas, there is a trailer-home family (Jack Black, Lukas Haas). In Las Vegas, a sleazy hotel entrepreneur (Jack Nicholson) is hatching a scheme for the biggest hotel on the Strip while his wife (Annette Bening) swears off booze.

But the main action is in the White House, where a gung-ho general (Rod Steiger), looking like Mussolini, and the first lady (Glenn Close) urge the prez (also played by Nicholson) to nuke the visitors posthaste, while a pipe-smoking scientific advisor (Pierce Brosnan) assures everyone of the Martians' undoubted civility and goodwill.

When the big day arrives, the Martian spokesthing assures the crowd that they come in peace—and then abruptly leads its cohorts in deep-frying the assembled humans with ray guns.

Script by British playwright Jonathan Gems, who worked closely with Burton in developing the storyline, serves up any number of sweetly subversive scenes, such as presidential advisor Martin Short's use of the White House's Kennedy Room for his fateful assignation with the voluptuous Martian Girl (Lisa Marie). But the picture is lacking in the uproarious humor that might well have ensued from the material.

Creatures were computer-generated, and interact with utter precision with the human actors.

●

MARTIN

1978, 95 mins, US Ⓥ ⊙ col

Dir George A. Romero **Prod** Richard Rubinstein **Scr** George A. Romero **Ph** Michael Gornick **Ed** George A. Romero **Mus** Donald Rubinstein

Act John Amplas, Lincoln Maazel, Christine Forrest, Elayne Nadeau, Tom Savini (Braddock/Laurel)

Title character in *Martin* is a supposed 84-year-old vampire whose youthful visage has survived his escape from Romania through his contemporary journey to Braddock, PA, where grandfather Lincoln Maazel is determined to drive out "Nosferatu," with Martin as the last remaining relative afflicted with the family curse.

This urban vampire kills not with his teeth, but with prepackaged razor blades, neatly slicing veins and arteries for his mealtime pleasure.

Pittsburgh-based auteur George A. Romero is still limited by apparently low budgets. But he has inserted some sepia-toned flashback scenes of Martin in Romania that are extraordinarily evocative, and his direction of the victimization scenes shows a definite flair for suspense.

●

MARTY

1955, 93 mins, US Ⓥ ⊙ b/w

Dir Delbert Mann **Prod** Harold Hecht **Scr** Paddy Chayefsky **Ph** Joseph LaShelle **Ed** Alan Crosland, Jr. **Mus** Roy Webb, George Bassman **Art** Edward S. Haworth, Walter Simonds

Act Ernest Borgnine, Betsy Blair, Esther Minciotti, Augusta Ciolli, Joe Mantell, Karen Steele (Hecht-Lancaster/United Artists)

Based on Paddy Chayefsky's teleplay, and screenplayed by the author, *Marty* has been fashioned into a sock picture. It's a warm, human, sometimes sentimental and an enjoyable experience. Although filmed on a modest budget (reportedly about $300,000), there is no evidence of any stinting in the production values.

Basically, it's the story of a boy and girl, both of whom consider themselves misfits in that they are unable to attract members of the opposite sex. The boy is sensitively played by Ernest Borgnine and the girl is beautifully played by Betsy Blair.

Chayefsky has caught the full flavor of bachelor existence in a Bronx Italian neighborhood. The meetings at a bar and grill, the stag-attended dances, the discussions about girls and "what do we do tonight?" poser ring with authenticity.

1955: Best Picture, Director, Actor (Ernest Borgnine), Screenplay

NOMINATIONS: Best Supp. Actor (Joe Mantell), Supp. Actress (Betsy Blair), B&W Cinematography, B&W Art Direction

●

MARUSA NO ONNA

(A TAXING WOMAN)

1987, 127 mins, Japan Ⓥ ⊙ col

Dir Juzo Itami **Prod** Yasushi Tamaoki, Seigo Hosogoe **Scr** Juzo Itami **Ph** Yonezo Maeda **Ed** Akira Suzuki **Mus** Toshiyuki Honda **Art** Shuji Nakamura

Act Nobuko Miyamoto, Tsutomu Yamazaki, Masahiko Tsugawa, Hideo Murato, Shuji Otaki, Daisuke Yamashita (Itami/New Century)

The taxing woman of the title is that in two respects. First of all, she is a tax inspector, and a most dedicated one, but she is also taxing, since she never tires or lets go of her prey, once she has set her sights on him. The victim, in this case, is a hood operating adult motels and crooked real estate deals.

In the tradition of the American thriller, but far more humorously put, the heroine is single, exclusively dedicated to her job, a tough cookie in remarkably feminine wrapping. Nobuko Miyamoto, who plays the part, happens to be Itami's wife, and she fits the role to perfection. Her running duel with Tsutomu Yamazaki, as the limping gangster she chases, holds plenty of twists and surprises, as new plots and tricks for beating the tax rap are introduced and one by one unveiled by the law.

Tighter than his first film, *The Funeral*, and better constructed than *Tampopo*, *The Taxing Woman* drives relentlessly forward, mixing social satire with action and sex, if anything piling it a bit too much for one film, and that in spite of the fact Itami says he used barely one-tenth of the material he collected in his extensive research.

●

MARVIN'S ROOM

1996, 98 mins, US Ⓥ ⊙ col

Dir Jerry Zaks **Prod** Scott Rudin, Jane Rosenthal, Robert De Niro **Scr** Scott McPherson **Ph** Piotr Sobocinski **Ed** Jim Clark **Mus** Rachel Portman **Art** David Gropman

Act Meryl Streep, Leonardo DiCaprio, Diane Keaton, Robert De Niro, Hume Cronyn, Gwen Verdon (Tribeca/Miramax)

The most interesting aspect of *Marvin's Room*, an intimate exploration of familial sacrifice and love, is observing Diane Keaton, Meryl Streep and Leonardo DiCaprio effectively submerge their idiosyncratic talents and personas in an effort to portray ordinary, down-to-Earth individuals.

Originally produced by Chicago's Goodman Theatre in 1990, and later in New York, *Marvin's Room* is a personal play by Scott McPherson, who died of AIDS in 1992, at the age of 33. Thematically, the narrative bears strong resemblance to Beth Henley's *Crimes of the Heart* and Arthur Miller's *The Price*.

Bessie (Keaton) is a sensitive, middle-aged woman in Orlando, FL, taking care of her dying father, Marvin (Hume Cronyn), and eccentric aunt (Gwen Verdon). Her younger sister Lee (Streep) is a tough divorcee, raising rebellious Hank (DiCaprio) and quieter brother Charlie (Hal Scardino). The two sisters have not spoken or written to each other for 20 years. A reunion of sorts is forced upon them when Bessie is diagnosed by Dr. Wally (Robert De Niro) as having leukemia.

Truly collaborating, rather than competing, Keaton and Streep render brilliant performances. Rest of the cast is flawless, including a back-in-form DiCaprio as the troubled teen who hits it off with his aunt.

1996: NOMINATION: Best Actress (Diane Keaton)

•

MARY OF SCOTLAND

1936, 123 mins, US Ⓥ ⊙ b/w

Dir John Ford ***Prod*** Pandro S. Berman ***Scr*** Dudley Nichols ***Ph*** Joseph H. August ***Ed*** Jane Loring ***Mus*** Nathaniel Shilkret ***Art*** Van Nest Polglase, Carroll Clark

Act Katharine Hepburn, Fredric March, Florence Eldridge, Douglas Walton, John Carradine, Robert Barrat (RKO)

When RKO set about the task of transmuting this Maxwell Anderson-Theatre Guild play to the screen, it had two possibilities, Could have softened the story and played up the business of a woman who threw away her kingdom for love and thus sold the picture as sheer entertainment; or it could have taken the hard way, telling the story beautifully, artistically, delicately, with meticulous attention to detail and portrayal. Having decided to do it the latter way, there can be nothing but credit to the production.

The really curious point about the film is its casting. On the face of it, Katharine Hepburn would seem to be the wrong choice for the character of the Scots queen. She is nowhere as hard as she should be, she nowhere shows the strength of courage and decision that the school-books talk of. And that is all in the film's favor because it humanizes it all.

Fredric March as Hepburn's vis-a-vis in the role of the swashbuckling Bothwell is a natural and excellent choice, playing the slapdash earl to the hilt. Florence Eldridge as Elizabeth is again a questionable choice from a strict historical standpoint. She, too, turns in such a fine acting job as to convince quite definitely of the wisdom of it.

In handling the photography and physical production, Ford put emphasis on shadows, several times achieving surprisingly strong effects.

•

MARY POPPINS

1964, 140 mins, US Ⓥ ⊙ col

Dir Robert Stevenson ***Prod*** Walt Disney ***Scr*** Bill Walsh, Don Da Gradi ***Ph*** Edward Colman ***Ed*** Cotton Warburton ***Mus*** Irwin Kostal (sup.) ***Art*** Carroll Clark, William H. Tuntke, Tony Walton

Act Julie Andrews, Dick Van Dyke, David Tomlinson, Glynis Johns, Hermione Baddeley, Ed Wynne (Walt Disney)

Disney has gone all-out in his dream-world rendition [from the books by P. L. Travers] of a magical Engish nanny who one day arrives on the East Wind and takes over the household of a very proper London banker.

Besides changing the lives of everyone therein, she introduces his two younger children to wonders imagined and possible only in fantasy. Among a spread of outstanding songs [by Richard M. and Robert B. Sherman] perhaps the most unusual is "Chim-Chim-Cher-ee," sung by Dick Van Dyke, which carries a haunting quality. Dancing also plays an important part in unfolding the story and one number, the Chimney-Sweep Ballet, performed on the roofs of London and with Van Dyke starring, is a particular standout. For sheer entertainment, a sequence mingling live-action and animation in which Van Dyke dances with four little penguin-waiters is immense.

Julie Andrews's first appearance on the screen is a signal triumph and she performs as easily as she sings, displaying a fresh type of beauty nicely adaptable to the color cameras. Van Dyke, as the happy-go-lucky jack-of-all-trades, scores heavily, the part permitting him to showcase his wide range of talents.

1964: Best Actress (Julie Andrews), Song ("Chim-Chim-Cher-ee"), Original Musical Scoring, Editing, Visual Effects

NOMINATIONS: Best Picture, Director, Adapted Screenplay, Color Cinematography, Color Costume Design, Color Art Direction, Adapted Music Score, Sound

•

MARY, QUEEN OF SCOTS

1972, 128 mins, UK/US ▭ col

Dir Charles Jarrott ***Prod*** Hal B. Wallis ***Scr*** John Hale ***Ph*** Christopher Challis ***Ed*** Richard Marden ***Mus*** John Barry ***Art*** Terence Marsh

Act Vanessa Redgrave, Glenda Jackson, Patrick McGoohan, Timothy Dalton, Nigel Davenport, Trevor Howard (Universal)

A large cast of excellent players appears to good advantage under the direction of Charles Jarrott. Superior production details and the cast help overcome an episodic, rambling story.

Mary Stuart (Vanessa Redgrave) emerges as a romantic, immature but idealistic young woman. Her perilous position was repeatedly confounded by the machinations of half-brother (later King) James Stuart (played by Patrick McGoohan), the blunt but well-meant efforts of eventual husband and lover Lord Bothwell (Nigel Davenport), the paranoid homosexual, and bisexual inclinations of second husband Henry Darnley (Timothy Dalton), and the low-key, amiable clerical advisor, David Riccio (Ian Holm).

Elizabeth (Glenda Jackson) in contrast had a well-oiled machine of intrigue: advisor William Cecil (Trevor Howard), a power-hungry lover Robert Dudley (Daniel Massey), and the corrupt cooperation of McGoohan and other Scottish factions.

The result of such a dramatic imbalance renders Redgrave's character that of a storm-tossed waif, while Jackson benefits from a far more well-defined character.

The face-to-face confrontations between the two women are said to be historically inaccurate. The script almost has to have one, and these brief climactic encounters are electric.

1971: NOMINATIONS: Best Actress (Vanessa Redgrave), Costume Design, Art Direction, Original Score, Sound

•

MARY REILLY

1996, 108 mins, US Ⓥ col

Dir Stephen Frears ***Prod*** Ned Tanen, Nancy Graham Tanen, Norma Heyman ***Scr*** Christopher Hampton ***Ph*** Philippe Rousselot ***Ed*** Lesley Walker ***Mus*** George Fenton ***Art*** Stuart Craig

Act Julia Roberts, John Malkovich, George Cole, Michael Gambon, Kathy Staff, Glenn Close (Tri-Star)

Atempting a Gothic-romance slant on the legend of Jekyll and Hyde, *Mary Reilly* has plenty of production polish but little of the dramatic force and erotic spark needed to vivify a tale of the famous split personality and his young chambermaid. Christopher Hampton's tepid and unfocused adaptation of Valerie Martin's novel (fans of Jekyll/Hyde creator Robert Louis Stevenson will probably be relieved that he receives nary a mention here) is the obvious source of many problems.

In the era of Jack the Ripper and gaslight, Mary (Julia Roberts) is a new addition to the household staff of Dr. Jekyll (John Malkovich), a saturnine recluse. The doctor begins to take the maid into his confidence, putting her in a privileged position that increasingly riles the staff's crusty head, Mr. Poole (George Cole).

Mary eventually reveals a horrific childhood incident in which her father locked her in a cupboard with a ravenous rat. Implicitly, that trauma left the young woman with a divided image of men that is eventually mirrored in her employer, who cryptically informs his servants that they are to tolerate the nocturnal ramblings of his new assistant, Mr. Hyde.

Script devotes entirely too much time to turgid exposition and never develops the parallels between Mary's mindset and Jekyll's beyond the rudimentary stage. Roberts tries hard and manages a convincing plaintiveness, but such a plain Jane is hardly her strong suit, and she gets little help from Malkovich.

•

MARY SHELLEY'S FRANKENSTEIN

See: Frankenstein (1994)

•

MASH

1970, 116 mins, US Ⓥ ⊙ ▭ col

Dir Robert Altman ***Prod*** Ingo Preminger ***Scr*** Ring Lardner, Jr. ***Ph*** Harold E. Stine ***Ed*** Danford B. Greene ***Mus*** Johnny Mandel ***Art*** Jack Martin Smith, Arthur Lonergan

Act Donald Sutherland, Elliott Gould, Tom Skerritt, Sally Kellerman, Jo Ann Pflug, Robert Duvall (20th Century-Fox/Aspen)

A Mobile Army Surgical Hospital (MASH), two minutes from bloody battles on the 38th Parallel of Korea, is an improbable setting for a comedy, even a stomach-churning, gory, often tasteless, but frequently funny black comedy [from the novel by Richard Hooker].

Elliott Gould, Donald Sutherland and Tom Skerritt head an extremely effective, low-keyed cast of players whose skillful subtlety eventually rescue an indecisive union of script and technique.

Gould is the totally unmilitary but arrogantly competent, supercool young battlefield surgeon, a reluctant draftee whose credo is let's get the job done and knock off all this Army muck.

The sardonic, cynical comments of the doctors and nurses patching and stitching battle-mangled bodies and casually amputating limbs before sending their anonymous patients out may be distasteful to some. It has the sharp look of reality when professionals become calloused from working 12 hours at a stretch to keep up with the stream of casualties from the battlefield.

1970: Best Adapted Screenplay

NOMINATIONS: Best Picture, Director, Supp. Actress (Sally Kellerman), Editing

•

MASK

1985, 120 mins, US Ⓥ ⊙ col

Dir Peter Bogdanovich ***Prod*** Martin Starger ***Scr*** Anna Hamilton Phelan ***Ph*** Laszlo Kovacs ***Ed*** Barbara Ford ***Art*** Norman Newberry

Act Cher, Sam Elliott, Eric Stoltz, Estelle Getty, Richard Dysart, Laura Dern (Universal)

Based on a true story, *Mask* is alive with the rhythms and textures of a unique life. Rocky Dennis (Eric Stoltz) is a 16-year-old afflicted with a rare bone disease which has ballooned his head to twice its normal size and cast the shadow of an early death over him.

Rocky is one of those rare individuals who has a vitality and gift for life and the emphasis here is not on dying, but living. The irony of the title is that his feelings are exposed far more than is customary and his experiences are intensified rather than dulled.

One of the accomplishments of *Mask* is the fullness of the environment it creates. Foremost in that portrait is Rocky's mother Rusty (Cher) and her motorcycle-gang friends.

Both in the background and foreground, *Mask* draws a vivid picture of life among a particular type of lower-middle-class Southern California whites.

Much of the credit for keeping the film from tripping over must go to the cast, especially Stoltz, who, with only his eyes visible behind an elaborate makeup job, brings a lively, life-affirming personality to his role without a trace of self-pity. Equally fine is Cher, who perfectly suggests a hard exterior covering a wealth of conflicting and confused feelings.

1985: Best Makeup

•

MASK, THE

1994, 101 mins, US Ⓥ ⊙ col

Dir Charles Russell ***Prod*** Bob Engelman ***Scr*** Mike Werb ***Ph*** John Leonetti ***Ed*** Arthur Coburn ***Mus*** Randy Edelman ***Art*** Craig Stearns

Act Jim Carrey, Cameron Diaz, Peter Riegert, Peter Greene, Amy Yasbeck, Richard Jeni (New Line)

Lean, mean and green, there's nothing mechanical or rote about this offbeat romantic adventure [from a screen story by Michael Fallon and Mark Verheiden]. This showcase for the talents of Jim Carrey is adroitly directed, viscerally and visually dynamic, and just plain fun.

In the fictional burg of Edge City, good-hearted Stanley Ipkiss (Carrey) works doggedly as a loan officer at a major bank. While his buddy and a couple of babes glide into the exclusive Coco Bongo Club Stan gets the proverbial heave-ho. Driving back to his dreary apartment, the dejected sap spies what he thinks is a body floating in the river. He dives into the polluted waters only to discover a carved face mask attached to a mass of flotsam.

But when he returns home and tries on the relic, drab mild-mannered Stanley morphs into a confident whirlwind of color. In his new guise, the Mask, he definitely provides the edge in Edge City.

The dazzling special effects come as close as humanly possible to replicating the mayhem and invention of '40s Warner Bros. cartoons. The title character literally bounces off walls, and when he spies his dream girl Tina Carlyle (Cameron Diaz), his jaw puts a dent in the floor boards. The glitch is that Tina is the moll of gangster Dorian Tyrel (Peter Greene).

Diaz is a real find as the femme fatale who's just looking for the decent thing to do. Charles Russell, hitherto a genre director, maintains a cartoon style to the violence that's quite suitable for all audiences.

1994: NOMINATION: Best Visual Effects

•

MASK OF DIMITRIOS, THE

1944, 96 mins, US b/w

Dir Jean Negulesco ***Prod*** Henry Blanke ***Scr*** Frank Gruber ***Ph*** Arthur Edeson ***Ed*** Frederick Richards ***Mus*** Adolph Deutsch ***Art*** Ted Smith

Act Sydney Greenstreet, Zachary Scott, Faye Emerson, Peter Lorre, Victor Francen, George Tobias (Warner)

Backgrounded with international intrigues, *The Mask of Dimitrios* has an occasional element of suspense, but those moments are comparatively few.

Dimitrios, which traces the year-long international criminal career of one Dimitrios Makropoulos (played by Zachary Scott), has the benefit of a good cast headed by Sydney Greenstreet and Peter Lorre, but it is mostly a conversational piece that too frequently suggests action in the dialog where, actually, the film itself practically has none.

Talky script [from the novel *A Coffin for Dimitrios* by Eric Ambler] slows the pace to a walk. Greenstreet and Lorre are capital as a criminal and mystery writer, respectively, while Scott gives a plausible performance as the titular character. The rest are mainly bits.

•

MASK OF FU MANCHU, THE

1932, 66 mins, US Ⓥ ⦿ b/w

Dir Charles Brabin ***Scr*** Irene Kuhn, Edgar Allan Woolf, John Willard ***Ph*** Tony Gaudio ***Ed*** Ben Lewis ***Art*** Cedric Gibbons

Act Boris Karloff, Lewis Stone, Karen Morley, Charles Starrett, Myrna Loy, Jean Hersholt (M-G-M)

Fu Manchu's latest mission is discovery of the tomb of Genghis Khan. Possession of the mask and sword of Genghis would give Fu the leadership of the East. Then he could lead his subjects on to victory in the Western world, with ultimate extermination of the white race which he fanatically despises.

Fu (Boris Karloff) has a daughter (Myrna Loy) who's not so pleasant herself. After pop is through torturing the best looking white men for his own purpose, daughter gets 'em for hers. She has the biggest boudoir couch this side of Peking, and pop doesn't object.

So that Fu doesn't get to the late Genghis's paraphernalia first, Scotland Yard dispatches a museum expedition to the spot. After that it's a contest over the tomb's contents. Just as Lewis Stone, as Inspector Nayland Smith of Scotland Yard, is about to be lowered into the cavernous mouths of a troupe of starving crocodiles he manages to escape.

Everybody is handicapped by the story and situations [from the story by Sax Rohmer]. It's strange how bad such troupers as Stone and Jean Hersholt can look when up against such an assignment as this.

•

MASK OF ZORRO, THE

1998, 136 mins, US Ⓥ ⦿ ▭ col

Dir Martin Campbell ***Prod*** Doug Claybourne, David Foster ***Scr*** John Eskow, Ted Elliott, Terry Rossio ***Ph*** Phil Meheux ***Ed*** Thom Noble ***Mus*** James Horner ***Art*** Cecilia Montiel

Act Antonio Banderas, Anthony Hopkins, Catherine Zeta-Jones, Stuart Wilson, Matt Letscher, Maury Chaykin (Amblin/TriStar)

The return of the legendary swordsman is well served by a grandly mounted production in the classical style. Somewhat overlong pic lacks the snap and concision that would have put it over the top as a bang-up entertainment, but it's closer in spirit to a vintage Errol Flynn or Tyrone Power swashbuckler than anything that's come out of Hollywood in quite some time.

Character of the mysterious Robin Hood/Scarlet Pimpernel figure who fights aristocratic oppressors in Old California was a household name from the time of his creation by police reporter and pulp fiction writer Johnston McCulley in 1919, and the appearance the next year of the silent film *The Mark of Zorro*, with Douglas Fairbanks, Sr.

Pic [from a screen story by Ted Elliott, Terry Rossio and Randall Jahnson] favors dashing adventure, dramatic and political intrigue, well-motivated characters and romance between mightily attractive leads over fashionable cynicism, cheap gags, over-stressed contemporary relevance and sensation for sensation's sake.

Zorro is the aristocratic Don Diego de la Vega (Anthony Hopkins). With the battle against colonial Spanish rule won, Don Diego resolves to hang up his mask and devote himself to his wife and baby daughter, Elena. But outgoing Spanish governor Montero (Stuart Wilson) kidnaps Elena and throws Don Diego into a dungeon.

Twenty years later, Montero is back with a devious scheme to buy Alta California. Now old and gray, Don Diego is on the point of assassinating Montero when he spots Elena (Catherine Zeta-Jones), who has been raised believing Montero is her father. He recruits an outlaw, Alejandro Murrieta (Antonio Banderas), and teaches him everything he knows, as the reincarnation of Zorro.

Thesping by all the principals is on the money. Mexican locations are alternately stark and lustrous.

•

MASQUE OF THE RED DEATH, THE

1964, 86 mins, UK Ⓥ ⦿ ▭ col

Dir Roger Corman ***Prod*** George Willoughby ***Scr*** Charles Beaumont, R. Wright Campbell ***Ph*** Nicolas Roeg ***Ed*** Ann Chegwidden ***Mus*** David Lee ***Art*** Robert Jones

Act Vincent Price, Hazel Court, Jane Asher, David Weston, Patrick Magee, Nigel Green (Anglo Amalgamated)

Roger Corman has garmented his film, lensed in England, with production values. His color camerawork, his sets, music and plot unfoldment itself—if the latter is vague and a bit involved it still fits into the pattern intended—establish an appropriate mood for pic's tale of terror and in addition it's evident Corman doesn't take his subject [based on a story by Edgar Allan Poe] too seriously.

Vincent Price is the very essence of evil, albeit charming when need be, and as film progresses the dark workings of his mind are stressed, tortuously intent on evil as a follower of the Devil. He plays Prince Prospero, a tyrannical power in Spain in the Middle Ages, who seizes a young girl and tries to make her choose between his saving the life of her beloved or her father, even as the Red Death is killing off most of his impoverished serfs. A strange and uninvited guest to the Bacchanalian orgy he is staging for his noble guests stalks through the festivities to transform the Masque Ball into a Dance of Death.

•

MASQUERADE

1965, 102 mins, UK col

Dir Basil Dearden ***Prod*** Michael Relph ***Scr*** William Goldman, Michael Relph ***Ph*** Otto Heller ***Ed*** John Gutheridge ***Mus*** Philip Green

Act Cliff Robertson, Jack Hawkins, Marisa Mell, Christopher Witty, Bill Fraser, Michel Piccoli (United Artists)

Michael Relph and Basil Dearden have had themselves a ball with *Masquerade*, for once forgetting the sociological themes which they often blend with their dramas, and turning out a clever, tongue-in-cheek spoof of the cloak-and-dagger yarns.

Relph and William Goldman have jettisoned much of the earnestness of the Victor Canning novel, *Castle Minerva*, retaining mainly the plotline and characters.

The story involves kidnapping, disguised identity, macabre doings in a travelling circus, a mysterious Spanish girl and escape from an eerie castle.

The British Foreign Office hires Jack Hawkins and Cliff Robertson for a daring mission. Hawkins is an ex-war colonel and hero. In this film, he obviously relishes being able to spoof the sort of stiff-upper-lip roles that so often he has to play seriously. Robertson is an American soldier of fortune who is down on his luck. Their job is to abduct the young heir to the throne of a Near East state and keep him under wraps for a few weeks until he comes of age and is able to sign a favourable oil concession to Britain.

•

MASQUERADE

1988, 91 mins, US Ⓥ ⦿ col

Dir Bob Swaim ***Prod*** Michael I. Levy ***Scr*** Dick Wolf ***Ph*** David Watkin ***Ed*** Scott Conrad ***Mus*** John Barry ***Art*** John Kasarda

Act Rob Lowe, Meg Tilly, Doug Savant, Kim Cattrall, John Glover, Dana Delany (M-G-M/Levy)

Masquerade, set in the Hamptons among the genteel with their weathered mansions and racing yachts, is like many poor-little-rich-girl stories; a beautiful backdrop and dreamy settings aren't enough to compensate for uninvolving characters caught in an unsuspenseful scheme.

Meg Tilly's womanizing, drunkard stepfather (John Glover) is in on a plot with Rob Lowe who, unbeknownst to her, is intent upon securing her hand in marriage so that he and his buddy will be set for life.

In the beginning, Lowe is a rake, the cocky captain of the racing boat *Obsession* while at the same time making it with the boat owner's much younger wife (Kim Cattrall). Tilly's just out of a Catholic women's college, innocent and apparently chaste.

It seems the Hamptons is not the bucolic haven it's cracked up to be. The police take their oath as peace officers to heart—that is, not upsetting the influential and wealthy community that pads the wallets for off-duty cops moonlighting at ritzy parties.

That leaves the snooping to an eager rookie (Doug Savant), seemingly wanting to protect the interests of Tilly, the girl he's always loved, as she takes the fall for a murder she didn't commit.

•

MASSACRE IN ROME

1973, 103 mins, Italy Ⓥ col

Dir George Pan Cosmatos ***Prod*** Carlo Ponti ***Scr*** Robert Katz, George Pan Cosmatos ***Ph*** Marcello Gatti ***Ed*** Francoise Bonnot, Roberto Silvi ***Mus*** Ennio Morricone ***Art*** Arrigo Berschi

Act Richard Burton, Marcello Mastroianni, Leo McKern, John Steiner, Delia Boccardo (Champion)

Massacre in Rome depends on its dramatic documentary flavor for a number of spellbinding sequences and its polemical shafts at Vatican reticence in resisting the massacre of 300 Italian hostages in reprisal for a partisan assault on a German storm troop detachment in Rome.

The film generally hews close to the controversial book, *Death in Rome*, by Robert Katz. Screenplay veers from the facts as Katz originally researched and presented them, with minor fictional treatment in a few characters, but does not detract from the overriding moral treatment involved in the wholesale slaughter of innocents, many of them Jews, in the Ardeatine Caves on the outskirts of Rome.

Richard Burton as Germany security forces commander Col. Kappler gets a richer portrait than his superiors and subordinates.

•

MASTER GUNFIGHTER, THE

1975, 121 mins, US ▭ col

Dir Frank Laughlin [= Tom Laughlin] ***Prod*** Philip L. Parslow ***Scr*** Harold Lapland ***Ph*** Jack A. Marta ***Ed*** William Reynolds, Danford Greene ***Mus*** Lalo Schifrin ***Art*** Albert Brenner

Act Tom Laughlin, Ron O'Neal, Lincoln Kilpatrick, GeoAnn Sosa, Barbara Carrera, Victor Campos (Billy Jack)

A curious blend of amateurish plotting and slick production values, Tom Laughlin's *The Master Gunfighter* also presents an ambiguous moral attitude toward the old West. The oater, attractively lensed on northern California locations, alternates sermonizing with gunfights and sword fights.

The Laughlin character talks like a liberal but behaves like a reactionary, and therein lies the confusion. It's a throwback to an earlier age of swashbuckling, but the blend with contemporary bleeding-heart attitudes makes the film seem hypocritical.

Action fans will find a good quota of kicks if they can sit through the turgid passages.

Ron O'Neal is Laughlin's chief antagonist, but doesn't arouse much interest as a character. In the lead femme roles, GeoAnn Sosa is spunky and charming, but Barbara Carrera betrays her fashion model background with her blank beauty.

Laughlin's wife, Delores Taylor, gets exec producer credit, and their nine-year-old son Frank Laughlin is billed as director.

•

MASTER OF BALLANTRAE, THE

1953, 88 mins, US Ⓥ col

Dir William Keighley ***Scr*** Herb Meadow, Harold Medford ***Ph*** Jack Cardiff ***Ed*** Jack Harris ***Mus*** William Alwyn ***Art*** Ralph Brinton

Act Errol Flynn, Roger Livesey, Anthony Steel, Beatrice Campbell, Yvonne Furneaux, Felix Aylmer (Warner)

Robert Louis Stevenson's novel provides a tailor-made vehicle for Errol Flynn. Picture was filmed mostly in Scotland, and the backgrounds are a colorful addition to the period values and escapism.

Character development in the plotting is elementary but the handling gets the most out of the script and the competent cast to sharpen the romantic values of the 18th-century adventure yarn.

Flynn's customary heroics are brought off with debonair dispatch, whether it's wooing the girls, duelling or engaging in mass battle. He's seen as Jamie Durrisdeer, heir to the Scottish estate of Ballantrae, who joins a Stuart rebellion against the King of England, becomes a fugitive after the rebels are put down and flees to the West Indies with Irish adventurer Roger Livesey, believing he had been betrayed to the British by his brother.

Livesey is colorful and humorous as Flynn's chief partner in the swashbuckling. Beatrice Campbell is gracious and beautiful as Lady Alison. Yvonne Furneaux, a girl with whom Flynn pitches some extra-curricular wooing, and Gillian Lynne, a pirate's dancing-girlfriend, also provide femme beauty.

•

MASTER OF THE ISLANDS

SEE: THE HAWAIIANS

•

MASTER RACE, THE

1944, 94 mins, US Ⓥ b/w

Dir Herbert J. Biberman ***Prod*** Robert S. Golden ***Scr*** Herbert J. Biberman, Anne Froelick, Rowland Leigh ***Ph*** Russell Metty

Ed Ernie Leadlay *Mus* Roy Webb *Art* Albert S. D'Agostino, Jack Okey
Act George Coulouris, Osa Massen, Stanley Ridges, Lloyd Bridges, Nancy Gates, Morris Carnovsky (RKO)

Eddie Golden originally selected the title as a likely one for a picture, and then searched for a yarn [by director Herbert J. Biberman] to pin it to in order to dramatically show the arrogance and synthetic character of the barbaric Nazis. He selected a period when the German armies were fleeing in disorder, and the final unconditional surrender of the Nazi minions.

Picture opens with clips of the D-Day invasion of June 6 for brief footage, and then swings to headquarters of George Coulouris, member of the German general staff, where he tells assemblage of German officers that the war is lost and they are to proceed according to individual instructions to points designated to create dissension among the peoples of the liberated countries to further destroy Europe so that the self-styled master race can again rise to rule the continent.

•

MASTERS OF THE UNIVERSE
1987, 106 mins, US Ⓥ ⦿ col
Dir Gary Goddard *Prod* Menahem Golan, Yoram Globus *Scr* David Odell *Ph* Hanania Baer *Ed* Anne V. Coates *Mus* Bill Conti *Art* William Stout
Act Dolph Lundgren, Frank Langella, Meg Foster, Billy Barty, Courteney Cox, Chelsea Field (Cannon)

All elements are of epic proportions in this *Conan-Star Wars* hybrid ripoff, based on the bestselling line of children's toys. Epitome of Good takes on Epitome of Evil for nothing less than the future of the Universe, and the result is a colossal bore.

Dolph Lundgren's He-Man is an impressive physical specimen, the ultimate warrior epitomizing all that is good and defending the honor of inhabitants of the planet Eternia. On the dark side is the hideously made up Frank Langella, as Skeletor. He has captured the Sorceress of Greyskull Castle (Christina Pickles), locking her in a tubular energy field and absorbing her power, which evidently comes from Eternia's moonbeams.

Turns out the battle to control the future of universal power takes place at a used music store in a small town in California. He-Man and his allies are searching for a cosmic key that will unlock the Sorceress from her nasty gravity field. Key is discovered by Julie Winston (Courteney Cox, she of Bruce Springsteen's *Dancing in the Dark* video fame) and her musician boyfriend, Kevin (Robert Duncan McNeil). Makeup and costuming is universally good, special effects uninspiring.

•

MATADOR
1986, 102 mins, Spain Ⓥ ⦿ col
Dir Pedro Almodovar *Prod* Andres Vicente Gomez (exec.) *Scr* Jesus Fererro, Pedro Almodovar *Ph* Angel Luis Fernandez *Ed* Pepe Salcedo *Mus* Bernardo Bonezzi *Art* Roman Arango, Jose Morales, Josep Rosell
Act Assumpta Serna, Antonio Banderas, Nacho Martinez, Eva Cobo, Julieta Serrano, Carmen Maura (Iberoamericana)

In *Matador*, Pedro Almodovar displays more polished filmmaking technique, but moves away from social commentary for a frenzied feeding on themes of carnal and blood obsession. The film's pulsing sexuality and mock mystery structure could hook specialty audiences, but those unfamiliar with Spanish society may not fully appreciate some of pic's corrosive, satirical subtexts.

Angel (Antonio Banderas), an emotionally repressed 21-year-old who lives with his conservative harridan of a mother, secretly attends the bullfighting school of Diego (Nacho Martinez), a gored-into-retirement ex-champion matador with the sexual appetite of a lusty bull. Diego supplements his relationship with the gorgeous but vacuous fashion model Eva (Eva Cobo) with diversionary flings, hardcore bondage porn and "snuff" videos and, as it transpires, the occasional murder of pretty girls whom he buries on the grounds of his opulent estate in suburban Madrid.

Frustrated in his attempt to win the respect of his hero maestro, Angel one night attempts to rape the matador's girlfriend, but fails in humiliating fashion. When young girls are reported missing, Angel confesses to their murders and is taken into custody while the police search for evidence. Angel is assigned a feminist lawyer, Maria (Assumpta Serna), who, it turns out, has the greatest obsession of all for the fallen matador.

Almodovar unfolds this convoluted plot with zigzagging surrealism and a careening, sordidly erotic energy that effectively undermines the culturally institutionalized repression targeted by the filmmaker. Serna and Martinez stand out as victims of psycho-sexual passion gone amok, while supporting performances are very effective.

•

MATA HARI
1931, 90 mins, US Ⓥ b/w
Dir George Fitzmaurice *Prod* [uncredited] *Scr* Benjamin Glazer, Leo Birinski, Doris Anderson, Gilbert Emery *Ph* William Daniels *Ed* Frank Sullivan *Mus* [uncredited] *Art* Cedric Gibbons
Act Greta Garbo, Ramon Novarro, Lionel Barrymore, Lewis Stone, C. Henry Gordon, Karen Morley (M-G-M)

Greta Garbo, Ramon Novarro, Lionel Barrymore and Lewis Stone—the Metro Tragedy Four—dominate the whole affair, making the picture, as a picture, very secondary.

It needs its cast names at all times, being a yarn which can't stand up for long on its own gams. Though Garbo is sexy and hot in a less subtle way this time, and though the plot goes about as far as it can in situation warmth, the story presents nothing sensational. Its few attempts at power are old style and all have been used before in similar trite spy stories.

Garbo does a polite cooch to Oriental music as a starter and in the same number makes a symbolic play for a huge idol, with the hips in motion all the while. The finish is a neatly masked strip with Greta's back to the lens.

Two other torrid moments later in the running are given to Garbo and Novarro. Both times they turn out the lights.

Mata Hari's method for grabbing enemy info, if this scenario is authentic, was to get 'em in the bedroom and keep 'em interested, while an assistant operative snatches the papers.

Barrymore and Stone are playing what, for them, are minor parts. Barrymore, as a broken general who loses his honor and finally his life through the glamorous Mata Hari, succeeds in inserting a punch in his moments of despair. But Stone is under wraps with a semivillainous assignment that doesn't warrant his ability.

•

MATCHMAKER, THE
1958, 100 mins, US Ⓥ ⦿ b/w
Dir Joseph Anthony *Prod* Don Hartman *Scr* John Michael Hayes *Ph* Charles Lang, Jr. *Ed* Howard Smith *Mus* Adolph Deutsch *Art* Hal Pereira, Roland Anderson
Act Shirley Booth, Anthony Perkins, Shirley MacLaine, Paul Ford, Robert Morse, Wallace Ford (Paramount)

Based on the Thornton Wilder Broadway hit, Shirley Booth takes the Ruth Gordon stage role of "marriage counsellor," dominating character in this yarn of 1884. Its period unfoldment permits added opportunity for laughs, some of the belly genre. The Yonkers screenplay catches every nuance of the situation of the widowed Booth ostensibly seeking a wife for the grasping Yonkers merchant (Paul Ford) while adroitly plotting to capture him for her own. Use of "asides" by various principals, speaking directly into the camera, peppers the action.

Most of the story unreels in New York, where Ford goes from nearby Yonkers to propose to Shirley MacLaine, a man-hungry milliner, and to meet a sexpot promised by Booth, who against his will has taken over Ford's romantic interests. Following Ford are the two overworked clerks in his general store (Anthony Perkins and Robert Morse) who pool their resources and determine to live it up in the big city, with 10 bucks between them.

Booth is no less than superb in her role, draining part of comedic possibilities. Perkins's switch to farce is also a bright experience. Ford is immense as the romantically inclined but tight small-towner, and MacLaine is pert and lovely. Morse, from the original Broadway cast, amusingly enacts Perkins's pardner.

•

MATEWAN
1987, 130 mins, US Ⓥ ⦿ col
Dir John Sayles *Prod* Peggy Rajski, Maggie Renzi *Scr* John Sayles *Ph* Haskell Wexler *Ed* Sonya Polonsky *Mus* Mason Daring *Art* Nora Chavooshian
Act Chris Cooper, Will Oldham, Mary McDonnell, Bob Gunton, James Earl Jones, Kevin Tighe (Cinecom/Film Gallery/Red Dog)

Matewan is a heartfelt, straight-ahead tale of labor organizing in the coal mines of West Virginia in 1920 that runs its course like a train coming down the track.

Among the memorable characters is Joe Kenehan (Chris Cooper), a young union organizer who comes to Matewan to buck the bosses. With his strong face and Harrison Ford good looks, Cooper gives the film its heartbeat. Of the townfolk, 16-year-old Danny (Will Oldham) is already a righteous preacher and a seasoned union man who passionately takes up the working man's struggle. Director John Sayles adds some texture to the mix by throwing in Italian immigrants and black migrant workers who become converted to the union side.

Most notable of the black workers is "Few Clothes" Johnson (James Earl Jones), a burly good-natured man with a powerful presence and a quick smile. Jones's performance practically glows in the dark. Also a standout is Sayles veteran David Strathairn as the sheriff with quiet integrity who puts his life on the line.

1987: NOMINATION: Best Cinematography

•

MATINEE
1993, 99 mins, US Ⓥ ⦿ col
Dir Joe Dante *Prod* Michael Finnell *Scr* Charlie Haas *Ph* John Hora *Ed* Marshall Harvey *Mus* Jerry Goldsmith *Art* Steven Legler
Act John Goodman, Cathy Moriarty, Simon Fenton, Omri Katz, Lisa Jakub, Kellie Martin (Universal/Renfield)

Joe Dante lovingly re-creates the monster pics of his youth in *Matinee*, an okay film geared toward buffs that should have been much better. *Matinee* derives from a high concept (credited to Jerico and scripter Charlie Haas) in which the real-life fears of the 1962 Cuban missile crisis interact with the artificial fears of a horror film premiering at a Key West movie house.

Believably cast as a huckster/showman modeled after producer-director William Castle, John Goodman is previewing his new monster pic *Mant!* (Half Man, Half Ant, All Terror!) in hopes of impressing exhibitor Jesse White to book it at his 50-theater chain.

Film-in-a-film is a very accurate, hilarious black & white pastiche featuring (uncredited) genre vets Kevin McCarthy, Robert Cornthwaite (of the original *The Thing*) and William Shallert opposite Goodman's girlfriend Cathy Moriarty. Yet Dante lets his own film lapse into the excruciating clichés of both the "good teen" romances and the j.d. sagas of the '50s.

Even when the film gets bogged down in romantic drivel, there are enough clever in-jokes and well-remembered period details to keep buffs happy. Casting is accurate.

•

MATING GAME, THE
1959, 97 mins, US ▭ col
Dir George Marshall *Prod* Philip Barry, Jr. *Scr* William Roberts *Ph* Robert Bronner *Ed* John McSweeney, Jr. *Mus* Jeff Alexander
Act Debbie Reynolds, Tony Randall, Paul Douglas, Fred Clark, Una Merkel, Philip Ober (M-G-M)

Figure a combination of *You Can't Take It with You* and elements of *Tobacco Road*, and it is a pretty fair indication of what *The Mating Game* is about and how the jokes are played. This romantic farce is as broad as its CinemaScope projection.

The production is based on H. E. Bates's English novel, *The Darling Buds of May*, a light, farcical tilt at the welfare state in Britain. Adapted for the screen, it becomes an American situation chiefly involving free enterprise versus the internal revenue department.

Tony Randall plays a tax agent assigned to investigate the Maryland farm family headed by Paul Douglas and Una Merkel. Douglas gets Randall predictably drunk, and Randall is predictably smitten with one of the Douglas-Merkel offspring, hoydenish Debbie Reynolds. She is a toothsome child of nature who is taking care of the mating of the farm stock when she isn't wrestling in the hay with some of the livelier neighbor boys.

Most of this is foreseeable farce, and much of it is done with allusions to sex, regarding both humans and animals. Reynolds is very good. Randall, somewhat uncomfortable as a straight actor, is brilliant in his comedy scenes, particularly an athletic drunk sequence and its aftermath.

•

MATING SEASON, THE
1951, 101 mins, US b/w
Dir Mitchell Leisen *Prod* Charles Brackett *Scr* Charles Brackett, Walter Reisch, Richard Breen *Ph* Charles B. Lang, Jr. *Ed* Frank Bracht *Mus* Joseph J. Lilley *Art* Hal Pereira, Roland Anderson
Act Gene Tierney, John Lund, Miriam Hopkins, Thelma Ritter, Jan Sterling, Larry Keating (Paramount)

Nominal stars of the piece [suggested by a play by Caesar Dunn] are Gene Tierney and John Lund, but it is Thelma Ritter who glitters the brightest, having been given the pivotal character and choicest lines.

Bolstering the comedy considerably is the fact laughs are not based on situations that are too far-fetched, even though a plot springboard that finds a mother-in-law taking a maid's job in the home of her new daughter would seem to come under that heading. Scripters make it all seem perfectly logical, and the playing and direction strengthen that effect.

Lund, a factory clerk, ties up with Tierney, world traveler and intimate of diplomatic personages, in a love-at-first-sight marriage. Ritter, Lund's mother and a hamburger stand operator, hitchhikes to visit the new bride and groom but is taken for a domestic being sent to help out at the newlyweds' first party. She goes along with the situation and then decides to continue it over the opposition of Lund. Things are working fine until Miriam Hopkins, mother of Tierney, moves in.

1951: NOMINATION: Best Supp. Actress (Thelma Ritter)

•

MATRIX, THE

1999, 136 mins, US Ⓥ ⊙ ▭ col

Dir Andy Wachowski, Larry Wachowski ***Prod*** Joel Silver ***Scr*** Andy Wachowski, Larry Wachowski ***Ph*** Bill Pope ***Ed*** Zach Staenberg ***Mus*** Don Davis ***Art*** Owen Paterson

Act Keanu Reeves, Laurence Fishburne, Carrie-Anne Moss, Hugo Weaving, Gloria Foster, Joe Pantoliano (Silver/Warner)

It's Special Effects 10, Screenplay 0 for *The Matrix*, an eye-popping but incoherent extravaganza of morphing and superhuman martial arts.

After a stunning big-city opening in which a young woman named Trinity (Carrie-Anne Moss) outmaneuvers some pursuing agents, focus settles on a slacker-style software expert (Keanu Reeves) who's contacted by Trinity and led to the mysterious Morpheus (Laurence Fishburne), an alleged cult leader and terrorist who tells the recruit that he is The One, the savior, from some 2,000 years in the future.

The underground city of Zion is now the last bastion of humankind, which awaits The One to disrupt the Matrix, a power field controlled by humanoid computers that have created a "virtual" real world fed by laboratory-controlled human energy. This new world order is enforced by men in sunglasses led by Agent Smith (Hugo Weaving).

Cybertronically reconstituted with the name Neo, the software expert is ready to do battle with the forces that made the world what it has become. A full hour in, the script is still devoted to exposition, and never really gets on track. Things settle down into a muddle of showdowns resulting in deaths and resurrections that follow no rules, not even those specified by the film itself.

Chinese kung-fu and wire-stunt ace Yuen Wo-ping was engaged to choreograph the fight sequences, which are perhaps unsurpassed in an American film. Serious, sincere and low-key, Reeves gives it his all here physically. Beyond that, he brings no more or less than he ever does to a role. Pic was economically made in Australia for about $60 million.

1999: Best Film Editing, Sound, Sound Effects Editing, Visual Effects

•

MATTER OF INNOCENCE, A

SEE: PRETTY POLLY

•

MATTER OF LIFE AND DEATH, A
(US: STAIRWAY TO HEAVEN)

1946, 104 mins, UK col

Dir Michael Powell, Emeric Pressburger ***Prod*** Michael Powell, Emeric Pressburger ***Scr*** Michael Powell, Emeric Pressburger ***Ph*** Jack Cardiff ***Ed*** Reginald Mills ***Mus*** Allan Gray ***Art*** Alfred Junge

Act David Niven, Kim Hunter, Marius Goring, Roger Livesey, Raymond Massey, Richard Attenborough (Archers)

Like other Powell-Pressburger pictures, the striving to appear intellectual is much too apparent. Less desire to exhibit alleged learning, and more humanity would have resulted in a more popular offering.

For the first 10 minutes, apart from some pretentious poppycock, the picture looks like living up to its boosting. This is real cinema, then action gives way to talk, some of it flat and dreary. Story is set in this world (graced with Technicolor), and the Other World (relegated to dye monochrome) as it exists in the mind of an airman whose imagination has been affected by concussion.

Returning from a bomber expedition, Squadron-Leader David Niven is shot up. Last of the crew, minus a parachute, and believing the end is inevitable, before bailing out talks poetry and love over the radio to Kim Hunter, American WAC on nearby air station. Miraculously Niven falls into the sea, is washed ashore apparently unhurt, and by strange coincidence meets Kim. They fall desperately in love.

Meanwhile in the Other World there's much bother. Owing to delinquency of Heavenly Conductor Marius Goring, Niven has failed to check in, and Goring is despatched to this world to persuade Niven to take his rightful place and balance the heavenly books.

Obviously experimental in many respects, the designs for the Other World are a matter of taste, but with all their ingenuity Powell, Pressburger, and Alfred Junge could only invent a heaven reminiscent of the Hollywood Bowl and an exclusive celestial night club where hostesses dish out wings to dead pilots.

•

MAURICE

1987, 140 mins, UK Ⓥ ⊙ col

Dir James Ivory ***Prod*** Ismail Merchant ***Scr*** Kit Hesketh-Harvey, James Ivory ***Ph*** Pierre Lhomme ***Ed*** Katherine Wenning ***Mus*** Richard Robbins ***Art*** Brian Ackland-Snow

Act James Wilby, Hugh Grant, Rupert Graves, Denholm Elliott, Simon Callow, Billie Whitelaw (Merchant-Ivory)

Maurice, based on a posthumously published novel by E. M. Forster, is a well-crafted pic on the theme of homosexuality. Penned in 1914 but not allowed to be published until 1971 (a year after Forster's death) because of its subject matter, *Maurice* is not ranked among Forster's best work. Key opening scene has Maurice as a schoolboy on a beachside outing being lectured by his teacher (Simon Callow), in comically fastidious fashion, on the changes that will soon occur in his body with the onset of puberty.

Maurice Hall (James Wilby) is next seen grown up and attending Cambridge, where he meets handsome Clive Durham (Hugh Grant). Durham falls in love with him and though resisting at first Maurice later reciprocates, all on a platonic level.

Durham, under pressure from his mother (Judy Parfitt), gets married to a naive girl (Phoebe Nicholls) while Maurice finally physically consummates his homosexual inclination with Durham's young gamekeeper Alec Scudder (Rupert Graves).

Wilby as Maurice gives a workmanlike performance, adequate to the role but never soaring. He is far outshadowed by a superlative supporting cast.

1987: NOMINATION: Best Costume Design

•

MAVERICK

1994, 129 mins, US Ⓥ ⊙ ▭ col

Dir Richard Donner ***Prod*** Bruce Davey, Richard Donner ***Scr*** William Goldman ***Ph*** Vilmos Zsigmond ***Ed*** Stuart Baird ***Mus*** Randy Newman ***Art*** Tom Sanders

Act Mel Gibson, Jodie Foster, James Garner, Graham Greene, James Coburn, Alfred Molina (Icon/Warner)

This exuberant Western is a crowdpleaser that remains faithful to the genre while having a roaring good time sending up its conventions. The original *Maverick*, which aired on ABC from 1957–62, was a popular television staple with Jack Kelly and newcomer James Garner as lovable rogue gamblers. Garner subsequently dusted off his character in several television movies. In its new big-screen incarnation, Mel Gibson takes up the mantle with glee.

Jodie Foster as a sometimes treacherous temptress, Garner as a seasoned lawman and a rogues' gallery of characters are along for the ride.

Director Richard Donner serves it all up as one rollicking piece of dumb fun. But thanks to a keen, comical script by William Goldman and a sterling cast, it's smart dumb fun. Goldman has taken his cue from his own script of *Butch Cassidy and the Sundance Kid* and added dollops of *The Sting* for a tasty confection.

In flashback, we see Bret Maverick arriving in a small, scenic town to find a card game. He stumbles onto a table where the principals include the demure Annabelle Bransford (Foster) and a mean hombre named Angel (Alfred Molina). He walks away a winner but not without incurring Angel's wrath and Annabelle's lust—for his money.

The title role provides Gibson with a cocky, physical character that suits his persona. Foster—not an obvious choice for his sparring partner—throws herself into the comic, vampish role with abandon. It's an inspired pairing. Best of all is Garner, an unsung master of this type of droll fare. He seems more a kindred spirit, even father, to Gibson than his competitor or nemesis.

1994: NOMINATION: Costume Design

•

MAX DUGAN RETURNS

1983, 98 mins, US Ⓥ ⊙ col

Dir Herbert Ross ***Prod*** Herbert Ross, Neil Simon ***Scr*** Neil Simon ***Ph*** David M. Walsh ***Ed*** Richard Marks ***Mus*** David Shire ***Art*** Albert Brenner

Act Marsha Mason, Jason Robards, Donald Sutherland, Matthew Broderick, Dody Goodman, Sal Viscuso (20th Century-Fox)

Max Dugan Returns is a consistently happy comedic fable which should please romanticists drawn to a teaming of Neil Simon, Marsha Mason and Herbert Ross. Once more, Simon's pen turns to the problems of parental relationships—especially reunion after long estrangement—but largely leaves aside any heavy emotional involvement or rapid fire comedy.

Struggling to raise a 15-year-old son (Matthew Broderick) on a meagre teacher's salary, widow Mason maintains a wonderful attitude as her refrigerator breaks, her old car barely runs but gets stolen to boot and life generally never quite works. Broderick is a good kid who accepts her poor-but-honest morality very well. In addition, there's a budding romance with Donald Sutherland, an exceptionally intelligent detective who's investigating the theft of her car.

Out of a dark night, however, returns Max Dugan (Jason Robards), the father who abandoned Mason when she was nine years old. Dying of a heart ailment, Robards is carrying a satchel full of remorse and a suitcase crammed with cash left over from a checkered career in Las Vegas.

•

MAXIE

1985, 90 mins, US Ⓥ ⊙ col

Dir Paul Aaron ***Prod*** Carter De Haven ***Scr*** Patricia Resnick ***Ph*** Fred Schuler ***Ed*** Lynzee Klingman ***Mus*** Georges Delerue ***Art*** John Lloyd

Act Glenn Close, Mandy Patinkin, Ruth Gordon, Barnard Hughes, Valerie Curtin, Googy Gress (Orion/Aurora)

As forgettable as it is well-meaning, *Maxie* represents a stab at an old-fashioned sort of romantic fantasy, as well as first chance at a full-blown starring role for Glenn Close. A concoction like this needs lots of fizz, but the bubbly here has gone mostly flat, and what's left evaporates quickly.

Much of the credit for keeping it alive at all must go to Mandy Patinkin, who shows himself to be a good-looking leading man with a rare light touch for romantic comedy.

Based on the novel *Marion's Wall* by Jack Finney, *Maxie* tells the story of a dead person returning to inhabit the body of a living soul. Such is what happens to Close, the normal, cheerful wife of book specialist Patinkin. When he uncovers a message on the wall from a certain "Maxie" who lived in the 1920s, Patinkin becomes quite taken with the jazz-age flapper who bore a striking resemblance to his wife.

She has some very good comic moments, but Close may be too down-to-earth an actress for foolishness of this kind. The late Ruth Gordon, in her last film role, contributes another of her patented nutty neighbor turns.

•

MAXIMUM OVERDRIVE

1986, 97 mins, US Ⓥ ⊙ ▭ col

Dir Stephen King ***Prod*** Martha Schumacher ***Scr*** Stephen King ***Ph*** Armando Nannuzzi ***Ed*** Evan Lottman ***Mus*** AC/DC ***Art*** Giorgio Postiglione

Act Emilio Estevez, Pat Hingle, Laura Harrington, Yeardley Smith, John Short, Ellen McElduff (De Laurentiis)

Master manipulator Stephen King, making his directoral debut from his own script, fails to create a convincing enough environment to make the kind of nonsense he's offering here believable or fun.

King starts out with a small-town idyll soon disrupted by a mindless revolt of trucks. He collects a typical mix of rednecks, good old boys, restless youth, drifters and the decent folk in a small corner of North Carolina where they hole up at a truck stop as the trucks stampede.

Truck stop is run as if it were a feudal fiefdom, complete with arsenal, by redneck despot Pat Hingle who gives an amusing performance as a true screen swine. Also on hand is Emilio Estevez as a cook in bondage to Hingle by virtue of his probation from the pen, but he's gone to college and is really a good kid.

•

MAXIMUM RISK

1996, 100 mins, US Ⓥ ⊙ ▭ col

Dir Ringo Lam ***Prod*** Moshe Diamant ***Scr*** Larry Ferguson ***Ph*** Alexander Gruszynski ***Ed*** Bill Pankow ***Mus*** Robert Folk ***Art*** Steven Spence

Act Jean-Claude Van Damme, Natasha Henstridge, Zach Grenier, Jean-Hugues Anglade, Paul Ben-Victor, Frank Senger (Birnbaum-Diamant/Columbia)

Maximum Risk is a visceral delight that refuses to be deterred by niceties of plot or character consistency and prefers sweat to emotion. This full-tilt genre boogie is technically a cut above the average carnage saga.

Alain Moreau (Jean-Claude Van Damme) is a French *flic* confronted by [the body of] his deceased lookalike. The dead man's passport identifies him as New York City resident Mikhail Suverov. And yes, Mom (Stephane Audran) reveals, they were so poor she had to give up one of her twins for adoption and has harbored that secret until this terrible day.

Luckily, Alain's a fearless cop (and a martial arts master). Assuming his brother's identity, he heads for the Big Apple's Little Odessa. The good news is that Mikhail has a stunningly attractive girlfriend named Alex (Natasha Henstridge) and the bad news is that both the local Russian Mafia and corrupt FBI agents (Paul Ben-Victor, Frank Senger) want him dead.

Director Ringo Lam's U.S. studio debut looks like a high-gloss version of the potboilers he made in Hong Kong. The difference is time and money—additives that provide a dazzling sheen, heightened by Alexander Gruszynski's smooth camera style and a high polish from editor Bill Pankow. If newcomer Henstridge has dramatic qualities, they will have to be discovered in another movie. Van Damme, at least, is gaining poise in front of the camera to offset his limited dramatic range.

•

MAYERLING

1968, 140 mins, UK/France Ⓥ ▭ col

Dir Terence Young ***Prod*** Robert Dorfmann ***Scr*** Terence Young, Denis Cannan ***Ph*** Henri Alekan ***Ed*** Benedik Rayner ***Mus*** Francis Lai ***Art*** Georges Wakhevitch

Act Omar Sharif, Catherine Deneuve, James Mason, Ava Gardner, James Robertson Justice, Genevieve Page (Winchester/Corona)

Film misfires through a flattish script and uninspired performances by two leads, Omar Sharif and Catherine Deneuve. Director Terence Young has used two novels (*Mayerling* and *The Archduke* by Michael Arnold) and much historical background research as the basis for his theory on how Crown Prince Rudolf of Austria and his young baroness mistress met their deaths in the Royal Hunting Lodge at Mayerling in the late 19th century.

The screenplay rarely touches any heights of romantic ecstasy. The political background—the always shaky Austrian throne, the students' violent protests, court intrigue—is introduced promisingly at the beginning, but later gets swamped in the romantic story which is protracted, humorless, often hesitant and plodding.

Sharif shows fire as the arrogant, ambitious son of Emperor Franz-Josef, torn between a desire to get things moving on a new progressive scale, and his loyalty to Habsburg tradition.

His romance with Catherine Deneuve is a singularly flat and prosaic affair. Deneuve's performance is too demure. Ava Gardner makes an impact throughout.

•

MAYTIME

1937, 132 mins, US Ⓥ col

Dir Robert Z. Leonard ***Prod*** Hunt Stromberg ***Scr*** Noel Langley ***Ph*** Oliver T. Marsh ***Ed*** Conrad A. Nervig ***Mus*** Herbert Stothart (dir.) ***Art*** Cedric Gibbons

Act Jeanette MacDonald, Nelson Eddy, John Barrymore, Herman Bing, Tom Brown, Lynne Carver (M-G-M)

Maytime has so many fine qualities that its length, occasional lapses into the superfluous and betimes dull interludes will be acceptable. The vocal piece-de-resistance, of course, is the Sigmund Romberg waltz ballad, "Will You Remember?" perhaps better known as "Sweetheart, Sweetheart." This has been artfully backgrounded throughout the extended running time by Herbert Stothart.

The stars, Jeanette MacDonald and Nelson Eddy, are splendid in their vocal assignments. It's chiefly MacDonald's picture. She looks her best in the Napoleonic period costumes, and is charming in her makeup as the venerable old lady, with a slightly mysterious past, who finally opens up as she counsels the petulant Lynne Carver and Tom Brown on the wisdom of forsaking a career in favor of romance. Eddy carries through the worthy impression made by this pair in their past operetta successes. His robust baritone again nicely balances MacDonald's soprano.

Histrionically there is also John Barrymore in a fat supporting assignment as a somewhat dour mentor of the ambitious prima donna. The "Huguenots" operatic sequence (Meyerbeer, scored by Stothart) is one of the major vocal highlights. "Czaritza" is the original Stothart adaptation from Tchaikovsky's Fifth Symphony into a new Russian opera, libretto by Bob Wright and Chet Forrest. This is the major operatic interlude and MacDonald, Eddy and the Don Cossacks make the most of it, singing the French lyrics by Gilles Guilbert.

The light-brown sepia tinging, which Metro used in *Good Earth* (1936), is utilized in certain sequences, notably in the St. Cloud carnival scene and the "Maytime"—"Will You Remember?" waltz finale.

1937: NOMINATIONS: Best Score, Sound

•

M. BUTTERFLY

1993, 100 mins, US Ⓥ ⦿ col

Dir David Cronenberg ***Prod*** Gabriella Martinelli ***Scr*** David Henry Hwang ***Ph*** Peter Suschitzky ***Ed*** Ronald Sanders ***Mus*** Howard Shore ***Art*** Carol Spier

Act Jeremy Irons, John Lone, Ian Richardson, Annabel Leventon, Shizuko Hoshi, Richard McMillan (Geffen/Warner)

This butterfly just doesn't fly. Icy, surprisingly conventional and never truly convincing, David Cronenberg's screen version of David Henry Hwang's hit Broadway play gets all dressed up in fancy threads but goes nowhere, due to lack of chemistry and heat on the part of the two leads.

Inspired by the true story of a French diplomat in China during the 1960s who conducted an 18-year affair with a native man he always thought was a woman and who was later convicted of espionage, *M. Butterfly* worked onstage because of the artifice and distance created by the theatrical setting.

But as much as one tries to buy the notion that Jeremy Irons's Rene Gallimard is so smitten with John Lone's Song Liling that he overlooks the hefty frame, masculine fingers and moustache stubble beneath the makeup, it just doesn't wash.

Set in Beijing in 1964, tale begins with French Embassy accountant Gallimard being enchanted with Song Liling's performance of excerpts from Pucini's *Madame Butterfly*. Once Gallimard is promoted to vice consul, in which capacity he is privy to confidential intelligence, Song Liling is able to become an effective spy for the Communist regime. Seventy minutes in, action jumps to Paris 1968. Gallimard is soon revealed to be a burnt-out case. To his astonishment, Song Liling suddenly appears at his door.

Irons's sang-froid and dissolute air don't work for the role, and all the effort in the world can't prevent Lone from looking like a man in drag. Lensed in China, Hungary and France, this is Cronenberg's first film shot outside Canada.

•

MCBAIN

1991, 102 mins, US Ⓥ ⦿ col

Dir James Glickenhaus ***Prod*** J. Boyce Harman, Jr. ***Scr*** James Glickenhaus ***Ph*** Robert M. Baldwin, Jr. ***Ed*** Jeffrey Wolf ***Mus*** Christopher Franke ***Art*** Charles C. Bennett

Act Christopher Walken, Maria Conchita Alonso, Michael Ironside, Steve James, Jay Patterson, Thomas G. Waites (Shapiro Glickenhaus)

Boasting excellent production values, *McBain* is a silly action film that has the elements of an A-grade picture but fails to create an engrossing or believable narrative. Pic becomes a spoof of itself and the genre early on and never recovers.

Prolog has Chick Vennera and fellow soldiers rescuing POW Christopher Walken on the day the Vietnam War ended in 1973, so Walken owes him one. When Vennera is killed in an abortive coup of the Colombian government eighteen years later, Walken agrees to help Vennera's sister (Maria Conchita Alonso) overthrow the drug cartel–run dictatorship there and let the common people come to power.

Cartoonish action is amusing but never gripping. Walken appears awkward and bored with a stiff-upper-lip assignment more suited to director James Glickenhaus's 1980 *Exterminator* leading man Robert Ginty. The extreme earnestness of Alonso as the freedom fighter is overdone. There is no romance in the pic and zero chemistry between the two leads, a glaring deficiency. Filming in the Philippines instead of South America results in Filipino extras who definitely don't look authentic.

•

MCCABE & MRS. MILLER

1971, 121 mins, US Ⓥ ⦿ ▭ col

Dir Robert Altman ***Prod*** David Foster, Mitchell Brower ***Scr*** Robert Altman, Brian McKay ***Ph*** Vilmos Zsigmond ***Ed*** Louis Lombardo ***Mus*** Leonard Cohen ***Art*** Leon Ericksen

Act Warren Beatty, Julie Christie, Rene Auberjonois, William Devane, Shelley Duvall, Keith Carradine (Warner)

Robert Altman's *McCabe & Mrs. Miller* is a disappointing mixture. A period story about a small northwest mountain village where stars Warren Beatty and Julie Christie run the bordello, the production suffers from overlength; also a serious effort at moody photography which backfires into pretentiousness; plus a diffused comedy-drama plotline which is repeatedly shoved aside in favor of bawdiness.

Edmund Naughton's novel, *McCabe*, was shot around Vancouver under the title, *The Presbyterian Church Wager*, named for a fictional town. Rene Auberjonois is top-featured as a saloon-bordello owner whose monopoly on fun and games is broken by roving gambler Beatty. Christie becomes Beatty's partner in the flourishing enterprise.

Beatty seems either miscast or misdirected. His own youthful looks cannot be concealed by a beard, makeup, a grunting voice and jerky physical movements; the effect resembles a high-school thesp playing Rip Van Winkle. Christie on the other hand is excellent.

1971: NOMINATION: Best Actress (Julie Christie)

•

MCGUIRE, GO HOME!

SEE: THE HIGH BRIGHT SUN

•

MCHALE'S NAVY

1964, 93 mins, US Ⓥ ⦿ col

Dir Edward J. Montagne ***Prod*** Edward J. Montagne ***Scr*** Frank Gill, Jr., G. Carleton Brown ***Ph*** William Margulies ***Ed*** Sam E. Waxman ***Mus*** Jerry Fielding ***Art*** Russell Kimball, Alexander Golitzen

Act Ernest Borgnine, Joe Flynn, Tim Conway, Carl Ballantine, George Kennedy (Universal)

One wonders how America won the war in the Pacific, if the exploits of Lt. Cmdr. Quinton McHale and his PT-boat crew were typical of that dark period in U.S. history. But then, *McHale's Navy*, a full-length feature version of Revue's successful telepix series, doesn't attempt to prove any point.

Edward J. Montagne, producer and sometimes-director of vidpix, handles both chores in this longer color rendition and pulls out all the stops.

Like its original TV counterpart, action here depends upon outlandish situations in which McHale and his crew, who do things the "McHale" way first and the Navy's way second, get involved. In the present case, it's getting out of debt, first for getting themselves deeply in the red by restaging Australian horse race results for excitement-hungry Marines from week-old-but-track-fresh news sheets flown in, and again for dock damages inflicted by their runaway PT-boat.

Where pic is longest on yocks is the clowning of Joe Flynn, as Capt. Wallace Binghampton and McHale's immediate superior, and Tim Conway's hamming—there's no other word—as McHale's own exec and as naive a gent as ever fell down a ship's ladder.

•

MCKENZIE BREAK, THE

1970, 106 mins, US Ⓥ col

Dir Lamont Johnson ***Prod*** Jules Levy, Arthur Gardner, Arnold Laven ***Scr*** William Norton, Brian McKay ***Ph*** Michael Reed ***Ed*** Tom Rolf ***Mus*** Riz Ortolani ***Art*** Leon Ericksen

Act Brian Keith, Helmut Griem, Ian Hendry, Patrick O'Connell, Caroline Mortimer, Horst Janson (United Artists)

The McKenzie Break is a taut, classically crafted World War II POW escape drama with an original twist. This time it is the Germans, a corps of crack U-boat officers, led by Helmut Griem, breaking out of a camp in Scotland.

An imaginative, intelligent script (from a novel by Sidney Shelley), crackling direction by Lamont and strong, three-dimensional portrayals by Griem and Brian Keith, as a British intelligence officer trying to outguess and outmaneuver the Nazi, transform the film into a tense personal duel that maintains its suspense until the final frames.

Griem is hardly the stereotype brutal Nazi, but nevertheless he is a model Hitler youth risen to young U-boat captain. He runs the prison like a youth camp, keeping his British captors at bay with riots and demonstrations planned to the split second. It is all a cover-up, and training, for the escape.

•

MCLINTOCK!

1963, 127 mins, US Ⓥ ⦿ ▭ col

Dir Andrew V. McLaglen ***Prod*** Michael Wayne ***Scr*** James Edward Grant ***Ph*** William H. Clothier ***Ed*** Otho Lovering ***Mus*** Frank DeVol ***Art*** Hal Pereira, Eddie Imazu

Act John Wayne, Maureen O'Hara, Yvonne De Carlo, Patrick Wayne, Stefanie Powers (Batjac/United Artists)

McLintock!, most of all, is a John Wayne western. The style of the production is forked-tongue-in-cheek. Nucleus of yarn is the marital duel between Wayne, straight-shooting, rough-and-tumble, high-living, hard-drinking cattle baron whose town has been named after him, and Maureen O'Hara, who has more reservations than a Comanche real-estate agent.

Wayne is in his element, or home, home on the Waynge. O'Hara gives her customary high-spirited performance, although it's never quite clear what she's so darned sore about. Yvonne De Carlo is attractive as Wayne's cook, Stefanie Powers likewise as his college-educated daughter. Vying for the latter's affection are Patrick Wayne, who etches a likable characterization, and Jerry Van Dyke, who gives a skillfully oafish performance.

●

MCQ
1974, 115 mins, US Ⓥ ⊙ ▭ col
Dir John Sturges ***Prod*** Jules Levy, Arthur Gardner ***Scr*** Lawrence Roman ***Ph*** Harry Stradling, Jr. ***Ed*** William Ziegler ***Mus*** Elmer Bernstein ***Art*** Walter Simonds
Act John Wayne, Eddie Albert, Diana Muldaur, Colleen Dewhurst, Clu Gulager, Al Lettieri (Batjac/Warner)

McQ is a good contemporary crime-actioner filmed entirely in Seattle, with John Wayne discovering that his slain buddy was a member of a crooked police ring stealing dope evidence.

Featured as an aging bar waitress from whom Wayne obtains evidence, Colleen Dewhurst is outstanding in her two scenes.

McQ attracts and sustains continued interest from the opening frames, where William Bryant, after shooting two policemen, is himself revealed as one, just before being killed. Eddie Albert, as Wayne's superior, makes the usual knee-jerk response (arrest radical hippies) while Wayne suspects big time dope dealer Al Lettieri.

●

MCVICAR
1980, 111 mins, UK Ⓥ ⊙ col
Dir Tom Clegg ***Prod*** David Gideon Thomson, Jackie Curbishley ***Scr*** John McVicar, Tom Clegg ***Ph*** Vernon Layton ***Ed*** Peter Boyle ***Mus*** Jeff Wayne ***Art*** Brian Ackland-Snow
Act Roger Daltrey, Adam Faith, Cheryl Campbell, Steven Berkoff, Brian Hall, Ian Hendry (Curbishley-Baird/The Who)

Feature is a conscientious reconstruction of several crucial months in the life of John McVicar, who escaped from the high-security wing of an English prison where he was serving eight years for robbery with violence.

McVicar is the author of the book *McVicar by Himself*, which was used as the basis of the film.

Roger Daltrey projects a disquieting mix of danger and vulnerability. Moreover, his characterization goes a long way towards supplying the sense of a mind at work behind the uncompromising, bony face and the thuggish look in the eyes.

Tom Clegg's firm direction is unflamboyant. Although much of the drama certainly doesn't call for obtrusive style, there are moments when more panache would not have come amiss.

There's an excellent, humorous performance by Adam Faith as Probyn, and a chillingly manic one by Steven Berkoff, in a role modeled on an actual inmate.

●

ME AND MY GAL
1932, 79 mins, US b/w
Dir Raoul Walsh ***Scr*** Arthur Kober ***Ph*** Arthur Miller ***Ed*** Jack Murray ***Art*** Gordon Wiles
Act Spencer Tracy, Joan Bennett, Marion Burns, George Walsh, J. Farrell MacDonald (Fox)

A story [by Barry Conners and Philip Klein] about a cop, the waitress he finally marries and the girl's sister who gets tangled up with a rodman. That's about all.

Spencer Tracy makes a good cop. Joan Bennett doesn't make as good a hardboiled waitress but she gets by with it.

Picture is not altogether a dud through having some comedy. Highlights in this direction are a drunk fisherman and a send-up of *Strange Interlude* with asides by Tracy and Bennett in a make sequence. Picture is called *Strange Innertube*, with the dialog the only part getting somewhere.

Dialog throughout runs to wisecracking. It becomes more than ordinarily tiring because of its lack of originality, which together with the slow pace set by the action makes *Me and My Gal* a long 79 minutes. Plot meanders unimportantly to the point where a cop captures the gunman who has been making life miserable for his girl's sister after unwisely falling into his company. The menace is done by George Walsh, who has changed a lot since the old silent days and the athletic hero roles he played.

●

ME AND MY GAL
1942, 94 mins, US b/w
Dir Busby Berkeley ***Prod*** Arthur Freed ***Scr*** Richard Sherman, Fred Fincklehoffe, Sid Silvers ***Ph*** William Daniels ***Ed*** Ben Lewis ***Mus*** George Stoll (dir)
Act Judy Garland, George Murphy, Gene Kelly, Richard Quine, Horace McNally (M-G-M)

Story of vaudeville troupers before and during the First World War [from an original story by Howard Emmett Rogers] is obvious, naive and sentimental. It's also genuine and affectionate and lively.

Picture's title, of course, is taken from one of the song numbers, the oldie "For Me and My Gal." The tune that brings Judy Garland and Gene Kelly together, first as vaudeville team and ultimately as a romance, it gets a sock presentation in a song-and-dance routine by them and is used thereafter as a theme.

Garland is a knockout as the warm-hearted young song-and-dance girl, selling a number of the songs persuasively, getting by neatly in the hoofing routines with Kelly, and giving a tender, affecting dramatic performance. Kelly gives a vividly drawn portrayal of the song-and-dance man and imperfect hero.

●

MEAN MACHINE, THE
SEE: THE LONGEST YARD

●

MEAN SEASON, THE
1985, 103 mins, US Ⓥ ⊙ ▭ col
Dir Phillip Borsos ***Prod*** David Foster, Larry Turman ***Scr*** Leon Piedmont ***Ph*** Frank Tidy ***Ed*** Duwayne Dunham ***Mus*** Lalo Schifrin ***Art*** Philip Jefferies
Act Kurt Russell, Mariel Hemingway, Richard Jordan, Richard Masur, Joe Pantoliano, Richard Bradford (Orion)

Based on the novel, *In the Heat of the Summer*, by former *Miami Herald* crime reporter John Katzenbach, pic establishes solid Florida heat and humidity as the "mean" background to a series of murders that perversely link together the killer (Richard Jordan), and a Miami police reporter (Kurt Russell) who becomes the psychopath's personal spokesman.

Jordan is at his shrewdly crazed best, anchoring the movie with a felt terror, initially just through his offscreen voice as he manipulates the reporter over the phone and ultimately through his cunning.

Russell plays a reporter (production used the city room of the *Miami Herald*) who, credibly enough, gets swept away with all the national hype he's getting as the only man who can talk to the killer.

His live-in elementary school teacher, g.f., essayed rather uneventfully by Mariel Hemingway, grows outraged as the reporter succumbs to his own ego, to the killer's tantalizing calls, and to his increased stature as newsmaker.

●

MEAN STREETS
1973, 110 mins, US Ⓥ ⊙ col
Dir Martin Scorsese ***Prod*** Jonathan T. Taplin ***Scr*** Martin Scorsese, Mardik Martin ***Ph*** Kent Wakeford ***Ed*** Sid Levin
Act Robert De Niro, Harvey Keitel, David Proval, Amy Robinson, Richard Romanus, Cesare Danova (TPS/Warner)

In essence *Mean Streets* is an updated, downtown version of *Marty* (1955), with small-time criminality replacing those long stretches of beer-drinking in a Bronx bar. Four aging adolescents, all in their mid-20s but still inclined toward prankish irresponsibility, float among the lower-class denizens of Manhattan's Little Italy, struggling to make a living out of loan-sharking, the numbers game and bartending.

The hero, competently played by Harvey Keitel, is on the verge of taking over a restaurant for his vaguely Mafioso uncle (Cesar Danova in a compelling, deglamorized interpretation), but his climb to respectability is obstructed by his kinship with the troublemaking Robert De Niro and his budding love for De Niro's epileptic cousin, played rather confusingly by Amy Robinson.

Screenplay, instead of developing these characters and their complex interactions, remains content to sketch in their day-to-day happenings. But Scorsese is exceptionally good at guiding his largely unknown cast to near-flawless recreations of types. Outstanding in this regard is De Niro.

●

MEATBALLS
1979, 92 mins, Canada Ⓥ ⊙ col
Dir Ivan Reitman ***Prod*** Dan Goldberg ***Scr*** Len Blum, Dan Goldberg, Janis Allen, Harold Ramis ***Ph*** Don Wilder ***Ed*** Debra Karen ***Mus*** Elmer Bernstein ***Art*** David Charles
Act Bill Murray, Harvey Atkin, Kate Lynch, Russ Banham, Kristine DeBell (Paramount)

It's difficult to come up with a more cliché situation for a summer pic than a summer camp, where all the characters and plot turns are readily imaginable. That makes director Ivan Reitman's accomplishment all the more noteworthy.

Bill Murray limns a head counselor in charge of a group of misfit counselors-in-training. The usual types predominate: the myopic klutz, the obese kid who wins the pig-out contest, the smooth-talking lothario, and a bevy of comely lasses.

Scripters have managed to gloss over the stereotypes and come up with a smooth-running narrative that makes the camp hijinks part of an overall human mosaic. No one is unduly belittled or mocked, and *Meatballs* is without the usual grossness and cynicism of many contempo comedy pix.

●

MECHANIC, THE
1972, 100 mins, US Ⓥ ⊙ col
Dir Michael Winner ***Prod*** Robert Chartoff, Irwin Winkler, Lewis John Carlino ***Scr*** Lewis John Carlino ***Ph*** Richard Kline ***Ed*** Freddie Wilson ***Mus*** Jerry Fielding ***Art*** Rodger Maus
Act Charles Bronson, Keenan Wynn, Jan-Michael Vincent, Jill Ireland, Linda Ridgeway, Frank de Kova (United Artists)

A mechanic, in underworld parlance, is a highly skilled contract killer. Possibilities of limning such a character are realistically pointed up in this action-drenched gangster yarn burdened with an overly contrived plot development.

For the first few reels, footage is more a series of episodes—not always clear, at that—than carrying a sustained story line.

Credibility is sometimes further strained during first half of film when Bronson oscillates between a typical hood at work and lolling in a luxurious apartment far removed from world of crime.

Michael Winner keeps the tempo at fever pitch despite deficiencies of feature's opening sequences.

Bronson plays the son of a former gang leader cut down in his prime, left a fortune but still associated with crime as a hired executioner.

●

MEDICINE MAN
1992, 106 mins, US Ⓥ ⊙ ▭ col
Dir John McTiernan ***Prod*** Andrew G. Vajna, Donna Dubrow ***Scr*** Tom Schulman, Sally Robinson, [Tom Stoppard] ***Ph*** Donald McAlpine ***Ed*** Michael R. Miller ***Mus*** Jerry Goldsmith ***Art*** John Krenz Reinhart, Jr.
Act Sean Connery, Lorraine Bracco, Jose Wilker, Rodolfo De Alexandre, Angelo Barra Moreira (Hollywood/Cinergi)

An indelicate attempt to create some *African Queen*–style magic while curing cancer and saving the rain forests in the bargain, this jumbo-budget two-character piece suffers from a very weak script and a lethal job of miscasting.

Ponytailed and bearded, Sean Connery portrays a maverick biochemist who's been working in the Amazon for six years when his sponsoring company sends a researcher to his remote outpost to check up on him. The woman in question is played by Lorraine Bracco, whose screeching New York accent is so pronounced that Connery immediately starts calling her Bronx, and whose manner is so abrasive that it's a wonder Connery doesn't just toss her to the crocodiles.

In search of the rare blossoms for his cancer cure, Connery takes Bracco on a major E-ticket ride up a series of counterbalanced rope riggings to the treetops, affording a breathtaking view of the jungle. Nonetheless, their personal story remains grounded by banality relieved only by a trek through the forest that sees Bracco indulging in some high-spirited substance abuse and getting stuck on a branch hundreds of feet above a gorge.

Trying to show that he can do something other than action, which he does so well, helmer John McTiernan has not proved that he can. Jerry Goldsmith's score is thunderingly overbearing.

●

MEDITERRANEO
1991, 105 mins, Italy Ⓥ ⊙ col
Dir Gabriele Salvatores ***Prod*** Gianni Minervini, Mario Cecchi Gori, Vittorio Cecchi Gori ***Scr*** Vincenzo Monteleone ***Ph*** Italo Petriccione ***Ed*** Nino Baragli ***Mus*** Giancarlo Bigazzi, Mario Falagiani ***Art*** Thalia Istikopoulou
Act Diego Abatantuono, Claudio Bigagli, Giuseppe Cederna, Claudio Bisio, Gigio Alberti, Vanna Barba (Pentafilm/AMA)

Final installment of Gabriele Salvatores's road pic trilogy, *Mediterraneo* follows *Marrakech Express* and *Turne* in its exploration of the dreams and disappointments and eventual escape of the generation now pushing 40. The rabble rousing of 1968 becomes WWII, the heady idealism of the '70s becomes the Greek idyll, and the fizzled hopes of the '80s become the return to mamma Italia, at least for the central characters.

Eight Italian soldiers are sent to garrison a remote, strategically unimportant Greek island during World War II. As they adapt to island life, the delicate comic moments stay just on the right side of schlocky: one soldier mourns his beloved donkey, a burly boy falls quietly in love with the sergeant, two brothers and a shepherdess have a sexually spiritual menage a trois, and the group underdog and the local prostitute undergo a little courtship.

The film's conclusion slips unnecessarily into trite barbershop philosophizing as two of the soldiers, 40 years on, escape from their grand delusion by pulling up a chair to chop eggplants back at the island taverna.

The pic is rich in affectionate new slants on old Italo emblems like soccer, sex and snappy dressing. The ensemble work of the performers and crew give this pic much of its buoyancy. Setting is the tucked-away island of Kastellorizo in the Dodecanese.

1991: Best Foreign Language Film

•

MEDIUM, THE
1951, 85 mins, US Ⓥ b/w
Dir Gian-Carlo Menotti ***Prod*** Walter Lowendahl ***Scr*** Gian-Carlo Menotti ***Ph*** Enzo Serafin ***Ed*** Alexander Hammid ***Mus*** Gian-Carlo Menotti
Act Marie Powers, Anna Maria Alberghetti, Leo Coleman, Belva Kibler, Beverly Dame, Donald Morgan (Transfilm)

Composer-librettist Gian-Carlo Menotti, who surprised Broadway by turning out two successive operas, *The Medium* and *The Consul*, that became legit hits, turns film director and makes *The Medium* into an impressive pic. The work is limited by the fact that it is stark modern opera, all in song or recitative.

Menotti filmed the opus in Rome, utilizing Marie Powers and Leo Coleman from the original legit cast, and the 15-year-old Italian coloratura find, Anna Maria Alberghetti, in her film debut, for the third principal. Menotti is too fond of the camera, and too intent on trick angles and effects. He overworks the close-ups. But he comes up with some nifty shots that dovetail with the bizarre opus. Story is that of a shabby medium, Madame Flora (Powers), living with her daughter Monica (Alberghetti), and Toby, a mute gypsy waif they adopted (Coleman), and the seances they hold for gullible clients.

Mme. Flora, who is given to drink, disrupts one seance suddenly when she fancies someone's hand at her throat trying to choke her. She accuses her customers and then Toby of the deed, and when they deny it, is distraught. Fear of some supernatural power turning on her for her shams drives her further towards the bottle.

Although the picture was filmed in Italy, it has no particular locale, and is sung entirely in English. Sets are simple and costumes and makeup properly drab. Film shows a tightened budget without cheapness of quality.

1950: NOMINATION: Best Scoring of a Musical Picture

•

MEDIUM COOL
1969, 110 mins, US Ⓥ ⦿ col
Dir Haskell Wexler ***Prod*** Tully Friedman, Haskell Wexler ***Scr*** Haskell Wexler ***Ph*** Haskell Wexler ***Ed*** Verna Fields ***Mus*** Mike Bloomfield ***Art*** Leon Ericksen
Act Robert Forster, Verna Bloom, Peter Bonerz, Marianna Hill, Harold Blankenship, Charles Geary (Paramount/H&J)

Photographed in Chicago against the clamor and violence of the 1968 Democratic National Convention, where cast principals were on their own as they made their way through the crowds and police lines. Buildup to these later sequences frequently is confusing and motives difficult to fathom.

Director Haskell Wexler, in his first indie production, mixes "reality" with the "theatrical," his two chief protagonists a realistic TV newsreel cameraman and a young hillbilly mother come to Chicago with her young son. Wexler adopts a documentary approach which helps sustain the mood and his cast fits into this pattern.

Robert Forster is strongly cast as the lenser who refuses to become emotionally involved with any of his assignments until caught up in the injustice done to a Negro and while on TV assignment, falls in love with a young mother.

•

MEDUSA TOUCH, THE
1978, 110 mins, UK/France Ⓥ col
Dir Jack Gold ***Prod*** Anne V. Coates, Jack Gold ***Scr*** John Briley ***Ph*** Arthur Ibbetson ***Ed*** Anne V. Coates, Ian Crafford ***Mus*** Michael J. Lewis ***Art*** Peter Mullins
Act Richard Burton, Lino Ventura, Lee Remick, Harry Andrews, Marie-Christine Barrault, Michael Hordern (ITC/Coatesgold)

Another disaster film? Not exactly, even if at the end a London cathedral caves in, with many victims trapped underneath the rubble but with the Queen of England saved in the nick of time. These scenes, realistically treated and technically good, are among the highlights of this lavishly produced film [from the novel by Peter Van Greenaway].

John Morlar (Richard Burton) is attacked by an unknown intruder who bashes in his skull. Why? The man didn't seem to have a single enemy. Inspector Brunel is puzzled. Why a French detective instead of British? Apparently due to French financial participation in this film. In any case, it allows Lino Ventura to make his British film debut and very good he is.

Brunel finally discovers a clue leading to a psychiatrist played by Lee Remick. She had treated Morlar for reasons not stated at once.

It turns out that Morlar is not dead at all. His mind is fighting a desperate battle to survive. Even as a child, Morlar proved a very odd number indeed. His files relate to a vast series of disasters and apparently unsolved mysteries.

Director Jack Gold controls all the angles of this improbable story. Burton has some very effective moments too as does Remick.

•

MEETING VENUS
1991, 117 mins, UK Ⓥ ⦿ col
Dir Istvan Szabo ***Prod*** David Puttnam ***Scr*** Istvan Szabo, Michael Hirst ***Ph*** Lajos Koltai ***Ed*** Jim Clark ***Mus*** Daisy Boschan (cons.) ***Art*** Attila Kovacs
Act Glenn Close, Niels Arestrup, Erland Josephson, Moscu Alcalay, Macha Meril, Johanna Ter Steege (Enigma)

Glenn Close hits the high notes as a cool diva in *Meeting Venus*, but romantic comedy set in a strife-torn Paris opera house is knocked on the head by a central love story that's dumb and uninvolving.

Yarn opens in sprightly style with Budapest conductor (Niels Arestrup) flying in for a production of Wagner's *Tannhauser* at the fictional Opera Europa. After being introduced to polyglot staff, he soon realizes that "here you can be misunderstood in six languages." The internal politics make old Eastern Europe look like a summer camp.

He doesn't get any help from his lead soprano (Close), who initially dismisses him. Plot grinds to a halt halfway when Close suddenly takes a liking to the humbled Arestrup, and they're soon exchanging confidences between the sheets. Film ends with the chaotic first night of *Tannhauser* back in Paris.

What must have seemed on paper like a lighthearted satire on Euro-squabbling and the multilingual opera scene works okay in the opening rounds. Magyar helmer Istvan Szabo directed the same opera in Paris six years earlier and makes no secret that the pic was inspired by his experiences. Things start to go wrong when the Close-Arestrup affair gets serious.

•

MEET JOE BLACK
1998, 180 mins, US Ⓥ ⦿ col
Dir Martin Brest ***Prod*** Martin Brest ***Scr*** Ron Osborn, Jeff Reno, Kevin Wade, Bo Goldman ***Ph*** Emmanuel Lubezki ***Ed*** Joe Hutshing, Michael Tronick ***Mus*** Thomas Newman ***Art*** Dante Ferretti
Act Brad Pitt, Anthony Hopkins, Claire Forlani, Jake Weber, Marcia Gay Harden, Jeffey Tambor (City Light/Universal)

In half the time it takes to *Meet Joe Black*, many good films chart an entire life story. By contrast, this thoroughly overelaborated whimsy dawdles distractedly in delineating one man's confrontation with mortality, in the person of a handsome young stranger.

Martin Brest skated on thin ice but got away with it, at least with moviegoers, when he stretched his last film, *Scent of a Woman* (1992), out to 157 minutes. Here, he pushes his luck too far by extending a slim conceit to a full three hours. The film upon which it is based, Mitchell Leisen's 1934 Paramount release, *Death Takes a Holiday*, ran just 79 minutes, except that the new picture isn't a remake in any meaningful sense. Brest and his writers have taken just the central premise of Death assuming human form for a few days to get a taste of what life is like, and falling in love along the way

New York media tycoon William Parrish (Anthony Hopkins) begins hearing a strange, disembodied voice, and shortly suffers a heart seizure. The voice materializes in the guise of a visitor, who goes by the name of Joe Black (Brad Pitt), who informs the older man he can buy some time if he will act as his guide to all things earthly.

Thus begins a peculiar relationship in which the dazzingly blond Joe follows the powerful William on all his rounds. William's younger daughter, Susan (Claire Forlani), is determined to figure out who the mystery man is, and sure enough maneuvers him into her arms.

Hopkins plays with tremendous verve and sympathy, but the character seems impossibly idealized. Looking dashing and slightly impish at times, Pitt's Joe Black is an odd egg indeed. Forlani makes a limited impression. Luxuriously upholstered pic so thoroughly expresses the world of its wealthy characters that the money all but drips from the screen.

•

MEET JOHN DOE
1941, 129 mins, US Ⓥ ⦿ b/w
Dir Frank Capra ***Prod*** Frank Capra ***Scr*** Robert Riskin ***Ph*** George Barnes ***Ed*** Daniel Mandell ***Mus*** Dimitri Tiomkin ***Art*** Stephen Goosson
Act Gary Cooper, Barbara Stanwyck, Edward Arnold, Walter Brennan, Spring Byington, James Gleason (Capra/Warner)

Picture tells the story of the rehabilitation of a tramp exbaseball player who assents to the role of a puppet social reformer in the hands of a young woman columnist on a metropolitan newspaper.

The heroine, having been fired from her job through a change in the sheet's ownership, regains her place by inventing a fictitious John Doe as author of a letter of protest against the prevailing injustices of a political and social system which permits hunger in a land of plenty and idleness in a world where much remains to be accomplished. As earnest of his appeal he declares he will commit suicide on Christmas Eve in expiation for the sins of society.

The synthetic fabric of the story is the weakness of the production, despite the magnificence of the Frank Capra–directed superstructure. But Robert Riskin, who wrote the screenplay from an original story by Richard Connell and Robert Presnell, leaves the audience at the finale with scarcely more than the hope that some day selfishness, fraud and deceit will be expunged from human affairs.

1941: NOMINATION: Best Original Story

•

MEET ME AFTER THE SHOW
1951, 86 mins, US col
Dir Richard Sale ***Prod*** George Jessel ***Scr*** Mary Loos, Richard Sale ***Ph*** Arthur E. Arling ***Ed*** J. Watson Webb, Jr. ***Mus*** Lionel Newman (dir.) ***Art*** Lyle Wheeler, Joseph C. Wright
Act Betty Grable, Macdonald Carey, Rory Calhoun, Eddie Albert, Fred Clark, Lois Andrews (20th Century-Fox)

George Jessel has endowed this Betty Grable offering with five strong production numbers and six tunes to make it topnotch escapist musical entertainment that will please the song-and-dance fan. There's a delightfully bawdy air about some of the numbers and in the playing and direction to sharpen the chuckles.

Yarn [suggested by a story by Erna Lazarus and W. Scott Darling] concerns a star-producer, husband-wife team that breaks up after seven years of marriage because the missus suspects that hubby is chasing other gals. As the supposedly wronged wife, Grable feigns amnesia and goes back to the cheap Miami nightclub where hubby Macdonald Carey had first discovered her. Carey and Eddie Albert, longtime suitor of Grable, pursue her, and plenty of comedy touches are poured on for laughs as they try to protect her from a sea-loving nature boy, neatly portrayed by Rory Calhoun, and bring back her memory.

Tunes are all by Jule Styne and Leo Robin, and are good, although not particularly outstanding.

•

MEET ME AT THE FAIR
1952, 87 mins, US col
Dir Douglas Sirk ***Prod*** Albert J. Cohen ***Scr*** Irving Wallace ***Ph*** Maury Gertsman ***Ed*** Russell Schoengarth ***Mus*** Joseph Gershenson (dir.) ***Art*** Bernard Herzbrun, Eric Orborn
Act Dan Dailey, Diana Lynn, Chet Allen, Scatman Crothers, Hugh O'Brian, Carole Mathews (Universal)

The production has a period flavor featuring nostalgia and schmaltz against a 1904 setting. The old-fashioned drama [from the novel *The Great Companions* by Gene Markey, adapted by Martin Berkeley] revolves around an orphan kid who runs away from a grim institution, takes up with a medicine man, with his new friend charged with kidnaping. Before it's all over, the medicine man and the kid are mixed up in a political fight and eventually bring about reforms at the orphanage.

Best in the musical department is Carole Mathews doing "Bill Bailey" and the title number. She also works with Dan Dailey on "Remember the Time" and generally impresses.

Dailey is very likeable as the medicine man, giving the character a good-natured flavor that helps the film.

•

MEET ME IN ST. LOUIS
1944, 118 mins, US Ⓥ ⦿ col
Dir Vincente Minnelli ***Prod*** Arthur Freed ***Scr*** Irving Brecher, Fred F. Finklehoffe ***Ph*** George Folsey ***Ed*** Albert Akst ***Art*** Cedric Gibbons, Lemuel Ayers, Jack Martin Smith
Act Judy Garland, Margaret O'Brien, Mary Astor, Lucille Bremer, Tom Drake, Marjorie Main (M-G-M)

Meet Me in St. Louis is wholesome in story [from the book by Sally Benson], colorful both in background and its literal Technicolor, and as American as the World Series.

As Leon Ames plays the head of the Alonzo Smith clan it's a 1903 life-with-father. Mary Astor is the understanding and, incidentally, quite handsome mother as they worry about Judy Garland and Lucille Bremer, playing their daughters. Henry H. Daniels, Jr., is the self-sufficient brother, off to Princeton, but the romantic travail of the two older girls is the fundamental. Backgrounded are Marjorie Main, capital as the maid who almost bosses the household, and the still-gallant Harry Davenport, now 80-ish, who is grandpa.

It's the time of the St. Louis Fair, hence the title song, and everything that makes for the happy existence of a typical American family is skillfully panoramaed.

Seasonal pastorals, from summer into the next spring, take the Smith clan through their appealing little problems. Judy Garland's plaint about "The Boy Next Door" (played by Tom Drake); the Paul Jones dance routine to the tune of "Skip to My Lou"; the Yuletide thematic, "Have Yourself a Merry Christmas"; and the "Trolley Song," en route to the Fairgrounds, are four socko musical highlights. They have been intelligently highlighted and well-paced by director Vincente Minnelli.

Garland achieves true stature with her deeply understanding performance, while her sisterly running mate, Lucille Bremer, likewise makes excellent impact with a well-balanced performance.

1944: NOMINATIONS: Best Color Cinematograhy, Scoring of a Musical Picture, Song ("The Trolley Song")

•

MEET THE APPLEGATES
(AUSTRALIA: THE APPLEGATES)
1991, 82 mins, US Ⓥ ⦿ col
Dir Michael Lehmann ***Prod*** Denise Di Novi ***Scr*** Redbeard Simmons, Michael Lehmann ***Ph*** Mitchell Dubin ***Ed*** Norman Hollyn ***Mus*** David Newman ***Art*** Jon Hutman
Act Ed Begley, Jr., Stockard Channing, Cami Cooper, Bobby Jacoby, Dabney Coleman, Glenn Shadix (New World)

In his weird 1988 debut *Heathers*, Lehmann gave a bizarre twist to the usual portrayal of U.S. teen life. In this pic he takes an even more extreme approach to sending up American family life. In a bid to save the Brazilian rain forest from development, a family of giant beetles is sent to infiltrate American society and blow up a nuclear power station as a warning.

Chameleonlike, they assume the form of humans, and, learning from a *Fun with Dick and Jane* reader, become the average America family. Surrounded by temptations in a community-minded town in Ohio, the family soon degenerates, with Dick (Ed Begley, Jr.) having an affair, Jane (Stockard Channing) becoming obsessed with credit and alcohol, Johnny (Bobby Jacoby) turning into a dope dealer and Sally (Cami Cooper) becoming pregnant. Such a wacky premise could derail easily, but Lehmann handles it with humor and paces it well. Begley and company play it for all it's worth, and seem to be having a ball. Scenes of the Applegates becoming bugs (usually with disastrous consequences) are cleverly done.

•

MEET THE PARENTS
2000, 108 mins, US Ⓥ ⦿ col
Dir Jay Roach ***Prod*** Nancy Tenenbaum, Jane Rosenthal, Robert De Niro, Jay Roach ***Scr*** Jim Herzfeld, John Hamburg ***Ph*** Peter James ***Ed*** Jon Poll ***Mus*** Randy Newman ***Art*** Rusty James
Act Robert De Niro, Ben Stiller, Blythe Danner, Teri Polo, James Rebhorn, Jon Abrahams (Universal/DreamWorks)

The history of comedy is loaded with stories of earnest young men who need to prove their worth to prospective wives or parents-in-law. *Meet the Parents* actually has its genesis in one of them, a short film by comedian Greg Glienna, who shares story credit with Mary Ruth Clarke. In the yarn as developed, Greg Focker (Ben Stiller) systematically proves he's not worthy to wed the lovely Pam Byrnes (Teri Polo), with the latter's intimidating CIA vet father Jack (Robert De Niro) giving the young man all the rope he needs to hang himself. Pic pivots on a clash of cultures and class that is rigged against the interloper from the outset, and the accumulation of disasters and humiliations instigated and suffered by the sincere suitor is accompanied by a direct escalation in hilarity.

Disaster piles upon disaster as Greg is effortlessly put in his place by Debbie's medically eminent father and fiance, injures the bride-to-be in a fiercely competitive water volleyball game, floods the backyard wedding site with sewage by flushing a toilet he's been told not to touch, lets Jack's precious cat outside and nearly destroys the house trying to retrieve it. Greg is finally kicked out of the house an hour into the picture, leaving the young man to wonder if he really is as big a schnook as he's seemed for the past two days, and Jack to decide whether he's an impossibly overprotective father.

Although De Niro is not the first actor that comes to mind to play a WASPy patriarch, actor socks over his characterization of military man with an unerring BS detector via an amazing array of condescending and critical facial expressions and twists of phrase. On more familiar ground is Stiller, whose performance constitutes a virtual catalog of the varieties of schmuckdom and consequent embarrassment. Directed by Jay Roach with real comic verve and alertness to the humorous possibilities in every situation, pic verily races along without ever seeming forced or losing steam.

•

MEET WHIPLASH WILLIE
SEE: THE FORTUNE COOKIE

•

MELANCHOLIA
1989, 87 mins, UK/W. Germany Ⓥ col
Dir Andi Engel ***Prod*** Colin MacCabe ***Scr*** Andi Engel, Lewis Rodia ***Ph*** Denis Crossan ***Ed*** Christopher Roth ***Mus*** Simon Fisher Turner ***Art*** Jock Scott
Act Jeroen Krabbe, Susannah York, Ulrich Wildgruber, Jane Gurnett, Kate Hardie, Saul Reichlin (BFI/Lichtblick)

Despite a dauntingly uninviting title, *Melancholia* proves to be a stimulating contemporary thriller about an idealist from the 1960s who decides to take violent action in support of his long-submerged beliefs.

Jeroen Krabbe plays a German, Keller, long resident in London, who works as a critic, lives alone and drinks too much. He is aroused from his inertia by a phone call from Hamburg from Manfred, who asks him to assassinate Chilean torturer Vargas, currently visiting London.

Manfred later visits London to tell Keller the assassination is off: The Chilean can now be of use to "our side." Soon after, Keller is approached by Sarah Yelin (Jane Gurnett), a torture victim, whose husband was horribly murdered by Vargas. He makes up his mind and tracks down the Chilean.

The film raises questions about the use of violence to prevent further violence, and about the passivity of idealists. It doesn't play as a straight commercial thriller, but as a serious pic exploring provocative themes with intelligence.

Melancholia is the first film directed by Andi Engel, the German-born, London-based former critic who's best known as a distributor and exhibitor in Britain.

•

MELODY
1971, 103 mins, UK Ⓥ col
Dir Waris Hussein ***Prod*** David Puttnam ***Scr*** Alan Parker ***Ph*** Peter Suschitzky ***Ed*** John Victor Smith ***Mus*** The Bee Gees ***Art*** Roy Stannard
Act Jack Wild, Mark Lester, Tracy Hyde, Sheila Steafel, Roy Kinnear, Hilda Barry (Hemdale/Sagittarius)

Melody is the story of a couple of 10-year-olds who fall in love and want to get married.

Mark Lester and Tracy Hyde as the very young lovers persist on ogling each other in class, despite the taunts of their fellows. Later, they forthrightly present their marriage plans to their parents and teachers. Jack Wild, as their engaging friend, makes the kind of overt attempt to woo his buddy away from romance that no sane kid would be able to filter past his learned notions of the acceptable.

Screenwriter Alan Parker and director Waris Hussein are to be congratulated for attempting something that—whatever its surface strains on credulity—is a lot closer to what kids are about than the mush they're usually served at matinees.

The acting by the adults is intentionally exaggerated, as if seen through the kids' eyes, and the young people, for the most part, are both natural and appealing. Lester is a bit too cute and a trifle phony, but Hyde, in the title role, is more than acceptable—and Wild, an actor of remarkable intelligence and wit, runs off with the picture.

•

MELODY OF LIFE
SEE: SYMPHONY OF SIX MILLION

•

MELVIN AND HOWARD
1980, 93 mins, US Ⓥ ⦿ col
Dir Jonathan Demme ***Prod*** Art Linson, Don Phillips ***Scr*** Bo Goldman ***Ph*** Tak Fujimoto ***Ed*** Craig McKay ***Mus*** Bruce Langhorne ***Art*** Toby Rafelson
Act Paul Le Mat, Jason Robards, Mary Steenburgen, Michael J. Pollard, Dabney Coleman, Gloria Grahame (Universal)

A pungent fable about the elusiveness of the American Dream, *Melvin and Howard* is a richly textured, highly individualistic look at Melvin Dummar, a man in over his head both before and after becoming the beneficiary of $156 million via Howard Hughes's so-called Mormon will. Jonathan Demme's tour-de-force direction, the imaginative screenplay and top-drawer performances from a huge cast fuse in an unusual, original creation.

Dummar's chance encounter with a man representing himself as the reclusive tycoon occupies first reel or so and, despite Jason Robards's amusing portrait of Hughes as a grizzled old coot, pic takes awhile generating a full head of steam. As his two-time bride and divorcee Mary Steenburgen says, Melvin is a loser, and early footage focusing upon his inability to cope with family or jobs makes for somewhat uncertain p.o.v.

Film is exemplary for its rare concentration on the quality, and lack of it, in Middle American life, and incisive, if indirect, examination of the no-win syndrome for contemporary proletariat.

1980: Best Supp. Actress (Mary Steenburgen), Original Screenplay

NOMINATION: Best Supp. Actor (Jason Robards)

•

MEMENTO
2000, 116 mins, US Ⓥ ⦿ ▭ col
Dir Christopher Nolan ***Prod*** Suzanne Todd, Jennifer Todd ***Scr*** Christopher Nolan ***Ph*** Wally Pfister ***Ed*** Dody Dorn ***Mus*** David Julyan ***Art*** Patti Podesta
Act Guy Pearce, Carrie-Anne Moss, Joe Pantoliano, Mark Boone Jr., Stephen Tobolowsky, Harriet Sansom Harris (Team Todd/Newmarket)

A bravura tribute to the spirit of *Point Blank* and the importance of short-term memory, *Memento* deconstructs time and space with Einstein-caliber dexterity in the service of a delectably disturbing tale of revenge [from a short story by Jonathan Nolan]. Pic's aggressively nonlinear structure and subtle accretion of clues suggest a second viewing may yield additional rewards, although it's all there the first time around for attentive auds. This beautifully structured puzzle sustains its mystery until the punch-packing resolution of the final frames.

Opening credits show a hand holding a Polaroid photo of a bloodied dead man lying facedown on concrete. The photo "undevelops"—indicating the scene is being shown in reverse. It's an apt intro to a story told via backtracking and partial repetition, all meticulously layered to approximate the waking nightmare and endless conundrum of Leonard Shelby (Guy Pearce, with bleached blonde hair and an American accent).

If ever there was an unreliable narrator, Leonard is it. He can recall everything in his life until the night of the assault that left his wife dead and him with brain damage. Since then, he hasn't been able to make a memory "stick." Leonard has to write himself notes about everything, with the most crucial reminders concerning his mission—such as "John G. raped and murdered your wife"—tattooed on his skin. Unable to remember anyone he's met postassault, no matter how many times they've interacted, Leonard takes Polaroids of everyone he meets and jots captions on them. Leonard's curse is that even if he gets revenge, he won't remember it a few minutes later. His condition also puts a fresh, frequently comical, twist on elements like a chase scene: Leonard is running, but he can't recall whether he's doing the chasing or is being chased.

•

MEMOIRS OF AN INVISIBLE MAN
1992, 99 mins, US Ⓥ ⦿ ▭ col
Dir John Carpenter ***Prod*** Bruce Bodner, Dan Kolsrud ***Scr*** Robert Collector, Dana Olsen, William Goldman ***Ph*** William A. Fraker ***Ed*** Marion Rothman ***Mus*** Shirley Walker ***Art*** Lawrence G. Paull
Act Chevy Chase, Daryl Hannah, Sam Neill, Michael McKean, Stephen Tobolowsky, Jim Norton (Warner/Cornelius)

Main problem with this mildly entertaining special effects showcase proves as transparent as its title character—

namely that Chevy Chase, who can only play Chevy Chase, lacks leading-man qualities necessary to make this sort of Hitchcockian man-in-peril scenario work. Working from H. F. Saint's well-received novel, director John Carpenter and a trio of screenwriters go the espionage route with a comedy twist, but the film fails to fully satisfy on either level.

Chase is cast as a detached stock analyst turned invisible by a freak accident, who then becomes the quarry of a ruthless government agent (Sam Neill) out to exploit his unique gift for the CIA. The story plays as a cat-and-mouse game as Chase flees from his pursuers, in the process receiving help from a woman (Daryl Hannah) he met and became instantly enamored with just prior to the optical mishap.

Film departs from past explorations of the subject in two specific areas: the hero's clothes are rendered invisible as well, meaning he doesn't have to run about in the nude like cinematic predecessor Claude Rains; and anything he ingests stays visible within him, creating the rare opportunity at one point to see an invisible man upchuck. Hannah is asked to do little but look beautiful, and she obliges admirably. Neill and Michael McKean are notably underemployed as the one-dimensional bad guy and Chase's best friend.

•

MEMOIRS OF A SURVIVOR
1981, 117 mins, UK Ⓥ col
Dir David Gladwell ***Prod*** Michael Medwin, Penny Clark ***Scr*** Kerry Crabbe, David Gladwell ***Ph*** Walter Lassally ***Ed*** William Shapter ***Mus*** Mike Thorn
Act Julie Christie, Christopher Guard, Leonie Mellinger, Debbie Hutchins, Pat Keen, Nigel Hawthorne (EMI/Memorial/NFFC)

The film [from the novel by Doris Lessing] depicts Julie Christie as D, an attractive middle-aged woman living alone in the midst of the chaos occurring around her. She dreams of a Victorian time and can go through a wall to witness events.

A little girl, maybe her, is seen in the rich, gilded interiors adroitly given a candlelight feeling by lenser Walter Lassally. The mother is annoyed at not being able to read, work and find herself while the little girl is somewhat neglected by mom and her austere father who at one time contemplates her undraped body while she is asleep.

But reality is grim. A teenage girl is moved in with D and she takes care of her. The girl becomes involved with a young man trying to help vagrant children, living in an abandoned subway station. They have already killed one of his helpers and cannibalized others.

People are leaving the stricken city with some indications of an outside government that gives orders. Strife is not due to any atomic war but just communal life running down.

Christie emerges as a fine character player despite her still potent attractiveness. Director David Gladwell apparently did not have the budget to give a more solid look to the degenerating city.

•

MEMPHIS BELLE
1990, 106 mins, UK Ⓥ ⦿ col
Dir Michael Caton-Jones ***Prod*** David Puttnam, Catherine Wyler ***Scr*** Monte Merrick ***Ph*** David Watkin ***Ed*** Jim Clark ***Mus*** George Fenton ***Art*** Stuart Craig
Act Matthew Modine, Eric Stoltz, Tate Donovan, D. B. Sweeney, David Strathairn, John Lithgow (Enigma)

Offering a romanticized view of heroism drawn from the Hollywood war epic, *Memphis Belle* is unashamedly commercial. Its moral fabric is thinner than that of other David Puttnam productions.

Pic's subject is the 25th and final mission of the *Memphis Belle*, the most celebrated of the U.S. Air Force B-17 bombers. The plane flew 24 perfect missions, and its 25th became part of a massive p.r. drive to boost war-bond sales and morale.

The plane and its team are sent to Germany to drop one last load, setting the scene for suspense, tension, terror and a fitting celebration when all return safe and (almost) sound.

Large chunk of the film is set on the ground, providing adequate exposition of events and character to involve the audience in the mission. Played up is the fact that these 10 guys are barely out of their teens and don't see themselves as heroes.

Original footage from the 1944 documentary *Memphis Belle* by William Wyler, father of coproducer Catherine Wyler, is used for the guaranteed tearjerking scene, with letters from parents of dead soldiers read over it by the commanding officer, thoughtfully played by David Strathairn.

•

ME, MYSELF & IRENE
2000, 117 mins, US Ⓥ ⦿ col
Dir Bobby Farrelly, Peter Farrelly ***Prod*** Bradley Thomas, Bobby Farrelly, Peter Farrelly ***Scr*** Peter Farrelly, Mike Cerrone, Bobby Farrelly ***Ph*** Mark Irwin ***Ed*** Christopher Greenbury ***Mus*** Peter Yorn, Lee Scott ***Art*** Sidney J. Bartholomew Jr.
Act Jim Carrey, Renee Zellweger, Chris Cooper, Robert Forster, Richard Jenkins, Rob Moran (Conundrum/20th Century Fox)

The laughs roll out by the handfuls in *Me, Myself & Irene*, even if they aren't quite as convulsive or surprising as the public might be hoping for in this highly anticipated matchup of Jim Carrey and the Farrelly brothers. With Carrey playing the "dual" role of a split-personality Rhode Island state trooper, the generation's most physical and elastic comic actor has endless opportunities to strut his stuff. Funny as much of the action is, however, the approach feels rather less fresh, and the gross-outs seem more gratuitous and tossed in for effect than in *There's Something About Mary*.

Walking away with the hilarity honors are the three young performers—Anthony Anderson, Mongo Brownlee and Jerod Mixon—who play Carrey's three outsize, street-talking, Ivy League-destined black sons, fabulously written characters whose vulgarity doesn't prevent them from being by far the sweetest people onscreen.

After his impressive turns in two loftier, seriously themed pictures, *The Truman Show* and *Man on the Moon*, Carrey is back in time-tested manic form. Alternating his meek and menacing characters with glee, Carrey, who's decked out with a military-style crew cut, exults in blowing his performances up to a sort of epic comic-book stature, and he gets to do it twice here. Unfortunately, Renee Zellweger doesn't match up as a perfect foil. Her character somehow prompts the hitherto delightful actress to reveal a certain harsh and unpleasant side that becomes rather too dominant. Nor is her timing nearly as precise as Carrey's, which translates into her not always being in synch with his quicksilver transformations and rapid-fire utterances.

As was not the case in *Mary*, on this occasion the Farrellys allow the action to sag from time to time, and their comic aim is not as sure-fire. The really outrageous sexual humor is present, to be sure, but it has a certain dragged-in quality, as if the brothers had a gross-out quota to fill and inserted the penile/rectal/vaginal gags, so to speak, wherever they could.

•

MEN, THE
1950, 85 mins, US Ⓥ b/w
Dir Fred Zinnemann ***Prod*** Stanley Kramer ***Scr*** Carl Foreman ***Ph*** Robert de Grasse ***Ed*** Harry Gerstad ***Mus*** Dimitri Tiomkin
Act Marlon Brando, Teresa Wright, Everett Sloane, Jack Webb, Richard Erdman (United Artists)

In *The Men* producer Stanley Kramer turns to the difficult cinematic subject of paraplegics, so expertly treated as to be sensitive, moving and yet, withal, entertaining and earthy-humored.

From the opening shot, a tensely played battle scene where Lieutenant Wilozek (Marlon Brando) suffers his crushing wound, *The Men* maintains its pace and interest. Thereafter, the film centers on the overwhelming problems of paralyzed vets who must be convinced that their wounds are incurable and that they must yet fight their way to a useful existence. While the film personalizes the story of Wilozek and his fiancée (Teresa Wright), the camera's scope is broader.

Brando, who film-debuts as Wilozek, fails to deliver the necessary sensitivity and inner warmth.

1950: NOMINATION: Best Story & Screenplay

•

MENAGE
SEE: TENUE DE SOIREE

•

ME, NATALIE
1969, 110 mins, US col
Dir Fred Coe ***Prod*** Stanley Shapiro ***Scr*** A. Martin Zweiback ***Ph*** Arthur J. Ornitz ***Ed*** Sheila Bakerman ***Mus*** Henry Mancini ***Art*** George Jenkins
Act Patty Duke, James Farentino, Martin Balsam, Elsa Lanchester, Salome Jens, Nancy Marchand (Cinema Center)

Me, Natalie is the type of picture which might have gone overboard in contrivance and oversentimentality, in monotonous rendition of personal feelings of its title character. Instead, it is sensitive, often-poignant drama painted with a light touch of an ugly duckling trying to find her place in the scheme of things.

Patty Duke, in title role, delivers a warm, roundly developed characterization of a girl who all her life has tried to be pretty, and is keenly aware she isn't, nor ever will be.

The title character engages in a great deal of offscreen running commentary throughout the film, explaining her feelings and her philosophy, which gives audience an insight into her feelings without slowing the pace, generally held to an interesting temp.

As the mother, Nancy Marchand delivers a tremendous performance.

•

MEN DON'T LEAVE
1990, 113 mins, US Ⓥ ⦿ col
Dir Paul Brickman ***Prod*** John Avnet ***Scr*** Barbara Benedek, Paul Brickman ***Ph*** Bruce Surtees ***Ed*** Richard Chew ***Mus*** Thomas Newman ***Art*** Barbara Ling
Act Jessica Lange, Chris O'Donnell, Charlie Corsmo, Arliss Howard, Tom Mason, Joan Cusack (Geffen/Warner)

Men Don't Leave is a quietly moving tale of a widow (Jessica Lange) and her struggle to support her two sons in shabby Baltimore surroundings.

Suggested by Moshe Mizrahi's 1981 French film *La vie continue* with Annie Girardot, *Men Don't Leave* is directed by Paul Brickman.

The title misleadingly suggests a feminist tract, not the warmhearted comedy-drama this pic becomes after getting past the disjointed kitchen-sink melodrama of debt-ridden husband Tom Mason's death and Lange's selling of the family's suburban home. The move to Baltimore revives what seemed a terminally ill film and brings it compellingly to life. Playing the role at first with an unmodulated emotional glaze, the taciturn Lange is pulled back to life by the spirited behaviour of her boys, superbly played by newcomers Chris O'Donnell and Charlie Korsmo; by O'Donnell's sweet but loopy g.f. Joan Cusack, and by the engagingly offbeat b.f. Arliss Howard.

The film's dramatic heart is a sequence showing Lange, after losing her job in a blowup against restaurant boss Kathy Bates, descending into a catatonic state and refusing to leave her bed for days as the apartment turns into a quiet vision of hell. It's a scary piece of acting by Lange, beautifully directed by Brickman, and it turns a somewhat meandering film into a memorable emotional experience.

•

MEN IN BLACK
1997, 98 mins, US Ⓥ ⦿ col
Dir Barry Sonnenfeld ***Prod*** Walter F. Parkes, Laurie MacDonald ***Scr*** Ed Solomon ***Ph*** Don Peterman ***Ed*** Jim Miller ***Mus*** Danny Elfman ***Art*** Bo Welch
Act Tommy Lee Jones, Will Smith, Linda Fiorentino, Vincent D'Onofrio, Rip Torn, Tony Shalhoub (Amblin)

A witty and sometimes surreal sci-fi comedy, *Men in Black* is a wild knuckleball of a movie that keeps dancing in and out of the strike zone. This zippy curio feels something like *Ghostbusters* as if done by the Coen brothers.

Lowell Cunningham's violent, little-known early '90s comics, *The Men in Black*, were based on the premise of strait-laced G-men involved in a secret struggle against outer-space aliens. The film's fabulous first half-hour could scarcely be more droll in the way it establishes the methods of the top-secret INS Division 6 to combat the evil that walks covertly among us. For a while, the film is a rare example of successful mainstream surrealism, with bizarre sights presented as part of the landscape.

Unfortunately, it doesn't manage to sustain this level of inventiveness, going soft particularly around the middle as new partners agent K (Tommy Lee Jones) and J (Will Smith) set out on their cases and indulge in only somewhat offbeat procedures.

Barry Sonnenfeld, who lensed several of the Coen brothers' films before turning director with the *Addams Family* duo and *Get Shorty*, is ever-alert to the unusual comic touch that can enliven the material, though story could have been sustained better with more character development, particularly in the case of Smith's J. At a snappy 98 minutes, it is probably the shortest $100 million-plus picture on the books.

1997: Best Makeup (Rick Baker, David LeRoy Anderson)

NOMINATIONS: Best Original Comedy Score, Art Direction

•

MENG LONG GUO JIANG
(THE WAY OF THE DRAGON; WAY OF THE DRAGON; RETURN OF THE DRAGON)
1972, 100 mins, Hong Kong Ⓥ ▭ col
Dir Bruce Lee ***Prod*** Raymond Chow ***Scr*** Bruce Lee ***Ph*** Ho Lan-shan ***Ed*** Peter Cheung ***Mus*** Joseph Koo ***Art*** Chien Hsin
Act Bruce Lee, Nora Miao, Chuck Norris, Marisa Longo, Robert Wall, Whong In-sik (Golden Harvest/Concord)

Written and directed by Chinese chop-socky superstar, Bruce Lee, and filmed both in Hong Kong and Rome, *Dragon* is noteworthy more for the martial arts action than for narrative, which is all its fans probably want anyway.

Highlight is the exciting climax as Lee and an international karate champ (Chuck Norris) hired by the gangsters battle it out on one of the upper levels of the Colosseum. Another sequence carrying edge-of-the-seat thrills is a fight between Lee and half a dozen stalwarts in which he uses a pair of nunchakus for deadly effect.

•

MEN IN HER LIFE, THE

1941, 89 mins, US b/w

Dir Gregory Ratoff ***Prod*** Gregory Ratoff ***Scr*** Frederick Kohner, Michael Wilson, Paul Trivers ***Ph*** Harry Stradling, Arthur Miller ***Ed*** Francis D. Lyon ***Mus*** David Raksin

Act Loretta Young, Conrad Veidt, Dean Jagger, Otto Kruger, Ann Todd, John Shepperd (Columbia)

Eleanor Smith's novel of the 1860s, *Ballerina*, in providing basis for the tale, details the intensive training required to bring a ballet dancer to stardom—and her love life along the way. Loretta Young comes under the stern hand of elderly ballet master Conrad Veidt, marrying him in appreciation after a sensational debut, although in love with young John Shepperd. After Veidt's death, she marries shipping magnate Dean Jagger, and honeymoon tour of Europe finds her forgetting the stage life. But she returns to dancing for separation, and bears a daughter (Ann Todd), whom Jagger eventually finds and takes back to New York for proper rearing.

Gregory Ratoff overcomes much of the story immobility through carrying various dramatic episodes to dramatic peaks, and then veering away to the next sequence without holding on the climax. Ratoff also generates strong sympathy in the latter reels with the mother-love heart tugs for the absent child.

1941: NOMINATION: Best Sound

•

MEN IN WAR

1957, 102 mins, US Ⓥ b/w

Dir Anthony Mann ***Prod*** Sidney Harmon ***Scr*** Philip Yordan ***Ph*** Ernest Haller ***Ed*** Richard C. Meyer ***Mus*** Elmer Bernstein ***Art*** Lewis Jacobs

Act Robert Ryan, Aldo Ray, Robert Keith, Philip Pine, Vic Morrow, Nehemiah Persoff (Security/United Artists)

A two-fisted account of what happens to an infantry platoon in Korea is told with a general air of excitement, tension and action. Battle sequences, well-staged under Anthony Mann's direction, are all small-scale, but none the less deadly, as befits the plot and its few characters. The Philip Yordan scripting from Van Van Praag's novel, *Day Without End (Combat)*, does considerably well in overcoming the fact that there is much that is similar in warpix and the characters that inhabit them.

Robert Ryan, battle-weary lieutenant trying to get the remnants of his platoon back to battalion headquarters, and Aldo Ray, hostile, disrespectful sergeant from another company trying to get his combat-shocked colonel to safety, each score strongly. Robert Keith, the colonel, successfully carries off a role that requires only one word of dialog.

Where the film does stand out over the usual warpic is in its intelligent use of music. Elmer Bernstein composed and conducted the score, never trying to compete with the sounds of battle and thereby heightening the effect of many scenes.

•

MEN IN WHITE

1934, 81 mins, UK b/w

Dir Richard Boleslawski ***Prod*** Monta Bell ***Scr*** Waldemar Young ***Ph*** George Folsey ***Mus*** William Axt

Act Clark Gable, Myrna Loy, Jean Hersholt, Elizabeth Allen, Otto Kruger, C. Henry Gordon (M-G-M)

Men is a keenly sensitive translation of the [Sidney Kingsley] stage version to the screen. The story is familiar—the surgeon who gives his best energy to his profession and thus irritates the woman he is to marry and who suggests that she is rich enough to permit him to adapt his office hours to their social engagements. Eventually, she is led to realize the importance of the work.

There is a side plot in a nurse who in an excess of admiration for his skill virtually seduces him and who dies while seeking to avoid the consequence of that tryst.

The story permits Clark Gable to disclose a tenderness wholly foreign to the rough stuff he often does. He dominates the picture, though he has to share many scenes with Jean Hersholt. Myrna Loy is an excellent choice as Gable's society admirer and reacts perfectly to her assignment. Elizabeth Allen is excellent as the errant nurse.

•

MEN OF BOYS TOWN

1941, 107 mins, US Ⓥ b/w

Dir Norman Taurog ***Prod*** John W. Considine, Jr. ***Scr*** James Kevin McGuinness ***Ph*** Harold Rosson ***Ed*** Frederick F. Smith ***Mus*** Herbert Stothart

Act Spencer Tracy, Mickey Rooney, Lee J. Cobb, Larry Nunn, Bobs Watson, Darryl Hickman (M-G-M)

Like its predecessor *Boys Town*, this one carries socko entertainment for wide general appeal, including plenty of tearjerking and sentimental episodes to blur the eyes of the most calloused, and spotlighting the life work of Father Edward J. Flanagan in his enterprise devoted to rehabilitation of wayward boys.

Spencer Tracy again presents a sincere and human portrayal of the priest, while Mickey Rooney displays plenty of restraint in handling the assignment of the completely reformed boy who goes out briefly to practice the precepts of the school head. Lee J. Cobb, as the fund-raiser to keep the institution open, gives a fine performance.

Story introduces Larry Nunn into the institution. Kid is bitter because of the crippled back sustained in a reform school beating, and Rooney heads a group of boys to try to make him laugh again. The kindly Father Flanagan and a dog do the trick.

Picture hits a consistent gait, always pointing up the sentimental angles in its dramatic unfolding.

Direction by Norman Taurog again demonstrates his unique talents in handling boys and their varied characteristics.

•

MEN OF HONOR

2000, 129 mins, US Ⓥ ⊙ ▭ col

Dir George Tillman Jr. ***Prod*** Robert Teitel, Bill Badalato ***Scr*** Scott Marshall Smith ***Ph*** Anthony B. Richmond ***Ed*** John Carter ***Mus*** Mark Isham ***Art*** Leslie Dilley

Act Robert De Niro, Cuba Gooding Jr., Charlize Theron, Aunjanue Ellis, Hal Holbrook, David Keith (State Street/20th Century-Fox)

A feature-length recruiting poster for the U.S. Navy and for overcoming all obstacles through the force of sheer will, *Men of Honor* is a by-the-numbers inspirational biopic about the first black man to become a master chief diver. Full of easy-to-say, harder-to-do messages about never quitting and surmounting daunting obstacles, pic needs only a chorus of "Climb Every Mountain" to be complete. Still, Robert De Niro and Cuba Gooding Jr. are eminently watchable as, respectively, a cantankerous Southern training officer and a sharecropper's son who successfully navigates an obstacle course of institutional racism.

Script charts the trailblazing naval career of Carl Brashear, a poor Kentucky kid whose enthusiasm for swimming led him to enter the diving-school program in the postwar period when, even though the military was technically desegregated, all the cards were still stacked against anyone of his race trying to make it through. The man naturally inspires a great rooting interest, but the film's rah-rah nature and if-you're-tough-enough-you'll-win message simplify all the issues down to the most elementary level. One of the pic's moderate highlights is the diving program's final exam, which has been rigged against Brashear but which he manages to pass with exceptional stamina and perseverance.

For those in search of positive role models and films detailing little-known aspects of black and military history, or stressing the value of tenacity and hard work, pic has something to offer.

•

MEN OF TWO WORLDS
(US: WITCH DOCTOR)

1946, 109 mins, UK Ⓥ col

Dir Thorold Dickinson ***Scr*** Thorold Dickinson, Herbert W. Victor ***Ph*** Desmond Dickinson ***Ed*** Aben Jaggs ***Mus*** Arthur Bliss ***Art*** Tom Morahan

Act Eric Portman, Phyllis Calvert, Orlando Martins, Robert Adams, Cyril Raymond (Two Cities)

This ambitious Two Cities production, which enters the $4 million class, is honest, dull and in Technicolor. With the best intentions, it states the case for a scientific treatment of sleeping sickness among the African tribes as opposed to witchcraft and superstition. But it is a statement of the obvious.

Film was three years in production with delays that appear to have badly dented the screenplay. It began in 1943. Eight months were spent in Tanganyika choosing locations. On the way out a U-boat sank cameras and stock. Film unit was put ashore 1,000 miles from Lagos, where its only still camera was impounded. Slow convoys, bad weather, a strike of lab men in Hollywood, delays waiting for Technicolor equipment, all brought costly handicaps to the enterprise. Director Thorold Dickinson has done his best, but the result is a long stretch of mumbo-jumbo, unrelieved by imaginative treatment or pictorial thrills.

Randall, the district commissioner, plans to evacuate an African village to save the inhabitants from the man-killing tsetse fly. His assistant is Kisenga, a noble savage who has risen from ancestral swamps, found culture in England and gone back to his tribe as a musician and composer. He takes Randall's side in the fight against sleeping sickness, but the power of black magic in the hands of the local witch doctor, Magole (played with remarkable force by Orlando Martins), is too much for him.

•

MEN'S CLUB, THE

1986, 100 mins, US Ⓥ ⊙ col

Dir Peter Medak ***Prod*** Howard Gottfried ***Scr*** Leonard Michaels ***Ph*** John Fleckenstein ***Ed*** Cynthia Scheider, David Dresher, Bill Butler ***Mus*** Lee Holdridge ***Art*** Ken Davis

Act Roy Scheider, Frank Langella, Harvey Keitel, Treat Williams, Richard Jordan, David Dukes (Atlantic)

Those who think men are immature, destructive, insensitive and basically animals may find *The Men's Club* great fun. Others are likely to balk at the film's contrived and dated treatment of the battle between the sexes.

Film is a distasteful piece of work that displays the worst in men. Leonard Michaels's screenplay (from his novel) is all warts and no insight, full of self-loathing for the gender. In addition, filmmaking is as tired as the material. Pic plays like a stageplay, so static is Peter Medak's direction.

A group of friends nearing age 40 get together and for most of the film's 100 minutes the camera is on their heads talking. Leader of the group is Cavanaugh (Roy Scheider), supposedly a retired baseball star who looks too unhealthy to have ever played anything more strenuous than cards.

•

MEN WITHOUT WOMEN

1930, 76 mins, US b/w

Dir John Ford ***Scr*** John Ford, James Kevin McGuinness, Dudley Nichols ***Ph*** Joseph H. August ***Ed*** Paul Weatherwax ***Mus*** Peter Brunellin, Glen Knight ***Art*** William S. Darling

Act Kenneth MacKenna, Frank Albertson, Paul Page, Warren Hymer, Walter McGrail (Fox)

Story and characters are built up with uncanny shrewdness. It opens in Shanghai with a shore party of American gobs going whoopee in an enormous establishment of entertainment of various kinds, mostly a vast bar and many fluttering petticoats and kimonos.

Back to the ship some great views of a sub streaking out to sea at night in clouds of black smoke and weird light and water reflections. Sub is run down in a collision and goes to the bottom in 90 feet of water with all escape cut off, and here begins the sledge hammer situation that lasts to the finish. Finale is a whooping bit of flag waving.

Kenneth MacKenna, as Chief Torpedoman Burke, does nicely with a heroic lead, but the punch of the acting is the surprise comedy bits of a number of minor characters. It is these touches and the grim comedy of the lines that lift the picture out of melodrama to an illusion of reality.

•

MEN WITH WINGS

1938, 102 mins, US col

Dir William A. Wellman ***Prod*** William A. Wellman ***Scr*** Robert Carson ***Ph*** W. Howard Greene ***Ed*** Tommy Scott ***Mus*** W. Franke Harling, Gerard Carbonara

Act Fred MacMurray, Ray Milland, Louise Campbell, Andy Devine, Lynne Overman, Porter Hall (Paramount)

Men with Wings is a giant bomber from the Paramount hangar, designed on a lavish scale by the skilled air picture mechanic, William A. Wellman, and polished off beautifully in Technicolor. The action scenes, including a dogfight in the air, are exceptionally impressive.

While the romance, involving three people, is subjugated to the story of the development of aviation from Kitty Hawk, NC, in 1903 down to the present, the love interest is never left very far in the background. Story stems from the beginning of aviation when the Wright brothers got off the ground at Kitty Hawk 35 years ago. It opens on the refusal of a small-town editor to believe the story of a breathless reporter that he had just seen a man fly. History is that this reporter's story, placed on the wires and scooping the world, was used by only three newspapers when filed.

In this first scene the three kids of the picture, who grow up into Fred MacMurray, Ray Milland and Louise Campbell, are charmingly pictured in an effort to fly with a kite, successful as it happens.

Action progresses through various stages of Wellman's aviation cavalcade down to the last, MacMurray leaving his wife (Campbell) and baby again for the Sino-Jap war. Milland as disappointed suitor but faithful friend, plays his part with fine restraint, understanding and poise. The reckless but fairly likable character of the flier who can't stay down, done to a crisp by MacMurray is reminiscent of Gable in *Test Pilot*, which also contained the wife angle.

•

MEPHISTO

1981, 146 mins, Hungary/W. Germany Ⓥ col

Dir Istvan Szabo ***Scr*** Peter Dobai, Istvan Szabo ***Ph*** Lajos Koltai ***Ed*** Zsuzsa Csakany ***Mus*** Zdenko Tamassy (arr.) ***Art*** Jozsef Romvari

Act Klaus Maria Brandauer, Krystyna Janda, Ildiko Bansagi, Karin Boyd, Rolf Hoppe, Christine Harbort (Objektiv/Durniok)

Mephisto delves deeply into the actor as cultural pawn or as a symbol of the theatrical totalitarianism that Nazism was. Hungaro pic shows extraordinary period flair for the Germany of the 1920s and '30s, balanced acting by a multinational cast, and exemplary direction. Based loosely on Klaus Mann's book (in turn based on a real actor), film details a provincial actor's climb to fame before and during the Nazi period. Austrian actor Klaus Maria Brandauer is extraordinary as this flamboyant actor who uses women and marries the daughter of a noted pre-Nazi figure.

When the Nazis come to power, his wife leaves but he stays. He eventually becomes head of the National Theatre where he begins to subvert classic figures to Nazi outlooks, especially the Mephisto of Goethe's *Faust*, played romantically.

The sadistic Culture Minister who aided his meteoric rise takes him to the 1936 Olympic stadium, after the actor marries a popular actress, and makes him run around with spotlights trained on him. It is a brilliant dramatic ephiphany of the corruption of power, the unwitting collaboration due to ambition and survival rather than moral choice.

1981: Best Foreign Language Film

•

MEPHISTO WALTZ, THE

1971, 115 mins, US Ⓥ col

Dir Paul Wendkos ***Prod*** Quinn Martin ***Scr*** Ben Maddow ***Ph*** William W. Spencer ***Ed*** Richard Brockway ***Mus*** Jerry Goldsmith ***Art*** Richard Y. Hamen

Act Alan Alda, Jacqueline Bisset, Barbara Parkins, Bradford Dillman, William Windom, Curt Jurgens (20th Century-Fox/QM)

Based on the novel by Fred Mustard Stewart, pic follows in deadpan style the antics of a deranged concert pianist (Curt Jurgens), dying of leukemia whose lust for his daughter (Barbara Parkins) and devotion to devil worship destroy the marriage of writer Alan Alda and Jacqueline Bisset.

To revive his sexual prowess, Jurgens has Alda killed, then assumes his body. A trifle slow on the uptake, Bisset finally realizes something is amiss after her daughter dies under mysterious conditions. Alda-cum-Jurgens starts getting ruthless in bed, and the ex-husband of Parkins (Bradford Dillman) tells her (before being killed) of a monster child miscarried by Parkins and sired by her father.

Main fault is a tired script with more than a full quota of arch, laughable dialogue, spouted with relish by performers struggling to keep their heads above water.

•

MEPRIS, LE
(CONTEMPT; GHOST AT NOON)

1963, 100 mins, France/Italy Ⓥ ⦿ ▭ col

Dir Jean-Luc Godard ***Prod*** Carlo Ponti, Georges de Beauregard ***Scr*** Jean-Luc Godard ***Ph*** Raoul Coutard ***Ed*** Agnes Guillemot ***Mus*** Georges Delerue

Act Brigitte Bardot, Jack Palance, Fritz Lang, Michel Piccoli, Georgia Moll, Jean-Luc Godard (Rome Paris/Concordia/Champion)

Crossing Brigitte Bardot with an arty, personal director, ex-New Waver Jean-Luc Godard, was not a bad idea. Bardot appears, at last, as an actress in her own right with her trademark nude scenes not forced but aptly stemming from the plot.

Slim tale has Bardot married to a hack scriptwriter called in by an egotistical American producer to rewrite scenes on an epic he is making in Italy with Fritz Lang himself directing. Film details her sudden intimations of contempt for her husband because of a series of incidents. It ends in her beginning to give in to the assiduous courting of the producer.

Based on an Alberto Moravia novel [*A Ghost at Noon*], Godard still makes this a personally told tale. Though full of inside film talk, grandiloquent phrasings, sudden sharp elipses or quick repeat montage scenes of early incidents to make a point, this does have a decisive visual flair that lays bare the figures.

Bardot handles her lines well and displays a timing and presence scarcely seen in her more undraped pix.

Color is good if sometimes overindulged for mood effects.

•

THE MERCENARIES
SEE: DARK OF THE SUN

•

MERMAIDS

1990, 111 mins, US Ⓥ ⦿ col

Dir Richard Benjamin ***Prod*** Lauren Lloyd, Wallis Nicita, Patrick Palmer ***Scr*** June Roberts ***Ph*** Howard Atherton ***Ed*** Jacqueline Cambas ***Mus*** Jack Nitzsche ***Art*** Stuart Wurtzel

Act Cher, Bob Hoskins, Winona Ryder, Michael Schoeffling, Christina Ricci, Caroline McWilliams (Orion)

As eccentric mother-daughter films go, this one [from the novel by Patty Dann] falls into the same category as *Terms of Endearment*, with many of the same comedic pleasures and dramatic pitfalls.

Set in the early 1960s, *Mermaids* begins rousingly, introducing flamboyant Mrs. Flax (Cher) and her two daughters: confused Charlotte (Winona Ryder), 15, who is obsessed with Catholicism, and Kate (Christina Ricci), nine, who's obsessed with swimming.

Constantly on the move due to mother's vagabond ways, they soon relocate to a small New England town that brings with it new romantic entanglements. Mrs. Flax takes up with a lovelorn shoe salesman (Bob Hoskins), while Charlotte becomes enamored with a dreamy groundskeeper (Michael Schoeffling) from the local nunnery, conveniently situated just down the road.

Since she's unable to communicate with her wanton mother, Ryder's dialog is largely limited to voice-over confessions and pleas to God, often while staring intently, wordless and wide-eyed, at her mother or Joe (Schoeffling), the unsuspecting object of her near-crazed lust.

The delightful Ryder, billing notwithstanding, is really the star. Cher is also fine as the cavalier, self-centered mom, an equally amusing if less sympathetic character.

•

MERRILL'S MARAUDERS

1962, 98 mins, US Ⓥ ▭ col

Dir Samuel Fuller ***Prod*** Milton Sperling ***Scr*** Milton Sperling, Samuel Fuller ***Ph*** William Clothier ***Ed*** Folmar Blangsted ***Mus*** Howard Jackson ***Art*** [uncredited]

Act Jeff Chandler, Ty Hardin, Peter Brown, Andrew Duggan, Luz Valdez, Claude Akins (United States)

Jeff Chandler's last role, as Brigadier General Frank Merrill, is one of his best. The rugged, gray-thatched Chandler fits this role naturally and portrays one of World War II's most colorful personalities with a proper blend of military doggedness and personal humanity.

When Samuel Fuller—he was a GI in Europe—took his small cast and crew to the Philippines to shoot *Merrill's Marauders*, he did plenty of preliminary screening and, down the line, he got the results he wanted. After Chandler, this film owes much of its excellence to William Clothier's Technicolor photography, both in his feeling for cinematic design and his superb use of color.

Charlton Ogburn's book was a springboard only for the scenarists. They elaborated it into a screenplay that balances battle scenes with character-establishing vignettes and gives the subject-hero a closer contact with his men through playing his story against the background of their daily activities, their fixture of personalities.

Ty Hardin's Lieutenant Stockton is a stock character—the young, still oversensitive officer—but he conveys a tenderness, a sense of truth that keeps the role from seeming stereotyped.

•

MERRILY WE LIVE

1938, 90 mins, US b/w

Dir Norman Z. McLeod ***Prod*** Milton H. Bren ***Scr*** Eddie Moran, Jack Jevne ***Ph*** Norbert Brodine ***Ed*** William Terhune ***Mus*** Marvin Hatley (dir.) ***Art*** Charles D. Hall

Act Constance Bennett, Brian Aherne, Billie Burke, Alan Mowbray, Patsy Kelly, Ann Dvorak (Favorite/M-G-M)

It's all in the acting and directing. Director Norman Z. McLeod has the knack of building up gags until he has three or four racing each other to the big laugh. Most of the fun comes from a fine performance by Billie Burke, who plays a scatterbrain wife and mother in a family of irresponsibles.

Burke has a weakness for helping worthless humanity. Brian Aherne is welcomed to the fold. It happens he isn't a tramp at all, but a writer who forgot to shave on the morning his flivver broke down when he stops by to use the telephone. Once inside, he decides to stay.

In his calm and self-possessed manner he begins to bring some order out of the confusion in which the Kilbourne family lives. This leads to a romance with the elder daughter (Constance Bennett), and a timely word which clinches an important business deal for the head of the house. Bennett gives a good performance and appears in some striking costumes. Alan Mowbray, as the family butler, contributes to the hilarity, as do Patsy Kelly, in a small part, and Bonita Granville and Tom Brown.

1938: NOMINATIONS: Best Supp. Actress (Billie Burke), Cinematography, Art Direction, Sound, Song ("Merrily We Live")

•

MERRY ANDREW

1958, 103 mins, US ▭ col

Dir Michael Kidd ***Prod*** Sol C. Siegel ***Scr*** Isobel Lennart, I. A. L. Diamond ***Ph*** Robert Surtees ***Ed*** Harold F. Kress ***Mus*** Saul Chaplin ***Art*** William A. Horning, Gene Allen

Act Danny Kaye, Pier Angeli, Baccaloni, Noel Purcell, Robert Coote, Patricia Cutts (M-G-M)

Merry Andrew has a happy-go-chuckley attitude and some smart musical numbers set up by stand-out music and lyrics. Against this is the fact that the production does not always maintain its own set of very high comedy values, nor the pace of its initial scenes.

Michael Kidd, who makes his screen debut as a director, still has a lot to learn about comedy setups and this unsureness is made the more evident by the contrast of the narrative stretches with the brisk and imaginative manner in which Kidd has choreographed the musical numbers. Here he is on experienced ground and he shows it.

The romance and humor of the screenplay, based on a story by Paul Gallico, are based on the fact that Andrew, played by Danny Kaye, is anything but merry in the opening sequences. He is an instructor in a stuffy British boys' school, presided over by his martinet father (Noel Purcell) and engaged to cool and detached Patricia Cutts. Via his vocation (archeology) he gets mixed up with a family circus presided over by papa Baccaloni and featuring daughter Pier Angeli. This gives Kaye an opportunity to slap on the clown makeup and do several turns with handy circus props.

•

MERRY CHRISTMAS, MR. LAWRENCE

1983, 122 mins, UK Ⓥ col

Dir Nagisa Oshima ***Prod*** Jeremy Thomas ***Scr*** Nagisa Oshima, Paul Mayersberg ***Ph*** Toichiro Narushima ***Ed*** Tomoyo Oshima ***Mus*** Ryuichi Sakamoto ***Art*** Jusho Toda

Act David Bowie, Tom Conti, Ryuichi Sakamoto, Takeshi, Jack Thompson (Recorded Picture)

By no means an easy picture to deal with, this thinking man's version of *The Bridge on the River Kwai* makes no concessions to the more obvious commercial requirements, unless it is the selection of David Bowie, the pop star, for the leading dramatic role.

The strongest points of the script, penned by Nagisa Oshima and Paul Mayersberg from a novel [*The Seed and the Sower*] by South African author Laurens van der Post, are the philosophical and emotional implications, brought up in a careful and intricate comparison between Orient and Occident on every possible level. The weakest point is its construction, sturdy and compact up to the point when it has to use flashbacks in order to explain the British side of the allegory.

Set in a Japanese prisoner-of-war camp in Java, the plot has a Japanese captain, Yonoi (Ryuichi Sakamoto), trying to impose his own ideas of discipline, honor, order and obedience, in a clash with a British major, Celliers (Bowie), who represents the diametrically opposed train of thought.

The conflict between the two leading figures is better verbalized by Colonel Lawrence (Tom Conti), who lends his name to the film's title, and Hara (Takeshi), the Japanese sergeant whose popular origins allow him much more freedom of emotions.

•

MERRY-GO-ROUND
SEE: KORHINTA

•

MERRY WIDOW, THE

1925, 107 mins, US ⊗ b/w

Dir Erich von Stroheim ***Scr*** Erich von Stroheim, Benjamin Glazer, Marion Ainslee ***Ph*** Oliver T. Marsh ***Ed*** Frank E. Hull ***Art*** Cedric Gibbons, Richard Day

Act Mae Murray, John Gilbert, Roy D'Arcy, Josephine Crowell, George Fawcett, Tully Marshall (M-G-M)

Erich Von Stroheim turns out Mae Murray in the most gorgeous production [adapted from Franz Lehar's operetta] she has yet had. Murray has never previously looked as well as she does before Oliver Marsh's camera. Some of her closeups are nothing less than superb, while the lighting, practically throughout the entire picture, is a revelation.

Von Stroheim has eliminated a number of captions by symbolizing. Distinct credits are the freezing of rain upon a window to denote the passing of time, a royal funeral suggested through a corps of muffled drums descending a long flight of stairs, and the brilliant silhouetting of gems adorning Murray to the exclusion of her face and figure when gazed upon by the mercenary Prince.

•

MERRY WIDOW, THE

1934, 110 mins, US Ⓥ b/w

Dir Ernst Lubitsch ***Prod*** Ernst Lubitsch ***Scr*** Ernest Vajda, Samson Raphaelson ***Ph*** Oliver T. Marsh ***Ed*** Frances Marsh ***Mus*** Herbert Stothart (adapt.) ***Art*** Cedric Gibbons, Frederic Hope

Act Maurice Chevalier, Jeanette MacDonald, Edward Everett Horton, Una Merkel, George Barbier, Minna Gombell (M-G-M)

Ernst Lubitsch has here brought the field of operetta to the level of popular taste. Besides Lubitsch, the many involved include Ernest Vajda and Samson Raphaelson on the book; Herbert Stothart on the music; Richard Rodgers, Lorenz Hart and Gus Kahn on the 1934 lyrics. They are, 26 years after, the collaborators on the original *Widow* by Franz Lehar, Victor Leon and Leo Stein. Two or three new airs have been added, but the music still stands pat on Lehar—smartly so.

In his leads, Lubitsch picked a double plum out of the talent grab bag. Maurice Chevalier and Jeanette MacDonald both are aces as Danilo and Sonia. The former Paramount pair once again works beautifully in harness. Supporting players are in chiefly for comedy purposes, and include such expert vets as Edward Everett Horton, George Barbier, Una Merkel, Sterling Holloway and Herman Bing.

1934: Best Interior Decoration (Cedric Gibbons, Frederic Hope)

•

MESMER

1994, 107 mins, Germany/Canada/UK col

Dir Roger Spottiswoode ***Prod*** Wieland Schulz-Keil, Lance Reynolds, Robert Goodale ***Scr*** Dennis Potter ***Ph*** Elemer Ragalyi ***Ed*** Susan Shipton ***Mus*** Michael Nyman ***Art*** Jan Schulbach

Act Alan Rickman, Amanda Ooms, Gillian Barge, Jan Rubes, David Hemben, Anna Thalbach (Levergreen/Babelsberg/Accent/ Mayfair)

The wild, impressionistic view with which writer Dennis Potter assails the so-called age of reason in *Mesmer* seems barely containable on the big screen. And if it were not for the grounded, eccentric title performance by Alan Rickman, one imagines the entire film might defy gravity and spin out of earthly orbit.

Biography is the least of concerns in the film, which focuses on a few short years in the life of the 18th-century medical radical who ventured into such areas as hypnosis and harmonics before they had names.

The drama and humor come from the threat he poses to the establishment. Mesmer truly has the esteemed Viennese doctors working overtime to explain away his success. Aside from the cat-and-mouse game that structures the pic, Potter sullies the notion of reason and passion being wholly separate entities in Mesmer's questionable doctor-patient relationship with Maria Theresa (Amanda Ooms), the blind daughter of a wealthy businessman.

Rickman effects an eerie, otherworldly quality in his role. Support cast is uniformly strong, with Jan Rubes, normally cast in fatherly roles, chilling as the chief nemesis. Ooms is a striking presence in her first major English-speaking film.

•

MESSAGE, THE
(US: MOHAMMED, MESSENGER OF GOD)

1976, 179 mins, UK Ⓥ col

Dir Moustapha Akkad ***Prod*** Moustapha Akkad ***Scr*** H. A. L. Craig ***Ph*** Jack Hildyard ***Ed*** John Bloom ***Mus*** Maurice Jarre ***Art*** Norman Dorme, Abdel Mouneim Chukri

Act Anthony Quinn, Irene Papas, Michael Ansara, Johnny Sekka, Michael Forest, Damien Thomas (Filmco)

The Message, Moustapha Akkad's $17 million saga of the birth of the Islamic religion, bears favorable comparison as a religious epic. H.A.L. Craig's screenplay is remarkably literate, sometimes witty and ironic, but ultimately and perhaps inevitably simplistic.

The action snowballs from underground cell meetings by followers of Mohammad, through brutal harassment, expulsion from Mecca, pitched battles in the desert, and the final conquering pilgrimage back to Mecca. Throughout the narrative there is uncommon respect for the mind and the eye.

Ultimately it's a triumph for Akkad who welded a logistically sprawling epic into coherence. His crowd scenes are credible and the battle scenes superbly rendered.

•

MESSENGER: THE STORY OF JOAN OF ARC, THE (JEANNE D'ARC)

1999, 148 mins, France Ⓥ ⊙ ▭ col

Dir Luc Besson ***Prod*** Patrice Ledoux ***Scr*** Andrew Birkin, Luc Besson ***Ph*** Thierry Arbogast ***Ed*** Sylvie Landra ***Mus*** Eric Serra ***Art*** Hugues Tissandier

Act Milla Jovovich, John Malkovich, Faye Dunaway, Dustin Hoffman, Pascal Greggory, Vincent Cassel (Gaumont)

If you're going to do Joan of Arc, it helps to have an actress to play the leading role. Although Luc Besson tries to minimize the importance of this fact by making his Joan an action heroine and as much a neurotic teenager as a divinely driven national savior, the lack of a plausible leading lady is enough to sink what is otherwise an eye-catching, although heavily '90s style, telling of one of history's most frequently filmed stories.

While Besson steers a reasonable enough middle course in his interpretation of one of history's most singular and mystifying figures, and manages to make the story politically and militarily coherent, his now-estranged wife, Milla Jovovich, adds nothing to the journey other than her strikingly tall and skinny physique.

Script skirts the issue of how Joan developed a local reputation and gathered a following, but by the time she is 17 she is sufficiently known to be received by the Dauphin (John Malkovich), who cannot officially become King Charles VII until a coronation can take place in Rheims, which is held by the English. But Jovovich's overwrought rantings and bug-eyed expressions make Joan seem like a possessed lunatic, by no means a young lady a presumptive king would entrust with his army.

Besson thrusts the camera into the middle of furious fighting. The battle scenes are a feast for the eyes and rep the main reason to see the film on the big screen.

Performances overall are serviceable, if a bit ragged, with Americans mixing with variously accented Euros. Malkovich makes for a blithe and quicksilver Dauphin. Pic was mainly shot in the Czech Republic.

•

METEOR

1979, 103 mins, US Ⓥ ▭ col

Dir Ronald Neame ***Prod*** Arnold Orgolini, Theodore Parvin ***Scr*** Stanley Mann, Edmund H. North ***Ph*** Paul Lohmann ***Ed*** Carl Kress ***Mus*** Laurence Rosenthal ***Art*** Edward Carfagno

Act Sean Connery, Natalie Wood, Karl Malden, Brian Keith, Martin Landau, Trevor Howard (American International)

Meteor really combines several disasters in one continuous cinematic bummer. Along with the threat of a five-mile-wide asteroid speeding towards Earth, with smaller splinters preceding it, there's an avalanche, an earthquake, a tidal wave and a giant mudbath. All in all, special effects wizards Glen Robinson and Robert Staples, along with stunt coordinator Roger Greed, got a good workout.

Inevitably, topliners Sean Connery as an American scientist, Brian Keith as his Soviet counterpart, and Natalie Wood as the translator in between them, take a back seat to the effects.

Avalanche sequence is one of the best in memory, aided by the fact that producers were allowed to blow up a mountain in the Swiss Alps.

1979: NOMINATION: Best Sound

•

METEOR MAN, THE

1993, 99 mins, US Ⓥ ⊙ col

Dir Robert Townsend ***Prod*** Loretha C. Jones ***Scr*** Robert Townsend ***Ph*** John A. Alonzo ***Ed*** Adam Bernardi, Richard Candib, Andrew London, Pam Wise ***Mus*** Cliff Eidelman ***Art*** Toby Corbett

Act Robert Townsend, Marla Gibbs, Eddie Griffin, Robert Guillaume, James Earl Jones, Roy Fegan (Tinsel Townsend)

There's a universe that divides actor-director-writer Robert Townsend's debut, *Hollywood Shuffle*, and *The Meteor Man*. The seemingly hip, irreverent and street-savvy talent has evolved into a kinder, gentler, rather too polite storyteller who is oddly out of step with the times. This allegorical fantasy is a cute skit expanded out of all proportion for the big screen.

Set in Washington, DC, yarn centers on schoolteacher and aspiring musician Jefferson Reed (Townsend). An advocate of nonviolence and flight in the face of danger, one evening Jeff runs afoul of the peroxided Golden Lords and just barely escapes their clutches. Emerging from his hiding place, he walks into the path of a falling meteor fragment, and when he awakes realizes that he's gained superpowers. He's enlisted into service to clean up the streets in a uniform lovingly sewn by his mother.

The idea of a street-smart though awkward superhuman crime fighter ought to have been a rich mine from which to excavate laughs. But Townsend seems strangely out of place in this milieu. His characters are stereotypes culled from two decades of television viewing.

•

METROPOLIS

1927, 107 mins, Germany Ⓥ ⊙ ⊗ b/w

Dir Fritz Lang ***Prod*** Erich Pommer ***Scr*** Thea von Harbou ***Ph*** Karl Freund, Guenther Rittau ***Art*** Otto Hunte, Erich Kettelhut, Karl Vollbrecht

Act Alfred Abel, Gustav Froelich, Rudolf Klein-Rogge, Theodor Loos, Heinrich George, Brigitte Helm (UFA)

The long-awaited film for which UFA has been beating the gong for the last year. It is said to have cost 7 million marks (about $1.68 million), and the picture looks it. From a photographic and directorial standpoint it is something entirely original.

The weakness is the scenario by Thea von Harbou. It gives effective chances for scenes, but it actually gets nowhere. The scene is laid 100 years in the future, in the mighty city of Metropolis, a magnified New York. It is ruled by a millionaire, who lives in the upper city and whose son falls in love with a girl of the workers, who lives below in the city of the toilers. This girl is preaching goodwill to the workers in the catacombs below the city.

An inventor has discovered a way to make artificial human beings, and at the request of the millionaire gives this creation of his the form of the girl. She preaches destruction to the workers, and they destroy the machinery which regulates everything in the city. Only through the aid of the boy and the real girl can the children of the workers be saved from inundation in the lower city. The workers turn against the evil marionette and burn her on a scaffold.

Too bad that so much really artistic work was wasted on this manufactured story.

Brigitte Helm, in the leading feminine role, is a find. If she has really never acted before, Fritz Lang, directing, certainly did an extraordinary piece of work with her. Also Heinrich George, Fritz Rasp and Gustav Froelich deliver exceptional performances.

[In 1984 a tinted, reedited and newly scored version, running 87 mins., was issued by composer Giorgio Moroder.]

•

METROPOLITAN

1990, 98 mins, US Ⓥ ⊙ col

Dir Whit Stillman ***Prod*** Whit Stillman ***Scr*** Whit Stillman ***Ph*** John Thomas ***Ed*** Chris Tellefsen ***Mus*** Mark Suozzo, Tom Judson ***Art*** [uncredited]

Act Carolyn Farina, Edward Clements, Christopher Eigeman, Taylor Nichols, Alison Parisi (Westerly)

Filmmaker Whit Stillman makes a strikingly original debut with *Metropolitan*, a glib, ironic portrait of the vulnerable young heirs to Manhattan's disappearing debutante scene. Story centers on a set of East Side friends who dub themselves the SFRP (or "Sally Fowler Rat Pack," after the girl whose Park Avenue apartment they gather in) and, more amusingly, UHBs, for Urban Haute Bourgeoisie.

They drag into their number a newcomer, Tom (Edward Clements), who openly disapproves of them but nonetheless shows up every night for private gatherings after black-tie parties and dances. A self-serious but insensitive young man, Tom inspires the first-time love of Audrey (Carolyn Farina). Tom repeatedly humiliates her as he continues to pursue an old flame, Serena (Elizabeth Thompson).

Among the fine cast, Christopher Eigeman stands out as Nick, the funny, arrogant group leader who's as jovially self-aware and self-mocking as his new friend, Tom, is stilted and blind to himself.

Pic is a true independent production, financed by Stillman (who sold his Manhattan apartment) and several friends.

1990: NOMINATION: Best Original Screenplay

•

M. HIRE
SEE: MONSIEUR HIRE

•

MIAMI BLUES
1990, 99 mins, US Ⓥ ⊙ col
Dir George Armitage ***Prod*** Jonathan Demme, Gary Goetzman ***Scr*** George Armitage ***Ph*** Tak Fujimoto ***Ed*** Craig McKay ***Mus*** Gary Chang ***Art*** Maher Ahmad
Act Alec Baldwin, Fred Ward, Jennifer Jason Leigh, Nora Dunn, Charles Napier, Jose Perez (Orion/Tristes Tropiques)

Based on Charles Willeford's novel, this quirky and sometimes brutally funny film strings together terrific moments but never takes a point of view.

Junior (Alec Baldwin) blows into town, initiates a crime spree with a homicide detective's stolen badge and settles down with a simpleminded hooker named Susie (Jennifer Jason Leigh). The sense that Junior can go off at any time, and the explosive and graphic bursts of violence create tension throughout.

Baldwin is more than equal to the task, and his intense machismo and make-believe posturing bring to mind some of Robert De Niro's menace in *Taxi Driver*. Leigh also is wondrously odd, her eyebrows knitting in frustration at the simplest of questions, her drawl filled with rapture at the recipes she can concoct for her new beau.

Pic, however, is missing a key ingredient: a discernible plot. If it's the detective (Fred Ward) seeking to reclaim his badge, false teeth and gun, it's a wispy one at best.

•

MIAMI RHAPSODY
1995, 95 mins, US Ⓥ col
Dir David Frankel ***Prod*** Barry Jossen, David Frankel ***Scr*** David Frankel ***Ph*** Jack Wallner ***Ed*** Steven Weisberg ***Mus*** Mark Isham ***Art*** J. Mark Harrington
Act Sarah Jessica Parker, Gil Bellows, Antonio Banderas, Mia Farrow, Paul Mazursky, Kevin Pollak (Hollywood)

Miami Rhapsody plays like *Hannah and Her Sisters*, a very Woody Allen-ish comedy about the amorous travails of a family of neurotics. Light, effervescent and exceedingly colorful, directorial debut by TV and film writer Frankel offers no new insight into the human condition but glosses over it in beguilingly entertaining fashion.

Like any self-respecting neurotic, Gwyn (Sarah Jessica Parker) has as many reasons not to get married as she does to proceed, but still agrees to become engaged to her b.f. Matt (Gil Bellows). However, at the wedding of her promiscuous younger sister, Leslie (Carla Gugino), to football hunk Jeff (Bo Eason), Gwyn's father, Vic (Paul Mazursky), confides to her that he suspects that her mother Nina (Mia Farrow) is having an affair.

To Gwyn's dismay, Nina in short order confirms Vic's hunch, telling her daughter that she's seeing studly Cuban Antonio (Antonio Banderas), who happens to be Gwyn's infirm grandmother's male nurse.

Completing the circle of adultery and deception, Gwyn's brother, Jordan (Kevin Pollak), is ditching his pregnant wife, Terri (Barbara Garrick), in favor of his business partner's gorgeous mate (Naomi Campbell); Vic has been secretly seeing his travel agent (Kelly Bishop); and even the just-married Leslie is caught in the act with an ex-beau.

This is an outstanding, potentially star-making vehicle for Parker. Sexy and funny, caustic and vulnerable, she carries the pic in the zingy manner of the best comediennes. Pic's flavor of New York Jewish humour with tropical coloration and a Latin beat proves very distinctive, as if the Woodman and his friends had gone on an extended Florida vacation.

•

MICHAEL
1996, 105 mins, US Ⓥ ⊙ col
Dir Nora Ephron ***Prod*** Sean Daniel, Nora Ephron, James Jacks ***Scr*** Nora Ephron, Delia Ephron, Peter Dexter, Jim Quinlan ***Ph*** John Lindley ***Ed*** Geraldine Peroni ***Mus*** Randy Newman ***Art*** Dan Davis
Act John Travolta, Andie MacDowell, William Hurt, Bob Hoskins, Robert Pastorelli, Jean Stapleton (Alphaville/Turner)

John Travolta's charismatic screen presence is the only element that propels *Michael* over its rough narrative spots and scattered direction. In what must be a casting coincidence, though a logical extension of his role in *Phenomenon*, Travolta plays a heaven-sent angel who brings joy, love and redemption to a team of cynical and frustrated tabloid journalists.

Tale begins in the editorial offices of the *National Mirror*, a sleazy taboid run by feisty publisher Vartan Malt (Bob Hoskins). When rumor of an angel's existence reaches the magazine, bitter, down-on-his luck journalist Frank Quinlan (William Hurt) senses a front-page scoop, but his boss won't let him track the alleged angel by himself. Instead, he sends along Huey Driscoll (Robert Pastorelli), another troubled reporter, and Dorothy Winters (Andie MacDowell), a mysterious woman who claims to be an "angel expert."

Though no fewer than four scripters are credited [two of whom, Peter Dexter and Jim Quinlan, also wrote the original story], *Michael* is at once underwritten and overwritten. Rowdy, slapdash and unevenly directed, the movie is basically a collection of episodes tied together with a flimsy string.

•

MICHAEL COLLINS
1996, 132 mins, US Ⓥ ⊙ col
Dir Neil Jordan ***Prod*** Stephen Woolley ***Scr*** Neil Jordan ***Ph*** Chris Menges ***Ed*** J. Patrick Duffner, Tony Lawson ***Mus*** Elliot Goldenthal ***Art*** Anthony Pratt
Act Liam Neeson, Aidan Quinn, Stephen Rea, Alan Rickman, Julia Roberts, Ian Hart (Geffen/Warner)

Such is the catalog it presents of violence, vendettas, betrayals, vengeance, assassinations and insidious factionalism that *Michael Collins* intriguingly comes off as political history writ in the mode of the gangster film.

Staggeringly well made, the film possesses the *Reds* problem, except more so, in that it is a highly thought-out rendition of a difficult and, by now, obscure political struggle involving names unfamiliar to all but specialists. Having harbored this dream project since the early '80s, when he first wrote the script, Neil Jordan has clearly anticipated all of these potential barriers to audience acceptance. To a surprising degree, he has made *Michael Collins* a film of tremendous action, incident and momentum.

Michael Collins (Liam Neeson) was, in essence, a pioneer guerrilla warrior, a deliberately mysterious, rather subterranean figure who, after the failed Easter Rising of 1916, realized that any conventional fighting against the British was doomed to failure. Instead, he raised the Irish Volunteers, who staged stunning ambushes on the Brits, who had occupied Ireland since the 12th century.

Neeson is a compulsive dynamo as Collins with the actor seizing his part with a passion and boldness. Stephen Rea registers effectively as a surreptitious double agent, while Aidan Quinn and Julia Roberts [as Collins' best friend and shared girlfriend] are winning even as they play roles that remain insufficiently defined in the writing.

1996: NOMINATIONS: Best Cinematography, Original Dramatic Score

•

MICKEY
1918, 90 mins, US ⊗ b/w
Dir F. Richard Jones ***Prod*** Mack Sennett ***Scr*** J. G. Hawks ***Ph*** Frank Williams ***Mus*** Neil Moret
Act Mabel Normand, Wheeler Oakman, Lew Cody, Minta Durfee (Normand/Serrett)

Mickey and Mabel Normand are one and the same. With all her tomboy pranks and cutting up, she is a wonderful little actress.

The opening scenes are those of the usual cut-and-dry western. But this illusion is dispelled as soon as Normand makes her appearance. Mickey's garments consist of an old pair of trousers, patched, a heavy flannel undershirt and a discarded waistcoat, many sizes too large for her. She lives with her uncle and his squaw housekeeper. He is working a mine at the opening of the picture, getting very little pay dirt, and they are not even prosperous, but they are a happy trio.

But Mickey's life in the wild and woolly West comes to an end when her uncle receives an invitation to send her east to some relations, who have a country home on Long Island. She goes there, but when these folks learn Mickey has no money they put her to work. As a domestic she is a rank failure and disrupts the whole household.

Throughout the picture she does a number of daring and intrepid stunts. The photography adds special interest to the picture. The cast supporting Normand is splendid and the whole production [made two years earlier, in 1916] breezes along, with action every minute.

•

MICKEY BLUE EYES
1999, 103 mins, UK/US Ⓥ ⊙ col
Dir Kelly Makin ***Prod*** Elizabeth Hurley, Charles Mulvehill ***Scr*** Adam Scheinman, Robert Kuhn ***Ph*** Donald E. Thorin ***Ed*** David Freeman ***Mus*** Basil Poledouris ***Art*** Gregory Keen
Act Hugh Grant, James Caan, Jeanne Tripplehorn, Burt Young, James Fox, Joe Viterelli (Simian/Castle Rock)

Mickey Blue Eyes is an engaging, often very funny fish-out-of-water story that provides Hugh Grant with an excellent vehicle.

As Michael Felgate, a proper English auctioneer enamored of a schoolteacher (Jeanne Tripplehorn) who secretly happens to be a Mafia princess, Grant makes the most of his awkward, boyish, slightly bumbling screen persona and deftly pulls off stunts of amusing verbal and physical comedy.

Michael proposes to Gina who, terrified he'll be sucked into the family business, refuses. When Michael learns that Gina's uncle Vito "The Butcher" Graziosi (Burt Young) runs more than a mere delicatessen, he insists he is up to the challenge. But Vito has plans to implicate the auctioneer in a money-laundering scheme involving his son's atrocious surreal paintings (think Jesus with an Uzi).

In the film's most ribald sequence, prospective father-in-law Frank (James Caan) tries to school Michael in mobster lingo, only to hear him give a ridiculously British, upper-class twist to classic wise-guy banter.

Grant's part fits him like a custom-tailored Italian suit. Caan is a fine foil as the wise guy who wants his little girl to be happy, and Young makes an impressively intimidating, tight-lipped crime boss. Tripplehorn, for her part, doesn't get to do much other than look dejected, disapproving or disappointed, until she performs some eleventh-hour shenanigans that seem to have been designed to give her character a bit more credibility.

Canuck helmer Kelly Makin keeps things moving apace.

•

MICKEY ONE
1965, 93 mins, US Ⓥ ⊙ b/w
Dir Arthur Penn ***Prod*** Arthur Penn ***Scr*** Alan Surgal ***Ph*** Ghislain Cloquet ***Ed*** Aram Avakian ***Mus*** Eddie Sauter ***Art*** George Jenkins
Act Warren Beatty, Hurd Hatfield, Alexandra Stewart, Franchot Tone, Jeff Corey, Teddy Hart (Florin/Tatira/Columbia)

Mickey One could be described as a study in regeneration, but the screenplay is overloaded with symbolic gestures which obscure the main objectives of the plot.

Title character is a one-time top nitery comic who has been leading an extravagant life, getting mixed up with dames and gamblers. In a bid to get away from his past and start afresh, he assumes the identity of a Pole whose name is conveniently abbreviated to Mickey One. He gradually drifts back to the world of nightclubs, and in a sleazy West Chicago joint rediscovers the art of wowing an audience.

To this point, the plot develops reasonably smoothly and the few touches of symbolism are not entirely unacceptable. Thereafter, however, symbolism runs riot, occasionally to the point of pretentiousness.

Arthur Penn must accept his share of responsibility for the confused style and bewildering nature of the more obscure sequences. But in his main intention he is powerfully backed by Warren Beatty, who gives a commanding, though highly mannered, performance—a consistently dominating study of a man who lives in fear of his past.

•

MICKI + MAUDE
1984, 118 mins, US Ⓥ ⊙ ⊏⊐ col
Dir Blake Edwards ***Prod*** Tony Adams ***Scr*** Jonathan Reynolds ***Ph*** Harry Stradling ***Ed*** Ralph E. Winters ***Mus*** Lee Holdridge ***Art*** Rodger Maus
Act Dudley Moore, Amy Irving, Ann Reinking, Richard Mulligan, George Gaynes, Wallace Shawn (Columbia-Delphi III/BEE)

Micki + Maude is a hilarious farce. For his part, Dudley Moore is in top antic form, and Amy Irving has never been better.

Debuting screenwriter Jonathan Reynolds has constructed a farce of simple, classical proportions about a man who accidentally gets his wife and new girlfriend pregnant at virtually the same time.

The host of a silly TV show which does features on things like the food at an election-night celebration, Moore rarely gets to see his attorney wife (Ann Reinking) due to her hectic schedule, finding time only for a quickie in the back of a limousine.

On the job for his show, Moore meets comely Amy Irving, who easily seduces him on their next encounter. Premise is set up shortly thereafter, when both women announce that they are pregnant.

•

MIDDLE AGE CRAZY
1980, 89 mins, Canada Ⓥ col
Dir John Trent ***Prod*** Robert Cooper ***Scr*** Carl Kleinschmidt ***Ph*** Reginald Morris ***Ed*** John Kelly ***Mus*** Matthew McCauley ***Art*** Karen Bromley
Act Bruce Dern, Ann-Margret, Graham Jarvis, Helen Hughes, Deborah Wakeham (20th Century-Fox/Tormont)

Bobby Lee (Bruce Dern) is a successful building contractor on the verge of his 40th birthday. He is getting hung up on his milestone date as a result of his wife's persistence that he's still the old stud she married.

Constant reminders from friends and family on his dependability eventually drive him to change his style. He buys a Porsche, dresses up like a drugstore cowboy, and has a brief fling with a Dallas Cowgirl (Deborah Wakeham).

He finally decides family and responsibility aren't so bad after all. The revelation is pat and steeped in sentimentality. A quick resolution would have been more in keeping with the movie's acerbic wit.

Dern emerges a likable family man with deep reservations about his lot in life. The actor is equally convincing dressed in three-piece suits or denim and boots. Ann-Margret as his wife is also outstanding.

•

MIDDLE AGE SPREAD
1979, 94 mins, New Zealand col
Dir John Reid ***Prod*** John Barnett ***Scr*** Keith Aberdein ***Ph*** Alun Bollinger ***Ed*** Michael Horton ***Mus*** Stephen McCurdy
Act Grant Tilly, Donna Akersten, Dorothy McKegg, Bridget Armstrong, Bevan Wilson, Peter Sumner (Endeavour/NZ Film Commission)

Middle Age Spread centres on Colin (Grant Tilly), a college teacher whose promotion to principal coincides with a number of personal crises.

Not least are a widening girth, which has him jogging round the streets at night, and a tentative first-and-last affair with a much younger teaching colleague, Judy (Donna Akersten).

At a dinner party he hosts, with his increasingly sexually disinterested wife, Elizabeth (Dorothy McKegg), the morality and values of their tight-knit circle of friends are played out with deadly accuracy.

To his credit, director John Reid, one of the actors in the original stage presentation, has created a film that is not just a pale adaptation of the play.

•

MIDNIGHT
1939, 92 mins, US b/w
Dir Mitchell Leisen ***Prod*** Arthur Hornblow, Jr. ***Scr*** Charles Brackett, Billy Wilder ***Ph*** Charles Lang, Jr. ***Ed*** Doane Harrison ***Mus*** Frederick Hollander ***Art*** Hans Dreier, Robert Usher
Act Claudette Colbert, Don Ameche, John Barrymore, Francis Lederer, Mary Astor, Hedda Hopper (Paramount)

Story [from one by Edwin Justus Mayer and Franz Schulz] is light, but with a good share of humorous moments, many of them of the screwball variety. It's a slender thread, however, on which to tie series of incidents in adventures of a stranded showgirl in Paris.

After a flirtation with Don Ameche, Claudette Colbert crashes a musicale and poses as a countess. This leads to job for John Barrymore, in which she is to attract the amorous attentions of Francis Lederer away from Barrymore's wife, Mary Astor. For her assignment, Colbert is provided with elaborate wardrobe and a hotel suite.

Direction by Mitchell Leisen is generally satisfactory, although picture is slow in getting under way and has several spots that could be tightened. Editing shows sketchiness in several instances.

•

MIDNIGHT COWBOY
1969, 119 mins, US Ⓥ ⊙ col
Dir John Schlesinger ***Prod*** Jerome Hellman, John Schlesinger ***Scr*** Waldo Salt ***Ph*** Adam Holender ***Ed*** Hugh A. Robertson ***Mus*** John Barry (sup.) ***Art*** John Robert Lloyd
Act Dustin Hoffman, Jon Voight, Sylvia Miles, John McGiver, Brenda Vaccaro, Barnard Hughes (United Artists)

Midnight Cowboy is the sometimes amusing but essentially sordid saga of a male prostitute in Manhattan. Dustin Hoffman is cast as gimp-legged, always unshaven, cough-wracked petty chiseler who at first exploits and then befriends the stupid boy hustler from Texas. The title role is played by Jon Voight.

The film [from a novel by James Leo Herlihy] is full of un-nice people from bad environments. It is obsessed with mercenary sex and haunted by memories of cruel group ravishments. Indignity is endemic.

Voight travels north by bus through an America that is mocked in every sign along the road. After Voight's first unsuccessful attempts at hustling he is "befriended" by Hoffman. The two chums hide in a tenement marked for demolition, living on canned soup cooked over canned heat.

It is never easy to work up a liking for either of the two main bums in this pantheon of lost souls. The story begins by suggesting that male prostitutes offer themselves to women but the facts of the city soon establish that this is a homosexual market primarily. The boy hustler "consents" in a movie theatre and then is deadbeat out of the agreed price. Later, desperate for money to take his dying crony to Florida, the Texan brutalizes a pathetic, middle-aged whimpering homosexual in a hotel room.

Midnight Cowboy has a miscellany of competent bit players and a good deal of both sly and broad humor.

1969: Best Picture, Director, Adapted Screenplay

NOMINATIONS: Best Actor (Dustin Hoffman, Jon Voight), Supp. Actress (Slyvia Miles), Editing

•

MIDNIGHT EXPRESS
1978, 120 mins, UK/US Ⓥ ⊙ col
Dir Alan Parker ***Prod*** David Puttnam ***Scr*** Oliver Stone ***Ph*** Michael Seresin ***Ed*** Gerry Hambling ***Mus*** Giorgio Moroder ***Art*** Geoffrey Kirkland
Act Brad Davis, Randy Quaid, John Hurt, Bo Hopkins, Paul Smith, Mike Kellin (Casablanca/Columbia)

Midnight Express is a sordid and ostensibly true story about a young American busted [in 1970] for smuggling hash in Turkey and his subsequent harsh imprisonment and later escape. Cast, direction and production are all very good, but it's difficult to sort out the proper empathies from the muddled and moralizing screenplay which, in true Anglo-American fashion, wrings hands over alien cultures as though our civilization is absolutely perfect.

Oliver Stone is credited for adapting the book by Billy Hayes, young tourist who, in the midst of airline terrorism and world pressure on Turkey over drug farming, is discovered wearing a not-insignificant amount of hash strapped to his body. Brad Davis plays Hayes in a strong performance.

Acceptance of the film depends a lot on forgetting several things: he was smuggling hash; Turkey is entitled to its laws, and is no more guilty of penal corruption and brutality than, say, the U.S., U.K., France, Germany, etc; a world tourist can't assume that a helpful father (played well by Mike Kellin) is going to have the same clout with some midwestern politicians; nor can an American expect to be treated with kid gloves everywhere.

However, the script loads up sympathy for Davis, also fellow convicts Randy Quaid (a psycho character), John Hurt (a hard doper) and Norbert Weisser (playing the obligatory gay inmate), by making the prison authorities even worse.

1978: Best Adapted Screenplay, Original Score

NOMINATIONS: Best Picture, Director, Supp. Actor (John Hurt), Editing

•

MIDNIGHT IN THE GARDEN OF GOOD AND EVIL
1997, 155 mins, US Ⓥ ⊙ col
Dir Clint Eastwood ***Prod*** Clint Eastwood, Arnold Stiefel ***Scr*** John Lee Hancock ***Ph*** Jack N. Green ***Ed*** Joel Cox ***Mus*** Lennie Niehaus ***Art*** Henry Bunstead
Act Kevin Spacey, John Cusack, Jack Thompson, Alison Eastwood, Irma P. Hall, Paul Hipp (Malpaso/Warner)

Midnight in the Garden of Good and Evil is an outstanding lean film trapped in a fat film's body. Clint Eastwood's screen version of John Berendt's phenomenally successful nonfiction tome, about a sensational murder case in genteel, eccentric old Savannah, GA, vividly captures the atmosphere and memorable characters of the book. But the picture's aimless, sprawling structure and exceedingly leisurely pace finally weigh too heavily on its virtues.

Author stand-in John Kelso (John Cusack) checks into Savannah for a brief stay to report on the glittering Christmas party to be given by leading society figure Jim Williams (Kevin Spacey), a middle-aged bachelor who made his fortune in antiques. In the wee hours, Williams shoots and kills his violence-prone houseboy and lover, Billy Hanson (Jude Law).

As he tells it, the killing was self-defense but Williams is arrested and charged with murder. As Kelso switches gear from society reporter to chronicler of crime, the less reputable portion of Savannah's colorful social strat is revealed.

Especially through the second half, script evinces no gathering force, and instead of gradually narrowing the focus, director Eastwood continues to let the yarn just unravel.

Performances are mostly aces, beginning with Spacey's Williams, oozing with savoir-faire, urban confidence, silken wit and a vaguely sinister charm. Vet Aussie thesp Jack Thompson, his Southern accent fitting in perfectly with everyone else's, registers strongly as Williams's powerful attorney, as does Irma P. Hall as the voodoo priestess who delves deeply into life's mysteries. Cusack does OK with the always difficult role of the semi-involved observer of people more fascinating than he.

•

MIDNIGHT LACE
1960, 108 mins, US Ⓥ col
Dir David Miller ***Prod*** Ross Hunter, Martin Melcher ***Scr*** Ivan Goff, Ben Roberts ***Ph*** Russell Metty ***Ed*** Russell F. Schoengarth, Leon Barsha ***Mus*** Frank Skinner ***Art*** Alexander Golitzen, Robert Clatworthy
Act Doris Day, Rex Harrison, John Gavin, Myrna Loy, Roddy McDowall, Herbert Marshall (Universal)

In a Ross Hunter effort the emphasis is on visual satisfaction. The idea seems to be to keep the screen attractively filled. First and foremost, it is mandatory to have a lovely and popular star of Doris Day's calibre. She is to be decked out in an elegant wardrobe and surrounded by expensive sets and tasteful furnishings. This is to be embellished by highly dramatic lighting effects and striking hues, principally in the warmer yellow-brown range of the spectrum. The camera is to be maneuvered, whenever possible, into striking, unusual positions.

Basis of the fuss is, preferably, to be a melodrama, but a light, sophisticated comedy is an acceptable alternative.

In *Midnight Lace*, adapted from Janet Green's play, *Matilda Shouted Fire*, Day is victimized by what seems to be a crank on the telephone. Informed by a nagging, mysterious, persistent caller that her life is in jeopardy, she works herself into such a lather that others, Scotland Yard included, begin to believe her obsession is the myth of a neglected wife (husband, Rex Harrison, is constantly preoccupied with business matters).

Among the chief suspects are John Gavin, a construction gang foreman who makes phone calls in a neighborhood pub; Roddy McDowall, a spoiled young punk who can't keep his eyes off the heroine; and Herbert Marshall, treasurer in Harrison's firm who's having trouble paying off his bookie.

The effervescent Day sets some sort of record here for frightened gasps. Harrison is capable. Director David Miller adds a few pleasant little humorous touches and generally makes the most of an uninspired yarn.

•

MIDNIGHT MAN, THE
1974, 117 mins, US col
Dir Roland Kibbee, Burt Lancaster ***Prod*** Roland Kibbee, Burt Lancaster ***Scr*** Roland Kibbee, Burt Lancaster ***Ph*** Jack Priestley ***Ed*** Frank Morriss ***Mus*** Dave Grusin ***Art*** James D. Vance
Act Burt Lancaster, Susan Clark, Cameron Mitchell, Morgan Woodward, Harris Yulin, Joan Lorring (Universal)

The Midnight Man stars Burt Lancaster as a paroled ex-cop stumbling into a series of small-town murders. With Roland Kibbee, Lancaster adapted, produced and directed on some refreshingly different locations in South Carolina. The cluttered plot's twists and turns get tiring after 117 minutes, but the violence highlights are well motivated and discreetly executed.

Script derives from a David Anthony novel, *The Midnight Lady and the Mourning Man*. Lancaster, out on parole after killing his wife's lover, is reduced to a campus security job under the auspices of his longtime pal (Cameron Mitchell). Susan Clark is Lancaster's sexy parole officer. The murder of Catherine Bach, whose personal trauma was committed to a tape stolen from psychologist Robert Quarry, triggers an awful lot of storytelling.

•

MIDNIGHT RUN
1988, 122 mins, US Ⓥ ⊙ col
Dir Martin Brest ***Prod*** Martin Brest ***Scr*** George Gallo ***Ph*** Donald Thorin ***Ed*** Billy Weber, Chris Lebenzon, Michael Tronick ***Mus*** Danny Elfman ***Art*** Angelo Graham
Act Robert De Niro, Charles Grodin, Yaphet Kotto, John Ashton, Dennis Farina, Joe Pantoliano (City Lights)

Midnight Run shows that Robert De Niro can be as wonderful in a comic role as he is in a serious one. Pair him, a gruff ex-cop and bounty hunter, with straight man Charles Grodin, his captive, and the result is one of the most entertaining, best executed, original road pictures *ever*.

It's De Niro's boyish charm that works for him every time and here especially as the scruffy bounty hunter ready to do his last job in a low-life occupation. He's to nab a philanthropically minded accountant hiding out in Gotham (Grodin) who embezzled $15 million from a heroin dealer/Las Vegas mobster and return him to Los Angeles in time to collect a $100,000 fee by midnight Friday.

Kidnapping Grodin is the easy part; getting him back to the West Coast turns out to be anything but easy. The two guys, who can't stand each other, are stuck together for the duration of a journey neither particularly wants to be on.

Midnight Run is more than a string of well-done gags peppered by verbal sparring between a reluctant twosome; it is a terrifically developed script full of inventive, humorous twists made even funnier by wonderfully realized secondary characters.

•

MIDNIGHT STING
SEE: DIGGSTOWN

•

MIDSUMMER NIGHT'S DREAM, A
1935, 132 mins, US Ⓥ ⦿ b/w
Dir Max Reinhardt, William Dieterle ***Prod*** Henry Blanke ***Scr*** Charles Kenyon, Mary C. McCall, Jr. ***Ph*** Hal Mohr ***Ed*** Ralph Dawson ***Mus*** Erich Wolfgang Korngold (arr.) ***Art*** Anton Grot
Act James Cagney, Olivia de Havilland, Mickey Rooney, Victor Jory, Joe E. Brown, Dick Powell (Warner)

Question of whether a Shakespearean play can be successfully produced on a lavish scale for the films is affirmatively answered by this commendable effort. The familiar story of *A Midsummer Night's Dream*, half of which is laid in a make-believe land of elves and fairies, is right up the film alley technically.

The fantasy, the ballets of the Oberon and Titania cohorts, and the characters in the eerie sequences are convincing and illusion compelling. Film is replete with enchanting scenes, beautifully photographed and charmingly presented. All Shakespearian devotees will be pleased at the soothing treatment given to the Mendelssohn score. The women are uniformly better than the men. They get more from their lines. The selection of Dick Powell to play Lysander was unfortunate. He never seems to catch the spirit of the play or role. And Mickey Rooney, as Puck, is so intent on being cute that he becomes almost annoying.

There are some outstanding performances, however, notably Victor Jory as Oberon. His clear, distinct diction indicates what can be done by careful recitation and good recording; Olivia de Havilland, as Hermia, is a fine artist here; others are Jean Muir, Verree Teasdale and Anita Louise, the latter beautiful as Titania but occasionally indistinct in her lines.

1935: Best Cinematography, Editing

NOMINATION: Best Picture

•

MIDSUMMER NIGHT'S SEX COMEDY, A
1982, 88 mins, US Ⓥ col
Dir Woody Allen ***Prod*** Robert Greenhut ***Scr*** Woody Allen ***Ph*** Gordon Willis ***Ed*** Susan E. Morse ***Art*** Mel Bourne
Act Woody Allen, Mia Farrow, Jose Ferrer, Julie Hagerty, Tony Roberts, Mary Steenburgen (Orion)

Woody Allen's *A Midsummer Night's Sex Comedy* is a pleasant disappointment, pleasant because he gets all the laughs he goes for in a visually charming, sweetly paced picture, a disappointment because he doesn't go for more.

The time is the turn of the century, the place a lovely old farmhouse in upstate New York. Here, Wall St. stockbroker Allen spends his spare time inventing odd devices and trying to bed his own wife (Mary Steenburgen) who has turned cold.

Arriving for a visit—and also a wedding—are Steenburgen's cousin Jose Ferrer, a stuffy, pedantic scholar, and his bride to be (Mia Farrow), a former near-nympho who's decided to settle down with Ferrer's intellect.

Also arriving are Allen's best friend, who else but Tony Roberts, an amorous physician and his current short-term fling (Julie Hagerty), a nurse dedicated to the study of anatomy and all its possibilities.

With this daffy assortment and Allen's gift for laughlines, the picture can't avoid being fun, even at a rather leisurely pace in keeping with its times.

•

MIDSUMMER NIGHT'S DREAM, A
1999, 116 mins, US Ⓥ ⦿ ▭ col
Dir Michael Hoffman ***Prod*** Leslie Urdang, Michael Hoffman ***Scr*** Michael Hoffman ***Ph*** Oliver Stapleton ***Ed*** Garth Craven ***Mus*** Simon Boswell ***Art*** Luciana Arrighi
Act Kevin Kline, Michelle Pfeiffer, Rupert Everett, Stanley Tucci, Calista Flockhart, Anna Friel (Fox Searchlight/Regency)

A Midsummer Night's Dream is a whimsical, intermittently enjoyable but decidedly unmagical version of the Bard's wild romantic comedy. Set in Tuscany at the turn of the century, this modernist comedy features an impressive cast that elevates film above its flaws. Pic brims with ideas and promises, but suffers from a lack of coherent vision and an incongruous tone, the result of diverse acting styles from the Brit, American and French thesps.

Preparations for the wedding of Duke Theseus (David Strathairn) and Hippolyta (Sophie Marceau) are under way when the duke is forced to listen to the complaints of opposing sides in a dispute over an arranged marriage. The crusty Egeus (Bernard Hill) has promised his daughter Hermia (Anna Friel) to Demetrius (Christian Bale), but she loves Lysander (Dominic West). Hermia plans to elope with her lover, but her best friend, Helena (Calista Flockhart), who is in love with Demetrius, knows of the plot.

Also bound for the same forest is a band of the village's amateur players. Of the quintet of workmen, it's Bottom the Weaver (Kevin Kline) who's the most dilettante. The dark forest is home of the fairies, where the trickster Puck (Stanley Tucci) administers a powerful love potion that causes the participants to change and mix their partners in an outrageous manner. Puck becomes a pawn in the love games of the fairies' king and queen, Oberon and Titania (Rupert Everett, Michelle Pfeiffer).

There is not much chemistry between Pfeiffer and Everett, nor between Pfeiffer and Kline, particularly in their big love scene. Overall, the Brits give more resonant performances.

•

MIDWAY
(UK: BATTLE OF MIDWAY)
1976, 132 mins, US Ⓥ ⦿ col
Dir Jack Smight ***Prod*** Walter Mirisch ***Scr*** Donald S. Sanford ***Ph*** Harry Stradling, Jr. ***Ed*** Robert Swink, Frank J. Urioste ***Mus*** John Williams ***Art*** Walter Tyler
Act Charlton Heston, Henry Fonda, James Coburn, Glenn Ford, Hal Holbrook, Toshiro Mifune (Mirisch)

The June 1942 sea-air battle off Midway Island was a turning point in World War II. However, the melee of combat was the usual hysterical jumble of noise, explosion and violent death. *Midway* tries to combine both aspects but succumbs to the confusion.

Henry Fonda's performance as Pacific Fleet Commander Chester W. Nimitz towers over everything else.

The Midway battle followed the Mames Doolittle air raid on Tokyo in April 1942. The turnback of the Japanese navy effectively cleared the West Coast from attack, and gave the U.S. time enough to mobilize for the long road back across the Pacific.

•

MIGHTY APHRODITE
1995, 95 mins, US Ⓥ ⦿ col
Dir Woody Allen ***Prod*** Robert Greenhut ***Scr*** Woody Allen ***Ph*** Carlo DiPalma ***Ed*** Susan E. Morse ***Art*** Santo Loquasto
Act Woody Allen, Helena Bonham Carter, Mira Sorvino, Michael Rapaport, F. Murray Abraham, Claire Bloom (Sweetland/Miramax)

Woody Allen takes a comic, only slightly sceptical look at his compulsion to rescue wayward young women in *Mighty Aphrodite*, a zippy, frothy confection that emerges as agreeable middle-range Woody, dominated by a striking performance from Mira Sorvino as a sweet-tempered hooker who gets a break from an unexpected source.

After a surprising opening with a mock Greek chorus, Allen's middle-aged Lenny fulminates to his wife, Amanda (Helena Bonham Carter), and another couple against the idea of adopting children. Before the viewer can recover from the autobiographical implications of this tirade, Lenny and Amanda are bringing home an adopted infant son.

A few years down the line, Lenny is so impressed with his son that he decides the kid's real mom must be some kind of genius. With a little stealth, Lenny is able to track his prey, but instead of finding a saint with a 150 IQ, he learns that she's a prostitute apparently named Linda Ash, but who also goes by the memorable nom de porno of Judy Cum.

Lenny makes a date with Linda (Sorvino) and encounters an incredibly statuesque bimbo whose amiable nature prevails over her notable life scars. Lenny befriends this guileless young lady, learns that her greatest regret was giving up her baby, and resolves to help her change her life.

Bonham Carter, sporting an Allen-inflected American accent, looks pale and almost otherworldly. The film's biggest surprise and attraction is Sorvino. Hair dyed blondish, and talking dirty in a high-pitched, flatly uninflected voice, this exciting young actress goes way beyond the whore-with-a-heart-of-gold externals of the part in developing a deeply sympathetic and appealing character.

1995: Best Supporting Actress (Mira Sorvino)

NOMINATION: Best Original Screenplay

•

MIGHTY BARNUM, THE
1934, 87 mins, US b/w
Dir Walter Lang ***Prod*** Darryl F. Zanuck ***Scr*** Gene Fowler, Bess Meredyth ***Ph*** Peverell Marley ***Ed*** Allen McNeil, Barbara McLean ***Mus*** Alfred Newman ***Art*** Richard Day
Act Wallace Beery, Adolphe Menjou, Virginia Bruce, Rochelle Hudson, Janet Beecher, Tammany Young (Twentieth)

P. T. Barnum's life, the things he did and the things that were done to him up to the time of the inspiration for the circus that was to become Barnum & Bailey, proves engrossing if not sensational screen entertainment.

Opening on the scenes of the present day Barnum & Bailey show, the story turns back 100 years to the time when Barnum was operating a general store in New York. Earlier sequences are very meaty and compact, whereas in the second half the action slows a bit here and there.

Despite the danger of a split with his conservatively reared wife (Janet Beecher), Barnum (Wallace Beery) signs up Joyce Heth (Lucille La Verne), supposed nursemaid to George Washington, who's later exposed as a fake. Then Zorro, the bearded lady (May Boley), who double crosses him. He tries again, this time becoming so successful with Tom Thumb (George Brasno) and his little midget wife (Olive Brasno) that he brings Jenny Lind over (Virginia Bruce). His romance with the singer causes P. T. to neglect his museum of freaks as well as his wife.

Adolphe Menjou, playing the reformed drunk who is to become Bailey, is capital in his assignment, with Rochelle Hudson for charming love interest. Beecher gives a commendable performance. The Jenny Lind sequences are inclined to slow matters. Two soprano solos are included where one might have been enough. Bruce, in singing, appears to have the benefit of a dubbed-in voice.

•

MIGHTY DUCKS, THE
(UK/AUSTRALIA: CHAMPIONS)
1992, 101 mins, US Ⓥ ⦿ col
Dir Stephen Herek ***Prod*** Jordan Kerner, Jon Avnet ***Scr*** Steven Brill ***Ph*** Thomas Del Ruth ***Ed*** Larry Bock, John F. Link ***Mus*** David Newman ***Art*** Randy Ser
Act Emilio Estevez, Joss Ackland, Lane Smith, Heidi Kling, Josef Sommer, Joshua Jackson (Walt Disney)

The Mighty Ducks is a formulaic pic meant for children but actually focusing on a yuppie's struggle for redemption.

Emilio Estevez stars as an accomplished but arrogant Minneapolis lawyer who carelessly gets nailed on drunk driving charges. His stern boss cuts a deal for him to do community service instead of suffering the humiliation of court. Once Estevez meets the undisciplined, street-wise kids whom he must shape into a winning peewee hockey team, pic becomes predictable and mighty preachy.

Political correctness informs the film from the careful ethnic and gender composition of the hockey team to pic's value system: teamwork over aggressive individualism and concentration over strength. Schematic script contains a few inspired one-liners, but not enough to distract attention from plot machinery.

Helmer Stephen Herek endows a familiar story with a crisp look and swift tempo, seldom allowing sanctimonious tale to linger too long or gags to get too tiresome. In pic's second part, the pace is accelerated by skillful montages of hockey games.

•

MIGHTY JOE YOUNG
1949, 88 mins, US Ⓥ ⦿ b/w
Dir Ernest B. Schoedsack ***Prod*** John Ford, Merian C. Cooper ***Scr*** Ruth Rose ***Ph*** J. Roy Hunt ***Ed*** Ted Cheesman ***Mus*** Roy Webb ***Art*** James Basevi
Act Terry Moore, Ben Johnson, Robert Armstrong, Frank McHugh, Douglas Fowley, Regis Toomey (Arko/RKO)

Mighty Joe Young is fun to laugh at and with, loaded with incredible corn, plenty of humor, and a robot gorilla who becomes a genuine hero. The technical skill of the large staff of experts [led by Willis O'Brien and Ray Harryhausen] gives the robot life.

Plot [by Merian C. Cooper] deals with a gorilla, raised in the African jungle by a young girl. Both the girl and the giant ape are happy with their rusticating until a safari headed by Broadway producer Robert Armstrong arrives in the jungle. Armstrong immediately sees the possibilities of the ape and the girl.

The presentation by John Ford and Cooper pulls all stops in slugging away at audience risibilities while pointing up the melodramatic phases. It's this general air of tongue-in-cheek treatment that makes the corn palatable.

1949: Best Special Effects

●

MIGHTY JOE YOUNG
1998, 114 mins, US Ⓥ ⊙ ▭ col
Dir Ron Underwood ***Prod*** Ted Hartley, Tom Jacobson ***Scr*** Mark Rosenthal, Lawrence Konner ***Ph*** Don Peterman, Oliver Wood ***Ed*** Paul Hirsch ***Mus*** James Horner ***Art*** Michael Corenblith
Act Charlize Theron, Bill Paxton, Rade Serbedzija, Peter Firth, David Paymer, Regina King (Walt Disney)

Mighty Joe Young is wholesome, well-crafted family fare like Hollywood used to make. Disney's new version of the 1949 RKO film about an oversized African gorilla out of his element in urban America makes the most of modern technology, adding color, computer graphics and impressive animatronics to a rather predictable storyline.

Scientist Dr. Ruth Young (Linda Purl) and her young daughter, Jill (Mika Boorem), are studying the behavior of a family of apes in Tanzania. Among the gorillas is young Joe, whose rare genetic mutation makes him grow faster than his peers. Leading a pack of poachers is the evil Strasser (Rade Serbedzija), who plans to snatch the baby gorilla for sale on the black market. Suffering a fatal wound, Ruth tells her daughter to protect Joe.

Years pass, and the adult Jill (Charlize Theron) and Joe live in peace and seclusion on their mountain. Scientist Gregg O'Hara (Bill Paxton) stumbles onto evidence of Joe and his discovery prompts the poachers' return. Gregg persuades Jill to move the gorilla to a California wildlife preserve, where Joe [eventually] escapes and roams through Hollywood, inadvertently terrorizing dumbstruck throngs.

There's not a lot to be said for the acting, since the humans play second banana to the gorilla throughout. However, the leggy Theron emotes well on cue, especially given that she was often acting opposite a blue screen or mechanized arm.

Paxton brandishes the same scientist's self-assured swagger he trotted out in *Twister*. And Serbedzija [here credited as Sherbedgia] does a variation on the arch-villain he portrayed in *The Saint*.

Technical credits and production values are fine, with kudos to Hoyt Yeatman's visual effects and Rick Baker's realistically designed Joe.

●

MIGHTY MORPHIN POWER RANGERS THE MOVIE
1995, 95 mins, US Ⓥ ⊙ col
Dir Bryan Spicer ***Prod*** Haim Saban, Shuki Levy, Suzanne Todd ***Scr*** Arne Olsen ***Ph*** Paul Murphy ***Ed*** Wayne Wahrman ***Mus*** Graeme Revell ***Art*** Craig Stearns
Act Karan Ashley, Johnny Yong Bosch, Steve Cardenas, Jason David Frank, Amy Jo Johnson, David Yost (Saban/Toei)

Morphin mania appears to have cooled somewhat during the past year, as the novelty of the campy *Mighty Morphin Power Rangers* TV series has begun to wear off. The movie won't do much to reverse the trend. But the sci-fi adventure pic, which is much slicker than its small-screen counterpart, should please the millions of youngsters who remain addicted.

The Rangers are six teenage martial artists who moonlight as superheroes when they're not attending high school in Angel Grove, USA. Each has a color-coded uniform and Zord, a mystically powered, animal-shaped attack vehicle.

Individually, each Ranger can kick more butt than a dozen Ninja Turtles. Most of the battle scenes—and the rubber bogeymen—are lifted intact from a Japanese TV series, giving the show an undeniably amusing air of low-rent tackiness.

The special effects in the movie, shot in Australia, are a great deal more special. High point is a battle with two huge, brightly metallic insect creatures that thrash downtown Angel Grove. On just about every other level, however, the pic plays like an elongated version of a 30-minute episode. Dialogue is as corny as Kansas in August. The photogenic young actors are, well, sincere.

The plot involves the accidental unearthing of Ivan Ooze (Paul Freeman), a centuries-old villain who's bent on crushing Zordon (Nicholas Bell), the Rangers's mentor, and ruling the world. In order to save Angel Grove, the Rangers journey to a distant planet where a mysterious power source is hidden. There they are aided by Dulcea (Gabrielle Fitzpatrick), a warrior woman who wears what appears to be a Stone Age version of a string bikini.

There is plenty of slam-bang action here, but no genuine bloodshed. Some of the dialogue is difficult to hear over the din.

●

MIKE'S MURDER
1984, 97 mins, US Ⓥ col
Dir James Bridges ***Prod*** Kim Kurumada (exec.) ***Scr*** James Bridges ***Ph*** Reynaldo Villalobos ***Ed*** Jeff Gourson, Dede Allen ***Mus*** John Barry, Joe Jackson ***Art*** Peter Jamison
Act Debra Winger, Mark Keyloun, Darrell Larson, Brooke Alderson, Paul Winfield, Robert Crosson (Skyeway/Ladd)

After a protracted postproduction period, *Mike's Murder* proves an intriguing, if not entirely successful, suspenser and paranoid mood piece. Resolutely a small, serious film, pic was made quickly and cheaply by James Bridges during the summer of 1982. Reported negative reactions at sneaks in northern California prompted drastic recutting. In addition, a score written by pop musician Joe Jackson was all but discarded.

Mark Keyloun's Mike is a casual, off-and-on-again lover of Debra Winger. He's a tennis teacher who earns additional dough as a small-time drug dealer. Unfortunately, with his sideline activities come some unsavory characters, notably the uncouth, impulsive Peter, convincingly played by Darrell Larson. In short order, Keyloun is killed and Larson is informed by a former associate that he's "a dead man."

A modestly successful bank employee, Winger spurns friends' advice and begins investigating the realities of Mike's world, meeting some of his lawless friends and ultimately being threatened by the desperate Larson.With its consciously repetitive scenes of driving around Los Angeles streets, film attempts a contemplative approach to the material and mood of impending doom. The attempt is both interesting and admirable—up to a point. As usual, Winger is wonderful to watch at all times, but her character is something of a cipher, and lack of any psychological angle holds down the film's ultimate achievement.

●

MIKEY AND NICKY
1976, 119 mins, US Ⓥ col
Dir Elaine May ***Prod*** Michael Hausman ***Scr*** Elaine May ***Ph*** Victor J. Kemper, Lucien Ballard, Jerry File, Jack Cooperman ***Ed*** John Carter ***Mus*** John Strauss ***Art*** Paul Sylbert
Act Peter Falk, John Cassavetes, Ned Beatty, Rose Arrick, Carol Grace, William Hickey (Paramount)

Peter Falk and John Cassavetes star as two old friends whose relationship is falling apart; two hours later, it is apparent there never was a friendship to begin with.

Cassavetes is a low-level criminal marked for extinction by ganglord Sanford Meisner, who employs Ned Beatty as hit man. Cassavetes calls Falk to help him, though neither Cassavetes nor the audience is certain that Falk isn't part of the rub-out strategy. That's the superficial hook on which hangs the real story of human relationships and mutual abuse. The interplay between the stars is excellent, Cassavetes slowly but steadily digging his own grave as he reveals his shallowness in dealings with Falk, girlfriend Carol Grace (a beautiful performance) and estranged wife Joyce Van Patten (a brief but excellent characterization).

●

MILAGRO BEANFIELD WAR, THE
1988, 117 mins, US Ⓥ ⊙ col
Dir Robert Redford ***Prod*** Robert Redford, Moctesuma Esparza ***Scr*** David Ward, John Nichols ***Ph*** Robbie Greenberg ***Ed*** Dede Allen, Jim Miller ***Mus*** Dave Grusin ***Art*** Joe Aubel
Act Ruben Blades, Richard Bradford, Sonia Braga, Julie Carmen, John Heard, Melanie Griffith (Universal)

The Milagro Beanfield War is a charming, fanciful little fable built around weighty issues concerning the environment, the preservation of a cultural heritage and the rights of citizens versus the might of the dollar.

The director and his screenwriters, who adapted John Nichols's 1974 novel, adeptly juggle at least a dozen major characters in telling the story of how one man's decision to cultivate his land, which is coveted by outside developers intent upon building a resort, leads to a standoff between natives of the area and the big boys.

Redford and company have put a quirky twist on the material, investing it with a quasi-mystical aspect as well as some raw comedy.

Set in modern-day New Mexico, tale is set in motion when impoverished farmer Joe Mondrago (Chick Vennera) improperly diverts some water from a main irrigation channel onto his own modest plot of land in order to start up a beanfield. This little act of defiance stirs up the handful of activists in the affected village, notably garage owner Ruby Archuleta (Sonia Braga), who recruits dropped out radical attorney and newspaperman Charley Bloom (John Heard) to rally round the cause.

1988: Best Original Score

●

MILDRED PIERCE
1945, 109 mins, US Ⓥ ⊙ b/w
Dir Michael Curtiz ***Prod*** Jerry Wald ***Scr*** Ranald MacDougall ***Ph*** Ernest Haller ***Ed*** David Weisbart ***Mus*** Max Steiner ***Art*** Anton Grot
Act Joan Crawford, Jack Carson, Zachary Scott, Eve Arden, Ann Blyth, Bruce Bennett (Warner)

At first reading James M. Cain's novel of the same title might not suggest screenable material, but the cleanup job has resulted in a class feature, showmanly produced by Jerry Wald and tellingly directed by Michael Curtiz.

It skirts the censorable deftly, but keeps the development adult in dealing with the story of a woman's sacrifices for a no-good daughter. High credit goes to Ranald MacDougall's scripting for his realistic dialog and method of retaining the frank sex play that dots the narrative while making the necessary compromises with the blue-pencillers.

Story is told in flashback as Mildred Pierce is being questioned by police about the murder of her second husband. Character goes back to the time she separated from her first husband and how she struggled to fulfill her ambitions for her children.

The dramatics are heavy but so skillfully handled that they never cloy. Joan Crawford reaches a peak of her acting career in this pic. Ann Blyth, as the daughter, scores dramatically in her first genuine acting assignment. Zachary Scott makes the most of his character as the Pasadena heel, a talented performance.

1945: Best Actress (Joan Crawford)

NOMINATIONS: Best Picture, Supp. Actress (Eve Arden, Ann Blyth), Screenplay, B&W Cinematography

●

MILK MONEY
1994, 108 mins, US Ⓥ col
Dir Richard Benjamin ***Prod*** Kathleen Kennedy, Frank Marshall ***Scr*** John Mattson ***Ph*** David Watkin ***Ed*** Jacqueline Cambas ***Mus*** Michael Convertino ***Art*** Paul Sylbert
Act Melanie Griffith, Ed Harris, Michael Patrick Carter, Malcolm McDowell, Anne Heche, Casey Siemaszko (Paramount/Kennedy-Marshall)

The premise of *Milk Money* could curdle in your stomach, and the execution of the idea is just plain rancid. With a tip of the hat to the performers, this is a misguided comedy with Hall of Shame pedigree.

Three boys on the cusp of puberty raid their piggy banks and sell their vintage comic books to raise $103.26 and head for the big city to pay to see a real live naked lady. The naifs fall right into an urban scam but are saved from robbery at gunpoint by a good-hearted prostitute, V (Melanie Griffith).

She puts the tykes into her pimp's car and escorts them back to the suburbs. But after she drops off Frank (Michael Patrick Carter), the car stalls and she's stuck. Frank's dad, Tom (Ed Harris), is, of course, a lonely widower, and V is in mortal danger because she's inadvertently run off with a tankful of ill-gotten lucre that's already resulted in the murder of her "manager." The film is obvious, loud, mean-spirited and has its mind in the gutter.

●

MILKY WAY, THE
1936, 80 mins, US Ⓥ ⊙ b/w
Dir Leo McCarey ***Prod*** E. Lloyd Sheldon ***Scr*** Grover Jones, Frank Butler, Richard Connell ***Ph*** Al Gilks ***Ed*** LeRoy Stone
Act Harold Lloyd, Adolphe Menjou, Verree Teasdale, Helen Mack, William Gargan, George Barbier (Paramount)

The Milky Way with Harold Lloyd is a good laff picture. The role of the timid milk wagon route-man who is catapulted into pugilistic fame and fortune is almost made to order for Lloyd and he plays it to the hilt. Given the support of a sturdy stage original [by Lynn Root and Harry Clork], the cinematic treatment is bolstered with some highly effective business of its own.

Adolphe Menjou is his usual capital self as the harassed fight manager who finds himself with a dead herring on his hands when middle-weight champ William Gargan gets the headline razz. This results in Lloyd's buildup as The Killer. Verree Teasdale is sophisticated vis-à-vis for Menjou, serving as good counterbalance to the almost psychopathic mentor of the maulers. Because of Menjou's insomnia, a sleep-inducer becomes plausible business for some more highly effective comedy, including the Morpheus act that puts Gargan to sleep again and permits Lloyd to win on a technical k.o.

The Milky Way merits the final good results, for this production was plenty harried by the illnesses of Menjou, McCarey and Teasdale, necessitating considerable delay.

Lionel Stander as the dumb-cluck pug is in his element with that basso-profundo speech and the wild attack of a role that's suited for his peculiar backgrounding.

•

MILLENNIUM

1989, 108 mins, US Ⓥ ⦿ col

Dir Michael Anderson ***Prod*** Douglas Leiterman ***Scr*** John Varley ***Ph*** Rene Ohashi ***Ed*** Ron Wisman ***Mus*** Eric N. Robertson ***Art*** Gene Rudolf

Act Kris Kristofferson, Cheryl Ladd, Daniel J. Travanti, Robert Joy, Al Waxman, Lloyd Bochner (Gladden)

Millennium tries hard to combine sci-fi special effects and a love story, but unfortunately neither are convincing and the pic ends up looking like a failed pilot for a TV series. Veteran science-fiction director Michael Anderson does the best he can with a mediocre script.

Pic opens with an investigation of a mid-air collision between a 747 and a DC-10 with Bill Smith (Kris Kristofferson) leading the experts' probe of the crash. He meets Louise Baltimore (Cheryl Ladd), leader of a commando unit of women from 1,000 years in the future. The complicated remainder of the pic [shot in Canada] involves movement through time, the search for the powerful "stunner" and the future civilization's efforts to continue. Seems that world is peopled by a race that can't procreate.

Kristofferson gives the film his best shot and breathes some life into the tired lines, while Ladd sports many outfits and wacky hairstyles but lacks real passion. Daniel J. Travanti just has to look studious for a few scenes.

•

MILLER'S CROSSING

1990, 114 mins, US Ⓥ ⦿ col

Dir Joel Coen ***Prod*** Ethan Coen, Mark Silverman ***Scr*** Joel Coen, Ethan Coen ***Ph*** Barry Sonnenfeld ***Ed*** Michael Miller ***Mus*** Carter Burwell ***Art*** Dennis Gassner

Act Gabriel Byrne, Albert Finney, Marcia Gay Harden, Jon Polito, John Turturro, J. E. Freeman (Circle/Pedas-Barenholtz-Durkin)

Substance is here in spades, along with the twisted, brilliantly controlled style on which filmmakers Joel and Ethan Coen made a name. Story unspools in an unnamed Eastern city in the 1930s where dim but ambitious Italian gangster Johnny Caspar (Jon Polito) has a problem named Bernie Bernbaum (John Turturro). Caspar wants approval from the city's Irish political boss, Leo (Albert Finney), to rub out the cause of his complaint, but Leo's not giving in. He's fallen in love with Bernie's sister, Verna (Marcia Gay Harden), who wants Bernie protected. Leo's cool, brainy aide-de-camp Tom (Gabriel Byrne) sees that Leo is making a big mistake, and it's up to Tom to save him as his empire begins to crumble. The complication is that Tom also is in love with Verna, though he's loath to admit it.

Rarely does a screen hero of Tom's gritty dimensions come along, and Irishman Byrne brings him gracefully and profoundly to life. As portrayed by screen newcomer Harden, Verna has the verve and flintiness of a glory-days Bette Davis or Barbara Stanwyck.

Also outstanding is Finney as the big-hearted political fixer who usually has the mayor and the police chief seated happily across his desk. He's as cool in a spray of bullets as he is vulnerable in affairs of the heart.

Buffs will note cameos by director Sam Raimi, with whom the Coens collaborated on his *Evil Dead*, and Frances McDormand, who made her indelible debut in *Blood Simple*.

•

MILLION, LE

1931, 85 mins, France Ⓥ b/w

Dir Rene Clair ***Scr*** Rene Clair ***Ph*** Georges Perinal ***Ed*** Rene Le Henaff ***Mus*** Armand Bernard, Philippe Pares, Georges Van Parys ***Art*** Lazare Meerson

Act Annabella, Rene Lefebvre, Constantin Stroesco, Paul Ollivier, Odette Talazac, Vanda Greville (Tobis)

Story [from the play by Georges Berr and M. Guillemand] is that of an impecunious painter in love with a girl in the opera ballet. It is fanciful, with no attempt at probability, but is highly entertaining. Director Rene Clair has a new trick of having a tune with lyrics applying to a certain thought played during appropriate silent sequences. There is a song about remorse, or a song about helplessness, sung when the principals are in appropriate situations, but without the principals singing themselves.

Some of the tunes are catchy. Direction, photo and sound are excellent. Femme lead is by Annabella, vastly better than at the time of Abel Gance's *Napoleon*. She is a looker, acts well and her voices registers very clearly. Vanda Greville, English, does a foreign vamp with a strong accent. Cost of the film was fully $80,000.

•

MILLIONAIRE FOR CHRISTY, A

1951, 90 mins, US b/w

Dir George Marshall ***Prod*** Bert E. Friedlob ***Scr*** Ken Englund ***Ph*** Harry Stradling ***Ed*** Daniel Mandell ***Mus*** Victor Young

Act Fred MacMurray, Eleanor Parker, Richard Carlson, Una Merkel, Kay Buckley, Raymond Greenleaf (Thor/20th Century-Fox)

Eleanor Parker, as poor legal secretary, is sent to Los Angeles to notify Fred MacMurray, a syrupy radio philosopher, that he has inherited $2 million. Parker sees a chance to improve her financial condition and makes a pitch for MacMurray without knowing he is on the brink of marriage to Kay Buckley.

Complications are piled on heavily when the best man (Richard Carlson), a psychiatrist, walks out on the wedding and the knotting is postponed while MacMurray chases him, taking along an unwilling Parker, to the doc's La Jolla clinic. En route along the coast highway, MacMurray winds up in a fog on the beach.

It is at this point that the comedy [from a story by Robert Harari] socks over. Director George Marshall has staged a wow scene involving a big wave that dashes the principals around. Another bright bit of merriment comes when the pair are taken in by a group of Mexican section hands who are led to believe they are newlyweds because of a sign on MacMurray's car.

•

MILLIONAIRESS, THE

1960, 90 mins, UK Ⓥ ▭ col

Dir Anthony Asquith ***Prod*** Dimitri De Grunwald ***Scr*** Wolf Mankowitz ***Ph*** Jack Hildyard ***Ed*** Anthony Harvey ***Mus*** George van Parys

Act Sophia Loren, Peter Sellers, Alastair Sim, Vittorio De Sica, Dennis Price, Alfie Bass (20th Century-Fox)

This stylized pic has Sophia Loren at her most radiant, wearing a series of stunning Balmain gowns. George Bernard Shaw's Shavianisms on morality, riches and human relationship retain much of their edge, though nudged into a practical screenplay by Wolf Mankowitz.

Anthony Asquith's direction often is slow, but he breaks up the pic with enough hilarious situations to keep the film from getting tedious. A major fault is that the cutting of the film is mainly episodic, but against this, there is handsome artwork and the relish with which Jack Hildyard has brought his camera to work on them.

Briefly, the yarn concerns a beautiful, spoiled young heiress who has all the money in the world but can't find love. Her eccentric deceased old man has stipulated that she mustn't marry unless the man of her choice can turn $1,400 into $42,000 within three months. She cheats. Her first marriage flops, she contemplates suicide and then sets her cap for a dedicated, destitute Indian doctor running a poor man's clinic. He's attracted to her, but scared of her money and power.

Loren is a constant stimulation. She catches many moods. Sellers plays the doctor straight, apart from an offbeat accent, but he still manages to bring in some typical comedy touches.

•

MILLION DOLLAR MERMAID

1952, 115 mins, US Ⓥ col

Dir Mervyn LeRoy ***Prod*** Arthur Hornblow, Jr. ***Scr*** Everett Freeman ***Ph*** George J. Folsey ***Ed*** John McSweeney, Jr. ***Mus*** Adolph Deutsch (dir.) ***Art*** Cedric Gibbons, Jack Martin Smith

Act Esther Williams, Victor Mature, Walter Pidgeon, David Brian, Donna Corcoran, Jesse White (M-G-M)

This is a gaudy, conventional biopic based on the career of Australian swimmer Annette Kellerman, appropriately tagged "Million Dollar Mermaid."

Toppers of the flashy acquatics are the fountain and smoke numbers, imaginatively staged by Busby Berkeley and boldly splashed with Technicolor hues. The old New York Hippodrome is re-created for the production numbers, which include a brief ballet by Maria Tallchief as Pavlova.

Film opens with Kellerman (Esther Williams) as a crippled child in Australia who heals her legs in taking up swimming. After becoming amateur champ Down Under, she heads for London with her musician father (Walter Pidgeon), attracts the attention of Victor Mature, a sports promoter, who brings her to America.

1952: NOMINATION: Best Color Cinematography

•

MILLION POUND NOTE, THE

(US: MAN WITH A MILLION)

1954, 92 mins, UK Ⓥ col

Dir Ronald Neame ***Prod*** John Bryan ***Scr*** Jill Craigie ***Ph*** Geoffrey Unsworth ***Ed*** Clive Donner ***Mus*** William Alwyn ***Art*** Jack Maxsted, John Box

Act Gregory Peck, Jane Griffiths, Ronald Squire, Joyce Grenfell, Reginald Beckwith, Maurice Denham (Group)

Mark Twain's classic story of the penniless American who is given a million pound bank note in a wager and succeeds in keeping it intact for a month, makes gentle screen satire.

With Edwardian settings providing a fascinating background, the yarn suffers from the protracted exploitation of one basic joke. It is sustaining and amusing for a time, but there are very few single gags that can successfully hold up for 92 minutes. *Note* is not an exception. The plot is based on a bet between two brothers (Ronald Squire and Wilfrid Hyde White) that a man with a million pound bank note in his possession could live on the fat of the land for a month without having to break into it. The guinea pig for their wager is Gregory Peck, a penniless American stranded in London. And, sure enough, he finds this an open sesame to food, clothes, hotels and, naturally, society.

•

MILLIONS LIKE US

1943, 103 mins, UK b/w

Dir Frank Launder, Sidney Gilliat ***Prod*** Edward Black ***Scr*** Frank Launder, Sidney Gilliat ***Ph*** Jack Cox, Roy Fogwell ***Ed*** R. E. Dearing, Alfred Roome ***Mus*** Louis Levy (dir.) ***Art*** John Bryan

Act Eric Portman, Patricia Roc, Gordon Jackson, Anne Crawford, Basil Radford, Naunton Wayne (Gainsborough)

Film is designed as patriotic propaganda on the U.K. front, minus flag waving and such-like. Acting throughout is superior to the story, and is of such a high quality it ought to make almost any film script interesting. It would not be at all surprising if the creation of this abundance of histrionic talent was due to slickness of direction.

The main star (in point of reputation) is Eric Portman, who has a relatively small part, but gives to it a dignified and intelligent portrayal. The outstanding roles are Patricia Roc and Gordon Jackson—she a factory worker, and he a young airman. Their lovemaking is crudely simple, but so sincere as to lift it out of the commonplace. The list of players includes a pair of prominent artists who appeared in the writers' successful *The Lady Vanishes*, when they scored smartly as a couple of silly Englishmen. An attempt is made to reproduce them in this picture, but without the same success. It really is unfair to Basil Radford and Naunton Wayne.

•

MIMIC

1997, 105 mins, US Ⓥ ⦿ col

Dir Guillermo Del Toro ***Prod*** Bob Weinstein, B. J. Rack, Ole Bornedal ***Scr*** Matthew Robbins, Guillermo Del Toro, Matthew Greenberg, John Sayles ***Ph*** Dan Laustsen ***Ed*** Patrick Lussier ***Mus*** Marco Beltrami ***Art*** Carol Spier

Act Mira Sorvino, Jeremy Northam, Josh Brolin, Giancarlo Giannini, Charles S. Dutton, F. Murray Abraham (Dimension)

Mimic is a dark, dank and drippy sci-fi shocker that threatens to become something unusual before trailing off into ridiculousness. Any artistic ambition gradually becomes overwhelmed by increasingly mundane genre developments, leaving the picture by the end as nothing more than a standard-issue big-bug item.

Pic [from a story by Matthew Robbins and director Guillermo Del Toro, based on the short story by Donald A. Wolheim] in some ways resembles the gory, entrails-laden thrillers David Cronenberg made early in his career, not least due to its having been lensed principally in Toronto, doubling for New York City.

Gifted young scientist Susan Tyler (Mira Sorvino) introduces a new breed of insect into the city to eliminate the conventional cockroaches that she has determined are carrying a terrible epidemic in Manhattan. Three years later, however, the roaches come home to roost.

Various unsuspecting victims are gobbled up by the hungry, hard-shelled predators, which have the ability to transform themselves into human-like form. Leaving aside the question of how many species have ever evolved so dramatically within three years, Susan determines there is a colony of the ugly critters about. Remainder of the picture is mostly set in the dingy bowels of the subway, as Susan manages to escape from a roach nest and joins her scientist husband (Jeremy Northam), a fellow worker (Josh Brolin) and cop (Charles S. Dutton) to turn the tables on the angry, lip-smacking beasts.

Mexican director Guillermo Del Toro, who made a splash with his debut film, the offbeat 1993 Mexican vampire feature *Cronos*, clearly knows his way around the camera, but the shadowy eeriness winds up being just dull. Special insect effects are accomplished enough, if fleeting.

•

MIND BENDERS, THE
1963, 101 mins, UK b/w
Dir Basil Dearden ***Prod*** Michael Relph ***Scr*** James Kennaway ***Ph*** Denys Coop ***Ed*** John D. Guthridge ***Mus*** Georges Auric ***Art*** James Morahan
Act Dirk Bogarde, Mary Ure, John Clements, Michael Bryant, Wendy Craig, Edward Fox (Novus/Anglo-Amalgamated)

James Kennaway's original screenplay finds the peg for its bizarre plot in "reduction of sensation" experiments reportedly done both in the U.S. and Britain. By eliminating a subject's various senses by submerging him in an isolation tank a shortcut to brainwashing is achieved. Once the basic story pattern has been established, it moves into a fascinating study of how a man's mind can be twisted by a laboratory technique.

Suicide of elderly scientist Harold Goldblatt prompts an investigation by secret agent John Clements to determine whether military security has been violated. Clements suspects Goldblatt has turned traitor. But the scientist's associate, Dirk Bogarde, denies any treason has been committed and blames Goldblatt's death as a result of the experiments. Bogarde voluntarily submits to isolation to prove his theory. Under Basil Dearden's firm direction, the cast absorbingly captures suspense and gruesome space-age qualities frequently generated by Kennaway's script. Bogarde emerges as a dedicated scientist who shades his role with lots of realism. Mary Ure's portrayal of the spurned wife is a touching piece of thesping.

•

MINISTRY OF FEAR
1945, 84 mins, US b/w
Dir Fritz Lang ***Prod*** B. G. De Sylva (exec.) ***Scr*** Seton I. Miller ***Ph*** Henry Sharp ***Ed*** Archie Marshek ***Mus*** Victor Young ***Art*** Hans Dreier, Hal Pereira
Act Ray Milland, Marjorie Reynolds, Dan Duryea, Carl Esmond, Hillary Brooke, Alan Napier (Paramount)

Fritz Lang, a master at getting the most out of mystery, intrigue and melodrama, in his direction apparently didn't have his way from beginning to end on *Ministry of Fear*. Pic [from the novel by Graham Greene] starts out to be a humdinger, and continues that way for the most part, but when the roundup of the spy gang gets underway the situation becomes drawn out and elementary, marring the footage that preceded.

Ray Milland, in the role of an ex-asylum inmate, who is released after serving two years for the "mercy" killing of his incurable wife, gives a forthright performance. He is tossed into the midst of a spy chase when, in purchasing a ticket to London upon leaving the asylum, he is drawn to the crowds at a British fair and wins a cake by guessing its weight. The cake contains a capsule that one of the spies is to have delivered to other enemy agents.

•

MINIVER STORY, THE
1950, 104 mins, UK/US b/w
Dir H. C. Potter ***Prod*** Sidney Franklin ***Scr*** Ronald Millar, George Froeschel ***Ph*** Joseph Ruttenberg ***Ed*** Harold F. Kress, Alfred Junge ***Mus*** Miklos Rozsa ***Art*** Alfred Junge
Act Greer Garson, Walter Pidgeon, John Hodiak, Leo Genn, Cathy O'Donnell, Peter Finch (M-G-M)

No one seriously expected a second *Mrs. Miniver* when *The Miniver Story* was in the making. It is difficult to capture the magical quality of the original, and this trades on its predecessor's name and the drawing power of Greer Garson and Walter Pidgeon.

Opening with a strangely pallid reproduction of London on VE day, Mrs. Miniver finds herself caught in the exuberant melee following the news that the war is over. She has just come from a doctor, realizes she has not long to live and bravely determines to keep the news from her family.

Chief laurels go to Greer Garson who, even with the unmistakable signs of illness and mental stress, makes feasible the husband's claim that she looks as lovely as ever.

John Hodiak gives a fine clear-cut performance.

•

MINNIE AND MOSKOWITZ
1971, 114 mins, US col
Dir John Cassavetes ***Prod*** Al Ruban ***Scr*** John Cassavetes ***Ph*** Arthur J. Ornitz, Alric Edens, Michael Margulies ***Ed*** Fred Knudtson ***Mus*** Bo Harwood (sup.)
Act Gena Rowlands, Seymour Cassel, Val Avery, Timothy Carey, Katherine Cassavetes, John Cassavetes (Faces Music/Universal)

Gena Rowlands and Seymour Cassel play the title roles in *Minnie and Moskowitz*, an oppressive and irritating film in which a shrill and numbing hysteria of acting and direction soon kills any empathy for the loneliness of the main characters. John Cassavetes wrote and directed in his now-familiar, home-movie improvisational and indulgent style.

The characters in Cassavetes's script are the "little people" who inhabit kitchen-sink dramas. When such people exist in reality, they are leasebreakers, who lower property values, create Saturday night brawls and otherwise earn the total contempt of neighbors.

Cassavetes has laid on with a trowel the silicones of borderline personal psychosis. The principals live on the knife-edge of breakdown. Rowlands, fed up with a back-street affair with Cassavetes, unbilled as a married man whose wife, Judith Roberts, tries suicide, has a friend in coworker Elsie Ames but little more. Rescuing her from a tight situation with pushy blind date Val Avery, Seymour Cassel outdoes in boorishness anything Avery might have tried. Cassel makes King Kong look like Cary Grant.

•

MIRACLE, THE
1959, 121 mins, US [widescreen] col
Dir Irving Rapper ***Prod*** Henry Blanke ***Scr*** Frank Butler ***Ph*** Ernest Haller ***Ed*** Frank Bracht ***Mus*** Elmer Bernstein
Act Carroll Baker, Roger Moore, Walter Slezak, Vittorio Gassman, Katina Paxinou, Gustavo Rojo (Warner)

Warner Bros.'s multi-million dollar spectacle, though laid in the 19th century is a "biblical" subject with elements and approach of such films. The production has bullfights, military battles, lavish ballroom parties, music, dancing, gypsies and vaulted cathedrals echoing to choirs of nuns. It has about everything, in fact, except a genuinely spiritual story.

The Miracle was a costume special of the German stager Max Reinhardt. Its theme is the recurrent one in religious legend, of the god, goddess or angel who assumes human shape to intervene directly in the affairs of men.

According to the screenplay, based on Karl Vollmoeller's old play, Carroll Baker is a postulant at a Spanish convent when she falls in love with Roger Moore, a soldier in the future Duke of Wellington's army, then battling Napoleon in Spain. When she leaves the convent to follow Moore, the statue of the Virgin in the chapel comes down from its pedestal and assumes the form of the postulant. And Baker is off on various adventures.

Irving Rapper's direction is effective in the spacious exteriors, moving massed groupings with force and interest. It is less perceptive in the handling of individuals and their interaction. As for the theme itself, it is not exactly clear what "The Miracle" is supposed to do, other than give Baker a chance to gallivant about Europe in a variety of costumes.

•

MIRACLE, THE
1991, 96 mins, UK Ⓥ ⦿ col
Dir Neil Jordan ***Prod*** Stephen Woolley, Redmond Morris ***Scr*** Neil Jordan ***Ph*** Philippe Rousselot ***Ed*** Joke van Wijk ***Mus*** Anne Dudley ***Art*** Gemma Jackson
Act Beverly D'Angelo, Donal McCann, Niall Byrne, Lorraine Pilkington, J. G. Devlin, Kathleen Delaney (Palace/Promenade)

Irish writer-director Neil Jordan returns to his home turf with the small-scale romantic drama *The Miracle*, with uneven results.

Jimmy (Niall Byrne) is a musician and a dreamer who spends much of his time in the company of Rose (Lorraine Pilkington). Rose would like their relationship to become more intimate. Together they walk the streets of their small coastal town (Bray in County Wicklow), inventing romantic stories about the people who pass them by.

Jimmy never knew his mother and lives with his father (Donal McCann), a drunken musician. One day his eye is caught by an attractive American woman (Beverly D'Angelo) who's in town to perform in a local production of *Destry Rides Again*. He fantasizes a romantic liasion with her, but there are no prizes for guessing that she's really his long-lost mother. Like everything else in the film, the incest theme is tentatively handled. More interesting is Rose's relationship with a circus animal trainer (Mikkel Gaup).

D'Angelo exudes mature sexuality as the stranger in town, but McCann makes heavy weather of his role as the perpetually drunken father.

•

MIRACLE CAN HAPPEN, A
SEE: ON OUR MERRY WAY

•

MIRACLE IN MILAN
SEE: MIRACOLO A MILANO

•

MIRACLE IN SOHO
1957, 98 mins, UK Ⓥ b/w
Dir Julian Amyes ***Prod*** Emeric Pressburger ***Scr*** Emeric Pressburger ***Ph*** Christopher Challis ***Ed*** Arthur Stevens ***Mus*** Brian Easdale ***Art*** Carmen Dillon
Act John Gregson, Belinda Lee, Cyril Cusack, Rosalie Crutchley, Ian Bannen, Billie Whitelaw (Rank)

A rather slow moving sentimental yarn has been woven around the polyglot population in central London's Soho. It is a simple story that lacks punch and gives the impression that more could have been made of the colorful material.

A small side street of shops and cafés has been shut down for road repairs, and Mike, one of the working gang, proceeds to live up to his reputation as a wolf. He gets involved with an Italian family about to emigrate to Canada. The son wants to stay behind as he is in love with a barmaid. The elder daughter is reluctant to go as she has a chance to marry a prosperous café proprietor. The younger girl falls for Mike's charm, and stays behind, only to find he doesn't want her.

The repairing gang moves on, after their job is complete, but after the girl is left flat she prays in the nearby church, and Saint Anthony obliges with a miracle.

John Gregson never seems quite at home in rough clothes but makes a likeable personality of the roving Romeo, and Belinda Lee is simple and naive as the Anglicized Italian girl in love with him.

•

MIRACLE OF LIFE, THE
SEE: OUR DAILY BREAD

•

MIRACLE OF MORGAN'S CREEK, THE
1944, 101 mins, US Ⓥ ⦿ b/w
Dir Preston Sturges ***Prod*** [uncredited] ***Scr*** Preston Sturges ***Ph*** John F. Seitz ***Ed*** Stuart Gilmore ***Mus*** Leo Shuken, Charles Bradshaw
Act Eddie Bracken, Betty Hutton, Diana Lynn, William Demarest, Brian Donlevy, Akim Tamiroff (Paramount)

Morgan's Creek is the name of the town where the action takes place and the miracle, as director Preston Sturges terms it, is the birth to Eddie Bracken and Betty Hutton of a set of sextuplets.

Done in the satirical Sturges vein, and directed with that same touch, the story makes much of characterization and somewhat wacky comedy, plus some slapstick, with excellent photography figuring throughout. The Sturges manner of handling crowds and various miscellaneous characters who are almost nothing more than flashes in the picture, such as the small-town attorney and the justice of the peace, contribute enormously to the enjoyment derived.

However, some of the comedy situations lack punch, and the picture is slow to get rolling, but ultimately picks up smart pace and winds up quite strongly on the birth of the sextuplets with the retiring Bracken and Hutton as national heroes.

Bracken is a small-town bank clerk who yearns to get into uniform and is madly in love with Hutton. Getting out on an all-night party with soldiers, the latter wakes up to remember that she married a serviceman, but can't remember the name, what the spouse looked like, or anything except that they didn't give their right names.

Bracken does a nice job. Hutton and he make a desirable team. Among the supporting cast, largest assignment is that given William Demarest, small-town cop father of Hutton, who has his troubles with his daughters, the other being attractive Diana Lynn.

1944: NOMINATION: Best Original Screenplay

•

MIRACLE ON 34TH STREET
(UK: THE BIG HEART)
1947, 95 mins, US Ⓥ ⦿ b/w
Dir George Seaton ***Prod*** William Perlberg ***Scr*** George Seaton ***Ph*** Charles Clarke, Lloyd Ahern ***Ed*** Robert Simpson ***Mus*** Cyril J. Mockridge ***Art*** Richard Day, Richard Irvine
Act Maureen O'Hara, John Payne, Edmund Gwenn, Gene Lockhart, Natalie Wood, Thelma Ritter (20th Century-Fox)

So you don't believe in Santa Claus? If you want to stay a nonbeliever don't see *Miracle*.

Film is an actor's holiday, providing any number of choice roles that are played to the hilt. Edmund Gwenn's Santa Claus performance proves the best in his career, one that will be thoroughly enjoyed by all filmgoers. Straight romantic roles handed Maureen O'Hara and John Payne as costars also display pair to advantage.

Valentine Davies's story poses question of just how valid is the belief in Santa Claus. Gwenn, old man's home inmate, becomes Santy at Macy's Department Store, events pile up that make it necessary to actually prove he is the real McCoy and not a slightly touched old gent. Gwenn is a little amazed at all the excitement because he has no doubt that he's the real article.

Gene Lockhart's performance as judge is a gem, as is Porter Hall's portrayal of a neurotic personnel director for Macy's. Surprise moppet performance is turned in by little Natalie Wood as O'Hara's nonbelieving daughter who finally accepts Santy. It's a standout, natural portrayal.

1947: Best Supp. Actor (Edmund Gwenn), Original Story, Screenplay

NOMINATION: Best Picture

•

MIRACLE ON 34TH STREET

1994, 114 mins, US Ⓥ ⦿ col

Dir Les Mayfield ***Prod*** John Hughes ***Scr*** George Seaton, John Hughes ***Ph*** Julio Macat ***Ed*** Raja Gosnell ***Mus*** Bruce Broughton ***Art*** Doug Kraner

Act Richard Attenborough, Elizabeth Perkins, Dylan McDermott, Mara Wilson, Robert Prosky, J. T. Walsh (Hughes/20th Century-Fox)

There's no lack of Santa mentality in the remake of the Christmas chestnut *Miracle on 34th Street*. Writer/producer John Hughes has done minor and subtle tampering with the 1947 vintage holiday yarn, and that proves both an asset and a hindrance. While the time is now, Hughes and company have done little to contemporize the story's setting or attitude.

Through happenstance, one Kriss Kringle (Richard Attenborough) becomes the official Cole's Department Store Santa. Not only does he resemble the yuletide icon, he genuinely loves children and embodies the spirit of giving. And, oh yes, he just happens to be the real McCoy, so he says.

The trouble is that there are still folks who refuse to recognize the obvious. Dorey Walker (Elizabeth Perkins), the Cole's exec who hired him, is a prime example. Her steadfast belief that "truth is the most important thing" has also made her daughter, Susan (Mara Wilson), a five-year-old doubter. Mother and child become a significant test case for Kriss Kringle. When forces of evil at the discount store conspire to discredit him, his attorney (and Dorey devotee), Brian Bedford (Dylan McDermott), must prove him mentally sound.

Hughes and director Les Mayfield have a superb St. Nick in Attenborough. Not only is he the embodiment of decency, he's having a crackling good time bringing the character to Earth. The young Wilson is the other stellar standout, displaying a wisdom and precociousness that enliven material with a tendency toward the cute.

•

MIRACLE WOMAN, THE

1931, 90 mins, US b/w

Dir Frank Capra ***Prod*** Frank Capra ***Scr*** Jo Swerling, Dorothy Howell ***Ph*** Joseph Walker ***Ed*** Maurice Wright

Act Barbara Stanwyck, David Manners, Sam Hardy, Beryl Mercer, Russell Hopton, Charles Middleton (Columbia)

Film has two unusual aspects. One is its basic theme of an exposé on evangelism. The other is a punch sequence at the opening, perhaps the strongest scene the feature possesses.

Frank Capra's direction has practically wasted nothing as he traces the girl through her exhortatory racket to the thrill finish of a tabernacle blaze which, from the mob standpoint, has been exceedingly well handled. There isn't much doubt that Capra can do more with Barbara Stanwyck than any other director. Her performance here is splendid in unfolding plenty of fire, balanced by undertones of instinctive character softness and mood as she slowly falls in love with a blind boy who becomes one of her ardent followers [based on the play by John Mechan and Robert Riskin]. The punch start is a country church on a Sunday morning in which the ruling faction has decided to secure a new and younger minister.

Stanwyck is the deposed reverend's daughter who takes the pulpit to read her father's valedictory after 20 years of service. Halfway through the message she stops and sobbingly announces that her father died at this point. Follows her launching of a tirade, berating the church members for their action and shortcomings.

•

MIRACLE WORKER, THE

1962, 106 mins, US Ⓥ ⦿ b/w

Dir Arthur Penn ***Prod*** Fred Coe ***Scr*** William Gibson ***Ph*** Ernest Caparros ***Ed*** Aram Avakian ***Mus*** Laurence Rosenthal ***Art*** George Jenkins

Act Anne Bancroft, Patty Duke, Victor Jory, Inga Swenson, Andrew Prine (United Artists)

A celebrated television show, later a critical, artistic and popular hit on the stage, the Fred Coe production was directed by Arthur Penn, who staged the legit version, and stars Anne Bancroft and Patty Duke in the roles they introduced to Broadway.

Gibson's screenplay relates the story of the young Helen Keller and how, through the dedication, perseverance and courage of her teacher, Annie Sullivan, she establishes a means of communication with the world she cannot see or hear.

Where the picture really excels, outside of its inherent story values, is in the realm of photographic technique. It is here that director Penn and cameraman Ernest Caparros have teamed to create artful, indelible strokes of visual storytelling and mood-molding. The measured dissolves, focal shifts and lighting and filtering enrich the production considerably. Add to these attributes the haunting, often chilling, score by Laurence Rosenthal.

1962: Best Actress (Anne Bancroft), Supp. Actress (Patty Duke)

NOMINATIONS: Best Director, Adapted Screenplay, B&W Costume Design

•

MIRACOLO A MILANO (MIRACLE IN MILAN)

1951, 100 mins, Italy 559 Ⓥ ⦿ b/w

Dir Vittorio De Sica ***Scr*** Cesare Zavattini ***Ph*** Aldo Graziati ***Ed*** Eraldo Da Roma ***Mus*** Alessandro Cicognini ***Art*** Guido Fiorini

Act Emma Gramatica, Francesco Golisano, Paolo Stoppa, Brunella Bovo, Anna Carena, Guglielmo Barnabo (De Sica/ENIC)

Miracle in Milan, an involved and rambling screenplay, originally written by Cesare Zavattini in 1940 and later published as a novel entitled *Toto the Good*, contrasts sharply with the simplicity and warm humanity of [the same writer-director team's] *Bicycle Thief* and gives director Vittorio De Sica less opportunities to guide his thespers to those extremely human, heart-warming performances that are his specialty. Whereas *Thief* was aimed at the audience heart, *Miracle* is aimed at the brain.

An intellectual fairy tale played against a background of the sharp realities of present-day life, film tells the story of Toto (Francesco Golisano), an orphan boy with a good, innocent approach to life, who joins a colony of beggars in a shack village on the outskirts of Milan. When the rich owner of the land discovers oil under the village and tries to evict the beggars, Toto helps fight them off with the aid of a miraculous dove given him for his good qualities by a friendly fairy. The opening sequences, the foster-mother's funeral, Toto's arrival at the beggar village, the tramps' fight for heat on a cold wintry day, the innocent love of Toto and his girl, are among many superb moments, which confirm De Sica's talent. The sharp satire on the oil-greedy industrialist is handled in a broader, perhaps exaggerated manner, and pic is liberally sprinkled with intelligent humor, much of it ironic. Performances by pros and tyros alike are flawless. Technically difficult special effects by Ned Mann are satisfying if not always convincing.

•

MIRAGE

1965, 108 mins, US Ⓥ ⦿ b/w

Dir Edward Dmytryk ***Prod*** Harry Keller ***Scr*** Peter Stone ***Ph*** Joseph MacDonald ***Ed*** Ted J. Kent ***Mus*** Quincy Jones

Act Gregory Peck, Diane Baker, Walter Matthau, Kevin McCarthy, Jack Weston, Leif Erickson (Universal)

Mirage starts as a mystery, unfolds as a mystery, ends as a mystery. There are moments of stiff action and suspense but plot is as confusing as it is overly contrived.

Gregory Peck stars as an amnesiac trying to learn why he is the target for assassins. Story is about a man in NY who suddenly discovers he cannot remember any part of his past life. Returning to his apartment from a big office building that was suddenly without lights and where a prominent man plunged to his death from the 27th floor, he is confronted by a stranger holding a gun who informs him he's taking Peck to a man he has never heard of. Knocking the gunman out, he goes to the police to demand protection, only to discover he's a thoroughly confused man.

Edward Dmytryk in his taut direction keeps a tight rein on pace and manages vigorous movement in individual sequences, but cannot overcome script deficiencies. Peck's character is not clearly drawn but actor makes the most of what's offered him as a brooding man trying to save his life. Diane Baker flits in and out of plot as a mysterious figure whose true identity is never established.

•

MIRANDA

1948, 80 mins, UK b/w

Dir Ken Annakin ***Prod*** Betty E. Box ***Scr*** Peter Blackmore, Denis Waldock ***Ph*** Ray Elton ***Ed*** Gordon Hales ***Mus*** Temple Abady ***Art*** George Patterson

Act Glynis Johns, Googie Withers, Griffith Jones, John McCallum, Margaret Rutherford, David Tomlinson (Gainsborough)

Planning a holiday alone in Cornwall, Paul Marten, a fashionable doctor, is dragged out of his fishing boat to the sea bottom by Miranda, a lovely mermaid. Price for return to his home and wife is that he takes Miranda to London.

Everything [in this adaptation of Peter Blackmore's stage play] is rightly played for laughs and Glynis Johns makes the mermaid an attractive and almost credible creature. Griffith Jones is good as her serious sponsor. Googie Withers turns in a nice performance as his bewildered wife, and David Tomlinson and John McCallum do well as the love-struck swains.

•

MIRROR CRACK'D, THE

1981, 105 mins, UK Ⓥ ⦿ col

Dir Guy Hamilton ***Prod*** John Brabourne, Richard Goodwin ***Scr*** Jonathan Hales, Barry Sandler ***Ph*** Christopher Challis ***Ed*** Richard Mardon ***Mus*** John Cameron ***Art*** Michael Stringer

Act Angela Lansbury, Elizabeth Taylor, Kim Novak, Rock Hudson, Geraldine Chaplin, Tony Curtis (EMI)

EMI's third Agatha Christie mystery [from her novel *The Mirror Crack'd from Side to Side*] is a nostalgic throwback to the genteel British murder mystery pix of the 1950s.

Though Angela Lansbury is top-billed in the role of Christie's famed sleuth Jane Marple, the central part really is Elizabeth Taylor's. Taylor comes away with her most genuinely affecting dramatic performance in years as a film star attempting a comeback following an extended nervous breakdown.

The Taylor character and those close to her have been haunted by the memory of an apparently accidental catastrophe that proves to have been caused by one of the minor characters.

Taylor has an uproarious good time as she trades bitchy insults with Kim Novak. Adroit supporting performances are given by Tony Curtis, Rock Hudson as Taylor's husband and director, and Geraldine Chaplin.

•

MIRROR HAS TWO FACES, THE

1996, 126 mins, US Ⓥ ⦿ col

Dir Barbra Streisand ***Prod*** Barbra Streisand, Arnon Milchan ***Scr*** Richard LaGravenese ***Ph*** Dante Spinotti ***Ed*** Jeff Werner ***Mus*** Marvin Hamlisch ***Art*** Tom John

Act Barbra Streisand, Jeff Bridges, Pierce Brosnan, George Segal, Mimi Rogers, Lauren Bacall (Milchan-Barwood/Tri-Star)

The Mirror Has Two Faces is a vanity production of the first order. A staggeringly obsessive expression of the importance of appearances, good looks and being adored, Barbra Streisand's third directorial outing is also, incidentally, a very old-fashioned wish-fulfillment romantic comedy that has been directed and performed in the broadest possible manner.

Lushly produced fantasy is based on a 1958 French sudser [*Le miroir a deux faces*, directed by Andre Cayatte] which starred Michele Morgan as a homely woman who emerges as a beauty courtesy of plastic surgery, only to cause complications that result in her selfish husband killing the doctor who performed the operation.

Streisand and scripter have jettisoned both the knife and the murder and, for starters, have transformed the snivelling, boorish husband into hunky university prof Gregory (Jeff Bridges), who feels so desperate for a meaningful relationship not based on sex that he places a personals ad. He ends up on a "date" with fellow prof Rose Morgan (Streisand), who lives with her hovering mother (Lauren Bacall) and as much as admits she's officially an old maid when her high-glam sister (Mimi Rogers) marries for the third time, to James Bond . . . er, Alex (Pierce Brosnan), whom Rose secretly covets.

After three months (and an hour of screen time) Gregory proposes they get married, with no sex in the equation to mess things up. This isn't quite what Rose always dreamed about, but she agrees. After Gregory leaves on a European book tour, Rose has a complete makeover. When he returns, she tells him their old deal is off.

Bacall poses, rolls her eyes and snaps out the one-liners with consummate skill. But ultimately, of course, it is Streisand who is the subject of the director's uninterrupted gaze.

1996: NOMINATIONS: Best Supp. Actress (Lauren Bacall), Original Song ("I Finally Found Someone")

●

MISERABLES, LES

1934, 265 mins, France b/w

Dir Raymond Bernard ***Prod*** Raymond Borderie ***Scr*** Andre Lang, Raymond Bernard ***Ph*** J. Kruger ***Ed*** [uncredited] ***Mus*** Arthur Honegger ***Art*** Jean Perrier

Act Harry Bauer, Charles Vanel, Charles Dullin, Jean Servais, Odette Florelle, Josselyne Gael (Pathe/Natan)

Any ordinary film, when loaded with piled-on handicaps as in *Les Miserables*, would stagger and drop with a resounding flop. Holding it all together is the thespic strength of the great Harry Bauer, who supports this epic with a power strangely comparable to that of the Jean Valjean he plays. Bauer is powerful, disciplined, and moving in the lead role, while other lead and supporting players, Charles Dullin and Charles Vanel in particular, are far better than average. Raymond Bernard's sharp direction is constantly in evidence.

Story is still essentially a moral essay, with Valjean the reformed criminal who becomes the embodiment of good under the constant flagellation of a scrupulous conscience. Film opens with his release from prison and metamorphosis through the kindness of a Bishop. He rises to mayoralty of a town and subsequent wealth, only to be forced by his conscience to declare his criminal identity, thereby saving another from prison. He escapes the police to carry out a mission to care for a dying woman's daughter, Cosette (Josselyne Gael).

There is a gap of eight years, where the second portion of the film takes up in 1832, following the Bourbon reaccession of the French throne. Cosette falls in love with a young revolutionary who mans the barricades against royalist troops. Although he disapproves, Valjean finally effects their rescue and marriage, then dies.

Vanel, as Javert, the police inspector who constantly haunts Valjean, is excellent; Dullin plays a scurrilous innkeeper. Scenes of the abortive revolutionary attempts are outstanding, while camera work throughout is on a high plane. [Original version was in three parts—*Une tempete sous un crane* (101 mins.), *Les Thenardiers* (81 mins.) and *Liberte, liberte cherie* (83 mins.)—released a week apart in Paris in February 1934. In a brief notice, *Variety*'s reviewer described it as "heavy and slow, following book closely. Relatively little dialogue and lots of ponderous gesture, in best French manner. Remarkably good technically, and acting marvelous." Kept out of the American market because of 20th Century's version then in production, the film was first shown in the U.S. in October 1936 in a subtitled 162-min. version (with an intermission after Valjean's second toppling by Javert)—"an A-1 example of intelligent shearing" noted *Variety*'s reviewer. Above review is of a (poorly) subtitled 209-min. version released in the U.S. in December 1946, divided into two parts (*Jean Valjean* and *Cosette*) with an intermission.]

●

MISERABLES, LES

1935, 109 mins, US Ⓥ ⦿ b/w

Dir Richard Boleslawski ***Prod*** Darryl F. Zanuck ***Scr*** W. P. Lipscomb ***Ph*** Gregg Toland ***Ed*** Barbara McLean ***Mus*** Alfred Newman (dir.) ***Art*** Richard Day

Act Fredric March, Charles Laughton, Cedric Hardwicke, Rochelle Hudson, John Beal, Frances Drake (20th Century)

Les Miserables will satisfy the most exacting Victor Hugo followers, and at the same time please those looking only for entertainment, regardless of literary backgrounds. The task of boiling down the lengthy Hugo novel is accomplished by W. P. Lipscomb with no loss of flavor. The essence of the original is faithfully retained.

Fredric March makes the screen Jean Valjean a living version of the panegyrical character. He is the same persecuted, pursued, pitiable, but always admirale man that all readers of the book must visualize. Side by side with March, throughout the picture, is Charles Laughton, as Javert, the cop. His performance is much more on the quiet side, but equally powerful and always believable.

Valjean's service in the galley, to which he is sentenced for stealing a loaf of bread; Javert's pursuit of Valjean and his foster-daughter; the revolt of the French students; the race of Valjean, with the injured Marius on his shoulders, through the stinking sewers of Paris, all breathtaking action passages, are brilliantly managed.

1935: NOMINATIONS: Best Picture, Cinematography, Editing, Assistant Director (Eric Stacey)

●

MISERABLES, LES

1952, 105 mins, US b/w

Dir Lewis Milestone ***Prod*** Fred Kohlmar ***Scr*** Richard Murphy ***Ph*** Joseph La Shelle ***Ed*** Hugh Fowler ***Mus*** Alex North ***Art*** Lyle Wheeler, J. Russell Spencer

Act Michael Rennie, Debra Paget, Robert Newton, Edmund Gwenn, Sylvia Sidney, Cameron Mitchell (20th Century-Fox)

Victor Hugo's somber classic was previously lensed by the Fox Film Co. in 1919, again by Universal in 1927, United Artists had a release out in 1935 and there was a French production in 1936.

In the first episode, when Valjean is sentenced to 10 years as a galley slave for stealing a loaf of bread, director Lewis Milestone permits the players and scenes to cry out flamboyantly against such injustice and the stark miseries of a prison ship existence.

The film actually gets going when Valjean, released under parole, becomes a successful pottery owner after getting his first lesson in humanity from a kindly bishop, beautifully played by Edmond Gwenn. It is during this time that he aids Sylvia Sidney, a poor, dying woman, and takes in her daughter (Debra Paget).

Rennie does exceptionally well with his role, particularly after the convict ship episode.

●

MISERABLES, LES

1958, 217 mins, France ▭ col

Dir Jean-Paul Le Chanois ***Scr*** Rene Barjavel, Jean-Paul Le Chanois ***Ph*** Jacques Natteau ***Ed*** Emma Le Chanois

Act Jean Gabin, Bernard Blier, Bourvil, Daniele Delorme, Gianni Esposito, Serge Reggiani (Pathe/PAC)

The French, on the surface, have their first blockbuster in this pic, taken from the Victor Hugo novel, with plenty of stars and production values. But it follows the monumental book too closely. All the romantic coincidence is used, with the result that the pic lags as the various threads of two generations are tied up.

Main strength is Jean Gabin's thesping of Jean Valjean, the man who served 20 years for stealing a crust of bread and then devoted himself to a lifetime of good due to a priest's kindness. The implacable policeman Javert is well played by Bernard Blier.

Made mainly in East Germany [at DEFA Studio], the film gives a good reconstruction of the 19th-century Paris barricades, with the action and derring-do well rendered. But in all the pic is an overdrawn, plodding odyssey, with pruning in order.

Bourvil is standout as the avaricious enemy of Valjean, while the production is peppered with known names etching good smaller roles. Direction is academic, if competent, while the color is uneven until settling down on interiors.

●

MISERABLES, LES

1982, 187 mins, France Ⓥ ▭ col

Dir Robert Hossein ***Prod*** Dominique Harispuru (exec.) ***Scr*** Robert Hossein, Alain Decaux ***Ph*** Edmond Richard ***Ed*** Martine Baraque-Curie ***Mus*** Michel Magne, Andre Hossein ***Art*** Francois de Lamothe

Act Lino Ventura, Michel Bouquet, Evelyne Bouix, Christiane Jean, Jean Carmet, Francoise Seigner (GEF/SFPC/TF1/DD)

Robert Hossein's *Les Miserables* is a handsomely produced, but dramatically denatured adaptation of the famous Victor Hugo novel. In setting up this $10 million cinema/TV operation—three hours for theaters, six 52-minute episodes for TV in 1985—and in signing Hossein to direct a top-name cast headed by Lino Ventura, the producers appear to have made all the right investments. But what Hossein has produced is low on conventional entertainment value, inhibited by a solemn sense of high purpose. His massive stage extravaganzas (including a musical version of *Les Miserables*) have earned him a tremendous popular following, but he's allowed his deepening religious preoccupations to get the upper hand, and is only interested in translating the spiritual grandeur of the novel.

Given the often cursory treatment of certain scenes and characters in this cinema cut, one at times has the frustrating impression of watching a celluloid equivalent of a *Reader's Digest* condensation. Hossein and his coadaptor, historian Alain Decaux, have maintained the shell of the plot and its many famous setpieces, but scene after scene unfolds as if they were embarrassed by all the pity and fear, suspense and thrills, that Hugo thought a compatible vehicle for the sublime.

The anti-melodramatic style is better-suited to Ventura's dignified, if unmoving, Jean Valjean (though he glosses several crucial dramatic beats), and to Michel Bouquet's ramrod-rigid Javert, who speaks softly and carries a big stick. Two veterans glow briefly: Louis Seigner, as Monseigneur Myriel, and Fernand Ledoux, as Marius's crabby royalist guardian. Evelyne Bouix is adequate as the wretched Fantine, and Candice Patou (Mrs. Hossein) is touching as Eponine.

Many exteriors were shot in the old quarters of Sarlat and Bordeaux, and the barricades and sewer scenes were executed in the studios of SFPC, studio arm for French TV.

●

MISERABLES, LES

1995, 177 mins, France Ⓥ ⦿ ▭ col

Dir Claude Lelouch ***Prod*** Claude Lelouch ***Scr*** Claude Lelouch ***Ph*** Claude Lelouch, Philippe Pavans de Ceccatty ***Ed*** Helene de Luze ***Mus*** Francis Lai, Didier Barbelivien, Philippe Servain, Erik Berchot/Michel Legrand ***Art*** Jacques Bufnoir

Act Jean-Paul Belmondo, Michel Boujenah, Alessandra Martines, Annie Girardot, Philippe Leotard, Clementine Celarie (Les Films 13/TF1)

Hugely ambitious in both theme and scope and brimming with sheer delight in the medium, Claude Lelouch's three-hour *Les Miserables* is the summation of ideas and obsessions the helmer has pursued with increasing complexity during the past 15 years. Extrapolating characters and themes from Victor Hugo's 1862 novel and recycling them through the sieve of key events in the first half of the current century, this is the mightiest of Lelouch's humanist hymns.

Big in every way—some 100 roles, more than 5,000 extras, and 67 days of shooting—the $20 million film makes no concessions to changing cinematic styles or social mores, and parallels his 1982 *Bolero* in many ways.

There is no need to know the Hugo original beyond its broadest outlines: An average guy, imprisoned for a peccadillo, rebuilds his life but is dogged by an obsessive nemesis. Lelouch's saga kicks off with a New Year's ball welcoming in the 20th century, flashes forward to 1931 and 1942, and moves on through the D-Day invasion, the euphoria of the Allied victory (cf. *Bolero*), to the eventual reunion of the main characters in a joyous, end-piece waltz.

At heart the pic recapitulates an obsessive theme in the helmer's work: the conjunction of similar lives and stories, of parallel social/moral universes, separated only by time. Or, as the poet said, there's only a handful of yarns and this is all of them.

In the triple role of Valjean and Fortin *pere et fils*, Jean-Paul Belmondo gives one of the finest perfs of his career, his rubbery, weather-beaten physiognomy moving from moments of interior drama to cheerful optimism with surprising ease. Visually, the pic bristles with Lelouchian set pieces—a boxing match in a snow-covered courtyard, a D-Day landing that's a triumph of cutting and mobile lensing, and numerous dances in which the camera is a whirling participant in the action.

Pic is also a buff's delight, with homages to French classics from Jean Renoir's *La grande illusion* to Claude Autant-Lara's World War II blacketeer movie *La traversee de Paris*.

●

MISERY

1990, 107 mins, US Ⓥ ⦿ col

Dir Rob Reiner ***Prod*** Andrew Scheinman, Rob Reiner ***Scr*** William Goldman ***Ph*** Barry Sonnenfeld ***Ed*** Robert Leighton ***Mus*** Marc Shaiman ***Art*** Norman Garwood

Act James Caan, Kathy Bates, Frances Sternhagen, Richard Farnsworth, Lauren Bacall, Graham Jarvis (Castle Rock/Nelson)

Misery is a very obvious and very commercial gothic thriller, a functional adaptation of the Stephen King bestseller.

Basically a two-hander, *Misery* is the name of the 19th-century heroine of a series of gothic romances penned by James Caan. During the opening credits his car crashes on slippery Colorado roads, and Kathy Bates digs him out of the snow and wreckage.

A plump former nurse, she fixes up his severely injured legs and virtually holds him prisoner, incommunicado, for the rest of the film. As in the classic Robert Aldrich gothics like *What Ever Happened to Baby Jane?*, the fun comes from the ebb and flow nastiness of the two characters in a love/hate (often hate/hate) relationship.

Key plot gimmick is that Caan's killed off the profitable but hack-work Misery character, an act that turns adoring fan Bates against him and sets in motion her obsession that he resurrect the fictional character. Casting of Caan is effective, as his snide remarks and grumpy attitude are backed up by a physical dimension that makes believable his inevitable fighting back. Bates has a field day with her role, creating a quirky, memorable object of hate.

Tech credits on this $21 million pic are very good, including Reno-area location shots.

1990: Best Actress (Kathy Bates)

•

MISFITS, THE

1961, 124 mins, US Ⓥ ⊙ b/w

Dir John Huston ***Prod*** Frank E. Taylor ***Scr*** Arthur Miller ***Ph*** Russell Metty ***Ed*** George Tomasini ***Mus*** Alex North ***Art*** Stephen Grimes, William Newberry

Act Clark Gable, Marilyn Monroe, Montgomery Clift, Thelma Ritter, Eli Wallach (Seven Arts)

At face value, *The Misfits* is a robust, high-voltage adventure drama, vibrating with explosively emotional histrionics, conceived and executed with a refreshing disdain for superficial technical and photographic slickness in favor of an uncommonly honest and direct cinematic approach. Within this framework, however, lurks a complex mass of introspective conflicts, symbolic parallels and motivational contradictions, the nuances of which may seriously confound general audiences.

Clark Gable essays the role of a self-sufficient Nevada cowboy, a kind of last of the great rugged individualists, a noble misfit. Into his life ambles a woman (Marilyn Monroe) possessed of an almost uncanny degree of humanitarian compassion. Their relationship matures smoothly enough until Gable goes "mustanging," a ritual in which wild, "misfit" mustangs are rudely roped into captivity. Revolted by what she regards as cruel and mercenary, Monroe, with the aid of yet another misfit, itinerant, disillusioned rodeo performer Montgomery Clift, strives to free the captive horses.

The film is somewhat uneven in pace and not entirely sound in dramatic structure. Character development is choppy in several instances. The one essayed by Thelma Ritter is essentially superfluous and, in fact, abruptly abandoned in the course of the story. Eli Wallach's character undergoes a severely sudden and faintly inconsistent transition. Even Monroe's never comes fully into focus.

•

MISHIMA
A LIFE IN FOUR CHAPTERS

1985, 120 mins, US Ⓥ col

Dir Paul Schrader ***Prod*** Mata Yamamoto, Tom Luddy ***Scr*** Paul Schrader, Leonard Schrader, Chieko Schrader ***Ph*** John Bailey ***Ed*** Michael Chandler, Tomoyo Oshima ***Mus*** Philip Glass ***Art*** Eiko Ishioka

Act Ken Ogata, Kenji Sawada, Yasosuke Bando, Toshiyuki Nagashima (Zoetrope/Filmlink)

Paul Schrader's film *Mishima* is a boldly conceived, intelligent and consistently absorbing study of the Japanese writer and political iconoclast's life, work and death.

The most famous of contemporary Japanese novelists to Westerners, Yukio Mishima was also a film actor and director and leader of a militant right-wing cult bent upon restoring the glory of the emperor. He became forever notorious in 1970 when, accompanied by a few followers, he entered a military garrison in Tokyo, "captured" a general, delivered an impassioned speech to an assembly and then committed *seppuku* (ritual suicide).

Instead of pretending to deliver a fully factual, detailed biopic, director Paul Schrader, his co-screenwriter and brother Leonard and other collaborators have opted to combine relatively realistic treatment of some aspects of Mishima's life, particularly his final day, with highly stylized renditions of assorted semi-autobiographical literary works (*Temple of the Golden Pavilion, Kyoko's House* and *Runaway Horses*) in an effort to convey key points about the man's personality and credos.

Pacing sometimes lags, particularly in the fictional interludes, and uninitiated audiences may be confused at times. Production itself, however, is stunning, and performances, led by that of Ken Ogata as the adult Mishima, are authoritative and convincing. [Pic is in Japanese with English subtitles, and narration read by Roy Scheider.]

•

MISS FIRECRACKER

1989, 102 mins, US Ⓥ ⊙ col

Dir Thomas Schlamme ***Prod*** Fred Berner ***Scr*** Beth Henley ***Ph*** Arthur Albert ***Ed*** Peter C. Frank ***Mus*** David Mansfield ***Art*** Kristi Zea

Act Holly Hunter, Mary Steenburgen, Tim Robbins, Alfre Woodard, Scott Glenn, Trey Wilson (Corsair)

Holly Hunter reprises her stage role [in Beth Henley's play *The Miss Firecracker Contest*] as Carnelle, a former goodtime girl whose dream is to win the local Miss Firecracker contest in her hometown of Yazoo City, MS. Her cousin (Mary Steenburgen) won the crown over a decade earlier, and against all odds Carnelle makes it to the finals as an alternate.

Miss Firecracker is peopled with oddball characters, notably Tim Robbins as Steenburgen's free spirit brother and Alfre Woodard as the black seamstress assigned to fabricate Carnelle's contest costume.

Putting the show over with a bang is Hunter, the epitome of energy in a tailor-made feisty role. She very accurately judges the line between high and low camp in her climactic tapdance for the talent contest, entertaining but just klutzy enough to be authentic.

Steenburgen and Woodard are consistent scene-stealers here, former dead-on as a Southern belle putting on airs and latter revivifying ethnic stereotypes such as bugged-out eyes into a hilarious, original character.

•

MISSING

1982, 122 mins, US Ⓥ ⊙ col

Dir Constantin Costa-Gavras ***Prod*** Edward Lewis, Mildred Lewis ***Scr*** Constantine Costa-Gavras, Donald Stewart ***Ph*** Ricardo Aronovich ***Ed*** Francoise Bonnot ***Mus*** Vangelis ***Art*** Peter Jamison

Act Jack Lemmon, Sissy Spacek, Melanie Mayron, John Shea, Charles Cioffi, David Clennon (Universal)

Although the country in question is never named, the subject here is unequivocally that of U.S. involvement in the 1973 military coup in Allende's Chile.

Based on the true story of a young American, Charles Horman, who disappeared during the Chile coup, drama [from a book by Thomas Hauser] presents John Shea and Sissy Spacek as a vaguely counterculturish couple living in Santiago.

When Shea inexplicably disappears and Spacek can get nowhere in locating him, his father (Jack Lemmon) flies down to get heavy with U.S. government officials.

Real jolt of the picture, which comes across on an effective personal level due to its impact on Lemmon, derives from the premise that, when pressed, the U.S. government places the interests of business above those of individual citizens.

Lemmon is superior as a man facing up to issues he never wanted to confront personally. Edgy and belligerent most of the time, Spacek is more constrained but she's fully believable.

1982: Best Adapted Screenplay

NOMINATIONS: Best Picture, Actor (Jack Lemmon), Actress (Sissy Spacek)

•

MISSING IN ACTION

1984, 101 mins, US Ⓥ ⊙ col

Dir Joseph Zito ***Prod*** Menahem Golan, Yoram Globus ***Scr*** James Bruner ***Ph*** Joao Fernandes ***Ed*** Joel Goodman ***Mus*** Jay Chattaway ***Art*** Ladi Wilheim

Act Chuck Norris, M. Emmet Walsh, Lenore Kasdorf, James Hong, David Tress, Ernie Ortega (Cannon)

With the Philippines filling in for Vietnam jungles, with Chuck Norris kicking and firing away, with a likable sidekick in the black marketeering figure of M. Emmet Walsh, and with a touch of nudity in sordid Bangkok bars, writer James Bruner and director Joseph Zito have marshalled a formula pic with a particularly jingoistic slant: even though the war is long over, the Commies in Vietnam still deserve the smack of a bullet.

Norris plays a former North Vietnamese prisoner, an American colonel missing in action for seven years, who escapes to the U.S. and then returns to Vietnam determined to find MIAs and convince the world that Yanks are still imprisoned in Vietnam.

•

MISSION, THE

1986, 125 mins, UK Ⓥ ⊙ ▭ col

Dir Roland Joffe ***Prod*** Fernando Ghia, David Puttnam ***Scr*** Robert Bolt ***Ph*** Chris Menges ***Ed*** Jim Clark ***Mus*** Ennio Morricone ***Art*** Stuart Craig

Act Robert De Niro, Jeremy Irons, Ray McAnally, Liam Neeson, Aidan Quinn, Ronald Pickup (Goldcrest/Kingsmere/Enigma)

Spectacular scenery and an extraordinary high degree of production values can't conceal serious flaws in *The Mission*, Goldcrest's $23 million pic.

The script is based on a little-known but nonetheless intriguing historical incident in mid-18th century South America, pitting avaricious colonialists against the Jesuit order of priests. The fundamental problem is that the script is cardboard thin, pinning labels on its characters and arbitrarily shoving them into stances to make plot points.

The two principal actors, Robert De Niro and Jeremy Irons, work hard to animate their parts. But there is little to do. *The Mission* is probably the first film in which De Niro gives a bland, uninteresting performance.

The pic is set in 1750. Portugal and Spain are haggling over territorial boundaries which today cover those of Brazil, Paraguay and Argentina. Sitting in a refuge literally above the squabbling is a Jesuit mission established by Father Gabriel (Irons) as a safe place for native Indians. Spain would like Portugal to take over mission lands so it can continue its illicit slave trading unimpeded.

De Niro is cast as a slave trader, who invades what is to become mission territory to ensnare Indians for Spanish traders. He joins the Jesuits after he murders his brother (Aidan Quinn) for stealing his fiancée. His part following the conversion becomes strictly secondary to that of Irons.

Juicier performances come from the supporting players. Ray McAnally has great fun as the Cardinal who pulls the rug from under the missionaries to preserve significant Jesuit presence in Europe.

Director Roland Joffe has come up with some stunning scenes, using the impressive Cataratas del Iguazu to supreme advantage. On the downside, he botches the climactic battle scene when colonialists take over the mission. Pic was lensed over a 16-week period largely in Colombia and (for three weeks) at the Iguazu falls.

[Version reviewed was a 128-min. one—shown at the 1986 Cannes festival while pic was still in postproduction—featuring a final shot of McAnally staring playfully, enigmatically at the audience after the final extended credit crawl.]

1986: Best Cinematography

NOMINATIONS: Best Picture, Director, Costume Design, Art Direction, Editing, Original Score

•

MISSIONARY, THE

1983, 90 mins, UK Ⓥ ▭ col

Dir Richard Loncraine ***Prod*** Neville C. Thompson, Michael Palin ***Scr*** Michael Palin ***Ph*** Peter Hannan ***Ed*** Paul Green ***Mus*** Mike Moran ***Art*** Norman Garwood

Act Michael Palin, Maggie Smith, Trevor Howard, Denholm Elliott, Michael Hordern, Graham Crowden (HandMade)

Turn-of-the-century English gentry targeted in *The Missionary* remains good for laughs, especially in the hands of the talented Michael Palin. But Palin's script meanders wastefully across three separate story possibilities, never making full use of any of them.

As the Anglican title character called home to England, Palin has a brief encounter on the boat with Her Ladyship Maggie Smith who exhibits a keen interest in pagan fertility symbols. But the reverend's mind is on marriage to his childhood sweetheart (Phoebe Nicholls), whose most romantic thoughts center on how well she has managed to file and crossfile his letters for 10 years.

Once in London, Palin is assigned by Bishop Denholm Elliott to start a slum mission for "fallen women." And here comes Smith with the seed money Palin needs, provided he's friendly in return since her married life with stuffy Trevor Howard is a bit empty.

•

MISSION: IMPOSSIBLE

1996, 110 mins, US Ⓥ ⊙ ▭ col

Dir Brian De Palma ***Prod*** Tom Cruise, Paula Wagner ***Scr*** David Koepp, Robert Towne ***Ph*** Stephen H. Burum ***Ed*** Paul Hirsch ***Mus*** Danny Elfman ***Art*** Norman Reynolds

Act Tom Cruise, Jon Voight, Emmanuelle Beart, Henry Czerny, Jean Reno, Ving Rhames (Paramount)

All *Mission: Impossible* had to do was not self-destruct. Mission accomplished. Does it ignite? Not really, but Tom Cruise's first adventure as a producer has just enough high-tech firepower, old-fashioned star power and a director who knows how to harness it all. The new *Mission: Impossible* latches onto things it should have left to the '60s: a lack of passion, humor or sense of fun. No James Bond wit here—or Bruce Willis smirk, for that matter. *Mission: Impossible* just might be the most dour sexless piece of escapism in memory.

Cruise stars as Ethan Hunt, a hotshot member of an elite, unnamed U.S. intelligence group. A former Russian spy is planning the theft of a computer disk containing the true identities of the world's top undercover agents, and the team's mission, should they choose to accept it, is to interrupt the crime. It all takes place at some black-tie embassy affair in Kiev.

Suffice it to say that everything goes wrong, with only Cruise's Hunt and Emmanuelle Beart's Claire surviving.

The mission (like the first 15 minutes of the movie) is a setup, and with Hunt alive his own agency decides that he must be a mole. Cruise's character spends the bulk of the film running from his former cohorts, led by agency boss Kittridge (Henry Czerny). More often than not, the various twists and turns are less ingenious than simply confusing.

That doesn't matter much, though, when the film's set pieces kick into gear. Best scene involves a break-in by Hunt and his new gang at the agency's headquarters. The film's climax atop the speeding Chunnel train packs an excitement lacking through much of the rest of the film.

•

MISSION: IMPOSSIBLE 2

2000, 123 mins, US Ⓥ ⊙ ▭ col

Dir John Woo ***Prod*** Tom Cruise, Paula Wagner ***Scr*** Robert Towne ***Ph*** Jeffrey L. Kimball ***Ed*** Christian Wagner, Steven Kemper ***Mus*** Hans Zimmer ***Art*** Tom Sanders

Act Tom Cruise, Dougray Scott, Thandie Newton, Ving Rhames, Richard Roxburgh, John Polson, Brendan Gleeson, Rade Sherbedgia, Anthony Hopkins (Paramount)

Even more empty a luxury vehicle than its predecessor, *M:I 2* pushes the envelope in terms of just how much flashy packaging an audience will buy when there's absolutely nada inside.

To call this chapter *Mission: Implausible* would be a heinous understatement. The big action set pieces (invariably in slo-mo, amid picturesque showers of sparks, glass, flames and dust) are so outrageously overcooked they induced preview-aud laughter, as did, in a different vein, the whole heroine-as-doe-eyed-sacrificial-lamb development.

Everything seems solemnly cardboard, without distinguishing human detail: Scott's handsome baddie is just a walking snarl in nice clothes; the oft-sensational Newton (*Beloved, Besieged*) is reduced to sultry pouts; Rhames struggles to interface intensely with computer screens and audio remotes; the plague-germ-in-the-hands-of-terrorists conceit sports no fresh wrinkles to alleviate its rote familiarity. Plot "twists" consist of little more than characters peeling off latex masks over and over: Surprise! It's really (blank). And you thought (blank) was dead!

As disappointing as the script's lack of cleverness and the director's bombast-overkill is this sequel's continued inability to give Cruise a real character. Ethan Hunt is just a by-numbers invincible superspy, forever eluding point-blank bullet hails, walking unscathed from kabooms that hurl extras into space, or deploying the perfect gadget at just the right unforeseeable moment. Does he have a past? Any opinions? Idiosyncrasies? Of course, he *does* have Tom Cruise's smashing good looks and pearly self-confidence. But even his stellar charisma doesn't render his sexual chemistry with Newton more credible than his dangling off a cliff.

•

MISSION TO MARS

2000, 112 mins, US Ⓥ ⊙ ▭ col

Dir Brian De Palma ***Prod*** Tom Jacobson ***Scr*** Jim Thomas, John Thomas, Graham Yost ***Ph*** Stephen H. Burum ***Ed*** Paul Hirsch ***Mus*** Ennio Morricone ***Art*** Ed Verreaux

Act Gary Sinise, Tim Robbins, Don Cheadle, Connie Nielsen, Jerry O'Connell, Kim Delaney, Armin Mueller-Stahl (Jacobson/Touchstone)

Dull and eventually ludicrous while trying to be moving and profound, Brian De Palma's first venture into the airless void aspires to join the small but distinguished club of spiritually inspiring sci-fiers that includes *The Day the Earth Stood Still, 2001: A Space Odyssey* and *Close Encounters of the Third Kind,* films in which human contact with otherworldly intelligence is benign and hopeful rather than hostile and horrific. But the vacuum created by the elimination of normal genre elements, including thrills and suspense, hasn't been filled with adequate substitutes, leaving the film floating through dead space; most accurate ad line for this one would be a riff on a previous sci-fi come-on: "In outer space, no one can hear you scream . . . of boredom."

There was probably a hopelessly irreconcilable conflict of sensibilities from the beginning, as the script by Jim and John Thomas (*Predator*) and Graham Yost (*Speed*) has an emotional sincerity and philosophical optimism utterly at odds with De Palma's flamboyant determinism. This is a film that needed real heart to have a prayer of making viewers overlook its fundamental shortcomings and just go along for the ride. Unfortunately, De Palma is one of the most baroque and dispassionate of American directors, and he cheats this story not only through his coldness but by purposely jettisoning sequences that could at least have provided visual thrills, such as takeoffs and landings, which under the tame circumstances here would have been high points.

Thesping by the talented leads is inoffensive but generally bland, although on more than one occasion the actors seem to have only the barest clue as to what special effects they're acting with or against. Spacecraft interiors have a strong *2001* look, the Martian surface has been aptly rendered by red-filtered second-unit shots of the Jordanian desert around Petra, and Ennio Morricone's score goes straight for the story's intended emotional impact via alternately wistful and majestic motifs.

•

MISSION TO MOSCOW

1943, 123 mins, US b/w

Dir Michael Curtiz ***Prod*** Robert Buckner ***Scr*** Howard Koch ***Ph*** Bert Glennon ***Ed*** Owen Marks ***Mus*** Max Steiner

Act Walter Huston, Ann Harding, Oscar Homolka, Gene Lockhart, Eleanor Parker, Helmut Dantine (Warner)

Film is of a highly intellectual nature, requiring constant attention and thought if it is to be fully appreciated. It is pretty much in the nature of a lengthy monologue, with little action.

It is truly a documentary; Hollywood's initial effort at living history. Every character is the counterpart of an actual person. Real names are used throughout—Roosevelt, Churchill, Stalin, Davies, Litvinov, et al. and the casting is aimed for physical likeness to the person portrayed. The jolting realism of the likenesses is far from the least of the picture's interesting aspects.

Outstanding in the tremendous cast are Walter Huston as Davies, Ann Harding as Mrs. Davies, Oscar Homolka as Litvinov, Gene Lockhart as Molotov, Barbara Everest as Mrs. Litvinov, Vladimir Sokoloff as Kalinin, and Dudley Field Malone as Churchill.

Film follows pretty much in chronological order from the time of Roosevelt's appointment of the progressively minded, capitalist-corporation lawyer Joseph E. Davies to the post of ambassador to Russia.

Manner of presentation of the film is the use of Huston's voice off-screen, employing the first person, to describe his tours and many of the events. Then, where the action permits, the film lapses into regular direct dialog among the characters on the screen.

1943: NOMINATION: Best B&W Art Direction

•

MISSISSIPPI

1935, 80 mins, US b/w

Dir A. Edward Sutherland ***Prod*** Arthur Hornblow, Jr. ***Scr*** Francis Martin, Herbert Fields, Claude Binvon, Jack Cunningham ***Ph*** Charles Lang ***Ed*** Chandler House ***Art*** Hans Dreier, Bernard Herzbrun

Act Bing Crosby, W. C. Fields, Joan Bennett, Queenie Smith, Gail Patrick, Paul Hurst (Paramount)

Paramount obviously couldn't make up its mind what it wanted to do with this film; it's rambling and hokey. For a few moments it's sheer farce, for a few moments it's romance. And it never jells.

Story [by Booth Tarkington] comes off the shelf. It was produced at least twice previously; first silent entitled *The Fighting Coward* (1924) and next as a talker for Buddy Rogers under its stage title, *Magnolia*. This time it has been completely written over, but gagged up too much. Some of the lines are funny, but that isn't enough. W. C. Fields works hard throughout the film and saves it, giving it whatever entertainment value it has.

The Bing Crosby part was written with Lanny Ross in mind and even when he's singing it's no go.

Three songs in the film and all good, although leaving something to be desired. That, too, is a production fault and not traceable to Rodgers & Hart. All three numbers are slow, dreamy tunes for Crosby to sing.

Joan Bennett is the girl, but doesn't get a chance to do much outside of looking pretty. Gail Patrick smiles nicely in the first reel only.

•

MISSISSIPPI BURNING

1988, 125 mins, US Ⓥ ⊙ col

Dir Alan Parker ***Prod*** Frederick Zollo, Robert F. Colesberry ***Scr*** Chris Gerolmo ***Ph*** Peter Biziou ***Ed*** Gerry Hambling ***Mus*** Trevor Jones ***Art*** Philip Harrison, Geoffrey Kirkland

Act Gene Hackman, Willem Dafoe, Frances McDormand, Brad Dourif, R. Lee Ermey, Gailard Sartain (Orion)

Though its credibility is undermined by a fanciful ending, *Mississippi Burning* captures much of the truth in its telling of the impact of a 1964 FBI probe into the murders of three civil rights workers.

Story follows the FBI men (Gene Hackman and Willem Dafoe) who've been sent down to Jessup, MS, to investigate the disappearance of three voter activists, one black and two white Jews. The two run into resistance from both the guilty parties and the blacks, who've been terrorized into silence. It's the fearless Dafoe who wears a hole through the wall and Hackman who knows what to do on the other side. Dafoe gives a disciplined and noteworthy portrayal of Ward, who squelches his emotions as his moral indignation burns. But it's Hackman who steals the picture as Anderson, a messily sympathetic man who connects keenly but briefly with the people. Glowing performance of Frances McDormand as the deputy's wife who's drawn to Hackman is an asset both to his role and the picture.

Parker pushes the picture along at a fervent clip, with the character scenes back-to-back with chases or violence.

1988: Best Cinematography

NOMINATION: Best Picture, Director, Actor (Gene Hackman), Supp. Actress (Frances McDormand), Editing, Sound

•

MISSISSIPPI GAMBLER, THE

1953, 99 mins, US col

Dir Rudolph Mate ***Prod*** Ted Richmond ***Scr*** Seton I. Miller ***Ph*** Irving Glassberg ***Ed*** Edward Curtiss ***Mus*** Frank Skinner

Act Tyrone Power, Piper Laurie, Julie Adams, John McIntire, Paul Cavanaugh, John Baer (Universal)

Opening finds Tyrone Power ready to start a career as an honest-dealing riverboat gambler. As he is ready to take off for the trip to New Orleans, dockside incidents team him with John McIntire, a card dealer, and acquaints him with Piper Laurie, spitfire Southern belle, and her brother (John Baer). Power is a big winner with his straight card-play and breaks Baer while arousing the enmity of crooked gambler Ralph Dumke. Power and McIntire jump ship, and they make their way to New Orleans, where Power seeks to further acquaint himself with Laurie. It is during this waiting romantic game that the film slows, with an occasional quickening scene, such as an abortive gun duel that brands Baer a coward and further complicates Power's suit for the sister, and a few riverboat scenes, in one of which Power is responsible for Baer's death.

Power carries off the romantic requirements with ease, looks good in his fencing scenes and otherwise takes good care of what action he is given. Laurie is nice to look at in the period costumes, while Adams, in a rather thankless role, fails to come off either photogenically or performance-wise. McIntire's old gambler does a lot to help carry things along, and Cavanaugh is excellent.

•

MISSISSIPPI MASALA

1992, 118 mins, US Ⓥ ⊙ col

Dir Mira Nair ***Prod*** Michael Nozik, Mira Nair ***Scr*** Sooni Taraporevala ***Ph*** Ed Lachman ***Ed*** Roberto Silvi ***Mus*** L. Subramaniam ***Art*** Mitch Epstein

Act Denzel Washington, Sarita Choudhury, Roshan Seth, Sharmila Tagore, Charles S. Dutton, Joe Seneca (Cinecom/Mirabi)

Indian director Mira Nair's tragicomedy is less passionate and disturbing than many U.S. pics dealing with race relations. *Mississippi Masala* is handled with a light touch.

The dramatic opening, set in Uganda in 1972, shows a middle-class Indian family forced to leave when Idi Amin takes power. A liberal lawyer (Roshan Seth) who has defended blacks in court, his wife (Sharmila Tagore) and little daughter, Mina, catch the last plane out under an eerie, threatening state of siege.

Story jumps to present-day Mississippi, where the family has settled. Nair skillfully depicts an interracial small town where there's a minor traffic accident involving a white redneck, black youth Demetrius (Denzel Washington) and a pretty Indian girl, the grown-up Mina (Sarita Choudhury). Mina and Demetrius are attracted to each other right away. Washington is savvy and attractive as the enterprising carpet cleaner destined for a brighter future. Choudhury is a discovery as the Americanized Mina, who calls herself a kind of masala (mixed spices). Together, they carry the film smoothly and agreeably.

•

MISS JULIE

SEE: FROKEN JULIE

•

MISSOURI BREAKS, THE

1976, 126 mins, US Ⓥ col

Dir Arthur Penn ***Prod*** Elliott Kastner, Robert M. Sherman ***Scr*** Thomas McGuane ***Ph*** Michael Butler ***Ed*** Jerry Greenberg, Stephen Rotter, Dede Allen ***Mus*** John Williams ***Art*** Albert Brenner

Act Marlon Brando, Jack Nicholson, Kathleen Lloyd, Randy Quaid, Frederic Forrest, Harry Dean Stanton (United Artists)

The environment is the Montana headlands of the Missouri River, where pioneer John McLiam is range boss, local political muscle and pretty well master of the territory. Enter Jack Nicholson, leader of the area's horse thieves, out to avenge a colleague's death while facilitating his work by buying a ranch near the McLiam property as a rest stop for stolen horses.

Finally comes Marlon Brando, vicious frontier hired gun, engaged by McLiam to ferret out the Nicholson gang.

The trouble with *The Missouri Breaks* is that one is seriously drawn to it on its upfront elements, but leaves with a depressing sense of waste. As a film achievement it's corned beef and ham hash.

•

MISS SADIE THOMPSON

1953, 90 mins, US Ⓥ ⊙ col

Dir Curtis Bernhardt ***Prod*** Jerry Wald ***Scr*** Harry Kleiner ***Ph*** Charles Lawton, Jr. ***Ed*** Viola Lawrence ***Mus*** George Duning ***Art*** Carl Anderson

Act Rita Hayworth, Jose Ferrer, Aldo Ray, Russell Collins, Peggy Converse, Charles Bronson (Columbia/Beckworth)

Rain, the stage play which John Colton made from W. Somerset Maugham's story about sex, sin and salvation in the tropics, is back for a third try as a motion picture. This time it's a modernized version fancied up with 3-D and Technicolor.

The production uses an authentic island background for the story, the lensing having been done in Hawaii, so the presentation has a lush tropical look.

In this treatment, Sadie is a shady lady chased out of a Honolulu bawdy house by Davidson, a man determined to keep sin out of the islands. She dodges deportation to San Francisco, where she's wanted for another rap, by taking a ship for New Caledonia. Enroute, the ship is quarantined at an island occupied mostly by Marines.

The dramatic pacing of Curtis Bernhardt's direction achieves a frenzied jazz tempo, quite in keeping with the modernization, and most of the performances respond in kind, especially that of Rita Hayworth. She catches the feel of the title character well, even to braving completely deglamorizing makeup, costuming and photography to fit her physical appearance to that of the bawdy, shady lady that was Sadie Thompson. Less effective is Jose Ferrer's Alfred Davidson, no longer a missionary bigot but a straight layman bigot. Missing under the change is the religious fanaticism that motivated and made understandable the original Freudian character. Aldo Ray, playing Sergeant O'Hara, the Marine who makes an honest woman of Sadie, is good.

1953: NOMINATION: Best Song ("Blue Pacific Blues")

•

MISS TATLOCK'S MILLIONS

1948, 99 mins, US b/w

Dir Richard Haydn ***Prod*** Charles Brackett ***Scr*** Charles Brackett, Richard L. Breen ***Ph*** Charles B. Lang, Jr. ***Ed*** Everett Douglas ***Mus*** Victor Young ***Art*** Hans Dreier, Franz Bachelin

Act John Lund, Wanda Hendrix, Barry Fitzgerald, Monty Woolley, Robert Stack (Paramount)

Basically, story and characters are much to-do about nothing, but the pace is fast, the dialog flip and sophisticated, and the playing expert. This gives the material a surface brightness that makes it look better than it is.

Haydn's directorial debut is creditable. He sets up his characters and situations to keep the chuckles rolling from the broad antics. Plot [based on the play, *Oh! Brother*, by Jacques Deval] concerns a screwball family and the idiot heir to millions, with a number of tangent ramifications that keep the fun pot boiling.

John Lund and Wanda Hendrix team brightly in the principal roles and film receives major assists from Barry Fitzgerald, Monty Woolley, Ilka Chase and others.

Haydn has given considerable footage to a display of the brawn of Lund and Robert Stack, romantic rivals, even to the point of neglecting Hendrix in a bathing suit. In addition to directing Haydn cuts himself in for a very funny bit as an eccentric lawyer, using the name of Richard Rancyd.

•

MISTER FROST

1990, 104 mins, France/UK Ⓥ ⊙ col

Dir Philippe Setbon ***Prod*** Xavier Gelin ***Scr*** Philippe Setbon, Brad Lynch ***Ph*** Dominique Brenguier ***Ed*** Ray Lovejoy ***Art*** Max Berto

Act Jeff Goldblum, Alan Bates, Kathy Baker, Roland Girand, Jean-Pierre Cassel, Daniel Gelin (Hugo/AAA)

Mister Frost is a tepid thriller about a mass murderer who claims to be the devil himself. Jeff Goldblum is a seemingly cordial country gentleman (in England, apparently) who casually confesses to police to having tortured and murdered no less than 24 men, women and children, buried on his property.

Most of the story is set in a clinic "somewere in Europe" where Goldblum breaks his silence to communicate with lady psychiatrist Kathy Baker. Yes, he's Satan in person, he tells her, and he's fuming mad because modern psychiatry has cheated him out of authorship in 20th century evil. Now he wants to make a comeback and has chosen Baker as his agent. None of this is particularly terrifying or gripping, especially since Gallic writer-helmer Philippe Setbon is incapable of creating any suspenseful doubt about whether Goldblum is indeed Satan, or merely a dangerous schizophrenic with psychic and hypnotic powers.

•

MISTER MOSES

1965, 115 mins, US ▭ col

Dir Ronald Neame ***Prod*** Frank Ross ***Scr*** Charles Beaumont, Monja Danischewsky ***Ph*** Oswald Morris ***Ed*** Phil Anderson, Peter Wetherley ***Mus*** John Barry

Act Robert Mitchum, Carroll Baker, Ian Bannen, Alexander Knox, Raymond St. Jacques, Orlando Martins (United Artists)

The Biblical Moses, in a manner, has been updated for this Frank Ross production, switching the plot to an American diamond smuggler leading an African tribe to a promised land. Director Ronald Neame has taken every advantage of fascinating African terrain for his unusual adventure yarn from Max Catto's novel.

Film takes its motivation from orders by the district commissioner for a village, threatened by flood waters of a new dam being constructed, to evacuate. The religious-minded chief, who has heard the story of Moses from a missionary and his daughter who live with the tribe, refuses to take his people in helicopters to be provided for purpose, because the Bible says the children of Israel, when they went to their promised land, took their animals with them. No animals, no go.

Robert Mitchum, a medicine-man who smuggles diamonds, is set down in this ticklish situation, a guy known as Dr. Moses. The chief hails him as the true Moses who will lead them to a special government preserve.

•

MISTER QUILP

1975, 117 mins, UK col

Dir Michael Tuchner ***Prod*** Helen M. Strauss ***Scr*** Louis Kamp, Irene Kamp ***Ph*** Christopher Challis ***Ed*** John Jympson ***Mus*** Anthony Newley ***Art*** Elliot Scott

Act Anthony Newley, David Hemmings, David Warner, Michael Hordern, Paul Rogers, Jill Bennett (Avco Embassy)

Mister Quilp is a sprightly musical version of Charles Dickens's *The Old Curiosity Shop*.

Anthony Newley, a corrupt lender in league with fringe lawyer David Warner and latter's sister Jill Bennett, harasses shopowner Michael Hordern and granddaughter Sarah Jane Varley, both rescued in time by arrival of Paul Rogers, Hordern's wealthy long-lost brother.

Peter Duncan, as Varley's admirer, David Hemmings as a likable boulevardier, Mona Washbourne as a delightful traveling show operator who befriends the fleeing Varley and Hordern, Sarah Webb as a plaintive street urchin, Philip Davis as Newley's whipping boy and Yvonne Antrobus as Newley's long-suffering wife all complement the main plot line.

Casting is uniformly excellent.

•

MISTER ROBERTS

1955, 120 mins, US Ⓥ ▭ col

Dir John Ford, Mervyn LeRoy ***Prod*** Leland Hayward ***Scr*** Frank Nugent, Joshua Logan ***Ph*** Winton Hoch ***Ed*** Jack Murray ***Mus*** Franz Waxman ***Art*** Art Loel

Act Henry Fonda, James Cagney, William Powell, Jack Lemmon, Betsy Palmer, Ward Bond (Orange/Warner)

Thomas Heggen's salty comedy about life aboard a navy cargo ship had no trouble moving from the printed page to the stage [in a play by Heggen and Joshua Logan]. Figuring importantly in the sock manner with which it all comes off on the screen is the directorial credit shared by John Ford and Mervyn LeRoy, the former having had to bow out because of illness midway in production.

Henry Fonda, who scored on the stage in the title role, repeats in the picture as the cargo officer who resented not being in the thick of the fighting in the Pacific during World War II.

James Cagney is simply great as the captain of the ship. William Powell tackles the role of ship's doctor with an easy assurance that makes it stand out and Jack Lemmon is a big hit as Ensign Pulver.

1955: Best Supp. Actor (Jack Lemmon)

NOMINATIONS: Best Picture, Sound

•

MISUNDERSTOOD

1984, 91 mins, US Ⓥ col

Dir Jerry Schatzberg ***Prod*** Tarak Ben Ammar ***Scr*** Barra Grant ***Ph*** Pasqualino De Santis ***Ed*** Marc Laub ***Mus*** Michael Hoppe ***Art*** Joel Schiller

Act Gene Hackman, Henry Thomas, Rip Torn, Huckleberry Fox, Maureen Kerwin, Susan Anspach (Accent/Keith Barish)

Misunderstood, a somber and largely unsentimental study of a rift and ultimate reconciliation between father and son, is a "remake and adaptation" of Luigi Comencini's 1967 Italian pic *Incompreso*.

New version places former postwar black marketeer and now shipping magnate Gene Hackman in a palatial home in Tunisia. His wife has just died, and Hackman has a tough time breaking the news to his seven- or eight-year-old son Henry Thomas. In his opinion, his other son, Huckleberry Fox, is simply too young to comprehend what's happened. When his relative Rip Torn suggests Hackman is too stern with the boys, that he expects too much of them, the latter protests he's trying to treat Thomas like a grown-up.

Ultimately, Thomas is seriously injured in a fall, and he and Hackman finally break through to each other.

•

MITT LIV SOM HUND
(MY LIFE AS A DOG)

1985, 100 mins, Sweden Ⓥ ⊙ col

Dir Lasse Hallstrom ***Prod*** Waldemar Bergendahl (exec.) ***Scr*** Lasse Hallstrom, Brasse Brannstrom, Pelle Berglund, Reidar Jonsson ***Ph*** Jorgen Persson, Rolf Lindstrom ***Ed*** Susanne Linnman, Christer Furubrand ***Mus*** Bjorn Isfalt ***Art*** Lasse Westfelt

Act Anton Glanzelius, Anki Liden, Tomas von Bromssen, Manfred Serner, Melinda Kinnaman, Ing-Marie Carlsson (Svensk Filmindustri)

Lasse Hallstrom's fifth feature effort in 10 years, *My Life As a Dog* is an exquisite look at childhood, based loosely on Reidar Jonsson's 1983 novel about a rural-provincial 12-year-old equivalent of J. D. Salinger's Holden Caulfield.

Hallstrom obviously put a lot of personal recollections into his telling of Ingemar Johansson, who has a hard time adjusting to the atmosphere of his beloved mother's house. She is bedridden with a terminal illness, but also given to temper tantrums. To secure the mother her peace and quiet, the boy is sent away to some relatives in a rural community near the famous Boda glassworks.

When his mother eventually dies, Ingemar finds elbowroom for his mischief when settling permanently with his soccer-playing, glassblower uncle, an amiable prankster himself, in a cozily tolerant household of no-nonsense love and happiness. The year of the action is 1959, when the boy's countryman-namesake won over Floyd Patterson in the world boxing champion fight.

Getting down on his knees to bark and to feign barking turns out to be the boy's best means of getting around various moments of crisis.

Otherwise, he is endowed with a charm so obvious that nobody can quite help loving him. As played by amateur Anton Glanzelius, dark-haired, slant-eyed and with a mouth of a multitude of expressions, there is nothing slick or cute about this Ingemar as there is nothing maudlin nor prearranged about the whole film.

•

MIXED NUTS

1994, 97 mins, US Ⓥ ⊙ col

Dir Nora Ephron ***Prod*** Paul Junger Witt, Tony Thomas, Joseph Hartwick ***Scr*** Nora Ephron, Delia Ephron ***Ph*** Sven Nykvist ***Ed*** Robert Reitano ***Mus*** George Fenton ***Art*** Bill Groom

Act Steve Martin, Madeline Kahn, Robert Klein, Anthony LaPaglia, Juliette Lewis, Rob Reiner (Tri-Star)

The holiday spirit goes into life-threatening cardiac arrest with the Christmas-themed comedy *Mixed Nuts*. Based on a French hit [movie, Jean-Marie Poire's 1982 *Le pere Noel est une ordure*], it's lost something crucial in translation.

Philip (Steve Martin) operates the Venice, CA, help line Lifesavers. In fact, the crew manning the phones could stand a little bit of counseling. Blanch Munchnik (Madeline

Kahn) is a tart-tongued widow and Catherine (Rita Wilson) is repressed.

The landlord has served notice on the service unless it can come up with a large chunk of dough. Somewhere in the mix, there's a parade of weirdos on the line and in the office. A pregnant woman (Juliette Lewis) blows hot and cold about her goof-off, ex-con boyfriend (Anthony LaPaglia); an Amazonian transvestite (Liev Schreiber) is looking for a dance partner; and a ukulele-playing delivery boy (Adam Sandler) is just plain irritating.

Director/coscripter Nora Ephron pitches the humor at a cacophonous level and displays the comedic equivalent of two left feet in evolving an absurdist, slapstick yarn. Truly alarming is watching some fine performers, including Kahn and LaPaglia, at their very worst.

•

MOANA

1926, 69 mins, US Ⓥ ⦿ ⊗ b/w

Dir Robert Flaherty ***Prod*** R. J. Flaherty, F. H. Flaherty ***Scr*** Robert Flaherty, Julian Johnson ***Ph*** Robert Flaherty (Paramount)

A magnified travel film, it's interesting and has been well done, but there's no story, and a travelog is a travelog.

The Flahertys were responsible for *Nanook of the North*. Here they have delved into the southern climes for their subject matter. A subtitle states that the men lingered with the Samoans for two years in order to win the confidence of the tribe and get the inside native stuff.

The action contains a couple of modified laughs and holds some exceptionally eye-filling rugged shorelines, with the surf pounding. The spearing of fish, the capture of a giant turtle in the water by two swimmers and the riding of the breakers by a homemade skiff provide the major "action" scenes.

•

MOB, THE

1951, 87 mins, US b/w

Dir Robert Parrish ***Prod*** Jerry Bresler ***Scr*** William Bowers ***Ph*** Joseph Walker ***Ed*** Charles Nelson ***Mus*** George Duning ***Art*** Cary Odell

Act Broderick Crawford, Betty Buehler, Richard Kiley, Neville Brand, Ernest Borgnine, Matt Crowley (Columbia)

Broderick Crawford is fine as a cop who poses as a hood to overthrow racketeers who've been shaking down dock workers on the waterfront. Fist fights, gunfire and some salty dialog and sexy interludes involving Crawford with Lynne Baggett enliven the proceedings considerably.

Crawford, altar-bound, gets called back to track the responsible party down, the victim being a brother cop. Difficult-to-find trail leads him to New Orleans and back to his starting point, California, right into the police department itself.

Scripter William Bowers has studded the Ferguson Findley original [novel *Waterfront*] with some logically developed clues designed to throw the customers off the track. It's definitely a surprise when the true culprit is exposed.

Betty Buehler is thoroughly sympathetic as Crawford's girlfriend, and Baggett and Jean Alexander as manbait planted to distract Crawford from his pursuits spark the distaff end expertly.

•

MO' BETTER BLUES

1990, 127 mins, US Ⓥ ⦿ col

Dir Spike Lee ***Prod*** Spike Lee ***Scr*** Spike Lee ***Ph*** Ernest Dickerson ***Ed*** Sam Pollard ***Mus*** Bill Lee ***Art*** Wynn Thomas

Act Denzel Washington, Spike Lee, Wesley Snipes, Joie Lee, Cynda Williams, Giancarlo Esposito (40 Acres & a Mule/Universal)

Personal rather than social issues come to the fore in *Mo' Better Blues*, a Spike Lee personality piece dressed in jazz trappings that puffs itself up like *Bird* but doesn't really fly. More focused on the sexual dilemmas of its main character than on musical themes, pic might well be subtitled *He's Gotta Have It*.

Pic's fabulous opening sequence, in which the camera does a sensual pan of jazz images—a horn, a man's ear, his mouth—raises expectations for a definitive film on jazz and an ambitious step forward for Lee. But the script unfolds to notes from a different scale: basically the same unique but limited range Lee has drawn on before.

Contempo tale stars Denzel Washington as Bleek Gilliam, a self-absorbed New York horn player who leads a jazz quintet on a roll at a trendy Manhattan club called Beneath the Underdog. The diminutive Lee plays Giant (as in "giant pain in the ass," one character observes), Bleek's ne'er-do-well friend who's found a precarious niche as the band's manager. Joie Lee (Lee's sister) and Cynda Williams play the women who compete for Bleek's attention. Also overlooked by the self-centered trumpeter is his sax player, Shadow (Wesley Snipes, in a standout perf). But if *Mo' Better* is soft in the center, the characters in and around the band and the nightclub provide winning entertainment.

•

MOBSTER, THE

SEE: I, MOBSTER

•

MOBSTERS

1991, 104 mins, US Ⓥ ⦿ col

Dir Michael Karbelnikoff ***Prod*** Steve Roth ***Scr*** Michael Mahern, Nicholas Kazan ***Ph*** Lajos Koltai ***Ed*** Scott Smith, Joe D'Augustine ***Mus*** Michael Small ***Art*** Richard Sylbert

Act Christian Slater, Patrick Dempsey, Richard Grieco, F. Murray Abraham, Lara Flynn Boyle, Anthony Quinn (Universal)

Mobsters resembles a cart-before-the-horse case of putting marketing ahead of filmmaking, as the seemingly can't-miss premise of teen-heartthrob gangsters gets lost in self-important direction, a shoddy script and muddled storytelling.

The narrative is amazingly confused in light of its simplicity: two Italian and two Jewish kids from the ghetto team up in the 1920s and get into organized crime, gradually finding themselves caught between two dons. Story [by coscripter Michael Mahern] is based on the real-life exploits of mob boss Lucky Luciano (Christian Slater) and confederates Meyer Lansky (Patrick Dempsey), Bugsy Siegel (Richard Grieco) and Frank Costello (Costas Mandylor).

True highlights come from its longer-toothed characters, with Anthony Quinn's lusty portrayal of Don Masseria and F. Murray Abraham as the Yiddish-spouting no-goodnik Arnold Rothstein.

First-time director Michael Karbelnikoff occasionally betrays his roots in TV commercials, particularly with a ludicrous, gauzily shot love scene between showgirl Lara Flynn Boyle and Slater that closely resembles a perfume ad.

[For pic's U.K. release the handle *The Evil Empire* was added to posters.]

•

MOBY DICK

1930, 70 mins, US b/w

Dir Lloyd Bacon ***Scr*** J. Grubb Alexander ***Ph*** Robert Kurrle

Act John Barrymore, Joan Bennett, Lloyd Hughes, May Boley, Walter Long (Warner)

The Sea Beast was a money picture for Warners in 1926. [This sound remake, using the title of Herman Melville's original novel, again stars John Barrymore.]

Moby Dick is just as smart as ever, but Barrymore is smarter. He's got a better whale to work with this time. And Moby Dick deserves his finish, after Barrymore has chased him over seven seas for seven years because of that leg bite.

Back home the demure Joan Bennett, who could never grow old out in New Bedford, waits for her whaling boyfriend to return.

Moby Dick is stirring, even if you don't believe in whales. And this one's said to have cost Warners $120,000, with or without teeth.

•

MOBY DICK

1956, 116 mins, UK Ⓥ ⦿ col

Dir John Huston ***Prod*** John Huston ***Scr*** Ray Bradbury, John Huston ***Ph*** Oswald Morris, Freddie Francis ***Ed*** Russell Lloyd ***Mus*** Philip Stainton ***Art*** Ralph Brinton

Act Gregory Peck, Richard Basehart, Leo Genn, Harry Andrews, Orson Welles, Bernard Miles (Moulin/Warner)

Costly weather and production delays on location in Ireland and elsewhere enlarged the bring-home price on John Huston's *Moby Dick* to as high as $5 million.

Moby Dick is interesting more often than exciting, faithful to the time and text [of the Herman Melville novel] more than great theatrical entertainment. Essentially it is a chase picture and yet not escaping the sameness and repetitiousness that often dulls the chase formula. It was astute of Huston to work out a print combining color and black-and-white calculated to capture the sombre beauties of New Bedford, circa 1840, and its whaling ways.

Orson Welles appears early and briefly as a local New Bedford preacher who delivers a God-fearing sermon on Jonah and the whale. Welles turns in an effective bit of brimstone exhortation, appropriate to time and place.

Gregory Peck hovers above the crew, grim-faced and hate-obsessed. He wears a stump leg made of the jaw of a whale, and he lives only to kill the greatest whale of all, the white-hided super-monster Moby Dick, the one which had chewed off his leg. Peck's Ahab is not very "elemental." It is not that he fails in handling the rhetoric. Actually he does quite well with the stylized speech in which Melville wrote and which Ray Bradbury and Huston have preserved in their screenplay. It's just that Peck often seems understated and much too gentlemanly for a man supposedly consumed by insane fury.

•

MODEL SHOP

1969, 90 mins, US col

Dir Jacques Demy ***Prod*** Jacques Demy ***Scr*** Jacques Demy, Adrien Joyce ***Ph*** Michel Hugo ***Ed*** Walter Thompson ***Mus*** Spirit ***Art*** Kenneth A. Reid

Act Anouk Aimee, Gary Lockwood, Alexandra Hay, Carol Cole, Severn Darden, Tom Fielding (Columbia)

French filmmaker Jacques Demy brings a fresh look at L.A. and American youth, plus a revealing eye for the character and feel of the sprawling California city.

And it is a work of love in its attitude toward the city and its characters. Demy can be sentimental, sans bathos or mawkishness, and comes up with a day in the life of a 26-year-old youthful drifter whose one romantic interlude is a step in coping with his life.

There is not much story here, but rather a revealing series of incidents that serve as a backdrop for a poetic tale of human disarray, fleeting comprehension and a surface gentleness that belies an underlying discontent and groping for meaning, love and aim by its disparate but well-mimed characters.

•

MODERN ROMANCE

1981, 93 mins, US Ⓥ ⦿ col

Dir Albert Brooks ***Prod*** Andrew Scheinman, Martin Shafer ***Scr*** Albert Brooks, Monica Johnson ***Ph*** Eric Saarinen ***Ed*** David Finfer ***Mus*** Lance Rubin ***Art*** Edward Richardson

Act Albert Brooks, Kathryn Harrold, Bruno Kirby, Jane Hallaren, James L. Brooks, George Kennedy (Columbia)

Given room to roam as star, director and cowriter, Columbia Pictures obviously hoped that comedian Albert Brooks might break through like Woody Allen. But Allen, too, started slowly and this is only Brooks's second feature after the critically acclaimed but commercially weak *Real Life*.

Simplicity and veracity of his story are a plus. Without excessive complications, he plays a nice-enough young fellow who cannot make a permanent commitment to his girlfriend, sympathetically portrayed by the beautiful and talented Kathryn Harrold. At first, he dumps her, then immediately regrets it and goes crazy trying to get her back. Succeeding in that, he starts aggravating her with jealousies.

Many scenes play far beyond the laughs they're worth. At the same time, Harrold doesn't get to round out her part quite as much as she should. One thing Brooks does well, however, is pepper the bit parts with interesting characters who all have a point to make, most particularly Bruno Kirby as his best friend.

When he isn't fretting about his personal life, Brooks plays a film editor cutting a low-budget sci-fi pic with Kirby for director James L. Brooks (no relation). The brief examination of the cutting room is hilarious as they first patch up a scene with George Kennedy hamming it up in true low-budget style as Zoron the space leader.

•

MODERNS, THE

1988, 126 mins, US Ⓥ ⦿ col

Dir Alan Rudolph ***Prod*** Carolyn Pfeiffer, David Blocker ***Scr*** Alan Rudolph, Jon Bradshaw ***Ph*** Toyomichi Kurita, Jan Kiesser ***Ed*** Debra T. Smith, Scott Brock ***Mus*** Mark Isham ***Art*** Steven Legler

Act Keith Carradine, Linda Fiorentino, John Lone, Wallace Shawn, Genevieve Bujold, Geraldine Chaplin (Alive/Nelson)

The artistic world of Paris in the 1920s comes to life as if in a lustrous dream in *The Moderns*, a romantic's lush vision of a group of expatriate Americans at a time and place of some of the century's most tumultuous creative activity.

There is Nick Hart (Keith Carradine) who, at 33, is viewed suspiciously for not having made it yet as an artist. Oiseau (Wallace Shawn), a gossip columnist for the *Tribune*, who dreams only of going to Hollywood; Bertram Stone (John Lone), an elegant, rich, philistine art dealer with a disturbing violent streak; his wife, Rachel (Linda Fiorentino), with whom Nick has a past and, he hopes, a future; and Hemingway himself (Kevin J. O'Connor), who amusingly careens through the action in varying states of inebriation, trying out titles for a new book.

Also critical to the assorted personal equations are Libby (Genevieve Bujold), an impoverished gallery owner with values diametrically opposed to those of Stone, and Nathalie (Geraldine Chaplin), a patroness of the arts who convinces Nick to execute some spectacular forgeries.

Carradine has never been better, as he conveys the strong feelings he has for art and his estranged wife as well as the diffidence that has set in due to years of frustration and lack of recognition. Lone is the picture of disciplined decadence, a magnetic figure who commands fascination, and Fiorentino is ideal as the gorgeous American of a prosaic background over whom men may lose their hearts, mind and lives.

•

MODERN TIMES

1936, 85 mins, US Ⓥ b/w

Dir Charles Chaplin ***Prod*** Charles Chaplin ***Scr*** Charles Chaplin ***Ph*** Rollie Totheroh, Ira Morgan ***Ed*** [uncredited] ***Mus*** Charles Chaplin ***Art*** Charles D. Hall, Russell Spencer

Act Charles Chaplin, Paulette Goddard, Henry Bergman, Stanley Sandford, Chester Conklin, Hank Mann (United Artists)

Whatever sociological meanings some will elect to read into *Modern Times,* there's no denying that as a cinematic entertainment Chaplin's first picture since *City Lights* (1931) is wholesomely funny.

The pathos of the machine worker who suffers temporary derangement, as he tightens the bolts on a factory treadmill to a clocklike tempo, gives way to a series of similarly winning situations. In each the victim of circumstance meets temporary frustration, almost inevitably resulting in a ride in Black Maria. When finally achieving what promises to be a semblance of economic security the menace, in the form of the law, enters to arrest Paulette Goddard as a refugee vagrant.

Modern Times is as 100 percent a one-man picture as probably is possible. Chaplin the pantomimist stands or falls by his two years' work. Dialog is almost negligible. And when the music [conducted by Alfred Newman, arranged by Edward Powell and David Raksin] is inadequate, Chaplin frankly recourses to plain titles.

Goddard, a winsome waif attired almost throughout in short, ragged dress, registers handily. Chaplin's old standbys, notably Henry Bergman (also an assistant director), Chester Conklin, Hank Mann and Allan Garcia, contribute nicely.

•

MODESTY BLAISE

1966, 118 mins, UK Ⓥ col

Dir Joseph Losey ***Prod*** Joseph Janni ***Scr*** Evan Jones ***Ph*** Jack Hildyard ***Ed*** Reginald Beck ***Mus*** John Dankworth ***Art*** Richard MacDonald

Act Monica Vitti, Terence Stamp, Dirk Bogarde, Harry Andrews, Michael Craig, Scilla Gabel (Janni)

Modesty Blaise is one of the nuttiest, screwiest pictures ever made. Not merely a spy spoof, based on a book and a comic strip about a femme James Bond–type, the colorful production gives the horse laugh to many different film plots and styles. Fine direction and many solid performances are evident.

Evan Jones has concocted a wacky screenplay, most immediately derived from the English comic strip by Peter O'Donnell and Jim Holdaway, which propels Blaise, played by Monica Vitti, into a British government espionage scheme. Heading the opposition is Dirk Bogarde, an effete international criminal, while Vitti is aided by longtime sidekick, bedhopping Terence Stamp.

Vitti's English is adequate for her part; her body English, however, transcends all language barriers. Stamp is good, and appropriately animated. Bogarde's jaded urbanity is very good, and all other players register in solid support.

•

DIE MOERDER SIND UNTER UNS
(THE MURDERERS ARE AMONGST US)

1946, 80 mins, Germany b/w

Dir Wolfgang Staudte ***Scr*** Wolfgang Staudte ***Ph*** Friedl Behn-Grund, Eugen Klagemann ***Mus*** Ernst Roters

Act Hildegard Knef, Wilhelm Borchert, Arno Paulsen, Robert Forsch, Albert Johann, Erna Sellner (Defa)

This first postwar German production is a serious film concerned with the knotty problem of the individual German's guilt for Nazism. While not fully successful, either as drama or ideology, film is marked by superb camera and montage technique recalling some of the first-rate German productions before the Nazi era.

Framed against the ruins of Berlin, story is concerned with a young medico haunted into drunkenness by the memory of mass executions that were ordered by his captain in Poland. When the doctor once again meets the captain, now a kindly family man, he determines to kill the war criminal. At the last moment, however, the doctor's sweetheart intervenes.

Basic flaw of this film is the slow pace with which the story unfolds. Shallow sentimentalism in the romantic passages between the doctor and his girlfriend also is damaging to this otherwise adult production.

Although made in the Russian zone of Germany, the film is not weighted with heavy-handed propaganda. On the contrary, all the questions which it raises are left unanswered.

Especially standout roles are turned in by Wilhelm Borchert, as the doctor, Armo Paulsen, as the captain, and Hildegard Knef, as the girl.

Good score also contributes importantly to the film's sombre quality.

•

MOGAMBO

1953, 115 mins, US Ⓥ col

Dir John Ford ***Prod*** Sam Zimbalist ***Scr*** John Lee Mahin ***Ph*** Robert Surtees, Freddie Young ***Ed*** Frank Clarke ***Mus*** [none] ***Art*** Alfred Junge

Act Clark Gable, Ava Gardner, Grace Kelly, Donald Sinden, Eric Pohlmann, Laurence Naismith (M-G-M)

The lure of the jungle and romance get a sizzling workout in *Mogambo* and it's a socko package of entertainment, crammed with sexy two-fisted adventure.

While having its origin in the Wilson Collison play [*Red Dust*], this remake is fresh in locale and characterizations switching from the rubber plantations of Indo-China to the African veldt and updating the period.

John Lee Mahin's dialog and situations are unusually zippy and adult. Ava Gardner feeding a baby rhino and elephant, and her petulant storming at a pet boa constrictor to stay out of her bed, are good touches.

The romantic conflict boils up between the principals during a safari into gorilla country, where an anthropologist and his wife plan to do research. Clark Gable is the great white hunter leading the party. Gardner is the girl on the prowl for a man, and who has now settled on Gable. To get him she has to offset the sweeter charms of Grace Kelly, the wife, who also has become smitten with the Gable masculinity and is ready to walk out on Donald Sinden, the unexciting anthropologist. For the second time in Metro history, a picture has been made without a music score (*King Solomon's Mines* was the first) and none is needed as the sounds of the jungle and native rhythms are all that are required.

1953: NOMINATIONS: Best Actress (Ava Gardner), Supp. Actress (Grace Kelly)

•

MOLL FLANDERS

1996, 123 mins, US Ⓥ ⦿ ⌑ col

Dir Pen Densham ***Prod*** John Watson, Richard B. Lewis, Pen Densham ***Scr*** Pen Densham ***Ph*** David Tattersall ***Ed*** Neil Travis, James R. Symons ***Mus*** Mark Mancina ***Art*** Caroline Hanania

Act Robin Wright, Morgan Freeman, Stockard Channing, John Lynch, Aisling Corcoran, Brenda Fricker (Trilogy/M-G-M)

English lit majors might not recognize the story—writer-director Densham uses Daniel Defoe's 1722 novel as only the most basic of blueprints, snatching bits and pieces from other historical sources and his own imagination to fashion a picaresque tale, by turns romantic and gritty, of a fiercely intelligent woman forever at odds with her lowly station in 18th-century London.

Born to a convicted thief who was hanged immediately after giving birth, Moll is sent to a nunnery. She escapes to the harsh streets of London and is taken in by kindly Mrs. Mazzawatti (Brenda Fricker). That phase, too, proves short-lived, so it's on to the next adventure, and the picture moves into its most vividly realized stretch as Moll arrives on the doorstep of Mrs. Allworthy (Stockard Channing), the greedy madam of a classy whorehouse. Moll quickly moves from servant to prostitute, believing she'll find a husband among the house's wealthy clients. Channing, in a screen appearance that finally captures the actress's considerable stage presence, has a fine time with Mrs. Allworthy, a Dickensian character who makes Fagin seem like a child welfare worker. But it's Wright who holds together the film's swinging moods, her Moll moving from youthful exuberance to despair and, reawakened by love, on to something between resignation and hope. She's convincing at every turn.

Production designer Caroline Hanania does a credible job of turning Ireland, where *Moll* was filmed, into the chaotic mess that was London in the 1700s.

•

MOLLY AND ME

1945, 76 mins, US Ⓥ b/w

Dir Lewis Seiler ***Prod*** Robert Bassler ***Scr*** Leonard Praskins, Roger Burford ***Ph*** Charles Clarke ***Ed*** John McCafferty ***Mus*** Cyril Mockridge ***Art*** Lyle R. Wheeler, Albert Hogsett

Act Gracie Fields, Monty Woolley, Roddy McDowall, Reginald Gardiner (20th Century-Fox)

Inauspicious title cloaks a pleasant comedy-drama. It is neatly studded with belly-laugh material as well as effective bits of pathos. Above all, it holds an excellent all-round cast topped by Gracie Fields, Monty Woolley, Roddy McDowall and Reginald Gardiner.

Story, with an English locale, opens with a jobless music hall entertainer (Fields) taking job as a housekeeper. She revitalizes a gloomy household, discharges a parasitical group of thieving servants, makes the place seem like home to the motherless boy, and finally brings about an understanding between father and son.

Interwoven is an ancient scandal concerning the runaway wife of the one-time politician (Woolley) who has been persuaded to stand for parliament again when his errant wife returns with blackmail as her objective. Unbeknown to the politician Fields scares the woman out of England by framing a phoney murder in her hotel room. The slender motif [from a novel by Frances Marion] has been nicely developed with corking individual performances.

•

MOLLY MAGUIRES, THE

1970, 124 mins, US Ⓥ ⦿ ⌑ col

Dir Martin Ritt ***Prod*** Martin Ritt, Walter Bernstein ***Scr*** Walter Bernstein ***Ph*** James Wong Howe ***Ed*** Frank Bracht ***Mus*** Henry Mancini ***Art*** Tambi Larsen

Act Sean Connery, Richard Harris, Samantha Eggar, Frank Finlay, Anthony Zerbe, Bethel Leslie (Paramount/Tamm)

The Molly Maguires, based on a Pennsylvania coal miners' rebellion of the late 19th century, is occasionally brilliant. Sean Connery, Richard Harris and Samantha Eggar head a competent cast.

Story background ("suggested" by an Arthur H. Lewis book) depicts Irish immigrants existing in the sort of company-captivity common to other American industries of the period. Employer abuses had led to unsuccessful strikes, after which the workers spawned an underground militant group.

Story is primarily that of Harris, hired by the mine-owners to infiltrate the workers' ranks. Connery is a rebel leader. Eggar appears occasionally for some light romantic interludes with Harris.

1970: NOMINATION: Best Art Direction

•

MOM AND DAD SAVE THE WORLD

1992, 88 mins, US Ⓥ ⦿ col

Dir Greg Beeman ***Prod*** Michael Phillips ***Scr*** Chris Matheson, Ed Solomon ***Ph*** Jacques Haitkin ***Ed*** W. O. Garret, Michael Jablow ***Mus*** Jerry Goldsmith ***Art*** Craig Stearns

Act Teri Garr, Jeffrey Jones, Jon Lovitz, Thalmus Rasulala, Wallace Shawn, Eric Idle (Warner/HBO)

Little kids will find some infantile laughs in *Mom and Dad Save the World,* but adults will be looking at their watches during this silly sci-fi comedy. Teri Garr and Jeffrey Jones gamely struggle with inane dialogue as a California couple transported to a tacky-looking "planet of idiots."

With garish color, goofy-looking creatures in rubbery costumes and sets parodying old Flash Gordon serials, pic flaunts its modest budget with engaging candor. Basic trouble is with the script by *Bill & Ted* writers Chris Matheson and Ed Solomon, whose dumbness jokes are stretched too far.

Pic's obvious fun-poking at San Fernando suburbanites wears thin, but not as quickly as the smarmy antics of a half-witted emperor (Jon Lovitz). The adept comic actor chews the scenery here in an overextended part as the sadistic lout who's taken over the planet from Eric Idle's imprisoned king.

Conceiving a mad passion for Garr's ditzy Earthling after spying her through his telescope, Lovitz has her transported to the planet with Jones in their station wagon by electromagnetic beam.

Garr's blithe lack of alarm over her predicament helps her survive the pic with minimal damage.

•

MOMENT BY MOMENT

1978, 105 mins, US col

Dir Jane Wagner ***Prod*** Robert Stigwood ***Scr*** Jane Wagner ***Ph*** Philip Lathrop ***Ed*** John F. Burnett ***Mus*** Lee Holdridge ***Art*** Harry Horner

Act Lily Tomlin, John Travolta, Andra Akers, Bert Kramer, Shelley R. Bonus, Debra Feuer (Universal)

What seemed like inspired casting on paper, the teaming of John Travolta and Lily Tomlin, fails badly in execution.

The lion's share of the blame must go to writer-director (and long-time Tomlin collaborator) Jane Wagner, who concocted this improbable story of a Beverly Hills chic housewife whose marriage has gone sour, and who meets up with an insecure young drifter, with whom she has an affair. Insouciant and likable from the outset, Travolta pursues the distant Tomlin like a determined puppy dog—once he latches on, she can't shake him loose. The first half hour of the pic, with this unusual courtship, is appealing, and only makes what follows more of a letdown.

Approaching Trisha as if she was one of her stable theatrical creations, Tomlin never varies her nasal monotone, nor her imperturbable exterior. It's a one-note performance that frustrates the entire picture.

Not helping matters is Wagner's banal script, which has cliché piled atop cliché, and dialog that evokes embarrassing laughter.

•

MOMENT TO MOMENT
1966, 108 mins, US col
Dir Mervyn LeRoy ***Prod*** Mervyn LeRoy ***Scr*** John Lee Mahin, Alec Coppel ***Ph*** Harry Stradling ***Ed*** Philip W. Anderson ***Mus*** Henry Mancini ***Art*** Alexander Golitzen, Alfred Sweeney
Act Jean Seberg, Honor Blackman, Sean Garrison, Arthur Hill, Gregoire Aslan, Peter Robbins (Universal/Le Roy)

Mervyn LeRoy, who has tackled just about every type of film, returns to romantic melodrama in *Moment to Moment*, an unabashed sudser. A mild suspense story blending a wife's infidelity and amnesia, the film doesn't entirely jell for several reasons, mainly thin scripting, weak acting and LeRoy's own too-leisurely pace.

John Lee Mahin joined Alec Coppel in adapting latter's story [*Laughs with a Stranger*] about a happily married Yank wife, increasingly neglected by headshrinker hubby who is on the lecture circuit all over Europe while she and the kid remain on the Riviera. A U.S. naval officer has an affair with her, provoking a physical argument and a shooting.

Jean Seberg lacks dimension as the wife, even allowing for the script. In early scenes, an overly passive limning—which suggests jaded boredom instead of a well-adjusted spouse in a single fall from grace—robs the role of most sympathy.

•

MOMMIE DEAREST
1981, 129 mins, US Ⓥ ⦿ col
Dir Frank Perry ***Prod*** Frank Yablans ***Scr*** Frank Yablans, Frank Perry, Tracy Hotchner, Robert Getchell ***Ph*** Paul Lohmann ***Ed*** Peter E. Berger ***Mus*** Henry Mancini ***Art*** Bill Malley
Act Faye Dunaway, Diana Scarwid, Steve Forrest, Howard da Silva, Jocelyn Brando (Paramount)

This is Faye Dunaway as Joan Crawford and the results are, well, screen history. Dunaway does not chew scenery. Dunaway starts neatly at each corner of the set in every scene and swallows it whole, costars and all. Prior to her death, Crawford once commented that Dunaway was among the best of up-and-coming young actresses. Too bad Crawford isn't around to comment now. Too bad Crawford isn't around to comment on the whole endeavor.

Much has been written and said pro-and-con about Crawford since daughter Christina wrote the book on which this film is based. Whatever the truth, director Frank Perry's portrait here is sorry indeed, 129 minutes with a very pathetic and unpleasant individual.

The story is familiar: self-centerd, insecure and pressured movie queen adopts two babies for both love and personal aggrandizement. Growing up, the kids are battered between luxurious pampering and abuse, never finding real affection with mother, who finally dies and cuts them out of the will, reaching beyond the grave for final revenge.

As Christina, Diana Scarwid is okay, but unexceptional. Much better is little Mara Hobel as Christina the child, genuinely touching at times. Rutanya Alda is also fine as Crawford's long-suffering but loving assistant.

•

MO' MONEY
1992, 89 mins, US Ⓥ ⦿ col
Dir Peter Macdonald ***Prod*** Michael Rachmil ***Scr*** Damon Wayans ***Ph*** Don Burgess ***Ed*** Hubert C. de la Bouillerie ***Mus*** Jay Gruska ***Art*** William Arnold
Act Damon Wayans, Marlon Wayans, Stacey Dash, Joe Santos, John Diehl, Harry J. Lennix (Columbia/Wife N' Kids)

Damon Wayans and his younger brother, Marlon, make a terrific comedy team in *Mo' Money*. Loosely structured film has trouble meshing its very funny gag scenes with rough action footage, but it should earn mucho change from escapist fans.

Damon casts himself as a ne'er-do-well street punk who sets a poor role model for younger brother (Marlon). Their father was a cop who died in the line of duty, with his partner, Joe Santos, trying in vain to set the Wayans brothers on the right track.

To pursue a lovely romantic interest (Stacey Dash), Damon gets a job in the mailroom for her credit card company. Soon the Wayanses have cooked up a scam using uncanceled credit cards to finance a shopping spree. Coincidentally (and this is where Wayans's script falls apart), cop Santos is investigating a murder that's linked to a much larger credit card scam at the same company. Evil exec John Diehl is the ruthless mastermind who soon blackmails Damon into becoming his reluctant henchman.

Well-staged, showy and violent finale of Damon using his street smarts to act like his late father and collar the criminal is telegraphed too many reels ahead.

•

MONA LISA
1986, 104 mins, UK Ⓥ ⦿ col
Dir Neil Jordan ***Prod*** Stephen Woolley, Patrick Cassavetti ***Scr*** Neil Jordan ***Ph*** Roger Pratt ***Ed*** Lesley Walker ***Mus*** Michael Kamen ***Art*** Jamie Leonard
Act Bob Hoskins, Cathy Tyson, Michael Caine, Robbie Coltrane, Kate Hardie, Sammi Davis (HandMade/Palace)

The couple at the center of this wide and wayward romantic thriller are about as odd as you could find anywhere. George (Bob Hoskins), short in stature as well as intellect, is just out of prison. Simone (Cathy Tyson) is a tall, slender black whore who plies the poshest London hotels for her up-market trade. George gets a job driving Simone to her various assignations and finds himself falling in love with her. What follows is a pic that skillfully combines comedy and thriller, romance and sleaze. Simone takes advantage of George's feelings for her and assigns him to search for her missing girlfriend, a teenage blonde hooked on heroin and involved in the kinkier areas of the vice trade.

Hoskins gives another memorable performance as the earnest, dumb ex-con. Tyson brings charm and sensuality to the role of Simone and the rotund Robbie Coltrane is very funny as George's loyal friend. Michael Caine is around, too, in a generously self-effacing supporting role as a sinister, dangerous cockney vice king.

1986: NOMINATION: Best Actor (Bob Hoskins)

•

MONDO CANE
1962, 105 mins, Italy Ⓥ ⦿ col
Dir Gualtiero Jacopetti, Paolo Cavara, Franco Prosperi ***Scr*** Gualtiero Jacopetti ***Ph*** Antonio Climati, Benito Frattari ***Ed*** Gualtiero Jacopetti ***Mus*** Riz Ortolani, Nino Oliviero (Cineriz)

Various themes pop up along the way through this impressive, hard-hitting documentary feature, notably the cruel treatment inflicted on animals, including the human species. Vehicle is impressive on many counts: first, the material found on a round-the-world hunt; second, the juxtaposition of the various elements, sequences, and themes in order to provoke the viewer; third, the adult commentary which, in its original Italian version [spoken by Stefano Sibaldi], manages glibness, irony and satire without overdoing it.

While nearly all bits are patently real, there are two sequences (one concerning the slow death of all life on a Bikini atoll; the other depicting children polishing human skulls and bones in a Roman catacomb) which, despite assurances to the contrary, smack of staging.

Yet the total effect is grimly stimulating from the visual standpoint, depressing in the conclusions drawn. Whether one sides with his views or not, Gualtiero Jacopetti deserves credit for a shattering view of the world.

•

MONEY FOR NOTHING
1993, 100 mins, US Ⓥ ⦿ ▭ col
Dir Ramon Menendez ***Prod*** Tom Musca ***Scr*** Ramon Menendez, Tom Musca, Carol Sobieski ***Ph*** Tom Sigel ***Ed*** Nancy Richardson ***Mus*** Craig Safan ***Art*** Michelle Minch
Act John Cusack, Debi Mazar, Michael Madsen, Benicio Del Toro, Michael Rapaport, Maury Chaykin (Hollywood)

Money for Nothing is a predominantly serious film about a subject matter that seems rife with humor—an uneven true story about an out-of-work longshoreman who finds $1.2 million lying in the street.

John Cusack plays Joey Coyle, a none-too-bright, blue-collar guy who, at 26, is watching the American Dream slip by: He's living with his family in South Philadelphia, estranged from his girlfriend (Debi Mazar), and he can't even get his straight-arrow brother to give him work at the docks.

Joey finds a bundle of money that has fallen out of an armored car, and he starts dreaming of the good life. Unfortunately, his ill-advised use of the cash creates an easy trail for a local detective (Michael Madsen) to follow, while Joey gets in deeper and deeper over his head by trying to launder the loot through the mob.

Cusack plays essentially the same character he created in *Say Anything*—a directionless 20-something type with, for the most part, a good heart. His efforts to win back his gal prove endearing, although her reactions also convey the indecision that generally plagues the whole production.

•

MONEY PIT, THE
1986, 91 mins, US Ⓥ ⦿ col
Dir Richard Benjamin ***Prod*** Frank Marshall, Kathleen Kennedy, Art Levinson ***Scr*** David Giler ***Ph*** Gordon Willis ***Ed*** Jacqueline Cambas ***Mus*** Michel Colombier ***Art*** Patrizia Von Brandenstein
Act Shelley Long, Tom Hanks, Alexander Godunov, Maureen Stapleton, Joe Mantegna, Philip Bosco (Amblin)

The Money Pit is simply the pits. Shortly after the starring couple has bought a beautiful old house that quickly shows itself to be at the point of total disrepair, Tom Hanks says to Shelley Long, "It's a lemon, honey, let's face it." There is really very little else to be said about this gruesomely unfunny comedy.

Unofficial remake of the 1948 Cary Grant–Myrna Loy starrer *Mr. Blandings Builds His Dream House* begins unpromisingly and slides irrevocably downward from there.

Most of the scenes in this demolition derby begin with something or other caving in or falling apart, an event which is invariably followed by the two leads yelling and screaming at each other for minutes on end.

•

MONEY TRAIN
1995, 110 mins, US Ⓥ ⦿ col
Dir Joseph Ruben ***Prod*** Jon Peters, Neil Canton ***Scr*** Doug Richardson, David Loughery ***Ph*** John W. Lindley ***Ed*** George Bowers, Bill Pankow ***Mus*** Mark Mancina ***Art*** Bill Groom
Act Wesley Snipes, Woody Harrelson, Jennifer Lopez, Robert Blake, Chris Cooper, Joe Grifasi (Peters/Columbia)

In a wrinkle that feels fabricated by some packaging agent, Wesley Snipes and Woody Harrelson play foster brothers (there are plenty of jokes about the lack of a resemblance) who work as New York City transit cops. John (Snipes) is protective of Charlie (Harrelson), a free spirit who gets himself indebted to the mob in a high-stakes poker game and keeps aggravating their obsessive boss, Patterson (wildly overplayed by Robert Blake).

Though the two spend most of the movie chasing pickpockets and a crazed arsonist around the subway, Charlie keeps dreaming about robbing the money train—a subway car that collects all the revenue garnered from the transit system each day. The brothers also find their relationship strained as they vie for the attention of their new partner, Grace (Jennifer Lopez). It takes the movie more than 80 minutes before the main story line actually kicks in, as the story rolls along in confusing fashion, seemingly unable to settle on a direction.

Director Joseph Ruben doesn't bring much suspense to the proceedings, and the script [from a screen story by Doug Richardson] features a few laughs but plenty of completely inane and hackneyed dialogue. Pic's saving grace is Snipes, who really is the centerpiece of this ride, with Harrelson's character acting as the baggage within the framework of the story and in general.

•

MONEY TRAP, THE
1966, 91 mins, US ▭ b/w
Dir Burt Kennedy ***Prod*** Max E. Youngstein, David Karr ***Scr*** Walter Bernstein ***Ph*** Paul C. Vogel ***Ed*** John McSweeney ***Mus*** Hal Schaefer ***Art*** George W. Davis, Carl Anderson
Act Glenn Ford, Elke Sommer, Rita Hayworth, Ricardo Montalban, Joseph Cotten, Tom Reese (M-G-M)

A story of a policeman-turned-thief, *The Money Trap* is aptly named—but only as far as production coin is concerned. A cliché-plotted, tritely written script that is not to be believed could not be salvaged even by far better direction and performances.

Walter Bernstein's adaptation of a Lionel White novel has the kernel of a good drama about a contemporary problem, that of an underpaid gumshoe dazzled into dishonesty by the riches of the criminals whom he encounters. Nearly all interest in this angle is snuffed out by extraneous, unbelievable subplots.

Specifically, Glenn Ford is the cop, husband of Elke Sommer. They live in a splashy pad made possible by her father's will and stocks. When the latter pass a divvy, hard times loom. Wife's idea to economize: fire the servants.

Add Joseph Cotten, a medic who supposedly works for the Syndicate. When he kills a junkie accomplice and reports it as self-defense from a supposed burglary, Ford gets the theft idea, keeps it from Ricardo Montalban (his partner, who later finds out and wants in).

•

MONKEY BUSINESS
1931, 78 mins, US Ⓥ ⦿ b/w
Dir Norman Z. McLeod ***Prod*** [uncredited] ***Scr*** S. J. Perelman, Will B. Johnstone, Arthur Sheekman ***Ph*** Arthur L. Todd ***Ed*** [uncredited] ***Mus*** [uncredited] ***Art*** [uncredited]
Act Groucho Marx, Harpo Marx, Chico Marx, Zeppo Marx, Thelma Todd, Tom Kennedy (Paramount)

The usual Marx madhouse and plenty of laughs sprouting from a plot structure resembling one of those California bungalows, which spring up over night.

It starts with the foursome as stowaways on a class liner, and switches to shore as the quartet evenly divide up to become bodyguards for a couple of racketeers. Switch makes the only slow portion being like an intermission with the boys having to start all over again.

Leads to the kidnapping of one gangster's daughter (Ruth Hall) from a masquerade ball, with the finish a free-for-all between Zeppo (the youngest) and the heavy in a barn as Groucho gags his way from rafter to rafter and in and out of the hay.

Harpo's main sequence is a mix up in a Punch and Judy show evolving from a chase, while Groucho is always slipping through his double-meaning quips. Thelma Todd, a consistant eyeful, the subject of these cracks, with Rockcliffe Fellowes, who hasn't been around in some time, and Harry Woods as the well-dressed gangsters.

•

MONKEY BUSINESS
1952, 97 mins, US Ⓥ ⦿ b/w
Dir Howard Hawks ***Prod*** Sol C. Siegel ***Scr*** Ben Hecht, Charles Lederer, I.A.L. Diamond ***Ph*** Milton Krasner ***Ed*** William B. Murphy ***Mus*** Leigh Harline ***Art*** Lyle Wheeler, George Patrick
Act Cary Grant, Ginger Rogers, Charles Coburn, Marilyn Monroe, Hugh Marlowe, Larry Keating (20th Century-Fox)

Attempt to draw out a thin, familiar slapstick idea isn't carried off.

Story has Cary Grant as a matured research chemist, working on a formula to regenerate human tissue and using monkeys in his lab as guinea pigs for his elixir-of-youth experiments. Ginger Rogers is his amiable wife, still madly enough in love with him to forgive his absentmindedness.

One of the lab monkeys breaks loose, mixes up an assortment of chemical ingredients lying about, dumps the concoction into the watercooler. First Grant, then Rogers, drink from the cooler, and immediately get teenage notions, emotions and symptoms.

Grant plays the role sometimes as if his heart isn't completely in it. Rogers, looking beautiful, makes as gay a romp of it as she can. Marilyn Monroe's sex appeal is played up for all it's worth (and that's not inconsiderable), as she appears as a nitwit secretary.

•

MONKEYS, GO HOME!
1967, 101 mins, US Ⓥ col
Dir Andrew V. McLaglen ***Prod*** Ron Miller ***Scr*** Maurice Tombragel ***Ph*** William Snyder ***Ed*** Marsh Hendry ***Mus*** Robert F. Brunner ***Art*** Carroll Clark, John B. Mansbridge
Act Maurice Chevalier, Dean Jones, Yvette Mimieux, Bernard Woringer, Clement Harari (Walt Disney)

Set in France but filmed completely in Walt Disney's Studio, *Monkeys, Go Home* is an amusing comedy-romance in which Dean Jones, heir to an olive farm, provokes political and romantic complications when he decides to use chimpanzee labor. Maurice Chevalier heads the cast as a village priest. Film has the usual professional Disney blend of children, animals, humor and charm.

In adapting G. K. Wilkinson's novel [*The Monkeys*], Maurice Tombragel has effected a subtle introduction of an implied Cold War situation. Title is a play on the "Yankee Go Home" slogan, herein applied to Jones's monkeys who create a capitalist issue in a small French town.

Jones, always a good underplaying comedian, reacts adroitly to the script demands that he be, variously, frustrated, angry and moonstruck, all the while remaining completely likeable. Chevalier, a showbiz legend, scores in projecting a benign worldliness.

•

MONKEY SHINES
1988, 115 mins, US Ⓥ ⦿ col
Dir George A. Romero ***Prod*** Charles Evans ***Scr*** George A. Romero ***Ph*** James A. Contner ***Ed*** Pasquale Buba ***Mus*** David Shire ***Art*** Cletus Anderson
Act Jason Beghe, John Pankow, Melanie Parker, Joyce Van Patten (Orion)

Monkey Shines is a befuddled story about a man constrained from the neck down told by a director confused from the neck up.

Jason Beghe starts out as a very virile, able-bodied young man with everything going for him, an up-and-coming physical specimen much desired by girlfriend Janine Turner and fawned over by mother, Joyce Van Patten.

An accident robs Beghe of all physical ability below his jawline, leaving him despondently dependent on an array of technology.

As melodrama, this is all pretty good stuff and could have continued to a convincing conclusion. But by contract, inclination and reputation (not to mention the book [by Michael Stewart] the film's based on), Romero is a horror-film director.

So here comes Beghe's best friend John Pankow, a yuppie mad scientist busy at the nearby university slicing up the brain of a dead Jane Doe and injecting the hormones into monkeys to make them smarter.

To help his friend, Pankow volunteers one of his highly intelligent, chemically dependent capuchins to be trained by Melanie Parker to serve as Beghe's companion and helper. For a while, this all works beautifully. Until something dreadful happens.

•

MONKEY TROUBLE
1994, 95 mins, US Ⓥ ⦿ col
Dir Franco Amurri ***Prod*** Mimi Polk, Heidi Rufus Isaacs ***Scr*** Franco Amurri, Stu Krieger ***Ph*** Luciano Tovoli ***Ed*** Ray Lovejoy, Chris Peppe ***Mus*** Mark Mancina ***Art*** Les Dilley
Act "Finster," Thora Birch, Harvey Keitel, Mimi Rogers, Christopher McDonald, Kevin Scannell (New Line/Scott-Main)

Starring an adorably cute Capuchin monkey, which performs magnificent tricks, *Monkey Trouble* is a touching children's adventure that belongs among the great animal movies. With Harvey Keitel in a refreshingly different role and beautiful child-star Thora Birch, this sentimental family yarn boasts a superlative production.

Nine-year-old Eva Gregory (Birch) desperately wants a pet, but Mom (Mimi Rogers) thinks she's not mature and responsible enough to take care of one. Opportunity knocks when Shorty Kohn (Harvey Keitel), a gypsy hustler, loses his pet, a Capuchin monkey trained to entertain and lift the wallets and jewelry of the crowds along Venice Beach's boardwalk. Shorty, who's about to pull a big heist with two crooks, has abused his pet so much that the monkey really hates him.

This is the premise to an endearing children's fantasy that can be summed as "girl meets monkey, girl loses monkey, girl finds monkey." As can be expected, the good cast of adult actors mostly plays second banana roles, except for Keitel.

•

MON ONCLE
(MY UNCLE)
1958, 120 mins, France/Italy Ⓥ ⦿ col
Dir Jacques Tati ***Scr*** Jacques Tati, Jacques Lagrange, Jean L'Hote ***Ph*** Jean Bourgoin ***Ed*** Suzanne Baron ***Mus*** Alain Romans, Franck Barcellini ***Art*** Henri Schmitt
Act Jacques Tati, Jean-Pierre Zola, Alain Becourt, Adrienne Servanti, Lucien Fregis, Betty Schneider (Specta/Gray/Alter/Centauro)

Somewhat long for a comedy, Jacques Tati's film has inventiveness, gags, warmth and a "poetic" approach to satire. Film took two years to make. Tati has built it via comic juxtaposition of two ways of life—his, as the eccentric, independent uncle, alongside a super-modern, hygienic, materialistic brother-in-law.

Antiseptic house of Hulot's (Tati) relatives operates a myriad of time-saving but noisy electronic gadgets. Tati is the catalyst who unintentionally creates havoc. He wins over his nephew whose parents have no time for him and who is only really happy during the wonderful escapades with his uncle. But Tati is finally sent off to be a traveling representative of the brother-in-law's firm.

Satire is not barbed or vicious and everybody can laugh at it and themselves. There's expert blocking out of the characters, creative use of sound, and eschewing of all useless dialog. An English version is nine minutes shorter.

1958: Best Foreign Language Film

•

MONSIEUR BEAUCAIRE
1946, 90 mins, US b/w
Dir George Marshall ***Prod*** Paul Jones ***Scr*** Melvin Frank, Norman Panama ***Ph*** Lionel Lindon ***Ed*** Arthur Schmidt ***Mus*** Robert Emmett Dolan ***Art*** Hans Dreier, Earl Hedrick
Act Bob Hope, Joan Caulfield, Patric Knowles, Cecil Kellaway (Paramount)

Monsieur Beaucaire is a frantic, screwballish version of Booth Tarkington's costume novel of high adventure in the days of silk-stockinged heroes. As such it has plenty of giggles and a few solidly premised laughs.

With the script handed him, George Marshall's direction measures up. He knows his way around a broadly aimed gag or situation, and proves it by milking each to its limit. Therein lies a fault of *Beaucaire*. Many sequences that could have played out on their own merits are unnecessarily embellished and eventually detract from the basically amusing yarn about a court barber forced to impersonate royalty.

Bob Hope plays the French barber, Beaucaire, with all stops out, waltzes through trying situations and varied romances with a bravado that is his particular forte. It's all fun, but could have been even more so if treated with a bit less broadness.

•

MONSIEUR HIRE
(M. HIRE)
1989, 79 mins, France Ⓥ ⦿ ▭ col
Dir Patrice Leconte ***Prod*** Philippe Carcassonne, Rene Cleitman ***Scr*** Patrice Leconte, Patrick Dewolf ***Ph*** Denis Lenoir ***Ed*** Joelle Hache ***Mus*** Michael Nyman ***Art*** Yvan Maussion
Act Michel Blanc, Sandrine Bonnaire, Luc Thuillier, Andre Wilms (Cinea/Hachette Premiere/FR3)

Michel Blanc, the bald, diminutive funnyman, plays it utterly straight in *Monsieur Hire*, an unconvincing adaptation of a 1933 novel by Georges Simenon, first filmed as *Panique* by Julien Duvivier in 1946.

Simenon's novel [*Les fiancailles de M. Hire*], about a lonely misanthropic man framed for a murder by a ruthless pair of lovers and hounded to death by a mob of neighbors, has been watered down. Script virtually does away with the social background and the frightening depiction of mob violence, which figured prominently in Duvivier's film. Worse, M. Hire, the protagonist, a sleazy minor felon chez Simenon (and memorably protrayed by Michel Simon under Duvivier), has been morally sanitized. The character is, if not a model citizen, a basically conventional outsider who's always impeccably dressed, keeps a cage of pet white mice, and regularly visits a brothel.

He's transfixed by the attractive young woman Alice (Sandrine Bonnaire) who lives across the courtyard and who doesn't believe in curtains. When Alice realizes she is being watched, she begins coming on to the lovesick voyeur who offers to take her abroad away from her sordid life. Blanc does a creditable if not credible job as M. Hire in a dour, no-nonsense performance. Bonnaire gives some ambiguities and touching shadings to the two-faced girl. Luc Thuillier, however, has nothing much to do as Bonnaire's ne'er-do-well lover. Film apparently is the 50th motion picture adapted from Simenon.

•

MONSIEUR VERDOUX
1947, 122 mins, US Ⓥ b/w
Dir Charles Chaplin ***Prod*** Charles Chaplin ***Scr*** Charles Chaplin ***Ph*** Rollie Totheroh ***Ed*** Willard Nico ***Mus*** Charles Chaplin ***Art*** John Beckman
Act Charles Chaplin, Martha Raye, Isobel Elsom, Marilyn Nash, Irving Bacon, William Frawley (United Artists)

Comedy based on the characterization of a modern Parisian Bluebeard treads dangerous shoals indeed. Even if the accent were more effective, the fundamentals are unsound when it's revealed that Chaplin has been driven to marrying and murdering middling mesdames in order to provide for his ailing wife and their son of 10 years' marriage.

Chaplin generates little sympathy. His broad-mannered antics, as a many-aliased fop on the make for impressionable matrons; the telltale technique, a hangover from his bankteller's days, of counting the bundles of francs in the traditional nervous manner of rapid finger movement; the business of avoiding Martha Raye at that garden party, when he finally woos and wins Isobel Elsom; the neo–*American Tragedy* hokum in the rowboat-on-the-lake scene with Raye; the mixed bottles of poisoned wine [again Raye, with old-time musicomedy star Ada-May (Weeks) as the blowsy buxom blonde of a maid in support]; and all the rest of it is only spotty.

Chaplin's endeavor to get his "common man" ideology into the film militates against its comedy values. Point is that depressions in the economy force us into being ruthless villains and murderers, despite the fact we are actually kind and sympathetic.

Chaplin also rings in another of his favorite themes, his strong feelings against war.

Chaplin's direction is disjointed on occasion, although perhaps the natural enough result of a leisurely production schedule that ranged up to five years. Chaplin's score, however, is above par, fortifying the progression in no small measure.

1947: NOMINATION: Best Original Screenplay

•

MONSIGNOR
1982, 122 mins, US Ⓥ col
Dir Frank Perry ***Prod*** Frank Yablans, David Niven, Jr. ***Scr*** Abraham Polonsky, Wendell Mayes ***Ph*** Billy Williams ***Ed*** Peter E. Berger ***Mus*** John Williams ***Art*** John DeCuir
Act Christopher Reeve, Genevieve Bujold, Fernando Rey, Jason Miller, Joe Cortese, Adolfo Celi (20th Century-Fox/Yablans)

Lots of potential for a rare, absorbing, behind-the-scenes look at the Vatican is totally blown in *Monsignor*. Constructed as a scene-by-scene "expose" of all sorts of nefarious goings-on in post–Second World War Rome, the self-serious $12 million pic [from the novel by Jack Alain Leger] teeters on the brink of being an all-out-hoot through much of its running time.

Introductory sequences briefly limn Brooklyn boy Christopher Reeve's ordination and subsequent service as a military chaplain on the European front, where he commits his first major priestly sin by gunning down a bunch of Nazis.

Upon reaching Rome, brash kid makes a big impression on Papal assistant Fernando Rey and is given control over the financially ailing church's commissary. Reeve makes use of his position to strike a deal with Sicilian mafioso Jason Miller to share in black market profits.

The rising opportunist meets novice nun Genevieve Bujold, and it isn't long before the two bed down.

It's amazing that neither Abraham Polonsky nor Wendell Mayes, both outstanding screenwriters, didn't spot the most gaping fundamental flaw here, namely the lack of any convincing explanation why Reeve's character became a priest in the first place.

•

MONSTER IN A BOX
1991, 88 mins, UK Ⓥ col
Dir Nick Broomfield ***Prod*** Jon Blair ***Scr*** Spalding Gray ***Ph*** Michael Coulter ***Ed*** Graham Hutchings ***Mus*** Laurie Anderson ***Art*** Ray Oxley
Act Spalding Gray (Blair)

Spalding Gray struts his anecdotal stuff once again in *Monster in a Box*, a frisky follow-up to *Swimming to Cambodia* and film rendition of his 1990 stage hit.

Titular "Monster" is Gray's 1,800-page autobiography, *Impossible Vacation*. Starting his peregrinations in 1987, Gray recounts how celeb status after *Swimming* gave him plenty of excuses to procrastinate. The easy laughs come at the start: East Coaster Gray's barbed comments on Tinseltown, where execs invite him to "idea lunches" and CAA woos him in hyper meetings. Subsequent divertissements include Columbia Pictures' putting him on a U.S. fact-finding mission to Nicaragua (a comic horror show), AIDS hysteria in New York, a flying saucer project for HBO, taking *Swimming* to the Moscow fest and Gotham critics' trashing of his perf in Gregory Mosher's Broadway production of *Our Town*.

Pic was shot at London's Riverside Studios before a live aud (seen briefly at first and occasionally heard reacting).

•

MONTE CARLO
1930, 93 mins, US Ⓥ b/w
Dir Ernst Lubitsch ***Scr*** Ernest Vajda, Vincent Lawrence ***Ph*** Victor Milner ***Art*** Hans Dreier
Act Jack Buchanan, Jeanette MacDonald, ZaSu Pitts, Claud Allister (Paramount)

If it were not for Jeanette MacDonald there would be no picture, this despite the disappointing direction of Ernst Lubitsch and the talker debut of England's Jack Buchanan.

There are a couple of catchy songs among the several—"Always in All Ways" and "Give Me a Moment."

MacDonald plays well all of the time, at moments exceptionally. MacDonald's singing is also most acceptable.

Buchanan is just the usual sort of juve with closely plastered down hair, doing a ladies hairdresser, a role that hurts.

It's that sort of a story, common [from Hans Mueller's *Blue Coast*]. A count, to meet an unknown countess, maneuvers to get her hairdresser's job, which he does. Then he wins, he says, 200,000 francs to take her out of Monte Carlo hock. About that time, as they both see *Monsieur Beaucaire* in different boxes at the theater, she surmises he isn't a hairdresser. It needs 90 minutes of film to unravel that.

•

MONTE WALSH
1970, 99 mins, US Ⓥ ▭ col
Dir William A. Fraker ***Prod*** Hal Landers, Bobby Roberts ***Scr*** Lukas Heller, David Zelag Goodman ***Ph*** David M. Walsh ***Ed*** Dick Brockway ***Mus*** John Barry ***Art*** Al Brenner
Act Lee Marvin, Jeanne Moreau, Jack Palance, Mitch Ryan, Jim Davis, John "Bear" Hudkins (Cinema Center)

Monte Walsh is a listless, wandering story of the old American West, which takes too long to get moving. Lee Marvin stars as a taciturn roughneck whose tragic romance with Jeanne Moreau comes across as irrelevant digression in a confused story.

This film [from a novel by Jack Schaefer] attempts meaningful exposition of the reality of an aging cowboy. Unfortunately, it appears that Marvin was simply playing his image, while other thesps were going through uncertain motions, and nobody had an eye out for exactly what direction the film was supposed to be taking.

Moreau's scenes are more like padded inserts than vital plot turns. The basic feeble theme is what happened to prototype pioneers when Eastern money bought up ranches and began operating long-distance.

•

MONTH IN THE COUNTRY, A
1987, 96 mins, UK Ⓥ ⊙ col
Dir Pat O'Connor ***Prod*** Kenith Trodd ***Scr*** Simon Gray ***Ph*** Kenneth MacMillan ***Ed*** John Victor Smith ***Mus*** Howard Blake ***Art*** Leo Austin
Act Colin Firth, Kenneth Branagh, Natasha Richardson, Patrick Malahide, Richard Vernon (Euston)

A Month in the Country is a gentle but moving pic [from the novel by J. L. Carr] about two men recovering from the horrors of World War I during an idyllic summer in remote rolling English countryside.

Pic opens with Birkin (Colin Firth) arriving at the remote Yorkshire village of Oxgodby to uncover a medieval wall painting in the local church. There he meets Moon (Kenneth Branagh), who is excavating a grave outside the churchyard.

Both are tormented by their war experiences, but during a beautiful summer month they experience the tranquility of the idyllic community that gradually helps them come to terms with their problems.

Birkin falls in love with the wife (Natasha Richardson) of an unfriendly local vicar, but never lets on to her about his passion, while the Branagh character turns out to be a homosexual.

Firth and Branagh are talented young actors—especially Branagh who has great screen presence. Richardson looks slightly uncomfortable in a very understated role.

•

MONTY PYTHON AND THE HOLY GRAIL
1975, 89 mins, UK Ⓥ ⊙ col
Dir Terry Gilliam, Terry Jones ***Prod*** Mark Forstater ***Scr*** Graham Chapman, John Cleese, Terry Gilliam, Eric Idle, Terry Jones, Michael Palin ***Ph*** Terry Bedford ***Ed*** John Hackney ***Mus*** DeWolfe ***Art*** Roy Smith
Act Graham Chapman, John Cleese, Terry Gilliam, Eric Idle, Terry Jones, Michael Palin (Python)

Monty Python's Flying Circus, the British comedy group that gained fame via BBC-TV, send-up Arthurian legend, performed in whimsical fashion with Graham Chapman an effective straight man as King Arthur.

Story deals with Arthur's quest for the Holy Grail and his battles along the way with various villains and is basically an excuse for set pieces, some amusing, others overdone.

Running gags include lack of horses for Arthur and his men, and a lackey clicking cocoanuts together to make suitable hoof noises as the men trot along. The extravagantly gruesome fight scenes, including one which ends with a man having all four limbs severed, will get laughs from some and make others squirm.

•

MONTY PYTHON'S LIFE OF BRIAN
SEE: LIFE OF BRIAN

•

MONTY PYTHON'S THE MEANING OF LIFE
1983, 103 mins, UK Ⓥ ⊙ col
Dir Terry Jones ***Prod*** John Goldstone ***Scr*** Graham Chapman, John Cleese, Terry Gilliam, Eric Idle, Terry Jones, Michael Palin ***Ph*** Peter Hannan ***Ed*** Julian Doyle ***Mus*** Eric Idle, Terry Jones, Michael Palin, Graham Chapman, John Cleese, John du Prez, Dave Howman, Andre Jacquemin ***Art*** Harry Lange
Act Graham Chapman, John Cleese, Terry Gilliam, Eric Idle, Terry Jones, Michael Palin (HandMade)

Gross, silly, caustic, tasteless and obnoxious are all adjectives that alternately apply to *Monty Python's The Meaning of Life* though probably the most appropriate description would simply be funny.

Pic opens with an amusing short film of its own where elderly workers unite against their younger bosses and then segues to the real task—finding the meaning of life. Tracing the human existence from birth through death, the group touches on such areas as religion, education, marriage, sex and war in a way it was no doubt never taught in school or in the home. Though there are some rough spots along the way (some of the passages on war don't register) most of the sections get their maximum comedic punch by not being allowed to linger for too long.

The writing truly offers bits of comedic brilliance though, like any film of this nature, has a few duds mixed in.

•

MOON AND SIXPENCE, THE
1943, 89 mins, US Ⓥ col
Dir Albert Lewin ***Prod*** David L. Loew ***Scr*** Albert Lewin ***Ph*** John F. Seitz ***Ed*** George Hively, Richard L. Van Enger ***Mus*** Dimitri Tiomkin ***Art*** Gordon Wiles
Act George Sanders, Herbert Marshall, Doris Dudley, Steven Geray, Eric Blore, Florence Bates (United Artists)

Somerset Maugham's widely read novel has been made into an intriguing, distinctive screen vehicle. The story of an English stockbroker who reached for the moon and ultimately won fame as a painter, only just before his death, at times is reminiscent of *Citizen Kane*.

While Herbert Marshall figures importantly, as he retraces the story of the painter, it is really George Sanders's picture. He makes the strange life of the struggling artist live, and it's his outstanding screen role to date.

The episodes in the distant island of Tahiti are rich in tropical flavor. The Tahitian portion of the story offers startling contrast in humorous moments and in most impressive scenes of film.

Albert Lewin's direction is keenly intelligent, shifting readily from lighter, funny moments to the harshly dramatic. Camerawork of John F. Seitz is on the same high plane. Sepia tone is employed in all Tahiti parts of the film, with color used in last few scenes when Sanders's hut is burned.

1943: NOMINATION: Best Scoring of a Dramatic Picture

•

MOONFLEET
1955, 86 mins, US Ⓥ ⊙ ▭ col
Dir Fritz Lang ***Prod*** John Houseman ***Scr*** Jan Lustig, Margaret Fitts ***Ph*** Robert Planck ***Ed*** Albert Akst ***Mus*** Miklos Rozsa, Vicente Gomez ***Art*** Cedric Gibbons, Hans Peters
Act Stewart Granger, George Sanders, Joan Greenwood, Viveca Lindfors, Jon Whiteley, Liliane Montevecchi (M-G-M)

Costumed action, well-spiced with loose ladies and dashing rakehellies, is offered in *Moonfleet*. With mood and action the keynote of the John Houseman production, the direction by Fritz Lang plays both hard, developing considerable movement in several rugged action sequences without neglecting suspense. Period of the J. Meade Falkner novel is the 1750s.

Stewart Granger was a good choice for the dubious hero of the story, a high-living dandy who heads a gang of murderous smugglers headquartering in the English coastal village of Moonfleet. Yarn opens on a Macbeth note of cold, wild-swept moors, and scary, dark shadows, establishing an eerie flavor for the kickoff.

Later, it reminds of *Treasure Island* a bit when Granger and a small boy go through some highly imaginative adventures.

•

MOON IN THE GUTTER, THE
SEE: LA LUNE DANS LE CANIVEAU

•

MOON IS DOWN, THE
1943, 90 mins, US Ⓥ b/w
Dir Irving Pichel ***Prod*** Nunnally Johnson ***Scr*** Nunnally Johnson ***Ph*** Arthur Miller ***Ed*** Louis Loeffler ***Mus*** Alfred Newman
Act Cedric Hardwicke, Henry Travers, Lee J. Cobb, Peter Van Eyck (20th Century-Fox)

The story is the thing here and the way it's treated on casting, direction, sound and production justifies 20th-Fox's investment of $300,000 for the basic film rights [to John Steinbeck's novel]. Though lacking names that mean much to filmgoers, casting for every role is socko from Cedric Hardwicke down to the bit appearance by Dorothy Peterson.

Story of Norway's invasion and resulting undercover uprising is familiar. Here it becomes the fight of inhabitants to survive in all conquered lands. There's the punishing of obdurate citizens, the executions to halt sabotage and dropping of dynamite by "chute" to help this program with blasting of rail lines, bridges, radio, etc., finally bringing the mass hanging of top village officials.

Director Pichel also plays an innkeeper bit in the dramatic snub scene when all village celebrants leave soon after the arrival of the Nazi lieutenant, and proves he's still a polished screen performer.

•

MOONLIGHT AND VALENTINO
1995, 104 mins, US Ⓥ col
Dir David Anspaugh ***Prod*** Alison Owen, Eric Fellner, Tim Bevan ***Scr*** Ellen Simon ***Ph*** Julio Macat ***Ed*** David Rosenbloom ***Mus*** Howard Shore ***Art*** Robb Wilson King
Act Elizabeth Perkins, Whoopi Goldberg, Gwyneth Paltrow, Kathleen Turner, Jon Bon Jovi, Peter Coyote (Working Title)

Sharply observed, if a tad too earnest, *Moonlight and Valentino* is a sensitive comedy-drama about coming to terms with deeply personal loss and its bitter aftermath, with terrific female cast headed by a superlative Elizabeth Perkins.

Adapted by Ellen Simon from her semi-autobiographical stage play, story revolves around Rebecca Lott (Perkins), a young, attractive, happily married woman whose husband is hit by a car while jogging. Shellshocked and disoriented, she stubbornly refuses at first to acknowledge the "W" word (widow) to her eccentric best friend, Sylvie (Whoopi Goldberg).

In addition to Sylvie, Rebecca's support group includes Lucy (Gwyneth Paltrow), her neurotic, virginal younger sister, and Alberta (Kathleen Turner), their overbearing former stepmother. Sylvie fears that her hubby (unbilled Peter Coyote) will leave her. Lucy has her own hang-ups, including deep anxiety about her body and bashful apprehension about dating men.

Things begin to change in pic's second part, when, as a birthday present for Rebecca, Alberta hires a sexy house painter (Jon Bon Jovi) to "spruce up her siding." The presence of the mysterious hunk causes each of the four women to peel away her facade, confront her true identity—and ultimately share her innermost feelings and fantasies.

Though screenplay betrays its theatrical origins, Simon resists the temptation to construct the women as broad types (widow, virgin, divorcée and wife). Scripter also resists the temptation to emulate her famous father (Neil Simon) in his younger years, eschewing one-liners in favor of humor that stems directly from the intensely dramatic interactions.

These four actresses ignite the screen with so much power and charisma that one yearns for more ensemble scenes.

•

MOONLIGHTING
1982, 97 mins, UK Ⓥ ⦿ col
Dir Jerzy Skolimowski ***Prod*** Mark Shivas, Jerzy Skolimowski ***Scr*** Jerzy Skolimowski ***Ph*** Tony Pierce-Roberts ***Ed*** Barry Vince ***Mus*** Stanley Myers ***Art*** Tony Woollard
Act Jeremy Irons, Eugene Lipinski, Jiri Stanislaw, Eugeniusz Haczkiewicz (White)

Jerzy Skolimowski made this film in 18 weeks—apparently a meditation on what happened in Poland when the military took over in December 1981 as seen by a Pole in Britain at the time.

Four Poles are sent to London by their boss who owns a house there to fix it up. They go off a week before military law is declared. The boss, a corrupt Communist, owns a building company, and the four are headed by Jeremy Irons who is the only one who can speak English.

The crew wants to finish, buy things for their family, and go home. Irons pushes the work but then finds out about the military coup. He decides to keep it from the others. The men finally turn against him because of his overbearing attitude, and it develops Irons was never a member of Solidarity.

Film is inventive, though anecdotal.

•

MOONLIGHT SONATA
1937, 90 mins, UK Ⓥ b/w
Dir Lothar Mendes ***Scr*** Edward Knoblock, E. M. Delafield ***Ph*** Jan Stallich
Act Ignace Jan Paderewski, Charles Farrell, Marie Tempest, Barbara Green, Eric Portman, Graham Browne (Pall Mall)

Charming love story woven round the central personality of the world-famous pianist, Paderewski. For the highbrows there will probably not be enough of the maestro's genius—for the lowbrows, there will certainly be too much.

Locale is Sweden, where Charles Farrell, agent for a country estate, declares his love for Ingrid, granddaughter of the baroness, by whom he is employed. Forced landing by a passenger plane bound for Paris brings into the household for temporary hospitality three men, one of them Paderewski; another, a plausible, much-traveled gent of doubtful antecedents.

Baroness is honoured by the presence of the famous musician but soon distrusts the boastful young man-about-town. He makes a play for the young girl, who, having led a hermitlike existence, gets carried away by his worldliness and is hopelessly infatuated.

Charles Farrell has little to do but look on wistfully while his lady is alienated from him; Eric Portman gives a polished, scoundrelly performance; Barbara Greene is attractive and sincere as Ingrid; Marie Tempest, in her first screen role, is her usual delightful self. Of the aged maestro there can be no criticism; they wished to weave a story around him, and artistically and unpretentiously they have succeeded.

•

MOON OVER PARADOR
1988, 105 mins, US Ⓥ ⦿ col
Dir Paul Mazursky ***Prod*** Paul Mazursky ***Scr*** Leon Capetanos, Paul Mazursky ***Ph*** Donald McAlpine ***Ed*** Stuart Pappe ***Mus*** Maurice Jarre ***Art*** Pato Guzman
Act Richard Dreyfuss, Raul Julia, Sonia Braga, Jonathan Winters, Fernando Rey, Sammy Davis, Jr. (Universal)

Paul Mazursky's elaborate farce [from a story by Charles G. Booth] about the actor as imposter (here posing as dictator of the mythical Latin nation Parador) has moments of true hilarity emerging only fitfully from a ponderous production.

Pic has Richard Dreyfuss well cast as a fairly successful stage and film actor on a location shoot in the English-speaking Parador. He's given an offer he can't refuse by police chief Raul Julia to impersonate the just-deceased dictator.

Dreyfuss reluctantly adopts the role, but soon takes on the new persona in earnest after being coached by the dictator's sexy mistress Madonna (Sonia Braga in a flamboyant, delicious turn).

Ruse comes to a climax when Dreyfuss starts instituting reforms inimical to Julia and other powerful interests.

Dreyfuss's panache carries the film most of the way, ably played off Braga's lusty and glamourous character. Julia is very convincing as the stern local despot and Jonathan Winters makes the most of his transparent Ugly American role as a CIA man in Parador.

•

MOONRAKER
1979, 126 mins, UK Ⓥ ⦿ ▭ col
Dir Lewis Gilbert ***Prod*** Albert R. Broccoli ***Scr*** Christopher Wood ***Ph*** Jean Tournier ***Ed*** John Glen ***Mus*** John Barry ***Art*** Ken Adam
Act Roger Moore, Lois Chiles, Michael Lonsdale, Richard Kiel, Bernard Lee, Corinne Clery (United Artists/Eon)

Christopher Wood's script takes the characters exactly where they always go in a James Bond pic and the only question is whether the stunts and gadgets will live up to expectations. They do.

The main problem this time is the outer-space setting, which somehow dilutes the mammoth monstrosity that 007 must save the world from. One more big mothership hovering over earth becomes just another model intercut with elaborate interiors.

The visual effects, stuntwork and other technical contributions all work together expertly to make the most preposterous notions believable. And Roger Moore, though still compared to Sean Connery, clearly has adapted the James Bond character to himself and serves well as the wisecracking, incredibly daring and irresistible hero.

1979: NOMINATION: Best Visual Effects

•

MOON-SPINNERS, THE
1964, 118 mins, UK Ⓥ ⦿ col
Dir James Neilson ***Prod*** Bill Anderson ***Scr*** Michael Dyne ***Ph*** Paul Beeson, John Wilcox, Michael Reed ***Ed*** Gordon Stone ***Mus*** Ron Grainer ***Art*** Tony Masters
Act Hayley Mills, Eli Wallach, Peter McEnery, Joan Greenwood, Irene Papas, Pola Negri (Walt Disney)

With a mixture of American, English and Greek talents, engaged in a silly but zestful tale of villainy undone, told against some photogenic landscapes, *Moon-Spinners* naturally concentrates on Hayley Mills. With action the keyword in the loosely knit script [from Mary Stewart's novel] this keeps the young lady perpetually on the move. Her adventures into first puppy-love and feats of derring-do are accomplished with equal amounts of energy. She's never still long enough for her virtue or her life to be in danger.

Tale chiefly concerns two English females (Mills and Joan Greenwood) becoming involved in a jewel-theft adventure that concerns the Moon-Spinners, the Cretan inn where they're staying. The intrigue includes an odd but colorful assortment of local types headed by Eli Wallach, a most hissable villain, his sister (Irene Papas) and a young, mysterious Englishman (Peter McEnery).

Wallach comes off best by playing his villainy straight—vicious, unfeeling and rotten to the core. He'd willingly shoot his nephew to keep the boy's mother from ratting on him. Irene Papas, a superb Greek actress with a wonderfully expressive face, gives more dignity and feeling to her tiny role than it deserves.

•

MOONSTRUCK
1987, 102 mins, US Ⓥ ⦿ col
Dir Norman Jewison ***Prod*** Patrick Palmer ***Scr*** John Patrick Shanley ***Ph*** David Watkin ***Ed*** Lou Lombardo ***Mus*** Dick Hyman ***Art*** Philip Rosenberg
Act Cher, Nicolas Cage, Vincent Gardenia, Olympia Dukakis, Danny Aiello, Julie Bovasso (M-G-M)

Norman Jewison's film is a mostly appetizing blend of comedy and drama carried by snappy dialog and a wonderful ensemble full of familiar faces. Leads Cher and Nicolas Cage are both solid and appealing, but it's the pic's older lovers—especially the splendidly controlled Olympia Dukakis—who give *Moonstruck* its endearing spirit.

Cher is Loretta Castorini, a vaguely dour, superstitious widow who believes her previous marriage—she was wed at City Hall, her father didn't give her away, her husband was killed when he was hit by a bus—was felled by bad luck.

Film begins with her accepting a wedding proposal, on bended knee, from the altogether unprepossessing Johnny Cammareri (Danny Aiello), who shortly thereafter heads off to Sicily to be at the bedside of his dying mother.

Loretta, resigned to accepting mediocrity (she admits to her mother that she doesn't love Johnny) for the sake of security, receives a shock upon meeting his kid brother. Cage's Ronny is a brooding, vital, angry, barely contained force haunted by his past.

In Rose Castorini (Loretta's mother), Dukakis fleshes out a good, tired woman who is nothing less than mystified by the actions of her husband, and what her response should be. It's a warm, lyrical performance, that provides the finest moments in the film.

1987: Best Actress (Cher), Supp. Actress (Olympia Dukakis), Original Screenplay

NOMINATION: Best Picture, Director, Supp. Actor (Vincent Gardenia)

•

MOONTIDE
1942, 94 mins, US b/w
Dir Archie Mayo ***Prod*** Mark Hellinger ***Scr*** John O'Hara ***Ph*** Charles Clarke ***Ed*** William Reynolds ***Mus*** Cyril Mockridge, David Buttolph
Act Jean Gabin, Ida Lupino, Thomas Mitchell, Claude Rains, Jerome Cowan, Helen Reynolds (20th Century-Fox)

Much of the success of the film [from the 1940 bestseller by Willard Robertson] may hinge on reaction to Jean Gabin. He's a pleasing and able player, but fails to project warmth and personal feeling.

Gabin, known as an earthy player in France, is given just that type of role in *Moontide*. He's an itinerant dockworker who for years hasn't had a home and is chiefly interested in getting drunk. Until, that is, he rescues from the surf a hash-house waitress (Ida Lupino) intent on killing herself.

Moontide is a series of incidents, although the overall impression is of a single important event in a man's life. Despite the speed with which director Archie Mayo paints each incident, the total effect is one of slowness and lacking suspense. Mayo's artistic direction is too even-paced to provide the occasional kick that any story requires.

1942: NOMINATION: Best B&W Cinematography

•

MOONWALKER

1988, 93 mins, US Ⓥ ⊙ col

Dir Colin Chivers, Jerry Kramer, Will Vinton, Jim Blashfield ***Prod*** Dennis Jones, Jerry Kramer ***Scr*** David Newman ***Ph*** John Hora, Frederick Elmes, Crescenzo Notarille ***Ed*** David E. Blewitt ***Mus*** Bruce Broughton ***Art*** Michael Ploog, Bryan Jones, John Walker

Act Michael Jackson, Sean Lennon, Kellie Parker, Brandon Adams, Joe Pesci (Lorimar)

Moonwalker—also the title of a Michael Jackson autobiography—seems unsure of what it was supposed to be. At the center of the pic is the *Smooth Criminal* segment, a musical/dramatic piece full of dancing, schmaltzy kids, sci-fi effects and blazing machine guns [directed by Colin Chilvers, based on a story by Jackson]. Around it are really just numerous Jackson music videos with little or no linkage. Although quite enjoyable the whole affair does not make for a structured or professional movie.

Pic opens with a hi-tech concert footage of *Man in the Mirror* and then quickly switches to a rather indulgent retrospective of Michael Jackson's career featuring clips of old songs, shows and videos, this time featuring eight- to ten-year-old children dancing and miming the song, with Brandon Ames playing the Jackson part.

Next segment is *Speed Demon* with Jackson disguised as a rabbit chased by fans. Next up is *Leave Me Alone*, the most fascinating section, featuring comments about Jackson from the tabloids accompanied by expert animation by Jim Blashfield. *Smooth Criminal* blends into a live performance of Jackson singing the Beatles' song "Come Together."

•

MOON ZERO TWO

1969, 100 mins, UK Ⓥ col

Dir Roy Ward Baker ***Prod*** Michael Carreras ***Scr*** Michael Carreras ***Ph*** Paul Besson ***Ed*** Spencer Reeve ***Mus*** Don Ellis ***Art*** Scott MacGregor

Act James Olson, Catherine Schell, Warren Mitchell, Adrienne Corri, Bernard Bresslaw, Dudley Foster (Hammer)

Moon Zero Two [from an original story by Gavin Lyall, Frank Hardman and Martin Davison] never makes up its mind whether it is a spoof or a straightforward space-adventure yarn. Overall it's a fairly dull experience, despite some capable artwork and special effects.

Space travel has progressed by 2021, and the moon's virtually old hat. First man to set foot on Mars (James Olson) declines to work as a regular passenger pilot.

Final sequence offers a spot of excitement, but the whole film tends to limp. Moon City's airport, its Wild West saloon and other amenities are presumably meant to be satire but it doesn't come off.

Olson is a melancholy hero. Mitchell plays with tongue in cheek, Bernard Bresslaw as one of his thugs seems bewildered by the entire proceedings.

•

MORE

1969, 115 mins, Luxembourg col

Dir Barbet Schroeder ***Prod*** Dave Lewis, Charles Lachman ***Scr*** Barbet Schroeder, Paul Gegauff ***Ph*** Nestor Almendros ***Ed*** Denise De Casabianca ***Mus*** Pink Floyd

Act Mimsy Farmer, Klaus Grunberg, Heinz Engelmann, Michel Chanderli (Jet/Two World)

In his first pic director Barbet Schroeder shows an insight into [late 1960s] youths, be they American or Europeans, who have been labeled everything from beatnik to yippie. There is no attempt to go in for forced erotics, violence, nudity or titillating amoralism. He gives a feeling of how it is sans didactics or obviousness. Drug-taking is a part of it in this tale of a youth from Germany destroyed by it.

The German boy meets a pretty, independent American girl. They soon become lovers and he follows her to Ibiza, a Spanish island, where they have an idyll in a beach house.

Brilliantly shot in arresting hues, it escapes picturesqueness and delves into its characters with sympathy and ease, sans indulgence.

Mimsy Farmer reveals a potent personality and gives her role of the girl a tension, inner hurt and alienation.

•

MORE AMERICAN GRAFFITI

1979, 111 mins, US Ⓥ ⊙ ⌴ col

Dir B.W.L. Norton ***Prod*** Howard Kazanjian ***Scr*** B. W. L. Norton ***Ph*** Caleb Deschanel ***Ed*** Tina Hirsch ***Art*** Ray Storey

Act Candy Clark, Bo Hopkins, Ron Howard, Scott Glenn, Paul Le Mat, Charles Martin Smith (Universal/Lucasfilm)

More American Graffiti may be one of the most innovative and ambitious films of the last five years, but by no means is it one of the most successful. In trying to follow the success of George Lucas's immensely popular 1973 hit, writer-director B. W. L. Norton overloads the sequel with four wholly different cinematic styles to carry forward the lives of *American Graffiti*'s original cast.

While dazzling to the eye, the flirtation with split-screen, anamorphic, 16mm and 1:85 screen sizes does not justify itself in terms of the film's content.

Part of Norton's presumed goal, of course, is to show how the 1960s fractured and split apart. But without a dramatic glue to hold the disparate story elements together, *Graffiti* is too disorganized for its own good.

•

MORE THAN A MIRACLE

1967, 102 mins, Italy/France ⌴ col

Dir Francesco Rosi ***Prod*** Carlo Ponti ***Scr*** Tonino Guerra, Raffaele La Capria, Giuseppe Patroni Griffi, Francesco Rosi ***Ph*** Pasquale De Santis ***Ed*** Jolanda Benvenuti ***Mus*** Piero Piccioni ***Art*** Piero Poletto

Act Sophia Loren, Omar Sharif, Dolores Del Rio, Georges Wilson, Leslie French (M-G-M)

More Than a Miracle is a real curiosity: labelled in production notes as a "fairy tale for adults," the production tells a Cinderella story, with some heavy-handed anticlericalism and antimonarchism thrown in.

Although the fairy tale approach is evident the script defeats itself in part by going too far into reality. Omar Sharif, therefore, is not only handsome, but arrogant, willful, brutal to his servants; also, the beautiful Sophia Loren, looking a bit uneasy and out of place in peasant weeds, eventually berates Sharif publicly for oppression of the lower classes.

Pic's fatal flaw is vacillation between pure make-believe, which would have gone over to some degree, and corny political tract which is what one would imagine *Snow White* to be if produced by Russian filmmakers.

•

MORE THE MERRIER, THE

1943, 101 mins, US Ⓥ ⊙ b/w

Dir George Stevens ***Prod*** George Stevens ***Scr*** Robert Russell, Frank Ross, Richard Flourney, Lewis R. Foster ***Ph*** Ted Tetzlaff ***Ed*** Otto Meyer

Act Jean Arthur, Joel McCrea, Charles Coburn, Richard Gaines, Bruce Bennett, Frank Sully (Columbia)

A sparkling and effervescing piece of entertainment, *The More the Merrier*, is one of the most spontaneous farce-comedies of the wartime era. Although Jean Arthur and Joel McCrea carry the romantic interest, Charles Coburn walks off with the honors.

Story [by Frank Ross and Robert Russell] is premised on the housing conditions existing in wartime Washington. Coburn arrives in town and sublets half interest in Miss Arthur's minute apartment, and when he finds the girl without a boyfriend, conveniently picks up McCrea—Air Force sergeant in town to get orders for secret mission—to become partner in his share of the housing layout. Naturally complications ensue in hilarious fashion until Coburn backs out to watch the culmination of the romance he very effectively cooks up.

1943: Best Supp. Actor (Charles Coburn)

NOMINATION: Best Picture, Director, Actress (Jean Arthur), Original Story, Screenplay

•

MORE THINGS CHANGE, THE

1986, 95 mins, Australia col

Dir Robyn Nevin ***Prod*** Jill C. Robb ***Scr*** Moya Wood ***Ph*** Dan Burstall ***Ed*** Jill Bilcock ***Mus*** Peter Best ***Art*** Josephine Ford

Act Judy Morris, Barry Otto, Victoria Longley, Lewis Fitz-Gerald, Peter Carroll (Syme)

The More Things Change is a universally topical film about a modern marriage, told with humor and insight. It's also splendidly acted.

Connie (Judy Morris) and Lex (Barry Otto) are happily married with a small son. They've decided to opt out of the rat race, and have purchased a small but spectacularly beautiful farm two hours' drive from the city, but until the farm is self-sufficient one of them has to keep working. A live-in baby-sitter is the answer, and Connie engages Geraldine (Victoria Longley).

The viewer's expectations are, naturally, that Lex and Geraldine will have an affair, but Moya Wood's sharp screenplay is much more subtle than that, making this a film where all the characters are a pleasure.

•

MORGAN!

SEE: A SUITABLE CASE FOR TREATMENT

•

MORGAN (A SUITABLE CASE FOR TREATMENT)

SEE: A SUITABLE CASE FOR TREATMENT

•

MORITURI

(UK: THE SABOTEUR, CODE NAME—"MORITURI")

1965, 118 mins, US Ⓥ b/w

Dir Bernhard Wicki ***Prod*** Aaron Rosenberg ***Scr*** Daniel Taradash ***Ph*** Conrad Hall ***Ed*** Joseph Silver ***Mus*** Jerry Goldsmith ***Art*** Jack Martin Smith, Herman A. Blumenthal

Act Marlon Brando, Yul Brynner, Janet Margolin, Trevor Howard, Martin Benrath, Hans Christian Blech (20th Century-Fox)

Morituri is a Second World War sea drama of sometimes battering impact. Starring Marlon Brando and Yul Brynner, the production carries strong suspense at times and a brooding menace that communicates to the spectator.

Action takes place aboard a German blockade runner in 1942 en route from Yokohama to Bordeaux with a cargo of 7,000 tons of indispensable crude rubber for the Nazis, which the Allies also want. British put a man on the freighter with orders to disarm explosive charges by which the captain would scuttle his ship rather than allow capture.

Both Brando and Brynner contribute hard-hitting performances, Brando as the saboteur and Brynner as captain. Former, a German deserter threatened with return to Germany and certain death if he doesn't acquiesce to British demand, gives his impersonation almost tongue-in-cheek handling.

In top support, Trevor Howard is in briefly as a British Intelligence officer, and Martin Benrath makes the most of his role as exec officer, a Nazi who takes over the ship when Brynner becomes raging drunk.

1965: NOMINATIONS: Best B&W Cinematography, B&W Costume Design

•

MORNING AFTER, THE

1986, 103 mins, US Ⓥ ⊙ col

Dir Sidney Lumet ***Prod*** Bruce Gilbert ***Scr*** James Hicks ***Ph*** Andrzej Bartkowiak ***Ed*** Joel Goodman ***Mus*** Paul Chihara ***Art*** Albert Brenner

Act Jane Fonda, Jeff Bridges, Raul Julia, Diane Salinger, Richard Foronjy (Lorimar/American Filmworks)

Overwrought and implausible, *The Morning After* is a dramatic situation in search of a thriller plot. Jane Fonda stars as a boozy, washed-up actress who wakes up one morning next to a man with a dagger in his heart, and her efforts to cope with the dilemma are neither terribly suspenseful nor entertaining.

She removes any trace that she was ever present at the fellow's place, doesn't call the cops and heads for the airport, where she hooks up with friendly redneck Jeff Bridges, who gradually insinuates himself into her life.

Along the way, Fonda battles the bottle, succumbs to Bridges's charms and is forced into a divorce by estranged hubby but good chum Raul Julia, an outrageously successful Beverly Hills hairdresser who now wants to marry a Bel-Air heiress.

While attempting to build up tension, Fonda and director Sidney Lumet more often succeed in creating hysteria.

1986: NOMINATION: Best Actress (Jane Fonda)

•

MORNING GLORY

1933, 70 mins, US Ⓥ ⊙ b/w

Dir Lowell Sherman ***Prod*** Pandro S. Berman ***Scr*** Howard J. Green ***Ph*** Bert Glennon ***Ed*** William Hamilton ***Mus*** Max Steiner ***Art*** Van Nest Polglase, Chick Kirk

Act Katharine Hepburn, Douglas Fairbanks, Jr., Adolphe Menjou, Mary Duncan, C. Aubrey Smith, Don Alvarado (RKO)

Morning Glory isn't an entirely happy choice for Katharine Hepburn but the star provides a strong performance. This one is heavy on legit class and lacks action and sustained conflict.

Story [from the stage play by Zoe Akins] is at great pains to build up the charming character of a well-bred, utterly innocent country girl who comes to Broadway seeking footlight fame. No sooner is the thoroughly lovable figure built to completeness than the hapless little Cinderella is dragged through the mud of backstage casual amours. This happens less than midway of the footage, and thereafter the grip of an engaging story relaxes fatally. The fate of this bedraggled Cinderella becomes a matter of indifference.

Aside from its story defects, the picture is excellent in technique. Dialogue is pointed and terse, and the photography is magnificent. A first-rate supporting cast gives Hepburn invaluable cooperation, notably a fine, intelligent handling of the male lead by Douglas Fairbanks, Jr., and a characteristically suave performance by Adolphe Menjou.

1932/33: Best Actress (Katharine Hepburn)

•

MORNING GLORY

1993, 95 mins, US Ⓥ ⦿ col

Dir Steven Stern ***Prod*** Michael Viner ***Scr*** Charles Jarrott, Deborah Raffin ***Ph*** Laszlo George ***Ed*** Richard Benwick ***Mus*** Jonathan Elias ***Art*** David Hiscox

Act Christopher Reeve, Deborah Raffin, Lloyd Bochner, Nina Foch, Helen Shaver, J. T. Walsh (Dove Audio)

Morning Glory, toting a script with more clunks than the 1930s Ford its characters drive, plays like a TV miniseries rather than a feature pic. It's got some heart, a rustic tone and Superman star appeal of Christopher Reeve.

The story, based on LaVyrle Spencer's 1989 novel of the same name, shows sparks of originality, with Reeve as down-and-out, ex-con Will Parker who answers a newspaper classified ad for a husband. But weak scripting and a choppy, uninspired narrative turn the Depression-era yarn into a garbled collection of predictable soap opera scenes.

Recently widowed Elly Dinsmore (Deborah Raffin) is not looking for love, just someone to share the chores. Parker, broke and fresh from a murder rap, appears on her doorstep to take the "husband" job.

Then, as if imported from a different pic, Sheriff Reese Goodloe (J. T. Walsh) roughs up Parker and local floozy Lula Peaks (Helen Shaver) pesters him with seduction attempts. Suddenly Lulu's dead, the sheriff is mad and Parker is back in jail.

Reeve is a sturdy, if not stiff, leading man. Raffin, who coscripted and whose hubby, Michael Viner, produced, uses small, affected gestures and ticks to convey her questionable madness.

•

MOROCCO

1930, 90 mins, US Ⓥ ⦿ b/w

Dir Josef von Sternberg ***Prod*** [Hector Turnbull] ***Scr*** Jules Furthman ***Ph*** Lee Garmes, [Lucien Ballard] ***Ed*** [Sam Winston] ***Mus*** [Karl Hajer] ***Art*** [Hans Dreier]

Act Gary Cooper, Marlene Dietrich, Adolphe Menjou, Ullrich Haupt, Eve Southern, Francis McDonald (Paramount)

Morocco is too lightweight a story to be counterbalanced by the big-time direction given it. Marlene Dietrich has little opportunities in her first American talker. There's nothing to the picture, except what Josef von Sternberg gives it in direction, and that's giving it more than it's got.

The story [from the play *Amy Jolly* by Benno Vigny] is given a terrific kick early, when Dietrich arrives in Morocco to star in the concert hall. The first evening of her appearance she gives the key to her home to a legionnaire, Cooper. After that the rest is apple sauce, even to her joining the female followers of the troops to keep near her soldier.

Adolphe Menjou has a walkthrough role, done with his acknowledged suavity. Ullrich Haupt handles a minor role very nicely. Cooper plays excellently. He gets the precise spirit of his role.

1930/31: NOMINATIONS: Best Director, Actress (Marlene Dietrich), Cinematography, Art Direction

•

MORTAL KOMBAT

1995, 101 mins, US Ⓥ ⦿ col

Dir Paul Anderson ***Prod*** Lawrence Kasanoff ***Scr*** Kevin Droney ***Ph*** John R. Leonetti ***Ed*** Martin Hunter ***Mus*** George S. Clinton ***Art*** Jonathan Carlson

Act Robin Shou, Linden Ashby, Bridgette Wilson, Cary-Hiroyuki Tagawa, Talisa Soto, Christopher Lambert (Threshold/New Line)

The novel twists in this martial arts action-adventure are superb technical and visual effects, a tongue-in-cheek script and performers who can convey its mocking tone without stooping to the obvious.

The action revolves around a rather unusual tournament of champions. One side consists of the human league and the other is repped by the dark, unworldly forces of evil sorcerer Shang Tsung (Cary-Hiroyuki Tagawa). The latter group includes characters who can turn into serpents, throw spitballs of lethal ice or simply tower two stories high with four arms each with the strength to crush iron.

But the best of the flesh-and-blood crew are better than their seemingly impossible adversaries, thanks to superior intellect, an ability to adapt and the watchful tutelage of good sorcerer Rayden (Christopher Lambert). Still, in nine prior competitions, the denizens of Outworld have prevailed. If the nonhuman team prevails again, the populace of Earth becomes enslaved to the evil empire.

Director Paul Anderson and writer Kevin Droney effect a viable balance between exquisitely choreographed action and ironic visual and verbal counterpoint. There's a vain martial arts actor (Linden Ashby) burdened by press reports that he's a fraud; a tough drug task-force leader (Bridgette Wilson) who winds up chained to a pillar in a hopelessly silly dress; and a hero (Robin Shou) who's reluctant despite having been "chosen" to fight in Final Kombat.

Slickly stylish, pic tops its [video arcade] sources of inspiration with lush, crisp production values and exotic Thailand locales.

•

MORTAL PASSIONS

1989, 98 mins, US Ⓥ ⦿ col

Dir Andrew Lane ***Prod*** Gwen Field ***Scr*** Alan Moscowitz ***Ph*** Christian Sebaldt ***Ed*** Kimberley Ray ***Mus*** Parmer Fuller ***Art*** Tucker Johnston

Act Zach Galligan, Michael Bowen, Krista Errickson, Luca Bercovici, Sheila Kelley, David Warner (Gibraltar)

Delightfully silly beneath its earnestness, *Mortal Passions* revels in the amoral, murderous frustrations of a beautiful young wife (Krista Errickson) doing her best to bed and bounty any and all of the men in her life.

First, there's the likable rich husband (Zach Galligan), long on suicidal impulses and short on immediate career goals. Galligan suspects Errickson is having an affair. Indeed, being so innocent, he would be shocked to know what a tryst it is, with Errickson enthusiastically bound to the bedposts by her lounge-lizard boyfriend (Luca Bercovici) as the two of them plot murder.

The scene is undone by the appearance of Galligan's older brother (Michael Bowen), even more psychotically overprotective than they were when they were little. Errickson has an affair with him, too.

There is absolutely nothing predictable about this wonderful group of loonies, and director Andrew Lane never lets slip where he and the tightly wrapped script are taking them.

•

MORTAL STORM, THE

1940, 100 mins, US b/w

Dir Frank Borzage ***Scr*** Claudine West, Andersen Ellis, George Froeschel ***Ph*** William Daniels ***Ed*** Elmo Vernon ***Mus*** Edward Kane ***Art*** Cedric Gibbons, Wade B. Rubottom

Act Margaret Sullavan, James Stewart, Robert Young, Frank Morgan, Robert Stack, Bonita Granville (M-G-M)

The Mortal Storm is a slugging indictment of the political and social theories advanced by Hitler, a combination of entertainment and democratic preachment, based on a novel of the same name by Phyllis Bottome.

The locale is Germany, 1933, at the time when the paper-hanger gained control of the government. Through the lives of the members of the family of a university professor there is revealed the soul-crushing effect of Nazi regimentation. Sons turn from their parents, friends become deadly enemies, innocent elders are tossed into concentration camps.

Because the action takes place in the early years of the Hitler regime, the ending of the story provides its most potent wallop. Hero and heroine plan a dangerous escape over a snowbound and unguarded frontier pass in the Austrian Alps.

Performances are excellent. James Stewart is the courageous individualist who refuses to join the Nazi party, and Robert Young is the heavy. Frank Morgan draws a fine characterization of the non-Aryan professor. Irene Rich returns to films as mother of the unhappy family. Margaret Sullavan carries the romantic interest.

Pictorially, the film is a panorama of beautiful mountain scenes and finely photographed interiors.

•

MORTAL THOUGHTS

1991, 104 mins, US Ⓥ ⦿ col

Dir Alan Rudolph ***Prod*** John Fiedler, Mark Tarlov ***Scr*** William Reilly, Claude Kerven ***Ph*** Elliot Davis ***Ed*** Tom Walls ***Mus*** Mark Isham ***Art*** Howard Cummings

Act Demi Moore, Glenne Headly, Bruce Willis, John Pankow, Harvey Keitel, Billie Neal (Columbia/New Visions/Polar)

Two gals make a murderous mess of a bad situation in *Mortal Thoughts.* Played straight and for sympathy, tale of dark retaliation goes astray early on, despite the promise created at the outset by imaginative, energetic production and appealing performances.

Demi Moore and Glenne Headly play lifelong friends who run a blue-collar New Jersey beauty shop and remain closer to each other than to their husbands. Small wonder, since Moore's husband (John Pankow) is a boorish salesman, and Headley's wed to a thoroughly despicable, abusive lout (Bruce Willis).

Headly's running response is that he should die and she wants to kill him, but Moore never takes it seriously until Willis ends up with his throat cut and the two femmes have blood all over their hands.

Scripters play the whole thing out from a police interrogation room, where a detective (Harvey Keitel) hammers away at Moore to get at the real story, which unspools in flashbacks.

•

MOSCOW DOES NOT BELIEVE IN TEARS

SEE: MOSKVA SLEZAM NE VERIT

•

MOSCOW NIGHTS

1935, 77 mins, UK Ⓥ b/w

Dir Anthony Asquith ***Prod*** Alexis Granowski, Max Schach ***Scr*** Eric Seipmann, Anthony Asquith ***Ph*** Philip Tannura ***Ed*** William Hornbeck, Francis Lyon ***Art*** Vincent Korda

Act Harry Baur, Laurence Olivier, Penelope Dudley-Ward, Athene Seyler, Hay Petrie (Denham/London)

Moscow Nights is a triumph for director Anthony Asquith in that you are actually transported to Russia in 1916, and no book could give you a more vivid spectacle of things as they existed at that time. Not once is it deemed necessary to resort to comedy relief. It is really and truly a triumph of film direction.

Plot is conventional enough, but it is the atmosphere in which it is disclosed. A handsome young Russian officer (Laurence Olivier) is carried into a hospital in a delirious condition from war wounds. Upon regaining consciousness he discovers a celestial-looking Red Cross nurse in the person of Penelope Dudley-Ward, and falls hard. She is, however, engaged to a middle-aged war profiteer who pays off the mortgage on her parents' home. The profiteer boasts he was born a peasant and is still a peasant. Part is played by Harry Baur, a Continental actor, who brings to the role a dominance that always falls short of being repellent.

Laurence Olivier has looks, charm and acting ability. This is his first big opportunity, and he takes advantage of it to the full.

The supporting cast is of a very high order, notably Athene Seyler, Kate Cutler, Morton Selten and Hay Petrie.

•

MOSCOW ON THE HUDSON

1984, 115 mins, US Ⓥ ⦿ col

Dir Paul Mazursky ***Prod*** Paul Mazursky ***Scr*** Paul Mazursky, Leon Capetanos ***Ph*** Donald McAlpine ***Ed*** Richard Halsey ***Mus*** David McHugh ***Art*** Pato Guzman

Act Robin Williams, Maria Conchita Alonso, Cleavant Derricks, Alejandro Rey, Savely Kramarov, Elya Baskin (Columbia)

Moscow on the Hudson is a sweet, beautifully performed picture that unfortunately wanders around several patriotic themes.

Directed by Paul Mazursky with his usual unusual touches, *Moscow* would be in a lot of trouble without a superbly sensitive portrayal by Robin Williams of a gentle Russian circus musician who makes a sudden decision to defect while visiting the U.S.

As Mazursky sees it, Williams thus becomes one more in a flood of immigrants who still are coming to this country and discovering virtues that those already here many times forget. Of course, they also encounter the faults, as well.

The entire film is full of performers working way beyond the material. Cleavant Derricks is especially good. Maria Conchita Alonso is also spirited as Williams's Italian girlfriend.

•

MOSES

1975, 139 mins, Italy/UK Ⓥ col

Dir Gianfranco De Bosio ***Prod*** Vincenzo Labella ***Scr*** Anthony Burgess, Vittorio Bonicelli, Gianfranco De Bosio ***Ph*** Marcello Gatti ***Ed*** Gerry Hambling, Peter Boita, John

Guthridge, Alberto Gallitti, Fred Wilson ***Mus*** Ennio Morricone, Dov Seltzer ***Art*** Pierluigi Basile

Act Burt Lancaster, Anthony Quayle, Ingrid Thulin, Irene Papas, Mariangela Melato, William Lancaster (RAI/ITC)

Moses is another attempt at compressing a big slice of biblical drama, and the inevitable result is superficial storytelling. The film was impressively photographed in Israel and has Burt Lancaster in a restrained portrayal as the patriarch of the ancient Hebrews who leads them from Egyptian bondage to the promised land.

Pic strikes a reasonable balance between spectacle and narrative. But the net effect is one of flat earnestness, a tale more of tribute than of dimensional human saga.

Feature was "inspired" by the TV miniseries, *Moses, the Lawgiver*. Besides recutting, the theatrical edition assertedly contains much footage not included in the TV version.

Lancaster delivers his usual polished professionalism, arrayed in seasoned if undistinguished support are Anthony Quayle and Ingrid Thulin as his brother and sister, Irene Papas as his wife, and Laurent Terzieff as the young Egyptian monarch loathe to free his Jewish serfs.

•

MOSKVA SLEZAM NE VERIT
(MOSCOW DOES NOT BELIEVE IN TEARS)

1980, 145 mins, USSR Ⓥ col

Dir Vladimir Menshov ***Scr*** Valentin Chernych ***Ph*** Igor Slabnyevich ***Ed*** Yelena Mikhailova ***Mus*** Sergei Nikitin ***Art*** Said Menyalshchikov

Act Vera Alentova, Irina Muravyova, Raisa Ryazanova, Natalya Vavilova, Aleksei Batalov, Yuri Vasiliev (Mosfilm)

Three girls come to Moscow from the country to find new lives and challenges. Men outweigh politics and their work in factories. One ends up with an illegitimate child, another does not marry, and one has a good simple marriage.

It starts in 1958 and then goes to 1978. A bit sprawling, overlong and indulgent, film still has an easygoing attitude toward the more forthright love scenes, albeit covered up. It indicates there are class distinctions due to standing in the work hierarchy and brings in an almost overheroic, unassuming worker who wins over the unwed mother, now the director of a big factory.

Film is engagingly played and directed with ease. Perhaps a bit reminiscent of American romantic comedies of the 1930s, but without their more dynamic pacing, bite and tongue-in-cheek innocence.

1980: Best Foreign-Language Film

•

MOSQUITO COAST, THE

1986, 117 mins, US Ⓥ ⊙ col

Dir Peter Weir ***Prod*** Jerome Hellman ***Scr*** Paul Schrader ***Ph*** John Seale ***Ed*** Thom Noble ***Mus*** Maurice Jarre ***Art*** John Stoddart

Act Harrison Ford, Helen Mirren, River Phoenix, Jadrien Steele, Hilary Gordon, Rebecca Gordon (Warner)

It is hard to believe that a film as beautiful as *The Mosquito Coast* [adapted from the novel by Paul Theroux] can also be so bleak, but therein lies its power and undoing. A modern variation of *Swiss Family Robinson*, it starts out as a film about idealism and possibilities, but takes a dark turn and winds up questioning the very values it so powerfully presents. There's a stunning performance by Harrison Ford with firstrate film-making by Peter Weir.

Ford's Allie Fox is a world-class visionary with the power to realize his vision. He rants and raves against prepackaged, mass-consumed American culture and packs up his wife and four kids and moves them to a remote Caribbean island—the Mosquito Coast.

Fox transforms a remote outpost on the island into a thriving community equipped with numerous Rube Goldberg–like gadgets to harness the forces of nature and make life better for the inhabitants. For a while it's an idylic little utopian community, but the seeds of its downfall are present even as it thrives.

As Fox starts to unravel so does the film. None of the outside antagonists supplied by Paul Schrader's screenplay are fitting adversaries for Fox's genius.

•

MOSS ROSE

1947, 82 mins, US b/w

Dir Gregory Ratoff ***Prod*** Gene Markey ***Scr*** Jules Furthman, Tom Reed ***Ph*** Joe MacDonald ***Ed*** James B. Clark ***Mus*** David Buttolph ***Art*** Richard Day, Mark-Lee Kirk

Act Peggy Cummins, Victor Mature, Ethel Barrymore, Vincent Price, Margo Woode, Patricia Medina (20th Century-Fox)

Moss Rose is good whodunit. Given a lift by solid trouping and direction, melodrama is run off against background of early-day England that provides effective setting for theme of destructive mother love.

The screenplay was adapted by Niven Busch from the Joseph Shearing novel. It's a sombre story of a mother who kills to keep from losing her son. First death comes to music-hall girl romanced by Victor Mature. Latter is seen leaving the girl's room by Peggy Cummins, who protects Mature in turn for his taking her to visit his mother at a country estate. Next victim is Patricia Medina, Mature's proper fiancée.

Gregory Ratoff's direction develops considerable flavor to the period melodramatics. He gets meticulous performances from players in keeping with mood of piece. Cummins is unusually interesting: English pronunciation, at first broad and then becoming more educated, is a trick she uses to develop character of music-hall girl who uses her knowledge of murder to satisfy a childhood desire. It's a well-rounded portrayal. Mature handles his sombre character of a well-bred Englishman expertly.

•

MOST DANGEROUS GAME, THE
(UK: THE HOUNDS OF ZAROFF)

1932, 61 mins, US Ⓥ b/w

Dir Ernest B. Schoedsack, Irving Pichel ***Prod*** Merian C. Cooper, Ernest B. Schoedsack ***Scr*** James A. Creelman ***Ph*** Henry Gerrard ***Ed*** Archie F. Marshek ***Mus*** Max Steiner ***Art*** Carroll Clark

Act Joel McCrea, Fay Wray, Leslie Banks, Robert Armstrong, Steve Clemento, Noble Johnson (RKO)

Fantastic would-be thriller [from a story by Richard Connell] whose efforts at horrifying are not very effective.

A crazy Russian count (Leslie Banks), who derives more pleasure from hunting human beings than lions and tigers since a wild bull kicked him in the head, is this one's baby-scaring Frankenstein. He operates alone on a deserted tropical isle, using shipwreck victims for game. When he gets 'em he fattens 'em up. The routine then is to send them out on the jungle-like isle with a few hours' start.

It's a foregone cinch that Joel McCrea, as a big-game hunter on his way to India when tossed into the count's trap, will hand the man hunter a trimming. It looks for a moment like the count wins this one, too, when McCrea goes over the waterfall with a hunting dog at his throat.

The producers have heretofore specialized in animal films with a more or less natural background. This time they stick mostly to the studio, and although the swamp and jungle settings serve, considering the limitations, they're frequently obviously phoney. Banks grabs everything worth grabbing among performance honors. Fay Wray has no opportunity to be anything but decorative. With McCrea and Robert Armstrong (as a booze-guzzling simpleton) miscasting is evident.

•

MOST DANGEROUS MAN IN THE WORLD, THE
SEE: THE CHAIRMAN

•

MOTHER, JUGS & SPEED

1976, 95 mins, US Ⓥ ▭ col

Dir Peter Yates ***Prod*** Peter Yates, Tom Mankiewicz ***Scr*** Tom Mankiewicz ***Ph*** Ralph Woolsey ***Ed*** Frank P. Keller ***Art*** Walter Scott Herndon

Act Raquel Welch, Bill Cosby, Harvey Keitel, Allen Garfield, Larry Hagman, L. Q. Jones (20th Century-Fox)

The three titular characters are Bill Cosby, Raquel Welch, and Harvey Keitel, all very pleasant in their roles as ambulance drivers for company owner Allen Garfield. Their easygoing camaraderie, which provides a strong role for Welch, allows for many good behavioral moments.

The film starts off as pure farce but veers into tragedy when young driver Bruce Davison is killed by a junkie's shotgun.

Other supporting characters also suffer from the film's opportunistic grab-bag tendencies.

The film, based on a story by Stephen Manes and Tom Mankiewicz, remains oddly appealing despite its serious flaws—in many ways it's an accurate reflection of what really goes on in hustling ambulance outfits.

•

MOTHER LODE

1982, 101 mins, US Ⓥ col

Dir Charlton Heston ***Prod*** Fraser Clarke Heston ***Scr*** Fraser Clarke Heston ***Ph*** Richard Leiterman ***Ed*** Eric Boyd-Perkins ***Mus*** Ken Wannberg ***Art*** Douglas Higgins

Act Charlton Heston, Nick Mancuso, Kim Basinger, John Marley, Dale Wilson (Agamemnon)

As the title indicates, the consuming issue in *Mother Lode* is a search for gold. The picture is not without shortcomings, but is long on good performances, charismatic people in the three principal roles, compelling outdoor aerial sequences in the Cassiar Mountains of British Columbia and high-level suspense throughout.

The role of Silas McGee, the disreputable Scottish miner trying to protect his great secret find, is a switch to villainy for Charlton Heston, but he relishes the role and even makes a creditable pass at a thick Scottish brogue. Nick Mancuso, as the bush-pilot protagonist who would delve the secret location of the lode at any cost, is the character around which the suspense must swirl, and he manages to keep matters tense to the very end.

Kim Basinger, the only femme in the picture, provides the reason for some unusual plot twists, and comes across as a beauteous screen personality.

•

MOTHER'S BOYS

1994, 95 mins, US Ⓥ ⊙ col

Dir Yves Simoneau ***Prod*** Jack E. Freedman, Wayne S. Williams, Patricia Herskovic ***Scr*** Barry Schneider, Richard Hawley ***Ph*** Elliot Davis ***Ed*** Michael Ornstein ***Mus*** George S. Clinton ***Art*** David Bomba

Act Jamie Lee Curtis, Peter Gallagher, Joanne Whalley-Kilmer, Vanessa Redgrave, Luke Edwards, Joss Ackland (Miramax/Dimension)

Elegant style and amiable cast can't conceal the silliness of *Mother's Boys*, an unsuspenseful variation of the yuppie-in-peril thriller. Jamie Lee Curtis stars as the "mother from hell."

Set in LA, story [from Bernard Taylor's novel] begins as Jude (Curtis), an attractive woman who deserted her husband (Peter Gallagher) and three sons without any explanation, suddenly returns, determined to win back her family. Jude is convinced that her hubby still loves her, even though he is now attached to Callie (Joanne Whalley-Kilmer). When begging forgiveness and other "charming" strategies fail, Jude resorts to manipulating eldest son, Kes (Luke Edwards).

In pic's most controversial scene, she demonstrates to Kes in full nudity her scar from his birth, which she sees as a symbol of their special bond.

Film has an uninteresting beginning, an exploitative middle that actually cheats by genre standards, and a ludicrous climax that is borderline laughable. The few suspenseful moments generated by Canadian helmer Yves Simoneau are unfairly earned.

•

MOTHER WORE TIGHTS

1947, 107 mins, US col

Dir Walter Lang ***Prod*** Lamar Trotti ***Scr*** Lamar Trotti ***Ph*** Harry Jackson ***Ed*** J. Watson Webb, Jr. ***Mus*** Alfred Newman (dir.) ***Art*** Richard Day, Joseph C. Wright

Act Betty Grable, Dan Dailey, Mona Freeman, Connie Marshall, Vanessa Brown, Sara Allgood (20th Century-Fox)

Mother Wore Tights [based on the book by Mariam Young] is a familiarly styled Technicolor musical opus on the life and times of a song-and-dance team that knocked around the vaude circuits about the century's turn. Leisurely paced and loosely constructed as a series of undramatic vignettes, picture will appeal to patrons who prefer their nostalgia trowelled on thickly and sweetly.

Musical is severely limited by its long and mediocre score of tunes [by Mack Gordon, Josef Myrow], which are presented without any visual imaginative touches. Numerous hoofing sequences [staged by Seymour Felix and Kenny Williams] featuring Betty Grable and vis-à-vis Dan Dailey also fail to rate the heavy accent put on them by the footage. Chief drawback, however, is the rambling story, whose lack of both major and minor climaxes is made glaring by Walter Lang's deadpan direction and a script that pulls out all the stops in its use of clichés and sentimentalism.

Yarn, unfolding via simple flashbacks to the commentary of the hoofers' younger daughter, progresses through the various stages of the vaude team's career.

1947: Best Scoring for a Musical Picture

NOMINATIONS: Best Color Cinematography, Song ("You Do")

•

MOTOR PSYCHO

1965, 73 mins, US ⊙ b/w

Dir Russ Meyer ***Prod*** Russ Meyer ***Scr*** Russ Meyer, W. E. Sprague ***Ph*** Russ Meyer ***Ed*** Charles G. Schelling ***Mus*** Igo Kantor

Act Stephen Oliver, Haji, Alex Rocco, Holle K. Winters, Joseph Cellini, Thomas Scott (Eve)

Motor Psycho is a violent Russ Meyer production concerning three young bums on a rape-murder spree in a California desert town. Slick, well-made and initially absorbing, it features sex angles that kill the credibility of a script which itself is long on loose ends and short on moral compensation.

Stephen Oliver, Joseph Cellini and Thomas Scott are the vagrants who, within the first five minutes, have viciously beaten Steve Masters and raped his wife, Arshalouis Aivasian. Holle K. Winters is then assaulted while hubby, Alex Rocco, is down the road resisting the advances of busty Sharon Lee.

At length, Coleman Francis is beaten and accidently killed when the gang moves in on his younger wife, played by a gal named Haji. Rest of pic concerns Rocco's trackdown of the trio, in which he is joined by Haji, left for dead after Oliver shoots her.

Meyer's direction is good, while his interesting and crisp camerawork is excellent.

•

MOUCHETTE
1967, 85 mins, France Ⓥ b/w
Dir Robert Bresson ***Prod*** Anatole Dauman (exec.) ***Scr*** Robert Bresson ***Ph*** Ghislain Cloquet ***Ed*** Raymond Lamy ***Mus*** Jean Wiener ***Art*** Pierre Guffroy
Act Nadine Nortier, Jean-Claude Guilbert, Maria Cardinal, Paul Herbert, Jean Vimenet, Marie Susini (Argos/Parc)

A 14-year-old girl, a drudge in an impoverished alcoholic peasant family, is the heroine of this brilliant film. Her sullen defiance, her failure to connect with life and a final opting out via suicide are treated with clear and uncluttered insight.

Director-writer Robert Bresson has updated Georges Bernanos's prewar book [*Nouvelle histoire de Mouchette*]. Bresson's refusal to use professional actors also aids his treatment.

At school, the daughter is friendless and takes to heaving dirt at her classmates every time she gets out of school. Her only human contact comes through her rape, half consented to, by a local poacher. The death of her mother, and the hypocritical piousness of her father and villagers, seem to be felt by this wild little girl.

Everyday incidents take on an almost spiritual intensity in Bresson's controlled and incisive direction and handling of the players. Nadine Nortier has the animal ferocity and gentleness needed for the role.

•

MOULIN ROUGE
1928, 90 mins, UK ⊗ b/w
Dir E. A. Dupont ***Scr*** Harry Chandlee ***Ph*** Werner Brandes
Act Olga Tschechowa, Eve Gray, Jean Bradin, George Treville, Marcel Vibert (British International)

Well done, but overlong, it's a love complication with the young man falling for his fiancée's mother, the leading lady of the Moulin Rouge revue.

Except for occasional shots where the players' eyes are overshadowed with that persistent habit of European filmmakers to ignore the importance of proper make-up, *Moulin Rouge* is photographically good. Its principals are interesting personalities, notably Olga Tschechowa, who resembles Pola Negri but with more humor.

Some of the backstage stuff is done exceptionally well, better, in fact, than the usual Hollywood efforts to reproduce convincingly a musical stage show. On this angle alone and on the general richness and novelty of its background, *Moulin Rouge* will hold interest.

•

MOULIN ROUGE
1952, 118 mins, UK Ⓥ ⊙ col
Dir John Huston ***Scr*** John Huston, Anthony Veiller ***Ph*** Oswald Morris ***Ed*** Ralph Kemplen ***Mus*** Georges Auric ***Art*** Paul Sheriff
Act Jose Ferrer, Colette Marchand, Suzanne Flon, Zsa Zsa Gabor, Christopher Lee, Eric Pohlmann (Romulus)

Jose Ferrer endows with conviction the part of Toulouse-Lautrec, the cultured, gifted artist of Paris in the 1880s whose glaring deformity—a childhood accident impeded growth of his legs—repulses the women whom he constantly seeks.

John Huston's direction is superb in the handling of individual scenes. The can-can ribaldry, the frank depiction of streetwalkers, the smokey atmosphere of Parisian bistro life—they come through in exciting pictorial terms. Each scene has a framed appearance that richly sets off the action. And the Technicolor tinting captures the flamboyant aura of Montmartre.

But overall, the production, while of great scenic merit, requires some dramatic explosiveness. The story unfolds in a constantly minor-key tone.

Filmed in France and England, the pic is an adaptation of the bestselling novel by Pierre La Mure.

1952: Best Color Art Direction, Color Costume Design

NOMINATIONS: Best Picture, Director, Actor (Jose Ferrer), Supp. Actress (Colette Marchand), Editing

•

MOUNTAIN MEN, THE
1980, 102 mins, US Ⓥ ⊙ ▭ col
Dir Richard Lang ***Prod*** Martin Shafer, Andrew Scheinman ***Scr*** Fraser Clarke Heston ***Ph*** Michael Hugo ***Ed*** Eva Ruggiero ***Mus*** Michel Legrand ***Art*** Bill Kenney
Act Charlton Heston, Brian Keith, Victoria Racimo, Seymour Cassel, John Glover (Columbia)

Does anyone want to see Charlton Heston as Grizzly Adams? That's the question arising from Columbia's lethargic wilderness pic *The Mountain Men*.

Screenplay by star's son Fraser Clarke Heston is loaded with vulgarities that seem excessive for the genre, and scene after scene dwells on bloody hand-to-hand battles between Indians and the grizzled trappers played by Heston and sidekick Brian Keith.

Film takes ages to drag from one plot development to another, though the Indian battles are with sufficient regularity to keep the audience from snoozing. Basic storyline is Heston's courtly protection of runaway Indian squaw Victoria Racimo and the violent attempts by her former Indian mate Stephen Macht to win her back. It's a limp feature debut for director Richard Lang.

•

MOUNTAINS OF THE MOON
1990, 135 mins, US Ⓥ ⊙ col
Dir Bob Rafelson ***Prod*** Daniel Melnick ***Scr*** William Harrison, Bob Rafelson ***Ph*** Roger Deakins ***Ed*** Thom Noble ***Mus*** Michael Small ***Art*** Norman Reynolds
Act Patrick Bergin, Iain Glen, Fiona Shaw, Richard E. Grant, Peter Vaughan, Anna Massey (Carolco/Indieprod)

Bob Rafelson's *Mountains of the Moon* is an outstanding adventure film, adapted from William Harrison's book *Burton and Speke* and the journals of 19th-century explorers Richard Burton and John Hanning Speke. Without sacrificing the historical context this pic provides deeply felt performances and refreshing, offbeat humor.

Starting in 1854, pic documents duo's ill-fated first two expeditions to Africa, climaxing with Speke's discovery of what became named Lake Victoria, the true source of the Nile (though Speke could not prove same). Roger Deakins's gritty, realistic photography of rugged Kenyan locations contrasts with segments of cheery beauty back home in England between treks.

Rafelson brings expert detailing to the saga. The male bonding theme of the two explorers is forcefully and tastefully told. Besides its vivid presentation of the dangers posed by brutal, hostile African tribes, pic strongly develops its major themes of self-realization and self-aggrandizement.

As Speke, Scots actor Iain Glen creates sympathy for a wayward character. He resembles David Bowie on screen, a reminder that project originally was planned as a vehicle for British rock stars, including Bowie, until wiser heads prevailed.

•

MOURIR A MADRID
See: To Die in Madrid

•

MOURNING BECOMES ELECTRA
1947, 173 mins, US Ⓥ ⊙ col
Dir Dudley Nichols ***Prod*** Dudley Nichols ***Scr*** Dudley Nichols ***Ph*** George Barnes ***Ed*** Roland Gross, Chandler House ***Mus*** Richard Hageman ***Art*** Albert S. D'Agostino
Act Rosalind Russell, Michael Redgrave, Raymond Massey, Katina Paxinou, Leo Genn, Kirk Douglas (RKO)

Eugene O'Neill's post–Civil War version of the ancient Greek classic was at best "good for those who like that sort of thing." The success of the 1931 play proved that there were plenty who did—or who were drawn by the O'Neill name and/or a sense that they owed it to themselves aesthetically to see *Electra*.

Unfortunately, the picture—although still laden with tense drama—lacks much of the impact of the play. The five-hour play (plus an hour's intermission for dinner) seemed less long than the 2 hours and 53 minutes of picture, which is run without intermission.

Nichols, who produced, directed and wrote the adaptation for the screen, will rate a bow from the O'Neill lovers in that he has made no compromises. The picture is every bit as unrelenting in its detailing of family tragedy, brought on by the warping effect of Puritan conscience in conflict with human emotion, as was the play. Even the distorted Oedipus relationships are unflaggingly handled. Never is there concession to a smile or other relaxation from the hammering tragedy of murder, self-destruction and twisted, dramatic emotionalism. The legend has been set down in almost modern surroundings and given the locale and speech, the morals and manners of Civil War New England.

Performances are uniformly good, although they never rise beyond the drama that is inherent in the situations themselves. Too often the emoting consists of Rosalind Russell and Michael Redgrave popping their eyes. Outstanding are Raymond Massey and Henry Hull, the latter in the secondary role of an aged retainer.

1947: NOMINATIONS: Best Actor (Michael Redgrave), Actress (Rosalind Russell)

•

MOUSE THAT ROARED, THE
1959, 83 mins, UK Ⓥ col
Dir Jack Arnold ***Prod*** Walter Shenson ***Scr*** Roger MacDougall, Stanley Mann ***Ph*** John Wilcox ***Ed*** Raymond Poulton ***Mus*** Edwin Astley
Act Peter Sellers, Jean Seberg, David Kossoff, William Hartnell, Leo McKern, Macdonald Parke (Open Road/Columbia)

Screen satire can be as risky as a banana skin on a sidewalk. There are a few occasions when *The Mouse That Roared* gets oversmart, but on the whole it keeps its slight, amusing idea bubbling happily in the realms of straightforward comedy. It's a comedy in the old Ealing tradition.

The yarn [from the novel by Leonard Wibberly] concerns the Grand Duchy of Grand Fenwick, the world's smallest country, which relies for its existence on the export of a local wine to the U.S. When California bottles a cheaper, inferior imitation, Grand Fenwick is on verge of going broke. So the prime minister hits on the wily scheme of going to war against America, on the grounds that the loser in any war is invariably on the receiving end of hefty financial handouts from the winners.

But the invasion of NY by an army of 20 men with mail uniforms and bows and arrows goes awry.

Peter Sellers plays three roles in the film. He is the Grand Duchess Gloriana, the prime minister and also the hapless field marshal who upsets the prime minister's plans. Jean Seberg is pretty, but makes little impact, as the heroine. But there is useful work from William Hartnell, David Kossoff, Leo McKern and Macdonald Parke as a pompous American general. The sight of the completely deserted city is an awesome one and owes considerably to Jack Arnold's direction, and remarkable artwork and lensing.

•

MOVE OVER, DARLING
1963, 103 mins, US ▭ col
Dir Michael Gordon ***Prod*** Aaron Rosenberg, Martin Melcher ***Scr*** Hal Kanter, Jack Sher ***Ph*** Daniel L. Fapp ***Ed*** Robert Simpson ***Mus*** Lionel Newman ***Art*** Jack Martin Smith, Hilyard Brown
Act Doris Day, James Garner, Polly Bergen, Chuck Connors, Thelma Ritter, Fred Clark (20th Century-Fox)

Something old, something new, something borrowed, something blue is the nature of *Move Over, Darling*, a reproduction of the 1940 romantic comedy *My Favorite Wife*, which costarred Cary Grant and Irene Dunne.

Its complicated history is revealed in the writing credit: screenplay by Hal Kanter and Jack Sher based on a screenplay by Bella Spewack and Samuel Spewack from a story by Bella Spewack, Samuel Spewack and Leo McCarey. The "old" is the basic yarn about the guy who remarries five years after his first wife is thought to have perished only to have his first wife turn up alive and kicking at the outset of his honeymoon. The "new" are the chiefly lackluster embellishments tagged on. The "borrowed," to cite one example, is a telephone sequence that owes more than a little something to Shelley Berman. The "blue" isn't of a really offensive nature.

Doris Day and James Garner play it to the hilt, comically, dramatically and last, but not least (particularly in the case of the former), athletically. What is missing in their portrayals is a light touch—the ability to humorously convey with a subtle eyelash-bat or eyebrow-arch what it tends to take them a kick in the shins to accomplish. Others of prominence in the cast are Polly Bergen as the sexually-obsessed second wife (it's never really much of a contest between her and Day), Thelma Ritter as the understanding mother-in-law, and Chuck Connors as the male animal who shared the small island hunk of real estate alone with Day for five years.

•

MOVIE MOVIE
1978, 105 mins, US Ⓥ col
Dir Stanley Donen ***Prod*** Stanley Donen ***Scr*** Larry Gelbart, Sheldon Keller ***Ph*** Charles Rosher, Jr., Bruce Surtees ***Ed*** George Hively ***Mus*** Ralph Burns ***Art*** Jack Fisk
Act George C. Scott, Barbara Harris, Eli Wallach, Trish Van Devere, Red Buttons, Barry Bostwick (Warner)

Stanley Donen's *Movie Movie* is a clumsy attempt to spoof the kind of film fare encountered in pic houses of the 1930s and 1940s. The idea was patronizing in its conception, is a flatout embarrassment in its execution, and weak vehicle for George C. Scott and other principal talents involved.

The overlong, 105-minute feature is split into three parts: a black-and-white sendup of those boxing sagas where the slum youth fueled by earnest ambition gets catapulted to fame and riches (*Dynamite Hands*); a satire of a coming attractions trailer featuring a saga of World War I pilots; and finally, a shot-in-color takeoff of the making of a Flo Ziegfeld–type Broadway musical (*Baxter's Beauties of 1933*).

But instead of gently twitting the conventions of old Hollywood pot-boilers, *Movie Movie* tries to milk the clichés by observing and scorning them simultaneously. The conception is a mess, and it shows.

Things are so muddied that Donen tacked on, after the pic was shot, a prologue by George Burns telling the audience that yes, *Movie Movie* is intended as fun. Too bad Burns didn't stick around for the rest of the film.

•

MOVING TARGET, THE
SEE: HARPER

•

MR. & MRS. BRIDGE
1990, 124 mins, US Ⓥ ⊙ col
Dir James Ivory ***Prod*** Ismail Merchant ***Scr*** Ruth Prawer Jhabvala ***Ph*** Tony Pierce-Roberts ***Ed*** Humphrey Dixon ***Mus*** Richard Robbins ***Art*** David Gropman
Act Paul Newman, Joanne Woodward, Robert Sean Leonard, Kyra Sedgwick, Blythe Danner, Simon Callow (Cineplex Odeon/Merchant-Ivory/Halmi)

Mr. & Mrs. Bridge is an affecting study of an uppercrust Midwestern family in the late 1930s. Ruth Prawer Jhabvala has adapted two Evan S. Connell novels into a taut script. Books *Mrs. Bridge* (1959) and *Mr. Bridge* (1969) painted (from each spouse's point of view) a portrait of stuffy Kansas City lawyer Walter Bridge and his stifled wife, India, by a steady accretion of anecdotal detail. The screenplay presents a series of highly dramatic scenes in their lives, the payoffs among the novels' hundreds of brief chapters.

Central theme of India Bridge's gradual realization that her life has been crushed in her husband's shadow is strongly conveyed by Woodward in the role.

Casting of hubby Newman as her husband resonates in their intimate scenes, particularly a 1939 vacation to Paris when the Bridges briefly rekindle their romance, only to have it cut short by World War II.

Kyra Sedgwick is smashing as the Bridges's bohemian daughter who takes off for New York and an arts career.

1990: NOMINATION: Best Actress (Joanna Woodward)

•

MR. & MRS. SMITH
1941, 90 mins, US Ⓥ ⊙ b/w
Dir Alfred Hitchcock ***Prod*** Harry E. Edington (exec.) ***Scr*** Norman Krasna ***Ph*** Harry Stradling ***Ed*** William Hamilton ***Mus*** Edward Ward ***Art*** Van Nest Polglase, L. P. Williams
Act Carole Lombard, Robert Montgomery, Gene Raymond, Jack Carson, Philip Merivale, Lucile Watson (RKO)

Carole Lombard and Robert Montgomery are teamed successfully here in a light and gay marital farce, with accent on the laugh side through generation of continual bickering of the pair.

The Smiths (Lombard and Montgomery) are happily—though battlingly—married. A bantering question, "If you had to do it all over would you marry me" and the obvious husbandly reply of "No," starts things going. Advised that the three-year-old marriage is void because of legal technicalities, Mrs. Smith tosses Mr. Smith out of the house. Then the yarn develops into a runaround—with Mr. making continual stabs to recapture his wife, while his law partner, (Gene Raymond) is a ready victim of her advances aimed at inspiring jealousy.

Alfred Hitchcock pilots the story in a straight farcical groove—with resort to slapstick interludes or overplaying by the characters. Pacing his assignment at a steady gait, Hitchcock catches all of the laugh values from the above par script of Norman Krasna.

•

MR. ARKADIN
SEE: CONFIDENTIAL REPORT

MR. ASHTON WAS INDISCREET
SEE: THE SENATOR WAS INDISCREET

MR. BASEBALL
1992, 109 mins, US Ⓥ ⊙ ⌑ col
Dir Fred Schepisi ***Prod*** Fred Schepisi, Doug Claybourne, Robert Newmyer ***Scr*** Gary Ross, Kevin Wade, Monte Merrick ***Ph*** Ian Baker ***Ed*** Peter Honess ***Mus*** Jerry Goldsmith ***Art*** Ted Haworth
Act Tom Selleck, Ken Takakura, Aya Takanashi, Dennis Haysbert, Toshi Shioya, Kohsuke Toyohara (Walt Disney/Outlaw)

Universal's $40 million–plus pic's a tame look at the cultural differences that erupt from a surly Yank trying to adjust his strapping frame and bad attitude to the rigid strictures of Japanese sport and society.

Given the central character of Jack Elliot (Tom Selleck), former Yankee World Series MVP who's traded off to Japan to make way for a young prospect (played by White Sox star Frank Thomas), there's only one direction in which the story can go, and it does, as if by prescription: he arrives in Nagoya to play for the Chunichi Dragons, hates it, looks down on all these little men who play such a safe, conformist brand of baseball, bristles at his stern manager, then finally starts getting it together as he begins to accept the virtues of the harmonic Japanese approach.

Also, an interracial romance between Elliot and the beautiful, westernized Hiroko (Aya Takanashi), daughter of the Dragons's manager (Ken Takakura), stirs up prejudicial feelings within the family.

Selleck is utterly believable as the star, but even his broad shoulders can't carry the weight of the entire pic. All the Japanese remain one-dimensional.

•

MR. BILLION
1977, 91 mins, US Ⓥ col
Dir Jonathan Kaplan ***Prod*** Steven Bach, Ken Friedman ***Scr*** Ken Friedman, Jonathan Kaplan ***Ph*** Matthew F. Leonetti ***Ed*** O. Nicholas Brown ***Mus*** Dave Grusin ***Art*** Richard Berger
Act Terence Hill [= Mario Girotti], Valerie Perrine, Jackie Gleason, Slim Pickens, William Redfield, Chill Wills (Pantheon)

Terence Hill is charming as an Italian mechanic who inherits a fortune and has a hell of a time getting to Frisco in time to claim it. Valerie Perrine and Jackie Gleason are among those who try to fleece the innocent of his loot. There are many loose ends in the plot, and some choppy sequences, but the pic is brisk enjoyment.

The obvious inspiration for the film was Frank Capra's classic 1936 populist comedy-fantasy, *Mr. Deeds Goes to Town*, in which Gary Cooper inherited a fortune only to find himself besieged by greedy city slickers.

Director Jonathan Kaplan also borrows heavily from Alfred Hitchcock. The blend of Capra and Hitchcock doesn't always work, and the film often seems too much of an artificial film buff homage.

•

MR. BLANDINGS BUILDS HIS DREAM HOUSE
1948, 93 mins, US Ⓥ ⊙ b/w
Dir H.C. Potter ***Prod*** Norman Panama, Melvin Frank ***Scr*** Norman Panama, Melvin Frank ***Ph*** James Wong Howe ***Ed*** Harry Marker ***Mus*** Leigh Harline ***Art*** Albert S. D'Agostino, Carroll Clark
Act Cary Grant, Myrna Loy, Melvyn Douglas, Reginald Denny, Jason Robards, Lex Barker (Selznick/RKO)

Eric Hodgins's novel of the trials and tribulations of the Blandings, while building their dream house, read a lot funnier than they filmed. Norman Panama and Melvin Frank come through with a glossy lustre in handling physical production, but fail to jell the story into solid film fare in their dual scripting.

Film's opening pulls some standard sight gags that register strongly, helped by the business injected through H. C. Potter's direction. Script gets completely out of hand when unnecessary jealousy twist is introduced, neither advancing the story nor adding laughs.

Grant is up to his usual performance standard as Blandings, getting the best from the material, and Myrna Loy comes through with another of her screen wife assignments nicely. Melvyn Douglas, the lawyer friend of the family, gives it a tongue-in-cheek treatment. Trio's finesse and Potter's light directorial touch do much to give proceedings a lift.

•

MR. DEEDS GOES TO TOWN
1936, 115 mins, US Ⓥ ⊙ b/w
Dir Frank Capra ***Prod*** Frank Capra ***Scr*** Robert Riskin ***Ph*** Joseph Walker ***Ed*** Gene Havlick ***Mus*** Howard Jackson (dir.) ***Art*** Stephen Goosson
Act Gary Cooper, Jean Arthur, George Bancroft, Lionel Stander, Douglass Dumbrille, Raymond Walburn (Columbia)

Mr. Deeds Goes to Town needs the marquee draught of Gary Cooper, Jean Arthur and George Bancroft to make it really go to town. With a sometimes too thin structure [from a story by Clarence Budington Kelland], the players and director Frank Capra have contrived to convert *Deeds* into fairly sturdy substance. The farce is good-humored and the trouping and production workmanlike, but there are some lapses in midriff that cause considerable uncertainty.

The native Yankee shrewdness endowed Longfellow Deeds takes a male Pollyanna tack that skirts some dangerous shoals. A mug with a $20 million heritage should know how to be more practical about things and while scriptwriter Robert Riskin and Capra have managed to have him turn the tables more or less effectively in the trial before a lunacy commission, there are times when Cooper's impression is just a bit too scatterbrained for sympathetic comfort.

Capra's direction is more mundane than flighty. With machinating attorneys, false claimants to the estate, down-to-earth "jest folks," etc., it's to be expected that the general structure will be in like tune.

Deeds is a guy who plays a tuba in bed, slides down banisters, decides to give away his $20 million just like that, after John Wray in a theatrical hokum bit waves a gun at him, fortified with a quasi-communistic plea. Combined with some of the other lines and business accorded the male topper, audience credulity, despite the general lightness of the theme, becomes strained.

1936: Best Director

NOMINATIONS: Best Picture, Actor (Gary Cooper), Screenplay, Sound

•

MR. DESTINY
1990, 105 mins, US Ⓥ ⊙ col
Dir James Orr ***Prod*** James Orr, Jim Cruickshank, Susan B. Landau ***Scr*** James Orr, Jim Cruickshank ***Ph*** Alex Thomson ***Ed*** Michael R. Miller ***Mus*** David Newman ***Art*** Michael Seymour
Act James Belushi, Linda Hamilton, Michael Caine, Jon Lovitz, Hart Bochner, Rene Russo (Touchstone/Silver Screen Partners IV)

A heavy-handed, by-the-numbers fantasy about an ordinary Joe who thinks his life would have been different if he'd connected with that all-important pitch in a high school baseball game.

James Belushi plays small-town, white-collar working stiff Larry Burrows, who on his depressing 35th birthday stumbles into a bar where a mysterious, twinkly-eyed barman (Michael Caine) serves him up a "spilt milk" elixir that sends him spinning back in time to take another swat at that baseball.

He hits a home run, and his whole life turns out differently, just as he expected. But guess what? He's not any happier than he was before.

So what if he's married to the dishy prom queen (Rene Russo) and has become the absurdly wealthy president of a sports equipment company—the same one he slaved for in his other life. He misses his original wife (Linda Hamilton) and their unpretentious lifestyle, and whether it makes sense or not, he sets out to win her back.

•

MR. HOBBS TAKES A VACATION
1962, 115 mins, US Ⓥ ⌑ col
Dir Henry Koster ***Prod*** Jerry Wald ***Scr*** Nunnally Johnson ***Ph*** William C. Mellor ***Ed*** Marjorie Fowler ***Mus*** Henry Mancini ***Art*** Jack Martin Smith, Malcolm Brown
Act James Stewart, Maureen O'Hara, Fabian, John Saxon, Reginald Gardiner, Marie Wilson (20th Century-Fox)

Togetherness, all-American family style, is given a gently irreverent poke in the ribs in *Mr. Hobbs Takes a Vacation*.

This is a fun picture, although it misfires, chiefly in the situation development department.

Nunnally Johnson's screenplay, based on the novel, *Hobbs' Vacation*, by Edward Streeter, is especially strong in the dialogue area. The film is peppered with refreshingly sharp, sophisticated references and quips. But Johnson's screenplay falls down in development of its timely premise, leaving the cast and director Henry Koster heavily dependent on their own comedy resources in generating fun.

Hobbs (James Stewart) is a St. Louis banker who has the misfortune to spend his vacation at the seashore with 10 other members of his immediate family, setting up a series of situations roughly designed to illustrate the pitfalls of that grand old Yankee institution, the family reunion.

The picture has its staunchest ally in Stewart, whose acting instincts are so remarkably keen that he can instill amusement into scenes that otherwise threaten to fall flat. Some of the others in the cast, endowed with less intuitive gifts for light comedy, do not fare as well.

Maureen O'Hara is decorative as Mrs. Hobbs. Fabian struggles along in an undernourished romantic role, and warbles, with considerable uncertainty, an uninspired ditty, tagged *Cream Puff*, by Johnny Mercer and Henry Mancini, who has composed a satisfactory score for the film.

John Saxon is mired in a stereotypical role of a pompously dense intellect.

•

MR. HOLLAND'S OPUS
1995, 142 mins, US Ⓥ ⦿ ▭ col
Dir Stephen Merek ***Prod*** Ted Field, Michael Nolin, Robert W. Cort ***Scr*** Patrick Sheane Duncan ***Ph*** Oliver Wood ***Ed*** Trudy Ship ***Mus*** Michael Kamen ***Art*** David Nichols
Act Richard Dreyfuss, Glenne Headly, Jay Thomas, Olympia Dukakis, W. H. Macy, Alicia Witt (Interscope/PolyGram/Hollywood)

An idealized tribute to a charismatic teacher who has devoted his entire life to music appreciation, *Mr. Holland's Opus* has the same old-fashioned texture as *Goodbye, Mr. Chips*, the 1939 M-G-M classic that won Robert Donat an actor Oscar.

Covering 1965 to the present, tale concerns Glenn Holland (Richard Dreyfuss), a passionate composer who believes that his true calling is to write one memorable piece of music. Over the course of his life, however, Holland becomes a reluctant hero, a man who fulfills himself not at the piano, but at the blackboard.

Borrowing heavily from *It's a Wonderful Life*, script stresses the pleasures and rewards in life that are unplanned and unanticipated. Initially, Holland accepts his school job as a "backup" position that will give him free time to compose, never imagining that his next 30 years would be spent in the classroom. But Holland ultimately realizes his legacy as an inspirational teacher is just as important as his longed-for opus.

Rather tiresomely, saga switches back and forth from school to family life. At home, married to a most understanding and loving wife, Iris (Glenne Headly), Holland has to accept the sad, somewhat ironic realization that their only son, Cole, is deaf.

While Stephen Herek's film has an epic arc embracing the era's major political events (Vietnam, Nixon's resignation) and cultural traumas (John Lennon's assassination), it lacks epic vision. The narrative unfolds as a catalog of familiar, often clichéd episodes.

Dreyfuss is the kind of actor who has been getting better as he grows older, and here he acquits himself with a sensitive, honorable performance. The often underrated Headly lends fine support as the sensitive wife and mother.

Pic was shot in and around Portland, OR.

1995: NOMINATION: Best Actor (Richard Dreyfuss)

•

MR. HULOT'S HOLIDAY
SEE: LES VACANCES DE MONSIEUR HULOT

•

MR. JOHNSON
1990, 103 mins, US Ⓥ col
Dir Bruce Beresford ***Prod*** Michael Fitzgerald ***Scr*** William Boyd ***Ph*** Peter James ***Ed*** Humphrey Dixon ***Mus*** Georges Delerue ***Art*** Herbert Pinter
Act Maynard Eziashi, Pierce Brosnan, Edward Woodward, Beatie Edney, Denis Quilley (Fitzgerald)

Capitalism and colonialism intertwine like a two-headed snake in this ponderous but well-made film. Director Bruce Beresford's modestly scaled follow-up to Oscar winner *Driving Miss Daisy* suffers from a slow, marginally involving storyline.

Pic's foremost discovery is Nigerian actor Maynard Eziashi in the title role as a young African obsessed with British mores, resourcefully working outside the rigid limits of his colonial clerkship.

Johnson uses that knack to help his boss, Rudbeck (Pierce Brosnan), build a road connecting their small outpost to the outside world, though his consistent circumvention of proper channels eventually catches up with him and proves his downfall.

Working from a 1939 novel by Joyce Carey set in the 1920s, Beresford and writer William Boyd have delivered a film strangely devoid of emotion and lacking a clear point of view.

Brosnan's straight-legged bureaucrat proves so stiff and lifeless there's no sense of caring in any direction, toward either his wife (Beatie Edney) or Johnson. Edward Woodward injects much-needed life into the staid proceedings as a vulgar expatriate English shop owner, a boozy bigot.

•

MR. JONES
1993, 112 mins, US Ⓥ ⦿ col
Dir Mike Figgis ***Prod*** Alan Greisman, Debra Greenfield ***Scr*** Eric Roth, Michael Cristofer ***Ph*** Juan Ruiz Anchia ***Ed*** Tom Rolf ***Mus*** Maurice Jarre ***Art*** Waldemar Kalinowski
Act Richard Gere, Lena Olin, Anne Bancroft, Tom Irwin, Delroy Lindo, Bruce Altman (Rastar/Tri-Star)

Mixing therapy and romance is a no-no in real life, and it proves problematic as well as the subject of *Mr. Jones*. A high-energy performance by Richard Gere and an intensely brooding one from Lena Olin engage attentive viewer interest, but the stars are forced to overcompensate for a rather slow pace and lack of plot.

Gere's cocky charm carries the first half hour, as Jones, on a manic high, hands out hundred-dollar bills, tests out pianos at a music showroom, has a playful afternoon tryst with a blonde pickup at a fancy hotel and, in an amusingly audacious scene, marches down the aisle at a packed symphony hall in a burst of enthusiasm and shows the conductor a thing or two about conducting Beethoven.

This naturally gets him carted away as a loony, diagnosed as a bipolar manic depressive. But he's soon released, against the wishes of Dr. Libbie Bowen (Olin), who thinks the guy poses a real threat, particularly to himself. With nothing else going on, the screenwriters have doctor and patient fall in love. Script [from a screen story by Eric Roth] warms up the romance very slowly.

Gere's effervescence in his manic phase endows the film with an engaging energy, but one can never really see the character and forget the actor. Olin gives a deeply serious reading of an intelligent, somewhat brittle woman who trusts her intuition as much as her logical decisions.

•

MR. LUCKY
1943, 94 mins, US Ⓥ ⦿ b/w
Dir H. C. Potter ***Prod*** David Hempstead ***Scr*** Milton Holmes, Adrian Scott ***Ph*** George Barnes ***Ed*** Theron Warth ***Mus*** Roy Webb ***Art*** William Cameron Menzies
Act Cary Grant, Laraine Day, Charles Bickford, Gladys Cooper, Alan Carney, Henry Stephenson (RKO)

Cary Grant is a resourceful and opportunist gambling operator, figuring on outfitting his outlawed gaming ship for trip to Havana. But coin and draft registration balk his departure. Assuming name and a draft card of a dying 4-F, he launches drive to raise the moola and runs into society heiress Laraine Day. Pursuing her for romantic pitches, he lands as member of the war relief agency and proceeds to ply his con to help the outfit with supplies and boat charters.

Picture carries an authentic ring to operations of big-time gamblers, and it faithfully follows the professional premise of "never give the sucker a break, but never cheat a friend." Writer Milton Holmes, in selling his first screen original, hews closely to the lines of actual incidents rather than depending on synthetic dramatics to drop it into the groove of obvious cinematic dramatics.

•

MR. MAJESTYK
1974, 104 mins, US Ⓥ col
Dir Richard Fleischer ***Prod*** Walter Mirisch ***Scr*** Elmore Leonard ***Ph*** Richard H. Kline ***Ed*** Ralph E. Winters ***Mus*** Charles Bernstein ***Art*** [uncredited]
Act Charles Bronson, Al Lettieri, Linda Cristal, Lee Purcell, Paul Koslo, Alejandro Rey (Mirisch)

Mr. Majestyk makes a first-reel pretense of dealing with the thorny subject of migrant Chicano farm laborers, but social relevance is soon clobbered by the usual Charles Bronson heroics, here mechanically navigated by director Richard Fleischer.

Bronson, in a boringly stoic performance, plays a melon-grower whose fair labor practices are rewarded with a trumped-up assault charge that lands him in jail. During a shoot-out engineered by Mafia gangsters to free underworld killer Al Lettieri as prisoners are being moved from one jail to another, Bronson captures the hitman and offers to return Lettieri in exchange for his own freedom. Lettieri eventually escapes and vows revenge on Bronson.

The narrative makes little sense unless viewed as a study in pathology.

•

MR. MOM
1983, 91 mins, US Ⓥ ⦿ col
Dir Stan Dragoti ***Prod*** Lynn Loring, Lauren Shuler, Harry Colomby ***Scr*** John Hughes ***Ph*** Victor J. Kemper ***Ed*** Patrick Kennedy ***Mus*** Lee Holdridge ***Art*** Alfred Sweeney
Act Michael Keaton, Teri Garr, Frederick Koehler, Taliesin Jaffe, Courtney & Brittany White, Christopher Lloyd (Sherwood/20th Century-Fox)

The comic talents of Michael Keaton and Teri Garr are largely wasted in *Mr. Mom*, an unoriginal romantic comedy where breadwinner husband and homemaker wife switch roles.

Though Keaton and Garr occasionally manage to evoke some pathos and laughs, it's an uphill battle that is won solely on the strength of their individual personalities.

Keaton, close to perfection as the husband and father depressed by unemployment but always a sport with his family, is already a known bundle of comic energy. But he especially shines here in some more dramatic moments with his children.

Garr, as always, is a delight to watch though it would be nice to see her in a role where she wasn't someone's wife or mother. Still, her inspired double takes continue to say more than pages of dialogue while her keen timing helps somewhat in the more beleaguered scenes.

•

MR. MOTO IN DANGER ISLAND
SEE: DANGER ISLAND

•

MR. MOTO'S GAMBLE
1938, 71 mins, US b/w
Dir James Tinling ***Prod*** John Stone (exec.) ***Scr*** Charles Belden, Jerry Cady ***Ph*** Lucien Andriot
Act Peter Lorre, Keye Luke, Dick Baldwin, Lynn Bari, Douglas Fowley, Jayne Regan (20th Century-Fox)

Romance and comedy are well interwoven as Moto (Peter Lorre) solves a ring murder. Okay action, and the story is atmosphered with the usual fight game addicts, cops, gamblers, bookies and trainers, besides women. Lynn Bari and Jayne Regan divide the s.a. assignment.

Moto runs a school for sleuths. While attending a fight, one of the ring contestants is killed in action. Moto's chief assistants are his two unwittingly funny pupils, Wellington (Maxie Rosenbloom), and Lee Chan, son of Charlie Chan (Keye Luke). Rosenbloom as a dimwit trying to learn to be a cop surprises with the quality of his buffoonery. Dialog is okay and Keye Luke adds to the screwball comicalities.

Peter Lorre is beginning to look more at ease in the role of Moto [in the third of the series]. Bari is the newspaper gal heroine, but Regan also angles for the hero.

•

MR. MOTO'S LAST WARNING
1939, 71 mins, US Ⓥ b/w
Dir Norman Foster ***Prod*** Sol M. Wurtzel (exec.) ***Scr*** Philip MacDonald, Norman Foster ***Ph*** Virgil Miller ***Ed*** Norman Colbert ***Mus*** Samuel Kaylin (dir.) ***Art*** Bernard Herzbrun, Lewis Creber
Act Peter Lorre, Ricardo Cortez, Virginia Field, John Carradine, George Sanders, Joan Carol (20th Century-Fox)

This [sixth in the series] is one of the better Moto pictures. Cast in a colorful Egyptian background, yarn is replete with mystery and action. Strong supporting cast is chiefly notable for excellent comeback by Ricardo Cortez. Also creditable are Virginia Field, blonde, English importation; George Sanders, the heavy, also British; John Carradine as a secret service operative, and Robert Coote as a caricatured English tourist.

Peter Lorre, in the title role, agent of the International Police, and Cortez, as leader of a spy ring working for some unnamed country anxious to disrupt England and France's sphere of influence in the Near East, are the principal protagonists. Posing as a vaudeville ventriloquist, Cortez plots to blow up the French fleet as it steams into Port Said for maneuvers. Lorre, working as a Japanese shopkeeper, survives several attempts on his life, but ultimately frustrates the plot.

Photography, direction and editing are adequate.

•

MR. MOTO TAKES A CHANCE
1938, 57 mins, US b/w
Dir Norman Foster ***Prod*** Sol M. Wurtzel (exec.) ***Scr*** Lou Breslow, John Patrick ***Ph*** Virgil Miller ***Ed*** Nick DeMaggio ***Mus*** Samuel Kaylin (dir.) ***Art*** Albert Hogsett
Act Peter Lorre, Rochelle Hudson, Robert Kent, J. Edward Romberg, Chick Chandler, George Regas (20th Century-Fox)

Picture, which concerns the activities of two government secret agents, has trapdoors, poison air guns, hidden passages, machine guns, carrier pigeons, bolo knives and a generous assortment of jungle beasts. There are too many hairbreadth escapes and uncanny accomplishments for a regulation feature. It all smacks of serial style.

Film also is weakened because it gives Peter Lorre few chances. Instead, the plot has him double as a mysterious, wrinkled priest role, adding further mystification and little to the yarn.

Norman Foster's direction [of this fourth entry in the series] is far behind his earlier efforts. He also helped with the original story, along with Willis Cooper. What humor that is introduced is too forced. Many of the sly tricks, smart twists and suspense present in first pictures in this series are missing.

Lorre plays Mr. Moto and Rochelle Hudson, as the other secret agent, is acceptable. Robert Kent makes a passably good newsreel cameraman, while Chick Chandler manages to grab a few laughs as his assistant. J. Edward Bromberg is the pompous Oriental ruler.

•

MR. MOTO TAKES A VACATION
1939, 65 mins, US b/w
Dir Norman Foster ***Scr*** Philip MacDonald, Norman Foster ***Ph*** Charles Clarke ***Ed*** Norman Colbert
Act Peter Lorre, Joseph Schildkraut, Lionel Atwill, Virginia Field, John King, Iva Stewart (20th Century-Fox)

Enmeshed in unconvincing mystery melodramatics, latest of Moto series is a very weak effort, full of incongruities in both story development and direction.

On his vacation Moto follows the supposed crown of the Queen of Sheba from its discovery in Egyptian diggings until arrival in a San Francisco museum. Motivation is conveniently set up for jewel thieves to go after the sparklers, with Moto intuitively keeping them under observation until he captures the famed international crook when latter attempts to walk out of the museum with the crown.

Story unfolds in unconvincing manner, action swinging in and out of dark alleys and passages, winding up in darkened museum to generate mysterious and unrecognizable figures sneaking around to further confuse onlookers.

Peter Lorre, with regulation Moto calm assurance, capably handles role of the Nippon sleuth, doing the best he can with material at hand. Norman Foster has done better directing jobs in the past, and on previous Moto subjects. Movement is uneven, with fast-paced sequences too infrequent, and general unfolding draggy and confusing. [Pic was eighth and last of the original series.]

•

MR. MUSIC
1950, 110 mins, US b/w
Dir Richard Haydn ***Prod*** Robert L. Welch ***Scr*** Arthur Sheekman ***Ph*** George Barnes ***Ed*** Duane Harrison, Everett Douglas
Act Bing Crosby, Nancy Olson, Charles Coburn, Ruth Hussey, Robert Stack, Tom Ewell (Paramount)

Mr. Music is a variation of a backstage musical, utilizing a lazy songsmith as the central figure.

The heart interest is well carried forward by Nancy Olson as the serious-minded undergraduate turned secretary who becomes Bing Crosby's creative policewoman, so to speak, and gets him back into harness as a songwriter instead of running off to the golf course, hobnobbing with bookies, and the like.

Charles Coburn is the vet producer who needs a comeback show, and looks to Crosby's personal rehabilitation to achieve that.

The utilization of Peggy Lee, The Champions (Gower & Marge), Groucho Marx, the Merry Macs and Dorothy Kirsten gives the unfolding a proper lift in the right spots.

•

MR. NANNY
1993, 84 mins, US Ⓥ ⦿ col
Dir Michael Gottlieb ***Prod*** Bob Engelman ***Scr*** Edward Rugoff, Michael Gottlieb ***Ph*** Peter Stein ***Ed*** Earl Ghaffari, Michael Ripps, Amy Tompkins ***Mus*** David Johansen, Brian Koonin ***Art*** Don DeFina
Act Terry "Hulk" Hogan, Sherman Hemsley, Austin Pendleton, Robert Gorman, Madeline Zima, David Johansen (New Line)

Cross *Uncle Buck* with *Home Alone*, stir in the Hulkster, and you've got *Mr. Nanny*, a comedy-actioner that should entertain the under 12 and couch potato sets.

Excuse for a plot has "Hulk" Hogan as an ex-grappler whiling away days fishing in Florida. To help out his old trainer (Sherman Hemsley), he reluctantly takes a job as bodyguard to computer tycoon Austin Pendleton.

Twist is that Hogan, who loathes kids, has in reality been hired to protect Pendleton's brats (Robert Gorman, Madeline Zima), as well as double as nanny when the latest in a long line walks out. The anklebiters have been targeted for kidnapping by a psycho loon (David Johansen) who wants one of Pendleton's microchips.

Meat of the movie is the domestic war between the indestructible Hogan and the two kids, whose preferred reading is *Unusual Weapons of the Inquisition*. Telegraphed finale has everyone learning mutual respect and taking on Johansen and his heavies in a warehouse finale.

•

MR. NORTH
1988, 92 mins, US Ⓥ ⦿ col
Dir Danny Huston ***Prod*** Steven Haft, Skip Steloff, Tom Shaw ***Scr*** Janet Roach, John Huston, James Costigan ***Ph*** Robin Vidgeon ***Ed*** Roberto Silvi ***Mus*** David McHugh ***Art*** Eugene Lee
Act Anthony Edwards, Robert Mitchum, Lauren Bacall, Harry Dean Stanton, Anjelica Huston, Mary Stuart Masterson (Heritage/Goldwyn)

By cowriting and serving as executive producer, the late John Huston could be said to have passed the baton to son Danny Huston on *Mr. North*. Unfortunately, Danny has not only dropped the stick but tripped over his own feet in his feature film debut, a woefully flat affair which even a stellar cast cannot bring to life.

The 1973 novel by Thornton Wilder is a resolutely old-fashioned tale about an unusually gifted young man who stirs things up among the rich folk in Newport, RI, circa 1926.

Wilder's fanciful yarn has Theophilus North, a bright Yale graduate, arriving in the seaside bastion of old money and extravagance and making his way in society by magically curing the rich of what ails them, and charming them to boot.

All of this gains North a reputation as something of a savior, but doesn't go down too well with the pillar of the local medical community, who drags the shining fellow into court.

Anthony Edwards gives it a reasonable try in the leading role, his matter-of-factness in the face of extraordinary accomplishments proving rather appealing, but he can't singlehandedly rescue this waterlogged vessel.

•

MR. SATURDAY NIGHT
1992, 119 mins, US Ⓥ ⦿ col
Dir Billy Crystal ***Prod*** Billy Crystal ***Scr*** Billy Crystal, Lowell Ganz, Babaloo Mandel ***Ph*** Don Peterman ***Ed*** Kent Beyda ***Mus*** Marc Shaiman ***Art*** Albert Brenner
Act Billy Crystal, David Paymer, Julie Warner, Helen Hunt, Jerry Orbach, Ron Silver (Castle Rock/Face)

Bringing the fictional comedian he created eight years earlier to the big screen, Billy Crystal hits a double with *Mr. Saturday Night*. By turns relentlessly jokey and shamelessly schmaltzy, the actor-writer's directorial debut charts a sometimes unpleasant funnyman's long career in choppy, two-dimensional fashion, but delivers enough laughs and heart-tugging.

As a veteran who feels dead without an audience, Buddy (Crystal) says he's "got cancer of the career. It's inoperable." Flashbacks reveal that the stubborn comic was usually his own worst enemy, deliberately undercutting himself with his superiors and letting his emotions get the better of him.

Other than his career, the only thing of enduring importance to Buddy is his relationship with his brother, Stan, a gentle, kind soul (David Paymer, in a standout performance).

After Stan retires to Florida, Buddy decides to take on a new agent (waspy blonde Helen Hunt), who has never heard of any of the old-time comedy greats but nevertheless gets Buddy a chance at some top jobs, such as a possible starring role in a film by megadirector Larry Meyerson (Ron Silver).

It's basically all Crystal and Paymer's show, and they age very convincingly through the years.

1992: NOMINATION: Best Supp. Actor (David Paymer)

•

MRS. BROWN
1997, 103 mins, UK Ⓥ ⦿ col
Dir John Madden ***Prod*** Sarah Curtis ***Scr*** Jeremy Brock ***Ph*** Richard Greatrex ***Ed*** Robin Sales ***Mus*** Stephen Warbeck ***Art*** Martin Childs
Act Judi Dench, Billy Connolly, Geoffrey Palmer, Anthony Sher, Gerard Butler, Richard Pasco (Ecosse/BBC)

Mrs. Brown is a sensitive, richly detailed drama about the extraordinarily complex and intimate friendship Queen Victoria developed with her loyal servant John Brown, a relationship that scandalized the entire country and even threatened the stability of the crown.

Story begins in 1864, three years after Victoria (Judi Dench) has lost her beloved husband and mentor, Albert, and plunged into a deep and dizzying depression. Into this gloomy milieu enters Scottish servant Brown (Billy Connolly), the Royal Family's loyal hunting guide and horse caretaker. Down-to-earth and with no regard for protocol, Brown causes immediate upheaval in the court. Rumors of an affair begin to scandalize British society.

Brown is contrasted with Prime Minister Disraeli (Anthony Sher), a shrewd, charismatic politician who understands that it's the servant who holds the key to the queen's return to public life, an act that will once and for all terminate all rumors of an unseemly affair.

Director John Madden handles his chores far more impressively than he did in his last assignments (*Ethan Frome*, *Golden Gate*), employing an unobtrusive style that serves the drama effectively and allows his gifted thesps to develop highly modulated characterizations.

1997: NOMINATIONS: Best Actress (Judi Dench), Makeup

•

MRS. DOUBTFIRE
1993, 125 mins, US Ⓥ ⦿ ▭ col
Dir Chris Columbus ***Prod*** Marsha Garces Williams, Robin Williams, Mark Radcliffe ***Scr*** Randi Mayem Singer, Leslie Dixon ***Ph*** Donald McAlpine ***Ed*** Raja Gosnell ***Mus*** Howard Shore ***Art*** Angelo Graham
Act Robin Williams, Sally Field, Pierce Brosnan, Harvey Fierstein, Polly Holliday, Lisa Jakub (20th Century-Fox/Blue Wolf)

Although overly sappy in places and probably 20 minutes too long, this Robin Williams–in-drag vehicle [from the novel *Alias Mrs. Doubtfire* by Anne Fine] provides the comic a slick surface for doing his shtick, within a story possessing broad family appeal. Director Chris Columbus shrewdly brings together many of the same selling points as in his *Home Alone* movies, mixing broad comedic strokes with heavy-handed messages about the magical power of family.

While the concept screams *Tootsie*, the tone is more *Mr. Mom*. Williams plays flaky, unemployed actor Daniel who botches his son's birthday party and ends up getting tossed out by his wife (Sally Field). Limited to weekly visitation, Daniel and his brother (Harvey Fierstein), a gay makeup artist, hatch the plan of having him masquerade as a matronly nanny—the better to steal precious hours with his three adorable moppets.

The pic does reveal occasional inspiration in terms of sharp dialogue and in scenes of well-choreographed slapstick lunacy, among them an unexpected visit from a court-appointed supervisor and a crowning scene in which Daniel/Mrs Doubtfire fulfills two dinner engagements at the same time.

That said, *Mrs. Doubtfire*'s warm-fuzzy aspects prove a bit much, from the raspy Sally Brown voice on the wide-eyed youngest daughter (Mara Wilson) to the ham-fisted and plentiful "You're OK even if your parents aren't together" speeches. Greg Cannom warrants kudos for the amusing body makeup.

1993: Best Makeup

•

MR. SKEFFINGTON
1944, 126 mins, US Ⓥ ⦿ b/w
Dir Vincent Sherman ***Prod*** Philip G. Epstein, Julius J. Epstein ***Scr*** Philip G. Epstein, Julius J. Epstein ***Ph*** Ernest Haller ***Ed*** Ralph Dawson ***Mus*** Franz Waxman ***Art*** Robert Haas
Act Bette Davis, Claude Rains, Walter Abel, Richard Waring, George Coulouris, Marjorie Riordan (Warner)

Fitting Bette Davis like a silk glove, the same as the gowns that she wears to intrigue the male of the species in defiance of all the laws of good womanhood, in the part of the vainglorious, selfish wife and mother, *Mr. Skeffington* is not only another triumph for the Warner star but also a picture of terrific strength.

Philip G. and Julius J. Epstein, who have given the story fine production and backgrounds, also adapted the book [by "Elizabeth"] but locale it in America rather than in England.

The story moves steadily and smoothly, gathering much impact as it goes along, while also the dialog ranges from the smart to the trenchantly dramatic in limning the life of the woman who lived for her beauty but found that it wasn't of a lasting character.

Davis, playing the coquettish daughter of a once-wealthy family, progresses through the years from 1914 before World War I to the present, going with gradual changes from early girlhood to around 50 years when suddenly aging badly as result of illness.

Opposite Davis is the able Claude Rains, the successful Wall Street tycoon who goes blind and also prematurely ages as result of several years spent in a Nazi concentration camp following the beginning of World War II.

1944: NOMINATIONS: Best Actor (Claude Rains), Actress (Bette Davis)

•

MRS. MIKE

1949, 98 mins, US b/w

Dir Louis King ***Prod*** Samuel Bischoff, Edward Gross ***Scr*** Alfred Lewis Levitt, DeWitt Bodeen ***Ph*** Joseph Biroc ***Ed*** Paul Weatherwax ***Mus*** Max Steines

Act Dick Powell, Evelyn Keyes, J. M. Kerrigan, Angela Clarke (United Artists/Regal)

Mrs Mike [from the book by Benedict and Nancy Freedman] is the story of a Boston girl who married a mountie and goes into the wilderness of Canada's Northwest territory to live.

The performances are splendid. Evelyn Keyes particularly shines in the title role with a portrayal that has excellent emotional depth and just the right touch of humor. As her costar, Dick Powell is fine. He approaches his assignment as the conscientious mountie with understanding. He also supplies the narrative that bridges the footage.

Considerable stress is laid on wilderness perils and the tragedies that befall pioneers. The emotional gamut abounds in childbirth, epidemics, amputation and death, all experiences encountered by the real-life Mrs. Michael Flannigan when she took to the northwoods in 1905.

•

MRS. MINIVER

1942, 133 mins, US Ⓥ ⊙ b/w

Dir William Wyler ***Prod*** Sidney Franklin ***Scr*** Arthur Wimperis, George Froeschel, James Hilton, Claudine West ***Ph*** Joseph Ruttenberg ***Ed*** Harold F. Kress ***Mus*** Herbert Stothart ***Art*** Cedric Gibbons, Urie McCleary

Act Greer Garson, Walter Pidgeon, Teresa Wright, May Whitty, Reginald Owen, Henry Wilcoxon (M-G-M)

Superbly catching the warmth and feeling of Jan Struther's characters in her bestselling book of sketches, *Mrs. Miniver,* Metro has created out of it a poignant story of the joys and sorrows, the humor and pathos of middle-class family life in wartime England.

Its one defect, not uncommon with Metro's prestige product, is its length. It gets about three-quarters of the way through and begins floundering, like a vaude act that doesn't know how to get off the stage.

In addition, the film, in its quiet yet actionful way, is, probably entirely unintentionally, one of the strongest pieces of propaganda against complacency to come out of the war.

When Mrs. Miniver's husband is summoned from his bed at 2 A.M. to help rescue the legions of Dunkirk, when her son flies out across the Channel each night, when she frightenedly captures a sick and starving German pilot who bears resemblance to her own boy, *Mrs. Miniver* truly brings the war into one's own family.

Greer Garson, with her knee-weakening smile, and Walter Pidgeon, almost equally personable, are the Minivers. Scarcely less engaging or capable are young Teresa Wright as their daughter-in-law and Richard Ney in the difficult role of their son.

It's impossible to praise too highly William Wyler's direction, which hits only one or two false notes throughout the lengthy presentation. His is clearly the understanding heart to whom these are not actors, but people living genuine joy and sorrow and fear and doubt.

1942: Best Picture, Director, Actress (Greer Garson), Supp. Actress (Teresa Wright), Screenplay, B&W Cinematography

NOMINATION: Best Actor (Walter Pidgeon), Supp. Actor (Henry Travers), Supp. Actress (May Whitty), Editing, Sound, Special Effects

•

MR. SMITH GOES TO WASHINGTON

1939, 126 mins, US Ⓥ ⊙ b/w

Dir Frank Capra ***Prod*** Frank Capra ***Scr*** Sidney Buchman ***Ph*** Joseph Walker ***Ed*** Gene Havlick, Al Clark ***Mus*** Dimitri Tiomkin ***Art*** Lionel Banks

Act Jean Arthur, James Stewart, Claude Rains, Edward Arnold, Thomas Mitchell, Guy Kibbee (Columbia)

Frank Capra goes to Washington in unwinding the story [by Lewis R. Foster], and in so doing provides a graphic picture of just how the national lawmakers operate. Capra never attempts to expose political skullduggery on a wide scale. He selects one state political machine and after displaying its power and ruthlessness, proceeds to tear it to pieces.

Stewart is a most happy choice for the title role, delivering sincerity to a difficult part that introduces him as a self-conscious idealist, but a stalwart fighter when faced with a battle to overcome the ruthless political machine of his own state. Jean Arthur is excellent as the wisely cynical senatorial secretary who knows the political ropes of Washington.

Replica of the Senate chamber provides a fine set for the filibustering episode.

1939: Best Original Story

NOMINATIONS: Best Picture, Director, Actor (James Stewart), Supp. Actor (Harry Carey), Screenplay, Art Direction, Editing, Score, Sound

•

MRS. MUNCK

1995, 90 mins, US Ⓥ col

Dir Diane Ladd ***Prod*** Barbara Boyle, Michael Taylor ***Scr*** Diane Ladd ***Ph*** James Glennon ***Ed*** Maysie Hoy ***Mus*** Leonard Rosenman ***Art*** James Allen

Act Diane Ladd, Bruce Dern, Kelly Preston, Shelly Winters, Jim Walton, Scott Fisher (Viacom)

Screen veteran Diane Ladd's helming bow is a campily claustrophobic two-hander about lost love and misperceived intentions that wears out its welcome after a bouncy start.

Ladd, who also scripted [from Ella Leffland's novel], toplines as the recently widowed title character, now ready for a new lodger. Rose Munck's selection of her wheelchair-bound father-in-law—the richest man in town—is not as sensible as it seems. You see, her relatives don't realize she had a lengthy affair with mean old Mr. Leary (Ladd ex, Bruce Dern) when he was in his married 40s and she was a naive teen. They even had a baby.

Once he's through her front door, the white gloves come off, and Munck indulges in a nonstop revenge fantasy, including knives, insults and open threats—all in a weird attempt to "heal" the crippled geezer.

Maybe *Misery* loves company, but few viewers will be thrilled by this attempt to blend the macabre with slapstick violence and earnest psychological melodrama. Ultimately, the results play more like an episode of *Love, American Style* written by Harold Pinter and directed by Lina Wertmuller.

The pic is enlivened substantially by Dern's stalwart performance, even if he never for a second looks 25 years older than Ladd.

•

MRS. PARKER AND THE VICIOUS CIRCLE

1994, 123 mins, US Ⓥ ⊙ col

Dir Alan Rudolph ***Prod*** Robert Altman ***Scr*** Alan Rudolph, Randy Sue Coburn ***Ph*** Jan Kiesser ***Ed*** Suzy Elmiger ***Mus*** Mark Isham ***Art*** Francois Seguin

Act Jennifer Jason Leigh, Matthew Broderick, Campbell Scott, Peter Gallagher, Jennifer Beals, Andrew McCarthy (Altman)

A striking performance by Jennifer Jason Leigh provides the centerpiece for *Mrs. Parker and the Vicious Circle,* a highly absorbing but naggingly patchy look at the acerbic writer Dorothy Parker and her cohorts at the legendary Algonquin Round Table. Alan Rudolph's latest dramatic mosaic is a natural sibling to *The Moderns,* his previous examination of a 1920s artistic milieu.

Parker left behind a legacy of often lacerating theater and literary reviews, tart poetry and numerous screenplays (including the original 1937 *A Star Is Born*). Contrast between the sadness and disappointment of Parker's personal and creative life, and the exhilaration of important friendships and glittering social swirl, that gives this film its poignance.

Screenplay begins with Parker (Leigh) in Hollywood in 1937. Drenched in weariness and evident self-loathing for having sold out, she is prompted by a young admirer to reflect on the "colorful" days beginning 18 years before in New York City.

Her husband, Eddie (Andrew McCarthy), reveals himself to be a morphine addict, and hardly Dorothy's match upstairs. At *Vanity Fair,* she and the other writers, including Robert Benchley (Campbell Scott) wear their salaries around their necks to protest their measly wages, and she is soon fired. Dorothy launches into a passionate affair with rakish newspaperman Charles MacArthur (Matthew Broderick), but it ends badly. At the heart of the picture is the intense but carefully platonic friendship between Mrs. Parker and Mr. Benchley, as they nearly always call each other. Married with two sons, Benchley is an editor and drama critic; the lovely relationship between the two lends the film an emotional purity that stands in relief to Parker's other unsatisfactory relationships.

All this is fine as far as it goes, but the picture ends very abruptly, with the proper connection never made between her declining condition in New York and her subsequent Hollywood career. Shot in Montreal, pic is a real treat physically.

•

MRS. PARKINGTON

1944, 123 mins, US b/w

Dir Tay Garnett ***Prod*** Leon Gordon ***Scr*** Robert Thoeren, Polly James ***Ph*** Joseph Ruttenberg ***Ed*** George Boemler ***Mus*** Bronislau Kaper ***Art*** Cedric Gibbons, Randall Duell

Act Greer Garson, Walter Pidgeon, Edward Arnold, Agnes Moorehead, Peter Lawford, Dan Duryea (M-G-M))

Mrs. Parkington is a successful picture from any angle. Film version of Louis Bromfield's novel is an absorbing and warmful presentation of the history of an American empire builder. With Greer Garson and Walter Pidgeon topping a strong cast of competent performers, there's a smooth-flowing script despite the extended running time.

Story covers period from 1875 to 1938, with modern portion allowing for frequent flashbacks through the years. Garson is presented at opening as the grand old lady and head of the family and its huge fortune. Her brood of indolent, selfish and generally worthless grandchildren is a collection of strange characters; only sane one is great-grandchild Frances Rafferty, in love with a penniless engineer.

Critical situation, calling for pledging the family fortune to save stock-manipulator Edward Arnold from jail and disgrace of the family, is resolutely handled by the wise old lady. After establishing the family crisis, history of the founder of the fortune, Walter Pidgeon, is developed via series of numerous extended flashbacks as reminiscences of the old lady.

•

MRS. SOFFEL

1984, 110 mins, US Ⓥ col

Dir Gillian Armstrong ***Prod*** Edgar J. Scherick, Scott Rudin ***Scr*** Ron Nyswaner ***Ph*** Russell Boyd ***Ed*** Nicholas Beauman ***Mus*** Mark Isham ***Art*** Luciana Arrighi

Act Diane Keaton, Mel Gibson, Matthew Modine, Edward Herrmann, Trini Alvarado, Jennie Dundas (M-G-M)

The potential for a moving, tragic love story is clearly there, but *Mrs. Soffel* proves distressingly dull for most of its running time.

True story is set in Pittsburgh in 1901, and has Diane Keaton, as the wife of Allegheny County Prison warden, Edward Herrmann, recovering from a long illness and resuming her rounds of quoting scripture to prisoners. She quickly takes a special interest in two cons on Death Row, brothers Mel Gibson and Matthew Modine, who are waiting to be hung for a murder they were convicted of committing during a burglary.

Defying all reason, Keaton helps the brothers escape and thereby undergoes an instant transformation from respectable woman to fugitive outlaw.

Final act does carry something of a charge, but it's too long a ride getting there.

•

MRS. WINTERBOURNE

1996, 104 mins, US Ⓥ col

Dir Richard Benjamin ***Prod*** Dale Pollock, Ross Canter, Oren Koules ***Scr*** Phoef Sutton, Lisa-Maria Randano ***Ph*** Alex Nepomniaschy ***Ed*** Jacqueline Cambas, William Fletcher ***Mus*** Patrick Doyle ***Art*** Evelyn Sakash

Act Shirley MacLaine, Ricki Lake, Brendan Fraser, Miguel Sandoval, Loren Dean, Peter Gerety (A&M)

As calculated as the cries of "Go Ricki!" on its star's talk show, *Mrs. Winterbourne* is a sappy, old-fashioned and predictable vehicle for actress-turned-talk maven-turned-actress-again Ricki Lake that delivers requisite warmth but few laughs. Lake's ebullient charm and solid performances by Shirley MacLaine, Brendan Fraser and Miguel Sandoval provide some highlights.

Based on a novel [*I Married a Dead Man*] by Cornell Woolrich, pic, as written by Phoef Sutton (a *Cheers* alumnus) and Lisa-Maria Radano (*The Tracey Ullman Show*), is highly derivative—the most obvious similarity being to *While You Were Sleeping*.

Striving for a fairy-tale tone, story centers on Connie Doyle (Lake), a down-on-her-luck young woman—impregnated and abandoned by her lowlife boyfriend (Loren Dean)—who is wrongly believed to be the widow of a young man who was an heir to the Winterbourne family fortune.

Awakening in the hospital after a train crash that took the life of one of the Winterbournes and his wife, Connie realizes that keeping quiet can offer her infant son great opulence, as well as the family provided by matriarch Grace (MacLaine) and Bill (Fraser), Connie's dead "husband's" twin brother.

The brazen sentimentality at work here doesn't give the material much weight. Most of the laughs come courtesy of MacLaine's ailing Grace, who can't resist cigarettes or booze, and her loyal butler, Paco (Sandoval), whose machinations help bring together Connie and Bill.

•

MR. TOPAZE
(US: I LIKE MONEY)
1961, 95 mins, UK col
Dir Peter Sellers ***Prod*** Pierre Rouve ***Scr*** Pierre Rouve ***Ph*** John Wilcox ***Ed*** Geoffrey Foot ***Mus*** Georges Van Parys ***Art*** Don Ashton
Act Peter Sellers, Nadia Gray, Herbert Lom, Leo McKern, Martita Hunt, Billie Whitelaw (20th Century-Fox/De Grunwald)

Peter Sellers plays a kindly, dedicated and very poor schoolmaster in a little French town. His integrity is such that when he refuses to compromise over a pupil's report to satisfy the child's rich, influential grandmother he is fired by the arrogant headmaster. The gullible Sellers is soft-talked into becoming the front for a swindling business man, finds that he has been a pawn but by then has discovered the wicked ways of the world.

The film [from the play by Marcel Pagnol] falls into sharply contrasting moods. The early stages, with Sellers as the gentle, honest schoolmaster is crammed with sly humor.

As a director Sellers brings out some slick performances from his colleagues. Leo McKern tends to overplay the headmaster, yet his scenes with Sellers are lively exchanges. Billie Whitelaw, as the daughter, who Sellers shyly woos, has limited opportunities but does well with them. Michael Gough is splendid as a seedy schoolmaster who is devoted to Sellers. Herbert Lom plays the con man flashily and effectively.

•

MR. WONDERFUL
1993, 98 mins, US Ⓥ ⊙ col
Dir Anthony Minghella ***Prod*** Marianne Moloney ***Scr*** Amy Schor, Vicki Polon ***Ph*** Geoffrey Simpson ***Ed*** John Tintori ***Mus*** Michael Gore ***Art*** Doug Kraner
Act Matt Dillon, Annabella Sciorra, Mary-Louise Parker, William Hurt, Vincent D'Onofrio, David Barry Gray (Goldwyn)

This charming, almost sedate little romantic comedy, which is short on laughs but tinged with a pleasant European flavor courtesy of British director Anthony Minghella, offers an appealing array of characters lacking a villain or heavy—just a lot of well-meaning folks stumbling their way through life, trying to find a soul mate.

The hook, which almost makes *Mr. Wonderful* sound like the screwball comedy it's not, centers on the efforts of blue-collar worker Gus (Matt Dillon) to marry off his ex-wife, Leonora (Annabella Sciorra), as a means of escaping his alimony payments, only to rekindle his feelings for her in the process.

Unfortunately, Gus is already involved with Rita (Mary-Louise Parker), while Leonora—in the midst of an affair with her married professor (William Hurt)—reluctantly agrees to go on a few blind dates, eventually meeting a truly nice guy, Rita's friend Dominic (Vincent D'Onofrio).

Story begins almost sluggishly. When things pick up, it's clear that *Mr. Wonderful* has more to do with texture and character than its central premise.

What sets the pic apart is the richness of its characters and the top-to-bottom strength of its cast, with Dillon confused yet likable, both Sciorra and Parker radiantly appealing, and Hurt, D'Onofrio and various pals all crafting clear portraits.

•

MR. WRONG
1996, 96 mins, US Ⓥ ⊙ col
Dir Nick Castle ***Prod*** Marty Katz ***Scr*** Chris Matheson, Kerry Ehrin, Craig Munson ***Ph*** John Schwarzman ***Ed*** Patrick Kennedy ***Mus*** Craig Safan ***Art*** Doug Kraner
Act Ellen DeGeneres, Bill Pullman, Joan Cusack, Dean Stockwell, Joan Plowright, John Livingston (Mandeville/Touchstone)

Ellen has found a movie vehicle that's sui DeGeneres in *Mr. Wrong*. The saga of how the perfect mate evolves into the date from hell has an underlying darkness that may surprise and put off some of the actress' TV fans. But the hip, smart yarn has a bite not seen in American movies since *The War of the Roses*.

Martha Alston (DeGeneres), the thirtysomething producer of a morning chat show, is the victim of parental pressure. Mom and Dad have been unsubtly effective at getting the message across that it's time for Martha to settle down with a nice guy.

One evening in a local bar "he" steps up to the jukebox and plays "her" song—"I'm So Lonely I Could Cry." Whitman Crawford (Bill Pullman) looks like Gary Cooper and acts like a dreamboat. Martha cannot believe her luck.

Still, it doesn't take long for the cracks in the plaster to emerge. Whit's idea of fun is shoplifting—and, to prove his love, he'd literally snap off a finger. For Martha, the final straw is when she's taken to meet Mrs. Crawford (Joan Plowright), who grants her approval, based on criteria more commonly applied to horse breeding.

Pullman effects just the right balance of charm and dimwittedness. DeGeneres's comic timing and dramatic instincts fill the bigscreen in a way not apparent from her television work. Only Joan Cusack, as Whit's jealous ex-girlfriend, seems out of step in a role that's too loud and overstated for the general tenor of the piece.

•

MS. 45
(AKA: ANGEL OF VENGEANCE)
1981, 84 mins, US Ⓥ ⊙ col
Dir Abel Ferrara ***Prod*** Rochelle Weisberg ***Scr*** N. G. St. John ***Ph*** James Momel ***Ed*** Christopher Andrews ***Mus*** Joe Delia
Act Zoe Tamerlis, Steve Singer, Darlene Stuto, Jack Thibeau, Peter Yellen (Rochelle/Navaron)

Crisply told tale deals with a mute, stunningly attractive young woman worker (Zoe Tamerlis) in New York's garment district who is traumatized one night by (1) being raped in an alley on the way home and then (2) raped a second time by a burglar waiting in her apartment.

Killing the burglar in self-defense, she takes his gun and embarks on a vendetta of shooting down lecherous males. Ultimately her killing spree becomes undiscriminating in its victims.

By keeping the picture short and busy, Ferrara makes its far-fetched elements play. His shock material works mainly by suggestion but there are enough "gross" elements to separate thrill-seeking viewers from traditionalists.

•

MUCH ADO ABOUT NOTHING
1993, 110 mins, UK/US Ⓥ ⊙ col
Dir Kenneth Branagh ***Prod*** Stephen Evans, David Parfitt, Kenneth Branagh ***Scr*** Kenneth Branagh ***Ph*** Roger Lanser ***Ed*** Andrew Marcus ***Mus*** Patrick Doyle ***Art*** Tim Harvey
Act Kenneth Branagh, Michael Keaton, Robert Sean Leonard, Keanu Reeves, Emma Thompson, Denzel Washington (Renaissance/Goldwyn)

Kenneth Branagh returns to the high and, for him, safe ground of Shakespeare with *Much Ado About Nothing,* a spirited, winningly acted rendition of one of the Bard's most popular comedies.

Film is continuously enjoyable from its action-filled opening to the dazzling final shot. Only real drawback is pic's visual quality, which is unaccountably undistinguished, even ugly, especially considering the sun-drenched Tuscan location.

All should be well in the domain of Leonato (Richard Briers): the righteous Don Pedro (Denzel Washington) helps young Claudio (Robert Sean Leonard) woo and win Leonato's lovely daughter Hero (Kate Beckinsale), while the proudly unmarried Benedick (Branagh) and the feisty Beatrice (Emma Thompson) trade barbs with such zest their teaming is inevitable. But the fly in the ointment is the sulky, jealous Don John (Keanu Reeves), who falsely convinces Claudio of Hero's unfaithfulness on the eve of their wedding.

Branagh and Thompson bring appealing intelligence and verbal snap to their ongoing sparring. Looking almost as weird as Beetlejuice, Michael Keaton delivers a very alert, surprising turn as the malapropping constable Dogberry.

•

MUDLARK, THE
1950, 98 mins, UK Ⓥ b/w
Dir Jean Negulesco ***Prod*** Nunnally Johnson ***Scr*** Nunnally Johnson ***Ph*** Georges Perinal ***Ed*** Thelma Myers ***Mus*** William Alwyn ***Art*** C. P. Norman
Act Irene Dunne, Alec Guinness, Andrew Ray, Beatrice Campbell, Anthony Steel, Finlay Currie (20th Century-Fox)

Let there be no illusions about *The Mudlark*. It is not a great picture. But it is a good one.

The adventures of the young mudlark—a riverside waif who ekes out an existence by picking up scraps left on the mud-reaches of the Thames—who goes to Windsor in the hope of seeing Queen Victoria, makes an appealing and tender yarn [from the novel by Theodore Bonnet].

Rumors spread through London of a plot to assassinate the queen, but Her Majesty, still in mourning for her husband 15 years after his death, denies Disraeli (Alec Guinness) the right to make a statement in the House of Commons. But subsequently the prime minister uses the mudlark incident to win the sympathy of Parliament for reform legislation, as well as persuading the queen to come out of her retirement.

It is the teamwork of the three principal artists that is responsible, more than any other factor, for the success of the film.

1950: NOMINATION: Best B&W Costume Design

•

MUI DU DU XANH
(THE SCENT OF GREEN PAPAYA)
1993, 104 mins, France Ⓥ col
Dir Tran Anh Hung ***Prod*** Christophe Rossignon ***Scr*** Tran Anh Hung ***Ph*** Benoit Delhomme ***Ed*** Nicole Dedieu, Jean-Pierre Roques ***Mus*** Ton That Tiet ***Art*** Alain Negre
Act Tran Nu Yen-Khe, Lu Man San, Truong Thi Loc, Nguyen Anh Hoa, Vuong Hoa Hoi, Tran Ngoc Trung (Lazennec/SFP/La Sept)

An exquisite exploration of a Vietnamese servant girl's private world in '50s Saigon, *The Scent of Green Papaya* marks a striking feature bow by 30-year-old helmer Tran Anh Hung. French-funded movie was entirely shot in a studio outside Paris.

First hour, set in 1951, limns the everyday chores and small joys of Mui (Tran Nu Yen-Khe), a peasant girl engaged by a family headed by a feckless, spendthrift father. Working alongside old servant Thi (Nguyen Anh Hoa), she learns cooking and cleaning, plus the inner workings of the extended family. Mui slowly develops a secret liking for Khuyen (Vyong Hoa Hoi), a friend of the eldest son, Trung (Souvannavong Keo).

Pic's second seg, 10 years later, finds the family on hard times and Mui, now a true beauty, is sent to work at the house of Khuyen, a talented classical pianist. Though he has a flirtatious g.f., Khuyen starts to notice Mui's devotion, and love flowers.

It's a film of small events, often quietly humorous, that builds to a moving but undogmatic portrait of quiet female strength. Dialogue, especially in the second part, is sparse, with events often recounted simply through music and Hung's constantly tracking camera. Star of the movie is production designer Alain Negre's main set of the rambling family house and street outside, both with a natural, lived-in look and packed with detail.

1993: NOMINATION: Best Foreign Language Film

•

MUJERES AL BORDE DE UN ATAQUE DE NERVIOS
(WOMEN ON THE VERGE OF A NERVOUS BREAKDOWN)
1988, 87 mins, Spain Ⓥ ⊙ col
Dir Pedro Almodovar ***Prod*** Agustin Almodovar ***Scr*** Pedro Almodovar ***Ph*** Jose Luis Alcaine ***Ed*** Jose Salcedo ***Mus*** Bernardo Bonezzi
Act Carmen Maura, Antonio Banderas, Fernando Guillen, Julieta Serrano, Maria Barranco, Rossy de Palma (El Deseo/Lauren)

This often hilarious, irreverent and offbeat comedy is the most coherent young Spanish filmmaker Pedro Almodovar has limned thus far. The dilemma of a woman on the verge of a nervous breakdown after breaking up with a married man is fascinatingly treated in a comic vein.

Almodovar understands his women, and there always is underlying sympathy for them, even when he turns their personal tragedies into whimsy. Central character is Pepa, superbly played by the helmer's Muse, Carmen Maura. Using mostly the interior of her apartment as the scenario of the action, Almodovar introduces her zany girlfriend, then the son of the man who has jilted Pepa, his outraged wife, a second girlfriend, two policemen, a distaff lawyer and a gay taxi driver.

Pic winds after an amusing taxi vs. motorcycle race to the airport, where one of the "nervous" women is collared by the police after trying to shoot her husband (who had been Pepa's lover).

Good production values, crisp lensing, fine editing and mock-heroic music all add up to a thoroughly enjoyable film.

•

MULAN
1998, 88 mins, US Ⓥ ⊙ col
Dir Barry Cook, Tony Bancroft ***Prod*** Pam Coats ***Scr*** Rita Hsiao, Christopher Sanders, Philip Lazebnik, Raymond Singer, Eugenia Bostwick-Singer ***Ed*** Michael Kelly ***Mus*** Jerry Goldsmith ***Art*** Hans Bacher (Walt Disney)

Mulan plays out as a rich dramatic tapestry lightly stained by some strained comedy, rigorous political correctness and more adherence to Disney formula than should have been the case. About a tradition-bucking young woman in ancient China who disguises herself as a man to serve in the army, this is a female empowerment story par excellence.

Purportedly based on a Chinese legend that has many versions, tale [based on a story by Robert D. San Souci] is boldly set up by first-time directors Barry Cook, a 17-year-old vet of the studio, and Tony Bancroft, a character animator on several recent films.

As the marauding Huns, led by the ruthless Shan-yu (voiced by Miguel Ferrer), are invading the country and pushing over the Great Wall, Mulan (Ming-Na Wen, sung by Lea Salonga) is being prepared for presentation to a matchmaker. That night, however, Mulan dresses herself as a man and prepares to head for camp, which lands her among a motley crew of recruits commanded by a dashing young captain, Shang (B. D. Wong, sung by Donny Osmond).

Mulan remarkably saves the day, but when she is unmasked in victory's wake as a woman, she is spared by Shang only because she has saved his life. Just as the Emperor is presiding over celebrations at the Imperial Palace, the Huns manage to rise again, challenging the ostracized Mulan to ever greater feats of bravery and physical prowess.

From a design point of view *Mulan* is constantly stimulating, sometimes even striking. Musically, the strongest material is vet composer Jerry Goldsmith's scoring, which brings the drama to life much as it would a live-action film. Songs by Matthew Wilder, a rock composer and producer, and lyricist David Zippel, who worked on *Hercules*, are solid, if somewhat formulaic.

The standard comic and kid-friendly elements, notably the cutesy animals, seem incongruous. There is also a feeling of how every last plot turn, line and gesture has been weighed for its full dramatic, ideological and cultural impact.

•

MULHOLLAND FALLS
1996, 107 mins, US Ⓥ ⊙ col
Dir Lee Tamahori ***Prod*** Richard D. Zanuck, Lili Fini Zanuck ***Scr*** Pete Dexter ***Ph*** Haskell Wexler ***Ed*** Sally Menke ***Mus*** Dave Grusin ***Art*** Richard Sylbert
Act Nick Nolte, Melanie Griffith, Chazz Palminteri, Michael Madsen, Chris Penn, Treat Williams (M-G-M)

Mulholland Falls is a *Chinatown* wanna-be that comes up short in every department. Although loaded with talent on both sides of the camera, this sex-and-corruption-drenched mystery meller [from a screen story by Pete Dexter and Floyd Mutrux] about a big official cover-up in postwar LA simply feels underachieved.

Subject of a real-life bunch of elite cops called the "Hat Squad," four tough guys in the LAPD of the early 1950s known for their sartorial elegance, would appear to possess strong screen potential. Opening scene has group's bulldog leader Max Hoover (Nick Nolte) and his boys (Chazz Palminteri, Michael Madsen, Chris Penn) busting up a mob party and dumping one of them down a ravine off the avenue of the title. Hoover shortly becomes sidetracked by a professional crisis that cuts to the quick of his personal life. The body of beautiful young Allison Pond (Jennifer Connelly) is found facedown in the middle of a field, a fragment of radioactive glass embedded in her foot. Some home movies feature, among other things, the late young lady in some frisky sex play with Hoover.

Trail in the case eventually leads to a desert military base active in A-bomb tests, as the top brass there, nutty genius Gen. Timms (John Malkovich), also was involved with the busy Miss Pond. Timms welcomes Hoover, even if it's clear that there's more going on at the base than first meets the eye.

Dialogue lacks the snap that another polish or two might have added, and direction by New Zealander Lee Tamahori, in his first American film, lacks anything approaching the brute force of his powerful debut pic, *Once Were Warriors*. The great *Chinatown* production designer Richard Sylbert has been recruited to re-create his magic here, but it doesn't happen this time.

Nolte does a reasonable job of fashioning a full characterization of a heavy-hitting, stalwart cop. Palminteri functions rather one-dimensionally as his second banana, while Madsen and Penn are mysteriously bland.

Film features three unbilled cameos by name actors, most prominent of which is Bruce Dern, very good in one major scene as the chief of police. Turning up much more fleetingly are William Petersen, as a hood in the early going, and Rob Lowe.

•

MUMMY, THE
1933, 63 mins, US Ⓥ ⊙ b/w
Dir Karl Freund ***Prod*** Stanley Bergerman ***Scr*** John L. Balderston ***Ph*** Charles Stumar ***Art*** Willy Pogany
Act Boris Karloff, Zita Johann, David Manners, Edward Van Sloan, Arthur Byron, Bramwell Fletcher (Universal)

The Mummy [from a story by Nina Wilcox Putnam and Richard Schayer] has some weird sequences, and it is the first starring film for Boris Karloff.

Revival of the mummy comes comparatively early in the running time. The transformation of Karloff's Im-Ho-Tep from a claylike figure in a coffin to a living thing is the highlight.

The sequence in the museum with Im-Ho planning to kill Helen Grosvenor, of Egyptian heritage, to revive her ancient state, is too stagey. The mustiness of the tombs excavated is also oversuggestive of the Hollywood set.

Other members of the cast are made to figure as the puppets of Im-Ho and to carry over the dialog during the few times Karloff takes intermissions from the camera. Zita Johann is attractive, but always role-conscious, as Grosvenor.

•

MUMMY, THE
1999, 124 mins, US Ⓥ ⊙ ▭ col
Dir Stephen Sommers ***Prod*** James Jacks, Sean Daniel ***Scr*** Stephen Sommers ***Ph*** Adrian Biddle ***Ed*** Bob Ducsay ***Mus*** Jerry Goldsmith ***Art*** Allan Cameron
Act Brendan Fraser, Rachel Weisz, John Hannah, Arnold Vosloo, Kevin J. O'Connor, Jonathan Hyde (Alphaville/Universal)

This touring company *Indiana Jones* tries to have it both ways, by sending up the adventure genre for laughs while also going for some mild shocks, but finds the sand slipping through its fingers on both counts.

Except for the title and the idea of reviving an ancient Egyptian mummy after thousands of years, Stephen Sommers's $80 million extravaganza bears no relation to Karl Freund's 1932 Boris Karloff starrer, nor to Terence Fisher's 1959 Hammer film of the same name, other than that you shouldn't mess with antiquity if explicit warnings of dire consequences are printed right on the box.

Story proper is set in the mid-'20s, when Egyptology was all the craze. Yank soldier-explorer Rick O'Connell (Brendan Fraser) is rescued from the noose by Evelyn (Rachel Weisz), a bumbling librarian from the Museum of Antiquities who pals around with her maladroit brother (John Hannah). They set out down the Nile for Hamunaptra, the legendary burial site of priest Imhotep, who was mummified alive, the location of which only Rick knows.

This being the age of CGI, one can be assured that the mummy will assume numerous different forms. Upon first seeing light of day, he's a crusty old skeleton; as he dispatches victims, he acquires what he needs from them—eyes, a tongue, teeth and so on, until he's entirely restored and all but invulnerable.

Fraser is physically and temperamentally ideal for this sort of swashbuckling leading role, but he, like the film itself, never quite finds the proper seriocomic pitch. Buffoonery hardly seems like Weisz's natural domain.

1999: NOMINATION: Best Sound

•

MUMSY, NANNY, SONNY & GIRLY
(US: GIRLY)
1970, 101 mins, UK Ⓥ col
Dir Freddie Francis ***Prod*** Ronald J. Kahn ***Scr*** Brian Comport ***Ph*** David Muir ***Ed*** Tristam Cones ***Mus*** Bernard Ebbinghouse ***Art*** Maggie Pinhorn
Act Michael Bryant, Ursula Howells, Pat Heywood, Howard Trevor, Vanessa Howard, Robert Swann (Fitsroy)

An offbeat, low-key horror melodrama—a macabre combo of Disney and Hammer films, in which a lady, her maid and two kids kidnap and murder unsuspecting males.

Story is set in a country estate populated by mumsy Ursula Howells, nanny Pat Heywood, sonny Howard Trevor and girly Vanessa Howard. It's a quaint family, mannered in the niceties of civilized living, except that they get their kicks from kidnapping stray males.

The domestic status quo begins to fall apart after kidnapping playboy Michael Bryant, blackmailed into coming to the house on threats of accusing him of the murder of girlfriend Imogen Hassall.

Players acquit themselves admirably. Howells, Heywood and Howard are excellent, Bryant a bit less dynamic than he should have been.

•

MUPPET CHRISTMAS CAROL, THE
1992, 85 mins, US Ⓥ ⊙ col
Dir Brian Henson ***Prod*** Brian Henson ***Scr*** Jerry Juhl ***Ph*** John Fenner ***Ed*** Michael Jablow ***Mus*** Miles Goodman ***Art*** Val Strazovec
Act Michael Caine, Dave Goelz, Steve Whitmire, Jerry Nelson, Frank Oz, David Rudman (Walt Disney/Henson)

This adaptation of Charles Dickens's Christmas classic is not as enchanting or amusing as the previous entries in the Muppet series. But nothing can really diminish the late Jim Henson's irresistibly appealing characters.

Closely following the Dickens story, *The Muppet Christmas Carol* is structured around Scrooge's encounters with the Ghosts of Christmas Past, Present and Yet to Come.

Michael Caine is perfectly cast as the nasty Scrooge, though his role is too dominant. Muppets take the other roles: Kermit the Frog (Steve Whitmire) becomes abused bookkeeper Bob Cratchit, Miss Piggy (Frank Oz) is his wife, Emily, and the Great Gonzo (Dave Goelz) is transformed into Dickens himself. The latter's narration is often obtrusive, creating unnecessary distance between the viewer and the tale.

Production values are high as ever. Brian Henson docs a fluid, if not spectacular, job of direction. Paul Williams's pedestrian songs are repetitious.

•

MUPPET MOVIE, THE
1979, 98 mins, US Ⓥ ⊙ col
Dir James Frawley ***Prod*** Jim Henson ***Scr*** Jerry Juhl, Jack Burns ***Ph*** Isidore Mankofsky ***Ed*** Chris Greenbury ***Mus*** Paul Williams ***Art*** Joel Schiller
Act Charles Durning, Austin Pendleton, Scott Walker (ITC/Henson)

Jim Henson, Muppet originator, and Frank Oz, creative consultant, have abandoned the successful format of their vidshow, and inserted their creations into a well-crafted combo of musical comedy and fantasy adventure.

Result is a muppet update of *The Wizard of Oz*, with Kermit the Frog leading a motley Muppet troupe on the asphalt road to Hollywood. Script incorporates the zingy one-liners and bad puns that have become the teleseries' trademark.

Director James Frawley has a lot of fun with cinematic sleight-of-hand, including shots of Kermit pedalling a bicycle, the Muppets driving cars and trucks, and additional full-body camerawork.

The cogent storyline runs Kermit through a gamut of emotions, from self-doubt and bashful love to a moral showdown on the old *High Noon* set.

1979: NOMINATIONS: Best Adapted Score, Song ("The Rainbow Connection")

•

MUPPETS FROM SPACE
1999, 88 mins, US Ⓥ ⊙ col
Dir Tim Hill ***Prod*** Brian Henson, Martin G. Baker ***Scr*** Jerry Juhl, Joseph Mazzarino, Ken Kaufman ***Ph*** Alan Caso ***Ed*** Michael A. Stevenson, Richard Pearson ***Mus*** Jamshied Sharifi ***Art*** Stephen Marsh
Act Jeffrey Tambor, F. Murray Abraham, Rob Schneider, Josh Charles, Ray Liotta, David Arquette (Henson/Columbia)

The sixth full-length feature to showcase Jim Henson's immensely popular puppets is a modestly clever comedy in which nothing, not even the wild and crazy ravings of the unpredictable Animal, gets seriously out of hand.

Departing from the formula in the last two Muppet movies—*The Muppet Christmas Carol* (1992) and *Muppet Treasure Island* (1996)—the new franchise installment goes back to basics and places the title characters in a contemporary setting.

Bent-beaked Gonzo (voiced by Dave Goelz) begins to receive cryptic messages ("R U There") in his Capt. Alphabet breakfast cereal and snaps to the idea that maybe he's the offspring of extraterrestrials. When Miss Piggy (voiced by Frank Oz) lands a low-level job at a TV station, she eagerly uses Gonzo as her stepping-stone to replace a superstar reporter (Andie MacDowell) as the host of a "reality" series titled *UFO Mania*.

Unfortunately, Gonzo's on-the-air appearance attracts the attention of K. Edgar Singer (Jeffrey Tambor), chief of a government agency charged with capturing alien visitors. Agents grab Gonzo and transport him to the agency's headquarters, where Gonzo befriends some lab rats who are regularly tormented by a mad scientist (David Arquette). Even worse, Singer wants to remove Gonzo's brain for closer scrutiny.

Gonzo is suitably engaging in his first starring role, while roommate Rizzo the Rat (voiced by Steve Whitmire) provides wise-guy comic relief. Kermit (also Whitmire) remains, as always, serenely graceful under pressure. Miss Piggy is slightly less overbearing than usual.

•

MUPPETS TAKE MANHATTAN, THE
1984, 94 mins, US Ⓥ ⦿ col
Dir Frank Oz ***Prod*** David Lazer ***Scr*** Frank Oz, Tom Patchett, Jay Tarses ***Ph*** Robert Paynter ***Ed*** Evan Lottman ***Mus*** Ralph Burns ***Art*** Stephen Hendrickson
Act Jim Henson, Frank Oz, Dave Goelz, Steve Whitmire, Richard Hunt, Jerry Nelson (Tri-Star/Delphi II)

The Muppets Take Manhattan is a genuinely fun confection of old-fashioned entertainment.

Feature poses a hypothetical story [by Tom Patchett and Jay Tarses] of Kermit the Frog penning a successful senior variety show, *Manhattan Melodies*, at Danhurst College and deciding to take it to Broadway. A hit show will enable him to marry his sweetheart, Miss Piggy, but the Muppets find it difficult to find backing and split up to various towns, working at odd jobs to support themselves.

Format allows director Frank Oz to poke light fun at showbiz clichés while creating some comic tension as Kermit, working among rat (literally) waiters at a luncheonette, befriends the cute human daughter (Juliana Donald) of the immigrant owner (Louis Zorich), arousing Miss Piggy's uncontrollable jealousy. A wonderful subplot has Kermit struck with amnesia and becoming a bigshot at an ad agency.

Pic boasts effective cameos (though not as potent as the first film), best of which are Joan Rivers comfortably adlibbing with Miss Piggy (played by Oz) and Dabney Coleman doing slapstick as an unscrupulous producer.

1984: NOMINATION: Best Original Song Score

•

MUPPET TREASURE ISLAND
1996, 99 mins, US Ⓥ ⦿ col
Dir Brian Henson ***Prod*** Martin G. Baker, Brian Henson ***Scr*** Jerry Juhl, Kirk R. Thatcher, James V. Hart ***Ph*** John Fenner ***Ed*** Michael Jablow ***Mus*** Hans Zimmer ***Art*** Val Strazovec (Henson/Disney)

The venerabe *Treasure Island* gets Muppetized. This pirate adventure is a rollicking musical reworking of the Robert Louis Stevenson classic, bearing due credit to the original, albeit with liberal, furry embellishment. Though not quite a bull's-eye, *Muppet Treasure Island* has enough craft and goodwill to register with fans.

Young Jim Hawkins (Kevin Bishop) is an orphan working in a seaside tavern. The blustery, now land-locked Billy Bones (Billy Connolly) spins yet again the saga of a fabulous treasure buried on a remote island by Capt. Flint, who murdered his crew and died before he could return to dig it up. Bones's last act is to give the Hawkins lad Flint's hitherto unknown treasure map. Jim hightails it with tavern coworkers Gonzo the Great and Rizzo the Rat in search of a ship to take him to the remote atoll.

Kermit the Frog (performed by Steve Whitmire) assays the role of Capt. Smollett, the skipper of the ship. Aboard, and pivotal, is the seemingly decent, salt-of-the-earth John Silver (Tim Curry).

The story doesn't leave port—literally or figuratively—until Kermit arrives on the scene, and one has to wade through far too much narrative before Miss Piggy is introduced. Curry is as sturdy a Long John as ever roamed the movie screen, and a darn sight better singer than either Wally Beery or Robert Newton. But most of the original Barry Mann–Cynthia Weil songs have a sameness or recall earlier Muppet efforts.

•

MURDER
1930, 110 mins, UK Ⓥ ⦿ b/w
Dir Alfred Hitchcock ***Prod*** John Maxwell ***Scr*** Alfred Hitchcock, Alma Reville ***Ph*** Jack Cox ***Ed*** Emile de Ruelle, Rene Harrison ***Art*** John Mead
Act Herbert Marshall, Norah Baring, Phyllis Konstam, Edward Chapman, Miles Mander (British International)

Original title of this one was *Enter Sir John*. Based on the rather highbrow mystery yarn (by Clemence Dane), it tells how a girl is convicted of murder on circumstantial evidence and sentenced to death. One of the jurymen, an actor, sets to work to solve the crime.

Drawback of this type of development is that the biggest kick in the picture occurs in the earlier reels.

Well-photographed and mounted, it contains all the gadgets of the pet Alfred Hitchcock technique, from quick cutting to skillful dialog blending.

The dialog is very well written. Long episodes have clever satirical values as attacks on the conventional and lower-class English.

Acting is very good. Herbert Marshall beats the cast to it as the knighted actor who turns amateur detective. Norah Baring is sympathetic as the suspected girl.

•

MURDER AT 1600
1997, 107 mins, US Ⓥ ⦿ ▭ col
Dir Dwight Little ***Prod*** Arnold Kopelson, Arnon Milchan ***Scr*** Wayne Beach, David Hodgin ***Ph*** Steven Bernstein ***Ed*** Billy Weber, Leslie Jones ***Mus*** Christopher Young ***Art*** Nelson Coates
Act Wesley Snipes, Diane Lane, Daniel Benzali, Dennis Miller, Alan Alda, Ronny Cox (Warner)

Murder at 1600 is a trashy movie that's intermittently intriguing and enjoyable on its own terms, a shrewdly packaged entertainment cashing in on public curiosity—and increasing cynicism—about secret operations in the fortress of American power.

Pic tries to have it both ways. On the one hand, the script pushes viewers' buttons and feeds a sense of paranoia, but then finds ways to redeem the sanctity of the White House as an institution and restore faith in the decency of its occupants.

DC homicide detective Harlan Regis (Wesley Snipes) is a seasoned pro called to investigate the murder of Carla (Mary Moore), a young, beautiful secretary whose body is found by a housekeeper in a White House bathroom. Regis is reluctantly assisted by a laconic Secret Service agent, Nina Chance (Diane Lane), who's been ordered by her supervisor, the rigid and ultra-tough Nick Spikings (Daniel Benzali), to wrap the case as quickly and quietly as possible.

Murder mystery unfolds in the midst of a global political crisis that sharply divides the administration. President Jack Neil (Ronny Cox) is hesitant to take aggressive action against North Korea, which holds hostage some American soldiers.

At first, all the clues implicate the president's son (Tate Donovan), who slept with Carla just minutes before she was killed. Soon Regis realizes the situation is far more complex, dangerous and corrupt.

What makes the film involving in its first hour is a thick, multilayered plot, a rare sight in mainstream movies nowadays. Nonetheless, the last act turns the yarn from a thriller into a routine actioner, wildly implausible. Snipes lends a sarcastic edge to his character, whose one-liners provide useful comic relief.

•

MURDER AT THE VANITIES
1934, 95 mins, US Ⓥ b/w
Dir Mitchell Leisen ***Prod*** E. Lloyd Sheldon ***Scr*** Carey Wilson, Joseph Gollomb, Sam Hellman ***Ph*** Leo Tover
Act Carl Brisson, Victor McLaglen, Jack Oakie, Kitty Carlisle, Gertrude Michael, Gail Patrick (Paramount)

Herein they mix up the elements of a musical show and a murder mystery, with effective comedy to flavor, and come out with 95 minutes of entertainment [based on the play by Earl Carroll and Rufus King] that should genuinely satisfy.

Victor McLaglen is in charge of the investigation of a couple murders that tax his limited detective prescience. McLaglen shares with Jack Oakie the comedy burden and for each it's a strike.

Picture serves to bring out Carl Brisson, Danish actor who was brought over by Paramount to get his baptism in this quasi-musical. In addition to having an ingratiating personality and photographing well, the foreign import sells his songs for good results.

Brisson has Kitty Carlisle opposite him, but she's not one-half as important, more attention being directed to Brisson than anyone else. Together they do several numbers [lyrics and music by Arthur Johnston and Sam Coslow], the most effective being a seashore interlude in which the Earl Carroll girls as mermaids manipulate fans that simulate rolling waves.

Murders are well planted and cast logical suspicion in several directions. All of the action occurs backstage at what is represented as the Earl Carroll theatre (now the Casino), on opening night of a Carroll show. It's a backstage musical but different.

•

MURDER BY CONTRACT
1958, 80 mins, US b/w
Dir Irving Lerner ***Prod*** Leon Chooluck ***Scr*** Ben Simcoe ***Ph*** Lucien Ballard ***Ed*** Carlo Lodato ***Mus*** Perry Botkin ***Art*** Jack Poplin
Act Vince Edwards, Phillip Pine, Herschel Bernardi, Caprice Toriel, Michael Granger, Cathy Browne (Orbit)

Murder by Contract is the story of a paid killer. The production has the benefit of mounting suspense, after a haphazard opening, and the story is sufficiently interesting.

Interest centers around Claude (Vince Edwards), an unemotional executioner who takes on a major assignment in Los Angeles after handling several eastern commitments with speed and dispatch. His victim here is a woman, who is to testify against his underworld employer. Events are given slick motivation in the screenplay, as two efforts fail to kill the woman who is surrounded by guards in her palatial home. Edwards is strongly cast as the killer and provides a quiet menace, which pays off in audience attention. Direction by Irving Lerner is brisk as he persuasively guns his characters, several of whom are topnotch. Phillip Pine and Herschel Bernardi lend conviction as the killer's confederates, jittery because of the casualness with which he undertakes his assignment.

A standout music score by Perry Botkin, using only a guitar, which he plays to perfection, gives fine atmospheric backing.

•

MURDER BY DEATH
1976, 94 mins, US Ⓥ ⦿ col
Dir Robert Moore ***Prod*** Ray Stark ***Scr*** Neil Simon ***Ph*** David M. Walsh ***Ed*** Margaret Booth, John F. Burnett ***Mus*** Dave Grusin ***Art*** Stephen Grimes
Act Eileen Brennan, Peter Sellers, James Coco, Peter Falk, Alec Guinness, David Niven (Columbia)

Murder by Death is a very good silly-funny Neil Simon satirical comedy, with a super all-star cast cavorting as recognizable pulp fiction detectives gathered at the home of Truman Capote, wealthy hedonist fed up with contrived gumshoe plots.

Capote makes a good theatrical feature debut as an impish Sheridan Whiteside, deploying his guests in a confusing series of sketches in which separate player teams, then the ensemble display their flair for low-key screwball nuttiness.

The cast list reveals the adroit mating of performer to send-up prototype, plus Alec Guinness as Capote's butler, Nancy Walker as mute maid. Every single player conveys a casualness and off-handedness which, of course, is the mark of comedic excellence.

•

MURDER BY DECREE
1980, 120 mins, UK/Canada Ⓥ ⦿ col
Dir Bob Clark ***Prod*** Len Herberman ***Scr*** John Hopkins ***Ph*** Reg Morris ***Ed*** Stan Cole ***Mus*** Carl Zittrer, Paul Zaza ***Art*** Harry Pottle
Act Christopher Plummer, James Mason, Donald Sutherland, Genevieve Bujold, David Hemmings, Susan Clark (Ambassador/CFDC/Famous Players)

Murder by Decree is probably the best Sherlock Holmes film since the inimitable pairing of Basil Rathbone and Nigel Bruce in the 1940s series at Universal.

The film's charm derives mainly from John Hopkins's literal, deadpan script that makes no attempt either to mock or contemporize Sir Arthur Conan Doyle's literary creation.

Ironically, Christopher Plummer works against this recreation by presenting a Holmes who looks as if he's just returned from a Caribbean vacation. Next to James Mason, who may be the most delightful Watson ever to appear on celluloid, Plummer's blonde handsomeness seems especially foreign.

Holmes and Watson are not called in to help solve a series of murders linked to Jack the Ripper. Anthony Quayle, as the new topper at Scotland Yard, has his reasons for excluding them, as does Inspector David Hemmings.

•

MURDERERS ARE AMONGST US, THE
SEE: DIE MOERDER SIND UNTER UNS

•

MURDERERS' ROW
1966, 108 mins, US Ⓥ col
Dir Henry Levin ***Prod*** Irving Allen ***Scr*** Herbert Baker ***Ph*** Sam Leavitt ***Ed*** Walter Thompson ***Mus*** Lalo Schifrin ***Art*** Joe Wright
Act Dean Martin, Ann-Margret, Karl Malden, Camilla Sparv, James Gregory, Beverly Adams (Meadway-Claude/Columbia)

It's a wise film producer who knows his own success formula. About the only changes made by Irving Allen in his sequel (also from a novel by Donald Hamilton) to the successful *The Silencers* are in scenery, girls and costumes. The addition of Ann-Margret is notable for some abandoned choreography and a chance to use both of her expressions—the open-mouthed Monroe imitation and the slinky Theda Bara bit.

This time out, Dean Martin's secret agent has to trek to the Riviera to catch that bad old Karl Malden who's about to blow up Washington with a secret beam.

Director Henry Levin's stress on action takes the film out of the comedy range at times. Helm is, of course, given some ridiculous special weapons—this time, a delayed-reaction gun is worked to death (no pun intended). But whenever the viewer begins to take things seriously, Levin cuts back to a laugh bit (Martin ripping off Ann-Margret's miniskirt, which contains an explosive, and hurling it at a wall decorated with Frank Sinatra's picture).

•

MURDER, HE SAYS
1945, 89 mins, US b/w
Dir George Marshall ***Prod*** E. D. Leshin ***Scr*** Lou Breslow ***Ph*** Theodor Sparkuhl ***Ed*** LeRoy Stone ***Mus*** Robert Emmett Dolan ***Art*** Hans Dreier, William Flannery
Act Fred MacMurray, Helen Walker, Marjorie Main, Porter Hall (Paramount)

This one tosses logic out the window and devotes itself to broad slapstick. Laughs clock heavily and pace moves so swiftly audiences won't have a chance to discover it is a lot of to-do about nothing.

Script [from a story by Jack Moffitt] piles on the corn thickly in detailing story of the weird Fleagle family, outlaw hillbillies, and what happens to a Trotter Poll man, collecting rural data, when he crosses the Fleagles's path.

MacMurray is the Trotter man, sent into a mountain district to find out what has happened to previous Trotterites polling the section. It seems they have done okay until approaching the Fleagles, who don't like strangers and calmly bump them off.

Continuous chases, fights, etc., keep the issues in a mad shambles before MacMurray and Helen Walker barely escape with their lives.

MacMurray and Walker do creditably by their assignments. Marjorie Main finds role of Ma Fleagle little different from her usual uncouth blowsy parts and gives it her usual treatment.

•

MURDER, INC.
SEE: THE ENFORCER (1951)

•

MURDER, INC.
1960, 103 mins, US ▭ b/w
Dir Burt Balaban, Stuart Rosenberg ***Prod*** Burt Balaban ***Scr*** Irve Tunick, Mel Barr ***Ph*** Gaine Rescher ***Ed*** Ralph Rosenblum ***Mus*** Frank DeVol ***Art*** Dick Sylbert
Act Stuart Whitman, May Britt, Henry Morgan, Peter Falk, Sarah Vaughan, David J. Stewart (20th Century-Fox)

Professional killers of the crime syndicate headed by Albert Anastasia and Louis "Lepke" Buchalter were a scourge in the Depression era. They later became known as Murder, Inc. The screenplay (from the book by Burton Turkus and Sid Feder) takes a leisurely approach to its subject. The pace is too slow, the suspense only occasionally gripping. Moreover, the overall production lacks zing and tension.

Amidst the tawdry backgrounds of Brooklyn's Brownsville section, the script recounts how Lepke and the syndicate shook down the garment district, trucking business and sundry other legitimate enterprises through goon squads and hired killers. Caught in this vicious crime ring through little fault of their own are a young couple—dancer May Britt and singer Stuart Whitman.

With the possible exception of Peter Falk's portrayal of killer Abe Reles, scarcely any of the cast's performances could be rated as dynamic. His delineation sharply defines the brutal nature of the thug who was killed in a "fall" from Brooklyn's Half Moon Hotel while in "protective" custody of the NY police.

1960: NOMINATION: Best Supp. Actor (Peter Falk)

•

MURDER IN THE CATHEDRAL
1952, 140 mins, UK b/w
Dir George Hoellering ***Prod*** George Hoellering ***Scr*** T. S. Eliot ***Ph*** David Kosky ***Ed*** Anne Allnatt ***Mus*** Laszlo Lajtha ***Art*** Peter Pendrey
Act John Groser, Alexander Gauge, David Ward, George Woodbridge, Basil Burton, T. S. Eliot (Hoellering)

T. S. Eliot's legit play, *Murder in the Cathedral,* has been turned into a moving but very ponderous film.

Story of the life of Thomas Becket, the martyred Archbishop of Canterbury, unfolds too statically in the picture form. Eliot scripted this from his own play, but failed to add sufficient movement.

Plot details how the Archbishop courageously returns to England after seven years of voluntary exile rather than submit to the king's ambition to dominate the church.

Father John Groser, as Archbishop Becket, is impressive amidst the welter of wordage. Mark Dignam, Michael Aldridge, Leo McKern and Paul Rogers, as the four knights sent to destroy Becket, measure up to the high standard of the Old Vic, from which they were borrowed for this film.

•

MURDER IN THE FIRST
1995, 122 mins, US Ⓥ ⦿ col
Dir Marc Rocco ***Prod*** Marc Frydman, Mark Wolper ***Scr*** Dan Gordon ***Ph*** Fred Murphy ***Ed*** Russell Livingstone ***Mus*** Christopher Young ***Art*** Kirk M. Petruccelli
Act Christian Slater, Kevin Bacon, Gary Oldman, Embeth Davidtz, Bill Macy, Brad Dourif (Studio Canal Plus/Warner)

A terrific true story, a good script, some potent performances and overly fancy, show-off direction combine to mostly strong effect in *Murder in the First.* The tale of a convict's hellacious punishment in solitary on Alcatraz in the late 1930s and a young attorney's attempt to expose the unspeakable conditions within America's most famous prison, pic has a visceral impact and an underdog appeal.

Film version of the horrible ordeal of prisoner Henri Young was in the works for many years. This is a classic anti-Establishment picture, and its ideal time would have been the 1970s, perhaps with Hal Ashby directing Jack Nicholson as Young.

An opening mock-newsreel relates the escape attempt of four Alcatraz cons in 1938. Of the two survivors, Young (Kevin Bacon) is thrown naked into the hellhole beneath the prison. He spends three years there before killing the other survivor, who had finked on his partners.

Young is charged with first degree murder and is transferred to a San Francisco jail. The thankless job of handling this open-and-shut case falls to tyro public defender James Stamphill (Christian Slater), who ends up using the case to accuse Alcatraz and, by extension, the government's entire prison system.

Bacon delves deeply into the part to give a very impressive performance. Slater brings probing energy to the fact finding sections, but goes over the top too soon and too often during the trial stage. Gary Oldman makes a strong showing in his few scenes as the fastidious but sadistic associate warden. Alcatraz locations and outstanding production design give a strong sense of time and place.

•

MURDER IN THORNTON SQUARE, THE
SEE: GASLIGHT (1944)

•

MURDER MOST FOUL
1964, 90 mins, UK Ⓥ b/w
Dir George Pollock ***Prod*** Ben Arbeid ***Scr*** David Pursall, Jack Seddon ***Ph*** Desmond Dickinson ***Ed*** Ernest Walter ***Mus*** Ron Goodwin ***Art*** Frank White
Act Margaret Rutherford, Ron Moody, Charles Tingwell, Andrew Cruickshank, Dennis Price, Francesca Annis (M-G-M)

Margaret Rutherford brings considerable assurance to the third Agatha Christie thriller to cast the doughty old-timer in the role of Miss Marple, the eccentric amateur sleuth.

Miss Marple is the lone member of a murder jury who holds out for acquittal. Armed only with her experience in amateur mystery theatricals, she proceeds to unsnarl the case and prove herself far more professional than the investigating police.

The picture [from the novel *Mrs. McGinty's Dead*] for all its comedy delight and charm does not quite hold up to its predecessors. Miss Marple begins to wear a little thin as she retraces many of the same comedy situations and even some similar dialogue.

Stringer Davis again plays the confused partner with a charming personality performance and Charles Tingwell completes the trio as the young inspector who ends up with the credit for solving the crime even though he flails Miss Marple all the way.

•

MURDER, MY SWEET
(UK: FAREWELL MY LOVELY)
1945, 92 mins, US Ⓥ b/w
Dir Edward Dmytryk ***Prod*** Adrian Scott ***Scr*** John Paxton ***Ph*** Harry J. Wild ***Ed*** Joseph Noriega ***Mus*** Roy Webb ***Art*** Albert S. D'Agostino, Carroll Clark
Act Dick Powell, Claire Trevor, Anne Shirley, Otto Kruger, Mike Mazurki, Miles Mander (RKO)

Murder, My Sweet, a taut thriller about a private detective enmeshed with a gang of blackmailers, is as smart as it is gripping.

Plot ramifications may not stand up under clinical study, but suspense is built up sharply and quickly. In fact, the film gets off to so jet-pulsed a start that it necessarily hits a couple of slow stretches midway as it settles into uniform groove. But interest never flags, and the mystery is never really cleared up until the punchy closing.

Director Edward Dmytryk has made few concessions to the social amenities and has kept his yarn stark and unyielding. Story [from the novel *Farewell, My Lovely* by Raymond Chandler] begins with a private dick hired by an ex-convict to find his one-time girlfriend.

Performances are on a par with the production. Dick Powell is a surprise as the hard-boiled copper. The portrayal is potent and convincing. Claire Trevor is as dramatic as the predatory femme, with Anne Shirley in sharp contrast as the soft kid caught in the crossfire.

•

MURDER ON MONDAY
SEE: HOME AT SEVEN

•

MURDER ON THE ORIENT EXPRESS
1974, 127 mins, UK Ⓥ ⦿ col
Dir Sidney Lumet ***Prod*** John Brabourne, Richard Goodwin ***Scr*** Paul Dehn ***Ph*** Geoffrey Unsworth ***Ed*** Anne V. Coates ***Mus*** Richard Rodney Bennett ***Art*** Tony Walton
Act Albert Finney, Lauren Bacall, Ingrid Bergman, Sean Connery, Vanessa Redgrave, Richard Widmark (EMI)

Murder on the Orient Express is an old-fashioned film. Agatha Christie's 1934 Hercule Poirot novel has been filmed for the first time in a bygone film style as it seems to be some treasure out of a time capsule. Albert Finney and a monstrously large cast of names give the show a lot of class and charm.

Finney is outstanding as Poirot, his make-up, wardrobe and performance a blend of topflight theater. The mysterious death of Richard Widmark triggers Finney's investigation at the behest of Martin Balsam, a railroad executive who hopes the crime can be solved before the snowbound train is reached by rescuers.

Amidst fades, repeated cuts to exterior train shots and all those other wonderful film punctuation devices Finney interrogates the passengers.

1974: Best Supp. Actress (Ingrid Bergman)

NOMINATIONS: Best Actor (Albert Finney), Adapted Screenplay, Cinematography, Costume Design, Original Dramatic Score

•

MURDER SHE SAID
1961, 86 mins, UK Ⓥ b/w
Dir George Pollock ***Prod*** George H. Brown ***Scr*** David Pursall, Jack Seddon ***Ph*** Geoffrey Faithfull ***Ed*** Ernest Walter ***Mus*** Ron Goodwin ***Art*** Harry White
Act Margaret Rutherford, Arthur Kennedy, Muriel Pavlow, James Robertson Justice, Charles Tingwell, Thorley Walters (M-G-M)

The spectacle of a grandmotherly amateur criminologist outsleuthing the skeptical, methodical professionals provides most of the fun in this somewhat unconvincing, but most followers of the whodunit.

According to the screenplay, from an adaptation by David Osborn of the Agatha Christie novel, *4.50 from Paddington,* Margaret Rutherford witnesses a murder transpiring in the compartment of a passing train. Since the police do not believe her story, and being an avid reader of mystery fiction, she takes it upon herself to solve the case, planting herself as maid within the household of the chief suspects.

The George H. Brown production is weak in the motivation area, and there's a sticky and unnecessary parting shot in which Rutherford nixes an absurd marriage proposal from the stingy, irascible patriarch of the house (James Robertson Justice), but otherwise matters purr along at a pleasant clip.

•

MURDERS IN THE RUE MORGUE
1932, 60 mins, US Ⓥ b/w
Dir Robert Florey ***Scr*** Tom Reed, Dale Van Every, John Huston ***Ph*** Karl Freund
Act Bela Lugosi, Sidney Fox, Leon Ames, Bert Roach, Brandon Hurst, Noble Johnson (Universal)

Edgar Allan Poe wouldn't recognize his story, which drops everything but the gorilla killer and the title, completely changes the characters, motives and developments, and is sexed up to the limit. In place of the cool detective whose calculating method was the model for the Sherlock Holmeses and Arsene Lupins that followed, this version's hero is a young medical student who mixes romance with science.

The cast's other scientist, a loony Dr. Mirakle played in Bela Lugosi's customary fantastic manner, is an evolution bug who seeks to prove a vague fact by mixing the blood of his captive gorilla with that of Parisian women. The murders—three real and one almost—are results of his fiendish transfusions.

First meeting of the young medico and his sweetheart with Dr. Mirakle and his caged gorilla occurs at the doc's side show. The brute snatches the girl's bonnet and from then on by intimation it's shown that the gorilla desires her.

The real threat is the constant possiblity of the gorilla capturing the girl. Sidney Fox overdraws the sweet ingenue to the point of nearly distracting an audience from any fear it might have for her.

•

MURIEL
OU LE TEMPS D'UN RETOUR
1963, 120 mins, France Ⓥ col
Dir Alain Resnais ***Scr*** Jean Cayrol ***Ph*** Sacha Vierny ***Ed*** Kenout Peltier, Eric Pluet ***Mus*** Hans Werner Henze ***Art*** Jacques Saulnier
Act Delphine Seyrig, Jean-Pierre Kerien, Nita Klein, Jean-Baptiste Thierre, Claude Sainval, Laurence Badie (Argos/Alpha/Pleiade/Eclair/Dear)

As in Alain Resnais's previous pix, *Hiroshima Mon Amour* and *Last Year in Marienbad,* memory and the weighing of an important past event on the characters seem to be the keystone of the film. A fortyish woman, living in a small town with her stepson, invites an old lover, whom she has not seen in 20 years, to come to see her. He appears accompanied by a 20-year-old mistress whom he passes off as his niece. The stepson is suffering from an experience during the recent Algerian war when a fellow soldier tortured an Arab girl called Muriel.

There can be no denying Resnais's brilliance in his rapid cutting, which replaces camera movement, plus maintenance of a mood and knowing use of color. But an attempt to add mystery to the pic by the man being tracked down by his abandoned wife's brother in the end makes this tale a pretentious one. The characters are forced to stand for things that are above their abilities.

Delphine Seyrig etches a mannered but acceptable portrait of the almost spinsterish widow who cannot cope with herself or her memories. Others are adequate in both simple and complex roles.

•

MURIEL'S WEDDING
1994, 105 mins, Australia/France Ⓥ col
Dir P. J. Hogan ***Prod*** Lynda House, Jocelyn Moorhouse ***Scr*** P. J. Hogan ***Ph*** Martin McGrath ***Ed*** Jill Bilcock ***Mus*** Peter Best ***Art*** Patrick Reardon
Act Toni Collette, Bill Hunter, Rachel Griffiths, Jeanie Drynan, Gennie Nevinson Brice, David Van Arkle (House & Moorhouse/CiBy 2000)

Muriel's Wedding is an aesthetically crude ugly-duckling fantasy that is shrewdly designed as a lowbrow audience pleaser.

First-time writer/director P. J. Hogan establishes poor Muriel (Toni Collette) as, in her own words, "stupid, fat and useless." The overweight 22-year-old high school dropout is savaged by her father (Bill Hunter) for not even being able to type. After a resort vacation where she hooks up with g.f. Rhonda (Rachel Griffiths) to do a lip-synched Abba routine in a club, the young ladies move to Sydney.

In a series of unlikely and bizarre plot developments, Rhonda contracts cancer, which provides the chance for Muriel to care for her and thus build some self-worth; her father becomes embroiled in a financial scandal as well as an extramarital affair; and Muriel fulfills at least the externals of her fantasy by marrying a hunky South African swimmer.

Most of the action is played for broad laughs, and Hogan demonstrates the ability to generate them, even if the humor is base and often cruel, making fun of people's looks and ineptitude. Visual style highlights the crassest elements of middle-class Aussie lifestyle, with an emphasis on vulgar color schemes, bad clothes and touristic consumerism.

•

MURMUR OF THE HEART
SEE: LE SOUFFLE AU COEUR

•

MURPHY'S LAW
1986, 100 mins, US Ⓥ ⦿ col
Dir J. Lee Thompson ***Prod*** Pancho Kohner ***Scr*** Gail Morgan Hickman ***Ph*** Alex Phillips ***Ed*** Peter Lee Thompson, Charles Simmons ***Mus*** Marc Donahue, Valentine McCallum ***Art*** William Cruse
Act Charles Bronson, Kathleen Wilhoite, Carrie Snodgress, Robert F. Lyons, Angel Tompkins, Richard Romanus (Cannon)

Murphy's Law, a very violent urban crime meller, is tiresome but too filled with extreme incident to be boring.

Title refers not only to the w.k. axiom that, "Whatever can go wrong will go wrong," but to Bronson's personal version of it: "Don't **** with Jack Murphy." Title character (played by Charles Bronson) is an LA cop who's down but not quite out, a tough loner whose main companion in life is his flask now that his wife has left him.

Murphy's life is shaken up even more when the ex-wife and numerous others around him are mowed down. Booked for the crimes, he escapes handcuffed to a foul-mouthed female street urchin (Kathleen Wilhoite), and after many more bodies hit the deck, he clears his name by tracking down killer Carrie Snodgress.

•

MURPHY'S ROMANCE
1985, 107 mins, US Ⓥ ⦿ col
Dir Martin Ritt ***Prod*** Laura Ziskin ***Scr*** Harriet Frank, Jr., Irving Ravetch ***Ph*** William A. Fraker ***Ed*** Sidney Levin ***Mus*** Carole King ***Art*** Joel Schiller
Act Sally Field, James Garner, Brian Kerwin, Corey Haim, Dennis Burkley, Georgann Johnson (Columbia)

Director Martin Ritt has just the right touch to keep *Murphy's Romance,* a fairly predictable love story, from lapsing into gushy sentimentality of clichés. Unfortunately, this sweet and homey picture, which casts two very decent actors (Sally Field and James Garner) in two very decent roles, falls far short of compelling filmmaking.

Field plays a divorced mother who is determined to make a living as a horse trainer on a desolate piece of property on the outskirts of a one-street town in rural Arizona. On practically her first day in the area, she meets Murphy, a widower who is the town's pharmacist and local good guy. He takes a liking to her almost immediately, but it isn't much later until her n'er-do-well former husband, Brian Kerwin, rides back into her life.

What unfolds is how the Field, Garner and Kerwin triangle is resolved with Field leaning toward Garner the whole time.

1985: NOMINATIONS: Best Actor (James Garner), Cinematography

•

MURPHY'S WAR
1971, 108 mins, UK Ⓥ ▭ col
Dir Peter Yates ***Prod*** Michael Deeley ***Scr*** Stirling Silliphant ***Ph*** Douglas Slocombe ***Ed*** Frank P. Keller, John Glen ***Mus*** John Barry ***Art*** Disley Jones
Act Peter O'Toole, Sian Phillips, Philippe Noiret, Horst Janson, John Hallam, Ingo Mogendorf (Dimitri de Grunwald)

Peter O'Toole, playing an Irishman for the first time does so with a gleaming zest that brings nerve and style to this wartime anecdote. It was shot mainly in a remote uncomfortable part of Venezuela's Orinoco River and director Peter Yates has brought out every ounce of the discomfort of the location.

Film opens with World War II drawing to a sluggish close. A German U-Boat torpedoes an armed merchantman and all survivors are bumped off, except, apparently, O'-Toole, one of the ship's aviation mechanics.

He is rescued by a French oil engineer (Philippe Noiret) who wants nothing more than to lie doggo till the war's over, but he takes O'Toole to a nearby Quaker mission where he's nursed by the missionary-nurse, played by Sian Phillips.

Another survivor is brought to the mission but is killed by the Germans. Before his death he pleads with O'Toole to find his wrecked plane and keep it out of enemy hands. The Mad Murphy has a better idea. He decides to patch it up and blow the submarine to the high heavens.

•

MUSCLE BEACH PARTY
1964, 94 mins, US Ⓥ ⦿ ▭ col
Dir William Asher ***Prod*** James H. Nicholson, Robert Dillon ***Scr*** Robert Dillon ***Ph*** Harold Wellman ***Ed*** Eve Newman ***Mus*** Les Baxter ***Art*** Lucius O. Croxton
Act Frankie Avalon, Annette Funicello, Luciana Paluzzi, John Ashley, Don Rickles, Jody McCrea (American International)

This is American International's follow-up to *Beach Party,* its flick of a year earlier. The novelty of surfing has worn off, leaving in its wake little more than a conventional teenage-geared romantic farce with songs.

The clash of three factions at a beach site sets off the romantic, comedic and musical fireworks. At one end is a group of youthful surfers. At another is a band of Atlasian musclemen. Catalyst is a wealthy, fickle contessa. Whenever the story bogs down, which it does quite often, someone runs into camera range and yells "surf up!"

Frankie Avalon and Annette Funicello top the cast and do most of the singing. The film introduces Little Stevie Wonder, a lad who can really wail. Peter Lorre puts in an unbilled appearance.

•

MUSIC BOX
1989, 123 mins, US Ⓥ ⦿ ▭ col
Dir Constantin Costa-Gavras ***Prod*** Irwin Winkler ***Scr*** Joe Eszterhas ***Ph*** Patrick Blossier ***Ed*** Joele Van Effenterre ***Mus*** Philippe Sarde ***Art*** Jeannine Claudia Oppewall
Act Jessica Lange, Armin Mueller-Stahl, Frederic Forrest, Donald Moffat, Lukas Haas, Cheryl Lynn Bruce (Carolco)

Jessica Lange plays an accomplished Chicago defense attorney, Ann Talbot, who must defend her own father (Armin Mueller-Stahl) in extradition proceedings when he's accused of having committed war crimes in Hungary during World War II.

Slowly losing her conviction as to her father's innocence, Lange's character pulls out all the stops, including the political connections of her former father-in-law, to try to exonerate her dad.

Even the film's accounts of Holocaust atrocities prove for the most part strangely unaffecting under Joe Eszterhas's limp dialog and Constantin Costa-Gavras's stodgy direction, which relies on a concussive score to try to create tension where there is none.

1989: NOMINATION: Best Actress (Jessica Lange)

•

MUSIC LOVERS, THE
1971, 122 mins, UK Ⓥ ▭ col
Dir Ken Russell ***Prod*** Ken Russell ***Scr*** Melvyn Bragg ***Ph*** Douglas Slocombe ***Ed*** Michael Bradsell ***Mus*** Andre Previn (dir.) ***Art*** Natasha Kroll
Act Richard Chamberlain, Glenda Jackson, Max Adrian, Christopher Gable, Izabella Telezynska, Kenneth Colley (United Artists)

There is frequently, but not always, a thin line between genius and madness. By going over that line and unduly emphasizing the mad and the perverse in their biopic of the 19th-century Russian composer Peter Ilyich Tchaikovsky, producer-director Ken Russell and scripter Melvyn Bragg lose their audience. The result is a motion picture that is frequently dramatically and visually stunning but more often tedious and grotesque.

Richard Chamberlain, bushy-bearded and eyes constantly brimming with tears, plays the homosexual, irrationally romantic composer, and Glenda Jackson the neurotic trollop he tragically marries. Their performances are more dramatically bombastic than sympathetic, or sometimes even believable.

Instead of a Russian tragedy, Russell seems more concerned with haunting the viewers' memory with shocking scenes and images. The opportunity to create a memorable and fluid portrait of the composer has been sacrificed for a musical Grand Guignol.

Christopher Gable plays Count Anton Chiluvsky, presumably Chamberlain's true love, as a faun-eyed social butterfly; Izabella Telezynska is the composer's patroness, a wealthy middle-aged widow who loves him but whose own romantic fantasies demand that they never meet but merely correspond by letter, although he lives in luxury on her estate.

•

MUSIC MAN, THE
1962, 151 mins, US Ⓥ ⦿ ▭ col
Dir Morton DaCosta ***Prod*** Morton DaCosta ***Scr*** Marion Hargrove ***Ph*** Robert Burks ***Ed*** William Ziegler ***Mus*** Ray Heindorf (arr.) ***Art*** Paul Groesse
Act Robert Preston, Shirley Jones, Buddy Hackett, Hermione Gingold, Paul Ford (Warner)

Allowing something of slowness at the very start and the necessities of establishing the musical way of telling a story, plus the atmosphere of Iowa in 1912, that's about the only criticism of an otherwise building, punching, handsomely dressed and ultimately endearing super-musical.

Call this a triumph, perhaps a classic, of corn, small-town nostalgia and American love of a parade. Dreamed up in the first instance out of the Iowa memories of Meredith Willson, fashioned into his first legit offering with his long radio musicianship fully manifest therein, the transfer to the screen has been accomplished by Morton DaCosta, as producer-director.

DaCosta's use of several of the original Broadway cast players is thoroughly vindicated. Paul Ford is wonderfully fatuous as the bumptious mayor of River City. Pert Kelton shines with warmth and humanity as the heroine's earthy mother.

But the only choice for the title role, Robert Preston, is the big proof of showmanship in the casting. Warners might have secured bigger screen names but it is impossible to imagine any of them matching Preston's authority, backed by 883 stage performances.

1962: Best Adapted Music Score

NOMINATIONS: Best Picture, Color Costume Design, Color Art Direction, Editing, Sound

•

•

MUSIC OF THE HEART
1999, 124 mins, US Ⓥ ⦿ col
Dir Wes Craven ***Prod*** Marianne Maddalena, Susan Kaplan, Alan Miller, Walter Scheuer ***Scr*** Pamela Gray ***Ph*** Peter Deming ***Ed*** Patrick Lussier ***Mus*** Mason Daring ***Art*** Bruce Miller
Act Meryl Streep, Aidan Quinn, Angela Bassett, Cloris Leachman, Gloria Estefan, Josh Pais (Craven/Maddalena/Miramax)

Horrormeister Wes Craven makes an abrupt U-turn with *Music of the Heart*, a gloriously sentimental true-life drama in which Meryl Streep offers another indelible portrayal, this time as a deserted wife who manages to make a fresh start in life by teaching violin to underprivileged kids in East Harlem. Building to a re-creation of the famous Carnegie Hall Fiddlefest in which the children played alongside such luminaries as Isaac Stern and Itzhak Perlman, pic is not for cynics.

Based on the 1996 AA–nominated documentary *Small Wonders* by Allen and Lana Miller, recalls famous pics in which a dedicated teacher is able to break through to classrooms of bored or antisocial children—think of *Blackboard Jungle; To Sir, with Love*; and *Mr. Holland's Opus*, just for starters.

In 1988, music-loving Navy wife Roberta Guaspari (Streep) was dumped by her husband. Traumatized, the middle-class Roberta tearfully keeps hoping he'll return, until forced by her acerbic mother (Cloris Leachman) to reenter the workforce. She re-acquaints with old school friend Brian Sinclair (Aidan Quinn), who recalls her childhood love of the violin and arranges an introduction with Janet Williams (Angela Bassett), the principal of a school in East Harlem.

Roberta proposes she teach violin within the school's music department. Warned by the school's cynical music teacher (Josh Pais) that most of the kids have attention spans that don't go past do-re-mi, Roberta nevertheless perseveres.

Streep, who claims never to have seen a Craven film before working on this one, adds another real-life character to her CV. Bassett is effective as the school's overworked principal.

1999: NOMINATIONS: Best Actress (Meryl Streep), Original Song

•

MUTINY ON THE BOUNTY
1935, 132 mins, US Ⓥ ⦿ b/w
Dir Frank Lloyd ***Prod*** Albert Lewin (assoc.) ***Scr*** Talbot Jennings, Jules Furthman, Carey Wilson ***Ph*** Arthur Edeson ***Ed*** Margaret Booth ***Mus*** Herbert Stothart ***Art*** Cedric Gibbons, Arnold Gillespie
Act Clark Gable, Charles Laughton, Franchot Tone, Dudley Digges, Donald Crisp, Movita (M-G-M)

This one is Hollywood at its very best. For plot the scenarists have used, with some variations, the first two books of the Charles Nordhoff–James Hall Norman trilogy on the mutiny of Fletcher Christian.

Beginnings of the first book and the picture are pretty much the same, as are the details up to the arrival of the hunted mutineers on Pitcairn's Island. Picture ends there, omitting the third book almost entirely.

First hour or so of the film leads up, step by step, to the mutiny, with a flexible "story" backgrounding some thrilling views of seamanship on a British man-o'-war in the early 18th century, and the cruel Capt Bligh's inhuman treatment of his sailors.

Bligh, through the cruelties he performs and due to the faithful portrait drawn by Charles Laughton, is as despicable a character as has ever heavied across a screen.

Laughton, Clark Gable and Franchot Tone are all that producer Al Lewin and director Frank Lloyd could have wished for in the three key roles. Laughton is magnificent. Gable, as brave Fletcher Christian, fills the doc's prescription to the letter. Tone, likeable throughout, gets his big moment with a morality speech at the finish, and makes the most of it.

1935: Best Picture

NOMINATIONS: Best Director, Actor (Clark Gable, Charles Laughton, Franchot Tone), Screenplay, Editing, Score

•

MUTINY ON THE BOUNTY
1962, 185 mins, US Ⓥ ⦿ ⊏⊐ col
Dir Lewis Milestone, [Marlon Brando, Carol Reed] ***Prod*** Aaron Rosenburg ***Scr*** Charles Lederer ***Ph*** Robert L. Surtees ***Ed*** John McSweeney, Jr. ***Mus*** Bronislau Kaper ***Art*** George W. Davis, J. McMillan Johnson
Act Marlon Brando, Trevor Howard, Richard Harris, Hugh Griffith, Richard Haydn, Tarita (M-G-M/Arcola)

Metro's 1962 version of *Mutiny on the Bounty*, after some two years of gestation and strenuous labor pains, emerges a physically superlative entertainment. It may be somewhat short of genuine dramatic greatness, but it is often overwhelmingly spectacular in Technicolor and Ultra Panavision 70. The new $8 million edition is generally superior to Metro's 1935 Academy Award winner.

Marlon Brando as Fletcher Christian and Trevor Howard as Capt. Bligh etch their own brilliant entries in the *Bounty*'s log. Brando in many ways gives the finest performance of his career. While Howard is always hot on his heels, the Britisher does not have the same range of character growth.

Brando boards as a foppish aristocrat, with more arrogance than true gentlemanly breeding, but underneath the veneer there is the steel of a Royal Navy officer. The struggle within Christian as he suffers humiliation by his captain before the crew is brilliantly suggested as well as projected.

Director Lewis Milestone has come up with some terrific scenes, from opening a man's back by laying on the whip to fighting wind, cold, snow, rain, towering seas and a murderous, runaway cask in the hold. This is a superb blending of direction, photography and special effects artistry.

Milestone, who often shot as Charles Lederer turned out pages of script [from the novel by Charles Nordhoff and James Norman Hall], time and again had to reshoot scenes for one reason or another. Milestone also experienced long lapses in filming and continuity but can take some pride in a job well done.

Intermission comes after the visit to Tahiti, where the native gals frolic and generously entertain their fairskinned, if not always handsome, visitors. Tarita (Taritatumi Teriipaia) is a 19-year-old native who plays the island chieftan's daughter. She is adequate to the demands of the role.

The mutiny on the homeward voyage gets the film off to a rousing second start. However, the climatic sequences on Pitcairn, where Christian determines to return home and attempt to justify seizure of Bligh's command before injuries aboard the blazing *Bounty* end his life, having a diminishing dramatic effect.

The *Bounty*'s crew includes some fine actors, notably Richard Harris as a seaman accused of stealing a head of cheese. Richard Haydn also has some good moments as the botanist in search of the breadfruit plant.

1962: NOMINATIONS: Best Picture, Color Cinematography, Color Art Direction, Editing, Original Music Score, Song ("Follow Me"), Special Effects

•

MUTTERS COURAGE
(My Mother's Courage)
1996, 88 mins, Germany/UK/Austria ⊏⊐ col
Dir Michael Verhoeven ***Prod*** Michael Verhoeven ***Scr*** Michael Verhoeven ***Ph*** Michael Epp, Theo Bierkes ***Ed*** David Freeman ***Mus*** Julian Nott, Simon Verhoeven ***Art*** Wolfgang Hundhammer
Act Pauline Collins, Ulrich Tukur, Natalie Morse, Heirbert Sasse, Robert Giggenbach, Buddy Elias (Sentana/Little Bird/Wega)

German filmmaker Michael Verhoeven returns to the subject of the Holocaust in his latest outing, *My Mother's Courage*. Based on writer George Tabori's recollection of his Jewish mother's plight in Nazi-held Budapest of 1944, it's an odd vignette of the war in which fate and fancy overcome the usual grim landscape.

In its simplest sense, the picture is one day in the life of Elsa Tabori (Pauline Collins). A woman who's boundlessly chipper, she remains confident her husband, a newspaper editor, will be released from prison. However, she's detained by two old neighbors and told she is among the Jews to be deported to some unknown destination.

But the logical arc and oft-told tragic scenario do not occur, and Elsa Tabori became a hero virtually by default.

Verhoeven is not unmindful of the story's bizarre quality and employs a number of Brechtian devices to that end. George Tabori pops up in contemporary and historical scenes as a commentator. (Pic was filmed in contemporary Prague).

Collins captures the blithe naivete of the woman but has little else to play. The real standout is Ulrich Tukur as a Nazi officer saddled with the job of supervising the deportation, yet aware that it is morally unfathomable.

[Version reviewed was a 92-min. English-language one shown at the 1995 Toronto fest. This was later replaced by an 88-min. German version, preemed at the 1996 Berlin fest.]

•

MY BEAUTIFUL LAUNDRETTE
1985, 97 mins, UK Ⓥ ⦿ col
Dir Stephen Frears ***Prod*** Sarah Radclyffe, Tim Bevan ***Scr*** Hanif Kureishi ***Ph*** Oliver Stapleton ***Ed*** Mick Audsley ***Mus*** Hans Zimmer, Stanley Myers ***Art*** Hugo Luczyc Wyhowski
Act Daniel Day-Lewis, Gordon Warnecke, Saeed Jaffrey, Roshan Seth, Shirley Anne Field, Derrick Branche (Working Title/SAF/Channel Four)

Tale of profiteering middle-class Pakistani capitalists making a fortune out of unscrupulous wheeling and dealing in an impoverished London.

Focus is on two youths, friends from schooldays. Johnny is a working-class white whose punkish mates are members of the National Front. Omar lives with his left-leaning widower father in a rundown house by the railway line.

When the film begins, Omar is given a menial job by his wealthy uncle, Nasser. He likes young Omar and gives him a rundown laundrette that he and Johnny convert into a veritable palace of a place, complete with video screens. Meanwhile, a repressed love blossoms between Omar and Johnny, adding tension to the already volatile racial situation.

As always, director Stephen Frears does a superb job of work when given a good script, and this is a very good script. It's peopled with interesting characters, allowing for a gallery of fine performances and situations.

1986: NOMINATION: Best Original Screenplay

•

MY BEST FRIEND'S WEDDING
1997, 105 mins, US Ⓥ ⦿ ⊏⊐ col
Dir P. J. Hogan ***Prod*** Jerry Zucker, Ronald Bass ***Scr*** Ronald Bass ***Ph*** Laszlo Kovacs ***Ed*** Garth Craven, Lisa Fruchtman ***Mus*** James Newton Howard ***Art*** Richard Sylbert
Act Julia Roberts, Dermot Mulroney, Cameron Diaz, Rupert Everett, Philip Bosco, M. Emmet Walsh (Predawn/TriStar)

Anchored by skilled comedienne Julia Roberts, this skewered variation on jealousy and the wrong woman doing battle in the aisles is a winning balance of the familiar and the novel.

The premise is simple and appealing. Julianne (Roberts), a successful writer of culinary guides, believes her best friend and former lover, sportswriter Michael (Dermot Mulroney), is about to propose marriage, a prospect that fills her with dread. But Michael has no intention of tying the knot . . . with her. He's been smitten by heiress Kimmy (Cameron Diaz) and wants Julianne to be part of the wedding party in Chicago.

Julianne tells her friend and editor, George (Rupert Everett), she's off to break it up by hook or by crook. Kimmy would appear to be no match for Julianne's devices. She's unworldly, vulnerable and sincere. However, every plot to demean the imminent bride backfires.

While the film has its antic moments (and a handful of cleverly integrated musical segs), it's far more soberminded than the usual film of this ilk. The characters grapple with their feelings and, without sacrificing the entertainment quotient, *My Best Friend's Wedding* gets the Psych 101 seal of approval.

Roberts's character is commanding yet out of control, a tasty combo she devours with gusto and artistry. Similar kudos to Diaz, a performer who has a powerful physical presence that runs counter to a chameleon-like emotional range. Mulroney is good in the thankless role as object of desire. Much more fun is Everett as Roberts's gay editor, who makes great sport of it when she pretends they're engaged to make Michael jealous.

1997: NOMINATION: Best Original Comedy Score

•

MY BEST GIRL
1927, 64 mins, US Ⓥ ⊗ b/w
Dir Sam Taylor ***Prod*** Mary Pickford ***Scr*** Hope Loring, Allen McNeil, Tim Whelan ***Ph*** Charles Rosher ***Art*** John Schulze

Act Mary Pickford, Charles "Buddy" Rogers, Sunshine Hart, Lucien Littlefield, Carmelita Geraghty (Pickford/United Artists)

Plenty of hoke in this Mary Pickford [based on a novel by Kathleen Norris]. It's the old tear-behind-the-smile, clean, wholesome, family type of fun.

Mary is the brains and character of an incompetent, shiftless but well-meaning family. The father is a mail carrier, a creature of habit and pressure. The mother, like certain women characters in Dickens, has a penchant for funerals—anybody's and all funerals. The other sister is a hotsy-totsy, and keeps company with a shady gent.

Mary is a stock girl in the five-and-ten. She falls in love with a new clerk, not knowing he is the son of the owner. The boy is betrothed to a society miss, but the father insists he makes some sort of a showing in the store before engagement is announced.

The cast is good. Charles Rogers overcomes his good looks with a display of naturalistic humanness. Pickford is her usual sweet and likable self.

•

MY BLUE HEAVEN

1950, 96 mins, US col

Dir Henry Koster *Prod* Sol C. Siegel *Scr* Lamar Trotti, Claude Binyon *Ph* Arthur E. Arling *Ed* James B. Clarke *Mus* Alfred Newman

Act Betty Grable, Dan Dailey, David Wayne, Jane Wyatt, Mitzi Gaynor (20th Century-Fox)

In *My Blue Heaven* the television's theater stage and the face of the video tube provide the locale for some highly entertaining goings-on by Betty Grable and Dan Dailey. They're unfortunately involved with an overly sticky plot.

Yarn has the two stars just moving over from their niche on radio to TV. They are anxious for a baby. Moved by the happy Pringle family (David Wayne/Jane Wyatt), they try to adopt a baby. This gives the scripters an opportunity to get into considerable detail on both the legal and illegal sides of the adoption business.

While Grable and Dailey offer their capable standard brands of song-and-dance, the real eye-catcher of the pic is a lush brunette youngster making her initial screen appearance. She's Mitzi Gaynor. She's long on terping and vocalizing.

•

MY BLUE HEAVEN

1990, 95 mins, US Ⓥ ⦿ col

Dir Herbert Ross *Prod* Herbert Ross, Anthea Sylbert *Scr* Nora Ephron *Ph* John Bailey *Ed* Stephen A. Rotter *Mus* Ira Newborn *Art* Charles Rosen

Act Steve Martin, Rick Moranis, Joan Cusack, Melanie Mayron, Carol Kane, Bill Irwin (Hawn-Sylbert/Warner)

Steve Martin and Rick Moranis do the mismatched pair o' guys shtick in *My Blue Heaven,* a lighthearted fairy tale. But scripter Nora Ephron's fish-out-of-water premise isn't funny enough to sustain a whole picture. Martin plays Vinnie, an incorrigible Italian-American criminal who teaches the white-bread citizens of a suburban town how to loosen up and have fun. Moranis plays Barney Coopersmith, a stiff-necked FBI agent who's assigned to settle mobster Martin into a new life "somewhere in America" as part of a government witness-protection program.

Life in a brand-new subdivision is too placid for Vinnie, who immediately starts getting involved in illegal mischief that brings him into the jurisdiction of the ultrastraight district attorney Hannah Stubbs (Joan Cusack). It's a mess for Moranis, who has to keep getting Vinnie out of the d.a.'s clutches so that he can testify in a New York mob murder trial.

Pic takes some satirical pot-shots at life in the have-a-nice-day suburban bubble, but beyond that it twiddles its thumbs waiting for the mob trial.

•

MY BODYGUARD

1980, 97 mins, US Ⓥ col

Dir Tony Bill *Prod* Don Devlin *Scr* Alan Ormsby *Ph* Michael D. Margulies *Ed* Stu Linder *Mus* Dave Grusin *Art* Jackson de Govia

Act Chris Makepeace, Adam Baldwin, Matt Dillon, Ruth Gordon, John Houseman, Craig Richard Nelson (20th Century-Fox/Simon/Market Street)

In his directorial debut, Tony Bill assembles a truly remarkable cast of youngsters with little or no previous acting experience.

Chris Makepeace is superb as the slightly built kid coming anew to a Chicago high school dominated by extortionist gang leader Matt Dillon, also terrific in his part.

Adam Baldwin is a standoffish, uncommunicative brute rumored throughout the school to be a psychotic weirdo who has killed cops and other kids. Dillon and gang use the rumors to demand payment from smaller fellows for "protection" from Baldwin.

But Makepeace will not pay up and takes his lumps until befriended by Baldwin, thereby beginning a warm friendship that leads to surprising turns in the plot.

Technically, picture sometimes shows the threads of low-budget shooting, but the distractions are minor.

•

MY BOYFRIEND'S BACK

1993, 84 mins, US Ⓥ ⦿ col

Dir Bob Balaban *Prod* Sean S. Cunningham *Scr* Dean Lorey *Ph* Mac Ahlberg *Ed* Michael Jablow *Mus* Harry Manfredini *Art* Michael Hanan

Act Andrew Lowery, Traci Lind, Danny Zorn, Edward Herrmann, Mary Beth Hurt, Austin Pendleton (Touchstone)

Bob Balaban's *My Boyfriend's Back* is an idiotic offbeat comedy about an obsessive teenage love. Scripter Dean Lorey sets his quirky fantasy in a white picket-fenced small town meant to look like a Norman Rockwell painting with a touch of David Lynch.

Missy (Traci Lind), the most attractive and desirable girl of her class, has a b.f. (Matthew Fox), but is obsessively pursued by Johnny Dingle (Andrew Lowery), a shy daydreaming classmate. Dingle stages a robbery at the convenience store where Missy is working so he can save her life. But the ill-conceived caper backfires and he loses his life. The relentless Dingle then comes back from the dead—as a frail and decaying zombie.

Napkin-thin pic starts falling apart in the first reel, as soon as Dingle is buried, and then keeps unraveling in an unremitting stream of false notes, which includes body parts falling off, cannibalism, vampirism and lynching. Balaban's direction repeats ideas and jokes more effectively used in his 1989 *Parents*.

•

MY BRILLIANT CAREER

1979, 98 mins, Australia Ⓥ ▭ col

Dir Gillian Armstrong *Prod* Margaret Fink *Scr* Eleanor Witcombe *Ph* Don McAlpine *Ed* Nick Beauman *Mus* Nathan Waks *Art* Luciana Arrighi

Act Judy Davis, Sam Neill, Wendy Hughes, Robert Grubb, Pat Kennedy, Max Cullen (New South Wales/ GUO)

This Australian film is a charming look [from the book by Miles Franklin] at 19th-century rural days in general and the stirrings of self-realization and feminine liberation in the persona of a headstrong young girl who wants to go her own way.

Judy Davis is fine as an ugly duckling who blossoms into an independent writer and refuses to give into the ritual and place reserved for women at the time which was, namely, marriage.

She resists marriage to write her book and go on with her own life. Perhaps the last part of her servitude with the farmer and his family is forced. But there is a rightness in tone in delving into the hidebound society and early flaunting of its taboos by an engaging girl.

1980: NOMINATION: Best Costume Design

•

MY CHAUFFEUR

1986, 97 mins, US Ⓥ ⦿ col

Dir David Beaird *Prod* Marilyn J. Tenser *Scr* David Beaird *Ph* Harry Mathias *Ed* Richard E. Westover *Mus* Paul Hertzog *Art* C. J. Strawn

Act Deborah Foreman, Sam J. Jones, Sean McClory, Howard Hesseman, E. G. Marshall (Crown)

David Beaird avowedly set out to imitate the screwball comedies of the 1930s and 1940s and has succeeded admirably, thanks to adorably spunky Deborah Foreman and her stuffy foil, Sam J. Jones. They make quite a pair.

Foreman is a real find, fitting into the mold of Goldie Hawn, Carole Lombard and Claudette Colbert. She not only can say a lot when saying nothing, she's a real pro when it comes to combining high-tuned dialogue with physical action.

Summoned mysteriously by a millionaire limo company owner (E. G. Marshall), Foreman takes a job as a driver, much to the objections of a wonderful assortment of chauvinistic chauffeurs who want to maintain their male-dominated domain.

She gets the impossible assignments, including Jones, a spoiled, domineering industrialist who is, unknown to her, Marshall's son.

Romance gradually blossoms.

•

MY COUSIN RACHEL

1952, 98 mins, US b/w

Dir Henry Koster *Prod* Nunnally Johnson *Scr* Nunnally Johnson *Ph* Joseph La Shelle *Ed* Louis Loeffler *Mus* Franz Waxman *Art* Lyle Wheeler, John De Cuir

Act Olivia de Havilland, Richard Burton, Audrey Dalton, Ronald Squire, George Dolenz, John Sutton (20th Century-Fox)

A dark, moody melodrama, with emphasis on tragedy, has been fashioned from Daphne du Maurier's bestseller, *My Cousin Rachel.*

Olivia de Havilland endows the title role with commanding histrionics. Opposite her is Richard Burton, debuting in Hollywood pictures. He creates a strong impression in the role of a love-torn, suspicious man.

The story, set in early 19th-century England, tells of a young man with a deep affection for the foster father who had raised him. When the foster father marries a distant cousin he has met while touring Italy to escape the rigors of winter in Cornwall, the young man is beset with jealousy. This later turns to suspicion and hate when he receives letters that indicate his beloved relative is being poisoned by the bride.

1952: NOMINATIONS: Best Supp. Actor (Richard Burton), B&W Cinematography, B&W Costume Design, B&W Art Direction

•

MY COUSIN VINNY

1992, 119 mins, US Ⓥ ⦿ col

Dir Jonathan Lynn *Prod* Dale Launer, Paul Schiff *Scr* Dale Launer *Ph* Peter Deming *Ed* Tony Lombardo *Mus* Randy Edelman *Art* Victoria Paul

Act Joe Pesci, Ralph Macchio, Marisa Tomei, Mitchell Whitfield, Fred Gwynne, Lane Smith (20th Century-Fox)

Joe Pesci puts in a lovable underdog turn as a hopelessly inept lawyer battling to prove himself in his first case. Tale has coarse Brooklynite Pesci called upon by family members to help his college-age cousin Bill (Ralph Macchio) out of a jam in the Deep South.

Seems Bill and his pal Stan (Mitchell Whitfield) were mistakenly nabbed for the murder of a store clerk. The lovable loser lawyer and his mouthy but beautiful girlfriend, Lisa (Marisa Tomei), must go to Alabama to extricate the pair. Their secret weapon will be Vinny's talent for argument, demonstrated for the audience in a latenight set-to with Tomei. Pic's running joke is that Vinny can't stay awake in court. Tomei, sashaying through the proceedings as kind of a sexy hood ornament, creates a buoyant chemistry with her combative b.f. Macchio and Whitfield are stuck in poorly drawn roles. Filmed mostly in Monticello, GA, pic is somewhat disappointing in production aspects.

1992: Best Supp. Actress (Marisa Tomei)

•

MY DARLING CLEMENTINE

1946, 97 mins, US Ⓥ ⦿ b/w

Dir John Ford *Prod* Samuel G. Engel *Scr* Samuel G. Engel, Winston Miller *Ph* Joe MacDonald *Ed* Dorothy Spencer *Mus* Alfred Newman *Art* James Basen, Lyle R. Wheeler

Act Henry Fonda, Linda Darnell, Victor Mature, Walter Brennan, Cathy Downs, Ward Bond (20th Century-Fox)

Trademark of John Ford's direction is clearly stamped on the film with its shadowy lights, softly contrasted moods and measured pace, but a tendency is discernible toward stylization for stylization's sake. At several points, the pic comes to a dead stop to let Ford go gunning for some arty effect.

Major boost to the film is given by the simple, sincere performance of Henry Fonda. Script doesn't afford him many chances for dramatic action, but Fonda, as a boomtown marshal, pulls the reins taut on his part, charging the role and the pic with more excitement than it really has. Playing counterpoint to Fonda, Victor Mature registers nicely as a Boston aristocrat turned gambler and killer.

Femme lead is held down by Linda Darnell although Cathy Downs plays the title role. As a Mexican firebrand and dancehall belle, Darnell handles herself creditably while the camera work does the rest in highlighting her looks. Downs, in the relatively minor role of Clementine, a cultured Bostonian gal who is in love with Mature, is sweet and winning.

Story opens with the killing of Fonda's brother while they are en route to California on a cattle-herding job. Fonda is offered, and takes, the post of sheriff in a bad man's town in an effort to track down the killers. Crossing paths with Mature in a saloon, Fonda suspects him at first but both become very chummy as Mature is revealed to be a talented surgeon who escaped to a dangerous life because he suffered from consumption.

●

MY DINNER WITH ANDRE
1981, 110 mins, US Ⓥ ⊙ col
Dir Louis Malle ***Prod*** George W. George, Beverly Karp ***Scr*** Wallace Shawn, Andre Gregory ***Ph*** Jeri Sopanen ***Ed*** Suzanne Baron ***Mus*** Allen Shawn
Act Wallace Shawn, Andre Gregory (Andre)

My Dinner with Andre is something of a film stunt, consisting almost entirely of a conversation over dinner between two theatrical acquaintances. Though conforming to the aloof, cooly observant mode of director Louis Malle's previous pics, *Andre* is really authored by its two players, Wallace Shawn and Andre Gregory, doubling as screenwriters. Shawn, a cherubic figure roughly playing himself as a sometime playwright and actor, is the audience surrogate, even bookending the film with his voiceover narration accompanying tracking shots of him on the streets of New York City. Somewhat apprehensive, he has dinner at a posh restaurant with Andre, portrayed also semi-autobiographically by theater director Andre Gregory.

What ensues is an overlong but mainly captivating conversation, consisting largely of stream of consciousness monologs by Gregory. Where the picture fails is in its lack of balance between the two protagonists. For the first half, Shawn is acceptable in closeup inserts, reacting or just listening to Gregory. However, in the second half Gregory begins making philosophical conclusions, which require response or rebuttal and Shawn's haltingly expressed "little guy" comebacks are inadequate and type his entire performance as comedy relief.

●

MY DOG SKIP
2000, 95 mins, US Ⓥ ⊙ col
Dir Jay Russell ***Prod*** Broderick Johnson, Andrew A. Kosove, Mark Johnson, John Lee Hancock ***Scr*** Gail Gilchriest ***Ph*** James L. Carter ***Ed*** Harvey Rosenstock, Gary Winter ***Mus*** William Ross ***Art*** David J. Bomba
Act Frankie Muniz, Diane Lane, Luke Wilson, Kevin Bacon, Caitlin Wachs, Bradley Coryell (Alcon/Warner)

The perennial boy-and-his-dog story receives elegiac treatment in a tender, if overly sentimental, version of Mississippi author Willie Morris' 1995 boyhood memoir. Alternately evoking rich, reflective memories of the 1940s Deep South and succumbing to obvious nostalgia and drama to keep things pumping for a contempo aud, this is superior family entertainment, flaws and all.

While Morris' adult voice makes an immediate presence, care of Harry Connick Jr.'s *Thin Red Line*-like narration, story tries to establish young Willie (Frankie Muniz) as an 8-year-old weakling, endlessly pummeled by neighborhood bullies. Willie's only pal is sports stud Dink Jenkins (Luke Wilson). But Dink is of draft age and quickly goes off to fight Hitler. Mother Ellen (Diane Lane), though, lifts Willie's spirits with a birthday gift of Skip, a smart, rambunctious English fox terrier (six Jack Russells superbly trained by Mathilde De Cagny and William S. Grisco). Father Jack (Kevin Bacon), who lost a leg in the Spanish Civil War and is overly protective of his only son, at first doesn't allow Skip to stay, warning Ellen that dogs die and are thus "a heartbreak waiting to happen." In one of pic's rare adult exchanges, Ellen counters that taking responsibility for a pet is a way for their son to grow up. Ensuing chain of episodes proves Ellen correct, in sometimes effective, sometimes obvious ways.

While pic is glorious in displays of pure, unabashed Americana, as when the boy simply trots through the Ol'Miss woods with loyal Skip, it seriously falters when things turn dramatic or cute. Dink's inglorious discharge for cowardice is effectively conveyed through town rumormongering, but eventual confrontation between Willie and his hero falls far short of the mark, as do awkward action set pieces involving moonshiners. Willie's parents also curiously vanish from much of pic—a loss, given the combined talents of Lane and Bacon. Under Jay Russell's direction, pic's shifts from dark to ultra-whimsical are too sudden, making cutaways and bits involving Skip's darling side nearly as manipulative as the William Ross score drowning in Copland-esque sap.

Yarn's denouement is exceptionally affecting. No less moving is Muniz, able to convey a wide range of feelings with uncommonly natural ease.

●

MY FAIR LADY
1964, 170 mins, US Ⓥ ⊙ ⊐ col
Dir George Cukor ***Prod*** Jack L. Warner ***Scr*** Alan Jay Lerner ***Ph*** Harry Stradling ***Ed*** William Ziegler ***Mus*** Andre Previn (sup.) ***Art*** Gene Allen
Act Audrey Hepburn, Rex Harrison, Stanley Holloway, Wilfrid Hyde White, Gladys Cooper, Jeremy Brett (Warner)

The great longrun stage musical made by Lerner & Loewe (and Herman Levin) out of the wit of Bernard Shaw's play *Pygmalion* has been transformed into a stunningly effective screen entertainment. *My Fair Lady* has riches of story, humor, acting and production values far beyond the average big picture. Warner paid $5.5 million for the rights alone. Care and planning shine in every detail and thus cast a glow around the name of director George Cukor. The original staging genius of Moss Hart cannot be overlooked as a blueprint for success. But like all great films *My Fair Lady* represents a team of talents. Rex Harrison's performance and Cecil Beaton's design of costumes, scenery and production are the two powerhouse contributions. [For contractual reasons, Beaton was credited with production design, but this was in fact done by art director Gene Allen.]

This is a man-bullies-girl plot with story novelty. An unorthodox musical without a kiss, the audience travels to total involvement with characters and situation on the rails of sharp dialog and business. The deft segues of dialog into lyric are superb, especially in the case of Harrison.

Only incurably disputatious persons will consider it a defect of *Lady* on screen that Julie Andrews has been replaced by the better known Miss H. She is thoroughly beguiling as Eliza though her singing is dubbed by Marni Nixon.

Stanley Holloway repeats from the Broadway stage version. Again and again his theatrical authority clicks. How this great English trouper takes the basically "thin" and repetitious, "With a Little Bit O' Luck" and makes it stand up as gaiety incarnate.

Everyone in the small cast is excellent. Mona Washbourne is especially fine as the prim but compassionate housekeeper. Wilfrid Hyde White has the necessary proper gentleman quality as Pickering and makes a good foil for Harrison. Gladys Cooper brings aristocratic common sense to the mother of the phonetics wizard.

A certain amount of new music by Frederick Loewe and added lyrics by Alan Jay Lerner are part of the adjustment to the cinematic medium. But it is the original stage score that stands out.

[Original roadshow presentations featured an intermission after 102 mins., after Eliza and Higgins leave for the ball.]

1964: Best Picture, Director, Actor (Rex Harrison), Color Cinematography, Color Art Direction, Sound, Adapted Musical Scoring, Color Costume Design

NOMINATIONS: Best Supp. Actor (Stanley Holloway), Supp. Actress (Gladys Cooper), Adapted Screenplay, Editing

●

MY FATHER, THE HERO
1994, 90 mins, US/France Ⓥ ⊙ col
Dir Steve Miner ***Prod*** Jacques Bar, Jean-Louis Livi ***Scr*** Francis Veber, Charlie Peters ***Ph*** Daryn Okada ***Ed*** Marshall Harvey ***Mus*** David Newman ***Art*** Christopher Nowak
Act Gerard Depardieu, Katherine Heigl, Dalton James, Lauren Hutton, Faith Prince, Stephen Tobolowsky (Touchstone/Cite/Film Par Film/DD

In an intriguing twist, French megastar Gerard Depardieu reprises a role he played in a 1991 French feature, *Mon pere, ce heros*, for a U.S. version of the same story.

Depardieu stars as an absentee father who takes his willful, resentful 14-year-old daughter, Nicole (Katherine Heigl), on a tropical vacation, only to have her concoct a lie about Dad being her lover to impress a slightly older boy (Dalton James).

That simple premise provides a fertile planting ground for comedy, as word of the liaison spreads among the hotel's increasingly outraged vacationers and staff, who view the oblivious Andre (Depardieu) as the worst sort of dirty old man. Nicole, meanwhile, keeps amplifying her story to keep the charade—and, in her eyes, the boy's interest—alive, eventually recruiting her father into the act.

As with his most recent feature, *Forever Young*, director Steve Miner gets the most out of formulaic material, working from a script based on writer-director Gerard Lauzier's original. Depardieu, having been over this terrain before, is perfect as the bewildered dad, while the lovely Heigl—previously seen in *King of the Hill*—brings the right mix to her role as innocent, boy-crazy coquette and compulsive liar all in one.

The Bahamas location itself also plays a major role, with cameraman Daryn Okada's vistas of crystal-blue water and stark white beaches.

●

MY FAVORITE BLONDE
1942, 78 mins, US b/w
Dir Sidney Lanfield ***Prod*** Paul Jones ***Scr*** Don Hartman, Frank Butler ***Ph*** William Mellor ***Ed*** William O'Shea ***Mus*** David Buttolph
Act Bob Hope, Madeleine Carroll, Gale Sondergaard (Paramount)

Madeleine Carroll is ideally cast as a British agent who involves vaudevillian Bob Hope into a helter-skelter coast-to-coast hop from Broadway to Hollywood.

The blend of a secret scorpion (containing the revised flying orders for a convoy of Lockheed bombers headed for Britain) with the wacky semi-backstage atmosphere, an al fresco plumbers' picnic, Nazi spies, etc., has been well kneaded by the authors (from a story by Melvin Frank and Norman Panama) and director Sidney Lanfield alike.

Producer Paul Jones and director Lanfield permit themselves a conceit when Bing Crosby is seen idling at a picnic bus station. Crosby directs the lammister Hope and Carroll toward the picnic grounds. As Hope gives Crosby one of those takes, he muses, "No, it can't be." That's all, and it's one of the best laughs in a progressively funny film.

●

MY FAVORITE BRUNETTE
1947, 87 mins, US Ⓥ ⊙ b/w
Dir Elliott Nugent ***Prod*** Daniel Dare ***Scr*** Edmund Beloin, Jack Rose ***Ph*** Lionel Lindon ***Ed*** Ellsworth Hoagland ***Mus*** Robert Emmett Dolan ***Art*** Hans Dreier, Earl Hedrick
Act Bob Hope, Dorothy Lamour, Peter Lorre, Lon Chaney, John Hoyt, Reginald Denny (Paramount/Hope)

Bob Hope, the sad sack would be sleuth; Hope, the condemned prisoner, nerving out his imminent quietus with unhappy bravado; and Hope, the pushover, squirming uneasily under a chemical yen for the potent Dorothy Lamour charms—it's familiar stuff but still grist for the yock mills. One long flashback is the device employed. Credits segue into a scene depicting Hope as a condemned murderer being groomed for the gas chamber. To reporters gathered to record his early demise, Hope relates his tale of woe—which at the outset has him as a baby photographer whose frustrated urge toward gumshoeing has inspired the invention of a special keyhole camera.

When Hope's next-door neighbor, a private eye, leaves town requesting Hope to tend his office, the comic's usual pot of trouble rises to a simmer. He tangles with Lamour in a fantastic snarl involving a mysterious map (concealed by Hope in a drinking cup container) and Lamour's missing uncle who's been snatched by a gang of international criminals headed by that familiar lawbreaker, Peter Lorre.

Curtain rings down on a solid rib. Hope's impatient executioner turns out to be—you guessed it—Bing Crosby. To which Hope cracks: "That guy will take any part." Another pretty conceit that comes off is the use of Alan Ladd in a bit part as the next-door detective.

●

MY FAVORITE SPY
1951, 93 mins, US b/w
Dir Norman Z. McLeod ***Prod*** Paul Jones ***Scr*** Edmund Hartmann, Jack Sher, Hal Kanter ***Ph*** Victor Milner ***Ed*** Frank Bracht ***Mus*** Victor Young ***Art*** Hal Pereira, Roland Anderson
Act Bob Hope, Hedy Lamarr, Francis L. Sullivan, Arnold Moss, John Archer, Luis Van Rooten (Paramount)

My Favorite Spy is in the same general pattern of other Bob Hope *My Favorite* films, scattering chuckles through the footage, with an occasional howler. Ably partnering is Hedy Lamarr, lending herself to the knockabout pace with a likeable loss of dignity.

Norman Z. McLeod guides the breezy plot [by Edmund Beloin and Lou Breslow] with a reasonably consistent speed and manages to make the zany doings fairly easy to follow. Hope, as a burley comic, is talked into doubling for an international spy so the U.S. government can get hold of plans for a pilotless plane. Dispatched to Tangiers with $1 million in a money belt, the masquerading Hope is met by Lamarr, another spy employed by a rival government agent (Francis L. Sullivan).

From here on, the script involves the comic in a wild and woolly free-for-all of danger, escape, lovely girls and chase that help fill out the film's 93 minutes.

●

MY FAVORITE WIFE
1940, 88 mins, US Ⓥ ⊙ b/w
Dir Garson Kanin ***Prod*** Leo McCarey ***Scr*** Sam Spewack, Bella Spewack, Leo McCarey ***Ph*** Rudolph Mate ***Ed*** Robert Wise ***Mus*** Roy Webb ***Art*** Van Nest Polglase, Mark-Lee Kirk

Act Irene Dunne, Cary Grant, Randolph Scott, Gail Patrick, Ann Shoemaker, Scotty Beckett (RKO)

Irene Dunne and Cary Grant pick up the thread of marital comedy at about the point where they left off in *The Awful Truth*. With these two stars working again with Leo McCarey, a surefire laughing film is guaranteed. McCarey is the producer of the new picture, which is directed by Garson Kanin, who filled in for McCarey when the latter was on the hospital list after an auto smashup.

Plot of the new film [by Leo McCarey and Bella and Samuel Spewack] is pretty thin in spots and it is distinctly to the credit of the players and Kanin that they can keep the laughs bouncing along. In this connection they have able assistance from Randolph Scott and Gail Patrick.

It's a pretty hard yarn to believe at the beginning when Dunne turns up at home after seven years' absence from her husband and two small children, who were infants when she left on a South Sea exploration. She was shipwrecked and tossed up on one of those invisible Pacific islands. She returns, therefore, as a female Enoch Arden, arriving on the day her husband has remarried. Of course, if anyone had mentioned the truth to the new wife (Patrick) the story would have been over right then and there before it gets underway. Nor does Dunne mention that Scott was the sole other survivor of the monsoon, and that he had come back to civilization with her.

1940: NOMINATIONS: Best Original Story, B&W Art Direction, Original Score

•

MY FAVORITE YEAR

1982, 92 mins, US Ⓥ ⊙ col

Dir Richard Benjamin ***Prod*** Michael Gruskoff ***Scr*** Norman Steinberg, Dennis Palumbo ***Ph*** Gerald Hirschfeld ***Ed*** Richard Chew ***Mus*** Ralph Burns ***Art*** Charles Rosen

Act Peter O'Toole, Mark Linn-Baker, Jessica Harper, Joseph Bologna, Bill Macy, Lainie Kazan (Brooksfilms/Gruskoff)

An enjoyable romp through the early days of television, *My Favorite Year* [from a story by Dennis Palumbo] provides a field day for a wonderful bunch of actors headed by Peter O'Toole in another rambunctious, stylish starring turn.

Looking exquisitely ravaged, O'Toole portrays a legendary Hollywood star in the Errol Flynn mold who, in 1954, the year of the title, agrees to make his TV debut on *The Comedy Cavalcade*. O'Toole is put in the hands of young comedy writer Mark Linn-Baker for safekeeping, latter's sole responsibility being to keep his idol sober enough to make it through the performance a few days later.

Fully cognizant of the kid's mission, flamboyant star behaves himself for awhile, but finally falls way off the wagon after enduring a dinner party at the Brooklyn home of Linn-Baker's mother. It's madcap farce from then on.

Linn-Baker is quite appealing and engagingly energetic in an excellent screen debut. Jessica Harper is fine as a spunky staffer, Joseph Bologna is wonderfully tyrannical as the show's star, Bill Macy is particularly funny as an agonized writer and Lainie Kazan hilariously overdoes the Jewish mother bit.

1982: NOMINATION: Best Actor (Peter O'Toole)

•

MY FIRST WIFE

1984, 95 mins, Australia Ⓥ col

Dir Paul Cox ***Prod*** Jane Ballantyne, Paul Cox ***Scr*** Paul Cox, Bob Ellis ***Ph*** Yuri Sokol ***Ed*** Tim Lewis ***Art*** Asher Bilu

Act John Hargreaves, Wendy Hughes, Lucy Angwin, Anna Jemison, David Cameron, Charles Tingwell (Dofine)

A lacerating, emotionally exhausting drama about a marriage breakup, *My First Wife* manages to breathe new life into familiar material.

Director Paul Cox and coscripter Bob Ellis ring a few changes. This 10-year marriage is collapsing because the wife (Wendy Hughes) not the husband (John Hargreaves) is having an affair, and it's the husband who desperately wants her back, willing to forgive and forget everything if only she'll return to him.

At the same time, Helen, who is obviously still very fond of him but no longer wants to live with him, can only stand by helplessly as he gradually loses his grip. Also at stake is their young daughter, Lucy, whom Helen unquestioningly believes should live with her.

Pic rings utterly true, with no false sentimentality, no firm ending.

•

MY FOOLISH HEART

1949, 98 mins, US Ⓥ b/w

Dir Mark Robson ***Prod*** Samuel Goldwyn ***Scr*** Julius J. Epstein, Philip G. Epstein ***Ph*** Lee Garmes ***Ed*** Daniel Mandell ***Mus*** Victor Young ***Art*** Richard Day

Act Dana Andrews, Susan Hayward, Kent Smith, Lois Wheeler, Jessie Royce Landis, Robert Keith (Goldwyn)

My Foolish Heart ranks among the better romantic films.

Picture gets off on the right foot with a script that is honest and loaded with dialog that is alive. The screenplay [based on a story in *The New Yorker* by J. D. Salinger] progresses through several different stages of emotion.

Plotting opens in 1949, and finds Susan Hayward at the tailend of an unhappy, wartime marriage with Kent Smith. Before she has a chance to pass on a part of her unhappiness to Smith, the sight of an old gown arouses memories and takes her back to 1941 when she was enfolded in romance with Dana Andrews.

Hayward's performance is a gem, displaying a positive talent for capturing reality. Opposite her, Andrews's slightly cynical character of a young man at loose ends comes to life and earns him a strong credit.

1949: NOMINATIONS: Best Actress (Susan Hayward), Song ("My Foolish Heart")

•

MY FORBIDDEN PAST

1951, 71 mins, US b/w

Dir Robert Stevenson ***Prod*** Polan Banks ***Scr*** Marion Parsonnet ***Ph*** Harry J. Wild ***Ed*** George C. Shrader ***Mus*** Frederick Hollander ***Art*** Albert S. D'Agostino, Al Herman

Act Robert Mitchum, Ava Gardner, Melvyn Douglas, Lucile Watson, Janis Carter, Gordon Oliver (RKO)

This costume drama hasn't much in the way of strong entertainment. It's a period piece, laid in early New Orleans, that makes much to-do about bloodlines and first family snobbery, with a few s.a. tidbits thrown in for exploitation.

Ava Gardner physically lives up to title implications, but her role is obvious and never socks enough to be believable. Robert Mitchum, as a young medical professor whom she wants, is required only to deliver a wooden performance, but his personality does give it some lift.

A romance between Barbara (Gardner) and Mark (Mitchum) is broken up by the former's cousin, Paul (Melvyn Douglas). Mitchum, on the rebound, marries Corrine (Janis Carter).

The script, based on Leopold Atlas's adaptation of Polan Banks's novel *Carriage*, has Barbara suddenly become the heir to a fortune left by the bad ancestor. She uses her money to bribe Paul to break up Mark's marriage.

Douglas's character has a Desperate Desmond quality, so overstated as to be ludicrous. Carter does what is demanded of her character, and Lucile Watson is Gardner's stuffy aunt who rules the family with an iron hand. On the technical side, the picture has been well dressed.

•

MY FRIEND FLICKA

1943, 89 mins, US Ⓥ col

Dir Harold Schuster ***Prod*** Ralph Dietrich ***Scr*** Lillie Hayward ***Ph*** Dewey Wrigley ***Ed*** Robert Fritch ***Mus*** Alfred Newman

Act Roddy McDowall, Preston Foster, Rita Johnson, Jeff Corey, James Bell (20th Century-Fox)

Basic theme, necessarily limited in appeal since it's the story of the influence of a wild pony (Flicka) on the lives and philosophy of a small family group, required all the topnotch production values, which the producer provided.

Fine color photography, capable performances by Roddy McDowall, Preston Foster, Rita Johnson and, of course, the magnificent horses, are assets. Essentially it's the story of a daydreaming youngster's longing for a colt of his own, the boy's complete transformation once his rancher-father fulfills his desire, and the trials and tribulations in taming and nursing the filly back to health.

•

MY GAL SAL

1942, 101 mins, US col

Dir Irving Cummings ***Prod*** Robert Bassler ***Scr*** Seton I. Miller, Darrell Ware, Karl Tunberg ***Ph*** Ernest Palmer ***Ed*** Robert Simpson ***Mus*** Alfred Newman (dir) ***Art*** Richard Day, Joseph C. Wright

Act Rita Hayworth, Victor Mature, John Sutton, Carole Landis, Phil Silvers, James Gleason (20th Century-Fox)

Theodore Dreiser's biography of his songwriting brother, Paul Dresser, parades a number of popular tunes of the 1890s—several with specially staged production numbers—to round out a fairly entertaining piece of filmusical entertainment.

Dresser's life is far from sugar-coated in its cinematic unreeling. Young Paul (Victor Mature) is picked up as the youth who runs away from home to pursue a musical career rather than study for the ministry. After a short stretch as entertainer with a cheap medicine show, and an intimate association with Carole Landis, he finally tosses over the small time for a whirl at the big town of New York.

There's too much footage consumed in unnecessary episodes and incidents that might have been historically correct for the times, but not important to a straight line presentation of a musical drama. Although Mature gives a solid performance as the songwriter, it's Rita Hayworth who catches major attention from her first entrance.

1942: Best Color Art Direction

NOMINATION: Best Scoring of a Musical Picture

•

MY GEISHA

1962, 119 mins, US Ⓥ ⊙ ▭ col

Dir Jack Cardiff ***Prod*** Steve Parker ***Scr*** Norman Krasna ***Ph*** Shunichiro Nakao ***Ed*** Archie Marshek ***Mus*** Franz Waxman ***Art*** Hal Pereira, Arthur Lonergan, Makoto Kikuchi

Act Shirley MacLaine, Yves Montand, Edward G. Robinson, Robert Cummings, Yoko Tani, Tatsuo Saito (Paramount/Sachiko)

Although hampered by a transparent plot, a lean and implausible one-joke premise and a tendency to fluctuate uneasily between comedy and drama, the picture has been richly and elaborately produced on location in Japan, cast with perception and a sharp eye for marquee juxtaposition.

A certain amount of elementary but traditionally evasive information on the Japanese geisha girl weaves helpfully through Norman Krasna's brittle screenplay about an American film actress (Shirley MacLaine) who blithely and vainly executes a monumental practical joke on her insecure director-husband (Yves Montand) by masquerading as a Geisha to win the part of "Madame Butterfly" in his arty production of same in Japan. Just as the comedy is about to peter out, there is a radical swerve into sentiment and moral significance. Montand, abruptly (and at long last) cognizant of what is transpiring, and deeply hurt, proposes B-girl monkeyshines, to his bewildered G-girl wife, and the marriage seems about to go to H.

MacLaine gives her customary spirited portrayal in the title role, yet skillfully submerges her unpredictably gregarious personality into that of the dainty, tranquil geisha for the bulk of the proceedings. Montand has his moments.

1962: NOMINATION: Best Color Costume Design

•

MY GIRL

1991, 102 mins, US Ⓥ ⊙ col

Dir Howard Zieff ***Prod*** Brian Grazer ***Scr*** Laurice Elehwany ***Ph*** Paul Elliott ***Ed*** Wendy Greene Bricmont ***Mus*** James Newton Howard ***Art*** Joseph T. Garrity

Act Dan Aykroyd, Jamie Lee Curtis, Macaulay Culkin, Anna Chlumsky, Richard Masur, Griffin Dunne (Imagine)

Plenty of shrewd commercial calculation went into concocting the right sugar coating for this story of an 11-year-old girl's painful maturation, but chemistry seems right.

Set in an idealized Anytown, USA, supposed to be in Pennsylvania but filmed in Florida, pic can afford to be relatively oblivious to events unfolding in 1972 because the man of the house (Dan Aykroyd) essentially stopped living a decade before. The widower mortician takes barely a passing interest in the doings of his daughter, Vada (Anna Chlumsky), an exceedingly bright girl who enrolls in an adult education poetry course because she has a crush on the teacher (Griffin Dunne) and expresses her severe, Woody Allen–like hypochondria by regularly bursting in on a local doctor.

Things change around the funeral home when Dad hires a sexy hippie (Jamie Lee Curtis) to apply makeup to cadavers. Vada spends most of her time with an engaging neighbor (Macaulay Culkin), and although a bit young for a real romance, the two experience their first kiss together.

It's a rough summer for an 11-year-old, but director Howard Zieff paints it in the manner of a watercolor of a youthful idyll. First-time screenwriter Laurice Elehwany's script neatly handles a number of details but on larger matters falls into predictable patterns.

Performers are highly simpatico.

•

MY GIRL 2

1994, 99 mins, US Ⓥ ⊙ col

Dir Howard Zieff ***Prod*** Brian Grazer ***Scr*** Janet Kovalcik ***Ph*** Paul Elliott ***Ed*** Wendy Greene Bricmont ***Mus*** Cliff Eidelman ***Art*** Charles Rosen

Act Dan Aykroyd, Jamie Lee Curtis, Anna Chlumsky, Austin O'Brien, Richard Masur, Christine Ebersole (Imagine/Columbia)

My Girl 2 is pleasant, painless and, as sequels go, genuinely ambitious in its efforts to be a continuation rather than just a retread of its surprise-hit 1991 predecessor.

Set two years after *My Girl*, in 1974, opening scenes return to original pic's setting, the fictitious town of Madison, PA, with same lead actors reprising central roles. Precocious Vada (Anna Chlumsky), now 13, still lives with her father, Harry (Dan Aykroyd), operator of the town's funeral parlor. Harry has married g.f. and coworker Shelly (Jamie Lee Curtis).

After a leisurely paced but amiable start, *My Girl 2* leaves Madison (and Aykroyd and Curtis) and moves to Los Angeles, where Vada wants to research her mother's past for a school project. In L.A., she stays with Uncle Phil (Richard Masur), a mechanic who's living with g.f./boss Rose (Christine Ebersole) and her young teenage son, Nick (Austin O'Brien).

Her investigation puts her in contact with a by-the-book cop (well played by Keone Young), a sickly poet (a witty turn by Aubrey Morris) and a self-absorbed film director (a nifty cameo by Richard Beymer).

My Girl 2 is often mildly amusing, and never less than engaging, but it lacks a strong narrative drive. Director Howard Zieff, who helmed the original, places a great deal of stock in the charm of his players, and they rarely let him down. Even without the presence of Macaulay Culkin, whose character was killed off in the original pic, *My Girl 2* has enough going for it to entertain and satisfy.

•

MY HEROES HAVE ALWAYS BEEN COWBOYS

1991, 106 mins, US col

Dir Stuart Rosenberg ***Prod*** Martin Poll, E. K. Gaylord II ***Scr*** Joel Don Humphreys ***Ph*** Bernd Heinl ***Ed*** Dennis M. Hill ***Mus*** James Horner

Act Scott Glenn, Kate Capshaw, Ben Johnson, Balthazar Getty, Tess Harper, Gary Busey (Gaylord-Poll)

An earnest family drama of *Rocky*-esque inspirational values, independently produced modern oater is a predictable tale of an aging, aching cowpoke's shot at redemption. It bears many similarities to Sam Peckinpah's fine, neglected 1972 feature *Junior Bonner*.

This time, it's Scott Glenn's turn out of the gate, playing H. D. Dalton, a journeyman rider who returns from Texas to his family in Oklahoma, only to find it in a fractured state. His father, Jesse (Ben Johnson), has been moved to an old folks' home by sister Cheryl (Tess Harper) and brother-in-law Clint (Gary Busey), who hope to sell off the compound. H. D.'s former girlfriend Jolie (Kate Capshaw) has lost her husband and is faced with raising two children alone.

H. D. spirits his Dad back home, where the two men renew their lifelong tense, bickering relationship, and takes up once again with Jolie. When Jesse is injured, pressure mounts on H. D. to make some big bucks fast. Directed in straightforward manner by Stuart Rosenberg, pic casts its lot with the underdog in true American fashion, but is bland and unexciting.

•

MY HUSTLER

1967, 79 mins, US b/w

Dir Chuck Wein, Andy Warhol ***Prod*** Andy Warhol ***Scr*** Chuck Wein, Andy Warhol ***Ph*** Andy Warhol

Act Paul America, Ed Hood, John McDermott, Genevieve Charbon, Joseph Campbell, Dorothy Dean (Warhol)

For all the technical blunders, *My Hustler* possesses some narrative fascination for those with sufficiently strong stomachs and/or psyches. A young boy, hired for the weekend by a wealthy Fire Island homo through the "Dial-a-Hustler Service," is fought over by the aging deviate, a girl from next door, and another hustler well past his prime.

What makes the film morbidly absorbing is not the tenuous storyline—which, in the best NY Underground tradition, is never resolved—but the detail with which gay life is documented. [Shorter version premiered in 1966.]

The camera remains stationary for long stretches (one static take lasts a full 30 minutes), and what motion Warhol does employ consists of headache-inducing zooms and wobbly pans. The sound reproduction is so poor as not to deserve the epithet "amateur"; volume level suggests an aural rollercoaster, about a third of the dialog is muffled, and lip sync is off for most of the film.

•

MY LEARNED FRIEND

1943, 80 mins, UK b/w

Dir Basil Dearden ***Prod*** Michael Balcon ***Scr*** Angus Macphail, John Dighton ***Ph*** Wilkie Cooper ***Ed*** Charles Hasse ***Mus*** Ernest Irving

Act Will Hay, Claude Hulbert, Mervyn Johns (Ealing)

An amusing vehicle for Will Hay, minus his former stooges. This time his associate is Claude Hulbert as a budding lawyer sacked for failing to convict Hay on a charge of writing begging letters.

Picture is slickly directed, never drags, and has a plausible excuse for many comic and improbable incidents. A released convict has it in for Hay, in reality a disbarred lawyer, for failing to save him from a forgery sentence, and with a maniacal look implies he intends rubbing out six people responsible for his incarceration, from the judge down to Hay himself.

Highlight is a chase to prevent Big Ben from striking 12, when a mechanical device set by the unhinged avenger will blow up the House of Lords, to whose final judgment he was not allowed to appeal. Clever photography, showing the trio dodging around the interior workings of the famous clock and clinging by their eyebrows to the face and hands suspended over Westminster, makes for hilarious excitement.

•

MY LEFT FOOT: THE STORY OF CHRISTY BROWN

1989, 98 mins, UK col

Dir Jim Sheridan ***Prod*** Noel Pearson ***Scr*** Shane Connaughton, Jim Sheridan ***Ph*** Jack Conroy ***Ed*** J. Patrick Duffner ***Mus*** Elmer Bernstein ***Art*** Austen Spriggs

Act Daniel Day-Lewis, Ray McAnally, Brenda Fricker, Ruth McCabe, Fiona Shaw, Cyril Cusack (Granada)

First and foremost, *My Left Foot* is the warm, romantic and moving true story of a remarkable man: the Irish writer and painter Christy Brown, born with cerebral palsy into an impoverished family. That it features a brilliant performance by Daniel Day-Lewis and a fine supporting cast lifts it from mildly sentimental to excellent.

At his birth, Christy's parents are told their child would be little more than a vegetable, but through his mother's insistence that he fit in with family life, he shows intelligence and strength inside his paralyzed body.

The older Christy amazes his family by writing the word "mother" on the floor with a piece of chalk gripped in his left foot. He goes on to become an artist—still using that left foot and is helped by therapist Fiona Shaw, with whom he falls in love.

All performances are on the mark in this perfect little film [from Brown's own novel]. Brenda Fricker, as his loving and resilient mother, is excellent, as is the late Ray McAnally as his bricklayer father. *My Left Foot* is not a sad film. In fact, there is a great deal of humor in Day-Lewis's Brown.

1989: Best Actor (Daniel Day-Lewis), Best Supp. Actress (Brenda Fricker)

NOMINATIONS: Best Picture, Director, Adapted Screenplay

•

MY LIFE

1993, 114 mins, US col

Dir Bruce Joel Rubin ***Prod*** Jerry Zucker, Bruce Joel Rubin, Hunt Lowry ***Scr*** Bruce Joel Rubin ***Ph*** Peter James ***Ed*** Richard Chew ***Mus*** John Barry ***Art*** Neil Spisak

Act Michael Keaton, Nicole Kidman, Bradley Whitford, Queen Latifah, Haing S. Ngor, Michael Constantine (Columbia)

Writer Bruce Joel Rubin's fascination with death knows no temporal bounds. It reached back from the grave in *Ghost* and struck out into the future in *Jacob's Ladder*. *My Life*, his directorial debut, is his most cozy brush with the final journey. It's an emotional, spiritual odyssey centered on a man confronting terminal cancer and, coincidentally, the birth of his first child. The sincere, often touching story tugs shamelessly at the heartstrings.

The writer-director's conceit is a videotape being prepared by Bob Jones (Michael Keaton) for his unborn child. His wife (Nicole Kidman) gently cajoles him into seeing a healer (Haing S. Ngor), and it is at these sessions that he begins to get in touch with what's really ailing him: his roots. We discover that his seething hostility toward his father (Michael Constantine) was so intense, changing his name was his least vengeful act.

There's nothing essentially wrong with the manipulative nature of *My Life*. Rubin's inexperience, however, makes his footprints a lot more obvious than those of others who have walked down this road before.

Keaton gives a textured performance that goes a long way to smooth the narrative's rough edges. Kidman, Ngor, Constantine and Bradley Whitford all register with emotional work.

•

MY LIFE AS A DOG

SEE: MITT LIV SOM HUND

•

MY LIFE TO LIVE

SEE: VIVRE SA VIE FILM EN DOUZE TABLEUX

•

MY LITTLE CHICKADEE

1940, 83 mins, US b/w

Dir Edward Cline ***Prod*** [Lester Cowan] ***Scr*** Mae West, W. C. Fields ***Ph*** Joseph Valentine ***Ed*** Edward Curtiss ***Mus*** Frank Skinner ***Art*** Jack Otterson, Martin Obzina

Act Mae West, W. C. Fields, Joseph Calleia, Dick Foran, Ruth Donnelly, Magaret Hamilton (Universal)

Universal catches Mae West on a delayed rebound from Paramount, teaming her with W. C. Fields for a hefty package of lusty humor. Picture marks return of West to the screen after two years absence.

The familiar Westian swagger, drawl, wisecracks and innuendos are all included, likewise the typical Fields routines and quick-triggered comments. Sequences in which the pair work together are reduced to a minimum. Script setup is a continual series of episodes, first with West and then Fields.

Story is a reverse twist to *Destry Rides Again* and with western frontier locale, is reminiscent of *Destry*. West, returning from a complete course in a Chicago dance hall, has a way with men. A masked bandit falls in love with her, which eventually drums her out of the town. Meeting Fields, whom she believes rich, aboard the train, she promotes a fake marriage ceremony. Pair hit the next frontier settlement, where Fields is inducted into job of sheriff, and West tosses her charms around rather freely.

My Little Chickadee has been turned in on a moderate budget compared to outlays for the West starrers previously under the Paramount banner.

•

MY MAN GODFREY

1936, 93 mins, US b/w

Dir Gregory La Cava ***Prod*** Charles R. Rogers ***Scr*** Morrie Ryskind, Eric Hatch ***Ph*** Ted Tetzlaff ***Ed*** Ted Kent ***Mus*** Charles Previn (dir.) ***Art*** Charles D. Hall

Act William Powell, Carole Lombard, Alice Brady, Gail Patrick, Eugene Pallette, Alan Mowbray (Universal)

William Powell and Carole Lombard are pleasantly teamed in this splendidly produced comedy. Story is balmy, but not too much so, and lends itself to the sophisticated screen treatment of Eric Hatch's novel.

Lombard has played screwball dames before, but none so screwy as this one. Her whole family, with the exception of the old man, seem to have been dropped on their respective heads when young. Into this punchy society tribe walks Powell, a former social light himself who had gone on the bum over a woman and is trying to become a man once more in butler's livery. He straightens out the family, as well as himself. Alice Brady, as the social mother in whom the family's psychopathic ward tendencies seemingly originate, does a bangup job with another tough part. Gail Patrick, as Lombard's sparring partner-sister, is excellent. Eugene Pallette, as the harassed father, and Mischa Auer, in a gigolo role, a beautiful piece of sustained comedy playing and writing, are both fine.

1936: NOMINATIONS: Best Director, Actor (William Powell), Actress (Carole Lombard), Supp. Actor (Mischa Auer), Supp. Actress (Alice Brady), Screenplay

•

MY MAN GODFREY

1957, 92 mins, US col

Dir Henry Koster ***Prod*** Ross Hunter ***Scr*** Everett Freeman, Peter Bermeis, William Bowers ***Ph*** William Daniels ***Ed*** Milton Carruth ***Mus*** Frank Skinner ***Art*** Alexander Golitzen, Richard H. Riedel

Act June Allyson, David Niven, Jessie Royce Landis, Robert Keith, Eva Gabor, Martha Hyer (Universal)

Updated version of *My Man Godfrey* is a pretty well-turned-out comedy with June Allyson and David Niven recreating the original Carole Lombard–William Powell star roles. Ross Hunter's production of the butler to an eccentric New York family of wealth who helps straighten them out, meanwhile recipient of the affections of the younger daughter, manages to pack plenty of lusty humor in the fast 92 minutes.

Where film misses is in the Niven character of butler. The screenplay drags him in by the heels in too fabricated a character—a former Austrian diplomat in the U.S. via illegal entry. Again, the scripters hit upon too ready a solution of the Allyson-Niven romance after Niven has been deported.

Director Henry Koster deftly handles his characters in their comedic paces and succeeds in establishing an aura of screwiness in keeping with the 1936 version. Niven is a particular standout in his helping the family back on their feet after bankruptcy faces them.

Jessie Royce Landis as the wacky society mother registers a definite hit, Martha Hyer as the arrogant elder sister is stunning and Robert Keith ably portrays the father faced with ruin.

•

MY MOTHER'S COURAGE
SEE: MUTTERS COURAGE

•

MY NAME IS IVAN
SEE: IVANOVO DYETSTVO

•

MY NAME IS JULIA ROSS
1945, 64 mins, US b/w
Dir Joseph H. Lewis ***Prod*** Wallace MacDonald ***Scr*** Muriel Roy Bolton ***Ph*** Burnett Guffey ***Ed*** James Sweeney, Henry Batista ***Mus*** Mischa Bakaleinikoff ***Art*** Jerome Pycha, Jr.
Act Nina Foch, May Whitty, George Macready, Roland Varno, Anita Bolster, Doris Lloyd (Columbia)

Mystery melodrama with a psychological twist runs only 64 minutes but it's fast and packed with tense action throughout. Acting and production (though apparently modestly budgeted) are excellent.

New face is Nina Foch, who has looks and talent, while rest of cast is backed notably by May Whitty, George Macready and Roland Varno.

Story [from the novel *The Woman in Red* by Anthony Gilbert] is of gal hired fraudulently as secretary to wealthy English dowager. Purpose of hiring is to impose a murder scheme in which the dowager's son is implicated. The story has its implausibilities, but general conduct of pic negates those factors for overall click results.

Whitty gives creditable performance, so does Macready as her psychiatric son. Others in support acquit themselves well. Joseph H. Lewis directed for pace, and he achieves it all the way.

•

MY NIGHT AT MAUD'S
SEE: MA NUIT CHEZ MAUD

•

MY OWN PRIVATE IDAHO
1991, 102 mins, US Ⓥ ⊙ col
Dir Gus Van Sant ***Prod*** Laurie Parker ***Scr*** Gus Van Sant ***Ph*** Eric Alan Edwards, John Campbell ***Ed*** Curtiss Clayton ***Mus*** Bill Stafford ***Art*** David Brisbin
Act River Phoenix, Keanu Reeves, James Russo, William Richert, Rodney Harvey, Chiara Caselli (New Line)

Rather less than the sum of its often striking parts, Gus Van Sant's appealingly idiosyncratic look at a pair of very different young street hustlers is one of those ambitious, overreaching disappointments that is more interesting than some more conservative successes.

Taking his title from a B-52s song, Van Sant begins his crooked yarn on a straight Idaho highway, where the scruffy outcast Mike (River Phoenix) succumbs to his affliction of narcolepsy and has visions of his lost home and mother. In Seattle, Mike is a sex-for-hire boy, a sensitive but raw youth who will go both ways but has the unfortunate habit of passing out on the job.

Mike's cohort and soon-to-be best friend is Scott (Keanu Reeves). The wealthy son of Portland's mayor, Scott is clearly hanging with the boys as an act of teenage rebellion against his family.

Then Van Sant makes a sudden, fatal shift in tone and style. The dialog begins sounding arch, the acting style becomes strangely theatrical and, for a while, the film becomes a modern, gay adaptation of Shakespeare's *Henry IV, Part I*.

Shakespearean side of the story falls short due to Reeves's very narrow range as an actor. Phoenix cuts a believable, sometimes compelling figure of a young man urgently groping for definition in his life. For a story about two gay hustlers, film deals very little with sex.

•

MY PAL GUS
1952, 83 mins, US b/w
Dir Robert Parrish ***Prod*** Stanley Rubin ***Scr*** Fay Kanin, Michael Kanin ***Ph*** Leo Tover ***Ed*** Robert Fritch ***Mus*** Leigh Harline
Act Richard Widmark, Joanne Dru, Audrey Totter, George Winslow, Regis Toomey, Joan Banks (20th Century-Fox)

Richard Widmark is a bon-bon manufacturer too busy to devote much time to his small son. As a result, the kid is a problem child who eventually lands in the progressive school operated by Joanne Dru. Little Winslow takes to the teacher, so does Dad, and things are well on their way toward the schoolmarm becoming his new mother when Audrey Totter, Widmark's ex-wife, appears on the scene.

Totter reveals her Mexican divorce is invalid and demands Widmark give up his community property half of his wealth for a valid divorce.

Widmark is very good as the tough, rags-to-riches father, showing both good comedy feeling as well as the more touchingly dramatic flavor required in the final scenes when he tries to take his kid to a mother who doesn't want him.

•

MYRA BRECKINRIDGE
1970, 94 mins, US Ⓥ ✉ col
Dir Michael Sarne ***Prod*** Robert Fryer ***Scr*** Michael Sarne, David Giler ***Ph*** Richard Moore ***Ed*** Danford B. Greene ***Mus*** Lionel Newman (sup.) ***Art*** Jack Martin Smith, Fred Harpman
Act Mae West, John Huston, Raquel Welch, Rex Reed, Farrah Fawcett, Roger C. Carmel (20th Century-Fox)

The film version of Gore Vidal's Hollywood-themed transsexual satire starts off promisingly, but after a couple of reels plunges straight downhill under the weight of artless direction.

As a lecherous female agent, Mae West after an absence from the screen of over 26 years provides some funny moments though her part is very short. John Huston, as drama school promoter Buck Loner, is good, while title-roled Raquel Welch—like the film, good at the beginning—has been let down as story progresses to the point where she alone must (but cannot) keep it going.

With David Giler, director Michael Sarne adapted Vidal's novel in such a way as to (1) create some expository interest, (2) abandon the players to carry the ball, and (3) hype the pacing by clip inserts, motivated and otherwise, as unreal and artificial as silicone injections.

•

MY REPUTATION
1946, 93 mins, US b/w
Dir Curtis Bernhardt ***Prod*** Henry Blanke ***Scr*** Catherine Turney ***Ph*** James Wong Howe ***Ed*** David Weisbart ***Mus*** Max Steiner ***Art*** Anton Grot
Act Barbara Stanwyck, George Brent, Eve Arden, Warner Anderson (Warner)

With the emphasis on a woman's struggle within herself over the ethics of behavior following her husband's death, this WB dramatization of the Clare Jaynes novel *Instruct My Sorrows* is okay.

Pic's greatest difficulty is getting started, scripter Catherine Turney and megger Curtis Bernhardt taking such pains to build up their characterizations that it is 35 minutes before George Brent hits the screen and causes the pace to pick up a bit.

Story emphasis is on psychological conflict rather than action. It attempts to picture the dilemma in the mind of an attractive young widow (Stanwyck) as she balances the demands of community and family convention against her desire to live her life as she sees it—namely, an affair with a rather attractive wolf in wolf's clothing.

Unfortunately, the script fails to demonstrate the deftness, which is necessary to present a conflict like this. It takes extreme skill to make all the needed points with a minimum of footage and to keep things moving on the screen.

•

MY SISTER EILEEN
1942, 97 mins, US ⊙ b/w
Dir Alexander Hall ***Prod*** Max Gordon ***Scr*** Joseph Fields, Jerome Chodorov ***Ph*** Joseph Walker ***Ed*** Viola Lawrence ***Mus*** Morris Stoloff
Act Rosalind Russell, Brian Aherne, Janet Blair, Richard Quine, June Havoc, Jeff Donnell (Columbia)

Adaptors Joseph Fields and Jerome Chodorov obviously liked their stage play [adapted from *New Yorker* stories by Ruth McKenney], for in translating it to the screen they've retained virtually the entire format, including all the key dialog. About all they've done has been to fill out the various chinks in the story, which had been excluded by the limitations of the single-set play.

In Alexander Hall's direction, the pacing is fast and smooth, with constant use of sight gags and comedy situations. Most of the action still takes place in the Greenwich Village basement studio-apartment, with a crescendo of exaggerated events breaking out near and in the place.

Rosalind Russell's performance as authoress Ruth is an effective blend of curtness and warmth.

1942: NOMINATION: Best Actress (Rosalind Russell)

•

MY SISTER EILEEN
1955, 106 mins, US ⊙ ✉ b/w
Dir Richard Quine ***Prod*** Fred Kohlmar ***Scr*** Blake Edwards, Richard Quine ***Ph*** Charles Lawton, Jr. ***Ed*** Charles Nelson ***Mus*** Morris Stoloff (sup.), George Duning (adapt.) ***Art*** Walter Holscher
Act Janet Leigh, Jack Lemmon, Betty Garrett, Bob Fosse, Kurt Kasznar, Richard York (Columbia)

Scripters have turned out a simplified filmusical, in that the tunes and dances come naturally to situations and are not overly staged. Thus, the problems that befall two sisters from Ohio, who come to New York to seek fame as a writer and actress respectively play naturally, even with some broadening for comedy. Richard Quine's direction keeps things gay and mostly moving at a spirited pace. Latter helps when some of the situations tend to be repetitious.

Two major assets in the trouping and funnying are Betty Garrett, as Ruth Sherwood, who pens sister's romantic adventures, and Jack Lemmon, as Bob Baker, the young publisher and would-be wolf who successfully romances Ruth. Seconding this pair are Janet Leigh, very attractive as the little sister, and [choreographer] Bob Fosse, the shy soda jerk.

None of the songs is from the stage tuner [*Wonderful Town*] having been cleffed by Jule Styne and Leo Robin especially for the picture. While not particularly standout, the numbers are mostly pleasant.

•

MY SIX CONVICTS
1952, 104 mins, US b/w
Dir Hugo Fregonese ***Prod*** Stanley Kramer ***Scr*** Michael Blankfort ***Ph*** Guy Roe ***Ed*** Gene Havlick ***Mus*** Dimitri Tiomkin ***Art*** Edward Ilou
Act Millard Mitchell, Gilbert Roland, John Beal, Marshall Thompson, Alf Kjellin, Henry Morgan (Kramer/Columbia)

My Six Convicts, the bestseller about the experiences of a prison psychologist, comes to the screen as mighty satisfying entertainment. As did the tome by Donald Powell Wilson, the film makes humans of the imprisoned men, and deals with them with whimsical humor and intelligent understanding. It's no regular prison drama of the common type.

Picture gets underway with the arrival at prison of John Beal, who is to establish, on trial, a psychological system for rehabilitating convicts. It's not until Millard Mitchell's safe cracker decides to try out the new doc that Beal is able to get going. The easy life in the psycho office soon attracts Gilbert Roland's mobster and killer; Marshall Thompson's alcoholic taking a rap for a girl; Alf Kjellin sentenced for an unarmed holdup; Henry Morgan's psycopathic killer; and Jay Adler's embezzler.

Mitchell and Roland split trouping honors about equally for cast standouts.

•

MY STEPMOTHER IS AN ALIEN
1988, 108 mins, US Ⓥ ⊙ col
Dir Richard Benjamin ***Prod*** Ronald Parker ***Scr*** Jerico, Herschel Weingrod, Timothy Harris, Jonathan Reynolds ***Ph*** Richard H. Kline ***Ed*** Jacqueline Cambas ***Mus*** Alan Silvestri ***Art*** Charles Rosen
Act Dan Aykroyd, Kim Basinger, Jon Lovitz, Alyson Hannigan, Joseph Maher (Weintraub)

My Stepmother Is an Alien is a failed attempt to mix many of the film genres associated with the "alien" idea into a sprightly romp.

Dan Aykroyd, as a rumpled, overweight, widower scientist, foils one of his own experiments using lightning and a high-powered satellite dish, which results in a signal reaching beyond our galaxy to a planet in peril.

Soon afterward, a flying saucer lands on a Southern California beach and two aliens alight. They come in the form of quintessential American beauty Kim Basinger in a slinky red sheath dress with an alien-buddy-mentor (the snake, voice courtesy of Ann Prentiss) hiding in her purse. Their mission is to get Aykroyd to repeat his experiment, which will save their planet. It is the lengths to which Basinger is expected to go wending her way into Aykroyd's otherwise nerdy suburban lifestyle that is supposed to levitate this fish-out-of-water story to comedic heights.

•

MYSTERIOUS ISLAND
1962, 100 mins, UK Ⓥ ⊙ col
Dir Cy Endfield ***Prod*** Charles H. Schneer ***Scr*** John Prebble, Daniel Ullman, Crane Wilbur ***Ph*** Wilkie Cooper ***Ed*** Frederick Wilson ***Mus*** Bernard Herrmann ***Art*** Bill Andrews
Act Michael Craig, Joan Greenwood, Michael Callan, Gary Merrill, Herbert Lom, Percy Herbert (Columbia)

Produced in England under Cy Endfield's vigorous direction, the film illustrates the strange plight that befalls three

Union soldiers, a newspaperman and a Rebel who, in 1865, escape the siege of Richmond in the inevitable Jules Verne balloon and return to land on an island in the remote South Seas, where they encounter, in chronological order: (1) a giant crab, (2) a giant bird, (3) two lovely shipwrecked British ladies of average proportions, (4) a giant bee, (5) a band of cutthroat pirates, (6) Captain Nemo's inoperative sub, (7) Captain Nemo.

The screenplay, from Verne's novel, winds with a staple of the science-fantasy melodrama—an entire volcanic isle sinking into the sea as the heroes and heroines beat a hasty retreat.

Dramatically the film is awkward, burdened with unanswered questions and some awfully ineffectual giant animals, but photographically it is noteworthy for the Super-dynamation process and special visual effects by Ray Harryhausen.

•

MYSTERIOUS LADY, THE

1928, 83 mins, US Ⓥ ⊗ b/w

Dir Fred Niblo ***Scr*** Bess Meredyth, Marion Ainslee, Ruth Cummings ***Ph*** William Daniels ***Ed*** Margaret Booth

Act Greta Garbo, Conrad Nagel, Gustav von Seyffertitz, Edward Connelly, Richard Alexander, Albert Pollet (M-G-M)

Secret service story [based on Ludwig Wolff's novel *War in the Dark*] involving a Russian feminine spy and an Austrian officer. Using up 83 minutes to unload this yarn is ridiculous.

Productionally it is very nice. Court balls, hundreds of uniforms, big interiors and beneath the surface much intrigue. Tania (Greta Garbo) has engineered her way into the heart of Karl (Conrad Nagel) but he turns on her when his uncle says she's a spy. For that Tania grabs some Austrian plans and Karl is court martialed and stripped of his uniform.

The secret service unc extracts him from prison so he can trail Tania to Warsaw. Posing as a musician, Karl finally finds his former sweetheart who gives evidence that he's still aces with her by returning the plans a fellow Austrian officer has slipped Gen. Alexandroff (Gustav von Seyffertitz), in pursuit of Tania for years. The general becomes so wise that Tania shoots him.

Inasmuch as the opening title includes that familiar phrase, "Vienna before the war," little else need be said. Garbo has done and is capable of better work.

•

MYSTERIOUS MR. MOTO

1938, 61 mins, US b/w

Dir Norman Foster ***Prod*** Sol M. Wurtzel (exec.) ***Scr*** Philip MacDonald, Norman Foster ***Ph*** Virgil Miller ***Ed*** Norman Colbert ***Mus*** Samuel Kaylin (dir.) ***Art*** Bernard Herzbrun, Lewis Creber

Act Peter Lorre, Mary Maguire, Henry Wilcoxon, Erik Rhodes, Harold Huber, Leon Ames (20th Century-Fox)

This time Mr. Moto (Peter Lorre) of the oily tongue and suave detection traps a gang of international murderers under circumstances that even baffles a beleaguered Scotland Yard. He's a one-man Hawkshaw who performs miracles, these not excluding the way he escapes from traps laid for him, from flocks of hoodlums, from gunfire, and from wet feet, or a head cold. Nothing can touch him, that also going for romance.

The story is hackneyed and the dialog isn't brilliant but the vital element in pictures of this kind, action, is in evidence in abundance.

Norman Foster, who directed, also collaborated on the original story and adaptation with Philip MacDonald. Neither the story nor the direction arouse any discussion concerning genius though getting high enough of a rating not to flunk.

Lorre is standard by now [in the fifth of the series] as the detective character but he's too much this side of requirements to engage in the fisticuffs handed him in this one. As a Eurasian girl, Karen Sorrell is an interesting screen type but held down on dialog. Henry Wilcoxon rather colorlessly does a steel mogul from Czechoslovakia, while Mary Maguire plays the secretary who's in love with him.

•

MYSTERY OF THE WAX MUSEUM, THE

1933, 78 mins, US Ⓥ ⊙ col

Dir Michael Curtiz ***Scr*** Don Mullaly, Carl Erickson ***Ph*** Ray Rennahan ***Ed*** George Amy ***Art*** Anton Grot

Act Lionel Atwill, Fay Wray, Glenda Farrell, Frank McHugh, Allen Vincent (Warner)

Technicolor horror-mystery production cofeaturing Lionel Atwill, Fay Wray, Glenda Farrell and Frank McHugh who struggle about as effectively as Michael Curtiz, the director, with a loose and unconvincing story, to manage a fairly decent job along *Frankenstein* and *Dracula* lines. Loose ends never quite jell but it's one of those artificial things.

Atwill is the maniacal custodian of the London wax museum whose fanatic enterprise with his transplanted museum on American soil leads Farrell, as the sob sister, to unearth this weird yarn, McHugh this time is the city ed. Wray and Allen Vincent are almost negligible in minor romantic background.

•

MYSTERY SCIENCE THEATER 3000: THE MOVIE

1996, 73 mins, US Ⓥ col

Dir Jim Mallon ***Prod*** Jim Mallon ***Scr*** Michael J. Nelson/Trace Beaulieu, Jim Mallon/Kevin Murphy, Mary Jo Pehl/Paul Chaplin, Bridget Jones ***Ph*** Jeff Stonehouse ***Ed*** Bill Johnson ***Mus*** Billy Barber ***Art*** Jef Maynard

Act Michael J. Nelson, Trace Beaulieu, Kevin Murphy, Jim Mallon, John Brady (Best Brains)

Just like the cable TV series that spawned it, *Mystery Science Theater 3000: The Movie* is cheap, silly fun, a barrage of one-liners aimed at a risible old picture by one human and two robots who constitute an onscreen audience.

Mystery Science Theater 3000 was born in Minneapolis in 1988, ran for 22 shows there, and the following year was picked up by HBO's Comedy Channel, which later merged with Viacom's Ha! into Comedy Central. The now-canceled series' staple has always been bad, low-budget 1950s sci-fi epics, but for the group's first feature, the creators actually picked a moderately revered and amply budgeted one, Universal's 1955 release *This Island Earth*.

The *Mystery Science* framework remains the same, with mad scientist Dr Clayton Forrester (longtime cast member and writer Trace Beaulieu) subjecting space traveler Mike Nelson (writer Michael J. Nelson) and his robot pals, the bulb-headed Tom Servo (writer Kevin Murphy) and the birdlike Crow T. Robot (Beaulieu) to an awful movie in an attempt to dominate them.

The threesome are constantly on view in silhouette along the bottom of the screen, needling it mercilessly throughout. Humor ranges from lots of mild gay innuendo about the male characters' "real" relationship to comments on the cheesy special effects and even inside industry jokes.

•

MYSTERY TRAIN

1989, 113 mins, US Ⓥ ⊙ col

Dir Jim Jarmusch ***Prod*** Jim Stark ***Scr*** Jim Jarmusch ***Ph*** Robby Muller ***Ed*** Melody London ***Mus*** John Lurie ***Art*** Dan Bishop

Act Masatoshi Nagase, Youki Kudoh, Nicoletta Braschi, Elisabeth Bracco, Joe Strummer, Rick Aviles (JVC/MTI)

Wholly financed by Japanese electronics giant JVC, a first for an American production, *Mystery Train* is a three-episode pic handled by indie writer-director Jim Jarmusch in his usual playful, minimalist style.

It could be almost dubbed "Memphis Stories," as this is Jarmusch's tribute to the city of Elvis and other musical greats.

Characteristically, the director explores the crumbling, decaying edges of the city through the eyes of foreigners: Japanese teenagers, an Italian widow and a British punk.

Story one, *Far from Yokohama,* intros teenagers Jun (Masatoshi Nagase) and Mitzuko (Youki Kudoh), who arrive by train, do a puzzling guided tour of Sun Studio (they can't understand a word the guide says), sit awed in front of a statue of Presley and check into the Arcade Hotel. Story two, *A Ghost,* features Nicoletta Braschi as Luisa, in Memphis to take her deceased husband's body back to Rome. She checks into the Arcade and meets talkative DeeDee (Elisabeth Bracco) in the lobby. Final segment, *Lost in Space,* picks up the story of abandoned Brit Johnny (Joe Strummer), who goes on a drunken binge with DeeDee's brother (Steve Buscemi) and a black friend (Rick Aviles). Johnny shoots a liquor store clerk, and the trio hides out in the Arcade; next morning, trying to stop Johnny from shooting himself, Buscemi gets shot in the leg.

•

MYSTIC PIZZA

1988, 104 mins, US Ⓥ ⊙ col

Dir Donald Petrie ***Prod*** Mark Levinson, Scott Rosenfelt ***Scr*** Amy Jones, Perry Howze, Randy Howze, Alfred Uhry ***Ph*** Tim Suhrstedt ***Ed*** Marion Rothman, Don Brochu ***Mus*** David McHugh ***Art*** David Chapman

Act Annabeth Gish, Julia Roberts, Lili Taylor, Vincent D'Onofrio, William R. Moses, Adam Storke (Goldwyn)

Mystic Pizza is a deftly told coming-of-age story [by Amy Jones] about three young femmes as they explore their different destinies, mostly through romance; it's genuine and moving.

Title refers to a pizza parlor in the heavily Portuguese fishing town of Mystic, CT, where three best friends, two of them sisters, are working the summer after high-school graduation, all on the verge of pursuing different directions in life.

Jojo (Lili Taylor) apparently is headed for marriage to high-school sweetheart Bill (Vincent D'Onofrio), but the idea terrifies her, while he's all for it.

Of the two sisters, Daisy (Julia Roberts) is a vamp who's after the good life and knows how to use her looks, while Kat (Annabeth Gish) is the "perfect" one—headed for college on an astronomy scholarship. Unlike her sister, she's not too savvy about men, and falls for the married man (William Moses) she baby-sits for, with painful results.

Script is remarkably mature in its dealings with teens. Characters are funny and vulnerable but capable of shaping their lives, and script artfully weaves in themes of class, destiny and friendship.

•

MY UNCLE

SEE: MON ONCLE

NADINE
1987, 83 mins, US Ⓥ ⊙ col
Dir Robert Benton ***Prod*** Arlene Donovan ***Scr*** Robert Benton ***Ph*** Nestor Almendros ***Ed*** Sam O'Steen ***Mus*** Howard Shore ***Art*** Paul Sylbert
Act Jeff Bridges, Kim Basinger, Rip Torn, Gwen Verdon, Glenne Headly, Jerry Stiller (Tri-Star/Delphi Premier)

Nadine is an innocuous souffle from writer-director Robert Benton so lightweight that in the end one can't help wondering where the film is. Set in Austin in 1954, Benton tries to get by on Texas charm but the recipe of screwball comedy and small-town thriller fails to jell.

Jeff Bridges and Kim Basinger are husband and wife on the verge of divorce drawn together again by a suspicious killing. As Vernon Hightower, proprietor of the unsuccessful Bluebonnet saloon, Bridges has a smile and an excuse for every mishandled situation. As Nadine, Basinger is a kvetch with a twang, who gives manicures in the local beauty parlor.

Things get going when Basinger witnesses the murder of two-bit photographer Raymond Escobar (Jerry Stiller) who happens to have in his possession some "art" shots of Nadine, thereby giving her a motive for the killing. The real meat of the matter are some photos for a proposed highway that Escobar has gotten his hands on and local mobster Buford Pope (Rip Torn) wants back at any cost.

Pope is the only truly interesting character here and the film comes alive when he's on the screen.

•

NADJA
1994, 95 mins, US b/w
Dir Michael Almereyda ***Prod*** Mary Sweeney, Amy Hobby ***Scr*** Michael Almereyda ***Ph*** Jim Denault ***Ed*** David Leonard ***Mus*** Simon Fisher Turner ***Art*** Kurt Ossenfort
Act Suzy Amis, Galaxy Craze, Martin Donovan, Peter Fonda, Karl Geary, Elina Lowensohn (Kino Link)

Vampires stalk the netherworld of the downtown New York scene of *Nadja*, a lovely idea for a film that's been beautifully executed but slips too far off its narrative tracks to get where it wants to go. Lowbudgeter is stunningly lensed in a mixture of black-and-white 35mm and Pixelvision and featuring one of the sexiest female vampires ever to bare her teeth onscreen.

The darkly mysterious, extravagantly beautiful Nadja (Elina Lowensohn) picks up a guy in a bar and later feasts upon him. Nadja next meets young Lucy (Galaxy Craze), with whom she unexpectedly falls in love. Lucy, it turns out, is married to Jim (Martin Donovan), whose uncle, Dr. Van Helsing (Peter Fonda), has killed Nadja's father and is now after the alluring young woman and her twin brother, Edgar (Jared Harris), who is in the care of private nurse Cassandra (Suzy Amis).

After creating such promise through the intriguing setup of stuning twin vampires in trendy, nocturnal Gotham, it's disappointing that Almereyda develops narrative butterfingers, letting the storyline become too diffuse and cutting among too many principal characters.

In his film *Another Girl, Another Planet*, Almereyda pioneered the use of the toy Pixelvision video camera, and he has reprised its use here in scenes that relate to the vampire state of mind. Technical work overall is fancy and impressive.

•

NAKED
1993, 131 mins, UK Ⓥ col
Dir Mike Leigh ***Prod*** Simon Channing-Williams ***Scr*** Mike Leigh ***Ph*** Dick Pope ***Ed*** Jon Gregory ***Mus*** Andrew Dickson ***Art*** Alison Chitty
Act David Thewlis, Lesley Sharp, Katrin Cartlidge, Greg Cruttwell, Claire Skinner, Peter Wight (Thin Man/Film Four)

A Stygian comedy on '90s London social angst, Mike Leigh's *Naked* will come as a major surprise to those reared on lighter fare like *Life Is Sweet* and *High Hopes*. Shot through with sudden, psychotic mood shifts, from comedy to violence to, finally, a strangely moving love story, pic dwarfs everything the director has yet done.

Center of Leigh's script—as with prior movies—is an unemployed philosopher-bum, Johnny (David Thewlis), who's fled south from Manchester and initially stays with former g.f. Louise (Lesley Sharp). After bedding her loopy flatmate, punkette Sophie (Katrin Cartlidge), he suddenly ups and leaves on a weird nocturnal odyssey on the streets of London.

Naked plays lighter than it reads, thanks to wonderful straight-faced thesping of Leigh's dry, humour-filled script. Anchored by a confident tour de force from Thewlis, perfs by the hand-chosen cast mesh splendidly, with Cartlidge (recalling the Jane Horrocks character in *Life*) delivering a

wonderful array of one-liners. Dialogue is four-letter stuff all the way.

•

NAKED AND THE DEAD, THE
1958, 131 mins, US Ⓥ ▭ col
Dir Raoul Walsh ***Prod*** Paul Gregory ***Scr*** Denis Sanders, Terry Sanders ***Ph*** Joseph LaShelle ***Ed*** Arthur P. Schmidt ***Mus*** Bernard Herrmann ***Art*** Ted Haworth
Act Aldo Ray, Cliff Robertson, Raymond Massey, Lili St. Cyr, Barbara Nichols, Richard Jaeckel (RKO)

The film bears little more than surface resemblance to the hard-hitting Norman Mailer novel of the same title. It catches neither the spirit nor the intent of the original yarn and thus becomes just another war picture, weighed with some tedious dialog sporadically lifted from the book.

The characters go through the motions, hating themselves, hating each other, hating the jungle war that flares around them.

The action sequences come in spurts, but when they do, lenser Joseph LaShelle sees to it that they impress and the dangers of the jungle warfare become vividly real. Unfortunately, a good deal of the footage is taken up with the platoon moving up a mountain or down a mountain, crossing rivers, etc. and, after a while, these scenes begin to wear thin.

Aldo Ray plays the frustrated, bitter and sadistic Sergeant Croft. It's not a very plausible part in the first place, and the strenuous efforts to "explain" him (his wife, Barbara Nichols, has been unfaithful) don't help. Ray plays this beefy character with gusto and certain raw power.

As the playboy whom the general picks as his aide, Cliff Robertson turns in a slick performance. He's good in his verbal encounters with the general, whom he eventually defies, but lacks conviction once he's assigned to lead the Croft platoon on its final sortie.

•

NAKED CITY, THE
1948, 94 mins, US b/w
Dir Jules Dassin ***Prod*** Mark Hellinger ***Scr*** Albert Maltz, Malvin Wald ***Ph*** William Daniels ***Ed*** Paul Weatherwax ***Mus*** Miklos Rozsa, Frank Skinner ***Art*** John F. DeCuir
Act Barry Fitzgerald, Howard Duff, Dorothy Hart, Don Taylor, Ted De Corsia (Universal)

Naked City is a boldly fashioned yarn [by Malvin Wald] about eastside, westside; about Broadway, the elevated, Fifth Avenue; about kids playing hop-skip-and-jump; about a populace of 8 million—about a blond beaut's mysterious murder in an Upper Westside apartment house.

Hellinger's off-screen voice carries the narrative. At the very opening he describes New York, with the aid of a mobile camera, and its teeming humanity. Kids at play, subway straphangers, street vendors on Orchard Street. Then that blonde with a questionable background who is mysteriously murdered. The kind of a story that Hellinger, one of the great tabloid crime reporters of the bathtub-gin era, used to write.

In this pic there are no props. A Manhattan police station scene was photographed in the police station; a Lower Eastside cops-and-robbers chase was actually filmed in the locale; the ghetto and its pushcarts were caught in all their realism.

Throughout, despite its omniscient, stark melodrama, there has been no sight lost of an element of humor. Barry Fitzgerald, as the film's focal point, in playing the police lieutenant of the homicide squad, strides through the role with tongue in cheek, with Don Taylor as his young detective aide.

1948: Best B&W Cinematography, Editing

NOMINATION: Best Motion Picture Story

•

NAKED EARTH, THE
1958, 96 mins, UK ▭ b/w
Dir Vincent Sherman ***Prod*** Adrian Worker ***Scr*** Milton Holmes ***Ph*** Erwin Hillier ***Ed*** Russel Lloyd ***Mus*** Arthur Benjamin ***Art*** Terence Verity
Act Richard Todd, Juliette Greco, Finlay Currie, John Kitzmiller, Laurence Naismith, Christopher Rhodes (Fox/Foray)

The Naked Earth is a thoroughly well-made film that peeks into the heart of Africa and comes out with a captivating actress in Juliette Greco. It also presents a twinkling performance by Richard Todd and an excellent photographic record of a bird picking the teeth of a crocodile.

Tale is set in a forsaken section of the darkest continent at the end of the 19th century. It's a story of man's struggle against nature, a bout in which he loses every round but still wins the fight. Todd, an Irishman looking for new wealth, treks to the African hinterlands to launch a farming effort with an old friend he's to meet there. When he finds the friend has been devoured by one of the feared crocodiles, he and the dead friend's female companion get married for convenience, then plant tobacco for profit. Bad luck with his plants pushes Todd into the gloomy rivers to stalk the treacherous crocodiles for their valued skins.

Greco has the humor and sarcasm of an Anna Magnani, and, to top that, a totally sensuous appeal. John Kitzmiller, as the native friend, and Finlay Currie, as a missionary, are excellent. The Milton Holmes script, from his own story, is skillfully constructed and sustains interest with a minimum of involvement.

•

NAKED EDGE, THE
1961, 99 mins, US b/w
Dir Michael Anderson ***Prod*** Walter Seltzer, George Glass ***Scr*** Joseph Stefano ***Ph*** Erwin Hillier ***Ed*** Gordon Pilkington ***Mus*** William Alwyn ***Art*** Carmen Dillon
Act Gary Cooper, Deborah Kerr, Eric Portman, Diane Cilento, Hermione Gingold, Peter Cushing (United Artists/Pennebaker-Baroda)

The picture that winds up Gary Cooper's long list of credits is a neatly constructed, thoroughly professional little suspense meller. Based on Max Ehrlich's novel, *First Train to Babylon*, Joseph Stefano's screenplay casts Cooper as an American businessman living in London who, coincidentally to the murder of his business partner (and the disappearance of a couple of hundred thousand dollars), happens to make a killing on the stock market, which funds he uses to make an even bigger fortune.

When, five years later, a blackmailer in the form of Eric Portman turns up to accuse her husband of the murder, Deborah Kerr remembers that Cooper, after all, had been the key prosecution witness at the murder trial and had come into a lot of money quite suddenly. The lady's further investigations confirm her suspicions.

Kerr suffers very prettily in a highly emotional role. Cooper, perhaps because he must appear to be enigmatic most of the time, gives a less successful performance. The picture, filmed entirely in London, utilizes some fine British supporting people.

•

NAKED EYE, THE
1957, 71 mins, US col
Dir Louis Clyde Stoumen, W. S. Van Dyke ***Prod*** Louis Clyde Stoumen ***Scr*** Louis Clyde Stoumen ***Ph*** Louis Clyde Stoumen, Benjamin Doniger ***Ed*** Louis Clyde Stoumen ***Mus*** Elmer Bernstein
(Camera Eye)

The Naked Eye is aptly subtitled a film about the fun and art of photography. Millions of shutterbugs also will find it an engrossing 71 minutes of what can be done with photography, both from the examples of the artists shown and from the equally outstanding production-photography job done by Louis Clyde Stoumen.

Stoumen uses a unique technique he calls photographic animation, along with live action documentary filming, to impart action to stills. Abetting this feeling of movement is an extremely good narration job by Raymond Massey and a most effective background score by Elmer Bernstein.

Footage covers the history of photography, without getting uninterestingly academic, while concentrating on several notable examples of the photographic art, each with story narrative to hold the interest.

•

NAKED GUN, THE: FROM THE FILES OF POLICE SQUAD!
1988, 85 mins, US Ⓥ ⊙ col
Dir David Zucker ***Prod*** Robert K. Weiss ***Scr*** Jerry Zucker, Jim Abrahams, David Zucker, Pat Proft ***Ph*** Robert Stevens ***Ed*** Michael Jablow ***Mus*** Ira Newborn ***Art*** John J. Lloyd
Act Leslie Nielsen, George Kennedy, Priscilla Presley, Ricardo Montalban, O. J. Simpson, Nancy Marchand (Paramount)

The Naked Gun is crass, broad, irreverent, wacky fun—and absolutely hilarious from beginning to end.

Subtitled *From the Files of Police Squad!*, based on ill-fated too-hip-for-TV series a few seasons earlier, comedy from the crazed Jerry Zucker, Jim Abrahams, David Zucker yock factory is chockablock with sight gags.

Leslie Nielsen is the clumsy detective reprising his TV role and George Kennedy his straight sidekick who wreaks havoc in the streets of L.A. trying to connect shipping magnate and socialite Ricardo Montalban with heroin smuggling.

Scintilla of a plot weaves in an inspired bit of nonsense with Queen Elizabeth II lookalike Jeannette Charles as the target for assassination at a California Angels's baseball games, where she stands up and does the wave like any other foolish-looking fan, plus a May-December romance between Nielsen and vapid-acting Priscilla Presley whose exchanges of alternatingly drippy or suggestive dialog would make great material for a soap parody.

●

NAKED GUN 33: THE FINAL INSULT

1994, 82 mins, US Ⓥ ⦿ col

Dir Peter Segal ***Prod*** Robert K. Weiss, David Zucker ***Scr*** Pat Proft, David Zucker, Robert LoCash ***Ph*** Robert Stevens ***Ed*** Jim Symons ***Mus*** Ira Newborn ***Art*** Lawrence G. Paull

Act Leslie Nielsen, Priscilla Presley, George Kennedy, O. J. Simpson, Fred Ward, Kathleen Freeman (Paramount)

Paramount's third spin of *The Naked Gun* is loaded with the usual barrage of irreverent, politically incorrect and virtually nonstop gags. This latest platter offers some killers, perhaps the most inspired being its *The Untouchables* spoof that precedes the credits. Those keeping track, however, will also see references, seldom subtle, to such diverse sources as *Thelma & Louise*, *White Heat* and *The Crying Game*. The latest is thinner in the plot department than the others. Police squad detective Frank Drebin (Leslie Nielsen) has retired and taken to the domestic life, while his wife prosecutes child-support cheats. Frank gets talked into returning to the force, going undercover to bunk up with a terrorist (Fred Ward) and the terrorist's mob, including his snarling mother (Kathleen Freeman) and bombshell girlfriend (supermodel Anna Nicole Smith).

By now Nielsen, Priscilla Presley and the other regs can virtually mail in their performances, which give shameless mugging a good name. Ward's an effective bad guy, while Smith's wonder-of-modern-engineering outfits almost prompt one to ignore that, based on this perf, she should probably stick to modeling.

●

NAKED GUN 2½, THE: THE SMELL OF FEAR

1991, 85 mins, US Ⓥ ⦿ col

Dir David Zucker ***Prod*** Robert K. Weiss ***Scr*** David Zucker, Pat Proft ***Ph*** Robert Stevens ***Ed*** James Symons, Chris Greenbury ***Mus*** Ira Newborn ***Art*** John J. Lloyd

Act Leslie Nielsen, Priscilla Presley, George Kennedy, O. J. Simpson, Robert Goulet, Richard Griffiths (Paramount)

The Naked Gun 2½ is at least two-and-a-half times less funny than its hilarious 1988 progenitor. But even if the laugh machine isn't operating at top efficiency, it still cranks out a few choice bits of irreverent lunacy.

Clothesline plot, designed to make the most of director David Zucker's environmental concerns, has bad guy Robert Goulet kidnapping the president's wheelchair-bound energy czar and replacing him with a lookalike who will endorse continued heavy reliance on oil, coal and nuclear power.

Case sees Lt. Frank Drebin (Leslie Nielsen) catching up with his erstwhile inamorata (Priscilla Presley) who, we learn, dumped him two years earlier. After an amusing rendezvous in a truly blue jazz boite, pair communes soulfully over a potter's wheel in a send-up of *Ghost*, and Drebin doesn't seem threatened by a newspaper headline that announces, "Elvis Spotted Buying Condo in Aspen."

Nielsen seems just a tad more self-aware than he was in the original. Whereas O. J. Simpson, who reappears here as the hapless Nordberg, took the brunt of physical abuse in the first *Naked Gun*, that honor in the sequel falls to Margery Ross, whose Barbara Bush hardly goes a minute without taking a nasty fall or hit.

●

NAKED JUNGLE, THE

1954, 95 mins, US Ⓥ ⦿ col

Dir Byron Haskin ***Prod*** George Pal ***Scr*** Philip Yordan, Ranald MacDougall ***Ph*** Ernest Laszlo ***Ed*** Everett Douglas ***Mus*** Daniele Amfitheatrof ***Art*** Hal Pereira, Franz Bachelin

Act Eleanor Parker, Charlton Heston, Abraham Sofaer, William Conrad, Romo Vincent, Douglas Fowley (Paramount)

There's a lot of the tried-and-found-true romantic drama formula in *The Naked Jungle*, an interesting feature that mixes in jungle adventure with a science-fiction touch dealing with an invading army of ants that think. Man-against-ant fight was described in the December 1938 issue of *Esquire* (Carl Stephenson's *Leiningen versus the Ants*).

The familiar names of Eleanor Parker and Charlton Heston occupy the star spots. For Parker it is a particularly good characterization, warm and human. Heston hits his stride about the halfway mark after his character opens up and becomes more human and understandable. Up to that time he plays the part with a sombre heaviness that is too forbidding. This is the only mistake in Byron Haskin's otherwise smart, suspense—building and actionful direction.

A mail-order bride comes from New Orleans to bed with a man, without femme experience, who has spent 15 years hewing a profitable plantation and palatial home out of the jungles of South America. As the conflict of this marital situation moves forward to a not unexpected climax, the threat of the ant invasion takes over. The dread soldier ants of South America organize in a purposeful march and descend on the plantation. Abraham Sofaer scores as the plantation owner's chief servant, as does William Conrad, jungle-wise commissioner; Douglas Fowley, medicine man; Leonard Strong, a native; and Norma Calderon, very appealing as the native girl assigned to care for the bride.

●

NAKED KISS, THE

1965, 90 mins, US ⦿ b/w

Dir Samuel Fuller ***Prod*** Samuel Fuller ***Scr*** Samuel Fuller ***Ph*** Stanley Cortez ***Ed*** Jerome Thoms ***Mus*** Paul Dunlap ***Art*** Eugene Lourie

Act Constance Towers, Anthony Eisley, Michael Dante, Virginia Grey, Patsy Kelly, Marie Devereux (Allied Artists/Firks)

Good Samuel Fuller programmer about a prostie trying the straight route, *The Naked Kiss* is primarily a vehicle for Constance Towers. Hooker angles and sex perversion plot windup are handled with care, alternating with handicapped children "good works" theme.

Action starts fast with brawl between hardened prostie Kelly (Towers) and cheating pimp who shaved her head, after which she takes to sticks, where she promptly makes it with local cop Griff. Role is played routinely throughout by Anthony Eisley.

Pic bogs down at this point in cliches, as hooker rejects berth in nearby red-lighter run by an effective hard-bitten Virginia Grey, instead taking up rehabilitation of crippled children under wing of Patsy Kelly who makes the most of her few lines.

Towers's overall effect is good, director Fuller overcoming his routine script in displaying blonde looker's acting range.

●

NAKED LUNCH

1991, 115 mins, Canada/UK Ⓥ ⦿ col

Dir David Cronenberg ***Prod*** Jeremy Thomas ***Scr*** David Cronenberg ***Ph*** Peter Suschitzky ***Ed*** Ronald Sanders ***Mus*** Howard Shore ***Art*** Carol Spier

Act Peter Weller, Judy Davis, Ian Holm, Julian Sands, Roy Scheider, Monique Mercure (Thomas)

William S. Burroughs's notorious, and notoriously unfilmable, novel *Naked Lunch* has landed in the right hands. Stretching himself with each new work, David Cronenberg has come up with a fascinating, demanding, mordantly funny picture.

A cult novel since its publication in 1959, Burroughs's non-narrative novel represented the literary equivalent of a Heironymous Bosch painting, a profane, outrageous explosion of riffs dominated by drugs, gay sex and a surreal evocation of society's control mechanisms.

At the center of this chilly emotional spiral is William Lee (Burroughs's alter ego and early pseudonym), an insect exterminator in New York City circa 1953. Lee (Peter Weller) lives in quiet squalor with his wife (Judy Davis) until, on a bug drug high, he accidently shoots her while playing *William Tell*.

Breaking into a hallucinatory state, Lee escapes to the realm of Interzone, an imaginatively demented rendition of Tangier heavily populated by artist addicts, homosexuals and secret agents, where he is able to begin writing, even if what he is writing are "reports" over which he seems to have no actual control.

Weller is a superb Burroughs stand-in, strongly holding center screen while not actually doing much. Supporting cast is diverse and outstanding. Dissuaded from actually shooting in Tangier by the outbreak of the 1991 Gulf War, Cronenberg's team has memorably created an artificial world almost entirely on stages.

●

NAKED PREY, THE

1966, 86 mins, US Ⓥ ⦿ ▭ col

Dir Cornel Wilde ***Prod*** Cornel Wilde ***Scr*** Clint Johnston, Don Peters ***Ph*** H.A.R. Thomson ***Ed*** Roger Cherrill ***Mus*** Andrew Tracey (adv.) ***Art*** [uncredited]

Act Cornel Wilde, Gert Van Der Berg, Ken Gampu, Patrick Mynhardt, Bella Randles, Morrison Gampu (Theodora/Persson)

Filmed entirely in South Africa, *The Naked Prey* is a story of a white man's survival under relentless pursuit by primitive tribesman. Told with virtually no dialog, the story embodies a wide range of human emotion, depicted in actual on-scene photography that effects realism via semi-documentary feel.

The basic story is set in the bush country of a century ago, where safari manager Cornel Wilde and party are captured by natives offended by white hunter Gert Van Der Berg. All save Wilde are tortured in some explicit footage that is not for the squeamish, while he is given a chance to survive—providing he can exist while eluding some dedicated pursuers.

Action then roves between the macroscopic and the microscopic; that is, from long shots of the varying bush country, caught in beautiful soft tones by H.A.R. Thomson's camera, where man is a spot on the landscape, all the way down to minute animal life, in which the pattern of repose, pursuit, sudden death and then repose matches that of Wilde and the natives.

Ken Gampu, film and legit actor in South Africa, is excellent as the leader of the pursuing warriors.

1966: NOMINATION: Best Original Story & Screenplay

●

NAKED RUNNER, THE

1967, 104 mins, UK Ⓥ ▭ col

Dir Sidney J. Furie ***Prod*** Brad Dexter ***Scr*** Stanley Mann ***Ph*** Otto Heller ***Ed*** Barrie Vince ***Mus*** Harry Sukman ***Art*** Peter Proud

Act Frank Sinatra, Peter Vaughan, Derren Nesbitt, Nadia Gray, Toby Robins, Inger Stratton (Warner/Sinatra)

From a Francis Clifford novel, writer Stanley Mann has fashioned a dullsville script, based on premise that British Intelligence cannot assign one of its own to murder a defector to Russia.

Instead, Frank Sinatra, a Second World War spy now a businessman-widower, is dragooned into service, and by events, deliberately staged, is goaded into killing the defector. Not only British Intelligence, but anybody's intelligence, is likely to be affronted by this potboiler.

Sinatra, whose personal magnetism and acting ability are unquestioned, is shot down by script. Peter Vaughan overacts part as the British agent.

●

NAKED SPUR, THE

1953, 91 mins, US Ⓥ col

Dir Anthony Mann ***Prod*** William H. Wright ***Scr*** Sam Rolfe, Harold Jack Bloom ***Ph*** William Mellor ***Ed*** George White ***Mus*** Bronislau Kaper ***Art*** Cedric Gibbons, Malcolm Brown

Act James Stewart, Janet Leigh, Robert Ryan, Ralph Meeker, Millard Mitchell (M-G-M)

This is a taut outdoor melodrama made to order for the western action addict who likes rugged dramatics delivered without dilution. Film has been tersely produced with no waste motion in getting the violence of the original screen story on film.

Plot deals with the violence to which greed spurs the oddly assorted characters caught up in the story. James Stewart is after Robert Ryan, an outlaw killer, so he can collect a $5,000 reward and start a ranch. As he corners the killer in the mountains after a long, arduous chase, he is joined by Millard Mitchell, an old prospector, and Ralph Meeker, who has just been dishonorably discharged from the Union Army.

They aid in the capture and determine to share in the reward, so it is a party at cross-purposes that starts the long trek back. During the journey, Ryan sets his captors against each other and, to further his aims at escape, uses Janet Leigh, an outlaw's daughter, to stir up trouble between Stewart and Meeker, both of whom are attracted to the girl.

The rugged beauty of the Colorado mountain location where film was shot is splendidly shown by William Mellor's cameras.

1953: NOMINATION: Best Story & Screenplay

●

NAKED TANGO
1990, 93 mins, US Ⓥ col
Dir Leonard Schrader ***Prod*** David Weisman ***Scr*** Leonard Schrader ***Ph*** Juan Ruiz-Anchia ***Ed*** Lee Percy, Debra McDermott ***Mus*** Thomas Newman ***Art*** Anthony Pratt
Act Vincent D'Onofrio, Mathilda May, Esai Morales, Fernando Rey, Cipe Lincovsky, Josh Mostel (Sugarloaf/Gotan)

Tango equals sex equals death in writer-director Leonard Schrader's fatally dark exploration of the 1920s tango underworld. The genesis for *Tango* was found among Argentine writer Manuel Puig's unpublished manuscripts about the Buenos Aires underworld of the '20s. The film is credited onscreen as "inspired by" the late playwright.

Production casts French actress Mathilda May as Stephanie, restless new bride of a wealthy elderly Argentine judge (Fernando Ray). She slips her leash while on board a ship bound for Buenos Aires and trades identities with a waif who has just hurled herself overboard. May learns she is now Alma, a Polish mail-order bride bound for a rendezvous with her future husband on the docks.

He proves to be the handsome young Zico (Esai Morales), part of a wealthy Jewish household, and the future looks pleasant. But Zico is actually a gangster and a pimp who runs a tango bordello with his mercenary, coldhearted mother (Cipe Lincovsky) and aloof, brutal "tango king" brother, Cholo (Vincent D'Onofrio).

Alma murders the first john they send her; after that the pic becomes a sort of underlit gangster chase thriller as the local mafia, known as the Black Hand, demands a sacrifice for the killing.

First-time director Schrader (brother of Paul) has put a vivid and specific vision on the screen, but his boldness with high melodrama is somewhat diminished by the sometimes-clumsy gangster action scenes.

•

NAKED UNDER LEATHER
SEE: THE GIRL ON A MOTORCYCLE

•

NAME OF THE ROSE, THE
1986, 130 mins, W. Germany/Italy/France Ⓥ ⦿ col
Dir Jean-Jacques Annaud ***Prod*** Bernd Eichinger ***Scr*** Andrew Birkin, Gerard Brach, Howard Franklin, Alain Godard ***Ph*** Tonino Delli Colli ***Ed*** Jane Seitz ***Mus*** James Horner ***Art*** Dante Ferretti
Act Sean Connery, F. Murray Abraham, Christian Slater, Michel Lonsdale, Ron Perlman, Valentina Vargas (Neue Constantin/Cristaldifilm/Ariane/ZDF)

The Name of the Rose is a sorrowfully mediocre screen version of Umberto Eco's surprise international bestselling novel.

Confusingly written and sluggishly staged, this telling of a murder mystery in a 14th-century abbey has been completely flubbed by director Jean-Jacques Annaud and his team of four (credited) screenwriters, as they struggle even to get the basics of the story up on the screen.

Tale has English Franciscan monk Sean Connery and his novice Christian Slater arriving at an Italian abbey in preparation for a conclave. After a series of murders at the massive edifice Connery, in the style of an aspiring Sherlock Holmes, undertakes an investigation of the deaths while more delegates continue to arrive.

One of the latecomers is F. Murray Abraham, an inquisitor who sees Satan behind every foul deed and who threatens to condemn his old rival Connery due to the latter's insistence on seeking a rational solution to the crimes.

Connery lends dignity, intelligence and his lovely voice to the proceedings. His performance, however, along with some tantalizing E. M. Escher–style labyrinths in the interior of the abbey, are about the only blessings.

•

NANA
1934, 87 mins, US b/w
Dir Dorothy Arzner ***Prod*** Samuel Goldwyn ***Scr*** Willard Mack, Harry Wagstaff Gribble ***Ph*** Gregg Toland ***Ed*** Frank Lawrence ***Mus*** Alfred Newman (dir.) ***Art*** Richard Day
Act Anna Sten, Phillips Holmes, Lionel Atwill, Richard Bennett, Mae Clarke, Muriel Kirkland (Goldwyn/United Artists)

Sam Goldwyn brilliantly launches a new star in a not so brilliant vehicle. Anna Sten has beauty, glamour, charm, histrionic ability (although there are a couple of moments that seemed a bit beyond her), and s.a.

The script is a very free adaptation of Emile Zola's famous novel. Much care is evident to make it as circumspect as possible and yet maintain its color and allure, which is the basis of this transition of a Parisian gamine to music hall heights.

It ends on a tragic note with a suicide by the glorified gamine who takes this way out to reunite the two brothers, Phillips Holmes whom she loves, and Lionel Atwill, his maturer kin, who has coveted her and who subsequently patronizes her when the younger brother is transferred with his regiment to Algiers.

In between there is Richard Bennett as the great Greiner, the master showman, who decides to clay this new unglorified model into the toast of the revue halls.

Sten's likening to Marlene Dietrich becomes inevitable. Her throaty manner of singing "That's Love" (the sole Rodgers-Hart song in the film) brings that home even more forcibly, apart from her light dialectic Teutonic brogue and the same general aura in personality. The Dorothy Arzner style of direction likewise recalls the Sternberg-Mamoulian technique employed in Dietrich's behalf.

•

NANCY GOES TO RIO
1950, 99 mins, US Ⓥ col
Dir Robert Z. Leonard ***Prod*** Joe Pasternak ***Scr*** Sidney Sheldon ***Ph*** Ray June ***Ed*** Adrienne Fazan ***Mus*** George Stoll (dir.)
Act Jane Powell, Ann Sothern, Barry Sullivan, Carmen Miranda, Louis Calhern (M-G-M)

Nancy Goes to Rio is all that a light, glittering musical should be. Producer Joe Pasternak has framed his production with nine tunes and a group of production numbers.

Plot setup for the melange of song and dance [based on a story by Jane Hall, Frederick Kohner and Ralph Block] deals with the theatrical family of Ann Sothern. Mom goes to Rio to rest and study a new play. Daughter is chosen for the play, and dashes to Rio to tell of her good fortune. She finds Sothern set on doing the show and holds off her own good news long enough for some side-bar complications to come to a boil.

Director Robert Z. Leonard doesn't allow pace to falter or any heavy moments to creep in on the escapist setup. Nick Castle's dance staging helps the physical values.

•

NANNY, THE
1965, 93 mins, UK Ⓥ b/w
Dir Seth Holt ***Prod*** Jimmy Sangster ***Scr*** Jimmy Sangster ***Ph*** Harry Waxman ***Ed*** James Needs, Tom Simpson ***Mus*** Richard Rodney Bennett ***Art*** Edward Carrick
Act Bette Davis, Wendy Craig, Jill Bennett, James Villiers, William Dix, Pamela Franklin (Hammer)

It's not necessary to be an astute student to guess that Bette Davis as a middle-aged Mary Poppins in a fairly fraught household will eventually be up to no good. Which immediately sets the odds against screenwriter Jimmy Sangster and director Seth Holt. But, in fairness, the balance of power between Davis, posing as a devoted nanny, and William Dix as a knowing youngster who hates Davis's innards, is so skillfully portrayed to make *The Nanny* a superior psycho-thriller.

It's an added plus to the pic [from the novel by Evelyn Piper] that neither writer nor director teeters over the edge into hysterics, and the cast has cottoned on and helped to build up the suspense gently but with a steely pricking of the nerve ends.

Yarn, briefly, concerns the relationship between nanny Davis and Master Joey (Dix) which is less than cordial. He comes out of a school for the unstable to which he has been sent when his baby sister is found drowned in the bath. He insists it was nanny's fault, but, of course, the adults don't believe him.

Davis handles her assignment with marked professionalism, and copes with plenty of know-how competition. Wendy Craig is fine as a weak, fond young mama whose nerves are shot to pieces by the household happenings.

•

NANOOK OF THE NORTH
1922, 55 mins, US Ⓥ b/w
Dir Robert Flaherty ***Scr*** Robert Flaherty, Carl Stearns Clancy ***Ph*** Robert Flaherty ***Ed*** Herbert Edwards (1947) ***Mus*** Rudolf Schramm (1947)

Nanook of the North is the granddaddy (or the Eskimo equivalent) of all documentaries and widely extolled as the classic in its field. Despite the comparatively primitive technique and the natural difficulties of shooting a film in the frozen Hudson Bay wastelands, every minute of *Nanook* lives up to its reputation.

Yarn holds tremendous interest in detailing the life of an Eskimo family through the seasons of the year.

Ralph Schoolman's narrative hits the proper note. It treats the Eskimos with dignity, yet with a sense of humor, and it never gets pompous.

Berry Kroeger likewise sticks to a simple, friendly, yet thoroughly dignified style in speaking the narration.

•

NAPOLEON
1927, 300 mins, France Ⓥ ⦿ ▭ b/w
Dir Abel Gance ***Ph*** Jules Kruger, Leonce-Henry Burel ***Ed*** Abel Gance, Marguerite Beauge, Henriette Pinson ***Mus*** Arthur Honegger ***Art*** Alexandre Benois, Pierre Schildknecht
Act Albert Dieudonne, Abel Gance, Antonin Artaud, Gina Manes, Daniel Burret, Suzanne Bianchetti (Westi/Societe Generale des Films)

French-made super-production by Abel Gance, dealing with the earlier life of Napoleon Bonaparte, particularly episodes of the French Revolution, was released at the Paris Opera as a special gala in favor of local charitable organizations assisting war victims.

The scenario deals with historical facts in the life of the future emperor up to the war in Italy, before he even became First Consul. The picture does not include the period when the hero was known to history as Napoleon I.

The opera showing was a triumph and there is every sign of *Napoleon* being a universal success. The triple screen, whereby (in certain portions of the picture for war scenes) the screen is increased to thrice the ordinary size caused a sensation for the lay public. The extended vision is obtained by projecting three reels from separate lanterns on three screens, the pictures synchronizing.

Details of the execution were given out for press use, wherein we are told the French government provided 5,000 troops, as supers, for the episode depicting the siege of Toulon, and the rallying of the famous army in Italy. Rock salt estimated at over a ton was used to imitate hail and half a ton of boric acid as snow. Though no deaths were to be deplored during the making of the picture, in which thousands maneuvered with fire arms, many accidents occurred, 220 claims having since been filed with the insurance companies.

The rain during the siege of Toulon is somewhat exaggerated, but the scenes during the Revolution are particularly impressing.

Albert Dieudonne in the title role is excellent. A special score by Arthur Honegger, of the new school of music grade, accompanies.

It is a splendid achievement but still needs careful pruning. [Pic was initially shown in the U.S. in a 70-min. version in 1929, released by M-G-M.]

•

NARAYAMA BUSHI-KO
(THE BALLAD OF NARAYAMA)
1958, 98 mins, Japan ▭ col
Dir Keisuke Kinoshita ***Scr*** Keisuke Kinoshita ***Ph*** Hiroshi Kusuda ***Ed*** Yoshi Sugihara ***Mus*** Tameharu Endo (arr.) ***Art*** Kisaku Ito
Act Kinuyo Tanaka, Teiji Takahashi, Yuko Mochizuki, Seiji Miyaguchi, Yunosuke Ito, Danko Ichigawa (Shochiko)

Distasteful story and slow pace are basic strikes against pic, despite moments of great poetry and top acting by all concerned, and especially by Kinuyo Tanaka, in the leading role.

Plot concerns a 69-year-old widow, Orin (Tanaka), who must settle her family affairs and find a wife for her son before the law of the land forces her to the hills to die on reaching the age of 70. When all is done and her great-grandchild is on the way, her son reluctantly carries her up the mountain to her peaceful death in the snow, which has just begun to fall to speed her on her way. Theme of hunger also permeates entire pic.

To further director Keisuke Kinoshita's semitheatrical style, speaker commentary and song, lighting effects, and stage-like scenic changes are used to span sequences. Entire pic is studio-shot to achieve this.

Pace is deliberately slow, and Japanese weakness for violence is seen in a shot in which the old woman knocks out her teeth, supposedly to still her hunger.

•

NARAYAMA BUSHI-KO
(US: THE BALLAD OF NARAYAMA)
1983, 130 mins, Japan col
Dir Shohei Imamura ***Prod*** Jiro Tomoda ***Scr*** Shohei Imamura ***Ph*** Masao Toshizawa ***Ed*** Hajime Okayazu ***Mus*** Shinichiro Ikebe
Act Ken Ogata, Sumiko Sakamoto, Takeshiro Aki, Seiji Kurasaki, Junko Takada, Kaoru Shimamori (Toei/Imamura)

Shohei Imamura's *The Ballad of Narayama* is excellently crafted, strongly acted and directed, and well shot.

Focus is on the now-past Japanese custom of taking their elderly to the mountains to die: in this case, a determined 69-year-old woman, portrayed convincingly by actress Sumiko Sakamoto, 47, who puts her own family in order and, though healthy, demands to be left on the mountain well before she becomes infirm. Her eldest son protests, but leaves her to the elements.

Imamura shows village life with all its gossip, friendship and abrupt violence and adds a few raw sex scenes that add rather than detract. Pic is a shade long for its telegraphed plot, but for those who take the time there are rewards.

The characters are a mixed bag: a shy elder son who must marry first, a second son who loses his lover when her family proves to be criminals and is buried alive by the village folk, and a third roisterous son who in a counterpoint subplot has sex with another of the village's old ladies.

•

NARROW MARGIN, THE
1952, 71 mins, US Ⓥ ⊙ b/w
Dir Richard Fleischer ***Prod*** Stanley Rubin ***Scr*** Earl Felton ***Ph*** George E. Diskant ***Ed*** Robert Swink ***Mus*** [none] ***Art*** Albert S. D'Agostino, Jack Okey
Act Charles McGraw, Marie Windsor, Jacqueline White, Gordon Gebert, Queenie Leonard, Don Beddoe (RKO)

A standard amount of cops-and-robber melodramatics are stirred up most of the time in *The Narrow Margin*. Plot falls apart at the climax, but regulation thriller tricks, tersely played, carry the story [by Martin Goldsmith and Jack Leonard] along sufficiently.

Two Los Angeles detectives (Charles McGraw and Don Beddoe) are sent to Chicago to escort the widow of a racketeer to the Coast for testimony before the grand jury. Beddoe is killed and McGraw starts back with Marie Windsor, closely pursued by gangsters who want to keep the widow from testifying. Chase makes for some excitement aboard the train as McGraw keeps outwitting the crooks.

Trouping is competent, with McGraw showing up excellently in his tight-lipped, terse cop portrayal. Windsor impresses the most among the femmes.

1952: NOMINATION: Best Motion Picture Story

•

NARROW MARGIN
1990, 97 mins, US Ⓥ ⊙ ▭ col
Dir Peter Hyams ***Prod*** Jonathan A. Zimbert ***Scr*** Peter Hyams ***Ph*** Peter Hyams ***Ed*** James Mitchell ***Mus*** Bruce Broughton ***Art*** Joel Schiller
Act Gene Hackman, Anne Archer, James B. Sikking, J. T. Walsh, M. Emmet Walsh, Susan Hogan (Carolco)

Spectacular stunt work and Canadian locations punch up the train thriller *Narrow Margin*, but feature remake is too cool and remote to grab the viewer. Richard Fleischer's trim 1952 classic for RKO had a negative cost of only $230,000, while the remake logs in at $21 million. That extra bread shows up on screen in impressive production values but filmmaker Peter Hyams fails to make his story involving.

Basic plotline is retained in the new version. In the Charles McGraw role, Gene Hackman plays a deputy d.a. delivering key witness Anne Archer to testify against gangster Harris Yulin. Hackman's teammate, cop M. Emmet Walsh, is killed leaving Hackman and Archer to escape from a helicopter of armed heavies. They flee to a train headed across remote stretches of Canada and have to play cat and mouse with the thugs (led by evil James B. Sikking) who've boarded the train to eliminate them.

Hackman adds panache to a one-dimensional role. Archer is stuck with a nothing part, given barely one monolog to express her character's feelings. Curiously there is no sex or suggestion of romance in the film.

•

NASHVILLE
1975, 157 mins, US Ⓥ ⊙ ▭ col
Dir Robert Altman ***Prod*** Robert Altman ***Scr*** Joan Tewkesbury ***Ph*** Paul Lohmann ***Ed*** Sidney Levin, Dennis Hill ***Mus*** Richard Baskin
Act Ned Beatty, Karen Black, Keith Carradine, Geraldine Chaplin, Shelley Duvall, Henry Gibson (Paramount/ABC)

One of the most ambitious, and more artistically, successful, "backstage" musical dramas, Robert Altman's *Nashville* is strung on the plot thread of a George Wallace–type pre-presidential campaign in which the interactions of 24 principal characters are followed over the period of a few days in the country music capitol of America.

Outstanding among the players are Henry Gibson, as a respected music vet with an eye on public office; Ronee Blakely, in a great film debut as a c&w femme star on the brink of nervous collapse; Gwen Welles, drawing tears from stone as a pitiably untalented waitress who undergoes the humiliation of stripping at a stag party for a chance to sing.

Among some real life cameos are Elliott Gould and Julie Christie, both as themselves on p.a. tours.

Nashville is one of Altman's best films, free of the rambling insider fooling around that sometimes mars entire chunks of every second or third picture. When he navigates rigorously to defined goals, however, the results are superb.

1975: Best Song ("I'm Easy")

NOMINATION: Best Picture, Director, Supp. Actress (Ronee Blakely, Lily Tomlin)

•

NASTY HABITS
1976, 98 mins, UK Ⓥ col
Dir Michael Lindsay-Hogg ***Prod*** Robert Enders ***Scr*** Robert Enders ***Ph*** Douglas Slocombe ***Ed*** Peter Tanner ***Mus*** John Cameron ***Art*** Robert Jones
Act Glenda Jackson, Melina Mercouri, Geraldine Page, Sandy Dennis, Anne Jackson, Anne Meara (Bowden)

A witty, intelligent screenplay [from Muriel Spark's novella *The Abbess of Crewe*] leaves no doubts that this is the Watergate circus transposed to a convent, complete with Machiavellian intrigues and power plays, sexual hanky-panky, visiting plumbers, hypocritical television chats, national and international political play, roving ambassadors, and so on.

Told straight, it's all about the battle for power in a Philly convent once the aged abbess dies, an all-stops-out dirty scrap which pits establishment against young lib "outsiders" who want a change. Glenda Jackson is superb, making her role as the scheming climber unerringly her own. Only one actress nearly bests her: Edith Evans in a memorable cameo, the actress's last stint in a distinguished legit-pic career.

•

NATIONAL LAMPOON'S ANIMAL HOUSE
1978, 109 mins, US Ⓥ ⊙ col
Dir John Landis ***Prod*** Matty Simmons, Ivan Reitman ***Scr*** Harold Ramis, Douglas Kenney, Chris Miller ***Ph*** Charles Correll ***Ed*** George Folsey, Jr. ***Mus*** Elmer Bernstein ***Art*** John J. Lloyd
Act John Belushi, Tim Matheson, John Vernon, Verna Bloom, Tom Hulce, Donald Sutherland (Universal)

Steady readers of the *National Lampoon* may find *National Lampoon's Animal House* a somewhat soft-pedalled, punches-pulled parody of college campus life circa 1962. However, there's enough bite and bawdiness to provide lots of smiles and several broad guffaws.

Writers have concocted a pre-Vietnam college confrontation between a scruffy fraternity and high-elegant campus society. Interspersed in the new faces are the more familiar John Vernon, projecting well his meany charisma here as a corrupt dean; Verna Bloom, Vernon's swinging wife; Cesare Danova, the Mafioso-type mayor of the college town; Donald Sutherland as the super-hip young professor in the days when squares were still saying "hep."

Of no small and subtle artistic help is the score by Elmer Bernstein which blithely wafts "Gaudeamus Igitur" themes amidst the tumult of beer "orgies," neo-Nazi ROTC drills, cafeteria food fights and a climactic disruption of a traditional Homecoming street parade.

Among the younger players, John Belushi and Tim Matheson are very good as leaders of the unruly fraternity, while James Daughton and Mark Metcalf are prominent as the snotty fratmen, all of whom, quite deliberately, look like Nixon White House aides.

•

NATIONAL LAMPOON'S CHRISTMAS VACATION
1989, 97 mins, US Ⓥ ⊙ col
Dir Jeremiah Chechik ***Prod*** John Hughes ***Scr*** John Hughes ***Ph*** Thomas Ackerman ***Ed*** Jerry Greenberg ***Mus*** Angelo Badalamenti ***Art*** Stephen Marsh
Act Chevy Chase, Beverly D'Angelo, Randy Quaid, Diane Ladd, John Randolph, E. G. Marshall (Warner/Hughes)

Solid family fare with plenty of yucks, *National Lampoon's Christmas Vacation* is Chevy Chase and brood doing what they do best. Despite the title, which links it to previous pics in the rambling *Vacation* series, this third entry is firmly rooted at the Griswold family homestead, where Clark Griswold (Chase) is engaged in a typical over-reaching attempt to give his family a perfect, old-fashioned Christmas.

Acidic contrast to his fanatical focus on family comes from next-door neighbors Todd and Margot (Nicholas Guest and Julia Louis-Dreyfus) as a pair of suave young urbanites repelled by Chase's behavior. Script gets off some zingers at their lifestyles, too.

A group piece in which the ensemble keeps growing as relatives arrive, pic really gains momentum when Randy Quaid shows up as redneck ne'er-do-well cousin, Eddie, driving an RV that looks like a septic tank on wheels.

For the most part, helmer Jeremiah Chechik makes an adept debut, injecting plenty of energy and spirit.

•

NATIONAL LAMPOON'S CLASS REUNION
1982, 84 mins, US Ⓥ ⊙ col
Dir Michael Miller ***Prod*** Matty Simmons ***Scr*** John Hughes ***Ph*** Phil Lathrop ***Ed*** Richard C. Meyer, Ann Mills ***Mus*** Peter Bernstein, Mark Goldenberg ***Art*** Dean Edward Mitzner
Act Gerrit Graham, Michael Lerner, Fred McCarren, Miriam Flynn, Stephen Furst, Marya Small (ABC)

It took them two tries and more than four years to come up with another National Lampoon picture after the hugely successful *Animal House*. Result, *National Lampoon's Class Reunion* gets sidetracked almost immediately thanks to a harebrained lunatic-on-the-loose plot in which the 1972 graduating class's high school is turned into the semblance of a haunted house.

Motley crew here includes former wiseacre Gerrit Graham, who's now become a snooty yacht salesman; Fred McCarren, a do-gooder with such a sparkling personality that no one can remember him; Miriam Flynn, a Little Miss Prim whose mind seems best suited to ordering refreshments for a sorority punch party; Stephen Furst, who gives the late John Belushi a run for his money in the girth department but not on the laugh meter.

Coming off a bit better are Marya Small as a blind nymphomaniac and Shelley Smith, who looks smashing in her silver evening gown and gets to do Diana Ross singing "Stop! In the Name of Love." Even guest star Chuck Berry seems at less than his best performing a quick medley in the early going.

•

NATIONAL LAMPOON'S EUROPEAN VACATION
1985, 94 mins, US Ⓥ ⊙ col
Dir Amy Heckerling ***Prod*** Matty Simmons ***Scr*** John Hughes, Robert Klane ***Ph*** Bob Paynter ***Ed*** Pembroke J. Herring ***Mus*** Charles Fox ***Art*** Bob Cartwright
Act Chevy Chase, Beverly D'Angelo, Jason Lively, Dana Hill, Eric Idle, Victor Lanoux (Warner)

Most imaginative stroke is the passport-stamped credit sequence that opens this sequel to the 1983 *National Lampoon's Vacation*. Story [by John Hughes] of a frenetic, chaotic tour of the Old World, with Chevy Chase and Beverly D'Angelo reprising their roles as determined vacationers, is graceless and only intermittently lit up by lunacy and satire.

As the family of characters cartwheel through London, Paris, Italy and Germany—with the French deliciously taking it on the chin for their arrogance and rudeness—director Amy Heckerling gets carried away with physical humor while letting her American tourists grow tiresome and predictable. Structurally, the film unfolds like a series of travel brochures.

Uneven screenplay never sails, and it's left to Chase to fire up the film. His character is actually rather sympathetic—if boorish—in his insistence on turning every Continental moment into a delight (scanning Paris, he shouts, "I want to write, I want to paint, I got a romantic urge!").

•

NATIONAL LAMPOON'S LOADED WEAPON 1
1993, 83 mins, US Ⓥ ⊙ col
Dir Gene Quintano ***Prod*** Suzanne Todd, David Willis ***Scr*** Don Holley, Gene Quintano ***Ph*** Peter Deming ***Ed*** Christopher Greenbury, Neil Kirk ***Mus*** Robert Folk ***Art*** Jaymes Hinkle
Act Emilio Estevez, Samuel L. Jackson, Jon Lovitz, Tim Curry, Kathy Ireland, William Shatner (New Line)

More an imitation than a parody, this would-be comedy is very short on laughs. Premise is spoofing Richard Donner's three *Lethal Weapon* movies right down to copying their logo.

Ostensible plotline [by Don Holley and Tori Tellem] has evil general William Shatner (allowed to ham it up disturbingly by director Gene Quintano) and goofy-accented henchman Tim Curry in a scheme involving cocaine and Girl Scout cookies. Investigation begins when cop Whoopi Goldberg (one of the few uncredited cameos) is murdered. Emilio Estevez is teamed with Goldberg's ex-partner Samuel L. Jackson, earmarked for the Danny Glover role.

The re-creation of scenes from *L.W.* movies includes Jackson's pretty daughter Danielle Nicolet playing footsie with Estevez from film 1 and Estevez comparing scars with heroine Kathy Ireland á la Rene Russo in film 3.

Film digresses at length with Kathy Ireland and an uncredited actress both playing Sharon Stone in *Basic Instinct* for some cheap potshots.

•

NATIONAL LAMPOON'S SENIOR TRIP
1995, 91 mins, US Ⓥ col
Dir Kelly Makin ***Prod*** Wendy Grean ***Scr*** Roger Kumble, I. Marlene Protat ***Ph*** Francios Protat ***Ed*** Stephen Lawrence ***Mus*** Steve Bartek ***Art*** Gregory Keen

Act Matt Frewer, Valerie Mahaffey, Lawrence Dane, Tommy Chong, Jeremy Renner, Rob Moore (Alliance)

There was a time when the *National Lampoon* name on a movie meant something, back in the days of *Animal House* and *Vacation*. Now it means a witless item that is hurried through its theatrical window on its way to cable and homevid.

Story involves a bunch of seniors in an Ohio high school (actually shot in Canada) whose detention assignment is to write a letter to the president of the United States about why the educational system has failed. The president is impressed and invites the kids to Washington. There, a manipulative senator (Lawrence Dane) sees their arrival as an opportunity to use the moronic teens to embarrass his political rival.

To his credit, Matt Frewer, as the principal, manages to flesh out his character to two dimensions; most of the rest of the cast are simply playing one-joke stick figures. Tommy Chong is the burnt-out bus driver known as *Red* because of his fondness for horse tranquilizers, while Valerie Mahaffey is the mousy teacher who is really a tigress. Kevin McDonald does add some life as a crazed crossing guard obsessed with *Star Trek*.

•

NATIONAL LAMPOON'S VACATION

1983, 96 mins, US Ⓥ ⊙ col

Dir Harold Ramis ***Prod*** Matty Simmons ***Scr*** John Hughes ***Ph*** Victor J. Kemper ***Ed*** Pem Herring ***Mus*** Ralph Burns ***Art*** Jack Collis

Act Chevy Chase, Beverly D'Angelo, Anthony Michael Hall, Imogene Coca, Randy Quaid, John Candy (Warner)

National Lampoon's Vacation is an enjoyable trip through familiar comedy landscapes.

Chevy Chase is perfectly mated with Beverly D'Angelo as an average Chicago suburban couple setting out to spend their annual two-week furlough. Determined to drive, Chase wants to take the two kids to "Walley World" in California. She would rather fly.

Despite home-computer planning, this trip is naturally going to be a disaster from the moment Chase goes to pick up the new car. No matter how bad this journey gets—and it gets pretty disastrous—Chase perseveres in treating each day as a delight, with D'Angelo's patient cooperation. His son, beautifully played by Anthony Michael Hall, is a help, too.

Vacation peaks early with the family's visit to Cousin Eddie's rundown farm, rundown by the relatives residing there. As the uncouth cousin, Randy Quaid almost steals the picture.

Credit director Harold Ramis for populating the film with a host of well-known comedic performers in passing parts.

•

NATIONAL VELVET

1944, 125 mins, US Ⓥ ⊙ col

Dir Clarence Brown ***Prod*** Pandro S. Berman ***Scr*** Theodore Reeves, Helen Deutsch ***Ph*** Leonard Smith ***Ed*** Robert J. Kern ***Mus*** Herbert Stothart ***Art*** Cedric Gibbons, Urie McCleary

Act Mickey Rooney, Donald Crisp, Elizabeth Taylor, Anne Revere, Angela Lansbury, Reginald Owen (M-G-M)

National Velvet is a horse picture with wide general appeal. The production also focuses attention on a new dramatic find—moppet Elizabeth Taylor.

Backgrounded in England, it tells of a former jockey (Mickey Rooney) who's become embittered through circumstances and plans to steal from a family that befriends him. But the family's 11-year-old daughter, Velvet, softens him.

From this point on, early in the film, Velvet becomes the dominant character in the story [from the novel by Enid Bagnold]. The kid is nuts about horses. When a neighbor raffles off an unmanageable brute he's unable to handle she wins it on tickets paid for by Rooney. Over the objections of both Rooney and her father, nag is entered in the greatest race in England, the Grand National Sweepstakes.

Story is told with warmth and understanding. There is much detail, in this direction, between husband and wife; between Velvet and her mother and between the two kids, especially when Rooney confesses to an abiding fear of horses ever since he rode in a sweepstakes which ended in another jockey's death.

1945: Best Supp. Actress (Anne Revere), Editing

NOMINATION: Best Director, Color Cinematography, Color Art Direction

•

NATURAL, THE

1984, 134 mins, US Ⓥ ⊙ col

Dir Barry Levinson ***Prod*** Mark Johnson ***Scr*** Robert Towne, Phil Dusenberry ***Ph*** Caleb Deschanel ***Ed*** Stu Linder ***Mus*** Randy Newman ***Art*** Angelo Graham, Mel Bourne

Act Robert Redford, Robert Duvall, Glenn Close, Kim Basinger, Wilford Brimley, Barbara Hershey (Tri-Star)

The Natural is an impeccably made, but quite strange, fable about success and failure in America. Robert Redford plays an aging rookie who takes the baseball world by storm in one season while dealing with demons from his past and present.

While remaining faithful to Bernard Malamud's 1952 novel in many regards, scenarists have drastically altered some major elements. Film thereby has become the story of the redemption of a born athlete whose life didn't unfold as anticipated.

Opening sequences present farmboy Roy Hobbs showing natural skill as a ballplayer and, upon the death of his father, carving his own magical bat, dubbed "Wonderboy" from the wood of a lightning-struck tree.

Some years later, Hobbs, now in the person of Redford, leaves for Chicago, and raises the eyebrows of ace sportswriter and cartoonist Robert Duvall when he strikes out the majors' greatest hitter (Joe Don Baker) in an impromptu exhibition.

Redford is perfectly cast as the wary, guarded Hobbs. The female characters leave behind a bad taste, however, since they schematically and simplistically stand for the archaic angel-whore syndrome. Whenever he goes for harlots like Barbara Hershey or Kim Basinger, Redford is in big trouble, from which he must be rescued by Glenn Close.

1984: NOMINATIONS: Best Supp. Actress (Glenn Close), Cinematography, Art Direction, Original Score

•

NATURAL BORN KILLERS

1994, 116 mins, US Ⓥ ⊙ col

Dir Oliver Stone ***Prod*** Jane Hamsher, Don Murphy, Clayton Townsend ***Scr*** David Veloz, Richard Rutowski, Oliver Stone ***Ph*** Robert Richardson ***Ed*** Hank Corwin, Brian Berdan ***Mus*** Budd Carr (exec. prod.) ***Art*** Victor Kempster

Act Woody Harrelson, Juliette Lewis, Robert Downey, Jr., Tommy Lee Jones, Rodney Dangerfield, Tom Sizemore (Ixtlan/New Regency/Warner)

Natural Born Killers is a heavy duty acid trip, quite possibly the most hallucinatory and anarchic picture made at a major Hollywood studio in at least 20 years. A scabrous look at a society that promotes murderers as pop culture icons, as well as a scathing indictment of a mass media establishment that caters to and profits from such star-making, this is Oliver Stone's most exciting work to date strictly from a filmmaking point of view.

A rare Stone film in that it's neither historically rooted nor written originally by him, *Killers* still shows the bloody fingerprints of its original author, Quentin Tarantino, who receives story credit only, although Stone has supplied a thick layer of sociopolitical commentary readily recognizable as his own.

Film is divided into two halves, the first of which lays out the crazy three weeks during which the lead couple gun down 52 people out West, the second of which presents the insane media circus which surrounds their incarceration, a live in-prison interview, a riot, and their subsequent amazing escape.

Mickey (Woody Harrelson) and Mallory (Juliette Lewis) kill for the sake of their great love for each other, they say, and the film's psychological ambitions never get much deeper than that. In an audacious comic conceit, flashbacks show Mallory's previous family life literally in sitcom terms, as meanie Dad (Rodney Dangerfield) bullies and molests her before hunky escaped con Mickey comes along to rescue her and launch their killing spree, à la *Badlands*, by mowing down her folks.

Their capture sends the picture into an even higher gear, as the irrepressible Wayne Gale (Robert Downey, Jr.) intends to capture his highest ratings with a live interview on Super Bowl Sunday. The unhinged good ol' boy warden (Tommy Lee Jones) has brought in a tough law enforcer (Tom Sizemore) to figure out a way to eliminate Mickey and Mallory in-house, but Mickey's survival instinct prevails.

The sheer amount of carnage is numbingly enormous, even though its stylized, sometimes even cartoon-like quality makes the killing much less shocking than in more realistic contexts. Visually, the film is a sensation, resembling a demonically clever light show at a late '60s rock concert. The narrative is related in color 35mm, black-and-white, 8mm and video, and at different speeds.

Performers are uniformly pushed to the brink, Harrelson and Lewis are all lust (blood and sex) and no conscience as the pretty couple "naturally born bad." Jones is broader than he's ever been as the sweaty, lip-smacking warden none too grand at his job. Standout perf comes from Downey.

•

NAUGHTY BUT NICE

1939, 90 mins, US b/w

Dir Ray Enright ***Prod*** [Sam Bischoff] ***Scr*** Richard Macaulay, Jerry Wald ***Ph*** Arthur L. Todd ***Ed*** Thomas Richards ***Mus*** Ray Heindorf (arr.), Leo F. Forbstein (dir.) ***Art*** Max Parker

Act Ann Sheridan, Dick Powell, Gale Page, Helen Broderick, Ronald Reagan, Allen Jenkins (Warner)

Naughty but Nice has a good quota of laughs and is generally bright, despite a plot at which cynical Tin Pan Alley habitues might look askance. This being Dick Powell's finale for Warner's, the studio gives Ann Sheridan No. 1 costar billing. Film title is not particularly consistent with story content.

Powell is a professional composer who finds himself a commercial songsmith, especially when partnered with Gale Page's lyrics. Sheridan is the slight menace here, a mike siren who would break up the songwriting team just to be cut in on his future songs.

An insidious rum drink is a plot essential. Mistaken for lemonade, it sends the staid Powell into hi jinks and front-page notoriety as a let's-tear-the-joint-down-kid, whenever he is taken into a nitery atmosphere and fed these high voltage beverages.

•

NAUGHTY MARIETTA

1935, 105 mins, US Ⓥ ⊙ b/w

Dir W. S. Van Dyke ***Prod*** Hunt Stromberg ***Scr*** J. L. Mahin, Frances Goodrich, Albert Hackett ***Ph*** William Daniels ***Ed*** Blanche Sewell ***Mus*** Herbert Stothart (adapt.)

Act Jeanette MacDonald, Nelson Eddy, Frank Morgan, Elsa Lanchester, Douglass Dumbrille, Joseph Cawthorne (M-G-M)

An adaptation of the Victor Herbert operetta [book and lyrics by Rida Johnson Young] which the singing of Jeanette MacDonald and Nelson Eddy must carry. Much of the original score, plus a couple of added tunes [lyrics by Gus Kahn], is included. There are nine songs, but only one reprise, a martial tune from Eddy and his warriors.

This operetta tells of a group of girls the French government has endowed before they sail to Louisiana, there to find husbands and build up that colony. The princess (MacDonald) escapes with this group from her tyrannical uncle and the aged suitor he has selected. In New Orleans she falls in love with the captain of the mercenaries (Eddy) and again escapes for a happy finish.

The comedy being insufficient to sustain this much footage, with no especially exciting action, provides serious handicaps. Although Marietta may have been naughty in 1910, if she's still naughty it's her secret.

MacDonald sings particularly well and is favored with fine recording and exceptional photography. She also carries her share of the story capably and in her lighter moments gives a hint of what might be.

Picture marks the full-length debut of Eddy who reveals a splendid and powerful baritone with the distinct asset for the camera of not being breathy. Eddy is a tall, nice-looking boy who previously, briefly, appeared in a couple of Metro films. In this picture he sings so often that the script calls for his kidding himself about it.

Frank Morgan does a routine governor, with an eye for an ankle, dominated by his wife. Elsa Lanchester is the wife with an unattractive tendency to mug her points.

1935: Best Sound Recording

NOMINATION: Best Picture

•

NAVIGATOR, THE

1924, 60 mins, US ⊗ b/w

Dir Donald Crisp, Buster Keaton ***Scr*** Jean Havez, Clyde Bruckman, Joe Mitchell ***Ph*** Elgin Lessley, Byron Houck ***Art*** Fred Gabourie

Act Buster Keaton, Kathryn McGuire, Frederick Vroom (Metro-Goldwyn)

Buster Keaton's comedy is spotty. That is to say it's both commonplace and novel, with the latter sufficient to make the picture a laugh getter.

The film is novel in that it has Keaton in a deep-sea diving outfit with the camera catching him underwater for comedy insertions. There's a possibility of doubling during some of the action, but close-ups are registered under water that reveal Keaton, personally, behind the glass within the helmet.

There's an abundance of funny business in connection with Keaton's going overboard to fix a propellor shaft and a thrill has been inserted through the comedian getting mixed up with a devilfish.

The actual story carries little weight. It has Keaton as a wealthy young man being matrimonially rejected by the girl. Having secured passage to Hawaii, he unknowingly boards a deserted steamship selected to be destroyed by foreign and warring factions. The girl's father, owner of the vessel, visits the dock, is set upon by the rogues who are bent on casting the liner adrift, and when the girl goes to her parent's rescue she is also caught on board with no chance of a return to land. The entire action practically takes place on the deserted ship, with the girl (Kathryn McGuire) and Keaton the only figures.

•

NAVIGATOR, THE: A MEDIEVAL ODYSSEY

1988, 93 mins, Australia/New Zealand Ⓥ col

Dir Vincent Ward ***Prod*** John Maynard ***Scr*** Vincent Ward, Kelly Lyons, Geoff Chapple ***Ph*** Geoffrey Simpson ***Ed*** John Scott ***Mus*** Davood A. Tabrizi ***Art*** Sally Campbell

Act Bruce Lyons, Chris Haywood, Hamish McFarlane, Marshall Napier, Noel Appleby, Paul Livingston (Arenafilm/NZ Film Investment Corp)

The Navigator is remarkable because of its absorbing story that links medieval fears and fortunes to our times, while confirming director Vincent Ward as an original talent.

The story begins in Cumbria in 1348, the year of the Black Death. Young Griffin (Hamish McFarlane) is anxious for the return of his beloved, much-older brother Connor (Bruce Lyons) from the outside world. He is haunted by a dream about a journey, a quest to a great cathedral in a celestial city, and a figure about to fall from a steeple.

When his brother returns to the village with tales of impending doom, the two brothers, with four comrades, set out on the journey fired by Griffin's prophetic dream. It takes them to a city of the late 1980s and on a mission against time if their village is to be saved.

The formidable skills of Ward are shown in the way his story works, not only as adventure, but as the love story of two brothers and a parable of faith and religion.

Geoffrey Simpson's photography—stark black and white for the Cumbrian sequences, color for the enactment of Griffin's dream and visions—is of the highest order, with score by Iranian composer Davood Tabrizi (domiciled in Sydney) empathetic with the whole.

•

NAVY LARK, THE

1959, 82 mins, UK ▭ b/w

Dir Gordon Parry ***Prod*** Herbert Wilcox ***Scr*** Sid Colin, Laurie Wyman ***Ph*** Gordon Dines ***Ed*** Basil Warren ***Mus*** James Moody, Tommy Reilly ***Art*** Jim Morahan

Act Cecil Parker, Ronald Shiner, Leslie Phillips, Elvi Hale, Nicholas Phipps, Cardew Robinson (20th Century-Fox)

The Navy Lark, based on a click BBC radio series, is the oldie about a "forgotten" naval base on an island off the South Coast of Britain. They're having a high old time feathering their nests with illicit smuggling and other rackets. The skipper's involved in fishing. His No. 1 yen is a pretty Wren officer's blonde charms. Suddenly higher authority decides that the minesweeping unit is redundant and from then on chaos breaks out as they scheme to avoid being posted elsewhere.

Only occasionally does the comedy creak. Then director Gordon Parry has the good fortune to have on hand some skilled performers who hold the fort. These include Cecil Parker, a master of the art of bumbling; Nicholas Phipps, as the probing senior officer constantly on the receiving end of indignity; Ronald Shiner, who boisterously can play a wily petty officer in his sleep; Cardew Robinson, extremely good as an over-diligent war correspondent, and Leslie Phillips, as a philandering second officer.

On the distaff side there are a number of comely femmes who are mostly around to decorate the scene. Elvi Hale, as a Wren officer who causes the love light in Phillips's eye, has the brightest opportunity.

•

NAVY SEALS

1990, 113 mins, US Ⓥ ⊙ col

Dir Lewis Teague ***Prod*** Brenda Feigen, Bernard Williams ***Scr*** Chuck Pfarrer, Gary Goldman ***Ph*** John A. Alonzo ***Ed*** Don Zimmerman ***Mus*** Sylvester LeVay ***Art*** Guy J. Comtois, Veronica Hadfield

Act Charlie Sheen, Michael Biehn, Joanne Whalley-Kilmer, Rick Rossovich, Cyril O'Reilly, Bill Paxton (Orion)

Nifty performances make this routine action flick better than it probably has a right to be. Playing to the *Rambo* mentality by focusing on an elite naval-attack group kicking tail around the globe, the film won't be a favorite of peaceniks or any Arab antidefamation leagues.

The film begins with a full-blown assignment and repeatedly sends the group out on elaborate suicide missions, showcasing plenty of gee-whiz gimickry in the process.

That first mission involves freeing U.S. personnel from terrorists who, it turns out, have access to handheld stinger missiles. The Navy Seals must subsequently locate the missiles and then eliminate them, aided (preposterously) by a beautiful TV reporter (Joanne Whalley-Kilmer).

Michael Biehn displays plenty of quiet determination, while Charlie Sheen cuts loose as a borderline psycho whose maverick style and cat-and-mouse games with death occasionally endanger fellow team members.

Director Lewis Teague brings real flair to much of the action, though the messy, overlong finale—set, no less, in the ravaged streets of Beirut—gets way out of hand.

•

NAZARIN

1959, 94 mins, Mexico Ⓥ ⊙ b/w

Dir Luis Bunuel ***Prod*** Manuel Barbachano Ponce ***Scr*** Luis Bunuel, Julio Alejandro, Emilio Carballido ***Ph*** Gabriel Figueroa ***Ed*** Carlos Savage ***Mus*** [none] ***Art*** Edward Fitzgerald

Act Francisco Rabal, Marga Lopez, Rita Macedo, Jesus Fernandez, Ignacio Lopez Tarso, Ofelia Guilmain (Ponce)

A priest unfrocks himself and takes to the road to live on alms when he is implicated by the law for harboring a prostitute after she had killed another one. However, he is followed in his pilgrimage by the escaped prostitute and a woman who has been left by a lover. Film [from the novel by Benito Perez Galdos] details their wanderings and attempts to help humanity and their constant rebuffs, until the priest realizes one must love humanity first, before one can be a human being or a priest.

Film abounds in a profound feeling for man. There are grotesque scenes. One involves a dwarf who falls in love with the prostie. There are also scenes of a plague.

This is a difficult but rewarding pic. Acting is excellent, as are technical aspects. Director Luis Bunuel's mastery of his theme and subject make this an unusual offbeater.

•

NEAR DARK

1987, 95 mins, US Ⓥ ⊙ col

Dir Kathryn Bigelow ***Prod*** Steven-Charles Jaffe ***Scr*** Eric Red, Kathryn Bigelow ***Ph*** Adam Greenberg ***Ed*** Howard Smith ***Mus*** Tangerine Dream ***Art*** Stephen Altman

Act Adrian Pasdar, Jenny Wright, Lance Henriksen, Bill Paxton, Jenette Goldstein, Tim Thomerson (De Laurentiis)

Near Dark achieves a new look in vampire films. Highpowered but pared down, slick but spare, this is a tale that introduces the unearthly into the banality of rural American existence.

Nervous, edgy opening has sharp young cowboy Adrian Pasdar hooking up with Jenny Wright, a good-looking new girl in town not averse to some nocturnal roistering as long as she gets home by dawn.

Wright soon welcomes Pasdar into her "family," a bunch of real low-down boys and girls that would have done Charles Manson proud. Led by the spidery Lance Henriksen, the gang hibernates by day, but at night scours the vacant landscapes in search of prey.

Script by Kathryn Bigelow and Eric Red is cool and laconic, and the evildoers essentially come off as some very nasty bikers who kill for sport as well as necessity.

Main point of interest will be the work of Bigelow, who has undoubtedly created the most hard-edged, violent actioner ever directed by an American woman.

•

NECESSARY ROUGHNESS

1991, 108 mins, US Ⓥ col

Dir Stan Dragoti ***Prod*** Mace Neufeld, Robert Rehme ***Scr*** Rick Natkin, David Fuller ***Ph*** Peter Stein ***Ed*** John Wright, Steve Mirkovich ***Mus*** Bill Conti ***Art*** Paul Peters

Act Scott Bakula, Hector Elizondo, Robert Loggia, Harley Jane Kozak, Larry Miller, Fred Dalton Thompson (Paramount)

This gridiron comedy piles up clichés the way Notre Dame racks up yardage, with an option-variety screenplay that promiscuously pitches the story in multiple directions. Essentially, this is a football version of the equally contrived and only slightly less hokey baseball comedy *Major League*.

Seemingly unable to settle on a single-wing hackneyed storyline, the filmmakers float at least three—a 34-year-old quarterback seeks to belatedly claim his college glory days, a female kicker joins a football team and a team of "real" students is assembled after a major college program is disbanded for recruiting violations—but basically settle on the former, with Scott Bakula carrying the ball.

The hurdles Bakula faces include wooing his attractive journalism prof (Harley Jane Kozak) and outwitting the priggish dean (Larry Miller), who's intent on punting the football program off-campus once and for all.

Director Stan Dragoti, who doesn't take the material too seriously, draws several procedure penalties for the horribly corny finale, slow-motion shots during the closing football game and for letting the air out of the ball with some long lulls in the action.

•

NED KELLY

1970, 101 mins, UK Ⓥ col

Dir Tony Richardson ***Prod*** Neil Hartley ***Scr*** Tony Richardson, Ian Jones ***Ph*** Gerry Fisher ***Ed*** Charles Rees ***Mus*** Shel Silverstein ***Art*** Jocelyn Herbert

Act Mick Jagger, Diane Craig, Clarissa Kaye, Frank Thring, Mark McManus, Allen Bickford (Woodfall)

Ned Kelly is basically an outback western in which director and coscripter Tony Richardson's simplicity becomes a pretension of its own. It is a film to which one applies the damning word "interesting."

In the 1870s Australia was a brutal frontier, settled by Irish, English and Scots convicts and their descendants. In the film, the convict stock are continually harassed by the English police troopers and the settlers' ranging cattle and horses impounded by the authorities on the slightest pretext. Unable to exist otherwise, Kelly and the other Irishmen turn to rustling.

Mick Jagger is a natural actor and performer with a wide range of expressions and postures at his instinctive command. Given whiskers, that gaunt, tough pop hero face takes on a classic hard bitten frontier look that is totally believable for the role. However, he has no one to play to. Jagger's Clyde has no Bonnie, his Sundance Kid has no Butch Cassidy.

•

NEEDFUL THINGS

1993, 120 mins, US Ⓥ ⊙ col

Dir Fraser C. Heston ***Prod*** Jack Cummins ***Scr*** W. D. Richter ***Ph*** Tony Westman ***Ed*** Rob Kobrin ***Mus*** Patrick Doyle ***Art*** Douglas Higgins

Act Max von Sydow, Ed Harris, Bonnie Bedelia, Amanda Plummer, J. T. Walsh, Ray McKinnon (Castle Rock/Columbia)

Fraser C. Heston (yes, Charlton's son) certainly had the plate set for his feature directing debut, working from a script by W. D. Richter (*The Adventures of Buckaroo Banzai*) based on a Stephen King bestseller about the devil opening a curio shop in a seemingly benign small town.

Set appropriately in King's fictitious Castle Rock, ME, the story has similarities to everything from the *Friday the 13th* TV series to Ray Bradbury's *Something Wicked This Way Comes.*

Fatherly looking Leland Gaunt (Max von Sydow) is the proprietor of Needful Things, a new shop providing objects to the town's residents in exchange for each doing him "a favor." Gaunt successfully uses those prankish deeds to prey on petty jealousies and set the good people homicidally at each other's throats. Only the town sheriff (Ed Harris) seems to realize something is rotten in the state of Maine, while even his fiancée (Bonnie Bedelia) falls under Gaunt's promise-fulfilling spell.

Heston employs a too-slow buildup to an explosion of mayhem that incorporates gruesome violence with awkward attempts at dark humor. The actors suffer from the same schizophrenia, with Harris playing things perfectly straight while many other performers (among them J. T. Walsh as an embezzling town elder) are cartoonishly over the top.

•

NEGOTIATOR, THE

1998, 138 mins, US Ⓥ ⊙ ▭ col

Dir F. Gary Gray ***Prod*** David Hoberman, Arnon Milchan ***Scr*** James DeMonaco, Kevin Fox ***Ph*** Russell Carpenter ***Ed*** Christian Wagner ***Mus*** Graeme Revell ***Art*** Holger Gross

Act Samuel L. Jackson, Kevin Spacey, David Morse, Ron Rifkin, John Spencer, J. T. Walsh (Regency/Mandeville/New Regency/Warner)

The teaming of Samuel L. Jackson and Kevin Spacey, in perfectly fitting roles that call for a battle of wits and wills, proves to be a shrewd piece of casting, and the best element of *The Negotiator.* Inspired by a real case involving the St. Louis police, this action thriller gives the familiar premise of a falsely accused man, who's forced to violate the law in order to prove his innocence, enough twists and turns to make it an engaging experience, though pic is slightly impaired by an overlong, overbaked production.

Working with a bigger budget than in his New Line movies *Friday* and *Set It Off*, F. Gary Gray demonstrates that he can handle a large-scale production with numerous action set pieces.

The partner of Danny Roman (Jackson), top hostage negotiator of the Chicago police, is assassinated minutes before he was supposed to meet Roman to disclose vital info. about embezzlement within their department. Caught at the scene of the crime, Roman becomes prime suspect.

With his entire world destroyed, Roman resorts to a desperate gambit: he takes his nemesis, Insp. Terence Niebaum (J. T. Walsh), two assistants and Commander Frost (Ron Rifkin) as hostages. Roman demands that Chris Sabian (Spacey), a respected negotiator from another precinct, be brought in to mediate. As the cover-up reaches further into the upper echelons, it's only a matter of time before the two negotiators join forces.

Jackson and Spacey rise to the occasion and, in a series of confrontations, manage to excel without outshining one another. The mostly male supporting cast is superb. Ace lenser Russell Carpenter and the rest of the technical crew give the film a high sheen. Pic is dedicated to Walsh, who died in 1998.

•

NEGRO SOLDIER, THE
1944, 42 mins, US b/w
Dir Frank Capra ***Scr*** Carlton Moss
Act Carlton Moss (War Dept)

A two-fisted plea for tolerance, told simply, honestly and conscientiously, is the 42-minute documentary, *The Negro Soldier*, made by the War Department under the supervision of Col. Frank Capra.

Production was handled by a crew of 14 U.S. Army technicians and Carlton Moss, Negro author, who scripted and plays the leading role of the pastor. Group visited more than 30 camps and reportedly took two years to complete the picture.

Facts are presented about the Negro that are not generally known to the average person. Pertinently, the role of the Negro soldier, from Crispus Attucks, mulatto hero of the Boston Massacre in 1770, to Robert Brooks, first American soldier to die in World War II. The Negro Minute Men at Lexington and Concord during the Revolutionary War—Peter Salem, who fought at Bunker Hill; Prince Whipple, who was with Washington when he crossed the Delaware, and the hundreds of other Negroes who shared the hardships of Valley Forge—are screened vividly.

In dramatic sequence the film tells of the Negro sailors who were with Perry at Lake Erie; soldiers who fought with Stonewall Jackson at New Orleans; and it also dwells on the Mass 54th Regiment of volunteers in the Civil War.

But the main part of *The Negro Soldier* deals with his activities during the Second World War. An enlisted man is picked up and followed through basic training, additional fundamentals, and through actual combat. These scenes, and those showing Negro WACs in training, drive home the picture's message harder than anything else caught by the army cameras.

•

NEIGHBORS
1981, 94 mins, US Ⓥ ⊙ col
Dir John G. Avildsen ***Prod*** Richard D. Zanuck, David Brown ***Scr*** Larry Gelbart ***Ph*** Gerald Hirschfield ***Ed*** John G. Avildsen, Jane Kurson ***Mus*** Bill Conti ***Art*** Peter Larkin
Act John Belushi, Kathryn Walker, Cathy Moriarty, Dan Aykroyd (Columbia)

Essentially the story of *Neighbors* focuses on staid suburbanite John Belushi who is slowly being driven crazy by his new, nutsy neighbors—a dyed blond, goon Dan Aykroyd and his smooth, sexually scintillating wife Cathy Moriarty. The new couple take over his car, his bank account, his house and even his family while at the same time making it seem like Belushi is a stick-in-the mud poor sport for not going along with it.

Larry Gelbart's script [from the novel by Thomas Berger] seems content to leave it at that, yet both he and director John G. Avildsen take great pains to throw in some serious reminders of just how pathetic the lives of each of these characters are, including the fun-loving neighbors. Consequently, other than a few laughs, the reason for the film is a little puzzling.

Ultimately it is Belushi and Aykroyd that make the picture work. When they hit the comedic mark, as they more often than not do here, nothing else seems to matter.

•

NELL
1994, 113 mins, US Ⓥ ⊙ ▭ col
Dir Michael Apted ***Prod*** Renee Missel, Jodie Foster ***Scr*** William Nicholson, Mark Handley ***Ph*** Dante Spinotti ***Ed*** Jim Clark ***Mus*** Mark Isham ***Art*** Jon Hutman
Act Jodie Foster, Liam Neeson, Natasha Richardson, Richard Libertini, Nick Searcy, Robin Mullins (Egg/20th Century-Fox)

The unusual but somewhat dramatically proscribed story of a young woman raised apart from civilization in the North Carolina backwoods, *Nell* seems rather too aware of its studied artfulness and sensitivity as it dramatizes the effort of two doctors to establish a connection with the outcast, who speaks her own language.

Working in his semi-anthropological *Gorillas in the Mist* mode, director Michael Apted moves deep into the Smoky Mountains to unfold the story of Nell (Jodie Foster), who at the outset is left alone in a remote lakeside cabin when her mother dies. Nell speaks in a unique way due to her mother's stroke-induced speech impediments.

Nell is fortunate in being found by an independent-minded doctor, Jerome Lovell (Liam Neeson). The medical authorities at Charlotte University want to hospitalize this prize specimen, but Lovell manages to win a stay of three months. But no sooner does he pitch a tent near Nell's cabin than psychologist Paula Olsen (Natasha Richardson) turns up in a houseboat to do her own monitoring of Nell's behavior.

Foster's performance relies in great measure upon techniques of movement, dance and mime. Nowhere is this more apparent than in some of the film's most haunting sequences, which have the two visitors spying on her while she cavorts nude in Isadora Duncan fashion on rocks and in the water under the moonlight.

The script, based on Mark Handley's play *Igioglossia*, generally sidesteps overly didactic melodrama. All the same, the film bogs down a bit in the late stages when resolution is required. Foster delivers with full credibility except for the courthouse climax. But the major weight of the film falls upon Neeson's broad shoulders, and he carries it splendidly.

1994: NOMINATION: Best Actress (Jodie Foster)

•

NELL GWYN
1935, 85 mins, UK b/w
Dir Herbert Wilcox ***Prod*** Herbert Wilcox ***Scr*** Miles Malleson ***Ph*** Frederick A. Young ***Ed*** Merrill White ***Mus*** Philip Braham (dir.) ***Art*** L. P. Williams
Act Anna Neagle, Cedric Hardwicke, Jeanne De Casalis, Lawrence Anderson, Miles Malleson, Esme Percy (British & Dominions/United Artists)

In toto it's a generally unsympathetic saga of a 17th-century music-hall trollop which requires a specially produced prologue to square existing moral standards and the Hays office. It opens in a hovel with the English bailiffs dispossessing a hag in her early 30s (Nell Gwyn of history died at 36), which is obviously primed to point the bromide that sin is its own worst reward.

As the bailiffs are reminiscing on the glory that was Gwyn, the flashback takes up the adventures of a colorful hussy who captured the fancy of King Charles II in an English music hall, becoming intimately associated with him, and in spiteful manner besting the Duchess of Portsmouth (capably played by Jeanne De Casalis), the king's favorite until the king sees Nell.

The medieval backgrounds contribute not a little charm; also more than a little dullness. That goes for the stilted dialog after the manner of Samuel Pepys, which is the scripting motivation.

Cedric Hardwicke, as King Charles, lends to his assignment the necessary regal poise and dignity. Anna Neagle's hoydenish personality fits her role. De Casalis, if a bit broad and physically unprepossessing as a favorite inamorata, endows the part with the proper amount of restraint.

•

NELLY & MONSIEUR ARNAUD
(NELLY & MR. ARNAUD)
1995, 105 mins, France/Italy/Germany Ⓥ ⊙ col
Dir Claude Sautet ***Prod*** Alain Sarde ***Scr*** Claude Sautet, Yves Ulmann ***Ph*** Jean-Francois Robin ***Ed*** Jacqueline Thiedot ***Mus*** Philippe Sarde ***Art*** Carlos Conti
Act Emmanuelle Beart, Michel Serrault, Jean-Hugues Anglade, Charles Berling, Daniele Lebrun, Michael Lonsdale (Sarde/TF1/Cecchi Gori/Prokino

Three years after *A Heart in Winter*, Gallic maestro Claude Sautet comes up with another exquisitely woven tapestry of emotions that dare not speak their name in *Nelly & Mr. Arnaud*. Marked by pointillist playing from Emmanuelle Beart and Michel Serrault, as a young woman and older man whose emotional orbits seem almost willfully out of synch, the movie is essentially an extended conversation whose delights can be savored at the dialogue and observational levels.

Beart plays Nelly, 25, who one day meets the emotionally remote but gentlemanly Arnaud (Serrault), a retired magistrate in his mid-60s who spontaneously offers her a loan to help out. Arnaud, who's penning his memoirs, later offers Nelly work as a typist at his apartment office. Meanwhile, she's courted by Arnaud's publisher, Vincent (Jean-Hugues Anglade), a relationship that increasingly irks Arnaud. Nelly rebels against Arnaud's seeming arrogance and possessiveness but eventually returns to their working relationship and, after Vincent dumps her, their friendship.

By distilling the pair's relationship into a series of conversations, mostly in Arnaud's apartment, Sautet studiously avoids the expected course of a May-December romance. As in the best of his previous pics, Sautet is more interested in the what-could-have-happened than the what-actually-has.

Beart not only holds her own opposite Serrault in the dialogue exchanges but also proves surprisingly touching in the pic's key emotional moments. Other perfs are well-rounded throughout, particularly Anglade's ruthless charmer and Michael Lonsdale's McGuffin-like mystery man from Arnaud's past.

•

NELLY & MR. ARNAUD
SEE: NELLY & MONSIEUR ARNAUD

•

NELSON AFFAIR, THE
SEE: BEQUEST TO THE NATION

•

NEON BIBLE, THE
1995, 92 mins, US/UK Ⓥ ▭ col
Dir Terence Davies ***Prod*** Elizabeth Karlsen, Olivia Stewart ***Scr*** Terence Davies ***Ph*** Mick Coulter ***Ed*** Charles Rees ***Mus*** Robert Lockhart (arr.) ***Art*** Phil Messina
Act Gena Rowlands, Jacob Tierney, Diana Scarwid, Drake Bell, Denis Leary, Leo Burmeister (Miramax/Channel 4/Scala)

Terence Davies has left his native Liverpool far behind but has retained the themes and style of his two fine British films, *Distant Voices Still Lives* and *The Long Day Closes* in *The Neon Bible*, a beautifully crafted but thin and self-conscious tale about a dysfunctional family living in rural Georgia in the 1940s.

The film opens promisingly with Mick Coulter's elegant Scope camera moving in on 15-year-old David (Jacob Tierney) as he travels by train away from the valley where he's lived all his life. Flashbacks return to five years earlier, when Aunt Mae (Gena Rowlands) came to live with David's parents, the dirt-poor Frank (Denis Leary) and Sarah (Diana Scarwid). A former small-time showgirl well past her prime, Mae fascinates the boy and becomes his constant companion, to the strong disapproval of his volatile father.

Frank enlists when war breaks out, and never returns, driving Sarah to the edge of insanity. The teenage David finishes school and gets a job in a general store; a brief courtship of a pretty girl leads, frustratingly, to nothing; and when Mae is offered a singing job in Nashville and decides to move away, David is left to care for his suicidal mother.

For about the first half hour, Davies and his superb creative team weave a potent spell. The gliding camera, the use of popular songs of the era, the backwater community that evokes the town in Charles Laughton's *The Night of the Hunter*, the disarming performances and the elegant direction all combine to exert a distinctive magic. But, starting with a poorly staged revival meeting sequence, things start to go wrong; Davies's grip slackens, and the artifice overwhelms the perilously slim storyline.

•

NEPTUNE FACTOR, THE
1973, 98 mins, Canada Ⓥ ▭ col
Dir Daniel Petrie ***Prod*** Sanford Howard ***Scr*** Jack DeWitt ***Ph*** Harry Makin ***Ed*** Stan Cole ***Mus*** Lalo Schifrin, William McCauley ***Art*** Dennis Lynton Clark, Jack McAdam
Act Ben Gazzara, Yvette Mimieux, Walter Pidgeon, Ernest Borgnine, Donnelly Rhodes (Quadrant/Bellevue-Pathe)

The Neptune Factor is an undersea sci-fi potboiler loaded with interesting technology and kindergarten plotting. Production, made in Canada, has a dull script, dreary direction by Daniel Petrie and a cast of familiar names for whom audiences may feel some embarrassment.

Script traces the rescue of some underwater scientists whose sea-bottom lab is hurled into an ocean crevasse by an earthquake. The action lurches from the surface control ship where Walter Pidgeon and Yvette Mimieux are anxious observers, to the underwater rescue vehicle, skippered by Ben Gazzara, whose crew includes Ernest Borgnine and Donnelly Rhodes, fellow scientists of the lost crew who are determined to find them.

Gazzara's role demands he project cool concern most of the time; Borgnine, Pidgeon and the others give it the old college try.

•

NEPTUNE'S DAUGHTER
1949, 92 mins, US Ⓥ col
Dir Edward Buzzell ***Prod*** Jack Cummings ***Scr*** Dorothy Kingsley ***Ph*** Charles Rosher ***Ed*** Irvine Warburton ***Mus*** Frank Loesser
Act Esther Williams, Red Skelton, Ricardo Montalban, Betty Garrett, Keenan Wynn, Xavier Cugat (M-G-M)

Neptune's Daughter is a neat concoction of breezy, light entertainment. It combines comedy, songs and dances into an amusing froth. Star sparkplugs are Esther Williams and Red Skelton. Williams's bathing beauty and Skelton's comedy make for a pleasing combination that does much to get over the pleasant, but fluffy, story.

Top tune of the Frank Loesser score is "Baby, It's Cold Outside," dueted by Williams and Ricardo Montalban, and, for comedy, by Skelton and Garrett.

Story thread holding the antics together concerns itself with a bathing suit designer-manufacturer-model, Williams; her business partner, Keenan Wynn; her dumbdora sister, Betty Garrett; and Skelton, a masseur for a polo club.

Film includes a number of beautifully staged water sequences.

1949: Best Song ("Baby, It's Cold Outside")

•

NET, THE
1995, 112 mins, US Ⓥ ⦿ col
Dir Irwin Winkler ***Prod*** Irwin Winkler, Rob Cowan ***Scr*** John Brancato, Michael Ferris ***Ph*** Jack N. Green ***Ed*** Richard Halsey ***Mus*** Mark Isham ***Art*** Dennis Washington
Act Sandra Bullock, Jeremy Northam, Dennis Miller, Diane Baker, Wendy Gazelle, Ken Howard (Columbia)

Riddled with more coincidences and implausibilities than Hitchcock permitted himself in his entire career, *The Net* still gets by as a reasonably suspenseful, very *au courant* thriller. Irwin Winkler's first directorial outing without Robert De Niro at the top of the cast trades effectively on time-tested female-in-jeopardy gambits.

Sandra Bullock plays Angela Bennett, a cuddly computer nerd who freelances out of her Venice, CA, home. On the eve of her first vacation in six years, a colleague sends her a new program through which she is strangely able to access some highly restricted government files.

Angela heads off to Mexico, where she meets a smooth-talking British hacker, Jack Devlin (Jeremy Northam). But it soon develops that he's more interested in her unique diskette than in her mind or body. Even if she manages to save her life, Angela still loses her identity. Robbed of all ID, she's issued a return visa to the U.S. under a different name and arrives home to discover that not only has her house been put up for sale, but she's wanted by the police.

Situation follows the Hitchcockian formula of placing an ordinary person in extraordinary circumstances, and Angela is, to her detriment, the Woman Who Knew Too Much. The thriller locales are typical and reminiscent of any number of old pics but the suspense is neatly achieved.

Bullock again provides highly accessible, viewer-friendly entry to a story. Her costar, more than any single actor, is the very active computer graphics, deftly done and pretty easy to follow even for the computer illiterate.

•

NETWORK
1976, 121 mins, US Ⓥ ⦿ col
Dir Sidney Lumet ***Prod*** Howard Gottfried ***Scr*** Paddy Chayefsky ***Ph*** Owen Roizman ***Ed*** Alan Heim ***Mus*** Elliot Lawrence ***Art*** Philip Rosenberg
Act Faye Dunaway, William Holden, Peter Finch, Robert Duvall, Wesley Addy, Ned Beatty (M-G-M/UA)

Paddy Chayefsky's absurdly plausible and outrageously provocative original script concerns media running amok. Sidney Lumet's direction is outstanding.

This is a bawdy, stops-out, no-holds-barred story of a TV network that will, quite literally, do anything to get an audience.

The fictional TV network, United Broadcasting System, has been acquired by a conglomerate headed by Ned Beatty, whose hatchet man, Robert Duvall, succeeds to operating control. Peter Finch, the passé evening news anchorman is about to get the heave. To the dismay of all, Finch announces his own axing, becoming an instant character.

Finch's on-the-air freakout suggests to Faye Dunaway that she turn the news into a gross entertainment package. It works, of course.

1976: Best Actor (Peter Finch), Actress (Faye Dunaway), Supp. Actress (Beatrice Straight), Original Screenplay

NOMINATION: Best Picture, Director, Actor (William Holden), Supp. Actor (Ned Beatty), Cinematography, Editing

•

NEVADA SMITH
1966, 131 mins, US Ⓥ ⦿ ▭ col
Dir Henry Hathaway ***Prod*** Henry Hathaway ***Scr*** John Michael Hayes ***Ph*** Lucien Ballard ***Ed*** Frank Bracht ***Mus*** Alfred Newman ***Art*** Hal Pereira, Tambi Larsen, Al Roelofs
Act Steve McQueen, Karl Malden, Brian Keith, Arthur Kennedy, Suzanne Pleshette, Raf Vallone (Paramount/Embassy/Solar)

A good story idea—boy avenging his murdered parents and maturing in the process—is stifled by uneven acting, often lethargic direction, and awkward sensation-shock values. Overlength serves to dull the often spectacular production values.

John Michael Hayes scripted in routine fashion a story and screenplay based on a character from Harold Robbins's *The Carpetbaggers*. Hayes's yarn is not a sequel, but a predecessor work, in that it is centered on the Nevada Smith character who acted as guardian to Jonas Cord, Jr., the youthful antihero of *Carpetbaggers*.

Steve McQueen is the young half-Indian boy whose parents are brutally murdered by Karl Malden, Arthur Kennedy and Martin Landau. Vowing revenge, McQueen sets off to kill them all. Brian Keith plays the elder Jonas Cord, then an itinerant gunsmith, who befriends the greenhorn and teaches him armed self-defense.

Henry Hathaway's uneven direction alternates jarring, overbearing fisticuffs with exterior footage as spectacular in some cases as it is dull in others.

•

NEVER A DULL MOMENT
1943, 60 mins, US b/w
Dir Edward Lilley ***Prod*** Howard Benedict ***Scr*** Mel Ronson, Stanley Roberts ***Ph*** Charles Van Enger ***Ed*** Paul Landron ***Mus*** Hans J. Salter
Act Harry Ritz, Al Ritz, Jimmy Ritz, Frances Langford, Mary Beth Hughes, Jack LaRue (Universal)

Familiar story is used principally as background for the Ritzes' shenanigans, variety numbers and Langford's neat warbling. Ritz Bros. pose as Chicago mobsters, taking job at a NY nightclub under the impression they've been hired on their vaude rep as "the Three Funny Bunnies." When they learn that Mary Beth Hughes is a femme pickpocket hired by the nitery operator to pass the stolen jewels to them, the wacky trio attempts to duck out. Romance concerns the nightclub singer (Frances Langford) and a socialite.

The nitery sequences offer the excuse to introduce the Igor-Pogi ballroom team and Rogers Dancers, both excellent. Production values are remarkably lavish for this type of picture. Jack LaRue, one of the nightclub's strong-arm boys, goes in for some comedy, but still remains the toughie menace.

•

NEVER A DULL MOMENT
1950, 89 mins, US Ⓥ ⦿ b/w
Dir George Marshall ***Prod*** Harriet Parsons ***Scr*** Lou Breslow, Doris Anderson ***Ph*** Joseph Walker ***Ed*** Robert Swink ***Mus*** Frederick Hollander
Act Irene Dunne, Fred MacMurray, William Demarest, Andy Devine, Gigi Perreau, Natalie Wood (RKO)

Never a Dull Moment doesn't always live up to its title in telling the story of a smooth femme songwriter who falls in love with a western rancher and goes to his impoverished acreage to make a home. George Marshall's direction is a great help in selling the physical business that goes with the comedy, and where scripting isn't strong he still manages chuckles for the average audience.

Incidents build to a point where Irene Dunne, as the songsmith, accidentally kills the prize bull of cantankerous William Demarest, a neighbor on whom Fred MacMurray depends for water. The married couple quarrel, she takes off for the east and tunecleffing, but finds there's no inspiration now.

Demarest has little to do other than be grumpy. Andy Devine adds some comedy as MacMurray's friend. Gigi Perreau and Natalie Wood are good as the little girls. Three songs are spotted in the footage, all written by Kay Swift, who authored the novel on which the script was based.

•

NEVER CRY WOLF
1983, 105 mins, US Ⓥ ⦿ col
Dir Carroll Ballard ***Prod*** Lewis Allen, Jack Couffer, Joseph Strick ***Scr*** Curtis Hanson, Sam Hamm, Richard Kletter ***Ph*** Hiro Narita ***Ed*** Peter Parasheles, Michael Chandler ***Mus*** Mark Isham ***Art*** Graeme Murray
Act Charles Martin Smith, Brian Dennehy, Zachary Ittimangnaq, Samson Jorah, Hugh Webster, Martha Ittimangnaq (Walt Disney)

Never Cry Wolf is a story about the life and times of white wolves in the Arctic. Based on a bestseller by Farley Mowat (an autobiographical account of the popular writer's experiences as a government biologist in the Canadian Northwest), pic was two years in production in the wilds of the Yukon and Alaska, and it measures up to the promise Ballard amply provided in his first feature, *The Black Stallion*.

The stretch of location shooting in and around Dawson City, Yukon, and Nome, Alaska, tried the talents of the entire crew, from the documentarist Ballard to actor Charles Martin Smith in the role of the young biologist Tyler.

The story is simple: idiotically simple. Biologist Tyler is sent to survive in the Arctic while investigating whether the predatory wolf is responsible for the gradual disappearance of the caribou herds. A friendly but reticent Eskimo, Ootek (Zachary Ittimangnaq), fortunately happens by the helpless biologist's stakeout in the dead of winter to rescue him. Then begins the study of the white wolf. Biologist Tyler, in some of the wittiest, funniest, and most human scenes in the film, comes to know his research quarry quite intimately.

The most praise goes to the imagery of this poetic fiction-documentary as fashioned by Ballard, cameraman Hiro Narita and soundman Alan R. Splet. Yet the magic of the film is in that quaint comic performance rendered by thesp Smith. He's the Goofy of the Walt Disney nature series.

•

NEVERENDING STORY, THE
1984, 94 mins, W. Germany Ⓥ ⦿ ▭ col
Dir Wolfgang Petersen ***Prod*** Bernd Eichinger, Dieter Geissler ***Scr*** Wolfgang Petersen, Herman Weigel ***Ph*** Jost Vacano ***Ed*** Jane Seitz ***Mus*** Klaus Doldinger, Giorgio Moroder ***Art*** Rolf Zehetbauer
Act Noah Hathaway, Barret Oliver, Tami Stronach, Moses Gunn, Patricia Hayes, Sydney Bromley (Neue Constantin)

Wolfgang Petersen's *The NeverEnding Story* is a marvelously realized flight of pure fantasy.

With the support of top German, British and U.S. technicians and artists plus a hefty $27 million budget (highest for any film made outside the U.S. or Russia), Wolfgang Petersen has improved on pic's immediate forebear, Jim Henson/Frank Oz's 1982 *The Dark Crystal*, by avoiding too much unrelieved strangeness.

Film opens with a little boy, Bastian (Barret Oliver), "borrowing" a strange-looking book from a local bookstore and holing up in the school attic to read.

Book, titled *The Neverending Story*, depicts a world known as Fantasia, threatened by an advancing force called The Nothing (represented by storms) which is gradually destroying all. To save Fantasia, an ailing empress (Tami Stronach) sends for a young warrior from among the plains people, Atreyu (Noah Hathaway) to go on a quest to find a cure for her illness.

Filming at and backed by Munich's Bavaria Studios, *Story* benefits from special effects technicians working overtime to create a new-look world.

•

NEVERENDING STORY II: THE NEXT CHAPTER, THE
1990, 89 mins, Germany/US Ⓥ ⦿ ▭ col
Dir George Miller ***Prod*** Dieter Geissler ***Scr*** Karin Howard ***Ph*** Dave Connell ***Ed*** Peter Hollywood, Chris Blunden ***Mus*** Robert Folk ***Art*** Bob Laing, Gotz Weidner
Act Jonathan Brandis, Kenny Morrison, Clarissa Burt, Alexandra Johnes, Martin Umbach, John Wesley Shipp (Geissler/Scriba/Deyhle/Warner)

Follow-up, produced by Germans based in Munich with location filming in Canada, Argentina, Australia, France and Italy, is a natural, since first film directed by Wolfgang Petersen only covered half of Michael Ende's classic novel.

Part II utilizes a whole new cast (except for Thomas Hill, reprising as Koreander the bookseller) to depict adventures in the imaginary world of Fantasia. Main innovation is that young hero Bastian joins his fantasy counterpart Atreyu in a heroic trek in search of the childlike empress locked in her Ivory Tower in Fantasia, rather than just reading about him.

Another improvement is the inclusion of a delicious villainess, dark beauty Clarissa Burt as Xayide, who suckers Bastian into making numerous wishes, each time losing a bit of his memory in return.

Film is effective in its own right, but as with most sequels, it lacks freshness. American actress Burt is any adolescent boy's fantasy seductress. Rest of the cast is adequate, but a letdown compared with the original's.

•

NEVERENDING STORY III, THE
1994, 95 mins, Germany Ⓥ ⦿ col
Dir Peter Macdonald ***Prod*** Dieter Geissler, Tim Hampton ***Scr*** Jeff Lieberman ***Ph*** Robin Vidgeon ***Ed*** Michael Bradsell ***Mus*** Peter Wolf ***Art*** Rolf Zehetbauer
Act Jason James Richter, Melody Kay, Freddie Jones, Jack Black, Ryan Bollman, Carole Finn (CineVox/Babelsberg/Geissler)

The Neverending Story lives up to its title in the worst way possible with this third outing, a charmless, desperate reworking of the franchise that might just as well be subtitled *Bastian Goes to High School*. Clearly aimed at a generation of moppets with one finger on the fast-forward button, lame effort throws over the magical charm of the 1984 original and darker fantasy of the 1990 sequel for a semi-hip yarn patched together by a marketing committee.

Central character, Bastian (Jason James Richter), is now on the edge of puberty and moved home with his father. Dad's new wife Jane (Tracey Ellis) is an eager-to-please happy homemaker with a sharp-tongued pubescent daughter, Nicole (Melody Kay). At school, Bastian is bullied by a bunch of senior punks called the Nasties.

Bastian takes refuge in the school library, coincidentally run by Mr. Koreander (Freddie Jones, taking over Thomas Hill's role in the first two pix), the antiquarian bookseller. Bastian wishes himself back into the dream world of Fantasia, courtesy of Jim Henson's Creature Shop. But when the Nasties get a hold of the tome and start filling it with their own warped imagination, Fantasia starts to crumble. Fantasia's child empress (now blossomed into the shapely Julie Cox) begs him to get the book back from the bad guys.

Showing every sign of lack of confidence in its original premise, this latest installment [from a screen story by Karin Howard] tries to have it all ways, thoroughly Americanizing the modern setting, stirring in a heap of hip, high school dialogue, and relegating the Fantasia sequences to little more than a collection of cuddly toys pitched somewhere between *The Wizard of Oz* and *Return of the Jedi*.

Helmer Peter Macdonald (*Rambo III*) does a pro job, and effects (supervised by Brit veteran Derek Meddings) are generally good, on a par with the earlier entries though not this time in widescreen.

•

NEVER GIVE AN INCH
SEE: SOMETIMES A GREAT NOTION

•

NEVER GIVE A SUCKER AN EVEN BREAK
(UK: WHAT A MAN)
1941, 70 mins, US Ⓥ ⦿ b/w
Dir Edward Cline ***Scr*** John T. Noville, Prescott Chaplin ***Ph*** Charles Van Enger ***Ed*** Arthur Hilton ***Mus*** Frank Skinner
Act W. C. Fields, Gloria Jean, Margaret Dumont, Susan Miller, Franklin Pangborn (Universal)

W. C. Fields parades his droll satire and broad comedy in this takeoff on eccentricities of film making—from personal writings of the original story by Fields under nom de plume of Otis Criblecoblis. It's a hodgepodge of razzle-dazzle episodes, tied together in disjointed fashion but with sufficient laugh content for the comedian's fans.

Story focuses attention on Fields and his presentation of an imaginative script for his next picture at Esoteric Studios. In series of cutbacks depicting wild-eyed action as read by producer Franklin Pangborn, Fields horseplays in a plane, dives out to land on a mountain plateau safely, and finally leaves the studio to embark on a crashing auto chase.

Fields is Fields throughout. He wrote the yarn for himself, and knew how to handle the assignment. Picture is studded with Fieldsian satire and cracks—many funny and several that slipped by the blue-pencil squad. Byplay and reference to hard liquor is prominent throughout.

•

NEVER LET ME GO
1953, 94 mins, UK/US Ⓥ b/w
Dir Delmer Daves ***Prod*** Clarence Brown ***Scr*** Ronald Millar, George Froeschel ***Ph*** Robert Krasker ***Ed*** Frank Clarke ***Mus*** Hans May ***Art*** Alfred Junge
Act Clark Gable, Gene Tierney, Bernard Miles, Richard Haydn, Belita, Kenneth More (Metro-British)

Adapted from a novel [*Came the Dawn*] by Roger Bax, yarn focuses attention on the problem of Soviet brides. Clark Gable plays an American newspaperman who weds a Russian ballerina (Gene Tierney), but is forced to leave her behind in Moscow, although having secured an exit visa.

Separation takes place after the newspaperman had made his own contribution to the Cold War, and finds himself persona non grata with the Soviet authorities. Back in Washington, he tries his hand at wire-pulling without success, and finally comes to London to tackle Molotov, who is attending a four-power conference.

Plot reeks of implausibility, but this is compensated by bold direction, nimble scripting and lively performances and there is suspense and action in good measure. As an added feature, there is an attractive ballet sequence in which Tierney is partnered by Anton Dolin.

Gable's interpretation of the newspaperman is sure, solid and confident; Tierney makes an admirable and attractive romantic partner. Bernard Miles is in fine form as a Cornish boat-builder who sails a tub through the Baltic, and Richard Haydn, as Gable's British partner, scores in an excellent drunk scene when he is feted by Soviet officials.

•

NEVER LOVE A STRANGER
1958, 91 mins, US Ⓥ b/w
Dir Robert Stevens ***Prod*** Harold Robbins, Richard Day ***Scr*** Harold Robbins, Richard Day ***Ph*** Lee Garmes ***Ed*** Sidney Katz ***Mus*** Raymond Scott ***Art*** Leo Kerz
Act John Drew Barrymore, Lita Milan, Robert Bray, Steve McQueen, R. G. Armstrong (Allied Artists)

This New York locationed melodrama is so ineptly, unprofessionally done, especially in its handling of such volatile subjects as race and religion, that it has nothing else to recommend it.

John Drew Barrymore plays a young man raised in a Catholic orphanage who discovers when he is almost grown that his parents were Jewish. Under the law, he must be removed to the jurisdiction of an orphanage of his own faith. Young Barrymore is already involved with hoodlum elements and, feeling rejection by the orphanage that has been his home and parents, takes the final plunge into the gangster world.

Barrymore does an able job with his role although he is repeatedly sabotaged by a story that is persistently old hat in its approach to religion, gangsterism and unwed mothers, the three chief plot threads.

•

NEVER ON SUNDAY
SEE: POTE TIN KYRIAKI

•

NEVER SAY NEVER AGAIN
1983, 137 mins, US Ⓥ ⦿ ▭ col
Dir Irvin Kershner ***Prod*** Jack Schwartzman ***Scr*** Lorenzo Semple, Jr., [Dick Clement, Ian La Frenais] ***Ph*** Douglas Slocombe ***Ed*** Robert Lawrence, Ian Crafford ***Mus*** Michel Legrand ***Art*** Philip Harrison, Stephen Grimes
Act Sean Connery, Klaus Maria Brandauer, Max von Sydow, Barbara Carrera, Kim Basinger, Alec McCowen (Taliafilm)

After a 12-year hiatus, Sean Connery is back in action as James Bond. The new entry marks something of a retreat from the far-fetched technology of many of the later Bonds in favor of intrigue and romance. Although it is not acknowledged as such, pic is roughly a remake of the 1965 *Thunderball*. World-threatening organization SPECTRE manages to steal two U.S. cruise missiles and announces it will detonate their nuclear warheads in strategic areas unless SPECTRE's outrageous ransom demands are met.

In short order, Bond hooks up with dangerous SPECTRE agent Fatima Blush (Barbara Carrera), who makes several interesting attempts to kill her prey, and later makes the acquaintance of Domino (Kim Basinger), g.f. of SPECTRE kingpin Largo (Klaus Maria Brandauer), who enjoys the challenge presented by the secret agent as long as he thinks he holds the trump card.

What clicks best in the film is the casting. Klaus Maria Brandauer makes one of the best Bond opponents since very early in the series. Carrera lets out all the stops, while Basinger is luscious as the pivotal romantic and dramatic figure. And then, of course, there's Connery, in fine form and still very much looking the part.

•

NEVER SO FEW
1959, 126 mins, US Ⓥ ⦿ ▭ col
Dir John Sturges ***Prod*** Edmund Grainger ***Scr*** Millard Kaufman ***Ph*** William H. Daniels ***Ed*** Ferris Webster ***Mus*** Hugo Friedhofer ***Art*** Hans Peters, Addison Hehr
Act Frank Sinatra, Gina Lollobrigida, Peter Lawford, Steve McQueen, Richard Johnson, Paul Henreid (Canterbury/M-G-M)

Never So Few is one of those films in which individual scenes and sequences play with verve and excitement. It is only when the relation of the scenes is evaluated, and their cumulative effect considered, that the threads begin to unravel like an old, worn sock.

The locale of the screenplay, based on Tom T. Chamales's book, is Burma during World War II. Frank Sinatra is the iconoclastic, ruggedly individualistic commander of a small British-American task force. The bulk of his force is made up of native Kachin troops. He is idolized by them and his Occidental troops. Chief action of the film has Sinatra leading a foray against a Japanese position near the Chinese border in which some of his men are ambushed by a Nationalist Chinese group out for plunder.

Sinatra's romantic interest is Gina Lollobrigida, looking like about $15 million, who has been the pampered mistress of mystery man Paul Henreid. She will abandon her plush life with Henreid and go back to Indianapolis with Sinatra, she says.

Steve McQueen has a good part, and he delivers with impressive style. Richard Johnson, a British actor, is also a standout. *Never So Few* did its principal photography on the Metro lot and on domestic locations, but it has some effective Ceylon photography that is neatly blended.

•

NEVER TAKE SWEETS FROM A STRANGER
1960, 81 mins, UK b/w
Dir Cyril Frankel ***Prod*** Anthony Hinds ***Scr*** John Hunter ***Ph*** Freddie Francis ***Ed*** Jim Neels ***Mus*** Elizabeth Lutyens
Act Gwen Watford, Patrick Allen, Felix Aylmer, Niall MacGinnis, Alison Leggatt, Bill Nagy (Hammer)

The yarn is set in Canada. Though filmed in Britain, the Canadian atmosphere is remarkably well conveyed. It deals with a senile, psychopathic pervert (Felix Aylmer) with a yen for little girls. When he persuades two innocent little girls to dance naked in front of him in exchange for candy, the English parents of one of them decide to take him to court. Unfortunately, they do not realize that he is the local big shot, the man who has helped to build the Canadian town to its prosperity and power.

Gwen Watford and Patrick Allen, as the distraught parents, and Alison Leggatt, as a wise, understanding grandmother, lead a cast which is directed with complete sensitivity by Cyril Frankel. Both Watford and Allen are completely credible while Leggatt, well-served by John Hunter's script, is outstanding.

Aylmer, who doesn't utter a word throughout the film, gives a terrifying acute study of crumbling evil, while Bill Nagy, as his son, is equally effective.

•

NEVER TALK TO STRANGERS
1995, 86 mins, US Ⓥ col
Dir Peter Hall ***Prod*** Andras Hamori, Jeffrey R. Neuman, Martin J. Wiley ***Scr*** Lewis Green, Jordan Rush ***Ph*** Elemer Ragalyi ***Ed*** Roberto Silvi ***Mus*** Pino Donaggio ***Art*** Linda Del Rosario, Richard Paris
Act Rebecca De Mornay, Antonio Banderas, Dennis Miller, Len Cariou, Harry Dean Stanton, Beau Starr (Alliance)

Never Talk to Strangers is a reasonably entertaining but largely uninspired erotic thriller that's too much a chip off the *Fatal Attraction/Sea of Love* block. The promise of high-impact bedroom aerobics featuring sexy stars Rebecca De Mornay and Antonio Banderas will generate some interest, but the fully clothed drama isn't nearly as enthralling as the steamy scenes.

There are two especially titillating scenes, including one that makes innovative use of a steel cage, and [U.S. distrib.] TriStar has trimmed some footage—apparently mostly of a naked Banderas—from the second heavy-duty sex bout. The uncut version will be seen in most other territories. Running time is reportedly the same in both versions, as replacement footage was inserted in the U.S. cut.

Yarn rolls with cool criminal psychiatrist Dr. Sarah Taylor (De Mornay) interviewing angry accused serial killer Max Cheski (Harry Dean Stanton). In a development right out of *Sea of Love*, Taylor bumps into mysterious-but-attractive stranger Toni Ramirez (Banderas) in the supermarket wine aisle. Before you can say Cabernet Sauvignon, the shy, distrustful shrink is off tasting wine at the suitably spooky loft of the self-described "surveillance consultant."

The near-hysterical shrink hires a private investigator to tail Ramirez. After Taylor's upstairs neighbor Cliff (Dennis Miller) gets clobbered with a lead pipe, the identity of the stalker is revealed in a surprise ending that will severely stretch the credulity of most viewers.

De Mornay and Banderas provide further evidence that they're not lacking in the big-screen sex-appeal department. Peter Hall does an efficient job moving the story along and manages to temper the thriller plotting with some in-depth drama.

•

NEVER TOO LATE

1965, 104 mins, US col

Dir Bud Yorkin *Prod* Norman Lear *Scr* Sumner Long *Ph* Philip Lathrop *Ed* William Ziegler *Mus* David Rose *Art* Edward Carrere

Act Paul Ford, Connie Stevens, Maureen O'Sullivan, Jim Hutton, Jane Wyatt, Lloyd Nolan (Tandem/Warner)

Outstanding direction and acting give full life to this well-expanded legiter about an approaching-menopause wife who becomes pregnant to the chagrin of hubby, spoiled-brat daughter, and freeloading son-in-law. Comedy ranges from sophisticated to near-slapstick, all handled in top form.

Sumner Arthur Long adapted his play which, though essentially a one-joke affair, he has filled out with exterior sequences which enhance, rather than pad. While the result is a family pic, it's not a potpourri of fluff.

Paul Ford and Maureen O'Sullivan are smartly reteamed in their Broadway roles of small town Massachusetts parents, settled in middle-age habits until wife's increasing fatigue is diagnosed as pregnancy. O'Sullivan looks great and handles light comedy with a warm, gracious flair.

Ford carries the pic as the flustered father-to-be, saddled with the sly grins of neighbors, the incompetency of son-in-law Jim Hutton, and the domestic bumblings of daughter Connie Stevens.

•

NEVINOST BEZ ZASTITE
(INNOCENCE UNPROTECTED)

1968, 78 mins, Yugoslavia Ⓥ col

Dir Dusan Makavejev *Scr* Dusan Makavejev *Ph* Branko Perak *Ed* Ivanka Vukasovic *Mus* Vojislav Kostic *Art* Dusan Makavejev

Act Dragoljub Aleksic, Ana Miloslavljevic, Vera Jovanovic, Bratoljub Grigorijevic, Ivan Zivkovic, Pera Milosavljevic (Avala)

This Yugoslav pic is a curious mixture of facts and fiction, newsreel footage, the remainder being from an old privately made film of 1942 vintage. If the latter had been skedded into the cinemas, it would have been the first Serbian feature pic. But the German occupation came along and the creator, an acrobat by the name of Dragoljub Aleksic, had to operate secretly.

The acrobat made the film about himself in occupied Belgrade. It's the story of a comely, if sad orphan, Nada (Ana Milosavljevic), who's driven by her shameless stepmother (Vera Jovanovic) into the arms of the rich and ugly Petrovic (Bratoljub Grigorijevic). But her true love belongs to the acrobat, who saves her after many heroic deeds.

The print of this film was confiscated by the Germans, and after the war discovered by the Yugoslavs. Director Dusan Makavejev searched for the acrobat and then put the old feature pic together via a documentary-type framework. Also, he added color to the old pic.

The outcome is both amusing and interesting. It has value as a documentary but also gives the viewer the chance to laugh at an old amateur feature pic.

•

NEW ADVENTURES OF DON JUAN, THE
SEE: ADVENTURES OF DON JUAN

•

NEW ADVENTURES OF TARZAN, THE

1935, 71 mins, US Ⓥ b/w

Dir Edward Kull, W. F. McGaugh *Scr* Charles F. Royal *Ph* Ernest F. Smith, Edward Kull

Act Herman Brix, Ula Holt, Frank Baker, Dale Walsh, Don Castello, Lewis Sargent (Burroughs-Tarzan)

Despite skillful cutting job, this picture, taken from 12-episode serial, remains of serial caliber. In only a few instances, where it attempts to ape highlights of other Tarzan features, does it do justice to story material at hand [novels by Edgar Rice Burroughs, whose own company produced, with adaptation by Charles F. Royal and Edwin H. Blum].

Adventures take Tarzan into Guatemalan jungles in search of a missing friend, winding up in mad dash for Lost Goddess filled with valuable gems. Then the animal stuff with the hero triumphant. Battle with natives is closest thing to realism in pic.

Whole sequences in which hardly a word is spoken. Maybe that's for the best since the dialog is pretty corny. Camera crew does well enough with wild beast and scenic shots.

Herman Brix is an athletic Tarzan who struggles manfully with absurdities of the dialog. Don Castello, as the villainous Raglan, makes the most of his role. Dale Walsh's biggest contribution is her screams. [See also *Tarzan and the Green Goddess*, 1938, produced by the same company.]

•

NEW AGE, THE

1994, 110 mins, US Ⓥ col

Dir Michael Tolkin *Prod* Nick Wechsler, Keith Addis *Scr* Michael Tolkin *Ph* John H. Campbell *Ed* Suzanne Fenn *Mus* Mark Mothersbaugh *Art* Robin Standefer

Act Peter Weller, Judy Davis, Patrick Bauchau, Corbin Bernsen, Jonathan Hadary, Patricia Heaton (Warner/Regency/Alcor/Ixtlan

At one point in *The New Age*, the terminally stylish post-yuppie couple played by Peter Weller and Judy Davis put on their fanciest threads in order to commit double suicide, but can't go through with it. Like them, Michael Tolkin's film gets all dressed up but doesn't quite know where to go.

Peppy opening scenes have upscale El Lay denizens Peter and Katherine Witner (Weller, Davis) losing the big-buck jobs that have enabled them to live the high life in the Hollywood Hills through the face-the-music early '90s. In bad shape as a couple, Peter and Katherine begin fooling around openly and then agree to separate while still living under the same roof.

As their lives collapse around them, the two seek salvation elsewhere; Katherine in New Age spirituality, Peter tentatively in the kinky club scene and ultimately in phone sales.

Together again after their outstanding pairing in *Naked Lunch*, Weller and Davis search for as many nuances to nerve-wracked edginess as they can while remaining remote at their cores. Lots of attention has been lavished on ultra-trendy locations, sets and clothes, although John Campbell's lensing manages to make everyone look pretty wasted and unattractive.

•

NEW BABYLON, THE
SEE: NOVI VAVILON

•

NEW CENTURIONS, THE
(UK: PRECINCT 45—LOS ANGELES POLICE)

1972, 103 mins, US Ⓥ ⊙ col

Dir Richard Fleischer *Prod* Irwin Winkler, Robert Chartoff *Scr* Stirling Silliphant *Ph* Ralph Woolsey *Ed* Robert C. Jones *Mus* Quincy Jones *Art* Boris Leven

Act George C. Scott, Stacy Keach, Jane Alexander, Scott Wilson, Rosalind Cash, Erik Estrada (Columbia)

The New Centurions is a somewhat unsatisfying film. Story [from Joseph Wambaugh's novel] largely avoids like the plague any real confrontation with the gray areas of modern-day citizen-police interactions which are at the seat of unrest.

George C. Scott dominates the first 76 minutes, starring as the old-time cop with a paradoxical philosophy. He sees nothing wrong in applying some pragmatic justice at the street level (there are several good, sometimes amusing episodes in this regard); at the same time, he is obviously blind to the realization that laws are contemporary reflections of transient attitudes which, every few generations, undergo a major flushing out.

Also starring is Stacy Keach. The nature of the plot necessarily makes Keach second banana to Scott. After Scott retires from the force, the film falls off in impact.

•

NEW JACK CITY

1991, 97 mins, US Ⓥ ⊙ col

Dir Mario Van Peebles *Prod* Doug McHenry, George Jackson *Scr* Thomas Lee Wright, Barry Michael Cooper *Ph* Francis Kenny *Ed* Steven Kemper *Mus* Michel Colombier *Art* Charles C. Bennett

Act Wesley Snipes, Ice-T, Mario Van Peebles, Allen Payne, Judd Nelson, Chris Rock (Jackson-McHenry)

Filmmakers pull off a provocative, pulsating update on gangster pics with this action-laden epic about the rise and fall of an inner city crack dealer. Strongest element is the anger and disgust directed squarely at drug dealers.

Drawn from articles about real drug kingpins in *California* magazine and the *Wall Street Journal*, pic presents the fictional story [by Thomas Lee Wright] of Nino Brown (Wesley Snipes), who in 1986 foresees the potential of crack and by 1989 has built an empire around it. Term "New Jack" was coined by journalist Barry Michael Cooper, pic's co-writer, to describe modern urban street life.

After Nino takes over an apartment building, brutally ejecting the tenants, police detective Stone (played by the director) recruits undercover cops Scotty (rap artist Ice-T) and Peretti (Judd Nelson) to bring him in.

It's clear from the start the filmmakers are out to blow the audiences away with pic's jacked-up hyperactive pace. Camera style is restless and aggressive. Problems of narrative flow mar the second half, with events jumping around without setup. Nonetheless, pic, filmed on location mostly in Harlem and the Bronx for $8.5 million, has a seat-of-the-pants energy guaranteed to sweep its target audience along.

•

NEW JERSEY DRIVE

1995, 95 mins, US col

Dir Nick Gomez *Prod* Larry Meistrich, Bob Gosse *Scr* Nick Gomez *Ph* Adam Kimmel *Ed* Tracy S. Granger *Mus* Dawn Soler (sup.) *Art* Lester Cohen

Act Sharron Corley, Gabriel Casseus, Saul Stein, Gwen McGee, Andre Moore, Donald Adeosun Faison (40 Acres & a Mule)

As an in-your-face evocation of what it's like to be young and living in an urban combat zone, *New Jersey Drive* could scarcely be more vivid and immediate. At the same time, lack of a discernible point of view on this out-of-control lawlessness and mayhem until the final minutes is a nagging problem throughout, leaving the viewer nowhere to put one's concerns or sympathies.

Nick Gomez's very low budget first film, *Laws of Gravity*, did no business but attracted critical attention for its visceral camera style and evident street smarts. Working on a considerably better-funded scale with the support of exec producer Spike Lee, Gomez [from a screen story by him and Michael Marriott] has fashioned a world where random crime is a lifestyle and nothing-to-lose kids respect nothing and no one.

At the center of things is Jason (Sharron Corley), a black teenager who lives with his mother and sister in the toughest part of Newark. Jason mostly follows the lead of his closest friend, a shaven-headed wise guy named Midget (Gabriel Casseus) who seems to need to steal cars the way a junkie needs a fix. The conflict between the local hoods and the cops escalates into a war neither side can win.

Pic's strongest suit is its realism. On the verbal side, much of the dialogue is so up-to-the-minute idiomatic that it almost sounds like another language.

•

NEW LEAF, A

1971, 102 mins, US Ⓥ col

Dir Elaine May *Prod* Joe Manduke *Scr* Elaine May *Ph* Gayne Rescher *Ed* Fredric Steinkamp, Donald Guidice *Art* Richard Fried

Act Walter Matthau, Elaine May, Jack Weston, George Rose, William Redfield, James Coco (Paramount)

Walter Matthau is both broad and satirically sensitive and Elaine May has gotten off some sharp and amusing dialog in her screenplay. It's sophisticated and funny, adroitly put together for the most part. May complained in a court action that final cuts were not hers and she would prefer not to have identity as the director.

Matthau is the marriage-aloof middle-ager who's running out of his inheritance because of high living and who has to come upon a rich wife to sustain himself. Rich wife turns out to be unglamorous May. The director and cosmetician have made May about as sexy as an Alsophiplia Grahamicus, which is a new leaf she has cultivated in her role as botanist. A new leaf is also something that Matthau turns over because after he weds May he decides, rather than kill her, to take care of her like the fine character he hadn't been in the past.

William Redfield fits in as the exasperated lawyer who has difficulty in conveying to Matthau that one doesn't drive a Ferrari and live in a luxurious townhouse when one is broke. James Coco is Uncle Harry, to whom Henry goes for a loan, which is provided on condition that Henry pay it back in six weeks or pay 10 times the principal.

•

NEW LIFE, A

1988, 104 mins, US Ⓥ ⊙ col

Dir Alan Alda *Prod* Martin Bregman *Scr* Alan Alda *Ph* Kelvin Pike *Ed* William Reynolds *Mus* Joseph Turrin *Art* Barbara Dunphy

Act Alan Alda, Ann-Margret, Hal Linden, Veronica Hamel, John Shea, Beatrice Alda (Paramount)

Perhaps trying to break his image as the most conscientiously nice guy of the latter half of the 20th century, Alan Alda has tried to give himself an edge in *A New Life*. As the newly divorced Steve Giardino, he is loud, obnoxious, neurotic, argumentative and manic; he also has permed hair and a beard, smokes, drinks hard liquor rather than wine, and eats red meat instead of chicken and fish.

After some 20 years of marriage, New Yorkers Alda and Ann-Margret decide to call it quits. Alda's screenplay follows the two equally as each endures the predictably excruciating blind dates, singles parties and matchups.

They are tenacious and game, and some months later each meets an attractive new prospect, she a dreamy, younger TriBeCa sculptor (John Shea), he a sharp and similarly younger doctor (Veronica Hamel).

All the actors have the upper-middle-class mannerisms down pat, and make for perfectly agreeable company despite the familiarity of the terrain. Shot mainly in Toronto, pic looks and sounds good.

•

NEWS BOYS, THE
SEE: NEWSIES

•

NEWSFRONT
1978, 110 mins, Australia Ⓥ ⦿ col
Dir Phillip Noyce ***Prod*** David Elfick ***Scr*** Phillip Noyce ***Ph*** Vince Monton ***Ed*** John Scott ***Mus*** William Motzing ***Art*** Lissa Coote
Act Bill Hunter, Gerard Kennedy, Angela Punch, Wendy Hughes, Chris Hayward, John Ewart (Palm Beach)

Set in an historically turbulent period for Australia (1949–56), *Newsfront* deals with the lives of movie newsreel cameramen and uses the events in which they are involved as a sort of microcosmic view of how, in a very short period of time, the country underwent remarkable socio-political change.

The approach is interesting and the film benefits greatly from two central strengths: history and Bill Hunter (as Len Maguire). In his feature film debut, director Phillip Noyce demonstrates his ability to deal with actors, narrative, and choreograph background activity.

By clever merging of b&w newsreel footage and scenario-inspired monochromatic sequences, he moves his film into and out of actuality and fiction in such a way as often to blur the edges so well that it frequently takes a conscious effort to detect the blend-point. This is especially true in one of his major set-pieces, re-creating the disastrous floods in the Maitland area in the early 1950s.

Plot [from an original screenplay by Bob Ellis, based on a concept by David Elphick] concerns the rivalry between two competing newsreel companies: Len works for the plodding, traditionally valued, Aussie-owned Cinetone, and ambitious brother Frank (Gerard Kennedy) has left them to run the go-ahead, pushy, Yank-owned Newsco.

Acting performances are all fine, particularly Angela Punch as the embittered wife, John Dease as the voiceover man, and Chris Hayward as the brash Britisher who gets a job as a camera assistant.

•

NEWSIES
(UK: THE NEWS BOYS)
1992, 121 mins, US Ⓥ ⦿ ▭ col
Dir Kenny Ortega ***Prod*** Michael Finnell ***Scr*** Bob Tzudiker, Noni White ***Ph*** Andrew Laszlo ***Ed*** William Reynolds ***Mus*** J.A.C. Redford ***Art*** William Sandell
Act Christian Bale, David Moscow, Luke Edwards, Ann-Margret, Ele Keats, Robert Duvall (Walt Disney)

They should have filmed the pitch meeting for this project: "Hey, guys, I found a story I bet nobody's ever thought of making: How about a movie on the 1899 New York newsboys' strike? Robert Duvall's got a hole in his schedule; he could play Pulitzer." "Great! But let's get Ann-Margret and a lot of cute kids and make a musical!"

A strange cross between *Oliver!* and Samuel Fuller's *Park Row*, *Newsies* was made with care and affection by choreographer-turned-director Kenny Ortega. But the writers have created cardboard cutouts instead of flesh-and-blood characters.

Composer Alan Menken, whose music works hard at being rousing, badly misses lyricist Howard Ashman, his late partner: Jack Feldman's lyrics here are relentlessly banal and unmemorable.

Cast has pleasant but ordinary voices, and it's only in the vigorous, *West Side Story*–style dancing, choreographed by Ortega and Peggy Holmes, that the film sporadically comes alive. Ortega avoids the MTV fragmentation that's de rigeur in musicals today.

Christian Bale plays the leader of the newsboys' walkout against the penny-pinching Pulitzer (bearded Robert Duvall). He's a charismatic figure, with a compelling blend of brashness and vulnerability. Duvall is a cartoon figure of ranting hard-heartedness as publisher of the *N.Y. World*. Ann-Margret's Jenny Lind-like thrush, an improbable ally of the boys, is shoehorned into the film to provide s.a. in a male-dominated story.

•

NEW YEAR'S DAY
1989, 89 mins, US Ⓥ col
Dir Henry Jaglom ***Prod*** Judith Wolinsky ***Scr*** Henry Jaglom ***Ph*** Joey Forsyte
Act Maggie Jakobson, Gwen Welles, Melanie Winter, Henry Jaglom, Milos Forman, Michael Emil (International Rainbow)

An undifferentiated extension of the same themes, concerns and artistic strategies featured in Henry Jaglom's previous films, *New Year's Day* is nonetheless notable for introducing a luminous new actress, Maggie Jakobson.

Jaglom again stars as a depressed Me Generation obsessive who returns to New York from Los Angeles in the midst of a midlife crisis.

Arriving on New Year's morning, Jaglom finds his apartment still occupied by three young ladies who thought they had until the end of the day to vacate the premises. Instead of booting them out, Jaglom immediately imposes himself upon their most personal concerns, especially those of Jakobson, whose boyfriend continues to fool around with other women throughout the open house the trio holds on their last day as roommates.

Lots of people show up for a drink or two in the course of the day, including Jakobson's parents and shrink, helmer's brother Michael Emil as a randy "psychosexologist," and director Milos Forman.

•

NEW YORK CONFIDENTIAL
1955, 87 mins, US b/w
Dir Russell Rouse ***Prod*** Clarence Greene ***Scr*** Russell Rouse, Clarence Greene ***Ph*** Edward Fitzgerald ***Ed*** Grant Whytock ***Mus*** Joseph Mullendore ***Art*** Fernando Carrere
Act Broderick Crawford, Richard Conte, Marilyn Maxwell, Anne Bancroft, J. Carrol Naish (Warner)

Among crime exposés, *New York Confidential* stacks up as one of the better-made entries, thanks to a well-fashioned story and good performances by a cast of familiar names. While a tough, no-punches-pulled melodrama, it relies more on logical development for effect than on unsoundly motivated bare-knuckles action.

Story [suggested by Jack Lait and Lee Mortimer's book] tells of the rise of Richard Conte, ambitious triggerman, in the big syndicate said to control all crime under the chairmanship of Broderick Crawford.

Conte does a top-notch job of making a cold-blooded killer seem real, and Crawford is good as the chairman of the crime board, as is Marilyn Maxwell as his girlfriend. Anne Bancroft, showing continuing progress and talent, scores with a standout performance of Crawford's unhappy daughter.

•

NEW YORK, NEW YORK
1977, 153 mins, US Ⓥ ⦿ col
Dir Martin Scorsese ***Prod*** Irwin Winkler, Robert Chartoff ***Scr*** Earl MacRauch, Mardik Martin ***Ph*** Laszlo Kovacs ***Ed*** Irving Lerner, Marcia Lucas, Tom Rolf, B. Lovitt ***Mus*** Ralph Burns (sup.) ***Art*** Boris Leven
Act Liza Minnelli, Robert De Niro, Lionel Stander, Barry Primus, Mary Kay Place, Georgie Auld (United Artists)

Taking Liza Minnelli and Robert De Niro from their first meeting after VJ Day, film proceeds slowly and deliberately through their struggle to make it as a band singer and saxophonist and as a marriage in which her voice is early acclaimed while his music is ahead of its time. The two are making it pretty good until her pregnancy sidelines her.

Though still professing enduring love, the couple breaks up with the birth of the baby and the film lurches forward several years. Now she's a big film star, banging out the new numbers by John Kander and Fred Ebb, and the 1950s have brought his style into vogue and he's a big name, too, if not as big as she.

In a final burst from Old Hollywood, Minnelli tears into the title song and it's a wowser. [In 1989, an uncut 163-min. version was released on home video, including the musical number *Happy Endings*]

•

NEW YORK STORIES
1989, 123 mins, US Ⓥ ⦿ col
Dir Martin Scorsese, Francis Coppola, Woody Allen ***Prod*** Robert Greenhut ***Scr*** Richard Price, Francis Coppola, Sofia Coppola, Woody Allen ***Ph*** Nestor Almendros, Vittorio Storaro, Sven Nykvist ***Ed*** Thelma Schoonmaker, Barry Malkin, Susan E. Morse ***Mus*** Carmine Coppola, Kid Creole and the Coconuts ***Art*** Kristi Zea, Dean Tavoularis, Santo Loquasto
Act Nick Nolte, Rosanna Arquette, Heather McComb, Talia Shire, Woody Allen, Mia Farrow (Touchstone)

New York Stories showcases the talents of three of the modern American cinema's foremost auteurs, Martin Scorsese, Francis Coppola and Woody Allen. Scorsesé's is aimed at serious-minded adults, Coppola's at children, and Allen's at a more general public looking for laughs.

Scorsese's *Life Lessons* gets things off to a pulsating start, as Nestor Almendros's camera darts, swoops and circles around Nick Nolte and Rosanna Arquette as they face the end of an intense romantic entanglement. The leonine Nolte plays a an abstract painter unprepared for a major gallery opening three weeks away. Announcing that she's had a fling, Arquette, Nolte's lover and artistic protégeé, agrees to stay on in his loft as long as she no longer has to sleep with him.

At 33 minutes, Coppola's *Life without Zoe* is the shortest of the three, but that is still not nearly short enough. Vignette is a wispy urban fairy tale about a 12-year-old girl who, because her parents are on the road most of the time, basically lives alone at the ritzy Sherry Netherland Hotel.

Happily, Woody Allen salvages matters rather nicely with *Oedipus Wrecks*, about the Jewish mother syndrome. When Allen takes shiksa girlfriend Mia Farrow home for dinner, he winces as mama assails him for choosing a blonde with three kids. Allen's fondest wish—that his mother just disappear—comes true when a magician literally loses her in the course of a trick.

•

NEXT KARATE KID, THE
1994, 104 mins, US ⦿ col
Dir Christopher Cain ***Prod*** Jerry Weintraub ***Scr*** Mark Lee ***Ph*** Laszlo Kovacs ***Ed*** Ronald Roose ***Mus*** Bill Conti ***Art*** Walter P. Martishuis
Act Noriyuki "Pat" Morita, Hilary Swank, Michael Ironside, Constance Towers, Chris Conrad, Arsenio Trinidad (Columbia)

The franchise is still kicking—but not very high—in *The Next Karate Kid*, in which a troubled teenage girl is transformed from bratty rebel into confident martial artist.

Boston dweller Louisa (Constance Towers) has her hands full with granddaughter Julie (Hilary Swank), whose parents were killed in a car crash. Having witnessed Julie's swift reflexes in averting a near-accident, wise Mr. Miyagi, played again by Noriyuki "Pat" Morita, embarks on a low-key mission to rescue the floundering 17-year-old via karate. Wholesome apprenticeship tale has its scattered moments of humor and insight but lacks sustained verve.

Morita excels as one cool, compassionate dude who always finds a way to recycle conflict and adversity into spiritual growth. Athletic Swank is gratingly cranky at the outset and a tad too enthusiastic once she shapes up. Chris Conrad is appealing as the kindly hunk who admires Julie's independent spirit. There's not much karate action compared with previous three pix.

•

NEXT MAN, THE
1976, 108 mins, US Ⓥ col
Dir Richard C. Sarafian ***Prod*** Martin Bregman ***Scr*** Mort Fine, Alan R. Trustman, David M. Wolf, Richard C. Sarafian ***Ph*** Michael Chapman ***Ed*** Aram Avakian, Robert Q. Lovett, Nina Feinberg ***Mus*** Michael Kamen ***Art*** Gene Callahan
Act Sean Connery, Cornelia Sharpe, Albert Paulsen, Adolfo Celi, Marco St. John, Ted Beniades (Artists Entertainment)

The Next Man emerges more a slick travesty with political overtones than the cynical suspense meller it was designed to be. The project apparently grew out of an interesting proposition—a major oil-producing nation breaks with the Middle Eastern oil cartel to join forces with Israel to assure technological development and peace.

Pic is based on an original story by Alan R. Trustman and David M. Wolf. No less than four writers compiled the screenplay and it shows.

Briefly, Sean Connery plays a peace-mongering Saudi Arabian diplomat, dispatched to the UN to plead a case for Israeli cooperation. For such arrant revisionism he is plagued by a network of Arab terrorists in whose employ is a beautiful, wealthy playgirl, friskily portrayed by Cornelia Sharpe.

•

NEXT OF KIN
1989, 108 mins, US Ⓥ ⦿ col
Dir John Irvin ***Prod*** Les Alexander, Don Enright ***Scr*** Michael Jenning ***Ph*** Steven Poster ***Ed*** Peter Honess ***Mus*** Jack Nitzsche ***Art*** Jack T. Collis

Act Patrick Swayze, Liam Neeson, Adam Baldwin, Helen Hunt, Andreas Katsulas, Michael J. Pollard (Lorimar/Warner)

Interesting wrinkle in Michael Jenning's screenplay, uncredited [based on a script by Jenning and pic's associate producer, Jeb Stuart] is a mixing and matching of two ethnic strains of the vendetta: backwoods Appalachian version and revenge Sicilian style.

These plot threads are set in motion when Bill Paxton, a Kentucky boy from the hills now working in Chicago, is ruthlessly murdered by mafia enforcer Adam Baldwin as part of a strongarm move in the vending machines racket. Paxton's older brother, Patrick Swayze, is a Chicago cop determined to find the killer.

Interfering with Swayze's efforts is the old-fashioned "eye for an eye" vengeance demanded by eldest brother Liam Neeson. Picture climaxes with an elaborate war in a Chicago cemetery between Baldwin's mafioso and Neeson's Kentucky kin, matching automatic weaponry with primitive (but reliable) crossbows, hatchets, snakes and knives.

•

NEXT STOP, GREENWICH VILLAGE

1976, 111 mins, US Ⓥ col

Dir Paul Mazursky ***Prod*** Paul Mazursky ***Scr*** Paul Mazursky ***Ph*** Arthur Ornitz ***Ed*** Richard Halsey ***Mus*** Bill Conti ***Art*** Phil Rosenberg

Act Lenny Baker, Shelley Winters, Ellen Greene, Lois Smith, Christopher Walken, Dori Brenner (20th Century-Fox)

Next Stop, Greenwich Village is a very beautiful motion picture. Writer-director Paul Mazursky's gentle and touching film is a sort of young adult's *American Graffiti*.

An outstanding cast of New York players, plus Shelley Winters in one of the most superb characterizations of her career, gives the film a wonderful humanity and credibility.

Lenny Baker heads the cast in an excellent depiction of a young Brooklyn boy aiming for an acting career; quite naturally, pop Mike Kellin and mom Winters have their doubts—she being more than willing to articulate them. But Baker, like Don Quixote, sets forth on his quest.

Baker's new life centers around a group of arresting people: Ellen Greene, his girl; Christopher Walken, lothario-playwright; Dori Brenner, the type of girl who hides her sensitivities in kookiness; Antonio Fargas, the gay equivalent of Brenner's character and so on.

In dark hair, Winters has managed to escape her near-formula mother role into new creative territory.

•

NEXT VOICE YOU HEAR . . . , THE

1950, 82 mins, US b/w

Dir William A. Wellman ***Prod*** Dore Schary ***Scr*** Charles Schnee ***Ph*** William Mellor ***Ed*** John Dunning ***Mus*** David Raksin ***Art*** Cedric Gibbons, Eddie Imazu

Act James Whitmore, Nancy Davis, Gary Gray, Lillian Bronson, Art Smith, Tom D'Andrea (M-G-M)

This unusual picture experience, so beautifully handled in the understanding writing, direction and playing, was suggested by George Sumner Albee's story of what happens to the peoples of the world when God reminds them that there is more to life than what they are getting out of it. In writing it for the screen, Charles Schnee pinpoints the message on the more intimate level of the small family and its reaction to the voice that speaks out to the universe each evening for six days.

Voice socks its preachment without preaching. There's no Holy Joe pulpiting. Footage carries a hearty load of warm, earthy humor that adds to the potency of the storytelling.

James Whitmore and Nancy Davis are average Americans, living a quiet life and enjoying the small pleasures permitted by their income. They have a son (Gary Gray) and another child is on the way. One night a voice suddenly speaks out from the radio, a voice that is heard all over the world.

William A. Wellman's direction turns scene after scene into actual slices of life. Davis's obvious pregnancy, the little bits of business between her and Whitmore, and with young Gray, ring true. There is Whitmore's regular morning adventure with his car and a traffic cop. His friends at the factory (Tom D'Andrea, Jeff Corey) are real, as are Art Smith as the grumpy boss, and Lillian Bronson as the frigid maiden aunt.

•

NIAGARA

1953, 89 mins, US Ⓥ ⦿ col

Dir Henry Hathaway ***Prod*** Charles Brackett ***Scr*** Charles Brackett, Walter Reisch, Richard Breen ***Ph*** Joe MacDonald ***Ed*** Barbara McLean ***Mus*** Sol Kaplan ***Art*** Lyle R. Wheeler, Maurice Ransford

Act Marilyn Monroe, Joseph Cotten, Jean Peters, Casey Adams, Denis O'Dea, Richard Allan (20th Century-Fox)

Niagara is a morbid, clichéd expedition into lust and murder. The atmosphere throughout is strained and taxes the nerves with a feeling of impending disaster. Focal point of all this is Marilyn Monroe, who's vacationing at the Falls with hubby Joseph Cotten.

A Korean War vet, Cotten is emotionally disturbed and his eye-filling blonde wife deliberately goes out of her way to irritate him. She flaunts her physical charms upon mere strangers, taunts him with disparaging remarks and has a clandestine affair in progress with Richard Allan.

These incidents are noticed by Jean Peters and Casey Adams. A honeymooning couple, they're stopping at the same cabins, and it's only too obvious that they'll be involved in the events to come. First, a plot of Monroe and Allan to kill Cotten backfires when the latter shoves his attacker over the Falls. Cotten then hunts down Monroe and strangles her. Now, pure theatrics take over.

The camera lingers on Monroe's sensuous lips, roves over her slip-clad figure and accurately etches the outlines of her derriere as she weaves down a street to a rendezvous with her lover. As a contrast to the beauty of the female form is another kind of nature's beauty—that of the Falls. The natural phenomena have been magnificently photographed on location.

•

NIBELUNGEN, DIE: KRIEMHILDS RACHE
(KRIEMHILD'S REVENGE; THE SHE DEVIL)

1924, 97 mins, Germany Ⓥ ⦿ ⊗ b/w

Dir Fritz Lang ***Prod*** Erich Pommer ***Scr*** Fritz Lang, Thea von Harbou ***Ph*** Karl Hoffmann, Guenther Rittau ***Art*** Otto Hunte, Erich Kettelhut, Karl Vollbrecht

Act Margarethe Schoen, Rudolf Klein Rogge, Rudolf Rittner, Hans Adalbert von Schlettow, Georg August Koch (Decla-Bioscop)

This sequel to *Siegfried* is a partial rehash and follow-up. The formerly beautiful Kriemhild is not so comely, physically as well as mentally overcome with the desire for vengeance. To advance her purpose Kriemhild weds the distorted Attila, King of the Huns. As queen of that domain she avenges the death of her beloved Siegfried, but not without herself meeting death in the end.

There is little or no action until Kriemhild departs for the land of the Huns. Opening sequences are the closing portions of *Siegfried*, from the death scene on. Out of all that comes nothing but a remembrance of much mugging.

The typical fantastic settings are notable and look like a lot of money. With its overabundance of slow motion and overly written subtitles [both English and German, one atop another, in the version released in the U.S. in 1928, reviewed here] it would be a better picture if cut to 15 or 20 minutes. The battle stuff, in short subject form, would make it playable.

•

NIBELUNGEN, DIE: SIEGFRIEDS TOD
(SIEGFRIED)

1924, 110 mins, Germany Ⓥ ⦿ ⊗ b/w

Dir Fritz Lang ***Prod*** Erich Pommer ***Scr*** Fritz Lang, Thea von Harbou ***Ph*** Karl Hoffmann, Guenther Rittau ***Mus*** Hugo Reisenfeld (U.S. only) ***Art*** Otto Hunte, Erich Kettelhut, Karl Vollbrecht

Act Paul Richter, Margarethe Schoen, Hanna Ralph, Bernhard Goetzke, Theodor Loos, Hans Adalbert von Schlettow (Decla-Bioscop)

The first part of this two-sectioned film, centered about the Nibelungen legends, appeared under the title of *Siegfried*, and was received with respect if not with acclaim. This film, directed by Fritz Lang, is the result of almost two years' work.

Not a single scene in the whole 16 reels was taken outdoors; all exteriors were built and photographed in a studio. Even the Germans had to admit that, as a whole, they found it rather boresome. The present version is somewhat different [from the story known from Wagner's *Ring* opera], leaning more heavily on the original folk tales.

Siegfried, the son of King Siegmund of the Netherlands, forges a sword and sets out to win Kriemhild of Burgund, of whose beauty he has heard tell. On the way he kills a dragon, in whose blood he bathes himself, thus making himself unwoundable.

Siegfried arrives at Worms, on the Rhine, where King Gunther agrees to grant the request if Siegfried will help him win Queen Brunhilde of Isenland, who can only be won by the most powerful hero. They set out together, and Gunther, with the aid of Siegfried, wins the queen as his bride.

The cast all do competently, and in some cases exceptionally. Especially to be mentioned are the King Gunther of Theodor Loos, the Hagen of Hans Schlettow, and the Brunhilde of Hanna Ralph. Paul Richter fulfills at least the physical requirements of his part as Siegfried.

The star is unquestionably Otto Hunte, who designed the scenery, and was brilliantly supported by the photography of Karl Hoffmann. Lang's direction is consistent, and achieves plasticity, dignity, and very nearly power.

•

NICE GIRL LIKE ME, A

1969, 90 mins, UK Ⓥ col

Dir Desmond Davis ***Prod*** Roy Millichip ***Scr*** Anne Piper, Desmond Davis ***Ph*** Gil Taylor, Manny Wynn ***Ed*** Ralph Sheldon ***Mus*** Pat Williams ***Art*** Ken Bridgeman

Act Barbara Ferris, Harry Andrews, Gladys Cooper, Bill Hinnant, James Villiers, Fabia Drake (Partisan/Levine)

On the death of her father, Candida (Barbara Ferris) goes to live with two gorgon aunts and escapes them to go to Paris to study languages. Her first tutor is a young student who picks her up and, after a brief idyllic affair, she is pregnant. Back home she confides in Savage (Harry Andrews), a gruff, kindly man who was caretaker to her late father.

She kids her aunts that she is minding the babe for a friend and nips off to Venice to continue her linguistic "studies." There, a hip young American picks her up and, pronto, she's carrying a second child.

Screenplay is light and gently amusing but not too cynically flip or gooey and director Davis keeps the film on a non-serious, yet perceptive level.

Ferris is a pleasantly attractive combo of intelligent approach and charm, Andrews is dependable as ever.

•

NICHOLAS AND ALEXANDRA

1971, 185 mins, UK Ⓥ ⦿ ⌑ col

Dir Franklin J. Schaffner ***Prod*** Sam Spiegel ***Scr*** James Goldman, Edward Bond ***Ph*** Freddie Young ***Ed*** Ernest Walter ***Mus*** Richard Rodney Bennett ***Art*** John Box

Act Michael Jayston, Janet Suzman, Harry Andrews, Irene Worth, Jack Hawkins, Laurence Olivier (Columbia)

Sam Spiegel comes up with a rarity: the intimate epic, in telling the fascinating story of the downfall of the Romanovs.

The tone is set from the opening sequences depicting the birth of the Russian Emperor and Empress's first boy and heir to the Romanov throne, followed closely by the tragic discovery that the child is hemophilic.

Slowly, intrusively, the viewers get to know more about the dominant Alexandra and the frequently vacillating Nicholas, whom she influences in misguided political decisions.

Complicating factors, of course, are the growing unrest of the Russian people, culminating in the confused revolution, the constant, distracting worry about the "bleeding" Czarevitch and, most of all, the dominant influence on the Empress of Rasputin, without whose occult, hypnotic presence she feels the heir will die.

Scripter James Goldman (with an assist from Edward Bond) has provided literate, sparse dialog in fashioning a crystal clear picture of a confused and confusing period. Certainly, as in the Robert K. Massie book, there's a feel here for tragically opposed worlds both heading blindly on a collision course towards the inevitable bloody clash.

Michael Jayston makes a most believable Nicholas, while Janet Suzman is also just right in the perhaps more difficult role of the Empress.

1971: Best Art Direction, Costume Design

NOMINATIONS: Best Picture, Actress (Janet Suzman), Cinematography, Orignal Music Score

•

NICHOLAS NICKLEBY

1947, 108 mins, UK Ⓥ b/w

Dir Alberto Cavalcanti ***Prod*** Michael Balcon ***Scr*** John Dighton ***Ph*** Gordon Dines ***Ed*** Leslie Norman ***Mus*** Lord Berners ***Art*** Michael Relph

Act Derek Bond, Cedric Hardwicke, Sally Ann Howes, Sybil Thorndike, Cyril Fletcher, Stanley Holloway (Ealing)

To make an entertaining film of this Dickens classic needed more courage than producer Michael Balcon shows. He should have thought first of the millions who care little or nothing whether any particular character or episode is missing as long as the picture does no violence to the author and is entertaining.

The 52 characters of the original prove too much for the scriptwriter. Some minor characters have been left out, and

Gride has become amalgamated with Ralph at the end, but the screenplay is more in the nature of a condensation into a series of scenes. And that's the way it appears on the screen.

Nicholas's adventures with the Crummies family has an old ham actor grandly played by Stanley Holloway. The stage scenes are amusing, but they do little to further the main story and, as an interlude, they slow down what action there might be. Scenes in Dotheboys Hall, which should have been among the most memorable, are slovenly, untidy and cramped.

For some reason, Alfred Drayton, who otherwise gives a fine performance, makes Wackford Squeers a brutish Cockney thug. His forbidding consort, played by Sybil Thorndike, obviously comes from a slightly better family.

Casting any Dickens film is an unenviable chore and Balcon has made as good a job as most producers. Derek Bond brings manly grace to the title role, but betrays inexperience. Nor does Sally Ann Howes, sweet and simple as Kate, rise to her big occasion when her wicked uncle uses her as a decoy to attract his immoral clients.

•

NICKELODEON
1976, 121 mins, US Ⓥ col
Dir Peter Bogdanovich ***Prod*** Irwin Winkler, Robert Chartoff ***Scr*** W. D. Richter, Peter Bogdanovich ***Ph*** Laszlo Kovacs ***Ed*** William Carruth ***Mus*** Richard Hazard ***Art*** Richard Berger
Act Ryan O'Neal, Burt Reynolds, Tatum O'Neal, Brian Keith, Stella Stevens, John Ritter (Columbia)

Peter Bogdanovich's film is an okay comedy-drama about the early days of motion pictures. Story begins with a group of barnstorming filmmakers in the pre-feature film era, later segues to the adolescence of the industry.

Stars include Ryan O'Neal, struggling lawyer who literally stumbles into directing; Burt Reynolds, roustabout who becomes a leading man; Tatum O'Neal, enterprising California country girl who makes money renting things to the fledgling production units sent here to escape the goon squads of the Motion Picture Patents Co. trust; Brian Keith, composite pioneer mogul; and Stella Stevens as an early leading lady.

The O'Neals, Reynolds, Keith and Stevens all engage interest, attention and affection.

•

NICK OF TIME
1995, 89 mins, US Ⓥ col
Dir John Badham ***Prod*** John Badham ***Scr*** Patrick Sheane Duncan ***Ph*** Roy H. Wagner ***Ed*** Frank Morriss ***Mus*** Arthur B. Rubenstein ***Art*** Philip Harrison
Act Johnny Depp, Christopher Walken, Charles S. Dutton, Peter Strauss, Roma Maffia, Gloria Reuben (Paramount)

Using real time as its gimmick, this OK but undistinguished thriller takes a simple Hitchcockian premise and milks things about as well as it can, given its confines, before a rather silly and abrupt conclusion.

Getting right into the action, pic features Johnny Depp as recently widowed father Gene Watson, arbitrarily drafted to kill the governor of California by a shady man (Christopher Walken) who takes his young daughter as hostage. The challenge: carry out the act in 90 minutes or his daughter dies.

Watson endeavors to warn the governor (Marsha Mason) but finds various members of her entourage involved in the scheme. As a result, he's forced to enlist the aid of various hotel personnel, including a grumpy shoeshine man (Charles S. Dutton).

As the action continues, the story begins to lose credibility, with the conspiracy plot becoming thick enough to look for Oliver Stone's name in the credits.

It's welcome that *Nick of Time* proves to be a relatively small-scale film set almost entirely within Los Angeles's Bonaventure Hotel. Still, the format also makes the movie feel a bit claustrophobic and humdrum.

Depp tries his hand at an everyday Joe with solid results. Walken brings trademark venom to his role, while Dutton livens up the proceedings as best he can.

•

NICO
SEE: ABOVE THE LAW

•

NIGHT, THE
SEE: LA NOTTE

•

NIGHT AMBUSH
SEE: ILL MET BY MOONLIGHT

•

NIGHT AND DAY
1946, 120 mins, US Ⓥ col
Dir Michael Curtiz ***Prod*** Arthur Schwartz ***Scr*** Charles Hoffman, Leo Townsend, William Bowers ***Ph*** Peverell Marley, William V. Skall ***Ed*** David Weisbart ***Mus*** Ray Heindorf (arr.), Leo F. Forbstein (dir.), Max Steiner ***Art*** John Hughes
Act Cary Grant, Alexis Smith, Monty Woolley, Jane Wyman, Dorothy Malone, Mary Martin (Warner)

Night and Day is a filmusical, based on the career of Cole Porter. It's to the credit of director Mike Curtiz and the combined scripters that they weighed the fruitful elements so intelligently, and kept it all down as much as they did. Wisely, all steered clear of making this a blend of "and then I wrote" and a Technicolored songplug unspooling.

Here's a guy to whom nothing more exciting happens than that he's born to millions and stays in a "rut" for the rest of his career by making more money. The plot, per se, therefore is static on analysis but paradoxically it emerges into a surprisingly interesting unfolding. A real-life ambulance driver in World War I, Porter is shown with the French army. Alexis Smith plays the nurse whom he marries; she's previously introduced as of an aristocratic family. And thereafter, save for a fall off a spirited steed, which caused Porter much real-life suffering because of broken legs which never set properly, the footage of *Night and Day* is a succession of hit shows and hit songs.

The tunes are chronologically mixed up a bit—a cinematic license with which none can be captious—and the romantic story line takes the accent principally in that Smith seeks to get her husband away from the mad show biz whirl of London and Broadway.

1946: NOMINATION: Best Scoring of a Musical Picture

•

NIGHT AND THE CITY
1950, 96 mins, UK/US b/w
Dir Jules Dassin ***Prod*** Samuel G. Engel ***Scr*** Jo Eisinger ***Ph*** Max Greene ***Ed*** Nick De Maggio, Sidney Stone ***Mus*** Franz Waxman ***Art*** C. P. Norman
Act Richard Widmark, Gene Tierney, Googie Withers, Hugh Marlowe, Francis L. Sullivan, Herbert Lom (20th Century-Fox)

Night and the City is an exciting, suspenseful melodrama, produced in London [from a novel by Gerald Kersh], which is the story of a double-crossing heel who finally gets his just desserts. In this role, Richard Widmark scores a definite hit. And he has excellent support right down the line. Gene Tierney was cast for name value only.

Jules Dassin, in his direction, manages extraordinarily interesting backgrounds, realistically filmed to create a feeling both of suspense and mounting menace.

Widmark plays a London hustler willing to do anything to be somebody. He finally sees an opportunity in going into partnership with the father of London's top wrestling promoter—and setting up his own wrestling enterprise, depending upon promoter's love for his father to make a go of it. Idea backfires.

•

NIGHT AND THE CITY
1992, 98 mins, US Ⓥ ⊙ col
Dir Irwin Winkler ***Prod*** Jane Rosenthal, Irwin Winkler ***Scr*** Richard Price ***Ph*** Tak Fujimoto ***Ed*** David Brenner ***Mus*** James Newton Howard ***Art*** Peter Larkin
Act Robert De Niro, Jessica Lange, Cliff Gorman, Alan King, Jack Warden, Eli Wallach (Penta/Tribeca)

Night and the City is a skilled, if not entirely psychologically convincing, remake of the 1950 film noir classic of the same name. Lively performances, pungent NYC atmosphere and abundance of dramatic incident keep this story of an irrepressible lowlife hustler ripping along.

Playing a frenetic, wired character right up his alley, Robert De Niro stars as Harry Fabian, a longtime ambulance-chasing lawyer who conceives the big time scheme to promote "the return of people's boxing" with a night of fights featuring sharp locals. But boxing promoter Boom Boom Grossman (Alan King), a genial tough guy, doesn't take kindly to Harry horning in.

Harry recruits Boom Boom's estranged brother Al (Jack Warden), a grizzled former prizefighter, and Eli Wallach's retired moneyman. He also counts on an investment from his good friend Phil (Cliff Gorman), a bar owner, but at the same time proceeds to lure away Phil's wife Helen (Jessica Lange).

Richard Widmark's Fabian in the original film (set in London) was very credibly a young American who remained in Europe after the war and tried to con his way through a foreign, hostile system. De Niro's Harry pushes just as brazenly, but fact that he's in his late 40s creates a credibility gap.

Gene Tierney's role in the first version, an add-on to the script at the behest of Darryl Zanuck, doesn't exist here. Story's ending has also been altered, to less powerful effect.

No particular sexual spark is indicated between De Niro and Lange, nor does Lange's laid-back performance suggest any reasons for her behavior.

In a nice gesture, pic is dedicated to Jules Dassin, director of the orginal film.

•

NIGHT AT THE OPERA, A
1935, 93 mins, US Ⓥ ⊙ b/w
Dir Sam Wood ***Prod*** [Irving G. Thalberg] ***Scr*** George S. Kaufman, Morrie Ryskind ***Ph*** Merritt B. Gerstad ***Ed*** William LeVanway ***Mus*** Herbert Stothart ***Art*** Cedric Gibbons, Ben Carre, Edwin B. Willis
Act Groucho Marx, Harpo Marx, Chico Marx, Kitty Carlisle, Sig Ruman, Allan Jones (M-G-M)

Story [by James Kevin McGuinness] is a rather serious grand opera satire in which the comics conspire to get a pair of Italian singers a break over here. For their foils the Marxes have Walter King and Sig Ruman as heavies, Robert Emmett O'Connor as a pursuing flatfoot, and Margaret Dumont to absorb the regulation brand of Groucho insults.

Although King also doubles on the vocals, Kitty Carlisle and Allan Jones do most of the singing as the love interest.

Groucho and Chico in a contract-tearing bit, the Marxes with O'Connor in a bed-switching idea, and a chase finale in the opera house are other dynamite comedy sequences, along with a corking build-up by Groucho while riding to his room on a trunk. The backstage finish, with Harpo doing a Tarzan on the fly ropes, contains more action than the Marxes usually go in for, but it relieves the strictly verbal comedy and provides a sock exit.

•

NIGHTBREED
1990, 99 mins, US Ⓥ ⊙ col
Dir Clive Barker ***Prod*** Gabriella Martinelli ***Scr*** Clive Barker ***Ph*** Robin Vidgeon ***Ed*** Richard Marden, Mark Goldblatt ***Mus*** Danny Elfman ***Art*** Steve Hardie
Act Craig Sheffer, Anne Bobby, David Cronenberg, Charles Haid, Hugh Ross (Morgan Creek)

Writer-director Clive Barker's *Nightbreed* is a mess. Self-indulgent horror pic [from his novel *Cabal*] could be the *Heaven's Gate* of its genre, of obvious interest to diehard monster fans but a turnoff for mainstream audiences.

Barker's inverted story premise is not explained until halfway through the picture: the last survivors of shapeshifters (legendary monsters including vampires and werewolves) are huddled below ground in a tiny Canadian cemetery near Calgary called Midian, trying to avoid final extinction.

Hero Craig Sheffer is plagued by nightmares and heads there in hopes of becoming a monster, while his nutty shrink (David Cronenberg) is on a messianic mission to destroy the undead critters. Sheffer's normal girlfriend (Anne Bobby) tags along. Pic presents unrelated sequences of gore and slashing until the ridiculously overproduced finale.

Chief casting gimmick is giving the lead baddie role to revered Canadian director Cronenberg. Horror cultists might enjoy his soft-spoken, monotone performance and in-jokes, but others will merely wonder why a professional actor was cheated out of a salary.

•

NIGHTCOMERS, THE
1972, 96 mins, UK Ⓥ ⊙ col
Dir Michael Winner ***Prod*** Michael Winner ***Scr*** Michael Hastings ***Ph*** Robert Paynter ***Ed*** Freddie Wilson ***Mus*** Jerry Fielding
Act Marlon Brando, Stephanie Beacham, Thora Hird, Verna Harvey, Christopher Ellis, Harry Andrews (Scimitar)

The Nightcomers is one of those atmosphere-drenched thrillers in which a semblance of surface decorum and respectability hides a multitude of aberrations beneath. This one, penned by Michael Hastings and inspired by the characters in Henry James's *The Turn of the Screw*, has a hand-tailored starring appearance by Marlon Brando.

Two recently orphaned children live alone on a British country estate with their nurse, a housekeeper and a gardener, Quint. It's the last named (played by Brando) who fascinates the boy and girl to such a degree that his instinctive actions, mysterious manners, homespun philosophizing becomes their (only) guide and lifeline.

His sado-carnal affair with the otherwise prim and bourgeois nurse, glimpsed in fleshly violent action by the fascinated boy, is similarly aped by youngsters, as are other aspects of couple's love-hate relationship which, in their unknowing innocence, they adopt and idealize. When the housekeeper decides to fire both nurse and gardener, the children plot to keep them together—forever—by killing them both.

•

NIGHT CROSSING

1981, 106 mins, UK Ⓥ col

Dir Delbert Mann ***Prod*** Tom Loetch ***Scr*** John McGreevey ***Ph*** Tony Imi ***Ed*** Gordon D. Denner ***Mus*** Jerry Goldsmith ***Art*** Rolf Zehetbauer

Act John Hurt, Jean Alexander, Glynnis O'Connor, Beau Bridges, Ian Bannen, Kay Walsh (Walt Disney)

There's plenty of drama hiding in this tale of two families' daring escape from East to West Germany by homemade hot-air balloon, but this Disney production can't find much of it. Unbelievable mix of actors from different nations is forced to deliver one bad line after another.

Story is a dramatic natural, as two construction workers, fed up with life behind the Iron Curtain, conspire to fashion a giant balloon out of household fabric and pilot it over the forbidding, heavily guarded half-mile zone between the two Germanys. First attempt doesn't quite make it but, despite fact that the secret police begin sniffing their trail, they try again, with suspenseful, successful results.

It all happened in 1978–79 and everything about it would indicate the potential for a grippingly serious family adventure pic. But script so seriously stumbles in the exposition stage that recovery is difficult even in the close-call climax.

•

NIGHT FLIGHT

1933, 89 mins, US b/w

Dir Clarence Brown ***Prod*** Clarence Brown ***Scr*** Oliver H. P. Garrett ***Ph*** Oliver T. Marsh ***Mus*** Herbert Stothart

Act John Barrymore, Helen Hayes, Clark Gable, Lionel Barrymore, Robert Montgomery, Myrna Loy (M-G-M)

It's a competently done saga [from the 1931 Prix Femina novel by Antoine de Saint-Exupery] of commercial flying which, while essentially a "man's picture," will likewise hold the femmes. The woman's angle comes from the mental stress on behalf of their menfolk, who are braving the aerial elements, and the heart tug is the necessity of speed to hasten serum across a continent to a stricken city suffering an epidemic of infantile paralysis.

The locale revolves about the Trans-Andean European Mail service, which spans South America and punchily gets over the great danger the flyers experience in crossing the Andes. As a story it's all rather simple but the veracity of detail and the other elements entailed [aerial photography by Elmer Dyer and Charles Marshall] make it an outstanding production.

Clark Gable is almost wholly superfluous as a flyer. Robert Montgomery lends a little more color. The two women (Helen Hayes and Myrna Loy), apart from their mental travail for their husbands, likewise deliver at a minimum. John Barrymore this time is the more forceful of the freres, being importantly cast as the ruthless managing director of the air service. Lionel Barrymore is altogether a vague characterization.

•

NIGHT HAS A THOUSAND EYES

1948, 80 mins, US b/w

Dir John Farrow ***Prod*** Endre Bohem ***Scr*** Barre Lyndon, Jonathan Latimer ***Ph*** John F. Seitz ***Ed*** Eda Warren ***Mus*** Victor Young ***Art*** Hans Dreier, Franz Bachelin

Act Edward G. Robinson, Gail Russell, John Lund, Virginia Bruce, William Demarest (Paramount)

Suspense is the dominating element in this thriller which follows a man who can foresee the future. Told in flashback form, story starts with Gail Russell about to commit suicide by jumping from a trestle onto a track in front of onrushing train, in terror after having been told by Edward G. Robinson, the diviner, that she will meet a violent death within a few days.

Events in natural order then are narrated by Robinson, from time he learned he was gifted—or damned—with his inner sight to opening events, and occurrences that follow leading up to strong climax.

John Farrow's sure directorial hand is seen throughout unfolding of picture, scripted melodramatically by Barre Lyndon and Jonathan Latimer [from a novel by Cornell Woolrich].

•

NIGHTHAWKS

1981, 99 mins, US Ⓥ ⦿ col

Dir Bruce Malmuth ***Prod*** Martin Poll ***Scr*** David Shaber ***Ph*** James A. Contner ***Ed*** Christopher Holmes ***Mus*** Keith Emerson ***Art*** Peter Larkin

Act Sylvester Stallone, Billy Dee Williams, Lindsay Wagner, Persis Khambatta, Nigel Davenport, Rutger Hauer (Universal)

Nighthawks is an exciting cops and killers yarn with Sylvester Stallone to root for and cold-blooded Rutger Hauer to hate.

Off and running right from the beginning, director Bruce Malmuth presents a vulnerable woman on a dark NY street about to be mugged. Suddenly the guys with the knives discover the woman is Stallone, on decoy duty and backed up by partner Billy Dee Williams.

While Stallone is doing his best to rid Gotham's streets of riffraff, Hauer is introduced in London as one of the most wanted and most murderous terrorists in the world, a crafty, intelligent killer who has fully rationalized his cause to justify blowing up department stores full of innocent victims, including children. This is an American film debut for Holland's top actor and he plays the part expertly, matching Stallone scene for scene.

Hauer comes to NY accompanied by equally evil Persis Khambatta and pursued by Nigel Davenport, a terrorist expert from Interpol who recruits the assistance of Stallone and Williams.

Though there's never much doubt how the duel will end, the climax is nonetheless surprising and totally satisfying, topping the energy of the previous pursuit.

•

NIGHT IN CASABLANCA, A

1946, 85 mins, US Ⓥ b/w

Dir Archie Mayo ***Prod*** David L. Loew ***Scr*** Joseph Fields, Roland Kibbee ***Ph*** James Van Trees ***Ed*** Gregg C. Tallas ***Mus*** Werner Janssen ***Art*** Duncan Cramer

Act Groucho Marx, Harpo Marx, Chico Marx, Lois Collier, Lisette Verea, Charles Drake (United Artists)

This isn't the best the Marx Bros have made but it's a pretty funny farce.

Postwar Nazi intrigue in Casablanca is the theme, having to do with the handsome French flyer who is under a cloud because of Nazi skullduggery dealing with European loot cached in the Hotel Casablanca. When three of the hotel's managers get bumped off in rapid succession, Groucho gets the nod. Chico runs the Yellow Camel Co. and Harpo is his mute pal who later breaks the bank in the hotel's casino and stumbles on the Nazi gold through a mishap with the lift.

Against the desert background of French provincial political bungling and Nazi chicanery the Marxes get off some effective comedy, and some of it not so. The brighter spots are the clown fencing duel; the frustrated tryst between Groucho and Lisette Verea, running from suite to suite, with portable phonograph, champagne cooler, etc; the sequence with the packing cases and clothes closet, prior to the getaway; and finally the air-autotruck chase, winding up back in the same jail from whence all escaped.

•

NIGHTMARE

1964, 83 mins, UK ▭ b/w

Dir Freddie Francis ***Prod*** Jimmy Sangster ***Scr*** Jimmy Sangster ***Ph*** John Wilcox ***Ed*** James Needs ***Mus*** Don Banks ***Art*** Bernard Robinson, Don Mingaye

Act David Knight, Moira Redmond, Brenda Bruce, Jennie Linden (Hammer)

Best features of this highly contrived chiller is the direction and lensing (by Freddie Francis and John Wilcox respectively) of the atmosphere of a house where eerie things happen in the way of shadows, significant noises and the fleeting appearances of a phantomlike woman in white.

Jennie Linden's mother was committed to an asylum when the child was 14, after stabbing her husband. This preys on the child's mind and she is convinced that she may have inherited a streak of madness. She certainly is the victim of bad dreams.

She is taken from school to her home where she is apparently safely guarded by the attention of an adoring housekeeper (Irene Richmond), her school mistress (Brenda Bruce), her young guardian (David Knight) and a nurse (Moira Redmond), posing as a companion. But Knight and Redmond are clandestine lovers. Their attempts to prey on the mind of the girl are elaborately worked out and, though highly incredible, serve as a workmanlike plot for such a modest thriller.

•

NIGHTMARE ALLEY

1947, 110 mins, US b/w

Dir Edmund Goulding ***Prod*** George Jessel ***Scr*** Jules Furthman ***Ph*** Lee Garmes ***Ed*** Barbara McLean ***Mus*** Cyril J. Mockridge ***Art*** Lyle R. Wheeler, J. Russell Spencer

Act Tyrone Power, Joan Blondell, Coleen Gray, Helen Walker, Ian Keith, Mike Mazurki (20th Century-Fox)

Nightmare Alley is a harsh, brutal story [based on the novel by William Lindsay Gresham] told with the sharp clarity of an etching.

The film deals with the roughest phases of carnival life and showmanship. Tyrone Power is Stan Carlisle, reform school graduate, who works his way from carney roustabout to big-time mentalist and finally to important swindling in the spook racket. Ruthless and unscrupulous, he uses the women in his life to further his advancement, stepping on them as he climbs.

Most vivid of these is Joan Blondell as the girl he works for the secrets of the mindreading act. Coleen Gray is sympathetic and convincing as his steadfast wife and partner in his act and Helen Walker comes through successfully as the calculating femme who topples Power from the heights of fortune back to degradation as the geek in the carney. Ian Keith is outstanding as Blondell's drunken husband.

•

NIGHTMARE BEFORE CHRISTMAS, THE

SEE: TIM BURTON'S THE NIGHTMARE BEFORE CHRISTMAS

•

NIGHTMARE ON ELM STREET, A

1984, 91 mins, US Ⓥ ⦿ col

Dir Wes Craven ***Prod*** Robert Shaye ***Scr*** Wes Craven ***Ph*** Jacques Haitkin ***Ed*** Rick Shaine ***Mus*** Charles Bernstein ***Art*** Greg Fonseca

Act John Saxon, Ronee Blakley, Heather Langenkamp, Amanda Wyss, Johnny Depp, Robert Englund (New Line/Media Home/Smart Egg)

A Nightmare on Elm Street is a highly imaginative horror film that provides the requisite shocks to keep fans of the genre happy.

Young teenagers in a Los Angeles neighborhood are sharing common nightmares about being chased and killed by a disfigured bum in a slouch hat who has knives for fingernails. It turns out that years ago, the neighborhood's parents took deadly vigilante action against a child murderer, who apparently is vengefully haunting their kids.

With original special effects, the nightmares are merging into reality, as teens are killed under inexplicable circumstances.

Writer-director Wes Craven tantalizingly merges dreams with the ensuing wakeup reality but fails to tie up his thematic threads satisfyingly at the conclusion.

•

NIGHTMARE ON ELM STREET, PART 2: FREDDY'S REVENGE, A

1985, 84 mins, US Ⓥ ⦿ col

Dir Jack Sholder ***Prod*** Robert Shaye, Sara Risher ***Scr*** David Chaskin ***Ph*** Jacques Haitkin ***Ed*** Arline Garson, Bob Brady ***Mus*** Christopher Young ***Art*** Mick Strawn

Act Mark Patton, Kim Myers, Robert Rusler, Clu Gulager, Hope Lange, Robert Englund (New Line/Heron/Smart Egg)

Beneath its verbose title, Jack Sholder's follow-up to Wes Craven's 1984 hit is a well made though familiar reworking of demonic horror material.

Screenplay basically makes a sex change on Craven's original: A teenage boy, Jesse Walsh (Mark Patton) is experiencing the traumatic nightmares previously suffered by a young girl, Nancy Thompson. Walsh's family has moved into Thompson's house, five years after the events outlined in the first film.

The slouch-hatted, long-steel-fingernails-affixed, disfigured monster Freddy (Robert Englund) is attempting to possess Walsh's body in order to kill the local kids once more and, judging from the film's body count, is quite successful.

Episodic treatment is punched up by an imaginative series of special effects. The standout is a grisly chest-burster setpiece.

Mark Patton carries the show in the central role as not quite a nerd, but strange enough to constitute an outsider presence. Kim Myers scores as his sympathetic girlfriend, surmounting her obvious teen lookalike for Meryl Streep image.

•

NIGHTMARE ON ELM STREET 3: DREAM WARRIORS, A

1987, 96 mins, US Ⓥ ⦿ col

Dir Chuck Russell ***Prod*** Robert Shaye ***Scr*** Wes Craven, Bruce Wagner, Chuck Russell, Frank Darabont ***Ph*** Roy H. Wagner ***Ed*** Terry Stokes, Chuck Weiss ***Mus*** Angelo Badalamenti ***Art*** Mick Strawn, C. J. Strawn

Act Heather Langenkamp, Patricia Arquette, Larry Fishburne, Priscilla Pointer, Craig Wasson, Robert Englund (New Line/Heron/Smart Egg)

With input from the original's creator, Wes Craven [who also co-wrote the screen story with Bruce Wagner], *3* shifts its focus away from the homely neighborhood horror to a setting of seven nightmare-plagued teens under the care of medicos Priscilla Pointer (instantly hissable) and Craig Wasson (decidedly miscast).

Heather Langenkamp, young heroine of the first film in the series, returns as an intern assigned to the ward. She's been using an experimental dream-inhibiting drug to keep her wits about her and proposes using it on the kids.

While everyone is stewing in their juices, pic is mainly focused on the violent special effects outbursts of Freddy Krueger (ably limned under heavy makeup by Robert Englund), the child murderer's demon spirit who seeks revenge on Langenkamp and the other Elm St. kids for the sins of their parents.

Debuting director Chuck Russell elicits poor performances from most of his thesps, making it difficult to differentiate between pic's comic relief and unintended howlers.

●

NIGHTMARE ON ELM STREET 4: THE DREAM MASTER, A

1988, 93 mins, US Ⓥ ⊙ col

Dir Renny Harlin ***Prod*** Robert Shaye, Rachel Talalay ***Scr*** Brian Helgeland, Scott Pierce ***Ph*** Steven Fierberg ***Ed*** Michael N. Knue, Chuck Weiss ***Mus*** Craig Safan ***Art*** Mick Strawn, C. J. Strawn

Act Robert Englund, Lisa Wilcox, Rodney Eastman, Danny Hassel, Andras Jones, Tuesday Knight (New Line/Heron/Smart Egg)

Imaginative special effects highlight the fourth entry in the series. As before, Freddy's out for revenge on the kids of Elm Street for their parents' having murdered him after he killed several children in the first place. Freddy's conjured up in the kids' nightmares and a clever plot [by William Kotzwinkle and Brian Helgeland] has him rapidly (and unexpectedly) dispensing with the surviving kids, only to extend his mayhem to their friends, starting with Alice (Lisa Wilcox).

Wilcox in the lead role gives a solid performance ranging from vulnerable to resourceful, as she gains strength from her departed friends to do battle with Freddy.

Robert Englund, receiving star billing for the first time, is delightful in his frequent incarnations as Freddy, delivering his gag lines with relish and making the grisly proceedings funny.

●

NIGHTMARE ON ELM STREET: THE DREAM CHILD, A

1989, 89 mins, US Ⓥ ⊙ col

Dir Stephen Hopkins ***Prod*** Robert Shaye, Rupert Harvey ***Scr*** Leslie Bohem ***Ph*** Peter Levy ***Ed*** Chuck Weiss, Brent Schoenfeld ***Mus*** Jay Ferguson ***Art*** C. J. Strawn

Act Robert Englund, Lisa Wilcox, Kelly Jo Winter, Danny Hassel, Erika Anderson, Nick Mele (New Line/Heron/Smart Egg)

Fifth edition of the hit *Nightmare* series is a poorly constructed special effects showcase. Pic's storyline [by John Skipp, Craig Spector and Leslie Bohem] dovetails closely with Parts 3 and 4: Alice (Lisa Wilcox, surviving from last pic) learns that the vengeful monster Freddy Krueger (steady Robert Englund) is now preying on her friends, materializing through the dreams of the fetus she's carrying.

New title character is Jacob (Whitby Hertford), 10-year-old dream child who reps what Alice's child will become and is the focus of her war with Freddy. Key to battling the monster is contacting the spirit of Freddy's mom (Beatrice Boepple), a nun who committed suicide following his birth.

Unfortunately, Aussie helmer Stephen Hopkins adopts a music-video approach, delaying the boring exposition for several reels and usually cutting away from climaxes to destroy much of the film's impact. Acting is highly variable. Saving grace is the series of spectacular special effects set pieces featuring fanciful makeup, mattes, stopmotion animation and opticals.

●

NIGHT MOVES

1975, 99 mins, US Ⓥ col

Dir Arthur Penn ***Prod*** Robert M. Sherman ***Scr*** Alan Sharp ***Ph*** Bruce Surtees ***Ed*** Dede Allen, Stephen A. Rotter ***Mus*** Michael Small ***Art*** George Jenkins

Act Gene Hackman, Jennifer Warren, Edward Binns, Susan Clark, James Woods, Melanie Griffith (Hiller-Layton/Warner)

Night Moves is a paradox: a suspenseless suspenser, very well cast with players who lend sustained interest to largely synthetic theatrical characters.

Minor LA detective Hackman is hired by faded actress Janet Ward to find runaway teenage daughter Melanie Griffith. He becomes enmeshed in the Florida smuggling operations of John Crawford (Griffith's stepfather), whose classy mistress Jennifer Warren indirectly helps Hackman's own reconciliation with wife Clark, herself dallying out of loneliness with Harris Yulin. Stuntmen Edward Binns and Anthony Costello, and mechanic Woods, provide a link between the Hollywood and Florida environments. Far more meritorious than the play are the players. Hackman works well with everyone.

●

NIGHT MUST FALL

1964, 99 mins, UK b/w

Dir Karel Reisz ***Prod*** Karel Reisz, Albert Finney ***Scr*** Clive Exton ***Ph*** Freddie Francis ***Ed*** Philip Barnikel ***Mus*** Ron Grainer ***Art*** Timothy O'Brien

Act Albert Finney, Susan Hampshire, Mona Washbourne, Sheila Hancock, Michael Medwin (M-G-M)

Artfully composed and strikingly photographed, this British-manufactured reproduction of Metro's 1937 shock-suspense thriller lacks the restraint, clarity and subtlety of its forerunner but makes up, to some degree, in cinematic flamboyance what it lacks in dramatic tidiness and conviction.

Albert Finney's performance as the cunning madman is vivid and explosive, and it might not be too far from wrong to suppose that the entire project may have germinated out of his desire to tackle the character.

Vagueness in key dramatic junctures hampers the new version, constructed around the skeleton of Emlyn Williams's stage play.

That story lapses and irregularities seem less than drastic is a tribute to the dazzling execution and a batch of tangy performances. Finney, in the role first played so well by Robert Montgomery, is fascinating to watch as his dispositions shift with maniacal rootlessness. It's an inventive, stimulating portrayal by a gifted actor. Yet Finney's thespic thunder is often stolen by Mona Washbourne's masterful delineation of the lonely "invalid" who becomes his victim.

●

NIGHT NURSE

1931, 73 mins, US Ⓥ ⊙ b/w

Dir William A. Wellman ***Scr*** Oliver H. P. Garrett, Charles Kenyon ***Ph*** Barney McGill ***Ed*** Edward M. McDermott ***Art*** Max Parker

Act Barbara Stanwyck, Ben Lyon, Joan Blondell, Charlotte Merriam, Charles Winninger, Clark Gable (Warner)

Night Nurse is a conglomeration of exaggerations, often bordering on serial dramatics. Reason for audience indifference is somewhat guttural. Barbara Stanwyck as the flip gal who knows pretty much what it's all about at the time she applies as an apprentice and cleans up on whatever details may be missing after donning the uniform. Meanwhile, there's a half-hearted attempt at love interest between the star and Ben Lyon as a mysterious male lead.

Director William A. Wellman hasn't done much with this chaotic subject [from the novel by Dora Macy] other than to slip through a few laughs in the slang dialog between the two nurses, who are a couple of pretty well-baked femmes when they start, and thereby cut short their chances for sympathy.

Clark Gable goes through socking everybody, including Stanwyck, and is finally done away with by inference. What legitimate performances crop up in the footage seem to belong to Joan Blondell and Charlie Winninger as the hospital head. Stanwyck plays her dancehall type of a girl on one note throughout and is shy of shading to lend her performance some color.

●

NIGHT OF THE COMET

1984, 95 mins, US Ⓥ col

Dir Thom Eberhardt ***Prod*** Andrew Lane, Wayne Crawford ***Scr*** Thom Eberhardt ***Ph*** Arthur Albert ***Ed*** Fred Stafford ***Mus*** David Richard Campbell ***Art*** John Muto

Act Robert Beltran, Catherine Mary Stewart, Kelli Maroney, Sharon Farrell, Mary Woronov, Geoffrey Lewis (Atlantic)

Night of the Comet is a successful pastiche of numerous science fiction films, executed with an entertaining, tongue-in-cheek flair that compensates for its absence of originality.

Comet closely resembles in structure the prototype for end-of-the-world cinema, Arch Obeler's 1951 Columbia feature *Five*. When nearly everyone is out watching the arrival of a comet, a few lucky people are indoors protected by steel walls from the comet's deadly rays. [Premise of course recalls *The Day of the Triffids*.] Survivors regroup and fight amongst themselves, attracted by an automated LA radio station signal.

Baddies are scientists led by Geoffrey Lewis and Mary Woronov. They're rounding up unaffected survivors, draining them of their blood to perform tests to come up with a serum before they gradually turn into disfigured monsters, a number of which are prowling the city's streets (à la *Omega Man*).

Other key plot elements are liberally lifted from *Dawn of the Dead* (and its shopping mall locale), *The Andromeda Strain*, and even a gender switch on Roger Corman–Robert Towne's *Last Woman on Earth*.

While SF fans are busy sorting out the influences, filmmaker Thom Eberhardt (whose previous feature was the minor *Sole Survivor*) creates a visually arresting B-picture in the neon-primary colors of the cult hit *Liquid Sky*.

Much of the film is played straight, but what makes the picture work is a light-hearted approach, typified by the reaction of one of the heroines during a suspenseful, dangerous last reel scene. Suddenly reunited with her sister she exclaims: "What a great outfit!"

As the resourceful sisters, Catherine Mary Stewart and Kelli Maroney are delightful, providing, respectively, a believably feisty battler who can beat up monsters and a new, improved Valley Girl (pic was produced by Atlantic's *Valley Girl* creators and features frequent plugola on-screen for that film).

●

NIGHT OF THE FOLLOWING DAY, THE

1969, 93 mins, UK col

Dir Hubert Cornfield ***Prod*** Hubert Cornfield ***Scr*** Hubert Cornfield, Robert Phippeny ***Ph*** Willi Kurout ***Ed*** Gordon Pilkington ***Mus*** Stanley Myers ***Art*** Jean Boulet

Act Marlon Brando, Richard Boone, Rita Moreno, Pamela Franklin, Jess Hahn (Universal/Gina)

The Night of the Following Day begins as an intriguing, offbeat kidnap drama, but soon shifts emphasis to delineating the freaked-out characters of its principals, and ends abruptly on a cop-out note.

Lionel White's book, *The Snatchers*, has been adapted into a rambling stew of deliberate and accidental black comedy and melodrama. Pamela Franklin is the prop focal character, a young woman kidnapped for ransom by Marlon Brando, Richard Boone, Rita Moreno and Jess Hahn.

A lot of effective and moody camerawork by Willi Kurout, combined with the good promise of the first reel and Brando's excellent physical appearance and dynamism, wash out as each character loses sympathy and interest. Even Franklin, ostensibly the victim of the piece, is forgotten for long periods.

●

NIGHT OF THE GENERALS

1967, 148 mins, UK/France Ⓥ ⊙ ▭ col

Dir Anatole Litvak ***Prod*** Sam Spiegel ***Scr*** Joseph Kessel, Paul Dehn ***Ph*** Henri Decae ***Ed*** Alan Osbiston ***Mus*** Maurice Jarre ***Art*** Alexandre Trauner

Act Peter O'Toole, Omar Sharif, Tom Courtenay, Donald Pleasence, Charles Gray, Joanna Pettet (Columbia/Horizon)

With an important theme about the nature of guilt and the promise of a teasing battle of wits, this is an interesting feature that lets the tension run slack, being afflicted with galloping inflation of its running time.

Plot opens in Nazi-occupied Warsaw in 1942, with a prostie being brutally murdered and the killer being recognized as wearing the uniform of a German general. But that's the only clue for Major Grau (Omar Sharif), the Military Intelligence man in charge of the hunt, and he establishes that only three brasshats could have committed the crime, having insufficient alibis.

One is Tanz (Peter O'Toole), a ruthless and devoted Nazi who destroys a quarter of Warsaw as an exercise in discipline. Another is Kahlenberge (Donald Pleasence), a cynical opportunist who has few scruples, but plenty of ingenuity. And the third suspect is the pompous Galber (Charles Gray).

Adapted from Hans Helmut Kirst's bitter novel, the story is told in flashback and the technique adds to the somewhat languid effect. But the chief factor militating against conviction is the central performance by O'Toole, which lacks the firm savagery Tanz seems to require.

●

NIGHT OF THE HUNTER, THE

1955, 93 mins, US Ⓥ ⊙ b/w

Dir Charles Laughton ***Prod*** Paul Gregory ***Scr*** James Agee ***Ph*** Stanley Cortez ***Ed*** Robert Golden ***Mus*** Walter Schumann ***Art*** Hilyard Brown

Act Robert Mitchum, Shelley Winters, Lillian Gish, Billy Chapin, Peter Graves, James Gleason (Gregory/United Artists)

The relentless terror of Davis Grubb's novel got away from Paul Gregory and Charles Laughton in their translation of *Night of the Hunter*. This start for Gregory as producer and Laughton as director is rich in promise but the completed product, bewitching at times, loses sustained drive via too many offbeat touches that have a misty effect.

Straight storytelling without the embellishments, it would seem, might have rammed home with frightening force the horror of this man's diabolical quest of a hanged murderer's $10,000 which he wants to use in serving his fancied Lord. It builds fine with suspense ingredients to a fitting climax.

Robert Mitchum intermittently shows some depth in his interpretation of the preacher but in instances where he's crazed with lust for the money, there's barely adequate conviction.

•

NIGHT OF THE IGUANA, THE

1964, 117 mins, US Ⓥ ⦿ b/w

Dir John Huston ***Prod*** Ray Stark ***Scr*** Anthony Veiller, John Huston ***Ph*** Gabriel Figueroa ***Ed*** Ralph Kemplen ***Mus*** Benjamin Frankel ***Art*** Stephen Grimes

Act Richard Burton, Ava Gardner, Deborah Kerr, Sue Lyon, James Ward, Grayson Hall (M-G-M/Seven Arts)

This Ray Stark production is rich in talents. Performances by Richard Burton, Ava Gardner and Deborah Kerr are superlative in demanding roles. Direction by John Huston is resourceful and dynamic as he sympathetically weaves together the often vague and philosophical threads that mark Tennessee Williams's writing.

Unfolds mainly in a ramshackle Mexican seacoast hotel where Burton, an unfrocked minister and now guide of a cheap bus tour, takes refuge from his latest flock, a group of complaining American schoolteachers who refuse to believe he actually is a preacher who lost his church. Frankness in dealing with his emotional problems as first he is pursued by a young sexpot in the party, then his involvement with the aggressive, man-hungry hotel owner and a sensitive, itinerant artist travelling with her 97-year-old grandfather, produces compassionate undertones finely realized in situations evoking particular interest.

Burton has stature in the difficult portrayal of the Reverend T. Lawrence Shannon, a part without glamour yet touched with magical significant force as he progresses to the point of a near-mental crackup. Gardner, in the earthy role of Maxine Faulk, the proprietress, is a gutsy figure as she makes her play for the depraved ex-minister, turning in a colorful delineation. Kerr lends warm conviction as the spinster who lives by idealism and her selling of quick sketches, a helpless creature yet endowed with certain innate strength.

1964: Best B&W Costume Design

NOMINATIONS: Best Supp. Actress (Grayson Hall), B&W Cinematography, B&W Art Direction

•

NIGHT OF THE JUGGLER

1980, 100 mins, US Ⓥ col

Dir Robert Butler ***Prod*** Jay Weston ***Scr*** Bill Norton, Sr., Rick Natkin ***Ph*** Victor J. Kemper ***Ed*** Argyle Nelson ***Mus*** Artie Kane ***Art*** Stuart Wurtzel

Act James Brolin, Cliff Gorman, Richard Castellano, Abby Bluestone, Dan Hedaya, Julie Carmen (Columbia)

Night of the Juggler is a relentlessly preposterous picture which never gives its cast a chance to overcome director Robert Butler's passion for mindless action.

This is supposed to be the story [from a novel by William P. McGivern] of James Brolin's frantic pursuit of a kidnapper who grabs his daughter and takes off with her in a car.

But who cares if the performers are never allowed to make the characters come true?

As a frustrated, racist psychotic seeking revenge for the deterioration of his Bronx neighborhood, Cliff Gorman is trapped by the script's needs for him to be so loony you might actually believe in him.

Technically, each individual shot was approached with intense concentration on the craft of filmmaking. Which is exactly what's wrong with the picture.

•

NIGHT OF THE LIVING DEAD

1968, 90 mins, US Ⓥ ⦿ b/w

Dir George A. Romero ***Prod*** Russell Streiner, Karl Hardman ***Scr*** John A. Russo, George A. Romero ***Ph*** George A. Romero

Act Judith O'Dea, Russell Streiner, Duane Jones, Karl Hardman, Keith Wayne (Image Ten)

Although pic's basic premise is repellent—recently dead bodies are resurrected and begin killing human beings in order to eat their flesh—it is in execution that the film distastefully excels.

No brutalizing stone is left unturned: crowbars gash holes in the heads of the living dead, monsters are shown eating entrails, and—in a climax of unparalleled nausea—a little girl kills her mother by stabbing her a dozen times in the chest with a trowel.

The rest of the pic is amateurism of the first order. Pittsburgh-based director George A. Romero appears incapable of contriving a single graceful setup, and his cast is uniformly poor.

Both Judith O'Dea and Duane Jones are sufficiently talented to warrant supporting roles in a backwoods community theater, but Russell Streiner, Karl Hardman, Keith Wayne and Judith Ridley do not suggest that Pittsburgh is a haven for undiscovered thespians.

John A. Russo's screenplay is a model of verbal banality and suggests a total antipathy for his characters.

•

NIGHT OF THE LIVING DEAD

1990, 89 mins, US Ⓥ ⦿ col

Dir Tom Savani ***Prod*** John A. Russo, Russ Steiner ***Scr*** George A. Romero ***Ph*** Frank Prinzi ***Ed*** Tom Dubensky ***Mus*** Paul McCollough ***Art*** James Feng

Act Tony Wood, Patricia Tallman, Tom Towles, McKee Anderson, William Butler, Katie Finnerman (21st Century)

The original producers of *Night of the Living Dead* have remade their own cult classic in a crass bit of cinematic grave-robbing. The only legitimate reason to remake the 1968 film would have been to improve its effects and sub-$200,000 budget, although the dimly shot black-&-white images were far creepier than any of its color progeny.

The story faithfully follows the original except for the bonehead decision to replace the ending with a "meaningful" twist that reeks of pretentiousness.

The plot still involves seven people trapped in a farmhouse fending off hordes of walking corpses intent on devouring them. Never explained is what animated the bodies in the first place, although a solid bash to the brain deanimates them.

The hero still is Ben (Tony Wood), and the bad guy still is a middle-aged businessman named Harry (Tom Towles) who holes up in the basement with his wife and daughter. The one beefed-up role is that of the female lead (Patricia Tallman), who reveals a Rambo-esque bent.

•

NIGHT ON EARTH

1992, 130 mins, US Ⓥ ⦿ col

Dir Jim Jarmusch ***Prod*** Jim Jarmusch ***Scr*** Jim Jarmusch ***Ph*** Frederick Elmes ***Ed*** Jay Rabinowitz ***Mus*** Tom Waits ***Art*** [uncredited]

Act Winona Ryder, Gena Rowlands, Giancarlo Esposito, Armin Mueller-Stahl, Beatrice Dalle, Roberto Benigni (JVC/Locus Solus)

Jim Jarmusch's existential comedy *Night on Earth* is an easy-to-take followup to his previous pic *Mystery Train*. Beginning with an outer-space shot gradually zeroing in on planet Earth, the director covers in five separate segments his favorite theme of lonely people interacting but ultimately facing the great void alone.

From this cosmic perspective he examines brief encounters between taxi drivers and their late-night fares. Opening LA segment is pic's weakest, as tomboyish cabbie Winona Ryder is matched against her patrician passenger Gena Rowlands. Contrasting with this is a powerful finale, set in Helsinki with actors from the troupe of the Kaurismaki brothers. Matti Pellonpaa is genuinely moving as a cabbie pouring out his tragic story to a trio of drunken guys. It's a tale of faith and love unrewarded.

En route to this somber finish, Jarmusch provides ebullient comedy in two winning routines: the hilarious and unlikely team (in matching floppy winter hats) of Giancarlo Esposito and Armin Mueller-Stahl in New York as well as a goofy, all-stops-out monologue by Roberto Benigni as a Roman cabbie confessing to a back-seat priest about his sexual exploits with pumpkins and a sheep named Lola.

Parisian segment is an unsettling encounter between a bitter blind woman (Beatrice Dalle) and her Ivory Coast–transplanted driver Isaach De Bankole. Filming in the languages of each city results in a feature about sixty percent English subtitled.

•

NIGHT ON THE TOWN, A

SEE: ADVENTURES IN BABYSITTING

•

NIGHT PASSAGE

1957, 90 mins, US ▭ col

Dir James Neilson ***Prod*** Aaron Rosenberg ***Scr*** Borden Chase ***Ph*** William Daniels ***Ed*** Sherman Todd ***Mus*** Dimitri Tiomkin ***Art*** Alexander Golitzen, Robert Clatworthy

Act James Stewart, Audie Murphy, Dan Duryea, Dianne Foster, Elaine Stewart, Brandon de Wilde (Universal)

This taut, well-made and sometimes fascinating western is the first use of Technicolor's new widescreen, anamorphic process, Technirama. Borden Chase has fashioned a script around two brothers—James Stewart, decent, upright; Audie Murphy, wild, a deadly gunman. The Technirama process gives new depth and definition, said to combine the principles of both VistaVision and CinemaScope. Pic was lensed in the Durango-Silverton region of Colorado.

Plot carries a railroad-building backdrop. Stewart is a former railroad employee recalled to help transport the payroll to rail's-end, previous attempts to take the money through to rebelling workers having been stymied when outlaw gang conducts series of raids. He becomes involved with gang during a train holdup.

Both stars deliver sound portrayals, Murphy making up in color Stewart's greater footage. Dan Duryea is immense as outlaw chief who isn't quite certain whether he can outdraw Murphy, a wizard with a gun.

•

NIGHT PEOPLE

1954, 93 mins, US ▭ col

Dir Nunnally Johnson ***Prod*** Nunnally Johnson ***Scr*** Nunnally Johnson ***Ph*** Charles G. Clarke ***Ed*** Dorothy Spencer ***Mus*** Cyril Mockridge ***Art*** Hanns Kuhnert, Theo Zwierski

Act Gregory Peck, Broderick Crawford, Anita Bjork, Rita Gam, Walter Abel, Buddy Ebsen (20th Century-Fox)

This is a top-notch, exciting cloak-and-dagger thriller, modernly paced and with a contemporary feel. An added touch is CinemaScope, making it the first updated meller in that medium. Nunnally Johnson gets a clean triple for his smart handling of the production, direction and scripting.

The screenplay is based on a story by Jed Harris and Thomas Reed, which tells of the kidnapping of a young American soldier and how a CIC officer manages to get him back safely to the western zone by being quicker-witted than the GI's captors and their agents. Peck plays the colonel, Van Dyke, and how he brings off the rescue makes for plenty of suspense-laden, and credibly conceived footage, since he has to fool the East Berlin Reds; the hangover Nazis working with them; handle Leatherby (Broderick Crawford), stateside industrial tycoon who has come to Berlin to rescue his son; and placate the State Department, which wants no illegal trafficking that might have serious international repurcussions. Chief heavy in the melodrama is ably enacted by Anita Bjork, who through most of her footage appears to be a friendly agent trying to help Van Dyke.

A still battle-scarred Berlin provides interesting backgrounds for the melodramatics. The stereophonic sound is not allowed to distract except in opening and closing shots, when it booms out noisily.

•

NIGHT PORTER, THE

1974, 115 mins, US/Italy Ⓥ ⦿ col

Dir Liliana Cavani ***Prod*** Robert Gordon Edwards, Esae De Simone ***Scr*** Liliana Cavani, Italo Moscati ***Ph*** Alfio Contin ***Ed*** Franco Arcalli ***Mus*** Daniele Paris

Act Dirk Bogarde, Charlotte Rampling, Philippe Leroy, Gabriele Ferzetti, Isa Miranda, Amedeo Amadio (United Artists)

Liliana Cavani deals with the ambivalent relationship between a concentration camp victim (Charlotte Rampling) and her torturer-lover (Dirk Bogarde) in a strange, brooding tale. There is a touch of *Last Tango in Paris* in this love affair that does not take society or other people into much account.

It has an apartment, albeit furnished, and the couple trapped there, serving for their trysts in Vienna of 1957. They meet accidentally, but the past and a group of still-ardent Nazis force them to revert to their camp relationship.

Bogarde is an ex-Storm Trooper who now works as a night porter. He belongs to a group who have managed to be acquitted by doing away with witnesses and destroying evidence. It's a gritty look at concentration camp quirks, but transposed to a strange drama. Bogarde treads intelligently through his role of an unbalanced man.

•

NIGHT SHIFT

1982, 105 mins, US Ⓥ ⦿ col

Dir Ron Howard ***Prod*** Brian Grazer ***Scr*** Lowell Ganz, Babaloo Mandel ***Ph*** James Crabe ***Ed*** Robert J. Kern, Daniel P. Hanley, Mike Hill ***Mus*** Burt Bacharach ***Art*** Jack Collis

Act Henry Winkler, Michael Keaton, Shelley Long, Gina Hecht, Pat Corley, Bobby DiCicco (Ladd)

Nerdy Henry Winkler is a meek attendant at the city morgue who is the kind of person who'd rather eat a plate of poisonous mushrooms than offend the chef who served them. His life is a mess. To compound matters, he must work the night shift with Looney Tune Michael Keaton—the type of guy who talks nonstop as he blasts rock songs on the radio while dancing up and down the aisles.

At the same time, Winkler befriends Shelley Long, the perennial "nice girl hooker" who just happens to live next door and happens to have just lost her pimp. It's not long before Winkler and Keaton devise a scheme to act as pimps for Long using the morgue as a base of operation.

Though the plotline hardly sounds like a family film, this is probably the most sanitized treatment of pimps and prostitution audiences will ever see.

None of this much matters, because director Ron Howard and screenwriters Lowell Ganz and Babaloo Mandel, all TV veterans, are only bent on giving the audience a good time.

•

NIGHT THEY RAIDED MINSKY'S, THE

1968, 100 mins, US Ⓥ col

Dir William Friedkin ***Prod*** Norman Lear ***Scr*** Arnold Schulman, Sidney Michaels, Norman Lear ***Ph*** Andrew Laszlo ***Ed*** Ralph Rosenblum ***Mus*** Charles Strouse ***Art*** William Eckart, Jean Eckart

Act Jason Robards, Britt Ekland, Norman Wisdom, Forrest Tucker, Harry Andrews, Joseph Wiseman (United Artists/Tandem)

Norman Lear's period peek at a peculiarly American form of entertainment—burlesque—is most successful in its art direction and nostalgic recapturing of New York's Lower East Side during its most hoydenish period.

So easily does Norman Wisdom dominate the many scenes he's in, that the other cast members suffer by comparison, particularly leading man Jason Robards, who's cast as the top banana in the Minsky burlesque theatre. One fault with this highly colorful and fast-moving comedy film is that it jumps about so much in its storytelling. Characters are introduced, then never developed.

Lear was able, during NY location filming, to talk the city into forestalling the demolion of an entire block on the East Side until he had used it for background footage.

Britt Ekland is lovely as the Amish girl who not only rebels against the restrictions of her religious background and a tyrannical father, but does so with a strip sequence that titillates the screen audience almost as much as it does the onscreen audience.

•

NIGHT TIDE

1961, 85 mins, US Ⓥ ⦿ b/w

Dir Curtis Harrington ***Prod*** Aram Kantarian ***Scr*** Curtis Harrington ***Ph*** Vilis Lapenieks ***Ed*** Jodie Copelan ***Mus*** David Raksin ***Art*** Paul Mathison

Act Dennis Hopper, Linda Lawson, Gavin Muir, Luana Anders (American International/Filmgroup-Virgo)

Curtis Harrington, onetime avant-garde filmmaker and assistant to Jerry Wald, made this first feature on an indie basis. Film mixes a love affair with the supernatural. If Harrington displays a good flair for narration and mounting, his feel for mood, suspense and atmospherics is not too highly developed.

A sailor on leave meets a girl who works as a mermaid in a side show on the amusement pier in Venice, California. It develops into love but there is a strangeness in her comportment. Her guardian tells the sailor that he had found her on a Greek island and brought her to the U.S. and that she is really a mermaid. It also develops that two men she had been with were found drowned. The sailor is bewildered, but when she almost kills him during skin diving he manages to escape while she disappears.

Dennis Hopper is acceptably bewildered by his plight while Linda Lawson has the exotic looks for the psychotic siren.

•

NIGHT TO REMEMBER, A

1958, 123 mins, UK Ⓥ b/w

Dir Roy Ward Baker ***Prod*** William MacQuitty ***Scr*** Eric Ambler ***Ph*** Geoffrey Unsworth ***Ed*** Sidney Hayers ***Mus*** William Alwyn ***Art*** Alex Vetchinsky

Act Kenneth More, Honor Blackman, Anthony Bushell, Ronald Allen, Robert Ayres, Jill Dixon (Rank)

Producer and director have done an honest job in putting the tragic sinking of the *Titanic* in 1912 on the screen with an impressive, almost documentary flavor. With around 200 speaking roles in the pic, few of the actors are given much chance to develop as characters. Even Kenneth More, in the star role, is only part of a team. The ship itself is the star.

The story tells how the "unsinkable" new ship set out for the U.S. on the night of 14 April 1912, how it struck an iceberg and sank in less than three hours with 1,302 people drowned and only 705 survivors. The film takes only 37 minutes less than the time of the actual disaster.

The errors and confusion which played a part in the drama are brought out with no whitewashing. Although many of the passengers and crew come vividly to life, there is no attempt to hang a fictional story on any of them. Technically, director Roy Baker does a superb job in difficult circumstances. His direction of some of the panic scenes during the manning of the lifeboats—of which there were not nearly enough to accommodate all on board—is masterly. Eric Ambler's screenplay [from Walter Lord's book], without skimping the nautical side of the job, brings out how some people kept their heads and others became cowards.

Others who manage to make impact are Laurence Naismith as the skipper; Anthony Bushell, captain of the rescue ship; Kenneth Griffith and David McCallum, as a couple of radio operators; Tucker McGuire, as a hearty American woman; George Rose, as a bibulous ship's baker, Michael Goodliffe, as the designer of the ship; and Frank Lawton, as the chairman of the White Star Line.

•

NIGHT TRAIN TO MUNICH

1940, 95 mins, UK Ⓥ b/w

Dir Carol Reed ***Prod*** Edward Black ***Scr*** Sidney Gilliat, Frank Launder ***Ph*** Otto Kanturek ***Ed*** R. E. Dearing, Michael Gordon ***Mus*** Louis Levy (dir.) ***Art*** Alex Vetchinsky

Act Margaret Lockwood, Rex Harrison, Paul Henreid, Basil Radford, Naunton Wayne, Felix Aylmer (Gaumont-British)

Made by the same British studio that turned out *The Lady Vanishes*, the film also has the same general subject matter, the same screenplay writers, Margaret Lockwood in the femme lead, and even makes similar use of Basil Radford and Naunton Wayne as two tourist Englishmen with a ludicrous interest in cricket.

Much of the film's merit obviously stems from the compact, propulsive screenplay by Sidney Gilliat and Frank Launder, and the razor-edge direction of Carol Reed. Story by Gordon Wellesley opens in the tense days of August 1939 with a Nazi espionage agent in London recapturing two Czechs who have escaped from a concentration camp, an aged armor-plate inventor and his pretty daughter. A British Secret Service operative follows them to Berlin and, after an exciting sequence of events during which war is declared, escapes with them into Switzerland.

Yarn is not only told without a single letdown, but it actually continues to pile up suspense to a nerve-clutching pitch. The headlong chase and escape at the end is a time-tested melodramatic device superbly handled.

Reed's direction is worthy of the best thrillers of Edgar Wallace, for whom he was for many years stage manager. Lockwood is an appealing heroine and her performance is direct and persuasive. Rex Harrison is properly suave as the ubiquitous British operative, while Paul Henreid is rightly cold as the treacherous Gestapo agent, Radford and Wayne repeat their goofy Britisher performances of *The Lady Vanishes* and again click. There are countless touches of atmosphere and comedy that add immeasurable flavor and zest to the picture.

•

NIGHT UNTO NIGHT

1949, 84 mins, US b/w

Dir Don Siegel ***Prod*** Owen Crump ***Scr*** Kathryn Scola ***Ph*** Peverell Marley ***Ed*** Thomas Reilly ***Mus*** Franz Waxman

Act Ronald Reagan, Viveca Lindfors, Broderick Crawford, Rosemary DeCamp (Warner)

Night Unto Night ventures into a dramatic theme rarely more than hinted at on the screen—epilepsy.

Picture's major strength comes from the performance of Viveca Lindfors, but it is not enough to carry the film. She projects emotion realistically, and with sex appeal. Ronald Reagan's performance suffers in comparison to his costar's, and lacks depth.

Plot of the Philip Wylie novel, scripted by Kathryn Scola, brings together a young man, who has just learned he is suffering from epilepsy, and a woman, still grieving over the loss of her husband.

Don Siegel's direction is strained and strives too much for dramatic effects with the more mechanical elements of the production.

Broderick Crawford tops the featured players as an artist friend of the dramatic couple.

•

NIGHT WARNING

1983, 94 mins, US Ⓥ col

Dir William Asher ***Prod*** Stephen Breimer, Eugene Mazzola ***Scr*** Stephen Breimer, Alan Jay Glueckman, Boon Collins ***Ph*** Robbie Greenberg ***Ed*** Ted Nicolaou ***Mus*** Bruce Langhorne

Act Jimmy McNichol, Susan Tyrrell, Bo Svenson, Marcia Lewis, Julia Duffy, Britt Leach (S2D Associates/Royal American)

Night Warning is a fine psychological horror film. As the maniacally possessive aunt and guardian of a 17-year-old boy, Susan Tyrrell gives a tour de force performance.

Billy (Jimmy McNichol) is a basketball player at high school who has been brought up by his aunt Cheryl (Tyrrell) after his parents died in a car crash (great stunt footage) 14 years ago. An old maid, Cheryl is overprotective, opposing Billy's desire to go to college in Denver on a hoped-for athletic scholarship to be with his girlfriend.

Cheryl maintains a candlelit memorial to an old boyfriend in the basement. The film's horror content begins (replete with slow-motion violence and plenty of blood) when she kills a young TV repairman after failing to seduce him. Cop on the case Detective Carlson (Bo Svenson) is very closed-minded, ignoring the facts and insisting on linking the crime to a homosexual basketball coach, making Billy the prime suspect instead of his aunt.

•

NIGHT WATCH

1973, 105 mins, UK Ⓥ col

Dir Brian G. Hutton ***Prod*** Martin Poll, George W. George, Barnard Straus ***Scr*** Tony Williamson, Evan Jones ***Ph*** Billy Williams ***Ed*** John Jympson ***Mus*** John Cameron ***Art*** Peter Murton

Act Elizabeth Taylor, Laurence Harvey, Billie Whitelaw, Robert Lang, Tony Britton, Bill Dean (Brut)

Lucille Fletcher's *Night Watch* isn't the first average stage play to be turned into a better-than-average film. Astute direction and an improved cast more than help.

Elizabeth Taylor dominates the doings. Director Brian G. Hutton makes the most of the suggested violence in the film and that is where it remains, suggested, until a brouhaha among the film's three principals at the end.

The switch ending is, actually, telegraphed by a disclosure made by the police inspector and the scripters are guilty of dragging one or two small red herrings across the trail. The biggest demand on credibility is believing that anyone in his right mind would want to leave the beautiful Taylor for the likes of Billie Whitelaw, an excellent actress but no prime example of feminine pulchritude. It suggests madness on the part of husband Laurence Harvey (first-rate in the role).

Besides the star-billed threesome, the most impressive performance is that of Robert Lang as the more-than-inquisitive bachelor neighbor.

•

NIGHT WE NEVER MET, THE

1993, 99 mins, US Ⓥ ⦿ col

Dir Warren Leight ***Prod*** Michael Peyser ***Scr*** Warren Leight ***Ph*** John Thomas ***Ed*** Camilla Toniolo ***Mus*** Evan Lurie ***Art*** Lester Cohen

Act Matthew Broderick, Annabella Sciorra, Kevin Anderson, Jeanne Tripplehorn, Justine Bateman, Michael Mantell (Miramax)

A quintessential New York movie, *The Night We Never Met* takes a novel premise and develops it in fits and starts.

Debuting filmmaker Warren Leight has come up with an offbeat notion: time-sharing a Greenwich Village apartment by days of the week. Hissable yuppie Kevin Anderson is behind the scheme, wanting two nights out a week with his buddies while living with patrician fiancée Justine Bateman.

One customer is Matthew Broderick, moping over losing his performance artist girlfriend Pastel (Jeanne Tripplehorn, spoofing a familiar downtown type). Third tenant is frustrated housewife Annabella Sciorra, who uses it to get away from her dense husband (Michael Mantell).

Plot is set in motion when Anderson switches one of his designated days with Broderick but doesn't update the posted schedule, causing Sciorra to confuse the two guys. Wonderfully atmospheric use of New York locations and familiar characters brings *Night* to life. Unfortunately, it's not really so much an ensemble piece as a film of alternating casts or vignettes.

•

NIJINSKY

1980, 125 mins, UK Ⓥ col

Dir Herbert Ross ***Prod*** Nora Kaye, Stanley O'Toole ***Scr*** Hugh Wheeler ***Ph*** Douglas Slocombe ***Ed*** William Reynolds ***Mus*** John Lanchberry ***Art*** John Blezard

Act Alan Bates, George De La Pena, Leslie Browne, Alan Badel, Janet Suzman, Ronald Pickup (Hera)

In *Nijinsky*, Herbert Ross and scripter Hugh Wheeler have constructed nothing less than a male-to-male romantic tragedy. The film takes the form of a broad flashback covering only two critical years (1912–13) in the young dancer's early 20s.

Beginning with his mentor-lover Sergei Diaghilev (Alan Bates), the period charts Nijinsky's gradual allegiance to a wealthy homosexual patron—brilliantly etched by Alan Badel; and the successful attempt of Hungarian aristocrat Romola de Pulsky (Leslie Browne) to catch Nijinsky on his briefly heterosexual rebound from Diaghilev.

Central theme of Wheeler's script is that Diaghilev's obsessive love for Nijinsky clouded his otherwise shrewd taste, showmanship and business sense.

George De La Pena has the intensity and ambiguous sexual aura to make him a credible Nijinsky.

•

NIKITA
(LA FEMME NIKITA)
1990, 115 mins, France/Italy Ⓥ ⦿ ▭ col
Dir Luc Besson ***Scr*** Luc Besson ***Ph*** Thierry Arbogast ***Ed*** Olivier Mauffroy ***Mus*** Eric Serra ***Art*** Dan Weil
Act Anne Parillaud, Jean-Hugues Anglade, Tcheky Karyo, Jeanne Moreau, Jean Reno, Jean Bouise (Gaumont/Tiger)

After the waterlogged mysticism of *The Big Blue*, Gaumont's wonderboy director Luc Besson is back on terra firma in *Nikita*. It's an absurd, shrill, ultraviolent but soft-centered urban thriller about a pretty, young, cop-killing junkie who's re-educated as a crack secret service agent, with license to kill.

Anne Parillaud is Nikita, a punk drug fiend who survives a police assault when her mad-dog band burgles a neighborhood pharmacy. Sentenced to life imprisonment for having cold-bloodedly executed one of the cops, Parillaud is drugged and wakes up in a cell where she is offered a second chance by an intelligence officer (Tcheky Karyo) in charge of her training.

Parillaud seems resigned to her fate until she meets an easygoing, affectionate supermarket cashier (Jean-Hugues Anglade) whom she picks up, romances and shacks up with. The idyll is complicated by the facade she must maintain and the dangerous periodic assignments. Parillaud (aka Mme. Besson) does her frenetic best to make Nikita something resembling a human being. But she remains a totally uninteresting figment of Besson's blinkered movieland imagination, especially when she's in the company of Karyo and Anglade, who provide balance to her overacting.

Jeanne Moreau provides a touch of class in a small role as over-the-hill agent who tutors Parillaud in feminine graces. Jean Reno, a Besson faithful, plays a killer with stone-faced parodic panache.

•

NIL BY MOUTH
1997, 128 mins, UK Ⓥ ⦿ col
Dir Gary Oldman ***Prod*** Luc Besson, Douglas Urbanksi, Gary Oldman ***Scr*** Gary Oldman ***Ph*** Ron Fortunato ***Ed*** Brad Fuller ***Mus*** Eric Clapton ***Art*** Hugo Luczyc-Wyhowski
Act Ray Winstone, Kathy Burke, Charlie Creed-Miles, Laila Morse, Edna Dore, Chrissie Cotterill (SE8 Group)

Rough, tough but with an underlying generosity toward its characters, Gary Oldman's *Nil by Mouth* is an impressive writing-helming debut, a perf-driven portrait of a dysfunctional London working-class family, which often plays like Ken Loach sans the politics. Godfathered by French director Luc Besson, with whom Oldman made both *Leon* and *The Fifth Element*, pic is clearly a personal film for the 39-year-old thesp.

Characters are presented with no introduction, as if familiar already; language is super-ripe, with a record use of words beginning with "f" and "c,"; and Oldman shows a preference for close-ups and medium close-ups.

Tight-knit family is made up of Raymond (Ray Winstone), brutish, foul-mouthed husband of Val (Kathy Burke) and brother-in-law of young Billy (Charlie Creed-Miles), with whom he has an edgy relationship. Also around are Val and Billy's mother (Laila Morse) and her mother (Edna Dore).

When Raymond kicks Billy out, the young kid, who has a drug habit, is forced to survive outside the family circle, apart from clandestine visits when Raymond is not around. After being absent for a good portion of the movie's middle, Raymond returns with a vengeance, savagely beating the pregnant Val and prompting a show of female solidarity.

Winstone, a former boxer, dominates the film with an intensely focused performance. Though the movie stands on its performances, Oldman has wrapped them in an edgy directorial style that alternates between hand-held, *verite* lensing and moments of remarkable stillness, such as Raymond's attempt to apologize to Val.

•

NINE ½ WEEKS
1986, 113 mins, US Ⓥ ⦿ col
Dir Adrian Lyne ***Prod*** Antony Rufus Isaacs, Zalman King ***Scr*** Patricia Knop, Zalman King, Sarah Kernochan ***Ph*** Peter Biziou ***Ed*** Tom Rolf, Caroline Biggerstaff ***Mus*** Jack Nitzsche ***Art*** Ken Davis
Act Mickey Rourke, Kim Basinger, Margaret Whitton, David Margulies, Christine Baranski, Karen Young (PSO/Kimmel/Barish/Jonesfilm/Galactic/Triple Ajaxxx)

Only and entire raison d'etre for this screen adaptation of Elizabeth McNeill's novel would be to vividly present the obsessive, all-consuming passion between a successful Wall Street type and a beautiful art gallery employee, who embark upon an intense love affair that lasts as long as the title indicates.

The film is about the crazy, overwhelming attachment they have with one another, and nothing else. Therefore, the virtual absence of anything interesting happening between them—like plausible attraction, exotic, amazing sex, or, God forbid, good dialogue—leaves one great big hole on the screen for two hours.

Mickey Rourke is less than totally convincing as a big businessman, but Kim Basinger is the film's one saving grace, as she manages to retain a certain dignity.

[A 117-min. version was released theatrically in Europe, and in 1987 on homevideo.]

•

NINE HOURS TO RAMA
1963, 125 mins, US ▭ col
Dir Mark Robson ***Prod*** Mark Robson ***Scr*** Nelson Gidding ***Ph*** Arthur Ibbetson ***Ed*** Ernest Walker ***Mus*** Malcolm Arnold ***Art*** Elliot Scott
Act Horst Buchholz, Jose Ferrer, Valerie Gearon, Don Borisenko, Robert Morley, Dione Baker (20th Century-Fox)

At the core, this dramatization of circumstances surrounding the assassination of Mahatma Gandhi is an achievement of insight and impact. The success of a drama focusing its attention on the assassin of a great man is to make the character of the killer dimensional and clearly motivated. This is achieved in the screenplay from Stanley Wolpert's novel and bolstered by Horst Buchholz's virile portrayal of the perpetrator.

Action of the drama takes place in the nine-hour span culminating with the fatal measure, with several flashback passages to illustrate the incidents of the past that contributed to the unstable frame of mind of the young man.

The story falls down in its development and clarification of certain key secondary characters. A married woman (Valerie Gearon) for whom the killer-to-be has fallen does not make very much sense. And her abrupt metamorphosis from sophisticated lady of the world to devout woman of India in the final scene is both superfluous and dramatically awkward.

Several other important characters, too, are poorly defined, among them the assassin's unwilling accomplice (Don Borisenko), a baffling Indian politico (Robert Morley) and an impulsive prostitute (Diane Baker).

Buchholz delivers a performance of intensity and conviction. Jose Ferrer is excellent as a desperately concerned and conscientious police superintendent guarding Gandhi against disheartening odds. An astonishingly accurate personification of the latter is etched by J. S. Casshyap.

•

NINE LIVES OF FRITZ THE CAT, THE
1974, 76 mins, US Ⓥ col
Dir Robert Taylor ***Prod*** Steve Krantz ***Scr*** Fred Halliday, Eric Monte, Robert Taylor ***Ph*** Ted C. Bemiller, Greg Heschong ***Ed*** Marshall M. Borden ***Mus*** Tom Scott and the LA Express
(American International)

Fritz the Cat is back again. The synthetic troublemaker and dilettante revolutionary was a trifle anachronistic when he first hit the screens in 1972. He is even more so in *The Nine Lives of Fritz the Cat*. The animated production utilizes several random flashback and flash-forward sequences within the framework of Fritz being chewed out by his wife and lapsing into reveries.

Somewhat forced and dated humor, not too well fluffed up by a frenzied and compulsive hip storytelling style, cartoon feature will please teenage mentalities.

Fact that period flashbacks—to Hitler's last days, to the Depression 1930s—and to a futuristic separate black state, among other segments, are the body of the plot, seems to suggest a lack of current timeliness.

•

NINE MONTHS
1995, 102 mins, US Ⓥ ⦿ col
Dir Chris Columbus ***Prod*** Anne Francois, Chris Columbus, Mark Radcliffe, ***Scr*** Chris Columbus ***Ph*** Donald McAlpine ***Ed*** Raja Gosnell ***Mus*** Hans Zimmer ***Art*** Angelo P. Graham
Act Hugh Grant, Julianne Moore, Tom Arnold, Joan Cusack, Jeff Goldblum, Robin Williams (1492/20th Century-Fox)

Nine Months is an innocuously funny, audience-pleasing comedy very much tailored around the cuddly charm and boyish good looks of Hugh Grant, the British actor who hit it big in *Four Weddings and a Funeral*.

Based on a French feature [the 1994 *Neuf Mois*, written and directed by Patrick Braoude] that was successful on its home turf but never made it into U.S. release, Americanized version has veered away from the original's concentration on the comic physical side of effects of pregnancy as well as its critique of hospital conditions and medical practice.

Grant stars as consummate yuppie Samuel Faulkner, a breezy young man who's got it all—red Porsche, San Francisco apartment with a bay view and a lovely girlfriend of five years, Rebecca Taylor (Julianne Moore). When Rebecca announces she's pregnant, Samuel runs his fancy car off the road in shock.

Unable to summon the nerve to tell his beloved he simply doesn't want the kid, Samuel starts suffering from discarded-mate/praying mantis nightmares. Rebecca stomps out and moves in with her new best friend, Gail (Joan Cusack), the latter's boorish husband, Marty (Tom Arnold), and their three monster kids.

Samuel tries to revive his bachelor ways at the encouragement of swinger pal Sean (Jeff Goldblum). But watching a video of his sprout in utero, he realizes it's time to grow up and smell the diapers.

All the film's humor and sentiments play right into the most commonly held "family values," so this will hardly be the ticket for someone looking for something edgy, sophisticated or hip.

Grant does lay on the mugging and facial contortions a bit thick at times, but his debonair manner and appealing personality do a lot to put the film over. Moore is winsome and just serious enough as Grant's well-matched mate, while Goldblum, Arnold and Cusack supply effective shtick. A hilariously malaprop Robin Williams has a field day as a newly arrived medic from Russia who has previously treated only animals.

•

1984
1956, 90 mins, UK b/w
Dir Michael Anderson ***Prod*** N. Peter Rathvon ***Scr*** William P. Templeton, Ralph Bettinson ***Ph*** C. Pennington Richards ***Ed*** Bill Lewthwaite ***Mus*** Malcolm Arnold ***Art*** Terence Verity
Act Michael Redgrave, Edmond O'Brien, Jan Sterling, David Kossoff, Mervyn Johns, Donald Pleasence (Holiday/Associated British)

A sinister glimpse of the future as envisaged by George Orwell, *1984* is a grim, depressing picture. The action takes place after the first atomic war, with the world divided into three major powers.

London, the setting for the story, is the capital of Oceania and is run by a ruthless regime, the heads of which are members of the inner party while their supporters are in the outer party. There are ministries of Love and Thought, anti-sex leagues and record divisions where the speeches of the great are rewritten from time to time to suit the needs of contemporary events.

The story is built around the illegal romance of two members of the outer party, Edmond O'Brien and Jan Sterling.

Orwell's picture of the ultimate in totalitarian ruthlessness is faithfully presented. Television "eyes" keep a day-and-night watch on party members in their homes and TV screens are to be found everywhere, blurting out the latest reports on the endless wars with rival powers.

•

NINETEEN EIGHTY-FOUR
1984, 120 mins, UK Ⓥ ⦿ col
Dir Michael Radford ***Prod*** Simon Perry ***Scr*** Michael Radford ***Ph*** Roger Deakins ***Ed*** Tom Priestley ***Mus*** Dominic Muldowney [later replaced by Eurythmics] ***Art*** Allan Cameron
Act John Hurt, Richard Burton, Suzanna Hamilton, Cyril Cusack, Gregor Fisher, James Walker (Virgin/Umbrella)

In this unremitting downer, writer-director Michael Radford introduces no touches of comedy or facile sensationalism to soften a harsh depiction of life under a totalitarian system as imagined by George Orwell in 1948.

Richard Burton is splendid as inner-party official O'Brien. Ironically, his swan song performance as the deceptively gentle spur to Winston Smith's "thought-crimes," and then as the all-knowing interrogator who takes on the attributes of a father-figure to the helpless man whom he is intent on destroying, is something new in Burton's repertoire.

Also strong is Suzanna Hamilton as Julia, who is the other agent of Smith's downfall. John Hurt as Winston Smith holds center stage throughout.

•

1941
1979, 118 mins, US Ⓥ ⊙ ▭ col
Dir Steven Spielberg ***Prod*** Buzz Feitshans ***Scr*** Robert Zemeckis, Bob Gale ***Ph*** William A. Fraker ***Ed*** Michael Kahn ***Mus*** John Williams ***Art*** Dean Edward Mitzner
Act Dan Aykroyd, Ned Beatty, John Belushi, Toshiro Mifune, Nancy Allen, Robert Stack (Universal/Columbia/A-Team)

Billed as a comedy spectacle, Steven Spielberg's *1941* is long on spectacle, but short on comedy. The Universal-Columbia Pictures co-production is an exceedingly entertaining, fast-moving revision of 1940s war hysteria in Los Angeles spawned by the bombing of Pearl Harbor, and boasts Hollywood's finest miniature and special effects work seen to date.

Fact that 82 cast members are specifically credited, along with more than 160 crew and tech personnel in a six minute end credits crawl, should be ultimate validation that film is a collaborative work. However, the vision on the screen is director Steven Spielberg's, who moves his actors, sets, props and cameras with the efficiency of a creative field marshal.

Screenwriters, who concocted the outlandish storyline with exec producer John Milius, are also daring in their attempt to intertwine five or six different distinct storylines into one coherent tale.

Dan Aykroyd is very impressive in his feature debut as the serious army sergeant, but his former *Saturday Night Live* cohort John Belushi turns in a snarling, obnoxious performance.

Real cast standouts are Bobby DiCicco, who spends the pic wrestling pretty Dianne Kay away from horny soldier Treat Williams; Robert Stack as a bemused general; Nancy Allen as the airborne inamorata of Tim Matheson; Wendie Jo Sperber as a frustrated femme; and Joseph P. Flaherty as a croony '40s emcee.

Christopher Lee and Toshiro Mifune also excel as the bickering Axis powers determined to destroy the only thing of value in Los Angeles, Hollywood.

It hardly matters that the actual Great Los Angeles Air Raid took place on Feb. 26, 1942, and not Dec. 13, 1941, nor that some of the racist consequences of that are given short shrift. [In 1996 a 146-min. de facto director's cut was released on home video.]

1979: NOMINATIONS: Best Cinematography, Sound, Visual Effects

•

1900
SEE: NOVECENTO

•

1969
1988, 90 mins, US Ⓥ ⊙ col
Dir Ernest Thompson ***Prod*** Daniel Grodnik, Bill Badalato ***Scr*** Ernest Thompson ***Ph*** Jules Brenner ***Ed*** William Anderson ***Mus*** Michael Small ***Art*** Marcia Hinds
Act Robert Downey, Jr., Kiefer Sutherland, Bruce Dern, Mariette Hartley, Winona Ryder, Joanna Cassidy (Atlantic)

Affecting memories and good intentions don't always add up to good screen stories, and such is the case in *1969*, one of the murkiest reflections on the Vietnam War era yet, notwithstanding good performances all around and bright packaging of Kiefer Sutherland and Robert Downey, Jr., in the leads.

Director-screenwriter Ernest Thompson (*On Golden Pond*) has a wonderful feel for the relationships. It's only when it comes time to deliver a screen-size story that things go goofy.

College students and best pals Scott (Sutherland) and Ralph (Downey) have adopted a lifestyle in sharp contrast to the buttoned-down mores of their families in a small Maryland town 83 miles away. When they hitchhike home, there's conflict, particularly between Scott and his older brother Alden (Christopher Wynne, in an extremely unsympathetic turn), who's shipping out for the war.

Story is not exactly gripping. Instead, it's a mild trip down memory lane as the two hit the road in a psychedelic van to taste America in their last "summer of innocence."

Sutherland gives one of his best and most natural performances, and Downey is very good in a role that's similar to his *Less Than Zero* junkie, but gives him less to work with. Joanna Cassidy gives a top-notch performance as Ralph's spunky, effervescent and slightly liberated mother, and Winona Ryder is a scene-stealer as younger sister Beth, who's the only one with any ideas.

•

9/30/55
(AKA: SEPTEMBER 30, 1955)
1977, 101 mins, US ⊙ ▭ col
Dir James Bridges ***Prod*** Jerry Weintraub ***Scr*** James Bridges ***Ph*** Gordon Willis ***Ed*** Jeff Gourson ***Mus*** Leonard Rosenman ***Art*** Robert Luthardt
Act Richard Thomas, Susan Tyrrell, Deborah Benson, Lisa Blount, Tom Hulce, Dennis Quaid (Universal)

Title is the date of the car-crash death of James Dean, and James Bridges's original script tells of the impact on Richard Thomas, starring in an excellent performance as a small-town Arkansas college kid whose life is permanently transformed by the incident.

Thomas is superb as the kid whose entire attitude undergoes a change when news of Dean's death is heard on the radio. Girlfriend Deborah Benson partially shares the grief, but not as much as Lisa Blount, a freakier chick.

Together with chums Tom Hulce, Dennis Christopher, Dennis Quaid and Mary Kai Clark, Thomas helps commemorate Dean's demise with booze and mock-occult mysticism, leading to a prank on other students.

Susan Tyrrell is outstanding as Blount's flamboyant mother.

•

NINE TO FIVE
1980, 110 mins, US Ⓥ ⊙ col
Dir Colin Higgins ***Prod*** Bruce Gilbert ***Scr*** Colin Higgins, Patricia Resnick ***Ph*** Reynaldo Villalobos ***Ed*** Pembroke J. Herring ***Mus*** Charles Fox ***Art*** Dean Mitzner
Act Jane Fonda, Lily Tomlin, Dolly Parton, Dabney Coleman, Sterling Hayden, Elizabeth Wilson (IPC/20th Century-Fox)

Anyone who has ever worked in an office will be able to identify with the antics in *Nine to Five*. Although it can probably be argued that Patricia Resnick and director Colin Higgins's script [from a story by Resnick] at times borders on the inane, the bottom line is that this picture is a lot of fun.

Story concerns a group of office workers (Lily Tomlin the all-knowing manager who trained the boss but can't get promoted, Jane Fonda the befuddled newcomer, and Dolly Parton the alluring personal secretary) who band together to seek revenge on the man who is making their professional lives miserable.

Tomlin comes off best in the most appealing role as the smart yet under-appreciated glue in the office cement.

Parton makes a delightful screen debut in a role tailored to her already well-defined country girl personality. Surprisingly, Fonda, initiator of the project, emerges as the weakest.

1980: NOMINATION: Best Song ("Nine to Five")

•

99 AND 44/100% DEAD
1974, 97 mins, US Ⓥ ▭ col
Dir John Frankenheimer ***Prod*** Joe Wizan ***Scr*** Robert Dillon ***Ph*** Ralph Woolsey ***Ed*** Harold F. Kress ***Mus*** Henry Mancini ***Art*** Herman Blumenthal
Act Richard Harris, Edmond O'Brien, Bradford Dillman, Ann Turkel, Constance Ford, Chuck Connors (20th Century-Fox)

99 and 44/100% Dead starts like a house on fire, with directorial style to burn, but self-incinerates within its first half-hour. Thereafter, audience endures a pointless hour of "bitter ashes, which the offended taste with spattering noise rejected" to use Milton's famous line. Director John Frankenheimer struggles with Robert Dillon's sophomoric, repulsive screenplay about gang warfare, but pyrrhic victory eludes him.

Hired killer Richard Harris enters a mythical, futuristic city "on the beginning of the third day of the War" and hunts down mob kingpin Bradford Dillman for rival gangster Edmond O'Brien's peace of mind.

For a short while Dillon seems to have parody on his mind. Unfortunately, Dillon has neither the wit nor the invention to sustain this tone for more than a few reels.

•

NINGEN NO JOKEN I–II
(THE HUMAN CONDITION; THE HUMAN CONDITION, PART I: NO GREATER LOVE)
1959, 208 mins, Japan Ⓥ ▭ b/w
Dir Masaki Kobayashi ***Prod*** Shigera Wakasuki ***Scr*** Zenzo Matsuyama, Masaki Kobayashi ***Ph*** Yoshio Miyajima ***Ed*** Keiichi Uraoka ***Mus*** Chuji Kinoshita ***Art*** Kazue Hirataka
Act Tatsuya Nakadai, Michiyo Aratama, So Yamamura, Eitaro Ozawa, Akira Ishihama, Shinji Nambara (Shochiku)

This is unique as a social document but pretty slow going as film entertainment. Picture's main claim to fame is that it's the first to be seen this side which portrays the Japanese war machine as seen by Japanese. The drama [from six-volume novel by Jumpei Gomikawa] is candid and stark; unfortunately, it is also lightly motivated, overlong and haphazardly edited. [Version reviewed was a 138-min. one for U.S. release in 1959.]

Story is set in 1943 with southern Manchuria as its locale. Protagonist is an idealistic young Japanese, Kaji (Tatsuya Nakadai), who takes a post as a labor overseer at an isolated mine (it looks like coal, but nobody says) to escape army service. Troubles arise when the guy tries to improve the lot of the labor force and objects to the treatment given to 600 Chinese POWs who are brought in to dig. Irony is that he eventually finds himself despised by his fellow countrymen and hated by the workers whom he has tried to help.

Valid theme is detailed to the point of tedium. More sensational aspects include a couple of sequences featuring "comfort girls" (brought in to comfort the workers and thus to make them more docile) and one scene of the beheading of several prisoners.

Technically the picture is first-rate. Widescreen black-and-white lensing is very good.

•

NINGEN NO JOKEN III–IV
(THE HUMAN CONDITION, PART II: THE ROAD TO ETERNITY)
1960, 181 mins, Japan Ⓥ ▭ b/w
Dir Masaki Kobayashi ***Prod*** Shigera Wakasuki ***Scr*** Zenzo Matasuyama, Masaki Kobayashi ***Ph*** Yoshio Miyajima ***Ed*** Keiichi Uraoka ***Mus*** Chuji Kinoshita ***Art*** Kazue Hirataka
Act Tatsuya Nakadai, Michiyo Aratama, Keiji Sada, Hideo Kisho, Jun Tatara, Kei Sato (Shochiku)

This is the second part of Masaki Kobayashi's great and monumental trilogy concerning the dilemma of a young Japanese who is forced to play a part in war, yet is the loser whichever side he takes.

Completed early in 1960, part begins with a quick summary of what took place in the preceding film, ending with the solitary figure of Kaji (Tatsuya Nakadai) leaving for service in the army.

The mentality of the Imperial Army of Japan, the brutalities and stupidities of army life, the way men act when facing violent death, and the way men are reduced to bestiality by killing and primitive treatment, are the elements which make this slow-moving tragedy of the human condition so compelling and piercing.

Part is remarkably self-contained and needs no explanations from its companion pictures to make its story-points clear.

•

NINGEN NO JOKEN V–VI
(THE HUMAN CONDITION, PART III: A SOLDIER'S PRAYER)
1961, 190 mins, Japan Ⓥ ▭ b/w
Dir Masaki Kobayashi ***Prod*** Shigera Wakasuki ***Scr*** Zenzo Matasuyama, Masaki Kobayashi ***Ph*** Yoshio Miyajima ***Ed*** Keiichi Uraoka ***Mus*** Chuji Kinoshita ***Art*** Kazue Hirataka
Act Tatsuya Nakadai, Michiyo Aratama, Taketoshi Naito, Keijiro Morozumi, Yusuke Kawazu, Kyoko Kishida (Shochiku)

Completed in late 1961, *A Soldier's Prayer* shows the final disillusionment in the three-year agony of the simple Japanese soldier who endures much, only to end by losing everything.

Sick and weary, Kagi (Tatsuya Nakadai) gives himself up to the Russians, under the impression that the conquerors will surely dispense a more humane rule than the Imperial Japanese. But once again his illusions are shattered. The Russians, like the Japanese, also rape the women, are also brutalized by war. In the prison camp he finds himself under the heel of Japanese officers, who act just as they did before they lost the war.

Kagi, forced to kill once more to avenge the death of a friend, breaks out of the camp, and with failing strength attempts to continue his journey to his wife. In his hand he clutches a dumpling as a gift.

Kobayashi's control [in the trilogy] of his material, his exposition of the theme, his manipulation of the cast, all give clarity to the mission of Kagi, who sets out from the clear tranquility of a simple life to make a frightening descent into Hell. If there is any weakness in the writing or playing of the part of Kagi, it is that he seems to lack spiritual motivation.

•

NINJA III: THE DOMINATION
1984, 95 mins, US Ⓥ col
Dir Sam Firstenberg ***Prod*** Menahem Golan, Yoram Globus ***Scr*** James R. Silke ***Ph*** Hanania Baer ***Ed*** Michael J. Duthie, Ken Bornstein ***Mus*** Udi Harpaz, Misha Segal, Buddy Royston, Mike Mercury ***Art*** Elliot Ellentuck
Act Sho Kosugi, Lucinda Dickey, Jordan Bennett, David Chung, Dale Ishimoto, James Hong (Cannon)

With *Ninja III* producers reunite members of the team that made their second entry in the martial arts series about the more deadly cousins of the Samurai. The new outing into the never-never land of the world's trickiest controlled violence is done with quite a twist.

The twist has several quite humorous aspects, the least of which being that most of the Ninja action is performed by a woman (Lucinda Dickey).

From time to time she bewilders her police officer boyfriend by unconsciously taking over the spirit of an evil Ninja on a visit to Arizona to carry on his wholesale killing of the police force.

Sho Kosugi is the Good Ninja who finally helps the American girl out of her predicament so she can return to her regular pastime.

•

NINOTCHKA
1939, 111 mins, US Ⓥ ⊙ b/w
Dir Ernst Lubitsch ***Prod*** Ernst Lubitsch ***Scr*** Charles Brackett, Billy Wilder, Walter Reisch ***Ph*** William Daniels ***Ed*** Gene Ruggiero ***Mus*** Werner Heymann ***Art*** Cedric Gibbons, Randall Duell
Act Greta Garbo, Melvyn Douglas, Bela Lugosi, Sig Ruman, Felix Bressart, Ina Claire (M-G-M)

Selection of Ernst Lubitsch to pilot Garbo in her first light performance in pictures proves a bull's-eye.

The punchy and humorous jabs directed at the Russian political system and representatives, and the contrast of bolshevik receptiveness to capitalistic luxuries and customs, are displayed in farcical vein, but there still remains the serious intent of comparisons between the political systems in the background [based on an original story by Melchior Lengyel].

Three Russian trade representatives arrive in Paris to dispose of royal jewels "legally confiscated." Playboy Melvyn Douglas is intent on cutting himself in for part of the jewel sale. Tying up the gems in lawsuit for former owner, Ina Claire, Douglas is confronted by special envoy Garbo who arrives to speed the transactions. Douglas gets romantic, while Garbo treats love as a biological problem.

1939: NOMINATIONS: Best Picture, Actress (Greta Garbo), Original Story, Screenplay

•

NINTH CONFIGURATION, THE
1980, 105 mins, US Ⓥ ⊙ col
Dir William Peter Blatty ***Prod*** William Peter Blatty ***Scr*** William Peter Blatty ***Ph*** Gerry Fisher ***Ed*** T. Battle Davis, Peter Lee-Thompson, Roberto Silvi ***Mus*** Barry DeVorzon ***Art*** Bill Malley, J. Dennis Washington
Act Stacy Keach, Scott Wilson, Jason Miller, Neville Brand, Moses Gunn, Robert Loggia (Warner)

The Ninth Configuration is an often confusing story concerning the effects of a new "doctor" on an institution for crazed military men which manages to effectively tie itself together in the end. Problem is the William Peter Blatty film takes entirely too long to explain itself.

Blatty makes his directorial debut here in addition to performing, producing and writing from his own novel.

Stacy Keach limns an army colonel who has been brought stateside to play psychiatrist to a compound of disturbed military men. From the beginning it's apparent Keach is infinitely more disturbed than any of the men he is supposed to be treating, making the actor's monotone, robotlike state unbearably grating on the nerves only minutes after his appearance.

•

NINTH GATE, THE
1999, 127 mins, France/Spain Ⓥ ⊙ ▭ col
Dir Roman Polanski ***Prod*** Roman Polanski ***Scr*** Enrique Urbizu, John Brownjohn, Roman Polanski ***Ph*** Darius Khondji ***Ed*** Herve de Luze ***Mus*** Wojciech Kilar ***Art*** Dean Tavoularis
Act Johnny Depp, Frank Langella, Lena Olin, Emmanuelle Seigner, Barbara Jefford, Jack Taylor (RP/Orly/TF1/Kino Vision/Origen)

Roman Polanski's *The Ninth Gate* is a sardonic detective thriller peppered with carefully crafted pleasures, not the least of which is a snide approach to wealthy people with a decadent streak. This is really a shaggy devil story [from one of Spain's all-time bestsellers, Arturo Perez-Reverte's *El Club Dumas*] whose giddy, ironic tone may throw viewers expecting a scary movie.

When powerful New Yorker Boris Balkan (Frank Langella), hell-bent on completing his collection of rare books concerning Lucifer, commissions ambitious young broker Dean Corso (Johnny Depp) to track down two special tomes, the lad has a devil of a time completing his assignment.

Pic's always assured, baroquely funny tone is set in opening sequence, in which an elderly gentleman in a book-lined study pens a suicide note before hanging himself. His widow, Liana Telfer (Lena Olin), doesn't know yet that her late spouse (played by ace art director Willy Holt, who designed Polanski's *Bitter Moon*) sold one of his most valuable books—one of only three known copies of *The Nine Gates of the Kingdom of Shadows*—to a fellow collector the day before.

If your story calls for a street-smart American who might be able to beat erudite Europeans at their own centuries-old game, Depp is a good choice. Olin does her determined hellcat routine with gusto, Langella convinces even in pic's loonier moments, and Shakespearean vet Barbara Jefford is terrific as a baroness in Paris.

Darius Khondji's widescreen lensing on location in France, Portugal and Spain is fine.

•

NIXON
1995, 190 mins, US Ⓥ ⊙ ▭ col
Dir Oliver Stone ***Prod*** Clayton Townsend, Oliver Stone, Andrew G. Vajna ***Scr*** Stephen J. Rivele, Christopher Wilkinson, Oliver Stone ***Ph*** Robert Richardson ***Ed*** Brian Berdan, Hank Corwin ***Mus*** John Williams ***Art*** Victor Kempster
Act Anthony Hopkins, Joan Allen, Powers Boothe, Ed Harris, Bob Hoskins, E. G. Marshall (Illusion/Cinergi/Hollywood)

Adding one more panel to his obsessional film portrait of American traumas of the 1960s and early 1970s, Oliver Stone now attempts to put his finger on the self-destructive demons deep within Richad Nixon's character, to decidedly mixed results. *Nixon* far overstays its welcome with an increasingly tedious final hour devoted largely to slogging through the minutiae of Watergate.

Stone and his writers have covered most of the bases of Nixon's life—his impoverished, religiously strict Quaker upbringing in rural California, his sometimes strained marriage and remoteness as a father, his political ups and downs and amazing central role in several of the key dramas of this century.

Beginning with the cause and effect of Watergate, pic slides back in time to Nixon's loss to JFK in the 1960 election and finally back to 1925, with young Dick Nixon in Whittier. Storytelling jumps around willy-nilly in the early going, vaulting ahead to 1962 and Nixon's humiliating loss in the California gubernatorial race and his promise to wife Pat that he'll retire forever from public life.

On it goes, through Nixon's dubious Cuban criminal connections that led to his links with the Watergate plumbers, his complicity with J. Edgar Hoover and his winning the presidency on the promise of ending the Vietnam War.

Anthony Hopkins is physically and vocally just not entirely convincing, and one never really forgets that this is an actor giving his best impression of a terribly famous man. The same could be said for nearly everyone else in the enormous cast, no matter how well they perform. The one performer who cuts deeper is Joan Allen, who gives her Pat Nixon a surprising dimensionality and often touching humanity.

Technically, film is impressive, with some of the White House sets modified from *The American President*. But the mixing of 35mm, videolike images, black-and-white and docu footage, so effective in *JFK* and *Natural Born Killers*, seems more arbitrary here.

1995: NOMINATIONS: Best Actor (Anthony Hopkins), Supporting Actress (Joan Allen), Original Screenplay, Original Dramatic Score

•

NOAH'S ARK
THE STORY OF THE DELUGE
1928, 135 mins, US b/w
Dir Michael Curtiz ***Prod*** Darryl F. Zanuck ***Scr*** Darryl F. Zanuck, Anthony Goldeway, De Leon Anthony ***Ph*** Hal Mohr, Barney McGill ***Mus*** Louis Silvers
Act Dolores Costello, George O'Brien, Noah Beery, Guinn Williams, Paul McAllister, Myrna Loy (Warner)

Noah's Ark has touches reminiscent of *Ten Commandments*, *King of Kings*, *Wings*, *The Big Parade* and quite a few other [1920s] screen epics. Better than $1.5 million was reported to have been spent on this film.

The Warner staff show everything conceivable under the sun—mobs, mobs and mobs; Niagaras of water; train wreck; war aplenty; crashes; deluges and everything. Nothing is missed from 'way back when folks thought that praying to the real God instead of Jehovah was the right thing until Noah got the message from above that it was not.

The story opens with scenes showing what is left of the world after the big deluge. It then drifts into the age where folks worshipped the Golden Calf and their lust for gold. It flashes modern to the extent of bringing to the fore the selfish motives of man. A flash is shown of the stock exchange in New York on a panicky day. A guy gets bumped off.

Then they hop to Europe. The scene is the Orient Express from Constantinople to Paris just as the First World War is in the air. There are folks of every nationality on the train. War is the topic.

Talk does not enter into the picture until after the first 35 minutes. It starts with love scene between George O'Brien and Dolores Costello and then brings in talk by Wallace Beery, Paul McAllister and Guinn Williams. The Costello voice hurts the impression made by her silent acting.

Beery is great as the Russian spy and as the King. McAllister, an old stage trouper, has a hard job with biblical quotations which are overdone. Voice okay but talk just a bit too much.

•

NOBI
(FIRES ON THE PLAIN)
1959, 100 mins, Japan Ⓥ ▭ b/w
Dir Kon Ichikawa ***Prod*** Masaichi Nagata ***Scr*** Natto Wada ***Ph*** Setsuo Kobayashi ***Ed*** Hiroaki Fujii ***Mus*** Yasushi Akutagawa ***Art*** Atsuji Shibata
Act Eiji Funakoshi, Mantaro Ushio, Yoshihiro Hamaguchi, Osamu Takizawa, Mickey Curtis, Asao Sano (Daiei)

This downbeat but fervent pic goes much further than the accepted war masterpieces in detailing humanity in crisis, and the spark left in one man. Production one of the most searing comments on war yet made.

Story covers the defeat and rout of the Imperial Japanese army during the Philippines campaign in the last World War. A ragged remnant is warned the Americans will slaughter them, and so start a trek through the jungles to the sea. It is all seen through one tubercular Japanese soldier whose approaching death has put him above it all. He manages to maintain a semblance of humanity to keep him from sinking to the cannibalism of many of his fellow soldiers.

Taken from a novel [by Shohei Ooka], director Kon Ichikawa has knit this into a visual tour de force in which man's inhumanity to man is denoted as he sinks into an animal void. The widescreen is well utilized and the acting exemplary. The only criticism might be a certain literary quality in the handling of the lead character, many of whose actions are not always clear. But it is a bone hard, forthright film.

•

NOBODY LIVES FOREVER
1946, 100 mins, US b/w
Dir Jean Negulesco ***Prod*** Robert Buckner ***Scr*** W. R. Burnett ***Ph*** Arthur Edeson ***Ed*** Rudi Fehr ***Mus*** Adolph Deutsch ***Art*** Hugh Reticker
Act John Garfield, Geraldine Fitzgerald, Walter Brennan, Faye Emerson, George Coulouris (Warner)

Nobody Lives Forever is the old gangster reformation theme. John Garfield is seen as a drafted mobster being released after years in the service and with plenty of heroic medals to indicate his fighting ability. Script by W. R. Burnett [from his own novel] follows writer's bent for putting down on paper more melodramatic elements of U.S. gang life and con men.

Garfield, intent on a long vacation from war duties, is talked into taking a wealthy widow for a large slice of her inheritance. Plot moves along towards its objective with all the obviousness of such a theme. The gangster falls for the gal he's trying to take.

John Garfield carries most of the weight of the story on capable shoulders. His performance gives picture considerable lift.

•

NOBODY RUNS FOREVER
(US: THE HIGH COMMISSIONER)
1968, 101 mins, UK Ⓥ col
Dir Ralph Thomas ***Prod*** Betty E. Box ***Scr*** Wilfred Greatorex ***Ph*** Ernest Steward ***Ed*** Ernest Hosler ***Mus*** Georges Delerue ***Art*** Anthony Woollard
Act Rod Taylor, Christopher Plummer, Lilli Palmer, Camilla Sparv, Daliah Lavi, Clive Revill (Rank)

Undemanding entertainment. A melodrama with political undertones which has tension and intrigue yet doesn't lose sight of its main purpose, to examine the relationship of two decent men in a rough situation. Storyline, based on Jon

Cleary's novel *The High Commissioner*, is workmanlike, though some of its possibilities are glibly skated over, dialogue is crisp and persuasive and most of the lead players are believable.

Rod Taylor is cast as an Australian police officer who is sent to London to arrest the Australian High Commissioner on a charge of murdering his first wife. The Commissioner (Christopher Plummer) is holding peace talks in London and courteously, but obstinately, refuses to go back to Australia until his mission is completed.

Taylor becomes reluctantly involved as bodyguard and the job becomes trickier as he becomes more convinced that the commissioner is not guilty.

As the cop, Taylor gives a thoroughly likeable and credible performance as a man clinging to his duty. Plummer is excellent as the courteous, but tough-minded and idealistic commissioner.

•

NOBODY'S FOOL

1986, 107 mins, US Ⓥ ⊙ col

Dir Evelyn Purcell ***Prod*** James C. Katz, Jon S. Denny ***Scr*** Beth Henley ***Ph*** Mikhail Suslov ***Ed*** Dennis Virkler ***Mus*** James Newton Howard ***Art*** Jackson DeGovia

Act Rosanna Arquette, Eric Roberts, Mare Winningham, Jim Youngs, Louise Fletcher (Island/Katz-Denny)

Nobody's Fool features kookiness without real comedy, romance without magic.

Rosanna Arquette, a small-town western girl, attends dutifully to her burned-out mother and bratty younger brother as she tries to forget the public shame and ridicule she endured when she impulsively stabbed her old beau in a restaurant. She is as insecure as can be when Eric Roberts, the lighting technician with a visiting theatrical troupe, begins quietly noticing her.

Arquette's performance, like the film, features hits and misses, yet there is something frequently moving about the character's scattershot approach to emotional salvation. Roberts, more subdued than usual, effectively registers the impulses of a young man who thinks he can save Arquette from her prospective dismal fate.

•

NOBODY'S FOOL

1994, 110 mins, US Ⓥ ⊙ col

Dir Robert Benton ***Prod*** Scott Rudin, Arlene Donovan ***Scr*** Robert Benton ***Ph*** John Bailey ***Ed*** John Bloom ***Mus*** Howard Shore ***Art*** David Gropman

Act Paul Newman, Jessica Tandy, Bruce Willis, Melanie Griffith, Dylan Walsh, Pruitt Taylor Vince (Paramount/Cinehaus)

Nobody's Fool is a gentle, flavorsome story of a loose-knit dysfunctional family whose members essentially include every glimpsed citizen of a small New York town. Fronted by a splendid performance from Paul Newman as a spirited man who has made nothing of his life, Robert Benton's character-driven film is sprinkled with small pleasures.

Newman's Sully is the odd man out in North Bath, NY, a fitfully employed 60-year-old construction worker and handyman who is reduced to boarding with his elderly eighth-grade teacher, Miss Beryl (Jessica Tandy), pursuing futile legal action assisted by a lawyer, Wirf (Gene Saks), who never wins a case and having the village idiot, Rub Squeers (Pruitt Taylor Vince), as his best friend. His closest soulmate is probably the sexy Toby (Melanie Griffith), but she's married, however unhappily, to Carl (Bruce Willis), the stingy manager of Tip Top Construction.

After the apparent randomness of the opening reels, which portray Sully's cheerfully adversarial relationship with much of life, Benton has adapted Richard Russo's novel in such a way that the film accrues strength through the sprouting of carefully planted seeds. Sully's long-running feud with the local cop finally lands him in jail, and a visit to what had been his father's home, now boarded up, ends up providing some hope for the future.

Playing 10 years younger than his real age with no problem, Newman delivers one of his most engaging performances in years, the sort of old coot to be found in every small town. In her second-to-last role, Tandy has some ominous initial lines, saying "I've got a feeling God's creeping in on me. I've got a feeling this is the year he'll lower the broom." She's very good, as always, and the film is dedicated to her.

Willis, who curiously is not billed in the front credits nor in the print art, delivers a tangy turn.

1994: NOMINATIONS: Actor (Paul Newman), Adapted Screenplay

•

NOBODY WAVED GOODBYE

1964, 80 mins, Canada b/w

Dir Don Owen ***Prod*** Roman Kroitor, Don Owen ***Scr*** Don Owen ***Ph*** John Spotton ***Ed*** John Spotton, Donald Ginsberg ***Mus*** Eldon Rathburn

Act Peter Kastner, Julie Biggs, Claude Rae, Toby Tarnow, Charmion King, Ron Taylor (National Film Board of Canada)

This is a simple story, simply told, about a couple of Toronto juves, the boy typically smart-alecky, the girl attractive, decent and naive. From truancy and petty offenses, the road is downhill until by fadeout the young couple is split, the girl pregnant, and the boy having to decide whether to go back and face the music for theft while there's still time to rehabilitate himself.

It's not a flawless film by any means. Some of the dialogue is dull. The acting in instances is bordering on bush league. The camera work veers to the pretentious. By and large, however, even if the story line becomes hokey and a little soap-operaish in content, the film could be a winner.

Peter Kastner and Julie Biggs have high and low points in the leads, but they're naturally charming enough to get away with momentary lapses in their performance.

•

NOCTURNE

1946, 86 mins, US Ⓥ ⊙ b/w

Dir Edwin L. Marin ***Prod*** Joan Harrison ***Scr*** Jonathan Latimer ***Ph*** Harry J. Wild ***Ed*** Elmo Williams ***Mus*** Leigh Harline ***Art*** Albert S. D'Agostino, Robert Boyle

Act George Raft, Lynn Bari, Virginia Huston, Joseph Pevney (RKO)

Nocturne is a detective thriller with action and suspense plentiful and hard-bitten mood of story sustained by Edwin L. Marin's direction. There's some confusion towards windup in pulling all threads of tale together but this was apparently due to editing problem in keeping footage to tight 86 minutes' running time.

George Raft is seen as hardboiled detective lieutenant whose stubbornness leads to uncovering a murder previously tagged a suicide. He gives his usual, slow-paced, tough touch to assignment to make it thoroughly effective. Costar Lynn Bari, a prime suspect through much of the footage, turns in a capable job. Virginia Huston is interesting as Bari's songstress sister and sings three tunes.

Plot has Edward Ashley, composer, found dead in his swank Hollywood home, an apparent suicide. Police accept theory, all but Raft, who can't believe the Ashley character is type to shoot himself in middle of composing tune.

•

NOISES OFF

1992, 104 mins, US Ⓥ ⊙ col

Dir Peter Bogdanovich ***Prod*** Frank Marshall ***Scr*** Marty Kaplan ***Ph*** Tim Suhrstedt ***Ed*** Lisa Day ***Mus*** Phil Marshall (adapt.) ***Art*** Norman Newberry

Act Carol Burnett, Michael Caine, Denholm Elliott, Julie Hagerty, Marilu Henner, Christopher Reeve (Touchstone/Amblin)

Michael Frayn's [1982] play centered on a theatrical company bumbling through the British provinces in a silly sex comedy, *Nothing On*. With the first act taken up with a disastrous dress rehearsal, Frayn's coup de theatre came in the second act, when the curtain came up on the behind-the-scenes shenanigans of a feuding cast. Third act was devoted to a presentation of the play so lax that most of the lines were ad libbed.

In Marty Kaplan's smart adaptation, the company is an American troupe working toward a New York opening. Action is framed—and the acts are divided—by director Michael Caine fretting outside a Broadway theater during the opening-night performance. Otherwise, Kaplan and director Peter Bogdanovich are faithful to their source.

Thesps include Carol Burnett as a slovenly housekeeper; John Ritter as a real estate agent planning to give sexy Nicollette Sheridan a personal tour of the bedroom; Christopher Reeve and Marilu Henner as the owners of the home who slip back into Britain from their tax haven in Spain; and Denholm Elliott as an inept burglar.

Bogdanovich has judged his approach to the material astutely, resisting impulses toward comic overkill or transferring focus away from the stage. He takes his cue from the actors, and the camera is always in the right place.

•

NOMADS

1985, 92 mins, US Ⓥ col

Dir John McTiernan ***Prod*** George Pappas, Cassian Elwes ***Scr*** John McTiernan ***Ph*** Steven Ramsey ***Ed*** Michael John Bateman ***Mus*** Bill Conti ***Art*** Marcia Hinds

Act Lesley-Anne Down, Pierce Brosnan, Anna-Maria Montecelli, Frances Ray, Jeannie Elias, Alan Alitry (Cinema International/Kastner)

Nomads avoids the more obvious ripped-guts devices in favor of dramatic visual scares. Director John McTiernan even has some kind of a love interest in his story without cluttering up the plot with sticky romance or strained eroticism. In fact, everything seems to come naturally in a tale that even has the supernatural ring true.

Pierce Brosnan plays French anthropologist Pommier who intends to settle in LA with his wife Niki (Anna-Maria Montecelli), when flesh-and-blood (seemingly) Evil Spirits of nomads he once studied in arctic and desert regions materialize to haunt him. They now look like death-pale punkers.

The acting of Brosnan and Lesley-Anne Down (as a doctor) is the more effective for being restrained. Singer Adam Ant is seen as one of the Nomads.

•

NO MAN OF HER OWN

1932, 75 mins, US Ⓥ ⊙ b/w

Dir Wesley Ruggles ***Scr*** Maurine Watkins, Milton H. Gropper ***Ph*** Leo Tover

Act Clark Gable, Carole Lombard, Dorothy Mackaill, Grant Mitchell, George Barbier, Elizabeth Patterson (Paramount)

Title is borrowed from the Val Lewton best-seller, *No Bed of Her Own*, which was originally bought for Clark Gable and Miriam Hopkins. After considerable trouble adapting the Lewton story for the screen and for Will Hays's okay, it was decided to turn out another story [by Edmund Goulding and Benjamin Glazer] under the *No Man of Her Own* title. Since then, Hopkins stamped her feet at Par and Carole Lombard was cast for the part opp Gable.

Gable is a swank card gyp who hits the trail heavy for the women, but in his supporting company, from Lombard down, Paramount doesn't cheat him at all. It is largely the good cast, direction and some of the comedy arising mostly out of the wisecracks that makes *No Man of Her Own* acceptable film fare.

Gable was under loan to Par for this one, his first away from the Metro apron-strings.

Story revolves around a crooked gambler who marries a small-town girl on a bet and finally does time in order to clear the mud off his feet for her.

•

NO MAN OF HER OWN

1950, 97 mins, US b/w

Dir Mitchell Leisen ***Prod*** Richard Maibaum ***Scr*** Sally Benson, Catherine Turney ***Ph*** Daniel L. Fapp ***Ed*** Alma Macrorie ***Mus*** Hugo Friedhofer ***Art*** Hans Dreier, Henry Bumstead

Act Barbara Stanwyck, John Lund, Phyllis Thaxter, Lyle Bettger, Jane Cowl, Milburn Stone (Paramount)

No Man of Her Own combines an adult love story with melodrama, runs off with the intensity of a full-bloom soap opera, and is altogether satisfying screen dramatics [from the novel *I Married a Dead Man* by Cornell Woolrich, writing as William Irish].

Barbara Stanwyck does a beautiful job of portraying the heroine, a girl who has been kicked out by her lover after becoming pregnant. She takes advantage of a train accident to assume the identity of a fellow passenger killed in the wreck and moves in with the latter's in-laws to assure her son a home and the love of good people. Her happiness is threatened when the ex-lover tracks her down.

John Lund wraps up his role as the man who falls in love with a girl he believes to be the widow of his dead brother. It's a fine job.

•

NO MAN'S LAND

1987, 106 mins, US Ⓥ ⊙ col

Dir Peter Werner ***Prod*** Joseph Stern, Dick Wolf ***Scr*** Dick Wolf ***Ph*** Hiro Narita ***Ed*** Steve Cohen ***Mus*** Basil Poledouris ***Art*** Paul Peters

Act Charlie Sheen, D. B. Sweeney, Randy Quaid, Lara Harris, Bill Duke, R. D. Call (Orion)

No Man's Land is a stylish thriller about a lower-class rookie cop becoming caught up in the fast-lane high life of the filthy rich car thief he's assigned to nail.

Charlie Sheen and D. B. Sweeney are both extremely effective as two young men, barely into their 20s, whose diametrically opposed backgrounds make for a dynamic and ultimately deadly relationship.

Sweeney is assigned by boss Randy Quaid to take a job at a Porsche garage that doubles as a "chop shop," where stolen cars are broken up and reassembled as untraceable new vehicles. Quaid suspects the wealthy owner, Sheen, of having killed another policeman, and Sweeney, despite his total inexperience, is supposed to get the goods on him.

A little joyriding and partying with the handsome, crafty Sheen easily seduces Sweeney into taking a softer view of illegal activity. He comes to like Sheen a lot and, furthermore, gets sexually involved with the latter's beautiful sister (Lara Harris).

Scenarist Dick Wolf is a vet of both *Hill Street Blues* and *Miami Vice* and both influences turn up here, as he has carefully worked out the script to offer opportunities for the character nuances of the first show and the flash of the second.

•

NO MERCY

1986, 105 mins, US Ⓥ ⦿ col

Dir Richard Pearce ***Prod*** D. Constantine Conte ***Scr*** Jim Carabatsos ***Ph*** Michel Brault ***Ed*** Jerry Greenberg, Bill Yahraus ***Mus*** Alan Silvestri ***Art*** Patrizia Von Brandenstein

Act Richard Gere, Kim Basinger, Jeroen Krabbe, George Dzundza, Gary Basaraba, William Atherton (Tri-Star Delphi IV & V)

Despite some graphically brutal violence and a fair bit of "too-cool" police jargon, *No Mercy* turns out to be a step above most other films in this blooming genre of lone-cop-turned-vigilante stories.

Eddie Jillette (Richard Gere) and his partner Joe Collins (Gary Basaraba) get wind of a contract to kill a Louisiana crime overlord. They go undercover as the hit men, but find they are dealing with a much bigger, much deadlier fish as Collins is murdered brutally. Jillette has only one lead in tracking his partner's murder, a mysterious blonde (Kim Basinger).

From the native, wild beauty of the Louisiana swamplands to the steamy, colourful French quarter of New Orleans, the film is a tightly woven piece.

Credit also goes to Gere, now sporting a noticeably older, grayer look, who manages to bring that maturity to his often typecast roles of the angry young man.

•

NONE BUT THE BRAVE

1965, 105 mins, US/Japan Ⓥ ⦿ ▭ col

Dir Frank Sinatra ***Prod*** Frank Sinatra, Kikumaru Okuda ***Scr*** John Twist, Katsuya Susaki ***Ph*** Harold Lipstein ***Ed*** Sam O' Steen ***Mus*** John Williams ***Art*** LeRoy Deane

Act Frank Sinatra, Clint Walker, Tommy Sands, Bill Dexter, Tony Bill, Tatsuya Mihashi (Artanis/Tokyo Eiga-Toho)

Marking the first joint screen venture actually filmed by an American and Japanese company in the U.S., *None but the Brave* manages a high level of interest via its unusual premise and action-adventure backdrop.

Frank Sinatra, who also stars with Clint Walker and produces, makes his directorial bow and is responsible for some good effects in maintaining a suspenseful pace. The compact and mostly tense screenplay tells its story [by Kikumaru Okuda] through the eyes of a Japanese lieutenant, commanding a small detachment of troops forgotten on an uncharted South Pacific island where an American plane carrying U.S. Marines crash lands.

A truce is arranged by the Japanese commander and Walker, the American pilot and senior officer, after Sinatra, as a pharmacist's mate, amputates the leg of one of the Japanese soldiers wounded in a skirmish with the Americans. Americans' radio is believed destroyed in the crash, and with no means of communication for the Japanese it seems that both sides are destined to sweat out the war on the island.

Sinatra appears only intermittently, his character only important in the operation scene which he enacts dramatically.

•

NONE BUT THE LONELY HEART

1944, 110 mins, US Ⓥ b/w

Dir Clifford Odets ***Prod*** David Hempstead ***Scr*** Clifford Odets ***Ph*** George Barnes ***Ed*** Roland Gross ***Mus*** Hanns Eisler ***Art*** Albert S. D'Agostino, Jack Okey

Act Cary Grant, Ethel Barrymore, Barry Fitzgerald, June Duprez, Jane Wyatt, Dan Duryea (RKO)

With the sotto voce accent on any social significance, *Heart* [from Richard Llewellyn's novel] emerges as a medley of simple romance in London's east side, interspersed with a little melodrama. The meller phase doesn't bestir matters until almost an hour and a half from scratch when the limey hoodlums hijack Ike Weber's pawnshop and beat up the kindly loan broker.

Cary Grant starts as a shiftless cockney who lets his struggling mother (Ethel Barrymore) fend for herself with her small, secondhand shop beneath their dingy home until the pawnbroker-friend (well underplayed by Konstantin Shayne) tips him off that his mother is dying of cancer. When Grant sees the light and decides to cease vagabonding, he becomes an almost model son. An expert clock and furniture repairer and piano-tuner, he helps make his mother's little business thrive until he himself gets mixed up with the mob, while the mother succumbs to the temptations of dealing in stolen goods.

1944: Best Supp. Actress (Ethel Barrymore)

NOMINATIONS: Best Actor (Cary Grant), Editing, Scoring of a Dramatic Picture

•

NO, NO, NANETTE

1940, 96 mins, US b/w

Dir Herbert Wilcox ***Prod*** Herbert Wilcox ***Scr*** Ken Englund ***Ph*** Russell Metty ***Ed*** Elmo Williams ***Mus*** Vincent Youmans

Act Anna Neagle, Richard Carlson, Victor Mature, Roland Young, Helen Broderick, ZaSu Pitts (Suffolk/RKO Radio)

Musical comedies rarely have much story. That's all right, no one expects them to. Plot is compensated for in a hit tune show by good music. That's an elementary show business lesson taught in a class that producer Herbert Wilcox must have skipped. In making a film version of the 1925 Broadway hit [by Frank Mandel, Otto Harbach, Vincent Youmans and Emil Nyltray], Wilcox saves all the book but very little of the music. "Tea for Two" and "I Want to Be Happy," as well as the title tune, "No, No, Nanette" have been reduced to virtually incidental music.

Even at that, Wilcox has been fortunate. *Nanette* has a pretty good plot as musical comedy plots go. He has erred, however, in complicating it instead of simplifying it, as was needed. Wilcox has been lavish, however, in instilling production values in *Nanette* and there's no denying, despite their age, the lilt of the Vincent Youmans tunes.

Anna Neagle, as the little Miss Fix-It who sparks the film, is passable. Roland Young, with accustomed facility, tops the cast-appeal. Runners-up are Helen Broderick and ZaSu Pitts, which makes it clear that all the honors go to the older generation. Neagle and the youngsters, Richard Carlson, Victor Mature and Eve Arden, show to no advantage against such a trio of comedy vets.

Yarn finds Young a gay oldster with a penchant for making people happy, particularly pretty girls, by promising them help to get ahead in their fields. Neagle, as Young's niece, sets about getting each of the femmes the things she wants, thus keeping from Young's wife the sordid details. Mature is a theatrical producer and Carlson an artist. Nanette works on each to take the troublemaking females under their wings and save the family honor.

•

NOOSE HANGS HIGH, THE

1948, 77 mins, US b/w

Dir Charles Barton ***Prod*** Charles Barton ***Scr*** John Grant, Howard Harris ***Ph*** Charles Van Enger ***Ed*** Harry Reynolds ***Mus*** Walter Schumann ***Art*** Edward L. Ilou

Act Lou Costello, Bud Abbott, Cathy Downs, Joseph Calleia, Leon Errol (Eagle Lion)

The Noose Hangs High gives Abbott & Costello full opportunity to display their fine slapstick art.

Routines, despite their age, have a freshness that wallops the risibilities in the artful hands of the comics. All of the gags are good with several that reach the acme of hilarious nonsense. Such a one is the on-and-off pants routine, a display of apt timing and high comedy talent. Another is the oldie, "you can't be here," played to top results.

A lot of writers had their hands in the plotting, but the story line is only a thread upon which to hang the A&C routines. Pic kicks off with window-washing setup that has the boys fumbling on a high window ledge. From there it moves into a mistaken-identity theme, involving comics with gambling syndicate and a missing $50,000 bet.

•

NORA PRENTISS

1947, 110 mins, US b/w

Dir Vincent Sherman ***Prod*** William Jacobs ***Scr*** N. Richard Nash ***Ph*** James Wong Howe ***Ed*** Owen Marks ***Mus*** Franz Waxman ***Art*** Anton Grot

Act Ann Sheridan, Kent Smith, Bruce Bennett, Robert Alda, Rosemary DeCamp, John Ridgely (Warner)

Nora Prentiss is an overlong melodrama, a story of romance between a married man and a girl. But it's never quite believable. Ann Sheridan makes much of her role but the production has unsympathetic slant for leads and a lack of smoothness. Background is San Francisco and New York, with authentic footage of both sites a physical aide.

Yarn [by Paul Webster and Jack Sobell] concerns a stuffy, middle-aged doctor who falls in love with a night-club singer. To follow his love to New York, the doctor fakes death, destroying the body of a patient who had died in his office and assuming latter's identity. This fact traps him later when he's arrested for the killing himself. Plot is supposedly based on actual insurance case history, but script is full of holes that make for featherweight motivation.

Sheridan is the singer, and has two tunes to warble. As the doctor, Kent Smith is okay dramatically in a part that doesn't hold much water. Bruce Bennett, costarred, has little to do as a medico friend of Smith's.

•

NORMA RAE

1979, 113 mins, US Ⓥ ⦿ ▭ col

Dir Martin Ritt ***Prod*** Tamara Asseyev, Alex Rose ***Scr*** Irving Ravetch, Harriet Frank ***Ph*** John A. Alonzo ***Ed*** Sidney Levin ***Mus*** David Shire ***Art*** Walter Scott Herndon

Act Sally Field, Beau Bridges, Ron Leibman, Pat Hingle, Gail Strickland, Lonny Chapman (20th Century-Fox)

Norma Rae is that rare entity, an intelligent film with heart. Films about unions haven't always fared well at the box office, but that didn't deter director Martin Ritt and screenwriters from updating the traditional management-labor struggles to a sharp contemporary setting. Now the battle is being waged in Southern textile mills, where the din of the machinery is virtually unbearable, and workers either go deaf or suffer the consumptive effects of "brown lung" disease.

Ron Leibman arrives on the scene as a New York-based labor organizer, who picks Sally Field as his most likely convert. This unlikely pairing of Jewish radicalism and Southern miasma is the core of *Norma Rae*, and is made real and touching by the individual performances of Leibman and Field.

The pacing is fresh and never laggard, and *Norma Rae* virtually hums right along.

1979: Best Actress (Sally Field), Song ("It Goes Like This")

NOMINATIONS: Best Picture, Adapted Screenplay

•

NORTE, EL
(THE NORTH)

1983, 139 mins, US Ⓥ col

Dir Gregory Nava ***Prod*** Anna Thomas ***Scr*** Gregory Nava, Anna Thomas ***Ph*** James Glennon ***Ed*** Betsy Blankett

Act Zaide Silvia Gutierrez, David Villalpando, Ernest Gomez Cruz, Alicia del Lago, Eraclio Zepeda, Stella Quan (American Playhouse/Independent)

An American Playhouse production for public television, *El Norte* is the first epic in the history of American independents. Each section in the three-part film lasts approximately 45 minutes.

The Guatemalan seg has a folkloric character about it. We are introduced to a closely knit family in a picturesque setting, but the paradise is deceiving. The 1982 military coup by dissident army officers has led to a wave of political violence and terror, whereupon some 200,000 Guatemalans have sought refuge in Mexico or elsewhere "to the north" (thus the film's title).

The Mexican seg deals with a brother and sister, the two surviving members of the Guatemalan Indian family, on their way north in search of a contact, who might help them to cross the border illegally into California. They are now facing abject poverty with only prostitution and ghetto slavery open as options. This is the strongest of the three parts.

The American seg finds the brother and sister living as Mexican illegals in Los Angeles, he as a waiter in a plush restaurant and she, first as a sweatshop assistant and then as a servant for a rich family. The ending ties all the threads together while offering a new dramatic twist of its own.

If all this sounds familiar, then accept the epic as a freestyle updating of John Steinbeck's *The Grapes of Wrath*. Perhaps it is too much of a tearjerker in the long run. However, it is beautifully lensed and comes across as a kind of giant Renaissance canvas.

•

NORTH, THE

SEE: EL NORTE

•

NORTH

1994, 88 mins, US Ⓥ col

Dir Rob Reiner ***Prod*** Rob Reiner, Alan Zweibel ***Scr*** Alan Zweibel, Andrew Scheinman ***Ph*** Adam Greenberg ***Ed*** Robert Leighton ***Mus*** Marc Shaiman ***Art*** J. Michael Riva

Act Elijah Wood, Bruce Willis, Jon Lovitz, Matthew McCurley, Alan Arkin, Dan Aykroyd (Castle Rock)

Rob Reiner's *North* is a shaggy-dog tale of a boy who "divorces" his parents and goes on an arduous trek to find his ideal mother and father. Rather than creating a modern *Wizard of Oz*, this noble misfire just barely manages to pull back the curtain and reveal the man manipulating the image.

The single-named title character (Elijah Wood) is the perfect preteen, but his interaction with work-obsessed parents (Jason Alexander, Julia Louis-Dreyfus) is increasingly having a negative impact on his psyche. So he goes to his "private place"—a chair store in a mall—to think it out. There he meets a man dressed in an Easter bunny suit (Bruce Willis) who listens to his problem. North's action throws his parents into simultaneous comas, and an eccentric judge (Alan Arkin) rules that North must reconcile with his family or find suitable new parents within two months, otherwise he will be remanded to an orphanage. The boy travels the globe in his quest.

Tech credits are smooth, and Reiner even pulls off a fantasy song-and-dance sequence that suggests *North* might have made a dandy musical.

•

NORTH BY NORTHWEST

1959, 136 mins, UK Ⓥ ⊙ col

Dir Alfred Hitchcock ***Prod*** Alfred Hitchcock ***Scr*** Ernest Lehman ***Ph*** Robert Burks ***Ed*** George Tomasini ***Mus*** Bernard Herrmann ***Art*** Robert Boyle, William A. Horning

Act Cary Grant, Eva Marie Saint, James Mason, Jessie Royce Landis, Leo G. Carroll, Martin Landau (M-G-M)

North by Northwest is the Alfred Hitchcock mixture—suspense, intrigue, comedy, humor. Seldom has the concoction been served up so delectably. Hitchcock uses actual locations—the Plaza in New York, the Ambassador East in Chicago, Grand Central Station, the 20th Century Limited, United Nations headquarters in Manhattan, Mount Rushmore National Monument, the plains of Indiana. One scene, where the hero is ambushed by an airplane on the flat, sun-baked prairie, is a brilliant use of location.

Cary Grant brings technique and charm to the central character. He is a Madison Avenue man-about-Manhattan, sleekly handsome, carelessly twice-divorced, debonair as a cigarette ad. The story gets underway when he's mistaken for a U.S. intelligence agent by a pack of foreign agents headed by James Mason. The complications are staggering but they play like an Olympic version of a three-legged race.

Grant's problem is to avoid getting knocked off by Mason's gang without tipping them that he is a classic case of the innocent bystander. The case is serious, but Hitchcock's macabre sense of humor and instinct for romantic byplay never allows it to stay grim for too long. Suspense is deliberately broken for relief and then skillfully re-established.

Eva Marie Saint dives headfirst into Mata Hari and shows she can be unexpectedly and thoroughly glamorous. She also manages the difficult impression of seeming basically innocent while explaining how she becomes Mason's mistress. Mason, in a rather stock role, is properly forbidding.

Robert Burks's photography, whether in the hot yellows of the prairie plain, or the soft green of South Dakota forests, is lucid and imaginatively composed. It is the first Metro release in VistaVision. Bernard Herrmann's score is a tingling one, particularly in the Mount Rushmore sequences, but light where mood requires.

1959: NOMINATIONS: Best Original Story & Screenplay, Color Art Direction, Editing

•

NORTH DALLAS FORTY

1979, 119 mins, US Ⓥ ⊙ ▭ col

Dir Ted Kotcheff ***Prod*** Frank Yablans ***Scr*** Frank Yablans, Ted Kotcheff, Peter Gent ***Ph*** Paul Lohmann ***Ed*** Jay Kamen ***Mus*** John Scott ***Art*** Alfred Sweeney

Act Nick Nolte, Mac Davis, Charles Durning, Dabney Coleman, Dayle Haddon, Bo Svenson (Paramount)

It's no surprise that the National Football League refused to cooperate in the making of *North Dallas Forty*. The production is a most realistic, hard-hitting and perceptive look at the seamy side of pro football.

What distinguishes this screen adaptation of Peter Gent's bestseller is the exploration of a human dimension almost never seen in sports pix. Most people understand that modern-day athletes are just cogs in a big business wheel, but getting that across on the screen is a whole different matter. And in large measure, that success is due to a bravura performance in the lead role by Nick Nolte.

Ted Kotcheff keeps the action flowing smoothly, and has perfectly captured the locker-room intensity and post-game letdown that never shows up on the tube.

•

NORTHERN PURSUIT

1943, 93 mins, US Ⓥ b/w

Dir Raoul Walsh ***Prod*** Jack Chertok ***Scr*** Frank Gruber, Alvah Bessie ***Ph*** Sid Hickox ***Ed*** Frank Killifer ***Mus*** Adolph Deutsch

Act Errol Flynn, Julie Bishop, Helmut Dantine, John Ridgely, Gene Lockhart, Tom Tully (Warner)

This one combines the elements of Nazi spies with the lusty and vigorous adventures of a Canadian Northwest mountie. Yarn pits Errol Flynn as a heroic mountie against Nazi flyer Helmut Dantine, who's been dropped in the Hudson Bay region by a sub for a war mission in Canada. But Dantine is captured in the wild snow country by Flynn and John Ridgely, with Flynn devising plan to gain confidence of the flyer to smash spy ring.

Snow-blanketed north is a fresh background for staging a Nazi spy chase; and full advantage is taken to blend the scenery with the dramatics. Particularly effective is the process photography with several spectacular shots. At opening is the surfacing of the sub in the ice-covered waters; later a snow avalanche.

Both script [from a story by Leslie T. White], and direction by Raoul Walsh, are in keeping with the best traditions of outdoor melodramatics.

•

NORTH SEA HIJACK
(US: FFOLKES)

1980, 99 mins, UK Ⓥ col

Dir Andrew V. McLaglen ***Prod*** Elliott Kastner ***Scr*** Jack Davies ***Ph*** Tony Imi ***Ed*** Alan Strachan ***Mus*** Michael J. Lewis ***Art*** Bert Davey

Act Roger Moore, James Mason, Anthony Perkins, Michael Parks, Jack Watson (Universal)

The biggest attraction is the banter between Roger Moore and the various types with whom he comes in conflict during his preparations to save a hijacked supply ship.

A misogynistic but dedicated frogman, whose private crew of frogmen are the only seeming rescuers of the ship, Moore is today's ideal male chauvinistic pig. And delights in it. He doesn't even mind telling the British Prime Minister (a lady, of course) what he thinks of the situation.

He's ably supported by James Mason as a by-the-book admiral. Mason is also given star billing and almost builds his role into deserving it, but Anthony Perkins and especially Michael Parks certainly belong below the title.

•

NORTH STAR, THE

1943, 105 mins, US Ⓥ b/w

Dir Lewis Milestone ***Prod*** Samuel Goldwyn ***Scr*** Lillian Hellman ***Ph*** James Wong Howe ***Ed*** Daniel Mandell ***Mus*** Aaron Copland

Act Anne Baxter, Dana Andrews, Walter Huston, Walter Brennan, Farley Granger, Erich von Stroheim (RKO)

Samuel Goldwyn as the producer and Lillian Hellman, the writer, team to tell of the Nazi invasion of the Soviet Union. As entertainment, however, there's too much running time consumed before the film actually gets into its story and, in parts, it is seemingly a too-obviously contrived narrative detailing the virtues of the Soviet regime.

Setting the background for the actual climax is a long and sometimes tedious one. The early parts of the film are almost always colorful in depicting the simple life of the villagers around whom this story revolves, but it's a question of too premeditatedly setting a stage of a simple, peace-loving people who, through the bestiality of the enemy, are driven to an heroic defense that must, in time, become legendary. For this is the story of the Soviet people as seen through the eyes of a small village.

Hellman's story, when she finally gets around to it, is a parallel one, dealing with a picnic group that's suddenly called on to rush arms through the German lines to their guerrilla comrades when the sudden invasion catches them unawares while on a walking trip. It is an exciting tale from here on in.

1943: NOMINATIONS: Best Original Screenplay, B&W Cinematography, B&W Art Direction, Scoring of a Dramatic Picture, Sound, Special Effects

•

NORTH TO ALASKA

1960, 122 mins, US Ⓥ ⊙ ▭ col

Dir Henry Hathaway ***Prod*** Henry Hathaway ***Scr*** John Lee Mahin, Martin Rackin, Claude Binyon ***Ph*** Leon Shamroy ***Ed*** Dorothy Spencer ***Mus*** Lionel Newman ***Art*** Duncan Cramer, Jack Martin Smith

Act John Wayne, Stewart Granger, Ernie Kovacs, Fabian, Capucine, Mickey Shaughnessy (20th Century-Fox)

North to Alaska is a good-humored, old-fashioned, no-holds-barred, all-stops-out northern, a kind of rowdy second cousin to a not-very-adult western. It's the sort of easy-going, slaphappy entertainment that must be accepted in absolutely the right spirit to be fully appreciated.

The screenplay (based on *Birthday Gift*, an unproduced play by Lazlo Fodor, adapted from an idea by John Kafka) takes an instantly recognizable yarn and wisely plays it for laughs. It's the story of the successful Alaskan gold prospector who transports a girl from Seattle north to Alaska for his lovesick partner, then proceeds to fall in love with her, she with him.

The three brawls director Henry Hathaway has staged are classics of the cinemmatic art of make-believe pugilistics. The first, at the outset of the film, is danced off amidst a barroom full of gushing beer keys. Second, highlighted by a mistaken piece of strategy in which star John Wayne unleashes a rail wagon down a steep incline at his foes but forgets to get out of it himself, is staged in a thorough water setting. Third, at the tail-end of the picture, is one big mud-bath.

Wayne and Ernie Kovacs share comedy honors. Director Hathaway ought to have curbed some of the excess zeal exhibited by Fabian and Stewart Granger.

Art directors have selected some fine Alaskan-looking sites in four areas of California and dressed them up with sets faithful to the popular notion of that northern frontier at the turn of the century.

•

NORTH WEST FRONTIER
(US: FLAME OVER INDIA)

1959, 129 mins, UK Ⓥ ▭ col

Dir J. Lee Thompson ***Prod*** Marcel Hellman ***Scr*** Robin Estridge ***Ph*** Geoffrey Unsworth ***Ed*** Freddie Wilson ***Mus*** Mischa Spoliansky ***Art*** Alex Vetchinsky

Act Kenneth More, Lauren Bacall, Herbert Lom, Wilfrid Hyde White, I. S. Johar, Ursula Jeans (Rank)

From a smash opening to quietly confident fade, *North West Frontier* is basically the ageless chase yarn, transferred from the prairie to the sun-baked plains of India and done with a spectacular flourish [adapted from a screenplay by Frank Nugent, based on an original story by Patrick Ford and Will Price]. Handled with tremendous assurance by J. Lee Thompson, the film is reminiscent of the same director's *Ice Cold in Alex*, with an ancient locomotive replacing the ambulance in that desert war story and with hordes of beturbaned tribesmen substituting for the Nazi patrols.

Time is the turn of the century when the English still held sway in India. Kenneth More plays an officer ordered to take a boy prince, sacred figurehead to the Hindus, to safety in the teeth of Moslems. In company with an assorted group, More makes his getaway from a besieged citadel in a makeshift coach drawn by a worn-out locomotive. Throughout, the cast serves the job expertly, More coming through as solid and dependable if a shade too unemotional. Lauren Bacall scores with a keen delineation of the prince's outspoken nurse. Herbert Lom is first-rate as a journalist. I. S. Johar is the hit of the picture as the Indian railroad man.

•

NORTH WEST MOUNTED POLICE

1940, 125 mins, US col

Dir Cecil B. DeMille, Arthur Rosson, Eric Stacey ***Prod*** Cecil B. DeMille ***Scr*** Alan LeMay, Jesse Lasky, Jr., C. Gardner Sullivan ***Ph*** Victor Milner, W. Howard Greene ***Ed*** Anne Bauchens ***Mus*** Victor Young ***Art*** Hans Dreier, Roland Anderson

Act Gary Cooper, Madeleine Carroll, Preston Foster, Paulette Goddard, Robert Preston, George Bancroft (Paramount)

The story is founded upon an incident of insurrection and bloodshed which took place in and around Regina in 1885, when Canadian troops finally subdued a settlers' discontent and revolt.

With that much fact to start from, scripters weave a story which has its exciting moments, a reasonable and convincing romance and a hero who is a pure Texan from down near the Rio Grande. Gary Cooper is the man from the South, and although Canadian uprisings are none of his business (he is one of the Texas Rangers on search for a murderer) he finds himself in the middle of gunplay before the end of the second reel.

Preston Foster as the sergeant-leader of the redcoats gets the better of Cooper in the contest for Madeleine Carroll. Foster has the girl and Cooper has George Bancroft, the heavy, tied up with his lariat and on his way back home. Before that takes place there are innumerable plot complications involving Paulette Goddard, a half-breed vixen; Robert Preston, one of the mounted who faltered in outpost duty; Walter Hampden, a big Indian chief; and Akim Tamiroff and Lynne Overman, who stage their own private duel of marksmanship, which is hilarious.

Interesting novelty is an introductory soundtrack talk by DeMille in which he recounts the historical basis for the film.

1940: Best Editing

NOMINATIONS: Best Color Cinematography, Color Art Direction, Original Score, Sound

•

NORTHWEST PASSAGE

1940, 125 mins, US Ⓥ ⊙ col

Dir King Vidor ***Prod*** Hunt Stromberg ***Scr*** Laurence Stallings, Talbot Jennings ***Ph*** Sidney Wagner, William V. Skall ***Ed*** Conrad A. Nervig ***Mus*** Herbert Stothart ***Art*** Cedric Gibbons, Malcolm Brown

Act Spencer Tracy, Robert Young, Walter Brennan, Ruth Hussey, Nat Pendleton, Donald McBride (M-G-M)

Northwest Passage, which hit a negative cost of nearly $2 million, is a fine epic adventure. The picture carries through only the first half of the novel [by Kenneth Roberts] and is so designated in the main title. The title is misleading from an historical standpoint as it only covers the one expedition through upper New York state to the St. Lawrence territory where the village of a hostile tribe is wiped out.

Spencer Tracy is brilliantly impressive as the dominating and driving leader of Rogers' Rangers, a band of 160 trained settlers inducted into service to clean up the hostile tribes to make homes and families safe. Robert Young, as the Harvardian who joins the Rangers to sketch Indians, has a more virile role than others assigned him and turns in a fine performance. Walter Brennan provides a typically fine characterization as the friend of Young.

There's a peculiar fascination in the unfolding of the historical narrative and adventure of the inspired band on the march to and from the Indian village. It's a continual battle against natural hazards, possible sudden attacks by ambushing enemies, and a display of indomitable courage to drive through swamps and over mountains for days at a time without food. It's grim and stark drama of those pioneers who blazed trails through the wilderness to make living in this country safe for their families and descendants.

1940: NOMINATION: Best Color Cinematography

•

NOSFERATU

SEE: NOSFERATU EINE SYMPHONIE DES GRAUENS

•

NOSFERATU EINE SYMPHONIE DES GRAUENS

(NOSFERATU; NOSFERATU THE VAMPIRE)

1922, 70 mins, Germany Ⓥ ⊙ ⊗ b/w

Dir F. W. Murnau ***Scr*** Henrik Galeen ***Ph*** Fritz Arno Wagner

Act Max Schreck, Alexander Granach, Gustav von Wangenheim, Greta Schroeder, Karl Schnell, Ruth Landshoft (Parana)

Story is claimed to have been inspired by [Bram Stoker's novel] *Dracula*. Action details the forages of a nobleman who is dead yet alive, making nighttime raids on human beings and compelling them to become subservient to him by sucking the blood from their necks, often plaguing them to death. His especial delight is a pretty woman.

Murnau proved his directorial artistry in *Sunrise* for Fox about three years earlier, but in this picture he's a master artisan demonstrating not only a knowledge of the subtler side of directing but in photography.

One shot of the sun cracking at dawn is an eye filler. Among others of extremely imaginative beauty is one which takes in a schooner sailing in a rippling stream photographed in such a manner that it has the illusion of color. Empty shattering buildings photographed to suggest the desperate desolation brought on by the vampire is extremely effective symbolism.

Max Schreck as the vampire is an able pantomimist and works clocklike, his makeup suggesting everything that's goose pimply.

•

NOSFERATU THE VAMPIRE

SEE: NOSFERATU

•

NO SMALL AFFAIR

1984, 102 mins, US Ⓥ ⊙ col

Dir Jerry Schatzberg ***Prod*** William Sackheim ***Scr*** Charles Bolt, Terence Mulcahy ***Ph*** Vilmos Zsigmond ***Ed*** Priscilla Nedd, Eve Newman, Melvin Shapiro ***Mus*** Rupert Holmes ***Art*** Robert Boyle

Act Jon Cryer, Demi Moore, George Wendt, Peter Frechette, Elizabeth Daily, Ann Wedgeworth (Columbia-Delphi II)

No Small Affair is an okay coming-of-age romance [from a screen story by Charles Bolt] in which the believability of the leading characters far outweighs that of many of the situations in which the script places them.

Film is set in San Francisco and has Jon Cryer as a 16-year-old who's precocious in still photography but not much else, being difficult socially and unresponsive to girls his own age.

By chance, he snaps a shot of a sharp looking gal (Demi Moore) by the waterfront and, by chance again, he finds her singing in a seedy North Beach nightspot. In a selfless effort to give her sluggish career a boost, he spends his entire life savings and gets her photo placed on top of 175 SF taxicabs.

Ultimately, she is invited to L.A. by a record company and, before she leaves, the inevitable occurs.

•

NOSTRADAMUS

1995, 118 mins, UK/Germany Ⓥ col

Dir Roger Christian ***Prod*** Edward Simons, Harold Reichebner ***Scr*** Knut Boeser, Piers Ashworth ***Ph*** Denis Crossan ***Ed*** Alan Strachan ***Mus*** Barrington Pheloung ***Art*** Peter J. Hampton

Act Tcheky Karyo, F. Murray Abraham, Rutger Hauer, Amanda Plummer, Julia Ormond, Assumpta Serna (Allied Entertainments/Vereinigte)

A gaudy tableau on an epic scale, *Nostradamus* is a disappointingly conventional biopic about the noted medieval scholar/prophet. Designed as a monument, this costume drama exhibits most of the sorrows of international productions: a rambling narrative, anachronistic language and an unsuccessful blend of accents and acting styles.

While focusing on the life of the famous philsopher/scientist, Michel de Nostradame (1503–66), there's no doubt that the filmmakers see strong contemporary relevance in the tale of a man who devoted his life to fighting the ravaging ills of 16th-century Europe: uncontrollable plagues, a conservative medical establishment and the terror of the Inquisition.

Born Jewish, he managed to survive the Inquisition, the plague and the devastating death of his first wife, Marie (Julia Ormond), who shared his interest in science, to marry a second wife, Anne (Assumpta Serna), and establish another family.

Filming in Romania, France and England, novice director Roger Christian (the accomplished art director on *Alien* and *Star Wars*) endows his pic with lush visuals (kudos to lenser Denis Crossan), but he's unable to find the core of the story, and, after the first reel, pic loses its dramatic focus and momentum.

In the lead, handsome French thesp Tcheky Karyo acquits himself with a decent performance. Of the large international cast, Rutger Hauer is effective as a mad monk, F. Murray Abraham is for once effectively cast as the hero's mentor, and Amanda Plummer is so weird as Catherine de Medici that her lines almost sound campy.

•

NOT AS A STRANGER

1955, 135 mins, US b/w

Dir Stanley Kramer ***Prod*** Stanley Kramer ***Scr*** Edna Anhalt, Edward Anhalt ***Ph*** Franz Planer ***Ed*** Fred Knudtson ***Mus*** George Antheil ***Art*** Rudolph Sternad, Howard Richmond

Act Olivia de Havilland, Robert Mitchum, Frank Sinatra, Gloria Grahame, Broderick Crawford, Charles Bickford (United Artists)

Producer Stanley Kramer, a man with a penchant for offbeat choices, took Morton Thompson's best-selling novel of a young doctor as the occasion of his own directorial debut.

Some of the most interesting characterizations appear only in the second story (out of three). Charles Bickford comes near to stealing the picture. Gloria Grahame, as a neurotic widow with lots of money, also stands out, though the part is much changed from the novel and never too clear in her motivations.

Frank Sinatra is another of the players who comes close to doing a little picture stealing. And what about the hero of the story? He's Robert Mitchum and he's considerably over his acting depth. Though some scenes come off fairly well, Mitchum is poker-faced from start to finish.

1955: NOMINATION: Best Sound

•

NOTHING BUT THE BEST

1964, 99 mins, UK col

Dir Clive Donner ***Prod*** David Deutsch ***Scr*** Frederic Raphael ***Ph*** Nicolas Roeg ***Ed*** Fergus McDonell ***Mus*** Ron Grainer ***Art*** Reece Pemberton

Act Alan Bates, Denholm Elliott, Harry Andrews, Millicent Martin (Domino/Anglo Amalgamated)

This stylish British comedy takes a sly, penetrating peek at the social climbing upper classes that use the Old School tie, social connections, well-padded bank balances and the Smart Set background to further their material ambitions.

It is ruthless in its unpeeling of the dubious foibles and mannerisms of its characters, none of whom fails to have an axe to grind. It's the story of an ambitious young man of humble background who, excited by the glitter of money, business power and an entry into the fascinating world of Hunt Balls, Ascot, smart restaurants, shooting, hunting, fishin' and the rest of the trappings, lies, bluffs, smiles, cheats, loves, and smoothtalks his way to marrying the boss' daughter, and doesn't stop at murder en route.

Alan Bates, showing a previously unexplored vein of comedy, is first class as the dubious hero. This is a measured, confident performance that appeals even when he is behaving at his worst. Many of the top scenes are those with Denholm Elliott who, in fact, turns in the best acting of the lot.

•

NOTHING BUT TROUBLE

1944, 69 mins, US b/w

Dir Sam Taylor ***Prod*** B. F. Zeidman ***Scr*** Russell Rouse, Ray Golden ***Ph*** Charles Salerno, Jr., ***Ed*** Conrad A. Nervig ***Mus*** Nathaniel Shilkret ***Art*** Cedric Gibbons, Harry McAfee

Act Stan Laurel, Oliver Hardy, Mary Boland, Philip Merivale, Henry O'Neill, David Leland (M-G-M)

Story, contrasting employment void in 1932 with big demand for help in 1944, seems to have something, but after the introductory reels it gets lost in the shuffle. It then veers into a prop setup for the stars to revive the clowning they have done for years, with little new added.

In the depression era Laurel and Hardy, descendants of a long line of cooks and butlers, are seeking employment against great odds. When convinced there isn't a job to be had in America, they hit off on a tour of foreign lands.

Same situash obtains there, and they return to America in the lush era of employment. They are grabbed by Mary Boland, social-climber, to handle chores at a dinner she and her husband, Henry O'Neill, are giving in honor of David Leland, who plays the boy regent of a mythical kingdom.

•

NOTHING BUT TROUBLE

1991, 94 mins, US Ⓥ ⊙ col

Dir Dan Aykroyd ***Prod*** Robert K. Weiss ***Scr*** Dan Aykroyd ***Ph*** Dean Cundey ***Ed*** Malcolm Campbell, James Symons ***Mus*** Michael Kamen ***Art*** William Sandell

Act Chevy Chase, Dan Aykroyd, John Candy, Demi Moore (Warner/Applied Action)

First-time director Dan Aykroyd might have once parodied this sort of wretched excess in his "bad-cinema" sketches on *Saturday Night Live*. Premise, stripped to the bone, had potential: a faceless drive-through town seems to have no resident except the cop who miraculously appears to pinch unsuspecting drivers.

The one-joke starter is then taken to absurd extremes as four Manhattan yuppies get shanghaied to the village of Valkenvania, where a demented old judge (Aykroyd, in heavy makeup) metes out executioner-style justice over moving violations.

The story [by Peter Aykroyd] turns into an extended maze with Chevy Chase and Demi Moore as the principal Nintendo-ized targets running through one tepid peril after another, while mouthing banal wisecracks. It's a good bet a film is in trouble when the highlight comes from seeing John Candy in drag.

•

NOTHING PERSONAL

1995, 86 mins, UK Ⓥ col

Dir Thaddeus O'Sullivan ***Prod*** Jonathan Cavendish, Tracey Seaward ***Scr*** Daniel Mornin ***Ph*** Dick Pope ***Ed*** Michael Parker ***Mus*** Philip Appleby ***Art*** Mark Geraghty

Act Ian Hart, John Lynch, James Frain, Michael Gambon, Gary Lydon, Ruaidhri Conroy (Little Bird/Channel 4)

An uncompromising depiction of the cult of sectarian violence that has in the past created civil war in Northern Ireland, *Nothing Personal* is a totally riveting drama rigorously directed by Thaddeus O'Sullivan.

Action is set in Belfast 20 years ago, when both sides were trying to forge a truce as a way out of the escalating bloodshed. O'Sullivan and screenwriter Daniel Mornin, working from his book *All Our Fault*, carefully depict the different levels of command within a Loyalist (i.e., pro-British) paramilitary group, from their bluff leader (Michael Gambon) down to members of a trigger-happy gang who bring unrelenting violence to the city streets.

This particular unit is nominally led by Kenny (James Frain), who sees himself as a soldier in the anti-IRA struggle, but the unit is effectively run by the hotheaded Ginger (Ian Hart), a fanatical bigot for whom the only good Catholic is a dead one. The fanatical Protestants are contrasted with a Catholic, Liam Kelly (John Lynch), who isn't an IRA member and deplores the violence, trying only to make a life for himself and his two children.

This is a far superior film to O'Sullivan's previous *December Bride*. The fine cast give flawless performances. Filmed on location in Dublin, pic has a totally authentic feel.

•

NOTHING SACRED
1937, 75 mins, US Ⓥ ⦿ col
Dir William A. Wellman ***Prod*** David O. Selznick ***Scr*** Ben Hecht ***Ph*** W. Howard Greene ***Ed*** Hal C. Kern, James E. Newcom ***Mus*** Oscar Levant ***Art*** Lyle Wheeler
Act Carole Lombard, Fredric March, Charles Winninger, Walter Connolly, Sig Ruman, Frank Fay (Selznick)

Ben Hecht wrote the adaptation for *Sacred* from the James H. Street magazine story detailing the experiences of a village beauty who becomes the center of a fantastic newspaper circulation stunt which justifies itself in the belief, unfounded, that the girl has only a short time to live. Hecht handles the material breezily and pungently, poking fun in typical manner of half-scorn at the newspaper publisher, his reporter, doctors, the newspaper business, phonies, suckers, and whatnot.

For added value there is tinting by Technicolor which greatly enhances its pictorial charm. The running time is only 75 minutes, making this a meaty and well-edited piece of entertainment from start to finish. There are no lagging moments.

Fredric March does the reporter behind the dizzy ride given Carole Lombard by a sucker-victimized New York which thinks she already has one foot in the grave. Walter Connolly bristles with importance from a comedy viewpoint as March's publisher-boss. Charles Winninger does the rural medico who hates newspapers but not booze.

•

NO TIME FOR COMEDY
1940, 98 mins, US b/w
Dir William Keighley ***Prod*** Hal B. Wallis, Robert Lord ***Scr*** Julius J. Epstein, Philip G. Epstein ***Ph*** Ernest Haller ***Ed*** Owen Marks ***Mus*** Heinz Roemheld ***Art*** John Hughes
Act James Stewart, Rosalind Russell, Genevieve Tobin, Charles Ruggles, Allyn Joslyn, Louise Beavers (Warner)

S. N. Behrman's Broadway success starred Katharine Cornell. Rosalind Russell, in the same part, endows it with skill equal to that of her predecessor. Combined with a deftness for handling comedy and a class type of beauty which is plenty well demonstrated right here, Russell emerges as a player of unusual dignity and authority.

Stewart is pretty much the same Mr. Smith who went to Washington. Cast in a role which was obviously tailored to his measure, he is top-notch in the characterization of the boyish playwright from the sticks who arrives in Manhattan with a map after detouring by way of the Grand Canyon because there was an excursion train running there.

All other members of the cast except one, Genevieve Tobin, are equally effective. Set to play the fluffy matron, such a skillfully drawn characterization that only equally skillful acting can keep it on the right side of the fine line demarcating comedy from burlesque, Tobin frequently misses her footing. At least part of the blame must devolve on William Keighley, whose direction otherwise is equal to the story.

Stewart is a young newspaper reporter from the midwest who writes a play in which Russell is being starred on Broadway. The author is needed to make revisions, which for the first time brings him to the big city about which he has written so knowingly. He and Russell just naturally get entangled and enter on domestic bliss. In this state Stewart authors four comedy successes in four years when enter the villainess (Genevieve Tobin).

She convinces him he's wasting time on comedy when he could be doing great plays and by swallowing this mouthwash he not only turns out a tragedy—in more ways than one—but thinks he has fallen for Tobin. Ever-loving wifey, in the meantime, has taken up with Tobin's husband (Charlie Ruggles) as a matter of convenience.

•

NO TIME FOR LOVE
1944, 83 mins, US b/w
Dir Mitchell Leisen ***Prod*** Fred Kohlmar ***Scr*** Claude Binyon ***Ph*** Charles Lang, Jr. ***Ed*** Alma Macrorie ***Mus*** Victor Young
Act Claudette Colbert, Fred MacMurray, Ilka Chase, Ruth Havoc, Richard Haydn, Paul McGrath (Paramount)

Escapist is the word, and *No Time for Love* is just that, in spades. Starring Claudette Colbert and Fred MacMurray in a Claude Binyon screenplay [adapted by Warren Duff from a story by Robert Lees and Fred Rinaldo] that's heavily loaded for laughs, this pic is rather obviously contrived in some of its situations, but there's no denying a sufficiency of crack dialogue—and the laughs that go with it. Mitchell Leisen handles both the production and direction reins, giving *No Time* both barrels on each count.

Story concerns a famous femme photographer for a national picture magazine (Colbert), and the complications that evolve when, on an assignment to lens a tunnel construction project, she meets up with a sandhog (MacMurray).

From there on the basic story is pretty much pretense, but the laughs come fast, and the performances by Colbert and MacMurray are capital.

Colbert emphasizes her flair for comedy and doesn't spare herself either in relegating her usual sartorial elegance for the sake of serious story values, as indicated in the climactic scene when she gets spilled into a lake of spewing mud from a tunnel cave-in.

1944: NOMINATION: Best B&W Art Direction

•

NOTORIOUS
1946, 101 mins, US Ⓥ ⦿ b/w
Dir Alfred Hitchcock ***Prod*** Alfred Hitchcock ***Scr*** Ben Hecht ***Ph*** Ted Tetzlaff ***Ed*** Theron Warth ***Mus*** Roy Webb ***Art*** Albert S. D'Agostino, Carroll Clark
Act Cary Grant, Ingrid Bergman, Claude Rains, Louis Calhern, Reinhold Schunzel, Moroni Olsen (RKO)

Production and directorial skill of Alfred Hitchcock combine with a suspenseful story and excellent performances to make *Notorious* force entertainment.

The Ben Hecht scenario carries punchy dialog but it's much more the action and manner in which Hitchcock projects it on the screen that counts heaviest. Of course the fine performances by Cary Grant, Ingrid Bergman and Claude Rains also figure. The terrific suspense maintained to the very last is also an important asset.

Story deals with espionage, the picture opening in Miami in the spring of 1946. Bergman's father has been convicted as a German spy. Yarn shifts quickly to Rio de Janeiro, where Bergman, known to be a loyal American, unlike her father, is pressed into the American intelligence service with a view to getting the goods on a local group of German exiles under suspicion.

Inducted into espionage through Cary Grant, an American agent with whom she is assigned to work. Bergman, because she loves Grant, doesn't want to go through with an assignment to feign love for Claude Rains, head of the Brazilian Nazi group.

1946: NOMINATIONS: Best Supp. Actor (Claude Rains), Original Screenplay

•

NOTORIOUS GENTLEMAN
SEE: THE RAKE'S PROGRESS

•

NOTORIOUS LANDLADY, THE
1962, 127 mins, US b/w
Dir Richard Quine ***Prod*** Fred Kohlmar ***Scr*** Larry Gelbart, Blake Edwards ***Ph*** Arthur Arling ***Ed*** Charles Nelson ***Mus*** George Duning ***Art*** Cary Odell
Act Kim Novak, Jack Lemmon, Fred Astaire, Lionel Jeffries, Estelle Winwood, Maxell Reed (Columbia)

The Notorious Landlady is a comedy-suspense melodrama somewhat akin in essence and style to *Arsenic and Old Lace*. Unlike its distant theatrical ancestor, however, the Fred Kohlmar production is neither sound enough as a mystery nor consistently merry enough as a comedy.

Screenplay, from a story by Margery Sharp, deals with the plight of a Yankee foreign diplomat (Jack Lemmon) newly arrived from London, who becomes implicated in some confusing homicidal shenanigans involving his landlady (Kim Novak). Seems the landlady is suspected of having done in her husband, who has disappeared. In the midst of the budding Novak-Lemmon romance, the "dead" hubby shows up, only to be plugged for real by his wife.

Although the mystery plot is completely contrived and doesn't hold together, and the comedy comes only in occasional clusters and is largely manufactured on the spot by the resourceful Lemmon, the screenplay does have some bright and witty lines.

Novak's latitude of expression remains narrow, but coupled with her sexy attitude and natural physical endowments, it gets her by in the role. Fred Astaire is adequate as Lemmon's diplomat employer. Supporting cast, almost entirely British, is accomplished.

•

NO TREES IN THE STREET
1959, 98 mins, UK b/w
Dir J. Lee Thompson ***Prod*** Frank Godwin ***Scr*** Ted Willis ***Ph*** Gilbert Taylor ***Ed*** Richard Best ***Mus*** Laurie Johnson ***Art*** Robert Jones
Act Sylvia Syms, Herbert Lom, Ronald Howard, Stanley Holloway, Joan Miller, Melvyn Hayes (Associated British)

Ted Willis is a writer with a sympathetic eye for problems of the middle and lower classes. Again teamed up with director J. Lee Thompson, his *No Trees in the Street* plays out a seamy slice of life in a London slum 20 years ago. Film is played on a violently strident note. Willis hammers home the point that people are more important than places.

The slim storyline shows how the various larger-than-life characters face up to the challenge of the Street. The drab blowsy mother (Joan Miller) who has given up long ago. Her daughter (Sylvia Syms), longing to get away from it with her young brother, but lacking the resources or the courage. The boy racketeer (Herbert Lom), who has made money by shady activities and now ruthlessly rules the Street.

Syms gives a moving performance as the gentle girl who refuses to marry the cheap racketeer just to escape. Lom, as the opportunist who dominates the street, is sufficiently suave and unpleasant. Stanley Holloway is a bookmaker's tout with the cheerful philosophy that the world's gone mad.

•

NOTTE, LA
(THE NIGHT)
1961, 125 mins, Italy/France Ⓥ b/w
Dir Michelangelo Antonioni ***Prod*** Emanuele Cassuto ***Scr*** Michelangelo Antonioni, Ennio Flaiano, Tonino Guerra ***Ph*** Gianni Di Venanzo ***Ed*** Eraldo Da Roma ***Mus*** Giorgio Gaslini ***Art*** Piero Zuffi
Act Marcello Mastroianni, Jeanne Moreau, Monica Vitti, Bernhard Wicki, Maria Pia Luzi, Rosy Mazzacurati (Nepi/Silva/Sofitedip)

This engrossing film's story [by director Michelangelo Antonioni] is a superficially simple one. After 10 years of marriage, a popular writer and his wife begin to realize their affair is nearing breaking point. She's bored, has had an extra-marital fling with a family friend who has just died suddenly, leaving her even more despondent. Pic covers one day and a night. And when dawn breaks up the party which the couple is attending, habit, fear, loneliness and sorrow bring them together again in one last desperate act of love.

Jeanne Moreau walks off with acting honors in a carefully modulated, masterful performance as the wife. Monica Vitti is fine as a would-be distraction for the husband. Latter is played well by Marcello Mastroianni, though the script gives the wife the choicest acting morsels. A brief but effective cameo is contributed by Bernhard Wicki as the dying friend whose death triggers the couple's thoughts and actions.

Slow pace fits the mood admirably. The technical credits, from the mood-setting lensing by Gianni Di Venanzo to the apt music by Giorgio Gaslini, are outstanding in this difficult but stimulating picture.

•

NOTTING HILL
1999, 123 mins, UK Ⓥ ⦿ ⌑ col
Dir Roger Michell ***Prod*** Duncan Kenworthy ***Scr*** Richard Curtis ***Ph*** Michael Coulter ***Ed*** Nick Moore ***Mus*** Trevor Jones ***Art*** Stuart Craig
Act Julia Roberts, Hugh Grant, Hugh Bonneville, Emma Chambers, James Dreyfus, Rhys Ifans (Notting Hill/PolyGram)

It's slick, it's gawky, it's 10 minutes too long, and it's certainly not *Four Weddings and a Funeral, Part 2*, either in construction or overall tone. But *Notting Hill*, the second outing of scripter Richard Curtis, producer Duncan Kenworthy and actor Hugh Grant, has buckets to spare of that rarest screen commodity—genuine, engaging charm—plus a cast and production values that fully deliver when the chips are down.

Toplined in style by Grant and Julia Roberts, this is a romantic comedy couched as a modern fairytale, about a shy London bookseller who falls for a Hollywood megastar (and vice versa). Clearly aware of the sophomore curse, Kenworthy and Curtis have preserved elements of the first pic (glamorous Yank, gauche Brit hero, a circle of his friends) but gone for a more straight-arrow storyline, less ensemble playing and a good, old-fashioned princess-and-a-commoner love story that's like a late-'90's London-set version of *Roman Holiday*.

Unspectacular life of William Thacker (Grant) changes one day when Anna Scott (Roberts), the planet's most famous actress, walks in alone and buys a book. Both Grant and Roberts manage to shed enough of their movie personas to establish the beginnings of a screen chemistry that becomes vital as the film progresses.

Only after more coincidental meetings, spread over a year and a half, does the on-off relationship resolve itself. A crucial late-on line, heartbreakingly delivered by Roberts, unlocks a reservoir of emotion that's been held at bay by both the plot machinations and the thesps' restrained perfs, and powers the movie to its cliffhanger ending.

•

NOT WITH MY WIFE, YOU DON'T!
1966, 118 mins, US b/w
Dir Norman Panama ***Prod*** Norman Panama ***Scr*** Norman Panama, Larry Gelbert, Peter Barnes ***Ph*** Charles Lang, Jr. ***Ed*** Aaron Stell ***Mus*** John Williams ***Art*** Edward Carrere
Act Tony Curtis, Virna Lisi, George C. Scott, Carroll O'Connor, Richard Eastham, Eddie Ryder (Warner)

Not With My Wife, You Don't! is an outstanding romantic comedy about a U.S. Air Force marriage threatened by jealousy as an old beau of the wife returns to the scene. Zesty scripting, fine performances, solid direction and strong production values sustain hilarity throughout.

Story sets up Tony Curtis and George C. Scott as old Korean conflict buddies whose rivalry for Virna Lisi is renewed when Scott discovers that Curtis won her by subterfuge. The amusing premise is thoroughly held together via an unending string of top comedy situations, including domestic squabbles, flashback, and an outstanding takeoff on foreign pix.

Curtis is excellent as the husband whose duties as aide to Air Force General Carroll O'Connor create the domestic vacuum into which Scott moves with the time-tested instincts of a proven, and non-marrying, satyr.

•

NOT WITHOUT MY DAUGHTER
1991, 114 mins, US Ⓥ ⊙ col
Dir Brian Gilbert ***Prod*** Harry J. Ufland, Mary Jane Ufland ***Scr*** David W. Rintels ***Ph*** Peter Hannan ***Ed*** Terry Rawlings ***Mus*** Jerry Goldsmith ***Art*** Anthony Pratt
Act Sally Field, Alfred Molina, Sheila Rosenthal, Roshan Seth, Sarah Badel, Mony Rey (Pathe/Ufland)

True story of Betty Mahmoody is a harrowing one by any standard. Married to Iranian doctor Moody who has lived in the U.S. for 20 years, she reluctantly agrees to accompany him back to Teheran in 1984 to visit his family, only to be told at the end of two weeks that he has decided to remain in Iran.

As related in the by-the-numbers screenplay [from Mahmoody's book, with William Hoffer], Iran turns Moody from a civilized, sophisticated gent into an intolerant monster within a fortnight. Not only is Betty restricted to the home, but she can't use the phone, has her passport taken away, and is told that her daughter will be raised as a Muslim. After nearly two years of staggering suffering, Betty finally manages to make contact with an underground of helpful Iranians who offer to smuggle her and her daughter over the mountains into Turkey, a perilous episode in itself.

With Israel, of all places, standing in for Iran, the film manages to strongly convey how strange and off-putting a truly alien culture can be to an average American. Biggest problem is Moody's abrupt transition from sensitive husband to violent tyrant; there is little the gifted actor Alfred Molina can do to clarify psychological issues ignored by the script.

Sally Field has the stage to herself to engage the audience's sympathy, and this she does with an earnest, suitably emotional performance as a rather typically sincere, middle-class American.

•

NOVECENTO
(1900)
1976, 320 mins, Italy/France/W. Germany Ⓥ ⊙ col
Dir Bernardo Bertolucci ***Prod*** Alberto Grimaldi ***Scr*** Bernardo Bertolucci, Franco Arcalli, Giuseppe Bertolucci ***Ph*** Vittorio Storaro ***Ed*** Franco Arcalli ***Mus*** Ennio Morricone ***Art*** Ezio Frigerio
Act Burt Lancaster, Robert De Niro, Sterling Hayden, Gerard Depardieu, Dominique Sanda, Stefania Sandrelli (PEA/Artistes Associes/Artemis)

Bernardo Bertolucci spent three years to coauthor, prepare and direct this epic film. *1900* has a total running time of five hours and 20 minutes, 163 minutes before the break and 157 minutes to curtain. Bertolucci's ambitious generational canvas is elaborately constructed. One pattern is cyclical—childhood summer, ravages of war and fascism in fall and winter, and time of hope and liberation in spring. Spine of the saga, however, is the dialectical interlock of two families—landowners and sharecroppers—from 1900 to Italy's liberation in 1945. An insignificant epilogue projects the class conflict to present day.

Within this framework, Bertolucci introduces a patriarchal landowner, Alfredo Berlinghieri (Burt Lancaster) and an equally sturdy family head, Leo Dalco (Sterling Hayden). Berlinghieri and Falco polarize the intricate genealogies, the social chasms and the human overlap in a lyric opening, ripe with Bertolucci nostalgia for the magical naturalism and folk culture of his Emilia region at the turn of the century.

Awkward then deepening friendship of the two grandsons, Alfredo (Robert De Niro) and Olmo (Gerard Depardieu), opens an arc that spans the entire film. Highlight sequence is the first strike of farmhands (1908). End of World War I and homecoming of Alfredo and Olmo renews ties and conflicts as mechanization reaches the countryside.

As fascism takes power, Alfredo inherits the farm estate and marries Ada (Dominique Sanda), an urban beauty. Olmo marries a militant schoolteacher who dies in childbirth. He becomes a Communist and is forced to flee. With the liberation, Olmo returns and the peasants fleetingly take over.

Hayden's role as a farmworker bridging two centuries comes off as the crowning effort of his long career. Lancaster and Depardieu are key cast cogs, while a sober De Niro is somewhat overshadowed by a role condemning him to passivity. Donald Sutherland is evil enough as the fascist chief but is outplayed by Laura Betti as his wife. [Paramount released a 248-min. English version in the U.S.]

•

NOVEMBER MEN, THE
1993, 98 mins, US Ⓥ ⊙ col
Dir Paul Williams ***Prod*** Rodney Byron Ellis, Paul Williams ***Scr*** James Andronica ***Ph*** Susan Emerson ***Ed*** Chip Brooks ***Mus*** Scott Thomas Smith
Act P. W. Williams [= Paul Williams], James Andronica, Leslie Bevis, Beau Starr, Rod Ellis, Robert Davi (Rohd House/Sun Lion)

The November Men is the ultimate in conspiratorial presidential assassination films. The slyly comic saga marks the welcome return of filmmaker Paul Williams, who carved out a niche two decades ago with such films as *Out of It* and *Dealing*. It works well as both thriller and black comedy.

The filmmaking is wild and unconventional, as befits the subject matter. Noted Oliver Stone–like cineaste Arthur Gwenlyn (Williams) is mad as hell there hasn't been an assassin from the left in recent American history. In the months leading up to the 1992 U.S. elections, he rolls up his sleeves, mortgages the house and adopts guerrilla tactics to get his little epic off the ground.

His girlfriend and collaborator, Elizabeth (Leslie Bevis), isn't even particularly sure he isn't serious about taking the fiction into a more realistic arena. Duggo (James Andronica), a disgraced Marine, is horrified about the movie plot but desperate for any kind of work. Others in the cast and crew appear to have different and personal scenarios in mind.

None of this would work without the fierce, airtight wacko logic of Gwenlyn's pursuit. Up to the very last moment, one remains unsure whether the movie's assassination script is only a movie or some horrible extreme of ego and dementia.

•

NOVI VAVILON
(THE NEW BABYLON)
1929, 110 mins, USSR ⊗ b/w
Dir Grigori Kozintsev, Leonid Trauberg ***Scr*** Grigori Kozintsev, Leonid Trauberg ***Ph*** Andrei Moskvin, Yevgeni Mikhailov ***Mus*** Dmitri Shostakovich ***Art*** Yevgeni Enei
Act Yelena Kuzmina, Pyotr Sobolevsky, D. Gutman, Sophie Magarill, Sergei Gerasimov, Andrei Kostrichkin (Sovkino)

A teetotaler will be doubtful of his own sobriety after sitting through *The New Babylon*. So restless is the direction that this film has only the vestige of continuity. Faces, feet, mud, singers, soldiers, guns. Projected time and again.

Babylon is described in the subtitles as the name of a department store. The owner (D. Gutman) is allowed plenty of footage in which to sip liquor monotonously or adjust his top hat. Nearest line to the story is an extemporaneous romance suddenly springing up between the soldier Jean and a sales girl. Between the triple exposures the couple are brought together.

At the crucial period Jean is with the Nationals who, licked by the Prussians, are now dealing with the Commune, the political faction within. At the finis, Jean and the store girl are again brought together. He is her grave digger and she is one of the targets for the firing squad.

Picture claims it follows episodically events in the Franco-Prussian war and Commune activities in 1871.

•

NOW AND FOREVER
1934, 83 mins, US b/w
Dir Henry Hathaway ***Prod*** Louis D. Lighton ***Scr*** Vincent Lawrence, Sylvia Thalberg ***Ph*** Harry Fischbeck ***Ed*** Ellsworth Hoagland ***Art*** Hans Dreier, Robert Usher
Act Gary Cooper, Carole Lombard, Shirley Temple, Guy Standing, Charlotte Granville, Gilbert Emery (Paramount)

Now and Forever has Shirley Temple. It also has Gary Cooper and Carole Lombard, who almost make the unbelievable romantic crook yarn [by Jack Kirkland and Melville Baker] ring true—not forgetting Guy Standing's admirable performance as a debonair renegade.

It's another version of *Little Miss Marker*, the Temple child being Cooper's offspring by a former marriage. His impossibly supercilious socialite in-laws want to keep the child away from the roving renegade of a father's influence and he sees a $75,000 bankroll in that. Only Cooper forgets his hunger for economic wherewithal and resumes practical custody of the baby.

After turning a little grand larceny in New York for a $5,000 stake, the action shifts to Paris and Juan-les-Pins. (It opened in Shanghai, impressing the constant on-the-hop battles which the romantically newly wedded pair, Cooper and Lombard, have had with the minions of the law.)

If some of Temple's allotted dialog is a bit sophisticated for a tot, she, too, offsets any captiousness by the thoroughly winsome manner of celluloid histrionics.

•

NOW AND THEN
1995, 96 mins, US Ⓥ col
Dir Lesli Linka Glatter ***Prod*** Suzanne Todd, Demi Moore ***Scr*** I. Marlene King ***Ph*** Ueli Steiger ***Ed*** Jacqueline Cambas ***Mus*** Cliff Eidelman ***Art*** Gershon Ginsburg
Act Christina Ricci, Thora Birch, Gaby Hoffmann, Ashleigh Aston Moore, Demi Moore, Rosie O'Donnell (Moving Pictures)

Formulaic comedy-drama about teens coming of age in 1970 has the novelty of being mostly about girls rather than boys. But that's not enough to keep the pic—which even its makers describe as "a *Stand by Me* for girls"—from seeming like a return trip to familiar ground.

Maiden effort of Demi Moore's production company, pic obviously is a low-paying labor of love for all involved, including grownup stars Moore, Melanie Griffith, Rosie O'Donnell and Rita Wilson. But the adults do little more than provide marquee allure in brief bookending scenes that add little to rest of the pic.

For the most part, *Now and Then* is a showcase for four fine actresses in their early teens: Christina Ricci (*Casper*), Thora Birch (*Patriot Games*), Gaby Hoffmann (*Sleepless in Seattle*) and newcomer Ashleigh Aston Moore (no relation to Demi). They winningly play 12-year-old best friends who share confidences and misadventures during the summer of 1970.

Ricci is first among equals as Roberta, a sharp-witted tomboy who's amusingly unsettled by her budding attraction to a cute neighbor boy. (None too plausibly, she grows up to be the smartmouthed doctor played by Rosie O'Donnell.) Birch is Tina, a flashy little dynamo who's already rehearsing her Oscar acceptance speech. She grows up to be the much-married actress played by Melanie Griffith, which seems about right. Ashleigh Aston Moore is Chrissy, an easily flustered prude who grows up to be the equally flustery and prudish Rita Wilson. And Hoffmann is Samantha, a wise-beyond-her-years philosopher. As grownup Samantha, a blocked writer, Moore provides pic's melancholy narration.

•

NO WAY OUT
1950, 106 mins, US b/w
Dir Joseph L. Mankiewicz ***Prod*** Darryl F. Zanuck ***Scr*** Joseph L. Mankiewicz, Lesser Samuels ***Ph*** Milton Krasner ***Ed*** Barbara McLean ***Mus*** Alfred Newman ***Art*** Lyle Wheeler, George W. Davis
Act Richard Widmark, Linda Darnell, Stephen McNally, Sidney Poitier, Joanne Smith, Harry Bellaver (20th Century-Fox)

Race riot hysteria is the theme of the original script. Story is told with words rather than action. There is one brief sequence of rioting, but that doesn't come until after 60-odd minutes of dialogue buildup. The racial question is forceably raised when two hoodlum brothers are brought into the prison ward injured in a gunfight. The Negro doctor takes over and one of the brothers dies during examination. The other brother, slum-bred with all the prejudices of such an environment, charges the doctor with murder. Equally prejudiced, a group of Negroes turn on the hoods.

Richard Widmark's work as the vindictive brother is exaggerated just enough. Stephen McNally does compelling work. Sidney Poitier is splendid.

1950: NOMINATION: Best Story & Screenplay

•

NO WAY OUT
1987, 116 mins, US Ⓥ ⦿ ▭ col
Dir Roger Donaldson ***Prod*** Laura Ziskin, Robert Garland ***Scr*** Robert Garland ***Ph*** John Alcott ***Ed*** Neil Travis ***Mus*** Maurice Jarre ***Art*** Dennis Washington
Act Kevin Costner, Gene Hackman, Sean Young, Will Patton, Howard Duff, George Dzundza (Orion)

No Way Out is an effective updating and revamping of the 1948 film noir classic *The Big Clock*, also based on Kenneth Fearing's novel of that name.

Film is set primarily in the Pentagon, with heroic Kevin Costner cast as a Lt. Commander assigned to the Secretary of Defense (Gene Hackman), acting as liaison to the CIA under Hackman's right-hand man Will Patton. Costner has a torrid love affair with good-time girl Sean Young ended when she is murdered by her other lover, Hackman. Costner recognizes his boss in the shadows but Hackman sees only an unidentified figure. Hackman starts a cover-up to find the unidentified man he saw leaving the apartment. Costner is put in charge of the top-security investigation to catch himself.

Costner is extremely low key while Hackman glides through his role and Patton dominates his scenes overplaying his villainous hand. Young is extremely alluring as the heroine.

•

NO WAY TO TREAT A LADY
1968, 108 mins, US Ⓥ col
Dir Jack Smight ***Prod*** Sol C. Siegel ***Scr*** John Gay ***Ph*** Jack Priestley ***Ed*** Archie Marshek ***Mus*** Stanley Myers ***Art*** Hal Pereira, George Jenkins
Act Rod Steiger, Lee Remick, George Segal, Eileen Heckart, Murray Hamilton, Michael Dunn (Paramount)

Entertaining suspense film neatly laced with mordant humor. Stronger, more appropriate direction could have pushed the film into the category of minor classic.

Plotline casts Rod Steiger as a psychotic theatrical entrepreneur who takes to strangling drab middle-aged women as a means of working out his hangups over his dead mother. He employs a variety of disguises, accents and mannerisms for each murder.

Steiger relishes the multiple aspect of his part, and audiences should equally relish his droll impersonations of an Irish priest, German handyman, Jewish cop, middle-aged woman, Italian waiter and homosexual hairdresser.

Assigned to capture the lunatic ladykiller is a mother-smothered cop, played to perfection by George Segal. With an excellent cast and a very good screenplay, *No Way to Treat a Lady* comes close to the quality of the best British films of the 1950s.

•

NOW BARABBAS WAS A ROBBER
1949, 87 mins, UK b/w
Dir Gordon Parry ***Prod*** Anatole de Grunwald ***Scr*** Anatole de Grunwald ***Ph*** Otto Heller ***Ed*** Gerald Turney-Smith ***Mus*** George Melachrino
Act Richard Greene, Cedric Hardwicke, Kathleen Harrison, Ronald Howard, Stephen Murray, Richard Burton (Warner)

The odd assortment of men who make up a prison community are the central characters in *Now Barabbas Was a Robber*, adapted from the successful West End play by William Douglas Home. The pic rarely moves outside its prison setting but the gloomy atmosphere is frequently relieved by human touches from the guards and inmates.

There is no connected plot in the accepted sense but the film is focused on a number of the prisoners with an occasional flashback to indicate how they landed up inside.

The camera adroitly switches from one to the other, cleverly achieving sympathy for the unhappy prisoners. Handling of the death-cell sequences is a model of restraint.

•

NOWHERE TO RUN
1993, 94 mins, US Ⓥ ⦿ col
Dir Robert Harmon ***Prod*** Craig Baumgarten, Gary Adelson ***Scr*** Joe Eszterhas, Leslie Bohem, Randy Feldman ***Ph*** David Gribble ***Ed*** Zach Staenberg, Mark Helfrich ***Mus*** Mark Isham ***Art*** Dennis Washington
Act Jean-Claude Van Damme, Rosanna Arquette, Kieran Culkin, Ted Levine, Tiffany Taubman, Joss Ackland (Columbia)

Action hero Jean-Claude Van Damme takes a career step backward in *Nowhere to Run*, a relentlessly corny and shamelessly derivative vehicle. Dog-eared project has a story credited to Joe Eszterhas and his *Jagged Edge* director Richard Marquand (who died in 1987), with its central loner role modeled after the Alan Ladd classic *Shane*.

Van Damme is a bank robber who hides out on Rosanna Arquette's farm. She's a widow (the major plot change from *Shane*) with two young kids (Kieran Culkin—younger brother of Macaulay—and Tiffany Taubman). They glimpse Van Damme bathing nude in a nearby lake, and before long mama Arquette has seduced the handsome stranger.

The next day the quartet are at the dinner table matter-of-factly discussing Van Damme's penis size and, with many reels to go, *Nowhere to Run* has self-destructed. But patchwork plot continues, with Arquette pressured by evil land developer Joss Ackland to sell her homestead.

At every key moment, Van Damme pops up, comic-strip style, to display his heroism, but his bread-and-butter fight scenes are so one-sided there's no catharsis in them.

•

NOW, VOYAGER
1942, 117 mins, US Ⓥ ⦿ b/w
Dir Irving Rapper ***Prod*** Hal B. Wallis ***Scr*** Casey Robinson ***Ph*** Sol Polito ***Ed*** Warren Low ***Mus*** Max Steiner ***Art*** Robert Haas
Act Bette Davis, Paul Henreid, Claude Rains, Bonita Granville, Gladys Cooper, Ilka Chase (Warner)

Now, Voyager, an excursion into psychiatry, is almost episodic in its writing. It affords Bette Davis one of her superlative acting roles, that of a neurotic spinster fighting to free herself from the shackles of a tyrannical mother. A spinster still recalling the frustration of a girlhood love.

The first scenes show Davis as dowdy, plump and possessed of a phobia that fairly cries for the ministrations of a psychiatrist. Treatment by the doctor, played by Claude Rains, transforms the patient into a glamorous, modish, attractive woman who soon finds herself, after long being starved for love.

The yarn's major love crisis focuses on Davis and Paul Henreid, the latter unable to upset the conventions of a complicated marital life. The remote satisfaction of their love, via the emotionally unstable daughter of Henreid, upon whom Davis lavishes a mother's attention, is, perhaps, a rather questionable conclusion, but it's the kind of drama [from a novel by Oliver Higgins Pronty] that demands little credibility.

Henried neatly dovetails and makes believable the sometimes-underplayed character of the man who finds love too late. As the curer of Davis's mental ills, Rains gives his usual restrained, above-par performance. Gladys Cooper is the domineering mother, weighted by Boston's Back Bay traditions and she's also within her metier.

1942: Best Score for a Dramatic Picture

NOMINATIONS: Best Actress (Bette Davis), Supp. Actress (Gladys Cooper)

•

NOW YOU SEE HIM, NOW YOU DON'T
1972, 88 mins, US Ⓥ col
Dir Robert Butler ***Prod*** Ron Miller ***Scr*** Joseph L. McEveety ***Ph*** Frank Phillips ***Ed*** Cotton Warburton ***Mus*** Robert F. Brunner ***Art*** John B. Mansbridge, Walter Tyler
Act Kurt Russell, Cesar Romero, Joe Flynn, Jim Backus, William Windom, Michael McGreevey (Walt Disney)

Virtually all the key creative elements which early in 1970 made *The Computer Wore Tennis Shoes* encore superbly in *Now You See Him, Now You Don't* [from a story by Robert L. King]. Discovery of a fluid which makes people and objects invisible provides the inventive plot peg for uproarious golf games and car chase sequences involving students, professors, police and criminals.

Encoring players include Kurt Russell, this time as a college student who accidentally discovers the invisible potion, Michael McGreevey as his sidekick, Joe Flynn as a befuddled dean, Cesar Romero as a local gangster who plans to foreclose on the school to make it a gambling casino-hotel, and Richard Bakalyan as Romero's right-hand flunkie.

Flynn's camping is a major comedy prop as the story develops. To raise mortgage money, he enters a golf game with philanthropist Jim Backus, and aided by the invisible students scores many holes-in-one and a host of laughs. Romero later steals the magic fluid to rob a bank, cueing a climactic car chase which comes across with spectacularly funny impact.

•

NOZ W WODZIE
(KNIFE IN THE WATER)
1962, 95 mins, Poland Ⓥ b/w
Dir Roman Polanski ***Scr*** Roman Polanski, Jerzy Skolimowski, Jakub Goldberg ***Ph*** Jerzy Lipman ***Ed*** Halina Prugar ***Mus*** Krzysztof T. Komeda ***Art*** Boleslaw Kamykowski
Act Leon Niemczyk, Jolanta Umecka, Zygmunt Malanowicz (Kamera)

Middle-aged cocksureness, arrogance and incomprehension versus teenage revolt, with a young woman as a sort of arbiter, is the theme of this lively and inventive little pic.

A couple driving along a deserted road to the sea almost run over a young man. The driver is a self-absorbed husband, the woman his pretty, irritated young wife, and the hitchhiker a teenager.

The husband, out of sheer patronizing good will, invites him to come sailing on their boat. Pic is then concerned with the boat ride and the subtle battle of personalities between the men and the wife's amused onlooking.

For a first pic, director Roman Polanski shows a flair for simple character revelation and wit. He sometimes overindulges, and charges the affair with gratuitous bits, but manages to keep up interest. Its social side is soft-pedaled.

•

NUIT AMERICAINE, LA
(DAY FOR NIGHT)
1973, 120 mins, France/Italy Ⓥ ⦿ col
Dir Francois Truffaut ***Scr*** Francois Truffaut, Jean-Louis Richard, Suzanne Schiffman ***Ph*** Pierre-William Glenn ***Ed*** Yann Dedet, Martine Barraque ***Mus*** Georges Delerue ***Art*** Damien Lanfranchi
Act Jacqueline Bisset, Valentina Cortese, Dani, Alexandra Stewart, Jean-Pierre Aumont, Jean-Pierre Leaud (Films du Carrosse/PECF/PIC)

Francois Truffaut turns to filmmaking itself for his story. From the first day's shooting to the last, he mixes comedy and intimations of drama but keeps it mainly a love letter to the cinematic art, more pointedly commercial films.

Here are loving observations, charming if familiar characterizations, and an ease in intertwining the story and the film within the story. Witty and avoiding any undue whimsy or self-indulgence, Truffaut plays the director of the film underway and makes it clear this is his life's love.

There are no highbrow attempts to work in parallels between the film being made and the film the viewer sees. It is just a job.

Jacqueline Bisset is amiable as the American star with her problems of a Hollywood childhood and theatrical mother behind her. Valentina Cortese is remarkable as an aging star who goes on despite a sick son. Jean-Pierre Aumont is charming as the aging leading man who wants to adopt a young man.

The members of the crew are played with engaging candor. Jean-Pierre Leaud, Truffaut's alter ego in his semi-biog pix, is a sort of spoiled young man who brings on the crises in the film.

1973: Best Foreign Language Film

•

NUN AND THE BANDIT, THE
1992, 92 mins, Australia Ⓥ col
Dir Paul Cox ***Prod*** Paul Ammitzboll, Paul Cox ***Scr*** Paul Cox ***Ph*** Nino Martinetti ***Ed*** Paul Cox ***Mus*** Tom E. Lewis, Norman Kaye ***Art*** Neil Angwin
Act Gosia Dobrowolska, Chris Haywood, Victoria Eagger, Charlotte Hughes Haywood, Norman Kaye, Tom E. Lewis (Illumination/Film Victoria/AFFC)

Marking a departure for Aussie auteur Paul Cox, *The Nun and the Bandit* is adapted from a book and set in the primal Australian bush, far from the claustrophobic interiors of his earlier films. Cox has updated E. L. Grant's kidnap thriller set in the 1930s to what appears to be the '50s, playing down the thriller elements in favor of a brittle character study.

Kidnappers are led by Michael Shanley (Chris Haywood), disaffected nephew of prominent citizen George Shanley (Norman Kaye). Michael devises an impromptu, harebrained scheme to hold the rich man's young granddaughter (played by the daughter of Haywood and Wendy Hughes, Charlotte Hughes Haywood) for ransom. The child is snatched when she is with her aunt, Sister Lucy (Gosia Dobrowolska), a Polish nun visiting her sickly sister (Eva Sitta), the girl's mother.

The bulk of the film plays as a two-hander between the frightened, unworldly nun and the strange "bandit" who refuses to rape his victim but demands that she "be nice" to him. Cox leaves it up to the viewer to decide what happens between the two.

Cox regulars Dobrowolska and Haywood give their usual standout performances. Kaye excels as the charmingly unscrupulous capitalist. Pic has very fine production values belying the modest budget.

•

NUNS ON THE RUN
1990, 90 mins, UK Ⓥ ⊙ col
Dir Jonathan Lynn ***Prod*** Michael White ***Scr*** Jonathan Lynn ***Ph*** Michael Garfath ***Ed*** David Martin ***Mus*** Yello, Hidden Faces ***Art*** Simon Holland
Act Eric Idle, Robbie Coltrane, Camille Coduri, Janet Suzman, Doris Hare, Tom Hickey (HandMade)

Like Jack Lemmon and Tony Curtis in the Billy Wilder classic *Some Like It Hot*, Eric Idle and Robbie Coltrane are motivated by fear for their lives to dress in women's garb. New pic has rival British and Chinese gangs trying to recover two suitcases full of illicit cash.

Idle and Coltrane make a wonderful pair of dumbbells, both in and out of their habits. Both are oddly believable as nuns, even while writer/director Jonathan Lynn mines all the expected comic benefits of drag humor. Idle and Coltrane are a lookout and a getaway driver for believable nasty London crime lord Robert Patterson. Their desire to escape their surroundings and the lure of easy cash backfire ominously, and they take refuge in a convent school run by Janet Suzman.

The constant double entendres are done with wit and the slapstick is mostly agreeable and efficiently directed, although the sight gags about Camille Coduri's extreme myopia are pushed a little far on occasion. Coduri otherwise is sweet and endearing in the Marilyn Monroe part.

•

NUN'S STORY, THE
1959, 149 mins, US Ⓥ ⊙ col
Dir Fred Zinnemann ***Prod*** Henry Blanke ***Scr*** Robert Anderson ***Ph*** Franz Planer ***Ed*** Walter Thompson ***Mus*** Franz Waxman ***Art*** Alexandre Trauner
Act Audrey Hepburn, Peter Finch, Edith Evans, Peggy Ashcroft, Dean Jagger, Mildred Dunnock (Warner)

Fred Zinnemann's production is a soaring and luminous film. Audrey Hepburn has her most demanding film role, and she gives her finest performance. Despite the seriousness of the underlying theme, *The Nun's Story* [from the book by Kathryn C. Hulme] has the elements of absorbing drama, pathos, humor, and a gallery of memorable scenes and characters. The struggle is that of a young Belgian woman (Hepburn) to be a successful member of an order of cloistered nuns. The order (not specified) is as different from the ordinary "regular guy" motion picture conception of nuns as the army is from the Boy Scouts. Its aim is total merging of self. Although the story is confined chiefly to three convents, in Belgium and the Congo, the struggle is fierce. Hepburn, attempting to be something she is not, is burned fine in the process.

One of the consistent gratifications is the cast. In addition to Edith Evans as the Mother Superior, who might have been a Renaissance prelate, there is Peggy Ashcroft, another convent superior, but less the dignitary, more the anchorite. Mildred Dunnock is a gentle, maiden aunt of a nun; Patricia Collinge, a gossipy cousin.

Peter Finch and Dean Jagger are the only males in the cast of any stature. Finch, as an intelligent, attractive agnostic, conveys a romantic attachment for Hepburn, but in terms that can give no offense. Jagger is Hepburn's perturbed loving father but contributes a valuable facet on the story.

Despite the seeming austerity of the story, Zinnemann has achieved a pictorial sweep and majesty. Franz Planer's Technicolor photography has a Gothic grace and muted splendor, Franz Waxman's score is a great one, giving proper place to cathedral organs and Congo drums.

1959: NOMINATIONS: Best Picture, Director, Actress (Audrey Hepburn), Adapted Screenplay, Color Cinematography, Scoring of a Dramatic Picture, Sound

•

NUOVO CINEMA PARADISO
(CINEMA PARADISO)
1988, 155 mins, Italy/France Ⓥ ⊙ col
Dir Giuseppe Tornatore ***Prod*** Franco Cristaldi ***Scr*** Giuseppe Tornatore ***Ph*** Blasco Giurato ***Ed*** Mario Morra ***Mus*** Ennio Morricone ***Art*** Andrea Crisanti
Act Philippe Noiret, Salvatore Cascio, Marco Leonardi, Jacques Perrin, Agnese Nano, Brigitte Fossey (Cristaldi/Films Ariane)

A colorful, sentimental trip through the happy days when the Italo film biz wasn't in a perennial "crisis," this *Amarcord* about a marvelous Sicilian hardtop and a boy who loves the movies boasts eye-catching technical work and a solid cast. Young helmer Giuseppe Tornatore (*The Professor*) is an able storyteller who knows the value of cute kids and easy emotion. Beneath the schmaltz lie buried a lot of good ideas.

Clocking in at an overlong $2^1/_2$ hours (cut from three), film divides into three parts, corresponding to the three ages of cineaste-hero Salvatore. As an adorable 10-year-old moppet (first-timer Salvatore Cascio), the boy sneaks into the parochial Paradise Cinema to watch a priest (Leopoldo Trieste) snip out all the kissing scenes. He worms his way into the heart of crusty peasant projectionist Alfredo (a well-balanced Philippe Noiret) who speaks in film dialogue.

With Alfredo the cinema is magic—like the night he regales patrons unable to get into a Toto comedy with a free show beamed on a wall in the piazza. Mid-show, the old nitrate film catches fire and destroys the theatre.

Second part shows Salvatore as a teenager in love with a blonde banker's daughter (Agnese Nano). Last, and least satisfying, is Salvatore as white-haired Jacques Perrin, now a famous (what else?) film director. He returns to Sicily for Alfredo's funeral and finds his long lost love, now played by Brigitte Fossey.

Top-notch lensing by Blasco Giurato and sets by Andrea Crisanti (the cinema itself is a small masterpiece) create a strong atmosphere. Ennio Morricone's score reinforces the sugary sentiment that defaces the film. [Pic's international success was in a 123-min. version in which the third part of the story was heavily cut. A 167-min. version, *Cinema Paradiso: The Special Edition* was released in the UK in 1993.]

1988: Best Foreign Language Film

•

NURSE BETTY
2000, 108 mins, US Ⓥ ⊙ ▭ col
Dir Neil Labute ***Prod*** Gail Mutrux, Steve Golin ***Scr*** John C. Richards, James Flamberg ***Ph*** Jean Yves Escoffier ***Ed*** Joel Plotch, Steven Weisberg ***Mus*** Rolfe Kent ***Art*** Charles Breen
Act Renee Zellweger, Morgan Freeman, Chris Rock, Greg Kinnear, Aaron Eckhart, Tia Texada (Propaganda-ab'strakt-IMF/Gramercy)

In the darkly comic *Nurse Betty*, Neil LaBute puts aside the intense explorations of misogyny that dominated his earlier films *(In the Company of Men, Your Friends & Neighbors)* and immerses himself in a lighter romantic fable that deals with the collision of fantasy and reality. As a small-town waitress stuck in a bad marriage but determined to make her dreams come true, a terrific Renee Zellweger heads a superlative cast.

First scene shows Kansas waitress Betty (Zellweger) more interested in daytime soap *A Reason to Love* than in serving her customers. The popular TV show offers escape from her bleak reality; back home, Betty has to endure the company of her no-good car salesman hubby, Del (Aaron Eckhart). While watching that day's soap episode, Betty hears her favorite character, Dr. David Ravell, say, "I know there's someone special out there for me." It's a line that she repeats over and over, and that provides the stimulus to what turns out to be a life-changing experience.

Opportunity knocks when a drug deal between Del and two hit men, Charlie (Morgan Freeman) and his easily excitable protege, Wesley (Chris Rock), goes horrendously, fatally awry. Del winds up on the wrong end of a gun in a gratuitous violent scene that recalls the Coen brothers' movies. Traumatized by the savagery that she's accidentally witnessed, Betty assumes the soap's persona of Nurse Betty and is set on returning to the love of her life, Dr. Ravell. Betty leaves Kansas in a borrowed 1997 Buick, failing to realize that it contains the stuff her husband's killers are looking for. Rest of tale is conveyed through cross-cutting between Betty's personal adventures and the duo of killers chasing her.

Centerpiece, and what gives pic its heart, is the encounter between Betty and George McCord (Greg Kinnear), who plays Dr. Ravell, and his acidic writer-producer, Lyla (Allison Janney). George thinks that Betty would like to get a part in his soap, only to realize that she's after something bigger than that. As pic explores, in many variations, the question of whether life imitates art or vice versa, the lines between fantasy and reality blur.

Few actresses can convey the kind of honesty and humanity that Zellweger does here—it's hard to imagine the film without her dominant, thoroughly credible performance. A dizzying array of secondary performers gives the movie a frenzied, funny texture.

•

NUTS
1987, 116 mins, US Ⓥ ⊙ col
Dir Martin Ritt ***Prod*** Barbra Streisand ***Scr*** Tom Topor ***Ph*** Andrzej Bartkowiak ***Ed*** Sidney Levin ***Mus*** Barbra Streisand ***Art*** Joel Schiller
Act Barbra Streisand, Richard Dreyfuss, Maureen Stapleton, Karl Malden, Eli Wallach, Robert Webber (Barwood/Ritt)

Based on the stageplay by Tom Topor, *Nuts* presents a premise weighted down by portentous performances. Issue of society's right to judge someone's sanity and the subjectivity of mental health is not only trite, but dated. While film ignites sporadically, it succumbs to the burden of its own earnestness.

As Claudia Draper, an upper-crust New York kid who has gone off the deep end into prostitution, Barbra Streisand is good, but it's too much of a good thing. For the most part it's a heroic performance, abandoning many of the characteristic Streisand mannerisms while she allows herself to look seedy. Streisand is flamboyantly, eccentrically crazy in a way that implies she is just a spirited woman society is trying to crush.

Richard Dreyfuss as Streisand's reluctant public defender is by far the film's most textured character, giving a performance that suggests a world of feeling and experience not rushing to gush out at the seams.

Arrested for killing her high-priced trick, it is Dreyfuss's job to convince a preliminary hearing that Streisand is mentally competent enough to stand trial with little help from her and against her parents' wishes.

•

NUTTY PROFESSOR, THE
1963, 107 mins, US Ⓥ ⊙ col
Dir Jerry Lewis ***Prod*** Ernest D. Glucksman ***Scr*** Jerry Lewis, Bill Richmond ***Ph*** W. Wallace Kelley ***Ed*** John Woodcock ***Mus*** Walter Scharf ***Art*** Hal Pereira, Walter Tyler
Act Jerry Lewis, Stella Stevens, Del Moore, Kathleen Freeman, Howard Morris (Paramount/Lewis)

The Nutty Professor is not one of Jerry Lewis's better films. Although attractively mounted and performed with flair by a talented cast, the production is only fitfully funny. Too often the film bogs down in pointless, irrelevant or repetitious business, nullifying the flavor of the occasionally choice comic capers and palsying the tempo and continuity of the story.

The star is cast as a meek, homely, accident-prone chemistry prof who concocts a potion that transforms him into a handsome, cocky, obnoxiously vain "cool cat" type. But the transfiguration is of the Jekyll-Hyde variety in that it wears off, restoring Lewis to the original mold, invariably at critical, embarrassing moments.

Another standard characteristic of the Lewis film is its similarity to an animated cartoon, especially noticeable on this occasion in that the professor played by Lewis is a kind of live-action version of the nearsighted Mr Magoo.

Musical theme of the picture is the beautiful refrain "Stella by Starlight." By starlight or any other light, Stella is beautiful—Stella Stevens, that is, who portrays the professor's student admirer. Stevens is not only gorgeous, she is a very gifted actress. This was an exceptionally tough assignment, requiring of her almost exclusively silent reaction takes, and Stevens has managed almost invariably to produce the correct responsive expression. On her, even the incorrect one would look good.

•

NUTTY PROFESSOR, THE
1996, 95 mins, US Ⓥ ⊙ col
Dir Tom Shadyac ***Prod*** Brian Grazer, Russell Simmons ***Scr*** David Sheffield, Barry W. Blaustein, Tom Shadyac, Steve Oedekerk ***Ph*** Julio Macat ***Ed*** Don Zimmerman ***Mus*** David Newman ***Art*** William Elliott
Act Eddie Murphy, Jada Pinkett, James Coburn, Larry Miller, Dave Chappelle, John Ales (Imagine/Universal)

He's not really kooky, but Eddie Murphy's reworking of Jerry Lewis's 1963 film *The Nutty Professor* is an apt and comic update of the Jekyll/Hyde formula. It's Murphy's most assured work in some time.

Eschewing the revenge-of-the-nerds theme of the Lewis original, the new version casts its title hero as a blimp-size pedagogue. Sherman Klump (Eddie Murphy) is a goodhearted, slightly absent-minded tub of lard conducting molecular research experiments at a fictional university. His goal is to find a solution that will make you thin, and he's making significant strides towards that end with his lab hamsters.

But the sedentary life that is his custom gets shaken with the arrival of Carla (Jada Pinkett), a comely grad student impressed by his work and seemingly undaunted by his girth. Sherman's own self-image is at a decided low. The college dean (Larry Miller) has threatened to kill him if he alienates a big-bucks donor (James Coburn), and his rambunctious, unschooled family goads him endlessly about his job and bachelorhood.

The sober side of pic stands in sharp contrast to fitfully related sequences featuring the Klump brood. Murphy plays both of Sherman's parents, his grandma and brother. They are staccatos of well-observed, painfully funny jibes that perk up the proceedings.

What's left of the supporting cast is also strong. Miller is at his obsequious best, and Pinkett, again unrecognizable from any previous role, demonstrates that her range ranks her among the most versatile young performers in movies.

1996: Best Makeup (Matthew W. Mungle, Deborah La Mia Denaver)

•

NUTTY PROFESSOR II: THE KLUMPS
2000, 106 mins, US Ⓥ ⊙ col

Dir Peter Segal ***Prod*** Brian Grazer ***Scr*** Barry W. Blaustein, David Sheffield, Paul Weitz, Chris Weitz ***Ph*** Dean Semler ***Ed*** William Kerr ***Mus*** David Newman ***Art*** William Elliott

Act Eddie Murphy, Janet Jackson, Larry Miller, John Ales, Richard Gant, Anna Maria Horsford (Imagine/Universal)

Offering incontrovertible proof that more is less, *Nutty Professor II: The Klumps* tries too hard to do too much to top its 1996 smash-hit predecessor. Raucous family gatherings in *The Nutty Professor* had Eddie Murphy playing five different characters at the same crowded dinner table. All are back and each gets a bigger slice of the action as the sequel shamelessly attempts to exploit and expand the most crowd-pleasing bits and pieces of the original. Sherman Klump is the nominal hero of the story, once again distracted by romantic longings as he toils on modern miracles of science, and once again winningly played by Murphy. Trouble is, there isn't enough of the big lug in the sequel, because his attention-grabbing relatives repeatedly upstage him.

At first, the special effects are so eye-poppingly prodigious that it's easy to overlook the repetitiveness of the plotting and the coarseness of the humor. The interactions among the Klump quintet are smooth, seamless and often downright astonishing, especially when one Eddie Murphy addresses another Eddie Murphy, then turns to embrace yet a third Eddie Murphy, who in turns says something to a fourth and a fifth. Since it's so easy to accept the illusion of five separate and distinct characters, the novelty value of that illusion starts to wane about a third of the way into *Nutty Professor II*.

Once you stop marveling at the high-tech trickery (special makeup effects: Rick Baker, visual effects supervisor: Jon Farhat), you begin to notice how much of the movie relies on jokes about flatulence, sexual dysfunction, animal excrement and the indefatigable horniness of Granny Klump, to say nothing of a gag involving the anal rape of a college dean (Larry Miller) by a chemically enhanced hamster.

Buddy Love also returns. An errant gene that is the last remaining trace of Sherman Klump's own private Mr. Hyde inadvertently mutates with a strand of dog hair and the result is a brave new Buddy who likes to chase cats, play fetch and sniff the air for traces of lovely ladies. But even with his canine accoutrements, Buddy simply isn't as funny the second time around. For that matter, neither are the Klumps.

OBCHOD NA KORZE
(THE SHOP ON MAIN STREET; A SHOP ON THE HIGH STREET)
1964, 125 mins, Czechoslovakia Ⓥ ⊙ b/w
Dir Jan Kadar, Elmar Klos ***Scr*** Elmar Klos, Jan Kadar, Ladislav Grosman ***Ph*** Vladimir Novotny ***Mus*** Zdenek Liska
Act Jozef Kroner, Frantisek Zvarik, Ida Kaminska, Hanna Slivkova, Martin Holly (Barrandov)

Racism is looked at deeply and provocatively in this revealing film. During the last World War, a small town in Slovakia was turned into a crucible Fascist state by the Nazis. Locals run everything and there are no Germans in sight. It concerns a not too pretty and mean little man who harbors a resentment against the local Nazis though he does nothing about it.

His own brother-in-law is the town police head and he is given the right to take over the store of an old Jewish woman by his relative when plans for deporting the Jews are well developed. She has lost her husband in the last war and all that is left is this little drygoods shop.

When the deportations start she is somehow forgotten and he decides he will do something to hide her. The end has him going through divided outlooks about what to do, wanting to help her, yet fearing reprisals.

This is all done with a non-rancorous flair sans any hysterical overtone. This makes it even more poignant. It becomes a statement on how anti-Semitism can be bred by oversight, plain laziness or general apathy. Directors Jan Kadar and Elmar Klos have built this carefully, and have given a good feel of the times and personalities before the drama erupts.

Ida Kaminska, a noted Polish actress from the Warsaw Yiddish Theatre, has the right blend of charm and aging dignity. Josef Kroner also gives life to the little man in his moments of decision.

1965: Best Foreign Language Film

●

OBJECTIVE, BURMA!
1945, 142 mins, US Ⓥ b/w
Dir Raoul Walsh ***Prod*** Jerry Wald ***Scr*** Ranald MacDougall, Lester Cole ***Ph*** James Wong Howe ***Ed*** George Amy ***Mus*** Franz Waxman ***Art*** Ted Smith
Act Errol Flynn, Henry Hull, William Prince, James Brown, George Tobias, Warner Anderson (Warner)

Yarn [from an original story by Alvah Bessie] deals with a paratroop contingent dropped behind the Japanese lines in Burma to destroy a radar station. The chutists achieve their objective, but while returning to a designated spot to be picked up by planes and flown back to the base, they're overtaken by Japs. Then follows a series of exciting experiences by the troopers against overwhelming odds.

The film has considerable movement, particularly in the early reels, and the tactics of the paratroopers are authentic in their painstaking detail. However, while the scripters have in the main achieved their purpose of heightening the action, there are scenes in the final reels that could have been edited more closely.

Flynn gives a quietly restrained performance as the contingent's leader, while supporting players who also perform capably are Henry Hull, as a war correspondent; William Prince, James Brown, George Tobias, Dick Erdman and Warner Anderson.

1945: NOMINATIONS: Best Original Story, Editing, Scoring of a Dramatic Picture

●

OBJECT OF BEAUTY, THE
1991, 101 mins, US/UK Ⓥ col
Dir Michael Lindsay-Hogg ***Prod*** Jon S. Denny ***Scr*** Michael Lindsay-Hogg ***Ph*** David Watkin ***Ed*** Ruth Foster ***Mus*** Tom Bahler ***Art*** Derek Dodd
Act John Malkovich, Andie MacDowell, Lolita Davidovich, Rudi Davies, Joss Ackland, Bill Paterson (Avenue/BBC)

The Object of Beauty is a throwback to the romantic comedies of Swinging London cinema, but lacks the punch of the best of that late 1960s genre.

John Malkovich toplines as a ne'er-do-well holed up in a swank London hotel with mate Andie MacDowell. Everyone assumes the two of them are married, but MacDowell is still hitched to estranged hubbie Peter Riegert.

Plot concerns the title object, a small Henry Moore figurine that MacDowell received from Riegert as a present and which Malkovich desperately wants to sell or use for an insurance scam to cover his hotel tab and ongoing business reverses.

Key script contrivance has a deaf-mute maid (Rudi Davies), newly hired at the hotel, becoming obsessed with the Moore sculpture and stealing it for a keepsake.

Malkovich ably brings out the unsympathetic nature of his antihero, but the script doesn't help him much. The viewer will instantly side with MacDowell, whose natural beauty is augmented here by a feisty violent streak whenever Malkovich steps over the line (which is frequent). Result is a mildly diverting but empty picture.

●

OBLONG BOX, THE
1969, 91 mins, UK Ⓥ ⊙ col
Dir Gordon Hessler ***Prod*** Gordon Hessler ***Scr*** Lawrence Huntington, Christopher Wicking ***Ph*** John Coquillon ***Ed*** Max Benedict ***Mus*** Harry Robinson ***Art*** George Provis
Act Vincent Price, Christopher Lee, Alastair Williamson, Hilary Dwyer, Harry Baird (American-International)

This 13th Edgar Allan Poe entry turned out by AIP is a story of witchcraft, retribution and revenge, with half a dozen daintily carved up stiffs lying around with blood flowing to serve as fare for stronger appetites.

It is the tale of a man, terribly mutilated by African savages, kept chained by his brother (Vincent Price) in a gloomy 19th-century English manor house, his escape and embarkation upon a series of murders as he extracts payment for certain "debts." What these debts are isn't exactly clear.

Price as usual overacts, but it is an art here to fit the mood and piece and as usual Price is good in his part. Alastair Williamson as the brother is called upon for some strange goings-on but acquits himself well and Christopher Lee likewise scores as a doctor who becomes involved with Williamson.

●

O BROTHER, WHERE ART THOU?
2000, 106 mins, US Ⓥ ⊙ ▭ col
Dir Joel Coen ***Prod*** Ethan Coen ***Scr*** Ethan Coen, Joel Coen ***Ph*** Roger Deakins ***Ed*** Roderick Jaynes, Tricia Cooke ***Mus*** T Bone Burnett ***Art*** Dennis Gassner, Richard Johnson
Act George Clooney, John Turturro, Tim Blake Nelson, Charles Durning, John Goodman, Michael Badalucco, Holly Hunter (Working Title)

A musically tinged riff on *The Odyssey* set in the Depression-era Deep South, *O Brother, Where Art Thou?* is a charming, if lightweight, Coen brothers escapade flecked by plenty of visual and performance grace notes. Picaresque tale of three cons in flight from life on a chain gang is more memorable for its fantastic moments than for its somewhat insubstantial cumulative impact.

While the film's epigraph and inspiration come from Homer, its title derives from Preston Sturges' film-biz classic *Sullivan's Travels*, in which the successful director played by Joel McCrea wants to abandon comedy to make a socially conscious drama about the Human Condition called *O Brother, Where Art Thou*? While appropriating the handle, the Coens aren't about to fall into the trap of pretentiousness themselves, crafting instead a seriocomedy that makes a fanciful tour of an old Mississippi in which kismet and good bluegrass music prevail over racism and criminality.

Working with their customary tonal precision and immaculate craftsmanship, the Coens release into the wilds three escaped criminals, with the leader, Everett Ulysses McGill (George Clooney), telling his cronies Pete (John Turturro) and Delmar (Tim Blake Nelson) that he knows where $1.2 million is buried. One eventful encounter follows another as the boys make their way across the lushly verdant landscapes, which have been photographed by Roger Deakins in slightly washed-out and burnished hues that are a constant delight.

Lack of irony and complexity in the wrap-up may be a shortcoming, but it also points up the welcome absence of condescension and ridicule in the film's portrait of dimwits, con men, rednecks and country folk. Most of the characters, including the three leads, may be dumb, misguided and delusional, but they are also engaging and straightforward, to be enjoyed for the colorful oddballs they are.

Not for the first time recalling Clark Gable in his looks and line delivery, Clooney clearly delights in embellishing Everett's vanity and in delivering the Coens' carefully calibrated, high-toned dialogue.

●

OBSESSION
(US: THE HIDDEN ROOM)
1949, 96 mins, UK Ⓥ ▭ b/w
Dir Edward Dmytryk ***Prod*** N. A. Bronsten ***Scr*** Alec Coppel ***Ph*** C. Pennington Richards, Robert Day ***Ed*** Lilo Carruthers ***Mus*** Nino Rota
Act Robert Newton, Sally Gray, Naunton Wayne, Phil Brown (Rank/Independent Sovereign)

Powerful suspense is the keynote of Edward Dmytryk's first British directorial effort and a strong dramatic situation has been developed from Alec Coppel's ill-fated stage play *A Man About a Dog*, which ran for only a few nights.

A straightforward situation is presented in which a doctor plans the "perfect" murder of his wife's American lover. Firstly the victim is confined in chains and the intention is to keep him alive while the hue and cry is on. If suspicion should fall on the doctor he could always produce the missing person.

In the early stages the pace could be quickened, but the whole atmosphere becomes tense when the official Scotland Yard inquiries begin. Naunton Wayne as the Yard superintendent is an example of perfect casting and his nonchalant manner deserves particular praise.

●

OBSESSION
1976, 98 mins, US Ⓥ ⊙ col
Dir Brian De Palma ***Prod*** George Litto, Harry N. Blum ***Scr*** Paul Schrader ***Ph*** Vilmos Zsigmond ***Ed*** Paul Hirsch ***Mus*** Bernard Herrmann ***Art*** Jack Senter
Act Cliff Robertson, Genevieve Bujold, John Lithgow, Sylvia "Kuumba" Williams, Wanda Blackman (Columbia)

Obsession is an excellent romantic and nonviolent suspense drama starring Cliff Robertson and Genevieve Bujold, shot in Italy and New Orleans.

Paul Schrader's script [from a story by him and Brian De Palma] is a complex but comprehensible mix of treachery, torment and selfishness. Robertson is haunted with guilt for the death of wife Bujold and child Wanda Blackman, both kidnapped in 1959.

Sixteen years later, on a trip abroad, he sees a lookalike to Bujold, and gets swept away with this new girl. John Lithgow, as Robertson's business partner, is not happy with these events.

Robertson's low-key performance is as crucial to the manifold surprise impact as Bujold's versatile, sensual and effervescent charisma.

1976: NOMINATION: Best Original Score

●

O. C. AND STIGGS
1987, 109 mins, US Ⓥ col
Dir Robert Altman ***Prod*** Robert Altman, Peter Newman ***Scr*** Donald Cantrell, Ted Mann ***Ph*** Pierre Mignot ***Ed*** Elizabeth Kling ***Mus*** King Sunny Ade & His African Beats ***Art*** Scott Bushnell
Act Daniel H. Jenkins, Neill Barry, Paul Dooley, Jane Curtin, Ray Walston, Dennis Hopper (M-G-M/UA)

Loosely based on a story in *National Lampoon*, pic is an anarchistic jab at the insurance business and any other American institution that happens to be handy. In his best work such as *Nashville* and *MASH*, Robert Altman was able to weave together an array of sights and sounds into a distinctive social commentary. In *O. C. and Stiggs* the structure comes apart and what's left is mostly random silliness. Plot [by Tod Carroll and Ted Mann] has something to do with O. C. (Daniel H. Jenkins) and Stiggs's (Neill Barry) efforts to extract a pound of flesh from Arizona insurance magnate Randall Schwab (Paul Dooley) in revenge for cancelling the old age insurance of O. C.'s grandfather (Ray Walston).

Along for the ride through the desert heartland is Schwab's drunken wife (Jane Curtin), Stiggs's lecherous father (Donald May) and birdbrained mother (Carla Borelli), a shell-shocked Vietnam vet (Dennis Hopper) and a horny high school nurse (Tina Louise), to name just a few.

In spite of the shortcomings and tedium of the production, there are moments when it becomes evident there is a vision and talent behind all the nonsense. Performances are uniformly good, with Dennis Hopper once again excelling as a madman. [Pic was finished in 1984 but not released until 1987.]

●

OCEAN'S ELEVEN

1960, 127 mins, US Ⓥ ▭ col

Dir Lewis Milestone ***Prod*** Lewis Milestone ***Scr*** Harry Brown, Charles Lederer ***Ph*** William H. Daniels ***Ed*** Philip W. Anderson ***Mus*** Nelson Riddle ***Art*** Nicolai Remisoff

Act Frank Sinatra, Dean Martin, Sammy Davis, Jr., Peter Lawford, Angie Dickinson, Richard Conte (Warner)

Although basically a no-nonsense piece about the efforts of 11 ex-war buddies to make off with a multi-million dollar loot from five Vegas hotels, the film is frequently one resonant wisecrack away from turning into a musical comedy. Laboring under the handicaps of a contrived script, an uncertain approach and personalities in essence playing themselves, the production never quite makes its point, but romps along merrily unconcerned that it doesn't.

Coincidence runs rampant in the screenplay, based on a story by George Clayton Johnson and Jack Golden Russell. Set in motion on the doubtful premise that 11 playful, but essentially law-abiding wartime acquaintances from all walks of life would undertake a job that makes the Brinks' hoist pale by comparison, it proceeds to sputter and stammer through an interminable initial series of scrambled expository sequences.

Acting under the stigma of their own flashy, breezy identities, players such as Frank Sinatra, Dean Martin, Sammy Davis, Jr., and Peter Lawford never quite submerge themselves in their roles, nor try very hard to do so. At any rate, the pace finally picks up when the daring scheme is set in motion.

The dialog is sharp, but not always pertinent to the story being told. And director Lewis Milestone has failed to curb a tendency toward flamboyant but basically unrealistic behaviour, as if unable to decide whether to approach the yarn straight or with tongue-in-cheek.

•

OCTAGON, THE

1980, 103 mins, US Ⓥ ⦿ col

Dir Eric Karson ***Prod*** Joel Freeman ***Scr*** Leigh Chapman ***Ph*** Michel Hugo ***Ed*** Dann Cahn ***Mus*** Dick Halligan ***Art*** James Schoppe

Act Chuck Norris, Karen Carlson, Lee Van Cleef, Tadashi Yamashita, Carol Bagdasarian, Art Hindle (American Cinema)

A bizarre plot involving the Ninja cult of Oriental assassins with international terrorism provides plenty of chances for Chuck Norris and other martial arts experts to do their stuff, and pic has a nicely stylized look with excellent lensing and music.

Screenwriter Leigh Chapman, working from a story she wrote with Paul Aaron, weaves a wildly incredible but entertaining tale of retired martial arts champ Norris being recruited by wealthy Karen Carlson to rub out the terrorists who have earmarked her for death. Norris gets involved when he realizes his nemesis is Tadashi Yamashita, his sworn enemy from their youthful days as chopsocky pupils.

The vendetta culminates in a pitched battle at the octagonal training compound of the Ninja cult, a school for terrorists of all types.

•

OCTOBER

SEE: OKTYABR

•

OCTOBER MAN, THE

1947, 95 mins, UK Ⓥ b/w

Dir Roy Ward Baker ***Prod*** Eric Ambler ***Scr*** Eric Ambler ***Ph*** Erwin Hillier ***Ed*** Alan L. Jaggs ***Mus*** William Alwyn ***Art*** Alex Vetchinsky

Act John Mills, Joan Greenwood, Edward Chapman, Joyce Carey, Kay Walsh, Catherine Lacey (Two Cities)

Author of many thrillers, Eric Ambler makes his debut as producer of his own script, and a fine beginning it is, with John Mills in top form and a grand all-round cast. Unlike the usual Ambler story, this is not a whodunit or spy story. It's a study of the conflict in the mind of a mentally sick man, not absolutely certain that he hasn't committed murder.

John Mills plays Jim Ackland, an industrial chemist who suffers from a brain injury following an accident in which the child of a friend is killed. He blames himself for the child's death, and develops suicidal tendencies. Released from hospital, he is warned of a possible relapse unless he takes things easy. He returns to work and lives in a suburban hotel inhabited by a small cross-section of the community—retired business men, fussy old women, young people struggling for a job—some well-meaning and some viciously stupid.

Molly (Kay Walsh), a fashion model, is being ruthlessly pursued by Peachey (Edward Chapman), a retired wolf. In a tight corner she borrows a check from Jim, who has only met her once. The following day Molly is found murdered and Jim is suspected.

This bare outline, which omits the somewhat superimposed love affair between Jim and Jenny Carden (Joan Greenwood), can't do justice to the development and treatment of the yarn, nor to the unusual angles. The dialogue is taut and adult, and the direction by Roy [Ward] Baker, onetime assistant to Hitchcock, is imaginative. Only defect is the tempo. For a suspense pic it sometimes lacks pace.

•

OCTOPUSSY

1983, 130 mins, UK Ⓥ ⦿ ▭ col

Dir John Glen ***Prod*** Albert R. Broccoli ***Scr*** George MacDonald Fraser, Richard Maibaum, Michael G. Wilson ***Ph*** Alan Hume ***Ed*** John Grover, Peter Davies, Henry Richardson ***Mus*** John Barry ***Art*** Peter Lamont

Act Roger Moore, Maud Adams, Louis Jourdan, Kristina Wayborn, Kabir Bedi, Steven Berkoff (Eon/United Artists)

Storyline concerns a scheme by hawkish Russian General Orlov (Steven Berkoff) to launch a first-strike attack with conventional forces against the NATO countries in Europe, relying upon no nuclear retaliation by the West due to weakness brought about by peace movement in Europe.

Orlov is aided in his plan by beautiful smuggler Octopussy (Maud Adams), her trader-in-art-forgeries underling Kamal (Louis Jourdan) and exquisite assistant Magda (Kristina Wayborn). James Bond (Roger Moore, in his sixth entry) is set on their trail when fellow agent 009 (Andy Bradford) is killed at a circus in East Berlin.

Trail takes Bond to India (lensed in sumptuous travelogue shots) where he is assisted by local contact Vijay (tennis star Vijay Amritraj in a pleasant acting debut). Surviving an impromptu *Hounds of Zaroff* tiger hunt turned manhunt and other perils, Bond pursues Kamal to Germany for the hair-raising race against time conclusion.

Film's high points are the spectacular aerial stuntwork marking both the pre-credits teaser and extremely dangerous-looking climax.

•

ODD ANGRY SHOT, THE

1979, 90 mins, Australia Ⓥ col

Dir Tom Jeffrey ***Prod*** Tom Jeffrey, Sue Milliken ***Scr*** Tom Jeffrey ***Ph*** Don McAlpine ***Ed*** Brian Kavanagh ***Mus*** Michael Carlos ***Art*** Bernard Hides

Act Graham Kennedy, John Hargreaves, John Jarratt, Bryan Brown, Graeme Blundell (Samson)

Australia's involvement in the Vietnamese war created a political and moral dichotomy in the country such as hadn't been seen since the question of conscription at the time of World War I. If anything, Tom Jeffrey's *The Odd Angry Shot* could be said to be cathartic.

The film concenrates on a group of Aussie volunteers. Special Air Service troops, militarily as elite as the Yanks' Special Forces, but in this view, at least, rather more bawdy than the Americans as depicted in *The Deer Hunter*. It is the same futile war, but what Jeffrey has expressed faithfully is the pragmatism and essential hope-of-survival of the troops on the ground.

Jeffrey has been helped immeasurably by his cameraman, Don McAlpine, who worked as a news cameraman in Vietnam. There is no agonizing political or moral message, and Jeffrey maintains the basic good humor of the guys at a very believable pitch.

•

ODD COUPLE, THE

1968, 105 mins, US Ⓥ ⦿ ▭ col

Dir Gene Saks ***Prod*** Howard W. Koch ***Scr*** Neil Simon ***Ph*** Robert B. Hauser ***Ed*** Frank Bracht ***Mus*** Neal Hefti ***Art*** Hal Pereira, Walter Tyler

Act Jack Lemmon, Walter Matthau, John Fiedler, Herb Edelman, David Sheiner, Larry Haines (Paramount)

The Odd Couple, Neil Simon's smash legit comedy, has been turned into an excellent film starring Jack Lemmon and Walter Matthau. Simon's somewhat expanded screenplay retains the broad, as well as the poignant, laughs inherent in the rooming together of two men whose marriages are on the rocks.

Teaming of Lemmon and Matthau has provided each with an outstanding comedy partner. As the hypochondriac, domesticated and about-to-be-divorced Felix, Lemmon is excellent. Matthau also hits the bull's-eye in a superior characterization.

Carrying over from the legit version with Matthau are Monica Evans and Carole Shelley, the two English girls from upstairs, and John Fiedler, one of the poker game group which, until Lemmon moved in, revelled in cigarette butts, clumsy sandwiches, and other signs of disarray.

New to the plot is opening scene of Lemmon bumbling in suicide attempts in a Times Square flophouse. By the time he arrives at Matthau's apartment, his amusing misadventures have caused a wrenched back and neck. Staggered main titles help prolong this good intro.

1968: NOMINATIONS: Best Adapted Screenplay, Editing

•

ODD MAN OUT

(US: GANG WAR)

1947, 116 mins, UK Ⓥ ⦿ b/w

Dir Carol Reed ***Scr*** F. L. Green, R. C. Sherriff ***Ph*** Robert Krasker ***Ed*** Fergus McDonnell ***Mus*** William Alwyn ***Art*** Ralph Brinton

Act James Mason, Robert Newton, Robert Beatty, Kathleen Ryan, F. J. McCormick, Cyril Cusack (Two Cities)

Accent in this film [based on the novel by F. L. Green] is on art with a capital A. Carol Reed has made his film with deliberation and care, and has achieved splendid teamwork from every member of the cast. Occasionally too intent on pointing his moral and adorning his tale, he has missed little in its telling.

Story is set in a city in Northern Ireland and takes place between 4 pm and midnight on a winter's day. Johnnie, leader of an organization, sentenced for gun running, has broken jail and is hiding with his girl Kathleen. He plans a holdup on a mill to obtain funds, and although deprecating violence, he takes a gun. During the holdup he accidentally kills a man, is badly wounded himself, and the driver of the car panics, leaving Johnnie to fend for himself. Bleeding, he stumbles through the city trying to hide from the police.

For Mason, two-thirds of the film is silent. From the moment he is wounded he has few lines and has to drag himself along, a hunted man with a fatal wound. It is hardly his fault that, in this passive character that expresses little more than various phases of pain and occasional delirium, he is less effective than he could be.

Making her screen debut, Kathleen Ryan reveals undoubted ability and much promise. Graduate of the Abbey and Gate theatres, this 24-year-old redhead was "discovered" in Ireland by Reed, who coached and trained her for this part.

1947: NOMINATION: Best Editing

•

ODDS AGAINST TOMORROW

1959, 96 mins, US ⦿ b/w

Dir Robert Wise ***Prod*** Robert Wise ***Scr*** John O. Killens, Nelson Gidding ***Ph*** Joseph Brun ***Ed*** Dede Allen ***Mus*** John Lewis ***Art*** Leo Kerz

Act Harry Belafonte, Robert Ryan, Shelley Winters, Ed Begley, Gloria Grahame (HarBel/United Artists)

On one level, *Odds Against Tomorrow* is a taut crime melodrama. On another, it is an allegory about racism, greed and man's propensity for self-destruction. Not altogether successful in the second category, it still succeeds on its first.

The point of the screenplay, based on a novel of the same name by William P. McGivern, is that the odds against tomorrow coming at all are very long unless there is some understanding and tolerance today. The point is made by means of a crime anecdote, a framework not completely satisfactory for cleanest impact.

Harry Belafonte, Robert Ryan and Ed Begley form a partnership with plans to rob a bank with a haul estimated to total $150,000. An ill-matched trio, their optimistic plans are dependent on the closest teamwork. Belafonte, a horse-playing nightclub entertainer, is something of an adolescent. Ryan is a psychotic. Begley, as an ex-cop fired for crookedness, has learned from that experience only not to get caught.

Director Robert Wise has drawn fine performances from his players. It is the most sustained acting Belafonte has done. Ryan makes the flesh crawl as the fanatical bigot. Begley turns in a superb study of a foolish, befuddled man who dies, as he has lived, without knowing quite what he has been involved in.

Shelley Winters etches a memorable portrait, and Gloria Grahame is poignant in a brief appearance. Joseph Brun's black and white photography catches the grim spirit of the story and accents it with some glinting mood shots. John Lewis's music backs it with a neurotic, edgy, progressive jazz score.

•

ODESSA FILE, THE

1974, 128 mins, UK/W. Germany Ⓥ ⦿ ▭ col

Dir Ronald Neame ***Prod*** John Woolf, John R. Sloan ***Scr*** Kenneth Ross, George Markstein ***Ph*** Oswald Morris ***Ed*** Ralph Kemplen ***Mus*** Andrew Lloyd Webber ***Art*** Rolf Zehetbauer

Act Jon Voight, Maximilian Schell, Maria Schell, Mary Tamm, Derek Jacobi, Shmuel Rodensky (Columbia)

The Odessa File is an excellent filmization of Frederick Forsyth's novel of a reporter who tracks down former Nazi SS officers still undetected in 1960s Germany.

Jon Voight's accidental reading of the diary of a suicide (a Jewish survivor of Nazi prison camps) leads to his attempted infiltration of Odessa, a secret network of SS veterans who have maintained their cover in diverse positions in postwar commerce and government.

Voight's immediate search is for Maximilian Schell, a quest inhibited by secret Odessa officials, but facilitated by Israeli intelligence agents who also get on his tail.

As Voight establishes his credentials in a superb grilling by Noel Willman, his girl (Mary Tamm) is under close surveillance by Odessa-affiliated police, and Klaus Lowitsch is dispatched to kill him.

•

ODE TO BILLY JOE
1976, 105 mins, US Ⓥ col
Dir Max Baer ***Prod*** Max Baer, Roger Camras ***Scr*** Herman Raucher ***Ph*** Michel Hugo ***Ed*** Frank E. Morriss ***Mus*** Michel Legrand ***Art*** Philip Jefferies
Act Robby Benson, Glynnis O'Connor, Joan Hotchkis, Sandy McPeak, James Best, Terence Goodman (Warner)

Ode to Billy Joe is a superbly sensitive period romantic tragedy, based on Bobbie Gentry's 1967 hit song lyric. Robby Benson is excellent as Billy Joe McAllister, and Glynnis O'Connor is outstanding as his Juliet.

The time is 1953. O'Connor and Benson are both emerging into fumbling sexual awareness, written and acted in a way to bring out all of the humor, heart and horniness that attends on such matters. O'Connor's parents, sensationally played by Sandy McPeak and Joan Hotchkis, have a wary but loving eye out for her.

The puppy love affair unfolds smoothly as it is interwoven with family, church, work and community functions, all of which establish the people as real, loving folk and create a magnificent dramatic environment.

•

ODETTE
1950, 123 mins, UK b/w
Dir Herbert Wilcox ***Prod*** Herbert Wilcox ***Scr*** Warren Chetham-Strode ***Ph*** Max Greene ***Ed*** Bill Lewthwaite ***Mus*** Anthony Collins ***Art*** William C. Andrews
Act Anna Neagle, Trevor Howard, Marius Goring, Peter Ustinov, Bernard Lee (British Lion)

The film recaptures all the essential details of Odette's adventures as a secret agent in France during the last war. In the production of a factual story of this type [from the book by Jerrard Tickell], presentation inevitably tends to be a bit jerky. Herbert Wilcox's facile direction mainly succeeds in overcoming this difficulty. Logically, too, he has used French or German dialog when justified.

Acting is uniformly good. Anna Neagle puts all she's got into the playing of Odette. Trevor Howard gives a smooth and confident interpretation of Capt. Peter Churchill, the British agent whom she subsequently marries. Marius Goring plays the counter-espionage officer with a genuine conviction while Peter Ustinov gives one of his best performances as the secret radio operator.

•

OEDIPUS THE KING
1968, 97 mins, UK col
Dir Philip Saville ***Prod*** Michael Luke ***Scr*** Michael Luke, Philip Saville ***Ph*** Walter Lassally ***Ed*** Paul Davies ***Mus*** Yanni Christou ***Art*** Yanni Migadis
Act Christopher Plummer, Orson Welles, Lilli Palmer, Richard Johnson, Cyril Cusack (Rank/Crossroads)

This version of Sophocles's play deals fairly superficially with the bare bones of the tragic story of the king, dragged down to degradation after having discovered that, unwittingly, he has murdered his father and married and had children by his mother.

It is filmed with dignity, extremely well directed and excellently acted by a small cast of fine thesps.

Director Philip Saville and, indeed, the translation do not harp so melodramatically on the tragic sequences. Done with restraint, physical action is confined mainly to the assassination of Laius and a recap. Nor is the translation sonorously heavy but retains a dignified poetry.

Christopher Plummer as Oedipus gives a sterling performance. His early clashes with his brother-in-law (Richard Johnson) are striking and the latter's performance is a useful foil to Plummer's.

Lilli Palmer, as the ill-fated Jocasta, does not fully bring out the tragic personality until the final bitter scene, and Orson Welles is unusually subdued, but all the more effective, as Tiresias, the blind prophet of doom.

The film is superbly lensed with the greens and browns making a soft, yet bleak backdrop to the somber action.

•

OF A THOUSAND DELIGHTS
SEE: VAGHE STELLE DELL'ORSA

•

OFFENCE, THE
1973, 112 mins, US/UK Ⓥ col
Dir Sidney Lumet ***Prod*** Denis O'Dell ***Scr*** John Hopkins ***Ph*** Gerry Fisher ***Ed*** John Victor Smith ***Mus*** Harrison Birtwistle ***Art*** John W. Clark
Act Sean Connery, Trevor Howard, Vivien Merchant, Ian Bannen, Derek Newark, Peter Bowles (United Artists/Tantallon)

There's a powerful confrontation of authority and accused between police sergeant Sean Connery and suspected child molester Ian Bannen in Sidney Lumet's *The Offence*. A brilliant scene, however, does not in itself make for a brilliant overall feature.

This often cold and dreary tale is about the self-realization of a veteran police officer that his own mind contains much of the evil with which he is confronted daily. Indeed, his willing accumulation of brutality and violence-packed incidents is recognized almost immediately by Bannen and it is not long before accuser becomes the accused.

However, the lengthy lead-up to this important scene is played against dreary backgrounds and with colorless people.

•

OFFICER AND A GENTLEMAN, AN
1982, 126 mins, US Ⓥ ⦿ col
Dir Taylor Hackford ***Prod*** Martin Elfand ***Scr*** Douglas Day Stewart ***Ph*** Donald Thorin ***Ed*** Peter Zinner ***Mus*** Jack Nitzsche ***Art*** Philip M. Jefferies
Act Richard Gere, Debra Winger, Louis Gossett, Jr., David Keith, Lisa Blount, Lisa Eilbacher (Lorimar)

An Officer and a Gentleman deserves a 21-gun salute, maybe 42. Rarely does a film come along with so many finely drawn characters to care about.

Officer belongs to Louis Gossett, Jr., who takes a near-cliché role of the tough, unrelenting drill instructor and makes him a sympathetic hero without ever softening a whit.

The title refers to the official reward awaiting those willing to endure 13 weeks of agony in Naval Aviation Officer Candidate School, whose initial aim—via Gossett—is to wash out as many hopefuls as possible before letting the best move on to flight training.

Pic is a bit muddled, via flashback, in setting up Richard Gere's motives for going into the training. Suffice to say he did not enjoy a model childhood. On leave, Gere meets Debra Winger, one of the local girls laboring at a paper mill and hoping for a knight in naval officer's uniform to rescue her from a life of drudgery. It's another fetching little slut role for Winger and she makes the most of it.

A secondary romance involves Gere's friend and fellow candidate (David Keith), who takes a tumble for Winger's friend (Lisa Blount), another slut but not so fetching.

1982: Best Supp. Actor (Louis Gossett, Jr.), Original Song ("Up Where We Belong")

NOMINATIONS: Best Actress (Debra Winger), Original Screenplay, Editing, Original Score

•

OFFICIAL STORY, THE
SEE: LA HISTORIA OFICIAL

•

OFF LIMITS
1953, 87 mins, US Ⓥ b/w
Dir George Marshall ***Prod*** Harry Tugend ***Scr*** Hal Kanter, Jack Sher ***Ph*** J. Peverell Marley ***Ed*** Arthur Schmidt ***Mus*** Van Cleave ***Art*** Hal Pereira, Walter Tyler
Act Bob Hope, Mickey Rooney, Marilyn Maxwell, Eddie Mayehoff, Stanley Clements, Jack Dempsey (Paramount)

Bob Hope's brash, smart-aleck comedy is turned loose on the army for an entertaining 87 minutes of nonsense that has plenty of laugh appeal.

Hope is his boastful self as manager-trainer of Stanley Clements, lightweight fighter who has just moved up to the championship. When Clements is drafted, Hope's gangster partners, headed by Marvin Miller, make him enlist to watch over the fighter. Hope, much to his disgust, is fit despite his efforts to get a psycho discharge.

Mickey Rooney enters the picture as a draftee eager to have Hope make him into a fighter. From then on it's a case of stringing Rooney along while trying to get next to Maxwell, who doesn't like fighters or fight managers, and convincing Eddie Mayehoff, a rulebook Military Policeman, that Hope is not completely hopeless.

Hope fans will find their favorite comic in fine form. Rooney's role is his best in some time, and Mayehoff is delightful as the rule-quoting MP.

•

OFF LIMITS
(UK: SAIGON)
1988, 102 mins, US Ⓥ ⦿ col
Dir Christopher Crowe ***Prod*** Alan Barnette ***Scr*** Christopher Crowe, Jack Thibeau ***Ph*** David Gribble ***Ed*** Douglas Ibold ***Mus*** James Newton Howard ***Art*** Dennis Washington
Act Willem Dafoe, Gregory Hines, Fred Ward, Amanda Pays, Kay Tong Lim, Scott Glenn (20th Century-Fox)

Off Limits is a well-crafted story that explores the underbelly of 1968 Saigon well enough as two undercover detectives (Willem Dafoe, Gregory Hines) go about to solve a string of prostitute murders by a high-ranking army officer. While the plot and characterizations are well worked out, what this production lacks is enough pizzazz to distinguish it from others of this genre.

Dafoe and Hines stick together like glue, working diligently in the sticky Saigon heat with equally racist attitudes about "gooks" and "slopes." Dafoe is a little more hot-tempered and Hines only slightly less intense.

This is much more a civilian story that only twice puts the action out in the country where the bombs are exploding. As such, with the exception of one scene where a sadist colonel, whom Dafoe and Hines suspect of being the sicko murderer, is pushing Vietcong out of a helicopter, lensing could have been accomplished on the backlot.

Director Christopher Crowe has tried to make a tough picture with sensitivity, though it's the former that mostly prevails. Dafoe has a platonic affection for a nun (Amanda Pays) who counsels prostitutes and takes care of their children. Fred Ward is particularly good as the partners' superior, Master Sgt. Dix.

•

OFFRET
(THE SACRIFICE)
1986, 150 mins, Sweden/France Ⓥ ⦿ col
Dir Andrei Tarkovsky ***Prod*** Katinka Farago ***Scr*** Andrei Tarkovsky ***Ph*** Sven Nykvist ***Ed*** Andrei Tarkovsky, Michal Leszczylowski ***Mus*** Watazumido Shuso ***Art*** Anna Asp
Act Erland Josephson, Susan Fleetwood, Allan Edwall, Sven Wolter, Gudrun Gisladottir, Valerie Mairesse (SFI/Argos)

The Sacrifice, which writer-director Andrei Tarkovsky calls "as Russian a film as any other made by me," is primarily a Swedish production with Swedish dialogue. It takes place in and around a house on the desolate and marshy coastal plains of a Swedish island in the Baltic Sea adjacent to the Soviet Union. Although decidedly overlong, the doomsday film is Tarkovsky's most generally accessible work.

Film concerns a middle-aged intellectual, Alexander (Erland Josephson), whose birthday dinner is interrupted by what is obviously the nuclear Big Bang, although it is seen (an icy light followed by near darkness) rather than heard. A mailman (Allan Edwall), of philosophical bent and knowledge, advises him to go sleep with a local witch and use her innocence to seek atonement for the sins of mankind.

Alexander follows the mailman's advice. But first he sinks to his knees and promises God to leave behind all his worldly possessions, including his young and cherished son, if the world may be allowed, so to speak, another lease on life. Alexander burns down his own house. He is considered looney by the survivors and is taken away, destined for the nuthouse.

All Tarkovsky's pet images and sounds—e.g., water dripping into stale pools, black & white flashbacks of decay and disaster, Japanese art and lifestyles—are emulated to heighten film's aesthetic values. And there is Sven Nykvist's camera wizardry with ultralong takes, and lighting that provides a sheen to even the most somber frames.

•

OF HUMAN BONDAGE
1934, 83 mins, US Ⓥ ⦿ b/w
Dir John Cromwell ***Prod*** Pandro S. Berman ***Scr*** Lester Cohen ***Ph*** Henry W. Gerrard ***Ed*** William Morgan ***Mus*** Max Steiner ***Art*** Van Nest Polglase, Carroll Clark
Act Leslie Howard, Bette Davis, Frances Dee, Kay Johnson, Reginald Denny, Alan Hale (Radio)

Basically, it's an obvious and familiar theme [from the novel by W. Somerset Maugham]. The unrequited love of the art-medical student, inhibited and clubfooted to the degree that he stumbles physically, mentally and spiritually, commands respect and sympathy. But as the footage unreels, the feeling grows that he's pretty much of a clunk to go the hard way he does for the strumpet who treats him so shabbily.

Leslie Howard tries hard to mellow his assignment. But somehow he misses at times because the script is too much against him. Perhaps Bette Davis is to blame. She plays her free 'n' easy vamp too well, so that it negates any audience sympathy for the gentle Howard.

Reginald Denny and Alan Hale get over a couple of lusty innings as males on the hunt who know how to handle gals of her type. Reginald Owen, too, milks his assignment.

Locales are Paris and London, chiefly London, with Davis in Cockney dialect throughout.

•

OF HUMAN BONDAGE

1946, 100 mins, US b/w

Dir Edmund Goulding ***Prod*** Henry Blanke ***Scr*** Catherine Turney ***Ph*** Peverell Marley ***Ed*** Clarence Kolster ***Mus*** Erich Wolfgang Korngold ***Art*** Hugh Reticker, Harry Kelso

Act Eleanor Parker, Paul Henreid, Alexis Smith, Edmund Gwenn, Janis Paige, Patric Knowles (Warner)

Somerset Maugham story has been given excellent period mounting to fit early London background, is well-played and directed in individual sequences, but lacks overall smoothness.

Top roles go to Eleanor Parker, as the tart; Paul Henreid, the sensitive artist-doctor; and Alexis Smith, novelist. A third femme love interest is Janis Paige. Three femmes represent various loves that enter the life of Henreid, frustrated artist, but major interest is concentrated on character played by Parker and how she affects Henreid's happiness.

Edmund Goulding's direction gets good work out of the cast generally and helps interest although most of major characters carry little sympathy, Parker's work is excellent, as is Henreid's depiction of the self-pitying cripple. Smith's role has been edited to a comparatively small part.

•

OF HUMAN BONDAGE

1964, 98 mins, UK Ⓥ b/w

Dir Ken Hughes, Henry Hathaway ***Prod*** James Woolf ***Scr*** Bryan Forbes ***Ph*** Oswald Morris ***Ed*** Russell Lloyd ***Mus*** Ron Goodwin ***Art*** John Box

Act Kim Novak, Laurence Harvey, Robert Morley, Siobhan McKenna, Roger Livesey, Jack Hedley (Seven Arts/M-G-M)

There was the Leslie Howard/Bette Davis 1934 version of this story and the 1946 entry starring Paul Henried and Eleanor Parker. This stab, with Laurence Harvey and Kim Novak, will not erase the memories. For those who come fresh to *Of Human Bondage*, this perceptive but highly introspective yarn by Somerset Maugham may seem a hard-to-take slab of period meller.

The pic had a ruffled nascency, due primarily to clashes of opinion among top brass. Henry Hathaway quit to let in Ken Hughes as director and it's bruited that the star duo did not always see eye-to-eye on the chore in hand.

Story concerns a withdrawn, young medical student very conscious of his clubfoot who manages to become a doctor in London's East End despite being totally besotted with the tawdry charms of a promiscuous waitress.

Allowing for the fact that Bryan Forbes's screenplay is light on humor, Harvey nevertheless plays the role in such a stiff, martyred manner as to forfeit any sympathy or liking in the audience.

The role that made Davis doesn't serve the same purpose for Novak. Yet she gamely tackles a wide range of emotions and seems to be far more aware of the demands of her role than is her costar.

Collectors of cinema trivia will notice, with interest, the fleeting appearances by highly paid scriptwriter Forbes as a student-extra without any lines, an inexplicable throwback to his earlier business of being an actor.

•

OF HUMAN HEARTS

1938, 100 mins, US b/w

Dir Clarence Brown ***Prod*** John W. Considine, Jr. ***Scr*** Bradbury Foote ***Ph*** Clyde DeVinna ***Ed*** Frank E. Hull ***Mus*** Herbert Stothart ***Art*** Cedric Gibbons, Harry Oliver, Edwin B. Willis

Act Walter Huston, James Stewart, Beulah Bondi, Guy Kibbee, Charles Coburn, John Carradine (M-G-M)

Frontier life in a village on the banks of the Ohio river in the days preceding the Civil War is the background against which Clarence Brown tells the story of a mother's sacrifice for the career of an ungrateful son.

Brown is said to have cherished the idea of producing this story for some time. Screenplay is based on Honore Morrow's story *Benefits Forgot*, published nearly a score of years earlier.

A meaner, more selfish, bigoted and ornery group never existed than these villagers, into whose midst comes a preacher of the Gospel with his wife and 12-year-old son. They had promised him $400 a year to be custodian of their souls, then cut the allowance to $250 and some cast-off clothing for his dependents.

The preacher accepts these terms with humility. The son, however, rebels against the petty tyranny and selfishness of the neighbors.

Latter part of the film relates the boy's brilliant success as a surgeon in the Union army, and his neglect for his mother, now widowed.

Walter Huston is the zealous circuit riding preacher, a man of uncompromising principle. Beulah Bondi is the wife and mother, and she shades the transitions of age with convincing acting. Gene Reynolds first appears as the son, a role played by James Stewart in the later scenes.

Chief cause for disappointment with the film is its slow pace, and the defeatist mood of the story.

1938: NOMINATION: Best Supp. Actress (Beulah Bondi)

•

OF MICE AND MEN

1939, 104 mins, US Ⓥ ⊙ b/w

Dir Lewis Milestone ***Prod*** Hal Roach ***Scr*** Eugene Solow ***Ph*** Norbert Brodine ***Ed*** Bert Jordan ***Mus*** Aaron Copland ***Art*** Nicolai Remisoff

Act Burgess Meredith, Lon Chaney, Jr., Betty Field, Charles Bickford, Roman Bohnen, Bob Steele (Roach/United Artists)

Under skillful directorial guidance of Lewis Milestone, the picture retains all of the forceful and poignant drama of John Steinbeck's original play and novel, in presenting the strange palship and eventual tragedy of the two California ranch itinerants. In transferring the story to the screen, scripter Eugene Solow eliminated the strong language and forthright profanity. Despite this requirement for the Hays whitewash squad, Solow and Milestone retain all of the virility of the piece in its original form.

As in the play, all of the action takes place on the San Joaquin valley barley ranch. George and Lennie catch on as hands. Former's strange wardship of the half-wit possessed of Herculean strength is never quite explained—in fact he wonders himself just why. George keeps Lennie close to him always—continually fearful that the simpleton will kill someone with his brute power. The pair plan to buy a small ranch of their own, where Lennie can raise rabbits, when disaster strikes.

Despite the lack of boxoffice names in the cast setup, the players have been excellently selected. Burgess Meredith is capital as George, and Lon Chaney, Jr., dominates throughout with a fine portrayal of the childlike giant. Betty Field is the sexy wife who encourages approaches from the ranch workers; Bob Steele is her jealous and hard hitting husband.

1939: NOMINATIONS: Best Picture, Original Score, Sound

•

OF MICE AND MEN

1992, 110 mins, US Ⓥ ⊙ col

Dir Gary Sinise ***Prod*** Russ Smith, Gary Sinise ***Scr*** Horton Foote ***Ph*** Kenneth MacMillan ***Ed*** Robert L. Sinise ***Mus*** Mark Isham ***Art*** David Gropman

Act John Malkovich, Gary Sinise, Ray Walston, Casey Siemaszko, Sherilyn Fenn, John Terry (M-G-M)

Well-mounted and very traditional, *Of Mice and Men* honorably serves John Steinbeck's classic story of two Depression-era drifters without bringing anything new to it.

First published in 1937, the novel has had continued life as a Broadway play, a Hollywood film starring Lon Chaney, Jr., and Burgess Meredith, and a 1980 stage piece at Chicago's Steppenwolf Theater that featured John Malkovich and Gary Sinise, who repeat their roles here.

Set in a lonely world of itinerant men in 1930, intelligent adaptation begins with George and Lennie fleeing a posse of dogs and armed men across the sun-baked California countryside. They have jobs lined up at a farm near Soledad. George (Sinise) is a quick-witted man of few but well-chosen words with no family or money to his name. His only charge is Lennie (Malkovich), a lumbering simpleton who has the mind of a child but the strength of an ox.

Dramatic gears start turning when belligerent farm boss son Curley (Casey Siemaszko) starts picking on Lennie. Before long, son's lovely, lonely wife (Sherilyn Fenn) begins hanging around the bunkhouse and barn, seemingly with an eye for George.

Captured in lovely, burnished hues by lenser Kenneth MacMillan and evocatively realized by production designer David Gropman, pic could not look more different from the studio-bound Lewis Milestone rendition of more than 50 years ago. Performances are sterling.

•

OH DAD, POOR DAD, MAMMA'S HUNG YOU IN THE CLOSET, AND I'M FEELIN' SO SAD

1967, 86 mins, US Ⓥ col

Dir Richard Quine ***Prod*** Ray Stark, Stanley Rubin ***Scr*** Ian Bernard ***Ph*** Geoffrey Unsworth ***Ed*** Warren Low, David Wages ***Mus*** Neal Hefti ***Art*** Phil Jeffries

Act Rosalind Russell, Robert Morse, Barbara Harris, Hugh Griffith, Jonathan Winters, Lionel Jeffries (Paramount)

Producers have labored mightily to bring forth a mouse. Rosalind Russell is the emasculating mother of Robert Morse, sired by Jonathan Winters who is dead, but stuffed and carried around by his widow as she and son travel about. Barbara Harris is the nymphet chippie who puts the make on Morse so successfully that he kills her in a psycho-substitution for his ma. Hugh Griffith is an aging lecher eyed by Russell as her next victim.

Despite multi-colored wigs and a game attempt, Russell falls flat. Morse has an appealing, winsome quality which certain film roles will fit, but not this one. Harris does rather well, however, and Griffith is up to the demands of his role. Winters gets the best comedy material, but it clashes with the rest. Film was shot on Jamaica locations, which adds color, but to no avail.

•

O. HENRY'S FULL HOUSE

1952, 116 mins, US b/w

Dir Henry Hathaway, Howard Hawks, Henry King, Henry Koster, Jean Negulesco ***Prod*** Andre Hakim ***Scr*** Richard Breen, Walter Bullock, Ivan Goff, Ben Roberts, Lamar Trotti ***Ph*** Lloyd Ahern, Lucien Ballard, Milton Krasner, Joe MacDonald ***Ed*** Nick De Maggio, Barbara McLean, William B. Murphy ***Mus*** Alfred Newman

Act Charles Laughton, Marilyn Monroe, Richard Widmark, Anne Baxter, Fred Allen, Jeanne Crain (20th Century-Fox)

This ties together five of O. Henry's classics into a full house of entertainment that has something for all tastes. The five classics are tied together by John Steinbeck's narration.

The Cop and the Anthem gets the quintet off to an enjoyable 19-minute start as Charles Laughton milks the fat part of Soapy, the gentleman bum who tries unsuccessfully to get arrested so he can spend the winter months in a warm jail.

The Clarion Call is a 22-minute excursion into melodrama with a twist. Dale Robertson plays the cop with a conscience who must arrest Richard Widmark, an old pal gone wrong and to whom he owes a debt.

The Last Leaf plunges into dramatics for 23 minutes, with Anne Baxter, Jean Peters and Gregory Ratoff keeping it emotionally sure. It's the tale of a girl, without the will to live because of an unhappy love affair, who believes she will die when the last leaf falls from a vine outside her window.

Fred Allen, Oscar Levant and young Lee Aaker keep amusing a highly burlesqued takeoff on *The Ransom of Red Chief*, the comedy saga of two city slickers who make the mistake of kidnapping for ransom the hellion son of a backwoods Alabama rich farmer. It's broad fun as directed by Howard Hawks.

Picture closes with a choice little account of that tender story of young love, *The Gift of the Magi*, splendidly trouped by Jeanne Crain and Farley Granger.

•

OH! FOR A MAN

SEE: WILL SUCCESS SPOIL ROCK HUNTER?

•

OH, GOD!

1977, 97 mins, US Ⓥ col

Dir Carl Reiner ***Prod*** Jerry Weintraub ***Scr*** Larry Gelbert ***Ph*** Victor Kemper ***Ed*** Bud Molin ***Mus*** Jack Elliott ***Art*** Jack Senter

Act George Burns, John Denver, Teri Garr, Donald Pleasence, Ralph Bellamy, William Daniels (Warner)

Oh, God! is a hilarious film which benefits from the brilliant teaming of George Burns, as the Almighty in human form, and John Denver, sensational in his screen debut as a supermarket assistant manager who finds himself a suburban Moses.

Carl Reiner's controlled and easy direction of a superb screenplay and a strong cast makes the Jerry Weintraub production a warm and human comedy.

An Avery Corman novel is the basis for Larry Gelbart's adaptation which makes its humanistic points while taking gentle pokes at organized Establishment religions, in particular the kind of fund-raising fundamentalism epitomized by

Paul Sorvino. Teri Garr is excellent as Denver's perplexed but loyal wife.

1977: NOMINATION: Best Adapted Screenplay

•

OH, GOD! BOOK II
1980, 94 mins, US col
Dir Gilbert Cates ***Prod*** Gilbert Cates ***Scr*** Josh Greenfeld, Hal Goldman, Fred S. Fox, Seaman Jacobs, Melissa Miller ***Ph*** Ralph Woolsey ***Ed*** Peter E. Berger ***Mus*** Charles Fox ***Art*** Preston Ames
Act George Burns, Suzanne Pleshette, David Birney, Louanne, John Louie, Howard Duff (Warner)

Oh, God! Book II is not a sequel to the hit 1977 release but rather an alternate approach to the same basic premise: what would happen if God were to appear to an ordinary person with instructions to "spread my message." Absence this time of John Denver, his chemistry with lead George Burns, and the original's solid comedy material lead to a bland, unstimulating film.

Script [from a story by Josh Greenfeld] has a pleasant moppet (Louanne) meeting God (Burns) in the lounge of a Chinese restaurant. It seems that Burns has decided to enlist a child "with belief in things you can't see" to remind people that God is still around. Since Louanne's dad (David Birney) is an adman, she sets out to concoct a slogan which will "make God a household name."

Burns is fine once again, a master of the throwaway line and well-suited to tone down the religious philosophy in the script. More screen time, however, is allotted to debuting Louanne, a pleasant and talented youngster who holds one's sympathy. Suzanne Pleshette and David Birney as her estranged parents are effective in limited roles.

•

OH, GOD! YOU DEVIL
1984, 96 mins, US col
Dir Paul Bogart ***Prod*** Robert M. Sherman ***Scr*** Andrew Bergman ***Ph*** King Baggot ***Ed*** Randy Roberts, Andy Zall ***Mus*** David Shire ***Art*** Peter Wooley
Act George Burns, Ted Wass, Ron Silver, Roxanne Hart, Eugene Roche, Robert Desiderio (Warner)

After two turns as an amusing Supreme Being, George Burns proves to be an equally diverting demon in *Oh God! You Devil*. Director Paul Bogart and writer Andrew Bergman have let Burns loose as Lucifer and relegated Burns as God to little more than a cameo.

Bergman's plot is unashamedly Faustian: struggling musician Ted Wass is desperate for the break that will bring happiness and afford parenthood for him and wife Roxanne Hart. Bad Burns picks up Wass's wail and a deal is soon struck. Burns switches him with an already reigning rock star (Robert Desiderio) whose own pact with the devil has run out.

Unhappily, the story didn't need to get this involved and it winds up constantly trying to pull the picture apart, working against the comedy. By the time Burns as God heeds Wass's plea for salvation, it's almost too much for even Him to iron out satisfactorily.

Ron Silver does an excellent rendition of a hotshot record company executive and Eugene Roche is delightful as the hopeless agent who's originally in charge of Wass's failing career.

•

OH, MR. PORTER!
1937, 84 mins, UK b/w
Dir Marcel Varnel ***Prod*** Edward Black ***Scr*** J.O.C. Orton, Val Guest, Marriott Edgar ***Ph*** Arthur Crabtree ***Ed*** R. E. Dearing, Alfred Roome ***Mus*** Louis Levy (dir.) ***Art*** Alex Vetchinsky
Act Will Hay, Moore Marriott, Graham Moffatt, Sebastian Smith, Percy Walsh, Agnes Lauchlan (Gainsborough)

A railway comedy [story by Frank Launder], reminiscent of *The Ghost Train* (1931), written around the comic personality of Will Hay, supported by his very "aged" and very "young" foils.

An amiable misfit, with a brother-in-law in the railway company, is sent as a last resort to a tiny, obscure village in Ireland as stationmaster, where his family hope to be rid of him. Finding a decrepit clerk and fat-boy porter the only occupants of the station, where no train ever stops, the newcomer tries to convert the ramshackle dump into something worthy of his dignity.

He senses a sinister atmosphere, in that his predecessors have either disappeared mysteriously, or gone nutty. Tracking a lost excursion to a disused tunnel and derelict line, the dauntless stationmaster discovers the supposedly ghostly crew are gun-runners about to get over the border.

No love interest to mar the comedy, as far as the juvenile mind is concerned, and the whole thing is amusing, if overlong.

•

O.H.M.S.
(US: YOU'RE IN THE ARMY NOW)
1937, 87 mins, UK b/w
Dir Raoul Walsh ***Prod*** [uncredited] ***Scr*** Lesser Samuels, Ralph Bettinson, Austin Melford, Bryan Wallace ***Ph*** Roy Kellino ***Ed*** Charles Saunders ***Mus*** Louis Levy (dir.) ***Art*** Edward Metzner
Act Wallace Ford, John Mills, Anna Lee, Grace Bradley, Frank Cellier, Peter Croft (Gaumont-British)

Not much to get excited about. Takes off from a fetching theme, but that nothing much eventuates can largely be blamed on a dour and flabby script.

Wallace Ford is a lively enough personality in the central role. Narrative poses him as a petty American racketeer who flees to England from a threatened rap for murder. There he turns to the army as a hideout, enlisting as from Canada. With occasional touches of humor, picture relates his doings as a recruit, adding romance to the proceedings by making Ford the third corner in a play for the sergeant-major's daughter (Anna Lee). His rival, and a good natured one, is his barracks sidekick (John Mills).

Complications develop when Ford's former showgirl flame from the States pops up. Ford stows away on a ship and finds himself occupying the same vessel as his regiment bound for China. The girl is also aboard. Picture goes melodramatic for the final reel.

•

OH . . . ROSALINDA!!
1955, 101 mins, UK col
Dir Michael Powell, Emeric Pressburger ***Prod*** Michael Powell, Emeric Pressburger ***Scr*** Michael Powell, Emeric Pressburger ***Ph*** Christopher Challis ***Ed*** Reginald Mills ***Mus*** Frederick Lewis (dir.) ***Art*** Hein Heckroth
Act Michael Redgrave, Mel Ferrer, Anton Walbrook, Dennis Price, Anthony Quayle, Ludmilla Tcherina (ABPC)

An opera converted to the screen inevitably loses much in transit, the result being, of necessity, half fantasty, half screen reality. In this instance, the story of *Die Fledermaus* is brought up-to-date and set in Vienna on the eve of her restoration as a sovereign state, still under the control of the four occupying powers. It is a lavish production, highly diverting and spectacular.

Anton Walbrook, as malignant compere Dr. Falke, takes the audience into his confidence preceding the opening of the story, explaining the progress of a malicious practical joke he is perpetrating. To accentuate the staginess and improbability of the story, sets are exaggerated in sugarcake dressing and the famous songs given new lyrics [by Dennis Arundell] to fit the modern sphere.

The captivating Rosalinda (Ludmilla Tcherina), married to a French officer, is pursued by an old flame, a U.S. officer, and is caught in compromising conditions by an escort guard who mistakes him for her husband, due for barrack detention. To save her reputation, her lover allows himself to be jailed while she goes to a masked ball given by the Russian commandant and flirts outrageously with her husband.

Michael Redgrave [singing his own part] has an adequate lightness of touch as the Gallic philanderer. Tcherina shows more of her person than her personality as his gay wife, with her role attractively sung by Sari Barabas.

Mel Ferrer [sung by Alexander Young] is dashing as the persistent American wooer, and Anthony Quayle [singing his own part] supplies the requisite somber touch to the character of the Russian officer who mellows under the influence of champagne and dames. [Walbrook's singing is dubbed by Walter Berry.]

•

OH! WHAT A LOVELY WAR
1969, 144 mins, UK col
Dir Richard Attenborough ***Prod*** Brian Duffy, Richard Attenborough ***Scr*** [Len Deighton] ***Ph*** Gerry Turpin ***Ed*** Kevin Connor ***Mus*** Alfred Ralston ***Art*** Don Ashton
Act Ralph Richardson, Laurence Olivier, John Gielgud, John Mills, Michael Redgrave, Vanessa Redgrave (Paramount/Accord)

Richard Attenborough's debut as a film director can be labelled with such debased showbiz verbal coinage as fabulous, sensational, stupendous, etc. It also happens to be dedicated, exhilarating, shrewd, mocking, funny, emotional, witty, poignant and technically brilliant.

A satire on war in which the songs are an integral part of the message, it was shot entirely on location, in and around Brighton [based on Joan Littlewood's Theatre Workshop production, by Charles Chilton and members of the original cast, after a stage treatment by Ted Allan].

Oh! What a Lovely War is an indictment of war which never relies on violence. Sudden, brutal death in combat is omitted and far more effectively, is rammed home by the symbol of poppies for each death.

The film is a kick in the pants for jingoism, false heroics, vanity and stupidity in high places. It never lessens or denigrates the bravery of those who took part, but brilliantly pinpoints the collective stupidity that made such a holocaust possible. The familiar wartime songs, sentiment, humor and satire are all incorporated, but Attenborough has never allowed any to stretch a mood beyond its capacity.

The film is seen through the eyes and family life of the humble Smith family, whose sons all go to war and are senselessly killed.

•

OIL FOR THE LAMPS OF CHINA
1935, 110 mins, US b/w
Dir Mervyn LeRoy ***Prod*** [Robert Lord] ***Scr*** Laird Doyle ***Ph*** Tony Gaudio ***Ed*** William Clemens ***Mus*** Leo F. Forbstein (dir.) ***Art*** Robert M. Haas
Act Pat O'Brien, Josephine Hutchinson, Jean Muir, Lyle Talbot, John Eldredge, Donald Crisp (Cosmopolitan/Warner)

This story, in book form, was a bestseller for over a year and caused a lot of talk. In transferring it to screen the filmers have taken many liberties, so that it evolves as a choppy, long, and sometimes confused yarn.

Alice Tisdale Hobart's original was an indictment of a great oil company for its subjugation of its employees. Film switches that around to a man's blind struggle against mistreatment, dishonesty in officials, personal misfortune, and rank deception on the part of his officers, with nothing more than faith in "the company" as his wand.

Story is laid practically entirely in China. The Atlantis Oil Company has sent Pat O'Brien over there to sell oil to the Chinese. Because he's saving the company some money, his first baby dies in childbirth. Because his best friend has lost a minor sales contract, he fires him, etc. Comes the revolution. The rebels try to take a few thousand dollars of the company's money so he risks his life, sees his assistant shot, is badly wounded himself, and is in a hospital for months. But he saves the $15,000. When he's out of the hospital he's rewarded by being demoted.

•

OKLAHOMA!
1955, 142 mins, US col
Dir Fred Zinnemann ***Prod*** Arthur Hornblow, Jr. ***Scr*** Sonya Levien, William Ludwig ***Ph*** Robert Surtees ***Ed*** Gene Ruggiero (70mm), George Boemler (35mm) ***Mus*** Jay Blackton (sup.), Robert Russell Bennett (arr.), Adolph Deutsch (adapt.) ***Art*** Oliver Smith
Act Gordon MacRae, Gloria Grahame, Gene Nelson, Charlotte Greenwood, Shirley Jones, Rod Steiger (Magna)

The innovative musical comedy magic that Richard Rodgers and Oscar Hammerstein II first created when The Theatre Guild produced their *Oklahoma!* [in 1943] has been captured and, in some details, expanded in the film version. The tunes ring out with undiminished delight. The characters pulsate with spirit. The Agnes De Mille choreography makes the play literally leap.

The wide screen used for the Todd-AO process adds production scope and visual grandeur, capturing a vista of blue sky and green prairie that can be breathtaking.

Heading the cast, Gordon MacRae as Curly, and Shirley Jones as Laurey make a bright, romantic pair. The entire cast goes through its paces with verve and spirit. If the singing is good, the acting just fine, top honors go to De Mille and her dancers.

After all's said and done, the main burden still falls on MacRae and Jones. MacRae not only looks the part of Curly, he acts it out with a modicum of theatrics. He cuts a clean-cut figure and he delivers his songs in grand style.

1955: Best Sound Recording, Scoring of a Musical Picture

NOMINATIONS: Best Color Cinematography, Editing

•

OKLAHOMA CRUDE
1973, 108 mins, US col
Dir Stanley Kramer ***Prod*** Stanley Kramer ***Scr*** Marc Norman ***Ph*** Robert Surtees ***Ed*** Folmar Blangsted ***Mus*** Henry Mancini ***Art*** Alfred Sweeney
Act George C. Scott, Faye Dunaway, John Mills, Jack Palance, William Lucking, Harvey Jason (Columbia)

Oklahoma Crude is a dramatically choppy potboiler about oil wildcatting in 1913.

Faye Dunaway plays a bitter woman determined to bring in an oil well on her own, aided by Rafael Campos, an Indian laborer. John Mills, aiming to help her out after years of parental abandonment, recruits George C. Scott from the hobo jungles. The three of them (Campos is killed off early) joust with Jack Palance, snarling provocateur of the oil trust which wants Dunaway's property.

Since Oklahoma today does not resemble 1913, director Stanley Kramer found a great location in Stockton, California, but the solid impact of that choice is often negated by erratic special effects work.

Scott hunkers around chewing the scenery, but occasionally the interplay with Dunaway is momentarily touching. Mills does well, but Palance's caricature destroys the chance for a good, tough characterization.

•

OKTYABR
(OCTOBER; TEN DAYS THAT SHOOK THE WORLD)

1928, 115 mins, USSR Ⓥ ⊙ ⊗ b/w

Dir Sergei Eisenstein, Grigori Alexandrov ***Scr*** Sergei Eisenstein, Grigori Alexandrov ***Ph*** Eduard Tisse, Vladimir Nilsen, Vladimir Popov ***Ed*** Sergei Eisenstein ***Mus*** Edmund Meisel [added for German release] ***Art*** Vasili Kovrigin

Act Vasili Nikandrov, N. Popov, Boris Livanov, Eduard Tisse (Sovkino)

Sergei Eisenstein's classic evocation of the Bolshevik Revolution, *October* is epic filmmaking that shows Eisenstein's strengths and weaknesses. Eisenstein himself considered *October* a failure, and abandoned to posterity no less than four divergent versions (not including the sundry watered-down export copies invariably released as *Ten Days That Shook the World*).

Commissioned for the 10th anni festivities of the 1917 Revolution, *October* was held up for release for months while Eisenstein, under orders from Stalin, cut out the many episodes of his film concerning Leon Trotsky, who was expelled from the Communist Party as film was being completed.

Film has been criticized for its lack of clarity and often idiosyncratic interpretation of the major events leading from the deposition of the czar in the February Revolution to the Bolshevik seizure of power eight months later.

For all its incoherence, *October* carries the spectator on a tidal wave of stunning imagery, with such high points as the tragically dispersed workers' demonstration in Petrograd and the climactic, brilliantly sustained siege of the Winter Palace (said to be much more spectacular than the original event).

No praise of Eisenstein's visual mastery can be complete without mention of his inventive chief cameraman Eduard Tisse.

Eisenstein's often playful experiments in intellectual montage are not always his forte here. Though the famous satiric passage on Prime Minister Kerensky's symbolic rise to power in the Provincial Government still is cinematically sharp, other sequences are long-winded and hermetic.

[Version reviewed was a composite of two variant prints dictated by German composer Edmund Meisel's original sheet music, shown on pic's 50th anni. Original version ran approx. 110 mins.]

•

OLD ACQUAINTANCE

1943, 110 mins, US b/w

Dir Vincent Sherman ***Prod*** Henry Blanke ***Scr*** John Van Druten, Lenore Coffee ***Ph*** Sol Polito ***Ed*** [uncredited] ***Mus*** Franz Waxman ***Art*** John Hughes

Act Bette Davis, Miriam Hopkins, Gig Young, John Loder, Dolores Moran, Philip Reed (Warner)

Bette Davis and Miriam Hopkins were schoolgirl chums. With former leaving home town to carve literary career, while latter settles to happy marriage to John Loder, Davis returns for lecture and, as guest of former pal, finds her with child and writer of hot sexy novels which she agrees to read and submit to publishers.

Eight years later, Hopkins is a successful pop novelist and hits New York with Loder and daughter for opening of Davis's play. Latter sees pending breakup of marriage, tries to prevent it, even though Loder tells of his walkout and real love for her.

Next episode unfolds another 10 years, with Loder now an army major, renewing acquaintance with Davis, but latter is being romanced by Gig Young, 10 years her junior. Moving swiftly to involvement, dramatics tosses young daughter into arms of Young, Loder is engaged to another woman, and the two schoolgal chums find themselves together and alone for mutual companionship.

John Van Druten and Lenore Coffee have devised fine script from the [former's 1940] original play, deftly molding it to particular dramatic talents of Hopkins-Davis, while Vincent Sherman provides fine directing job.

•

OLD BOYFRIENDS

1979, 103 mins, US Ⓥ ⊙ col

Dir Joan Tewkesbury ***Prod*** Edward R. Pressman, Michele Rappaport ***Scr*** Paul Schrader, Leonard Schrader ***Ph*** William A. Fraker ***Ed*** Bill Reynolds ***Mus*** David Shire ***Art*** Peter Jamison

Act Talia Shire, Richard Jordan, Keith Carradine, John Belushi, John Houseman, Buck Henry (Avco Embassy)

The premise of *Old Boyfriends* is an intriguing and universal one, the fantasy of revisiting lovers out of an individual's past.

Script is contemporary and grounded in realism, right down to the shifting morals which have marked male-female relationships in the past. In this case, the femme (Talia Shire) is a clinical psychologist who roots into her past after a failed suicide attempt.

Shire's odyssey takes her across America to old beaux including her college sweetheart (Richard Jordan), high school romance (John Belushi) and first adolescent love (Keith Carradine). The experience proves to be disquieting.

A protege of Robert Altman, novice director Joan Tewkesbury, who scripted his *Nashville*, employs similar loosely narrative techniques, with the Shire character holding together the series of set pieces.

•

OLD DARK HOUSE, THE

1932, 74 mins, US b/w

Dir James Whale ***Prod*** Carl Laemmle, Jr. ***Scr*** Benn W. Levy, [R. C. Sherriff] ***Ph*** [Arthur Edeson] ***Ed*** [Clarence Kolster] ***Art*** [Charles D. Hall]

Act Boris Karloff, Melvyn Douglas, Charles Laughton, Gloria Stuart, Lillian Bond, Ernest Thesiger (Universal)

The [original J. B.] Priestley novel must have been a bit more plausible than as evidenced in the cinematic transition. But regardless, it has all the elements for horror and thriller exploitation, including as it does a mad brute butler (Boris Karloff), insanity, ghosts in the family closets, sex, romance, not to mention the titular setting in a storm-torn Welsh mountain retreat.

Let one stop and think but a few seconds about what's happened on the screen and there'd be no picture; hence, it's been the somewhat too difficult task of the Laemmle studio to pile on trick after trick. For it's a certainty that the average mortal, despite the raging elements without, would have carried on in the storm at any price, or camped out in their motor, rather than sit in for an evening with the eccentric Femm family or their insane butler, Morgan.

Among the performances, Karloff with a characteristically un-drawing-room physical getup, by no means impresses as a sissy by stature, demeanor and surliness. Gloria Stuart gives excellent account of herself, although that extreme decolletage is rather uncalled for considering the locale. Charles Laughton turns in one of his usually top-notch performances as the Lancashire knight. Melvyn Douglas is rather hit and miss under the circumstances, and that stable tete-a-tete with Lillian Bond, who is satisfactory up until that point, makes it a bit worse.

•

OLD DRACULA
SEE: VAMPIRA

•

OLD ENOUGH

1984, 91 mins, US Ⓥ col

Dir Marisa Silver ***Prod*** Dina Silver ***Scr*** Marisa Silver ***Ph*** Michael Ballhaus ***Ed*** Mark Burns ***Mus*** Julian Marshall ***Art*** Jeffrey Townsend

Act Sarah Boyd, Rainbow Harvest, Neill Barry, Danny Aiello, Susan Kingsley, Roxanne Hart (Silverfilm)

The tale of friendship between two young girls of widely different social backgrounds, *Old Enough* has just the right balance of humor and insight to connect with audiences.

Produced and directed by sisters Dina and Marisa Silver, the project evolved from Utah's Sundance Institute for Independent Filmmakers. Nonetheless, the simple story and modest-budgeted effort need make no excuses for finished product.

Story centers on 12-year-old Lonnie Sloan (Sarah Boyd) from an upper-class New York City family and slightly older Karen Bruckner (Rainbow Harvest) from blue-collar background. Both are at important emotional turning points when they meet on the street of the widely divergent economic neighborhood. It is an easily understandable attraction of opposites.

The mix of fresh faces and a few seasoned pros in cast all register indelibly. Both Boyd and Harvest have burden of carrying the film, which they accomplish with ease.

•

OLD FASHIONED WAY, THE

1934, 69 mins, US b/w

Dir William Beaudine ***Prod*** William LeBaron ***Scr*** Garnett Weston, Jack Cunningham ***Ph*** Benjamin Reynolds ***Mus*** Harry Revel ***Art*** [John Goodman]

Act W. C. Fields, Joe Morrison, Judith Allen, Jan Duggan, Nora Cecil, Baby LeRoy (Paramount)

Made to order for W. C. Fields and permitting him to do his old cigar-box juggling among other things, *The Old Fashioned Way* is light comedy material that will please the Fields followers.

A repertoire troupe of the days when *The Drunkard* and *East Lynne* were big draws serves as the background and the small town of Bellefontaine, O, is the locale. It is here that the Great McGonigle, who heads the rep company, runs into all kinds of difficulties, most of them of a financial origin.

At the outset the troupe is on the way to the next stand, Bellefontaine. Train sequences provide some pretty good laughs from the beginning as McGonigle skips a summons and accidentally falls heir to an upper berth, not to mention the reception at Bellefontaine he mistakingly believes to be in his honor.

Joe Morrison is worked in for songs with suitable spots provided for him during the *Drunkard* sequence. Morrison's voice registers well and on the love interest he carries himself through satisfactorily. Romantic side of the story [by Charles Bogle (= W. C. Fields)] treated lightly but has its place as fitted in, Judith Allen holding up the other end adequately.

•

OLD GRINGO

1989, 119 mins, US Ⓥ ⊙ col

Dir Luis Puenzo ***Prod*** Lois Bonfiglio ***Scr*** Aida Bortnik, Luis Puenzo ***Ph*** Felix Monti ***Ed*** Juan Carlos Macias, William Anderson, Glen Farr ***Mus*** Lee Holdridge ***Art*** Stuart Wurtzel

Act Jane Fonda, Gregory Peck, Jimmy Smits, Patricio Contreras, Jenny Gago (Fonda/Columbia)

Based on Carlos Fuentes's novel *Gringo Viejo*, the complex psychological tableau makes it easy to see why Jane Fonda plopped herself in the plum role of 40-ish spinster-on-the-run Harriet Winslow. She is swept up by accident in the Mexican Revolution and swept off her feet by a charismatic general in Pancho Villa's popular front.

A rakish Jimmy Smits as Gen. Arroyo is superbly cast. He conveys the cocksure yet sensitive machismo and motivations of his character's torment between the revolution he lives and the woman he loves.

As the embittered, sardonic journalist Ambrose Bierce, Gregory Peck has found a role that suits him to a T. He portrays the world-weary Bierce with relish and wit.

The paternalistic figure in a nebulous love triangle with Fonda and Smits, Peck exudes a sympathetic mien despite his crusty exterior. His best moments come long before the denouement, and the film's wittiest lines are his alone.

•

OLD MAID, THE

1939, 92 mins, US Ⓥ ⊙ b/w

Dir Edmund Goulding ***Prod*** Hal B. Wallis ***Scr*** Casey Robinson ***Ph*** Tony Gaudio ***Ed*** George Amy ***Mus*** Max Steiner ***Art*** Robert Haas

Act Bette Davis, Miriam Hopkins, George Brent, Donald Crisp, Jane Bryan, James Stephenson (Warner)

Film version of the Pulitzer prize play [by Zoe Akins from a novel by Edith Wharton] sticks pretty close to the original development and dialog. Therein lies a handicap to success of the piece on the screen. It's stagey, somber and generally confusing fare.

Story opens during the Civil War days. Miriam Hopkins loves George Brent, but, when he fails to return after two years, prepares to marry rich James Stephenson. Brent arrives on the wedding day and is comforted by Bette Davis, younger cousin of Hopkins. Brent goes to war and is killed, leaving Davis with a child.

Skipping over 15 years, household is presented in complex antagonism between the two cousins, now matronly.

Davis provides a strong portrayal in the title role. Hopkins provides a strong contrast as the motherly matron.

•

OLD MAN AND THE SEA, THE

1958, 86 mins, US Ⓥ ⊙ col

Dir John Sturges ***Prod*** Leland Hayward ***Scr*** Peter Viertel ***Ph*** James Wong Howe, Floyd Crosby, Tom Tutwiler ***Ed*** Arthur

P. Schmidt *Mus* Dimitri Tiomkin *Art* Art Loel, Edward Carrere

Act Spencer Tracy, Felipe Pazos, Harry Bellaver (Warner)

Ernest Hemingway's introspective one-episode novelette, *The Old Man and the Sea*, is virtually a one-character film, the spotlight being almost continuously on Spencer Tracy as the old Cuban fisherman who meets his final test in his tremendous struggle with the huge marlin.

The picture has power, vitality and sharp excitement as it depicts the gruelling contest between man and fish. It is exquisitely photographed and skillfully directed. It captures the dignity and the stubborness of the old man, and it is tender in his final defeat.

And yet it isn't a completely satisfying picture. There are long and arid stretches, when it seems as if producer and director were merely trying to fill time.

It is Tracy's picture from beginning to end. One could quarrel with his interpretation of the old man. There are moments when he is magnificent and moving, and others when he seems to move in a stupor. It is, on the whole, a distinguished and impressive performance, ranging from the old man's pursuit of the fish, to hooking him, to the long chase and the final slashing battle.

In a supporting part, Felipe Pazos plays the boy who loves the old man and understands him. It is a very appealing and tender performance. Harry Bellaver has a small role as the tavern owner who sympathizes with the old man and, with the rest of the village, learns to admire him for his catch.

John Sturges directs with a view to keeping the essential values intact. It's not his fault that the basic material simply doesn't sustain interest throughout 86 minutes.

1958: Best Scoring of a Dramatic Picture

NOMINATIONS: Best Actor (Spencer Tracy), Color Cinematography

•

OLD YELLER

1957, 83 mins, US Ⓥ ⦿ col

Dir Robert Stevenson *Prod* Walt Disney *Scr* Fred Gipson, William Tunberg *Ph* Charles P. Boyle *Ed* Stanley Johnson *Mus* Oliver Wallace *Art* Carroll Clark

Act Dorothy McGuire, Fess Parker, Tommy Kirk, Kevin Corcoran, Chuck Connors (Walt Disney)

Disney organization's flair for taking a homely subject and building a heartwarming film is again aptly demonstrated in this moving story set in 1869 of a Texas frontier family and an old yeller dog. Based on Fred Gipson's novel of same tag, this is a careful blending of fun, laughter, love, adventure and tragedy.

Emphasis is laid upon animal action, including squirrels, jackrabbits, buzzards and newborn calves as well as more rugged depictions. Packed into film's tight footage is the 115-pound dog's fight with a huge bear, its struggle with a marauding wolf and battle with a pack of wild hogs.

•

OLEANNA

1994, 89 mins, US Ⓥ col

Dir David Mamet *Prod* Patricia Wolff, Sarah Green *Scr* David Mamet *Ph* Andrzej Sekula *Ed* Barbara Tulliver *Mus* Rebecca Pidgeon *Art* Kate Conklin

Act William H. Macy, Debra Eisenstadt (Bay Kinescope)

David Mamet's *Oleanna* comes with all the trappings of political correctness that the playwright and filmmaker so obviously abhors. It's a tale of sexual tension in the workplace (here, academia) in which a common situation is propelled into the stuff of tragedy.

Hewing to the structure of his play, Mamet's first act finds a professor, John (William H. Macy), in conference in his office with Carol (Debra Eisenstadt), a failing student. John is burned out. His teaching prowess is spent and he feels hopelessly shackled to family and convention but afraid to confront the fact that he wants to bail out and start over, unencumbered. So Carol is a challenge, a conceit and a diversion. He spends more time grappling with her inability to comprehend than he should.

In the second act, John has asked Carol to his office. In the brief interim, she's made accusations of sexual harrassment against him to the tenure committee. He's now in jeopardy of losing all those material things he railed against in the first act. He's ready to apologize. But as low as he's willing to stoop, John isn't ready to accept that the accusations are fact simply because the committee has accepted them. John's not guilty of anything on Carol's hysterical laundry list. Mamet makes that very clear—too clear, in fact, leaving little dramatic ambiguity.

"Oleanna" is apparently a reference to a bygone utopian community. Still, one can't help suspect a more perverse derivation—an opaque reference to oleander, the poisonous shrub. With an obvious villain in Carol, the subject of sexual harrassment gets hopelessly lost.

Eisenstadt is shrill as Carol. Macy fares little better in a part that largely demands a lot of preening.

•

OLIVER!

1968, 140 mins, UK Ⓥ ⦿ ▭ col

Dir Carol Reed *Prod* John Woolf *Scr* Vernon Harris *Ph* Oswald Morris *Ed* Ralph Kemplen *Mus* Johnny Green (dir.) *Art* John Box

Act Ron Moody, Shani Wallis, Oliver Reed, Harry Secombe, Mark Lester, Jack Wild (Columbia/Romulus)

This $10 million pic is a bright, shiny, heartwarming musical, packed with songs and lively production highspots. Lionel Bart's [1960] stage musical hit is adroitly opened out by director Carol Reed.

Oliver! goes with a cheerful swing, leading up to a strong dramatic climax when Bill Sikes gets his comeuppance. Mark Lester, as the workhouse waif who finds happiness after a basinful of scary adventures, is a frail Oliver, with a tremulous, piping singing voice, but he's vigorous and mischievous enough, and is sufficiently dewy-eyed and angelic to captivate the audience.

The youngsters are natural scene-stealers but major honors go to a diminutive 15-year-old, Jack Wild, who plays the Artful Dodger with knowing cunning and impudent self-confidence.

Ron Moody's Fagin lacks some of the malignance usually associated with the role of the wily old rascal though he shows sudden flashes of evil temper. He riotously squeezes every morsel of fun out of his tuition scenes with the little pickpockets.

Bart's familiar songs, such as "Food, Glorious Food," "Consider Yourself," "I'd Do Anything" and "Oom-Pah-Pah" are as fresh as ever.

1968: Best Picture, Director, Art Direction, Sound, Scoring of a Musical Picture, Honorary Award (Onna White, for choreography)

NOMINATIONS: Best Actor (Ron Moody), Supp. Actor (Jack Wild), Adapted Screenplay, Cinematography, Costume Design, Editing

•

OLIVER'S STORY

1978, 92 mins, US Ⓥ col

Dir John Korty *Prod* David V. Picker *Scr* Erich Segal, John Korty *Ph* Arthur Ornitz *Ed* Stuart H. Pappe *Mus* Francis Lai *Art* Robert Gundlach

Act Ryan O'Neal, Candice Bergen, Nicola Pagett, Edward Binns, Benson Fong, Ray Milland (Paramount)

Love Story is a tough act to follow, but *Oliver's Story* manages to hold its own. The continuation of Erich Segal's tale of fated lovers gets a sensitive and moving treatment from director and coscripter (with Segal) John Korty.

Oliver's Story begins with the burial of Jenny Cavalleri Barrett, whose death closed out the first pic. Ryan O'Neal, working as a lawyer in a prestigious New York firm, is burdened by a sense of despair and loneliness, along with a liberal dose of self-pity.

Enter Candice Bergen as the Bonwit heir in Bonwit Teller, the flip side in looks and disposition to the Jenny character created by Ali MacGraw. Their meeting is one of those coincidences that only occur in films, but Korty and Segal plot the relationship with a sureness that proves to be highly endearing.

The most moving segments come, ironically, not out of the O'Neal-Bergen encounters, but from a few brief scenes between O'Neal and Ray Milland, who encores as his wealthy banker father. It's a tribute to both performances and Korty's direction that this most basic of conflicts is resolved here in a genuinely satisfying manner.

•

OLIVER TWIST

1948, 116 mins, UK Ⓥ ⦿ b/w

Dir David Lean *Prod* Ronald Neame *Scr* David Lean, Stanley Haynes *Ph* Guy Green *Ed* Jack Harris *Mus* Arnold Bax *Art* John Bryan

Act Robert Newton, Alec Guinness, Kay Walsh, Francis L. Sullivan, John Howard Davies, Anthony Newley (Cineguild)

From every angle this is a superb achievement. Dickens's devotees may object to condensing of the story and omission of some of the minor characters. But what is left still runs close to two hours.

One of its merits is the absence of considerable unnecessary dialog, the child Oliver having the fewest lines ever allotted to so prominent a character. He has the wistful air of the typical Dickens waif and heads almost faultless casting.

Camerawork is on an exceptionally high level. Opening shots of a storm-swept sky and heavy clouds give an eerie quality that immediately grips the imagination. Josephine Stuart's delineation of a woman in labor pains, dragging herself across rain-sodden fields to a distant light that spells sanctuary, is unparalleled in its poignant realism.

Alec Guinness gives a revoltingly faithful portrait of Fagin and Kay Walsh extracts just the right amount of viciousness overcome by pity in her delineation of Nancy. Robert Newton is a natural for the brutish Sikes and gets every ounce out of his opportunities.

•

O LUCKY MAN!

1973, 176 mins, UK Ⓥ col

Dir Lindsay Anderson *Prod* Michael Medwin, Lindsay Anderson *Scr* David Sherwin *Ph* Miroslav Ondricek *Ed* David Gladwell, Tom Priestley *Mus* Alan Price *Art* Jocelyn Herbert

Act Malcolm McDowell, Ralph Richardson, Rachel Roberts, Arthur Lowe, Helen Mirren, Dandy Nichols (Memorial/SAM)

No less than an epic look at society is created in Lindsay Anderson's third and most provocative film. It is in the form of a human comedy on a perky, ambitious but conformist young man using society's ways to get to the top.

Malcolm McDowell, though practically onscreen throughout, displays a solid grasp of character and nuances. He is first a salesman, then guinea pig to science, assistant to a great business tycoon, railroaded to prison as a fall guy, converted to near saintliness, almost martyred and then returned to conformism by an almost mystical reaching of understanding through a Zen-Buddhist-like happening.

The film bows to various film greats but always assimilated to Anderson's own brand of epic comedy. The music and songs of Alan Price also add by underlining and counterpointing the action.

Ralph Richardson gives his pointed aplomb to the rich man and as a wise old tailor who gives the hero a golden suit; Rachel Roberts is a sexy personnel chief, rich society mistress and a poverty row housefrau who commits suicide with expert balance in all. In fact, all are good, especially Helen Mirren as the way-out rich girl and Arthur Lowe as an unctous African potentate.

•

OLVIDADOS, LOS
(THE YOUNG AND THE DAMNED)

1950, 88 mins, Mexico Ⓥ b/w

Dir Luis Bunuel *Prod* Oscar Dancigers *Scr* Luis Bunuel, Luis Alcoriza *Ph* Gabriel Figueroa *Ed* Carlos Savage *Mus* Rodolfo Halffter *Art* Edward Fitzgerald

Act Alfonso Mejia, Roberto Cobo, Estela Inda, Miguel Inclan, Efrain Arauz, Mario Ramirez (Ultramar)

Film is an objective, unrelenting closeup of life among some delinquents in a Mexican slum.

Director Luis Bunuel, famous for his surrealist pix, has cast his eye on a cancerous aspect of society, and made a jolting pic. Boys are presented as a group who grow up without any moral conceptions or responsibilities. Film offers no hope except in sweeping social changes.

Bunuel has filled his pic with such symbols as a terrifying blind man, donkeys bearing dead bodies, and bloody battles. Gabriel Figueroa gives it a fine contrasty lensing that helps mood. Acting by a group of unknowns is uniformly good.

•

OMAR KHAYYAM

1957, 101 mins, US b/w

Dir William Dieterle *Scr* Barre Lyndon *Ph* Ernest Laszlo *Ed* Everett Douglas *Mus* Victor Young *Art* Hal Pereira, Joseph MacMillan Johnson

Act Cornel Wilde, Michael Rennie, Debra Paget, Raymond Massey, John Derek, Yma Sumac (Paramount)

Static cumbersomeness of some sets of the romantic love duets between Cornel Wilde and Debra Paget flaw this spectacular; but well-staged battle and court intrigue sequences speed up the pace and hold interest.

Barre Lyndon script sets forth Omar (Wilde) as an oriental equivalent of the later Renaissance man—poet, lover, scholar, scientist and court counsellor—all in one. Lyndon weaves romance between Omar and wife (Paget) of the ruling Shah (Raymond Massey), against intrigue in court and the machinations of the murderous and mysterious Eastern cult of Assassins, not to mention 11th-century warfare between Persian and Byzantine empires. Sprinkled throughout are recitations from the Rubaiyat.

•

OMEGA MAN, THE
1971, 98 mins, US col
Dir Boris Sagal ***Prod*** Walter Seltzer ***Scr*** John William Corrington, Joyce H. Corrington ***Ph*** Russell Metty ***Ed*** William Ziegler ***Mus*** Ron Grainer ***Art*** Arthur Loel, Walter M. Simonds
Act Charlton Heston, Anthony Zerbe, Rosalind Cash, Paul Koslo, Lincoln Kilpatrick, Eric Laneuville (Warner)

The Omega Man is an extremely literate science fiction drama starring Charlton Heston as the only survivor of a worldwide bacteriological war, circa 1975. Thrust of the well-written story [adapted from Richard Matheson's novel] is Heston's running battle with deranged survivors headed by Anthony Zerbe.

The deserted streets of LA through which Heston drives by day while Zerbe's eye-sensitive mutants hide until nightfall, provide low-key but powerful emphasis on what can and does happen when the machinery of civilized society grinds to a halt.

An Oriental missile war has caused a worldwide plague. Zerbe, formerly a TV newscaster, has become the leader of the mutants, whose extreme reaction to the science which caused the disaster has led to wanton destruction of cultural and scientific objects. Rosalind Cash provides romantic interest for Heston as a member of another band of rural survivors not yet under Zerbe's control.

•

OMEN, THE
1976, 111 mins, US col
Dir Richard Donner ***Prod*** Harvey Bernhard ***Scr*** David Seltzer ***Ph*** Gilbert Taylor ***Ed*** Stuart Baird ***Mus*** Jerry Goldsmith ***Art*** Carmen Dillon
Act Gregory Peck, Lee Remick, David Warner, Billie Whitelaw, Patrick Troughton, Harvey Stephens (20th Century-Fox)

Suspenser starring Gregory Peck and Lee Remick as the unwitting parents of the Antichrist. Richard Donner's direction is taut. Players all are strong.

There's enough exposition of the Book of Revelation to educate on the spot a person from another civilization. As for any religious commitment needed, that problem is minimal; the only premise one must accept is that the fallen Lucifer remains a very strong supernatural being.

Peck, well cast as a career American ambassador, is convinced by Italian priest Martin Benson to substitute another hospital baby for the one wife Remick lost in childbirth. Five years later, strange things begin to happen.

At various points, portents of Satanism emerge, underscored (or, rather, overscored) by Jerry Goldsmith's heavy music.

1976: Best Original Score

NOMINATION: Best Song ("Ave Satani")

•

ON A CLEAR DAY YOU CAN SEE FOREVER
1970, 129 mins, US col
Dir Vincente Minnelli ***Prod*** Howard W. Koch ***Scr*** Alan Jay Lerner ***Ph*** Harry Stradling ***Ed*** David Bretherton ***Mus*** Nelson Riddle (arr.) ***Art*** John DeCuir
Act Barbra Streisand, Yves Montand, Bob Newhart, Larry Blyden, Simon Oakland, Jack Nicholson (Paramount)

[Based on the Alan Jay Lerner–Burton Lane 1965 Broadway musical], the story line, without the gimmick of reincarnation, is pure soapsuds.

Barbra Streisand is a chain-smoker so addicted that she doesn't fly because "I'm afraid of the No Smoking sign." She is engaged to Larry Blyden, a business school student in the upper 2 percent of his class who is so square that he is selecting a future employer on the basis of the pension plan.

To stop smoking before an important dinner with the personnel recruiter from Chemical Foods Inc., Streisand crashes a medical school class in hypnotism taught by Yves Montand. He accidentally discovers that she has extra-sensory perception. Under hypnosis, she becomes an aristocratic femme fatale with whom Montand falls in love.

•

ONCE AROUND
1991, 114 mins, US col
Dir Lasse Hallstrom ***Prod*** Amy Robinson, Griffin Dunne ***Scr*** Malia Scotch Marmo ***Ph*** Theo Van De Sande ***Ed*** Andrew Mondsheim ***Mus*** James Horner ***Art*** David Gropman
Act Richard Dreyfuss, Holly Hunter, Danny Aiello, Laura San Giacomo, Gena Rowlands, Roxanne Hart (Universal/Cinecom)

Vast opportunities for unbearable quantities of sentimentality are fortunately squelched in *Once Around*, an intelligently engaging domestic comedy-drama. U.S. debut by Lasse Hallstrom, director of the widely loved 1985 Swedish hit *My Life As a Dog*, keenly delineates how a woman finding happiness with a man for the first time paradoxically involves the serious deterioration of relations within her close-knit family.

Story is hung upon numerous family rituals—weddings, dinners, birthdays, baptisms, funerals—and opening sees thirty-something Holly Hunter being badgered about her marital prospects at the wedding of sister Laura San Giacomo.

Rebuffed by her b.f. (coproducer Griffin Dunne in a neat cameo), Hunter flees chilly Boston for the Caribbean, where she instantly is swept off her feet by irrepressible, vulgar, tireless, wealthy condominium salesman Richard Dreyfuss.

Brightest strategy is forcing the viewer to experience Hunter's family's acceptance of Dreyfuss. His sheer relentlessness darkens the mood and thickens the complexity of the situation, removing the film from the real of the feel-good Hollywood formula.

Danny Aiello (as the father), brightest in an excellent cast, invests all his scenes with evident emotional and mental deliberation. Hunter has many nice moments. San Giacomo and Gena Rowlands (as the mother) are very much on the money.

•

ONCE A THIEF
1965, 106 mins, US b/w
Dir Ralph Nelson ***Prod*** Jacques Bar ***Scr*** Zekial Marko ***Ph*** Robert Burks ***Ed*** Fredric Steinkamp ***Mus*** Lalo Schifrin ***Art*** George W. Davis, Paul Groesse
Act Alain Delon, Ann-Margret, Van Heflin, Jack Palance, John Davis Chandler, Jeff Corey (M-G-M)

Once a Thief packs both violence and young married love in unfolding of its theme, aptly titled, about an ex-con trying to go straight, but constantly harassed by a vengeful cop.

Once a Thief has a San Francisco setting, where lenser Robert Burks makes interesting use of Chinatown and North Beach locations to backdrop story of $1 million platinum robbery and ultimate violent demise of each member of the five-man gang that pulled the job. Alain Delon not too unwillingly is pulled into the plot when he finds his wife, Ann-Margret, working in a cheap nightclub so they may live.

Delon delivers strongly. He's the romantic type who excels also in rugged action. Ann-Margret, too, is first-rate in her role. Van Heflin, as a police inspector who thinks Delon once shot him, and Jack Palance, as Delon's gangster brother, also star.

Heflin, as Delon's nemesis effectively plays the relentless police officer, and Palance, with less footage, similarly scores.

•

ONCE IN PARIS
1978, 100 mins, US
Dir Frank D. Gilroy ***Prod*** Frank D. Gilroy, Manny Fuchs, Gerard Croce ***Scr*** Frank D. Gilroy ***Ph*** Claude Saunier ***Ed*** Robert Q. Lovett ***Mus*** Mitch Leigh
Act Wayne Rogers, Gayle Hunnicutt, Jack Lenoir, Philippe March, Clement Harari, Tanya Lopert (Gilroy)

Writer-director Frank Gilroy has come up with a highly personalized tale of a rough around-the-edges Yank screenwriter's relationship with a worldly chauffeur and a beauteous British aristocrat. Gilroy's developed the triad in subtle, believable, intelligent and often humorous fashion making *Once in Paris* a super film.

Shot entirely in Paris, with a French crew, the pic gets maximum mileage from its three principals: Wayne Rogers, Gayle Hunnicutt, and Jack Lenoir.

Michael Moore (Rogers) is a scenarist travelling to Paris for the first time to salvage a film script. He is met at the airport and immediately informed that the chauffeur (Lenoir) is a bad egg (he has served time for manslaughter) and will be replaced tout de suite.

The driver stays, of course, and develops a strong friendship with the writer. The writer eventually has an affair with the British aristocrat (Hunnicutt) in Paris on business—she just happens to occupy the hotel suite adjoining the scripter's.

•

ONCE IS NOT ENOUGH
(AKA: JACQUELINE SUSANN'S ONCE IS NOT ENOUGH)
1975, 121 mins, US col
Dir Guy Green ***Prod*** Howard W. Koch ***Scr*** Julius J. Epstein ***Ph*** John A. Alonzo ***Ed*** Rita Roland ***Mus*** Henry Mancini ***Art*** John DeCuir
Act Kirk Douglas, Alexis Smith, David Janssen, George Hamilton, Melina Mercouri, Gary Conway (Paramount)

Jacqueline Susann's final novel, *Once Is Not Enough*, gallumphs to the screen as a tame potboiler. Kirk Douglas heads as a fading film producer devoted to daughter Deborah Raffin, so much so that he marries wealthy Alexis Smith to pay for the daughter's lifestyle.

Raffin resists the casual sexuality epitomized by George Hamilton, wealthy young man-about-town, and stumbles into a genuine love for David Janssen, a fading author who can't get it on in many areas of life anymore. Brenda Vaccaro plays a kooky magazine editor who tries to help Raffin.

Opulent production credits put the shallow dramaturgy even more to shame. Henry Mancini's lush romantic score is appropriate.

1975: NOMINATION: Best Supp. Actress (Brenda Vaccaro)

•

ONCE MORE, MY DARLING
1949, 92 mins, US b/w
Dir Robert Montgomery ***Prod*** Joan Harrison ***Scr*** Robert Carson, Oscar Saul ***Ph*** Franz Planer ***Ed*** Ralph Dawson ***Mus*** Elizabeth Firestone
Act Robert Montgomery, Ann Blyth, Jane Cowl, Lillian Randolph (Universal/Neptune)

As director and star, Robert Montgomery functions capably in both positions, except for a tendency to hold some early, talky sequences a bit too long. Otherwise, he gives the picture deft direction and first-class comedy playing, keeping the amusement quota strong.

Robert Carson based the script on his *SatEvePost* yarn, "Come Be My Love." It's bolstered with zingy dialogue and situations that contribute to the fun punch. Montgomery is seen as an attorney-actor who is called up from his inactive army reserve status for a special assignment. His undercover job is to woo a young heiress (Ann Blyth) and track down the man who has given her several pieces of "liberated" Nazi jewelry.

Blyth shows a bent for comedy and tickles the risibilities with her furious wooing of the man who was supposed to make the romantic pitch.

•

ONCE MORE, WITH FEELING
1960, 92 mins, US col
Dir Stanley Donen ***Prod*** Stanley Donen ***Scr*** Harry Kurnitz ***Ph*** Georges Perinal ***Ed*** Jack Harris ***Mus*** Muir Mathieson (arr.) ***Art*** Alexander Trauner
Act Yul Brynner, Kay Kendall, Geoffrey Toone, Maxwell Shaw, Gregory Ratoff, Mervyn Johns (Columbia)

The bright, entertaining touches of producer-director Stanley Donen breeze through *Once More, With Feeling* like an allegro, making a good Broadway play into a better motion picture. It's a smart, perfectly cast comedy.

Kay Kendall died less than three months after *Once More* was completed. Her eyes clouded with tears, Kendall blows away a kiss in her final scene, the sentiment seeming peculiarly prophetic. However, the picture of the actress through the rest of the film is one of life and of a spirited performer.

As a pompous sympathy conductor with a love of fine music that surpasses his participation in mundane existence, Yul Brynner has strength and humor, adeptly playing sly appeal against defiant arrogance. Together, he and Kendall make an overwhelming screen couple.

Harry Kurnitz wrote the screenplay from his own play, moved the setting from the United States to Europe and has come up with a scriptful of witty dialogue and amusing situations.

The conflict finds Brynner at odds with the world. He makes great music, but he can't get along with his musicians or the orchestra's board of trustees, and his pretty wife (Kendall) must soothe feelings all the way around. Eventually she has enough of her egomaniac husband, leaves him and decides to marry a physicist.

In support of the stars, Gregory Ratoff is excellent as the agent, prone to absurd comparisons and remarkably able to keep the warring mates in hand.

•

ONCE UPON A CRIME
1992, 94 mins, US col
Dir Eugene Levy ***Prod*** Dino De Laurentiis ***Scr*** Charles Shyer, Nancy Meyers, Steve Kluger ***Ph*** Giuseppe Rotunno ***Ed*** Patrick Kennedy ***Mus*** Richard Gibbs ***Art*** Pier Luigi Basile
Act John Candy, James Belushi, Cybill Shepherd, Sean Young, Richard Lewis, Ornella Muti (De Laurentiis)

SCTV alum Eugene Levy makes his feature-film directing debut with a film that, ironically, would have provided ample fodder for a Second City spoof as a group of U.S. stars chews its way through Italy and France in search of a movie.

The action is fittingly spurred along by a dog, as an out-of-work actor (Richard Lewis) and just-jilted woman (Sean Young) find a stray dachshund and trek from Rome to Monte Carlo to collect the $5,000 reward for its return. But the pair find the dog's owner murdered and get implicated in the crime, as do a compulsive gambler (John Candy), a too-ugly American (James Belushi) and his neglected wife (Cybill Shepherd).

Tech credits are significantly better than the action, with splashy costumes and sets as well as a jaunty score by Richard Gibbs.

•

ONCE UPON A HONEYMOON

1942, 116 mins, US Ⓥ ⦿ b/w

Dir Leo McCarey ***Prod*** Leo McCarey ***Scr*** Sheridan Gibney ***Ph*** George Barnes ***Ed*** Tharon Warth ***Mus*** Robert Emmett Dolan

Act Ginger Rogers, Cary Grant, Walter Slezak, Albert Dekker, Albert Basserman (RKO)

Producer-director Leo McCarey develops hit tale at a decidedly slow pace, and despite the overlength footage, succeeds in holding attention most of the way through.

Story picks up Ginger Rogers as a naive golddigger and former stripper from Flatbush in Vienna on the eve of her wedding to influential Nazi (Walter Slezak). Cary Grant, American war correspondent, meets her and falls in love, following the honeymooning couple through eastern Europe until he convinces Rogers her husband is Hitler's finger man.

In deliberately focusing attention on Rogers and Grant, McCarey spends much time on development of incidents, with result that there's an overload of dialogue and too much footage devoted to secondary sequences. Even with these drawbacks, picture holds together in good shape.

•

ONCE UPON A TIME IN AMERICA

1984, 227 mins, US Ⓥ ⦿ col

Dir Sergio Leone ***Prod*** Arnon Milchan ***Scr*** Leonardo Benvenuti, Piero De Bernardi, Enrico Medioli, Franco Arcalli, Franco Ferrini, Sergio Leone, Stuart Kaminsky ***Ph*** Tonino Delli Colli ***Ed*** Nino Baragli ***Mus*** Ennio Morricone ***Art*** Carlo Simi, James Singelis

Act Robert De Niro, James Woods, Elizabeth McGovern, Treat Williams, Tuesday Weld, Burt Young (Ladd)

Once Upon a Time in America arrives as a disappointment of considerable proportions. Sprawling $32 million saga of Jewish gangsters over the decades is surprisingly deficient in clarity and purpose, as well as excitement and narrative involvement.

Pic opens with a series of extraordinary violent episodes. It's 1933 and some hoods knock off a girlfriend and some cohorts of "Noodles" (Robert De Niro), while trying to track down the man himself.

Then, action shifts to 1968, when the aging De Niro (superior makeup job) returns to New York after a 35-year absence and reunites with a childhood pal, Fat Moe (Larry Rapp). De Niro is clearly on a mission relating to his past, and his later discovery of a briefcase filled with loot for a contract is obviously a portent of something big to come.

Leone's pattern of jumping between time periods isn't at all confusing and does create some effective poetic echoes, but also seems arbitrary at times and, because of the long childhood section, forestalls the beginning of involvement.

Quiet and subtle throughout, De Niro and his charisma rep the backbone of the picture but, despite frequent threats to become engaging, Noodles remains essentially unpalatable.

•

ONCE UPON A TIME IN THE WEST

1969, 165 mins, Italy/US Ⓥ ⦿ ▭ col

Dir Sergio Leone ***Prod*** Fulvio Morsella ***Scr*** Sergio Leone, Sergio Donati, Mickey Knox ***Ph*** Tonino Delli Colli ***Ed*** Nino Baragli ***Mus*** Ennio Morricone ***Art*** Carlo Simi

Act Henry Fonda, Claudia Cardinale, Jason Robards, Charles Bronson, Gabriele Ferzetti, Lionel Stander (Paramount/Rafran/San Marco)

Henry Fonda and Jason Robards relish each screen minute as the heavies, and Charles Bronson plays Clint Eastwood's "man with no name" role.

Leone's story here [from one by Dario Argento, Bernardo Bertolucci and himself], presented in broad strokes through careful interconnection of set-piece action, focuses on the various reactions of four people—the three male leads, plus Claudia Cardinale, extremely effective as a fancy lady from New Orleans—to the idea of garnering extreme wealth via ownership of a crucial watertown on the route of the transcontinental railroad.

The paradoxical, but honest "fun" aspect of Leone's previous preoccupation with elaborately stylized violence is here unconvincingly asking for consideration in a new "moral" light. This means that Leone's own special talent for playing with film ideas gets lost in a no-man's land of the merely initiative.

•

ONCE WERE WARRIORS

1994, 99 mins, New Zealand Ⓥ col

Dir Lee Tamahori ***Prod*** Robin Scholes ***Scr*** Riwia Brown ***Ph*** Stuart Dryburgh ***Ed*** Michael Horton ***Mus*** Murray Grindley, Murray McNabb ***Art*** Michael Kane

Act Rena Owen, Temuera Morrison, Mamaengaroa Kerr-Bell, Julian "Sonny" Arahanga, Taungaroa Emile, Rachael Morris (Communicado)

The barren lives of members of an urban Maori family are rigorously exposed in this rugged and painful picture, based on Alan Duff's novel, which was a Kiwi bestseller. It's one of the best to emerge from New Zealand in quite a while.

First-time director Lee Tamahori has done a marvelous job in depicting the day-to-day horror of the Heke family, which is held together only by its women, the sorely tried Beth and her eldest daughter, 16-year-old Grace. Beth comes from a noble Maori family, who disapproved of her marriage to Jake Heke some 18 years earlier.

Out of work, he spends his welfare money boozing at a bar with his mates and getting into fights, and he regularly brings a crowd home for more drinking and eating. Jake's fiery temper has estranged him from eldest son Nig, who has left home to join a tough street gang; the younger children despise him, too, because he regularly beats Beth when he's drunk.

Pic would be unrelentingly downbeat if not for the magnetic performances of the lead players and for the fact that, despite the drinking and violence, the relationship between Beth and Jake is, against the odds, a warm one.

•

ON DANGEROUS GROUND

1951, 82 mins, US Ⓥ ⦿ b/w

Dir Nicholas Ray ***Prod*** John Houseman ***Scr*** A. I. Bezzerides ***Ph*** George E. Diskant ***Ed*** Roland Gross ***Mus*** Bernard Herrmann ***Art*** Albert S. D'Agostino, Ralph Berger

Act Ida Lupino, Robert Ryan, Ward Bond, Charles Kemper, Anthony Ross, Sumner Williams (RKO)

Lack of definition in characters is chief flaw in writing, with Nicholas Ray, who also directed, and A. I. Bezzerides sharing the blame for their adaptation of the Gerald Butler novel, *Mad with Much Heart*.

There's not much Robert Ryan can do with the character of a cop made tough by the types with whom he is brought into contact, nor does Ida Lupino have much opportunity as a blind girl who presumably softens Ryan's character.

First half of the footage is given over to Ryan's mental travail as a city prowl car cop who favors plenty of roughness for those he arrests. In fact, this ready use of fists eventually gets him assigned out of town to aid a county sheriff hunt down a madman who has killed a little girl. Trail leads to a lonely farmhouse where Ryan and Ward Bond, playing the father of the murder victim, encounter Lupino. The killer is her mentally deficient kid brother (Sumner Williams) whom she has hidden out.

Ray manages to inject an occasional bit of excitement into the yarn, and had the psychotic touches been elimated in the script, film could have qualified as okay, even if grim, melodrama.

•

ON DEADLY GROUND

1994, 101 mins, US Ⓥ ⦿ ▭ col

Dir Steven Seagal ***Prod*** Steven Seagal, Julius R. Nasso, A. Kitman Ho ***Scr*** Ed Horowitz, Robin U. Russin ***Ph*** Ric Waite ***Ed*** Robert Ferretti, Don Brochu ***Mus*** Basil Poledouris ***Art*** William Ladd Skinner

Act Steven Seagal, Michael Caine, Joan Chen, John C. McGinley, R. Lee Ermey, Shari Shattuck (Warner)

This filigree thriller with eco trappings and a decibel and body count that strains mind and matter is a vanity production parading as a social statement. It nonetheless has enough sound, fury and flash to satisfy the action crowd who have propped up Steven Seagal's career.

Seagal is a Red Adair–style trouble shooter and fire quasher for Aegis Oil Co. in Alaska. After imploding one fire, he comes to the alarming discovery that it was preventable. The greed of chairman Michael Jennings (Michael Caine) is responsible for the orders to install substandard equipment.

As Taft is of pure heart—and graphically beats the crap out of bigots and bullies on several occasions to make that point—he shifts sides to the noble, if primitive Inuit. The holy people recognize him as the Spirit Warrior and soon he is in mortal combat with the forces of evil from the corporate world.

Seagal, both as actor and director, filches heavily from *Billy Jack*. However, this is a pale facsimile. He lacks Tom Laughlin's acting technique and the ability behind the camera to keep the story simple and direct. Horrifying rumors of a concluding 10-minute speech proves unfounded, with that turn whittled down to a near four-minute infomercial about being good to Mother Nature.

Work of the supporting cast ranges from uncomfortable (Caine) to loony (John C. McGinley's heavy) to improbable (Joan Chen as an Inuit activist).

•

ONE BORN EVERY MINUTE

SEE: THE FLIM-FLAM MAN

•

ONE DAY IN THE LIFE OF IVAN DENISOVICH

1972, 100 mins, UK/Norway Ⓥ ⦿ col

Dir Caspar Wrede ***Prod*** Caspar Wrede ***Scr*** Ronald Harwood ***Ph*** Sven Nykvist ***Ed*** Thelma Connell ***Mus*** Arne Nordheim ***Art*** Per Schwab

Act Tom Courtenay, Espen Skjonberg, James Maxwell, Alfred Burke, Eric Thompson, John Cording (Group W/Norsk)

Based on the novel by Alexander Solzhenitsyn, *One Day in the Life of Ivan Denisovich* is a tribute to the inherent dignity of man and his ability to maintain his humanity under seemingly impossible conditions.

Though faithful to the novel, the film emerges as strangely unmoving. *Life* chronicles a "good" day for Ivan Denisovich, a prisoner in the eighth year of a 10-year sentence at a Siberian labor camp. The day is filled with small victories over the system. He does not fall ill, he manages to cop some extra food and tobacco, finds a hacksaw blade, builds a cinderblock wall and retires without incurring the wrath of his keepers.

Sincerity (and austerity) of the production, lensed expertly under fierce conditions in Norway by Sven Nykvist, cannot compensate for Caspar Wrede's lackluster direction and a script so sparse it almost seems nonexistent. Considering what they have to work with, the performers are fine, especially Courtenay, who captures a mix of wiliness and childlike enthusiasm that is consistently convincing.

•

ONE DEADLY SUMMER

SEE: L'ETE MEURTRIER

•

ONE-EYED JACKS

1961, 141 mins, US Ⓥ ⦿ col

Dir Marlon Brando ***Prod*** Frank P. Rosenberg ***Scr*** Guy Trosper, Calder Willingham, [Stanley Kubrick, Sam Peckinpah] ***Ph*** Charles Lang, Jr. ***Ed*** Archie Marshek ***Mus*** Hugo Friedhofer ***Art*** Hal Pereira, J. McMillan Johnson

Act Marlon Brando, Karl Malden, Pina Pellicer, Katy Jurado, Ben Johnson, Slim Pickens (Paramount/Pennebaker)

Charles Neider's novel, *The Authentic Death of Hendry Jones*, is the source of the tellingly direct screenplay. It is the brooding, deliberate tale of a young man (Marlon Brando) consumed by a passion for revenge after he is betrayed by an accomplice (Karl Malden) in a bank robbery, for which crime he spends five years (1880–85) in a Mexican prison.

His vengeful campaign leads him to the town of Monterey, where Malden has attained respectability and the position of sheriff, but romantic entanglements with Malden's stepdaughter (Pina Pellicer) persuade Brando to abandon his intention until the irresistibility of circumstance and Malden's own irrepressible will to snuff out the living evidence of his guilt draws the two men into a showdown.

It is an oddity of this film that both its strength and its weakness lie in the area of characterization. Brando's concept calls, above all, for depth of character, for human figures endowed with overlapping good and bad sides to their natures. In the case of the central characters—his own, Malden's, Pellicer's—he is successful. But a few of his secondary people have no redeeming qualities—they are simply arch-villains.

Brando creates a character of substance, of its own identity. It is an instinctively right and illuminating performance. Another rich, vivid variable portrayal is the one by Malden. Katy Jurado is especially fine as Malden's wife. Outstanding in support is Ben Johnson as the bad sort who leads Brando to his prey.

The $5 to $6 million production, framed against the turbulent coastline of the Monterey peninsula and the shifting sands and mounds of the bleak Mexican desert, is notable for its visual artistry alone.

1961: NOMINATION: Best Color Cinematography

•

ONE FALSE MOVE
1991, 105 mins, US Ⓥ ⦿ col
Dir Carl Franklin ***Prod*** Jesse Beaton, Ben Myron ***Scr*** Billy Bob Thornton, Tom Epperson ***Ph*** James L. Carter ***Ed*** Carole Kravetz ***Mus*** Terry Plumeri ***Art*** Gary T. New
Act Bill Paxton, Cynda Williams, Billy Bob Thornton, Michael Beach, Jim Metzler, Earl Billings (IRS Media)

Scenes of grimly realistic drug-related slayings set a nihilistic tone at the outset of *One False Move*, which shocks but grows progressively more involving.

Offbeat scenario features an attractive young woman (Cynda Williams), who's escaped from rural Arkansas but fallen into very bad company in LA. Her b.f. (Billy Bob Thornton) and his accomplice (Michael Beach), both vicious killers, are after a big cache of cash and cocaine.

They hit the road for Houston, where they plan to offload the drugs on a dealer. Also on the itinerary is a promised trip to small-town Arkansas to visit the baby Williams left behind.

Working for the most part in straightforward style, director Carl Franklin achieves considerable suspense by pitting the frailties of each party against the other.

Director, veteran of three Roger Corman films and a recent American Film Institute grad, allows the characters time to unfold in ways that considerably deepen story interest. Despite time and budget constraints in the approximately $2 million shoot, the pic in its finer passages has qualities many studio pix would covet.

•

ONE FINE DAY
1996, 108 mins, US Ⓥ ⦿ col
Dir Michael Hoffman ***Prod*** Lynda Obst ***Scr*** Terrel Seltzer, Ellen Simon ***Ph*** Oliver Stapleton ***Ed*** Garth Craven ***Mus*** James Newton Howard ***Art*** David Gropman
Act Michelle Pfeiffer, George Clooney, Mae Whitman, Alex D. Linz, Charles Durning, Ellen Greene (Fox 2000/20th Century-Fox)

One Fine Day is a pretty ideal baby-boomer romance. Made with the right breezy insouciance and performed with consummate flair and sexy star allure by Michelle Pfeiffer and George Clooney, this lively confection spins on one of the central domestic dilemmas of the era: how to balance kids and a career.

In tried-and-true romantic comedy tradition, Melanie (Pfeiffer) and Jack (Clooney) "meet cute" and are antagonistic from the outset. Divorced Jack, a hard-hitting *Daily News* columnist, is abruptly put in charge of his five-year-old daughter (Mae Whitman). Same-aged Sammy (Alex D. Linz), divorced architect Melanie's son, is missing a day-long school trip on a ferry. Thus are the two parents stuck with their kids for the day.

Jack is in the middle of an erupting City Hall controversy. Melanie has a major presentation to make for a big-bucks urban development; her hypochondriacal boss is so phobic of kids that Melanie hasn't even been able to admit she has one. And so it goes throughout the day, with accident-prone Sammy causing a succession of little disasters, and his defiant, I-can-do-it-alone mother finally agreeing to let the despised, egotistical Jack help her out a bit.

Pfeiffer, in an excellent, well-judged performance, plays Melanie as enough of a hard-headed, disagreeable workaholic that one initially believes she might remain impervious to anything Jack has to offer. Clooney, in his second post-*E.R.* stardom feature, makes it all look easy. He's the rare major actor who, like Clark Gable, holds equal appeal for men and women.

The emotional undercurrents remain uninsistent until the very end, when they finally, if gently, hook in. By fade-out, pic conveys a sweet quality that mostly overrides the time-squeezed contrivances of the plotting.

•

ONE FLEW OVER THE CUCKOO'S NEST
1975, 133 mins, US Ⓥ ⦿ col
Dir Milos Forman ***Prod*** Saul Zaentz, Michael Douglas ***Scr*** Lawrence Hauben, Bo Goldman ***Ph*** Haskell Wexler, Bill Butler, William Fraker ***Ed*** Richard Chew, Lynzee Klingman, Sheldon Kahn ***Mus*** Jack Nitzsche ***Art*** Paul Sylbert
Act Jack Nicholson, Louise Fletcher, William Redfield, Dean Brooks, Scatman Crothers, Danny DeVito (Fantasy)

One Flew Over the Cuckoo's Nest is brilliant cinema theatre. Jack Nicholson stars in an outstanding characterization of asylum antihero McMurphy, and Milos Forman's direction of a superbly cast film is equally meritorious.

The film is adapted from Ken Kesey's novel, the 1963 Broadway legit version of which, by Dale Wasserman, starred Kirk Douglas.

The $3 million film traces the havoc wreacked in Louise Fletcher's zombie-run mental ward when Nicholson (either an illness faker or a free spirit) displays a kind of leadership which neither Fletcher nor the system can handle.

The major supporting players emerge with authority: Brad Dourif (in a part played on Broadway by Gene Wilder), the acne-marked stutterer whose immature sexual fantasies are clarified on the night of Nicholson's aborted escape; Sidney Lassick, a petulant auntie; Will Sampson, the not-so-dumb Indian with whom Nicholson effects a strong rapport; and William Redfield, the overintelligent inmate.

The film's pacing is relieved by a group escape and fishing boat heist, right out of Mack Sennett, and some stabs at basketball in which Nicholson stations the tall Indian for telling effect. This in turn make the shock therapy sequences awesomely potent.

1975: Best Picture, Director, Actor (Jack Nicholson), Actress (Louise Fletcher), Adapted Screenplay

NOMINATIONS: Best Supp. Actor (Brad Dourif), Cinematography, Editing, Original Score

•

ONE FOOT IN HEAVEN
1941, 106 mins, US b/w
Dir Irving Rapper ***Prod*** Hal B. Wallis ***Scr*** Casey Robinson ***Ph*** Charles Rosher ***Ed*** Warren Low ***Mus*** Max Steiner
Act Fredric March, Martha Scott, Beulah Bondi, Gene Lockhart, Elisabeth Fraser, Harry Davenport (Warner)

A warm and human preachment for godliness, this biography of a Methodist minister is from the bestseller by Hartzell Spence. About the only faults with the picture are its slowness in the first half and the tendency of director Irving Rapper to skip over the hectic postwar depression years. Most of the dramatic wallop is contained in the last 40 minutes, or when the Rev. Spence (Fredric March) is in conflict with the wealthy element in his Denver congregation.

Spence, originally a medical student, comes to religion through listening to an evangelist. He takes his fiancée (Martha Scott) from her opulent Canadian home to his first parish in an Iowa mud-road town. This is the beginning of a trek through similar parishes with the Spences undergoing various privations. They raise three children, likably played by Frankie Thomas, Elisabeth Fraser and Casey Johnson.

March and Scott are both splendid in their roles. The stars carry the brunt of the story, although the cast is both populous and excellent.

1941: NOMINATION: Best Picture

•

ONE FROM THE HEART
1982, 101 mins, US Ⓥ ⦿ col
Dir Francis Coppola ***Prod*** Gray Frederickson, Fred Roos, Armyan Bernstein ***Scr*** Armyan Bernstein, Francis Coppola ***Ph*** Vittorio Storaro ***Ed*** Arne Goursaud, Rudi Fehr, Randy Roberts ***Mus*** Tom Waits ***Art*** Dean Tavoularis
Act Frederic Forrest, Teri Garr, Nastassja Kinski, Raul Julia, Lainie Kazan, Harry Dean Stanton (Zoetrope)

Francis Coppola's *One from the Heart* is a hybrid musical romantic fantasy, lavishing giddy heights of visual imagination and technical brilliance onto a wafer-thin story of true love turned sour, then sweet.

Set against an intentionally artificial fantasy version of Las Vegas—with production designer Dean Tavoularis's studio-recreated casino strip, desert outposts and even the Vegas airport easily the film's best-paid and most dazzling stars—the film quite simply plots the breakup, separate dalliances and eventual happy ending of a pair of five-year lovers (Frederic Forrest and Teri Garr) over the course of a single Independence Day.

He meets a sultry, exotic circus girl (Nastassja Kinski); she's swept away by a suave Latino singing waiter (Raul Julia).

With cheerful intermittent turns by Harry Dean Stanton as Forrest's best friend and partner, and Lainie Kazan as Garr's blowsy, sentimental barmaid buddy, the film's focus turns almost exclusively on Forrest's mounting efforts to win back Garr.

1982: NOMINATION: Best Original Song Score

•

ONE GOOD COP
1991, 105 mins, US Ⓥ ⦿ col
Dir Heywood Gould ***Prod*** Laurence Mark ***Scr*** Heywood Gould ***Ph*** Ralf Bode ***Ed*** Richard Marks ***Mus*** David Foster, William Ross ***Art*** Sandy Veneziano
Act Michael Keaton, Rene Russo, Anthony LaPaglia, Kevin Conway, Rachel Ticotin, Tony Plana (Hollywood/Silver Screen Partners IV)

Michael Keaton plays a staunchly decent cop who's as close to his longtime partner (Anthony LaPaglia) as he is to his fashion designer wife (Rene Russo). When widowed LaPaglia gets killed in an heroic attempt to save a woman's life, Keaton and Russo take in his three orphaned little girls and decide they want to keep them.

But the authorities seem rather eager to take them away and Keaton's crowded digs can't accommodate a family, so he winds up on a wrong-side-of-the law stunt to come up with enough money to be a hero at home.

The drug-dealer villains and inner-city skirmishes here are standard issue, and pic's basic parameters are only a cut above telefilm fare. Still, it's the skill with which the writer-director works the audience into the palm of his hand that makes this a crowd-pleaser.

Keaton demonstrates remarkable range and dexterity, giving his best performance since *Clean and Sober* [1988], and soulful LaPaglia projects a toned-down version of the same true-hearted qualities that made him so winning in *Betsy's Wedding* [1990].

•

ONE HOUR TO DOOMSDAY
SEE: CITY BENEATH THE SEA

•

ONE HOUR WITH YOU
1932, 75 mins, US ⦿ b/w
Dir Ernst Lubitsch ***Prod*** Ernst Lubitsch ***Scr*** Samson Raphaelson ***Ph*** Victor Milner ***Mus*** Oscar Strauss, Richard A. Whiting
Act Maurice Chevalier, Jeanette MacDonald, Genevieve Tobin, Charles Ruggles, Roland Young, George Barbier (Paramount)

It's a 100% credit to all concerned, principally Ernst Lubitsch on his production and direction, which required no little courage to carry out the continuity idea. The unorthodoxy concerns Maurice Chevalier's interpolated, confidential asides to his audience, in the *Strange Interlude* manner, although in an altogether gay spirit. Chevalier periodically interrupts the romantic sequence to come downscreen for a close-up to intimately address the "ladies and gentlemen" as to his amorous problems.

It starts first with the opening scene in the Bois de Boulogne of Paris where Chevalier and his bride (Jeanette MacDonald) of three years are caught necking. The gendarme won't believe it's legal so they retire to their home where, in a boudoir scene, Chevalier interrupts just in time for that first aside to tell the audience that they really are married. From then on Genevieve Tobin in an obvious "make" role completes the triangle, with Chevalier periodically soliloquizing in a chatty, intimate manner (taking the audience into his marital confidence, so to speak) on what he is to do under the circumstances.

The excellent script [from the play by Lothar Schmidt] is replete with many niceties and touches which Lubitsch has skillfully dovetailed, without overdoing the detail. On top of that, Jeanette MacDonald is a superb vis-a-vis for the star, intelligently getting her song lyrics over in a quiet, chatty manner.

1931/32: NOMINATION: Best Picture

•

ONE HUNDRED AND ONE DALMATIANS
1961, 79 mins, US Ⓥ col
Dir Wolfgang Reitherman, Hamilton Luske, Clyde Geronimi ***Prod*** Walt Disney ***Scr*** Bill Peet ***Ed*** Donald Halliday, Roy M. Brewer, Jr. ***Mus*** George Burns ***Art*** Ken Anderson (Walt Disney)

While not as indelibly enchanting or inspired as some of the studio's most unforgettable animated endeavors, this is nonetheless a painstaking creative effort. There are some adults for whom 101—count 'em—dalmatians is about 101 dalmatians too many, but even the most hardened, dogmatic pooch-detester is likely to be amused by several passages in this story.

Bill Peet's screen yarn, based on the book by Dodie Smith, is set in London and concerned with the efforts of Blighty's four-legged population to rescue 99 dognapped pups from the clutches of one Cruella De Ville, a chic up-to-date personification of the classic witch. The concerted effort is successful thanks to a canine sleuthing network

("Twilight Bark") that makes Scotland Yard an amateur outfit by comparison.

Film purportedly is the $4 million end product of three years of work by some 300 artists. It benefits from the vocal versatility of a huge roster of "voice" talents, including Rod Taylor, J. Pat O'Malley and Betty Lou Gerson. There are three songs by Mel Leven, best and most prominent of which is "Cruella De Ville."

•

101 DALMATIANS
1996, 103 mins, US Ⓥ ⊙ ▭ col
Dir Stephen Herek ***Prod*** John Hughes, Ricardo Mestres ***Scr*** John Hughes ***Ph*** Adrian Biddle ***Ed*** Trudy Ship ***Mus*** Michael Kamen ***Art*** Assheton Gorton
Act Glenn Close, Jeff Daniels, Joely Richardson, Joan Plowright, Hugh Laurie, Mark Williams (Great Oaks/Walt Disney)

Glenn Close and the lead dogs are great, but a key conceptual decision and a less-than-inspired climax prevent Disney's live-action *101 Dalmatians* from being the cat's meow.

Set contemporaneously but in a London with a feel of decades ago, tale gets of to a terrific start, as the attraction betwen the Dalmatians of American computer game designer Roger (Jeff Daniels) and fashion designer Anita (Joely Richardson) brings their masters together into instantaneous marriage. Canine lovebirds Pongo and Perdy are soon expecting, as are their human counterparts.

Disgusted by the latter development, Anita's boss, the outlandish, fearsome fashion-world diva Cruella DeVil (Close) is more intrigued by the prospect of some little doggies for her latest creation, an authentic Damlatian coat. In short order the pups are kidnapped and spirited to a distant old mansion, where 84 other Dalmatians await a cruel fate.

Where the film misses its biggest bet is in depriving the animals of the voices they had in the 1961 animated version. In the post-*Babe* era, the dogs could have been given the same capacity for verbal expression, but, alas, they just bark, whimper and gowl.

Fully conversant with the grande dame persona after her turn on-stage [in the LA production of Andrew Lloyd Webber's musical *Sunset Boulevard*] as Norma Desmond, Close is like Bette Davis and Joan Crawford combined as the fashion-plate witch, delivering show-stopping line readings that are simply non-pareil.

Film in general is appointed as luxuriously as a Rolls.

•

102 DALMATIANS
2000, 100 mins, US Ⓥ ⊙ col
Dir Kevin Lima ***Prod*** Edward S. Feldman ***Scr*** Kristen Buckley, Brian Regan, Bob Tzudiker, Noni White ***Ph*** Adrian Biddle ***Ed*** Gregory Perter ***Mus*** David Newman ***Art*** Assheeton Gorton
Act Glenn Close, Ioan Gruffudd, Alice Evans, Tim McInerny, Ian Richardson, Gerard Depardieu (Walt Disney)

More is not merrier in an overly strenuous sequel to the live-action remake of the animated classic that plays like a pale reworking of its predecessor, a perhaps appropriate result for a film that sports 56 people credited as "spot removal artists."

Basic dynamic of this spotty dog tale once more pivots on fashion-plate Cruella's demented desire to create a unique Dalmatian-skin coat. Told that she will forfeit her entire fortune if she ever lapses into her old ways, Cruella (Glenn Close) reports to her probation officer, Chloe (Alice Evans), a Dalmatian owner who becomes involved with the mild-mannered Kevin (Ioan Gruffudd), who operates a perilously underfunded animal rescue home. Like a fox magnanimously assuming responsibility for a henhouse, the convicted dognapper underwrites the decrepit shelter and appoints it in her customary lavish style. Rededicating herself to evil, Cruella teams up with a loony French fashion designer, Jean Pierre Le Pelt (a thatch-topped, crazy-eyed Gerard Depardieu, not in his finest hour), to kidnap the many Dalmatians that have now come under her purview and spirit them off to Paris to be transformed into haute couture.

The undoubted star among the new generation of pups is Oddball, an all-white puppy that must have taxed the abilities of all of those spot removers. Also helpful is Waddlesworth, a hyper-chatty green-winged macaw that thinks it's a dog and is provided a lively voice by Eric Idle.

Given the virtually identical setup to the original and similar action involving animal and human pursuit of purloined pups to a remote outpost, it's inevitable that the climax has a twice-baked flavor. Here and elsewhere, director Kevin Lima hits all the obvious notes hard, and must be held to account for indulging so much hammy mugging from his cast, particularly from Depardieu. Close herself goes further over the top than before.

•

ONE HUNDRED MEN AND A GIRL
1937, 85 mins, US b/w
Dir Henry Koster ***Prod*** Joe Pasternak ***Scr*** Bruce Manning, Charles Kenyon, James Mulhauser ***Ph*** Joseph Valentine ***Ed*** Bernard W. Burton ***Mus*** Charles Previn (dir.) ***Art*** John Harkrider
Act Deanna Durbin, Adolphe Menjou, Alice Brady, Eugene Pallette, Mischa Auer, Leopold Stokowski (Universal)

Deanna Durbin is a bright, luminous star in her second picture, *One Hundred Men and a Girl*. Its originality rests on a firm and strong foundation, craftsmanship which has captured popular values from Wagner, Tchaikovsky, Liszt, Mozart and Verdi.

Universal wisely gives her excellent support in Leopold Stokowski, director of the Philadelphia symphony orchestra, who plays a lengthy film role with surprising ease and conviction, and Adolphe Menjou, who is in a role quite different from his usual type of parts. In addition to these two, Alice Brady breezes thru a short sequence in high glee, and Eugene Pallette, Mischa Auer and Billy Gilbert have important things to do and do them well.

The "hundred men" of the title are members of a symphony orchestra of unemployed musicians whom Durbin is organizing and managing. Hans Kraly is credited with the original story.

Idea is that the unemployed artists in order to get sponsorship for a radio contract must obtain a conductor with an outstanding name of wide radio appeal. Stokowski, completing his regular subscription season, is unapproachable, but rebuffs which would discourage Napoleon mean nothing to the youngster.

Durbin, to Stokowski accompaniment, sings Mozart's "Exultate" and the aria "Libiamo ne" from *Traviata*.

1937: Best Score

NOMINATIONS: Best Picture, Original Story, Editing, Sound

•

ONE IN A MILLION
1936, 92 mins, US b/w
Dir Sidney Lanfield ***Prod*** Raymond Griffith ***Scr*** Leonard Praskins, Mark Kelly ***Ph*** Edward Cronjager ***Ed*** Robert Simpson ***Mus*** Louis Silvers (dir.)
Act Sonja Henie, Adolphe Menjou, Jean Hersholt, Ned Sparks, Don Ameche, Ritz Bros. (20th Century-Fox)

A very entertaining, adroitly mixed concoction of romance, music, comedy and skating introduces to film audiences Olympic figure-skating champion Sonja Henie. Walking off with the laurels during 1936 at the games in Germany, the little Scandinavian wizard of the ice was placed under contract by 20th-Fox. A sweet demeanor, engaging personality, an intriguing Scandinavian accent and an abundance of poise are among her assets.

In *One in a Million* Henie wears the skates a good part of the time, giving various exhibitions that are Pavlovaesque on frozen water.

Jack Haskell staged the numbers on ice. Some are very simple with Henie alone on the ice, while others are not too elaborate, with male and female chorus, also on skates, for production atmosphere. The big number is at Madison Square Garden, which ends the picture cold on Henie's final routine without letting her fall into Don Ameche's arms as a topper.

Adolphe Menjou is the head of a theatrical troupe, a sort of Ziegfeld. Seeing Henie do her stuff, he immediately gets busy to exploit her. Menjou has many good opportunities, and opposite him Arline Judge makes a good heckler as the wife. Ameche figures as the newspaperman, opposite Henie, who protects her against Menjou.

•

ONE IS A LONELY NUMBER
1972, 97 mins, US Ⓥ col
Dir Mel Stuart ***Prod*** Stan Margulies ***Scr*** David Seltzer ***Ph*** Michel Hugo ***Ed*** David Saxon ***Mus*** Michel Legrand ***Art*** Walter M. Simonds
Act Trish Van Devere, Monte Markham, Janet Leigh, Melvyn Douglas, Jane Elliot, Jonathan Lippe (M-G-M)

One Is a Lonely Number is an excellent contemporary drama about the big and little problems affecting a divorced woman.

Trish Van Devere is the focal point of the story [from one by Rebecca Morris]. Suddenly abandoned by husband Paul Jenkins, she is forced into self-reliance for the first time in her life. It isn't always easy. But Van Devere does get help, principally from the kindness of old store-keeper Melvyn Douglas; professional man-hater Janet Leigh; Jane Elliot, the heroine's best friend; and Maurice Argent, manager of the neighborhood swimming pool where she finds employment as a life guard.

Van Devere, strikingly beautiful, projects a credible warmth, depth of character and a great deal of ladylike sensuality. Her romantic scenes with Monte Markham are as tasteful as they are most arousingly erotic.

•

ONE MAN MUTINY
SEE: THE COURT-MARTIAL OF BILLY MITCHELL

•

ONE MILLION B.C.
(UK: MAN AND HIS MATE)
1940, 80 mins, US Ⓥ ⊙ b/w
Dir Hal Roach, Hal Roach, Jr. ***Prod*** Hal Roach ***Scr*** Mickell Novak, George Baker, Joseph Frickert, Grover Jones ***Ph*** Norbert Brodine ***Ed*** Ray Snyder ***Mus*** Werner R. Heymann ***Art*** Charles D. Hall, Nicolai Remisoff
Act Victor Mature, Carole Landis, Lon Chaney, Jr., John Hubbard, Mamo Clark, Nigel de Brulier (Roach/United Artists)

One Million B.C. looks something like A.D. 1910; it's that corny. Except for the strange-sounding grunts and monosyllabic dialog, it is also another silent. Hal Roach, who spent a lifetime making comedies, goes to the other extreme as producer of the prehistoric spectacle, filmed in Nevada. D. W. Griffith was associated with Roach in production of the film at the beginning but withdrew following dissension concerning casting and other angles. His name does not appear in the credits.

There isn't much sense to the action nor much interest in the characters. Majority of the animals fail to impress but the fight between a couple of lizards, magnified into great size, is exciting and well photographed. The ease with which some of the monsters are destroyed by man is a big laugh, notably the way one is subdued with a fishing spear. Knocking off a giant iguana is another audience snicker.

On occasion, also, the actions of the characters, including Victor Mature, bring a guffaw. He plays the part oxlike and the romantic interest, with Carole Landis on the other end, fails to ignite. Chaney, Jr., carves a fine characterization from the role of a tribal chieftain.

The story, pretty thin, relates to the way common dangers serve to wash up hostilities between the Rock and Shell clans, with a note of culture developed by the heroine (Landis) who astonishes the lads of the stone age when she sees to it that the women are to be served first, and the roast dinosaur (or whatever it is) is cut off in hunks with a rock knife, instead of torn off by the hands.

1940: NOMINATIONS: Best Original Score, Special Effects

•

ONE MILLION YEARS B.C.
1966, 100 mins, UK Ⓥ ⊙ col
Dir Don Chaffey ***Prod*** Michael Carreras ***Scr*** Michael Carreras ***Ph*** Wilkie Cooper ***Ed*** James Needs, Tom Simpson ***Mus*** Mario Nascimbene ***Art*** Robert Jones
Act Raquel Welch, John Richardson, Percy Herbert, Robert Brown, Martine Beswick, Jean Wladon (Hammer)

Biggest novelty gimmick is that, despite four writers on screenplay [Mickell Novak, George Baker and Joseph Frickert from 1940 screenplay *One Million B.C.*, plus producer Michael Carreras], dialog is minimal, consisting almost entirely of grunts. Raquel Welch here gets little opportunity to prove herself an actress but she is certainly there in the looks department.

Don Chaffey does a reliable job directorially, but leans heavily on the ingenious special effects in the shape of prehistoric animals and a striking earthquake dreamed up by Ray Harryhausen. Simple idea of the film is of the earth as a barren, hostile place, one million years B.C., inhabited by two tribes, the aggressive Rock People and the more intelligent, gentler Shell People.

John Richardson plays a Rock man who is banished after a fight with his gross father (Robert Brown). Wandering the land, battling off fearful rubber prehistoric monsters, he comes across the Shell People and falls for Welch, one of the Shell handmaidens. The two go off together to face innumerable other hazards.

•

ONE NIGHT OF LOVE
1934, 98 mins, US Ⓥ ⊙ b/w
Dir Victor Schertzinger ***Scr*** S. K. Lauren, James Gow, Edmund North ***Ph*** Joseph Walker ***Mus*** Victor Schertzinger (adapt.), Louis Silvers
Act Grace Moore, Tullio Carminati, Lyle Talbot, Mona Barrie, Jessie Ralph, Luis Alberni (Columbia)

One Night of Love is basically an operatic film. It's the fact that the film is human, down to earth, that helps most. Even the operatic excerpts have all been carefully picked for popular appeal.

Story [by Dorothy Speare and Charles Beahan] is one of those convenient little yarns spun around the career of a singer (Grace Moore). She fails to win a radio contest so goes to Europe on her own, has usual student struggles, sings in a café, is discovered by Tullio Carminati, a great singing teacher. He drives her, mesmerizes her, makes her into a star. She falls in love with him, is jealous of another girl singer, and almost upsets the applecart at the last minute of success at the Metropolitan debut in New York.

It's all handled carefully. Carminati, as the teacher-lover, is a perfect choice and manages to ease himself into a lot more attention than might be expected. Lyle Talbot is the other man for Moore and Mona Barrie is the other girl. Both do well enough. Jessie Ralph is excellent as the housekeeper.

1934: Best Score, Sound Recording

NOMINATIONS: Best Picture, Director, Actress (Grace Moore), Editing

•

ONE NIGHT STAND

1984, 94 mins, Australia Ⓥ col

Dir John Duigan ***Prod*** Richard Mason ***Scr*** John Duigan ***Ph*** Tom Cowan ***Ed*** John Scott ***Mus*** William Motzing ***Art*** Ross Major

Act Tyler Coppin, Cassandra Delaney, Jay Hackett, Saskia Post, Midnight Oil (Edgley)

It's New Year's Eve on a hot summer night in Sydney. Over a transistor radio comes the news nobody thought was possible: nuclear war has broken out in Europe and North America, and bombs have already dropped on U.S. facilities in Australia: Everyone is warned to stay where they are. Thus begins a long, long night.

Pic builds inexorably to a truly shattering climax, yet doesn't rely on special effects or histrionics. Duigan seems to suggest that, in Australia at least, the world will end not with a bang nor exactly a whimper, but with a puzzled question-mark.

It's a daring approach but overall, and despite some rather strident acting early on, it does work.

•

ONE NIGHT STAND

1995, 92 mins, US Ⓥ col

Dir Talia Shire ***Prod*** Alida Camp ***Scr*** Marty Casella ***Ph*** Arthur Albert ***Ed*** Jim Prior ***Mus*** David Shire ***Art*** Rusty Smith

Act Ally Sheedy, A. Martinez, Frederic Forrest, Don Novello, Diane Salinger, Gina Hecht (Concorde/New Horizons)

Talia Shire's long-in-the-works debut feature starts promisingly enough with an intriguing exploration of the sexuality of a lonely and frustrated woman, but eventually develops into a banal and familiar thriller involving murder and incest.

Commercial designer Michelle "Micky" Sanderson (Ally Sheedy), a lonely and frustrated divorcée, yearns for some excitement and knows that her insistent boss (Don Novello) won't be able to supply it. One night, visiting a bar with some femme colleagues, Micky allows herself to be picked up by a complete stranger (A. Martinez), who takes her back to his apartment for a hot night of sex.

Next morning, Micky wakes up alone in an empty apartment and discovers from the owner, Josslyn (Frederic Forrest), that the place is up for lease. She becomes obsessed with finding her dream lover again. From this point on, the film becomes much less interesting, as screenplay tilts into familiar Frightened Lady territory when Micky discovers that his first wife, whom he claims died in a car accident, was actually murdered.

Forrest gives such an embarassingly over-the-top performance that he throws the whole film out of whack. Sheedy, however, is fine in a gutsy portrayal.

•

ONE NIGHT STAND

1997, 102 mins, US Ⓥ ⊙ col

Dir Mike Figgis ***Prod*** Mike Figgis, Annie Stewart, Ben Myron ***Scr*** Mike Figgis ***Ph*** Declan Quinn ***Ed*** John Smith ***Mus*** Mike Figgis ***Art*** Waldemar Kalinowski

Act Wesley Snipes, Nastassja Kinski, Ming-Na Wen, Robert Downey, Jr., Kyle MacLachlan, Amanda Donohoe (Red Mullet/New Line)

As fluid, loose and seductive as the languid jazz riffs with which Mike Figgis underscores its moods, *One Night Stand* is a complex, almost existential take on relationships and reassessing life choices.

The project originated from a script by Joe Eszterhas, reportedly sold for $3 million. Figgis, however, has tossed out everything but the title, the basic structure and the central idea of a casual sexual encounter with long-term seismic results. Eszterhas receives no credit on the finished film.

Tryst of the title takes place while successful Los Angeles–based commercials director Max (Wesley Snipes) is back in his native New York on a job and to patch up his ruptured friendship with gay performance artist Charlie (Robert Downey, Jr.) who has AIDS. Max meets Karen (Nastassja Kinski) and the couple eventually cross the line during the shocked intimacy that follows a violent mugging attempt.

Returning to L.A. the next morning, Max squirms guiltily in front of his wife, Mimi (Ming-Na Wen). Profoundly altered by the New York experience, Max begins to pull back from the soullessness of his sellout job and his shallow social circle.

Max returns to New York a year later to be with Charlie, now hospitalized. The real bombshell drops when Max, now accompanied by Mimi, unexpectedly meets Karen.

Conclusion feels wrong in its neat symmetry but, regardless, this is the work of a filmmaker firmly in control and not afraid to take risks. Like Downey, Snipes has rarely been better: his sleek masculinity is arrestingly paired with the dreamy poise of Kinski. Interestingly, no issue is made of the interracial dynamics; Max was originally written for Nicolas Cage.

•

ONE OF OUR AIRCRAFT IS MISSING

1942, 100 mins, UK Ⓥ b/w

Dir Michael Powell ***Prod*** John Corfield, Michael Powell, Emeric Pressburger ***Scr*** Emeric Pressburger, Michael Powell ***Ph*** Ronald Neame ***Ed*** David Lean ***Art*** David Rawnsley

Act Godfrey Tearle, Eric Portman, Hugh Williams, Bernard Miles, Pamela Brown, Hay Petrie (British National)

Aircraft is a full-length feature dealing with the flight of a crew of bombers which start from England to raid Stuttgart. The squadron all returns safely, except one which hits an obstruction and is entirely demolished. Then follows the story of what happened to the airmen.

The aforesaid bomber is returning from its raid on Stuttgart when it is hit and the crew tries to limp home. But over Holland they're compelled to bail out, landing in Dutch (occupied) territory, where the people protect them and give them disguises.

The six members of the Wellington are played by Godfrey Tearle, Eric Portman, Hugh Williams, Bernard Miles, Hugh Burden and Emrys Jones. A lot of Dutch people are recruited as natives of Holland, all of them excellent, not to mention Hay Petrie as the burgomaster. With the exception of Pamela Brown, all arrive solidly. Script, production, direction and photography are splendid.

1942: NOMINATIONS: Best Original Screenplay, Special Effects

•

ONE ON ONE

1977, 98 mins, US Ⓥ b/w

Dir Lamont Johnson ***Prod*** Martin Hornstein ***Scr*** Robby Benson, Jerry Segal ***Ph*** Donald M. Morgan ***Ed*** Robbe Roberts ***Mus*** Charles Fox ***Art*** Sherman Loudermilk

Act Robby Benson, Annette O'Toole, G. D. Spradlin, Gail Strickland, Melanie Griffith, James G. Richardson (Warner)

A trite and disappointing little film about a Los Angeles college basketball player. It follows the formula about the underdog-turned-hero but fails to ignite the emotions.

Robby Benson has an inarticulate, bumbling presence in this film as he blunders through the commercialized world of college athletics. His awkward performance slows down the film badly and makes it hard to empathize with him, despite the usually potent plot cliche of the little guy fighting back.

It's unbelievable that this nebbish would be pursued by such mature and attractive women as Annette O'Toole and Gail Strickland, both of whom have extended and embarrassing romantic scenes with Benson.

•

ONE POTATO, TWO POTATO

1964, 102 mins, US b/w

Dir Larry Peerce ***Prod*** Sam Weston ***Scr*** Raphael Hayes, Orville H. Hampton ***Ph*** Andrew Laszlo ***Ed*** Robert Fritch ***Mus*** Gerald Fried

Act Barbara Barrie, Bernie Hamilton, Richard Mulligan, Marti Merika, Robert Earl Jones (Cinema V/Weston-Bowalco)

Made in Ohio on a subscription basis for a reported $250,000, this is a tender, tactful look at miscegenation that speaks in human rather than polemic terms.

Set in a midwest U.S. location (northern tier), it deals with a seemingly well-adjusted young Negro office worker who meets a young white divorcée who has a little girl. Their idyll grows slowly and gently as both react on normal planes with the color no apparent problem.

Then along comes the woman's first husband who has made his fortune after leaving her and demands the custody of the little girl. A sympathetic judge locates the girl in a good home, since he feels that as long as prejudice exists the little girl's life could be touched by it. All this is helped by fine delineation of character and added help from some new faces and the on-the-spot lensing.

Barbara Barrie has a striking presence and manages to mix integrity with need to etch a firm, moving character as the woman who finally finds the right man only to have her child taken away on racist principles. Bernie Hamilton is taking as the Negro husband who suddenly finds his manhood and very human liberty threatened by something that prevents him being a complete man.

Director Larry Peerce, for his first pic, has wisely told his story without many heavy symbolical and overdramatic embellishments.

1964: NOMINATION: Best Original Story & Screenplay

•

ONE SPY TOO MANY

1966, 101 mins, US col

Dir Joseph Sargent ***Prod*** David Victor ***Scr*** Dean Hargrove ***Ph*** Fred Koenekamp ***Ed*** Henry Berman ***Mus*** Gerald Fried ***Art*** George W. Davis, Merrill Pye

Act Robert Vaughn, David McCallum, Rip Torn, Dorothy Provine, Leo G. Carroll, Yvonne Craig (Arena/M-G-M)

Expanded from a *Man from U.N.C.L.E.* TV two-parter, *One Spy Too Many* zips along at a jazzy spy thriller pace.

Action and gadgetry are hung on a slender plot. Alexander, played by Rip Torn, is out to take over the world in the fashion of his Greek namesake. He hoists from the U.S. Army Biological Warfare Division a tankful of its secret "will gas," leaving a Greek inscription in the lab.

International espionage agents Robert Vaughn and David McCallum begin to pursue Alexander and are joined in their efforts by his wife (Dorothy Provine), who is attempting to reach her husband in order to have him sign her divorce papers.

•

ONE TOUCH OF VENUS

1948, 81 mins, US Ⓥ ⊙ b/w

Dir William A. Seiter ***Prod*** Lester Cowan ***Scr*** Harry Kurnitz, Frank Tashlin ***Ph*** Franz Planer ***Ed*** Otto Ludwig ***Mus*** Ann Ronell ***Art*** Bernard Herzbrun, Emrich Nicholson

Act Robert Walker, Ava Gardner, Dick Haymes, Eve Arden, Olga San Juan, Tom Conway (Universal)

One Touch of Venus comes to the screen as a pleasant comedy fantasy. Ava Gardner steps into the top ranks as the goddess, Venus. Hers is a sock impression, bountifully physical and alluring, delivered with a delightfully sly instinct for comedy. Three of the songs from the original [1943] stage musical have been used, with new lyrics [by Ann Ronell].

Plot, briefly, covers the romantic adventures of a department store window dresser (Robert Walker), who, in a completely pixilated moment, kisses a statue of Venus and brings her to life for 24 hours. Those are eventful hours; Venus's aura of love casts a spell over all, bringing couples together and spreading happiness of romance. The script by Harry Kurnitz and Frank Tashlin [based on S. J. Perelman's book of the musical, suggested by F. Anstey's *The Tinted Venus*] is punctuated with snappy dialogue and funny situations.

Walker delivers a gifted comedy performance. Eve Arden, the store owner's glib secretary, gives another of her punchy deliveries. Musical high spots please the ear and best is "Speak Low," from the original Kurt Weill–Ogden Nash score, reprised several times.

•

ONE, TWO, THREE

1961, 115 mins, US Ⓥ ⊙ ▭ b/w

Dir Billy Wilder ***Prod*** Billy Wilder ***Scr*** Billy Wilder, I. A. L. Diamond ***Ph*** Daniel L. Fapp ***Ed*** Daniel Mandell ***Mus*** Andre Previn (arr.) ***Art*** Alexandre Trauner

Act James Cagney, Horst Buchholz, Pamela Tiffin, Arlene Francis, Lilo Pulver, Howard St. John (Mirisch)

Billy Wilder's *One, Two, Three* is a fast-paced, high-pitched, hard-hitting, lighthearted farce crammed with topical gags and spiced with satirical overtones. Story is so furiously quick-witted that some of its wit gets snarled and smothered in overlap. But total experience packs a considerable wallop.

James Cagney is the chief exec of Coca-Cola's West Berlin plant whose ambitious promotion plans are jeopardized when he becomes temporary guardian of his stateside superior's wild and vacuous daughter. The girl (Pamela Tiffin) slips across the border, weds violently anti-Yankee Horst Buchholz, and before long there's a bouncing baby Bolshevik on the way. When the home office head man decides to visit his daughter, Cagney masterminds an elaborate masquerade that backfires.

The screenplay, based on a one-act play by Ferenc Molnar, is outstanding. It pulls no punches and lands a few political and ideological haymakers on both sides of the Brandenburg Gate.

Cagney proves himself an expert farceur with a glib, full-throttled characterization. Although some of Buchholz's delivery has more bark than bite, he reveals a considerable flair for comedy. Pretty Tiffin scores with a convincing display of mental density.

Another significant factor in the comedy is Andre Previn's score, which incorporates semi-classical and period pop themes (like *Saber Dance* and "Yes, We Have No Bananas") to great advantage throughout the film.

1961: NOMINATION: Best B&W Cinematography

•

ONE WAY PENDULUM

1965, 90 mins, UK b/w

Dir Peter Yates ***Prod*** Michael Deeley ***Scr*** N. F. Simpson ***Ph*** Denys Coop ***Ed*** Peter Taylor ***Mus*** Richard Rodney Bennett ***Art*** Reece Pemberton

Act Eric Sykes, George Cole, Julia Foster, Jonathan Miller, Peggy Mount, Mona Washbourne (Woodfall)

Adapted from his own play by N. F. Simpson, what there is of a plot deals with an eccentric British family whose antics resemble normal behavior as Salvador Dali resembles Grandma Moses.

Papa (Eric Sykes) seeks change from his humdrum existence as an insurance clerk by erecting a do-it-yourself replica of the Old Bailey in his living room, only to find a trial underway when he gets it finished; the mother (Alison Leggatt repeating her stage role), seemingly the sane one, goes along with her oddly behaved family until she adds her own bit by engaging a charwoman (Peggy Mount) not to clean, but to eat the family's leftovers.

Nearly rational is daughter (Julia Foster), whose only concern is for what she considers a physical deformity—her arms don't reach her knees.

Peter Yates directs with a technique that treats comedy as deadly serious and is responsible for much of the antic spirit that keeps the film animated during most of its chaotic run.

•

ONE WILD NIGHT

SEE: CAREER OPPORTUNITIES

•

ONE WOMAN'S STORY

SEE: THE PASSIONATE FRIENDS

•

ON GOLDEN POND

1981, 109 mins, US Ⓥ ⦿ col

Dir Mark Rydell ***Prod*** Bruce Gilbert ***Scr*** Ernest Thompson ***Ph*** Billy Williams ***Ed*** Robert L. Wolfe ***Mus*** Dave Grusin ***Art*** Stephen Grimes

Act Katharine Hepburn, Henry Fonda, Jane Fonda, Dabney Coleman, Doug McKeon (Universal/ITC/IPC)

Without question, these are major, meaty roles for Katharine Hepburn and Henry Fonda, and there could have been little doubt that the two would work superbly together. Fact that Ernest Thompson's 1978 play backs away from the dramatic fireworks that might have been mutes overall impact of the piece, but sufficient pleasures remain.

Fonda, a retired professor, and Hepburn arrive at their New England cottage to spend their 48th summer together. He's approaching his 80th birthday and, while it's clear that his wife is thoroughly familiar with his crotchety act, his mostly intentional rudeness and irascibility make life difficult for others in his vicinity.

At the half-hour point, along come daughter Jane Fonda, future son-in-law Dabney Coleman and latter's son Doug McKeon. Coleman manages a stand-off with the elder Fonda, but Jane is clearly still terrified of her dad, suffering from lingering feelings of neglect and inferiority.

The film's most moving interlude, a near-death scene, is saved for the end, and both Fonda (pere) and Hepburn are miraculous together here, conveying heartrending intimations of mortality which are doubly powerful due to the stars' venerable status.

1981: Best Actor (Henry Fonda), Actress (Katharine Hepburn), Adapted Screenplay

NOMINATIONS: Best Picture, Director, Supp. Actress (Jane Fonda), Cinematography, Editing, Score, Sound

•

ON HER MAJESTY'S SECRET SERVICE

1969, 139 mins, UK Ⓥ ⦿ ▭ col

Dir Peter Hunt ***Prod*** Harry Saltzman, Albert R. Broccoli ***Scr*** Richard Maibaum, Simon Raven ***Ph*** Michael Reed ***Ed*** John Glen ***Mus*** John Barry ***Art*** Syd Cain

Act George Lazenby, Diana Rigg, Telly Savalas, Ilse Steppat, Gabriele Ferzetti, Bernard Lee (United Artists)

Film of breakneck physical excitement and stunning visual attractions in which George Lazenby replaced Sean Connery as James Bond.

Lazenby is pleasant, capable and attractive in the role, but he suffers in the inevitable comparison with Connery. He doesn't have the latter's physique, voice and saturnine, virile looks.

The baddie's hideout is perched on the peak of a Swiss alp, part Playboy Penthouse, part Frankenstein's laboratory, and part cave of the mountain troll. There, Telly Savalas is experimenting with biological warfare to take over the world, under the guise of its being a research institute for treating allergies.

In *Service* Bond finds his true love, Diana Rigg, coolly beautiful, intelligent, sardonic, and his equal in bed, on skis, driving hellbent on icy mountain roads, and with a few karate chops of her own.

•

ONIBABA
(THE HOLE)

1965, 103 mins, Japan Ⓥ ⦿ b/w

Dir Kaneto Shindo ***Prod*** Hisao Itoya, Setsuo Noto, Tamotsu Minato ***Scr*** Kaneto Shindo ***Ph*** Kiyomi Kuroda ***Ed*** Toshio Enoki ***Mus*** Hikaru Hayashi ***Art*** Shindo

Act Nobuko Otowa, Jitsuko Yoshimura, Kei Sato, Jukichi Uno, Taiji Tonomura (Kindai/Tokyo)

Raw fare is sometimes high adventure and exciting, at other times dull in its so-called symbolism. Too often, it turns out to be a potpourri of ravenous eating and blatant sex.

Basic plot shows an elderly woman and her daughter-in-law, stranded without any means of support, during the civil wars of 16th-century Japan. They live among the reeds, many of them grown higher than their heads. When wounded, exhausted warriors wander in, the women kill them. The victims are stripped of their weapons and clothing, which they sell in return for food. They live undisturbed until Hachi (Kei Sato) returns from the fighting with news that the older woman's son, husband of the younger woman, is dead.

Hachi immediately tries to lure the younger femme to his hut for nightly trysts. He succeeds, and the older woman tries to halt the affair.

Nobuko Otowa is superb as the older woman, while Jitsuko Yoshimura contribs an excellent characterization as the daughter-in-law, especially in the "romantic" sequences. Sato is well cast as the former farmer youth.

•

ONION FIELD, THE

1979, 122 mins, US Ⓥ ⦿ col

Dir Harold Becker ***Prod*** Walter Coblenz ***Scr*** Joseph Wambaugh ***Ph*** Charles Rosher ***Ed*** John W. Wheeler ***Mus*** Eumir Deodato ***Art*** Brian Eatwell

Act John Savage, James Woods, Ted Danson, Ronny Cox, Franklyn Seales, Priscilla Pointer (Avco Embassy/Black Marble)

A highly detailed dramatization of a true case, *The Onion Field* deals in its two hours with death and guilt; and the manipulation of the judicial system to pervert justice.

Set in 1963, two plainclothes cops on patrol in Hollywood stop a couple of suspicious-looking punks in a car. In a swift moment one of the bad guys pulls a gun and the cops are disarmed and kidnapped. They are taken to an onion field miles away and one is brutally murdered. The second makes his escape. The two killers are quickly arrested but each claims the other did the killing.

On this confusion the trials and retrials drag on for years. Concurrently the survivor goes through bouts of guilt and is forced to resign from the force.

James Woods as the near-psychotic Powell is chillingly effective, creating a flakiness in the character that exudes the danger of a live wire near a puddle.

•

ONLY ANGELS HAVE WINGS

1939, 120 mins, US Ⓥ b/w

Dir Howard Hawks ***Prod*** Howard Hawks ***Scr*** Jules Furthman ***Ph*** Joseph Walker, Elmer Dyer ***Ed*** Viola Lawrence ***Mus*** Manuel Maciste, Dimitri Tiomkin

Act Cary Grant, Jean Arthur, Richard Barthelmess, Rita Hayworth, Thomas Mitchell, Sig Ruman (Columbia)

In *Only Angels Have Wings*, Howard Hawks had a story to tell and he has done it inspiringly well. Cary Grant is boss of the kindly Dutchman's decrepit airline. Grant takes up the planes only when it's too hazardous for the others. If the Dutchman can fly the mails regularly he's set for a juicy contract.

Jean Arthur is an American showgirl en route to Panama. She's excellent for the assignment.

Subplot has Richard Barthelmess coming on the scene with Rita Hayworth as his wife.

Baranca is the basic setting of this subtropical aviation romance [from an original story by Hawks] where treacherous mountain crags, capricious rainstorms and the like do their utmost to worst the mail plane service.

The Grant-Arthur cynicism and unyielding romantics are kept at a high standard.

1939: NOMINATION: Best Special Effects

•

ONLY GAME IN TOWN, THE

1970, 113 mins, US Ⓥ col

Dir George Stevens ***Prod*** Fred Kohlmar ***Scr*** Frank D. Gilroy ***Ph*** Henri Decae ***Ed*** John W. Holmes, William Sands, Pat Shade ***Mus*** Maurice Jarre ***Art*** Herman Blumenthal

Act Elizabeth Taylor, Warren Beatty, Charles Braswell, Hank Henry (20th Century-Fox)

The Only Game in Town is a rather mixed blessing. Elizabeth Taylor and Warren Beatty star as two Vegas drifters who find love with each other. Film was shot at Studios de Boulogne in Paris, with second unit work in Las Vegas for some key exteriors.

Beatty delivers an engaging performance as a gambling addict, working off his debts as a saloon pianist for Hank Henry.

Frank D. Gilroy's script [based on his play] permits both stars to shine in solo and ensemble moments of hope, despair, recrimination, and sardonic humor. But the drama develops too sluggishly.

Montage sequences of Vegas niteries, all well shot and cut, break up the pacing, but also emphasize the dramatic vamping even more so, an inevitable result.

•

ONLY THE LONELY

1991, 102 mins, US Ⓥ ⦿ col

Dir Chris Columbus ***Prod*** John Hughes, Hunt Lowry ***Scr*** Chris Columbus ***Ph*** Julio Macat ***Ed*** Raja Gosnell ***Mus*** Maurice Jarre ***Art*** John Muto

Act John Candy, Maureen O'Hara, Ally Sheedy, Kevin Dunn, Milo O'Shea, Anthony Quinn (20th Century-Fox/Hughes)

A lower-key *Marty* for the 1990s, *Only the Lonely* is a charming and well-observed romantic comedy about a single Chicago cop (John Candy) trying to break free from his smothering Irish mom (Maureen O'Hara, in her welcome return to the screen after 20 years). Performances are delightfully true and never descend into bathos or cheap sentiment.

O'Hara uses her native Dublin accent and her feistiest no-nonsense style to convey the mean-spirited, bigoted personality of Rose Muldoon. This flinty immigrant widow, who's bullied her son all his life, routinely spews out invective against Italians, Greeks, Poles and Jews.

Candy is a sweet-natured fellow who yearns for something more out of life but is afraid to ask for it. His best friend (James Belushi) and his brother (Kevin Dunn) want him to stay single and everyone treats him like an overgrown baby. When he meets a shy mortuary cosmetician (Ally Sheedy), Candy begins to assert himself in ways that drive his mother to new lows of tart-tongued nastiness.

The neighborhood is enjoyably populated with such serio-comic types as the silver-tongued denizens of O'Neill's pub (Bert Remsen and Milo O'Shea), and O'Hara's devastatingly sexy next-door neighbor (Anthony Quinn) whom she scorns as a "Typical Greek" for besieging her with passion: "Come to my bed. You will never leave."

•

ONLY THE VALIANT
1951, 104 mins, US Ⓥ ⦿ b/w
Dir Gordon Douglas ***Prod*** William Cagney ***Scr*** Edmund H. North, Harry Brown ***Ph*** Lionel Lindon ***Ed*** Walt Hannemann, Robert S. Seiter ***Mus*** Franz Waxman
Act Gregory Peck, Barbara Payton, Ward Bond, Gig Young, Lon Chaney, Jr., Neville Brand (Cagney/Warner)

In this cavalry yarn unfolding in the wild Apache country of the old west, great pains have been exerted to provide interesting characters. Gregory Peck plays a martinet, an army captain who lives strictly by the rulebook; consequently, although regarded as a fine soldier he is greatly disliked by his men. Plot revolves around his leading a detachment of men to an outpost which guards the only pass by which the Apaches can cross the mountain.

Indians are known to be on the verge of attacking an undermanned garrison, and Peck and his troopers are to try to hold the pass until an expected reinforcement of 400 men arrive.

Peck makes the most of a colorful role. Ward Bond, in a Victor McLaglen–type of tough-and-hearty army corporal, scores in one of his outstanding performances.

•

ONLY TWO CAN PLAY
1962, 106 mins, UK Ⓥ b/w
Dir Sidney Gilliat ***Prod*** Leslie Gilliat ***Scr*** Bryan Forbes ***Ph*** John Wilcox ***Ed*** Thelma Connell ***Mus*** Richard Rodney Bennett ***Art*** Albert Witherick
Act Peter Sellers, Mai Zetterling, Virginia Maskell, Richard Attenborough, Kenneth Griffiths (British Lion)

Kingsley Amis's novel, *That Uncertain Feeling*, has had some of its cool sting extracted for the film version, but the result is a lively, middle-class variation along the lines of *The Seven Year Itch*.

Some of the humor is over-earthy and slightly lavatory, and the film never fully decides whether it is supposed to be light comedy, farce or satire. But it remains a cheerful piece of nonsense with some saucy dialogue and situations capably exploited by Sellers and his colleagues.

He is a member of the staff of a Welsh public library, a white-collar job. He is fed up and frustrated with the eternal prospect of living in a shabby apartment with a dispirited wife, two awful kids, peeling wallpaper, erratic plumbing and a dragon of a landlady. Into his drab life floats the bored, sexy young wife of a local bigwig and she makes a play for Sellers.

The fact that she can influence her spouse to get Sellers a promotion is hardly in Sellers's mind. But what is in his mind never gets a chance of jelling. Their attempts at mutual-seduction are thwarted by babysitting problem, sudden return of the husband, intrusion of a herd of inquisitive cows when attempting a nocturnal roll.

Sellers adds another wily characterization to his gallery. His problems as frustrated lover carry greater weight because, from the beginning, he does not exaggerate or distort the role of the humble little librarian with aspirations. Mai Zetterling and Virginia Maskell provided effective contrasts as the two women in his life.

•

ONLY WHEN I LARF
1968, 103 mins, UK col
Dir Basil Dearden ***Prod*** Len Deighton, Brian Duffy ***Scr*** John Salmon, Patrick Tilley ***Ph*** Anthony Richmond ***Ed*** Fergus McDonell ***Mus*** Ron Grainer ***Art*** John Blezard
Act David Hemmings, Richard Attenborough, Alexandra Stewart, Nicholas Pennell, Terence Alexander, Melissa Stribling (Paramount)

Only When I Larf is a pleasant little joke, based on a Len Deighton novel and rather less complicated than some of his other work, with sound, unfussy direction and witty, observed thesping.

Filmed in London, New York and Beirut, it has Richard Attenborough, David Hemmings and Alexandra Stewart as a con-trio. Situation arises whereby Attenborough and Hemmings fall out and seek to doublecross each other.

Mood is admirably set with the gang pulling off a slickly planned con trick in a New York office. Talk is minimal, though the script opens up into a more gabby talkfest later, but dialogue is usually pointed and crisp.

Attenborough plays an ex-brigadier and takes on various guises. His brigadier is a masterly piece of observation and the whole film has Attenborough at his considerable comedy best. Hemmings is equally effective as the discontented young whiz-kid lieutenant and Stewart, with little to do, manages to look both efficient and sexy.

•

ONLY WHEN I LAUGH
(UK: IT HURTS ONLY WHEN I LAUGH)
1981, 120 mins, US Ⓥ ⦿ col
Dir Glenn Jordan ***Prod*** Roger M. Rothstein, Neil Simon ***Scr*** Neil Simon ***Ph*** David M. Walsh ***Ed*** John Wright ***Mus*** David Shire ***Art*** Albert Brenner
Act Marsha Mason, Kristy McNichol, James Coco, Joan Hackett, David Dukes, Kevin Bacon (Columbia)

Patrons expecting a skin-deep laughfest may be surprised at the unusually somber shadows and heavy dramatics that make their way into this tale (a reworking of Neil Simon's short-lived legit play, *The Gingerbread Lady*), though abundant humor still shines through.

Marsha Mason delivers a bravura performance as the film's centerpiece, a divorced actress who returns from a three-month drying out session at an alcoholic clinic to face a revitalized career both on the legit boards and as a mother to her long-estranged, 17-year-old daughter, well-played here by Kristy McNichol.

Core of the film is McNichol's attempt to reestablish a full-time relationship with her mother, despite latter's previously boozy neglect and frequent social embarrassment. Storyline details Mason's juggling of those demands, along with the potential for renewed romance and career success (with former lover David Dukes, who's written their stormy affair into a strong Broadway vehicle for her).

The one-on-one encounters between Mason and McNichol, ranging from sisterly tomfoolery to intense emotional battling, are particularly strong. Their final scene of family rapprochement is not unrealistically rosy.

1981: NOMINATIONS: Best Actress (Marsha Mason), Supp. Actor (James Coco), Supp. Actress (Joan Hackett)

•

ONLY YESTERDAY
1933, 105 mins, US b/w
Dir John M. Stahl ***Prod*** Carl Laemmle, Jr. ***Scr*** Arthur Richman, George O'Neill, William Hurlbut ***Ph*** Merritt Gerstad ***Ed*** Milton Carruth ***Mus*** [uncredited] ***Art*** Charles D. Hall
Act Margaret Sullavan, John Boles, Edna May Oliver, Billie Burke, Benita Hume, Reginald Denny (Universal)

Introducing to the screen Margaret Sullavan, trained in legit, this picture is as auspicious a launching as could be asked by any performer. Universal says the picture was suggested by Frederick Lewis Allen's book, a volume of contemporary reminiscences. That has nothing to do with the story except that the yarn starts in 1917 during the war, and ends in 1929 just as Wall Street laid that egg.

It is the irony of the heroine's life to be twice seduced by the same man but not recognized by him. A lapse of 12 years has wiped the man's memory clean but to the woman, in her middle 30s, her love for the man is as pristine as when she first surrendered.

A secondary role by Billie Burke glistens like a diamond. She is Aunt Julia, the broadminded New Yorker who takes care of the girl and her child. Later, Aunt Julia takes herself a husband (Reginald Denny). A couple of delightful comedy sequences with Denny playing the piano and Burke singing off-key provide natural laughs.

The lad with the faulty memory, but okay for all of that, is John Boles, a tenor who turns out to be a dependable dramatic leading man.

•

ONLY YOU
1994, 108 mins, US Ⓥ ⦿ col
Dir Norman Jewison ***Prod*** Norman Jewison, Cary Woods, Robert N. Fried, ***Scr*** Diane Drake ***Ph*** Sven Nykvist ***Ed*** Stephen Rivkin ***Mus*** Rachel Portman ***Art*** Luciana Arrighi
Act Marisa Tomei, Robert Downey, Jr., Bonnie Hunt, Joaquim De Almeida, Fisher Stevens, Billy Zane (Tri-Star/Yorktown)

Norman Jewison tries to revive some of the *Moonstruck* magic, via a side trip through *Sleepless in Seattle*, in *Only You*, a puff of romantic comedy set in a storybook Italy and populated by characters who believe in pursuing their amorous destinies as long as it involves staying in five-star hotels.

As a child, Faith is informed by both a Ouija board and a fortune-teller that her man of destiny will be named Damon Bradley. Fourteen years later, Faith (Marisa Tomei), a Pittsburgh schoolteacher, is set to marry straight-and-narrow podiatrist Dwayne (John Benjamin Hickey) when an old friend of Dwayne's calls in his regrets for not being able to attend the wedding, since he's leaving for Venice that very day. Oh yes, his name is Damon Bradley.

Faith immediately spins into orbit at this and rushes to the airport with best friend Kate (Bonnie Hunt). In Rome, through a mix-up and a lie, Faith comes to believe that a friendly Yank (Robert Downey, Jr.) is Damon Bradley. By morning, the smitten young man has to admit that he's actually named Peter. Peter realizes that the only way he can keep Faith in the country, and his chances alive, is to help her find the real Damon and hope for the best.

Jewison knows exactly where the laugh and welling-up buttons are that will hook the audience into this middle-class fairy-tale-come-true, and has smartly cast it with engaging personalities. Tomei comes on a little strong for some tastes, but her enthusiasm and ordinary-gal quality will get most viewers rooting for her. Downey is spirited and winning in one of the more conventional roles he's played to date. Hunt has most of the good lines and delivers them with expert timing.

•

ON MOONLIGHT BAY
1951, 94 mins, US col
Dir Roy Del Ruth ***Prod*** William Jacobs ***Scr*** Jack Rose, Melville Shavelson ***Ph*** Ernest Haller ***Ed*** Thomas Reilly ***Art*** Douglas Bacon
Act Doris Day, Gordon MacRae, Jack Smith, Leon Ames, Rosemary DeCamp, Mary Wickes (Warner)

On Moonlight Bay is a nostalgic comedy-romance of the 1915–17 period that takes a slice from Booth Tarkington's *Alice Adams* and another from his *Penrod* stories to frame the likeable characters against a small-town family setting. In keeping with the period, only one new song is used, and that fits the costumed background.

Doris Day is seen as the 18-year-old tomboyish daughter of Leon Ames and Rosemary DeCamp and the sister of puckish kid brother, Billy Gray. Day transitions from tomboy to dating miss when she meets Gordon MacRae after papa has moved his family to a new neighborhood, and the plot carries the principals through typical involvements, romantic and family, before pop finally consents to a marriage.

All of the characters are good for some hefty laughs, and Del Ruth's direction and the writing supply plenty of touches that keep punching the risibilities and jogging nostalgic memory. Highly hilarious moments include Day's first dance date with MacRae, and the two powder puffs aiding nature, until a violent embrace nearly asphyxiates MacRae in a cloud of talc.

•

ON MY WAY TO THE CRUSADES, I MET A GIRL WHO . . .
1968, 93 mins, Italy/US col
Dir Pasquale Festa Campanile ***Prod*** Francesco Mazzei ***Scr*** Luigi Magni, Larry Gelbart ***Ph*** Carlo Di Palma ***Ed*** Chas Nelson ***Mus*** Riz Ortolami ***Art*** Piero Poletto
Act Tony Curtis, Monica Vitti, Nino Castelnuovo, Hugh Griffith, John Richardson, Ivo Garrani (Julia/Warner/Seven Arts)

It's a mystery why Warner/Seven Arts abandoned the Italian title, *The Chastity Belt*, even briefly, for the long tongue-twisting title used outside of Italy but there's plenty of entertainment in this release. Set in the Middle Ages, Larry Gelbart provides an extra measure of modern, romantic candor. When bumpkin-type provincial noble Guerrando (Tony Curtis) is knighted to become a crusade draftee, he gets a castle, the tax-collecting concession and the right to have affairs with all eligible soft-bosomed femininity in his fief. Only holdout is Boccadoro (Golden Lips) played by Monica Vitti, an emancipated forest wench.

To safeguard his prize, Guerrando locks his chaste spouse into a chastity belt, puts the key into his pocket and heads out across the drawbridge. The indignant medieval feminist is determined to get even.

Director Pasquale Festa Campanile fluctuates between classy ribald satire and stock burlesque.

It is safe to assume that the original English version will further lighten some of the medieval clinkers that show here and there and tighten slack moments.

Curtis and Vitti are not at their best but the latter is much more at home in her role.

•

ON OUR MERRY WAY
(AKA: A MIRACLE CAN HAPPEN)
1948, 107 mins, US b/w
Dir King Vidor, Leslie Fenton ***Prod*** Benedict Bogeaus, Burgess Meredith ***Scr*** Laurence Stallings, Lou Breslow ***Ph*** Edward Cronjager, Joseph Biroc, Gordon Avil, John Seitz, Ernest Laszlo ***Ed*** James Smith ***Mus*** Heinz Roemheld ***Art*** Ernst Fegte, Duncan Cramer
Act Burgess Meredith, Paulette Goddard, Fred MacMurray, James Stewart, Dorothy Lamour, Henry Fonda (United Artists)

The fact that this attempt at whimsy doesn't always come off is incidental; just look at the names! The pic opens with a pair of surefire names like Goddard and Meredith and in bed, too.

Then Stewart, Fonda, and Harry James. Plus Lamour and Victor Moore, in a Hollywood satire, or how the sarong became famous. Followed by Fred MacMurray and William Demarest. All in episodic sequences detailing what an inquiring reporter encounters when he seeks to have answered the question of how a child influenced the lives of a group of selected adults.

Meredith is the reporter, so-called. Actually he's only a classified-ad solicitor for a newspaper. But he's lied to his recent bride; he's told her he's the inquiring reporter. Through a subterfuge, however, he assumes the mantle of the paper's actual I. R., a longtime ambition, for just this one question.

The cast couldn't have been better. The story's execution falters because a scene here and there is inclined to strive too much for its whimsical effect. But Meredith responds capitally to the mood of the character he plays, being given more of a chance to do so than any of the other stars. [Originally reviewed at a New York sneak preview under the title *A Miracle Can Happen*.]

•

ON THE AVENUE

1937, 90 mins, US Ⓥ b/w

Dir Roy Del Ruth ***Prod*** Gene Markey (assoc.) ***Scr*** Gene Markey, William Conselman ***Ph*** Lucien Andriot ***Ed*** Allen McNeil ***Mus*** Arthur Lange (dir.) ***Art*** William Darling, Mark-Lee Kirk

Act Dick Powell, Madeleine Carroll, Alice Faye, Ritz Bros., George Barbier, Alan Mowbray (20th Century-Fox)

On the Avenue is no sock but has attractive personalities in Dick Powell, Madeleine Carroll, Alice Faye, and the ever-funny Ritz Brothers. It needs, however, all the tuneful support it can get from the Irving Berlin score.

Avenue tells of Powell starred in his own revue which satirizes "the richest girl in the world" (Carroll). In pique, she eventually buys up the entire production just to jazz up a romantic (stage) scene for Powell. The breakup scene of the romance revolves around the madcap Ritzes doing a scat version of "O Chi-Chornia."

Alice Faye is almost a walk-through as the unrequited backstage amour de Powell but she socks 'em with "This Year's Kisses" and "Slumming on Park Avenue." George Barbier glares through the proceedings as the papa of the richest girl in the world whom Powell caricatures onstage.

•

ON THE BEACH

1959, 134 mins, US Ⓥ b/w

Dir Stanley Kramer ***Prod*** Stanley Kramer ***Scr*** John Paxton ***Ph*** Giuseppe Rotunno ***Ed*** Frederic Knudtson ***Mus*** Ernest Gold ***Art*** Rudolph Sternad

Act Gregory Peck, Ava Gardner, Fred Astaire, Anthony Perkins, Donna Anderson, John Tate (United Artists)

On the Beach is a solid film of considerable emotional, as well as cerebral, content. But the fact remains that the final impact is as heavy as a leaden shroud. The spectator is left with the sick feeling that he's had a preview of Armageddon, in which all contestants lost.

John Paxton, who did the screenplay from Nevil Shute's novel, avoids the usual cliches. There is no sergeant from Brooklyn, no handy racial spokesmen. Gregory Peck is a U.S. submarine commander. He and his men have been spared the atomic destruction because their vessel was submerged when the bombs went off.

The locale is Australia and the time is 1964. Nobody remembers how or why the conflict started. "Somebody pushed a button," says nuclear scientist Fred Astaire. Australia, for ill-explained reasons, is the last safe spot on earth. It is only a matter of time before the radiation hits the continent and its people die as the rest of the world has died.

In addition to Peck and Astaire, the other chief characters include Ava Gardner, a pleasure-bent Australian; and a young Australian naval officer and his wife, Anthony Perkins and Donna Anderson. All the personal stories are well-presented. The trouble is it is almost impossible to care with the implicit question ever-present—do they live?

The cast is almost uniformly excellent. Peck and Gardner make a good romantic team in the last days of the planet. Perkins and Anderson evoke sympathy as the young couple. Fred Astaire, in his first straight dramatic role, attracts considerable attention.

1959: NOMINATIONS: Best Editing, Scoring of a Dramatic Picture

•

ON THE BLACK HILL

1988, 116 mins, UK Ⓥ col

Dir Andrew Grieve ***Prod*** Jennifer Howarth ***Scr*** Andrew Grieve ***Ph*** Thaddeus O'Sullivan ***Ed*** Scott Thomas ***Mus*** Robert Lockhart ***Art*** Jocelyn James

Act Mike Gwilym, Robert Gwilym, Bob Peck, Gemma Jones, Nesta Harris (BFI/Film Four/British Screen)

A low-budget drama about Welsh hill farmers may not sound broadly appealing, but Andrew Grieve's *On the Black Hill* is a remarkably moving and entertaining film [from the novel by Bruce Chatwin] offering a fascinating view of life in the border country between Wales and England.

Pic follows the Jones family from 1895–1980, but mainly centers around twin brothers Benjamin and Lewis Jones (played by brothers Mike and Robert Gwilym). It is through their inseparability, and the traumas and humor that inspires, that the story is told.

Bob Peck and Gemma Jones are excellent as the Welsh farming couple, and the pic ably displays the hardship of their life. The Gwilyms perform well and are especially good in the twins' later years.

•

ON THE RIVIERA

1951, 89 mins, US Ⓥ col

Dir Walter Lang ***Prod*** Sol C. Siegel ***Scr*** Valentine Davies, Phoebe Ephron, Henry Ephron ***Ph*** Leon Shamroy ***Ed*** J. Watson Webb, Jr. ***Mus*** Alfred Newman (dir.) ***Art*** Lyle Wheeler, Leland Fuller

Act Danny Kaye, Gene Tierney, Corinne Calvet, Marcel Dalio, Sig Ruman, Clinton Sundberg (20th Century-Fox)

Danny Kaye is an American entertainer working the Riviera with his French girlfriend (Corinne Calvet). When he realizes his striking resemblance to a French aviation hero, he creates a new number to spotlight the hero's lothario doings.

Kaye is called in to double for the aviator at an important party from which the latter had been called by business. Gene Tierney is the beautiful wife of the flier and is wise to the impersonation, but the glib script, loaded with fast and furious dialogue quips, introduces enough complications so that before the evening is over she's not sure.

Full range of the Kaye talent is used, both in the music-comedy divisions and in straight performance. It's a wow delivery he gives.

Four tunes, three of which are used to back the potent production numbers, were cleffed by Sylvia Fine to show off the Kaye talent for fun-making.

•

ON THE TOWN

1949, 97 mins, US Ⓥ ⦿ col

Dir Gene Kelly, Stanley Donen ***Prod*** Arthur Freed ***Scr*** Adolph Green, Betty Comden ***Ph*** Harold Rosson ***Ed*** Ralph E. Winters ***Mus*** Lennie Hayton (dir.), Conrad Salinger (arr.) ***Art*** Cedric Gibbons, Jack Martin Smith

Act Gene Kelly, Frank Sinatra, Betty Garrett, Ann Miller, Jules Munshin, Vera-Ellen (M-G-M)

The pep, enthusiasm and apparent fun the makers of *On the Town* had in putting it together comes through to the audience and gives the picture its best asset.

Gene Kelly, Frank Sinatra and Jules Munshin are the three sailors on a 24-hour leave in New York. Betty Garrett, Ann Miller and Vera-Ellen are the three femmes who wind up with the navy.

Picture is crammed with songs and dance numbers. Picture kicks off and ends with "New York, New York." Tune is used in the beginning as a musical backing for a montage of three curious sailors prowling the city's points of interest. It gets the film off to a fascinating start and the style and pacing is continued.

Based on their 1944 musical play [from an idea by Jerome Robbins], the Adolph Green–Betty Comden script puts the players through light story paces as a setup for 10 tunes and dances.

Roger Edens, associate producer, did the music for the six new tunes and lyrics are by Green and Comden. Latter team, with Leonard Bernstein, did the four original numbers ["New York, New York," "Miss Turnstiles" dance, "Come Up to My Place," and "A Day in New York" ballet].

1949: Best Scoring of a Musical Picture

•

ON THE WATERFRONT

1954, 108 mins, US Ⓥ ⦿ b/w

Dir Elia Kazan ***Prod*** Sam Spiegel ***Scr*** Budd Schulberg ***Ph*** Boris Kaufman ***Ed*** Gene Milford ***Mus*** Leonard Bernstein ***Art*** Richard Day

Act Marlon Brando, Karl Malden, Lee J. Cobb, Rod Steiger, Pat Henning, Eva Marie Saint (Columbia/Horizon)

Longshore labor scandals serve as the takeoff point for a flight into fictionalized violence concerning the terroristic rule of a dock union over its coarse and rough, but subdued, members.

Budd Schulberg's script was based on his own original which in turn was "suggested" by the Malcolm Johnson newspaper articles. Schulberg greatly enhanced the basic story line with expertly turned, colorful and incisive dialog.

Under Elia Kazan's direction, Marlon Brando puts on a spectacular show, giving a fascinating, multifaceted performance as the uneducated dock walloper and former pug, who is basically a softie with a special affection for his rooftop covey of pigeons and a neighborhood girl back from school. Eva Marie Saint has enough spirit to escape listlessness in her characterization.

Story opens with Brando unwittingly setting the trap for the murder of a longshoreman who refuses to abide by the "deaf and dumb" code of the waterfront.

Lee J. Cobb is all-powerful as the one-man boss of the docks. He looks and plays the part harshly, arrogantly and with authority. Another fine job is executed by Karl Malden as the local Catholic priest who is outraged to the point that he spurs the revolt against Cobb's dictatorship.

Rod Steiger is a good choice as Brando's brother for both incline toward the hesitant manner of speech that has been especially identified with Brando. Steiger is Cobb's "educated" lieutenant who is murdered when he fails to prevent Brando from blabbing to the crime probers.

1954: Best Picture, Director, Actor (Marlon Brando), Supp. Actress (Eva Marie Saint), Story & Screenplay, B&W Cinematography, B&W Art Direction, Editing

NOMINATIONS: Best Supp. Actor (Lee J. Cobb, Karl Malden, Rod Steiger), Scoring of a Dramatic Picture

•

OPEN CITY

SEE: ROMA, CITTA APERTA

•

OPENING NIGHT

1978, 144 mins, US Ⓥ ⦿ col

Dir John Cassavetes ***Prod*** Al Ruban ***Scr*** John Cassavetes ***Ph*** Tom Ruban ***Ed*** Tom Cornwell ***Mus*** Bo Harwood ***Art*** Brian Ryman

Act Gena Rowlands, Ben Gazzara, John Cassavetes, Joan Blondell, Paul Stewart, Zohra Lampert (Faces)

With *Opening Night*, John Cassavetes, the cinematic poet of middle-class inner turmoil, explores the angst-ridden world of a famous actress on the brink of breakdown. Preparing a difficult role in a Broadway play, she witnesses the accidental death of a devoted fan, a traumatic event which causes her to reexamine her personal and professional relationships.

Gena Rowlands turns in another virtuoso performance as the troubled actress. Cassavetes's highly personal work will please his coterie of enthusiasts, but for general audiences it will be viewed as shrill, puzzling, depressing and overlong.

As with his other films, Cassavetes, who wrote and directed, puts a slice of life under the microscope. Across the board, he culls stunning performances from the entire cast, especially Joan Blondell as the writer whose play is being mounted. But it is such a demanding work, so draining, that one must question whether more than a handful of moviegoers are interested in the effort.

•

OPERATION CROSSBOW

1965, 118 mins, US Ⓥ ▭ col

Dir Michael Anderson ***Prod*** Carlo Ponti ***Scr*** Richard Imrie, Derry Quinn, Ray Rigby ***Ph*** Erwin Hillier ***Ed*** Ernest Walter ***Mus*** Ron Goodwin ***Art*** Elliot Scott

Act Sophia Loren, George Peppard, Trevor Howard, John Mills, Tom Courtenay, Richard Johnson (M-G-M)

Operation Crossbow is a sometimes suspenseful war melodrama said to be based upon British attempts to find and destroy Germany's development of new secret weapons—long-range rockets—in the early days of the Second World War. Ambitiously filmed in Europe and boasting production values which may seem to catch the spirit of the monumental effort, what the Carlo Ponti production lacks primarily is a cohesive story line [by Duilio Coletti and Vittorio Petrilli].

Sophia Loren is in for little more than a bit, albeit a key character in one sequence. George Peppard plays the chief protagonist in this rambling tale of a British espionage mission, whose members impersonate German scientists believed dead, sent to locate and transmit information on the underground installation where Nazis are working on their deadly project.

Peppard acquits himself satisfactorily although unexplained is his flawless command of German so he can impersonate a German scientist.

•

OPERATION PETTICOAT
1959, 124 mins, US Ⓥ ⊙ col
Dir Blake Edwards ***Prod*** Robert Arthur ***Scr*** Stanley Shapiro, Maurice Richlin ***Ph*** Russell Harlan ***Ed*** Ted J. Kent, Frank Gross ***Mus*** David Rose ***Art*** Alexander Golitzen, Robert E. Smith
Act Cary Grant, Tony Curtis, Joan O'Brien, Dina Merrill, Gene Evans, Arthur O'Connell (Granart/Universal)

Operation Petticoat has no more weight than a sackful of feathers, but it has a lot of laughs. Cary Grant and Tony Curtis are excellent, and the film is directed by Blake Edwards with a slam-bang pace.

The time is December 1941, and the locale is the Philippines. Grant is the commander of a wheezy old submarine which he gets operational through his conniving junior officer (Curtis). In a series of improbable but acceptable situations [suggested by a story by Paul King and Joseph Stone], the sub takes on as passengers five army nurses, a couple of Filipino families (including expectant mothers) and a goat.

Grant is a living lesson in getting laughs without lines. In this film, most of the gags play off him. Curtis is a splendid foil, and his different style of playing meshes easily with Grant's. David Rose's score is especially bright, helping the comedy without getting coy.

1959: NOMINATION: Best Original Story & Screenplay

•

OPERATION UNDERCOVER
SEE: REPORT TO THE COMMISSIONER

•

OPTIMISTS OF NINE ELMS, THE
(US: THE OPTIMISTS)
1974, 110 mins, UK Ⓥ col
Dir Anthony Simmons ***Prod*** Adrian Gaye, Victor Lyndon ***Scr*** Anthony Simmons, Tudor Gates ***Ph*** Larry Pizer ***Ed*** John Jympson ***Mus*** George Martin ***Art*** Robert Cartwright
Act Peter Sellers, Donna Mullane, John Chaffey, David Daker, Marjorie Yates (Cheetah/Sagittarius)

Pic is a romanticized, Anglicized variant on [Vittorio De Sica's 1952 Italian classic] *Umberto D*, with Peter Sellers playing an aging vaudevillian whose meager income derives from sidewalk minstrelling with his equally weary trained mutt. He tentatively befriends an eleven-year-old girl and her six-year-old brother, opening their poverty-clouded eyes to a world of magical dreams while they offer him the blessing of human contact.

It all sounds like goo, and the film's last half-hour verges perilously close. But even at its worst *The Optimists* is acceptable family fare, and for much of its first 80 minutes it engagingly achieves a sense of fantasy.

Director-coscripter Anthony Simmons (on whose novel *The Optimists of Nine Elms* screenplay is based) obviously understands and relishes the unique world of childhood.

•

ORCA
1977, 92 mins, US Ⓥ ⊙ ▭ col
Dir Michael Anderson ***Prod*** Luciano Vincenzoni ***Scr*** Luciano Vincenzoni, Sergio Donati ***Ph*** Ted Moore ***Ed*** Ralph E. Winters, John Bloom, Marion Rothman ***Mus*** Ennio Morricone ***Art*** Mario Garbuglia
Act Richard Harris, Charlotte Rampling, Will Sampson, Bo Derek, Keenan Wynn, Robert Carradine (De Laurentiis)

Orca is man-vs-beast nonsense. Some fine special effects and underwater camera work are plowed under in dumb storytelling.

Richard Harris is a shark-hunting seafarer who incurs the enmity of a superintelligent whale after harpooning the whale's pregnant mate. We learn all about the whales from Charlotte Rampling, ever at the ready with scientific exposition, occasional voiceover and arch posing.

Assorted supporting players include Will Sampson, who complements Rampling's pedantic dialog with ancient tribal lore; Peter Hooten, Bo Derek and Keenan Wynn, a part of the Harris boat crew; Scott Walker as menacing leader of village fishermen who wish Harris would just leave their whale-harassed town.

•

ORDINARY PEOPLE
1980, 123 mins, US Ⓥ ⊙ col
Dir Robert Redford ***Prod*** Ronald L. Schwary ***Scr*** Alvin Sargent ***Ph*** John Bailey ***Ed*** Jeff Kanew ***Mus*** Marvin Hamlisch ***Art*** Phillip Bennett, J. Michael Riva
Act Donald Sutherland, Mary Tyler Moore, Judd Hirsch, Timothy Hutton, Elizabeth McGovern, M. Emmet Walsh (Paramount/Wildwood)

A powerfully intimate domestic drama, *Ordinary People* represents the height of craftsmanship across the board. Robert Redford stayed behind the camera to make a remarkably intelligent and assured directorial debut that is fully responsive to the mood and nuances of the astute adaptation of Judith Guest's best seller.

While not ultimately downbeat or despairing, tale of a disturbed boy's precarious tightrope walk through his teens is played out with tremendous seriousness. Pic possesses a somber, hour-of-the-wolf mood, with characters forced to definitively confront their own souls before fade-out.

Dilemma is of a youth who has recently attempted suicide in remorse for not having saved his older brother from drowning.

Redford keenly evokes the darkly serene atmosphere of Chicago's affluent North Shore and effectively portrays this WASP society's predilection for pretending everything is okay even when it's not.

1980: Best Picture, Director, Supp. Actor (Timothy Hutton), Adapted Screenplay

NOMINATIONS: Best Actress (Mary Tyler Moore), Supp. Actor (Judd Hirsch)

•

ORFEU NEGRO
(BLACK ORPHEUS)
1959, 100 mins, France Ⓥ ⊙ col
Dir Marcel Camus ***Prod*** Sacha Gordine ***Scr*** Jacques Viot, Marcel Camus ***Ph*** Jean Bourgoin ***Ed*** Andree Feix ***Mus*** Luis Bonfa, Antonio Carlos Jobim
Act Breno Mello, Marpessa Dawn, Lea Garcia, Lourdes De Oliveira, Adhemar Da Silva (Gordine)

With a background of the pulsating, colorful Rio carnival in Brazil, a reenactment of the Orpheus legend is executed in this vehicle [based on Vinicius De Moraes's play]. This time they are Negroes and there is a clever transposition of the tragedy to modern times.

Eurydice (Marpessa Dawn) is a girl who comes to visit her cousin in the city in order to escape from a man trying to kill her after she turned him down. However, she is pursued by him (disguised as Death) in a carnival getup. She meets Orpheus, a streetcar conductor who is engaged to another girl. They fall in love but she is killed inadvertently by Orpheus. The descent into Hades is smartly engineered at a revival meeting when her voice comes through from an old, possessed woman.

Pic is somewhat cerebral, being mainly helped by the fresh playing of the cast, especially Yank actress Dawn. Color is excellent, and director Marcel Camus gives this movement.

1959: Best Foreign Language Film

•

ORGANIZATION, THE
1971, 105 mins, US Ⓥ col
Dir Don Medford ***Prod*** Walter Mirisch ***Scr*** James R. Webb ***Ph*** Joseph Biroc ***Ed*** Ferris Webster ***Mus*** Gil Melle ***Art*** George B. Chan
Act Sidney Poitier, Barbara McNair, Gerald S. O'Loughlin, Sheree North, Fred Beir, Allen Garfield (United Artists)

Sidney Poitier is back for third time around as Virgil Tibbs, the San Francisco homicide lieutenant, faced this time with combatting a worldwide dope syndicate.

The screenplay, generally highly polished, is a bit hazy occasionally in development, and Don Medford establishes a fast tempo in his lively direction. Pic's opening is a gem as stage is set for consequent action, skillfully enacted and drivingly constructed.

It's a heist of a furniture factory—front for crime ring—and seizure of $5 million in heroin by a group of young people taking law into their own hands to try to halt the drug sale that has been ruining the lives of relatives and friends. Tibbs is assigned case when the murdered body of the factory manager is found.

Poitier is confronted by a serious problem in police ethics as group calls him in, admitting robbery but denying the murder. Group asks his assistance, leaving them free to operate while they try their own methods.

•

ORIGINAL GANGSTAS
1996, 98 mins, US Ⓥ col
Dir Larry Cohen ***Prod*** Fred Williamson ***Scr*** Aubrey Rattan ***Ph*** Carlos Gonzalez ***Ed*** David Kern, Peter B. Ellis ***Mus*** Vladimir Horunzhy ***Art*** Elayne Barbara
Act Fred Williamson, Jim Brown, Pam Grier, Paul Winfield, Richard Roundtree, Ron O'Neal (Po'Boy/Orion)

They're back . . . and they're bad. *Original Gangstas* is a return to the so-called blaxploitation pics of the 1970s. Even if there are no direct homages to *Shaft*, *Cleopatra Jones* or *Super Fly*, the very presence of such performers as Jim Brown, Fred Williamson and Pam Grier serves as an echo of that era. Eschewing parody, this two-fisted urban gang drama is solid action entry.

Set in Gary, IN—the nation's homicide capital—contempo yarn kicks off with a basketball hustle that goes sour. The gang shoots the wrong shopkeeper—he's the papa of John Bookman (Williamson), a former bad boy made good coaching pro football in L.A. Bookman rides into town and claims his turf. He enlists his former buddies to help him quell the terror. The only thing slowing down the process is a knee-jerk, liberal attitude toward mediation on the part of some community leaders.

There's a sense of elation as law is tossed aside in favor of justice. The film's Magnificent Five admittedly move a bit slower than the vintage warriors of the Old West, but they're no less lethal. It's particularly gratifying to see Brown back before the cameras in a major role, as the original victim's biological father. Mom is played winningly by Grier.

•

ORLACS HAENDE
(HANDS OF ORLAC)
1925, 80 mins, Austria Ⓥ ⊗ b/w
Dir Robert Wiene ***Scr*** Ludwig Nerz ***Ph*** Guenther Krampf, Hans Andreschin ***Art*** Stefan Wessely
Act Conrad Veidt, Alexandra Sorina, Fritz Strassny, Paul Askenas, Carmen Cartellieri, Fritz Kortner (Pan)

Were it not for Conrad Veidt's masterly characterization, *The Hands of Orlac* [from the novel by Maurice Renard] would be an absurd fantasy in the old-time mystery-thriller class. As the musician who learns that the hands he lost in a train wreck have been supplanted by those from a man guillotined for a murder, Veidt keeps his audience highly tensed in spots.

Drab photography and over-footage devoted to long gloomy hallways make for repetition. Poorly titled, the picture is hopelessly complicated until the latter half of the last reel. Not until then is it discovered that a character assumed to be an apparition of the murderer has framed the man who was executed and has perpetrated the second killing, which he endeavored to place on the musician with the dead man's hands.

The salvaging of a train wreck by torchlight is one of the production's most vivid sequences.

•

ORLANDO
1993, 93 mins, UK/Russia/Italy/France/Netherlands Ⓥ ⊙ col
Dir Sally Potter ***Prod*** Christopher Sheppard ***Scr*** Sally Potter ***Ph*** Alexei Rodionov ***Ed*** Herve Schneid ***Mus*** Bob Last ***Art*** Ben van Os, Jan Roelfs
Act Tilda Swinton, Billy Zane, Lothaire Bluteau, John Wood, Charlotte Valandrey, Quentin Crisp (Adventure/Lenfilm/Mikado/Rio/Sigma)

Overcoming European coproduction pitfalls, *Orlando* provides exciting, wonderfully witty entertainment with glorious settings and costumes and Tilda Swinton's sock performance in the title role.

Virginia Woolf's 1928 novel is structured around the intriguing notion of a character who lived for 400 years, changing sex in the course of time. Orlando is a youth who, in 1600, becomes the favorite of Queen Elizabeth I and lives to tell the tale well into the 20th century.

Though she's really too feminine to pass for a man in pic's first half, Swinton is extraordinary as the eponymous Orlando, who frequently, in witty asides to the camera, takes the audience into his/her confidence.

The cast is uniformly strong, with Billy Zane very effective as a manly Yank and Quentin Crisp looking exactly right as the aging Queen Elizabeth.

Logistically, pic looks rich and expensive, with St. Petersburg locations standing in for medieval London in winter. Pic was also shot in Uzbekistan.

1993: NOMINATIONS: Best Art Direction, Costume Design

•

ORPHANS
1987, 120 mins, US Ⓥ ⊙ col
Dir Alan J. Pakula ***Prod*** Alan J. Pakula ***Scr*** Lyle Kessler ***Ph*** Donald McAlpine ***Ed*** Evan Lottman ***Mus*** Michael Small ***Art*** George Jenkins
Act Albert Finney, Matthew Modine, Kevin Anderson, John Kellogg (Lorimar)

The inherent dramatic insularity of Lyle Kessler's play about two urban outcast brothers and the Mephistophelian gangster who transforms their hermetic world is driven by the inspired energies of its principal cast.

Treat (Matthew Modine) and Phillip (Kevin Anderson) live in isolated squalor. Treat is a violent sociopath who ventures into New York to steal and scavenge. Phillip is a recluse terrified of the world outside the house and the physically dominant older brother who keeps him there, a virtual prisoner of fear.

Control of self and one's destiny is the gospel of Harold (Albert Finney), a hard-drinking mobster whom Treat lures from a saloon to the house one night with the intention of holding him hostage for ransom. The tables are quickly turned, however, when the mysterious but expansive gunman offers these destitute marginals an opportunity for big money and a spiffy new life.

Modine does all he can to dominate the picture in a tangibly physical performance that seems to use madness as its method and to succeed on these terms more often than not. Anderson portrays Phillip with great sensitivity and an aching pathos that's free of mannered affectation. Finney permits himself to anchor the center between these two extremes.

•

ORPHANS OF THE STORM

1921, 170 mins, US Ⓥ ⊙ ⊗ b/w

Dir D. W. Griffith ***Prod*** D. W. Griffith ***Scr*** Marquis de Trolignac [= D. W. Griffith] ***Ph*** Hendrik Sartov, Paul Allen, G. W. Bitzer ***Ed*** James Smith, Rose Smith ***Art*** Charles M. Kirk, Edward Scholl

Act Lillian Gish, Dorothy Gish, Joseph Schildkraut, Frank Losee, Katherine Emmett, Morgan Wallace (Griffith/United Artists)

D. W. Griffith has tossed two orphans onto the tempestuous sea of the French Revolution and uses the ride-to-the-rescue for a finale, with an orphan under the guillotine and "Danton five miles away." This scene is drawn out agonizingly but does not let down in any spot.

The cavalry ride through the town, the storming of the moated guillotine gates, the last-minute reprieve and the hesitating release trigger on the guillotine all make for a dramatic final reel with a Griffith thrill that will compensate those who are not won by the unbelievable fidelity of the entire film historically.

The plot [based on the French play *Les Deux Orphelines*, by D'Ennery and Cormon] carries the two orphan girls, one blind, into Paris. Dorothy Gish is the blind girl, and this step from comedienne roles into a role of unlimited emotional possibilities reveals new capabilities in the less famous of the two Gish girls.

•

ORPHEE
(ORPHEUS)

1950, 95 mins, France Ⓥ ⊙ b/w

Dir Jean Cocteau ***Prod*** Andre Paulve ***Scr*** Jean Cocteau ***Ph*** Nicolas Hayer ***Ed*** Jacqueline Sadoul ***Mus*** Georges Auric ***Art*** Jean D'Eaubonne

Act Jean Marais, Marie Dea, Francois Perier, Maria Casares, Juliette Greco, Edward Dhermitte (Palais Royal)

Pic is a highly personalized, modernistic production, a poetic interpretation of the Orpheus myth transposed to modern times. The modern Orpheus is a Left Bank poet (Jean Marais) envied by his fellow writers. He becomes enamored of a strange princess depicted as in reality, Death (Maria Casares). From then on, the plot follows the general Orpheus fable.

Jean Cocteau's scripting and directing give the film its proper key of unworldliness. Though slow at times, the special effects are expertly handled. Lensing is lucid and editing gives fine rhythm to pic.

Marais etches a fine portrait as the tortured Orpheus, and the enigmatic Casares is perfect as Death. Francois Perier as Heurtebise, and Marie Dea as Eurydice, round out the stellar spots well.

•

OSCAR, THE

1966, 122 mins, US Ⓥ col

Dir Russell Rouse ***Prod*** Clarence Greene ***Scr*** Harlan Ellison, Russell Rouse, Clarence Greene ***Ph*** Joseph Ruttenberg ***Ed*** Chester W. Schaeffer ***Mus*** Percy Faith ***Art*** Hal Pereira, Arthur Lonegan

Act Stephen Boyd, Elke Sommer, Milton Berle, Eleanor Parker, Joseph Cotten, Jill St. John (Greene-Rouse)

This is the story of a vicious, bitter, first-class heel who rises to stardom on the blood of those close to him. Without a single redeeming quality, part played by Stephen Boyd is unsympathetic virtually from opening shots.

Clarence Green as producer and Russell Rouse as director are unrelenting in their development of the character, in screenplay on which they collabed with Harlan Ellison [based on Richard Sale's novel], and they make handsome use of the Hollywood background.

Boyd is surrounded by some offbeat casting which adds an interesting note. Milton Berle switches to dramatic role as a top Hollywood agent, and Tony Bennett, the singer, portrays a straight character, Boyd's longtime friend victimized by the star in his battle for success.

Boyd makes the most of his part, investing it with an audience-hate symbol which he never once compromises. Elke Sommer, as his studio-designer wife who is another of his victims, is chief distaff interest in a well-undertaken portrayal. Eleanor Parker excels in the rather thankless role of a studio talent scout and dramatic coach who discovers Boyd in NY.

An arresting impression is made by Hedda Hopper, playing herself.

1966: NOMINATIONS: Best Color Costume Design, Color Art Direction

•

OSCAR

1991, 109 mins, US Ⓥ ⊙ col

Dir John Landis ***Prod*** Leslie Belzberg ***Scr*** Michael Barrie, Jim Mulholland ***Ph*** Mac Ahlberg ***Ed*** Dale Beldin ***Mus*** Elmer Bernstein ***Art*** Bill Kenney

Act Sylvester Stallone, Ornella Muti, Don Ameche, Peter Riegert, Tim Curry, Vincent Spano (Touchstone)

Oscar is an intermittently amusing throwback to gangster comedies of the 1930s. While dominated by star Sylvester Stallone and heavy doses of production and costume design, pic is most distinguished by sterling turns by superb character actors.

Verbally adept script by TV comedy writers Michael Barrie and Jim Mulholland is based on a 1958 French play of the same name by Claude Magnier that was turned into a 1967 film starring Louis de Funes and directed by Edouard Molinaro. Set virtually entirely in Stallone's mansion, antics have an inescapably stagebound feel.

Manic proceedings unfold within a four-hour time period on the morning when legendary hood Angelo "Snaps" Provolone (Stallone) will officially go straight by entering the banking business. Snaps is rudely awakened on his big day by his young accountant (Vincent Spano), who brashly announces he needs a big raise so he can afford to marry the gangster's daughter (Marisa Tomei).

This sets in motion a domestic tempest involving two more potential husbands for the daughter, her surprise announcement she's pregnant, the arrival of another woman who claims to be Snaps's daughter and the mixing up of three identical black bags.

Stallone does no more than a serviceable job in getting across the humor. But pic's a pleasure around the edges through the casting of Don Ameche and Eddie Bracken, not to mention Yvonne DeCarlo and, in an opening scene cameo as Snaps's father, Kirk Douglas.

•

OSCAR AND LUCINDA

1997, 132 mins, Australia/US Ⓥ ⊙ ▭ col

Dir Gillian Armstrong ***Prod*** Robin Dalton, Timothy White ***Scr*** Laura Jones ***Ph*** Geoffrey Simpson ***Ed*** Nicholas Beauman ***Mus*** Thomas Newman ***Art*** Luciana Arrighi

Act Ralph Fiennes, Cate Blanchett, Ciaran Hinds, Tom Wilkinson, Richard Roxburgh, Clive Russell (Dalton/Fox Searchlight)

Oscar and Lucinda is a truly poetic movie, a Victorian-era romance revolving around two eccentric soulmates, reckless dreamers and gamblers. Faithfully adapted from Peter Carey's 1988 novel, story is told in one long flashback from the p.o.v. of Oscar's great grandson, who recounts the peculiar events leading to his birth.

Pic's first part, which depicts Oscar and Lucinda's respective childhoods, is too literary, relying heavily on voiceover narration. Film gains momentum when the mature Oscar goes to Oxford to train as a minister, where he realizes once again he "simply does not fit." Oscar's fateful meeting with Lucinda takes place on board a ship, when he determines to become a missionary in the Australian outback. Their unusual relationship inevitably leads to gossip, scandal and controversy.

Ralph Fiennes renders an astoundingly nuanced performance. Newcomer Cate Blanchett also excels as the fiery, self-reliant female industrialist.

1997: NOMINATION: Best Costume Design

•

OSCAR WILDE

1960, 98 mins, UK b/w

Dir Gregory Ratoff ***Prod*** William Kirby ***Scr*** Jo Eisinger ***Ph*** Georges Perinal ***Ed*** Tony Gibbs ***Mus*** Kenneth V. Jones

Act Robert Morley, Phyllis Calvert, John Neville, Ralph Richardson, Dennis Price, Alexander Knox (Vantage)

This black-and-white version of the story of the poet-playwright-wit whose tragic downfall on homosexual charges was a scandal in Victorian times hit London screens just five days before *The Trials of Oscar Wilde*, a color job. It was produced swiftly but shows no signs of technical shoddiness, even though it was being edited up to a couple of hours before screening for the press.

Georges Perinal's lensing is effective and the atmosphere of Victorian London, Paris and the court scenes has been faithfully caught. The literate screenplay draws heavily on both Wilde's own epigrams and wisecracks but also on the actual documented evidence in the two celebrated court cases.

The picture starts unsatisfactorily but comes vividly to life when the court proceedings begin. The opening sequences are very sketchy and merely set the scene of Wilde as a celebrated playwright and his first meeting with the handsome father-hating young Lord Alfred Douglas, an association which was to prove his downfall.

Gregory Ratoff, as director, swiftly gets into his stride after the aforesaid uneasy start and, though the film is over-talky and over-stagey, it is a good and interesting job of work.

Robert Morley, who once made an effective stage Oscar Wilde, looks perhaps a little too old for the role but he gives a very shrewd performance, not only in the rich relish with which he delivers Wilde's bon mots but also in the almost frighteningly pathetic way in which he crumbles and wilts in the dock.

Ralph Richardson is also in memorable form as the brilliant Queen's Counsel, Sir Edward Carson, who mercilessly strips Wilde in court with his penetrating questions.

•

OSSESSIONE

1942, 140 mins, Italy Ⓥ ⊙ b/w

Dir Luchino Visconti ***Scr*** Luchino Visconti, Mario Alicata, Giuseppe De Santis, Gianni Puccini ***Ph*** Aldo Tonti, Domenico Scala ***Ed*** Mario Serandrei ***Mus*** Giuseppe Rosati ***Art*** Gino Franzi

Act Clara Calamai, Massimo Girotti, Juan De Landa, Dhia Cristiani, Elio Marcuzzo, Vittorio Duse (ICI)

Made in 1942 during the war, this film, based on James M. Cain's novel *The Postman Always Rings Twice*, ran afoul of Fascist blue pencils and was radically cut before release. Copyright troubles—the Cain novel was owned by Metro—kept it shelved until 1959, when pic was reviewed in Paris, its first official foreign showing. Version was an incomplete, 112-min. one. It emerges a grim tale that rings true in character.

Director Luchino Visconti has made this essentially Yank hardboiled tale completely Italian by unfolding it without any recourse to suspense or glibness. Its personages are brought into their tragic position by their own characters and their impoverished milieu.

The original storyline is followed as a semiliterate tramp falls for the young wife of an old tavern keeper. This leads to their murdering him, and they turn to distrusting each other to a final ironic climax. Stark lensing and excellent acting give this banal slice-of-life tale almost tragic proportions. Sound is not up to par but other technical credits are. Acting is exemplary.

•

OSTERMAN WEEKEND, THE

1983, 102 mins, US Ⓥ ⊙ col

Dir Sam Peckinpah ***Prod*** Peter S. Davis, William N. Panzer ***Scr*** Alan Sharp, Ian Masters ***Ph*** John Coquillon ***Ed*** Edward Abroms, David Rawlins ***Mus*** Lalo Schifrin ***Art*** Robb Wilson King

Act Rutger Hauer, John Hurt, Craig T. Nelson, Dennis Hopper, Chris Sarandon, Burt Lancaster (Davis-Panzer/20th Century-Fox)

Sam Peckinpah's *The Osterman Weekend* is a competent, professional but thoroughly impersonal meller which reps initial adaptation of a Robert Ludlum tome for the big screen.

CIA chief Burt Lancaster, who harbors presidential ambitions, recruits operative John Hurt to convince powerful TV journalist Rutger Hauer that several of his closest friends are actually Soviet agents. Hauer is about to host an annual weekend get-together with his buddies and their wives.

After Hurt has equipped the California ranch house with a warehouse-full of sophisticated surveillance gear, Hauer warily bids welcome to his guests, who include: hot-tempered financier Chris Sarandon and his sexually unsatisfied wife (Cassie Yates); writer and martial arts expert Craig T. Nelson; doctor Dennis Hopper, and his wife, cocaine addict Helen Shaver.

After a videotape foul-up, the pals get wind of Hauer's suspicions of them, and the domestic situation rapidly deteriorates.

Hauer is solid as the off-balance but determined protagonist. Hurt effectively plays most of his role isolated from the others in his video command post, and Lancaster socks over his bookend cameo as the scheming CIA kingpin.

•

OSTRE SLEDOVANE VLAKY
(CLOSELY WATCHED TRAINS; CLOSELY OBSERVED TRAINS)

1966, 92 mins, Czechoslovakia Ⓥ ⦿ b/w

Dir Jiri Menzel ***Scr*** Bohumil Hrabal, Jiri Menzel, Vaclav Nyvlt ***Ph*** Jaromir Sofr ***Ed*** Jirina Lukesova ***Mus*** Jiri Sust ***Art*** Oldrich Borack

Act Vaclav Neckar, Jitka Bendova, Vladimir Valenta, Libuse Havelkova, Josef Somr, Alois Vachek (Barrandov)

Without being vulgar or tasteless, this Czech production mixes comedy, drama and the most delicate love sequences against the background of the German Occupation and the Czech resistance during the last days of WWII.

The locale is a small railway station somewhere in Bohemia. There are only a few people around: the old stationmaster who is mainly concerned with his small cattle; the adjunct whose main interest is the opposite sex; and the apprentice Hrma, a clumsy young lad who's still rather shy when it comes to making love to a girl. But he's eventually given practice by an attractive female resistance fighter who doesn't hesitate to spend a night with him.

The 28-year-old Jiri Menzel registers a remarkable directorial debut. His sense for witty situations is as impressive as his adroit handling of the players. A special word of praise must go to Bohumil Krabal, the creator of the literary original; the many amusing gags and imaginative situations are primarily his. The cast is composed of wonderful types down the line.

1967: Best Foreign Language Film

•

OTAC NA SLUZBENOM PUTU
(WHEN FATHER WAS AWAY ON BUSINESS)

1985, 135 mins, Yugoslavia Ⓥ col

Dir Emir Kusturica ***Prod*** Mirza Pasic (exec.) ***Scr*** Abdulah Sidran ***Ph*** Vilko Filac ***Ed*** Andrija Zafranovic ***Mus*** Zoran Simjanovic ***Art*** Predrag Lukovan

Act Moreno De Bartolli, Miki Manojlovic, Mirjana Karanovic, Mustafa Nadarevic, Mira Furlan, Predrag Lakovic (Forum)

Emir Kusturica's second feature is set in Sarajevo during the troubled years following Tito's break with Stalin and the Soviet Cominform, from 1948 to 1952. Former partisans and wishful believers in the Communist future could be arbitrarily accused of Stalinism and (whether guilty or innocent) chucked into work-correction camps for the duration.

Pic is seen through the eyes of six-year-old Malik (Moreno De Bartolli), and it's his rather witty commentary on the events about him that sets the tone of this finely etched tragicomedy. Malik sees his father Mesa (Miki Manojlovic) always away on business trips, but what he doesn't know (until the final scenes) is that he's a brusque and lusty Lothario with a yen for the girls.

The twist of fate comes when a girlfriend of the father turns her erstwhile lover over to the local police inspector during a fit of jealousy. Mesa is picked up at night and packed off to the salt mines, so to speak. As a result, his wife Sena (Mirjana Karanovic) has to suffer through three miserable years as a seamstress at home to make ends meet.

Pic scores as a film of irony and sarcasm, imbued with "human comedy" tenderness—rendered much in the style of Czech comedies during the mid-1960s.

•

OTHELLO

1952, 91 mins, Morocco b/w

Dir Orson Welles ***Prod*** Orson Welles ***Scr*** Orson Welles ***Ph*** Anchise Brizzi, G. R. Aldo, Georgo Fanto, Obadan Troiani, Roberto Fusi ***Ed*** Jean Sacha, Renzo Lucidi, John Shepridge ***Mus*** Angelo Francesco Lavagnino, Alberto Barberis ***Art*** Alexandre Trauner

Act Orson Welles, Micheal MacLiammoir, Suzanne Cloutier, Robert Coote, Hilton Edwards, Fay Compton (Mercury)

After three years in the making, Orson Welles unveiled his *Othello* at the Cannes Film Festival in April 1952 to win the top award. Film is an impressive rendering of the Shakespearean tragedy.

Beginning is catchy in lensing, plasticity and eye appeal, but a bit murky in development. After the marriage of Othello and Desdemona over the protests of her father, the film takes a firm dramatic line and crescendos as the warped Iago brings on the ensuing tragic results. The planting of the jealousy seed in Othello is a bit sudden, but once it takes hold, the pic builds in power until the final death scene.

Micheal MacLiammoir is good as Iago, the jealous, twisted friend whose envy turns to hate and murder. Orson Welles gives the tortured Moor depth and stature.

Footage shot in Italy and Morocco is well matched photographically. Standout scenes are the murder of Roderigo in a Moroccan bath as the chase weaves through the steamy air and ends in general skewering and mayhem.

•

OTHELLO

1995, 124 mins, US/UK Ⓥ ⦿ col

Dir Oliver Parker ***Prod*** Luc Roeg, David Barron ***Scr*** Oliver Parker ***Ph*** David Johnson ***Ed*** Tony Lawson ***Mus*** Charlie Mole ***Art*** Tim Harvey

Act Laurence Fishburne, Irene Jacob, Kenneth Branagh, Nathaniel Parker, Michael Maloney, Anna Patrick (Dakota/Imminent/Castle Rock/Columbia)

This rendition of *Othello* takes its place alongside the Mel Gibson *Hamlet* as a pared down, straightforward, respectable screen version of the Bard. Colorful and intimate production is relatively conventional and unremarkable as an interpretation, but is well performed by its two male leads and clearly staged and enunciated for ready comprehension by a mass audience.

Laurence Fishburne's only previous contact with Shakespeare was reciting the "To be or not to be" soliloquy in the 1980 film *Willie & Phil*, but he tackles the challenging role head-on and grapples successfully with its eloquent language and churning emotions. With the text slashed nearly in half by first-time director Oliver Parker, a British actor and longtime Clive Barker cohort who has played both Iago and Roderigo in stage productions of the play, this *Othello* comes off as an elemental tale of passion, jealousy, treachery and murder, with few adornments, shot in straight-ahead style on Italian locations.

The dynamics of suspicion, jealousy and loathing in 16th-century Venice are swiftly delineated at the outset, as Othello's elopement with the beautiful Desdemona (Irene Jacob) spurs the resentment of her nobleman father, and the general's promotion of Cassio (Nathaniel Parker) over his faithful longtime aide Iago (Kenneth Branagh) sets the latter on a vengeful vendetta.

Whereas the men sail through the verse with verve and sureness, Jacob, while a lovely object of Othello's desire, simply can't get her mouth around the Elizabethan dialogue. Passionate scenes between Othello and Desdemona are rather hotter than usual. The few crowd scenes, however, look a bit threadbare and awkwardly managed.

•

OTHER, THE

1972, 108 mins, US Ⓥ col

Dir Robert Mulligan ***Prod*** Robert Mulligan ***Scr*** Tom Tryon ***Ph*** Robert L. Surtees ***Ed*** Folmar Blangsted, O. Nicholas Brown ***Mus*** Jerry Goldsmith ***Art*** Albert Brenner

Act Uta Hagen, Diana Muldaur, Chris Udvarnoky, Martin Udvarnoky, Norma Connolly, Victor French (20th Century-Fox)

The apparently sluggish opening reels of *The Other* subsequently justify themselves among many other mind-engrossing plot twists in this occult shocker. The film [written by actor Tom Tryon from his first novel] is an outstanding example of topflight writing structure and dialog, enhanced to full fruition by a knowing director.

On a small Connecticut farm in 1935 a tragedy-stricken family is plagued further with a series of deaths. The story unfolds around, and from the viewpoint of, Diana Muldaur's two young identical twin sons, expertly played by 10-year-olds Chris and Martin Udvarnoky. Martin is aloof, introverted, and a downbeat influence on Chris, whose more normal juvenile attributes and fantasies are nurtured lovingly by Hagen.

Tryon and Mulligan have seeded the story with many clues and visible occasions for misjudgment.

•

OTHER PEOPLE'S MONEY

1991, 101 mins, US Ⓥ ⦿ col

Dir Norman Jewison ***Prod*** Norman Jewison, Ric Kidney ***Scr*** Alvin Sargent ***Ph*** Haskell Wexler ***Ed*** Lou Lombardo ***Mus*** David Newman ***Art*** Philip Rosenberg

Act Danny DeVito, Gregory Peck, Penelope Ann Miller, Piper Laurie, Dean Jones, Tom Aldredge (Warner/Yorktown)

Danny DeVito does a very entertaining star turn as a delicious personification of the greedy and heartless 1980s, but there is a softening of Jerry Sterner's biting theatrical success and problematic casting.

First produced in 1987 and launched on a long run off-Broadway two years later with Kevin Conway and Mercedes Ruehl in the leads, acidly comic play effectively illustrated the vulnerability of old-fashioned virtues embodied in family-run, locally owned companies when preyed upon by takeover vultures looking for asset-rich firms.

Big time Wall Street operator Lawrence Garfield (DeVito) sets his sights on a venerable old company run by folksy "Jorgy" Jorgenson (Gregory Peck) amid the beautiful turning leaves of Rhode Island. Jorgy is inclined to ignore the threat but is convinced to call in Kate Sullivan (Penelope Ann Miller), a sharp young lawyer and daughter of his longtime assistant and companion (Piper Laurie).

Winning the game is the bottom line for the wily Larry, but he is also extremely taken with the foxy, deliberately provocative Kate, and the two perform a teasing tango in which he holds the upper hand in biz smarts, but she holds the sexual reins. Constant maneuvers and one-upsmanship ploys constitute good, peppery drama, and the strongly etched settings, both in Manhattan and New England, provide a vivid backdrop for this drama of capitalistic conflict.

Peck and Laurie give perfectly good performances. More crucially, Miller comes off about 10 years too young to play Kate. She looks more like a law student than an experienced corporate attorney.

•

OTHER SIDE OF MIDNIGHT, THE

1977, 165 mins, US Ⓥ col

Dir Charles Jarrott ***Prod*** Frank Yablans ***Scr*** Herman Raucher, Daniel Taradash ***Ph*** Fred J. Koenekamp ***Ed*** Donn-Cambern, Harold F. Kress ***Mus*** Michel Legrand ***Art*** John DeCuir

Act Marie-France Pisier, John Beck, Susan Sarandon, Raf Vallone, Clu Gulager, Christian Marquand (20th Century-Fox)

The film is directed in somewhat predictable style by Charles Jarrott. The script [from the novel by Sidney Sheldon] seems awkwardly pulled together, making for some weird time jumps in the 1939–47 period even with the help of sequence subtitles.

Inducted early into a life of making it on her body, Marie-France Pisier sleeps her way up to international film star status, all the while paying out money to follow John Beck.

Beck meanwhile meets Susan Sarandon in Washington, DC, and marries her before going off to the Pacific theater of war. Sarandon has enough troubles in his absence, but when he comes back, her pull with boss Clu Gulager lands Beck lots of jobs.

Pisier, from the mansions of rich Greek Raf Vallone, fixes it so Beck has to turn to work abroad, hiring on as her pilot so she can degrade him.

Players, script and director have not failed the project in this regard; Michel Legrand's score is appropriately goopy.

1977: NOMINATION: Best Costume Design

•

OTHER SIDE OF THE MOUNTAIN, THE
(UK: WINDOW IN THE SKY)

1975, 101 mins, US Ⓥ col

Dir Larry Peerce ***Prod*** Edward S. Feldman ***Scr*** David Seltzer ***Ph*** David M. Walsh ***Ed*** Eve Newman ***Mus*** Charles Fox ***Art*** Philip Abramson

Act Marilyn Hassett, Beau Bridges, Belinda J. Montgomery, Nan Martin, William Bryant, Dabney Coleman (Universal/Filmways)

This is a heartwarming love story—the true-life tale of a desperately injured 19-year-old girl skier with such love for life she beats her way back to a future of hope.

It's based on the tragic experience of Jill Kinmont, a Bishop, CA, girl who was a shoo-in for a berth on the 1956 Winter Olympics team until she suffered her near-fatal accident while racing down the slopes in the Snow Cup Race at Alta, Utah.

Script is from the biographical book, *A Long Way Up*, by E. G. Valens, and personal reminiscences of the victim.

Film is a standout in every department, perfect casting, fine acting, sensitive direction, imaginative photography and general overall production all combining to give unusual strength to subject matter.

1975: NOMINATION: Best Song ("Richard's Window")

•

OTLEY
1969, 90 mins, UK Ⓥ col
Dir Dick Clement ***Prod*** Bruce Cohn Curtis ***Scr*** Ian La Frenais ***Ph*** Austin Dempster ***Ed*** Richard Best ***Mus*** Stanley Myers ***Art*** Carmen Dillon
Act Tom Courtenay, Romy Schneider, Alan Badel, James Villiers, Leonard Rossiter (Columbia)

Otley seeks to break away from overdone Ian Fleming-like spy tales [of the period]. It focuses on exploits of bumbling "everyman type" thrust into the espionage game.

Storyline is pegged around Tom Courtenay unfortuitously present at an acquaintance's London flat, when the latter is bumped off. It soon evolves that the recently deceased was a defector from a gang of state secret smugglers, and now all parties concerned think that Courtenay somehow knew as much as his late friend.

Because of this, he is first kidnapped and beaten up by Romy Schneider and her cohorts, then after bumbling his way out of their clutches, he is caught by the opposing side and bounced about by them.

In seeking to avoid overheroics as well as the pitfalls of parody, the film has an uneasy lack of a point of view and fails to focus viewer's attention on any particular character or plotline philosophy.

•

OUR DAILY BREAD
(UK: THE MIRACLE OF LIFE)
1934, 74 mins, US Ⓥ ⊙ b/w
Dir King Vidor ***Prod*** King Vidor ***Scr*** King Vidor, Elizabeth Hill Vidor ***Ph*** Robert Planck ***Ed*** Lloyd Nossler ***Mus*** Alfred Newman
Act Karen Morley, Tom Keene, John Qualen, Barbara Pepper (Viking/United Artists)

King Vidor, who has the nerve to do unusual things, has here brought to the screen a story which deals with a throng of unemployed who take up squatter rights on an abandoned farm and turn it into a thriving communal collective project. On the way they have various difficulties chiefly from that ghoulish visitor of farmlands, the drought.

When the drought has just about withered the corn, and the young leader (Tom Keene) of the collectives is nuts over a blonde strumpet (Barbara Pepper), the colony is aroused from the abyss of despondency for one last effort.

It's a glorification of human willpower driving man beyond ordinary feats of endurance. Primitive, forceful, real and moving.

•

OUR DANCING DAUGHTERS
1928, 86 mins, US Ⓥ b/w
Dir Harry Beaumont ***Scr*** Marion Ainslee, Ruth Cummings ***Mus*** William Axt, David Mendoza
Act Joan Crawford, John Mack Brown, Dorothy Sebastian, Anita Page, Kathlyn Williams, Nils Asther (M-G-M/Cosmopolitan)

This jazz epic [from Josephine Lovett's newspaper serial] follows the title, is sumptuously mounted, gets plenty of playing from three girls and is sufficiently physically teasing.

Add to that headwork in direction which doesn't show the younger generation doing impossible things, except in one instance, and a story that marries off the juvenile to the scheming flapper before he gets back to the frank and daring but honest heroine.

It's mainly because of Joan Crawford and Anita Page who seesaw for cast honors, although someone ought to have tipped the camera boys to stop shooting Anita in profile on closeups or mediums.

The boyishly figured Crawford has seldom looked better than in this one. She's both heavy and light on clothes and strictly for the camera either way.

Page is given her major spot down next to closing in a lengthy drunk sequence to which she gives abundant authenticity and which ends in her death after a fall down a flight of stairs.

Dorothy Sebastian is close behind as the wronged girl with the fiery husband. She especially registers in scenes opposite Nils Asther and has a couple of spots with Crawford which aren't hard to watch.

•

OUR GIRL FRIDAY
(US: THE ADVENTURES OF SADIE)
1953, 88 mins, UK col
Dir Noel Langley ***Prod*** George Minter, Noel Langley ***Scr*** Noel Langley ***Ph*** Wilkie Cooper ***Ed*** John Seabourne ***Mus*** Ronald Binge ***Art*** Fred Pusey
Act Joan Collins, George Cole, Kenneth More, Robertson Hare, Hermione Gingold, Hattie Jacques (Renown)

Three men and a girl stranded on a desert island should be an obvious vehicle for a spicy, sexy comedy, but this British effort does not quite come up to expectations. The story [from Norman Lindsay's novel, *The Cautious Amorist*] has its moments of fun but the dialogue is often flat and forced. Much of the film was lensed in the Spanish island of Mallorca.

After a collision at sea, Joan Collins finds herself on a desert island with George Cole, a journalist; Kenneth More, a ship's stoker; and Robertson Hare, an insufferable professor. For the sake of harmony, the three men make a pact not to make a pass at the girl, but two of them, Cole and Hare, rapidly succumb to her charms.

There is some lively competition among the two swains for the privilege of being alone with the girl. These incidents are the mainstay of the film's humor and inevitably cause the joke to be a little protracted. There is a delightful guest portrayal, taking only a couple of minutes of screen time, from Hermione Gingold.

•

OUR HOSPITALITY
1923, 81 mins, US Ⓥ ⊙ ⊗ b/w
Dir Buster Keaton, John G. Blystone ***Scr*** Jean Havez, Joseph A. Mitchell, Clyde Bruckman ***Ph*** Elgin Lessley, Gordon Jennings ***Art*** Fred Gabourie
Act Buster Keaton, Natalie Talmadge, Buster Keaton, Jr., Joseph Keaton, Kitty Bradbury (Schenck/Metro)

This is an unusual comedy picture, a novelty melange of dramatics, low comedy, laughs and thrills. Jean Havez has built up a comedy masterpiece about as serious a subject as a feud.

The feud between the McKays and Canfields starts dramatically in a prolog showing the double shooting of a McKay and a Canfield. The McKay baby is taken north by the widow to remove him from the environment. He grows to manhood in the northern home of his aunt, but is summoned back to his old home to claim an inheritance.

This brings the story up to 1830 and allows for a trip on a railroad train of that period that is a comedy classic.

William McKay (Buster Keaton) meets Virginia Canfield (Natalie Talmadge Keaton) on the train. Unknown to each other, the girl invites him to her house for dinner. Her two brothers and father have sworn to kill him, but their code will not allow them to kill him in the house.

The picture is splendidly cast, flawlessly directed and intelligently photographed. The usual low comedy and slapstick have been modified and woven into a consistent story that is as funny as it is entertaining.

•

OUR MAN FLINT
1966, 107 mins, US Ⓥ ⊙ ▭ col
Dir Daniel Mann ***Prod*** Saul David ***Scr*** Hal Fimberg, Ben Starr ***Ph*** Daniel L. Fapp ***Ed*** William Reynolds ***Mus*** Jerry Goldsmith ***Art*** Jack Martin Smith, Ed Graves
Act James Coburn, Lee J. Cobb, Gila Golan, Edward Mulhare, Benson Fong, Shelby Grant (20th Century-Fox)

This Saul David production is a dazzling, action-jammed swashbuckling spoof [from a story by Hal Fimberg] of Ian Fleming's valiant counter-spy; he's given more tools and gimmicks to pursue his craft as he tracks down and destroys the perpetrators of a diabolical scheme to take over the world.

James Coburn takes on the task of being surrounded by exotically undraped beauts and facing dangers which would try any man. But he comes through unscathed, helped by a dandy little specially designed lighter which has 83 separate uses, including such items as being a derringer, two-way radio carrying across oceans, blowtorch, tear gas bomb, dart gun, you name it.

Assignment comes to him when three mad scientists threaten the safety of the world by controlling the weather, and he's selected by ZOWIE (Zonal Organization on World Intelligence Espionage) as the one man alive who can ferret them out before they can put their final threatened plan into work.

Lee J. Cobb has a field day as the exasperated American rep and head of ZOWIE who cannot keep Flint in line according to recognized standards for espionage.

•

OUR MAN IN HAVANA
1960, 111 mins, UK ▭ b/w
Dir Carol Reed ***Prod*** Carol Reed ***Scr*** Grahame Greene ***Ph*** Oswald Morris ***Ed*** Bert Bates ***Mus*** Hermand Deniz ***Art*** John Box
Act Alec Guinness, Burl Ives, Maureen O'Hara, Ernie Kovacs, Noel Coward, Ralph Richardson (Columbia)

Based on the Grahame Greene novel, scripted by that author, directed by Carol Reed, shot mainly in colorful Cuba and acted by a star-loaded cast headed by Alec Guinness, this turns out to be polished, diverting entertainment, brilliant in its comedy but falling apart towards the end when undertones of drama, tragedy and message crop up.

Story concerns a mild-mannered and not very successful vacuum cleaner salesman in Havana who needs extra money to send his daughter to finishing school in Switzerland. Against his will he is persuaded to become a member of the British secret service. To hold down his job, he is forced to invent mythical subagents and concoct highly imaginative, fictitious reports which he sends back to London. They are taken so seriously that two assistants are sent to help him, and the web of innocent deceit that he has spun gradually mounts up to sinister and dramatic consequences.

Greene has scripted his novel fairly faithfully, though the Catholic significance is only lightly brought into the film. Reed sometimes lets the story become woolly but has expert control of a brilliant cast. Guinness is a perfect choice for the reluctant spy role, giving one of his usual subtle, slyly humorous studies.

But the standout thesping comes from Noel Coward. From his first entrance, which is immediately after the credits, he dominates every scene in which he appears. He plays the boss of the Caribbean network.

Another performance which steals a lot of thunder from Guinness is that of Ralph Richardson, who is Coward's boss stationed in London.

•

OUR MOTHER'S HOUSE
1967, 104 mins, UK/US col
Dir Jack Clayton ***Prod*** Jack Clayton ***Scr*** Jeremy Brooks, Haya Harareet ***Ph*** Larry Pizer ***Ed*** Tom Priestley ***Mus*** Georges Delerue ***Art*** Reece Pemberton
Act Dirk Bogarde, Margaret Brooks, Pamela Franklin, Louis Sheldon Williams, John Gugolka, Mark Lester (Heron/M-G-M)

Our Mother's House, a film about children but not to be considered in any way a kiddie pic, is a well made look at family life and parenthood by seven destitute moppets. Dirk Bogarde stars in an excellent performance as their long-lost legal father, who is not the total heel he seems; nor, for that matter, are the kids all angels.

Julian Gloag's novel has been adapted into a good screenplay which develops neatly the accelerated maturing of children after the death of their long-ailing mother (Annette Carell).

Latter, object of adulation, is buried in the back yard, eldest child Margaret Brooks imposing her belief on others that this will eliminate orphanage fears. To all except eldest son Louis Sheldon Williams, she conceals existence of a father, Bogarde.

•

OUR RELATIONS
1936, 72 mins, US Ⓥ ⊙ b/w
Dir Harry Lachman ***Prod*** Hal Roach, Stan Laurel ***Scr*** Charles Rogers, Jack Jevne, Richard Connell, Felix Adler ***Ph*** Rudolph Mate ***Mus*** Leroy Shield
Act Stan Laurel, Oliver Hardy, Betty Healy, Daphne Pollard, Sidney Toler, James Finlayson (Roach/M-G-M)

Stan Laurel does himself proud on his first fling as a producer. For one thing, both Laurel & Hardy get plenty of chances to talk and the dialogue handed them is considerably above par. Picture is deftly gagged, with the slapstick routine nicely contrasted with the saner moments.

Our Relations is based on a short story [*The Money Box* by W. W. Jacobs] published in 1903 but it is doubtful if the author would recognize the screen version. Principal reason is that the plot has been subordinated for laugh purposes, with every move concocted to popular appeal.

Most of mix-ups involve instances of mistaken identity, with the twin brothers of Laurel & Hardy wandering into situations that obviously contain dynamite for the unsuspecting victims. Outstanding sequences are the phone booth episode with three men packed in and the climactical one where the two clowns sway along the dock with their feet embedded in cement forms.

•

OUR TOWN
1940, 89 mins, US Ⓥ b/w
Dir Sam Wood ***Prod*** Sol Lesser ***Scr*** Thornton Wilder, Frank Craven, Harry Chandlee ***Ph*** Bert Glennon ***Ed*** Sherman Todd ***Mus*** Aaron Copland ***Art*** William Cameron Menzies, Harry Horner
Act William Holden, Martha Scott, Fay Bainter, Beulah Bondi, Thomas Mitchell, Frank Craven (Lesser/United Artists)

The film version of Thornton Wilder's Pulitzer prize play *Our Town* is an artistic offering, utilizing the simple and philosophical form of the stage piece, excellently written, directed, acted and mounted.

The film version retains the story and essentials of the play. Developed at a deliberately slow tempo, the simple and unhurried life of a rural New England village of 2,200 souls is unfolded without attempt to point up dramatic highlights.

The tale is divided into three periods, 1901, 1904, and 1913. It's a plain and homey exposition of life, romance, marriage and death in the New Hampshire town. More explicitly, it concerns the intimacies of two families, the adolescent and matured romance and married life of a boy and girl. Tragic ending of the play is switched for picture purposes, the girl taking a nightmare excursion through the village graveyard and visions of death while going through childbirth. The ethereal expedition, running about five minutes, is the one false note in the picture.

Lesser drew heavily on the original stage cast for the film version. Martha Scott delivers a sincerely warm portrayal as the girl, displaying a wealth of ability and personality. In addition, Arthur Allen and Doro Merande are from the stage group in their original roles, Allen particularly effective in his brief professor appearance describing the geographic structure of the countryside.

William Holden is fine as the boy; Fay Bainter and Beulah Bondi provide excellent mother portrayals; while Thomas Mitchell and Guy Kibbee are prominent as heads of the two households.

1940: NOMINATIONS: Best Picture, Actress (Martha Scott), B&W Art Direction, Original Score, Sound

•

OUR WIFE
1941, 92 mins, US b/w
Dir John M. Stahl ***Prod*** John M. Stahl ***Scr*** F. J. Wolfson ***Ph*** Franz F. Planer ***Ed*** Gene Mavlick ***Mus*** Leo Shuken
Act Melvyn Douglas, Ruth Hussey, Ellen Drew, Charles Coburn, John Hubbard (Columbia)

Despite the triangular familiarity with the basic story, director John Stahl bisects it with a moderate admixture of satirical and dramatic ingredients generating from the battle of a man's divorced wife and new interest to snare him for the future. Many feminine wiles and catty scratchings are paraded along the line in the open warfare, all providing audience amusement and enlightenment.

Composer-musician Melvyn Douglas, drowning sorrows of his recent unhappy marriage, meets Ruth Hussey, her father Charles Coburn, and brother John Hubbard, on a cruise off Panama. Family group are all medical scientists, and try to straighten out Douglas before he disembarks at Havana. Accepting his offer to use his Long Island home while they are in New York, Douglas quickly falls in love with Hussey.

Her companionship inspires him to compose a concerto which is performed at a symphony concert for acclaim. His new fame brings back the divorced wife, who decides to regain him from the opposition.

Stahl's direction proceeds at a bumpy pace at times, while in other sections he zips along at a good speed.

•

OUTBREAK
1995, 127 mins, US Ⓥ ⊙ col
Dir Wolfgang Petersen ***Prod*** Arnold Kopelson, Wolfgang Petersen, Gail Katz ***Scr*** Laurence Dworet, Robert Roy Pool ***Ph*** Michael Ballhaus ***Ed*** Stephen Rivkin ***Mus*** James Newton Howard ***Art*** William Sandell
Act Dustin Hoffman, Rene Russo, Morgan Freeman, Kevin Spacey, Cuba Gooding, Jr., Donald Sutherland (Warner)

Rather like the mutated virus that propels its story, *Outbreak* starts out as one movie and becomes another before it's over. While the first one is considerably more frightening and plausible than the second, the entire film has been put together with such skill and attention to viewer excitement that audiences will readily swallow the whole enchilada without a burp.

Smashing opening sequence shows the ravaging effects of a mystery virus on a mercenary camp in Zaire in 1967. Two men in insulated hooded suits, whose faces are unseen but who sound amazingly like Donald Sutherland and Morgan Freeman, proceed with a scorched-earth approach to eradicating the disease and any trace of its victims.

Jump to the present, and when another instance of such a devastating plague is detected in a Zairian village, ace army medic Col. Sam Daniels (Dustin Hoffman) is sent in, along with associates Casey Schuler (Kevin Spacey) and the green but highly trained Maj. Salt (Cuba Gooding, Jr.), to assess the damage. Daniels is convinced that the virus could spread to the United States, or anywhere else, at any time, and so informs his ex-wife, Robby (Rene Russo), also an infectious disease expert.

In a breathless, disturbingly credible stretch of narrative, pic indelibly shows how the virus's "host," an African monkey, is captured in the jungle, transported by a sailor to San Francisco and, ultimately, released into the Californean wild. At the same time, the army higher-ups who conspired to cover up the virus's history dating back to the '60s pull the "nosy bastard" Col. Daniels off the case, anxious to keep things quiet.

Director Wolfgang Petersen demonstrates a smooth stylistic savvy that keeps the film highly absorbing from beginning to end. Questions, holes and implausabilities are lost in the rearview mirror before one can sort them out mentally.

With all the running around he's required to do, this isn't one of Hoffman's deeper or quirkier performances, but his Everyman quality is welcome in the heroic part. Russo is convincingly professional as a smart, humane doctor, while Spacey weighs in with some wry comic relief.

•

OUTCAST OF THE ISLANDS
1952, 102 mins, UK b/w
Dir Carol Reed ***Prod*** Carol Reed ***Scr*** William Fairchild ***Ph*** John Wilcox, Ted Scaife ***Ed*** Bert Bates ***Mus*** Brian Easdale ***Art*** Vincent Korda
Act Ralph Richardson, Trevor Howard, Robert Morley, Kerima, Wendy Hiller, George Coulouris (London/British Lion)

Picture is based on the Joseph Conrad story, but the screenplay fails to capture the authentic atmosphere of the Far East in which the story is set. The backgrounds are genuine enough, but the plot is loosely constructed and the editing occasionally episodic.

The outcast is played by Trevor Howard. He is saved from the police, after being involved in a swindle, by the captain of a trading vessel who takes him to his island outpost. There, he doublecrosses his friend, tricks his partner and falls in love with the daughter of the blind tribal chief.

Within that outline, the film concentrates on developing the shifting character of the outcast as a man without honor, without principle and without friends, yet having a devouring passion for the native girl.

Ralph Richardson, polished and dignified as usual, gives a sterling performance as the captain of the trading boat. Robert Morley chalks up another success as the captain's partner.

•

OUTFIT, THE
1973, 102 mins, US Ⓥ col
Dir John Flynn ***Prod*** Carter De Haven ***Scr*** John Flynn ***Ph*** Bruce Surtees ***Ed*** Ralph E. Winters ***Mus*** Jerry Fielding ***Art*** Tambi Larsen
Act Robert Duvall, Karen Black, Joe Don Baker, Robert Ryan, Timothy Carey, Richard Jaeckel (M-G-M)

In *The Outfit* two relatively small time outside-the-law characters, stylishly handled by Robert Duvall and Joe Don Baker, drive off into the credits laughing gleefully. In their wake they leave countless stiffs, including crime-syndicate topper Robert Ryan, Duvall's girlfriend (Karen Black), and a batch of other broken-boned face-smashed individuals who were caught up in pair's vengeance-motivated assault on organized crime.

John Flynn's simple screenplay [from a novel by Richard Stark, pen name for Donald E. Westlake] focuses on Duvall's explosive compulsion to square things with the mobsters who killed his brother as reprisal for their ripping off a bank controlled by the syndicate.

Flynn keeps the pace extremely fast and engaging. Duvall and Baker work smoothly together. Joanna Cassidy makes an attractive screen bow as Ryan's wife.

•

OUT FOR JUSTICE
1991, 91 mins, US Ⓥ ▭ col
Dir John Flynn ***Prod*** Steven Seagal, Arnold Kopelson ***Scr*** David Lee Henry ***Ph*** Ric Waite ***Ed*** Robert A. Ferretti, Donald Brochu ***Mus*** David Michael Frank ***Art*** Gene Rudolf
Act Steven Seagal, William Forsyth, Jerry Orbach, Jo Champa, Shareen Mitchell, Sal Richards (Warner)

Out for Justice harbors an incredibly simple vengeance plot loaded with enough macho sadism to satiate the action genre's bloodthirsty fans.

This time Steven Seagal plays an Italian cop pursuing the killer of his partner, who's gunned down in broad daylight just after the opening credits. Seagal relentlessly pursues the murderous, drugged-out Richie (William Forsythe), dispatching his henchmen in brutal encounters in a butcher shop, pool hall and his own apartment that make the LAPD's brutality seem tame.

Director John Flynn does a fair job of keeping the minimal storyline crawling along well enough to justify all the mayhem. Too bad the climactic confrontation doesn't justify the build-up. Stuntwork, however, is first-rate, and Seagal remains a convincing action figure.

•

OUTLAND
1981, 109 mins, US Ⓥ ⊙ ▭ col
Dir Peter Hyams ***Prod*** Richard A. Roth ***Scr*** Peter Hyams ***Ph*** Stephen Goldblatt ***Ed*** Stuart Baird ***Mus*** Jerry Goldsmith ***Art*** Philip Harrison
Act Sean Connery, Peter Boyle, Frances Sternhagen, James B. Sikking, Kika Markham, Clarke Peters (Warner/Ladd)

Outland is something akin to *High Noon* in outer space, a simple good guys-bad guys yarn set in the future on a volcanic moon of Jupiter.

While there are several mile-wide plot holes and one key underdeveloped main character, the film emerges as a tight, intriguing old-fashioned drama that gives audiences a hero worth rooting for.

It's clear from the beginning that newly arrived marshal Sean Connery is going to have his hands full. Soon into the action, a miner takes it upon himself to enter the deadly moon atmosphere without his spacesuit and literally fries before the audience's eyes.

Connery soon finds out that the miners are growing crazy due to an amphetamine they are taking that makes them produce more, but eventually destroys their brains. It doesn't take long to figure out that his rival (Peter Boyle), the smug general manager who basically runs the colony's operations, is involved in supplying the drug.

Writer-director Peter Hyams falls just short of providing the exciting payoff to the conflicts he so painstakingly sets up throughout the picture.

1981: NOMINATION: Best Sound

•

OUTLAW, THE
1943, 124 mins, US Ⓥ ⊙ b/w
Dir Howard Hughes ***Prod*** Howard Hughes ***Scr*** Jules Furthman ***Ph*** Gregg Toland ***Ed*** Wallace Grissell ***Mus*** Victor Young
Act Jack Buetel, Jane Russell, Thomas Mitchell, Walter Huston (Howard Hughes)

Beyond sex attraction of Jane Russell's frankly displayed charms, picture, according to accepted screen entertainment standards, falls short. Plot is based on legend Billy the Kid wasn't killed by the law but continued to live on after his supposed death.

Pace is series of slow-moving incidents making up continuous chase as directed by Howard Hughes and isn't quickened by the two hours running time, but slowness is not so much a matter of length as a lack of tempo in individual scenes.

This variation of the checkered film career of Billy the Kid has the outlaw joining forces with legendary Doc Holliday, played by Walter Huston, to escape the pursuing Sheriff Pat Garrett (Thomas Mitchell). Mixing strangely into the kid's life is Rio, Latin charmer, as portrayed by Russell.

Sex seldom rears its beautiful head in simonpure prairie dramas, but since this is an unorthodox, almost burlesque, version of tried and true desert themes, anything can and often does happen.

•

OUTLAW BLUES
1977, 100 mins, US Ⓥ col
Dir Richard T. Heffron ***Prod*** Steve Tish ***Scr*** B. W. L. Norton ***Ph*** Jules Brenner ***Ed*** Danford B. Greene, Scott Conrad ***Mus*** Charles Bernstein, Bruce Langhorne ***Art*** Jack Marty
Act Peter Fonda, Susan Saint James, John Crawford, James Callahan, Michael Lerner, Steve Fromholz (Warner)

Script takes Peter Fonda from prison, where he has developed a musical ability, to Texas in pursuit of James Callahan, C&W name who has stolen the title song from Fonda.

Accidental shooting of Callahan in a scuffle launches a manhunt for Fonda by police chief John Crawford, mayoral candidate not about to be embarrassed at election time.

Susan Saint James, one of Callahan's singing group, beds and befriends Fonda and, by clever p.r., makes him a major new platter star to be reckoned with by Michael Lerner, a music biz sharpie.

The film revolves into a series of chases, interweaved with some okay songs which Fonda is said to have sung himself. Story opts for the laughs and smiles which come easily in abundance.

•

OUTLAW JOSEY WALES, THE

1976, 135 mins, US Ⓥ ⦿ col

Dir Clint Eastwood ***Prod*** Robert Daley ***Scr*** Phil Kaufman, Sonia Chernus ***Ph*** Bruce Surtees ***Ed*** Ferris Webster ***Mus*** Jerry Fielding ***Art*** Tambi Larsen

Act Clint Eastwood, Chief Dan George, Sondra Locke, Bill McKinney, John Vernon, Paula Trueman (Warner)

The screenplay [based on the book *Gone to Texas* by Forrest Carter] is another one of those violence revues, with carnage production numbers slotted every so often and intercut with Greek chorus narratives by John Vernon and Chief Dan George.

Clint Eastwood is a Civil War era farmer whose family is murdered by brigands led by Bill McKinney; Vernon is a fellow counter-guerrilla who is tricked into surrendering his men; George is an old Indian whom Eastwood encounters on the long trail of earthly retribution.

Eastwood's character meanders through the Middle West, disposing of antagonists by the dozen aided at times by George, Sam Bottoms, romantic interest Sondra Locke, latter's granny Paula Trueman and others.

1976: NOMINATION: Best Original Score

•

OUT OF AFRICA

1985, 150 mins, US Ⓥ ⦿ col

Dir Sydney Pollack ***Prod*** Sydney Pollack ***Scr*** Kurt Luedtke ***Ph*** David Watkin ***Ed*** Fredric Steinkamp, William Steinkamp, Pembroke Herring, Sheldon Kahn ***Mus*** John Barry ***Art*** Stephen Grimes

Act Meryl Streep, Robert Redford, Klaus Maria Brandauer, Michael Kitchen, Malick Bowens, Joseph Thiaka (Universal)

At two-and-a-half hours, *Out of Africa* certainly makes a leisurely start into its story. Just short of boredom, however, the picture picks up pace and becomes a sensitive, enveloping romantic tragedy.

Getting top billing over Robert Redford, Meryl Streep surely earns it with another engaging performance. Still, the film rarely comes to life except when Redford is around.

Ably produced and directed by Sydney Pollack, *Africa* is the story of Isak Dinesen, who wrote of her experiences in Kenya. Though Dinesen (real name: Karen Blixen) remembered it lovingly, hers was not a happy experience. Pic opens in 1914.

With one landscape after another, Pollack and lenser David Watkin prove repeatedly, however, why she should love the land so, but at almost travelog drag.

Eventually, Streep and husband Klaus Maria Brandauer split, leaving an opening for Redford to move in. True love follows, but not happiness because he's too independent to be tied down by a marriage certificate.

1985: Best Picture, Director, Adapted Screenplay, Cinematography, Art Direction, Sound, Original Score

NOMINATIONS: Best Actress (Meryl Streep), Supp. Actor (Klaus Maria Brandauer), Costume Design, Editing

•

OUT OF SEASON

1975, 90 mins, UK Ⓥ col

Dir Alan Bridges ***Prod*** Eric Bercovici, Reuben Bercovitch ***Scr*** Eric Bercovici, Reuben Bercovitch ***Ph*** Arthur Ibbetson ***Ed*** Peter Weatherly ***Mus*** John Cameron ***Art*** Robert Jones

Act Vanessa Redgrave, Cliff Robertson, Susan George, Edward Evans, Frank Jarvis (EMI/Lorimar)

Virtually a three-hander, *Out of Season* boasts topnotch performances by Vanessa Redgrave, Cliff Robertson and Susan George, a taut script and first-rate direction.

Though basic plot is that old chestnut about the dark stranger returning—after 20 years away—to visit an isolated hotel in an English seaside town, its handling is expert enough to avoid most of the pitfalls of the genre. And so is the acting.

Director Alan Bridges displays his ability to develop and hold obsessive situations, all hints and innuendos, and this Ping-Pong match of the affections often has the suspense of a whodunit as audience tries to guess next move by the entangled mother, daughter, lover trio.

•

OUT OF SIGHT

1998, 122 mins, US Ⓥ ⦿ col

Dir Steven Soderbergh ***Prod*** Danny DeVito, Michael Shamberg, Stacy Sher ***Scr*** Scott Frank ***Ph*** Elliot Davis ***Ed*** Anne V. Coates ***Mus*** David Holmes ***Art*** Gary Frutkoff

Act George Clooney, Jennifer Lopez, Ving Rhames, Don Cheadle, Dennis Farina, Albert Brooks (Jersey/Universal)

A sly, sexy, vastly entertaining film version of Elmore Leonard's playful novel, this reflexively witty crime caper boasts the sort of bright, snappy dialog that's rarely heard in a mainstream picture. In the leading roles, George Clooney and Jennifer Lopez create a blissful chemistry that will make viewers root for their flawed characters and eccentric romance.

Director Steven Soderbergh, who became poster child for the new American independent cinema with *sex, lies, and videotape* (1989), stumbled through a decade of small, idiosyncratic films, searching for the right material to bring out his talent. *Out of Sight* reveals Soderbergh in peak form.

First reel introduces the colorful gallery of characters, beginning with Jack Foley (Clooney), an ex-con about to perform yet another bank robbery. A dead car battery leads to his imprisonment in Florida.

The next, masterfully orchestrated sequence depicts a prison break that goes hilariously awry. It just happens that Deputy Federal Marshal Karen Sisco (Lopez) is on the premises while the action occurs. Foley's pal, Buddy Bragg (Ving Rhames), prevents Sisco from using her gun, and Foley manages to escape safely. The mismatched Foley and Sisco begin their courtship in the tight space of a car's trunk, where they share their values—and love for movies. It soon becomes obvious that their paths will criss cross and fates intertwine.

The densely rich yarn is more character than plot-driven. Scripter Scott Frank, who also adapted *Get Shorty*, and Soderbergh understand that Leonard's forte lies in his sharp, nonjudgmental characterizations and authentic lingo of lowlifes who are nonetheless appealing.

Not since *Boogie Nights* has a Hollywood movie had so many characters and seemed so perfectly cast.

[Michael Keaton, reappearing in his *Jackie Brown* FBI getup, and Samuel L. Jackson also make uncredited appearances.]

•

OUT OF THE BLUE

1980, 94 mins, Canada Ⓥ col

Dir Dennis Hopper ***Scr*** Leonard Yakir, Gary Jules Jouvenat ***Ph*** Marc Champion ***Ed*** Doris Dyck ***Mus*** Tom Lavin

Act Linda Manz, Sharon Farrell, Dennis Hopper, Raymond Burr, Don Gordon (Robson Street)

Dennis Hopper directs and stars in this terse drama of what the 1970s drug culture and dregs of the counterculture would have wrought on those easy riders who got off their bikes and tried to conform.

Linda Manz has tart authority as a streetwise 15-year-old. She had been in a terrible accident while driving with Hopper, her father, who plowed into a school bus stalled in the middle of the road, killing many of the kids.

Hopper has been sentenced to five years in prison. He has become a hero to his daughter, who has fantasized the late Elvis Presley into another hero.

Dramatically economical, pic captures urban overcrowding, personal problems and violence but sans excess. Hopper reportedly took over direction after film started but worked with the writer on changes to fit his own personal outlooks.

•

OUT OF THE PAST
(UK: BUILD MY GALLOWS HIGH)

1947, 95 mins, US Ⓥ ⦿ b/w

Dir Jacques Tourneur ***Prod*** Warren Duff ***Scr*** Geoffrey Homes [= Daniel Mainwaring] ***Ph*** Nicholas Musuraca ***Ed*** Samuel E. Beetley ***Mus*** Roy Webb ***Art*** Albert S. D'Agostino, Jack Okey

Act Robert Mitchum, Jane Greer, Kirk Douglas, Rhonda Fleming, Richard Webb, Steve Brodie (RKO)

Out of the Past is a hardboiled melodrama [from the novel by Geoffrey Homes] strong on characterization. Direction by Jacques Tourneur pays close attention to mood development, achieving realistic flavor that is further emphasized by real life settings and topnotch lensing by Nicholas Musuraca.

Plot depicts Robert Mitchum as a former private detective who tries to lead a quiet, small-town life. Good portion of story is told in retrospect by Mitchum when his past catches up with him. Hired by a gangster to find a girl who had decamped with $40,000 after shooting the crook, Mitchum crosses her path in Acapulco, falls for her himself and they flee the gangster together.

Mitchum gives a very strong account of himself. Jane Greer as the baby-faced, charming killer is another lending potent interest. Kirk Douglas, the gangster, is believable and Paul Valentine makes role of henchman stand out. Rhonda Fleming is in briefly but effectively.

•

OUT OF TOWNERS, THE

1970, 97 mins, US Ⓥ ⦿ col

Dir Arthur Hiller ***Prod*** Paul Nathan ***Scr*** Neil Simon ***Ph*** Andrew Laszlo ***Ed*** Fred Chulack ***Mus*** Quincy Jones ***Art*** Charles Bailey

Act Jack Lemmon, Sandy Dennis, Sandy Baron, Anne Meara, Robert Nichols, Ann Prestiss (Paramount/Jalem)

The Out of Towners is a total delight. Neil Simon's first modern original screen comedy stars Jack Lemmon and Sandy Dennis, an Ohio couple who become disillusioned with big-city life, New York style.

Lemmon and Dennis come to NY on one of those expense paid executive suite job interviews. In the course of 24 hours, they are stacked-up over the airport; diverted to Boston; lose their luggage; ride a food-less train to strikebound and rainy NY; lose their Waldorf reservations; get held up; become involved in a police chase; escape mugging in Central Park; flee a mounted cop; and are asked to leave a church because of a TV rehearsal. Among other things.

Dennis and Lemmon are superb in comedy characterizations.

•

OUT-OF-TOWNERS, THE

1999, 92 mins, US Ⓥ ⦿ col

Dir Sam Weisman ***Prod*** Robert Evans, Teri Schwartz, Robert Cort, David Madden ***Scr*** Marc Lawrence ***Ph*** John Bailey ***Ed*** Kent Beyda ***Mus*** Marc Shaiman ***Art*** Ken Adam

Act Steve Martin, Goldie Hawn, Mark McKinney, John Cleese, Oliver Hudson (Paramount)

At once warmer and rowdier than its 1970 predecessor, Sam Weisman's updated remake of *The Out-of-Towners* is a pleasantly amusing comedy that showcases first-rate comic thesping and nimble slapstick shtick by Steve Martin and Goldie Hawn. Working from Marc Lawrence's more softhearted rewrite of Neil Simon's original screenplay, Weisman and his well-cast leads go through their paces with solid professionalism.

While remaining true to the basic outline of Simon's script, screenwriter Lawrence—fresh from his *Forces of Nature* success—puts his own imprint on the material, changing everything from the age of lead characters to the overall tone of the story. This offers a more affectionately romanticized view of Manhattan, even as the remake provides just as much reason for the Ohio visitors to have second thoughts about relocating there.

Martin and Hawn play Henry and Nancy Clark, a long-married couple forced to cope with empty-nest blues after their youngest child (Oliver Hudson, Hawn's real-life son) jets off to college. Henry is newly unemployed, a fact he has concealed from Nancy when he's beckoned to New York for a job interview.

The remake is aggressively upbeat—the Clarks don't merely survive, they thrive in the Big Apple—and indicates that the quality of life has drastically improved since 1970. Maybe that's why New York Mayor Rudy Giuliani agreed to play himself in a cameo role.

•

OUTRAGE

1950, 79 mins, US b/w

Dir Ida Lupino ***Prod*** Collier Young, Malvin Wald ***Scr*** Collier Young, Malvin Wald, Ida Lupino ***Ph*** Archie Stout ***Ed*** Harvey Manger ***Mus*** Paul Sawtell

Act Mala Powers, Tod Andrews, Robert Clarke, Raymond Bond, Lilian Hamilton, Rita Lupino (RKO/Filmakers)

Rape and its effect on the victim and her loved ones set up the melodramatic plot. However, handling of the theme is more interested in the events that transpire afterwards.

Mala Powers impresses as the victim. She is a young girl, engaged to a clean-cut young man. After working late one night, she is violated while going home. The whispering and knowing looks that come later from the small-town folks force her to run away.

Ida Lupino directed from a script written with Collier Young and Malvin Wald, co-producers. Her handling of the earlier sequences packs a hefty punch. In the latter sequences, when Powers is beginning to find herself, the pace is deliberate, almost idyllic.

While made on a tight budget, the production manages very good values.

•

OUTRAGE, THE

1964, 95 mins, US b/w

Dir Martin Ritt ***Prod*** A. Ronald Lubin ***Scr*** Michael Kanin ***Ph*** James Wong Howe ***Ed*** Frank Santillo ***Mus*** Alex North ***Art*** George W. Davis, Tambi Larsen

Act Paul Newman, Laurence Harvey, Claire Bloom, Edward G. Robinson, William Shatner, Howard da Silva (M-G-M)

The Outrage is adapted from the Fay and Michael Kanin Broadway play, *Rashomon*, which in turn was based on the Japanese film production of same tab. It is the story of a killing of a Southern gentleman and the rape of his wife by a bloodthirsty bandit, told through the eyes of the three protagonists and then by a disinterested eye witness, each version differing.

Script unfolds in the American Southwest in the 1870s, a neat metamorphosis from the 12th-century Japan of the play and original Nipponese pic. Bandit character is retained, but the samurai character becomes a Southern gentleman of fine family (Laurence Harvey) who is travelling through the West with his wife (Claire Bloom) when set upon by a Mexican outlaw (Paul Newman).

Plot takes its form, opening on platform of a deserted railroad station as a prospector and a preacher, who is leaving the town a disillusioned man, recite to con man Edward G. Robinson the trial of the outlaw a few days previously, when three people testify to three totally different accounts of what "actually" happened.

Newman as the violent and passionate killer plays his colorful character with a flourish and heavy accent. Harvey has little to do in first three accounts except remain tied to a tree, his turn coming in fourth when the prospector tells how he and bandit are shamed by the wife into fighting for her. Bloom, who appeared in Broadway play, has her gamut during the four versions of her ravishment, running from pure innocence to her demand to the outlaw to kill her husband so she can go with her new lover. In all, she delivers strongly, turning glibly from drama to comedy.

•

OUTRAGEOUS FORTUNE

1987, 100 mins, US col

Dir Arthur Hiller ***Prod*** Ted Field, Robert Cort ***Scr*** Leslie Dixon ***Ph*** David M. Walsh ***Ed*** Tom Rolf ***Mus*** Alan Silvestri ***Art*** James D. Vance

Act Shelley Long, Bette Midler, Peter Coyote, Robert Prosky, John Schuck, George Carlin (Touchstone/Interscope)

Outrageous Fortune is well crafted, old-fashioned entertainment that takes some conventional elements, shines them up and repackages them as something new and contemporary. It's a traditional male buddy film that has substituted women, and the main plot device is that the two heroines are sleeping with the same man. Bette Midler and Shelley Long collide even before their affections do in an acting class given by the eminent Russian director Stanislov Korenowski (Robert Prosky). Long is a wealthy, spoiled dilettante while Midler last starred in *Ninja Vixens*. When the audience learns they're sharing the same man (Peter Coyote) before they do, it's a delicious moment complete with one image-shattering sight gag.

The film takes off as a chase picture with the girls following Coyote to New Mexico to demand a decision. They're not the only ones looking for him. It seems the CIA is hot on his trail, as is the KGB. To top things off, it turns out Korenowski is a Russian agent first and a director second.

Even when Leslie Dixon's script sags and becomes a bit repetitious in the long New Mexico chase section, Midler and Long are never less than fun to watch.

•

OUTRIDERS, THE

1950, 93 mins, US col

Dir Roy Rowland ***Prod*** Richard Goldstone ***Scr*** Irving Ravetch ***Ph*** Charles Schoenbaum ***Ed*** Robert J. Kern ***Mus*** Andre Previn

Act Joel McCrea, Arlene Dahl, Barry Sullivan, Claude Jarman, Jr., James Whitmore, Ramon Novarro (M-G-M)

The Outriders is sturdy meat for the action fan. Principal motivation of script is a $1 million gold robbery.

Joel McCrea, Barry Sullivan and James Whitmore are Confederate soldiers who escape from the Yankees, join up with a gang of renegade rebel raiders. They are dispatched to New Mexico to figure an angle to lead a wagon train of gold slated for the Yanks into an ambush. They join the train when they help beat off an Indian attack. Before the ambush destination is reached McCrea has fallen for a comely widow (Arlene Dahl).

Roy Rowland's direction packs a wallop. Some scenes are alive with tingling suspense, such as the crossing of a raging river at high flood.

•

OUTSIDER, THE

1979, 128 mins, US col

Dir Tony Luraschi ***Scr*** Tony Luraschi ***Ph*** Ricardo Aronovitch ***Ed*** Catherine Kelber ***Mus*** Ken Thorne ***Art*** Franco Fumagalli

Act Craig Wasson, Sterling Hayden, Patricia Quinn, Niall O'Brien, T. P. McKenna, Ray McAnally (Paramount/Cinematic Arts)

The Outsider represents the first attempt to get behind the incessant headlines and into the minds and motives at work on one of the longest-fought terrorist campaigns of the times—through an intelligent fictional story with an Irish setting.

A measure of the effectiveness of Craig Wasson's performance, as a young Irish-American inflamed to join the IRA by his grandfather's (Sterling Hayden) tales of fighting the Brits in the religion-charged cause of Irish nationalism, is that by the time he finally leaves Ireland as a disillusioned fugitive he looks—without artifice—10 years older.

What he's escaped is a neatly plotted double trap by both the IRA and British army.

The strength of Tony Luraschi's features debut lies in its restraint.

•

OUTSIDERS, THE

1983, 91 mins, US col

Dir Francis Coppola ***Prod*** Fred Roos, Gray Frederickson ***Scr*** Kathleen Knutsen Rowell ***Ph*** Stephen H. Burum ***Ed*** Anne Goursaud ***Mus*** Carmine Coppola ***Art*** Dean Tavoularis

Act C. Thomas Howell, Matt Dillon, Ralph Macchio, Patrick Swayze, Rob Lowe, Emilio Estevez (Zoetrope)

Francis Coppola has made a well acted and crafted but highly conventional film out of S. E. Hinton's popular youth novel, *The Outsiders*. Although set in the mid-1960s, pic feels very much like a 1950s drama about problem kids.

Screenplay is extremely faithful to the source material, even down to having the film open with the leading character and narrator, C. Thomas Howell, reciting the first lines of his literary effort while we see him writing them.

But dialog which reads naturally and evocatively on the page doesn't play as well onscreen, and there's a decided difficulty of tone during the early sequences, as Howell and his buddies (Matt Dillon and Ralph Macchio) horse around town, sneak into a drive-in and have an unpleasant confrontation with the Socs, rival gang from the well-heeled part of town.

When the Socs attack Howell and Macchio in the middle of the night, latter ends up killing a boy to save his friend, and the two flee to a hideaway in an abandoned rural church. It is during this mid-section that the film starts coming to life, largely due to the integrity of the performances by Howell and Macchio.

Howell is truly impressive, a bulwark of relative stability in a sea of posturing and pretense. Macchio is also outstanding as his doomed friend, and Patrick Swayze is fine as the oldest brother forced into the role of parent.

•

OUTWARD BOUND

1930, 83 mins, US b/w

Dir Robert Milton ***Prod*** [Jack L. Warner] ***Scr*** J. Grubb Alexander ***Ph*** Hal Mohr ***Ed*** Ralph Dawson ***Mus*** Erno Rapee, Louis Silvers (dirs.) ***Art*** [uncredited]

Act Leslie Howard, Douglas Fairbanks, Jr., Beryl Mercer, Dudley Digges, Helen Chandler, Alec B. Francis (Warner)

If a half-real, half-allegorical idea with a psychology midriff can be put on the screen in as intelligent a manner as this, then films have a wide future in an educational direction. On that score this film may be considered a laboratory experiment for the rest of the film world to ponder over and learn.

Two of the players, Beryl Mercer and Leslie Howard, are from the original cast on Broadway in 1924. Before that, the play [by Sutton Vane] had a London run [starting in September 1923].

The story is suggestive of the stage play, *Liliom*. It's that allegorical theme of going before an examiner (Dudley Digges) in Heaven. In *Liliom* they go to Heaven in a railroad train; here, a steamship.

The boy and the girl—"half-ways" held between death and life—are always or nearly always in the distance. The boy and the girl are neither sinners nor saints in the full sense. But they sought death and carry their secret along with a suspense that's worthy of the production and the theme.

The bully big man of the business world and the supercilious snob of a woman with a past try to ritz death. The boy and girl don't know what it's all about.

Director Robert Milton, coming from the stage, has built a good start but he had a stage play to do it with. Helen Chandler is still the same sobbing contralto and suits her role.

•

OVERBOARD

1987, 112 mins, US col

Dir Garry Marshall ***Prod*** Anthea Sylbert, Alexandra Rose ***Scr*** Leslie Dixon ***Ph*** John A. Alonzo ***Ed*** Dov Hoenig, Sonny Baskin ***Mus*** Alan Silvestri ***Art*** James Shanahan, Jim Dultz

Act Goldie Hawn, Kurt Russell, Edward Herrmann, Katherine Helmond, Michael Hagerty, Roddy McDowall (M-G-M)

Overboard is an uninspiring, unsophisticated attempt at an updated screwball comedy that is brought down by plodding script and a handful of too broadly drawn characters. Only element that occasionally lifts pic is the work of the redoubtable Goldie Hawn, who gives a gem of a performance.

Hawn plays Joanna Stayton, a millionaire wife who decides it's time to have her yacht's closet remodeled. On deck comes Kurt Russell as carpenter Dean Proffitt, whose performance doesn't seem to go beyond affable or angry. She fires him and, shortly thereafter, pushes him overboard.

Her comeuppance is the kind of revenge only found in film—Joanna falls off the boat trying to retrieve her wedding rock, and washes back on the Elk Cove shore with a nasty case of amnesia. Proffitt sees her on TV and devises a scheme to claim her as his wife Annie.

There is little to do but sit back and admire Hawn's performance, as she splendidly transforms herself from rich bitch to caring wife. Supporting roles are mostly pedestrian, except for a sweet, funny turn by Michael Hagerty, as Russell's best friend and a graduate of the John Candy School of Cinematic Oafishness.

•

OVERLANDERS, THE

1946, 91 mins, UK/Australia b/w

Dir Harry Watt ***Prod*** Michael Balcon ***Scr*** Harry Watt ***Ph*** Osmond Borradaile ***Ed*** Leslie Norman ***Mus*** John Ireland

Act Chips Rafferty, John Nugent Hayward, Daphne Campbell, Jean Blue (Ealing)

Producer Michael Balcon sent director Harry Watt to Australia with a mandate to make a picture representative of that continent. Watt spent five months soaking up the atmosphere. In the Federal Food Office, Controller Murphy explained of the greatest mass migration of cattle the world has ever known to get them out of reach of a probable Jap landing. Across 2,000 miles of heat and dust, drovers had battled with 500,000 head of cattle. Watt decided this would be the film's theme.

Story begins in 1942 at the tiny town of Wyndham, where meat works are destroyed, personnel evacuated, and Chips Rafferty, boss cattle drover, is told to shoot 1,000 head of prime beasts. He decides instead to overland them across 2,000 miles of tough going.

Epic trip lasts 15 months, and the adventures are graphic. Highlights are the breaking-in of wild horses when their own had died from poison weed; the stampede with the men facing a charge of maddened cattle and the forced march across a mountain path with a sheer drop on one side.

•

OVERLORD

1975, 85 mins, UK b/w

Dir Stuart Cooper ***Prod*** James Quinn ***Scr*** Stuart Cooper, Christopher Hudson ***Ph*** John Alcott ***Ed*** Jonathan Gili ***Mus*** Paul Glass

Act Brian Stirner, Davyd Harries, Nicholas Ball, Julie Neesam, Sam Sewell (Imperial War Museum)

Overlord concentrates on a British youngster's World War II blitztime induction into the army, his brief training period and his early D-day death.

Pic has a lovely reminiscent feel for its period and the deceptively peaceful at-home backdrop to the war in the buildup phase to the Allied invasion of the Continent, with bombers taking off from the green fields of England, convoys of invasion troops crossing silent villages and, as a foretaste of deadlier things to come, rarely seen footage of dummy run rehearsals conducted along the coasts of Britain, eerily dramatic when glimpsed in hindsight on later events.

Youth's indoctrination is very skillfully melded with real footage. U.S. director Stuart Cooper gives it the right understated, unheroic feel.

•

OVER THE BROOKLYN BRIDGE

1984, 106 mins, US col

Dir Menahem Golan ***Prod*** Menahem Golan, Yoram Globus ***Scr*** Arnold Somkin ***Ph*** Adam Greenberg ***Ed*** Mark Goldblatt ***Mus*** Pino Donaggio ***Art*** John Lawless

Act Elliott Gould, Margaux Hemingway, Sid Caesar, Burt Young, Shelley Winters, Carol Kane (City)

Over the Brooklyn Bridge is producer-director Menahem Golan's love letter to New York City: a warm and pleasant romance similar to the type of films topliner Elliott Gould used to make in the early 1970s.

Screenplay by Arnold Somkin is short on laughs but very effective. Gould stars as Alby Sherman, owner of a Brooklyn eatery who dreams of buying a posh restaurant on the East Side in midtown Manhattan. His love affair with an aristocratic Catholic girl from Philadelphia (Margaux Hemingway) raises the ire of his Jewish family, particularly the patriarch Uncle Benjamin (Sid Caesar), a women's underwear manufacturer who would rather have Alby marry his fourth cousin Cheryl (Carol Kane).

Gould and Hemingway are solid in the central roles, with standout support from a large cast. Caesar is very funny as a man who tries to run everyone else's lives for them. Kane is delightfully droll as the virginal intellectual whose demure exterior hides a rather kinky fantasy-sex life.

•

OVER THE TOP

1987, 93 mins, US Ⓥ ⦿ ▭ col

Dir Menahem Golan ***Prod*** Menahem Golan, Yoram Globus ***Scr*** Stirling Silliphant, Sylvester Stallone ***Ph*** David Gurfinkel ***Ed*** Don Zimmerman, James Symons ***Mus*** Giorgio Moroder ***Art*** James Schoppe

Act Sylvester Stallone, Robert Loggia, Susan Blakely, Rick Zumwalt, David Mendenhall, Chris McCarty (Cannon)

Sylvester Stallone muscles his way to the top of the heap in a beefy world of armwrestling in *Over the Top*. Routinely made in every respect, melodrama [from a story by Gary Conway and David C. Engelbach] concerns itself as much with a man's effort to win the love of his son as it does with macho athletics.

Stallone, as a down-on-his-luck trucker named Lincoln Hawk, appears out of the blue to fetch his son when the latter graduates from military academy. Absent from both the kid's and mama Susan Blakely's lives for years, Stallone proposes a get-to-know-you truck ride back home to Los Angeles.

Little Michael (David Mendenhall) doesn't make things especially easy for his papa, his military rigidity and formality providing a formidable barrier. At truckstops along the way, Stallone introduces his son to the thrills of armwrestling, and Michael's transformation from spoiled intellectual snot to future regular guy is well underway.

Stallone is sincere and soulful as a "father who messed up pretty bad" and just wants his kid back, Mendenhall is a likable tyke, and justice is served in the end.

•

OWL AND THE PUSSYCAT, THE

1970, 98 mins, US Ⓥ ⦿ ▭ col

Dir Herbert Ross ***Prod*** Ray Stark ***Scr*** Buck Henry ***Ph*** Harry Stradling ***Ed*** Margaret Booth ***Mus*** Richard Halligan ***Art*** Robert Wightman

Act Barbra Streisand, George Segal, Robert Klein, Allen Garfield, Roz Kelly, Jacques Sandulescu (Columbia)

A zany, laugh-filled story of two modern NY kooks who find love at the end of trail of hilarious incidents.

Bill Manhoff's 1954 play, adapted here by Buck Henry, has been altered in that, as originally cast, one of the principals was white, the other black (on Broadway, Alan Alda and Diana Sands). Here it's two Bronx-Brooklyn Caucasian types, with Barbra Streisand giving it a Jewish Jean Arthur treatment and George Segal as an amiable, low-key foil.

The story is basically that of the out-of-work quasi-model and the struggling writer who cut up and down apartment corridors and in public to the astonishment of all others.

Streisand is a casual hooker, who first confronts Segal after he has finked on her activities to building superintendent Jacques Sandulescu. Their harangues then shift to apartment of buddy Robert Klein who decides it is better to leave with gal Evelyn Lang than lie awake listening.

One of her old scores turns out to be Jack Manning, Segal's intended father-in-law, but that plot turn blows up his affair and leads into the excellent climax we have been waiting for.

•

OX-BOW INCIDENT, THE

1943, 75 mins, US Ⓥ ⦿ b/w

Dir William A. Wellman ***Prod*** Lamar Trotti ***Scr*** Lamar Trotti ***Ph*** Arthur Miller ***Ed*** Allen McNeil ***Mus*** Cyril J. Mockridge

Act Henry Fonda, Dana Andrews, Mary Beth Hughes, Anthony Quinn, Jane Darwell, Harry Davenport (20th Century-Fox)

Screen version of the best-selling book [by Walter Van Tilburg Clark] depends too much on the hanging theme, developing this into a brutal closeup of a Nevada necktie party. Hardly a gruesome detail is omitted. Where the pleading by the three innocent victims doubtlessly was exciting on the printed page, it becomes too raw-blooded for the screen. Chief fault is that the picture overemphasizes the single hanging incident of the novel, and there's not enough other action.

Western opus follows the escapades of two cowboys, played by Henry Fonda and Henry Morgan, in town after a winter on the range. They are tossed into the turmoil of the usually quiet western community which is aroused by the report of a cattleman's slaying by rustlers. A buddy of the supposedly slain rancher stirs the pot-boiling, and a posse is formed to get the culprits and handle them "western style." Remainder of story concerns efforts of the few law-abiding gentry to halt the lynching.

Fonda measures up to star rating, as one of the few level-headed cowhands. His brief scene with Mary Beth Hughes, the flashy belle of the village, following her sudden marriage, is top-flight. He helps hold together the loose ends of the rather patent plot.

1943: NOMINATION: Best Picture

•

OXFORD BLUES

1984, 93 mins, UK/US Ⓥ ⦿ col

Dir Robert Boris ***Prod*** Cassian Elwes, Elliott Kastner ***Scr*** Robert Boris ***Ph*** John Stanier ***Ed*** Patrick Moore ***Mus*** John DuPrez ***Art*** Terry Pritchard

Act Rob Lowe, Ally Sheedy, Amanda Pays, Julian Sands, Julian Firth, Alan Howard (Winkast/M-G-M)

At heart, *Oxford Blues* is really *Rocky Goes to College*. Though source material is M-G-M's 1938 Robert Taylor starrer, *A Yank at Oxford*, treatment is decidedly modern. Director-writer Robert Boris fails to establish a consistent tone to make his fairytale story believable.

In the original film, Lionel Barrymore borrows the cash to send athlete son Taylor over to Oxford. In *Oxford Blues*, Lowe, a valet at the Dunes Hotel in Vegas, hustles the money at the crap table from a stake put up by an older woman (Gail Strickland) who picks him up. Nick's real reason for going to England is not to crew and certainly not for an education (students never seem to study in this film), but to chase his dreamgirl, aristocrat covergirl Lady Victoria (Amanda Pays). Climax proves the hero has the right stuff to get the girl. Only the girl turns out to be another American (Ally Sheedy). Must be a moral in there somewhere.

Lowe is suitably nasty as the streetwise Nick in a way that often passes for charm in films like this.

PACIFIC HEIGHTS
1990, 102 mins, US Ⓥ ⦿ col
Dir John Schlesinger ***Prod*** Scott Rudin, William Sackheim ***Scr*** Daniel Pyne ***Ph*** Dennis E. Jones ***Ed*** Mark Warner ***Mus*** Hans Zimmer ***Art*** Neil Spisak
Act Melanie Griffith, Matthew Modine, Michael Keaton, Mako, Nobu McCarthy, Laurie Metcalf (Morgan Creek)

The specter of a menace who invades one's home turf and can't be ousted is universally disturbing, and director John Schlesinger goes all out to make this creepy thriller-chiller as unsettling as it needs to be.

Story has babes-in-the-woods home buyers Patty (Melanie Griffith) and Drake (Matthew Modine) spending their every dime to restore an 1883 Victorian house in San Francisco, counting on the income from two downstairs apartments to meet the mortgage.

A nice Asian couple takes the one-bedroom, but the studio falls to reptilian Michael Keaton, who smooth talks Modine into handing over a key without money up front. After he "takes possession," it becomes clear they'll never see a dollar from this unnerving man. They encounter the shock of a legal system that's always on the renter's side.

First-time film scripter Daniel Pyne sets up a menacing cat-and-mouse game as sociopath Keaton plays the system to his advantage, finally provoking Modine into attacking him so he can go after his assets with a lawsuit. But pic loses its grip when it tips over into psycho-chiller territory.

Griffith lights up the screen as the kittenish but in-control Patty who lets her instincts be her guide when she takes off after Keaton on a one-woman crusade for justice.

•

PACIFIC PALISADES
1990, 94 mins, France col
Dir Bernard Schmitt ***Prod*** Bernard Verley, Lise Fayolle ***Scr*** Marion Vernoux, Bernard Schmitt ***Ph*** Martial Barrault ***Ed*** Gilbert Namiand ***Mus*** Jean-Jacques Goldman, Roland Romanetti
Act Sophie Marceau, Adam Coleman Howard, Anne Curry, Virginia Capers, Toni Basil (BVF/Sandor)

Pacific Palisades is a transatlantic romance bringing Sophie Marceau to America for a change of climate (physical and emotional). She's in for some surprises, but the audience isn't. First feature by prize-winning vidclip helmer Bernard Schmitt sinks into the tar pits of culture shock cliches.

Marceau is a dissatisfied Parisian waitress who heads for LA on a bum job offer and finds herself living alone in a large modern suburban house. She's quickly exasperated and bored. Then she gets involved with the Canadian boyfriend (Adam Coleman Howard) of a Yank actress she initially was to have flown in with.

Despite the platitudes and plot inconsistencies, film is charmingly acted by Marceau in her first (mostly) English-lingo role. Howard is okay as the romantic interest whose idea of a hot date is a group outing to a hockey game.

•

PACK, THE
1977, 99 mins, US Ⓥ col
Dir Robert Clouse ***Prod*** Fred Weintraub, Paul Heller ***Scr*** Robert Clouse ***Ph*** Ralph Woolsey ***Ed*** Peter E. Berger ***Mus*** Lee Holdridge
Act Joe Don Baker, Hope Alexander-Willis, Richard B. Shull, R. G. Armstrong, Ned Wertimer, Bibi Besch (Warner)

The Pack is a well-made and discreetly violent story of a pack of wild dogs menacing residents of a remote island.

The production, with Robert Clouse scripting Dave Fisher's novel and also directing, stars Joe Don Baker as a marine biologist who leads the humans' defense.

Strong story peg is habit of summer vacationers to abandon pets, but in this case, the stranded mutts band together in ferocious attack on people.

Clouse's attention to lighting and shadow adds an extra eerie feel to the proceedings. Fast cutaways from dog attacks create an unseen horror that makes for more fear than explicit footage otherwise might have achieved.

Given the simplistic script demands, Baker is very good. Hope Alexander-Willis, in film debut, comes across okay.

•

PACKAGE, THE
1989, 108 mins, US Ⓥ ⦿ col
Dir Andrew Davis ***Prod*** Beverly J. Camhe, Tobie Haggerty ***Scr*** John Bishop ***Ph*** Frank Tidy ***Ed*** Don Zimmerman, Billy Weber ***Mus*** James Newton Howard ***Art*** Michel Levesque
Act Gene Hackman, Joanna Cassidy, Tommy Lee Jones, John Heard, Dennis Franz, Pam Grier (Orion)

Smartly written, sharply played and directed at a cracking pace that never sacrifices clarity for speed, *The Package* is an enormously satisfying political thriller.

Poised and professional as ever, Gene Hackman is perfectly cast as a career army officer, escorting a troublesome soldier (Tommy Lee Jones) Stateside to stand trial. When this "package" (the military term for the person being delivered) takes a powder, Hackman visits the man's estranged wife—and soon realizes the package is posing as someone he's not.

When the woman turns up murdered—and Hackman's under house arrest for the killing—the action really heats up. He turns to his ex-wife (Joanna Cassidy), also an army officer. Soon she finds herself behind the eight ball along with her ex.

The film's grand finale—in which various forces are seen converging on a Chicago hotel to either kill or prevent a killing—is very effective. You know exactly where each character is in relation to the other in this very complex piece of staging.

In the brief but pivotal title role, Jones shows it's possible to play an out-of-control psychopath without turning into a gargoyle. Cassidy is as smooth as ever.

•

PACK UP YOUR TROUBLES
1932, 70 mins, US Ⓥ b/w
Dir George Marshall, Raymond McCarey ***Prod*** Hal Roach ***Scr*** H. M. Walker ***Ph*** Art Lloyd ***Ed*** Richard Currier
Act Stan Laurel, Oliver Hardy, Donald Dillaway, Jacquie Lyn, Mary Carr, James Finlayson (M-G-M)

Seventy minutes of slapstick is a tall order for Laurel & Hardy and they hardly fill it. It's one of those hokum war farces with the numbskull L&H jazzing up the army as hapless rookies.

There's also a wartime buddy's girl baby whom the well-meaning L&H endeavor to return to her grandparents, a Mr. and Mrs. Smith. Trying to identify the Smiths through the city directory constitutes a major portion of that sort of pseudo-comedy.

One wonders why it wasn't kept to the confines of the usual twin-reeler as in the past.

•

PAD (AND HOW TO USE IT), THE
1966, 86 mins, US col
Dir Brian G. Hutton ***Prod*** Ross Hunter ***Scr*** Thomas C. Ryan, Ben Starr ***Ph*** Ellsworth Fredericks ***Ed*** Milton Carruth ***Mus*** Russ Garcia ***Art*** Alexander Golitzen
Act Brian Bedford, Julie Sommars, James Farentino, Edy Williams, Nick Navarro, Pearl Shear (Universal)

The Private Ear, which made up one half of the Peter Shaffer play, *The Private Ear and the Public Eye*, was a short but observant look at loneliness and the aborted effort of one shy male to communciate with the opposite sex. Ross Hunter's screen adaptation, thanks almost entirely to Shaffer's original dialog and the recreation by Brian Bedford of the shy young man he played in the New York production, recaptures much of the humor, compassion and wisdom of the legit production.

While the setting has been switched from an English flat to a Los Angeles rooming house, there is, basically, little difference between the storyline of the play and the film. Necessary expansion shows scenes only referred to in the play and adds a few extraneous characters. There is first rate playing by Julie Sommars as the gauche girl he covets and James Farentino as the Lothario friend who wrecks the timid type's plans.

•

PADRE PADRONE
1977, 114 mins, Italy Ⓥ col
Dir Paolo Taviani, Vittorio Taviani ***Prod*** Giuliani De Negri ***Scr*** Paolo Taviani, Vittorio Taviani ***Ph*** Mario Masini ***Ed*** Roberto Perpignani ***Mus*** Egisto Macchi ***Art*** Giovanni Sbarra
Act Omero Antonutti, Saverio Marioni, Marcella Michelangeli, Fabrizio Forte (RAI/Cinema Srl)

Made almost entirely on location in the backwoods of Sardinia (except for a few scenes in Pisa), this little low-budget film for TV—wisely sponsored by RAI-2—is a probe of unusual dimension into the deformation of young Sardinians compelled by local economics and the mystics of genealogy to sacrifice childhood and adolescence as sheep herders in the high country. The film is based freely on the autobiographical expose by Gavino Ledda.

Around the initiation of a seven-year-old boy into the lonely life of sheep herder until his triumphant rift at the age of 20 with a remarkably overbearing father-patriarch (Omero Antonutti), the Taviani brothers have for the most part succeeded in adapting a miniature epic. When Saverio Marioni takes over from moppet Fabrizio Forte to bring the boy herder into focus as an adolescent and young man, the film blurs slightly without losing its dimension—highlighted by a first brush with strangers and an accordion, the revolt of the community's young people who emigrate in a body to Germany.

In a long final part, accenting the boy's iron will to learn right up to a high school diploma, the final showdown between patriarch and rebel son is perhaps a more consequent narrative.

•

PAGEMASTER, THE
1994, 75 mins, US Ⓥ ⦿ col
Dir Joe Johnston, Maurice Hunt ***Prod*** David Kirschner, Paul Gertz, Michael R. Joyce ***Scr*** David Casci, David Kirschner, Ernie Contreras ***Ph*** Alexandra Gruszynski ***Ed*** Roy Forge Smith ***Mus*** James Horner ***Art*** Gay Lawrence, Valeria Ventura
Act Macaulay Culkin, Christopher Lloyd, Ed Begley, Jr., Mel Harris (20th Century-Fox)

Built on a wispy premise better suited to the realm of TV, *The Pagemaster* plays like a slickly produced afternoon special. More than anything else, *Pagemaster* comes off as propaganda for the public library, with even its most hummable song providing a pro-social message about reading and using one's imagination.

The simplest of childhood fantasies, the story [by David Kirschner and David Casci] begins in the world of live action before our chronically frightened hero, Richard (Macaulay Culkin), with the help of a mysterious librarian (Christopher Lloyd), gets transported into an animated world where fictional characters come to life—led on his journey by book-sized companions Adventure (voiced by Patrick Stewart), Fantasy (Whoopi Goldberg) and Horror (Frank Welker).

Through the world of books, Richard encounters an array of famous fictional characters and perils while trying to make it to the "Exit" sign, which will provide his means of escape.

The problem is that after introducing these characters—Captain Ahab, Long John Silver, Dr. Jekyll/Mr. Hyde, etc.—the filmmakers don't have anything to do with them, other than the sort of madcap chase with Mr. Hyde that feels plucked from an old Bugs Bunny cartoon.

Technically, the animation, overseen by one-time Disney animator Maurice Hunt (*The Black Cauldron*), is fluid if perhaps a bit too dark and brooding, though it does offer some impressive flourishes to go with James Horner's typically rousing score.

•

PAGE MISS GLORY
1935, 92 mins, US b/w
Dir Mervyn LeRoy ***Prod*** Robert Lord ***Scr*** Delmer Daves, Robert Lord ***Ph*** George Folsey ***Ed*** William Clemens ***Mus*** Leo F. Forbstein (dir.) ***Art*** Robert Haas
Act Marion Davies, Pat O'Brien, Dick Powell, Mary Astor, Frank McHugh, Patsy Kelly (Cosmopolitan/Warner)

Same deficiency as in the play [by Joseph Schrank and Philip Dunning] occurs—the obvious. The farcical situations telegraph each ensuing denouement yards ahead. But the same fast and furious tempo, as in the play, does much to offset this fault. It's really a comedy Cinderella theme.

Marion Davies is the hotel chambermaid who is catapulted into being "Down Glory," the mythical non-existent, composite beauty who cops a contest. Pat O'Brien and Frank McHugh are the broken-down promoters (slang for chiselers, although harmless guys in the main) who engineer the photographic compo girl into a $2,500 cash prize and a flock of offers.

When besieged by commercial sponsors for endorsements and newspapermen for interviews, Davies unconsciously walks from the metamorphosis from the femme de chambre into the No. 1 U.S. beaut. The farcical complications pile on with O'Brien (Chick Wiley) extricating himself ingeniously with each turn.

Davies does well by her generous comedy opportunities. Dick Powell, as a goofy stunt flyer, is well nigh wasted, virtually dragged in for his "Page Miss Glory" title song [by Harry Warren and Al Dubin] duet with the star.

•

PAINTED VEIL, THE
1934, 83 mins, US Ⓥ b/w
Dir Richard Boleslawski ***Prod*** Hunt Stromberg ***Scr*** John Meehan, Salka Viertel, Edith Fitzgerald ***Ph*** William Daniels ***Ed*** Hugh Wynn ***Mus*** Herbert Stothart ***Art*** Cedric Gibbons, Alexander Toluboff, Edwin B. Willis
Act Greta Garbo, Herbert Marshall, George Brent, Warner Oland, Jean Hersholt, Beulah Bondi (M-G-M)

From almost any standpoint, *The Painted Veil* is a bad picture. It's clumsy, dull and long-winded. It's mostly the fault of the scripters. Yarn is so confused in the telling as to be almost hopeless. It deviates considerably from the original W. Somerset Maugham tale; that wouldn't be so bad if well done, but it emerges as neither film nor novel. Yarn has Greta Garbo as the daughter of a Viennese professor (Jean Hersholt). A doctor in China (Herbert Marshall) comes a-visiting, asks her to marry him and she does, largely, it's indicated, because she wants to see China. Once they get to China she sits down to a constant and dangerous routine of wearing cockeyed hats that are an absolute menace.

She meets George Brent, who doesn't seem to mind the hats. He flatters her for a while, then manages to get in a kiss. Hubby Marshall finds out, so he goes into the interior of China to clear up a bad cholera plague and drags her along, the idea seemingly being that maybe both of them will catch the disease and die.

Garbo is but fair, although she doesn't get much chance to emote. Acting honors really go to Marshall.

•

PAINT YOUR WAGON
1969, 166 mins, US Ⓥ ⦿ ▭ col
Dir Joshua Logan ***Prod*** Alan Jay Lerner ***Scr*** Alan Jay Lerner, Paddy Chayefsky ***Ph*** William A. Fraker ***Ed*** Robert C. Jones ***Mus*** Nelson Riddle (arr.) ***Art*** John Truscott
Act Lee Marvin, Clint Eastwood, Jean Seberg, Ray Walston, Harve Presnell, Tom Ligon (Paramount)

Paint Your Wagon is the tale of a gold mining town in California in the 1840s—before it became a state and before there were many "good" women in the territory.

Main story centers around a menage a trois. Lee Marvin, his pardner Clint Eastwood, and Marvin's wife (Jean Seberg) are the trio.

Director Joshua Logan has captured best the vastness and beauty of the country; the loneliness of men in womenless societies.

What the $17 million-plus film (from the 1951 Lerner-Loewe Broadway musical) lacks in a skimpy story line it makes up in the music and expert choreography. There are no obvious "musical numbers." All the songs, save one or two, work neatly, quietly and well into the script. The actors used their own voices, which are pleasant enough and add to the note of authenticity.

1969: NOMINATION: Best Adapted Music Score

•

PAISA
(PAISAN)
1946, 124 mins, Italy Ⓥ b/w
Dir Roberto Rossellini ***Prod*** Roberto Rossellini, Rod Geiger ***Scr*** Sergio Amidei, Federico Fellini, Roberto Rossellini ***Ph*** Otello Martelli ***Ed*** Eraldo Da Roma ***Mus*** Renzo Rossellini ***Art*** [uncredited]
Act Carmela Sazio, Dots Johnson, Maria Michi, Harriet White, Bill Tubbs, Dale Edmonds (OFI/FFP/Capitani)

Paisan (meaning "fellow-countryman") comprises six episodes as Yank and British troops battle their way northward to push the Nazis out of Sicily and Italy. They are tied together in semi-documentary fashion by an off-screen narrator pointing out on an onscreen map the successive waves that took the Allies from Sicily to the valley of the Po. Sequences are otherwise unconnected.

Most of the film's quality must be credited to young Italian writer-director-producer Roberto Rossellini's feeling for people and his ability to put them in an atmosphere of reality. Aside from a director's sensitivity to his characters, Rossellini knows the technical tricks of getting desired effects with the camera, lighting, mood and location. Rossellini achieves part of his effect by the mingling of professional and non-professional actors in his cast in such a way that it's often impossible to tell which is which.

Initial episode, in Sicily, is the night of the landing there, with an American—Joe from Jersey (Robert Von Loon)—left by his squad leader to guard an Italian girl in a deserted castle. In Naples, a Negro MP (Dots Johnson) has his shoes stolen by an Italian urchin while he sleeps. Rome sequence is the best of the lot. A prostitute (Maria Michi) picks up a GI (Gar Moore) and takes him to her room. He lies on her bed too drunk to do anything but babble of the fresh, sweet girl who befriended him with a drink of water when his tank burst into the city six months earlier.

In Florence, there's a chase by an American nurse and a partisan through German lines. It's more tense and breathtaking than any staged by maestro Alfred Hitchcock himself. At the Gothic line, three chaplains—a Catholic, Protestant and Jew—are overnight guests in a Franciscan monastery. Final sequence, in the Po Valley, has a group of O.S.S. and British Intelligence men working with partisans behind German lines.

•

PAISAN
SEE: PAISA

•

PAJAMA GAME, THE
1957, 101 mins, US Ⓥ ⦿ ▭ col
Dir George Abbott, Stanley Donen ***Prod*** George Abbott, Stanley Donen ***Scr*** George Abbott, Richard Bissell ***Ph*** Harry Stradling ***Ed*** William Ziegler ***Mus*** Nelson Riddle, Buddy Bregman (arr.) ***Art*** Malcolm Bert
Act Doris Day, John Raitt, Carol Haney, Eddie Foy, Jr., Reta Shaw, Barbara Nichols (Warner)

The inherent mobility and fluidity of *Pajama Game* as a stage property was such that this almost faithful transmutation into celluloid required little physical enhancement [of the Richard Adler-Jerry Ross 1954 musical]. But the filmmakers have not slighted the opportunities for size and scope when occasion warranted.

If the film version contains a shade more of social significance in the labor-engagement hassle, which was the springboard of the original Richard Bissell novel, *7-1/2 Cents*, from which stems the romantic conflict between pajama factory superintendent John Raitt (who created the original stage role) and "grievance committee chairman" Doris Day, it is a plus value because of the sturdy book.

Raitt is properly serious as the earnest factory executive and earnestly smitten with the blonde and beauteous Day. Day, always authoritative with a song, makes her chore even a shade more believable than Raitt. Carol Haney, recreating her soubret role opposite Eddie Foy, Jr. (also of the original stage cast), whams with "Steam Heat," aided by Buzz Miller (stage original) and Kenneth LeRoy (substituting for Peter Gennaro of the Broadway cast).

•

PAJAMA PARTY
1964, 82 mins, US Ⓥ ▭ col
Dir Don Weis ***Prod*** James H. Nicholson, Samuel Z. Arkoff, Anthony Carras ***Scr*** Louis M. Heyward ***Ph*** Floyd Crosby ***Ed*** Fred Feitshans, Eve Newman ***Mus*** Les Baxter ***Art*** Daniel Haller
Act Tommy Kirk, Annette Funicello, Elsa Lanchester, Jody McCrea, Buster Keaton, Dorothy Lamour (American International)

Exuberance of youth guns the action which twirls around a personable young Martian—Tommy Kirk—arriving on Earth to pave the way for an invasion. He lands during a swimming party tossed by an eccentric wealthy widow (Elsa Lanchester), and immediately falls for Annette Funicello, girlfriend of widow's lug nephew (Jody McCrea).

Funicello displays an engaging presence and registers solidly. Kirk likewise shows class and Lanchester projects a rather zany character nicely, McCrea hams it up the way he should for such a part. Buster Keaton, playing an Indian, and Dorothy Lamour, dress store manager, sock over their roles.

•

PALEFACE, THE
1948, 91 mins, US Ⓥ ⦿ col
Dir Norman Z. McLeod ***Prod*** Robert L. Welch ***Scr*** Edmund Hartmann, Frank Tashlin, Jack Rose ***Ph*** Ray Rennahan ***Ed*** Ellsworth Hoagland ***Mus*** Victor Young ***Art*** Hans Dreier, Earl Hedrick
Act Bob Hope, Jane Russell, Robert Armstrong, Iris Adrian, Robert Watson (Paramount)

The Paleface is a smart-aleck travesty on the west, told with considerable humor and bright gags. Bob Hope has been turned loose on a good script.

Hope isn't all the film has to sell. There's Jane Russell as Calamity Jane, that rough, tough gal of the open west whose work as a government agent causes Hope's troubles, but whose guns save him from harm and give him his hero reputation. She makes an able sparring partner for the Hope antics, and is a sharp eyeful in Technicolor.

"Buttons and Bows" is top tune of the score's three pop numbers. Jay Livingston and Ray Evans cleffed and Hope renders as a plaintive love chant to Russell.

Script poses an amusing story idea—Hope as a correspondence school dentist touring the west in a covered wagon. He's having his troubles, but they're nothing compared to the grief that catches up with him when Calamity Jane seduces him into marriage so she can break up a gang smuggling rifles to the Indians.

1948: Best Song ("Buttons and Bows")

•

PALE RIDER
1985, 115 mins, US Ⓥ ⦿ ▭ col
Dir Clint Eastwood ***Prod*** Clint Eastwood ***Scr*** Michael Butler, Dennis Shryack ***Ph*** Bruce Surtees ***Ed*** Joel Cox ***Mus*** Lennie Niehaus ***Art*** Edward Carfagno
Act Clint Eastwood, Michael Moriarty, Carrie Snodgress, Christopher Penn, Richard Dysart, Richard Kiel (Malpaso/Warner)

As he did in his Sergio Leone trilogy, Clint Eastwood portrays a nameless drifter, here called "Preacher," who descends into the middle of a struggle between some poor, independent gold prospectors and a big company intent upon raping the beautiful land for all it's worth.

Borrowing from *Shane*, "Preacher," so dubbed because he initially appears wearing a clerical collar, moves in with a group consisting of earnest Michael Moriarty, his somewhat reluctant lady friend Carrie Snodgress and her pubescent daughter Sydney Penny.

Preach pulls the threatened community together and inspires them to fight for their rights to the land rather than give up.

It's all been seen before, but Eastwood serves it up with authority, fine craftsmanship and a frequent sense of fun. This film is graced not only by an excellent visual look and confident storytelling, but by a few fine performances, led by Eastwood's own.

•

PAL JOEY
1957, 112 mins, US Ⓥ ⦿ col
Dir George Sidney ***Prod*** Fred Kohlmar ***Scr*** Dorothy Kingsley ***Ph*** Harold Lipstein ***Ed*** Viola Lawrence, Jerome Thoms ***Mus*** Morris Stoloff (sup.), Nelson Riddle, George Duning (arr.) ***Art*** Walter Holscher
Act Rita Hayworth, Frank Sinatra, Kim Novak, Barbara Nichols, Bobby Sherwood, Hank Henry (Columbia/Essex-Sidney)

Pal Joey is a strong, funny entertainment. Dorothy Kingsley's screenplay, from John O'Hara's book, is skillful rewriting, with colorful characters and solid story built around the Richard Rodgers and Lorenz Hart songs. Total of 14 tunes are intertwined with the plot, 10 of them being reprised from the original. Others by the same team of cleffers are "I Didn't Know What Time It Was," "The Lady Is a Tramp," "There's a Small Hotel" and "Funny Valentine."

Kingsley pulled some switches in shaping the [1940] legiter for the screen. Given a buildup to star status is the chorine from Albuquerque who becomes Joey's prey; Rita Hayworth (in the Vivienne Segal role) does the "Zip" number that had been done by the herein-eliminated newspaper gal. There's not much terping, and the finale is happy ending stuff. Frank Sinatra is potent. He's almost ideal as the irreverent, free-wheeling, glib Joey, delivering the rapid-fire cracks in a fashion that wrings out the full deeper-than-pale blue comedy potentials. Point might be made, though, that it's hard to figure why all the mice fall for this rat. Kim Novak is one of the mice (term refers to the nitery gals) and rates high as ever in the looks department but her turn is pallid in contrast with the forceful job done by Sinatra.

Hayworth, no longer the ingenue, moves with authority as Joey's sponsor and does the "Zip" song visuals in such fiery, amusing style as to rate an encore. Standout of the score is "Lady Is a Tramp." It's a wham arrangement and Sinatra gives it powerhouse delivery.

1957: NOMINATIONS: Best Costume Design, Art Direction, Editing, Sound Recording

•

PALLBEARER, THE
1996, 97 mins, US Ⓥ ⦿ col
Dir Matt Reeves ***Prod*** Jeffrey Abrams, Paul Webster ***Scr*** Jason Katims, Matt Reeves ***Ph*** Robert Elswit ***Ed*** Stan Salfas ***Mus*** Stewart Copeland ***Art*** Robin Standefer
Act David Schwimmer, Gwyneth Paltrow, Michael Rapaport, Toni Collette, Carol Kane, Michael Vartan (Miramax)

Aside from its blatant appropriation of themes, situations and even shots from *The Graduate*, *The Pallbearer* is a passably entertaining seriocomedy about the dawning of adulthood for some, uh, graduates who don't quite know what to do with their lives. Appealing performances by David Schwimmer and Gwyneth Paltrow go a long way toward putting over this very slightly offbeat tale of twentysomethings trying to find their way.

Without a job a year out of college and still living with mom in Brooklyn, affable oaf Tom Thompson (Schwimmer) gets a call out of the blue from a Ruth Abernathy (Barbara Hershey), asking him to serve as a pallbearer at the funeral of her son, with whom Tom supposedly went to high school. He doesn't even remember her boy, but obliges.

His circle of friends is limited to his old high school pals Scott (Michael Vartan) and Brad (Michael Rapaport) and their respective girlfriends Cynthia (Toni Collette) and Lauren (Bitty Schram), so he is caught off guard by the reappearance of the lovely Julie DeMarco (Gwyneth Paltrow). Once he sees her, he's a goner all over again. But before Tom can get anywhere with Julie, the grieving Mrs. Abernathy seduces the young man. *The Pallbearer* is nowhere near as barbed or witty as the earlier pic, and it doesn't convey anything particular about the Zeitgeist of its period, a crucial factor in the huge success of *The Graduate*. Reeves's film speaks for the large number of people in their 20s who still live with their parents, but otherwise could have taken place just about anytime and anyplace.

●

PALM BEACH STORY, THE

1942, 96 mins, US Ⓥ ⦿ b/w

Dir Preston Sturges ***Prod*** Paul Jones ***Scr*** Preston Sturges ***Ph*** Victor Milner ***Ed*** Stuart Gilmore ***Mus*** Victor Young ***Art*** Hans Dreier, Ernst Fegte

Act Claudette Colbert, Joel McCrea, Mary Astor, Rudy Vallee, William Demarest, Sig Arno (Paramount)

This Preston Sturges production is packed with delightful absurdities. Claudette Colbert comes through with one of her best light comedy interpretations. She's strikingly youthful and alluring as the slightly screwball wife of five years standing, who, after seeing husband Joel McCrea out of debt, suddenly decides to seek a divorce, adventure and a bankroll for the husband she leaves behind.

Tongue-in-cheek spoofing of the idle rich attains hilarious proportions in scenes where Rudy Vallee, as John D. Hackensacker the Third, proposes to the errant wife and later woos her by singing to her to the accompaniment of a privately hired symphony orch big enough to fill the Radio City Music Hall pit.

McCrea plays it straight, for the most part, as the husband intent on winning his wife back.

●

PANDORA AND THE FLYING DUTCHMAN

1951, 122 mins, UK col

Dir Albert Lewin ***Prod*** Albert Lewin ***Scr*** Albert Lewin ***Ph*** Jack Cardiff ***Ed*** Ralph Kemplen ***Mus*** Alan Rawsthorne ***Art*** John Bryan

Act James Mason, Ava Gardner, Nigel Patrick, Sheila Sim, Marius Goring, Mario Cabre (Kaufman/Lewin)

Albert Lewin produced, directed and did the story and script, keeping this film on an almost unrelieved level of somber depression.

Lewin set his story in 1930 and filmed it on the coast of Spain. He gets into it with a flashback to explain the bodies of a man and woman found by fishermen off the coast.

Thanks to the pesence of James Mason, the film has at least one distinctive histrionic touch. He plays the Dutchman of the title, a sea captain who, back in the 17th century, had been condemned to sail the oceans of the world until he found a woman willing to die for love. When this miracle occurs, his soul can find salvation.

Ava Gardner fares less distinctively as the girl who falls in love with this restless shade during one of the occasional brief periods allotted him to take on human form. Standout quality of the production is Jack Cardiff's color photography.

●

PANDORA'S BOX

SEE: DIE BUECHSE DER PANDORA

●

PANIC IN NEEDLE PARK, THE

1971, 110 mins, US Ⓥ col

Dir Jerry Schatzberg ***Prod*** Dominick Dunne ***Scr*** Joan Didion, John Gregory Dunne ***Ph*** Adam Holender ***Ed*** Evan Lottman ***Art*** Murray P. Stern

Act Al Pacino, Kitty Winn, Alan Vint, Richard Bright, Kiel Martin, Michael McClanathan (20th Century-Fox)

The Panic in Needle Park is a total triumph. Gritty, gutsy, compelling, and vivid to the point of revulsion, it is an overpowering tragedy about urban drug addiction. Director Jerry Schatzberg in only his second film becomes a major talent, while Al Pacino and Kitty Winn are terrific as a heroin-doomed couple.

Dominick Dunne produced on the streets of N.Y. a drama so real that the persons and situations seem to have been caught in a documentary. James Mills's novel has been superbly adapted. The dialog is raw and uncompromising, yet artistic in its tragic-sardonic-ironic context.

Winn, introduced as a post-abortion discard of artist Raul Julia, takes up with Pacino, a drug pusher whose pretense of non-addiction soon fades away. She learns, and fast, the ropes of a strung-out world filled with young derelicts who steal, love, cheat, befriend and betray. This world is a jungle, ruled by instinctive addiction and passion, and it's just around everyone's corner now.

Pacino, after a brief mannered introduction, settles into his key role with terribly effective results. Winn is smash.

●

PANIC IN THE CITY

1968, 96 mins, US col

Dir Eddie Davis ***Prod*** Earle Lyon ***Scr*** Eddie Davis, Charles E. Savage ***Ph*** Alan Stensvold ***Ed*** Terrell O. Morse ***Mus*** Paul Dunlap ***Art*** Paul Sylos, Jr.

Act Howard Duff, Linda Cristal, Stephen McNally, Nehemiah Persoff, Anne Jeffreys, Oscar Beregi (United)

Panic in the City posits that a Communist operative in the U.S., acting independently of his Russian superiors, should be able to collect the material to construct an atomic bomb in Los Angeles. The panic of the title—there is talk of evacuating the city—never really happens thanks to the ingenious efforts of Howard Duff, an agent of the "National" Bureau of Investigation.

It's all done perfunctorily and without any real distinction, but the low budget, necessitating real locations, makes possible the use of a great deal of L.A.

Nehemiah Persoff rather hysterically portrays the Commie fanatic, while Anne Jeffreys is his accomplice.

There are some sparks from Oscar Beregi's Czech scientist who assembles the bomb. Motorcycle vet Dennis Hopper has brief role of a murderer. Development of the story is workmanlike enough, but disbelief sets in after Persoff goes batty by disobeying his superiors and deciding to explode the bomb.

●

PANIC IN THE STREETS

1950, 92 mins, US Ⓥ b/w

Dir Elia Kazan ***Prod*** Sol C. Siegel ***Scr*** Richard Murphy ***Ph*** Joe MacDonald ***Ed*** Harmon Jones ***Mus*** Alfred Newman ***Art*** Lyle Wheeler, Maurice Ransford

Act Richard Widmark, Paul Douglas, Barbara Bel Geddes, Jack Palance, Zero Mostel (20th Century-Fox)

This is an above-average chase meller. Tightly scripted and directed, it concerns the successful attempts to capture a couple of criminals, who are germ carriers, in order to prevent a plague and panic in a large city. The plague angle is somewhat incidental to the cops-and-bandits theme.

Story [by Edna and Edward Anhalt, adapted by Daniel Fuchs] opens harshly with three thieves stalking a man for his money and killing him to obtain it. The man has just arrived in New Orleans illegally and is suffering from bubonic plague. His murderers, unknown to themselves, pick it up from him. The plot then concerns the efforts of the police, prodded by an alert Health Service officer, to locate and capture the slayers.

There is vivid action, nice human touches and some bizarre moments. Jack Palance gives a sharp performance.

1950: Best Motion Picture Story

●

PANIC IN YEAR ZERO

1962, 92 mins, US ▭ b/w

Dir Ray Milland ***Prod*** Lou Rusoff, Arnold Houghland ***Scr*** Jay Simms, John Morton ***Ph*** Gil Warrenton ***Ed*** William Austin ***Mus*** Les Baxter ***Art*** Daniel Haller

Act Ray Milland, Jean Hagen, Frankie Avalon, Mary Mitchel, Joan Freeman (American-International)

The aftermath of a nuclear attack is the subject pursued by this serious, sobering and engrossing film. The screenplay advances the theory that, in the event of a sudden wholesale outbreak of nuclear warfare, civilization will swiftly deteriorate into a decentralized society of individual units, each necessarily hostile in relations with all others as part of a desperate struggle for self-preservation.

A family unit of four—father, mother and two teenaged children—is followed here in the wake of a series of initial nuclear blasts destroying Los Angeles and four other major U.S. cities (excluding Washington—a rather astonishing oversight on the part of the unspecified enemy). The family is followed to an isolated cave in the hills where, thanks to the father's negative ingenuity, it remains until it is safe to come out.

Ray Milland manages capably in the dual task of director and star (he's the resourceful father), but it's safe to observe that he'd probably have done twice as well by halving his assignment, one way or the other.

●

PANTHER

1995, 124 mins, US Ⓥ col

Dir Mario Van Peebles ***Prod*** Preston Holmes, Mario Van Peebles, Melvin Van Peebles ***Scr*** Melvin Van Peebles ***Ph*** Eddie Pei ***Ed*** Earl Watson ***Mus*** Stanley Clark ***Art*** Richard Hoover

Act Kadeem Hardison, Bokeem Woodbine, Joe Don Baker, Courtney B. Vance, Tyrin Turner, Marcus Chong (PolyGram/Working Title)

Panther, a fictionalized telling of some incidents in the life of the Black Panthers, represents a gloss on history for the ennobling benefit of its protagonists. Simplified when it should be complex, and sanitized when moral ambiguity doesn't suit its ideological agenda, this Van Peebles father-and-son collaboration seems tailored to glorify the positive aspirations of the late-'60s black power movement to an audience that wasn't even born then.

Film is motivated by a desire to nail the FBI for its relentless efforts to destabilize and destroy the Panthers, a campaign driven by J. Edgar Hoover's obsession with them and his labeling of the group as Public Enemy No. 1. To this end, the tale's central character is the fictional one of Judge (Kadeem Hardison), a young man in his early 20s who witnesses the police oppression of blacks on the streets of Oakland and begins siding with firebrands such as his friend Tyrone (Bokeem Woodbine), Huey Newton (Marcus Chong) and Bobby Seale (Courtney B. Vance).

But Judge, a reasonable fellow, is tagged early on by local authorities as a potential spy, someone they can squeeze for help in their attempt to infiltrate the group. Judge ends up as the classic man in the middle.

Screenwriter Melvin Van Peebles, whose incendiary 1971 feature *Sweet Sweetback's Song* established him as the godfather of black American cinema, has his hands full cramming all the necessary historical incidents into the two-hour drama. But the case against the FBI comes off as very strong indeed.

While the filmmakers go after the authorities with claws bared, they pull them in all the way where the Panthers are concerned. The approach amounts to a whitewash.

Pic is peppered with brief cameos, including one by Melvin Van Peebles as a jail inmate. Physically, at least, Mario Van Peebles is less than ideally cast as Stokely Carmichael. Frequent shifting between color and black-and-white feels arbitrary.

●

PAPER, THE

1994, 110 mins, US Ⓥ ⦿ col

Dir Ron Howard ***Prod*** Brian Grazer, Frederick Zollo ***Scr*** David Koepp, Stephen Koepp ***Ph*** John Seale ***Ed*** Daniel Hanley, Michael Hill ***Mus*** Randy Newman ***Art*** Todd Hallowell

Act Michael Keaton, Robert Duvall, Glenn Close, Marisa Tomei, Randy Quaid, Jason Robards (Imagine/Universal)

A rambunctious look at a day in the life of a struggling New York tabloid, *The Paper* is Paddy Chayefsky lite. With every member of the all-star staff battling personal life crises as they race to put the next edition to bed, Ron Howard's pacy meller can't help but generate a fair share of humor, excitement and involvement, even if it veers off the tracks in the final reels with some contrived, over-the-top theatrics.

The *New York Sun* is established as a financially precarious sheet (in the mold of the real-life *Post* and *Daily News*) desperately trying to hold head above water in tough economic times, even if it remains the sixth-largest daily in the nation. Setting the wheels and presses in motion this hot summer day is the brutal murder of a pair of white men in a parked car. The paper's forces mobilize to fan the city's racial tensions.

But, as they used to say, there are 8 million stories in the naked city, and this movie's got a few of them. Under pressure from his mucho pregnant wife, Martha (Marisa Tomei), to get a better-paying job, Metro editor Henry Hackett (Michael Keaton) halfheartedly interviews at the snooty *NY Sentinel* (read *Times*), where he sneaks a look at the note pad of his would-be boss (Spalding Gray) and steals some key info for the *Sun*.

Crusty old-school editor Bernie White (Robert Duvall) gets the bad news about his prostate cancer and, after trying to reconcile with his resentful daughter (Jill Hennessy), leaves the paper in the hands of managing editor Alicia Clark (Glenn Close), who finds the time for a hotel quickie with her lover and prepares for a showdown over her contract with her publisher (Jason Robards).

Howard is handsomely helped by his uniformly talented actors, all of whom snap out the lines, good and bad, like the crafty pros they are, even if they aren't hitting any unfamiliar notes.

1994: NOMINATION: Best Original Song ("Make Up Your Mind")

•

PAPER CHASE, THE

1973, 111 mins, US Ⓥ ⊙ col

Dir James Bridges ***Prod*** Robert C. Thompson, Rodrick Paul ***Scr*** James Bridges ***Ph*** Gordon Willis ***Ed*** Walter Thompson ***Mus*** John Williams ***Art*** George Jenkins

Act Timothy Bottoms, Lindsay Wagner, John Houseman, Graham Beckel, Edward Herrmann (20th Century-Fox)

The Paper Chase has some great performances, literate screenwriting, sensitive direction and handsome production.

The tale of a young law school student, confused by his professional calling vs. his inner evolution as a human being, seems timeless yet dated, too narrowly defined for broad audience empathy, and too often a series of sideways-moving (though entertaining) thespian declamations.

James Bridges directs his own adaptation of the novel by John Jay Osborn, Jr. Timothy Bottoms is excellent as the puzzled law student, Lindsay Wagner is very good as his girl, and John Houseman, the veteran legit and film producer-director-writer, is outstanding as a hard-nosed but urbane law professor.

The three players constitute the pervading plot triangle—Houseman the classroom dictator, Bottoms the uncertain supplicant, and Wagner, who plays Houseman's daughter.

1973: Best Supp. Actor (John Houseman)

NOMINATIONS: Best Adapted Screenplay, Sound

PAPER HEARTS

1993, 90 mins, US Ⓥ ⊙ col

Dir Rod McCall ***Prod*** Rod McCall, Catherine Wanek ***Scr*** Rod McCall ***Ph*** Barry Markowitz ***Ed*** Curtis Edge ***Mus*** George S. Clinton ***Art*** Susan Brand

Act Sally Kirkland, James Brolin, Pamela Gidley, Kris Kristofferson, Laura Johnson, Michael Moore (King-Moonstone)

A feminist streak informs Rod McCall's directorial feature debut *Paper Hearts*, a modest, sensitive and often touching family drama that poignantly dissects the effects of a dissolving marriage.

Sally Kirkland stars as Jenny Stevenson, an attractive, middle-aged woman separated from her scoundrel womanizer of a husband, Henry (James Brolin), who left her a mountain of debts. Jenny tries to hold onto the house she inherited, now on the verge of foreclosure.

The family's disparate members reunite for one stormy and fateful weekend, during which Kirkland's youngest daughter (Renee Estevez) gets married. Brolin is actually scheming to get the house. The oldest daughter (Pamela Gidley), a music student in New York, also shows up. McCall acquits himself better as writer than as director, endowing his story with a coherent female point of view. The moody, often somber film consists of brief scenes, usually confrontations between two characters. Regrettably, the big climactic scene is overly melodramatic.

•

PAPERHOUSE

1989, 92 mins, UK Ⓥ ⊙ col

Dir Bernard Rose ***Prod*** Sarah Radclyffe, Tim Bevan ***Scr*** Matthew Jacobs ***Ph*** Mike Southon ***Ed*** Dan Rae ***Mus*** Hans Zimmer, Stanley Myers ***Art*** Frank Walsh, Ann Tilby

Act Charlotte Burke, Ben Cross, Glenne Headly, Elliott Spears, Gemma Jones, Sarah Newbold (Working Title)

Paperhouse is the thinking person's *A Nightmare on Elm Street*. A riveting fantasy film, centering on the vivid dreams and nightmares of an 11-year-old girl [from Catherine Starr's novel], it heralds a new director of talent in Bernard Rose.

Anna (Charlotte Burke), psychologically disturbed, perhaps because of the frequent long absences from home of her beloved father (Ben Cross), has become a discipline problem at school via her bossy, unappealing ways. While undergoing minor punishment, she faints and finds herself by a strange house on a cliff-top, a house similar to one she'd earlier drawn on paper.

Gradually, she discovers that as she embellishes the drawing, she can enter the house in her dreams. Between her dreams, Anna discovers her kindly doctor (Gemma Jones) is treating a dying boy who seems to be identical to a boy in the house.

There's no violence in this film, but there's considerable suspense and tension. Crucial to the film's success is a superb soundtrack, with a strong music score, but also heightened sound effects of great impact.

•

PAPER MASK

1990, 118 mins, UK Ⓥ ⊙ col

Dir Christopher Morahan ***Prod*** Christopher Morahan ***Scr*** John Collee ***Ph*** Nat Crosby ***Ed*** Peter Coulson ***Mus*** Richard Harvey ***Art*** Caroline Hanania

Act Paul McGann, Amanda Donohoe, Frederick Treves, Tom Wilkinson, Barbara Leigh-Hunt, Jimmy Yuill (Film Four/Granada/British Screen)

Christopher Morahan's taut suspense thriller, from John Collee's novel about a young man who gets away with posing as an emergency room doctor in a British hospital, raises provocative questions about human pretense and the ruses of professional survival.

Pic focuses on a dissatisfied hospital worker, Matthew (Paul McGann), who seizes the chance to assume the identity of a promising young doctor after the other man dies in a car crash and his papers fall into Matthew's hands. Befriended by a competent and sympathetic nurse (Amanda Donohoe), he survives day by day. But the stakes are dramatically raised when he accidentally kills a doctor's wife with an overdose of anesthesia. To his astonishment, the hospital protects him, and in turn, itself.

Highly entertaining as a thriller-chiller, film is equally engrossing on a psychological level as it is always some aspect of the typically self-absorbed beings surrounding him that allows Matthew to pull off his deception.

•

PAPER MOON

1973, 101 mins, US Ⓥ ⊙ b/w

Dir Peter Bogdanovich ***Prod*** Peter Bogdanovich ***Scr*** Alvin Sargent ***Ph*** Laszlo Kovacs ***Ed*** Verna Fields ***Art*** Polly Platt

Act Ryan O'Neal, Tatum O'Neal, Madeline Kahn, John Hillerman, P. J. Johnson, Randy Quaid (Directors/Paramount/Saticoy)

Ryan O'Neal stars as a likeable con artist in the Depression midwest, and his real-life daughter, Tatum O'Neal, is outstanding as his nine-year-old partner in flim-flam. Joe David Brown's novel, *Addie Pray*, was the basis for Alvin Sargent's adaptation.

O'Neal arrives late at the funeral of a woman who was, or wasn't (as he claims), his wife, who has left a child of undetermined parentage but most determined character. Figuring to promote some fast money from locals for the kid, O'Neal finds the child more than adept in the shifty arts of selling Bibles to widows. Locked in uneasy but increasingly affectionate partnership, the O'Neals wend their way through the Kansas-Missouri farmlands.

Prominent among the large cast is Madeline Kahn, excellent as a carny stripper who captivates Ryan O'Neal. Tatum O'Neal makes a sensational screen debut.

1973: Best Supp. Actress (Tatum O'Neal)

NOMINATIONS: Best Supp. Actress (Madeline Kahn), Adapted Screenplay, Sound

•

PAPER TIGER

1975, 101 mins, UK Ⓥ ▭ col

Dir Ken Annakin ***Prod*** Euan Lloyd ***Scr*** Jack Davies ***Ph*** John Cabrera ***Ed*** Alan Pattillo ***Mus*** Roy Budd ***Art*** Herbert Smith

Act David Niven, Toshiro Mifune, Hardy Kruger, Ando, Jeff Corey, Irene Tsu (Shalako/Maclean)

Paper Tiger recalls the plots of vintage Shirley Temple vehicles in its cutesy relationship between English tutor David Niven and an 11-year-old Japanese moppet (Ando), kidnapped together during turmoil in [Kulagong, a fictitious] Southeast Asian country.

Ando, like Temple, is dimpled, plucky, clever, and more resourceful than any of the adults in the story. He has a fresh, engaging personality, and it isn't his fault the camera moons over him at every opportunity. Niven tries hard to breathe subtlety into his coward-turned-hero role, but is impeded by the lame screenplay and plodding direction. Toshiro Mifune, playing Ando's ambassador father, acts like his mind is elsewhere.

•

PAPILLON

1973, 150 mins, US Ⓥ ⊙ ▭ col

Dir Franklin J. Schaffner ***Prod*** Robert Dorfmann, Franklin J. Schaffner ***Scr*** Dalton Trumbo, Lorenzo Semple, Jr. ***Ph*** Fred Koenekamp ***Ed*** Robert Swink ***Mus*** Jerry Goldsmith ***Art*** Anthony Masters

Act Steve McQueen, Dustin Hoffman, Victor Jory, Don Gordon, Anthony Zerbe, Robert Deman (Allied Artists)

Henri Charriere's story of confinement in, and escape from, the infamous French Guiana prison colony was that of an ordeal. So is Franklin J. Schaffner's film version. For 150 uninterrupted minutes, the mood is one of despair, brutality, and little hope.

The script is very good within its limitations, but there is insufficient identification with the main characters. Steve McQueen, for example, says he has been framed for murdering a pimp; we do not see the injustice occur, hence have insufficient empathy.

Dustin Hoffman plays an urbane counterfeiter, a white collar criminal whose guilt is beyond question. Hoffman does an excellent job in portraying his character's adaptation to the corruptibilities of prison life.

The film begins with co-adaptor Dalton Trumbo (in an unbilled bit) addressing the latest shipload of prisoners consigned to the South American jungle horrors. He informs them they are henceforth non-human baggage. The oppressive atmosphere is so absolutely established within the first hour of the film that, in a sense, it has nowhere to go for the rest of the time.

The $13 million film was shot mostly in Spain and in Jamaica.

1973: NOMINATION: Best Original Score

•

PARADINE CASE, THE

1947, 131 mins, US Ⓥ b/w

Dir Alfred Hitchcock ***Prod*** David O. Selznick ***Scr*** David O. Selznick ***Ph*** Lee Garmes ***Ed*** Hal C. Kern ***Mus*** Franz Waxman ***Art*** J. McMillan Johnson

Act Gregory Peck, Ann Todd, Charles Laughton, Charles Coburn, Louis Jourdan, Alida Valli (RKO/Selznick)

The Paradine Case offers two hours and 11 minutes of high dramatics. Plot concerns murder of a blind man by his wife so she can marry her lover. Her attorney, believing in her not guilty plea, fights for her life. Himself infatuated with his client, the barrister plots and schemes to defeat justice but as dramatic events are brought out, the truth is revealed. There are no flashback devices to clutter the trial and the audience gradually is let in on the facts, as is the court, as the hearing proceeds and emotions take hold. Charles Laughton gives a revealing portrait of a gross, lustful nobleman who presides at the trial.

Alfred Hitchcock's penchant for suspense, unusual atmosphere and development gets full play. There is a deliberateness of pace, artful pauses and other carefully calculated melodramatic hinges upon which he swings the story and players. Selznick wrote the screenplay, adapted from the Robert Hichens novel by Alma Reville and James Bridie. It is a job that puts much emphasis on dialog and it's talk that punches. A very mobile camera helps give a feeling of movement to majority of scenes confined to the British courtroom as Hitchcock goes into the unfoldment of the highly dramatic murder trial.

Gregory Peck's stature as a performer of ability stands him in good stead among the extremely tough competition. As the barrister who defends Alida Valli, charged with the murder of her husband, he answers every demand of a demanding role. Ann Todd delights as his wife, giving the assignment a grace and understanding that tug at the emotions.

1947: NOMINATION: Best Supp. Actress (Ethel Barrymore)

•

PARADISE

1991, 110 mins, US Ⓥ ⊙ col

Dir Mary Agnes Donoghue ***Prod*** Scott Kroopf, Patrick Palmer ***Scr*** Mary Agnes Donoghue ***Ph*** Jerzy Zielinski ***Ed*** Eva Gardos, Debra McDermott ***Mus*** David Newman ***Art*** Evelyn Sakash, Marcia Hinds

Act Melanie Griffith, Don Johnson, Elijah Wood, Thora Birch, Sheila McCarthy, Louise Latham (Touchstone)

Writer Mary Agnes Donoghue debuts as a film director with her careful adaptation of a 1987 French drama *Le grand chemin* [written and directed by Jean-Loup Hubert]. Story focuses on 10-year-old Elijah Wood, sent by his pregnant mom (Eve Gordon) to spend a school vacation in the sleepy town of Paradise. Melanie Griffith and husband Don Johnson, who are mysteriously cold to each other, take care of the boy. There's a third reel revelation that the death of their three-year-old son in 1987 has driven a wedge between them.

The boy is befriended by nine-year-old Thora Birch, and film gently follows their pranks and adventures in an idyllic natural setting. Duo have in common the absence of a father; Wood's is supposedly away at sea while Birch's is a roller-skating instructor in a nearby town.

Donoghue shows impressive self-assurance for a first-time helmer in not rushing the pace or overdoing the maudlin elements of this material. Birch is irresistible as the wise little girl, whose gestures and body language are a treat throughout the picture. Wood underplays and is very natural.

Johnson and Griffith co-star for the first time with effective overtones of a longstanding off-screen relationship (married twice). Both are deglamorized for their character roles and are convincing as a rustic, unsophisticated couple.

•

PARADISE ALLEY
1978, 107 mins, US Ⓥ ⊙ col
Dir Sylvester Stallone ***Prod*** John F. Roach, Ronald A. Suppa ***Scr*** Sylvester Stallone ***Ph*** Laszlo Kovacs ***Ed*** Eve Newman ***Mus*** Bill Conti ***Art*** John W. Corso
Act Sylvester Stallone, Kevin Conway, Anne Archer, Armand Assante, Lee Canalito, Tom Waits (Force Ten/Universal)

Paradise Alley is *Rocky* rewritten by Damon Runyon. Set in New York's Hell's Kitchen area during the 1940s, it tells the uplifting tale of three brothers, played by Sylvester Stallone, Armand Assante, and Lee Canalito, and how they literally wrestle their way out of the ghetto. It's an upbeat, funny, nostalgic film populated by colorful characters, memorable more for their individual moments than for their parts in the larger story.

Stallone proves a number of points with this film. First, that he's a very capable director with a keen eye for casting. Second, he has a charming comic presence.

Paradise Alley shows off, once again, Stallone's ability as a writer. His sense of plot is old-fashioned—but it's also very commercial. The basic element is a hopeful loser who wants desperately to be a winner and triumphs.

The plot of this film is almost a throwaway. Three brothers, a dumb, beefy ice man (Canalito), a bitter crippled war veteran (Assante) and Stallone, the con man, all want to escape the slums. Stallone decides that Canalito's muscles in a wrestling ring are their ticket uptown. [A two-minute longer version was issued on homevideo.]

•

PARADISE FOR THREE
1938, 75 mins, US b/w
Dir Edward Buzzell ***Prod*** Sam Zimbalist ***Scr*** George Oppenheimer, Harry Ruskin ***Ph*** Leonard Smith ***Ed*** Elmo Veron ***Mus*** Edward Ward
Act Frank Morgan, Robert Young, Mary Astor, Edna May Oliver, Florence Rice, Reginald Owen (M-G-M)

There's a laugh a minute in *Paradise for Three*, a genuinely funny farce which is played humorously by a cast that knows how to stir the risibles. Screenplay is taken from Erich Kaestner's novel *Three Men in the Snow*.

Yarn recounts the adventures of a prosperous continental soap manufacturer (Frank Morgan) who wins a prize in his own radio slogan contest and proceeds to sneak a fortnight's vacation under an assumed name in a mountain winter resort. He gets into some comical scrapes, including a breach of promise suit. What starts out to be a frolic develops complications that are fresh and amusing.

Mary Astor is the adventuress who becomes the nemesis of the multimillionaire. Her acting is delightful and her good looks are accentuated by some attractive costumes. Romantic interest is furnished by Robert Young and Florence Rice.

•

PARADISE, HAWAIIAN STYLE
1966, 87 mins, US Ⓥ col
Dir Michael Moore ***Prod*** Hal Wallis ***Scr*** Allan Weiss, Anthony Lawrence ***Ph*** W. Wallace Kelley ***Ed*** Warren Low ***Mus*** Joseph J. Lilley ***Art*** Hal Pereira, Walter Tyler
Act Elvis Presley, Suzanna Leigh, James Shigeta, Donna Butterworth, Marianna Hill, Irene Tsu (Paramount)

Hal Wallis, who first brought Elvis Presley to the screen in 1956 and once before locationed in Hawaii (*Blue Hawaii*, 1961), returns singer to the island state in this gaily begarbed and flowing musical.

Light script by Allan Weiss and Anthony Lawrence, based on former's original, serves more as a showcase for Presley's wares than as plottage but suffices to sock over the Presley lure. Star plays an airplane pilot with girl trouble, who loses one job after another when he becomes innocently embroiled. His troubles continue after he and James Shigeta team up for inter-island ferrying, with usual romanantic entanglements, fights and outbursts of song.

Michael Moore, making his directional bow after seven years with Wallis as an assistant, maintains a breezy pace and manages good performances from his cast.

•

PARADISE LAGOON
SEE: THE ADMIRABLE CRICHTON

•

PARALLAX VIEW, THE
1974, 102 mins, US Ⓥ ▭ col
Dir Alan J. Pakula ***Prod*** Alan J. Pakula ***Scr*** David Giler, Lorenzo Semple, Jr. ***Ph*** Gordon Willis ***Ed*** John W. Wheeler ***Mus*** Michael Small ***Art*** George Jenkins
Act Warren Beatty, Hume Cronyn, William Daniels, Paula Prentiss, Anthony Zerbe, Kenneth Mars (Paramount/Gus)

The Parallax View is a partially-successful attempt to take a serious subject—a nationwide network of political guns for hire—and make it commercially palatable to the popcorn trade—via chases, fights, and lots of exterior production elements.

The adaptation of Loren Singer's novel follows newshawk Warren Beatty in his discovery of an assassination complex involving a security organization (called the Parallax Corp.) which deliberately seeks out social misfits, dispatched by clients to murder political figures of various persuasions.

The story begins with the murder of Senator Bill Joyce, followed by the official investigation, after which many witnesses begin to die. Paula Prentiss, very good as a prototype TV newshen, finally gets Beatty's interest aroused before her mysterious death.

Pakula's production and direction are lavish in physical details.

•

PARAMOUNT ON PARADE
1930, 101 mins, US col
Dir Dorothy Arzner, Victor Heerman, Ernst Lubitsch, A. Edward Sutherland, Otto Brower, Edwin H. Knopf, Lothar Mendes, Edmund Goulding, Rowland V. Lee, Victor Schertzinger, Frank Tuttle ***Ph*** Harry Fishbeck, Victor Milner ***Ed*** Merrill White ***Art*** John Wenger
Act Maurice Chevalier, Jean Arthur, Gary Cooper, Clara Bow, Jack Oakie, George Bancroft (Paramount)

Paramount on Parade links together with almost incredible smoothness achievements from the smallest technical detail to the greatest artistic endeavor. Interspersed throughout the 20 numbers are 11 songs, the work of 13 writers. Technicolor is used in seven of the numbers.

In color, setting and gracefulness of players and direction, the "Dream Girl" number is outstanding. But even with all the competition Maurice Chevalier comes through in first place. He is featured in three numbers and in two of these renders the song hits of the production. "Sweeping the Clouds Away" is sung by him. Before this Chevalier appears in a sketch called "A Park in Paris," which presents him as a gendarme among springtime activities.

Jack Oakie and Zelma O'Neal do a tapping special, in a gym. Clara Bow, in sailor garb, does her regular on the navy.

•

PARANOIAC
1963, 80 mins, UK ⊙ ▭ b/w
Dir Freddie Francis ***Prod*** Anthony Hinds ***Scr*** Jimmy Sangster ***Ph*** Arthur Grant ***Ed*** James Needs ***Mus*** Elizabeth Lutyens ***Art*** Bernard Robinson
Act Janette Scott, Oliver Reed, Liliane Brousse, Alexander Davion, Maurice Denham (Hammer)

Paranoiac marks the directorial debut of Freddie Francis, British cameraman. Lack of experience proves no handicap for Francis, however, as he sculpts a suspenseful and smartly paced opus out of Jimmy Sangster's effective screenplay.

Plot is a reworking of the imposter-heir swindle bit in which someone poses as a long-lost member of a family who just happens to turn up in time to claim a tidy inheritance. The phoney is impersonating a young man believed by members of his family to have committed suicide when a boy, following the death of his parents. His sister deeply misses him but his brother wouldn't mind it at all if the sister vanished too so he could have all the loot for himself. In fact he tries to convince his sister and their aunt that she's nuts so they'll pack her off and leave him with the inheritance all to himself.

Oliver Reed plays the scheming brother with demonic skill, blending bits of spoiled brat and sneaky madman for a menacing portrayal. Janette Scott is pretty and disarming as the sister and emotes credibly. Alexander Davion makes a fine baddie-turned-hero, thesping with ease and believability.

•

PARAPLUIES DE CHERBOURG, LES
(THE UMBRELLAS OF CHERBOURG) Ⓥ col
1964, 95 mins, France/W. Germany
Dir Jacques Demy ***Prod*** Mag Bodard ***Scr*** Jacques Demy ***Ph*** Jean Rabier ***Ed*** A. M. Cotret, M. Teisseire ***Mus*** Michel Legrand ***Art*** Bernard Evein
Act Catherine Deneuve, Nino Castelnuovo, Anne Vernon, Marc Michel, Ellen Farmer, Mireille Perrey (Parc/Madeleine/Beta)

It takes nerve to make a pic in which all dialog is sung. Also, there is no dancing and this is not a filmed operetta or opera.

Director-writer Jacques Demy went to the port town of Cherbourg to make this simple tale of a boy and girl in love. He is depicted leaving for the army, with said girl pregnant, and she giving in to her mother's blandishments and marrying a well-heeled suitor. He comes back and finally marries a childhood friend and they see each other briefly one Christmas night as both go back to their regular lives.

Seemingly banal and sentimental on the surface, Demy has avoided these aspects by tasteful handling and the right balance in emotion, compassion and narrative. Pic becomes touching without being mawkish, simple sans being trite, and lovely to look at.

Michel Legrand has supplied a richly tuneful score that serves as a sharp counterpart to help story points and enhance the moods. The bright sets and the excellent color work are also assets.

Catherine Deneuve, a winsome-looking type that other directors have forced to act, here is allowed to be herself. She etches a fine portrait of a 16-year-old in love. Nino Castelnuovo has presence and poise as the boy. The dubbed voices, done in playback and recorded before shooting started, are all fitting for the various characters.

The title stems from an umbrella store owned by the girl's mother.

•

PARASITE
1982, 85 mins, US Ⓥ ▭ col
Dir Charles Band ***Prod*** Charles Band ***Scr*** Alan Adler, Michael Shoob, Frank Levering ***Ph*** Mac Ahlberg ***Ed*** Brad Arensman ***Mus*** Richard Band ***Art*** Pamela Warner
Act Robert Glaudini, Demi Moore, Luca Bercovici, James Davidson, Al Fann, Vivian Blaine (Embassy)

Parasite is a low-budget monster film which utilizes the 3-D process to amplify its shock effects.

Set in 1992, tale has a skimpy sci-fi peg of scientist Dr. Paul Dean (Robert Glaudini) attempting to neutralize a strain of parasite he has developed for the government. Morbid premise is that the large, wormlike parasite is in his abdomen growing while he studies another specimen, racing to somehow avert his own death and save the world from millions of offspring.

Pic's raison d'etre is a set of frightening mechanical and sculpted monster makeup effects by Stan Winston. Convincing gore and sudden plunges at the camera are enhanced by Stereo Vision 3-D filming. Otherwise *Parasite* is lethargic between its terror scenes, making it a test of patience for all but the fanatical followers of horror cheapies.

•

PARASITE MURDERS, THE
SEE: SHIVERS

•

PAR-DELA LES NUAGES
(BEYOND THE CLOUDS)
1996, 104 mins, France/Italy/Germany col
Dir Michelangelo Antonioni, Wim Wenders ***Prod*** Stephane Tchalgadjieff, Philippe Carcassone ***Scr*** Tonino Guerra, Michelangelo Antonioni, Wim Wenders ***Ph*** Alfio Contini, Robby Muller ***Ed*** Claudio Di Mauro, Peter Przygodda, Luciano Segura ***Art*** Thierry Flamand
Act John Malkovich, Kim Rossi Stuart, Ines Sastre, Sophie Marceau, Fanny Ardant, Peter Weller (Sunshine/Cine. B/France 3/Cecchi Gori/Road Movies)

Beyond the Clouds might be the most intimate, personal film Michelangelo Antonioni has made, but it may also be his least significant, his first feature in 13 years after a stroke in 1985 left him practically unable to speak or write. This landmark production, laced with a top-drawer cast of Euro thesps, is a leaky boat whose slow artiness is more sleep-inducing than insightful.

Film opens [in a frame story directed by Wim Wenders] with a film director (John Malkovich) descending from the clouds in a plane. Like a benevolent, omniscient angel (a favorite Wenders motif), he spies on and recounts the tormented love affairs of various couples. The body of Tonio Guerra's screenplay is directed by Antonioni and is based on four short-short stories from Antonioni's book *That Bowling Alley on the Tiber River*.

In the first episode, *Chronicle of a Love That Never Was*, handsome young traveler Silvano (Kim Rossi Stuart) encounters a young woman, Carmen (Ines Sastre), in a provincial hotel in Ferrara, Italy. Two years pass before they meet again, but this time Silvano deliberately chooses to vanish.

In *The Girl, the Crime*, Malkovich is wandering around off-season Portofino when he is struck by a pretty girl (Sophie Marceau) who works in a boutique. As a conversation opener, she tells him she killed her father; then they end up in bed.

Paris is the setting of *Don't Try to See Me Again*, where another young woman (Chiara Caselli) strikes up a conversation with a stranger (Peter Weller). The next thing you know, they have been lovers for three years, and Weller's wife (Fanny Ardant) is threatening to leave him.

In the final round, *This Body of Mud*, a boy in Aix-en-Provence (Vincent Perez) is so desperate to pick up a girl (Irene Jacob) on the street that he follows her to Mass. Nothing doing: she is already in love with God.

A brief intermezzo, filmed by Wenders, shows Marcello Mastroianni painting in a field, observed by Jeanne Moreau, who teases him about making mere "copies" of nature.

Another sign of Wenders's affection for his colleague is his generosity in stepping into the film basically as a standby director for the 82-year-old Antonioni, at the behest of the producers and insurance companies. The fine cast barely has a chance to emerge. Ardant and Jacob leave the most lasting impression.

[Version reviewed was a 113-min. "last work print" preemed at the 1995 Venice festival.]

•

PARDON MY PAST
1945, 89 mins, US b/w
Dir Leslie Fenton ***Scr*** Earl Felton, Karl Kamb ***Ph*** Russell Metty ***Ed*** Otho Lovering, Richard Heermance ***Mus*** Dimitri Tiomkin ***Art*** Bernard Herzbrun
Act Fred MacMurray, Marguerite Chapman, Akim Tamiroff, William Demarest, Rita Johnson, Harry Davenport (Columbia/Mutual)

Pardon My Past is a topnotch comedy [from a story by Patterson McNutt and Harlan Ware] packing plenty of fun for all types of audiences. It's a comedy of mistaken identity and frustration. Fred MacMurray and William Demarest are just-discharged GIs enroute to Wisconsin to start a mink farm with their service savings. MacMurray is mistaken for a rich playboy by a gambler who tries to collect an old debt.

MacMurray's dual role is deftly handled so that the two characters he portrays never actually meet on the screen, which makes for a more satisfactory solution of the old double-exposure problems. Actor contributes an ace performance in his best style under Leslie Fenton's smart direction. Dry wit and dumbness of the Demarest character are also good for many a chuckle. Harry Davenport, as the grandfather soured on his worthless kin, is also topnotch.

•

PARDON MY SARONG
1942, 83 mins, US b/w
Dir Erle C. Kenton ***Prod*** Jules Levey ***Scr*** True Boardman, Nat Perrin, John Grant ***Ph*** Milton Krasner ***Ed*** Arthur Hilton ***Mus*** Charles Previn (dir.)
Act Bud Abbott, Lou Costello, Virginia Bruce, Lionel Atwill, Robert Paige, William Demarest (Universal/Mayfair)

Abbott and Costello starrer is one continual chase, with the boys displaying their familiar routines and antics for plenty of laughs en route. In addition to the broad horseplay of the two comedians, picture has six song numbers.

Chase gets away right at the opening, with the two comics heading west in a Chicago municipal bus bound for the Coast. Gags and routines are dropped plentifully along the route, until boys switch to a sailing yacht. This lands them on a South Sea island as locale for further horseplay.

Despite the fact that many of the gag sequences have been filmed many times before, the spontaneous and expertly timed deliveries by Abbott and Costello dress them up in new regalia for cinch laugh reaction.

Director Erle Kenton, veteran of Hollywood's comedy scene, pulls many an oldie out of the files for the boys to romp around with merrily.

•

PARDON US
1931, 56 mins, US Ⓥ ⊙ b/w
Dir James Parrott ***Prod*** Hal Roach ***Scr*** H. M. Walker ***Ph*** George Stevens ***Ed*** Richard Currier
Act Stan Laurel, Oliver Hardy, Walter Long, James Finlayson, June Marlowe (Roach/M-G-M)

Another two-reel idea on a six-reel frame with the usual strain resulting. *Pardon Us* proves nothing for Laurel and Hardy.

First 20-odd minutes are brimming with solid laughs. During that period the film is technically in the two-reel short class. What's in it seems funny. Just after the quarter-hour mark of so the hokum starts kicking itself in the back.

Opening is an excellent piece of comedy business. Boys are jotting down a recipe outside a malt and hop store. They decide to make some beer. Laurel's idea is to sell what they don't drink. In the next scene they're being waltzed into jail.

Second best laugh comes pretty early and nothing else that follows deserves to be in the same scenario. This is when the two attempt to get comfortable in a single upper berth in the cell.

Only girl is on for only three or four minutes and speaks about a dozen words in all. She's June Marlowe, playing the warden's daughter.

•

PARENTHOOD
1989, 124 mins, US Ⓥ ⊙ col
Dir Ron Howard ***Prod*** Brian Grazer ***Scr*** Lowell Ganz, Babaloo Mandel ***Ph*** Donald McAlpine ***Ed*** Michael Hill, Daniel Hanley ***Mus*** Randy Newman ***Art*** Todd Hallowell
Act Steve Martin, Mary Steenburgen, Dianne Wiest, Jason Robards, Rick Moranis, Tom Hulce (Imagine/Universal)

An ambitious, keenly observed, and often very funny look at one of life's most daunting passages, *Parenthood*'s masterstroke is that it covers the range of the family experience, offering the points of view of everyone in an extended and wildly diverse middle-class family. At its center is overanxious dad Steve Martin, who'll try anything to alleviate his eight-year-old's emotional problems, and Mary Steenburgen, his equally conscientious but better-adjusted wife.

Rick Moranis is the yuppie extreme, an excellence-fixated nerd who forces math, languages, Kafka and karate on his three-year-old girl, to the distress of his milder wife (Harley Kozak).

Dianne Wiest is a divorcee and working mother whose rebellious teens (Martha Plimpton and Leaf Phoenix) dump their anger in her lap.

Jason Robards is the acidic patriarch of the family whose neglectful fathering made his eldest son (Martin) grow up with an obsession to do better. The old man is forced to take another shot at fatherhood late in life when his ne'er-do-well, 27-year-old son (Tom Hulce) moves back in.

1989: NOMINATIONS: Best Supp. Actress (Dianne Wiest), Song ("I Love to See You Smile")

•

PARENTS
1989, 82 mins, US Ⓥ ⊙ col
Dir Bob Balaban ***Prod*** Bonnie Palef ***Scr*** Christopher Hawthorne ***Ph*** Ernest Day, Robin Vidgeon ***Ed*** Bill Pankow ***Mus*** Angelo Badalamenti, Jonathan Elias ***Art*** Andris Hausmanis
Act Randy Quaid, Mary Beth Hurt, Sandy Dennis, Bryan Madorsky, Juno Mills-Cockell, Kathryn Grody (Vestron)

Parents is your typical anthropological analysis of cannibalism in 1950s suburbia. First feature from actor Bob Balaban, who has worked behind the camera on shorts and in TV, delights in its evocation of plastic suburbia, highlighting the bad-taste clothes and furniture that look vaguely fashionable today.

Most of the action takes place in the home of the Laemles, where Dad (Randy Quaid) lords it over little Michael (Bryan Madorsky) while Mom (Mary Beth Hurt) mostly busies herself in the kitchen. Michael suffers from recurring nightmares, and is sent to see the in-house psychologist-social worker (Sandy Dennis).

It's pretty clear to the viewer early on that Mom and Dad are up to something very nasty, so it's only a matter of time, quite laboriously spent, until the folks attempt to indoctrinate little Michael in their peculiar tastes.

There is not enough weight or complexity to the material to justify the serious approach, and while the potential for considerable black comedy exists, Balaban only scratches the surface. The laughs never come. Shot in Toronto, pic conveys the desired look.

•

PARENT TRAP, THE
1961, 129 mins, US Ⓥ ⊙ col
Dir David Swift ***Prod*** Walt Disney ***Scr*** David Swift ***Ph*** Lucien Ballard ***Ed*** Philip W. Anderson ***Mus*** Paul Smith ***Art*** Carroll Clark, Robert Clatworthy
Act Hayley Mills, Maureen O'Hara, Brian Keith, Charles Ruggles, Una Merkel, Leo G. Carroll (Walt Disney)

David Swift, whose writing, direction and appreciation of young Hayley Mills's natural histrionic resources contributed so much to *Pollyanna*, repeats the three-ply effort on this excursion, with similar success. Swift's screenplay, based on Erich Kastner's book, *Das doppelte Lottchen*, describes the nimble-witted method by which identical twin sisters (both played by Mills) succeed in reuniting their estranged parents after a 14-year separation during which the sisters were parted, unbeknownst to them, in opposite parental camps.

Mills seems to have an instinctive sense of comedy and an uncanny ability to react in just the right manner. Overshadowed, but outstanding in his own right, is Brian Keith as the father. Maureen O'Hara's durable beauty makes the mother an extremely attractive character.

1961: NOMINATIONS: Best Editing, Sound

•

PARIS BELONGS TO US
SEE: PARIS NOUS APPARTIENT

•

PARIS BLUES
1961, 98 mins, US Ⓥ b/w
Dir Martin Ritt ***Prod*** Sam Shaw ***Scr*** Walter Bernstein, Irene Kamp, Jack Sher ***Ph*** Christian Matras ***Ed*** Roger Dwyre ***Mus*** Duke Ellington ***Art*** Alexandre Trauner
Act Paul Newman, Joanne Woodward, Sidney Poitier, Louis Armstrong, Diahann Carroll, Serge Reggiani (Pennebaker/Diane)

This reflects to some extent in form and technique the influence of the restless young Paris cinema colony, the environment in which the film was shot. But within its snappy, flashy veneer is an undernourished romantic drama of a rather traditional screen school.

The screenplay, based on a novel by Harold Flender, relates the romantic experiences of two expatriate U.S. jazz musicians (Paul Newman and Sidney Poitier) and two American girls (Joanne Woodward and Diahann Carroll) on a two-week vacation fling in Paris. The men fall in love with the girls, then must weigh their philosophies and careers against their amour.

The screenplay [from an adaptation by Lulla Adler] fails to bring any true identity to the four characters. As a result, their relationships are vague and superficial. The film is notable for Duke Ellington's moody, stimulating jazz score. There are scenes when the drama itself actually takes a back seat to the music, with unsatisfactory results insofar as dialog is concerned. Along the way there are several full-fledged passages of superior Ellingtonia such as "Mood Indigo" and "Sophisticated Lady," and Louis Armstrong is on hand for one flamboyant interlude of hot jazz.

1961: NOMINATION: Best Scoring of a Musical Picture

•

PARIS BY NIGHT
1989, 101 mins, UK Ⓥ col
Dir David Hare ***Prod*** Patrick Cassavetti ***Scr*** David Hare ***Ph*** Roger Pratt ***Ed*** George Akers ***Mus*** Georges Delerue ***Art*** Anthony Pratt
Act Charlotte Rampling, Michael Gambon, Robert Hardy, Iain Glen, Jane Asher, Niamh Cusack (British Screen/Zenith/Film Four/Greenpoint-Pressman)

David Hare's second feature as a director is a handsomely produced, rather cold drama about the fall of a femme politician.

Although Clara Paige is at the top of the ladder, a high-profile, pro-Thatcher, Tory politico and member of the European parliament, she still finds other people's lives more attractive than her own. Her husband, Gerald (an MP), is a drunk she's come to despise.

On a high-level trip to Paris she meets with a young British businessman, Wallace, and starts an affair with him. Late at night, by the Seine, she's walking along when she sees Michael. Certain he's followed her, and that he's her anonymous caller, she tips him into the river, where he drowns.

What follows involves Clara's attempts to cover up her crime and her gradual realization that Michael, after all, was neither a blackmailer nor her telephone caller.

Hare handles it all with dry, often witty, precision, but with a slightly academic style. Iain Glen is miscast as the lover, and hardly comes across as a candidate for a passionate love affair.

•

PARIS CALLING
1941, 93 mins, US b/w
Dir Edwin L. Marin ***Prod*** Benjamin Glazer ***Scr*** Benjamin Glazer, Charles S. Kaufman ***Ph*** Milton Krasner ***Ed*** Edward Curtiss ***Mus*** Richard Hageman
Act Elisabeth Bergner, Randolph Scott, Basil Rathbone, Gale Sondergaard, Lee J. Cobb, Charles Arnt (Universal)

Smash, spy melodrama, with the background of France just after the Germans crashed Paris and immediately thereafter, *Paris Calling* offers Elisabeth Bergner in perhaps her top screen characterization (also her initial film made in U.S.) as well as Randolph Scott and Basil Rathbone. With Bergner as the wealthy Frenchwoman who later serves her country as an underground operative, the romance between her and Scott, a Texan serving in the RAF, is kept warm without losing the main plot thread—activity of the French loyalists working underground and in league with Great Britain.

Director Edwin Marin builds powerful suspense, first as the Texan RAF husky evades capture and later when Bergner extricates herself from carefully laid traps of the Nazis.

Besides Bergner's superb work as the Frenchwoman turned spy in her country's cause, Scott checks in with a superior performance as the devil-may-care RAF-er from Texas.

•

PARIS EXPRESS
SEE: THE MAN WHO WATCHED TRAINS GO BY

•

PARIS NOUS APPARTIENT
(PARIS BELONGS TO US)
1960, 140 mins, France b/w
Dir Jacques Rivette ***Scr*** Jacques Rivette, Jean Gruault ***Ph*** Charles Bitsch ***Ed*** Denise de Casabianca ***Mus*** Philippe Arthuys
Act Betty Schneider, Gianni Esposito, Francoise Prevost, Daniel Crohem, Francois Maistre, Jean-Claude Brialy (AJYM/Carrosse)

The last of the New Wave films, in that it is the final one from the group of highbrow pic critics-turned-filmmakers, this uses a vague suspense theme and budding love story around a tale of a supposedly perking world totalitarian takeover by some sort of secret organization. This turns out to be a fiction in the mind of a psychotic American ex-journalist who had to leave the U.S. for political reasons.

All this is overblown, making it pretentious, slow-moving and fairly confused. It takes much too long to tell its over-complicated story. A young girl (Betty Schneider) comes to Paris and her brother intros her into a Bohemian group. She is taken by an intense young theatrical director (Gianni Esposito) trying to put on a Shakespearean play with practically no money. She joins the troupe and hears he is in danger from some sort of organization. Pic then follows the girl's quest to find out what the danger is. The emptiness and sordidness of the group is supposedly shown up through this search.

Rivette took two years to make the production and was given money by fellow "wavers" to finish it. Acting is uneven, with Schneider not up to conveying the anguish and emotions of a fairly innocent young girl caught up in a big city. Others acquit themselves adequately, with Esposito especially effective as the idealistic, if weak, theatrical man.

•

PARIS, TEXAS
1984, 150 mins, W. Germany/France Ⓥ ⊙ col
Dir Wim Wenders ***Prod*** Don Guest ***Scr*** Sam Shepard ***Ph*** Robby Muller ***Ed*** Peter Przygodda ***Mus*** Ry Cooder ***Art*** Kate Altman
Act Harry Dean Stanton, Nastassja Kinski, Dean Stockwell, Aurore Clement, Hunter Carson, Bernhard Wicki (Road/Argos)

Paris, Texas is a "road movie"—an odyssey, if you will. It's a man's journey to self-recognition. But what really impresses is the vision of writer-playwright Sam Shepard, upon whose *Motel Chronicles* short stories the original script was inspired and partially based.

Pic is the story of a man, Travis, wandering aimlessly along the Texas-Mexican border. Travis's brother in Los Angeles, Walt, is a billboard artist who took in the hero's boy four years ago when the mother literally left him on their doorstep.

Travis decides to win back the love of his son. Once he has done so, the pair's then off to Houston to find the missing mother, who works in a lonely-hearts kind of strip-joint.

Dean Stockwell as Walt is a standout, while Harry Dean Stanton as Travis only comes alive in the interim segments when he recovers his taste for humanity. Nastassja Kinski is hampered in a part that drags the film out interminably during a duolog with Stanton at the end.

•

PARIS TROUT
1991, 100 mins, US Ⓥ ⊙ col
Dir Stephen Gyllenhaal ***Prod*** Frank Konigsberg, Larry Sanitsky ***Scr*** Pete Dexter ***Ph*** Robert Elswit ***Ed*** Harvey Rosenstock ***Mus*** David Shire ***Art*** Richard Sherman
Act Dennis Hopper, Barbara Hershey, Ed Harris, Ray McKinnon, Tina Lifford, Darnita Henry (Viacom)

Pete Dexter's haunting novel about an unspeakable crime in a simple Southern town circa 1949 is brought masterfully to life in *Paris Trout*, a mesmerizing, morbidly fascinating tale, with outstanding performances by Dennis Hopper, Barbara Hershey and Ed Harris.

Trouble begins when a young black man (Eric Ware) signs a note to buy a used car from Trout (Hopper). When the worthless car is wrecked the same day, he drops it off at Trout's store, declaring he won't pay. Trout and a hired gun head out to the "hollow" to settle the debt. When the black man runs off, they enter the house and unload their pistols into his terrified mother and 12-year-old sister.

After his horrified wife (Hershey) visits the dying child at the clinic, Trout begins to humiliate and abuse her. He hires the town's crack lawyer (Harris) to defend him, but the attorney becomes more and more disturbed by the case and Trout's lack of remorse.

Hopper, beefy and aged for the role and sporting a clipped redneck haircut, gives an extraordinary portrayal of the tortured madman. Hershey is marvelous in a mature, nuanced perf as the compassionate spouse struggling to maintain dignity.

•

PARIS WHEN IT SIZZLES
1964, 108 mins, US Ⓥ col
Dir Richard Quine ***Prod*** Richard Quine, George Axelrod ***Scr*** George Axelrod ***Ph*** Charles Lang, Jr. ***Ed*** Archie Marshek ***Mus*** Nelson Riddle ***Art*** Jean D'Eaubonne
Act William Holden, Audrey Hepburn, Gregoire Aslan, Raymond Bussieres, Christian Duvaleix (Paramount)

Paris When It Sizzles fizzles. The Richard Quine-George Axelrod production is a romantic comedy that, as Axelrod himself describes the story-within-a-story that weaves through the film, is "contrived, utterly preposterous and totally unmotivated."

Axelrod's 108-minutes of marshmallow-weight hokum is concerned with the evolution of a romantic relationship between a somewhat broken-down, middle-aged screenwriter (William Holden) and his Tessie the Typist, an adorable Givenchy wenchy also known as Audrey Hepburn. Their affair is more or less paralleled in the creative ramblings of Holden's mind as he dreams up an artificial cloak-and-dagger screenplay.

The basic error in this film seems to be the artificiality of the shell in which the takeoffs are encased.

Prettiest image by far is Hepburn, a refreshingly individual creature in an era of the exaggerated curve. Holden handles his assignment commendably. Both give a lot more than they have gotten. Chipping in extended, uncredited cameos are Tony Curtis and Noel Coward, with smaller bits in the same vein by Mel Ferrer and Marlene Dietrich. The singing voices of Fred Astaire and Frank Sinatra are heard, former in a chorus of "That Face," latter singing one line of a tune in a parody of main titles that is one of the more amusing passages of the film.

•

PARRISH
1961, 140 mins, US col
Dir Delmer Daves ***Prod*** Delmer Daves ***Scr*** Delmer Daves ***Ph*** Harry Stradling, Sr. ***Ed*** Owen Marks ***Mus*** Max Steiner ***Art*** Leo K. Kuter
Act Troy Donahue, Claudette Colbert, Karl Malden, Dean Jagger, Connie Stevens, Diane McBain (Warner)

Parrish is a long, plodding account of man *vs.* monopoly in Connecticut's tobacco game.

Based on the novel by Mildred Savage, director Delmer Daves's screenplay is something of a cross between a rich man's *Tobacco Road* and a poor man's *A Place in the Sun*. Troy Donahue essays the title role of a poor young man who emerges from a laborer's toil in the Connecticut tobacco fields to challenge the dynasty of mighty land baron Karl Malden.

A number of romantic entanglements crop up to complicate this basic conflict, not the least of which are Donahue's bat-of-an-eyelash love affairs with Malden's daughter (Sharon Hugueny), his arch rival's (Dean Jagger's) daughter (Diane McBain) and a loose field girl (Connie Stevens) who gives illegitimate birth to the child of Malden's son (Hampton Fancher). Then there is the supreme complication: Malden's marriage to Donahue's mother (Claudette Colbert).

Donahue is handsome and has his moments, but lacks the animation and projection that is required to bring the title character, curiously vacant and elusive as written, into clearer focus. The picture's three principal veterans—Colbert, Malden and Jagger—do well, particularly Malden in spite of the exaggerated nature of his role.

•

PARTING GLANCES
1986, 90 mins, US Ⓥ col
Dir Bill Sherwood ***Prod*** Yoram Mandel, Arthur Silverman ***Scr*** Bill Sherwood ***Ph*** Jacek Laskus ***Ed*** Bill Sherwood ***Art*** John Loggia
Act Richard Ganoung, John Bolger, Steve Buscemi, Adam Nathan, Patrick Tull (Rondo)

Parting Glances is bracingly forthright and believable in its presentation of an all-gay world within contempo New York City. Set within a 24-hour period, Bill Sherwood's highly sophisticated pic centers around a series of farewell events for Robert (John Bolger), good-looking boyfriend of ultra-yuppie Michael (Richard Ganoung). Robert, for reasons finally discovered by his lover, is leaving for a stint in Kenya, which will bring about the interruption, if not the end, of a six-year relationship.

Intertwined with this is Michael's very responsible dealing with his former lover Nick (Steve Buscemi), a caustic, cynical rock musician who has recently learned that he has AIDS.

Fortunately, film indulges in no special pleading, merely regarding the disease as another fact of gay life.

•

PARTNERS
1976, 96 mins, Canada Ⓥ col
Dir Don Owen ***Prod*** Chalmers Adams, Don Owen ***Scr*** Norman Snider, Don Owen ***Ph*** Marc Champion ***Ed*** George Appleby ***Mus*** Murray McLauchlan
Act Denholm Elliott, Hollis McLaren, Michael Margotta, Lee Broker, Judith Gault, Robert Silverman (Clearwater)

Partners is a love story played off against a background of unscrupulous methods used by an American multinational firm interested in buying out a large Canadian pulp and paper firm controlled by a very old moneyed family. Don Owen brings it off with élan and a few mystifying moments along the way.

A thief and dope smuggler, played with macho vigor by Michael Margotta, gets romantically and sexually involved with the daughter of the pulp and paper firm's owner and takes her along running dope across the U.S.-Canada border.

Aside from Margotta, a fine performance by Denholm Elliott, and a jail scene vignette by actress Jackie Burroughs as a prostitute, the acting rarely rises above the superficial.

•

PARTNERS
1982, 93 mins, US Ⓥ col
Dir James Burrows ***Prod*** Aaron Russo ***Scr*** Francis Veber ***Ph*** Victor J. Kemper ***Ed*** Danford B. Greene ***Mus*** Georges Delerue ***Art*** Richard Sylbert
Act Ryan O'Neal, John Hurt, Kenneth McMillan, Robyn Douglass, Jay Robinson, Denise Galik (Paramount)

Screenwriter/exec producer Francis Veber, who scored by spoofing one segment of the homosexual lifestyle in *La Cage aux Folles* and its sequel, this time tries to transfer his approach to a contemporary American setting. This production could loosely be termed *The Odd Couple Turns Gay and Joins the Police Force*, ultimately runs one very tired joke into the ground.

Essentially, this is the story of straight, macho detective Ryan O'Neal and closeted gay police office clerk John Hurt—an odd pair forced by their superior to go undercover and pose as a homosexual couple in order to trap the murderer of a male model.

Naturally, all the gays they encounter seem to either putter around displaying their limp wrists or swoon the moment O'Neal walks into a room. Hurt tries to be a crime solver, but is infinitely more content to bake a soufflé or stare doe-eyed at O'Neal as he adoringly serves him breakfast in bed.

•

PARTY, THE
1968, 98 mins, US Ⓥ ⊙ ▭ col
Dir Blake Edwards ***Prod*** Blake Edwards ***Scr*** Blake Edwards, Tom Waldman, Frank Waldman ***Ph*** Lucien Ballard ***Ed*** Ralph Winters ***Mus*** Henry Mancini ***Art*** Fernando Carrere

Act Peter Sellers, Claudine Longet, Marge Champion, Steve Franken, Fay McKenzie (United Artists)

All the charm of two-reel comedy, as well as all the resulting tedium when the concept is distended to 10 reels, is evident in *The Party*. The one-joke script, told in laudable, if unsuccessful, attempt to emulate silent pix technique, is dotted with comedy ranging from drawing-room repartee to literally, bathroom vulgarity.

Peter Sellers is a disaster-prone foreign thesp, who, in an amusing eight-minute prolog to titles, fouls up an important Bengal Lancer–type film location. His outraged producer (Gavin MacLeod) blackballs him to studio chief J. Edward McKinley, but, in a mixup, Sellers gets invited to a party at McKinley's home.

Production designer Fernando Carrere has done an outstanding job in creating, on the one set used, a super-gauge house of sliding floors, pools, centralized controls and bizarre trappings.

Besides Sellers, most prominent thesps are Claudine Longet, the romantic interest, and Steve Franken as a tipsy butler. Eventually it all becomes a big yawn.

•

PARTY GIRL

1930, 73 mins, US Ⓥ b/w

Dir Victor Halperin ***Prod*** Edward Halperin ***Scr*** Monte Katterjohn, George Draney, Victor Halperin ***Ph*** Henry Cronjager, Robert Newhard ***Ed*** Russell Schoengarth

Act Douglas Fairbanks, Jr., Jeanette Loff, Judith Barrie, Marie Prevost (Halperin)

Marie Prevost is the pip party eyeful of joy. She is classified as "A" and "popular" on her index card, with her party salary $100 nightly. Playing the party route shows on Prevost. She has a masseuse after each one.

Jeanette Loff is a former party girl gone straight and now the sec to a big business house, the head of which doesn't believe it is required to have dames at parties to boost sales. Almeda Fowler as Maude Lindsay, the boss of the call shop, says businessmen have found these parties are the best salesmen.

So the son of the proper businessman gets tangled up with two party girls, the one in his father's office and another who frames him. Douglas Fairbanks, Jr., is the juve soused college boy. Does all right, as do the girls and the entire cast.

•

PARTY GIRL

1958, 99 mins, US Ⓥ ⦿ ⌑ col

Dir Nicholas Ray ***Prod*** Joe Pasternak ***Scr*** George Wells ***Ph*** Robert Bronner ***Ed*** John McSweeney, Jr. ***Mus*** Jeff Alexander ***Art*** William A. Horning, Randall Duell

Act Robert Taylor, Cyd Charisse, Lee J. Cobb, John Ireland, Claire Kelly, Corey Allen (Euterpe/M-G-M)

Party Girl is a straight melodrama of gangster days in [early 1930s] Chicago, played straight. There is no effort to understand the phenomenon or to relate it to the times.

Robert Taylor plays a crippled lawyer, mouthpiece for gangster boss Lee J. Cobb. Taylor uses his disability to play on the sympathies of juries to get the mobster underlings, such as John Ireland, free of murder and mayhem charges he knows they are guilty of. He begins to be disturbed about his way of life when he meets Cyd Charisse, a dancer at a nightclub who picks up a little money occasionally at parties. Taylor sees he cannot censure Charisse for making money out of the mobs when he is doing the same thing himself. Taylor's breaking point comes when he is called on by Cobb to defend a psychopath mobster (Corey Allen). The screenplay, based on a story by Leo Katcher, is intelligent and convincing, and Nicholas Ray's direction is good within the limits of the action.

Taylor carries considerable conviction as the attorney, suave and virile. Charisse's character has little background to supply her with any acting exercise, but she is interesting and, in two fine dance numbers, exciting. Lee J. Cobb contributes another of his somewhat flamboyant characterizations.

•

PASCALI'S ISLAND

1989, 104 mins, UK Ⓥ ⦿ col

Dir James Dearden ***Prod*** Eric Fellner ***Scr*** James Dearden ***Ph*** Roger Deakins ***Ed*** Edward Marnier ***Mus*** Loek Dikker ***Art*** Andrew Mollo

Act Ben Kingsley, Charles Dance, Helen Mirren, George Murcell, Sheila Allen, Nadim Sawalha (Avenue/Initial)

Intrigue on a Turkish-occupied Greek island in 1908 is the theme of this mildly exotic British pic [based on the novel by Barry Unsworth] which, despite an eye-catching but mannered central performance from Ben Kingsley, looms as too languid and remote to make much impact.

Kingsley plays Pascali, a seedy little Turkish spy who's lived on the small island of Nisi for 20 years. The ever-watchful agent is a very minor cog in the crumbling Ottoman Empire, yet is filled with self-importance. Sexually ambivalent, he carries a half-hearted torch for a comely, middle-aged Austrian painter, Lydia (Helen Mirren).

Enter Charles Dance as Bowles, a bronzed British adventurer professing to be an archeologist, actually planning to loot the island of its ancient treasures. Before long he's involved in an affair with Lydia, observed by the frustrated and jealous Pascali who is, perhaps, even more attracted to Bowles than to the woman. The stage is set for a final-reel tragedy.

Kingsley gives a technically impressive performance as the frustrated, bitter spy, but his mannerisms are becoming bothersome. Best is Mirren who still can disrobe to play a love scene with elegance and style; she brings much-needed warmth to an otherwise cold pic.

•

PASSAGE TO INDIA, A

1985, 163 mins, UK/US Ⓥ ⦿ col

Dir David Lean ***Prod*** John Brabourne, Richard Goodwin ***Scr*** David Lean ***Ph*** Ernest Day ***Ed*** David Lean ***Mus*** Maurice Jarre ***Art*** John Box

Act Judy Davis, Victor Banerjee, Peggy Ashcroft, James Fox, Alec Guinness, Nigel Havers (Columbia/HBO)

Fourteen years after his last film, David Lean returned to the screen with *A Passage to India*, an impeccably faithful, beautifully played and occasionally languorous adaptation of E. M. Forster's classic novel about the clash of East and West in colonial India.

Tale is set in 1928, a curious fact in that Forster's enduring novel was penned four years earlier. A young woman, Judy Davis, is taken from England to India by Peggy Ashcroft with the likely purpose of marrying the older woman's son Nigel Havers, the city magistrate of fictitious Chandrapore.

Intelligent and well brought up, Davis is not exactly a rebel, but chafes at the limitations and acute snobbery of the ruling British community.

Breaking the general rule against racial intermingling, local medic Victor Banerjee invites the ladies on an expedition to the nearby Marabar caves, an excursion which ends in tragedy when a bloodied Davis returns to accuse the bewildered, devastated Banerjee of having attempted to rape her in one of the caves.

Lean has succeeded to a great degree in the tricky task of capturing Forster's finely edged tone of rational bemusement and irony.

The outstanding set of performances here is led by Ashcroft, a constant source of delight as the wonderfully independent and frank Mrs. Moore, and Davis, an Australian actress who has the rare gift of being able to look very plain (as the role calls for) at one moment and uncommonly beautiful at another.

1984: Best Supp. Actress (Peggy Ashcroft), Original Score

NOMINATIONS: Best Picture, Director, Actress (Judy Davis), Adapted Screenplay, Cinematography, Costume Design, Art Direction, Editing, Sound

•

PASSAGE TO MARSEILLE

1944, 110 mins, US Ⓥ b/w

Dir Michael Curtiz ***Prod*** Hal B. Wallis ***Scr*** Casey Robinson, Jack Moffitt ***Ph*** James Wong Howe ***Ed*** Owen Marks ***Mus*** Max Steiner ***Art*** Carl Jules Weyl

Act Humphrey Bogart, Michele Morgan, Claude Rains, Sydney Greenstreet, Peter Lorre, Philip Dorn (Warner)

Yarn [from a novel by Charles Nordhoff and James Norman Hall], dedicated to the Fighting French, unwinds in a series of flashbacks, as related by a French liaison officer (Claude Rains) to an American newspaperman (John Loder), who seeks background for a story dealing with activities of those Frenchmen who are fighting, and flying, on the side of the Allies. Rains goes back many months in the telling, when a ship he was on picked up a group of men in a lifeboat in the Atlantic. The survivors admit, when pressed, that they are escaped prisoners from Devil's Island, who wish to return to France to fight for their country.

After the rescue, the freighter settles down to its normal routine, continuing back to Marseille, its destination, only to be disturbed again when the wireless crackles with the news of French surrender to the Nazis. The captain of the ship (Victor Francen) secretly orders its course changed toward England, but not before the fascist wireless operator radios the ship's position to a German patrol bomber.

Humphrey Bogart, as Matrac, a journalist whose opposition to the appeasers at the time of Munich resulted in his conviction on a trumped up charge of murder and treason and his banishment to Devil's Island, gives a forthright performance as one of the escaped convicts rescued by the freighter.

But the best job of all is done by Rains. Not only does he have the biggest part in the picture, but he captures practically all the acting honors in a film filled with good acting.

•

PASSENGER, THE

1975, 123 mins, US Ⓥ ⌑ col

Dir Michelangelo Antonioni ***Prod*** Carlo Ponti ***Scr*** Mark Peploe, Peter Wollen, Michelangelo Antonioni ***Ph*** Luciano Tovoli ***Ed*** Franco Arcali, Michelangelo Antonioni ***Art*** Piero Poletto

Act Jack Nicholson, Maria Schneider, Jenny Runacre, Ian Hendry (M-G-M)

Jack Nicholson plays a seasoned TV newsman, adjusted to established limits yet conscious of his inadequacy in probing through the grim truth. Death of a British adventurer in a small north African hotel becomes a last chance for the newsman to scrap his own anguished identity and take on the mission of the dead man.

His new probe becomes a showdown with the merciless revolutionary currents and countercurrents in today's world.

It is not quite clear what part of Nicholson is courageous involvement in third world liberation, what part is a reaction to the disinterested passion of youth for justice or the ironic attrition of feared exposure by his estranged wife in London.

Nicholson plays the character with personal flair, as penetrating as Antonioni's handling of the film.

•

PASSENGER 57

1993, 83 mins, US Ⓥ ⦿ col

Dir Kevin Hooks ***Prod*** Lee Rich, Dan Paulson, Dylan Sellers ***Scr*** David Loughery, Dan Gordon ***Ph*** Mark Irwin ***Ed*** Richard Nord ***Mus*** Stanley Clarke ***Art*** Jaymes Hinkle

Act Wesley Snipes, Bruce Payne, Tom Sizemore, Alex Datcher, Bruce Greenwood, Elizabeth Hurley (Warner)

Passenger 57 is a reasonably saucy action tale that runs out of gas before landing.

At least the filmmakers have the good sense to acknowledge the scenario's absurdity when an airline exec questions the logic, after the fact, of transporting a known hijacker (Bruce Payne) by air.

With his henchmen disguised as crew members, Payne seizes the jet, murdering the FBI agents and pilot. That leaves it to newly hired airline security expert Wesley Snipes (cutting his teeth as a big-time action hero) to try and stop them, however burdened by the inconvenient emotional baggage of having watched his wife's murder under similar circumstances.

Snipes seems to relish his opportunity to play this cross between John Shaft and *Die Hard*'s John McClane, but script [from Stewart Raffill and Dan Gordon's story] doesn't give him much room to operate. Payne's hissable villain contributes greatly to maintaining the film's intensity.

•

PASSION

1982, 87 mins, France/Switzerland Ⓥ col

Dir Jean-Luc Godard ***Prod*** Alain Sarde ***Scr*** Jean-Luc Godard ***Ph*** Raoul Coutard ***Ed*** Jean-Luc Godard

Act Hanna Schygulla, Michel Piccoli, Isabelle Huppert, Jerzy Radziwilowicz, Laszlo Szabo, Jean-Francois Stevenin (Sara/Sonimage/Films A2/Film & Video)

Passion is a return to Jean-Luc Godard's talky, quirky films where dialog often vied with commentary. As is usual, both are irritating, but good visual ideas abound if taken at face value.

He managed to get a batch of international names for small roles, like German star Hanna Schygulla playing a motel owner dawdling with men, much to Frenchman Michel Piccoli's annoyance. There is also the inevitable Isabelle Huppert and the Polish actor from Andrzej Wajda's *Man of Iron*, Jerzy Radziwilowicz.

There is a video film being made by the Pole which imitates great paintings and old myths. Everybody has trouble but Godard insists the plan should work as Huppert tries to get back to her job after being sacked.

Godard's visuals are fine as usual but whether it will grip new audiences is chancy. However, Godard does not care and goes his way.

•

PASSIONATE FRIENDS, THE
(US: ONE WOMAN'S STORY)

1949, 91 mins, UK b/w

Dir David Lean ***Prod*** Ronald Neame ***Scr*** Eric Ambler ***Ph*** Guy Green ***Ed*** Geoffrey Foot ***Mus*** Richard Addinsell ***Art*** John Bryan

Act Ann Todd, Claude Rains, Trevor Howard, Betty Ann Davies, Isabel Dean (Cineguild)

Polished acting, masterly direction and an excellent script put *The Passionate Friends* in the top rank of class British productions. Eric Ambler's screenplay takes many liberties with the original H. G. Wells novel [adapted by David Lean and Stanley Haymes], but he has built up a powerful dramatic situation on the triangle drama.

For the first half hour the story is related by means of a series of flashbacks, which inclines to some confusion, but it soon settles down to straightforward presentation with none of the dramatic effect being lost in the telling.

Ann Todd rises to new heights as the girl who forswears love for security and wealth. Hers is a flawless portrayal and ranks with the best seen in British pictures. Claude Rains, in the role of the banker husband, is a model of competence and Trevor Howard brings vigor and polish to the part of the lover.

•

PASSIONATE PLUMBER, THE
1932, 73 mins, US b/w
Dir Edward Sedgwick ***Scr*** Laurence E. Johnson, Ralph Spence
Act Buster Keaton, Jimmy Durante, Irene Purcell, Polly Moran, Gilbert Roland, Mona Maris (M-G-M)

Nonsensical slapstick story derived somehow from Frederick Lonsdale's *Her Cardboard Lover*. There is some comedy of merit in this flimsy scenario, stretched from a natural two-reel length to fill a full-length spool, and it isn't necessary to gaze beyond the cast to find the source. But the cast and the laughs are constantly obliged to fight the plot and motives; unfortunately the plot wins the battle, contrary to the picture's best interests.

Not until the plate-tossing finish does the story catch up with the playing in effectiveness. Up to then Jimmy Durante and Buster Keaton are compelled to carry the burden alone.

While Durante and Keaton are cross-firing for laughs the rest is momentarily laid aside, and when the chief laugh grabbers return to the theme, they don't mix.

Polly Moran hasn't much to do, which is the picture's biggest disappointment.

•

PASSION DE JEANNE D'ARC, LE
(US: THE PASSION OF JOAN OF ARC)
1928, 114 mins, France ⦿ ⊗ b/w
Dir Carl Dreyer ***Scr*** Carl Dreyer, Joseph Delteil ***Ph*** Rudolph Mate ***Art*** Hermann Warm, Jean Hugo
Act Maria Falconetti, Eugene Silvain, Antonin Artaud, Maurice Schutz, Andre Berly, Michel Simon (SGF)

Here is a deadly tiresome picture that merely makes an attempt to narrate without sound or dialog an allegedly written recorded 15th or 16th century trial of Joan of Arc for witchery, leading to her condemnation and burning at the stake.

One grows terribly weary of seeing her judges reappear, of the long series of captioned questions and answers, of Joan double-crossed, and of Joan doing a long-distance burning sequence, with the French mobs as inserts. Totally a cheaply economic film as a product.

There is some photographic value through the continuous allure of whole-screen closeups of faces only, mostly of the hard-visaged elderly men in cloistered costumes. They look like stone images brought to life.

In appearance, Joan is at all times immobile in countenance and always staring into the camera when she isn't washing tears off her face.

•

PASSION FISH
1992, 134 mins, US Ⓥ ⦿ col
Dir John Sayles ***Prod*** Sarah Green, Maggie Renzi ***Scr*** John Sayles ***Ph*** Roger Deakins ***Ed*** John Sayles ***Mus*** Mason Daring ***Art*** Dan Bishop, Diana Freas
Act Mary McDonnell, Alfre Woodard, David Strathairn, Vondie Curtis-Hall, Nora Dunn, Sheila Kelley (Atchafalaya)

John Sayles charts the long road back from physical and emotional debilitation in *Passion Fish*, a sympathetic if somewhat deliberate and over-long intimate study of two women emerging from their protective shells.

Mary McDonnell plays May-Alice, a TV soap star who becomes paralyzed from the waist down in an accident she suffers en route to getting her legs waxed in New York. Retreating to her childhood womb, she installs herself in the deserted family home in Louisiana's Cajun Country and nastily rejects a succession of nurses until Chantelle (Alfre Woodard) comes along.

Understandably bitter, May-Alice sinks into a daily grind of drinking and non-stop TV watching. Not for long willing to tolerate maid status, Chantelle soon throws out the booze and forces her employer to shape up. But Chantelle is fighting demons of her own.

Interludes between the two men (David Strathairn and Vondie Curtis-Hall) invigorate the picture and provide a way to introduce a welcome dose of local color. Other relief, comic and otherwise, comes in the form of visits from a couple of bird-brained former schoolmates of May-Alice, three soap actresses from Gotham and the show's producer.

Sayles edited this one solo, and might have profited by advice to keep this small-scaled drama under two hours. Title refers to some tiny fish that Strathairn's character finds in the belly of a large fish he catches.

1992: NOMINATIONS: Best Actress (Mary McDonnell), Original Screenplay

•

PASSION OF JOAN OF ARC, THE
SEE: LE PASSION DE JEANNE D'ARC

•

PASSOVER PLOT, THE
1976, 108 mins, US/Israel Ⓥ col
Dir Michael Campus ***Prod*** Wolf Schmidt ***Scr*** Millard Cohan, Patricia Knop ***Ph*** Adam Greenberg ***Ed*** Dov Hoenig ***Mus*** Alex North ***Art*** Kuli Sander
Act Harry Andrews, Hugh Griffith, Zalman King, Donald Pleasence, Scott Wilson, Dan Ades (Atlas/Golan-Globus)

A disappointing film based on Hugh J. Schonfield's tampering-with-orthodoxy revisionist 1960s book on the life of Jesus Christ, *The Passover Plot*. The physically handsome production drains the vitality out of the Christ story through verbiage and overacting.

Schonfield's retelling of the New Testament depicts Jesus (or "Yeshua," the Hebraic name used in the book and film) as a political revolutionary who contrives his own crucifixion as a plot against the Roman establishment.

Zalman King's Yeshua is an angry young man with little of the warmth and folk humor the character displays in the Bible texts. Far from seeming disrespectful, the film in fact errs on the side of excessive respect.

1976: NOMINATION: Best Costume Design

•

PASSPORT TO FAME
SEE: THE WHOLE TOWN'S TALKING

•

PASSPORT TO PIMLICO
1949, 84 mins, UK Ⓥ b/w
Dir Henry Cornelius ***Prod*** Michael Balcon ***Scr*** T.E.B. Clarke ***Ph*** Lionel Banes ***Ed*** Michael Truman ***Mus*** Georges Auric ***Art*** Roy Oxley
Act Stanley Holloway, Barbara Murray, Raymond Huntley, Paul Dupuis, Jane Hylton, Hermione Baddeley (Ealing)

Sustained, lightweight comedy scoring a continual succession of laughs. Story describes what happens when a wartime unexploded bomb in a London street goes off and reveals ancient documents and treasure which make the territory part of the duchy of Burgundy. Ration cards are joyfully torn up and customs barriers are put up by British.

The theme is related with a genuine sense of satire and clean, honest humor. The principal characters are in the hands of experienced players with Stanley Holloway leading the new government, Raymond Huntley the bank manager turned Chancellor of the Exchequer, Hermione Baddeley as the shopkeeper and Sydney Tafler as the local bookmaker.

1949: NOMINATION: Best Story & Screenplay

•

PASSWORD IS COURAGE, THE
1962, 116 mins, UK ⊏⊐ b/w
Dir Andrew L. Stone ***Prod*** Andrew L. Stone, Virginia Stone ***Scr*** Andrew L. Stone ***Ph*** Davis Boulton ***Ed*** Noreen Ackland, Virginia Stone
Act Dirk Bogarde, Maria Perschy, Alfred Lynch, Nigel Stock, Reginald Beckwith (M-G-M)

Andrew L. Stone's screenplay, based on a biog of Sergeant-Major Charles Coward by John Castle, has pumped into its untidy 116 minutes an overdose of slapstick humour. Result is that what could have been a telling tribute to a character of guts and initiative, the kind that every war produces, lacks conviction.

Coward (Dirk Bogarde), a breezy, likeable character, becomes a prisoner of war and is dedicated to sabotaging and humiliating his German captors. As senior soldier in Stalag 8B, he rallies the other men to escape so that they can get back to fighting the Nazis. Coward's main problem is to make contact with the Polish underground to get maps, money, etc., before escaping through a 280-foot tunnel, which the prisoners have laboriously built.

Bogarde gives a performance that is never less than competent, but never much more. The best male performance comes from Lynch, as Corporal Pope, a philosophical soldier devoted to Coward. He is a composite of several characters in Coward's actual story. Maria Perschy, a personable Hungarian girl making her first appearance in a British film, brings some glamor to the film as the underground worker.

•

PAT AND MIKE
1952, 94 mins, US Ⓥ ⦿ b/w
Dir George Cukor ***Prod*** Lawrence Weingarten ***Scr*** Ruth Gordon, Garson Kanin ***Ph*** William Daniels ***Ed*** George Boemler ***Mus*** David Raksin ***Art*** Cedric Gibbons, Urie McCleary
Act Spencer Tracy, Katharine Hepburn, Aldo Ray, William Ching, Sammy White, George Mathews (M-G-M)

The smooth-working team of Spencer Tracy and Katharine Hepburn spark the fun in *Pat and Mike*. Hepburn is quite believable as a femme athlete taken under the wing of promoter Tracy. Actress, as a college athletic instructor engaged to eager-beaver prof William Ching, enters an amateur golf tournament to prove to herself and to Ching that she is good. Deed attracts the attention of Tracy, who quick-talks her into signing a pro contract for a number of sports.

Film settles down to a series of laugh sequences of training, exhibitions and cross-country tours in which Hepburn proves to be a star.

Tracy is given some choice lines in the script and makes much of them in an easy, throwaway style that lifts the comedy punch.

1952: NOMINATION: Best Story & Screenplay

•

PATCH OF BLUE, A
1965, 105 mins, US Ⓥ ⦿ ⊏⊐ b/w
Dir Guy Green ***Prod*** Pandro S. Berman ***Scr*** Guy Green ***Ph*** Robert Burks ***Ed*** Rita Roland ***Mus*** Jerry Goldsmith ***Art*** George W. Davis, Urie McCleary
Act Sidney Poitier, Shelley Winters, Elizabeth Hartman, Wallace Ford, Ivan Dixon, Elisabeth Fraser (M-G-M/Berman)

A Patch of Blue is a touching contemporary melodrama, relieved at times by generally effective humor, about a blind white girl, rehabilitated from a dreary home by a Negro. Film has very good scripting plus excellent direction and performances, including an exceptional screen debut by Elizabeth Hartman as the gal.

Director Guy Green adapted Elizabeth Kata's *Be Ready with Bells and Drums*, and the ending, while positive, isn't sudsy. Hartman gives a smash interpretation to the role, and progresses most believably from an uneducated, unwanted and home-anchored maiden, to an upbeat, firmer grasp on what is to be her sightless maturity.

Sidney Poitier is excellent as he becomes her first true friend and gives her some self-assurance. She, of course, doesn't know he is Negro. The domestic situation is grim, with Shelley Winters very good as Hartman's sleazy mother. Vet character actor Wallace Ford, Winters's dad, effectively blends personal frustration, shame and disappointment in his own daughter and pity for Hartman in limited footage.

1965: Best Supp. Actress (Shelley Winters)

NOMINATIONS: Best Actress (Elizabeth Hartman), B&W Cinematography, B&W Art Direction, Original Music Score

•

PATERNITY
1981, 94 mins, US Ⓥ ⦿ col
Dir David Steinberg ***Prod*** Lawrence Gordon, Hank Moonjean ***Scr*** Charlie Peters ***Ph*** Bobbie Byrne ***Ed*** Donn Cambern ***Mus*** David Shire ***Art*** Jack Collis
Act Burt Reynolds, Beverly D'Angelo, Paul Dooley, Elizabeth Ashley, Lauren Hutton (Paramount)

There are several funny bits in *Paternity*, a harmless enough romantic comedy that strangely has its strongest laughs in its least important scenes. But the basic story of a successful 44-year-old man who decides to fulfill his desire for fatherhood by pacting with a woman to have his child never comes across with much punch.

The idea behind the film is a charming one and Reynolds manages to evoke the sensitivity needed to make his character's desires seem believable. Charlie Peters's script comes through in odd moments, usually in the form of witty visual asides superfluous to the primary action.

Much of the latter is also due to the hand of first time director David Steinberg, whose style clearly owes to his wonderfully snide point of view as a successful stand-up comic.

While Reynolds and D'Angelo make a nice enough onscreen couple, they just don't provide the sparks needed to light up a romantic comedy.

•

PAT GARRETT & BILLY THE KID

1973, 106 mins, US Ⓥ ⦿ ▭ col

Dir Sam Peckinpah ***Prod*** Gordon Carroll ***Scr*** Rudy Wurlitzer ***Ph*** John Coquillon ***Ed*** Roger Spottiswoode, Garth Craven, Robert L. Wolfe, Richard Halsey, David Berlatsky, Tony de Zarraga ***Mus*** Bob Dylan ***Art*** Ted Haworth

Act James Coburn, Kris Kristofferson, Bob Dylan, Richard Jaeckel, Katy Jurado, Jason Robards (M-G-M)

"It feels like times have changed," mutters James Coburn as gunman-turned-sheriff Pat Garrett, now hot on the trail of erstwhile buddy, Billy the Kid (Kris Kristofferson).

Coburn offers more of his smiles as testimony to the wizardry of Old West dentistry, while Kristofferson ambles through his role with solid charm. Neither conveys the psychological tension felt between the two men whose lives diverge after years of camaraderie.

Bob Dylan makes his dramatic film debut in a part so peripheral (or so abridged by six film editors) as to make his appearance a trivial cameo. His acting is limited to an embarrassing assortment of tics, smirks, shrugs, winks and smiles.

The editing, faulted by the director, conceals the reported postproduction tinkering but also reduces such players as Jason Robards, Richard Jaeckel and Katy Jurado to walk-on status. [Peckinpah's original 122-min. cut was finally released in 1989.]

•

PATHER PANCHALI

1955, 112 mins, India Ⓥ ⦿ b/w

Dir Satyajit Ray ***Scr*** Satyajit Ray ***Ph*** Subrata Mitra ***Ed*** Dulal Dutt ***Mus*** Ravi Shankar ***Art*** Bansi Chandragupta

Act Kanu Bannerjee, Karuna Bannerjee, Subir Bannerjee, Uma Das Gupta (State of West Bengal)

Film justly won the "most human document award" at the 1956 Cannes Film Fest, unveiling a mature film talent in director Satyajit Ray.

Film [from the novel by Bibhuti Bannerjee, *Little Song of the Road*] poetically and lyrically unfolds a tender but penetrating tale of coming of age in India, a land of poverty but also of spiritual hope. Two adolescents, a boy and his sister, grow in this atmosphere. The film fuses all aspects of pic-making into a moving whole that shows India perceptively for the first time to a Western audience.

The treatment of old age is one of the most profound ever seen on the screen. An old woman lives and dies among the budding children with a dignity and beauty that counterpoints the growth and experiences of the children. Acting, lensing and all other aspects are masterfully orchestrated by Ray into a document on life in India.

[Pic's world preem was at New York's Museum of Modern Art in 1955. Its Calcutta premiere was in early 1956.]

•

PATHS OF GLORY

1957, 87 mins, US Ⓥ ⦿ b/w

Dir Stanley Kubrick ***Prod*** James B. Harris ***Scr*** Stanley Kubrick, Calder Willingham, Jim Thompson ***Ph*** George Krause ***Ed*** Eva Kroll ***Mus*** Gerald Fried ***Art*** Ludwig Reiber

Act Kirk Douglas, Ralph Meeker, Adolphe Menjou, George Macready, Wayne Morris, Richard Anderson (Bryna/Harris-Kubrick/United Artists)

Paths of Glory [based on the novel by Humphrey Cobb] is a starkly realistic recital of French army politics in 1916 during World War I. While the subject is well-handled and enacted in a series of outstanding characterizations, it seems dated and makes for grim screen fare.

Story nub revolves around decision of the General Staff for a military unit commanded by George Macready, a general of the old school, to take an objective held for two years by the Germans. Knowing full well the impossibility of such an assault because of lack of manpower and impregnability of the position, the general nevertheless orders Kirk Douglas, colonel in command of the regiment, to make the suicidal attempt.

When his men either are driven back by enemy fire or are unable to leave the trenches, an unjust charge of cowardice against the men is lodged by the general and Douglas is ordered to arrange for three men to be selected to stand court-martial, as an object lesson to the whole army.

Stanley Kubrick in his taut direction catches the spirit of war with fine realism, and the futile advance of the French is exciting. He draws excellent performances, too, right down the line. Douglas scores heavily in his realization that his is a losing battle against the system, and Macready as the relentless general instilled with the belief that an order is an order, even if it means the death of thousands, socks over what may be regarded his most effective role to date.

•

PATRICK

1978, 110 mins, Australia Ⓥ col

Dir Richard Franklin ***Prod*** Antony I. Ginnane, Richard Franklin ***Scr*** Everett de Roche ***Ph*** Don McAlpine ***Ed*** Edward Queen-Mason ***Mus*** Brian May ***Art*** Leslie Binns

Act Susan Penhaligon, Robert Helpmann, Rod Mullinar, Bruce Barry, Julia Blake, Helen Heminway (Australian International)

Psychokinesis is a subject that can usually be relied upon to create some spectacular effects on screen, and as a result, occasionally the story and characters become subordinated. Not so with *Patrick*, which is more a study in character reactions.

The denominative Patrick is introduced as a matricide who, after having done away with mom and her lover, is next seen in the intensive care section in a state of chronic, advanced—and, we're told—irreversible catatonic reaction: "160 pounds of limp meat hanging off a comatosed brain," says Dr. Roget (Robert Helpmann).

Kathy Jacquard (Susan Penhaligon) is a recently estranged wife who returns to nursing to support herself. At Roget's clinic, as the newest member of the staff, she's given Patrick to watch over.

The patient falls in love with his nurse, which would be okay if he only had tonsillitis and was normal: Patrick is polyplegic and homicidal and possessed of this really terrific sixth sense which he uses spitefully. The inert (and uncredited) lead, with help from Richard Franklin's shrewd direction, creates an incredible menace while the thesps surrounding him go through their action.

•

PATRICK THE GREAT

1945, 86 mins, US Ⓥ col

Dir Frank Ryan ***Prod*** Howard Benedict ***Scr*** Bertram Millhauser, Dorothy Bennett ***Ph*** Frank Redman ***Ed*** Ted J. Kent ***Mus*** Hans J. Salter ***Art*** John B. Goodman, Abraham Grossman

Act Donald O'Connor, Peggy Ryan, Frances Dee, Donald Cook, Eve Arden (Universal)

Donald O'Connor and Peggy Ryan as a song-and-dance team with romantic ups and downs help mightily to make *Patrick the Great* [from a story by Jane Hall, Frederick Block and Ralph Block] a diverting musical. It's not the tops in entertainment but has several listenable songs and a pleasing little story.

The story is built around Donald Cook, a musical comedy star, and young O'Connor as his stagestruck son, plus Ryan who, in addition to having theatrical ambitions, is also plenty sweet on O'Connor. Virtually all of the action takes place at a mountain lodge where O'Connor mistakenly thinks Frances Dee, an authoress, has fallen in love with him.

The cast supporting O'Connor and Ryan fit well into the pattern of the story with both Dee and Cook giving well-turned performances.

•

PATRIOT, THE

1928, 108 mins, US b/w

Dir Ernst Lubitsch ***Scr*** Hans Kraley, Julian Johnson ***Ph*** Bert Glennon ***Mus*** Domenico Savino, Gerard Carbonara ***Art*** Hans Dreier

Act Emil Jannings, Lewis Stone, Florence Vidor, Neil Hamilton, Harry Cording, Vera Voronina (Paramount)

Many elements combine to give *The Patriot* a valid claim to greatness. The magnificent performance of Emil Jannings as the mad Czar Paul alone. Besides Jannings the production has a whole array of assets. Story value is excellent, cast is almost flawless and the physical production is rich in beauty and fine graphic background.

Time is the late 18th century, and locale the richly picturesque atmosphere of the Russian court under Czar Paul, the insane emperor of all the Russias, idiot-monster of Nero-like proportions. Surrounded by murderous plots, the only creature the madman trusts is his minister of war, Count Pahlen (Lewis Stone).

The role of Pahlen is really the star part, and it is only Jannings's genius that holds up the character of the Czar. Stone gives a balanced and polished performance. Pahlen is pictured as a suave man of the world rather than the paragon of virtue as legendary heroes are usually presented. Character comes on the screen without heroics.

Pictorially the production is full of magnificent bits. One of the sets is the vast palace courtyard and long shots of soldiers moving through its intricate vistas, columns of foot soldiers with galloping horsemen weaving around dim corners and streaking across the snow-covered spaces, are stunning effects.

Sound effects are managed inconspicuously. There is no dialog.

1928/29: Best Writing

NOMINATIONS: Best Picture, Director, Actor (Lewis Stone), Art Direction

•

PATRIOT, THE

2000, 164 mins, US Ⓥ ⦿ ▭ col

Dir Roland Emmerich ***Prod*** Dean Devlin, Mark Gordon, Gary Levinsohn ***Scr*** Robert Rodat ***Ph*** Cabel Deschanel ***Ed*** David Brenner ***Mus*** John Williams ***Art*** Kirk M. Petruccelli

Act Mel Gibson, Heath Ledger, Joely Richardson, Jason Isaacs, Chris Cooper, Tcheky Karyo, Tom Wilkinson (Mutual/Centropolis/Columbia)

Corny and melodramatic as it is, *The Patriot* still manages to do something few films have done—to tell a story of the American Revolutionary War that has some emotional pull and isn't stuffy and dull. German helmer Roland Emmerich's take on the struggle to form the first true democracy since the ancient Greeks is told in broad strokes and at considerable length. But, with one exception, it wisely focuses upon common folk rather than prominent figures, and makes a sincere effort to address some of the complex currents and vexing issues that faced the men who decided to take up arms against the British.

Ambitious screenplay by Robert Rodat unmistakably brands itself as a product of its era with its very Baby Boomerish fetishism about family; children and the family unit were certainly sacrosanct in the old Hollywood, but in historical films of no previous period did characters fuss as sentimentally about the well-being of young 'uns as they're doing now.

Mel Gibson forcefully socks over the two prime components of his role, the deeply caring dad who would just like to watch his children grow up in peace, and the vengeful, crafty warrior capable of great brutality. Aussie thesp Heath Ledger makes an entirely believable son for such a father, cutting a dashing figure with style and seriousness. Jason Isaacs stakes a claim as a legitimate heir to the Alan Rickman/Jeremy Irons tradition of ruthless British villains, while Tom Wilkinson adroitly creates a satisfyingly complex portrait of the tragically deluded aristocrat Cornwallis.

•

PATRIOT GAMES

1992, 116 mins, US Ⓥ ⦿ ▭ col

Dir Phillip Noyce ***Prod*** Mace Neufeld, Robert Rehme ***Scr*** W. Peter Iliff, Donald Stewart ***Ph*** Donald M. McAlpine, Stephen Smith, James Devis ***Ed*** Neil Travis, William Hoy ***Mus*** James Horner ***Art*** Joseph Nemec III

Act Harrison Ford, Anne Archer, Patrick Bergin, Sean Bean, Thora Birch, James Fox (Paramount)

Mindless, morally repugnant and ineptly directed to boot, *Patriot Games* is a shoddy follow-up to Par's 1990 hit *The Hunt for Red October*. Also based on a bestselling Tom Clancy novel about intrepid CIA analyst Jack Ryan, the ultra-violent, fascistic, blatantly anti-Irish film stars a dour Harrison Ford.

Ford's Ryan, at the onset, has left the CIA to teach naval history at Annapolis. A visit to London with his family places him in the middle of an attack on a high British official (James Fox) by what Ford later identifies as "some ultra-violent faction of the IRA." His rescue of Fox and killing of one attacker makes him the quarry of a revengeful, ice-blooded IRA man (Sean Bean).

The case is sentimentally loaded by painting the IRA faction as monsters who don't hesitate to attack Ford's wife (Anne Archer) and daughter (Thora Birch) as part of Bean's vendetta.

Director Phillip Noyce is way out of his depth here, relying on tight close-ups that eliminate visual and social context and incoherently handling action sequences in the would-be spectacular climax.

•

PATSY, THE

1928, 64 mins, US ⊗ b/w

Dir King Vidor ***Scr*** Ralph Spence ***Ph*** John F. Seitz

Act Marion Davies, Orville Caldwell, Marie Dressler, Del Henderson, Lawrence Gray, Jane Winton (M-G-M)

Barry Conners's stage play has been converted with liberal license into a dandy laugh picture. Marion Davies does some really great comedy work. Many of the laughs come from the subtitles, with about half taken verbatim or with slight changes from the play. Ralph Spence gets sole credit for the title job, but should split credit with Conners.

The picture follows loosely the general story of *The Patsy*, that of a younger sister who is imposed upon by an older sister and her mother, who favors the butterfly daughter. Pop takes sides with The Patsy, being somewhat of a patsy himself.

Efforts of the younger girl to attract the attention of the man who is courting her sister forms the basis of the comedy and plot. Toward the end, with a generous employment of screen liberty, Davies does a series of imitations of Pola Negri, Mae Murray and Lillian Gish. The imitations are great and reveal Davies as a skillful comic.

•

PATSY, THE

1964, 100 mins, US Ⓥ ⦿ col

Dir Jerry Lewis ***Prod*** Ernest D. Glucksman ***Scr*** Jerry Lewis, Bill Richmond ***Ph*** Wallace Kelley ***Ed*** John Woodcock ***Mus*** David Raksin ***Art*** Hal Pereira, Cary Odell

Act Jerry Lewis, Ina Balin, Everett Sloane, Phil Harris, Keenan Wynn, Peter Lorre (Paramount)

The Patsy's slim story line has its ups and downs, sometimes being hilarious, frequently unfunny.

Premise of a group of film professionals—a producer, director, writer-gagman, press agent and secretary—who have lost their star in a plane disaster and find another meal ticket by grabbing a hotel bellboy and building him to stardom, is an okay device for situations but lacks development—which might have made a better comedy.

Jerry Lewis also directs in the part, and as the patsy of this pack of hangers-on he indulges in his usual mugging and clowning, good for guffaws and enough nonsensical anticking to appeal to juve audiences especially.

Lewis as the simple-minded Stanley, "discovered" as he is delivering ice to the forlorn group wondering how to salvage their own positions, socks over his customary brand of broad and nutty humor and gets good backing right down the line. Everett Sloane as the producer, Peter Lorre the director, Phil Harris the gagman, Keenan Wynn the p.a., and Ina Balin the secretary, deliver soundly.

Hedda Hopper plays herself in a nice scene, and others playing themselves in cameo roles are Ed Wynn, Rhonda Fleming, George Raft, Mel Tormé.

•

PATTI ROCKS

1987, 87 mins, US Ⓥ col

Dir David Burton Morris ***Prod*** Gwen Field, Gregory M. Cummins ***Scr*** David Burton Morris, Chris Mulkey, John Jenkins, Karen Landry ***Ph*** Gregory M. Cummins ***Ed*** Gregory M. Cummins ***Mus*** Doug Maynard ***Art*** Charlotte Whitaker

Act Chris Mulkey, John Jenkins, Karen Landry (Film Dallas)

An often bitingly humorous expose of the male ego accomplished dramatically in one night, *Patti Rocks* is a quintessential American independent production, and a very good one.

Film opens with the phrase "Twelve years later . . . ," a cute reference to David Burton Morris's first feature, *Loose Ends*, which involved the same leading characters but is in no way mandatory viewing for appreciating the follow-up.

Patti Rocks picks up Billy (Chris Mulkey), a working stiff who seems to be refusing to grow up even though he's into his thirties with a wife and two kids. During the cold Christmas season in Minnesota, Billy shanghais his old buddy Eddie (John Jenkins), a garage foreman, to drive with him to a distant town to help him tell a woman he's "knocked up" that he's hitched and that she ought to have an abortion.

Eddie ends up sitting in the passenger seat for hours as Billy delivers a torrential monolog of ever-escalating sexual boasts and fantasies. The tone changes dramatically, however, once the boys reach the home of Patti Rocks. Too chicken-hearted to break the news to her himself, Billy sends Eddie into her bedroom to do the job, and that's when the twists are added.

Made on a frugal $350,000 budget, film is totally dialog and performance oriented, and stands up well on both counts. Unknown thesps are not charismatic, but are vividly believable as regular folk who are both evasive and brutally frank about sex and life.

•

PATTON

1970, 170 mins, US Ⓥ ⦿ ▭ col

Dir Franklin J. Schaffner ***Prod*** Frank McCarthy ***Scr*** Francis Coppola, Edmund H. North ***Ph*** Fred Koenekamp ***Ed*** Hugh S. Fowler ***Mus*** Jerry Goldsmith ***Art*** Urie McCleary, Gil Parrondo

Act George C. Scott, Karl Malden, Michael Bates, Karl Michael Vogler, Edward Binns, Lawrence Dobkin (20th Century-Fox)

War is hell, and *Patton* is one hell of a war picture.

George C. Scott's title-role performance is outstanding and the excellent direction of Franklin J. Schaffner lends realism, authenticity, and sensitivity without ever being visually offensive, excessive or overdone in any area. *Patton* is an amazingly brilliant depiction of men in war, revealing all facets of their character. [Script is based on factual material from *Patton: Ordeal and Triumph* by Ladislas Farago and *A Soldier's Story* by Omar N. Bradley.]

Film begins in North Africa, just before Gen. George S. Patton, Jr. takes over command in 1943 of an American component of an Anglo-American unit, decimated by German attack. It ends after the surrender of Germany, and Patton's relief from an occupation command because of embarrassing statements contrary to civilian and Allied policy.

1970: Best Picture, Director, Actor (George C. Scott, declined award), Original Story & Screenplay, Art Direction, Sound, Editing

NOMINATIONS: Best Cinematography, Original Score, Visual Effects

•

PATTY HEARST

1988, 108 mins, US Ⓥ ⦿ col

Dir Paul Schrader ***Prod*** Marvin Worth ***Scr*** Nicholas Kazan ***Ph*** Bojan Bazelli ***Ed*** Michael R. Miller ***Mus*** Scott Johnson ***Art*** Jane Musky

Act Natasha Richardson, William Forsythe, Ving Rhames, Frances Fisher, Jodi Long (Atlantic/Zenith)

Patty Hearst puts forth much less than its pretensions. Frequently wrapped in surrealistic stylization, film manages only to tell Hearst's side of her kidnapping ordeal.

Paralleling Hearst's book *Every Secret Thing*, on which Nicholas Kazan based the script, story quickly recounts Hearst's early life and picks up cinematically with her kidnapping.

Stuffed into a closet and blindfolded for nearly 50 days, Hearst is subjected to verbal abuse by the deranged band of self-styled revolutionaries that called themselves the Symbionese Liberation Army. By the time Hearst is offered her freedom or membership in the SLA, one is bound to accept that the latter was chosen at least as much for survival as for any other motive.

In portraying Hearst, Natasha Richardson—daughter of Vanessa Redgrave and director Tony Richardson—is quite effective. She manages to convey all the sympathy clearly intended.

•

PAWNBROKER, THE

1965, 112 mins, US Ⓥ ⦿ b/w

Dir Sidney Lumet ***Prod*** Roger H. Lewis, Philip Langner ***Scr*** Morton Fine, David Friedkin ***Ph*** Boris Kaufman ***Ed*** Ralph Rosenblum ***Mus*** Quincy Jones ***Art*** Richard Sylbert

Act Rod Steiger, Geraldine Fitzgerald, Brock Peters, Thelma Oliver, Jaime Sanchez, Marketta Kimbrell (Landau/Allied Artists)

The Pawnbroker [based on the novel by Edward Lewis Wallant] is a painstakingly etched portrait of a man who survived the living hell of a Nazi concentration camp and encounters further prejudice when he runs a pawnshop in Harlem.

Rod Steiger plays the embittered pawnbroker, and his personal credo is a reflection of his past experiences. He has lost his faith in God, the arts and sciences, he has no discriminatory feelings against white or colored man, but regards them all as human scum. Such is the character of the man whose pawnshop is actually a front for a Negro racketeer, whose main income comes from the slums and brothels.

There is little plot in the regular sense, but a series of episodes spanning just a few days of the present, which recall many harrowing experiences of the past. Some are absorbing, but others seem to lack the dramatic punch for which the director must have strived.

By the very nature of the subject, the pic is dominated by Steiger, and indeed virtually must stand or fall by his performance. He knows most of the tricks of the trade, and puts them to good use.

Although appearing only in three scenes, Geraldine Fitzgerald makes a deep impression as a welfare worker who almost succeeds in getting through to him, but at the last moment he refuses to weaken.

1965: NOMINATION: Best Actor (Rod Steiger)

•

PAYBACK

1999, 110 mins, US Ⓥ ⦿ ▭ col

Dir Brian Helgeland ***Prod*** Bruce Davey ***Scr*** Brian Helgeland, Terry Hayes ***Ph*** Ericson Core ***Ed*** Kevin Stitt ***Mus*** Chris Boardman ***Art*** Chris Boardman

Act Mel Gibson, Gregg Henry, Maria Bello, Deborah Kara Unger, David Paymer, Bill Duke (Icon/Paramount)

Structured more like an action thriller than the moody noir of its source material [Richard Stark's novel *The Hunter*], *Payback* is not an embarrassment, but it's not distinguished either. Tailored to Mel Gibson's screen qualities, pic is such a loose reworking of John Boorman's dazzling 1967 noir, *Point Blank*, that it hardly qualifies as a remake.

In the new yarn, which is moved from Alcatraz and a diffuse, alienating Los Angeles to Chicago's urban jungle, Porter (Gibson in the Lee Marvin role) and partner Val (Gregg Henry) engage in a heist that goes smoothly enough. But Val steals Porter's share and his druggie wife, Lynn (Deborah Kara Unger), and shoots Porter.

Porter is reborn with one obsessive motivation: retribution. His efforts take him into the city's underworld, dominated by a secretive syndicate called the Outfit. Scripters present Porter as a brutally murderous thief who'll do anything to get his money back, but also a man with an inner code of honor—a gunslinger in the Old West tradition.

Pandering to Gibson's fans, the film vacillates between the dark and sinister and the comic and whimsical, with funny one-liners that change the morbid, metaphysical tone of the story. Reflecting the zeitgeist, *Payback* is more graphically violent than *Point Blank*: Some of the torture scenes approach the level of *Reservoir Dogs*. Yarn also expands role of Rosie, Porter's former flame (Angie Dickinson in Boorman's pie, and decently acted here by *ER*'s Maria Bello).

Holding the episodic, occasionally disjointed picture on his shoulders, Gibson renders a decent performance, nothing more.

•

PAY IT FORWARD

2000, 122 mins, US Ⓥ ⦿ col

Dir Mimi Leder ***Prod*** Steven Reuther, Peter Abrams, Robert Levy ***Scr*** Leslie Dixon ***Ph*** Oliver Stapleton ***Ed*** David Rosenbloom ***Mus*** Thomas Newman ***Art*** Leslie Dilley

Act Kevin Spacey, Helen Hunt, Haley Joel Osment, Jay Mohr, James Caviezel, Jon Bon Jovi, Angie Dickinson (Tapestry/Warner)

An inherently inspirational, issue-driven drama centered on three emotionally battered people who challenge their personal limitations and in the process develop the possibility of changing society itself, *Pay It Forward* is an unusual film [from the novel by Catherine Ryan Hyde] that intelligently avoids numerous potential pitfalls even if its central earnestness is ultimately inescapable.

Capturing the attention of young Trevor McKinney (Haley Joel Osment) and the class as a whole on the first day of seventh grade, social studies teacher Eugene Simonet (Kevin Spacey) delivers a bracing argument on behalf of knowing something about the world in order to be able to cope with it once they're out on their own, then ups the ante with an extra-credit, yearlong assignment: "Think of an idea to change our world—and put it into action."

A latchkey kid whose father has taken off and whose mother works two jobs, Trevor first has the idealistic notion of giving shelter to a homeless drug addict, Jerry (James Caviezel). This doesn't go down too well with his mom, Arlene (Helen Hunt), an alcoholic barmaid.

Eugene's problems are both more apparent and concealed. A fastidious, bespectacled fellow, he has serious scars over most of his face. It becomes increasingly clear that this is a man whose orderly manner and professional confidence cork a barrelful of hurt and anguish.

Trevor remains dedicated to his idea that people should "pay it forward"—rather than "paying back" for favors already done. Working things out mathematically, Trevor figures that if one person were to help three people, and those three each helped three people and so on, the snowball effect would soon be felt. On a purely selfish level, Trevor is motivated to find a father, and makes humorously transparent efforts to push Eugene and his mother together.

Unbenownst to any of them, the idea of "pay it forward" has begun seeping into the outside world. Startling conclusion is upsetting but feels apt in its muted echo of the origins of Christianity, with a motley band of disciples being the ones to spread the Word to a world that may or may not be ready to hear it.

Spacey creates another indelible characterization. Willing to look like a fright with horrible bleached hair and generally classless getup, Hunt is on firm ground in a role that inevitably recalls her single mom in *As Good as It Gets*. And Osment truly is as good as it gets where kid thesps are concerned; endearing but never cloying, he brings the requisite brightness, determination, hurt and optimism to a multifaceted role.

•

PAYMENT ON DEMAND
1951, 90 mins, US b/w
Dir Curtis Bernhardt ***Prod*** Jack H. Skirball, Bruce Manning ***Scr*** Bruce Manning, Curtis Bernhardt ***Ph*** Leo Tover ***Ed*** Harry Marker ***Mus*** Victor Young ***Art*** Albert S. D'Agostino, Carroll Clark
Act Bette Davis, Barry Sullivan, Jane Cowl, Kent Taylor, Betty Lynn, Frances Dee (Skirball-Manning/RKO)

In exploring the topical subject of husband and wife, parents of two grown daughters, who find themselves on the marital rocks, *Payment on Demand* makes a point of avoiding the pitfalls of soap opera fiction in which emotional and physical crises are developed in rapid succession. Bette Davis is in top form. Her interpretation of the overly ambitious wife, whose unscrupulousness leads to the marital collapse, has great believability. Part of the husband, who stuns Davis with the announcement he wants a divorce, is the sympathetic role, and Barry Sullivan handles it neatly and with a quiet dignity.

Adding color and flavor to the drama is the appearance of Jane Cowl, as the aging, pathetic divorcee struggling for happiness in a Port-au-Prince villa in company of a young artist protege.

•

PCU
1994, 79 mins, US Ⓥ ⦿ col
Dir Hart Bochner ***Prod*** Paul Schiff ***Scr*** Adam Leff, Zak Penn ***Ph*** Reynaldo Villalobos ***Ed*** Nicholas C. Smith ***Mus*** Steve Vai ***Art*** Steven Jordan
Act Jeremy Piven, Chris Young, Jon Favreau, David Spade, Sarah Trigger, Jessica Walter (20th Century-Fox)

Screenwriters Adam Leff and Zak Penn, who garnered some notoriety in 1993 for providing the story for *Last Action Hero*, have concocted a rowdy new comedy, *PCU*, that's a boisterous if not uproariously funny look at political correctness as it afflicts college campuses.

Leff and Penn have set their yarn at the fictional Port Chester University, no doubt standing in for Wesleyan, their alma mater. It's a campus divided into so many protest groups that students have no time to attend classes. At the center is a coed gang whose anarchic leader, Droz (Jeremy Piven), encourages any form of offensive and bizarre behavior. Into this chaos arrives Tom (Chris Young), a handsome pre-freshman unprepared for life on the treacherous campus, which is torn apart by Rand (David Spade), a spoiled brat who leads the wealthy Republican fraternity; the Womynists, headed by a humorless feminist; and other militant clubs.

PCU tries to capture the comic energy and surreal fun that pix like *House Party* and *National Lampoon's Animal House* had. But despite some memorable vignettes, most of the jokes are rather mild. In his feature directorial debut, actor Hart Bochner shows some visual flair and a sense of tempo.

•

PEACEMAKER
1990, 90 mins, US Ⓥ ⦿ col
Dir Kevin S. Tenney ***Prod*** Andrew Lane, Wayne Crawford ***Scr*** Kevin S. Tenney ***Ph*** Thomas Jewitt ***Ed*** Dan Duncin ***Mus*** Dennis Michael Tenney ***Art*** Rob Sissman
Act Robert Forster, Lance Edwards, Hilary Shephard, Robert Davi, Bert Remsen (Gibraltar/Mentone)

Peacemaker is an unexpected gem, a sci-fi action thriller that really delivers the goods despite an apparent low budget.

Inventive plot is a tale of two humanoid aliens (Robert Forster and Lance Edwards) who crash-land on Earth. One is an intergalactic serial killer, the other a police officer, or peacemaker. A simple set-up, except for one complication: both claim to be the cop.

Both aliens attempt to enlist the aid of assistant medical examiner Hilary Shepard, hoping she can help them find the key to the one functional space rover that survived their crash landing.

Peacemaker is a stunt extravaganza, a nonstop, fast-paced assemblage of chases, shootouts and explosions building to an impressive climax. Pic has a big-budget look throughout.

•

PEACEMAKER, THE
1997, 123 mins, US Ⓥ ⦿ ▭ col
Dir Mimi Leder ***Prod*** Walter Parkes, Branko Lustig ***Scr*** Michael Schiffer ***Ph*** Dietrich Lohmann ***Ed*** David Rosenbloom ***Mus*** Hans Zimmer ***Art*** Leslie Dilley
Act George Clooney, Nicole Kidman, Marcel Iures, Alexander Baluev, Rene Medvesek, Gary Werntz (DreamWorks)

This long-anticipated first release from DreamWorks Pictures is an uncommonly dour and even grim action thriller that globetrots as diversely as a James Bond film but offers a very limited view politically, emotionally and dramatically. George Clooney and Nicole Kidman aren't quite lustrous enough to get this lavish entry across on star power alone.

A member of the Bosnian parliament is assassinated and nine nuclear weapons stolen from a train. Western intelligence naturally takes a quick interest in the incident, and thrust together to piece things out are scientist Dr. Julia Kelly (Kidman) and U.S. Army Special Forces Lt. Col. Thomas Devoe (Clooney).

Their first stop is Vienna, where Kelly witnesses the cutthroat brutality with which the old spy game can be played. Film's third major action sequence is when Devoe stops a truck bearing the world's most dangerous, illicit merchandise headed for the Iranian border. Unfortunately, one of the stolen bombs has already disappeared, which send the heroes to New York City.

The finale, which looks as though it must have shut down half of Manhattan's East Side to shoot, is reasonably impressive but ends with a hackneyed race with time to save at least part of the civilized world from a nuclear holocaust.

Based on [an article] by investigate political journalists Andrew and Leslie Cockburn, script alternates between information conveyance and shouted commands. Clooney and Kidman are mainly asked to keep moving.

•

PEAU DOUCE, LA
(SOFT SKIN; SILKEN SKIN)
1964, 118 mins, France Ⓥ ⦿ b/w
Dir Francois Truffaut ***Scr*** Francois Truffaut, Jean-Louis Richard ***Ph*** Raoul Coutard ***Ed*** Claudine Bouche ***Mus*** Georges Delerue
Act Jean Desailly, Francoise Dorleac, Nelly Benedetti, Daniel Ceccaldi, Jean Lanier, Paule Emanuele (Films du Carrosse/SEDIF)

Heretofore full of free-wheeling inventiveness, Francois Truffaut now goes in for a clean, uncluttered study of a man's first extra-marital affair in 12 years that leads to tragedy.

Film details the matter-of-fact home life of a semi-successful highbrow magazine editor and lecturer who one day becomes enamored of an airline hostess. He manages to get a date with her and love comes quickly, and is carried on when they get back to Paris. The wife senses something wrong and catches him in a lie.

One of the flaws in the pic is that the three rather colorless people suddenly do unusual things without any sort of preparation. The film's almost classic treatment makes them jolting rather than dramatically right.

But Truffaut does show that he can make a solidly carpentered film like anybody else. There are some irrepressibly witty scenes. Direction is sharp and lensing has the clear gradations and compositions to fit this prosaic pic. Francoise Dorleac has the feckless quality for the girl, while Jean Desailly has the reserve and phlegmatic qualities of a supposedly set man who succumbs to the flesh. Nelly Benedetti is more unlclear as the seemingly settled housewife.

•

PEEPER
1975, 87 mins, US ▭ col
Dir Peter Hyams ***Prod*** Irwin Winkler, Robert Chartoff ***Scr*** W. D. Richter ***Ph*** Earl Rath ***Ed*** James Mitchell ***Mus*** Richard Clements ***Art*** Albert Brenner
Act Michael Caine, Natalie Wood, Kitty Winn, Thayer David, Liam Dunn, Dorothy Adams (20th Century-Fox)

Peeper is flimsy whimsy. In the can for a year after being made under the title *Fat Chance*, director Peter Hyams's limp spoof of a 1940s private-eye film stars Michael Caine as a fumbling gumshoe and Natalie Wood as a member of a mysterious wealthy family. Even in the cutdown 87-minute release version, the extremely handsome production shows far more care in physical details than artistic ones.

Keith Laumer's novel *Deadfall* (not to be confused with a 1968 Bryan Forbes film of that name, coincidentally starring Caine) was altered in tone and time by scripter W. D. Richter. Mimic artist Guy Marks opens the film by a Humphrey Bogart reading of the main credits over footage of a mysterious figure in an alley.

Story gets underway with Michael Constantine hiring Caine to find his long lost daughter so she will get his money. But comic assassins Timothy Agoglia Carey and Don Calfa keep popping up doing bad numbers on people.

Caine's search involves him with the odd Prendergast family, where bedridden neurotic mother Dorothy Adams, daughters Wood and Kitty Winn (one of whom may be Constantine's kid), and uncle Thayer David and household fixture Liam Dunn complicate the plot.

•

PEEPING TOM
1960, 109 mins, UK Ⓥ col
Dir Michael Powell ***Prod*** Michael Powell ***Scr*** Leo Marks ***Ph*** Otto Heller ***Ed*** Noreen Ackland ***Mus*** Brian Easdale, Wally Stott, Freddie Phillips ***Art*** Arthur Lawson
Act Karl Boehm, Moira Shearer, Anna Massey, Maxine Audley, Shirley Anne Field, Jack Watson (Anglo-Amalgamated/Powell)

Anglo-Amalgamated unloaded around $560,000 on making *Peeping Tom*, the biggest load of coin it had ever invested in one picture. It's as well, for stripped of its color and some excellent photography plus imaginative direction by Michael Powell, the plot itself would have emerged as a shoddy yarn.

Story concerns a young man who, as a boy, was used as a guinea pig by his father [played by Powell himself], a noted professor studying the symptoms of fear. The boy grows up to become an insane killer obsessed with the desire to photograph the terror on the faces of his victims as he kills them. He also has an unhealthy craving for peeping at young lovers, hence the title. In between these activities, he has a regular job as an assistant cameraman in a film studio and a part time job of photographing saucy pictures.

This mixed-up young man is played rather stolidly by Karl Boehm. It is more the fault of the screenplay than the actor himself that one gets only a very superficial glimpse into the workings of his mind. Anna Massey is charming as the girl who is one of his tenants and befriends him before she realizes that he is a killer. Maxine Audley, as her blind mother, tackles a difficult, unrewarding role very well.

Brenda Bruce has a few good moments at the beginning of the film as a streetwalker who is his first victim while Moira Shearer is effective as another of his victims, an ambitious bit player who is murdered while he is pretending to give her a screen test on a deserted studio lot.

Powell has directed with imagination but he might well have tightened up the story line. The standout feature of *Peeping Tom* is some fascinating photography by Otto Heller, particularly in the film studio sequences. His use of color and shadow is most effective. Heller does much to give *Peeping Tom* a veneer which the story by Leo Marks does not entirely deserve.

•

PEE-WEE'S BIG ADVENTURE
1985, 90 mins, US Ⓥ ⦿ col
Dir Tim Burton ***Prod*** Robert Shapiro, Richard Gilbert Abramson ***Scr*** Phil Hartman, Paul Reubens, Michael Varhol ***Ph*** Victor J. Kemper ***Ed*** Billy Weber ***Mus*** Danny Elfman ***Art*** David L. Snyder
Act Pee-wee Herman [= Paul Reubens], Elizabeth Daily, Mark Holton, Diane Salinger, Judd Omen, Jon Harris (Aspen/Shapiro)

Children should love the film and adults will be dismayed by the light brushstrokes with which Paul Reubens (one of three credited screenwriters, but star-billed under his stage name, Pee-wee Herman) suggests touches of Buster Keaton and Eddie Cantor.

Pee-wee wakes up in a children's bedroom full of incredible toys, slides down a fire station-like brass pole, materializing in his trademark tight suit with white shoes and red bow-tie, proceeds to make a breakfast a la Rube Goldberg, and winds up in a front yard that looks like a children's farm.

It's a delicious bit, with Reubens making noises like a child, walking something like Chaplin, and remarkably drawing for adult viewers the joys and frustrations of being a kid. Rest of narrative deals with Pee-wee's unstoppable pursuit of his prized lost bicycle, a rambling kidvid-like spoof.

•

PEGGY SUE GOT MARRIED
1986, 104 mins, US Ⓥ ⦿ col
Dir Francis Coppola ***Prod*** Paul R. Gurian ***Scr*** Jerry Leichtling, Arlene Sarner ***Ph*** Jordan Cronenweth ***Ed*** Barry Malkin ***Mus*** John Barry ***Art*** Dean Tavoularis
Act Kathleen Turner, Nicolas Cage, Barry Miller, Catherine Hicks, Joan Allen, Kevin J. O'Connor (Rastar/Tri-Star Delphi IV & V)

First-time scriptwriters have written a nice mix of sap and sass for Peggy Sue's (Kathleen Turner) character, a melancholy mother of two facing divorce who gets all dolled up in her 1950s-style ballgown to make a splash at her 25th high school reunion.

Sure enough, she's selected Prom Queen. In all the excitement, she collapses on stage—finding herself revived as an 18-year-old high school senior of the class of 1960.

Almost immediately, she realizes she's returned to her youth with all the knowledge and experience learned as an adult, quickly figuring out that she can alter the course of her future life by changing certain crucial decisions she made as a teenager.

The most important relationship for her is with steady boyfriend Charlie (Nicolas Cage), who she eventually marries, has two children by and only later seeks to divorce because of his infidelity.

What makes this treatment unique is that the jokes aren't so much derivative of pop culture, but are instead found in the learned wisdom of a middle-aged woman reacting to her own teenage dilemmas.

1986: NOMINATIONS: Best Actress (Kathleen Turner), Cinematography, Costume Design

•

PEG O' MY HEART

1923, 106 mins, US ⊗ b/w

Dir King Vidor ***Scr*** Mary O'Hara ***Ph*** George Barnes

Act Laurette Taylor, Mahlon Hamilton, Russell Simpson, Ethel Grey Terry, Nigel Barrie, Lionel Belmore (Metro)

Peg on the screen isn't the full, rich racy character she was on the stage [in the play by J. Hartley Manners], but still stands head and shoulders over almost any comedienne the screen has. Laurette Taylor does a unique piece of work here. New to the camera, she masters that pitiless instrument by sheer naturalness and abandon.

She looks 20 and acts 16 with an exquisite grace that is memorable. Except for her deft and dainty comedy, the picture might be pretty tepid. But this consummate actress makes the little imp of O'Connell live.

Metro and director King Vidor have done handsomely by the production. It has some exquisite settings, authentic scenic background taken abroad, and interiors done in the best form.

It was inevitable perhaps that there would be changes, but it is not easy to see that it was necessary to resurrect Peg's father and drag him through nearly a reel of picture at the start and bring him back for the finale. Peg gains sympathy from being an orphan. What was gained but footage to give her an absent but protective father?

•

PEKING EXPRESS

1951, 85 mins, US b/w

Dir William Dieterle ***Prod*** Hal B. Wallis ***Scr*** John Meredyth Lucas ***Ph*** Charles B. Lang, Jr. ***Ed*** Warren Low, Stanley Johnson ***Mus*** Dimitri Tiomkin ***Art*** Hal Pereira, Franz Bachelin

Act Joseph Cotten, Corinne Calvet, Edmund Gwenn, Marvin Miller, Benson Fong, Soo Young (Paramount)

An excellent coating of intrigue and action against an Oriental background provides *Peking Express* with enough thriller melodramatics to satisfy action-minded audiences.

Considerable of the action [from a story by Harry Hervey, adapted by Jules Furthman] takes place aboard the Peking Express on a run between Shanghai and Peking. Aboard are Joseph Cotten, U.N. doctor on his way to operate on the head of the Nationalist underground; Corinne Calvet, adventuress and old flame of Cotten's; Edmund Gwenn, a priest; Marvin Miller, black market operator; and Benson Fong, rabid Commie newspaperman.

Action becomes rapid when Miller tips his hand, has his bandits seize the train and the principal passengers to hold as hostages so he can secure the release of his son from the underground.

Cotten does a credible job of his character, keeping it unassuming but forceful. Calvet makes an interesting charmer, and Gwenn is excellent as the old priest. Miller's Chinese heavy is expertly forced for hisses. Fong impresses strongly as the reporter, a role that takes him away from his usual light-comedy characters.

•

PELICAN BRIEF, THE

1993, 141 mins, US Ⓥ ⊙ ▭ col

Dir Alan J. Pakula ***Prod*** Alan J. Pakula, Pieter Jan Brugge ***Scr*** Alan J. Pakula ***Ph*** Stephen Goldblatt ***Ed*** Tom Rolf, Trudy Ship ***Mus*** James Horner ***Art*** Philip Rosenberg

Act Julia Roberts, Denzel Washington, Sam Shepard, John Heard, Tony Goldwyn, James B. Sikking (Warner)

With perfect casting and stellar work by writer-producer-director Alan J. Pakula that eliminates most of the John Grisham novel's flaws, *The Pelican Brief* is a taut, intelligent thriller that succeeds on almost every level. Playing a part written with her in mind, Julia Roberts is sensational as law student-on-the-run Darby Shaw, and Denzel Washington proves her equal in a laudable example of color-blind casting.

The story opens with two Supreme Court justices murdered on the same night by a contract killer (Stanley Tucci). Engrossed by the bizarre events, 24-year-old Tulane law student Darby researches and drafts a brief detailing an obscure case that could provide inspiration for the dual murders.

Darby's professor boyfriend, Thomas Callahan (Sam Shepard, in a solid cameo) passes the brief along to a friend at the FBI (John Heard). When Thomas's car explodes, the game of cats-and-mouse is on—with both the government and the perpetrators pursuing Darby, even as the president (Robert Culp) and his chief of staff (Tony Goldwyn) fret that the conspiracy could implicate the White House. Pushed to the limit, Darby contacts newspaper reporter Gray Grantham (Washington), already chasing the story through an anonymous source.

Pakula does a remarkable job weaving and making sense of these complex strands. With all the descriptions of a long-legged, red-haired beauty in the book, it's not hard to figure out who Grisham had in mind, and Roberts is simply terrific. Washington also impresses as Gray, whose personality remained vague in the novel.

•

PELLE EROBREREN
(PELLE THE CONQUEROR)

1987, 160 mins, Denmark/Sweden Ⓥ ⊙ col

Dir Bille August ***Prod*** Per Holst ***Scr*** Bille August, Per Olov Enquist, Bjarne Reuter ***Ph*** Jorgen Persson, Rolf Lindstrom, Soren Berthelin, Fritz Schroder ***Ed*** Janus Billeskov Jansen ***Mus*** Stefan Nilsson ***Art*** Anna Asp

Act Max von Sydow, Pelle Hvenegaard, Erik Paske, Bjorne Granath, Axel Strobye, Astrid Villaume (Holst/Svensk Film-industri)

Pelle the Conqueror is a feature film of epic proportions and a relentlessly unsentimental look at life among the haves and, primarily, the have-nots on a big turn-of-the-century farm. Writer-helmer Bille August avoids larger social issues and stays firmly down on the farm with the story culled from episodes in the first, and best, volume of Danish Nobel Prize winner Martin Andersen Nexo's trilogy, an early classic in world socialist literature.

Film is a record of what happened when Lasse, an elderly and widowed farmer (Max von Sydow), and his young son Pelle (Pelle Hvenegaard) join a boatload of immigrants to escape from impoverished rural Sweden to the Land Of Plenty of their dreams, Denmark's Baltic island of Bornholm. On Bornholm, Lasse, possessor of visions and dreams but essentially broken of spirit, comes to terms with a life of near-slavery as the lowliest tender of the farm's cows, while Pelle, during two years of misery and abuse, learns to trust mainly himself. He comes of age in more ways than one, casts off his chains and sets out, in time-honored style (a lone figure crossing the snowy fields), to conquer the world.

The Danish-Swedish cast has von Sydow offering his career's apex as Lasse, with his long horse's face lit by the minutest registrations of hope and despair. Younger Hvenegaard plays Pelle with never a hint of being coached beyond what comes naturally and true. The other characters who populate August's large canvas have stock characteristics enough to float a TV soap.

1988: Best Foreign Language Film

•

PELLE THE CONQUEROR

SEE: PELLE EROBREREN

•

PENDULUM

1969, 101 mins, US Ⓥ ⊙ col

Dir George Schaefer ***Prod*** Stanley Niss ***Scr*** Stanley Niss ***Ph*** Lionel Lindon ***Ed*** Hugh S. Fowler ***Mus*** Walter Scharf ***Art*** Walter M. Simonds

Act George Peppard, Jean Seberg, Richard Kiley, Charles McGraw, Madeleine Sherwood, Robert F. Lyons (Columbia)

Although the end result is a somewhat routine crime meller, *Pendulum* attacks head-on the issue of individual liberties under the U.S. Constitution vs. society as a whole. An excellent basic plot strain has been weakened by potboiler elements.

The root idea is a nifty. George Peppard is a police hero who rode to fame on the rape-murder conviction of Robert F. Lyons. But some sloppy gumshoe work precipitated a U.S. Supreme Court reversal, and ultimate dismissal of charges against the accused.

Then, Peppard himself is suspected of the murder of his wife (Jean Seberg) and becomes a victim of a society, and its keepers, who, while mouthing the principle that an accused is innocent until he's proven guilty, tends to think along reverse lines.

•

PENELOPE

1966, 94 mins, US ▭ col

Dir Arthur Hiller ***Prod*** Arthur Loew, Jr. ***Scr*** George Wells ***Ph*** Harry Stradling ***Ed*** Rita Roland ***Mus*** John Williams ***Art*** George W. Davis, Preston Ames

Act Natalie Wood, Ian Bannen, Dick Shawn, Peter Falk, Jonathan Winters, Lila Kedrova (M-G-M)

Penelope is one of those bright, delightfully wacky comedies. It's got a good—if light—basic plot premise and plenty of glib laugh lines and situations.

Script by George Wells [from a novel by E. V. Cunningham] gives full sway to the story of a young wife whose hobby is larceny. Arthur Hiller's deft direction takes advantage of the intended spirit and seizes upon every opportunity for a romp.

Film opens with a little old lady holding up a bank and getting away with $60,000 a few hours after bank's official opening. She turns out to be Natalie Wood, married to the bank's prexy (Ian Bannen) and disguised with a rubber mask which she doffs, along with a distinguishing yellow suit, the in the ladies' washroom.

Wood does a nimble job and turns in a gay performance as well as being a nice clotheshorse for Edith Head's glamorous fashions. Bannen is properly stuffy as her spouse. As the psychoanalyst Dick Shawn is in his element in one of his zany characterizations and Peter Falk socks over his role as police lieutenant assigned to the bank case.

•

PENITENTIARY

1979, 99 mins, US Ⓥ col

Dir Jamaa Fanaka ***Prod*** Jamaa Fanaka ***Scr*** Jamaa Fanaka ***Ph*** Marty Ollstein ***Ed*** Betsy Blankett ***Mus*** Frankie Gaye ***Art*** Adel Mazen

Act Leon Isaac Kennedy, Thommy Pollard, Hazel Spears, Badja Djola, Gloria Delaney, Chuck Mitchell (Gross)

A tough, disturbing and relatively uncompromising look at contemporary prison life, *Penitentiary* is a solid third feature for Jamaa Fanaka and rates as one of the "blackest" pictures to come along since the blaxploitation trend waned.

Circumstantial evidence lands lanky, streetwise Leon Isaac Kennedy in prison. Balance of power in his cell block, largely inhabited by blacks, is dictated by brute force, with the meanest, toughest inmates lording it over the smaller (read sensitive) ones with their fists. Bottom line in prison relationships is sexual power, and Kennedy avoids the dreaded fate of being used as a "girl" only by beating up his cellmate.

The brutal realities of prison life are rendered with extreme believability, and a welcome lack of preachiness or liberal posturing.

•

PENNIES FROM HEAVEN

1981, 107 mins, US Ⓥ ⊙ col

Dir Herbert Ross ***Prod*** Nora Kaye, Herbert Ross ***Scr*** Dennis Potter ***Ph*** Gordon Willis ***Ed*** Richard Marks ***Art*** Ken Adam, Fred Tuch, Bernie Cutler

Act Steve Martin, Bernadette Peters, Christopher Walken, Jessica Harper, Tommy Rall, John McMartin (M-G-M/Hera)

Adapted by Dennis Potter from his acclaimed six-part, 1978 BBC series of the same name, film deliberately alienates viewer from the first scene, which presents an unpleasant Steve Martin attempting to force morning sex on his mousy, unhappy wife, Jessica Harper.

Martin is a sheet-music salesman in Depression-ridden Chicago of 1934 whose "real" life consists of one squalid little scene after another: He makes virginal schoolteacher Bernadette Peters pregnant, after which she loses her job and becomes a streetwalker in the employ of pimp Christopher Walken.

Worked into this lugubrious, neo-Brechtian tragedy are more than a dozen musical numbers of grave opulence. Purpose is to illustrate the idealism and innocence to which Martin presumably aspires, with the vivid contrast between the sunny escapism of 1930s song lyrics and the somber dispiritedness of the era from whence they came.

Almost as if he were directing Pinter, Herbert Ross has actors speak a line, then wait two beats before delivering the next phrase. Technique smothers such ordinarily lively performers as Martin, Peters and Harper. In short, this reportedly $19 million esoteric item is *Penny Gate*.

1981: NOMINATIONS: Best Adapted Screenplay, Costume Design, Sound

•

PENNY SERENADE

1941, 110 mins, US Ⓥ b/w

Dir George Stevens ***Prod*** George Stevens ***Scr*** Morrie Ryskind ***Ph*** Joseph Walker ***Ed*** Otto Meyer ***Mus*** Morris Stoloff

Act Irene Dunne, Cary Grant, Beulah Bondi, Edgar Buchanan, Ann Doran (Columbia)

Here's the story. Irene Dunne and Cary Grant adopt a six-week-old baby and raise her until she is six, when she dies, after a brief illness. Then they adopt a boy of two.

That's all, but the telling of it from an excellently written screenscript by Morrie Ryskind, who found inspiration from a *McCall's* magazine story by Martha Cheavens, occupies nearly two hours, in the course of which there are tenderness, heartthrob, comedy and good, old-fashioned, gulping tears. Half a dozen times the yarn approaches the saccharine, only to be turned back into sound, human comedy-drama.

Produced with less skill and acted with less sincerity, *Penny Serenade* might have missed the mark by a mile, but George Stevens's direction and the excellence of the stars' playing make the film.

1941: NOMINATION: Best Actor (Cary Grant)

•

PENTHOUSE

1933, 90 mins, US b/w

Dir W. S. Van Dyke ***Prod*** Hunt Stromberg ***Scr*** Frances Goodrich, Albert Hackett ***Ph*** Lucien Andriot, Harold Rosson

Act Warner Baxter, Myrna Loy, Charles Butterworth, Mae Clarke, Phillips Holmes, C. Henry Gordon (M-G-M)

It's a sugarcoated gang story, but worked out indirectly, the underworld plot developing as secondary to a romantic tale, two rather surefire elements teamed in a rather shrewd treatment. Development has capital comedy incident and some of the most likable characters of underworld pictures.

Action revolves around three characters: a rich lawyer with a taste for criminal cases; the gangster he saves from the chair; and the girl who appears to help him clear a society friend, framed in a killing by a rival gang chief. Finish is elaborately prepared.

The adaptation [from the novel by Arthur Somers Roche] has been well done. Interest is splendidly centered and never gets out of focus as it frequently does in arranging scattered book material into screen form. Warner Baxter turns in one of his usual workmanlike performances, while Myrna Loy reveals new skill in the management of light scenes—light on the surface but with the inference of tenseness in the background.

•

PENTHOUSE, THE

1967, 90 mins, UK col

Dir Peter Collinson ***Prod*** Harry Fine ***Scr*** Peter Collinson ***Ph*** Arthur Lavis ***Ed*** John Thumper ***Mus*** John Hawksworth ***Art*** Peter Mullins

Act Suzy Kendall, Terence Morgan, Tony Beckley, Norman Rodway, Martine Beswick (Tahiti-Twickenham/Compton)

Story is one of those claustrophobic items which find hero and heroine trapped in an isolated apartment with a pair of deranged hoodlums alternating physical and mental bouts of sadism as they break down the couple's resistance.

But it's not what goes on but how it's developed that raised this item above the level of other orgy-chiller entries. Peter Collinson's script [from the play *The Meter Man* by C. Scott Forbes] and direction work hand-in-hand like a precision watch in milking a situation or line to the utmost before segueing, after a pause for breath, to the next crescendo build-up.

The quality of the lines and the subtle-yet-powerful impact of their content, plus the superbly controlled delivery by the cast, make this a compelling—if at times inevitably distasteful—glimpse at some of the seamier characteristics of the human being.

•

PEOPLE AGAINST O'HARA, THE

1951, 101 mins, US b/w

Dir John Sturges ***Prod*** William H. Wright ***Scr*** John Monks, Jr. ***Ph*** John Alton ***Ed*** Gene Ruggiero ***Mus*** Carmen Dragon ***Art*** Cedric Gibbons, James Basevi

Act Spencer Tracy, Pat O'Brien, Diana Lynn, John Hodiak, Eduardo Ciannelli, James Arness (M-G-M)

A basically good idea for a film melodrama [from a novel by Eleazar Lipsky] is cluttered up with too many unnecessary side twists and turns, and the presentation is uncomfortably overlong.

Plot premise finds Spencer Tracy, practicing civil law after pressure of criminal cases had driven him to the bottle, taking on the defense of James Arness, a young man he has known since a boy, who has been charged with murder. Arness has been neatly framed for the killing, and asst. district attorney John Hodiak sees it as a cinch case. Despite careful work by Tracy, he loses the case to Hodiak.

Arness is convicted, but Tracy does not give up and finally convinces Hodiak and homicide policeman Pat O'Brien there is still a chance to prove the frame.

The picture has a number of very good performances, sparked by the always sound Tracy. O'Brien, Hodiak and Diana Lynn, latter doing Tracy's daughter, have comparatively shorter footage, but each comes through excellently.

•

PEOPLE THAT TIME FORGOT, THE

1977, 90 mins, US Ⓥ col

Dir Kevin Connor ***Prod*** John Dark ***Scr*** Patrick Tilley ***Ph*** Alan Hume ***Ed*** John Ireland, Barry Peters ***Mus*** John Scott ***Art*** Maurice Carter

Act Patrick Wayne, Doug McClure, Sarah Douglas, Dana Gillespie, Thorley Walters, Shane Rimmer (American International)

Story of a small party headed by Patrick Wayne seeking a marooned World War I naval hero north of the ice barrier in the Arctic. Film is second in Edgar Rice Burroughs's *Lost World* trilogy lensed in the Canary Islands and in Britain.

Special effects predominate the action as Wayne and his group leave their ship in a 1918 amphibian through ice-cluttered water and perilously lift over towering ice peaks, are attacked by a giant pterodactyl and forced to crash-land on the dusty island of Caprona. Again, special effects add to the suspense as the group encounter all manner of hair-raising beasties and erupting fire in braving the dangers of the cavemen in an attempt to find their quarry.

•

PEOPLE UNDER THE STAIRS, THE

1991, 102 mins, US Ⓥ ⊙ col

Dir Wes Craven ***Prod*** Marianne Maddalena, Stuart M. Besser ***Scr*** Wes Craven ***Ph*** Sandi Sissel ***Ed*** James Coblentz ***Mus*** Don Peake ***Art*** Bryan Jones

Act Brandon Adams, Everett McGill, Wendy Robie, A. J. Langer, Ving Rhames, Sean Whalen (Alive)

A pretense of social responsibility and most of the necessary tension get lost in a combination of excessive gore and over-the-top perfs in *The People Under the Stairs*. Writer-director Wes Craven sneaks in a post-Reagan era message about haves and have-nots by making his hero a 13-year-old ghetto kid. Pic's still an old-style haunted house film with spooky couple Everett McGill and Wendy Robie terrorizing their teen daughter (A. J. Langer) and keeping a horde of ashen youths locked in the basement.

Stumbling into the ample vulgarity within those walls is the aptly nicknamed Fool (Brandon Adams), brought along by his sister's b.f. to rob the place since the strange couple also are the boy's landlords on the verge of evicting the family.

House of horrors includes cannibalism, McGill cavorting around in a leather suit and a blood-crazed Rottweiler. Cartoonish villains quickly thaw pic's initial chill, in the process trivializing the more serious issues (child abuse, poverty) that might have been raised.

•

PEOPLE WILL TALK

1951, 109 mins, US b/w

Dir Joseph L. Mankiewicz ***Prod*** Darryl F. Zanuck ***Scr*** Joseph L. Mankiewicz ***Ph*** Milton Krasner ***Ed*** Barbara McLean ***Mus*** Alfred Newman (dir.) ***Art*** Lyle Wheeler, George W. Davis

Act Cary Grant, Jeanne Crain, Finlay Currie, Hume Cronyn, Walter Slezak, Sidney Blackmer (20th Century-Fox)

Curt Goetz's play and film, *Dr. Praetorius*, was used by Joseph L. Mankiewicz as the basis for his screenplay, and the script reflects his construction skill at melding drama. Serious aspects of the play, concerning a doctor who believes illness needs more than just medicinal treatment, have been brightened with considerable humor, and the camera adds enough scope to help overcome the fact that the picture's legit origin is still sometimes apparent.

Cary Grant is the doctor and Jeanne Crain the medical student who are the principals mixed up in the plot. Grant, facing charges of conduct unbecoming to his profession, finds time to become interested in Crain when she faints during a classroom lecture. He discovers she is pregnant, but when she tries to commit suicide, he proclaims the diagnosis a mistake and marries her.

Climax is hung on Grant's trial by the college board, and its more serious touches are carefully leavened with a lightness that makes it more effective.

Grant and Crain turn in the kind of performances expected of them and their work receives top support from the other members of the largish cast.

•

PEOPLE VS. LARRY FLYNT, THE

1996, 127 mins, US Ⓥ ⊙ ▭ col

Dir Milos Forman ***Prod*** Oliver Stone, Janet Yang, Michael Hausman ***Scr*** Scott Alexander, Larry Karaszewski ***Ph*** Philippe Rousselot ***Ed*** Christopher Tellefsen ***Mus*** Thomas Newman ***Art*** Patrizia von Brandenstein

Act Woody Harrelson, Courtney Love, Edward Norton, James Cromwell, Crispin Glover, James Carville (Ixtlan/Columbia)

A vastly entertaining lesson in the importance of the First Amendment, Milos Forman's first picture in seven years [since *Valmont*, 1989] uses the shenanigans and occasional serious gestures of an unabashed pornographer to serve up a roller-coaster ride across the sociopolitical landscape as it turned from anything-goes irreverence in the early '70s to the hypocritical self-righteousness of the Reagan years. Along the way, it also tells a poignant love story, one sparked by a sensational performance by rock star Courtney Love.

Penned by Scott Alexander and Larry Karaszewski (*Ed Wood*), picture quickly sketches the essentially unwitting rise to riches of poor Kentucky backwoods boy Larry Flynt (Woody Harrelson) with *Hustler* magazine. While still running sleazy Cincinatti strip clubs, he takes up with one of his dancers, Althea (Love), who is quite willing to share other women with him and stands by him through the years despite some insane provocations.

Flynt's life takes a radical turn when he becomes a born-again Christian, but the conflict disappears when Flynt is gunned down outside a Georgia courthouse, paralyzing him from the waist down. Shot full of mind-numbing drugs, Flynt and Althea spent the next few years holed up in a Hollywood mansion. But while Flynt has the willpower to kick his drug dependency, his wife does not. Though devastated, Flynt rebounds with the most significant action of his life, his battle with Moral Majority leader Jerry Falwell (Richard Paul).

Harrelson's quite agreeable lead performance takes the clear position that there was no grand scheme in Flynt's mind, and he was not seized by noble or patriotic ideals in his court fights. But Love is the revelation here, as she delivers an impulsive, nakedly emotional, quicksilver turn that brings the central romance alive whenever she's on screen.

1996: NOMINATIONS: Best Actor (Woody Harrelson), Director

•

PEPE LE MOKO

1937, 90 mins, France Ⓥ b/w

Dir Julien Duvivier ***Scr*** Roger Ashelle, Julien Duvivier, J. Constant, Henri Jeanson ***Ph*** Jules Kruger, Marc Fossard ***Ed*** Marguerite Beauge ***Mus*** Vincent Scotto, Mohamed Iguerbouchen ***Art*** Jacques Krauss

Act Jean Gabin, Mireille Balin, Line Noro, Lucas Gridoux, Gabriel Gabrio, Charpin (Paris)

Fugitive from the law takes refuge in Casablanca's native quarter to head a huge theft ring, only to kill himself because he cannot leave with the white woman with whom he is in love. Role is Jean Gabin's meat, and he masticates it well.

Support, headed by Mireille Balin and Line Noro, is of high standard, while the simple story [from a novel by Roger Ashelle] is directed with dexterity, to make the whole a commendable finished product, but the scissors could have been used a bit more severely.

Aided by his grandfather (Saturnin Fabre), evaluator of stolen property, Gabin neatly molds the character of a hardened criminal who holds both his white and native enemies at bay by brutality and harshness, mixed with the proper amount of kindness. All attempts on the part of the French authorities to lure him into the open have failed.

Gabin's troubles start when the police descend on the quarter to capture him. A tourist (Mireille Balin) is separated from her party during the raid and is taken into Gabin's hangout by Gridoux, native policeman, for safety. He intrigues her; she interests him.

Interesting movement holds through the entirety. Life in the native quarter, with its squalor and intrigues, is particularly well presented and photographed.

[Pic was remade by U.S. producer Walter Wanger as *Algiers*, released in 1938, and by Universal as a musical, *Casbah*, in 1948.]

•

PEREZ FAMILY, THE

1995, 112 mins, US Ⓥ ⊙ col

Dir Mira Nair ***Prod*** Michael Nozic, Lydia Dean Pilcher ***Scr*** Robin Swicord ***Ph*** Stuart Dryburgh ***Ed*** Robert Estrin ***Mus*** Alan Silvestri (sup.) ***Art*** Mark Friedberg

Act Marisa Tomei, Alfred Molina, Anjelica Huston, Chazz Palminteri, Trini Alvarado, Celia Cruz (Samuel Goldwyn)

An enormously likeable ensemble, headed by Marisa Tomei and Anjelica Huston, struggles hard to give the proper color, texture and mood to *The Perez Family*, Mira Nair's serio-comic exploration of Cuban immigrants in Miami at the time of the 1980 Mariel boatlift.

Based on Christie Bell's popular novel, adapted to the screen by Robin Swicord (*Little Women*), *The Perez Fam-*

ily chronicles the entangled lives and romances of Cuban immigrants as they forge a new existence—and new families.

For two decades, Juan Raul Perez (Alfred Molina) has patiently endured hard prison life by dreaming about a reunion with his wife, Carmela (Anjelica Huston), who's had to raise their daughter, Teresa (Trini Alvarado), alone in Miami.

Finally free and on board a boat to the promised land, Juan meets Dottie Perez (Marisa Tomei), a spunky prostitute who proudly claims, "I'm like Cuba, used by many, conquered by no one." Once they arrive in the U.S., the immigration authorities erroneously list Juan and Dottie, who have the same surname, as a married couple. An indefatigable survivor, Dottie takes advantage of Juan's frustration, realizing that if they want to stay in America they'll have to become a family.

A major problem is the film's relentless incoherent, often soft gaze at its characters. Attempting to make at once a charmingly freewheeling and socially poignant movie, director Nair can't find the right balance among the tale's multiple facets.

Tomei is a spunky, attractive performer who has the audience on her side, but it's still hard to determine whether she can carry a movie. In contrast, the usually reliable Huston underacts, rendering one of her most low-key performances.

•

PERFECT
1985, 120 mins, US Ⓥ ⊙ ▭ col
Dir James Bridges ***Prod*** James Bridges ***Scr*** Aaron Latham, James Bridges ***Ph*** Gordon Willis ***Ed*** Jeff Gourson ***Mus*** Ralph Burns ***Art*** Michael Haller
Act John Travolta, Jamie Lee Curtis, Anne De Salvo, Marilu Henner, Laraine Newman, Jann Wenner (Columbia/Delphi III)

Perfect pretends to be an old-fashioned love story dressed up in leotards, but more than anything else, it's a film about physical attraction. Set in the world of journalism, pic is guilty of the sins it condemns—superficiality, manipulation and smugness.

Formula is really quite simple—a man must prove his worth to a reluctant woman—but problems with the plot and profession it's set in keep the affair from flowering.

Jamie Lee Curtis is an ex–Olympic-class swimmer turned aerobics instructor who was burned by a reporter and must be thawed out before she can enter into a relationship with star Travolta.

John Travolta is the heat, but before she can accept him, he must prove himself a decent fellow, something the film never really succeeds in doing. Character is a semi-autobiographical version of writer Aaron Latham, who based the script on a searing story he originally wrote for *Rolling Stone* and now seems to be exorcising here, feeling guilty for his ruthlessness.

Travolta cannot rescue his character, and he remains basically an unsympathetic figure. Curtis does cut quite a figure in her numerous aerobic outfits, and she does communicate a certain wounded pride and appeal.

•

PERFECT COUPLE, A
1979, 110 mins, US ▭ col
Dir Robert Altman ***Prod*** Robert Altman ***Scr*** Robert Altman, Allan Nicholls ***Ph*** Edmond L. Koons ***Ed*** Tony Lombardo ***Mus*** Allan Nicholls (prod.)
Act Paul Dooley, Marta Heflin, Titos Vandis, Belita Moreno, Henry Gibson, Dimitra Arliss (20th Century-Fox/Lion's Gate)

Immensely likeable in some parts, and a complete turn-off in others, *Perfect Couple* reaffirms both Robert Altman's intelligence and his inaccessibility. The same theme turns up again here: the struggle of individuals to deal with forces and circumstances beyond their control. In this instance, it's two different family structures. The linear family has Alex Theodopoulos (Paul Dooley) imprisoned in a suffocating, old-world Greek clan. Flip side is Sheila Shea (Marta Heflin), an elfin singer locked into a rock group/commune.

The couple meets through a videotape dating service (the kind of institution Altman loves to poke fun at) and have an on-again, off-again relationship complicated by both families.

•

PERFECT FRIDAY
1970, 94 mins, UK Ⓥ col
Dir Peter Hall ***Prod*** Jack Smith ***Scr*** Anthony Grenville-Bell, C. Scott Forbes ***Ph*** Alan Hume ***Ed*** Rex Pyke ***Mus*** John Dankworth ***Art*** Terence Marsh
Act Ursula Andress, David Warner, Stanley Baker, Patience Collier, T. P. McKenna, David Waller (Sunnymede)

No one else can steal $1 million with quite the flair of the British. A caper in point is *Perfect Friday* with Ursula Andress, Stanley Baker, and David Warner as a triangle of totally amoral thieves in a charming, ingenious and sexy bank job, tightly masterminded to the split-second, by director Peter Hall.

Andress and Warner play a casually-married couple, a vain, self-centered, modish and jet-setting playboy English lord and his Swiss wife, who live now, pay later, but at the moment are thoroughly bankrupt.

The gorgeously undressed Andress spends a great deal of the footage at maximum exposure, but also demonstrates a flair for low-key comedy. Warner is superb as the foppish young lord.

•

PERFECT MURDER, A
1998, 105 mins, US Ⓥ ⊙ col
Dir Andrew Davis ***Prod*** Arnold Kopelson, Anne Kopelson, Christopher Mankiewicz, Peter Macgregor-Scott ***Scr*** Patrick Smith Kelly ***Ph*** Dariusz Wolski ***Ed*** Dennis Virkler, Dov Hoenig ***Mus*** James Newton Howard ***Art*** Philip Rosenberg
Act Michael Douglas, Gwyneth Paltrow, Viggo Mortensen, David Suchet, Sarita Choudhury, Constance Towers (Kopelson/Warner)

A Perfect Murder, based on the play [by Frederick Knott] and subsequent [1954] Hitchcock film *Dial M for Murder*, freely adapts a lesser work by the master and only serves to prove that even that minor bygone film is superior to high gloss, misconceived modernization. The notion of a crime of passion executed with icy precision has been superseded by issues of commerce and rendered a cold and cynical piece.

Emily (Gwyneth Paltrow) is married to commodities trader Stephen Taylor (Michael Douglas) but romantically entangled with bohemian painter David Shaw (Viggo Mortensen). On the pretense of buying some artwork, Stephen visits David at his loft and confronts him with a dossier that includes jail time and a series of past scams.

Stephen's willing to forgive and forget if David will do him one favor—he'd like him to murder Emily. He'll also throw in $500,000 for David's trouble. And he's made it just a touch easier by carefully plotting out a way of doing it.

The dilemma in this *Perfect Murder* is its singular failure at creating a rooting interest for a character or situation. Once David is exposed and agrees to the conspiracy, he's lost our sympathy. Stephen lacks even the irrational passion of jealousy, driven to homicide solely by the allure of Emily's gelt. The targeted woman suffers overly from being the cover model for smart woman, dumb choices. Her vulnerability wears thin as she habitually fails to grasp the obvious.

What's chiefly out of kilter is the pic's leaden seriousness. Hitchcock played against the gravity of murder with bright colors and personalities; director Andrew Davis concocts an inky tone throughout that embraces the lighting, costumes and David's paintings.

•

PERFECT STORM, THE
2000, 129 mins, US Ⓥ ⊙ ▭ col
Dir Wolfgang Petersen ***Prod*** Paula Weinstein, Wolfgang Petersen, Gail Katz ***Scr*** Bill Wittliff ***Ph*** John Seale ***Ed*** Richard Francis-Bruce ***Mus*** James Horner ***Art*** William Sandell
Act George Clooney, Mark Wahlberg, John C. Reilly, Diane Lane, William Fichtner, John Hawkes, Allen Payne, Mary Elizabeth Mastrantonio, Karen Allen (Baltimore Spring Creek/Warner)

Wolfgang Petersen made a classic underwater film with *Das Boot*, but he doesn't fare nearly as well on the surface with *The Perfect Storm*. An attempt to do on the high seas what *Twister* did on great open spaces on land, this adaptation of Sebastian Junger's bestseller about some Gloucester, Massachusetts, fishermen's battle with the storm of the century boasts a physical enormity courtesy of heavy digital effects work. But the yarn's emotional undercurrents never take hold, resulting in a picture that leaves one thinking less about the fates of the characters than about how the actors had to spend most of their working days soaking wet.

The location photography of the town that inspired Kipling's *Captains Courageous* and the characters' scruffy grooming, constant drinking and smoking and heavy preoccupations with earnings establish the working-class milieu solidly enough. But the emotional links and desires, along with the motivational notations and behavioral ticks in Bill Wittliff's screenplay are perfunctory and undeveloped, as if they were items to be ticked off a checklist.

There are sequences of notable tension before the final onslaught, but even here, one watches the action with heart and mind unquickened by genuine suspense, due to the mild involvement in character and the haphazard nature of the incidents and the way in which they are conveyed.

With the exception of John C. Reilly, who in his full beard looks like a cuddly rat who would be at home on any vessel, cast is merely adequate. By the second half, the men are reduced to shouting almost all their lines to be heard over the watery din, while the dressed-down but ever-fetching Diane Lane leads the group of worrying women on the home front.

Industrial Light & Magic's special effects work is extensive and no doubt state of the art when it comes to the exceedingly difficult task of reproducing water by digital means. But even after one becomes accustomed to the rough weather's computerized look, the sense of artifice remains, which may account for some of the sense of emotional remove. James Horner's churning score never goes away, at least in the final hour.

•

PERFECT STRANGERS
1945, 100 mins, US b/w
Dir Alexander Korda ***Prod*** Alexander Korda ***Scr*** Clemence Dane, Anthony Pelissier ***Ph*** Georges Perinal ***Ed*** E. B. Jarvis ***Mus*** Clifton Parker ***Art*** Vincent Korda
Act Robert Donat, Deborah Kerr, Glynis Johns, Ann Todd, Roland Culver (London)

Perfect Strangers is a perfect stranger to modern technique, real life and smooth running. It appears too much like a museum piece.

The story is that of a young worker and his suburban wife, who find themselves respectively in the Royal Navy and the Wrens with the war's outbreak. Both benefit physically and mentally from the change. Donat shaves his moustache: Deborah Kerr puts on lipstick. Neither expects to like the other when they meet again but they do.

It's the type of yarn [an original story by Clemence Dane] that offers many possibilities of drama and situation, but all have been missed in this film. First you see Donat getting fit; then you see Kerr getting fit. Then you see Donat dancing; then you see Kerr dancing. Then you hear Donat telling his friends how dreary Kerr is; then you hear Kerr telling her friends how dreary Donat is. It seems to go on and on like this.

•

PERFECT STRANGERS
1950, 87 mins, US Ⓥ b/w
Dir Bretaigne Windust ***Prod*** Jerry Wald ***Scr*** Edith Sommer ***Ph*** J. Peverell Marley ***Ed*** David Weisbart ***Mus*** Leigh Harline
Act Ginger Rogers, Dennis Morgan, Thelma Ritter, Margalo Gillmore, Anthony Ross (Warner)

Cramming the Ben Hecht–Charles MacArthur legiter, *Ladies and Gentlemen*, into a fast-stepping film was a tough trick. It has been done admirably by scripter Edith Sommer and slammed home forcefully by director Bretaigne Windust.

Stars are spotted as jurors in a murder trial. Dennis Morgan is a married man with two children, Ginger Rogers a divorcee. They fall in love. Margalo Gillmore, whose husband has deserted her, holds out for the death sentence because the accused had asked his wife for a divorce before she was pushed, or fell, from a cliff. Suspense mounts neatly, hand-in-glove with the love story, to a gripping climax.

Picture is a top credit for producer Jerry Wald—different, provocative, adult. Morgan and Rogers are in top form.

•

PERFECT WORLD, A
1993, 137 mins, US Ⓥ ⊙ ▭ col
Dir Clint Eastwood ***Prod*** Mark Johnson, David Valdes ***Scr*** John Lee Hancock ***Ph*** Jack N. Green ***Ed*** Joel Cox, Ron Spang ***Mus*** Lennie Niehaus ***Art*** Henry Bumstead
Act Kevin Costner, Clint Eastwood, Laura Dern, T. J. Lowther, Keith Szarabajka, Leo Burmester (Warner/Malpaso)

Star Kevin Costner and director Clint Eastwood deliver lean, finely chiseled work in *A Perfect World*, a somber, subtly nuanced study of an escaped con's complex relationship with an abducted boy that carries a bit too much narrative flab for its own good.

This is a disturbing, intimate, noirish road movie paradoxically lensed in widescreen across the vast, sunbaked Texas landscape, its impact made through oblique dialog and the finesse of performance rather than by broad action and suspense.

Story centers on Butch Haynes (Costner), a lifelong loser toughened up by many years in the pen. Butch and his nasty partner Terry (Keith Szarabajka) break out of the joint on Halloween night in 1963, commandeer a car and, after briefly terrorizing a family, make off with 7-year-old Phillip Perry (T. J. Lowther) as a hostage.

Quickly taking up the chase is Texas Ranger Red Garnett (Eastwood), a seasoned, instinctive pro who gets saddled with an unwanted contingent of man hunters, including Laura Dern's state criminologist and Bradley Whitford's odious sharpshooter.

Film is strongest in building the erratic, potent and unusually complicated link between man and boy. Film's major surprise is Costner's performance, which trades in taciturnity for major dividends. As the kid, Lowther is exceptionally good, achingly conveying the contradictory feelings his experience with Butch summons up.

Pic would have benefited from at least 20 minutes of tightening, nearly all in the police scenes. Fact that tale is set three weeks before JFK's fateful trip to Dallas is fortunately not belabored.

•

PERFORMANCE
1971, 102 mins, UK Ⓥ ⦿ col
Dir Donald Cammell, Nicolas Roeg ***Prod*** Sandy Lieberson ***Scr*** Donald Cammell ***Ph*** Nicolas Roeg ***Ed*** Antony Gibbs, Brian Smedley-Aston ***Mus*** Jack Nitzsche ***Art*** John Clark
Act James Fox, Mick Jagger, Anita Pallenberg, Michele Breton, Ann Sidney, John Bindon (Goodtimes/Warner)

James Fox, Mick Jagger and Anita Pallenberg star in a crime meller, laced with needless, boring sadism and dull, turnings-off sex angles. Fox is a hood who finally gets the heat put on him; he hides in a house owned by Jagger, entrenched in freaky atmosphere with Pallenberg and Michele Breton. Fox finally is found out, there's a phoney sadness to the climax, and it all runs out after a too-long 102 minutes.

Randy Newman conducted the Jack Nitzsche music, overall a good sound. Co-director Nicolas Roeg's lensing is tricky, the characters gamey, the dialog dull, performances flat, impact none.

•

PERIL
SEE: PERIL EN LA DEMEURE

•

PERIL EN LA DEMEURE
(PERIL; DEATH IN A FRENCH GARDEN)
1985, 100 mins, France Ⓥ ⦿ col
Dir Michel Deville ***Prod*** Emmanuel Schlumberger ***Scr*** Michel Deville, Rosalinde Damamme ***Ph*** Martial Thury ***Ed*** Raymonde Guyot ***Art*** Philippe Combastel
Act Christophe Malavoy, Nicole Garcia, Michel Piccoli, Anemone, Richard Bohringer, Anais Jeanneret (Gaumont/Elefilm/TF1)

Peril is a sleek drama of eroticism and murder from Michel Deville, who is finally earning the commercial success that has evaded his last few films, including *Deep Water*, a failed attempt to adapt a Patricia Highsmith novel. Based on a French novel [Rene Belletto's *Sur la terre comme au ciel*], *Peril* finds the tone of disturbing ambiguity and perversity missing in *Deep Water*, though the conventional, overexplicit denouement dilutes the overall effect. Still for most of its length, pic intrigues by its camera virtuosity, cryptic dialog and shadowy characterizations.

Christophe Malavoy is David, an unsuspecting guitar instructor hired by a well-heeled suburban couple, Julia and Graham Tombsthay (Nicole Garcia, Michel Piccoli), to give lessons to their teenage daughter. Latter (Anais Jeanneret) is nubile and seemingly attracted to Malavoy, but mother is quicker on the sexual draw and beds the young man in no time, visiting him at his Paris loft.

David drifts on the erotic currents, not overly concerned with the apparent complicity of Julia's husband or the prying of a voyeuristic neighbor (Anemone). Complications arise when videocassette recordings of their trysts are mailed to the lovers.

A new element in the drama comes in the form of Daniel, a professional killer (Richard Bohringer), who saves David from a mugger and befriends him, apparently out of homosexual impulse. Daniel soon admits he has a contract out on Graham, and warns David about his involvement.

Deville's direction is stealthy and stylish, aided by Martial Thury's gliding camera and Raymonde Guyot's sly editing, which enforce the feeling of deepening insecurity. Fine use of limpid themes by Brahms, Schubert and Granados offer contrast to the unsettling events.

•

PERILS OF PAULINE, THE
1947, 93 mins, US Ⓥ col
Dir George Marshall ***Prod*** Sol C. Siegel ***Scr*** P. J. Wolfson, Frank Butler ***Ph*** Ray Rennahan ***Ed*** Arthur Schmidt ***Mus*** Robert Emmett Dolan ***Art*** Hans Dreier, Roland Anderson
Act Betty Hutton, John Lund, Constance Collier, William Demarest, Billy De Wolfe, Frank Faylen (Paramount)

Betty Hutton is tip-top in the title role, giving distinction to antics of early day picture-making and four bright tunes [by Frank Loesser]. It's a funfest for the actress and she makes the most of it.

Pointing up many solid laughs are sequences depicting old open-air stages on which all variety of entertainment was ground out side by side in utter confusion. George Marshall draws heavily on his long picture experience to make it all authentic and garners himself a top credit for surefire direction.

Screenplay [from a story by P. J. Wolfson, "with a salute to Charles W. Goddard who wrote the original serial"] purports to show how Pearl White, early-day serial queen, got her start in silent films. Scripters carry her from a New York sweatshop to a traveling stock company and then into pictures with credible writing. Romance angle is the only apparent hoke factor in script but it, too, blends well with overall high entertainment level.

John Lund co-stars as a ham stock actor who is loved by the cliffhanger queen. Choice performances are delivered by Constance Collier, as the character actress, and William Demarest, as the silent director.

1947: NOMINATION: Best Song ("I Wish I Didn't Love You So")

•

PERIOD OF ADJUSTMENT
1962, 112 mins, US ▭ b/w
Dir George Roy Hill ***Prod*** Lawrence Weingarten ***Scr*** Isobel Lennart ***Ph*** Paul C. Vogel ***Ed*** Fredric Steinkamp ***Mus*** Lyn Murray ***Art*** George W. Davis, Edward Carfagno
Act Anthony Franciosa, Jane Fonda, Jim Hutton, Lois Nettleton, John McGiver (M-G-M)

Period of Adjustment is lowercase Tennessee Williams, but it also illustrates that lowercase Williams is superior to the uppercase of most modern playwrights.

Jane Fonda–Jim Hutton and Lois Nettleton–Anthony Franciosa are two teams whose emotional instability is explored. The togetherness of the first couple—newlyweds—is threatened by the insecurity of the afflicted groom, whose periodically severe outbreaks of the shakes are the manifestation of a long-standing complex wherein he feels compelled to hide behind a false he-man facade for fear of being found inadequate or below par at the supreme sexual moment.

Relations of the second pair are impaired by a more routine issue—in-law interference—coupled with the wife's accurate knowledge she was wed for money, not love—an original mercenary motive dissolved, however, after six years of marriage. Doesn't sound very funny, but there are spurts and flashes of good fun, both in dialog and situation.

Fonda gives an animated performance and makes an impression, but there are times when animation lapses into over-animation, stripping the character of believability. Hutton does generally well by the part of the afflicted husband. Franciosa has the meatiest part, and plays it to the hilt, creating an appealing, attractive, masculine person. Nettleton is solid as the gradually more desirable wife. George Roy Hill's direction has peaks and valleys.

1962: NOMINATION: Best B&W Art Direction

•

PERMANENT RECORD
1988, 91 mins, US Ⓥ ⦿ col
Dir Marisa Silver ***Prod*** Frank Mancuso, Jr. ***Scr*** Jarre Fees, Alice Liddle, Larry Ketron ***Ph*** Frederick Elmes ***Ed*** Robert Brown ***Mus*** Joe Strummer ***Art*** Michel Levesque
Act Alan Boyce, Keanu Reeves, Michelle Meyrink, Jennifer Rubin, Pamela Gidley, Lou Reed (Paramount)

A look at how a bunch of high schoolers try to deal with the suicide of their class's most promising member, pic is populated by profoundly unrewarding characters doing and saying utterly uninteresting things. The only potentially distinguished one of the lot is David (Alan Boyce), who is the best-looking, smartest and possibly a talented composer. At the same time, David is prone to inexplicable bouts of doubt, anguish and indecision, until he finally just plunges off a cliff into the sea. Shocking event forces everyone to face their own insecurity and vulnerability, but it is especially painful to Chris, David's best friend, who looked up to him as a shining example for his own comparatively aimless, irresponsible life.

Chris's gradual coming to grips with his sense of self gives the film its only point of interest, largely due to Keanu Reeves's performance, which opens up nicely as the drama progresses. Boyce is appealing enough as the doomed bright boy, and Richard Bradford contributes a highly sympathetic turn as the school principal. All the girls are vapid dips.

•

PERSECUTION
1974, 92 mins, UK Ⓥ col
Dir Don Chaffey ***Prod*** Kevin Francis ***Scr*** Robert B. Hutton, Rosemary Wootten, Frederick Warner ***Ph*** Kenneth Talbot ***Ed*** Mike Campbell ***Mus*** Paul Ferris ***Art*** Jack Shampan
Act Lana Turner, Ralph Bates, Trevor Howard, Olga Georges-Picot, Suzan Farmer, Patrick Allen (Tyburn)

In this British-made gothic suspenser, Lana Turner toplines as a sick-in-the-head mother who has killed her husband and goes on to blight her bastard son's life, ultimately seeing that his child and marriage are destroyed before she herself ends up an ironic corpse. It's all heavy with Freud-laden symbols.

The old-fashioned meller is riddled with ho-hum and sometimes laughably trite scripting. Also, very tame in the shock horror department. Under the circumstances, Turner's performance as Carrie, the perverted dame of the English manor, has reasonable poise.

As told partly in flashback, Turner's sadistic saga originates when her husband (Patrick Allen), discovering she's pregnant from an affair, dumps her down a staircase, leaving her with a lame leg. She avenges the experience by killing hubby. Deeply embittered, she starves the bastard son for love that she lavishes instead on her pet cat.

There isn't much animation to Ralph Bates as the grown-up edition of the tormented son. Suzan Farmer is okay as his wife, and Olga Georges-Picot is physically right as the prostie hired by Turner to seduce Bates and break up his marriage.

•

PERSECUTION AND ASSASSINATION OF JEAN-PAUL MARAT AS PERFORMED BY THE INMATES OF THE ASYLUM OF CHARENTON UNDER THE DIRECTION OF THE MARQUIS DE SADE, THE
(AKA: MARAT/SADE)
1967, 115 mins, UK/US ⦿ col
Dir Peter Brook ***Prod*** Michael Birkett ***Scr*** Adrian Mitchell ***Ph*** David Watkin ***Ed*** Tom Priestley ***Mus*** Richard Peaslee ***Art*** Sally Jacobs
Act Ian Richardson, Patrick Magee, Glenda Jackson, Clifford Rose, Michael Williams, Susan Williamson (Marat Sade/United Artists)

As a theatrical production in London and New York, the Royal Shakespeare Company's version, under Peter Brook's direction, of Peter Weiss's play has elements to make it impressive and stunning, also horrific and repellent. There were consummate performances, eye-filling spectacle, weighty natural verse, engrossing drama, burlesque (in its pristine sense), and, above all, startling originality. As a film directed and acted by the same director and cast, the result is somewhat less.

Ostensibly "a play within a play," written by De Sade, story centers on a single action—the murder of the revolutionary leader Jean-Paul Marat by Charlotte Corday while he issued dictums to the people of Paris from his bathtub. The action, however, is hysterically performed by the inmates until their excitation reaches an intolerable pitch, and each segment of the action is periodically aborted just short of Pandemonium by lengthy arguments between the paranoiac Marat and the egomaniacal De Sade over their conflicting views of man *vs.* society and vice versa.

In the end, Marat is murdered, the action completed, and total mayhem ensues. The inmates assault their keepers and the audience and their barely supressed capacity for violence is released.

Paradoxically, though film is supposed to be a more "intimate" medium, the play is more remote on film. The gain, however, is that the viewer's attention is riveted on the speeches.

Performances are uniformly excellent. There are several moments in the film that make the hair bristle and skin crawl.

•

PERSONA
1966, 84 mins, Sweden Ⓥ ⦿ b/w
Dir Ingmar Bergman ***Scr*** Ingmar Bergman ***Ph*** Sven Nykvist ***Ed*** Ulla Ryghe ***Mus*** Lars Johan Werle ***Art*** Bibi Lindstrom
Act Bibi Andersson, Liv Ullmann, Margaretha Krook, Gunnar Bjornstrand, Jorgen Lindstrom (Svensk Filmindustri)

There is no denying the absorbing theme and the perfection in direction, acting, editing and lensing. Pic is hypnotic in its first part, as stark black-and-white imagery tells of a noted actress who has suddenly stopped dead during a performance of a Greek tragedy and has refused to talk since. She is tended by a nurse and they are finally sent off to a beach island house together under orders of a psychiatrist.

Here the roles suddenly seem reversed, for the nurse talks about herself, and just about strips herself bare. The patient listens, reacts, and it is she giving solace; there is even a hint of love. There follows a sudden whiplash scene as the nurse abuses her out of pride. The nurse even lets her step on a piece of glass she has seen but not picked up. Here Bergman suddenly resorts to a Brechtian bit by simulating a ripping of the pic and then a burning.

Bibi Andersson's distraught, knowing, naive, helpful and then resentful performance of the nurse is a tour de force, and Liv Ullmann has the right luminous, questioning and sometimes impenetrable face and projection for the part of the beauteous but mute actress. At the end their faces photographically fuse.

Bergman has come up with probably one of his most masterful films technically and in conception, but also one of his most difficult ones.

•

PERSONAL BEST

1982, 122 mins, US Ⓥ col

Dir Robert Towne ***Prod*** Robert Towne ***Scr*** Robert Towne ***Ph*** Michael Chapman ***Ed*** Bud Smith, Ned Humphreys, Jere Huggins, Jacqueline Cambas, Walt Mulconery ***Mus*** Jack Nitzsche, Jill Fraser ***Art*** Ron Hobbs

Act Mariel Hemingway, Scott Glenn, Patrice Donnelly, Kenny Moore, Jim Moody, Luana Anders (Geffen/Warner)

Personal Best offers audiences a lot to like in solid characterizations, plus some shock that is a Robert Towne trademark. What they probably won't share, however, is his tedious fascination with physical perfection.

At his best, Towne handily overcomes the surface distractions of a lesbian relationship between two track stars (Mariel Hemingway and Patrice Donnelly). Though sometimes graphic, their intimacy is never self-conscious and Towne's sensitive pen creates two entirely believable characters in search of affection.

Towne is equally adept at drawing the two male characters, Scott Glenn as tough, domineering coach, and Kenny Moore, an ex-Olympic jock who becomes Hemingway's cushion once her crush on Donnelly is done.

Unfortunately, the vibrant personal scenes among these four are set against various track-and-field preparations for the Olympic trials. Towne has a love of slow motion that's employed as if he's afraid you might miss one, rippling muscle. Worse than that, when people aren't exercising, they are often talking about exercising.

•

PERSONAL PROPERTY

1937, 88 mins, US b/w

Dir W. S. Van Dyke ***Prod*** John W. Considine, Jr. ***Scr*** Hugh Mills, Ernest Vajda ***Ph*** William Daniels ***Ed*** Ben Lewis ***Mus*** Franz Waxman

Act Jean Harlow, Robert Taylor, Reginald Owen, Una O'Connor, Henrietta Crossman, E. E. Clive (M-G-M)

Personal Property is just a good two-reel farce [from the play *Man in Possession* by H. N. Harwood] padded rather too thinly into a feature. It is well-enough directed and acted but situations which might have been funny are slightly flattened out.

Just why Metro should believe there is any entertainment in a close-up of Robert Taylor taking a bath is rather hard to say. He follows this with a scene in which he puts a nail-file to work.

Jean Harlow is hoydenish and coy in her own inimitable style. She wears some striking costumes which clearly convey the ideas which the designer had in mind. There is more of Harlow on display when she's all dressed up than some girls reveal in their step-ins.

The plot? Well, Taylor gets himself the job of a sheriff's officer and moves into Harlow's London house as custodian of her person and her possessions. The idea is that she resents his presence. He stays around a couple of days—and nights. The picture is about what doesn't happen.

•

PERSONALS, THE

1982, 90 mins, US Ⓥ ⊙ col

Dir Peter Markle ***Prod*** Patrick Wells ***Scr*** Peter Markle ***Ph*** Peter Markle, Greg Cummins ***Ed*** Stephen E. Rivkin ***Mus*** Will Sumner

Act Bill Schoppert, Karen Landry, Paul Elding, Michael Laskin, Vicki Dakil, Chris Forth (New World)

With a neutral title and a cast of unknowns, *The Personals* has little going for it other than that it's a terrific little picture.

Entire cast make their feature film debut, along with writer-director Peter Markle. Markle's story really isn't all that profound, but it's told with sincerity and humor.

Bill Schoppert is a true discovery as an average, balding, career-minded and funny fellow whose equally nice wife feels neglected and leaves him for another man. Reluctantly tossed back into the singles world. Schoppert resorts to placing a personal ad in a newspaper.

Initial result is a hilarious date with pushy Vicki Dakil, but he perseveres until he connects with Karen Landry, another neatly unassuming actress, and the result is love.

•

PERSONAL SERVICES

1987, 105 mins, UK Ⓥ ⊙ col

Dir Terry Jones ***Prod*** Tim Bevan ***Scr*** David Leland ***Ph*** Roger Deakins ***Ed*** George Akers ***Mus*** John Du Prez ***Art*** Hugo Luczyc Wyhowski

Act Julie Walters, Alec McCowen, Shirley Stelfox, Danny Schiller, Tim Woodward, Peter Cellier (British Screen/Zenith)

For a pic about sex, *Personal Services* is remarkably unerotic. It deals with society's two-faced attitude to sex-for-sale in a humorous but essentially sad way, and is excellently acted and directed. Film is based on a real madam who became a household name as a result of a trial in 1986.

Pic tells the story of the transition of Christine Painter (a dominating performance by Julie Walters) from waitress to madam of Britain's most pleasant brothel, where the perversions are served up with a cooked breakfast and a cup of tea to follow. She looks after the aged and infirm along with eminent clients, none of whom has a kink her girls can't cater to.

Julie Walters plays Christine as a charmingly vulgar yet benign madam, whose brothel-keeping career seemingly comes to an end when the police raid her London house during a Christmas party. At her trial she recognizes the judge as one of her regular clients.

Alec McCowen is excellent as her friend and business partner, a former pilot who proudly boasts of a World War II record of 207 missions over enemy territory in "bra and panties."

•

PETE KELLY'S BLUES

1955, 95 mins, US Ⓥ ⊙ ▭ col

Dir Jack Webb ***Prod*** [uncredited] ***Scr*** Richard L. Breen ***Ph*** Hal Rosson ***Ed*** Robert M. Leeds ***Mus*** Matty Matlock (arr.) ***Art*** Harper Goff

Act Jack Webb, Janet Leigh, Edmond O'Brien, Peggy Lee, Andy Devine, Lee Marvin (Mark VII/Warner)

Jazz addicts (usually highly opinionated) may have a special interest in the musical frame. Beyond this special-interest factor is a melodramatic story that catches the mood of the Prohibition era. Jack Webb enacts a cornet player in a 1927 Kansas City speakeasy. Mostly it develops as a gangster picture (without the cops) with a Dixieland accompaniment.

Plot around which the music is woven has to do with the move-in into the band field by Edmond O'Brien, small-time bootlegger-racketeer, and the abortive efforts at resistance made by Webb to protect his small outfit. Webb's understatement of his character is good and Peggy Lee scores a personal hit with her portrayal of a fading singer taken to the bottle.

1955: NOMINATION: Best Supp. Actress (Peggy Lee)

•

PETE 'N' TILLIE

1972, 100 mins, US Ⓥ ▭ col

Dir Martin Ritt ***Prod*** Julius J. Epstein ***Scr*** Julius J. Epstein ***Ph*** John Alonzo ***Ed*** Frank Bracht ***Mus*** John Williams ***Art*** George Webb

Act Walter Matthau, Carol Burnett, Geraldine Page, Barry Nelson, Rene Auberjonois, Lee H. Montgomery (Universal)

Pete 'n' Tillie is a generally beautiful, touching and discreetly sentimental drama-with-comedy, starring Walter Matthau and Carol Burnett as two lonely near–middle-agers whose courtship, marriage, breakup and reunion are told with compassion through producer Julius J. Epstein's fine script and Martin Ritt's delicate direction.

Based on a Peter De Vries novella, *Witch's Milk*, screenplay neatly establishes the two main characters—Matthau as an awkward, pun-prone market researcher who covers his gaucheries with a sardonic veneer; and Burnett as a maturing woman beginning to harden into uneasy spinsterhood.

In particular, Burnett is the key to the film's viability by largely playing straight man to Matthau's ironies, so there is a smooth credible transition to the drama of later reels.

1977: NOMINATIONS: Best Supp. Actress (Geraldine Page), Adapted Screenplay

•

PETER IBBETSON

1935, 83 mins, US b/w

Dir Henry Hathaway ***Prod*** Louis D. Lighton ***Scr*** Vincent Lawrence, Waldemar Young ***Ph*** Charles Lang ***Ed*** Stuart Heisler ***Mus*** Ernst Toch ***Art*** Hans Dreier, Robert Usher

Act Gary Cooper, Ann Harding, John Halliday, Ida Lupino, Douglass Dumbrille, Doris Lloyd (Paramount)

From a technical standpoint, picture is just about tops, gaining so much weight in beauty and serenity that it almost overbears the incredulity of the story. George du Maurier wrote this story two generations earlier. It followed on his already successful first novel *Trilby* and was an even greater success. [Script also draws on the play by John Nathaniel Raphael.] Wallace Reid made a click film of it in the silent days.

Casting is not of the happiest. Gary Cooper was never meant to be a dreamy love-sick boy. When he tells the Duchess of Towers that she can't have things the way she wants them but the way he wants them, he's fine. When he lies dying in a stinking jail and dreams of wandering in Elysian lanes with his sweetheart—he's just not believable.

Ann Harding, on the other hand, as the duchess, is splendid. Ringlets have replaced the part down the center and the effect is startling. John Halliday is the duke, a bit here but expertly played. Ida Lupino has a bit as Agnes and most definitely impresses.

1935: NOMINATION: Best Score

•

PETER PAN

1953, 76 mins, US Ⓥ ⊙ col

Dir Hamilton Luske, Clyde Geronimi, Wilfred Jackson ***Prod*** Walt Disney ***Scr*** Ted Sears, Bill Peat, Joe Rinaldi, Erdman Penner, Winston Hibler, Milt Banta, Ralph Wright ***Mus*** Oliver Wallace

(Walt Disney)

James M. Barrie's childhood fantasy, *Peter Pan*, many times legit-staged, and previously filmed with live actors, is a feature cartoon of enchanting quality.

The music score is fine, highlighting the constant buzz of action and comedy, but the songs are less impressive than usually encountered in such a Disney presentation.

The Barrie plot deals familiarly with a little boy (Peter Pan) who refused to grow up, preferring to remain a pixie in Never Never Land, and a little girl (Wendy) under paternal orders to pass into young ladyhood.

Before she does, however, she has one more night of childhood and, with Peter, Tinker Bell, and her two young brothers, John and Michael, pays a visit to the land of chimerical fantasy wherein dwell the comically dreadful Captain Hook; the toadying Smee, who fawningly tends the pirate; the basso-voiced Indian chief; the popeyed, tick-tocking crocodile; and the beautiful mermaids and lost boys.

The voice of young Bobby Driscoll, and cartoon animation in his likeness, sell the Peter Pan character. Equally good are the voices of Kathryn Beaumont as Wendy; Hans Conried as the villainous Hook and the exasperated father, Mr. Darling, and Bill Thompson as the fawning Smee. Tom Conway dulcetly intones the narrated story bridges.

•

PETERSEN

1974, 103 mins, Australia Ⓥ col

Dir Tim Burstall ***Prod*** Tim Burstall ***Scr*** David Williamson ***Ph*** Robin Copping ***Ed*** David Bilcock ***Mus*** Peter Best ***Art*** Bill Hutchinson

Act Jack Thompson, Jacki Weaver, Joey Hohenfels, Amanda Hunt, George Mallaby, Arthur Dignam (Hexagon)

Tony Petersen (Jack Thompson) is an ex-electrician at university in pursuit of an arts degree. Married with two children, he's carrying on an affair with Patricia who, besides being a tutor in English at the university is also the wife of the Associate Professor of English who is responsible for Petersen's studies.

Women find Petersen irresistible, and the attraction is mutual. He even actively participates in a public sex act protest by the University Women's Liberationists.

Plotwise pic is not too strong but has several meaningful meanderings. It contains some of playwright David Williamson's best writing yet. He's more disciplined and doesn't let the action get farcically out of hand and displays depths of sensitivity, humanity and gentleness mostly lacking previously.

•

PETER'S FRIENDS

1992, 100 mins, UK/US Ⓥ ⊙ col

Dir Kenneth Branagh ***Prod*** Kenneth Branagh ***Scr*** Rita Rudner, Martin Bergman ***Ph*** Roger Lanser ***Ed*** Andrew Marcus ***Mus*** Gavin Greenaway (dir.) ***Art*** Tim Harvey

Act Kenneth Branagh, Emma Thompson, Stephen Fry, Hugh Laurie, Rita Rudner, Imelda Staunton (Renaissance/Channel 4/Goldwyn)

Already called a British *Big Chill*, Kenneth Branagh's third feature is a sometimes funny, often cloying entertainment about old friends who experience a year's worth of crises in two days.

Script confines the action almost entirely to the country estate of Peter (Stephen Fry), a witty, charmingly dissolute young aristocrat who invites his college theatrical friends for a New Year's reunion. In a manner that smacks of both stage comedy and sitcoms, the various characters are paraded forward with their most humorous traits front and center.

Playing an insecure egotist and fitness freak who secretly raids the fridge, co-writer Rita Rudner has given herself a lion's share of the good bits and she carries off the Joan Collins-ish role in high style. As her tag-along hubby who has deserted the U.K. for L.A., Branagh is slyly humorous, but a hollow character.

Most appealing are the ditzy Thompson, whose sudden transformation into a glamorpuss by Rudner and subsequent quickie affair are nevertheless jarring; Phyllida Law as the mansion's dignified, longtime housekeeper; and Fry as the affable host.

•

PETE'S DRAGON

1977, 134 mins, US Ⓥ ⦿ col

Dir Don Chaffey ***Prod*** Ron Miller ***Scr*** Malcolm Marmorstein ***Ph*** Frank Phillips ***Ed*** Gordon D. Brenner ***Mus*** Irwin Kostal (sup.) ***Art*** John B. Mansbridge, Jack Martin Smith

Act Helen Reddy, Jim Dale, Mickey Rooney, Red Buttons, Shelley Winters, Sean Marshall (Walt Disney)

Pete's Dragon is an enchanting and humane fable which introduces a most lovable animal star (albeit an animated one). Budgeted at $11 million, it was the most expensive film in the history of the Disney Studios, besting *Mary Poppins* by $4.5 million.

The pic's story line is just a shell. This is a star vehicle and the headliner has been created with love and care by Disney animators, headed by Ken Anderson and Don Blyth.

Elliott, the dumpy, clumsy, 12-foot-tall mumbling dragon with the ability to go instantly invisible and the misfortune of setting the idyllic Maine town of Passamaquoddy even farther back into the early 20th century, is a triumph.

1977: NOMINATIONS: Best Adapted Score, Song ("Candle on the Water")

•

PETRIFIED FOREST, THE

1936, 75 mins, US Ⓥ b/w

Dir Archie Mayo ***Scr*** Charles Kenyon, Delmer Daves ***Ph*** Sol Polito ***Ed*** Owen Marks ***Art*** John Hughes

Act Leslie Howard, Bette Davis, Humphrey Bogart, Genevieve Tobin, Dick Foran, Joseph Sawyer (Warner)

The picture sticks closely to the legit script by Robert E. Sherwood. Playing the roles they created in the stage version are Leslie Howard and Humphrey Bogart—the former a soul-broken, disillusioned author, seeking, by wayfaring, to find some new significance in living, and the latter a killer, harried and surrounded by pursuers, revealing in his last moments a bewildered desperation which is not far removed from that of the writer.

The scenes in which the desperado holds court, as he awaits his own doom, over the group in the little Arizona gas station-barbecue stand are packed with skillfully etched drama and embroidered with appropriate touches of comedy.

Impressively enacted is the romance between Howard and Bette Davis which comes to flowering under the lowering brows and guns of the killer. The girl, daughter of the desert oasis' owner, longs for foreign climes and a chance to develop her talents as a painter. Howard, wishing to make this longing a reality, strikes a bargain with the gunman.

Davis gives a characterization that fetches both sympathy and admiration. Bogart's menace leaves nothing wanting. Well placed are the comedy relief bits which are allotted Charles Grapewin.

Warners made two endings for this picture. The happy ending had Howard recovering.

•

PET SEMATARY

1989, 102 mins, US Ⓥ ⦿ col

Dir Mary Lambert ***Prod*** Richard P. Rubinstein ***Scr*** Stephen King ***Ph*** Peter Stein ***Ed*** Michael Hill, Daniel Hanley ***Mus*** Elliot Goldenthal ***Art*** Michael Z. Hanan

Act Dale Midkiff, Fred Gwynne, Denise Crosby, Brad Greenquist, Michael Lombard (Paramount)

Pet Sematary marks the first time Stephen King has adapted his own book for the screen, and the result is undead schlock dulled by a slasher-film mentality—squandering its chilling and fertile source material.

The story hinges on a small family that comes to New England, moving into a vintage Americana house alongside a truck route. When Louis Creed (Dale Midkiff) finds his daughter's cat dead along the road, his elderly neighbor Jud (Fred Gwynne) takes him to a hidden Indian burial ground that brings the beast back to life.

The quiet madness that gradually leads Louis to try and bring a person back via the same process—despite the repeated warnings of a friendly ghost—isn't apparent in Mary Lambert's hastily assembled narrative.

King appears in a cameo as a minister presiding over a funeral. He also introduces some wan, recurrent humor in the form of the reappearing and grisly ghost (Brad Greenquist).

•

PET SEMATARY TWO

1992, 100 mins, US Ⓥ ⦿ col

Dir Mary Lambert ***Prod*** Ralph S. Singleton ***Scr*** Richard Outten ***Ph*** Russell Carpenter ***Ed*** Tom Finan ***Mus*** Mark Governor ***Art*** Michelle Minch

Act Edward Furlong, Anthony Edwards, Clancy Brown, Jared Rushton, Darlanne Fluegel, Lisa Waltz (Paramount)

Pet Sematary Two is about 50% better than its predecessor, which is to say it's not very good at all. The latest incarnation relies more on gore than genuine chills and is sorely lacking in subtlety.

The story opens with the accidental death of an actress (Darlanne Fluegel) in front of her teenage son (Edward Furlong). Dad (Anthony Edwards) and son move to a small town, where the boy has to grapple with his loneliness and the obligatory school bully (Jared Rushton). Jeff (Furlong) befriends another boy (Jason McGuire) whose tyrannical stepfather (Clancy Brown) guns down the kid's dog. Duo take the beast to the "pet sematary," an ancient Indian burial ground rumored to revive the dead, subsequently repeating the process on the stepfather and setting up the inevitable question about tempting the forces of nature by awakening mom.

Director Mary Lambert (reprising her duties from the 1989 release) again errs by setting much of the action around the cemetery in daylight, although the pacing is significantly better than the first pic. Makeup and special effects are topnotch.

•

PETTICOAT PIRATES

1961, 87 mins, UK Ⓥ col

Dir David Macdonald ***Prod*** Gordon L. T. Scott ***Scr*** Lew Schwarz, Charlie Drake ***Ph*** Gilbert Taylor ***Ed*** Ann Chegwidden ***Mus*** Don Banks ***Art*** Robert Jones

Act Charlie Drake, Anne Heywood, Cecil Parker, John Turner, Maxine Audley, Thorley Walters (Associated British)

Film has a flimsy, screwball but acceptable theme for a comedy-farce. Wren Officer Anne Heywood and the 150 girls under her command are piqued. On the grounds that anything men can do, Wrens can do better they maintain the right to serve at sea in warships. When the plan is turned down by the authorities they raid a frigate, imprison the skeleton crew and set off to sea, where they take part in an exercise between British and U.S. fleets.

These goings-on are mainly an excuse for pocket-sized television comedian Charlie Drake (in his second cinema vehicle) to masquerade as a Wren and for the main decks of the frigate to be turned into a sun-bathing parade, with the girls stripped down to their scanties.

The screenplay [from a story by T. J. Morrison] is flabby and dialog mainly flat. Heywood looks pretty, but unconvincing as the chief raider. Cecil Parker offers another of his well-timed studies in pomposity while John Turner makes a stalwart, pleasant hero.

•

PETULIA

1968, 103 mins, UK Ⓥ col

Dir Richard Lester ***Prod*** Raymond Wagner ***Scr*** Lawrence B. Marcus ***Ph*** Nicolas Roeg ***Ed*** Antony Gibbs ***Mus*** John Barry ***Art*** Tony Walton

Act Julie Christie, George C. Scott, Richard Chamberlain, Arthur Hill, Shirley Knight, Pippa Scott (Petersham-Wagner)

Petulia is an excellent romantic drama featuring the brief encounter of Julie Christie and George C. Scott. The bittersweet story vies for prominence with much commentary on materialistic aspects of society. Producer Raymond Wagner has complemented the story with strong production values, mainly from the Frisco locations.

Based on a John Haase novel, *Me and the Arch Kook Petulia*, the plot turns on the hectic, sometimes ecstatic affair between Christie, unhappy wife of sadistically weak Richard Chamberlain and Scott, just divorced from Shirley Knight and currently squiring Pippa Scott.

Arthur Hill and Kathleen Widdoes play a couple who try to patch things up between Knight and Scott, and Joseph Cotten has a few key scenes as Chamberlain's indulgent, overpowering father.

Scott's performance, in the face of a plot and film structure which could have relegated him to a reactive posture, is excellent. The natural emphasis is on Christie, who turns in a vital, versatile performance.

•

PEYTON PLACE

1957, 166 mins, US Ⓥ ▭ col

Dir Mark Robson ***Prod*** Jerry Wald ***Scr*** John Michael Hayes ***Ph*** William Mellor ***Ed*** David Bretherton ***Mus*** Franz Waxman

Act Lana Turner, Hope Lange, Lee Philips, Lloyd Nolan, Arthur Kennedy, Russ Tamblyn (20th Century-Fox)

In leaning backwards not to offend, producer and writer have gone acrobatic.

On the screen is not the unpleasant sex-secret little town against which Grace Metalious set her story. These aren't the gossiping, spiteful, immoral people she portrayed. There are hints of this in the film, but only hints.

Under Mark Robson's direction, every one of the performers delivers a top-notch portrayal. Performance of Diane Varsi particularly is standout as the rebellious teenager Allison, eager to learn about life and numbed by the discovery that she is an illegitimate child. Also in top form in a difficult role is Hope Lange, stepdaughter of the school's drunken caretaker. As Varsi's mother, Lana Turner looks elegant and registers strongly.

Lee Philips is another new face as Michael Rossi, the school principal who courts the reluctant Turner. Pleasant looking, Philips has a voice that is at times high and nasal. Opposite Varsi, Russ Tamblyn plays Norman Page, the mama's boy, with much intelligence and appealing simplicity.

Robson's direction is unhurried, taking best advantage of the little town of Camden, ME, where most of the film was shot.

1957: NOMINATIONS: Best Picture, Director, Actress (Lana Turner), Supp. Actor (Arthur Kennedy, Russ Tamblyn), Supp. Actress (Hope Lange, Diana Varsi), Adapted Screenplay, Cinematography

•

PHANTASM

1979, 90 mins, US Ⓥ ⦿ col

Dir Don Coscarelli ***Prod*** D. A. [= Don] Coscarelli ***Scr*** Don Coscarelli ***Ph*** Don Coscarelli ***Ed*** Don Coscarelli ***Mus*** Fred Myrow, Malcolm Seagrave ***Art*** S. Tyer

Act Michael Baldwin, Bill Thornbury, Reggie Bannister, Kathy Lester, Angus Scrimm (Avco Embassy)

Pic opens with 13-year-old Mike Pearson (Michael Baldwin), who foolishly disobeys his older brother's orders not to attend the funeral of a close friend who, unbeknownst to everyone, was really stabbed by a woman after the two made love in a cemetery. Mike hides in the bushes during the ceremony and later happens to eye the villainous tall man (Angus Scrimm) loading the casket into a car.

Once inside the mausoleum, the fun begins, with Mike treated to a quite grisly murder courtesy of a futuristic flying silver sphere and the wrath of the tall man, who doesn't cotton to the kid's curiosity. Film then follows Mike, brother Jody (Bill Thornbury) and company as they attempt to unravel exactly what is going on.

Strong point of the feature is that it's played for both horror and laughs.

•

PHANTASM II

1988, 90 mins, US Ⓥ ⦿ col

Dir Don Coscarelli ***Prod*** Robert. A. Quezada ***Scr*** Don Coscarelli ***Ph*** Daryn Okada ***Ed*** Peter Teschner ***Mus*** Fred Myrow ***Art*** Philip J. C. Duffin

Act James Le Gros, Reggie Bannister, Angus Scrimm, Paula Irvine, Samantha Phillips (Universal)

Phantasm II is an utterly unredeeming, full-gore sequel to the original nine years earlier. The special effects horrors run amok here, with slimy, hissing apparitions constantly erupting from the bodies of the afflicted.

Story involves the morbid obsessions of two psychically connected teens, Mike (James Le Gros) and Liz (Paula Irvine). The pair are tortured in their dreams by The Tall Man (Angus Scrimm, reprising the role), a ghoulish mortician who wreaks evil via flying spheres that carve up people's faces.

Working out of his Morningside Mortuary, The Tall Man robs graves and hauls away corpses via a band of dwarves whose costumes look suspiciously like those of the Jawas in *Star Wars*.

All of this might be a hoot if molded in the right spirit, but in writer-director Don Coscarelli's hands it's incredibly morbid and meaningless.

•

PHANTOM, THE

1996, 100 mins, US Ⓥ ⊙ ▭ col

Dir Simon Wincer ***Prod*** Robert Evans, Alan Ladd, Jr. ***Scr*** Jeffrey Boam ***Ph*** David Burr ***Ed*** O. Nicholas Brown ***Mus*** David Newman ***Art*** Paul Peters

Act Billy Zane, Kristy Swanson, Treat Williams, Catherine Zeta Jones, James Remar, Cary-Hiroyuki Tagawa (Village Roadshow)

While it hardly stands to vanquish the celluloid incarnations of Superman and Batman, this version of an older cartoon crusader's exploits does have a pleasingly astute sense of its place in the great scheme of things pulp. Pic brings a light touch to appealingly old-fashioned action material.

The Phantom admirably avoids any temptation to modernize or complicate a hero who became a prototype for many that would follow when Hearst cartoonist Lee Falk introduced him in 1936.

Story opens with four fedora-wearing thugs braving the island's jungle to steal a mysterious metal skull. The Phantom (Billy Zane) swoops in to thwart the heist, but unavoidably lets the main miscreant go free. White-collar master criminal Xander Drax (Treat Williams) has been trying to acquire the legendary Skulls of Touganda, which supposedly have magical powers when united.

The Gotham politico investigating Drax can't follow the evidence all the way to Bengalla, so he sends his niece, Diana Palmer (Kristy Swanson), who arrives only to be quickly taken prisoner by Drax henchman Quill (James Remar) and the vixenish Sala (Catherine Zeta Jones). Aided by his trusty wolf, Devil, the Phantom plucks Diana from the villains' grasp.

While there's little distinctive about pic's style, helmer Simon Wincer does a capable job drawing together elements that require lots of stuntwork and special effects, and filming in several far-flung locales including remote parts of Thailand, which contributed a hefty share of eye-grabbing scenery. Like much of the surrounding film, Zane's masked hero is unapologetically two-dimensional, and he's nicely matched by Swanson's Girl Scout of a heroine. The baddies come across more vividly. The standouts here are Remar, Zeta Jones and, especially, Williams.

•

PHANTOM FIEND, THE

SEE: THE LODGER (1932)

•

PHANTOM LADY

1944, 83 mins, US b/w

Dir Robert Siodmak ***Prod*** Milton Feld (exec.) ***Scr*** Bernard C. Schoenfeld ***Ph*** Woody Bredell ***Ed*** Arthur Hilton ***Mus*** Hans J. Salter ***Art*** John B. Goodman, Robert Clatworthy

Act Franchot Tone, Ella Raines, Alan Curtis,, Elisha Cook, Jr. (Universal)

Phantom Lady [based on the novel by Cornell Woolrich] is an expertly contrived, suspenseful mystery meller developing along unusual cinematic lines. Catching and holding attention at the opening sequence, it rolls through a maze of episodes to allow a femme amateur detective to unravel a strange murder.

Plot has Alan Curtis picking up a strange woman in a bar, and he takes her to a show. During the evening his wife is murdered, and he eventually is convicted on circumstantial evidence when he cannot find or identify his woman companion of the night, whose main distinguishing feature is an odd hat creation. While Curtis is facing execution, secretary Ella Raines embarks on sleuthing tour to find the woman with the hat.

Picture is the first producer chore for Joan Harrison, who was associated with producer-director Alfred Hitchcock for eight years as secretary, reader and scripter. *Phantom Lady* demonstrates that the pupil absorbed much of Hitchcock's technique in displaying screen suspense.

•

PHANTOM OF THE OPERA, THE

1925, 101 mins, US Ⓥ ⊙ ⊗ b/w & col

Dir Rupert Julian ***Scr*** [Raymond Schrock, Elliott J. Clawson, Tom Reed] ***Ph*** [Virgil Miller] ***Ed*** [Maurice Pivar] ***Art*** [Charles D. Hall]

Act Lon Chaney, Mary Philbin, Norman Kerry, Arthur Edmund Carewe, Gibson Gowland, John Sainpolis (Universal)

It's reported the production cost approached $1 million, including over $50,000 for retakes, far above Universal's expectations. It's not a bad film from a technical viewpoint, but revolving around the terrifying of all inmates of the Grand Opera House in Paris by a criminally insane mind (Lon Chaney) behind a hideous face, the combination (from the novel by Gaston Leroux) makes a Welsh rarebit look foolish as a sleep destroyer.

The love angle is in the persons of an understudy (Mary Philbin) whom the Phantom cherishes while she is also the sole thought of her military lover (Norman Kerry).

The girl is twice abducted by the Phantom to his cellar retreat, and the finish is built up by the pulling of levers, concealed buttons, etc., to make active secret doors, heat chambers, flooding passages and other appropriate devices. However, the kick of the picture is in the unmasking of the Phantom by the girl. It's a wallop.

Kerry is a colorless hero, Philbin contents herself with being pretty and becoming terrorized at the Phantom, and Chaney is either behind a mask or grimacing through his fiendish makeup.

•

PHANTOM OF THE OPERA, THE

1930, 89 mins, US Ⓥ col

Dir Rupert Julian, Edward Sedgwick, (sound sequences) Ernst Laemmle ***Scr*** Elliott J. Clawson, Frank McCormack, Tom Reed ***Ph*** Charles Van Enger ***Ed*** Gilmore Walker, Edward Sedgwick ***Art*** Charles D. Hall, Ben Carre

Act Lon Chaney, Mary Philbin, Norman Kerry, Snitz Edwards, Arthur Edmund Carewe, Virginia Pearson (Universal)

In taking the old negative of *Phantom of the Opera*, U has even reproduced off-screen the voice of Lon Chaney in a few spots, besides scenes with Norman Kerry, Mary Philbin and others.

Dialog starts at the beginning. The big scene leading to the finish and capture of the Phantom is silent action. Synchronized score accompanies throughout with sound effects added to former silent scenes and singing obviously dubbed in for solos. This is particularly noticeable in a sequence where Philbin does a *Faust* favorite. Only scenes in color are a few of the opera and a masque ball but they are okay.

Only substitution in cast is Edward Martindel, talking the part played formerly by John Sainpolis. Others who appeared in the original picture, including John Miljan, are out through cutting of lesser scenes.

•

PHANTOM OF THE OPERA

1943, 92 mins, US Ⓥ ⊙ col

Dir Arthur Lubin ***Prod*** George Waggner ***Scr*** Eric Taylor, Samuel Hoffenstein ***Ph*** Hal Mohr, W. Howard Greene ***Ed*** Russell Schoengarth ***Mus*** Edward Ward ***Art*** Alexander Golitzen, John B. Goodman

Act Nelson Eddy, Susanna Foster, Claude Rains, Jane Farrar, Hume Cronyn, J. Edward Bromberg (Universal)

Phantom of the Opera is far more of a musical than a chiller, though this element is not to be altogether discounted, and holds novelty appeal. Story is about the mad musician who haunts the opera house and kills off all those who are in his protegee's way towards becoming the headliner.

Tuneful operatic numbers and the splendor of the scenic settings in these sequences, combined with excellent group and solo vocalists, count heavily. Nelson Eddy, Susanna Foster and Jane Farrar (niece of operatic star Geraldine Farrar) score individually in singing roles and provide marquee dressing. Third act from [Friedrich von Flotow's opera] *Martha* and two original opera sketches based on themes from Chopin and Tchaikovsky have been skillfully interwoven.

Outstanding performance is turned in by Claude Rains as the musician who, from a fixation seeking to establish the heroine as a leading opera star, grows into a homicidal maniac. Eddy, Foster, and Edgar Barrier, as the Parisian detective, are awkward in movement and speech, though much like opera performers restricted by their medium.

1943: Best Color Cinematography, Color Art Direction

NOMINATIONS: Best Scoring of a Musical Picture, Sound

•

PHANTOM OF THE OPERA, THE

1962, 84 mins, UK Ⓥ ⊙ col

Dir Terence Fisher ***Prod*** Anthony Hinds ***Scr*** John Elder ***Ph*** Arthur Grant ***Ed*** James Needs, Alfred Cox ***Mus*** Edwin Astley ***Art*** Bernard Robinson, Don Mingaye

Act Herbert Lom, Heather Sears, Thorley Walters, Michael Gough, Edward De Souza (Hammer)

Herbert Lom somewhat precariously follows in the macabre footsteps of Lon Chaney and Claude Rains. Switched to a London Opera House background, lushed up in color, with a new character, a dwarf rather confusingly brought in to supplement the sinister activities of the Phantom, it still provides a fair measure of goose pimples to combat some potential unwanted yocks.

Basically, the story remains the same. Baleful goings-on backstage at the opera which suggest that the place is invaded by evil spirits. The evil spirit is, of course, the Phantom but he turns out to be a rather more sympathetic character than of old and much of his malignance is now switched to a new character, the dwarf, played effectively by Ian Wilson.

However, the atmosphere of brooding evil still works up to some effective highlights, with the terror of the heroine (Heather Sears) paramount, the bewilderment of the hero (Edward De Souza) and the eerie personality of the Phantom still motivating the action.

•

PHANTOM OF THE OPERA, THE

1989, 90 mins, US Ⓥ ⊙ col

Dir Dwight H. Little ***Prod*** Harry Alan Towers ***Scr*** Duke Sandefur ***Ph*** Elemer Ragalyi ***Ed*** Charles Bornstein ***Mus*** Misha Segal ***Art*** Tivada Bertalan

Act Robert Englund, Jill Schoelen, Alex Hyde-White, Bill Nighy, Stephanie Lawrence (21st Century)

Not only are audiences unlikely to confuse this competent but flatly directed in Budapest production with Andrew Lloyd Webber's stage musical, or the classic Lon Chaney's silent, it also has precious little to do with Gaston Leroux's novel.

Opening in contemporary New York, this *Phantom* [based on a screenplay by Gerry O'Hara] starts with its heroine being hit on the head by a sandbag and mentally transported back to the mid-19th century for the bulk of the plot.

Set in London, rather than the Paris of *Phantom* tradition, this rendition seems faithful in broad outline to the original, save for the fact that its tragic antihero is a Jack the Ripper–style maniac who apparently would rather kill the young soprano to whom he's devoted than kiss her.

Running about encased in makeup that makes him appear a kind of Jack Palance gone to seed, Robert England is his usual broad self. Yet gorehounds are bound to be disappointed. As the object of his decidedly mixed emotions, Jill Schoelen is pretty but vapid.

•

PHANTOM OF THE PARADISE

1974, 91 mins, US Ⓥ ⊙ col

Dir Brian De Palma ***Prod*** Edward R. Pressman ***Scr*** Brian De Palma ***Ph*** Larry Pizer ***Ed*** Paul Hirsch ***Mus*** Paul Williams ***Art*** Jack Fisk

Act Paul Williams, William Finley, Jessica Harper, George Memmoli, Gerrit Graham (Pressman-Williams/20th Century-Fox)

Phantom of the Paradise is a very good horror comedy-drama about a disfigured musician haunting a rock palace. Brian De Palma's direction and script makes for one of the very rare "backstage" rock story pix, catching the garishness of the glitter scene in its own time.

The story takes novice songwriter William Finley through the despair of being ripped off by Paul Williams (excellent as a composite rock entrepreneur mogul), framed into prison, disfigured by an accident, and nearly betrayed anew by Williams who ostensibly sought reconciliation with Finley after the latter began haunting the Paradise rock house. Part of phantom Finley's motivation is his distant love of Jessica Harper, whom he wants to sing his music in Williams's rock cantata production.

All the principals come across extremely well, especially Harper.

1974: NOMINATION: Best Adapted Score

•

PHANTOM OF THE RUE MORGUE

1954, 83 mins, US col

Dir Roy Del Ruth ***Prod*** Henry Blanke ***Scr*** Harold Medford, James R. Webb ***Ph*** Peverell Marley ***Ed*** James Moore ***Mus*** David Buttolph

Act Karl Malden, Claude Dauphin, Patricia Medina, Steve Forrest, Allyn McLerie, Veola Vonn (Warner)

The horror in *Phantom of the Rue Morgue* is more to be taken lightly than seriously, since the shocker quality in Edgar Allen Poe's chiller tale, *Murders in the Rue Morgue*, has been dimmed considerably by the passage of time.

Murders and gory bodies abound in the Henry Blanke production, which gives fulsome attention to the bloody violence loosed by the title's phantom.

The script follows regulation horror lines in getting the Poe yarn on film and Roy Del Ruth's direction also is standard. Performances by Karl Malden, Claude Dauphin, Patricia Medina, Steve Forrest and the others fall into the same groove and none manages to rise above the material. Malden is the mad scientist who has his trained ape destroy all pretty girls who spurn him. After Allyn McLerie, Veola Vonn and Dolores Dorn have died violent deaths, the rather stupid police inspector played by Dauphin figures Forrest, young professor of psychology, is the guilty party.

The 3-D color lensing by Peverell Marley is good, and puts the turn-of-the-century Paris scenes on display to full advantage.

•

PHANTOM PRESIDENT, THE
1932, 78 mins, US b/w
Dir Norman Taurog ***Scr*** Walter DeLeon, Harlan Thompson ***Ph*** David Abel
Act George M. Cohan, Claudette Colbert, Jimmy Durante, George Barbier, Sidney Toler, Louise MacKintosh (Paramount)

A political satire holding a full share of laughs, it's about the first of its type for the screen, certainly as to the musical comedy vein. A lot of smart stuff packed into this footage including a gem of an opening sequence which is done in meter and kids the country's general condition.

For George M. Cohan it suffices to say that this is his first picture and maybe his last. For pictures such as these, light and frothy, he brings nothing to the screen which it has not already at hand. With Claudette Colbert wasted in an inconsequential role, it leaves everything up to Jimmy Durante. They evidently just let Durante alone and allowed him to play his scenes about as he pleased.

The story [from a novel by G. F. Worts] has Cohan playing a dual role. As T. K. Blair he's the colorless banker whom his party would make president but fears it can't because of his lack of personality. In playing Peter Varney, the medicine show man, Cohan is unquestionably happier with circumstances bringing about his substituting for Blair during the pre-election campaign. Mixed into this is the girl (Colbert) who senses something different when in the presence of Varney, but who can't figure it out. With Blair planning to rid himself of Varney, Colbert intervenes and it's the banker who's whisked from the scene on election day and Varney coasts to the White House.

Meanwhile there's Durante as Varney's helper who finally gains entrance to the convention hall and by the simple expedient of adapting his medicine show technique to the occasion stampedes his pal into the nomination. It's the high action mark of the film, done in rhythm and lyrics [by Richard Rodgers and Lorenz Hart] with the assembled delegates acting as the chorus.

•

PHAR LAP
1983, 118 mins, Australia Ⓥ ▭ col
Dir Simon Wincer ***Prod*** John Sexton ***Scr*** David Williamson ***Ph*** Russell Boyd ***Ed*** Tony Paterson ***Mus*** Bruce Rowland ***Art*** Laurence Eastwood
Act Tom Burlinson, Martin Vaughan, Judy Morris, Ron Leibman, Celia de Burgh, Vincent Ball (Edgley)

Phar Lap was a champion Australian racehorse, a legend in his own lifetime, who met a mysterious death in California in 1932.

Film's one flaw is its opening: It begins with Phar Lap's illness and death, and while every schoolboy in Australia knows this is how the story ended, a little suspense might have been retained for overseas viewers. However, once the flashbacks begin and Phar Lap's story is told, the film takes off.

Tom Burlinson is very effective as the shy stable boy who becomes devoted to the courageous horse. Martin Vaughan is impressive as the grimly determined trainer who leases the horse in the first place, as is Celia de Burgh, luminous as his loyal but neglected wife. Ron Leibman practically walks away with the picture as Davis, the smooth American horseowner, and Judy Morris is quietly effective as his naive, talkative wife.

•

PHASE IV
1974, 93 mins, US Ⓥ ⦿ col
Dir Saul Bass ***Prod*** Paul B. Radin ***Scr*** Mayo Simon ***Ph*** Dick Bush, Ken Middleton ***Ed*** Willy Kemplen ***Mus*** Brian Gascoigne ***Art*** John Barry
Act Nigel Davenport, Michael Murphy, Lynne Frederick, Alan Gifford, Robert Henderson, Helen Horton (Alced)

This one didn't get the bugs worked out before release. It's another in the Hollywood cycle of films based on every kind of creature enlarged by radiation. Today, the hot topic is ecology and the beasties have returned to normal size, but still bent on getting back at mankind.

In *Phase IV*, the ants are it. A couple of scientists (Nigel Davenport and Michael Murphy) set up an elaborate outpost in the desert to find out what the ants are up to and why.

Despite endless conversation and dial twirling, Davenport and Murphy never focus the story in any dramatic direction. Joining them as an ant attack refugee, Lynne Frederick only adds to the confusion.

Cinematically, the ants are never very menacing. Pic opens with an interminable segment inside an anthill. But photography is poor quality, looking like outtakes rejected by *National Geographic*.

•

PHENIX CITY STORY, THE
1955, 87 mins, US b/w
Dir Phil Karlson ***Prod*** Samuel Bischoff, David Diamond ***Scr*** Crane Wilbur, Dan Mainwaring ***Ph*** Harry Neumann ***Ed*** George White ***Mus*** Harry Sukman ***Art*** Stanley Fleischer
Act John McIntire, Richard Kiley, Kathryn Grant, Edward Andrews, Lenka Peterson, Biff McGuire (Allied Artists/Bischoff)

Vice, Southern style, gets the expose treatment in *Phenix City Story*. Production mostly hews to provable incident, with some coloring or rearrangement for dramatic emphasis. There's quite a bit of violence. Contemporary headlines and magazine articles have up-pointed conditions in this Alabama town, just across the Chattahoochee River from Columbus, Georgia, and the army's Fort Benning. Proximity of the latter contributed to the label of "the wickedest city in the U.S." hung on the Southern town, particularly during World War II.

A 13-minute prolog features radio-TV's Clete Roberts doing on-the-scene interviews with actual participants in the 1954 events, including the widow of Albert Patterson, the murdered candidate. This prolog stretches show's running time to 100 minutes, but it's up to the exhibitor whether or not it is used.

The downfall of Phenix City sin is woven around the return from overseas service of Richard Kiley with wife and two children to find his hometown still living up to its wicked reputation. Kiley plays John Patterson, the son of the murdered candidate, who was elected to the attorney general post by an aroused citizenry after the death of the father, ably depicted by John McIntire.

Edward Andrews plays Rhett Tanner, a menacing, entirely believable crime czar. Kathryn Grant is another who scores as Ellie Rhodes, a dealer in Tanner's joint.

Picture was lensed almost entirely in the actual locale, with hometown talent seen to quite an extent.

•

PHENOMENON
1996, 124 mins, US Ⓥ ⦿ ▭ col
Dir Jon Turteltaub ***Prod*** Barbara Boyle, Michael Taylor ***Scr*** Gerald DiPego ***Ph*** Phedon Papamichael ***Ed*** Bruce Green ***Mus*** Thomas Newman ***Art*** Garreth Stover
Act John Travolta, Kyra Sedgwick, Forest Whitaker, Jeffrey DeMunn, Robert Duvall, Richard Kiley (Touchstone)

The notion that human beings use something like just 10% of their brain capacity provides the springboard for *Phenomenon*, a movie that lives up to a similar fraction of its potential. The *Twilight Zone*–type premise, of a simple man who suddenly finds himself endowed with exceptional mental powers, generates some undeniable interest, with John Travolta's sympathetic performance as an Everyman transformed into a latter-day Einstein.

Director Jon Turteltaub has taken the easiest road, emerging with a soppy, soft-headed disease-of-the-week-style piece that sentimentalizes or opts out of every interesting issue the script raises.

George Malley (Travolta) is a small man in a small town, an agreeable auto mechanic who raises vegetables at his rural Northern California home but can't get a date for his 37th birthday party. Taking a break from the beer bash, he is struck down by a blinding light from the night sky, whereupon he returns to the party. Very quickly, however, he finds himself a changed man.

Despite all his accomplishments and unsullied likability, he still can't get anywhere with foxy single mom Lace (Kyra Sedgwick), but he keeps working on her. In the meantime, he cleverly fixes up his lonely-guy best friend, Nate (Forest Whitaker), just as he lands in hot water with the FBI. Travolta keeps things watchable, and Sedgwick is classy as the wary object of his affections, and Whitaker and (as a local doctor) Robert Duvall warmly fill out the emotional aspects of their decent, friendly characters.

•

PHFFFT
1954, 91 mins, US Ⓥ b/w
Dir Mark Robson ***Prod*** Fred Kohlmar ***Scr*** George Axelrod ***Ph*** Charles Lang ***Ed*** Charles Nelson ***Mus*** Frederick Hollander ***Art*** William Flannery
Act Judy Holliday, Jack Lemmon, Jack Carson, Kim Novak, Luella Gear, Donald Randolph (Columbia)

Title is the product of Walter Winchell's shell game with words—put "rift" under one cover, shake well, and it emerges "phffft" from another. Pic originally was written as a play (unproduced) by George Axelrod and was fashioned for the screen by the same author.

Phffft is a lightweight farce running from bed to verse. Judy Holliday and Jack Lemmon are the married couple whose bickering leads to the great divide of Reno. Each seeks to put the newly found freedom to exciting use via romantic pursuits in other directions.

Kim Novak gets across a zesty show as an accessible blonde out to cure Lemmon of the post-conubial blues. Jack Carson, as a bachelor wont to boast of his success in free-wheeling romance, registers colorfully. Holliday and Lemmon make an attractive combo. Femme star's bouts with the French language and psychiatry in addition to the agressive Carson are smartly played comedy.

•

PHILADELPHIA
1993, 122 mins, US Ⓥ ⦿ col
Dir Jonathan Demme ***Prod*** Edward Saxon, Jonathan Demme ***Scr*** Ron Nyswaner ***Ph*** Tak Fujimoto ***Ed*** Craig McKay ***Mus*** Howard Shore ***Art*** Kristi Zea
Act Tom Hanks, Denzel Washington, Jason Robards, Mary Steenburgen, Antonio Banderas, Ron Vawter (Tri-Star/Clinica Estetico)

This extremely well-made message picture about tolerance, justice and discrimination is pitched at mainstream audiences, befitting its position as the first major Hollywood film to directly tackle the disease of AIDS. Intelligent but too neatly worked out in its political and melodramatic details, pic is fronted by a dynamite lead performance from Tom Hanks.

Hanks stars as Andrew Beckett, a rising young attorney at a powerful Philadelphia law firm. But as soon as he's assigned to an extremely important case, he displays the first visible signs of AIDS. He's fired by the firm over a bit of alleged incompetence, but Andrew knows he was dismissed because of his illness.

Determined to spend the rest of his life, if necessary, fighting this gross injustice, Andrew, in desperation, is finally able to recruit Joe Miller (Denzel Washington), a somewhat flashy lawyer, as his attorney. He finally signs on, even if he still can't buy Andrew's lifestyle. By the time the trial begins, at the 45-minute point in the film, Andrew has lost weight and gone gray.

The screenplay has been extremely well worked out, but too much so, because every piece fits so perfectly that there are no rough edges, no moments when the raw, devastating reality of the situation registers with total force.

Pic's rainbow coalition of sympathies is impeccably tidy—Andrew's lawyer is black, his "partner" is Spanish (Antonio Banderas), one trial witness is a woman who contracted AIDS "innocently" through a transfusion, the defense attorneys are a woman and a black man, Andrew's family is unfailingly loving and supportive, and the bad guys are big-shot WASP lawyers anyone can root against. Still, Hanks makes it all hang together in a performance that constantly connects on the most basic human level.

1993: Best Actor (Tom Hanks), Original Song ("Streets of Philadelphia")

NOMINATIONS: Best Original Screenplay, Makeup, Song ("Philadelphia")

•

PHILADELPHIA EXPERIMENT, THE
1984, 102 mins, US Ⓥ col
Dir Stewart Raffill ***Prod*** Douglas Curtis, Joel B. Michaels ***Scr*** William Gray, Michael Janover ***Ph*** Dick Bush ***Ed*** Neil Travis ***Mus*** Ken Wannberg ***Art*** Chris Campbell
Act Michael Pare, Nancy Allen, Eric Christmas, Bobby Di Cicco, Kene Holliday, Louise Latham (New World/Cinema Group)

The Philadelphia Experiment had a lot of script problems in its development that haven't been solved yet, but final result is an adequate sci-fi yarn [story by Wallace Bennett, Don Jakoby]. Problems with the pic are common to all stories with a time-warp twist but director Stewart Raffill and writers have kept *Philadelphia* reasonably simple.

In 1943, Michael Pare and Bobby Di Cicco are sailors aboard a destroyer that's the center of a secret radar experiment which goes awry, throwing them into 1984, seemingly cross-circuited into another experiment. Befriended in the future by Nancy Allen, the pair obviously are a bit bemused at their surroundings before Di Cicco fades again into the past, leaving Pare to develop a romance with Allen and try to find his own way back in time.

•

PHILADELPHIA STORY, THE
1940, 112 mins, US Ⓥ ⊙ b/w
Dir George Cukor ***Prod*** Joseph L. Mankiewicz ***Scr*** Donald Ogden Stewart ***Ph*** Joseph Ruttenberg ***Ed*** Frank Sullivan ***Mus*** Franz Waxman ***Art*** Cedric Gibbons, Wade B. Rubottom
Act Cary Grant, Katharine Hepburn, James Stewart, Ruth Hussey, John Howard, Roland Young (M-G-M)

It's Katharine Hepburn's picture, but with as fetching a lineup of thesp talent as is to be found, she's got to fight every clever line of dialog all of the way to hold her lead. Pushing hard is little Virginia Weidler, the kid sister, who has as twinkly an eye with a fast quip as a blinker light. Ruth Hussey is another from whom director George Cukor has milked maximum results to get a neat blend of sympathy-winning softness under a python-tongued smart-alecknes. As for Cary Grant, James Stewart and Roland Young, there's little to be said that their reputation hasn't established. John Howard, John Halliday and Mary Nash, in lesser roles, more than adequately fill in what Philip Barry must have dreamt of when he wrote the 1939 play.

The perfect conception of all flighty but characterful Main Line socialite gals rolled into one, Hepburn has just the right amount of beauty, just the right amount of disarray in wearing clothes, just the right amount of culture in her voice—it's no one but Hepburn.

Story is localed in the very social and comparatively new (for Philly, 1860) Main Line sector in the suburbs of Quakertown. Hepburn, divorced from Grant, a bit of rather useless uppercrust like herself, is about to marry a stuffed-bosom man of the people (Howard). Grant, to keep Henry Daniell, publisher of the mags *Dime* and *Spy* (*Time* and *Life*, get it?) from running a scandalous piece about Hepburn's father (Halliday), agrees to get a reporter and photog into the Hepburn household preceding and during the wedding. Stewart and Hussey are assigned and Grant, whose position as ex-husband is rather unique in the mansion, manages to get them in under a pretext. Everyone, nevertheless, knows why Stewart and Hussey are there and the repartee is swift.

When the acid tongues are turned on at beginning and end of the film it's a laugh-provoker from way down. When the discussion gets deep and serious, however, on the extent of Hepburn's stone-like character, the verbiage is necessarily highly abstract and the film slows to a toddle.

1940: Best Actor (James Stewart), Screenplay

NOMINATIONS: Best Picture, Director, Actress (Katharine Hepburn), Supp. Actress (Ruth Hussey)

•

PHONE CALL FROM A STRANGER
1952, 96 mins, US Ⓥ b/w
Dir Jean Negulesco ***Prod*** Nunnally Johnson ***Scr*** Nunnally Johnson ***Ph*** Milton Krasner ***Ed*** Hugh Fowler ***Mus*** Franz Waxman ***Art*** Lyle Wheeler, J. Russell Spencer
Act Shelley Winters, Gary Merrill, Michael Rennie, Keenan Wynn, Bette Davis (20th Century-Fox)

A solidly based dramatic story idea has been brought off with a reasonable amount of success in *Phone Call From a Stranger*. Nunnally Johnson produced and did the script from a story by I.A.R. Wylie.

Plot concerns the survivor of an airplane crash who decides to call on the families of three people with whom he had become friends during the air trip that led up to the tragedy; hence the title. Before this stage of the story is reached, however, script does a topnotch job of slugging dramatics dealing with Gary Merrill's departure from home after his wife has made a mistake.

Shelley Winters does a good job of work on her flip character. Bette Davis's role as Wynn's bedridden wife occupies comparatively short footage but gives thespian strength to the film.

•

PHYSICAL EVIDENCE
1989, 99 mins, US Ⓥ ⊙ col
Dir Michael Crichton ***Prod*** Martin Ransohoff ***Scr*** Bill Phillips ***Ph*** John A. Alonzo ***Ed*** Glenn Farr ***Mus*** Henry Mancini ***Art*** Dan Yarhi
Act Burt Reynolds, Theresa Russell, Ned Beatty, Kay Lenz, Ted McGinley, Tom O'Brien (Columbia)

Burt Reynolds plays Joe Paris, a suspended detective who wakes up from a drunken binge to find himself the lead suspect in a murder investigation. His case is given to an assertive debutante (Theresa Russell) working in the public defender's office, whose obsession with the case begins to wreack havoc on her relationship with her yuppie, hot-tubbing stockbroker fiance (Ted McGinley).

Beyond that it's really anybody's guess as to what's going on, since the film [story by Steve Ransohoff] is so choppily assembled none of the various clues and innumerable suspects ever seem to lead anywhere. Another major shortcoming is the woeful miscasting of Russell as the young attorney. Even with her hair tightly pulled back into an unflattering bun (to be literally and symbolically let down in quieter moments), Russell's uncommon on-screen beauty proves a distraction.

•

PIANO, THE
1993, 120 mins, Australia/France Ⓥ ⊙ col
Dir Jane Campion ***Prod*** Jan Chapman ***Scr*** Jane Campion ***Ph*** Stuart Dryburgh ***Ed*** Veronika Jenet ***Mus*** Michael Nyman ***Art*** Andrew McAlpine
Act Holly Hunter, Harvey Keitel, Sam Neill, Anna Paquin, Kerry Walker, Genevieve Lemon (Chapman/Ciby 2000)

Jane Campion's fourth feature is a visually sumptuous and tactile tale of adultery set during the early European colonization of New Zealand, with Harvey Keitel daringly cast in the role of a passionately romantic lover, and Holly Hunter knockout as a woman physically unable to articulate her feelings.

Ada McGrath (Hunter) can hear, and can communicate in sign language through her young daughter, Fiona (Anna Paquin), but she can't talk. Apart from her child, Ada's most treasured possession is her piano. She's to marry a man she's never met, a pioneer settler (Sam Neill) in far-off New Zealand.

The marriage gets off to a bad start when Neill refuses to transport Ada's piano to his settlement. Later, he allows George Baines (Keitel) to take the piano. Baines, who has "gone native," offers to return the piano to her—if she gives him some lessons. These become stages in an increasingly erotic courtship.

Campion unfolds this striking story with bold strokes, including flashes of unexpected humor. The settlement is a chilly, muddy, rainswept place where civilization is barely making an impact. Hunter herself played solo piano and acted as piano coach on the production.

1993: Best Actress (Holly Hunter), Supp. Actress (Anna Paquin), Original Screenplay

NOMINATIONS: Best Picture, Director, Cinematography, Costume Design, Film Editing

•

PICCADILLY
1929, 92 mins, UK b/w
Dir E. A. Dupont ***Scr*** Arnold Bennett ***Ph*** Werner Brandes ***Ed*** J. N. McConaughty ***Mus*** Eugene Contie ***Art*** Alfred Junge
Act Gilda Gray, Jameson Thomas, Anna May Wong, King Ho Chang, Cyril Ritchard, Charles Laughton (British International)

Piccadilly is virtually silent despite a useless prolog. It may have been added and contains its only dialog, badly done.

This Arnold Bennett story is set in a cabaret in Piccadilly. The owner of the class joint digs up a dancer from the scullery. It's Anna May Wong, a dishwasher whom the proprietor catches dancing for her companions.

In the cabaret are a couple of ballroom dancers, with Gilda Gray one of them. Business commences to fade and the house staff concludes the male dancer must have been the draw. With trade shot, the proprietor remembers the girl downstairs, calls her up and dresses her up, then falls for her.

Gray is so peeved she calls upon the Chinese dancer. The two women meet after the owner leaves. The audience apparently sees Gray shoot Wong, as the latter unsheaths a dagger.

Music is the usual medley of pop dance stuff, with the cabaret set about the best thing in the production. Camerawork on close-ups is excellent.

•

PICKLE, THE
1993, 103 mins, US Ⓥ col
Dir Paul Mazursky ***Prod*** Paul Mazursky ***Scr*** Paul Mazursky ***Ph*** Fred Murphy ***Ed*** Stuart Pappe ***Mus*** Michel Legrand ***Art*** James Bissell
Act Danny Aiello, Dyan Cannon, Clotilde Courau, Shelley Winters, Barry Miller, Jerry Stiller (Columbia)

The Pickle is a vegetarian turkey. Self-indulgent story about a depressed, dispirited, middle-aged film director aims for comedy and poignance that never come, and feels wearily disenchanted and out of touch.

More than 20 years earlier, Paul Mazursky made *Alex in Wonderland*, an appealingly personal look at a creatively blocked filmmaker with a hit behind him. By contrast, the director in *The Pickle*, Harry Stone (Danny Aiello), has made a string of flops and is suffering convulsions of remorse over having sold out for the first time in his career.

Mazursky once again summons up memories of Fellini's *8½* by surrounding his melancholy protagonist with two ex-wives, a 22-year-old French girlfriend, daughter, son, granddaughter, mother, predatory female fan, publicist and journalist, among others. Harry abuses almost all of his loved ones.

Mazursky layers the mirthless tale with black and white flashbacks to Harry's youth in 1940s Brooklyn, as well as with bizarre snatches from the dreaded film-within-a-film, which concerns a space trip embarked upon by a giant pickle grown and launched by farm kids.

•

PICK-UP ARTIST, THE
1987, 81 mins, US Ⓥ ⊙ col
Dir James Toback ***Prod*** David L. MacLeod ***Scr*** James Toback ***Ph*** Gordon Willis ***Ed*** David Bretherton, Angelo Corrao ***Mus*** Georges Delerue ***Art*** Paul Sylbert
Act Molly Ringwald, Robert Downey, Dennis Hopper, Danny Aiello, Mildred Dunnock, Harvey Keitel (20th Century-Fox)

As long as this film sticks to what its title suggests, *The Pick-Up Artist* is a tolerably amusing comedy. But as soon as the compulsive skirt-chaser gets hooked on one girl, James Toback's long-gestating portrait of a one-track mind becomes bogged down in unconvincing plot mechanics.

Opening reels possess considerable buoyancy and zip, as makeout king Robert Downey cruises the streets of New York trying out his shtick on every pretty woman who crosses his path. Downey hits on Ringwald and quickly scores in his convertible, but predictably becomes intrigued by her apparent lack of interest in seeing him again.

Suddenly, he's got blinders on and finds himself assuming personal responsibility for some enormous gambling debts the mob expects delivered by high noon. Dennis Hopper once again plays a drunken, washed-up shell of his former self as Ringwald's irresponsible father, and Harvey Keitel is the threatening collector.

More responsible for the picture's deterioration than the unnecessary melodrama is Ringwald's thinly conceived character. Toback never lets the viewer in on what she really thinks and feels. Downey, in his first starring role, is brashly likeable, if perhaps too young, as the indefatigable but sincere ladies' man.

Warren Beatty developed the project and was listed as producer during shooting, but producer-of-record credit goes to Beatty's cousin, David L. MacLeod.

•

PICKUP ON SOUTH STREET
1953, 80 mins, US Ⓥ b/w
Dir Samuel Fuller ***Prod*** Jules Schermer ***Scr*** Samuel Fuller ***Ph*** Joe MacDonald ***Ed*** Nick De Maggio ***Mus*** Leigh Harline ***Art*** Lyle R. Wheeler, George Patrick
Act Richard Widmark, Jean Peters, Thelma Ritter, Murvyn Vye, Richard Kiley, Willis Bouchey (20th Century-Fox)

If *Pickup on South Street* makes any point at all, it's that there is nothing really wrong with pickpockets, even when they are given to violence, as long as they don't play footsie with Communist spies. Since this is at best a thin theme, *Pickup* for the most part falls flat on its face and borders on presumably unintended comedy.

Film's assets are partly its photography, which creates an occasional tense atmosphere, and partly the performance of Thelma Ritter, the only halfway convincing figure in an otherwise unconvincing cast. As Moe, the tired but sharp-tongued old woman who sells ties and habitually informs on her underworld pals in order to collect enough money for a decent "plot and stone," Ritter is both pathetic and amusing.

Story [by Dwight Taylor] has Richard Widmark picking Jean Peters's purse in the subway. In the wallet he lifts are films of a secret chemical formula obtained by a Commie spy ring. Widmark's act is observed by two federal agents who are shadowing Peters. Latter is instructed by her boyfriend-boss Richard Kiley to trace Widmark and get back the film.

Widmark is given a chance to repeat on his snarling menace characterization followed by a look-what-love-can-do-to-a-bad-boy act as Widmark's hard-boiled soul melts before Peters's romancing.

1953: NOMINATION: Best Supp. Actress (Thelma Ritter)

•

PICKWICK PAPERS, THE
1952, 109 mins, UK Ⓥ b/w
Dir Noel Langley *Prod* George Minter *Scr* Noel Langley *Ph* Wilkie Cooper *Ed* Anne V. Coates *Mus* Antony Hopkins *Art* Fred Pusey
Act James Hayter, James Donald, Nigel Patrick, Kathleen Harrison, Hermione Baddeley, Joyce Grenfell (Renown)

The adventures of Mr. Pickwick (James Hayter) and his henchmen have been deftly adapted for the screen by Noel Langley. By its adherence to the original, the film is naturally episodic in character.

The picture follows the members of the Pickwick Club on their adventurous tour across England in search of knowledge and human understanding. The encounter with Mr. Jingle (Nigel Patrick), the unscrupulous ne'er-do-well with the stilted turn of phrase; the famous literary fancy dress breakfast; the engagement of Sam Weller (Harry Fowler); the breach of promise suit brought against Mr. Pickwick by his former housekeeper and his subsequent sojourn in Fleet prison are among the incidents.

In manner and appearance Hayter gives the impression of being the genuine article. His fellow members of the Pickwick Club are admirably played.

•

PICNIC
1955, 115 mins, US Ⓥ ⦿ ▭ col
Dir Joshua Logan *Prod* Fred Kohlmar *Scr* Daniel Taradash *Ph* James Wong Howe *Ed* Charles Nelson, William A. Lyon *Mus* George Duning *Art* Jo Mielziner, William Flannery
Act William Holden, Rosalind Russell, Kim Novak, Betty Field, Susan Strasberg, Cliff Robertson (Columbia)

This is a considerably enlarged *Picnic*, introducing new scope and style in flow of presentation without dissipating the mood and substance of the legiter by William Inge. The boards-to-screen transplanters correctly refrained from making any basic changes. It's the story of a robust and shiftless show-off who, looking up an old college chum in a small town in Kansas, sets off various emotional responses among the small group of local inhabitants he encounters.

William Holden is the drifter, sometimes ribald, partly sympathetic and colorful and giving a forceful interpretation all the way.

Kim Novak is the town's No. 1 looker, and an emotional blank until muscle-man (and, to her, downtrodden) Holden proves an awakening force. Novak does right well.

Rosalind Russell, the spinster schoolteacher boarding with Novak's family, is standout.

1955: Best Color Art Direction, Editing

NOMINATIONS: Best Picture, Director, Supp. Actor (Arthur O'Connell), Scoring of a Dramatic Picture

•

PICNIC AT HANGING ROCK
1975, 115 mins, Australia Ⓥ ⦿ col
Dir Peter Weir *Prod* Jim McElroy, Hal McElroy *Scr* Cliff Green *Ph* Russell Boyd *Mus* Bruce Smeaton *Art* David Copping
Act Rachel Roberts, Dominic Guard, Vivian Gray, Helen Morse, Kirsty Child, Anne Lambert (SAFC)

On a warm St Valentine's Day in 1900 some schoolgirls from a boarding school in Victoria picnic at nearby Hanging Rock. Four girls venture forth on their own; one, Edith, falls asleep and wakes to find the other three have taken off their shoes and stockings and are climbing higher. The police are called to make an unsuccessful search. A young Englishman, Michael, also searches, spends the night alone by the rock and next day is found with a mysterious head wound but no memory of happenings. Later, one of the girls, Irma, is also found with a similar head wound and no memory of events.

Visually it probably is one of the most beautiful pix ever seen, with Aussie flora and fauna and wonderful blue skies. Everything has been carefully re-created with loving exactitude.

•

PICTURE OF DORIAN GRAY, THE
1945, 107 mins, US Ⓥ ⦿ b/w & col
Dir Albert Lewin *Prod* Pandro S. Berman *Scr* Albert Lewin *Ph* Harry Stradling *Ed* Ferris Webster *Mus* Herbert Stothart (dir.), [Mario Castelnuovo-Tedesco, Franz Waxman] *Art* Cedric Gibbons, Hans Peters
Act George Sanders, Hurd Hatfield, Donna Reed, Angela Lansbury, Peter Lawford, Lowell Gilmore (M-G-M)

The Picture of Dorian Gray, based upon the Oscar Wilde novel, represents an interesting experiment by Metro, reported to have cost over $2 million.

The morbid theme of the Wilde story is built around Gray: his contempt for the painting that was made of him, the fears of not retaining youth and, of course, the unregenerate depths to which Gray sinks. In the adaptation by Albert Lewin, much of the offscreen narration, explaining among other things what is going on in Gray's mind may be too much for most to grasp.

Hurd Hatfield is pretty-boy Gray. He plays it with little feeling, as apparently intended, though he should have aged a little toward the end. George Sanders, misogynistic of mind and a cynic of the first water, turns in a very commendable performance. It's he who upsets the romance, ostensibly serious on Gray's part, which has developed with a cheap music hall vocalist. She's Angela Lansbury, who registers strongly and very sympathetically.

[Original release prints included inserts in Technicolor.]

1945: Best B&W Cinematography

NOMINATIONS: Best Supp. Actress (Angela Lansbury), B&W Art Direction

•

PICTURE SHOW MAN, THE
1977, 99 mins, Australia col
Dir John Power *Prod* Joan Long *Scr* Joan Long *Ph* Geoff Burton *Ed* Nick Beauman *Mus* Peter Best *Art* David Copping
Act Rod Taylor, John Meillon, John Ewart, Harold Hopkins, Patrick Cargill, Yelena Zigon (Limelight)

The Picture Show Man has an old-fashioned endearing quality. The story of an itinerant purveyor of motion picture entertainment in the country areas of Australia in the 1920s, it's cute without being cloying, and episodic without being disjointed.

Based on an unpublished manuscript, Joan Long's script has enough characterization to allow the actors a fair go at establishing themselves, yet keeps them well-ordered enough to maintain the forward movement of the plot.

John Power's direction is firm without being thwarting and the result is that the good times being had on screen are conveyed to the audience and are affecting.

Rod Taylor's portrayal of the heavy is definitely lightweight.

•

PICTURE SNATCHER
1933, 70 mins, US b/w
Dir Lloyd Bacon *Scr* Allen Rivkin, P. J. Wolfson *Ph* Sol Polito
Act James Cagney, Ralph Bellamy, Patricia Ellis, Alice White, Ralf Harolde, Robert Emmett O'Connor (Warner)

Plenty of shoot-'em-up stuff, including some strong-arming and roughhouse tactics, this time in the guise of a technically legal and sympathetic cause—that of getting pictures of a woman being electrocuted, a crazy fireman shooting it out wih the cops, and the like.

James Cagney is a reformed hoodlum just out of stir after a three-year stretch. His yen to work on a newspaper finds him getting impossible pictures for a scurillous tab, the N.Y. *Graphic-News*, so identified. Among the highlights are the Ruth Snyder takeoff from the N.Y. *News* stunt in lensing that Sing-Sing execution via an ankle-strapped miniature camera. The crazy fireman shooting it out with the cops also harks back to a sensational tabloidized build-up in which a kid New York yegg figured notoriously.

Dominating it all—so much so that several loose ends are conveniently glossed over—is Cagney. He takes full advantage of the fly, crisp lines and situations, and a couple of the situashes are not Sunday school. It's all sex stuff. A moll and a double-dealing sobbie are the femme pursuers, while Cagney is chasing the honest cop's daughter. Patricia Ellis, as the ingenue, is a recent face with beaucoup possibilities. A piquant, youthful personality, she evidences also that she can manage a dramatic scene or two when necessary. Alice White, as the wise-cracking sobbie, is okay if not altogether sympathetic. Ralph Bellamy, as the city ed, sort of ups the average for male pulchritude in newspaper circles, but he's otherwise authentic throughout.

Story, an original by Danny Ahearn, suggests by the Cagney character name of Danny, something of an autobiographical import. It's a punchy, meaty yarn, properly peppered with topical highlights that never permit things to sag.

•

PIED PIPER, THE
1972, 90 mins, UK Ⓥ col
Dir Jacques Demy *Prod* David Puttnam, Sandy Lieberson *Scr* Andrew Birkin, Jacques Demy, Mark Peploe *Ph* Peter Suschitzky *Ed* John Trumper *Mus* Donovan *Art* Assheton Gorton
Act Jack Wild, Donald Pleasence, John Hurt, Donovan, Michael Hordern, Roy Kinnear (Sagittarius/Goodtimes)

The Pied Piper, based on the 14th-century legend from Hamelin, has been filmed by the sensitive Jacques Demy as a sort of somber fairy tale and allegory. The results are commendable in ambition but uneven in execution.

In recreating the story of the minstrel who leads the rats out of Hamelin, but then leads its children away when the politicians fail to keep a promise, the writers started with one of folklore's greatest pre-sold subjects. However, the script seems more a series of broad, arch, low-comedy vignettes without a clear emphasis.

As a result, Donovan, in the title role, is in and out of the story, as is Jack Wild, cast as the crippled boy whose alchemist patron, Michael Hordern, cannot convince the town's elders of the connection between Black Plague and rats.

•

PIERROT LE FOU
(CRAZY PETE)
1965, 110 mins, France/Italy Ⓥ ⦿ ▭ col
Dir Jean-Luc Godard *Prod* Georges de Beauregard *Scr* Jean-Luc Godard *Ph* Raoul Coutard *Ed* Francoise Colin *Mus* Antoine Duhamel *Art* [Pierre Guffroy]
Act Jean-Paul Belmondo, Anna Karina, Dirk Sanders, Raymond Devos, Graziella Galvani, Roger Dutoit (Rome Paris/SNCC)

Insider jokes, the use of objects to comment on a situation, and a mingling of the serious and comic—Jean-Luc Godard uses all of these devices here but the result is repetitive and precious rather than inventive and fresh.

A bored young man (Jean-Paul Belmondo) married to a rich woman one night goes off with the baby-sitter (Anna Karina) after a boring party. A dead man is found in her flat and they are soon on the run. After an idyllic time at the seashore, they get bored and hit the road and live by stealing, only to run into friends of hers.

Two gangs, repping Arab gun-runners and perhaps Israeli forces, fight it out and he gets embroiled. A cache of money is taken by the girl, who runs off with it and her so-called brother.

There is brilliant use of color in spots to mark the mood. There are also some seemingly spontaneous scenes of the two living off the land that are topflight Godard. But there is too much padding, and interspersed songs and fabricated scenes make up a compendium of all his stylistic tricks rather than a more coherent offbeater. [Pic is based on Lionel White's novel *Obsession*.]

Belmondo has the usual rugged verve as the bored, but dynamic, young man. Karina is delightful as an unpredictable, beguiling but finally deadly female.

•

PIGEON THAT TOOK ROME, THE
1962, 101 mins, US ▭ b/w
Dir Melville Shavelson *Prod* Melville Shavelson *Scr* Melville Shavelson *Ph* Daniel L. Fapp *Ed* Frank Bracht *Mus* Alessandro Cicognini *Art* Hal Pereira, Roland Anderson
Act Charlton Heston, Elsa Martinelli, Harry Guardino, Salvatore Baccaloni, Gabriella Pallotta, Brian Donlevy (Paramount)

Melville Shavelson functions as producer, director and writer and shows good control in all three categories. This is a good-fun comedy and there's no incongruity in the fact that the setting is authentic-looking World War II Italy. His adaptation of *The Easter Dinner*, a novel by Donald Downes, has a wacky story that plays out amusingly well. Interesting casting has to do with Charlton Heston, who's an American infantry officer assigned to a cloak-and-dagger role in Rome before the Nazis decide to leave and the Yanks walk in. It comes to be that homing pigeons represent his contact with the Allies. His birds provide an Easter dinner for a local and friendly family who do not know they're partaking of a part of "the American Air Force," as stated by one of the characters. Heston becomes replenished with German pigeons, gives them ankle bracelets with false war information, and one of these messengers heads unexpectedly to the Allies, instead of the enemy.

Heston plays the bewildered American officer with enough effectiveness to suggest that he can be at home with cinematic mischief. Harry Guardino is Heston's radio man, a sort of funny fellow sidekick who becomes enamored of a local girl who happens to be pregnant by previous misfortune.

Elsa Martinelli is Heston's romantic vis-à-vis, not one easily won over but eventually, of course, they go hand in hand.

1962: NOMINATION: Best B&W Art Direction

PILGRIMAGE
1933, 90 mins, US b/w
Dir John Ford ***Scr*** Philip Klein, Barry Connors, Dudley Nichols ***Ph*** George Schneiderman ***Ed*** Louis R. Loeffler ***Mus*** Samuel Kaylin (dir.)
Act Henrietta Crosman, Heather Angel, Norman Foster, Marian Nixon, Maurice Murphy, Lucille La Verne (Fox)

Story deals with the selfishness of mother love, but works out a new twist, dealing with the problem of a mother who stands in the way of her son's happiness with sympathetic treatment toward the woman.

Opening passages deal with the mother and her fatherless boy working an Arkansas farm. Restricted settings convey the idea of the narrow lives the people of the story are leading. Picture is full of similarly subtle touches.

Central character of Hannah Jessop is a compelling portrait: Willful, domineering and rooted in the land her pioneering forebears won from the wilderness. She's determined to hold her son to the farm and when the boy in rebellion determines to marry the girl of his choice, she gives him up to the World War draft board.

When he's killed in action and the girl, daughter of a neighboring ne'er-do-well, has a child, the old woman remains as unyielding and grim in her grief. A decade after, on a pilgrimage to the dead boy's grave in France, she sees the error of her ways.

Henrietta Crosman plays the Hannah character under wraps, leaving the impression of a reserve of power and vitality. Norman Foster gives to the son the earnest playing that has made him a standard in this type of role, while Marian Nixon deals with the deserted sweetheart well, a quiet, restrained treatment that fits beautifully into the story structure.

PILLOW BOOK, THE
1996, 123 mins, UK/Netherlands/France Ⓥ col
Dir Peter Greenaway ***Prod*** Kees Kasander ***Scr*** Peter Greenaway ***Ph*** Sacha Vierny ***Ed*** Chris Wyatt, Peter Greenaway ***Art*** Wilbert Van Dorp, Andree Putman, Emi Wada
Act Vivian Wu, Ewan McGregor, Yghi Oida, Ken Ogata, Hideko Yoshida, Judy Ongg (Woodline/Kasander & Wigman/Alpha)

Iconoclastic British helmer Peter Greenaway's fascination with the most arcane reaches of the world's art and literature is on full display in the dense yet enormously impressive *The Pillow Book*, uniquely bold and arresting depiction of exotic erotica, with inventive visual design and slow but inexorably logical plot development.

His response to 10th-century Japanese writer Sei Shonagon's *Pillow Book*, a compendium of lists, reminiscences, literary quotes and amorous adventures, is at first daunting but ultimately awesome and beautiful. Pic revolves around the erotic adventures of a young Japanese woman, Nagiko (played as an adult by Vivian Wu). Nagiko's birthdays are celebrated in a highly ritualized manner as her father (Ken Ogata), an impoverished writer and expert calligrapher, writes a sensuous birthday greeting on her face with brush and ink while her aunt reads passages from the Shonagon classic.

At the age of 18, Nagiko is persuaded to marry the nephew of her father's gay publisher. The frustrated young woman becomes obsessed with following in the footsteps of Shonagon, and when her husband burns her diaries, she leaves him and flees to Hong Kong. There she becomes a successful fashion model and begins searching out a series of lovers who are also calligraphers. None really satisfies her, however, until she meets an Englishman, Jerome (Ewan McGregor), with whom she falls in love.

The actors lend themselves generously to the director's heady vision, and bravely take part in some pretty explicit sequences. Wu is lovely as the intrepid heroine, McGregor impressive as the hedonistic Jerome.

PILLOW TALK
1959, 105 mins, US Ⓥ ▭ col
Dir Michael Gordon ***Prod*** Ross Hunter, Martin Melcher ***Scr*** Stanley Shapiro, Maurice Richlin ***Ph*** Arthur E. Arling ***Ed*** Milton Carruth ***Mus*** Frank DeVol ***Art*** Richard H. Riedel
Act Rock Hudson, Doris Day, Tony Randall, Thelma Ritter, Nick Adams, Julia Meade (Arwin/Universal)

Pillow Talk is a sleekly sophisticated production that deals chiefly with s-e-x. The principals seem to spend considerable time in bed or talking about what goes on bed, but the beds they occupy are always occupied singly. There's more talk than action, natch.

The plot (slight) of the amusing screenplay, from a story by Clarence Greene and Russell Rouse, is based on the notion that a telephone shortage puts Doris Day and Rock Hudson on a party line. Hudson is here a sophisticated man about town. Day displays a brace of smart Jean Louis gowns, and delivers crisply.

There is a good deal of cinema trickery in *Pillow Talk*. There are split screens; spoken thoughts by the main characters; and even introduction of background music orchestration for a laugh. It all registers strongly.

1959: Best Story & Screenplay

NOMINATIONS: Best Actress (Doris Day), Supp. Actress (Thelma Ritter), Color Art Direction, Scoring of a Dramatic Picture

PINK FLAMINGOS
1974, 95 mins, US Ⓥ col
Dir John Waters ***Scr*** John Waters ***Ph*** John Waters ***Ed*** John Waters
Act Divine, David Lochary, Mink Stole, Mary Vivian Pearce, Edith Massey, Danny Mills (Dreamland)

Divine, also known as Babs Johnson, is a 300-lb. drag queen of grotesque proportions who holds the title "the filthiest person in the world." Vying for the title are Connie and Raymond Marble, who kidnap girls, impregnate them, and sell the children to lesbian couples in order to finance "an inner city heroin ring" catering to high school students. Around the above premise spins the nitwit plot of the poorly lensed 16mm picture *Pink Flamingos*—one of the most vile, stupid and repulsive films ever made.

Divine's Mama Edie, a huge mountain of adipose tissue, inhabits a playpen in the mobile home and performs coprophagy on the fresh product of a miniature poodle while "How Much Is That Doggie in the Window" toodles on the soundtrack.

PINK FLOYD—THE WALL
1982, 99 mins, UK Ⓥ ⊙ ▭ col
Dir Alan Parker ***Prod*** Alan Marshall ***Scr*** Roger Waters ***Ph*** Peter Biziou ***Ed*** Gerry Hamblyn ***Art*** Gerald Scarfe
Act Bob Geldof, Christine Hargreaves, James Laurenson, Eleanor David, Bob Hoskins (M-G-M/United Artists/Tin Blue)

This $12 million production is not a concert film but an eye-popping dramatization of an audio storyline. Being a visual translation of a so-called "concept" album, pic works extremely well in carrying over the somber tone of the LP.

The music is the core of the film, vocals subbing for the usual film dialog. But there's little need for dialog, since the visual treats offered by animation director Gerald Scarfe and photography director Peter Biziou tell the story.

Story centers around a frustrated, burned-out but successful rock star (Pink) who is near-suicidal and on the verge of insanity. His wife has left him for another man because of the interminable amount of time Pink spends on the road. When he contacts her by telephone, only to have the other man answer, his self-destruct mechanism begins its slow burn. Powerful performance of Boomtown Rats lead singer Bob Geldof as Pink works to the pic's overall believability, despite its fantasy aura.

PINK PANTHER, THE
1964, 115 mins, US Ⓥ ⊙ ▭ col
Dir Blake Edwards ***Prod*** Martin Jurow ***Scr*** Maurice Richlin, Blake Edwards ***Ph*** Philip Lathrop ***Ed*** Ralph E. Winters ***Mus*** Henry Mancini ***Art*** Fernando Carrere
Act David Niven, Peter Sellers, Robert Wagner, Capucine, Claudia Cardinale, Brenda de Banzie (Mirisch/GE)

This is film-making as a branch of the candy trade, and the pack is so enticing that few will worry about the jerky machinations of the plot. Quite apart from the general air of bubbling elegance, the pic is intensely funny. The yocks are almost entirely the responsibility of Peter Sellers, who is perfectly suited as a clumsy cop who can hardly move a foot without smashing a vase or open a door without hitting himself on the head.

The Panther is a priceless jewel owned by the Indian Princess Dala (Claudia Cardinale), vacationing in the Swiss ski resort of Cortina. The other principals are introduced in their various habitats, before they converge on the princess and her jewel.

Sellers's razor-sharp timing is superlative, and he makes the most of his ample opportunities. His doting concern for criminal wife (Capucine), his blundering ineptitude with material objects, and his dogged pursuit of the crook all coalesce to a sharp performance, with satirical overtones.

David Niven produces his familiar brand of debonair ease. Robert Wagner has a somewhat undernourished role. Capucine, sometimes awkward and over-intense as if she were straining for yocks, is nevertheless a good Simone Clouseau.

1964: NOMINATION: Best Original Music Score

PINK PANTHER STRIKES AGAIN, THE
1976, 103 mins, UK Ⓥ ⊙ ▭ col
Dir Blake Edwards ***Prod*** Blake Edwards ***Scr*** Frank Waldman, Blake Edwards ***Ph*** Harry Waxman ***Ed*** Alan Jones ***Mus*** Henry Mancini ***Art*** Peter Mullins
Act Peter Sellers, Herbert Lom, Colin Blakely, Leonard Rossiter, Lesley-Anne Down, Burt Kwouk (United Artists)

The Pink Panther Strikes Again is a hilarious film about the further misadventures of Peter Sellers as Inspector Clouseau. Herbert Lom, Clouseau's nemesis in the police bureau, has had his character expanded into a Professor Moriarty–type fiend, which works just fine. This time around, Lom is introduced nearly cured of his nervous collapse. But Sellers has assumed Lom's old chief inspector job, and when Lom escapes, Sellers is assigned to the case. Lom kidnaps scientist Richard Vernon, who has a disappearing ray device; pitch is that Lom threatens world destruction unless Sellers is handed over to him for extermination.

Action proceeds smartly through plot-advancing action scenes, interleaved with excellent non-dialog sequences featuring Sellers and underscored superbly by Henry Mancini.

1976: NOMINATION: Best Song ("Come to Me")

PINK STRING AND SEALING WAX
1945, 93 mins, UK b/w
Dir Robert Hamer ***Prod*** Michael Balcon ***Scr*** Diana Morgan, Robert Hamer ***Ph*** Richard S. Pavey, R. Julius ***Ed*** Michael Truman ***Mus*** Norman Demuth ***Art*** Duncan Sutherland
Act Mervyn Johns, Mary Merrall, Gordon Jackson, Sally Ann Howes, Googie Withers, Catherine Lacey (Ealing)

Bringing the England of the Victorian period to life is the best thing *Pink String and Sealing Wax* accomplishes. The black, high-necked, rustling Sunday-best bombazines which the church-going women wear contrast violently with the billowing cleavages of the bad women. The unrelenting tyranny of the lord and master of the respectable family is offset by the free-and-easy beatings-up the naughty gals receive at the hands of Cagney-ish husbands and sweethearts. In giving this side of English life, the picture (based on the West End stage hit by Roland Pertwee) is tops.

The bit players turn in performances so bright one wonders how come they aren't in the top billing. Catherine Lacey as a gin drunkard is superb. John Carol's warned-off jockey who loves 'em and leaves 'em without batting an eye is as smooth as the greasy cowlick draped over his forehead. Garry Marsh as the booze hound proprietor of the pub whom Withers rubs out with strychnine is Bill Sykes come to life.

PINKY
1949, 102 mins, US Ⓥ b/w
Dir Elia Kazan ***Prod*** Darryl F. Zanuck ***Scr*** Philip Dunne, Dudley Nichols ***Ph*** Joe MacDonald ***Ed*** Harmon Jones ***Mus*** Alfred Newman
Act Jeanne Crain, Ethel Barrymore, Ethel Waters, William Lundigan (20th Century-Fox)

Pinky is the tag hung by Negroes on a member of their own race who is light-skinned enough to pass for white. In this case it is made clear that Jeanne Crain had passed herself off as ofay for a number of years while studying in Boston. However, when she returns to the home of her grandmother (Ethel Waters) in the south, the scripters always have her quickly reveal herself as Negro. That's what leads to the complications, romantic and dramatic.

"Pinky" is in love with a young doctor (William Lundigan) from New England who wants to marry her despite the color line.

Scripters have put a load of dramatic punch and a share of humor in the yarn [from a novel by Cid Ricketts Sumner].

Crain brings proper dignity and sincerity to her role, although she's not always convincing.

1949: NOMINATIONS: Best Actress (Jeanne Crain), Supp. Actress (Ethel Barrymore, Ethel Waters)

PINOCCHIO
1940, 87 mins, US Ⓥ ⊙ col
Dir Ben Sharpsteen, Hamilton Luske ***Prod*** Walt Disney ***Scr*** Ted Sears, Webb Smith, Joseph Sabo, Otto Englander, William Cottrell, Aurelius Battaglia, Erdman Penner ***Mus***

Leigh Harline
(Walt Disney/RKO)

Pinocchio is a substantial piece of entertainment for young and old. Both animation and photography are vastly improved over Walt Disney's first cartoon feature, *Snow White*. Animation is so smooth that cartoon figures carry impression of real persons and settings rather than drawings.

Extensive use of the Disney-developed multiplane camera (first used moderately for *Snow White*) provides some ingenious cartoon photography, allowing for camera movement similar to dolly shots. Most startling effect is the jumpy landscape as seen through the eyes of a leaping Jiminy Cricket.

Opening is similar to *Snow White*, establishing at the start that this is a fairy tale. Jiminy, witty, resourceful and effervescing cricket, displays the title cover and first illustrations of the book with a dialog description introducing the old woodcarver, Geppetto, and his workshop. Place abounds with musical clocks and gadgets, pet kitten and goldfish—and the completed puppet whom he names Pinocchio. Geppetto's wish for a son on the wishing star is granted when the Blue Fairy appears and provides life for the puppet; with Jiminy Cricket appointed guardian of latter's conscience. Pinocchio soon encounters villainous characters and his impetuous curiosity gets him into a series of escapades.

Cartoon characterization of Pinocchio is delightful, with his boyish antics and pranks maintaining constant interest. Jiminy Cricket is a fast-talking character providing rich humor with wisecracks and witticisms. Kindly old Geppetto is a definitely drawn character while several appearances of Blue Fairy are accentuated by novel lighting effects. Picture stresses evil figures and results of wrongdoing more vividly and to greater extent than *Snow White*, and at times somewhat overplays these factors for children. This is minor, however.

1940: Best Song ("When You Wish Upon a Star"), Original Score

•

PIN UP GIRL

1944, 85 mins, US Ⓥ ⦿ col

Dir H. Bruce Humberstone ***Prod*** William LeBaron ***Scr*** Robert Ellis, Helen Logan, Earl Baldwin ***Ph*** Ernest Palmer ***Ed*** Robert Simpson ***Mus*** Emil Newman, Charles Henderson (dir.) ***Art*** James Basevi, Joseph C. Wright

Act Betty Grable, John Harvey, Martha Raye, Joe E. Brown (20th Century-Fox)

This is one of those escapist filmusicals which makes no pretenses at ultra-realism, and if you get into the mood fast that it's something to occupy your attention for an hour and a half. It's all very pleasing and pleasant.

Producer William LeBaron, director H. Bruce Humberstone and the cast, scripters, et al., have treated *Pin Up Girl* in uniform spirit. The Missouri gal who crashes the party of a welcome-to-a-Guadalcanal-hero (John Harvey) in one of New York's top niteries brooks no plot examination.

Right from the start, when Betty Grable is almost trapped in her gate-crashing she poses as a musicomedy actress, mounts the rostrum pronto and Charlie Spivak picks up the music cue and it all comes out all right. Just like that!

Joe E. Brown as the cafe prop and Martha Raye as his jealous star carry the low comedy against which are backgrounded expert hoofology by the Condos Bros., Spivak's stuff, rollerskating routines and the military finale.

In Technicolor Grable is a looker in pastel shades and spades. The costumes of the spec numbers have likewise been contrived for ultra-sartorial resplendence. All combined it makes for merry movie moments.

•

PIRANHA

1978, 92 mins, US Ⓥ col

Dir Joe Dante ***Prod*** Jon Davison ***Scr*** John Sayles ***Ph*** Jamie Anderson ***Ed*** Mark Goldblatt, Joe Dante ***Mus*** Pino Donaggio ***Art*** Bill Mellin, Kerry Mellin

Act Bradford Dillman, Heather Menzies, Kevin McCarthy, Keenan Wynn, Dick Miller, Barbara Steele (New World)

Since the title characters in *Piranha* are never actually seen (there's lots of speeded-up nibbling, but no closeups of the deadly Brazilian river munchers), the pic utilizes a lot of red dye in the water, and an auditory effect for the gnawing that sounds like an air-conditioner on the fritz.

What is different about *Piranha* is the unusual number of victims. Not only is the requisite slew of cameo performers dispatched quickly (Keenan Wynn, Kevin McCarthy, Bruce Gordon), but an entire camp full of schoolchildren, and a holiday crowd at a lakeside resort get chomped. This is one film where the fish win.

Heather Menzies plays an aggressive femme searching for missing persons, who enlists backwoods recluse Bradford Dillman in her cause. When they stumble on mad doctor McCarthy's mountaintop lab, they unwittingly release a generation of super-hardy piranhas McCarthy was breeding for use in the Mekong Delta during the Vietnam war.

Barbara Steele turns up as a government scientist who hints the piranhas may be back for a sequel. Menzies is attractively competent, and Dillman does what he's supposed to, which isn't much. One yearns to have seen more of McCarthy and his lab, where a scaly homunculus is seen lurking about, but never explained.

•

PIRANHA II THE SPAWNING
(AKA: PIRANHA 2: FLYING KILLERS)

1983, 95 mins, Italy Ⓥ ⦿ col

Dir James Cameron ***Prod*** Chako van Leuwen, Jeff Schectman ***Scr*** H. A. Milton ***Ph*** Roberto D'Ettore Piazzoli ***Ed*** Roberto Silvi ***Mus*** Steve Powder

Act Tricia O'Neil, Steve Marachuk, Lance Henriksen, Ricky G. Paul, Ted Richert, Leslie Graves (Chako)

Made in 1981, this is a routine monster film, unrelated to Joe Dante's 1978 *Piranha*. Idiotic premise has U.S. government genetic engineering experiments creating a deadly form of grunions (hinted at being used in the Vietnam war). A missing canister of fertile eggs of these mutant fish (called piranha for horror fans' sake) turns up in the Caribbean resort of Club Elysium and the beasties start chewing up vacationers. Film's title refers to the grunions' annual mating ritual of spawning on the beach. Lame script pokes fun at the match of human and fishy mating rites. Nominal human interest plot has Club Elysium scuba diver Anne (Tricia O'Neil) teaming up with incognito biochemist Tyler (Steve Marachuk) to discover and blow up the fish, while her estranged husband Steve (Lance Henriksen) looks out for the welfare of the locals as the film's Roy Scheider-esque cop.

Exec producer Ovidio G. Assonitis follows up his similar made-in-America horror pics *Beyond the Door*, *Tentacles*, and *The Visitor* with an Italian-crewed film which easily passes as All-American. Special effects experts come up with convincing gore for the victims, but the monsters are laughably phoney.

•

PIRATE, THE

1948, 101 mins, US Ⓥ ⦿ col

Dir Vincente Minnelli ***Prod*** Arthur Freed ***Scr*** Albert Hackett, Frances Goodrich ***Ph*** Harry Stradling ***Ed*** Blanche Sewell ***Mus*** Lennie Hayton (dir.), Conrad Salinger (arr.) ***Art*** Cedric Gibbons, Jack Martin Smith

Act Judy Garland, Gene Kelly, Walter Slezak, Gladys Cooper, Reginald Owen, George Zucco (M-G-M)

The Pirate is escapist film fare. It's an eye and ear treat of light musical entertainment, garbing its amusing antics, catchy songs and able terping in brilliant color.

Gene Kelly and Judy Garland team delightfully in selling the dances and songs, scoring in both departments. The Cole Porter score is loaded with tunes that get over to the ear and the foot.

Adapted from the S. N. Behrman play, picture tells of the cloistered Latin girl about to fulfill an arranged wedding when she meets a travelling troupe of entertainers headed by Kelly. Title springs from fact that gal yearns for a fabulous pirate and sees him in the actor. Vincente Minnelli's direction is light and seems to poke subtle fun at the elaborate musical ingredients and plot. The fact that *The Pirate* never takes itself too seriously adds to enjoyment, giving sharp point to some of the dialog in the script.

1948: NOMINATION: Best Scoring of a Dramatic Picture

•

PIRATES

1986, 124 mins, France/Tunisia Ⓥ ▭ col

Dir Roman Polanski ***Prod*** Tarak Ben Ammar ***Scr*** Gerard Brach, Roman Polanski, John Brownjohn ***Ph*** Witold Sobocinski ***Ed*** Herve de Luze, William Reynolds ***Mus*** Philippe Sarde ***Art*** Pierre Guffroy

Act Walter Matthau, Damien Thomas, Richard Pearson, Cris Campion, Charlotte Lewis, Olu Jacobs (Carthago/Accent-Cominco)

Roman Polanski's *Pirates* is a decidedly underwhelming comedy adventure adding up to a major disappointment.

Pirates first was announced as a 1976 Polanski feature to star Jack Nicholson and Isabelle Adjani, before finally being produced (commencing in 1984) in Tunisia, Malta and the Seychelles, costing in excess of $30 million.

Walter Matthau gainfully essays the central role of Capt. Thomas Bartholomew Red, a peg-legged British pirate captain with plenty of Long John Silver in his manner. Teamed with a handsome young French sailor (Cris Campion), Red is captured by Don Alfonso (Damien Thomas), captain of the Spanish galleon *Neptune*.

In a series of turnabout adventures, Red causes the *Neptune*'s crew to mutiny, takes the niece (Charlotte Lewis) of the governor of Maracaibo hostage, and steals a golden Aztec throne from the Spaniards.

Casting is unimpressive, with Matthau unable to carry the picture single-handedly. Newcomer Campion projects a pleasant personality, more than can be said for Polanski's discovery Charlotte Lewis, thoroughly inexpressive here.

1986: NOMINATION: Best Costume Design

•

PIRATES OF PENZANCE, THE

1983, 112 mins, US Ⓥ ⦿ ▭ col

Dir Wilford Leach ***Prod*** Joseph Papp, Timothy Burrill ***Scr*** Wilford Leach ***Ph*** Douglas Slocombe ***Ed*** Anne V. Coates ***Mus*** William Elliott (arr.) ***Art*** Elliot Scott

Act Kevin Kline, Angela Lansbury, Linda Ronstadt, George Rose, Rex Smith, Tony Azito (Pressman/Universal)

Gilbert & Sullivan's durable *The Pirates of Penzance* has been turned into an elaborate screen musical by basically the same hands responsible for Joseph Papp's smash New York Shakespeare Festival and Broadway stage production, and result is a delight.

For the film, shot at Shepperton Studios in England, a charming artificiality of style was arrived at, which is most immediately apparent in Elliot Scott's beautifully witty production design.

Simple tale has orphan Rex Smith leaving, upon turning 21, the band of pirates with whom he's been raised. Upon hitting land, he encounters eight sisters and becomes smitten with one of them, Linda Ronstadt. Pirate King Kevin Kline is not about to let Smith go straight so easily, however, and informs him that, having been born on 29 February, he's actually only had five birthdays, and will therefore be obliged to remain with the gang until 1940 or so.

With the exception of Angela Lansbury, entertaining as the pirates' nursemaid and *aide-de-combat*, all principal cast members have repeated their Broadway performances here, and in exemplary fashion.

•

PIT AND THE PENDULUM

1961, 85 mins, US Ⓥ ▭ col

Dir Roger Corman ***Prod*** Roger Corman ***Scr*** Richard Matheson ***Ph*** Floyd Crosby ***Ed*** Anthony Carras ***Mus*** Les Baxter ***Art*** Daniel Haller

Act Vincent Price, John Kerr, Barbara Steele, Luana Anders, Antony Carbone, Patrick Westwood (American International)

Pit and the Pendulum is an elaboration of the short Poe classic about blood-letting in 16th-century Spain. The result is a physically stylish, imaginatively photographed horror film which, though needlessly corny in many spots, adds up to good exploitation.

The main problem is that Poe furnished scriptwriter Richard Matheson with only one scene—the spine-tingling climax—and Matheson has been hard put to come up with a comparably effective build-up to these last 10 or so minutes. He has removed the tale one generation beyond the time of the Spanish Inquisition (for reasons best known to himself) and contrived a plot involving an ill-fated nobleman slowly losing his mind because he thinks he accidentally buried his wife alive, just like his father did some years before—on purpose.

Actually Matheson's plotting isn't at all bad, but he has rendered it in some fruity dialog. If audiences don't titter, it's only because veteran star Vincent Price can chew scenery while keeping his tongue in his cheek.

While Matheson's script takes a good deal of time, including three extended flashbacks, to get to the denouement, it's almost worth it. The last portion of the film builds with genuine excitement to a reverse twist ending that might well have pleased Poe himself.

•

PIXOTE A LEI DO MAIS FRACO
(PIXOTE)

1981, 130 mins, Brazil Ⓥ col

Dir Hector Babenco ***Prod*** Sylvia B. Naves ***Scr*** Jorge Duran, Hector Babenco ***Ph*** Rodolfo Sanches (exec.) ***Ed*** Luiz Elias ***Mus*** John Neschling

Act Fernando Ramos Da Silva, Jorge Juliao, Gilberto Moura, Marilia Pera, Jardel Filho (Babenco/Embrafilme)

A trenchant, uncompromising look at Brazilian juvenile delinquents, *Pixote* is a social expose of the first order.

Although milieu of the urban jungle is sordid and situation depicted seems beyond hope even for the most idealistic reformers, director Hector Babenco has made this tragic drama come vividly, even excitingly, alive through the extraordinary performances of his non-pro cast of slum youngsters. Tale's primary focus is one Pixote, an abandoned boy with an oddly haunting face. Despite nominal instructional efforts within the "school," all anyone picks up there are more criminal ideas. After an hour in this almost unthinkable squalor, film follows a gang of four out into Sao Paulo and later Rio after their successful escape.

Ringleader is a self-styled "queen," nearing the critical age of 18, who involves the group in drug dealing through a tough black lover. Sent to Rio to sell some dope, the band falls in with local pimps and hookers and quickly progresses from petty crime to murder.

Babenco [inspired by Jose Louzeiro's book *Infancia dos Mortos*] working from a book by DeLouis Louza, displays no conventional liberal or sentimental instincts. Film is sufficiently dramatized and structured to lift it out of the realm of the docu-drama, but caught-in-the-act sense of reality is virtually total. Technically, film is just okay.

•

PLACE FOR LOVERS, A

1969, 88 mins, Italy/France col

Dir Vittorio De Sica ***Prod*** Carlo Ponti, Arthur Cohn ***Scr*** Julian Halevy, Peter Baldwin, Ennio De Concini, Tonino Guerra, Cesare Zavattini ***Ph*** Pasquale De Santis ***Ed*** Adriana Novelli ***Mus*** Maurice De Sica ***Art*** Piero Poletto

Act Faye Dunaway, Marcello Mastroianni, Caroline Mortimer, Karin Engh (M-G-M/Ponti-Cohn)

With five scripters freely adapting a play [*Amanti*, by Brunello Rondi and Renaldo Cabieri] the result is bound to lack decision and this romantic drama comes out at times as somewhat sudsy and flabby. But with Vittorio De Sica's direction, the eye-pleasing atmosphere of the Italian Alps and Marcello Mastroianni and Faye Dunaway a good team as a pair of ill-starred lovers, there's enough pull.

Dunaway arrives to stay at a deserted elegant villa near Venice. She phones Mastroianni and he hotfoots it to the villa. Without quite understanding what gives, he is in the sack with Dunaway before the night's out.

Situations are often lethargically introduced and dialog is frequently stagey and mannered. But De Sica gets full measure out of the love interest with its moody background. Dunaway looks beautiful and enticing and Mastroianni is pleasantly cast as the infatuated lover.

•

PLACE IN THE SUN, A

1951, 118 mins, US Ⓥ ⦿ b/w

Dir George Stevens ***Prod*** George Stevens ***Scr*** Michael Wilson, Harry Brown ***Ph*** William C. Mellor ***Ed*** William Hornbeck ***Mus*** Franz Waxman ***Art*** Hans Dreier, Walter Tyler

Act Montgomery Clift, Elizabeth Taylor, Shelley Winters, Anne Revere, Fred Clark, Raymond Burr (Paramount)

Theodore Dreiser's much-discussed novel of the 1920s, *An American Tragedy*, is here transposed to the screen for the second time by Paramount. The first version was made in 1930 by Josef Von Sternberg under the original title. This version, brought completely up to date in time and settings [and also based on Patrick Kearney's play from the novel], is distinguished beyond its predecessor in every way. Montgomery Clift, Shelley Winters and Elizabeth Taylor give wonderfully shaded and poignant performances.

Tale is of a poor and lonely boy and girl who find comfort in each other. Unhappily, while the girl progresses to real love of the boy, he finds love elsewhere in a wealthy lass of a social set to which he'd like to become a part. His first attachment is not easily broken off, however, because the girl discovers herself pregnant. When she appears at a mountain lake resort where he is spending his vacation with the femme who has by this time become his fiancee, his confused emotions lead him to take her into a boat with intention of drowning her.

Winters plays the poor gal, Taylor the rich one. Clift at times seems overly laconic.

1951: Best Director, Screenplay, B&W Cinematography, Scoring of a Dramatic Picture, Editing, B&W Costume Design.

NOMINATIONS: Best Picture, Actor (Montgomery Clift), Actress (Shelley Winters)

•

PLACES IN THE HEART

1984, 102 mins, US Ⓥ ⦿ col

Dir Robert Benton ***Prod*** Arlene Donovan ***Scr*** Robert Benton ***Ph*** Nestor Almendros ***Ed*** Carol Littleton ***Mus*** John Kander ***Art*** Gene Callahan

Act Sally Field, Lindsay Crouse, Ed Harris, Amy Madigan, John Malkovich, Danny Glover (Tri-Star)

Places in the Heart is a loving, reflective homage to his hometown by writer-director Robert Benton. Flawlessly crafted, Benton creates a full tapestry of life in Waxahachie, Texas, circa 1935, but filmgoers may find his understated naturalistic approach lacking in dramatic punch. Obviously drawing on his personal experiences and people he knew growing up, Benton remembers the rituals of everyday life: love, in all of its forms, birth and death.

Sally Field is solid in the lead role as a widowed mother, but she is not the strong unifying character that can tie the strands of Benton's script together.

Nestor Almendros's photography is not pretty, but high on feeling and atmosphere. It radiates a lived-in autumnal light.

1984: Best Actress (Sally Field), Original Screenplay.

NOMINATIONS: Best Picture, Director, Actor (John Malkovich), Supp. Actress (Lindsay Crouse), Costume Design

•

PLAGUE OF THE ZOMBIES, THE

1966, 90 mins, UK Ⓥ col

Dir John Gilling ***Prod*** Anthony Nelson-Keys ***Scr*** Peter Bryan ***Ph*** Arthur Grant ***Ed*** James Needs, Chris Barnes ***Mus*** James Bernard ***Art*** Bernard Robinson

Act Andre Morell, Diane Clare, John Carson, Brook Williams, Alexander Davion, Jacqueline Pearce (Hammer/Seven Arts)

Filmed at Ireland's Bray Studios, *The Plague of the Zombies* is a well-made horror programmer about strange happenings a century ago in a small town on the moors. Peter Bryan is credited with the script which brings Andre Morell, a distinguished medic professor, and daughter Diane Clare to the boondocks town where former pupil Brook Williams isn't having much luck in his new practice. A dozen people have died mysteriously, and local squire John Carson won't permit autopsies. Jacqueline Pearce, Williams's wife, isn't looking too good, either.

The formula scripting involves about 55 minutes of seeding with various unexplained incidents, followed by an explanation of the diabolical forces involved. Then in the last 35 minutes, the demons are foiled.

•

PLAINSMAN, THE

1937, 112 mins, US Ⓥ ⦿ b/w

Dir Cecil B. DeMille ***Prod*** Cecil B. DeMille ***Scr*** Waldemar Young, Lynn Riggs, Harold Lamb ***Ph*** Victor Milner, George Robinson ***Ed*** Anne Bauchens ***Mus*** George Anthei ***Art*** Hans Dreier, Roland Anderson

Act Gary Cooper, Jean Arthur, James Ellison, Charles Bickford, Helen Burgess, Porter Hall (Paramount)

The Plainsman is a big and a good western. It's cowboys and Indians on a broad, sweeping scale; not a *Covered Wagon* (1923) but majestic enough. Gary Cooper is Hickok, Jean Arthur is the historic Calamity Jane of his immediate associations, and James Ellison is a rather aggrandized Buffalo Bill. Opposite the latter is Helen Burgess as his bride. This perforce casts him as something of a musical comedy version of the plains scout whom history has pictured a much more grisly personality. The spec appeal is in the redskin warfare. The sequence with the near burning-at-the-stake of Hickok in Yellow Hand's camp is tingling and the soldiers' holding out for several days against an almost overwhelming horde of Comanches, with some corking charging-through-the-water action, is another. Scripting [based on data from stories by Courtney Ryley Cooper and Frank J. Wilstack] and editing stand out favorably. Arthur is particularly endowed with some punch lines and pungent expletives as the hardy daughter.

•

PLANES, TRAINS & AUTOMOBILES

1987, 93 mins, US Ⓥ ⦿ col

Dir John Hughes ***Prod*** John Hughes ***Scr*** John Hughes ***Ph*** Don Peterman ***Ed*** Paul Hirsch ***Mus*** Ira Newborn ***Art*** John W. Corso

Act Steve Martin, John Candy, Laila Robins, Michael McKean, Kevin Bacon, Dylan Baker (Paramount)

John Hughes has come up with an effective nightmare-as-comedy in *Planes, Trains & Automobiles*. Disaster-prone duo of Steve Martin and John Candy repeatedly recall a contemporary Laurel & Hardy as they agonizingly try to make their way from New York to Chicago by various modes of transport.

Man versus technology has been one of the staples of screen comedy since the earliest silent days, and Hughes makes the most of the format here packing as many of the frustrations of modern life as he can into this calamitous travelog of roadside America.

An ultimate situation comedy, tale throws together Martin, an ad exec, and Candy, a shower curtain ring salesman, as they head home from Manhattan to their respective homes in Chicago two days before Thanksgiving.

The problems start before they even get out of midtown. From there, it's a series of ghastly motel rooms, crowded anonymous restaurants, a sinister cab ride, an abortive train trip, an even worse excursion by rented car, some hitchhiking by truck, and, finally, a hop on the "El" before sitting down to turkey.

•

PLANET OF THE APES

1968, 112 mins, US Ⓥ ⦿ ▭ col

Dir Franklin J. Schaffner ***Prod*** Arthur P. Jacobs ***Scr*** Michael Wilson, Rod Serling ***Ph*** Leon Shamroy ***Ed*** Hugh S. Fowler ***Mus*** Jerry Goldsmith ***Art*** Jack Martin Smith, William Creber

Act Charlton Heston, Roddy McDowall, Kim Hunter, Maurice Evans, James Whitmore, Linda Harrison (Apjac/20th Century-Fox)

Planet of the Apes is an amazing film. A political-sociological allegory, cast in the mold of futuristic science-fiction, it is an intriguing blend of chilling satire, a sometimes ludicrous juxtaposition of human and ape mores, optimism and pessimism.

Pierre Boulle's novel, in which U.S. space explorers find themselves in a world dominated by apes, has been adapted by Michael Wilson and Rod Serling.

The totality of the film works very well, leading to a surprise ending. The suspense, and suspension of belief, engendered is one of the film's biggest assets.

Charlton Heston, leader of an aborted space shot which propels his crew 20 centuries ahead of earth, is a cynical man who eventually has thrust upon him the burden of reasserting man's superiority over all other animals. At fadeout, he is the new Adam.

Key featured players—all in ape makeup—include Roddy McDowall and Kim Hunter, Maurice Evans, James Whitmore and James Daly.

1968: Honorary Award (John Chambers, for makeup design)

NOMINATIONS: Best Costume Design, Original Music Score

•

PLATINUM BLONDE

1931, 82 mins, US b/w

Dir Frank Capra ***Scr*** Jo Swerling, Dorothy Howell, Robert Riskin ***Ph*** Joseph Walker ***Ed*** Gene Milford

Act Loretta Young, Robert Williams, Jean Harlow, Louise Closser Hale, Donald Dillaway, Reginald Owen (Columbia)

It's entertaining, has a lot of light, pleasing comedy and carries a cast that's tops. Robert Williams is a very likable character as a reporter who marries himself off to a snobbish society frail, and he plays it like a champ. Always displaying a fine screen presence and manner, Williams quickly ingratiates himself.

The newspaper background is prominent, and for once it's 100 percent natural. The managing editor (Edmund Breese) with his hollering, swearing, affability and pride is aces.

The picture is with Williams all the way. It gives him a great break, and a pip scene, when after marrying the snooty plat (Jean Harlow) he renounces the whole gang in stiff language, taking ozone with the sob sister who all along has wanted it that way. Loretta Young runs third on footage and is somewhat missed.

•

PLATOON

1986, 120 mins, US Ⓥ ⦿ col

Dir Oliver Stone ***Prod*** Arnold Kopelson ***Scr*** Oliver Stone ***Ph*** Robert Richardson ***Ed*** Claire Simpson ***Mus*** Georges Delerue ***Art*** Bruno Rubeo

Act Tom Berenger, Willem Dafoe, Charlie Sheen, Forest Whitaker, John C. McGinley, Kevin Dillon (Hemdale)

Platoon is an intense but artistically distanced study of infantry life during the Vietnam War. Writer-director Oliver Stone seeks to immerse the audience totally in the nightmare of the United States's misguided adventure, and manages to do so in a number of very effective scenes.

A Vietnam vet himself, Stone obviously had urgent personal reasons for making this picture, a fact that emerges instantly as green volunteer Charlie Sheen is plunged into the thick of action along the Cambodian border in late 1967.

Willem Dafoe comes close to stealing the picture as the sympathetic sergeant whose drugged state may even heighten his sensitivity to the insanity around him, and each of the members of the young cast all have their moments to shine.

1986: Best Picture, Director, Sound, Editing

NOMINATIONS: Best Supp. Actor (Tom Berenger, Willem Dafoe), Original Screenplay, Cinematography

•

PLAYBOYS, THE

1992, 110 mins, US Ⓥ col

Dir Gillies MacKinnon ***Prod*** William P. Cartlidge ***Scr*** Shane Connaughton, Kerry Crabbe ***Ph*** Jack Conroy ***Ed*** Humphrey Dixon ***Mus*** Jean-Claude Petit ***Art*** Andy Harris

Act Albert Finney, Aidan Quinn, Robin Wright, Milo O'Shea, Alan Devlin, Niamh Cusack (Goldwyn)

Pic started off with a hitch when originally cast star Annette Bening dropped out on the eve of production. Replacement Robin Wright (Mrs. Sean Penn) was a felicitous choice, in her best film acting to date. Story by Shane Connaughton, who co-scripted *My Left Foot*, concerns an Irish lass (Wright) in 1957 who's shamed by her fellow townsfolk for being an unwed mother.

A new love enters her life with the arrival of Milo O'Shea's troupe of traveling actors, The Playboys. Newest thesp in the company (Aidan Quinn) immediately impresses Wright and eventually beds her. Fly in the ointment is the local constable (Albert Finney) who has always been in love with Wright and explodes into violence.

This familiar pattern of headstrong girl and passions brimming beneath the surface is well-directed by first-time Scottish helmer Gillies MacKinnon, though the pace slows in middle reels as plot gives way to the troupe's enjoyable stage performances.

•

PLAY DIRTY

1969, 117 mins, UK ▭ col

Dir Andre de Toth ***Prod*** Harry Saltzman ***Scr*** Lotte Colin, Melvyn Bragg ***Ph*** Ted Scaife ***Ed*** Alan Osbiston ***Mus*** Michel Legrand ***Art*** Tom Morahan

Act Michael Caine, Nigel Davenport, Nigel Green, Harry Andrews, Bernard Archer (United/Lowndes)

Play Dirty is mainly the story of a small unit detailed to blow up a vital enemy fuel dump in the desert.

Main disappointment about the film [from an original story by George Marton] which has occasional crisp dialog and situations and two or three lively skirmishes is the performance of lead Michael Caine, who plays with an often tired and flat lack of expression which doesn't pump much blood into the dialog or action. He handles his role with intelligence but comes out second best to Nigel Davenport, a resourceful rogue with style.

Caine is cast as an inexperienced British army captain, detailed to lead reluctantly a small band of mercenaries into the desert to dispose of a vital enemy fuel dump.

Clash between Caine and Davenport is the main thread of the story and results in a fascinating relationship beween the two.

•

PLAYER, THE

1992, 123 mins, US Ⓥ ⊙ col

Dir Robert Altman ***Prod*** David Brown, Michael Tolkin, Nick Wechsler ***Scr*** Michael Tolkin ***Ph*** Jean Lepine ***Ed*** Geraldine Peroni ***Mus*** Thomas Newman ***Art*** Stephen Altman

Act Tim Robbins, Greta Scacchi, Fred Ward, Whoopi Goldberg, Peter Gallagher, Vincent D'Onofrio (Avenue)

The Player is the deep dish on Hollywood, 1992. Mercilessly satiric yet good-natured, this enormously entertaining slam dunk quite possibly is the most resonant Hollywood saga since the days of *Sunset Blvd.* and *The Bad and the Beautiful*.

Brilliantly scripted by Michael Tolkin from his own novel, plot hinges on a series of threatening postcards received by hotshot studio executive Griffin Mill (Tim Robbins) from an ignored screenwriter. Mill tracks down the man he suspects of being the sender—the garrulous writer David Kahane (Vincent D'Onofrio)—has a few drinks with the man and, in a fit of anger, accidentally kills him. Mill is able to continue his normal life of worrying about being edged out of the studio by the newly hired Larry Levy (Peter Gallagher).

The postcards keep coming, but Mill initiates a romance with his victim's sexy girlfriend, June (Greta Scacchi), then maneuvers brilliantly on a film project that provides *The Player* with its showstopping capper.

Center screen throughout, Robbins is superb as Mill. Whoopi Goldberg brings cheerful vigor to her surprising role of a Pasadena police detective. Scacchi gives the untearful girlfriend a contemporary, ambiguous amorality.

Glimpsed at restaurants, galas, parties, on the lot and just around, celebs from Cher, Nick Nolte, Anjelica Huston, Burt Reynolds, Susan Sarandon and Harry Belafonte to Jack Lemmon, Lily Tomlin, Elliott Gould, Rod Steiger and, hilariously, Julia Roberts and Bruce Willis, keep turning up. Made independently on a modest $8 million, the picture looks like plenty more.

1992: NOMINATION: Best Director, Screenplay Adaptation, Editing

•

PLAYERS

1979, 120 mins, US Ⓥ col

Dir Anthony Harvey ***Prod*** Robert Evans ***Scr*** Arnold Schulman ***Ph*** James Crabe ***Ed*** Randy Roberts ***Mus*** Jerry Goldsmith ***Art*** Richard Sylbert

Act Ali MacGraw, Dean-Paul Martin, Maximilian Schell, Pancho Gonzalez, Steve Guttenberg (Paramount)

Another love story in disguise, this time backgrounded against the tennis world, *Players* is disqualified by exec producer Arnold Schulman's wobbly script, a simpering performance by Ali MacGraw, and a preponderance of tennis footage.

Via backward glances, it's explained that Dean-Paul Martin, who at the film's beginning is pitted against Guillermo Vilas in the Wimbledon championships, rescues socialite Ali MacGraw from a car accident, is adopted by her, and eventually falls in love with her.

Only ace in *Players* is casting of Martin, who, in his first film role proves highly believable in both his tennis and dramatic scenes.

Excellent support is offered by Pancho Gonzalez in a recreation of his real-life role as a pro-turned-teacher.

•

PLAY IT AGAIN, SAM

1972, 84 mins, US Ⓥ ⊙ col

Dir Herbert Ross ***Prod*** Arthur P. Jacobs ***Scr*** Woody Allen ***Ph*** Owen Roizman ***Ed*** Marion Rothman ***Mus*** Billy Goldenberg ***Art*** Ed Wittstein

Act Woody Allen, Diane Keaton, Tony Roberts, Jerry Lacy, Susan Anspach, Jennifer Salt (Paramount/Apjac)

Woody Allen's 1969 legit comedy-starrer, *Play It Again, Sam*, has become on the screen 84 minutes of fragile fun. Allen and other key players from the stage version encore to good results. The placid direction of Herbert Ross keeps Allen in the spotlight for some good laughs, several chuckles and many smiles.

Allen's adaptation showcases his self-deprecating, and sometimes erratic, comedy personality. Ditched by wife Susan Anspach, who cannot stand his vicarious living of old Humphrey Bogart films, Allen is consoled by Diane Keaton and Tony Roberts, to the point that Keaton begins to fall for Allen. The interlude ends with a recreation of the final scene from Warners's *Casablanca*. Jerry Lacy is most effective as the Bogart phantom who drops in from time to time.

•

PLAY IT TO THE BONE

1999, 124 mins, US Ⓥ ⊙ ▭ col

Dir Ron Shelton ***Prod*** Stephen Chin ***Scr*** Ron Shelton ***Ph*** Mark Vargo ***Ed*** Paul Seydor, Patrick Flannery ***Mus*** Alex Wurman ***Art*** Claire Jenora Bowin

Act Antonio Banderas, Woody Harrelson, Lolita Davidovich, Tom Sizemore, Lucy Liu, Robert Wagner (Shanghai'd/Touchstone)

Ron Shelton's foray into the world of pugilists is a woefully under-realized story of small-time boxers enjoying perhaps their last moment in the spotlight. The hope that Shelton, long Hollywood's premier observer of sports, would bring fresh insight to "the sweet science" of the ring is unfulfilled on nearly every level. Pic is rife with scenes crying out for rewrites. Though Shelton has said that boxing is his favorite sport, he not only misses out on many aspects of the ultra-colorful culture of the ring, but his characteristically wry sense of humor has almost totally escaped him this time around. Shelton's patented combo of rough characters and good-natured observances remains intact, but it's at the service of an ultimately pointless story.

Failure of tone is evident from the beginning, when two contending middleweight fighters are KO'd by life, and promoter Joe Domino (Tom Sizemore) must find subs in a hurry to fill the opening card of the latest Mike Tyson bout at Vegas' Mandalay Bay Hotel, owned by the slick Hank Goody (Robert Wagner). Ex-middleweight contenders Cesar (Antonio Banderas) and Vince (Woody Harrelson), now reduced to sparring in a low-life LA gym, agree to fight each other for $50,000 each, with the winner earning a bid for the middleweight champ contest.

Contorted plotting has the guys urging Cesar's current and Vince's ex-g.f., Grace (Lolita Davidovich), to drive them in her lime-green muscle car, but she insists on taking the highway rather than the speedy interstate. Pic divides into two dissimilar halves, the first a dawdling road movie in which the threesome, none of whom is terribly interesting, unload backstory baggage, and the second half the fight itself. Pic delivers some powerful moments as Banderas and Harrelson throw their bodies and souls into some brutal, undisguised boxing.

Harrelson is burdened with the pic's worst stabs at comedy, but he effortlessly conveys a guy struggling day to day with the only life he knows. Banderas' biggest verbal outburst is in nonsubtitled Spanish, and he carries pic more with innate charisma than anything in the script. In her best performance since her breakthrough in Shelton's *Blaze*, Davidovich coaxes more passion and energy out of Grace than is on the page.

•

PLAY MISTY FOR ME

1971, 102 mins, US Ⓥ ⊙ col

Dir Clint Eastwood ***Prod*** Robert Daley ***Scr*** Jo Heims, Dean Riesner ***Ph*** Bruce Surtees ***Ed*** Carl Pingitore ***Mus*** Dee Barton ***Art*** Alexander Golitzen

Act Clint Eastwood, Jessica Walter, Donna Mills, John Larch, Clarice Taylor, Don Siegel (Universal/Malpaso)

When it's not serving as an overdone travelog for the Monterey Peninsula–Carmel home environment of star, producer and debuting director Clint Eastwood, *Play Misty for Me* is an often fascinating suspenser about psychotic Jessica Walter, whose deranged infatuation for Eastwood leads her to commit murder. For that 80% of the film which constitutes the story, the structure and dialog create a mood of nervous terror which the other 20 percent nearly blows away.

Walter gives a superior performance as an unusual woman whose eccentricities are killing. Eastwood has selected excellent support: John Larch as a detective who nearly solves the case; Clarice Taylor, outstanding as a housekeeper; James McEachin as Eastwood's fellow-deejay on a (real) local radio station; Irene Hervey as a potential benefactor driven off by Walter's insults and director Don Siegel as a friendly bartender.

•

PLAY TIME

1967, 145 mins, France Ⓥ col

Dir Jacques Tati ***Prod*** Rene Silvera (assoc.) ***Scr*** Jacques Tati, Jacques Lagrange ***Ph*** Jean Badal, Andreas Winding ***Ed*** Gerard Pollicand ***Mus*** Francis Lemarque ***Art*** Eugene Roman

Act Jacques Tati, Barbara Dennek, Georges Montant, John Abbey, Reinhardt Kolldehoff, Yves Barsacq (Specta)

Jacques Tati, with considerable renown as a personalized comic director-actor-writer via only three films, makes his fourth effort after an almost 10-year hiatus. Tati has come up with a big scale, gentle comedy about people (mainly tourists) in the growing new metallic and glass cities that resemble each other. Pic takes to the 70mm process with an extraordinary impressionistic outdoor set of a new Paris, and is an observant romp during a one-day stay of a group of tourists.

Here, Mr. Hulot (Tati) wanders into a glass and metal building ostensibly to see someone and just his presence turns all this modernism into fun. He gets mingled with a group of American tourists and this new modern world as he goes his almost wordless, innocent way.

He meets an old friend and is taken home where people literally live in glass houses. Hulot also gets into a new nitery-eatery, Royal Gardens, which is still being built as the customers arrive. He ends up unwittingly helping tear down the unfinished structure.

Tati is not an active satirist nor does he use slapstick. He has assimilated the greats but is an individual comic talent who builds meticulous gags founded on a gentle, anarchic individualism that is always sympathetic, personal and, above all, funny and constantly inventive. Dialog is just functional.

•

PLAZA SUITE

1971, 114 mins, US Ⓥ ⊙ col

Dir Arthur Hiller ***Prod*** Howard W. Koch ***Scr*** Neil Simon ***Ph*** Jack Marta ***Ed*** Frank Bracht ***Mus*** Maurice Jarre ***Art*** Arthur Lonergan

Act Walter Matthau, Maureen Stapleton, Barbara Harris, Lee Grant, Louise Sorel (Paramount)

Neil Simon's excellent adaptation of his 1968 Broadway hit stars Walter Matthau in three strong characterizations of comedy-in-depth, teamed separately with Maureen Stapleton, Lee Grant and Barbara Harris. Film opens with a 44-minute sketch featuring Stapleton as a nervous suburban wife who has taken her bridal suite at N.Y.'s Plaza Hotel while the paint dries at home. Hubby Matthau is a cool, jaded mate whose affair with secretary Louise Sorel is intuitively divined by the wife. Segment is the most dramatic, though filled with nervous comedy.

Middle episode is 33 minutes of lecherous farce, as Hollywood producer Matthau puts the make on Harris, a flame of 15 years past. She has become a reluctant matron of Tenafly, NJ. Some of the best laughs of the whole piece occur here.

Final 37 minutes involve father-of-the-bride Matthau, trying to coax frightened daughter Jenny Sullivan out of a locked hotel bathroom and into marriage to Thomas Carey. Grant is the harried mother. The comedy emphasis here is generally slapstick: rain-drenched clothes; torn tails and stockings; broken furniture.

Each of the femme stars is given much screen time and the result not only is excellent spotlighting of their own talents, but also an adroit restraint on Matthau's presence.

•

PLEASE DON'T EAT THE DAISIES
1960, 111 mins, US Ⓥ ▭ col
Dir Charles Walters ***Prod*** Joe Pasternak ***Scr*** Isobel Lennart ***Ph*** Robert Bronner ***Ed*** John MacSweeney ***Mus*** David Rose ***Art*** George W. Davis, Hans Peters
Act Doris Day, David Niven, Janis Paige, Spring Byington, Richard Haydn, Patsy Kelly (M-G-M)

Please Don't Eat the Daisies is a light and frothy comedy, and boff family fare. Pic is episodic—as was the book by Jean Kerr—a series of highly amusing incidents strung together by a rather loose story thread, but this circumstance doesn't militate against interest. Charles Walters's direction maintains terrific pace.

Plotline is based on the adventures of Doris Day and David Niven after he turns to newspaper drama criticking during which they are forced out of their Gotham apartment and buy a monstrosity in the country—70 miles from Broadway—where Day takes on community life while trying to modernize and make their new home livable. Janis Paige enters scene as a Broadway actress whom Niven pans in his very first review, which also incurs the enmity of his best friend, producer Richard Haydn.

Day delivers lustily and Niven makes hay with his critic's portrayal, for whom Paige goes on the make in a big way. Jack Weston also is good as a playwriting cabby.

•

PLEASURE OF HIS COMPANY, THE
1961, 114 mins, US col
Dir George Seaton ***Prod*** William Perlberg ***Scr*** Samuel Taylor ***Ph*** Robert Burks ***Ed*** Alma Macrorie ***Mus*** Alfred Newman ***Art*** Hal Pereira, Tambi Larsen
Act Fred Astaire, Debbie Reynolds, Lilli Palmer, Tab Hunter, Gary Merrill, Charles Ruggles (Paramount)

Samuel Taylor's screenplay, based on the Broadway comedy Cornelia Otis Skinner and he concocted, is the sort of property that rises or falls with the comic conduct of the cast and the calibre of the direction. George Seaton's direction, for the most part, indicates verve and humorous perception, letting down only briefly in the picture's lethargic midsection. Most of the performances are bright and keen-witted, and in one or two cases downright inventive.

Fred Astaire plays the role originated by Cyril Ritchard on the stage, that of the prodigal, middle-aged playboy papa who returns after a 15–20 year absence to visit his wealthy ex-wife (Lilli Palmer) and daughter (Debbie Reynolds) just prior to the latter's wedding. Balance of the film consists of a contest of sorts in which Astaire more or less vies with his daughter's fiance for her affection over the protestations of the shrewd, knowing Palmer and the vexations of her present husband.

It is Palmer who steals the show. Her reactions are responsible for the picture's strongest comedy wallops, and she comes through equally fine during the weaker sentimental passages. The venerable Astaire isn't very far behind.

•

PLEASURE SEEKERS, THE
1964, 106 mins, US ▭ col
Dir Jean Negulesco ***Prod*** David Weisbart ***Scr*** Edith Sommer ***Ph*** Daniel L. Fapp ***Ed*** Louis Loeffler ***Mus*** Lionel Newman ***Art*** Jack Martin Smith, Edward Carrere
Act Ann-Margret, Tony Franciosa, Carol Lynley, Gardner McKay, Pamela Tiffin, Gene Tierney (20th Century-Fox)

Twentieth-Fox's big 1954 grosser, *Three Coins in the Fountain*, is back in new dress as *The Pleasure Seekers*. Background has been switched to Madrid from Rome, but the basic plot structure fashioned around the romantic adventures of three American girls residing there still provides a happy storyline under the direction of Jean Negulesco, who also helmed *Fountain*.

Trio of young femme charmers—Ann-Margret, Carol Lynley and Pamela Tiffin—spice the events. Foiling for them romantically are Tony Franciosa, Gardner McKay and Andre Lawrence, and for complications Brian Keith.

There is the added plus of Ann-Margret warbling four songs cleffed by Sammy Cahn and James Van Heusen, catchy and well suited to the action. One, "Everything Makes Music When You're in Love," with actress clad in a brief bikini on a Spanish beach, affords a lively dance number.

Script by Edith Sommer based on the John H. Secondari novel interweaves the lives of the three girls who share the same Madrid apartment. Ann-Margret, ambitious to be a dancer and singer, is in love with Lawrence, a struggling Spanish doctor; Lynley, secretary to Keith, head of a big American news agency and a married man, carries a torch for him and later turns to McKay; Tiffin is all out for Franciosa, a wealthy Spanish playboy who offers everything but marriage.

Ann-Margret delivers what is perhaps her best performance to date and gets the most footage. Gene Tierney acquits herself capably as Keith's jealous wife.

•

PLENTY
1985, 124 mins, US/UK Ⓥ ⊙ ▭ col
Dir Fred Schepisi ***Prod*** Edward R. Pressman, Joseph Papp ***Scr*** David Hare ***Ph*** Ian Baker ***Ed*** Peter Honess ***Mus*** Bruce Smeaton ***Art*** Richard Macdonald
Act Meryl Streep, Charles Dance, Tracey Ullman, John Gielgud, Sting, Ian McKellen (RKO/Pressman)

A picture possessing a host of first-class pedigrees, *Plenty* emerges as an absorbing and fastidiously made adaptation of David Hare's acclaimed play, but also comes off as cold and ultimately unaffecting.

Hare's ambitious drama, first staged in London in 1978, charts the growing social malaise of Western Europe and, specifically, Great Britain, over the years following World War II. He does this through the character of Susan Traherne, a difficult, unsettled, neurotic young woman who moves from idealism to frustration and madness in her passage through a succession of bleak political and personal events.

Pic opens with Susan, played by Meryl Streep, involved in derring-do with the Resistance in France during the war. She has a brief affair with commando Sam Neill, and no man can ever displace Neill from her mind.

Personally and historically, it's all downhill from there. Action is set principally in the British diplomatic world, and moves across a stage backdropped by postwar economic difficulties, Coronation Year, the Suez crisis and further developments in the Middle East.

•

PLOT AGAINST HARRY, THE
1989, 80 mins, US Ⓥ b/w
Dir Michael Roemer ***Prod*** Robert Young, Michael Roemer ***Scr*** Michael Roemer ***Ph*** Robert Young ***Ed*** Terry Lewis, Georges Klotz ***Mus*** Frank Lewin ***Art*** Howard Mandel
Act Martin Priest, Ben Lang, Henry Nemo (King Screen)

The Plot Against Harry is hilarious and often poignant. It was shot in 1969 but was held up because of a lack of completion funding. B&W pic is a sociological fossil of manners, mores and life in the 1960s.

Harry Plotnick (Martin Priest), a small-time Jewish numbers racketeer, gets released from prison and expects to pick up the gambling circuit he ran in his old neighborhood. His loyal schlemiel assistant/chauffeur Max, in cruising through his old turf in Manhattan, makes him realize the world has changed, and blacks and Hispanics now have dibs on his area.

In a farcical accident, Harry hits the rear end of a car carrying his ex-wife Kay and his ex-brother-in-law Leo and wife. Without missing a beat, Kay introduces Harry to the daughter he never saw, Margie (now pregnant), and her husband Mel, in an almost touching encounter.

As the story unfolds, Harry is faced with a new world and the gnawing lures of the solid middle-class family life that he's always eschewed. The Plotnick family is boisterous, up-front, multilayered and Jewish in a way that Philip Roth would savor parodying. The cast is uniformly solid, delivering their sparklingly crisp dialog straight.

•

PLOUGH AND THE STARS, THE
1937, 72 mins, US b/w
Dir John Ford ***Prod*** Cliff Reid, Robert Sisk ***Scr*** Dudley Nichols ***Ph*** Joseph H. August ***Ed*** George Hiveley ***Mus*** Roy Webb
Act Barbara Stanwyck, Preston Foster, Barry Fitzgerald, Denis O'Dea, Arthur Shields, Una O'Conner (RKO)

Story is an account of the Irish rebellion in 1916, a sanguinary outburst which failed of its purpose because the people were divided in allegiance, many Irish at the time fighting in France. It depicts the Irish character in various shadings of comedy, tragedy, sacrifice, selfishness and stupidity.

So many changes have been made in adapting this Sean O'Casey play to the screen that the tragic original has been modified into a romantic melodrama. Primarily the screen version is a woman's starring picture calling for an actress of considerably more gifts than Barbara Stanwyck here possesses. The altered story is the familiar theme that the men do the fighting and the women the weeping.

The opening shows the struggle and grief in a young bride's heart when her husband is selected by the citizen army to be the commandant of the fighting forces in Dublin. She has no interest in the uprising to free Ireland. Her world is her home.

These Irish boys are good-looking, earnest and sincere. They take a tough licking but they're not quitters. Sympathy therefore is with the lads, which is one of the reasons Stanwyck has such a hard time holding up her end of the story.

In between there is humor and amusing characterization. Barry Fitzgerald has a joyful time in the role of Fluther, an Irish braggart. He is teamed with J. M. Kerrigan who is up to his usual high standard. Preston Foster, opposite Stanwyck, fits nicely and his brogue comes easily. Only Stanwyck, of the entire cast, does not go Irish.

•

PLOUGHMAN'S LUNCH, THE
1983, 100 mins, US Ⓥ col
Dir Richard Eyre ***Prod*** Simon Relph, Ann Scott ***Scr*** Ian McEwan ***Ph*** Clive Tickner ***Ed*** David Martin ***Mus*** Dominic Muldowney ***Art*** Luciana Arrighi
Act Jonathan Pryce, Tim Curry, Rosemary Harris, Frank Finlay, Charlie Dore, Bill Paterson (Greenpoint/Goldcrest/White)

Pic is set in the heartland of bourgeois England among its media creators and academic pontificators, and runs the period from the first spark of 1982's Falklands warlet to the victory speech of Prime Minister Margaret Thatcher at her party's gung ho autumn shindig.

But those events are only a backdrop to the multilayered story of a group of people who are either off the rails or suffering an acute lack of human commitment. It's a plot that could have turned out over-schematic, but Richard Eyre's strong directorial hand shows in delicately ambivalent performances from all players.

The film evidently springs from its author Ian McEwan's heart in characterizing the radio journalist played by Jonathan Pryce as lacking in virtue and understanding. His sins include political convictions that blow with the wind; neglect of a dying mother, leading on an older woman, and a fruitless infatuation with the TV researcher played by Charlie Dore.

Film reaches an astonishing climax during the Conservative party conference, where crew and cast filmed undercover.

•

PLYMOUTH ADVENTURE
1952, 104 mins, US col
Dir Clarence Brown ***Prod*** Dore Schary ***Scr*** Helen Deutsch ***Ph*** William Daniels ***Ed*** Robert J. Kern ***Mus*** Miklos Rozsa ***Art*** Cedric Gibbons, Urie McCleary
Act Spencer Tracy, Gene Tierney, Van Johnson, Leo Genn, Lloyd Bridges, Dawn Adams (M-G-M)

Metro has made *Plymouth Adventure*, the story of the *Mayflower*'s perilous voyage to America [from a novel by Ernest Gebler], a large-scale sea spectacle.

The production, ably executed, puts more emphasis on the voyage itself and the attendant dangers than on developing the characters into flesh-and-blood people.

To Spencer Tracy falls the chore of enacting Captain Christopher Jones, the tough, earthy master of the *Mayflower*. Gene Tierney is the tragic Dorothy Bradford and Leo Genn her husband, the William Bradford later to become the first governor of the new colony. Van Johnson is John Alden, the carpenter who ships on the voyage and later marries Priscilla Mullins, played by Dawn Addams. They are all competent.

1952: Best Special Effects

•

POCAHONTAS
1995, 87 mins, US Ⓥ ⊙ col
Dir Mike Gabriel, Eric Goldberg ***Prod*** James Pentecost ***Scr*** Carl Binder, Susannah Grant, Philip LaZebnick ***Ed*** H. Lee Petersen ***Mus*** Alan Menken ***Art*** Michael Giaimo (Walt Disney)

Disney's 33rd animated feature and its first drawn, so to speak, from an actual historic figure, *Pocahontas* hooks from the start, and all the studio's signature elements—spirited animal sidekicks; wise, not necessarily human, advisers; evil, bumbling villains; natural visas breathtakingly heightened—are all in place.

Pocahontas's father, the chief, wants her to marry the tribe's bravest warrior, but she's holding out for someone a little more exciting. Excitement arrives in the form of John Smith, an adventurer accompanying a band of brutish, greedy, stupid men under the command of brutish, greedy, stupid Gov. Ratcliffe.

For Smith and Pocahontas, it's pretty much love at first sight. He's ruggedly blond, and, as if that's not enough, he comes with Mel Gibson's voice. She is equally blessed, not only with beauty but with the singing voice of Judy Kuhn.

The Powhatans fear the well-armed Englishmen invading their turf. Like Maria, Pocahontas has been marked for betrothal to an outstanding member of her tribe; like Tony, John Smith was his clan's fiercest fighter until common sense—in this case, the natural beauty of the New World and the sight of Pocahontas—conspire to tame his heart.

The Powhatans have been created with considerable care. The chief (Russell Means) and the warrior he wants his daughter to marry, Kocoum (James Apaumut Fall), are both quite grave. Appropriately, there is not a tepee in sight (less appropriately, there's hardly a wigwam, either), and the tribe is uniformly at one with nature. The motherless (another Disney tradition) Pocahontas takes spiritual advice from a wise old widow (Linda Hunt), and her constant companions are a racoon and a hummingbird.

The Disney artists have created a vivid palette for the picture. The colors are intense and play with nature. The film's theme is the "Colors of the Wind," and the artists have taken that seriously: The Virginia air is always full of glimmering lights. The forests and mountains are majestically rendered, and some effects—sunlight through the forests, the falling water—are stunning.

1995: Best Original Musical or Comedy Score, Best Original Song ("Colors of the Wind")

NOMINATIONS: Original Musical or Comedy Score

•

POCKETFUL OF MIRACLES

1961, 136 mins, US Ⓥ ⦿ ▭ col

Dir Frank Capra ***Prod*** Frank Capra ***Scr*** Hal Kanter, Harry Tugend ***Ph*** Robert Bronner ***Ed*** Frank P. Keller ***Mus*** Walter Scharf ***Art*** Hal Pereira, Roland Anderson

Act Glenn Ford, Bette Davis, Hope Lange, Arthur O'Connell, Peter Falk, Edward Everett Horton (Franton)

The scenario, which alternates uneasily between wit and sentiment, is based on the 1933 *Lady for a Day*, which was adapted by Robert Riskin from a Damon Runyon story, and also directed by Frank Capra. It has to do with an impoverished apple-vender (Bette Davis) who would have her long lost daughter (Ann-Margret) believe that she is a lady of means. This is simple enough when the daughter is on the other side of the globe, but when she comes trotting over for a look-see, mama is in trouble.

Enter mama's favorite apple-polisher, influential Dave the Dude (Glenn Ford), who hastily sets up an elaborate masquerade with the aid of a horde of typical 1930s Runyon-esque hoodlums who are hard as nails on the surface, but all whipped cream on the inside.

The picture seems too long, considering that there's never any doubt as to the outcome, and it's also too lethargic, but there are sporadic compensations of line and situation that reward the patience. Fortunately Capra has assembled some of Hollywood's outstanding character players for the chore.

For the romantic leads, he has Ford and Hope Lange. As a comedy team, they are no James Stewart-Jean Arthur (probably Capra's most formidable star-pairing), but they get by—particularly Ford. Lange is more suitable for serious roles. Davis has the meaty role of "Apple Annie" and, except for a tendency to overemote in close-ups, she handles it with depth and finesse.

The best lines in the picture go to Peter Falk, who just about walks off with the film when he's on.

1961: NOMINATIONS: Best Supp. Actor (Peter Falk), Color Costume Design, Song ("Pocketful of Miracles")

•

POETIC JUSTICE

1993, 110 mins, US Ⓥ ⦿ col

Dir John Singleton ***Prod*** Steve Nicolaides, John Singleton ***Scr*** John Singleton ***Ph*** Peter Lyons Collister ***Ed*** Bruce Cannon ***Mus*** Stanley Clarke ***Art*** Keith Burns

Act Janet Jackson, Tupac Shakur, Regina King, Joe Torry, Tyra Ferrell, Roger Guenveur Smith (Columbia)

John Singleton's followup to *Boyz N the Hood* and the screen debut of Janet Jackson cannot sustain the scrutiny and expectation that inevitably follow a conspicuous first film. *Poetic Justice* is a hermetic inner-city love story elevated by resonant social commentary.

The film begins promisingly enough with the central character, Justice (Jackson), at the local drive-in with her boyfriend. The momentary idyll quickly disintegrates when a nabe hothead recognizes the young man as someone who crossed his path. The firebrand kills the beau while in the girl's embrace.

Justice, chastened by the incident, has cut herself off from the world outside the beauty salon where she works. Lucky (Tupac Shakur), the young letter carrier on the shop's route, attempts to break the ice with brittle consequences.

Things finally get into gear when Justice's planned trip from South Central L.A. to Oakland is fouled up by a dead car battery. Her friend Iesha (Regina King) arranges a last-minute ride with Chicago (Joe Torry) and his buddy from work. The pal turns out to be Lucky, the mailman.

Singleton proves himself an adept director, fascinated with the echoes beneath the narrative. But his writing skills are less assured. Jackson proves herself a natural in front of the camera in a thoughtful rather than dynamic performance. Shakur has the juicier part and turns in truly outstanding work.

1993: NOMINATION: Best Song ("Again")

•

POINT BLANK

1967, 92 mins, US Ⓥ ▭ col

Dir John Boorman ***Prod*** Judd Bernard, Robert Chartoff ***Scr*** Alexander Jacobs, David Newhouse, Rafe Newhouse ***Ph*** Philip H. Lathrop ***Ed*** Henry Berman ***Mus*** Johnny Mandel ***Art*** George W. Davis, Albert Brenner

Act Lee Marvin, Angie Dickinson, Keenan Wynn, Carroll O'Connor, John Vernon, Sharon Acker (M-G-M)

Point Blank is a violent, dynamic, thinly-scripted film. Lee Marvin stars as a double-crossed thief seeking vengeance, only to find he has again been used. Britisher John Boorman's first Hollywood pic is a textbook in brutality and a superior exercise in cinematic virtuosity. Richard Stark's novel *The Hunter* is the basis for the screenplay, in which first five minutes recap Marvin's betrayal by best pal John Vernon and wife (Sharon Acker). The space-time jumps are lucid, effective, inventive, fluid—and repetitive. A hurry-and-wait sensation grows on a viewer as, once transposed from one scene to another, a dramatic torpor ensues at times, except for the hypo of choreographed brutality.

The futility of revenge is exemplified by the cyclic pattern of Marvin's movements, and Boorman's frequent cuts to the past overmake the point.

•

POINT BREAK

1991, 122 mins, US Ⓥ ⦿ ▭ col

Dir Kathryn Bigelow ***Prod*** Peter Abrams, Robert L. Levy ***Scr*** W. Peter Iliff ***Ph*** Donald Peterman ***Ed*** Howard Smith ***Mus*** Mark Isham ***Art*** Peter Jamison

Act Patrick Swayze, Keanu Reeves, Gary Busey, Lori Petty, John McGinley, James LeGros (Largo)

A hare-brained wild ride through big surf and bad vibes, *Point Break* acts like a huge, nasty wave, picking up viewers for a few major thrills but ultimately grinding them into the sand via overkill and absurdity. What it lacks is subtlety, logic or any redeeming grace. "Too much testosterone here," says a femme surfer (Lori Petty), walking disdainfully away from a crude party. Comment fits.

Keanu Reeves plays a 25-year-old ex-footballer turned FBI agent who is assigned to penetrate the Southern California surf culture in search of some highly successful bank robbers. Partnered with a cranky veteran fed (Gary Busey), who naturally doesn't like him, Reeves has to first learn to surf, then gain the trust of a radical dude named Bodhi (Patrick Swayze) who mixes mystical vibes with fearless thrill-seeking.

Script [from a story by Rick King and W. Peter Iliff] tries to ride on the cockeyed relationship between these two rocketheads, but since they spend most of the pic trying to throttle or maim each other, it's not very interesting.

Director Kathryn Bigelow (*Blue Steel*) affects a hyperkinetic, agitated visual style that generates plenty of excitement. Actors, especially John McGinley as an FBI boss, behave as if injected with rocket fuel. One wonders if their heads had to be unscrewed from the ceiling after each take.

•

POINT OF NO RETURN
(UK/AUSTRALIA: THE ASSASSIN)

1993, 109 mins, US Ⓥ ⦿ ▭ col

Dir John Badham ***Prod*** Art Linson ***Scr*** Robert Getchell, Alexandra Seros ***Ph*** Michael Watkins ***Ed*** Frank Morriss ***Mus*** Hans Zimmer ***Art*** Philip Harrison

Act Bridget Fonda, Gabriel Byrne, Dermot Mulroney, Miguel Ferrer, Anne Bancroft, Harvey Keitel (Warner)

For those who saw Luc Besson's high-tech thriller *La Femme Nikita*, about a female criminal transformed into a government assassin, this soulless, efficiently slavish remake [of the 1990 French pic] is almost like watching it all over again.

But the premise remains a strong hook on which to peg a taut, straight-line action narrative. Sentenced to death for killing a cop in a robbery, a young drug-addicted punk (Bridget Fonda), here named Maggie, is given a chance to live, under the supervision of an agent named Bob (Gabriel Byrne). The elegant Amanda (Anne Bancroft) adds the feminine touch.

Having won her stripes, she is transferred from Washington to Venice, California, where she instantly seduces J. P. (Dermot Mulroney), the friendly young caretaker of her boardwalk apartment building. The nasty assignments keep coming, though, until her jobs get in the way of her pleasant personal life. Ending is a shade more upbeat and conventional than the French version.

Fonda acquits herself admirably in all departments. Byrne is low-key as Maggie's lovestruck Pygmalion, and Mulroney endows Maggie's beach-dwelling boyfriend with welcome humor and a comfortable naturalism. Most amusing turn comes from Harvey Keitel, who plays a ruthless hitman nicknamed the Cleaner as if pretending to be the Terminator.

Director John Badham offers no interpretation or distinctive p.o.v., but does get the requisite action up on the screen in a straightforward manner that's a degree less stylized and poetic than the original.

•

POISON

1991, 85 mins, US Ⓥ col

Dir Todd Haynes ***Prod*** Christine Vachon ***Scr*** Todd Haynes ***Ph*** Maryse Alberti, Barry Ellsworth ***Ed*** James Lyons, Todd Haynes ***Mus*** James Bennett ***Art*** Sarah Stollman

Act Edith Meeks, Millie White, Larry Maxwell, Susan Norman, Scott Renderer, James Lyons (Bronze Eye)

Todd Haynes's *Poison* is a conceptually bold, stylistically audacious first feature, a compelling study of different forms of deviance. Point of departure is the works of the late French writer Jean Genet: *Our Lady of the Flowers*, *Miracle of the Rose* and *Thief's Journal*. Haynes has composed three distinctive stories that constitute case studies of antisocial aberrations, shot them in three strikingly different styles and intercut them in surprisingly successful ways.

Hero takes up the case of a seven-year-old boy who, in blandest suburbia, murders his father. Arguably the weakest of the three story strands, but amusing enough withal, section features straight-on TV documentary-style interviews with the lad's mother, neighbors, teachers and classmates.

The vastly effective *Horror* uses a 1950s B-pic sci-fi approach to relate the sad story of a scientist who isolates the source of human sex drive, but, upon drinking the fluid, becomes horribly disfigured and murderous.

A direct representation of the Genet universe, *Homo* scrutinizes an obsessive relationship between a hardened criminal and a new arrival in a 1940s French prison. A mood of seething, violent homoeroticism permeates the proceedings, as one prisoner stalks another in an episode spiked with multiple glimpses of rear-entry intercourse and one of genital fondling.

•

POISON IVY

1992, 89 mins, US Ⓥ ⦿ col

Dir Katt Shea Ruben ***Prod*** Andy Ruben ***Scr*** Andy Ruben, Katt Shea Ruben ***Ph*** Phedon Papamichael ***Ed*** Gina Mittelman ***Mus*** David Michael Frank ***Art*** Virginia Lee

Act Tom Skerritt, Drew Barrymore, Sara Gilbert, Cheryl Ladd, Alan Stock, Jeanne Sakata (New Line)

Katt Shea Ruben's first film away from her Roger Corman training ground has Drew Barrymore as Ivy, a tarty-looking high-schooler who befriends the bookish, withdrawn Sylvie (Sara Gilbert). Before long, she's living in Sylvie's opulent Hollywood Hills home with dad (Tom Skerritt), a recovering alcoholic with a decided Humbert Humbert bent, and mom (Cheryl Ladd), who is slowly expiring from emphysema.

Methodically, the blond siren conquers not only all the family members, but the dog as well. Parading around in bedridden mom's fancy gowns, she gets dad so worked up that he takes to the bottle again, and the two appear to get it on while mom is lying passed out in bed next to them. Suicide, hints of lesbianism, murder, staged accidents and every other applicable melodramatic contrivance is dragged in. Unfortunate thesps take it all very seriously, while technical aspects are emptily polished. [Screen story by Melissa Godard and Peter Morgan.]

•

POKEMON
THE FIRST MOVIE
MEWTWO STRIKES BACK
1999, 75 mins, Japan/US Ⓥ ⦿ col
Dir Kunihiko Yuyama ***Prod*** Norman J. Grossfeld, Choji Yoshikawa, Tomoyuki Igarashi, Takemoto Mori ***Scr*** Takeshi Shudo ***Ph*** Hisao Shirai ***Ed*** Toshio Henmi, Yutaka Ito ***Mus*** Ralph Schuckett, John Loeffler ***Art*** Katsuyoshi Kanemura (Pikachu Project '98/Shogakukan/Kids WB!)

It's Pokemon's world, and we're just living in it—at least, until the next kiddie craze hits and these multitalented, evolutionary pocket monsters fade away to join Mutant Ninja Turtles and Mighty Morphin Power Rangers in the Hall of Fame of Retired Cartoon Superheroes.

This once-humble anime saga about a boy named Ash Ketchum and his self-made mission to become the world's greatest Pokemon master is a bloated and epic-sized departure from the rollicking adventures and subversive humor of the massively popular Japanese TV show [with characters created by Satoshi Tajiri]. Something is disturbingly different, and off, starting with pic's *Frankenstein*-themed prologue, when scientists discover that their efforts to bio-engineer the rarest Pokemon of all, Mew, have created a monster—Mewtwo.

Things get back on more familiar ground as picnicking Ash and his pals are interrupted by a rival, who, like Ash, is a Pokemon trainer with several pocket monsters of his own. Mysterious "mistress of the greatest No. 1 trainer" invites eager trainers to remote New Island. Ash and friends find themselves duped as the No. 1 trainer reveals himself to be Mewtwo. Little does Mewtow know, though, that the rare Mew has emerged from the sea and flies into the New Island lair.

The younger set loves the flat anime design, continued here from the series and game (wisely, Warner reportedly quashed the idea to add dimensional touches), and the only new visual elements include a certain sepulchral darkness in key scenes and digitized backgrounds which don't match the foregrounded art. Music lacks the emblematic "Pokemon" theme song.

•

POKEMON THE MOVIE 2000: THE POWER OF ONE
2000, 81 mins, Japan/US Ⓥ ⦿ col
Dir Kunihiko Yuyama ***Prod*** Norman J. Grossfeld, Choji Yoshikawa, Yukako Matsusasko, Takemoto Mori ***Scr*** Takeshi Shudo ***Ph*** Hisao Shirai ***Ed*** Jay Film ***Mus*** Ralph Shuckett, John Loeffler ***Art*** Katsuyoshi Kanemura (Pikachu Project '99/Shogakukan/Kids WB!)

Though Pokemania has settled into early middle age, the second feature-length installment [English adaptation by Norman J. Grossfeld, Michael Haigney] is a much more intense action vehicle for hero Ash Ketchum and his band of pocket monster trainers than its leaden, sometimes claustrophobic predecessor. Returning to ongoing saga's roots in the great outdoors, the new entry takes place on stormy seas, in turbulent skies and on rocky, volcanic islands.

Makers have clearly determined that the features, unlike the lighter, funkier tube item, must be aimed at young boys and their yen for action-adventure. Ash's gal-pal and fellow trainer Misty is relegated to the sidelines here, a fairly passive audience for Ash's grand exploits. Her biggest scenes involve modest cat fighting with a new female character, the cynical-turned-believing Melody, who seems to want to vie for Ash's attention. This goes nowhere, though, when the real action takes over. It tends to leave *Pokemon* girl fans without a true rooting interest of their own, which isn't the case in the TV version.

As per previous pic, *Pokemon 2000* assumes aud knowledge of this universe created by Satoshi Tajiri, but ironically contains a built-in critique of the collector's craze that defines the pop phenomenon for many. It comes in the form of Lawrence III, British baddie who flies around in a massive machine resembling the *Close Encounters* mothership (created in 3-D animation, a visual nuance new to *Pokemon* projects).

His goal is to capture the three key Poke-birds that rule the elements of fire, lightning and ice. Capturing this trio, Lawrence can also lure the powerful amphibious sea-air creature, Lugia, which controls deep sea currents and thus, global weather. Perhaps only in *Pokemon* could a moral be drawn between excessive collecting and global weather imbalance, but that's the dilemma Ash and his vacationing buddies fall into when Lawrence's chicanery unleashes storm sending their boats adrift.

New creatures added to the Pokemon stable are Lugia and Slowking, one changeable and majestic, the other static and slightly goofy, but not quite up to the cool scale of previous feature's nasty Mewtwo. It reflects difference in tone here from first pic—thankfully lighter, visually easier on the eye and more suited to the ultra-flat anime style.

Fans will be happy that the English-language voice casting hasn't strayed much from original vocal thesps, who all go for a sincerely serious tone that can be amusing if you take it in the right light.

•

POKOLENIE
(A GENERATION; LIGHT IN THE DARKNESS)
1955, 90 mins, Poland Ⓥ b/w
Dir Andrzej Wajda ***Prod*** Aleksander Ford ***Scr*** Bohdan Czeszko ***Ph*** Jerzy Lipman ***Ed*** Czeslaw Raniszewski ***Mus*** Andrzej Markowski ***Art*** Roman Mann
Act Tadeusz Lomnicki, Urszula Modrzynska, Tadeusz Janczar, Janusz Paluszkiewicz, Ryszard Kotas, Roman Polanski (WFF)

This pic is one of the most incisive of all Polish director Andrzej Wajda's films, despite the fact it was made in 1954 when there was more central governmental control of screen productions in Poland. [Film was reviewed at a Paris screening in 1962.]

Story [from the novel by Bohdan Czeszko] concerns a youth during the occupation of Poland in the last World War who comes to adulthood through love and adversity. Members of the old Polski governmental underground here are treated mainly as gangster types, with the Communists more humane and active.

Wajda's feeling for the period and heroism weld this so well it becomes a moving tale of youth in crisis. It is perfectly acted and directed, with technical credits tops.

•

POLICE
1985, 113 mins, France Ⓥ col
Dir Maurice Pialat ***Prod*** Emmanuel Schlumberger ***Scr*** Catherine Breillat, Sylvie Danton, Jacques Fieschi, Maurice Pialat ***Ph*** Luciano Tovoli ***Ed*** Yann Dedet ***Mus*** Henryk Mikolaj Gorecki ***Art*** Constantin Mejinsky
Act Gerard Depardieu, Sophie Marceau, Richard Anconina, Pascale Rocard, Sandrine Bonnaire, Franck Karoui (Gaumont/TF1)

Director Maurice Pialat subverts the mainstream thriller genre for a personal film that deliberately works against conventional expectations. Gaumont sank a reported FF25 million (nearly $3 million) into *Police*. Film was first announced as an adaptation of a Yank detective novel, *Bodies Are Dust* by P. J. Wolfson. Pialat suddenly dropped the idea and asked writer-scripter Catherine Breillat for an original screenplay, but then discarded most of what she came up with. Backed by a small battery of writers, the filmmaker improvised story development as production rolled.

Not surprising then that the film hasn't much of a plot. Pialat ruthlessly strips everything down to a deliberately anti-climactic study of an ill-fated romance between a cop and a drug dealer's girlfriend.

Gerard Depardieu gives a superb, buttressing performance as the flic, whose boisterous, macho manner hides an abyss of mediocrity and desperate loneliness. When off duty, he often knocks around with a shady young lawyer (Richard Anconina) and doesn't shun the company of hookers (one of them played by Sandrine Bonnaire).

It is also through Anconina that Depardieu gets closer to a young girl (Sophie Marceau), who has been arrested along with her Arab boyfriend during a drug raid. Depardieu begins to see her socially, and soon falls in love with her.

The first half of *Police* is vivid and vigorous, as the director situates his protagonist in his professional milieu. When the Depardieu-Marceau relationship comes to the fore (and story and secondary characters all but disappear) the film begins to unravel badly.

Film was the last production initiated at Gaumont by its former general manager, Daniel Toscan du Plantier.

•

POLICE ACADEMY
1984, 95 mins, US Ⓥ ⦿ col
Dir Hugh Wilson ***Prod*** Paul Maslansky ***Scr*** Neal Israel, Pat Proft, Hugh Wilson ***Ph*** Michael D. Margulies ***Ed*** Robert Brown, Zach Staenberg ***Mus*** Robert Folk ***Art*** Trevor Williams
Act Steve Guttenberg, G. W. Bailey, George Gaynes, Michael Winslow, Kim Cattrall, Bubba Smith (Warner/Ladd)

Police Academy at its core is a harmless, innocent poke at authority that does find a fresh background in a police academy. Women in the film, such as Kim Cattrall as an Ivy League–type and Leslie Easterbrook as a busty sergeant, have almost nothing to do. Marion Ramsey as a timid-voiced trainee is fine in the film's most vivid female part.

Co-writer Hugh Wilson, makes his feature film debut as director, and his scenes are short and fragmentary. He gets a fresh comic performance from Michael Winslow as a walking human sound effects system (the film's most appealing turn).

Through it all, Steve Guttenberg is a likeable rogue in a role that's too unflappable to set off any sparks.

•

POLICE ACADEMY 2: THEIR FIRST ASSIGNMENT
1985, 87 mins, US Ⓥ ⦿ col
Dir Jerry Paris ***Prod*** Paul Maslansky ***Scr*** Barry Blaustein, David Sheffield ***Ph*** James Crabe ***Ed*** Bob Wyman ***Mus*** Robert Folk ***Art*** Trevor Williams
Act Steve Guttenberg, Bubba Smith, David Graf, Michael Winslow, Bruce Mahler, Marion Ramsey (Warner/Ladd)

Follow-up features much of the original's cast but none of its key behind-the-scenes creative talent, save producer Paul Maslansky. Only actor to get any mileage out of this one is series newcomer Art Metrano, as an ambitious lieutenant bent upon taking over the department.

With the recruits assigned to saving the neighborhood from the grasp of marauding punks, Metrano does everything he can to make them fail, whereupon they exact some faintly amusing revenge upon him. Metrano somehow manages to shine in these murkiest of circumstances, and Michael Winslow has a couple of good moments doing his patented sound effects and engaging in some kung fu, complete with unsynchronized yells and screams.

•

POLICE ACADEMY 3: BACK IN TRAINING
1986, 82 mins, US Ⓥ ⦿ col
Dir Jerry Paris ***Prod*** Paul Maslansky ***Scr*** Gene Quintano ***Ph*** Robert Saad ***Ed*** Bud Molin ***Mus*** Robert Folk ***Art*** Trevor Williams
Act Steve Guttenberg, Bubba Smith, David Graf, Michael Winslow, Marion Ramsey, Leslie Easterbrook (Warner)

Cast of cartoon misfits is still basically intact and if *Police Academy 3* has any charm it's in the good-natured dopeyness of these people. No bones about it, these people are there to laugh at.

Leading the charge for the third time is Steve Guttenberg turning in another likable boy-next-door performance. His role, however, as the cute straight man seems a bit abbreviated, with the comic burden spread out among the cast. New additions Tim Kazurinsky and Bobcat Goldthwait as cadets are only intermittently amusing.

Plot has something to do with one of the two rival police academies being shut down by the penny-pinching governor (Ed Nelson). Bad guys led by Commandant Mauser (Art Metrano) try to sabotage the forces of virtue led by Commandant Lassard (George Gaynes).

•

POLICE ACADEMY 4: CITIZENS ON PATROL
1987, 87 mins, US Ⓥ ⦿ col
Dir Jim Drake ***Prod*** Paul Maslansky ***Scr*** Gene Quintano ***Ph*** Robert Saad ***Ed*** David Rawlins ***Mus*** Robert Folk ***Art*** Trevor William
Act Steve Guttenberg, Bubba Smith, Michael Winslow, David Graf, Sharon Stone, Leslie Easterbrook (Warner)

Police Academy 4 carries the banner of tasteless humor raised in the first three installments to new heights of insipidness. As usual, Steve Guttenberg leads the proceedings as Mahoney, the cute cop. Instead of just resembling a puppy dog, he actually imitates one at one point. Most of the regulars are back with Bobcat Goldthwait assuming a larger role as the moronic cop Zed, who spends most of his time chasing birdlike Officer Sweetchuck (Tim Kazurinsky). Bubba Smith growls his way through a few scenes and Leslie Easterbrook as the statuesque Officer Callahan gets to show off her talents as well.

Plot, such as it is, has something to do with Commandant Lassard's (George Gaynes) Citizens On Patrol program and attempts by archrival Captain Harris (G. W. Bailey) to make him look bad, a truly difficult task since collectively this police force barely has a triple digit IQ. Script is merely a collection of gags tied together by the slightest suggestion of a story.

•

POLICE ACADEMY 5: ASSIGNMENT MIAMI BEACH
1988, 90 mins, US Ⓥ ⦿ col
Dir Alan Myerson ***Prod*** Paul Maslansky ***Scr*** Stephen J. Curwick ***Ph*** Jim Pergola ***Ed*** Hubert De La Bouillerie ***Mus*** Robert Folk ***Art*** Trevor Williams
Act Matt McCoy, Janet Jones, George Gaynes, G. W. Bailey, Rene Auberjonois, Bubba Smith (Warner)

Miami field trip only brings a pastel backdrop to the insipid infighting of the boobs in blue.

The jokes are all on Capt. Harris (G. W. Bailey) this time out, as he makes a disastrous attempt to unseat

Cmdt. Lassard (George Gaynes), aging leader of this dunce-cap police academy, by pulling out a mandatory retirement clause. Lassard's last act is to address a Miami police convention, which gives his downhearted but loyal graduates an excuse to follow him there for some surfside antics.

At Miami airport, Lassard crosses paths with some excitable crooks, and in the old luggage switcheroo, ends up in possession of some diamonds they've heisted. The trio of baddies, led by Rene Auberjonois, spends the rest of the film trying to get them back from the blissfully unaware, graciously idiotic Lassard.

The usual crew—minus Steve Guttenberg or Bobcat Goldthwait, but with Tab Thacker, a Fat Albert look-alike, taking both seats—is ostensibly on vacation while in Miami.

•

POLICE ACADEMY 6: CITY UNDER SIEGE
1989, 83 mins, US Ⓥ ⊙ col
Dir Peter Bonerz ***Prod*** Paul Maslansky ***Scr*** Stephen J. Curwick ***Ph*** Charles Rosher, Jr. ***Ed*** Hubert De La Bouillerie ***Mus*** Robert Folk ***Art*** Thomas E. Azzari
Act Bubba Smith, David Graf, Michael Winslow, Leslie Easterbrook, Marion Ramsey, Lance Kinsey (Warner)

Commandant Lassard (George Gaynes) and his crack team are assigned to stop a wave of robberies, much to the chagrin of the cartoonish Captain Harris (G. W. Bailey). The crimes are committed by a trio with circus-like skills, keyed by a not-so-mysterious Mr. Big.

Director Peter Bonerz and writer Stephen J. Curwick (the latter taking his second *Academy* shift) both cut their teeth on TV sitcoms, and it shows. Rarely has a film cried out so desperately for a laugh track. Michael Winslow still has the funniest shtick with his seemingly limitless ability to perform vocal gymnastics—the film's only truly amusing moment coming when he nails one of the bad guys, first as a badly dubbed ninja, then a herky-jerky robot.

•

POLICE ACADEMY VII: MISSION TO MOSCOW
1994, 83 mins, US Ⓥ col
Dir Alan Metter ***Prod*** Paul Maslansky ***Scr*** Randolph Davis, Michele S. Chodos ***Ph*** Ian Jones ***Ed*** Denise Hill, Suzanne Hines ***Mus*** Robert Folk ***Art*** Frederic Weiler
Act George Gaynes, Michael Winslow, David Graf, Leslie Easterbrook, Christopher Lee, Ron Perlman (Warner)

It's been five years since Warner last wheeled out the boobs in blue, and the intervening span hasn't been kind. Seventh *Police Academy* stanza, with the gang taking on the Moscow mafia, is an inept, geriatric romp that's for completists only.

Law and order is breaking down in Moscow, where top mobster Konstantin Konali (Ron Perlman) has made millions from worldwide sales of a computer game. In desperation, top cop Rakov (Christopher Lee) rings his stateside pal Lassard (George Gaynes) who promptly announces, "Team, we're off to Russia—to kick many, many buttskies."

Excuse for a plot has Konali forcing a computer nerd (Richard Israel) to install a device in the game that will give him access to security systems for world domination. While Lassard slides off for some R&R, the troops go undercover.

Tech credits are on the cheesy side.

•

POLICE STORY 4: FIRST STRIKE
1996, 110 mins, HONG KONG Ⓥ ⊙ ▭ col
Dir Stanley Tong ***Prod*** Leonard Ho ***Scr*** Stanley Tong, Nick Tramontane, Greg Mellot, Tong ***Ph*** Jingle Ma ***Ed*** Peter Cheung, Yau Chi-wai ***Mus*** Nathan Wang ***Art*** Oliver Wong
Act Jackie Chan, Jackson Lou, Annie Wu, Bill Tung, Yuri Petrov, Nonna Grishajeva (Golden Harvest)

Jackie Chan dons his SuperCop mantle again in the Bondish actioner *First Strike*, a good-natured, high-energy showcase. Enlisted by the CIA, Jackie (Chan) is sent undercover to Ukraine to keep tabs on a woman (Nonna Grishajeva) acting as go-between in the transfer of nuclear secrets. The real perp is Jackson Tsui (Jackson Lou), a disaffected ex-agent who's working in concert with senior Russian intelligence honcho Col. Yegorov (Yuri Petrov).

The plot-dense opening section, set in the snow, is at times incomprehensible. The story doesn't find its footing until the action shifts to Australia, where Tsui's dying father has been the crime lord of Brisbane's Chinatown.

Pic's producers clearly have aimed to compete with studio blockbusters by providing comparable bang for the buck. The Russian winter offers ample opportunity for 007-style chase on skis, with parachuting assassins on Jackie's tail and a spectacular free-fall into icy waters.

There's also an extended, tongue-in-cheek homage to *Jaws* and *Thunderball*, with sharks and assassins in an underwater ballet in the aquarium where Tsui's sister (Annie Wu) works.

There's also plenty of Chan's signature acrobatic martial-arts wizardry to satisfy fans.

•

POLLYANNA
1960, 133 mins, US Ⓥ ⊙ col
Dir David Swift ***Prod*** George Golitzin (assoc.) ***Scr*** David Swift ***Ph*** Russell Harlan ***Ed*** Frank Gross ***Mus*** Paul Smith ***Art*** Carroll Clark, Robert Clatworthy
Act Jane Wyman, Hayley Mills, Richard Egan, Karl Malden, Nancy Olson, Adolphe Menjou (Walt Disney)

In Walt Disney's *Pollyanna* Hayley Mills's work more than compensates for the film's lack of tautness and, at certain points, what seems to be an uncertain sense of direction. That the incredibly pre-World War I confectionery character (the glad girl, she was called) emerges normal and believably lovable is a tribute to Mills's ability and to writer-director David Swift's sane sensible approach to the familiar character from Eleanor H. Porter's novel.

Pollyanna is the tale of the little 12-year-old girl who plays the "glad game" so well that she's soon got everyone she knows playing it. She's an orphan who lives with her aunt (Jane Wyman), the richest, most influential woman in a town which bears her name and sheepishly takes her advice and her charity. That is, until Pollyanna arrives.

Wyman, Richard Egan, Donald Crisp, Adolphe Menjou, Agnes Moorehead and Karl Malden are more than competent in key roles.

1960: Honorary Award (Hayley Mills)

•

POLTERGEIST
1982, 114 mins, US Ⓥ ⊙ ▭ col
Dir Tobe Hooper ***Prod*** Steven Spielberg, Frank Marshall ***Scr*** Steven Spielberg, Michael Grais, Mark Victor ***Ph*** Matthew F. Leonetti ***Ed*** Michael Kahn ***Mus*** Jerry Goldsmith ***Art*** James H. Spencer
Act Craig T. Nelson, JoBeth Williams, Beatrice Straight, Dominique Dunne, Oliver Robins, Heather O'Rourke (M-G-M)

Given the talents, *Poltergeist* is an annoying film because it could have been so much better. Certainly, the subject is interesting, a persistent parapsychological phenomenon that defies scientific explanation, yet refuses to go away.

But producer Steven Spielberg and the director Tobe Hooper don't really care. They're fully content to demonstrate how well they can create the physical manifestations, plus a lot of standard sideshow horrors.

But the story is truly stupid, though well-acted. Craig T. Nelson and JoBeth Williams are the parents, living almost wall-to-wall with their neighbors in a suburban development. But when the furniture starts to fly around the room and the big tree in the yard gets hungry for the kids nobody ever seems to notice. Here you have a house in the middle of the street going berserk in Dolby Stereo and nobody calls the cops. But Williams is terrific as the mother, at first amused by the strange goings-on in her kitchen and later terrified when cute little Heather O'Rourke disappears into the walls. And Zelda Rubinstein walks off with the film as the miniature lady who comes to cleanse the house.

1982: NOMINATIONS: Best Original Score, Sound Effects Editing, Visual Effects

•

POLTERGEIST II: THE OTHER SIDE
1986, 90 mins, US Ⓥ ⊙ ▭ col
Dir Brian Gibson ***Prod*** Mark Victor, Michael Grais ***Scr*** Mark Victor, Michael Grais ***Ph*** Andrew Laszlo ***Ed*** Thom Noble ***Mus*** Jerry Goldsmith ***Art*** Ted Haworth
Act JoBeth Williams, Craig T. Nelson, Heather O'Rourke, Oliver Robins, Zelda Rubinstein, Will Sampson (M-G-M)

It's another horrifying house party at the Freelings's in *Poltergeist II*. Sequel finds the poor Freeling family a year later penniless and slightly crazed after their Cuesta Verde house was obliterated by poltergeists.

When Gramma dies, little Carol Anne's play telephone spontaneously rings with a call from "the other side."

This time around, co-scripters Mark Victor and Michael Grais (who wrote the first *Poltergeist* with Steven Spielberg) have the focus of evil in human form, in the perfectly cast, since deceased, Julian Beck.

Unlike the first film that focused all the action around the innocent blond and persecuted Carol Anne (Heather O'Rourke), juiciest moments in *II* revolve around Craig Nelson playing a soppy drunk, a lustful husband (again to the warm JoBeth Williams), a loving father and a ghoulie-spewing monster.

1986: NOMINATION: Best Visual Effects

•

POLTERGEIST III
1988, 97 mins, US Ⓥ ⊙ col
Dir Gary Sherman ***Prod*** Barry Bernardi ***Scr*** Gary Sherman, Brian Taggert ***Ph*** Alex Nepomniaschy ***Ed*** Ross Albert ***Mus*** Joe Renzetti ***Art*** Paul Eads
Act Tom Skerritt, Nancy Allen, Heather O'Rourke, Zelda Rubinstein, Lara Flynn Boyle, Richard Fire (M-G-M)

As the third chapter unfolds, poor little Carol Anne (the late Heather O'Rourke) has had to move again. Her parents have shipped her off to live with her aunt and uncle (Nancy Allen and Tom Skerritt) in a brand-new Chicago high-rise. No sooner does Carol Anne move in than the mirrors start to crack and icebergs begin to form, not to mention the noise in her bedroom and the smoke that follows her down the hallway.

The family relationships are somewhat confused, but there's a teenage daughter (Lara Flynn Boyle) and her boyfriend (Kip Wenz) who get dragged into the basement floor with Carol Anne and a know-it-all school psychiatrist (Richard Fire), who may or may not have been dropped down the elevator shaft. Zelda Rubinstein is back as Tangina, the friendly psychic.

Director/co-writer Gary Sherman demonstrates absolutely no interest in whether this film ever has a modicum of meaning as he rushes from one special effect to another. Even there, Sherman arrives too late.

•

POLYESTER
1981, 94 mins, US Ⓥ col
Dir John Waters ***Prod*** John Waters ***Scr*** John Waters ***Ph*** David Insley ***Ed*** Charles Roggero ***Mus*** Chris Stein ***Art*** Vincent Peranio
Act Divine, Tab Hunter, Edith Massey, Mary Garlington, David Samson, Stiv Bators (New Line)

Baltimore-based underground filmmaker John Waters, famous for his midnight circuit hits like *Pink Flamingos*, surfaces in the pro ranks with *Polyester*, a fitfully amusing comedy of not so ordinary people. Waters's fabled shock tactics are toned down here.

Transvestite thesp Divine never steps out of character essaying the role of a housewife stuck with horrid children (Mary Garlington and Ken King), an unsympathetic husband (David Samson) and a truly evil mother (Joni Ruth White). As the episodic situation comedy unfolds, camp followers may enjoy Divine's eyerolling reactions but to the uninitiated most scenes play as overacted melodrama.

After a couple of silent teaser shots, Tab Hunter finally enters the picture after a full hour has elapsed. He is unable to fit into Waters's world, straining to overact and pull faces as the rest of the troupe and even extras do. His kissing Divine is about as offensive as film gets. With nudity and explicit sex and violence absent, *Polyester* strains for a marketing gimmick by introducing "Odorama." After a cute scientist-in-lab prolog explaining the process, cheap gimmick turns out to be a scratch and sniff card handed out to the viewer, keyed manually to numbers flashed on the screen periodically during the film. It's a far cry from the fumes in the theatre gimmicks of Walter Reade's 1959 AromaRama and Mike Todd, Jr.'s 1960 Smell-O-Vision.

•

PONTIAC MOON
1994, 107 mins, US Ⓥ ⊙ col
Dir Peter Medak ***Prod*** Robert Schaffel, Youssef Vahabzadeh ***Scr*** Finn Taylor, Jeffrey Brown ***Ph*** Thomas Kloss ***Ed*** Anne V. Coates ***Mus*** Randy Edelman ***Art*** Jeffrey Beecroft
Act Ted Danson, Mary Steenburgen, Ryan Todd, Eric Schweig, Cathy Moriarty, Lisa Jane Persky (Paramount)

Pontiac Moon is a sincere but tedious road movie that derives its title and inspiration from the Apollo landing/moonwalk in 1969. Pic's quirky, almost European flavor lends itself to a small, sensitive scale, but the filmmakers shoot for the stars and end up with a story that's more mundane than magical.

Katherine (Mary Steenburgen) hasn't ventured outside the house for seven years, and her husband, Washington (Ted Danson), an eccentric teacher, fears her phobias may be extending to their 11-year-old son (Ryan Todd), who isn't even allowed to ride in a car.

Seizing on the immenent moon landing to create "one perfect act," Washington decides to take the boy and his vintage Pontiac the 1,776 miles (no doubt additional symbolism regarding his declaration of independence) to Spires of the Moon National Park, which would push the car's mileage to 238,857—equaling the distance between the Earth and the moon.

The script does a half-baked job of developing period, as father and son encounter a Vietnam veteran Native American (Eric Schweig), hostile rednecks, a flirty waitress (Cathy Moriarty) and a bumbling local sheriff (John Schuck), the last sequence threatening to turn the pic ino a lightweight *Thelma & Louise*.

Director Peter Medak offers some nice touches but also hits some potholes along the road. Cutting back and forth between the Apollo landings and the story, the director tries too hard to create a sense of wonder.

•

PONY EXPRESS, THE
1925, 110 mins, US ⊗ b/w
Dir James Cruze ***Scr*** Walter Woods ***Ph*** Karl Brown ***Mus*** Hugo Riesenfeld
Act Betty Compson, Ricardo Cortez, Ernest Torrence, Wallace Beery, George Bancroft (Paramount)

Patriotic, expensive, pretentious, verbose and just fair—that describes *The Pony Express*. In plot this concerns the machinations of Senator Glen of California, and his attempt to establish an empire of that state and Sonora, Mexico. To this end, he plots to have the new pony express system "fixed" at Julesberg, Miss., so that any political news from the east which would have a bearing on his plans might be delayed.

The Pony Express has all the atmosphere in the world. Its production has been careful and elaborate, but the scenario and story are weak. Were it not for the comedy relief of Ernest Torrence and Wallace Beery, the whole thing would be tiresome. Ricardo Cortez has a good role here and plays it well, while Betty Compson and George Bancroft are others of the cast who do well. The film has its moments, but 110 minutes of running time is long.

•

POOKIE
SEE: THE STERILE CUCKOO

•

POOL OF LONDON
1951, 85 mins, UK b/w
Dir Basil Dearden ***Prod*** Michael Relph ***Scr*** Jack Whittingham, John Eldridge ***Ph*** Gordon Dines ***Ed*** Peter Tanner ***Mus*** John Addison ***Art*** Jim Morahan
Act Bonar Colleano, Susan Shaw, Renee Asherson, Earl Cameron, Moira Lister, Max Adrian (Ealing)

The story of *Pool of London* spans just 48 hours when a cargo ship is in the London docks. The plot goes off at various tangents before finally converging on the basic dramatic theme of a manhunt following a holdup, murder and jewel robbery.

The central character, played by Bonar Colleano, is an over-confident, over-exuberant seaman who makes a bit of side money by small-time smuggling. He is tempted into the big coin by a gang of jewel thieves. Before he gets back to his boat, he finds that he has become implicated in a murder hunt and that he has landed his best friend, a colored boy, with the incriminating evidence.

While the main story is being developed, the film traces the warm attachment of the Negro seaman for a white girl. Although this is tastefully done, it has no bearing on the plot.

Colleano's role is a natural for him. He lives the part of the swaggering sailor, sure of himself until the moment of crisis. Earl Cameron gives a restrained and dignified performance as his friend.

•

POOR COW
1967, 101 mins, UK Ⓥ col
Dir Ken Loach ***Prod*** Joseph Janni ***Scr*** Nell Dunn, Ken Loach ***Ph*** Brian Probyn ***Ed*** Roy Watts ***Mus*** Donovan ***Art*** Bernard Sarron
Act Carol White, Terence Stamp, John Bindon, Kate Williams, Queenie Watts, Malcolm McDowell (Vic/Anglo Amalgamated)

The film has a jolting opening, with Joy, the hapless heroine, shown in full detail giving birth to a baby, with the infant emerging from the womb in its natural state. This leads into a portrait of Joy, who has married a brutal crook (John Bindon) and, after he is nabbed by the cops, shacks up with another thief (Terence Stamp), a gentler type who is himself put inside.

The incidents of the plot are an excuse for an examination of promiscuous Joy. Left to fend for herself, she snatches happiness where she can find it.

Kenneth Loach uses an improvisatory technique in all this, and it largely works. Thesps were given the gist and trend of the dialog, and permitted to embroider it with their own words.

It is Carol White's film, and she scores with a flow of varied emotion, ranging from fetching happiness to a sudden spurt of tears in the final minutes, when she recalls straight to camera her affection for her baby.

•

POPE JOAN
1972, 101 mins, UK Ⓥ col
Dir Michael Anderson ***Prod*** Kurt Unger ***Scr*** John Briley ***Ph*** Billy Williams ***Ed*** Bill Lenny ***Mus*** Maurice Jarre ***Art*** Elliot Scott
Act Liv Ullmann, Trevor Howard, Lesley-Anne Down, Franco Nero, Olivia de Havilland, Maximilian Schell (Columbia/Big City)

Pope Joan deals with a female head of the Roman Catholic Church. Thanks to a screenplay that uses a modern-day story counterpart to suggest, apparently, that the theme is timely, this is too disjointed and rambling to make much sense.

The story is told as the ancient prototype of a modern female evangelist, torn between sex and salvation, whose religious fervor and bedroom capers more or less match those of her earlier counterpart. She's "adopted" in more ways than one by an artist-monk who eventually takes her to Greece as a male. They eventually wind up in Rome where her street preaching brings her to the attention of Leo XII, who takes her (him) on as a papal secretary, upped to cardinal and eventually his successor.

Liv Ullmann as Pope Joan carries the film with Maximilian Schell and Franco Nero trailing behind.

[Version reviewed is 132-minute one trade shown in New York. The 101-minute UK version omits all modern sequences.]

•

POPE MUST DIE, THE
(US: THE POPE MUST DIET)
1991, 97 mins, UK Ⓥ col
Dir Peter Richardson ***Prod*** Stephen Woolley ***Scr*** Peter Richardson, Pete Richens ***Ph*** Frank Gell ***Ed*** Katherine Wenning ***Mus*** Anne Dudley, Jeff Beck ***Art*** John Ebden
Act Robbie Coltrane, Beverly D'Angelo, Herbert Lom, Paul Bartel, Salvatore Cascio, Alex Rocco (Palace/British Screen)

Say no prayers for *The Pope Must Die*, a barbed comedy about an honest goofball who boots the mob out of the Vatican when he's mistakenly made top banana.

Scots comic Robbie Coltrane toplines as a priest who doubles as a car mechanic and rock musician in a rural Italian orphanage. When the pope kicks it in Rome, Father Dave Albinizi's name comes up thanks to a clerical error, and next thing he's riding around in the popemobile and dispensing blessings.

First to hit the cobblestones is the finance director (Alex Rocco), mob boss Herbert Lom's main inside man. But when Coltrane's ex-g.f. (Beverly D'Angelo) turns up and reveals they have a long-lost rock star son (Balthazar Getty), Rocco and his accomplice (Paul Bartel) inform the press.

Loosely based (like *The Godfather Part III*) on the Roberto Calvi banking scandal, yarn broadens out into a breezy satire of mob pictures and religious pics. Coltrane is solid (and physically right) as the ingenuous lead, but pace slackens when he's left to make the running. Rest of the cast play it in the fast lane.

Pic lensed in Yugoslavia under the dummy title *Sleeping with the Fishes*. End roller includes the blithe note: "Filmed entirely on location in Europe, not far from the Vatican."

•

POPE MUST DIET, THE
SEE: THE POPE MUST DIE

•

POPE OF GREENWICH VILLAGE, THE
1984, 120 mins, US Ⓥ ⊙ col
Dir Stuart Rosenberg ***Prod*** Gene Kirkwood ***Scr*** Vincent Patrick ***Ph*** John Bailey ***Ed*** Robert Brown ***Mus*** Dave Grusin ***Art*** Paul Sylbert
Act Eric Roberts, Mickey Rourke, Daryl Hannah, Geraldine Page, Kenneth McMillan, Tony Musante (United Artists)

The Pope of Greenwich Village, set in Manhattan's Italian community, is a near-miss in its transition from novel [by Vincent Patrick] to film, setting forth an offbeat slice-of-life tale of small-time guys involved in big trouble.

Key protagonists are two young buddies (distantly related), Charlie (Mickey Rourke), a supervisor in a restaurant where Paulie (Eric Roberts) works as a waiter. Both are heavily in debt and headed nowhere, with the usual pipe dreams of escape.

Fired from their jobs at film's outset due to a misdeed by Paulie, the two of them seek a way out via a crime caper initiated by Paulie, involving an older man, Barney (Kenneth McMillan), as safecracker.

1984: NOMINATIONS: Best Supp. Actress (Geraldine Page)

•

POPEYE
1980, 114 mins, US Ⓥ ⊙ col
Dir Robert Altman ***Prod*** Robert Evans ***Scr*** Jules Feiffer ***Ph*** Giuseppe Rotunno ***Ed*** Tony Lombardo ***Mus*** Harry Nilsson ***Art*** Wolf Kroeger
Act Robin Williams, Shelley Duvall, Ray Walston, Paul L. Smith, Paul Dooley, Linda Hunt (Paramount/Walt Disney)

It is more than faint praise to say that *Popeye* is far, far better than it might have been, considering the treacherous challenge it presented. But avoiding disaster is not necessarily the same as success.

To the eye, Robin Williams is terrifically transposed into the squinting sailor with the bulging arms. But to the ear, his mutterings are not always comprehensible.

Popeye comes to the quaint village of Sweethaven in search of a father who abandoned him and this is his underlying motivation as he first meets Olive Oyl and acquires his own abandoned baby, Swee'pea.

That's just too much for a cartoon to carry, even with some generally good songs and a wacky, colorfully created town. Shelley Duvall makes a delightful Olive Oyl and Paul L. Smith a perfectly jealous Bluto.

•

POPI
1969, 115 mins, US Ⓥ col
Dir Arthur Hiller ***Prod*** David B. Leonard ***Scr*** Tina Pine, Lester Pine ***Ph*** Andrew Laszlo ***Ed*** Anthony Ciccolini ***Mus*** Dominic Frontiere ***Art*** Robert Gundlach
Act Alan Arkin, Rita Moreno, Miguel Alejandro, Ruben Figueroa, John Harkins (United Artists)

Alan Arkin is cast as a Puerto Rican father, living in Spanish Harlem, whose fantastic plan to improve the lot of his two small sons backfires. Arkin is given too much free rein for his very personal style, and is sometimes guilty of working a scene, meant to be poignant or even dramatic, for a laugh, which he usually gets. The undecided mood of the film works against it for any lasting impression on the viewer. The character played by Arkin is the little man vs. the big odds and he does what he can with it but the story is too much for him.

Script is riddled with illogical loopholes, some of which, hopefully, will only be apparent to those familiar with the Spanish Harlem scene. Moreno is dropped midway through the film, but makes a good impression while she's on scene. If any viewer believes that Arkin would turn down such a doll, they'll believe the rest of the story.

•

POPIOL I DIAMENT
(ASHES AND DIAMONDS)
1958, 106 mins, POLAND Ⓥ b/w
Dir Andrzej Wajda ***Scr*** Jerzy Andrzejewski, Andrzej Wajda ***Ph*** Jerzy Wojcik ***Ed*** Halina Nawrocka ***Mus*** Jan Krenz ***Art*** Roman Mann
Act Zbigniew Cybulski, Ewa Krzyzewska, Adam Pawlikowski, Waclaw Zastrzezynski, Bogumil Kobiela, Jan Ciecierski (Kadr)

Taut thriller [from the novel by Jerzy Andrzejewski] about immediate postwar Poland also has a heavier theme of the futility of killing and violence. Its technical know-how, fine acting and directorial prowess make this an above-average drama.

It concerns two men told to kill a top Communist on the last day of the war. They represent the pre-war Polski ruling forces. Film details the eventual murder and the ironic death of the murderer.

Director Andrzej Wajda is masterly in composing atmosphere and gets fine performances, especially from Zbigniew Cybulski as the erratic young killer. But it is somewhat overdone in expressionistic bravura.

However, sharp direction, theme and insight into a changing Poland of the period lend it additional hypo factors.

•

POPPY
1936, 75 mins, US b/w
Dir A. Edward Sutherland ***Prod*** William LeBaron ***Scr*** Waldemar Young, Virginia Van Upp ***Ph*** William Mellor ***Ed*** Stuart Heisler ***Mus*** Gerard Carbonera ***Art*** Hans Dreier, Bernard Herzbrun

Act W. C. Fields, Rochelle Hudson, Richard Cromwell, Lynne Overman, Catherine Doucet (Paramount)

There's one thing that W. C. Fields will never be, and that's unfunny. He could get laughs with Hamlet's soliloquy, which is just about what he does in *Poppy* [from a play by Dorothy Donnelly]. Amidst the 19th-century melodramatics and the considerable sob stuff that goes with it, Fields manages to shake off the ill effects and get his laughs.

The role of Prof. Eustace McGargle, carnival guy, three-shell operator, medicine man and beloved rogue, is a setup for Fields. The juvenile romance, calling for mostly starry-eyed mutual admiration close-ups by Richard Cromwell and Rochelle Hudson, is just a series of interruptions between the Fields's comedy business. The section of the plot which provides the complications, via villainy, is more helpful, for it ushers in Catherine Doucet as a first-rate contrasting foil for Fields in some of his best moments.

•

PORGY AND BESS

1959, 136 mins, US col

Dir Otto Preminger ***Prod*** Samuel Goldwyn ***Scr*** N. Richard Nash ***Ph*** Leon Shamroy ***Ed*** Daniel Mandell ***Mus*** Andre Previn (dir.) ***Art*** Oliver Smith

Act Sidney Poitier, Dorothy Dandridge, Sammy Davis, Jr., Pearl Bailey, Brock Peters, Diahann Carroll (Columbia)

As screen entertainment, *Porgy and Bess* retains most of the virtues and some of the libretto traits of the folk opera.

A novel [by DuBose and Dorothy Heyward] first in 1925, it became a play in 1927, running 217 performances for the Theatre Guild. The opera version of 1935, also for the Guild, eked out only 124 performances. It was not until the revival, after composer George Gershwin's death, that *Porgy and Bess* came into its own. The melodrama of a 1905 Charleston waterfront slum, which might otherwise have been forgotten, was elevated into a world favorite.

Sidney Poitier makes him thoroughly believable, though when he opens his voice to sing it is Robert McPherrin. Bess, the incompletely regenerate floozie, is Dorothy Dandridge, but the voice is Adele Addison. (Neither voice gets screen credit.)

The love affair of this oddly-assorted pair has considerable humanity though Dandridge is perhaps too "refined" to be quite convincing as the split-skirt, heroin-sniffing tramp.

Otto Preminger manipulates the characters in the Catfish Row to develop as much tension and pathos as the screenplay (fairly close to the original text) allows.

Many of the old slum life details of the stage production have been faded down. The racial stereotype dangers have been sterilized. The handling of the music by conductor Andre Previn, including a three-minute overture before the story opens, is professional. Some liberties with the arrangements, in the de-operatizing direction, may irritate loyal followers of Gershwin who notice such matters.

1959: Best Scoring of a Musical

NOMINATIONS: Best Color Cinematography, Color Costume Design, Sound

•

PORK CHOP HILL

1959, 97 mins, US b/w

Dir Lewis Milestone ***Prod*** Sy Bartlett ***Scr*** James R. Webb ***Ph*** Sam Leavitt ***Ed*** George Boemler ***Mus*** Leonard Rosenman ***Art*** Nicolai Remisoff

Act Gregory Peck, Harry Guardino, Rip Torn, George Peppard, George Shibata, Woody Strode (United Artists/Melville)

Pork Chop Hill is a grim, utterly realistic story that drives home both the irony of war and the courage men can summon to die in a cause which they don't understand and for an objective which they know to be totally irrelevant.

King Company, commanded by Gregory Peck as Lt. Joe Clemons, is ordered to take Pork Chop Hill from the Chinese Reds and to hold it against attack. The time is the Korean War, and the irony of the situation is that (1) armistice negotiations at Panmunjon are virtually concluded, and (2) Pork Chop has absolutely no tactical importance. It must be taken simply because its loss means a loss of face on the part of the Americans in the eyes of the Communist negotiators.

Peck's performance as the company commander is completely believable. He comes through as a born leader, and yet it is quite clear that he has his moments of doubt and of uncertainty.

The accent on the combat is such that, besides Peck, the other men barely emerge as people. They look real, they sound real, but there's no chance to get to know them, though the picture makes it very clear that they all know that their objective is secondary at best.

•

PORKY'S

1981, 94 mins, Canada col

Dir Bob Clark ***Prod*** Don Carmody, Bob Clark ***Scr*** Bob Clark ***Ph*** Reginald H. Morris ***Ed*** Stan Cole ***Mus*** Carl Zittrer, Paul Zaza ***Art*** Reuben Freed

Act Dan Monahan, Mark Herrier, Wyatt Knight, Kim Cattrall, Alex Karras, Susan Clark (Simon/Astral Bellevue Pathe)

If, by chance, *Porky's* should prove to be Melvin Simon's swan song in the film industry, it will either be perceived as a thunderously rude exit or a titanic raspberry uttered to audiences everywhere.

Virtually every scene and dialog exchange constitutes a new definition of lewdness. Locker room humor reaches new heights (depths) here. Film cannot be faulted for lack of a driving force—simply, all these young Florida boys are itching to score and most of their time is spent in pursuit of said goal.

Title refers to a redneck establishment out in the Everglades known for its available women. After being embarrassingly turned away on their first visit, the boys return to wreak havoc on the joint, proving once and for all that violence will result when the sex drive is repressed.

•

PORKY'S II THE NEXT DAY

1983, 95 mins, US col

Dir Bob Clark ***Prod*** Don Carmody, Bob Clark ***Scr*** Roger E. Swaybill, Alan Ormsby, Bob Clark ***Ph*** Reginald H. Morris ***Ed*** Stan Cole ***Mus*** Carl Zittrer ***Art*** Fred Price

Act Dan Monahan, Wyatt Knight, Mark Herrier, Roger Wilson, Cyril O'Reilly, Tony Ganios (Simon-Reeves-Landsburg/Astral Bellevue/Pathe)

Plot follows in the grand tradition of many early rock 'n' roll quickies, in which self-righteous upholders of comic morality attempted to stomp out the threat posed by the new primitive music. Replacing Chuck Mitchell's Porky as the heavy here is Bill Wiley's bigoted Rev. Bubba Flavel, who makes a crusade out of shutting down the school's Shakespeare festival due to the lewdness he finds strewn throughout the Bard's work.

Enlisted in his cause is the ample girls' gym teacher Miss Balbricker and the local contingent of the Ku Klux Klan, who are each the victims of two of the film's three "big scenes." Everyone who saw it remembers "that scene" from the original. Here, some of the boys get back at Balbricker by sending a snake up into her toilet.

Director Bob Clark has not allowed success to lead him astray into the dreaded realm of good taste.

•

PORTE DES LILAS

1957, 95 mins, France/Italy b/w

Dir Rene Clair ***Scr*** Rene Clair, Jean Aurel ***Ph*** Robert Le Febvre ***Ed*** Louisette Hautecoeur, Arlette Lalande ***Mus*** Georges Brassens ***Art*** Leon Barsacq

Act Pierre Brasseur, Georges Brassens, Henri Vidal, Dany Carrel, Raymond Bussieres, Amedee (Filmsonor/Cinetel/Seca/Rizzoli

Rene Clair returns to the lower-class suburbs and milieu used for his best prewar pix. However, he has come up with a light tale which wavers between comedy and drama, making a slight, fragile pic.

A genial neighborhood good-for-nothing drunkard (Pierre Brasseur), living off his hard-working mother, and his friend, an itinerant singing troubadour (Georges Brassens) get saddled with a gangster (Henri Vidal) who has just killed three people. The killer stays on until he is discovered by a clever young girl (Dany Carrel). The gangster woos and wins her and tries to get her to steal money from her father.

The film's mixture of styles rarely allows for the achieving the balance of irony and comedy. Its story loopholes are not quite covered by the treatment.

Brasseur gives an astute portrait of the drifter. Brassens, a noted ballader, is too unsure of his lines to do much as the troubadour. However, he is okay when he sings. Carrel is a pert flirt but Vidal does not infuse the gangster with enough redeeming qualities.

•

PORTNOY'S COMPLAINT

1972, 101 mins, US col

Dir Ernest Lehman ***Prod*** Ernest Lehman, Sidney Beckerman ***Scr*** Ernest Lehman ***Ph*** Philip Lathrop ***Ed*** Sam O'Steen, Gordon Scott ***Mus*** Michel Legrand ***Art*** Robert F. Boyle

Act Richard Benjamin, Karen Black, Lee Grant, Jack Somack, Jeannie Berlin, Jill Clayburgh (Warner/Chenault)

The film version of *Portnoy's Complaint* is *not* trashy, tawdry, cheap, offensively vulgar, and pruriently titillating. Instead, it is a most effective, honest in context, necessarily strong and appropriately bawdy study in ruinous self-indulgence.

Besides adapting the Philip Roth novel into a lucid, balanced and moral screenplay, and producing handsomely on various locations, Ernest Lehman makes an excellent directorial debut. Richard Benjamin heads an outstanding cast.

Alexander Portnoy's hang-up derives from heterosexual masturbation fantasies, and the first 44 minutes constitute the slap-happy, kinky exposition of his development. But what the story then pulls an audience into is the inevitable consequence.

•

PORTRAIT OF JENNIE

1948, 86 mins, US b/w & col

Dir William Dieterle ***Prod*** David O. Selznick ***Scr*** Paul Osborn, Peter Berneis ***Ph*** Joseph August ***Ed*** [William Morgan, Gerald Wilson] ***Mus*** Dimitri Tiomkin ***Art*** J. McMillan Johnson, Joseph B. Platt

Act Joseph Cotten, Jennifer Jones, Ethel Barrymore, David Wayne, Lillian Gish, Cecil Kellaway (RKO/Selznick)

Portrait of Jennie is an unusual screen romance. The story of an ethereal romance between two generations is told with style, taste and dignity.

William Dieterle has given the story sensitive direction and his guidance contributes considerably toward the top performances from the meticulously cast players.

The script, by Paul Osborn and Peter Berneis, taken from Robert Nathan's novel, deals simply with an artist living in New York in the 1930s. His work lacks depth and it is only when he meets a strange child in the park one day that inspiration to paint people comes. The elfish quality of the child stimulates a sketch. It is appreciated by art dealers and he builds the child's physical being in his mind until the next time she appears he sees her as a girl just entering her teens. Her growth moves into college years and then as a graduate while he, meantime, is discovering she is a person who has been dead for years.

Jennifer Jones's performance is standout. Her miming ability gives a quality to the four ages she portrays—from a small girl through the flowering woman. Ingenuity in makeup also figures importantly in sharpening the portrayal. Joseph Cotten endows the artist with a top performance, matching the compelling portrayal by Jones.

[Original release prints featured a Technicolor sequence in the final reel.]

1948: Best Special Effects

NOMINATION: Best B&W Cinematography

•

PORTRAIT OF A LADY, THE

1996, 144 mins, US/UK col

Dir Jane Campion ***Prod*** Monty Montgomery, Steve Golin ***Scr*** Laura Jones ***Ph*** Stuart Dryburgh ***Ed*** Veronika Jenet ***Mus*** Wojciech Kilar ***Art*** Janet Patterson

Act Nicole Kidman, John Malkovich, Barbara Hershey, Mary-Louise Parker, Martin Donovan, Shelley Winters (Propaganda/PolyGram)

Jane Campion's *The Portrait of a Lady*, her much anticipated follow-up to *The Piano*, emerges as a literary adaptation of exceeding intelligence, beauty and concentrated artistry, but one that remains emotionally remote and perhaps unavoidably problematic dramatically. This highbrow melodrama [from Henry James's novel] about the misfortunes of a young American woman of privilege in Europe in the 1870s appeals to the head far more than to the heart.

Initial section, during which the beautiful, 23-year-old heroine, Isabel Archer (Nicole Kidman), rejects the idea of marriage out of hand and acquires a vast fortune that allows her to live as she likes, establishes a clear connection with Campion's previous headstrong, independent leading ladies.

But when she places herself in a cage through marriage to a manipulative, spirit-sapping man (John Malkovich), her life, as well as the film, loses definition and clarity. Wrap-up comes off as far too fuzzy and inconclusive in light of the intellectual surety with which pic begins, leaving the viewer perplexed by the story's arc and ultimate point.

Campion presents the story in a dark, lush, mysterious manner, using a style that perhaps relies overly upon close-ups and occasionally indulges in the exoticism of the foreign for its own sake.

Kidman is everything one could ask for as Isabel—bright, alert, optimistic. Malkovich's quirks and hard-to-read behavior work well for the deceptive Osmond, while

Barbara Hershey is excellent in her early scenes as Madame Merle, meant to represent woman at her best.

1996: NOMINATIONS: Best Supp. Actress (Barbara Hershey), Costume Designer (Janet Patterson).

•

POSEIDON ADVENTURE, THE

1972, 117 mins, US Ⓥ ⦿ ⌑ col

Dir Ronald Neame ***Prod*** Irwin Allen ***Scr*** Stirling Silliphant, Wendell Mayes ***Ph*** Harold E. Stine ***Ed*** Harold F. Kress ***Mus*** John Williams ***Art*** William Creber

Act Gene Hackman, Ernest Borgnine, Red Buttons, Carol Lynley, Roddy McDowall, Stella Stevens (Kent/20th Century-Fox)

The Poseidon Adventure is a highly imaginative and lustily-produced meller that socks over the dramatic struggle of 10 passengers to save themselves after an ocean liner capsizes when struck by a mammoth tidal wave created by a submarine earthquake.

It is a case of everything being upside down; in this reversed world of twisted ruin the principals' goal is the vessel's bottom where to break through may be some hope of survival.

The adaptation of the Paul Gallico novel plays up the tragic situation with a set of values which permits powerful action and building tension. Chief protagonist is played by Gene Hackman, as a free-talking minister who keeps his cool and assumes leadership of the small group.

1972: Best Song ("The Morning After"), Honorary Award (special visual effects)

NOMINATIONS: Best Supp. Actress (Shelley Winters), Cinematography, Costume Design, Art Direction, Editing, Original Score, Sound

•

POSSE

1975, 92 mins, US Ⓥ ⦿ ⌑ col

Dir Kirk Douglas ***Prod*** Kirk Douglas ***Scr*** William Roberts, Christopher Knopf ***Ph*** Fred J. Koenekamp ***Ed*** John W. Wheeler ***Mus*** Maurice Jarre ***Art*** Lyle Wheeler

Act Kirk Douglas, Bruce Dern, Bo Hopkins, James Stacy, Luke Askew, David Canary (Paramount/Bryna)

Posse is a good western, with Kirk Douglas as a cynical U.S. marshal who eventually stumbles on his own political ambitions while tracking thief Bruce Dern under a strident law-and-order platform.

Story is a sort of convoluted *High Noon*, in which self-assured Douglas, complete with his own gang of deputies, manipulates a cowardly town which in the end turns its back on him. Dern, very effective as an escaped robber, ultimately capitalizes on Douglas's disloyalty to his men and escapes anew with a fully-trained crew which easily adapts to lawlessness.

Bo Hopkins, Luke Askew, Bill Burton, Louie Elias and Gus Greymountain are good as Douglas's assistants whom he plans to dump after becoming a U.S. Senator from Texas.

•

POSSE

1993, 109 mins, US/UK Ⓥ ⦿ ⌑ col

Dir Mario Van Peebles ***Prod*** Preston Holmes, Jim Steele ***Scr*** Sy Richardson, Dario Scardapane ***Ph*** Peter Menzies, Jr. ***Ed*** Mark Conte ***Mus*** Michel Colombier ***Art*** Catherine Hardwicke

Act Mario Van Peebles, Stephen Baldwin, Charles Lane, Tiny Lister, Jr., Big Daddy Kane, Billy Zane (PolyGram/Working Title)

Begin with a reliable pursuit-and-revenge plotline, lay on a Sergio Leone look and flashback structure, stir in some John Ford community values and Sam Peckinpah violence, tag *The Magnificent Seven* on at the end and paint it black, and you've got *Posse*.

Engaged in the Spanish-American War in Cuba in 1898, a ragtag band including strong silent type Mario Van Peebles, bespectacled Charles Lane, giant Tiny Lister, Jr., cigar-chomping Tone Loc and irreverent white boy Stephen Baldwin, is betrayed by vicious, swashbuckling commanding officer Billy Zane, and flees the regiment with a large stash of gold. They also pick up a laconic riverboat gambler, Father Time (Big Daddy Kane).

The band finally arrives at Freemansville, a utopian black township. But venal nearby sheriff Richard Jordan and his Ku Klux Klan goons suddenly covet Freemansville, since it lies along a future railway route.

Eventful script packs in enough confrontations, fights and shootouts for several films, which will keep action fans happy. But neither the writers nor Van Peebles, in his second directorial outing, modulate the drama to maximize its impact.

•

POSSESSED

1947, 108 mins, US Ⓥ ⦿ b/w

Dir Curtis Bernhardt ***Prod*** Jerry Wald ***Scr*** Silvia Richards, Ranald MacDougall ***Ph*** Joseph Valentine ***Ed*** Rudi Fehr ***Mus*** Franz Waxman ***Art*** Anton Grot

Act Joan Crawford, Van Heflin, Raymond Massey, Geraldine Brooks, Stanley Ridges (Warner)

Joan Crawford cops all thesping honors in this production with a virtuoso performance as a frustrated woman ridden into madness by a guilt-obsessed mind. Actress has a self-assurance that permits her to completely dominate the screen even vis-à-vis such accomplished players as Van Heflin and Raymond Massey.

Heflin's part of a footloose engineer who romances his ladies with one eye on the railroad schedule is now drawn with equal sharpness. By sheer power of personal wit, however, Heflin infuses his role with charm and degree of credibility despite a lack of clear motivation for his behavior.

Unfolding via flashback technique, film opens with a terrific bang as the camera picks up Crawford wandering haggard and dazed through Los Angeles until she collapses. In the psychiatric ward of the local hospital, under narco-hypnosis, she relives the series of personal blows that ultimately reduced her to schizophrenia.

Despite its overall superiority, *Possessed* is somewhat marred by an ambiguous approach in Curtis Bernhardt's direction. Film vacillates between being a cold clinical analysis of a mental crackup and a highly surcharged melodramatic vehicle for Crawford's histrionics.

1947: NOMINATION: Best Actress (Joan Crawford)

•

POSSESSION

1981, 127 mins, France/W. Germany Ⓥ col

Dir Andrzej Zulawski ***Prod*** Marie-Laure Reyre ***Scr*** Andrzej Zulawski, Frederic Tuten ***Ph*** Bruno Nuytten ***Ed*** Marie-Sophie Dubus ***Mus*** Andrzej Korzynski ***Art*** Holger Gross

Act Isabelle Adjani, Sam Neill, Heinz Bennent, Margit Carstensen, Michael Hogben (Oliane/Marianne/Soma)

Possession starts on a hysterical note, stays there and surpasses it as the film progresses. There are excesses on all fronts: In supposedly ordinary married life and then occult happenings, intricate political skulduggery with the infamous Berlin Wall as background—they all abound in this horror-cum-political-cum-psychological tale.

Sam Neill, New Zealand actor, returns home after a long absence. He has been on some sort of secret mission. After an ambiguous report to a commission he goes home to find his wife (Isabelle Adjani) acting strangely.

Neill hires a detective who tracks Adjani to an old house and a strange apartment. The detective gains entry and sees some sort of monster [special effects by Carlo Rambaldi] before Adjani slashes his throat with a broken bottle. Another sleuth gets the same treatment, and a bizarre mass of entrails encompass the men after they are killed. Adjani is game as she plays the deranged, obsessed woman in high gear throughout. Pic's mass of symbols and unbridled, brilliant directing meld this disparate tale into a film that could get cult following on its many levels of symbolism and exploitation.

•

POSSESSION OF JOEL DELANEY, THE

1972, 105 mins, UK Ⓥ col

Dir Waris Hussein ***Scr*** Matt Robinson, Grimes Grice ***Ph*** Arthur Ornitz ***Ed*** John Victor Smith ***Mus*** Joe Raposo ***Art*** Peter Murton

Act Shirley MacLaine, Michael Hordern, Edmundo Rivera Alvarez, Robert Burr, Miriam Colon, David Elliott (ITC)

The Possession of Joel Delaney is an unusual occult thriller [based on Ramona Stewart's novel]. Pic centers on a chic East Side society divorcee (Shirley MacLaine) who harbors an inordinate affection for her brother, Joel (Perry King), and attempts to save him when he is possessed by the spirit of a Puerto Rican friend fond of ritual beheadings.

Script eschews any serious attempt to explain the subject matter in conventional psychiatric terms, coming down on the side of ethnically originated spiritualism. You believe it or you don't, ditto the rather murky sociological overtones that seem needlessly overemphasized. Script overextends the build-up, making the final quarter a bit anticlimactic and slowing the pace, but the presence of MacLaine smooths over the rough spots.

•

POSTCARDS FROM THE EDGE

1990, 101 mins, US Ⓥ ⦿ col

Dir Mike Nichols ***Prod*** Mike Nichols, John Calley ***Scr*** Carrie Fisher ***Ph*** Michael Ballhaus ***Ed*** Sam O'Steen ***Mus*** Howard Shore (sup.), Carly Simon ***Art*** Patrizia Von Brandenstein

Act Meryl Streep, Shirley MacLaine, Dennis Quaid, Gene Hackman, Richard Dreyfuss, Rob Reiner (Columbia)

Mike Nichols's film of Carrie Fisher's novel *Postcards from the Edge* packs a fair amount of emotional wallop in its dark-hued comic take on a chemically dependent Hollywood mother and daughter (Shirley MacLaine and Meryl Streep).

Streep's tour through Hollywood hell is signposted with many recognizable, on-target types: predatory macho creep (Dennis Quaid), sleazy business manager (Gary Morton), oafish producer (Rob Reiner), airheaded and round-heeled actress (Annette Bening) and sternly paternalistic director (Gene Hackman).

Refreshingly guileless in a role requiring casual clothing and no accent, Streep plays an overgrown child who's spent her life in her mother's shadow and has resorted to drugs to blunt her pain and boredom.

While casting of MacLaine in the role of an arch, ditzy, impossible stage mother is somewhat predictable, the actress gradually makes it her own until, stripped of her glamour in the climactic scene, she abandons the rampant egotism of the character to reveal the frightened creature underneath.

(Nichols insists, for the record, that the character isn't based on Fisher's mom, Debbie Reynolds, even though MacLaine's wickedly salacious memories of life at Louis B. Mayer's M-G-M might suggest otherwise.)

1990: NOMINATIONS: Best Actress (Meryl Streep), Song ("I'm Checkin' Out")

•

POSTINO, IL
(THE POSTMAN)

1994, 116 mins, Italy/France/Belgium Ⓥ ⦿ col

Dir Michael Radford ***Prod*** Mario Cecchi Gori, Vittorio Cecchi Gori, Gaetano Daniele ***Scr*** Anna Pavignano, Michael Radford, Furio Scarpelli, Giacomo Scarpelli, Massimo Troisi ***Ph*** Franco Di Giacomo ***Ed*** Roberto Perpignani ***Mus*** Luis Enrique Bacalov ***Art*** Lorenzo Baraldi

Act Massimo Troisi, Philippe Noiret, Maria Grazia Cucinotta, Linda Moretti, Renato Scarpa, Anna Buonaiuto (Penta/Esterno Mediterraneo/Blue Dahlia/K2T)

Late Italo actor Massimo Troisi bows out with an affecting performance in *The Postman*, a sad-sweet tale of a simple Mediterranean islander whose life is forever changed by his friendship with an exiled Chilean poet. The popular Neapolitan comic died in his sleep June 4, 1994, at age 41, a day after shooting wrapped at Cinecitta Studios.

Chilean writer Antonio Skarmeta's original novel, *Burning Patience*, inspired by his own exile in Berlin during the '80s, was set off the coast of Chile. Present version transfers the action to an unnamed Italian island during the early '50s, and makes several other major changes.

Troisi plays Mario, who dreams of wider horizons but lacks the intellectual ticket to reach them. When Communist Chilean poet Pablo Neruda (Philippe Noiret) arrives on the island after being granted sanctuary, Mario is hired as his personal postman. When Mario falls for sexy local barmaid Beatrice (Maria Grazia Cucinotta), Neruda becomes his councelor/father-confessor, smoothing the way past the girl's overprotective aunt (Linda Moretti) and trying to teach him to pen love poetry.

The first feature by British director Michael Radford since *White Mischief* in 1987, pic is essentially a two-hander between Troisi and Noiret, spending much of its length flip-flopping between chats at Neruda's cottage and Mario's musings back in the village. It's Troisi's show but, with little assistance from Radford's by-the-numbers direction, and a script that starts to become very diffused about halfway through, the bottom line is that it's a performance in a vacuum. Luis Enrique Bacalov's warm, tuneful score is a big help in giving the pic some emotional shape.

[Out of respect for the late actor, within Italy direction was credited to "Michael Radford, in collaboration with Massimo Troisi."]

1995: NOMINATIONS: Best Film, Director, Actor (Massimo Troisi), Screenplay Adaptation, Original Dramatic Score

•

POSTMAN, THE

SEE: IL POSTINO)

•

POSTMAN, THE
1997, 177 mins, US Ⓥ ⊙ ▭ col
Dir Kevin Costner *Prod* Jim Wilson, Steve Tisch, Kevin Costner *Scr* Eric Roth, Brian Helgeland *Ph* Stephen Windon *Ed* Peter Boyle *Mus* James Newton Howard *Art* Ida Random
Act Kevin Costner, Will Patton, Larenz Tate, Olivia Williams, James Russo, Daniel von Bargen (Tig/Warner)

A passionately expressed vision of what the United States was, and is meant to be, *The Postman* is a rare epic film that is actually about something. Film may be branded as reactionary by left-wingers but is a curiously antirugged-individualist statement that stresses the overriding importance of community.

Set in 2013 in the wake of a devastating war in which most of the U.S., including the government, is wiped out, this adaptation of David Brin's 1985 sci-fi novel quickly comes to feel more like a Western than anything else.

Costner's solitary wayfarer wanders the wasteland that is America and comes across a small community before being captured by a marauding band known as the Holnists, led by the strutting Gen. Bethlehem (Will Patton), a self-styled dictator who presides over an army and forced labor camp.

Making a daring escape, Costner's drifter comes across an abandoned old mail Jeep, puts on the uniform he finds there and, at a small town called Pineview, announces he is to deliver 15-year-old mail in his role as representative of the restored United States. The Postman wins over the skittish citizens simply because they need to believe in something. [Much later] he is forced into the role of a reluctant leader, a hero whose credentials are false but who represents the rebirth of the nation's democratic principles.

Pic has an undeniable streak of vanity but, despite the missteps, is played with general conviction. As a beautiful girl the Postman is asked to impregnate by her impotent husband, British newcomer Olivia Williams is a real find.

•

POSTMAN ALWAYS RINGS TWICE, THE
1946, 110 mins, US Ⓥ ⊙ b/w
Dir Tay Garnett *Prod* Carey Wilson *Scr* Harry Ruskin, Niven Busch *Ph* Sidney Wagner *Ed* George White *Mus* George Bassman *Art* Cedric Gibbons, Randall Duell
Act Lana Turner, John Garfield, Cecil Kellaway, Hume Cronyn, Audrey Totter, Leon Ames (M-G-M)

The Postman Always Rings Twice is a controversial picture. The approach to lust and murder is as adult and matter-of-fact as that used by James M. Cain in his book from which the film was adapted.

It was box-office wisdom to cast Lana Turner as the sexy, blonde murderess, and John Garfield as the foot-loose vagabond whose lust for the girl made him stop at nothing. Each give to the assignments the best of their talents. Development of the characters makes Tay Garnett's direction seem slowly paced during first part of the picture, but this establishment was necessary to give the speed and punch to the uncompromising evil that transpires.

As in Cain's book, there will be little audience sympathy for the characters, although plotting will arouse moments of pity for the little people too weak to fight against passion and the evil circumstances it brings. The script is a rather faithful translation of Cain's story of a boy and girl who murder the girl's husband, live through terror and eventually make payment for their crime. The writing is terse and natural to the characters and events that transpire.

Cecil Kellaway, the husband, is a bit flamboyant at times in interpreting the character. Hume Cronyn is particularly effective as the attorney who defends the couple for murder.

•

POSTMAN ALWAYS RINGS TWICE, THE
1981, 123 mins, US Ⓥ ⊙ col
Dir Bob Rafelson *Prod* Charles Mulvehill, Bob Rafelson *Scr* David Mamet *Ph* Sven Nykvist *Ed* Graeme Clifford *Mus* Michael Small *Art* George Jenkins
Act Jack Nicholson, Jessica Lange, John Colicos, Anjelica Huston, Christopher Lloyd, John P. Ryan (Northstar/Lorimar)

James M. Cain's 1934 novel attracted notoriety for its adulterous murder story, spiced with some fairly daring sequences for its day. Because of the Hays Office, Hollywood couldn't touch the property until 1946, when M-G-M released a sanitized version with Lana Turner and John Garfield—and even that was greeted by some shock. For this remake, Bob Rafelson said he would shoot as an X but cut to an R.

But the final cut is limited to some fairly heavy groping, explicit shots of Jack Nicholson massaging the front of Jessica Lange's panties and a view of his head between her legs, suggesting more than is ever witnessed.

Stripped of its excess, Cain's yarn is essentially a morality tale of a Depression drifter who comes to work for a beautiful young woman and her older Greek husband. Falling madly in lust, they murder the old man, escape justice and then get their desserts in an ironical twist at the end.

In the key roles, Nicholson and Lange are excellent, as is Michael Lerner as their defense attorney.

In Cain's novel, once the couple escape punishment in court, she dies in an auto accident and he is wrongly executed for her murder, thus providing the justice. Rafelson throws this away for an ending that's not so neat.

•

POSTO, IL
(THE JOB; THE SOUND OF TRUMPETS)
1961, 105 mins, Italy b/w
Dir Ermanno Olmi *Prod* Alberto Soffientini *Scr* Ermanno Olmi *Ph* Lamberto Caimi *Ed* Carla Colombo *Mus* Pier Emilio Bassi *Art* Ettore Lombardi
Act Sandro Panzeri, Loredana Detto, Tullio Kezich, Mara Revel, Bice Melegari, Corrado Aprile (The 24 Horses)

This is a little jewel of a picture made (for $55,000) as his first feature effort by Ermanno Olmi. Players are all non-pros but they and other facets of pic form a winning combo.

A youngster has just finished school and leaves his town for the big city to seek a job. After an exam, at which he meets a young girl to whom he takes a teenage fancy, they are both admitted. He serves a period of apprenticeship, then finally is seated at a desk of his own.

Plot is deceptively simple, but every frame of pic is rich with shadings and nuances. Olmi's keenly observant camera is of major assistance, as are his actors. His two leads, Alessandro Panseri and Loredana Detto, are almost incredibly good in their muted, underplayed roles, while all others in pic are equally well chosen and directed.

Pic filled with humorous passages and tongue-in-cheek observations of the daily scene. (There's a particularly funny sequence spoofing mental and physical tests by applicants.) Pic has no musical backdrop. Camerawork is standout, whether in hidden-camera street shots or in close-ups at home or office.

•

POT CARRIERS, THE
1962, 84 mins, UK b/w
Dir Peter Graham Scott *Prod* Gordon L. T. Scott *Scr* T. J. Morrison, Mike Watts *Ph* Erwin Hillier *Ed* Richard Best *Mus* Stanley Black *Art* Robert Jones
Act Ronald Fraser, Paul Massie, Carol Lesley, Dennis Price, Davy Kaye, Alfred Burke (Associated British)

This lively slice of life in jail is a moderately unpretentious job but it shrewdly captures the atmosphere of the locale, neatly blends comedy and drama and offers some sharp thesping. Screenplay has been adapted by T. J. Morrison and Mike Watts from the latter's play. Pic title is used to spotlight one of the supreme indignities of prison.

Paul Massie plays a first offender sentenced to a year's jail for grievous bodily harm, after slugging another man in a jealous tiff with his girlfriend. Assigned to the Kitchen Gang, he quickly settles down to the routine and joins in the "fiddling" which is highly organized among the prisoners, which mainly consists of stealing chow from the kitchens and swapping it for luxuries which another member of the gang lifts from the officers' mess.

In a large, mainly male cast, there are some notable bits of thesping, biggest impact being made by Ronald Fraser as the "trusty" who is the kingpin among the fiddlers. Paul Massie is a likeable, straightforward hero.

•

POTEMKIN, THE
SEE: BRONENOSETS 'POTYOMKIN'

•

POTE TIN KYRIAKI
(NEVER ON SUNDAY)
1960, 97 mins, Greece Ⓥ ⊙ b/w
Dir Jules Dassin *Prod* Jules Dassin *Scr* Jules Dassin *Ph* Jacques Natteau *Ed* Roger Dwyre *Mus* Manos Hadjidakis
Act Melina Mercouri, Jules Dassin, Georges Foundas, Titos Vandis, Mitsos Liguisos, Despo Diamantidou (Melina/Lopert)

United Artists has a catchy comedy in this philosophical romp about an intellectual but prudish American who tries to reform a jolly Greek prostitute. It has some fine scenery and enough entertainment, plus a colorful offbeat locale.

Pic serves to establish Greek actress Melina Mercouri who has a temperament that comes over well. It is a brilliant execution of a larger-than-life character which is the anchor and very reason for the pic.

Yank director Jules Dassin also wrote and plays the feckless American who almost ruins the life of this contented woman, and the simple people around her. Dassin is better with his behind-the-camera work because he does not quite instill the right note of naivete into his role. But he is adequate, with the Greek actors all natural and effective in other parts.

The racy, jangling music score, with local instruments, the bouzoukis, is also an asset. Film is mainly in English with some Greek talk bits.

•

POWER, THE
1968, 108 mins, US ⊙ ▭ col
Dir Byron Haskin *Prod* George Pal *Scr* John Gay *Ph* Ellsworth Fredricks *Ed* Thomas J. McCarthy *Mus* Miklos Rozsa *Art* George W. Davis, Merrill Pye
Act George Hamilton, Suzanne Pleshette, Richard Carlson, Yvonne De Carlo, Earl Holliman, Arthur O'Connell (M-G-M)

Somewhere along the way something misfired. What started out as an ingenious, imaginative sci-fi premise developed into a confusing maze of cloudy characters, motivations and events in its development.

George Pal's production carries plenty of suspense as audience hopefully awaits a logical conclusion, but in final wrap-up the spectator is left wondering what it's all about.

Screenplay, based on the Frank M. Robinson novel, is set among a group of scientists engaged in human endurance research. It is discovered that one among them has a super-intelligence, possibly a mind of the next evolution, so strong it controls the others' minds. As murder starts, George Hamilton, one of the scientists, undertakes to learn the identity of The Power, while himself a suspect by the police.

Byron Haskin's direction is limited by script but he manages tension as yarn builds to its finale. Hamilton is okay in his role and Suzanne Pleshette, in part of his geneticist girlfriend, is easy on the eye. Balance of cast are as good as roles will allow.

•

POWER
1986, 111 mins, US Ⓥ ⊙ col
Dir Sidney Lumet *Prod* Reene Schisgal, Mark Tarlov *Scr* David Himmelstein *Ph* Andrzej Bartkowiak *Ed* Andrew Mondshein *Mus* Cy Coleman *Art* Peter Larkin
Act Richard Gere, Julie Christie, Gene Hackman, Kate Capshaw, Denzel Washington, E. G. Marshall (Lorimar/Polar)

Not so much about power as about p.r., this facile treatment of big-time politics and media, featuring Richard Gere as an amoral imagemaker, revolves around the unstartling premise that modern politicians and their campaigns are calculatedly packaged for TV. In spite of relentless jet-propelled location hopping that helps to stave off boredom, *Power* never gets airborne.

Pete St. John (Gere) is a peripatetic public relations wiz whose services practically guarantee political success. His ex-wife (Julie Christie) and alcoholic former mentor Wilfred Buckley (Gene Hackman) both remember Pete when the kid had ideals. He's dumped them both but they still care for him. All that remains to be seen is if Pete will find some sort of redemption.

•

POWER AND THE GLORY, THE
1933, 73 mins, US b/w
Dir William K. Howard *Prod* Jesse L. Lasky *Scr* Preston Sturges *Ph* James Wong Howe *Mus* Louis De Francesco (dir.) *Art* Max Parker
Act Spencer Tracy, Colleen Moore, Ralph Morgan, Helen Vinson, Clifford Jones, Henry Kolker (Fox)

Jesse L. Lasky's production for Fox, is unique through its "narratage" style of cinematurgy. Its treatment has been consummately developed by director William K. Howard and scenarist Preston Sturges. The four principal characters are performed by Spencer Tracy, who has never done better; Colleen Moore, whose comeback is distinguished; Ralph Morgan, ever-effective; and Helen Vinson, at her best.

Film starts with its ending—the ecclesiastic services for the dead. Showing the finale of the life span of your central character is something that is by no means easy to offset. And that's where the "narratage" comes in. Morgan is the narrator, detailing the highlights in the career of his friend (Tracy) who, even in death, is much maligned.

Morgan undertakes to show that Tracy, who fought his way up from an ignorant, unschooled trackwalker to the presidency of railroads, and a tycoon of industry, was not the bad egg everybody painted. He argues that his strike-breaking methods, which cost many railroad workers' lives, had another element to it; that his turning out his first wife (Moore) in favor of Vinson might have had extenuating circumstances, etc.

It's well done in every respect. Casting right down the line is punchy for performance. Howard's direction is truly unique and distinguished. His favorite cameraman. James Wong Howe, manifests indubitable artistry.

•

POWER OF ONE, THE
1992, 111 mins, US Ⓥ ⦿ col
Dir John G. Avildsen ***Prod*** Arnon Milchan ***Scr*** Robert Mark Kamen ***Ph*** Dean Semler ***Ed*** John G. Avildsen ***Mus*** Hans Zimmer ***Art*** Roger Hall
Act Stephen Dorff, Armin Mueller-Stahl, Morgan Freeman, John Gielgud, Maria Marais, Simon Fenton (Regency/Canal Plus/Alcor)

Bryce Courtenay's South African coming-of-age novel is brought to the screen with mixed success in this lushly mounted production. On the one hand a captivating and inspiring tale of a boy's journey to courage amid searing injustice, pic often gives way to scenes of intense violence that are likely to bludgeon the very sensibilities it seeks to awaken. In 1930s Zimbabwe, young white P.K. is orphaned and sent to a boarding school. The only English boy among Afrikaaners, he is treated brutally, a victim of the bitter struggle among the two colonizing groups for control of South Africa. Kindly German composer and botanist Doc (Armin Mueller-Stahl) educates his mind, and dignified black prisoner Geel Piet (Morgan Freeman) teaches P.K. to defend himself in the boxing ring. Piet molds P.K. into a boxing champion and spreads word among the hundreds of other black prisoners that he's the legendary Rainmaker, come to make peace. As P.K. grows up (played admirably at age 18 by Californian Stephen Dorff), he decides to fulfill that destiny, defying the brutally racist regime.

Beautifully produced and gorgeously shot on location in Zimbabwe by lenser Dean Semler, picture has depth, dimension and first-rate casting.

•

POWER OF THE PRESS
1928, 62 mins, US ⊗ b/w
Dir Frank Capra ***Scr*** Fred C. Thompson ***Ph*** Ted Tetzlaff
Act Douglas Fairbanks, Jr., Jobyna Ralston, Robert Edeson, Mildred Harris, Dell Henderson, Wheeler Oakman (Columbia)

Exciting and insistently engaging melodrama with a light touch that lifts it out of the stencil class. While theatricalizing to an extent, the newspaper atmosphere is exceptionally restrained and reasonable for Hollywood.

Story hinges about a mayoralty election in which the candidate of the w.k. party of intelligence and morality is maneuvered into a disastrous political position by the candidate of vice and corruption. Having by his story ruined the virtuous candidate and disgraced the daughter, a young reporter (Douglas Fairbanks, Jr.), upon meeting the daughter socially, goes after the hidden aspects of the scandal and ends by exposing the whole kaboodle.

Fairbanks in ease and confidence belies his age and takes after his famous pop, never an introvert in the matter of self-assurance. Jobyna Ralston is attractive as the girl. A very suave and cold-blooded henchman of corruption is ably played by Wheeler Oakman.

•

PRAYER FOR THE DYING, A
1988, 107 mins, UK/US Ⓥ ⦿ col
Dir Mike Hodges ***Prod*** Peter Snell ***Scr*** Edmund Ward, Martin Lynch ***Ph*** Mike Garfath ***Ed*** Peter Boyle ***Mus*** Bill Conti ***Art*** Evan Hercules
Act Mickey Rourke, Bob Hoskins, Alan Bates, Sammi Davis, Liam Neeson, Alison Doody (PFD/Goldwyn)

A Prayer for the Dying is a disappointing thriller adapted from Jack Higgins's novel. Release version has been disowned by director Mike Hodges, who joined the project on short notice, succeeding Franc Roddam before shooting commenced. Pic was originally planned to be filmed a decade earlier, with Edward Dmytryk to direct and Robert Mitchum to star.

Mickey Rourke, styled with red hair and Irish brogue, portrays Martin Fallon, an IRA hitman who sees the light and flees to London. He reluctantly agrees to carry out a mob hit for gangster Jack Meehan (Alan Bates), but the killing is witnessed by priest Father Da Costa (Bob Hoskins).

Fallon confesses the murder to the priest, who refuses to identify Fallon to the police. Film becomes rather conventional at this point, with Fallon outwitting the gangsters, police and IRA hitmen (Liam Neeson, Alison Doody) hot on his case, aided by the sympathetic, blind niece of the priest, Anna (Sammi Davis).

Dying emerges as a cold, unexciting affair, lightened up only by Bates's funny overplaying of the villain. Rourke is convincing as the antihero and ably supported by Davis. As an IRA hit-lady, Doody looks more like a fashion model.

•

PREACHER'S WIFE, THE
1996, 124 mins, US Ⓥ ⦿ col
Dir Penny Marshall ***Prod*** Samuel Goldwyn ***Scr*** Nat Mauldin, Allan Scott ***Ph*** Miroslav Ondricek ***Ed*** Stephen A. Rotter, George Bowers ***Mus*** Hans Zimmer ***Art*** Bill Groom
Act Denzel Washington, Whitney Houston, Courtney Vance, Gregory Hines, Justin Pierre Edmund, Jenifer Lewis (Goldwyn/Touchstone)

Hope and love are the forces that can overcome life's travails according to *The Preacher's Wife*, a likable, modern musical fairy tale, based on the pleasantly appealing 1947 Samuel Goldwyn production *The Bishop's Wife*, transposed to an unnamed contempo New York–area setting.

The Rev. Henry Biggs (Courtney Vance) is in the throes of a crisis of confidence that is affecting every aspect of his personal and professional existence. Henry asks for divine intervention. Not only is his prayer heard, but help is sent in the form of a handsome angel (the wings, he says, are a bad literary cliché) named Dudley (Denzel Washington).

Though intelligently adapted, pic remains rooted in sentiments from another era. However, there still are plenty of timeless and modern elements for director Penny Marshall to explore. The rev.'s wife, Julia (Whitney Houston), is a considerably more strong-willed woman (and a better singer) that portrayed by Loretta Young [in the original]. It's also frankly more adult about sexual tension and jealousy than was the case when Cary Grant's angel and David Niven's minister tangled.

Houston remains more a presence than an actress, but she is extremely commanding all the same. Both male leads are exceptionally strong. Although some of Marshall's pacing and structure is a tad inelegant, camerawork and production design are pristine.

1996: NOMINATION: Best Original Musical Score

•

PRECINT 45—LOS ANGELES POLICE
SEE: THE NEW CENTURIONS

•

PREDATOR
1987, 107 mins, US Ⓥ ⦿ col
Dir John McTiernan ***Prod*** Lawrence Gordon, Joel Silver, John Davis ***Scr*** Jim Thomas, John Thomas ***Ph*** Donald McAlpine ***Ed*** John F. Link, Mark Helfrich ***Mus*** Alan Silvestri ***Art*** John Vallone
Act Arnold Schwarzenegger, Carl Weathers, Elpidia Carrillo, Bill Duke, Jesse Ventura, Sonny Landham (20th Century-Fox)

Predator is a slightly above-average actioner that tries to compensate for tissue-thin-plot with ever-more-grisly death sequences and impressive special effects.

Arnold Schwarzenegger plays Dutch, the leader of a vaguely defined military rescue team that works for allied governments. Called into a U.S. hot spot somewhere in South America, he encounters old buddy Dillon (Carl Weathers), who now works for the CIA.

The unit starts to get decimated in increasingly garish fashion by an otherworldly Predator. Enemy is a nasty, formidable foe with laser powers.

Schwarzenegger, while undeniably appealing, still has a character who's not quite real. While the painted face, cigar, vertical hair and horizontal eyes are all there, none of the humanity gets on the screen, partly because of the sparse dialog.

Weathers can't breathe any life into the cardboard character of Dillon, who goes from being unbelievably cynical to unbelievably heroic in about five minutes.

Director John McTiernan relies a bit too much on special effects "thermal vision" photography, in looking through the Predator's eyes, while trying to build tension before the blood starts to fly.

1987: NOMINATION: Best Visual Effects

•

PREDATOR 2
1990, 108 mins, US Ⓥ ⦿ col
Dir Stephen Hopkins ***Prod*** Lawrence Gordon, Joel Silver, John Davis ***Scr*** Jim Thomas, John Thomas ***Ph*** Peter Levy ***Ed*** Mark Goldblatt ***Mus*** Alan Silvestri ***Art*** Lawrence G. Paull
Act Danny Glover, Gary Busey, Ruben Blades, Maria Conchita Alonso, Bill Paxton, Kevin Peter Hall (20th Century-Fox)

While the film doesn't achieve the same thrills of the final 45 minutes of *Predator* in terms of overall excitement, it outdoes its first safari in start-to-finish hysteria. The real star is the pic's design. Writers don't waste much time on character development.

The setting is Los Angeles, 1997, where outgunned cops face hordes of Jamaican, Colombian and other assorted drug dealers who rule the streets. It's a balmy 109 degrees in the globally warmed basin, where Danny Glover heads a dedicated, ethnically mixed group of cops who are more than a little confused as the drug dealers start turning up dead in droves. The plot thickens when a fed (Gary Busey) comes in to take charge of the investigation.

Centerpiece is, again, a massive alien gifted with the strange weaponry and camouflage abilities like his kinsman that, it's told, had visited the planet 10 years earlier.

The pace of the film is absolutely frenetic. An awe-inspiring set in the closing sequence recalls the climactic moment in *Aliens*.

•

PRELUDE TO A KISS
1992, 106 mins, US Ⓥ ⦿ col
Dir Norman Rene ***Prod*** Michael Gruskoff, Michael I. Levy ***Scr*** Craig Lucas ***Ph*** Stefan Czapsky ***Ed*** Stephen A. Rotter ***Mus*** Howard Shore ***Art*** Andrew Jackness
Act Alec Baldwin, Meg Ryan, Kathy Bates, Ned Beatty, Patty Duke, Sydney Walker (20th Century-Fox)

Thanks to a magnetic cast and intelligent adaptation, *Prelude to a Kiss* has made a solid transfer from stage to screen. Craig Lucas's 1988 fairy-tale play about commitment and transcendent romantic love enjoyed a nice run on Broadway in 1990 after a limited period off-Broadway engagement with Alec Baldwin toplined.

Zippy opening reel nicely conveys the headiness of love's first stage. Peter (Baldwin) and Rita (Meg Ryan) meet sexily at a party and combust so quickly that they are in bed before they've even had a proper date.

They soon tie the knot at a lovely lakeside ceremony that turns curious with the arrival of a mysterious old man who asks to kiss the bride. Strangely drawn to the oldster, Rita agrees, then scarely knows what hit her.

During their Jamaica honeymoon, Rita doesn't seem at all like her old self. She flees back to her parents, leaving Peter to track down the old man whose ailing body now contains his wife's personality, and then to effect a retransference.

Lucas's overarching theme has to do with the spiritual prevailing over the physical, of the primacy of love no matter what the temporal obstacles.

Baldwin is a romantic lead both men and women can enjoy watching. Cuter-than-cute Ryan rambunctiously embodies the life force even when playing a basically aimless young woman, and pic suffers during her prolonged absence in the later stages.

Pic's title is derived from the Duke Ellington standard, and Howard Shore's original compositions have been combined with more than a dozen tunes of varied vintage to outstanding effect.

•

PRELUDE TO WAR
1943, 53 mins, US b/w
Dir Frank Capra
(US War Department)

First in the series of seven *Why We Fight* films produced for the U.S. War Dept. by Lt. Col. Frank Capra, of the Special Service Division, Army Service Forces, *Prelude to War* was originally intended for exclusive use in the Army's orientation courses. In piecing together the collection of clips—many of them released for the first time—giving the causes and events leading up to the present conflict, Capra has turned out a forceful, dramatic and ofttimes spectacular presentation. It's a triumph for Capra and those associated with him in the production of the film and is singularly outstanding for the War Dept.'s courage in placing great stress on this country's fatal error—of being lulled into a false sense of security by two oceans when the aggressor nations, as far back as 1931, were on the march.

Throughout Capra uses the technique of comparing the men and ideals of a free world and those of the slave world. As the U.S. was sinking its ships in a futile attempt to cement peace after the last war, the aggressor nations, with their inbred love of regimentation and discipline, were preparing to strike anew with newer and more powerful war machines and campaign of lies.

Particularly stirring is a marching sequence showing how, almost from infancy, the youth of Germany, Italy and Japan were being trained, drilled and regimented.

•

PRENOM CARMEN
(FIRST NAME: CARMEN)
1983, 85 mins, France Ⓥ col
Dir Jean-Luc Godard ***Prod*** Alain Sarde ***Scr*** Jean-Luc Godard, Anne-Marie Mieville ***Ph*** Raoul Coutard ***Ed*** Jean-Luc God-ard
Act Maruschka Detmers, Jacques Bonnaffe, Myriem Roussel, Christophe Odent, Jean-Luc Godard, Hyppolite Girardot (Sara/JLG)

As Jean-Luc Godard used contemplation of classical paintings to calmly counterpoint the fragmented cinematic prose-poetry style of his previous *Passion*, in *First Name: Carmen* he intersperses the main action throughout with close looks at the Quatuor Prat ensemble rehearsing and playing a series of Beethoven quartets. He also has Raoul Coutard's expert camera divert to shots of the sea and of Paris traffic. Film has no Bizet, but the title character is rather a gypsy, attached to a group of terrorists, working for an unnamed cause. Having held up a bank, Carmen (Maruschka Detmers) starts what develops into a love affair with the young cop, Joseph (Jacques Bonnaffe), who tried to stop her from getting away.

Carmen and Joseph occasionally go to bed with each other, but most of the time they just undress, fight, and dress again. There is some mayhem in the film, but it is always treated mostly as a joke: the chairwoman in the bank taking trouble not to disturb the dead bodies while she sweeps the floor clean of blood, or innocent bystanders just keeping their noses in their newspapers while large-scale killing goes on right next to them, etc.

There is, on the whole, more crude humor and less poetical-political philosophy than in most of Godard's earlier works. He calls his new film a Western. He originally wrote the title role for Isabelle Adjani, but the old-fashioned sultry look of Dutch replacement Maruschka Detmers serves Godard's purposes well.

•

PREPAREZ VOS MOUCHOIRS
(GET OUT YOUR HANDKERCHIEFS)
1977, 108 mins, France Ⓥ ⊙ col
Dir Bertrand Blier ***Scr*** Bertrand Blier ***Ph*** Jean Penzer ***Ed*** Claudine Merlin ***Mus*** Georges Delerue
Act Gerard Depardieu, Patrick Dewaere, Carole Laure, Riton, Michel Serrault, Eleonore Hirt (Ariane/CAPAC)

A rather bizarre mixture of gritty comedy, satire and delving into female status makes this a literary film. There is a lot of talk, sometimes good, but often edgy and too often pointless in lieu of a more robust visual dynamism and life.

Gerard Depardieu is first seen in close-up talking to his pretty but vacant-looking wife in a restaurant. He insists he loves her enough to give her to another man. He picks on a be-spectacled young man (Patrick Dewaere) and talks him into going with his wife. The wife (lovely Canadian thesp Carole Laure) accepts. But it does not quite work. The three go off to a summer camp run by Dewaere where there is a 13-year-old quiz kid picked on by the others. Laure warms to him and lets him sleep with her as her husband and suitor read books together. The boy, a long-haired, shrewd innocent, manages to tap her need for a child and uses it to become her lover.

Blier did the more anarchic tale of two semi-delinquents living on women and society, *Going Places*, which launched Dewaere and Depardieu. Now they do a sort of comedy team number rather than imbuing their roles with human insight. Film stays in the realm of ideas.

1978: Best Foreign Language Film

•

PRESENTING LILY MARS
1943, 106 mins, US Ⓥ b/w
Dir Norman Taurog ***Prod*** Joseph Pasternak ***Scr*** Richard Connell, Gladys Lehman ***Ph*** Joseph Ruttenberg ***Ed*** Albert Akst ***Mus*** George Stoll (dir.)
Act Judy Garland, Van Heflin, Fay Bainter, Marta Eggerth, Richard Carlson (M-G-M)

Presenting Lily Mars spotlights Judy Garland and Van Heflin in a stage Cinderella yarn that supplies minor switches to regulation formula, but mainly depends on performances, direction and musical mounting, to carry it through.

Story is a typical Cinderella tale, with Garland an aspiring and stagestruck youngster who attempts to catch attention of producer Van Heflin in a small Indiana town. She makes a pest of herself for 40 minutes of the running time until she follows him into New York, gets a job in his new show, and eventually falls in love with the producer. Heflin adequately handles the asignment of the young producer who eventually falls in love with Garland. Latter delivers in her usual effective style as the aspiring actress, putting across her numbers in top fashion.

Bob Crosby band is on for one tune in a nightspot where Garland heads for the mike to sing a song, while Tommy Dorsey and his ork appears for the finale accompaniment to song and dance by Miss Garland.

•

PRESIDENT'S ANALYST, THE
1967, 103 mins, US Ⓥ ▭ col
Dir Theodore J. Flicker ***Prod*** Stanley Rubin ***Scr*** Theodore J. Flicker ***Ph*** William A. Fraker ***Ed*** Stuart H. Pappe ***Mus*** Lalo Schifrin ***Art*** Pato Guzman
Act James Coburn, Godfrey Cambridge, Severn Darden, Joan Delaney, Pat Harrington, Barry McGuire (Paramount/Panpiper)

The President's Analyst is a superior satire on some sacred cows, principally the lightly camouflaged FBI, hippies, psychiatry, liberal and conservative politics—and the telephone company.

Inventive story peg—James Coburn starring as the personal analyst to the President of the U.S.—is fleshed out with hilarious incidents which zero in on, and hit, their targets.

William Daniels scores as an upper-middle-class compulsive liberal, whose family practices marksmanship, karate and eavesdropping because of right-wing neighbours.

Barry McGuire and Jill Banner are hippies, and Banner's sex scene with Coburn—in fields of flowers right out of some cosmetics teleblurb—is a comedy highlight in which several foreign and domestic spies kill each other off as they plot Coburn's demise.

•

PRESIDENT'S LADY, THE
1953, 96 mins, US Ⓥ b/w
Dir Henry Levin ***Prod*** Sol C. Siegel ***Scr*** John Patrick ***Ph*** Leo Tover ***Ed*** William B. Murphy ***Mus*** Alfred Newman ***Art*** Lyle R. Wheeler, Leland Fuller
Act Susan Hayward, Charlton Heston, John McIntire, Fay Bainter, Ralph Dumke (20th Century-Fox)

The dramatic story of a lady's influence on the life of a great man invariably makes for interesting filming, and in the case of Andrew Jackson, the seventh president of the United States, 20th-Fox has created a particularly moving narrative. Based on Irving Stone's bestselling novel, *Lady* covers more than 40 years in the life of the famed Indian-fighter and general.

It covers the period when the young Tennessee lawyer is Attorney General, through his battles with the Indians—and, more importantly, through the period of courting and marriage with Rachel Donelson Robards. It is the story of Jackson being forced to fight his way up the political ladder with the stigma of adultery plaguing him along the way. Through it all, Charlton Heston supplies the kind of ammunition to this film that is as loaded as any carbine slung across his broad shoulders. It is a forthright steely-eyed portrayal. Susan Hayward gives the pic a simple, sustained performance in addition to physical beauty. John McIntire plays Jackson's longtime friend and law partner, and he gives the role neat shading in a distinctly lesser role.

1953: NOMINATIONS: Best B&W Costume Design, B&W Art Direction

•

PRESIDIO, THE
1988, 97 mins, US Ⓥ ⊙ ▭ col
Dir Peter Hyams ***Prod*** D. Constantine Conte ***Scr*** Larry Ferguson ***Ph*** Peter Hyams ***Ed*** James Mitchell ***Mus*** Bruce Broughton ***Art*** Albert Brenner
Act Sean Connery, Mark Harmon, Meg Ryan, Jack Warden, Mark Blum, Jenette Goldstein (Paramount)

Sean Connery and Mark Harmon go head to head as an Army provost marshal and a San Francisco cop who clash jurisdictions and styles in the investigation of an MP's murder.

Naturally, there's a backstory—they'd locked horns earlier when Connery was Harmon's c.o. in the military—and a complication—Harmon gets involved with Connery's frisky and equally willful daughter (Meg Ryan).

Tug-of-war for dominance among the trio provides the interest in an otherwise ordinary crime story, as Harmon and Connery end up working to piece together clues in a convoluted smuggling caper.

Along the way there are three very splashy action sequences—a car chase through the army base and the streets of S.F., a footrace through crowded Chinatown and the final, treacherous shootout in a water bottling plant that becomes as hairy as the swamps of 'Nam.

•

PRESUMED INNOCENT
1990, 127 mins, US Ⓥ ⊙ col
Dir Alan J. Pakula ***Prod*** Sydney Pollack, Mark Rosenberg ***Scr*** Frank Pierson, Alan J. Pakula ***Ph*** Gordon Willis ***Ed*** Evan Lottman ***Mus*** John Williams ***Art*** George Jenkins
Act Harrison Ford, Brian Dennehy, Raul Julia, Bonnie Bedelia, Paul Winfield, Greta Scacchi (Mirage/Warner)

Honed to a riveting intensity by director Alan J. Pakula and featuring the tightest script imaginable, *Presumed Innocent* is a demanding, disturbing javelin of a courtroom murder mystery.

Hewing closely to Scott Turow's bestselling 1987 novel, the harrowing tale unfolds with nary a wasted step, as deputy prosecutor and family man Rusty Sabich (Harrison Ford) arrives at work to learn his beautiful colleague Carolyn Polhemus (Greta Scacchi) has been brutally murdered. Forced to lead the investigation by his longtime boss Raymond Horgan (Brian Dennehy), who's in a deep sweat over his re-election campaign, Sabich can scarcely admit he'd had an affair with the dead attorney. But his pained, steely cool wife (Bonnie Bedelia) knows, and she's none too sympathetic or forgiving about it.

Sabich is then confronted by rat-like ex-colleague Tommy Molto (Joe Grifasi), who's part of an opposing campaign for the chief prosecutor's office. Molto swears Sabich was at Carolyn's apartment the night of the murder. Before long Sabich is embroiled in a grand jury investigation that spurs his politically frightened boss to turn on him. With a sly, magnetic Raul Julia brought in as Sabich's crafty defense lawyer, one never knows, until pic's astonishing denouement, whether Sabich did the deed or not.

Ford, in a very mature, subtle, low-key performance, pulls off the difficult feat of making it impossible to be sure. Bedelia is wondrously controlled, and Scacchi, sans any hint of a European accent, is convincing and seductive.

•

PRET-A-PORTER
SEE: READY TO WEAR

•

PRETTY BABY
1978, 109 mins, US Ⓥ ⊙ col
Dir Louis Malle ***Prod*** Louis Malle ***Scr*** Polly Platt ***Ph*** Sven Nykvist ***Ed*** Suzanne Baron, Suzanne Fenn ***Mus*** Jerry Wexler ***Art*** Trevor Williams
Act Keith Carradine, Susan Sarandon, Brooke Shields, Frances Faye, Antonio Fargas, Gerrit Graham (Paramount)

The Louis Malle–Polly Platt collaboration on *Pretty Baby* has yielded an offbeat depiction of life in New Orleans's Storyville red-light district circa 1917, as experienced by a lifelong resident—a 12-year-old girl. The film is handsome, the players nearly all effective, but the story highlights are confined within a narrow range of ho-hum dramatization. The time of the plot is just before Josephis Davids, Secretary of the U.S. Navy, closed Storyville as a bad influence; the black musicians who found employment in the brothels there drifted north to Kansas City, Memphis and Chicago, later east to N.Y., and thereby changed forever the direction and the fabric of American popular music. But that potentially strong film plot is not what's here.

Instead, Malle and Platt [using material in *Storyville* by Al Rose] have created a placid milieu in the barrelhouse owned by Frances Faye. There, Susan Sarandon is one of the girls who, in residence, has given birth to a child, in this case Brooke Shields, who gives either an extraordinarily subtle or else a totally perplexed performance as a preteenager whose entire world is that of the brothel.

Keith Carradine is cast as a catatonic photographer who only likes to shoot portraits of the girls. Eventually Shields and Carradine live together, but the relationship ends when Sarandon, who left to marry a customer, returns in respectability to claim the underage child. That's it.

1978: NOMINATION: Best Adapted Score

•

PRETTY BOY FLOYD
1960, 96 mins, US b/w
Dir Herbert J. Leder ***Prod*** Monroe Sachson ***Scr*** Herbert J. Leder ***Ph*** Chuck Austin ***Ed*** Ralph Rosenblum ***Mus*** Del Sirino, William Sanford
Act John Ericson, Barry Newman, Joan Harvey, Carl York, Phil Kenneally (Le-Sac)

This is a grim, almost sadistic reworking of the tale of the Oklahoma farm boy who won fame and ill-fortune in the early 1930s. It points a glib moral (crime does not pay) without ever presenting anything more than a few superficial reasons for the phenomenon that Pretty Boy Floyd represented. Script says Floyd had a bad temper and was ignorant. Period.

John Ericson does a good job in the role and is backed by a competent group of New York actors, few of whom have been on the screen before. (Film was shot entirely at Gold Medal Studios in the Bronx.) Low budget of the pic shows through from time to time, but actually seems to help create an appropriately seedy and sordid atmosphere.

Script first picks up Floyd when he is making a desultory attempt to go straight as an oil-field worker. Bounced when it's revealed that he served time for armed robbery in St. Louis, Floyd picks up a life of crime again with an old cellmate. He soon branches out on his own and becomes the terror of the Middle West.

The film shows numerous of Floyd's bank holdups, as well as the famous "Kansas City Massacre," in which Floyd and two others gunned to death two FBI men and a policeman who were transferring a brother hood to prison. Same incident, as well as Floyd's eventual demise at the hands of the G-men, are in *The FBI Story*.

•

PRETTY IN PINK

1986, 96 mins, US Ⓥ ⊙ col

Dir Howard Deutch ***Prod*** Lauren Shuler ***Scr*** John Hughes ***Ph*** Tak Fujimoto ***Ed*** Richard Marks ***Mus*** Michael Gore ***Art*** John W. Corso

Act Molly Ringwald, Harry Dean Stanton, Jon Cryer, Andrew McCarthy, Annie Potts, James Spader (Paramount)

Pretty in Pink is a rather intelligent (if not terribly original) look at adolescent insecurities.

Like scores of leading ladies before her, Molly Ringwald is the proverbial pretty girl from the wrong side of the tracks, called to a motherless life with down-on-his-luck dad (Harry Dean Stanton) and the misfortune to have to attend high school where the rich kids lord it over the poor.

That's enough to make any young lady insecure, even before the wealthy nice guy (Andrew McCarthy) asks her to the senior prom. Teased by his rich pals for slumming, McCarthy is also a bundle of uncertainties. Moving predictably, none of this is unique drama. In the end, the wrong guy still gets the girl, which is a lesson youngsters might as well learn early.

•

PRETTY MAIDS ALL IN A ROW

1971, 95 mins, US col

Dir Roger Vadim ***Prod*** Gene Roddenberry ***Scr*** Gene Roddenberry ***Ph*** Charles Rosher ***Ed*** Bill Brame ***Mus*** Lalo Schifrin ***Art*** George W. Davis, Preston Ames

Act Rock Hudson, Angie Dickinson, Telly Savalas, John David Carson, Roddy McDowall, Keenan Wynn (M-G-M)

Pretty Maids All in a Row, Roger Vadim's first U.S.-made film, is apparently intended as a sort of genteel black murder-sex comedy. Gene Roddenberry's production careers through 95 minutes of juvenile double entendre and pratfall. Rock Hudson stars as a married high-school guidance counseller who gets to know his girl students in the academic and Biblical sense, and eventually has to kill several to keep them quiet. The unravelling of the murders (but not to an audience, which knows early what's up) parallels another story line: John David Carson's post-acne, pre-adult shy-guy character which blossoms under the careful attention of Angie Dickinson, the constant nymph. Carson does extremely well in the best-developed characterization in the script.

Whatever substance was in the original [novel by Francis Pollini] or screen concept has been plowed under, leaving only superficial, one-joke results.

•

PRETTY POISON

1968, 89 mins, US Ⓥ col

Dir Noel Black ***Prod*** Marshal Backlar, Noel Black ***Scr*** Lorenzo Semple, Jr. ***Ph*** David Quaid ***Ed*** William Ziegler ***Mus*** Johnny Mandel ***Art*** Jack Martin Smith, Harold Michelson

Act Anthony Perkins, Tuesday Weld, Beverly Garland, John Randolph, Dick O'Neill, Clarice Blackburn (20th Century-Fox)

Pretty Poison is an attempt at low-key psychological terror. Anthony Perkins, a mentally unhealthy resident of his own fantasies, finds in Tuesday Weld a more than willing pupil. Awkwardly begun and tediously developed, the film [from a novel by Stephen Geller] goes too much off the track.

A prolog and a quasi-epilog sequence establish Perkins as a disobedient parolee from confinement for arson-murder. Main body of the story, all shot on location in Massachusetts, concerns his play-acting and sexual playing with Weld, restless daughter of the widowed Beverly Garland. From an innocent-looking teenager, Weld progresses to a cold, pathological killer and betrayor, escaping justice while pitiable Perkins, probably less deranged than she, falls victim to her superior depravity.

Perkins does a creditable job in a difficult part. So much of his earlier dialog might lead to disastrous guffaws that merely avoiding this trap must be credited to him and the director.

•

PRETTY POLLY
(US: A MATTER OF INNOCENCE)

1967, 102 mins, UK col

Dir Guy Green ***Prod*** George W. George, Frank Granat ***Scr*** Willis Hall, Keith Waterhouse ***Ph*** Arthur Ibbetson ***Ed*** Frank Clarke ***Mus*** Michel Legrand ***Art*** Peter Mullins

Act Hayley Mills, Trevor Howard, Shashi Kapoor, Brenda de Banzie, Dick Patterson, Kalen Lui (Universal)

Hayley Mills (as Polly) goes on vacation with a rich, disagreeable aunt to Singapore. Frumpish, bespectacled and lumpily dressed, she timidly obeys her aunt's constant demands for attention and looks suitably badgered.

But the relation dies from taking a swim too soon after a heavy lunch, and this sparks off the transformation scene. Polly is encouraged by an Indian acting as guide and helpmate to have her hair done, exchange her glasses for contact lenses, and indulge in a riot of makeup. She emerges as a siren.

Derived from a Noel Coward short story—itself written in the vein of Somerset Maugham—the script goes all out for sentiment, and, on its undemanding level, achieves it.

•

PRETTY WOMAN

1990, 117 mins, US Ⓥ ⊙ col

Dir Garry Marshall ***Prod*** Arnon Milchan, Steven Reuther ***Scr*** J. F. Lawton ***Ph*** Charles Minsky ***Ed*** Priscilla Nedd ***Mus*** James Newton Howard ***Art*** Albert Brenner

Act Richard Gere, Julia Roberts, Ralph Bellamy, Jason Alexander, Laura San Giacomo, Hector Elizondo (Touchstone)

J. F. Lawton's formula screenplay owes plenty to *Pygmalion*, *Cinderella* and *The Owl and the Pussycat* in limning a fairy tale of a prostitute with a heart of gold who mellows a stuffy businessman.

Pic's first two reels are weak, as corporate raider Richard Gere is unconvincingly thrown together with streetwalker Julia Roberts when he seeks directions to Beverly Hills. Seducing this reluctant john, she's improbably hired by Gere to spend the week with him as escort since he's split up with his girlfriend. Her price tag is $3,000; film's cryptic shooting title was *3000*.

Film blossoms along with Roberts, when she doffs her unflattering Carol Channing blond wig to get natural and embark on a massively entertaining (and class-conscious) shopping adventure on Rodeo Drive. Roberts handles the transition from coarse and gawky to glamorous with aplomb.

Pic's casting is astute, with Gere underplaying like a sturdy ballet star who hoists the ballerina Roberts on his shoulders. Sexiest routine has Gere playing solo-jazz piano late at night in the hotel ballroom and joined for a tryst by Roberts. Supporting cast is outstanding.

1990: NOMINATION: Best Actress (Julia Roberts)

•

PRICK UP YOUR EARS

1987, 108 mins, UK Ⓥ ⊙ col

Dir Stephen Frears ***Prod*** Andrew Brown ***Scr*** Alan Bennett ***Ph*** Oliver Stapleton ***Ed*** Mick Audsley ***Mus*** Stanley Myers ***Art*** Hugo Luczyc Wyhowski

Act Gary Oldman, Alfred Molina, Vanessa Redgrave, Wallace Shawn, Julie Walters, Frances Barber (Civilhand/Zenith)

Though selling itself as a biography of controversial young British playwright Joe Orton, who was murdered in 1967, *Prick Up Your Ears* actually says very little about Orton the author, but deals almost totally with his relationship with Kenneth Halliwell, his lover and bludgeon killer.

Orton and Halliwell met at the Royal Academy of Dramatic Art. The inarticulate Orton fell for the seemingly sophisticated Halliwell, and for a while the pic dwells on Orton's promiscuity, at a time when homosexuality was still illegal in the U.K. Suddenly, after years of obscurity, Orton becomes an overnight success.

The script [based on the biography by John Lahr] is witty, the direction fluid, with one of the homosexual orgy scenes in a public toilet almost balletic, and the depiction of the lovers' life in their flat suitably claustrophobic.

Gary Oldman is excellent as Orton, right down to remarkable resemblance, while Alfred Molina creates both an amusing and tormented Halliwell. Vanessa Redgrave takes top honors, though, as a compassionate and benign agent.

•

PRIDE AND PREJUDICE

1940, 117 mins, US Ⓥ b/w

Dir Robert Z. Leonard ***Prod*** Hunt Stromberg ***Scr*** Aldous Huxley, Jane Murfin ***Ph*** Karl Freund ***Ed*** Robert J. Kern ***Mus*** Herbert Stothart ***Art*** Cedric Gibbons, Paul Groesse

Act Greer Garson, Laurence Olivier, Mary Boland, Edna May Oliver, Edmund Gwenn, Maureen O'Sullivan (M-G-M)

Metro reaches into the remote corners of the library bookshelf for this old-time novel about English society and the vicissitudes of a British mother faced with the task of marrying off five daughters in a limited market. *Pride and Prejudice* was written by Jane Austen in 1793. As a film it possesses little of general interest, except as a co-starring vehicle for Greer Garson and Laurence Olivier.

Any novel which survives more than a century possesses unusual qualities, and *Pride and Prejudice* qualifies chiefly because of the characterization of Elizabeth Bennet (Garson), eldest of the eligible sisters and a rather daring young woman with ideas of feminism far in advance of her contemporaries. In the screenplay she is trimmed to fit into a yarn about a family, rather than about an unusual and courageous girl. In consequence, the film is something less than satisfactory entertainment, despite lavish settings, costumes, and an acting ensemble of unique talent.

Olivier appears very unhappy in the role of Darcy, rich young bachelor, who is first spurned and then forgiven for his boorishness, conceit and bad manners.

There are some good performances. Mary Boland is a fluttering, clucking mother of a brood of young women whose aim is matrimony. Edna May Oliver, as the dominant Lady Catherine, comes on the scene late in the story and makes for some much needed merriment. Melville Cooper does a good comedy bit and the other Bennet sisters, as played by Maureen O'Sullivan, Ann Rutherford, Marsha Hunt and Heather Angel, provide charm and pulchritude.

1940: Best B&W Interior Decoration

•

PRIDE AND THE PASSION, THE

1957, 132 mins, US ⊙ Ⓥ col

Dir Stanley Kramer ***Prod*** Stanley Kramer ***Scr*** Edna Anhalt, Edward Anhalt ***Ph*** Franz Planer ***Ed*** Frederic Knudtson, Ellsworth Hoagland ***Mus*** George Antheil ***Art*** Fernando Carrere

Act Cary Grant, Frank Sinatra, Sophia Loren, Theodore Bikel, John Wengraf (United Artists)

This is Stanley Kramer's powerful production of C. S. Forester's sweeping novel, *The Gun*, about the Spanish "citizens' army" that went to battle against the conquering legions of the French in 1810. The picture was in preparation and production in Spain for a year and a half. It is the story of the band of guerillas who come upon an oversized cannon that is abandoned by the retreating Spanish army. All things revolve around the huge weapon; it becomes symbolic of the spirit and courage of the Spanish patriots and their leader (Frank Sinatra).

From this point on *Passion* focuses on this unlikely army seeking to make its way to the French stronghold at Avila against incredibly tall odds. Their ally is Cary Grant, a British naval officer assigned to retrieve the gun for use against Napoleon's forces.

Sophia Loren is Sinatra's sultry and inflammable mistress with beaucoup accent on the decollete. At first hostile toward Grant, she comes to recognize his pro-Spanish motives and veers to him romantically. They make for an engaging trio.

Top credit must go to the production. The panoramic, long-range views of the marching and terribly burdened army, the painful fight to keep the gun mobile through ravine and over waterway—these are major plusses.

•

PRIDE OF THE MARINES
(UK: FOREVER IN LOVE)

1945, 119 mins, US b/w

Dir Delmer Daves ***Prod*** Jerry Wald ***Scr*** Albert Maltz, Marvin Borowsky ***Ph*** Peverell Marley, Robert Burks ***Ed*** Owen Marks ***Mus*** Franz Waxman ***Art*** Leo Kuter

Act John Garfield, Eleanor Parker, Dane Clark, Ann Doran, John Ridgely, Rosemary DeCamp (Warner)

Pride of the Marines is a two-hour celluloid saga [from a story by Roger Butterfield] which as an entertainment film with a forceful theme, so punchy that its "message" aspects are negligible, is a credit to all concerned.

The simple story of Al Schmid, real-life Marine-hero of Guadalcanal, is the story of American patriotism and heroism which is unheroic in its simple forthrightness; American pride in defending our way of life; American guts; and also a distorted sense of foolish pride, born of stubbornness, when the blinded Al Schmid rebels at returning to his loved ones because he "wants nobody to be a seeing-eye dog for me." As unfolded it's a heart-tugging, sentimentally heroic tale. John Garfield as the brittle Al Schmid, ex-machinist now Marine-hero, albeit blinded, gives a vividly histrionic performance. He is buoyed plenty by Dane Clark and Anthony Caruso, with Eleanor Parker as the No. 1 femme.

1945: NOMINATIONS: Best Screenplay

•

PRIDE OF THE YANKEES, THE
1942, 120 mins, US Ⓥ ⦿ b/w
Dir Sam Wood ***Prod*** Sam Goldwyn ***Scr*** Jo Swerling, Herman J. Mankiewicz ***Ph*** Rudolph Mate ***Ed*** Daniel Mandell ***Mus*** Leigh Harline ***Art*** William Cameron Menzies
Act Gary Cooper, Teresa Wright, Babe Ruth, Walter Brennan, Dan Duryea, Elsa Jansen (RKO/Goldwyn)

Sam Goldwyn has produced a stirring epitaph on Lou Gehrig. For baseball and non-baseball fan alike, this sentimental, romantic saga of the NY kid who rose to the baseball heights and later met such a tragic end is well worth seeing. Clever fictionizing and underplaying of the actual sport in contrast to the more human, domestic side of the great ballplayer make the film good for all audiences.

Gary Cooper makes his Gehrig look and sound believable from the screen. To the credit of the screenwriters, and Paul Gallico who wrote the original, no attempt is made to inject color into the characterization of Gehrig. He's depicted for what he was, a quiet, plodding personality who strived for and achieved perfection in his profession.

1942: Best Editing

NOMINATIONS: Best Picture, Actor (Gary Cooper), Actress (Teresa Wright), Original Story, Screenplay, B&W Cinematography, B&W Art Direction, Scoring of a Dramatic Picture, Sound, Special Effects

•

PRIEST
1995, 105 mins, UK Ⓥ col
Dir Antonia Bird ***Prod*** George Faber, Josephine Ward ***Scr*** Jimmy McGovern ***Ph*** Fred Tammes ***Ed*** Sue Spivey ***Mus*** Andy Roberts ***Art*** Ray Langhorn
Act Linus Roache, Tom Wilkinson, Cathy Tyson, James Ellis, Robert Carlyle, John Bennett (BBC)

Priest is an absolutely riveting, made-for-BBC slice-of-life drama that's a controversial look at incest, gay love and the Catholic church. The pic is the first full-length feature from theater and TV vet Antonia Bird.

Father Greg (Linus Roache), a young priest brimming with lofty ideals, is in for a rude shock to his value system when he arrives in a tough, inner-city Liverpool parish. First there's his colleague Father Matthew (Tom Wilkinson), a middle-aged social activist prone to giving rabble-rousing, left-wing speeches from the pulpit. Even worse, Father Matthew is openly breaking his vows of celibacy and living with a woman.

But the young priest's naive sense of right-and-wrong soon begins to come apart at the seams. One night, he switches from his day-job robes into a leather jacket and heads out to a local gay bar, where he picks up a guy. The ethical horizon becomes even more cloudy when a young girl tells him in the confessional that her father is sexually abusing her. The priest feels he can't help the girl because it would break the seal of silence of the confession.

Roache will turn heads with his intense perf in a difficult role, and the rest of the cast get the job done with gritty flair. Liverpool writer Jimmy McGovern's script is refreshingly down-to-earth, and it's his willingness to generate laughs from even the direst situations that makes the pic so accessible.

•

PRIEST OF LOVE
1981, 125 mins, UK Ⓥ col
Dir Christopher Miles ***Prod*** Christopher Miles, Andrew Donally ***Scr*** Alan Plater ***Ph*** Ted Moore ***Ed*** Paul Davies ***Mus*** Joseph James ***Art*** Ted Tester, David Brockhurst
Act Ian McKellen, Janet Suzman, Ava Gardner, Penelope Keith, Jorge Rivero, John Gielgud (Milesian)

Priest of Love is an impressively mounted and acted biopic [from a book by Harry T. Moore] dealing with the later years in the life of author D. H. Lawrence. Reunited with screenwriter Alan Plater who wrote his filmization of Lawrence's *The Virgin and the Gypsy*, director Christopher Miles takes a somewhat removed and cool look at his subject.

Picture opens in 1924 with Lawrence (Ian McKellen), wife Frieda (Janet Suzman) and their friend Dorothy Brett (Penelope Keith) enroute to Taos, New Mexico, for a self-imposed exile at the home of art patroness Mabel Dodge Luhan (Ava Gardner). Back in Britain, his books have been banned by the censor Herbert Muskett (an effectively stern cameo by John Gielgud).

Key scenes involve the fearless duo pushing relentlessly for the truth in a sexual manifesto in literature and tasteful scenes indicating his bisexuality (with a youth nude bathing at an Italian seashore) and relentless selfishness in inviting Dorothy to bed and then spurning her suddenly.

Too infrequently seen in films, McKellen gives a bravura performance, all the more remarkable for its avoidance of easy empathy. Veteran of a one-woman show on stage as Frieda, Janet Suzman is given her head by Miles and turns in a flamboyant, explosive turn which prevents the film from being dominated by McKellen.

•

PRIMAL FEAR
1996, 129 mins, US Ⓥ ⦿ col
Dir Gregory Hoblit ***Prod*** Gary Lucchesi ***Scr*** Steve Shagan, Ann Biderman ***Ph*** Michael Chapman ***Ed*** David Rosenbloom ***Mus*** James Newton Howard ***Art*** Jeannine Oppewall
Act Richard Gere, Laura Linney, John Mahoney, Alfre Woodard, Frances McDormand, Edward Norton (Paramount)

A densely plotted, talky murder-case drama with some well-placed twists, *Primal Fear* resembles a high-end telefilm. Crammed with critical insights into the complicity, hypocrisy and compromises of big-city ruling elites and the selfishly misguided motives of celebrity attorneys, slickly produced film has plenty to say, but does so a bit insistently and obviously.

Pic marks the feature directorial debut of Gregory Hoblit, a nine-time Emmy winner for producing and directing the likes of *Hill Street Blues*, *L.A. Law* and *NYPD Blue*. Point-making approach here is similar to that of those involving, high-minded series.

Richard Gere plays Martin Vail, a hotshot Chicago lawyer who used to work for the state. When the popular archbishop of Chicago is gruesomely butchered in his bedroom, and one of his altar boys, Aaron (Edward Norton), a shy, former street kid, is instantly picked up fleeing, blood-soaked, from the scene, Vail, with the eagerness of an ambulance chaser, volunteers to represent him.

Aaron insists a third party did the awful deed. Vail brings in a shrink (Frances McDormand), to whom Aaron reveals a second personality, that of a vicious, violently tempered thug. This is the first surprise sprung in the well-crafted, if verbose, screenplay from a novel by William Diehl. Norton, a young theater actor, exhibits outstanding technique and range. Gere breezes through the cocksure portion of his role and is impressively forceful in several confrontation scenes. Laura Linney is excellent as the attractive prosecuter who likes to think she's tough enough for her job.

1996: NOMINATION: Best Supp. Actor (Edward Norton)

•

PRIMARY COLORS
1998, 143 mins, US Ⓥ ⦿ ▭ col
Dir Mike Nichols ***Prod*** Mike Nichols ***Scr*** Elaine May ***Ph*** Michael Ballhaus ***Ed*** Arthur Schmidt ***Mus*** Ry Cooder ***Art*** Bo Welch
Act John Travolta, Emma Thompson, Billy Bob Thornton, Kathy Bates, Adrian Lester, Maura Tierney (Universal/Mutual)

Frequently funny, wonderfully performed, eerily evocative of recent history and gratifyingly blunt in its assessment of what it takes to get to the top in modern American politics, pic also lacks something crucial at its center that prevents it from being an entirely credible portrait of its subject.

Mike Nichols and Elaine May have made a shrewd adaptation of the bestselling 1996 novel [published anonymously but later revealed to have been written by Joe Klein] about the first Clinton presidential campaign.

Opening scenes are near-brilliant in their precise focus and nuanced layering as the film indicates its potential as a densely textured portrait of a supremely persuasive manipulator of everyone who enters his sphere of influence.

Gov. Jack Stanton (John Travolta), from an unspecified Southern state, succeeds in convincing the skeptical Henry Burton (Adrian Lester), the bright grandson of a great civil rights pioneer, to become his deputy campaign manager. Invaluable to Stanton are his attractive and bracingly frank wife, Susan (Emma Thompson), and his close adviser Richard Jemmons (Billy Bob Thornton), a self-procalimed redneck who bluntly identifies his boss' Achilles heel: "The woman thing, that's the killer."

In order to dig up all the dirt before anyone else does, the team brings in the tenacious Libby Holden (Kathy Bates), a sassy, upfront lesbian who knows where all the bodies are buried.

Nichols keeps many balls in the air and continually reinforces his central theme in varied and subtle ways. But because Travolta has been able so uncannily to impersonate the real president, one is also forcibly reminded of what is missing from his characterization—intellectual distinction, the Rhodes Scholar side to the man, that can represent the first step toward an understanding of a man of such accomplishment.

•

PRIME CUT
1972, 86 mins, US Ⓥ ▭ col
Dir Michael Ritchie ***Prod*** Joe Wizan ***Scr*** Robert Dillon ***Ph*** Gene Polito ***Ed*** Carl Pingitore ***Mus*** Lalo Schifrin ***Art*** Bill Malley
Act Lee Marvin, Gene Hackman, Angel Tompkins, Gregory Walcott, Sissy Spacek, Janit Baldwin (Cinema Center)

Prime Cut is another contemporary underworld bloodletting, which is drawn, quartered and ground according to an overused recipe for hash.

Lee Marvin and Gene Hackman provide the dressing along with the scenery of Calgary.

Writer Robert Dillon sends collection-agent Marvin to Eddie Egan, a Chi gangster who no longer is getting his cut from Hackman, a Kansas cattle king who also deals in dope and girls, among whom are Sissy Spacek and Janit Baldwin.

Director Michael Ritchie moves the pawns about inventively and with sterile precision.

There are no serious dramatic demands made of the players. Marvin and Hackman do this sort of thing all the time. Spacek and Baldwin look good in their feature debut and Gregory Walcott is most effective as a supersadist.

•

PRIME OF MISS JEAN BRODIE, THE
1969, 116 mins, UK Ⓥ col
Dir Ronald Neame ***Prod*** Robert Fryer ***Scr*** Jay Presson Allen ***Ph*** Ted Moore ***Ed*** Norman Savage ***Mus*** Rod McKuen ***Art*** John Howell
Act Maggie Smith, Robert Stephens, Pamela Franklin, Gordon Jackson, Celia Johnson, Jane Carr (20th Century-Fox)

Maggie Smith's tour-de-force performance as a schoolteacher slipping into spinsterhood is one of several notable achievements in this sentimental and macabre personal tragedy.

Jay Presson Allen adapted her own play [based on a novel by Muriel Spark]. The story, set in 1930s Edinburgh, treats in a tenderly savage way the decline of an age-resisting schoolmarm who lives too vicariously through a select group of prodigy-stooges. The telling involves elements of warm humor, biting sarcasm, pity, contempt, betrayal, and despair.

Smith's performance is a triumph. Other cast principals, all of whom project excellent performances, include Robert Stephens, the art teacher, Pamela Franklin, cast as a mysteriously adult child and the eventual betrayor of Smith, and Gordon Jackson is impressive as the pitiable, gutless music teacher. Celia Johnson's key adversary role as the school head-mistress comes off magnificently.

1969: Best Actress (Maggie Smith)

NOMINATION: Best Song ("Jean")

•

PRINCE AND THE PAUPER, THE
1937, 115 mins, US Ⓥ b/w
Dir William Keighley ***Prod*** Robert Lord ***Scr*** Laird Doyle ***Ph*** Sol Polito ***Ed*** Ralph Dawson ***Mus*** Erich Wolfgang Korngold
Act Errol Flynn, Claude Rains, Henry Stephenson, Barton MacLane, Billy Mauch, Bobby Mauch (Warner)

Of all his stories, Mark Twain loved best *The Prince and the Pauper*. Produced with sincerity and lavishness, this film [from a dramatised version by Catherine C. Cushing] is a costume picture minus any romance whatsoever.

In this film are the Mauch Twins, in addition to Errol Flynn, who is at his best in romantic, swashbuckling roles. But there is no girl opposite Flynn. So it's just the story of the Tudor Prince who exchanges places with a beggar boy, and regains his throne on Coronation Day through the heroism of a dashing soldier of fortune.

Such interest as the film contains could have been heightened by some drastic trimming in the early scenes, so that Flynn's entrance might have been moved up. He does Miles Hendon with the proper dash and spirit. The Mauch boys play their contrasting parts with earnestness if not too much skill. Claude Rains as Hertford; Montagu Love as Henry VIII, and Barton MacLane as John Canty, are fiercely melodramatic. It doesn't seem that William Keighley, in his direction, has captured sufficient sympathy for the two youngsters to compensate for the romantic loss in having no fiancee for Flynn.

•

PRINCE AND THE PAUPER, THE *(US: CROSSED SWORDS)*
1977, 121 mins, UK Ⓥ col
Dir Richard Fleischer ***Prod*** Pierre Spengler ***Scr*** George Macdonald Frazer ***Ph*** Jack Cardiff ***Ed*** Ernest Walter ***Mus*** Maurice Jarre ***Art*** Tony Pratt
Act Oliver Reed, Raquel Welch, Mark Lester, Ernest Borgnine, George C. Scott, Rex Harrison (Salkind)

Some of the irony and wit of Mark Twain's original fable about an English prince's switch with his poor look-alike has been lost or subdued, but this edition of *The Prince and the Pauper* [from an original screenplay by Berta Dominguez and Pierre Spengler, based on Twain's novel] still makes for satisfactory entertainment.

Lester as the prince trades identities with Mark Lester the pauper and is then banished from the castle and launched into an eye- and heart-opening odyssey around medieval England, finding it to be no Camelot but a land of wretched, poor and persecuted.

As the pauper, meantime, he not only swoons over young Lady Jane but also breathes a refreshing humanity into the court of ruthless King Henry.

•

PRINCE AND THE SHOWGIRL, THE
1957, 117 mins, US Ⓥ col
Dir Laurence Olivier ***Prod*** Laurence Olivier ***Scr*** Terence Rattigan ***Ph*** Jack Cardiff ***Ed*** Jack Harris ***Mus*** Richard Addinsell ***Art*** Roger Furse
Act Marilyn Monroe, Laurence Olivier, Sybil Thorndike, Richard Wattis, Jeremy Spenser, Paul Hardwick (Monroe/Warner)

This first indie production of Marilyn Monroe's company is a generally pleasant comedy, but the pace is leisurely. Filmed in London with a predominantly British cast, the film is not a cliche Cinderella story as its title might indicate.

Based on Terence Rattigan's play *The Sleeping Prince*, the story takes place in London in 1911 at the time of the coronation of King George V. Laurence Olivier and his entourage, including his son, the boy king of the Balkan country, and the queen dowager, Olivier's mother-in-law, come to London for the ceremonies. The regent's roving eye alights on Monroe and the British Foreign Office, apprehensive of the delicate balance of power in the Balkan area, makes a determined effort to give the regent what he wants.

To Olivier's credit as producer, director and performer, he achieves the utmost from his material. His own performance as the stuffy regent is flawless. The part of the seemingly naive showgirl is just right for Monroe; she shows a real sense of comedy and can command a laugh with her walk or with an expression. Sybil Thorndike is excellent as the hard-of-hearing not-quite-there dowager; Jeremy Spenser, who bears a remarkable resemblance to Sal Mineo, is appropriately serious as the young king, and Richard Wattis is properly harassed as the British Foreign office representative.

•

PRINCE JACK
1984, 100 mins, US Ⓥ col
Dir Bert Lovitt ***Prod*** Jim Milio ***Scr*** Bert Lovitt ***Ph*** Hiro Narita ***Ed*** Janice Hampton ***Mus*** Elmer Bernstein ***Art*** Michael Corenblith
Act Robert Hogan, James F. Kelly, Kenneth Mars, Lloyd Nolan, Cameron Mitchell, Robert Guillaume (LMF)

Prince Jack is an ambiguous little indie mock documentary about key events and private encounters during the Kennedy years. The ambiguity lies in writer-director Bert Lovitt's wavering between depicting Jack Kennedy as a tough wheeler-dealer and a politician of the grandest vision.

Towards the end, the Cuban missile crisis is solved with Martin Luther King as a go-between.

King is made to be the only thoroughly likable and almost all-around popular guy in this feature, and he is played with cool and quiet charm by Robert Guillaume.

It would seem that the greater policy decisions are depicted fairly correctly (Ole Miss, The Bay of Pigs), while most of the Inner Sanctum private talks in the Oval Office of the White House are obviously based on hearsay and guesswork.

•

PRINCE OF DARKNESS
1987, 101 mins, US Ⓥ ⊙ ▭ col
Dir John Carpenter ***Prod*** Larry Franco ***Scr*** Martin Quatermass [= John Carpenter] ***Ph*** Gary B. Kibbe ***Ed*** Steve Mirkovich ***Mus*** John Carpenter, Alan Howarth ***Art*** Daniel Lomino
Act Donald Pleasence, Jameson Parker, Victor Wong, Lisa Blount, Dennis Dun, Susan Blanchard (Alive/Universal)

The Great Satan doesn't just reside in man's heart of darkness. Instead he lives in an opposite dimension, and manifests himself in this world in . . . bugs. That's about the extent of the horror that John Carpenter conjures up in *Prince of Darkness*.

Carpenter spends so much time turning the screws on the next scare that he completely forsakes his actors, who are already stranded with a shoddy script.

Story takes place in L.A., where physics prof Birack (Victor Wong) takes his graduate class to an abandoned church in the middle of the city. He's summoned there by a priest (Donald Pleasence, who seems to have some secret sorrow), who has discovered inside the church a secret canister, guarded for hundreds of years by a forgotten sect of the Catholic church, the Brotherhood of Sleep.

Canister itself, which is supposed to be the embodiment of all evil, mostly looks like a green slime lava lamp. It starts sliming various students and turning them into zombies, so they can go out and wreak even more havoc.

None of the ensemble really stand out, with lovers Jameson Parker and Lisa Blount never getting a real chance to develop their relationship, and Dennis Dun's Walter completely robbed of his charm through his stilted delivery of equally wooden lines.

•

PRINCE OF EGYPT
1998, 97 mins, US Ⓥ ⊙ col
Dir Brenda Chapman, Steve Hickner, Simon Wells ***Prod*** Penney Finkelman Cox, Sandra Rabins ***Scr*** Philip LaZebnik ***Ed*** Nick Fletcher ***Mus*** Hans Zimmer ***Art*** Darek Gogol (DreamWorks)

Far more than a cartoon rendering of a much-beloved Bible story, DreamWorks' four-years-in-the-making *The Prince of Egypt* proves an outstanding artistic achievement that, along with *Antz*, further ups the ante in high-stakes feature animation. At once rich in historic and character detail and full of eye-popping tableaux, this new spin on the Moses saga admirably refuses to play down to little ones with farcical time-outs—no talking camels or Sphinx-like Siamese, if you please.

An oft-described labor of love for DreamWorks cofounder Jeffrey Katzenberg, who at Disney helped marshal *Beauty and the Beast* and *The Lion King*, this plays like an abbreviated, considerably less vulgar version of the story Cecil B. DeMille filmed twice.

A seamless combination of traditional animation and state-of-the-art CGI, with Semitic-flavored score by Hans Zimmer (*The Lion King*) and original songs by Stephen Schwartz (*Pocahontas*), pic opens masterfully with an audacious eight-minute musical prolog establishing both the majesty and ruthlessness of ancient Egypt.

Central conflicts emerge as Pharaoh (voiced by Patrick Stewart) reminds Rameses (Ralph Fiennes) of his duties as divine successor, and Moses (Val Kilmer), after a chance meeting with his slave sister, Miriam (Sandra Bullock), begins to question his own lineage.

The burning bush encounter and parting of the Red Sea don't disappoint here. Even more impressive is the plague-and-pestilence sequence, which unfolds eerily in monochromatic grays as a ghoulish coil snuffs the life from Egypt's first born.

At 97 minutes, pic is longer than most animated features, but darn-near brisk next to DeMille's nearly four-hour extravaganza. Appropriately, story ends with Moses delivering commandments, just short of DeMille's golden-calf orgy.

•

PRINCE OF FOXES
1949, 107 mins, US Ⓥ b/w
Dir Henry King ***Prod*** Sol C. Siegel ***Scr*** Milton Krims ***Ph*** Leon Shamroy ***Ed*** Barbara McLean ***Mus*** Alfred Newman ***Art*** Lyle Wheeler, Mark-Lee Kirk
Act Tyrone Power, Orson Welles, Wanda Hendrix, Everett Sloane, Katina Paxinou, Felix Aylmes (20th Century-Fox)

Prince of Foxes actually is a fictional incident in the history of the Italian Renaissance general Cesare Borgia, but too often it is slow and plodding in its exposition and execution.

Prince tells of Borgia's lust for power and desire to expand his empire. This he does with all the intrigue and knife-in-the-back knavery at his command.

The Borgiastic episode, despite its 16th-century background, has been conceived and executed in true Capone and Chicago tradition. As the murderous Cesare, Orson Welles is alternately glowering, reposing and diabolical.

Tyrone Power plays Orsini, who assumes the mantle of nobility to achieve social stature and ultimately bests Borgia when he deserts him to join the invaded duchy of the elderly Varano. Wanda Hendrix, as Varano's young wife, gives the weakest of the performances.

1949: NOMINATIONS: Best B&W Cinematography, B&W Costume Design

•

PRINCE OF PLAYERS
1955, 102 mins, US ▭ col
Dir Philip Dunne ***Prod*** Philip Dunne ***Scr*** Moss Hart ***Ph*** Charles G. Clarke ***Ed*** Dorothy Spencer ***Mus*** Bernard Herr-mann
Act Richard Burton, Maggie McNamara, John Derek, Raymond Massey, Charles Bickford, Elizabeth Sellars (20th Century-Fox)

Prince of Players is one of the handsomest and most perfectly composed CinemaScope productions to date. Produced by Philip Dunne, and also his first directing chore, pic tells a powerfully dramatic story of a great American actor of the past—Edwin Booth—and without overaccenting the issue, it weaves into its narrative also the tragic tale of Booth's brother, John Wilkes, who gained fame and infamy by assassinating Lincoln.

Prince is also a serious and for the most part outstandingly successful attempt to make the stage, and specifically Shakespeare, serve the purpose of the screen. There are excerpts, staged with skill and acted masterfully, from *Richard III*, *Romeo and Juliet*, *Hamlet* and *King Lear*.

In the part of Booth, Richard Burton proves why Britain's Old Vic rates him so highly. On stage and off, he etches a portrayal that stands out with its fire and strength.

Maggie McNamara has charm, even though her Juliet pales before the conviction of Burton. Their scene in the garden of a New Orleans brothel, humorous and yet tender and wistful, is a delight. John Derek as John Wilkes Booth comes up with a fine performance. Raymond Massey brings to the tragic figure of Junius Brutus Booth the elder a curious dignity which clashes with his drunk ravings.

•

PRINCE OF THE CITY
1981, 167 mins, US Ⓥ ⊙ col
Dir Sidney Lumet ***Prod*** Burtt Harris ***Scr*** Jay Presson Allen, Sidney Lumet ***Ph*** Andrzej Bartkowiak ***Ed*** John J. Fitzstephens ***Mus*** Paul Chihara ***Art*** Tony Walton
Act Treat Williams, Jerry Orbach, Bob Balaban, Lindsay Crouse, James Tolkan, Lance Henricksen (Warner/Orion)

The film is a concentrated, unrelievedly serious and cerebrally involving entry, exhaustively detailing the true-life saga of a Gotham detective who turned Justice Dept. informer to eke out widespread corruption in his special investigating unit during the 1960s.

Treat Williams is outstanding as the young, gung-ho cop who is courted by federal investigators and finds himself on a conscience-wracking approach-avoidance track that finally leads him to accept the informant role.

As Federal pressure for indictments mounts, however, matters quickly careen out of control and Williams is cajoled, manipulated and ultimately blackmailed into spilling everything, while friends spurn him or commit suicide, his protectors are promoted upstairs, Mafiosi attempt buying him off, then try bumping him off, and the Feds barely agree not to prosecute him for his own past sins.

Within a nightmarish, frequently Kafkaesque atmosphere of intense danger and uncontrollable conscience, the film paints a world where law and morality are only relative commodities.

Director Sidney Lumet is in firm control of the sprawling canvas, showing in spades his ability to harness intense energy and almost uniformly top-rate performances from a cannily cast stable of solid character actors.

1981: NOMINATION: Best Adapted Screenplay

•

PRINCE OF TIDES, THE
1991, 132 mins, US Ⓥ ⊙ col
Dir Barbra Streisand ***Prod*** Barbra Streisand, Andrew Karsch ***Scr*** Pat Conroy, Becky Johnston ***Ph*** Stephen Goldblatt ***Ed*** Don Zimmerman ***Mus*** James Newton Howard ***Art*** Paul Sylbert
Act Nick Nolte, Barbra Streisand, Blythe Danner, Kate Nelligan, Jeroen Krabbe, Melinda Dillon (Columbia/Barwood-Longfellow)

A deeply moving exploration of the tangled emotions of a dysfunctional Southern family, this lovingly crafted (though unevenly scripted) film of Pat Conroy's novel centers on Nick Nolte's performance of a lifetime. Bringing her usual strengths of character to her role as Nolte's psychiatrist/lover, Barbra Streisand marks every frame with the intensity and care of a filmmaker committed to heartfelt, unashamed emotional involvement with her characters.

Ex-teacher/coach Nolte is in a midlife crisis unusually chaotic even for a Nolte character. He's jobless, drinking too much and struggling with a disintegrating marriage to Blythe Danner.

Nolte's disturbed sister Melinda Dillon, a NY poet of some repute, has attempted suicide, and she lies catatonic in hospital restraints. Her brother is summoned north to help Streisand piece together the splintered mirror of her past. In the process, this emotionally guarded doctor finds herself not only becoming Nolte's surrogate mother but also crossing the professional line to emotional and sexual involvement.

Screenwriters underdevelop some characters (especially Dillon) while overdoing the boorishness of Streisand's musician husband (Jeroen Krabbe) and the "Golden Boy" subplot involving her violin-playing son (Jason Gould), who learns football from Nolte. But the heart of the film is the relationship between Nolte and Streisand, a creative sparring match doomed to go nowhere but leaves an indelible imprint on each.

1991: NOMINATIONS: Best Picture, Actor (Nick Nolte), Supp. Actress (Kate Nelligan), Adapted Screenplay, Cinematography, Original Score, Art Direction

•

PRINCESS AND THE PIRATE, THE

1944, 92 mins, US Ⓥ ⦿ col

Dir David Butler ***Prod*** Samuel Goldwyn ***Scr*** Don Hartman, Melville Shavelson, Everett Freeman ***Ph*** Victor Milner, William Snyder ***Ed*** Daniel Mandell ***Mus*** David Rose ***Art*** Ernst Fegte, McClure Capps

Act Bob Hope, Virginia Mayo, Walter Brennan, Walter Slezak, Victor McLaglen, Hugo Haas (RKO/Goldwyn)

Virginia Mayo is the princess, on the lam because she loves a commoner, and Victor McLaglen is the buccaneer of another century who steers his course to capture the beautiful princess as the richest prize yet of his career. Bob Hope is cast as the 18th-century smalltimer who does a protean act—"The Great Sylvester, Man of Seven Faces"—and is admittedly a coward. He wants nought of pirates, whereas the beauteous princess, who is also brave in face of direst danger, bolsters him throughout.

Action is replete with lawlessness in the West Indies, particularly in the dissolute governor's palace, and at the Bucket of Blood, a bistro with a definite Hell's Kitchen clientele where Hope and Mayo do their vaudeville specialty, with the expected comic results.

•

PRINCESS BRIDE, THE

1987, 98 mins, US Ⓥ ⦿ col

Dir Rob Reiner ***Prod*** Andrew Scheinman, Rob Reiner ***Scr*** William Goldman ***Ph*** Adrian Biddle ***Ed*** Robert Leighton ***Mus*** Mark Knopfler ***Art*** Norman Garwood

Act Cary Elwes, Mandy Patinkin, Chris Sarandon, Christopher Guest, Robin Wright, Peter Falk (Act III/20th Century-Fox)

Based on William Goldman's novel, this is a postmodern fairy tale that challenges and affirms the conventions of a genre that may not be flexible enough to support such horseplay.

It also doesn't help that Cary Elwes and Robin Wright as the loving couple are nearly comatose and inspire little passion from each other, or the audience.

Bound together by their love at tender age, young Westley (Elwes) then stableboy, falls in love with his beautiful mistress (Wright), but they're separated when he goes off to sea on a mission. After years of grieving for him she becomes betrothed to the evil Prince Humperdinck (Chris Sarandon) who masterminds her kidnapping to strengthen his own position in the kingdom.

First off, Westley must defeat a trio of kidnappers headed by the diminutive, but slimy, Wallace Shawn. His accomplices are the kind-hearted giant Fezzik (Andre The Giant) and Inigo Montoya, a Spanish warrior (Mandy Patinkin) out to avenge the murder of his father. Patinkin especially is a joy to watch and the film comes to life when his longhaired, scruffy cavalier is on screen.

1987: NOMINATION: Best Song ("Storybook Love")

•

PRINCESS CARABOO

1994, 96 mins, US/UK Ⓥ col

Dir Michael Austin ***Prod*** Andrew Karsch, Simon Bosanquet ***Scr*** Michael Austin, John Wells ***Ph*** Freddie Francis ***Ed*** George Akers ***Mus*** Richard Hartley ***Art*** Michael Howells

Act Phoebe Cates, Jim Broadbent, Wendy Hughes, Kevin Kline, John Lithgow, Stephen Rea (Beacon/Longfellow/Artisan)

Princess Caraboo is an airy bit of historical fluff. Based on a true story, the romantic comedy about a Pacific island princess in 1817 England who may not be for real could be considered Merchant Ivory Lite.

The great costumes and sets are more substantial than the plot and characters.

Princess Caraboo (Phoebe Cates) shows up in a country village unable to speak or write English, but slowly conveys a story of her kidnapping from a royal household and her swimming for safety from a pirate ship off the English coast. The Worralls (Jim Broadbent, Wendy Hughes) see the princess as a means to increase their wealth and prestige. Their problem is Gutch (Stephen Rea), a local reporter who is suspicious of the princess even as he finds himself falling in love.

Kevin Kline milks a supporting role as the Worrall's Greek butler for all it's worth, while John Lithgow is a standout in a featured turn as a skeptical academic.

Equally striking is the location shooting in Wales and western England, which brings the early 19th century to life. But the central story is cotton candy. Cates is charming but looks far too modern for the role.

•

PRINCESS O'ROURKE

1943, 92 mins, US b/w

Dir Norman Krasna ***Prod*** Hal B. Wallis ***Scr*** Norman Krasna ***Ph*** Ernest Haller ***Ed*** Warren Low

Act Olivia de Havilland, Robert Cummings, Charles Coburn, Jack Carson, Jane Wyman (Warner)

Princess O'Rourke is a spritely, effervescing and laugh-explosive comedy-romance. Credit for general sparkle and excellence of the picture must be tossed to Norman Krasna, who handled the writing and directing responsibilities. It's Krasna's initial directing assignment.

Krasna provides numerous humorous and novel twists to the tale of an American who falls in love with a girl after a whirlwind romance, and then discovers she's a refugee princess of European royalty. After approval for marriage has been given to cement relations of the two countries, the boy balks at renouncing his American citizenship.

Picture unfolds at a spontaneously fast pace, with Krasna studding the proceedings with toppling laughs most of the way. Final 20 minutes, when levity must be tossed aside for proper decorum within the walls of the White House, slows down considerably, but previous pace carries momentum through the romantic windup successfully.

Olivia de Havilland shines brightly as the girl, with Robert Cummings getting equal prominence for excellent portrayal of the airline pilot.

•

PRINCE VALIANT

1954, 100 mins, US Ⓥ ▭ col

Dir Henry Hathaway ***Prod*** Robert L. Jacks ***Scr*** Dudley Nichols ***Ph*** Lucien Ballard ***Ed*** Robert Simpson ***Mus*** Franz Waxman

Act James Mason, Janet Leigh, Robert Wagner, Debra Paget, Sterling Hayden, Victor McLaglen (20th Century-Fox)

The cartoon strip hero comes to the screen as a good offering for fans who dote on the fanciful derring-do of the Arthurian period.

Harold Foster's King Features strip gives an imaginative action basis for Robert L. Jacks's production guidance and the direction by Henry Hathaway. Although the picture comes in a bit overlength, the direction and Dudley Nichols's scripting combine to bring it off acceptably against some rather dazzling settings, including authentic castles and sites actually lensed in England.

Heading the star list is James Mason, who plays Sir Brack, pretender to King Arthur's throne. His dirty work is excellent, whether thinking up ambushes for Robert Wagner, in the title role, or engaging the young hero in joust or broadsword combat. The way he and Mason have at each other in the climaxing duel puts a topnotch action capper on the tale.

The plot finds Wagner in exile with his royal parents after their throne was seized by Primo Carnera. The Viking prince goes to King Arthur's court, becomes a squire to Sir Gawain, falls in love with Janet Leigh and, eventually, is able to put the finger on Mason as the mysterious Black Knight.

•

PRISON

1988, 102 mins, US Ⓥ ⦿ col

Dir Renny Harlin ***Prod*** Irwin Yablans ***Scr*** C. Courtney Joyner ***Ph*** Mac Ahlberg ***Ed*** Ted Nicolaou ***Mus*** Richard Band ***Art*** Phillip Duffin

Act Lane Smith, Viggo Mortensen, Chelsea Field, Andre De Shields, Lincoln Kilpatrick (Empire)

Starring as the prison in this rough penal pic with its special effects-laden horror story is the 87-year-old Wyoming State Penitentiary, which has attracted tourists rather than cons since 1981. The structure takes on all the menace of the house in *Amityville Horror* or hotel in *The Shining*.

The crumbling stone fortress is grounds for revenge because, as aged inmate Cresus (Lincoln Kilpatrick) points out toward the end, "things won't stay buried." It turns out that in 1964 guard Ethan Sharpe (Lane Smith) watched an innocent man fry in the electric chair.

Sharpe, now a warden, is appointed to the prison's helm despite recurrent nightmares brought on by a guilty conscience. The wronged convict's evil spirit is mad enough to eliminate a few of the new guards and inmates.

Viggo Mortensen plays Burke, a James Dean type antihero spared death but not a lot of bumps and bruises. His resemblance to the electrocuted con apparently is just a coincidence in the screenplay of producer Irwin Yablans's story.

•

PRISONER, THE

1955, 94 mins, UK Ⓥ b/w

Dir Peter Glenville ***Prod*** Vivian A. Cox ***Scr*** Bridget Boland ***Ph*** Reginald Wyer ***Ed*** Freddie Wilson ***Mus*** Benjamin Frankel ***Art*** John Hawkesworth

Act Alec Guinness, Jack Hawkins, Wilfrid Lawson, Jeannette Sterke, Ronald Lewis, Raymond Huntley (Columbia)

Closely following the Bridget Boland play, this British filmization retains the essentials of this stark and dramatic narrative with Alec Guinness repeating his original role of the cardinal held on a phoney charge of treason.

In her own adaptation, Boland has broadened the canvas of her subject, particularly to include background atmosphere of unrest in the capital while the cardinal is held without charge.

Peter Glenville's studied direction is a technical achievement, although the film just fails to achieve the anticipated emotional impact. The acting, however, is exceptionally high. The flawless performance by Guinness is matched by a superb portrayal by Jack Hawkins. But both of these stars find their equal in Wilfrid Lawson's interpretation of the jailor.

•

PRISONER OF SECOND AVENUE, THE

1974, 98 mins, US Ⓥ ▭ col

Dir Melvin Frank ***Prod*** Melvin Frank ***Scr*** Neil Simon ***Ph*** Philip Lathrop ***Ed*** Bob Wyman ***Mus*** Marvin Hamlisch ***Art*** Preston Ames

Act Jack Lemmon, Anne Bancroft, Gene Saks, Elizabeth Wilson, Florence Stanley, Macine Stuart (Warner)

Neil Simon's play *The Prisoner of Second Avenue* has Jack Lemmon and Anne Bancroft as a harried urban couple. The film is more of a drama with comedy, for the personal problems as well as the environmental challenges aren't really funny, and even some of the humor is forced and strident.

Lemmon has done prior Simon plots on the screen, and he has the same basic character down cold. Bancroft demonstrates a fine versatility in facing the script demands. Atop the couple's problems in their apartment comes Lemmon's axing after many years on the job.

Gene Saks, Elizabeth Wilson and Florence Stanley do well as Lemmon's brother and sisters, while Ed Peck, the hostile upstairs neighbor, and Ivor Francis, Lemmon's taciturn shrink, head a good supporting cast.

•

PRISONER OF SHARK ISLAND, THE

1936, 95 mins, US Ⓥ b/w

Dir John Ford ***Prod*** Darryl F. Zanuck ***Scr*** Nunnally Johnson ***Ph*** Bert Glennon ***Ed*** Jack Murray ***Mus*** Hugo Friedhofer, R. H. Bassett ***Art*** William Darling

Act Warner Baxter, Gloria Stuart, Claude Gillingwater, Arthur Byron, Harry Carey, Francis Ford (20th Century-Fox)

Warner Baxter as Dr Samuel A. Mudd, "America's Jean Valjean" of the post-Civil War hysteria, turns in a capital performance as the titular prisoner of "America's Devil's Island."

The sympathetic trouping of Gloria Stuart as Dr. Mudd's plucky wife who constantly endeavors to win back biased public favor for her unjustly condemned husband, plus the effective injection of a new kid charmer (Joyce Kay) as their baby daughter does much to achieve some mixed sympathies, but by and large it's a film for the men.

Not wholly a figment of Hollywood imagination, the saga of Dr. Mudd is founded on fact. Baxter's woes start when he unknowingly sets the broken leg of John Wilkes Booth, Lincoln's assassin. Accused of conspiracy in the crime, he is court-martialed and, of eight co-defendants, three are hung and Dr. Mudd is among those committed to Shark Island for life. Casting is tiptop. John Carradine stands out as a new face among especially sinister heavies, a highly effective villain. Frank McGlynn, Sr., in his Abraham Lincoln personation is, as ever, realistic in dignified portrayal and uncanny resemblance to the martyred liberator.

•

PRISONER OF ZENDA, THE

1922, 130 mins, US ⊗ b/w

Dir Rex Ingram ***Prod*** Rex Ingram ***Scr*** Mary O'Hara ***Ph*** John F. Seitz

Act Lewis Stone, Alice Terry, Robert Edeson, Stuart Holmes, Barbara La Marr, Lois Lee (Metro)

To say that Rex Ingram and a remarkably good company of screen players have made the very utmost of the possibilities of Anthony Hope's novel about sums up this venture. It is the kind of romance that never stales—fresh, genuine, simple and wholesome. Indeed this screen translation is more profoundly interesting than either the novel or the Edward Rose stage play.

Ingram built a spacious ballroom with an atmosphere of unobtrusive splendor. For once you get the illusion that it is a royal ball and not a movie mob scene.

Another bit of finesse is the choice of the hero and heroine, in Lewis Stone, who makes no pretence to Apollo-like beauty, and Alice Terry who makes a Princess Flavia of surpassing blonde loveliness in her regal robes.

The close-ups of all the characters are done in a misty dimness that gives them a remoteness that inspires the imagination. Some of the landscapes are handled in like manner and throughout the photography is marked.

•

PRISONER OF ZENDA, THE

1937, 100 mins, US Ⓥ b/w

Dir John Cromwell ***Prod*** David O. Selznick ***Scr*** John L. Balderston, Donald Ogden Stewart ***Ph*** James Wong Howe ***Ed*** Hal C. Kern, James E. Newcom ***Mus*** Alfred Newman ***Art*** Lyle Wheeler

Act Ronald Colman, Madeleine Carroll, Douglas Fairbanks, Jr., Mary Astor, David Niven, Raymond Massey (Selznick/United Artists)

Zenda is hokum of the 24-carat variety [from Anthony Hope's novel, dramatized by Edward Rose; script adaptation by Wells Root]; a sheer piece of romantic nonsense about a mythical European kingdom, a struggle for possession of a throne between a dissolute true heir and an ambitious step-brother with larcenous inclinations; a lovely blonde princess; a swashbuckling duke, who bends with the political wind, and a young Englishman, on his annual outing, who is persuaded to impersonate the king.

Cromwell's direction is excellent. His opening scenes in the Balkan capital are as casual as a travelog, and his players assume lifelike characterizations through a series of intimate, human situations.

Colman (who plays the dual role of Englishman and King) has the ability to make a full dress court uniform appear as comfortable as a suit of pajamas. He never trips over his sword, or loosens his collar for air.

Madeleine Carroll in all her blonde loveliness is quite receptive to impassioned protestations, so the romance has a touch of verity.

It's a close race between Colman and Fairbanks, Jr., who plays Rupert of Hentzau for top acting honours. Best femme part is the scheming Antoinette, which Mary Astor is inclined to underplay.

1937: NOMINATIONS: Best Art Direction, Score

•

PRISONER OF ZENDA, THE

1952, 100 mins, US Ⓥ col

Dir Richard Thorpe ***Prod*** Pandro S. Berman ***Scr*** John L. Balderston, Noel Langley ***Ph*** Joseph Ruttenberg ***Ed*** George Boemler ***Mus*** Alfred Newman ***Art*** Cedric Gibbons, Hans Peters

Act Stewart Granger, Deborah Kerr, James Mason, Louis Calhern, Jane Greer, Lewis Stone (M-G-M)

Fanciers of costumed swashbucklers will find this remake of the venerable *Prisoner of Zenda* a likeable version. The third time around for the yarn [adapted by Wells Root from the novel by Anthony Hope and dramatization by Edward Rose] this time it wears Tehnicolor dress, and has lavish physical appurtenances.

Plot deals with an Englishman who goes on a holiday to the small kingdom of Ruritania and gets involved in a royal impersonation and a love affair with a beautiful princess. Stewart Granger is the hero, dualing as the Englishman and the king he impersonates, and gives the roles the proper amount of dashing heroics.

Opposite him is Deborah Kerr, the lovely princess, and her looks and ability to wear period gowns are just what the part requires. James Mason scores as Rupert of Hentzau, making the character a rather likeable heavy.

Lewis Stone, who played the dual role in the original 1922 version of the story, appears briefly in this one as a cardinal.

•

PRIVATE AFFAIRS OF BEL AMI, THE

1947, 110 mins, US Ⓥ col

Dir Albert Lewin ***Prod*** David L. Loew ***Scr*** Albert Lewin ***Ph*** Russell Metty ***Ed*** Albrecht Joseph ***Mus*** Darius Milhaud ***Art*** Gordon Wiles

Act George Sanders, Angela Lansbury, Ann Dvorak, Frances Dee, John Carradine, Susan Douglas (Loew-Lewin)

Confronted with the old problem of cleaning up a classic novel to conform to strict censorship codes, the production outfit has come up with a scrubbed-face version of the complete scoundrel depicted in Guy de Maupassant's novel *Private Affairs of Bel Ami.* The title character pays for his sins by being killed in a duel which he brought on himself, in strict compliance with the production's code of "crime doesn't pay." Prosties, which had a feature part in the story, emerge as dancers of questionable character.

Entire tempo of the story is slow-paced. Director Albert Lewin's script builds up little sympathy for George Sanders, the Bel Ami of the piece, who climbs to the top of Paris social and political circles in the 1880s over the broken hearts of five women whom he uses to advance himself and then discards.

Cast is exceptionally strong and, under Lewin's skilled direction, is mostly responsible for the film's merits. Sanders plays it with the correct hammy touch, emoting with de Maupassant epigrams for sock effect. Angela Lansbury is beauteous and competent as the young widow with whom he's probably in love all the time. Ann Dvorak, Frances Dee, Susan Douglas, Katherine Emery and Marie Wilson all show well as the other women in his path. John Carradine, as the comrade, and Hugo Haas and Albert Basserman handle the male roles in okay fashion.

Painting of *The Temptation of Saint Anthony*, by Max Ernst, which forms one of the focal points of the story a la *Dorian Gray*, is flashed on the screen the first time it's shown in brilliant Technicolor for good effect. Darius Milhaud's score is excellent and Russell Metty's camera work, spotlighting shadows and gas-lit interiors, is good.

•

PRIVATE BENJAMIN

1980, 109 mins, US Ⓥ ⊙ col

Dir Howard Zieff ***Prod*** Nancy Meyers, Charles Shyer, Harvey Miller ***Scr*** Nancy Meyers, Charles Shyer, Harvey Miller ***Ph*** David M. Walsh ***Ed*** Sheldon Kahn ***Mus*** Bill Conti ***Art*** Robert Boyle

Act Goldie Hawn, Eileen Brennan, Armand Assante, Sam Wanamaker, Harry Dean Stanton, Robert Webber (Warner/Meyers-Shyler-Miller)

Goldie Hawn's venture in producing her own film is actually a double feature—one is a frequently funny tale of an innocent who is conned into joining the U.S. Army and her adventures therein; the other deals with the same innocent's personality problems as a Jewish princess with only an intermittent chuckle to help out.

The trouble may be with the use of too many screenwriters who have been told to always keep their star's image uppermost in their scribblings. But she's not so gifted that she can carry a heavy load of indifferent material on her own two little shoulders, without considerable sagging.

Another script problem is that the supporting characters are, even when they start out sympathetically, turned into unlikeable types.

1980: NOMINATIONS: Best Actress (Goldie Hawn), Supp. Actress (Eileen Brennan), Original Screenplay

•

PRIVATE FILES OF J. EDGAR HOOVER, THE

1977, 112 mins, US Ⓥ col

Dir Larry Cohen ***Prod*** Larry Cohen ***Scr*** Larry Cohen ***Ph*** Paul Glickman ***Ed*** Christopher Lebenzon ***Mus*** Miklos Rozsa ***Art*** Cathy Davis

Act Broderick Crawford, Jose Ferrer, Michael Parks, Ronee Blakely, Rip Torn, Celeste Holm (Larco)

According to Larry Cohen, who wrote, produced and directed this $3 million look at America's top cop, J. Edgar Hoover was a public relations gimmick. As a vindictive, puritanical paranoid he shipped agents off to Knoxville for reading *Playboy* magazine. Privately, he was a mama's boy and a homosexual who got his jollies by sitting in the dark with a bottle of bourbon and a tape recorder playing the sounds of a powerful government official's hotel liaisons.

This may be the motion picture industry's first historical horror story. Cohen has adopted two visual styles. There's the "backlot look" used to reenact great moments in J. Edgar Hoover's life, like the shooting of John Dillinger in front of the Biograph Theatre in Chicago and Hoover's first arrest.

Then there's the documentary look: Hoover in the FBI building; that's the real FBI building. Hoover in the apartment of his lifelong friend Lionel McCoy; that's the real McCoy's apartment.

He also knew enough to cast Broderick Crawford in the lead. As Hoover, the jowly Crawford turns in a fine performance. However, the remainder of the performances, starting with Michael Parks's Robert Kennedy, are grotesque attempts to mimic well known public officials.

•

PRIVATE FUNCTION, A

1984, 93 mins, UK Ⓥ col

Dir Malcolm Mowbray ***Prod*** Mark Shivas ***Scr*** Alan Bennett ***Ph*** Tony Pierce-Roberts ***Ed*** Barrie Vince ***Mus*** John Du Prez ***Art*** Stuart Walker

Act Michael Palin, Maggie Smith, Liz Smith, Denholm Elliott, Richard Griffiths, John Normington (HandMade)

Pic is set in 1947, at a time of national rejoicing over a royal wedding and hardship caused by food rationing. Plot evolves out of a plan hatched by a group of town notables to fatten up a secret pig for festive devouring on the wedding night.

Central characters are a husband and wife team played by Maggie Smith and Michael Palin. She's a bullying wife anxious to reach the social highspots in the Yorkshire village where he works as a foot doctor. Their domestic crises are made more complex and amusing by the presence of a greedy mother (Liz Smith) who lives in terror of being put away.

Director Malcolm Mowbray neatly orchestrates the resulting drama, and points up the class antagonisms at play.

•

PRIVATE LESSONS

1981, 87 mins, US Ⓥ ⊙ col

Dir Alan Myerson, [James Fargo] ***Prod*** R. Ben Efraim ***Scr*** Dan Greenburg ***Ph*** Jan De Bont ***Ed*** Fred Chulack

Act Sylvia Kristel, Howard Hesseman, Ron Foster, Eric Brown, Pamela Bryant, Ed Begley, Jr. (Jensen Farley)

Private Lessons is a novelty comedy limning an adolescent boy's introduction to sex via his worldly European housekeeper. Suffering from a rickety structure that reflects extensive production problems (James Fargo directed additional footage sans credit), picture has a sustained air of amorality which is quite unusual for U.S. films.

Story is set at a ritzy mansion in idyllic Arizona during summer vacation, with premise of Mr. Fillmore (Ron Foster) leaving orders that his beautiful housekeeper (Sylvia Kristel) initiate his 15-year-old son Philly (Eric Brown) to sex before he returns from a business trip.

Dan Greenburg's script from his own novel [*Philly*] is very effective in presenting an innocent youth's point-of-view confronted with the sexual stimuli that pervade modern society. Inability to flesh out this central notion into a feature-length screenplay is a pity, but *Private Lessons* should satisfy general audiences with its diversions of frequent nudity, softcore sex, dominant rock music score and gags.

As Philly, Brown successfully carries the picture with a warm performance. Kristel is a beautiful dream-woman, but play-acting role here does not tap her thesping abilities. Although Kristel bares her breasts frequently, an unmatched stunt double [Judy Helden] is used for her disconcertingly in several of the nude scenes.

•

PRIVATE LIFE OF DON JUAN, THE

1934, 89 mins, UK Ⓥ b/w

Dir Alexander Korda ***Prod*** Alexander Korda ***Scr*** Frederick Lonsdale, Lajos Biro ***Ph*** Georges Perinal, Robert Krasskor ***Ed*** Harold Young, Stephen Harrison ***Mus*** Mischa Spoliansky, Arthur Wimperis, Arthur Benjamin ***Art*** Vincent Korda

Act Douglas Fairbanks, Merle Oberon, Binnie Barnes, Joan Gardner, Benita Hume, Barry Mackay (London/United Artists)

Douglas Fairbanks's prime portrayal is as the antiquated knight who is finally disillusioned as the arch-heartbreaker when he must bow to his years and recognize that his amorous porch-climbing career is finis.

But the film holds more than that. There are many fine lights and shadings to get over the fact that the susceptible Seville femmes, who were not loath to two-timing their senors, had glorified Don Juan into an almost mythical figure.

Fairbanks is first introduced as a bit weary and slightly ill cavalier. All the faithful illusion is maintained to impress upon the viewer that he is still the potent Don Juan of history, excepting that he happens to have become a bit fatigued. His faithful retainer, his cook, his masseur, all his aides, are shown jealously watching over him.

There's even planted the premise of Fairbanks being irked with the wife (Benita Hume) whom, he complains, has been too possessive of late; so much so that it's been cramping his style.

Fairbanks, stacked beside some nifty lookers—Merle Oberon, Binnie Barnes, Joan Gardner, Hume, Patricia Hilliard, Diana Napier, Natalie Lelong (Princess Paley), Betty Hamilton, Toto Koopman, Spencer Trevor, Nancy Jones and Florence Wood—makes for an incongruous impression. Georges Perinal, Rene Clair's ace camera-grinder, in this, his first away from French productions, has fashioned some fine stuff.

•

PRIVATE LIFE OF HELEN OF TROY, THE
1927, 87 mins, US ⊗ b/w
Dir Alexander Korda ***Prod*** Carey Wilson ***Scr*** Carey Wilson ***Ph*** Lee Garmes, Sid Hickox ***Ed*** Harold Young
Act Maria Corda, Lewis Stone, Ricardo Cortez, George Fawcett, Alice White (First National)

Helen [based on the novel by John Erskine] is all comedy. Satirizing ancient myth in general and Helen's affairs particularly, the titles are topical, while the music is mainly based on pop dance tunes. Wheeling the giant wooden horse inside the gates of Troy is accomplished to the strains of "Horses, Horses, Horses," etc.

The film kids the husband-wife complex throughout, the king, following the conquest of Troy, making a beeline for Helen's dressmaker to destroy the shop. Meanwhile, he has been trying to go fishing since nine o'clock. When it looks as if Helen is about to take another vacation with her second prince, the king is convinced he's going to get in his trip, and that finishes the picture.

No battles and no slow spots. The action is lively all the way, with Maria Corda in various stages of slight clothing.

1927/28: NOMINATION: Best Engineering Effects

•

PRIVATE LIFE OF HENRY VIII, THE
1933, 96 mins, UK Ⓥ ⦿ b/w
Dir Alexander Korda ***Prod*** Alexander Korda ***Scr*** Lajos Biro, Arthur Wimperis ***Ph*** Georges Perinal ***Ed*** Harold Young, Stephen Harrison ***Mus*** Kurt Schroeder ***Art*** Vincent Korda
Act Charles Laughton, Binnie Barnes, Merle Oberon, Elsa Lanchester, Wendy Barrie, Robert Donat (London)

Unquestionably the perfect pick for the part, it must also be said that Charles Laughton is aided no little by the script, more generous to the character of Henry VIII than most of his biographers. The corpulent ruler is here made rather a jolly old soul and, for those who may have forgotten, it can be said that he had six wives, of whom the picture concerns itself with five. A couple are inclined to beat about the royal bush, so they thereby lose their heads for being promiscuous.

Laughton is happily supported right down the line, especially by Merle Oberon, Binnie Barnes, Robert Donat and Elsa Lanchester. The fair Barnes shares with Lanchester the major portion of footage devoted to the wives while Oberon is a British edition of Fay Wray.

Of comedy highlights audiences will probably like best the card game between Henry and Anne of Cleves (Lanchester), in which she takes him for almost half his kingdom, and the ruler at the banquet table. It being the open season for belching, Laughton demonstrates that he is equally as adept in this as at giving the 'berry [*If I Had a Million*, 1932].

1932/33: Best Actor (Charles Laughton)

NOMINATION: Best Picture

•

PRIVATE LIFE OF SHERLOCK HOLMES, THE
1970, 125 mins, UK Ⓥ ⦿ ▭ col
Dir Billy Wilder ***Prod*** Billy Wilder ***Scr*** Billy Wilder, I.A.L. Diamond ***Ph*** Christopher Challis ***Ed*** Ernest Walter ***Mus*** Miklos Rozsa ***Art*** Alexandre Trauner
Act Robert Stephens, Colin Blakely, Genevieve Page, Christopher Lee, Tomara Toumanova, Clive Revill (Mirisch/United Artists)

Billy Wilder's enterprise is a strange one because of its shift in directions from quite good satire to straight spy stuff. It is in large part old-fashioned, in that it's mile-wide and ancient-history Sherlock Holmes, but it's also handsomely produced and directed with incisiveness by Wilder.

Robert Stephens is the detective consultant, the man from Baker Street who fakes a story about his being not all masculine to duck out on an assignment from a Russian ballerina. But is he really faking? Stephens plays Sherlock in rather gay fashion under Wilder's tongue-in-cheek direction. Colin Blakely is Dr. John H. Watson; a performer who plays it broad and bright.

The dialog is crisp and amusing, Wilder and I.A.L. Diamond having a way with such matters.

•

PRIVATE LIVES
1931, 82 mins, US b/w
Dir Sidney Franklin ***Scr*** Hans Kraly, Richard Schayer, Claudine West ***Ph*** Ray Binger ***Ed*** Conrad A. Nervig
Act Norma Shearer, Robert Montgomery, Reginald Denny, Una Merkel, Jean Hersholt (M-G-M)

Sidney Franklin has followed the Noel Coward play closely with the addition of a number of interpolated scenes and the changing of the final locale from a Paris apartment to a Swiss chalet. Both Norma Shearer and Robert Montgomery capably handle themselves as the divorced couple who again run away together the night of their honeymoons with their newly acquired better halves. Both having tempestuous natures, their love making and quarreling is equally violent and the warfare is apt to start any time.

As the somewhat neurotic man in the case, Montgomery plays deftly and well. So does Shearer, but the medium of the screen has lost many of the laugh lines which did much to sustain the play. However, Franklin establishes and maintains a good pace after a rather slow start.

•

PRIVATE LIVES OF ELIZABETH AND ESSEX, THE
1939, 106 mins, US Ⓥ col
Dir Michael Curtiz ***Prod*** Hal B. Wallis (exec.) ***Scr*** Norman Reilly Raine, Aeneas MacKenzie ***Ph*** Sol Polito, W. Howard Greene ***Ed*** Owen Marks ***Mus*** Erich Wolfgang Korngold ***Art*** Anton Grot
Act Bette Davis, Errol Flynn, Olivia de Havilland, Vincent Price, Donald Crisp, Alan Hale (Warner)

The Private Lives of Elizabeth and Essex is a lavishly produced historical drama, the first picture to be released using the new fast Technicolor negative, and improved processing methods.

Bette Davis dominates the production at every turn as Elizabeth, virgin queen of England. Her delineation would indicate that Davis did much personal research.

Picture is a film version of Maxwell Anderson's [stage play] *Elizabeth the Queen*. Story details the intimate May-and-December love affair of youthful Lord Essex (Errol Flynn) and matronly Queen Elizabeth. Both are headstrong and stubborn; each is ambitious to rule England.

Picture has its slow spots, particularly the excursion of Essex to Ireland to subdue Tyrone (Alan Hale). At times the dialog becomes brittle, and direction grooves into stagey passages that could have been lightened. Minor shortcomings, however, in the general excellence of the production.

1939: NOMINATIONS: Best Color Cinematography, Color Art Direction, Score, Sound, Special Effects

•

PRIVATE NAVY OF SGT. O'FARRELL, THE
1958, 92 mins, US col
Dir Frank Tashlin ***Prod*** John Beck ***Scr*** Frank Tashlin ***Ph*** Alan Stensvold ***Ed*** Eda Warren ***Mus*** Harry Sukman ***Art*** Bob Kinoshita
Act Bob Hope, Phyllis Diller, Jeffrey Hunter, Mylene Demongeot, Gina Lollobrigida, Mako (NAHO)

The Private Navy of Sgt. O'Farrell is an okay, but crudely plotted comedy set in World War II, routinely directed by Frank Tashlin from his awkward screenplay.

Tashlin's script, from a John L. Greene–Robert M. Fresco story, has Bob Hope as one of these stock all-knowing, all-wise paternal non-coms, herein looking out for the morale of his troops. Site is a South Pacific island, around which the war and the action have detoured. Seems a cargo ship loaded with beer has been torpedoed, and Hope fears a dip in morale unless the booze is found.

Diller is a daffy civilian nurse, not quite the morale-lifter Hope had anticipated. Jeffrey Hunter is a junior naval officer. Gina Lollobrigida is an old Hope sweetie with whom he split in a flashback to a Hawaiian beach rendezvous, moments before the Pearl Harbor attack. She pops up again—goddess-ex-machina—adrift on a raft, with niece Mylene Demongeot.

References to Bing Crosby (appearing in an old clip), a takeoff on the Burt Lancaster–Deborah Kerr beach scene in *From Here to Eternity* and satirical subtitles, plus occasional good gags from assorted players, make the 92 minutes sporadically enjoyable.

•

PRIVATE POTTER
1963, 89 mins, UK b/w
Dir Caspar Wrede ***Prod*** Ben Arbeid ***Scr*** Ronald Harwood, Caspar Wrede ***Ph*** Arthur Lavis ***Ed*** John Pomeroy ***Mus*** George Hall
Act Tom Courtenay, James Maxwell, Ralph Michael, Brewster Mason, Ronald Fraser, Mogens Wieth (M-G-M)

This film is an egghead pic that doesn't quite come off. Yarn has a strong, imaginative idea but tails away inconclusively and falls between two stools, not quite arty, not quite commercial.

Tom Courtenay plays an inexperienced young soldier who screams in terror while on patrol that is tracking down a terrorist leader on a Mediterranean island. As a result, the mission misfires and a colleague is killed. The young soldier excuses himself with the plea that he saw a vision of God. Question that arises is whether he is to be court-martialled for cowardice or whether, in fact, he did have this religious experience. And, if so, whether or not he should be punished.

It is the conflicting clash of army regulations and men's consciences which intrigue. But the young solider's character is never clearly defined and the film eventually flounders in speculation and conjecture.

Courtenay acts with some imagination but best performance comes from James Maxwell, as his commanding officer. Gradually he begins to believe in the lad's story and then his own conscience starts to interfere. Ralph Michael, as the padre; Brewster Mason, as the brigadier, who lives by army regulations; and Ronald Fraser, as a cheery doctor, also give vivid performances.

•

PRIVATE'S PROGRESS
1956, 102 mins, UK Ⓥ b/w
Dir John Boulting ***Prod*** John Boulting, Roy Boulting ***Scr*** Frank Harvey, John Boulting ***Ph*** Eric Cross ***Ed*** Anthony Harvey ***Mus*** John Addison
Act Richard Attenborough, Dennis Price, Terry-Thomas, Ian Carmichael, Peter Jones, William Hartnell (Charter/British Lion)

As a lighthearted satire on British army life during the last war, *Private's Progress* has moments of sheer joy based on real authenticity. But it is not content to rest on satire alone and introduces an unreal melodramatic adventure which robs the story of much of its charm. The Boulting Brothers obviously felt there must be some point to the plot and they've added an adventure tailpiece in which a War Office brigadier invades enemy territory to bring back valuable art treasures to Britain.

The basic comedy, however, derives from the depiction of the typical misfit into the army way of life. Ian Carmichael is shown as the earnest university student who interrupts his studies to join the forces. He is a lamentable failure.

Many weaknesses of the yarn are surmounted by the allround performances of the cast. Carmichael does remarkably well. Richard Attenborough is in confident mood as a private who soon gets to know his way around. Dennis Price gives a smooth study as the brigadier.

•

PRIVATE WORLDS
1935, 84 mins, US b/w
Dir Gregory La Cava ***Prod*** Walter Wanger ***Scr*** Lynn Starling ***Ph*** Leon Shamroy ***Ed*** Aubrey Scotto
Act Claudette Colbert, Charles Boyer, Joan Bennett, Joel McCrea, Helen Vinson, Samuel S. Hinds (Paramount)

Set against a morbid background, that of a mental hospital, *Private Worlds* skirts the clinical and the laboratory aspects, emphasizes the romanticism and the melodramatics.

Director Gregory La Cava has done a highly sensitized transmutation of Phyllis Bottome's 1934 bestseller of the same name, and Lynn Starling rates a bouquet for the equally careful adaptation.

The sanatorium where psychiatrists Claudette Colbert, Charles Boyer and Joel McCrea are thrown together is kept in a sufficiently country-clubby atmosphere without becoming unfaithful to authenticity. The mental maelstroms which some of the patients must meet are introduced solely for allegorical purpose, as the instance where Dr. Jane Everest (Colbert) copes with Big Boy Williams, playing a burly inmate in an ugly mood. Colbert's performance is among her tops. She manifests her usual restraint and intelligently gets across the spirit of her own little "private world"—that of nurturing a romance with a shadow of the past, a boy who lost his life in the war.

Charles Boyer's private world has been the shielding of his murderess-sister (capably played by Helen Vinson) who, although acquitted, is seemingly guilty of the "fall" which took the life of his best friend, her husband.

Joel McCrea's private world as co-worker with Colbert and his unintentional neglect of his domestic life is similarly depicted in intelligent vein. Joan Bennett as his wife is at her dramatic best.

•

PRIVILEGE
1967, 103 mins, UK Ⓥ col
Dir Peter Watkins ***Prod*** John Heyman ***Scr*** Norman Bogner ***Ph*** Peter Suschitzky ***Ed*** John Trumper ***Mus*** Mike Leander ***Art*** Bill Brodie

Act Paul Jones, Jean Shrimpton, Mark London, William Job (Rank-Universal/World-Film/Memorial)

In *Privilege*, Paul Jones, erstwhile singer with the Manfred Mann Group, makes his acting debut. Maybe it's the fault of writer, director or both but Jones plays the role of the bewildered, disillusioned singer on one note of unanimated distaste.

Trouble with *Privilege* is that it cannot make up its mind whether it's a crusading film for the intelligentsia or a snide, "with it" comedy.

A coalition government encourages the violence of the act of pop idol Steve Shorter (Jones) as a means of guiding the violence of Britain's youth into controllable channels. Then, cynically, it's decided that his image must be changed and he is taken from the ordinary scene of putting over national-interest commercials and selling consumer goods to his worshipping fans and exploited by the Church as a kind of godlike hot gospeller.

But the best angles of the pic are those which turn a cynical and only too accurate searchlight on the pop music scene and those who batten on a minimal talent, plus the gullibity of the fans.

•

PRIZE, THE

1963, 135 mins, US Ⓥ ▭ col

Dir Mark Robson *Prod* Pandro S. Berman *Scr* Ernest Lehman *Ph* William H. Daniels *Ed* Adrienne Fazan *Mus* Jerry Goldsmith *Art* George W. Davis, Urie McCleary

Act Paul Newman, Edward G. Robinson, Elke Sommer, Diane Baker, Micheline Presle, Gerard Oury (M-G-M/Roxbury)

Stockholm during Nobel week is the setting for Irving Wallace's smorgasbord novel. In Ernest Lehman's Hitchcockeyed screenplay, seven selected prizewinners convene to receive the award. The man from literature (Paul Newman) senses something amiss in the behavior and physique of the man from physics (Edward G. Robinson), proceeds to snoop around for clues and ends up in a wild goose chase, with himself as the goose who almost gets cooked.

The Prize is a suspense melodrama played for laughs. Trouble is the basic comedy approach clashes with the political-topical framework of the story. Although limited as a comic actor and confronted here with a rather difficult and unsubstantial character to portray, Newman tackles his task with sufficient vivacity to keep an audience concerned for his welfare and amused by his antics. Robinson achieves a persuasive degree of contrast in his dual role.

Elke Sommer, as an attache who gets attached to Newman, hasn't a very scintillating role, but has the looks to make that a secondary issue.

Mark Robson's direction generates a lot of excitement, humor and suspense in spots, but this is offset by hokey elements, occasional exaggerations and stripping of dramatic gears as the film fluctuates between its incompatible components.

•

PRIZE OF ARMS, A

1962, 105 mins, UK b/w

Dir Cliff Owen *Prod* George Maynard *Scr* Paul Ryder *Ph* Gilbert Taylor, Gerald Gibbs *Ed* John Jympson *Mus* Robert Sharples *Art* Jim Morahan, Bernard Sarron

Act Stanley Baker, Helmut Schmid, Tom Bell, Tom Adams, Anthony Bate (RLC/British Lion)

Stanley Baker's carefully laid scheme for knocking off a $700,000 army payroll seems unnecessarily complicated. This seems to shriek out for mishaps. But Paul Ryder's screenplay [from an original story by Nicolas Roeg and Kevin Kavanagh] is smoothly efficient even though audiences are too often left in the dark about details. Baker plays an ex-army captain who has been cashiered for Black Market activities in Hamburg. While in the army he has dreamed up a perfect plan for revenge (and to get rich). He has enlisted the help of Helmut Schmid, an explosives expert, and Tom Bell, a daring but edgy young man.

Baker learns that an army is preparing to go abroad at the time of the Suez crisis. He realizes that when troops are on the move abroad they have to take money with them. The trio plan to hijack the dough while the forces are moving towards the docks.

Baker, Schmid and Bell play the three leads confidently, with Baker particularly on the ball in the type of harsh tough part that he plays so often and so well. But the thesping of the three stars is given greater impact by the strength of a long list of character and feature actors as officers, other ranks, detectives, etc.

•

PRIZE OF GOLD, A

1955, 96 mins, UK col

Dir Mark Robson *Prod* Irving Allen, Albert R. Broccoli *Scr* John Paxton *Ph* Ted Moore *Ed* William Lewthwaite *Mus* Malcolm Arnold

Act Richard Widmark, Mai Zetterling, Nigel Patrick, George Cole, Donald Wolfit, Joseph Tomelty (Warwick/ Columbia)

A Prize of Gold is a taut suspense thriller unfolded against vividly interesting Berlin-London backgrounds.

Based on Max Catto's novel of the same title, the script details the hijacking of gold bullion being air-transported from Berlin to London. The writing lays a good foundation for the climaxing action, switching from lightly humorous handling in the first half to tight excitement in the latter half and Mark Robson's direction projects it all strongly with the aid of the topnotch cast.

Richard Widmark is an American sergeant stationed in the British sector of Berlin who turns larcenous when Mai Zetterling, a refugee with whom he has fallen in love, needs funds to transport a group of war-displaced children for whom she is caring to South America and a new life.

•

PRIZZI'S HONOR

1985, 129 mins, US Ⓥ ⊙ col

Dir John Huston *Prod* John Foreman *Scr* Richard Condon, Janet Roach *Ph* Andrzej Bartkowiak *Ed* Rudi Fehr, Kaja Fehr *Mus* Alex North *Art* Dennis Washington

Act Jack Nicholson, Kathleen Turner, Robert Loggia, William Hickey, John Randolph, Anjelica Huston (ABC)

John Huston's *Prizzi's Honor* packs love, sex, and murder—and dark comedy—into a labyrinthine tale.

Based on the novel by Richard Condon, plot centers on the tragic-comedy that results when a hit man for a powerful crime family (Jack Nicholson) falls hard for a svelte blonde (Kathleen Turner) who turns out to be his female counterpart in hired killings.

Picture is a stretch for Nicholson, who speaks in a street-tough, accented gangster-ese that initially takes some getting used to, but shortly becomes totally convincing. Turner manages to use her loveliness to jolting results when she finally turns her gun on a pair of victims in an apartment hallway.

Even more monstrous, in a deceptive way, is the character played by Anjelica Huston, who is the black sheep of the powerful clan, but who maneuvers the plot in insidious ways, all of them tied to the fact that she harbors a lost love for Nicholson.

1985: Best Supp. Actress (Anjelica Huston)

NOMINATIONS: Best Picture, Director, Actor (Jack Nicholson), Supp. Actor (William Hickey), Adapted Screenplay, Costume Design, Editing

•

PROBLEM CHILD

1990, 81 mins, US Ⓥ ⊙ col

Dir Dennis Dugan *Prod* Robert Simonds *Scr* Scott Alexander, Larry Karaszewski *Ph* Peter Lyons Collister *Ed* Daniel Hanley, Michael Hill *Mus* Miles Goodman *Art* George Costello

Act John Ritter, Jack Warden, Michael Oliver, Gilbert Gottfried, Amy Yasbeck, Michael Richards (Imagine)

Universal took a step in the right direction by whittling *Problem Child* down to just 81 minutes but didn't go far enough. The studio should have excised another 75 minutes and released this unbelievable mess as a short. (Several characters listed in the credits never show upon screen.)

John Ritter and Amy Yasbeck play a yuppie couple determined to have a child, primarily so they can be invited to the neighbors' birthday parties for their own kids. Unable to conceive themselves, they get suckered into adopting round-faced Junior (Michael Oliver), a child repulsive enough to make nuns cheer when he's taken from their care. The major subplot has Junior becoming pen pals with a serial killer (Michael Richards) who busts out of prison to see him, leading to a kidnapping and chase that makes *Smokey and the Bandit* look like *Citizen Kane*.

The film marks an atrocious bigscreen debut for actor and episodic TV director Dennis Dugan. The most offensive character is Yasbeck's shrill, status-conscious wife.

•

PROBLEM CHILD 2

1991, 91 mins, US Ⓥ col

Dir Brian Levant *Prod* Robert Simonds *Scr* Scott Alexander, Larry Karaszewski *Ph* Peter Smokler *Ed* Lois Freeman-Fox *Mus* David Kitay *Art* Maria Caso

Act John Ritter, Michael Oliver, Jack Warden, Laraine Newman, Amy Yasbeck, Ivyann Schwan (Universal/Imagine)

At times this poor version of a sitcom seems written by five-year-olds for five-year-olds, so much so that one suspects its script was fingerpainted.

The plot has Ben (John Ritter) and Junior (Michael Oliver) moving to a new town of cloying divorcees, as Junior grapples with his fear of losing his adopted dad by reverting to various revolting if not terribly funny habits.

A second "problem child," a little girl (Ivyann Schwan, from *Parenthood*), eventually teams up with Junior to try to bring his lonely dad together with her sheepish mom (Amy Yasbeck).

The most depressing aspect of the film stems from seeing Ritter and Laraine Newman, playing a rich femme fatale with her own desires on Ben, struggling against such fastidiously inane material. Oliver remains an annoying child actor who mugs constantly.

Pic also suffers from a cheap look all the way around, including jokes using a stuffed dog that's supposed to be a real dog and an obviously styrofoam rock.

•

PROCES DE JEANNE D'ARC
(THE TRIAL OF JOAN OF ARC)

1962, 65 mins, France b/w

Dir Robert Bresson *Prod* Agnes Delahaie *Scr* Robert Bresson *Ph* Leonce-Henry Burel *Ed* Germaine Artus *Mus* Francis Seyrig *Art* Pierre Charbonnier

Act Florence Carrez, Jean-Claude Fourneau, Marc Jacquier, Roger Honorat, Jean Gillibert, Andre Regnier (Delahaie)

Joan of Arc is judged again in this austere version of the trial and burning of the 15th-century French saint. Director-author Robert Bresson has relied on trial and rehabilitation transcripts. This sober, clean pic is both revealing and sedate.

Vehicle relies on the play of questions and answers, done mainly in medium shots, to achieve an insight into Joan of Arc's (Florence Carrez) character. Using non-actors, there are no false dramatics. This unveils another side of the oft-filmed tale, and the state and church politics of that century.

She is seen as a direct, dedicated girl trying to show that her tasks were real and from the Lord. In the background are the English, who want her destroyed to do away with her myth, and the Church collaborating. Her burning is done with a minimum of effect but with heightened feeling.

•

PRODIGAL, THE

1955, 117 mins, US Ⓥ ⊙ ▭ col

Dir Richard Thorpe *Prod* Charles Schnee *Scr* Maurice Zimm *Ph* Joseph Ruttenberg *Ed* Harold F. Kress *Mus* Bronislau Kaper

Act Lana Turner, Edmund Purdom, Louis Calhern, Audrey Dalton, Neville Brand, Taina Elg (M-G-M)

Metro's treatment of the Parable of the Prodigal Son (from Luke XV) is a bigscale spectacle, making overwhelmingly lavish use of sets, props, CinemaScoped Eastman Color and a well-populated cast. End result of all this flamboyant polish, however, is only fair entertainment.

The brief 22 verses which tell the story of the prodigal who wanders from his home in pursuit of the high priestess of Astarte have been stretched to one hour and 57 minutes.

With rather empty characters to portray in the screenplay, from the adaptation by Joe Breen, Jr., and Samuel James Larsen, the performances by Lana Turner, as the high priestess; Edmund Purdom, the prodigal; Louis Calhern, the high priest of Baal; and most of the others in the huge cast are hollow and generally uninteresting. Almost the only note of character warmth is to be found in the romance between the mute runaway slave (James Mitchell) and the high priestess slave (Taina Elg).

Most of the screen plot takes place in pagan Damascus, where the prodigal is busy spending his third of his father's wealth trying to win the priestess away from her pagan gods to be his wife. It's a standoff, though, because he will not give up his God, Jehovah. The pagan revelry and temple maidens dedicated to love come off tamely in the film. So do the love scenes between Turner and Purdom.

•

PRODUCERS, THE

1968, 100 mins, US Ⓥ ⊙ col

Dir Mel Brooks *Prod* Sidney Glazier *Scr* Mel Brooks *Ph* Joseph Coffey *Ed* Ralph Rosenblum *Mus* John Morris *Art* Charles Rosen

Act Zero Mostel, Gene Wilder, Kenneth Mars, Estelle Winwood, Dick Shawn, Christopher Hewett (Embassy)

Mel Brooks has turned a funny idea into a slapstick film, thanks to the performers, particularly Zero Mostel.

Playing a Broadway producer of flops who survives (barely) by suckering little old ladies, he teams with an emotionally retarded accountant portrayed by Gene Wilder in a scheme to produce a flop. By selling 25,000 percent of production, they figure to be rich when it flops. For the twist, the musical comedy *Springtime for Hitler*, penned by a shell-shocked Nazi, is a smash.

The film is unmatched in the scenes featuring Mostel and Wilder alone together, and several episodes with other actors are truly rare. When the producers approach the most atrocious director on Broadway, they find Christopher Hewett in drag exchanging catty comments with his secretary (Andreas Voutsinas).

Estelle Winwood is a winner as a salacious little old lady, and Kenneth Mars has his moments as the Nazi scripter.

1968: Best Original Story & Screenplay

NOMINATION: Best Supp. Actor (Gene Wilder)

•

PROFESSIONAL, THE
SEE: LEON

•

PROFESSIONALS, THE
1966, 116 mins, US Ⓥ ⦿ ▭ col
Dir Richard Brooks ***Prod*** Richard Brooks ***Scr*** Richard Brooks ***Ph*** Conrad Hall ***Ed*** Peter Zinner ***Mus*** Maurice Jarre ***Art*** Edward Haworth
Act Burt Lancaster, Lee Marvin, Robert Ryan, Jack Palance, Claudia Cardinale, Ralph Bellamy (Columbia)

The Professionals is a well-made actioner, set in 1917 on the Mexican-U.S. border, in which some soldiers of fortune rescue the reportedly kidnapped wife of an American businessman. Exciting explosive sequences, good overall pacing and acting overcome a sometimes thin script.

Richard Brooks's adaptation of Frank O'Rourke's novel, *A Mule for the Marquesa*, depicts the strategy of Lee Marvin and cohorts, sent by gringo Ralph Bellamy into the political turmoil of Mexico to rescue his missing wife, Claudia Cardinale, known to be secreted in the brigand village of Jack Palance. Latter only a few years earlier had achieved a transient victory in the Revolution with the help of Marvin and Burt Lancaster.

Quiet and purposeful, Marvin underplays very well as the leader of the rescue troop. Robert Ryan, who loves animals, is in the relative background, as is Woody Strode, Negro-Indian scout and tracker.

Lancaster is the most dynamic of the crew, as a lighthearted but two-fisted fighter.

1966: NOMINATIONS: Best Director, Adapted Screenplay, Color Cinematography

•

PROJECTED MAN, THE
1967, 77 mins, UK ▭ col
Dir Ian Curteis ***Prod*** John Croydon, Maurice Foster ***Scr*** John C. Cooper, Peter Bryan ***Ph*** Stanley Pavey ***Ed*** Derek Holding ***Mus*** Kenneth V. Jones ***Art*** Peter Mullins
Act Mary Peach, Bryant Haliday, Norman Wooland, Ronald Allen, Derek Farr, Tracey Crisp (MLC/Compton)

Prof. Steiner (Bryant Haliday), whose experiments involve converting objects to energy and reforming them elsewhere, is in conflict with Dr. Blanchard (Norman Wooland), his superior at a research foundation. Latter is being forced by a third party to see that the experiments fail. After an important demonstration is sabotaged, Steiner is told the project will be dismantled.

Anxious to continue, he attempts to project himself into a visiting scientist's living room but an accident causes him to miss target, become facially disfigured and possessed with an electrical charge that is fatal on contact.

Screenplay [from a screen story by Frank Quattrocchi] is a mosaic compiled from other films but the pieces hang together fairly well, though the origin and motives of the third party (Derrick de Marney) are never fully explained. Happily, the characters do not fall prey to the usual cliches. Deformed scientist Steiner is "angry" but not "insane," and retains his human personality, killing only from fear or sense of justice.

Acting is generally good, though Tracey Crisp's secretary is simply a sexy ingenue. Director Ian Curteis fills the Techniscope screen with compositions inspired by Sidney Furie's *Ipcress File* style that keep the film visually lively without resorting to outright imitation. Lighting sharply selects or outlines objects and the costume and setting colors are chosen with an eye for subtle contrast.

•

PROJECT X
1987, 108 mins, US Ⓥ ⦿ col
Dir Jonathan Kaplan ***Prod*** Walter F. Parkes, Lawrence Lasker ***Scr*** Stanley Weiser ***Ph*** Dean Cundey ***Ed*** O. Nicholas Brown ***Mus*** James Horner ***Art*** Lawrence G. Paull
Act Matthew Broderick, Helen Hunt, Bill Sadler, Johnny Ray McGhee, Jonathan Stark, Robin Gammell (20th Century-Fox)

If nothing else, *Project X* is the ultimate film for monkey lovers. Some quite endearing chimpanzees share center stage with Matthew Broderick for nearly two hours here, and while they, and he, are engaging enough to watch, picture lets its manipulative strings show too clearly.

Broderick plays a wayward Air Force pilot who, as punishment, is sent to play zookeeper at the Strategic Weapons Research Center, where intelligent chimps are trained for top secret and, it transpires, fatal experiments involving the effects of radiation.

Brightest of the little hairy ones is Virgil, an orphan who was taught sign language under a university program. When Virgil is put on the line, Broderick feels compelled to act and end the seemingly needless experiments.

Director Jonathan Kaplan keeps the proceedings [from a screen story by Stanley Weiser and Lawrence Lasker] amiable enough, and has covered the monkeys' actions with loving care and skillful attention, which cannot have been easy. Broderick is rightly more subdued here than in some recent performances, and supporting cast is discreetly effective.

•

PROMISE, THE
(AKA: FACE OF A STRANGER)
1979, 97 mins, US Ⓥ ▭ col
Dir Gilbert Cates ***Prod*** Fred Weintraub, Paul Heller ***Scr*** Gary Michael White ***Ph*** Ralph Woolsey ***Ed*** Peter E. Berger ***Mus*** David Shire ***Art*** William Sandell
Act Kathleen Quinlan, Stephen Collins, Beatrice Straight, Laurence Luckin, Michael O'Hare, Bibi Besch (Universal)

The title of this romantic melodrama, has to do with a buried necklace and the promise of undying love and faith in each other made by a young architectural student and a girl student.

The girl is severely injured in an auto accident and the boy is unconscious for some time, during which his mother—a female building tycoon—persuades the girl to undergo some very expensive plastic surgery and seek a new life elsewhere. She tells her son the girl is dead.

The scene changes to California. The girl, a promising artist, has for reasons known only to herself, switched to photography. She's an overnight success and is sought by the young architect who's building a medical center. Does he recognize her?

Kathleen Quinlan is pretty convincing as the painter/photographer and a new, very handsome, young leading man is added to the Hollywood scene with Stephen Collins as the architect.

1979: NOMINATION: Best Song ("I'll Never Say Goodbye")

•

PROMISED LAND
(AKA: YOUNG HEARTS)
1988, 100 mins, US Ⓥ ⦿ col
Dir Michael Hoffman ***Prod*** Rick Stevenson ***Scr*** Michael Hoffman ***Ph*** Ueli Steiger, Alexander Gruszynski ***Ed*** David Spiers ***Mus*** James Newton Howard ***Art*** Eugenio Zanetti
Act Jason Gedrick, Kiefer Sutherland, Meg Ryan, Tracy Pollan, Googy Gress, Deborah Richter (Wildwood/Oxford)

Promised Land is a pregnant drama about aimless Middle American lives that never delivers. Produced in Utah near where it was developed at the Sundance Institute, pic covers familiar, unexciting ground as it looks at four thoroughly unremarkable young people who never come close to getting things together.

Writer-director Michael Hoffman starts his story off on the basketball court, where Davey (Jason Gedrick) wins the game for the high school home team, much to the delight of friend and admirer Danny (Kiefer Sutherland) and g.f. Mary (Tracy Pollan).

Within two years, Gedrick's life consists of making the rounds of sleepy Ashville as a cop in a squad car, and Pollan has matured at college. By contrast, the bashful Sutherland has left town to find himself, only to return with a bride, hellcat Bev (Meg Ryan), whom he married three days after meeting her. Once she arrives in Ashville to meet the folks, this outsider brings senseless tragedy to the group of old friends.

Many scenes are extended to the point that all potential dramatic tension is drained out of them. A cattle prod would have been a useful tool on the set, as the actors show boundless earnestness and little energy except for Ryan, whose role calls for her to be dangerously wild and reckless in a sexy, silly way, something she manages just fine.

•

PROMISE HER ANYTHING
1966, 96 mins, UK/US col
Dir Arthur Hiller ***Prod*** Stanley Rubin ***Scr*** William Peter Blatty ***Ph*** Douglas Slocombe ***Ed*** John Shirley ***Mus*** Lyn Murray ***Art*** Wilfrid Shingleton
Act Warren Beatty, Leslie Caron, Bob Cummings, Keenan Wynn, Hermione Gingold, Lionel Stander (Seven Arts/Stark)

Promise Her Anything is a light, refreshing comedy-romance, set in Greenwich Village but filmed in England, which satirizes both child psychology and nudie pix in a tasteful, effective manner. Well-paced direction of many fine performances, generally sharp scripting and other good production elements add up to a satisfying comedy.

An Arne Sultan–Marvin Worth story has been adapted into what is basically a romantic triangle. Leslie Caron, with a precocious baby boy but no hubby, hopes to connect with her employer, child psychologist Bob Cummings who, in private life, abhors moppets. Caron's neighbor (Warren Beatty) wants her, although he is careful to conceal his profession–making mail-order nudie films.

Director Arthur Hiller has overcome a basic problem: specifically, that Caron and Beatty are not known as film comics. His fine solution has been to spotlight baby Michael Bradley in the first 30 minutes, when Caron is establishing an easy audience rapport, while Beatty slides into a likeable groove via energetic tumbles and other manifestations of youthful enthusiasm.

•

PROMISES IN THE DARK
1979, 115 mins, US Ⓥ col
Dir Jerome Hellman ***Prod*** Jerome Hellman ***Scr*** Lorin Mandel ***Ph*** Adam Holender ***Ed*** Bob Wyman ***Mus*** Leonard Rosenman ***Art*** Walter Scott Herndon
Act Marsha Mason, Kathleen Beller, Ned Beatty, Susan Clark, Michael Brandon, Paul Clemens (Orion)

Producer-director Jerome Hellman has admirably attempted to focus attention on the death of a young cancer victim. Major problem remains not the promises physician Marcia Mason makes to her terminally-ill patient (Kathleen Beller) but the premise itself. No matter how well acted (and thesping here is superior) or mounted, a story that spends two hours watching a pretty young girl expire is just not most people's idea of a good time.

Screenplay pulls no punches, and medical realism is heightened to an extent that damages the film more than it helps. Beller injures her leg in the pic's opening sequence, and after that, it's an endless array of emergency rooms, surgery theatres and bed-ridden shots as the cancer spreads throughout her body.

Set up as counterpoint to the distress Beller, boyfriend Paul Clemens, and parents Ned Beatty and Susan Clark undergo is the courtship of divorced Mason by radiologist Michael Brandon. Mason, who is given the central focus by Helman's serivative direction, never really allows the audience to share in her conflicting emotions.

Rest of cast is first-rate, particularly Beller (whose "why me" speech is heart-wrenching). Hellman's direction seems to have been inspired by two colleagues he's frequently worked with, Hal Ashby and John Schlesinger.

•

PROM NIGHT
1980, 91 mins, US Ⓥ ⦿ col
Dir Paul Lynch ***Prod*** Peter Simpson ***Scr*** William Gray ***Ph*** Robert New ***Ed*** Brian Ravok ***Mus*** Carl Zittrer, Paul Zaza ***Art*** Reuben Freed
Act Leslie Nielsen, Jamie Lee Curtis, Casey Stevens, Eddie Benton (Simcom)

Borrowing shamelessly from *Carrie* and any number of gruesome exploitationers pic [from a story by Robert Gunza, Jr.] manages to score a few horrific points amid a number of sagging moments.

It opens with the falling death of a 10-year-old girl brought on by unmerciful teasing on the part of four of her peers. It's six years later and prom night for the surviving kiddies and each is slated to meet an unsavory fate due to past exploits—unbeknownst to anyone.

Once the masked killer gets going it becomes a guessing game of who is the ax-wielding avenger and which, if any, victims will escape.

Director Paul Lynch seems to capture the spirit of the genre here, but spends a little too much time setting up each murder, thus eliminating some suspense.

•

PROMOTER, THE
SEE: THE CARD

•

PROOF
1991, 86 mins, Australia Ⓥ col
Dir Jocelyn Moorhouse *Prod* Lynda House *Scr* Jocelyn Moorhouse *Ph* Martin McGrath *Ed* Ken Sallows *Mus* Not Drowning, Waving *Art* Patrick Reardon
Act Hugo Weaving, Genevieve Picot, Russell Crowe, Heather Mitchell, Jeffrey Walker, Frank Gallacher (House & Moorhouse)

Proof is an intriguing psychological drama structured around the contradictory character of a blind photographer, a striking debut from writer-director Jocelyn Moorhouse.

Intriguing premise has a blind man required to rely on the information of others, and what if those people don't tell the truth? Blind from birth, Martin (Hugo Weaving) never really believed his mother (Heather Mitchell) was telling him the truth about the world around him. Now in his 30s, Martin lives alone, his only company a seeing-eye dog and Celia (Genevieve Picot), the young woman who comes to clean his house and do his shopping.

She has become infatuated with Martin, but he keeps her firmly at arm's length. Enter Andy (Russell Crowe), a guileless young man who works in an Italian restaurant Martin frequents. Celia decides to get at Martin through Andy.

Moorhouse builds up a good deal of sexual tension among the three characters, aided by a trio of excellent performances. Pic is also not without humor.

•

PROPHECY
1979, 102 mins, US Ⓥ ▭ col
Dir John Frankenheimer *Prod* Robert L. Rosen *Scr* David Seltzer *Ph* Harry Stradling Jr *Ed* Tom Rolf *Mus* Leonard Rosenman *Art* William Craig Smith
Act Talia Shire, Robert Foxworth, Armand Assante, Richard Dysart, Victoria Racimo, Tom McFadden (Paramount)

Director John Frankenheimer has made a frightening monster movie that people could laugh at for generations to come, complete with your basic big scary thing, cardboard characters and a story so stupid it's irresistible.

Once again, the real villain is Careless Mankind. Only this time, it isn't Atomic Fallout that's creating giant ants and killer cockroaches but Industrial Pollution.

Among the performers, only Armand Assante as an Indian leader gets half a chance to show his talent and Talia Shire is reduced to a whining wimp. Leonard Rosenman's score cheats constantly, building to frightening moments that don't happen.

•

PROSPERO'S BOOKS
1991, 124 mins, UK/France Ⓥ col
Dir Peter Greenaway *Prod* Kees Kasander *Scr* Peter Greenaway *Ph* Sacha Vierny *Ed* Marina Bodbyl *Mus* Michael Nyman *Art* Ben Van Os, Jan Roelfs
Act John Gielgud, Michael Clark, Michel Blanc, Roland Josephson, Isabelle Pasco, Tom Bell (Allarts/Cinea/Camera/Penta

With more visual stimulation than a dozen normal films, Peter Greenaway's *Prospero's Books* is an intellectually and erotically rampaging meditation on the arrogance and value of the artistic process. The product of a feverish, overflowing imagination, this almost impossibly dense take on *The Tempest* displays both the director's audacious brilliance and lewd extravagance at full tilt.

The playwright's tale is presented basically intact, but Greenaway's underlying gambit is to make Prospero (John Gielgud) the author of his own story. Through the use of exquisite calligraphy, the old man's writing is made vivid on the screen, and the device opens the way to Gielgud himself to supply the voices for many of the supporting characters, who are sometimes also voiced by Gielgud and another thesp simultaneously.

Shot entirely indoors in Amsterdam, the production is stunning from every physical point of view. As always, Michael Nyman's vaulting, repetitive, lyrical score plays a major part in the effectiveness of a Greenaway film. Greenaway here ventures into new cinematic territory through the use of high-definition video (which accounts for the unusual 1.77:1 aspect ratio) and the Quantel Paintbox.

•

PROTECTOR, THE
1985, 95 mins, US Ⓥ ⦿ col
Dir James Glickenhaus *Prod* David Chan *Scr* James Glickenhaus *Ph* Mark Irwin *Ed* Evan Lottman *Mus* Ken Thorne *Art* William F. De Seta, Oliver Wong
Act Jackie Chan, Danny Aiello, Roy Chiao, Victor Arnold, Kim Bass, Richard Clarke (Golden Harvest/Warner)

Jackie Chan and Danny Aiello head for Hong Kong to track down a drug kingpin who has kidnapped the daughter of his estranged business partner.

A furious barroom shootout at the outset is immediately followed by a speedboat chase in New York harbor that rivals James Bond pictures for elaborate thrills.

What also puts matters on the right track is the tongue-in-cheek humor running throughout. Chan and Aiello both sail through the farfetched action with insouciance and aplomb as they infuriate their superiors by wreaking havoc wherever they go and knock off enough baddies to momentarily put a dent in Hong Kong's population figures.

Chan indulges in almost superhuman acrobatics every 15 minutes or so, running up walls, pole-vaulting and swinging from sampan to sampan in the harbor and generally putting his karate expertise to good use.

•

PROTOCOL
1984, 96 mins, US Ⓥ ⦿ col
Dir Herbert Ross *Prod* Anthea Sylbert *Scr* Buck Henry *Ph* William A. Fraker *Ed* Paul Hirsch *Mus* Basil Poledouris *Art* Bill Malley
Act Goldie Hawn, Chris Sarandon, Richard Romanus, Andre Gregory, Gail Strickland, Cliff De Young (Warner)

Goldie Hawn's insistence on Saying Something Important takes a lot of the zip out of *Protocol*, but the light comedy still has its moments for the forgiving.

One big problem here is an oh-so-obvious effort to reinvent the formula that boosted *Private Benjamin* to the heights. Here she's a sweet, unsophisticated cocktail waitress hurdled into the unfamiliar world of Washington diplomacy and Mideast travail.

In *Benjamin*, Hawn's main adversary was a woman captain (Eileen Brennan) and ill-intentioned men; here, it's Gail Strickland as a devious, plotting protocol officer and more ill-intentioned men.

Formula doesn't work as well in *Protocol*, partly because Strickland and gang aren't as much fun to foil as Brennan's bunch was.

•

PROUD ONES, THE
1956, 94 mins, US ▭ col
Dir Robert D. Webb *Prod* Robert L. Jacks *Scr* Edmund North, Joseph Petracca *Ph* Lucien Ballard *Ed* Hugh S. Fowler *Mus* Lionel Newman
Act Robert Ryan, Virginia Mayo, Jeffrey Hunter, Robert Middleton, Walter Brennan, Arthur O'Connell (20th Century-Fox)

20th-Fox has an exceptionally well-presented outdoor drama in *The Proud Ones*. A credible story with excellent dramatic values, direction that sharpens them and builds suspense, and strong performances by an able cast are among the entertainment assets of this well-thought-out production.

Robert Ryan, Jeffrey Hunter and Robert Middleton are the male cast toppers. Playing a marshal who knows his business, a young man who has not yet determined where he is going, and a gambling saloon operator, respectively, the trio responds exactly right to Robert D. Webb's forceful direction. For femme interest, Virginia Mayo stars, and she gives the pic a performance asset as the girl who loves the marshal.

Script, from the novel by Verne Athanas, provides believable shadings to the characters and situations as the plot moves through a dramatic study of a Kansas frontier town suddenly become rich and riotous with the entry of the railroad and trail herds. How Ryan works out his personal and duty obligations, proves that sometimes the use of a gun is necessary, and wins over a young man to his side in the climaxing battle with the town's evil forces, is suspensefully and engrossingly presented.

•

PROUD REBEL, THE
1958, 100 mins, US Ⓥ col
Dir Michael Curtiz *Prod* Samuel Goldwyn, Jr. *Scr* Joe Petracca, Lillie Hayward *Ph* Ted McCord *Ed* Aaron Stell *Mus* Jerome Moross *Art* McClure Capps
Act Alan Ladd, Olivia de Havilland, Dean Jagger, David Ladd, Cecil Kellaway, John Carradine (Buena Vista)

Warmth of a father's love and faith, and the devotion of a boy for his dog, are the stand-out ingredients of this suspenseful and fast-action post-Civil War yarn. Michael Curtiz, too, has achieved fine feeling in his direction of the screenplay, based on an original by James Edward Grant, and is backed by some fine color photography.

It's the characterizations that hold forth most strongly, topped perhaps by the very appealing performance of David Ladd, star's 11-year-old son who plays Alan Ladd's boy in the pic. Youngster has been shocked mute during Union forces' sacking of Atlanta during the war, when he saw his mother killed and his home destroyed by fire, and it's Alan Ladd's dogged wandering of the land to find a doctor who can cure his son which motivates plot.

Action unfolds in a small Southern Illinois community, where Ladd is drawn into a fight with the two sons of Dean Jagger, a big sheep-raiser; the payment of his fine after his arrest by Olivia de Havilland, a lonely farm-woman whose property is coveted by Jagger; and Ladd working out this fine on the farm.

•

PROVIDENCE
1977, 110 mins, France Ⓥ col
Dir Alain Resnais *Prod* Action Films-SFP *Scr* David Mercer *Ph* Ricardo Arnovitch *Ed* Albert Jurgenson *Mus* Miklos Rozsa *Art* Jacques Saulnier
Act Dirk Bogarde, Ellen Burstyn, John Gielgud, David Warner, Elaine Stritch, Cyril Luckham (Action/SFP)

A striking amalgam of the literary and theatrical approach in scripting; that is, sharp talk, highblown scenes of personal revelation and general politico asides; has been turned into an unusual visual tour-de-force by French director Alain Resnais.

It is a riveting pic pictorially, offering dense insights into the flights of imagination of a supposedly dying writer of perhaps some faddish fame.

The style is impeccable as the film sashays from the novelist's feverish, drunken ramblings about his new novel, putting his family into it, and commenting on them.

John Gielgud's mellifluous or impassioned delivery as the writer is extraordinary; as well as Dirk Bogarde as the son, a cold, internally wounded man who cannot show emotion.

•

PROWLER, THE
1951, 92 mins, US b/w
Dir Joseph Losey *Prod* S. P. Eagle [= Sam Spiegel] *Scr* Hugo Butler *Ph* Arthur Miller *Ed* Paul Weatherwax *Mus* Lyn Murray *Art* Boris Leven
Act Van Heflin, Evelyn Keyes, John Maxwell, Katherine Warren, Emerson Treacy, Madge Blake (Horizon/Eagle)

Combination of illicit love, murder and premarital relations makes *The Prowler* a bawdy, daring story [from an original story by Robert Thoeren and Hans Wilhelm].

Van Heflin makes the most of an unsympathetic role, that of a cop who steals the love of a woman (Evelyn Keyes) who had called the police when she saw a prowler peering through her bathroom window. Keyes, as the woman, wife of an all-night disk jockey, also has an unsympathetic part, as a gal wooed and won by Heflin behind her husband's back.

Pic builds to an exciting climax in a desert ghost town, where Heflin has taken Keyes, now his wife, to have her baby in order to avoid publicity.

•

PRUDENCE AND THE PILL
1968, 92 mins, US col
Dir Fielder Cook *Prod* Kenneth Harper, Ronald J. Kahn *Scr* Hugh Mills *Ph* Ted Moore *Ed* Norman Savage *Mus* Bernard Ebbinghouse *Art* Wilfrid Shingleton
Act Deborah Kerr, David Niven, Judy Geeson, David Dundas, Vickery Turner, Hugh Armstrong (20th Century-Fox)

Deborah Kerr and David Niven team as a couple which winds up married to others.

Hugh Mills wrote the book, and adapted it for films. Basic flaw in the screenplay, which the generally excellent acting and direction cannot entirely overcome, is the rambling from one set of interesting characters to another.

Obvious attempt was to incorporate a lot of unique personalities, all affected by the pill and changing sex customs, but the result is a lack of unity. The whole film, then, is less than the sum of its parts.

Film is more than a one-joke script—the secret switching of birth control pills so that the wrong people get pregnant—and to the credit of the pic, this is not a tasteless recurring incident.

Title art designed by Richard Williams is a great sendoff to the film, in its semi-Victorian atmosphere on which modern characters intrude. The parallel between old-fashioned genteel marriage and contemporary assaults thereon, is drawn most cleverly.

•

PSYCHO
1960, 109 mins, US Ⓥ ⦿ b/w
Dir Alfred Hitchcock *Prod* Alfred Hitchcock *Scr* Joseph Stefano *Ph* John L. Russell *Ed* George Tomasini *Mus* Bernard Herrmann *Art* Joseph Hurley, Robert Clatworthy

Act Anthony Perkins, Janet Leigh, Vera Miles, John Gavin, Martin Balsam, John McIntire (Paramount)

Alfred Hitchcock is up to his clavicle in whimsicality and apparently had the time of his life in putting together *Psycho*. He's gotten in gore, in the form of a couple of graphically depicted knife murders, a story that's far out in Freudian motivations, and now and then injects little amusing plot items that suggest the whole thing is not to be taken seriously.

Anthony Perkins is the young man who doesn't get enough exorcise (repeat exorcise) of that other inner being. Among the victims are Janet Leigh, who walks away from an illicit love affair with John Gavin, taking with her a stolen $40,000, and Martin Balsam, as a private eye who winds up in the same swamp in which Leigh's body also is deposited.

John McIntire is the local sheriff with an unusual case on his hands, and Simon Oakland is the psychiatrist. Perkins gives a remarkably effective in-a-dream kind of performance as the possessed young man. Others play it straight, with equal competence.

Joseph Stefano's screenplay, from a novel by Robert Bloch, provides a strong foundation for Hitchcock's field day. And if the camera, under Hitchcock's direction, tends to over-emphasize a story point here and there, well, it's forgivable.

1960: NOMINATIONS: Best Director, Supp. Actress (Janet Leigh), B&W Cinematography, B&W Art Direction

•

PSYCHO

1998, 109 mins, US Ⓥ ⊙ col

Dir Gus Van Sant ***Prod*** Brian Grazer, Gus Van Sant ***Scr*** Joseph Stefano ***Ph*** Christopher Doyle ***Ed*** Amy Duddleston ***Mus*** Danny Elfman (adapt.) ***Art*** Tom Foden

Act Vince Vaughn, Anne Heche, Julianne Moore, Viggo Mortensen, William H. Macy, Robert Forster (Imagine/Universal)

A faithful-unto-slavish remake of the 1960 Hitchcock classic, pic contains nothing to outrage or offend partisans of the original, yet neither does it stand to add much to their appreciation. And as for introducing a new generation to the granddaddy of all slasher films, forget about it: To the *Scream* kids, sincerity is out anyway, and the thrills here are strictly old hat.

The reason the conceit backfires is that the original depended on narrative surprises that can't possibly be surprising now, and on material that's long since lost its power even to raise an eyebrow (Hitch's single most shocking move was to show a toilet flushing, which had never been done in a major studio film).

This *Psycho* is not a "shot by shot" re-creation of the original [as initially publicized]. It's a largely faithful "scene by scene" restaging in which many shots of the original, especially the most famous and striking, are copied. This *Psycho* is in color (ably shot by ace Aussie [via East Asia] lensman Christopher Doyle), which reduces the dream-like mood as well as the schematic visual rigor of Hitchcock's design.

Although director Gus Van Sant shot on the same Universal lot and kept to the original's brisk six-week schedule, the result feels looser and more prone to fresh air.

The film's most famous scene, the shower-knife-murder, Van Sant restages with slightly more nudity and realism and at what seems like a slightly more protracted length.

Vince Vaughn's awkwardness as Norman only proves the extraordinary skill and subtlety of Anthony Perkins's work for Hitchcock. Anne Heche ends up a pale, vapid, slightly vulgar shadow of Janet Leigh's brilliant, hard-edged original. Two bright spots in the cast are William H. Macy, whose Arbogast has presence, dimension and believable quirkiness, and Robert Forster, who does a surprisingly good job in the thankless role of the psychiatrist. Danny Elfman's new rendition of Bernard Herrmann's legendary score is first rate.

•

PSYCHO II

1983, 113 mins, US Ⓥ col

Dir Richard Franklin ***Prod*** Hilton A. Green ***Scr*** Tom Holland ***Ph*** Dean Cundey ***Ed*** Andrew London ***Mus*** Jerry Goldsmith ***Art*** John W. Corso

Act Anthony Perkins, Vera Miles, Meg Tilly, Robert Loggia, Dennis Franz, Hugh Gillin (Universal/Oak Industries)

Psycho II is an impressive, 23-years-after followup to Alfred Hitchcock's 1960 suspense classic.

New story, set 22 years later, has Norman Bates (Anthony Perkins) released from a mental institution on the petition of his psychiatrist, Dr. Raymond (Robert Loggia), over the objections of Lila Loomis (Vera Miles) whose sister he murdered (Janet Leigh in the first film). Securing a job as cook's assistant at a local diner, Bates is befriended by a young waitress Mary (Meg Tilly) who moves into his house as an empathetic companion. A series of mysterious murders ensue, beginning with the killing of the obnoxious manager Toomey (Dennis Franz), who has turned the Bates family business into a hot-sheets motel.

Director Richard Franklin deftly keeps the suspense and tension on high while doling out dozens of shock-of-recognitions shots drawn from the audience's familiarity with *Psycho*.

Reprising his famous role, Perkins is very entertaining, whether stammering over the pronunciation of "cutlery" or misleading the audience in both directions as to his relative sanity.

•

PSYCHO III

1986, 96 mins, US Ⓥ ⊙ col

Dir Anthony Perkins ***Prod*** Hilton A. Green ***Scr*** Charles Edward Pogue ***Ph*** Bruce Surtees ***Ed*** David Blewitt ***Mus*** Carter Burwell ***Art*** Henry Bumstead

Act Anthony Perkins, Diana Scarwid, Jeff Fahey, Roberta Maxwell, Hugh Gillin, Lee Garlington (Universal)

A few amusing little notions are streched to the point of diminishing returns in *Psycho III*.

Opening sequence is a full-fledged homage to Alfred Hitchcock's *Vertigo* and helps set the comic, in-joke tone of the rest of the picture. Unhappy novice Diana Scarwid is all set to jump from a church belltower but, in an effort to save her, one of the nuns falls to her death instead.

Scarwid flees in distress, is given a ride through the desert by aspiring musician Jeff Fahey, and where should the unlikely and unsuspecting duo wind up but the Bates Motel.

The whole enterprise is dependent almost entirely upon self-referential incidents and attitudes for its effect, and it eventually becomes wearying.

Main pleasure of the picture stems from Anthony Perkins's amusing performance.

•

PSYCHOMANIA

1964, 90 mins, US b/w

Dir Richard L. Hilliard ***Prod*** Del Tenney ***Scr*** Robin Miller ***Ph*** Louis McMahon ***Ed*** Robert Q. Lovett ***Mus*** W. L. Holcombe

Act Lee Philips, Shepperd Strudwick, James Farentino, Jean Hale, Lorraine Rogers, Sylvia Miles (Emerson)

Psychomania is a low-budget, well-done shocker with a tightly knit plot and a believable surprise ending.

Lee Philips does a fine acting job as the karate-expert artist from a family with a psychotic background, who gets involved in a pair of bizarre murders. Shepperd Strudwick and James Farentino are believable as the lawyer and tough motorcycle hood respectively.

Richard Hilliard's realistic direction and Louis McMahon's excellent camerawork help build the suspense of Robin Miller's screenplay to a satisfyingly real ending. Some of the dialog shows good imagination.

Probably with a bigger budget, film could have been an excellent psychodrama.

•

PSYCH-OUT

1968, 88 mins, US Ⓥ ⊙ col

Dir Richard Rush ***Prod*** Dick Clark ***Scr*** E. Hunter Willett, Betty Ulius ***Ph*** Leslie Kovacs ***Ed*** Ken Reynolds ***Mus*** Ronald Stein ***Art*** Leon Ericksen

Act Susan Strasberg, Dean Stockwell, Jack Nicholson, Bruce Dern, Adam Roarke, Henry Jaglom (American International)

Psych-Out is an above average programmer about San Francisco hippies. Thin story line—girl seeking lost brother—is sufficient as the medium for a series of incidents, including drug-induced hallucinations, all directed in excellent fashion by Richard Rush. Production is strong on realistic location values, as well as special effects.

Script follows Susan Strasberg on her search for far-out brother Bruce Dern. Dean Stockwell is a disenchanted hippie, while Jack Nicholson is a swinger tending towards a romantic interest in Strasberg.

Most principals register strong impact, Strasberg via reaction, Nicholson via action, and Stockwell through a combination of both. Dern's flamboyant performance is partly justified by script.

Rush's direction is quite exceptional. Considering what coin he had to play with, it is worthy of 20 times the apparent budget.

There are a lot of songs in the film, many quite good, by The Strawberry Alarm Clock and The Seeds.

•

PUBERTY BLUES

1981, 97 mins, Australia Ⓥ ▭ col

Dir Bruce Beresford ***Prod*** John Long, Margaret Kelly ***Scr*** Margaret Kelly ***Ph*** Don McAlpine ***Ed*** Bill Anderson ***Mus*** Les Gock ***Art*** David Copping

Act Nell Schofield, Jad Capelja, Geoff Rhoe, Tony Hughes, Sandy Paul (Limelight)

Puberty Blues is a leisurely, entertaining tale about a group of teenagers fumbling, fighting and fretting their way through adolescence.

Puberty Blues is based on a book of the same name, published in 1979, by Sydney teenagers Kathy Lette and Gabrielle Carey, who also wrote for local newspapers and magazines under the intriguing pseudonym, the Salami Sisters.

Set in the middle-class suburb of Cronulla, one of Sydney's southern beaches, the story focusses on Debbie and Sue, two girls of fairly average looks, intelligence and upbringing. Opening passages show them falling in with one of the school gangs, cheating in exams, smoking in the toilets, getting drunk, and pairing off with boyfriends.

Film gains more momentum when Debbie fears she is pregnant, her boyfriend Garry cannot cope, he seeks refuge in heroin, and dies of an overdose. To offset the bleakness, the pic is laced with Debbie's witty observations and humorous interludes.

Working with a young, inexperienced cast, Beresford has drawn some remarkable performances. Nell Schofield, 17, is particularly impressive as Debbie, an intuitive player with tangible screen presence.

•

PUBLIC ACCESS

1993, 89 mins, US Ⓥ ⊙ col

Dir Bryan Singer ***Prod*** Kenneth Kokin ***Scr*** Christopher McQuarrie, Bryan Singer, Michael Feit Dougan ***Ph*** Bruce Douglas Johnson ***Ed*** John Ottman ***Mus*** John Ottman ***Art*** Jan Sessler

Act Ron Marquette, Dina Brooks, Burt Williams, Larry Maxwell, Charles Kavanaugh, Brandon Boyce (Cinemabeam/Tokuma)

Public Access represents a disturbing, dramatically cloudy, technically proficient feature debut from young helmer Bryan Singer. This very low-budget study of malaise lurking beneath the tranquil surface of a typical small American town is serious-minded and bounces around some provocative ideas, but is vague about important matters as key story points, motivation and overriding theme.

Handsome, flinty and disconcertingly creepy, Whiley Pritcher (Ron Marquette) takes a room in a small boarding house in the sleepy community of Brewster run by the grizzled former mayor (Burt Williams) and immediately takes air time on the local public access channel, where he launches a call-in show dubbed *Our Town*, and poses the simple question, "What's wrong with Brewster?"

Whiley becomes an immediate local celebrity. While beginning a romance with sincere librarian Rachel (Dina Brooks), he takes some heat from locals for getting involved in matters he knows nothing about. Polite, smiling and affable in public, Whiley allows neither other characters nor the audience behind his steely persona—he's a man with no known background, psychology or motivation.

What Singer and his co-scenarists seem to be getting at is a critique of Reagan-era greed, hypocrisy and antihumanism, as well as a commentary on the power of the media and its ability to distract the public from issues with attractive surfaces.

Technically, the production is impressive, especially considering the $250,000 budget and 18-day schedule. Individual sequences are very well staged, shot and edited, and confrontation scenes carry a fair measure of tension.

•

PUBLIC ENEMY, THE
(UK: ENEMIES OF THE PUBLIC)

1931, 83 mins, US Ⓥ ⊙ b/w

Dir William A. Wellman ***Scr*** Harvey Thew ***Ph*** Dev Jennings ***Ed*** Edward M. McDermott ***Mus*** David Mendoza (dir.) ***Art*** Max Parker

Act James Cagney, Edward Woods, Donald Cook, Joan Blondell, Jean Harlow, Beryl Mercer (Warner)

There's no lace on this picture. It's raw and brutal. It's lowbrow material given such workmanship as to make it highbrow. To square everything there's a foreword and postscript moralizing on the gangster as a menace to the public welfare.

Pushing a grapefruit into the face of the moll (Mae Clarke) with whom he's fed up, socking another on the chin for inducing him to her for the night while he's drunk, and spitting a mouthful of beer into the face of a speakeasy proprietor for using a rival's product are a few samples of James Cagney's deportment as Tom, a tough in modern gangster's dress.

The story [by Kubec Glasmon and John Bright] traces him and Matt (Edward Woods) from street gamins in 1909 as a couple of rowdy neighbourhood boys. Titles then designate lapses in time of 1915, 1917 and finally 1920. During this interim they've killed a cop on their first big job, and both kids are set to go the hard way.

The comedy in the picture, as well as the rough stuff, is in the dialog and by-play with the dames who include, besides Clarke, Joan Blondell and Jean Harlow. Harlow better hurry and do something about her voice. She doesn't get the best of it alongside Clarke and Blondell, who can troupe.

1930/31: NOMINATION: Best Original Story

•

PUBLIC EYE, THE

1992, 98 mins, US Ⓥ ⦿ col

Dir Howard Franklin ***Prod*** Sue Baden-Powell ***Scr*** Howard Franklin ***Ph*** Peter Suschitzky ***Ed*** Evan Lottman ***Mus*** Mark Isham ***Art*** Marcia Hinds-Johnson

Act Joe Pesci, Barbara Hershey, Stanley Tucci, Jerry Adler, Jared Harris, Gerry Becker (Universal)

A down-and-dirty subject gets the velvet glove treatment in *The Public Eye*. Playing a 1940s tabloid crime photographer (based on w.k. shutterbug Weegee) who yearns for respectability and a little love, Joe Pesci creates an involving character, but almost everything about Howard Franklin's solo directorial debut is muted and moody where it should be bold and brash.

Franklin wrote the screenplay nine years earlier before making a name for himself with scripts to *Someone to Watch Over Me*, *The Name of the Rose* and *Quick Change*, which he co-directed with Bill Murray.

Called in to do a favor for beautiful Kay Levitz (Barbara Hershey), a glamorpuss who has inherited an exclusive nightclub from her wealthy late husband, Bernzy (Pesci) is flattered by her apparent serious interest in his book proposal. As a result, he allows himself to get involved in a power struggle between two N.Y. mob factions when his whole career has been based on a philosophy of not playing favorites.

In all respects, the film looks great, but that's the main problem. With terrific production design evoking wartime N.Y. (location work was done in Cincinnati and Chicago) and gorgeous lensing, pic approaches physical beauty of a Coen Bros. or David Cronenberg film. Unfortunately, this is entirely counterproductive to the style that would have been appropriate for the tabloid subject matter.

•

PUBLIC HERO NO. 1

1935, 91 mins, US b/w

Dir J. Walter Ruben ***Prod*** Lucien Hubbard ***Scr*** Wells Root ***Ph*** Gregg Toland ***Mus*** Edward Ward

Act Lionel Barrymore, Jean Arthur, Chester Morris, Joseph Calleia, Paul Kelly, Lewis Stone (M-G-M)

Rates with the best of the G-men pictures. Joseph Spruin-Calleia's screen debut is auspicious. Curtailed to Joseph Calleia, this legit recruit does a consummate job as the arch-menace into whose confidence the G-man has wormed himself.

Action [from a story by J. Walter Rubin and Wells Root] opens fast and tense on how a prison break is plotted and successfully achieved. It develops that it's all part of the scheme to get Sonny (Calleia) out of confinement on a relatively minor rap in order that Chester Morris (pseudo-convict, and co-conspirator with Calleia in the break) might ferret out the Purple Gang's retreat. That's the first indication that Morris is a Fed.

Lionel Barrymore as a dipsomaniac medico who is sympathetic with the mobsters so long as he's kept in constant liquid saturations gives a memorable performance as a sometimes lovable, ever professionally competent but tragic figure of a surgeon who might have been great if not for the booze.

Jean Arthur's introduction to the scene is plausible and her playing further cinches it. Paul Kelly as the G chief and the rest of the support more than make their contributions stand up.

•

PUGNI IN TASCA, I
(FISTS IN THE POCKET)

1965, 105 mins, Italy b/w

Dir Marco Bellocchio ***Prod*** Enzo Doria ***Scr*** Marco Bellocchio ***Ph*** Alberto Marrama ***Ed*** A. Margiatti ***Mus*** Ennio Morricone ***Art*** Gisella Longo

Act Lou Castel, Paola Pitagora, Marino Mase, Liliana Gerace, Pier Luigi Troglio, Jennie McNeill (Doria)

A provincial family with some money lives in a big house. Two brothers are epileptic, the mother is blind, the sister acts much more childish than her age (early twenties), and one normal, older brother runs this strange household.

One of the epileptics (Lou Castel) seems sane but gets the idea that if the more unstable elements of the family are eliminated (his mother and a retarded brother), things would be better. He commits both crimes when the chance presents itself. He even seduces his sister, who finally becomes aware of his crimes and is paralyzed in a fall. Now he even thinks of doing away with her.

Director Marco Bellocchio displays expert tact in first laying out this inbred sickly family in their daily unrestrained lives. Film is photographed with sharp definition, with acting extremely well balanced to keep this from falling into only the clinical or shocking.

Castel, a Swedish-Italo youth, has the roughhewn looks to make his character always revealing, sometimes pathetic, disturbing but never gratuitous. Paola Pitagora is a lovely if slightly unbalanced beauty. Others are also fine in this offbeat, sometimes shocking but never forced look at an inverted family that engenders its own doom.

•

PULP

1972, 95 mins, UK Ⓥ col

Dir Mike Hodges ***Prod*** Michael Klinger ***Scr*** Mike Hodges ***Ph*** Ousama Rawi ***Ed*** John Glen ***Mus*** George Martin ***Art*** Patrick Downing

Act Michael Caine, Mickey Rooney, Lionel Stander, Lizabeth Scott, Nadia Cassini, Dennis Price (Three Michaels/United Artists)

A crime fictionalist (Michael Caine) reluctantly enters the reality of his own fantasies in *Pulp*, a reasonably entertaining piece of rococo recall [shot on Malta], at its best as visual camp. The joke isn't an easy one to sustain, but it's part of the film's appeal that writer-director Mike Hodges doesn't flog it.

Caine is hired by a faded screen tough guy (Mickey Rooney) to ghost his memoir, and the plottage thereafter hinges on a scandal in the star's past involving elements of the local shady set. Having previously hushed things up, they now fear Rooney means to spill the beans in his book, hence they contract his murder. Caine is naturally compelled not to turn tail but to see the mystery and danger through.

Hodges's dialog is appropriately crisp and often witty, though it's the sight gags that work best—a throwaway salute to Bogart or the camp interior of Rooney's island villa, fitted out for the insecure narcissist that he was.

Caine, solo billed above the title, delivers his usual attractive turn, albeit with more than a whiff of hangover from one of Len Deighton's spy plots. There's also a deft bit by Dennis Price as a shaggy Englishman, and newcomer Nadia Cassini is featured as Rooney's sexy satrap.

•

PULP FICTION

1994, 153 mins, US Ⓥ ⦿ ▭ col

Dir Quentin Tarantino ***Prod*** Lawrence Bender ***Scr*** Quentin Tarantino ***Ph*** Andrzej Sekula ***Ed*** Sally Menke ***Mus*** Karyn Rachtman (sup.) ***Art*** David Wasco

Act John Travolta, Samuel L. Jackson, Uma Thurman, Harvey Keitel, Tim Roth, Amanda Plummer (A Band Apart/Jersey)

A spectacularly entertaining piece of pop culture, *Pulp Fiction* is the *American Graffiti* of violent crime pictures. Following up on his reputation-making debut, *Reservoir Dogs*, Quentin Tarantino makes some of the same moves here but on a much larger canvas, in a context set by delicious dialogue and several superb performances.

As did *Reservoir Dogs*, new pic begins in a coffee shop, with a young couple who call each other Pumpkin and Honey Bunny (Tim Roth, Amanda Plummer) chattering away before deciding to hold up the place.

Next sequence also feels like familiar territory, as two hit men, Vincent and Jules (John Travolta, Samuel L. Jackson), bump off some kids who didn't play straight with crime lord Marsellus (Ving Rhames). Vincent, as a courtesy, takes his boss's statuesque wife, Mia (a dark-haired Uma Thurman), out for a night on the town. This "date" occasions the picture's biggest set piece, an amazing outing to a giant 1950s-themed restaurant/club.

An hour in, pic becomes even more audacious, as Tarantino leads the audience deeper into uncharted territory with Bruce Willis, as a boxer named Butch, on the run for his life. Some of the earlier characters begin to drop back into the story, and gradually a grand design starts falling into place.

Buffs will have a field day with the bold, confident style of the film [based on stories by Tarantino and Roger Avary] and with the cinematic points of reference. Jackson possibly has the showiest opportunities. Travolta, sporting long hair and an earring, is also terrific, especially during his ambiguous outing with Thurman. Willis is all coiled tension and self-control. Keitel has tasty fun as a criminal efficiency expert.

1994: Original Screenplay

NOMINATIONS: Best Picture, Director, Actor (John Travolta), Supp. Actor (Samuel L. Jackson), Supp. Actress (Uma Thurman), Film Editing

•

PUMPING IRON

1977, 85 mins, US Ⓥ ⦿ col

Dir George Butler, Robert Fiore ***Prod*** George Butler, Jerome Gary ***Scr*** George Butler ***Ph*** Robert Fiore ***Ed*** Larry Silk, Geof Bartz ***Mus*** Michael Small

Act Arnold Schwarzenegger, Lou Ferrigno, Matty Ferrigno, Ken Waller, Franco Columbu, Mike Katz (Cinema 5)

The life of a bodybuilder who takes himself seriously is, ultimately, as lonely as that of a ballet dancer. He knows that if he's serious about his profession it means a daily, dedicated routine of exercises so that any gains won are not lost.

What this film documentary, based on George Butler and Charles Gaines's book, *Pumping Iron*, does not tell the viewer, however, is what lies beyond the peak of success.

The most fascinating aspect of this film is the dedicated training that turns average-built young men (frequently they refer to themselves as weaklings in their early youth) into superbly created physical edifices.

The film, while spotlighting Arnold Schwarzenegger, also treats with other competitors, preparing for the Mr. Universe and Mr. Olympia contests.

•

PUMPING IRON II: THE WOMEN

1985, 107 mins, US Ⓥ ⦿ col

Dir George Butler ***Prod*** George Butler ***Scr*** Charles Gaines, George Butler ***Ph*** Dyanna Taylor, Craig Perry ***Ed*** Paul Barnes, Susan Crutcher, Jane Kurson ***Mus*** David McHugh, Michael Montes

Act Lori Bowen, Carla Dunlap, Bev Francis, Rachel McLish, Kris Alexander, Lydia Cheng (Pumping Iron/White Mountain)

This enjoyable, slickly conceived documentary on the subculture of women's bodybuilding could have been better had director George Butler tempered his penchant for camera's eye detachment with some analytical and repertorial sweat.

Although he succeeds fairly well in exploiting the inherent drama of the 1983 Caesars Palace World Cup Championship for women bodybuilders, Butler is too content to let the alluring amazons speak for themselves on the film's central question: what is femininity and how far many women go in liberating themselves from stereotypes before confronting immovable cultural resistance?

The question is embodied graphically by Australian power-lifter Bev Francis, whose awesome, spectacularly mannish physique will be matched in a great flex-off against the wiry, compelling developed bodies of the best "feminine" bodybuilders. These include smug, shrewd defending champ Rachel McLish; the appealingly articulate Carla Dunlap, who's the only black woman in the group; and Lori Bowen, a humble girl from Texas who idolizes the aloof McLish and plans to use her prize money to free her boyfriend from his male go-go dancer's gig.

•

PUMPKIN EATER, THE

1964, 118 mins, UK b/w

Dir Jack Clayton ***Prod*** James Woolf ***Scr*** Harold Pinter ***Ph*** Oswald Morris ***Ed*** James Clark ***Mus*** Georges Delerue ***Art*** Edward Marshall

Act Anne Bancroft, Peter Finch, James Mason, Cedric Hardwicke, Richard Johnson, Eric Porter (Columbia/Romulus)

Harold Pinter's screenplay is based on a witty novel by Penelope Mortimer, and his script vividly brings to life the principal characters in this story of a shattered marriage, though Pinter's resort to flashback technique is confusing in the early stages. Jack Clayton's direction gets off to a slow, almost casual start, but the pace quickens as the drama becomes more intense.

Anne Bancroft is exceptionally good. She plays the mother of several young children who leaves her second husband to marry Peter Finch, a scriptwriter with a promising career ahead. And as he succeeds in his work, so she becomes aware of his increasing infidelities and she becomes a case for psychiatric treatment. The role may sound conventional enough, but not as played by Bancroft; she adds a depth and understanding which puts it on a higher plane.

Peter Finch's performance is a mature intrepretation, and always impressive. To him, casual infidelities are the natural prerequisites of a successful writer.

Notwithstanding the scope offered by those two roles, James Mason stands out in a much smaller part. He plays a deceived husband with a sinister, malevolent bitterness, to provide one of the acting highlights of the picture.

1964: NOMINATION: Best Actress (Anne Bancroft)

•

PUMP UP THE VOLUME
1990, 105 mins, US/Canada Ⓥ ⊙ col
Dir Allan Moyle ***Prod*** Rupert Harvey, Sandy Stern ***Scr*** Allan Moyle ***Ph*** Walt Lloyd ***Ed*** Wendy Bricmont, Ric Keeley, Kurt Hathaway ***Art*** Bruce Bolander
Act Christian Slater, Samantha Mathis, Ellen Greene, Scott Paulin, Cheryl Pollack, Annie Ross (New Line/SC Entertainment)

Writer-director Allan Moyle's story about a shy high school student who galvanizes an Arizona suburb with a rebellious pirate radio show has rambunctious energy and defiant attitude.

Christian Slater is first-rate as a bright but alienated student who feels trapped and disconnected in a suburban "whitebread land" where "everything is sold out." Everything includes his father (Scott Paulin), a former 1960s radical who has bought into the yuppie dream. Slater's rebellious late-night broadcasts soon make him a hero and stir up the dormant anger of other alienated kids. But one night his talk-radio antics go out of control.

Moyle resolves things in favor of love and justice, but his ending resolutely refuses to sell out the movie's angry stance against complacency. Slater handles numerous monolog scenes with conviction and charisma. Newcomer Samantha Mathis (as Nora, who falls in love with Slater's disembodied voice) and Paulin show a good grasp of their characters.

•

PUNCH AND JUDY MAN, THE
1963, 96 mins, UK b/w
Dir Jeremy Summers ***Prod*** Gordon L. T. Scott ***Scr*** Philip Oakes, Tony Hancock ***Ph*** Gilbert Taylor ***Ed*** Gordon Pilkington ***Mus*** Derek Acott, Don Banks
Act Tony Hancock, Sylvia Syms, Ronald Fraser, Barbara Murray, John Le Mesurier, Hugh Lloyd (Macconkey)

Tony Hancock's second film produces many amusing sequences, but it fails to jell. Story line is too slight. Result is a series of spasmodic incidents which Hancock has, largely, to carry on his own personality, despite being surrounded by some first-class character actors.

Hancock plays a Punch and Judy man at a seaside resort which is ruled over by a snobbish mayor. Hancock's marriage is foundering, since he fights the snobbery while his social climbing wife (Sylvia Syms) is anxious for him to mend his ways so that she can move into the local big league. Climax is the gala held to celebrate the 60th anni of the resort.

Director Jeremy Summers makes good use of the closeup to put over Hancock's expressive mug, and devotees of the comic will get a generous quota of giggles. But either Summers or the editor, or maybe both, have failed to keep the film on a taut and even keel.

Syms, as Hancock's disgruntled wife, takes her few opportunities avidly. Ronald Fraser shines as the officious mayor. Eddie Byrne chips in with a neat cameo as an ice cream assistant and Barbara Murray, as a socialite and guest of honor at the gala, pinpoints once more that she is a sadly underrated femme in pix.

•

PUNCHLINE
1988, 128 mins, US Ⓥ ⊙ col
Dir David Seltzer ***Prod*** Daniel Melnick, Michael Rachmil ***Scr*** David Seltzer ***Ph*** Reynaldo Villalobos ***Ed*** Bruce Green ***Mus*** Charles Gross ***Art*** Jack DeGovia
Act Sally Field, Tom Hanks, John Goodman, Mark Rydell, Kim Greist, Pam Matteson (Columbia)

Despite its title, *Punchline* is not a comedy. It's an uneven melodrama where Tom Hanks exhibits flashes of brilliance as a caustically tongued stand-up comic in a strange, undefinable romance with protege Sally Field. Hanks is the real reason to see the film and those who enjoyed watching him in *Big* will find a different, more realized comedian.

Punchline opens up the unfunny backstage world of stand-up comics by zeroing in on the lives and motivations of two very different people—Hanks as Steven Gold, a failing medical student who derives his humor from his experiences with cadavers and other things, and Field as Lilah, a Jersey housefrau and achingly bad novice comic with an unfulfilled desire to make people laugh.

Writer-director David Seltzer has tapped into one of the more intriguing subcultures of the entertainment world, here a place called the Gas Station in Manhattan where club owner Romeo (Mark Rydell) gives almost anyone a break.

There's a dark side to Hanks's character, which makes his time on stage more than superficially entertaining. Field supposedly brings out his soft side, playing the most unlikely of romantic interests—a styleless 40ish mom of two kids. How she manages to escape her claustrophobic existence playing wife to a traditionally minded insurance salesman husband (John Goodman) to try her schtick with the other wannabes is never quite believable.

The production overall manages to keep its audience off-center with surprisingly unpredictable moments—notably when Rydell is on the scene trying to keep things or his comics together.

•

PUNISHER, THE
1990, 90 mins, US/Australia Ⓥ ⊙ col
Dir Mark Goldblatt ***Prod*** Robert Kamen ***Scr*** Boaz Yakin ***Ph*** Ian Baker ***Ed*** Tim Wellburn ***Mus*** Dennis Dreith ***Art*** Norma Moriceau
Act Dolph Lundgren, Louis Gossett Jr., Jeroen Krabbe, Kim Miyori, Bryan Marshall, Nancy Everhard (New World)

With origins in a Marvel Comics character, *The Punisher* is, as might be expected, two-dimensional. The Punisher has killed 125 people before the film even begins, and the ensuing 90 minutes are crammed with slaughters of every conceivable kind. Pic was the only product of the New World offshoot Down Under.

Story involves an ex-cop whose wife and children were murdered by the mafia in New York. He hides from civilization in the city's sewers and for five years he's been killing the various heads of the mob families in nonstop vengeance.

Another party comes to play—the Japanese mafia headed by the glamorous, stony cold Lady Tanaka. The Punisher is quite content to see his enemies slaughter each other until the Japanese kidnap the locals' children.

Dolph Lundgren looks just as if he's stepped out of a comic book. Thankfully, he breezes through the B-grade plot with tongue firmly placed in cheek.

•

PUNISHMENT PARK
1971, 88 mins, US col
Dir Peter Watkins ***Scr*** Peter Watkins ***Ph*** Joan Churchill ***Ed*** Peter Watkins ***Mus*** Paul Motian
Act Paul Alelyanes, Carmen Argenziano, Stan Armsted, Harold Beaulieu, Jim Bohan, Kerry Cannon (Francoise)

Like the same director's *The War Game*, this pic apparently is set in the indeterminate future. It is presented in the guise of a live TV documentary complete with camera jerks, microphones and lights in full view.

Escalation of Asian wars is pre-supposed with intensified tensions between the larger international powers and the increase of anti-war propaganda and demonstrations of draft evaders.

Those youthful rebels coming before tribunals on conscientious and other grounds are given the choice of serving penal sentences or a three-days endurance test in Punishment Park, situated in Southern California. The rules are that "corrective groups" are given three days to reach, on foot, an American flag 57 miles away. They are allowed two to three hours' start, after which the National Guard hounds them out. If they manage to reach the flag in the alloted time they will be given their freedom. The journey they have to traverse is over desert territory in temperatures rising above the 100-degree mark by day and cold by night. The pic deftly switches back and forth from the members of one such corrective group, the armed forces and seven different offenders being tried by a quasi-judicial tribunal.

•

PUPPET ON A CHAIN
1971, 98 mins, UK Ⓥ col
Dir Geoffrey Reeve ***Prod*** Kurt Unger ***Scr*** Alistair MacLean ***Ph*** Jack Hildyard ***Ed*** Bill Lenny ***Mus*** Piero Piccioni
Act Sven-Bertil Taube, Barbara Parkins, Alexander Knox, Patrick Allen, Vladek Sheybal, Penny Casdagli (Unger)

Puppet on a Chain could be remembered as the film with the speedboat chase. Don Sharp, who was engaged specially to direct this sequence, has in no way spared the boats as the hero relentlessly pursues the villain through the canals of Amsterdam. Regrettably the standard of this sequence is not reflected in the rest of the film.

Sven-Bertil Taube plays a U.S. narcotics agent seeking the headquarters of a drug syndicate in Amsterdam aided by his outcover assistant, Maggie (Barbara Parkins). Wherever they go sudden death is never far behind. The trail leads to a religious order and an island castle.

Alistair MacLean scripted his own story. There is all the action, implausible happenings, violent rough housing and mystery that distinguishes so much of his work, but he has created little sympathy for the characters.

•

PURE COUNTRY
1992, 112 mins, US Ⓥ col
Dir Christopher Cain ***Prod*** Jerry Weintraub ***Scr*** Rex McGee ***Ph*** Richard Bowen ***Ed*** Jack Hofstra, Robin Katz ***Mus*** Steve Dorff ***Art*** Jeffrey Howard
Act George Strait, Lesley Ann Warren, Isabel Glasser, Kyle Chandler, John Doe, Rory Calhoun (Warner/Weintraub)

Though this slick-looking paean to down-home values often undercuts its own message, *Pure Country* is an effective vehicle for amiable country star George Strait. Screenplay mingles corn with knowing satire of the hollowness of stardom, but the heartfelt romantic chemistry between Strait and Texas ranch gal Isabel Glasser carries the day.

Strait's Dusty feels like a sham in his gussied-up show and wants to get back to basics, while his desperate manager Lesley Ann Warren fools the public by having her young stud (Kyle Chandler) lip-sync in his place.

Strait, who looks like a more wholesome version of the late Warren Oates, doesn't have much acting range, but he is convincing as someone who would just as soon chuck it all to settle down on Glasser's ranch.

Glasser's freshly scrubbed, weatherbeaten beauty and forthright country charm stand in starkly loaded contrast to the twitchy, overheated neuroticism of Warren, who archly vamps in a role that cries out for Elizabeth Ashley to camp it up.

•

PURE HELL OF ST. TRINIAN'S, THE
1960, 94 mins, UK Ⓥ b/w
Dir Frank Launder ***Prod*** Frank Launder, Sidney Gilliat ***Scr*** Sidney Gilliat, Frank Launder, Val Valentine ***Ph*** Gerald Gibbs ***Ed*** Thelma Connell ***Mus*** Malcolm Arnold
Act Cecil Parker, Joyce Grenfell, George Cole, Thorley Walters, Irene Handl, Eric Barker (Hallmark/Tudor)

Ronald Searle's familiar cartoon characters come to life in yet another St. Trinian's School romp, which is well up to standard.

Current yarn gets off to a flying start with the girls burning down the school and being brought to trial at the Old Bailey. But to the horror of the police and the Ministry of Education they are acquitted. This is partly because the judge does not miss the most beautiful blonde in the sixth form (Julie Alexander), but also because of the intervention of a strange professor who offers to start a new St. Trinian's and give the girls a fresh start. He turns out to be a dubious character mixed up with a racket for supplying glamor girls to an Oriental Emir as wives for his numerous sons.

Dialog is brisk and the film is directed at a sufficiently swift pace to keep the fun moving steadily.

In a large cast, Cecil Parker, as the professor; Irene Handl, as his assistant; Dennis Price, Thorley Walters, Eric Barker and Raymond Huntley all provide polished comedy studies. Joyce Grenfell is once again the prim policewoman in love with the superintendent. George Cole repeats his familiar performance as Flash Harry, who runs a matrimonial agency on behalf of the Sixth Form

•

PURPLE HEART, THE
1944, 90 mins, US Ⓥ b/w
Dir Lewis Milestone ***Prod*** Darryl F. Zanuck ***Scr*** Jerome Cady ***Ph*** Arthur Miller ***Ed*** Douglas Biggs ***Mus*** Alfred Newman ***Art*** James Baseri, Lewis Creber
Act Dana Andrews, Richard Conte, Farley Granger, Sam Levene, Tala Birell (20th Century-Fox)

The celluloid version of the tragic events which followed the capture of eight of the American flyers who bombed Tokyo is an intensely moving piece, spellbinding though gory at times, gripping and suspenseful for the most part. Scenes depicting, by inference, the tortures which the American boys were subjected to, strike home with terrific impact. About a dozen individual performances are outstanding, with acting honors being shared fairly evenly among all the principals in the drama.

Under Darryl Zanuck's production guidance and Lewis Milestone's deft direction, Jerome Cady's script emerges as taut, swift-paced fare.

The story is about eight captured American flyers on trial before a Jap civil court on a murder rap, charged with purposely bombing and machine-gunning Jap civilians. Protests by Lt. Wayne Greenbaum (Sam Levene) that civil courts have no jurisdiction over military prisoners and that the proceedings constitute a violation of the Geneva Convention are ignored. Action takes place mainly in the Jap courtroom, with war correspondents from Axis nations only admitted.

•

PURPLE HEARTS

1984, 115 mins, US col

Dir Sidney J. Furie ***Prod*** Sidney J. Furie ***Scr*** Rick Natkin, Sidney J. Furie ***Ph*** Jan Kiesser ***Ed*** George Grenville ***Mus*** Robert Folk ***Art*** Francisco Balangue

Act Ken Wahl, Cheryl Ladd, Stephen Lee, David Harris, Cyril O'Reilly, Lane Smith (Ladd)

Purple Hearts is a systematically simple love story set against the Vietnam War, with the action largely overwhelming the romantic time-outs.

Ken Wahl is a handsome young and dedicated doctor in Vietnam where he meets a beautiful young and dedicated nurse (Cheryl Ladd). They fall in love. Between kisses, they assure each other that they hope one day to return Stateside and do medical good together forever. But then he's killed—but no he isn't—and then she's killed—but (fill in the blank)—and it looks like they may never live happily ever after. Wahl is solid in the lead and Ladd hangs in there in a less demanding part.

•

PURPLE PLAIN, THE

1954, 100 mins, UK col

Dir Robert Parrish ***Prod*** John Bryan ***Scr*** Eric Ambler ***Ph*** Geoffrey Unsworth ***Ed*** Clive Donner ***Mus*** John Veale ***Art*** Jack Maxstead

Act Gregory Peck, Win Min Than, Bernard Lee, Maurice Denham, Lyndon Brook, Brenda de Banzie (Two Cities)

The combined writing talents of novelist H. E. Bates and scripter Eric Ambler produce a fine dramatic vehicle for Gregory Peck's second British-made film which is set in the Burmese jungle in the last days of the war.

After vividly establishing the atmosphere and developing the principal characters, the action switches from the airstrip to mountainous terrain held by the Japs into which Peck has crashed his plane while on a routine flight with his navigator (Lyndon Brook) and a fellow officer (Maurice Denham). From that point the entire incident concentrates on their attempts to get out with Peck in an obstinate mood and insisting that they should not wait by the wreckage for help but should try and reach water.

There are some very tender scenes played in a neighbouring village community in which Peck begins a romantic entanglement with Win Min Than, an exotic yet restrained Burmese beauty. The backgrounds, filmed in Ceylon, are lensed in lush Technicolor.

•

PURPLE RAIN

1984, 104 mins, US col

Dir Albert Magnoli ***Prod*** Robert Cavallo, Joseph Ruffalo, Steven Fargnoli ***Scr*** Albert Magnoli, William Blinn ***Ph*** Donald E. Thorin ***Ed*** Albert Magnoli, Ken Robinson ***Mus*** Michel Colombier ***Art*** Ward Preston

Act Prince, Apollonia Kotero, Morris Day, Olga Karlatos, Clarence Williams III, Jerome Benton (Warner/Purple)

Playing a character rooted in his own background, and surrounded by the real-life members of his Minneapolis-based musical "family," rock star Prince makes an impressive feature film debut in *Purple Rain*, a rousing contemporary addition to the classic backstage musical genre.

Director Albert Magnoli gets a solid, appealing performance from Prince, whose sensual, somewhat androgynous features are as riveting on film as they are on a concert stage. Femme love interest Apollonia Kotero is a beautiful, winsome presence.

Custom-tailored vehicle for the rocker spins the familiar tale of a youngster who escapes the sordid confines of his family life through music, ultimately becoming the better man and musician.

1984: Best Original Song Score

•

PURPLE ROSE OF CAIRO, THE

1985, 82 mins, US col

Dir Woody Allen ***Prod*** Robert Greenhut ***Scr*** Woody Allen ***Ph*** Gordon Willis ***Ed*** Susan E. Morse ***Mus*** Dick Hyman ***Art*** Stuart Wurtzel

Act Mia Farrow, Jeff Daniels, Danny Aiello, Dianne Wiest, Van Johnson, Zoe Caldwell (Orion)

Tale is a light, almost frivolous treatment of a serious theme, as Woody Allen here confronts the unalterable fact that life just doesn't turn out the way it does (or did) in Hollywood films. For all its situational goofiness, pic is a tragedy, and it's too bad Allen didn't build up the characters and drama sufficiently to give some weight to his concerns.

Allen introduces Depression-era waitress Mia Farrow, a hopeless film buff so consumed by motion picture gossip and fantasies she can barely hold down her job.

Her husband (Danny Aiello) is a complete boor, so she spends all her free time seeing films over and over again until Tom Baxter (Jeff Daniels), a character in a fictional RKO epic *The Purple Rose of Cairo*, stops the action, starts speaking to Farrow directly from the screen, and, fed up with repeating the same action time after time, steps out of the film and asks to be shown something of real life.

Mia Farrow is excellent again under Allen's direction, and at certain times (especially when lying to her husband) begins to sound like him.

Jeff Daniels is okay as the bland 1930s adventurer come to life, although he's rather restricted by role's unavoidable thinness.

1985: NOMINATION: Best Original Screenplay

•

PURSUED

1947, 100 mins, US b/w

Dir Raoul Walsh ***Prod*** Milton Sperling ***Scr*** Niven Busch ***Ph*** James Wong Howe ***Ed*** Christian Nyby ***Mus*** Max Steiner ***Art*** Ted Smith

Act Teresa Wright, Robert Mitchum, Judith Anderson, Dean Jagger, Harry Carey, Jr., John Rodney (Warner/United States)

Pursued is potent frontier days western film fare. Standout in picture is suspense generated by the original script and Raoul Walsh's direction. It builds the western gunman's death walk to high moments of thrill and action. Strong casting also is a decided factor in selling the action wares. Production makes use of natural outdoor backgrounds supplied by New Mexico scenery, lending air of authenticity that is fully captured by the camera.

There are psychological elements in the script, depicting the hate that drives through a man's life and forces him into unwanted dangers. Robert Mitchum is the victim of that hate, made to kill and fear because of an old family feud. His role fits him naturally and he makes it entirely believable. Teresa Wright upholds the femme lead with another of her honestly valued, talented portrayals that register sincerity.

Plot motivation stems from feuding between the Callums and the Rands. Feud starts when Dean Jagger, a Callum, wipes out Mitchum's family because a Callum girl dared love Mitchum's father.

Among memorable moments is the stalking of Mitchum by the Callums as he spends his wedding night with a bride who also had just tried to kill him.

•

PURSUIT OF D. B. COOPER, THE

1981, 100 mins, US col

Dir Roger Spottiswoode ***Prod*** Daniel Wigutow, Michael Taylor ***Scr*** Jeffrey Alan Fiskin ***Ph*** Harry Stradling, Charles F. Wheeler ***Ed*** Allan Jacobs, Robbe Roberts ***Mus*** James Horner ***Art*** Preston Ames

Act Robert Duvall, Treat Williams, Kathryn Harrold, Ed Flanders, Paul Gleason, R. G. Armstrong (PolyGram/Universal)

A decade earlier, "D. B. Cooper"—whoever he really was—did indeed excite the nation by taking over a jet with a fake bomb, demanding $200,000 and then parachuting out the back door, never to be seen again. That tale could still make an exciting picture.

Unfortunately, director Roger Spottiswoode and writer Jeffrey Alan Fiskin [adapting the book *Free Fall* by J. D. Reed] choose to invent a totally specious yarn that begins with Treat Williams leaping from the plane. Apparently, he landed in an episode of *The Dukes of Hazzard*, complete with banjos and Waylon Jennings in the background.

The airline's insurance agent (Robert Duvall) just happens to be Williams's former Green Beret instructor and naturally suspects who the culprit is. Paul Gleason is also a fellow Green Beret, now wearing a black hat, who also suspects who got the money.

Duvall and Gleason venture upon separate pursuits while Williams drops by the homestead to gather up his suffering wife (Kathryn Harrold) to go escaping with him. The resulting endless chases have the cinematic value of a laundry dryer.

Begun by director John Frankenheimer, continued by director Buzz Kulik and finally finished by Spottiswoode, *Cooper* must have once had something that attracted such normally fine performers as Duvall, Williams and Harrold.

•

PURSUIT OF THE GRAF SPEE

SEE: THE BATTLE OF THE RIVER PLATE

•

PUSHING TIN

1999, 124 mins, US col

Dir Mike Newell ***Prod*** Art Linson ***Scr*** Glen Charles, Les Charles ***Ph*** Gale Tattersall ***Ed*** Jon Gregory ***Mus*** Anne Dudley ***Art*** Bruno Rubeo

Act John Cusack, Billy Bob Thornton, Cate Blanchett, Angelina Jolie, Vicki Lewis, Jake Webber (Linson/Regency/Fox 2000)

Pushing Tin makes for a lively flight most of the way, but then coasts in on its approach toward a routine landing. This punchy and involving look at the cowboys who form the seemingly crazed fraternity of air traffic controllers benefits from its privileged peek at a fresh milieu and from some fine character detailing by the four leading players. Unfortunately, story's tension climaxes a half-hour before the film is over.

[Based on the article *Something's Got to Give* by Darcy Frey], script by writer-producers of *Cheers* and *Taxi* attempts to create a sense of camaraderie among the well-paid but stressed-out workers who sit at their radar screens on Long Island to guide 7,000 planes a day to Gotham's three international airports. But just two of them emerge with any depth: Nick Falzone (John Cusack), the self-confessed ace of the team, and Russell Bell (Billy Bob Thornton) a new arrival from out West whose Zenlike cool unnerves Nick.

Nick's wife, Connie (Cate Blanchett), conscientiously dabbles in classes to improve herself. But Russell's voluptuous young wife, Mary (Angelina Jolie), dresses like a tart and has a weakness for booze. Nick can't resist taking advantage of Mary's drunken vulnerability one evening. The erotic/paranoid/competitive tension among Nick and Connie and Russell and Mary is deliciously sustained until Nick is undone at home by Connie's learning the truth, and at the office by Russell's becoming a media hero.

The biggest surprise is Blanchett, the Aussie actress, who adds more layers to her performance than anyone else. *Pushing Tin* is slang for the controllers' job of directing planes into flight patterns.

•

PUSSYCAT ALLEY

SEE: THE WORLD TEN TIMES OVER

•

PUTNEY SWOPE

1969, 84 mins, US b/w

Dir Robert Downey ***Scr*** Robert Downey ***Ph*** Gerald Cotts ***Ed*** Bud Smith ***Mus*** Charley Cuva ***Art*** Gary Weist

Act Stanley Gottlieb, Allen Garfield, Arnold Johnson, Laura Greene, Ramon Gordon (Herold)

What happens when black militants take over a large Manhattan advertising agency is the basis for a comic satire on black racial identity and the dollar sign on the American altar of success.

The situations include political caricature, but disappointedly nothing much beyond marginal interest occurs. The comedy is only intermittently funny and the satire is mostly shallow and obvious.

Putney Swope is the only black member of an ad agency. By happenstance he is elected to head the firm after the previous chairman dies. Director Robert Downey's sense of the ridiculous is employed in a spotty, punchline kind of comic usage. The sharp individual parts do not build to anything and the film, as a piece, is more often dull than exciting, less revealingly witty then merely clever.

•

PUZZLE OF A DOWNFALL CHILD

1970, 104 mins, US col

Dir Jerry Schatzberg ***Prod*** Paul Newman, John Foreman ***Scr*** Adrien Joyce [= Carolyn Eastman] ***Ph*** Adam Holender ***Ed*** Evan Lottman ***Mus*** Michael Small ***Art*** Richard Bianchi

Act Faye Dunaway, Barry Primus, Viveca Lindfors, Barry Morse, Roy Scheider (Universal)

Puzzle of a Downfall Child, stars Faye Dunaway as a confused high-fashion model with severe emotional problems, most never resolved. Unfortunately, the film is marked by cinema-verite chic though Dunaway makes the most of a tour-de-force opportunity.

Plot takes a riches-to-rags course, Dunaway entering as the latest hot model, insecure in frustrating relationships with photographer Barry Primus and well-to-do Roy Scheider. Dunaway tells her story to Primus in flashback in her seacoast cabin refuge from mental breakdown, professional decline and personal unfulfillment.

The character first garners wholesome pity, but the plot development soon banishes her to bathos and finally boredom.

•

PYGMALION

1938, 96 mins, UK Ⓥ ⊙ b/w

Dir Anthony Asquith, Leslie Howard ***Prod*** Gabriel Pascal ***Scr*** George Bernard Shaw, W. P. Lipscomb, Cecil Lewis ***Ph*** Harry Stradling ***Ed*** David Lean ***Mus*** Arthur Honegger ***Art*** Laurence Irving, John Bryan

Act Wendy Hiller, Leslie Howard, Wilfrid Lawson, Marie Lohr, Scott Sunderland, Jean Cadell (Pascal)

Smartly produced, this makes an excellent job of transcribing George Bernard Shaw, retaining all the key lines and giving freshness to the theme. The speed of the first half contrives to show up the anticlimax, the play subsequently petering out in a flood of clever talk. But it's still a Cinderella story, which is one of the most reliable subjects for drama.

Leslie Howard's performance is excellent in its comedy. It's vital and at times dominating. Wendy Hiller carries off a difficult part faultlessly. She never loses sight of the fact that this is a guttersnipe on whom culture has been imposed; the ambassador's reception, where she moves like a sleepwalker, is eloquent of this, and even in the final argument the cockney is always peeping through the veneer.

Wilfred Lawson's Doolittle is only a shadow of the part G. B. S. wrote, but his moral philosophies could obviously not have been put on the screen in toto without gumming up the action. As it is he presents a thoroughly enjoyable old reprobate.

1938: Best Adaptation, Screenplay (George Bernard Shaw)

NOMINATIONS: Best Picture, Actor (Leslie Howard), Actress (Wendy Hiller)

•

PYROMANIAC'S LOVE STORY, A

1995, 94 mins, US Ⓥ col

Dir Joshua Brand ***Prod*** Mark Gordon ***Scr*** Morgan Ward ***Ph*** John Schwartzman ***Ed*** David Rosenbloom ***Mus*** Rachel Portman ***Art*** Dan Davis

Act William Baldwin, John Leguizamo, Sadie Frost, Erika Eleniak, Michael Lerner, Joan Plowright (Hollywood)

Highly reminiscent of *Moonstruck* and other works written by John Patrick Shanley, *A Pyromaniac's Love Story* is a modern-day fairy tale with a bemused appreciation of romantic love, blazing passions and other human follies. Television vet Joshua Brand (*St. Elsewhere*, *Northern Exposure*) has assembled a sparkling ensemble cast for his debut effort as a feature helmer.

Plot revolves around a mysterious fire that razes a bakery in a multi-ethnic, inner-city neighborhood. Initially, pastry boy Sergio Cuccio (John Leguizamo) fears his beloved employer, Mr. Linzer (Armin Mueller-Stahl), has torched the place to avoid a humiliating bankruptcy. But Sergio quickly learns the real culprit is the hot-blooded, mood-swinging son of a successful businessman.

Mr Lumpke (an unbilled Richard Crenna) offers Sergio $25,000 to take the rap for his son, Garet (William Baldwin). Sergio seriously considers the deal as it will enable him to see the world with the young woman of his dreams, Hattie (Sadie Frost), a spirited waitress with a serious case of wanderlust.

Things get complicated when Linzer insists on making his own confession. But the real complications arise only when, 30 minutes into the pic, Garet makes his first on-screen appearance.

Pic was shot on location in Toronto. For a welcome change, however, the city is not used as a stand-in for New York or some other specific U.S. locale

Q
(UK: Q—THE WINGED SERPENT; AKA: THE WINGED SERPENT)
1982, 92 mins, US Ⓥ col
Dir Larry Cohen ***Prod*** Larry Cohen ***Scr*** Larry Cohen ***Ph*** Fred Murphy ***Ed*** Armand Lebowitz ***Mus*** Robert O. Ragland
Act Michael Moriarty, Candy Clark, David Carradine, Richard Roundtree, Lee Louis, Malachy McCourt (Larco)

Larry Cohen's tale of a religious bird of prey terrorizing New York City has wit, style and an above average script for the genre.

Story centers on Michael Moriarty, an ex-junkie who drives getaway cars for the mob. He takes refuge in the Chrysler Building's summit, where he stumbles onto the title character's lair complete with a large unhatched egg.

In the meantime, the green bird has been having a merry feed of workmen and apartment dwellers in the city's high rises. Policeman David Carradine links the arrival of the monster to a series of bizarre ritual killings where the victims are literally skinned alive.

Q has great fun mixing realistic settings with political satire and a wild yarn. Writer-director Cohen has a bagful of tricks and a wild sense of the bizarre to lend the project.

The picture belongs to the bird and Moriarty, and the latter assays his loser with relish.

•

Q&A
1990, 132 mins, US Ⓥ ⦿ col
Dir Sidney Lumet ***Prod*** Arnon Milchan, Burtt Harris ***Scr*** Sidney Lumet ***Ph*** Andrzej Bartkowiak ***Ed*** Richard Cirincione ***Mus*** Ruben Blades ***Art*** Philip Rosenberg
Act Nick Nolte, Timothy Hutton, Armand Assante, Patrick O'Neal, Lee Richardson, Jenny Lumet (Regency/Odyssey)

Director Sidney Lumet grabs a tiger by the tail with *Q&A*, a hard-hitting thriller that takes on weighty topics of racism and corruption in the New York City justice system.

Working from Edwin Torres's novel, Lumet has scripted in concise, suspenseful fashion, opening with cop Nick Nolte ruthlessly killing a Latino drug dealer outside an after-hours club and then intimidating witnesses on the scene. As his first job as a new assistant d.a., Timothy Hutton is summoned by his cooly evil boss Patrick O'Neal (a man with unbridled political ambitions) to do a routine investigation, writing up a Q&A with Nolte and other principal players. He's obviously the fall guy. Key to film's success is how the case gradually uncovers new layers of corruption and insidious racism, with escalating awareness (and danger) for Hutton.

Nolte is outstanding, bringing utter conviction to the stream of racist and sexist epithets that pour from his good ole boy lips.

•

QIUJU DA GUANSI
(THE STORY OF QIU JU)
1992, 99 mins, Hong Kong Ⓥ col
Dir Zhang Yimou ***Prod*** Ma Fung-kwok (exec.) ***Scr*** Liu Heng ***Ph*** Chi Xiaoning, Yu Xiaoqun ***Ed*** Du Yuan ***Mus*** Zhao Jiping ***Art*** Cao Jiuping
Act Gong Li, Lei Kesheng, Ge Zhijun, Liu Peiqi, Yang Liuchun (Sil-Metropole)

Adapted from a novel [Chen Yuanbin's *The Wan Family's Lawsuit/Wan jia susong*] set in rural China, *The Story of Qiu Ju* marks Chinese director Zhang Yimou's first contempo story, and as such lacks the exotic visual pageantry that was big attraction in his prior pics. Yet this simple, repetitive tale has a mesmerizing quality able to hook audiences from beginning to end.

Zhang leading lady Gong Li forgoes glamor to play a round, pregnant peasant, Qiu Ju. Her young husband (Liu Peiqi) is laid up after a fight with the village head (Lei Kesheng) in which he received a debilitating kick in the groin. Qiu Ju makes up her mind that the village chief must apologize; this the old man, who's as stubborn as she, refuses to do. Qiu Ju thus embarks on a series of pilgrimages to get justice done. Local mediators and then the city court judges don't understand that it's a question of principles. They just rule the village chief must pay damages, which Qiu Ju couldn't care less about. In a final twist, Qiu Ju tastes a very bitter victory.

High-pitched songs punctuate the fable-like tale with authentic local music. Cinematography shifts from panoramas of majestic mountains and bustling city-scapes to intimate family scenes. Many of the strikingly authentic crowd shots were snatched by using a hidden camera.

•

Q PLANES
1939, 82 mins, UK b/w
Dir Tim Whelan ***Prod*** Irving Asher, Alexander Korda ***Scr*** Ian Dalrymple, Brock Williams, Jack Whittingham, Arthur

Wimperis ***Ph*** Harry Stradling ***Mus*** Muir Mathieson (dir.) ***Art*** Vincent Korda
Act Laurence Olivier, Ralph Richardson, Valerie Hobson (Harefield/London)

Q Planes is an aviation picture, but not heavy on heroics. Even in the final rescue sequence, melodramatically carried to the timber line of hokum, there is a refreshing tongue-in-cheek attitude. Whole thing is bright, breezy and flavorsome. Starts off as a newsreel, showing government buildings and streets in London.

The acting honors go—and at a gallop—to Ralph Richardson, playing a Scotland Yard eccentric. Director Tim Whelan is entitled to full credit for a generally fast-paced and well-integrated entertainment.

Plot concerns the use of a salvage ship anchored at sea to capture army airplanes on their test flights. All of the crew speak with German accents and little doubt is left as to who the villains are.

Valerie Hobson, as a newspaperwoman and sister of the Scotland Yard eccentric, provides the romantic touch.

•

Q—THE WINGED SERPENT
SEE: Q

•

QUADROPHENIA
1979, 120 mins, UK Ⓥ ⦿ col
Dir Franc Roddam ***Prod*** Roy Baird, Bill Curbishley ***Scr*** Dave Humphries, Martin Stellman, Franc Roddam ***Ph*** Brian Tufano ***Ed*** Mike Taylor ***Mus*** Pete Townshend ***Art*** Simon Holland
Act Phil Daniels, Mark Wingett, Toyah Wilcox, Sting, Leslie Ash (The Who)

Set in 1963, when rival image-cults among young Britishers led to a wave of crowd-fights in normally staid seaside resorts, the picture [based on the record album *Quadrophenia* by Pete Townshend] plots the plight of one pill-popping, fashion-mad "Mod" who abandons himself completely to the gang-identity.

After fighting the enemy "Rockers" (denoted by black leather, motorbikes and beer) in a disorderly clash on Brighton beach, and being arrested for the cause, he swiftly discovers the hollowness of the whole image thing.

It's a tribute to helmer Franc Roddam's simple, restrained direction that the downbeat ending, when the jobless, exhausted kid is left in the advanced state of schizophrenia implied by the title, succeeds in being climactic.

Sting, as the weekend super-Mod whose image collapses when he's revealed to work as a bellhop, cuts a slick dash in the dancehall sequences.

•

QUAI DES ORFEVRES
1947, 110 mins, France b/w
Dir Henri-Georges Clouzot ***Prod*** Roger de Venloo ***Scr*** Henri-Georges Clouzot, J. Ferry ***Ph*** Armand Thirard ***Ed*** Charles Bretoneiche ***Mus*** Francis Lopez ***Art*** Maz Douy
Act Louis Jouvet, Simone Renant, Bernard Blier, Suzy Delair, Pierre Larquey, Charles Dullin (Majestic)

Quai des Orfevres, being for the French the equivalent of what Scotland Yard is for the British, indicates clearly that this is a detective meller [from the novel *Legitime Defense* by S. A. Steeman]. In every respect it is outstanding.

The murder on which the investigation hangs is but an excuse for the story, which combines a character study of a show business couple, detective work most realistically staged in authentic sets of police headquarters.

Louis Jouvet, as the star, does not enter the picture until it has rolled some time. It opens showing Suzy Delair, an ambitious small-time torch singer, making overtures to a banker who can star her overnight, despite the jealousy of her husband. Delair is of the Mae West type. Jouvet does his part of the poor but honest detective with his usual peculiar mannerisms, but in exemplary manner. Bernard Blier, as the weak husband whom jealousy makes a potential murderer, brings out everything in the character.

Simone Renant, as the photographer who is the couple's best friend, is very plausible. Charles Dullin, legit actor who specializes in character parts, is suitably repulsive as the picture-maker. Pierre Larquey is the honest taxi driver whom the police methods compel to turn informant in spite of himself.

Direction by Henri-Georges Clouzot takes full advantage of every possible opportunity to bring out character and manages to keep the tempo at a fast clip all the time.

•

QUALITY STREET
1937, 84 mins, US Ⓥ ⦿ b/w
Dir George Stevens ***Prod*** Pandro S. Berman ***Scr*** Mortimer Offner, Allan Scott ***Ph*** Robert de Grasse ***Ed*** Henry Berman ***Mus*** Roy Webb
Act Katharine Hepburn, Franchot Tone, Eric Blore, Fay Bainter, Cora Witherspoon, Joan Fontaine (RKO)

Of a dramatic texture which never was too strong even in the theatre, *Quality Street* is a theatrical memory involving Maude Adams in a J. M. Barrie piece. It was not rated among her best. Incredibly romantic and farcical, the idea of a 30-year-old woman deceiving her sweetheart into believing she is her own niece of 16 was tough going for the horse-and-buggy patrons of 1901.

It is a film full of effort. The settings are of a charming London residential spot, the gardens are charmingly arranged, and the costumes are charming beyond description. The dialog tries to be charming, too. The men in the cast, headed by Franchot Tone, are soldiers in England's army which smashed Napoleon. They're not so charming as quaint. Napoleon must have been a pushover and history is all wrong.

Working from a script possessing neither imagination nor ingenuity, George Stevens is limited in his direction.

1937: NOMINATION: Best Score

•

QUARE FELLOW, THE
1962, 90 mins, UK b/w
Dir Arthur Dreifuss ***Prod*** Anthony Havelock-Allan ***Scr*** Arthur Dreifuss ***Ph*** Peter Hennessy ***Ed*** Gitta Zadek ***Mus*** Alexander Faris ***Art*** Ted Marshall
Act Patrick McGoohan, Sylvia Syms, Walter Macken, Harry Brogan, Dermot Kelly, Marie Kean (British Lion)

Based on Brendan Behan's play [adapted by Jacqueline Sundstrom and director Arthur Dreifuss], this is an all-out protest against capital punishment. It is downbeat entertainment but honest and has the benefit of a sterling cast, virtually all Irish. It has also been shot entirely in a Dublin prison and on location.

Patrick McGoohan is a young man from the Irish backwoods who takes up his first appointment as a jail warder with lofty ideals. Criminals must be punished for the sake of society is his inflexible theory and that also embraces capital punishment. But when he arrives he is shaken by the prison atmosphere.

Two men are awaiting the noose. One is reprieved but hangs himself. That shakes McGoohan. He meets the young wife (Sylvia Syms) of the other murderer and his convictions totter still more when he hears precisely what caused her husband to murder his brother. Mostly, though, he is influenced by a veteran warder (Walter Macken) who believes that capital punishment is often a worse crime than the original offence. *The Quare Fellow* (Irish prison slang for a guy due to be topped) is mostly a study of men's conscience and convictions. Such thin storyline as there is hinges on whether the murderer will be reprieved.

The film, a mixture of grim humor and cynical starkness, brings out the clamminess and misery of prison life, and is helped by the grey lensing of Peter Hennessy.

•

QUARTET
1948, 120 mins, UK Ⓥ b/w
Dir Ken Annakin, Arthur Crabtree, Harold French, Ralph Smart ***Prod*** Antony Darnborough ***Scr*** R. C. Sherriff ***Ph*** Ray Elton, Reg Wyer ***Ed*** A. Charles Knott, Jean Barker ***Mus*** John Greenwood ***Art*** George Provis, Cedric Dalve
Act Basil Radford, Naunton Wayne, Dirk Bogarde, George Cole, Cecil Parker, Nora Swinburne (Rank/Gainsborough)

Of the four stories [from originals by Somerset Maugham] that make up the film, the first and last are the most intriguing. *The Facts of Life* [directed by Ralph Smart] is a superbly told piece of a 19-year-old who disregards his father's advice on his first trip to Monte Carlo and outwits an obvious adventuress, and *The Colonel's Lady* [directed by Ken Annakin] is a delightful yarn of a colonel's wife

(Nora Swinburne) who causes much embarrassment to her husband (Cecil Parker) by the publication of a book of verse purporting to describe her romantic experiences.

The intermediate two, while lacking the high level of the first and last, are certainly more than potboilers. An undergraduate son (Dirk Bogarde) of a member of the landed gentry, who hopes to become a professional pianist, provides the melodramatic theme of *The Alien Corn* [directed by Harold French], while *The Kite* [directed by Arthur Crabtree] is an unusual story of a simple young man (George Cole), very much under his mother's domination, who put his kite-flying before his wife and cheerfully goes to gaol when she wrecks his latest invention.

•

QUARTET
1981, 100 mins, UK/France col
Dir James Ivory ***Prod*** Ismael Merchant, Jean-Pierre Mahot de la Querantonnais ***Scr*** Ruth Prawer Jhabvala ***Ph*** Pierre Lhomme ***Ed*** Humphrey Dixon ***Mus*** Richard Robbins ***Art*** Jean-Jaques Caziot
Act Alan Bates, Maggie Smith, Isabelle Adjani, Anthony Higgins, Suzanne Flon, Pierre Clementi (Merchant Ivory/Lyric)

Quartet is an elegant tale of a pretty, innocent but resilient woman set in the Paris of the late 1920s. Director James Ivory takes his usual aloofly observant distance and the film's love triangle loses some drastic impetus. The seething Paris bohemian backdrop of the era is used only in a token way.

Isabelle Adjani is married to a young Pole who, arrested when he gets mixed up in nefarious art dealings, is sentenced to a year in prison. She is left alone and penniless. A noted English agent, played by Alan Bates with massive solemnity, had taken a shine to her after meeting her in the expatriate circles of Paris residents. He asks her to move in with him and his wife.

The latter is an edgy, middle-aged painter limned with asperity by Maggie Smith. Other girls had stayed there and she indulged her husband's sensuality to keep him. Adjani at first spurns Bates's advances but gives in though she still loves her husband.

Overall, a low-key film. Based on Jean Rhys's book, the script uses her spare style.

•

QUATERMASS AND THE PIT
(US: 5,000,000 YEARS TO EARTH)
1968, 98 mins, UK col
Dir Roy Ward Baker ***Prod*** Anthony Nelson Keys ***Scr*** Nigel Kneale ***Ph*** Arthur Grant ***Ed*** James Needs, Spencer Reeve ***Mus*** Tristram Cary ***Art*** Bernard Robinson, Ken Ryan
Act James Donald, Andrew Keir, Barbara Shelley, Julian Glover, Duncan Lamont, Bryan Marshall (Hammer)

A long-dormant tribe from Mars, accidentally liberated by a London excavation, forms a good story peg but routine, somewhat distended development blunts impact of this British-made programmer.

Nigel Kneale's original script again turns on the Prof. Quatermass character, essayed by Andrew Keir, this time embroiled with a stuffy colonel (Julian Glover) when a scientist (James Donald) discovers skeletons in a London subway expansion. Evil demons, brain waves and sketchy visions of a dying Mars civilization, plus some great special effects work, provide plot complications. Given the predictable science-vs-military conflicts, and the introduction of Barbara Shelley as a female scientist (like Jean Parker and Ellen Drew in other years), film manages to retain interest through suspenseful (if not always clear) exposition of the mysterious creatures. Roy Ward Baker's direction is professional.

•

QUATERMASS EXPERIMENT, THE
(US: THE CREEPING UNKNOWN)
1955, 81 mins, UK b/w
Dir Val Guest ***Prod*** Anthony Hinds ***Scr*** Val Guest, Richard Landau ***Ph*** Jimmy Harvey ***Ed*** James Needs ***Mus*** James Bernard ***Art*** J. Elder Wills
Act Brian Donlevy, Jack Warner, Richard Wordsworth, David King-Wood, Gordon Jackson, Lionel Jeffries (Hammer)

Taken from a BBC television play, *The Quatermass Experiment* is an extravagant piece of science fiction, based on the after-effects of an assault on space by a rocket ship. Despite its obvious horror angles, production is crammed with incident and suspense.

Brian Donlevy (in the title role) is the scientist who designs a new rocket that is sent hurtling into space with three men on board. It crash lands in a small English village, with only one survivor. The mystery is what happened to the other two who have disappeared without trace although the rocket ship remained air sealed.

This is unrelieved melodrama. It draws its entertainment from a series of wildly improbable happenings. There is an occasional over-plus of horror closeups of the victims.

Donlevy plays the scientist with a grim and ruthless conviction.

•

QUATERMASS 2
(US: ENEMY FROM SPACE)
1957, 84 mins, UK b/w
Dir Val Guest ***Prod*** Anthony Hinds ***Scr*** Nigel Kneale, Val Guest ***Ph*** Gerald Gibbs ***Ed*** James Needs ***Mus*** James Bernard ***Art*** Bernard Robinson
Act Brian Donlevy, John Longden, Sidney James, Bryan Forbes, William Franklyn, Vera Day (Hammer)

Production stars Brian Donlevy as an English scientist engaged in interplanetary research. He suddenly stumbles upon a hush-hush government project on the moorlands where it's announced that synthetic food is being produced, but actually its operations are being directed by an enemy from space, working to take over the earth. Yarn unfolds in fine confusion, Donlevy in some way managing to destroy the project.

Val Guest's direction is as uncertain as script on which he collabs with Nigel Kneale [author of original story], with the result that all characters are stodgy. Donlevy is supported by John Longden, as a Scotland Yard inspector trying to help; Sidney James, a newspaper reporter; William Franklyn, a lab assistant, and Bryan Forbes, another assistant who comes under the out-of-this-world spell.

Special effects are imaginative.

•

QUATRE CENTS COUPS, LES
(THE 400 BLOWS)
1959, 98 mins, France b/w
Dir Francois Truffaut ***Scr*** Francois Truffaut, Marcel Moussy ***Ph*** Henri Decae ***Ed*** Marie-Josephe Yoyotte ***Mus*** Jean Constantin ***Art*** Bernard Evein
Act Jean-Pierre Leaud, Claire Maurier, Albert Remy, Guy Decomble, Patrick Auffay, Georges Flamant (Carrosse/SEDIF)

Offbeat pic gets deep into the life of a 12-year-old boy, his disorientation with school and parents, and his final commitment to, and escape from, an institution. It eschews conventional blames and emerges an engaging, moving film.

Boy has a mother who cheats on his weak father. One day he runs off when, to explain a truancy, he suddenly makes up a tale that his mother is dead. He steals something and is committed to an institution as his parents wash their hands of him. Pic ends with his dash to freedom.

Moppets are well-handled and adults properly one-dimensional in this astute look at the child's world. Young director Francois Truffaut [scripting from his own original story] still lacks form and polish but emerges an important new director here. Technical qualities are uneven but blend with the meandering but sensitive look at a child's world and revolt.

•

QUEEN CHRISTINA
1933, 100 mins, US b/w
Dir Rouben Mamoulian ***Prod*** Walter Wanger ***Scr*** S. N. Behrman, Salka Viertel, H. M. Harwood ***Ph*** William Daniels ***Ed*** Blanche Sewell ***Mus*** Herbert Stothart ***Art*** Alexander Toluboff
Act Greta Garbo, John Gilbert, Ian Keith, Lewis Stone, Elizabeth Young, C. Aubrey Smith (M-G-M)

Chief fault with *Christina* is its lethargy. It is slow and ofttimes stilted. This is perhaps good cinematic motivation to establish the contrast between the queen, who has been reared as a boy to succeed to the Swedish throne, and the episode in the wayside inn where she shares her room with the new Spanish envoy who had mistaken her for a flip Nordic youth.

The buildup of the romance fol-de-rol, after the major climactic clinch, is a bit DeMille-Stroheim. Greta Garbo, in this sequence, for example, consumes beaucoup footage caressing sundry pieces of furniture, fixtures and plaques in the room, in a self-expressed purpose of memorizing every aspect thereof and when John Gilbert asks her, "What are you doing?" sympathetically, the audience isn't quite as understanding.

The background is an obviously romantic admixture of history and fiction [story by Salka Viertel and Margaret P. Levino], touching lightly on the protestations of the A.D. 1600 Protestant Sweden's nationals against their queen's alliance with a Catholic from Spain. Gilbert is the Spanish envoy who has come to Stockholm on the expressly diplomatic and amorous mission of asking for the queen's hand in marriage to his king, the Spanish ruler.

Garbo's performance is too often apace of the script's lethargy, but as often, and more, in glamorous keeping with the romantic highlights. Her regal impression is convincing, which counts for plenty.

That goes for almost every character, from the humble peasants who are called upon to manifest their deep-rooted loyalty to the Crown in words, to the members of the royal court.

•

QUEEN KELLY
1929, 96 mins, US b/w
Dir Erich von Stroheim ***Prod*** Gloria Swanson ***Scr*** Erich von Stroheim ***Ph*** Gordon Pollock, Paul Ivano ***Ed*** Viola Lawrence ***Mus*** Adolph Tandler ***Art*** Harold Miles
Act Gloria Swanson, Seena Owen, Walter Byron, Wilhelm von Brincken, Madge Hunt, Wilson Benge (Gloria/United Artists)

Queen Kelly, which Erich von Stroheim originally wrote as *The Swamp*, was the director's eighth silent picture and was undertaken at the behest of Gloria Swanson. Best guess is that Stroheim's full scenario would have played for at least five hours' running time. Film was in production less than three months, from 1 November 1928 to 21 January 1929, when Swanson, finally fed up with her director's excesses, told financier Joseph Kennedy to shut it down after an expenditure of $800,000.

Since *Queen Kelly* was shot in sequence, what exists of it plays very smoothly and coherently up through its arbitrary, but dramatically valid, conclusion. Set in the sort of fin-de-siecle Ruritanian principality usually favored by the director, tale presents the mad young Queen Regina (Seena Owen) forcing the playboy Prince Wolfram (Walter Byron) into a royal marriage.

Far from resigned to a life of amorous activity, Wolfram encounters a troup of convent girls while on cavalry drill in the country and, in a legendary scene, meets Kitty Kelly (Gloria Swanson).

As planned by the director, film would have continued ever-deeper into grand melodrama until, coming full circle, Kitty would truly have become Queen Kelly along with Wolfram, displacing Regina on the throne.

Version of the film released minimally in Europe and South America in the early 1930s ended with Kitty successfully committing suicide. Footage of her in a bordello in German East Africa was not discovered until 1963. The music score by Adolph Tandler, which was written for Swanson's 1931–32 version, was discovered on a nitrate soundtrack for use in this edition. [Version reviewed is a complete-as-possible reconstruction in 1985.]

•

QUEEN MARGOT
(SEE: LA REINE MARGOT)

•

QUEEN OF OUTER SPACE
1958, 80 mins, US col
Dir Edward Bernds ***Prod*** Ben Schwalb ***Scr*** Charles Beaumont ***Ph*** William Whitley ***Ed*** William Austin ***Mus*** Marlin Skiles ***Art*** David Milton
Act Zsa Zsa Gabor, Eric Fleming, Laurie Mitchell, Paul Birch, Patrick Waltz, Barbara Darrow (Allied Artists)

Most of the female characters in *Queen of Outer Space* look like they would be more at home on a Minsky runway than the Cape Canaveral launching pad, but Ben Schwalb's production [based on a story by Ben Hecht] is a good-natured attempt to put some honest sex into science-fiction.

The year is 1985, and Eric Fleming, Patrick Waltz and Dave Willock are U.S. officers in charge of a space ship assigned to check on an American satellite space station. They are deflected from their course by mysterious energy rays from the planet Venus, where their ship is eventually wrecked. Taken prisoner by a malignant queen (Laurie Mitchell), they are about to be destroyed, when they are rescued by a pro-masculine group headed by Zsa Zsa Gabor.

The cast is predominantly feminine and attractively garbed in the brief raiment that appears to be customary on other planets. Gabor makes a handsome leading lady, romanced by Fleming and the others lend the necessary ingredients to their roles.

•

QUEEN OF SPADES, THE
1949, 95 mins, UK b/w
Dir Thorold Dickinson ***Prod*** Anatole de Grunwald ***Scr*** Rodney Ackland, Arthur Boys ***Ph*** Otto Heller, Gus Drisse, Val Stewart ***Ed*** Hazel Wilkinson ***Mus*** Georges Auric ***Art*** Oliver Messel
Act Anton Walbrook, Edith Evans, Yvonne Mitchell, Ronald Howard (Associated British Pathe)

Opulence of Imperial Russia at the beginning of the 19th century provides a colorful background for this filmization of Alexander Pushkin's short story, which brings to the screen a legend of gambling and intrigue.

Central character in the story is a captain of the Engineers. He cannot afford to gamble but is prepared to stake his all on a secret formula believed to have been passed on to a certain countess. Countess dies, but believing he has received a message from the dead, the captain goes to a gambling table and challenges his rival in love.

Outstanding performance comes from Edith Evans, making her screen debut. Her interpretation of the old grotesque countess is almost terrifying in its realism, and she dominates the screen from her first entry until her death. Anton Walbrook, and Ronald Howard as his rival in love, lack color.

•

QUENTIN DURWARD
(UK: THE ADVENTURES OF QUENTIN DURWARD)
1955, 101 mins, US col
Dir Richard Thorpe ***Prod*** Pandro S. Berman ***Scr*** Robert Ardrey ***Ph*** Christopher Challis ***Ed*** Ernest Walter ***Mus*** Bronislau Kaper ***Art*** Alfred Junge
Act Robert Taylor, Kay Kendall, Robert Morley, George Cole, Alec Clunes, Duncan Lamont (M-G-M)

This lively film version of Walter Scott's *Quentin Durward* finds knighthood again in bloom with enough dash and costumer derring-do to make fans of swashbucklers happy. Excellent photographic use of English castles, French chateaus and broad sweeps of fields and forests in actual overseas settings is made in the production, from an adaptation by George Froeschel.

Robert Taylor dons armor to fight for fair lady and honor, though gunpowder is replacing lance and he finds it difficult to maintain his ideals among the treachery and court intrigue into which the plot plunges him. He's been dispatched to France from Scotland to look over a prospective bride for his aged uncle. He falls in love with the lady himself, but nobly remembers his mission.

Knighthood becomes Taylor and he carries off the heroics with the proper postures. Opposite him romantically is Kay Kendall. Robert Morley stands out as the scheming Louis XI who will resort to any unscrupulous act to keep peace in France. Others in the predominantly British cast do well.

•

QUERELLE
1982, 120 mins, W. Germany/France Ⓥ col
Dir Rainer Werner Fassbinder ***Scr*** Rainer Werner Fassbinder ***Ph*** Xaver Schwarzenberger ***Ed*** Juliane Lorenz ***Mus*** Peer Raben ***Art*** Rolf Zehetbauer
Act Brad Davis, Franco Nero, Jeanne Moreau, Laurent Malet, Hanno Poschl, Gunther Kaufman (Planet/Gaumont)

The last film of Rainer Werner Fassbinder is, unfortunately, disappointing. His attempt to put the mystical homosexual world of French writer Jean Genet on film is ultimately tedious.

There is curio value in this strange tale of a young sailor, Querelle, who fascinates all who come in contact with him but who seems more absorbed in himself.

It seems to be set in the 1930s but is timeless and stylized. A boat on which Querelle works pulls into a port in Brest, France. Film is all studio work without any pretense at realism. It ties up at a jetty which has a bar and a bordello run by Jeanne Moreau. Querelle, played with a sort of dreamlike intensity by Brad Davis, is soon mixed up in this strange world.

•

QUEST, THE
1996, 103 mins, US Ⓥ ⦿ col
Dir Jean-Claude Van Damme ***Prod*** Moshe Diamant ***Scr*** Stuart Klein, Paul Mones ***Ph*** David Gribble ***Ed*** John F. Link ***Mus*** Randy Edelman ***Art*** Steve Spence
Act Jean-Claude Van Damme, Roger Moore, James Remar, Janet Gunn, Jack McGee, Abdel Qissi (Touchstone)

Jean-Claude Van Damme's *The Quest* is a decidedly mixed bag, a self-consciously old-fashioned swashbuckling adventure that insistently aims at a primary target audience of boys and young adolescents. Blend of genres and styles is diverting without being truly absorbing or engaging.

Van Damme plays Chris Dubois, an honest, idealistic street criminal who embarks on an odyssey of self-discovery that literally spans the globe, from the slums of New York City to the mysterious magic of Tibet's Lost City.

Beginning in '20s New York in darkly lit scenes that are meant to evoke *Oliver Twist*, Dubois is forced to leave his surrogate family of orphaned children. Kidnapped and enslaved by gun smugglers, Dubois is rescued by a classic rapscallion pirate, Dobbs (Roger Moore), and his fat right-hand man, Harry (Jack McGee), who in turn sell him in servitude to Khao (Aki Aleong), Muay Thai island's master of kickboxing, who trains him in the martial arts. Moore plays his role with characteristic cool but with a tad of over-the-top campiness.

A beautiful blond reporter, Carrie (Janet Gunn), is thrown into the mix to provide romantic interest for Dubois; for yet another hue, the humdrum tale brings in Maxie (James Remar), the world heavyweight boxing champion, who's both a threat and a challenge for Dubois. Culminating in the Lost City, Dubois's odyssey becomes a test of honor and manhood in the mythic "Ghan-gheng," an ancient winner-take-all competition.

Having choreographed his own battles and stunts for years, Van Damme's move into the director's chair is not a surprising development. Framed by a contempo prologue and epilogue, *The Quest* is not badly directed or executed.

•

QUEST FOR FIRE
1981, 97 mins, France/Canada Ⓥ ⦿ col
Dir Jean-Jacques Annaud ***Prod*** Denis Heroux, John Kemeny, Jacques Dorfmann, ***Scr*** Gerard Brach ***Ph*** Claude Agostini ***Ed*** Yves Langlois ***Mus*** Philippe Sarde ***Art*** Brian Morris
Act Everett McGill, Rae Dawn Chong, Ron Perlman, Nameer El Kadi, Gary Schwartz, Kurt Schiegel (ICC/Belstar/Stephan)

Jean-Jacques Annaud's *Quest for Fire* is an engaging prehistoric yarn that happily never degenerates into a club and lion skin spinoff of *Star Wars* and resolutely refuses to bludgeon the viewer with facile or gratuitous effects.

Despite four years of effort, a $12 million budget, grueling location shooting in Kenya, Scotland, Iceland and Canada, hundreds of masks and costumes and a herd of difficult elephants (making their screen apperance as mammoths), Annaud and his collaborators have brought off a polished entertainment.

Technical advisor Anthony Burgess invented special primitive jargons for the occasion, which are used in moderation and don't jar comically on the ears.

Gerard Brach's screenplay is loosely based on Jean-Henri Rosny the Elder's *La guerre du feu* (1911), a classic of French language popular literature. He also introduces a female character as a major dramatic and emotional pivot.

Three warriors of a primitive homo sapiens tribe are sent out to find a source of fire after their old pilot lights are extinguished during an attack by a group of unneighborly Neanderthals. After numerous adventures they find a fire amongst a cannibal tribe, but also learn how to produce it when they are led to an advanced human community by a young girl whom they've saved from the cannibals.

Everett McGill, New York stage actor Ron Perlman, and Turkish-born Nameer El Kadi etch engaging portraits as the three early homo sapiens, but the best performance comes from 20-year-old Rae Dawn Chong (daughter of comic Tommy Chong), unaffectedly radiant as the tribal nymphet who teaches them how to make a fire and eventually mates with McGill (after showing him how to make love face-to-face).

1982: Best Makeup

•

QUICK AND THE DEAD, THE
1995, 105 mins, US Ⓥ ⦿ col
Dir Sam Raimi ***Prod*** Joshua Donen, Allen Shapiro, Patrick Markey ***Scr*** Simon Moore ***Ph*** Dante Spinotti ***Ed*** Pietro Scalia ***Mus*** Alan Silvestri ***Art*** Patrizia von Brandenstein
Act Sharon Stone, Gene Hackman, Russell Crowe, Leonardo DiCaprio, Tobin Bell, Lance Henriksen (IndieProd/Tri-Star)

The bloodthirsty spirit of the Roman Circus invades the Old West in *The Quick and the Dead*, an ill-flavored concoction that tastes like warmed-over spaghetti. The zoom shots, glaring sun, closeups of eyes, unerring marksmanship, costume fetishism, brooding silences, revenge motif, flashbacks and pseudo-Morricone score, among many other stylistic flourishes, mark this as an elaborate tribute to the late Italian maestro, Sergio Leone.

But *The Quick and the Dead* feels utterly unauthentic from the moment Sharon Stone, playing a stranger named Ellen, rides into the hell-hole called Redemption and signs up to take part in an annual tournament in which the town's citizens basically kill each other off in a series of gun duels.

Presiding over this slaughter like a mad emperor from his red velvet chair is Herod (Gene Hackman), who not only rules the town but, as the territory's fastest gun, wins the competition every year.

Also dragged to the arena is Cort (Russell Crowe), Herod's former partner in crime who's now gotten religion. The wild card here is Ellen, who talks trash, belts back the booze with the best of them and can even hold her own in a fight, but most of the time skulks around looking tense and nervous in her designer duds.

Pic is dedicated to the late Woody Strode, who makes his final screen appearance here with the briefest of bits in the early going.

•

QUICK CHANGE
1990, 88 mins, US Ⓥ ⦿ col
Dir Howard Franklin, Bill Murray ***Prod*** Robert Greenhut, Bill Murray ***Scr*** Howard Franklin ***Ph*** Michael Chapman ***Ed*** Alan Heim ***Mus*** Randy Edelman, Howard Shore ***Art*** David Gropman
Act Bill Murray, Geena Davis, Randy Quaid, Jason Robards, Bob Elliott, Philip Bosco (Warner/Devoted)

Bill Murray delivers a smart, sardonic and very funny valentine to the rotten Apple in *Quick Change*. Pic became Murray's directing debut (he shares the chores with screenwriter Howard Franklin) after he and Franklin became too attached to the project to bring anyone else in. Material, based on Jay Cronley's book, is neither ambitious nor particularly memorable, but it's brought off with a sly flair that makes it most enjoyable.

Murray plays a fed-up New Yorker who enlists his girlfriend (Geena Davis) and lifelong pal (Randy Quaid) in a bank heist so they can get outta town. Hold-up, which nets $1 million and a very nice watch, sets off a carnival of police and crowd reaction in the New York streets, but none of it flaps the dynamite-rigged Murray.

With Jason Robards as a crusty police inspector who's as crazily sharp as *Twin Peaks* agent Cooper, pic offers some crazy little setpieces in a manic game of chase. Pic is so thick with gritty, tired, scuzzy N.Y. atmosphere viewer wants to scrape it off the skin.

Only in the final reel do things feel broadly contrived, concurrent with pic's move from N.Y. locations to a Florida soundstage for airport shooting.

•

QUICK MILLIONS
1931, 69 mins, US b/w
Dir Rowland Brown ***Scr*** Courtenay Terrett, Rowland Brown, John Wray ***Ph*** Joseph August ***Ed*** Harold Schuster ***Art*** Duncan Cramer
Act Spencer Tracy, Marguerite Churchill, Sally Eilers, Robert Burns, John Wray, Warner Richmond (Fox)

Another gangster story, but written down to the bone and directed for everything it contains.

For continuity and cutting the studio handed Brown a bonus of $1,000. It's Rowland Brown's first picture. Previously he was a Fox contract writer. His co-author on this story, like himself, is a former newspaper reporter. Courtenay Terrett once wrote a story called *Only Saps Work*, and Paramount took it along with Terrett.

The background of *Quick Millions* is similar and takes the eye through a cleverly knit panorama of racketeering as the yoke is laid on big business interests.

Story, after a fashion, gives an inside on how racketeers prey on organized business. In brief, it recounts the tale of a tough truck driver, with ideas, who climbs to the top, even socially, through forcing contractors into the right corner, only to topple from his throne at the hands of rival gangsters after turned down by the girl, a contractor's daughter. Simple, but the force, interest, suspense and the benefit of capable workmanship.

Spencer Tracy is excellent. Sally Eilers looks well at all times, and that's about all she has to do. Marguerite Churchill, as the former sweetheart, has the better of it from a script viewpoint. Robert Burns, Warner Richmond and George Raft are good gangster types. Contractor racket victim John Wray, who did the added dialog, oke.

•

QUIET AMERICAN, THE
1958, 120 mins, US b/w
Dir Joseph L. Mankiewicz ***Prod*** Joseph L. Mankiewicz ***Scr*** Joseph L. Mankiewicz ***Ph*** Robert Krasker ***Ed*** William Hornbeck ***Mus*** Mario Nascimbene ***Art*** Rino Mondinelli
Act Audie Murphy, Michael Redgrave, Claude Dauphin, Giorgia Moll, Kerima, Bruce Cabot (United Artists/Figaro)

In adapting Graham Greene's bitter and cynical *The Quiet American* into a motion picture, Joseph L. Mankiewicz has allowed himself the luxury of turning the screen into a debating society. It might have paid off had he retained the central character of the American in the book who, in Greene's version, represented all the determined bungling of American foreign policy. As it turns out, the film—shot in Vietnam and at Cinecitta Studios in Rome—is an overlong, overdialogued adaptation, concerned with the pros and cons of a Third Force in Asia.

Story follows the line of the book, but with the all-important difference that the character of the American, played without much depth by Audie Murphy, has been drained of meaning, giving the whole picture a pro-American slant. Murphy here doesn't represent the U.S. government, but merely works for a private U.S. aid mission. In other words, his ideas of a Third Force standing between Communism and French Colonialism are his own.

It's one long flashback from the moment Murphy is found murdered and Michael Redgrave, playing a British correspondent, is asked by French inspector Claude Dauphin to identify him. Dauphin gradually unspools the sometimes obscure story.

Love interest in the film is pretty newcomer Giorgia Moll who lives with Redgrave but leaves him for the younger Murphy. Running throughout is the clashing of views between Redgrave and Murphy.

Redgrave's moody portrayal of the neurotic aging Britisher hiding personal anxieties under a mask of cynicism makes the whole thing worthwhile.

The Quiet American has been photographed skillfully, though the number of scenes showing off Vietnam (the story is laid in 1952, before the partition) isn't very large.

•

QUIET DAYS IN CLICHY

1970, 100 mins, Denmark b/w

Dir Jens-Jorgen Thorsen ***Scr*** Jens-Jorgen Thorsen ***Ph*** Jesper Hom ***Ed*** Anker ***Mus*** Country Joe McDonald, Ben Webster, Andy Sunstrom

Act Louise White, Paul Valjean, Wayne John Rodda, Ulla Lemvigh-Muller, Susanne Krage (SBA)

This is a true-to-the-letter re-telling of Henry Miller's memoir about Montmartre life, with very little food and many, many women.

Director Jens-Jorgen Thorsen shows both technical skill and madcap humor and, furthermore, knows more than a little about the loneliness dimension of Miller's work.

Paul Valjean looks like the popular image of Henry Miller, easygoing, nice, lecherous, hungry and full of fun. Among the girls who indulge in unlimited frontal nudity, Louise White, Ulla Lemvigh-Muller and Susanne Krage have the rather spectacular achievement of making the audience remember their faces as well as their bodies.

•

QUIET EARTH, THE

1985, 100 mins, New Zealand Ⓥ ⊙ col

Dir Geoff Murphy ***Prod*** Don Reynolds, Sam Pillsbury ***Scr*** Bill Baer, Bruno Lawrence, Sam Pillsbury ***Ph*** James Bartle ***Ed*** Michael Horton ***Mus*** John Charles ***Art*** Rick Kofoed

Act Bruno Lawrence, Alison Routledge, Peter Smith (Cinepro/Pillsbury)

One of New Zealand's top directors, Geoff Murphy has taken a man-alone theme and turned it imaginatively to strong and refreshing effect in *The Quiet Earth*.

Plot centers on scientist Zac Hobson (Bruno Lawrence) who wakes one morning to discover he is alone in the world. A global top-secret energy project he has been working on has malfunctioned and altered the fabric of the universe. While humanity appears to be wiped out, all its materialistic trappings remain. For a time, Zac lives out his fantasies. Then begins a search for other survivors. He finds two—a woman, Joanne (Alison Routledge), and a man, Api (Peter Smith). The emotions unleashed by this trio in their struggle for survival propels the story, which has an intriguing mystical dimension, to a shattering conclusion.

The film is notable for high production values. Acting isn't far behind. Lawrence, a veteran of NZ films turns in a performance that is funny and moving, while Maori actor Smith makes a bold debut. But it is Alison Routledge who is the real find. Possessing a special, delicate, Madonna-like beauty, she invests Joanne with sparky intelligence and strength.

•

QUIET MAN, THE

1952, 129 mins, US Ⓥ ⊙ col

Dir John Ford ***Prod*** John Ford, Merian C. Cooper ***Scr*** Frank S. Nugent ***Ph*** Winton C. Hoch ***Ed*** Jack Murray ***Mus*** Victor Young ***Art*** Frank Hotaling

Act John Wayne, Maureen O'Hara, Victor McLaglen, Barry Fitzgerald, Ward Bond, Mildred Natwick (Argosy/Republic)

This is a robust romantic drama of a native-born's return to Ireland. Director John Ford took cast and cameras to Ireland to tell the story [by Maurice Walsh] against actual backgrounds.

Wayne is the quiet man of the title, returning to the land of his birth to forget a life of struggle and violence. In Inisfree, Wayne buys the cottage where he was born, immediately arousing the ire of Victor McLaglen, a well-to-do farmer who wanted the property himself.

His next mistake is to fall for Maureen O'Hara, McLaglen's sister. Custom decrees the brother must give consent to marriage, so Wayne's suit is hopeless until newly made friends are able to trick McLaglen long enough to get the ceremony over with. Safely married, Wayne finds himself with a bride but not a wife.

Despite the length of the footage, film holds together by virtue of a number of choice characters, the best of which is Barry Fitzgerald's socko punching of an Irish type. Wayne works well under Ford's direction, answering all demands of the vigorous, physical character.

1952: Best Director, Color Cinematography

NOMINATIONS: Best Picture, Supp. Actor (Victor McLaglen), Screenplay, Color Art Direction, Sound

•

QUIET ROOM, THE

1996, 91 mins, Australia/Italy Ⓥ col

Dir Rolf de Heer ***Prod*** Domenico Procacci, Rolf de Heer ***Scr*** Rolf de Heer ***Ph*** Tony Clark ***Ed*** Tania Nehme ***Mus*** Graham Tardif ***Art*** Fiona Paterson

Act Celine O'Leary, Paul Blackwell, Chloe Ferguson, Phoebe Ferguson (Vertigo/Fandango)

Rolf de Heer's audacious film takes the viewer into the mind of a seven-year-old girl whose parents are separating. Heer's acute insights into a child's mentality and speech patterns, his bold visual design and the quite amazing performance of Chloe Ferguson, his young protagonist, will rivet audiences.

Most of the action takes place in two rooms, the brightly painted bedroom of an unnamed girl and the bedroom of her parents next door. In addition, the entire film is seen from the child's perspective; the viewer is given no information other than that available to her. When her parents talk to her, the girl remains silent but answers then in her thoughts, achieved by means of voiceover.

The drawings she spends so much time creating vividly reflect her hopes and fears, but the adults are unable to read the messages she's sending them. She plays with Barbie dolls, experiments with an ordinary supermarket egg she hopes will hatch into a baby chick and lies in bed at night afraid of the panthers that might come to get her. And all the time she ponders why adults fail to understand her.

All technical credits are highly professional, with cinematographer Tony Clark giving the film a bold, bright look.

•

QUIGLEY DOWN UNDER

1990, 119 mins, US Ⓥ ⊙ ▭ col

Dir Simon Wincer ***Prod*** Stanley O'Toole ***Scr*** John Hill ***Ph*** David Eggby ***Ed*** Adrian Carr, Peter Burgess ***Mus*** Basil Poledouris ***Art*** Ross Major

Act Tom Selleck, Laura San Giacomo, Alan Rickman, Chris Haywood, Ron Haddrick, Tony Bonner (M-G-M/Pathe)

Quigley Down Under is an exquisitely crafted, rousing western made in Oz.

Script was written for Steve McQueen in the 1970s, then developed in 1984, Rick Rosenthal to helm; project was reactivated in 1986 with Lewis Gilbert scheduled to direct.

Tom Selleck is in the title role as a sharp-shooter from the American West who answers villain Alan Rickman's ad and heads to Fremantle in Western Australia. Quigley is informed that he's been hired to kill aborigines with his long-range, custom-made rifle as part of Rickman's campaign of genocide, encouraged by the local authorities. Selleck's violent response to the request begins a vendetta is which Rickman has him left for dead in the middle of nowhere. Along for the ensuing survival trek is Laura San Giacomo, a fellow American haunted by the death of her child in a Comanche raid.

Selleck has his best bigscreen casting so far here (not counting the missed opportunity to be Indiana Jones). He's thoroughly convincing with his custom-made rifle and low-key manner. San Giacomo comes into her own as the feisty heroine. Rickman is a perfectly cast hissable villain.

•

QUILLER MEMORANDUM, THE

1966, 103 mins, UK Ⓥ ▭ col

Dir Michael Anderson ***Prod*** Ivan Foxwell ***Scr*** Harold Pinter ***Ph*** Erwin Hiller ***Ed*** Freddie Wilson ***Mus*** John Barry ***Art*** Maurice Carter

Act George Segal, Alec Guinness, Max von Sydow, Senta Berger, George Sanders, Robert Helpmann (Rank)

The Quiller Memorandum, based on a novel by Adam Hall (pen name for Elleston Trevor) and with a screenplay by Harold Pinter, deals with the insidious upsurge of neo-Nazism in Germany. It relies on a straight narrative storyline, simple but holding, literate dialog and well-drawn characters.

Set largely on location in West Berlin, it has George Segal brought back from vacation to replace a British agent who has come to a sticky end at the hands of a new infiltrating group of Nazis. His job is to locate their headquarters. He does this in a lone-wolf way, refusing to be hampered by bodyguards. En route he has some edgy adventures.

Segal plays Quiller with a laconic but likeable detachment, underlining the loneliness and lack of relaxation of the agent, who cannot even count on support from his own side. Alec Guinness never misses a trick in his few scenes as the cold, witty fish in charge of Berlin sector investigations. Max von Sydow plays the Nazi chief quietly but with high camp menace.

•

QUILLS

2000, 123 mins, US/UK Ⓥ ⊙ col

Dir Philip Kaufman ***Prod*** Julia Chasman, Nick Wechsler, Peter Kaufman ***Scr*** Doug Wright ***Ph*** Rogier Stoffers ***Ed*** Peter Boyle ***Mus*** Stephen Warbeck ***Art*** Martin Childs

Act Geoffrey Rush, Kate Winslet, Joaquin Phoenix, Michael Caine, Billie Whitelaw, Patrick Malahide (Industry Entertainment-Walrus & Associates/Fox Searchlight)

The eternal struggle between unbridled personal expression and society's impulse to censor receives an engaging, if not galvanizing, airing in *Quills*. Brimming with colorful incident, juicy confrontations and layers of irony, Philip Kaufman's intelligently boisterous screen version of Doug Wright's successful play about the Marquis de Sade maintains a sharp focus on the notorious writer's compulsive creativity during his long imprisonment at the Charenton asylum. At the same time, the film lacks an edge of danger or excitement that might have brought the subject alive in more than a cerebral way.

The notorious Marquis (Geoffrey Rush) is being held prisoner at a relatively benign institution where its most famous inmate enjoys the luxury of a furnished apartment, complete with a velvet-draped bedchamber and large collections of books and erotica. Giving vent to his physical frustration in a torrent of scabrous writing, the Marquis smuggles his prose to the outside world courtesy of a lovely young laundress, Madeleine (Kate Winslet), a virginal girl fascinated by the Marquis but unwilling to submit to his raging desires. His incendiary book *Justine* is published and achieves such notoriety that it even comes to the attention of Napoleon. In the wake of the emporor's disgust with *Justine*, doctor-cum-torturer Royer-Collard (Michael Caine) is dispatched to bring the Marquis into line. Royer-Collard's draconian methods meet resistance from Charenton's overseer, Abbe Coulmier (Joaquin Phoenix), a liberal-minded, good-looking young priest whose progressive notions include allowing the Marquis to write and stage theatricals featuring the asylum's assorted loonies.

Rush gives the Marquis a full-blooded reading fueled by acid, blood and lust. Still, the piece shies away from presenting the worst side of the author. His vicious cruelty and torturous inventions are sidestepped. In the end, this Marquis de Sade is more a depraved but witty gentleman than a truly rapacious, even murderous beast, which takes some of the edge off the dramatic parallel to Royer-Collard and, in an important sense, reduces his genuinely dangerous stature.

•

QUINTET

1979, 118 mins, US Ⓥ col

Dir Robert Altman ***Prod*** Robert Altman ***Scr*** Frank Barhydt, Robert Altman, Patricia Resnick ***Ph*** Jean Boffety ***Ed*** Dennis M. Hill ***Mus*** Tom Pierson ***Art*** Leon Ericksen

Act Paul Newman, Vittorio Gassman, Fernando Rey, Bibi Andersson, Brigitte Fossey, Nina Van Pallandt (Lion's Gate)

Here's another one for Robert Altman's inner circle.

In one of the few obvious points about the picture [based on a story by Altman, Lionel Chetwynd and Patricia Resnick], the title refers to a game popular in some future city (Montreal?) that's slowly dying in a new Ice Age. Though the finer details are anybody's guess, the game involves five players trying to eliminate each other, plus a sixth who comes late to the board.

Paul Newman arrives in the city with his young pregnant bride (Brigitte Fossey) and finds some of the citizens playing the game for real, with Fernando Rey as referee. After losing his bride to a bomb, Newman is drawn into the game.

Before it's over, there have been two bloody throat slashings, a hand bursting open in a fire and one vigorous stabbing.

•

QUIZ SHOW

1994, 130 mins, US Ⓥ ⊙ col

Dir Robert Redford ***Prod*** Robert Redford, Michael Jacobs, Julian Krainin, ***Scr*** Paul Attanasio ***Ph*** Michael Ballhaus ***Ed*** Stu Linder ***Mus*** Mark Isham ***Art*** Jon Hutman

Act John Turturro, Rob Morrow, Ralph Fiennes, Paul Scofield, David Paymer, Hank Azoria (Wildwood/Baltimore/Hollywood)

A national scandal that arguably inflicted an early wound on the American postwar moral fiber is smoothly dramatized in Robert Redford's *Quiz Show*, with colorful, bright characters playing out a lamentable true-life scenario against the lively backdrop of '50s television and the vibrant New York City of the era.

Redford and screenwriter Paul Attanasio [working from Richard N. Goodwin's book *Remembering America: A Voice from the Sixties*] telescope history rather severely in squeezing the events of the three years into a matter of months. But if the film lacks an edge of excitement and daring, the story still proves strongly engrossing.

Set in 1958, pic sweeps the viewer into a live broadcast of the NBC game show *Twenty-One*. King of *Twenty-One* is Herbie Stempel (John Turturro), a brainy, ill-mannered Jewish grad student from Queens. The show's producer, Dan Enright (David Paymer), asks Stempel to take a dive for a large fee, thus allowing the handsome, brilliant, patrician Charles Van Doren (Ralph Fiennes), to be crowned.

Van Doren goes along with the ruse, persuaded that it's been done that way all along and no one will ever know. But shadowing it all is young Dick Goodwin (Rob Morrow), a similarly bright Harvard grad holding down a Washington entry-level job on the House Subcommittee on Legislative Oversight. Goodwin scours Gotham checking things out for himself.

Quiz show sequences are craftily done, and New York in the city's heyday of the '50s is deftly evoked. Turturro, who put on considerable poundage for the role, is a perfect Stempel—pushy, nervous, uncouth. Morrow captures a quiet wryness along with Goodwin's intelligence and drive, but his Boston accent ranges all up and down the Eastern seaboard. Similarly, Fiennes cuts a winning figure as Van Doren, but he can't keep his English accent suppressed for long.

1994: NOMINATIONS: Best Picture, Director, Supp. Actor (Paul Scofield), Adapted Screenplay

•

QUO VADIS

1951, 171 mins, US Ⓥ col

Dir Mervyn LeRoy ***Prod*** Sam Zimbalist ***Scr*** John Lee Mahin, S. N. Behrman, Sonya Levien ***Ph*** Robert Surtees, William V. Skall ***Ed*** Ralph E. Winters ***Mus*** Miklos Rozsa ***Art*** Cedric Gibbons, William Horning, Edward Carfagno

Act Robert Taylor, Deborah Kerr, Leo Genn, Peter Ustinov, Patricia Laffan, Finlay Currie (M-G-M)

Quo Vadis is a super-spectacle in all its meaning. That there are shortcomings [in this fourth version of the tale] even Metro must have recognized and ignored in consideration of the project's scope. The captiousness about the story line, some of the players' wooden performances in contrast to the scenery-chewing of Peter Ustinov (Nero), are part and parcel of any super-spectacular.

The contrast, of course, is sharp in that Leo Genn's slick underplaying makes Ustinov's sybarite conception of Nero that much more out of focus with realities. But the Polish novelist, Henryk Sienkiewicz, intended to contrast the glory that was Rome and the splendor that was Nero's court with the travails of the early Christians.

While the Romans worship their idols and vestal virgins, while Nero rules a still-lush if decadent court in its final stage of cowardice, wickedness and degeneracy, Robert Taylor is shown leading his victorious Roman troops down the Appian Way. Deborah Kerr, as a Christian hostage, is the vis-a-vis. Genn, as the suave Petronius, who constantly derides the stupid Nero, has Marina Berti, a beauteous slave girl, as his romantic opposite.

There are no ups and downs on the spectacular values that comprise the Circus of Nero, the profligate court scenes, the marching armies, the racing chariots, the burning of Rome, the shackled captives under Roman rule, the pagan ceremonies, the secret Christian meetings, the gladiators unto the death to amuse Nero's court, and the climax as the Christian martyrs face the unleashed lions in the great Circus of Nero.

1951: NOMINATIONS: Best Picture, Supp. Actor (Leo Genn, Peter Ustinov), Color Cinematography, Color Costume Design, Color Art Direction, Editing, Scoring of a Dramatic Picture

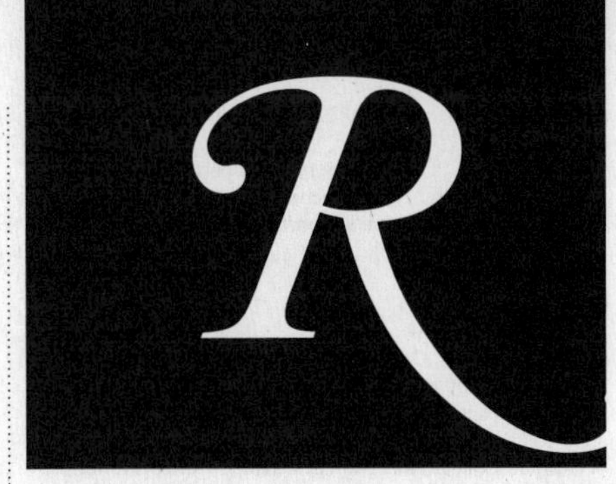

RABID
1977, 91 mins, Canada Ⓥ col
Dir David Cronenberg ***Prod*** John Dunning ***Scr*** David Cronenberg ***Ph*** Rene Verzier ***Ed*** Jean Lafleur ***Mus*** Ivan Reitman (sup.) ***Art*** Claude Marchand
Act Marilyn Chambers, Frank Moore, Joe Silver, Howard Ryshpan, Patricia Gage, Susan Roman (Dibar/Cinema Entertainment)

Rabid, as the dictionary explains means both "affected with rabies" and "extremely violent." Using both definitions, *Rabid*, is so accurately titled that this one word tells all. Here is an extremely violent, sometimes nauseating, picture about a young woman affected with rabies, running around Montreal infecting others.

Marilyn Chambers, the Whilone Procter & Gamble Ivory Snow girl turned porno film actress, plays the infected one—sort of a cross between Typhoid Mary with rabies and a vampire.

On the one side in the urban jungle are human animals, foaming at the mouth, biting each other in shopping malls, operating rooms and subway cars. On the other side are animals of another sort shooting down those salivating the green foam.

•

RACE WITH THE DEVIL
1975, 88 mins, US Ⓥ col
Dir Jack Starrett ***Prod*** Wes Bishop ***Scr*** Wes Bishop, Lee Frost ***Ph*** Robert Jessup ***Ed*** Alan Jacobs ***Mus*** Leonard Rosenman
Act Peter Fonda, Warren Oates, Loretta Swit, Lara Parker, R. G. Armstrong, Clay Tanner (20th Century-Fox)

A follow-up to *Dirty Mary Crazy Larry*, this meller includes the requisite road chases and other hyped-up thrills, some of them slickly executed by director Jack Starrett. Otherwise the production is a sloppy, cynical blend of secondhand plot elements.

Patchwork screenplay also uses story elements from horror pix as it pits vacationing Peter Fonda, Warren Oates and their wives Lara Parker and Loretta Swit against a horde of rampaging Satanists in the Texas backwoods. Pic seems to be trying at times for an archetypal confrontation between middle-American values, as repped by the couples in their fortress-like motor home, and bizarre counter-culture elements. The film's action highlight is a slam-bang duel between the camper and several trucks, but generally the pic is done with perfunctory TV-like stylelessness.

Oates does his usual believably gritty job with the meagre character material here. Fonda is less dreamy than usual, though still without evoking much interest.

•

RACHEL AND THE STRANGER
1948, 92 mins, US Ⓥ ⊙ b/w
Dir Norman Foster ***Prod*** Richard H. Berger ***Scr*** Waldo Salt ***Ph*** Maury Gertsman ***Ed*** Les Millbrook ***Mus*** Roy Webb ***Art*** Albert S. D'Agostino, Jack Okey, Walter E. Keller
Act Loretta Young, William Holden, Robert Mitchum, Gary Gray, Tom Tully, Sara Haden (RKO)

Mood of the picture is pleasant but is so even that interest isn't too strong. Dangers of pioneering in a wilderness, vaguely referred to as the northwest, could have been more excitingly depicted. Single incident of excitement—a strong one—is put off until the finale and has a socko Indian raid on a settler's homestead in the wilds.

Otherwise, narrative maintains its even pace in telling story of a pioneer who buys a bride to do the chores and teach niceties of life to his motherless son. The bride is only a servant until a hunter, friend of the groom, appears and makes a play for her.

William Holden enacts the dour settler, so deeply in love with his dead wife he fails to appreciate, or even notice, the charms of his new bondswoman bride. Loretta Young has only two costume changes and her makeup is true to role, but she makes some glamour shine through. Robert Mitchum is the aimlessly wandering hunter.

•

RACHEL PAPERS, THE
1989, 95 mins, UK Ⓥ col
Dir Damian Harris ***Prod*** Andrew S. Karsch ***Scr*** Damian Harris ***Ph*** Alex Thomson ***Ed*** David Martin ***Mus*** Chaz Jenkel ***Art*** Andrew McAlpine
Act Dexter Fletcher, Ione Skye, Jonathan Pryce, James Spader, Bill Patterson, Michael Gambon (Initial/Longfellow)

Charles Highway is a 19-year-old with no money problems who maps out his sexual conquests via his desktop. He meets beautiful American Rachel Noyce, also 19. It's love at first sight, but she already has a boyfriend.

After a bit of frustration, he sends her a funny love message on videotape, and she comes around. They have a steamy, passionate affair, of which he tires all too soon. They part. End of story.

The basic material is as old as the hills, but Martin Amis, who wrote the original novel some 15 years earlier, explored it in fresh directions. Director Damian Harris isn't able to capture the book's special charms, and resorts to having his young hero address the camera to keep the viewer in the picture. Unfortunately, Dexter Fletcher is rather too self-conscious here, and makes Charles a less than endearing hero. On the other hand, Ione Skye seizes her chances as Rachel and gives a glowingly sensual performance. Their lengthy love scenes together, often in a bathtub, are certainly steamy.

•

RACHEL, RACHEL
1968, 101 mins, US Ⓥ col
Dir Paul Newman ***Prod*** Paul Newman ***Scr*** Stewart Stern ***Ph*** Gayne Rescher ***Ed*** Dede Allen ***Mus*** Jerome Moross ***Art*** Robert Gundlach
Act Joanne Woodward, James Olson, Kate Harrington, Estelle Parsons, Donald Moffatt, Terry Kiser (Warner/Seven Arts)

Rachel, Rachel is a low-key melodrama starring Joanne Woodward as a spinster awakening to life. Produced austerely by Paul Newman, who also directs with an uncertain hand, it marks Newman's feature debut in these non-acting capacities. Offbeat film moves too slowly to an upbeat, ironic climax.

Margaret Laurence's novel, *A Jest of God*, has been adapted into an episodic, halting screenplay which not only conveys the tedium of Woodward's adult life but also, unfortunately, takes its time in so doing.

There is very little dialog—most of which is very good—but this asset makes a liability out of the predominantly visual nature of the development, which in time seems to become redundant, padded and tiring.

James Olson, a childhood friend who has returned for a visit, provides Woodward with an alternative. Believing herself pregnant by Olson, she determines to have the child.

Direction is awkward. Were Woodward not there film could have been a shambles.

1968: NOMINATIONS: Best Picture, Actress (Joanne Woodward), Supp. Actress (Estelle Parsons), Adapted Screenplay.

•

RACING WITH THE MOON
1984, 108 mins, US Ⓥ ⊙ col
Dir Richard Benjamin ***Prod*** Alain Bernheim, John Kohn ***Scr*** Steven Kloves ***Ph*** John Bailey ***Ed*** Jacqueline Cambas ***Mus*** Dave Grusin ***Art*** David L. Snyder
Act Sean Penn, Elizabeth McGovern, Nicolas Cage, John Karlen, Rutanya Alda, Kate Williamson (Paramount)

Racing with the Moon is a sweet, likable film that doesn't contain the usual commercial elements normally expected these days in youth pics. Working in a more straightforward, serious mode, Richard Benjamin confirms the directorial promise he displayed in *My Favorite Year*, and Sean Penn and Elizabeth McGovern are good as the romantic leads.

Time frame is Christmas of 1942, and Penn and his rowdy buddy Nicolas Cage have just a few weeks left until they join the Marines. Penn becomes dazzled by a new face (McGovern) in the California coastal town, whom he takes to be a rich girl since she lives up in the "Gatsby" mansion. While Cage, a wrong-side-of-the-tracks type, gets his g.f. pregnant, and after a disastrous, but wonderfully staged, attempt to hustle some sailors at pool, Penn forces himself to enlist McGovern's help in raising $150 for an abortion for his friend's gal.

First-time scenarist Steven Kloves has created two nice leading characters, nicely essayed by Penn and McGovern. Benjamin shows a consistently generous attitude toward his characters and an inclination to emphasize their most exemplary traits.

•

RACKET, THE
1928, 70 mins, US ⊗ b/w
Dir Lewis Milestone ***Prod*** Howard Hughes ***Scr*** Harry Behn, Del Andrews, Bartlett Cormack, Eddie Adams ***Ph*** Tony Gaudio ***Ed*** Tom Miranda
Act Thomas Meighan, Marie Prevost, Louis Wolheim, George Stone, John Darrow, Skeets Gallagher (Paramount/Caddo)

A good story, plus good direction, plus a great cast and minus dumb supervision, is responsible for another great underworld film.

Thomas Meighan has his best role in years as Captain McQuigg, and Louis Wolheim, as Nick Scarsi, adds to a screen rep that has already labeled him the best character heavy, the one-eyed monster has ever pecked at.

The Racket, like all great pictures, started with a great yarn [from Bartlett Cormack's play] and a director alive to its possibilities. It grips your interest from the first shot to the last, and never drags for a second. It's another tale of the underworld, a battle of wills and cunning between an honest copper and a gorilla who has the town in his lap.

Tom Miranda was given wide latitude with slang and gun chatter and the result is the most authentic set of titles that have graced an underworld picture to date. The gorillas talk as they should and not as some lame-brained obstructionist thinks they should. They don't go to jail—they go to the can—and without those diagrams the average super wants with any title in vernacular.

And shades of Beverly Hills, there's no love interest! Imagine a hero who doesn't cop a moll in the last ten feet.

Boy, page the millenium!

1927/28: NOMINATION: Best Picture

•

RACKET, THE
1951, 89 mins, US Ⓥ ⊙ b/w
Dir John Cromwell ***Prod*** Edmund Grainger ***Scr*** William Wister Haines, W. R. Burnett ***Ph*** George E. Diskant ***Ed*** Sherman Todd ***Mus*** Constantin Bakaleinikoff (dir.) ***Art*** Albert S. D'Agostino, Jack Okey
Act Robert Mitchum, Lizabeth Scott, Robert Ryan, William Talman, Ray Collins, Joyce MacKenzie (RKO)

This remake of Bartlett Cormack's old play has been handled to emphasize clearcut action and suspense and the casting is just right to stress the rough and ready toughness in the script.

Robert Mitchum is the honest police captain pitted against Robert Ryan, the mobster, and both dominate the picture with forceful credible performances that add a lot of interest. Further masculine attention is gained through the strong work of William Talman as a rookie cop, the pairing of Ray Collins and William Conrad as crooked politicians, and other assorted male casts.

Development is enlivened with some solid thriller sequences, such as a rooftop fight between Mitchum and a gunman, careening autos and crashes, and gunplay between the forces of good and evil.

Femme interest is at a minimum, but Lizabeth Scott, as a nitery singer does what she has to do well.

•

RADIO DAYS
1987, 85 mins, US Ⓥ ⊙ col
Dir Woody Allen ***Prod*** Robert Greenhut ***Scr*** Woody Allen ***Ph*** Carlo Di Palma ***Ed*** Susan E. Morse ***Mus*** Dick Hyman (sup.) ***Art*** Santo Loquasto
Act Mia Farrow, Seth Green, Julie Kavner, Josh Mostel, Michael Tucker, Dianne Wiest (Orion)

Although lacking the bite and depth of his best work, *Radio Days* is one of Woody Allen's most purely entertaining pictures. It's a visual monolog of bits and pieces from the glory days of radio and the people who were tuned in.

Rockaway Beach, a thin strip of land on the outskirts of New York City is where young Joe (Seth Green) and his family live in not-so splendid harmony and for entertainment and escape to listen to the radio. Set at the start of World War II, it's a world of aunts and uncles all living on top of each other and the magical events and people, real and imagined, that forever shape one's young imagination.

Radio Days is not simply about nostalgia, but the quality of memory and how what one remembers informs one's present life.

Dianne Wiest is delicious as an aunt who is desperate to find a husband but somehow keeps meeting Mr. Wrong. The robust Masked Avenger is, in real life, the diminutive Wallace Shawn. Mia Farrow is a none-too-bright cigaret girl with a yen for stardom who magically transforms her life.

1987: NOMINATIONS: Best Original Screenplay, Art Direction

•

RADIO FLYER
1992, 113 mins, US Ⓥ ⊙ ▭ col
Dir Richard Donner ***Prod*** Lauren Schuler-Donner ***Scr*** David Mickey Evans ***Ph*** Laszlo Kovacs ***Ed*** Stuart Baird ***Mus*** Hans Zimmer ***Art*** J. Michael Riva
Act Lorraine Bracco, John Heard, Adam Baldwin, Elijah Wood, Ben Johnson, Tom Hanks (Columbia/Stonebridge)

Radio Flyer is a film one would like to like more. Underdeveloped screenplay about two boys' fantasy of escape from an abusive stepfather is sometimes moving but too often distant and literal-minded.

David Mickey Evans started the pic in June 1990 with Rosanna Arquette as the mother, but the first time writer-director was soon fired. Production shut down before new director Richard Donner moved the setting of the late 1960s story from L.A. to rustic northern California.

Film builds a quiet sense of dread as the boys, who feel they can't confide in their distracted mother (Lorraine Bracco), spend as little time as possible in a home that has become a purgatory. Elijah Wood, the older, has a believable mixture of strength and timidity in his attempts to protect Joseph Mazzello from the (mostly off-screen) beatings by their drunken stepfather (Adam Baldwin). Mazzello, terrific as Baldwin's stoic victim, gives the film much of its intermittent emotional power. Pic, however, has a feeling of distance reinforced by some major screenplay gaps and by heavy-handed narration read by unbilled Tom Hanks. As the grown-up Wood, Hanks bookends the film by telling his own sons what happened to their uncle. Only pic's last part, with the boys building and launching their flying machine, has a magical feeling.

•

RADIOLAND MURDERS
1994, 108 mins, US Ⓥ ⊙ col
Dir Mel Smith ***Prod*** Rick McCallum, Fred Roos ***Scr*** Willard Huyck, Gloria Katz, Jeff Reno, Ron Osborn ***Ph*** David Tattersall ***Ed*** Paul Trejo ***Mus*** Joel McNeely ***Art*** Gavin Bocquet
Act Brian Benben, Mary Stuart Masterson, Ned Beatty, George Burns, Scott Michael Campbell, Brion James (Lucasfilm/Universal)

George Lucas collaborated previously with screenwriters Willard Huyck and Gloria Katz on *Howard the Duck*, and in terms of recalling that fiasco, *Radioland Murders* does pretty much everything but quack. A wild farce with more than 100 speaking parts, pic offers scant appeal to the MTV generation and is too frenetic for anyone who might appreciate its Golden-Age-of-Radio setting.

Billed as a "romantic mystery-comedy," *Radioland* wants to be a cross between *Clue* and a Marx Bros movie, with perhaps a pinch of *Radio Days* and the short-lived TV show *On the Air* thrown in for good measure.

Director Mel Smith (*The Tall Guy*) struggles to make sense of the scattershot screenplay [from a screen story by exec. producer Lucas].

Set in 1939, all the action takes place during the debut night of a new radio network, WBN, emanating from a Chicago studio. One of the writers, Roger (Brian Benben), is seeking to woo back his estranged wife (Mary Stuart Masterson), the owner's assistant. Soon, however, matters become a bit grim, as various staffers turn up dead, each time preceded by a cackling, "Shadow"-like voice coming from somewhere in the building. Roger soon finds himself a suspect, trying to solve the mystery.

For the most part, *Radioland* feels like a theme-park ride without an exit—rolling out a non-stop barrage of stale sight gags and snappy repartee that's both cliche-ridden and sorely lacking in snap. Masterson gets to be plucky and not much else, while Benben plays a character similar to his persona in the HBO series *Dream On*.

•

RAFFERTY AND THE GOLD DUST TWINS
1975, 91 mins, US Ⓥ ▭ col
Dir Dick Richards ***Prod*** Michael Gruscoff, Art Linson ***Scr*** John Kaye ***Ph*** Ralph Woolsey ***Ed*** Walter Thompson ***Mus*** Artie Butler ***Art*** Joel Schiller
Act Alan Arkin, Sally Kellerman, Mackenzie Phillips, Alex Rocco, Charles Martin Smith, Harry Dean Stanton (Warner)

Rafferty and the Gold Dust Twins is another sterile Warner Bros. comedy-drama about the "little people" of America, as seen through the eyes of Beverly Hills and Upper Manhattan. Alan Arkin stars as a loutish bumbler, fraudulently kidnapped by Sally Kellerman and teenager Mackenzie Phillips, into an odyssey through many lower class southwest locations.

Arkin's stereotyped Everyman clod meshes awkwardly with spaced-out Kellerman's formula characterization, thereby throwing interest by default to Phillips (the mature moppet of *American Graffiti*) in another good streetwise role).

Harry Dean Stanton in a very good part as an embittered yahoo, and Charlie Martin Smith (also from *Graffiti*) are among the more effective supporting players.

•

RAFFLES
1930, 70 mins, US b/w
Dir Harry D'Arrast, George Fitzmaurice ***Prod*** Samuel Goldwyn ***Scr*** Sidney Howard ***Ph*** George Barnes, Gregg Toland ***Ed*** Stuart Heisler ***Art*** William Cameron Menzies, Park French
Act Ronald Colman, Kay Francis, David Torrence, Frances Dade, Alison Skipworth, Bramwell Fletcher (Goldwyn)

The old-fashioned artifices of the [original 1899 novel *The Amateur Cracksman* by E. W. Hornung and its subsequent dramatization] are incidental. The essence of its interest is a rascal so captivating that you are pleased to see him emerge triumphant, though guilty, from his brush with Scotland Yard.

Picture version capitalizes such instinctive feeling, by actually having the defeated Inspector K. McKenzie take his final trimming with a philosophical grin.

Kay Francis is a happy choice—an actress with that suggestion of reserve vitality that makes her stand out strongly.

Comedy sequences supplied by Alison Skipworth and Frederick Kerr, the sentimental British dowager and her absurd spouse, have a good deal of freshness and reality. In like manner, the picture's atmosphere impresses as thoroughly authentic.

1929/30: NOMINATION: Best Sound

•

RAFFLES
1939, 70 mins, US b/w
Dir Sam Wood, William Wyler ***Prod*** Samuel Goldwyn ***Scr*** John Van Druten, Sydney Howard ***Ph*** Gregg Toland ***Ed*** Sherman Todd ***Mus*** Victor Young ***Art*** James Basevi
Act David Niven, Olivia de Havilland, May Whitty, Dudley Digges, Douglas Walton, Lionel Pape (Goldwyn)

Previous Goldwyn production of *Raffles* had Ronald Colman and Kay Francis as main figures in the romantic motivation to dovetail with the crook angle. Here, however, script concentrates on cat-and-mouse by-play between Scotland Yard inspector Mackenzie (Douglas Digges) and the elusive cracksman (David Niven), with the romantic interludes of minor importance. Present version also lacks the sparkle and good humor of the original with Colman.

As weekend guest of Lord and Lady Melrose (Lionel Pape, May Whitty) Raffles discovers his buddy and brother of his sweetheart needs funds quickly to prevent being cashiered from the army. Under the nose of the Scotland Yard inspector, he plans to pilfer the hostess' necklace, but eventually finds he has to lift the gems from a thief who had the same idea.

The E. W. Hornung tale [*The Amateur Cracksman*] has moments of interest and suspense in its present telling, but overall is able to generate only slight reaction for a familiar yarn. Niven is adequate as Raffles, with Digges providing interesting, amusing and important characterization as the inspector. Olivia de Havilland has slight footage as the romantic interest opposite Niven.

Raffles has been given Class A production values throughout, but on the entertainment side its a lower A.

•

RAGE
1966, 103 mins, US/Mexico Ⓥ ▭ col
Dir Gilberto Gazcon ***Prod*** Gilberto Gazcon ***Scr*** Teddi Sherman, Gilberto Gazcon, Fernando Mendez ***Ph*** Rosalio Solano ***Ed*** Carlos Savage, Walter Thompson ***Mus*** Gustavo Cesar Carreon
Act Glenn Ford, Stella Stevens, David Reynoso, Armando Silvestre, Ariadna Wellter, Jose Elias Moreno (Schenck/Jalisco)

Rage, a joint Mexican-American production lensed entirely below the Border, is a moderately interesting story of a doctor's frantic race against time to reach a hospital for the Pasteur treatment against rabies.

Glenn Ford and Stella Stevens are the only Americans in cast, balance recruited wholly from Mexican ranks. Although Mexican-made, pic was shot in English.

Ford plays a guilt-ridden physician half-bent upon self-destruction, haunted by memory of the death of his wife and child, for which he blames himself. His base of operations is a construction camp practically in the wilderness. Nipped by his pet dog, he finds later it has rabies, and figures he has only about 48 hours to reach a medical center where he may be treated. With Stevens, a hooker who has been in the camp, he races thru desert and mountain in an attempt to reach the hospital.

Good suspense is worked up in situation and writer-director Gilberto Gazcon maintains mood realistically. Ford etches a rugged characterization, particularly as panic begins to take hold in what appears to be a hopeless effort in reaching the hospital in time.

•

RAGE
1972, 99 mins, US Ⓥ col
Dir George C. Scott ***Prod*** Fred Weintraub ***Scr*** Philip Friedman, Dan Kleinman ***Ph*** Fred Koenekamp ***Ed*** Michael Kahn ***Mus*** Lalo Schifrin ***Art*** Frank Sylos
Act George C. Scott, Richard Basehart, Martin Sheen, Barnard Hughes, Nicolas Beauvy, Paul Stevens (Warner/Weintraub)

Rage is a sluggish, tired and tiring melodrama, starring George C. Scott, in his directorial debut, as a father wreaking vengeance for the death of his son after a chemical warfare experiment accident. Though largely a western states exterior film, the plot is a stagey, talky effort reminiscent of a 1950s TV anthology drama.

Writers start on a promising track—establishing widower Scott's relationship with son Nicolas Beauvy, and engendering suspense when the boy and the family cattle suddenly begin to drop like flies. Even further, the efforts of the U.S. Army and other government officials to hush the goof from press and Scott are dramatized in an all-too-credible way. But the story resolution becomes a shambles as Scott begins killing and blowing up installations.

•

RAGE IN HARLEM, A
1991, 108 mins, US Ⓥ ⊙ col
Dir Bill Duke ***Prod*** Stephen Woolley, Kerry Boyle ***Scr*** John Toles-Bey, Bobby Crawford ***Ph*** Toyomichi Kurita ***Ed*** Curtiss Clayton ***Mus*** Elmer Bernstein ***Art*** Steven Legler
Act Forest Whitaker, Gregory Hines, Robin Givens, Zakes Mokae, Danny Glover, John Toles-Bey (Palace/Miramax)

Director Bill Duke has brought a stylish sheen to *A Rage in Harlem*, but his mix of comedy and violence in the Chester Himes period crime tale is dubious. Many will be turned off by the excessive bloodshed, but the fine cast keeps the pic watchable.

Though not promoted as such, *Rage* is a followup to the Himes film adaptations *Cotton Comes to Harlem* (1970) and *Come Back, Charleston Blue* (1972). Here the novelist's cynical police detective protagonists Coffin Ed Johnson and Grave Digger Jones are relegated to secondary parts as the criminals take centerstage.

The raffish humor that made *Cotton Comes to Harlem* so delightful is only fitfully present. Co-producer Forest Whitaker, as an innocent mortuary accountant sucked into a plot involving stolen gold transported to 1956 Harlem from Mississippi, provides amiable but overdone antics in the lead role.

Pudgy mama's boy Whitaker keeps large pictures of Jesus and his stolid mother framed over his bed, occasioning jokes that become progressively less funny. And when he falls for Southern siren Robin Givens, he falls predictably hard. Givens holds the screen with assurance, though she works a bit too hard at the coy and sultry bits.

•

RAGE OF PARIS, THE
1938, 75 mins, US Ⓥ b/w
Dir Henry Koster ***Prod*** B. G. DeSylva ***Scr*** Bruce Manning, Felix Jackson ***Ph*** Joseph Valentine ***Mus*** Charles Previn (dir.)
Act Danielle Darrieux, Douglas Fairbanks, Jr., Mischa Auer, Louis Hayward, Helen Broderick (Universal)

Universal successfully launches Danielle Darrieux, young French star of unusual beauty and charm, in a written-to-order story.

Nothing more exacting is required than to play a light comedy role in one of those adjacent bedroom farces. She is quite stunning in evening gowns and furs, and very cute and intriguing in oversize pajamas. Her musical French accent is pleasant to the ear and capitalized humorously in the dialog.

Story is about a French girl who is having difficulty finding a model's job in New York. Helen Broderick, older and experienced in the ways of life and men, takes her in charge, and with Mischa Auer, hotel headwaiter, connives a campaign to get the young woman a rich husband. Louis Hayward is the object of their conspiracy, but Douglas Fairbanks, Jr. interferes and threatens to expose the canard.

There are several excellent sequences—an opening in which Darrieux, mistaking Fairbanks for a commercial photographer seeking models to pose undraped, starts to take off her clothes in his office; a scene at the opera when

Hayward and Fairbanks whisper confidences to the astonished annoyance of spectators; and a bedroom duet delightfully played by the stars.

•

RAGE TO LIVE, A

1965, 101 mins, US b/w

Dir Walter Grauman ***Prod*** Lewis J. Rachmil ***Scr*** John T. Kelley ***Ph*** Charles Lawton ***Ed*** Stuart Gilmore ***Mus*** Nelson Riddle ***Art*** James Sullivan

Act Suzanne Pleshette, Bradford Dillman, Ben Gazzara, Peter Graves, Bethel Leslie, James Gregory (Mirisch/United Artists)

In this banal transfer from tome to film, the characters in John O'Hara's *A Rage to Live* have retained their two-dimensional unreality in a country-club setting. Nympho heroine goes from man to man amidst corny dialog and inept direction which combine to smother all thesps.

Director Walter Grauman achieves little with the players, nor does he attempt to hype visual interest via technical gimmicks.

Thesps share the guilt. Suzanne Pleshette misses as the nympho who is dressed to the nines in an eye-catching Howard Shoup wardrobe. Bradford Dillman, the love in her life (as opposed to the men in her bed), is wasted on Roverboy lines. Ben Gazzara, the boy-who-worked-his-way-up, has little of the animal magnetism which is supposed to have rocked the pair's marriage boat.

1965: NOMINATION: Best B&W Costume Design

•

RAGGEDY MAN

1981, 94 mins, US Ⓥ ⦿ col

Dir Jack Fisk ***Prod*** Burt Weissbourd, William D. Wittliff ***Scr*** William D. Wittliff ***Ph*** Ralf Bode ***Ed*** Edward Warschilka ***Mus*** Jerry Goldsmith ***Art*** John Lloyd

Act Sissy Spacek, Eric Roberts, Sam Shepard, William Sanderson, Tracey Walter, Henry Thomas (Universal)

Directed by husband Jack Fisk (his first feature), Sissy Spacek plays a spunky divorcee, struggling to raise two young boys and stuck in a hopeless job as a small-town telephone operator tied to the switchboard in her house.

The setting is Texas in 1944 and Fisk, along with art director John Lloyd and costumer Joe I. Tompkins, has done a superb job in creating a faithful environment, down to the smallest detail. (Fisk was previously an art director.)

Enter sailor Eric Roberts in a rainstorm, knocking on the door to use the phone. After a night on the porch, Roberts spends a warm-hearted day with Spacek and the lads (Henry Thomas and Carey Hollis, Jr.). Gradually, warmth turns to heat in Spacek's bed.

Roberts is a terrific match for Spacek and their building romance sparkles. But she abruptly sends him packing and, after a tearful farewell, Roberts is seen no more.

With Roberts gone, the film turns mean as William Sanderson and Tracey Walter—both ably playing their redneck roles—make their move on Spacek. This is standard stuff and hardly worth Spacek's talents.

•

RAGGEDY RAWNEY, THE

1988, 102 mins, UK Ⓥ col

Dir Bob Hoskins ***Prod*** Bob Weis ***Scr*** Bob Hoskins, Nicole De Wilde ***Ph*** Frank Tidy ***Ed*** Alan Jones ***Mus*** Michael Kamen ***Art*** Jiri Matolin

Act Bob Hoskins, Dexter Fletcher, Zoe Nathanson, Dave Hill, Ian Dury, Zoe Wanamaker (HandMade)

Bob Hoskins brings to the screen an intriguing and particularly insightful perspective on the horrors suffered by the innocent amidst warfare.

Heading an ensemble cast as Darky, Hoskins plays the gritty leader of a gypsy-like band of refugees on the run from a war purposely set in an unspecified period somewhere in Europe.

A young soldier named Tom (Dexter Fletcher) deserts after an attack on his unit sends him into a panic.

By the time he catches up with Darky, et al, Tom is deemed to be a "rawney"—a person who is half-mad and half-magic. The film then opens its direct passageway into this closed community of near medieval attitudes, with fears of evil spirits and the unknown.

•

RAGING BULL

1980, 119 mins, US Ⓥ ⦿ col

Dir Martin Scorsese ***Prod*** Irwin Winkler, Robert Chartoff, Peter Savage ***Scr*** Paul Schrader, Mardik Martin ***Ph*** Michael Chapman ***Ed*** Thelma Schoonmaker ***Art*** Gene Rudolf

Act Robert De Niro, Cathy Moriarty, Joe Pesci, Frank Vincent, Nicholas Colasanto (United Artists)

Martin Scorsese makes pictures about the kinds of people you wouldn't want to know. In his mostly b&w biopic of middleweight boxing champ Jake La Motta, *Raging Bull*, the La Motta character played by Robert De Niro is one of the most repugnant and unlikeable screen protagonists in some time.

But the boxing sequences are possibly the best ever filmed, and the film captures the intensity of a boxer's life with considerable force.

Scorsese excels at whipping up an emotional storm but seems unaware that there is any need for quieter, more introspective moments in drama.

The relentless depiction of the downward slide of La Motta from a trim contender in 1941 to a shockingly bloated slob introducing strippers in a sleazy nightclub in 1964 has the morbid quality of a German expressionist film. By the time De Niro—who actually gained 50 pounds for the latter scenes—sits at a dressing-room mirror looking at his puffy face, he's become as grotesque as Emil Jannings in *The Blue Angel*. Aside from the customary genre plot of a boxer selling out to the mob, what seems to be on the minds of Scorsese and his screenwriters is an exploration of an extreme form of Catholic sadomasochism.

1980: Best Actor (Robert De Niro), Editing

NOMINATIONS: Best Picture, Director, Supp. Actor (Joe Pesci), Supp. Actress (Cathy Moriarty), Cinematography, Sound

•

RAGING MOON, THE
(US: LONG AGO TOMORROW)

1971, 110 mins, UK Ⓥ col

Dir Bryan Forbes ***Prod*** Bruce Cohn Curtis ***Scr*** Bryan Forbes ***Ph*** Tony Imi ***Ed*** Timothy Gee ***Mus*** Stanley Myers ***Art*** Robert Jones

Act Malcolm McDowell, Nanette Newman, Georgia Brown, Bernard Lee, Gerald Sim, Michael Flanders (M-G-M/EMI)

The Raging Moon is a tender love story [from a novel by Peter Marshall] woven round a delicate situation, but it has some good tangy dialog and some funny situations.

Early situations are broad and a bit bawdy but purpose is to establish the rough-and-ready character of the young hero (a bit of a yobbo, though with a yearning to write) and his background. He's a carefree boy with the birds, crazy about football and with little respect for his elders. Injured in a football match he loses the use of his legs. He lands up in a home for cripples. He's surly, resentful and a pain to the rest of the inmates who've learned to live with their misfortune. But at the home he meets and falls in love with a girl who has been wheelchaired for six years. Slowly, their relationship blossoms.

Bryan Forbes's dialog is punchy, perceptive and very understanding of human problems. He has also worked up an excellent cast. Malcolm McDowell handles the two or three facets of the hero with strong facility. Nanette Newman has a stunning warmth and radiance that communicates.

•

RAGMAN'S DAUGHTER, THE

1972, 94 mins, UK col

Dir Harold Becker ***Prod*** Harold Becker, Souter Harris ***Scr*** Alan Sillitoe ***Ph*** Michael Seresin ***Ed*** Antony Gibbs ***Mus*** Kenny Clayton ***Art*** David Brockhurst

Act Simon Rouse, Victoria Tennant, Patrick O'Connell, Leslie Sands, Rita Howard, Brian Murphy (Penelope/Harpoon)

Slow-paced but poignant pic based on an Alan Sillitoe novel which captures both the lyricism and grime of the Nottingham area. Carefully avoiding the pitfalls of the motorcycle thug genre, director Harold Becker weaves a bittersweet love affair between a petty teenage thief and the daughter of a wealthy rag dealer. Touches of humor and implied social comment, plus imaginative location lensing, give a ring of authenticity and honesty.

Both Simon Rouse and Patrick O'Connell, as the younger and older Tony, put in superb, convincing jobs of thesping as outcasts of society. Sillitoe steers clear of moralizing, and even social issues inherent in the relationship between the protagonists is made subservient to a broader concern for lost youth and the joys of yesteryear.

•

RAGTIME

1981, 155 mins, US Ⓥ ⦿ col

Dir Milos Forman ***Prod*** Dino De Laurentiis ***Scr*** Michael Weller ***Ph*** Miroslav Ondricek ***Ed*** Anne V. Coates, Antony Gibbs, Stanley Warnow ***Mus*** Randy Newman ***Art*** John Graysmark

Act James Cagney, Brad Dourif, Elizabeth McGovern, Pat O'Brien, Donald O'Connor, Mandy Patinkin (Paramount/De Laurentiis)

The page-turning joys of E. L. Doctorow's bestselling *Ragtime*, which dizzily and entertainingly charted a kaleidoscopic vision of a turn-of-century America in the midst of intense social change, have been realized almost completely in Milos Forman's superbly crafted screen adaptation.

Within a myriad of characters who include the likes of Evelyn Nesbit, Stanford White, Booker T. Washington and J. Pierpont Morgan, the film charts the syncopated social forces that truly ushered in 20th-century America by pivoting them around a nameless upper-crust family unexpectedly caught up in the maelstrom.

Overriding focus of the film is on the travails of a fictional black ragtime pianist (Howard E. Rollins), whose common-law wife (Debbie Allen) is taken in by The Family after she abandons her newborn child in their garden.

Juggling the scores of characters that Doctorow intertwined in his quirky blend of historical and fictional people and events, Forman and scripter Michael Weller were forced into some occasional truncation and short-cutting, but ultimately win the chess game hands down.

1981: NOMINATIONS: Best Supp. Actor (Howard E. Rollins), Supp. Actress (Elizabeth McGovern), Adapted Screenplay, Cinematography, Costume Design, Art Direction, Score, Song ("One More Hour")

•

RAIDERS OF THE LOST ARK

1981, 115 mins, US Ⓥ ⦿ col

Dir Steven Spielberg ***Prod*** Frank Marshall ***Scr*** Lawrence Kasdan ***Ph*** Douglas Slocombe ***Ed*** Michael Kahn ***Mus*** John Williams ***Art*** Norman Reynolds

Act Harrison Ford, Karen Allen, Denholm Elliott, Paul Freeman, Ronald Lacey, John Rhys-Davies (Paramount)

Raiders of the Lost Ark is the stuff that raucous Saturday matinees at the local Bijou once were made of, a crackerjack fantasy-adventure. Steeped in an exotic atmosphere of lost civilizations, mystical talismans, gritty mercenary adventurers, Nazi arch-villians and ingenious death at every turn, the film is largely patterned on the serials of the 1930s, with a large dollop of Edgar Rice Burroughs.

Story [by George Lucas and Philip Kaufman] begins in 1936 as Indiana Jones (Harrison Ford), an archeologist and university professor who's not above a little mercenary activity on the side, plunders a South American jungle tomb. He secures a priceless golden Godhead, only to have it snatched away by longtime archeological rival Paul Freeman, now employed by the Nazis.

Back in the States, Ford is approached by U.S. intelligence agents who tell him the Nazis are rumored to have discovered the location of the Lost Ark of the Covenant (where the broken 10 Commandments were sealed). The ark is assumed to contain an awesome destructive power. Ford's mission is to beat the Germans to the ark.

Director Steven Spielberg has deftly veiled proceedings in a sense of mystical wonder that makes it all the more easy for viewers to suspend disbelief and settle back for the fun.

1981: Best Art Direction, Sound, Editing, Visual Effects, Sound Effects Editing

NOMINATIONS: Best Picture, Director, Cinematography, Score

•

RAILWAY CHILDREN, THE

1970, 108 mins, UK Ⓥ col

Dir Lionel Jeffries ***Prod*** Robert Lynn ***Scr*** Lionel Jeffries ***Ph*** Arthur Ibbetson ***Ed*** Teddy Darvas ***Mus*** Johnny Douglas ***Art*** John Clark

Act Dinah Sheridan, Bernard Cribbins, William Mervyn, Iain Cuthbertson, Jenny Agutter, Sally Thomsett (EMI)

Story, from E. Nesbit's w.k. novel set in the Edwardian age, concerns a well-to-do family whose life's turned upside down when the father (something in the Foreign Office) is unjustly jailed. The family, in straitened circumstances, go to live on the Yorkshire moors.

They soon adapt to the new life, make friends with the goodhearted villagers, and particularly with a well-to-do gent whom they enlist to help clear their father.

The village is near a railway and this becomes the center of their activities with the local porter and general railway factotum becoming one of their most useful allies.

Much of the film's success depends on the trio of children. Eldest is played with grave confidence by snub-nosed Jenny Agutter.

•

RAIN

1932, 92 mins, US Ⓥ b/w

Dir Lewis Milestone ***Prod*** Lewis Milestone ***Scr*** Maxwell Anderson, Lewis Milestone ***Ph*** Oliver Marsh ***Ed*** W. Duncan Mansfield ***Art*** Richard Day

Act Joan Crawford, Walter Huston, William Gargan, Guy Kibbee, Walter Catlett, Beulah Bondi (Milestone/United Artists)

It turns out to be a mistake to have assigned the Sadie Thompson role to Joan Crawford. The dramatic significance of it all is beyond her range. As for producer-director Lewis Milestone's shortcomings as an entrepreneur, the outcome is equally to be laid at his doorstep [in this version of the play by John Cotton and C. Randolph from the story by W. Somerset Maugham].

The 92 minutes to achieve the climactic finale, where the salvationist succumbs to the flesh, is too long a period to reach the fairly obvious. It then becomes the burden of the Sadie Thompson, Davidson (Walter Huston) and other characters to sustain matters through their own personal impressions. And it's all so talky.

Apart from that, Milestone goes in for the impressionistic rain thing too much with camera angles.

Huston must have felt as ridic as were some of his lines when he had to utter them during production.

Joan Crawford's getup as the light lady is extremely bizarre. Pavement pounders don't quite trick themselves up as fantastically as all that.

•

RAINBOW, THE

1989, 112 mins, US Ⓥ ⊙ col

Dir Ken Russell **Prod** Ken Russell **Scr** Ken Russell, Vivian Russell **Ph** Billy Williams **Ed** Peter Davies **Mus** Carl Davis **Art** Luciana Arrighi

Act Sammi Davis, Paul McGann, Amanda Donohoe, Christopher Gable, David Hemmings, Glenda Jackson (Vestron)

The Rainbow was D. H. Lawrence's fourth novel and concludes with the sexual awakening of Ursula Brangwen, whose story was continued in *Women in Love*. The current film reps a prequel to director Ken Russell's earlier one, in which Jennie Linden played Ursula, and Glenda Jackson won an Oscar as her sister Gudrun.

Concentrating on the last section of the novel, Russell charts the spasmodic, often brutal maturation of Ursula (Sammi Davis), a country girl at the turn of the century. Ursula's very out-of-the-ordinary sexual initiation comes at the persuasive hands of her swimming instructor, the strikingly beautiful Winnifred (Amanda Donohoe), one of Lawrence's patented free spirits.

Rebelling against her parents, Ursula moves to London to take a lowly position as a grade school teacher. Before long, she finds herself attracted to a man, the career soldier Anton (Paul McGann), who is mostly occupied fighting the Boer War. Despite the rough deflowering, Ursula's feelings grow into love before coming to grips with her full nature and rushing off to the adventures that will be *Women in Love*.

The Rainbow finds Russell working in a most restrained, classical style. The director, who wrote the script with his wife Vivian, plainly identifies and sympathizes with his heroine's fierce search for independence.

Davis, who came to the fore as the man-hungry teenager in *Hope and Glory*, throws herself into Ursula with all the physical and emotional energy she can muster. Donohoe is absolutely on the money as the liberated Winnifred. McGann makes Anton too languid and remote to get excited about.

•

RAINING STONES

1993, 90 mins, UK Ⓥ col

Dir Ken Loach **Prod** Sally Hibbin **Scr** Jim Allen **Ph** Barry Ackroyd **Ed** Jonathan Morris **Mus** Stewart Copeland **Art** Martin Johnson

Act Bruce Jones, Julie Brown, Ricky Tomlinson, Tom Hickey, Gemma Phoenix, Jonathan James (Parallax/Film Four)

Repeating more or less the same formula as their 1991 success *Riff-Raff*, director Ken Loach and writer Jim Allen come up trumps with *Raining Stones*, a sad-funny portrayal of working class stiffs battling the recession in northern England.

Pic, set in Manchester suburb of Middleton, centers on Bob (Bruce Jones), an out-of-work plumber who desperately needs money to pay for the expensive white dress he feels his small daughter deserves for her first communion. His attempts to earn much-needed cash include the bizarre (rustling a sheep and selling pieces of mutton at the local pub) to the comic (going door to door offering to fix faulty drains) to the dangerous (borrowing money from a loan shark).

Loach and Allen alternate comedy (some of it spoken in broad enough Manchester accents to warrant the use of subtitles) with suspense and tragedy. Jones is perfectly cast as the rumpled hero and Ricky Tomlinson (the guy caught in the bath in *Riff-Raff*) is a scream as his loyal, sardonic friend.

The title is derived from a comment made by Bob's socialist father-in-law: "When you're a worker, it rains stones seven days a week."

•

RAINMAKER, THE

1956, 121 mins, US Ⓥ ⊙ col

Dir Joseph Anthony **Prod** Hal Wallis **Scr** N. Richard Nash **Ph** Charles Lang, Jr. **Ed** Warren Low **Mus** Alex North **Art** Hal Pereira, Walter Tyler

Act Burt Lancaster, Katharine Hepburn, Wendell Corey, Lloyd Bridges, Earl Holliman, Cameron Prud'homme (Paramount)

The N. Richard Nash play has been fashioned into a solid screen entertainment. With Burt Lancaster turning in perhaps his most colorful performance and Katharine Hepburn offering a free-wheeling interpretation of a spinster in search of romance, the adaptation is a click show all around.

Nash's own screenplay stays close to the original, establishing the title character right at the start and then moving into the story of how the smooth-talking fraud pretends to bring rain to a drought-stricken ranch area. It's humorously and imaginatively done against unusually effective sets.

Locale is the southwestern town of Three Point where Lancaster sets out to pick up $100 on his promise of bringing a vitally-needed downpour. He comes into contact with rancher Cameron Prud'homme and his family, comprising Hepburn as the daughter, two sons, Lloyd Bridges, who's stern and practical, and Earl Holliman, a clumsy, likeable youngster.

That's the setup. Lancaster, although he's obviously a con artist, is permitted to live in Prud'homme's tack house and work his rain magic. He convinces Hepburn that she's pretty, and not plain as Bridges insists.

1956: NOMINATIONS: Best Actress (Katharine Hepburn), Scoring of a Dramatic Picture

•

RAINMAKER, THE
(AKA: JOHN GRISHAM'S THE RAINMAKER)

1997, 135 mins, US Ⓥ ⊙ ▭ col

Dir Francis Coppola **Prod** Michael Douglas, Steven Reuther, Fred Fuchs **Scr** Francis Coppola **Ph** John Toll **Ed** Barry Malkin, Melissa Kent **Mus** Elmer Bernstein **Art** Howard Cummings

Act Matt Damon, Claire Danes, Jon Voight, Mary Kay Place, Mickey Rourke, Danny DeVito (Constellation/Paramount)

As carefully constructed, handsomely crafted and flavorsomely acted as a top-of-the-line production from Hollywood's studio era, this story of a young Southern lawyer taking on an evil insurance giant exerts an almost irresistible David and Goliath appeal.

Authoring a script on his own for the first time in a very long while, Francis Ford Coppola [with Michael Herr writing the narration] has adhered to the essential dramatic crescendos important to any John Grisham tale, climaxing inevitably in a major courtroom scene in which the little (and young and attractive) guy takes on the establishment or big money or simply long odds.

Memphis law school grad Rudy Baylor (Matt Damon) goes to work for the aptly named Bruiser Stone (Mickey Rourke), a slimy operator. From Bruiser's shameless leg man Deck Schifflet (Danny DeVito), Rudy learns the basics of ambulance-chasing, which is how he meets Kelly Riker (Claire Danes), hospitalized after being beaten by her husband with a baseball bat.

Rudy has also generated clients on his own, including Dot Black (Mary Kay Place), whose son Donny Ray (Johnny Whitworth) is dying of leukemia. The poor family's insurance company has rejected all eight attempts to secure coverage for Donny Ray's care. Breaking away from Bruiser just as the Feds close in, Rudy and Deck place all their bets on the Blacks. At the slightest threat of being taken to court, the insurance company's slick lawyer, Leo F. Drummond (Jon Voight), offers to settle.

Coppola seems bent on leavening the melodrama with as many laughs as possible, and they are generally honest and well-earned. Towering over DeVito, Damon adroitly shades Rudy's transformation from greenhorn to legal eagle. Voight makes for a super-smooth villain. Production values are immaculate.

•

RAIN MAN

1988, 140 mins, US Ⓥ ⊙ col

Dir Barry Levinson **Prod** Mark Johnson **Scr** Ronald Bass, Barry Morrow **Ph** John Seale **Ed** Stu Linder **Mus** Hans Zimmer **Art** Ida Random

Act Dustin Hoffman, Tom Cruise, Valeria Golino, Jerry Molen, Jack Murdock (Guber-Peters/United Artists)

Raymond Babbitt (Dustin Hoffman) is an autistic savant, a person extremely limited in some mental areas and extremely gifted in others. His younger brother, hard-driving luxury car dealer Charlie Babbitt (Tom Cruise), has his limitations too—mostly in the areas of kindness and understanding.

Unaware of Raymond's existence until his estranged father dies, Charlie is brought up short when he learns the old man's entire $3 million fortune has been willed to his brother.

Charlie shanghais him, without regard for his welfare, into a cross-country trip to L.A., dangling a Dodger game as bait. Meanwhile, he threatens Raymond's guardian, the bland Dr. Bruner (Jerry Molen), with a custody battle unless he hands over half the fortune.

Director Barry Levinson lingers long on the road trip segment, building the relationship between the brothers degree by degree. Result is lightly engrossing.

By the last third, pic [based on a story by Barry Morrow] becomes quite moving as these two very isolated beings discover a common history and deep attachment.

It's a mature assignment for Cruise and he's at his best in the darker scenes. Hoffman achieves an exacting physical characterization of Raymond, from his constant nervous movements to his rigid, hunched shoulders and childish gait.

1988: Best Picture, Director, Actor (Dustin Hoffman), Original Screenplay

NOMINATIONS: Best Cinematography, Editing, Original Score, Art Direction

•

RAIN PEOPLE, THE

1969, 101 mins, US Ⓥ col

Dir Francis Coppola **Prod** Bart Patton, Ronald Colby **Scr** Francis Coppola **Ph** Wilmer Butler **Ed** Blackie Malkin **Mus** Ronald Stein **Art** Leon Ericksen

Act James Caan, Shirley Knight, Robert Duvall, Marya Zimmet, Tom Aldredge (Warner/Seven Arts/Coppola)

Writer-director Francis Coppola, scrutinizing the flight of a neurotic young woman and her efforts to assist a brain-damaged ex-football player, has developed an overlong, brooding film incorporating some excellent photography. Often lingering too long on detail to build effects, he manages to lose character sympathy.

Shirley Knight, in a neurotic panic because she dreads the ties of domesticity, runs away from her Long Island home and husband. She phones him from the Pennsylvania Turnpike to tell him she is pregnant and has to get away from home.

She picks up James Caan, an ex-football hero whose brain was damaged in a college game, who is hitchhiking to West Virginia to work for the father of a girlfriend from school.

•

RAINS CAME, THE

1939, 100 mins, US b/w

Dir Clarence Brown **Prod** Darryl F. Zanuck **Scr** Philip Dunne, Julien Josephson **Ph** Arthur Miller **Ed** Barbara McLean **Mus** Alfred Newman **Art** William Darling, George Dudley

Act Myrna Loy, Tyrone Power, George Brent, Brenda Joyce, Nigel Bruce, Maria Ouspenskaya (20th Century-Fox)

Liberties have been taken with [Louis Bromfield's] original novel, resulting in switching some of the original characterizations or intent, but under production code restrictions, and to conform with the mass market of film entertainment, it merges as a competent job.

True, Myrna Loy's Lady Esketh isn't the trollop of the original. True, the romantic Major (Dr.) Rama Safti (Tyrone Power) was more of a symbol of the new India in the book, than triangular link as in this film. True, also, that the romantic antics by the stellar trio and Brenda Joyce (opposite George Brent), and the tropical earthquake that well nigh wrecks the mythical domain of Ranchipur, are more Zanuck than Bromfield. But it is good cinematurgy.

Newcomer Joyce, 18-year-old Los Angeles high school "find" cast as the daughter of social-climbing missionaries, rings the bell throughout with a consistent performance as a forthright romantic adolescent, stuck on Brent. Latter is the wastrel, of good British family, who has been dawdling in Ranchipur for years on an art assignment.

His best friend is the enlightened young Safti, who is blind to any romantic deviations, in his intensive medical duties, until Loy comes on the scene.

The simple heroics following the quake are more effective than the earth-rending sequences themselves. On montage, Fred Sersen rates a bow for his special effects.

1939: Best Special Effects

NOMINATIONS: Best Art Direction, Editing, Sound, Original Score

RAINS OF RANCHIPUR, THE
1955, 104 mins, US col
Dir Jean Negulesco *Prod* Frank Ross *Scr* Merle Miller *Ph* Milton Krasner *Ed* Dorothy Spencer *Mus* Hugo Friedhofer *Art* Lyle Wheeler, Addison Hehr
Act Lana Turner, Richard Burton, Fred MacMurray, Joan Caulfield, Michael Rennie, Eugenie Leontovich (20th Century-Fox)

Louis Bromfield's *The Rains Came*, brought to the screen once before by 20th-Fox in 1939, is filmed this time with Lana Turner as the titled trollop.

However, the cast itself hardly comes alive. Only sturdy performances are turned in by Richard Burton and Eugenie Leontovich.

Turner, as Edwina (Lady Esketh), has the role of a temptress down pat, perhaps too much so. She's good in a couple of scenes, indifferent in most of them and almost embarrassing in some. Burton's portrayal of Dr. Safti, the dedicated Indian doctor, who falls in love with Turner, has strength and conviction and is underplayed intelligently. As the Maharani, Leontovich has dignity, and the scenes between her and Burton are definite assets to the picture.

1955: NOMINATION: Best Special Effects

RAINTREE COUNTY
1957, 187 mins, US col
Dir Edward Dmytryk *Prod* David Lewis *Scr* Millard Kaufman *Ph* Robert Surtees *Ed* John Dunning *Mus* Johnny Green *Art* William A. Horning, Urie McCleary
Act Montgomery Clift, Elizabeth Taylor, Eva Marie Saint, Nigel Patrick, Lee Marvin, Rod Taylor (M-G-M)

Raintree County, one of the biggest and costliest (estimated at $5 million) productions from Metro since its release of David O. Selznick's *Gone With the Wind*, was lensed via the Camera 65 process (65 mm negative is used and reduced to 35 mm for release prints). It is a study of emotional conflicts set against the Civil War turmoil, and done with pictorial sweep.

Story unfolds against a background of historic events—the war, Abraham Lincoln's election, the Northern abolition movement, Southern secession, etc. Metro shot on location near Danville, KY, for the most part.

The setting at the start is Raintree County, Indiana, where Montgomery Clift and Eva Marie Saint are blissfully in love and looking ahead to life together. Elizabeth Taylor, whose troubled mind is later revealed, comes as a visitor from New Orleans and woos Clift away from Saint and into marriage.

They take up residence in the Deep South where the slavery issue is exposed to Clift, who abhors it, and the couple return to Raintree. At first distressed by the upheaval of the times, Taylor eventually becomes insane. Taking her young son with her, she runs again to her native Dixie. Clift enters the Union Army.

Under Edward Dmytryk's direction, this adaption of Ross Lockridge, Jr.'s novel unfolds fairly interestingly but slowly. Picture lacks highlight material; even the war scenes don't quite have the necessary impact and the relationship between Taylor and Clift could have been charged up more.

1957: NOMINATIONS: Best Actress (Elizabeth Taylor), Costume Design, Art Direction, Score

RAISE THE RED LANTERN
SEE: DA HONG DENGLONG GAO GAO GUA

RAISE THE TITANIC
1980, 102 mins, UK col
Dir Jerry Jameson *Prod* William Frye *Scr* Adam Kennedy *Ph* Matthew F. Leonetti *Ed* J. Terry Williams, Robert F. Shugrue *Mus* John Barry *Art* John F. DeCuir
Act Jason Robards, Richard Jordan, Alec Guinness, David Selby, Anne Archer, M. Emmet Walsh (ITC)

Raise the Titanic wastes a potentially intriguing premise with dull scripting, a lackluster cast, laughably phony trick work, and clunky direction. Half of the running time (at least) is devoted to underwater miniature shots of submarines and other apparatus trying to dislodge the long-lost luxury liner *Titanic* from its deepsea resting place.

The ridiculously expository screenplay [adapted by Eric Hughes from the novel by Clive Cussler] repeatedly explains what will happen, why it's happening, and how it's going to happen.

The actors adopt various strategies for coping with their unspeakable dialog and cardboard characterizations. Alec Guinness provides a dramatic highlight with a lovely scene as a retired old salt who served on the *Titanic*'s crew.

RAISING ARIZONA
1987, 94 mins, US col
Dir Joel Coen *Prod* Ethan Coen, Mark Silverman *Scr* Ethan Coen, Joel Coen *Ph* Barry Sonnenfeld *Ed* Michael R. Miller *Mus* Carter Burwell *Art* Jane Musky
Act Nicolas Cage, Holly Hunter, Trey Wilson, John Goodman, William Forsythe, Frances McDormand (Circle/Pedas-Barenholtz)

Pic is the Coen Brothers' twisted view of family rearing in the American heartlands and as full of quirky humor and off-the-wall situations as their debut effort, *Blood Simple*. The film captures the surrealism of everyday life. Characters are so strange here that they seem to have stepped out of late-night television, tabloid newspapers, talk radio and a vivid imagination.

Nicolas Cage and Holly Hunter are the off-center couple at the center of the doings. Cage is a well-meaning petty crook with a fondness for knocking off convenience stores. Hunter is the cop who checks him into prison so often that a romance develops.

They soon learn marriage is "no Ozzie and Harriet Show" and when she learns she can't have kids or adopt them, they do the next logical thing—steal one.

Loosely structured around a voice-over narration by Cage, *Raising Arizona* is as leisurely and disconnected as *Blood Simple* was taut and economical. While film is filled with many splendid touches and plenty of yocks, it often doesn't hold together as a coherent story.

While Cage and Hunter are fine as the couple at sea in the desert, pic sports at least one outstanding performance from John Goodman as the con brother who wants a family too.

RAISING CAIN
1992, 95 mins, US col
Dir Brian De Palma *Prod* Gale Anne Hurd *Scr* Brian De Palma *Ph* Stephen H. Burum *Ed* Paul Hirsch, Bonnie Koehler, Robert Dalva *Mus* Pino Donaggio *Art* Doug Kraner
Act John Lithgow, Lolita Davidovich, Steven Bauer, Frances Sternhagen, Gregg Henry, Mel Harris (Universal/Pacific Western)

Brian De Palma's modest-budget ($11 million) thriller *Raising Cain* is a superficial, often risible, exercise in pure aesthetics. As a showcase for John Lithgow's acting talents and a visual tour de force, the film may delight the director's most camp followers.

Though there are plenty of nods to Hitchcock's 1960 *Psycho* here, De Palma's point of departure is Michael Powell's classic *Peeping Tom* (also released in 1960), in which a scientist experimented on his young son, causing him to grow up as a psychotic killer.

Lithgow portrays both scientist and son, among several other contrasting roles, in an impressive display of surface acting skills.

Film begins promisingly with daylit horror, as the meek Carter (Lithgow) turns suddenly sinister, attacking a family friend (Teri Austin) to kidnap her young son. Out of nowhere his alter ego, twin brother Cain, pops up to save the day and take over Carter's identity. Carter and Cain are rounding up five kids, including Carter's daughter, for their dad who's returned to America to complete his experiments.

Pic loses its footing midway through with the introduction of a spoofed romantic subplot involving Carter's wife Lolita Davidovich and her old flame, Steven Bauer. Using awkwardly inserted (on purpose) and very showy flashbacks, De Palma deconstructs his narrative and has trouble gaining momentum.

RAKE'S PROGRESS, THE
(US: NOTORIOUS GENTLEMAN)
1945, 110 mins, UK b/w
Dir Sidney Gilliat *Prod* Sidney Gilliat, Frank Launder *Scr* Sidney Gilliat, Frank Launder *Ph* Wilkie Cooper, Jack Asher *Ed* Thelma Myers *Mus* William Alwyn *Art* Norman Arnold
Act Rex Harrison, Lilli Palmer, Godfrey Tearle, Jean Kent, Griffith Jones (Individual)

This is probably one of the finest films to come out of a British studio. Superb as Rex Harrison and Lilli Palmer are, their individual performances are equalled by many others in the big cast. The script is racy in dialogue.

Direction by Sidney Gilliat who with Frank Launder, also wrote [from a story by Val Valentine] and produced the picture, is virtually flawless. The independent company [Individual Productions] was formed by Gilliat and Launder when these two experienced scriptwriters got tired of working for a salary and threw up their jobs with Gainsborough.

RALLY 'ROUND THE FLAG, BOYS!
1958, 106 mins, US col
Dir Leo McCarey *Prod* Leo McCarey *Scr* Claude Binyon, Leo McCarey *Ph* Leon Shamroy *Ed* Louis Loeffler *Mus* Cyril J. Mockridge *Art* Lyle Wheeler, Leland Fuller
Act Paul Newman, Joanne Woodward, Joan Collins, Jack Carson, Dwayne Hickman, Tuesday Weld (20th Century-Fox)

This is a bedroom farce of split-level thinking in split-level housing. The film version of Max Shulman's bestseller is unmistakably a Leo McCarey picture. Some of the gags are elaborate and as carefully timed as a dance sequence.

The plot is simple. Paul Newman and Joanne Woodward are the couple (two children), living in Fairfield County, Conn. They have, in the delicate phrase, drifted apart. Newman is all for drifting right back, but Woodward is so busy organizing their town into a community as neat, tidy and efficient as their modern kitchen, she can't find the time. Enter the Temptress, or third angle of triangle. She is Joan Collins.

McCarey is working here with players—Newman, Woodward and Collins—who did only incidental film comedy up to this one. They are called upon to slam into opening doors, swing from chandeliers, do the dropped pants bit (in Newman's case), takes and double-takes. Jack Carson, of course, is a past-master at the slow burn and volcanic reaction, and more than holds his own.

RAMBLING ROSE
1991, 113 mins, US col
Dir Martha Coolidge *Prod* Renny Harlin *Scr* Calder Willingham *Ph* Johnny Jensen *Ed* Steven Cohen *Mus* Elmer Bernstein *Art* John Vallone
Act Laura Dern, Robert Duvall, Diane Ladd, Lukas Haas, John Heard, Kevin Conway (Midnight Sun)

Calder Willingham's memoir [novel] of the South, *Rambling Rose* is a funny and moving tale of an oversexed young woman from the wrong side of the tracks.

Rose (Laura Dern) starts her life as maid to the family of Robert Duvall and Diane Ladd in a small Georgia town in 1935. It turns out that rumors of her having been forced into prostitution at a tender age are true. Both Duvall and his 13-year-old son Lukas Haas are immediately taken by Dern's raw sexuality, yet it is the boy who nearly has his first conquest with her when Dern innocently gets in bed with him one night in a funny and risque scene.

Duvall is a proper gentleman, rejecting Dern's attempt at seduction and quickly adopting a fatherly concern for her. Family matriarch Ladd (Dern's real-life mom) is a Yankee educated at Columbia U. who also takes Dern under her wing. Main source of conflict is Dern's promiscuous activities, which cause young men to loiter outside the house at all hours.

Dern's naturalness in a very eccentric role confirms the promise of her earlier work. Duvall and Ladd play off each other to perfection.

Director Martha Coolidge and her technical crew have re-created the detail and texture of Southern life with great feeling at Carolco's Wilmington, NC, studio.

1991: NOMINATIONS: Best Actress (Laura Dern), Supporting Actress (Diane Ladd)

RAMBO
FIRST BLOOD PART II
1985, 95 mins, US col
Dir George Pan Cosmatos *Prod* Buzz Feitshans *Scr* Sylvester Stallone, James Cameron *Ph* Jack Cardiff *Ed* Mark Goldblatt, Mark Helfrich *Mus* Jerry Goldsmith *Art* Bill Kenney
Act Sylvester Stallone, Richard Crenna, Charles Napier, Julia Nickson, Steven Berkoff, Martin Kove (Tri-Star)

This overwrought sequel to the popular *First Blood* (1982) is one mounting fireball as Sylvester Stallone's special operations veteran is sprung from a prison labor camp by his former Green Beret commander (Richard Crenna) to find POWs in Vietnam.

That the secret mission is a cynical ruse by higher-ups which is meant to fail heightens Stallone's fury while touching off a provocative political theme: a U.S. government that wants to forget about POWs and accommodate the public at the same time.

The charade on the screen, which is not pulled off, is to accept that the underdog Rambo character, albeit with the help of an attractive machine-gun wielding Vietnamese girl

(Julia Nickson), can waste hordes of Vietcong and Red Army contingents enroute to hauling POWs to a Thai air base in a smoking Russian chopper with only a facial scar (from a branding iron-knifepoint) marring his tough figure.

Steven Berkoff is a twisted and nominally chilly Russian advisor, but his performance is essentially the same nasty thing he did in *Octopussy* and *Beverly Hills Cop*.

1985: NOMINATION: Best Sound Effects Editing

•

RAMBO III

1988, 101 mins, US Ⓥ ⦿ ⌑ col

Dir Peter Macdonald ***Prod*** Buzz Feitshans ***Scr*** Sylvester Stallone, Sheldon Lettich ***Ph*** John Stanier ***Ed*** James Symons, Andrew London, O. Nicholas Brown, Edward A. Warschilka ***Mus*** Jerry Goldsmith ***Art*** Billy Kenney

Act Sylvester Stallone, Richard Crenna, Marc de Jonge, Kurtwood Smith, Spiros Focas (Carolco)

Rambo III stakes out a moral high ground for its hero missing or obscured in the previous two pictures. In the Soviets' heinous nine-year occupation of Afghanistan, this mythic commando and quintessential outsider is enlisted in a cause that—glasnost notwithstanding—is indisputably righteous.

Indeed, as this chapter opens, the character of John Rambo has been demilitarized and transported to exotic self-exile in Thailand, where he lives in a Buddhist monastery and supports himself by engaging in slam-bang mercenary martial arts contests.

Richard Crenna has come halfway around the world to Bangkok to ask Stallone for payback—Rambo's participation in a clandestine operation to destroy a "brutal" Russian general who rules a remote province in occupied Afghanistan.

The battle scenes in *Rambo III* are explosive, conflagratory tableaux that make for wrenching, frequently terrifying viewing. Always at ground zero in the chaos is Rambo—gloriously, inhumanly impervious to fear and danger—whose character is inhabited by Stallone with messianic intensity.

•

RAMPAGE

1987, 97 mins, US Ⓥ col

Dir William Friedkin ***Prod*** David Salven ***Scr*** William Friedkin ***Ph*** Robert D. Yeoman ***Ed*** Jere Huggins ***Mus*** Ennio Morricone ***Art*** Buddy Cone

Act Michael Biehn, Alex McArthur, Nicholas Campbell, Deborah Van Valkenburgh, John Harkins, Art Lafleur (De Laurentiis)

Anthony Fraser (Michael Biehn) is the assistant district attorney in charge of the major crimes division and is handed a grisly murder case by his boss with orders to go for the death penalty. The case involves a psychopath named Charles Reece (Alex McArthur) who has killed five people, mutilating four of them and drinking their blood. Fraser doesn't want the case because he's against the death penalty.

Writer-director William Friedkin [adapting the novel by William P. Wood] elects to explore the frustration of the legal system's insanity defense. He refuses to present an easy out to the dilemma. Even Dr. Keddie (John Harkins), as the defense's chief psychiatrist, is given his moment to defend his position.

The cast is top notch all around with Biehn (once cast as a crazed killer in *The Fan*) suggesting the anguish beneath the cool exterior of his prosecutor. Deborah Van Valkenburgh brings some depth to the supporting role of Biehn's wife. As Reece, McArthur appears dangerous and unstable but remains opaque, so we—like the lawyers and the doctors—can never be completely sure if he knew what he was doing when he committed the murders.

•

RAMROD

1947, 94 mins, US Ⓥ b/w

Dir Andre de Toth ***Prod*** Harry Sherman ***Scr*** Jack Moffitt, Graham Baker, Cecile Kramer ***Ph*** Russell Harlan, Harry Redmond ***Ed*** Sherman A. Rose ***Mus*** Adolph Deutsch ***Art*** Lionel Banks

Act Veronica Lake, Joel McCrea, Preston Foster, Lloyd Bridges, Charles Ruggles, Don DeFore (United Artists/Enterprise)

Ramrod is a good western with above-par names. The title stands for ranch foreman and Joel McCrea is the ramrod of Veronica Lake's ranch. The challenge starts when the cattlemen would stop sheepherding in this cowtown of the 1870s.

Preston Foster runs the cow-country, with acquiescence of Charlie Ruggles whom his daughter (Lake) defies when she throws the gauntlet to Foster. Arleen Whelan is the honest homespun seamstress to whom McCrea finally turns, and in between there is the volatile Don DeFore as the hero's aide and Donald Crisp as the honest sheriff who is another victim of Foster's men.

The femme angles give more than ordinary substance to this western which otherwise has its usual assortment of gunplay, hard-riding, skullduggery and the inevitable chase for the finale.

•

RAN

1985, 161 mins, Japan/France Ⓥ ⦿ ⌑ col

Dir Akira Kurosawa ***Prod*** Masato Hara, Serge Silberman ***Scr*** Akira Kurosawa, Hideo Oguni, Masato Ide ***Ph*** Takao Saito ***Mus*** Toru Takemitsu ***Art*** Yoshiro Muraki, Shinobu Muraki

Act Tatsuya Nakadai, Satoshi Terao, Jinpachi Nezu, Daisuke Ryu, Mieko Harada, Peter (Herald Ace/Nippon Herald/Greenwich)

Akira Kurosawa has turned once again to Shakespeare for source material, just as he did nearly 30 years earlier when *Macbeth* became the memorable *Throne of Blood*. At age 75, the director has made his most costly epic to date, and it's a dazzlingly successful addition to his distinguished career.

The basis of *Ran* (literally *Chaos*) is *King Lear*, but with a few minor modifications. Chief of these is that the old king's offspring are now three sons rather than three daughters, though all the basic motivations of the original remain intact.

On his 70th birthday, Lord Hidetora announces he's passing authority on to his eldest son, Taro; when his youngest, Saburo, who genuinely cares for his father, violently protests, he's banished. Subsequently, Taro treats his father shamefully, as does the middle son, Jiro, and eventually the two join forces to attack their father's castle.

Kurosawa starts the film in a leisurely way as he sets up the drama and intros the principal characters, but from the very beginning his use of bold color and dynamic camera angles indicates a master at the peak of his powers. The two major battle sequences, the first about an hour into the film, the second providing the climax, are superbly staged.

In addition to these genuinely enthralling sequences, Kurosawa provides gripping drama and intrigue in the court scenes. Changing the sexes of the king's heirs provides not only fine roles for three excellent actors, but also gives Mieko Harada, as the evil, scheming Lady Kaede (who goads first one brother then another into war and destruction), the opportunity to play an unforgettable character role, a role similar to that of Lady Macbeth in *Throne of Blood*. Tatsuya Nadadai, in superb makeup, is the king, and it's a tribute to this relatively young actor that he's so convincing in the role. In the part of the fool, the king's loyal jester, Peter, a well-known Japanese transvestite, is startling and touching.

•

RANCHO DELUXE

1975, 93 mins, US Ⓥ col

Dir Frank Perry ***Prod*** Elliott Kastner ***Scr*** Thomas McGuane ***Ph*** William A. Fraker ***Ed*** Sid Katz ***Mus*** Jimmy Buffett ***Art*** Michael Haller

Act Jeff Bridges, Sam Waterston, Elizabeth Ashley, Charlene Dallas, Slim Pickens, Harry Dean Stanton (United Artists)

Rancho Deluxe becomes an amiable, lightweight comedy featuring Jeff Bridges and Sam Waterston as two modern day drifters living hand-to-mouth on illegal pickings from big-time rancher Clifton James.

Perry's location film has a very good cast and an easy charm. But the humor is too throwaway when it isn't laid on with a trowel.

Script has Bridges and Waterston (his Indian pal) besting pompous James in minor ripoffs. James hires Slim Pickens to roust the rustlers, while the boys corrupt ranch hands Harry Dean Stanton and Richard Bright into a major heist plan.

The film has a kind of relaxed pointlessness and a measure of dainty bawdiness, and the presence of some good players. Bridges's indefatigable charisma is in good shape to the very end.

•

RANCHO NOTORIOUS

1952, 89 mins, US Ⓥ ⦿ col

Dir Fritz Lang ***Prod*** Howard Welsch ***Scr*** Daniel Taradash ***Ph*** Hal Mohr ***Ed*** Otto Ludwig ***Mus*** Emil Newman ***Art*** Wiard Ihnen

Act Marlene Dietrich, Arthur Kennedy, Mel Ferrer, Gloria Henry, William Frawley, Jack Elam (Fidelity)

This Marlene Dietrich western has some of the flavor of the old outdoor classics (like the actress's own onetime *Destry Rides Again*) without fully capturing their quality and magic. The characters play the corny plot [original story by Silvia Richards] straight; directing keeps the pace lively and interesting, and the outdoor shots, abetted by the constant splash of color, are eye-arresting. Dietrich is as sultry and alluring as ever.

Plot, starting off in a little Wyoming town in the 1870s, finds a young femme brutally assaulted and killed on the eve of her wedding and her embittered cowboy lover (Arthur Kennedy) riding off to find and kill the unknown murderer. The trail first leads to Frenchy Fairmount (Mel Ferrer), a flashy outlaw, and then to Chuck-a-Luck, the ranch run by Altar Keane (Dietrich), one-time fabulous saloon entertainer.

Dietrich is a dazzling recreation of the oldtime saloon mistress, and handles her song, "Get Away, Young Man," with her usual throaty skill.

•

RANDOM HARVEST

1942, 125 mins, US Ⓥ ⦿ b/w

Dir Mervyn LeRoy ***Prod*** Sidney Franklin ***Scr*** Claudine West, George Froeschel, Arthur Wimperis ***Ph*** Joseph Ruttenberg ***Ed*** Harold F. Kress ***Mus*** Herbert Stothart ***Art*** Cedric Gibbons, Randall Duell

Act Ronald Colman, Greer Garson, Philip Dorn, Susan Peters, Henry Travers, Reginald Owen (M-G-M)

The film transcription of James Hilton's novel *Random Harvest*, under Sidney Franklin's production and Mervyn LeRoy's direction, achieves much more than average importance.

Ronald Colman plays Charles Rainier, prosperous Briton who loses his memory as result of shellshock in the First World War. As the film opens he is a mental case in an asylum where efforts are being made to restore his memory. He wanders off, eluding officers of the sanatorium.

Colman gives a fine performance but is not quite the romantic type that he was years ago. In fact, he looks older than he should have been for film expediency.

Greer Garson, more charming and seductive than ever, is an important mainstay of the picture. Essaying a highly sympathetic role, she overshadows Colman.

1942: NOMINATIONS: Best Picture, Director, Actress (Susan Peters), Screenplay, B&W Art Direction, Scoring of a Dramatic Picture

•

RANDOM HEARTS

1999, 133 mins, US Ⓥ ⦿ col

Dir Sydney Pollack ***Prod*** Sydney Pollack, Marykay Powell ***Scr*** Kurt Luedtke ***Ph*** Philippe Rousselot ***Ed*** William Steinkamp ***Mus*** Dave Grusin ***Art*** Barbara Ling

Act Harrison Ford, Kristin Scott Thomas, Charles S. Dutton, Bonnie Hunt, Dennis Haysbert, Sydney Pollack (Rastar/Mirage/Columbia)

An ideal rainy-day matinee attraction for well-to-do ladies of a certain age, Sydney Pollack's immaculately crafted anachronism hearkens back, in its relative restraint and civility, to the likes of *Brief Encounter*.

In fact, the story, based on a 1984 novel by Warren Adler [adaptation by Darryl Ponicsan], is about the retroactive discovery of adultery, but it's a realization that haunts the protagonists throughout the film's protracted running time.

Sgt. Dutch Van Den Broeck (Harrison Ford), of the Internal Affairs division of the Washington, DC, police force, lives in exceedingly pleasant suburban comfort with a beautiful wife. When Dutch hears of the crash of a Miami-bound airliner, he thinks nothing of it. Similarly, Kay Chandler (Kristin Scott Thomas), a patrician congresswoman from New Hampshire, has no idea that her husband was headed for Florida.

Dutch and Kay react very differently to the news of their spouses' deaths: Kay with emotional denial and the pragmatic calculation of a born politician who finds her tragedy appears to be helping her bid for reelection. When Kay joins Dutch in a quick visit to Miami to observe the seductive setting for what they've learned was a long-term affair between their mutual mates, the media picks up the scent.

It's all very adult, very serious and very legitimate; it's also laborious, remote and strangely uninvolving for the audience. An ear-studded Ford delivers all his lines with a flat stoicism. Scott Thomas, sporting an American accent, is aggravatingly, and intentionally, off-putting through the early going.

•

RANSOM!
1956, 101 mins, US Ⓥ b/w
Dir Alex Segal ***Prod*** Nicholas Nayfack ***Scr*** Cyril Hume, Richard Maibaum ***Ph*** Arthur E. Arling ***Ed*** Ferris Webster ***Mus*** Jeff Alexander
Act Glenn Ford, Donna Reed, Leslie Nielsen, Juano Hernandez, Robert Keith, Richard Gaines (Nayfack/M-G-M)

After twice being staged live on television as *Fearful Decision*, this kidnap melodrama has made its way to the theatrical films as *Ransom!* The big screen impact's not as sharp as was the television's. Still, it has a quota of tension-arousing scenes—a couple of which are really potent.

The dramatic meat that was good for 54 minutes on TV gets ground mighty thin during the film's hour and 41 minutes. Alex Segal, who did the TV directorial chore, repeats here, but he and scripters (also TV) Cyril Hume and Richard Maibaum provide weak filler material.

Production shows what happens to a happy family and, in some respects, to a town, when the family's small son is kidnapped and held for $500,000 ransom. The father can and does raise the money as he's a prosperous industrialist, but the switch comes when he decides not to pay the ransom and goes on television to tell the watching kidnapper why. The ransom is to become blood money for the kidnapper's capture, dead or alive, if the child's not returned unharmed.

Ford is splendid as the father, David Stannard, a role that takes full advantage of his talent for projection. The direction fails to get much out of Donna Reed [as his wife, Edith] that can be felt and most of the other players, too, seem at odds with the characters they play, leaving it to Ford to carry off the show. One exception is Juano Hernandez's understanding butler. His big scene is when he comforts the father while the latter wonders if his decision was the right one after it is believed the boy is dead.

Clear, sharp lensing heads up the generally good technical credits.

•

RANSOM
(US: THE TERRORISTS)
1975, 97 mins, UK Ⓥ col
Dir Caspar Wrede ***Prod*** Peter Rawley ***Scr*** Paul Wheeler ***Ph*** Sven Nykvist ***Ed*** Thelma Connell ***Mus*** Jerry Goldsmith ***Art*** Sven Wickman
Act Sean Connery, Ian McShane, Norman Bristow, John Cording, Isabel Dean, William Fox (Lion/20th-Century Fox)

Sean Connery is billed above the title as the head of a government security agency trying to cope with plane-hijacking terrorists. Rather curiously, Connery works for the government of "Scandinavia," not Norway where most of the pic was filmed, but in any event at no time does he lose his Scottish brogue.

The terrorists are holding the British ambassador in exchange for their own release and that of some cohorts held by Britain. A squad of accomplices headed by Ian McShane commandeer a loaded passenger jet as it lands at Oslo, and the cat and mouse game begins.

As a match of wits, the ensuing tale doesn't amount to much. But along with plot ingenuity, what's glaringly missing is even the briefest of exploration of the terrorists and their psychology.

•

RANSOM
1996, 120 mins, US Ⓥ ⦿ col
Dir Ron Howard ***Prod*** Scott Rudin, Brian Grazer, B. Kipling Hagopian ***Scr*** Richard Price, Alexander Ignon ***Ph*** Piotr Sobocinski ***Ed*** Dan Hanley, Mike Hill ***Mus*** James Horner ***Art*** Michael Corenblith
Act Mel Gibson, Rene Russo, Gary Sinise, Delroy Lindo, Lili Taylor, Liev Schreiber (Grazer-Rudin/Touchstone)

A crackerjack thriller with some unusually tasty plot twists, *Ransom* pays plenty of entertaining dividends. Mel Gibson very effectively stars in a made-to-order role as a wealthy business exec who eventually must take matters into his own hands to rescue his kidnapped son.

Pic is based on a 1956 M-G-M release of the same name, directed by Alex Segal, who had previously helmed the Cyril Hume–Richard Maibaum story for live television. These origins may help account for the fact that the basic plot is considerably better constructed than the great majority of thrillers these days.

A self-made man who runs the nation's fourth-largest airline, Tom Mullen (Gibson) is an I-Did-It-My-Way type who has settled into Upper East Side comfort and respectability with his wife, Kate (Rene Russo), and son, Sean (Brawley Nolte). On an outing in Central Park, nine-year-old Sean vanishes. In short order, Tom is contacted by a voiceover e-mail demanding $2 million within 48 hours.

Ringleader is a renegade cop (Gary Sinise), whose knowledge of technology and police techniques is so complete that he can thwart all attempts to trace him. Also in on the job are his g.f. (Lili Taylor), two grungy brothers (Liev Schreiber, Donnie Wahlberg) and another lowlife (Evan Handler). Tom takes the risky maneuver of going on TV, withdrawing the ransom and offering it instead as bounty for the head of the kidnapper.

Picture's most intriguing subtext lies in the fact that the rich, sympathetic leads are played by big movie stars, while the villains are largely portrayed by icons of the low-budget independent cinema. Are the filmmakers trying to tell us something?

Pic has a resplendent professional sheen that is nicely offset by the hard-edged Gotham locations and rough, abruptly erupting action.

[A 139-min. version was released on homevideo in 1997.]

•

RAPA NUI
1994, 107 mins, US Ⓥ ⦿ col
Dir Kevin Reynolds ***Prod*** Kevin Costner, Jim Wilson ***Scr*** Kevin Reynolds, Tim Rose Price ***Ph*** Stephen Windom ***Ed*** Peter Boyle ***Mus*** Stewart Copeland ***Art*** George Liddle
Act Jason Scott Lee, Esai Morales, Sandrine Holt, Eru Potaka-Dewes, George Henare, Zac Wallace (Tig/Majestic)

Rapa Nui looks very much like an act of cinematic folly, a wacky anthropological adventure staged on a grand scale and filmed in obviously difficult and inhospitable circumstances. It's more of a guilty pleasure than a satisfying movie experience.

Robin Hood director Kevin Reynolds initiated this project after seeing an ethnographic docu about Easter Island, the world's most remote inhabited island. Screenplay, which he concocted with Britisher Tim Rose Price, speculates on the creation of the moai, the mysterious giant statues scattered over the barren terrain, and on what happened to the original islanders prior to the arrival of the Dutch on Easter Sunday, 1722.

Pic unfolds some 40 years before the Europeans landed, when the island's inhabitants were divided between the ruling Long Ear nobility and the enslaved Short Ears. Every year, a contest is held among the Long Ear clans to decide who will rule for the next year. The competition consists of a kind of Ironman race.

For 20 years, the race has been won by the same clan, led by Ariki-mau (Eru Potaka-Dewes). The old man is now sick but determined to win again via his grandson, Noro (Jason Scott Lee). The race is excitingly staged and filmed, including the inevitable shark attack.

Reynolds decided to shoot on Easter Island, with additional shooting and post-production in Australia. The result certainly looks spectacular. Dramatically, pic is more problematic, with sometimes laughable moments.

•

RAPE OF MALAYA, THE
SEE: A TOWN LIKE ALICE

•

RAPID FIRE
1992, 95 mins, US Ⓥ ⦿ col
Dir Dwight H. Little ***Prod*** Robert Lawrence ***Scr*** Alan McElroy ***Ph*** Ric Waite ***Ed*** Gib Jaffe ***Mus*** Christopher Young ***Art*** Ron Foreman
Act Brandon Lee, Powers Boothe, Nick Mancuso, Raymond J. Barry, Kate Hodge, Tzi Ma (20th Century-Fox)

Brandon Lee, American-born son of the legendary chopsocky hero Bruce Lee, acquits himself well in his first lead role in a U.S. film, *Rapid Fire*, as a pacifist college student forced to become a killing machine. Director Dwight H. Little expertly handles implausible but entertaining action sequences that keep the pic lively despite a schlocky plot [from a story by Cindy Cirile and Alan McElroy] and cardboard characterizations.

Thankfully devoid of standard hunk narcissism, young Lee manages to maintain audience sympathy despite having to surrender his ideals and annihilate hordes of bad guys (stock Mafia and Oriental types) on behalf of Chicago cop Powers Boothe.

Boothe, enjoyable as a lower-budget Clint Eastwood type, works out of an abandoned bowling alley, does illegal wiretapping and coldly uses Lee as bait in his 10-year-old vendetta against heroin-dealing bigwigs Tzi Ma and Nick Mancuso.

The script unwisely does away with Mancuso after only an hour. The tension slackens in the last section and even a budding sexual relationship between Lee and Boothe's macho female partner Kate Hodge can't make up for it.

•

RAPTURE, THE
1991, 102 mins, US Ⓥ ⦿ col
Dir Michael Tolkin ***Prod*** Nick Wechsler, Nancy Tenenbaum, Karen Koch ***Scr*** Michael Tolkin ***Ph*** Bojan Bazelli ***Ed*** Suzanne Fenn ***Mus*** Thomas Newman ***Art*** Robin Standefer
Act Mimi Rogers, Patrick Bauchau, David Duchovny, Kimberly Cullum, Dick Anthony Williams, Will Patton (New Line)

An unexpectedly serious investigation into spiritual malaise and religious fanaticism, *The Rapture* has difficulty walking the line between profundity and pretentiousness. Film nevertheless stands as a singular feature debut for writer-director Michael Tolkin, who demonstrates more talent than judgment.

Mimi Rogers plays Sharon, a beautiful young woman with no direction. She lives on the sexual edge in L.A. with her amoral b.f. (Patrick Bauchau), and in one of their group gropes meets Randy (David Duchovny). Her hot affair with him pushes her to peer into the spiritual abyss, which leads her to the Bible, prayer and ultimate acceptance of the Lord. Six years later, now a fervently devout married couple, Sharon and Randy are raising their daughter in the belief that the end is nigh. Sharon absconds with her daughter to the desert, where she awaits the rapture, the ultimate fulfillment of her religious beliefs that will unite her with her husband and God.

Centerscreen throughout, Rogers reduces everyone else in range to pawns and delivers one of those soul-baring turns that is both impressive and almost too much. Also notable is Bojan Bazelli's luminous lensing.

•

RARE BREED, THE
1966, 97 mins, US Ⓥ ▭ col
Dir Andrew V. McLaglen ***Prod*** William Alland ***Scr*** Ric Hardman ***Ph*** William H. Clothier ***Ed*** Russell F. Schoengarth ***Mus*** John Williams ***Art*** Alexander Golitzen, Alfred Ybarra
Act James Stewart, Maureen O'Hara, Brian Keith, Juliet Mills, Don Galloway, David Brian (Universal)

Based on the actual intro of white-faced Hereford cattle from England to the U.S. western ranges, *The Rare Breed* is a generally successful fictionalized blend of violence, romance, comedy, inspiration and oater Americana.

Ric Hardman's good—if overly wide-ranging—script takes as a point of departure the phasing out of the longhorn by the "rare" (circa 1884) Hereford stock from England. As the drama unfolds, rugged animal survival problems dissolve into human conflicts.

For almost half of the running time the plot concerns the stubborn determination of widowed Maureen O'Hara and daughter Juliet Mills to deliver a bull for breeding purposes. Opposing factors include James Stewart, intially a drifter who agrees, although reluctantly, to swindle the gals via Alan Caillou's bribe, with two conspirators, Jack Elam and Harry Carey, Jr.

Second half is virtually another pic, with quietly-stubborn O'Hara pitted against Brian Keith in a sort of Anna-and-the-King-of-Siam byplay.

•

RASHOMON
1950, 88 mins, Japan Ⓥ ⦿ b/w
Dir Akira Kurosawa ***Prod*** Jingo Minoru, Masaichi Nagata ***Scr*** Shinobu Hashimoto, Akira Kurosawa ***Ph*** Kazuo Miyagawa ***Mus*** Fumio Hayasaka ***Art*** So Matsuyama
Act Toshiro Mifune, Masayuki Mori, Machiko Kyo, Takashi Shimura, Minoru Chiaki, Kichijiro Ueda (Daiei)

Unveiled at the Venice film fest [in August 1951], this caused a flurry in critical circles for its brilliance of conception, technique, acting and its theme of passion.

Set in 12th-century Japan, pic [based on two stories by Ryunosuke Akutagawa] paints a fascinating story of a killing told through the eyes of the three protagonists and then by an eyewitness. Each one differs. A seedy bandit sees a Samurai warrior leading his comely wife through the forest. He overpowers the warrior and seduces the wife. It all ends in facesaving harikiri by the husband.

Direction is excellent. Shot completely outdoors, the camerawork is flawless. Toshiro Mifune gives a sterling performance as the vermin-ridden bandit. Machiko Kyo supplies a role of dramatic intensity as the wife. Masayuki Mori lends an impassive, glowering presence to the part of the husband. Lesser characters are good.

1951: Best Foreign Language Film

•

RASPUTIN THE MAD MONK
1966, 92 mins, UK Ⓥ ▭ col
Dir Don Sharp ***Prod*** Anthony Nelson-Keys ***Scr*** John Elder [= Anthony Hinds] ***Ph*** Michael Reed ***Ed*** James Needs, Roy Hyde ***Mus*** Don Banks ***Art*** Bernard Robinson

Act Christopher Lee, Barbara Shelley, Richard Pasco, Francis Matthews, Suzan Farmer, Renee Asherson (Hammer)

Producer Anthony Nelson-Keys had scripter John Elder take a somewhat fanciful (and unbelievable) approach to the subject of Russia's bad boys. As a result, the dastardly villain has been given some attributes that are certainly colorful. Christopher Lee's Rasputin is completely in character—huge, deep-voiced, compelling stare. He's a proper rascal.

Religious aspects of l'affaire Rasputin are skimmed over, the only two dignitaries portrayed as colorless and dull. Of the Russian court, the Czarina (Renee Asherson) and the Czarevitch (Robert Duncan) are the only Romanoffs shown, the plot revolving (after the monk's entry into court affairs, accredited to his hypnotic influence over a lady-in-waiting) on a revenge plot by the would-be fiance (Nicholas Pennell) of the seduced lady-in-waiting (Barbara Shelley). His principal accomplices are an alcoholic doctor (Richard Pasco), and an Army officer (Francis Matthews), whose sister (Suzan Farmer) has been lined up as Rasputin's next victim.

•

RATBOY
1986, 104 mins, US Ⓥ col
Dir Sondra Locke *Prod* Fritz Manes *Scr* Rob Thompson *Ph* Bruce Surtees *Ed* Joel Cox *Mus* Lennie Niehaus *Art* Edward Carfagno
Act Sondra Locke, Robert Townsend, Christopher Hewett, Larry Hankin, Sydney Lassick, Gerrit Graham (Malpaso)

Yet another picture about how a semi-human, quasi-alien being just can't fit in among earthlings, *Ratboy* can boast of some modest virtues, but is simply too mild on all counts to carry much impact. Oddball first feature from Sondra Locke, who also stars as an out-of-work journalist, deals with eccentric, desperate individuals but in a rather straightforward, unobsessed manner.

The origins of the title character are never investigated or explained. Indeed, after the terrified little bugger is trapped by some transients, he is just blithely manipulated and used by a succession of hustlers who can't put their greed and self-interests on hold long enough to even inquire where the tiny one came from or how he got that way.

Acting tends to the broad side, and Ratboy's nose twitching is cute.

•

RATTLE OF A SIMPLE MAN
1964, 96 mins, UK Ⓥ b/w
Dir Muriel Box *Prod* William Gell *Scr* Charles Dyer *Ph* Reg Wyer *Ed* Frederick Wilson *Mus* Stanley Black *Art* Robert Jones
Act Harry H. Corbett, Diane Cilento, Thora Hird, Michael Medwin, Charles Dyer, Hugh Futcher (Associated British)

Most of the charm and tenderness that occasionally illuminated Charles Dyer's successful play has been lost in this coarsened, fatuous film. Only a lively, vivid performance by Diane Cilento in a contrived role holds much interest, though a sound cast does spartan work in juggling the sparse material. Dyer, has broadened his intimate little play for the benefit of the screen and has heaved most of its values into the trash can.

A bunch of football fans from the North of England, characteristically drawn as noisy, boozing, lecherous nitwits, comes to London for the Cup Final and a night out among the sleazy bright lights. One of them (Harry H. Corbett), a particularly gormless, repressed, mother-ridden oaf, is conned into a bet with his pals. He wagers his motorbike that he'll have an affair with a goodlooking, blonde tart that he picks up in a Soho drinking club.

The bedroom rendezvous is a pitiable farce in which he fails to take the opportunities cheerfully flung at him by the goodtime girl. Instead he weaves dreams of real love about the goldenhearted little prostie.

•

RAVEN, THE
1935, 60 mins, US Ⓥ ⦿ b/w
Dir Louis Landers *Prod* David Diamond *Scr* David Boehm *Ph* Charles Stumar *Ed* Albert Akst *Mus* Gilbert Harland *Art* Albert S. D'Agostino
Act Boris Karloff, Bela Lugosi, Irene Ware, Lester Matthews, Samuel S. Hinds, Inez Courtney (Universal)

A good horror flicker. Just vaguely "suggested" by the Edgar Allen Poe classic, the adaptation wanders not a little, but the basic romance is wisely kept to the fore, and Bela Lugosi, as the psycopathic medico to whom Irene Ware is indebted for her life contributes the shocker aspects forcibly.

Boris Karloff again goes into a plastic cast as a horrible example of disfigurement, this serving as the means whereby Lugosi bends him to his will, with the promise of corrective plastic surgery later on, as his reward for doing the dirty deeds.

After a hectic reel or so in the torture chamber where collapsible rooms grind victims to bits and a descending sword of Damocles threatens extermination within 15 minutes, Lugosi becomes the victim of one of his most Machiavellian devices.

•

RAVEN, THE
1963, 85 mins, US Ⓥ ⦿ ▭ col
Dir Roger Corman *Prod* Roger Corman *Scr* Richard Matheson *Ph* Floyd Crosby *Ed* Ronald Sinclair *Mus* Les Baxter *Art* Daniel Haller
Act Vincent Price, Peter Lorre, Boris Karloff, Hazel Court, Olive Sturgess, Jack Nicholson (American International)

Edgar Allan Poe might turn over in his crypt at this nonsensical adaptation of his immortal poem, but audiences will find the spooky goings-on of a flock of 15th century English sorcerers a corn-pop of considerable comedic dimensions.

The screenplay is a skillful, imaginative narrative of what comes to pass when there comes a rapping at magician Vincent Price's chamber-door by a raven—who else but Peter Lorre, a fellow magician, transformed by another sorcerer (Boris Karloff).

Roger Corman as producer-director takes this premise and develops it expertly as a horror-comedy climaxing with Price and Karloff engaging in a duel to the death in the black arts, each a master of the craft. Special effects figure prominently.

Hazel Court as Price's sexy and conniving spouse, Olive Sturgess, his daughter, and Jack Nicholson, Lorre's son, lend effective support.

•

RAVEN'S END
SEE: KVARTERET KORPEN

•

RAW DEAL
1986, 106 mins, US Ⓥ ⦿ ▭ col
Dir John Irvin *Prod* Martha Schumacher *Scr* Gary M. DeVore, Norman Wexler *Ph* Alex Thomson *Ed* Anne V. Coates *Mus* Cinemascore *Art* Giorgio Postiglione
Act Arnold Schwarzenegger, Kathryn Harrold, Sam Wanamaker, Paul Shenar, Robert Davi, Ed Lauter (De Laurentiis/International)

Comic book crime meller suffers from an irredeemably awful script, and even director John Irvin's engaging sense of how absurd the proceedings are can't work an alchemist's magic.

Bald exposition sees former FBI man, Arnold Schwarzenegger, now rather implausibly a southern sheriff, recruited to infiltrate Chicago's biggest mob, which has been rubbing out men scheduled to testify against it. The big man impresses kingpin Sam Wanamaker with his brain and lieutenant Paul Shenar (as well as tarty Kathryn Harrold) with his brawn, and soon wins himself a job with the gang.

Cast members do what's necessary, but have all been seen to better advantage on other occasions.

•

RAWHIDE
1951, 87 mins, US Ⓥ b/w
Dir Henry Hathaway *Prod* Samuel G. Engel *Scr* Dudley Nichols *Ph* Milton Krasner *Ed* Robert Simpson *Mus* Sol Kaplan *Art* Lyle Wheeler, George W. Davis
Act Tyrone Power, Susan Hayward, Hugh Marlowe, Dean Jagger, Edgar Buchanan, Jack Elam (20th Century-Fox)

Maximum suspense for a western is generated in this Tyrone Power–Susan Hayward costarrer. Despite a strongly told story, however, picture isn't the proper vehicle for Power, who is wasted in part and comes off second best to a number of other players.

Power and Hayward are held prisoners at a stagecoach station in the early west by Hugh Marlowe, an escaped murderer from a prison in the territory, and his three companions, who are waiting to rob the eastbound stage next day which carries $100,000 in gold. Power is employed at station, and Hayward is there with her infant niece only until she can catch the next stage east.

Acting honors are about evenly divided between femme star and Marlowe, both in hardboiled parts. Jack Elam, too, fares particularly favorably as woman-hungry escaped con, member of Marlowe's pack, and Edgar Buchanan, Dean Jagger and George Tobias likewise are effective. Power is never permitted a chance as a hero.

•

RAZORBACK
1984, 94 mins, Australia Ⓥ ⦿ ▭ col
Dir Russell Mulcahy *Prod* Hal McElroy *Scr* Everett De Roche *Ph* Dean Semler *Ed* Bill Anderson *Mus* Iva Davies *Art* Bryce Walmsley
Act Gregory Harrison, Arkie Whiteley, Bill Kerr, Chris Haywood, David Argue, Judy Morris (McElroy & McElroy)

A razorback is a particularly nasty species of feral pig, vicious and brainless, which is found in Australia's outback. Production involves a giant of the species which runs amok with spectacular abandon.

Screenplay by Everett De Roche, an experienced writer of thrillers, from a book by Peter Brennan, starts with a bang: Jake Cullen (Bill Kerr) is minding his grandchild in his isolated homestead when the place is attacked by the unseen porker who wounds the old man and disappears with the infant.

The distraught granddad is brought to trial for killing the kid, but acquitted, and he becomes obsessed with getting the giant beast. Enter Judy Morris who plays an American TV journalist who arrives in this remote spot to do a story on the slaughter of the kangaroos. She becomes the next victim of the razorback. But her husband, Carl (Gregory Harrison), doesn't believe she fell down a mine shaft, the story put out by the locals.

The plot may be a bit familiar, but *Razorback* is no quickie: it's an extremely handsome production, beautifully shot by Dean Semler.

•

RAZOR'S EDGE, THE
1946, 146 mins, US Ⓥ b/w
Dir Edmund Goulding *Prod* Darryl F. Zanuck *Scr* Lamar Trotti *Ph* Arthur Miller *Ed* J. Watson Webb *Mus* Alfred Newman *Art* Richard Day, Nathan Juran
Act Tyrone Power, Gene Tierney, John Payne, Anne Baxter, Clifton Webb, Herbert Marshall (20th Century-Fox)

The Razor's Edge has everything for virtually every type of film fan. Fundamentally it's all good cinematurgy. It's a moving picture that moves.

The romance is more than slightly on the sizzling side. Tyrone Power, as the flyer who can't find himself, is always seeking goodness and spurns the easy life offered him by the more than casually appealing Gene Tierney. It reaches a climax after they play the Paris nitery belt from Montmartre to Montparnasse, and when back in Chicago she loses sight of him and marries John Payne there is the unashamed confession of a lasting love which Power spurns.

For all its pseudo-ritualistic aura the film is fundamentally a solid love story. Tierney is the almost irresistibly appealing femme and completely depicts all the beauty and charm endowed her by Maugham's characterization. Anne Baxter walks off with perhaps the film's personal bit as the dipso, rivaled only by Clifton Webb's effete characterization as the dilettante rich uncle.

Herbert Marshall introduces a new cinematic technique—as it was in the original novel—of playing the author W. Somerset Maugham who thus integrates himself into the story by name identity instead of the conventional first-person (but invariably fictitiously identified) characterization.

1946: Best Supp. Actress (Anne Baxter)

NOMINATIONS: Best Picture, Supp. Actor (Clifton Webb), B&W Art Direction

•

RAZOR'S EDGE, THE
1984, 128 mins, US Ⓥ ⦿ ▭ col
Dir John Byrum *Prod* Robert P. Marcucci, Harry Brenn *Scr* John Byrum, Bill Murray *Ph* Peter Hannan *Ed* Peter Boyle *Mus* Jack Nitzsche *Art* Philip Harrison
Act Bill Murray, Theresa Russell, Catherine Hicks, Denholm Elliott, James Keach, Peter Vaughan (Columbia)

Conceived as a major career departure for comic star Bill Murray, *The Razor's Edge* emerges as a minimally acceptable adaptation of W. Somerset Maugham's superb 1944 novel. Tonally inconsistent and structurally awkward, film does develop some dramatic interest in the second half, but inherent power of the material is never realized. This is the film that Murray insisted Columbia let him make if he appeared in *Ghost Busters*.

Film opens with a happy-go-lucky Murray preparing to set sail for the European conflict. When it's over, he is no longer certain he wants to marry his intended, pretty chatterbox Catherine Hicks. While his old friends are being destroyed by the stock market crash, he's finally finding inner peace in the Himalayas.

The full-fledged arrival of Theresa Russell into the story livens things up considerably. A former friend from the

States, Russell has descended to a routine of drugs, drink and hooking in Paris's underworld, from which Murray resolves to rescue her. Hicks conspires to wreck their planned marriage, and ends by doing much worse than that.

Most of the time, it seems that director John Byrum and Murray have all they can handle just getting the basic plot developments up on the screen. Regretfully absent is any sense of time passing, of spiritual and emotional feeling being deepened.

Chicago-area scenes were shot in Europe, and Paris locationing has yielded little in the way of local color or atmosphere. The trip to India was worth it, though.

•

REACH FOR GLORY

1962, 80 mins, UK b/w

Dir Philip Leacock ***Prod*** John Kohn, Jud Kinberg ***Scr*** John Kohn, Jud Kinberg ***Ph*** Bob Huke ***Ed*** Freddie Wilson ***Mus*** Bob Russell ***Art*** John Blezard

Act Michael Anderson, Jr., Martin Tomlinson, Oliver Grimm, Harry Andrews, Kay Walsh (Gala/Blazer)

In this tale about a group of adolescent boys at a military school in Britain during the last war, the themes of racism, war hate and its effect on youth, conscientious objection and the consequences of parental weakness on youth are all touched on.

Film is well meaning, tightly and economically made but still lacks the edge of the necessary impact. Result is a diffuse pic which is interesting but does not emerge a heavyweight.

A group of London youths chafe in a country school to which they have been evacuated. The war fills them with dreams of glory and a desire for action that is unfortunately turned to gang warfare, spartan, cabalistic rituals, anti-Semitism and general unruliness. Into this comes a refugee Jewish boy from Germany.

Shame at conscientious objectors is also worked in via a brother of one of the boys and false accusations of budding homosexuality.

•

REACH FOR THE SKY

1956, 136 mins, UK Ⓥ b/w

Dir Lewis Gilbert ***Prod*** Daniel M. Angel ***Scr*** Lewis Gilbert ***Ph*** Jack Asher ***Ed*** John Shirley ***Mus*** John Addison ***Art*** Bernard Robinson

Act Kenneth More, Muriel Pavlow, Lyndon Brook, Lee Patterson, Alexander Knox, Dorothy Alison (Rank/Pinnacle)

First and foremost, this is a story of courage, showing a man's triumph over physical disability and every obstacle raised to curtail his normal activities. Adapted from the biography [*The Story of Douglas Bader*] by his fellow pilot Paul Brickhill, it covers the career of Douglas Bader who, after losing both legs in a plane crash while stunting, succeeds in rejoining the RAF to become a Wing Commander in the last world war and one of the aces in the Battle of Britain.

From the cocky young recruit's first day at the training station through all the gay comradeship and hazards of flying, Kenneth More (Bader) depicts with unerring skill the humor, friendliness and supreme fortitude of one of the war's most honored heroes.

His determination to take up life where it nearly left off and return to the only job he knows, is shown without heroics. And this enhances its dramatic value. Every Air Force taboo on his disability is finally overcome and he gets airborne again with the outbreak of war.

Lyndon Brook plays the staunch friend who has to break the news to Bader of his affliction. Alexander Knox is quietly effective as the surgeon.

•

READER, THE

SEE: LA LECTRICE

•

READY TO WEAR (PRET-A-PORTER)

1994, 132 mins, US Ⓥ ⦿ ▭ col

Dir Robert Altman ***Prod*** Robert Altman ***Scr*** Robert Altman, Barbara Shulgasser ***Ph*** Pierre Mignot, Jean Lepine ***Ed*** Geraldine Peroni ***Mus*** Michel Legrand ***Art*** Stephen Altman

Act Sophia Loren, Marcello Mastroianni, Julia Roberts, Tim Robbins, Kim Basinger, Stephen Rea (Miramax)

Robert Altman's latest ensemble extravaganza has all the style, glitz and head-turning star power of an A-list party—and about as much substance. With its focus fragmented among 31 featured players and countless background figures, the film relies upon surface tics and bits of business to sketch the hectic week when fashion designers trot out their latest collections in Paris. While pic is eye-catching and fitfully amusing, net effect proves frivolous and ephemeral, closer to the director's *Health* and *A Wedding* than to *Nashville* or *Short Cuts*.

Action is set in a very visible Paris, and Marcello Mastroianni's mysteriously furtive character provides the springboard for what passes for a dramatic thread in the checkerboard scenario. Most significantly, he hops out of a limo when his companion (Jean-Pierre Cassel), head of the host French fashion commission, gags to death on a sandwich. The unknown man's flight and jump into the Seine lead people to suspect that Cassel has been deliberately killed, setting up a fabricated "murder" plot that is so much nonsense.

His glamorous widow (Sophia Loren), who hated him, becomes the figurehead of the week's events while his top designer mistress (Anouk Aimee), and her son (Rupert Everett), are facing the prospect of selling their label to a Texas boot tycoon (Lyle Lovett).

Mastroianni makes off with the suitcase of an American sports reporter (Tim Robbins), who is kept in Paris to cover the Cassel murder case and, poor fellow, is forced to share a room with another reporter (Julia Roberts). Supplying the scorecard for the rest of the assembled tastemakers is a fashion reporter (Kim Basinger), who interviews everyone as they arrive.

Designers and models themselves get relatively short shrift, with the exception of Richard E. Grant's ultra-effete hand-waver and Forest Whitaker's down-to-earth designer, who happen to be an item. As a trendy photog, Stephen Rea is rather amusing in his smug sadism.

Serving as the film's spectacle, of course, are the fashion shows themselves, which have a fascination all their own. Several major designers were responsible for the creations on view, contributing to the pic's authenticity.

•

REAL GENIUS

1985, 104 mins, US Ⓥ ⦿ ▭ col

Dir Martha Coolidge ***Prod*** Brian Grazer ***Scr*** Neal Israel, Pat Proft, Peter Torokvei ***Ph*** Vilmos Zsigmond ***Ed*** Richard Chew ***Mus*** Thomas Newman ***Art*** Josan F. Russo

Act Val Kilmer, Gabe Jarret, Michelle Meyrink, William Atherton, Jonathan Gries, Patti D'Arbanville (Tri-Star)

Real Genius is *Police Academy* with brains. Setting the proceedings at a think tank for young prodigies seems a curious choice as most of the humor of the film comes out of character rather than place. Val Kilmer, punning his way through his senior year at Pacific Tech, is hardly convincing as a world-class intellect.

Plot [by Neal Israel, Pat Proft] about creating a portable laser system for the Air Force under the tutelage of campus creep Professor Hathaway (William Atherton) has the authority of an old Abbott and Costello film. Theme about the exploitation of these youthful minds is lost in a sea of sight gags.

What lifts the production above the run-of-the-mill is swift direction by Martha Coolidge, who has a firm grasp over the manic material.

•

REAL GLORY, THE

1939, 95 mins, US Ⓥ b/w

Dir Henry Hathaway ***Prod*** Samuel Goldwyn ***Scr*** Jo Swerling, Robert R. Presnell ***Ph*** Rudolph Mate ***Ed*** Daniel Mandell ***Mus*** Alfred Newman ***Art*** James Basevi

Act Gary Cooper, Andrea Leeds, David Niven, Broderick Crawford, Reginald Owen, Kay Johnson (Goldwyn)

Gary Cooper is in uniform in *The Real Glory*, this time as a U.S. Army lieutenant in the medical corps, stationed at some remote spot called Fort Mysang, in the Philippines. The time is 1906, when American expeditionary troops were evacuating, and native command was taking over the newly won possessions. Moro uprisings, guerrilla warfare, cholera epidemics and fancy exhibitions of inhuman cruelty are the frame against which an innocuous melodramatic yarn [from a novel by Charles L. Clifford] is told.

As a vehicle for Cooper, *Real Glory* offers him a chance to perform some unusual feats of gallantry, over a wide terrain. He is probably the busiest medical officer the army ever produced. And he takes all his assignments in his long stride. En route, romantic interest is established with the daughter of his ailing captain.

•

REALITY BITES

1994, 98 mins, US Ⓥ ⦿ col

Dir Ben Stiller ***Prod*** Danny DeVito, Michael Shamberg ***Scr*** Helen Childress ***Ph*** Emmanuel Lubezki ***Ed*** Lisa Churgin ***Mus*** Karl Wallinger ***Art*** Sharon Seymour

Act Winona Ryder, Ethan Hawke, Ben Stiller, Janeane Garofalo, Steve Zahn, Swoosie Kurtz (Jersey)

Reality Bites begins as a promising and eccentric tale of contemporary youth but evolves into a banal love story as predictable as any lush Hollywood affair. While one can commend tyro director Ben Stiller for some adroit work with actors, he's yet to display much grasp of narrative.

The story centers on four recent Texas college grads, including valedictorian Lelaina Pierce (Winona Ryder). Her parting comment to the class and parents is that the answer is, "There is no answer."

Such aimlessness infects these lives. Her roomie Vickie (Janeane Garofalo) manages a heavy-denim clothing store, while Troy (Ethan Hawke) and Sammy (Steve Zahn) appear to have no profession. Lelaina's work, as a television intern on a chatty morning show with a two-faced host (John Mahoney), seems very adult in comparison.

Script employs the quite labored device of having the heroine meet a romantic interest in a fender bender. Michael (Stiller) is a high-strung exec on an MTV-style cable web. The device descends into a three-way sexual tension, with Troy the third point in the mix.

Shrill and obvious, *Reality Bites* quickly turns blunt and dull. The screenplay telegraphs virtually every character move. Ryder maintains her dignity in a thankless role. She is genuine when all around her is patently synthetic.

•

REAL MCCOY, THE

1993, 104 mins, US Ⓥ ⦿ col

Dir Russell Mulcahy ***Prod*** Martin Bregman, Willi Baer, Michael S. Bregman ***Scr*** William Davies, William Osborne ***Ph*** Denis Crossan ***Ed*** Peter Honess ***Mus*** Brad Fiedel ***Art*** Kim Colefax

Act Kim Basinger, Val Kilmer, Terence Stamp, Gailard Sartain, Zach English, Raynor Scheine (Universal)

This Kim Basinger vehicle about a female bank robber isn't bad but gets where it's going very slowly. Basinger and Val Kilmer generate little romantic chemistry, and the action is uninspired. Former video director Russell Mulcahy offers little flash in what turns out to be a standard caper pic with a dose of old-fashioned motherhood thrown in for calculated good measure.

Just paroled after six years in prison, cat burglar Karen McCoy (Basinger) tries to get out of the safe-cracking biz, but big-time criminal Jack Schmidt (Terence Stamp) kidnaps her son (Zach English) as a means of compelling her to knock off an Atlanta bank.

Karen's lone ally is J. T. (Kilmer), a none-too-bright small-timer whose m.o. includes robbing convenience stores with a faulty gun and stealing Betamax equipment, apparently unaware that virtually nobody uses it anymore.

Mulcahy's direction provides scant suspense, and the final bank job doesn't blaze any trails for anyone who's seen caper movies. Similarly, the payoff may satisfy the undemanding, but most viewers will see it coming a mile off.

•

RE-ANIMATOR

1985, 86 mins, US Ⓥ ⦿ col

Dir Stuart Gordon ***Prod*** Brian Yuzna ***Scr*** Dennis Paoli, William J. Norris, Stuart Gordon ***Ph*** Mac Ahlberg ***Ed*** Lee Percy ***Mus*** Richard Band ***Art*** Robert A. Burns

Act Jeffrey Combs, Bruce Abbott, Barbara Crampton, Robert Sampson, David Gale, Gerry Black (Re-Animated)

Re-Animator is based on an H. P. Lovecraft tale [*Herbert West—The Re-Animator*] about a crazy scientist who brings dead bodies back to life with a special serum. Trouble is, they come back violent and ready to kill.

Herbert West (Jeffrey Combs) is the inventor who, like horror film scientists from time immemorial, is too batty to realize the consequences of his actions. Romantic leads are Bruce Abbott and Barbara Crampton, latter a looker who, at the pic's climax, is strapped naked to a lab table as an object of the lust of a hateful admirer, who by this time literally has lost his head.

Pic has a grisly sense of humor, and sometimes is *so* gross and over the top the film tips over into a bizarre comedy.

•

REAP THE WILD WIND

1942, 124 mins, US Ⓥ b/w

Dir Cecil B. DeMille ***Prod*** Cecil B. DeMille ***Scr*** Alan LeMay, Charles Bennett, Jesse Lasky, Jr. ***Ph*** Victor Milner, William V. Skall ***Ed*** Anne Bauchens ***Mus*** Victor Young ***Art*** Hans Dreier, Roland Anderson

Act Ray Milland, John Wayne, Paulette Goddard, Raymond Massey, Robert Preston, Susan Hayward (Paramount)

Reap the Wild Wind is a melodrama of Atlantic coastal shipping in the windjammer days, 100 years ago. It is a film possessing the spectacular sweep of colorful backgrounds which characterize the Cecil DeMille type of screen entertainment.

After a short foreword by DeMille, the picture opens with scenes of a hurricane, shipwreck and struggle for bounty among the salvage workers. This melodramatic tempo is too swift to be maintained. Various angles of plot and contest necessarily must be introduced. The pacing is uneven.

Towards the end, however, the action quickens. There is a unique filming of an undersea battle between a giant squid, of octopus descent, and the two male protagonists. Despite its obvious make-believe, it is shrewd filming, realistic and thrilling.

The production is a visual triumph. Some of the marine scenes are breathtaking. There is skillful blending of process photography.

1942: Best Special Effects

NOMINATIONS: Best Color Cinematography, Color Art Direction

•

REAR WINDOW
1954, 112 mins, US Ⓥ ⊙ col
Dir Alfred Hitchcock ***Prod*** Alfred Hitchcock ***Scr*** John Michael Hayes ***Ph*** Robert Burks ***Ed*** George Tomasini ***Mus*** Franz Waxman ***Art*** Hal Pereira, Joseph MacMillan Johnson
Act James Stewart, Grace Kelly, Wendell Corey, Thelma Ritter, Raymond Burr, Judith Evelyn (Paramount)

A tight suspense show is offered in *Rear Window*, one of Alfred Hitchcock's better thrillers. Hitchcock combines technical and artistic skills in a manner that makes this an unusually good piece of murder mystery entertainment. A sound story by Cornell Woolrich and a cleverly dialoged screenplay provide a solid basis for thrill-making.

Hitchcock confines all of the action to a single apartment-courtyard setting and draws nerves to snapping point in developing the thriller phases of the plot.

James Stewart portrays a news photographer confined to his apartment with a broken leg. He passes the long hours by playing Peeping Tom on the people who live in the other apartments overlooking the courtyard. In one of the apartments occupied by Raymond Burr and his invalid, shrewish wife Stewart observes things that lead him to believe Burr has murdered and dismembered the wife.

Adding to the grip the melodrama has on the audience is the fact that virtually every scene is one that could only be viewed from Stewart's wheelchair, with the other apartment dwellers seen in pantomime action through the photog's binoculars or the telescopic lens from his camera.

The production makes clever use of natural sounds and noises throughout.

1954: NOMINATIONS: Best Director, Screenplay, Color Cinematography, Sound

•

REBECCA
1940, 130 mins, US Ⓥ ⊙ b/w
Dir Alfred Hitchcock ***Prod*** David O. Selznick ***Scr*** Robert E. Sherwood, Joan Harrison ***Ph*** George Barnes ***Ed*** Hal C. Kern, James E. Newcom ***Mus*** Franz Waxman ***Art*** Lyle Wheeler
Act Laurence Olivier, Joan Fontaine, George Sanders, Judith Anderson, Nigel Bruce, Reginald Denny (Selznick/United Artists)

Picture is noteworthy for its literal translation of Daphne du Maurier's novel to the screen, presenting all of the sombreness and dramatic tragedy of the book.

Alfred Hitchcock pilots his first American production with capable assurance and exceptional understanding of the motivation and story mood. Despite the psychological and moody aspects of the tale throughout its major footage, he highlights the piece with several intriguing passages that display inspired direction.

Laurence Olivier provides an impressionable portrayal as the master of Manderley, unable to throw off the memory of his tragic first marriage while trying to secure happiness in his second venture. Joan Fontaine is excellent as the second wife, carrying through the transition of a sweet and vivacious bride to that of a bewildered woman marked by the former tragedy she finds hard to understand.

Supporting cast has been selected with careful attention to individual capabilities. Judith Anderson is the sinister housekeeper and confidante of the former wife; George Sanders is personable in portrayal of the despicable Jack Flavell; and Reginald Denny is Crawley, the estate manager and pal of Olivier. Florence Bates provides many light moments in the early portion as a romantically inclined dowager.

1940: Best Picture, B&W Cinematography

NOMINATIONS: Best Director, Actor (Laurence Olivier), Actress (Joan Fontaine), Supp. Actress (Judith Anderson), Screenplay, B&W Art Direction, Editing, Original Score, Special Effects

•

REBECCA OF SUNNYBROOK FARM
1917, 74 mins, US ⊙ ⊗ b/w
Dir Marshall Neilan ***Scr*** Frances Marion ***Ph*** Walter Stradling
Act Mary Pickford, Eugene O'Brien, Helen Jerome Eddy, Charles Ogle, Marjorie Daw, Mayme Kelso (Artcraft)

Rebecca of Sunnybrook Farm moves along in perfect unison, devoid of padding, minus the wastage of one foot of film, engrossing and impressive, yet with perfect accord in its relation to suspense and cumulative appeal.

In adapting the Kate Douglas Wiggin book for the screen, Frances Marion wrought well. The original story has been retained, with the necessary elaboration. Compared with the dramatic production, which was excellently done, the screen version seems magnitudinous. The story is of Rebecca, a member of a large family, who is sent to the home of her aunts for rearing, ultimately inheriting their estate, and, incidentally, marrying the finest young man in the town. It attained its great popularity through its fidelity in picturing the atmosphere of New England.

Mary Pickford plays as she never played before, varying lights and shades to elicit the major interest, tearful at one moment and laughing the next. Her support is flawless, embodying many artists of repute.

•

REBECCA OF SUNNYBROOK FARM
1938, 80 mins, US Ⓥ ⊙ b/w
Dir Allan Dwan ***Prod*** Raymond Griffith ***Scr*** Karl Tunberg, Don Ettlinger ***Ph*** Arthur Miller ***Ed*** Allen McNeil ***Mus*** Arthur Lange (dir.) ***Art*** Bernard Herzbrun, Hans Peters
Act Shirley Temple, Randolph Scott, Jack Haley, Gloria Stuart, Helen Westley, Bill Robinson (20th Century-Fox)

Shirley Temple proves she's a great little artist in this one. The rest of it is synthetic and disappointing. Why they named it *Rebecca of Sunnybrook Farm* is one of those mysteries. The only resemblance to Kate Douglas Wiggins's charming comedy is a load of hay, a litter of pigs and Bill Robinson's straw hat.

More fitting title would be *Rebecca of Radio City*. The story is about a talented stage child who wins a broadcasting moppet contest, then is lost to the advertising agency in the shuffle and rediscovered at Aunt Mirandy's farm. The supporting characters, mostly unsympathetic, over-drawn and exaggerated, are familiar types.

Randolph Scott and Jack Haley try to get some excitement and suspense into the search for Shirley. Slim Summerville and Helen Westley manage a few laughs from the old situation of sulking sweethearts.

•

REBECCA'S DAUGHTERS
1992, 94 mins, Germany/UK Ⓥ col
Dir Karl Francis ***Prod*** Chris Sievernich ***Scr*** Guy Jenkin ***Ph*** Russ Walker ***Ed*** Roy Sharman ***Mus*** Rachel Portman ***Art*** Ray Price
Act Peter O'Toole, Paul Rhys, Joely Richardson, Keith Allen, Simon Dormandy, Dafydd Hywel (Astralma Erste/Rebecca's Daughters/Delta)

Peter O'Toole goes way over the top and stays there in *Rebecca's Daughters*, an irresistible period romp about Welsh peasants taking on the English taxmen. Script is based on a screenplay commissioned in 1948 from Dylan Thomas but never produced.

Set in southern Wales in 1843, yarn opens with Anthony Raine (Paul Rhys) returning from service in India with thoughts of childhood sweetheart Rhiannon (Joely Richardson) uppermost on his mind. He soon gets wise, however, to the peasants' problems, including a tollgate tax levied by drunken lord of the manor (O'Toole).

With Rhiannon playing hard to get, he dresses up as a mysterious masked avenger, Rebecca (modeled on the Bible figure whose offspring rose up against their oppressors), to win her back and right local wrongs. He's soon leading a hit squad of yokels in drag who turn the tables on a snotty English captain (Simon Dormandy) in nocturnal raids.

Main competition to O'Toole in the histrionics department is Dormandy, excellent as the crazed English captain. Bulk of pic's $6 million budget was raised by producer from private German investors.

•

REBEL, THE
(US: CALL ME GENIUS)
1961, 105 mins, UK col
Dir Robert Day ***Prod*** W. A. Whittaker ***Scr*** Alan Simpson, Ray Galton ***Ph*** Gilbert Taylor ***Ed*** Richard Best ***Mus*** Frank Cordell ***Art*** Robert Jones
Act Tony Hancock, George Sanders, Paul Massie, Margit Saad, Gregoire Aslan, Irene Handl (Associated British)

Tony Hancock's TV writers, Alan Simpson and Ray Galton, scripted this, and they knew their man's idiosyncracies intimately. He's the little man, slightly at war with himself and his fellows, but quick to grasp an opportunity for getting on.

In *The Rebel*, he is a downtrodden London city clerk, fed up with the daily round, and with a yen to be a sculptor. Unfortunately, he's very unskilled. Eventually, he blows his top, throws away his job and sets up shop as an existentialist painter in Paris. He talks himself into being accepted on the Left Bank as the leader of a new movement in art. Then an art connoisseur. He exhibits the paintings of Hancock's roommate, thinking they are Hancock's work. The misfit becomes a national figure.

Among several amusing scenes are those when Hancock revolts against his office boss, an existentialist Left Bank party, Hancock's visit to the yacht of a Greek millionaire where he is commissioned to sculpt the tycoon's vamp wife, a colorful carnival party aboard the yacht and Hancock "painting" a picture by daubing paint on a canvas and then bicycling over it.

•

REBELLION
SEE: JOI-UCHI

•

REBEL WITHOUT A CAUSE
1955, 111 mins, US Ⓥ ⊙ ▭ col
Dir Nicholas Ray ***Prod*** David Weisbart ***Scr*** Stewart Stern ***Ph*** Ernest Haller ***Ed*** William Zeigler ***Mus*** Leonard Rosenman ***Art*** William Wallace
Act James Dean, Natalie Wood, Corey Allen, Sal Mineo, Dennis Hopper, Jim Backus (Warner)

Here is a fairly exciting, suspenseful and provocative, if also occasionally far-fetched, melodrama of unhappy youth on another delinquency kick. The film presents a boy whose rebellion against a weakling father and a shrewish mother expresses itself in boozing, knife-fighting and other forms of physical combat and testing of his own manhood.

Although essentially intent upon action, director Nicholas Ray, who sketched the basic story, does bring out redeeming touches of human warmth. There is as regards the hero, if not as regards the highschool body generally, a better-than-average-for-a-psychological thriller explanation of the core of confusion in the child.

James Dean is very effective as a boy groping for adjustment to people. His actor's capacity to get inside the skin of youthful pain, torment and bewilderment is not often encountered.

Natalie Wood as the girl next door also shows teenage maladjustment. She, too, asks more of her father than he can give.

1955: NOMINATIONS: Best Supp. Actor (Sal Mineo), Supp. Actress (Natalie Wood), Motion Picture Story

•

RECKLESS
1935, 95 mins, US Ⓥ b/w
Dir Victor Fleming ***Prod*** David O. Selznick ***Scr*** P. J. Wolfson ***Ph*** George Folsey ***Ed*** Margaret Booth ***Mus*** Herbert Stothart (sup.) ***Art*** Cedric Gibbons, Merrill Pye, Edwin B. Willis
Act Jean Harlow, William Powell, Franchot Tone, May Robson, Rosalind Russell, Mickey Rooney (M-G-M)

Reckless is a hodgepodge of melodrama, backstage and quasi-musical. It includes a cinematic recreation [from a story by Oliver Jeffries] of a recent newspaper melodrama involving a torch songstress and a posthumous heir to a tobacco fortune, but it's a rambling affair in toto.

Direction is as haphazard as the story. The showfolk are ridiculously white-washed and the socialites are made out consistently caddish. It's one of those things.

From the moment the infatuated Franchot Tone buys out the whole evening's performance and sops up champagne in the audience while solo-appreciating the performance, up until the elopement, which culminates in his suicide, it's ever make-believe. William Powell is an equally vague character. A combination sportsman-philanthropist, he's subsequently influential enough to b.r. the musical comedy which spells the girl's professional comeback.

Instead of a torcher, Jean Harlow is a dancer, yet for the climactic situation she's the fulcrum of a dramatic song number—strongly reminiscent of the real-life counterpart. Rosalind Russell as a jilted girl and Robert Light as her brother alone make their chores ring true.

•

RECKLESS
1995, 91 mins, US Ⓥ col
Dir Norman Rene *Prod* Amy J. Kaufman *Scr* Craig Lucas *Ph* Frederick Elmes *Ed* Michael Berenbaum *Mus* Stephen Endelman *Art* Andrew Jackness
Act Mia Farrow, Scott Glenn, Mary Louise Parker, Tony Goldwyn, Eileen Brennan, Stephen Dorff (Goldwyn)

If weird were automatically wonderful, *Reckless* would be a nonpareil delight. But this twisted fairy tale is a grossly misfired entertainment that squanders the talents of all involved.

One magical Christmas eve, Rachel (Mia Farrow) is told by her repentant husband, Tom (Tony Goldwyn), that the noise downstairs isn't Santa but a contract killer. He pushes her out the window, and in flight she hooks up with Lloyd (Scott Glenn) and his crippled, mute companion, Pooty (Mary Louise Parker).

Pooty can actually speak, and makes the fugitive wife swear to keep her secret. Lloyd has a dark past that's in sharp contrast to his present gentle ways. Rachel basically remains above it all until Tom recognizes her on a quiz show and tracks her down.

The most interesting characters are those played by Glenn and Parker, who disappear midway through the film. Eileen Brennan then pops in as a defrocked nun, but she can't compensate for their absence in pic's later stages.

Director-writer team of Norman Rene and Craig Lucas couldn't get the material to work onstage, and celluloid proves to be an equally inhospitable medium for this quirky fare. Filmed as if it were a make-believe world, pic's heightened sense of unreality only serves to remind of *Reckless*'s stage origins.

•

RECKLESS KELLY
1993, 94 mins, Australia Ⓥ ⊙ col
Dir Yahoo Serious *Prod* Yahoo Serious, Warwick Ross *Scr* Yahoo Serious, David Roach, Warwick Ross, Lulu Serious *Ph* Kevin Hayward *Ed* Yahoo Serious, David Roach, Robert Gibson, Antony Gray *Mus* Yahoo Serious, Tommy Tycho *Art* Yahoo Serious, Graham "Grace" Walker
Act Yahoo Serious, Melora Hardin, Alexei Sayle, Hugo Weaving, Kathleen Freeman, John Pinette (Serious)

Australian comic Yahoo Serious's second outing, produced on a far larger budget, is full of ideas and nonsense but short on geniune laughs and zest.

Starting from the engaging premise that the spirit of Australia's legendary outlaw Ned Kelly (1855-80) lives on in one of his descendents, Serious puts the new Ned Kelly (himself) and family on an island paradise.

Kelly motorbikes to Sydney, where he robs the bank owned by evil Sir John (Hugo Weaving), who hires Brit military expert Alexei Sayle and plots to sell Kelly's island to the Japanese. Needing a quick $1 million, Kelly heads for the "land of opportunity for outlaws," America, accompanied by actress girlfriend Robin Banks (get it?), charmingly played by Melora Hardin. In Hollywood, they are spotted by schlock producer (John Pinette) and starred in a Vegas-based B-picture.

There are a lot of ideas here and a brash, go-for-it style. But star-helmer-co-writer-editor-designer Serious seems to have taken on too many chores: his own perf suffers and the script continually builds to punchlines that, when they come, fall flat.

•

RECKLESS MOMENT, THE
1949, 81 mins, US b/w
Dir Max Ophuls *Prod* Walter Wanger *Scr* Henry Garson, Robert W. Soderberg *Ph* Burnett Guffey *Ed* Gene Havlick *Mus* Hans J. Salter *Art* Cary Odell
Act James Mason, Joan Bennett, Geraldine Brooks, Henry O'Neill, Shepperd Strudwick, David Bair (Columbia)

A tense melodrama projecting good mood and suspense has been fashioned out of Elisabeth Sanxay Holding's *Ladies Home Journal* yarn, *The Blank Wall* [adaptation by Mel Dinelli and Robert E. Kent]. Matter-of-fact technique used in the script and by Max Ophuls's direction doesn't permit much warmth to develop for the characters. Production gains in authentic values by using the seaside resort of Balboa and commercial sections of Los Angeles.

Plot wrings out suspense in its concern with a mother who becomes involved in murder and blackmail to save her daughter from the consequences of a romance with an unsavory older man.

James Mason's ability as an actor makes his assignment as a blackmailer very substantial and Joan Bennett shows up exceptionally well in a part that is tinged with coldness despite the fact it deals with a mother's concern and Henry O'Neill is good as the grandfather.

•

RECKONING, THE
1970, 109 mins, UK col
Dir Jack Gold *Prod* Ronald Shedlo *Scr* John McGrath *Ph* Geoffrey Unsworth *Ed* Peter Weatherley *Mus* Malcolm Arnold *Art* Ray Simm
Act Nicol Williamson, Rachel Roberts, Ann Bell, Zena Walker, Paul Rogers, Gwen Nelson (Columbia)

The Reckoning is the story of a ruthless man, who rises from a Liverpool slum to the upper strata of cutthroat big business in London. Actually a character study of a man totally without morals or ethics, it is interesting in its treatment and for Nicol Williamson's performance in a hard-hitting role.

Filmed in story's actual locale, script is based on Patrick Hall's novel, *The Harp That Once*.

Scene segues from fashionable London, where Williamson, as an ambitious and aggressive businessman, is married to a woman he doesn't love and is stymied from rising in his job by politics, to Liverpool. He is called there when his father is dying.

Williamson is entirely believable in his part, displaying a dominant personality and a flair for punching over his role.

Rachel Roberts is realistic as a married woman Williamson picks up at a wrestling match the night his father dies.

•

RED AND THE WHITE, THE
SEE: CSILLAGOSOK KATONAK

•

RED BADGE OF COURAGE, THE
1951, 60 mins, US Ⓥ b/w
Dir John Huston *Prod* Gottfried Reinhardt *Scr* John Huston *Ph* Harold Rosson *Ed* Ben Lewis *Mus* Bronislau Kaper *Art* Cedric Gibbons, Hans Peters
Act Audie Murphy, Bill Mauldin, John Dierkes, Royal Dano, Arthur Hunnicutt, Douglas Dick (M-G-M)

This is a curiously moody, arty study of the psychological birth of a fighting man from frightened boy, as chronicled in Stephen Crane's novel *The Red Badge of Courage*.

Pic follows two figures during the days of the War Between the States. They are Audie Murphy, the youth who goes into his first battle afraid but emerges a man, and Bill Mauldin, on whom the same fears and misgivings have less sensitive impact.

Rather than any clearly defined story line, picture deals with a brief few hours of war and the effect it has on the few characters with which the script is concerned. Within the limited format, director John Huston artfully projects the characters to capture a seemingly allegorical mood of all wars and the men involved in them. His battle scene staging has punch and action, and his handling of the individual players makes them stand out. Narration, taken directly from the text of Crane's story, does a great deal to make clear the picture's aims.

There is an unbilled guest appearance by Andy Devine as a cheery soldier who lets God do his worrying, and it makes a single scene stand out.

•

RED BEARD
SEE: AKAHIGE

•

RED DANUBE, THE
1950, 119 mins, US b/w
Dir George Sidney *Prod* Carey Wilson *Scr* Gina Kaus, Arthur Wimperis *Ph* Charles Rosher *Ed* James E. Newcom *Mus* Miklos Rozsa
Act Walter Pidgeon, Ethel Barrymore, Peter Lawford, Angela Lansbury, Janet Leigh, Louis Calhern (M-G-M)

In *The Red Danube* [from the novel *Vespers in Vienna* by Bruce Marshall], Metro aims a haymaker at Soviet repatriation methods in Europe and general Communist ideology, but the punch lands short of the mark. Film might have been rescued by a more winning portrayal of its pro-democratic forces. But Walter Pidgeon, who limns a British army colonel engaged in fulfilling the western allies' commitment to repatriate forcibly all refugees from Russia, is hamstrung for too many reels by calloused and blundering doings. His adjutant, Peter Lawford, is depicted as a peculiarly capricious character.

Scene of the struggle is Vienna, circa 1945, where Pidgeon is billeted in a convent. Here much tedious religious talk is generated between the colonel, a professed unbeliever, and the mother-superior (Ethel Barrymore) on the pros and cons of organized religion.

Chief pawn is a ballerina (Janet Leigh) beloved by Lawford. Pidgeon turns over the ballerina on the promise she will not be mistreated.

1950: NOMINATION: Best B&W Art Director

•

RED DAWN
1984, 114 mins, US Ⓥ ⊙ col
Dir John Milius *Prod* Buzz Feitshans, Barry Beckerman *Scr* Kevin Reynolds, John Milius *Ph* Ric Waite *Ed* Thom Noble *Mus* Basil Poledouris *Art* Jackson De Govia
Act Patrick Swayze, C. Thomas Howell, Ron O'Neal, William Smith, Powers Booth, Charlie Sheen (United Artists/Valkyrie)

Red Dawn charges off to an exciting start as a war picture and then gets all confused in moralistic handwriting, finally sinking in the sunset.

Sometime in the future, the United States stands alone and vulnerable to attack, abandoned by its allies. Rather than an all-out nuclear war Soviet and Cuban forces bomb selectively and then launch a conventional invasion across the southern and northwest borders.

Dawn takes place entirely in a small town taken by surprise by paratroopers. Grabbing food and weapons on the run, a band of teens led by Patrick Swayze and C. Thomas Howell makes it to the nearby mountains as the massacre continues below.

Swayze, Howell and the other youngsters are all good in their parts.

•

RED DESERT
SEE: IL DESERTO ROSSO)

•

RED DUST
1932, 83 mins, US Ⓥ b/w
Dir Victor Fleming *Prod* [uncredited] *Scr* John Lee Mahin *Ph* Harold Rosson *Ed* Blanche Sewell *Mus* [uncredited] *Art* Cedric Gibbons
Act Clark Gable, Jean Harlow, Gene Raymond, Mary Astor, Donald Crisp, Tully Marshall (M-G-M)

Familiar plot stuff, but done so expertly it almost overcomes the basic script shortcomings and the familiar hot-love-in-the-isolated-tropics theme [from the play by Wilson Collison].

This time it's a rubber plantation in Indo-China, bossed by Clark Gable. Jean Harlow is the Sadie Thompson of the territory. Enter Gene Raymond and Mary Astor on Raymond's initial engineering assignment. Gable makes a play for Astor and it looks like the young husband will have his ideals shattered when circumstances cause Gable to send them both back to a more civilized existence, with more conventional standards, leaving Harlow as a more plausible (and, for audience purposes, more acceptable) playmate.

It's as simple as all that, basically. Astor is oke in the passive virtuous moments, but falls down badly on the clinches, sustained only by Gable. As the putteed, unshaven he-man rubber planter Gable's in his element, sustaining an unsympathetic assignment until it veers about a bit.

Harlow's elementary conception of moral standards, so far as the decent kid explorer (Raymond) is concerned, sort of gilds her lily of the fields assignment. She plays the light lady to the limit, however, not overdoing anything.

•

RED-HEADED WOMAN
1932, 74 mins, US Ⓥ b/w
Dir Jack Conway *Scr* Anita Loos *Ph* Harold Rosson *Ed* Blanche Sewell
Act Jean Harlow, Chester Morris, Lewis Stone, Leila Hyams, Una Merkel, Henry Stephenson (M-G-M)

The outstanding fact is that M-G-M has turned out an interesting dissertation on a thoroughly provocative subject. Jean Harlow, hitherto not highly esteemed as an actress, gives an electric performance.

Ethics of the subject are sufficient to make a church deacon gulp and stammer. Heroine (Harlow) is a home wrecker, a vicious vamp and a destroyer of peace, and the wages of sin in her case are paid in the final close-up in strange and wonderful coin.

Picture is handled with a curious blending of bluntness and subtlety. Some of the "vamping" sequences, and there are plenty of them, are torrid. But the overall effect is conveyed with a great deal of fancy skating over very thin ice and its very candor is disarming.

•

RED HEAT

1988, 103 mins, US Ⓥ ⊙ col

Dir Walter Hill ***Prod*** Walter Hill, Gordon Carrol ***Scr*** Harry Kleiner, Walter Hill, Troy Kennedy Martin ***Ph*** Matthew F. Leonetti ***Ed*** Freeman Davies, Carmel Davies, Donn Aron ***Mus*** James Horner ***Art*** John Vallone

Act Arnold Schwarzenegger, James Belushi, Peter Boyle, Ed O'Ross, Larry Fishburne, Gina Gershon (Carolco/Lone Wolf/Oak)

Red Heat [from a screen story by Walter Hill] has earned a place in the history books as the first entirely American-produced film to have been permitted to lens in Russia, even if location work was essentially limited to establishing shots.

Entire early Moscow section (shot mostly in Budapest) establishes the notion that one of the prices the East will pay for opening up is an increase in the Western disease of drug dealing. A particularly loathesome practitioner in the field named Viktor (Ed O'Ross) manages to slip through the fingers of the Red Army's top enforcer (guess who) and heads for Chicago.

In full uniform, Arnold Schwarzenegger arrives at O'Hare Airport, where he is greeted by two working stiffs from the Chicago Police Dept., James Belushi and Richard Bright. Belushi is assigned to keep tabs on the terminator as the latter tracks down Viktor.

Schwarzenegger, who when he dons a green suit is dubbed "Gumby" by Belushi, is right on target with his characterization of the iron-willed soldier, and Belushi proves a quicksilver foil.

•

RED HOUSE, THE

1947, 100 mins, US Ⓥ b/w

Dir Delmer Daves ***Prod*** Sol Lesser ***Scr*** Delmer Daves ***Ph*** Bert Glennon ***Ed*** Merrill White ***Mus*** Miklos Rozsa ***Art*** McClure Capps

Act Edward G. Robinson, Lon McCallister, Judith Anderson, Allene Roberts, Julie London, Rory Calhoun (United Artists)

The Red House is an interesting psychological thriller [based on the novel by George Agnew Chamberlain], with its mood satisfactorily sustained throughout the pic. Film, however, has too slow a pace, so that the paucity of incident and action stands out sharply, despite good performances by Edward G. Robinson, Judith Anderson, Allene Roberts, Lon McCallister and others.

Film has a simple, rustic quality in scripting, setting and characterization.

Pic, however, is built on a single thread, and takes too long in getting to its climax. It ends on something of a macabre note, and throughout it has several false touches—a muscle-brained young woodsman being in possession of $750; entrusting the money to a flighty girl to buy him a bond with it, etc.

Robinson has supplied himself with a fat part that suits his talents and to which he gives his best efforts. He's cast as a farmer, living with a sister and an adopted daughter in an isolated area of a small community, further withdrawn from the community by his strange, gloomy moods. Part of his property is a wooded area to which no one can go; the farmer even employs a young woodsman to keep trespassers out by gunfire if necessary. A young hired hand comes to work on the farm, is intrigued by the wooded area, and enters it, to meet with several mishaps.

•

RED LINE 7000

1965, 118 mins, US Ⓥ col

Dir Howard Hawks ***Prod*** Howard Hawks ***Scr*** George Kirgo ***Ph*** Milton Krasner ***Ed*** Stuart Gilmore, Bill Brame ***Mus*** Nelson Riddle

Act James Caan, Laura Devon, Gail Hire, Charlene Holt, John Robert Crawford, Marianna Hill (Paramount)

Script by George Kirgo, based on a story by director Howard Hawks, centers on three sets of characters as they go about their racing and lovemaking. Trio of racers are members of a team operating out of Daytona, Fla., their individual lives uncomplicated until three femmes fall in love with them. In a thrilling climax, one of the drivers, overcome with jealousy, causes another to crash but miraculously his life is saved.

Making excellent impressions are Laura Devon, Gail Hire and Marianna Hill, as girlfriends of the three daredevils of the track. James Caan, John Robert Crawford and James Ward in these roles are effective.

Hawks is on safe ground while his cameras are focused on race action. His troubles lie in limning his various characters in their more intimate moments. Title refers to an engine speed beyond which it's dangerous to operate a race car, perhaps symbolic of what Hawks wanted to achieve in the emotions of his players.

•

RED PLANET

2000, 106 mins, US Ⓥ ⊙ ▭ col

Dir Antony Hoffman ***Prod*** Mark Canton, Bruce Berman, Jorge Saralegui ***Scr*** Chuck Pfarrer, Jonathan Lemkin ***Ph*** Peter Suschitzky ***Ed*** Robert K. Lambert, Dallas S. Puett ***Mus*** Graeme Revell ***Art*** Owen Paterson

Act Val Kilmer, Carrie-Anne Moss, Tom Sizemore, Benjamin Bratt, Simon Baker, Terence Stamp (Canton/Warner)

As dull and arid as a hike through the desert, which is essentially what the film documents, *Red Planet* purports to be the most "realistic" account of an interplanetary journey ever put on screen, but that's no excuse for its staggering lack of dramatic incident and narrative excitement.

Red Planet is ploddingly prosaic and only commands viewer attention with sporadically nifty special effects, such as a space capsule's bounce landing on the rocky mountain Martian surface and the menacing antics of a robot dog, and the spectacular landscapes provided by Wadi Rum in Jordan (familiar from *Lawrence of Arabia*) and Coober Pedy in the Australian Outback.

Otherwise, there's astonishingly little going on in this tale of six astronauts sent to Mars in 2050 to—what else?—save the human race from eco-suicide. The six-month trip to Mars is dispatched with merciful economy, but still lasts long enough to make clear that the filmmakers haven't bothered to re-imagine the future in any interesting ways: The spacecraft interior design remains rooted in the look established by *2001: A Space Odyssey* 32 years ago, while the dialogue and musical tastes precisely express turn-of-the-millennium styles.

For presumably carefully selected professionals on a joint mission of overweening cosmic importance, this bunch is a motley crew with a pronounced lack of cohesion and camaraderie; given the shared jeopardy and imminent death they face at any moment, they're strangely at each others' throats much of the time.

Picture does boast a more "real"—that is, nondigital—look than many other recent effects-driven films. Technically the film cannot be faulted; if only that held in the creative area as well. Constrained in space suits throughout, the thesps have little to do but look stressed and declaim functional dialogue.

•

RED PLANET MARS

1952, 87 mins, US b/w

Dir Harry Horner ***Prod*** Anthony Veiller ***Scr*** John L. Balderston, Anthony Veiller ***Ph*** Joseph Biroc ***Ed*** Francis D. Lyon ***Mus*** Mahlon Merrick ***Art*** Charles D. Hall

Act Peter Graves, Andrea King, Walter Sande, Herbert Berghof, Marvin Miller, Willis Bouchey (Melaby/United Artists)

Despite its title, *Red Planet Mars* takes place on terra firma, sans space ships, cosmic rays or space cadets. It is a fantastic concoction [from a play by John L. Balderston and John Hoare] delving into the realms of science, politics, religion, world affairs and Communism.

Pic's main theme deals with a scientist (Peter Graves) who has managed to achieve radio contact with Mars. Messages from the planet cause all sorts of havoc on earth. The Martians, it appears, have prolonged the life span to 300 years and use cosmic power for energy. As a result of this news and the contact with Mars, mere earth dwellers fear that these secrets will soon be forwarded to earth and will change the entire economic structure of the globe.

Despite the hokum dished out, the actors concerned turn in creditable performances.

•

RED PONY, THE

1949, 89 mins, US Ⓥ ⊙ col

Dir Lewis Milestone ***Prod*** Lewis Milestone ***Scr*** John Steinbeck ***Ph*** Tony Gaudio ***Ed*** Harry Keller ***Mus*** Aaron Copland ***Art*** Nicolai Remisoff

Act Myrna Loy, Robert Mitchum, Louis Calhern, Shepperd Strudwick, Peter Miles, Margaret Hamilton (Republic/Feldman-Milestone)

Lewis Milestone's filmization of a novelette by John Steinbeck has been pieced together with taste and fidelity. It has, however, stumbled over one obstacle. The secondary theme, an attempt to etch the emotional complexities of the grownups that surround the boy is slack-paced and sketchily drawn.

Boy-and-pony theme owes much of its compassion and winning graces to a fine and sensitive performance by Peter Miles. As Billy Buck, the hired man, Robert Mitchum underscores a likeable role.

Neither Myrna Loy nor Shepperd Strudwick are as satisfactory as the boy's parents. Since it is their lot to go through some pretty tedious bits of business, script and direction are undoubtedly more at fault than their thesping efforts.

•

RED RIVER

1948, 126 mins, US Ⓥ ⊙ b/w

Dir Howard Hawks, Arthur Rosson ***Prod*** Howard Hawks ***Scr*** Borden Chase, Charles Schnee ***Ph*** Russell Harlan ***Ed*** Christian Nyby ***Mus*** Dimitri Tiomkin ***Art*** John Datu Arensma

Act John Wayne, Montgomery Clift, Joanne Dru, Walter Brennan, Coleen Gray, John Ireland (Monterey)

Howard Hawks's production and direction give a masterful interpretation to a story of the early west and the opening of the Chisholm Trail, over which Texas cattle were moved to Abilene to meet the railroad on its march across the country.

Also important to *Red River* is the introduction of Montgomery Clift. Clift brings to the role of Matthew Garth a sympathetic personality that invites audience response.

Hawks has loaded the film with mass spectacle and earthy scenes. His try for naturalness in dialog between principals comes off well. The staging of physical conflict is deadly, equalling anything yet seen on the screen. Picture realistically depicts trail hardships; the heat, sweat, dust, storm and marauding Indians that bore down on the pioneers. Neither has Hawks overlooked sex, exponents being Joanne Dru and Coleen Gray.

Picture is not all tough melodrama. There's a welcome comedy relief in the capable hands of Walter Brennan. He makes his every scene stand out sharply, leavening the action with chuckles while maintaining a character as rough and ready as the next.

Sharing co-director credit with Hawks is Arthur Rosson. The pair have staged high excitement in the cattle stampedes and other scenes of mass action.

1948: NOMINATIONS: Best Motion Picture Story, Editing

•

RED ROCK WEST

1993, 97 mins, US Ⓥ ⊙ col

Dir John Dahl ***Prod*** Sigurjon Sighvatsson, Steve Golin ***Scr*** John Dahl ***Ph*** Mark Reshovsky ***Ed*** Scott Chestnut ***Mus*** William Orvis ***Art*** Rob Pearson

Act Nicolas Cage, Denis Hopper, Lara Flynn Boyle, J. T. Walsh, Timothy Carhart, Dan Shor (PFE/Propaganda)

A wry thriller with a keen edge, *Red Rock West* is a sprightly, likable noirish yarn. Centered on a case of mistaken identity, the internecine plot becomes progressively more complex without losing its sense of fun. Essentially a bumbler, Michael (Nicolas Cage) finds himself in a nest of vipers and only through dumb luck manages to elude getting bitten. Michael has headed to the oil fields of Wyoming on the promise of a job. In the town of Red Rock he's presumed to be a hired gun commissioned to rub out the wife of a local barkeep.

The saloon owner, Wayne (J. T. Walsh), wafts the long green in front of Michael's nose, and the near destitute man takes a deep whiff. Playing along for a moment, he confronts the woman (Lara Flynn Boyle) only to have the original offer doubled. He grabs it but decides to bail out before things get worse. Of course, nothing's that easy.

The ping-pong plot, concocted by writer-director John Dahl, is not to be taken seriously or metaphorically. It owes more to hard-boiled thrillers of the 1940s, albeit with a very large tongue-in-cheek quotient. Dahl, who earlier made the slick, steamy *Kill Me Again*, demonstrates an affection and understanding of the genre.

•

REDS

1981, 200 mins, US Ⓥ ⊙ col

Dir Warren Beatty ***Prod*** Warren Beatty ***Scr*** Warren Beatty, Trevor Griffiths ***Ph*** Vittorio Storaro ***Ed*** Dede Allen, Craig McKay ***Mus*** Stephen Sondheim, Dave Grusin ***Art*** Richard Sylbert

Act Warren Beatty, Diane Keaton, Jerzy Kosinski, Jack Nicholson, Maureen Stapleton, Edward Herrmann (Paramount)

Warren Beatty's *Reds* is a courageous and uncompromising attempt to meld a high-level socio-political drama of ideas with an intense love story, but it is ultimately too ponderous.

More than just the story of American journalist-activist John Reed's stormy romantic career with writer Louise Bryant, a kinetic affair backdropped by pre-World War I radicalism and the Russian Revolution, the film is also, to its eventual detriment, structured as a Marxist history lesson.

First half of the film, though it takes an inordinant amount of time and detail to do it, does an intelligent job of setting both the political and emotional scene. Beginning in 1915, Reed (Beatty) is introduced as an idealistic reporter of decidedly radical bent who meets Portland writer Bryant (Diane Keaton) and persuades her to join him in New York within a tight-knit radical intellectual salon that includes the likes of playwright Eugene O'Neill (Jack Nicholson), anarchist-feminist Emma Goldman (Maureen Stapleton) and radical editor Max Eastman (Edward Herrmann).

Their on-again, off-again affair—which challenges their respective claims of emotional liberation—survives Keaton's brief fling with Nicholson and they marry.

But Beatty's inability to resist the growing socialist bandwagon strains them yet again and Keaton ships off to cover the French battlefront and begin life afresh. En route to cover the upcoming conflagration in Russia, Beatty persuades her to join him—in professional, not emotional status—and in Petrograd, the revolutionary fervor rekindles their romantic energies as well.

Reds bites off more than an audience can comfortably chew. Constant conflicts between politics and art, love and social conscience, individuals versus masses, pragmatism against idealism, take the form of intense and eventually exhausting arguments that dominate the script by Beatty and British playwright Trevor Griffiths.

As director, Beatty has harnessed considerable intensity into individual confrontations but curiously fails to give the film an overall emotional progression.

1981: Best Director, Supp. Actress (Maureen Stapleton), Cinematography

NOMINATIONS: Best Picture, Actor (Warren Beatty), Actress (Diane Keaton), Supp. Actor (Jack Nicholson), Original Screenplay, Costume Design, Art Direction, Editing, Sound

•

RED SALUTE
(AKA: RUNAWAY DAUGHTER; HER ENLISTED MAN; ARMS AND THE GIRL)
1935, 77 mins, US b/w
Dir Sidney Lanfield ***Prod*** Edward Small ***Scr*** Humphrey Pearson, Manuel Seff ***Ph*** Robert Planck ***Ed*** Grant Whytock ***Mus*** [uncredited] ***Art*** John DuCasse Schulze
Act Barbara Stanwyck, Robert Young, Hardie Albright, Ruth Donnelly, Cliff Edwards, Gordon Jones (Reliance)

Stripped of its anti-Red angle, *Red Salute* resolves itself down to a weak take-off of *It Happened One Night*. While it is studded here and there with pungent humor, after the first few rounds the rough, wisecracking exchange between Barbara Stanwyck and Robert Young begins to pall.

Preachment which *Salute* seeks to espouse stems from the agitation against war by student groups on various college campuses. Into this topical idea is woven the story of a young radical orator (Hardie Albright) who is loved by the general's daughter (Stanwyck), the efforts of her father to keep them apart, and the new romance that comes into her life when an enlisted man (Young) goes AWOL to help her escape from Mexico and back to her lover.

Stanwyck does a crack job at holding interest. Another telling performance is that of Young as the reckless soldier who pulls many a misdemeanor, including the kidnaping of a tourist trailer and its owner, while pursued by border police. Showing by Albright is as all-sided as the political arguments that the script [from a story by Humphrey Pearson] assigns him to voice on the platform.

During the first day's showing at the Rivoli, N.Y., patriots and youths allied with the anti-war National Student League climaxed their contending rounds of applause, hissing and booing with several fist fights. Out on the sidewalk girl and boy Student Leaguers distributed handbills urging a boycott of the picture

•

RED SCORPION
1989, 102 mins, US Ⓥ ⦿ col
Dir Joseph Zito ***Prod*** Jack Abramoff ***Scr*** Arne Olsen ***Ph*** Joao Fernandes ***Ed*** Daniel Loewenthal ***Mus*** Jay Chattaway ***Art*** Ladislav Wilheim
Act Dolph Lundgren, M. Emmet Walsh, Al White, T. P. McKenna, Carmen Argenziano, Brion James (Shapiro Glickenhaus)

Red Scorpion is a dull, below-average action pic, lensed in Swaziland. Out-of-date screenplay [from a story by Robert Abramoff, producer Jack Abramoff, and Arne Olsen] has Scandinavian star Dolph Lundgren playing a Russian special services officer ordered by his nasty commander (Irish thesp T. P. McKenna) to kill the rebel leader of a fictional African country. Lundgren fails in his mission and is tortured by Cubans.

Under the guidance of a knowing, mystical bushman (Regopstaan, obviously patterned on the hero of *The Gods Must Be Crazy*) who tattoos a scorpion on Dolph's chest, Lundgren realizes the commies are oppressing the Africans. Anticlimax has this Nordic giant leading the otherwise defeated rebels to defeat the combined Russian/Cuban might.

Joseph Zito's sluggish direction lingers on nonessentials. Tediousness could have been alleviated by dropping at least a reel's worth of trekking across the African desert. Lundgren provides little more than sustained beefcake.

•

RED SHOES, THE
1948, 134 mins, UK Ⓥ ⦿ col
Dir Michael Powell, Emeric Pressburger ***Prod*** Michael Powell, Emeric Pressburger ***Scr*** Michael Powell, Emeric Pressburger ***Ph*** Jack Cardiff ***Ed*** Reginald Mills ***Mus*** Brian Easdale ***Art*** Hein Heckroth
Act Anton Walbrook, Marius Goring, Moira Shearer, Leonide Massine, Robert Helpmann, Ludmilla Tcherina (Archers)

For the first 60 minutes, this is a commonplace backstage melodrama, in which temperamental ballerinas replace the more conventional showgirls.

Then a superb ballet of the Red Shoes, based on a Hans Andersen fairy tale, is staged with breathtaking beauty outclassing anything that could be done on the stage. It is a colorful sequence, full of artistry, imagination and magnificence. The three principal dancers, Moira Shearer, Leonide Massine and Robert Helpmann, are beyond criticism.

Then the melodrama resumes, story being about the love of a ballerina for a young composer thus incurring the severe displeasure of the ruthless Boris Lermontov, guiding genius of the ballet company.

Although the story may be trite, there are many compensations, notably the flawless performance of Anton Walbrook, whose interpretation of the role of Lermontov is one of the best things he has done on the screen. Shearer, glamorous redhead, shows that she can act as well as dance, while Marius Goring, polished as ever, plays the young composer with enthusiasm.

Other assets that can be chalked up are the wide variety of interesting locations—London, Paris, Monte Carlo, magnificent settings, firstclass Technicolor and some brilliant musical scores played by the Royal Philharmonic Orchestra with Thomas Beecham as conductor.

1948: Best Color Art Direction, Score for a Dramatic Picture

NOMINATIONS: Best Picture, Motion Picture Story, Editing

•

RED SONJA
1985, 89 mins, US Ⓥ ⦿ ⊏⊐ col
Dir Richard Fleischer ***Prod*** Christian Ferry ***Scr*** Clive Exton, George MacDonald Fraser ***Ph*** Giuseppe Rotunno ***Ed*** Frank J. Urioste ***Mus*** Ennio Morricone ***Art*** Danilo Donati
Act Brigitte Nielsen, Arnold Schwarzenegger, Sandahl Bergman, Paul Smith, Ernie Reyes Jr., Ronald Lacey (De Laurentiis/Famous)

Red Sonja [based on stories by Robert E. Howard] returns to those olden days when women were women and the menfolk stood around with funny hats on until called forth to be whacked at.

Except, of course, for Arnold Schwarzenegger, whose Kalidor creation has just enough muscles to make him useful to the ladies, but not enough brains to make him a bother, except that he talks too much.

To her credit in the title role, Brigitte Nielsen never listens to a word he has to say, perhaps because he has an unfortunate tendency to address her as "Sony-uh." Nielsen wants to revenge her sister and find the magic talisman all on her own with no help from Kalidor, though she does think it's kind of cute when he wades into 80 guys and wastes them in an effort to impress her.

•

RED SUN
1971, 115 mins, France Ⓥ ⦿ col
Dir Terence Young ***Prod*** Robert Dorfmann ***Scr*** L. Koenig, D. B. Petitclerc, W. Roberts, L. Roman ***Ph*** Henri Alekan ***Ed*** Johnny Dwyre ***Mus*** Maurice Jarre
Act Charles Bronson, Ursula Andress, Toshiro Mifune, Alain Delon, Capucine (Corona/Oceania)

East is East and West is West, but the twain meet in this actionful oater with Japanese actor Toshiro Mifune matching sword and wits with Yank Charles Bronson and Frenchman Alain Delon.

Mifune is a Samurai accompanying the Japanese ambassador in a trek across the West to Washington in the mid-19th century to deliver a jeweled, golden sword to the U.S. president. On the way the train is held up by Bronson and Delon, but the latter double-crosses Bronson and also kills a Samurai friend of Mifune and takes the sword. Mifune's code requires he find the sword and kill Delon.

Mifune is his towering, glowering self in his rich samurai garb and his sword matches the guns. Bronson is relaxed and effective as the bandit with some honor within his own life. Ursula Andress is decorative as the wily prostie, out to make a killing to get out of her life of bondage.

Young lays on the action and blood with some interludes in the growing friendship between Bronson and Mifune.

•

RED TENT, THE
1971, 121 mins, Italy/USSR Ⓥ ⦿ col
Dir Mikhail Kalatozov ***Prod*** Franco Cristaldi ***Scr*** Ennio De Concini, Richard Adams ***Ph*** Leonid Kalashnikov ***Ed*** Peter Zinner ***Mus*** Ennio Morricone ***Art*** Giancarlo Bartolini Salimboni, David Vinitsky
Act Sean Connery, Claudia Cardinale, Hardy Kruger, Peter Finch, Massimo Girotti, Luigi Vannucchi (Vides/Mosfilm)

This first Italo-Russian co-production deals with the 1928 rescue of an Italian Polar expedition stranded by a dirigible crash. Some spectacularly beautiful Arctic footage, plus an exciting personal story of survival, make the production compelling and suspenseful.

Framework of the script is metaphysical; a sort of rugged adventure yarn in a Jean-Paul Sartre setting. Peter Finch plays General Nobile, an Italian Arctic explorer who is lost in the North Atlantic wastes. Years later, his nightmares about the incident summon up phantoms of those involved with him.

Sean Connery plays Roald Amundsen, a fellow explorer who died in search for Finch; Claudia Cardinale plays a nurse who was in love with one of Finch's crew; and Hardy Kruger is a daredevil rescue pilot whose motivations in rescuing Finch before his men creates an international scandal.

Connery plays an aged man very convincingly. Kruger and Cardinale supply key plot motivations, but the heaviest burden is on Finch; he is excellent in a characterization which demands many moods, many attitudes.

•

REF, THE
(UK: HOSTILE HOSTAGES)
1994, 93 mins, US Ⓥ ⦿ col
Dir Ted Demme ***Prod*** Ron Bozman, Richard LaGravenese, Jeff Weiss ***Scr*** Richard LaGravenese, Marie Weiss ***Ph*** Adam Kimmel ***Ed*** Jeffrey Wolf ***Mus*** David A. Stewart ***Art*** Dan Davis
Act Denis Leary, Judy Davis, Kevin Spacey, Robert J. Steinmiller, Jr., Glynis Johns, Raymond J. Barry (Touchstone)

Don Simpson and Jerry Bruckheimer's first production for Disney is a high-concept comedy [from a screen story by coscripter Marie Weiss] that mixes O. Henry's chestnut *Ransom of Red Chief* with touches of *Home Alone* and Bunuel's *Exterminating Angel*. *The Ref* mines a few laughs from the case of a high-strung cat burglar named Gus (Denis Leary), who, after a bungled second-story job on Christmas Eve, grabs Connecticut yuppie couple Caroline (Judy Davis) and Lloyd (Kevin Spacey) as hostages while he plots his escape.

The plot-driving problem is that these are two of the most grating, unrelentingly angry neurotics one could find in this otherwise placid L.L. Bean–couture paradise. Gus essentially becomes hostage to their bickering, as his hapless, largely offscreen partner in crime, Murray (Richard Bright), tries over the course of the evening to get an escape plan under way.

Co-scripted and co-produced by Richard LaGravenese, whose *The Fisher King* screenplay also mixed up seemingly disparate elements of black humor, contemporary social and psychological dysfunction with a life-affirming fade-out, *The Ref* works virtually none of the miracles of his previous mix 'n' match effort.

Davis is essentially retreading her earlier shrewish role in Woody Allen's corrosive *Husbands and Wives*, while Spacey fills out his Milquetoast-becomes-a-man role serviceably.

•

REFLECTING SKIN, THE
1990, 93 mins, UK Ⓥ col
Dir Philip Ridley ***Prod*** Dominic Anciano, Ray Burdis ***Scr*** Philip Ridley ***Ph*** Dick Pope ***Ed*** Scott Thomas ***Art*** Rick Roberts

Act Viggo Mortensen, Lindsay Duncan, Jeremy Cooper, Sheila Moore, Duncan Fraser, David Longworth (Fugitive)

In this pretentious essay in the grotesque, British newcomer Philip Ridley shows technical ability and a macabre sense of humor, but the script's abnormal situations and morbid characters pall quickly and leave little more than a bad aftertaste.

Set in grassroots America of the 1950s (film was shot in Canada), story describes how a young boy persecutes and catalyzes the death of a young widow whom he thinks is a vampire with bloodthirsty aims on his elder brother.

Nobody in the story is normal. The boy has a penchant for sadistic practical jokes, mom is hysterically obsessed with odors and dad, a service station operator with a history of pederasty, commits suicide (by gasoline immolation) when accused of sodomy and murder of his son's friend.

The lovers (widow and brother) are bent too. Latter is clearly disturbed by his recent military service in the Pacific, while the widow, a British woman whose rube husband hung himself, is a necrophile fetishist.

Ridley tops things off with some twisted religious symbolism, such as the fossilized fetus the boy finds in a barn and befriends. Tech credits, notably Dick Pope's striking color images, are fine.

•

REFLECTIONS IN A GOLDEN EYE
1967, 109 mins, US Ⓥ ⊙ ▭ col
Dir John Huston ***Prod*** Ray Stark ***Scr*** Chapman Mortimer, Gladys Hill ***Ph*** Aldo Tonti ***Ed*** Russell Lloyd ***Mus*** Toshiro Mayuzumi ***Art*** Stephen Grimes
Act Elizabeth Taylor, Marlon Brando, Brian Keith, Julie Harris, Robert Forster, Zorro David (Warner/Seven Arts)

Carson McCullers's novel, *Reflections in a Golden Eye*, about a latent homosexual U.S. Army officer in the pre Second World War period, has been turned into a pretentious melodrama by director John Huston.

Adaptation features six disparate characters: Marlon Brando, the latent homosexual; his wife, Elizabeth Taylor, a practicing heterosexual—practicing with Brian Keith, whose own wife, Julie Harris, once cut off her breasts with scissors after unfortunate childbirth; Robert Forster, young fetishist and exhibitionist; Zorro David, Harris's fey houseboy.

Also prominent are a host of sex symbols, and some salty expressions. Brando struts about and mugs as the stuffy officer, whose Dixie dialect is often incoherent. Taylor is appropriately unaware of her husband's torment. Her dialect also obscures some vital plot points.

The most outstanding and satisfying performance is that of Brian Keith. This versatile actor is superb as the rationalizing and insensitive middle-class hypocrite.

•

REFLECTIONS ON A CRIME
1994, 96 mins, US Ⓥ col
Dir Jon Purdy ***Prod*** Gwen Field, Barbara Klein, Carol Dunn Trussel, ***Scr*** Jon Purdy ***Ph*** Teresa Medina ***Ed*** Norman Buckley ***Mus*** Parmer Fuller ***Art*** Arlan Jay Vetter
Act Mimi Rogers, Billy Zane, John Terry, Kurt Fuller, Lee Garlington, Nancy Fish (Concorde/Saban)

A full-bore star turn by Mimi Rogers, playing a glamorous killer about to take the chair, is the main selling point for this slickly made, intellectually empty character study. Sharp style on a mini-budget and uncompromising seriousness lend some distinction to Jon Purdy's first feature.

Rogers toplines as Regina, convicted of killing her pompous husband because "divorce would have broken his heart." From this flimsy bit of moral ambiguity, writer/helmer Purdy fashions a claustrophobic, execution-eve face-off between Rogers and young "media junky" guard Colin (Billy Zane), who has bribed his way into her holding cell.

Rogers then spins her tale of the events leading up to the fatal encounter, some repeated from every angle, with the only twist that hubby is dispatched by different means each time.

That sounds intriguing on paper, but Purdy's leaden hand guarantees hard labor for all involved. B-meister Roger Corman exec. produced, and the gratuitous ogling of Rogers's body (or her body double) is certainly more Russ Meyer than Chantal Akerman.

•

REFORM SCHOOL GIRLS
1986, 94 mins, US Ⓥ ⊙ col
Dir Tom deSimone ***Prod*** Jack Cummins ***Scr*** Tom deSimone ***Ph*** Howard Wexler ***Ed*** Michael Spence ***Mus*** Tedra Gabriel ***Art*** Becky Block
Act Linda Carol, Wendy O. Williams, Pat Ast, Sybil Danning, Charlotte McGinnis, Sherri Stoner (New World)

Reform School Girls don't have it so bad. For one thing, they don't have to wear uniforms—or much else for that matter. They talk dirty, play dirty and are allowed to take long, long showers.

Busty Wendy O. Williams, who made a name for herself as the headbanging lead singer of the rock group, The Plasmatics, continues her trashy theatrics here as a leather-clad lesbian who reigns terror over the other girls serving time at Pridemore Juvenile Facilities.

Supported by her gang of "death rockers," Williams intimidates each new arrival into submission until she encounters fresh-faced Jenny (Linda Carol), who is bent on countering corruption at Pridemore.

Every character is a caricature, from the rifle-toting, Bible-quoting warden (Sybil Danning) to the lineup of lovelies who parade as reform school girls.

Pat Ast, as the cantankerous and corpulent head matron, and Williams play their rotten roles to the hilt and get most of the juicy lines.

•

REGARDING HENRY
1991, 107 mins, US Ⓥ ⊙ col
Dir Mike Nichols ***Prod*** Mike Nichols, Scott Rudin ***Scr*** Jeffrey Abrams ***Ph*** Giuseppe Rotunno ***Ed*** Sam O'Steen ***Mus*** Hans Zimmer ***Art*** Tony Walton
Act Harrison Ford, Annette Bening, Bill Nunn, Mikki Allen, Donald Moffat, Nancy Marchand (Paramount)

A subtle emotional journey impeccably orchestrated by director Mike Nichols and acutely well acted, *Regarding Henry* has a back-to-basics message that's bound to strike a responsive chord in the troubled aftermath of the 1980s. In a way, the pic is a variation on the old story of the husband who goes down to the corner for a pack of cigarettes and never comes back.

The controlling, intolerant Henry Turner (Harrison Ford) who steps out of his Manhattan brownstone late one night for a pack of Merits, only to become the victim of a mindless, hysterical violence, is certainly not the same man who has to be coaxed back home from the hospital after a lengthy rehabilitation. Henry has to start from scratch to regain such basic capacities as how to read, take a walk or make love to his wife.

The grace of the script by 23-year-old Jeffrey Abrams is that it doesn't contrive a practical alternative for Henry. The change in his character is story enough. On the other hand, there is the dimension contributed by Annette Bening's interpretation of an elegant society wife who bravely becomes Henry's truest friend when his former confidence deserts him.

In a role as far removed as possible from her cunning Myra in *The Grifters*, Bening sets a shining new standard of performance. Ford operates with his usual first-rate precision, pushing the super-competent Henry slyly into the realm of humor, and suggesting the physical timidity and mental struggles of the debilitated Henry without overdoing it.

•

REGLE DU JEU, LA
(THE RULES OF THE GAME)
1939, 113 mins, France Ⓥ ⊙ b/w
Dir Jean Renoir ***Scr*** Jean Renoir, Karl Koch, Camille Francois ***Ph*** Jean Bachelet ***Ed*** Marguerite Houlet-Renoir ***Mus*** Roger Desormieres (arr.) ***Art*** Eugene Lourie
Act Nora Gregor, Jean Renoir, Dalio, Roland Toutain, Paulette Dubost, Gaston Modot (NEF)

La Regle du Jeu is one of those controversial pix bound to elicit much comment but definitely lacking in marquee strength. It's advertised as a comic film "called upon to open new horizons for the French cinema, taking its inspiration from a new school."

As an experiment it's interesting, but Jean Renoir, who directs, wrote the scenario and dialog, and takes a leading role, has made a common error: he attempts to crowd too many ideas into 80 minutes of film fare, resulting in confusion. Also weak is Nora Gregor, the former Princess Starhemberg, whose accent is far from pleasing and her acting stilted.

Tale concerns transatlantic flyer Andre Jurieux (Roland Toutain), who confesses to his buddy, Octave (Jean Renoir), that he's frantically in love with the Marquise (Gregor). Whimsical Octave wants to see the love affair carried out to its denouement and arranges for a hunting party at the Marquis's (Dalio) chateau.

Here begins a series of screwy situations. The Marquis discovers that he loves his wife and decides to give up his mistress, played by Mila Parely. But the latter has other ideas. Andre then attempts to rush the Marquise into running away with him. To complicate matters, Paulette Dubost, as the Marquise's maid, and wife of the gamekeeper (Gaston Modot), carries on a high-powered flirtation with the Marquis's valet (Carette). All of which continues into a dizzier whirl of infidelities.

Dalio, Carette, Toutain and Renoir are excellent. Modot is commendable. All minor roles are adequate. Photography is nifty and score pleasant.

[Renoir's original 113-min. version was cut before release to 100 mins, and in the furore after release to 80 mins. Version reviewed is the latter, just prior to the pic's withdrawal. Original version, reconstituted, was preemed at 1959 Venice festival.]

•

REINCARNATION OF PETER PROUD, THE
1975, 104 mins, US Ⓥ ⊙ col
Dir J. Lee Thompson ***Prod*** Frank P. Rosenberg ***Scr*** Max Ehrlich ***Ph*** Victor J. Kemper ***Ed*** Michael Anderson ***Mus*** Jerry Goldsmith ***Art*** Jack Martin Smith
Act Michael Sarrazin, Jennifer O'Neill, Margot Kidder, Cornelia Sharpe, Paul Hecht, Tony Stephano (American International)

Reincarnation of Peter Proud embodies all the thrills of Max Ehrlich's bestseller, plus an oustandingly rich performance from Margot Kidder. Only weakness still is story's sudden and unsatisfactory ending. Michael Sarrazin from the start almost, realizes that some unknown person is within him. Tracing scenes from his dreams, he ventures to small Massachusetts town where Kidder had murdered philandering husband, briefly but ably played by Stephano.

Sarrazin is best in contending with the semi-incestuous love affair that develops between him and Jennifer O'Neill. Her best moments, too, come in the clinches that do-don't take place between two obviously attracted, and otherwise eligible, young lovers.

•

REINE MARGOT, LA
(QUEEN MARGOT)
1955, 125 mins, France/Italy col
Dir Jean Dreville ***Scr*** Abel Gance, Jean Camp, Paul Andreota ***Ph*** Roger Hubert, Henri Alekan ***Ed*** Gabriel Rongier
Act Jeanne Moreau, Armando Francioli, Francoise Rosay, Henri Genes, Daniel Ceccaldi, Louis de Funes (Vendome/Lux)

Still another historical fresco from the color spec cycle of the Franco-Italian production setup, this is reminiscent of oldie costumers with intercutting between various climaxes, and keeping most history in the bedroom.

This [adaptation of Alexandre Dumas's novel] concerns the impetuous Margot (Jeanne Moreau), daughter of Catherine (Francoise Rosay) and brother of Charles IX (Robert Porte), who is married to the Huguenot prince (Andre Versini) in order to form a bulwark for the king and ward off trouble. However, right after the marriage, the king calls for the massacre of the Huguenots and a bloodbath follows. During this debacle, a handsome count stumbles into Margot's boudoir. It is, of course, love after the first fright. Then intrigue builds.

Moreau is an engaging feline actress but is miscast for nudie roles. Remainder of the cast is fine, with Rosay a scheming Catherine and Porte a properly unpredictable king. Massacre has its share of bloodiness, with the nudity and love scenes not sparing the anatomy. Production is opulent and decorative.

•

REINE MARGOT, LA
(QUEEN MARGOT)
1994, 161 mins, France/Germany/Italy Ⓥ ⊙ col
Dir Patrice Chereau ***Prod*** Claude Berri ***Scr*** Daniele Thompson, Patrice Chereau ***Ph*** Philippe Rousselot ***Ed*** Francois Gedigier, Helene Viard ***Mus*** Goran Bregovic ***Art*** Richard Peduzzi, Olivier Radot
Act Isabelle Adjani, Daniel Auteuil, Jean-Hughes Anglade, Vincent Perez, Virna Lisi, Dominique Blanc (Renn/France 2/DA/NEF/Degeto/WMG/RCS

The grandiose *Queen Margot* aspires to the mantle of Shakespearean tragedy but plays more like bad Grand Guignol theater. Sprawling, bloody costumer about the dastardly deeds of 16th-century French royalty is a frenzy of religious conflict, personal betrayal, raw passion and enough killing for all three parts of *The Godfather*. Celebrated theater and opera director Patrice Chereau plays the swirling action to the highest balcony, encouraging his actors to emote and gesticulate without restraint.

In a France dominated by the Italian exile Catherine de Medici (Virna Lisi) and nominally ruled by her son Charles IX (Jean-Hugues Anglade), a gesture is made toward peace through the arranged marriage of the Catholic Margot (Isabelle Adjani), Charles's sister, and the Protestant Henri of Navarre (Daniel Auteuil).

Almost at once, the rulers at the Louvre decide that the Protestants must be wiped out, resulting in the St

Bartholomew's Day massacre that saw perhaps 6,000 killed in Paris on Aug. 23-24, 1572. Henri advisedly converts to Catholicism, while Margot is awakened amorously by the dashing Protestant La Mole (Vincent Perez), who is protected by his lover before embarking abroad to gather an army to fight the treacherous papists.

Beyond the disagreeableness of all the characters and their behavior, a chief problem is that Margot is basically a sideline player. Similarly, Henri is an annoyingly ineffectual type until he surprisingly intervenes on behalf of the king. La Mole is a standard-issue heroic lover type without a distinctive personality.

Chereau and his co-scenarist no doubt had in mind parallels to modern Europe, where Catholics and protestants still fight and religious intolerance is once again resulting in slaughter. But the focus is almost exclusively on the carnage rather than on understanding it.

Physically, pic has been executed on the grandest scale on locations in France and Portugal. Still, Philippe Rousselot's exceedingly mobile camera stays in claustrophobically tight on the characters much of the time.

[Outside France, pic was released in a 143-min. "international version" at the behest of its U.S. distributor, though the original version was subsequently issued on video in the U.K. in 1996.]

●

REIVERS, THE

1969, 107 mins, US Ⓥ ▭ col

Dir Mark Rydell ***Prod*** Irving Ravetch ***Scr*** Irving Ravetch, Harriet Frank, Jr. ***Ph*** Richard Moore ***Ed*** Thomas Stanford ***Mus*** John Williams ***Art*** Charles Bailey, Joel Schiller

Act Steve McQueen, Sharon Farrell, Rupert Crosse, Mitch Vogel, Clifton James, Will Geer (Duo)

The Reivers is a nice bawdy film, sort of Walt Disney with an adult rating. Imagine a charming nostalgia-soaked family-type film about a winsome 11-year-old in turn-of-the-century Mississippi who gets himself cut up in a Memphis bordello defending the good name of a lovely professional lady. The film is an adaptation [narrated by Burgess Meredith] of William Faulkner's last novel.

Mitch Vogel, as the kid, is appealing, subtle and sensitive, hovering between freckle-faced moppet and sexual puberty.

He is led astray by the family handyman and resident rogue Steve McQueen who gives a lively ribald characterization. Completing the triumvirate of "Reivers," an old word that means "thieves," is Rupert Crosse. He is a humorously light-hearted but sardonically mocking dude. In a gleaming gold Winton Flyer the three steal off to Memphis, and the end of innocence for the boy.

1969: NOMINATIONS: Best Supp. Actor (Rupert Crosse), Original Music Score

●

REKOPIS ZNALEZIONY W SARAGOSSIE
(THE SARAGOSSA MANUSCRIPT)

1964, 175 mins, Poland b/w

Dir Wojciech J. Has ***Scr*** Tadeusz Kwiatkowski ***Ph*** Mieczyslaw Jahoda ***Ed*** [uncredited] ***Mus*** Krzysztof Penderecki ***Art*** Jerzy Skarzynski, Tadeusz Myszorek

Act Zbigniew Cybulski, Slawomir Lindner, Franciszek Pieczka, Barbara Krafftowna, Leon Niemczyk, Elzbieta Czyzewska (Kamera)

Jack-in-the-box pic [from the 1814 novel by Jan Potocki] with stories within stories, adult costumer follows a young Spanish captain into a series of adventures while reason and magic strive for his soul. Though filled with the trappings of 18th-century Spain, much derring-do, and exotic and occult adventures, its appeal is more intellectual than swashbuckling.

A young captain wanders into an inn that appears deserted but he meets two Moorish beauties and is told he is a descendant of an important family and has many missions to fulfill before he has proven himself. Meetings with many people follow, whose stories have some bearing on him, or clarify an idea.

He meets a man possessed of demons, has trouble with the Inquisition, is subjected to many tales by a magician trying to win his soul while a rationalist also fights for it.

Film's main appeal is its expert stylization, imaginative period recreations and gutsy playing by a big cast, with bouncy and valorous Zbigniew Cybulski as the man on the quest.

[Version reviewed is the complete one shown at the 1965 Venice fest. Outside Poland, pic is generally available in a 124-min. version.]

●

RELENTLESS

1989, 92 mins, US Ⓥ ⊙ col

Dir William Lustig ***Prod*** Howard Smith ***Scr*** Jack T. D. Robinson [= Phil Alden Robinson] ***Ph*** James Lemmo ***Ed*** David Kern ***Mus*** Jay Chattaway ***Art*** Gene Abel

Act Judd Nelson, Robert Loggia, Leo Rossi, Meg Foster, Patrick O'Bryan, Angel Tompkins (Cinetel)

Relentless is a riveting, splendidly acted suspense thriller. Phil Alden Robinson's fresh and invigorating script strikes a careful balance in focusing not just on maniacal killer Judd Nelson's murderous escapades but also putting at film's center the story of dedicated cop Leo Rossi and his supportive wife Meg Foster.

Format follows a pure Hitchcock suspense pattern: the audience immediately knows that Nelson is the so-called "Sunset Killer," murdering L.A. denizens seemingly at random and leaving snotty messages for the police on telephone book pages.

Rossi is a recently promoted police detective anxious to go all out to find the killer while his experienced partner (Robert Loggia in a solid turn) moves slowly. Climax set at Rossi's home is spellbinding, with excellent visual imagery to round off the story in satisfying fashion.

Director William Lustig keeps the screws tightened for an exciting, sometimes scary ride, while allowing for considerable warmth to be generated in the idiosyncratic family scenes involving Rossi, Foster and their young son.

●

RELUCTANT DEBUTANTE, THE

1958, 96 mins, US Ⓥ ▭ col

Dir Vincente Minnelli ***Prod*** Pandro S. Berman ***Scr*** William Douglas Home ***Ph*** Joseph Ruttenberg ***Ed*** Adrienne Fazan ***Mus*** Eddie Warner (arr.) ***Art*** A. J. d'Eaubonne

Act Rex Harrison, Kay Kendall, John Saxon, Sandra Dee, Angela Lansbury, Diane Clare (M-G-M/Avon)

The Reluctant Debutante is refreshing and prettily dressed, a colorful, saucy film version of the William Douglas home stage trifle.

Debutante is the story of London's social "season," a time when bright and not-too-bright 17-year-olds make their debuts in society, carrying on at one deb's ball after another. Rex Harrison and Kay Kendall, as newly married on screen as off, invite his American daughter (by a former marriage) for a British visit that results in the girl's coming out socially.

As played by Sandra Dee, the teenager is bored with English stiffs but falls madly for an American drummer (John Saxon) who's tabbed with a most dubious reputation. Mixed-up telephone calls, embarrassing situations and advances—both wanted and unwanted—follow with rapidity.

Harrison is suavely disturbed as the father. Dee proves a rather good actress who maintains a lively character throughout, and Saxon lends a fine boyish charm to the proceedings. But it's really Kendall's picture, and she grabs it with a single wink. She's flighty and well-meaning, snobbish and lovable.

●

RELUCTANT DRAGON, THE

1941, 73 mins, US col

Dir Alfred Werker, Hamilton Luske ***Prod*** Walt Disney ***Scr*** Ted Sears, Al Perkins, Larry Clemmons, Bill Cottrell, Harry Clork ***Ph*** Bert Glennon, Winton Hoch ***Ed*** Paul Weatherwax ***Mus*** Frank Churchill, Larry Morey ***Art*** Gordon Wiles

Act Robert Benchley, Frances Gifford, Buddy Pepper, Nana Bryant, Claud Allister, Barnett Parker (Walt Disney)

Ever a trail-hewer, Walt Disney has once more created a film entirely different from anything before. The film, in its essentials, is a trip through the Disney plant—interspersed with cartoon shorts to insure the picture's appeal. Aside from the introductory sequences in Disney's *Fantasia*, this is the first film to combine cartoons and humans on a large scale.

Pic opens with Robert Benchley's wife (Nana Bryant) reading Kenneth Grahame's famed fairy tale, *The Reluctant Dragon*. She rags Benchley into calling on Disney to sell it to him. Even after he is admitted to the studio, Benchley "escapes" from his guide (Buddy Pepper) so that he won't have to face Disney.

His "escape" takes him into strange doors and strange rooms. In his stumbling through the plant, Benchley (and the audience) sees some eight operations in the making of cartoons, plus three full shorts and hunks of a number of other Disney features in work, notably *Bambi*.

Cartoons [directed by Hamilton Luske] include *Baby Weems, How to Ride a Horse* and *The Reluctant Dragon*. Many of the performers in the live action portions are Disney employees doing their actual jobs, although virtually all of the speaking parts are handled by professionals.

Beginning of the film is in black and white. It cleverly shifts into Technicolor [photographed by Winton Hoch] when Benchley gets to the camera room where the color work is done. Direction keeps the live action zipping along. If there's any slowness, it's in the cartoon division.

●

REMAINS OF THE DAY, THE

1993, 135 mins, US/UK Ⓥ ⊙ ▭ col

Dir James Ivory ***Prod*** Mike Nichols, John Calley, Ismail Merchant ***Scr*** Ruth Prawer Jhabvala ***Ph*** Tony Pierce-Roberts ***Ed*** Andrew Marcus ***Mus*** Richard Robbins ***Art*** Luciana Arrighi

Act Anthony Hopkins, Emma Thompson, James Fox, Christopher Reeve, Peter Vaughan, Hugh Grant (Columbia/Merchant Ivory)

All the meticulousness, intelligence, taste and superior acting that one expects from Merchant Ivory productions have been brought to bear on *The Remains of the Day*. This curious, cloistered piece, which examines the life of a very proper English butler who sacrifices anything resembling a personal life in total dedication to his master's needs, is continuously absorbing, but lacks the emotional resonance that would have made it completely satisfying, despite top performances from Anthony Hopkins and Emma Thompson.

Based on the 1989 Booker Prize-winning novel by Kazuo Ishiguro, faithfully adapted by Ruth Prawer Jhabvala, story begins with the aging butler Stevens (Hopkins) traveling across Britain to see his former co-worker, Miss Kenton (Thompson). Stevens's employer at the palatial Darlington Hall is now an American ex-Congressman, Mr. Lewis (Christopher Reeve), and in the course of his journey, Stevens recalls life at the great estate in its heyday during the 1930s.

Stevens places dignity and decorum at the top of life's values and his own emotional needs at the bottom. The latter are tested a bit in his relationship over several years with Miss Kenton. Nothing can ruffle Stevens, not even the death of his father (Peter Vaughan), who inconveniently expires during a major political conference hosted by Lord Darlington (James Fox) who harbors German sympathies.

Hopkins creates a superbly observed and nuanced Stevens. Pic also reps another career highlight for Thompson, who expertly reveals the conflicting feelings of her conventional, if occasionally spirited character. If the ending feels emotionally flat it isn't the fault of the lead actors, but of the script's somewhat lumpy construction, which causes the film to seem to evaporate rather than conclude.

1993: NOMINATIONS: Best Picture, Director, Actor (Anthony Hopkins), Actress (Emma Thompson), Original Score, Adapted Screenplay, Art Direction, Costume Design

●

REMBRANDT

1936, 85 mins, US Ⓥ b/w

Dir Alexander Korda ***Prod*** Alexander Korda ***Scr*** Carl Zuckmayer, June Head, Arthur Wimperis ***Ph*** Georges Perinal ***Ed*** William Hornbeck, Francis Lyon ***Mus*** Geoffrey Toye ***Art*** Vincent Korda

Act Charles Laughton, Gertrude Lawrence, Elsa Lanchester, Edward Chapman, Walter Hudd, Roger Livesey (London)

An idealized film biography of the life of the famous painter. Story begins at the height of Rembrandt's fame, during his lifetime, and carries on to his solitary, poverty-stricken old age. Despite a cast of two score principals, it is a one-part production, with but one scene in the entire film in which the star does not play the central character. It was an inspiration to film many of the scenes with a suggestion of the lighting for which Rembrandt is famous in his paintings.

Forty principals were requisitioned from the best artists the British legitimate stage has to offer. If some of them, like Gertrude Lawrence and Elsa Lanchester, stand out from the others, it is only because they have more extensive and showier roles.

Despite all this artistic and technical assistance, Charles Laughton is far from satisfactory. According to the story, he is never interested in anything relating to finance or the ordinary rules of domestic economy. The only tragic things in his life are the deaths of his two wives. On neither occasion does Laughton express the overwhelming sorrow the story calls for.

●

REMEMBER MY NAME

1978, 95 mins, US col

Dir Alan Rudolph ***Prod*** Robert Altman ***Scr*** Alan Rudolph ***Ph*** Tak Fujimoto ***Ed*** Thomas Walls, William A. Sawyer ***Mus*** Alberta Hunter

Act Geraldine Chaplin, Anthony Perkins, Moses Gunn, Berry Berenson, Jeff Goldblum, Tim Thomerson (Lion's Gate)

Remember My Name is an attempt to make what Alan Rudolph calls a "contemporary blues fable." Whatever the generic goal, the end product is an incomprehensible melange of striking imagery, obscure dialog, a powerful score, and a script that doesn't know how to go from A to B.

Anthony Perkins is a construction worker married to Berry Berenson. Geraldine Chaplin arrives on the scene and begins a petty harassment of the couple, which gradually turns more sinister.

It develops that Chaplin is an ex-convict, recently sprung from a 12-year sentence for murder. She got a job in a nearby five-and-dime store managed by Jeff Goldblum (whose mother is still doing time), where she terrorizes store clerk Alfre Woodard and Goldblum. Chaplin also gets a room in a rundown apartment building managed by Moses Gunn, with whom she has a brief liaison.

If done on a traditional, linear level, *Remember My Name* might have induced some interest as a moderate chiller with emotional undertones. In Rudolph's infuriatingly oblique style, however, it becomes an irritating and puzzling affair that insults, rather than teases, the viewer.

•

REMEMBER THE DAY
1941, 95 mins, US b/w
Dir Henry King ***Prod*** William Perlberg ***Scr*** Tess Slesinger, Frank Davis, Allan Scott ***Ph*** George Barnes ***Ed*** Barbara McLean ***Mus*** Alfred Newman
Act Claudette Colbert, John Payne, John Shepperd, Anne Revere, Douglas Croft (20th Century-Fox)

Remember the Day is a warmly human drama depicting the basic American way of life—skillfully assembled to generate exacting audience attention in one of the best examples of well-rounded filmplay fabrication. With Claudette Colbert niftily handling her assignment and assisted by exceptionally capable support, direction and script, picture is an "A" attraction.

Story [from a play by Philo Higley and Philip Dunning] is slightly reminiscent of *Goodbye, Mr Chips*. In *Remember the Day* it's a femme schoolteacher who holds the spotlight; but there's still the neat admixture of happiness and semi-tragedy in her involvement in a brief romance that upsets the puppy-love adoration of a teenage pupil she has become interested in to generate his interests into proper hobbies and channels.

•

REMEMBER THE NIGHT
1940, 93 mins, US b/w
Dir Mitchell Leisen ***Prod*** Mitchell Leisen ***Scr*** Preston Sturges ***Ph*** Ted Tetzlaff ***Ed*** Doane Harrison ***Mus*** Frederick Hollander ***Art*** Hans Dreier, Roland Anderson
Act Barbara Stanwyck, Fred MacMurray, Beulah Bondi, Elizabeth Patterson, Willard Robertson, Sterling Holloway (Paramount)

Preston Sturges's original screenplay depends mainly on individual sequences and bright situations rather than the overall effect of the story itself. Here is a tale of a girl crook (Barbara Stanwyck) who becomes enmeshed in the law after lifting a bracelet from a store. Deputy district attorney Fred MacMurray is assigned to prosecute, even though he plans to leave for Xmas holidays with his mother in Indiana. When defense attorney pulls a surprise, young d.a. has trial continued for two weeks, and girl has to remain in jail in the interim. MacMurray suffers pangs of conscience and gets her out on bail. When he finds her home is also in Indiana, he takes her along on the trip.

Picture is highlighted in numerous instances by some deft telling in the script and fine piloting by director Mitchell Leisen to lift the yarn from commonplace and trite category.

Stanwyck turns in a fine performance. MacMurray is impressive as the serious-minded prosecutor, but loosens up for the comedy stretches. Beulah Bondi and Elizabeth Patterson, MacMurray's mother and aunt, respectively, provide good characterizations, and Sterling Holloway scores as the hick hired hand.

•

REMEMBER THE TITANS
2000, 113 mins, US Ⓥ ⦿ ▭ col
Dir Boaz Yakin ***Prod*** Jerry Bruckheimer, Chad Oman ***Scr*** Gregory Allen Howard ***Ph*** Philippe Rousselot ***Ed*** Michael Tronick ***Mus*** Trevor Rabin ***Art*** Deborah Evans
Act Denzel Washington, Will Patton, Donald Faison, Wood Harris, Ryan Hurst, Ethan Suplee (Technical Black/Disney)

As earnest and well-intentioned as any Stanley Kramer movie, *Remember the Titans* grapples with the civil rights struggle with an almost cartoonlike simplicity and naivete. Using the true story of the forced integration of a 1971 Virginia high school football team to show how we can all get along if race and background are put aside for the sake of the common goal of scoring touchdowns, this high-minded sports drama attempts to merge the boldfaced thematic seriousness of something like Kramer's *The Defiant Ones* with the macho swagger of *Top Gun*.

Framed by the funeral service for one Titan player 10 years later, script zeroes in on how it went down at T. C. Williams High in Alexandria, Virginia, when blacks were introduced to the previously all-white school. Because training begins in the summer, the football program is integrated well before any black student sets foot in a classroom, and the process gets off to a poor start as far as the community is concerned when a black coach from South Carolina, Herman Boone (Denzel Washington), is brought in to replace a revered and successful white coach, Bill Yoast (Will Patton).

Aside from its message-waving, pic dedicates itself to entertaining the audience via its military-style whip-'em-into-shape training antics. Although he's denied the salty dialogue that ordinarily comes with the territory (just as the countless racist characters on view are never allowed to say the *n*-word in this decidedly family-oriented film), Washington seems to relish playing such a kick-butt authoritarian figure; the film depicts his tough medicine as just what it takes to cleanse these young men of their mutual suspicions and boiling blood. It's an engaging performance, even if half of his lines are platitudes and the rest orders and instructions.

Patton and Ryan Hurst (as hostile white All-American team captain Gerry Bertier) effectively play the two white characters whose gradual coming around symbolizes the dawning of understanding that, the film posits, everyone will need to experience if society is to improve.

•

REMODELING HER HUSBAND
1920, 65 mins, US ⊗ b/w
Dir Lillian Gish ***Scr*** Dorothy Elizabeth Carter
Act Dorothy Gish, James Rennie, Marie Burke, Downing Clarke, Frank Kingdon (New Art/Paramount)

This feature will be liked by film fans but not particularly because of the story or the picturization of it, but through the exquisite comedy Dorothy Gish offers.

The picture seems to be a real Gish family affair, with Dorothy starring and Lillian directing. Much is made of the latter in a title leader, which sets forth that this day is one where woman is asserting herself in all the arts, and therefore it is time she undertook the direction of pictures.

But Lillian does not qualify as a particularly strong directress in this production. The story may have had something to do with that. It is not a world beater but with the action that Dorothy supplies it gets by with laughs.

James Rennie, who plays opposite the star, is the only member of the supporting cast who seems to have more than a "bit" to do. The others while acceptable fail to show often enough to get a line on them. It is a picture that is Dorothy Gish, hook, line and sinker, and it would sink if it weren't for her.

•

REMO
UNARMED AND DANGEROUS
SEE: REMO WILLIAMS—THE ADVENTURE BEGINS . . .

•

REMO WILLIAMS: THE ADVENTURE BEGINS . . .
(UK: REMO—UNARMED AND DANGEROUS)
1985, 121 mins, US Ⓥ ⦿ col
Dir Guy Hamilton ***Prod*** Larry Spiegel ***Scr*** Christopher Wood ***Ph*** Andrew Laszlo ***Ed*** Mark Melnick ***Mus*** Craig Safan ***Art*** Jackson De Govia
Act Fred Ward, Joel Grey, Wilford Brimley, J. A. Preston, Kate Mulgrew, Charles Cioffi (Orion)

Remo Williams is a poor man's James Bond with a dash of two or three other popular genres thrown in for good measure. The film [based on *The Destroyer* series by Richard Sapir and Warren Murphy] never seems to know where it's going and, when the smoke has cleared, doesn't seem to have got there either.

Williams (Fred Ward) is sort of a proletarian Bond—a New York City cop recruited for some secret government agency (headed by Wilford Brimley) supposedly working undercover for the President himself. What levity occurs in the film is mostly reserved for the long middle section in which Remo is placed under the tutelage of the last living master of the Korean martial art Sinanju.

The relationship between Remo and Chiun (Joel Grey) is an adult version of *The Karate Kid*. Small feats such as walking on water and dodging bullets are simply routine for the great man.

Charles Cioffi as an arms manufacturer in cahoots with the military is a cardboard heavy surrounded by a supply of bumbling bad guys. Thrown in for a slight romantic interest is Kate Mulgrew as an honest officer stumbling on the nefarious plot.

1985: NOMINATION: Best Makeup

•

RENAISSANCE MAN
1994, 129 mins, US Ⓥ ⦿ col
Dir Penny Marshall ***Prod*** Sara Colleton, Elliot Abbott, Robert Greenhut ***Scr*** Jim Burnstein ***Ph*** Adam Greenburg ***Ed*** George Bowers, Battle Davis ***Mus*** Hans Zimmer ***Art*** Geoffrey Kirkland
Act Danny DeVito, Gregory Hines, James Remar, Cliff Robertson, Lillo Brancato, Jr., Stacey Dash (Cinergi-Parkway/Touchstone)

What looks like *Stripes* in its TV campaign actually has more in common with *Dead Poets Society* or even *To Sir with Love*, featuring Danny DeVito as the reluctant teacher of eight dense-but-good-hearted Army recruits.

This bittersweet comedy needed a clearer focus, or a more ruthless hand in the editing room. Highlights are too often followed by lulls of inactivity or feel-good moments that cause the narrative to drag.

DeVito plays Bill Rago, an advertising executive who suddenly loses his job and is forced to take a temporary gig teaching a group of Army underachievers. The idea, not warmed to by the group's sergeant (Gregory Hines), is that having more smarts will make the group better soldiers. Uncertain where to begin, Rago stumbles onto the idea of teaching the kids Shakespeare, gradually winning them over and becoming involved in their various hard-luck stories.

DeVito is such an engaging character that *Renaissance Man* generates its share of laughs, and the filmmakers have done a terrific job casting the eight recruits with fresh faces who bring the film an inordinate amount of energy. Lillo Brancato, Jr., emerges as the principal scene-stealer, playing the Brooklyn-born Benitez, but Kadeem Hardison is also a hoot, and rapper Mark Wahlberg (aka Marky Mark), making his movie debut, has the properly addled look of a good ol' country boy.

On the flip side, both Hines and James Remar seem miscast (their roles probably could have been flip-flopped) as the stern drill sergeant and overworked captain, failing to provide strong foils for DeVito.

•

RENDEZVOUS
1935, 96 mins, US b/w
Dir William K. Howard ***Prod*** Lawrence Weingarten ***Scr*** Bella Spewack, Samuel Spewack, P. J. Wolfson, George Oppenheimer ***Ph*** William Daniels ***Ed*** Hugh Wynn ***Mus*** William Axt
Act William Powell, Rosalind Russell, Binnie Barnes, Lionel Atwill, Cesar Romero, Samuel S. Hinds (M-G-M)

Another chill-and-chuckle play scoring a bullseye. Yarn was developed by Bella and Sam Spewack from a novel [*American Black Chamber*] by Herbert O. Yardley, in the War Department intelligence office during the war.

William Powell is puzzle editor of a Washington newspaper who quits to enlist in the army. The day before he leaves he meets Rosalind Russell, whose uncle is one of the under-secretaries of war. Love develops in the speedy fashion of those times and she persuades her uncle that Powell will be more useful in decoding messages than in shooting at the enemy. The comedy is cleverly worked into the action and becomes a part of it instead of an interpolation, and herein lies its success. Interest is never diverted from the thread of the story.

Powell is at ease as the nonchalant decoder who can face danger with a grin and teams perfectly with Russell. She has both looks and intelligence, playing the wilful girl with delightful spirit.

•

RENEGADES
1989, 106 mins, US Ⓥ ⦿ col
Dir Jack Sholder ***Prod*** David Madden ***Scr*** David Rich ***Ph*** Phil Meheux ***Ed*** Caroline Biggerstaff ***Mus*** Michael Kamen ***Art*** Carol Spier
Act Kiefer Sutherland, Lou Diamond Phillips, Jami Gertz, Rob Knepper, Bill Smitrovich, Floyd Westerman (Morgan Creek/Interscope)

Renegades offers some rollercoaster thrills thanks to Jack Sholder's full-throttle direction but ultimately exhausts itself with unrelenting bedlam.

Kiefer Sutherland plays Buster, an undercover cop chasing a baddie who's stolen $2 million in diamonds. In the process, Marino (Rob Knepper) kills the brother of Hank (Lou Diamond Phillips) and makes off with an ancient spear, an artifact sacred to their Lakota Indian tribe. Phillips must recover it to satisfy his father, throwing him together with Sutherland, who's intent on exposing the "dirty cop" working with the gang because *his* father was ousted from the force with a blemished record.

Story resembles an earlier quest film, *Red Sun*, which cast Charles Bronson as a gunslinger shackled with a stone-faced Samurai (Toshiro Mifune) jointly pursuing the bad guy who swiped Mifune's ceremonial sword.

There's some terrific action, to be sure, which should come as no surprise to anyone who saw Sholder's impressive sleeper *The Hidden*. The frenetic pace, however, provides scant opportunity to flesh out the two leads, let alone any of the supporting cast.

•

RENT-A-COP

1988, 95 mins, US Ⓥ ⦿ col

Dir Jerry London ***Prod*** Raymond Wagner ***Scr*** Dennis Shryack, Michael Blodgett ***Ph*** Giuseppe Rotunno ***Ed*** Robert Lawrence ***Mus*** Jerry Goldsmith ***Art*** Tony Masters

Act Burt Reynolds, Liza Minnelli, James Remar, Richard Masur, Dionne Warwick, Bernie Casey (Kings Road)

Pic, a cheesy little crime thriller, starts off promisingly as a sort of follow-up to Burt Reynolds's *Sharky's Machine*, with him working again with fellow cop Bernie Casey on a big drug bust. Nutcase James Remar wipes everybody out except Reynolds, who is suspected of being crooked and bounced from the force.

He gets work as a "rent-a-cop," undercover (dressed as a Santa Claus) in a department store. In an awkwardly staged but key subplot, Liza Minnelli, as a Chicago hooker, has been saved from Remar by Reynolds and now attaches herself to him for protection.

Reynolds looks bored and is boring here, with an ill-fitting toupe that is downright embarrassing from one closeup angle. Minnelli is a lot of fun as the flamboyant prostie. Dionne Warwick is thoroughly wasted here as head of a call-girl ring. Remar is laughably hammy as the narcissistic killer.

•

REPLACEMENT KILLERS, THE

1998, 86 mins, US Ⓥ ⦿ ▭ col

Dir Antoine Fuqua ***Prod*** Brad Grey, Bernie Brillstein ***Scr*** Ken Sanzel ***Ph*** Peter Lyons ***Ed*** Jay Cassidy ***Mus*** Harry Gregson-Williams ***Art*** Naomi Shohan

Act Chow Yun-fat, Mira Sorvino, Michael Rooker, Jurgen Prochnow, Kenneth Tsang, Til Schweiger (Brillstein-Grey/WCG/Columbia)

A Westernization of the Hong Kong movies of Chow Yun-fat, here making his American debut, and exec producers John Woo and Terence Chang, this mechanical effort is studied rather than heartfelt.

Chow is on familiar ground as John Lee, a hired gun with a debt to pay to Manhattan-transplanted Asian crime czar Terence Wei (Kenneth Tsang). His final mission is to murder the seven-year-old boy of the cop (Michael Rooker) responsible for the death of Wei's son during a botched drug transaction. However, in a sequence that seems like a variation on the opening scene of Woo's *Face/Off*, a crisis of conscience prevents him from pulling the trigger.

On the way to the airport for his return to Shanghai, he contacts master forger Meg Coburn (Mira Sorvino) to get a phony passport. But Wei's trigger men descend and Lee and Cobun begin their long flight, pursued through New York discos, restaurants and a car wash.

First-time feature director Antoine Fuqua, a hot musicvid and commercials helmer, and scripter Ken Sanzel have obviously studied every slo-mo sequence and violently choreographed ballet of blood Hong Kong has served up in recent years.

The performances, too, have a rote quality. Chow is an elegant, soulful presence but he still needs significant quality time with a voice coach. Sorvino is once again in macha form, though for most of the pic's running time she fires off rounds of ammunition without coming close to doing physical injury. German star Til Schweiger's talents are squandered in the thankless role of one of the title characters.

•

REPLACEMENTS, THE

2000, 118 mins, US Ⓥ ⦿ col

Dir Howard Deutch ***Prod*** Dylan Sellers ***Scr*** Vince McKewin ***Ph*** Tak Fujimoto ***Ed*** Bud Smith, Seth Flaum ***Mus*** John Debney ***Art*** Dan Bishop

Act Keanu Reeves, Gene Hackman, Orlando Jones, Jon Favreau, Brooke Langton, Rhys Ifans (Bel Air/Warner)

Pic is a frankly formulaic but agreeably funny comedy about the has-beens, wannabes and never-weres recruited by team owners during a strike by pro footballers. By-the-numbers script obviously is based on the true-life misadventures of replacement players employed during the 1987 NFL strike. That no one in *Replacements* ever mentions the real-world precedent only adds to the air of unreality that permeates this feel-good fantasy.

The striking players in general, and snide quarterback Eddie Martel (Brett Cullen) in particular, are unflatteringly tarred by the same brush: They are "a bunch of bitchy millionaires" (according to team owner Edward O'Neil, played by Jack Warden) who have lost their passion for the sport. On the other hand, the game, not the fame, is still the most important thing for replacement players such as Shane Falco (Keanu Reeves), a once-promising college quarterback whose spirit was broken by a devastating Sugar Bowl loss. When veteran coach Jimmy McGinty (Gene Hackman) is plucked from retirement to assemble a replacement team for the Washington Sentinels, the underemployed Falco is at the top of a very short list of potential recruits. You have to accept that the other pickup players on the ersatz Sentinels lineup will be a sitcom-flavored, demographics-conscious mix of aggressively colorful oddballs, eccentrics and hair-trigger brutes.

On the sidelines, chief cheerleader Annabelle Farrell (Brooke Langton) tries to assemble a new squad of limber lovelies—evidently, the regular cheerleaders went out on strike, too—and winds up settling for a crew of hot-to-trot lap dancers.

Although nearly two hours long, The *Replacements* takes a brisk trot over familiar territory and never seems padded or unduly protracted. Director Howard Deutch manages to make even the hoariest of cliches acceptable, if not entirely credible, by moving full speed ahead.

•

REPO MAN

1984, 94 mins, US Ⓥ ⦿ col

Dir Alex Cox ***Prod*** Jonathan Wacks, Peter McCarthy ***Scr*** Alex Cox ***Ph*** Robby Muller ***Ed*** Dennis Dolan ***Mus*** Steven Hufsteter, Humberto Larriva ***Art*** J. Rae Fox, Lynda Burbank

Act Harry Dean Stanton, Emilio Estevez, Olivia Barash, Tracey Walter, Sy Richardson, Vonetta McGee (Edge City/Universal)

Repo Man has the type of unerring energy that leaves audiences breathless and entertained. While the title, referring to the people who repossess cars from those behind on their payments, might suggest a low-budget, gritty, realistic venture, the truth exists somewhat on the other end of the spectrum.

The more conventional aspects of the script deal with an aimless young man, wonderfully underplayed by Emilio Estevez, who falls in with a crowd of repo men and takes to the "intense" lifestyle with ease.

Director-writer Alex Cox establishes the offbeat nature of the film from the start. In the opening scene, a state trooper stops a speeder and on a routine check of his trunk is blasted by a flash of light leaving him merely a smoldering pair of boots. This aspect of the story, centering on a 1964 Chevy Malibu, begins to have significance only later.

The initial plot thrust involves Otto Maddox (Estevez) and Bud (Harry Dean Stanton), the veteran repo man who teaches him the ropes. However, these are certainly tame facets as a story of alien invaders evolves. The ever reliable Stanton turns in yet another indelible portrait of a seamy lowlife while Estevez registers as a charismatic and talented actor. [A TV version, prepared by Cox himself, runs 99 mins.]

•

REPORT TO THE COMMISSIONER
(UK: OPERATION UNDERCOVER)

1975, 112 mins, US Ⓥ col

Dir Milton Katselas ***Prod*** Mike Frankovich ***Scr*** Abby Mann, Ernest Tidyman ***Ph*** Mario Tosi ***Ed*** David Blewitt ***Mus*** Elmer Bernstein ***Art*** Robert Clatworthy

Act Michael Moriarty, Yaphet Kotto, Susan Blakely, Hector Elizondo, William Devane, Richard Gere (United Artists)

Report to the Commissioner is a superb suspense drama of the tragic complexities of law enforcement.

Based on the novel by James Mills, it tells in flashback why Michael Moriarty, an idealistic new dectective, is being harassed to provide an alibi for the death of Susan Blakely, an undercover narc killed accidentally in the pad she shares with bigtime dealer Tony King. Hector Elizondo and Michael McGuire are medium-level detectives whose ambitions overcome their adherence to procedure, and lay the foundations for Moriarty's unexpected fate. Yaphet Kotto, in an outstanding performance, is Moriarty's senior partner. Richard Gere is very good as a small-time pimp.

•

REPOSSESSED

1990, 84 mins, US Ⓥ ⦿ col

Dir Bob Logan ***Prod*** Steve Wizan ***Scr*** Bob Logan ***Ph*** Michael Margulies ***Ed*** Jeff Freeman ***Mus*** Charles Fox ***Art*** Shay Austin

Act Linda Blair, Ned Beatty, Leslie Nielsen, Anthony Starke, Lana Schwab, Thom J. Sharp (New Line)

Nonstop silliness keeps this frightless spoof of *The Exorcist* entertaining enough to keep an undemanding audience happy. Linda Blair, her teeth and hair encrusted with green gunk, once again plays the devil's host. Leslie Nielsen plays the priest pulled out of retirement to battle Satan. This time the rematch is staged on national TV.

Blair is a housewife who prepares (what else?) split-pea soup for her suburban family until Satan flies out of the television during an evangelist show and takes possession of her soul. Earnest young priest Anthony Starke is called in to help, but he's no match for swivel-neck, so Nielsen has to be persuaded.

No joke is too tasteless, no gag too weak, as the script romps along trying to pad its thin premise out to feature-length. Starke more than holds up his end as the timid clergyman, and Ned Beatty and Lana Schwab are a hoot as the evangelists. Production values are fairly generous.

•

REPULSION

1965, 104 mins, UK Ⓥ b/w

Dir Roman Polanski ***Prod*** Gene Gutowski ***Scr*** Roman Polanski, Gerard Brach, David Stone ***Ph*** Gilbert Taylor ***Ed*** Alastair McIntyre ***Mus*** Chico Hamilton ***Art*** Seamus Flannery

Act Catherine Deneuve, Ian Hendry, John Fraser, Patrick Wymark, Yvonne Furneaux, Renee Houston (Compton/Tekli)

Repulsion is a classy, truly horrific psychological drama in which Polish director Roman Polanski draws out a remarkable performance from young French thesp, Catherine Deneuve. Polanski, who wrote the original screenplay with Gerard Brach, uses his technical resources and the abilities of his thesps to build up a tense atmosphere of evil.

A notable plus is Polanski's use of sound. There are two brief sequences, for instance, when the young heroine tosses in her bed as she listens to the muted sound of her sister and her lover in the next room. The moans and ecstatic whimperings of the love act is a dozen times more effective and sensual than any glimpse of the lovers in bed.

Deneuve is a youngster working in a beauty shop, a deliberately sharp contrast to the drab apartment which she shares with her flighty elder sister. The girl is sexually repressed, deeply attracted to the thought of men but at the same time loathing the thought of them. Her daydreaming grows into erotic sexual fantasies, and when her sister and boyfriend leave her for a few days while they go on an Italian vacation, her loneliness and imagination take hold and insanity sets in.

Deneuve, without much dialog, handles a very difficult chore with insight and tact. John Fraser plays her would-be boyfriend likeably.

•

REQUIEM FOR A HEAVYWEIGHT
(UK: BLOOD MONEY)

1962, 85 mins, US b/w

Dir Ralph Nelson ***Prod*** David Susskind ***Scr*** Rod Serling ***Ph*** Arthur J. Ornitz ***Ed*** Carl Lerner ***Mus*** Laurence Rosenthal ***Art*** Burr Smidt

Act Anthony Quinn, Jackie Gleason, Mickey Rooney, Julie Harris, Stanley Adams, Cassius Clay (Columbia)

Rod Serling's poignant portrait of the sunset of a prize-fighter has lost some of its dramatic weight in the transition from the very small to the very large screen. However, it still packs considerable punch as a character study, although its action has slowed to where the plot padding is often obvious.

Some of the casting, no doubt done for authenticity and atmosphere, has boomeranged. Julie Harris plays her employment counselor as though she never really believed in the character. Casting actual boxing personalities is atmospheric but distracting and often ludicrous, particularly an amateurish bit by Jack Dempsey.

The performances of Quinn and Gleason are equally matched and carry the picture, no small chore. Quinn's punchy, inarticulate behemoth is so painfully natural that one winces when he feels pain, whether to his body or his feelings. Gleason is amazingly fine. He's weak, crafty, shiftly and still a little pathetic.

Mickey Rooney, hampered with some bad makeup, is warm and sympathetic as Army, the trainer, but doesn't really shine except for one card-playing scene. It's the only funny bit in the pic and he steals it from under Gleason's nose. The plot contains some glaring implausibilities.

•

RESCUERS, THE

1977, 76 mins, US Ⓥ col

Dir Wolfgang Reitherman, John Lounsbery, Art Stevens ***Prod*** Wolfgang Reitherman ***Scr*** Larry Clemmons, Ken Anderson, Vance Gerry, David Michener, Burny Mattinson, Frank Thomas, Fred Lucky, Ted Berman, Dick Sebast *Ed* James Melton, Jim Koford *Mus* Artie Butler *Art* Don Griffith (Walt Disney)

Four years of work were invested on this $7.5 million production and the expense, care, and expertise shows.

An admirably simple story [suggested by *The Rescuers* and *Miss Bianca* by Margery Sharp] about two mice (voiced by Bob Newhart and Eva Gabor) who embark on a quest to rescue a kidnapped orphan girl (Michelle Stacy) from the clutches of an evil witch (Geraldine Page).

There's real terror in the story, and the Gothic setting of the swamp where the girl is held captive; the maudlin pitfalls of the plot are avoided through deft use of humor, and the plucky character of the young captive.

Among the most memorable sequences are two hilarious ascents by a goofy bird named Orville, who takes the mice on their rescue mission.

1977: NOMINATION: Best Song ("Someone's Waiting for You")

•

RESCUERS DOWN UNDER, THE
1990, 74 mins, US Ⓥ ⦿ col
Dir Hendel Butoy, Mike Gabriel *Prod* Thomas Schumacher *Scr* Jim Cox, Karey Kirkpatrick, Byron Simpson, Joe Ranft *Ph* John Aardal, Chris Beck, Mary E. Lescher, Gary W. Smith, Chuck Warren *Ed* Michael Kelly *Mus* Bruce Broughton *Art* Maurice Hunt (Walt Disney)

This sort-of sequel to the 1977 hit *The Rescuers* boasts reasonably solid production values and fine character voices. Too bad they're set against such a mediocre story that adults may duck.

The bare-bones storyline hinges on a little boy who inexplicably cavorts with animals in Dolittle-esque fashion, including a huge golden eagle, a species apparently indigenous to the Aussie Outback. The bird is the prey of an evil hunter, McLeach (voiced by George C. Scott), who kidnaps the boy, resulting in a round-the-world call for those fearless mice of the Rescue Aid Society to come a-runnin'.

From there it's a simple quest pic, as mice Bernard (Bob Newhart), Miss Bianca (Eva Gabor) and guide Jake (Tristan Rogers) fumble their way through the jungle, with Bernard poised to pop the question to his rodent love only to be interrupted by one threat after another.

The film is not a musical. Instead, the producers have gone the action-adventure route, adding comic relief based largely on an awkward albatross named Wilbur (John Candy). Bruce Broughton augments the action immeasurably with his strongest score since *Silverado*.

•

RESERVOIR DOGS
1992, 105 mins, US Ⓥ ⦿ ▭ col
Dir Quentin Tarantino *Prod* Lawrence Bender *Scr* Quentin Tarantino *Ph* Andrzej Sekula *Ed* Sally Menke *Mus* Karyn Rachtman (sup.) *Art* David Wasco
Act Harvey Keitel, Tim Roth, Michael Madsen, Chris Penn, Steve Buscemi, Lawrence Tierney (Live America)

A show-off piece of filmmaking that put debut writer-director Quentin Tarantino on the map, *Reservoir Dogs* is an intense, bloody, in-your-face crime drama about a botched robbery and its aftermath, colorfully written in vulgar gangster vernacular and well played by a terrific cast.

Strikingly shot and funny opening scene has eight criminals at breakfast arguing about the true meaning of Madonna's "Like a Virgin." Script fractures very cleverly into an intricate flashback structure that mixes the post-robbery mess with telling character and plot details from the planning stages.

To put it chronologically, crime kingpin Lawrence Tierney and son Chris Penn recruit six pros to whom they assign false, color-themed names, so that no one will know anything about the others. The diamond heist at an L.A. jewelry store goes awry, however, when it becomes apparent the cops have been tipped off.

Hotheaded Harvey Keitel takes his injured cohort, Tim Roth, to a hideout where they are soon joined by Steve Buscemi. As they ponder who the rat may have been, in comes psychotic Michael Madsen with a hostage cop. This launches the bloodbath for real.

Tarantino's complex plot construction works very well, relieving the warehouse setting's claustrophobia. Dialogue is snappy, imaginative and loaded with threats, and the director, presumably with the help of Keitel, has assembled a perfect cast.

•

RESTLESS YEARS, THE
1958, 86 mins, US ▭ b/w
Dir Helmut Kautner *Prod* Ross Hunter *Scr* Edward Anhalt *Ph* Ernest Laszlo *Ed* Al Joseph *Mus* Joseph Gershenson *Art* Alexander Golitzen, Philip Barber
Act John Saxon, Sandra Dee, Teresa Wright, James Whitmore, Luana Patten, Margaret Lindsay (Universal)

A touching account of adolescence and some of its problems as compounded by adult density, *The Restless Years* is based on Patricia Joudry's play, *Teach Me How to Cry*. In almost the first line of dialog, Sandra Dee is described as an illegitimate child. Her problems arise out of this and the fact that her unwed mother (Teresa Wright) has never recovered from the desertion by the father.

Everyone in town, apparently, knows the story except Dee. The girl begins to grow up when a new boy in town (John Saxon), who doesn't know or doesn't care about local gossip and prejudice, meets her and falls in love. His life is complicated by his luckless father (James Whitmore) who has come back to his home town to achieve the success that has eluded him elsewhere.

It is a period piece, with the dressmaker mother of an illegitimate child, and would have been more plausible if it had been played in period. But granting this, it has a feeling of poetry and sensitivity. Dee gives the picture its strongest sense of reality.

•

RESTORATION
1995, 118 mins, US Ⓥ ⦿ col
Dir Michael Hoffman *Prod* Cary Brokaw, Andy Paterson, Sarah Ryan Black *Scr* Rupert Walters *Ph* Oliver Stapleton *Ed* Garth Craven *Mus* John Newton Howard *Art* Eugenio Zanetti
Act Robert Downey, Jr., Sam Neill, David Thewlis, Polly Walker, Meg Ryan, Ian McKellen (Segue/Avenue/Miramax)

Resplendent in its evocation of teeming, gaudy, plague-stricken 17th-century England, *Restoration* earns an instant place in contempo screen history for converting a reported $18.5 million budget into a lavish, old-school period epic. Sweeping yet intimate drama boasts an exemplary cast headed by Robert Downey, Jr., who does bravura work as a wastrel physician.

In 1660, the Stuart monarchy, restored to the throne after a decade of dour Puritan rule, unleashes a long pent-up torrent of hedonistic and intellectual energies. Embodying both, Robert Merivel (Downey) is a doctor who devotes more passion to whoring than to his patients, despite the warnings of his father and the example of his colleague and best friend, John Pearce (David Thewlis).

Summoned to the palace, Merivel finds himself a favored courtier of King Charles II (Sam Neill). When the king bids him, as a ruse, to marry the royal mistress but not, under any circumstances, fall in love with her, Merivel approaches a precipice. And falls. Celia (Polly Walker), his gorgeous but untouchable wife, scorns him as the sodden fool he has become.

Besides slipping in tone from engagingly ribald to earnest, pic's latter stages prove the downside of picaresque stories: the unfolding episodes can feel more arbitrary than necessary, leaving the characters more as pawns of chance (or authorial whimsy) than architects of their own fates.

Director Michael Hoffman handles his fine cast with a consistency that also distinguishes pic's visual elegance and striking re-creation of England during one of its most tumultuous periods.

1995: Best Art Direction, Costume Design

•

RESURRECTION
1980, 103 mins, US Ⓥ col
Dir Daniel Petrie *Prod* Renee Missel, Howard Rosenman *Scr* Lewis John Carlino *Ph* Mario Tosi *Ed* Rita Roland *Mus* Maurice Jarre *Art* Paul Sylbert
Act Ellen Burstyn, Sam Shepard, Richard Farnsworth, Roberts Blossom (Universal)

Resurrection, an unusual supernatural drama about a faith healer, gives Ellen Burstyn a shot at a tour-de-force performance, but never comes into strong enough focus dramatically or philosophically. The overly prosaic style of director Daniel Petrie and the underdeveloped screenplay inhibit her from exerting her full range of emotions.

She begins as a housewife who gives her husband a sports car, only to have it cause his death in a crash which leaves her legs paralyzed. During her laborious recovery period, she discovers that her close brush with death has given her the power of healing by the laying on of hands. There is commendably little sensationalism, but not enough thoughtful exploration. Petrie's filming makes the pic resemble a soap opera.

1980: NOMINATIONS: Best Actress (Ellen Burstyn), Supp. Actress (Eva Le Gallienne)

•

RETREAT, HELL!
1952, 94 mins, US Ⓥ b/w
Dir Joseph H. Lewis *Prod* Milton Sperling *Scr* Milton Sperling, Ted Sherdeman *Ph* Warren Lynch *Ed* Folmar Blangsted *Mus* William Lava *Art* Edward Carrerre
Act Frank Lovejoy, Richard Carlson, Russ Tamblyn, Anita Louise, Ned Young, Lamont Johnson (United States/Warner)

The fighting Marines get a film salute in *Retreat, Hell!*, a topnotch war drama blending some celluloid rah-rah with tense action, and generally enacted with effectiveness. Title is lifted from the historic remark credited to Gen Oliver P. Smith: "Retreat, hell! We're just advancing in a different direction."

Film has a personal equation, detailing the broader battle action through its effect on cast principals such as Frank Lovejoy, battalion commander; Richard Carlson, a "retread" captain from World War II called away from a happy home life to take up arms again; Russ Tamblyn, youthful enlistee who wants to carry on a family tradition of service in the Marine Corps; and Ned Young, a Marine regular.

Joseph H. Lewis's direction guides the footage quickly and interestingly.

•

RETURN FROM THE ASHES
1965, 108 mins, UK ▭ b/w
Dir J. Lee Thompson *Prod* J. Lee Thompson *Scr* Julius Epstein *Ph* Christopher Challis *Ed* Russell Lloyd *Mus* John Dankworth *Art* Michael Stringer
Act Maximilian Schell, Samantha Eggar, Ingrid Thulin, Herbert Lom, Talitha Pol, Vladek Sheybal (Mirisch)

Return from the Ashes does not always reach its mark as a thriller. The production, filmed in England, carries the makings of a suspenseful melodrama but in development is early contrived.

The screenplay based on a novel by Hubert Monteilhet builds around a plot for the perfect murder by an unscrupulous Polish chess master married to one woman and in love with her stepdaughter. Set in Paris at the close of Second World War, when the wife, a Jewess, returns from tortured internment in Dachau to find her husband living with the younger woman, plottage concerns the Pole's passion for money as he does away first with one, then the other femme, to accomplish his goal.

Thompson, who also directs, establishes a tense mood frequently, but level of interest suffers from character fuzziness which occasionally clouds the issue.

Maximilian Schell delivers strongly in a blackhearted role, lending credence to the character through constantly underplaying his scenes. Samantha Eggar displays dramatic aptitude as the amoral stepdaughter, Fabi, whose entry into her bath provides one of the highlights of the film.

•

RETURN FROM WITCH MOUNTAIN
1978, 93 mins, US Ⓥ col
Dir John Hough *Prod* Ron Miller, Jerome Courtland *Scr* Malcolm Marmorstein *Ph* Frank Phillips *Ed* Bob Bring *Mus* Lalo Schifrin *Art* John B. Mansbridge, Jack Senter
Act Bette Davis, Christopher Lee, Kim Richards, Ike Eisenmann, Jack Soo, Anthony James (Walt Disney)

Kim Richards and Ike Eisenmann reprise their roles from *Escape to Witch Mountain* (1975) as sister and brother from another world, this time back on Earth for a vacation, courtesy of space traveler Uncle Bene (Denver Pyle). Siblings get a quick test of their psychic powers as mad scientist Christopher Lee and accomplice Bette Davis are testing their mind-control device on henchman Anthony James—when Eisenmann saves James from falling off a building by anti-gravity display, Lee sees the youngster as his meal ticket to world power.

Film is basically a chase caper, as Richards tries to find her brother, aided by a junior bunch of Dead End Kids, Christian Juttner, Brad Savage, Poindexter and Jeffrey Jacquet. Despite an extrasensory link between the siblings (they communicate via telepathy, and can also make objects move at will), Lee has Eisenmann strait-jacketed with his device, so he can use youngster's "molecular reorganization" powers to his own purposes.

Eisenmann and Richards have matured considerably since original. Lee makes one of the best Disney villains in years, but Davis doesn't quite click as his partner in crime.

•

RETURN OF A MAN CALLED HORSE, THE
1976, 125 mins, US Ⓥ ⦿ ⊏⊐ col
Dir Irvin Kershner ***Prod*** Terry Morse Jr. ***Scr*** Jack De Witt ***Ph*** Owen Roizman ***Ed*** Michael Kahn ***Mus*** Laurence Rosenthal ***Art*** Stewart Campbell
Act Richard Harris, Gale Sondergaard, Geoffrey Lewis, Bill Lucking, Jorge Luke, Claudio Brook (United Artists)

The Return of a Man Called Horse is a visually stunning sequel, again starring Richard Harris as an English nobleman who this time returns to the American west to save his adopted Indian tribe from extinction.

Irvin Kershner's film is handsome, leisurely, placid to the point of being predictable but dotted with some action highlights; in particular, Harris encores a physical torture-ritual, explicit enough to drive some audiences to the concession stand.

Jack De Witt wrote the original *Horse* script from a Dorothy M. Johnson story, published in 1950 in the old *Collier's* mag.

De Witt herein has extended the story, bringing Harris back west again to find his tribe wasted and dispossessed by land poacher Geoffrey Lewis.

•

RETURN OF DR. FU MANCHU, THE
1930, 73 mins, US b/w
Dir Rowland V. Lee ***Scr*** Florence Ryerson, Lloyd Corrigan ***Ph*** Archie J. Stout
Act Warner Oland, Neil Hamilton, Jean Arthur, O. P. Heggie, William Austin, Evelyn Hall (Paramount)

Another chapter in the lurid melodramatic series made more or less from the detective stories by Sax Rohmer, English writer. As a picture it's absurd.

Picture has a brisk opening. Fu Manchu (Warner Oland) having been apparently killed in the previous picture, it became necessary to bring him to life again in an elaborate Chinese funeral. The archdemon escapes from his own coffin by a spring door, while an Oriental attendant is sealing the casket with molten lead. He takes up the trail of Dr. Petrie all over and the story becomes a checker game between the wily Celestial and the super detective, Nayland Smith.

Picture has a nicely staged wedding scene with Jean Arthur looking remarkably beautiful as the bride. Neil Hamilton does all that is possible to hold up the puppet role of the hero and O. P. Heggie is once more the super-human cool Inspector Nayland Smith.

•

RETURN OF FRANK JAMES, THE
1940, 92 mins, US Ⓥ ⦿ col
Dir Fritz Lang ***Prod*** Kenneth Macgowan ***Scr*** Sam Hellman ***Ph*** George Barnes, William V. Skall ***Ed*** Walter Thompson ***Mus*** David Buttolph ***Art*** Richard Day, Wiard B. Ihnen
Act Henry Fonda, Gene Tierney, Jackie Cooper, John Carradine, Henry Hull, J. Edward Bromberg (20th Century-Fox)

Jesse James, under the sponsorship of 20th Century-Fox, was murdered a year ago by those cowards, the Ford brothers. This season, with vengeance rankling in his breast, Jesse's older brother, Frank, returns to even the score. That he does, in obedience to Sam Hellman's script, but it's pretty slow stuff in the telling. Frank's no cinematic match for Jesse, which appears to be Will Hays's fault more than anyone else's. Rule 16a in the book is that a bad man can't be a hero. Which leaves Hellman in the paradoxical position of having Frank responsible for deaths of three men who never so much as tasted a single slug from his six-shooter. Effort to put wings on Frank is too much. Angelic aspect bogs the plot and instead of flying it can do no better than plod for a slow 92 minutes.

From standpoint of production and cast, Darryl Zanuck has spared nary a horse. It's filled with ah-evoking outdoor scenes and nostalgically impressive western streets and indoor sets. Henry Fonda, underplaying Jesse James's older brother, Frank, in typical quiet style, is impressive; Jackie Cooper, as his kid buddy, shows a maturing dramatic sense although the pout is still there; Henry Hull, as a southern newspaper editor, overacts like no one else can, but is tremendously appealing despite it; John Carradine is a duly hissable villain as Bob Ford; J. Edward Bromberg earns laughs as a dumb railroad detective; and Donald Meek, Eddie Collins and George Barbier are, as usual, good for smiles.

Only member of the cast with whom fault can be found is Gene Tierney, making her film debut. Tierney's plenty pretty but for oomph she just isn't. Playing the role of a naive gal reporter to whom Frank takes a fancy, she seems to just lack what it takes to make an impression on the screen.

•

RETURN OF SWAMP THING, THE
1989, 88 mins, US Ⓥ ⦿ col
Dir Jim Wynorski ***Prod*** Ben Melniker, Michael Uslan ***Scr*** Derek Spencer, Grant Morris ***Ph*** Zoran Hockstalter ***Ed*** Leslie Rosenthal ***Mus*** Church Cirino ***Art*** Robb Wilson King
Act Louis Jourdan, Heather Locklear, Sarah Douglas, Dick Durock, Ace Mask, Joey Sagal (Lightyear)

The Return of Swamp Thing is scientific hokum without the fun. Second attempt to film the DC Comics character will disappoint all but the youngest critters.

They may be entertained by watching crossbred creatures squirm helplessly or buy into the Swamp Thing's (Dick Durock) instant love for Heather Locklear. He's a plant; she's a vegetarian.

Pic is set against a backdrop of evil where Dr. Arcane (Louis Jourdan) has turned the disco-looking basement of his antebellum mansion into a mutant lab inhabited by failed experiments as he tries to discover the genetic equivalent of the Fountain of Youth.

The Swamp Thing escaped, but most of his more unfortunate distant cousins of the Petri dish have not, like the cockroach/man stuck on his back flailing his legs while Drs. Lana Zurrell and Rochelle (Sarah Douglas and Ace Mask, respectively) lament another misfire.

Locklear arrives at the scene to confront Jourdan, her evil stepfather, who has never quite adequately explained her mother's mysterious death. It doesn't take a genius to figure out Mom's fate, though it takes the dense Locklear character an hour and a half.

•

RETURN OF THE DRAGON
SEE: MENG LONG GUO JIANG

•

RETURN OF THE FLY
1959, 78 mins, Ⓥ ⦿ ⊏⊐ b/w
Dir Edward L. Bernds ***Prod*** Bernard Glasser ***Scr*** Edward L. Bernds ***Ph*** Brydon Baker ***Ed*** Richard C. Meyer ***Mus*** Paul Sawtell, Bert Shefter ***Art*** Lyle R. Wheeler, John Mansbridge
Act Vincent Price, Brett Halsey, John Sutton, David Frankham, Dan Seymour, Danielle De Metz (20th Century-Fox)

Return of the Fly was conceived and executed as a sequel to *The Fly* in order to cash in on the latter's reputation as a grosser. With justice, it will be unfavorably compared with the first, which was a superior horror film.

The sequel's amateurishly contrived plot picks up at the death of the inventor's widow, who had been acquitted of murdering him. Vincent Price, the only actor carried over from the original, explains to the inventor's now-grown son, played by Brett Halsey, the plot of the other picture.

What follows is one unmotivated episode after another, loosely tied to the theme that the son, in following in his father's footsteps, will come to the same bad end. Suspense is attempted by making the son's assistant a traitor who is trying to steal the secret of the "matter transmitter." Horror is achieved when the assistant uses the device to scramble a policeman's corpse with a guinea pig and to scramble the inventor's scientist son with a fly.

Considering the script's limitations, the cast does fairly well. The picture is technically slick and the special effects—for which no credit is given—are good.

•

RETURN OF THE JEDI
1983, 133 mins, US Ⓥ ⦿ ⊏⊐ col
Dir Richard Marquand ***Prod*** Howard Kazanjian ***Scr*** Lawrence Kasdan, George Lucas ***Ph*** Alan Hume ***Ed*** Sean Barton, Marcia Lucas, Duwayne Dunham ***Mus*** John Williams ***Art*** Norman Reynolds
Act Mark Hamill, Harrison Ford, Carrie Fisher, Billy Dee Williams, Anthony Daniels, Peter Mayhew (Lucasfilm/20th Century-Fox)

Jedi is the conclusion of the middle trilogy of George Lucas's planned nine-parter and suffers a lot in comparison to the initial *Star Wars* [1977], when all was fresh. One of the apparent problems is neither the writers nor the principal performers are putting in the same effort.

Telegraphed in the preceding *The Empire Strikes Back* [1980], the basic dramatic hook this time is Mark Hamill's quest to discover—and do something about—the true identity of menacing Darth Vader, while resisting the evil intents of the Emperor (Ian McDiarmid).

Hamill is not enough of a dramatic actor to carry the plot load here, especially when his partner in so many scenes is really little more than an oversized gas pump, even if splendidly voiced by James Earl Jones.

Even worse, Harrison Ford, who was such an essential element of the first two outings, is present more in body than in spirit this time, given little to do but react to special effects. And it can't be said that either Carrie Fisher or Billy Dee Williams rise to previous efforts. But Lucas and director Richard Marquand have overwhelmed these performer flaws with a truly amazing array of creatures, old and new, plus the familiar space hardware.

1983: Best Special Visual Effects

NOMINATIONS: Best Art Direction, Original Score, Sound, Sound Editing

•

RETURN OF THE LIVING DEAD, THE
1985, 90 mins, US Ⓥ ⦿ col
Dir Dan O'Bannon ***Prod*** Tom Fox ***Scr*** Dan O'Bannon ***Ph*** Jules Brenner ***Ed*** Robert Gordon ***Mus*** Matt Clifford ***Art*** William Stout
Act Clu Gulager, James Karen, Don Calfa, Thom Mathews, Beverly Randolph, John Philbin (Hemdale/Fox)

Early on here, one character asks another if he's seen the original *Night of the Living Dead*, then goes on to explain that the 1968 film altered the facts concerning a real-life zombie attack on the local populace.

Virtually the entire action of the rather threadbare production [from a story by Rudy Ricci, John Russo and Russell Streiner] shuttles among three locations—a medical supply warehouse, where numerous zombies have been sent by the Army; a nearby mortuary; and an adjacent cemetery, where a bunch of punks frolic before being chased out by corpses risen from their graves.

From then on, it's the same old story, as unusually vigorous, athletic zombies besiege the motley bunch of human beings holed up in the vicinity and eat the brains of anyone they get their hands on.

Director Dan O'Bannon deserves considerable credit for creating a terrifically funny first half-hour of exposition, something in which he is greatly aided by the goofball performance of James Karen as a medical supply know-it-all.

•

RETURN OF THE LIVING DEAD PART II
1988, 89 mins, US Ⓥ ⦿ col
Dir Ken Weiderhorn ***Prod*** Tom Fox ***Scr*** Ken Weiderhorn ***Ph*** Robert Elswit ***Ed*** Charles Bornstein ***Mus*** J. Peter Robinson
Act James Karen, Thom Mathews, Michael Kenworthy, Marsha Dietlein, Dana Ashbrook, Philip Bruns (Greenfox/Lorimar)

Billed as a comedy/horror flick, *Return of the Living Dead Part II* is neither scary nor funny and adds salt in the wound with an obnoxious soundtrack of grating rock music.

This time a canister falls off an army truck and three kids—including Jesse Wilson (Michael Kenworthy)—discover it. Curiosity leads Jesse's two friends to fool around with a few buttons and suddenly a weird fog spews from the container, awakening a ghoul who is packed inside as neatly as tuna fish.

As the fog spreads, it is a call to arms for the occupants of a cemetery, unleashing a throng of decaying cadavers. The balance of the film is a prolonged chase scene as these creatures pursue Jesse, Lucy (Marsha Dietlein), Tom (Dana Ashbrook) and Doc (Philip Bruns) through the streets of a small town.

The overall effects of *Living Dead* is supposed to be tongue-in-cheek but turns out to be foot in mouth as dialogue seems aimed at four-year-olds. The only saving grace in a totally misguided effort is the performance of character actor Bruns who is quite funny as the slightly off-the-wall doctor.

•

RETURN OF THE LIVING DEAD III
1993, 97 mins, US Ⓥ ⦿ col
Dir Brian Yuzna ***Prod*** Gary Schmoeller, Brian Yuzna ***Scr*** John Penney ***Ph*** Gerry Lively ***Ed*** Christopher Roth ***Mus*** Barry Goldberg ***Art*** Anthony Tremblay
Act Mindy Clarke, J. Trevor Edmond, Kent McCord, Sarah Douglas, James T. Callahan, Basil Wallace (Trimark)

Playing it straight, sans humor, *Return of the Living Dead III* departs from the first two films of the horror series that began in 1985. In an effort to capture the youth market, this B-pic emphasizes a love story gone awry at the expense of constructing a scary plot.

Tale begins with two attractive lovebirds, Curt (J. Trevor Edmond) and Julie (Mindy Clarke), sneaking into his father's army research lab, where experiments are conducted with Trioxin, a chemical capable of bringing the dead back to life, which was introduced in the series' first installment. When Julie dies in a tragic motorcycle accident, the heartbroken Curt is determined to keep her alive by exposing her to the "magical" chemical.

Serving as background is the yarn of Curt's insensitive father (Kent McCord), about to be relieved from his top-ranking position by the Pentagon's new female chief (Sarah Douglas). Most of the pic consists of special effects that include piercing, vampirism and cannibalism. Pic boasts the dubious achievement of using five different special effects experts—the superior Sam Raimi's *Army of Darkness* reportedly held the previous record of a four-memeber crew. This may be why, after the story reaches its climax and resolution, pic goes on for another act, entirely composed of special effects.

•

RETURN OF THE MUSKETEERS, THE

1989, 94 mins, UK/France/Spain Ⓥ col

Dir Richard Lester ***Prod*** Pierre Spengler ***Scr*** George MacDonald Fraser ***Ph*** Bernard Lutic ***Ed*** John Victor Smith ***Mus*** Jean-Claude Petit ***Art*** Gil Parrondo

Act Michael York, Oliver Reed, Frank Finlay, C. Thomas Howell, Richard Chamberlain, Kim Cattrall (Burrill/Film debroc/Cine 5/Iberoamericana

In 1974 Richard Lester boosted his then-flagging career with *The Three Musketeers* and its sequel *The Four Musketeers*, lavish swashbucklers with a comic touch. His attempt at a comeback is, sadly, a stillborn event which looks as tired as its re-assembled cast.

It's 20 years since the four musketeers ordered the execution of the evil Milady De Winter. But now King Charles is dead, and his son Louis, a 10-year-old, reigns with his mother (a reprise by Geraldine Chaplin).

D'Artagnan (Michael York) is assigned to bring together his three former comrades to fight for the Queen and Cardinal. He quickly recruits Porthos (Frank Finlay) and Athos (Oliver Reed), together with the latter's son, Raoul (C. Thomas Howell); however, Aramis (Richard Chamberlain), now a womanizing Abbe, is reluctant to join the band.

There follows a complicated and sometimes hard to follow plot [from Alexandre Dumas's *Twenty Years After*] involving a failed attempt to rescue King Charles I of England from execution. According to this, the executioner of the king was actually Justine (Kim Cattrall), evil daughter of Milady, who's intent on avenging herself on the four musketeers who she blames for the death of her mother.

Pic is dedicated to Roy Kinnear, whose accidental death during production must have cast a pall over the entire project.

•

RETURN OF THE PINK PANTHER, THE

1975, 115 mins, UK Ⓥ ⊙ ⌴ col

Dir Blake Edwards ***Prod*** Blake Edwards ***Scr*** Frank Waldman, Blake Edwards ***Ph*** Geoffrey Unsworth ***Ed*** Tom Priestley ***Mus*** Henry Mancini ***Art*** Peter Mullins

Act Peter Sellers, Christopher Plummer, Catherine Schell, Herbert Lom, Peter Arne, Gregoire Aslan (United Artists)

The Return of the Pink Panther establishes Peter Sellers once again as the bane of the existence of chief detective Herbert Lom, who is forced to reinstate Sellers when the Pink Panther diamond is stolen from its native museum by a mysterious burglar.

Suspicion falls on Christopher Plummer, ostensibly retired phantom jewel thief who decides he must catch the real culprit to save himself. Catherine Schell plays Plummer's wife, who turns out to be a decoy in more ways than one.

Sellers's work takes him into contact with Peter Arne and Gregoire Aslan, native police under pressure from general Peter Jeffrey to find the gem: with befuddled concierge Victor Spinetti and perplexed bellboy Mike Grady, both at a posh Swiss resort hotel; and periodically with his valet Cato, played by Burt Kwouk.

All hands seem to be having a ball, especially Schell, whose unabashed amusement at Clouseau's seduction attempts often matches an audience's hilarity.

•

RETURN OF THE SECAUCUS SEVEN

1980, 110 mins, US Ⓥ col

Dir John Sayles ***Prod*** Jeffrey Nelson, William Aydelott ***Scr*** John Sayles ***Ph*** Austin de Besche ***Ed*** John Sayles ***Mus*** K. Mason Daring

Act Mark Arnott, Gordon Clapp, Maggie Cousineau, Brian Johnston, Adam LeFevre, John Sayles (Salsipuedes)

John Sayles has fashioned an admirable postmortem of the 1960s student left. Virtually the whole cast and crew make their feature debut here, and while not all the work is on an entirely professional level, earnestness and intelligence of the enterprise carry the day.

Structured like a well-built three-act play, drama is set at eight-year reunion of seven student activists who were arrested together in Secaucus, NJ, on their way to a Washington demonstration. As old cohorts and a few new companions gather at the New Hampshire farm of one of the couples, complicated history of romantic relationships within the group begins to be unravelled. A diagram of past and present liaisons would prove as dense as that for any soap opera.

Film is virtually wall-to-wall talk, all of it interesting and much of it rather witty.

•

RETURN OF THE SEVEN

1966, 95 mins, US Ⓥ ⌴ col

Dir Burt Kennedy ***Prod*** Ted Richmond ***Scr*** Larry Cohen ***Ph*** Paul Vogel ***Ed*** Bert Bates ***Mus*** Elmer Bernstein ***Art*** Jose Alguero

Act Yul Brynner, Robert Fuller, Julian Mateos, Warren Oates, Claude Akins, Elisa Montes (Mirisch)

Filmed in Spain by Mirisch, *Return of the Seven* is an unsatisfactory followup to John Sturges's *The Magnificent Seven*. Yul Brynner, sole holdover thesp, stars in a plodding cliche-ridden script.

Dreary screenplay reunites Brynner and two other members of the Sturges septet—Robert Fuller evidently in the old Steve McQueen part, and Julian Mateos filling the former Horst Buchholz role—when the latter is dragooned by Emilio Fernandez, psychotic Mexican rancher who enslaves local farmers to rebuild a village. Four new characters are recruited—girl-chasing Warren Oates, brooding Claude Akins, suave Virgilio Texeira and juvenile Jordan Christopher, latter in a dim dramatic feature debut.

Under Burt Kennedy's limp direction, players walk through their predictable dialog while rescuing Mateos, and provoking the long-awaited showdown with Fernandez. Elisa Montes is okay as Mateos's wife, and Fernando Rey is competent in a thankless role of a prayer-mumbling priest.

•

RETURN OF THE SOLDIER, THE

1982, 102 mins, UK Ⓥ col

Dir Alan Bridges ***Prod*** Anne Skinner, Simon Relph ***Scr*** Hugh Whitemore ***Ph*** Stephen Goldblatt ***Ed*** Laurence Mery Clark ***Mus*** Richard Rodney Bennett ***Art*** Luciana Arrighi

Act Julie Christie, Alan Bates, Glenda Jackson, Ann-Margret, Ian Holm, Frank Finlay (Brent Walker)

Alan Bates comes home from World War I with shell shock and is partly amnesiac. He does not remember his wife, played by Julie Christie with overdone snobbishness, but does recall a lower-class girl (Glenda Jackson) he loved as a young man and his doting cousin, latter played with feeling by Ann-Margret.

Christie allows Bates to see Jackson, now married and a bit dowdy. However the love is still there. A psychiatrist warns that bringing Bates back to normal might be dangerous, for he is probably concealing the tragedy of the death of his child from himself.

Stereotyped characters may have been more alive when the book [by Rebecca West] was written castigating the hollowness of a certain British class system. Today it is more quaint than anything else and fails to find the depth in these people to make them timeless.

•

RETURN OF THE TEXAS CHAINSAW MASSACRE, THE

1995, 102 mins, US Ⓥ col

Dir Kim Henkel ***Prod*** Robert Kuhn ***Scr*** Ken Henkel ***Ph*** Levie Isaacks ***Ed*** Sandra Adair ***Art*** Debbie Pastor

Act Renee Zellweger, Matthew McConaughey, Robert Jacks, Tony Perenski, Joe Stevens, Lisa Newmeyer (Return)

Not so much a sequel as an unofficial remake, Kim Henkel's *The Return of the Texas Chainsaw Massacre* manages the difficult feat of being genuinely scary and sharply self-satirical all at once. Pic may be too restrained in its violence to satisfy the full-bore gore hounds.

In his first effort as a feature director, writer Henkel (who co-wrote Tobe Hooper's original 1974 horror classic) is borderline sadistic when it comes to sustaining a mood of high voltage dread. Even some jaded horror fans will find it hard to take many extended scenes in which the threat of sudden, lethal brutality seems just a scream away.

Renee Zellweger (*Love and a .45*) stars as Jenny. On the night of her senior prom, she and three friends take the wrong turn down a dark country road and wind up terrorized by Vilmer (Matthew McConaughey), a homicidal towtruck driver. Jenny seeks refuge in the secluded office of Darla (Tony Perenski), a voluptuous, silicone-enhanced real estate agent who's fond of flashing her breasts at uninvited visitors. Unfortunately, Darla is in league with Vilmer. Even more unfortunately, both Darla and Vilmer are in league with Leatherface (Robert Jacks), the chainsaw-wielding maniac who, in Henkel's revisionist version of the story, has a lot in common with the gender-bending killer in *The Silence of the Lambs*.

Until it begins to fall apart in the last reel, *Return* is adept at keeping its audience in a constant state of jumpiness as Jenny tries to escape the old dark house where the Leatherface clan resides.

McConaughey goes way, way over the top with his mood swinging menace and trip-wire temper. Zellweger makes Jenny the most formidable scream queen since Jamie Lee Curtis went legit.

•

RETURN TO OZ

1985, 110 mins, US Ⓥ ⊙ col

Dir Walter Murch ***Prod*** Paul Maslansky ***Scr*** Walter Murch, Gill Dennis ***Ph*** David Watkin ***Ed*** Leslie Hodgson ***Mus*** David Shire ***Art*** Norman Reynolds

Act Nicol Williamson, Jean Marsh, Fairuza Balk, Piper Laurie, Matt Clark, Sean Barrett (Walt Disney/Silver Screen Partners II)

Return to Oz is an astonishingly somber, melancholy and, sadly, unengaging trip back to a favorite land of almost every American's youth. Straight dramatic telling of little Dorothy's second voyage to the Emerald City [based on *The Land of Oz* and *Ozma of Oz* by L. Frank Baum] employs an amusement park–full of imaginative characters and special effects, but a heaviness of tone and absence of narrative drive prevent the flights of fancy from getting off the ground.

Opening finds Dorothy back at home in Kansas but unable to sleep because of disturbing memories of her recent trip. Reacting harshly, Aunt Em and Uncle Henry decide the girl has become deranged and send her to a clinic to receive electroshock therapy from sinister nurse Jean Marsh and doctor Nicol Williamson.

After nearly a half-hour of these nightmarish goings-on, Dorothy and her talking chicken Billina are delivered to Oz, but not a very inviting section of it. Landed on the edge of the Deadly Desert, Dorothy soon discovers the Yellow Brick Road in disrepair, the Emerald City in ruins and her companions from the previous trip turned to stone.

Along the way, as before, Dorothy accumulates some helpful friends.

1985: NOMINATION: Best Visual Effects

•

RETURN TO PARADISE

1953, 90 mins, US col

Dir Mark Robson ***Prod*** Theron Warth ***Scr*** Charles Kaufman ***Ph*** Winton C. Hoch ***Ed*** Daniel Mandell ***Mus*** Dimitri Tiomkin

Act Gary Cooper, Roberta Haynes, Barry Jones, Moira MacDonald, John Hudson (Aspen)

The simplicity of authentic Samoan settings provides a strong, appealing background for this leisurely, idyllic, romantic drama, based on the *Mr. Morgan* portion of James A. Michener's bestselling *Return to Paradise*.

Gary Cooper protrays Morgan, a casual soldier of fortune taking his ease in the unhurried life of the island paradises. On one atoll where he decides to stay awhile, an island beauty attracts his attention to set the romance of the piece. For conflict there is the domination of the island and the natives by a missionary, a man who has forgotten the Bible teaches more than hellfire and damnation.

Cooper's delivery of the foot-loose South Seas wanderer is in his easy-going, understated style of histrionics and just right for the character and for the mood aimed by Mark Robson's direction. Opposite him is Roberta Haynes as the native girl, Maeva. Barry Jones makes his portrayal of the zealot, Pastor Cobbett, a performance gem. Moira MacDonald, three-quarters Polynesian and recruited in Samoa for the role, has natural appeal as the daughter.

Music is an important part of the production both in the native numbers recorded in the islands, where all of the lensing took place, and that cleffed by Dimitri Tiomkin.

•

RETURN TO PEYTON PLACE

1961, 123 mins, US Ⓥ ⌴ col

Dir Jose Ferrer ***Prod*** Jerry Wald ***Scr*** Ronald Alexander ***Ph*** Charles G. Clarke ***Ed*** David Bretherton ***Mus*** Franz Waxman ***Art*** Jack Martin Smith, Hans Peters

Act Carol Lynley, Jeff Chandler, Eleanor Parker, Mary Astor, Tuesday Weld, Robert Sterling (20th Century-Fox)

Basically *Return to Peyton Place* is a high-class soap opera. The screenplay preserves the nature of Grace Metalious's novel, alternately building three or four separate but related story veins into individual crescendos, then welding the moving parts into a single grand climax in which everything falls neatly into place.

The basic stories are: (1) Carol Lynley's, as the tyro novelist whose close-to-home fiction produces civic repercussions and whose romantic relations with her editor-publisher (Jeff Chandler) accelerate her maturity; (2) Tuesday Weld's, as the emotionally-troubled girl whose past misfortunes are soothed when Lynley's book sheds new light into the matter; and (3) Mary Astor's, as a super-possessive Peyton Place mother who attempts to wreck the marriage of her son.

Jose Ferrer's direction of this material is deliberate, but restrained and perceptive. The cast is a blend of polished veterans and young players. The lovely Lynley does a thoroughly capable job, although a shade more animation would have been desirable. But it is the veteran Astor who walks off with the picture.

•

RETURN TO THE BLUE LAGOON
1991, 100 mins, US Ⓥ col
Dir William A. Graham ***Prod*** William A. Graham ***Scr*** Leslie Stevens ***Ph*** Robert Steadman ***Ed*** Ronald J. Fagan ***Mus*** Basil Poledouris ***Art*** Jon Dowding
Act Milla Jovovich, Brian Krause, Lisa Pelikan, Courtney Phillips, Garette Patrick Ratcliff, Nana Coburn (Columbia/Price)

Return to the Blue Lagoon is a pointless spinoff of the 1980 hit, which was itself a remake of a 1949 British pic. Leslie Stevens's script [based on Henry DeVere Stacpoole's novel *The Garden of God*] has the original's leading characters found dead in a tiny boat along with their young son, who has survived the journey in fine shape.

But the tyke is soon put out to sea again to escape an outbreak of cholera on board the rescue ship and, along with straightlaced American Lisa Pelikan and her little daughter, washes up on the same tropical island his parents inhabited. Once the budding beauties hit adolescence and assume the bodies of international model Milla Jovovich and TV hunk Brian Krause, they are disturbed to find that "nothing's the same."

For propriety's sake, they marry, then they splash about a lot as they begin what promises to be a very long honeymoon. Only conflict crops up in the form of a visiting ship, which provides all sorts of trouble.

Vet TV director William A. Graham is content to stick to pretty pictures rather than create a strong feeling for isolated life through the accretion of telling detail. Jovovich manages to project some good sense and resilience along with her cover girl beauty; the 15-year-old Soviet native makes a decent impression in her first bigscreen leading role. Krause looks like he's straight off the Southern California beaches. Pic was lensed on Taveuni in the Fiji archipelago.

•

REUBEN, REUBEN
1983, 101 mins, US Ⓥ col
Dir Robert Ellis Miller ***Prod*** Walter Shenson, Julius J. Epstein ***Scr*** Julius J. Epstein ***Ph*** Peter Stein ***Ed*** Skip Lusk ***Mus*** Billy Goldenberg ***Art*** Peter Larkin
Act Tom Conti, Kelly McGillis, Roberts Blossom, Cynthia Harris, E. Katherine Kerr, Joel Fabiani (20th Century-Fox/Taft Entertainment)

About a leching, alcoholic Scottish poet making the New England campus circuit, *Reuben, Reuben* is exceptionally literate, with lines that carom with wit from the superb adaptation by Julius J. Epstein of a 1964 Peter De Vries novel [and the play *Spofford* by Herman Shumlin]. Epstein, with De Vries's blessing, merged three separate stories in the novel into the character of the rascal poet on the slide.

Helmsman Robert Ellis Miller draws solid performances from debuting actress Kelly McGillis, whose chic blond Vassar looks interestingly contrast, in this case, with her character's farmyard roots. She becomes the all-consuming obsession of Tom Conti as he lurches from one bottle and bed to another. Two of his sexual conquests on the poet's college town circuit are nicely and avariciously played by Cynthia Harris and E. Katherine Kerr.

But the film is a tour-de-force act for Conti (in his first U.S.-made film) and he captures the vulnerability of a man whose plunge into darkness suggests the emotional time most closely associated with 4 a.m.

1983: NOMINATIONS: Best Actor (Tom Conti), Adapted Screenplay

•

REUNION
1942, 101 mins, US b/w
Dir Jules Dassin ***Prod*** Joseph L. Mankiewicz ***Scr*** Jan Lustig, Marvin Borowsky, Marc Connolly ***Ph*** Robert Planke ***Ed*** Elmo Veron ***Mus*** Franz Waxman
Act Joan Crawford, John Wayne, Philip Dorn, Reginald Owen, Albert Basserman, John Carradine (M-G-M)

Reunion is another one of those dramas cooked up about the subjugation of the French by the German conquerors. Starting out with some promise, it falls apart at the halfway point. Attempts to generate a hot triangular romance with Joan Crawford as the pivot prove very tepid.

Story [from an original by Ladislas Bus-Fekete] opens just prior to move-in of the Germans to Paris, with rich playgirl Crawford engaged to French patriot and arms manufacturer Philip Dorn. On fall of the city, girl discovers that her intended is a renegade cooperating to the fullest with the Nazis. Disillusioned, she hides John Wayne, who has eluded the Gestapo, and gradually falls in love with him.

Direction by Jules Dassin lacks smoothness in pace, and dwells too long in many spots on character development and minor incidents.

•

REUNION
1989, 110 mins, France/W. Germany/UK Ⓥ col
Dir Jerry Schatzberg ***Prod*** Anne Francois ***Scr*** Harold Pinter ***Ph*** Bruno de Keyzer ***Ed*** Martine Barraque ***Mus*** Philippe Sarde ***Art*** Alexandre Trauner
Act Jason Robards, Christian Anholt, Samuel West, Francois Fabian, Maureen Kewin, Barbara Jefford (Ariane/FR3/NEF/Vertriebs/CLG/Tac/Arbo/Maran

This enormously impressive film ranks as one of the best of countless pics dealing with the rise of Nazism in Germany in the early 1930s.

Based on Fred Uhlman's autobiographical novel, drama is set in Stuttgart in 1933 and deals with the growing friendship between two schoolboys from different backgrounds: Hans (Christian Anholt), son of a Jewish doctor and World War I vet who, till now, was considered a pillar of the community; and the aristocratic Konrad (Samuel West), who's led a sheltered life, taught by private tutors, and who finds himself stimulated by the intelligent, sensitive Hans.

At the beginning of the year, portents of what's to come are few: small groups of Nazis march in the streets; a friend advises Hans's father to leave before Hitler takes over. Gradually, as the year progresses, the Fascist movement takes hold.

The long central part of the film is framed by a present-day narrative in which Hans, now Henry Strauss (Jason Robards), decides to return to Stuttgart to locate his parents' grave and to discover what happened to his old friend.

Director Jerry Schatzberg has made what probably is his best film to date, a sober, thoughtful pic that recreates a seemingly authentic world of 56 years ago.

•

REVENGE
1990, 124 mins, US Ⓥ ⊙ ▭ col
Dir Tony Scott ***Prod*** Hunt Lowry, Stanley Rubin ***Scr*** Jim Harrison, Jeffrey Fiskin ***Ph*** Jeffrey Kimball ***Ed*** Chris Lebenzon ***Mus*** Jack Nitzsche ***Art*** Michael Seymour, Benjamin Fernandez
Act Kevin Costner, Anthony Quinn, Madeleine Stowe, Sally Kirkland, James Gammon, Miguel Ferrer (New World/Rastar)

This far-from-perfect rendering of Jim Harrison's shimmering novella has a romantic sweep and elemental power that ultimately transcend its flaws. It's a contempo tale of a doomed love triangle in lawless Mexico.

As J. Cochran, a hotshot Navy pilot who retires after 12 years, Kevin Costner heads down to Puerto Vallarta for recreation at the home of a wealthy sportsman friend, Tibey (Anthony Quinn) and is right away smitten with his host's gorgeous and unhappy wife Miryea (Madeleine Stowe). Despite his friend's graciousness and reputation as a cold-blooded killer, Cochran takes the suicide plunge into passion, running off with Miryea for a sexual idyll.

The much-fiddled-with footage was eventually pasted into its current form, and though much is lost, the tale's simplicity, grace and subtlety shine through. All three elements of the love triangle are compelling, and as a crucial fourth character Mexico performs radiantly.

Stowe is a great screen beauty and is certainly a match for Costner's charisma. The magnificent Quinn as a political puppeteer is so rich and sympathetic that he threatens to steal away the audience despite his brutality.

•

REVENGE OF FRANKENSTEIN, THE
1958, 89 mins, UK Ⓥ col
Dir Terence Fisher ***Prod*** Anthony Hinds ***Scr*** Jimmy Sangster, H. Hurford Janes ***Ph*** Jack Asher ***Ed*** Alfred Cox, James Needs ***Mus*** Leonard Salzedo ***Art*** Bernard Robinson
Act Peter Cushing, Francis Matthews, Eunice Gayson, Michael Gwynn, John Welsh, Lionel Jeffries (Hammer)

Made by the same team as *The Curse of Frankenstein*, this is a high grade horror film.

Peter Cushing, as the famed medical experimenter, is still determined to make a monster, although that is not how he would put it. Despite official pressure, Frankenstein is again collecting bits of bone and tissue, muscle and blood, to put together a man of his creation. Again he succeeds, but again something goes wrong and his creature—through brain damage—becomes a cannibal, slavering blood and saliva.

The production is a rich one. The screenplay is well-plotted, peopled with interesting characters, aided by good performances from Francis Matthews as Cushing's chief assistant and others.

•

REVENGE OF THE CREATURE
1955, 82 mins, US ▭ b/w
Dir Jack Arnold ***Prod*** William Alland ***Scr*** Martin Berkeley ***Ph*** Charles S. Welbourne ***Ed*** Paul Weatherwax ***Mus*** Herman Stein ***Art*** Alexander Golitzen, Alfred Sweeney
Act John Agar, Lori Nelson, John Bromfield, Robert P. Williams, Nestor Paiva (Universal)

Revenge of the Creature, sequel to *Creature from the Black Lagoon*, is a routine shocker that doesn't get much of a boost from the 3-D treatment.

The fellow who plays the scaly monster in the film certainly rates top billing. Expertly made up, he's the only one who looks and acts believable. Fact that he only roars and has no speaking lines helps since the script cooked up by Martin Berkeley is hardly on the expert side. There's an unusual volume of dialog that serves mostly to bridge the gaps between the action sequences.

There are too few of those, but some of them are staged with sock effect, with or without 3-D. Underwater scenes involving the gillman, have been directed by Jack Arnold for shock value and they build up tension nicely. Cast performs its routine chores in routine fashion.

•

REVENGE OF THE NERDS
1984, 90 mins, US Ⓥ ⊙ col
Dir Jeff Kanew ***Prod*** Ted Field, Peter Samuelson ***Scr*** Steve Zacharias, Jeff Buhai ***Ph*** King Baggot ***Ed*** Alan Baisam ***Mus*** Thomas Newman ***Art*** James L. Schoppe
Act Robert Carradine, Anthony Edwards, Ted McGinley, Bernie Casey, Julia Montgomery (Interscope)

Simple-minded romp about a group of freshmen outcasts doesn't qualify for the dean's list, but *Revenge of the Nerds* shows more than enough smarts to deserve passing grades.

From the outset the nerds, who have learned to feel more at home talking computers and grade point average, get a "real-world" education from the upperclass fraternity of jocks. They suffer constant humiliations from the older students and ultimately decide to fight back.

Led by hometown buddies Lewis (Robert Carradine) and Gilbert (Anthony Edwards), the nerds rent a house and form their own frat. But breaking into the school's Greek fraternity group will not come easily because the council is chaired by Stan (Ted McGinley), a member of the jock frat, and his g.f. Betty (Julie Montgomery), enemies of the nerds and sticklers for the rules.

Though the picture features extensive cardboard stereotypes, belching and other bad taste humor, director Jeff Kanew moves the action [from a screen story by Tim Metcalfe, Miguel Tejeda-Flores, Steve Zacharias and Jeff Buhai] swiftly to a convincing payoff. There's also ample t&a along the way.

•

REVENGE OF THE NINJA
1983, 88 mins, US Ⓥ col
Dir Sam Firstenberg ***Prod*** Menahem Golan, Yoram Globus ***Scr*** James R. Silke ***Ph*** David Gurfinkel ***Ed*** Michael J. Duthie, Mark Helfrich ***Mus*** Rob Walsh, W. Michael Lewis, Laurin Rinder ***Art*** Paul Staheli
Act Sho Kosugi, Keith Vitali, Virgil Frye, Arthur Roberts, Mario Gallo, Grace Oshita (Cannon)

Revenge of the Ninja is an entertaining martial arts actioner, following up *Enter the Ninja* (1981) but lacking that film's name players and Far East locale.

After a brief intro set in Japan, where Cho Osaki (Sho Kosugi) witnesses most of his family wiped out by black-clad ninjas, action shifts to an unidentified U.S. locale (filmed in Salt Lake City) six years later.

Osaki, with his surviving child and its grandma, runs a gallery featuring imported Japanese dolls, which unbeknownst to him is a front for heroin smuggling run by his pal Braden (Arthur Roberts). Braden is involved with an unscrupulous U.S. mobster Caifano (Mario Gallo). Revenge occurs when Braden kills grannie, kidnaps the child

Kane (Kane Kosugi) and later kills Osaki's best friend, martial arts expert Dave Hatcher (Keith Vitali). Fine fight choreography by Kosugi, including fast and often funny moves by him, keeps the film cooking.

REVENGE OF THE PINK PANTHER
1978, 98 mins, US Ⓥ ⦿ col
Dir Blake Edwards ***Prod*** Blake Edwards ***Scr*** Frank Waldman, Ron Clark, Blake Edwards ***Ph*** Ernest Day ***Ed*** Alan Jones ***Mus*** Henry Mancini ***Art*** Peter Mullins
Act Peter Sellers, Herbert Lom, Dyan Cannon, Robert Webber, Burt Kwouk, Paul Stewart (United Artists)

Revenge of the Pink Panther isn't the best of the continuing film series, but Blake Edwards and Peter Sellers on a slow day are still well ahead of most other comedic filmmakers.

This time out, Sellers tracks down an international drug ring. Herbert Lom also encores as Sellers's nemesis and Dyan Cannon is delightful as the resourceful discarded mistress of dope smuggler industrialist Robert Webber.

The screenplay, from an Edwards story, is a paradoxical embarrassment of riches: Sellers, faithful servant Burt Kwouk, Lom, Cannon, etc., each alone and also in various combinations, are too much for a simple story line. The result is that the plot roams all over the map, trying to cover all the bases but in totality adding up to less than the parts.

REVERSAL OF FORTUNE
1990, 120 mins, US Ⓥ ⦿ col
Dir Barbet Schroeder ***Prod*** Edward R. Pressman, Oliver Stone, Elon Dershowitz, ***Scr*** Nicholas Kazan ***Ph*** Luciano Tovoli ***Ed*** Lee Percy ***Mus*** Mark Isham ***Art*** Mel Bourne
Act Jeremy Irons, Glenn Close, Ron Silver, Anabella Sciorra, Uta Hagen, Fisher Stevens (Warner/Shochiku Fuji/Sovereign)

Reversal of Fortune turns the sensational Claus von Bulow case into a riveting film. The story [from the book by Alan Dershowitz] of the Newport society figure's trial, conviction and acquittal on appeal for the attempted murder of his wealthy wife is presented here in an absorbing, complex mosaic.

Jeremy Irons gives a memorable performance as the inscrutable European blueblood emigre. Cast in perfect apposition is Ron Silver, seizing with dynamic gusto the role of a career as von Bulow's passionately idealistic but streetwise defense attorney, Harvard law professor Dershowitz.

Glenn Close is typically excellent in the smaller but pivotal role of Sunny von Bulow, who narrates the story and appears in flashbacks. On one level, *Reversal of Fortune* deals with the impossibility of knowing the truth about the unknowable. Was von Bulow guilty of injecting his wife with a near-fatal dose of insulin? Was he framed by Sunny's maid (Uta Hagen) or family? Or did the profoundly unhappy woman attempt suicide?

On other levels, it is a finely detailed manners study of the superwealthy, a drama of conflicting principles and values and an engrossing legal detective story.

1990: Best Actor (Jeremy Irons)

NOMINATIONS: Best Director, Adapted Screenplay

REVOLUTION
1986, 125 mins, UK/Norway Ⓥ ⦿ col
Dir Hugh Hudson ***Prod*** Irwin Winkler ***Scr*** Robert Dillon ***Ph*** Bernard Lutic ***Ed*** Stuart Baird ***Mus*** John Corigliano ***Art*** Assheton Gorton
Act Al Pacino, Donald Sutherland, Nastassja Kinski, Joan Plowright, Steven Berkoff, Annie Lennox (Goldcrest/Viking)

Watching *Revolution* is a little like visiting a museum—it looks good without really being alive. The film doesn't tell a story so much as it uses characters to illustrate what the American Revolution has come to mean. Despite attempting to reduce big events to personal details, *Revolution* rarely works on a human scale.

While the intimate story of Tom Dobb (Al Pacino) and his son Ned (Dexter Fletcher, Sid Owen as young Ned) and Tom's love for renegade aristocrat Daisy McConnahay (Nastassja Kinski) is full of holes, the larger canvas is staged beautifully.

Unfortunately, against this well-drawn background the small story that is meant to serve as a way into the drama for viewers looks too much like an historical reenactment.

Performances fail to elevate the material with only Pacino, Fletcher and Owen giving their characters a personal touch. Donald Sutherland is wasted and distant as an English officer, partially because it is nearly impossible to understand what he's saying through his thick brogue.

REWARD, THE
1965, 91 mins, US col
Dir Serge Bourguignon ***Prod*** Aaron Rosenberg ***Scr*** Serge Bourguignon, Oscar Millard ***Ph*** Joe MacDonald ***Ed*** Robert Simpson ***Mus*** Elmer Bernstein ***Art*** Jack Martin Smith, Robert Boyle
Act Max von Sydow, Yvette Mimieux, Efrem Zimbalist, Jr., Gilbert Roland, Emilio Fernandez, Nino Castelnuovo (Arcola/20th Century-Fox)

The Reward for a fugitive and its effects on a group thrown together by fate comprise the theme of this moody, somewhat uneven, desert meller. Some good acting and excellent production values bolster a plot that fizzes out in the final reel.

Director Serge Bourguignon and Oscar Millard adapted Michael Barrett's tome which crash-lands crop duster Max von Sydow in a boondocks Mexican town coincident with the passing through of Efrem Zimbalist, Jr., latter on the lam from a murder rap and accompanied by Yvette Mimieux. Sydow cues police inspector Gilbert Roland to the price on Zimbalist's head, and the slow chase is on, leading to uneventful and unresisted capture. About 40 percent of the film has elapsed before plot begins to move when brutal, sadistic police sergeant Emilio Fernandez finds out there's a reward and starts to dominate the group.

Sydow gives a lethargic performance despite a role that is basically passive. He talks little, then in guttural tones, but mostly reacts sluggishly to events.

RHAPSODY IN BLUE
1945, 130 mins, US Ⓥ ⦿ b/w
Dir Irving Rapper ***Prod*** Jesse L. Lasky ***Scr*** Howard Koch, Elliot Paul ***Ph*** Sol Polito, Merritt Gerstad ***Ed*** Folmer Blangsted ***Mus*** Leo F. Forbstein (dir.) ***Art*** Anton Grot, John B. Hughes
Act Robert Alda, Joan Leslie, Alexis Smith, Charles Coburn, Oscar Levant, Albert Basserman (Warner)

Those who knew George Gershwin and the Gershwin saga may wax slightly vociferous at this or that miscue, but as cinematurgy, designed for escapism and entertainment, no matter the season, *Rhapsody in Blue* can't miss.

The years have certainly lent enhancement to his music, and the glib interplay of names such as Otto Kahn, Jascha Heifetz, Maurice Ravel, Walter Damrosch and Rachmaninov (all of whom are impersonated) lend conviction to the basic yarn [from a story by Sonya Levien] of the New York East Side boy whose musical genius was to sweep the world.

Robert Alda plays Gershwin and makes him believable. Herbert Rudley as Ira Gershwin is perhaps more believable to the initiate, looking startlingly like the famed lyricist brother of the composer, but young Alda, a newcomer, makes his role tick as the burningly ambitious composer who is constantly driving himself.

Oscar Levant as Oscar Levant can't miss, and he doesn't here. He has the meatiest, brilliant lines and whams over the titular *Rhapsody in Blue* and Concerto in F with virtuosity and authority as befits a real-life confidante of the late composer.

1945: NOMINATIONS: Best Scoring of a Musical Picture, Sound

RHINESTONE
1984, 111 mins, US Ⓥ ⦿ col
Dir Bob Clark ***Prod*** Howard Smith, Marvin Worth ***Scr*** Phil Alden Robinson, Sylvester Stallone ***Ph*** Timothy Galfas ***Ed*** Stan Cole, John Wheeler ***Mus*** Dolly Parton ***Art*** Robert Boyle
Act Sylvester Stallone, Dolly Parton, Richard Farnsworth, Ron Leibman, Tim Thomerson, Steven Apostle Pec (20th Century-Fox)

Effortlessly living up to its title, *Rhinestone* is as artificial and synthetic a concoction as has ever made its way to the screen.

Directed in low-down, good-spirited vulgar fashion by Bob Clark, film is a genuine oddball [from a screen story by Phil Alden Robinson, based on the song "Rhinestone Cowboy" by Larry Weiss]. Sylvester Stallone's character, that of a Gotham cabbie whom singer Dolly Parton bets she can turn into a convincing country crooner in two weeks' time, is like no one ever encountered on earth before.

Uncouth loudmouth has no discernible talents whatsoever, so it's an uphill battle when Parton takes him down home to Tennessee to try to pump some real country feeling into his bulging veins.

Neither Stallone nor Parton stray at all from their past personae.

RICH AND FAMOUS
1981, 117 mins, US Ⓥ ⦿ col
Dir George Cukor ***Prod*** William Allyn ***Scr*** Gerald Ayres ***Ph*** Don Peterman ***Ed*** John F. Burnett ***Mus*** Georges Delerue ***Art*** Jan Scott
Act Jacqueline Bisset, Candice Bergen, Meg Ryan, David Selby, Hart Bochner, Michael Brandon (M-G-M)

While not without its problems, *Rich and Famous* is an absorbing drama of some notable qualities, the greatest of which is a gutsy, fascinating and largely magnificent performance by Jacqueline Bisset. Tale delineating the friendship of two smart, creative ladies over a period of two decades makes for "women's picture" in the best sense of the term.

Plot dynamics of Gerald Ayres's imaginative, very modern updating of John Van Druten's 1940 play *Old Acquaintance* rather closely follow those of Warner Brothers's solid 1943 film version, which starred Bette Davis and Miriam Hopkins. Bisset and Bergen essay college chums whose lives intersect at crucial points over the years.

A recurrent spot in which the pic seems to miss its potential is the occasional confrontation scene in which the ladies have at it in shouting catfights. These abusive sessions invariably deal with the essence of their relationship, but they have been directed at such a fast pace that the emotional depth charges fizzle out on the surface.

For a bright, sophisticated piece such as this, particularly one under the guidance of the irrepressibly elegant Goerge Cukor, the somewhat harsh, murky visual style is suprising. Cukor took over the production on short notice when original director Robert Mulligan was replaced after four days' lensing (none of the latter's footage remains).

RICHARD III
1955, 160 mins, UK Ⓥ col
Dir Laurence Olivier, Anthony Bushell ***Prod*** Laurence Olivier ***Scr*** Laurence Olivier ***Ph*** Otto Heller ***Ed*** Helga Cranston ***Mus*** William Walton ***Art*** Roger Furse, Carmen Dillon
Act Laurence Olivier, John Gielgud, Claire Bloom, Ralph Richardson, Alec Clunes, Stanley Baker (London)

The Bard pulled no punches in his dramatization of *Richard III*, and Laurence Olivier's film likewise portrays him as a ruthless and unscrupulous character, who stops at nothing to obtain the throne. The murder of his brother Clarence (John Gielgud), the betrayal of his cousin, Buckingham (Ralph Richardson), the suffocation of the princes in the Tower are among the unscrupulous steps in the path of Richard's crowning, which are staged with lurid, melodramatic conviction.

At all times Shakespeare's poetry, impeccably spoken by this outstanding cast, heightens the dramatic atmosphere. The production, and notably Roger Furse's decor, is consistently spectacular. The climactic battle sequences rival the pageantry of *Henry V*.

Running Olivier's performance a very close second is Richardson's scheming Buckingham. Another distinguished performance is contributed by Gielgud as Clarence.

1956: NOMINATION: Best Actor (Laurence Olivier)

RICHARD III
1996, 105 mins, UK/US Ⓥ ⦿ col
Dir Richard Loncraine ***Prod*** Lisa Katselas Pare, Stephen Bayly ***Scr*** Ian McKellen, Richard Loncraine ***Ph*** Peter Biziou ***Ed*** Paul Green ***Mus*** Trevor Jones ***Art*** Tony Burrough
Act Ian McKellen, Annette Bening, Jim Broadbent, Robert Downey, Jr., Nigel Hawthorne, Kristen Scott Thomas (First Look/United Artists)

Spirited acting, machine-gun pacing and ominous Art Deco settings combine to rousing effect in this *Richard III*, a surefire crowd pleaser among recent Shakespeare movies. Adapting an acclaimed British stage production, director Richard Loncraine and star Ian McKellen do the Bard a favor by transferring his most celebrated royal thug from the Middle Ages to the no-less blood-soaked 1930s.

Loncraine and McKellen have condensed Shakespeare's second-longest play, which can run four hours onstage. Lots of text is simply deep-sixed, yet the cutting is so intelligently done that it both aids the pace and sometimes makes meanings and character relationships clearer than they are in Olivier's celebrated 1955 movie, which is longer by 5 minutes.

Tale opens with a war scene, implied by the play, in which Richard's forces overwhelm a rival HQ and he shoots and kills Prince Edward. Action then shifts to a victory gala where, after a big-band version of Marlowe's "Come live with me and be my love," Richard takes the stage and begins his "winter of our discontent" monologue as a speech, then completes it privately in a nearby lavatory, speaking to the camera. McKellen's Richard is less the Machiavellian monster of some versions and more the craftiest of organization men. A vivid, finely honed characterization, it receives top-notch support, especially in Jim Broadbent's pliant Buckingham, Nigel Hawthorne's credulous Clarence and Kristin Scott Thomas's conflicted Lady Anne.

Casting Americans Annette Bening and Robert Downey, Jr., as Queen Elizabeth and her brother makes sense for characters who are foreign-born, and Bening does standout work in the larger role, giving the queen the presence of a woman who could hold her own against the usurping Richard.

1995: NOMINATIONS: Best Art Direction, Costume Design

•

RICHARD PRYOR . . . HERE AND NOW

1983, 94 mins, US Ⓥ col

Dir Richard Pryor ***Prod*** Bob Parkinson, Andy Friendly ***Scr*** Richard Pryor ***Ph*** Vincent Singletary, Kenneth A. Patterson, Joe Epperson, Tom Geren, Johnny Simmons, Dave Landry ***Ed*** Raymond Bush ***Art*** Anthony Sabatino, William Harris

Act Richard Pryor (Columbia/Indigo)

As a concert film, *Richard Pryor . . . Here and Now* should attract and please those who appreciate him as a stand-up comic. But beyond the ample laughs, there is a beautiful monolog that's so painfully acute it would entrance even those who never laugh at his other stuff.

His third concert film, *Here and Now* is a mixture of the ones done before and after the fire that almost killed him. Drug-free and still grateful for a second chance, Pryor remains much more mellow, but less self-examining and contemplative than in *Live on the Sunset Strip* (1982).

Some of the hostility and bite have returned, though well under control. On top of the laughs, he also displays a deepening sympathy for those doomed by substances.

•

RICHARD PRYOR LIVE ON THE SUNSET STRIP

1982, 82 mins, US Ⓥ col

Dir Joe Layton ***Prod*** Richard Pryor ***Scr*** Richard Pryor ***Ph*** Haskell Wexler ***Ed*** Sheldon Kahn ***Mus*** Harry R. Betts ***Art*** Michael Baugh

Act Richard Pryor (Columbia/Rastar)

This is not a film in any respect, except to note the medium Richard Pryor's stand-up routine was captured on in two nights at the Palladium in 1981. Director Joe Layton and cameraman Haskell Wexler make no noticeable contributions and often fail to solve the problems of concert lensing.

But Pryor is truly amazing and that's all that counts. After a number of roles in successful pictures, he brings an acting ability to his stage routine that enhances his well-established talent for caricature. What this allows him to do is pull the audience into moments of genuine emotion, then clobber them suddenly with a hilarious switch.

By far the best comes with a candid discussion of his drug addiction that culminates in the freebase explosion that almost killed him.

•

RICHIE RICH

1994, 95 mins, US Ⓥ ⦿ col

Dir Donald Petrie ***Prod*** Joel Silver, John Davis ***Scr*** Tom S. Parker, Jim Jennewein ***Ph*** Don Burgess ***Ed*** Malcolm Campbell ***Mus*** Alan Silvestri ***Art*** James Spencer

Act Macaulay Culkin, John Larroquette, Edward Herrmann, Jonathan Hyde, Christine Ebersole, Stephi Lineburg (Silver/Warner)

Decently crafted but oddly charmless, *Richie Rich* isn't likely to jump-start the fading superstardom of aging child star Macaulay Culkin.

Based on the popular Harvey comic books (and subsequent cartoon spin-offs), pic casts Culkin in the title role as the world's richest 12-year-old. How rich is he? Well, he has Reggie Jackson for a baseball coach, Claudia Schiffer for a personal trainer and his very own McDonald's in a room of his family's sprawling mansion.

Through the intervention of Cadbury (Jonathan Hyde), his loyal manservant, Richie is able to find some working-class kids to pal around with. His new buddies prove to be valuable allies when Lawrence Van Dough (John Larroquette), a Rich Industries executive, attempts a hostile takeover of the Rich fortune.

Script, from a story by Neil Tolkin, calls for Richie, Cadbury and Richie's new buddies (led by appealing newcomer Stephi Lineburg) to invade the Rich manor to rescue Richie's parents. It's actually quite true to the adventurous spirit of the original comic books.

Still, there's something mechanical and soulless about all the slam and bang action that overwhelms this pic during the last half hour. Culkin is clearly too mature for his role, Larroquette offers a generous slice of well-seasoned hamminess as the villain of the piece, while Hyde is even better as the very proper Cadbury.

•

RICH IN LOVE

1993, 105 mins, US Ⓥ ⦿ col

Dir Bruce Beresford ***Prod*** Richard D. Zanuck, Lili Fini Zanuck ***Scr*** Alfred Uhry ***Ph*** Peter James ***Ed*** Mark Warner ***Mus*** Georges Delerue ***Art*** John Stoddart

Act Albert Finney, Jill Clayburgh, Kathryn Erbe, Kyle MacLachlan, Piper Laurie, Ethan Hawke (M-G-M/Zanuck)

The creative team that brought *Driving Miss Daisy* to the screen fails to conjure up similar magic with *Rich in Love*. Despite a luminous performance by Kathryn Erbe, the story of a South Carolina teen's coming of age in a dysfunctional family seems overly familiar and dramatically diffuse.

Daisy playwright/scriptwriter Alfred Uhry, recruited by producers to adapt a novel by Josephine Humphreys, has a fine ear for Southern dialog that's colorful but not too arch. But this languidly paced film follows a meandering narrative line that seems to have trouble coming to its point.

Is it a story about the shattering effect of divorce on Erbe and her aimless, recently retired father (Albert Finney)? Not really, since they eventually adapt quite well to life without mom (Jill Clayburgh), who briefly pops in and out of the film without making much of an impression.

Finney fits into his Charleston accent like an old shoe, but he's working here with an unfocused character and using his technical virtuosity to carry it along. The unglamorized but compellingly watchable Erbe commendably avoids punching obvious emotional buttons.

A brief romantic interlude with Kyle MacLachlan, Yankee husband of her neurotic older sister (Suzy Amis), never develops into much of anything because his character is so amorphous.

Pic is dedicated to composer Georges Delerue, who died shortly after completing this score.

•

RICOCHET

1991, 97 mins, US Ⓥ ⦿ ▭ col

Dir Russell Mulcahy ***Prod*** Joel Silver, Michael Levy ***Scr*** Steven de Souza ***Ph*** Peter Levy ***Ed*** Peter Honess ***Mus*** Alan Silvestri ***Art*** Jaymes Hinkle

Act Denzel Washington, John Lithgow, Ice T, Kevin Pollak, Lindsay Wagner, Victoria Dillard (HBO/Silver)

A taut, twisty urban suspenser powered by the spring-loaded performance of Denzel Washington in his first major action role, *Ricochet* has a nasty streak and a tendency toward implausible excess.

Washington plays an ambitious young cop who nails a vicious hit man (John Lithgow), putting him behind bars just as his own career begins an upward spiral. The pathological killer plots his revenge for seven years, watching the gifted cop become district attorney and acquire a loving family and a promising political future. When Lithgow finally breaks out of jail, he's armed with a diabolical plan to wreak havoc on everything his nemesis has attained.

Tension is sustained by skillful cutting between the two opposite lives and full-bore performances on both ends of the seesaw. Plot kicks into high gear once the killer gets loose to pursue his prey.

Screenplay [from a story by Fred Dekker and Menno Meyjes] offers unusually good dialog for the smooth-talking Washington and a number of scenes to savor. Pic threatens to become truly absorbing as Lithgow's brilliant revenge scheme unfolds, but *Ricochet* soon abandons cleverness in favor of spectacle.

•

RIDE 'EM COWBOY

1942, 84 mins, US b/w

Dir Arthur Lubin ***Prod*** Alex Gottlieb ***Scr*** True Boardman, John Grant ***Ph*** John W. Boyle ***Ed*** Phillip Cahn ***Mus*** Charles Previn (dir.)

Act Bud Abbott, Lou Costello, Dick Foran, Anne Gwynne, John Mack Brown (Universal)

Typical Abbott and Costello film fare whose title and background of a dude ranch out West are only props set up to display the usual broadly burlesqued antics of the pair. There are a number of slick sequences in which Abbott and Costello parade their comedic abilities to the maximum, and excellent timing of delivery refurbishes some old routines sufficiently to get them over for a reprise.

Adding some musical numbers, Universal endeavors to raise the production value of this one over its predecessors, but it all adds up to the same thing—when A&C are off the screen, interest in the proceedings lags. The two comics are picked up in New York as a couple of peanut and hot dog vendors at a rodeo show and are quickly shunted West to join up as cowhands on a dude ranch. Every prop and background around the place is utilized for slapstick antics of the pair.

•

RIDE IN THE WHIRLWIND

1966, 82 mins, US Ⓥ ⦿ col

Dir Monte Hellman ***Prod*** Monte Hellman, Jack Nicholson ***Scr*** Jack Nicholson ***Ph*** Gregory Sandor ***Mus*** Robert Drasnin ***Art*** James Campbell

Act Cameron Mitchell, Jack Nicholson, Millie Perkins, Katherine Squire, George Mitchell, Harry Dean Stanton (Proteus)

Monte Hellman's *Ride in the Whirlwind* is a flat, woodenly acted western with mild suspense that never grabs. Part of the fault is with Jack Nicholson's script, which is little more than a promising plotline rather than a fully developed scenario. Nicholson also plays the lead, but since Nicholson the writer has little to say, Nicholson the actor has even less.

Hellman never exploits the full potential of the situations. A trio of uncommunicative saddle tramps—Nicholson, Cameron Mitchell, Tom Filer—stumble on a motley gang holed up in a mountain shack after a stagecoach robbery. For reasons never adequately explained, the one-eyed gang leader is downright cordial to the cowpokes.

They spend the night, and in the morning find themselves surrounded by a posse of vigilantes that is going to string them up first and ask questions later.

In the getaway Filer is shot down and Mitchell and Nicholson have to climb up a sheer canyon.

Not one of the characters emerges from the flatness of the screen, and to a man they move and talk like animated cigar store Indians.

•

RIDE LONESOME

1959, 74 mins, US ▭ col

Dir Budd Boetticher ***Prod*** Budd Boetticher ***Scr*** Burt Kennedy ***Ph*** Charles Lawton, Jr. ***Ed*** Jerome Thoms ***Mus*** Heinz Roemheld ***Art*** Robert Peterson

Act Randolph Scott, Karen Steele, Pernell Roberts, James Best, Lee Van Cleef, James Coburn (Ranown/Columbia)

Ride Lonesome has Randolph Scott as a bounty hunter whose interest in a young murderer (James Best) seems to be solely the money he will collect for his delivery. Along the way, he picks up a young widow (Karen Steele), and two feckless outlaws (Pernell Roberts and James Coburn). Soon Best's brother (Lee Van Cleef) is trailing them with his own band, intent on rescuing Best.

Ride Lonesome has several good plots and subplots going for it, creating a chase melodrama that is often a chase-within-a-chase. Scriptwriter Burt Kennedy has used genuine speech of the frontier and some offhand, often rather grim humor, to give the screenplay additional interest where the pursuit portions necessarily lag. Boetticher and his cast handle it well, only occasionally overreaching in brief scenes where Steele's sex seems stressed beyond reason.

Scott does a good job as the taciturn and misunderstood hero, but the two standouts are Best as the giggling killer and Roberts as the sardonic outlaw who wants to get away to a new start.

•

RIDE THE HIGH COUNTRY
(UK: GUNS IN THE AFTERNOON)

1962, 94 mins, US Ⓥ ⦿ ▭ col

Dir Sam Peckinpah ***Prod*** Richard E. Lyons ***Scr*** N. B. Stone, Jr. ***Ph*** Lucien Ballard ***Ed*** Frank Santillo ***Mus*** George Bassman ***Art*** George W. Davis, Leroy Coleman

Act Randolph Scott, Joel McCrea, Mariette Hartley, Edgar Buchanan, Ron Starr, Warren Oates (M-G-M)

The old saying "you can't make a silk purse out of a sow's ear" rings true for Metro-Goldwyn-Mayer's artistic western *Ride the High Country*. It remains a standard story, albeit with an interesting gimmick and some excellent production values.

Scott and McCrea play their ages in roles that could well be extensions of characters they have each played in countless earlier films. They are quick-triggered ex-lawmen, former famed "town-tamers" whom life has passed by and who are now reduced to taking jobs as guards for a gold shipment. They engage in one last battle—over a woman and involving a youth who epitomizes their own youth.

It is Sam Peckinpah's direction, however, that gives the film greatest artistry. He gives N. B. Stone, Jr.'s script a measure beyond its adequacy, instilling bright moments of sharp humor and an overall significant empathetic flavor.

•

RIDE, VAQUERO

1953, 91 mins, US col

Dir John Farrow ***Prod*** Stephen Ames ***Scr*** Frank Fenton ***Ph*** Robert Surtees ***Ed*** Harold F. Kress ***Mus*** Bronislau Kaper ***Art*** Cedric Gibbons, Arthur Lonergan

Act Robert Taylor, Ava Gardner, Howard Keel, Anthony Quinn, Kurt Kasznar, Jack Elam (M-G-M)

Locale of the production is southwest Texas, a territory around Brownsville, that is under the thumb of a group of outlaw gangs controlled by Anthony Quinn and his lieutenant (Robert Taylor). When Howard Keel tries to found a cattle empire and brings in settlers, the outlaws fight back, knowing they will be through if civilization comes to the land.

John Farrow's direction stirs up plenty of violent action as he plays off the story. While the script is a bit vague in development of some of the personalities, overall effect is okay for the outdoor fan, although more critical audiences would have liked less obscurity. Keel brings Ava Gardner, his bride, to his new homestead, only to find it a smoking ruin as the result of a Quinn-directed raid. Keel builds again, stronger this time, after he fails to unite the townspeople and the sheriff against the outlaw. When the new home is ready, Quinn's forces attack.

Taylor is very good in selling the quiet menace of his character, and Quinn stands out as the flamboyant outlaw leader. Gardner provides physical beauty to a character that is not as well-stated as it could have been. Keel does well by his determined, foolhardy character.

•

RIDE WITH THE DEVIL

1999, 138 mins, US Ⓥ ⦿ ▭ col

Dir Ang Lee ***Prod*** Ted Hope, Robert Colesberry, James Schamus ***Scr*** James Schamus ***Ph*** Frederick Elmes ***Ed*** Tim Squyres ***Mus*** Mychael Danna ***Art*** Mark Friedberg

Act Skeet Ulrich, Tobey Maguire, Jewel, Jeffrey Wright, Simon Baker, Jonathan Rhys Meyers (Good Machine/Universal)

A complex and divisive time in American history is painted in admirably expressive shades of gray in *Ride with the Devil*. Impressing once again with the diversity of his choices of subject matter and milieu, director Ang Lee has made a brutal but sensitively observed film about the fringes of the Civil War, about the families and neighbors who were divided among themselves along the Missouri-Kansas border.

In the anarchic world of Southern-sympathizing Bushwhackers and pro-Union Jayhawkers, it is never easy to know who might be ally or enemy, and the conflict is more often personal and haphazard rather than militarily organized.

Jack Bull Chiles (Skeet Ulrich) is a product of oldstyle Southern life. His close friend Jake Roedel (Tobey Maguire), however, is the son of a poor German immigrant who, like most of his class, fervently backs the North, so Jake's decision to join the ad hoc Bushwhackers after the outbreak of hostilities puts him into fateful conflict with his father.

Among the two young men's colleagues are confidant leader Black John (James Caviezel), mistrustful psychotic Pitt Mackeson (Jonathan Rhys Meyers) and young gentleman George Clyde (Simon Baker). When the men hole up for a while in a woodshed, a self-possessed woman, Sue Lee (Jewel), brings them provisions and Jack initiates a romance with her.

Intelligent script, based on Daniel Woodrell's 1987 novel *Woe to Live On*, also pays gratifying attention to linguistic niceties. On the downside, story softens and slows considerably as the men retreat increasingly from the action. Maguire, Ulrich and Wright capably handle the principal parts.

•

RIDICULE

1996, 102 mins, France Ⓥ ▭ col

Dir Patrice Leconte ***Prod*** Gilles Legrand, Frederic Brillion, Philippe Carcassonne ***Scr*** Remi Waterhouse, Michel Fessler, Eric Vicaut ***Ph*** Thierry Arbogast ***Ed*** Joelle Hache ***Mus*** Antoine Duhamel ***Art*** Ivan Maussion

Act Charles Berling, Jean Rochefort, Fanny Ardant, Judith Godreche, Bernard Giraudeau, Bernard Dheran (Epithete/Cinea/France 3)

Resplendent and intelligent from start to finish, *Ridicule* strikes a winning balance between humor and heart as it pillories an era in France (the court of Louis XVI, circa 1780) when wit was the most valuable currency and a man's fortune and reputation could be made or undone on the strength of a single remark.

Engineer Gregoire Ponceludon de Malavoy (Charles Berling) is baron of an estate where the peasants are dropping (literally) like flies, felled by diseases that breed in the murderous swamps. Gregoire sets out from the provinces to plead his case at Versailles.

Gregoire is befriended by a near-penniless physician, the Marquis de Bellegarde (Jean Rochefort). Bellegarde knows the ins and outs of establishing favor at Versailles but also maintains a more down-to-earth home life with his daughter, Mathilde (Judith Godreche), a bright lass on the brink of loveless union.

All Gregoire has to do is steer clear of humiliation as he works his way up to an audience with the king while sorting out his carnal attraction to powerful Madame de Blayac (Fanny Ardant) versus his love for Mathilde. Thesps are terrific. Nasty characters abound in the pithy script but they are never less than human and well-observed. Stage-trained Berling fits the bill as the Candide-like interloper who is both attracted to and repelled by the heady, elitist atmosphere at court. Costumes and hairdos evoke the era without calling undue attention to themselves.

1996: NOMINATION: Best Foreign Language

•

RIDING HIGH

1943, 89 mins, US col

Dir George Marshall ***Prod*** Fred Kohlmar ***Scr*** Walter DeLeon, Arthur Phillips, Art Arthur ***Ph*** Karl Struss, Harry Hallenberger ***Ed*** LeRoy Stone ***Mus*** Victor Young

Act Dorothy Lamour, Dick Powell, Victor Moore, Gil Lamb, Cass Daley (Paramount)

Lots of ingredients for a b.o. musical are in this one, and George Marshall makes the most of a rather flimsy framework. An ex-burlesque principal (Dorothy Lamour) lands back at her father's ill-fated silver mine out in Arizona when her show folds. She finds that mining engineer Dick Powell is also back after trying unsuccessfully to sell stock in the same mine. Lamour takes a job at the elaborate Dude Ranch cabaret, run by Cass Daley, in order to help her dad.

Victor Moore fits snugly into the counterfeiter role, his droll witticisms being solid throughout. Opening poker game sequence, an oldie, is given a new twist, but is topped by the series of succeeding gags. Cass Daley makes the grade in her rough-and-ready part of Dude Ranch owner, on the make for Moore. Her mugging is held to a minimum except in the "Willie, the Wolf of the West" comedy song-dance number, played with all stops out. Containing many bits from her vaude act, it's a howl. Powell is Powell again, but managing to carry the romance with Lamour nicely.

•

RIFF-RAFF

1991, 92 mins, UK Ⓥ col

Dir Ken Loach ***Prod*** Sally Hibbin ***Scr*** Bill Jesse ***Ph*** Barry Ackroyd ***Ed*** Jonathan Morris ***Mus*** Stewart Copeland ***Art*** Martin Johnson

Act Robert Carlyle, Emer McCourt, Jimmy Coleman, Ricky Tomlinson, Willie Ross, Derek Young (Parallax/Film Four)

Riff-Raff, a sprightly ensemble comedy about workers on a London building site, will surprise those who think Brit helmer Ken Loach can crank out only political items. Semi-improvised pic is strong on yucks and easy to digest.

Central character is Stevie (Robert Carlyle), a young Glaswegian just out of stir, who's come south and got a job converting a closed-down hospital into luxury apartments. His co-workers are from all over—Liverpudlians, Geordies (natives of Newcastle), West Indians. They're breaking every regulation in the book and running scams on the side. Home is a squat in a dingy council block.

After Stevie meets Susan (Emer McCourt), a drifter from Belfast who's trying to make it as a singer, they move in together and make a go of it in the big city. Story yo-yos between their fragile relationship and the shenanigans on the building site.

Fruity script by onetime laborer Bill Jesse (who died in 1990 just before the pic was completed) catches the wise-cracking flavor of navvy repartee. Comedic tone also spills over into the love story. Thesping by no-name cast is strong and clearly benefits from Loach's insistence that all actors have building-site experience.

•

RIFIFI

SEE: DU RIFIFI CHEZ LES HOMMES

•

RIGHT CROSS

1950, 89 mins, US b/w

Dir John Sturges ***Prod*** Armand Deutsch ***Scr*** Charles Schnee ***Ph*** Norbert Brodine ***Ed*** James E. Newcom ***Mus*** David Raksin

Act June Allyson, Dick Powell, Ricardo Montalban, Lionel Barrymore, Teresa Celli (M-G-M)

A breezy style brightens up the drama in *Right Cross* and makes it good entertainment.

Ricardo Montalban portrays a champion prizefighter who carries a chip on his shoulder because he is a Mexican. There's a neat shift of the social problem, the persecution being Montalban's own and not the result of any prejudice from what he terms the *gringos*.

June Allyson is Montalban's manager, carrying on for her crippled dad (Lionel Barrymore). There's quite a spitfire romance between the femme and her champ that nearly founders on his belief he has to continue as champ and get rich or lose her.

Talk is glib, light at the proper moment and tough elsewhere. Montalban looks impressive in the ring and wears his barechest well.

•

RIGHT STUFF, THE

1983, 193 mins, US Ⓥ ⦿ col

Dir Philip Kaufman ***Prod*** Irwin Winkler, Robert Chartoff ***Scr*** Philip Kaufman ***Ph*** Caleb Deschanel ***Ed*** Glenn Farr, Lisa Fruchtman, Stephen A. Rotter, Douglas Stewart, Tom Rolf ***Mus*** Bill Conti ***Art*** Geoffrey Kirkland

Act Sam Shepard, Scott Glenn, Ed Harris, Dennis Quaid, Fred Ward, Barbara Hershey (Ladd Company)

The Right Stuff is a humdinger. Full of beauty, intelligence and excitement, this big-scale look at the development of the U.S. space program and its pioneering aviators provides a fresh, entertaining look back at the recent past. Film version of Tom Wolfe's best-selling revisionist history was some three years in the making.

Tale spans 16 years, from ace test pilot Chuck Yeager's breaking of the sound barrier over the California desert to Vice President Johnson's welcoming of the astronauts to their new home in Houston with an enormous barbecue inside the Astrodome. Telling takes over three hours, but it goes by lickety-split under Philip Kaufman's direction and is probably the shortest-seeming film of its length ever made.

Emblematic figure here is Yeager, played by a taciturn Sam Shepard. As the ace of aces who was passed by for astronaut training due to his lack of college degree, Yeager, for Kaufman as for Wolfe, is the embodiment of "the right stuff," that ineffable quality that separates the men from the boys, so to speak.

1983: Best Original Score, Editing, Sound (Mark Berger, Tom Scott, Randy Thom, David MacMillan), Sound Editing

NOMINATIONS: Best Picture, Supporting Actor (Sam Shepard), Cinematography, Art Direction

•

RIKKY AND PETE

1988, 101 mins, Australia Ⓥ ⦿ col

Dir Nadia Tass ***Prod*** Nadia Tass, David Parker ***Scr*** David Parker ***Ph*** David Parker ***Ed*** Ken Sallows ***Mus*** Phil Judd, Eddie Raynor ***Art*** Josephine Ford

Act Stephen Kearney, Nina Landis, Tetchie Agbayani, Bill Hunter, Bruno Lawrence, Bruce Spence (United Artists/Cascade)

Rikky and Pete has a clutch of potentially interesting characters and a promising story line; but the characters are inadquately developed, and the plotting doesn't live up to expectations.

Pete is an inventor in Melbourne. For reasons barely specified, Pete is in the middle of a vendetta with a burly police officer (Bill Hunter) who's out to get him; his sister, Rikky, meanwhile, is tired of her latest beau (Lewis Fitzgerald) and of singing to unappreciative audiences in a bar. They take off in their mother's magnificent Bentley for the outback.

They arrive in a mining town and strike it rich. Pete has an affair with a pretty Filipino girl (Tetchie Agbayani), but winds up in prison, where the pursuing cop finally locates him.

Stephen Kearney gives Pete plenty of raffish charm, and Nina Landis has a warm personality as Rikky. Unfortunately, their roles remain sketchy. Landis suffers particularly, since a romance with miner Bruno Lawrence is suggested but never followed through, leaving a void in the film. Nadia Tass directs with a very deliberate pace, which drags the film down.

•

RING, THE

1927, 106 mins, UK Ⓥ ⊙ ⊗ b/w

Dir Alfred Hitchcock ***Scr*** Alma Reville, Alfred Hitchcock ***Ph*** Jack Cox ***Art*** C. Wilfred Arnold

Act Carl Brisson, Lillian Hall-Davis, Ian Hunter, Forrester Harvey, Gordon Harker, Harry Terry (B.I.P.)

Hailed as the greatest British film yet produced, this picture merited unusual attention for many reasons. It was the first offer from Elstree after the studios were taken over and reorganized by British International Productions. It was, at last, the performance of the long-deferred "promise" of Alfred Hitchcock.

Carl Brisson is overshadowed by the acting of the heavy, Ian Hunter. He is a first-rate film actor with an engaging he-man personality and a strong flapper appeal.

Gordon Harker, on the screen for the first time, nearly steals this one as a hard-boiled cynical trainer. His sense of screen comedy is acute and restrained at the same time and he makes his points with lips and eyes in a notable fashion.

Hitchcock gets more out of Lilian Hall-Davis than any Continental director and at times makes her reminiscent of Lya de Putti. But the story gives her a rather unsympathetic and incredulous role and her sudden revulsion in favor of friend and husband is not too convincing.

•

RING, THE

1952, 79 mins, US Ⓥ b/w

Dir Kurt Neumann ***Scr*** Irving Shulman ***Ph*** Russell Harlan ***Ed*** Bruce B. Pierce ***Mus*** Herschel Burke Gilbert

Act Gerald Mohr, Rita Moreno, Lalo Rios, Robert Arthur, Robert Osterloh, Jack Elam (King Bros/United Artists)

Efforts of a young boxer to fight his way up from preliminaries to main-bout stature provides a stock setting for a well-spun yarn [from a novel by Irving Shulman] of discrimination on the Coast against the Mexican-Americans.

Accent is on realism. Pic pinpoints the discriminatory line without relying on any hysterical sequences. The message hits home with such effectively underplayed scenes as tourists gazing at "those lazy Mexicans," brush-off of a group of Mexican-American boys by a waitress in a Beverly Hills eatery and the turndown of a young couple at a skating rink gate because it wasn't "Mexican Night." The prizefighting scenes, too, are executed graphically.

Cast is headed by Gerald Mohr, the manager; Lalo Rios, the boxer; and Rita Moreno.

•

RING OF BRIGHT WATER

1969, 107 mins, UK Ⓥ col

Dir Jack Couffer ***Prod*** Joseph Strick ***Scr*** Jack Couffer, Bill Travers ***Ph*** Wolfgang Suschitzky ***Ed*** Reginald Mills ***Mus*** Frank Cordell ***Art*** Ken Ryan

Act Bill Travers, Virginia McKenna, Roddy McMillan, Jameson Clark, Jean Taylor-Smith (Palomar)

Bill Travers and Virginia McKenna followed up their success in *Born Free* with an engaging film about an otter. It is a semi-documentary, based on Gavin Maxwell's autobiographical bestseller, *Ring of Bright Water*.

Story concerns a London civil servant, anxious to get out of the rat race to write. He makes his decision when he acquires Mij, a young otter, as a pet and finds that keeping the charming but mischievous mammal in a London apartment is frought with headaches. So he and Mij depart for a lonely coastal village in the Highlands where they settle down contentedly in a ramshackle crofter's cottage.

Travers and McKenna unselfishly subdue their performances to the star demands of the lolloping young rascal, Mij, but keep the interest firmly alive by their tactful playing.

•

RING OF SPIES

1964, 90 mins, UK b/w

Dir Robert Tronson ***Prod*** Leslie Gilliat ***Scr*** Frank Launder, Peter Barnes ***Ph*** Arthur Lavris ***Ed*** Thelma Connell ***Art*** Norman Arnold

Act Bernard Lee, William Sylvester, Margaret Tyzack, David Kossoff, Thorley Walters (British Lion)

In 1961 British spies were sentenced to long spells of forced reflection for their part in the Portland Spy Case. This film purports to give "the inside story" of the case. Instead, it merely presents a realistic documentary of the surface events leading up to the uncovering of the spies.

Henry Houghton (Bernard Lee) is sacked from the British Embassy at Warsaw as a bad security risk. He is transferred to Records at the Portland Underwater Weapons Establishment. With a chip on his shoulder and a desire for easy money he is readily blackmailed into borrowing secret documents from Portland. He inveigles a respectable spinster, who is in charge of the safe keys, to help him. Gordon Lonsdale, the Russian contact, passes the info on to a middle-aged couple in the suburbs who are ostensibly book dealers. They ingeniously transmit it by shortwave to Russia.

Lee and Margaret Tyzack play the dupes with conviction, William Sylvester is a suave, formidable Lonsdale and David Kossoff and Nancy Nevinson successfully complete the quintet as the fake book dealers.

•

RINGS ON HER FINGERS

1942, 85 mins, US Ⓥ b/w

Dir Rouben Mamoulian ***Prod*** Milton Sperling ***Scr*** Ken Englund ***Ph*** George Barnes ***Ed*** Barbara McLean ***Mus*** Cyril Mockridge

Act Henry Fonda, Gene Tierney, Laird Cregar, Spring Byington (20th Century-Fox)

Parading a vacuous story that gets no assistance on the directing end, *Rings on Her Fingers* is a lightweight film that tumbles and stumbles along in boresome fashion to emerge as misfit entertainment.

Story [from an original by Robert Pirosh and Joseph Schrank] is of Cinderella texture, without benefit of originality in either its unfolding or direction. Gene Tierney is a store clerk plucked by confidence operators Laird Cregar and Spring Byington for a whirl as cute decoy for their shakedowns of rich victims. Henry Fonda, an accountant vacationing in California with savings of $15,000 to buy a sailboat, gets caught in the net and clipped.

Picture is filled with vapid situations that stretch the credulity of audiences, and fails entirely in attempts to get over lightness and smart situations along the route. Frequent clinches of Fonda and Tierney do little more than consume footage. He fails to emerge from the mesh of story difficulties and static direction.

•

RIO BRAVO

1959, 140 mins, US Ⓥ ⊙ col

Dir Howard Hawks ***Prod*** Howard Hawks ***Scr*** Jules Furthman, Leigh Brackett ***Ph*** Russell Harlan ***Ed*** Folmar Blangsted ***Mus*** Dimitri Tiomkin ***Art*** Leo K. Kuter

Act John Wayne, Dean Martin, Ricky Nelson, Angie Dickinson, Walter Brennan, Ward Bond (Armada)

Rio Bravo is a big, brawling western. Script, based on the B. H. McCampbell short story, gets off to one of the fastest slam-bang openings on record. Within 90 seconds Wayne, a fast-shooting sheriff, is clubbed, another man knocked out and a third man murdered.

Plot thereafter revolves around Wayne's attempts to hold the murderer, brother of the most powerful rancher in the area, until the arrival some days hence of the U.S. marshal. He's up against the rancher utilizing gunman tactics to free the jailed killer.

Producer-director Howard Hawks makes handsome use of force in logically unravelling his hard-hitting narrative, creating suspense at times and occasionally inserting lighter moments to give variety. Wayne delivers a faithful portrayal of the peace officer who must fight his battle with the aid of only two deputies. One of these is Dean Martin, his ex-deputy who attempts to kick a two-year drunk to help his friend. The other deputy is Walter Brennan, a cantankerous old cripple assigned to guard the prisoner in the jail.

In for distaff interest and with more legitimate footage than usual in a western is Angie Dickinson, a looker fashioned into an important key character who delivers in every way.

•

RIO CONCHOS

1964, 105 mins, US Ⓥ ▭ col

Dir Gordon Douglas ***Prod*** David Weisbart ***Scr*** Joseph Landon, Clair Huffaker ***Ph*** Joe MacDonald ***Ed*** Joseph Silver ***Mus*** Jerry Goldsmith ***Art*** Jack Martin Smith, William Creber

Act Richard Boone, Stuart Whitman, Anthony Franciosa, Jim Brown, Wende Wagner, Edmond O'Brien (20th Century-Fox)

Rio Conchos is a big, tough, action-packed slam-bang western with as tough a set of characters as ever rode the sage. It is Old West adventure at its best.

Producer David Weisbart has woven fanciful movement along with lush settings via on-the-spot color lensing in Arizona. To this, Gordon Douglas has added his own version of what a lusty western should be in the direction, getting the most from a batch of colorful characters. Music score by Jerry Goldsmith is a particularly valuable asset in striking a fast mood from the opening scene.

Script by Joseph Landon and Clair Huffaker, adapted from latter's novel, limns the quest of four men for 2,000 stolen repeating rifles that a group of former Confederate soldiers have been running to the Apaches. Quartet is composed of Stuart Whitman, a cavalry captain, who heads the party; Richard Boone, an ex-reb who hates Apaches; Tony Franciosa, a Mexican gigolo-type killer whom the army was about to hang; and Jim Brown, a cavalry corporal. Their destination is the camp of a demented Confederate gunrunner (Edmond O'Brien) who wants vengeance on the North for the South's defeat.

Whitman acquits himself excellently in his tough role but interest principally lies in characters played by Boone and Franciosa, both killers and a director's dream. Brown, too, handles himself well, and Vito Scotti, as a laughing bandit, registers particularly in his brief menacing role before being killed.

•

RIO GRANDE

1950, 105 mins, US Ⓥ b/w

Dir John Ford ***Prod*** John Ford, Merian C. Cooper ***Scr*** James Kevin McGuinness ***Ph*** Bert Glennon ***Ed*** Jack Murray ***Mus*** Victor Young ***Art*** Frank Hotaling

Act John Wayne, Maureen O'Hara, Ben Johnson, Claude Jarman, Jr., Harry Carey, Jr., Victor McLaglen (Republic/Argosy)

Rio Grande is filmed outdoor action [based on a *Saturday Evening Post* story by James Warner Bellah] at its best, delivered in the John Ford manner. John Wayne's devotion to military oath had led him, some 15 years back, to destroy the plantation home of his southern-born wife during the War Between the States. He is now a lonely man, fighting Indians in the West. To his fort comes his young son, Claude Jarman, Jr., whom he has not seen in 15 years.

Into this setup of rugged living, endangered daily by marauding Indians, comes Maureen O'Hara, Wayne's estranged wife, determined to take the son back.

Comedy touches are introduced by Victor McLaglen as the top sergeant, a role he has performed in other Ford pictures.

•

RIO LOBO

1970, 114 mins, US Ⓥ ⊙ col

Dir Howard Hawks ***Prod*** Howard Hawks ***Scr*** Leigh Brackett, Burton Wohl ***Ph*** William Clothier ***Ed*** John Woodcock ***Mus*** Jerry Goldsmith ***Art*** Robert Smith

Act John Wayne, Jorge Rivero, Jennifer O'Neill, Jack Elam, Chris Mitchum, Victor French (Malabar/Cinema Center)

Rio Lobo is the sort of western that John Wayne and producer-director Howard Hawks do in their sleep. But by no stretch of nostalgia does it match such previous Wayne-Hawks epics as *Red River* or *Rio Bravo*.

Leigh Brackett and Burton Wohl's script, based on Wohl's story, is by the numbers. In the Civil War, Wayne is a Union colonel—an ex–Texas Ranger, of course—who keeps losing army gold shipments to Confederate guerrillas led by Jorge Rivero and Chris Mitchum. He captures them, but they won't tell him who the traitors are who have been tipping them off about the gold.

From then on it is the same plot that has been worked over since the silent days of Bronco Billy, with no new surprises.

Hawks's direction is as listless as the plot.

•

RIO RITA

1929, 135 mins, US col

Dir Luther Reed ***Prod*** William LeBaron ***Scr*** Luther Reed ***Mus*** Harry Tierney

Act Bebe Daniels, John Boles, Bert Wheeler, Robert Woolsey, Dorothy Lee, George Renevant (RKO)

Ziegfeld's [1927] stage *Rio Rita* [with songs by Harry Tierney and Joe McCarthy], from which the screenplay was adapted, had a national fame but played comparatively little territory in the legit.

The picture is in black-and-white except for the ballroom portion, handsomely colored by Technicolor.

In casting, the picture is perfect, with the paralyzer Bebe Daniels. She hogs the talker, although anyone will agree that John Boles as the ranger captain is entitled to a word of credit, both for a splendid canned voice and his playing.

In comedy it's Bert Wheeler first, with Robert Woolsey next, while Dorothy Lee stands second to Daniels. Wheeler and Woolsey are the only members of the stage company on the screen. George Renevant as the heavy General Ravenoff does a good villain.

The story is familiar, that of a captain of the Texan Rangers seeking a bandit over the border and falling in love, with the attendant incidents, sometimes melodramatic.

•

RIO RITA
1942, 91 mins, US Ⓥ ⊙ b/w
Dir S. Sylvan Simon ***Prod*** Pandro S. Berman ***Scr*** Richard Connell, Gladys Lehman ***Ph*** George Folsey ***Ed*** Ben Lewis ***Mus*** Herbert Stothart (dir)
Act Bud Abbott, Lou Costello, Kathryn Grayson, John Carroll, Patricia Dane, Tom Conway (M-G-M)

Like all Abbott and Costello entries. Without them it would be so much celluloid. So far as the oft-filmed version of the former Ziegfeld stage musical is concerned, Metro uses but the original title song and the "Rangers" number.

Script relies principally on a Nazi espionage story. The plot has to do with mysterious radiocasts to a foreign power; the manager (Tom Conway) of the heroine's (Kathryn Grayson) hotel is really a Nazi spy; his girlfriend Patricia Dane is (or isn't) a G-woman in disguise (the plot's confusing on this point), and Abbott and Costello, along with hero John Carroll, save the day in the nick. It's that kind of a plot.

Director S. Sylvan Simon has spaced the A&C nonsensities with a good sense of timing to properly break up the hoke. There are a couple of reprises on some of the business, but withal the 91 minutes pace well.

•

RIOT
1968, 96 mins, US col
Dir Buzz Kulik ***Prod*** William Castle ***Scr*** James Poe ***Ph*** Robert B. Hauser ***Ed*** Edwin H. Bryant ***Mus*** Christopher Komeda ***Art*** Paul Sylbert
Act Jim Brown, Gene Hackman, Mike Kellin, Gerald S. O'Loughlin, Ben Carruthers (Paramount)

Riot is a good prison programmer produced with authenticity inside Arizona State Prison. Jim Brown and Gene Hackman are leaders of a convict revolt which paralyzes prison routine and unleashes some violent passions. Buzz Kulik's direction is better in the forward plot thrusts than in the many repetitious stretches, not at all alleviated by a pedestrian ballad reprised much too often.

Ex-convict Frank Elli's book, *The Riot*, has been adapted into a wandering script which lacks a definite cohesion. Concept vacillates between apparent attempt to tell a straightforward escape story, and temptation to linger and exploit violence. No social document, this; but not a potboiler, either.

Hackman, Mike Kellin and a freaked-out psychotic con, played by Ben Carruthers, launch a minor riot as prelude to escape.

Brown's immensely strong screen presence is manifest. Hackman gives the best performance as an equivocating, cynical manipulator of crowd psychology. Carruthers is too unrestrained.

•

RIOT IN CELL BLOCK 11
1954, 80 mins, US ⊙ b/w
Dir Don Siegel ***Prod*** Walter Wanger ***Scr*** Richard Collins ***Ph*** Russell Harlan ***Ed*** Bruce B. Pierce ***Mus*** Herschel Burke Gilbert
Act Neville Brand, Emile Meyer, Frank Faylen, Leo Gordon, Robert Osterloh, Paul Frees (Allied Artists)

Riot in Cell Block 11 is a hard-hitting, suspenseful prison thriller. The pros and cons of prison riots are stated articulately in the Richard Collins screen story, and producer Walter Wanger uses a realistic, almost documentary, style to make his point for needed reforms in the operation of penal institutions.

The picture doesn't use formula prison plot. There's no inmate reformed by love or fair treatment, nor unbelievable boy-meets-girl, gets-same angle. Nor are there any heroes and heavies of standard pattern. Instead, it deals with a riot, how it started and why, what was done to halt it, the capitulations on both sides.

The points for reform made in the Wanger production cover overcrowded housing, poor food, the mingling of mentally well and mentally sick prisoners, the character-corroding idleness of men caged in cell blocks.

A standout performance is given by Emile Meyer, the warden who understands the prisoners' problems.

•

RISE OF CATHERINE THE GREAT, THE
(US: CATHERINE THE GREAT)
1934, 95 mins, UK Ⓥ ⊙ b/w
Dir Paul Czinner ***Prod*** Alexander Korda ***Scr*** Arthur Wimperis, Lajos Biro, Melchior Lengyel ***Ph*** Georges Perinal ***Ed*** Harold Young, Stephen Harrison ***Mus*** Muir Mathieson ***Art*** Vincent Korda
Act Douglas Fairbanks, Jr., Elisabeth Bergner, Flora Robson, Gerald du Maurier, Irene Vanbrugh, Joan Gardner (London)

A nice rather than a good-looking girl, with beautiful eyes, Elisabeth Bergner charms as she progresses and is altogether believable as the minor German princess of moderate circumstances summoned to Russia by the Empress Elizabeth to wed her erratic nephew, the Grand Duke Peter, sometimes called Peter the Impossible. The throne needs an heir. Theatrical license has been liberally taken. This story makes the marriage the culmination of the blue-blooded Cinderella's childhood dream and almost places her upon the throne despite herself, except that she rises to meet the obligation upon realizing how unequipped her dissolute husband is to meet the responsibility.

Bergner's scene with the dying empress (Flora Robson) is a gem of expert playing by both women and there are other highlight sequences, particularly a banquet, which stand out for direction, portrayal and dialog. The story is principally in the hands of Bergner, Robson and Douglas Fairbanks, Jr. Robson gives a fine performance, while Fairbanks's definition of the fuming Peter is one of the best he has ever done. *Catherine* is reported to have cost close to $400,000 which, for England, is the theoretical equivalent of a $1 million Hollywood effort. It is certainly one of the most expensive pictures ever made there.

•

RISING SUN
1993, 129 mins, US Ⓥ ⊙ col
Dir Philip Kaufman ***Prod*** Peter Kaufman ***Scr*** Philip Kaufman, Michael Crichton, Michael Backes ***Ph*** Michael Chapman ***Ed*** Stephen A. Rotter, William S. Scharf ***Mus*** Toru Takemitsu ***Art*** Dean Tavoularis
Act Sean Connery, Wesley Snipes, Harvey Keitel, Cary-Hiroyuki Tagawa, Kevin Anderson, Mako (20th Century-Fox/Walrus)

Rising Sun waters down the more contentious aspects of Michael Crichton's controversial bestseller about Japanese influence in the United States, while remaining faithful to its mechanical plotting and superficial characterizations.

A thriller spurred by the murder of a white party girl at the opening of a Japanese office tower in Los Angeles, Crichton's novel ruffled feathers due to its alleged Japan-bashing, its blunt discussion of Japanese mores, aggressive and exclusionary business practices and purportedly racist attitudes.

Lt. Web Smith (Wesley Snipes), a liaison officer with the LAPD, is advised to bring with him a man of both legendary and slightly dubious status within the force, Detective John Connor (Sean Connery), who is so expert on the Japanese that he is suspected of having been co-opted by them.

The cops' leads point to Japanese playboy Eddie Sakamura (Cary-Hiroyuki Tagawa), who was involved with the dead girl and with her that night. But critical surveillance tape of the murder scene would seem to have been doctored to alter the identities of the people who appear to have been present.

Crichton's structure tiresomely flip-flops investigative scenes with interludes of the men driving through the wet night as Connor imparts his wisdom to his less experienced partner.

Idea of casting a black actor as Lt. Smith, who was white in the novel, hasn't altered matters much. Compared to some of his earlier performances, Snipes seems lax and unfocused here. Detective Connor was reputedly written with Connery in mind, and the brawny veteran thesp brings plenty of authoritative, fatherly appeal to the role, issuing sage aphorisms.

•

RISKY BUSINESS
1983, 96 mins, US Ⓥ ⊙ col
Dir Paul Brickman ***Prod*** Jon Avnet ***Scr*** Paul Brickman ***Ph*** Reynaldo Villalobos, Bruce Surtees ***Ed*** Richard Chew ***Mus*** Tangerine Dream ***Art*** William J. Cassidy
Act Tom Cruise, Rebecca DeMornay, Curtis Armstrong, Bronson Pinchot, Raphael Sbarge, Joe Pantoliano (Geffen)

Risky Business is like a promising first novel, with all the pros and cons that come with that territory.

High schooler Tom Cruise could literally be a next-door neighbor to Timothy Hutton in *Ordinary People* on Chicago's affluent suburban North Shore. That changes virtually overnight, however, when he meets sharp-looking hooker Rebecca DeMornay. On the lam from her slimy pimp, she shacks up in Cruise's splendid home while his parents are out of town and, since he's anxious to prove himself as a Future Enterpriser in one of his school's more blatantly greed-oriented programs, convinces him to make the house into a bordello for one night.

Ultimately, pic seems to endorse the bottom line, going for the big buck. In fact, not only is Cruise rewarded financially for setting up the best little whorehouse in Glencoe, but it gets him into Princeton to boot. Writer-director Paul Brickman can therefore be accused of trying to have it both ways, but there's no denying the stylishness and talent of his direction.

•

RITA, SUE AND BOB TOO
1987, 95 mins, UK Ⓥ ⊙ col
Dir Alan Clarke ***Prod*** Sandy Lieberson ***Scr*** Andrea Dunbar ***Ph*** Ivan Strasburg ***Ed*** Stephen Singleton ***Mus*** Michael Kamen ***Art*** Leo Huntingford
Act Michelle Holmes, Siobhan Finneran, George Costigan, Lesley Sharp, Willie Ross, Patti Nicholls (Film Four/Umbrella/British Screen)

Rita, Sue and Bob Too is a sad-funny comedy about sex and life in the Yorkshire city of Bradford.

Rita and Sue are two schoolgirls who sometimes babysit for a well-off couple, Bob and Michelle. In the film's opening sequence, the odious yet somehow charming Bob, a real-estate agent, gives the girls a lift home, but stops off first on the moors above the city and without preliminaries, proposes sex with them. The girls are agreeable, with Sue taking the first turn on the reclining seat in Bob's Rover.

Immediately screenwriter Andrea Dunbar [who adapted the film from her own plays *The Arbor* and *Rita, Sue and Bob Too*] injects a completely convincing mixture of raunchy comedy and sadness.

Rita and Sue, splendidly played by Siobhan Finneran and Michelle Holmes, are pathetic figures as they trip along in their tight miniskirts, but they're lively and funny. George Costigan makes Bob a charming character, despite his ingrained seediness.

•

RITZ, THE
1976, 90 mins, US Ⓥ col
Dir Richard Lester ***Prod*** Denis O'Dell ***Scr*** Terrence McNally ***Ph*** Paul Wilson ***Ed*** John Bloom ***Mus*** Ken Thorne ***Art*** Phillip Harrison
Act Jack Weston, Rita Moreno, Jerry Stiller, Kaye Ballard, F. Murray Abraham, Paul B. Price (Warner)

Depending on where one's taste lies, *The Ritz* is either esoteric farce for the urban cosmopolite, or else one long tasteless and anachronistic 1950-ish "gay" joke, shot at England's Twickenham Studios in 25 days. Terrence McNally adapted his 1975 play about assorted mistaken identities and hang-ups in a N.Y. gay steambath (including Broadway cast originals).

McNally's story has Weston fingered for rubout by dying father-in-law George Coulouris. Escaping from the midwest, Jack Weston heads for a notorious Gotham gay bath, figuring that avenging brother-in-law Jerry Stiller will never find him.

But the plan doesn't figure on the gangland family's diversified business interests, nor on the ingenuity of Weston's wife, played by Kaye Ballard.

Classic farce construction provides the expected physical action.

•

RIVER, THE
1938, 30 mins, US ⊙ b/w
Dir Pare Lorentz ***Scr*** Pare Lorentz ***Ph*** Stacy Woodward, Floyd Crosby, Willard Van Dyke ***Ed*** Pare Lorentz ***Mus*** Virgil Thompson
(Farm Security Administration)

This is the second film produced by the Farm Security Administration, previous one having been *The Plough That Broke the Plains*, also written and directed by Pare Lorentz, with musical score by Virgil Thomson. It's a more arresting, more compelling job than the previous effort, although still failing to encompass the subject entirely.

Documentary pic seeks to tell the story of the Mississippi River, its sources, its majestic course, its destination, its uses and abuse by heedless man, and its relentless retaliation.

As the narrator [Thomas Chalmers] states, the Mississippi is the most nearly perfect river in the world, and something of that mighty quality infests the film. Film impressively depicts the beauty and the power of the river, how it has been squandered and destroyed, how terrible has been the inevitable result. But it fails to tie its interrelated parts into a whole that is entirely clear or convincing. It skips from fact to fact, argument to argument, but doesn't quite weave a perfect pattern. Thomson's score, blended from symphonic sources, ballads, spirituals and original compositions, highlights the film dramatically. Narrative is vividly effective, being a composite of straight description and exposition and poetic prose.

•

RIVER, THE
1951, 99 mins, India/US col
Dir Jean Renoir ***Prod*** Kenneth McEldowney ***Scr*** Rumer Godden, Jean Renoir ***Ph*** Claude Renoir ***Ed*** George Gale ***Mus*** M. A. Partha Sarathy ***Art*** Eugene Lourie
Act Nora Swinburne, Esmond Knight, Arthur Shields, Thomas E. Breen, Patricia Walters, Adrienne Corri (Oriental-International/United Artists)

Jean Renoir's *The River* is a sort of animated geographic, in color, of life on the Ganges River in West Bengal. It is a distinctive story of adolescent love, with a philosophy that life flows on just as the river.

This is a beautiful picture, and certainly neither Technicolor nor India ever looked better. Throughout it is ablaze with vivid, contrasting colors. But one never feels the real India and rather suspects that this is a highly glamorized version.

The story tells how the life of a British family (the family runs a jute mill) is interrupted by the appearance of one Capt. John on a visit to his cousin, Mr. John, a neighbor. Two young teenagers fall as madly in love with Capt. John, who lost a leg in the last war, as their newly awakened emotions will allow. But Capt. John is too busy being a lost soul to take them seriously.

Although the drama too frequently seems merely an afterthought, a sort of excuse upon which to build a lush panorama of India, the characters are completely credible. Exception is Thomas Breen as Capt. John. He has the appearance of one who might excite the immature emotions of the three young ladies, but hasn't the ability to appear convincing. Outstanding is Radha, whose ritual dance of love with the god Krishna highlights the pic.

•

RIVER, THE
1984, 122 mins, US col
Dir Mark Rydell ***Prod*** Edward Lewis, Robert Cortes ***Scr*** Robert Dillon, Julian Barry ***Ph*** Vilmos Zsigmond ***Ed*** Sidney Levin ***Mus*** John Williams ***Art*** Charles Rosen
Act Mel Gibson, Sissy Spacek, Shane Bailey, Becky Jo Lynch, Scott Glenn, Don Hood (Universal)

The River puts fundamental American values to the test in a society that has come unglued. Stripped down to the bare essentials few people actually ever come into contact with, pic remains a rather private ordeal observed from the outside looking in. There is a victory at the end, but not a sense of lasting triumph.

Setting the tone is the Garvey family battling the floodwaters of the river to save their farm. Farmers are forced to sell off their land with hungry wolf businessman Joe Wade (Scott Glenn) waiting to pick up the pieces.

Glenn, as the silver-spoon kid and Spacek's former lover, is the film's most complex creation. Though he is the malignancy behind much of the farmers' troubles, director Mark Rydell allows him to maintain a level of humanity.

1984: NOMINATIONS: Best Actress (Sissy Spacek), Cinematography, Original Score, Sound, Special Achievement Award (Sound Effects Editing)

•

RIVER OF GRASS
1994, 75 mins, US col
Dir Kelly Reichardt ***Prod*** Jesse Hartman, Kelly Reichardt ***Scr*** Kelly Reichardt ***Ph*** Jim Denault ***Ed*** Larry Fessenden
Act Lisa Bowman, Larry Fessenden, Dick Russell (Plan B)

An outlaw-lovers-on-the-run saga in which the leads don't commit a crime, fall in love or ever hit the road, *River of Grass* is a modern, ennui-laden film noir turned inside out and filmed in bright colors under the Florida sun.

New York writer-director Kelly Reichardt returned to her native area of suburban Miami to make her first feature, and she clearly knows her way around the neighborhood as well as around film conventions.

A terminally bored housewife, Cozy (Lisa Bowman) doesn't know what to do with herself until she meets Lee (Larry Fessenden), an entropy specialist who still lives at home at 29 and whose ambition is to "just drink." Lee has come into possession of a gun found on the road, one lost by Cozy's detective (and jazz drummer) father, Jimmy (Dick Russell). When Cozy accidentally fires the gun, she and Lee believe they've shot a black man and bolt to a motel to decide what to do. Bowman and Fessenden (who also edited) occasionally generate some deadpan humor but generally make for lackluster centers of attention. Russell gives the father, desperate to recover his weapon, some welcome style and pizzazz. With the tiniest of budgets at their disposal, filmmakers have gotten a reasonably good-looking picture on the screen.

•

RIVER OF NO RETURN
1954, 90 mins, US col
Dir Otto Preminger ***Prod*** Stanley Rubin ***Scr*** Frank Fenton ***Ph*** Joseph LaShelle ***Ed*** Louis Loeffler ***Mus*** Cyril J. Mockridge
Act Robert Mitchum, Marilyn Monroe, Rory Calhoun, Tommy Rettig, Murvyn Vye, Douglas Spencer (20th Century-Fox)

The striking beauties of the Canadian Rockies co-star with the blonde charms of Marilyn Monroe and the masculine muscles of Robert Mitchum in *River of No Return*.

The competition between scenic splendors of the Jasper and Banff National Parks and entertainment values finds the former finishing slightly ahead on merit, although there's enough rugged action and suspense moments to get the production through its footage. In between the high spots, Otto Preminger's directorial pacing is inclined to lag, so the running time seems overlong.

Mitchum and Tommy Rettig, playing father and son, pull Monroe and Rory Calhoun from a river that races by their wilderness farm. Calhoun is trying to get to a settlement to file a gold claim he has won dishonestly at cards and Monroe is along because she expects to marry him. Calhoun steals Mitchum's horse and gun and rides off, leaving the others at the mercy of warring Indians. Man, woman and boy take to the river on a raft to escape the redskins.

•

RIVER RUNS THROUGH IT, A
1992, 123 mins, US col
Dir Robert Redford ***Prod*** Robert Redford, Patrick Markey ***Scr*** Richard Friedenberg ***Ph*** Philippe Rousselot ***Ed*** Lynzee Klingman, Robert Estrin ***Mus*** Mark Isham ***Art*** Jon Hutman
Act Craig Sheffer, Brad Pitt, Tom Skerritt, Brenda Blethyn, Emily Lloyd, Edie McClurg (Columbia)

A skilled, careful adaptation of a much-admired story, *A River Runs Through It* is a convincing trip back in time to a virtually vanished American West, as well as a nicely observed family study. Old-fashioned, literary and restrained, it's Robert Redford's third directorial outing.

Published in 1976, the poetic, elegiac novella traces Norman Maclean's relationship with his wilder, younger brother Paul in Montana against the backdrop of fly-fishing, used as a metaphor for achieving a state of grace in life.

Arcing gracefully from 1910 to 1935, tale reveals the love and stability within the proud Maclean family, but also the inability to transform that love into the help Paul needs to save his life.

Performances are thoughtful and well-judged. Craig Sheffer brings well-tempered nuances to Norman. With the showiest role, Brad Pitt shines, his smoldering James Dean–ish looks and recklessness encompassing both Paul's charm and doom. Tom Skerritt discreetly reveals the loving core inside the reedy exterior of the boys' preacher father.

Exquisitely lit and lensed, pic gives a strong physical sense of the majestic mountains and brilliant rivers of Montana.

1992: Best Cinematography

NOMINATIONS: Best Screenplay Adaptation, Original Score

•

RIVER'S EDGE
1986, 99 mins, US col
Dir Tim Hunter ***Prod*** Sarah Pillsbury, Midge Sanford ***Scr*** Neal Jimenez ***Ph*** Frederick Elmes ***Ed*** Howard Smith, Sonya Sones ***Mus*** Jurgen Knieper ***Art*** John Moto
Act Crispin Glover, Keanu Reeves, Ione Skye, David Roebuck, Dennis Hopper, Leo Rossi (Hemdale)

Tim Hunter's *River's Edge* is an unusually downbeat and depressing youth pic.

The setting is a small town, presumably in Oregon. Pic opens with 12-year-old Tim destroying his kid sister's doll and then spotting high schooler Samson sitting on the riverbank with the naked body of a girl he's just murdered. Tim's reaction is to steal a couple of cans of beer for the killer.

But they're really nice at heart, the film seems to be saying. They have to cope with broken homes and the threat of the Bomb, otherwise they wouldn't be so hopeless.

As group leader Layne, Crispin Glover could have used more restraint: He gives a busy, fussy performance. Others in the cast are more effective, with young Joshua Miller particularly striking as the awful child, Tim.

•

RIVER WILD, THE
1994, 111 mins, US col
Dir Curtis Hanson ***Prod*** David Foster, Lawrence Turman ***Scr*** Denis O'Neill ***Ph*** Robert Elswit ***Ed*** Joe Hutshing, David Brenner ***Mus*** Jerry Goldsmith ***Art*** Bill Kenney
Act Meryl Streep, Kevin Bacon, David Strathairn, Joseph Mazzello, John C. Reilly, Benjamin Bratt (Turman-Foster/Universal)

The characters and the audience take a wild ride in *The River Wild*, a tense, sharply made thriller about a family held hostage during a river rafting vacation. Pic marks a career watershed for Meryl Streep, outstanding as a buff white-water rafter who has it all over the men around her.

Looking robust and glowing with healthy color, Streep is first glimpsed sculling at sunset in Boston, where her character, Gail, lives with architect hubby Tom (David Strathairn), two kids and a dog. Gail, son Roarke (Joseph Mazzello), whose tenth birthday the vacation out West is celebrating, and Fido are virtually hopping aboard their raft when Tom belatedly joins them.

Gail, who grew up amidst these spectacular mountains, used to be a river guide and knows its every twist and turn, a fact seized upon by a trio of supposed fishermen, led by the friendly Wade (Kevin Bacon), when their guide mysteriously disappears. It turns out that the pack Wade is carrying contains $250,000 that he and Terry robbed from a cattle auction. They've also already killed two men.

First-time screenwriter Denis O'Neill and director Curtis Hanson tighten the screws skillfully after Wade takes charge. The cat-and-mouse game continues suspensefully until the climactic encounter with the Gauntlet rapids, where Nature effectively becomes an unknown third force in the battle of wits.

Production materials state that Streep did 90% of the rapids work herself, but film makes it look as though she did it all. Bacon proves insidiously effective as a boyish baddie, and John C. Reilly's white trash sidekick reps the film's most forceful reminder of its closest precursor, *Deliverance*.

•

ROAD GAMES
1981, 100 mins, Australia col
Dir Richard Franklin ***Prod*** Richard Franklin ***Scr*** Everett De-Roche ***Ph*** Vincent Monton ***Ed*** Edward McQueen-Mason ***Mus*** Brian May ***Art*** Jon Dowding
Act Stacy Keach, Jamie Lee Curtis, Marion Edward, Grant Page, Bill Stacey (Quest)

Road Games is an above-average suspenser concerning an offbeat truck driver who winds up stalking a murderer. Stacy Keach's characterization of the amusing, poetry-spouting man is particularly endearing but the film builds all too effectively to a rather disappointing climax.

Keach limns an independent trucker in Melbourne assigned to deliver a major shipment of pork to Perth. Amid cracking jokes, concocting stories about the inhabitants of passing cars and fantasizing about pretty girls (all to the deadpan of his pet dog), he becomes suspicious of the driver of a green van.

Through a series of clues he begins to realize the guy is actually a killer of young women the police have been looking for. Neither the police nor anyone else will listen to Keach so he eventually decides to get the guy himself.

Jamie Lee Curtis appears midway through as an heiress hitchhiker who befriends Keach while looking for some diversion from everyday life.

•

ROAD HOME, THE
SEE: LOST ANGELS

•

ROAD HOUSE
1948, 95 mins, US b/w
Dir Jean Negulesco ***Prod*** Edward Chodorov ***Scr*** Edward Chodorov ***Ph*** Joseph LaShelle ***Ed*** James B. Clark ***Mus*** Cyril J. Mockridge ***Art*** Lyle R. Wheeler, Maurice Ransford

Act Ida Lupino, Cornel Wilde, Celeste Holm, Richard Widmark, O. Z. Whitehead, Robert Karnes (20th Century-Fox)

Framed within a realistically intimate roadhouse setting, yarn [by Margaret Gruen and Oscar Saul] reconstructs the triangle with an arrestingly psychotic twist supplied by Richard Widmark. For most of the way, director Jean Negulesco hurdles the script's over-length and internal weaknesses by building up conflict out of character studies of the principals. But the film finally bogs down in a lack of incident until a climatic shot-in-the-arm revives interest.

At the center of the story, turning in one of the best performances of her career, is Ida Lupino, playing a low-down blues warbler who finds herself in the middle between Widmark and Cornel Wilde. Widmark, the roadhouse operator, has a powerful yen for the singer but she prefers his general manager, Wilde.

Lupino's standout performance is highlighted by her first-rate handling of a brace of blues numbers. Her gravel-toned voice lacks range but has the more essential quality of style, along the lines of a femme Hoagy Carmichael.

•

ROAD HOUSE

1989, 114 mins, US Ⓥ ⦿ col

Dir Rowdy Herrington ***Prod*** Joel Silver ***Scr*** David Lee Henry, Hilary Henkin ***Ph*** Dean Cundey ***Ed*** Frank Urioste, John Link ***Mus*** Michael Kamen

Act Patrick Swayze, Kelly Lynch, Sam Elliott, Ben Gazzara, Marshall Teague, Julie Michaels (United Artists/Silver)

With *Road House*, United Artists hot-wires Patrick Swayze a star vehicle shackled by a couple of flat tires in the script department. Ill-conceived and unevenly executed, pic essentially is a Western—a loner comes in to clean up a bar, of all things, and ends up washing and drying the whole town—but its vigilante justice, lawlessness and wanton violence feel ludicrous in a modern setting.

A club owner (Kevin Tighe) recruits Dalton (Swayze) to clean up his bar, which is frequented by lowlifes and bikers. At first, Dalton avoids fighting when possible yet carries a big rep—including the label of having killed a man.

Road House degenerates into a seemingly endless series of fistfights, egged on by bad guy Brad Wesley (Ben Gazzara), who runs the town. The wispy subplot involves a flat romantic attachment for Dalton by a leggy and beautiful local doctor (Kelly Lynch), who turns up with thick glasses and her hair in a bun.

Director Rowdy Herrington has a flair for lensing the fisticuffs—especially a particularly brutal encounter between Swayze and Wesley's top mugger (Marshall Teague). But there's just far too much of it.

•

ROAD TO BALI

1952, 91 mins, US Ⓥ col

Dir Hal Walker ***Prod*** Harry Tugend ***Scr*** Frank Butler, Hal Kanter, William Morrow ***Ph*** George Barnes ***Ed*** Archie Marshek ***Mus*** Joseph J. Lilley (dir.) ***Art*** Hal Pereira, Joseph McMillan Johnson

Act Bob Hope, Bing Crosby, Dorothy Lamour, Murvyn Vye, Peter Coe, Leon Askin (Paramount)

Bing Crosby, Bob Hope and Dorothy Lamour are back again in another of Paramount's highway sagas, with nonsensical amusement its only destination. Five songs are wrapped up in the production.

Needing a job, Crosby and Hope hire out to Murvyn Vye, a South Seas island prince, as divers, sail for Vye's homeland and meet Princess Lamour, which is excuse enough for her to sing "Moonflowers," later reprised as the finale tune.

There's no story to speak of in the script [from a story by Frank Butler and Harry Tugend] but the framework is there on which to hang a succession of amusing quips and physical comedy dealing with romantic rivalry and chuckle competition between the two male stars. It also permits some surprise guest star appearances, such as the finale walk-on of Jane Russell; Humphrey Bogart pulling the African Queen through Africa.

•

ROAD TO EL DORADO, THE

2000, 89 mins, US Ⓥ ⦿ col

Dir Eric "Bibo" Bergeron, Don Paul ***Prod*** Bonne Radford, Brooke Breton ***Scr*** Ted Elliott, Terry Rossio ***Ed*** Vicki Hiatt ***Mus*** Hans Zimmer, John Powell ***Art*** Christian Schellewald (DreamWorks)

An animated combo of the old Bob Hope–Bing Crosby *Road* pictures and *The Man Who Would Be King*, DreamWorks' third major feature cartoon is a strained and pallid concoction with six of the least memorable songs Elton John and Tim Rice have written. Five years in production, epic buddy picture went through two sets of directors and numerous evolving concepts, arriving finally at a middle ground between outright romp and a serious take on the conquistadors in the New World.

Whenever *El Dorado* threatens to get serious, it backs off, retreating into loud shenanigans between its two mischievous heroes, complete with annoyingly anachronistic mannerisms. Dark-haired Tulio (voiced by Kevin Kline) and blond-maned Miguel (Kenneth Branagh) are Spanish rascals placed aboard one of Cortes's ships headed across the Atlantic in 1519. With Cortes's noble horse, they escape in a lifeboat and wash up on a beautiful beach.

Quickly captured by imposing bronze-skinned natives, the boys think their goose is cooked upon arrival at the fabled city of gold, El Dorado. But the coming of such "gods," as they are perceived to be, has been prophesied, and Tulio and Miguel are installed in exclusive quarters atop one of the city's many pyramids. Local babe Chel (Rosie Perez) is on to their game and blackmails the pair into including her in their plan to escape El Dorado with a bounty of gold. Although there is a local chief (Edward James Olmos), he, along with the rest of the community, is dominated by high priest Tzekel-Kan (Armand Assante), who gradually becomes skeptical of the white stranger's presumed divinity.

Far too much time is devoted to the two charlatans' silly arguments about how and if they're going to pull off their charade, and to contretemps concerning Chel. By contrast, one of the script's more promising elements—Miguel's sudden surge of feeling for the local citizens and their gentle lifestyle—is given unduly short shrift.

Kline and Branagh give boisterous, spirited readings to their characters, even if script provides them with few shadings or interesting traits. Assante registers strongly as the powerful priest. But the Chel character is so contemporary, and in a vulgar way to boot, as to be incredible and off-putting, and Perez's urbanite voicing doesn't help.

Visual design is colorful, sometimes attractive but never breathtaking.

•

ROAD TO GLORY, THE

1936, 103 mins, US Ⓥ b/w

Dir Howard Hawks ***Prod*** Nunnally Johnson ***Scr*** Joel Sayre, William Faulkner ***Ph*** Gregg Toland ***Ed*** Edward Curtiss ***Mus*** Louis Silvers ***Art*** Hans Peters

Act Fredric March, Warner Baxter, June Lang, Lionel Barrymore, Gregory Ratoff, John Qualen (20th Century-Fox)

Fredric March, Warner Baxter and June Lang constitute the war-front triangle. Barrymore is the veteran soldier who refuses to be sent back of the lines by his son (Baxter), chief in command, and who finds sympathetic alliance in March, a French lieutenant.

As romantic war stuff, *The Road to Glory* is a bit too obvious and stylized. But it's the highly competent production treatment which elevates it to big league company.

Glory is actually a remake of *Croix de Bois* (Wooden Crosses), French-made film (Pathe-Natan) of some years earlier, which Fox bought and scrapped for America, principally because of the battlefront stuff. Winnie Sheehan utilized some of it for his *The World Moves On* in 1934.

Baxter as the nerve-racked captain and March as his equally efficient lieutenant are capital, as are Lionel Barrymore and Gregory Ratoff. Latter makes his impersonation of the orderly a standout performance. Lang manifests potentialities, although her banged hairdo and general fullness of the way she wears her hair militate against a completely favorable impression.

•

ROAD TO HONG KONG, THE

1962, 91 mins, UK/US Ⓥ b/w

Dir Norman Panama ***Prod*** Melvin Frank ***Scr*** Norman Panama, Melvin Frank ***Ph*** Jack Hildyard ***Ed*** Alan Osbiston, John Victor Smith ***Mus*** Robert Farnon ***Art*** Roger Furse

Act Bing Crosby, Bob Hope, Joan Collins, Dorothy Lamour, Robert Morley, Felix Aylmer (United Artists/Melnor)

The seventh *Road* comedy, after a lapse of seven years, takes the boys on a haphazard trip to a planet called Plutonius, though this only happens as a climax to some hilarious adventures in Ceylon and Hong Kong.

It's almost useless to outline the plot. But it involves Crosby and Hope as a couple of flop vaudevillians who turn con men. Somewhere along the line, Hope loses his memory and that, in a mysterious manner, leads them to involvement with a mysterious spy (Joan Collins), a secret formula and a wacky bunch of thugs called the Third Echelon, led by Robert Morley. The script is spiced with a number of private jokes (golf, Hope's nose, Crosby's dough, reference to gags from previous *Road* films) but not enough to be irritating. Major disappointment is Joan Collins, who though an okay looker, never seems quite abreast of the comedians. Lamour plays herself as a vaude artist who rescues the Crosby-Hope team from one of their jams.

As guest artists, Frank Sinatra and Dean Martin help to round off the film. David Niven appears for no good reason, while the best interlude is that of Peter Sellers. He plays a native medico, examining Hope for amnesia and it is a brilliantly funny cameo.

•

ROAD TO MOROCCO

1942, 83 mins, US Ⓥ b/w

Dir David Butler ***Prod*** Paul Jones (assoc.) ***Scr*** Frank Butler, Don Hartman ***Ph*** William C. Mellor ***Ed*** Irene Morra ***Art*** Hans Dreier, Robert Usher

Act Bing Crosby, Bob Hope, Dorothy Lamour, Anthony Quinn, Vladimir Sokoloff, Dona Drake (Paramount)

Morocco is a bubbling spontaneous entertainment without a semblance of sanity; an uproarious patchquilt of gags, old situations and a blitz-like laugh pace that never lets up for a moment. It's Bing Crosby and Bob Hope at their best, with Dorothy Lamour, as usual, the pivotal point for their romantic pitch.

The story's absurdities, all of which are predicated on Crosby and Hope as shipwrecked stowaways cast ashore on the coast of North Africa, at no time weave a pattern of restraint. It's just a madcap holiday for the fun-makers.

The scripters, along with everyone else associated with the production, must surely have realized, of course, that the yarn couldn't be played straight. The result is some unorthodox filmmaking that finds both male stars making dialogistic asides that kid, for instance, some of the film's "weaknesses" or, in other cases, poke fun at various objects that aren't even remotely associated with the picture.

1942: NOMINATIONS: Best Original Screenplay, Sound

•

ROAD TO RIO

1947, 100 mins, US Ⓥ b/w

Dir Norman Z. McLeod ***Prod*** Daniel Dare ***Scr*** Edmund Beloin, Jack Rose ***Ph*** Ernest Laszlo ***Ed*** Ellsworth Hoagland ***Mus*** Robert Emmett Dolan (dir.) ***Art*** Hans Dreier, Earl Hedrick

Act Bing Crosby, Bob Hope, Dorothy Lamour, Gale Sondergaard, Frank Faylen, Joseph Vitale (Paramount)

There are no talking animals in this to prep uproarish see-hear gags, but a capable substitute is a trumpet that blows musical bubbles. Stunt pays off as one of a number of top, hard-punching laugh-getters. Norman Z. McLeod's direction blends the music and comedy into fast action and sock chuckles that will please followers of the series.

Bing Crosby and Bob Hope repeat their slaphappy characters in the Edmund Beloin-Jack Rose plot. Opening establishes the boys, as usual, in trouble and broke. When they set a circus on fire, pair escape by taking refuge on a ship heading for Rio. It doesn't take them long to discover a damsel in distress (Dorothy Lamour) and action centers around their efforts to save her from a wicked aunt and a forced marriage.

1947: NOMINATION: Best Scoring of a Musical Picture

•

ROAD TO SINGAPORE

1940, 84 mins, US Ⓥ b/w

Dir Victor Schertzinger ***Prod*** Harlan Thompson ***Scr*** Don Hartman, Frank Butler ***Ph*** William C. Mellor ***Ed*** Paul Weatherwax ***Mus*** Victor Young (dir.) ***Art*** Hans Dreier, Robert Odell

Act Bing Crosby, Dorothy Lamour, Bob Hope, Charles Coburn, Judith Barrett, Anthony Quinn (Paramount)

Initial teaming of Bing Crosby and Bob Hope in *Road to Singapore* provides foundation for continuous round of good substantial comedy of rapid-fire order, swinging along at a zippy pace. Contrast is provided in Crosby's leisurely presentation of situations and dialog, in comparison to the lightning-like thrusts and parries of Hope. Neat blending of the two brands accentuates the comedy values for laugh purposes.

Story [by Harry Hervey] is a light framework on which to drape the situations for Crosby and Hope, with Dorothy Lamour providing decorative character of a native gal in sarong-like trappings. Crosby is the adventurous son of a shipping magnate, who refuses to sit behind a desk. He walks out on both father and a socialite fiancée to ship to the South Seas with sailor-buddy Hope. Lamour moves in with the pair, and from there on it's a happy mixture of both making passes for the native beauty, while they struggle to raise the necessary coin to live in comfort on the island. Crosby eventually gets the girl, but not until the trio romps through some zany adventures.

•

ROAD TO UTOPIA

1946, 90 mins, US Ⓥ ⦿ b/w

Dir Hal Walker ***Prod*** Paul Jones ***Scr*** Norman Panama, Melvin Frank ***Ph*** Lionel Lindon, Gordon Jennings, Farciot Edouart ***Ed*** Stuart Gilmore ***Mus*** Leigh Harline ***Art*** Hans Dreier, Roland Anderson

Act Bing Crosby, Bob Hope, Dorothy Lamour, Robert Benchley, Hillary Brooke, Douglass Dumbrille (Paramount)

Bob Benchley is cut into an upper corner of various shots making wisecracks, first being that "this is how not to make a picture." Others are in the same groove, while additional off-the-path gags include Bob Hope and Dorothy Lamour in a kissing scene, topped by Hope's aside to the audience: "As far as I'm concerned the picture is over right now." Another is a guy walking across a scene asking Bing Crosby and Hope where Stage 8 is.

Action is laid in the Klondike of the gold rush days. On their way there, scrubbing decks because they'd lost their money, Crosby and Hope come upon a map leading to a rich gold mine. It had been stolen from Lamour's father by two of the toughest badmen of Alaska. Lamour goes to the Klondike in search of them.

Technically picture leaves nothing to be desired. Paul Jones, producer, and Hal Walker, who directed, make a fine combination in steering and in the production value provided. Performances by supporting cast are all good.

1946: NOMINATION: Best Original Screenplay

•

ROAD TO WELLVILLE, THE

1994, 120 mins, US Ⓥ ⦿ col

Dir Alan Parker ***Prod*** Alan Parker, Armyan Bernstein, Robert F. Colesberry ***Scr*** Alan Parker ***Ph*** Peter Biziou ***Ed*** Gerry Hambling ***Mus*** Rachel Portman ***Art*** Brian Morris

Act Anthony Hopkins, Bridget Fonda, Matthew Broderick, John Cusack, Dana Carvey, Lara Flynn Boyle (Dirty Hands/Beacon/Columbia)

A satire of health fanaticism in turn-of-the-century America, *The Road to Wellville* is a curiosity of the first order. Amusing without being particularly funny, and not especially involving in terms of its characters or melodrama, Alan Parker's unzipped cereal comedy is more something to gape at in wonderment.

Based on T. Coraghessan Boyle's 1992 historically based novel, physically resplendent picture takes a comical look at the shenanigans perpetrated in the name of good health at the Battle Creek Sanitarium, circa 1907. Founded by the Seventh Day Adventists, the impeccably appointed lakeside spa has become the personal laboratory of Dr. John Harvey Kellogg (Anthony Hopkins), who thunders on to his affluent clients about the evils of meat, smoking, alcohol and sex, and the virtues of Bulgarian yogurt and frequent enemas.

Among those arriving to take the cure this fall season are Will and Eleanor Lightbody (Matthew Broderick, Bridget Fonda), an attractive young couple. Also turning up in the Michigan boomtown is Charles Ossining (John Cusack), who hopes to strike it rich by producing a successful new cornflake breakfast food. His crooked partner, Bender (Michael Lerner), however, has squandered the investment money.

The film proves as energetic as its central character as it documents the vibrating machines, electric blankets, dunkings and dousings, current-fed baths and rear-end probings endorsed by Kellogg, as well as the genitally stimulating belt and "womb manipulation" practised by the doctor's more erotically inclined competitors.

But the lack of compelling or inventive narrative incidents, coupled with characters who inspire no more than lukewarm enthusiasm, leaves the second half flailing about. Hopkins's Kellogg remains a one-dimensional figure devoid of character development or personal quest.

•

ROAD TO ZANZIBAR

1941, 89 mins, US Ⓥ b/w

Dir Victor Schertzinger ***Prod*** Paul Jones ***Scr*** Frank Butler, Don Hartman ***Ph*** Ted Tetzlaff ***Ed*** Alma Macrorie ***Mus*** Victor Young (dir.) ***Art*** Hans Dreier, Robert Usher

Act Bing Crosby, Bob Hope, Dorothy Lamour, Una Merkel, Jean Marsh, Eric Blore (Paramount)

Zanzibar is Paramount's second coupling of Bing Crosby, Bob Hope and Dorothy Lamour. Although picture has sufficient comedy situations and dialog between its male stars, it lacks the compactness and spontaneity of its predecessor.

The story framework [by Don Hartman, Sy Bartlett] is pretty flimsy foundation for hanging the series of comedy and thrill situations concocted for the pair. It's a fluffy and inconsequential tale, with Crosby-Hope combo doing valiant work to keep up interest.

Pair are stranded in South Africa, with Crosby the creator of freak sideshow acts for Hope to perform. With his saved passage money back to the States, Crosby buys a diamond mine, which is quickly sold by Hope for profit. Then pair start out on strange safari with Lamour and Una Merkel, pair of Brooklyn entertainers, pursuing a millionaire hunter. Comedy episodes generally lack sparkle and tempo, and musical numbers [staged by Le Roy Prinz] are also below par for a Crosby picture.

•

ROAD TRIP

2000, 91 mins, US Ⓥ ⦿ col

Dir Todd Phillips ***Prod*** Daniel Goldberg, Joe Medjuck ***Scr*** Todd Phillips, Scot Armstrong ***Ph*** Mark Irwin ***Ed*** Sheldon Kahn ***Mus*** Mike Simpson ***Art*** Clark Hunter

Act Breckin Meyer, Seann William Scott, Amy Smart, Paulo Costanzo, D. J. Qualls, Rachel Blanchard (Montecito/DreamWorks)

Anal probe jokes. Sperm bank jokes. Jokes about toe-sucking, Viagra-fueled erections, eating live mice and doing unspeakably vulgar things to French toast. No doubt about it: When it comes to gross-out humor, *Road Trip* is even grosser than *American Pie*. Much more exuberantly funny than its generic title might indicate, *Road Trip* focuses on the rude, crude and occasionally lewd behavior of four college pals on a cross-country misadventure.

At New York's Ithaca College, chronic under-achiever Josh (Breckin Meyer) assumes his suddenly incommunicado girlfriend, Tiffany (Rachel Blanchard), must be misbehaving while attending college in far-off Austin, Texas. Deeply wounded, Josh has a terrific night of whoopee with the beautiful Beth (Amy Smart), who impulsively records the evening's festivities on videotape. The next morning, Josh discovers that Tiffany was coping with a family tragedy and that one of his roomies has accidentally mailed the Beth-does-Josh video to Tiffany.

Frantic to retrieve the tape before Tiffany receives it, Josh sets out for Austin, accompanied by three friends: E. L. (Seann William Scott), a wild-eyed party animal; Rubin (Paulo Costanzo), a cerebral stoner; and Kyle (D. J. Qualls), a reedy geek. The travelers wreck their car, lose most of their money and nearly cause an unpleasant incident at an African-American college frat house. Desperation leads to improvisation: The guys steal a bus from a school for the blind, earn some quick money as sperm donors and even fortuitously find a way for Kyle to be relieved of his virginity.

The anything-goes comedy isn't nearly as politically incorrect as it seems at first glance. The filmmakers want to have their *American Pie* and eat it, too, so they nimbly avoid stereotyping while rolling out the raunch. At the African-American frat house, for example, the four white leads, not their bemused black hosts, serve as the butts of broad jokes. And the female characters, even the less-than-virginal ones, are what feminists might describe as "empowered," in that they always are the ones to decide who gets to do what, when and how during close contacts. Indeed, the filmmakers are quite generous in rewarding anyone with a healthy sex drive, even when the reward calls for upending audience expectations regarding how this kind of comedy usually resolves itself.

•

ROAD WARRIOR, THE

SEE: MAD MAX 2

•

ROAR

1981, 102 mins, US ▭ col

Dir Noel Marshall ***Prod*** Noel Marshall, Charles Sloan, Jack Rattner ***Scr*** Noel Marshall ***Ph*** Jan De Bont ***Mus*** Dominic Frontiere ***Art*** Joel Marshall

Act Tippi Hedren, Noel Marshall, John Marshall, Melanie Griffith, Jerry Marshall, Kyalo Mativo (Marshall)

The noble intentions of director-writer-producer Noel Marshall and his actress-wife Tippi Hedren shine through the faults and shortcomings of *Roar*, their 11-year, $17 million project—touted as the most disaster-plagued pic in Hollywood history.

Given the enormous difficulties during production—a devastating flood, several fires, an epidemic that decimated the feline cast and numerous injuries to actors and crew, it's a miracle that the pic was completed. Here is a passionate plea for the preservation of African wildlife meshed with an adventure-horror tale which aims to be a kind of *Jaws* of the jungle. If it seems at times more like *Born Free* gone berserk, such are the risks of planting the cast in the bush (actually the Marshalls's ranch in Soledad Canyon in California), surrounded by 150 untrained lions, leopards, tigers, cheetahs and other big cats, not to mention several large and ill-tempered elephants.

Thin plot has Hedren and her three children trekking to Africa to reunite with Marshall, an eccentric scientist who's been living in a three-story wooden house in the jungle with his feline friends, an experiment to show that humans and beasts can happily coexist.

Hedren and her daughter Melanie Griffith have proved their dramatic ability elsewhere: here they and their costars are required to do little more than look petrified.

•

ROARING TWENTIES, THE

1939, 106 mins, US Ⓥ ⦿ b/w

Dir Raoul Walsh ***Prod*** Hal B. Wallis (exec.) ***Scr*** Jerry Wald, Richard Macaulay, Robert Rossen ***Ph*** Ernest Haller ***Ed*** Jack Killifer ***Mus*** Ray Heindorf (arr.) ***Art*** Max Parker

Act James Cagney, Priscilla Lane, Humphrey Bogart, Gladys George, Frank McHugh, Paul Kelly (Warner)

This is a partially true gangster melodrama from the pen of Mark Hellinger. As a seasoned Broadway columnist Hellinger well remembered the dizzy times that gave birth to such illegal hot spots as the Hotsy-Totsy, Dizzy, Black Bottom, etc. Above all, he had intimate knowledge of the El Fay, the Del Fey and the Guinan clubs, and the Texas Guinan–Larry Fay operation thereof. He has thinly disguised them as the central figures of this yarn, in a good many instances spilling some inside facts, but the blow-off (for the sake of better picture entertainment) is certainly fictionized.

Because of James Cagney and the story's circumstances, *The Roaring Twenties* is reminiscent of *Public Enemy*. Story and dialog are good. Raoul Walsh turns in a fine directorial job; the performances are uniformly excellent.

•

ROBBERY

1967, 114 mins, UK Ⓥ col

Dir Peter Yates ***Prod*** Stanley Baker, Michael Deeley ***Scr*** Edward Boyd, Peter Yates, George Markstein ***Ph*** Douglas Slocombe ***Ed*** Reginald Beck ***Mus*** Johnny Keating ***Art*** Michael Seymour

Act Stanley Baker, Joanna Pettet, James Booth, Frank Finlay, Barry Foster, William Marlowe (Oakhurst)

This precision-tooled suspense thriller turns many of the traditional ingredients that usually go into this kind of film inside out and manages to come up with a tight, well-paced, highly entertaining pic [from a treatment by Gerald Wilson].

For a brisk start there's a car robbery and the maneuvers of the robbers in London streets consume the first 20 minutes, during which there is [virtually] no dialog but a thumping good score by Johnny Keating which adds to the unexplained incidents. The cleverly executed theft is followed by a roller-coaster car chase.

Peter Yates directs with a sense of authenticity and detail which makes the viewer both detached and increasingly curious concerning the various incidents involved in blueprinting and executing the robbery of £3 million from a British mail train.

•

ROBBERY UNDER ARMS

1957, 99 mins, UK Ⓥ col

Dir Jack Lee ***Prod*** Joseph Janni ***Scr*** Alexander Baron, W. P. Lipscomb ***Ph*** Harry Waxman ***Ed*** Manuel Del Campo ***Mus*** Matyas Seiber ***Art*** Alex Vetchinsky

Act Peter Finch, Ronald Lewis, Laurence Naismith, Maureen Swanson, David McCallum, Jill Ireland (Rank)

Set in Australia of 100 years earlier, *Robbery Under Arms* is a well-made straightforward drama. The story, based on a Victorian novel [by Rolf Boldrewood] has Peter Finch as Captain Starlight, a virile, likeable rogue who runs a gang of bushrangers. In search of adventure, Ronald Lewis and David McCallum join the gang, which includes their father. When the two attempt to break away and lead honest lives they find that they've lost their chance.

Jack Lee's direction splendidly captures the Australian atmosphere. He indulges in no frills. Lee is admirably supported by lenser Harry Waxman who fills the screen with sweeping camerawork, suggesting the vastness of the Australian canvas.

In the star role, Finch has a comparatively small role but he plays it with a swagger which is highly effective. Good opportunities are given to the brothers, Lewis and McCallum. The distaff side plays second fiddle to the men in this action meller, but Maureen Swanson, in an undeveloped role as a fiery, possessive young woman who sets her amorous sights on Lewis, has a real opportunity.

•

ROBE, THE
1953, 135 mins, US Ⓥ ⦿ ▭ col
Dir Henry Koster *Prod* Frank Ross *Scr* Philip Dunne *Ph* Leon Shamroy *Ed* Barbara McLean *Mus* Alfred Newman *Art* Lyle R. Wheeler, George W. Davis
Act Richard Burton, Jean Simmons, Victor Mature, Michael Rennie, Jay Robinson, Dean Jagger (20th Century-Fox)

The Robe was 10 years coming, first under RKO aegis when producer Frank Ross was there. It is a big picture in every sense of the word. One magnificent scene after another, under the [new] anamorphic CinemaScope technique, unveils the splendor that was Rome and the turbulence that was Jerusalem at the time of Christ on Calvary.

The homespun robe worn by Jesus is the symbol of Richard Burton's conversion when the Roman tribune realizes he carried out the crucifixion of a holy man at Pontius Pilate's orders. Victor Mature is the Greek slave for whom Burton outbid the corrupt Caligula (Jay Robinson), the Roman prince regent.

Lloyd C. Douglas's original bestseller is a fictionized novel of Scriptural times, and thus Jean Simmons is cast as the love interest who, as the ward of the Emperor Tiberius (Ernest Thesiger), spurns her destiny as the betrothed of the Prince Regent for the love of Marcellus Gallio (Burton).

The performances are consistently good. Simmons, Burton and Mature are particularly effective, and Betta St. John, Dean Jagger, Michael Rennie, Torin Thatcher and Ernest Thesiger likewise stand out in the other more prominent roles. Jeff Morrow's heavy is good, and the sword duel between him and Burton a highlight.

The slave market, the freeing of the Greek slave from the torture rack, the Christians in the catacombs, the dusty plains of Galilee, the Roman court splendor and that finale "chase" (with the four white steeds charging head-on into the camera creating a most effective 3-D illusion) are standouts.

The Robe reportedly cost $4.5 million, of which close to $1 million may date back to producer Frank Ross's investiture under the original RKO banner. With or without the hidden charges it looks almost all of it.

1953: Best Color Art Direction, Color Costume Design

NOMINATIONS: Best Picture, Actor (Richard Burton), Color Cinematography

•

ROBERTA
1935, 105 mins, US Ⓥ ⦿ b/w
Dir William A. Seiter *Prod* Pandro S. Berman *Scr* Jane Murfin, Sam Mintz *Ph* Edward Cronjager *Ed* William Hamilton *Mus* Max Steiner (dir.) *Art* Van Nest Polglase, Carroll Clark
Act Irene Dunne, Fred Astaire, Ginger Rogers, Randolph Scott, Helen Westley, Victor Verconi (RKO)

Roberta is musical picture-making at its best—fast, smart, good-looking and tuneful. The original [1933 Broadway musical's] chief assets were fine music [by Jerome Kern] and good taste. The picture retains both of these and accumulates a stronger story and better gait along the way.

When not dancing in *Roberta* Fred Astaire is trying for laughs, and he can light comedy with the best of them. In Ginger Rogers, Astaire has an ideal partner. Rogers dances well enough to be able to hold her own in the stepping numbers, which is something when dancing with Astaire. Irene Dunne looks like a million and sings like just as much. Biggest weakness in the stage *Roberta* was in the story [by Otto Harbach, from the novel by Alice Duer Muller]. It isn't changed much in the adaptation, but new dialog [by Allan Scott and Glenn Tryon] marks the difference.

As in the original version, the footballer still comes over to Paris with his pal's Indiana jazz band and inherits his devoted aunt's gown emporium. A nightclub side provides the necessary elbow room to allow for the Astaire and Astaire-Rogers dancing and singing.

Jerome Kern's "Smoke Gets in Your Eyes" is good enough to rate its preferred spot in the picture's score. Added to the Kern-Harbach compositions from the show are some highly listenable tunes by the same team plus Dorothy Fields and Jimmy McHugh.

•

ROBIN AND MARIAN
1976, 106 mins, UK Ⓥ col
Dir Richard Lester *Prod* Denis O'Dell *Scr* James Goldman *Ph* David Watkin *Ed* John Victor Smith *Mus* John Barry *Art* Michael Stringer
Act Sean Connery, Audrey Hepburn, Robert Shaw, Richard Harris, Nicol Williamson, Denholm Elliott (Columbia/Rastar)

Robin and Marian is a disappointing and embarrassing film: disappointing, because Sean Connery, Audrey Hepburn, the brilliant Robert Shaw, Richard Harris and a screenplay by James Goldman ought to add up to something even in the face of Richard Lester's flat direction; embarrassing, because the incompatible blend of tongue-in-cheek comedy, adventure and romance gives the Robin Hood–revisited film the grace and energy of a geriatrics' discotheque.

Connery's Robin and Nicol Williamson's Little John return to England after Harris's King Richard dies abroad; back home, Shaw's Sheriff of Nottingham is still in office, now nominally subservient to nobleman Kenneth Haigh, who was appointed by Ian Holm's bad King John. Hepburn's Marian has retired to a nunnery, eventually becoming Mother Superior there when Robin didn't return from the Crusades.

The idea of picking up the Robin Hood legend 20 years later seems okay at first consideration, but Goldman and Lester never got beyond the premise.

•

ROBIN AND THE 7 HOODS
1964, 123 mins, US Ⓥ ⦿ ▭ col
Dir Gordon Douglas *Prod* Frank Sinatra *Scr* David R. Schwartz *Ph* William H. Daniels *Ed* Sam O'Steen *Mus* Nelson Riddle (dir.) *Art* LeRoy Deane
Act Frank Sinatra, Dean Martin, Sammy Davis, Jr., Peter Falk, Bing Crosby, Barbara Rush (Warner/P-C)

Robin and the 7 Hoods is a spoof on gangster pix of bygone days sparked by the names of Frank Sinatra, Dean Martin and Bing Crosby. The daffy doings of Chicago's hoodlums during the Prohibition era in a battle for leadership of the rackets backdrops action which usually is on the slightly wacky side.

Scripter David R. Schwartz takes the legend of Robin Hood and his merry men and retailors it loosely to the frolickings of Sinatra and his pack. In some measure the parallel is successful, at least as basis for a premise which gives the plot a gimmick springboard as Sinatra, as Robbo, the good-hearted hood, takes from the rich to give to the poor.

Yarn opens in 1928 with the gangster kingpin of the day—Edward G. Robinson doing a cameo bit here—guest of honor at a lavish birthday party. After a sentimental rendition of "For He's a Jolly Good Fellow" by the assembled company of hoods, they shoot Robinson dead. Thereafter it's for grabs as Peter Falk has himself elected as the new Number One, and Sinatra arrives to warn him to keep out of his territory.

Performance-wise, Falk comes out best. His comic gangster is a pure gem. Sinatra, of course, is smooth and Crosby in a "different" type of role rates a big hand.

1964: NOMINATIONS: Best Adapted Musical Score, Song ("My Kind of Town")

•

ROBIN HOOD
1922, 125 mins, US Ⓥ ⊗ b/w
Dir Allan Dwan *Prod* Douglas Fairbanks *Scr* Elton Thomas [= Douglas Fairbanks], Lotta Woods *Ph* Arthur Edeson *Ed* William Nolan *Art* Wilfred Buckland, Irvin J. Martin, Edward M. Langley
Act Douglas Fairbanks, Wallace Beery, Sam De Grasse, Enid Bennett, Paul Dickey, William Lowery (Fairbanks/United Artists)

Archery, and when knights were bold while villains were cold, and that is *Robin Hood.*

Robin Hood is a great production but not a great picture. It just misses being great through a slow, long opening, in the days of Richard the Lionheart and his first crusade.

The prettiness of the sets of Robin Hood's lair in Sherwood Forest, the picturesqueness of his band of outlaws who were for their king and against his villainous brother, Prince John; the breadth of the settings throughout; the stunts by Douglas Fairbanks when he gets going; the superb supporting cast; the castle—that's *Robin Hood* and why it is a good picture. It holds you tense in the Robin Hood portion and lets you down badly when it's about Richard.

•

ROBIN HOOD
1991, 104 mins, UK/US Ⓥ ⦿ col
Dir John Irvin *Prod* Sarah Radclyffe *Scr* Sam Resnick, John McGrath *Ph* Jason Lehel *Ed* Peter Tanner *Mus* Geoffrey Burgon *Art* Austen Spriggs
Act Patrick Bergin, Uma Thurman, Jurgen Prochnow, Edward Fox, Jeroen Krabbe, Owen Teale (Working Title/20th Century-Fox)

Despite solid production values and a few extremely good moments, this awkwardly depicted *Robin Hood* may disturb those sentimentally attached to the original 1938 Michael Curtiz–directed classic. Tinkering with the lore, the pic's tone unflatteringly recalls the worst flippant aspects of Richard Lester's *Musketeers* films.

This story [by Sam Resnick] has nobleman Robert Hode (Patrick Bergin) giving spoils to the poor as an afterthought. Having already turned to crime, he thinks the gesture could be just the one to protect his hide. The one wrinkle that does work is Uma Thurman's scrappy, sexy Maid Marian, a woman who battles alongside the men.

The reworked legend has Saxon noble Hode disenfranchised by his one-time friend Daguerre (Jeroen Krabbe), the Norman who holds sway over the area. After an encounter with Little John (David Morrissey), Hode and his compatriot (Owen Teale) join the ranks of a group of thieves—hidden in caves rather than the trees of Sherwood Forest—ultimately leading the group in rebellion against Daguerre and Prochnow's foppish baron.

The lack of major action sequences is surprising in light of the resumes of director John Irvin and exec producer John McTiernan. Costumes and sets solidly capture the 12th century time period, muted with autumnal tones.

[Version reviewed was the 180-minute telemovie broadcast on U.S. TV May 13, 1991.]

•

ROBIN HOOD: MEN IN TIGHTS
1993, 102 mins, US Ⓥ ⦿ col
Dir Mel Brooks *Prod* Mel Brooks *Scr* Mel Brooks, J. David Shapiro, Evan Chandler *Ph* Michael D. O'Shea *Ed* Stephen Rivkin *Mus* Hummie Mann *Art* Roy Forge Smith
Act Cary Elwes, Richard Lewis, Roger Rees, Amy Yasbeck, Tracey Ullman, Mel Brooks (Brooksfilms/20th Century-Fox)

Pic marks a return to the wild, anarchic scatological comedies that made Mel Brooks a marquee name around the world. It is a film for both his diehard fans and a new generation who know Mad Mel only from legend. In 1975 he covered the territory in the television series *When Things Were Rotten*. Here he has managed to mangle the legend so that it essentially resembles his biggest hit, *Blazing Saddles*.

Tale involves nobleman Robin of Loxley (Cary Elwes), who ventures with King Richard to the Crusades. He escapes and returns to England, where he finds the kingdom in disarray in the hands of Prince John (Richard Lewis) and his evil henchman, renamed here the Sheriff of Rottingham (Roger Rees). Adopting outlaw ways, Robin also finds romance with Maid Marian (Amy Yasbeck).

Friar Tuck has been reinvented for Brooks to play as Rabbi Tuckman, and the characters include a black foreign-exchange student and plenty of anachronistic modern references.

The manic ensemble is grounded by Elwes's virtually straight-faced interpretation of Robin with a glib assuredness that hits the target dead center. Rather slier is Yasbeck's Marian, who gets great comic effect from being the girl too good to be true. The supporting cast features many members of Brooks's stock company.

•

ROBIN HOOD PRINCE OF THIEVES
1991, 138 mins, US Ⓥ ⦿ col
Dir Kevin Reynolds *Prod* John Watson, Pen Densham, Richard B. Lewis *Scr* Pen Densham, John Watson *Ph* Doug Milsome *Ed* Peter Boyle *Mus* Michael Kamen *Art* John Graysmark
Act Kevin Costner, Morgan Freeman, Mary Elizabeth Mastrantonio, Christian Slater, Alan Rickman, Sean Connery (Morgan Creek)

Kevin Costner's *Robin Hood* is a Robin of wood. Murky and uninspired, this $50 million rendition bears evidence of the rushed and unpleasant production circumstances that were much reported upon. At the same time, this seriously intended, more realistically motivated revision of the Robin myth may have diminished the hero, but it hasn't destroyed him. Lackluster script, from a story by Pen Densham, begins in the year 1194 in Jerusalem, where Robin leads a prison uprising and escapes with a Moor, Azeem (Morgan Freeman). Retreating from the Crusades, the pair head for England, where they find that Robin's father has been slain by the Sheriff of Nottingham (Alan Rickman), who is attempting to eliminate all resistance and perhaps make a play for the throne in the absence of King Richard.

To avenge his father's death, Robin joins up with Little John and the latter's band of outsiders in a safe enclave in Sherwood Forest. Major setpiece is the sheriff's attack on the outlaws' hippie-like compound, which decimates the group. But Robin is able to lead a counterattack on Nottingham Castle.

The best that can be said for Costner's performance is that it is pleasant. At worst, it can be argued whether it is more properly described as wooden or cardboard.

Looking beautiful and sporting an accent that comes and goes, Mary Elizabeth Mastrantonio makes a sprightly, appropriately feisty Marian. Of the Americans, Christian Slater is most successful at putting on an English accent, and he has some spirited moments as Will Scarlett. As the "painted man" who accompanies Robin in gratitude for his life having been saved, Freeman is a constant, dominant presence. As the sheriff, Rickman goes way over the top, emoting with facial and vocal leers. It's a relief whenever this resourceful thesp is on-screen, such is the energy and brio he brings to the proceedings. An unbilled Sean Connery shows up at the very end as King Richard to give his blessing to Robin and Marian's marriage.

1991: NOMINATION: Best Original Song ("(Everything I Do) I Do It for You")

•

ROBOCOP

1987, 103 mins, US Ⓥ ⦿ col

Dir Paul Verhoeven ***Prod*** Arne Schmidt ***Scr*** Edward Neumeier, Michael Miner ***Ph*** Jost Vacano ***Ed*** Frank J. Urioste ***Mus*** Basil Poledouris ***Art*** William Sandell

Act Peter Weller, Nancy Allen, Ronny Cox, Kurtwood Smith, Dan O'Herlihy, Miguel Ferrer (Davison)

RoboCop is a comic book movie that's definitely not for kids. The welding of extreme violence with four-letter words is tempered with gut-level humor and technical wizardry.

Roller-coaster ride begins with the near-dismemberment of recently transferred police officer Murphy (Peter Weller) to the southern precinct of the Detroit Police Dept. in the not-too-distant future.

There are three organizations inextricably wound into Detroit's anarchical society—the police, a band of sadistic hoodlums, and a multinational conglomerate which has a contract with the city to run the police force.

Weller is blown to bits just at the time an ambitious junior exec at the multinational is ready to develop a prototype cyborg—half-man, half-machine programmed to be an indestructable cop. Thus Weller becomes RoboCop, unleashed to fell the human scum he encounters, not the least among them his killers.

As sicko sadists go, Kurtwood Smith is a well-cast adversary. Nancy Allen as Weller's partner (before he died) provides the only warmth in the film, wanting and encouraging RoboCop to listen to some of the human spirit that survived inside him. *RoboCop* is as tightly worked as a film can be, not a moment or line wasted.

1987: Special Award (sound effects editing)

NOMINATIONS: Best Editing, Sound

•

ROBOCOP 2

1990, 118 mins, US Ⓥ ⦿ col

Dir Irvin Kershner ***Prod*** Jon Davison ***Scr*** Frank Miller, Walon Green ***Ph*** Mark Irwin ***Ed*** William Anderson ***Mus*** Leonard Rosenman ***Art*** Peter Jamison

Act Peter Weller, Nancy Allen, Dan O'Herlihy, Belinda Bauer, Tom Noonan, Galyn Gorg (Orion/Tobor)

This ultraviolent, nihilistic sequel has enough technical dazzle to impress hardware fans, but obviously no one in the Orion front office told filmmakers that less is more.

The future is represented by a crumbling Detroit (actually filmed, like the original, in Texas), dominated by Dan O'Herlihy's Omni Consumer Products company. He's set to foreclose on loans and literally take possession of Motown. Standing in his way is a loose cannon, drug magnate/user Tom Noonan, whose goal is to flood society with designer versions of his drug Nuke.

Peter Weller as RoboCop must defeat both factions while effeminate mayor Willard Pugh gets in the way. Noonan is reconstituted as Robocop 2 by O'Herlihy's sexy assistant Belinda Bauer, providing the film's final half hour of great special effects as an end in themselves.

Gabriel Damon as a precocious 12-year-old gangster is the best thing in the picture.

•

ROBOCOP 3

1993, 104 mins, US Ⓥ ⦿ col

Dir Fred Dekker ***Prod*** Patrick Crowley ***Scr*** Frank Miller, Fred Dekker ***Ph*** Gary B. Kibbe ***Ed*** Bert Lovitt ***Mus*** Basil Poledouris ***Art*** Hilda Stark

Act Robert John Burke, Nancy Allen, Rip Torn, John Castle, Jill Hennessy, CCH Pounder (Universal)

This latest widget off the *RoboCop* assembly line is a bit better than the first sequel, which amounts to damnation with faint praise. Limiting the gore, but not the carnage, pic remains a cluttered, nasty exercise that seems principally intent on selling action figures.

Robert John Burke replaces Peter Weller—star of the first two films—in the title role of the murdered cop who returns as a crime-fighting cyborg. This time, ubiquitous conglomerate OCP is trying to evict poor tenants from a run-down neighborhood to erect Delta City, a pet project of the massive Japanese corporation run by tycoon villain Kanemitsu (Mako) that now owns the company.

Director Fred Dekker (*The Monster Squad*) wrote the screenplay with comic-book writer-illustrator Frank Miller—who also scripted the series' second installment—and helps bring some flashes of broad humor to the otherwise dour proceedings.

The marketing gurus seem to be working overtime, introducing an orphaned, computer-hacking moppet (Remy Ryan) to try reaching a younger demographic and, for their older brothers, a dishy doctor (Jill Hennessy) who also joins the Robocause.

The series' enduring stars remain Rob Bottin's knockout RoboCop suit and Basil Poledouris's musical score.

•

ROBOT MONSTER

1953, 62 mins, US Ⓥ ⦿ b/w

Dir Phil Tucker ***Prod*** Phil Tucker ***Scr*** Wyott Ordung ***Ph*** Jack Greenhalgh ***Ed*** Bruce Schoengarth ***Mus*** Elmer Bernstein

Act George Nader, Claudia Barrett, Selena Royle, Gregory Moffett, John Mylong, Pamela Paulson (Three Dimensional)

Judged on the basis of novelty, as a showcase for the Tru-Stereo Process, *Robot Monster* comes off surprisingly well, considering the extremely limited budget ($50,000) and schedule on which the film was shot.

The Tru-Stereo Process (3-D) utilized here is easy on the eyes, coming across clearly at all times. To the picture's credit no 3-D gimmicks were employed.

Beating Arch Oboler's *Five* [1951] by one survivor, yarn here concerns itself with the last six people on earth—all pitted against a mechanical monster called Ro-Man, sent from another planet whose "people" are disturbed by strides being made on earth in the research fields of atomic development and space travel.

Sextet—a famed scientist, his wife, assistant, daughter and two children—are protected from Ro-Man's supersonic death ray by antibiotic serum.

Of the principals, George Nader, as the aide who falls in love with and eventually marries the scientist's daughter in a primitive ceremony, fares the best. Selena Royle also comes across okay, but of the others the less said the better.

•

ROB ROY

(AKA: ROB ROY, THE HIGHLAND ROGUE)

1954, 81 mins, UK Ⓥ col

Dir Harold French ***Prod*** Perce Pearce ***Scr*** Lawrence E. Watkin ***Ph*** Guy Green ***Ed*** Geoffrey Foot ***Mus*** Cedric Thorpe Davie ***Art*** Geoffrey Drake

Act Richard Todd, Glynis Johns, James Robertson Justice, Michael Gough, Finlay Currie, Eric Pohlmann (Walt Disney)

Rob Roy is a lively swashbuckling meller. The synopsis explicitly states that the film is not based on the Walter Scott novel, but is founded entirely on history and legend.

History has been conveniently romanticized to provide a boisterous and rollicking epic of the revolt of the Scottish clans against the English monarchy. Central character is played by Richard Todd, who takes the part of the adventurous Rob Roy MacGregor with a surprise virility. It is he who leads the clan against the redcoats, who is responsible for a siege of the king's fort, and who eventually secures an amnesty for all the MacGregors.

The battle scenes have a vividness of their own and the stamp of realism is appreciated when it is known that Highland forces were loaned for these scenes. The misty highlands have been effectively photographed and the overall background provides the right touch of atmosphere.

While Todd has the stellar role, which he confidently grips, there is a fine all-round standard. Glynis Johns, as the innkeeper's daughter, admirably provides the romance with a performance of honest sincerity. At the head of the name feature cast, James Robertson Justice stands out with his warm portrayal of the one-time secretary of state who brings Rob Roy to the King's court.

•

ROB ROY

1995, 139 mins, US Ⓥ ⦿ ▭ col

Dir Michael Caton-Jones ***Prod*** Peter Broughan, Richard Jackson ***Scr*** Alan Sharp ***Ph*** Karl Walter Lindenlaub ***Ed*** Peter Honess ***Mus*** Carter Burwell ***Art*** Assheton Gorton

Act Liam Neeson, Jessica Lange, John Hurt, Tim Roth, Eric Stoltz, Andrew Keir (Talisman/United Artists)

An old-fashioned epic about honor, righteousness and fidelity, *Rob Roy* comes fully to life only when it is portraying outright treachery and venality. This handsome, not unappealing look at a Scottish legend of nearly 300 years ago is a fair way too solemn, wooden and dour for its own good, and feels oddly of another era.

The real Robert Roy MacGregor was a cattle drover and sometime thief who, upon becoming an outlaw and fugitive in 1713 due to a dispute with his former benefactor, the Marquis of Montrose, emerged as something of a folk hero to the poor local clansmen.

Liam Neeson cuts an imposing figure as he strides across the mountains to apprehend some cattle poachers. Nor is there any reason to suspect that he is anything other than a loving husband to his lusty wife, Mary (Jessica Lange), and a decent risk when he arranges to borrow £1,000 from Montrose (John Hurt) to purchase more cattle.

But when Rob Roy falls victim to the evil scheming of Montrose's factotums Killearn (Brian Cox) and Cunningham (Tim Roth), the latter a foppish, obsequious British opportunist who murders Rob Roy's friend McDonald (Eric Stoltz) and steals the money, the humorlessly dashing Scot becomes the object of a pointedly violent manhunt led by the sadistic Cunningham, who orders a rape-and-pillage expedition on the family farm after Rob Roy takes to the hills.

Lacking is any clear sense of Rob Roy's importance beyond the specific matter of fighting back against the rather arbitrary nastiness of Montrose and the outright villainy of Killearn and Cunningham. Rather, Rob Roy makes no end of high-minded speeches about the importance of honor and the sanctity of his word, and these quickly become wearisome. By contrast, the scenes involving Roth's unctuous Cunningham are a wild delight. The character manages to keep topping himself in the area of amoral acts, running the gamut of sins.

NOMINATIONS: Best Supporting Actor (Tim Roth)

•

ROB ROY, THE HIGHLAND ROGUE

SEE: ROB ROY

•

ROCCO AND HIS BROTHERS

SEE: ROCCO E I SUOI FRATELLI

•

ROCCO E I SUOI FRATELLI

(ROCCO AND HIS BROTHERS)

1960, 180 mins, Italy/France Ⓥ ⦿ b/w

Dir Luchino Visconti ***Prod*** Goffredo Lombardo ***Scr*** Luchino Visconti, Suso Cecchi D'Amico, Pasquale Festa Campanile, Massimo Franciosa, Enrico Medioli ***Ph*** Guiseppe Rotunno ***Ed*** Mario Serandrei ***Mus*** Nino Rota ***Art*** Mario Garbuglia

Act Alain Delon, Renato Salvatori, Annie Girardot, Katina Paxinou, Roger Hanin, Claudia Cardinale (Titanus/Marceau/Cocinor)

With all its faults, this is one of the top achievements of the year in Italy. Plot [from Giovanni Testori's novel *Il ponte della ghisolfa*, adapted by Luchino Visconti, Vasco Pratolini and Suso Cecchi D'Amico] deals with a south Italian family's trek to the big northern city of Milan, where it intends to start a new life, and of its slow disintegration as its members go their own way. It's plotted in the form of an epic poem, each stanza dedicated to a member of the group.

Rocco is the all-good brother who falls for the same girl, Nadia, a prostitute, as his brother Simone does. He reluctantly gives her up, but the affair ends tragically anyway, with Simone killing Nadia. Other brothers break off and live honest lives on their own while Rocco is tormented by the tragedy and wishes only to return to the land where he was born.

Scripting shows numerous hands at work, yet all is pulled together by Visconti's dynamic and generally tasteful direction. Occasionally, as in the near-final revelation to the family of Simone's crime, the action gets out of hand and comes close to melodrama.

Yet the impact of the main story line, aided by the sensitive, expertly guided playing of Alain Delon as Rocco, Annie Girardot as the prostie, and Renato Salvatori as Simone, is great. Katina Paxinou at times is perfect, at others she is allowed to act too theatrically and off-key. Lensing by Guiseppe Rotunno of the northern metropolis is realistically harsh, in key with the action.

•

ROCK, THE

1996, 136 mins, US Ⓥ ⦿ ▭ col

Dir Michael Bay ***Prod*** Don Simpson, Jerry Bruckheimer ***Scr*** David Weisberg, Douglas S. Cook, Mark Rosner [Dick Clement, Ian La Frenais] ***Ph*** John Schwartzman ***Ed*** Richard Francis-Bruce ***Mus*** Nick Glennie-Smith, Hans Zimmer ***Art*** Michael White

Act Sean Connery, Nicolas Cage, Ed Harris, Michael Biehn, William Forsythe, David Morse (Hollywood)

The Rock is inescapably entertaining, a high-octane, kick-butt actioner that dresses up a far-fetched premise out of a Steven Seagal movie with top-flight actors and an ultra-slick package. This final outing from the Simpson-Bruckheimer team has the strutting, souped-up, hardware-fetishizing personality of their signature productions.

A tense tale of rebel military officers who take over Alcatraz Island and threaten to unleash rockets on San Francisco unless their demands are met, this is a pure popcorn picture. The yarn has its share of gaping holes and jaw-dropping improbabilities, but director Michael Bay sweeps them all aside with his never-take-a-breath pacing.

Opening stretch is given over to the perpetrator of the dastardly scheme, Brigadier Gen. Hummel (Ed Harris), a veteran of every U.S. military engagement since Vietnam. With an elite unit of like-minded mutineers, Hummel absconds with a bunch of rockets loaded with deadly VX liquid gas, takes 81 hostages from a tour group on Alcatraz and promises to launch the missiles on the Bay Area unless Washington forks over $100 million from a secret slush fund within 40 hours.

The only man who can save the day is John Patrick Mason (Sean Connery), a former SAS operative who was secretly imprisoned for making off with J. Edgar Hoover's most closely held secrets. Officially, Mason doesn't exist, but he is nonetheless compelled to lead a team of Navy SEALs underwater to Alcatraz, with FBI biochemical weapons expert Stanley Goodspeed (Nicolas Cage).

Bay, who debuted with the same producers' *Bad Boys* in 1995, seems right at home with the macho posturing, tough talk and military logistics. Connery trades winningly on his sophisticated, elegant sense of cool, and Cage proves equally engaging as a sort of goofy chemical-set geek who must rise to the occasion of proving he's a man among the he-men elite. Harris is similarly outstanding, conveying the discipline but also the thought and weight behind his extreme decisions.

Film is dedicated to Don Simpson [who died in January 1996, aged 52].

1996: NOMINATION: Best Sound

•

ROCK AROUND THE CLOCK
1956, 76 mins, US Ⓥ b/w
Dir Fred F. Sears ***Prod*** Sam Katzman ***Scr*** Robert Kent, James B. Gordon ***Ph*** Benjamin H. Kline ***Ed*** Saul A. Goodkind, Jack W. Ogilvie ***Mus*** Fred Karger (sup.)
Act Bill Haley and The Comets, The Platters, Tony Martinez and His Band, Freddie Bell and His Bellboys, Alan Freed, Lisa Gaye (Clover/Columbia)

Rock Around the Clock takes off to a bouncy little beat and never lets up for 76 minutes of foot-tapping entertainment. Bill Haley and The Comets set the beat with nine of their record favorites, including the title tune, "Razzle Dazzle," "Happy Baby," "See You Later, Alligator," "Rudy's Back" and others. Freddie Bell and His Bellboys are on for two solid numbers, "Giddy Up, Ding Dong" and "We're Gonna Teach You to Rock."

Fred F. Sears's direction has excellent pace and keeps interest going with a story that tells how a band manager finds the Haley Comets in the mountains and brings dancing back to ballrooms throughout the country. Johnny Johnston is likeable as the manager, while Alix Talton is a cool chick as a big band booker who tries unsuccessfully to get her matrimonial hooks in him. Film is a particularly strong showcasing for Lisa Gaye, who plays the rock and roll dancer with The Comets. Her terping's good and that figure the dance costumes display commands added interest.

•

ROCKETEER
SEE: THE ROCKETEER

•

ROCKETEER, THE
(UK: ROCKETEER; AUSTRALIA: THE ADVENTURES OF THE ROCKETEER)
1991, 108 mins, US Ⓥ ⊙ ⊏⊐ col
Dir Joe Johnston ***Prod*** Lawrence Gordon, Charles Gordon, Lloyd Levin ***Scr*** Danny Bilson, Paul De Meo ***Ph*** Hiro Narita ***Ed*** Arthur Schmidt ***Mus*** James Horner ***Art*** Jim Bissell
Act Bill Campbell, Jennifer Connelly, Alan Arkin, Timothy Dalton, Paul Sorvino, Ed Lauter (Walt Disney/Gordon)

Based on a comic ["graphic novel" by Dave Stevens] unveiled in 1981, this $40 million adventure fantasy puts a shiny polish on familiar elements: airborne hero, damsel in distress, Nazi villains, 1930s Hollywood glamor, and dazzling special effects. [Screen story by Danny Bilson, Paul De Meo and William Dear]

Elaborate opening sequence has an ace pilot (Bill Campbell) testing a new racing plane over L.A. skies in 1938 while, on the ground below, hoods and Feds in speeding cars shoot it out after robbery of a mysterious device.

Developed by none other than Howard Hughes, the invention makes its way into the pilot's hands, but it's coveted by a dashing star of swashbuckling films who also happens to be a dedicated Nazi (Timothy Dalton). Although he has hired thugs led by Paul Sorvino to recover the priceless device, Dalton has his own ideas about getting at Campbell through his gorgeous g.f. (Jennifer Connelly).

The object of intense interest is a portable rocket pack which, if strapped to one's back, can send its wearer zipping around almost as fast, if not as quietly, as Superman.

Newcomer Campbell exhibits the requisite grit and all-American know-how, but the lead role is written with virtually no humor or subtext. Those around him come off to better advantage, notably Dalton as the deliciously smooth, insidious Sinclair; Sorvino and Alan Arkin, with the latter as the Rocketeer's mentor; Terry O'Quinn as Hughes; and the lovely, voluptuous Connelly.

•

ROCKING HORSE WINNER, THE
1949, 96 mins, UK Ⓥ b/w
Dir Anthony Pelissier ***Prod*** John Mills ***Scr*** Anthony Pelissier ***Ph*** Desmond Dickinson ***Ed*** John Seabourne ***Mus*** William Alwyn
Act Valerie Hobson, John Howard Davies, Ronald Squire, John Mills, Hugh Sinclair, Charles Goldner (Two Cities)

There has rarely been a more faithful adaptation of an original, with the exception of the ending, which was added at the request of the censor.

In following the original D. H. Lawrence short story, Anthony Pelissier, who scripted as well as directed, has developed the story of an extravagant mother as seen through the eyes of a sensitive child. How to raise the cash to bring the family out of debt and anxiety is the problem preying on the youngster's mind.

Then, gradually, the boy realizes he has a facility for picking winners in horse races and in secret association with the family handyman, later joined by a sporting uncle, has an astonishing run of good luck.

John Howard Davies plays the sensitive lad with a skill and sincerity which would do credit to a seasoned trouper. Valerie Hobson is fine as the mother.

•

ROCK, PRETTY BABY
1956, 89 mins, US Ⓥ b/w
Dir Richard Bartlett ***Prod*** Edmond Chevie ***Scr*** Herbert Margolis, William Raynor ***Ph*** George Robinson ***Ed*** Frederick Y. Smith ***Mus*** Henry Mancini
Act Sal Mineo, John Saxon, Luana Patten, Edward C. Platt, Fay Wray, Rod McKuen (Universal)

Universal liberally sprinkled this entry with rock 'n' roll tunes, offering a total of 17 musical numbers. As an added appeal for the teenage set, U cast the picture with a group of vigorous youngsters, including Sal Mineo, a semi-established teenage hero; John Saxon, an aspirant for teen laurels; and Luana Patten, an all-American type bluejeaner.

Rock, Pretty Baby must be judged for the purpose it was made—to cash in on the rock 'n' roll frenzy. If considered from any other standpoint, the picture is dull and embarrassing.

No juvenile delinquency is involved. The youngsters come from fairly well-to-do parents and live in nice neighborhoods.

Saxon, as an 18-year-old high-school senior, wants to follow a career in music and become a band leader. His father—a physician—can't see it that way and wants his son to follow in his footsteps. That's the basic conflict.

As the budding leader of a combo, Saxon and his colleagues have the opportunity to break out in song and instrumentals at the drop of a hat. Fay Wray, of *King Kong* fame, makes a charming and understanding mother, and Edward C. Platt is properly stern as the confused father.

•

ROCKY
1976, 119 mins, US Ⓥ ⊙ col
Dir John G. Avildsen ***Prod*** Irwin Winkler ***Scr*** Sylvester Stallone ***Ph*** James Crabe ***Ed*** Richard Halsey, Scott Conrad ***Mus*** Bill Conti ***Art*** Bill Cassidy
Act Sylvester Stallone, Talia Shire, Burt Young, Carl Weathers, Burgess Meredith, Thayer David (United Artists)

Sylvester Stallone stars in his own screenplay about a minor local boxer who gets a chance to fight a heavyweight championship bout. Stallone's title character is that of a near-loser, a punchy reject scorned by gym owner Burgess Meredith, patronized by local loan shark Joe Spinell, rebuffed by plain-Jane Talia Shire, whose brother, Burt Young, keeps engineering a romantic match.

Rocky would have remained in this rut, had not heavyweight champ Carl Weathers come up with the Bicentennial gimmick of fighting a sure ringer, thereby certifying the American Dream for public consumption. During all this, Stallone brings out the best in Shire, exposes the worst in Young and generally gets his life together.

1976: Best Picture, Director, Editing

NOMINATIONS: Best Actor (Sylvester Stallone), Actress (Talia Shire), Supp. Actor (Burgess Meredith, Burt Young), Story & Screenplay, Best Song ("Gonna Fly Now"), Sound

•

ROCKY II
1979, 119 mins, US Ⓥ ⊙ col
Dir Sylvester Stallone ***Prod*** Irwin Winkler, Robert Chartoff ***Scr*** Sylvester Stallone ***Ph*** Bill Butler ***Ed*** Danford B. Greene, Stanford C. Allen, James D. Mitchell, Christopher V. Holmes ***Mus*** Bill Conti ***Art*** Richard Berger
Act Sylvester Stallone, Talia Shire, Burt Young, Carl Weathers, Burgess Meredith (United Artists)

Rocky II follows much the same theme as its predecessor—that is, fighter Rocky Balboa's path to a stab at the heavyweight crown. In its boxing and training scenes *Rocky II* packs much of the punch the original did, complete with an exciting pugilistic finale that's even better than its predecessor.

However, in an attempt to tell the new story—that of Rocky's adjustment to near-success and an attempt to lead a non-boxing life—the plot tends to drag and the picture takes on a murky quality.

Luckily, director, actor and scripter Sylvester Stallone and producers Irwin Winkler and Robert Chartoff know from experience audiences love to root for the underdog and have concocted an irresistible final 30 minutes.

1982: NOMINATION: Best Original Song ("Eye of the Tiger")

•

ROCKY III
1982, 99 mins, US Ⓥ ⊙ col
Dir Sylvester Stallone ***Prod*** Irwin Winkler, Robert Chartoff ***Scr*** Sylvester Stallone ***Ph*** Bill Butler ***Ed*** Don Zimmerman, Mark Warner ***Mus*** Bill Conti ***Art*** William J. Cassidy
Act Sylvester Stallone, Carl Weathers, Mr. T, Talia Shire, Burt Young, Burgess Meredith (United Artists)

The real question with *Rocky III* was how Sylvester Stallone could twist the plot to make an interesting difference. He manages.

Revisiting the champ three years after the big victory, we find him and wife Talia Shire happily married with a son, a big house, lots of money and media attention after successfully defending his title 10 times.

But Clubber Lang, menacingly and beautifully played by Mr. T, is also tough and hungry for a title shot. Ailing Burgess Meredith tells Stallone he's no longer a match for T and should retire gracefully. But Stallone insists on proving himself and quickly goes down for the count under T's hammering.

Though lion-hearted and iron-jawed, it's obvious now that Stallone has never been a very skilled boxer. But Carl Weathers steps in to teach and train him, if Stallone can work up the will.

As usual, Stallone the writer-director is less successful in handling all the dramatic interims than staging the battles.

•

ROCKY IV
1985, 91 mins, US Ⓥ ⊙ col
Dir Sylvester Stallone ***Prod*** Robert Chartoff, Irwin Winkler ***Scr*** Sylvester Stallone ***Ph*** Bill Butler ***Ed*** Don Zimmerman, John W. Wheeler ***Mus*** Vince DiCola ***Art*** Bill Kenney
Act Sylvester Stallone, Talia Shire, Burt Young, Carl Weathers, Brigitte Nielsen, Dolph Lundgren (United Artists)

Sylvester Stallone is really sloughing it off shamelessly in *Rocky IV*, but it's still impossible not to root for old Rocky Balboa to get up off the canvas and whup that bully one more time.

Beyond its visceral appeal, *Rocky IV* is truly the worst of the lot, though Stallone himself is more personable in this one and that helps. Dolph Lundgren is the most contrived opponent yet and that hurts.

Lundgren, an almost inhuman giant fighting machine created in Russian physical-fitness labs, comes to the U.S.

to challenge the champ, but is first taken on by Apollo Creed (Carl Weathers), anxious to prove himself one last time.

So it's on to Moscow where, surprise, surprise, it's going to take a lot of training to get Stallone in shape for the Soviet. Though it really makes no difference, the story gets truly dumb at this point. Lundgren, according to the digital readout, has developed a punch of 2,000 p.s.i., which should be enough to send Rocky back to Philadelphia without a plane. Once the fight starts, however, there's no way Rocky fans can resist getting caught up in it, predictable and preposterous though it be.

•

ROCKY V

1990, 104 mins, US Ⓥ ⦿ col

Dir John G. Avildsen ***Prod*** Irwin Winkler, Robert Chartoff ***Scr*** Sylvester Stallone ***Ph*** Steven Poster ***Ed*** John G. Avildsen, Michael N. Knue ***Mus*** Bill Conti ***Art*** William J. Cassidy

Act Sylvester Stallone, Talia Shire, Burt Young, Sage Stallone, Burgess Meredith, Tommy Morrison (United Artists)

When the underdog always wins he's not much of an underdog anymore, and the narrative cartwheels Sylvester Stallone has turned over the years to put Rocky in that position have peeled away the novelty.

So it is with *Rocky V*. Stallone again scripted and continues to evince a thudding lack of storytelling subtlety, sinking to a new low with the ending, which seems inspired by championship wrestling.

Stallone positively goes wild with clichés here: Rocky left broke by mismanagement of his fortune, a Don King–like promoter (Richard Gant) pressuring Rocky to fight again, strained relations between Rocky and his son (real-life son Sage) because of Rocky's tutelage of a young boxer (Tommy Morrison) who ultimately turns on him.

The central problem is that Rocky suffers brain damage from his various beatings in the ring, making it risky for him ever to fight again. Burt Young has his moments as the slobbish Paulie. Talia Shire has become shrill and annoying as Adrian. Gant is perfectly hissable as Duke. Boxer-turned-actor Morrison is serviceable as the ham-fisted heavy. Bill Conti's score remains the series' greatest asset.

•

ROCKY HORROR PICTURE SHOW, THE

1975, 100 mins, UK/US Ⓥ col

Dir Jim Sharman ***Prod*** Michael White ***Scr*** Jim Sharman, Richard O'Brien ***Ph*** Peter Suschitzky ***Ed*** Graeme Clifford ***Mus*** Richard Hartley (arr.) ***Art*** Brian Thomson

Act Tim Curry, Susan Sarandon, Barry Bostwick, Richard O'Brien, Jonathan Adams, Little Nell [= Nell Campbell] (White/20th Century-Fox)

The Rocky Horror Picture Show is adapted from a rock stage musical of same title [by Richard O'Brien] set in a spooky castle deep in the heart of Ohio. Into it on a rain-swept night stumble affianced Janet and Brad, wholesome straights, hoping to find a telephone, but finding instead the earthy lair of some weirdos from the planet Transylvania. Chief freak therein is the bisexual Frank N. Furter, played with relish by Tim Curry, who first seduces Janet (Susan Sarandon) and then conquers Brad (Barry Bostwick).

The plot mixture also includes Curry's "monster" creation, rippling-muscled Rocky; a revenging scientist; Riff Raff (O'Brien), Curry's hunchbacked lackey; and assorted groupies of which Magenta and Columbia (Patricia Quinn and Nell Campbell) are most prominent.

Overall, however, most of the jokes that might have seemed jolly fun on stage now appear obvious and even flat. The sparkle's gone.

•

ROGER AND ME

1989, 90 mins, US Ⓥ ⦿ col

Dir Michael Moore ***Prod*** Michael Moore ***Ph*** Chris Beaver, John Prusak, Kevin Rafferty, Bruce Schermer ***Ed*** Wendey Stanzler, Jennifer Berman

(Dog Eat Dog)

Roger and Me is a cheeky and smart indictment against General Motors for closing its truck plant in Flint, MI, throwing 30,000 employees out of work and, as a result, leaving many neighborhoods abandoned. Michael Moore, a Flint native who recalls the prosperous "Great American Dream" days of his 1950s childhood, launches a one-man documentary crusade to bring GM chairman Roger Smith back to town. He wants Smith to see the human tragedy caused by the plant closing.

He interviews fired workers, shows decaying houses across the city and two grandiose schemes to reactivate the town: the opening of a Hyatt Regency hotel and a huge shopping mall. Both fail quickly for lack of business. Tourists don't come to Flint.

Intercut are scenes of the town's rich, who seem oblivious to the plight of their fellow citizens and wonder what the fuss is about.

Pic is one-sided, for sure, but Moore makes no pretense otherwise. The irony of the title pervades the piece.

•

ROLLERBALL

1975, 129 mins, US Ⓥ ⦿ col

Dir Norman Jewison ***Prod*** Norman Jewison ***Scr*** William Harrison ***Ph*** Douglas Slocombe ***Ed*** Antony Gibbs ***Mus*** Andre Previn (sup.) ***Art*** John Box

Act James Caan, John Houseman, Maud Adams, John Beck, Moses Gunn, Pamela Hensley (United Artists)

Norman Jewison's sensational futuristic drama about a world of Corporate States stars James Caan in an excellent performance as a famed athlete who fights for his identity and free will. The $5 million film was made in Munich and London.

The year is 2018, and the world has been regrouped politically to a hegemony of six conglomerate cartels. There is total material tranquility: no wars, no poverty, no unrest—and no personal free will and no God.

The ingenious way of ventilating human nature's animal-violence residual content is the world sport of rollerball, a combination of roller derby, motorcycle racing and basketball where violent death is part of the entertainment. Caan is a long-standing hero of the sport, becoming dangerously popular. He is ordered to retire. He refuses. Tilt.

The very fine music track was supervised and conducted by Andre Previn, utilizing excerpts from Bach, Shostakovich, Tchaikovsky and Albinoni/Giazotto, plus original Previn work which included the corporate anthems which begin each game.

The performances of the principals are uniformly tops. Besides the great work of Caan, John Houseman and Ralph Richardson (as head of the corporation), John Beck is excellent as the model yahoo jock. As the women in Caan's life, Maud Adams, Pamela Hensley and Barbara Trentham step right out of today's deodorant and cosmetics teleblurbs—just the way they're supposed to be when life imitates consumer advertising imagery.

•

ROLLERCOASTER

1977, 119 mins, US Ⓥ ▭ col

Dir James Goldstone ***Prod*** Jennings Lang ***Scr*** Richard Levinson, William Link ***Ph*** David M. Walsh ***Ed*** Edward A. Biery, Richard Sprague ***Mus*** Lalo Schifrin ***Art*** Henry Bumstead

Act George Segal, Richard Widmark, Timothy Bottoms, Henry Fonda, Harry Guardino, Susan Strasberg (Universal)

Timothy Bottoms is a subdued maniac with a plan to blackmail $1 million from a group of amusement park owners.

Pic's plot is simple and uncluttered. There is a madman on the loose, one with a thorough knowledge of bombs, roller coasters and electronics. From a short scene early on, there is a hint that he served in Vietnam, which is supposed to partly account for his instability. His sole objective is cash.

Bottoms and the man trying to outsmart him (George Segal) are adversaries who develop a mutual respect and, in a sense, a rapport. Pic's taut opening 20 minutes depict the major catastrophe—bombing of a roller-coaster track and the subsequent derailing of the cars. The roller-coaster rides are the picture's highlights and they are fabulous.

•

ROLLING THUNDER

1977, 99 mins, US Ⓥ ⦿ col

Dir John Flynn ***Prod*** Lawrence Gordon ***Scr*** Paul Schrader, Heywood Gould ***Ph*** Jordon Croneweth ***Ed*** Frank P. Keller ***Mus*** Barry DeVorzon ***Art*** Steve Berger

Act William Devane, Tommy Lee Jones, Linda Haynes, Lisa Richards, Dabney Coleman, James Best (AIP)

Excellent cast performs well, but not well enough, and Paul Schrader's story is strong, but not strong enough. In sum, it neither rolls nor thunders.

With co-scripter Heywood Gould, Schrader follows an embittered loner to a bloody conclusion. After eight years of torture as a prisoner of war, William Devane returns to a grateful San Antonio where he receives a hero's welcome, except at home where his wife, Lisa Richards, has fallen in love with his friend (Lawrason Driscoll).

But neither the good nor the ill has much impact on Devane, who left all emotion behind in the prison camp. And even though he has a hard time animating a wooden character, Devane succeeds in making the first half of the picture the best, creating a believable reflection of the difficult adjustments of real POWs.

Unfortunately, formula clichés start to creep in when the bad guys, led by James Best, break into Devane's house in search of silver dollars. The crooks fire off a few shots and leave the Devane family for dead. But he survives and goes off in search of the killers of his wife and son. Along the way enlisting the help of Tommy Lee Jones, who was with him in Vietnam, and Linda Hanes, a loving barmaid.

Jones is also good, but is stuck with a stoic role similar to Devane's while remaining much less clearly motivated. As the devoted war groupie, Haynes racks up an exceptionally fine feature credit, projecting a liveliness, warmth and vulnerability that explains her presence at Devane's side more than Jones's.

•

ROLLOVER

1981, 118 mins, US Ⓥ ▭ col

Dir Alan J. Pakula ***Prod*** Bruce Gilbert ***Scr*** David Shaber ***Ph*** Giuseppe Rotunno ***Ed*** Evan Lottman ***Mus*** Michael Small ***Art*** George Jenkins

Act Jane Fonda, Kris Kristofferson, Hume Cronyn, Josef Sommer, Bob Gunton, Jodi Long (Orion/Warner)

Although elegantly appointed and possessed of a provocative theme, *Rollover* is a fundamentally disappointing political-romantic thriller [from a story by David Shaber, Howard Kohn and David Weir] set in the rarified world of international high finance.

Coiffed and gowned to the hilt, Jane Fonda plays a former film star whose corporate big-wheel husband is mysteriously murdered. Bank troubleshooter Kris Kristofferson is called in to try to right the ailing firm, quickly begins consoling the widow by night as well as by day and soon accompanies her to Saudi Arabia to firm a deal for venture capital, which, while giving Fonda the board chairmanship, also hands the Arabs the final financial trump card.

Eventually transpires that the Arabs decide not to "roll over," or redeposit, their huge sums in the bank, which sends the banking community, Wall Street and the entire international financial network into chaos.

It's a scary theme, and Pakula's previously displayed expertise at conveying pervasive paranoia triggered by massive conspiracies at high levels is perfectly in tune with the story's aims. But there's a certain lack of reality, cued in part by numerous melodramatic contrivances.

•

ROMA, CITTA APERTA
(OPEN CITY; ROME, OPEN CITY)

1945, 100 mins, Italy Ⓥ b/w

Dir Roberto Rossellini ***Scr*** Sergio Amidei, Federico Fellini, Roberto Rossellini ***Ph*** Ubaldo Arata ***Ed*** Eraldo Da Roma ***Mus*** Renzo Rossellini ***Art*** R. Megna

Act Vito Annichiarico, Nando Bruno, Aldo Fabrizi, Harry Feist, Anna Magnani, Maria Michi (Excelsa)

This is a human, credible story [by Sergio Amidei and Alberto Consiglio] of the fine behavior of the "little people" during the German occupation of Rome.

Climax to series of intrigues and adventures of these little people in getting money and information and other assistance to the underground comes during a Gestapo raid on a block of workingmen's houses. Gestapo agents carry off the key underground leader, and shoot his girl as she runs after the truck that takes him off to prison. There is a nasty torture scene at prison.

This much of the film is standard hero and villain stuff. But what makes picture good is the story of other characters involved in the tragedy. Aldo Fabrizi does superb job of portraying the understanding priest who carries money bound in scholarly looking volumes across the lines, smuggles ammunition under his priest's robes and inspires the hero with courage in the final ordeal.

Top performance is turned in by Anna Magnani as Pina, the hero's girl. Despite grimness of plot, there are several little touches of humor. Much of the humor in Italian dialects will be lost in dubbing.

•

ROMANCE

1930, 76 mins, US Ⓥ b/w

Dir Clarence Brown ***Scr*** Bess Meredyth, Edwin Justus Mayer ***Ed*** Hugh Wynn, Leslie F. Wilder ***Art*** Cedric Gibbons

Act Greta Garbo, Lewis Stone, Gavin Gordon, Elliott Nugent, Florence Lake (M-G-M)

When Garbo gargles on the low ones it's hard to accept her as the operatic high soprano an off-screen singer presents her to be, but the picture [from the play *Signora Cavallini* by Edward Sheldon] is Garbo all the way.

Director Clarence Brown again uses her very nicely in a part that might have easily been overacted. A French opera star with a past falls in love with a holy and wealthy young

American preacher—in America. Her rep is generally known but the boy love laughs that off. The uncle of the good girl the preacher-boy is to wed was himself the French woman's ex-master.

Though the story occurs in the 1860s, action starts and finishes with a prolog and epilog, on a modern New Year's Eve. An old bishop, who was Garbo's lover those years ago, is telling his grandson about it.

•

ROMANCE OF A HORSETHIEF
1971, 101 mins, US col
Dir Abraham Polonsky ***Prod*** Gene Gutowski ***Scr*** David Opatoshu ***Ph*** Piero Portalupi ***Ed*** Kevin Connor ***Mus*** Mort Shuman ***Art*** Otto Pischinger
Act Yul Brynner, Eli Wallach, Jane Birkin, Oliver Tobias, Lainie Kazan, Serge Gainsbourg (Allied Artists)

Allied Artists hasn't spared the coin in giving this period comedy a lush production, but a large cast and extensive location shooting can't salvage a lifeless script made even flatter by Abraham Polonsky's derivative direction.

Set in Poland (but shot in Yugoslavia), pic centers on a small rural community of Jewish peasants who live off the offtimes illegal horse trade. Town is ruled by Cossack-in-exile Stoloff (Yul Brynner), who maintains a love-hate relationship with its residents, including horsethief Kifke (Eli Wallach), his madam ladylove Estusha (Lainie Kazan) and his protege Zanvill (Oliver Tobias). When the town's horses are commandeered by Stoloff in the name of Tsar Nicholas, the people begin to stir under his oppressive boot, sparked by Zanvill's girlfriend Naomi (Jane Birkin), just returned from a French finishing school where she learned the gentle art of revolution.

The international cast, sporting a babble of accents, always seems to be making a movie, and not having a bad time of it. Film's best performances come from Birkin, who strikes an appropriate note of naive commitment to revolution, and Tobias, in his first major role.

Director Polonsky plays everything on too low a key and the result is a sluggish 101 minutes too padded with pointless dissolves and minor idyllic set pieces.

•

ROMANCING THE STONE
1984, 105 mins, US Ⓥ ⦿ ▭ col
Dir Robert Zemeckis ***Prod*** Michael Douglas, Jack Brodsky, Joel Douglas ***Scr*** Diane Thomas ***Ph*** Dean Cundey ***Ed*** Donn Cambern, Frank Morriss ***Mus*** Alan Silvestri, Eddy Grant ***Art*** Lawrence G. Paull
Act Michael Douglas, Kathleen Turner, Danny DeVito, Zack Norman, Alfonso Arau, Manuel Ojeda (El Corazon/20th Century-Fox)

Living alone with her cat, Kathleen Turner writes romantic novels and cries over the outcome, assuring friend Holland Taylor that one day the writer's life will pick up for real.

Naturally, Turner receives a package mailed from South America just ahead of sister's phone call that she's been kidnapped and will die if Turner doesn't deliver the contents of the package south of the border as soon as possible.

Heading for the jungles in her high heels, Turner is like a lot of unwitting screen heroines ahead of her, guaranteed that her drab existence is about to be transformed—probably by a man, preferably handsome and adventurous. Sure enough, Michael Douglas pops out of the jungle. The expected complications are supplied by the kidnappers, Danny DeVito and Zack Norman.

1984: NOMINATION: Best Editing

•

ROMAN HOLIDAY
1953, 118 mins, US Ⓥ ⦿ b/w
Dir William Wyler ***Prod*** William Wyler ***Scr*** Ian McLellan Hunter, John Dighton ***Ph*** Franz Planer, Henri Alekan ***Ed*** Robert Swink ***Mus*** Georges Auric ***Art*** Hal Pereira, Walter Tyler
Act Gregory Peck, Audrey Hepburn, Eddie Albert, Hartley Power, Harcourt Williams, Margaret Rawlings (Paramount)

This William Wyler romantic comedy-drama [from a story by Dalton Trumbo] is the Graustarkian fable in modern dress, plus the Cinderella theme in reverse. He times the chuckles with a never-flagging pace, puts heart into the laughs, endows the footage with some boff bits of business and points up some tender, poignant scenes in using the smart script and the cast to the utmost advantage.

The aged face of the Eternal City provides a contrast to the picture's introduction of a new face, Audrey Hepburn, British ingenue who made an impression with the legit-goers in *Gigi*. Gregory Peck, in the role of American newspaperman, figures importantly in making the picture zip along engrossingly. Eddie Albert makes a major comedy contribution as a photog who secretely lenses the princess during the 24 hours she steals away from the dull court routine.

The fine script deals with a princess who rebels against the goodwill tour she is making of Europe after arriving in Rome. The adventures she encounters with Peck during the day and evening are natural and amusing. After this day of fun is over the princess and the reporter are in love, but each knows nothing can come of the Roman holiday.

All the interiors, except those in the Palazzos Brancaccio and Colonna, were lensed in Rome's Cinecitta Studios, while exteriors put on film many landmarks of the city.

1953: Best Actress (Audrey Hepburn), Motion Picture Story [awarded to Ian McLellan Hunter, in place of blacklisted Dalton Trumbo], B&W Costume Design (Edith Head)

NOMINATIONS: Best Picture, Director, Supp. Actor (Eddie Albert), Screenplay, B&W Cinematography, B&W Art Direction, Editing

•

ROMANOFF AND JULIET
1961, 103 mins, US ▭ col
Dir Peter Ustinov ***Prod*** Peter Ustinov ***Scr*** Peter Ustinov ***Ph*** Robert Krasker ***Ed*** Renzo Lucidi ***Mus*** Mario Nascimbene ***Art*** Alexandre Trauner
Act Peter Ustinov, Sandra Dee, John Gavin, Akim Tamiroff, Suzanne Cloutier, John Phillips (Universal)

Some of the satiric toxin has gone out of Peter Ustinov's *Romanoff and Juliet* in its cinemetamorphosis, but enough of the comic chemistry remains. Ustinov has managed not only to retain the lion's share of his tongue-in-cheek swing at political hyprocisy, diplomatic pomposity and general 20th-century lack of harmony or philosophical perspective, but he has added several noteworthy observations.

His performance as the general of Concordia, a tiny mock republic feverishly wooed by Russia and the U.S. to solicit its vital U.N. vote, is a beautiful blend of outrageous mugging and sly comment. When he's on, the picture's at its best. Sandra Dee and John Gavin costar as daughter and son of the U.S. and Russian ambassadors to Concordia, whose romance and marriage ultimately blots out the political crisis, representing Ustinov's love-and-laughter platform for harmonious international relations.

•

ROMAN SCANDALS
1933, 93 mins, US Ⓥ b/w
Dir Frank Tuttle, Busby Berkeley ***Prod*** Samuel Goldwyn ***Scr*** George S. Kaufman, Robert Sherwood, William Anthony McGuire, Arthur Sheekman, Nat Perrin, George Oppenheimer ***Ph*** Ray June, Gregg Toland ***Ed*** Stuart Heisler ***Art*** Richard Day
Act Eddie Cantor, Ruth Etting, Gloria Stuart, David Manners, Verree Teasdale, Edward Arnold (Goldwyn/United Artists)

Comedy high spots and moments of exotic beauty in production retrieve a sometimes ineffective Eddie Cantor vehicle. Subject matter is the hokiest kind of hoke.

Best of the bits has Cantor as the Roman emperor's food taster trying to stall off the queen's plot to poison her royal spouse and struggling at the same time with a stubborn attack of hiccoughs. Hilarity of Cantor's buffoonery lies in the dignity of the stately surroundings of the Roman court and the straight playing of the supporting cast.

Background of imperial Rome is made to order for spectacle, and the producer has made the most of it. There is a long sequence in a swank Roman women's bath, elaborated and built for pictorial effect to the last extreme. This sequence is the elaborate incidental to one of the song numbers, "Keep Young and Beautiful," which gets a remarkably intricate build-up for the Cantor rendering in blackface.

Cantor is almost constantly on the screen for all of the hour and a half, and it's practically impossible for any funmaker to sustain top speed that length of time.

David Manners stands out in the cast, one of the few Hollywood actors who can look genuine in Roman toga. His satisfying playing of the leading straight role does a lot to sharpen the comedy angle. Gloria Stuart and Verree Teasdale in the top femme parts make an eyeful, the one blonde and the other brunette.

•

ROMAN SPRING OF MRS. STONE, THE
1962, 103 mins, UK Ⓥ col
Dir Jose Quintero ***Prod*** Louis de Rochemont ***Scr*** Gavin Lambert ***Ph*** Harry Waxman ***Ed*** Ralph Kemplen ***Mus*** Richard Addinsell ***Art*** Roger Furse
Act Vivien Leigh, Warren Beatty, Coral Browne, Jill St. John, Lotte Lenya, Jeremy Spenser (Warner)

Vivien Leigh is the star of this gloomy, pessimistic portrait of the artist as a middle-aged widow, from Tennessee Williams's only novel. She portrays a lonely, uncertain ex-actress who has given up her profession and her past to settle in Rome following the sudden death of her wealthy husband. However reluctantly, she soon falls prey to the interests of the fortune-hunting parasites and pimps of Rome who seek monetary rewards in return for romantic favors.

But Leigh has the misfortune to fall in love with her "young man" (Warren Beatty), who convincingly feigns amour, then flutters away on another attractive assignment provided by agent-panderer Lotte Lenya. Leigh gives an expressive, interesting delineation—projecting intelligence and femininity, as always. Mrs. Stone, however, is no Blanche DuBois. There's less to work with. Although every once in a while a little Guido Panzini creeps into his Italo dialect and Marlon Brando into his posture and expression, Beatty gives a fairly convincing characterization of the young, mercenary punk-gigolo. Lenya is frighteningly sinister as the cunning pimpette.

1962: NOMINATION: Best Supp. Actress (Lotte Lenya)

•

ROMANTIC ENGLISHWOMAN, THE
1975, 115 mins, UK/France Ⓥ col
Dir Joseph Losey ***Prod*** Daniel M. Angel ***Scr*** Thomas Wiseman, Tom Stoppard ***Ph*** Gerry Fisher ***Mus*** Richard Hartley ***Art*** Richard MacDonald
Act Glenda Jackson, Michael Caine, Helmut Berger, Beatrice Normand, Nathalie Delon, Michel Lonsdale (DIAL/Meric-Matalon)

Joseph Losey has concocted a low-key, sitcom-type pic [from the book by Thomas Wiseman] using the familiar theme of an unsatisfied, well-heeled married woman with a child on a romantic escapade.

Glenda Jackson plays in her clipped, cold way as she is off to the German bath and gambling site of Baden-Baden at the start of the pic. There she notices Helmut Berger, who is noted as smuggling in heroin, which he inanely stashes in a rain drain and which is later washed away. In Britain the husband, Michael Caine, invites him to stay. Eventually she and Berger are caught necking by Caine and she runs off after Berger.

Pic remains disappointing in its cocktail of satire, intrigue and romantic comedy-drama that does not quite jell.

•

ROME EXPRESS
1932, 94 mins, UK b/w
Dir Walter Forde ***Prod*** Michael Balcon ***Scr*** Sidney Gilliat, Clifford Grey, Frank Vosper, Ralph Stock ***Ph*** Gunther Krampf ***Ed*** Frederick Y. Smith ***Mus*** [uncredited] ***Art*** A. L. Mazzei
Act Conrad Veidt, Esther Ralston, Joan Barry, Cedric Hardwicke, Frank Vosper, Hugh Williams (Gaumont-British)

The acting and casting call attention to *Rome Express*. A combination of *Grand Hotel* and *Shanghai Express*, nevertheless it is original in conception and execution. Casting is superb and the players all excellent.

Conrad Veidt does an unusually good job as Zurta, a criminal, and Frank Vosper makes a human being of Jolif, the head of the French Sûreté. Story is laid entirely on a train which travels out of Paris. Veidt and Hugh Williams are adventurers chasing Donald Calthrop, who double-crossed them after stealing a famous painting. Also on the train are Joan Barry and Harold Huth, married but not traveling with their legal mates; Esther Ralston, a film star, and her American manager, Finlay Currie; Cedric Hardwicke, a philanthropist, and his secretary (Eliot Makeham); and Vosper, head of the French police. Search for the picture leads to murder, with all those above named involved. Theft, murder and explanation unravel before the train ends its run.

•

ROMEO AND JULIET
1936, 130 mins, US Ⓥ b/w
Dir George Cukor ***Prod*** Irving Thalberg ***Scr*** Talbot Jennings ***Ph*** William Daniels ***Ed*** Margaret Booth ***Mus*** Herbert Stothart ***Art*** Cedric Gibbons, Oliver Messel
Act Norma Shearer, Leslie Howard, John Barrymore, Edna May Oliver, Basil Rathbone, C. Aubrey Smith (M-G-M)

Romeo and Juliet is a faithful and not too imaginative translation to the screen of the William Shakespeare play.

Romeo and Juliet is a love-story tragedy, requiring precise pace in order that the beauty of its poetry shall be thoroughly grasped. The fine lyric qualities have been retained, and from that point of view there is every reason to laud the production as successful. In accomplishing this worthy purpose, however, the tempo is a beat or two slower than the familiar methods of modern storytelling.

Surprisingly few liberties have been taken with the original text. Preparation for the screen was confined chiefly to condensation. Norma Shearer adds an important portrait to her gallery of roles. She never conveys the impression that she is getting a great kick out of the part, and her restraint aids her conception of the characterization of the daughter of the Capulets, a child of 14.

The famous balcony love scene with Leslie Howard is played sincerely and beautifully. She makes the final tragic moments of the play convincing and moving.

Against her childlike figure, Howard and Ralph Forbes, rival suitors, appear years her senior. Howard's Romeo is a forthright young man of considerable determination, rather than a headstrong, impassioned young lover. But what illusion is lost in looks, Howard adequately makes up in speech. His lines are clearly spoken.

After a rather hesitant beginning John Barrymore makes a real, live person out of Mercutio. His opening scenes are hurried, noisy and indistinct. But the passages preceding and following the fatal duel with Basil Rathbone (Tybalt) are exciting and thrilling. Barrymore plays in the grand manner, which the part allows.

1936: NOMINATIONS: Best Picture, Actress (Norma Shearer), Supp. Actor (Basil Rathbone), Art Direction

•

ROMEO AND JULIET

1968, 138 mins, UK/Italy Ⓥ ⊙ col

Dir Franco Zeffirelli ***Prod*** Anthony Havelock-Allan, John Brabourne ***Scr*** Franco Brusati, Masolino D'Amico, Franco Zeffirelli ***Ph*** Pasquale De Santis ***Ed*** Reginald Mills ***Mus*** Nino Rota ***Art*** Renzo Mongiardino

Act Leonard Whiting, Olivia Hussey, John McEnery, Milo O'Shea, Pat Heywood, Michael York (Verona/De Laurentiis/British Home Entertainment)

Shot entirely in Italy, director Franco Zeffirelli has conjured up a very good eyeful, with splendid use of color in costumes and backgrounds.

Street and fight sequences give film plenty of movement, allied with bold effective cuts in the Bard's text. Zeffirelli has tried, and often succeeds, in giving the film an up-to-date feeling.

Neither Olivia Hussey nor Leonard Whiting has the experience, looks or vital personality to rise to the pinnacles of the star-cross'd lovers. Dramatic highlights are stilted and much of the verse flat to the ear. Rarely will audiences be moved to throat-gulping by the plight of the young couple.

For all Hussey's prettiness and Whiting's shy charm it is clear that they do not understand one tenth of the meaning of their lines and it is a drawback from which the film cannot recover. The young leads are surrounded by some excellent pro performers, which helps them, but also shows up their inadequacies.

1968: Best Cinematography, Costume Design (Danilo Donati)

NOMINATIONS: Best Picture, Director

•

ROMEO + JULIET
(AKA: WILLIAM SHAKESPEARE'S ROMEO + JULIET)

1996, 120 mins, US Ⓥ ⊙ ▭ col

Dir Baz Luhrmann ***Prod*** Gabriella Martinelli, Baz Luhrmann ***Scr*** Craig Pearce, Baz Luhrmann ***Ph*** Donald M. McAlpine ***Ed*** Jill Bilcock ***Mus*** Craig Armstrong, Marius de Vries, Nellee Hooper ***Art*** Catherine Martin

Act Leonardo Di Caprio, Claire Danes, Brian Dennehy, John Leguizamo, Pete Postlethwaite, Paul Sorvino (Bazmark/20th Century-Fox)

The most aggressively modern, assertively trendy adaptation of Shakespeare ever filmed, this version can serve as a litmus test for any viewer's willingness to accept extreme stylistic attitudinizing as a substitute for the virtues of traditional storytelling; anyone unwilling to accept Mercutio as a black disco diva in drag had best stay away.

[Australian director] Baz Luhrmann transports the Montagues and Capulets to Verona Beach and a violent contemporary world dominated by designer guns, customized cars and incessant music. Result is simultaneously striking and silly. Although arresting in spots, it falls far short of bringing out the full values of the play, and doesn't approach the emotional resonance of Franco Zeffirelli's immensely popular 1968 screen version.

Playing Romeo as a James Dean-ish brooder, Leonardo DiCaprio brings youthful energy to the role but seems neither like his parents' son nor much like one of the gang he runs with. He gets his speeches out without undue embarrassment but, unlike with Claire Danes, they don't seem second-nature to him. Her Juliet, from the moment she appears, is the picture of youthful purity, spontaneity and romantic readiness. Her scenes, both with and apart from Romeo, also stand as a welcome relief from the unrelenting cacophony of the rest of the picture.

Despite the Miami-like ambience, pic was largely shot in Mexico City, with additional Veracruz sites.

1996: NOMINATION: Best Art Direction

•

ROMEO IS BLEEDING

1993, 108 mins, UK/US Ⓥ ⊙ col

Dir Peter Medak ***Prod*** Hilary Henkin, Paul Webster ***Scr*** Hilary Henkin ***Ph*** Dariusz Wolski ***Ed*** Walter Murch ***Mus*** Mark Isham ***Art*** Stuart Wurtzel

Act Gary Oldman, Lena Olin, Annabella Sciorra, Juliette Lewis, Roy Scheider, Will Patton (Working Title/PFE)

The blood and grunge run thick on the mean streets in *Romeo Is Bleeding*. This heavy dose of ultra-violent neo-noir gives Gary Oldman a face-first trip through the gutter that would make Mickey Rourke drool, but the far-fetched plotting eventually goes so far over the top that pic flirts with inventing a new genre of film noir camp.

Oldman's New York police sergeant, Jack Grimaldi, does his job on the organized crimes task force while accepting payoffs from the mob. He also has it both ways in the sack, knowing his lovely wife (Annabella Sciorra) awaits him at home while he makes time with his sultry mistress (Juliette Lewis).

But that is before he meets a member of a Moscow crime family, Mona Demarkov (Lena Olin), who has just been nabbed after wiping out some Feds and a government witness. Grimaldi is entrusted with guarding her at a safe house but she's got him disarmed and sexually compromised before the Feds even arrive to pick her up.

Screenwriter and co-producer Hilary Henkin has delivered some pungent dialogue, vivid characters and wild scenes, and director Peter Medak has responded by creating a stylishly warped environment for it all. One of pic's prime motives would seem to be the creation of the most astoundingly, memorably vicious and sexy female villains in movie history. With her deep, husky voice and intimations of limitless depravity, Olin would convince anyone that she has already chewed up and spat out the men of one empire and is working on her second.

•

ROME, OPEN CITY

SEE: ROMA, CITTA APERTA

•

ROMMEL—DESERT FOX

SEE: THE DESERT FOX

•

ROMPER STOMPER

1992, 92 mins, Australia Ⓥ ⊙ col

Dir Geoffrey Wright ***Prod*** Daniel Scharf, Ian Pringle ***Scr*** Geoffrey Wright ***Ph*** Ron Hagen ***Ed*** Bill Murphy ***Mus*** John Clifford White ***Art*** Steven Jones-Evans

Act Russell Crowe, Daniel Pollock, Jacqueline McKenzie, Alex Scott, Leigh Russell, Daniel Wyllie (Seon)

Romper Stomper is a *Clockwork Orange* without the intellect. In many ways genuinely appalling, pic centers on a gang of moronic neo-Nazi skinheads who regularly do battle with Melbourne's Vietnamese community. Russell Crowe gives a powerful performance as skinhead leader Hando, a brute with a veneer of charm whose bible is *Mein Kampf*. The late Daniel Pollock is also impressive as Davey, his friend and lieutenant. Gang is joined by Gabe (Jacqueline McKenzie), a spaced-out drug addict whose father (Alex Scott) has abused her in an incestuous relationship. When gang attacks Vietnamese in the process of purchasing the skinheads' favorite bar, the "gooks" (as they're called) counterattack with a large force, driving the skinheads from their warehouse base in a long, brutally violent battle sequence.

Pic is well acted and directed with a certain slickness.

•

ROMY AND MICHELE'S HIGH SCHOOL REUNION

1997, 91 mins, US Ⓥ ⊙ col

Dir David Mirkin ***Prod*** Laurence Mark ***Scr*** Robin Schiff ***Ph*** Reynaldo Villalobos ***Ed*** David Finfer ***Mus*** Steve Bartek ***Art*** Mayne Berke

Act Mira Sorvino, Lisa Kudrow, Janeane Garofalo, Alan Cumming, Julia Campbell, Mia Cottet (Touchstone)

First feature by vet TV writer-director-producer David Mirkin looks like a peroxided *Clueless* wanna-be straggling along to the party two years after it's over. Desperately uncertain in tone and able to generate only sporadic laughs, pic decks out its meager story of revenge and comeuppance with a vulgar, flashy shimmer.

Best friends since high school and roommates for a decade since, Romy (Mira Sorvino) and Michele (Lisa Kudrow), with their died blond manes, gaudy wardrobes and vapid small talk, are virtual caricatures of Hollywood bimbos, but they somehow haven't even managed to be successful in that role. Romy, a cashier at a BevHills Jaguar repair shop, seems marginally brighter than her friend.

As the two confront the prospect of returning to Tucson for their 10th high school reunion, the deluded dolls furiously work out at the gym, urgently try to score boyfriends and, in Michele's case, find a job, before they realize they can just pretend they've got some. It's all just a buildup to the trip to Arizona and their grand scheme to pass themselves off as the fabulously rich inventors of Post-its, a deception uncovered by the class cynic and curmudgeon (Janeane Garofalo).

Sorvino and Kudrow get off some good, blank takes and the occasional dumb line readings that will provoke mirth among those with an easy appetite for the comedy of recognition. Garofalo, as a misfit ironically named Heather, lets loose with some zingers that put her at the head of the class.

•

RONDE, LA

1950, 109 mins, France Ⓥ b/w

Dir Max Ophuls ***Prod*** Sacha Gordine ***Scr*** Jacques Natanson, Max Ophuls ***Ph*** Christian Matras ***Ed*** Leonide Azar ***Mus*** Oscar Strauss ***Art*** Jean D'Eaubonne

Act Anton Walbrook, Simone Signoret, Serge Reggiani, Simone Simon, Daniel Gelin, Danielle Darrieux (Gordine)

Max Ophuls's first European chore in 15 years, *La Ronde* is a fantasy on various varieties of love affairs [from the play *Reigen* by Arthur Schnitzler]. A raconteur leads the audience through a series of affairs by a group of people, the plethora of situations making the pic ponderous in its present state.

The raconteur's first character is a streetwalker who meets a soldier for a brief moment and then he is called back to the barracks. The soldier next meets a lovely chambermaid whom he loves and leaves. The raconteur then leads her into an adventure with a sensitive young student. The student in turn has an affair with a married woman. It goes on and on, but that is the basic format of the yarn.

Ophuls has used a dearth of close-ups, brilliant decor playing a vital part. Film gains an opulence in the expert lensing of Christian Matras. There is much filming through carved glass, linen, silks and mirrors to create the aura of romance.

Anton Walbrook is properly suave as the raconteur. Danielle Darrieux and Daniel Gelin are standouts as the wife and amorous student.

•

RONDE, LA
(CIRCLE OF LOVE)

1964, 110 mins, France Ⓥ ▭ col

Dir Roger Vadim ***Prod*** Robert Hakim, Raymond Hakim ***Scr*** Jean Anouilh ***Ph*** Henri Decae ***Ed*** Victoria Mercanton

Act Jean-Claude Brialy, Jane Fonda, Anna Karina, Catherine Spaak, Francine Berge, Marie Dubois (Paris/Interopa)

Arthur Schnitzler's play on turn-of-the-century morals and sex and standing gets still another film this time around by Robert and Raymond Hakim, who produced the first one in 1950. But this is no remake, with early 1900s Vienna replaced by the Paris of 1914 on the eve of the First World War. It shapes as an almost classic French film, insouciant, elegant, witty and one-track in its series of seductions as love is handed from one character to another until the round is completed when the last meets the first.

Roger Vadim's direction stresses the cluttered and cozy decors of the era. His treatment of love is almost modest, to give this a sort of comedic air rather than an ironic undertone.

A prostie and a soldier have a brief fling, with the soldier seducing a maid who is then taken over by the son of the house. He goes on to a young married woman, then to a girl he has picked up, etc. It all ends with the prostitute again, as he has a drunken night out.

Jane Fonda is especially beguiling and deceptively naive as the philandering wife, while Anna Karina is a right, waif-like maid. Marie Dubois has the underlying good nature, under a vulgar exterior, as the sentimental prostie. Catherine Spaak depicts an adroit blending of innocence and guile as an emancipated young woman. Francine Berge displays a knowing mixture of sexual appetite and discreet longing as an actress. The men are mainly foils.

Also worth mentioning are Maurice Binder's expertly conceived titles.

•

RONIN
1998, 118 mins, US Ⓥ ⊙ ▭ col
Dir John Frankenheimer ***Prod*** Frank Mancuso, Jr. ***Scr*** J. D. Zeik, Richard Weisz [Úvid Mamet] ***Ph*** Robert Fraisse ***Ed*** Tony Gibbs ***Mus*** Elia Cmiral ***Art*** Michael Z. Hanan
Act Robert De Niro, Jean Reno, Natascha McElhone, Stellan Skarsgard, Sean Bean, Michael Lonsdale (FGM/United Artists)

Ronin reps a pleasurable throwback to the sort of gritty, low-tech international thriller that was a staple of the '60s. Even though the characters are virtual cut-outs and the story is ultimately without much meaning or resonance, the film offers enough potent action, intriguing shifting loyalties and scenic French locations to hold the interest.

Beginning on a shadowy Montmartre street as the scruffy Sam (Robert De Niro) arrives for an appointment at a seedy bar, plot snaps to attention as Irish ringleader Deidre (Natascha McElhone) presides over a planning meeting for an ambush to retrieve a mysterious briefcase from some criminals.

Gang consists of the usual cross-section of specialists: American expert strategist Sam, French coordinator Vincent (Jean Reno), German electronics and surveillance whiz Gregor (Stellan Skarsgard), Yank driver Larry (Skipp Sudduth) and British weapons advisor Spence (Sean Bean).

Throughout the fast-moving yarn, it's only a matter of who's the most clever and who can lay final claim to the all-important briefcase, a genuine McGuffin whose contents are unknown. The first major setpiece, a nocturnal face-off by the Seine that erupts into a huge shootout, is excitingly handled, whereupon the action shifts to the South of France.

De Niro and Gallic star Reno are well matched, with the weight of having seen and done it all showing everywhere on their faces except in their eyes, which retain impudent, amused twinkles. Skarsgard is chillingly good as the cagiest poker player of the bunch, while McElhone is alluringly mysterious as the organizer who dispenses orders received from the occasionally glimpsed mastermind played by Jonathan Pryce.

Title refers to the 47 ronin of Japanese legend, Samurai who became solitary agents wandering the land after their leader was killed.

•

ROOKIE, THE
1990, 121 mins, US Ⓥ ⊙ ▭ col
Dir Clint Eastwood ***Prod*** Howard Kazanjian, Steven Siebert, David Valdes ***Scr*** Boaz Yakin, Scott Spiegel ***Ph*** Jack N. Green ***Ed*** Joel Cox ***Mus*** Lennie Niehaus ***Art*** Judy Cammer
Act Clint Eastwood, Charlie Sheen, Raul Julia, Sonia Braga, Tom Skerritt, Lara Flynn Boyle (Malpaso/Warner)

Overlong, sadistic and stale even by the conventions of the buddy pic genre, Clint Eastwood's *The Rookie* is actually *Dirty Harry 5 ½*, since Eastwood's tough-as-nails cop Nick Pulovski could just as easily be named Harry Callahan, and his penchant for breaking in partners (and getting them killed) is a holdover from Harry's first three patrols. This time, however, the troubles lie in partner Charlie Sheen, a rich kid working out childhood guilt and hostility against his parents by playing policeman. Pair pursues a stolen-car ring operated by ruthless thief Raul Julia and sweaty henchwoman Sonia Braga (in a nearly non-verbal role). Pulovski is taken hostage, and Sheen's character has to find himself by, essentially, disregarding all conventional legal channels and destroying as much property as possible.

The normally brilliant Julia lapses into and out of a bad German accent, Braga has just a window-dressing bad-girl role, and *Twin Peaks*'s Lara Flynn Boyle is Sheen's blandly drawn girlfriend. Eastwood the actor seems rightfully bored with the material, while Sheen continues to hammer away at his own tough-guy rep with only marginal success.

•

ROOKIE OF THE YEAR
1993, 103 mins, US Ⓥ ⊙ col
Dir Daniel Stern ***Prod*** Robert Harper ***Scr*** Sam Harper ***Ph*** Jack N. Green ***Ed*** Donn Cambern, Raja Gosnell ***Mus*** Bill Conti ***Art*** Steven Jordan
Act Gary Busey, Albert Hall, Amy Morton, Dan Hedeya, Bruce Altman, Eddie Bracken (20th Century-Fox)

Rookie of the Year aspires to be a pint-sized "It's a Wonderful Field of Dreams," and largely succeeds in minor league fashion.

The premise is engaging. Preteen Henry Rowengarter (Thomas Ian Nicholas) is your typical single-parented, enthusiastic baseball-playing Chicago kid who's unaware of life's cruelties. Then the accident happens. When a school bully goads him into going for a high pop fly, in his headlong zeal Henry fails to notice a loose baseball in his path. Tripping on the orb, he's sent skyward, falling with a thud and breaking his arm.

Months later, when his cast is removed, Henry discovers the fracture has healed in a curious way. His tendons have tightened, allowing him to hurl a ball faster than a speeding bullet. Circumstance brings this to the attention of his beloved Chicago Cubs. Soon the contracts are signed and the pee-wee player is rapidly on his way to delivering his franchise a berth in the World Series.

Essentially a one-gag premise, Sam Harper's screenplay valiantly attempts to enhance the yarn by fleshing out the characters and injecting broad splashes of madcap comedy. It connects more often than it fans in the hands of rookie director Daniel Stern, who lacks seasoning to ground the fantasy in a realistic setting.

The principal cast shines. Youngster Thomas Ian Nicholas has a winning personality. Also strong are the ever-reliable Gary Busey as the pitcher edging into over-the-hill status, and Amy Morton, who, with little script help, provides the modern mum with old-fashioned warmth and new-era independence. John Candy provides an uncredited turn as an announcer.

•

ROOM AT THE TOP
1959, 117 mins, UK Ⓥ ⊙ b/w
Dir Jack Clayton ***Prod*** John Woolf, James Woolf ***Scr*** Neil Paterson ***Ph*** Freddie Francis ***Ed*** Ralph Kemplen ***Mus*** Mario Nascimbene
Act Laurence Harvey, Simone Signoret, Heather Sears, Donald Wolfit, Donald Houston, Hermione Baddeley (Remus)

Room at the Top, based on John Braine's bestselling novel, is an adult, human picture. Neil Paterson's literate, well-molded screenplay is enhanced by subtle, intelligent direction from first-timer Jack Clayton and a batch of top-notch performances.

Laurence Harvey takes a job as an accountant in the local government offices of a North Country town. He is an alert young man with a chip on his shoulder because of his humble background. He quickly finds that the small town is virtually controlled by a self-made millionaire and is dominated by those with money and power. Harvey is determined to break down this class-consciousness and sets his cap at the millionaire's daughter. At the same time he is irresistibly drawn to an unhappily married Frenchwoman (Simone Signoret) with whom he has a violent affair. The Clayton touch produces some fine scenes. These include the young girl's first capitulation to Harvey, the manner in which the millionaire stresses his power over the young upstart, the love scenes between Harvey and Simone Signoret and their quarrel and parting. Above all, Clayton never loses the authentic "small town" atmosphere.

Harvey makes a credible figure of the young man, likeable despite his weaknesses, torn between love and ambition, and he brings strength and feeling to his love scenes with Signoret. She gives, perhaps, the best performance in a capital all-round cast. Heather Sears has less opportunity as the young girl.

1959: Best Actress (Simone Signoret), Adapted Screenplay

NOMINATIONS: Best Picture, Director, Actor (Laurence Harvey), Supp. Actress (Hermione Baddeley)

•

ROOM FOR ONE MORE
1952, 97 mins, US b/w
Dir Norman Taurog ***Prod*** Henry Blanke ***Scr*** Jack Rose, Melville Shavelson ***Ph*** Robert Burks ***Ed*** Alan Crosland, Jr. ***Mus*** Max Steiner ***Art*** Douglas Bacon
Act Cary Grant, Betsy Drake, George Winslow, Iris Mann, Clifford Tatum, Jr., Lurene Tuttle (Warner)

A happy combination of good humor and warm drama has been put together with neat results in *Room for One More*.

Cary Grant and Betsy Drake make a smart star team to head up this story of a real-life couple who open hearts and home to unfortunate children. Themselves Mr. and Mrs., Grant and Drake spark the film with the humor it needs without neglecting honest tugs at the heart.

Yarn tells of the Roses, financially insecure and with three youngsters of their own, bringing into their uninhibited family life two children whom life's hard knocks are rapidly warping beyond repair. One is a sullen girl of 13, already scarred beyond her years because of being unwanted anywhere. The other is a crippled boy, already on his way toward being a mean, retarded citizen.

•

ROOMMATES
1995, 108 mins, US Ⓥ ⊙ col
Dir Peter Yates ***Prod*** Ted Field, Scott Kroopf, Robert W. Cort ***Scr*** Max Apple, Stephen Metcalfe ***Ph*** Mike Southon ***Ed*** John Tintori ***Mus*** Elmer Bernstein ***Art*** Dan Bishop
Act Peter Falk, D. B. Sweeney, Julianne Moore, Jan Rubes, Frankie Faison, Ellen Burstyn (Interscope/PFE/Hollywood)

Roommates is an exceedingly mild story of the emotional tug of war between a lovably cantankerous old codger and the grandson he raises to maturity. Agreeably humorous at times and less squishily sentimental than it might have been, Peter Yates's generational tale goes down painlessly but hasn't much flavor or substance.

Script [from a screen story by Max Apple] scans some thirty years in the lives of ancient Rocky Holeczek (Peter Falk) and his grandson, Michael (D. B. Sweeney). Orphaned at five, Michael is taken in by his gruff granddad, an old Polish-American coot in Pittsburgh who works as a baker.

When Michael, at 25, becomes a hospital intern at Ohio State and Rocky, by now spryly approaching 100, is evicted from his longtime home, the oldster has no choice but to come live with the kid in Columbus. More serious is Rocky's objection to Michael's incipient relationship with Beth (Julianne Moore), a lovely social worker with a very wealthy mother (Ellen Burstyn). Being a good boy, Michael does the only thing he can—he marries the girl. Thereafter, Michael and Beth have two kids, illness finally strikes the indefatigable Rocky, and much worse tragedy hits the door of the family.

The main artistic and commercial attraction is Falk's old-age performance. With bald pate, trim mustache and leathery skin, the actor looks a bit like a diminutive version of Brando's elderly Godfather. Sweeney is energetic but a bit opaque as Michael, while Moore is just plain sweet as his sweetheart.

NOMINATION: Best Makeup

•

ROOM SERVICE
1938, 76 mins, US Ⓥ ⊙ b/w
Dir William A. Seiter ***Prod*** Pandro S. Berman ***Scr*** Morrie Ryskind ***Ph*** J. Roy Hunt ***Ed*** George Crone ***Mus*** Roy Webb (dir.) ***Art*** Van Nest Polglase, Al Herman
Act Groucho Marx, Chico Marx, Harpo Marx, Lucille Ball, Ann Miller, Frank Albertson (RKO)

Room Service with the Marx Bros. will satisfy on the laugh score. There may be captious ones who'll miss (1) Groucho's standard rasslin' with a femme via-á-vis; (2) Harpo's harp solo; (3) Chico's equally standard pianology. But the Marxes have a more staple story structure upon which to hang their buffoonery.

The minimization of the musical highlights naturally points up Groucho's comedy all the more. But running a close second is Donald MacBride, from the original George Abbott play production [by John Murray and Allen Boretz] re-creating his role of the bombastic hotel executive. MacBride well-nigh steals all of his scenes, adroitly foiled by Cliff Dunstan (also of the Broadway original) as the distrait hotel manager who has permitted the shoestring impresario (Groucho Marx) to camp a stranded troupe of 22 in his hostelry and run up a $1,200 tab.

Frank Albertson is the trusting young playwright from Oswego; Lucille Ball and Ann Miller are virtually walk-throughs as the femme vis-à-vis with Groucho and Albertson.

•

ROOM WITH A VIEW, A
1986, 115 mins, UK Ⓥ ⊙ col
Dir James Ivory ***Prod*** Ismail Merchant ***Scr*** Ruth Prawer Jhabvala ***Ph*** Tony Pierce-Roberts ***Ed*** Humphrey Dixon ***Mus*** Richard Robbins ***Art*** Gianni Quaranta, Brian Ackland-Snow
Act Maggie Smith, Helena Bonham Carter, Denholm Elliott, Julian Sands, Daniel Day Lewis, Simon Callow (Merchant-Ivory/Goldcrest)

A thoroughly entertaining screen adaptation of novelist E. M. Forster's comedy of manners about the Edwardian English upper class at home and abroad, distinguished by superb ensemble acting, intelligent writing and stunning design.

Set in 1907, *A Room With a View* moves between a pensione in Florence, Italy, where a well-to-do young English lady, Lucy Honeychurch (Helena Bonham Carter) is traveling on the type of compulsory horizon-broadening tour that was the prerogative of her class, chaperoned by her fussy, punctilious aunt Charlotte (Maggie Smith), and the insular Surrey countryside where she lives with her mother (Rosemary Leach). James Ivory's direction makes what might have been a talky period piece in lesser hands a consistently engaging study of the mores and morality of a bygone time.

1986: Best Adapted Screenplay, Art Direction, Costume Design (Jenny Beavan, John Bright)

NOMINATIONS: Best Picture, Director, Supp. Actor (Denholm Elliott), Supp. Actress (Maggie Smith), Cinematography

•

ROOSTER COGBURN

1975, 107 mins, US Ⓥ ⦿ ▭ col

Dir Stuart Millar ***Prod*** Hal B. Wallis ***Scr*** Martin Julien ***Ph*** Harry Stradling, Jr. ***Ed*** Robert Swink ***Mus*** Laurence Rosenthal ***Art*** Preston Ames

Act John Wayne, Katharine Hepburn, Anthony Zerbe, Richard Jordan, John McIntyre, Strother Martin (Universal)

Rooster Cogburn has the exciting charisma of John Wayne and Katharine Hepburn, plus the memories of Wayne's Oscar-winning performance in *True Grit*.

The title is based on the character from Charles Portis's novel *True Grit*, which picks up judge John McIntyre after another trigger-happy foul-up. But outlaw Richard Jordan and gang, aided by Anthony Zerbe, Wayne's onetime scout, is acting up, causing several deaths including that of preacher Jon Lormer, survived by spinster daughter Hepburn and Indian lad Richard Romancito. Latter pair join reinstated marshal Wayne to track down the bad guys.

A little artfulness, a little creativity, a little subtlety could work wonders. Like Jordan not chewing up the scenery like a silent pix heavy. Like Hepburn and Wayne not doing a frontier version of The Bickersons. Like not shoe-horning *The African Queen* plot line into this script.

•

ROOSTERS

1993, 93 mins, US Ⓥ col

Dir Robert M. Young ***Prod*** Susan Block-Reiner, Norman I. Cohen, Kevin Reidy ***Scr*** Milcha Sanchez-Scott ***Ph*** Reynaldo Villalobos ***Ed*** Arthur Coburn ***Mus*** David Kilay

Act Edward James Olmos, Sonia Braga, Maria Conchita Alonso, Danny Nucci, Sarah Lassez, Valente Rodriguez (American Playhouse/WMG)

Centering on a classic father-son conflict, *Roosters* is an absorbing family drama marked by Freudian symbolism and the fatalism of a Greek tragedy. Superb acting, particularly by Sonia Braga, almost makes up for the lack of sustained dramatic interest and some rough shifts between the film's realistic scenes and its more poetic ones.

Narrative, set in the Southwest, begins with the coming home of Gallo Morales (Edward James Olmos), a legendary breeder of fighting cocks, after seven years in prison for manslaughter. His return is anxiously anticipated by his sturdy wife, Juana (Braga), 20-year-old son Hector (Danny Nucci) and, especially, adolescent daughter Angela (Sarah Lassez). Also living in the house is Chata (Maria Conchita Alonso), Gallo's sister, whose overt sensuality soon ignites her libidinous nephew.

The conflict that haunts and eventually tears the family apart revolves around a prize-fighting cock that Hector inherited from his grandfather, to the utmost resentment of his father, for whom the cock is a symbol of his macho, patriarchal power.

Adapting her 1987 stage hit to the screen, Milcha Sanchez-Scott has opened up her compelling play without sacrificing its dramatic intensity. However, in pic's second part, a few of the one-on-one scenes reveal the theatrical origins of the material.

•

ROOTS OF HEAVEN, THE

1958, 130 mins, US ▭ col

Dir John Huston ***Prod*** Darryl F. Zanuck ***Scr*** Romain Gary, Patrick Leigh-Fermor ***Ph*** Oswald Morris ***Ed*** Russell Lloyd ***Mus*** Malcolm Arnold ***Art*** Stephen Grimes, Raymond Gabutti

Act Errol Flynn, Juliette Greco, Trevor Howard, Eddie Albert, Orson Welles, Herbert Lom (20th Century-Fox)

The Roots of Heaven has striking pictorial aspects, some exciting performances and builds to a pulsating climax of absorbing tension. Unfortunately, these plus factors almost all come in the second half of the picture.

The locale of the screenplay, from Romain Gary's novel, is French Equatorial Africa. Trevor Howard, whose presence is never completely explained, is launching a campaign to save the elephants of Africa. He believes they are threatened with extinction from big game hunters, ivory poachers and the encroachment of civilization. When he tries to get signers of his petition to outlaw the killings, he is rebuffed on all fronts.

Howard gets only two signatures. One is from Errol Flynn, an alcoholic British ex-officer, and the other is from Juliette Greco, a prostitute. So Howard decides on a campaign of harassment of the huntes and his counterattack attracts the attention of a safari-ing American TV personality, Orson Welles; a Danish scientist, Friedrich Ledebur; a German nobleman, Olivier Hussenot; and some natives who propose to use Howard as a symbol of their own resistance to colonial law and practice.

Director John Huston has staged his exterior scenes superbly. Full advantage is taken here of the arduous African locations. Howard gives a fine performance and is responsible for conveying as much as comes across of the tricky theme. Flynn plays the drunken officer competently but without suggesting any latent nobility or particular depth. Greco is interesting without being very moving. Orson Welles in a brief bit (reportedly done as a favor to producer Darryl F. Zanuck) is a pinwheel of flashing vigor, his evil to be lamented.

•

ROPE

1948, 80 mins, US Ⓥ ⦿ col

Dir Alfred Hitchcock ***Prod*** [Alfred Hitchcock, Sidney Bernstein] ***Scr*** Arthur Laurents ***Ph*** Joseph Valentine, William V. Skall ***Ed*** William H. Ziegler ***Mus*** [David Buttolph] ***Art*** Perry Ferguson

Act James Stewart, John Dall, Farley Granger, Cedric Hardwicke, Constance Collier, Joan Chandler (Transatlantic)

Hitchcock could have chosen a more entertaining subject with which to use the arresting camera and staging technique displayed in *Rope*. Theme is of a thrill murder, done for no reason but to satisfy a sadistical urge and intellectual vanity. Plot has its real-life counterpart in the infamous Loeb-Leopold case, and is based on the play by Patrick Hamilton [adapted by Hume Cronyn].

Feature of the picture is that story action is continuous without time lapses. Action takes place within an hour-and-a-half period and the film footage nearly duplicates the span, being 80 minutes. It is entirely confined to the murder apartment of two male dilettantes, intellectual morons who commit what they believe to be the perfect crime, then celebrate the deed with a ghoulish supper served to the victim's relatives and friends from atop the chest in which the body is concealed.

To achieve his effects, Hitchcock put his cast and technicians through lengthy rehearsals before turning on a camera.

James Stewart, as the ex-professor who first senses the guilt of his former pupils and nibbles away at their composure with verbal barbs, does a commanding job. John Dall stands out as the egocentric who masterminds the killing and ghoulish wake. Equally good is Farley Granger as the weakling partner in crime.

•

ROSALIE

1937, 123 mins, US Ⓥ b/w

Dir W. S. Van Dyke ***Prod*** William Anthony McGuire ***Scr*** William Anthony McGuire ***Ph*** Oliver T. Marsh ***Ed*** Blanche Sewell ***Mus*** Herbert Stothart (dir.)

Act Nelson Eddy, Eleanor Powell, Frank Morgan, Edna May Oliver, Ray Bolger, Ilona Massey (M-G-M)

A stage play once confined within the liberal proscenium of the New Amsterdam theatre (NY), where Marilyn Miller scintillated for the Ziegfeld management, *Rosalie* breaks through the chrysalis of celluloid as a mammoth fantasy.

Nelson Eddy is a line-plunging West Point cadet-baritone; Eleanor Powell, a dancing Balkan princess; Frank Morgan and Edna May Oliver, amusing musical comedy king and queen; and a light operetta story. Opening shots (from the newsreels) show 80,000 cheering maniacs at an Army-Navy football game. Down on the field Eddy intercepts a pass, changes his pace, dodges a tackler and scores for Army.

Scene changes to a Vassar dormitory, where Powell is telling her classmates that Eddy is a conceited young man whom she never wishes to see again. Soon, however, she hears his voice in a serenade. They make a date to meet at festival time in the Balkan capital, come next spring.

It is in the festival scenes that *Rosalie* really shows its cinematic girth. Setting for the peasants' folk dances seems as big as Soldiers' Field, Chicago, which means there are hundreds of Albertina Rasch dancers, thousands of costumed extras and innumerable others. In the midst of this ensemble Powell does an acrobatic tap atop some massive drums.

While the gaiety is at its height, the red menace of revolution breaks out. The royal family and household escape to America by steamship. Eddy decides to fly back to West Point in his airplane. The distinguished visitors are entertained at the Academy, where Powell masquerades as a cadet.

Cole Porter has written new music and lyrics. Ray Bolger, a good comedian and rated tops among legit dancers, is the real discovery in *Rosalie*. His humor is clean, unforced and spontaneous.

•

ROSARY MURDERS, THE

1987, 105 mins, US Ⓥ ⦿ col

Dir Fred Walton ***Prod*** Robert G. Laurel, Michael Mihalich ***Scr*** Elmore Leonard, Fred Walton ***Ph*** David Golia ***Ed*** Sam Vitale ***Mus*** Bobby Laurel, Don Sebesky

Act Donald Sutherland, Charles Durning, Josef Sommer, Belinda Bauer, James Murtaugh, John Danelle (First Take)

A string of a half-dozen murders committed by someone with a grudge against the Catholic Church, his victims being nuns and priests in a Detroit parish, is lacking in suspense or dramatic buildup, and what should have been the final climatic sequences are as flat as a holy wafer.

Pic [from the novel by William X. Kienzle] revolves mostly around a priest, Father Koesler, who sets about trying to solve the murders while the police seem to be twiddling their thumbs. The priest turns sleuth after the murderer drops a few clues to him during a confessional box session. As a man of the cloth, latter can't tip off the police or probable victims because of his secrecy vows.

Donald Sutherland puts in a good performance as the liberal-minded investigating priest, and Charles Durning is fine as the hard-line father superior.

•

ROSE, THE

1979, 134 mins, US Ⓥ ⦿ ▭ col

Dir Mark Rydell ***Prod*** Marvin Worth ***Scr*** Bill Kerby, Bo Goldman ***Ph*** Vilmos Zsigmond ***Ed*** Robert L. Wolfe ***Mus*** Paul A. Rothchild ***Art*** Richard MacDonald

Act Bette Midler, Alan Bates, Frederic Forrest, Harry Dean Stanton, Barry Primus, David Keith (20th Century-Fox)

Producers haven't flinched from picking the scabs off the body of 1960s rock 'n' roll. While there are certainly similarities to the tragic story of Janis Joplin, *The Rose* emerges as its own self-contained tale. What's puzzling is that the screenwriters have chosen to dwell solely on the downward career spiral of Bette Midler's character, known on and offstage as The Rose.

Revolving around the star are various satellites, including boyfriend Frederic Forrest, manager Alan Bates and road manager Barry Primus. Result is an ultra-realistic look at the infusion of money, sex, drugs and booze into the simple process of singing a song, a chore Midler does faultlessly in several excellent concert sequences.

1979: NOMINATIONS: Best Actress (Bette Midler), Supp. Actor (Frederic Forrest), Editing, Sound

•

ROSEBUD

1975, 126 mins, US ▭ col

Dir Otto Preminger ***Prod*** Preminger ***Scr*** Erik Lee Preminger ***Ph*** Denys Coop ***Ed*** Peter Thornton ***Mus*** Laurent Petitgirard ***Art*** Michael Seymour

Act Peter O'Toole, Richard Attenborough, Cliff Gorman, Claude Dauphin, John V. Lindsay, Peter Lawford (United Artists)

Political tumult story, involving Palestine Liberation Organization terrorist kidnapping, is a bland and unexciting film. Peter O'Toole heads the cast as a Briton, secret agenting for the U.S., who sorts out the crisis.

An episodic collage of long sequences which crosscut between the yacht heist of five young wealthy girls, and the efforts of their families and police to track down their kidnappers. O'Toole (who replaced Robert Mitchum after shooting began) is recruited from his CIA cover as a *Newsweek International* reporter to locate the girls and the PLO group. O'Toole's is among the few strong performances, but that isn't saying much. As a foreign policy document, *Rosebud* at least will not cause controversy, because as a motion picture, it's a crashing bore.

•

ROSELAND
1977, 103 mins, US Ⓥ col
Dir James Ivory ***Prod*** Ismail Merchant ***Scr*** Ruth Prawere Jhabvala ***Ph*** Ernest Vincze ***Ed*** Humphrey Dixon, Richard Schmiechen ***Mus*** Michael Gibson
Act Teresa Wright, Lou Jacobi, Christopher Walken, Louise Kirtland, Geraldine Chaplin, Helen Gallagher (Merchant-Ivory)

There is romance to the notion that our buildings will outlast us, that our passions will be seen and remembered within the walls while we go on our way to our just desserts. That is the emotional underpinning of *Roseland*, a clean, well-lighted ballroom of New York's West Side.

Standout is Lilia Skala, playing an elderly German woman with the bearing of Bismarck, who confides to her sleepy Peabody (a Roseland dance) partner, David Thomas, that she has had to do cleaning and work as a cook at Schrafft's to pay her way.

Second tale of a gigolo, nicely crafted by Christopher Walken, is of his failure to separate himself from Joan Copeland, excellent in her portrayal of a lonely and dying woman now buying what her faded glamor once commanded.

•

ROSE-MARIE
1936, 110 mins, US Ⓥ ⦿ b/w
Dir W. S. Van Dyke ***Prod*** Hunt Stromberg ***Scr*** Frances Goodrich, Albert Hackett, Alice Duer Miller ***Ph*** William Daniels ***Ed*** Blanche Sewell ***Mus*** Rudolf Friml, Herbert Stothart (dir.) ***Art*** Cedric Gibbons, Joseph Wright, Edwin B. Willis
Act Jeanette MacDonald, Nelson Eddy, James Stewart, Reginald Owen, Allan Jones, Alan Mowbray (M-G-M)

Strong impression left by the Jeanette MacDonald–Nelson Eddy twain in *Naughty Marietta* (1935) is surpassed in *Rose-Marie*, Metro's operatic western. Sturdy stage libretto by Otto Harbach and Oscar Hammerstein II is further enhanced by the scope of the cinematic treatment. There is a wholly satisfying blend of sophisticated behind-the-opera-scenes temperament with the Great Outdoors stuff which comprises much of the ensuing footage as Eddy pursues MacDonald's scapegrace brother.

Score by Rudolf Friml and Herbert Stothart, the latter also Metro studio musical director (also contributing the maestro-ing on this production), has survived more than a decade since its premiere at the Imperial Theatre on Broadway 2 September 1924. The classic "Indian Love Call" as it re-echoes through the "Canadian" woodlands (actual location at Lake Tahoe on the Cal.-Nev. border, and very beautiful) means more than it ever did in its stage original. Eddy's balladeering of the titular "Rose-Marie" as he paddles MacDonald on the trek for the escaped criminal (her brother) is likewise photographically and in other respects enhanced. The waltz song from *Romeo and Juliet* is the legit operatic opener [staged by William von Wymetal], wherein Allan Jones, who warbles a nifty tenor on his own, is MacDonald's vocal vis-á-vis. Femme star has a solo opportunity with "Pardon Me, Madame" (Gus Kahn's lyric interpolation).

There is a nine-minute prologue to the film, with the Metro orchestra, under the direction of symphony conductor Alfred Wallerstein, playing the *Poet and Peasant* overture.

•

ROSE MARIE
1954, 106 mins, US ▭ col
Dir Mervyn LeRoy ***Prod*** Mervyn LeRoy ***Scr*** Ronald Millar, George Froeschel ***Ph*** Paul Vogel ***Ed*** Harold F. Kress ***Mus*** Georgie Stoll (dir.)
Act Ann Blyth, Howard Keel, Fernando Lamas, Bert Lahr, Marjorie Main, Joan Taylor (M-G-M)

Rose Marie, a perennial operetta favorite since first presented on Broadway in 1924, is dished up as a lavish CinemaScope production complete with stereophonic sound. The views of the forests, the lakes and the mountains are breathtaking. Unfortunately, operetta plot of yesteryear is sweet and occasionally sad, but with little substance. Mervyn LeRoy, who produced and directed, has fine-looking leads in Ann Blyth, Howard Keel and Fernando Lamas, but they fail to instill much verve or enthusiasm to the proceedings. The bright moments of the film are offered by Marjorie Main and Bert Lahr, who provide some welcome comedy relief. Lamentably, Lahr is not given enough screen time.

Blyth is seen as the backwoods French-Canadian gal who has to choose between Howard Keel, the Mountie, and Lamas, "the ornery-but-no-killer" trapper. Keel magnanimously releases her from any obligations and she rides off into the woods to join Lamas.

There is one dance production number, staged by Busby Berkeley, an Indian festival dance completely lacking in authenticity but nevertheless an effective eye-catcher.

•

ROSEMARY'S BABY
1968, 134 mins, US Ⓥ ⦿ col
Dir Roman Polanski ***Prod*** William Castle ***Scr*** Roman Polanski ***Ph*** William Fraker ***Ed*** Sam O'Steen, Bob Wyman ***Mus*** Christopher Komeda ***Art*** Richard Sylbert
Act Mia Farrow, John Cassavetes, Ruth Gordon, Sidney Blackmer, Maurice Evans, Ralph Bellamy (Paramount)

Several exhilarating milestones are achieved in *Rosemary's Baby*, an excellent film version of Ira Levin's diabolical chiller novel. Writer-director Roman Polanski has triumphed in his first U.S.-made pic. The film holds attention without explicit violence or gore.

Mia Farrow and John Cassavetes, a likeable young married couple, take a flat in a run-down New York building. Ralph Bellamy, an obstetrician prescribing some strange prenatal nourishment for Farrow and Maurice Evans, Farrow's sole ally, who dies a mysterious death, as well as Charles Grodin, enter the plot at adroit intervals.

The near-climax—Farrow has been drugged so as to conceive by Satan—and the final wallop make for genuine cliff-hanger interest.

Farrow's performance is outstanding. Cassavetes handles particularly well the difficult projection of a husband as much in love with his wife as with success. Neighbour Ruth Gordon is pleasantly unrestrained in her pushy self-interest, quite appropriate herein, while other principals score solidly.

1968: Best Supp. Actress (Ruth Gordon)

NOMINATION: Best Adapted Screenplay

•

ROSENCRANTZ & GUILDENSTERN ARE DEAD
1991, 118 mins, UK Ⓥ col
Dir Tom Stoppard ***Prod*** Michael Brandman, Emanuel Azenberg ***Scr*** Tom Stoppard ***Ph*** Peter Biziou ***Ed*** Nicolas Gaster ***Mus*** Stanley Myers ***Art*** Vaughan Edwards
Act Gary Oldman, Tim Roth, Richard Dreyfuss, Iain Glen, Joanna Roth, Donald Sumpter (Brandenberg)

Marking his debut as director, playwright Tom Stoppard takes two marginal characters from Shakespeare's *Hamlet* and places them at the center of a comedy-drama, while the major characters of the play—Hamlet, Ophelia, Claudius and the rest—are only part of the background.

Rosencrantz and Guildenstern are never certain about what's going on in Elsinore. They overhear crucial conversations and encounters, they talk briefly to the King and to Hamlet, and, in the end, they accompany Hamlet on a voyage to England, but they're never a part of the central drama. Stoppard's 1967 play has been seen as a mixture of Samuel Beckett and Shakespeare, but on film, he adds cinematic references so that the two protagonists, with their endless word games, come across as a mixture of Abbott and Costello (the "Who's On First" routine) and Laurel and Hardy (with the clumsy Rosencrantz forever annoying and frustrating the superior Guildenstern). There's also a touch of Monty Python in the zaniness of the characters and their verbal and visual antics.

Gary Oldman and Tim Roth are splendid in their roles. Oldman plays his character as a shrewd simpleton, and Roth plays his as a man who thinks he's clever, but really isn't. Also giving a formidable performance is Richard Dreyfuss as the leader of a band of strolling players.

•

ROSE OF WASHINGTON SQUARE
1939, 90 mins, US b/w
Dir Gregory Ratoff ***Prod*** Nunnally Johnson (assoc.) ***Scr*** Nunnally Johnson ***Ph*** Karl Freund ***Ed*** Louis Loeffler ***Mus*** Louis Silvers (dir.) ***Art*** Richard Day, Rudolph Sternad
Act Tyrone Power, Alice Faye, Al Jolson, William Frawley, Joyce Compton, Hobart Cavanaugh (20th Century-Fox)

Of the three co-stars this is Al Jolson's picture. But it's not much of a film musical. It's primarily a story deficiency. Nunnally Johnson did the screenplay and production, although original by John Larkin and Jerry Horwin is as much to blame.

A major, solo title emphasizes that the plot structure is fictional. However, the Fannie Brice–Nicky Arnstein saga is an incidental to a show business romance where Al Jolson (billed as Ted Cotter, but he might just as well have been called Jolson) is the altruistic patron of the beauteous and talented Alice Faye. She in turn is stuck on the wrong-guy character played by Tyrone Power.

Faye is still plenty on the s.a. side, excepting for a few camera angles that don't flatter her chin-line. Power's vacillating characterization is a missout.

•

ROSE TATTOO, THE
1955, 117 mins, US Ⓥ ⦿ b/w
Dir Daniel Mann ***Prod*** Hal Wallis ***Scr*** Tennessee Williams ***Ph*** James Wong Howe ***Ed*** Warren Low ***Mus*** Alex North ***Art*** Hal Pereira, Tambi Larsen
Act Anna Magnani, Burt Lancaster, Marisa Pavan, Ben Cooper, Jo Van Fleet, Virginia Grey (Paramount)

The Rose Tattoo creates a realistic Italiano atmosphere in the bayou country of the south, establishes vivid characters with one glaring exception and dwells upon a story that is important only because it gives its key character a jumping-off point for fascinating histrionics.

Anna Magnani gives *Tattoo* its substance; she's spellbinding as the signora content with the memory of the fidelity of her husband until she discovers he had a blonde on the side before his banana truck carried him to death.

The characters inspire little sympathy. Magnani has animalistic drive and no beauty. Burt Lancaster, as the village idiot by inheritance, is called upon to take on a role bordering on the absurd.

Otherwise Daniel Mann does fine in the directing. He provides pace where some situations might have been static.

1955: Best Actress (Anna Magnani), B&W Cinematography, B&W Art Direction

NOMINATIONS: Best Picture, Supp. Actress (Marisa Pavan), B&W Costume Design, Editing, Scoring of a Dramatic Picture

•

ROTTEN TO THE CORE
1965, 89 mins, UK ▭ b/w
Dir John Boulting ***Prod*** Roy Boulting ***Scr*** Jeffrey Dell, Roy Boulting, John Warren, Len Heath ***Ph*** Freddie Young ***Ed*** Teddy Darvas ***Mus*** Michael Dress ***Art*** Alex Vetchinsky
Act Anton Rodgers, Eric Sykes, Charlotte Rampling, Ian Bannen, Avis Bunnage, Dudley Sutton (BLC/Boulting)

Big-time crime is the main target of the Boulting Brothers' latest piece of satirical joshing, with army and police figuring in the story. It provides a reasonable ration of yocks and amusing situations but these have to struggle against some dim passages. The Boulting Brothers' knives are less sharp than customary.

Idea hinges on the appeal of Prime Minister Harold Wilson to adapt scientific methods to 1965 big business and industry. And this the Boultings have applied to the activities of a gang of crooks whose young boss (Anton Rodgers) has set his beady eye on hijacking an army payroll worth nearly $3 million. Rodgers, known as "Duke," assembles his gang under the front of running a health resort hospital near the army camp. Rodgers shows versatility in four or five characterizations but it needed a comedy character actor to dominate the laugh sequences. Eric Sykes is largely wasted in the role of a private eye, which fails to jell.

The Boultings put their faith in an unknown girl (Charlotte Rampling) as the Duke's moll. She is quite easy on the eye but lacks the experience and personality.

•

ROUGE
SEE: INJI KAU

•

ROUGH CUT
1980, 112 mins, US Ⓥ ⦿ col
Dir Don Siegel ***Prod*** David Merrick ***Scr*** Francis Burns [= Larry Gelbart] ***Ph*** Freddie Young ***Ed*** Doug Stewart ***Mus*** Nelson Riddle ***Art*** Ted Haworth
Act Burt Reynolds, Lesley-Anne Down, David Niven, Patrick Magee, Joss Ackland, Timothy West (Paramount)

Rough Cut emerges as an undistinctive, frothy romantic comedy that will charm a few and probably miss the eye of many. Love match of Burt Reynolds and Lesley-Anne Down works only in selected spots and frame of the story, intrigue over a $30 million diamond heist, is hard-pressed to sustain interest.

Blake Edwards was originally scheduled to direct the picture for David Merrick in 1977 with Larry Gelbart scripting and Reynolds top-lining. Edwards eventually bowed out and Reynolds took on other films until Don Siegel was signed to helm in 1979. Siegel was fired and re-hired by Merrick and pic finally wound.

Trouble began when Merrick decided he wanted a new ending and Siegel insisted he had the final cut. Result was Merrick hiring Robert Ellis Miller to shoot a fourth finale.

Problem seems to lie in much of the dialog, which comes across as both wooden and contrived. Reynolds and Down do what they can but their attempts at witty banter never appear natural.

•

ROUGH NIGHT IN JERICHO

1967, 102 mins, US ⊏⊐ col

Dir Arnold Laven ***Prod*** Martin Rackin ***Scr*** Sydney Boehm, Marvin H. Albert ***Ph*** Russell Metty ***Ed*** Ted J. Kent ***Mus*** Don Costa ***Art*** Alexander Golitzen, Frank Arrigo

Act Dean Martin, George Peppard, Jean Simmons, John McIntire, Slim Pickens, Don Galloway (Universal)

Most unusual aspect about this production is offbeat casting of Dean Martin as a heavy without a single redeeming quality. George Peppard is the hero. Both are embroiled in a bloody and violent western.

Plotwise, *Rough Night in Jericho* frequently carries a nebulous story line, particularly in limning the actions of Martin, onetime lawman turned vicious town boss. Screenplay, an adaptation of Marvin H. Albert's novel *The Man in Black*, is lacking in the suspense one expects from a big league western but regulation action is there in good measure.

Peppard plays a former deputy U.S. marshal who becomes involved in the affairs of the town of Jericho—and Martin—when he arrives with John McIntire, onetime marshal whom he once served under. Latter has come to help Jean Simmons save her stage line, coveted by Martin, who also wants its femme owner.

•

ROUNDERS

1998, 120 mins, US Ⓥ ⦿ ⊏⊐ col

Dir John Dahl ***Prod*** Joel Stillerman, Ted Demme ***Scr*** David Levien, Brian Koppelman ***Ed*** Scott Chestnut ***Mus*** Christopher Young ***Art*** Rob Pearson

Act Matt Damon, Edward Norton, John Turturro, Gretchen Mol, Famke Janssen, John Malkovich (Spanky/Miramax)

Rounders wins a few hands but doesn't walk off with the whole pot. Intermittently engaging but dramatically slack, this tale of a law student's discovery of his true calling as a world-class poker player is more interesting around the edges than it is at its core, thanks to the dull nature of the lead character played by Matt Damon.

Knitted together by some often effective first-person narration, script kicks off with confident college boy Mike McDermott (Damon) losing his life savings by pushing his luck in a game against a crafty Russian hood and New York club owner, Teddy KGB (John Malkovich). Nine months later, Mike is dutifully hitting his law books, but g.f. Jo's (Gretchen Mol) antennae are raised by the release from prison of Worm (Edward Norton), Mike's wise-ass old friend whom she suspects will quickly lead her mate astray once again.

The dramatic ante is upped midway through when a debt-collecting thug named Grama (Michael Rispoli) puts the squeeze on Worm. When Grama tells them to fork over $15,000 in five days or else, the pair go on a sleepless binge of games that concludes with a showdown with Teddy KGB.

Supporting cast does a lot to bring matters to life, notably Malkovich, has a grand old time hamming it up as the thickly accented Russian card master, John Turturro as a normal guy who just happens to support his family by gambling, and Norton as the impulsive bad boy who can't help himself.

Unfortunately, the writers didn't give their leading character any emotional dimension or compelling characteristics. Mike tends to just let things happen to him, whether it's his girlfriend leaving him or Worm luring him back to the table or into a web of debt.

John Dahl applies a smooth directorial hand but pic lacks the bite and sense of insidiousness found in his earlier work, and the big card games don't convey the expected tension and excitement.

•

'ROUND MIDNIGHT

1986, 133 mins, France/US Ⓥ ⦿ ⊏⊐ col

Dir Bertrand Tavernier ***Prod*** Irwin Winkler ***Scr*** Bertrand Tavernier, David Rayfiel ***Ph*** Bruno de Keyzer ***Ed*** Armand Psenny ***Mus*** Herbie Hancock ***Art*** Alexandre Trauner

Act Dexter Gordon, Francois Cluzet, Gabrielle Haker, Sandra Reaves-Phillips, John Berry, Martin Scorsese (Little Bear/PECF/Warner)

'Round Midnight is a superbly crafted music world drama in which Gallic director Bertrand Tavernier pays a moving dramatic tribute to the great black musicians who lived and performed in Paris in the late 1950s. The $3 million film is dedicated to jazz giants Bud Powell and Lester Young, the composite inspiration for the story's central personage.

With his American co-scripter, David Rayfiel, Tavernier has placed deftly the themes of cultural roots, affinities and distances at the heart of the screenplay ["inspired by incidents in the lives of Francis Paudras and Bud Powell"], which dramatizes the friendship between an aging jazz saxophonist, who has accepted an engagement at the legendary Blue Note club in Saint-Germain-des-Pres, and a passionate young French admirer who is ready to make personal sacrifices to help his idol.

Tavernier cast a non-professional in the central role: Dexter Gordon, the 63-year-old jazz veteran whom Tavernier has long admired. With his hoarse, hesitant diction and his lanky shuffle, Gordon fills the part of the world-weary artist with his own jagged warmth.

Film is no less a treat for the eye as for the ear. Shot almost entirely in the Epinay studios north of Paris, production is vividly designed by veteran Alexandre Trauner.

1986: Best Original Score

NOMINATION: Best Actor (Dexter Gordon)

•

ROXANNE

1987, 107 mins, US Ⓥ ⦿ ⊏⊐ col

Dir Fred Schepisi ***Prod*** Michael Rachmil, Daniel Melnick ***Scr*** Steve Martin ***Ph*** Ian Baker ***Ed*** John Scott ***Mus*** Bruce Smeaton ***Art*** Jack DeGovia

Act Steve Martin, Daryl Hannah, Rick Rossovich, Shelley Duvall, Michael J. Pollard, Damon Wayans, Fred Willard, Michael J. Pollard (Columbia/Melnick/LA Films)

As a reworking of Edmond Rostand's play *Cyrano de Bergerac*, the only reason to see the film is for a few bits of inspired nonsense by Steve Martin as the nosey lover. Written by Martin to suit his special talent for sight gags, this Cyrano, called CB here, is just a wild and crazy guy with a big nose and a gift for gab.

The central plot device of the play, in which a true love writes letters to help another suitor with the same woman he doesn't love as much, is here adapted to a small ski community in Washington State where Martin is fire chief.

The film is barely underway when Roxanne (Daryl Hannah) is out of her clothes and locked out of her house. When CB comes to the rescue it's love at first sight, but his enlarged proboscis disqualifies him as a serious suitor, or so he thinks.

Instead, Roxanne turns her attentions to Chris (Rick Rossovich), a new recruit on the fire department who is all but rendered dumb in front of women. Eventually, Roxanne learns Rossovich is only after her body and realizes Martin loves her truly.

Aussie director Fred Schepisi, who has elsewhere handled much rougher material, does a professional job of creating a breezy atmosphere, but in the end it's hopelessly sappy stuff.

•

ROXIE HART

1942, 72 mins, US b/w

Dir William A. Wellman ***Prod*** Nunnally Johnson ***Scr*** Nunnally Johnson ***Ph*** Leon Shamroy ***Ed*** James B. Clark ***Mus*** Alfred Newman

Act Ginger Rogers, Adolphe Menjou, George Montgomery, Lynne Overman, Nigel Bruce, Phil Silvers (20th Century-Fox)

Maurine Watkins's play [*Chicago*] of a girl who basks in the publicity spotlight for a brief period when accused of murder is broadly embellished via the screenplay by Nunnally Johnson and direction by William Wellman.

Picture aims solely for adult attention. Ginger Rogers is the girl who stands trial for murder committed by her husband, after getting buildup on publicity values by cynical crime reporter Lynne Overman. Banner-lined all over town, Roxie becomes an enthusiastic stooge for the press, court and slick mouthpiece (Adolphe Menjou).

Ginger Rogers does well as the tough girl who is dazzled by the sudden attention, but seems to overdo her characterization at several points. Menjou is excellent as the theatric and wily criminal mouthpiece who craftily steers the judge and jury to the proper verdict.

•

ROYAL FLASH

1975, 121 mins, UK Ⓥ col

Dir Richard Lester ***Prod*** David B. Picker, Denis O'Dell ***Scr*** George McDonald Fraser ***Ph*** Geoffrey Unsworth ***Ed*** John Victor Smith ***Mus*** Ken Thorne ***Art*** Terence Marsh

Act Malcolm McDowell, Alan Bates, Florinda Bolkan, Oliver Reed, Britt Ekland, Lionel Jeffries (20th Century-Fox)

Royal Flash is a royal pain. Richard Lester's formula period comedy style [adapted by George MacDonald Fraser from his novel], as enduring as it is not particularly endearing, achieves its customary levels of posturing silliness.

Malcolm McDowell, fleeing a bordello raid, falls in with Florinda Bolkan, playing Lola Montez, in turn alienating Oliver Reed's Otto von Bismarck. The latter, with accomplice Alan Bates and hit men Lionel Jeffries and Tom Bell, force McDowell to impersonate a Prussian nobleman for purposes of marriage to duchess Britt Ekland. Complex political, sexual and survival strategies lurch the plot forward.

The players are as competent as the film allows, and their work in other films is proof of their talent.

•

ROYAL HUNT OF THE SUN, THE

1969, 121 mins, UK ⦿ ⊏⊐ col

Dir Irving Lerner ***Prod*** Eugene Frenke, Philip Yordan ***Scr*** Philip Yordan ***Ph*** Roger Barlow ***Ed*** Peter Parasheles ***Mus*** Marc Wilkinson ***Art*** Eugene Lourie

Act Robert Shaw, Christopher Plummer, Nigel Davenport, Michael Craig, Leonard Whiting, Andrew Keir (Rank)

Based on Peter Shaffer's rich, imaginative play, *Royal Hunt of the Sun* is a film that's striking in many ways, visually and literately.

It has many plusses, notably a standout duo of performances by Robert Shaw and Christopher Plummer and some very sound supporting and an intelligent top-drawer script by Philip Yordan.

Story concerns General Francisco Pizarro, Spanish soldier of fortune who for the third time penetrates Peru, the Land of the Sun, in search of the Kingdom of Gold. He leads a small, ill-equipped band with which to tackle the forces of the Inca.

Shaw powerfully portrays the conquistador and his varying and complicated moods of violence, sadness, despair, anger and puzzlement. Plummer is particularly outstanding in the tricky role of King Atahuallpa, though not always entirely audible due to the curious accent he affects.

•

ROYAL SCANDAL, A

1945, 94 mins, US b/w

Dir Otto Preminger ***Prod*** Ernst Lubitsch ***Scr*** Edwin Justus Mayer, Bruno Frank ***Ph*** Arthur Miller ***Ed*** Dorothy Spencer ***Mus*** Alfred Newman ***Art*** Lyle R. Wheeler, Mark-Lee Kirk

Act Tallulah Bankhead, Charles Coburn, Anne Baxter, William Eythe, Vincent Price, Mischa Auer (20th Century-Fox)

A Royal Scandal is a highly hilarious comedy with superb performances by Tallulah Bankhead and Charles Coburn, in particular, and the wit of the original play by Lajos Biro and Melchior Lengyel.

This version of Catherine the Great's saga turns out to be a farce of real proportions, although never eclipsing the Czarina as an extremely vigorous personality, surrounded by palace intrigue and a parade of lovers. Ernst Lubitsch and director Otto Preminger have neatly interwoven the court intrigue with her w.k. amorous proclivities. The stream of captains of the palace guards is pointed up somewhat briskly.

Yarn concentrates on impetuous William Eythe, who has ridden three days and nights to warn the Czarina about two plotting generals. Because he admittedly is not tired after his strenuous ride, Catherine ignores his impetuosity and slight dumbness to have him await a nocturnal interview. That this interview is successful is borne out by subsequent events.

•

ROYAL WEDDING
(UK: WEDDING BELLS)

1951, 93 mins, US Ⓥ ⦿ col

Dir Stanley Donen ***Prod*** Arthur Freed ***Scr*** Alan Jay Lerner ***Ph*** Robert Planck ***Ed*** Albert Akst ***Mus*** Johnny Green (dir.)

Act Fred Astaire, Jane Powell, Peter Lawford, Sarah Churchill, Keenan Wynn, Albert Sharpe (M-G-M)

This is an engaging concoction of songs and dances in a standard musical framework, brightly dressed in color to show off its physical attributes.

Score uses up nine tunes to back the singing and terping, and two of the numbers are sock enough to almost carry the picture by themselves. They are Astaire's solo dance on a ceiling, upside down, and the teaming with Powell in a sort of Frankie-and-Johnny-apache-hepcat presentation that will click with audiences.

The ceiling stepping to the Burton Lane–Alan Jay Lerner "You're All the World to Me" combines technical magic and Astaire's foot wizardry into a potent novelty. "How Could You Believe Me" sets up the earthy Astaire-Powell delivery of the other outstanding musical sequence.

Light plot sees Astaire and Powell as a brother-sister team of Broadway musical stars. They go to London to open their show during the period when preparations are being made for the royal marriage. In between presentation of the musical numbers, Astaire falls in love with Sarah Churchill, show hoofer, and Powell catches the love bug from Peter Lawford, an English lord-romeo.

1951: NOMINATION: Best Song ("Too Late Now")

•

R.P.M.
REVOLUTIONS PER MINUTE
1970, 92 mins, US Ⓥ col
Dir Stanley Kramer ***Prod*** Stanley Kramer ***Scr*** Erich Segal ***Ph*** Michel Hugo ***Ed*** William A. Lyon ***Mus*** Barry DeVorzon, Perry Botkin, Jr. ***Art*** Robert Clatworthy
Act Anthony Quinn, Ann-Margret, Gary Lockwood, Paul Winfield, Graham Jarvis, Alan Hewitt (Columbia)

Subtitled "Revolutions Per Minute," this campus crisis meller slowly spins its improbable wheels to the climactic production number involving a student riot.

Anthony Quinn stars as a harassed college president, Ann-Margret is his plot-irrelevant young mistress, and Gary Lockwood is a student radical. The treatment is déjà vu, Eric Segal's script is replete with glib one-liners but lacking real story fibre, and Kramer's direction is dull.

Quinn is introduced as a 53-year-old professor, risen to his post from Spanish Harlem and popular with his students. At the outset, the current college head has thrown in the towel as students have occupied the Administration Building, housing a big computer.

Lockwood and Paul Winfield are the radical student leaders.

•

RUBY
1977, 84 mins, US Ⓥ col
Dir Curtis Harrington ***Prod*** George Edwards ***Scr*** George Edwards, Barry Schneider ***Ph*** William Mendenhall ***Ed*** Bill Magee ***Mus*** Don Ellis ***Art*** Tom Rasmussen
Act Piper Laurie, Stuart Whitman, Roger Davis, Janit Baldwin, Crystin Sinclaire, Paul Kent (Dimension/Krantz)

In the cookbook school of filmmaking *Ruby* is strictly leftovers. Begin with a hunk of the occult. Add a cup of 1950s nostalgia, some hard-boiled detective, a dash of camp from old horror movies and sprinkle with violence.

Most of the pic's action takes place around Ruby's Drive-In. Piper Laurie is the onetime gun moll and wife of a big-time mobster. She now owns a drive-in staffed by "associates" of her dead husband. He was gunned down 16 years ago when someone finked on him, but his spirit is back to haunt the drive-in.

He gets the job done: a projectionist is strangled with film; a concession stand attendant stuffed into a soda machine; and the dead mobster's daughter afflicted with a case of the shaking bed.

Performances are generally poor.

•

RUBY
1992, 110 mins, US Ⓥ ⊙ col
Dir John Mackenzie ***Prod*** Sigurjon Sighvatsson, Steve Golin ***Scr*** Stephen Davis ***Ph*** Phil Meheux ***Ed*** Richard Trevor ***Mus*** John Scott ***Art*** David Brisbin
Act Danny Aiello, Sherilyn Fenn, Arliss Howard, Tobin Bell, David Duchovny, Richard C. Sarafian (PolyGram/Propaganda)

Danny Aiello and Sherilyn Fenn's earnest, first-rate performances can't overcome strewed story elements of this otherwise well-put-together drama [from Stephen Davis' play *Love Field*]. Highly fictionalized bio of the club owner and small-time hood who killed Lee Harvey Oswald points a finger at organized crime and rogue elements within the CIA as the parties responsible for bringing Camelot to a crashing end.

The fiction stems in large part from Ruby's relationship with a stripper (Fenn) who, it's revealed at the end, is a composite of various characters. Ruby starts to be drawn in when he's sent to Cuba to kill an imprisoned Mafia don (Marc Lawrence) but instead turns on the con who sent him, in the process being drawn back into big-league mob activities.

The problem with *Ruby* is that it plays too much like TV docudrama and, to paraphrase Winston Churchill, ends up a mystery wrapped in a riddle. Aiello is terrific as Ruby, a tough outsider who never quite was. Fenn turns in a performance hotter than a cup of *Twin Peaks* java as the power-seeking stripper, looking Monroe-like with her platinum blond locks and classic features.

•

RUBY CAIRO
(Aka: Deception)
1993, 110 mins, US/Japan Ⓥ ⊙ col
Dir Graeme Clifford ***Prod*** Lloyd Phillips, Haruki Kadokawa ***Scr*** Robert Dillon, Michael Thomas ***Ph*** Laszlo Kovacs ***Ed*** Caroline Biggerstaff, Paul Rubell ***Mus*** John Barry, Robert Randles ***Art*** Richard Sylbert
Act Andie MacDowell, Liam Neeson, Viggo Mortensen, Jack Thompson, Jeff Corey, Miriam Reed (Kadokawa)

Ruby Cairo is an old-fashioned Yank-in-Europe mystery-adventure [from a screen story by Robert Dillon] that squanders an interesting cast headed by Andie MacDowell and Liam Neeson. Too bad everyone forgot to pack a script along with their passports and sunscreen.

MacDowell plays the wife of Viggo Mortensen, who runs an aircraft salvage company directly under a flight path to LAX. One day, while he's off in Mexico, she receives a packet with some teeth inside, and hotfoots it to Veracruz to inspect the remains of his plane and supposed body.

Realizing he's still alive and done a runner, she sets off tracking him down. The trail leads from Panama and the Bahamas to Berlin, Athens and Cairo, where with the help of food aid worker Liam Neeson she uncovers a scam smuggling a chemical for making poison gas inside grain shipments. This could have played either as a romantic comedy-thriller or as a long-limbed drama of betrayed love. Under Graeme Clifford's unfocused direction, it keeps promising both but ends up neither. Where the reported $24 million budget went is anyone's guess.

•

RUBY GENTRY
1952, 82 mins, US Ⓥ b/w
Dir King Vidor ***Prod*** Joseph Bernhard ***Scr*** Silvia Richards ***Ph*** Russell Harlan ***Ed*** Terry Morse ***Mus*** Heinz Roemheld
Act Jennifer Jones, Charlton Heston, Karl Malden, Tom Tully, James Anderson, Josephine Hutchinson (Bernhard-Vidor/20th Century-Fox)

This is a bold, adult drama laying heavy stress on sex, a story of fleshy passions in the tidewater country of North Carolina.

Vidor belts over the blatantly sensual Arthur Fitz-Richard story. It's a sordid type of drama, with neither Jennifer Jones nor Charlton Heston gaining any sympathy in their characters.

Story starts with the animal attraction between Jones, from the wrong side of the tracks, and Heston, purse-poor southern gent who willingly trifles in the swamp but for marriage chooses Phyllis Avery's wealthy, properly bred girl, so he can rebuild his family fortunes.

With a legal mating with Heston impossible, Jones turns to the friendship of Malden and his bedridden wife (Josephine Hutchinson). After the latter dies, she accepts Malden's proposal and they are married. Society refuses to accept his bride.

Jones goes through much of the footage in skintight Levis, of which she and careful camera angles and lighting make the most.

•

RUBY IN PARADISE
1993, 115 mins, US Ⓥ col
Dir Victor Nunez ***Prod*** Sam Gowan, Peter Wentworth (exec.) ***Scr*** Victor Nunez ***Ph*** Alex Vlacos ***Ed*** Victor Nunez ***Mus*** Charles Engstrom ***Art*** John Iacovelli
Act Ashley Judd, Todd Field, Bentley Mitchum, Allison Dean, Dorothy Lyman, Betsy Dowds (Full Crew/Say Yeah)

A wonderfully expressive character study exhibiting a thoughtfulness and concern for real life rare in American cinema, *Ruby in Paradise* rewards the care put into it and the patience it asks of audiences. After an eight-year layoff from filmmaking after *A Flash of Green*, Victor Nunez has returned with a film of gentle, intelligent qualities, vividly portraying a young woman's inner life. He is incalculably aided by the extraordinary central performance of Ashley Judd. Attractive, poised and possessed of a gravity that is immensely appealing, this new actress (the younger daughter of country singer Naomi Judd) manages to rivet one's attention even when she is doing nothing.

Beginning by showing her escape from small-town Tennessee, tale lands Ruby in Panama Beach City, a tourist town on Florida's "redneck Riviera." Ruby finds a job in a local souvenir shop owned by a businesslike woman whose good-looking but shallow son Ricky (Bentley Mitchum) ranks himself the local roue.

Ruby sleeps with him, but later develops a more meaningful romance with Mike (Todd Field), a smart biker who works in the local tree nursery. The two seem good together, but Ruby holds back.

There is always the possibility of condescension when sophisticated filmmakers take on working-class characters, but *Ruby* hits very close to the mark in evoking everyday life.

•

RUDYARD KIPLING'S THE JUNGLE BOOK
SEE: THE JUNGLE BOOK

•

RUGGLES OF RED GAP
1923, 89 mins, US ⊗ b/w
Dir James Cruze ***Scr*** Walter Woods, Anthony Coldeway ***Ph*** Karl Brown
Act Edward Everett Horton, Ernest Torrence, Lois Wilson, Fritzi Ridgeway, Charles Ogle, Louise Dresser (Paramount)

Here is a great comedy novel [by Harry Leon Wilson] made into a delightful feature picture. The adaptation is literal in that it reproduces the effect of the original story with no forced interpolations and a full use of the material. The acting is a triumph of teamwork.

Ernest Torrance's Cousin Egbert is a gem, a bit of comic characterization that hasn't a suspicion of clowning. Edward Horton's Ruggles is a fitting companion piece. This most British of British valets is almost as good fun in the film as in the book.

One of the things that go to make the whole picture delightful is the absence of hokum. Ruggles is as far from the familiar comic picture of the English valet as could be. He is just an embarrassed automaton hedged about by his own class consciousness and prejudices and stunned by the strange people he is thrown among. He is actually a likeable human being.

Lois Wilson plays "the Kenner woman" with her invariable charm while Louise Dresser is abundantly convincing as the formidable Mrs. Ellie, wife and general manager of Cousin Egbert.

•

RUGGLES OF RED GAP
1935, 90 mins, US Ⓥ b/w
Dir Leo McCarey ***Prod*** Arthur Hornblow, Jr. ***Scr*** Walter De Leon, Harlan Thompson, Humphrey Pearson ***Ph*** Alfred Gilks ***Ed*** Edward Dmytryk ***Mus*** Ralph Rainger ***Art*** Hans Dreier, Robert Odell
Act Charles Laughton, Mary Boland, Charles Ruggles, ZaSu Pitts, Roland Young, Leila Hyams (Paramount)

Leo McCarey has turned out a fast and furiously funny film which is a perfect example of what smart handling behind the camera can do. Original novel [by Harry Leon Wilson] has been made as a film twice before, once by Essanay (1918) and by Paramount (1923). But this time the yarn is handled from a completely fresh standpoint—with gratifying results.

Story is a bit dated. It plants Elmer (Charlie Ruggles) and his wife (Mary Boland) in Paris. They play poker with the Earl of Burnstead (Roland Young) and win his butler, Ruggles (Charles Laughton). They take him back to Red Gap, state of Washington. There Ruggles is mistaken for a British army captain and becomes a celebrity. That gives him the idea of freedom and standing on his own. He falls in love with Mrs. Judson (ZaSu Pitts) and opens a restaurant.

Laughton turns in a performance that will surprise some and widen his appeal by far. He's played comedy before (*Henry VIII*), but here he is doing it differently. It's not satire; it's not a pathological character study. Just plain comedy.

1935: NOMINATION: Best Picture

•

RULES OF ENGAGEMENT
2000, 128 mins, US Ⓥ ⊙ ▭ col
Dir William Friedkin ***Prod*** Richard D. Zanuck, Scott Rudin ***Scr*** Stephen Gaghan ***Ph*** Nicola Pecorini, William Fraker ***Ed*** Augie Hess ***Mus*** Mark Isham ***Art*** Robert Laing
Act Tommy Lee Jones, Samuel L. Jackson, Guy Pearce, Bruce Greenwood, Blair Underwood, Philip Baker Hall (Paramount)

Rules of Engagement is a nuts-and-bolts, ramrod-straight military thriller that uses a distinctly unsavory case to defend the honor of the U.S. Marines' way of life. The specifics of the situation, from a story by former Marine infantry commander and Secretary of the Navy James Webb, may be distinct from other screen military mellers but the dynamics—the honor of the military view vs. the incomprehension and hostility of civilians—are pretty familiar.

With angry crowds besieging the American embassy in Yemen, Col. Terry Childers (Samuel L. Jackson) commands three Marine choppers, which are sent to rescue the cowering ambassador (Ben Kingsley), his wife (Anne Archer) and son. Childers only barely manages to spirit out the government representative in the nick of time. But the fighting continues, Marines start to be killed, and Childers finally gives the order to start firing into the crazed crowd.

The result is an international scandal: Eighty-three Arabs are dead, including many women and children, with scores more wounded. The transparently evil National Security Adviser, William Sokal (Bruce Greenwood), demands that the blame for the slaughter be placed squarely on Col. Childers for giving illegal orders, so as to take responsibility off the United States in general. Rightly sensing he's being hung out to dry, Childers asks his old buddy Col. Hays Hodges (Tommy Lee Jones) to represent him at the court-martial. Final 45 minutes are devoted to the trial, in which callow bulldog prosecutor Maj. Mark Biggs (Guy Pearce) relentlessly attacks Childers's alleged recklessness and makes him look pretty bad.

Rules of Engagement gives fresh meaning to the term "narrative cinema," since there is essentially nothing else here. Hodges is divorced with a grown son and once had "a drinking problem," but that's all the information about him provided by either the script or Jones's recessive performance. Jackson has even less to work with, since Childers is defined only as Pure Marine—no family, no psychology, no nothing.

Picture's outlook on the events it depicts is strictly legalistic, never broadening to assume anything resembling a political, moral or philosophical position. All performances are as narrowly defined as the storytelling approach.

•

RULES OF THE GAME, THE
SEE: LA REGLE DU JEU

•

RULING CLASS, THE
1972, 154 mins, UK Ⓥ ⦿ col
Dir Peter Medak ***Prod*** Jules Buck, Jack Hawkins ***Scr*** Peter Barnes ***Ph*** Ken Hodges ***Ed*** Ray Lovejoy ***Mus*** John Cameron ***Art*** Peter Murton
Act Peter O'Toole, Alastair Sim, Arthur Lowe, Harry Andrews, Coral Browne, Michael Bryant (Keep/Avco Embassy)

Peter Medak's *Ruling Class*, based on Peter Barnes's play of same name and scripted by the author, is a biting indictment of the so-called upper strata (British and/or other) of the old school tie thing. Barnes's amusing but hard-hitting script doesn't tell as well as it plays in recounting the rise to the House of Lords of the allegedly insane 14th Earl of Gurney, who very topically believes he's J.C. and whose unamused family wants him back in the nuthouse—once he's fathered the child through which they hope to get their greedy hands back on the estate the Earl has unexpectedly inherited.

Symbols are up for grabs, of course, but pic avoids usual message film pitfalls in coming across almost throughout with amusing tongue-in-cheek finesse alternating with hilarious stretches.

1972: NOMINATION: Best Actor (Peter O'Toole)

•

RUMBLE FISH
1983, 94 mins, US Ⓥ b/w
Dir Francis Coppola ***Prod*** Fred Roos, Doug Claybourne ***Scr*** S. E. Hinton, Francis Coppola ***Ph*** Stephen H. Burum ***Ed*** Barry Malkin ***Mus*** Stewart Copeland ***Art*** Dean Tavoularis
Act Matt Dillon, Mickey Rourke, Diane Lane, Dennis Hopper, Diana Scarwid, Vincent Spano (Zoetrope)

Rumble Fish is another Francis Coppola picture that's overwrought and overthought with camera and characters that never quite come together in anything beyond consistently interesting. Beautifully photographed in black and white by Stephen H. Burum, the picture [from the novel by S. E. Hinton] really doesn't need all the excessive symbolism Coppola tries to cram into it.

For those who want it, however, *Fish* is another able examination of teenage alienation, centered around two brothers who are misfits in the ill-defined urban society they inhabit.

One, Matt Dillon, is a young tough inspired to no-good purposes by an older brother, Mickey Rourke, once the toughest but now a bit of an addled eccentric, though remaining a hero to neighborhood thugs.

Dillon and Rourke turn in good performances, as does Dennis Hopper as their drunken father and Diane Lane as Dillon's dumped-on girlfriend. Title and a lot of the symbolism stem from Siamese fighting fish (photographed in color composite shots) which are unable to coexist with their fellows, or even an image of themselves.

•

RUMBLE IN THE BRONX
SEE: HUNG FAN KUI

•

RUNAWAY
1984, 100 mins, US Ⓥ ⦿ ▭ col
Dir Michael Crichton ***Prod*** Michael Rachmil ***Scr*** Michael Crichton ***Ph*** John A. Alonzo ***Ed*** Glenn Farr ***Mus*** Jerry Goldsmith ***Art*** Douglas Higgins
Act Tom Selleck, Cynthia Rhodes, Gene Simmons, Kirstie Alley, Stan Shaw, Joey Cramer (Tri-Star/Delphi III)

Tom Selleck, with a cop's short haircut and playing a workaday stiff who's afraid of heights, cuts a less dashing but more accessible figure in *Runaway* than in prior pictures. However, this Michael Crichton robotic nightmare is so trite that the story seems lifted from Marvel Comics, with heat-seeking bullets and a villain so bad he would be fun if the film wasn't telling us to take this near-futuristic adventure with a straight face.

Selleck's femme police partner Cynthia Rhodes, is an overachiever and formula romantic foil to Selleck, who's a single parent raising a son. Departure may be fresh for Selleck but the comparative lack of his trademarked sardonic humor does cost the pic.

•

RUNAWAY BRIDE
1999, 116 mins, US Ⓥ ⦿ ▭ col
Dir Garry Marshall ***Prod*** Ted Field, Tom Rosenberg, Scott Kroopf, Robert Cort ***Scr*** Josann McGibbon, Sara Parriott ***Ph*** Stuart Dryburgh ***Ed*** Bruce Green ***Mus*** James Newton Howard ***Art*** Mark Friedberg
Act Julia Roberts, Richard Gere, Joan Cusack, Hector Elizondo, Rita Wilson, Paul Dooley (Interscope/Paramount/Touchstone)

Having waited nine years before following up their 1990 smash *Pretty Woman*, Julia Roberts, Richard Gere and director Garry Marshall score again with *Runaway Bride*, an ultra-commercial mainstream romantic comedy that delivers all the laughs and smiles it intends to.

Even though the film has all the earmarks of a highly tailored package—2 studios, 10 producers, roles molded specifically for major stars—the central idea is quite clever and appealing, and the charm meter is turned up all the way.

Journalist Ike Graham (Gere) heads for Hale, MD, to get the full story about a Maryland woman with the chronic habit of leaving fiancés at the altar. Approaching her fourth attempted wedding, to high-school sports coach Bob (Christopher Meloni), Maggie Carpenter (Roberts) is none too happy to have Ike cozying up to her father (Paul Dooley).

Ike gets around, interviewing everyone about Maggie, especially her first two jilted beaux. Ike also points out to Maggie's best friend, Peggy (Joan Cusack), that Maggie is being quite flirtatious with Peggy's husband. At pic's halfway point, Maggie agrees to cooperate with the writer, which leads to prolonged proximity, which in turn leads to the unavoidable recognition of mutual attraction.

Roberts has a perfect role in Maggie, an open, lovable, slightly neurotic but capable girl-next-door. She can be goofy, sporty or amorous with ease. Perhaps realizing that she's prettier than he is, Gere drops the preening, posing, self-satisfied air he affects when he's the biggest star in a picture. Technically, pic looks immaculate on the widescreen.

•

RUNAWAY DAUGHTER
SEE: RED SALUTE

•

RUNAWAY TRAIN
1985, 111 mins, US Ⓥ ⦿ col
Dir Andrei Konchalovsky ***Prod*** Menahem Golan, Yoram Globus ***Scr*** Djordje Milicevic, Paul Zindel, Edward Bunker ***Ph*** Alan Hume ***Ed*** Henry Richardson ***Mus*** Trevor Jones ***Art*** Stephen Marsh
Act Jon Voight, Eric Roberts, Rebecca DeMornay, Kyle T. Heffner, John P. Ryan, T. K. Carter (Cannon/Northbrook)

Runaway Train is a sensational picture. Wrenchingly intense and brutally powerful, Andrei Konchalovsky's film rates as a most exciting action epic and is fundamentally serious enough to work strongly on numerous levels.

An exercise in relentless, severe tension, tale begins with a prison drama, then never lets up as it follows two escaped cons as they become inadvertent passengers on some diesel units that run out of control through the Alaskan wilderness.

The two desperate men, who find themselves joined by a young lady, are tracked throughout their headlong journey by railroad officials bent on avoiding a crash.

Jon Voight brilliantly portrays a two-time loser determined never to return to prison after his third breakout.

Pic is based upon [an unfilmed] screenplay by Akira Kurosawa, and bears imprint of the renowned Japanese director.

Younger con Eric Roberts impressively manages to hold his own under the demanding circumstances, and Rebecca DeMornay works herself well into the essentially all-male surroundings.

1985: NOMINATIONS: Best Actor (Jon Voight), Supp. Actor (Eric Roberts), Editing

•

RUN FOR THE SUN
1956, 98 mins, US ▭ col
Dir Roy Boulting ***Prod*** Harry Tatelman ***Scr*** Dudley Nichols, Roy Boulting ***Ph*** Joseph LaShelle ***Ed*** Fred Knudtsen ***Mus*** Fred Steiner
Act Richard Widmark, Trevor Howard, Jane Greer, Peter Van Eyck, Carlos Henning, Juan Garcia (Russ-Field)

Film is a chase feature in practically all phases. Jane Greer, news mag staffer, comes to Mexico to find Richard Widmark, writer-adventurer, to find why he's given up writing. She falls for her news quarry and then the plane in which she is flying with him crashes in the jungle. The couple is rescued by Trevor Howard and Peter Van Eyck, a mysterious pair. When Widmark discovers their true identities as war criminals hiding out from trial and punishment, it becomes a murderous game through the jungle.

The four principals enact their roles exceptionally well. Pic is based on Richard Connell's story *The Most Dangerous Game* [filmed in 1932], but there is virtually no resemblance to that old thriller in the final results.

•

RUNNERS
1983, 110 mins, UK Ⓥ col
Dir Charles Sturridge ***Prod*** Barry Hanson ***Scr*** Stephen Poliakoff ***Ph*** Howard Atherton ***Ed*** Peter Coulson ***Mus*** George Fenton ***Art*** Arnold Chapkis
Act James Fox, Jane Asher, Kate Hardie, Robert Lang, Eileen O'Brien, Ruti Simon (Hanstoll/Goldcrest)

There are a lot of interesting ideas in *Runners*, but they're never really shaped into a coherent film. It's evident that directing *Brideshead Revisited*, the rambling TV series with which helmer Charles Sturridge secured international acclaim, was not the best education in cinematic structure.

The meandering plot follows a father, played by James Fox, who searches for his daughter long after everyone else, including his wife, have given up. Tracking her down to a car hire firm, rather than some perverse religious sect as he had expected, he is horrified at her reluctance to return.

Along the way, the father strikes up with a woman from a different social class who is hunting for her son. There are some interesting nuances in this relationship, but eventually it is the trival details of the hunt that dominate the screen.

One is two thirds of the way through the film before the question is even raised of why this girl fled. Fox and Jane Asher give as much to the roles as they can.

•

RUNNER STUMBLES, THE
1979, 99 mins, US Ⓥ col
Dir Stanley Kramer ***Prod*** Stanley Kramer ***Scr*** Milan Stitt ***Ph*** Laszlo Kovacs ***Ed*** Pembroke J. Herring ***Mus*** Ernest Gold ***Art*** Al Sweeney, Jr.
Act Dick Van Dyke, Kathleen Quinlan, Maureen Stapleton, Ray Bolger, Tammy Grimes, Beau Bridges (Stanley Kramer)

Based on an actual murder case in 1927 where a priest was accused of killing a nun he was in love with, subject matter is celibacy in the Catholic church, and presented in such a way that, at times, it appears like the best of the old-fashioned 1940s tearjerkers complete with overly lush sound track.

Yet *Runner* ultimately emerges as more than melodrama because director Stanley Kramer puts equal emphasis on the priest (Dick Van Dyke) and how he grapples with his love for God and this woman (Kathleen Quinlan) in his life.

Throughout, the film is paced by fine performances, especially Van Dyke as Father Rivard, Quinlan as Sister Rita and Maureen Stapleton as Van Dyke's housekeeper.

•

RUNNING MAN, THE
1963, 103 mins, UK ▭ col
Dir Carol Reed ***Prod*** Carol Reed ***Scr*** John Mortimer ***Ph*** Robert Krasker ***Ed*** Bert Bates ***Mus*** William Alwyn
Act Laurence Harvey, Lee Remick, Alan Bates, Felix Aylmer, Eleanor Summerfield (Columbia)

The story of the man who poses as dead in order that his "widow" can pick up the insurance money is not exactly new. But director Carol Reed makes it holding entertainment.

Based on Shelley Smith's novel *Ballad of a Running Man*, John Mortimer has written a smart script, with the three principal characters well delineated. Interiors were shot at Ardmore Studios, Ireland, but main locations were lensed in Spain.

Film opens with a memorial service for Laurence Harvey, believed drowned following a glider accident. Solemnly his wife (Lee Remick) accepts the sympathy of friends. But soon Harvey turns up, larger than life, and sets in motion their plan to collect $140,000.

The claim goes through and the wife joins Harvey in Spain where she finds that he has assumed the identity of an Australian millionaire and is already plotting to pull off another insurance swindle.

Harvey has a role that suits him admirably, allowing him to run the gamut of many moods. Remick is also admirable as the young, pretty wife. Hers is a difficult part suggesting acute tension as she wavers between Harvey and Alan Bates, who has fallen for her and to whom she gives in one afternoon.

Bates, in the less flashy role of an insurance agent, ostensibly playing detective, is first class. He plays on a quiet, yet strong, note and is a most effective contrast to the flamboyance of Harvey.

•

RUNNING MAN, THE
1987, 101 mins, US Ⓥ ◉ col
Dir Paul Michael Glaser ***Prod*** Tim Zinnemann, George Linder ***Scr*** Stephen E. de Souza ***Ph*** Tom Del Ruth ***Ed*** Mark Roy Warner, Edward A. Warschilka, John Wright ***Mus*** Harold Faltermeyer ***Art*** Jack T. Collis
Act Arnold Schwarzenegger, Maria Conchita Alonso, Richard Dawson, Yaphet Kotto, Jim Brown, Jesse Ventura (Tri-Star/Taft/Barish/HBO

Pic, based on a novel by Richard Bachman (Stephen King), opens in 2017 when the world, following a financial collapse, is run by a police state, with TV a heavily censored propaganda tool of the government. Arnold Schwarzenegger is Ben Richards, a helicopter pilot who disobeys orders to fire on unarmed people during an L.A. food riot. He's slapped in prison and escapes 18 months later with pals Yaphet Kotto and Marvin J. McIntyre.

Producer-host of the popular TV game show *The Running Man*, Damon Killian (Richard Dawson) orders Richards up as his next contestant and he is duly captured and made a runner in this lethal (and fixed) gladiatorial contest for the masses.

Format works only on a pure action level, with some exciting, but overly repetitious, roller-coaster style sequences of runners hurtling into the game through tunnels on futuristic sleds. Bloated budget was $27 million.

Schwarzenegger sadistically dispatches the baddies, enunciating typical wisecrack remarks (many repeated from his previous films), but it's all too easy, despite the casting of such powerful presences as Jim Brown and former wrestlers Jesse Ventura and Prof. Toru Tanaka.

•

RUNNING ON EMPTY
1988, 116 mins, US Ⓥ ◉ col
Dir Sidney Lumet ***Prod*** Amy Robinson, Griffin Dunne ***Scr*** Naomi Foner ***Ph*** Gerry Fisher ***Ed*** Andrew Mondshein ***Mus*** Tony Mottola ***Art*** Philip Rosenberg
Act Christine Lahti, River Phoenix, Judd Hirsch, Martha Plimpton, Jonas Arby, L. M. Kit Carson (Lorimar/Double Play)

The continuing shock waves emitted by the cataclysmic events of the 1960s are dramatized in fresh and powerful ways in *Running On Empty*, a complex, turbulent tale told with admirable simplicity. Film successfully operates on several levels—as study of the primacy of the family unit, an anguished teen romance, a coming-of-age story and a look at what happened to some political radicals a generation later.

The two central adult characters are Weathermen-like urban bombers who have been living underground since 1971.

Arthur and Annie Pope (Judd Hirsch and Christine Lahti) have been on the FBI's most-wanted list since bombing a university defense research installation, an act that blinded a janitor. Their life since then has required them to be as unobtrusively middle-class as possible, and to be able to pick up and leave for a new destination on a moment's notice. Son Danny (River Phoenix), now 17, is quickly recognized by the local music teacher as an exceptionally promising pianist, and is nudged along toward an eventual audition for Juilliard. At the same time, Danny slowly commences an edgy but potent first love with the teacher's daughter Lorna (Martha Plimpton).

Superior screenplay keeps the focus intimate, forcing the head of the family to face the prospect of the family's breakup so that his son can pursue his own talents and interests.

1988: NOMINATIONS: Best Supp. Actor (River Phoenix), Original Screenplay

•

RUNNING SCARED
1986, 106 mins, US Ⓥ ◉ ▭ col
Dir Peter Hyams ***Prod*** David Foster, Lawrence Turman ***Scr*** Gary DeVore, Jimmy Huston ***Ph*** Peter Hyams ***Ed*** James Mitchell ***Mus*** Rod Temperton ***Art*** Albert Brenner
Act Gregory Hines, Billy Crystal, Steven Bauer, Darlanne Fleugel, Joe Pantoliano, Jimmy Smits (M-G-M/Turman-Foster)

Set in dead of winter in Chicago, *Running Scared* is an ultra-hip cop picture, shot in gritty style by Peter Hyams, that plays like a combination of *Beverly Hills Cop* and *Hill Street Blues*.

Gregory Hines and Billy Crystal are undercover cops too cool for words, guys who risk their necks by the hour without a hint of fear, chase women together at night and feel smugly superior to their cohorts in the force. Hines and Crystal are concerned particularly with aborting the career of aspiring Spanish godfather Jimmy Smits, a ruthless thug whose favorite film undoubtedly would be *Scarface*.

Plot [by Gary DeVore] is no more original or eventful than an average police TV show, so it must sink or swim on the moment-by-moment cleverness of the dialog and the behavioral talents of Hines and Crystal. Fortunately, these elements prove formidable. Nonstop banter between the two stars is rowdy, intimate, natural and often very funny. Hyams keeps most of it fresh, including the action ending, staged within one of Chicago's architectural spectacles, the cavernous, glass-enclosed Illinois State Building.

•

RUN OF THE ARROW
1957, 86 mins, US Ⓥ ▭ col
Dir Samuel Fuller ***Prod*** Samuel Fuller ***Scr*** Samuel Fuller ***Ph*** Joseph Biroc ***Ed*** Gene Fowler, Jr. ***Mus*** Victor Young ***Art*** Albert S. D'Agostino, Jack Okey
Act Rod Steiger, Sarita Montiel, Brian Keith, Ralph Meeker, Jay C. Flippen, Charles Bronson (RKO/Globe)

Yankee-hating Southerner goes west after the Civil War to join the Sioux in their uprising against the U.S. Slow in takeoff, action becomes pretty rough at times.

Production is strong on visual values to bolster Samuel Fuller's sometimes meandering screenplay highlighting Rod Steiger as Southerner taken into the tribe after he survives the run-of-the-arrow torture ordeal. Forceful use is made of Indians and their attacks on the whites to give unusual color to feature, which additionally has Sarita Montiel, Spanish actress, in as Steiger's Indian wife [dubbed by Angie Dickinson].

On debit side, Steiger frequently lapses from Southerner into Irish dialect, and footage occasionally is impeded by irrelevant sequences. Steiger is never sympathetic and character itself is not clearly defined, though actor endows his character with vigor.

•

RUN SILENT, RUN DEEP
1958, 93 mins, US Ⓥ b/w
Dir Robert Wise ***Prod*** Harold Hecht ***Scr*** John Gay ***Ph*** Russell Harlan ***Ed*** George Boemler ***Mus*** Franz Waxman ***Art*** Edward Carrere
Act Clark Gable, Burt Lancaster, Jack Warden, Brad Dexter, Don Rickles, Nick Cravat (United Artists/Hecht-Hill-Lancaster)

Run Silent, Run Deep is a taut, exciting drama of submarine warfare in the Pacific during the Second World War. Observant viewers may recognize overtones of *Moby Dick* and *The Caine Mutiny* in the screenplay from the novel by Capt. Edward L. Beach. Clark Gable is seen as a staunchly dedicated, hard-driving submarine commander with a single-minded purpose—to seek out and destroy a Japanese Akikaze destroyer which he holds responsible for sinking his previous sub.

His one-track dedication leads to charges of cowardice and incompetency which results in what seems like a "mutiny" on the part of Burt Lancaster, his tough executive officer who is resentful of Gable for taking over the command he had expected and who is in disagreement with Gable's tactics.

The submarine action is particularly effective and provides a sense of participation as the men sweat out depth charges and fire from enemy destroyers and planes. The miniature photography is especially good.

RUN WILD, RUN FREE
1969, 100 mins, UK col
Dir Richard C. Sarafian ***Prod*** John Danischewsky ***Scr*** David Rook ***Ph*** Wilkie Cooper ***Ed*** Geoffrey Foot ***Mus*** David Whitaker ***Art*** Ted Tester
Act John Mills, Sylvia Syms, Bernard Miles, Mark Lester, Gordon Jackson, Fiona Fullerton (Irving Allen)

This sensible and sensitive film is handled with care and obvious affection. Heavy on the melodrama and profound in the study of characters through outstanding performances by John Mills and Mark Lester, feature is an honestly moving film.

Young Lester registers an excellent performance as an introverted, psychosomatically mute lad growing up on the moors of England. Lester's meeting with a wild, white colt concurrent with his initial acquaintance with moorman Mills, a retired army colonel, provides a setup for interaction beween the three that is basis for the film. David Rook's film adaptation of his own novel [*The White Colt*] is particularly good in that it sentimentalizes without getting sticky and his concise dialogue and sensible placement of incidents eliminates any story lag.

•

RUSH
1991, 120 mins, US Ⓥ ◉ col
Dir Lili Fini Zanuck ***Prod*** Richard D. Zanuck ***Scr*** Pete Dexter ***Ph*** Kenneth MacMillan ***Ed*** Mark Warner ***Mus*** Eric Clapton ***Art*** Paul Sylbert
Act Jason Patric, Jennifer Jason Leigh, Sam Elliott, Max Perlich, Gregg Allman, William Sadler (Zanuck)

Moral ambiguity that has plagued America since the 1960s is given a harrowing probe in this tale of undercover narcs who succumb to the temptation in their midst. Head-swiveling directorial debut of Lili Fini Zanuck lays out a tough masculine scenario [based on Kim Wozencraft's book] in a way that is always emotionally riveting.

A bearded Jason Patric stars as Jim, an earthy, direct, Texas narcotics cop who sees a spark in rookie Kristen (Jennifer Jason Leigh), a fresh-scrubbed comer who's serious about making a difference. Kristen soon finds Jim has a disturbing way of getting too involved in his work. Kirsten tries to draw the line, but she's already too emotionally involved with Jim, who's become her lover, and the strange, secret and intoxicating rituals of drug buys and the underworld.

Set in the early 1970s, when America was struggling to reinvent itself after the shattering events of the 1960s, pic depicts a culture in which morality is one big gray area. *Rush* benefits from outstanding lead performances and an uncannily accurate picture of its time and place.

•

RUSH HOUR
1998, 98 mins, US Ⓥ ◉ col
Dir Brett Ratner ***Prod*** Roger Birnbaum, Arthur Sarkissian, Jonathan Glickman ***Scr*** Jim Kouf, Ross Lamanna ***Ph*** Adam Greenberg ***Ed*** Mark Helfrich ***Mus*** Lal Schifrin ***Art*** Robb Wilson King
Act Jackie Chan, Chris Tucker, Tom Wilkinson, Elizabeth Pena, Philip Baker Hall, Mark Rolston (New Line)

Jackie Chan scores his biggest American-produced hit with *Rush Hour*, a frankly formulaic but raucously entertaining action comedy that comes equipped with the additional marquee lure of up-and-comer Chris Tucker.

Some Chan purists may be disappointed. The fight scenes are shorter and slightly less plentiful, and the death-defying stunts—which, as usual, Chan performs without a double—are kept to a minimum. Tucker also brings it down a few notches, and comes across as much looser and funnier than he did in 1997's *Money Talks*—which, like current pic, was directed by Brett Ratner.

Tucker's manic, motor-mouth style of comedy is an effective counterbalance to Chan's rapid-fire acrobatics. Whether their characters are bickering or bonding, the two stars bring out the best in each other.

Maverick Detective James Carter (Tucker) yearns to join the FBI, and thinks he's gotten a big break when his disapproving chief (Philip Baker Hall) assigns him to the bureau for a major case. But the feds simply want Carter to "baby-sit" Hong Kong supercop Det.-Insp. Lee (Chan), who has flown to L.A. to help his old friend the Chinese consul (Tzi Ma) recover his abducted 11-year-old daughter (Julia Hsu).

Working from a serviceable script [from a screen story by coscripter Ross Lamanna], Ratner gives the two leads ample opportunity to bounce humorously off each other. A peroxided Ken Leung provides some forebodingly silken menace as Sang, the chief kidnapper, who proves to be almost as lethal as the Hong Kong cop when it comes to martial arts mayhem.

Chan and vet stunt coordinator Terry Leonard choreograph some full-throttle action sequences to keep the party lively. In a few scenes, the editing works against Chan by breaking up the flow of his frenzied physicality. Otherwise, tech credits are first rate.

●

RUSH TO JUDGMENT
1967, 122 mins, US b/w
Dir Emile de Antonio ***Prod*** Mark Lane, Emile de Antonio ***Scr*** Mark Lane ***Ph*** Robert Primes ***Ed*** Daniel Drasin (Impact Films/Judgment)

Lawyer Mark Lane, whose "brief for the defense" of Lee Harvey Oswald was in the number one non-fiction best-seller position for several months, converted his material into a film of the same name, *Rush to Judgment*. For many it will seem a convincing pic, opening up severe doubts about the thoroughness and even integrity of the Warren Commission's investigation into the assassination of President Kennedy.

Rush to Judgment is sober and unexcited, making its points with quiet and controlled definiteness, sans hysterics or frenzied accusations. Lane and collaborator Emile de Antonio have let their material present itself, utilizing wryness as their main weapon to sow seeds of doubt. Point of the film is neatly summed up by one interviewee: "The Warren Commission, I think, had to report in their book what they wanted the world to believe . . . It had to read like they wanted it to read. They had to prove that Oswald did it alone."

●

RUSSIA HOUSE, THE
1990, 123 mins, US Ⓥ ⦿ ▭ col
Dir Fred Schepisi ***Prod*** Paul Maslansky, Fred Schepisi ***Scr*** Tom Stoppard ***Ph*** Ian Baker ***Ed*** Peter Honess ***Mus*** Jerry Goldsmith ***Art*** Richard MacDonald
Act Sean Connery, Michelle Pfeiffer, Roy Scheider, James Fox, Klaus Maria Brandauer, Ken Russell (Pathe)

John le Carre's glasnost-era espionage novel has been turned into intelligent adult entertainment, but somber tone, utter lack of action and sex, and complexity of plot tilts this mainly to upscale audience. The film is the first U.S. non-coproduction to be shot substantially in the USSR.

Sean Connery plays Barley Blair, a boozy, inconoclastic London publisher to whom a highly sensitive manuscript is sent via a Moscow book editor named Katya (Michelle Pfeiffer). Intercepted by British authorities, the text, authored by a leading physicist, purports to lay out the facts about Soviet nuclear capabilities in devastating detail.

Over his protestations, Blair is sent to Moscow in his role as prospective publisher to meet the writer, the mysterious Dante (Klaus Maria Brandauer), determine his reliability and put more questions to him. His intermediary is the beautiful Katya, with whom he falls in love. As the flawed, unreliable publisher, Connery is in top form. Pfeiffer's Katya is a much more guarded figure. Her Russian accent proves very believable but she has limited notes to play.

Most of the supporting roles are one-dimensional British or U.S. intelligence types, but James Fox, Roy Scheider, John Mahoney and Michael Kitchen embody them solidly and with wit when possible. Director Ken Russell amusingly hams it up as an impishly aggressive spy master. Brandauer is strong as always in his brief appearance as the charismatic Dante.

●

RUSSIANS ARE COMING! THE RUSSIANS ARE COMING!, THE
1966, 124 mins, US Ⓥ ⦿ ▭ col
Dir Norman Jewison ***Prod*** Norman Jewison ***Scr*** William Rose ***Ph*** Joseph Biroc ***Ed*** Hal Ashby, J. Terry Williams ***Mus*** Johnny Mandel ***Art*** Robert F. Boyle
Act Carl Reiner, Eva Marie Saint, Alan Arkin, Brian Keith, Jonathan Winters, Theodore Bikel (Mirisch/United Artist)

The Russians Are Coming! The Russians Are Coming! is an outstanding Cold War comedy depicting the havoc created on a mythical Massachusetts island by the crew of a grounded Russian sub.

Nathaniel Benchley's novel *The Off-Islanders* got its title from New England slang for summer residents, herein top-featured Carl Reiner, wife Eva Marie Saint, and their kids, Sheldon Golomb and Cindy Putnam. Basically, story concerns aftermath of an accidental grounding of the Russian sub by overly curious skipper Theodore Bikel, who sends Alan Arkin ashore in charge of a landing party to get a towing boat. The wild antics which follow center around sheriff Brian Keith, sole resident who manages to keep cool except when arguing with Paul Ford, firebrand civil defense chief (self-appointed) who arms himself to repel the "invasion" with a sword and an American Legion cap.

Arkin, in his film bow, is absolutely outstanding as the courtly Russian who kisses a lady's hand even as he draws a gun.

English music hall vet Tessie O'Shea, also in film debut, is very good as the island's telephone operator who contributes to the spread of the "invasion" rumors, and her scenes with Reiner, in which they are lashed together and attempt to escape, is a comedy highlight.

1966: NOMINATIONS: Best Picture, Actor (Alan Arkin), Adapted Screenplay, Editing

●

RUTHLESS
1948, 104 mins, US Ⓥ b/w
Dir Edgar G. Ulmer ***Prod*** Arthur S. Lyons ***Scr*** S. K. Lauren, Gordon Kahn ***Ph*** Bert Glennon ***Ed*** Francis D. Lyon ***Mus*** Werner Janssen ***Art*** Frank Sylos
Act Zachary Scott, Louis Hayward, Diana Lynn, Sydney Greenstreet, Lucille Bremer, Martha Vickers (Producing Artists)

Despite a sextet of name players, *Ruthless* is a victim of clichéd and outmoded direction and of weary dialogue to which no actor could do justice.

Practically the entire yarn stems from the mental reflections of Louis Hayward, one-time partner of powerful financier Zachary Scott. Early sequences show how Scott moved from a poor environment to a position of prestige and wealth by a "what-makes-Zachary-run" technique. Picture boils down to a character study of Scott.

Performances are handicapped by the direction of Edgar G. Ulmer.

Adaptation from the Dayton Stoddart novel, *Prelude to Night*, is involved and confusing. Plot's denouement is also telegraphed long before the finale.

Hayward contribs a fair interpretation of Scott's associate, who eventually breaks from him. Diana Lynn, in a dual role, is wistful and appealing as a pawn in Scott's affections. Sydney Greenstreet, cast as a utilities magnate who's ousted by Scott, tends to overact.

●

RUTHLESS PEOPLE
1986, 93 mins, US Ⓥ ⦿ col
Dir Jim Abrahams, David Zucker, Jerry Zucker ***Prod*** Michael Peyser ***Scr*** Dale Launer ***Ph*** Jan DeBont ***Ed*** Arthur Schmidt ***Mus*** Michel Colombier ***Art*** Donald Woodruff
Act Danny DeVito, Bette Midler, Judge Reinhold, Helen Slater, Anita Morris, Bill Pullman (Touchstone)

Ruthless People is a hilariously venal comedy about a kidnapped harridan whose rich husband won't pay for her return.

In short, impoverished couple Judge Reinhold and Helen Slater kidnap Bel-Air princess Bette Midler because her mercenary husband, played by Danny DeVito, has ripped off Slater's design for spandex miniskirts. There is much, much more to it than that, as screenwriter Dale Launer cleverly builds twist upon complication to a point where practically everyone in the cast is writhing in frustration and mystification as they wonder whether their latest opportunistic scheme is going to work. Midler, when first glimpsed, is an absolute fright who looks like a cross between Cyndi Lauper and Divine. After terrorizing her kidnappers, she embarks upon an energetic self-improvement program, and not surprisingly emerges with the upper hand.

●

RYAN'S DAUGHTER
1970, 194 mins, UK Ⓥ ⦿ ▭ col
Dir David Lean ***Prod*** Anthony Havelock-Allan ***Scr*** Robert Bolt ***Ph*** Freddie Young ***Ed*** Norman Savage ***Mus*** Maurice Jarre ***Art*** Stephen Grimes
Act Robert Mitchum, Trevor Howard, Sarah Miles, Christopher Jones, John Mills, Leo McKern (M-G-M/Faraway)

Ryan's Daughter is a brilliant enigma, brilliant, because director David Lean achieves to a marked degree the daring and obvious goal of intimate romantic tragedy along the rugged geographical and political landscape of 1916 Ireland; an enigma, because overlength of perhaps 30 minutes serves to magnify some weaknesses of Robert Bolt's original screenplay, to dissipate the impact of the performances, and to overwhelm outstanding photography and production.

Robert Mitchum gives a stolid performance as an aloof widower, a schoolteacher returning from a Dublin trip to whom Sarah Miles pours out her conception of love. United in marriage, pair never achieve a full sexual-spiritual union—he is 20 years her senior, she is immature. Arrival of shell-shocked Christopher Jones to take over the British occupation garrison cues an illicit affair.

As the townsfolk become more scandalized by the affair between Jones and Miss Miles, she is eventually stripped and shorn as an adulterer and a wrongly convicted informer.

Trevor Howard gives an assured performance as a knowing local priest; John Mills might be a technical tour de force as a Quasimodo-like town idiot, but the character is overdrawn and often jarring to storytelling; other supporting players, many drawn from the Irish stage, are very good.

1970: Best Supp. Actor (John Mills), Cinematgraphy

NOMINATIONS: Best Actress (Sarah Miles), Sound

SABOTAGE
1936, 76 mins, UK Ⓥ ⊙ b/w

Dir Alfred Hitchcock ***Prod*** Michael Balcon ***Scr*** Charles Bennett, Ian Hay, Helen Simpson, E. V. H. Emmett ***Ph*** Bernard Knowles ***Ed*** Charles Frend ***Mus*** Louis Levy ***Art*** Otto Werndorff, Albert Jullion

Act Sylvia Sydney, Oscar Homolka, Desmond Tester, John Loder, Joyce Barbour, Matthew Boulton (Gaumont-British)

Competent and experienced hand of the director is apparent throughout this production, which is a smart one and executed in a business-like manner from start to finish.

But the story, somehow, seems outmoded. Joseph Conrad was never a dramatist, and his novels were dependent altogether upon his genius for descriptive writing. Film play [from Conrad's novel *The Secret Agent*] is, therefore, more or less obscure in plot.

It revolves around a secret organization which hires people to plant bombs in crowded sections of London, but the reason for their desire to systematically blow up innocent persons is not made clear. Film thus just misses being great.

Oscar Homolka's performance of the harassed victim of the sabotage organization into whose clutches he has fallen is a brilliant piece of character acting. Sylvia Sydney seems to have been circumscribed by plot deficiency.

•

SABOTEUR
1942, 100 mins, US Ⓥ ⊙ b/w

Dir Alfred Hitchcock ***Prod*** Frank Lloyd ***Scr*** Peter Viertel, Joan Harrison, Dorothy Parker ***Ph*** Joseph Valentine ***Ed*** Otto Ludwig ***Mus*** Frank Skinner ***Art*** Jack Otterson

Act Priscilla Lane, Robert Cummings, Norman Lloyd, Otto Kruger, Murray Alper, Alma Kruger (Universal)

Saboteur is a little too self-consciously Hitchcock. Its succession of incredible climaxes, its mounting tautness and suspense, its mood of terror and impending doom could have been achieved by no one else. That is a great tribute to a brilliant director. But it would be a greater tribute to a finer director if he didn't let the spectator see the wheels go round, didn't let him spot the tricks—and thus shatter the illusion, however momentarily.

Like all Hitchcock films, *Saboteur* is excellently acted. Norman Lloyd is genuinely plausible as the ferret-like culprit who sets the fatal airplane factory fire. Robert Cummings lacks variation in his performance of the thick-headed, unjustly accused worker who crosses the continent to expose the plotters and clear himself; but his directness and vigor partly redeem that shortcoming.

There is the customary Hitchcock gallery of lurid minor characters, including a group of circus freaks, a saboteur whose young son has the macabre habit of breaking his toys, and a monstrous butler with a sadistic fondness for a blackjack.

•

SABOTEUR, CODE NAME — "MORITURI", THE
SEE: MORITURI

•

SABRINA
(UK: SABRINA FAIR)
1954, 112 mins, US Ⓥ ⊙ b/w

Dir Billy Wilder ***Prod*** Billy Wilder ***Scr*** Billy Wilder, Samuel Taylor, Ernest Lehman ***Ph*** Charles Lang ***Ed*** Arthur Schmidt ***Mus*** Frederick Hollander ***Art*** Hal Pereira, Walter Tyler

Act Humphrey Bogart, Audrey Hepburn, William Holden, Walter Hampden, John Williams, Martha Hyer (Paramount)

A slick blend of heart and chuckles makes *Sabrina* a sock romantic comedy. Script is long on glibly quipping dialog, dropped with a seemingly casual air, and broadly played situations. The splendid trouping delivers them in style. Leavening the chuckles are tugs at the heart.

Basically, the plot's principal business is to get Audrey Hepburn, daughter of a chauffeur in service to an enormously wealthy family, paired off with the right man. She's always been in love with playboy William Holden, but ends up with Humphrey Bogart, the austere, businessman brother.

The fun is in the playing. Bogart is sock as the tycoon with no time for gals until he tries to get Hepburn's mind off Holden. The latter sells his comedy strongly, wrapping up a character somewhat offbeat for him. Hepburn again demonstrates a winning talent for being "Miss Cinderella."

1954: Best B&W Costume Design

NOMINATION: Best Director, Actress (Audrey Hepburn), Screenplay, B&W Cinematography, B&W Art Direction, Costume Design (Edith Head)

•

SABRINA
1995, 127 mins, US Ⓥ ⊙ col

Dir Sydney Pollack ***Prod*** Scott Rudin, Sydney Pollack ***Scr*** Barbara Benedek, David Rayfiel ***Ph*** Giuseppe Rotunno ***Ed*** Frederic Steinkamp ***Mus*** John Williams ***Art*** Brian Morris

Act Harrison Ford, Julia Ormond, Greg Kinnear, John Wood, Nancy Marchand, Richard Crenna (Mirage/Sandollar/Paramount)

This new *Sabrina* is more fizzle than fizz. Although the revamping of one of Audrey Hepburn's most enchanting vehicles has its share of diverting scenes and dialog, especially in the first half, Sydney Pollack and his writers have uncomfortably tilted this Cinderella story of a young woman's romantic blossoming toward being the tale of a workaholic tycoon's midlife crisis, to less than scintillating results. Billy Wilder's original 1954 film, made simultaneously with the production of Samuel Taylor's source play on Broadway with Margaret Sullivan and Joseph Cotten in the leading roles, may not rank as one of his very best, but has a witty sparkle and, most crucially, Hepburn at her most incomparable.

Julia Ormond's Sabrina not only doesn't come close to Hepburn's, but is singularly colorless, dour and lacking in inner spark.

Romantic comedy elements of the opening reels (save the Paris stuff) just get by on the strength of the dialog, which veers increasingly from the source as the story moves along, as well as some lively playing, notably by Greg Kinnear (as playboy David Larrabee) and Nancy Marchand (as his no-nonsense mother), and the undeniable appeal of the glittering settings and overall story.

Latter half offers few laughs, however, as it shifts to the realm of drama.

1995: NOMINATIONS: Original Musical or Comedy Score, Original Song ("Moonlight")

•

SABRINA FAIR
SEE: SABRINA

•

SACRIFICE, THE
SEE: OFFRET

•

SADDLE THE WIND
1958, 84 mins, US ⌑ col

Dir Robert Parrish ***Prod*** Armand Deutsch ***Scr*** Rod Serling ***Ph*** George J. Folsey ***Ed*** John McSweeney, Jr. ***Mus*** Elmer Bernstein ***Art*** William A. Horning, Malcolm Brown

Act Robert Taylor, Julie London, John Cassavetes, Donald Crisp, Charles McGraw, Royal Dano (M-G-M)

Armand Deutsch's production is the story of a wrong kid, a real bad one, dangerous as he is charming, that is as germane to today's headlines as it was when the restless gunslingers roamed the west. Rod Serling's screenplay [from a screen story by Thomas Thompson] is colorful and exciting and director Robert Parrish has kept it keyed high for a fast, exciting picture. Robert Taylor, Julie London and John Cassavetes act out this tale of compulsive evil against the magnificent location backgrounds of the Colorado Rockies.

Taylor plays Steve Sinclair, a retired gunman, sick of death and sick to death of guns. He is farming the lush valley presided over by Donald Crisp, patriarchal landowner who has given Taylor his chance to foreswear violence and bring up his orphaned, much-younger brother, John Cassavetes. But Cassavetes is one of those young men to whom a gun is more exciting than a beautiful woman, even though he does bring back saloon singer Julie London from a trip to the big city. He also brings back a hair-triggered six-shooter and proceeds to prove his manhood, not with London, but with the gun.

Taylor gives a lot of ruggedness to his role, still gentle and loving with the kid brother. London, who also sings the lyrical title song by Jay Livingston and Ray Evans, gets exceptional believability into her part, somewhat hackneyed, as the dance hall girl who really wants to settle down. Cassavetes has a tendency to be rather mannered but his intensity gives great conviction.

•

SADIE MCKEE
1934, 90 mins, US Ⓥ b/w

Dir Clarence Brown ***Prod*** Lawrence Weingarten ***Scr*** John Meehan ***Ph*** Oliver T. Marsh ***Ed*** Hugh Wynn ***Mus*** William Axt (dir.) ***Art*** Cedric Gibbons, Fredric Hope, Edwin B. Willis

Act Joan Crawford, Gene Raymond, Franchot Tone, Edward Arnold, Esther Ralston, Akim Tamiroff (M-G-M)

Sadie McKee is the Cinderella theme all over again, plus an s.a. angle through the stellar player of the titular role encountering three major romances in the persons of the featured male trio in support—Franchot Tone, Gene Raymond and Edward Arnold.

Basically it's the story [from the *Liberty* magazine serial by Vina Delmar] of the housemaid (Joan Crawford) who marries the boss of the manor, but not until after he comes humbly to her, and after she has experienced turbulent affairs with the other two.

That her major attachment to Arnold is obviously a mercenary marriage is sufficiently well built up to make it almost sympathetic, in view of the goading of the supercilious young master (Tone) of the household in which Sadie's mother is the cook.

Raymond is cast as the No. 1 sweetie who, according to Tone, is a no-good guy, but who is the major romance interest even after he runs out with a vaudeville single (well played by Esther Ralston).

The playing is expert throughout, so much so that in its realism it perhaps makes the star suffer a bit, particularly at the hands of Arnold whose bluff, constantly inebriated performance almost steals the picture.

•

SADIE THOMPSON
1928, 94 mins, US Ⓥ ⊙ ⊗ b/w

Dir Raoul Walsh ***Scr*** Raoul Walsh, C. Gardner Sullivan ***Ph*** Oliver Marsh, George Barnes, Robert Kurrle ***Ed*** C. Gardner Sullivan ***Art*** William Cameron Menzies

Act Lionel Barrymore, Gloria Swanson, Blanche Friderici, Raoul Walsh, Charles Lane, Florence Midgley (United Artists)

Program credits make no reference to *Rain* the play, the picture having been adapted from the "original story" by W. Somerset Maugham. However, the presentation conveys the idea of *Rain* by a stereoptican downpour effect prior to and through the opening titles.

The scene in which Hamilton enters Sadie's room during the night is not more than barely hinted at, finishing with Lionel Barrymore standing at the door. For a few previous feet is shown his mental struggle to overcome Sadie's physical attraction for him, but nothing more than a faltering hand reaching out to stroke her hair is flashed.

Sadie's costume, her struggle to articulate above and over a wad of rum and her familiarity with the Marines is sufficient to establish her character at the beginning. But there's likely to be a wide difference of opinion on Gloria Swanson's interpretation of the role.

Barrymore's performance is okay and Raoul Walsh, assuming the double duties of actor and director, does well by both. He plays O'Hara with whom Sadie eventually sails away. Charles Lane makes a minor bit count, and Blanche Friderici rises to her occasion late in the running.

1927/8: NOMINATIONS: Best Actress (Gloria Swanson), Cinematography

•

SAFE PLACE, A
1971, 94 mins, US col

Dir Henry Jaglom ***Prod*** Bert Schneider ***Scr*** Henry Jaglom ***Ph*** Dick Kratina ***Ed*** Pieter Bergema

Act Tuesday Weld, Orson Welles, Jack Nicholson, Philip Proctor, Gwen Welles, Dov Lawrence (BBS/Columbia)

Tuesday Weld is the child-like woman in whose silly pussycat consciousness the backward, forward, now it's now, now it isn't now action takes place. In her one clear decision she is casually cruel to the young man (Philip Proctor) who adores her while receptive to the curiously charming drop-by-without-calling stud played by Jack Nicholson.

Weld has many scenes in the park with an itinerant magician, supposedly a father image. Of the many weirdo roles played in his time by Orson Welles this may be the prize example.

Unrelated to the story in Weld's head is hippie girl's rambling account of her feelings adroitly soliloquized by

Gwen Welles. This is rather touching, quite lucid and uninterrupted, though wildly neurotic.

All this deliberate experimentation puts a heavy burden upon the viewer. Hardly a scene is fully played out, hardly an explanation provided. It would seem that writer-director Henry Jaglom has plunged in over his own depth. It is like a gymnastic symphony conductor over-personalizing the music.

•

SAFETY LAST
1923, 77 mins, US Ⓥ ⊗ b/w
Dir Fred Newmeyer, Sam Taylor ***Scr*** Hal Roach, Sam Taylor, Tim Whelan, H. M. Walker ***Ph*** Walter Lundin ***Ed*** Thomas J. Crizer ***Art*** Fred Guiol
Act Harold Lloyd, Mildred Davis, Bill Strother, Noah Young, Westcott B. Clarke, Mickey Daniels (Roach)

This Harold Lloyd high-class low comedy has thrills as well as guffaws. It leads up to big shrieks through Lloyd apparently climbing the outside wall to the top or 12th floor of a building, probably in Los Angeles. This bit is chockerblock with trick camera work but skillfully done. The comedy business of the department store where Lloyd is a clerk nearly equals the remainder.

Lloyd as a small-town boy leaves his sweetheart in the country, going to the city and obtains a $15-a-week position as a counter jumper. Back home the girl receives a little cheap piece of jewelry and believes Lloyd has made the great success he said he would in the big city. Upon the advice of her mother she goes there.

Lloyd, in an attempt to have her think he is the boss instead of a clerk, wanders into all kinds of complications. It leads up to the building climbing, a plan suggested by the clerk to the general manager as a means of obtaining publicity for the firm.

•

SAHARA
1943, 85 mins, US Ⓥ ⦿ ▭ b/w
Dir Zoltan Korda ***Prod*** Harry Joe Brown ***Scr*** John Howard Lawson, Zoltan Korda ***Ph*** Rudolph Mate ***Ed*** Charles Nelson ***Mus*** Miklos Rozsa
Act Humphrey Bogart, Bruce Bennett, Lloyd Bridges, Rex Ingram, J. Carrol Naish, Dan Duryea (Columbia)

Story background displays Libyan desert fighting in 1942, when the British were hurled back to the El Alamein line. It vividly focuses attention on exploits of an American tank crew headed by Humphrey Bogart to escape the onrushing Nazis, and battles against desert sands and lack of water.

Picture gets off to a fast start, with Bogart heading his 28-ton tank south on the desert in drive to regain the British lines. Along the way he picks up six Allied stragglers; Sudenese soldier Rex Ingram with latter's Italian prisoner, J. Carrol Naish; and a downed Nazi pilot (Kurt Krueger). Bogart pushes on with his assorted passengers to reach a water hole at an old desert fort which provides a trickle but enough to sustain the group. Nazi motorized battalion also heads for the water supply.

Script [adapted by James O'Hanlon from a story by Philip MacDonald] is packed with pithy dialog, lusty action and suspense, and logically and well-devised situations avoiding ultra-theatrics throughout. It's an all-male cast, but absence of romance is not missed in the rapid-fire unfolding of vivid melodrama.

1943: NOMINATIONS: Best Supp. Actor (J. Carrol Naish), B&W Cinematography, Sound

•

SAHARA
1983, 104 mins, US Ⓥ col
Dir Andrew V. McLaglen ***Prod*** Menahem Golan, Yoram Globus ***Scr*** James R. Silke ***Ph*** David Gurfinkel ***Mus*** Ennio Morricone ***Art*** Luciano Spadoni
Act Brooke Shields, Lambert Wilson, Horst Buchholz, John Rhys-Davies, Ronald Lacey, John Mills (Cannon)

Coproducer Menahem Golan reportedly hatched the idea for *Sahara* when Mark Thatcher, son of the British prime minister, disappeared in the desert during an international car rally.

An old-fashioned B-grade romantic adventure, directed in pedestrian fashion by Andrew V. McLaglen, *Sahara* is lamentably low on excitement, laughs and passion.

Screenplay, set in 1927, has Brooke Shields as heiress to a car company who promises her dying daddy that she'll win the world's toughest endurance rally driving the car he designed. Wily Brooke disguises herself as a man, complete with wig and moustache.

Soon after the race starts, she discards her disguise and reverts to Brooke the beautiful, only to receive a beating and a mouthful of sand when she's captured by Arab thug John Rhys-Davies. Handsome sheikh Lambert Wilson saves her from his clutches and falls mildly in love with her.

Director McLaglen and most everyone else treat it all tongue-in-cheek.

•

SAIGON
SEE: OFF LIMITS

•

SAIGON
1948, 93 mins, US b/w
Dir Leslie Fenton ***Prod*** P. J. Wolfson ***Scr*** P. J. Wolfson, Arthur Sheekman ***Ph*** John F. Seitz ***Ed*** William Shea ***Mus*** Robert Emmett Dolan ***Art*** Hans Dreier, Henry Bumstead
Act Alan Ladd, Veronica Lake, Wally Cassell, Douglas Dick, Morris Carnovsky (Paramount)

Alan Ladd fans and other followers of high adventure will like *Saigon*. It's strictly pulp-fiction stuff with a flair for good characterizations and plenty of action. P. J. Wolfson, in his production and co-scripting chore with Arthur Sheekman, has paid close attention to the little details that will catch audience interest.

Performers' characters are well-established and they know what to do with them under Leslie Fenton's able direction. Latter keeps the action high and the interest unflagging in telling the saga of three ex-army fliers who go adventuring in Saigon with a beautiful blonde.

There's a load of menacing and mysterious characters, a plane crash, a jungle boat ride and lushly backgrounded Saigon to point up action and intrigue before finale. Music score aids plotting, and camera work is sharp in depicting settings.

Ladd is at home as the ex-army flier, with Wally Cassell as a happy-go-lucky air sergeant, selling plenty of chuckles. Lake aptly fits the blonde siren role.

•

SAILOR BEWARE
1951, 104 mins, US b/w
Dir Hal Walker ***Prod*** Hal B. Wallis ***Scr*** James Allardice, Martin Rackin, John Grant ***Ph*** Daniel L. Fapp ***Ed*** Warren Low ***Mus*** Joseph J. Lilley (dir.) ***Art*** Hal Pereira, Henry Bumstead
Act Dean Martin, Jerry Lewis, Corinne Calvert, Marion Marshall, Robert Strauss, Leif Erickson (Paramount)

While this film version of the 1933 legit piece [by Kenyon Nicholson and Charles Robinson, adapted by Elwood Ullman] has been padded to an unnecessary 104 minutes, it has enough of the comics in hilarious routines to more than satisfy Dean Martin and Jerry Lewis's considerable following. Less emphasis on lightweight plotting and more on M&L would have made for better, overall comedy entertainment.

Martin and Lewis this time set out to scuttle the Navy. It's a cleaned-up version of the stage hit, and only a thread of that original is contained in the celluloid treatment.

There's an unbilled opening and closing appearance by Betty Hutton—referred to as Hetty Button—and Martin makes his vocal bid on four tunes by Mack David and Jerry Livingstone. There's the usual round of scenes depicting Navy training, plus a television broadcast involving the comics and screaming femmes, and other incidents that set up the sailors' bets that Lewis can't kiss Calvet, nitery entertainer, when their submarine reaches Honolulu. Marion Marshall is a WAVE who has struck a spark with Lewis because she uses no makeup to which the comic is allergic.

Running through what passes as a plot are Robert Strauss, tough petty officer who is the natural enemy of the comics; Leif Erickson, sub commander; and Don Wilson, jovial TV announcer.

•

SAILOR FROM GIBRALTAR, THE
1967, 89 mins, UK b/w
Dir Tony Richardson ***Prod*** Oscar Lewenstein, Neil Hartley ***Scr*** Christopher Isherwood, Don Magner, Tony Richardson ***Ph*** Raoul Coutard ***Ed*** Anthony Gibbs ***Mus*** Antoine Duhamel ***Art*** Marilena Aravantinou
Act Jeanne Moreau, Ian Bannen, Vanessa Redgrave, Zia Moyheddin, Hugh Griffith, Orson Welles (Lopert Pictures)

The novels of Marguerite Duras are frequently no more than lengthy short stories—and not too strong on the narrative side. With such interpreters as Christopher Isherwood and Tony Richardson (neither famous for clarity of intent) plus Don Magner, the ensuing screenplay is replete with repetitive sequences.

A Britisher (Ian Bannen) and his mistress (Vanessa Redgrave) are on an Italian holiday which quickly becomes evident will be their last. She's still hungry for him but he can't stand her but isn't brave enough to send her away.

When a mysterious woman on a yacht (Jeanne Moreau) crosses their path, his greed (both sexual and practical) provides the impetus to ditch his mistress and make a fast pass at the yachtswoman.

Orson Welles is wasted on a brief bit as an information peddler and Hugh Griffith is only slightly better as a white hunter and guide. Redgrave is touching and believably irritating in her brief role. The rest of the cast walk through their parts like somnambulists.

•

SAILOR'S RETURN, THE
1978, 112 mins, UK col
Dir Jack Gold ***Prod*** Otto Plaschkes ***Scr*** James Saunders ***Mus*** Carl Davis
Act Tom Bell, Shope Shodeinde, Mick Ford, Paola Dionisotti, George Costigan, Clive Swift (Ariel/NFFC)

Set in the early reign of Queen Victoria (1819–1901), story, adapted from David Garnett's novel, is about a sailor who returns home to England with a bride from the black Kingdom of Dahomey in West Africa. It's her dowry, a treasure of pearls, that sets them up in business with an inn for thirsty passers-by in a lush English countryside. But her color and the presence of a black son set them off from intolerant neighbors, despite some support from friends in the area.

Conflicts with the sailor's sister, the local pastor (who preaches hellfire), and prejudiced visitors to the inn lead to slow alienation in a foreign land.

Tom Bell scores as the sailor Targett, and Shope Shodeinde (a native Nigerian) as the African princess brings credibility but hardly sparkle to Tulip, a lively flower that must slowly wither in a foreign climate with the accumulation of disappointments and hostility.

•

SAILOR TAKES A WIFE, THE
1946, 92 mins, US b/w
Dir Richard Whorf ***Prod*** Edwin H. Knopf ***Scr*** Chester Erskine, Anne Morrison Chapin, Whitfield Cook ***Ph*** Sidney Wagner ***Ed*** Irvine Warburton ***Mus*** Johnny Green ***Art*** Cedric Gibbons, Edward Carfagno
Act Robert Walker, June Allyson, Hume Cronyn, Audrey Totter, Eddie "Rochester" Anderson (M-G-M)

The Sailor Takes a Wife stage play has been given light, broad screen treatment. Production isn't elaborate but has polish, the direction is smooth, and the cast gets the best from the comedy situations.

Robert Walker and June Allyson head the funning, making the antics and complications around which the plot revolves delightful. Story is on the light side and laughs are mostly situation, but Richard Whorf's direction keeps it on the move. Plot deals with a sailor and a girl who meet and marry, all in one evening, and subsequent efforts to adjust themselves to marital status.

Bride's first disappointment comes when her husband is discharged almost immediately, leaving her with a civilian instead of the hero she expected. Further complications develop when Walker, searching for a job, becomes entangled innocently with a romantically inclined foreign femme menace, brightly played by Audrey Totter.

•

SAILOR WHO FELL FROM GRACE WITH THE SEA, THE
1976, 104 mins, UK Ⓥ ▭ col
Dir Lewis John Carlino ***Prod*** Martin Poll ***Scr*** Lewis John Carlino ***Ph*** Douglas Slocombe ***Ed*** Anthony Gibbs ***Mus*** John Mandel ***Art*** Ted Haworth
Act Sarah Miles, Kris Kristofferson, Jonathan Kahn, Margo Cunningham, Earl Rhodes, Paul Tropea (Avco Embassy)

With a quartet of fine characters and performances, *The Sailor Who Fell From Grace With the Sea* could have ventured just about anywhere—except where writer-director Lewis John Carlino takes it in an effort to remain faithful to Yukio Mishima's novel.

Cultural differences still remain in this increasingly homogenized world and the prime problem with *Sailor* is trying to transfer decidedly Oriental ideas about honor, order and death into an English countryside.

Mishima's novel was about a Japanese widow who falls in love with a sailor. At first attracted to the sailor as an honorable symbol, her 13-year-old son defends him before his gang of idealistic schoolmates. But when the sailor leaves the sea to marry, the boy and his gang feel betrayed and plot to kill him to restore his purity.

On film, the story won't settle down with these upper-class young English lads.

•

SAINT, THE
1997, 116 mins, US col
Dir Phillip Noyce ***Prod*** David Brown, Robert Evans, William J. Macdonald, Mace Neufeld ***Scr*** Jonathan Hensleigh, Wesley Strick ***Ph*** Phil Meheux, Alex Thompson ***Ed*** Terry Rawlings ***Mus*** Graeme Revell ***Art*** Joseph Nemec III
Act Val Kilmer, Elisabeth Shue, Rade Serbedzija, Valery Nikolaev, Henry Goodman, Alun Armstrong (Paramount)

A generic suspenser that doesn't taste bad at first bite but becomes increasingly hard to swallow, *The Saint* comes off more as a pallid imitation of Paramount's Eurothriller *Mission: Impossible* than as anything resembling the further adventures of Leslie Charteris's charming rogue. Long-in-the-works, $70 million production offers only mild diversion before sinking in a murk of preposterous plotting.

That the original author's name nowhere appears on the film serves as a good indication of how important the source material has been to the present filmmakers.

Simon Templar (Val Kilmer), in Moscow and dressed like a high-tech cat burglar, breaks into a safe to steal a microchip important to Ivan Tretiak (Rade Serbedzija). Latter is a blowhard nationalist, a former communist and now Mafia-style billionaire who is planning to manipulate a heating-oil crisis in the frigid capital as a way to seize power. Templar gets away to England, where he is induced by the admiring Tretiak to nab a rumored breakthrough formula for cold-fusion developed by Yank scientist Dr. Emma Russell (Elisabeth Shue). He has little trouble seducing the smart but vulnerable "genius."

Up to his point, it looks like screenwriters Jonathan Hensleigh (*The Rock*) and Wesley Strick (*Cape Fear*) are striving to replace the suave, charming, very British Saint with a stateless soul who compensates for his profound identity crisis by assuming endless disguises. But the second hour descends into routine cat-and-mouse stuff as the Russian baddies chase the breathless couple all over Moscow.

Kilmer's Saint is mostly a cipher. Shue may be a vision, but she is not a vision one readily believes has solved the daunting challenge of cold fusion. [In pic's original preview version, prior to reshoots, her character was killed off before the end.]

Director Phillip Noyce keeps things moving at a brisk pace.

•

SAINT IN LONDON, THE
1939, 72 mins, UK b/w
Dir John Paddy Carstairs ***Prod*** William Sistrom ***Scr*** Lynn Root, Frank Fenton ***Ph*** Claude Friese-Greene ***Ed*** Douglad Robertson ***Mus*** Harry Acres (dir.) ***Art*** C. Wilfred Arnold
Act George Sanders, Sally Gray, David Burns, Gordon McLeod, Athene Seyler, Henry Oscar (RKO)

This is a workmanlike job. Previous *Saint* pix, with George Sanders in his standard role, were made in Hollywood.

Plot [from the story *The Million Pound Day* by Leslie Charteris] revolves around an organization of international counterfeiters. The Saint aids Scotland Yard in rounding up a gang that's ready to foist upon the public $5 million worth of banknotes printed in England for a Continental country. The Saint's chief assistants are Sally Gray and David Burns. Burns almost steals the picture with another inimitable hick crook role. Sanders is excellent, as usual.

Direction is alert, with some photography being excellent.

•

SAINT IN NEW YORK, THE
1938, 72 mins, US b/w
Dir Ben Holmes ***Prod*** William Sistrom ***Scr*** Charles Kaufman, Mortimer Offner ***Ph*** Joseph August, Frank Redman ***Ed*** Harry Marker
Act Louis Hayward, Kay Sutton, Sig Ruman, Jonathan Hale, Jack Carson (RKO)

A rugged gangster melodrama, highly fantastic in plot but intriguing, has been skillfully shaped from the Leslie Charteris novel about a modern Robin Hood whose dish is rubbing out baddies. It makes no pretentions to being more than a B picture.

Making a good team, Louis Hayward and Kay Sutton are romantically paired. Throughout the picture there are numerous murders, mostly the higher-ups in a mob of racketeers, but also there are some incredible escapes by the Saint. To some extent, Hayward has too much the appearance of a college freshman to suggest that his exploits in wiping out gangsters and escaping from tight pinches could be anything but imaginative.

Cast is made up chiefly of gangster characters, including Sig Ruman, who's excellent, Paul Guilfoyle, an old favorite, Jack Carson and Ben Welden. Jonathan Hale plays a police inspector whose part is highly fictional in character.

•

SAINT JACK
1979, 112 mins, US col
Dir Peter Bogdanovich ***Prod*** Roger Corman ***Scr*** Howard Sackler, Paul Theroux, Peter Bogdanovich ***Ph*** Robby Muller ***Ed*** William Carruth ***Art*** David Ng
Act Ben Gazzara, Denholm Elliott, James Villiers, Joss Ackland, Rodney Bewes, Lisa Lu (New World/Playboy/Shoals Creek-Copa de Oro)

Shot entirely on location in Singapore, the film (produced by Roger Corman, who gave Bogdanovich his start of *The Wild Angels* in 1964) is extremely well crafted, finely acted, and conjures up a positively intriguing milieu.

At bottom line, though, it's essentially a character study—Ben Gazzara excels as a pimp with a heart of gold—told in a mood that begins with a twinkling-eyed bawdiness, but becomes progressively more somber and even nihilistic.

Based on Paul Theroux's novel, the film is laid in 1971, putting its exclusive focus on Gazzara, an expatriate U.S. hustler-type who jumps ship and uses the cover of a local provision broker to operate a freelance prostitution ring.

The script is a good one, gutsy and sometime very funny.

•

SAINT JOAN
1957, 110 mins, US b/w
Dir Otto Preminger ***Prod*** Otto Preminger ***Scr*** Graham Greene ***Ph*** Georges Perinal ***Ed*** Helga Cranston ***Mus*** Mischa Spoliansky ***Art*** Roger Furse
Act Jean Seberg, Richard Widmark, Richard Todd, Anton Walbrook, John Gielgud, Felix Aylmer (United Artists)

Otto Preminger showed courage when he decided to make G. B. Shaw's *Saint Joan* into a film and to star an unknown of next to no theatrical experience in the role. Jean Seberg of Marshalltown, Iowa, makes a sincere effort, but her performance rarely rises above the level of the Iowa prairie.

Seberg is helped most by her appealing looks. She has a fresh, unspoiled quality and she photographs well. But Shaw's Joan is more than just an innocent country maiden.

In vivid contrast, Preminger surrounds her with a supporting cast that performs brilliantly. Richard Widmark plays the idiot Dauphin with gusto though he at times overacts the part. Richard Todd as Dunois; Anton Walbrook as Cauchon, the Bishop of Beauvais; and Felix Aylmer, the Inquisitor.

It is John Gielgud who stands out with a brilliant performance as the politically minded Earl of Warwick, determined to get Joan to the stake, though contemptuous of the Church's winded arguments of "heretic" versus "witch."

Graham Greene wrote the screenplay, and while it is somewhat toned down, and probably less anti-clerical than the Shaw original, it still retains the essentials of the Shaw classic.

•

SALAAM BOMBAY
1988, 113 mins, India col
Dir Mira Nair ***Prod*** Mira Nair ***Scr*** Sooni Taraporevala ***Ph*** Sandi Sissel ***Ed*** Barry Alexander Brown ***Mus*** L. Subramaniam
Act Shafik Syed, Sarfuddin Qurassi, Raju Barnad, Raghubir Yadav, Nana Patekar, Aneeta Kanwar (Mirabai)

A kind of Indian *Pixote* about kids living on the sidewalks of Bombay utilizing their wits, the story [by Mira Nair and Sooni Taraporevala] evolves around a young boy, Krishna, who leaves his home village, kicked out by his family who suspects him unjustly of stealing money.

He comes to the big city, hoping to make quickly the 500 rupees which would permit him to return home. Carrying tea in a Bombay slum for pimps and prostitutes, sleeping on a pile of rubble and learning the ways of the street and the means to survive, innocence gradually is beaten out of him by the circumstances.

Director Mira Nair, trained in America, is very much in control of her material, tells her story efficiently and has most of the cast, none of them real professionals, under total control. She indulges in some melodramatic explorations, however, dangerously verging on a romanticized Oriental tearjerker mood.

Superior camerawork and editing keep the story moving along briskly.

•

SALAIRE DE LA PEUR, LE
(THE WAGES OF FEAR)
1953, 155 mins, France/Italy b/w
Dir Henri-Georges Clouzot ***Prod*** Raymond Borderie, Henri-Georges Clouzot (execs.) ***Scr*** Henri-Georges Clouzot, Jerome Geronimi ***Ph*** Armand Thirard ***Ed*** Henri Rust, Madeleine Gug ***Mus*** Georges Auric ***Art*** Rene Renoux
Act Yves Montand, Charles Vanel, Peter Van Eyck, William Tubbs, Vera Clouzot, Falco Lulli (CICC/Filmsonor/Vera/Fono Roma

A harrowing odyssey of four derelicts inching two trucks loaded with nitroglycerine over a tortuous terrain puts this in the strong meat department with a downbeat theme of fear and its manifestations.

Early portion showing a group of outcasts in a torrid Central American outpost could be tightened a bit and some of the truck scenes could be trimmed, as they heap too much suspense on an already taut situation.

Story [from the novel by Georges Arnaud] shows a group of foreign tramps huddled in a small tropical village suffering from heat and boredom, and plotting some means of getting out. Into this comes an ex-gangster who is immediately lackeyed by Mario (Yves Montand), a young Frenchman. A chance to get away offers itself because an American oil company wants two trucks loaded with explosives driven to a well fire.

Director Henri-Georges Clouzot has given this rhythm and pacing that makes it seem shorter than it is. He catches the feeling of a dank tropic town and the attitude of the men in crisis. Montand is good as the young Frenchman who sees his idol's clay feet, while Charles Vanel etches an excellent portrait of an aging man feeling fear and resignation.

•

SALLY IN OUR ALLEY
1931, 77 mins, UK b/w
Dir Maurice Elvey ***Scr*** Basil Dean ***Ph*** Miles Malleson, Alma Reville, Archie Pitt
Act Gracie Fields, Ian Hunter, Florence Desmond, Fred Groves, Gibb McLaughlin (Associated Talking Pictures/Radio)

Gracie Fields doesn't exactly suggest sufficient sympathy to hold the romantic lead, but her eccentric singing and dialect-gagging records well.

Story [from the play *The Likes of 'Er* by Charles McEvoy] tells how a Lancashire girl refuses to marry because her boyfriend is reported killed in the war, although actually he isn't dead but pretends to be because he's crippled. She makes a hit serving and singing in a coffee shop.

Atmosphere is good generally. Introduction of the songs is resourceful and some of the gags are quite good. Dialogue is pert on English comedy lines. But the whole canvas is very small and the footage seems very long.

Fields is just Fields as in vaude, but lacking aggressiveness. Ian Hunter has more repose and acting ability than the rest, while newcomer Florence Desmond troupes well in an utterly unsympathetic role.

•

SALLY, IRENE AND MARY
1925, 58 mins, US b/w
Dir Edmund Goulding ***Scr*** Edmund Goulding ***Ph*** John Arnold ***Ed*** Harold Young ***Art*** Cedric Gibbons, Merrill Pye
Act Constance Bennett, Joan Crawford, Sally O'Neill, William Haines, Henry Kolker (M-G-M)

Transplanted to the screen, this book for a musical show is rather trashy chorus-girl stuff. It's not a good picture.

Dealing with Broadway's backstage angle, the script doesn't ring true. Director Edmund Goulding has given the production one lavish stage setting for a full-stage Charleston number, but has fallen into the pitfall of having every member of the audience applaud as soon as the curtain starts to ascend.

Sally is the "kept woman" of the trio; Irene can't make up her mind whether to choose a "chaser" or a boy with honorable intentions, and Mary is the innocent miss who nearly loses Sally her de luxe flat when the latter's money man takes a tumble in her favor.

Constance Bennett gives the one genuine performance in the picture as Sally, and suffers because of an unsympathetic role. Joan Crawford makes a silly girl of Irene, with whom interest is lost when she falls for he of the evil intent, and it's doubtful if there ever has been a chorus girl such as Sally O'Neill has been instructed to play in depicting Mary, fresh and too dizzy.

•

SALLY, IRENE AND MARY
1938, 86 mins, US b/w
Dir William A. Seiter ***Prod*** Darryl F. Zanuck ***Scr*** Harry Tugend, Jack Yellen ***Ph*** Peverell Marley ***Ed*** Walter Thompson ***Mus*** Arthur Lange (dir.) ***Art*** Bernard Herzbrun, Rudolph Sternad
Act Alice Faye, Tony Martin, Fred Allen, Jimmy Durante, Gregory Ratoff, Joan Davis (20th Century-Fox)

Sally, Irene and Mary is another in the Darryl F. Zanuck formula of vaudscreen musicals, skillfully blending the variety components and dovetailing them into an amiable entertainment [from an original story by Karl Tunberg and Don Ettlinger, suggested by a play by Edward Dowling and Cyrus Wood].

Fred Allen marks his second big league picture work since he became a radio name. He foils with and for Jimmy Durante, both proving an efective team throughout with a running gag sequence.

It's the vocal prowess of Tony Martin and Alice Faye, Mr. and Mrs. in private life and the romance interest here, that does much to sustain the interest.

Gregory Ratoff as an amorous baron, the gangling Joan Davis with her standard comedy hokum, notably a gypsy sequence, Durante as a white wing gone impresario, and a runaway showboat (finale) are the comedy highlights. Plus of course Allen's own staccato line-reading, cast as a shoestring agent. He's foiled principally in this respect by Louise Hovick, née Gypsy Rose Lee, doing a sleeker, brunet Mae West.

•

SALLY OF THE SAWDUST

1925, 104 mins, US Ⓥ ⊗ b/w

Dir D. W. Griffith ***Scr*** Forrest Halsey ***Ph*** Harry Fischbeck ***Ed*** James Smith ***Art*** Charles M. Kirk

Act Carol Dempster, W. C. Fields, Alfred Lunt, Erville Alderson, Effie Shannon (Griffith/United Artists)

D. W. Griffith is down to common picture making in this one. It is strange to witness a Griffith film directed by him in a straight manner. As W. C. Fields made his legit stage hit in the musical *Poppy* as the carnival showman, so does he here scream his screen debut as a film funny man in *Sally*. And Fields plays them as well as on the stage. He gives a smoothness to his comedy stuff that cannot be missed.

Griffith follows the stage story but sparsely. The director slips in pathos and sentiment in his masterly manner without too much of either, but he allows the comedy to go at full tilt.

Sally is an orphan, her mother a gentlewoman from New England, having married a theatrical man against her parents' wishes. When her mother dies, Prof. McGargle takes charge of Sally, bringing her up as his daughter with the girl unaware of her parentage.

•

SALOME

1922, 75 mins, US ⊗ b/w

Dir Charles Bryant ***Scr*** Peter M. Winters ***Ph*** Charles Van Enger ***Mus*** Ulderico Marcelli ***Art*** Natacha Rambova

Act Nazimova, Rose Dione, Mitchell Lewis, Nigel de Brulier (Nazimova/Allied)

A highly fantastic *Salome* is that which Nazimova presents on the screen. It is far from the *Salome* Oscar Wilde penned.

The picture is done with a decidedly modernistic touch. Picturesquely it is very pretty as to lightings, setting and photography, but there ends about all that can be said in praise. *Nazimova in Facial Expressions*, with Salome as the background, would have been much better billing for the picture.

Other than the facial contortions there is little to the picture, likewise little to her costume. The heroic figures are given a decided appearance of effeminacy and the slaves of color are beefy instead of muscular. The settings, however, are well worked out and make a really worth background for the action, such as it is.

•

SALOME

1953, 102 mins, US Ⓥ col

Dir William Dieterle ***Prod*** Buddy Adler ***Scr*** Harry Kleiner ***Ph*** Charles Lang ***Ed*** Viola Lawrence ***Mus*** George Duning, Daniele Amfitheatrof ***Art*** John Meehan

Act Rita Hayworth, Stewart Granger, Judith Anderson, Cedric Hardwicke, Alan Badel, Charles Laughton (Columbia/Beckworth)

The story by Jesse L. Lasky, Jr., and the screenplay by Harry Kleiner change and embroider the Biblical tale of the girl who danced for King Herod and caused the beheading of John the Baptist. More their own interpretation than a factual chronicle of the religious story, it is a vehicle especially slanted for Rita Hayworth.

Film opens by establishing King Herod's superstitious fear of John the Baptist and his protection of the prophet, despite the insistence of his queen, Herodias, that the holy man be slain for talking against the throne. Opening also finds Salome, Herod's stepdaughter, banished from Rome because Caesar's nephew wants to marry her. During the trip back to Galilee, she vents her spite against all Romans on Commander Claudius, played by Stewart Granger, even though they are attracted to each other. Salome finds Galilee in a state of unrest and, egged on by her wicked mother, Herodias, tries to enlist Claudius's aid in doing away with the prophet.

Hayworth, who has never been better photographed, injects excellent dramatic values and wears the clinging Roman costumes to advantage. Her dance, staged by Valerie Bettis, packs plenty of s.a. Granger gives an easy, assured masculine portrayal to his central role, and when he and Miss Hayworth are on together the picture has a decided lift.

•

SALT OF THE EARTH

1954, 94 mins, US Ⓥ ⦿ b/w

Dir Herbert J. Biberman ***Prod*** Paul Jarrico ***Scr*** Michael Wilson ***Ph*** [uncredited] ***Ed*** [uncredited] ***Mus*** Sol Kaplan

Act Rosaura Revueltas, Juan Chacon, Will Geer, David Wolfe, Mervin Williams, David Sarvis (Independent/International Union of Mine, Mill & Smelter Worker)

Salt of the Earth is a good, highly dramatic and emotion-charged piece of work that tells its story straight. It is, however, a propaganda picture which belongs in union halls rather than theaters.

It is a bitter tale that Michael Wilson has concocted and the large cast acts it out with a conviction that obviously didn't require much prompting. The story concerns Mexican miners in a small New Mexican mining community, Zinc Town. A series of mine accidents prompts a strike. The company attempts to break it via acts of intimidation that include arrest and brutality.

Director Herbert J. Biberman was one of the Unfriendly Ten who served a five-month jail sentence for contempt of Congress. Producer Paul Jarrico also was in trouble with Congress.

Yet as a piece of film artistry, *Salt* achieves moments of true pictorial excellence. Rosaura Revueltas, a Mexican actress playing the wife of the strike leader, gives a taut, impressive performance that has real dimension. Juan Chacon, a union leader in real life, turns in a creditable acting job.

Biberman's direction achieves distinctive quality. He concentrates on misery and violence and anger with a stark determination and a flair for realism that is designed to do much more than rouse sympathy.

•

SALT ON OUR SKIN

1993, 110 mins, Germany/France/Canada Ⓥ ⦿ col

Dir Andrew Birkin ***Prod*** Bernd Eichinger, Martin Moszkowicz ***Scr*** Andrew Birkin, Bee Gilbert ***Ph*** Dietrich Lohmann ***Ed*** Dagmar Hirtz ***Mus*** Klaus Doldinger ***Art*** Jean-Baptiste Tard

Act Greta Scacchi, Vincent D'Onofrio, Anais Jenneret, Petra Berndt, Claudine Auger, Rolf Illig (Constantin)

Salt on Our Skin is an old-fashioned weepie about mismatched lovers whose rare, passionate encounters over 30 years make both their lives worth living.

Couple's odyssey is told in flashback and v.o. by the 40ish Greta Scacchi. Refreshing twist here is that Scacchi follows her heart as well as her intellect.

Shortly after discovering true ecstasy in Vincent D'Onofrio's arms in the late 1950s, Scacchi discovers Camus, Sartre and—bingo!—Simone de Beauvoir's *The Second Sex*. When D'Onofrio proposes, Scacchi assures him it could never work: she's a restless intellectual, he's a hunky fisherman, and a future cannot be built on sex alone. They part but end up trysting every so often.

Based on Benoite Groult's 1988 bestseller [*Les vaisseaux du coeur*], which was hailed for its frank descriptions of female sexual desire, conventional pic relies on the two leads' personalities and does not innovate. The heat and devotion between the real-life couple are convincing. (They also starred in Gillian Armstrong's 1991 *Fires Within*.)

•

SALT TO THE DEVIL

SEE: GIVE US THIS DAY

•

SALUTE OF THE JUGGER, THE

(US: THE BLOOD OF HEROES)

1989, 102 mins, Australia Ⓥ col

Dir David Peoples ***Prod*** Charles Roven ***Scr*** David Peoples ***Ph*** David Eggby ***Ed*** Richard Francis-Bruce ***Mus*** Todd Boekelheide ***Art*** John Stoddart

Act Rutger Hauer, Joan Chen, Vincent D'Onofrio, Anna Katarina, Delroy Lindo, Hugh Keays-Byrne (Kings Road)

It's the first feature directed by screenwriter David Peoples (*Blade Runner*, *Leviathan*) and he's provided himself with a murky, familiar screenplay about a band of wandering "juggers." They're futuristic gladiators, led by the deeply scarred Sallow (Rutger Hauer), who was once a member of the League, the ruling elite, but who was banished over a misdemeanor. Now Sallow is determined to challenge the League's juggers and regain his position.

His own team (which includes Vincent D'Onofrio, Delroy Lindo and Anna Katarina) is augmented by a feisty peasant girl, Kidda (Joan Chen), who proves invaluable in the climactic confrontation with the League's team, which is headed by the giant Gonzo (Max Fairchild).

Plot development is slim. Much of running time is given over to the game itself, which seems to have no rules except that the winning team places the skull of a dog atop a pointed stick.

Hauer, whose character loses an eye halfway through the pic, gives Sallow a certain presence, but doesn't extend himself. Chen comes off best with a graceful performance as Kidda: her moves in the game sequences are often quite beautiful in the midst of all the ugliness. Pic was shot on desert locations near the mining town of Coober Pedy, South Australia, as well as in studios in Sydney.

•

SALVADOR

1986, 123 mins, US Ⓥ ⦿ col

Dir Oliver Stone ***Prod*** Gerald Green, Oliver Stone ***Scr*** Oliver Stone, Richard Boyle ***Ph*** Robert Richardson ***Ed*** Claire Simpson ***Mus*** Georges Delerue ***Art*** Bruno Rubeo

Act James Woods, James Belushi, Michael Murphy, John Savage, Elpidia Carrillo, Tony Plana (Hemdale)

The tale of American photojournalist Richard Boyle's adventures in strife-torn Central America, *Salvador* is as raw, difficult, compelling, unreasonable, reckless and vivid as its protagonist.

James Woods portrays the real-life Boyle, who at the outset is shown to be at his lowest ebb as a virtual bum and professional outcast in San Francisco.

With no particular prospects, he shanghais fun-loving buddy James Belushi for the long drive down to (El) Salvador, where Woods has left behind a native girlfriend and where he thinks he might be able to pick up some freelance work.

The film has an immediacy, energy and vividness that is often quite exciting, and the essential truth of much of what director Oliver Stone has put on display will prove bracing for many viewers.

1986: NOMINATIONS: Best Actor (James Woods), Original Screenplay

•

SALVATORE GIULIANO

1961, 125 mins, Italy b/w

Dir Francesco Rosi ***Prod*** Franco Cristaldi ***Scr*** Francesco Rosi, Suso Cecchi D'Amico, Enzo Provenzale, Franco Solinas ***Ph*** Gianni Di Venanzo ***Ed*** Mario Serandrei ***Mus*** Piero Piccioni

Act Salvo Randone, Frank Wolff, Federico Zardi, Pietro Cammarata (Lux/Vides/Galatea)

An outstanding film has been fashioned by Francesco Rosi using the story of Sicilian bandit Giuliano as a pretext for a historical, political, and social document of its times (the late 1940s and early 1950s), and of the island setting (Sicily) which made it possible.

Though the pic has many moments of suspense and excitement as it tells the Giuliano story and all that went with it, it is by no means the usual bandit-gendarme yarn. In fact, one rarely if ever catches a close-up of the notorious outlaw who made national and international headlines in the post-war years.

Tale is told in flashback, beginning with a graphic re-enactment of Giuliano's death (shot by his best friend, then again by the police, who claimed credit for the deed), and the ending when still another gang member, who betrayed, is shot during a recent Sicilian night.

Of the name players, Salvo Randone does an outstanding job as the judge charged with the impossible job of seeking clear-cut justice for those involved, gang members and not. Frank Wolff, an American, is standout as Gaspare Pisciotta, Giuliano's right-hand man.

All of the pic was shot on location in Giuliano's home territory. An extra nod must go also to Piero Piccioni's fine musical scoring.

•

SAME TIME, NEXT YEAR

1978, 119 mins, US Ⓥ ⦿ col

Dir Robert Mulligan ***Prod*** Walter Mirisch, Morton Gottlieb ***Scr*** Bernard Slade ***Ph*** Robert Surtees ***Ed*** Sheldon Kahn ***Mus*** Marvin Hamlisch ***Art*** Henry Bumstead

Act Ellen Burstyn, Alan Alda, Ivan Bonar (Universal)

Same Time, Next Year is a textbook example of how to successfully transport a stage play to the big screen. The production of Bernard Slade's play, sensitively directed by Robert Mulligan, is everything you'd want from this kind of film. And it features two first-class performances by Ellen Burstyn and Alan Alda.

The picture opens in 1951 at a resort in northern California. Burstyn, a 24-year-old Oakland housewife, and Alda, a 27-year-old accountant from New Jersey, meet over dinner, get along and have a fling. The next morning they wake up in the same bed, talk about what's happened, realize that while they're both happily married with six children between them, they're in love.

They make a pact to meet at the same resort every year, which is just what they do and is just what the film is about. We see the two every five or six years as they adjust to the changes time brings.

What always remains through the years is the deep affection the two share. It's nice to see a film about two people who like each other this deeply.

1978: NOMINATIONS: Best Actress (Ellen Burstyn), Adapted Screenplay, Cinematography, Song ("The Last Time I Felt Like This")

•

SAMMA NO AJI
(AN AUTUMN AFTERNOON)

1962, 113 mins, Japan col

Dir Yasujiro Ozu ***Prod*** Shizuo Yamanuchi ***Scr*** Yasujiro Ozu, Kogo Noda ***Ph*** Yuhara Atsuta ***Ed*** Yoshiyasu Hamamura ***Mus*** Takanobu Saito ***Art*** Tatsuo Hamada

Act Shima Iwashita, Shinichiro Mikami, Keiji Sata, Mariko Okada, Nobuo Nakamura, Chishu Ryu (Shochiku)

This view of contemporary middle-class life in Japan is too leisurely paced, too sentimental in design and its humorous social comments too infrequent.

Screenplay tells the story of a bourgeois widower's adjustment to coming old age, the departure of his children into marriage, and the changes in a society which has apparently been very good to him. It's a gentle, nostalgic view of life which director Yasujiro Ozu draws, with some intrusively stark, abrupt camera techniques which are almost always inappropriate.

Director intercuts between characters in a single scene, and between scenes, with the same tempo, totally eschewing anything that resembles a dissolve or slow fade. This might be effective depicting tension or violence but interrupts the flow of *Autumn Afternoon*. Also intrusive are a schmaltzy musical score and the vivid Agfacolor.

The picture is nicely acted throughout, and does have its comic and affecting moments. There is one extremely funny scene in which the widower, who had been a captain of a destroyer during the war, meets an old shipmate who speculates on what might have happened if Japan had won the war: "We'd be sitting in New York right now, listening to the real thing (jazz). They'd all be wearing wigs and playing hot tunes on the samisen."

•

SAMMY AND ROSIE GET LAID

1987, 100 mins, UK Ⓥ ⦿ col

Dir Stephen Frears ***Prod*** Tim Bevan, Sarah Radclyffe ***Scr*** Hanif Kureishi ***Ph*** Oliver Stapleton ***Ed*** Mick Audsley ***Mus*** Stanley Myers ***Art*** Hugo Lyczyc Wyhowski

Act Shashi Kapoor, Frances Barber, Claire Bloom, Ayub Khan Din, Roland Gift, Wendy Gazelle (Working Title)

Cynical and brutally unsentimental in outlook, *Sammy and Rosie Get Laid* brings the force of an accelerated cinematic attack to bear upon its complex thematic juxtaposition of sexual warfare, cross-cultural dislocation, racism and the ruthlessness of power.

With relentless momentum director Stephen Frears unfolds the story of Sammy (Ayub Khan Din), the hedonistic, thoroughly English son of a prominent Pakistani politician. Sammy, who scrapes out a living as an accountant, lives in a dangerous and decaying black neighborhood with his wife Rosie (Frances Barber), a sexually adventurous feminist journalist.

Change enters their lives with the arrival of Rafi (Shashi Kapoor), Sammy's long-lost father who has been forced to flee his political enemies in Pakistan. Rafi attempts to buy his way back into the affection of his son and that of a beautiful and sensitive Englishwoman, Alice (Claire Bloom) whom he also cruelly abandoned in his self-centered quest for power in the East.

Frears levitates the film's harsh realism with a fantastical counterpoint in touches like the ghost of a tortured labor leader who haunts Rafi from the outset, and a band of gypsy buskers who serenade the ongoing anarchy.

•

SAMMY GOING SOUTH
(US: A BOY TEN FEET TALL)

1963, 128 mins, UK ▭ col

Dir Alexander Mackendrick ***Prod*** Michael Balcon ***Scr*** Denis Cannan ***Ph*** Edwin Hillier ***Ed*** Jack Harris ***Mus*** Tristram Cary

Act Edward G. Robinson, Fergus McClelland, Constance Cummings, Harry H. Corbett, Paul Stassino, Zia Moyheddin (British Lion/Bryanston Seven Arts)

Pic is based on an uneasy, incredible idea [from a novel by W. H. Canaway]. A 10-year-old youngster (Fergus McClelland) is orphaned when his parents are killed in an air raid during the Suez crisis. In a blur he remembers that he has an Aunt Jane in Durban and that Durban is in the South. So he sets out, armed only with a toy compass.

He meets a Syrian peddler who sees in the kid a chance of a reward from Aunt Jane. He meets a rich American tourist but escapes her greedy clutches. Not until he meets up with a grizzled old diamond smuggler (Edward G. Robinson) does the film flicker into some spark of human interest. The old man and the moppet strike up a splendid friendship. Mackendrick's films usually strike an attitude and have intuition on points of views. Relationships between his key characters are usually more clearly defined and worked on than in this. With the exception of Robinson, looking like a slightly junior Ernest Hemingway, and Paul Stassino, as a glib crook of a guide, the others are cardboard.

•

SAMOURAI, LE
(THE SAMURAI)

1967, 105 mins, France/Italy col

Dir Jean-Pierre Melville ***Scr*** Jean-Pierre Melville, Georges Pellegrin ***Ph*** Henri Decae, Jean Charvein ***Ed*** Yolande Maurette ***Mus*** Francois de Roubaix ***Art*** Francois de Lamothe

Act Alain Delon, Nathalie Delon, Cathy Rosier, Francois Perier, Michel Boisrond (Filmel/Borderie/TCP/Fida

Jean-Pierre Melville has a great knowledge and fondness for Yank pix, especially gangster items. Here he uses an American book [by Joan McLeod] on a hired killer and transposes it to France for a curiously hybrid pic. It almost seems to be an American film dubbed into French, with some strange effects in altering the French scene to appear American, in such things as night clubs, sordid little hotels, police lineups and the general comportment of the personages.

It is intermittently successful. Without a true French gangster core that would breed this sort of automaton killer, Melville extends it to try to compare him to the Japanese Samurai dedicated to military codes.

Alain Delon has the empty agate eyes, cold demeanor and implacable presence for the glacial killer who manages to spark love in a part-time kept woman, and becomes the prey of a dedicated, unswerving police inspector. Melville does wring some suspense as the killer tries to gun down his ex-employers and is also being hounded by the police.

Nathalie Delon is somewhat too frigid as the killer's mistress while Cathy Rosier has presence and poise as a comely pianist. Francois Perier, a comedian, is cast against type as the almost fanatical inspector but manages to acquit himself acceptably.

•

SAMSON AND DELILAH

1950, 120 mins, US Ⓥ ⦿ col

Dir Cecil B. DeMille ***Prod*** Cecil B. DeMille ***Scr*** Jesse L. Lasky, Jr., Fredric M. Frank ***Ph*** George Barnes ***Ed*** Anne Bauchens ***Mus*** Victor Young ***Art*** Hans Dreier, Walter Tyler

Act Hedy Lamarr, Victor Mature, George Sanders, Angela Lansbury, Henry Wilcoxon, Russ Tamblyn (Paramount)

Cecil B. DeMille has again dipped into the Bible for his material, made appropriately dramatic revisions in the original, and turned up with a DeMille-size smash.

The scriptwriters have woven from the abbreviated biblical telling of the Samson legend [from original treatments by Harold Lamb and Vladimir Jabotinsky] a lusty action story with a heavy coating of torrid-zone romance. Dozens of bit players and extras in tremendous, sweeping sets give size to the picture.

Victor Mature fits neatly into the role of the handsome but dumb hulk of muscle that both the Bible and DeMille make of the Samson character. Hedy Lamarr never has been more eye-filling and makes of Delilah a convincing minx. George Sanders gives a pleasantly light flavor of satirical humor to the part of the ruler, while Henry Wilcoxon is duly rugged as the military man.

The picture is claimed to have cost $3 million and looks well like it might have run considerably more than that.

1950: Best Color Art Direction, Color Costume Design (Edith Head)

NOMINATION: Best Color Cinematogrphy, Scoring of a Dramatic Picture, Special Effects

•

SAMURAI, THE
SEE: LE SAMOURAI)

•

SAMURAI REBELLION
SEE: JOI-UCHI

•

SAN ANTONIO

1945, 110 mins, US Ⓥ col

Dir David Butler ***Prod*** Robert Buckner ***Scr*** Alan LeMay, W. R. Burnett ***Ph*** Bert Glennon ***Ed*** Irene Morra ***Mus*** Max Steiner ***Art*** Ted Smith

Act Errol Flynn, Alexis Smith, S. Z. Sakall, Victor Francen, Paul Kelly (Warner)

Here's a western in the old, old tradition. In forsaking both social significance and art for this excursion into days of yore, the storytellers cooked up what might well be some genuine history about the way in which one lone, honest hombre defeated the hordes of evil gathered in San Antonio (Texas) during the middle of last century.

Errol Flynn looks and acts right handsome as that hero. Paul Kelly and Victor Francen earn their villainous hisses.

Alexis Smith walks through the business beautifully. S. Z. "Cuddles" Sakall is funny as the luscious dame's manager, and the furniture in that saloon at San Antonio, where the final battle starts, gets smashed with breathtaking thoroughness.

•

SAND CASTLE, THE

1961, 70 mins, US col

Dir Jerome Hill ***Prod*** Jerome Hill ***Scr*** Jerome Hill ***Ph*** Lloyd Ahern ***Ed*** Julia Knowlton, Henri A. Sundquist ***Mus*** Alec Wilder

Act Barrie Cardwell, Laurie Cardwell, George Dunham, Maybelle Nash, Erica Speyer (De Rochemont/Noel)

This delightful, fanciful look at the world and its people as we might like them to be is the complete work of Jerome Hill, who previously made the notable documentary *Albert Schweitzer*.

A little boy and his sister (Barrie and Laurie Cardwell) start the day's activities as their mother leaves them on the beach to play. Slowly but in ever-increasing numbers, other people begin to arrive: the painter (George Dunham) who must change his picture as the people obscure his view; the eccentric old lady (Maybelle Nash) who brings her bird in its cage and sits beneath a large canopy; the angler, the diver, the fat man and the blonde who worship the sun.

Oblivious to them all, the boy starts to build a large sand castle in the shape of a fort, helped by his sister, who fetches driftwood and shells. The others gather round and admire his work. There is no dialog, only incidental and amusing conversation.

Nothing is overstated and none of the characters is overdrawn or derivative. The mood is always one of gentleness, charm and tranquility. As the afternoon ends everyone goes home and the boy and his sister fall asleep by their castle to dream (in color) of being within its walls where they meet cut-out puppets (also the work of Hill) of the people who were on the beach.

•

SAN DEMETRIO—LONDON

1943, 93 mins, UK b/w

Dir Charles Frend ***Prod*** Michael Balcon ***Scr*** Robert Hamer, Charles Frend ***Ph*** Ernest Palmer ***Ed*** Eily Boland ***Mus*** John Greenwood

Act Walter Fitzgerald, Mervyn Johns, Ralph Michael, Robert Beatty, Gordon Jackson (Ealing)

Whether wittingly or accidentally, the presentation of this epic tale of the British Merchant Marine omits the customary cast of characters in the screen credits. Thus does it emphasize the genuineness of the personalities concerned in the unfolding of a gripping drama.

So one prefers to believe the man who plays the skipper of the *San Demetrio* is Captain Waite in person, just as the tough, nameless Texan who joins the tanker in Galveston is a tough Texan imbued with the idea of Britain's needing help to win the war.

If the chief engineer—who performs miracles in the half-flooded, fire-swept engine room by not only restarting the engines, but by cooking a pailful of potatoes in live steam from a leaking valve—is not a c.e. in real life, it really doesn't make any difference. And this goes for all of them, from the bosun to the kid apprentice whose first voyage it is.

Much credit must go to Michael Balcon, the producer, and Charles Frend, who directed. How much F. Tennyson Jesse's official account on salvaging the *San Demetrio*, after she had been abandoned for two days and nights 900 miles from her port, helped Robert Hamer and the director in their writing of the script can only be surmised, but the dialog is unvaryingly authentic.

•

SANDERS OF THE RIVER

1935, 98 mins, UK Ⓥ b/w

Dir Zoltan Korda ***Prod*** Alexander Korda ***Scr*** Lajos Biro, Jeffrey Dell ***Ph*** Georges Perinal, Osmond Borrodaile, Louis Page ***Ed*** William Hornbeck, Charles Crichton ***Mus*** Mischa Spoliansky ***Art*** [Vincent Korda]

Act Paul Robeson, Leslie Banks, Nina Mae McKinney, Robert Cochrane, Martin Walker, Richard Grey (London)

Story of an African colony [Nigeria] is an immense production, done for the greater part with deft direction, played with distinction by two main characters. Leslie Banks and Paul Robeson carry the greater part of this tale of a British commissioner who rules an African sector through commanding both fear and respect.

The story [from the novel by Edgar Wallace] is simple. Sanders (Banks) is in charge of a large section in the British African possessions. He makes a minor chief of Bosambo (Robeson), an engaging fugitive from prison, revealing the excellence of his judgment of men. Mofolabo, known as "the old king," is in an inaccessible section of the district and gives much trouble. When Sanders goes out on leave to get married, rum runners send word through the district that Sanders is dead, inciting the king to fresh depredations. But Sanders has gone only as far as the coast when he hears of the trouble, and comes back.

There are some nicely staged mob scenes, mostly ceremonials, with a remarkable male muscle dancer and a small regiment of natives who appear to be genuine. Robeson gets two of the songs [lyrics by Arthur Wimperis], with the third going to Nina Mae McKinney, a lullaby set against a humming harmonic background.

•

SANDLOT, THE

1993, 101 mins, US Ⓥ ⦿ ▭ col

Dir David Mickey Evans ***Prod*** Dale de la Torre, William S. Gilmore ***Scr*** David Mickey Evans, Robert Gunter ***Ph*** Anthony Richmond ***Ed*** Michael A. Stevenson ***Mus*** David Newman ***Art*** Chester Kaczenski

Act Tom Guiry, Mike Vitar, Patrick Renna, Chauncey Leopardi, Karen Allen, James Earl Jones (20th Century-Fox)

The Sandlot is yet another wallow in the coming-of-age stakes circa 1962. Sweet and sincere, the film is also remarkably shallow, rife with incident and slim on substance.

Scotty Smalls (Tom Guiry) arrives in some quiet piece of Americana and is recruited into the neighborhood's ad-hoc baseball team despite—to use the boys' most withering reference—the fact he "plays like a girl."

Scotty's mentor is Benny Rodriguez (Mike Vitar), the most charismatic and best player on the block. Running beneath the surface is the promise of some cataclysmic event, foreshadowed in voice-over by the older Scotty (silently played by Arliss Howard and voiced by director David Mickey Evans, both uncredited) 30 years later.

The Sandlot pretends to be about something when it really just strings together loosely connected vignettes. Worse, the set pieces are familiar retreads. The adult roles provide solid cameos for James Earl Jones and Karen Allen.

•

SAND PEBBLES, THE

1966, 193 mins, US Ⓥ ▭ col

Dir Robert Wise ***Prod*** Robert Wise ***Scr*** Robert Anderson ***Ph*** Joseph MacDonald ***Ed*** William Reynolds ***Mus*** Jerry Goldsmith ***Art*** Boris Leven

Act Steve McQueen, Richard Attenborough, Richard Crenna, Candice Bergen, Marayat Andriane, Mako (Argyle/Solar/20th Century-Fox)

Out of the 1926 political and military turmoil in China, producer-director Robert Wise has created a sensitive, personal drama, set against a background of old-style U.S. Navy gunboat diplomacy. *The Sand Pebbles*, based on the novel by Richard McKenna, is a handsome production, boasting some excellent acting characterizations.

Steve McQueen looks and acts the part he plays so well—that of a machinist's mate with nine years of navy service. Richard Crenna likewise is authentic as the gunboat captain, a young lieutenant who speaks the platitudes of leadership with a slight catch in his throat, due to lack of practical experience.

The title derives from a language perversion of San Pablo, formal name of the gunboat on Yangtze River patrol. Among the crew is Richard Attenborough, very believable in his role as a sailor who falls in love with newcomer Marayat Andriane in a tragic bi-racial romance. Her performance is sensitive.

The major drawback to the film as a whole is a surfeit of exposition, mainly in the second half. Every scene is in itself excellent, but unfortunately the overall dramatic flow of the pic suffers in the end.

1966: NOMINATIONS: Best Picture, Actor (Steve McQueen), Supp. Actor (Mako), Color Cinematography, Color Art Direction, Editing, Original Music Score, Sound

•

SANDPIPER, THE

1965, 115 mins, US Ⓥ ▭ col

Dir Vincente Minnelli ***Prod*** Martin Ransohoff ***Scr*** Dalton Trumbo, Michael Wilson ***Ph*** Milton Krasner ***Ed*** David Bretherton ***Mus*** Johnny Mandel ***Art*** George W. Davis, Urie McCleary

Act Elizabeth Taylor, Richard Burton, Eva Marie Saint, Charles Bronson, Robert Webber, James Edwards (M-G-M/Filmways)

The Sandpiper is the story of a passing affair between an unwed nonconformist and a married Episcopalian minister who is headmaster of a private boys' school attended by femme's nine-year-old son. Original by Martin Ransohoff, who produced, is trite and often ponderous in its philosophizing by the two principals, and picture is further burdened by lack of any fresh approach. [Story adaptation by Irene and Louis Kamp.]

Under Vincente Minnelli's leisurely but dramatic direction, the screenplay opens on Elizabeth Taylor as a budding artist whose young son is taken away from her after lad's brush with the law and sent to the school run by Richard Burton. Latter becomes interested in her although ostensibly happily wed to Eva Marie Saint, mother of his twin teenage sons.

Burton probably comes off best with a more restrained performance, although Taylor plays well enough a role without any great acting demands.

Saint gets the most out of a comparatively brief appearance, most of her drama confined to her reaction upon Burton's confession. Morgan Mason, son of Pamela and James Mason, makes a nice impression as Taylor's son.

1965: Best Song ("The Shadow of Your Smile")

•

SANDRA

SEE: VAGHE STELLE DELL'ORSA

•

SANDS OF IWO JIMA

1949, 110 mins, US Ⓥ ⦿ b/w

Dir Allan Dwan ***Prod*** Edmund Grainger (assoc.) ***Scr*** Harry Brown, James Edward Grant ***Ph*** Reggie Lanning ***Ed*** Richard L. Van Enger ***Mus*** Victor Young ***Art*** James Sullivan

Act John Wayne, John Agar, Adele Mara, Forrest Tucker, Wally Cassell, Richard Webb (Republic)

This is a vast saga [by Harry Brown] of a marine platoon whose history is traced from its early combat training through its storming of Iwo Jima's beaches to the historic flag-raising episode atop the sandy atoll [on the morning of Feb. 23, 1945]. It's loaded with the commercial ingredients of blazing action, scope and spectacle, but it falls short of greatness because of its sentimental core and its superficial commentary on the war.

Best portions of this pic are the straight battle sequences, many of which were made up of footage taken at the actual fighting at Tarawa and Iwo Jima.

John Wayne stands head and shoulders above the rest of the cast, and not only physically, as the ruthlessly efficient marine sergeant. He draws a powerful portrait of a solider with the job of making plain joes into murdering machines.

1949: NOMINATIONS: Best Actor (Johm Wayne), Motion Picture Story, Editing, Sound

•

SANDS OF THE KALAHARI

1965, 119 mins, UK ▭ col

Dir Cy Endfield ***Prod*** Cy Endfield, Stanley Baker ***Scr*** Cy Endfield ***Ph*** Erwin Hillier ***Ed*** John Jympson ***Mus*** John Dankworth ***Art*** Seamus Flannery, George Provis

Act Stuart Whitman, Stanley Baker, Susannah York, Harry Andrews, Theodore Bikel, Nigel Davenport (Paramount/Levine)

Cy Endfield, co-producer, director and scripter of the long film (made almost entirely on location in Africa), wisely makes the camera as important as anyone in the cast, emphasizing the savagery that is throughout. Although Endfield has been lucky with his casting, some members too quickly betray symptoms of scenery chewing.

A planeload of assorted types crashes in the desert and the rest of the film deals with their efforts to survive. It's some time before a villain is unveiled and, even then, the viewer's faith gets a few shakes. Susannah York, as the only female in the cast, gets plenty of exposure. Stuart Whitman, a gunhappy survivalist, and Stanley Baker, a nondescript loser, are the only main characters. Unbilled but colorful are assorted natives, animals and insects.

Entertainment, pure and simple [from a novel by William Mulvihill], was evidently what the filmmakers aimed for and that's the target they hit.

•

SANDWICH MAN, THE

1966, 95 mins, UK Ⓥ col

Dir Robert Hartford-Davis ***Prod*** Peter Newbrook ***Scr*** Michael Bentine, Robert Hartford-Davis ***Ph*** Peter Newbrook ***Ed*** Peter Taylor ***Mus*** Mike Vickers

Act Michael Bentine, Dora Bryan, Harry H. Corbett, Bernard Cribbins, Diana Dors, Ian Hendry (Titan)

The Sandwich Man is like a documentary in drag. Michael Bentine, who wrote the screenplay with the director, Robert Hartford-Davis, seeks to give a picture of London and some of the way-out, curious behaviour of its inhabitants through the eyes of a sandwich-board man who, wandering the streets, has a load of opportunity of observing, and of getting implicated. Not a bad idea and, filmed on location entirely, it gives director and cameraman Peter Newbrook a swell chance of bringing London to life. But in the countdown, a film has either got to be a feature pic or a "doc" primarily.

A loosely scribed romance between a young car salesman and a model, and the fact that on this day Bentine's prize racing pigeon is competing in an important race are the only two highly slim "plotlines." For the remainder, Bentine (dressed as a dude sandwich-board man) wanders around observing the odd things happening around him.

Bentine has an amiable personality that deserves further screen exposure.

•

SAN FRANCISCO

1936, 115 mins, US Ⓥ ⦿ b/w

Dir W. S. Van Dyke ***Prod*** John Emerson, Bernard Hyman ***Scr*** Anita Loos ***Ph*** Oliver T. Marsh ***Ed*** Tom Held ***Mus*** Herbert Stothart ***Art*** Cedric Gibbons, Arnold Gillespie, Harry McAfee

Act Clark Gable, Jeanette MacDonald, Spencer Tracy, Jack Holt, Jessie Ralph, Ted Healy (M-G-M)

An earthquake, noisy and terrifying, is *San Francisco*'s forte. Quake occurs after more than an hour and up to then the picture is distinguished chiefly for its corking cast and super-fine production.

Story basically follows the outline traced previously by Warner's *Frisco Kid* and Goldwyn's *Barbary Coast* [both 1935], although this one tends more to the musical through the constant singing of Jeanette MacDonald.

Lone incongruous note is the remarkable survival of Clark Gable after a whole wall has toppled over on him. His survival is necessary, to complete the picture, but it might have been made easier to believe.

As were James Cagney and Edward G. Robinson before him, Gable is "king" of the Barbary Coast, and like his predecessors, his reformation is the essence of the plot [story by Robert Hopkins]. Only this guy is tougher; it takes the earthquake to cure him. As Blackie Norton he operates a prosperous gambling joint and beer garden. The closest friend of this godless soul is a priest, who doesn't try to reform Blackie but always hopes for the best.

MacDonald enters as a Denver choir singer who's in Frisco looking for work. From the show at Blackie Norton's she graduates to grand opera under the sponsorship of Blackie's political rival.

Spencer Tracy plays a priest, and it's the most difficult role in the picture. His slang—he calls Gable "mug" and "sucker" good-naturedly—is the sort usually associated with men of lesser spiritual quality.

1936: Best Sound Recording

NOMINATIONS: Best Director, Actor (Spencer Tracy), Original Story, Assistant Director (Joseph Newman)

•

SANG D'UN POETE, LE
(BLOOD OF A POET)
1932, 60 mins, France b/w
Dir Jean Cocteau ***Prod*** Vicomte de Nouailles ***Scr*** Jean Cocteau ***Ph*** Georges Perinal ***Ed*** Jean Cocteau ***Mus*** Georges Auric ***Art*** Jean D'Eaubonne
Act Lee Miller, Pauline Carton, Odette Talazac, Enrique Rivero, Jean Desbordes, Fernand Dichamps (Vicomte de Nouailles)

On the face of it, this film represents six reels of scraped-together footage from off the cutting room floor. A more vague or hopeless mess could not have resulted.

Director-writer Jean Cocteau is a Parisian poet, artist and author, one of the finest. He has been called "a mad genius." No sense to try and explain what happens in this picture. It's all silent footage with Cocteau personally explaining the action (in French) that's just as meaningless as the action itself.

Photography is okay but has nothing special to bring attention. The sets are terrible.

[At New York's Fifth Avenue Playhouse, where the film was reviewed in 1933, a lobby poster offered $25 for an explanation of the film's meaning.]

•

SANJURO
SEE: TSUBAKI SANJURO

•

SAN QUENTIN
1937, 70 mins, US b/w
Dir Lloyd Bacon ***Prod*** Samuel Bischoff ***Scr*** Peter Milne, Humphrey Cobb ***Ph*** Sid Hickox ***Ed*** William Holmes ***Art*** Esdras Hartley
Act Pat O'Brien, Humphrey Bogart, Ann Sheridan, Barton MacLane, Joseph Sawyer, Veda Ann Borg (Warner Bros.)

San Quentin is stark, authentic-looking prison melodrama that misses being big entertainment because of a love story that is none too strong and a plot [by Robert Tasker and John Bright] that is only moderately forceful.

Various scenes were made in and around the San Quentin pen. Those which are of the prison and not staged were shot at a distance so that no prisoners could be recognized.

The only time when the camera isn't in the prison or with Warner-hired players doing the convicts (large mobs having been used for some sequences), is when the story is with the girl, a café singer whose brother is in stir. Majority of the action is assigned to convicts and prison officials, guards, etc.

Romantic leads are Pat O'Brien and Ann Sheridan, while the girl's brother is Humphrey Bogart, a tough convict, and a guard of the old school is played by Barton MacLane. All turn in good jobs.

•

SAN QUENTIN
1946, 66 mins, US b/w
Dir Gordon Douglas ***Prod*** Martin Mooney ***Scr*** Lawrence Kimble, Arthur A. Ross, Howard J. Green ***Ph*** Frank Redman ***Ed*** Marvin Coil ***Mus*** Paul Sawtell ***Art*** Albert S. D'Agostino, Lucius O. Croxton
Act Lawrence Tierney, Barton MacLane, Harry Shannon, Marian Carr, Carol Forman, Richard Powers (RKO)

Gordon Douglas whips together this tale of reformation leagues within prisons with plenty of movement, spotting action and development without a slow moment. Lawrence Tierney, as a prisoner of San Quentin, now reformed and just discharged from honorable army service, acquits himself capably, making role believable all the way.

Plot frames its melodramatics around efforts of Harry Shannon, San Quentin warden, to keep his prisoners' welfare league going in the face of opposition. Taking a group of prisoners to San Francisco to speak to a newspaper club, Shannon is wounded and others killed when a supposedly reformed inmate arranges an escape. To clear the warden's plan and make life better for majority of prisoners Tierney goes on a manhunt for Barton MacLane, the killer.

•

SANSHO DAYU
(SANSHO THE BAILIFF; THE BAILIFF)
1954, 120 mins, Japan Ⓥ b/w
Dir Kenji Mizoguchi ***Prod*** Masaichi Nagata ***Scr*** Fuji Yahiro, Yoshikata Yoda ***Ph*** Kazuo Miyagawa ***Mus*** Fumio Hayasaka ***Art*** Kisaku Itoh
Act Kinuyo Tanaka, Kyoko Kagawa, Eitaro Shindo, Yoshiaki Hanayagi, Ichiro Sugai, Masao Chimizu (Daiei)

This elegant film [from the story by Ogai Mori] utilizes 11th-century Japan. It tells the story of a noble mother and her two children who are separated by river pirates. The latter sells the children to a tyrant, and the mother to a brothel. Film builds up a fine, well-ordered story as the children grow up but never forget their mother who tries desperately to escape to them. Legend, adventure and poetry fuse to make this engrossing, if overlong, film material.

Director Kenji Mizoguchi has given this a lacquered, fetching mounting. The big cast is all admirable. Kinuyo Tanaka is superb as the strong but self-effacing mother. Her two children are well played by Yoshiaki Hanayagi as the son and Kyoko Kagawa as the daughter. Lensing has the beauty and plasticity of most Japanese product. Editing is fine.

•

SANSHO THE BAILIFF
SEE: SANSHO DAYU

•

SANTA CLAUS
1985, 112 mins, US Ⓥ ⦿ ▭ col
Dir Jeannot Szwarc ***Prod*** Ilya Salkind, Pierre Spengler ***Scr*** David Newman ***Ph*** Arthur Ibbetson ***Ed*** Peter Hollywood ***Mus*** Henry Mancini ***Art*** Anthony Pratt
Act David Huddleston, Dudley Moore, John Lithgow, Judy Cornwell, Christian Fitzpatrick, Carrie Kei Heim (Salkind/Santa Claus)

Santa Claus is a film for children of all ages, but will probably skew best toward infancy or senility.

Oddly enough, even Scrooge himself might adore the first 20 minutes when *Santa* develops a charming attitude, lovely special effects and a magical feeling that the audience may indeed be settling down for a warm winter's eve.

After that, however, the picture becomes Santa Meets Son of Flubber or something in a mad rush to throw in whatever might appeal to anybody. Bah, humbug.

David Huddleston is a perfect Claus, first introduced several centuries ago as a woodcutter who delights in distributing Christmas gifts to village children. Wondrously, Mr. and Mrs. Claus awake to discover they are at the North Pole, where their arrival is excitedly hailed by elves led by Dudley Moore.

Moore manufactures a batch of bad toys and, sorry to have disappointed Santa, flees to 20th-century New York City, where he ends up working in a crooked toy factory run by John Lithgow, saddled with an absolutely horrible, cigar-sucking performance as a greedy corporate monster.

•

SANTA CLAUSE, THE
1994, 97 mins, US Ⓥ ⦿ col
Dir John Pasquin ***Prod*** Brian Reilly, Jeffrey Silver, Robert Newmyer ***Scr*** Leo Benvenuti, Steve Rudnick ***Ph*** Walt Lloyd ***Ed*** Larry Bock ***Mus*** Michael Convertino ***Art*** Carol Spier
Act Tim Allen, Judge Reinhold, Wendy Crewson, Eric Lloyd, David Krumholtz, Peter Boyle (Outlaw/Hollywood)

The sticky legal question of Disney's holiday movie boils down to the validity of the fine print on Old St. Nick's business card. It states that if you put on the "suit" you're stuck with the reindeer, the cookie-and-milk diet, the suite at the North Pole and, of course, delivering the gifts. That's *The Santa Clause*.

The hapless hero of the piece is ad exec Scott Calvin (Tim Allen), divorced from his wife and doing the split-custody holiday scene with son Charlie (Eric Lloyd). Except this year, a clatter arises from the roof, and when Scott investigates, he startles a red-suited gent who falls with a thud. That's when he passes along his card and Scott reluctantly dons the costume and, with Charlie, climbs aboard the Reindeermobile, grabs the list and goes to work.

When he wakes up the following morning in his suburban bed, he assumes the events of the previous night were all a dream. The humor in the screenplay centers on characters' reactions to the preposterous premise. Laura (Wendy Crewson), the ex-spouse, and her cloying new mate, headshrinker Neal Miller (Judge Reinhold), assume Scott's tall tale is a sort of revenge scenario. They turn the tables and have the court suspend Santa dad's visitation rights.

Director John Pasquin, in his feature debut, has the precarious task of rooting the tale, minimally, in movie reality. While the tyro talent demonstrates no great flair or invention, he does get the job done. This is abetted in no small measure by Allen, who is just as personable and likable on the big screen as he is on the tube.

•

SANTA FE TRAIL
1940, 110 mins, US Ⓥ ⦿ b/w
Dir Michael Curtiz ***Prod*** Hal B. Wallis (exec) ***Scr*** Robert Buckner ***Ph*** Sol Polito ***Ed*** George Amy ***Mus*** Max Steiner ***Art*** John Hughes
Act Errol Flynn, Olivia de Havilland, Raymond Massey, Ronald Reagan, Alan Hale, Van Heflin (Warner)

This is a thrilling saga of hard-bitten U.S. Army officers' fight to wipe out John Brown's marauding crew of Kansas's abolition days.

Newly made army officers learn on their way to the Leavenworth post why John Brown's operations have resulted in the region being known as "bloody" Kansas territory. There's a gunfight, a killing and escape of an abolitionist from the train. The West Pointers find their job cut out for them, two newcomers, Jeb Stuart (Errol Flynn) and George Custer (Ronald Reagan), being assigned to guard a freight caravan. From the bloody encounter they have with Brown and his renegade crew, the whole army troop finally is assigned the task of capturing him, "alive if possible."

Some historians may find fault with the way John Brown is pictured as a fanatic, religious zealot. However, this is tempered, with references to his basic ideas on slavery in U.S. being sound. Often made a villainous character, presence of Rader, his aide, who was kicked out of West Point, softens this because the ex-cadet always is more despicable. Scene where Brown frees the slaves through "the Underground Railroad" also modifies the character. Picture shrewdly does not take sides on the slave issue.

Flynn measures up to his heroic assignment. Olivia de Havilland forsakes pretty clothes for most of this film, sporting cowgirl garb in the scenes about Ft. Leavenworth. Raymond Massey makes the John Brown role the film's outstanding characterization.

•

SAPPHIRE
1959, 92 mins, UK Ⓥ col
Dir Basil Dearden ***Prod*** Michael Relph ***Scr*** Janet Green, Lukas Heller ***Ph*** Harry Waxman ***Ed*** John D. Guthridge ***Mus*** Philip Green ***Art*** Carmen Dillon
Act Nigel Patrick, Yvonne Mitchell, Michael Craig, Paul Massie, Bernard Miles, Earl Cameron (Rank)

Sapphire is a well-knit pic showing how the police patiently track down a murderer. But, though obviously inspired by 1958's outbreak of color-bar riots in London and Nottingham, it ducks the issue, refusing to face boldly up to the problem. It eventually adds up merely to another whodunit.

Victim of a savage murder in a London open space is attractive music student Sapphire (Yvonne Buckingham). The girl is revealed as having a dual personality. As well as being a student, she is also a good-time girl with a love for the bright lights. She is pregnant after an affair with a young man with a brilliant career as architect awaiting him.

Director Basil Dearden has a very effective cast. Nigel Patrick is fine as a suave, polite but ruthlessly efficient cop. Michael Craig, his assistant, is equally good as a less tolerant man who, for some unexplained reason, loathes coloured people. But perhaps the best performance of all is that of Earl Cameron as an intelligent, tolerant Negro doctor who is the brother of the slain girl. Cameron brings immense dignity to a small role.

•

SARABAND
SEE: SARABAND FOR DEAD LOVERS

•

SARABAND FOR DEAD LOVERS
(US: SARABAND)
1948, 96 mins, UK col
Dir Basil Dearden, Michael Relph ***Prod*** Michael Balcon ***Scr*** John Dighton, Alexander Mackendrick ***Ph*** Douglas Slocombe ***Ed*** Michael Truman ***Mus*** Alan Rawsthorne ***Art*** Jim Morahan, William Kellner
Act Stewart Granger, Joan Greenwood, Flora Robson, Francoise Rosay, Anthony Quayle, Frederick Valk (Ealing)

Colorful production, magnificent settings and costumes enhanced by unobtrusive use of Technicolor and a powerful melodramatic story of court intrigue at the House of Hanover in the early 18th century, add up to a first-rate piece of hokum entertainment.

Taken from Helen Simpson's novel, the screenplay sincerely captures the atmosphere of the period. It tells the poignant story of the unhappy Princess Dorothea, compelled to marry against her will the uncouth Prince Louis to strengthen his title to the kingship of England.

Without undue sentiment, and with emotion in the right key, the plot unfolds against the fascinating background of the Hanoverian court, with its intrigue and tragedies, its romances and miseries.

Reality is established by the excellent characterization of a well-chosen cast. Stewart Granger, as the Swedish Count Konigsmark, gives a performance that ranks with his best. Joan Greenwood is charming and colorful as the hapless Dorothea. Flora Robson is merciless as the arch intriguer at the court.

1949: NOMINATION: Best Color Art Direction

•

SARAFINA!

1992, 115 mins, South Africa Ⓥ col

Dir Darrell James Roodt ***Prod*** Anant Singh ***Scr*** William Nicholson, Mbongeni Ngema ***Ph*** Mark Vicente ***Ed*** Peter Hollywood, Sarah Thomas ***Mus*** Stanley Myers ***Art*** David Barkham

Act Leleti Khumalo, Whoopi Goldberg, Miriam Makeba, John Kani, Mbongeni Ngema (Distant Horizon/Ideal)

Opening up *Sarafina!* for the screen has given the popular musical a dimension it never had onstage. Powerfully lensed on location in Soweto, emotionally and politically impassioned piece effectively registers the antiapartheid movement's anger and hope in an infectious musical context, and has been imaginatively reconceived for film.

Mbongeni Ngema's theatrical production, a Broadway hit in 1988, was set principally at the township high school. Institution still serves as the symbolic center of the action.

Pic clicks in as students try to pursue such normal activities as getting an education and putting on a show under the strictures of emergency rule. Inspiring teacher Whoopi Goldberg gives an amusingly apt history lesson, but casting a pall over everything is a firebombing of the school.

The beautiful Sarafina, who idolizes Nelson Mandela, sees a fellow student she may fancy shot dead by police, participates in the rioting following the shooting of more blacks, takes part in the torching of a black officer who works for the whites, and is tortured in prison. Terrific songs by Ngema and Hugh Masekela propel the work at a fine clip and are exceedingly well performed and staged. Technical side of the film matches anything Hollywood could have done with much more money.

•

SARAGOSSA MANUSCRIPT, THE

SEE: REKOPIS ZNALEZIONY W SARAGOSSIE

•

SARATOGA

1937, 90 mins, US b/w

Dir Jack Conway ***Prod*** Bernard H. Hyman, John Emerson ***Scr*** Anita Loos, Robert Hopkins ***Ph*** Ray June ***Ed*** Elmo Veron ***Mus*** Edward Ward ***Art*** Cedric Gibbons, John S. Detlie

Act Jean Harlow, Clark Gable, Lionel Barrymore, Frank Morgan, Walter Pidgeon, Una Merkel (M-G-M)

Saratoga, a story of the thoroughbreds and the men and women who follow the horses around the circuit, is a glamorous comedy-drama which the late Jean Harlow was completing, as co-star with Clark Gable. The few scenes remaining to be made at the time of her death were photographed with an alternate in her part, and done with such skill that audiences will not easily distinguish the substitution.

Anita Loos and Robert Hopkins, who collaborated on *San Francisco*, have gone behind the scenes at racetracks and breeding farms to tell a story of human interest. Gable plays a bookmaker in a breezy, horsey manner. Harlow is the daughter in a family which has bred and raced horses for generations. She takes her small inheritance and wagers on the horses. She is prompted to this in an effort to win enough to repurchase the family breeding farm from Gable, who holds the mortgage to cover losses incurred by her father.

Harlow's performance is among her best. She has several rowdy comedy passages with Gable which are excellently done. The performances of Lionel Barrymore (as the grandfather), Una Merkel (an itinerant follower of the horses), and Frank Morgan (as a turf neophyte) are splendid.

•

SARATOGA TRUNK

1943, 135 mins, US b/w

Dir Sam Wood ***Prod*** Hal B. Wallis ***Scr*** Casey Robinson ***Ph*** Ernest Haller ***Ed*** Ralph Dawson ***Mus*** Max Steiner ***Art*** Joseph St. Amand

Act Gary Cooper, Ingrid Bergman, Flora Robson, Jerry Austin, John Warburton, Florence Bates (Warner)

Story has color, romance, adventure, and not a little s.a. Ingrid Bergman is the beautiful albeit calculating Creole, and Gary Cooper is very effective in the plausible role of a droll, gamblin' Texan who has the romantic hex on the headstrong Creole. Flora Robson is capitally cast as her body-servant and Jerry Austin does a bang-up job as the dwarf who, with the mulatto servant, make a strange entourage.

The 1875 period, and the New Orleans and Saratoga locales, combine into a moving story [from Edna Ferber's novel] as Bergman returns from Paris to avenge her mother's "shame." That this is a spurious sentimentality, considering she was born out of wedlock, and her father's family sought to banish her virtually to France, is beside the point. Bergman, as fetching in a brunette wig as in her natural lighter tresses, takes command in every scene. She sparks the cinematurgy, a vital plus factor considering Cooper's laconic personation, and the sultry reticence of her two curious servants.

The two major geographical segments—her native New Orleans and the fertile Saratoga—are replete with basic action and never pall.

1946: NOMINATION: Best Supp. Actress (Flora Robson)

•

SASAME YUKI
(THE MAKIOKA SISTERS)

1983, 140 mins, Japan Ⓥ col

Dir Kon Ichikawa ***Prod*** Tomoyuki Tanaka ***Scr*** Shinya Hidaka, Kon Ichikawa ***Ph*** Kiyoshi Hasegawa ***Ed*** Chizuko Nagata ***Mus*** Shinosuke Okawa ***Art*** Shinobu Muraki

Act Keiko Kishi, Yoshiko Sakuma, Sayuri Yoshinaga, Yuko Kotegawa, Juzo Itami, Koji Ishizaka (Toho)

Kon Ichikawa's *The Makioka Sisters* is based on one of the classics of Japanese literature by the celebrated writer Junichiro Tanizaki. This is a rambling family epic along the lines of Booth Tarkington's *The Magnificent Ambersons* and John Galsworthy's *The Forsyte Saga*. It makes for an elegant view of life in Japan a half-century ago.

A wealthy Osaka family, the Makiokas, owe their social standing to their recently deceased father. He has four daughters, two of them now married. The oldest, Tsuruko, is the legal heir, but of nothing to speak of save the home. The second oldest, Sachiko, is married to a salesman in a department store. It's at their modest home that the two younger sisters, Yukiko and Taeko, still unmarried, prefer to live.

The husband of Sachiko falls in love with the gentle, retiring Yukiko. Eventually, however, Yukiko finds a suitor she likes. But that, too, is complicated by the youngest falling in love with a poor and lowly bartender.

There is rich opportunity for ensemble acting—and it's here to perfection in Ichikawa's hands. Another aspect is the show of costumes, the compositional images of interiors of homes, and the catalog of emotions associated with Japanese manners—in other words, a certain reflection of a particular time and place in a not too distant past.

•

SASOM I EN SPEGEL
(THROUGH A GLASS DARKLY)

1961, 89 mins, Sweden Ⓥ b/w

Dir Ingmar Bergman ***Scr*** Ingmar Bergman ***Ph*** Sven Nykvist ***Ed*** Ulla Ryghe ***Mus*** Erik Nordgren ***Art*** P. A. Lundgren

Act Harriet Andersson, Gunnar Bjornstrand, Max von Sydow, Lars Passgard (Svensk Filmindustri)

Ingmar Bergman tells a story that is in many ways reminiscent of *Long Day's Journey Into Night*. Pic deals with four members of a family who are estranged through their inability to express feelings for each other. The action is limited to 24 hours. The time is the nightless Scandinavian summer and the setting is an isolated island in the Baltic. Not a pleasant film, it is a great one.

Main character is Karin (Harriet Andersson), who is suffering from a mental ailment. Released from a mental institution, she seeks the security of her childhood, the love of her father, David (Gunnar Bjornstrand), and her 17-year-old brother, Fredrick (Lars Passgard). She turns more and more away from her husband Martin (Max von Sydow), a doctor and instructor at a medical school.

In a boat for a day of fishing, Karin and her brother confide inner secrets to one another. The day of youthful fun-making comes to a tragic end when Karin madly seduces her brother.

The Bergman message comes at the end when David speaks personally to his son that he believes: "God exists in love, in every sort of love, maybe God is love."

1961: Best Foreign Language Film

•

SATAN BUG, THE

1965, 114 mins, US Ⓥ ⦿ ▭ col

Dir John Sturges ***Prod*** John Sturges ***Scr*** James Clavell, Edward Anhalt ***Ph*** Robert Surtees ***Ed*** Ferris Webster ***Mus*** Jerry Goldsmith ***Art*** Herman Blumenthal

Act George Maharis, Richard Basehart, Anne Francis, Dana Andrews, John Larkin, Richard Bull (Mirisch-Kappa)

The Satan Bug is a superior suspense melodrama and should keep audiences on the edge of their seats despite certain unexplained, confusing elements which tend to make plot at times difficult to follow.

Based on a novel by Ian Stuart (nom de plume for Britisher Alistair MacLean), producer-director John Sturges builds his action to a generally chilling pace after a needlessly slow opening which establishes America's experiments in bacteriological warfare at a highly secret top-security research installation in the desert. The scientist who develops the deadly virus known as the Satan Bug, so lethal it can cause instant death over great areas, is murdered and flasks containing the liquid mysteriously spirited out of the lab.

Script projects George Maharis as a former Army Intelligence officer recalled to find the virus before it can be put to the use threatened by a millionaire paranoiac who masterminded the theft and claims to hate war.

Maharis makes a good impression as the investigator, although his character isn't developed sufficiently due to overspeedy editing.

•

SATAN MET A LADY

1936, 74 mins, US Ⓥ b/w

Dir William Dieterle ***Scr*** Brown Holmes ***Ph*** Arthur Edeson ***Ed*** Warren Low ***Art*** Max Parker

Act Bette Davis, Warren William, Alison Skipworth, Arthur Treacher, Winifred Shaw, Marie Wilson (Warner)

This is an inferior remake of *The Maltese Falcon*, which Warner produced in 1931. Many changes have been made [to the novel by Dashiell Hammett], in story structure as well as title, but none is an improvement.

Bette Davis is dropped to featured billing rank in this one, on an equal basis with Warren William, and both under the title. But as for importance in the story, Davis has much less to do than at least one other femme member of the cast.

Where the detective of *Maltese Falcon* and his activities were natural and amusing, he and his satiric crime detection are now forced and unnatural.

Among items changed are the names of the characters as well as a few of the characters themselves. Sam Spade, played by Ricardo Cortez in the original, is now Ted Shane as played by Warren William. The plaster bird is now a ram's horn. There's hardly any mystery in this version. The comedy isn't strong enough to fill the bill.

William tries hard to be gay as the eccentric private cop and his performance is all that keeps the picture moving in many lagging moments. Marie Wilson has a tendency to muff her best chances through overstressing.

•

SATAN NEVER SLEEPS
(UK: THE DEVIL NEVER SLEEPS)

1962, 133 mins, US ▭ col

Dir Leo McCarey ***Prod*** Leo McCarey ***Scr*** Claude Binyon, Leo McCarey ***Ph*** Oswald Morris ***Ed*** Gordon Pilkington ***Mus*** Richard Rodney Bennett ***Art*** Tom Morahan

Act William Holden, Clifton Webb, France Nuyen, Athene Seyler, Martin Benson, Weaver Lee (20th Century-Fox)

China in its critical year of 1949 is the setting of the screenplay, from a novel by Pearl S. Buck. Cornered in this moment of imminent national alteration to Communism are two Catholic priests, played by Clifton Webb and William Holden, the latter adoringly but hopelessly pursued by a Chinese maiden (France Nuyen). The priests are soon imprisoned by the local People's Party leader (Weaver Lee), who also rapes the girl.

Lee eventually see the light when: (1) Nuyen gives birth to his child, (2) his parents are murdered by the Reds, (3) he is reprimanded and demoted for personal ambition and leniency. More occurs in the final 15 minutes of this picture than in the preceding 118.

Holden is a kind of leather-jacketed variation of Bing Crosby's sweatshirted Father O'Malley and Webb a wry, caustic version of Barry Fitzgerald's Father Fitzgibbon in Leo McCarey's *Going My Way* (1944). Nuyen plays vivaciously as the sweet nuisance. The villains are absurdly all black. Outdoor locations in England and Wales pass acceptably for China.

•

SATURDAY NIGHT AND SUNDAY MORNING

1960, 89 mins, UK Ⓥ ⦿ b/w

Dir Karel Reisz ***Prod*** Tony Richardson, Harry Saltzman ***Scr*** Alan Sillitoe ***Ph*** Freddie Francis ***Ed*** Seth Holt ***Mus*** Johnny Dankworth

Act Albert Finney, Shirley Anne Field, Rachel Roberts, Hylda Baker, Norman Rossington, Bryan Pringle (Woodfall/Bryanston)

Alan Sillitoe's novel is produced, directed and acted with integrity and insight. This is a good, absorbing but not very likeable film. The hero is a Nottingham factory worker who refuses to conform. He hates all authority but protests so blunderingly. His attitude is simple: "What I want is a good time. The remainder is all propaganda." Through the week he works hard at his lathe. In his spare time—Saturday night and Sunday morning (and a couple of evenings)—he comes into his own. Liquor and women.

Sillitoe does a good job with his first screenplay, though, necessarily, much of the motive and the thinking of his characters has been lost in the adaptation. Director Karel Reisz's experience in documentaries enables him to bring a sharp tang and authenticity to the film. The locations and the interiors have caught the full atmosphere of a Midland industrial town.

The central figure is cocky, violent and selfish, yet at times almost pathetically likeable. Albert Finney, in his first major screen performance, handles scenes of belligerence and one or two love scenes with complete confidence and is equally effective in quieter moments. On a par is the performance of Rachel Roberts as the married woman carrying on a hopeless affair with Finney. Shirley Anne Field, as the conventional young woman who eventually snares Finney, is appropriately pert.

•

SATURDAY NIGHT FEVER

1977, 119 mins, US Ⓥ ⦿ col

Dir John Badham ***Prod*** Robert Stigwood ***Scr*** Norman Wexler ***Ph*** Ralph D. Bode ***Ed*** David Rawlins ***Mus*** David Shire (adapt.) ***Art*** Charles Bailey

Act John Travolta, Karen Lynn Gorney, Barry Miller, Joseph Cali, Paul Pape, Bruce Ornstein (Paramount)

John Travolta stars as an amiably inarticulate N.Y. kid who comes to life only in a disco environment. The clumsy story lurches forward through predictable travail and treacle, separated by phonograph records (or vice versa). John Badham's direction is awkward.

Coloring-book plotlines [based on a story by Nik Cohn] give Travolta a bad homelife (Val Bisoglio's father is an ethnic horror story), a formula gang of buddies, an available "bad" girl (Donna Pescow), an elusive "good" girl (Karen Lynn Gorney), plus lots of opportunity to boogie on the dance floor and make out in automobile backseats. [Musical numbers choreographed by Lester Wilson.]

Between original music by Barry, Robin and Maurice Gibb plus David Shire, and familiar platter hits, the film usually has some rhythm going on in the background.

1977: NOMINATION: Best Actor (John Travolta)

•

SATURDAY NIGHT OUT

1964, 96 mins, UK b/w

Dir Robert Hartford-Davis ***Prod*** Robert Hartford-Davis ***Scr*** Donald Ford, Derek Ford ***Ph*** Peter Newbrook ***Ed*** Alastair McIntyre ***Mus*** Robert Richards ***Art*** Peter Proud

Act Heather Sears, Bernard Lee, Erica Remberg, Colin Campbell, Francesca Annis, Inigo Jackson (Compton Tekli)

Robert Hartford-Davis is a sound director, but *Saturday Night Out* falls apart mainly because of poor, undistinguished dialog and predictable situations. Several sailors in the Merchant Navy descend on London with 15 hours' shore leave and the film depicts their brief adventures. Since most of the folks involved are concerned mainly with the delights of dames and drink, the results are predictable and the gals-and-guzzle routine palls.

Astute businessman George Hunter (Bernard Lee) turns the tables on a blackmailing dame (Erica Remberg) and her cameraman "business partner"; seaman David Lodge makes a beeline for his regular London dockside popsy and spends the 15 hours with her; another (Inigo Jackson) gets crocked and clipped in a sleazy Soho drinking club, while his naive young pal gets involved with a young girl for whom he jumps ship to marry, John Bonney is picked up by an incredible beatnik girl (Heather Sears) and also falls in love somewhat incredibly.

None of these incidents provides ultra bite or excitement, though the Bernard Lee–Erica Remberg blackmailing affair has a mildly neat twist. Worst anecdote is also, regrettably, the longest, that in which Jackson makes a fool of himself in the drinking club.

Hartford-Davis has done a routine but uninspired job as director and producer. Perhaps the greatest disappointment in the film is the appearance of Sears, after a longish layoff, in a role which gives poor scope for her talent.

•

SATURDAY'S CHILDREN

1940, 97 mins, US b/w

Dir Vincent Sherman ***Prod*** Hal B. Wallis (exec) ***Scr*** Julius J. Epstein, Philip G. Epstein ***Ph*** James Wong Howe ***Ed*** Owen Marks ***Mus*** Adolph Deutsch ***Art*** Hugh Reticker

Act John Garfield, Anne Shirley, Claude Rains, Roscoe Karns, Lee Patrick, Dennie Moore (Warner)

Saturday's Children, Warner's latest remake of Maxwell Anderson's play of the '20s, still is good as human drama with comedy sidelights. Basic plot varies from Anderson's play, but still retains essential ingredients of youthful romance and young couple's tour through financial straits and marital difficulties which sends them to the verge of separation.

John Garfield delivers impressively as Rims Rosson, a slow-thinking youth who devises impractical inventions and is tricked into marriage. Anne Shirley is excellent as Bobby Halevy, the romantic girl and wife. This is the role, originally assigned to Jane Bryant, who reneged and retired when married, which was responsible for contract suspension of Olivia de Havilland by Warners on refusal to assume it, and resulted in an undisclosed newcomer being replaced by Shirley after an unsatisfactory two reels were shot.

Claude Rains is strong in the support as girl's plodding and sympathetically understanding father.

Story tells romance of Garfield and Shirley, with latter forcing the marriage proposal on eve of his departure for a big opportunity in the Philippines. Couple soon find the marital struggle tough when she loses her job and his income is inadequate. Script by the Epstein brothers develops story at a fast pace.

•

SATURN 3

1980, 88 mins, UK Ⓥ ⦿ col

Dir Stanley Donen ***Prod*** Stanley Donen ***Scr*** Martin Amis ***Ph*** Billy Williams ***Ed*** Richard Marden ***Mus*** Elmer Bernstein ***Art*** Stuart Craig

Act Farrah Fawcett, Kirk Douglas, Harvey Keitel, Ed Bishop, Douglas Lambert (Grade-Kastner)

Somewhere in deepest, darkest space, Kirk Douglas and Farrah Fawcett jog around through a space station that looks suspiciously like Bloomingdale's after closing. The pair are scientists doing important work, when bad guy Harvey Keitel shows up.

Douglas is sprightly, but he has to handle some pretty awful lines in this Martin Amis script [from a story by John Barry]. Keitel's dialog, if quoted, would be on a par.

Life goes on in this shopping mall of lights till Keitel builds Hector, the mad robot, whose tubes and hubcaps develop goose bumps for Farrah. Best scene in the entire effort is Hector's resurrection after he has been dismantled for being randy. The parts find each other and reconnect, which is more than this film does.

•

SATYRICON
(AKA: FELLINI–SATYRICON)

1969, 138 mins, Italy/France Ⓥ ⦿ col

Dir Federico Fellini ***Prod*** Alberto Grimaldi ***Scr*** Federico Fellini, Bernardino Zapponi, Brunello Rondi ***Ph*** Giuseppe Rotunno ***Ed*** Ruggero Mastroianni ***Mus*** Nino Rota, Ilhan Mimaroglu, Tod Dockstader, Andrew Rudin ***Art*** Danilo Donati, Luigi Scaccianoce

Act Martin Potter, Hiram Keller, Max Born, Capucine, Alain Cuny, Lucia Bose (PEA/Artistes Associes)

Federico Fellini presents an incredible fresco-like vision of Rome's social structure 2,000 years ago in which survival and pleasure were man's sole motivating forces. The $3 million film is as loosely segmented as the original classic Latin satire by Petronius. Fellini and his script collaborators adapted what they wanted from the surviving fragments of the original work and nibbled on other ancient legends and writings—or fictionalized—to complete.

The adventures of two young student vagabonds Encolpio (Martin Potter) and Ascilto (Hiram Keller)—both infatuated with a young boy, Gitone (Max Born)—constitute the bare continuity for a hallucinating view of Roman life.

Big sequence (overlength) is the phantasmagorical banquet of wealthy captain of commerce Trimalchio (Mari Romagnoli) also attended by Encolpio and his poet protector Eumolpus (Salvo Randone). Encolpio is then enslaved aboard ship of Tryphaena (Capucine) and her husband Lichas (Alain Cuny). After escaping to the mainland, Encolpio later finds himself in a labyrinth combatting a Minotaur. His life is spared and he is turned over to insatiable Ariadne, but is shattered to discover a sudden, mysterious impotence.

Pic is Fellini's break with the autobiographical in filmmaking. Dialogue in Italian is static and weighs on this vividly visual fresco. Here and there, footage needs explanation or definition.

Danilo Donati's production design and sets, set dressing and costumes are of award quality. Makeup is also brilliantly innovated by Rino Carbone. Potter and Keller acquit themselves in a difficult debut when the film is at its spectacular height during the first hour.

•

SAVAGE, THE

1953, 95 mins, US col

Dir George Marshall ***Prod*** Mel Epstein ***Scr*** Sydney Boehm ***Ph*** John F. Seitz ***Ed*** Arthur Schmidt ***Mus*** Paul Sawtell ***Art*** Hal Pereira, William Flannery

Act Charlton Heston, Susan Morrow, Peter Hanson, Joan Taylor, Richard Rober, Donald Porter (Paramount)

This tale of Indian fighting travels in fairly devious circles to relate a standard story [from a novel by L. L. Foreman]. However, it has excellent outdoor photography and liberal amounts of Indian fighting scenes.

Charlton Heston has a fairly confused role which forces the story to travel unnecessarily in circles. He plays Warbonnet, a white lad who has been brought up as an Indian following the massacre of his father by Crow Indians. Living with a tribe in the Sioux confederation, Heston knows how to knock off a Crow scalp, but his major problem comes when he has to choose on which side he'll fight in the impending war between the paleface and the Indians.

The femme interest is slight, with Susan Morrow as the belle of the army fort. Joan Taylor as an Indian maid is Morrow's major competition for Heston's affection.

Peter Hanson and Richard Rober do well in major white roles while Indians are staunchly portrayed by Ian MacDonald and Donald Porter. One of the more colorful enactments is by Milburn Stone as a corporal who befriends Heston.

•

SAVAGE EYE, THE

1959, 68 mins, US b/w

Dir Ben Maddow, Sidney Meyers, Joseph Strick ***Prod*** Edward Harrison ***Ph*** Jack Couffer, Helen Leavitt, Haskell Wexler ***Mus*** Leonard Rosenman

Act Barbara Baxley, Herschel Bernardi, Jean Hidey, Elizabeth Zemach (City)

Fascinating and uncompromising semi-documentary impressively put together as an obvious labor of love by three talented American filmmakers.

Story of a divorced woman's attempts to readjust to a single life affords an excellent opportunity to dissect some frightening and depressing panoramas of modern existence. From the woman's first arrival at a big-city airport (site of most of shooting is Los Angeles, but no effort has been made to establish a specific locale), pic moves into her first visual impressions of the city, its seamy side, its bars and drunks, its beauty parlors lined with elderly women, its store windows, and above all, its people.

Subsequent portions of the film feature, among other things, the detailed horror of a nose-bobbing operation, the bloodthirsty behaviour of men and women at boxing and wrestling matches, a detailed and critically observed striptease sequence, complete with leering spectators, a cruelly fascinating sequence shot during a faith-healing service, and a harrowing and nightmarish bit depicting a pervert's party.

Wealth of material is linked by presence of the key character, caught on her search for warmth and companionship, and by a spoken commentary (well-mouthed by Gary Merrill) in the form of a dialog between the woman and an imaginary poet.

Footage, shot over a span of several years, boasts much expertly and realistically photographed (some of it hidden-camera) material. It's slickly integrated and matched with recreated sequences to bring about a true-looking patina.

•

SAVAGE INNOCENTS, THE

1960, 111 mins, UK/Italy/US Ⓥ ▭ col

Dir Nicholas Ray ***Prod*** Joseph Janni, Maleno Malenotti ***Scr*** Nicholas Ray ***Ph*** Aldo Tonti, Peter Hennessy ***Ed*** Ralph Kemplen ***Mus*** Angelo Francesco Lavagnino ***Art*** Don Ashton

Act Anthony Quinn, Yoko Tani, Marie Jang, Francis De Wolff, Carlo Justini, Peter O'Toole (Rank/Appia/Paramount)

The Savage Innocents is a polyglot pic. Financial responsibility was carved up between Britain, America and Italy. Rank chipped in with a third of the $1.5 million budget and Pinewood studios and British technicians were used; Italy, through producer Maleno Malenotti, has a third stake; America (Paramount release) supplied the remainder. There's a Yank director and screenplay writer, Nicholas Ray; America's Anthony Quinn is the main star, while the [Japanese] femme lead Yoko Tani comes from Paris.

Remainder of the cast is drawn from various countries. Shooting, apart from Pinewood, took place in Hudson Bay and Greenland. Somewhere along the line Denmark gets an honorable mention among the credits.

Two undeniable things stand out. Art director and editor have done a standout job in matching and cutting so that it is virtually impossible to decide where Pinewood began and Canada came in. Secondly, the chief lensers have turned out some brilliant camerawork with color sweeping superbly across the widescreen.

The problem is whether the yarn [based on Hans Ruesch's novel *Top of the World*] stands up. For long sessions it is a documentary of life in the Eskimo belt. The story line is simple. It concerns a powerful, good-humored hunter (Quinn) who spends the early stages of the film deciding which of two young women he wishes to make his wife. Second half becomes melodrama when he accidentally murders a missionary.

The memorable moments are those of Quinn hunting down foxes, bears, seals, walruses and the majesty of the bleak wastes, the ice, the storms and primitive living conditions. The human element doesn't come out of it quite so well.

Quinn, mainly talking pidgin English-cum-Eskimo, comes out as an authentic Eskimo. Tani is a delight as the woman. Peter O'Toole is first-rate as a tough trooper.

•

SAVAGE MESSIAH
1972, 100 mins, UK col
Dir Ken Russell ***Prod*** Ken Russell ***Scr*** Christopher Logue ***Ph*** Dick Bush ***Ed*** Michael Bradsell ***Mus*** Michael Garrett ***Art*** George Lack, Derek Jarman
Act Dorothy Tutin, Scott Antony, Helen Mirren, Lindsay Kemp, Michael Gough, John Justin (Russfilm/M-G-M)

Offbeat in subject matter (the platonic yet deeply affectionate love of an extrovert young French sculptor, Henri Gaudier, for an introverted older woman, set early in this century) pic is distinctively Russellian in treatment as well, showing that the British director has lost none of his filmic impudence.

Not unexpectedly played with most stops out, and soundtrack decibels at upper limits, a potentially introverted tale [from H. S. Ede's book] is instead played broadly and with considerable panache, especially in having the artist portrayed as a physically strong and agile extrovert, and young to boot. A virtual unknown in his first pic role, Scott Antony rises beautifully to the challenge.

More expected, but enjoyable nevertheless, is Dorothy Tutin's astute and measured delivery as the object of the sculptor's affection, a would-be writer whose somber reasoning acts as counterpoint to his ebullience, while lending him inner strength. Helen Mirren is eye-filling and able as a women's lib type (and, incongruously, improvised full-frontal nude model as well), while a number of backdrop roles are colorfully filled by a large back-up cast.

As usual, there's more style than warmth in Russell's character relationships. It is only at the end, when one is brought up sharply by the (true-to-life) news of the sculptor's precocious demise, aged 23, in a World War II battle that some deep-down feeling comes into play.

•

SAVAGES
1972, 105 mins, US Ⓥ col
Dir James Ivory ***Prod*** Ismail Merchant ***Scr*** James Ivory, George Swift Trow, Michael O'Donoghue ***Ph*** Walter Lassally ***Ed*** Kent McKinney ***Mus*** Joe Raposo ***Art*** Charles E. White III, Michael Doret
Act Louis J. Stadlen, Anne Francine, Thayer David, Susan Blakely, Russ Thacker, Salome Jens (Angelika/Merchant-Ivory)

Savages, first U.S. film by producer Ismail Merchant and director James Ivory, is about members of a primitive tribe who are lured by the appearance of a rolling croquet ball to an old deserted mansion where they dress in clothes and take on "civilized" societal behavior, only to return to the forest and their primitive behavior the following morning.

The playing has flair and grace, sans woodenness from everyone, with Walter Lassally's excellently balanced b&w lensing for the primitive days and color for the so-called civilized times a great asset, as are the editing and music. The only carp might be a tendency to overplay an act.

But no denying an almost hypnotic charm and fascination in this offbeat, insouciant look at mankind and his climb to civilization and fall.

•

SAVAGE STREETS
1984, 93 mins, US Ⓥ ⊙ col
Dir Danny Steinmann ***Prod*** John C. Strong III ***Scr*** Norman Yonemoto, Danny Steinmann ***Ph*** Stephen Posey ***Ed*** Bruce Stubblefield, John O'Conner ***Mus*** Michael Lloyd, John D'Andrea ***Art*** Ninkey Dalton
Act Linda Blair, John Vernon, Robert Dryer, Johnny Venocur, Sal Landi, Scott Mayer (Savage Street)

Linda Blair toplines as Brenda, an L.A. girl who turns vigilante when her mute younger sister Heather (Linnea Quigley) is brutally gang-raped by a local gang of toughs.

Pic unfolds as a tough update of the juvenile delinquency B-pictures of the 1950s, incorporating ineffectual adult authorities (John Vernon as the hard-nosed but powerless high school principal), warring groups of dislikeable good kids and gangs of punks.

The uncensored approach pays off in deliciously vulgar dialog and well-directed confrontation scenes.

Blair emerges here as a tawdry, delightfully trashy sweater girl in a league with 1950s B-heroines such as Beverly Michaels, Juli Reding and Mamie Van Doren.

•

SAVE THE TIGER
1973, 99 mins, US Ⓥ ⊙ col
Dir John G. Avildsen ***Prod*** Steve Shagan ***Scr*** Steve Shagan ***Ph*** Jim Crabe ***Ed*** David Bretherton ***Mus*** Marvin Hamlisch ***Art*** Jack Collis
Act Jack Lemmon, Jack Gilford, Laurie Heineman, Normann Burton, Patricia Smith, Thayer David (Filmways)

Save the Tiger is an intellectual exploitation film which ostensibly lays bare the crass materialism of the age. Producer-writer Steve Shagan's script stars Jack Lemmon in an offbeat casting as a pitiable businessman trapped in his own lifestyle.

Partnered with Jack Gilford in the garment business, Lemmon finds his finances so strapped that he decides to hire a professional arsonist to have what used to be called "a successful fire" in one of his factories. This trauma occurs on fashion-show day, when lecherous out-of-town buyer Norman Burton demands some call-girl kinkiness and has a coronary attack.

The closest thing to a point of reference is in Gilford's character, who, after the successful fashion line showing, berates Lemmon's ethics. Latter makes a facile comeback, thereby returning the plot to its free-form, floating exploitation of seaminess.

There is a lot of mature, untapped ability on display in Lemmon's performance. Gilford delivers an outstanding performance, beyond the fact that his is the sole voice of sanity. Patricia Smith is excellent as Lemmon's wife.

1973: Best Actor (Jack Lemmon)

NOMINATIONS: Best Supp. Actor (Jack Gilford), Original Story & Screenplay

•

SAVING GRACE
1986, 112 mins, US Ⓥ ⊙ ▭ col
Dir Robert M. Young ***Prod*** Herbert F. Solow ***Scr*** David S. Ward ***Ph*** Reynaldo Villalobos ***Art*** Giovanni Natalucci
Act Tom Conti, Fernando Rey, Erland Josephson, Giancarlo Giannini, Donald Hewlett, Angelo Evans (Embassy)

This may be the first comedy ever about a Pope running away from office—for a short, private spree in the country among the real people whose shepherd he is supposed to be, sans the bureaucratic interference of the Vatican hierarchy.

Tom Conti may be a little young and literally too light on his feet to play a pope, but he is too good an actor not to make the best of it, eliciting lots of personal sympathy even when not quite convincing as a High Pontiff.

Fernando Rey, Erland Josephson and Donald Hewlett are an amusing trio of Cardinals covering for their boss in his absence. Giancarlo Giannini is effective as a mysterious goatherd of few words, and Angelo Evans displays plenty of vitality as a tough-acting kid with a good heart.

•

SAVING GRACE
2000, 94 mins, UK Ⓥ ⊙ ▭
Dir Nigel Cole ***Prod*** Mark Crowdy ***Scr*** Craig Ferguson, Mark Crowdy ***Ph*** John de Borman ***Ed*** Alan Strachan ***Mus*** Mark Russell ***Art*** Eve Stewart
Act Brenda Blethyn, Craig Ferguson, Martin Clunes, Tcheky Karyo, Jamie Forman, Bill Bailey (Homerun/Portman)

A spiritedly daft and droll gem of straight-faced lunacy, *Saving Grace* harvests a bumper crop of laughs from a plot revolving around a most unlikely marijuana farmer. Brenda Blethyn stars to perfection as Grace Trevethan, a cheery housewife and amateur horticulturist in a tiny town on the Cornish coast. Grace gets bad news from her solicitor: Her late husband amassed huge debts and, if she doesn't raise £300,000 ASAP, she stands to lose her lovely manor to creditors. So Grace is atypically receptive when Matthew (Craig Ferguson), her Scottish gardener, requests a touch of her green thumb as he raises some cannabis for private consumption. Together, the matron and the young Scotsman hatch a bold scheme to convert her orchid hothouse into an indoor marijuana farm.

Naturally, scads of other townspeople—including the local doctor (Martin Clunes), who's known to take a toke now and then—wise up to what's going on. Nicky (Valerie Edmond), Matthew's beautiful girlfriend, voices strong disapproval—and not just because she's pregnant with his child. But all of the other knowledgeable locals look the other way, except when they're admiring the dazzling light show provided nightly by Grace's illuminated hothouse.

The witty script provides a sufficient number of plot complications to keep things lively. Modest suspense is generated by the inquiries of a local constable (Ken Campbell), who's not as thick-witted as he seems, and the introduction of a French drug lord (Tcheky Karyo) who may not be as violent as he claims. Even so, *Saving Grace* is more character-driven than plot-propelled. The pic is generously sprinkled with off-the-wall eccentricities, and many of the funniest moments have nothing to do with the nominal story line. A pub owner and a patron debate the relative merits of Franz Kafka and Jackie Collins. The local vicar takes an unholy delight in late-night telecasts of Hammer horror pics. Two staid shopkeepers get blissfully, babblingly high when they inadvertently sample Grace's home-grown product. And the French drug lord (a nice piece of self-mockery by Karyo) takes inordinate pride in making a bad impression.

•

SAVING PRIVATE RYAN
1998, 169 mins, US Ⓥ ⊙ col
Dir Steven Spielberg ***Prod*** Steven Spielberg, Ian Bryce, Mark Gordon, Gary Levinsohn ***Scr*** Robert Rodat ***Ph*** Janusz Kaminski ***Ed*** Michael Kahn ***Mus*** John Williams ***Art*** Tom Sanders
Act Tom Hanks, Edward Burns, Tom Sizemore, Adam Goldberg, Matt Damon, Dennis Farina (Amblin/DreamWorks/Paramount)

Steven Spielberg's third World War II drama is a vivid, realistic and bloody portrait of armed conflict, as well as a generally effective intimate drama about a handful of men on a mission of debatable value in the middle of the war's decisive action.

Pic drops the audience onto a U.S. landing craft getting ready to unload the first GIs to hit the beach on June 6, 1944. Capt. John Miller (Tom Hanks) and his squad—Sgt. Horvath (Tom Sizemore), Pvts. Reiben (Edward Burns), Jackson (Barry Pepper), Mellish (Adam Goldberg) and Caparzo (Vin Diesel) and Medic Wade (Giovanni Ribisi)—painstakingly make it past the many obstacles and are finally able to take one of the enemy's concrete pillboxes on top of the bluff.

Nonstop action lasts 24 minutes, and every one of them is infinitely more intense than anything in the standard work on D-Day, *The Longest Day*.

But no sooner have Capt. Miller and his men paused for a smoke than they are ordered to try to locate a certain private, James Ryan, who parachuted into France the night before. The reason: his three brothers have all recently been killed in combat, and government policy dictates that he should return home lest his family be deprived of all its male offspring.

Robert Rodat's original screenplay thus transforms to a mission format. Even if its thematic elements are not as richly developed as they might be, and the story itself is somewhat irksome in its far-fetched, even contrived nature, the film packs a heavy emotional punch at many moments, as the tenuousness of life and the abruptness of loss assert themselves.

Cinematographer Janusz Kaminski has desaturated the color in a way that emphasizes the pale greens of the uniforms and landscapes, blue-grays of the water and skies, and flesh tones; in this context, the red of the blood always jumps out. Frequent handheld shots add to the intimacy and impact, while a shuttering device makes some of the action appears a bit jumpy, even pixilated.

•

SAY ANYTHING . . .
1989, 100 mins, US Ⓥ ⊙ col
Dir Cameron Crowe ***Prod*** Polly Platt ***Scr*** Cameron Crowe ***Ph*** Laszlo Kovacs ***Ed*** Richard Marks ***Mus*** Richard Gibbs, Anne Dudley, Nancy Wilson ***Art*** Mark Mansbridge

Act John Cusack, Ione Skye, John Mahoney, Lili Taylor, Amy Brooks, Lois Chiles (20th Century-Fox/Gracie)

Say Anything . . . is a half-baked love story, full of good intentions but uneven in the telling. Appealing tale of an undirected army brat proving himself worthy of the most exceptional girl in high school elicits a few laughs, plenty of smiles and some genuine feeling.

On the eve of high school graduation, bright but unremarkable student John Cusack decides he's just got to go out with "Miss Priss" (Ione Skye). Skye is doted upon by her divorced father (John Mahoney) and is headed for studies in England on a fellowship.

Cusack, who bunks with his nephew and sister (an unbilled appearance by real-life sister Joan Cusack), starts a friendship that slowly grows into something more. Conflict rears its head in a conventional way when Skye becomes torn between leaving for England and staying with her boyfriend.

Cusack and Skye's relationship develops nicely and believably, but Crowe has not written an entirely convincing character for the latter to play. Pic also has considerable structural problems, as many scenes feel unachieved.

Lois Chiles (unbilled) plays a scene as Skye's mother, and Eric Stoltz pops up briefly at a teen party.

•

SAY IT WITH SONGS
1929, 93 mins, US b/w
Dir Lloyd Bacon *Scr* Joe Jackson
Act Al Jolson, Davey Lee, Marian Nixon, Holmes Herbert, Fred Kohler, John Bowers (Warner)

With Al Jolson, *Say It with Songs* is a marked advancement for him as a screen player. It far overshadows *The Jazz Singer* or *The Singing Fool* in that respect.

Jolson is happily cast as a radio singer. Again the story [by Darryl F. Zanuck and Harvey Gates] has him married with a son, the same Davey Lee. Jolson, the kid, and Marian Nixon, as the wife and mother, are the picture.

The station announcer tries to make Marian Nixon. He is Jolson's best friend in the film. So that night while driving with the announcer toward the station, the radio singer lets him have it. The blow that does the trick sends the announcer against a stone cornice, and the husband-father gets life for manslaughter.

Al sings seven songs in all, four by DeSylva, Brown and Henderson. Much of the smoothness of the running is due to the direction by Lloyd Bacon. Nixon looks nice, in not a brilliant role.

•

SAYONARA
1957, 147 mins, US Ⓥ ⦿ ▭ col
Dir Joshua Logan *Prod* William Goetz *Scr* Paul Osborn *Ph* Ellsworth Fredricks *Ed* Arthur P. Schmidt, Philip W. Anderson *Mus* Franz Waxman *Art* Ted Haworth
Act Marlon Brando, Red Buttons, Ricardo Montalban, Patricia Owens, James Garner, Martha Scott (Warner)

Sayonara, based on the James A. Michener novel, is a picture of beauty and sensitivity. Amidst the tenderness and the tensions of a romantic drama, it puts across the notion that human relations transcend race barriers. Joshua Logan's direction is tops.

Though strongly supported, particularly by Red Buttons, it's Marlon Brando who carries the production. As Major Gruver, the Korean war air ace, Brando affects a nonchalant Southern drawl that helps set the character from the very start. He is wholly convincing as the race-conscious Southerner whose humanity finally leads him to rebel against army-imposed prejudice.

Story has combat-fatigued Brando transferred [in 1951] to Kobe for a rest and to meet his Stateside sweetheart (Patricia Owens), daughter of the commanding general of the area. They find things have changed and the sensitive, well-educated girl is no longer sure she wants to marry Brando. He in turn is upset because Airman Joe Kelly, played by Buttons, wants to marry a Japanese (Miyoshi Umeki).

Brando meets a beautiful Japanese actress-dancer (Miiko Taka) and gradually falls deeply in love with her. When Buttons and his wife, in desperation, commit suicide, Brando realizes that, regardless of the consequences, he must marry Taka.

Taka plays the proud Hana-ogi, the dedicated dancer, who starts by hating the Americans whom she sees as robbing Japan of its culture and ends in Brando's arms. Apart from being beautiful she's also a distinctive personality and her contribution rates high.

1957: Best Supp. Actor (Red Buttons), Supp. Actress (Miyoshi Umeki), Art Direction, Sound (Warner Bros. Sound Dept)

NOMINATIONS: Best Picture, Director, Actor (Marlon Brando), Adapted Screenplay, Cinematography, Editing

•

SCALPHUNTERS, THE
1968, 102 mins, US Ⓥ ▭ col
Dir Sydney Pollack *Prod* Jules Levy *Scr* William Norton *Ph* Duke Callaghan, Richard Moore *Ed* John Woodcock *Mus* Elmer Bernstein *Art* Frank Arrigo
Act Burt Lancaster, Shelley Winters, Telly Savalas, Ossie Davis, Armando Silvestre, Dabney Coleman (United Artists)

In artistic terms, *The Scalphunters* is hard to describe: a satirical, slapstick, intellectual drama, laced with civil rights overtones, and loaded with recurring action scenes. Burt Lancaster and Shelley Winters provide marquee dressing.

Story topcasts Lancaster as a fur trapper, robbed of his skins by Indian chief Armando Silvestre, who swaps cultured Negro ex-slave Ossie Davis. Telly Savalas heads a crew of scalphunters, with Winters as mistress to Savalas. Lancaster and Davis pursue the scalphunters.

The whole ensemble works to a remarkable degree. Lancaster and Davis work particularly well together, ditto Savalas and Winters. There are talky periods of slow pace, but they are terminated before undue damage has been done.

•

SCAMP, THE
1957, 88 mins, UK b/w
Dir Wolf Rilla *Prod* James Lawrie *Scr* Wolf Rilla *Ph* Freddie Francis *Ed* Bernard Gribble *Mus* Francis Chagrin *Art* Elven Webb
Act Richard Attenborough, Terence Morgan, Dorothy Alison, Jill Adams, Colin Petersen, Geoffrey Keen (Minter)

Based on Charlotte Hastings's play *Uncertain Joy*, this emerges as a run-of-the-mill domestic drama. It has a touch too much of sentimentality and many situations are implausible.

Richard Attenborough is a schoolmaster, and he and his doctor wife befriend a youngster (Colin Petersen) whose father, a drunken vaudeville actor, neglects the child and leaves him to run wild. When he goes on a tour of South America, he reluctantly leaves his son with Attenborough and his wife, who try to show the kid a new way of life. But he can't live down his background and the authorities order that he should be returned to his father, who has returned from tour with a new wife.

While there is plenty of scope in such a story for a good, meaty drama, *The Scamp* suffers from unimaginative direction by Wolf Rilla and a somewhat pedestrian script. But no praise can be too high for Petersen (who sprang to prominence in the film *Smiley*) as the 10-year-old scamp. Here is a natural.

•

SCANDAL
1989, 114 mins, UK Ⓥ ⦿ col
Dir Michael Caton-Jones *Prod* Stephen Woolley *Scr* Michael Thomas *Ph* Mike Molloy *Ed* Angus Newton *Mus* Carl Davis *Art* Simon Holland
Act John Hurt, Joanne Whalley-Kilmer, Bridget Fonda, Ian McKellen, Leslie Phillips, Britt Ekland (Palace)

In 1963 the sensational revelations that a good-time girl had been having affairs with a British cabinet minister and a Soviet naval attaché shocked the U.K. and helped bring down the Conservative government. *Scandal* reexamines the controversy.

Man-about-town Stephen Ward (John Hurt) meets young showgirl Christine Keeler (Joanne Whalley-Kilmer) and decides to transform her into a glamorous sophisticate.

Ward is delighted when Soviet naval attaché Ivanov (Jeroen Krabbe) takes a shine to Whalley-Kilmer, though at the same time cabinet minister John Profumo (Ian McKellen), the secretary of state for war, falls for her. Profumo is forced to resign and Ward is eventually arrested and charged with living on the earnings of prostitutes.

Hurt is excellent as the charming but shallow Ward. Whalley-Kilmer looks the part, but seems happier with the humorous and ironic parts of the script. American Bridget Fonda—with an admirable British accent—is perfect.

•

SCANDAL AT SCOURIE
1953, 89 mins, US col
Dir Jean Negulesco *Prod* Edwin H. Knopf *Scr* Norman Corwin, Leonard Spigelgass, Karl Tunberg *Ph* Robert Planck *Ed* Ferris Webster *Mus* Daniele Amfitheatrof *Art* Cedric Gibbons, Wade B. Rubottom
Act Greer Garson, Walter Pidgeon, Donna Corcoran, Agnes Moorehead, Arthur Shields (M-G-M)

Plot is laid in Canada, and it's a gentle tale of a young Catholic orphan who wins the hearts of a childless Protestant couple and the community, but not without causing plenty of commotion that makes for chuckles, drama and tears. Jean Negulesco's direction gets the best from the script, which was based on a story by Mary McSherry.

As the orphan, little Donna Corcoran sparks the story. After having accidentally caused a fire that destroyed the Catholic orphanage in which she resides, she and the other children are loaded on a train for a cross-country junket and stops, during which nuns try to find new homes for the youngsters. At Scourie, a Protestant community, Corcoran wanders away, encounters Greer Garson, the wife of Walter Pidgeon, town merchant and political figure, and charms her. Political opponents, chiefly Philip Ober, charge Pidgeon is using the girl to get the Catholic vote, resulting in both an indignant Garson and an infuriated Pidgeon publicly trouncing him.

•

SCANNERS
1981, 102 mins, Canada Ⓥ ⦿ col
Dir David Cronenberg *Prod* Claude Heroux *Scr* David Cronenberg *Ph* Mark Irwin *Ed* Ron Sanders *Mus* Howard Shore *Art* Carol Spier
Act Stephen Lack, Jennifer O'Neill, Patrick McGoohan, Michael Ironside, Lawrence Dane (Filmplan)

Scanners offers at least one literally eye-popping moment and another that can only be called mind-blowing.

A variation on the pod people of *Invasion of the Body Snatchers* in that they cannot readily be distinguished from normal humans, scanners are telepathic curiosities who, like Sissy Spacek's Carrie, are able to zap people and things at will.

There are good scanners and bad scanners and one, Stephen Lack, who is in between and finds himself recruited by scientist Patrick McGoohan to infiltrate the evil group and track down the chief baddie, who has Hitlerian aspirations for his band of psychic gangsters.

Following the pattern of many effects-oriented low-budgeters, story settles into low gear after the opening reel, in which a man's head explodes on camera.

All this should give fans of David Cronenberg's previous pix their money's worth, although lack of any rooting interest vitiates any possible suspense and highly elegant visual style works against much shock value. Ending is also a bit puzzling.

•

SCARAMOUCHE
1923, 132 mins, US ⊗ b/w
Dir Rex Ingram *Scr* Willis Goldbeck *Ph* John F. Seitz *Ed* Grant Whytock *Mus* Ernst Litz
Act Ramon Novarro, Alice Terry, Lewis Stone, Lloyd Ingraham, Julia Swayne Gordon (Metro)

Rex Ingram's *Scaramouche* [from the novel by Rafael Sabatini] is a big feature. Comparisons cannot be made with his *Four Horsemen*, as it is an entirely different type of story.

Adhering closely to historical fact, the story tells of a youth in love with a titled lady, also sought by a marquis who holds domination over that portion of France. The boy sees his chum murdered in a duel by the marquis, the only explanation being given is that his friend, who was studying for the clergy, could talk too well. The story then carries the boy through the various stages of French history up to the breaking of the revolution in Paris.

Andre, the boy, is brought into the French Assembly. It is here that Ingram makes many truly worthwhile long shots, the galleries filled with the bedlam, the white-wigged aristocrats and then the deputies of the people.

Navarro's performance has a sincere boyishness coupled with natural good looks. Alice Terry not only is beautiful in the white wig and gowns of the period, but she gives a capable performance as well.

•

SCARAMOUCHE
1952, 115 mins, US Ⓥ ⦿ col
Dir George Sidney *Prod* Carey Wilson *Scr* Ronald Millar, George Froeschel *Ph* Charles Rosher *Ed* James E. Newcom *Mus* Victor Young *Art* Cedric Gibbons, Hans Peters
Act Stewart Granger, Eleanor Parker, Janet Leigh, Mel Ferrer, Henry Wilcoxon, Nina Foch (M-G-M)

Metro's up-to-date version of *Scaramouche* bears only the most rudimentary resemblance to its 1923 hit or to the Rafael Sabatini novel on which they both were based. Pic never seems to be quite certain whether it is a costume adventure drama or a satire on one.

The highly complex Sabatini plot has been greatly simplified for present purposes. It finds the French Revolution all but eliminated from the story, because of the inevitable Red analogy were the hero allowed to spout the 1789 theme of "Liberty, Equality, Fraternity."

Granger is a brash young man who is determined to avenge the death of a friend at the hand of nobleman Mel Ferrer, the best swordsman in France. Stewart Granger has to keep under cover until he gets in enough lessons with the weapon to take on Ferrer. Just in the nick, (a) he's elected to the French assembly, so he doesn't have to hide out anymore; (b) he discovers Janet Leigh is not his sister, so he can grab her; and (c) the marquis is really his brother. That leaves everyone mildly happy except Eleanor Parker, who, when last seen, is being hauled into a bedroom by Napoleon.

•

SCARECROW

1973, 112 mins, US col

Dir Jerry Schatzberg ***Prod*** Robert M. Sherman ***Scr*** Garry Michael White ***Ph*** Vilmos Zsigmond ***Ed*** Evan Lottman ***Mus*** Fred Myrow ***Art*** Al Brenner

Act Gene Hackman, Al Pacino, Dorothy Tristan, Ann Wedgeworth, Richard Lynch, Eileen Brennan (Warner)

Scarecrow is a periodically interesting but ultimately unsatisfying character study of two modern drifters. Gene Hackman is excellent as a paroled crook with determined plans for the future, but Al Pacino is shot down by the script, which never provides him with much beyond freaky second-banana status.

Script seems an attempt to update Runyonesque characters and situations to the seamy 1970s.

Hackman and Pacino meet in the California countryside. The former is gruff, eccentric, crude and volatile. The latter is likeable, weak, but sufficiently put together to return to Detroit to the wife and child he abandoned years earlier.

In their travels, pair encounter several extremely well-cast and most effective characters.

•

SCARECROW, THE

1982, 87 mins, New Zealand col

Dir Sam Pillsbury ***Prod*** Rob Whitehouse ***Scr*** Sam Pillsbury, Michael Heath ***Ph*** James Bartle ***Ed*** Ian John ***Mus*** Andrew Hagen, Morton Wilson, Phil Broadhurst ***Art*** Neil Angwin

Act Jonathan Smith, Daniel McLaren, Stephen Taylor, Des Kelly, Tracy Mann, John Carradine (Oasis/NZNFU)

As did the novel on which it is based, *The Scarecrow* sets up its own category, which is a kind of hillbilly Gothic thriller. The bizarre events are seen through the eyes of Ned, and the impact on a small New Zealand country township, circa 1953, of the quintessential evil stranger, embodied by the smooth-talking itinerant sideshow magician and hypnotist, Salter.

Evil the stranger may be, but he is also the flame that brings to the boil the town's stew of lust and perversion that has been simmering all along.

Events are commented upon by the offscreen voice of Ned, now grown older but still talking in the overblown phrases of a lad who has read too many cheap adventure thrillers. It is an effective part of this device, however, carried over from the original novel by Ronald Hugh Morrieson, that highly unpleasant undertones exist, such as necrophilia and senile sexuality.

The central role of Salter himself is given the full saturnine treatment by John Carradine, abetted by ominous lighting and sound effects at every turn.

•

SCARED STIFF

1953, 106 mins, US b/w

Dir George Marshall ***Prod*** Hal B. Wallis ***Scr*** Herbert Baker, Walter De Leon, Ed Simmons, Norman Lear ***Ph*** Ernest Laszlo ***Ed*** Warren Low ***Mus*** Leith Stevens ***Art*** Hal Pereira, Franz Bachelin

Act Dean Martin, Jerry Lewis, Lizabeth Scott, Carmen Miranda, Dorothy Malone, George Dolenz (Paramount)

Dean Martin and Jerry Lewis provide a freewheeling round of slapstick hilarity—the kind they do so well—in *Scared Stiff*, new version of the old Paul Dickey–Charles W. Goddard play [*The Ghost Breakers*]. Script has its chief setting on a lonely, zombie-haunted island off the coast of Cuba.

Preliminaries are concerned with Martin, a cabaret singer, and his awkward chum (Lewis) back in New York, where they get mixed up with a gangster's girl (Dorothy Malone) and, in fleeing a gangland ride, meet up with Lizabeth Scott, heiress to the island. M&L decide to go along with her as protection against mysterious men who are attempting to keep her from claiming her inheritance.

Oddly enough, a comedy highlight in the picture is handled by uncredited Frank Fontaine, playing a drunk who thinks Martin is a ventriloquist when he is caught talking to Lewis, hidden in a trunk at dockside. The comedy team is in its element in the story's slapstick harum-scarum. Scott handles herself niftily and Carmen Miranda shows up well. Malone's chores in the early footage are carried out delightfully as a gal who likes to kiss, even if it does displease her gangster boyfriend.

•

SCARFACE

1932, 90 mins, US b/w

Dir Howard Hawks ***Prod*** Howard Hughes ***Scr*** Ben Hecht, W. R. Burnett, John Lee Mahin, Seton I. Miller ***Ph*** Lee Garmes, L. William O'Connell ***Ed*** Edward Curtiss ***Mus*** Adolph Tandler, Gustav Arnheim ***Art*** Harry Olivier

Act Paul Muni, Ann Dvorak, Karen Morley, George Raft, Boris Karloff, Osgood Perkins (Hughes/United Artists)

Scarface contains more cruelty than any of its gangster picture predecessors, but there's a squarer for every killing. The blows are always softened by judicial preachments and sad endings for the sinners. There is none of *Public Enemy*'s tracing the mug from boyhood to blame the environment for the cause this time. Paul Muni is a bad one in the first spin of the spindle, murdering a gent while he (Muni) is still just an introductory shadow on the wall. He whistles an operatic aria before shooting his cannon, which signals when he's going to kill somebody from then on.

Plot traces the rise of Scarface from the position of bodyguard for an early district beer baron to the booze chief of the whole city. Along the way he overthrows his employer and later has him slain. He even cops the boss's girl. She's a wicked blonde with a love for gunmen and gunfire, and she of all the gang is left unpunished at the finish.

George Raft gets most of the sympathy for his Rinaldo. He talks little and habitually tosses a coin while doing most of his pal's private gat work. Karen Morley has to fight an apparently natural air of refinement to get into the moll atmosphere, but she makes her part sit up and talk. Ann Dvorak is okay as Scarface's kid sister.

•

SCARFACE

1983, 170 mins, US col

Dir Brian De Palma ***Prod*** Martin Bregman ***Scr*** Oliver Stone ***Ph*** John A. Alonzo ***Ed*** Jerry Greenberg, David Ray ***Mus*** Giorgio Moroder ***Art*** Ed Richardson

Act Al Pacino, Steven Bauer, Michelle Pfeiffer, Mary Elizabeth Mastrantonio, Robert Loggia, F. Murray Abraham (Universal)

Scarface is a grandiose modern morality play, excessive, broad and operatic at times. Film's origins lie in the 1932 Howard Hughes production directed by Howard Hawks and adapted by Ben Hecht from the novel by Armitage Trail. Contours of the saga are very similar to those of the original, as the nearly three-hour effort charts the rise and fall of an ambitious young thug who for awhile becomes the biggest shot in gangsterdom, but ultimately is just too dumb to stay at the top.

Docu prolog recounts how some 25,000 criminals entered the United States in 1980 during the boatlift from Mariel Harbor in Cuba. Among them, per this fiction, was one Tony Montana (Al Pacino), who impresses local Miami kingpin Robert Loggia. Thanks to the fact that he has nerves of steel and ice in his veins, Pacino moves up fast in the underworld and establishes a crucial personal link with Bolivian cocaine manufacturer Paul Shenar.

All this is brought off by scripter Oliver Stone and director Brian De Palma in efficient, sometimes stylish fashion.

Performances are all extremely effective, with Pacino leading the way. Michelle Pfeiffer does well with a basically one-dimensional role as a blonde WASP goddess. Shenar is oustanding as the cool, well-bred Bolivian.

•

SCARLET BUCCANEER, THE

SEE: SWASHBUCKLER

•

SCARLET EMPRESS, THE

1934, 104 mins, US b/w

Dir Josef von Sternberg ***Scr*** Manuel Komroff ***Ph*** Bert Glennon ***Ed*** [uncredited] ***Mus*** [John M. Leopold, W. Frank Harling (arr.)] ***Art*** [Hans Dreier, Peter Ballbusch, Richard Kollorsz]

Act Marlene Dietrich, John Lodge, Sam Jaffe, Louise Dresser, Maria Sieber, C. Aubrey Smith (Paramount)

The greatest trouble with *Scarlet Empress* is, at the same time, its greatest weakness. Josef von Sternberg becomes so enamoured of the pomp and flash values that he subjugates everything else to them. That he succeeds as well as he does is a tribute to his artistic genius and his amazingly vital sense of photogenic values.

Marlene Dietrich has never been as beautiful as she is here. Again and again she is photographed in close-ups, under veils and behind thin mesh curtains and always breathtakingly. But never is she allowed to become really alive and vital. She is as though enchanted by the immense sets through which she stalks.

She is first picked up as a baby and a cute touch has this sequence being acted by her baby, Maria Sieber. Then she's the young German princess affianced to the far-off Russian and sent to the foreign court. She is innocent, wide-eyed, unsuspecting. And, of course, she is an easy mark for all the viciousness and grossness she soon finds herself surrounded with. Wedded to the mad crown prince she is slowly driven into the arms of other men.

Film is claimed based on a diary of Catherine II which, perhaps, forgives its choppiness and episodic quality. Sternberg uses a minimum of dialog and goes back to the silent film method of titles to explain action.

•

SCARLET LETTER, THE

1926, 98 mins, US b/w

Dir Victor Seastrom ***Scr*** Frances Marion ***Ph*** Hendrik Sartov ***Ed*** Hugh Wynn ***Art*** Cedric Gibbons, Sidney Ullman

Act Lillian Gish, Lars Hanson, Henry B. Walthall, Karl Dane (M-G-M)

This latest MGM production [from Nathaniel Hawthorne's novel] starring Lillian Gish is gripping. Gish makes of Hester Prynne—the little English Puritan maid who married before coming to America, through the wishes of her father, a man she did not love expecting him to follow after—a really sympathetic character.

Hester and the Rev. Dimmesdale receive all the sympathy of the audience, but particularly through the toll that the little heroine is compelled to pay for loving. Lars Hanson, who plays the lead opposite the star, handles the role with a great deal of finesse. Others standing out are Karl Dane as Giles, and Marceline Corday as Mistress Hibbins. Henry B. Walthall plays the husband with a make-up suggestive of Shylock and mannerism much the same, though the reason for this is far from explained.

•

SCARLET LETTER, THE

1995, 135 mins, US col

Dir Roland Joffe ***Prod*** Roland Joffe, Andrew G. Vajna ***Scr*** Douglas Day Stewart ***Ph*** Alex Thomson ***Ed*** Thom Noble ***Mus*** John Barry ***Art*** Roy Walker

Act Demi Moore, Gary Oldman, Robert Duvall, Robert Prosky, Edward Hardwicke, Joan Plowright (Lightmotive/Allied Stars/Cinergi/Moving Pictures

The credits acknowledge that this new version of *The Scarlet Letter* has been "freely adapted from the novel by Nathaniel Hawthorne," which is one of the understatements of the year. Opening with what look like outtakes from *The Mission* and continuing with fat slices of *The Last of the Mohicans*, *The Crucible* and hothouse eroticism that's pure Hollywood, this borderline campy look at the Puritans is politically correct melodrama with sex on the brain.

As lugubriously and lubriciously directed by Roland Joffe, pic's first act is basically devoted to the headstrong Hester Prynne (Demi Moore) and Gary Oldman's repressed romantic reverend casting furtive looks at each other until they can't stand it any longer, while the remainder shows them suffering the extensive repercussions of their one night of passion. A very '90s take on a 1660s tale written in 1850, as a picture of early colonial life it's about as convincing as *Pocahontas*.

When Hester is finally forced to admit that she's pregnant, she's jailed until her daughter is born, after which she's released but forced to wear an embroidered red letter "A" for Adultery whenever she goes out in public. Who should turn up but her long-lost husband, Roger (Robert Duvall), who all this time has been dancing with wolves after having been captured by the local tribe.

Hawthorne's partly tragic ending has been junked in favor of one in which the Indians get to play the cavalry, no one dies who doesn't deserve to, and everyone who needs a comeuppance gets it.

Production has been lushly mounted, with the mostly Nova Scotian locations providing a plausible, if not entirely topographically accurate, substitute for Massachusetts.

•

SCARLET PIMPERNEL, THE

1934, 98 mins, UK b/w

Dir Harold Young ***Prod*** Alexander Korda ***Scr*** Lajos Biro, S. N. Behrman, Robert Sherwood, Arthur Wimperis ***Ph*** Harold

Rosson *Ed* William Hornbeck *Mus* Arthur Benjamin *Art* Vincent Korda
Act Leslie Howard, Merle Oberon, Raymond Massey, Nigel Bruce, Bramwell Fletcher, Joan Gardner (London)

An intriguing adaptation of a noted novel, the English-made *Pimpernel* is distinguished by a splendid cast and productional mounting that rates with Hollywood's best.

Leslie Howard's performance in the title role is not only up to the Howard standard, but so fine that an extraordinary production job was required to prevent this from being a monologue film.

As the Scarlet Pimpernel, an English nobleman who seeks to rescue the aristocrats of France from Robespierre's guillotine, Howard essays what amounts to a dual role. At home a foppish, affected clotheshorse; abroad, a gallant adventurer playing a dangerous game.

With the story in his favor, Howard has the acting edge all the way, so it was only by their own efforts that the supporting players could stand out. As Chauvelin, the villain of the piece, Raymond Massey turns in a gem of a performance.

Co-starred with Howard is Merle Oberon, the slant-eyed knockout. Portraying Lady Blakeley, a tragic young woman who nearly betrays her husband, Oberon is confined by script limitations to sad moments only. Enough of Baroness Orczy's novel is retained to make the picture plot recognizable to the book readers.

•

SCARLET STREET

1945, 96 mins, US Ⓥ b/w
Dir Fritz Lang *Prod* Walter Wanger *Scr* Dudley Nichols *Ph* Milton Krasner *Ed* Arthur Hilton *Mus* Hans J. Salter *Art* Alexander Golitzen
Act Edward G. Robinson, Joan Bennett, Dan Duryea, Margaret Lindsay, Rosalind Ivan, Jess Barker (Universal/Diana)

Fritz Lang's production and direction ably project the sordid tale of the romance between a milquetoast character and a gold-digging blonde. Script [based on the French novel and play *La Chienne* by Georges la Fouchardiere] is tightly written by Dudley Nichols and is played for sustained interest and suspense by the cast.

Edward G. Robinson is the mild cashier and amateur painter whose love for Joan Bennett leads him to embezzlement, murder and disgrace. Two stars turn in top work to keep the interest high, and Dan Duryea's portrayal of the crafty and crooked opportunist whom Bennett loves is a standout in furthering the melodrama.

•

SCARY MOVIE

2000, 88 mins, US Ⓥ ⊙ ▭ col
Dir Keenen Ivory Wayans *Prod* Eric L. Gold, Lee R. Mayes *Scr* Shawn Wayans, Marlon Wayans, Buddy Johnson, Phil Beauman, Jason Friedberg, Aaron Seltzer *Ph* Francis Kenny *Ed* Mark Helfrich *Mus* David Kitay *Art* Lawrence F. Pevec
Act Shawn Wayans, Marion Wayans, Cheri Oteri, Shannon Elizabeth, Anna Faris, Jon Abrahams (Wayans Bros.)

Keenen Ivory Wayans' gleefully gross and exuberantly smutty *Scary Movie* is a zany scattershot spoof of teen horror pics, high-school sex comedies and assorted pop-culture phenomena, unbounded by taste, inhibition or political correctness.

There is something like a plot to connect the assorted sight gags, satirical bits, rude remarks and sketch-comedy episodes. But the slender narrative (think *Scream* meets *I Know What You Did Last Summer*, with a side order of *American Pie*) is never allowed to get in the way of a cheap laugh or an inspired non sequitur. *Scary Movie* remains sufficiently flexible and loosely knit to encompass references to *The Usual Suspects, The Sixth Sense, Dawson's Creek, Amistad* (don't ask) and *The Matrix*. Unlike most spoofs of this helter-skelter sort, *Scary Movie* manages an impressively huge score in the hit-or-miss gag ratio.

Director Wayans sets the tone during the opening minutes. Hell, he sets it during the first 30 seconds, when Carmen Electra, playing a character named—wink-wink, nudge-nudge—Drew, passes gas while on the phone with a mad killer. Shortly after, the slasher arrives to bury his knife in her bountiful bosom. When he removes the blade, however, he finds the point is embedded in a breast implant. Much of the rest of the pic proceeds in the same anything-goes vein. At least two gags involving male genitalia—especially one that uses an erect penis as an offensive weapon—are shocking but explosively funny.

The well-cast leads appear ready for anything—which, considering what they're asked to do, is a very good thing—but their unbridled enthusiasm never devolves into self-conscious campiness. They're funny largely because they seem to take everything so seriously.

•

SCENE OF THE CRIME

1949, 91 mins, US Ⓥ b/w
Dir Roy Rowland *Prod* Harry Rapf *Scr* Charles Schnee *Ph* Paul C. Vogel *Ed* Robert J. Kern *Mus* Andre Previn
Act Van Johnson, Arlene Dahl, Gloria de Haven, Norman Lloyd (M-G-M)

The Metro lot has etched on celluloid a taut, tough and often relentless picture of the backroom activities of a detective team on the hunt for a murderer in *Scene of the Crime*.

On the score of diversified characterizations and generally believable dialog, *Scene* is as good as the best. Its dramatis personae give the film broad cross-sectional lift. It has its serious limitations, though, via a generous dose of cinematic clichés and a story that periodically sacrifices clarity for pace.

This is the story of how a Los Angeles plainclothes lieutenant (Van Johnson) tracks the killers of a fellow cop regardless of where the chips may fall. Adding bone and grist to the story are important revelations of how Johnson lives.

The cast is uniformly expert. Johnson, for one, gains much from the script's canny refusal to limn him as a glamor boy.

•

SCENES FROM A MALL

1991, 87 mins, US Ⓥ ⊙ col
Dir Paul Mazursky *Prod* Paul Mazursky *Scr* Roger L. Simon, Paul Mazursky *Ph* Fred Murphy *Ed* Stuart Pappe *Mus* Marc Shaiman *Art* Pato Guzman
Act Bette Midler, Woody Allen, Bill Irwin, Daren Firestone, Rebecca Nickels, Paul Mazursky (Touchstone/Silver Screen Partners IV)

Paul Mazursky's 14th film as director is a cozy, insular middle-aged marital comedy that's about as deep and rewarding as a day of mall-cruising.

Talents of Bette Midler and Woody Allen seem misspent in roles as cuddly but squabbling spouses. Pic's title, a takeoff on Ingmar Bergman's *Scenes From a Marriage*, should be consumers' first clue as to what's in store.

Midler and Allen are a Hollywood Hills–dwelling twin-career couple of the 1990s. He's a successful sports lawyer; she's a psychologist who's written a high-concept book on how to renew a marriage. They pack their kids off for a ski weekend and head for the Beverly Center mall to spend their 16th anniversary indulging their every whim.

Allen drops the bombshell that he's just ended a six-month affair with a 25-year-old. Midler confesses to an ongoing affair with a Czechoslovakian colleague, played by Mazursky. These emotional storms never achieve any veracity. They seem like just another indulgence on the part of the pampered, secure spouses.

Pic shot exteriors at the Beverly Center and moved to a mall in Stamford, CT, for two weeks of interior filming. For the remainder, a huge, two-story replica mall was constructed at Kaufman Astoria Studios, NY, and 2,600 New York extras were outfitted in L.A. garb.

•

SCENES FROM THE CLASS STRUGGLE IN BEVERLY HILLS

1989, 102 mins, US Ⓥ ⊙ col
Dir Paul Bartel *Prod* J. C. Katz *Scr* Bruce Wagner *Ph* Steven Fierberg *Ed* Alan Toomayan *Mus* Stanley Myers *Art* Alex Tavoularis
Act Jacqueline Bisset, Ray Sharkey, Robert Beltran, Mary Woronov, Ed Begley, Jr., Wallace Shawn (North Street)

Scenes from the Class Struggle in Beverly Hills is a lewd delight. In top form here, director Paul Bartel brings a breezy, sophisticated touch to this utterly outrageous sex farce and thereby renders charming even the most scabrous moments in Bruce Wagner's very naughty screenplay [from a story by him and Bartel].

Script is structured in the manner of a classical French farce, and features more seductions and coitus interuptus than a season of soap operas. Hoity-toity divorcée Mary Woronov is having her house fumigated and so, with her sensitive son, checks in for the weekend next door at the home of former sitcom star Jacqueline Bisset, whose husband has just kicked the bucket.

Joining the menagerie of the filthy rich are Woronov's pretentious playwright brother Ed Begley, Jr., his brand-new sassy black wife Arnetia Walker, Woronov's crazed ex-husband Wallace Shawn, Bisset's precocious daughter Rebecca Schaeffer, "thinologist" Bartel and, in a surprisingly real apparition, Bisset's late hubby, Paul Mazursky.

Droll tone is set at the outset by the quaintly 1950s titles and Stanley Myers's witty score, and the comic champagne is kept bubbly with only the most momentary of missteps.

•

SCENT OF A WOMAN

1992, 157 mins, US Ⓥ ⊙ col
Dir Martin Brest *Prod* Martin Brest *Scr* Bo Goldman *Ph* Donald E. Thorin *Ed* William Steinkamp, Michael Tronick, Harvey Rosenstock *Mus* Thomas Newman *Art* Angelo Graham
Act Al Pacino, Chris O'Donnell, James Rebhorn, Gabrielle Anwar, Philip S. Hoffman, Richard Venture (Universal/City Light)

Of note for Al Pacino's theatrical, virtuoso star turn as a blind ex-military officer who introduces a greenhorn to the things of life, *Scent of a Woman* indulgently stretches a modest conceit well past the breaking point.

Universal release is based on a 1974 Italian film directed by Dino Risi [from Giovanni Arpino's novel *Il buio e il miele*]; it stands more as a reconceptualization than a remake. Oddly, original title was kept when it has next to nothing to do with anything.

Script takes the p.o.v. of teenager Charlie Simms (Chris O'Donnell), a straight-arrow student at a snooty Eastern boarding school. While the other boys head for Vermont to ski during Thanksgiving vacation, O'Donnell is obliged to earn a few bucks by caring for a sightless lieutenant colonel (Pacino) whose family is leaving for the long weekend.

Frank Slade is a feisty, combative, irascible, remarkably insightful character who holds on to a genuine, if embittered, lust for life. He whisks the reluctant Charlie to New York, where he intends to savor some of his favorite things one last time. Most of the action is confined to the pair's suite at the Waldorf-Astoria.

O'Donnell does pretty well holding his own, although for dramatic purposes the character stays the same.

Reportedly, two shorter versions of the film were tested at previews but went over less well with auds than the release cut.

1992: Best Actor (Al Pacino)

NOMINATIONS: Best Picture, Director, Screenplay Adaptation

•

SCENT OF GREEN PAPAYA, THE

SEE: MUI DU DU XANH

•

SCENT OF MYSTERY

1960, 125 mins, US ▭ col
Dir Jack Cardiff *Prod* Michael Todd, Jr. *Scr* William Roos *Ph* John Von Kotze *Mus* Mario Nascimbene
Act Denholm Elliott, Peter Lorre, Paul Lukas, Peter Arne, Beverley Bentley, Leo McKern (Todd)

Scent of Mystery is carefully planned to synchronize scents with action in the film. Unlike Aromarama, which hit the market (in Manhattan) first, the script is designed with the smells in mind. In the AromaRama presentation [Carlo Lizzani's *Behind the Great Wall*, 1959], a documentary dealing with Red China, the odors were added as an afterthought.

The dispensing systems are different. In Smell-O-Vision, developed by the Swiss-born Hans Laube, the odors are piped via plastic tubing—a mile of tubing at Chicago's Cinestage Theatre—to individual seats, the scents being triggered automatically by signals on the film's soundtrack. The Aromarama smells are conveyed through the theatre's regular air ventilating system. The Smell-O-Vision odors are more distinct and recognizable and do not appear to linger as long as those in Aromarama.

Reaction of those at the Smell-O-Vision premiere was mixed. Of those queried, not all claimed to have whiffed the some 30 olfactions said to have been distributed during the course of the film. A number of balcony smellers said the aroma reached them a few seconds after the action on the screen. Other balcony dwellers said they heard a hissing sound that tipped off the arrival of a smell. Among the smells that clicked were those involving flowers, the perfume of the mystery girl in the film, tobacco, orange, shoe polish, port wine (when a man is crushed to death by falling casks), baked bread, coffee, lavender, and peppermint.

Utilizing the 70-mm Todd Process, a similar but technically different process, from Todd-AO, the picture—with or without the smells—is a fun picture, expertly directed by Jack Cardiff. It has many elements that are derivative of a Hitchcock chase film, the late Mike Todd's *Around the World in Eighty Days*, and the Cinerama travelog technique. It wanders all over the Spanish landscape, covering fiestas, the running of the bulls ceremony, native dances, street scenes of Spanish cities and towns. The travelog is neatly integrated as part of the chase as Denholm Elliott, as a very proper Englishman on Spanish holiday, plays a sort of Don Quixote character who boldly stumbles through the cities and countryside as a self-appointed protector of a damsel in distress. He is accompanied by a philosophical taxi driver, neatly portrayed by Peter Lorre. Paul Lukas is properly sinister as a mysterious hired assassin. Cardiff has wisely directed the film with a tongue-in-cheek quality. Diana Dors is seen briefly (time and costume) on a Spanish beach and Elizabeth Taylor is present at the denouement in a non-speaking role. Although smell plays an important part in Elliott's uncovering of the villain, the audience need not necessarily be involved in the odor—the recognition of a man's tobacco.

•

SCHINDLER'S LIST
1993, 195 mins, US Ⓥ ⦿ col
Dir Steven Spielberg ***Prod*** Steven Spielberg, Gerald R. Molen, Branko Lustig ***Scr*** Steven Zaillian ***Ph*** Janusz Kaminski ***Ed*** Michael Kahn ***Mus*** John Williams ***Art*** Allan Starski
Act Liam Neeson, Ben Kingsley, Ralph Fiennes, Caroline Goodall, Jonathan Sagalle, Embeth Davidtz (Amblin/Universal)

After several attempts at making a fully realized, mature film, Steven Spielberg has finally put it all together in *Schindler's List*. This searing historical and biographical drama, about a Nazi industrialist who saved some 1,100 Jews from certain death in the concentration camps, evinces an artistic rigor and unsentimental intelligence unlike anything the world's most successful filmmaker has demonstrated before.

Taking their cue from Australian writer Thomas Keneally's 1982 book *Schindler's Ark*, Spielberg and scenarist Steven Zaillian keep as their main focus a man whose mercenary instincts only gradually turned him into an unlikely hero and savior.

The Nazis have completed their lightning conquest of Poland in September 1939, and Nazi Party member Oskar Schindler (the imposing Liam Neeson) arranges to run a major company that will be staffed by unpaid Jews. Itzhak Stern (Ben Kingsley) becomes his accountant and right-hand man. In near-documentary fashion and often using a dizzyingly mobile, handheld camera, Spielberg (who operated his own camera for many of these sequences) deftly sketches the descent of the Jews from refugee settlers in Krakow to their confinement within 16 square blocks by 1941, to the creation of a Plaszow Forced Labor Camp in 1942, to the brutal liquidation of the ghetto the following year.

In these sequences, the seed is planted for one of the picture's superbly developed great themes—that the matter of who lived and died was completely, utterly, existentially arbitrary.

Looming above the labor camp is the opulent chateau of Commandant Amon Goeth (Ralph Fiennes), as evil as any Nazi presented onscreen over the past 50 years, but considerably more complex and human than most. Schindler must use utmost diplomacy in dealing with Goeth and other top-ranking Nazis in order to get his way.

Despite its 3¼-hour length, the film moves forward with great urgency and is not a minute too long for the story it is telling and the amount of information it imparts. The only debatable choice is the brief color epilogue, which depicts many of the surviving "Schindler Jews" filing by his grave in Israel accompanied, for the most part, by the much younger actors who have portrayed them in the film. This smacks, on a certain level, of direct emotional manipulation.

1993: Best Picture, Director, Screenplay Adaptation, Cinematography, Film Editing, Original Score, Art Direction

NOMINATIONS: Best Actor (Liam Neeson), Supp. Actor (Ralph Fiennes), Costume Design, Sound, Makeup

•

SCHIZOPOLIS
1996, 99 mins, US col
Dir Steven Soderbergh ***Prod*** John Hardy ***Scr*** Steven Soderbergh ***Ph*** Steven Soderbergh
Act Steven Soderbergh, Betsy Brantley, David Jensen (Point 406)

Some combination of goof, provocation and willfully anarchic eruption, *Schizopolis* is a satire and critique of modern life so scattershot in its aim and techniques that it misses the mark more often than it hits. A no-budgeter made as a guerrilla project by Steven Soderbergh in Baton Rouge, LA, pic is a real head-scratcher that so insistently keeps jumping all over the place that it becomes impossible to pinpoint its intent.

Film had a world premiere as a "surprise" entry at the Cannes Film Festival as odd as its own nature. The picture bears no credits at all, either front or rear, except for a one-frame copyright card at the end that goes by so fast as to prove unreadable. Soderbergh, who wrote, directed and shot the film and plays the main role as well, is preferring to send the pic out as an "authorless text" to which audiences will bring no preconceived notions.

Schizopolis (title appears only on a character's T-shirt) is as mangy, indecipherable and from-the-hip as Soderbergh's previous films are precise, literate and meticulously calibrated. This would seem to be the work of someone in a conflicted and bilious frame of mind.

Pic starts out as an apparent satire of, and attack on, Scientology-like organizations. Munson (Soderbergh) is a functionary working on behalf of a movement called Eventualism, the guru of which is the uniquely selfish, mean-spirited T. Azimuth Schwitters. Focus then veers to the annoying antics of a weird exterminator in an orange suit and goggles named Elmo, whose aggressively promiscuous activities remain utterly unfathomable throughout the running time.

Along the way, characters begin speaking in different forms of gibberish, with Munson and his wife relating in a fitfully amusing techno-ese in which they might say hello by uttering "generic greetings." Technically, film is a hodgepodge that doesn't attempt to gloss over its made-on-the-run quality.

•

SCHOOL DAZE
1988, 120 mins, US Ⓥ ⦿ col
Dir Spike Lee ***Prod*** Spike Lee ***Scr*** Spike Lee ***Ph*** Ernest Dickerson ***Ed*** Barry Alexander Brown ***Mus*** Bill Lee ***Art*** Wynn Thomas
Act Larry Fishburne, Giancarlo Esposito, Tisha Campbell, Kyme, Joe Seneca, Spike Lee (40 Acres & a Mule/Columbia)

Filmgoers who admired the freshness and energy of Spike Lee's *She's Gotta Have It* are bound to be thrown by his follow-up *School Daze*. A loosely connected series of musical set-pieces exploring the experience of blackness at an all-black university, film is a hybrid of forms and styles that never comes together in a coherent whole. Surprising, too, is the almost dour tone of the film.

Story, such as it is, focuses on the conflict between the militant activists on campus and the goodtime boys of Gamma Phi Gamma fraternity which comes to a head during homecoming week. Leading the freshman pledges class and begging for acceptance is the diminutive Half-Pint (Spike Lee), caught between the demands of fraternity life and the responsibilities of being black advanced by his cousin Dap Dunlap (Larry Fishburne).

Making life miserable for Half-Pint is his pledge-master and Dap's arch rival Julian Eaves (Giancarlo Esposito). On the female side, it's the Gamma Rays versus the Jigaboos illustrating the tensions between the light-skinned, straight-haired blacks and the dark-skinned sisters.

As a director, Lee fails to strike the right note between realism and fantasy, and the heavy subject matter just falls with a thud. As an actor, however, Lee does a good job creating a sort of black babe in the woods.

•

SCHOOL FOR SCOUNDRELS OR HOW TO WIN WITHOUT ACTUALLY CHEATING
1960, 94 mins, UK Ⓥ b/w
Dir Robert Hamer ***Prod*** Hal E. Chester (exec.) ***Scr*** Patricia Moyes, Hal E. Chester ***Ph*** Erwin Hillier ***Ed*** Richard Best ***Mus*** John Addison ***Art*** Terence Verity
Act Ian Carmichael, Terry-Thomas, Alastair Sim, Janette Scott, Dennis Price, Peter Jones (Guardsman)

The gentle art of getting and remaining "one up" on the next fellow, so painstakingly chronicled by British humorist Stephen Potter in his series of books, is engagingly translated to the screen in this delicate English comedy. Those familiar with Potter's spoofs (*Lifemanship*, *Gamesmanship*, *Oneupmanship*) will get the biggest boot out of *School for Scoundrels*.

Although it is virtually impossible to capture Potter's many intimate ironies, the scenarists have successfully caught the essence of the author's maxim—"How to Win Without Actually Cheating" (as the film is subtitled).

Alastair Sim personifies the master lifeman down to the minutest detail—a brilliant performance. Ian Carmichael is a delight as the pitifully inept wretch who undergoes metamorphosis at Sim's finishing school for social misfits, and Terry-Thomas masterfully plummets from one-up to one-down as his exasperated victim.

Janette Scott, a fresh, natural beauty, charmingly plays the object of their attention. Unfortunately for Dennis Price and Peter Jones, they are involved in the weakest passage of the film—a none-too-subtle used car sequence that will disturb Potter purists.

•

SCIUSCIA
(SHOESHINE; SHOESHINE BOYS)
1946, 105 mins, Italy Ⓥ b/w
Dir Vittorio De Sica ***Prod*** Paolo W. Tamburella ***Scr*** Cesare Zavattini, Cesare Giulio Viola, Sergio Amidei, Adolfo Franci, Vittorio De Sica ***Ph*** Anchise Brizzi ***Mus*** Alessandro Cicognini
Act Rinaldo Smordoni, Franco Interlenghi, Carlo Ortensi, Aniello Mele, Emilio Cigoli (Alfa)

With the shoeshine boys of Rome's streets as background, this film is a preachment on Italian juvenile delinquency. Producers used real shoeshine boys and the absence of experienced actors works out okay. Scenes in Rome's jail emphasize the need for drastic reforms there.

Two bootblacks are the principal characters, the film showing their change from honest lads into bitter juvenile gangsters. Paolo W. Tamburella, producer, and Vittoria De Sica, director, deserve bulk of praise for this.

•

SCORCHERS
1992, 88 mins, UK Ⓥ ⦿ col
Dir David Beaird ***Prod*** Morrie Eisenman, Richard Hellman ***Scr*** David Beaird ***Ph*** Peter Deming ***Ed*** David Garfield ***Mus*** Carter Burwell ***Art*** Bill Eigenbrodt
Act Emily Lloyd, Jennifer Tilly, Leland Crooke, Faye Dunaway, James Earl Jones, Denholm Elliott (Goldcrest)

Writer-director David Beaird's beguiling stage play about a bawdy, rollicking wedding night in the Louisiana bayou makes an uneven transfer to film. Despite some pungent performances, *Scorchers* is hampered by a nervous visual tone and inexplicable production flaws.

Emily Lloyd plays a nervous 20-year-old virgin bride whose cajun wedding-night jitters are exacerbated by the community's lusty interest in the goings-on. Jennifer Tilly plays a preacher's daughter who can't get her husband to prefer her to the town whore (Faye Dunaway).

Film's flighty story eventually finds two successful places to roost—a bar and the bedroom in which Lloyd and her madly frustrated young husband (James Wilder) are counseled by Lloyd's father (Leland Crooke). Film suffers from a murky sound mix obscuring initial dialog, which already is difficult to make out with the Cajun accents.

•

SCORPIO
1973, 114 mins, US Ⓥ ⦿ col
Dir Michael Winner ***Prod*** Walter Mirisch ***Scr*** David W. Rintels, Gerald Wilson ***Ph*** Robert Paynter ***Ed*** Freddie Wilson ***Mus*** Jerry Fielding ***Art*** Herbert Westbrook
Act Burt Lancaster, Alain Delon, Paul Scofield, John Colicos, Gayle Hunnicutt, J. D. Cannon (Scimitar/United Artists)

Despite its anachronistic emulation of mid-1960s cynical spy mellers, *Scorpio* might have been an acceptable action programmer if its narrative were clearer, its dialogue less "cultured" and its visuals more straightforward.

Pic opens with the assassination of an Arab government official, but his identity and relationship to the protagonists remain puzzlements beyond the film's conclusion. Even more irritating is nearly total confusion about other characters' occupations or moral positions.

Ultimately, pic settles down into the usual is-he-or-isn't-he-a-double-agent gimmick, with CIA-blackmailed Alain Delon pursuing supposed Soviet defector Burt Lancaster from Washington to Europe. While ducking his would-be assassin, Lancaster takes refuge in the Viennese home of Paul Scofield, a Russian agent.

•

SCOTT JOPLIN
1977, 96 mins, US col
Dir Jeremy Paul Kagan ***Prod*** Stan Hough ***Scr*** Christopher Knopf ***Ph*** David M. Walsh ***Ed*** Patrick Kennedy ***Mus*** Scott Joplin ***Art*** William H. Hiney
Act Billy Dee Williams, Clifton Davis, Margaret Avery, Eubie Blake, Godfrey Cambridge, Seymour Cassel (Motown/Universal)

Universal Pictures owed a large debt to Scott Joplin—whose ragtime music was a key factor in the enormous success of *The Sting*—and the studio paid back the debt with *Scott Joplin*, a biopic starring Billy Dee Williams originally intended for TV.

Williams is fine, and the film has a lot of verve and intensity, but the story of Joplin's life is so grim it makes the film a real downer. *Scott Joplin* is buoyant fun for the first half but then becomes a harrowing ordeal when Joplin learns he has syphilis. He turns into a desperate wreck, forsaking his popular ragtime tunes to write an opera, "Treemonisha," which wasn't performed until 1975.

But the second half of the film makes too many wobbly jumps over periods of Joplin's life to satisfy dramatically.

•

SCOTT OF THE ANTARCTIC

1948, 111 mins, UK Ⓥ col

Dir Charles Frend ***Prod*** Michael Balcon ***Scr*** Walter Meade, Ivor Montagu, Mary Hayley Bell ***Ph*** Jack Cardiff, Osmond Borrodaile, Geoffrey Unsworth ***Ed*** Peter Tanner ***Mus*** Ralph Vaughan Williams ***Art*** Arne Akermark

Act John Mills, Harold Warrender, Derek Bond, Reginald Beckwith, James Robertson Justice, Kenneth More (Ealing)

Scott of the Antarctic should be not only a magnificent eye-filling spectacle but also a stirring adventure. But the director's affinity to the documentary technique robs the subject of much of its intrinsic drama.

Pic's greatest asset is the superb casting of John Mills in the title role. Obviously playing down the drama on directorial insistence, Mills's close resemblance to the famous explorer makes the character come to life.

Scott's discovery that he has been beaten in the race to the South Pole should be a piece of poignant and moving drama. Instead, the five members of the expedition look very resolute, and very British, and philosophically begin the long trail home. Although depicted with fidelity, the agonies of the explorers on their homeward trek are presented with inadequate dramatization, with the result that the audience isn't emotionally affected.

•

SCOUNDREL, THE

1935, 75 mins, US b/w

Dir Ben Hecht, Charles MacArthur ***Prod*** Ben Hecht, Charles MacArthur ***Scr*** Ben Hecht, Charles MacArthur ***Ph*** Lee Garmes ***Ed*** Arthur Ellis ***Mus*** George Antheil ***Art*** Walter E. Keller

Act Noel Coward, Julie Haydon, Stanley Ridges, Martha Sleeper, Hope Williams, Ernest Cossart (Paramount)

The film is something of an audible novel. Beaucoup dialog and much palaver, with a minimum of action. It's a talky, slow exposition for the first three reels or so, all tending to indicate what a rat Anthony Mallare (Noel Coward), publisher, is.

When Julie Haydon becomes the latest romantic vis-à-vis, the motivation illustrates the same shabby technique which sends a real romance into the gutter. Coward meets destruction when an equally self-centered, cynical individual (Hope Williams) treats him in kind, and he thus becomes the victim of a NY-Bermuda plane wreck.

Histrionically Coward has his moments, but there are others when most film fans may find it a bit difficult to remain content with just an English accent and a Continental flair of character. The illusion isn't always wholly there.

1935: NOMINATION: Best Original Story

•

SCOUT, THE

1994, 101 mins, US Ⓥ ⊙ col

Dir Michael Ritchie ***Prod*** Albert S. Ruddy, Andre E. Morgan ***Scr*** Andrew Bergman, Albert Brooks, Monica Johnson ***Ph*** Laszlo Kovacs ***Ed*** Don Zimmerman, Pembroke Herring ***Mus*** Bill Conti ***Art*** Stephen Hendrickson

Act Albert Brooks, Brendan Fraser, Dianne Wiest, Lane Smith, Anne Twomey, Michael Rapaport (20th Century-Fox)

Baseball fans won't get their needed fix with this virtually baseball-free baseball movie—an odd hybrid of broad comedy and a darker undercurrent of psychological drama.

The film—inspired by a *New Yorker* magazine article—is about a down-on-his-luck talent scout, Al (Albert Brooks), who discovers in the inner wilds of Mexico Steve Nebraska (Brendan Fraser), a fireball-throwing, ambidextrous dream come true. Al inks the kid to a multimillion-dollar deal with the New York Yankees.

What follows, however, is less about baseball than a sort of awkward reworking of *Of Mice and Men*, with Fraser as the potentially dangerous innocent and Brooks cast as the reluctant father figure, trying to keep the kid's head together just long enough to cash in on that lucrative contract.

Brooks and director Michael Ritchie (who last visited the ballpark with *The Bad News Bears*) never quite commit to either of the movie's disparate chords.

•

SCREAM

1996, 110 mins, US Ⓥ ⊙ ▭ col

Dir Wes Craven ***Prod*** Cary Woods, Cathy Konrad ***Scr*** Kevin Williamson ***Ph*** Mark Irwin ***Ed*** Patrick Lussier ***Mus*** Marco Beltrami ***Art*** Bruca Alan Miller

Act Neve Campbell, David Arquette, Courteney Cox, Matthew Lillard, Skeet Ulrich, Drew Barrymore (Woods/Dimension)

Director Wes Craven is on familiar turf with *Scream*. The setting is a small town, the protagonists are teens, and there's a psychotic killer on the prowl. The pic's chills are top-notch, but its underlying mockish tone won't please die-hard fans.

Home-alone high schooler Casey Becker (Drew Barrymore) answers the phone and the sinister caller coerces her to play a series of increasingly perilous games. Next on the unknown maniac's list is Sidney Prescott (Neve Campbell), whose mother was murdered by a similar-style fiend a year earlier. Aggressive tab TV reporter Gale Weathers (Courteney Cox) believes it's the same killer and that the man (currently on death row) fingered by Sidney for her mom's murder is innocent.

Craven and scripter Kevin Williamson have worked hard to gussy up well-trod territory. Though the material is more intelligent than the norm and has a unusual third-act twist, it also employs some very clunky stereotypes.

The fictional community of Woodsboro, CA, is normally a sleepy hamlet populated by callous teens and ineffectual adults. The kids can quote chapter and verse from Craven's *Nightmare on Elm Street*, *Halloween* and *Prom Night* to explain the killer's gestalt. The rules of movie horror—as delineated by a vid-store employee—make Billy (Skeet Ulrich), Sidney's boyfriend, a prime suspect.

Craven, in this film and his prior *New Nightmare*, displays a fascination with blurring the lines between reality and film. But *Scream* merely ponders copycat murders, something that occurs more often onscreen than in dozing towns.

[A 111-min. *Director's Cut*, with 20 seconds of extra footage, was released on homevideo in 1997.]

•

SCREAM 2

1997, 120 mins, US Ⓥ ⊙ ▭ col

Dir Wes Craven ***Prod*** Cathy Konrad, Marianne Maddalena ***Scr*** Kevin Williamson ***Ph*** Peter Deming ***Ed*** Patrick Lussier ***Mus*** Marco Beltrami ***Art*** Bob Ziembicki

Act David Arquette, Neve Campbell, Courteney Cox, Sarah Michelle Gellar, Jamie Kennedy, Laurie Metcalf (Konrad/Dimension)

There's no question that the filmmakers—all veterans of the phenomenally successful original—have not only thought long and hard about stepping back into familiar territory but have been ultra-diligent about keeping the second outing on course. This sequel is visceral, witty and appropriately redundant.

A handful of the original cast continue the story, relocated from Northern California to Windsor College in small-town Ohio. Sidney (Neve Campbell) and Randy (Jamie Kennedy) are students attempting to escape the notoriety created by last year's tabloid-sensation murder and mayhem. A book on the incident by reporter Gale Weathers (Courteney Cox) was a bestseller and has been adapted for the screen.

A young couple (Jada Pinkett, Omar Epps) attending the premiere of the movie become the first victims of a copycat killer. Sidney is thrown back into the limelight, Gale is assigned to the news story, and former deputy Dewey (David Arquette) flies cross-country to protect the imperiled young woman.

On the most mundane level, *Scream 2* is a flat-out chiller with a seemingly unstoppable knife-wielding murderer. But the picture aspires to a lot more than slasher fare. The house-of-mirrors structure has a more chilling underlying message about the consequences of confusing artifice with the real thing. When the identity of the killer is revealed, he tells his intended victims his defense will be that he was corrupted by violent images from movies and other popular media.

Film is a smooth piece of goods and cast is top-notch.

•

SCREAM 3

2000, 116 mins, US Ⓥ ⊙ ▭ col

Dir Wes Craven ***Prod*** Cathy Konrad, Kevin Williamson, Marianne Maddalena ***Scr*** Ehren Kruger ***Ph*** Peter Deming ***Ed*** Patrick Lussier ***Mus*** Marco Beltrami ***Art*** Bruce Alan Miller

Act David Arquette, Neve Campbell, Courteney Cox Arquette, Patrick Dempsey, Scott Foley, Lance Henriksen (Konrad/Dimension)

Much like *Scream* and *Scream 2*, the third installment slices and dices slasher-movie cliches with a serrated edge of self-reflexive satire. Most of the action revolves around the filming of—wink, wink, nudge, nudge—*Stab 3*, the second sequel to a pic based on the "real-life" events of the first *Scream*. A running gag involves repeated warnings to expect the unexpected because the last chapter in a trilogy *always* breaks the rule. To underscore that point, *Scream 3* begins by disposing of a prominent survivor from the first two pics. It's a cheeky touch, easily the most audacious thing in the scenario.

Sidney Prescott (Neve Campbell), the franchise's amazingly resourceful heroine, is reintroduced as a veritable hermit. She remains out of the loop throughout the first hour or so as pic focuses on the killings of *Stab 3* cast members.

Telejournalist Gale Weathers (Courteney Cox Arquette) sees another chance to elevate her profile when real murders interrupt the fake mayhem of *Stab 3*. She's uneasy about reuniting with ex-sweetheart Dewey Riley (David Arquette) and annoyed by the strident Method mannerisms of Jennifer Jolie (Parker Posey) who has been signed to play the Gale Weathers character—and who has hired Dewey as technical adviser and, ahem, bodyguard.

Publicity-conscious studio chiefs halt production on *Stab 3* in the wake of what appears to be copycat killings. It quickly becomes clear that yet another masked murderer is on the prowl—and, worse, that the actors may be killed in the same order that their characters die in the film.

Detective Kincaid (Patrick Dempsey) agrees to share info with Gale Weathers in order to figure out why all the victims are found with photos of Sidney Prescott's long-dead mother. Eventually, the plucky *Scream* queen comes out of hiding to take a more active role in the proceedings, arousing the bloodlust of a killer whose identity is a genuine surprise.

Clever touches include a cameo appearance by Carrie Fisher as an ex-starlet who's still bitter about not being cast in *Star Wars*. As usual, director Wes Craven generates serious suspense even while his characters comment on the plot mechanics employed to achieve that suspense. By now, Campbell, Arquette and Cox Arquette are perfectly attuned to Craven's wavelength and offer performances enhanced by self-mockery.

•

SCREAM OF STONE

1991, 105 mins, Germany/France/Canada Ⓥ col

Dir Werner Herzog ***Prod*** Walter Saxer ***Scr*** Hans-Ulrich Klenner, Walter Saxer ***Ph*** Rainer Klausmann, Herbert Raditschnig ***Ed*** Suzanne Baron ***Mus*** Ingram Marshall, Alan Lamb, Sarah Hopkins, Atahualpa Yupanqui ***Art*** Juan Santiago

Act Vittorio Mezzogiorno, Mathilda May, Stefan Glowacz, Brad Dourif, Donald Sutherland, Al Waxman (SERA/Molecule/Stock)

Ever in search of new mad adventurers to catch his fancy, Werner Herzog has found them among mountain climbers for his latest South American epic, *Scream of Stone*. While it does feature some spectacular mountain photography in an area of the world few will ever see firsthand, the dramatic and psychological aspects remain so obscure as to become silly.

Clumsy prolog introduces two champion climbers. Martin (Vittorio Mezzogiorno) is a young hotshot who, for two years running, has won a televised indoor event by scaling an artificial cliff. Roger (Stefan Glowacz), an older man and a quintessentially Herzogian figure, is the world-class climbing master who scoffs at Martin as a mere "acrobat." Roger accepts a challenge to climb what he regards as the toughest peak in the world, a needle-like peak in Patagonia that he has tried and failed to conquer twice before. Accompanied by journalist Donald Sutherland, the rivals and their entourages assemble in Argentina and commence to wait around for ideal conditions for their climb.

Pic is poorly, sometimes laughably acted by an international cast playing uniquely dour, shallow, self-absorbed characters. But once the cameras get above ground level, Herzog offers quite a bit worth looking at.

•

SCREWBALLS

1983, 90 mins, US Ⓥ col

Dir Rafal Zielinski ***Prod*** Maurice Smith ***Scr*** Jim Wynorski, Linda Shayne ***Ph*** Miklos Lente ***Ed*** Brian Ravok ***Mus*** Tim McCauley ***Art*** Sandra Kybartas

Act Peter Keleghan, Lynda Speciale, Alan Daveau, Kent Deuters, Jason Warren, Linda Shayne (New World)

Screwballs is a poor man's *Porky's*. This compendium of horny high school jokes set in 1965 is full of youthful exuberance and proves utterly painless to watch, but it is so close in premise and tone to its model that negative comparisons can't help but be drawn.

Five lads receive detentions for such infractions as posing as a doctor during girls' breast examinations and straying into the gals' locker room. Responsible for the boys' plight is snooty homecoming queen Purity Busch, evidently the only female virgin left at the school. Five guys dedicate themselves to de-purifying her, and remainder of the film describes their goon-like attempts on her innocence.

Film was lensed in Toronto, which can only make one wonder why all these studies of randy young Americans come from north of the border.

•

SCROOGE
1970, 118 mins, UK Ⓥ ⦿ ▭ col
Dir Ronald Neame ***Prod*** Robert H. Solo ***Scr*** Leslie Bricusse ***Ph*** Oswald Morris ***Ed*** Peter Weatherley ***Mus*** Leslie Bricusse ***Art*** Terry Marsh
Act Albert Finney, Alec Guinness, Edith Evans, Kenneth More, Laurence Naismith, Michael Medwin (Cinema Center/Waterbury)

Scrooge is a most delightful film in every way, made for under $5 million in direct costs at England's Shepperton Studios. Albert Finney's remarkable performance in the title role; executive producer Leslie Bricusse's fluid adaptation of the Charles Dickens classic, *A Christmas Carol*, plus his unobtrusive complementary music and lyrics; and Ronald Neame's delicately controlled direction, which conveys but does not force, all the inherent warmth, humor and sentimentality.

An excellent cast of key supporting players enhances both the artistry of the film and its universal appeal: Alec Guinness, as Marley's ghost and Edith Evans and Kenneth More, respectively, as the Ghosts of Christmas Past and Present.

Finney's performance as coldhearted Scrooge is a professional high-water mark.

1970: NOMINATIONS: Best Costume Design, Art Direction, Song Score, Song ("Thank You Very Much")

•

SCROOGED
1988, 101 mins, US Ⓥ ⦿ col
Dir Richard Donner ***Prod*** Richard Donner ***Scr*** Mitch Glazer, Michael O'Donoghue ***Ph*** Michael Chapman ***Ed*** Fredric Steinkamp, William Steinkamp ***Mus*** Danny Elfman ***Art*** J. Michael Riva
Act Bill Murray, Karen Allen, John Forsythe, John Glover, Carol Kane, Robert Mitchum (Paramount)

Scrooged is an appallingly unfunny comedy, and a vivid illustration of the fact that money can't buy you laughs. Its stocking spilling with big names and production values galore, this updating of Dickens's *A Christmas Carol* into the world of cutthroat network television is, one episode apart, able to generate only a few mild chuckles.

Scrooge here is an utterly venal network chief whose taste runs beneath the lowest common denominator, has no friends, sacks any underlings who dare to disagree with him and possesses a personal history based entirely upon having watched TV since infancy. Unfortunately for the film, things ring false from the start because Bill Murray's cruelty seems very arbitrary, unfunny and ultimately unconvincing.

Murray's network, IBC, is preparing to broadcast a live version of *A Christmas Carol* (with, in a good bit, Buddy Hackett as Scrooge), so it is against this backdrop that Murray's own journey through his past and toward his personal salvation takes place.

Lunatic taxi driver David Johansen spirits Murray back to his deprived childhood in 1955. By 1968, Murray is working as an office boy when he bumps into the idealistic Karen Allen and takes up with her. Within three years, however, the love of his life has left, and so starts Murray's ascent from portraying a dog on a kiddies' show into the top executive suite at the company.

Pic's comic highlight unquestionably is Carol Kane's appearance as the Ghost of Christmas Present. Kane dispenses verbal and physical punishment on her victim with sadistic glee.

1988: NOMINATION: Best Makeup

•

SCUM
1979, 96 mins, UK Ⓥ col
Dir Alan Clarke ***Prod*** Davina Belling ***Scr*** Roy Minton ***Ph*** Phil Meheux ***Ed*** Mike Bradsell ***Art*** Mike Porter
Act Ray Winstone, Mick Ford, John Judd, Phil Daniels (Boyd's)

Given that *Scum*, a relentlessly brutal slice of British reform school life, is strongly directed by Alan Clarke and acted with admirable conviction, it is a pity that the hard-hitting screenplay is more passionate tract than powerful entertainment.

Its appeal could have been wider with more dramatic light and shade, and its message more likely to find its mark if the basic point—that a youth penitentiary can kill, not cure—had been made through more investigative character-study, instead of via a catalogue of horrific events.

Significantly, the plot of a "trainee" (young offender) whose means of survival in the corrupt reformatory is to become top dog by meeting violence with violence started life as a BBC-TV play. Although filmed, it was never aired on account of its alleged bias and unpalatability.

•

SEA CHASE, THE
1955, 116 mins, US Ⓥ ⦿ ▭ col
Dir John Farrow ***Prod*** John Farrow ***Scr*** James Warner Bellah, John Twist ***Ph*** William Clothier ***Ed*** William Ziegler ***Mus*** Roy Webb
Act John Wayne, Lana Turner, David Farrar, Lyle Bettger, Tab Hunter, James Arness (Warner)

While seemingly equipped with all the elements for exciting screenfare, the picture never quite lives up to its promise, having overlooked gripping suspense, the one basic ingredient that would have made the difference. Thus, producer-director John Farrow and scripters turn a rather neat trick in making a chase picture without the suspenseful excitement of a chase, albeit based on Andrew Geer's novel of the pursuit of a nondescript German freighter from Australia to the North Sea by the British Navy.

The picture registers a kind of broad action as the rusty tub *Ergenstrasse* eludes its pursuers and, short of food and fuel, still manages to make its way almost to the Fatherland before being caught and sunk. The story brings out the trials and tribulations of the hard-driven crew, and the ingenuity of the skipper and his officers in keeping going when surrender would not have been too great a shame.

There is a romance woven in, between John Wayne, a German who despises Nazism but as captain of his ship still determines to bring it home, and Lana Turner, a Nazi spy and adventuress who has been no more than the term implies.

Wayne, as a he-man type, seems a little embarrassed in delivering some of the boy-girl talk that occurs as he, at first hating, gradually comes to love the spy aboard his freighter. Turner does her character well, developing it on as believable lines as the story permits.

•

SEA GULL, THE
1968, 141 mins, UK col
Dir Sidney Lumet ***Prod*** Sidney Lumet ***Ph*** Gerry Fisher ***Ed*** Alan Heim ***Art*** Tony Walton
Act James Mason, Vanessa Redgrave, Simone Signoret, David Warner, Harry Andrews, Denholm Elliott (Warner/Seven Arts)

The Sea Gull is a sensitive, well-made and abstractly interesting period pic. Downbeat eternal verities—frustration, unrequited love, etc.—are projected admirably by a cast featuring James Mason, Simone Signoret (both in memorable performances), Vanessa Redgrave and David Warner.

Setting is a rural Russian house, where bailiff Ronald Radd, his wife Eileen Herlie and daughter Kathleen Widdoes seek to create a pleasant climate for the final years of Harry Andrews, a retired official who apparently has endured a life of frustration. Andrews herein is a cliché, crotchety old fool. His performance is the poorest one in the film.

Signoret, Andrews's sister, has descended for a visit, trailed by her current lover, Mason, a popular hack writer. Redgrave, a neighborhood girl, becomes entranced with Mason.

The deliberate adherence to the Chekhov's script necessarily retains the somewhat old-fashioned character motivations and plot structures.

Director Sydney Lumet has created an appropriately somber mood.

•

SEA HAWK, THE
1924, 129 mins, US ⊗ b/w
Dir Frank Lloyd ***Scr*** J.G. Hawks, Walter Anthony ***Ph*** Norbert Brodine ***Ed*** Edward M. Roskam ***Art*** Stephen Goosson, Fred Gabourie
Act Milton Sills, Enid Bennett, Lloyd Hughes, Wallace MacDonald, Marc MacDermott, Wallace Beery (First National)

This picture has no end of entertainment value. It is just as thrilling and gripping as reading one of Rafael Sabatini's books; all of the punch of that author's writings has been brought to the screen.

There's action aplenty. It starts in the first reel and holds true to the last minute. Milton Sills, who is featured together with Enid Bennett, comes into his own in this production, and Bennett also scores tremendously. One must, however, not overlook Wallace Beery, a low comedy ruffian, who wades right through the story.

Frank Lloyd, who directed, is to be considered with the best that wield a megaphone. *The Sea Hawk* cost around $800,000. The properties used alone cost $135,000. The picture looks it.

•

SEA HAWK, THE
1940, 127 mins, US Ⓥ ⦿ b/w
Dir Michael Curtiz ***Prod*** Hal B. Wallis (exec.), Henry Blanke ***Scr*** Howard Koch, Seton I. Miller ***Ph*** Sol Polito ***Ed*** George Amy ***Mus*** Erich Wolfgang Korngold ***Art*** Anton Grot
Act Errol Flynn, Brenda Marshall, Claude Rains, Flora Robson, Donald Crisp, Alan Hale (Warner)

The Sea Hawk retains all of the bold and swashbuckling adventure and excitement of its predecessor, turned out for First National by Frank Lloyd in 1923. But the screenplay of the new version is expanded to include endless episodes of court intrigue during the reign of Queen Elizabeth that tend to diminish the effect of the epic sweep of the high seas dramatics. When the script focuses attention on the high seas and the dramatic heroics of the sailors who embarked on daring raids against Spanish shipping, the picture retains plenty of excitement.

Story traces the adventures of the piratical sea fighter (Errol Flynn), commander of a British sailing ship that preys on Spanish commerce in the late 16th century. Colorful and exciting sea battle at the start, when Flynn's ship attacks and sinks the galleon of the Spanish ambassador, comes too early and is never topped by any succeeding sequences. Then follows extensive internal politics of Elizabeth's court, with the queen secretly condoning Flynn's buccaneering activities.

Little credit can be extended to the overwritten script, with long passages of dry and uninteresting dialog, or to the slow-paced, uninspiring direction by Michael Curtiz. Errol Flynn fails to generate the fire and dash necessary to successfully put over the role of the buccaneer leader, although this lack might partially be attributed to the piloting. Flora Robson gets attention in the role of Queen Elizabeth.

The Sea Hawk is a big-budget production with reported cost set around $1.75 million. Expenditure is easily seen in the large sets, sweeping sea battles and armies of extras used with lavish display. From a production standpoint, the picture carries epic standards, but same cannot be said for the story.

1940: NOMINATIONS: Best B&W Art Direction, Score, Sound, Special Effects

•

SEANCE ON A WET AFTERNOON
1964, 116 mins, UK Ⓥ b/w
Dir Bryan Forbes ***Prod*** Richard Attenborough ***Scr*** Bryan Forbes ***Ph*** Gerry Turpin ***Ed*** Derek York ***Mus*** John Barry ***Art*** Ray Simm
Act Kim Stanley, Richard Attenborough, Nanette Newman, Patrick Magee, Mark Eden (Beaver)

This is a skillful and, on many counts, admirable picture. Bryan Forbes's writing and direction create an aptly clammy atmosphere and he's backed by some shrewd thesping.

Onus of the acting falls heavily on Kim Stanley and Richard Attenborough. Yet though she is an exciting actress to watch, she is much Method, and technicalities occasionally get in the way.

It throws extra responsibility on Attenborough as her weak, loving and downtrodden husband. Here is a splendid piece of trouping which rings true throughout.

The star is a medium of dubious authenticity, who inveigles her spouse into a nutty plan which she confidently believes will give her the recognition due to her. Idea is to "borrow" a child, make out it has been kidnapped, collect the ransom loot and wait for the story to pump up to front-page sensation. Then she aims to hold a seance and reveal clues which will enable the cops to find the child unharmed.

The film throughout is pitched in sombre key with much macabre reference to a son that the couple never had but in whom Stanley implicitly believes. The dankness of the house in which her shabby machinations evolve is well caught, thanks to deft artwork and Gerry Turpin's searching camera.

Forbes's well-written, imaginative script [from the novel by Mark McShane] is a study in grey, abetted by the fine lensing of Turpin. An exciting, ingenious high spot involves complicated production when Attenborough is due to collect the ransom money. It was shot with hidden cameras in Leicester Square and Piccadilly at London's busiest hour. Result is an air of intense, exciting realism. So realistic, in fact, that parts of it had to be reshot.

1964: NOMINATION: Best Actress (Kim Stanley)

•

SEA OF GRASS, THE
1947, 122 mins, US Ⓥ b/w
Dir Elia Kazan ***Prod*** Pandro S. Berman ***Scr*** Marguerite Roberts, Vincent Lawrence ***Ph*** Harry Stradling ***Ed*** Robert J.

Kern **Mus** Herbert Stothart **Art** Cedric Gibbons, Paul Groesse
Act Spencer Tracy, Katharine Hepburn, Robert Walker, Melvyn Douglas, Phyllis Thaxter, Edgar Buchanan (M-G-M)

Film is loaded with very superior acting and spectacular imaginative photography. Camerawork by Harry Stradling is particularly breathtaking in the outdoor sequences for the sense of space and correct feeling it gives to this drama of the New Mexico prairielands.

Story [from the novel by Conrad Richter] is built around the traditional American feud between cattlemen and farmers, with Spencer Tracy perfect as the iron-jawed leader in the ranchers' determined stand against the inevitable surge westward of the agriculturists whose hoes and fences cut into the ranges on which the huge herds are dependent.

Katharine Hepburn is pictured as a cultured St. Louis belle who goes to New Mexico to marry range-baron Tracy. His attachment is so great for the "sea of grass" that he has no understanding of his wife's feeling for the farm families whom he is forcing to starvation by illegally keeping them from the land. Melvyn Douglas, as a lawyer and judge, not only has a feeling for the farmers, but for Hepburn as well, and a natural amity grows between them.

Long arm of coincidence enters in when she finally leaves Tracy and runs into Douglas in Denver. In despair and confusion she gives herself up to him, only to turn remorseful the following day and decide to return to Tracy. A child is born and all concerned realize it is Douglas's not Tracy's. Tracy forces his wife to leave. There's never a surprise. Likewise, the clichéd dialog is frequently hard to accept.

•

SEA OF LOVE
1989, 112 mins, US Ⓥ ⦿ col
Dir Harold Becker **Prod** Martin Bregman, Louis A. Stoller **Scr** Richard Price **Ph** Ronnie Taylor **Ed** David Bretherton **Mus** Trevor Jones **Art** John Jay Moore
Act Al Pacino, Ellen Barkin, John Goodman, Michael Rooker, William Hickey, Richard Jenkins (Universal)

Sea of Love is a suspenseful film noir boasting a superlative performance by Al Pacino as a burned-out Gotham cop.

Handsome production benefits from a witty screenplay limning the bittersweet tale of a 20-year veteran NYC cop (Pacino) assigned to a case tracking down the serial killer of men who've made dates through the personal columns.

He teams up with fellow cop John Goodman to set a trap for the murderer. Clues point to a woman being the killer.

Early on, Ellen Barkin appears as one of the suspects, but after an initial rebuff Pacino is smitten with her and crucially decides not to get her fingerprints for analysis. Pic builds some hair-raising twists and turns as the evidence mounts pointing to her guilt, climaxing in a surprising revelation.

Pacino here brings great depth to the central role. A loner with retirement after 20 years facing him, this cop is a sympathetic, self-divided individual and Pacino makes his clutching at a second chance with femme fatale Barkin believable.

•

SEA OF SAND
(US: DESERT PATROL)
1958, 97 mins, UK b/w
Dir Guy Green **Prod** Robert S. Baker, Monty Berman **Scr** Robert Westerby **Ph** Wilkie Cooper **Ed** Gordon Pilkington **Mus** Clifton Parker **Art** Maurice Pelling, Alastair McIntyre
Act Richard Attenborough, John Gregson, Michael Craig, Vincent Ball, Percy Herbert, Barry Foster (Tempean)

Sea of Sand, it's claimed, is based on an original story by Sean Fielding, but there is nothing very original about it. It is a routine war adventure, with excellent all-round acting and taut direction by Guy Green.

Pic deals with the Long Range Desert Group on the eve of Alamein [in 1942]. Y Patrol is given the arduous task of blowing up one of the Nazis's biggest petrol dumps. Mission accomplished, the nine men fight their way back to base.

Shot entirely on location [in Tripolitania, Libya], director Green and cameraman Wilkie Cooper splendidly capture the remote loneliness of the vast desert, the heat, the boredom and the sense of pending danger. The screenplay is predictable, but the dialog is reasonably natural and the various characters are well drawn.

•

SEARCH, THE
1948, 105 mins, US Ⓥ b/w
Dir Fred Zinnemann **Prod** Lazar Wechsler **Scr** Richard Schweizer, David Wechsler, Paul Jarrico **Ph** Emile Berna **Ed** Hermann Haller **Mus** Robert Blum
Act Montgomery Clift, Aline MacMahon, Jarmila Novotna, Ewart G. Morrison, Ivan Jandl, Wendell Corey (M-G-M)

This simple film was made in the American zone of Germany, principally in and around the rubbled remains of Nuremberg. Only four of its actors are professionals, the others having been recruited on the spot.

The story is the familiar one of a family torn apart by the Nazis. This time the family is Czech. Only survivors are the mother and a nine-year-old boy, who are separated. Unable to differentiate between the beatings suffered from the Germans and the good intent of UNRRA's displaced persons workers, the lad runs away. His cap is found by a riverbank and it is assumed he has drowned. Actually, he lives amongst the rubble until hunger tempts him close enough to a GI for the soldier to catch him.

The four professionals in the cast are Montgomery Clift, as the GI, making his film debut following a Broadway break-in; Aline MacMahon, as the camp official, and as typical a social worker as one could put a finger on anywhere; Jarmila Novotna, Metropolitan Opera singer and herself a Czech, who plays the mother, and Wendell Corey.

1948: Best Motion Picture Story, Special Award (Ivan Jandl)

NOMINATIONS: Best Director, Actor (Montgomery Clift), Screenplay

•

SEARCH AND DESTROY
1995, 90 mins, US Ⓥ col
Dir David Salle **Prod** Ruth Charny, Dan Lupovitz, Elie Cohen **Scr** Michael Almereyda **Ph** Bobby Bukowski, Michael Spiller **Ed** Michelle Gorchow **Mus** Elmer Bernstein **Art** Robin Standefer
Act Griffin Dunne, Illeana Douglas, Dennis Hopper, Christopher Walken, John Turturro, Rosanna Arquette (New Image)

Visual artist David Salle's eagerly awaited premiere, *Search and Destroy* aspires to be an inventive black comedy of the absurd with sharp social commentary, but instead is a disappointing film with few bright moments and many more tedious ones. Major talent behind the cameras and a dream cast of eccentric actors only partially overcome the trappings of a misconceived film that is poorly directed.

Inevitable comparisons will be made with the far superior 1985 angst comedy *After Hours*, directed by Martin Scorsese, who co-executive produced this one [and cameos as a government accountant].

Griffin Dunne plays Martin Mirkhein, an ambitious Florida businessman sought by the IRS for tax evasion. Hearing the tax news for the first time, Martin's attractive wife (Rosanna Arquette), fed up with his chronic lying and abominable conduct, demands a separation.

Martin miraculously stumbles on the philosophy of Dr. Luther Waxling (Dennis Hopper), a self-help guru with a popular cable TV show. Martin flies to Dallas to propose making a movie out of his bestseller. But his initial attempts to meet the guru are rebuffed by Waxling's assistant, Roger (Ethan Hawke), and Marie (Illeana Douglas), his sexy receptionist.

Martin and Marie eventually elope to New York to pursue his obsessive dream. From then on, pic is structured as a madcap fantasy (with horror and violence) that throws Martin in one catastrophe after another. Adapting Howard Korder's stage play to the screen, scripter Michael Almereyda divides the tale into two chapters—*Search* and *Destroy*. The script's shortcomings would have been tolerated if pic were better directed, but first-time helmer Salle exhibits severe problems with tone and rhythm, resulting in a film that seldom finds its right tempo or proper mood.

•

SEARCHERS, THE
1956, 119 mins, US Ⓥ ⦿ col
Dir John Ford **Prod** C. V. Whitney **Scr** Frank S. Nugent **Ph** Winton C. Hoch **Ed** Jack Murray **Mus** Max Steiner **Art** Frank Hotaling, James Basevi
Act John Wayne, Jeffrey Hunter, Vera Miles, Ward Bond, Natalie Wood, Hank Worden (Whitney/Warner)

The Searchers is a western in the grand scale—handsomely mounted and in the tradition of *Shane*. The VistaVision-Technicolor photographic excursion through the southwest—presenting in bold and colorful outline the arid country and areas of buttes and giant rock formations—is eye-filling and impressive.

Yet *The Searchers* is somewhat disappointing. There is a feeling that it could have been so much more. Overlong and repetitious, there are subtleties in the basically simple story that are not adequately explained. There are, however, some fine vignettes of frontier life.

The picture [from the novel by Alan LeMay] involves a long, arduous trek through primitive country by two men in search of nine-year-old girl kidnapped by hostile Comanche Indians.

Wayne, the uncle of the kidnapped girl, is a bitter, taciturn individual throughout and the reasons for his attitude are left to the imagination of the viewer. His bitterness toward the Indians is understandable. They massacred his brother's family (except for the kidnapped girl) and destroyed the ranch. He feels the girl has been defiled by the Indians during her years with them and is determined to kill her. Wayne's partner in the search is Jeffrey Hunter, who is also involved in labored attempts at comic relief.

Wayne is fine in the role of hard-bitten, misunderstood, and mysterious searcher and the rest of the cast acquits itself well, notably Hunter and Vera Miles.

1956: NOMINATIONS: Best Editing, Original Musical Score

•

SEARCH FOR PARADISE
1957, 120 mins, US ▭ col
Dir Otto Lang **Prod** Lowell Thomas **Scr** Lowell Thomas, Otto Lang, Prosper Buranelli **Ph** Harry Squire, Jack Priestley **Ed** Lovel S. Ellis, Harvey Manger **Mus** Dimitri Tiomkin
Act Lowell Thomas, James S. Parker, Christopher Young (Cinerama)

The fourth Cinerama sticks almost slavishly to established formulae. Once more strange lands are "seen" by two selected "tourists," this time a make-believe air force major (Christopher Young) and sergeant (James S. Parker) who, at the payoff, decide that they'll sign up for another hitch, the air force itself being the ultimate paradise.

The beginning of the picture is cornily contrived. An Associated Press news machine is seen ticking out a bulletin that Lowell Thomas is one of three ambassadors just appointed to represent Washington at the coronation durbar of King Mahendra of Nepal.

The several stops of *Search* are all way-stations en route to Nepal. The picture centers upon the approach to and environs of the Himalayas, world's greatest peaks, truthfully described as a region of mystery, age, mysticism and Communistic intrigue.

Lowell picks up the major and the sarge in the Vale of Kashmir, a plausible paradise indeed, especially its Shalimar Gardens. The visit at Nepal is the big sequence. And a stunning display of oriental pomp it is. This segment is a genuine peep into dazzling fantasy and a true coup for Cinerama and Thomas.

•

SEARCHING FOR BOBBY FISCHER
1993, 110 mins, US Ⓥ ⦿ col
Dir Steven Zaillian **Prod** Scott Rudin, William Horberg **Scr** Steven Zaillian **Ph** Conrad L. Hall **Ed** Wayne Wahrman **Mus** James Horner **Art** David Gropman
Act Joe Mantegna, Max Pomeranc, Joan Allen, Ben Kingsley, Laurence Fishburne, Michael Nirenberg (Mirage/Paramount)

Based on a true story written by the father depicted in the film, *Searching for Bobby Fischer* focuses on Josh Waitzkin (Max Pomeranc), a relatively normal 7-year-old who possesses a stunning aptitude for chess. Max starts honing that talent, playing a sped-up form of the game known as "blitz" with street hustlers. Soon after, his father, Fred (Joe Mantegna), takes him to a chess coach (Ben Kingsley) who says that Josh could well be the second coming of Bobby Fischer, the legendary former chess champ.

Searching is at its best when exploring the tension between wanting to develop a child's abilities and allowing him to remain a child. Unfortunately, as scripter, debuting director Steven Zaillian (who wrote *Awakenings*) also feels compelled to throw in *Karate Kid*–type flourishes, a rather stale genre that doesn't lend itself all that well to chess. The narrative is ruthlessly edited, jumping around in a manner that skips needed exposition and abandons characters.

Zaillian does a better job with his actors. Mantegna adds to his portfolio with a fine, subdued performance as the suddenly driven father, while Joan Allen is strong as the protective mom. Newcomer Pomeranc is wonderfully real and wide-eyed as Josh, with a raspy voice and slight lisp recalling Linus from the *Peanuts* cartoons.

1993: NOMINATION: Best Cinematography

•

SEARCHING WIND, THE
1946, 107 mins, US b/w
Dir William Dieterle **Prod** Hal Wallis **Scr** Lillian Hellman **Ph** Lee Garmes **Ed** Warren Low **Mus** Victor Young **Art** Hans Dreier, Franz Bachelin
Act Robert Young, Sylvia Sidney, Ann Richards, Dudley Digges, Douglas Dick, Albert Basserman (Paramount)

Hal Wallis has produced a fine film from Lillian Hellman's Broadway success, presenting a searching indictment of the once weak-willed liberal, and appeasement policy of the U.S.

The film is an improvement on the Broadway play (Hellman scripted both) because it is more coherent, and better acted. Although the story is carried forward only till Mussolini's death, and much of it is a flashback to the days of the March on Rome in 1922, pic isn't dated.

Pic is story of a bewildered diplomat, stationed in Europe to report the significance of changing events to the U.S. State Dept., who fails to see importance of a Fascist takeover in Italy, the rise of Nazism in Germany, the Munich agreement, etc. His wife is mixing socially with the wrong people, the smug, satisfied set who are pulling the strings for these events, unaware of the cataclysmic results.

Tied up with the political is a personal story, the diplomat's marriage to the wrong woman and his constant love for the newspaper woman he should have wed.

Robert Young plays the diplomat with an honest sense of bewilderment and inadequacy toward forces he can't foresee or direct. Sylvia Sidney, as the prescient reporter, is not only unusually attractive but a superior actress. Ann Richards, as the wife, is also good.

●

SEA WOLF, THE
1941, 98 mins, US Ⓥ b/w
Dir Michael Curtiz ***Prod*** Henry Blanke (assoc.) ***Scr*** Robert Rossen ***Ph*** Sol Polito ***Ed*** George Amy ***Mus*** Erich Wolfgang Korngold ***Art*** Anton Grot
Act Edward G. Robinson, Ida Lupino, John Garfield, Alexander Knox, Gene Lockhart, Barry Fitzgerald (Warner)

Jack London's famous hellship sails for another voyage over the cinematic seas in this version of *The Sea Wolf*. Edward G. Robinson steps into the role of the callous and inhuman skipper, Wolf Larsen.

John Garfield signs on to the sailing schooner to escape the law. Ida Lupino (also a fugitive) and the mild-mannered novelist (Alexander Knox) are rescued from a sinking ferryboat in San Francisco bay. Robinson is the dominating and cruel captain who takes fiendish delight in breaking the spirits of his crew and unwilling passengers.

Robinson provides plenty of vigor and two-fisted energy to the actor-proof role of Larsen, and at times is overdirected. Garfield is the incorrigible youth whose spirit cannot be broken, and is grooved to his familiar tough characterization of previous pictures. Lupino gives a good account of herself in the rough-and-tumble goings on, but the romantic angle is under-stressed in this version.

Michael Curtiz directs in a straight line, accentuating the horrors that go on during the voyage of the *Ghost*.

●

SEA WOLVES, THE
THE LAST CHARGE OF THE CALCUTTA LIGHT HORSE
1980, 120 mins, UK Ⓥ col
Dir Andrew V. McLaglen ***Prod*** Euan Lloyd ***Scr*** Reginald Rose ***Ph*** Tony Imi ***Ed*** John Glen ***Mus*** Roy Budd ***Art*** Syd Cain
Act Gregory Peck, Roger Moore, David Niven, Trevor Howard, Barbara Kellermann, Patrick Macnee (Lorimar)

How a band of pip-pip British civilians rallied to King and country, tucked in their pot bellies and knocked out a German spy nest that was playing havoc with wartime Allied shipping in the Indian Ocean. Touted as "the last great untold action story of the war," film was scripted by Reginald Rose from James Leasor's novel *Boarding Party*.

Sea Wolves is unabashed flag-waving, a salute to the Calcutta Light Horse, a part-time regiment whose membership consisted mainly of colonial business types way past draft age but recruited as volunteers for the destruction of three German freighters interned in coastal waters off the then-neutral Portuguese colony of Goa.

Gregory Peck's a Britisher in this one, but the affected accent won't fool anyone. He and Roger Moore are regular army. The stiff-uppered civvy retreads, headed by David Niven, include Trevor Howard and Patrick Macnee.

●

SEBASTIAN
1968, 100 mins, UK Ⓥ col
Dir David Greene ***Prod*** Herbert Brodkin, Michael Powell ***Scr*** Gerald Vaughn-Hughes ***Ph*** Gerry Fisher ***Ed*** Brian Smedley-Aston ***Mus*** Jerry Goldsmith ***Art*** Wilfrid Shingleton
Act Dirk Bogarde, Susannah York, Lilli Palmer, John Gielgud, Janet Munro, Ronald Fraser (Paramount/Maccius)

Very good direction, acting and dialog are apparent in *Sebastian*, but a fatal flaw in basic plotting makes this production just a moderately entertaining Cold War comedy-drama.

The amusing, and not so amusing, pressures on persons who break foreign government secret codes are potent angles for a strong film, but, herein, the story touches so many bases that it never really finds a definite concept.

Leo Marks's original screen story, scripted by Gerald Vaughn-Hughes, depicts Dirk Bogarde as a daffy math genius in cryptography. Susannah York, a new recruit to the code force, breaks down his romantic reserve. Lilli Palmer, as a politically suspect coder, and John Gielgud, an Intelligence chief, add lustre. Janet Munro scores very well as a boozy fading pop singer who, with Ronald Fraser, attempts to compromise Bogarde's security clearance.

Despite all the plus elements, the film wanders about in its unfolding. Short, tight scenes of good exposition are broken by recurring transitional sequences which add up to an apparent padding effect.

●

SECOND BEST
1994, 105 mins, UK/US Ⓥ col
Dir Chris Menges ***Prod*** Sarah Radclyffe ***Scr*** David Cook ***Ph*** Ashley Rowe ***Ed*** George Akers ***Mus*** Simon Boswell ***Art*** Michael Howells
Act William Hurt, Chris Cleary Miles, Keith Allen, Prunella Scales, Jane Horrocks, John Hurt (Fron/Regency/Alcor)

The agonizing process by which a withdrawn man and his troubled adopted son grow to know and love each other is minutely charted in *Second Best*, nicely acted and dramatized in all its particulars but modest in its aim and achievement.

Novelist David Cook's acutely felt story revolves around the deprived emotional lives of 10-year-old James (Chris Cleary Miles) and the 42-year-old man who would adopt him, Graham Holt (William Hurt). James's mother is dead and his father (Keith Allen) is a long-term jailbird.

Graham is also motherless, and his father (Alan Cumming) is bedridden due to a stroke. A rumpled, withdrawn village postmaster, Graham has never had a significant emotional contact or sexual experience, but now has the sudden impulse to adopt a boy, which would be the first assertive thing he's done in his life.

To a large extent, pic depends upon performance to put it over. A seemingly unlikely choice to play an unworldly Welshman, Hurt lets his inwardness work to great benefit and creates a completely convincing and often touching characterization.

●

SECONDS
1966, 108 mins, US Ⓥ ⊙ b/w
Dir John Frankenheimer ***Prod*** Edward Lewis ***Scr*** Lewis John Carlino ***Ph*** James Wong Howe ***Ed*** Ferris Webster, David Newhouse ***Mus*** Jerry Goldsmith ***Art*** Ted Howarth
Act Rock Hudson, Salome Jens, John Randolph, Will Geer, Jeff Corey, Richard Anderson (Joel/Frankenheimer/Paramount)

U.S. suburbia boredom is treated in an original manner in this cross between a sci-fi opus, a thriller, a suspense pic and a parable on certain aspects of American middle-class life.

A middle-aged man has lost contact with his wife. His only daughter is married and gone. Even his work, which was his mainstay in life, seems to pall. Into this comes a strange call from a supposedly dead friend to come to a certain place.

He finds himself in a mysterious big business surgery corporation with some disquieting features of a room full of listless men. He is told he can be redone surgically to become a young man and start life over again. He decides to go through with it and after surgery wakes up as Rock Hudson.

This has some intriguing aspects on the yearning for youth and a chance to live life over again by many men. But this Faustian theme is barely touched on and the hero's tie with the past is also somewhat arbitrary. Film [from the novel by David Ely] does not quite come off as a thriller, sci-fi adjunct or philosophical fable.

[Pic's "European version," which has a slightly longer nude party sequence, was released on homevideo in 1997.]

●

SECRET AGENT
1936, 83 mins, UK Ⓥ ⊙ b/w
Dir Alfred Hitchcock ***Prod*** Michael Balcon ***Scr*** Charles Bennett, Ian Hay, Jesse Lasky, Jr. ***Ph*** Bernard Knowles ***Ed*** Charles Frend ***Mus*** Louis Levy (dir.) ***Art*** Otto Werndorff
Act Madeleine Carroll, Peter Lorre, John Gielgud, Robert Young, Percy Marmont, Lilli Palmer (Gaumont-British)

Secret Agent dallies much on the way but rates as good spy entertainment, suave story telling, and, in one particular case, brilliant characterization. This is the role of the "Mexican," a hired killer as played by Peter Lorre. Director Alfred Hitchcock has done well at lending the tale's grim theme [from the play by Campbell Dixon, based on the novel *Ashenden* by W. Somerset Maugham] with deftly fashioned humor, appropriate romantic interplay and some swell outdoor photography.

More critical element will find the part of Madeleine Carroll somewhat straining credulity. The film has her philandering at the game of espionage and out of sheer ineptitude pulling one of the major coups of the service. Likewise unconvincing is the overly sensitive conduct in which her co-spy (John Gielgud) indulges once he is bitten by love.

Production maintains an easygoing pace almost throughout, with most of the action cast against the background of the Swiss Alps. Gielgud is assigned to Switzerland to prevent a German spy from getting back into pro-German territory. To do the actual killing, Lorre, a Mexican with a juvenile sense of fun but a boundless enthusiasm for playing the knife upon humans, is sent along. Arriving on the scene, Gielgud finds that Carroll had been matched with him for the job, with the pair to pose as man and wife.

●

SECRET BEYOND THE DOOR . . .
1947, 98 mins, US Ⓥ b/w
Dir Fritz Lang ***Prod*** Fritz Lang ***Scr*** Silvia Richards ***Ph*** Stanley Cortez ***Ed*** Arthur Hilton ***Mus*** Miklos Rozsa ***Art*** Max Parker
Act Joan Bennett, Michael Redgrave, Anne Revere, Barbara O'Neil, Natalie Schafer (Universal/Diana)

Film carries the Diana Productions label, a combo of Walter Wanger, Fritz Lang and Joan Bennett who have been responsible for several other Diana thrillers. It is arty, with almost surrealistic treatment in camera angles, storytelling mood and suspense, as producer-director Lang hammers over his thrill points.

Co-starring with Bennett is Michael Redgrave. He disappoints as the man with an anti-woman complex who nearly murders his wife before finding out what his trouble is. Bennett is good as the rich, useless society girl who finds a love so strong she would rather die than give it up. Mental complexities of the principals makes it sometimes hard to sort out the various motivations used to spin the tale. It's based on a story by Rufus King, scripted by Silvia Richards. Such psychiatric tricks as mental cases who recoil at locked doors, lilacs, or become oddly stimulated by physical combat and looks are some of the suspense devices.

●

SECRET CEREMONY
1968, 109 mins, UK Ⓥ col
Dir Joseph Losey ***Prod*** John Heyman, Norman Priggen ***Scr*** George Tabori ***Ph*** Gerry Fisher ***Ed*** Reginald Beck ***Mus*** Richard Rodney Bennett ***Art*** Richard MacDonald
Act Elizabeth Taylor, Mia Farrow, Robert Mitchum, Peggy Ashcroft, Pamela Brown (Universal/WFS)

Robert Mitchum is featured in this macabre tale [from a short story by Marco Denevi] of mistaken identity, psychological and sexual needs, ultimate suicide and murder. Moody, leisurely developed and handsomely produced, it was made at England's Elstree Studios.

Mia Farrow, playing a wealthy, demented and incest-prone nympho, appears to have kidnapped Elizabeth Taylor, in the role of an aging prostitute. As things turn out, Taylor does not mind being mistaken for Farrow's deceased mother; instead, she gradually, but fitfully, eases into the child's desired mold. Only the return of Mitchum, the girl's stepfather with a libertine reputation, cues the revelation that Farrow is a sexual psychotic whose seduction of Mitchum helped ruin her mother's marriage.

Performances are generally good: Farrow's via an emphasis on facial expressions, Taylor's via a salutary toning down of her shrieking-for-speaking tendencies, and Mitchum's casual, stolid projection.

●

SECRET COMMAND
1944, 81 mins, US b/w
Dir A. Edward Sutherland ***Prod*** Phil Ryan ***Scr*** Roy Chanslor ***Ph*** Franz F. Planer ***Ed*** Viola Lawrence ***Mus*** Paul Sawtell ***Art*** Lionel Banks, Edward Jewell
Act Pat O'Brien, Carole Landis, Chester Morris, Ruth Warrick (Columbia/Terneen)

This is a lusty melodrama of counter-espionage around a large shipyard, with expert blending of action and suspense with spontaneous good humor resulting in solid entertainment.

Naval intelligence gets wind of Nazi sabotage plans at the large shipyard, and Pat O'Brien is sent in to get a job as a secret agent. He starts as a pilebuck on shift bossed by brother Chester Morris, and latter is not sold on O'Brien's tale of wife (Carole Landis) and two youngsters in bungalow—with family and housing conveniently supplied by Intelligence. Yarn weaves between the dramatics of tracing the Nazi saboteurs at the shipyards, and intimacies at home with O'Brien's newly acquired family setup.

O'Brien turns in a fine performance in the lead, with Landis and Ruth Warrick sharing femme spots in good style. Strong support is provided by Morris, Barton MacLane, Tom Tully and Wallace Ford.

•

SECRET FOUR, THE
SEE: THE FOUR JUST MEN

•

SECRET FOUR, THE
SEE: KANSAS CITY CONFIDENTIAL

•

SECRET GARDEN, THE
1949, 92 mins, US Ⓥ col
Dir Fred M. Wilcox ***Prod*** Clarence Brown ***Scr*** Robert Ardrey ***Ph*** Ray June ***Ed*** Robert J. Kern ***Mus*** Bronislau Kaper
Act Margaret O'Brien, Herbert Marshall, Dean Stockwell, Brian Roper, Gladys Cooper, Elsa Lanchester (M-G-M)

The Secret Garden is a yarn about kids and superficially, it would appear designed to entice them. Yet the allegorical and psychological implications that have been carried over from Frances Hodgson Burnett's book are clearly for the grown-up trade.

Margaret O'Brien is an orphan come to live with her uncle (Herbert Marshall). His wife died 10 years earlier and he has turned against the world in bitterness. He has a son (Dean Stockwell) who suffers from a paralysis of the legs and whom he keeps in bed.

Among Marshall's quirks is a phobia about anyone going into the garden. He keeps it locked until O'Brien finds a key and, with the aid of a neighbor boy (Brian Roper), secretly nurtures the neglected flowers and plants back to beauty.

The production throughout is on a lavish scale. Unfortunately, the performances do not equal it.

•

SECRET GARDEN, THE
1993, 101 mins, US Ⓥ ⊙ col
Dir Agnieszka Holland ***Prod*** Fred Fuchs, Fred Roos, Tom Luddy ***Scr*** Caroline Thompson ***Ph*** Roger Deakins ***Ed*** Isabelle Lorente ***Mus*** Zbigniew Preisner ***Art*** Stuart Craig
Act Kate Maberly, Heydon Prowse, Andrew Knott, Maggie Smith, Laura Crossley, John Lynch (Warner/American Zoetrope)

As the company did with *The Black Stallion* 14 years earlier, American Zoetrope has produced another exquisite children's classic in *The Secret Garden*, executed to near perfection in all artistic departments.

Best known of late as a Broadway musical, *The Secret Garden* has been a success ever since English-American author Frances Hodgson Burnett wrote it in 1911. A solid, darkly Gothic, psychologically slanted film version starring Margaret O'Brien was made by M-G-M in 1949, and the BBC and Hallmark Hall of Fame each produced telefilms of the metaphorical fantasy.

When her parents are killed in an Indian earthquake, 10-year-old orphan Mary Lennox (Kate Maberly) is sent to live in the gloomy, 100-room Yorkshire mansion of her reclusive uncle, Lord Craven (John Lynch). Craven ignores both Mary and his crippled son, Colin (Heydon Prowse), whose bedridden life is tyrannically run by the estate's housekeeper, Mrs. Medlock (Maggie Smith).

Rude and disagreeable at first, Mary soon becomes intrigued by the existence on the grounds of a secret garden that has supposedly never been entered since Lady Craven's death. In league with down-to-earth local boy Dickon (Andrew Knott), Mary begins nurturing the unkempt garden, just as she begins an edgy, illicit friendship with Colin. Using all British thesps of proper age (unlike the earlier Hollywood version, which seemed cast too old), Polish-born director Agnieszka Holland displays an unerring instinct for obtaining truthful performances from child actors. Smith gets off to a great start as Mrs. Medlock, gnawing chicken legs while transporting Mary across the forbidding moors, and brilliantly sustains the character of an all-seeing, dictatorial witch. Zbigniew Preisner's score is timelessly melodic.

•

SECRET HEART, THE
1946, 97 mins, US b/w
Dir Robert Z. Leonard ***Prod*** Edwin H. Knopf ***Scr*** Whitfield Cook, Anne Morrison Chapin ***Ph*** George Folsey ***Ed*** Adrienne Fazan ***Mus*** Bronislau Kaper ***Art*** Cedric Gibbons, Edward Garfagno
Act Claudette Colbert, June Allyson, Walter Pidgeon, Lionel Barrymore, Robert Sterling, Patricia Medina (M-G-M)

Heart is more than just a suspenseful thriller. Based on an original story by Rose Franken and William Brown Meloney, the film presents in honest fashion a tale of a young girl with a father fixation that might have been taken from an actual case history.

Tale revolves around a rich widow and her two stepchildren, a boy just out of the navy and a college-age girl. Latter, an excellent pianist, is in love with the memory of her father, who taught her to play. Her only interest, consequently, is to shut out the rest of the world by locking herself in a room and playing for him. On the advice of a psychiatrist, the widow takes her brood to the family farm where the father had committed suicide. There the girl begins to come out of her shell but then undergoes another deep emotional upset.

In a role that's a far cry from her usual song-and-dance parts, June Allyson gives out with what's undoubtedly the best emoting of her career. Claudette Colbert is fine as the young widow, with her flair for comedy helping to lighten the film's heavy mood. Walter Pidgeon, as the guy she's been in love with all the time, is his usual suave, competent self.

•

SECRET LIFE OF AN AMERICAN WIFE, THE
1968, 93 mins, US Ⓥ col
Dir George Axelrod ***Prod*** George Axelrod ***Scr*** George Axelrod ***Ph*** Leon Shamroy ***Ed*** Harry Gerstad ***Mus*** Billy May ***Art*** Jack Martin Smith
Act Walter Matthau, Anne Jackson, Patrick O'Neal, Edy Williams, Richard Bull (20th Century-Fox/Charlton)

The Secret Life of an American Wife, as the title might indicate, is a light sophisticated marital farce. Basic idea, which sometimes takes on the aspect of a French romp, takes a comedy look at sex in the person of a 34-year-old Connecticut wife who thinks she's gone to pot and lost all her appeal. More skillful development might have heightened impact of her deciding to do something about it, but overall the tale is amusing. George Axelrod production, which he also wrote and directed, actually is a one-woman show with a couple of male characters tossed in for necessary consequence.

Even when such a past master at comedy as Walter Matthau, in role of a top film star on whom Anne Jackson tries her wiles, enters, the unfoldment is focused on her.

Jackson is enticing as the wife of a public relations man, Patrick O'Neal, who must cater to his top client, Matthau, whenever latter comes to N.Y. from Hollywood for a round of frolic.

Matthau turns on all the faucets in his delineation of the thesp, who spends most of his scenes in pajama bottoms and a towel.

•

SECRET LIFE OF WALTER MITTY, THE
1947, 108 mins, US Ⓥ ⊙ col
Dir Norman Z. McLeod ***Prod*** Samuel Goldwyn ***Scr*** Ken Englund, Everett Freeman ***Ph*** Lee Garmes ***Ed*** Monica Collingwood ***Mus*** David Raksin ***Art*** George Jenkins, Perry Ferguson
Act Danny Kaye, Virginia Mayo, Boris Karloff, Fay Bainter, Ann Rutherford, Florence Bates (RKO/Goldwyn)

Some of the deepest-dyed Thurber fans may squeal since there's naturally considerable change from the famed short story on which the screenplay is built. There's a basic switch in the plot that has been concocted around the Mitty daydreams. Thurber's whole conception of Mitty was an inconsequential fellow from Perth Amboy, NJ, to whom nothing—but nothing—ever happened and who, as a result, lived a "secret life" via his excursions into daydreaming. In contrast, the picture builds a spy-plot around Mitty that is more fantastic than even his wildest dream.

Danny Kaye reveals a greater smoothness and polish thespically and a perfection of timing in his slapstick than has ever been evident in the past.

Exceedingly slick job is done on the segues from the real-life Mitty into the dream sequences. Mitty's fantasies carry him through sessions as a sea captain taking his schooner through a storm, a surgeon performing a next-to-impossible operation, an RAF pilot, a Mississippi gambler, a cowpuncher and a hat designer. They're all well-loaded with satire, as is the real-life plot with pure slapstick.

Virginia Mayo is the beautiful vis-à-vis in both the real-life spy plot, and the dreams. She comes a commendable distance thespically in this picture. Karloff wins heftiest yaks in a scene in which he plays a phony psychiatrist convincing Mitty he's nuts.

•

SECRET OF BLOOD ISLAND, THE
1965, 84 mins, UK Ⓥ col
Dir Quentin Lawrence ***Prod*** Anthony Nelson Keys ***Scr*** John Gilling ***Ph*** Jack Asher ***Ed*** James Needs, Tom Simpson ***Mus*** James Bernard ***Art*** Bernard Robinson
Act Barbara Shelley, Jack Hedley, Charles Tingwell, Bill Owen, Lee Montague, Patrick Wymark (Hammer)

The "secret" isn't one for long—a British female agent is shot down near a Jap prison camp in Malaya. The prisoners hide her and eventually help her to escape, not without some ensuing incidents that provide the necessary action.

Barbara Shelley manages to fool the Jap guards into thinking she's just another male prisoner much more easily than she does the audience. But when she's supposed to look dirty and sweaty (and this attention to detail is due to meticulous work by the technicians on the film), she looks properly soiled. None of the actors are ever seen out of character.

Besides Shelley, very good performances are given by Jack Hedley and Charles Tingwell as the leaders of the British prisoners and Bill Owen, Peter Welch, Lee Montague and Edwin Richfield as other prisoners. Among the Japanese roles, however, there isn't one convincing performance in the group.

•

SECRET OF MY SUCCESS, THE
1965, 112 mins, UK ▭ col
Dir Andrew L. Stone ***Prod*** Virginia Stone, Andrew L. Stone ***Scr*** Andrew L. Stone ***Ph*** David Boulton ***Ed*** Virginia Stone, Noreen Ackland ***Mus*** Lucien Cailliet, Derek New, Joao Baptista Laurenco, Christopher Stone
Act Shirley Jones, Stella Stevens, Honor Blackman, James Booth, Lionel Jeffries, Amy Dolby (M-G-M)

There are several capable players in *Secret of My Success*, many of them from the British studios. But the screenplay Andrew L. Stone has whipped up is too much of a handicap, and what might have been a bright, little British comedy turns out to be neither comedy nor melodrama.

Three almost separate yarns are employed to trace the rise of a lowly English town constable to position of ruler in a mythical Latin-American country.

Initial episode details how his understanding of a comely, little village dressmaker (Stella Stevens), while only a town constable, wins a promotion to police inspector. The curvaceous, red-haired Stevens puts this across despite all its implausibilities, such as hiding the body of her slain husband.

Booth's first big job as police inspector shows him becoming involved with a baroness. This little tale tells about the breeding of giant spiders until they become as big as oversized bulldogs—and large enough to crush a man to death.

Another sharp maneuver by his mother wins Booth the job of liaison officer to the president of Guanduria, Latin-American mythical land. By helping Shirley Jones, who is secretly plotting a revolution, he winds up as new ruler of this country.

•

SECRET OF MY SUCCE$S, THE
1987, 110 mins, US Ⓥ ⊙ col
Dir Herbert Ross ***Prod*** Herbert Ross ***Scr*** Jim Cash, Jack Epps, A. J. Carothers ***Ph*** Carlo Di Palma ***Ed*** Paul Hirsch ***Mus*** David Foster ***Art*** Edward Pisoni, Peter Larkin
Act Michael J. Fox, Helen Slater, Richard Jordan, Margaret Whitton, John Pankow, Christopher Murney (Rastar)

The Secret of My Success is a bedroom farce with a leaden touch, a corporate comedy without teeth. What it does have is Michael J. Fox in a winning performance as a likable hick out to hit the big time in New York.

Fresh off the bus from Kansas, Brantley Foster (Fox) doesn't want to return until he has a penthouse, jacuzzi, a beautiful girlfriend and a private jet he can go home in. His ideals are a yuppie's dream.

Fox encounters the predictable crime-infested corners of New York and his squalid apartment is furnished with roaches and rats. When he meets his dream girl (Helen Slater), he is literally thunderstruck.

After young Brantley lands a job in the mailroom of an anonymous NY corporation his big chance comes when he takes over an abandoned office and sets himself up as a young exec.

Fox, in spite of his inherent charm, lacks a genuine personality and is neither country bumpkin nor city sharpie. Consequently, the film lacks a consistent tone or style.

•

SECRET OF NIMH, THE
1982, 82 mins, US Ⓥ ⊙ col
Dir Don Bluth ***Prod*** Don Bluth, Gary Goldman, John Pomeroy ***Scr*** Don Bluth, Gary Goldman, John Pomeroy,

Will Finn *Ed* Jeffrey Patch *Mus* Jerry Goldsmith (M-G-M/United Artists)

The Secret of NIMH is a richly animated and skillfully structured film created by former Disney animators Don Bluth, Gary Goldman and John Pomeroy. As craft, their first feature film is certainly an homage to the best of an age ago. Every character moves fluidly and imaginatively against an extravaganza of detailed background and dazzling effects, all emboldened by fascinating colored textures.

The story is simple. A mother mouse (voiced by Elizabeth Hartman) is simply trying to find a new home for her brood before the old one is destroyed by spring plowing. Her task is complicated by the severe illness of a son, too sick to move.

Beyond that, the layers pile high. On the light side there's the comedy of Dom DeLuise as a clumsy crow who tries to help. At the worst are a pack of rats led for good and ill by Derek Jacobi, Peter Strauss and Paul Shenar, all influenced by some modern-day sci-fi mind-bending, mixed with old-fashioned sorcery. John Carradine also serves well as a menacing but helpful great owl, full of wisdom and woe.

•

SECRET OF ROAN INISH, THE

1994, 103 mins, US Ⓥ ⦿ col

Dir John Sayles *Prod* Sarah Green, Maggie Renzi *Scr* John Sayles *Ph* Haskell Wexler *Ed* John Sayles *Mus* Mason Daring *Art* Adrian Smith

Act Mick Lalley, Eileen Colgan, John Lynch, Jeni Courtney, Richard Sheridan, Cillian Byrne (Jones Entertainment)

John Sayles's *The Secret of Roan Inish* marks his entry into family-pic terrain, a crossing that draws pleasant, albeit unexciting, results and is short on the lush atmospherics its fanciful story cries for. Story (drawn from Brit author Rosalie K. Fry's juve novel *Secret of the Ron Mor Skerry*) has plucky 10-year-old Fiona (Jeni Courtney) shipped off by a hard-drinking, widowed dad to her grandparents' coastal home in post-World War II County Donegal. There she and teen cousin Eamon are drawn into their folkloric clan past—especially one ancestor's union with a half-human, half-seal "Selkie" (Susan Lynch).

Strange sights further pique Fiona's curiosity. She finally convinces grandfolk (Mick Lally, Eileen Colgan) to row out to Roan Inish, the nearby island home they've abandoned, in hopes of solving the puzzle of her infant brother Jamie.

Film captures hardscrabble life of this remote fishing culture, but lowkey direction and Haskell Wexler's handsome yet somber lensing could use more leavening touches to help script's fantastic side take flight. Jaunty soundtrack of traditional Celtic sounds sets an appropriate mood.

•

SECRET OF SANTA VITTORIA, THE

1969, 134 mins, US ▭ col

Dir Stanley Kramer *Prod* Stanley Kramer *Scr* William Rose, Ben Maddow *Ph* Giuseppe Rotunno *Ed* William Lyon, Earle Herdan *Mus* Ernest Gold *Art* Robert Clatworthy

Act Anthony Quinn, Anna Magnani, Virna Lisi, Hardy Kruger, Sergio Franchi, Giancarlo Giannini (United Artists)

The Secret of Santa Vittoria comes near being a dramatic knockout, so tempered with humor and understanding that it also becomes an idyll of war and Italian peasantry. Carrying charm, suspense, romance, the production offers Anthony Quinn at his seasoned best, a plot and unfoldment that holds the spectator.

Based on the Robert Crichton bestseller, its story—said to be true and to have become a legend—is simple. The people of a hill town in northern Italy are suddenly thrown into shock when apprised that a detachment of the retreating German army is to descend on their town to confiscate all their wine, their very life blood.

Screenplay painstakingly developes this conflict, to which Stanley Kramer's direction adds fascinating character evolvement and ingenious invention.

•

SECRET PEOPLE

1952, 96 mins, UK b/w

Dir Thorold Dickinson *Prod* Sidney Cole *Scr* Thorold Dickinson, Wolfgang Wilhelm *Ph* Gordon Dines *Ed* Peter Tanner *Mus* Roberto Gerhard *Art* William Kellner

Act Valentina Cortese, Serge Reggiani, Charles Goldner, Audrey Hepburn, Megs Jenkins, Athene Seyler (Ealing)

Secret People is a hackneyed story of political agents working against a tyrannical dictator, dressed up with all the familiar cliches to make a dull and rather confusing offering.

The yarn has a prewar setting, opening in London in 1930 with the arrival of two girls whose father has been killed by a European dictator. Story skips seven years, when the two girls together with the Italian cafe owner who has adopted them, spend a weekend in Paris. There, the older girl runs into the boy she left behind at home to carry on her father's work. He follows her to London, and compels her to act as an accomplice in an attempt on the dictator's life.

Audrey Hepburn, in a minor role combines beauty with skill, particularly in two dance sequences.

•

SECRET PLACES

1984, 96 mins, UK Ⓥ col

Dir Zelda Barron *Prod* Simon Relph, Ann Skinner *Scr* Zelda Barron *Ph* Peter MacDonald *Ed* Laurence Mery-Clark *Mus* Michel Legrand *Art* Eileen Diss

Act Marie-Therese Relin, Tara MacGowran, Claudine Auger, Jenny Agutter, Cassie Stuart, Anne-Marie Gwatkin (Skreba/Virgin)

Secret Places is a pleasing evocation of schoolgirl life in England during World War II.

Based on a novel by Janice Elliott, the film recounts the initially hostile response of a group of adolescents to the enrollment of Laura Meister, a German refugee, in their all-girl school. Gradually her exotically winning ways and intelligence secure her enrollment in the select circle which gathers in "secret places." Things turn sour, however, when a girl's father is killed in battle.

The plot relates the psychological pressures which lead to Laura's attempted suicide.

Marie-Therese Relin captures the gestures and looks of a girl whose emotional resilience conceals suffering. Tara MacGowran is right on as a repressed English girl.

•

SECRET POLICEMAN'S BALL, THE

1980, 91 mins, UK Ⓥ ⦿ col

Dir Roger Graef *Prod* Roger Graef, Thomas Schwalm *Ph* Ernest Vincze, Clive Tickner, Pascoe MacFarlane *Ed* Thomas Schwalm

Act John Cleese, Peter Cook, Eleanor Bron, Pete Townshend, Rowan Atkinson, Michael Palin (Document/Amnesty International)

Roger Graef's film record of the 1979 Amnesty International benefit show at Her Majesty's Theatre, London, is primarily aimed at the tube. John Cleese, Michael Palin and Terry Jones of the *Monty Python* team appear in various sketches; guitarist Pete Townshend plays acoustic versions of a couple of The Who's repertoire, joined on one by classical picker John Williams; Peter Cook (sans Dudley Moore) renders a takeoff of one of the local hits of 1979—the judge's summing-up in the trial of Liberal politician Jeremy Thorpe; and Billy Connolly, Clive James and Eleanor Bron, among others, contribute solo spots. All gave their services free.

There is no backstage material in *The Secret Policeman's Ball*, which is a disappointment. The earlier such venture, *Pleasure at Her Majesty's* [1976], included footage of hasty rehearsals and dressing-room neurosis, which leavened the laugh-lump with an extra dimension.

•

SECRET POLICEMAN'S OTHER BALL, THE

1982, 99 mins, UK Ⓥ ⦿ col

Dir Julien Temple *Prod* Martin Lewis, Peter Walker *Scr* Marty Feldman, Michael Palin, Martin Lewis, and members of the cast *Ph* Oliver Stapleton *Ed* Geoff Hogg

Act Rowan Atkinson, Alan Bennett, John Cleese, Billy Connolly, Victoria Wood, Eric Clapton (Amnesty International)

The second filmed record of the biannual Amnesty International fundraiser in London. *The Secret Policeman's Other Ball* is a thoroughly entertaining concert pic. As irreverent and clever as its title, show boasts comic talents from *Monty Python, Beyond the Fringe* and *Not the Nine O'Clock News* and therefore does require a taste for British humor. Some of the humor slides over into tastelessness, but most of it is rousing fun in the tradition of the groups from which these performers have sprung. Particularly hilarious are a *Top of the Form* quiz show takeoff in which the moderator gets the correct answers mixed up, and a deadpan, coming-out-of-the-closet sexual confession by Alan Bennett. [The film released in the U.S. under the title *The Secret Policeman's Other Ball* is a combination of footage from this pic and the previous one.]

•

SECRET RAPTURE, THE

1994, 96 mins, UK Ⓥ ⦿ col

Dir Howard Davies *Prod* Simon Relph *Scr* David Hare *Ph* Ian Wilson *Ed* George Akers *Mus* Richard Hartley *Art* Barbara Gosnold

Act Juliet Stevenson, Joanne Whalley-Kilmer, Penelope Wilton, Neil Pearson, Alan Howard, Robert Stephens (Channel 4/Greenpoint)

A broad family melodrama, *The Secret Rapture* is a fitfully successful adaptation (by the author) of the David Hare play. Making his film directing debut, the theater's Howard Davies provides an appropriate somber tone for the tale of blood rivalries and emotional manipulation. The film jettisons much of the play's politically specific underpinnings and bolsters the Shakespearean-style tragedy.

Isobel (Juliet Stevenson), whose father has recently died, is torn apart when she discovers her bereavement for the dead man isolates her from friends and family. Sister Marion (Penelope Wilton) remains icily detached, concerned only with the family fortunes. Their young stepmother, Katherine (Joanne Whalley-Kilmer), has inured herself to alcohol.

While Isobel grapples with a sense of loss, Marion is quick to establish her reign. Of course, the neat little package quickly unravels. Human frailties plague the orderliness Marion so fiercely attempts to create. Hare's screenplay delineates a frightening precision and alarming logic in the machinations that bring the principals to the breaking point. But the story's catharsis is never satisfyingly resolved.

Stevenson effects a powerful, strident and unpleasant pose that ultimately works against the material.

•

SECRETS & LIES

1996, 142 mins, France/UK Ⓥ ⦿ col

Dir Mike Leigh *Prod* Simon Channing-Williams *Scr* Mike Leigh *Ph* Dick Pope *Ed* Jon Gregory *Mus* Andrew Dickson *Art* Alison Chitty

Act Timothy Spall, Brenda Blethyn, Phyllis Logan, Marianne Jean-Baptiste, Claire Rushbrook, Ron Cook (CiBy 2000/Thin Man/Channel 4)

Mike Leigh's first film in three years has all the feel of a career-summarizing work. A return to his less stygian, pre-*Naked* style of dysfunctional dramatic comedy, but painted on a far more ambitious and serious canvas, *Secrets & Lies* is unquestionably a finely observed, deeply felt work, though with some nagging problems in pacing and structure.

Much like Woody Allen's *Crimes and Misdeameanors*, pic yo-yos between sequences of interior drama and classic observational humor, with the emphasis on the former. In its more intense sequences, often shot in long, tightly framed takes, *Secrets & Lies* is almost Leigh's version of *Scenes from a Marriage*.

Film opens gradually, with the funeral of the adoptive parents of a young black woman, Hortense (Marianne Jean-Baptiste), an optometrist with a yuppie-ish London lifestyle. One by one, we meet the other characters, either at work or at home: middle-aged factory worker Cynthia (Brenda Blethyn), who lives with her unsmiling, argumentative daughter, Roxanne (Claire Rushbrook), a road sweeper, in a terraced house in a working-class area; and Cynthia's younger bro, Maurice (Timothy Spall), a portrait photographer who's moved to an upscale, leafy suburb with his snooty wife, Monica (Phyllis Logan).

Plot driver is Hortense's decision, now that she's sans family, to discover her birth parents, not least when it emerges that her biological mother may have been white.

Blethyn (Brad Pitt's mom in *A River Runs Through It*) juggles the twin facets of her role with consummate skill. It's a complex performance—funny, pitiable and stereotypical, but very real. Spall's turn as Maurice will come as a surprise to those who know him best as the loony restaurateur in *Life Is Sweet*. Maurice emerges as the strongest and wisest of the pic's gallery of dysfunctional, a role bolstered by Spall's careful underplaying.

Despite its accomplishments, the pic doesn't sustain its length. Not enough new is brought to the table after the first few reels to justify some of the more extended heart-to-hearts, and the long-awaited birthday set piece is too swift in its resolution and too long coming (some 100 minutes in). At one point the pic almost grinds to a halt with the introduction of a completely extraneous character, the previous owner of Maurice's business.

1996: NOMINATIONS: Best Picture, Actress (Brenda Blethyn), Supp. Actress (Marianne Jean-Baptiste), Director, Original Screenplay

•

SECRET WAR OF HARRY FRIGG, THE
1968, 110 mins, US Ⓥ ▭ col
Dir Jack Smight ***Prod*** Hal Chester ***Scr*** Peter Stone, Frank Tarloff ***Ph*** Russell Metty ***Ed*** Terry Williams ***Mus*** Carlo Rustichelli ***Art*** Alexander Golitzen, Henry Bumstead
Act Paul Newman, Sylva Koscina, Tom Bosley, Andrew Duggan, John Williams, Werner Peters (Universal/Albion)

The Secret War of Harry Frigg is an amusing World War II comedy starring Paul Newman as a dumb army private sent to rescue five Axis-held Allied generals. Strong story premise, excellent supporting cast and generally good dialog work to smooth over sometimes static direction and sluggish pacing.

Frank Tarloff's original story, scripted by author and Peter Stone, concerns the exploits of the title character as he effects the eventual rescue of five top brass from Italian-German incarceration. Newman plays a perennial goof-off, who achieves a measure of self-confidence and maturity under pressure. Sympathy is with him all the way.

Carrying the main comedy load are the five captured generals—Andrew Duggan, Tom Bosley, John Williams, Charles D. Gray, Jacques Roux—plus their Italo captor, Vito Scotti, and James Gregory, the U.S. general. There are many smiles, and some strong laughs, in the pic, result of which audience will probably emerge feeling lifted, if never consistently nor hilariously diverted.

•

SECRET WAYS, THE
1961, 112 mins, US b/w
Dir Phil Karlson ***Prod*** Richard Widmark ***Scr*** Jean Hazlewood ***Ph*** Max Greene ***Ed*** Aaron Stell ***Mus*** John Williams ***Art*** Werner Schlichting, Isabella Schlichting
Act Richard Widmark, Sonja Ziemann, Charles Regnier, Walter Rilla, Howard Vernon, Senta Berger (Universal)

The Secret Ways emerges a ludicrous, imitative, unintentional parody of dozens of cloak-and-dagger pictures. Filmed in Europe by producer-star Richard Widmark, the production amounts to a sort of poor man's *Third Man*.

The undistinguished, astonishingly uninformative screenplay was adapted from the novel by Alistair MacLean. Widmark stars as an American adventurer-for-hire who hires out to rescue a noted scholar from behind the Iron Curtain in Hungary. He has a running skirmish with the Budapestiferous AVO (Hungarian Secret Police), but ultimately gets his man.

As directed by Phil Karlson, there are a few lively chase sequences but most of the film is burdened with suspicious eyeballing and unrealistically theatrical behavior.

•

SEDMIKRASKY
(DAISIES)
1966, 75 mins, Czechoslovakia col
Dir Vera Chytilova ***Prod*** Bohumil Smida, Ladislav Fikar ***Scr*** Ester Krumbachova, Vera Chytilova ***Ph*** Jaroslav Kucera ***Ed*** Miroslav Hajek ***Mus*** Jiri Sust, Jiri Slitr ***Art*** Karel Lier
Act Jitka Cerhova, Ivana Karbanova, Julius Albert (Barrandov)

Two zany young teenage girls are the focus of this extremely funny, witty and expertly fashioned film. The gals seem to live on men, do not work, and have no ties with society. Director Vera Chytilova has them as engaging but futile rebels or misfits who can never seem to fit into life.

In this, her second feature pic, Chytilova [working from a screen story by her and Pavel Juracek] harks back to early silent comedies and displays a remarkable control of filmic language, special effects and rhythm and sight gags.

The two girls are introduced sitting on a beach and seem to be like puppets. They are then seen at home in a mad pop-art atmosphere of cutouts on walls, flower arrangements on their beds, and strange eating habits. This is interlarded with their meetings with different types of men.

The two free-living madcaps never become annoying or silly because of the engaging treatment and playing. Color is subtle, pleasing and is a mix with sepia, tinting and inventive special effects that help the mood and atmosphere.

•

SEDUCTION OF JOE TYNAN, THE
1979, 107 mins, US Ⓥ ⊙ col
Dir Jerry Schatzberg ***Prod*** Martin Bregman ***Scr*** Alan Alda ***Ph*** Adam Holender ***Ed*** Evan Lottman ***Mus*** Bill Conti ***Art*** David Chapman
Act Alan Alda, Barbara Harris, Meryl Streep, Rip Torn, Melvyn Douglas (Universal)

Adroitly combining humor and intimate drama, *Joe Tynan* joins that list of exemplary Washington-set pix, including *Advise and Consent* and *The Best Man*.

In large part, the credit goes to Alan Alda, whose portrayal in the title role is no less complex and multifaceted than his screenplay. Joe Tynan is a familiar political figure: the young, handsome liberal senator who rides upward on the coattails of a few big media victories. Alda assumes the pasted-on smile, the hearty handshake and breezy confidence of a politico with immense ease. He seems to have been born for the role.

Less often explored is the price paid for such double-edged success, and this is where *Joe Tynan* excels. As Alda's intelligent and frustrated wife, Barbara Harris gives the performance of her career.

•

SEE NO EVIL
(UK: BLIND TERROR)
1971, 87 mins, US Ⓥ ⊙ col
Dir Richard Fleischer ***Prod*** Martin Ransohoff, Leslie Linder ***Scr*** Brian Clemens ***Ph*** Gerry Fisher ***Ed*** Thelma Connell ***Mus*** Elmer Bernstein ***Art*** John Hoesli
Act Mia Farrow, Dorothy Alison, Robin Bailey, Diane Grayson, Brian Rawlinson, Norman Eshley (Filmways)

Brian Clemens's script has Mia Farrow recuperating from a blinding horse riding accident at the home of Robin Bailey, his wife Dorothy Alison and daughter Diane Grayson. An innocently offended young punk slays the household while Farrow is riding with fiance Norman Eshley. Extremely good suspense is built and maintained as Farrow discovers the senseless murders, then outwits the murderer who has returned to recover a wrist bracelet.

Paul Nicholas, the murderer, is not seen facially until the climax though Gerry Fisher's lensing puts the mysterious character in an emphatic dormant posture throughout via shooting his boots and arrogant bodily mannerisms. Clemens's script seeds the plot with a thousand sock red herrings, but Farrow's lengthy travails in time become rather heavy on the meller side; all that's missing is for her to be trapped on an ice floe.

Farrow's performance as a blind girl is very convincing, grabbing and maintaining audience sympathy for her character.

•

SEE NO EVIL, HEAR NO EVIL
1989, 103 mins, US Ⓥ ⊙ col
Dir Arthur Hiller ***Prod*** Marvin Worth ***Scr*** Earl Barret, Arne Sultan, Eliot Wald, Andrew Kurtzman, Gene Wilder ***Ph*** Victor J. Kemper ***Ed*** Robert C. Jones ***Mus*** Stewart Copeland ***Art*** Robert Gundlach
Act Richard Pryor, Gene Wilder, Joan Severance, Kevin Spacey, Kirsten Childs, Anthony Zerbe (Tri-Star)

With Richard Pryor and Gene Wilder in the lead roles, *See No Evil, Hear No Evil* could only be a broadly played, occasionally crass, funny physical comedy [from a screen story by Earl Barret, Arne Sultan and Marvin Worth].

How the blind Pryor ends up working for the deaf Wilder at a Manhattan lobby newsstand really is inconsequential, since neither their first encounter, nor anything that follows, is believable for a minute, including the thing that binds them in the first place—how each denies his limitations.

While Wilder's back is turned, a customer is shot in the back. Pryor is out on the curb listening for the New York *Daily News* to make its morning drop—so he misses hearing anything inside.

By the time Wilder turns around, he's only able to catch a glimpse of the assailant's (Joan Severance) sexy gams. Pryor has missed it all, though he does manage to catch a whiff of Severance's perfume before she slips by him onto the crowded street.

The cops arrive and, in predictable fashion, arrest the only suspects around, the two numbskulls who couldn't possibly coordinate anything, much less a murder.

•

SEE YOU IN THE MORNING
1989, 119 mins, US Ⓥ ⊙ col
Dir Alan J. Pakula ***Prod*** Alan J. Pakula ***Scr*** Alan J. Pakula ***Ph*** Donald McAlpine ***Ed*** Evan Lottman ***Art*** George Jenkins
Act Jeff Bridges, Alice Krige, Farrah Fawcett, Drew Barrymore, Lukas Haas, Macaulay Culkin (Lorimar)

See You in the Morning is a bad dream for those who've admired Alan J. Pakula's best work.

Pakula produced, wrote and directed the semi-autobiographical story of a man torn between two families and two marriages.

Jeff Bridges is a Manhattan psychiatrist who tries earnestly to fit in with his new life with second wife Beth (Alice Krige) and her two kids, while remaining the most decent of dads to his own two kids. Their mother is played by Farrah Fawcett.

As dull as this sounds, it's even more boring to watch. At just under two hours, it seems nearly interminable.

Pakula tried too hard to make this into a romantic comedy. Bridges's character jokes to avoid talking about his feelings (some shrink!) while Krige is the guilt-ridden martyr type.

•

SEIZE THE DAY
1986, 93 mins, US Ⓥ ⊙ col
Dir Fielder Cook ***Prod*** Chiz Schultz ***Scr*** Ronald Ribman ***Ph*** Eric Van Haren Noman ***Ed*** Sidney Katz ***Mus*** Elizabeth Swados ***Art*** John Robert Lloyd
Act Robin Williams, Jerry Stiller, Joseph Wiseman, Glenne Headly, William Hickey, Tony Roberts (Learning in Focus)

The first film ever made based upon a Saul Bellow novel, *Seize the Day* can boast of earnest performances and intent, but is swamped in obviousness and the broadness of its brush strokes. Overwrought piece was made for television.

Having lost his job as a salesman, disappointed his girlfriend and allowed himself to be bled dry by his estranged wife, Tommy (Robin Williams in a "serious" starring role), who's pushing 40, returns to New York City to appeal to his father in an attempt at a new start.

Tommy finds heartlessness everywhere he turns. His father (Joseph Wiseman) is a successful doctor forever disappointed that his son didn't follow in his footsteps. The only one to take a positive interest in poor Tommy is Doc (Jerry Stiller), a physician of great alleged healing powers who in fact spends most of his time playing the commodities market.

The world of power here, in 1956, is made up exclusively of crusty old Jewish men who play cards and hang out at the steam bath, and it is not a pretty picture. Williams throws himself entirely into his character, and his desperation is palpable. Fielder Cook's direction is extremely literal, and lack of modulation is a major problem.

•

SEMI-TOUGH
1977, 107 mins, US Ⓥ ⊙ col
Dir Michael Ritchie ***Prod*** David Merrick ***Scr*** Walter Bernstein ***Ph*** Charles Rosher, Jr. ***Ed*** Richard A. Harris ***Mus*** Jerry Fielding ***Art*** Walter Scott Herndon
Act Burt Reynolds, Kris Kristofferson, Jill Clayburgh, Robert Preston, Bert Convy, Roger E. Mosley (United Artists)

Semi-Tough begins as a bawdy and lively romantic comedy about slap happy pro football players, then slows down to a too-inside putdown of contemporary self-help programs.

Stars Burt Reynolds, Kris Kristofferson and Jill Clayburgh are all excellent within the limits of the zigzag Walter Bernstein script and Michael Ritchie's ambivalent direction.

Dan Jenkins's book was adapted by Bernstein to tell of pals Reynolds and Kristofferson, members of a flashy team owned by eccentric Robert Preston, whose daughter (Clayburgh) roommates with the two guys. She tilts romantically towards Kristofferson, whose personality has become more assured after undergoing training by Bert Convy.

•

SENATOR WAS INDISCREET, THE
(UK: MR. ASHTON WAS INDISCREET)
1947, 86 mins, US Ⓥ b/w
Dir George S. Kaufman ***Prod*** Nunnally Johnson ***Scr*** Charles MacArthur ***Ph*** William Mellor ***Ed*** Sherman A. Rose ***Mus*** Daniele Amfitheatrof ***Art*** Bernard Herzbrun, Boris Leven
Act William Powell, Ella Raines, Arleen Whelan, Charles D. Brown, Peter Lind Hayes, Myrna Loy (Universal)

Director George S. Kaufman manifests pace and polish in a fast-moving bit of fluff [story by Edwin Lanham] about a flannel-mouth Solon whose presidential aspirations become complicated when he loses an incriminating diary wherein he had recorded every step taken by his political backers in the past 30 days. Topper finds William Powell (in the title role) in native South Seas garb and his "queen" is the unbilled Myrna Loy—a frank takeoff on the Crosby-Hope technique of "surprise" tongue-in-cheek fadeouts.

Powell does a fine job as the stuffy dimwit of a senator who was not stupid enough not to record his political machine's machinations. He uses that as a club over Charles D. Brown, who does a capital job as the bullying political boss. Ella Raines is the newspaper gal who rightly suspects Arleen Whelan got away with the diary as a favor to her beau, who too has political ambitions in opposition to the senator.

Casting is good down the line, and there are many nice little touches (such as that autographed, oversize postage stamp whereon George Washington "thanks" p.a. Peter Lind Hayes for "putting me on the stamp").

•

SENDER, THE
1983, 91 mins, US Ⓥ ⊙ col
Dir Roger Christian ***Prod*** Edward S. Feldman ***Scr*** Thomas Baum ***Ph*** Roger Pratt ***Ed*** Alan Strachan ***Mus*** Trevor Jones ***Art*** Malcolm Middleton
Act Kathryn Harrold, Zeljko Ivanek, Shirley Knight, Paul Freeman, Sean Hewitt, Harry Ditson (Paramount)

The Sender is a superbly crafted modern horror picture, credibly using telepathic communication as its premise for creating nightmarish situations.

Thomas Baum's screenplay concerns a suicidal young amnesiac (Zeljko Ivanek) near the fictional town of Corinth, Georgia. Taken to a psychiatric clinic, he establishes a telepathic link with his psychiatrist Gail Farmer (Kathryn Harrold), causing her to experience involuntarily his violent nightmares.

The "sender" cannot control his telepathic powers, and when Dr. Denman (Paul Freeman), Farmer's superior, subjects him to shock treatment and surgical experiments, he sends telepathic images of horror which disrupt the entire hospital. Farmer, who is visited by the sender's mysterious mother Jerolyn (Shirley Knight), tries to cure him.

Cast is good within script limitations, as Harrold represents an attractive, sympathetic heroine and Ivanek a mesmerizing, troubled youngster.

•

SEND ME NO FLOWERS
1964, 100 mins, US Ⓥ col
Dir Norman Jewison ***Prod*** Harry Keller ***Scr*** Julius Epstein ***Ph*** Daniel L. Fapp ***Ed*** J. Terry Williams ***Mus*** Frank DeVol ***Art*** Alexander Golitzen, Robert Clatworthy
Act Rock Hudson, Doris Day, Tony Randall, Paul Lynde, Hal March, Edward Andrews (Universal)

Send Me No Flowers doesn't carry the same voltage, either in laughs or originality, as Doris Day and Rock Hudson's two previous entries, *Pillow Talk* (1959) and *Lover Come Back* (1961).

Adapted from the Broadway play by Norman Barasch and Carroll Moore, the thin story line romps around Hudson, a hypochondriac, overhearing his doctor discussing the fatal symptoms of another patient and believing them to be his own. In the belief he has only a few weeks to live, he sets about trying to find a suitable man to take his place as Day's husband.

Norman Jewison in his direction weaves his characters in and out of this situation as skillfully as the script will permit, having the benefit, of course, of seasoned thesps in such roles. Day is quite up to the demands of her part, indulging in a bit of slapstick in the opening sequence as she's locked out of the house in her nightgown, arms loaded with eggs and milk bottles. Hudson plays his character nobly.

Tony Randall, costarred with the pair in the other two films, again plays Hudson's pal, this time his next door neighbor, who takes his friend's expected fate even harder than the soon-to-be-deceased and goes on a three-day drunk.

•

SENSATIONS OF 1945
1944, 85 mins, US Ⓥ b/w
Dir Andrew L. Stone ***Prod*** Andrew L. Stone ***Scr*** Dorothy Bennett, Andrew L. Stone ***Ph*** Peverell Morley, John J. Mescall ***Ed*** James E. Smith ***Mus*** Mahlon Merrick (dir) ***Art*** Charles Odds
Act Eleanor Powell, Dennis O'Keefe, C. Aubrey Smith, Eugene Pallette, Mimi Forsythe, Cab Calloway (United Artists)

Plot is one of those things. Eleanor Powell is the ambidextrous musicomedy dancer turned p.a. whose imagination cooks up spectacular ideas calling for lavish showmanship and Miss-Fixit technique which, however, almost always involves her deeper with Dennis O'Keefe. That's the ridic part of the plot. P.a.s capable of handling literary memoirs, promoting a Circus-in-the-Sky nitery, a Devil's Gorge ropewalking stunt, a Times Square jitterbugging melee, with assorted cabaret preems and musicomedy ventures in between, makes for a story which reads like a Ziegfeldian nightmare.

Despite the cold analysis of the curious plot motivation it all plays far more compellingly than this brief recounting would indicate. It's to producer-director Andrew L. Stone's credit that he has thus been able to jell the Woody Herman and Cab Calloway bands, the specialties of W. C. Fields (too brief), Sophie Tucker's two dandy numbers (with Teddy Shapiro omnipotently at the Steinway) and the crack boogie-woogieing of Dorothy Donegan.

•

SENSE AND SENSIBILITY
1995, 135 mins, US Ⓥ ⊙ col
Dir Ang Lee ***Prod*** Lindsay Doran ***Scr*** Emma Thompson ***Ph*** Michael Coulter ***Ed*** Tim Squyres ***Mus*** Patrick Doyle ***Art*** Luciana Arrighi
Act Emma Thompson, Alan Rickman, Kate Winslet, Hugh Grant, James Fleet, Harriet Walter (Mirage/Columbia)

This shrewd, highly humorous adaptation reps the first screenplay written by actress Emma Thompson, while this is the first entirely non-Chinese picture directed by Taiwanese helmer Ang Lee, who scored in the West with his second and third films, *The Wedding Banquet* and *Eat Drink Man Woman*. Both potentially long-shot bets have paid off in spades, a tribute to the talent acumen of producer Lindsay Doran and exec producer Sydney Pollack.

Deftly setting the stage in late 18th-century rural England, pic briskly delineates the suddenly reduced circumstances of widow Dashwood (Gemma Jones) and her three lovely daughters after the death of her husband. Eldest daughter Elinor (Thompson) is the sensible one, a bright, if emotionally stunted, woman widely regarded as an incipient spinster. Middle daughter Marianne (Kate Winslet), in her late teens, is quite the opposite, a reckless romantic who can't abide her sister's restrained propriety. Little sister Margaret (Emile Francois) is an 11-year-old tomboy.

The women are reliant for their social lives on the boisterous, conspiratorial Sir John Middleton (Robert Hardy) and his mother-in-law, Mrs. Jennings (the irrepressible Elizabeth Spriggs). The wealthy, brooding, middle-aged Col. Brandon (Alan Rickman) comes to call, but Marianne finds her romantic dreams come to life in the person of the dashing John Willoughby (Greg Wise).

Thompson's script manages the neat trick of preserving the necessary niceties and decorum of civilized behavior of the time while still cutting to the dramatic quick. But she and Lee have always kept an eye out for the comedic possibilities in any situation, assisted by a highly skilled cast of actors.

Crucially for such an elaborately dressed production, the characters all come thoroughly alive with their ready wits and pulsing emotions, overcoming the two-century gap with seeming effortlessness. Behind-the-scenes hands have crafted an exceedingly handsome production that is not overly plush.

1995: Best Screenplay Adaptation

NOMINATIONS: Best Picture, Actress (Emma Thompson), Best Supporting Actress (Kate Winslet), Cinematography, Original Dramatic Score, Costume Design

•

SENSO
(THE WANTON CONTESSA)
1954, 122 mins, Italy Ⓥ col
Dir Luchino Visconti ***Scr*** Luchino Visconti, Suso Cecchi D'Amico, Carlo Alianello, Giorgio Bassani, Giorgio Prosperi ***Ph*** G. R. Aldo, Robert Krasker ***Ed*** Mario Serandrei ***Mus*** Franco Ferrara (dir.) ***Art*** Ottavio Scotti
Act Alida Valli, Farley Granger, Massimo Girotti, Heinz Moog, Rina Morelli, Christian Marquand (Lux)

Senso is an elegant, expensively produced, period love story, set back in the Italian 1860s, and a stylist delight. Film [from the story by Camillo Boito] was originally shot with an English soundtrack, with dialog by Tennessee Williams and Paul Bowles.

Story, in which married Venetian aristocrat Countess Lidia (Alida Valli) falls for young Austrian officer Franz Mahler (Farley Granger), is intertwined with historical-political events of the period, the Austrian occupation, the anti-Austrian movement, the battle of Custoza, etc. Valli falls more and more in love with her officer while his interest is more financial than real.

She chases him, nevertheless, hides him from the Italians, helps him avoid combat, and treats him to a good life in a nearby city. When she finally catches up with him and finds he's also living with a new mistress, she goes mad and denounces him to authorities.

Luchino Visconti's direction is evident in every detail of the picture. His direction of Valli and Granger, his care for detail and backdrop atmosphere, for lighting and color, costumes and decor, his handling of the sweeping battle scenes help keep a shaky story together and give the film class.

Camera job by the late G. R. Aldo and Robert Krasker in Technicolor is among the best ever seen here, both in carefully lit interiors as well as on the many location settings in Venice and vicinity. Music, taken from Anton Bruckner's Seventh Symphony, is well chosen. In such a beautiful film, it seems a shame that the trimmings outshine the main dish (in this case the love story).

•

SENTINEL, THE
1977, 91 mins, US Ⓥ col
Dir Michael Winner ***Prod*** Michael Winner ***Scr*** Michael Winner ***Ph*** Dick Kratina ***Ed*** Bernard Gribble, Terence Rawlings ***Mus*** Gil Melle ***Art*** Philip Rosenberg
Act Chris Sarandon, Cristina Raines, Martin Balsam, John Carradine, Jose Ferrer, Ava Gardner (Universal)

The Sentinel is a grubby, grotesque excursion into religioso psychodrama, notable for uniformly poor performances by a large cast of familiar names and direction that is hysterical and heavy-handed. The story [from Jeffrey Knovitz's novel] is based on the familiar device of taking some innocent (in this case, Cristina Raines, whose performance is miserable), confronted with kooky situations and characters whose motives are unclear except that the innocent seems to be losing mental control.

Raines, cast as a fashion model, has some mighty formidable plot adversaries: fiance Chris Sarandon, amusingly trying to play a successful lawyer; weird neighbors like Burgess Meredith, in ludicrous overacting job; also pushy lesbian Sylvia Miles and lover Beverly D'Angelo.

•

SEPARATE LIVES
1995, 101 mins, US Ⓥ col
Dir David Madden ***Prod*** Mark Amin, Diane Nabatoff, Guy Reidel ***Scr*** Steven Pressfield ***Ph*** Kees Van Oostrum ***Ed*** Janice Hampton ***Mus*** William Olvis ***Art*** Bernt Capra
Act James Belushi, Linda Hamilton, Vera Miles, Elisabeth Moss, Drew Snyder, Mark Lindsay Chapman (Interscope/Trimark)

Top-billed James Belushi and Linda Hamilton (reunited for the first time since 1990's *Mr. Destiny*) are main attractions in a thinly plotted and tiresomely formulaic drama about murder, repressed memory and split personalities.

Hamilton plays Lauren Porter, a demure psychology professor who occasionally turns into Lena, her promiscuous, sexy alter ego. Fearing she may have killed someone during one of her split-personality perambulations, she seeks help from Tom Beckwith (Belushi), an ex-cop turned-psych student.

Despite Hamilton's raunchy talk and revealing outfits as Lena, there is very little overt sexiness in *Separate Lives*, and even less chemistry between the two leads.

•

SEPARATE TABLES
1958, 98 mins, US Ⓥ b/w
Dir Delbert Mann ***Prod*** Harold Hecht ***Scr*** Terence Rattigan, John Gay ***Ph*** Charles Lang, Jr. ***Ed*** Marjorie Fowler, Charles Ennis ***Mus*** David Raksin ***Art*** Harry Horner
Act Rita Hayworth, Deborah Kerr, David Niven, Wendy Hiller, Burt Lancaster, Gladys Cooper (United Artists/Hecht-Hill-Lancaster)

As a play, *Separate Tables* consisted of two separate vignettes set against the same English boarding house and served as an acting tour de force for Eric Portman and Margaret Leighton. Much of the appeal of Terence Rattigan's play was due to the remarkable change in characterization they were able to make as they assumed different roles in each of the segments. Rattigan and John Gay have masterfully blended the two playlets into one literate and absorbing full-length film.

Basically, story is a character study of a group of residents of the small British seaside town of Bournemouth, described in the film as a tourist spot in the summer and haven for the lonely and the desperate in the winter. The majority of the residents are tortured by psychological problems and unhappy pasts. As a phoney major, with a made-up Sandhurst background, David Niven gives one of the best performances of his career. Deborah Kerr is excellent as a plain, shy girl completely cowed by a domineering and strong mother, finely portrayed by Gladys Cooper.

A separate but integrated story concerns Burt Lancaster, Rita Hayworth and Wendy Hiller. As a writer hurt by life and living a don't-care existence at the out-of-the-way hotel, Lancaster turns in a shaded performance. Hayworth is equally good as his former wife whose narcissism and desire to dominate men leads to Lancaster's downfall. Hiller is the efficient manager of the hotel who finds her romance with Lancaster shattered on the arrival of his physically attractive and fashionable ex-wife.

1958: Best Actor (David Niven), Supp. Actress (Wendy Hiller)

NOMINATIONS: Best Picture, Actress (Deborah Kerr), Adapted Screenplay, B&W Cinematography, Scoring of a Dramatic Picture

•

SEPPUKU
(HARAKIRI)
1962, 135 mins, Japan ▭ b/w
Dir Masaki Kobayashi ***Prod*** Tatsuo Hosoya ***Scr*** Shinobu Hashimoto ***Ph*** Yoshio Miyajima ***Ed*** Hisashi Sagara ***Mus*** Toru Takemitsu ***Art*** Junichi Ozumi, Shigemasa Toda

Act Tatsuya Nakadai, Akira Ishihama, Shima Iwashita, Tetsuro Tamba, Rentaro Mikuni, Yoshio Inaba (Shochiku)

This stunning film is a sombre tragedy [from Yasuhiko Takiguchi's novel] giving off deep rage against militarism, political systems and beliefs that do not allow for a rational human outlook or future change.

In 17th century Japan, a powerful centralizing shogun breaks up various self-sufficient clans and creates a flock of rootless ronins, samurai sans masters, who roam the countryside. Some threaten to commit harakiri. One clan feels this is against the idealistic military shield of the samurai. When a young man comes begging, they decide to force him to perform it, with a wooden blade.

In comes an older samurai, and he, too, is allowed to commit harakiri. But the man who died atrociously turns out to be his son-in-law. Pic ends in carnage as the would-be harakiri victim takes on the whole house.

Director Masaki Kobayashi shows a sure hand in showing men being destroyed in a tragic setup that will eventually be changed but still creates these destinies.

This is not for the squeamish. Pic is technically audacious in its cutting on various levels of past and present. Its acting has the right stern, bigger-than-life quality.

•

SEPTEMBER
1987, 82 mins, US Ⓥ ⦿ col
Dir Woody Allen *Prod* Robert Greenhut *Scr* Woody Allen *Ph* Carlo D. Palma *Ed* Susan E. Morse *Art* Santo Loquasto
Act Denholm Elliott, Dianne Wiest, Mia Farrow, Elaine Stritch, Sam Waterston, Jack Warden (Orion)

September sees Woody Allen in a compellingly melancholy mood, as he sends four achingly unhappy younger people and two better adjusted older ones through a grim story drenched with Chekhovian overtones.

Set entirely within the lovely Vermont country home of Mia Farrow at summer's end, tale is constructed around a pattern of unrequited, mismatched infatuations that drive the high-strung, intellectual characters to distraction. Neighbor Denholm Elliott loves Farrow, Farrow is a goner for guest-house occupant Sam Waterston, and Waterston is nuts for Farrow's best friend Dianne Wiest, who is married. Also visting are Farrow's mother, a former screen star and great beauty played by Elaine Stritch, and the latter's husband, physicist Jack Warden.

So it goes, a merry-go-round of frustration, resentment, heartbreak, disappointment and bitterness, described in brittle, often piercing terms in Allen's dialog. Happily, the air is cleared on occasion by the outrageous Stritch, whose rowdy, forthright comments never fail to lighten the mood and provide genuine amusement.

This is the film Allen largely reshot with a significantly altered cast after feeling dissatisfied with his first version. Originally, Maureen O'Sullivan, Farrow's real mother, played the role finally filled by Stritch. Sam Shepard, then, briefly, Christopher Walken, had Waterston's part, and Elliott was first cast as the actress' husband, with Charles Durning in the role of the neighbor.

•

SEPTEMBER AFFAIR
1950, 91 mins, US Ⓥ ⦿ b/w
Dir William Dieterle *Prod* Hal Wallis *Scr* Robert Thoeren *Ph* Charles B. Lang *Mus* Victor Young
Act Joan Fontaine, Joseph Cotten, Francoise Rosay, Jessica Tandy, Robert Arthur, Fortunio Bonanova (Paramount)

Joan Fontaine, pianist, and Joseph Cotten, an engineer, are on the same plane bound for New York from Rome. Engine trouble forces the plane down in Naples. Both go sightseeing for a couple of hours.

They return to the airport just in time to see their plane roaring away overhead. More sightseeing together to Pompeii and Capri. They discover that the plane they were to have taken had crashed and that they are reported dead. They decide that since the world no longer believes they exist, they will start a new life together.

Fontaine gives a light touch to her role without becoming flirtatious. Cotten is always believable as the engineer who finds that running away from work and wife is not the answer to his restlessness and unhappiness.

•

SEPTEMBER 30, 1955
SEE: 9/30/55

•

SERGEANT, THE
1968, 107 mins, US col
Dir John Flynn *Prod* Richard Goldstone *Scr* Dennis Murphy *Ph* Henri Persin *Ed* Charles Nelson, Francoise Diot *Mus* Michel Magne *Art* Willy Holt
Act Rod Steiger, John Phillip Law, Ludmila Mikael, Frank Latimore, Elliott Sullivan (Warner/Seven Arts)

Dennis Murphy's novel reaches the screen as a moving production, filmed with sensitivity by debuting director John Flynn, and with robust, appropriately grim physical values. Rod Steiger's title-role performance is generally excellent, and John Phillip Law hits the mark, as the would-be mark.

To say that this is a story about a homosexual is like claiming that an iceberg floats completely on the surface of water. The pic is about a total, pervading enslavement of one person to another.

A five-minute prolog, in black-and-white for good contrast, establishes Steiger as a hero during the 1944 liberation of France. The heroic deed included the strangling of a helpless, disarmed German soldier. His death grip on the younger man betrays a latent homosexuality.

Time shifts under titles to 1952, with Steiger reporting as first sergeant at a U.S. base in rural France. He effectively seizes command, and works to shape up the slovenly unit. Law attracts Steiger's attention. Practically dragooned into the company office, Law falls increasingly under the thrall of Steiger.

Story threads are strongly woven, through Murphy's own fine adaptation of his book as well as Flynn's incisive direction.

•

SERGEANT RUTLEDGE
(AKA: THE TRIAL OF SERGEANT RUTLEDGE)
1960, 111 mins, US col
Dir John Ford *Prod* Willis Goldbeck, Patrick Ford *Scr* James Warner Bellah, Willis Goldbeck *Ph* Bert Glennon *Ed* Jack Murray *Mus* Howard Jackson *Art* Eddie Imazu
Act Jeffrey Hunter, Constance Towers, Billie Burke, Woody Strode, Carleton Young, Juano Hernandez (Warner)

Give John Ford a troop of cavalry, some hostile Indians, a wisp of story and chances are the director will come galloping home with an exciting film. *Sergeant Rutledge* provides an extra plus factor in the form of an offbeat and intriguing screenplay which deals frankly, if not too deeply, with racial prejudice in the post-Civil War era. Ford expertly blends the action-pictorial and the story elements to create lively physical excitement as well as sustained suspense about the fate of a Negro trooper who is accused of rape and double murder. Original tag on this picture was *Captain Buffalo*.

As the giant-sized Negro 1st sgt. who is eventually proven to be a victim of circumstantial evidence, Woody Strode gives an unusually versatile performance.

The screenplay is said to have a historical basis in that the U.S. 9th and 10th Cavalry of Negro troopers, commanded by white officers, fought skirmishes with the Apaches in Arizona after the Civil War. Whether the actual incident which forms the plot structure—the murder of the Commanding Officer of the 9th Cavalry and the rape-murder of his daughter—also is factual is not quite as important as that it plays well.

Story unfolds via a series of flashbacks from the court martial of Strode as witnesses describe his friendship with the dead white girl, his panicky desertion, the circumstances of his capture by the lieutenant (Jeffrey Hunter) who later volunteers as defense counsel. Most of the action flows out of the testimony of Constance Towers, the only sympathetic witness, whom Strode has saved from an Indian ambush.

•

SERGEANTS 3
1962, 113 mins, US ▭ col
Dir John Sturges *Prod* Frank Sinatra *Scr* W. R. Burnett *Ph* Winton Hoch *Ed* Ferris Webster *Mus* Billy May *Art* Frank Hotaling
Act Frank Sinatra, Dean Martin, Sammy Davis, Jr., Peter Lawford, Joey Bishop (United Artists)

Sergeants 3 is warmed-over *Gunga Din* a westernized version of that screen epic, with American-style Indians and Vegas-style soldiers of fortune. The essential differences between the two pictures, other than the obvious one of setting, is that the emphasis in *Gunga* was serious, with tongue-in-cheek overtone, whereas the emphasis in *Sergeants* is tongue-in-cheek, with serious overtones.

Although, unaccountably, no mention is made of the obvious source in the screen credits. W. R. Burnett's screenplay not only owes its existence to that story, but adheres to it faithfully, with one noteworthy exception—*Gunga* does not die for his heroism. It's peaches and cream all the way.

The "Big Three" of Sinatra, Martin and Lawford reenact the parts played in the original by Cary Grant, Victor McLaglen and Douglas Fairbanks, Jr.. Of the three, Martin seems by far the most animated and comfortable, Sinatra and Lawford coming off a trifle too businesslike for the irreverent, look-ma-we're-cavalrymen approach.

•

SERGEANT YORK
1941, 134 mins, US Ⓥ b/w
Dir Howard Hawks *Prod* Jesse L. Lasky, Hal B. Wallis *Scr* Abem Finkel, Harry Chandlee, Howard Koch, John Huston *Ph* Sol Polito *Ed* William Holmes *Mus* Max Steiner *Art* John Hughes
Act Gary Cooper, Walter Brennan, Joan Leslie, Ward Bond, Margaret Wycherly, George Tobias (Warner)

For more than 20 years studios sought permission to film the heroic World War deeds of Sergeant York. And for as long a period York refused the necessary cooperation for a film of his heroism on the early morning of 8 October 1918, when he single-handed killed 20 Germans and compelled the surrender of 132 of the enemy in the Argonne sector.

Lauded, praised, awarded the Congressional Medal of Honor, York side-stepped all proffers to benefit from the acclaim. He returned from army service to his home in Pall Mall, TN, where he devoted himself to farming and educational work.

It is film biography at its best. The writers have paid more attention to character, and the backgrounds and associations which create it, than to incident.

For Gary Cooper the role is made to order. He convincingly portrays the youthful backwoodsman, unruly as a youth, who in time gains mastery over his wildness. The romantic passages played with Joan Leslie are tender and human. But Cooper is best, perhaps, in the scenes of early camp training when his marksmanship, learned in the woods, attracts attention. Among the featured players the reliable Walter Brennan is splendid as the combination village pastor and storekeeper.

1941: Best Actor (Gary Cooper), Editing

NOMINATIONS: Best Picture, Director, Supp. Actor (Walter Brennan), Supp. Actress (Margaret Wycherly), Original Screenplay, B&W Cinematography, B&W Art Direction, Scoring of a Dramatic Picture, Sound

•

SERIAL MOM
1994, 93 mins, US Ⓥ ⦿ col
Dir John Waters *Prod* John Fiedler, Mark Tarlov *Scr* John Waters *Ph* Robert Stevens *Ed* Janice Hampton, Erica Huggins *Mus* Basil Poledouris *Art* Vincent Peranio
Act Kathleen Turner, Sam Waterson, Ricki Lake, Matthew Lillard, Mary Jo Catlett, Justin Whalin (Polar)

John Waters's latest expose of society's hypocrisies, normal people's naughty thoughts, and the secrets that lie behind suburbia's well manicured facades, is almost endearing in its cheeky irreverence, but also rather mild and scattershot in its satiric marksmanship. *Serial Mom* provokes chuckles and the occasional raised eyebrow rather than guffaws and gross-outs.

To all outward appearances, Baltimore hausfrau Beverly Sutphin (Kathleen Turner) is June Cleaver incarnate. An endlessly supportive wife to dentist Eugene (Sam Waterston), her family includes college-student daughter Misty (Ricki Lake), who has extensive boy problems, and high-schooler son Chip (Matthew Lillard), a gore-film junkie.

As soon as they all leave for the day, however, Beverly jumps into action. Once started, there's no stopping Beverly, who runs Misty's impolite boyfriend through with a fire poker and dispatches a couple for not flossing. In a nifty little Hitchcock homage, she clubs a woman over the head with a leg of lamb as she watches the movie *Annie*, all for not rewinding the videotapes she rents. By the time she's arrested and charged with murder, she has killed six people.

With its mockery of America's glorification of celebrity and luridly winking fascination with crime, *Serial Mom* is tolerably amusing as far as it goes, but Waters's distinctive humor could also be better amplified and sustained if it were goosed up by more stylized visuals.

As one with Waters's charming bad-boy spirit, Turner turns in a game, rambunctious star performance that hits the right note between satire and seriousness.

•

SERIOUS CHARGE
1959, 105 mins, UK b/w
Dir Terence Young *Prod* Mickey Delamar *Scr* Guy Elmes, Mickey Delamar *Ph* Georges Perinal *Ed* Reginald Beck *Mus* Leighton Lucas
Act Anthony Quayle, Sarah Churchill, Andrew Ray, Irene Browne, Percy Herbert, Cliff Richard (Eros)

Producer Mickey Delamar and director Terence Young do a smooth, conscientious job in transferring Philip King's play,

Serious Charge, to the screen. The screenplay is a literate piece of craftsmanship with plenty of shafts of quiet humor. It sticks very faithfully to the play. The plausible situation takes place in a small British town which is riddled with gossipmongers and juve delinquency. A new vicar arrives. He's a young good looking bachelor, athletic, sincere, keen and he tries to grapple with the situation. He comes up against a vindictive teenager who leads a local gang of small-time hoodlums. The kid frames the vicar by alleging a homo attack.

Anthony Quayle's well rounded portrayal of the vicar is sympathetic and gripping. He convincingly stresses the strained inner feelings of a man who feels that his reactions to the slander prove that he is not fitted for his calling. Sarah Churchill as the spinster who loves him has some good moments, particularly when she realizes how her action has compromised the man she loves. Andrew Ray gives a well observed performance and is a typical, credible juve delinquent. The film also introduces Cliff Richard, who sings a trio of useful beat songs.

•

SERPENT AND THE RAINBOW, THE
1988, 98 mins, US Ⓥ ⦿ col
Dir Wes Craven ***Prod*** David Ladd, Doug Claybourne ***Scr*** Richard Maxwell, A. R. Simoun ***Ph*** John Lindley ***Ed*** Glenn Farr, Peter Amundson ***Mus*** Brad Fiedel ***Art*** David Nichols
Act Bill Pullman, Cathy Tyson, Zakes Mokae, Paul Winfield, Brent Jennings, Michael Gough (Universal)

Wes Craven's *The Serpent and the Rainbow* is a better-than-average supernatural tale [inspired by Wade Davis's book] that offers a few good scares but gets bogged down in special effects. Film is intriguingly eerie as long as it explores the secrets of voodoo in a lush Haitian setting alive with mysteries of the spirit.

Dennis Alan (Bill Pullman), a Harvard anthropologist looking for a magic zombie powder at the behest of an American drug company, is sort of a second-rate Indiana Jones.

In Haiti, Alan gets involved with psychiatrist Marielle Celine (Cathy Tyson) who is battling the cumulative effects of deep-rooted black magic, religion and everyday mental illness.

Opposing the more progressive Marielle are the reactionary political and supernatural forces of police chief Dargent Peytraud, played with evil zeal by Zakes Mokae. Speaking out of the side of his gold-toothed mouth, Mokae walks a narrow line between being truly frightening and truly hilarious.

Special effects are well done, but fail to capture the creepy undercurrents of voodoo.

•

SERPENT OF THE NILE: THE LOVES OF CLEOPATRA
1953, 81 mins, US col
Dir William Castle ***Prod*** Sam Katzman ***Scr*** Robert E. Kent ***Ph*** Henry Freulich ***Ed*** Gene Havlick ***Mus*** Mischa Bakaleinikoff ***Art*** Paul Palmentola
Act Rhonda Fleming, William Lundigan, Raymond Burr, Jean Byron, Michael Ansara, Julie Newmar (Columbia)

Producer Sam Katzman dusts off some incidents in the life and loves of Cleopatra for mediocre results in *Serpent of the Nile*. Much of the difficulty is the lack of credibility in the script. Its treatment of Mark Anthony's rise to power following Caesar's assassination and subsequent fall, when subjected to the wiles of Cleopatra, is seldom convincing. This slice of Roman history is played straight.

Yarn has Raymond Burr, as Anthony, proposing an alliance between Rome and wealthy Egypt, which is ruled by Rhonda Fleming as Cleopatra. Thoroughly unscrupulous, she schemes to eliminate Burr and place herself on the throne of Rome. Her plan, however, is nipped by William Lundigan, Burr's lieutenant, who brings the Roman legions to Alexandria.

Burr's Anthony is a wishywashy individual whose love for drink and infatuation for Fleming makes him lose his sense of logic. She, on the other hand, fails to impress as the Egyptian beauty, primarily due to the stilted dialog. Lundigan, too, has his moments of vacillation. But, fortunately, his portrayal shows enough virility and drive to meet the combat requirements the role demands.

•

SERPENT'S EGG, THE
1977, 120 mins, W. Germany/US Ⓥ col
Dir Ingmar Bergman ***Prod*** Dino De Laurentiis ***Scr*** Ingmar Bergman ***Ph*** Sven Nykvist ***Ed*** Petra von Oelffen ***Mus*** Rolf Wilhelm ***Art*** Rolf Zehetbauer
Act Liv Ullmann, David Carradine, Gert Frobe, Heinz Bennent, James Whitmore (Rialto/De Laurentiis)

The Serpent's Egg, Ingmar Bergman's first English-language feature and his first film made outside his home country, bears the master's stamp right from the beginning in a superior collaboration with cinematographer Sven Nykvist and production designer Rolf Zehetbauer.

The latter has recreated a Berlin of a poverty-ridden, fear-stricken early 1920s that is much more than paint-deep. Also, Bergman makes his actors, with one fatal exception (David Carradine), work their individualities into the grandest of ensemble playing.

The Serpent's Egg lacks both the strength and depth of Bergman's major work. By going outwardly international, the master becomes perilously close to becoming shallow as well.

•

SERPICO
1973, 129 mins, US Ⓥ ⦿ col
Dir Sidney Lumet ***Prod*** Martin Bregman ***Scr*** Waldo Salt, Norman Wexler ***Ph*** Arthur J. Ornitz ***Ed*** Dede Allen, Richard Marks ***Mus*** Mikis Theodorakis ***Art*** Charles Bailey
Act Al Pacino, John Randolph, Jack Kehoe, Biff McGuire, Barbara Eda-Young, Cornelia Sharpe (De Laurentiis/Artists Entertainment)

Serpico is based on the actual experiences of an honest N.Y. policeman who helped expose corruption. Al Pacino's performance is outstanding. Sidney Lumet's direction adeptly combines gritty action and thought-provoking comment.

The real-life Frank Serpico, who climaxed an 11-year police career by blowing the lid on departmental corruption, told his story first through a book collaboration with Peter Maas.

Pacino dominates the entire film. His inner personal torment is vividly detailed, manifested first in the breakup of an affair with Cornelia Sharpe and later, much more terribly, in the wreck of his love for Barbara Eda-Young.

A very large cast exemplifies the assorted attitudes with which Pacino must deal.

1973: NOMINATIONS: Best Actor (Al Pacino), Adapted Screenplay

•

SERVANT, THE
1963, 117 mins, UK Ⓥ b/w
Dir Joseph Losey ***Prod*** Joseph Losey, Norman Priggen ***Scr*** Harold Pinter ***Ph*** Douglas Slocombe ***Ed*** Reginald Mills ***Mus*** John Dankworth ***Art*** Richard Macdonald
Act Dirk Bogarde, Sarah Miles, Wendy Craig, James Fox, Catherine Lacey, Richard Vernon (Springbok)

The Servant is for the most part strong dramatic fare, though the atmosphere and tension is not fully sustained to the end. Harold Pinter's screenplay based on the Robin Maugham novel is distinguished by its literacy and sharp incisive dialog.

Dirk Bogarde plays a manservant who is hired by a young and elegant man about town to run a house he has just bought in a fashionable part of London, and who, almost imperceptibly, begins to dominate his master. Up to the point where the servant gains supremacy, Joseph Losey's direction is first class, despite a few conventional shots which are used to gain effect. The last segment of the story, which puts some strain on credibility, is less convincing and, therefore, less satisfying. But the relationship of master and servant, with its underlying suggestion of homosexuality is sensitively handled.

Bogarde not only looks the part, but plays it with natural assurance. There is also a noteworthy performance from James Fox, who assuredly suggests the indolent young man about town. The two main femme roles are also expertly played, Sarah Miles making a highly provocative and sensuous maid, and Wendy Craig giving a contrasting study as the fiancee who is overwhelmed by events she cannot control.

•

SESAME STREET PRESENTS FOLLOW THAT BIRD
SEE: FOLLOW THAT BIRD

•

SET-UP, THE
1949, 72 mins, US Ⓥ b/w
Dir Robert Wise ***Prod*** Richard Goldstone ***Scr*** Art Cohn ***Ph*** Milton Krasner ***Ed*** Roland Gross ***Mus*** Constantin Bakaleinikoff (dir.) ***Art*** Albert S. D'Agostino, Jack Okey
Act Robert Ryan, Audrey Totter, George Tobias, Alan Baxter, Wallace Ford, Percy Helton (RKO)

Compact and suspenseful is RKO's *The Set-Up*, a boxing film which shows the seamier side of the fight racket [from the poem by Joseph Moncure March].

It throws the spotlight on 35-year-old washed-up heavyweight (Robert Ryan). Feeling that it's his lucky night, he wades through a four-rounder to kayo his opponent and spoil a match that had been fixed. But the story itself is not the peg that integrates *Set-Up* into a biting, pictorial analysis of pugilism; the film's values primarily lie in its unmerciless character studies. Under Robert Wise's skillful direction, the assorted ringside audience "types" give an added lustre of realism. Dressing-room hangers-on, rubdown boys and other pugs on the bill also come in for scalpel-like scrutiny.

•

SE7EN
1995, 127 mins, US Ⓥ ⦿ ▭ col
Dir David Fincher ***Prod*** Arnold Kopelson, Phyllis Carlyle ***Scr*** Andrew Kevin Walker ***Ph*** Darius Khondji ***Ed*** Richard Francis-Bruce ***Mus*** Howard Shore ***Art*** Arthur Max
Act Brad Pitt, Morgan Freeman, Gwyneth Paltrow, Kevin Spacey, R. Lee Ermey, Richard Roundtree (New Line)

An intensely claustrophobic, gut-wrenching thriller about two policemen's desperate efforts to stop an ingenious serial killer whose work is inspired by the seven deadly sins, this weirdly off-kilter suspenser goes well beyond the usual police procedural or killer-on-a-rampage yarn due to a fine script, striking craftsmanship and a masterful performance by Morgan Freeman.

David Fincher's second feature, after *Alien 3*, cuts against most expectations for this sort of genre piece: it's not a buddy picture; the murders themselves are not actually depicted; and the usual gritty big-city realism has been replaced by a highly stylized, borderline-arty visual conception that greatly cranks up the psychological and physical intensity of the drama, by first-time screenwriter Andrew Kevin Walker.

At the outset, world-weary veteran cop William Somerset (Freeman) and the cocky newcomer due to replace him, David Mills (Brad Pitt), can barely tolerate each other. Obliged to take the kid on his rounds, Somerset pursues an investigation of the death of an enormously obese man who appears to have exploded from eating too much.

The next day, an influential defense attorney is found gruesomely murdered, and when the words "Gluttony" and "Greed" are discovered, respectively, at the scenes, Somerset correctly predicts that there will be five more murders to cover: sloth, pride, lust, envy and wrath. The unidentified city in which the grisly yarn unravels is subject to heavy rain through the early days of the inquiry, which provides the first element in Fincher's channeling of images. Virtuoso French cinematographer Darius Khondji and production designer Arthur Max have sculpted a dark, murky world, parts of which are illuminated only by flashlight and much of the rest of which is suffused in a pea-soup green that defies penetration. The film has been hand-tooled with precision and to powerful effect.

Freeman's is a supremely nuanced, moving performance as the seasoned, bruised and solitary Somerset. This is screen acting at its best. Pitt turns in a determined, energetic, creditable job as the eager young detective. Gwyneth Paltrow gives as much human dimension as possible to her few scenes as Pitt's sensitive, uncertain wife.

Except for a chase sequence, pic features no overt violence, but the gruesome handiwork of the killer is shown in detail, in part courtesy of special makeup effects wiz Rob Bottin.

1995: NOMINATION: Film Editing

•

SEVEN BRIDES FOR SEVEN BROTHERS
1954, 102 mins, US Ⓥ ⦿ ▭ col
Dir Stanley Donen ***Prod*** Jack Cummings ***Scr*** Albert Hackett, Frances Goodrich, Dorothy Kingsley ***Ph*** George Folsey ***Ed*** Ralph E. Winters ***Mus*** Adolph Deutsch (dir.) ***Art*** Cedric Gibbons, Urie McCleary
Act Howard Keel, Jeff Richards, Russ Tamblyn, Tommy Rall, Jane Powell, Julie Newmar (M-G-M)

This is a happy, hand-clapping, foot-stomping country type of musical with all the slickness of a Broadway show. Johnny Mercer and Gene de Paul provide the slick, showy production with eight songs, all of which jibe perfectly with the folksy, hillbilly air maintained in the picture. Howard Keel's robust baritone and Jane Powell's lilting soprano make their songs extremely listenable.

A real standout is the acrobatic hoedown staged around a barn-raising shindig, during which six of the title's seven brothers vie in love rivalry with the town boys for the favor of the mountain belles. With tunes and terping taking up so much of the footage there isn't too much for Stanley Donen to do except direct the story bridges between the numbers.

It's the story of seven brothers living on a mountain farm. The eldest gets a bride and the others decide likewise, steal their maidens and after a snowed-in winter, the girls' parents mastermind a mass shot-gun wedding.

The long and the short of the teaming of Keel and Powell is that the pairing comes off very satisfactorily, vocally and otherwise. The brothers are all good, with Russ Tamblyn standing out in particular for performance and his dance work.

1954: Best Scoring of a Musical Picture

NOMINATIONS: Best Picture, Screenplay, Color Cinematography, Editing

•

SEVEN DAYS IN MAY

1964, 120 mins, US Ⓥ ⊙ b/w

Dir John Frankenheimer ***Prod*** Edward Lewis ***Scr*** Rod Serling ***Ph*** Ellsworth Fredricks ***Ed*** Ferris Webster ***Mus*** Jerry Goldsmith ***Art*** Cary Odell

Act Burt Lancaster, Kirk Douglas, Fredric March, Ava Gardner, Edmond O'Brien, Martin Balsam (Seven Arts/Joel)

A combination of competents has drawn from the novel of the same title a strikingly dramatic, realistic and provocatively topical film in *Seven Days in May*. Fletcher Knebel–Charles W. Bailey II's book detailed a military plot to overthrow the government of the United States "in the not-too-distant future."

What *Seven Days in May* undertakes is the proposition that extremists could reach the point where they'd try to uproot the present form of government. Such a man is Gen. James M. Scott, played with authority by Burt Lancaster. He's a member of the Joint Chiefs of Staff, burning with patriotic fervor and seeking to "save" the country from the perils of a just-signed nuclear pact with Russia. He enlists the support of fellow chiefs. Their plan of seizure is to be consummated in seven days in May. The performances are excellent down the line, under the taut and penetrating directorial guidance of John Frankenheimer. Kirk Douglas is masterfully cool and matter of fact as Scott's aide, utterly devoted until he comes to be suspicious. He goes to the president with information that has got to be checked out in those fateful seven days. Edmond O'Brien is standout as a Southern senator with an addiction to bourbon and an unfailing loyalty to the president. Ava Gardner works out well enough as the Washington matron who has had an affair with Lancaster and is amenable to a go with Douglas.

1964: NOMINATIONS: Best Supp. Actor (Edmond O'Brien), B&W Art Direction

•

SEVEN DAYS TO NOON

1950, 94 mins, UK b/w

Dir Roy Boulting, John Boulting ***Prod*** Roy Boulting, John Boulting ***Scr*** Frank Harvey, Roy Boulting ***Ph*** Gilbert Taylor ***Ed*** Roy Boulting, John Boulting ***Mus*** John Addison ***Art*** John Elphick

Act Barry Jones, Olive Sloane, Andre Morell, Sheila Manahan, Hugh Cross, Joan Hickson (London/Boulting)

Much of the pic was lensed on location in the London area. Focal point of the plot [by Paul Dehn and James Bernard] is an ultimatum sent to the prime minister by an atom scientist who becomes mentally deranged because his work is being used for destruction, not for mankind's benefit. He warns that unless atomic bomb production ceases by noon the following Sunday (the letter is received on the Monday morning), he will, himself, blow up all of London with a bomb he has stolen. Barry Jones's interpretation of the scientist is intelligent. His clearly defined portrait of the man no one understands is a moving piece of acting. Principal female role, which is generously filled with comedy lines, is taken by Olive Sloane. She plays a former showgirl with rare gusto.

1951: Best Motion Picture Story

•

711 OCEAN DRIVE

1950, 102 mins, US b/w

Dir Joseph M. Newman ***Prod*** Frank N. Seltzer ***Scr*** Richard English, Francis Swann ***Ph*** Franz Planer ***Ed*** Bert Jordan ***Mus*** Sol Kaplan ***Art*** Perry Ferguson

Act Edmond O'Brien, Joanne Dru, Donald Porter, Sammy White, Otto Kruger, Dorothy Patrick (Columbia)

Story concerns a telephone worker (Edmond O'Brien) with a knack for electrons who joins a syndicate and expands its operations with his inventions. When the syndicate chief is killed, he takes charge of the organization, and runs into the opposition of an eastern syndicate. The bigger outfit makes overtures which he rejects until he meets Joanne Dru, the wife of one of the eastern leaders.

Operations of the syndicates are given a realistic touch by the screenplay, and Joseph M. Newman's direction keeps action at a fast pace. O'Brien is excellent as the hot-tempered, ambitious young syndicate chief.

•

SEVEN LITTLE FOYS, THE

1955, 92 mins, US Ⓥ col

Dir Melville Shavelson ***Prod*** Jack Rose ***Scr*** Melville Shavelson, Jack Rose ***Ph*** John F. Warren ***Ed*** Ellsworth Hoagland ***Mus*** Joseph J. Lilley ***Art*** Hal Pereira, John Goodman

Act Bob Hope, James Cagney, Milly Vitale, Angela Clarke, George Tobias, Herbert Hayes (Paramount)

Bob Hope abandons the buffoon to go straight actor in biopicturing Eddie Foy, song-and-dance man of the vaudeville age.

From the opening when Foy vows he will always remain a single, professionally and maritally, even an audience unfamiliar with his life will know it won't be long. It isn't, and Milly Vitale, Italian film actress who does a fine job of portraying the Italian ballerina who marries Foy, is reason enough for him to change his mind. Their hit-and-miss life together is told with heart in the performances of Hope and Vitale.

A standout sequence is the appearance of James Cagney as George M. Cohan, a characterization he created with 1942 Academy Award-winning success in *Yankee Doodle Dandy*. He and Hope, in a Friars Club scene, toss the Shavelson-Rose lines back and forth for sock results and then turn in some mighty slick hoofing.

1955: NOMINATION: Best Story & Screenplay

•

SEVEN MINUTES, THE

1971, 115 mins, US Ⓥ col

Dir Russ Meyer ***Prod*** Russ Meyer ***Scr*** Richard Warren Lewis ***Ph*** Fred Mandl ***Ed*** Dick Wormell ***Mus*** Stu Phillips ***Art*** Rodger Maus

Act Wayne Maunder, Marianne McAndrew, Philip Carey, Edy Williams, Jay C. Flippen, Lyle Bettger (20th Century-Fox)

The hypocrisies of censorship and censors are no more evident than in today's world. Unfortunately, Irving Wallace's *The Seven Minutes* was a potboiler novel which averted the essense of the problem in resolving the story. Producer-director Russ Meyer, himself a censor-exploited as well as a censor-exploiting filmmaker, began with a story handicap and adds a few of his own. Meyer, obscures the issues in cardboard-caricatures of his heavies, with regular time-out for the sexually liberated dalliances which have been his stock in trade.

Large cast is headed by Wayne Maunder, attorney for Robert Moloney, bookstore owner busted by vice cop Charles Drake, Philip Carey, excellent as a d.a., is egged on by J. C. Flippen, a behind-the-scenes king-maker, to attack the book-within-a-book as the reason John Sarno brutally raped Yvonne D'Angers, though sadist Billy Durkin was really to blame. Lyle Bettger is the accused boy's father, and Marianne McAndrew is his secretary who shifts to Maunder's side.

Climax of the trial (Harold J. Stone presiding) is surprise appearance of Yvonne De Carlo, a semi-retired former film star who reveals she wrote the book in question many years ago, and concealed her past to insure a career.

Meyer's artistic eye remains most sure in composition and pacing. Far too little attention is paid to acting, and too much of the dialog seems one-take in nature. As usual, all femme castings are knockouts, including Edy Williams (Mrs. Meyer).

•

SEVEN NIGHTS IN JAPAN

1976, 104 mins, UK/France Ⓥ col

Dir Lewis Gilbert ***Prod*** Lewis Gilbert ***Scr*** Christopher Wood ***Ph*** Henri Decae ***Ed*** John Glen ***Mus*** David Hentschel

Act Michael York, Hidemi Aoki, Charles Gray, Ann Lonnberg, Eleonore Hirt, James Villiers (EMI/Paramount)

Seven Nights in Japan is a beautifully photographed pastiche bearing little true resemblance to the enigmatic life of bustling Tokyo, where it was lensed.

Simplistic plot details the implausible romance between a royal prince (Michael York) who is serving as a naval officer, and a petite Japanese bus guide (Hidemi Aoki) whom he meets when his ship visits Japan. There are also some ludicrous attempts to kill the prince made by a fanatical gang of bungling political cut-throats.

Christopher Wood's script is sadly lacking in humor and pace and the storyline can only be labeled corny and unreal. York's acting is suitably princelike although never exceptional while Aoki has occasional moments.

•

SEVEN-PER-CENT SOLUTION, THE

1976, 113 mins, UK Ⓥ ⊙ col

Dir Herbert Ross ***Prod*** Herbert Ross ***Scr*** Nicholas Meyer ***Ph*** Oswald Morris ***Ed*** William Reynolds, Chris Barnes ***Mus*** John Addison ***Art*** Ken Adam

Act Alan Arkin, Vanessa Redgrave, Robert Duvall, Nicol Williamson, Laurence Olivier, Joel Grey (Universal)

The Seven-Per-Cent Solution is an outstanding film. Producer-director Herbert Ross and writer Nicholas Meyer, adapting his novel, have fashioned a most classy period crime drama.

The concept is terrific, in that Sherlock Holmes (Nicol Williamson), while a patient of Sigmund Freud (Alan Arkin), becomes his analyst's partner as both apply their specialized abilities in the parallel solution of a kidnap crime. Simultaneously, there is resolved Holmes's own childhood trauma which has motivated his lifelong enmity towards Professor Moriarty.

The title takes its name from a dope mixture used by Holmes in his addiction. Dr Watson, faithful friend, gets Holmes's brother Mycroft (Charles Gray) and mild-mannered Moriarty (Laurence Olivier) to trick Holmes to Vienna where Freud can treat him.

Holmes agrees to a powerful withdrawal regimen, which dissolves story wise into the introduction of Vanessa Redgrave, a former Freud patient cured of her own addiction, but now apparently in relapse. Holmes becomes intrigued with Redgrave's plight, as does Freud, and both pursue the matter.

1976: NOMINATIONS: Best Adapted Screenplay, Costume Design

•

SEVEN SAMURAI, THE

SEE: SHICHININ NO SAMURAI

SEVEN SAMURAI

SEE: SHICHININ NO SAMURAI

•

SEVEN YEARS IN TIBET

1997, 139 mins, US Ⓥ ⊙ ▭ col

Dir Jean-Jacques Annaud ***Prod*** Jean-Jacques Annaud, John H. Williams, Iain Smith ***Scr*** Becky Johnston ***Ph*** Robert Fraisse ***Ed*** Noelle Boisson ***Mus*** John Williams ***Art*** At Hoang

Act Brad Pitt, David Thewlis, B. D. Wong, Mako, Danny Denzongpa, Victor Wong (Reperage/Vanguard-Applecross/Mandalay/TriStar)

Brad Pitt climbs lotsa mountains and meets the young Dalai Lama, but doesn't carry the audience with him for much of the odyssey. Despite some magnificent widescreen lensing and faultless ethnographic detail, director Jean-Jacques Annaud's true-life tale about a self-obsessed Austrian mountaineer who learns selflessness in the Himalayas rarely delivers at a simple emotional level.

Pic [from Heinrich Harrer's own book] starts with the hurdle of asking auds to identify with a ruthlessly self-absorbed member of the Nazi party, and the script by Becky Johnston (*The Prince of Tides*) rarely hits the heights of eloquence or poetry needed. Brad Pitt's Harrer remains a somewhat cold, one-dimensional cipher prior to finally meeting the young Dalai Lama. It's only then—well over an hour into the movie—that the picture starts to tread solid ground.

The blond, Aryan-looking Harrer is introduced in Austria, 1939, as he sets out with buddy Peter Aufschnaiter (David Thewlis) to conquer Nanga Parbat peak. The team fails in its mission and the group is interned by the British in a North Indian POW camp.

[After escaping in fall 1942,] the pair reach the closed kingdom of Tibet.

Pic emotional clout is largely thanks to the scenes between Harrer and Kundun, the boy Dalai Lama (Bhutanese actor Jamyang Jamtsho Wangchuk), which have zest and some welcome humor. Even here, however, Johnston's fragmented script doesn't really rise to the challenge. Too often you just long for the pic to cut loose from the ethnography and correct attitudes and go with the drama in old Hollywood style.

All of the reported $70 million budget is up on the screen: from p.d. At Hoang's clever use of Argentine locales and the foothills of the Andes for Tibet to Enrico Sabbatini's lived-in costumes.

•

SEVENTH CROSS, THE

1944, 111 mins, US Ⓥ b/w

Dir Fred Zinnemann ***Prod*** Pandro S. Berman ***Scr*** Helen Deutsch ***Ph*** Karl Freund ***Ed*** Thomas Richards ***Mus*** Roy Webb ***Art*** Cedric Gibbons, Leonid Vasian

Act Spencer Tracy, Signe Hasso, Hume Cronyn, Jessica Tandy, Agnes Moorehead, George Macready (M-G-M)

Cross tells the story of seven men who escape from a concentration camp, and it follows the death or capture of six of them. Upon their escape the camp's commandant has ordered seven trees stripped and crosses nailed to them. It is his plan, as each fugitive is caught, to pinion them to the crosses and let them die of exposure.

And so this becomes the story of the seventh cross—the one that was never occupied. It is the story of George Heisler, who makes good his escape amid a web of almost unbelievable circumstances. The sheer fancy, as he eludes the Gestapo at every turn, is gripping drama.

This is a film of fine performances. There are one or two characterizations that might possibly eclipse that of the central one, played by Spencer Tracy, who, as usual, underplays and gives one of his invariably creditable portrayals.

1944: NOMINATION: Best Supp. Actor (Hume Cronyn)

•

7TH DAWN, THE

1964, 123 mins, UK col

Dir Lewis Gilbert ***Prod*** Charles K. Feldman, Karl Tunberg ***Scr*** Karl Tunberg ***Ph*** Freddie Young ***Ed*** John Shirley ***Mus*** Riz Ortolani ***Art*** John Stoll

Act William Holden, Susannah York, Capucine, Tetsuro Tamba, Michael Goodliffe, Allan Cuthbertson (United Artists)

Set in the Malayan jungle, circa 1945, the pic uses as its background a three-way struggle between Communist-inspired Malayan terrorists, British governors and the people of Malaya along with outsiders who have vested interests in the country. All are interested in freedom for the place but their motives vary considerably.

Pivotal characters in the film each represent a faction, a fact which leads to some rather predictable problems and solutions as time passes. Personal relationships aren't helped much either by co-producer Karl Tunberg's screenplay, based on Michael Keon's novel *The Durian Tree*. Although the script moves fairly fluently through the action passages, harmful slowdowns develop during personal moments between the characters.

William Holden handles himself in credible fashion as a Yank co-leader of local guerilla forces during World War II who stays on after the war's end to become a major local land owner and who gets involved in the new politics because of his old-time friendshp for the leader of the Red terrorists, played by Tetsuro Tamba. Holden is further involved because of his mistress, a Malayan loyalist portrayed by Capucine. These three had worked together on the same side during the previous combat. For further plot there's the blonde and attractive daughter of the British governor, a role essayed by Susannah York.

•

7TH HEAVEN

1927, 115 mins, US ⊗ b/w

Dir Frank Borzage ***Scr*** Benjamin Glazer, Katherine Hilliker, H. H. Caldwell ***Ph*** Ernest Palmer ***Ed*** Katherine Hilliker, H. H. Caldwell ***Art*** William Darling, David Hall

Act Janet Gaynor, Charles Farrell, Ben Bard, David Butler, Marie Mosquini, Albert Gran (Fox)

7th Heaven [based on Austin Strong's play] is a great big romantic, gripping and red-blooded story told in a straight-from-the-shoulder way.

Director Frank Borzage is entitled to the blue ribbon for this one. He has made a great picture. Secondly, he has brought to the fore a little girl who has been playing parts in pictures for two years and made a real star out of her overnight—Janet Gaynor.

Borzage can also take credit for bringing Charles Farrell over the hurdles. David Butler comes into his own as Gobin. George Stone has his first shot at a part in the cinema. He plays the rat in the devoted and cringing fashion it should be.

There is not more than 2,500 feet of actual warfare in the film. Balance of the story is romance. A big punch is the march of the taxi cabs and trucks and pleasure cars with troops 30 miles from Paris to the Marne to stem the advance of the Germans.

This one cost Fox around $1.3 million and took over six months to make.

1927/28: Best Director, Actress (Janet Gaynor), Adaptation

NOMINATIONS: Best Picture, Interior Direction

•

SEVENTH HEAVEN

1937, 100 mins, US b/w

Dir Henry King ***Prod*** Raymond Griffith ***Scr*** Melville Baker ***Ph*** Merritt Gerstad ***Ed*** Barbara McLean ***Mus*** Louis Silvers (dir.)

Act Simone Simon, James Stewart, Jean Hersholt, Gregory Ratoff, Gale Sondergaard, J. Edward Bromberg (20th Century-Fox)

Tenderness of this Austin Strong play has been retained in a fine film production. *Seventh Heaven* is a romance that can stand another telling. Picture is a remake dating back to 1927 as a film and 1922 as a Broadway legit entry.

Simone Simon's is a mixed, and at times disturbing, performance. Frequent impression is that she's uncertain of the character. She is a pretty Diane, and not so much the beaten, bewildered, cringing slavey. The girl's early plight in this case fails to arouse but a meager amount of pity. What makes it still tougher for Simon (who follows Helen Menken [stage] and Janet Gaynor in the role) are the squeaks she emits as part of her more emotional sequences.

There are several scenes brilliantly mixed for poignancy and humor. Major credit for this is due James Stewart's firm grasp of his role and to Henry King's direction.

Even though the action slows up badly in the final two reels, production's pace as a whole is in keeping. Little of war is woven into the narrative, nor are the Armistice celebration scenes too obtrusive. From Jean Hersholt comes a wealth of understanding and patience. His is the part of the slum priest. Gregory Ratoff gets much comedy in the portrait of the taxi driver, while John Qualen, as the contented sewer rat, eases in a number of good-humored moments on his own. Gale Sondergaard, as Diane's dominant sister, registers a full amount of cruelty.

•

SEVENTH SEAL, THE

SEE: DET SJUNDE INSEGLET

•

SEVENTH VEIL, THE

1945, 94 mins, UK Ⓥ ⊙ b/w

Dir Compton Bennett ***Prod*** Sydney Box ***Scr*** Muriel Box, Sydney Box ***Ph*** Reginald Wyer, Bert Mason ***Ed*** Gordon Hales ***Mus*** Benjamin Frankel ***Art*** Jim Carter

Act James Mason, Ann Todd, Herbert Lom, Albert Lieven, Hugh McDermott (Sydney Box/Ortus)

Title refers to the screen every human uses to hurdle his innermost thoughts. Like Salome, ordinary people will remove one or two—or more veils for the benefit of friends, sweethearts, spouses. But unlike Salome, nobody ever sheds the seventh veil. How Ann Todd is made to do this is the backbone of the pic—and its achievement is filmed magnificently.

Apart from the engrossing story (of the merciless discipline to which a teenage, sensitive orphan is subjected by a grim bachelor guardian) as it surges swiftly to its tremendous climax, there is a feast of harmony by the London Symphony Orchestra, conducted by Muir Mathieson, accompanying an unidentified piano virtuoso [Eileen Joyce]—ostensibly Todd.

1946: Best Original Screenplay

•

SEVENTH VICTIM, THE

1943, 71 mins, US Ⓥ b/w

Dir Mark Robson ***Prod*** Val Lewton ***Scr*** Charles O'Neal, DeWitt Bodeen ***Ph*** Nicholas Musuraca ***Ed*** June Lockhert ***Mus*** Roy Webb ***Art*** Albert S. D'Agostino, Walter E. Keller

Act Kim Hunter, Tom Conway, Isabel Jewell, Jean Brooks, Evelyn Brent, Erford Gage (RKO)

A particularly poor script is the basis for the ills besetting this mystery melodrama. Even the occasional good performance can't offset this minor dualer.

Tom Conway has the lead, and while he's generally a satisfactory performer, he, too, can't extricate himself from the maze of circumstances that abound in this totally unbelievable hocus-pocus about a strange Greenwich Village coterie.

•

7TH VOYAGE OF SINBAD, THE

1958, 89 mins, UK Ⓥ ⊙ col

Dir Nathan Juran ***Prod*** Charles H. Schneer ***Scr*** Kenneth Kolb ***Ph*** Wilkie Cooper ***Ed*** Edwin Bryant, Jerome Thoms ***Mus*** Bernard Herrmann ***Art*** Gil Parrondo

Act Kerwin Mathews, Kathryn Grant, Richard Eyer, Torin Thatcher, Alec Mango, Danny Green (Morningside/Columbia)

Just about every trick in the book—including one called Dynamation, i.e. the animation of assorted monsters, vultures, skeletons, etc.—has been used to bring a vivid sort of realism to the various and terrifying hazards which Sinbad encounters on his voyage and in his battle with Sokurah the magician. Add to this a love story, interrupted when the princess Parisa is shrunk to inch-size by the magician, and what emerges is a bright, noisy package.

Kerwin Mathews makes a pleasant Sinbad, acting the part with more restraint than bravura; Kathryn Grant is pretty as the princess; Torin Thatcher has a fittingly evil look as the magician; Richard Eyer is cute as the Genie; Alec Mango has dignity as the Caliph.

But this isn't the sort of film in which performances matter much. It's primarily entertainment for the eye, and the action moves swiftly and almost without interruption. Ray Harryhausen, who was responsible for visual effects, emerges as the hero of this piece.

•

SEVEN UPS, THE

1973, 103 mins, US Ⓥ ⊙ col

Dir Philip D'Antoni ***Prod*** Philip D'Antoni ***Scr*** Albert Ruben, Alexander Jacobs ***Ph*** Urs Furrer ***Ed*** Jerry Greenberg, Stephen A. Rotter, John C. Horger ***Mus*** Don Ellis ***Art*** Ed Wittstein

Act Roy Scheider, Victor Arnold, Jerry Leon, Ken Kercheval, Tony Lo Bianco, Larry Haines (20th Century-Fox)

The Seven Ups is a serviceable dualer about some underground cops who get caught in a series of gangland kidnappings. Produced by debuting director Philip D'Antoni in NY, the film features, at midpoint, a complicated and extravagant car chase which must have taxed the ingenuity of the director and that of stunt coordinator Bill Hickman. Roy Scheider heads an okay cast in a fair script.

Plot finds Scheider, Victor Arnold, Jerry Leon and Ken Kercheval members of a special NYPD unit which operates in unorthodox methods. Tony Lo Bianco plays an informant who uses Scheider's loan shark list to set up his own kidnap operation.

Scheme backfires with Kercheval's surprise death. That event sets off Scheider into a spree of lawless law enforcement which on the screen always turns out right.

•

7 WOMEN

1965, 88 mins, US ⊙ ▭ col

Dir John Ford ***Prod*** Bernard Smith ***Scr*** Janet Green, John McCormick ***Ph*** Joseph LaShelle ***Ed*** Otho S. Lovering ***Mus*** Elmer Bernstein ***Art*** George W. Davis, Eddie Imazu

Act Anne Bancroft, Sue Lyon, Margaret Leighton, Flora Robson, Mildred Dunnock, Eddie Albert (M-G-M)

7 Women is a run-of-the-mill story of an isolated American mission in North China whose serenity is rudely shattered by a ravaging Mongolian barbarian and his band of cutthroats. Production is set in 1935, when the Chinese-Mongolian border was a lawless, violent land dominated by bandits, and takes its title from the seven femmes trapped in a mission and subjected to gross indignities.

John Ford directs from script based on a short story *Chinese Finale* by Norah Lofts and manages regulation treatment. While yarn attempts to tell the relationships of the septet—generally an uninteresting lot—most of the attention focuses necessarily upon Anne Bancroft, a recently arrived doctor whose worldly cynicism brings her into conflict with the rigid moral concepts of mission's head, portrayed by Margaret Leighton. Bancroft endows character with some authority, and Mike Mazurki is properly brutal as the huge bandit leader.

Leighton acquits herself well in an intolerant, self-righteous role.

•

7 WONDERS OF THE WORLD

1956, 120 mins, US ▭ col

Dir Ted Tetzlaff, Andrew Marton, Tay Garnett, Paul Mantz, Walter Thompson ***Prod*** Lowell Thomas ***Scr*** Prosper Buranelli, William Lipscomb ***Ph*** Harry Squire, Gayne Rescher ***Ed*** Harvey Manger, Jack Murray ***Mus*** Emil Newman, David Raksin, Jerome Moross (Stanley Warner/Cinerama)

While the titular *7 Wonders of the World* might be pointed to captiously as a misnomer, this third Cinerama production is a resourceful kickoff for an airlift from Manhattan through 32 countries in 120 minutes. The Sphinx and the Pyramids are pointed to as the sole remainders of the seven ancient wonders and the unfolding is a modern odyssey.

Emerging from the aerial hedgehop of local geographical closeups is a religioso pageantry which includes an exposition of Israel's renaissance; the final ceremonies of the Marian Year, culminating in the Papal blessing and a first-time lighting of Saint Peter's for motion pictures; and a curtsy to the Protestant church, back in the U.S. with a typical American countryside scene. Buddhist priests and Benares (India) temple dancers blend with scenes of African tribal dances and a glorified Japanese geisha line that looks more Leonidoff than authentic Fujiyama.

7 Wonders of the World is at its best when the old and the modern are shown in sharp juxtaposition.

•

SEVEN YEAR ITCH, THE

1955, 105 mins, US Ⓥ ⊙ ▭ col

Dir Billy Wilder ***Prod*** Billy Wilder, Charles K. Feldman ***Scr*** George Axelrod, Billy Wilder ***Ph*** Milton Krasner ***Ed*** Hugh

S. Fowler *Mus* Alfred Newman *Art* Lyle Wheeler, George W. Davis
Act Marilyn Monroe, Tom Ewell, Evelyn Keyes, Sonny Tufts, Robert Strauss, Victor Moore (20th Century-Fox)

The film version of *The Seven Year Itch* bears only a fleeting resemblance to George Axelrod's play of the same name on Broadway. The screen adaptation concerns only the fantasies, and omits the acts, of the summer bachelor, who remains totally, if unbelievably, chaste. Morality wins if honesty loses, but let's not get into that. What counts is that laughs come thick and fast, that the general entertainment is light and gay.

The performance of Marilyn Monroe is baby-dollish as the dumb-but-sweet number upstairs who attracts the eye of the guy, seven years married and restless, whose wife and child have gone off for the summer. The acting kudos belongs to Tom Ewell, a practiced farceur and pantomimist who is able to give entire conviction to the long stretches of soliloquy, a considerable test of Ewell's technique.

•

SEVERED HEAD, A
1971, 98 mins, UK col
Dir Dick Clement *Prod* Alan Ladd, Jr. *Scr* Frederic Raphael *Ph* Austin Dempster *Ed* Peter Weatherley *Mus* Stanley Myers *Art* Richard Macdonald
Act Lee Remick, Richard Attenborough, Ian Holm, Claire Bloom, Jennie Linden, Clive Revill (Winkast)

This is a very upper-class and intellectually snobbish film about "civilized copulation." It's based on Iris Murdoch's novel (subsequently dramatized by Murdoch and J. B. Priestley).

It's the writing, direction (by Dick Clement) and acting that gives it stylish panache. The mattress merry-go-round has a great game of musical chairs among its cast. Ian Holm plays Martin Lynch-Gibbon, a wine taster, with a mistress played by Jennie Linden. Holm's wife (Lee Remick), a predatory nympho, is having an affair with her husband's best friend, psychologist Richard Attenborough, who is also sexually involved with his sister, Claire Bloom ("She's only my half sister," he explains apologetically, but with little conviction).

Cast, all round, is very good, with Holm, the fall guy, excellent. Attenborough gives the psychiatrist a nicely humored pomposity, and Clive Revill, as Holm's sculptor brother, brings his usual breeziness to one of the few extrovert roles.

On the distaff side Remick makes the least impact, at times becoming tediously fluffy. Linden is strong and loving as the mistress who's shuffled around like a pawn and Bloom scores heavily as the menacing, enigmatic egghead.

•

SEX AND THE SINGLE GIRL
1964, 114 mins, US Ⓥ ⦿ col
Dir Richard Quine *Prod* William T. Orr *Scr* Joseph Heller, David R. Schwartz *Ph* Charles Lang *Ed* David Wages *Mus* Neal Hefti *Art* Cary Odell
Act Tony Curtis, Natalie Wood, Henry Fonda, Lauren Bacall, Mel Ferrer, Edward Everett Horton (Reynard/Warner)

Helen Gurley Brown's how-to-do-it book for single girls is takeoff point for story by Joseph Hoffman, scripted by Joseph Heller and David R. Schwartz. Natalie Wood is Dr. Helen Brown of International Institute of Advanced Marital and Pre-Marital Studies, who is target of scandal mag editor Tony Curtis. Curtis is bent on exposing her to be 23-year-old virgin without background for advising single girls about sex.

Curtis poses as his neighbor, Henry Fonda, who has monumental wife trouble, and goes to Wood for advice. Inevitably, they fall for one another with Wood ignorant of Curtis's identity as ogre out to ruin her career.

As usual in this type of farce, male and female leads have fewer comic lines than supporting players. But Curtis registers exceptionally well when detailing supposed marital problems to adviser. His timing in confessing to "inadequacies" shows great comic talent. And one of funniest bits in pic comes when poised, self-assured "Dr. Brown" finds she has romantic problem of own, crumples into tears and places long-distance call to "Mother."

Fonda and Bacall as warring husband and wife also serve up effective scenes as they battle over Fonda's nonexistent wild life as head of Sexy Sox Inc..

Edward Everett Horton shines as boss of Curtis's mag, who harangues aides to make publication "the most disgusting scandal sheet the human mind can recall."

•

SEX, LIES, AND VIDEOTAPE
1989, 101 mins, US Ⓥ ⦿ col
Dir Steven Soderbergh *Prod* Robert Newmyer, John Hardy *Scr* Steven Soderbergh *Ph* Walt Lloyd *Ed* Steven Soderbergh *Mus* Cliff Martinez *Art* Joanne Schmidt
Act James Spader, Andie MacDowell, Peter Gallagher, Laura San Giacomo (Outlaw)

This is a sexy, nuanced, beautifully controlled examination of how a quartet of people are defined by their erotic impulses and inhibitions.

Imaginatively presented opening intercuts the embarrassed therapy confessions of young wife Andie MacDowell with the impending arrival in town of James Spader, a mysterious stranger type who was a college chum of MacDowell's handsome husband (Peter Gallagher).

Given MacDowell's admissions that she and Gallagher are no longer having sex, it would seem that Spader is walking into a potentially provocative situation.

He drops a bombshell by revealing that he is impotent, seemingly scratching any developments on that end. Meanwhile Gallagher has been conducting a secret affair with his wife's sexy wild sister (Laura San Giacomo).

Pic is absorbing and titillating because nearly every conversation is about sex and aspects of these attractive people's relationships. Several steamy scenes between Gallagher and San Giacomo, and some extremely frank videotapes featuring women speaking about their sex lives, turn the temperature up even more.

Lensed on location in Baton Rouge, LA, for $1.2 million, production looks splendid.

1989: NOMINATION: Best Original Screenplay

•

SEXTETTE
1978, 91 mins, US Ⓥ col
Dir Ken Hughes *Prod* Daniel Briggs, Robert Sullivan *Scr* Herbert Baker *Ph* James Crabe *Ed* Argyle Nelson *Mus* Artie Butler *Art* James F. Claytor
Act Mae West, Timothy Dalton, Dom DeLuise, Tony Curtis, Ringo Starr, George Hamilton (Briggs-Sullivan)

Sextette is a cruel, unnecessary and mostly unfunny musical comedy. Mae West made the mistake in 1970 of returning to the screen after a 26-year absence in *Myra Breckenridge*, and she's blundered again.

The screenplay, based on a play by West, concerns a sexy Hollywood movie star who has married a young British nobleman. It's her sixth marriage and in the course of attempting to consummate the liaison she's interrupted by numbers four and five, fans, newspapermen, Rona Barrett, an American gymnastic team and a group of international diplomats meeting at her London hotel.

She's also in the middle of dictating her memoirs when the tape of her recorded autobiography gets out of her hands, a fate which could shorten her latest marriage.

West is on screen for most of the film, mostly attempting Mae West imitations and lip-syncing a series of undistinguished musical numbers. It's an embarrassing attempt at camp from the lady who helped invent the word.

Only Dom DeLuise is occasionally amusing as West's agent. The remainder of the cast—Tony Curtis as a Soviet delegate to the peace conference, Timothy Dalton as West's new husband, Ringo Starr and George Hamilton as former husbands, among others—hardly enhance their reputations.

•

S.F.W.
1995, 92 mins, US Ⓥ col
Dir Jefery Levy *Prod* Dale Pollock *Scr* Danny Rubin, Jefery Levy *Ph* Peter Deming *Ed* Lauren Zuckerman *Mus* Graeme Revell *Art* Eve Cauley
Act Stephen Dorff, Reese Witherspoon, Jake Busey, Joey Lauren Adams, Pamela Gidley, David Barry Gray (Gramercy)

A satirical spin through America's oft-reported fascination with celebrities, no matter how empty or facile, *S.F.W.* tries hard to juice up a subject that feels done to death.

When suburban teen buddies Cliff Spab (Stephen Dorff) and Joe Dice (Jack Noseworthy) zip into their local convenience store for a couple of brewskis, their typical night out on the 'burb is turned upside down. Waiting inside is a group of video camera-wielding terrorists who hold the two boys and three other customers hostage.

The gang demands that TV networks broadcast the tapes they're creating, but the lack of a political or financial explanation for their actions is only one of several key weaknesses of this caricature-laden adaptation of Andrew Wellman's novel.

Pic instead focuses on the after-effects of what turns into a 36-day ordeal that claims the lives of all the hostages except Spab and winsome uppercrust teen Wendy Pfister (Reese Witherspoon).

While director Jefery Levy, whose previous pix were *Drive* and *Inside Monkey Zetterland*, clearly sympathizes with his protagonist's ennui and confusion, *S.F.W.* fails to develop flesh-and-blood characters, and instead trades on tired filmic tricks that stack the deck at every turn.

•

SGT. BILKO
1996, 94 mins, US Ⓥ ⦿ col
Dir Jonathan Lynn *Prod* Brian Grazer *Scr* Andy Breckman *Ph* Peter Sova *Ed* Tony Lombardo *Mus* Alan Silvestri *Art* Lawrence G. Paull
Act Steve Martin, Dan Aykroyd, Phil Hartman, Glenne Headly, Daryl Mitchell, Max Casella (Imagine/Universal)

Even Steve Martin back in his wild-and-crazy mode can't breathe much life into *Sgt. Bilko*—a somewhat unlikely candidate for translation from the TV sitcom vaults to the bigscreen. *Bilko* can't really be much more than the series—the exploits of an unscrupulous army scam artist constantly looking for new ways to make a buck.

The plot has Bilko's nemesis, Maj. Thorn (Phil Hartman), coming to the base, seeking revenge on Bilko for a past indiscretion that nearly scuttled his career. Thorn not only wants to ruin Bilko's current setup but also to steal his girlfriend (Glenne Headly), whom Bilko has a bad habit of repeatedly leaving at the altar. Another thread finds Bilko trying to win over a straitlaced new addition to the unit, Wally (Daryl Mitchell).

Director Jonathan Lynn generally has a nice comic touch, but *Bilko* simply misfires on too many of its gags, often seeking to mask its deficiencies with a frenetic energy that's difficult even for Martin to maintain.

Among the other featured players, Dan Aykroyd, as Bilko's benignly ineffectual superior Col. Hall, amounts to window dressing, Hartman has played this smarmy character many times before and Headly is back in her Tess True-heart mode as the faithful, forgotten girlfriend. Tech credits are sharp.

•

SGT. PEPPER'S LONELY HEARTS CLUB BAND
1978, 111 mins, US Ⓥ ⦿ ▭ col
Dir Michael Schultz *Prod* Robert Stigwood *Scr* Henry Edwards *Ph* Owen Roizman *Ed* Christopher Holmes *Art* Brian Eatwell
Act Peter Frampton, Barry Gibb, Robin Gibb, Maurice Gibb, Frankie Howerd, Paul Nicholas (Universal)

Sgt. Pepper's Lonely Hearts Club Band will attract some grown-up flower children of the 1960s who will soon find the Michael Schultz film to be a totally bubblegum and cotton candy melange of garish fantasy and narcissism. The production crams nearly 30 songs, largely by The Beatles, into newly recorded versions tailored for stars Peter Frampton and The Bee Gees.

Plot has Frampton as the grandson of the earlier Sgt. Pepper who carries on the family band tradition with a modern-sound in partnership with The Bee Gees. Story introduces a lot of freakish characters out to steal the band's instruments which, somehow, make Heartland, USA, a dream of a small town. They don't succeed, though there's enough teeny-bopper-teasing naughtiness to amuse and thrill the target audience. Donald Pleasence, one of the heavies, plays a music biz wizard whose fictional trademark is that of producer Robert Stigwood's organization.

Near the end of the 111-minute film, when all wrongs have been righted, there's a celebrity olio in which many familiar names appear to be singing happily. The sound of this isn't any more lifelike than much of the preceding singing.

•

SHADOW, THE
1994, 107 mins, US Ⓥ ⦿ col
Dir Russell Mulcahy *Prod* Martin Bregman, Willi Baer, Michael S. Bregman *Scr* David Koepp *Ph* Stephen H. Burum *Ed* Peter Honess *Mus* Jerry Goldsmith *Art* Joseph Nemec III
Act Alec Baldwin, John Lone, Penelope Ann Miller, Ian McKellen, Peter Boyle, Tim Curry (Bregman-Baer/Universal)

Starting with the main title credits backed by Jerry Goldsmith's brooding score, *The Shadow* is clearly trying to mine the *Batman* lode, down to its impressive production design, somber tone and occasional flashes of high camp. However, *The Shadow*—which enjoyed its greatest success in radio in the '30s after being created in pulp novels—lacks the same visceral appeal. The end result is a hollow production design showcase.

Pic opens with its worst sequence, set in Tibet, illustrating how Lamont Cranston (Alec Baldwin) acquires his Shadow-y powers. Director Russell Mulcahy recovers with a stylish introduction of the character in New York.

The heart of the story involves a comic-book nemesis, Shiwan Khan (John Lone), a descendant of Genghis Khan who possesses the same mental powers as the Shadow. Influencing the mind of the noted if slightly daft scientist Reinhardt Lane (Ian McKellen), Khan decides to destroy New York, fashioning a pre-nuclear facsimile of an atomic bomb. Cranston, meanwhile, finds himself entangled with Lane's daughter, Margo (Penelope Ann Miller).

Mulcahy remains a gifted visual stylist but struggles with character and meanders when it comes to advancing a story—a challenge made more difficult thanks to the underdeveloped script by David Koepp (*Jurassic Park*).

Baldwin turns in a sturdy central performance, managing to bring some dimension and self-effacing humor to his role. Lone also provides a shrewd and formidable adversary. Other performances are either uneven or wildly over-the-top, particularly Miller's shameless vamping.

•

SHADOWLANDS
1994, 130 mins, UK/US Ⓥ ⦿ col
Dir Richard Attenborough ***Prod*** Richard Attenborough, Brian Eastman ***Scr*** William Nicholson ***Ph*** Roger Pratt ***Ed*** Lesley Walker ***Mus*** George Fenton ***Art*** Stuart Craig
Act Anthony Hopkins, Debra Winger, Edward Hardwicke, Michael Denison, John Wood, Peter Firth (Shadowlands/Spelling)

Anthony Hopkins delivers a towering performance in *Shadowlands*, a touching, somewhat fictionalized account of a late-in-life love between eminent English writer and scholar C. S. Lewis and Joy Gresham, an American poet. Set in the early 1950s, it's a quiet, pensive tale of two eccentric individuals whose personae, lifestyles and cultures couldn't have been more different.

A middle-aged bachelor, Lewis is a reserved, repressed intellectual who lives an orderly life with his brother Warnie (Edward Hardwicke). For years, he's been the literary hero of Gresham (Debra Winger), a feisty, straightforward American who decides to take her son Douglas (Joseph Mazzello) and visit him in London.

At first, the relationship is formal and restrained, but gradually it evolves into intimate friendship, romantic love and, ultimately, marriage.

Up to the last reel, the film resists sentimentality, but then it succumbs to a level of a slow, old-fashioned—even heavy-handed—melodrama that negates its earlier matter-of-fact tone.

It's a testament to the nuanced writing of William Nicholson, who adapted his stage play after successful productions in London and Broadway [and a TV adaptation for the BBC], that the drama works effectively on both personal and collective levels. The film's greatest achievement is that neither comes across as an abstraction of type. Coming off years of desultory and unimpressive movies, Winger at last plays a role worthy of her talent.

1993: NOMINATIONS: Best Actress (Debra Winger), Adapted Screenplay

•

SHADOW MAKERS
SEE: FAT MAN AND LITTLE BOY

•

SHADOW OF A DOUBT
1943, 106 mins, US Ⓥ ⦿ b/w
Dir Alfred Hitchcock ***Prod*** Jack H. Skirball ***Scr*** Thornton Wilder, Sally Benson, Alma Reville ***Ph*** Joseph Valentine ***Ed*** Milton Carruth ***Mus*** Dimitri Tiomkin ***Art*** John B. Goodman, Robert Boyle
Act Joseph Cotten, Teresa Wright, Macdonald Carey, Henry Travers, Patricia Collinge, Hume Cronyn (Skirball/Universal)

The suspenseful tenor of dramatics associated with director Alfred Hitchcock is utilized here to good advantage in unfolding a story [by Gordon McDonell] of a small town and the arrival of what might prove to be a murderer. Hitchcock poses a study in contrasts when the world-wise adventurer (Joseph Cotten) eludes police in Philadelphia to journey to his sister's home and family in the small California town of Santa Rosa. His deb-age niece (Teresa Wright), is not only named young Charlie after her uncle, but knows there's a mental contact somewhere along the line. Amid the typical small-town family life, she intuitively feels that Cotten has a guilty conscience, and finally ties the ends together to cast suspicion on him as a murderer and fugitive.

Hitchcock deftly etches his small-town characters and homey surroundings. Wright provides a sincere and persuasive portrayal as the girl, while Cotten is excellent as the motivating factor in the proceedings. Strong support is provided by Henry Travers, Patricia Collinge, Edna May Wonacott and Charles Bates. Hume Cronyn gets attention as the small-town amateur sleuth.

1943: NOMINATION: Best Original Story

•

SHADOW OF THE THIN MAN
1941, 97 mins, US Ⓥ ⦿ b/w
Dir W. S. Van Dyke ***Prod*** Hunt Stromberg ***Scr*** Irving Brecher, Harry Kurnitz ***Ph*** William Daniels ***Ed*** Robert J. Kern ***Mus*** David Snell ***Art*** Cedric Gibbons, Paul Groesse
Act William Powell, Myrna Loy, Barry Nelson, Donna Reed, Sam Levene, Alan Baxter (M-G-M)

Much of the farcical flavor which characterized the earlier *Thin Man* films is reclaimed in the new picture. On the sentimental side, William Powell and Myrna Loy get a great deal of fun from their first appearance as parents of a four-year-old son, who has a way of asking embarrassing questions. For excitement the couple find themselves in the middle of an investigation into racetrack gambling, in the course of which there are three homicides, half a dozen suspects and a bit of gunplay.

Harry Kurnitz has fashioned the story with a good deal of ingenuity, using the characters of the private detective and his wife, as created in the original yarn by Dashiell Hammett.

Sam Levene, as a police lieutenant, is particularly amusing. Stella Adler is a stunning blonde heavy, and the character bits by Lou Lubin, Joseph Anthony, Alan Baxter and Loring Smith add some reality to the seamy side of the action. With much to work with, W. S. Van Dyke has directed with speed.

•

SHADOW OF THE VAMPIRE
2000, 93 mins, UK/US Ⓥ ⦿
Dir E. Elias Merhige ***Prod*** Nicolas Cage, Jeff Levine ***Scr*** Steven Katz ***Ph*** Lou Bogue ***Ed*** Chris Wyatt ***Mus*** Dan Jones ***Art*** Assheton Gorton
Act John Malkovich, Willem Dafoe, Cary Elwes, John Aden Gillet, Eddie Izzard, Udo Kier, Catherine McCormack, Roman Vibert (Long Shot/Saturn/Lions Gate)

The first and arguably the greatest vampire film, F. W. Murnau's 1922 *Nosferatu*, is the subject of a much-belated, and stimulatingly warped, "making of" in *Shadow of the Vampire*. Wholly absorbing and inspired in parts, this carefully crafted curio dares to suggest that Murnau made a Faustian pact with an actual vampire to play the title role in exchange for the neck of the film's leading lady at production's end. Anchored by an astounding performance by Willem Dafoe as the tormented actor Max Schreck, director E. Elias Merhige's first professional feature is not nearly as weird as his strikingly original student thesis film, *Begotten*, a fest and cult hit in 1991. But pic skirts the edge of the wild side nonetheless in its examination of the "anything for art" mentality taken to the limit.

The highly aestheticized approach to filmmaking espoused by Murnau, the "difficult actor" syndrome seen in the extreme and the injection of vampirism into a historical undertaking involving prominent figures all provide intriguing grist for the mill. Add to that one of the more successful representations of the making of a classic film—a considerable feat in itself—and Merhige & Co. can be said to have mostly pulled off a daunting exercise.

Willem Dafoe has been skillfully made up to look amazingly like Schreck in the role—bald, pointy-eared and skeletal, with frighteningly prominent teeth and enormously long fingernails, which he sometimes clicks together in moments of nervous distress. Dafoe's uncanny impersonation becomes the film's primary source of fascination, as Schreck/Nosferatu insidiously takes over the production by pushing Murnau over the edge and threatening the very lives of the crew members.

With the mood shifting between mild dread and appalled amusement, *Shadow of the Vampire* is not entirely consistent; it might sound better than it sometimes plays, and it's never genuinely scary or emotionally implicating. After starting off strong, Murnau recedes as a full-blown character, and while John Malkovich does a reasonable job, the actor is not ideally cast as a director known for his aristocratic fastidiousness and enormous height.

•

SHADOW OF THE WOLF
1993, 112 mins, Canada/France Ⓥ col
Dir Jacques Dorfmann ***Prod*** Claude Leger ***Scr*** Rudy Wurlitzer, Evan Jones ***Ph*** Billy Williams ***Ed*** Francoise Bonnot ***Mus*** Maurice Jarre ***Art*** Wolf Kroeger
Act Lou Diamond Phillips, Toshiro Mifune, Jennifer Tilly, Bernard-Pierre Donnadieu, Donald Sutherland (Vision)

A story of survival, revenge and murder in the frozen north, *Shadow of the Wolf* has all the subtlety of a silent movie serial. Reportedly, at $30-plus million, the costliest Canadian production ever, this wilderness epic's oddball international cast enacts the tragic confrontation of native Americans and encroaching whites in the Arctic, circa 1935.

As fashioned here from the much honored source novel [Yves Theriault's *Agaguk*, adapted by David Milhaud], tale relates the maturation of a young Inuit Eskimo hunter (Lou Diamond Phillips) who, out of violent hatred for whites, is banished by his shaman father, impetuously kills a trader and, in company with the local beauty, forges a difficult life on the tundra. Eventually, everything comes full circle and Agaguk returns to the village to accept the mantle of maturity from his father. Unfortunately, the film borders on the laughable throughout due to dialog that erases the distinction between simple and simple-minded. One notable sequence has Agaguk jumping on board a speeding whale to escape his foes.

Phillips acts with a heavy seriousness that compounds the problems. As the compromised father, Japanese great Toshiro Mifune lends his imposing presence, but is obviously dubbed.

•

SHADOWS
1961, 84 mins, US ⦿ b/w
Dir John Cassavetes ***Prod*** Maurice McEndree, Seymour Cassel ***Scr*** [improvised] ***Ph*** Erich Kolmar ***Ed*** Len Appleson, Maurice McEndree ***Mus*** Charlie Mingus, Shifi Hadi ***Art*** Randy Liles, Bob Reeh
Act Lelia Goldoni, Ben Carruthers, Tony Ray, Hugh Hurd, Rupert Crosse, Tom Allen (McEndree-Cassel)

First made in 16mm as an exercise in improvisation by a group of actors directed by John Cassavetes, a w.k. thesp himself, *Shadows* was then filled out and blown up to 35mm under the supervision of two producers. It came in for $40,000, and a showing at the British Film Institute got it raves and an advance from British Lion of $25,000.

A brother and sister who look white have a brother who is completely Negro. The film dwells on the dramatic interludes in their lives and the inevitable race problems. The girl is 20 and unsure of her emotions until her first affair is marred by a cowardly reaction to the revelation of her color by her lover. The white-looking brother drifts through various adventures with too unanchored white friends, and the Negro brother is a singer accepting his fate of trying to work in low dive shows and getting along with his edgy sister and brother.

Nothing rings false in the film. Though the narrative is rambling it strikes solid truths and dimension in showing people living and reacting in a manner which is dictated from within rather than forced on them by a script. Pic, in its improvised form, has actors working from general situations within an agreed outline.

Lelia Goldoni has nervous charm, guile and vulnerability as the girl, Ben Carruthers possesses the sullen violence of solitude and indecision, and Hugh Hurd has warmth and understanding as the breadwinning brother. Cassavetes has given this form and a point of view without trying to solve anything but letting the characters express themselves. There is no attempt at technique but the story and action carries itself and New York is an essential part of this unique film.

•

SHADOWS AND FOG
1992, 86 mins, US Ⓥ ⦿ b/w
Dir Woody Allen ***Prod*** Jack Rollins, Charles H. Joffe ***Scr*** Woody Allen ***Ph*** Carlo Di Palma ***Ed*** Susan E. Morse ***Art*** Santo Loquasto
Act Woody Allen, Mia Farrow, John Malkovich, Madonna, Donald Pleasence, Jodie Foster (Orion)

Exquisitely shot in black and white, Woody Allen's *Shadows and Fog* is a sweet homage to German expressionist filmmaking and a nod to the content of socially responsible tales since narrative film began. Allen's fans will regard this as a nice try that falls short.

Mia Farrow and boyfriend John Malkovich are part of a traveling circus that has pitched its tent near an unnamed European town where rival bands of vigilantes roam the nighttime streets in search of a marauding strangler. When Farrow catches Malkovich cheating on her with the strongman's wife (Madonna in a murky cameo), she walks out into the fog where she is befriended by streetwalker Lily Tomlin.

Helmer throws in some Kafka (Allen's persecuted character is never sure what he's supposed to do), some evil (there's a killer on the loose, casting shadows in the fog), a spunky counterbalancing force (Mia Farrow) and a little magic.

Tomlin is good, and Julie Kavner also scores as a former Allen paramour. John Cusack hits all the right notes as a college student who cajoles Farrow into selling herself just once. Several top thesps, including Jodie Foster and Kathy Bates, have been caught in surprisingly ordinary (and brief) perfs.

•

SHADOW WARRIOR, THE
SEE: KAGEMUSHA

•

SHAFT
1971, 98 mins, US Ⓥ col
Dir Gordon Parks ***Prod*** Joel Freeman ***Scr*** John D. F. Black ***Ph*** Urs Furrer ***Ed*** Hugh A. Robertson ***Mus*** Isaac Hayes
Act Richard Roundtree, Moses Gunn, Gwenn Mitchell, Christopher St. John, Charles Cioffi, Lawrence Pressman (M-G-M)

Take a formula private-eye plot, update it with all-black environment, and lace with contemporary standards of on-and off-screen violence, and the result is *Shaft*. It is directed by Gordon Parks with a subtle feel for both the grit and the humanity of the script.

Ernest Tidyman's novel, adapted by himself and John D. F. Black, concerns the kidnap by the Mafia of Sherri Brewer, daughter of Harlem underworld boss Moses Gunn. Richard Roundtree, as a black Sam Spade, is hired by Gunn to find her. Understanding but tough white cop Charles Cioffi, whose outstanding characterization singlehandedly upgrades the plot from strictly racial polemic, works with Roundtree in avoiding a gangland confrontation which, to outsiders, would appear to be a racial war.

In his second feature film after a long career as a still photographer, Parks shows some excellent storytelling form, with only minor clutter of picture-taking-for-its-own-sake.

1971: Best Song ("Theme from Shaft").

NOMINATION: Best Original Score

•

SHAFT IN AFRICA
1973, 112 mins, US Ⓥ ▭ col
Dir John Guillermin ***Prod*** Roger Lewis ***Scr*** Stirling Silliphant ***Ph*** Marcel Grignon ***Ed*** Max Benedict ***Mus*** Johnny Pate ***Art*** John Stoll
Act Richard Roundtree, Frank Finlay, Vonetta McGee, Neda Arneric, Debebe Eshetu, Spiros Focas (M-G-M)

Shaft in Africa, third in the series, takes a new storytelling direction which gets it out of the well plowed inner-city ghetto rut. Richard Roundtree again stars as the black private eye, now infiltrating an Africa-to-Europe slave smuggling ring.

Script, from the Ernest Tidyman character trove, is surprisingly good. Dragooned by diplomat Cy Grant into cracking the slave ring, run by Frank Finlay and his nympho mistress Neda Arneric, Roundtree embarks on a series of journeys, in which he successively kills all assassins dispatched by Finlay through Debebe Eshetu, Grant's aide who is also in Finlay's employ. Vonetta McGee is Grant's daughter with whom Roundtree eventually connects, though her character is most awkwardly interwoven in the script.

•

SHAFT'S BIG SCORE!
1972, 105 mins, US Ⓥ ▭ col
Dir Gordon Parks ***Prod*** Roger Lewis, Ernest Tidyman ***Scr*** Ernest Tidyman ***Ph*** Urs Furrer ***Ed*** Harry Howard ***Mus*** Gordon Parks ***Art*** Emanuel Gerard
Act Richard Roundtree, Moses Gunn, Drew Bundini Brown, Joseph Mascolo, Kathy Imrie, Julius W. Harris (Shaft/ M-G-M)

Richard Roundtree again heads the cast as a swinging black private eye, caught between opposing criminal forces. This time around, there is a lot more production and nurturing of the project, not all of which is to the good, however.

Script finds Roundtree trapped in the double-dealings of Wally Taylor, who has killed partner Robert Kya-Hill for money. Moses Gunn is again excellent as a black mobster, and Joseph Mascolo is a white mobster eyeing Taylor's territory for a move-in. Julius W. Harris is a police detective who gives Roundtree his head to unravel the mess.

The first *Shaft* had a running-scared excitement not only in the characters, but also throughout the whole picture. The new film seems more self-conscious, contrived, ambitious and sluggish.

•

SHAG
1988, 100 mins, UK/US Ⓥ ⊙ col
Dir Zelda Barron ***Prod*** Stephen Wooley, Julia Chasman ***Scr*** Robin Swicord, Lanier Laney, Terry Sweeney ***Ph*** Peter Macdonald ***Ed*** Laurence Mery-Clark ***Art*** Buddy Cone
Act Phoebe Cates, Scott Coffey, Bridget Fonda, Annabeth Gish, Page Hannah, Robert Rusler (Palace/Hemdale)

As a dance flick, *Shag* suffers from an unexciting dance-style and so-so choreography but compensates with a fine young cast and likable story. Pic is set in South Carolina in 1963 and opens with three girls, Page Hannah, Annabeth Gish and Bridget Fonda, picking up pal Phoebe Cates for her last summer fling with the girls before she marries dull Tyrone Power, Jr..

They head for Myrtle Beach and the Sun Fun Festival, full of boys, beer, a beauty parade and shagging—the current dance craze. Within hours of their arrival Cates becomes fascinated by hunky Robert Rusler and plump Gish falls for preppy Scott Coffey.

The four female leads are excellent, though it is Fonda who exudes confidence and star quality and looks destined for great things. Of the guys, Coffey's character is the only one with any depth; the rest seem to play hunks, wimps or louts.

Acting-family connections are strong in *Shag*, including Bridget Fonda (daughter of Peter), Page Hannah (sister of Daryl) and Tyrone Power, Jr. (billed as "Junior" but son of star Tyrone Power and grandson of Tyrone Power, Sr.), though Annabeth Gish is no relation to the thesp sisters.

•

SHAGGY D.A., THE
1976, 91 mins, US Ⓥ col
Dir Robert Stevenson ***Prod*** Bill Anderson ***Scr*** Don Tait ***Ph*** Frank Phillips ***Ed*** Bob Bring, Norman Palmer ***Mus*** Buddy Baker ***Art*** John B. Mansbrough, Perry Ferguson
Act Dean Jones, Tim Conway, Suzanne Pleshette, Keenan Wynn, JoAnne Worley, Dick Van Patten (Walt Disney)

In *The Shaggy Dog*, teenager Tommy Kirk came into possession of a magical ring which periodically changed him into a sheepdog. Here, in Don Tait's script drawn from the same material, Felix Salten's *The Hound of Florence*, fledgling d.a. candidate Dean Jones suffers the same fate. Most of the brisk 91-minute film is physical comedy as Jones tries to escape embarrassing situations and to outwit villainous d.a. Keenan Wynn.

Jones is a pleasant light comedian whose style is perfectly suited to the WASPish world of Disney. As his wife, Suzanne Pleshette has her first film role in five years, and her beauty and intelligence livens a part that might have been dull without her.

Rounding out a large and able supporting cast are such people as Tim Conway, JoAnne Worley (in her film debut), Dick Van Patten, Hans Conreid, and in an unbilled cameo as a dogcatcher, the late Liam Dunn, who died before completing his part. Conway is particularly droll as a cloddish ice-cream salesman.

•

SHAGGY DOG, THE
1959, 101 mins, US Ⓥ ⊙ b/w
Dir Charles T. Barton ***Prod*** Bill Walsh (assoc.) ***Scr*** Bill Walsh, Lillie Hayward ***Ph*** Edward Colman ***Ed*** James D. Ballas ***Mus*** Paul Smith ***Art*** Carroll Clark
Act Fred MacMurray, Jean Hagen, Tommy Kirk, Annette Funicello, Tim Considine, Kevin Corcoran (Walt Disney)

The Shaggy Dog, said to be the first live action film by Walt Disney set in the present, is about what's called "shape-shifting." According to the screenplay suggested by Felix Salten's *The Hound of Florence*, there used to be a great deal of shifting of shapes, from man to beast and sometimes back.

There are a good many laughs on this simple premise and the script's exploitation of them. The only time the film falters badly is in its choice of a gimmick to get the boy-who-turns-into-a-dog turned back, for good and all, into a boy. According to the legend, it takes an act of heroism on the part of the shifting shape to be restored.

Fred MacMurray plays the father of the two boys, Tommy Kirk and Kevin Corcoran. MacMurray himself is a mailman physically allergic to dogs. Young Kirk accidentally transforms himself into a large, shaggy sheep dog when he comes into possession of a spellcasting ring once owned by the Borgias.

Where MacMurray has a good line, he shows that he has few peers in this special field of comedy. Jean Hagen, as his wife, is pretty and pleasant in a more or less straight role, while the two boys handle their comedy nicely.

•

SHAKE HANDS WITH THE DEVIL
1959, 104 mins, US b/w
Dir Michael Anderson ***Prod*** Michael Anderson ***Scr*** Ivan Goff, Ben Roberts ***Ph*** Erwin Hillier ***Ed*** Gordon Pilkington ***Mus*** William Alwyn ***Art*** Tom Morahan
Act James Cagney, Don Murray, Dana Wynter, Glynis Johns, Michael Redgrave, Sybil Thorndike (United Artists/ Pennebaker)

A strong and unusual story has been diluted in its telling. The theme is that those who "shake hands with the devil" often find they have difficulty getting their hands back. Two such, in the screenplay from the novel by Rearden Conner, are James Cagney and Don Murray. Against a background of the 1921 Irish Rebellion, Cagney is a professor of medicine at a Dublin university, and Murray, an American veteran of World War I, is his student. Cagney is also a "commandant" of the underground, and Murray's father, an Irish patriot, was killed while working with Cagney.

It is Cagney who wants to continue the terror when the leader of the Irish independence movement (Michael Redgrave) works out a treaty with the British that eventually leads to freedom.

The principals, paced by Cagney, are interesting and sometimes moving. But they seem posed against the Irish background, rather than part of it. The supporting cast looms larger than it should. Sybil Thorndike, for instance, as a titled Irish lady lending her name and fierce old heart to the cause, is fine. Redgrave has dignity and strength in his few scenes.

Erwin Hillier's camerawork is good, creating a grim, gray Ireland that is a natural setting for the sanguine struggle.

•

SHAKESPEARE IN LOVE
1998, 122 mins, US Ⓥ ⊙ col
Dir John Madden ***Prod*** David Parfitt, Donna Gigliotti, Harvey Weinstein, Edward Zwick, Marc Norman ***Scr*** Marc Norman, Tom Stoppard ***Ph*** Richard Greatrex ***Ed*** David Gamble ***Mus*** Stephen Warbeck ***Art*** Martin Childs
Act Joseph Fiennes, Gwyneth Paltrow, Geoffrey Rush, Judi Dench, Simon Callow, Colin Firth (Bedford Falls/Miramax/Universal)

With *Shakespeare in Love*, director John Madden does for adults what Baz Luhrmann did for teens in *Romeo + Juliet*—he makes Shakespeare accessible, entertaining and fun for modern audiences. Exquisitely acted, tightly directed and impressively assembled, this lively period piece is the kind of arty gem with potentially broad appeal.

While the film's storyline is labyrinthine, its premise is fairly simple: William Shakespeare (Joseph Fiennes) has writer's block and needs a muse to unlock his creative abilities. When he falls for the lovely Viola De Lesseps (Gwyneth Paltrow), his passion is released, and his ineptly titled *Romeo and Ethel, the Pirate's Daughter* becomes *Romeo and Juliet*.

But in true Shakespearean fashion, their romance is hampered by various complications: Viola is betrothed to another, the insufferable Lord Wessex (Colin Firth), and that union has been sanctioned by Queen Elizabeth (Judi Dench).

Set against the backdrop of London in 1593, pic presents a theatrical community in which Shakespeare is but one of several successful playwrights—including Christopher Marlowe, Thomas Kyd, Robert Greene and George Peele. Notoriously competitive with the then better-known Marlowe (*Dr. Faustus*), Shakespeare is striving to find his own creative niche.

Paltrow has a luminosity that makes Viola irresistible, and RSC-trained Fiennes endows Shakespeare with a likable humanity and romantic charm. The supporting cast is a dream. As the smarmy Wessex, Firth is hateful without overdoing the part. The unassailable Dench plays Elizabeth with gusto.

Madden keeps his cast together with the skill of a veteran, finding opportunities to let almost every actor shine. Richard Greatrex's lensing lends a refreshingly contempo feel to the proceedings.

•

SHAKESPEARE WALLAH
1965, 125 mins, India/US Ⓥ b/w
Dir James Ivory ***Prod*** Ismail Merchant ***Scr*** Ruth Prawer Jhabvala, James Ivory ***Ph*** Subrata Mitra ***Ed*** Amit Bose ***Mus*** Satyajit Ray
Act Shashi Kapoor, Felicity Kendal, Geoffrey Kendal, Laura Liddell, Madhur Jaffrey (Merchant Ivory)

Shakespeare Wallah is officially designated an Indian-American coproduction, though the official credits do not name the U.S. associates, apart from the Californian-born director, James Ivory.

The English language production is the story of a touring theatrical company specializing in Shakespearean production which has seen better days. It's a struggle to keep the company going which was founded by Tony and Carla Buckingham (Geoffrey Kendal and Laura Liddell) who are totally dedicated, and expect the same from all around, and particularly from their daughter Lizzie, who is currently enamored of an Indian playboy, who is also indulging in some extra-curricular activities with an Indian actress in the company.

The pace of the production is always too leisurely, and some of the Shakespearean excerpts could advantageously be cut. Nevertheless, there is a naive charm to the production.

There is also a very confident performance by Shashi Kapoor, as the Indian playboy. Felicity Kendal is a pert newcomer with an ingenuous style. Madhur Jaffrey ably completes the cast as the Indian actress.

•

SHALAKO

1968, 118 mins, UK Ⓥ ▭ col

Dir Edward Dmytryk ***Prod*** Euan Lloyd ***Scr*** J. J. Griffith, Hal Hopper, Scot Finch ***Ph*** Ted Moore ***Ed*** Bill Blunden ***Mus*** Robert Farnon ***Art*** Herbert Smith

Act Sean Connery, Brigitte Bardot, Stephen Boyd, Jack Hawkins, Peter Van Eyck, Honor Blackman (Kingston/De Grunwald)

Though purporting to take place in New Mexico during the 19th century, this $5 million film was actually shot on location in Almeria, Spain, but doesn't look it.

Based on Louis L'Amour's novel [adapted by Clarke Reynolds], it's a 19th-century story of an aristocratic, "dude" hunting safari from Europe which is led into Apache territory by its double crossing "white" hunter and given a hard time by the redskins.

Shalako (Sean Connery) comes across the camp when he rescues one of them (Brigitte Bardot) from Indians and has to pit his wits and resource, not only against the Apaches but against members of the expedition, before he manages to save the party from complete destruction. [Action sequences directed by Bob Simmons.]

Jealousy, obstinacy, greed and roguery all emotionally stir up trouble for the hunters.

The film is a slow starter while the various characters are being established and has an over-abrupt and inconclusive ending. Intriguing are the relationships between members of the hunting party.

•

SHALLOW GRAVE

1994, 91 mins, UK Ⓥ ⊙ col

Dir Danny Boyle ***Prod*** Andrew Macdonald ***Scr*** John Hodge ***Ph*** Brian Tufano ***Ed*** Masahiro Hirakubo ***Mus*** Simon Boswell ***Art*** Kave Quinn

Act Kerry Fox, Christopher Eccleston, Ewan McGregor, Keith Allen, Ken Stott, John Hodge (Figment/Film Four)

Blighty's new wave of knock-'em-dead filmers has a banner to march under with *Shallow Grave*, a tar-black comedy that zings along on a wave of visual and scripting inventiveness.

Main surprise is that this first feature of English TV director Danny Boyle manages to sustain its oddball humor and theatrical style without depending on non-stop eye-whacking tricks. First script by Glasgow-based doctor John Hodge (who cameos as a cop) keeps springing surprises until the final shot.

Story, set in modern-day Scotland, revolves around a trio of unlikely friends sharing a spacious top-floor apartment. Juliet (Kerry Fox) is a seemingly levelheaded nurse; David (Christopher Eccleston), a studiously boring accountant in a stuffy firm; and Alex (Ewan McGregor), a wild-side journalist on a local rag.

Juliet takes a shine to the rough-looking, mysterious Hugo (Keith Allen), who soon takes up residence but is found dead in bed, a suitcase stuffed with money. After shilly-shallying over what to do, the trio decides to chop up the cadaver, bury the bits and keep the loot—a sequence that sets the tone for the pic's several grisly comic set pieces.

Playing and casting are strong down the line. Of the central trio, Kiwi actress Fox rates special praise for her disarming portrayal of everyday madness. Superb set of the off-center apartment is a constant delight, with its color-coded rooms and its play with light.

•

SHALL WE DANCE

1937, 101 mins, US Ⓥ ⊙ b/w

Dir Mark Sandrich ***Prod*** Pandro S. Berman ***Scr*** Allan Scott, Ernest Pagano ***Ph*** David Abel ***Ed*** William Hamilton ***Mus*** Nathaniel Shilkret (dir.) ***Art*** Van Nest Polglase, Carroll Clark

Act Fred Astaire, Ginger Rogers, Edward Everett Horton, Eric Blore, Jerome Cowan, Ketti Gallian (RKO)

Shall We Dance, the seventh in the Astaire-Rogers series, is a standout because the script affords Astaire a legitimate excuse for a change of pace in his dancing, the comedy is solid, and this is the best cutting job an Astaire picture has enjoyed in a long time. This latter item is important as it had begun to look as if the studio couldn't decide whether Astaire was making musicals or operettas.

There have been others in the string which have had stronger tunes, superior punch laughs, and packed more dynamite in Astaire's own specialties, yet seldom have these ingredients been made to fit so evenly. All six songs [by George and Ira Gershwin], one more than usual, have been nicely spotted with no attempt to overplay any of them. Nor is there a bad ditty in the batch.

Basically the story [*Watch Your Step* by Lee Loeb and Harold Buchman, adapted by P. J. Wolfson] is of a ballet dancer (Astaire) who would rather be a hoofer. Romantically the script ties him into a complicated affinity with Ginger Rogers who is a musical comedy star. The rumors of their marriage grow to such proportion it forces them to secretly wed with the understanding of an immediate divorce. In locale the yarn starts in Paris, spends some time en route to the U.S. and finishes in New York.

Astaire's stock company has been reassembled, hence the comedy is in the hands of Edward Horton, as Astaire's manager, and Eric Blore, as a Manhattan maitre d'hotel.

1937: NOMINATIONS: Best Song ("They Can't Take That Away from Me")

•

SHAMPOO

1975, 109 mins, US Ⓥ ⊙ col

Dir Hal Ashby ***Prod*** Warren Beatty ***Scr*** Robert Towne, Warren Beatty ***Ph*** Laszlo Kovacs ***Ed*** Robert C. Jones ***Mus*** Paul Simon ***Art*** Richard Sylbert

Act Warren Beatty, Julie Christie, Goldie Hawn, Lee Grant, Jack Warden, Tony Bill (Columbia)

Late 1960s story about the ultimate emotional sterility and unhappiness of a swinger emerges as a mixed farcical achievement.

Warren Beatty is a Beverly Hills hairdresser who turns onto all his customers including Lee Grant, bored wife of Jack Warden (latter in turn keeping Julie Christie on the side), while Beatty's current top trick is Goldie Hawn.

All the excellent creative components do not add up to a whole. There are, however, strong elements in the film. Warden's performance is outstanding. He makes the most of a script and direction which gives his character much more dimension than the prototype cuckold. Also, Hawn's excellent delineation of a bubbly young actress has a solid undertone of sensitivity which culminates in her quiet dismissal of Beatty from her home and her heart.

1975: Best Supp. Actress (Lee Grant)

NOMINATIONS: Best Supp. Actor (Jack Warden), Original Screenplay, Art Direction

•

SHAMUS

1973, 98 mins, US Ⓥ ⊙ col

Dir Buzz Kulik ***Prod*** Robert M. Weitman ***Scr*** Barry Beckerman ***Ph*** Victor J. Kemper ***Ed*** Walter Thompson ***Mus*** Jerry Goldsmith ***Art*** Philip Rosenberg

Act Burt Reynolds, Dyan Cannon, John Ryan, Joe Santos, Georgio Tozzi, Ron Weyand (Columbia/Weitman)

Shamus is a confusing, hardbiting meller of a tough private eye. Burt Reynolds plays a rough-hewn and alert character who has turned to private investigation in his tough Brooklyn neighborhood instead of laying in with the mob. Filming was done on actual locations, which lends an emphatic authenticity to backgrounds.

Star carries the narrative niftily as he's called in by a multimillionaire to ferret out the indentity of the person who bumped off a man who stole a fortune in diamonds owned by a tycoon. But thereafter scripter Barry Beckerman drags in an assortment of mostly unexplained characters but some dandy rough work—and finales in a fine fog. Perhaps something was lost in translation to the screen.

•

SHANE

1953, 118 mins, US Ⓥ ⊙ col

Dir George Stevens ***Prod*** George Stevens ***Scr*** A. B. Guthrie, Jr., Jack Sher ***Ph*** Loyal Griggs ***Ed*** William Hornbeck, Tom McAdoo ***Mus*** Victor Young ***Art*** Hal Pereira, Walter Tyler

Act Alan Ladd, Jean Arthur, Van Heflin, Brandon de Wilde, Jack Palance, Ben Johnson (Paramount)

This is by no means a conventional giddyap oater feature, being a western in the truer sense and ranking with some of the select few that have become classics in the outdoor field.

Director George Stevens handles the story and players with tremendous integrity. Alan Ladd's performance takes on dimensions not heretofore noticeable in his screen work. Van Heflin commands attention with a sensitive performance, as real and earnest as the pioneer spirit he plays. The screenplay is A. B. Guthrie, Jr.'s first, as is the novel of Jack Schaefer.

Plot is laid in early Wyoming, where a group of farmer-settlers have taken land formerly held by a cattle baron. Latter resents this intrusion on the free land and the fences that come with the setting down of home roots. His fight is against Heflin chiefly, who is the driving force that keeps the frightened farmers together. Just when it seems the cattle man may eventually have his way, a stranger, known only as Shane, rides on to Heflin's homestead, is taken in and becomes one of the settlers, as he tries to forget his previous life with a gun.

Jean Arthur plays the role of Heflin's wife, who is attracted to the stranger. A standout is the young stage actor, Brandon de Wilde, who brings the inquisitiveness and quick hero worship of youth to the part of Heflin's son. Jack Palance, with short but impressive footage, is the hired killer.

Wyoming's scenic splendors against which the story is filmed are breathtaking. Sunlight, the shadow of rain storms and the eerie lights of night play a realistic part in making the picture a visual treat.

1953: Best Color Cinematography

NOMINATIONS: Best Picture, Director, Supp. Actor (Brandon de Wilde, Jack Palance), Screenplay

•

SHANGHAI EXPRESS

1932, 80 mins, US b/w

Dir Josef von Sternberg ***Prod*** [uncredited] ***Scr*** Jules Furthman ***Ph*** Lee Garmes ***Ed*** [uncredited] ***Mus*** W. Franke Harling ***Art*** Hans Dreier

Act Marlene Dietrich, Clive Brook, Anna May Wong, Warner Oland, Eugene Pallette, Lawrence Grant (Paramount)

Josef von Sternberg, the director, has made this effort interesting through a definite command of the lens. As to plot structure and dialog, *Shanghai Express* runs much too close to old meller and serial themes to command real attention. The finished product is an example of what can be done with a personality and photogenic face such as Marlene Dietrich possesses to circumvent a trashy story.

The script [from a story by Harry Hervey] relates how the heroine became China's most famed white prostitute, who meets her former English fiance (Clive Brook) on board train. The man has become a medical officer in the British Army. With a revolution going on, Warner Oland turns out to be the rebel leader, has the train held up and in looking for a hostage, to guarantee the return of his chief lieutenant captured by the Chinese forces, he picks Brook.

To save Brook's eyes being burned from his head, Shanghai Lily promises to become mistress of the revolutionary, leading to further misunderstandings between the central pair.

For counter-interest there is Eugene Pallette as an American gambler among the passengers, Louise Closser Hale as a prim boarding housekeeper, Gustav von Seyffertitz as a dope smuggling invalid, Lawrence Grant as a fanantical missionary, and Emile Chautard as a disgraced French officer wearing his uniform without authority. It can't be said that either Dietrich or Brook gives an especially good performance. The British actor is unusually wooden, while Dietrich's assignment is so void of movement as to force her to mild but consistent eye rolling.

1931/32: Best Cinematography

NOMINATIONS: Best Picture, Director

•

SHANGHAI GESTURE, THE

1942, 97 mins, US Ⓥ ⊙ b/w

Dir Josef von Sternberg ***Prod*** [Arnold Pressburger] ***Scr*** [Karl Vollmoeller], Geza Herczeg, Jules Furthman, Josef von Sternberg ***Ph*** Paul Ivano ***Ed*** Sam Winston ***Mus*** Richard Hageman ***Art*** Boris Leven

Act Gene Tierney, Victor Mature, Ona Munson, Walter Huston, Phyllis Brooks, Albert Basserman (Arnold)

Thirty-one film treatments on [John Colton's play] *Shanghai Gesture* were submitted without success to the Hays Office. Producer Arnold Pressburger finally slipped through a treatment for a go-ahead signal—to at least bring the original title and the Oriental background of the polyglot Asiatic metropolis to the screen.

Stripped of the sensational elements of *Gesture* at the time it was produced on the stage, the resultant film version is a rather dull and hazy drama of the Orient.

Mother Gin Sling (Ona Munson) is the operating brains of a gambling casino, case-hardened through her struggles up the ladder. When property in the district is bought up by Walter Huston, English financier, and the Mother is told to fold, she goes out to get the goods on her enemy in typical Oriental fashion. Result is Gin Sling's manipulation of Huston's daughter (Gene Tierney) onto a downward path; Gin Sling's accusation of his desertion years before; and his rebuttal that the girl she has ruined is actually her daughter.

Victor Mature, as the matter-of-fact Arab despoiler of Tierney's honor, provides a standout performance. Huston's abilities are lost in the jumble, while Munson cannot penetrate the mask-like makeup arranged for her characterization.

1942: NOMINATIONS: Best B&W Art Direction, Scoring of a Dramatic Picture

•

SHANGHAI NOON
2000, 110 mins, US Ⓥ ⦿ ▭ col
Dir Tom Dey ***Prod*** Roger Birnbaum, Gary Barber, Jonathan Glickman ***Scr*** Alfred Gough, Miles Millar ***Ph*** Dan Mindel ***Ed*** Richard Chew ***Mus*** Randy Edelman ***Art*** Peter J. Hampton
Act Jackie Chan, Owen Wilson, Lucy Liu, Brandon Merrill, Roger Yuan, Xander Berkeley (Birnbaum/Barber/Jackie Chan)

Yippie-ki-kung-fu! Jackie Chan rides tall in the saddle—when he isn't busy running up walls, bounding over bad guys and generally kicking up a fuss—in *Shanghai Noon*, a high-concept action-comedy. Owen Wilson (*Armageddon, Bottle Rocket*) adds to the fun with an immensely appealing breakthrough performance, and first-time feature helmer Tom Dey does a canny job of bringing out the best in each of his odd-couple leads.

Shanghai Noon may look like a conventional Western—Dan Mindel's impressive widescreen lensing would pass muster in any serious sagebrush saga—but pic most certainly isn't an old-fashioned cowboys-and-Indians story. For one thing, the cowboys are somewhat smaller than life: Chon (Chan) can barely manage to mount or dismount his horse, and Roy (Wilson) turns to outlawry only because he thinks being a bank robber is a cool way to attract girls. As for the Indians, the Sioux tribesmen on view here are rendered as bemused sophisticates, not bloodthirsty savages.

As usual, Chan is nothing less than poetry in motion, evidencing graceful exuberance in his physical comedy and cunning inventiveness in his fight scenes. At various points in *Shanghai Noon* he used horseshoes, tree limbs, moose antlers and even a sheriff's badge as props in combat. Appreciably more at ease with English than he seemed in *Rush Hour*, Chan radiates enough megawatt charisma to power a mid-size city, and gives the impression of someone who's generously sharing the fun while he's having the time of his life. Wilson is a perfect foil, reacting with equal measures of amusement and amazement each time Chan opens up a can of whup-ass on an outmatched opponent.

•

SHANGHAI SURPRISE
1986, 97 mins, UK/US Ⓥ ⦿ col
Dir Jim Goddard ***Prod*** John Kohn ***Scr*** John Kohn, Robert Bentley ***Ph*** Ernie Vincze ***Ed*** Ralph Sheldon ***Mus*** George Harrison, Michael Kamen ***Art*** Peter Mullins
Act Sean Penn, Madonna, Paul Freeman, Richard Griffiths, Philip Sayer (M-G-M/Handmade/Vista)

Tale [from the novel *Faraday's Flowers* by Tony Kenrick] is a phony, thoroughgoing concoction. A missionary (Madonna) enlists the services of a down-and-out, would-be adventurer (Sean Penn) to help her track down a substantial supply of opium that disappeared under mysterious circumstances a year before, in 1937, during the Japanese occupation of China.

The blood-stirring premise provides the excuse for any number of encounters with exotic and shady characters who would have been right at home in Warner Bros. foreign intrigue mellers of the 1940s.

But centerstage is the completely illogical relationship between the hustler and missionary. Penn seems game and has energy while Madonna can't for a moment disguise that her character makes no sense at all.

•

SHANGHAI TRIAD
SEE: YAO A YAO YAO DAO WAIPO QIAO

•

SHARKY'S MACHINE
1981, 119 mins, US Ⓥ ⦿ col
Dir Burt Reynolds ***Prod*** Hank Moonjean ***Scr*** Gerald Di Pego ***Ph*** William A. Fraker ***Ed*** William Gordean ***Mus*** Al Capps (arr.) ***Art*** Walter Scott Herndon
Act Burt Reynolds, Vittorio Gassman, Rachel Ward, Brian Keith, Charles Durning, Earl Holliman (Deliverance/Orion)

Directing himself in *Sharky's Machine*, Burt Reynolds has combined his own macho personality with what's popularly called mindless violence to come up with a seemingly guaranteed winner [from the novel by William Diehl].

Not surprisingly, Reynolds is "Sharky" and the "machine" is police parlance for a team of fellow cops working with him. They are all good policemen, but for one reason or another have been relegated to unchallenging assignments, mainly in the cesspool of the vice squad. But a hooker's murder brings Reynolds within sniffing distance of big time shenanigans involving gubernatorial candidate Earl Holliman, crime boss Vittorio Gassman and high-priced call girl Rachel Ward. Staking out Ward's apartment, actor Reynolds surrenders to an infatuation with her that director Reynolds has an intersting time developing.

By the time Reynolds gets a couple of fingers sliced off by Darryl Hickman & Co., all characterization is gone and it's just a matter then of who runs out of bullets first.

•

SHATTERED
1991, 98 mins, US Ⓥ ⦿ col
Dir Wolfgang Petersen ***Prod*** Wolfgang Petersen, John Davis, David Korda ***Scr*** Wolfgang Petersen ***Ph*** Laszlo Kovacs ***Ed*** Hannes Nikel, Glenn Farr, Richard Byard ***Mus*** Alan Silvestri ***Art*** Gregg Fonseca
Act Tom Berenger, Bob Hoskins, Greta Scacchi, Joanne Whalley-Kilmer, Corbin Bernsen, Theodore Bikel (Capella/Connexion/Geissler)

Shattered goes to pieces almost instantly. A far-fetched thriller about unlikable characters, Wolfgang Petersen's debut American feature aspires to Hitchcockian suspense and surprise, but the parade of hokey implausibilities puts the viewer off rather than drawing one in. Petersen assembled an attractive cast to populate his adaptation of Richard Neely's novel *The Plastic Nightmare*, a project he was contemplating even before his breakthrough success with *Das Boot* 10 years earlier. Unfortunately, the roles the actors fill are nearly all unappetizing or uninteresting, leaving the audience with no emotional investment in their fates.

A devastating car wreck leaves an upscale Bay Area real estate developer (Tom Berenger) a disfigured mess, although his wife (Greta Scacchi) escapes virtually unscathed. Although plastic surgery restores his good looks, husband's memory is a blank. Berenger eventually learns that he and his wife weren't getting along well before the accident and that she was having an affair with a certain Jack Stanton. Enter a private detective (Bob Hoskins), enlisted to help Berenger try to figure everything out.

Berenger manages character's outward anguish and bafflement but is not one who makes himself vulnerable enough to invite the viewer into his skin or mind. The evergorgeous Scacchi has the meatiest role, that of a scheming liar accustomed to always getting her way, but full, Bette Davis-style impact of the role is missed. Hoskins enlivens things as a p.i. who works out of a pet shop.

•

SHAWSHANK REDEMPTION, THE
1994, 142 mins, US Ⓥ ⦿ ▭ col
Dir Frank Darabont ***Prod*** Niki Marvin ***Scr*** Frank Darabont ***Ph*** Roger Deakins ***Ed*** Richard Francis-Bruce ***Mus*** Thomas Newman ***Art*** Terence Marsh
Act Tim Robbins, Morgan Freeman, Bob Gunton, William Sadler, Clancy Brown, James Whitmore (Castle Rock/Columbia)

There's a painstaking exactness to *The Shawshank Redemption* that is both laudable and exhausting. The 19 years that the film's protagonist spends behind prison walls is a term shared by the audience. It's vivid, grueling and painful, and passes with the appropriate tedium and sudden bursts of horror that one imagines reflect the true nature of incarceration.

The saga begins in 1947, when bank vice president Andy Dufresne (Tim Robbins) goes on trial for the murder of his wife and her lover. Circumstantial evidence proves enough to land him in Shawshank Prison with two concurrent life sentences.

While it's unquestionably Andy's story, the chronicle is related in voice over by "Red" (Morgan Freeman), a lifer who's set himself up as someone who can get "things" from the outside. He marvels at the new man's tenacity, knowing intrinsically that Andy is different and that he likes him, quirks and all.

Soon Andy is put to work in all manner of financial activity. He is Warden Norton's (Bob Gunton) crown jewel and the source of both an enhanced public image for the man and a quietly acquired personal fortune. But the warden cannot afford to have Andy paroled. The man knows too much, and he is too valuable an asset.

Writer/director Frank Darabont adapts his source material [Stephen King's short novel] with sly acuity. It's a fiendishly clever construct in which seemingly oblique words or incidents prove to have fierce resonance. Central to the film's success is a riveting, unfussy performance from Robbins. Freeman has the showier role, allowing him a grace and dignity that come naturally.

1994: NOMINATIONS: Best Picture, Actor (Morgan Freeman), Adapted Screenplay, Cinematography, Film Editing, Sound, Original Score

•

SHE
1935, 96 mins, US ⦿ b/w
Dir Irving Pichel, Lansing C. Holden ***Prod*** Merian C. Cooper ***Scr*** Ruth Rose, Dudley Nichols ***Ph*** J. Roy Hunt ***Ed*** Ted Cheesman ***Mus*** Max Steiner ***Art*** Van Nest Polglase, Al Herman
Act Helen Gahagan, Randolph Scott, Helen Mack, Nigel Bruce, Gustav von Seyffertitz, Samuel Hinds (RKO)

Ruth Rose adapted H. Rider Haggard's novel and did a smooth job. Story blame belongs with the basic yarn and not with the treatment. There are scenes that skirt the twilight zone of the horse laugh.

In the bowels of the earth is the mythical land of Kor. Its she-monster ruler (Helen Gahagan) has the gift and the curse of eternal life. All these hundreds of years she has been waiting for her lover to come back reincarnated. Meanwhile the embalmed corpse of the original lover (whom she killed in a jealous tantrum) lies in state until his counterpart, a grandson 15 generations removed (Randolph Scott), shows up.

Queenie is pretty excited and gets rid of the corpse intending to spend the next two or three milleniums with Sonny Boy the second. But she loses out to the sweet young thing from Main Street (Helen Mack) who has tumbled into the Kor country with Sonny Boy and the inevitable scientist (Nigel Bruce).

The ceremonials, bacchanals, ballets and executions provide the materials for a psychopathic pipe-dream. Some of the sequences are stunning, merging sound effects, camera angles, imaginative costuming [by Aline Bernstein and Harold Miles] and Benjamin Zemach's socky choreography.

On the performance end Cahagan cops honors. It was wise casting to pick a face not well known to the screen audience. But it's not an actor's picture. It's a cameraman's triumph, an art director's picnic and a dancing master's joy.

•

SHE
1965, 105 mins, UK ⦿ ▭ col
Dir Robert Day ***Prod*** Michael Carreras ***Scr*** David T. Chantler ***Ph*** Harry Waxman ***Ed*** James Needs, Eric Boyd-Perkins ***Mus*** James Bernard ***Art*** Robert Jones
Act Ursula Andress, Peter Cushing, Bernard Cribbins, John Richardson, Rosenda Monteros, Christopher Lee (Hammer)

Fourth filming of H. Rider Haggard's fantasy adds color and widescreen to special effects, all of which help overcome a basic plot no film scripter has yet licked.

Ursula Andress is sole-starred as the immortal She, cold-blooded queen Ayesha of a lost kingdom who pines for return of the lover she murdered eons ago. In David T. Chantler's okay script, it turns out that John Richardson is the look-alike lover, footloose in Palestine after the First World War with buddies Peter Cushing and Bernard Cribbins.

High priest Christopher Lee and servant girl Rosenda Monteros are emissaries who spot Richardson's resemblance, triggering a desert trek by the three men to Kuma land. Cushing and Cribbins keep their senses, while Richardson falls under Andress's spell.

Director Robert Day's overall excellent work brings out heretofore unknown depths in Andress's acting. Role calls for sincere warmth as a woman in love, also brutal cruelty as queen, and she convinces.

All other players are good in routine roles, particularly Monteros as the competing love interest who loses her man and her life. Christopher Lee is also effective as the loyal priest whom Ayesha kills.

•

SHE DEVIL, THE
SEE: DIE NIBELUNGEN KRIEMHILDS RACHE

•

SHE-DEVIL
1989, 99 mins, US Ⓥ ⦿ col
Dir Susan Seidelman ***Prod*** Jonathan Brett, Susan Seidelman ***Scr*** Barry Strugatz, Mark R. Burns ***Ph*** Oliver Stapleton ***Ed*** Craig McKay ***Mus*** Howard Shore ***Art*** Santo Loquasto
Act Meryl Streep, Roseanne Barr, Ed Begley, Jr., Linda Hunt, Sylvia Miles, Elizabeth Peters (Orion)

A dark and gleeful revenge saga set in a world of unfaithful husbands and unfair standards of beauty, *She-Devil* [from Fay Weldon's novel *The Life and Loves of a She Devil*] offers a unique heroine in Ruth Patchett (Roseanne Barr), a dumpy but dedicated housewife afflicted with a conspicuous facial mole and an uninterested husband (Ed Begley, Jr.). When Begley, an accountant, strays into the arms of a fabulously wealthy and affected romance novelist (Meryl Streep), Barr puts up with it—to a point.

However, when Begley, bags more or less packed, sets her blood boiling with crude put-downs, Barr clicks into an inspired attack mode, first by blowing up the house, then by dumping off the children at his love nest on her way to Whereabouts Unknown, then by ingeniously dismantling his career.

The casting is a real coup, with Barr going her everywoman TV persona one better by breaking the big screen heroine mold, and Streep blowing away any notion that she can't be funny.

•

SHE DONE HIM WRONG
1933, 65 mins, US Ⓥ b/w
Dir Lowell Sherman ***Prod*** [uncredited] ***Scr*** Harvey Thew, John Bright ***Ph*** Charles Lang ***Ed*** [uncredited] ***Mus*** Ralph Rainger ***Art*** [uncredited]
Act Mae West, Cary Grant, Owen Moore, Gilbert Roland, Noah Beery, Sr., David Landau (Paramount)

Atmospherically, *She Done Him Wrong* is interesting since it takes audiences back to the 1890s and inside a Bowery free-and-easy, but mostly following a few highlights in the career of Diamond Lou, nee Lil.

Director Lowell Sherman turns in a commendable job. He tackles the script with a tongue-in-cheek attitude that takes nothing too seriously, and he restrains Mae West from going too far.

The locale, the clothes and the types are interesting, and so is West in her picture hats, straight jacket gowns and with so much jewelry that she looks like a Knickerbocker ice plant.

Deletions in the script from its original 1928 legit form [*Diamond Lil* by Mae West] are few, with only the roughest of the rough stuff out. White slavery angle is thinly disguised, with the girls instead shipped to Frisco to pick pockets. Character titles are changed only slightly, such as from Lil to Lou, etc. The swan bed is in, but for a flash only, with West doing her stuff on the chaise lounge in this version. Numerous ex-vaudevillians besides West in the cast, including Cary Grant, the soul-saver; Fuzzy Knight, who whips a piano, and Grace La Rue. The latter, who headlined when West was chasing acrobats in the No. 2 spot, has a bit. Rafaela Ottiano, who does Rita, is a carry-over from the original legit cast.

With this strong line-up and others, including Gilbert Roland, Noah Beery, David Landau and Owen Moore as background, they're never permitted to be anything more than just background. West gets all the lens gravy and full figure most of the time.

1932/33: NOMINATION: Best Picture

•

SHEIK, THE
1921, 100 mins, US Ⓥ ⊗ b/w
Dir George Melford ***Scr*** Monte M. Katterjohn ***Ph*** William Marshall
Act Anges Ayres, Rudolph Valentino, Adolphe Menjou, Walter Long, Lucien Littlefield, George Waggner (Paramount)

Edith M. Hull's novel, preposterous and ridiculous as it was, won out because it dealt with every caged woman's desire to be caught up in a love clasp by some he-man who would take the responsibility and dispose of the consequences, but Monte M. Katterjohn's scenario hasn't even that to recommend it. He has safely deleted most of the punch, and what they missed George Melford manages by inept direction of the big scenes.

Lady Diana has gone alone into the desert with a native guide only to be captured by a young sheik and he detains her in his palace of a tent, and that is all.

The acting could not be worse than the story, but it is bad enough. Valentino is revealed as a player without resource. He depicts the fundamental emotions of the Arabian sheik chiefly by showing his teeth and rolling his eyes, while Agnes Ayres looks too matronly to lend much kick to the situation in which she finds herself.

•

SHE'LL BE WEARING PINK PAJAMAS
1985, 90 mins, UK Ⓥ col
Dir John Goldschmidt ***Prod*** Tara Prem, Adrian Hughes ***Scr*** Eva Hardy ***Ph*** Clive Tickner ***Ed*** Richard Key ***Mus*** John du Prez ***Art*** Colin Pocock
Act Julie Walters, Anthony Higgins, Jane Evers, Janet Henfrey, Paula Jacobs, Penelope Nice (Film Four/Pink Pajamas)

She'll Be Wearing Pink Pajamas is about a group of British women from mixed backgrounds who gather together, awkwardly at first, but eventually confide in each other and reveal their innermost secrets and problems.

After a slightly off-key opening, in which the characters are introed, we're into the setting of an outdoor survival course for women only, a week-long exercise designed to push the participants physically as far as they can go. The intimate discussions that follow take place against outdoor backgrounds, filmed in England's beautiful Lake District, as the women ford streams, climb mountains, canoe, swing on ropes, or go on a marathon hike.

There's one man around (Anthony Higgins), but he's almost an intrusion. The women are a lively and well differentiated lot, and there is a bevy of fine actresses playing them. Standout is Julie Walters as a bouncy type who proves surprisingly weak in the crunch.

•

SHELTERING SKY, THE
1990, 137 mins, UK/ITALY Ⓥ ⊙ ⊏⊐ col
Dir Bernardo Bertolucci ***Prod*** Jeremy Thomas ***Scr*** Mark Peploe, Bernardo Bertolucci ***Ph*** Vittorio Storaro ***Ed*** Gabriella Cristiani ***Mus*** Ryuichi Sakamoto, Richard Horowitz ***Art*** Gianni Silvestri
Act John Malkovich, Debra Winger, Campbell Scott, Jill Bennett, Timothy Spall, Eric Vu-An (Thomas)

Paul Bowles's classic 1949 novel of a journey into emptiness has been visualized with intense beauty by the creative team of *The Last Emperor*. But those who haven't read the book will be left bewildered.

John Malkovich and Debra Winger play Port and Kit Moresby, Americans traveling without destination or itinerary in postwar North Africa. Their 10-year marriage is unraveling while their opportunistic companion, Tunner (Campbell Scott), looks on.

They press on through Tangiers, Niger and Algeria, moving with a perverse sense of purpose further from comfort, ego and the signposts of the familiar. Pic boils down to the existential love story between Kit and Port, who are groping through the ruins of their infidelities toward whatever is left between them when all is lost.

In a marvelous directorial conceit, Bowles himself, 80 years old, watches his characters from a seat in a Tangiers cafe.

Malkovich is an excellent choice as Port, his shifting, centaur-like physicality filling in for the interior life the screen can't provide. Aside from her resemblance to writer Jane Bowles, who inspired Kit, Winger is less interesting to watch.

At the end, familiar language completely disappears, as shell-shocked Kit wanders into the desert and becomes a sex slave to the wandering Tuareg leader Belqassim (played by Eric Vu-An of the Paris Ballet).

•

SHENANDOAH
1965, 105 mins, US Ⓥ ⊙ col
Dir Andrew V. McLaglen ***Prod*** Robert Arthur ***Scr*** James Lee Barrett ***Ph*** William H. Clothier ***Ed*** Otho Lovering ***Mus*** Frank Skinner ***Art*** Alexander Golitzen, Alfred Sweeney
Act James Stewart, Doug McClure, Glenn Corbett, Patrick Wayne, Rosemary Forsyth, Katharine Ross (Universal)

Shenandoah centers upon one person, a sort of behind-the-scenes glimpse of one man's family in Virginia during the Civil War.

Screenplay focuses on Stewart, a prosperous Virginia farmer in 1863 who completely ignores the strife raging around him. A widower, he has raised his family of six sons and one daughter to be entirely self-contained. Not believing in slavery, he wants no part in a war based upon it, providing the conflict does not touch either his land or his family. When his youngest, a 16-year-old boy whose mother died giving birth and who therefore occupies a particular spot in the father's heart, is captured as a Reb by Unionists, the farmer then makes the war his own business.

Stewart, seldom without a cigar butt in the corner of his mouth, endows his grizzled role with warm conviction.

Battle sequences are well integrated with the family's efforts to lead a normal life, and Andrew McLaglen is responsible for some rousing hand-to-hand action between the Blue and the Grey.

1965: NOMINATION: Best Sound

•

SHERIFF OF FRACTURED JAW, THE
1958, 100 mins, UK Ⓥ ⊏⊐ col
Dir Raoul Walsh ***Prod*** Daniel M. Angel ***Scr*** Arthur Dales ***Ph*** Otto Heller ***Ed*** John Shirley ***Mus*** Robert Farnon ***Art*** Bernard Robinson
Act Kenneth More, Jayne Mansfield, Robert Morley, Ronald Squire, Henry Hull, Bruce Cabot (20th Century-Fox)

The starring combo of Jayne Mansfield and Kenneth More merge like bacon and eggs, and the result is a wave of yocks. Raoul Walsh directs this cheerful skit about the wild, woolly west with vigor and pace. He gives little time to remind the audience that many of the situations are predictable and that the brisk screenplay [from a short story by Jacob Hay] occasionally needs an upward jolt from the skill of the leading thesps.

Yarn starts off in London at the turn of the century. More has inherited a fading gunsmith business. Reading that there is a spot of bother in the Wild West he decides that that's the place to sell his guns. So this dude salesman (walking stick, brown derby and strictly West End suiting) nonchalantly sets off with some samples, and all the confidence in the world.

It's not long before he is up to his surprised eyebrows in trouble. He becomes involved with Injuns, two warring sets of cowboys and with Mansfield, the pistol-packing boss of a saloon. He is conned into becoming the sheriff of the one-horse town of Fractured Jaw.

More's immaculate throwaway line of comedy gets full rein. With polite manners, impeccable accent and a brash line of action, he leaves the locals in doubt as to whether he is the biggest fool or the bravest man ever to hit their territory. Mansfield gives More hearty support, looks attractive and sings two or three numbers very well.

•

SHERLOCK, JR.
1924, 48 mins, US ⊗ b/w
Dir Buster Keaton ***Scr*** Jean Havez, Joseph Mitchell, Clyde Bruckman ***Ph*** Elgin Lessley, Byron Houck ***Art*** Fred Gabourie
Act Buster Keaton, Kathryn McGuire, Ward Crane, Joseph Keaton (Keaton/Metro)

This Buster Keaton feature length comedy is about as unfunny as a hospital operating room.

The picture has all the old hoke in the world in it. That ranges from a piece of business with a flypaper to a money-changing bit and, for added good measure, a chase. There are, in fact, two chases; but neither can for a single second hold a candle to Harold Lloyd. In comparison they appear child's play.

There is one piece of business, however, that is worthy of comment. It is the bit where Buster as a motion-picture machine operator in a dream scene walks out of the booth and into the action that is taking place on the screen of the picture that he is projecting. That is clever. The rest is bunk.

•

SHE'S GOTTA HAVE IT
1986, 100 mins, US Ⓥ ⊙ b/w
Dir Spike Lee ***Prod*** Shelton J. Lee ***Scr*** Spike Lee ***Ph*** Ernest Dickerson ***Ed*** Spike Lee ***Mus*** Bill Lee ***Art*** Wynn Thomas
Act Tracy Camilla Johns, Redmond Hicks, John Terrell, Spike Lee, Raye Dowell, Joie Lee (40 Acres & a Mule)

This worthy but flawed attempt to examine an independent young woman of the 1980s was lensed, in Super 16mm, in 15 days but doesn't appear jerrybuilt.

All the elements of an interesting yarn are implicit here—save one: a compelling central figure (played by Tracy Camilla Johns). The young woman who's the focus of the pic is, clearly, trying to find herself. She juggles three beaus, fends off a lesbian's overtures and consults a shrink to determine if she's promiscuous or merely a lady with normal sexual appetites.

The three beaus, an upscale male model, a sensitive sort and a funny street flake, all essayed nicely by, respectively, John Terrell, Spike Lee and Redmond Hicks, serve to keep the scenario moving with interest.

•

SHE'S HAVING A BABY
1988, 106 mins, US Ⓥ ⊙ col
Dir John Hughes ***Prod*** John Hughes ***Scr*** John Hughes ***Ph*** Don Peterman ***Ed*** Alan Heim ***Mus*** Stewart Copeland, Nicky Holland ***Art*** John W. Corso
Act Kevin Bacon, Elizabeth McGovern, Alec Baldwin, Isabel Lorca, William Windom, Cathryn Damon (Paramount)

She's Having a Baby is an oddly uneven and quasi-serious look into the angst of the early years of a contemporary marriage that parallels TV's *thirtysomething*. There are many comedic setups which, if they were with less architypically drawn characters, might have delivered the laughs with the refreshingly innocent joy that has been the hallmark of other John Hughes pics.

In the lead role, Kevin Bacon is enthusiastic and believable, but even his energy can't carry what boils down to a fairly limp story told from his p.o.v. about buying into the comfortable suburban dream possibly before his time.

Bacon ties the knot with teenage sweetheart Kristy (Elizabeth McGovern) and begins to fantasize about what he's going to be missing out on as a married man from the moment they take their vows. It soon becomes evident why Bacon is endlessly dreaming: take away his imaginings and his home life is dull indeed.

For one thing, he's got a stepford wife for a mate. McGovern is so uncomplicated and unabashedly adoring towards her husband, it gets one wondering what such a bright guy is doing with her. Bacon's wayward buddy Davis (Alec Baldwin) shows up too infrequently to spar with his good chum and ruffle McGovern's feathers by bringing along just the kind of girl she would loathe.

•

SHE'S THE ONE
1996, 96 mins, US Ⓥ ⦿ ▭ col
Dir Edward Burns ***Prod*** Ted Hope, James Schamus, Edward Burns ***Scr*** Edward Burns ***Ph*** Frank Prinzi ***Ed*** Susan Graef ***Mus*** Tom Petty ***Art*** William Barklay
Act Jennifer Aniston, Maxine Bahns, Edward Burns, Cameron Diaz, John Mahoney, Mike McGlone (Good Machine/Marlboro Road Gang)

There's charm to burn in *She's the One*, Ed Burns's sophomore romantic comedy. Very much in the vein of his award-winning *The Brothers McMullen*, this outing is a decided step forward artistically and technically, endowed with a refreshing honesty and poignancy.

Once again the focus is family. Mickey Fitzpatrick (Burns) is an emotionally fried cab driver who marries Hope (Maxine Bahns) after a couple of days of whirlwind romance. Francis (Mike McGlone) married childhood sweetheart Renee (Jennifer Aniston), got a respectable job on Wall Street and, despite success and security, has the driving need to compete with and best Mickey. The battleground between the brothers is represented by Heather (Cameron Diaz), who is supposed to wed Mickey but is carrying on an affair with Francis.

Burns is a natural-born filmmaker. There's no sign of artifice in his style. His graceful, unfussy visuals and fluid editing lend facility to material prone to drift into the complex and cumbersome.

The picture also is blessed with a uniformly strong cast. Both Diaz and Aniston revel in the opportunity to flesh out familiar types and imbue them with more than just comic dimension. [As the brothers' father] John Mahoney, rarely offered a major part in movies, demonstrates his consummate skill as a mature actor. McGlone humanizes an essentially unpleasant character with aplomb; Bahns radiates a kinetic energy, but it's the filmmaker himself who emerges as the most significant screen presence, assured and centered.

•

SHE WORE A YELLOW RIBBON
1949, 103 mins, US Ⓥ ⦿ col
Dir John Ford ***Prod*** John Ford, Merian C. Cooper ***Scr*** Frank Nugent, Laurence Stallings ***Ph*** Winton Hoch ***Ed*** Jack Murtay ***Mus*** Richard Hageman ***Art*** James Basevi
Act John Wayne, Joanne Dru, John Agar, Ben Johnson, Victor McLaglen, Mildred Natwick (RKO/Argosy)

She Wore a Yellow Ribbon is a western meller done in the best John Ford manner.

Drama [from James Warner Bellah's story] of the undermanned U.S. Cavalry post far out in the Indian country is centered on a veteran captain about to retire. It develops into a saga of the cavalry, its hard-bitten men, loyal wives and usual intrigues. The tale moves along easily as it shows how the troop surmounts the Indian peril. There's hardly a breather from the time the audience is tipped that John Wayne is soon retiring as cavalry captain til he finalizes his last dramatic moment.

Wayne wears well in this somewhat older characterization. He makes the officer an understanding, two-fisted guy without overdoing it. Victor McLaglen gives the production tremendous lift as the whisky-nipping non-com.

1949: Best Color Cinematography

•

SHICHININ NO SAMURAI
(THE SEVEN SAMURAI; SEVEN SAMURAI; THE MAGNIFICENT SEVEN)
1954, 200 mins, Japan Ⓥ ⦿ b/w
Dir Akira Kurosawa ***Prod*** Shojiro Motoki ***Scr*** Shinobu Hashimoto, Hideo Oguni, Akira Kurosawa ***Ph*** Asakazu Nakai ***Ed*** Fumio Yanoguchi ***Mus*** Fumio Hayasaka ***Art*** So Matsuyama
Act Takashi Shimura, Toshiro Mifune, Yoshio Inaba, Seiji Miyaguchi, Minoru Chiaki, Daisuke Kato (Toho)

High adventure and excitement are stamped all over this solid-core film about a group of seven Samurai warriors who save a little village from annihilation at the hands of a group of bandits in 15th-century Japan. Besides the well manned battlescenes, the pic has a good feeling for characterization and time.

Bandits are waiting to attack an isolated village as soon as the rice is ripe. Some of the men go to look for help and run into a sage old Samurai warrior who consents to help them. Then follows a series of deft bits as the seven men are gathered and head for the village to prepare defenses, train the men, and get ready for the onslaught. They finally vanquish the bandits but not without losses.

Director Akira Kurosawa has given this a virile mounting. It is primarily a man's film, with the brief romantic interludes also done with taste. Each character is firmly molded. Toshiro Mifune as the bold, hairbrained but courageous warrior weaves a colossal portrait. He dominates the picture although he has an extremely strong supporting cast.

Lensing is excellent, as is editing in bundling together the immense footage and making its battle scenes monumental and exciting. Music is also helpful in mood, vacillating between western and eastern themes for telling effect.

[Version reviewed was 161-min. international one, first shown at 1954 Venice festival.]

•

SHINE
1996, 105 mins, Australia Ⓥ col
Dir Scott Hicks ***Prod*** Jane Scott ***Scr*** Jan Sardi ***Ph*** Geoffrey Simpson ***Ed*** Pip Karmel ***Mus*** David Hirschfelder ***Art*** Sally Campbell
Act Geoffrey Rush, Armin Mueller-Stahl, Noah Taylor, Lynn Redgrave, John Gielgud, Googie Withers (Momentum)

In *Shine*, director Scott Hicks and writer Jan Sardi unfold an unconventional biopic about a brilliant young pianist who is driven to the edge of madness by his monstrously protective father and, as an adult, finds unexpected redemption thanks to an astonishingly understanding woman.

Hicks and Sardi have tackled tricky material here: their Australian protagonist, David Helfgott (Geoffrey Rush), is very much alive and has a growing rep as an unconventional concert pianist in parts of Europe. His extraordinary life is intelligently charted here.

His demanding father, Peter Helfgott (Armin Mueller-Stahl), a Polish Jew whose family was wiped out in the Holocaust, drives his son to achieve greatness as a pianist, but is too proud, and too poor, to give him the tuition he clearly needs.

Befriended by an elderly writer, Katharine Prichard (Googie Withers, delightful) he wins a scholarship to study at the London College of Music. Under the tutelage of Professor Cecil Parkes (a lovely performance from 91-year-old John Gielgud), David blossoms. But, at the moment of his triumph, he collapses onstage and, rejected by his father, spends 15 years in a psychiatric hospital.

The last act of this extraordinary bio intros Gillian (Lynn Redgrave), a middle-aged astrologer and divorcee who meets David by chance and eventually marries him, giving him the support and encouragement he needs to resume his concert career.

The real-life Helfgott plays the piano for his screen counterparts.

1996: Best Actor (Geoffrey Rush)

NOMINATIONS: Best Picture, Director, Supp. Actor (Armin Mueller-Stahl), Screenplay, Editing, Music

•

SHINING, THE
1980, 142 mins, US Ⓥ ⦿ col
Dir Stanley Kubrick ***Prod*** Stanley Kubrick ***Scr*** Stanley Kubrick, Diane Johnson ***Ph*** John Alcott ***Ed*** Ray Lovejoy ***Mus*** Wendy Carlos, Rachel Elkind ***Art*** Roy Walker
Act Jack Nicholson, Shelley Duvall, Danny Lloyd, Scatman Crothers, Barry Nelson, Anne Jackson (Warner)

With everything to work with, director Stanley Kubrick has teamed with jumpy Jack Nicholson to destroy all that was so terrifying about Stephen King's bestseller.

In his book, King took a fundamental horror formula—an innocent family marooned in an evil dwelling with a grim history—and built layers of ingenious terror upon it. The father is gradually possessed by the demonic, desolate hotel.

With dad going mad, the only protection mother and child have is the boy's clairvoyance—his "shining"—which allows him an innocent understanding and some ability to outmaneuver the devils. But Kubrick sees things his own way, throwing 90 percent of King's creation out.

The crazier Nicholson gets, the more idiotic he looks. Shelley Duvall transforms the warm sympathetic wife of the book into a simpering, semi-retarded hysteric.

[Version reviewed ran 146 mins. Kubrick cut pic soon after its premiere.]

•

SHINING THROUGH
1992, 132 mins, US Ⓥ ⦿ ▭ col
Dir David Seltzer ***Prod*** Howard Rosenman, Carol Baum ***Scr*** David Seltzer ***Ph*** Jan De Bont ***Ed*** Craig McKay ***Mus*** Michael Kamen ***Art*** Anthony Pratt
Act Michael Douglas, Melanie Griffith, Liam Neeson, Joely Richardson, John Gielgud, Francis Guinan (20th Century-Fox)

An old-fashioned women's picture that could pass for a television movie except for its lavish trappings, this oddly titled melodrama [from Susan Isaac's novel] turns out to be little more than a big, brassy Hallmark card with a World War II backdrop, combining shameless romance with predictable spy intrigue.

Melanie Griffith plays Linda Voss, a half-Jewish, half-Irish woman, circa 1940, who goes to work for a mysterious attorney (Michael Douglas) who turns out to be a spy for the U.S. government. The two become lovers, and despite his reluctance, Linda, a lower-class girl hired because of her fluent German, is ultimately sent to Berlin, as a spy, infiltrating the house of a German honcho (Liam Neeson).

Along the way, she hooks up with several Germans working undercover for the U.S., including the code-named Sunflower (John Gielgud) and a young woman of privilege (Joely Richardson).

There's a fair degree of tension as the spy antics draw to a close, but the flashback structure diffuses some of it because it's the aged Linda, after all, who's recounting the tale.

The dialog doesn't make any effort to capture that era, and Griffith's spunky secretary, despite appealing moments, seems more a 1990s working girl than a 1940s working-class girl.

Douglas has less to work with as the robotic soldier whose heart is turned to mush.

•

SHIP OF FOOLS
1965, 148 mins, US Ⓥ ⦿ b/w
Dir Stanley Kramer ***Prod*** Stanley Kramer ***Scr*** Abby Mann ***Ph*** Ernest Laszlo ***Ed*** Robert C. Jones ***Mus*** Ernest Gold ***Art*** Robert Clatworthy
Act Vivien Leigh, Simone Signoret, Jose Ferrer, Lee Marvin, Oskar Werner, Elizabeth Ashley (Columbia)

Director-producer Stanley Kramer and scenarist Abby Mann have distilled the essence of Katherine Anne Porter's bulky novel in a film that appeals to the intellect and the emotions.

As screen entertainment *Ship of Fools* is intelligent and eminently satisfying most of the time. The human cargo aboard the German ship *Vera* sailing from Vera Cruz to Bremerhaven (1933) is a cross-section of mass humanity that a landlubber can encounter in any metropolis.

All of the principals give strong performances from the aggressive interpretation by Jose Ferrer as a loathsome disciple of the emerging Hitlerian new order to Vivien Leigh as a fading American divorcee who gets her kicks out of leading on admirers and throwing cold water on their burning desires.

Of equal importance to the main stream of this drama, and also astutely attuned, are the contributions by Simone Signoret in the role of La Condesa and Oskar Werner as Dr. Schumann, the ship's doctor. Also impressive are George Segal and Elizabeth Ashley as young lovers whose intellects and emotions seem to be always warring against the animal magnetism that draws them together.

1965: Best B&W Cinematography, B&W Art Direction.

NOMINATIONS: Best Picture, Actor (Oskar Werner), Actress (Simone Signoret), Supp. Actor (Michael Dunn), Adapted Screenplay, B&W Costume Design

•

SHIP WAS LOADED, THE
SEE: CARRY ON ADMIRAL

•

SHIPWRECK
SEE: THE SEA GYPSIES

•

SHIRLEY VALENTINE
1989, 108 mins, UK Ⓥ ⦿ col
Dir Lewis Gilbert ***Prod*** Lewis Gilbert ***Scr*** Willy Russell ***Ph*** Alan Hume ***Ed*** Lesley Walker ***Mus*** George Hadjinasios, Willy Russell ***Art*** John Stoll
Act Pauline Collins, Tom Conti, Alison Steadman, Julia McKenzie, Joanna Lumley, Bernard Hill (Paramount)

Shirley Valentine is an uneven but generally delightful romantic comedy that has as its lead the irresistible Pauline Collins.

Collins *is* Shirley Valentine, the perfect match of actress and character. She starred in the one-woman show for more than a year on stage, first in a London West End production, then on Broadway. The legit work was a monolog in which

Collins, a middle-aged Liverpool housewife who yearns to drink "a glass of wine in a country where the grape is grown," described other characters and gave them life through her fanciful imagery.

In Willy Russell's film adaptation, *Shirley Valentine* becomes a full-blown location shot with those and other characters now cast as separate speaking parts, mostly by other terrific British actors. Tom Conti is barely recognizable here playing a very convincing swarthy Greek tavern keeper whose specialty is the romantic sail to a secluded cove. Shirley Valentine-Bradshaw, the mildly sour Liverpool housewife, was more entertaining than Shirley Valentine, the contented reborn woman. Even so, it would be impossible not to smile along with this very happy person as the curtain/sunset falls.

1989: NOMINATIONS: Best Actress (Pauline Collins), Song ("The Girl Who Used to Be Me")

•

SHIVERS
(AKA: THEY CAME FROM WITHIN; THE PARASITE MURDERS)
1975, 88 mins, Canada Ⓥ col
Dir David Cronenberg ***Prod*** Ivan Reitman ***Scr*** David Cronenberg ***Ph*** Robert Saad ***Ed*** Patrick Dodd ***Mus*** Ivan Reitman (sup.) ***Art*** Erla Gliserman
Act Paul Hampton, Joe Silver, Lynn Lowry, Alan Migicovsky, Susan Petrie, Barbara Steele (DAL/Reitman)

Shivers, a low-budget Canadian production, is a silly but moderately effective chiller about creeping parasites that systematically (and comically) "infect" an entire highrise population with nothing less than sexual hysteria.

Premise of pic is a bit shaky. A mad doctor who believes in matter over mind has implanted in his teenage mistress a strange parasite that brings out the basest of human impulses. He's not the only one she fools around with, so before long, the "disease" is spreading like crazy. The star of the movie is special effects and makeup man Joe Blasco, whose bloody, disgusting-looking crawlers are seen climbing out of people's throats as well as highrise plumbing to attack innocents.

•

SHOCK CORRIDOR
1963, 101 mins, US Ⓥ ⦿ b/w & col
Dir Samuel Fuller ***Prod*** Samuel Fuller ***Scr*** Samuel Fuller ***Ph*** Stanley Cortez, [Samuel Fuller] ***Ed*** Jerome Thoms ***Mus*** Paul Dunlap ***Art*** Eugene Lourie
Act Peter Breck, Constance Towers, Gene Evans, James Best, Hari Rhodes, Larry Tucker (Allied Artists)

Samuel Fuller's thin plot has a newspaperman (Peter Breck) contriving, with the aid of a psychiatrist no less, to get himself committed to a mental ward in order to identify a murderer known only to the inmates and whom the police have been unable to detect.

Within all this lurks three points about Americana, each embodied in characters the fourth-estater encounters in the hospital. A Communist-brainwashed and subsequently disgraced Korean war vet (James Best) is the mouthpiece through which Fuller pleads for greater understanding of such unfortunate individuals.

Likewise, a Negro (Hari Rhodes) supposed to have been the first to attend an all-white Southern university serves to make the point that it takes enormous emotional stamina to play the role of the martyr in social progress. And the character of a renowned physicist (Gene Evans) whose mind has deteriorated into that of a six-year-old enables Fuller to get in some digs against bomb shelters and America's participation in the space race.

But all these points go for naught because the film is dominated by sex and shock superficialities. Among the gruelling passages are a striptease and an attack on the hero in a locked room by half-a-dozen nymphos.

The dialog is unreal and pretentious, and the direction is heavyhanded, often mistaking sordidness for realism. The performers labor valiantly, but in vain. Those most prominent are Breck, who really gets his lumps and earns his pay, and Constance Towers as his stripper girlfriend.

[Original prints included documentary color sequences shot on 16mm by Fuller himself.]

•

SHOCKER
1989, 110 mins, US Ⓥ ⦿ col
Dir Wes Craven ***Prod*** Marianne Maddalena, Barin Kumar ***Scr*** Wes Craven ***Ph*** Jacques Haitkin ***Ed*** Andy Blumental ***Mus*** William Goldstein ***Art*** Cynthia Kay
Act Michael Murphy, Peter Begg, Mitch Pileggi, Cami Cooper, Richard Brooks, Dr. Timothy Leary (Alive/Universal)

At first glance (or at least for the first 40 minutes) *Shocker* seems a potential winner, an almost unbearably suspenseful, stylish and blood-drenched ride courtesy of writer-director Wes Craven's flair for action and sick humour.

As it continues, however, the camp aspects simply give way to the ridiculous while failing to establish any rules to govern the mayhem. The result is plenty of unintentional laughs.

The obtuse story has Horace Pinker (Mitch Pileggi), already a mass killer of several families, slaying the foster family of Jonathan (Peter Berg) and his police captain father (Michael Murphy). Jonathan "sees" the events in a prescient dream that indicates he's linked to the murderer.

That leads the police to Pinker's door, and after a series of misadventures he's caught and executed. But Horace lives on after the execution as a disembodied malevolent spirit who strikes out by possessing others.

•

SHOCKPROOF
1949, 78 mins, US b/w
Dir Douglas Sirk ***Scr*** Helen Deutsch, Samuel Fuller ***Ph*** Charles Lawton, Jr. ***Ed*** Gene Havlick ***Mus*** George Duning
Act Cornel Wilde, Patricia Knight, John Baragrey, Esther Minciotti, Howard St. John (Columbia)

Shockproof is a patly told tale of the parole system with a strong romantic thread.

Yarn is wrapped up in a good production dress that uses Los Angeles locales to stress semi-documentary flavor. While never credible, story does point up the standard melodramatics and good playing to keep it all interesting.

Douglas Sirk's direction moves at an excellent pace. Plot deals with probationary work, with Cornel Wilde as one of the officers in the local bureau. A paroled murderess, Patricia Knight, is assigned to his care, and story is based on what happens to him and the girl when love moves into their lives.

Situations come together with pat coincidences that don't make for credence.

Wilde does well by his assignment, and Knight brings a strong personality and s.a to her part.

•

SHOESHINE
SEE: SCIUSCIA

•

SHOESHINE BOYS
SEE: SCIUSCIA

•

SHOES OF THE FISHERMAN, THE
1968, 162 mins, US Ⓥ ⌑ col
Dir Michael Anderson ***Prod*** George Englund ***Scr*** John Patrick, James Kennaway ***Ph*** Erwin Hillier ***Ed*** Ernest Walter ***Mus*** Alex North ***Art*** George W. Davis, Edward Carfagno
Act Anthony Quinn, Laurence Olivier, Oskar Werner, David Janssen, Vittorio De Sica, Leo McKern (M-G-M)

Anthony Quinn plays a future Pope of Russian extraction who would, if necessary, strip the Roman Catholic Church of its material wealth in order to avoid nuclear world war. Occasionally awkward script structure and dialog, and overall sluggish pacing do not substantially blunt the impact of the basic story (from Morris L. West's novel), as interpreted by an excellent international cast.

It starts with Quinn as a 20-year inmate of a Siberian slave labor camp, and ends with his public Coronation promise as the new Pope to spend the Church's wealth.

Laurence Olivier, as the Russian premier, had ordered Quinn's release from religious persecution, and ultimate dispatch to Rome.

Quinn's performance is excellent. That experience-lined face suggests 20 years of Siberian enslavement, even if the script has him returning to urbane society with a bit too much facility.

Olivier, along with Frank Finlay and Clive Revill, are superior in projecting not unsympathetic Russian politicians.

1968: NOMINATIONS: Best Art Direction, Original Music Score

•

SHOGUN
1981, 150 mins, US Ⓥ ⦿ col
Dir Jerry London ***Prod*** Eric Bercovici ***Scr*** Eric Bercovici ***Ph*** Andrew Laszlo ***Ed*** Bill Luciano, Jerry Young, Benjamin A. Weissman, Donald R. Rode ***Mus*** Maurice Jarre ***Art*** Joseph R. Jennings
Act Richard Chamberlain, Toshiro Mifune, Yoko Shimada, Alan Badel, Michael Hordern, John Rhys-Davies (Paramount)

In *Shogun*, East meets West in a period clash of swords and culture, but with scarcely the wit, style, dramatic tension or plausibility to justify a running time of 150 tiresome minutes for this spinoff from the James Clavell novel as recut from the eight-hour Paramount TV miniseries.

Richard Chamberlain and Toshiro Mifune are top-featured in this bilingual (and subtitled) tale of 17th-century Japanese political intrigue with praiseworthy professioal dignity, the former as a shipwrecked Englishman, the latter as one of the tribal chieftains vying for the title and power of shogun, or supreme Godfather. The whole shebang was lensed on locations in Japan.

Yoko Shimada projects a Dresden-doll appeal as an aristocratic lady who, besides helping Chamberlain bridge the culture gap, enters into forbidden love, thereby telegraphing her doom.

Producer Eric Bercovici's script on the big screen proves only too diffuse and confusing to do anything like justice to either the romance, any other relationship or indeed the wider canvas of betrayal, barbarism and warlord ritual posturing.

•

SHOOT FIRST
1953, 88 mins, UK b/w
Dir Robert Parrish ***Prod*** Raymond Stross ***Scr*** Eric Ambler ***Ph*** Stan Parey ***Ed*** Russell Lloyd ***Mus*** Hans May ***Art*** Ivan King
Act Joel McCrea, Evelyn Keyes, Herbert Lom, Roland Culver, Marius Goring, Frank Lawton (United Artists)

Eric Ambler's screenplay of the Geoffrey Household novel, *A Rough Shoot*, has Joel McCrea stumbling into the role of a British counterspy, aiding Herbert Lom, a real cloak-and-dagger character, and his boss (Roland Culver), of the British secret service. Foreign agents, they've learned, plan to fly in a spy on McCrea's farm, and McCrea, his wife (Evelyn Keyes) and Lom greet the plane and smuggle off the spy, posing as his English confederates.

Plan is to get to London, have him meet his contact and then arrest the pair. But the real agents, led by Marius Goring, along with the police, who want McCrea on suspicion of murder, make a chase out of it that doesn't let up in suspense until the last minute.

McCrea is excellent as the colonel forced by circumstances into the counterplot, and Keyes is appealing and believable as his wife. Lom scores as the swashbuckling counterspy, making a completely engaging character out of what's intended as a caricature. Goring scores as the fanatic foreign agent, and Karl Stepanek is excellent as his brutal sidekick.

Robert Parrish's inventive direction keeps the story moving at a rapid pace.

•

SHOOTING PARTY, THE
1984, 106 mins, UK Ⓥ col
Dir Alan Bridges ***Prod*** Geoffrey Reeve ***Scr*** Julian Bond ***Ph*** Fred Tammes ***Ed*** Peter Davies ***Mus*** John Scott ***Art*** Morley Smith
Act Edward Fox, Cheryl Campbell, James Mason, Dorothy Tutin, John Gielgud, Frank Windsor (Reeve)

A handsome historical homage to the proprieties and values of pre-First World War landed aristocracy in England, *The Shooting Party* revolves around a holiday spent on an estate in 1913, as an era ends.

Julian Bond's adaptation of the novel [by Isabel Colegate] incorporates enough to make a promising miniseries.

James Mason as Sir Randolph is as world-weary as he is tired of his genuinely tiresome guests. Thesp credits resemble a Who's Who of the British stage, with John Gielgud eclipsing the gentry in a brief appearance as a pamphleteering defender of animal rights, opposed to slaughter as amusement.

Director Alan Bridges is very good at handling a story that tries to distinguish between the nobility and what is truly noble.

•

SHOOTIST, THE
1976, 99 mins, US Ⓥ ⦿ col
Dir Don Siegel ***Prod*** Mike Frankovich, William Self ***Scr*** Miles Hood Swarthout, Scott Hale ***Ph*** Bruce Surtees ***Ed*** Douglas Stewart ***Mus*** Elmer Bernstein ***Art*** Robert Boyle
Act John Wayne, Lauren Bacall, Ron Howard, Bill McKinney, James Stewart, Richard Boone (De Laurentiis)

The Shootist stands as one of John Wayne's towering achievements. Don Siegel's terrific film is simply beautiful, and beautifully simple, in its quiet, elegant and sensitive telling of the last days of a dying gunfighter at the turn of the century. Wayne and Lauren Bacall are both outstanding.

The time is 1901. Wayne a prairie-hardened gunfighter, rides into the new century where Carson City is in segue to modern civilization. Saloon shootouts still occur; Hugh O'Brian's card dealing is still not to be challenged.

Wayne's trip is to town doctor James Stewart, who confirms a cancer diagnosis. Atop this comes an emerging tenderness between Wayne and Bacall which is articulated in careful politeness and the artful exchange of expressions that evoke memories of great silent films.

1976: NOMINATION: Best Art Direction

●

SHOOT THE MOON
1982, 124 mins, US Ⓥ col
Dir Alan Parker ***Prod*** Alan Marshall ***Scr*** Bo Goldman ***Ph*** Michael Seresin ***Ed*** Gerry Hambling ***Art*** Geoffrey Kirkland
Act Albert Finney, Diane Keaton, Karen Allen, Peter Weller, Dana Hill, Viveka Davis (M-G-M)

A number of high-powered artists fail to coalesce their talents in *Shoot the Moon* a grim drama of marital collapse which proves disturbing and irritating by turns.

Noisy pic belongs almost entirely to toplined Albert Finney and Diane Keaton, who play affluent serious writer and housewife, respectively, and parents of four girls. First act is devoted to couple hitting absolute rock bottom, with nothing to do but for Finney to walk out into the arms of g.f. Karen Allen.

Attempting to handle the situation in civilized fashion, pair agrees that Finney can spend a reasonable amount of time with the girls, which allows Finney to catch glimpses of his wife's slow-cooking affair with a construction worker.

Forced to "control" himself much of the time, Finney is a walking time bomb, exploding horrendously on one occasion before the climax when he beats his most troublesome daughter. Stripped of most of her charm and sometimes brutally photographed, Keaton is more erratic.

●

SHOOT THE PIANIST
SEE: TIREZ SUR LE PIANISTE

●

SHOOT THE PIANO PLAYER
SEE: TIREZ SUR LE PIANISTE

●

SHOOT TO KILL
(UK: DEADLY PURSUIT)
1988, 110 mins, US Ⓥ ⊙ col
Dir Roger Spottiswoode ***Prod*** Ron Silverman, Daniel Petrie, Jr. ***Scr*** Harv Zimmel, Michael Burton, Daniel Petrie, Jr. ***Ph*** Michael Chapman ***Ed*** Garth Craven, George Bowers ***Mus*** John Scott ***Art*** Richard Sylbert
Act Sidney Poitier, Tom Berenger, Kirstie Alley, Clancy Brown, Richard Masur, Andrew Robinson (Touchstone/Silver Screen Partners III)

Everybody, including the audience, gets a good workout in *Shoot to Kill*, a rugged, involving manhunt adventure [story by Harv Zimmel] in which a criminal leads his pursuers over what is perhaps the most challenging land route out of the United States.

Sidney Poitier establishes his authority immediately as a veteran FBI man in San Francisco who, despite handling the crisis with calm assuredness, cannot prevent the getaway of a jewel thief who kills hostages on a foggy night on Frisco Bay.

Another shooting of a similar type takes Poitier up to the Pacific Northwest, where he is forced to engage the services of tough backwoodsman Tom Berenger to lead him up into the mountains to apprehend the villain before he makes it over the border into Canada.

A self-styled macho hermit, Berenger considers Poitier a cityfied softy incapable of making it in the mountains. This sets up a cliched enmity between the two men that one knows will have to be broken down, but not without some predictable jibes at Poitier's awkwardness outdoors and some revelations of Berenger's own vulnerabilities.

Poitier, 63 when the film was shot, looks little more than 40. The actor's directness and easiness on the screen are refreshing, his humor self-deprecating and understated.

Berenger solidly fills the bill as the confident mountain man, and Kirstie Alley, despite the extreme limitations of her role, proves entirely believable as his female counterpart. British Columbia locations give the film tremendous scenic impact.

●

SHOP AROUND THE CORNER, THE
1940, 97 mins, US Ⓥ ⊙ b/w
Dir Ernst Lubitsch ***Prod*** Ernst Lubitsch ***Scr*** Samson Raphaelson ***Ph*** William Daniels ***Ed*** Gene Ruggiero ***Mus*** Werner R. Heymann ***Art*** Cedric Gibbons, Wade B. Rubottom
Act Margaret Sullavan, James Stewart, Frank Morgan, Joseph Schildkraut, Sara Haden, Felix Bressart (M-G-M)

Although picture carries the indelible stamp of Ernst Lubitsch at his best in generating humor and human interest from what might appear to be unimportant situations, it carries further to impress via the outstanding characterizations by Margaret Sullavan and James Stewart in the starring spots. Sullavan's portrayal is light and fluffy—in contrast to the seriousness of Stewart in both business and romance. The supporting cast is very well-balanced. In the compact group is Frank Morgan, as the owner-operator of the small gift shop in Budapest, and his staff including Joseph Schildkraut, Sara Haden, Felix Bressart, William Tracy, Inez Courtney and Charles Smith.

The story [based on Nikolaus Laszlo's play] might be termed a small edition of *Grand Hotel*, with practically all of the action taking place in the small shop. Stewart, senior clerk, confides to Bressart that he is corresponding with a girl (Sullavan) through a newspaper ad, and takes the affair with the unknown very seriously. Sullavan arrives to apply for a job and, after being turned down by Stewart, is hired by Morgan.

From that point on it's an intimate tale of the store and its workers. Story swings along at fast pace.

●

SHOP ON MAIN STREET, THE
SEE: OBCHOD NA KORZE

●

SHOP ON THE HIGH STREET, A
SEE: OBCHOD NA KORZE

●

SHOPPING
1994, 106 mins, UK Ⓥ ⊙ col
Dir Paul Anderson ***Prod*** Jeremy Bolt ***Scr*** Paul Anderson ***Ph*** Tony Imi ***Ed*** David Stiven ***Mus*** Barrington Pheloung ***Art*** Max Gottlieb
Act Sadie Frost, Jude Law, Sean Pertwee, Fraser James, Marianne Faithfull, Sean Bean (Impact/Film Four)

An all-style, no-content attitudinal actioner, *Shopping* is as blank-minded as its vapidly rebellious leading characters. Set in a vaguely futuristic Britain exclusively populated by valueless kids and fascistic police, this slick, sleek and empty joyless ride is immediately unhinged by its lack of credible forces of opposition; there's nothing colliding here except cars.

At the outset, when 19-year-old pretty boy Billy (Jude Law) is being released, he's asked, "What's prison taught you, Billy?" He replies, "Don't get caught," and that's as philosophical as the picture gets. Without missing a beat, Billy and his partner, Jo (Sadie Frost), steal and trash a BMW in a profound bit of anti-yuppie crime. Billy is intent upon regaining his status as top dog in his anarchic world, which he can do by stealing cars and "shopping."

This plot setup opens the door on an orgy of extravagant destruction, spurred on by Billy's macho battle with Tommy (Sean Pertwee) and tempered only by Jo's growing desire to take Billy away from all this. Along with aping American actioners, tyro writer-director Paul Anderson, who comes out of TV, would appear to aspire to the mantle of the British Luc Besson, as his faith in the power of heavy atmospherics and thick style seems unlimited.

Newcomer Law seems more like a candidate for a British technorock group than screen stardom, and Frost, fresh from *Dracula*, strikes a tough-girl pose throughout. Marianne Faithfull pops up momentarily as the proprietress of a video arcade, while Jonathan Pryce is obliged to supply world-weary opposition as a police chief.

●

SHOPWORN ANGEL, THE
1928, 80 mins, US b/w
Dir Richard Wallace ***Scr*** Howard Estabrook, Albert Shelby LeVino
Act Nancy Carroll, Gary Cooper, Paul Lukas (Paramount)

Once in a long while the formula picture factories in Hollywood turn out a glamorous gem such as this [from a story by Dana Burnet], stirring, finely drawn, and so beautifully presented that the critical faculties declare a holiday. Nancy Carroll and Gary Cooper contribute excellent work. Both seem natural and lifelike.

As the showgirl Daisy living with the worldly sophisticate (Paul Lukas), with nothing to worry over except booze headaches and bawling the dance director when asked to come to rehearsals on time, Carroll never strays from type. She's hard, smart and strong-willed.

The soldier boy, William Tyler (Cooper), is from Texas where he never saw a show girl or a skyscraper first hand. He bumps into Daisy accidentally, is driven to camp in her limousine, and then brags to the gang. She later weakens enough to get the soldier out of the mess. Only two dialog sequences in the picture, both highly effective. First is the marriage ceremony; Cooper has a few brief lines. In the second the dance director is putting the chorus through the paces; Carroll has a few lines here and also sings. The girl's voice records surprisingly well.

Lukas, a Hungarian imported by Paramount over a year ago, is a smooth, most nonchalant and likeable heavy.

●

SHOPWORN ANGEL, THE
1938, 85 mins, US b/w
Dir H. C. Potter ***Prod*** Joseph L. Mankiewicz ***Scr*** Waldo Salt ***Ph*** Joseph Ruttenberg ***Ed*** W. Donn Hayes ***Mus*** Edward Ward ***Art*** Cedric Gibbons, Joseph C. Wright, Edwin C. Willis
Act Margaret Sullavan, James Stewart, Walter Pidgeon, Hattie McDaniel, Nat Pendleton, Alan Curtis (M-G-M)

Original of *Shopworn Angel* first appeared about 20 years earlier as a *Sat Eve Post* story by Dana Burnet. Paramount filmed it (partly in sound) in 1928, with Nancy Carroll, Gary Cooper and Paul Lukas.

In general, this remake follows the original story with reasonable faithfulness. It's still the wartime yarn about the crafty Broadway chorine who meets a Texas rookie on his way to France and, when he falls for her, marries him rather than disillusion him. Latter pair had their first strong parts in the production and it established their reps as well as cleaned up financially. The present version seems a softer one, without the stark edges of the original and as a result less absorbing. Instead of the cool schemer played by Nancy Carroll, the chorine is now generous and warm-hearted. The girl's lover is no longer the menace of the earlier version, but is now the typical Walter Pidgeon man-who-doesn't-get-the-girl.

It is only occasional credible screen drama. As the girl, Margaret Sullavan turns in a powerful performance. Her playing is pliant, has depth and eloquence.

James Stewart is a natural enough rookie but there's little characterization in his performance.

●

SHORT CIRCUIT
1986, 98 mins, US Ⓥ ⊙ ⌑ col
Dir John Badham ***Prod*** David Foster, Lawrence Turman ***Scr*** S. S. Wilson, Brent Maddock ***Ph*** Nick McLean ***Ed*** Frank Morriss ***Mus*** David Shire ***Art*** Dianne Wager
Act Ally Sheedy, Steve Guttenberg, Fisher Stevens, Austin Pendleton, G. W. Bailey, Brian McNamara (Tri-Star/PSO)

Short Circuit is a hip, sexless sci-fi sendup featuring a Defense Dept. robot who comes "alive" to become a pop-talking peacenik. Robot is the one-dimensional No. 5, the ultimate weapon designed by playful computer whiz Dr Newton Crosby (Steve Guttenberg).

By a fluke, No. 5 gets short-circuited and begins to malfunction. It finds itself outside the high-security Nova compound in a chase that lands it on top of a natural foods catering truck and under the influence of its sweet but tough animal-loving owner, Stephanie (Ally Sheedy). Scripters get credit for some terrific dialog that would have been a lot less disarming if not for the winsome robot and Sheedy's affection for it. Guttenberg plays his best goofy self.

●

SHORT CIRCUIT 2
1988, 110 mins, US Ⓥ ⊙ col
Dir Kenneth Johnson ***Prod*** David Foster, Lawrence Turman, Gary Foster ***Scr*** S. S. Wilson, Brent Maddock ***Ph*** John McPherson ***Ed*** Conrad Buff ***Mus*** Charles Fox ***Art*** Bill Brodie
Act Fisher Stevens, Michael McKean, Cynthia Gibb, Jack Weston, Tim Blaney, Dee McCafferty (Turman-Foster/Tri-Star)

Mild and meek, *Short Circuit 2* has an uncomplicated sweetness as a successful followup to the original robot kiddie comedy.

"Johnny Five" makes his way to the Big City, where protector Fisher Stevens struggles to make ends meet hawking toy models of his mechanical wonder on the street.

Cutie-pie store employee Cynthia Gibb needs to bring a novel item to her shelves, and sends Stevens and self-styled entrepreneur Michael McKean into instant action by ordering 1,000 of the little buggers for the Christmas season. Underhanded banker Jack Weston has some other ideas for the tireless automaton, scheming to kidnap it and press it into service stealing some priceless jewels from a safe deposit box.

Although derivative, the robot, made up of all manner of spare electronic parts, remains charming, and kids will undoubtedly find delightful scenes in which No. 5 jumps around from place to place and sails through the air amid the skyscrapers of Toronto.

The film is set in a generic U.S. metropolis, complete with American flags and a citizenship swearing-in ceremony. However, the city is constantly recognizable as Toronto.

•

SHORT CUTS
1993, 184 mins, US Ⓥ ⊙ ▭ col
Dir Robert Altman ***Prod*** Cary Brokaw ***Scr*** Robert Altman, Frank Barhydt ***Ph*** Walt Lloyd ***Ed*** Geraldine Peroni ***Mus*** Mark Isham ***Art*** Stephen Altman
Act Andie MacDowell, Tim Robbins, Chris Penn, Julianne Moore, Anne Archer, Jack Lemmon (Avenue/Spelling)

Exploding 10 of Raymond Carver's spare stories and minimally drawn characters onto the screen with startling imagination, Robert Altman has made his most complex and full-bodied human comedy since *Nashville*. Crisscrossing 22 significant characters, this is a bemused contemplation of the unaccountable way people behave when fate deals them unexpected hands, embracing everything from slapstick comedy to devastating tragedy.

They include married couple Bruce Davison and Andie MacDowell, whose young son is hit by a car driven by waitress Lily Tomlin, a trailer park denizen whose marriage to chauffeur Tom Waits has hit choppy water. Attending to the injured boy is doctor Matthew Modine, who still wonders if artist wife Julianne Moore had an affair a few years back. They meet married couple Anne Archer, who works as a clown at children's parties, and Fred Ward at a concert and invite them to dinner, but first Ward is due to take a fishing trip with buddies Buck Henry and Huey Lewis, during which they make the shocking discovery of a dead woman's body in the water.

Performing at the concert is classical cellist Lori Singer, a loner whose mother Annie Ross sings jazz and ballads at a local club. Among the hangout's habitues are pool serviceman Chris Penn and wife Jennifer Jason Leigh, who indelibly gives phone sex from home while feeding her kids, and their friends Robert Downey, Jr., a special-effects makeup artist, and Lili Taylor, who make the most of a housesitting opportunity.

Medfly chopper pilot Peter Gallagher has split from wife Frances McDormand, who in turn has been having an affair with L.A. cop Tim Robbins, whose wife Madeleine Stowe models for Moore.

As in any multi-episode film, some vignettes work better than others. The price it pays for being an observant character piece, rather than narrative-driven, is that its length is fully felt.

Altman and lenser Walt Lloyd keep the camera alertly moving but simple, often starting with establishing shots, then closing in on the actors. Editor Geraldine Peroni has done a stupendous job juggling the story lines, never losing sight of one for too long, and expertly judging when to resume another.

Mark Isham's effective score is abetted by a torrent of source music, notably Ross's throaty jazz vocals and Singer's cello playing. For the record, the Carver stories drawn upon are "Jerry and Molly and Sam," "Will You Please Be Quiet, Please?," "Collectors," "Neighbours," "A Small Good Thing," "So Much Water So Close to Home," "They're Not Your Husband," "Vitamins" and "Tell the Women We're Going," and the narrative poem "Lemonade."

1993: NOMINATION: Best Director

•

SHORT FILM ABOUT KILLING, A
SEE: DEKALOG

•

SHORT FILM ABOUT LOVE, A
SEE: DEKALOG

•

SHOT IN THE DARK, A
1964, 103 mins, US Ⓥ ⊙ ▭ col
Dir Blake Edwards ***Prod*** Blake Edwards ***Scr*** Blake Edwards, William Peter Blatty ***Ph*** Christopher Challis ***Ed*** Ralph E. Winters, Bert Bates ***Mus*** Henry Mancini ***Art*** Michael Stringer
Act Peter Sellers, Elke Sommer, Herbert Lom, George Sanders, Graham Stark, Douglas Wilmer (Mirisch/United Artists)

Based upon the French farce authored by Marcel Achard and adapted to the American stage by Harry Kurnitz, director Blake transforms Peter Sellers's role from a magistrate, whose activities were limited to judicial chambers, into Inspector Clouseau, where more movement and greater area are possible. "Give me 10 men like Clouseau, and I could destroy the world!" his superior exclaims in despair, summing up the character played by Sellers, sent to investigate a murder in the chateau of a millionaire outside Paris.

When this chief inspector, portrayed by Herbert Lom, attempts to take him off the case, powers above return him to his investigations which revolve about chief suspect Elke Sommer, a French maid, whom the dick is convinced is innocent.

The chores takes him to a nudist camp, a tour of Parisian nightclubs, where dead bodies are left in his wake, and to his apartment, where one of the funniest seduction scenes ever filmed unfolds to the tune of three in a bed and an exploding time bomb. It's never completely clear whether the detective solves his case in a windup that doesn't quite come off.

Sometimes the narrative is subordinated to individual bits of business and running gags but Sellers's skill as a comedian again is demonstrated, and Sommer, in role of the chambermaid who moves all men to amorous thoughts and sometimes murder, is pert and expert. Lom gives punch and humor to star's often distraught superior, George Sanders lends polish as the millionaire and Graham Stark excels as Sellers's deadpan assistant.

•

SHOULDER ARMS
1918, 36 mins, US ⊗ b/w
Dir Charles Chaplin ***Prod*** Charles Chaplin ***Scr*** Charles Chaplin ***Ph*** Rollie Totheroh ***Mus*** Charles Chaplin
Act Charles Chaplin, Edna Purviance, Sydney Chaplin, Loyal Underwood, Henry Bergman, Albert Austin (First National)

In *Shoulder Arms* Chaplin is a doughboy. At the finish he captures the Kaiser, Crown Prince and Hindenburg.

At the opening he is the most awkward member of an awkward drilling squad. His trouble with his feet is terrific. After a long hike, Chaplin has heroic dreams of what he accomplishes as a private in the trenches over there.

Chaplin wrote and directed the story. His camouflage as a small tree, during which he runs through a wood is one of the best and most original pieces of comedy work ever put on a screen. There is some slapstick, laughably worked in, also pie-throwing with limburger cheese substituted. That occurs in the trenches.

The trenches are good production bits. There is fun also in the dug-out, with the water, and a floating candle burning one of the boys' exposed toes.

Shoulder Arms includes much more action than generally found in a Chaplin comedy. With Chaplin in uniform without his derby hat and cane, it says that Charlie Chaplin is a great film comedian.

•

SHOUT
1991, 89 mins, US Ⓥ ⊙ col
Dir Jeffrey Hornaday ***Prod*** Robert Simonds ***Scr*** Joe Gayton ***Ph*** Robert Brinkmann ***Ed*** Seth Flaum ***Mus*** Randy Edelman ***Art*** William F. Matthews
Act John Travolta, James Walters, Heather Graham, Richard Jordan, Linda Fiorentino, Scott Coffey (Universal)

Shout is a 1950s rock 'n' roll fantasy that tries to have it all ways at once and winds up sorely out of tune. Set in an isolated hamlet on the Texas plains, film purports to be about the liberating effect of the birth of rock 'n' roll, but as producers have not secured rights to any signature songs of that era, musical mix sounds wildly inauthentic.

Broadly etched tale is about a home for wayward and orphaned boys. Kid with the worst attitude (James Walters) clashes with the grim and heavy-handed headmaster (Richard Jordan), who espouses a regimen of hard labor and calisthenics.

Along comes a music teacher (John Travolta), a hepcat ahead of his time who indoctrinates the boys in the forbidden pleasures of rock 'n' roll. On the side, he's making time with the owner (Linda Fiorentino) of a dance club on the wrong side of the tracks and former flame of the town sheriff.

It's the kind of hokey scenario that would fly only if aided by a camp sense of humor or the promise of a good musical number about to break out, and neither of these are present. Music and dance elements are used naturalistically, as in *La Bamba*, but rather sparingly.

Only Travolta bothers to put on a Texas accent, and his thick, nuanced emoting clashes with the unadorned delivery of the others. In all, ill-thunk scenario seems slung together by amateurs. The culprits are producer Robert Simonds (both *Problem Child* pics) and first-time director Jeffrey Hornaday (*Flashdance* choreographer).

•

SHOUT, THE
1978, 87 mins, UK Ⓥ col
Dir Jerzy Skolimowski ***Prod*** Jeremy Thomas ***Scr*** Michael Austin, Jerzy Skolimowski ***Ph*** Mike Molloy ***Ed*** Barrie Vince ***Mus*** Rupert Hine, Anthony Banks, Michael Rutherford ***Art*** Simon Holland
Act Alan Bates, Susannah York, John Hurt, Robert Stephens, Tim Curry, Julian Hough (Recorded Picture)

Polish director Jerzy Skolimowski has been able to create a gripping film [from a story by Robert Graves] that holds attention most of the way through its economical length. It probes a couple beset by a catalyst that breaks their seemingly surface contentment. Film is told by Alan Bates during a cricket match in an asylum.

Bates, a tramp-like figure, accosts a man (John Hurt) outside a church one day. It is a small town and Bates gets invited to dinner and stays. He tells strange tales of how he lived with Australian aborigines and killed his own children when he left and how he learned how to cast various spells, especially a shout that can kill.

Flash forwards indicate Bates will disrupt the couple with one problem of the man apparently dallying with the wife of the local shoemaker. Hurt is an electronic music composer and his work counterpoints Bates's shout in a way. The story builds as the listener becomes apprehensive. It crescendos as Bates, in the tale, reduces the wife to his whims.

•

SHOUT AT THE DEVIL
1976, 147 mins, UK Ⓥ ⊙ ▭ col
Dir Peter Hunt ***Prod*** Michael Klinger ***Scr*** Wilbur Smith, Stanley Price, Alastair Reid ***Ph*** Mike Reed ***Ed*** Michael Duthie ***Mus*** Maurice Jarre ***Art*** Syd Cain
Act Lee Marvin, Roger Moore, Barbara Parkins, Ian Holm, Rene Kolldehoff, Horst Janson (Hemdale)

A nice sprawling, basic, gutsy and unsophisticated film, which displays its reported $7 million budget on nearly every frame.

Based on a Wilbur Smith (*Gold*) novel, the script is a pastiche of almost every basic action-suspense ingredient known to the cinema. Exotic tropical settings, man-eating crocodiles, air and sea combat, shipwreck, big game hunting, natives on a rampage, ticking time bombs, rape and fire, malaria, they're all there and then some.

Basic ingredients have to do with a successful attempt to put permanently out of action a crippled World War I German battle cruiser holed up for repairs in a remote South East African river delta. The oddball opposites-attract relationship between Lee Marvin and Roger Moore generally works very well indeed, and the constantly imbibing Irisher and the contrastingly "straight" Britisher make good foils. The motivating love story linking Moore and Barbara Parkins is rarely involving and convincing.

•

SHOW BOAT
1936, 110 mins, US Ⓥ ⊙ b/w
Dir James Whale ***Prod*** Carl Laemmle Jr ***Scr*** Oscar Hammerstein II ***Ph*** John J. Mescall ***Ed*** Ted Kent, Bernard Burton ***Mus*** Victor Baravelle (dir.) ***Art*** Charles D. Hall
Act Irene Dunne, Allan Jones, Charles Winninger, Paul Robeson, Helen Morgan, Helen Westley (Universal)

Show Boat, Universal's second talkerized version, is a smash film musical. Basic tender romance [from Edna Ferber's novel] between Magnolia (Irene Dunne) and Gaylord Ravenal (Allan Jones), romantic wastrel of the Mississippi river banks, has been most effectively projected by this reproduction of the classic [1927] Edna Ferber–Oscar Hammerstein II–Jerome Kern operetta.

The now classic songs, "Make Believe," "Ol' Man River," "Can't Help Lovin' That Man," "Why Do I Love You," "Bill" and "You Are Love," as the duet thematic have been retained and three new numbers, all in a novelty vein, have been added.

Dunne and Jones are superb in the roles originally created by Norma Terriss and Howard Marsh. Charles Winninger in his original Captain Andy role is, as ever, engaging; Helen Morgan is the same Julie as in the Ziegfeld original; Paul Robeson has Jules Bledsoe's basso opportunities with "Ol' Man River"; Helen Westley has the original Edna Mae Oliver assignment and delivers adequately, if a bit morosely, lacking the subtle brittleness of the Oliver interpretation.

Dunne maintains the illusion of her Magnolia throughout—from her own secluded girlhood; into sudden stardom on the Cotton Blossom; and later, as a more mature artist, carrying the torch for the disappeared Ravenal and rearing her own child into professional prominence.

Robeson's "Ol' Man River" is perhaps the single song highlight, although some may be captious a bit over the camera angles illustrating "Totin' the Bales" and "Landing in Jail."

•

SHOW BOAT
1951, 107 mins, US Ⓥ ⊙ col
Dir George Sidney ***Prod*** Arthur Freed ***Scr*** John Lee Mahin ***Ph*** Charles Rosher ***Ed*** John Dunning ***Mus*** Adolph Deutsch (dir.) ***Art*** Cedric Gibbons, Jack Martin Smith

Act Kathryn Grayson, Howard Keel, Ava Gardner, Joe E. Brown, Marge Champion, Gower Champion (M-G-M)

Show Boat started beguiling audiences back in 1927, when it was first brought to the Broadway stage after a Philadelphia tryout. Since then, in many legit versions and in two previous film treatments, it has continued that beguilement.

There has been no tampering with the basic line of the Edna Ferber novel, from which Jerome Kern and Oscar Hammerstein II did the original musical. There are a few changes in this latest film version, the first in color, and an introduction of the finale in a time span much shorter than the original.

"Ol' Man River," "Make Believe," "Why Do I Love You," "You Are Love," "My Bill," and "Can't Help Lovin' That Man" are Kern tunes that lose nothing in the passing of the years. With voices of such show-tune ableness as Kathryn Grayson and Howard Keel to sing them they capture the ear and tear at the emotions.

Grayson is a most able Magnolia, the innocent show boat girl who runs off with the dashing gambler (Keel), finds her marriage wrecked by his love of lady chance, goes back to the show boat to have her child and then reconciles with the wandering mate after a few years.

Ava Gardner is the third star, bringing to her role of Julie, the mulatto who is kicked off the *Cotton Blossom* because of early Southern prejudice, all the physical attributes it needs to attract attention. [Actress's singing voice was dubbed by Annette Warren.]

There is an amazing amount of freshness instilled into the picture by Marge and Gower Champion, young dance team who handle the roles of Ellie May and Frank Schultz, show boat terpers. The other big song moment is William Warfield's rich baritoning of "Ol' Man River."

1951: NOMINATIONS: Best Color Cinematography, Scoring of a Musical Picture

•

SHOWGIRLS

1995, 131 mins, US col

Dir Paul Verhoeven **Prod** Alan Marshall, Charles Evans **Scr** Joe Eszterhas **Ph** Jost Vacano **Ed** Mark Goldblatt, Mark Helfrich **Mus** David A. Stewart **Art** Allan Cameron

Act Elizabeth Berkley, Kyle MacLachlan, Gina Gershon, Robert Davi, Alan Rachins, William Shockley (United Artists/Chargeurs/Carolco)

The only positive thing there is to say about *Showgirls* is that the sensibility of the film perfectly matches that of its milieu. Impossibly vulgar, tawdry and coarse, this much-touted major studio splash into NC-17 waters is akin to being keel-hauled through a cesspool, with sharks swimming alongside.

Hot young babe Nomi Malone (Elizabeth Berkley) hitches a ride for Vegas. Once there, she has the good fortune of being rescued by the only decent, unexploitative person in all of Vegas, Molly (Gina Ravera), who takes her in at her modest trailer-park home.

Through Molly, who's a costumer, Nomi gets to glimpse the gaudy "Goddess" show at the Stardust and to briefly meet its star, Cristal Connors (Gina Gershon). This world holds Nomi's dream, but for the moment she's got to endure working at Cheetahs strip joint. Aspiring choreographer James Smith (Glenn Plummer) intermittently tries to strike up a friendship.

Nomi is finally able to escape Cheetahs for a spot in the Stardust dance troupe. Cristal, who gives Nomi plenty of long, lingering looks, becomes incensed by the woman's power play of sleeping with her man, Zack (Kyle MacLachlan), and vetoes Nomi's new gig as her understudy, whereupon Nomi pushes Cristal down some stairs backstage, breaking her hip. For good measure, there's a brutal gang-bang rape of Molly.

Pic wobbles between the risible and the merely unconvincing throughout. For all the time spent backstage, no effort is made to convey a credible or detailed picture of the lives of the (mostly) women who populate this world. Worse is that, with the exception of Molly and, to a lesser extent, James (the film's two black characters), everyone in the picture is a selfish, heartless, unsympathetic user.

As Berkley plays her, Nomi is harsh, graceless and quickly tiresome. Gershon has a little fun with her queen-of-the-fleshpot role. Tech contributions are suitably gaudy and ostentatious.

•

SHOW PEOPLE

1928, 63 mins, US b/w

Dir King Vidor **Scr** Wanda Tuchock, Ralph Spence **Ph** John Arnold **Ed** Hugh Wynn **Art** Cedric Gibbons

Act Marion Davies, William Haines, Dell Henderson, Paul Ralli, Tenen Holtz, Harry Gribbon (M-G-M)

As an entertainment *Show People* is a good number. It has laughs, studio atmosphere galore, intimate glimpses of various stars, considerable Hollywood geography, and just enough sense and plausibility to hold it together.

As a document of Hollywood it presents some peculiar angles. When Peggy Pepper (Marion Davies) gets the w.k. swell head she is seen to be the complacent girlfriend of her leading man, an insufferably conceited stuffed shirt. The odd part of this leading man character is that he (Paul Ralli) looks, dresses and acts like John Gilbert, star of the company which produced the picture. The satire seems pretty sharply pointed at times.

Davies is obviously mimicking the peculiar pucker of the lips identified with Mae Murray, former M-G-M star. However, at other times the story suggests the career of Gloria Swanson, particularly with emphasis upon the custard pie gal becoming an emotional actress. Bebe Daniels is also suggested.

•

SHUTTERED ROOM, THE

1966, 99 mins, UK col

Dir David Greene **Prod** Phillip Hazelton **Scr** D. B. Ledrov, Nathaniel Tanchuck **Ph** Ken Hodges **Ed** Brian Smedley-Aston **Mus** Basil Kirchin **Art** Brian Eatwell

Act Gig Young, Carol Lynley, Oliver Reed, Flora Robson, William Devlin, Bernard Kay (Seven Arts)

With a good quota of shudders and a neat suggestion of evil throughout, this is an efficient entry in a somewhat old-fashioned vein of melodrama. Although supposedly taking place in New England, the locations are blatantly British scenery.

Susannah Kelton (Carol Lynley) has inherited an old millhouse on a remote island, and turns up there with husband Mike (Gig Young) to take possession. A prolog already has warned that there's a mad dame locked up in an upper story. Ethan (Oliver Reed), who heads a mischievous gang of layabouts, surveys her with a morose and lascivious eye.

The script is adequate in the plotting but feeble in the dialog department, sparking off untoward laughs in the wrong places. Lynley is competently scared throughout. And Reed brings a brooding touch of lechery to the over-excited Ethan.

•

SHY PEOPLE

1987, 118 mins, US col

Dir Andrei Konchalovsky **Prod** Menahem Golan, Yoram Globus **Scr** Gerard Brach, Andrei Konchalovsky, Marjorie David **Ph** Chris Menges **Ed** Alain Jakubowicz **Mus** Tangerine Dream **Art** Steve Marsh

Act Jill Clayburgh, Barbara Hershey, Martha Plimpton, Merritt Butrick, John Philbin, Don Swayze (Cannon)

Cosmopolitan writer Diana Sullivan (Jill Clayburgh) lives in splendid disharmony in New York with her teenage daughter Grace (Martha Plimpton). Clayburgh is totally in her element as a spoiled middle-age woman trying to cope with her too-hip daughter.

They are soon out of their element, though, when they travel to Louisiana. It is not simply a case of invaders from civilization soiling a pure culture; story is deepened by the exploration of family ties. What they find when they arrive is Ruth Sullivan (Barbara Hershey), the matriarch of a family of three sons, one of whom is kept in a cage and another retarded, plus a pregnant daughter (Mare Winningham).

Director Andrei Konchalovsky and cinematographer Chris Menges offer a slow and seductive descent into this world of alligators and primordial beauty.

Clayburgh gives one of her best performances and seems right at home with the ticks and self-centered mannerisms of a modern woman. Plimpton nearly steals the show with her mixture of girlish brashness and suggestive sexuality.

•

SIBLING RIVALRY

1990, 88 mins, US col

Dir Carl Reiner **Prod** David V. Lester, Don Miller, Liz Glotzer **Scr** Martha Goldhirsh **Ph** Reynaldo Villalobos **Ed** Bud Molin **Mus** Jack Elliott **Art** Jeannine Claudia Oppewall

Act Kirstie Alley, Bill Pullman, Carrie Fisher, Jami Gertz, Scott Bakula, Sam Elliott (Castle Rock/Nelson)

In her first solo-starring vehicle, Kirstie Alley—who plays the creatively stifled wife of a stuffy young doctor (Scott Bakula)—comes into her own with a flamboyant, highly physical performance. Her adulterous hop in the sack with mystery hunk Sam Elliott results in his death by heart attack after strenuous lovemaking. What follows involves three sets of siblings: Alley and her slightly ditzy younger sister and rival (Jami Gertz); weird vertical blinds salesman Bill Pullman as the black sheep younger brother of upwardly mobile cop Ed O'Neil; and the massive clan of doctors comprising Bakula, his sister (Carrie Fisher) and brother (Elliott).

The surprise that Elliott turns out to be Alley's brother-in-law is effectively developed and launches several hilarious setpieces. Pullman and Alley are united in crime after Pullman thinks *he* accidentally killed Elliott with his vertical blinds equipment. Both he and Alley attempt to cover up the fatality as a suicide.

Though the rushed happy ending doesn't ring true, *Sibling Rivalry* creates a cheerful mood from morbid material. Carl Reiner directs swiftly and efficiently, getting maximum yocks out of borderline vulgar content.

•

SICILIAN, THE

1987, 115 mins, US col

Dir Michael Cimino **Prod** Michael Cimino, Joann Carelli **Scr** Steve Shagan **Ph** Alex Thomson **Ed** Francoise Bonnot **Mus** David Mansfield **Art** Wolf Kroeger

Act Christopher Lambert, Terence Stamp, Joss Ackland, John Turturro, Barbara Sukowa, Ray McAnally (Gladden/Beckerman)

The Sicilian represents a botched telling of the life of post-war outlaw leader Salvatore Giuliano. Just who contributed to what parts of the botching remain a mystery, since uncredited hands cut 30 minutes from the version director Michael Cimino delivered. [The 145-minute version was later released on video, and theatrically in Europe.]

Cimino seems to be aiming for an operatic telling of the short career of the violent 20th-century folk hero [based on Mario Puzo's novel], but falls into an uncomfortable middle ground between European artfulness and stock Hollywood conventions.

Saga served as the basis of Francesco Rosi's 1962 *Salvatore Giuliano*, and has at its core a popular young man who, working from the mountains, employs increasingly excessive means to further his dream of achieving radical land distribution from the titled estate owners to the peasants. Giuliano unhesitatingly kills anyone he thinks has betrayed him, and maintains a semi-adversarial, curiously equivocal relationship with both the Catholic Church and the all-powerful Mafia.

In the lead, Christophe (billed in U.S. projects as Christopher) Lambert betrays little inner conflict or sense of thought, and simply does not make Giuliano interesting.

Coming off by far the best is Joss Ackland, who makes the Mafia chieftain a warm, sympathetic man one enjoys being around. Richard Bauer makes a strong impression as an adviser and go-between for Giuliano and the Mafia, and Giulia Boschi is strikingly, seriously beautiful as the hero's wife.

•

SID AND NANCY

1986, 111 mins, UK col

Dir Alex Cox **Prod** Eric Fellner **Scr** Alex Cox, Abbe Wool **Ph** Roger Deakins **Ed** David Martin **Mus** The Pogues, Pray for Rain **Art** Andrew McAlpine

Act Gary Oldman, Chloe Webb, David Hayman, Drew Schofield, Debby Bishop, Tony London (Embassy/Zenith/Initial)

Sid and Nancy is the definitive pic on the punk phenomenon. The sad, sordid story of Sid Vicious, a lead member of The Sex Pistols, and his relationship with his American girlfriend, Nancy Spungen, is presented by Alex Cox without flinching. Authenticity is the film's major asset.

It's a world of drugs and booze, with sex lagging behind in interest for the most part. But grim as much of the film is, it's not without humor. With his unwashed hair sticking out at all angles, his pale face and brash British accent, Gary Oldman fits the part like a glove. Chloe Webb doesn't spare her looks as the ravaged, shrill Nancy. Both actors are beyond praise.

The film's dialog is extremely rough, the settings sordid, the theme of wasted lives (and talent?) depressing. But *Sid and Nancy* is a dynamic piece of work, which brings audiences as close as possible to understanding its wayward heroes.

•

SIDDHARTHA

1972, 95 mins, US col

Dir Conrad Rooks **Prod** Conrad Rooks **Scr** Conrad Rooks **Ph** Sven Nykvist **Ed** Willy Kemplen **Mus** Hemanta Kumar **Art** Malcolm Golding

Act Shashi Kapoor, Simi Garewal, Romesh Sharma, Pincho Kapoor, Zul Vellani, Amrik Singh (Lotus)

Conrad Rooks's second pic, *Siddhartha*, based on the 1922 book by Hermann Hesse, takes place 2,500 years ago in

India. It is about a well-to-do young Brahmin who feels he must leave home and find himself and also echoes a man questing for nirvana in a confused society.

Rooks has chosen to give this a surface elegance which sometimes robs the film of its needed earthiness and sensuality in its love angle and more robustness in detailing the vagaries of social aspects and values at the time. But it does have a fine photographic beauty in the hands of Swedish lenser Sven Nykvist.

Siddhartha, after leaving his father, roams with a friend for years, with a group of holy men. Then he meets a great teacher who preaches the need for one's own way to inner harmony who may be the Buddha himself.

•

SIDEKICKS

1993, 100 mins, US Ⓥ ⊙ col

Dir Aaron Norris ***Prod*** Don Carmody ***Scr*** Don Thompson, Lou Illar ***Ph*** Joao Fernandes ***Ed*** David Rawlins, Bernard Weiser ***Mus*** Alan Silvestri ***Art*** Reuben Freed

Act Chuck Norris, Beau Bridges, Jonathan Brandis, Mako, Julia Nickson-Soul, Joe Piscopo (Gallery)

Imagine a cross between *The Karate Kid* and *The Secret Life of Walter Mitty*, and you'll know what to expect from *Sidekicks*, an off-beat family-audience opus from, of all people, action star Chuck Norris.

Norris's presence dominates pic, but the lead character is a daydreaming teen (Jonathan Brandis), an asthmatic outsider who's mocked by many of his peers, harassed by most of his teachers, and ignored by his computer-programmer dad (Beau Bridges). So the boy seeks refuge in heroic fantasies where he is the brave and resourceful sidekick of his favorite action movie hero (Norris).

Film is peppered with moderately clever daydream sequences modeled after (and featuring brief excerpts from) such Norris movies as *Missing in Action*, *Lone Wolf McQuade* and *The Hit Man*.

Coached by the sage uncle (Mako) of his only compassionate teacher (Julia Nickson-Soul), Brandis quickly picks up enough martial arts skill to compete in a karate tournament against his school's worst bully (a punkish John Buchanan).

Brandis is appealing and persuasively intense; Danica McKellar is passably sweet as a classmate who feels sorry for, then falls for him.

•

SIEGE, THE

1998, 116 mins, US Ⓥ ⊙ ⊗ col

Dir Edward Zwick ***Prod*** Lynda Obst, Edward Zwick ***Scr*** Lawrence Wright, Menno Meyjes, Edward Zwick ***Ph*** Roger Deakins ***Ed*** Steven Rosenblum ***Mus*** Graeme Revell ***Art*** Lilly Kilvert

Act Denzel Washington, Annette Bening, Bruce Willis, Tony Shalhoub, Sami Bouajila, David Proval (20th Century-Fox)

A potentially provacative idea is played out to diminishing returns in *The Siege*. Opening reels concerning the FBI's efforts to thwart terrorists in New York City possess some grit, power and verve. But as the stakes mount and Bruce Willis marches onto the scene as a power-hungry general carried away with his exercise of martial law, Edward Zwick's attempt to extend recent history into a hypothetical nightmare scenario descends into stock, generalized action and almost cartoon-like confrontations.

With its tense standoffs, bleached images, edgy cutting and the can-do professionalism of the characters, first act has some crackle and pop, as FBI Terrorism Task Force chief Anthony Hubbard (Denzel Washington) mobilizes his Gotham-based team to get to the bottom of a bomb threat and hostage situation.

Much of the early going consists of cat-and-mouse pursuits through Brooklyn's ethnic neighborhoods. In the process, Hub crosses paths, and trades barbs, with undercover National Security Agency operative Elise Kraft (Annette Bening), a Middle East specialist. In the long run the two agents need each other to crack a difficult case.

When a massive explosion at a Broadway theater wipes out scores of Manhattan culturati, the attacks come at an alarming pace. Washington demands action, and Gen. William Devereaux (Willis) heads the massive force deployed on the streets of Manhattan and Brooklyn when the president declares martial law.

The Arabs, who are strictly cardboard-cutouts, are bad enough, but Willis's tough-guy general single-handedly changes the character of the film from an ambitious, serious-minded thriller to a one-dimensional "my cojones are bigger than yours" bazooka-fest.

Lead performances are as good as the limited range of the film will allow. Massive scenes of traffic gridlock, police action and troops marching must have repped a pain in the neck for filmmakers and New Yorkers alike.

•

SIEGE OF SIDNEY STREET, THE

1960, 93 mins, UK ⊏⊐ b/w

Dir Robert S. Baker, Monty Berman ***Prod*** Robert S. Baker, Monty Berman ***Scr*** Jimmy Sangster, Alexander Baron ***Ph*** Robert S. Baker, Monty Berman ***Ed*** Peter Bezencenet ***Mus*** Stanley Black ***Art*** William Kellner

Act Donald Sinden, Nicole Maurey, Kieron Moore, Peter Wyngarde, Leonard Sachs, T. P. McKenna (Mid-Century)

This turns out to be quite a lively version of a gangster episode that had the East End of London on its ears early in 1911. It's a re-vamp [from a story by Jimmy Sangster] of the celebrated incident when a gang of Russians brought out the police and the army before they could be smoked out of their hideout in Sidney Street.

In straightforward fashion, this shows Donald Sinden as a dedicated police officer who patiently tracks down the gang of Russian patriots, led by a character named Peter the Painter (Peter Wyngarde). They robbed allegedly to gain funds for their cause, which was anarchy. By disguising himself as a down-and-outer, Sinden eventually gets the thugs penned up.

The result was one of the bloodiest gangster scenes that London has ever known. The East End of London in 1911 is vividly brought to life, direction is sound without being overemphasized while the final siege is an exciting sock climax.

Wyngarde gives an alert, strong portrayal of the quiet but ruthless top gangster. Kieron Moore, a trigger-happy lieutenant, and Leonard Sachs, as an older but equally devoted member of the cause, are also first-rate.

Sinden, as the cop, tends to play much on same note, but his is a comparatively colorless role compared with those of the Russo thugs.

•

SIEGFRIED

SEE: DIE NIBELUNGEN

SIEGFRIEDS TOD

•

SIESTA

1987, 97 mins, US/UK Ⓥ ⊙ col

Dir Mary Lambert ***Prod*** Gary Kurfirst, Chris Brown ***Scr*** Patricia Louisianna Knop ***Ph*** Bryan Loftus ***Ed*** Glenn A. Morgan ***Mus*** Marcus Miller ***Art*** John Beard

Act Ellen Barkin, Gabriel Byrne, Julian Sands, Isabella Rossellini, Martin Sheen, Jodie Foster (Lorimar/Siren/Palace)

First feature film by Mary Lambert, best known for her Madonna videos, is a densely packed portrait of a beautiful, disturbed woman at the end of her rope. Told in a fragmented, time-jumping style, this subjective, hallucinatory recollection of a five-day descent into hell sustains intense interest throughout, to a great extent because of Ellen Barkin's extravagantly fine performance in the leading role.

In its elaborate, jigsaw-puzzle way, film [from the novel by Patrice Chaplin] tells of how Barkin, a daredevil skydiver, impulsively leaves her home and husband in Death Valley for a quick trip to Spain to find the man she still loves, trapeze artist Gabriel Byrne, who also has married someone else, Isabella Rossellini.

Although due back in California imminently for a big commercial payday, Barkin lets her desire for Byrne prolong her Spanish sojourn past the deadline. She falls in with a dissolute, aimless English crowd led by Julian Sands and Jodie Foster and finally becomes utterly lost and delirious, helpless at the hands of filthy-minded taxi driver Alexei Sayle.

Byrne puts on a continuous smoldering act as the sought-after lover, Martin Sheen is all congenial American hype as Barkin's abandoned husband, and Jodie Foster, as a snooty but friendly socialite, has fun with a British accent.

•

SIGN OF THE CROSS, THE

1932, 115 mins, US b/w

Dir Cecil B. DeMille ***Prod*** Cecil B. DeMille ***Scr*** Waldemar Young, Sidney Buchman ***Ph*** Karl Struss ***Ed*** Anne Bauchens ***Mus*** Rudolph Kopp

Act Fredric March, Claudette Colbert, Elissa Landi, Charles Laughton, Ian Keith (Paramount)

Religion triumphant over paganism. And the soul is stronger than the flesh. Religion gets the breaks, even though its followers all get killed in this picture. It's altogether a moral victory.

For example, the handsome Prefect of Rome (Fredric March) sees that he can't get to first base with the Christian maiden (Elissa Landi), so he calls in the village temptress, Ancaria (Joyzelle Joyner), for help. Ancaria is described as the hottest gal in town. "The most versatile" is the phrase used. She uses her arts on Landi. In the street the other Christian martyrs are marching to their doom, singing hymns bravely as they go. Their chants disrupts and finally drowns out the temptress's routine, and she strikes the unmoved Landi in the face. Then, having lost, she walks.

Besides Ancaria, there is Charles Laughton's expert Nero, who doubles as the degenerate emperor and musical pyromaniac as Rome burns. Most of the last half is taken up with a bloody festival staged by crazy Caesar in the arena.

Cast is uniformly good, but only one exceptional performance is registered. That's Laughton's. With utmost subtlety and a minimum of effort he manages to get over his queer character before his first appearance is a minute old.

Claudette Colbert [as Poppaea] and Landi and March and Ian Keith [as Tigellinus] are called upon chiefly to look their parts, and they manage. Frequently some badly written and often silly dialog holds them down.

1932/33: NOMINATION: Best Cinematography

•

SIGN OF THE PAGAN

1954, 91 mins, US ⊏⊐ col

Dir Douglas Sirk ***Prod*** Albert J. Cohen ***Scr*** Oscar Brodney, Barre Lyndon ***Ph*** Russell Metty ***Ed*** Al Clark ***Mus*** Frank Skinner, Hans J. Salter ***Art*** Alexander Golitzen, Emrich Nicholson

Act Jeff Chandler, Jack Palance, Ludmilla Tcherina, Rita Gam, Jeff Morrow, George Dolenz (Universal)

Unlike most screen spectacles, *Sign of the Pagan*'s running time is a tight 91 minutes, in which the flash of the Roman Empire period is not permitted to slow down the telling of an interesting action story.

Plot [from a story by Oscar Brodney] deals with Attila the Hun, the Scourge of God, and his sweep across Europe some 1,500 years ago. Particularly noteworthy is the treatment of the barbarian in writing and direction, and in the manner in which Jack Palance interprets the character. Instead of a straight, all-evil person, he is a human being with some good here and there to shade and make understandable the bad. Douglas Sirk's direction of the excellent script catches the sweep of the period portrayed without letting the characters get lost in spectacle. Representing good in the plot is Jeff Chandler, centurion made a general by his princess, Ludmilla Tcherina, to fight off Attila's advancing hordes.

With Palance scoring so solidly in his role of Attila, he makes the other performers seem less colorful, although Chandler is good as Marcian.

•

SIGN O' THE TIMES

1987, 85 mins, US Ⓥ col

Dir Prince ***Prod*** Robert Cavallo, Joseph Ruffalo, Steven Fragnoli ***Ph*** Peter Sinclair, Jerry Watson ***Ed*** Steve Purcell ***Mus*** Billy Youdelman, Susan Rogers (sup.) ***Art*** Leroy Bennett (Cavallo Ruffalo & Fragnoli)

Following his disastrous, hubris-drenched fling as a leading man in the non-musical, glossy b&w fantasy *Under the Cherry Moon*, Prince Rogers Nelson of Minneapolis wisely has returned with a polychromatic concert performance film that should draw anyone who got a charge of out his classic rock 'n' roll romance pic *Purple Rain*.

Shot on location at a music hall in Rotterdam and at the musician's studio in Minnesota, *Sign O' the Times* is a filmed treatment of Prince's touring show of 14 songs from his hit lp of the same name. Defiantly carnal in the face of AIDS-era safe sexiness, the Prince revue is set in a *film noir* fantasy zone where the come-hither blinking of gaudy neon honky-tonk signs flashes over an idealized back-alley netherworld. There, strong-willed, Nautilus-sinewed, lascivious women—lissom gladiatrixes of rock 'n' roll bloodsport—challenge the sexual imperatives of Princely machismo.

Posing, pouting and pirouetting with androgynous abandon, pushing his guitar into ethereal, upper-register soundstorms and giving supple voice to songs of sensual and emotional free-fall in an anomic contemporary world, Prince provides musicvideo addicts with a pure fix of visual and aural synchronicity.

•

SILENCE, THE

SEE: TYSTNADEN

•

SILENCE OF THE LAMBS, THE

1991, 118 mins, US Ⓥ ⊙ col

Dir Jonathan Demme ***Prod*** Edward Saxon, Kenneth Utt, Ron Bozman ***Scr*** Ted Tally ***Ph*** Tak Fujimoto ***Ed*** Craig McKay ***Mus*** Howard Shore ***Art*** Kristi Zea

Act Jodie Foster, Anthony Hopkins, Scott Glenn, Ted Levine, Brooke Smith, Diane Baker (Orion/Strong Heart)

Skillful adaptation of Thomas Harris's bestseller intelligently wallows in the fascination for aberrant psychology and perverse evil.

Sharp script charts tenacious efforts of young FBI recruit Clarice Starling (Jodie Foster) to cope with the appalling challenges of her first case. Confounded by a series of grotesque murders committed by someone known only as "Buffalo Bill," bureau special agent Jack Crawford (Scott Glenn) asks his female protege to seek the help of the American prison system's No. 1 resident monster in fashioning a psychological profile of the killer.

Dr. Hannibal Lecter (Anthony Hopkins) has been kept in a dungeon-like cell for eight years, and while officious doctors and investigators can get nothing out of him, he is willing to play ball with his attractive new inquisitor. Lecter gives Starling clues as to the killer's identity in exchange for details about her past.

Just as it seems the noose is tightening around the killer, Lecter, in a remarkably fine suspense sequence, manages an unthinkable escape.

Plot is as tight as a coiled rattler. Foster fully registers the inner strength her character must summon up. Scott Glenn is a very agreeable surprise as the FBI agent who takes a chance by putting his young charge on the case. Hopkins, helped by some highly dramatic lighting, makes the role the personification of brilliant, hypnotic evil, and the screen jolts with electricity whenever he is on.

1991: Best Picture, Director, Actor (Anthony Hopkins), Actress (Jodie Foster), Adapted Screenplay

NOMINATIONS: Best Editing, Sound

•

SILENCERS, THE

1966, 103 mins, US Ⓥ ⦿ col

Dir Phil Karlson ***Prod*** Irving Allen ***Scr*** Oscar Saul ***Ph*** Burnett Guffey ***Ed*** Charles Nelson ***Mus*** Elmer Bernstein ***Art*** Joe Wright

Act Dean Martin, Stella Stevens, Daliah Lavi, Victor Buono, Arthur O'Connell, Cyd Charisse (Meadway/Claude)

Dean Martin—as Matt Helm, ace of the American counterespionage agency, ICE—succeeds in a kind of lover-boy way in taking his place up there with such stalwarts as Sean Connery, James Coburn and David Niven. Produced by Irving Allen and directed by Phil Karlson, both utilizing shock technique, the fastdriving screenplay is based on two of Donald Hamilton's Matt Helm books, *The Silencers* and *Death of a Citizen*.

Plot focuses on a Chinese agent (Victor Buono) who masterminds a ring that plans to divert a U.S. missile so it will destroy Alamogordo, New Mexico, thus creating wide devastation and atomic fallout leading perhaps to global war. All Matt Helm has to do is halt this catastrophe. Starring with Martin are Stella Stevens and Daliah Lavi. Stevens does herself proud as a mixed-up living doll who can stumble over her own shadow. Lavi is a femme fatale, Martin's ever-lovin' spymate who comes up with a big surprise for him. The glamor department is further repped by Cyd Charisse as a dancer killed by the mob as she's dancing.

•

SILENT ENEMY, THE

1958, 112 mins, UK Ⓥ b/w

Dir William Fairchild ***Prod*** Bertram Ostrer ***Scr*** William Fairchild ***Ph*** Otto Heller ***Ed*** Alan Osbiston ***Mus*** William Alwyn ***Art*** Bill Andrews

Act Laurence Harvey, Dawn Addams, Michael Craig, John Clements, Gianna Maria Canale, Arnoldo Foa (Romulus)

The Silent Enemy [from the book *Commander Crabb* by Marshall Pugh] tells the remarkable story of Lieutenant Crabb, a young naval bomb disposal officer, whose exploits in leading frogmen against the Italians earned him a George Medal. It makes smooth, impressive drama, done without heroics, but with excitement.

Laurence Harvey arrives in Gibraltar in 1941 to tackle the Italian menace that is striking successfully at key shipping in the area. With courage and determination, he becomes an experienced diver. Harvey is brash, intolerant of red tape, but fired with drive.

Without permission, Harvey and Michael Craig, one of the seamen, slip across to Spain and discover that the enemy base is in an interned Italian ship. The hull has been converted so that the frogmen can come and go underwater without being seen.

The impatience of the men as they wait to strike, the rigorous training and, above all, the feeling of men doing a thankless and arduous job with a quiet sense of duty are all admirably portrayed. The remarkable underwater scenes give this polished film a sock impact.

•

SILENT FALL

1994, 100 mins, US Ⓥ col

Dir Bruce Beresford ***Prod*** James A. Robinson ***Scr*** Akiva Goldsman ***Ph*** Peter James ***Ed*** Ian Crafford ***Mus*** Stewart Copeland ***Art*** David Bomba

Act Richard Dreyfuss, Linda Hamilton, John Lithgow, J. T. Walsh, Ben Faulkner, Liv Tyler (Morgan Creek/Warner)

An awkward synthesis of autism as a clinical problem and family abuse as a social issue, *Silent Fall* is a well crafted murder mystery that unfortunately is short on excitement and genuine suspense.

Richard Dreyfuss plays Jake Rainer, a once-prominent psychiatrist. Jake is forced out of his profession and emotional stupor when a bizarre double murder occurs at the Warden's estate. There are no obvious clues, but there are the two witnesses: Tim Warden (Ben Faulkner), an autistic 9-year-old boy, and his overly protective sister (Liv Tyler).

At first, he's reluctant to get involved, which gives his wife (Linda Hamilton) plenty of ammunition for accusing him of being a failure. It's only when his rival, the stern Dr. Harlinger (John Lithgow), subjects Tim to his notorious authoritarian treatment that Jake takes the child under his wing.

After an hour or so, pic changes gears and turns into a rather conventional thriller. As such, it depends on offering twists and revelations, and the chief problem is that pic provides so many clues that it's possible to unravel the killer's identity long before the finale.

Dreyfuss renders one of his more restrained and effective performances, holding the entire picture together. It's refreshing to see the muscled Hamilton in a non-action pic, but as Jake's suffering wife, she plays a thankless role.

•

SILENT MOVIE

1976, 86 mins, US Ⓥ ⦿ col

Dir Mel Brooks ***Prod*** Michael Hertzberg ***Scr*** Mel Brooks, Ron Clark, Rudy DeLuca, Barry Levinson ***Ph*** Paul Lohmann ***Ed*** John C. Howard, Stanford C. Allen ***Mus*** John Morris ***Art*** Al Brenner

Act Mel Brooks, Marty Feldman, Dom DeLuise, Bernadette Peters, Sid Caesar, Harold Gould (20th Century-Fox)

It took a lot of chutzpah for Mel Brooks to make *Silent Movie* a film with only one word of dialog in an almost non-stop parade of sight gags. Brooks, Marty Feldman, and Dom DeLuise head the cast as a has-been director and his zany cronies, conning studio chief Sid Caesar into making their silent film as a desperate ploy to prevent takeover of the studio by the Engulf & Devour conglomerate, headed by villainous Harold Gould. The parallels with realities are drolly satiric.

The slender plot of *Silent Movie* [from a story by Ron Clark] is basically a hook for slapstick antics, some feeble and some very fine (notably a wonderful nightclub tango with Anne Bancroft). Harry Ritz, Charlie Callas, Henny Youngman and the late Liam Dunn are standouts.

•

SILENT PARTNER, THE

1979, 103 mins, Canada Ⓥ ⦿ col

Dir Daryl Duke ***Prod*** Joel B. Michaels, Stephen Young ***Scr*** Curtis Hanson ***Ph*** Billy Williams ***Mus*** Oscar Peterson ***Art*** Trevor Williams

Act Susannah York, Christopher Plummer, Elliott Gould, Celine Lomez, Ken Pogue, John Candy (EMC)

The *Silent Partner* is one of the films that run the gamut from intrigue to violence. Filmed entirely in Toronto, it's an independently financed film which won six Canadian Film Awards.

Christopher Plummer plays the villain for a change—a bank robber. Elliott Gould is a bank clerk who finds out that Plummer, dressed in a Santa Claus suit, plans a robbery. Susannah York is a bank employee under pressure from Plummer and newcomer Celine Lomez is a cohort of Plummer.

The story [from the novel *Think of a Number* by Anders Bodelson] has Gould, a teller in a branch office, get suspicious when it is the Christmas season and the bank is filled with shoppers. The robber hits and Gould's alertness inspires him to hide $50,000 in a lunch box with the police believing that the robber has all the loot.

•

SILENT RAGE

1982, 100 mins, US Ⓥ ⦿ col

Dir Michael Miller ***Prod*** Anthony B. Unger ***Scr*** Joseph Fraley ***Ph*** Robert Jessup, Neil Roach ***Ed*** Richard C. Meyer ***Mus*** Peter Bernstein, Mark Goldenberg ***Art*** Jack Marty

Act Chuck Norris, Ron Silver, Steven Keats, Toni Kalem, William Finley, Brian Libby (Unger/Topkick)

Silent Rage seems as if it were made with a demographics sampler entitled "10 Sleazy Ways to Cash in on the Exploitation Market." The result is a combination horror-kung-fu-oater-woman-in-peril-mad-scientist film with more unintentional laughs than possible in the space of 100 minutes.

The scenario goes something like this—a sweaty, crazy young man chops a woman and another man to death. Our hero of the day, Chuck Norris (the sheriff), catches him but the guy is shot by some overanxious law enforcers.

The run-of-the-mill crime story? Of course not. One of the hospital surgeons happens to be a mad scientist who has been working on a formula to speed up the human healing process. All he needs is a human guinea pig. Now we have a murderer who is not only crazy but indestructible.

•

SILENT RUNNING

1972, 89 mins, US Ⓥ ⦿ col

Dir Douglas Trumbull ***Prod*** Michael Gruskoff ***Scr*** Deric Washburn, Michael Cimino, Steven Bocho ***Ph*** Charles F. Wheeler ***Ed*** Aaron Stell ***Mus*** Peter Schickele ***Art*** [uncredited]

Act Bruce Dern, Cliff Potts, Ron Rifkin, Jesse Vint (Universal)

Silent Running depends on the excellent special effects of debuting director Douglas Trumbull and his team and on the appreciation of a literate but broadly entertaining script. Those being the highlights, they are virtually wiped out by the crucial miscasting of Bruce Dern. As a result, the production lacks much dramatic credibility and often teeters on the edge of the ludicrous.

Dern and three clod companions man a space vehicle in a fleet of airships containing vegetation in case the earth again can support that type of life. But the program is scuttled, all hands are recalled, but Dern decides to mutiny. In the process, he kills his three shipmates and goes deeper into space. His only companions are two small robots, whose life-like qualities are rather touching.

•

SILENT TONGUE

1993, 106 mins, France/US Ⓥ ⦿ ▭ col

Dir Sam Shepard ***Prod*** Carolyn Pfeiffer, Ludi Boeken ***Scr*** Sam Shepard ***Ph*** Jack Conroy ***Ed*** Bill Yahraus ***Mus*** Patrick O'Hearn ***Art*** Cary White

Act Alan Bates, Richard Harris, Dermot Mulroney, River Phoenix, Sheila Tousey, Jeri Arredondo (Canal Plus/Belbo/Alive)

Sam Shepard transplants a couple of his famously dysfunctional families to the Old West in *Silent Tongue*, a bizarre, meandering and, finally, maddening mystic-oater, the first Western financed entirely with French money.

The sins of the fathers are distinctly visited upon the sons in this loosely knit yarn, with the characters literally haunted by the ghosts of those they wronged. Result is an unpalatable combination of prairie melodrama, Greek tragedy, Japanese ghost tale and traveling minstrel show, staged with little sense of style and cinematic rhythm.

Richard Harris arrives in search of Alan Bates, a drunken Irish charlatan of the first order. Bates had sold Harris his half-Indian daughter (Sheila Tousey), who married Harris's son (River Phoenix). Tousey has since died in childbirth, driving Phoenix to the brink of madness. Hoping to cure his son's delirium, Harris kidnaps Bates's second daughter (Jeri Arredondo) and takes her back to Phoenix.

The dialog is mostly rambling and unmemorable and, in the case of Bates and his brogue-tinted blustering, indecipherable.

•

SILENT TOUCH, THE

1993, 100 mins, UK/Poland/Denmark Ⓥ ⦿ col

Dir Krzysztof Zanussi ***Prod*** Mark Forstater ***Scr*** Peter Morgan, Mark Wadlow ***Ph*** Jaroslav Zamojda ***Ed*** Marek Denys ***Mus*** Wojciech Kilar ***Art*** Ewa Braun

Act Max von Sydow, Lothaire Bluteau, Sarah Miles, Sofie Grabol, Aleksander Bardini, Peter Hesse Overgaard (Forstater/Tor/Metronome)

After years of directing brilliant and complex Polish films, Krzysztof Zanussi has helmed a simple and moving breakthrough pic about a crotchety old composer coaxed out of retirement by an inspired musicologist and a sweet young muse.

Max von Sydow delivers a definitive performance as a silenced classic composer and Holocaust survivor who reblossoms from a miserable old drinker into a meticulous artist when Stefan (Lothaire Bluteau) arrives as "guardian angel." Casting is superb, though Sarah Miles's stiff delivery (in the wife role) is pic's drawback.

Bluteau (*Jesus of Montreal*) does his usual low-key routine to perfection as the Polish music student who becomes obsessed with a melody he hears in his sleep (thesp's Quebecois accent is a non-issue in the film). Stefan tracks down von Sydow in Copenhagen and, after much (believable) resistance, convinces him to compose a complex symphony on his neglected piano. Love interests take fascinating twists as loyal wife Miles reluctantly accepts her husband's music secretary (Danish thesp Sophie Grabol, a fresh screen presence) as his young lover.

•

SILKEN SKIN
SEE: LA PEAU DOUCE

•

SILK STOCKINGS
1957, 117 mins, US Ⓥ ⊙ ⊏⊐ col
Dir Rouben Mamoulian ***Prod*** Arthur Freed ***Scr*** Leonard Gershe, Leonard Spigelgass ***Ph*** Robert Bronner ***Ed*** Harold F. Kress ***Mus*** Andre Previn (dir.), Conrad Salinger (arr.) ***Art*** William A. Horning, Randall Duell
Act Fred Astaire, Cyd Charisse, Janis Paige, Peter Lorre, Jules Munshin, Joseph Buloff (M-G-M)

Silk Stockings has Fred Astaire and Cyd Charisse, the music of Cole Porter and comes off as a top-grade musical version of Metro's 1939 *Ninotchka*. Adapted from the [1955] Broadway musical adaptation of same tag, film has two new Porter songs and a total of 13 numbers. Astaire enacts an American film producer in Paris who falls for the beautiful Commie when she arrives from Moscow to check on the activities of three Russian commissars.

Rouben Mamoulian in his deft direction maintains a flowing if over-long course. Musical numbers are bright, inserted naturally, and both Astaire and Charisse shine in dancing department, together and singly. Choreography is by Hermes Pan (Astaire numbers) and Eugene Loring (others).

Janis Paige shares top honors with the stars for a knock-'em-dead type of performance, George Tobias has a few good moments as a Commie chief, and commissar trio Peter Lorre, Jules Munshin and Joseph Buloff are immense.

•

SILKWOOD
1983, 128 mins, US Ⓥ ⊙ col
Dir Mike Nichols ***Prod*** Mike Nichols, Michael Hausman ***Scr*** Nora Ephron, Alice Arlen ***Ph*** Miroslav Ondricek ***Ed*** Sam O'Steen ***Mus*** Georges Delerue ***Art*** Patrizia Von Brandenstein
Act Meryl Streep, Kurt Russell, Cher, Craig T. Nelson, Diana Scarwid, Fred Ward (ABC)

A very fine biographical drama, *Silkwood* concerns Karen Silkwood, a nuclear materials factory worker who mysteriously died just before she was going to blow the whistle on her company's presumed slipshod methods and cover-ups.

A lowdown, spunky and seemingly uneducated Southern gal whose three kids live elsewhere with their father, Silkwood works long hours at a tedious job which presents the constant threat of radiation contamination. Her home life is rather more unconventional, as she shares a rundown abode with two coworkers, b.f. Kurt Russell and a lesbian friend, Cher. The complexion of their domestic life takes a turn when blonde cowgirl beautician Diana Scarwid moves in with Cher, and at work, Silkwood finds herself increasingly at odds with management after she becomes involved with a union committee fighting decertification of the union at the plant.

Silkwood's death in 1974 was officially ruled an accident, but the story became a cause celebre in the media and among anti-nuke proponents.

1983: NOMINATIONS: Best Director, Actress (Meryl Streep), Supp. Actress (Cher), Original Screenplay, Editing

•

SILVERADO
1985, 132 mins, US Ⓥ ⊙ ⊏⊐ col
Dir Lawrence Kasdan ***Prod*** Lawrence Kasdan ***Scr*** Lawrence Kasdan, Mark Kasdan ***Ph*** John Bailey ***Ed*** Carol Littleton ***Mus*** Bruce Broughton ***Art*** Ida Random
Act Kevin Kline, Scott Glenn, Kevin Costner, Danny Glover, John Cleese, Rosanna Arquette (Columbia)

Rather than relying on legendary heroes of Westerns past, writer-director Lawrence Kasdan with his brother Mark have used their special talent to create a slew of human scale characters against a dramatic backdrop borrowing from all the conventions of the genre. *Silverado* strikes an uneasy balance between the intimate and naturalistic with concerns that are classical and universal.

Drifters Paden (Kevin Kline) and Emmett (Scott Glenn) join fates in the desert and follow their destiny to Silverado where they tangle with the McKendrick clan. Along the way they meet up with Glenn's gun happy brother Jake (Kevin Costner) who they break from a jail guarded by Sheriff Langston (John Cleese).

Modern element in the stew is introduction of Danny Glover, an itinerant black returning to Silverado to rejoin what's left of his family. On the other side of the fence is arch villain Cobb, sheriff of Silverado and puppet of the McKendricks. As Cobb, Brian Dennehy is an actor born to be in Westerns, so powerful is his sense of destruction. Other performances, especially Kline and Glenn, are equally strong. Real rewards of the film are in the visuals and rarely has the West appeared so alive, yet unlike what one carries in his mind's eye. Ida Random's production design is thoroughly convincing in detail.

1985: Best Original Score, Sound

•

SILVER BEARS
1978, 113 mins, US Ⓥ col
Dir Ivan Passer ***Prod*** Alex Winitsky, Arlene Sellers ***Scr*** Peter Stone ***Ph*** Anthony Richmond ***Ed*** Bernard Gribble ***Mus*** Claude Bolling ***Art*** Edward Marshall
Act Michael Caine, Cybill Shepherd, Louis Jourdan, Stephane Audran, Tom Smothers, David Warner (Columbia)

Director Ivan Passer has assembled a rather talented squad of performers, then marched them through a minefield, losing all hands in an attack on an uncertain objective.

Michael Caine goes to Switzerland to set up a bank for mobster Martin Balsam, with the help of Louis Jourdan running swindle one against them. Caine and Jourdan get involved with Stephane Audran and David Warner's swindle two silver-mine in Iran.

Adapted from Paul E. Erdman's novel about international finance, Peter Stone's script keeps the air filled with multimillion dollar figures, confounded hourly but yielding no interest.

Unceasingly cynical, the film lacks a single sympathetic character worth caring about. Everybody lies; everybody swindles; and all the bad guys—and girl—win in the end.

•

SILVER CHALICE, THE
1954, 142 mins, US Ⓥ ⊏⊐ col
Dir Victor Saville ***Prod*** Victor Saville ***Scr*** Lesser Samuels ***Ph*** William V. Skall ***Ed*** George White ***Mus*** Franz Waxman ***Art*** Rolf Gerard, Boris Leven
Act Virginia Mayo, Pier Angeli, Jack Palance, Paul Newman, Natalie Wood, Joseph Wiseman (Warner)

Like the Thomas B. Costain book, the picture is overdrawn and sometimes tedious, but producer-director Victor Saville still manages to instill interest in what's going on, and even hits a feeling of excitement occasionally.

The picture introduces Newman who handles himself well before the cameras. Helping his pic debut is Pier Angeli, and it is their scenes together that add the warmth to what might otherwise have been a cold spectacle.

The plot portrays the struggle of Christians to save for the future the cup from which Christ drank at the Last Supper. On the side of the Christians is a Greek sculptor, played by Newman, who is fashioning a silver chalice to hold the religious symbol. On the side of evil are the decadent Romans, ruled over by an effete Nero, and Simon, the magician (a real character), played by Jack Palance, who wants to use the destruction of the cup to further his own rise to power.

1954: NOMINATIONS: Best Color Cinematography, Scoring of a Dramatic Picture

•

SILVER CITY
1984, 101 mins, Australia Ⓥ ⊏⊐ col
Dir Sophia Turkiewicz ***Prod*** Joan Long ***Scr*** Thomas Keneally, Sophia Turkiewicz ***Ph*** John Seale ***Ed*** Don Saunders ***Mus*** William Motzig ***Art*** Igor Nay
Act Gosia Dobrowolska, Ivar Kants, Anna Jemison, Steve Bisley, Debra Lawrance, Ewa Brok (Limelight)

A passionate love story set against a background of postwar European immigration into Australia is the theme of *Silver City*, an extremely handsome production which introduces vibrant new actress Gosia Dobrowolska.

She plays Nina, a young Polish girl who arrives, bereaved and alone, in Australia in 1948 and becomes one of thousands of citizens of so-called Silver City, a migrant camp outside Sydney. There she meets a fellow Pole, Julian, a former law student, and falls in love with him although he's married to one of her best friends.

This is a film for anyone who has ever left the country of their birth to start a new life in a strange land.

The background to this affair is vividly etched in. Director Sophia Turkiewicz, came to Australia from Poland aged three with her mother, which has provided her with rich material for her first feature.

•

SILVER DREAM RACER
1980, 111 mins, UK Ⓥ ⊏⊐ col
Dir David Wickes ***Prod*** Rene Dupont ***Scr*** David Wickes ***Ph*** Paul Beeson ***Ed*** Peter Hollywood ***Mus*** David Essex, John Cameron (dir.) ***Art*** Malcolm Middleton
Act David Essex, Beau Bridges, Cristina Raines, Harry H. Corbett, Diane Keen, Lee Montague (Rank)

It's about motorcycle racing. But among all the biking footage in a yarn about a "revolutionary" prototype which challenges and, natch, licks all world championship comers, there's not one memorable shot of the machine in action.

That's a big pity, as the model—a genuine prototype built by Britisher Barry Hart—will certainly whet the appetites of two-wheel fans. But the film's action sequences prove generally disappointing.

Plot [from an original story by Michael Billington] is routine, but no worse than many, and the acting does favors for the dialog. Popstar David Essex is a natural as the ingenuous-looking Cockney fellow who can turn on a sneer when needed. Beau Bridges is fine as the loud-mouthed American Goliath against whom David pits his derided British mount.

•

SILVER STREAK
1976, 113 mins, US Ⓥ ⊙ col
Dir Arthur Hiller ***Prod*** Thomas L. Miller, Edward K. Milkis ***Scr*** Colin Higgins ***Ph*** David M. Walsh ***Ed*** David Bretherton ***Mus*** Henry Mancini ***Art*** Alfred Sweeney
Act Gene Wilder, Jill Clayburgh, Richard Pryor, Patrick McGoohan, Ned Beatty, Clifton James (20th Century-Fox)

While falling short of its comedy promise (except when Richard Pryor is on the screen), *Silver Streak* is an okay adventure comedy starring Gene Wilder on the lam from crooked art thieves aboard a transcontinental train.

Wilder, mild-mannered book executive, boards a train for a leisurely trip from Los Angeles to Chicago. Jill Clayburgh, in adjoining compartment, works for an art scholar whose research will expose the fakery of Patrick McGoohan, urbane and despicable villain of the George Sanders–Basil Rathbone school.

Only when Pryor enters the film is there some long-overdue snap and zest. Wilder and Pryor are great together.

1976: NOMINATION: Best Sound

•

SIMPLE MEN
1992, 106 mins, US/UK Ⓥ col
Dir Hal Hartley ***Prod*** Ted Hope, Hal Hartley ***Scr*** Hal Hartley ***Ph*** Michael Spiller ***Ed*** Steve Hamilton ***Mus*** Ned Rifle ***Art*** Dan Ouellette
Act Robert Burke, William Sage, Karen Sillas, Elina Lowensohn, Martin Donovan, John MacKay (Zenith/American Playhouse/True Fiction)

Hal Hartley's *Simple Men* is a beautifully realized American art film. Tale of two brothers' search for their renegade father, and the major life change one of them experiences, possesses exceptional literary and cinematic qualities, as well as emotional resonance new for the director.

Startling opening sequence has small-time criminal Bill McCabe (Robert Burke) doubly betrayed by his g.f., who runs off with their mutual partner and stiffs him of his loot. Meanwhile Bill's father (John MacKay), a radical anarchist on the run, has apparently escaped somewhere on Long Island. Bill's younger brother Dennis (William Sage) is anxious to track the old man down.

Bill announces to his brother how he plans to behave with the next woman he meets. He will calculatedly remain aloof. But the drama takes on a significant new dimension when the fellows meet Kate (Karen Sillas), a lovely, divorced earth mother type who runs a homey rural inn. At the same time, Dennis encounters a sexy young Romanian woman (Elina Lowensohn) who turns out to be his father's lover.

Thesps are a constant pleasure to watch. No matter how arbitrary or bizarre some of Hartley's ploys seem at first, pic is so carefully constructed that they all resurface to pay off in the end.

•

SIMPLE STORY, A
SEE: UNE HISTOIRE SIMPLE

•

SIMPLE TWIST OF FATE, A
1994, 106 mins, US Ⓥ col
Dir Gillies MacKinnon ***Prod*** Ric Kidney ***Scr*** Steve Martin ***Ph*** Andrew Dunn ***Ed*** Humphrey Dixon ***Mus*** Cliff Edelman ***Art*** Andy Harris
Act Steve Martin, Gabriel Byrne, Laura Linney, Catharine O'Hara, Alana Austin, Alyssa Austin (Touchstone)

The pairing of Steve Martin and 19th-century novelist George Eliot seems about as likely an artistic union as Oliver Stone adapting Louisa May Alcott. Yet *A Simple Twist of Fate*—inspired by *Silas Marner*—betrays no telltale strains of clashing sensibilities. Martin leavens the material somewhat, but this is a faithful, heartfelt, somber piece about family and responsibility.

Pic's twist involves the proverbial child abandoned at the doorstep. Dour, reclusive furniture-maker Michael McCann (Martin) finds meaning in his life through his care of an infant girl. The baby's biological dad is John Newland (Gabriel Byrne), the wealthiest man in the county, who is primed for a political career.

Over the course of a decade, we see the girl, Mathilda (Alana Austin), evolve into a bright, precocious child. Her blossoming also brings out the best in McCann. But Newland finds himself becoming increasingly possessive. Eventually, he goes to court to win back custody in a bitterly contested trial.

Byrne gives a multitextured performance as the villain of the piece. Austin is genuinely winning as the girl, and Laura Linney, as Byrne's show wife, conveys a much-appreciated intelligence and depth. Overall, it is a polished, adult film.

•

SINBAD AND THE EYE OF THE TIGER
1977, 112 mins, US Ⓥ ⦿ col
Dir Sam Wanamaker ***Prod*** Charles H. Schneer, Ray Harryhausen ***Scr*** Beverley Cross ***Ph*** Ted Moore ***Ed*** Roy Watts ***Mus*** Roy Budd ***Art*** Geoffrey Drake
Act Patrick Wayne, Taryn Power, Margaret Whiting, Jane Seymour, Patrick Troughton, Kurt Christian (Columbia)

The plot [by Beverley Cross and Ray Harryhausen] takes Patrick Wayne, as Sinbad, on a quest to free a prince (Damien Thomas) from the spell of evil sorceress Margaret Whiting. Thomas has quite a dilemma, in that he's turned into a baboon and is fast losing all vestiges of human behavior.

Along for the odyssey are a couple of young cuties (Taryn Power and Jane Seymour) who keep their modest demeanor while wearing scanty outfits. The plot scenes are hammy beyond belief. Whiting is a particular offender with her all-stops-out villainy.

When the fantasy creatures have center stage, the film is enjoyable to watch. Such beasties as skeletons, a giant bee and an outsized walrus, are marvelously vivified by Ray Harryhausen.

Most of the studio work was done in England, with locations in Spain, Malta and the Mediterranean.

•

SINBAD THE SAILOR
1947, 116 mins, US Ⓥ ⦿ col
Dir Richard Wallace ***Prod*** Stephen Ames ***Scr*** John Twist ***Ph*** George Barnes ***Ed*** Sherman Todd, Frank Doyle ***Mus*** Roy Webb ***Art*** Albert S. D'Agostino, Carroll Clark
Act Douglas Fairbanks, Jr., Maureen O'Hara, Walter Slezak, Anthony Quinn, Jane Greer, George Tobias (RKO)

The sterling adventures of Sinbad as a sailing man and as a romancer are garbed in brilliant color in this RKO production.

Cast values match production elegance. Douglas Fairbanks, Jr., matches do-and-dare antics of his father. He measures up to the flamboyance required to make Sinbad a dashing fictional hero. Maureen O'Hara lends shapely presence as the heroine.

Story concerns Sinbad's mythical eighth adventure wherein he seeks a fabulously rich island and the love of an Arabian Nights beauty. Major production fault is that dialog and main story points are obscure, making intelligent following of plot difficult. Principal opponents to Sinbad's search are Walter Slezak and Anthony Quinn. Former's character is never clearly explained, and latter's role also is obscured in the writing.

•

SINCE YOU WENT AWAY
1944, 158 mins, US Ⓥ ⦿ b/w
Dir John Cromwell ***Prod*** David O. Selznick ***Scr*** David O. Selznick ***Ph*** Stanley Cortez, Lee Garmes ***Ed*** Hal C. Kern ***Mus*** Max Steiner ***Art*** William L. Pereira
Act Claudette Colbert, Jennifer Jones, Joseph Cotten, Shirley Temple, Monty Woolley, Robert Walker (Selznick)

As David O. Selznick screenplayed his own production, from Margaret Buell Wilder's [adaptation of her own] book, *Since You Went Away* is a heartwarming panorama of human emotions, reflecting the usual wartime frailties of the thoughtless and the chiseler, the confusion and uncertainty of young ideals and young love, all of it projected against a background of utterly captivating home love and life in the wholesome American manner.

Claudette Colbert is the attractive, understanding mother of Jennifer Jones, 17, and Shirley Temple, in her earliest teens, all of whom adore their absent husband and father, Timothy, a captain off to the wars. The father is never shown; only his photo in officer's uniform, along with closeups of other domestic memorabilia.

True, Selznick's continuity has given director John Cromwell an episodic script, but it is this narrative form which makes for so much audience-appeal. Each sequence is a closeup, a character study, a self-contained dramalet.

1944: Best Score for a Dramatic Picture.

NOMINATIONS: Best Picture, Actress (Claudette Colbert), Supp. Actor (Monty Woolley), Supp. Actress (Jennifer Jones), B&W Cinematography, B&W Art Direction, Editing, Special Effects

•

SINFUL DAVEY
1969, 95 mins, UK col
Dir John Huston ***Prod*** William N. Graf ***Scr*** James R. Webb ***Ph*** Freddie Young, Edward Scaife ***Ed*** Russel Lloyd ***Mus*** Ken Thorne ***Art*** Stephen Grimes
Act John Hurt, Pamela Franklin, Nigel Davenport, Ronald Fraser, Robert Morley, Anjelica Huston (Mirisch)

Sinful Davey is a bland, lethargic period comedy about a 19th-century teenage highwayman. A competent cast and a good James R. Webb screenplay are shot down by the club-footed, forced direction of John Huston, who seems to think that comedy is chatter, alternating with pratfall running and jumping.

Webb, it is said, discovered the ancient diary of David Haggart, subject of the piece, and the writer has, indeed, fashioned a good episodic story.

John Hurt has the title role, and other principal players include Nigel Davenport, a dedicated cop and Ronald Fraser and Fidelma Murphy, as Hurt's two genial associates in a series of daring robberies. The script and cast, plus uniformly excellent below-the-line staffers are present, but the project founders on Huston's work.

•

SING, BOY, SING
1936, 90 mins, US b/w
Dir Sidney Lanfield ***Prod*** B. G. De Sylva ***Scr*** Milton Sperling, Jack Yellen, Harry Tugend ***Ph*** Peverell Marley ***Ed*** Barbara McLean ***Mus*** Louis Silvers (dir.)
Act Alice Faye, Adolphe Menjou, Gregory Ratoff, Ted Healy, Patsy Kelly, Michael Whalen (20th Century-Fox)

Ritz Bros., long in vaude, make their debut in this musical. They are a riot. After 20th-Fox saw them in this picture they were resigned. Ritzes are in the opening shot, sending the picture off to a flying start, doing a medley routine, heavily clowned up, that's mainly built around "Music Goes 'Round."

Ritzes are cast into the story as performers, which is true, also, of Alice Faye, Ted Healy, Patsy Kelly and Tony Martin. Adolphe Menjou plays an actor with a Shakespearean complex and a lust for liquor. He is obviously doing a caricature of John Barrymore.

The story has Gregory Ratoff trying to get off coffee and cakes by selling Faye to the air lanes. Eventually he is trying to sell Menjou with Faye, with his difficulties opening up an avenue for situations that can't help but land. Menjou's craving for baby rum, which he thinks is South American brandy, becomes funny.

•

SINGER NOT THE SONG, THE
1961, 132 mins, UK Ⓥ col
Dir Roy Ward Baker ***Prod*** Roy Ward Baker ***Scr*** Nigel Balchin ***Ph*** Otto Heller ***Ed*** Roger Cherrill ***Mus*** Philip Green ***Art*** Alex Vetchinsky
Act Dirk Bogarde, John Mills, Mylene Demongeot, Laurence Naismith, Eric Pohlmann, John Bentley, Leslie French (Rank)

As a dialectic discussion hinged on the Roman Catholic religion, this can only be accepted as flippant. As a romantic drama, it must be agreed that it is glossy, but over-contrived. Yet, somehow, the thesping of the two principals, John Mills and Dirk Bogarde, prevents the screen version of Audrey Erskine Lindop's novel (shot in Spain) from falling between these two spacious schools.

Mills is a dedicated Roman Catholic priest who comes to the tiny community of Quantana, Mexico, to replace an older priest who is worn out from battling with the murderous, marauding gang of bandits led by Anacleto (Bogarde). To intimidate the newcomer, Bogarde's gang sets out on a series of murders by the alphabetical method.

Priest Mills, resolutely deciding to break Bogarde's power, shows a struggle in which the two gain mutual respect, though their religious opinions clash badly. The unscrupulous, cynical bandit realizes, though in a manner not explained very convincingly, that a local belle (Mylene Demongeot) is in love with the priest and he with her. He uses this knowledge to create a situation that puts the priest in a moral dilemma. Mills and Bogarde have some excellent acting encounters, though their accents, like those of many others, strike odd notes in the Mexican atmosphere.

•

SINGING FOOL, THE
1928, 105 mins, US b/w
Dir Lloyd Bacon ***Scr*** Joseph Jackson, C. Graham Baker ***Ph*** Byron Haskin
Act Al Jolson, Betty Bronson, Josephine Dunn, Reed Howes, Edward Martindel, Arthur Houseman (Warner/Vitaphone)

There are seven songs sung by Al Jolson, four seemingly new, with one, "Sonny Boy," plugged as the theme number, sung by Jolson at three different points. Others are "Keep Smiling at Trouble," "Golden Gate," "Rainbow Round My Shoulder," "Spaniard Who Blighted My Life," "Sitting on Top of the World" and "It All Depends on You."

Al meets two women in the picture and talks to both of them. Both talk back. Josephine Dunn doesn't talk so well, and she looks pretty steely-hearted, even for a blonde. Betty Bronson talks a little better, but Joe Jackson's dialog is no smash. Little David Lee playing the Jolsons's kid is a perfect wonder. He plays sick, dead, happy, asleep, affectionate and sad, and talks. The story opens in a side street slab called Blackie Joe's, where Jolson is a singing waiter and Dunn the soubret. Jolson goes for the blonde, but she tells him she's off any waiter, even after he has written a song for her that she won't read. So he sings it to her on the floor. It is "It All Depends on You." A Broadway producer is in the joint. That's it.

•

SINGING NUN, THE
1966, 96 mins, US Ⓥ ⦿ ▭ col
Dir Henry Koster ***Prod*** John Beck, Hayes Goetz ***Scr*** Sally Benson, John Furia, Jr. ***Ph*** Milton Krasner ***Ed*** Rita Roland ***Mus*** Harry Sukman ***Art*** George W. Doris, Urie McCleary
Act Debbie Reynolds, Ricardo Montalban, Greer Garson, Agnes Moorehead, Chad Everett, Katharine Ross (M-G-M)

The Singing Nun, patently designed to cash in on the story of the Belgian nun Soeur Sourire and her song "Dominique," carries an expectancy not always realized. Fictionized approach to the truelife character—necessitated by agreement with Catholic church authorities not to make pictures autobiographical—resultantly loses in the transition, and while there are engaging musical interludes what emerges is slight and frequently slow-moving.

The production unfolds mostly in the small Samaritan House, situated in a slum section of Brussels, where the young Dominican nun carries on her work with children and study preparatory to an African missionary assignment. In this role, Debbie Reynolds expertly warbles a dozen numbers to her own guitar accompaniment, some nine of the songs composed by the Belgian sister.

1966: NOMINATION: Best Adapted Musical Score

•

SINGIN' IN THE RAIN
1952, 102 mins, US Ⓥ ⦿ col
Dir Gene Kelly, Stanley Donen ***Prod*** Arthur Freed ***Scr*** Adolph Green, Betty Comden ***Ph*** Harold Rosson ***Ed*** Adrienne Fazan ***Mus*** Lennie Hayton (dir.) ***Art*** Cedric Gibbons, Randall Duell
Act Gene Kelly, Donald O'Connor, Debbie Reynolds, Jean Hagen, Millard Mitchell, Cyd Charisse (M-G-M)

Musical has pace, humor and good spirits a-plenty, in a breezy, good-natured spoof at the film industry itself. The 1927 era, with advent of the talkies, lends itself to some hilarious slapstick, of which the film takes excellent advantage.

Story has Gene Kelly and Jean Hagen as a team of romantic film favorites of the silents, and the studio's problem of translating their popularity to the talkies because of Hagen's high-pitched, squeaky voice. Problem is complicated further by Kelly falling in love with a nitery chorine (Debbie Reynolds), and Hagen's jealous tantrums and knifings. Donald O'Connor plays the boyhood pal and early-vaude days teammate of Kelly, as well as his present studio mentor.

Kelly's dancing is standout, whether in the "Singin' in the Rain" and other solos; in the duo dance numbers with O'Connor, such as the vaudeville routine, "Fit As a Fiddle," or the diction lesson, or in trios with O'Connor and Reynolds as in "Good Morning." Reynolds is a pretty, pert minx, with a nice singing voice and fine dancing ability. O'Connor has the film's highspot with a solo number, "Make 'Em Laugh." The guy appears to kill himself with his acrobatics and pratfalls over a cluttered studio set.

1952: NOMINATIONS: Best Supp. Actress (Jean Hagen), Scoring of a Musical Picture

•

SINGLES
1992, 99 mins, US Ⓥ ⊙ col
Dir Cameron Crowe ***Prod*** Cameron Crowe, Richard Hashimoto ***Scr*** Cameron Crowe ***Ph*** Ueli Steiger ***Ed*** Richard Chew ***Mus*** Paul Westerberg ***Art*** Stephen Lineweaver
Act Bridget Fonda, Campbell Scott, Kyra Sedgwick, Sheila Kelley, Jim True, Matt Dillon (Atkinson-Knickerbocker/Warner)

This younger version of *The Big Chill* is a straightforward story about young adults who live separate and intertwined lives in a Seattle apartment building. They often share their secrets directly with the audience and their bodies with each other.

Linda (superbly played by Kyra Sedgwick) becomes the link between the audience and parallel comedies. Her first romantic catastrophe sets the stage for the many hilarious horror stories—and feats of desperation—that follow, including her budding love story with honest, earnest, cool dude Steve (Campbell Scott).

Bridget Fonda turns in a stunning performance as dipsy Janet, in love with hopelessly bad guitar player Cliff (Matt Dillon, doing a great job as a brain-dead, self-centered, second-rate musician). Their story unfolds amidst various singles' crises, including Debbie Hunt's (Sheila Kelley) dating video search for a man. Any man.

There's no shortage of tender moments in this comedy, and former rock journalist Cameron Crowe cleverly transforms "real" problems into crackerjack material.

•

SINGLE STANDARD, THE
1929, 73 mins, US Ⓥ d b/w
Dir John S. Robertson ***Scr*** Josephine Lovett, Marion Ainslee ***Ph*** Oliver Marsh ***Ed*** Blanche Sewell ***Art*** Cedric Gibbons
Act Greta Garbo, Nils Asther, John Mack Brown, Dorothy Sebastian, Lane Chandler, Robert Castle (M-G-M)

Although Greta Garbo, as Arden Stuart, is meant to throw off the cloak of conventionalism for free plunges, the actress is almost unfeline in her brazen directness. The star keeps well wrapped throughout.

Garbo's impulsive rush to the chauffeur hits as too quick a stepping out of character and too sudden a drop for a moral aspect that had been fairly high. The chauffeur deliberately wrecking his boss's car, and killing himself after the conquest, is an illogically sincere interpretation.

Greta lets a couple of months elapse after the tragedy before she is impelled to seek another victim. This time it is the over-gifted Packy Cannon, a regular villager with a Rockefeller fountain of dough. Asther is Packy. He does not lend the sailor-artist-boxer role the John Gilbertine touch.

This is followed by a regular film trip through the South Seas with plenty of stretching and necking. Finally even Packy tires. This permits Garbo and the picture to go in for matrimony with a mild but virile man (John Mack Brown) who gives her the son that kills off moral turpitude.

•

SINGLE WHITE FEMALE
1992, 107 mins, US Ⓥ ⊙ col
Dir Barbet Schroeder ***Prod*** Barbet Schroeder ***Scr*** Don Roos ***Ph*** Luciano Tovoli ***Ed*** Lee Percy ***Mus*** Howard Shore ***Art*** Milena Canonero
Act Bridget Fonda, Jennifer Jason Leigh, Steven Weber, Peter Friedman, Stephen Tobolowsky (Columbia)

Director Barbet Schroeder has made a calculated attempt to cross an acutely observed character study with a slasher pic. But despite excellent lead performances and numerous memorable scenes, *Single White Female* feels like two different movies in one.

Giving her unfaithful b.f. the heave, smart, upwardly mobile designer/software expert Bridget Fonda takes waify Jennifer Jason Leigh in to share her attractive Upper West Side flat. They become instant best friends, and the needy Leigh seems reassured by Fonda's vow she'll never take her cheating man back.

Even after Fonda returns to her errant lover (Steven Weber) and becomes engaged, the ways in which Leigh tries to nicely insinuate herself into the "family" remain beautifully observed and psychologically true.

But pic [from John Lutz's novel *SWF Seeks Same*] gradually tilts in the direction of a production line thriller, until finally assuming the full personality of a Hollywood killing machine. Turning point arrives when Leigh gets her hair cut and dyed just like Fonda's pert carrot-top.

Most of pic's virtues are subtle, while the flaws are blatant. Under Schroeder's careful guidance, both Fonda and Leigh play with an ease and unselfconsciousness that are bracingly refreshing. Some of their scenes together feature a casual intimacy rare in U.S. films.

•

SINK THE BISMARCK!
1960, 97 mins, UK Ⓥ ⊙ ▭ b/w
Dir Lewis Gilbert ***Prod*** John Brabourne ***Scr*** Edmund H. North ***Ph*** Christopher Challis ***Ed*** Peter Hunt ***Mus*** Clifton Parker ***Art*** Arthur Lawson
Act Kenneth More, Dana Wynter, Carl Mohner, Laurence Naismith, Karel Stepanek, Maurice Denham (20th Century-Fox)

Sink The Bismarck! is a first-rate film re-creation of a thrilling historical event. The screenplay is taken from a book by C. S. Forester. It concentrates almost entirely on three playing areas. These are the subterranean London headquarters of the British admiralty, where the battle is plotted and directed; aboard the Germans' "unsinkable" battleship, the *Bismarck;* and on board the various British vessels called into pursuit of the Nazi raider.

The film opens with the chilling news that the *Bismarck* has escaped the British naval blockade and is loose in the North Atlantic. After it sinks the *Hood*, considered the greatest battleship in the world, it appears nothing can stop it from rendezvousing with its sister ships holed up at Brest.

Some of the dialog is a little high-flown, with the British at times too aware of the historical importance of the event. The Germans, on the other hand, tend to be Nazi caricatures.

Kenneth More plays the British captain who directs the battle to catch the *Bismarck* with his customary and effective taciturnity. Dana Wynter is a helpful note as the WREN officer who is his aide. Carl Mohner manages some character as the German officer commanding the Bismarck.

•

SIN OF HAROLD DIDDLEBOCK, THE
1947, 90 mins, US Ⓥ b/w
Dir Preston Sturges ***Prod*** Preston Sturges ***Scr*** Preston Sturges ***Ph*** Robert Pittock ***Ed*** Tom Neff ***Mus*** Werner Heymann ***Art*** Robert Usher
Act Harold Lloyd, Raymond Walburn, Franklin Pangborn, Margaret Hamilton, Edgar Kennedy (California)

Attired in the same straw hat and black-rimmed specs in his silent flickers, neither Harold Lloyd's person nor his comedy has changed much. As an added lure, director Preston Sturges has incorporated into the first 10 minutes of the film an actual sequence from Lloyd's *The Freshman* which the comedian made in 1923.

Film segues expertly from the *Freshman* footage to the new product, showing Raymond Walburn, as an enthusiastic alumnus now head of a top ad agency, promising Lloyd a job for having won the game. Lloyd takes the job after graduation but is stuck immediately into a minor bookkeeper's niche, where he remains forgotten for 22 years. Walburn finally remembers him long enough to fire him—which is where the fun starts.

Abetted by some excellent dialog from Sturges's pen, Lloyd handles his role in his usual funny fashion. One sequence, in which he dangles from a leash 80 stories above the sidewalk, with the other end of the leash tied to a nervous lion, is standout.

•

SINS OF RACHEL CADE, THE
1960, 123 mins, US col
Dir Gordon Douglas ***Prod*** Henry Blanke ***Scr*** Edward Anhalt ***Ph*** J. Peverell Marley ***Ed*** Owen Marks ***Mus*** Max Steiner ***Art*** Leo K. Kuter
Act Angie Dickinson, Peter Finch, Roger Moore, Errol John, Woody Strode, Juano Hernandez (Warner)

One of filmdom's favorite stamping grounds, the Belgian Congo, is the setting for some familiar bwana monkeyshines in *The Sins of Rachel Cade*. Although it is an earnest and workmanlike effort, nothing very novel or enlightening occurs in the Henry Blanke production, which is based upon Charles Mercer's popular novel [*Rachel Cade*] about a spinster missionary.

Chief conflict of the film is the heroine's (Angie Dickinson) inner emotional turmoil in which her religious principles debate against her natural sexual impulses. Arriving in the Congo, she dramatically persuades the region's "left wing" element to adopt the Christian philosophy, but has a deuce of a time practising what she has been preaching when a handsome RAF doctor (Roger Moore) arrives by unscheduled plane crash.

Dickinson is generally persuasive, although a trifle too composed in spots. Peter Finch, a convincing low-pressure performer, makes the most of his role. Moore is handsome, but far too British sounding to score in the part of an American, even a Yank from Boston.

Direction by Gordon Douglas is nowhere near as perceptive as it should be. There is also a distracting tendancy to jam the lens right into the pupils of the heroine's eye.

•

SIRENS
1994, 94 mins, Australia/UK Ⓥ ⊙ col
Dir John Duigan ***Prod*** Sue Milliken ***Scr*** John Duigan ***Ph*** Geoff Burton ***Ed*** Humphrey Dixon ***Mus*** Rachel Portman ***Art*** Roger Ford
Act Hugh Grant, Tara Fitzgerald, Sam Neill, Elle Macpherson, Portia de Rossi, Kate Fischer (Samson/Radclyffe/Sirens)

Sirens is a deliciously sexy and hedonistic comedy of morals and manners, with the formidable presence of Australian supermodel Elle Macpherson, who is seen regularly in the buff in her featured role as an artist's model. Though the story is fictional, it's based on real characters and situations.

In the early 1930s, artist Norman Lindsay (Sam Neill) became embroiled in a controversy over an etching, *The Crucified Venus*. Oxford graduate, the Rev. Anthony Campion (Hugh Grant), journies to Lindsay's home in the Blue Mountains to convince him the painting must be removed.

Campion, who considers himself a bit of a free thinker, and his young, naive wife, Estella (Tara Fitzgerald), arrive to find the unrepentant artist living with his wife/model, Rose (Pamela Rabe), and three models. Sheela (Macpherson) and Pru (Kate Fischer) enjoy flaunting their frequent nudity, while the younger and shyer Giddy (Portia de Rossi) refuses to disrobe for a new painting, *Sirens*, on which Lindsay is working.

Director-writer John Duigan injects plenty of humor into this sensual saga, and particularly has fun with Australia's fauna and with the way the local mountain folk behave toward the outrageous Lindsays and their houseguests.

•

SIROCCO
1951, 98 mins, US Ⓥ ⊙ b/w
Dir Curtis Bernhardt ***Prod*** Robert Lord ***Scr*** A. I. Bezzerides, Hans Jacoby ***Ph*** Burnett Guffey ***Ed*** Viola Lawrence ***Mus*** George Antheil ***Art*** Robert Peterson
Act Humphrey Bogart, Marta Toren, Lee J. Cobb, Everett Sloane, Gerald Mohr, Zero Mostel (Santana)

This melodrama goes back to 1925 and the war between French occupation troops and the Syrians in Damascus. Visual presentation interestingly depicts the locale, and it is given excellent low-key lensing in keeping with the yarn, but story deals with sordid characters with little redeeming uplift, even in the climactic stretch.

Humphrey Bogart is a gunrunner and profiteer, constantly keeping ahead of the French intelligence commanded by Lee J. Cobb. He is thrown in contact with Marta Toren, a girl no better than she should be who is being kept by Cobb, and goes on the make for her. She's interested, seeing a chance to escape to Cairo, but Cobb outsmarts the fleeing pair, gets the goods on Bogart and forces him to establish contact with the Syrian leader so Cobb can try to negotiate a truce.

The script, based on Joseph Kessel's novel *Coup de Grace*, attempts to show some reform on the part of the Bogart character after Cobb seems certain to be killed by the Syrians. Reformation takes the form of Bogart carrying ransom money for Cobb's release.

•

SISTER ACT
1992, 100 mins, US Ⓥ ⊙ col
Dir Emile Ardolino ***Prod*** Teri Schwartz ***Scr*** Joseph Howard ***Ph*** Adam Greenberg ***Ed*** Richard Halsey ***Mus*** Marc Shaiman ***Art*** Jackson DeGovia
Act Whoopi Goldberg, Maggie Smith, Harvey Keitel, Bill Nunn, Mary Wickes, Kathy Najimy (Touchstone)

Blessed with the from-on-high concept of Whoopi Goldberg bringing rock 'n' roll to a nuns' chorus, this infectious little throwaway—originally seen as a vehicle for Bette Midler—has a warm-hearted story and engaging premise.

Goldberg plays Deloris, a Reno lounge singer who witnesses a murder by her mobster b.f. Vince (Harvey Keitel) and ends up on the lam. The detective (Bill Nunn) trying to bust Vince pops Deloris into a San Francisco convent for safekeeping, where one-time Catholic school girl promptly outrages the mother superior (Maggie Smith).

Deloris and the movie find their respective callings about halfway in when she's asked to take over the convent's dreadful choir, introducing 1960s rock to the nuns through adapted renditions of "My Guy" (becoming "My God").

It's a divine concept, and after a weak start director Emile Ardolino (*Dirty Dancing, Three Men and a Little Lady*) milks it for all the laughs it's worth, while deriving requisite warmth from Goldberg and Smith's solid performances.

•

SISTER ACT 2 : BACK IN THE HABIT

1993, 106 mins, US Ⓥ ⦿ col

Dir Bill Duke ***Prod*** Dawn Steel, Scott Rudin ***Scr*** James Orr, Jim Cruickshank, Judi Ann Mason ***Ph*** Oliver Wood ***Ed*** John Carter, Pem Herring, Stuart Pappe ***Mus*** Miles Goodman ***Art*** John DeCuir, Jr.

Act Whoopi Goldberg, Kathy Najimy, Barnard Hughes, Mary Wickes, James Coburn, Maggie Smith (Touchstone)

Two trips to the convent is one too many. Suffering a bad case of sequelitis, this *Sister Act* follow-up is too formulaic and frequently pauses to sermonize at the expense of entertaining.

The major shift involves the setting—a run-down high school as opposed to a decrepit convent, a milieu seemingly designed to allow the filmmakers to push an agenda counselling youths to stay in school, which would be fabulous if this were a public service announcement.

The action opens with Deloris (Whoopi Goldberg) headlining in Vegas. Almost immediately, however, she's doing the nun thing again at the request of the Mother Superior (Maggie Smith), who needs help reaching her young flock. The lone menace this time around is rather pallid, coming in the form of an officious administrator (James Coburn) intent on closing the school. Deloris turns the rather tame group of kids into a choir in a nebulous effort to save good ol' St. Francis.

Director Bill Duke and writers devote themselves to reaching the younger audience segment at the expense of keeping the narrative moving. The action gets bogged down, for example, in a subplot involving the talented Rita (impressive newcomer Lauryn Hill), whose mother (Sheryl Lee Ralph) objects to her joining the choir.

•

SISTERS

SEE: SOME GIRLS

•

SISTERS, THE

1938, 95 mins, US b/w

Dir Anatole Litvak ***Prod*** Anatole Litvak ***Scr*** Milton Krims ***Ph*** Tony Gaudio ***Ed*** Warren Low ***Mus*** Max Steiner ***Art*** Carl Jules Weyl

Act Errol Flynn, Bette Davis, Anita Louise, Ian Hunter, Donald Crisp, Beulah Bondi (Warner)

Adapted from Myron Brinig's bestseller, this film has the sweep of a virtual cavalcade of early 20th-century American history. Plot starts out with three sisters, daughters of a small Montana town druggist, getting ready for a dance, staged to hear returns on the national election that swept Roosevelt into a second term as president. It closes four years later as the same family prepares again for another election ball, this time to hail Taft as new president.

Totally different marriages of the three girls are clearly set out, with highlights in their wedded lives taking the happy sisters often close to the brink of matrimonial smashup but always managing to surmount trying difficulties.

Most of the interest centres on Louise (Bette Davis) who elopes with Frank Medlin (Errol Flynn), sports scribe. This case of love-at-first sight works out satisfactorily until the newspaperman, hampered by domestic ties and unwillingness to buckle down as an author, takes to heavy imbibing.

Davis turns in one of her most scintillating performances. Flynn's happy-go-lucky reporter is a vivid portrayal although his slight English accent seems incongruous. Anita Louise makes a delightful flirty daughter who finally weds the elderly wealthy man in her community while Jane Bryan is adequate as the more conservative sister who decides that safety in matrimony is represented by the dull town banker's son.

•

SISTERS

1973, 92 mins, US Ⓥ col

Dir Brian De Palma ***Prod*** Edward R. Pressman ***Scr*** Brian De Palma, Louisa Rose ***Ph*** Gregory Sandor ***Ed*** Paul Hirsch ***Mus*** Bernard Herrmann ***Art*** Gary Weist

Act Margot Kidder, Jennifer Salt, Charles Durning, William Finley, Lisle Wilson, Barnard Hughes (American International)

Sisters is a good psychological murder melodrama, starring Margot Kidder as the schizoid half of Siamese twins, and Jennifer Salt as a news hen driven to terror in her investigation of a bloody murder. Brian De Palma's direction emphasizes exploitation values which do not fully mask script weakness.

Kidder, paired with Lisle Wilson on a TV game show (neatly satirized in opening scene), later invites him over for the night. Next morning, in a nervous state and after a voiceover dialog in French with another person never seen, Kidder slashes Wilson with a butcher knife.

Salt views the murdered man's agonies from a nearby window, and doggedly pursues the case despite incredulity of detective Dolph Sweet but with assistance of private eye Charles Durning.

•

SITTING DUCKS

1979, 90 mins, US Ⓥ col

Dir Henry Jaglom ***Prod*** Meira Attia Dor ***Scr*** Henry Jaglom ***Ph*** Paul Glickman ***Mus*** Richard Romanus

Act Michael Emil, Zack Norman, Patrice Townsend, Richard Romanus, Irene Forrest, Henry Jaglom (Sunny Side Up)

Rather loopy story serves basically to provide a framework for several fabulous character riffs and to give a little momentum to any number of enjoyable crazy situations.

Two small-time hustlers make off with loot siphoned off from a gambling syndicate for which one works, and majority of the running time is devoted to their haphazard drive down the eastern seaboard to reach a plane that will carry them to a life of kings in Central America.

Along the way, hyped-up pair, acted in a marvel of improvisational style by Michael Emil and Zack Norman, meet up with two young ladies who hitch on for the wild ride.

Interplay among the four constitutes the meat of the film, and every line and every scene springs spontaneously off the screen as if they're being played for the first time.

•

SITTING PRETTY

1933, 80 mins, US b/w

Dir Harry Joe Brown ***Prod*** Charles R. Rogers ***Scr*** Jack McGowan, S. J. Perelman, Lou Breslow ***Ph*** Milton Krasner ***Art*** Lyle Wheeler, Leland Fuller

Act Jack Oakie, Jack Haley, Ginger Rogers, Thelma Todd, Gregory Ratoff, Lew Cody (Paramount)

Sitting Pretty's assets are a youthful trio of leads, some fast dialog, a swell score and direction that hits a pace from the start and sustains it to the finish.

The good old triangle provides a foundation for the action [from a story suggested by Nina Wilcox Putnam]. But that foundation is neatly upholstered by the cast, the music, the girls and the staging. Story takes Jack Oakie and Jack Haley to Hollywood as a songwriting team. Back in New York they're told to go west by Mack Gordon, who plays a music publisher in the film and who, with his partner Harry Revel, wrote the score. Ginger Rogers slips in as a kind-hearted lunch-wagon proprietress whom the boys happen to touch while hitchhiking westward.

For Oakie it's quite familiar ground; again he's the fresh guy who goes swell-headed from success, then becomes a nice but deflated fellow at the finish. For Haley this is his first really important screen assignment. Rogers hasn't an opportunity to get a good lick at the ball, being hemmed in by story limitations, but she looks good.

Gregory Ratoff plays a Hollywood agent, and through this dialectician and Lew Cody, as a picture producer, the dialog gets in some satirical inside studio stuff that's broad enough to be understood by almost anybody.

•

SITTING TARGET

1972, 93 mins, UK Ⓥ col

Dir Douglas Hickox ***Prod*** Barry Kulick ***Scr*** Alexander Jacobs ***Ph*** Ted Scaife ***Ed*** John Glen ***Mus*** Stanley Myers ***Art*** Jonathan Barry

Act Oliver Reed, Jill St. John, Ian McShane, Edward Woodward, Frank Finlay, Freddie Jones (M-G-M)

Sitting Target is a picture of brutish violence. Its story of a British prison break by a hardened, jealousy-ridden convict to kill the wife he believes unfaithful has been recounted with no holds barred.

The screenplay [from a novel by Laurence Henderson] sometimes is difficult to follow, but Douglas Hickox's tense direction keeps movement at top speed. Obsession of con to get to his wife, who has revealed she is pregnant and wants a divorce, is a motivating theme—built with growing suspense. Jill St. John becomes the sitting target for Oliver Reed as the convicted murderer who smashes his way to freedom and stalks his prey.

Actual scenes lensed in two Irish prisons give film a grimly authentic atmosphere and the escape of Reed and two other cons is spectacularly depicted.

•

SIX DAYS SEVEN NIGHTS

1998, 101 mins, US Ⓥ ⦿ ▭ col

Dir Ivan Reitman ***Prod*** Ivan Reitman, Wallis Nicita, Roger Birnbaum ***Scr*** Michael Browning ***Ph*** Michael Chapman ***Ed*** Sheldon Kahn, Wendy Greene Bricmont ***Mus*** Randy Edelman ***Art*** J. Michael Riva

Act Harrison Ford, Anne Heche, David Schwimmer, Jacqueline Obradors, Temuera Morrison, Allison Janney (Northern Lights/Touchstone)

A passable romantic comedy in which enforced proximity makes the heart grow fonder, this old-fashioned popcorn picture is agreeably breezy and colorful, but lacks the pizzazz and star chemistry of a genre ancestor such as *Romancing the Stone*. Anne Heche is the best thing in the picture.

Star Harrison Ford plays a South Pacific cargo pilot, Quinn Harris, who becomes stranded on a deserted island with a neurotic, high-powered New York magazine editor, Robin Monroe (Heche). Things become physical when Robin gets a snake up her pants in a pool of water and insists that Quinn gets it out. But that's about as risque as pic gets—until Robin's fiance, Frank (David Schwimmer), [waiting for her on a nearby isle,] starts spending a lot of time at the hotel bar with Quinn's sexpot g.f., Angelica (Jacqueline Obradors).

Just when it appears that Robin is too irremediably urban to cope with the Robinson Cruso lifestyle, she starts coming around, pitching in to prove herself to Quinn. First-time scenarist Michael Browning's script generates mild conflict and a few laughs. But dialogue is hardly memorable and characters are far from indelible.

Ford and Heche make a tolerable team—decent enough company for the quick, bouncy ride the film provides. Ford is predictably assured and light on his feet but not all that interesting in the part, while Heche is the live wire who keeps things sparking to the limited extent they do. By contrast, Schwimmer delivers annoyingly one-note shtick. Obradors is easy on the eyes, the only other supporting part of note.

Shot mainly on the Hawaiian island of Kauai, pic has the lush look expected of such fare. But there are too many shots in which the sky has obviously been computer enhanced, and the film is almost quaint in the way the artificiality of studio-shot scenes contrasts with location work.

•

SIX DEGREES OF SEPARATION

1993, 111 mins, US Ⓥ ⦿ ▭ col

Dir Fred Schepisi ***Prod*** Fred Schepisi, Arnon Milchan ***Scr*** John Guare ***Ph*** Ian Baker ***Ed*** Peter Honess ***Mus*** Jerry Goldsmith ***Art*** Patrizia von Brandenstein

Act Stockard Channing, Will Smith, Donald Sutherland, Ian McKellen, Mary Beth Hurt, Bruce Davison (Maiden Movies/New Regency/M-G-M)

The connection between any two people in the world—so we are told in *Six Degrees of Separation*—is no farther than a half-dozen human associations away. Scientific sociology aside, the screen version of John Guare's award-winning stage hit is an elaborate mousetrap where getting caught can be delightful fun. But the central scam dissipates into self-analysis and moralization.

The tale within a tale is related by the Kittredges (Stockard Channing, Donald Sutherland), chic Fifth Avenue folk who deal and speculate in high-society art. They have an incredible story to relate about a young black man who arrived at their doorstep late one evening bleeding from a knife wound and claiming to have been a mugging victim. Identifying himself as Paul (Will Smith), a friend and classmate of their children at Harvard, he enters their life for a moment.

Posing as the son of Sidney Poitier, he captivates the couple and a visiting friend (Ian McKellen). Next morning Paul flees. The Kittredges simply must get to the root of why anyone would go to such elaborate lengths to create such an elegant ruse for no tangible profit.

The promise of an exciting journey is run aground by rather routine, banal explanations. Pic is in essence an examination of artifice. On that level it has few equals. It is a choice, elegant production, pristine in its craft and attention to detail.

1993: NOMINATION: Best Actress (Stockard Channing)

•

SIXTEEN CANDLES
1984, 93 mins, US Ⓥ ⊙ col
Dir John Hughes ***Prod*** Hilton A. Green ***Scr*** John Hughes ***Ph*** Bobby Byrne ***Ed*** Edward Warschilka ***Mus*** Ira Newborn ***Art*** John W. Corso
Act Molly Ringwald, Anthony Michael Hall, Michael Schoeffling, Paul Dooley, Justin Henry, Liane Curtis (Universal)

Cream puff of a teen comedy about the miseries of a girl turning 16 turns out to be an amiable, rather goldilocked film. Tone of the film, despite some raw language, brief nudity in the shower and carnage at a high school party, actually suggests the middle America of a Norman Rockwell *Saturday Evening Post* cover.

For the girls, there's Molly Ringwald as the film's angst-ridden centerpiece. Ringwald is engaging and credible. For the boys, there's a bright, funny performance by Anthony Michael Hall, a hip freshman wimp called Ted the Geek. There's also a darkly handsome high school heartbreak kid (Michael Schoeffling), a merciful brisk pace, some quick humor (visual and verbal), and a solid music track.

•

SIXTH AND MAIN
1977, 103 mins, US col
Dir Christopher Cain ***Prod*** Christopher Cain ***Scr*** Christopher Cain ***Ph*** Hilyard John Brown ***Ed*** Ken Johnson ***Mus*** Bob Summers
Act Leslie Nielsen, Roddy McDowall, Beverly Garland, Leo Penn, Joe Maross, Bard Stevens (National Cinema)

Sixth and Main is a very professionally made lowbudgeter which succeeds to a great extent in exploring the emotions underneath the skin of the cliche skid row character. Christopher Cain wrote, produced and directed the pic, starring Leslie Nielsen as a talented dropout and Roddy McDowall as a crippled street person.

The film is earthy without being vulgar, though script at times veers too far into the preachy and meller literary realm.

Plot takes Beverly Garland, a slumming literary type, to downtown L.A. to absorb atmosphere for a book. She stumbles onto Nielsen, who hardly ever speaks but lives in a junked trailer full of promising manuscripts. With help from literary critic Joe Maross, she tries to promote Nielsen as a new find.

•

6TH DAY, THE
2000, US, 124 mins Ⓥ ⊙ ▭ col
Dir Roger Spottiwoode ***Prod*** Mike Medavoy, Arnold Schwarzenegger, Jon Davison ***Scr*** Cormac Wibberley, Marianne Wibberley ***Ph*** Pierre Mignot ***Ed*** Mark Conte, Dominique Fortin, Michel Arcand ***Mus*** Trevor Rabin ***Art*** James Bissell, John Willett
Act Arnold Schwarzenegger, Tony Goldwyn, Michael Rapaport, Michael Booker, Sarah Wynter, Robert Duvall (Davison-Columbia/Phoenix)

The 6th Day is a mostly standard-issue latter-day Arnold Schwarzenegger actioner spiked with a creepily plausible cloning angle.

Clones of all kinds have popped up in countless sci-fi films in recent years, but rarely have they played as central, or credible, a role as they do in this otherwise formulaic story set in a near-future in which human cloning is illegal but is practiced surreptitiously by a heinous biotech corporation. Adventure helicopter pilot Adam Gibson (Schwarzenegger) is in some respects a traditionalist throwback: he drives a '50s Cadillac and believes in "the natural process of life—you're born, you live and you die."

He and his partner Hank (Michael Rapaport) consent to a fancy finger-printing and eyesight-testing process requested by genetic engineering tycoon Drucker (Tony Goldwyn). When Adam soon thereafter returns home to attend his birthday party, he finds an exact duplicate of himself already celebrating with his family and friends. Mild-mannered homebody Adam is instantly forced into action-hero mode, pursued by Drucker's goons on a wild chase into the night.

Scenarists concoct numerous requisite action scenes, which enable Schwarzenegger to do what comes naturally, even if he now does it rather less roughly and with some hesitation. In a surprisingly direct (and intentionally humorous) commentary on the recent brouhaha over screen violence, and the star's own desire to tone it down, Adam is going after some villains when he remarks, re his daughter, "I don't want to expose her to any graphic violence. She already gets enough of that from the media." All the same, there's plenty of it here, even though it's more generalized and far less bloody than equivalent combat would have produced in the past.

As routinely staged and shot in a kind of gloomy eternal night that all too closely resembles the nocturnal funk of *End of Days*, the action scenes prove functional, if uninspired, and are generally trumped in interest by the way the film works pointed, provocative and legitimate views of cloning issues into a genre format.

•

633 SQUADRON
1964, 94 mins, UK Ⓥ ⊙ ▭ col
Dir Walter Grauman ***Prod*** Cecil F. Ford ***Scr*** James Clavell, Howard Koch ***Ph*** Ted Scaife, John Wilcox ***Ed*** Bert Bates ***Mus*** Ron Goodwin ***Art*** Michael Stringer
Act Cliff Robertson, George Chakiris, Maria Perschy, Harry Andrews, Donald Houston, Michael Goodliffe (Mirisch)

Cinematically, *633 Squadron* is a spectacular achievement, a technically explosive depiction of an RAF unit's successful but costly mission to demolish an almost impregnable Nazi rocket fuel installation in Norway. The production, filmed in its entirety in England, contains some rip-roaring aerial action. Unfortunately, this technical prowess is not matched by the drama it adorns.

The characters of the scenario from the novel by Frederick E. Smith are somewhat shallowly drawn and fall into rather familiar war story molds and behavior patterns.

Cliff Robertson skillfully rattles off the leading assignment, that of a Yank wing commander whose squadron is chosen for the dangerous mission. George Chakiris is adequate though miscast and rather colorless as a Norwegian resistance leader who is to pave the way for the vital bombing raid. Maria Perschy supplies decorative romantic interest as Chakiris's sister and eventually Robertson's girl.

•

SIXTH SENSE, THE
1999, 107 mins, US Ⓥ ⊙ col
Dir M. Night Shyamalan ***Prod*** Frank Marshall, Kathleen Kennedy, Barry Mendel ***Scr*** M. Night Shyamalan ***Ph*** Tak Fujimoto ***Ed*** Andrew Mondshein ***Mus*** James Newton Howard ***Art*** Larry Fulton
Act Bruce Willis, Toni Collette, Olivia Williams, Haley Joel Osment, Donnie Wahlberg, Glenn Fitzgerald (Spyglass/Hollywood)

A terrific last-minute twist goes a fair way toward redeeming *The Sixth Sense*, a mostly ponderous tale of paranormal communication across the River Styx.

Ten-minute prologue has the Philadelphia home of child psychologist Dr. Malcolm Crowe (Bruce Willis) and his wife, Anna (Olivia Williams), broken into by a mental case (Donnie Wahlberg) who, after accusing the doctor of having failed him, shoots Malcolm before turning the gun on himself.

The following autumn, Malcolm takes an interest in the case of an eight-year-old boy, Cole Sear (Haley Joel Osment), the unusually bright son of sorely taxed single mother Lynn (Toni Collette). Cole is obsessed with toy soldiers, prone to violent free-association writing, able to envision what happened in places years before and, most crucial, capable of seeing and hearing the dead.

Gradually, Cole's visions increase—people hanging from the rafters of his school, a kid with the back of his head blown away, a teenage girl from the neighborhood dying.

But Philadelphia-based writer-director M. Night Shyamalan keeps the dramatic temperature low throughout, an approach that attempts to make mood and state-of-mind the content of the film but that results in a lot of downtime.

Acting is in tune with the general understatement. Osment, who played Forrest Gump, Jr., is the standout here, reminding with his straight-faced intelligence of some exceptional British moppet thesps over the years. Willis is at his most subdued. Williams and Collette are okay in the seriously circumscribed female parts.

1999: NOMINATIONS: Best Picture, Director, Original Screenplay, Supp. Actor (Haley Joel Osment), Supp. Actress (Toni Collette), Editing

•

SIX WEEKS
1982, 107 mins, US Ⓥ ⊙ ▭ col
Dir Tony Bill ***Prod*** Peter Guber, Jon Peters ***Scr*** David Seltzer ***Ph*** Michael D. Margulies ***Ed*** Stu Linder ***Mus*** Dudley Moore ***Art*** Hilyard Brown
Act Dudley Moore, Mary Tyler Moore, Katherine Healy, Shannon Wilcox, Bill Calvert, Joe Regalbuto (PolyGram/Universal)

A sort of moppet *Love Story*, *Six Weeks* is an unabashed tearjerker aimed directly at the hearts of the mass audience.

Story [from the novel by Fred Mustard Stewart] for the most part takes place in the rarified, monied atmosphere of upper-class L.A. and N.Y. as leukemia-stricken Katherine Healy is the 12-year-old daughter of cosmetics tycoon Mary Tyler Moore and has admittedly had all the advantages in life, except for a father.

Daddy figure comes along in the person of California congressional candidate Dudley Moore. Healy takes an immediate shine to the likable politician, so much so that she insists upon working for his campaign.

In the middle of his campaign, Moore chucks everything for a whirlwind weekend in Gotham, where he "miraculously" manages to get ballet-addict Healy cast in a children's production of *The Nutcracker*.

Such material could have been insufferable, but scripter David Seltzer and Tony Bill, displaying growing assurance in his second directorial outing, have generally stayed on the tightrope between shameless emotional manipulation and undue restraint.

•

SJUNDE INSEGLET, DET
(THE SEVENTH SEAL)
1957, 95 mins, Sweden Ⓥ ⊙ b/w
Dir Ingmar Bergman ***Scr*** Ingmar Bergman ***Ph*** Gunnar Fischer ***Ed*** Lennart Wallen ***Mus*** Erik Nordgren ***Art*** P. A. Lundgren
Act Max von Sydow, Gunnar Bjornstrand, Bengt Ekerot, Nils Poppe, Bibi Andersson, Ake Fridell (Svensk Filmindustri)

Director-writer Ingmar Bergman has a morality play in this tale of a returning crusader in the 14th century who keeps Death at bay, via a chess game, while he tries to find out the meaning of life. Film has superior technical narrative, impressive lensing and thesping.

The knight (Max von Sydow) comes back to his home, which is in the grip of the black plague. The re-creation of medieval times is evocative in its bawdiness, superstition, cruelty and humanity. It spreads out an awesome canvas of human cupidity and purity. Characters abound with vitality, and Bergman wraps this into an absorbing film.

The chess game with Death (Bengt Ekerot) is interspersed with his meeting with a family of itinerant mountebanks whom he feels are worth saving, and even Death seems to coincide with this thought as all fall before his coming except them.

•

SKIDOO
1968, 97 mins, US ▭ col
Dir Otto Preminger ***Prod*** Otto Preminger ***Scr*** Doran William Cannon ***Ph*** Leon Shamroy ***Ed*** George Rohre ***Mus*** Harry Nilsson ***Art*** Robert E. Smith
Act Jackie Gleason, Carol Channing, Frankie Avalon, Fred Clark, Michael Constantine, Frank Gorshin (Sigma/Paramount)

Skidoo opens and closes in clever fashion, but in between, Otto Preminger's film is a dreary, unfunny attempt at contemporary comedy. Screenplay is a sort of updated Damon Runyon plot, in which allegedly lovable, old-time gangster types are foiled by hippies. Static photography and tame editing compound a weak script.

Jackie Gleason and Carol Channing are respectable marrieds, long since retired from their gang. Plot starts to shuffle along when Cesar Romero and Frankie Avalon, reps of a syndicate headed by Groucho Marx, insist Gleason does one more torpedo job. Mark this time is old-pal Mickey Rooney, living rather nicely in prison and about to spill the beans to politically motivated crime crusader Peter Lawford.

The domestic situation also is complicated by daughter Alexandra Hay's new beau, Indian-garbed hippie John Phillip Law. Principals also include warden Burgess Meredith, guard Fred Clark (his last pic), and cons Michael Constantine and Frank Gorshin.

Film prods from scene to scene in one-two-three-kick, one-two-three-kick monotone. *Skidoo* patronises young and old alike, which is pretty much like cutting off both legs before a track meet.

•

SKIN DEEP
1978, 103 mins, New Zealand Ⓥ col
Dir Geoff Steven ***Prod*** John Maynard ***Scr*** Piers Davies, Roger Horrocks, Geoff Steven ***Ph*** Leon Narby
Act Jim Macfarlane, Ken Blackburn, Alan Jervis, Grant Tilly, Bill Johnson, Arthur Wright (Phase Three)

Skin Deep, New Zealand's long-awaited breakthrough film, is a soberly-paced but absorbing tale of a small country town which is making its bid, via a publicity campaign, to attract tourists and industry. When a masseuse is imported from the nearest big city and Vic's Gym becomes a massage parlor and sauna the inevitable happens. Many local males are anxious to try the parlor-style sex that previously they had only read about, and the respectable matrons pressure the police to shutter the den of vice.

An excellent script and three-dimensional characters flesh out this skeleton. Central to the theme and payoff is Sandra Ray (Deryn Cooper), the masseuse who, though she still emits plenty of erotic voltage, has had enough of the sex side of the business.

Leading the parade of straying husbands on the prowl for parlor extras is Bob Warner, (Ken Blackburn) chairman of the fund-raising group, the town's leading business man and the first to run for cover when the squeeze comes on the massage establishment.

•

SKIN DEEP

1989, 101 mins, US Ⓥ ⊙ col

Dir Blake Edwards ***Prod*** Tony Adams ***Scr*** Blake Edwards ***Ph*** Isidore Mankofsky ***Ed*** Robert Pergament ***Mus*** Ivan Neville, Don Grady ***Art*** Rodger Maus

Act John Ritter, Vincent Gardenia, Alyson Reed, Joel Brooks, Julianne Phillips, Raye Hollitt (Morgan Creek/BECO)

Blake Edwards's *Skin Deep* finds the director centering again on the trials and tribulations of his favourite kind of character—the charming, womanizing sot. Fortunately, he freshens up his trademark formula by satirizing the most contemporary of current social practices: safe sex.

John Ritter is a dissipated writer with writer's block who is always to be found with a drink in his hand and an eye on a potential sexual conquest.

Ritter is married to a pretty (and pretty dull) newscaster (Alyson Reed) who is smart enough, however, to boot her husband out when she finds him in bed with her hairdresser (Julianne Phillips).

Revenge is sweet and Ritter gets his due in any number of silly and embarrassing situations which he handles with nearly perfect comic timing.

•

SKIN GAME, THE

1931, 85 mins, UK Ⓥ b/w

Dir Alfred Hitchcock ***Prod*** John Maxwell ***Scr*** Alfred Hitchcock, Alma Reville ***Ph*** Jack Cox, Charles Martin ***Ed*** Rene Harrison, A. Gobbett

Act Edmund Gwenn, Jill Esmond, John Longden, C. V. France, Helen Haye, Frank Lawton (BIP)

With Alfred Hitchcock its director, more was expected. The story appears to be run through in a straight style as though closely following John Galsworthy's London stage hit.

The playing is exceptional, both men and women. Edmund Gwenn, Phyllis Konstam, Jill Esmond and C. V. France will be accepted likely as the best performers, and into that group must go Helen Haye who is the best. Haye plays the elderly aristocratic wife.

Galsworthy wrote way over the head of the peasants for this one. Story is of a retired Englishman who sold his estate to a Scotsman. The buyer broke his word not to eject tenants on the estate and not to further build on a factory site. So the aristocratic family called it a "skin game." To assert the family's moral rights and enforce the verbal obligation, the wife (Haye) connives to uncover the past of the Scotsman's daughter-in-law.

•

SKIPPY

1931, 85 mins, US b/w

Dir Norman Taurog ***Scr*** Joseph L. Mankiewicz, Norman McLeod, Don Marquis

Act Jackie Cooper, Robert Coogan, Mitzi Green, Jackie Searl, Willard Robertson, Enid Bennett (Paramount)

All credit to the kid players, director Norman Taurog, and the adapters for taking Percy Crosby's newspaper comic strip [co-written with Sam Mintz] and making it readable and moving in scenario form.

When Skippy (Jackie Cooper) is so sorely depressed over the death of his poor kid-pal's dog, he turns down supper and goes up to his bed to cry. The two kids had tried so hard to dig up the coin for his release from the moronic dogcatcher's pound.

To get the $3 for the license they tried everything from staging a show and running out on the musicians after promoting a buck from Mitzi Green to let her play the lead, to selling lemonade for a cent a drink. When Skippy's father gives him the promised bike to ease his sorrow, Skippy trades it for Mitzi's dog. Sooky (Robert Coogan) already had gotten a new mutt meanwhile, making it a bad deal for Skippy, but Skippy's father makes the ending happy.

Cooper's playing could not be improved upon. He does everything well, never camera-conscious and never suggesting it's only a picture. The small and young Coogan boy is cute in every sense. His voice jibes with his looks and manner so well it makes him doubly cute. In contributing some valuable "heavy" aid to this talker, Jackie Searl plays his boyish assignment as well as John Barrymore ever played a lover.

1930/31: Best Director

NOMINATIONS: Best Picture, Actor (Jackie Cooper), Adapted Screenplay, Writing (Joseph L. Mankiewicz, Sam Mintz)

•

SKIP TRACER

1977, 93 mins, Canada b/w

Dir Zale Dalen ***Prod*** Laara Dalen ***Ph*** Ron Oreiux

Act David Petersen (Highlights/CFDC)

Skip Tracer, as its title implies, is an account of the methods of persons employed to recover automobiles, television sets, furniture or whatever on which the time-purchase buyers have defaulted.

Film emerges as one of the best ever turned out in British Columbia, though none of the players are known and all were recruited from Vancouver legit stage troupes. Film was made on a low budget of $145,000.

David Petersen is the central figure, the poker-faced, epitome of a hardhearted, alibi-contemptuous sleuth. Supporting players also believable.

There is a slow pace and a lack of action, but the film involves the viewer.

•

SKIRTS AHOY!

1952, 109 mins, US Ⓥ col

Dir Sidney Lanfield ***Prod*** Joe Pasternak ***Scr*** Isobel Lennart ***Ph*** William C. Mellor ***Ed*** Cotton Warburton ***Mus*** George Stoll (dir.) ***Art*** Cedric Gibbons, Daniel B. Cathcart

Act Esther Williams, Joan Evans, Vivian Blaine, Barry Sullivan, Keefe Brasselle, Margalo Gillmore (M-G-M)

Three femmes join the WAVES, after varied romantic troubles, and quickly run through a recruiting pitch depicting a rather fanciful life among distaff sailors. Plot is an adequate support for the typical musical comedy material most of the time, with seven tunes by Ralph Blane annd Harry Warren.

Femme trio is made up of Esther Williams as a rich girl who left her groom at the altar; Vivian Blaine, shopgirl whose matrimonial urge is continually frustrated by duty assignments for her sailor boyfriend; and Joan Evans, who has been deserted at the altar by a hesitant fiance. As the Great Lakes Training Base medical officer, Barry Sullivan rates the most of the little tossed to the actors in the cast. Williams has two okay swim numbers. For added help, there's a very good guest star turn by Debbie Reynolds and Bobbie Van to that oldie, "Oh, By Jingo!"

•

SKYJACKED

1972, 100 mins, US ▭ col

Dir John Guillermin ***Prod*** Walter Seltzer ***Scr*** Stanley R. Greenberg ***Ph*** Harry Stradling, Jr. ***Ed*** Robert Swink ***Mus*** Perry Botkin, Jr. ***Art*** Edward C. Carfagno

Act Charlton Heston, Yvette Mimieux, James Brolin, Claude Akins, Jeanne Crain, Susan Dey (M-G-M)

Charlton Heston and Yvette Mimieux star as pilot and stewardess respectively of a jetliner seized by James Brolin. John Guillermin's fastpaced direction makes the most of a large group of top performers. Stanley R. Greenberg's adaptation of David Harper's novel, *Hijacked*, establishes early and sustains throughout the diverse personal interactions of literally dozens of characters. The dramatic device of trapping a motley group is a venerable but effective blueprint, herein made all the more compelling by a contemporary social phenomenon. Heston is a most effective leader as the plane captain suddenly faced with a lipstick-scrawled demand for a course change to Anchorage, Alaska, where Claude Akins as a ground controller heightens the suspense of a delicate landing maneuver.

•

SKYLARK

1941, 92 mins, US b/w

Dir Mark Sandrich ***Prod*** Mark Sandrich ***Scr*** Allan Scott ***Ph*** Charles Lang, Jr. ***Ed*** LeRoy Stone ***Mus*** Victor Young

Act Claudette Colbert, Ray Milland, Brian Aherne, Binnie Barnes, Walter Abel (Paramount)

Posing the problem of a wife who finds—on their fifth wedding anniversary—that her husband is absorbed in business and taking his marital relations for granted, *Skylark* proceeds to develop a sparkling farce.

Picture carries several basic changes in story structure from Samson Raphaelson's original tale which appeared as a *Sat Eve Post* serial, a book and play. But revisions are decidedly advantageous in the transposition to the screen.

Under skillful guidance of Mark Sandrich as producer-director, story unfolds at a zestful pace, accentuating the comedic episodes to the utmost.

Claudette Colbert's performance of the wife (stage role created by Gertrude Lawrence), around whom the motivation revolves, is of high merit, and player takes advantage of every line and situation for delightful exposition. Ray Milland is topnotch as the business-absorbed advertising executive; Brian Aherne catches attention as the suave "other man."

•

SKY RIDERS

1976, 91 mins, US Ⓥ ▭ col

Dir Douglas Hickox ***Prod*** Terry Morse, Jr. ***Scr*** Jack DeWitt, Stanley Mann, Garry Michael White ***Ph*** Ousama Rawi ***Ed*** Malcolm Cooke ***Mus*** Lalo Schifrin ***Art*** Terry Ackland-Snow

Act James Coburn, Susannah York, Robert Culp, Charles Aznavour, Werner Pochath, Zou Zou (20th Century-Fox)

Hang gliding stunts provide most of the interest in *Sky Riders* filmed in Greece. The political terrorism story line is a familiar one and the screenplay is synthetic formula stuff, but the stunt work is good. The simple plot has footloose pilot James Coburn masterminding the rescue of Susannah York and her two children after bungling police operation led by Charles Aznavour doesn't produce results.

The film provoked an international incident when a Greek electrician died in an explosion accident. Ironically, no one was seriously injured in the aerial scenes. Producer Terry Morse, Jr., was arrested, exec producer Sandy Howard was detained in Greece for several weeks, and a $250,000 out-of-court settlement was made.

•

SKY WEST AND CROOKED
(US: GYPSY GIRL)

1966, 102 mins, UK Ⓥ col

Dir John Mills ***Prod*** Jack Hanbury ***Scr*** Mary Hayley Bell, John Prebble ***Ph*** Arthur Ibbetson ***Ed*** Gordon Hales ***Mus*** Malcolm Arnold ***Art*** Carmen Dillon

Act Hayley Mills, Ian McShane, Laurence Naismith, Geoffrey Bayldon, Annette Crosbie, Norman Bird (Rank)

It's a family affair with Hayley Mills starring, poppa John Mills doing his first directorial stint and his wife Mary (who writes professionally as Mary Hayley Bell), sharing the screenplay with John Prebble from her own story.

Hayley Mills portrays a village girl who is a misfit because of simplicity, the result of an accident which resulted in the death of her boy playmate and her own wounding.

The adults around the village tolerantly regard her as slightly idiotic, with her morbid obsession with death which causes her to be at her happiest when playing in the local graveyard and in burying dead pets in consecrated ground.

This naive yarn is rescued from bathos by the evident sincerity of both star and director and by a very convincing portrayal of village life, highlighted by some excellent photography by Arthur Ibbetson. John Mills has played safe in his first directing experiment and the result, while often stodgy, suggests that he knows his way around a directorial chair.

•

SLACKER

1991, 97 mins, US Ⓥ col

Dir Richard Linklater ***Prod*** Richard Linklater ***Scr*** Richard Linklater ***Ph*** Lee Daniel ***Ed*** Scott Rhodes ***Art*** Denise Montgomery, Debbie Pastor

Act Richard Linklater, Mark James, Stella Weir, John Slate, Louis Mackey, Joseph Jones (Detour)

Slacker is one of the freshest independent films to come along in some time, but because of non-narrative, non-characterization approach, film won't be to all tastes. Set in one day, the action shifts fluidly from one character to another as people walk around town, hang out in cafes, speechify and lay raps on each other.

Highly idiosyncratic and original in approach, pic was produced on a shoestring budget in Austin, Texas, in the summer of 1989 and was seen in a slightly different version in 1990 at festivals in Seattle, Dallas and Munich.

Title refers to a new species of beatnik or hippie that, from the evidence presented here, has some humor and wants to be committed to some ideal, although members could use a strong dose of reality along with their espresso to perk them up a bit. People on display are nearly all white and in their 20s.

There's the young man (director Richard Linklater himself) who opens the film by regaling a diffident cab driver with his theories of alternate realities. Arriving at his destination, he notices a woman who has been run over, whereupon the action switches to the woman's disturbed son, who apparently committed the crime. And so it goes with a population consisting of political conspiracy freaks, out-of-work musicians, car fanatics, anarchists, idle girls, would-be philosophers and proselytizers of many persuasions.

Linklater springs these seemingly random encounters together with a fluid, on-the-move style. Basic problem, given the absence of storyline, is that interest quickly rises and falls by virtue of who happens to be on screen.

•

SLAM DANCE
1987, 99 mins, US/UK Ⓥ col
Dir Wayne Wang ***Prod*** Rupert Harvey, Barry Opper ***Scr*** Don Opper ***Ph*** Amir Mokri ***Ed*** Lee Percy ***Mus*** Mitchell Froom ***Art*** Eugenio Zanetti
Act Tom Hulce, Mary Elizabeth Mastrantonio, Virginia Madsen, Millie Perkins, Adam Ant, Harry Dean Stanton (Island/Zenith/Sho)

Slam Dance is like junk food. It's brightly packaged, looks good and satisfies the hunger for entertainment, but it isn't terribly nourishing or well-made.

Tom Hulce is underground cartoonist C. C. Drood, a man whose life has come apart cheerfully at the seams. He's separated from his wife (Mary Elizabeth Mastrantonio) and daughter (Judith Barsi), though he still imagines them back together as a family.

Drood's the kind of man who never lets a little thing like marriage stand in the way of a good time or a hot romance with the beautiful and mysterious Yolande (Virginia Madsen). Only one day Yolande turns up dead and Drood's the prime suspect.

Mastrantonio is lovely as always, but without direction. Madsen fares even worse and has virtually nothing to do but look glamorous in a few scenes.

Adam Ant decorates the screen as Drood's two-timing buddy, but basically he's just along for the ride. What really holds the film together is Hulce's loosey-goosey performance which sets the tempo for the action.

•

SLAP SHOT
1977, 123 mins, US Ⓥ ⊙ col
Dir George Roy Hill ***Prod*** Robert J. Wunsch, Stephen Friedman ***Scr*** Nancy Dowd ***Ph*** Victor Kemper ***Ed*** Dede Allen ***Mus*** Elmer Bernstein ***Art*** Henry Bumstead
Act Paul Newman, Strother Martin, Michael Ontkean, Jennifer Warren, Lindsay Crouse, Jerry Houser (Universal)

Like the character played by Paul Newman in *Slap Shot*, director George Roy Hill is ambivalent on the subject of violence in professional ice hockey. Half the time Hill invites the audience to get off on the mayhem, the other half of the time he decries it.

Screenwriter Nancy Dowd, who drew on the experiences of her hockey-playing brother Ned Dowd (pic's tech advisor and a bit player), had the originality to deal with an offbeat milieu that has been rarely treated by American films.

What Dowd seems to have had in mind was a satire of American rowdyism, as brought out in the adolescent antics of this sleazy minor league Pennsylvania hockey team, of which Newman is player-coach.

Interspersed with the roughhouse rink action are scenes delineating the confused sexual liaisons of Newman and the others.

•

SLAUGHTERHOUSE-FIVE
1972, 104 mins, US Ⓥ ⊙ col
Dir George Roy Hill ***Prod*** Paul Monash ***Scr*** Stephen Geller ***Ph*** Miroslav Ondricek ***Ed*** Dede Allen ***Mus*** Glenn Gould ***Art*** Alexander Golitzen, George Webb
Act Michael Sacks, Ron Leibman, Eugene Roche, Sharon Gans, Valerie Perrine, Roberts Blossom (Universal/Vanadas)

Slaughterhouse-Five is a mechanically slick, dramatically sterile commentary about World War II and afterward, as seen through the eyes of a boob Everyman. Director George Roy Hill's arch achievement emphasizes the diffused cant to the detriment of characterizations, which are stiff, unsympathetic and skin-deep.

Stephen Geller's adaptation of Kurt Vonnegut, Jr.'s novel *Slaughterhouse-Five or The Children's Crusade* is in an academic sense fluid and lucid. Michael Sacks in his screen debut plays Billy Pilgrim, the luckless loser who always seems to be in the wrong place at the wrong time. The story jumps around from its beginning in World War II where as a dumb draftee Pilgrim becomes a prisoner of war in Germany.

In the postwar period, Pilgrim moves into the orbits of overweight wife and predictable offspring.

•

SLAUGHTER ON TENTH AVENUE
1957, 103 mins, US b/w
Dir Arnold Laven ***Prod*** Albert Zugsmith ***Scr*** Lawrence Roman ***Ph*** Fred Jackman ***Ed*** Russell F. Schoengarth ***Mus*** Herschel Burke Gilbert (arr.) ***Art*** Alexander Golitzen, Robert E. Smith
Act Richard Egan, Jan Sterling, Dan Duryea, Julie Adams, Walter Matthau, Charles McGraw (Universal)

Slaughter on Tenth Avenue, the title of Richard Rodgers's ballet music from *On Your Toes*, is effectively employed for a hard-hitting and commendable film about racketeering on the New York waterfront. The picture is adapted from a book entitled *The Man Who Rocked the Boat* by William J. Keating and Richard Carter.

Since Keating was a N.Y. assistant district attorney whose true-life experiences with waterfront gangs are recorded in the book, the film has a quiet, documentary flavor and contains a minimum of the false heroics that usually appear in pictures of this type.

The story presents Richard Egan as Keating, a young assistant d.a. who has been assigned to a shooting case stemming from waterfront conflicts. Mickey Shaughnessy, an honest longshoreman, is shot because of his efforts to eliminate the gangster elements from the docks. Shaughnessy, his wife (Jan Sterling) and his supporters at first follow the underworld code of not revealing the identity of the triggermen. However, Keating is persistent.

Egan is convincing as the at-first-wide-eyed and then tough assistant DA from the Pennsylvania coal country. Sterling is excellent as Shaughnessy's tough yet tender and understanding wife.

•

SLAVE SHIP
1937, 90 mins, US b/w
Dir Tay Garnett ***Prod*** Darryl F. Zanuck ***Scr*** Sam Hellman, Lamar Trotti, Gladys Lehman, William Faulkner ***Ph*** Ernest Palmer ***Mus*** Alfred Newman
Act Warner Baxter, Wallace Beery, Elizabeth Allan, Mickey Rooney, George Sanders, Jane Darwell (20th Century-Fox)

While a lot of the acting and motivation reeks of the phoney, *Slave Ship* is so effectively mounted and shot through with action that it stands up.

Director Tay Garnett passes up no known artifice for intensifying the gymnastic implications of ship fighting. He has his bullet-struck sailors popping off from the halyards, the crow's nest and where not. The dives these extras take make an Olympiad in themselves.

As a couple of the last of the slave runners, Warner Baxter and Wallace Beery move along elementary grooves, the former going from one tight spot to another, and the latter playing his dumb, sentimental scalawag to the hilt. Elizabeth Allan carves out a telling performance where it has to do with romantic interludes. Mickey Rooney also bats out a neat score, accounting for most of the film's scanty allotment of comedy as the cabin boy.

Most of the action [from the novel by George S. King] is laid aboard the barque *Albatross*. Ill-fated from the day she is launched, the ship finally comes into the ownership of Baxter who, with Beery as his first mate and partner, puts her in the trade of smuggling slaves from Africa to America.

•

SLEEPER
1973, 88 mins, US Ⓥ ⊙ col
Dir Woody Allen ***Prod*** Jack Grossberg ***Scr*** Woody Allen, Marshall Brickman ***Ph*** David M. Walsh ***Ed*** Ralph Rosenblum ***Mus*** Woody Allen ***Art*** Dale Hennesy
Act Woody Allen, Diane Keaton, John Beck, Mary Gregory, Don Keefer, Don McLiam (United Artists)

Woody Allen's *Sleeper*, is a nutty futuristic comedy, with Allen brought back to life 200 years hence to find himself a wanted man in a totally regulated society. Diane Keaton again plays his foil, and both are hilarious. The Dixieland music score [played by Allen with the Preservation Hall Jazz Band and New Orleans Funeral & Ragtime Orchestra] is just one more delightful non sequitur.

Story opens with Bartlett Robinson and Mary Gregory, two underground scientists, restoring Allen to life from a two-century deep freeze after sudden death from a minor operation. Allen is hunted as an alien. In the course of avoiding capture he becomes first a robot servant to Keaton, later her captor, then rescuer, finally her lover in a fadeout clinch. The film is loaded with throwaway literacy and broad slapstick, and while it fumbles the end, the parade of verbal and visual amusement is pleasant as long as it lasts.

The star teaming resembles, on a much more advanced basis, the Bob Hope pix of the 1940s in which he starred with some gorgeous leading women in a series of improbable but delightful escapades.

•

SLEEPERS
1996, 152 mins, US Ⓥ ⊙ ▭ col
Dir Barry Levinson ***Prod*** Barry Levinson, Steve Golin ***Scr*** Barry Levinson ***Ph*** Michael Ballhaus ***Ed*** Stu Linder ***Mus*** John Williams ***Art*** Kristi Zea
Act Kevin Bacon, Robert De Niro, Dustin Hoffman, Jason Patric, Brad Pitt, Minnie Driver (Propaganda/Baltimore/PolyGram)

Owing a lot to Martin Scorsese's New York films about petty gangsters and goodfellas, *Sleepers*, based on Lorenzo Carcaterra's controversial semi-autobiography, is shrewdly packaged to appeal to a mass audience, though its revenge theme carries a questionable message.

Basically an ensemble piece, pic is notable for being the first to costar two of the top actors of their generation, Robert De Niro and Dustin Hoffman, who give solid performances as a fatherly priest and washed-up attorney. Hoffman's is the lesser role, but the actor makes the most of his material.

Levinson's best films have focused on friendship, and friendship proves to be the central theme of this evocative tale of four Hell's Kitchen teenagers—Shakes, Michael, John and Tommy—whose lives are irreparably changed by one foolhardy moment of recklessness in the summer of '67, when a thoughtless incident involving a quick-tempered Greek hot dog vendor results in a near-fatal accident. The boys are sentenced to a Dickensian hell-hole where chief guard Nokes (Kevin Bacon) proves to be a sadistic pedophile.

About one hour into the film, the action abruptly shifts to the fall of 1981. Shakes (Jason Patric) is now a journalist and Michael (Brad Pitt) an assistant d.a., while John (Ron Eldard) and Tommy (Billy Crudup) are street-smart drug dealers and killers. Revenge theme kicks in when John and Tommy happen across Nokes.

As in *A Time to Kill*, the assumption here is that because the crimes against the four youths were truly terrible, the avenging of those crimes outside the legal system is perfectly in order.

Production values are tiptop. John Williams contributes another solid score.

1996: NOMINATION: Best Original Dramatic Score

•

SLEEPERS, THE
SEE: LITTLE NIKITA

•

SLEEPING BEAUTY
1959, 75 mins, US Ⓥ ⊙ ▭ col
Dir Clyde Geronimi (sup.) ***Prod*** Walt Disney ***Scr*** Erdman Penner ***Ed*** Roy M. Brewer, Jr., Donald Halliday ***Mus*** George Bruns (adapt.)(Walt Disney)

Sleeping Beauty, adapted from the Charles Perrault version of the fairy tale (and reportedly costing $6 million), is no surprise in its familiar outlines. It's the story of Princess Aurora, who is put under a spell at birth by the bad fairy, Maleficent. She is to prick her finger on a spinning wheel and die before she grows up. But the good fairies, Flora, Fauna and Merryweather, are able to amend the curse. The princess shall not die, but shall fall into a deep sleep. She will be awakened by her true love, Prince Philip.

Mary Costa's rich and expressive voice for the title character gives substance and strength to it. The music is an adaptation of Tchaikovsky's *Sleeping Beauty* ballet, and it is music—where adapted for song—that requires something more than just a pleasant voice. Bill Shirley, as the prince, contributes some good vocal work. His cartoon character is considerably more masculine than Disney heroes usually are. Some of the best parts of the picture are those dealing with the three good fairies, spoken and sung by Verna Felton, Barbara Jo Allen and Barbara Luddy.

The picture was shot in Technirama and Technicolor, and then, when completed, printed for 70mm on special printer lenses developed for Disney by Panavision. Disney gives credit to more than 70 contributors on *Sleeping Beauty*. Clyde Geronimi was supervising director, and Eric Larson, Wolfgang Reitherman and Les Clark, the sequence directors.

1959: NOMINATION: Best Scoring of a Musical Picture

•

SLEEPING DOGS
1977, 107 mins, New Zealand Ⓥ col
Dir Roger Donaldson ***Prod*** Roger Donaldson ***Scr*** Ian Mune, Arthur Baysting ***Ph*** Michael Sarasin ***Ed*** Ian John ***Mus*** Murray Grindlay
Act Sam Neill, Bernard Kearns, Nevan Rowe, Ian Mune, Ian Watkin, Don Selwyn (Aardvark)

Sleeping Dogs has sharp directional flair evident, particularly in the action segments, taut performances by the large cast and a handsome technical gloss in all departments.

When the pictures are left to tell the story they do it with great visual impact. The script is less successful.

The story is a political thriller [from the novel *Smith's Dream* by Karl Stead], set in New Zealand of the near future, and sees the small democracy taken over by the rightist party in power, via rigged shooting at a street demonstration. Overnight a police state is set up, and a counter-revolutionary force of freedom-fighters starts hitting back. As Smith, Sam Neill is natural. He projects the right intensity for a man caught up in an Orwellian nightmare.

•

SLEEPING WITH THE ENEMY
1991, 98 mins, US Ⓥ ⦿ col
Dir Joseph Ruben ***Prod*** Leonard Goldberg ***Scr*** Ronald Bass ***Ph*** John W. Lindley ***Ed*** George Bowers ***Mus*** Jerry Goldsmith ***Art*** Doug Kraner
Act Julia Roberts, Patrick Bergin, Kevin Anderson, Elizabeth Lawrence, Kyle Secor (20th Century-Fox)

In *Sleeping with the Enemy*, a chilling look at marital abuse gives way to a streamlined thriller [from the novel by Nancy Price] delivering mucho sympathy for imperiled heroine Julia Roberts and screams aplenty as she's stalked by her maniacal husband.

Laura (Roberts) appears to be a perfect doll wife dwelling in an isolated Cape Cod beach manse with successful financial consultant Martin (Patrick Bergin). In fact, he's an overbearing control freak. She's actually been plotting her escape for a long time. One night she gets her chance, slipping off a sailboat during a storm and swimming ashore while her husband believes she's drowned.

But Martin comes up with enough peculiar clues to believe he's been had. Soon after Laura, who's renamed herself Sara Waters, is ensconced in an idyllic Iowa college town and forging a friendship with a sweet-natured drama teacher (Kevin Anderson), the menacing Martin is on the trail. Ironically, it's Laura's poor, blind, stroke-ridden mother (Elizabeth Lawrence) who points Martin toward her door, and once there in indulges some unique forms of fetishistic terrorism.

Roberts is terrific in a layered part. Anderson brings an edge to the nice-guy-next-door role, and the dark, dashing Bergin is chillingly twisted.

•

SLEEPLESS IN SEATTLE
1993, 104 mins, US col
Dir Nora Ephron ***Prod*** Gary Foster ***Scr*** Nora Ephron, David S. Ward, Jeff Arch ***Ph*** Sven Nykvist ***Ed*** Robert Reitano ***Mus*** Marc Shaiman ***Art*** Jeffrey Townsend
Act Tom Hanks, Meg Ryan, Bill Pullman, Ross Malinger, Rosie O'Donnell, Gaby Hoffmann (Tri-Star)

Having achieved her greatest success writing *When Harry Met Sally . . .*, director-cowriter Nora Ephron tries a slightly new riff on that theme in this shamelessly romantic comedy [from a screen story by Jeff Arch]. Pic delivers ample warmth and some explosively funny moments. Sam (Tom Hanks) is still grieving over the death of his wife (Carey Lowell, seen in flashback) when his son Jonah (Ross Malinger) phones a latenight radio call-in show saying he thinks the solution is for dad to remarry. Sam reluctantly gets on the line and ends up spilling his guts. Among those listening is Annie (Meg Ryan), a just-engaged newspaper reporter whose husband-to-be, Walter (Bill Pullman), is sensible but not very exciting. She finds herself increasingly obsessed with "Sleepless in Seattle," Sam's on-air handle.

For all the enjoyable flourishes, and there are many, Ephron keeps pausing to remind us that this is a movie, making it hard for anyone to really get lost in the story. And since the big question isn't "if," but "when" and "how," the film loses considerable momentum about two-thirds through before rallying for a heart-tugging finale.

Hanks certainly figures to increase his stock as a well-rounded actor and not just a comic, while Ryan essentially plays the same character as *Sally*, with pleasing if predictable results.

1993: NOMINATIONS: Best Original Screenplay, Song ("A Wink and a Smile")

•

SLEEP, MY LOVE
1948, 94 mins, US b/w
Dir Douglas Sirk ***Prod*** Charles (Buddy) Rogers, Ralph Cohn ***Scr*** St. Clair McKelway, Leo Rosten ***Ph*** Joseph Valentine ***Ed*** Lynn Harrison ***Mus*** Rudy Schrager ***Art*** William Ferrari
Act Claudette Colbert, Robert Cummings, Don Ameche, Hazel Brooks, George Coulouris, Raymond Burr (United Artists)

Sleep, My Love manages a fair share of suspense and adds up to okay melodrama. Plot gets off to a strong start and windup is high melodrama that brings off the finale on a fast note.

Basic story is the familiar one of the man who wants to kill off his wealthy wife so he can marry the sex trollop. Development, however, brings in some new angles.

Claudette Colbert is the healthy, wealthy wife who is being stealthily drugged by husband Don Ameche. Under drugged hypnosis, she is made to do strange things that indicate a mental crackup. Opener has her awakening on a train to Boston, unable to explain how it happened. Next she sees a strange, sinister character who gives her a phony psychoanalysis.

Douglas Sirk paces his direction neatly in handling the not always smooth script by St. Clair McKelway and Leo Rosten [based on the novel by Leo Rosten].

•

SLEEPWALKERS
1992, 91 mins, US Ⓥ ⦿ col
Dir Mick Garris ***Prod*** Mark Victor, Mark Grais, Nabeel Zahid ***Scr*** Stephen King ***Ph*** Rodney Charters ***Ed*** O. Nicholas Brown ***Mus*** Nicholas Pike ***Art*** John DeCuir, Jr.
Act Brian Krause, Madchen Amick, Alice Krige, Jim Haynie, Cindy Pickett, Ron Perlman (Ion/Victor & Grais)

Stephen King's *Sleepwalkers* is an idiotic horror potboiler. New approach to the vampire legend is really a variation on TriStar's 1988 flop *The Kiss*. Brian Krause and mom Alice Krige are incestuous monsters called Sleepwalkers who survive by draining the life force from virgin girls.

Film takes place in sleepy Travis, IN, where Krause is the new kid in school claiming to be a transfer student. He romances beautiful classmate Madchen Amick, resulting in a pretentious date-rape scene in which Amick is saved from a fate worse than death *and* worse than rape. King's screenplay has no internal logic and relies wholly on stupid gimmicks like the monsters' ability to become invisible and their vulnerability to cats. The potential pathos of Krause and Krige as perhaps the last lonely members of their breed is undeveloped.

Many noted genre directors (Joe Dante, Tobe Hooper) as well as King himself have pointless cameo roles. Even Amick's name "Tanya Robertson" seems like a pun on sexy actress Tanya Roberts. Cast is physically appealing and could have generated some sympathy if permitted.

•

SLEEP WITH ME
1994, 85 mins, US Ⓥ col
Dir Rory Kelly ***Prod*** Michael Steinberg, Roger Hedden, Eric Stoltz ***Scr*** Duane Dell'Amico, Roger Hedden, Neal Jimenez, Joe Keenan, Rory Kelly, Michael Steinberg ***Ph*** Andrzej Sekula ***Ed*** David Moritz ***Mus*** David Lawrence ***Art*** Randy Eriksen
Act Craig Sheffer, Eric Stoltz, Meg Tilly, Joey Lauren Adams, Parker Posey, Quentin Tarantino (Castleberg/August)

Sleep with Me is as erratic as only a film with six writers can be. Initially cloying and cliched, group portrait of twentysomethings in romantic disarray slowly gathers interest as things build to a dramatic head. Rory Kelly's first feature bears decided similarities to *Bodies, Rest & Motion*, with which it shares talent in the producing, writing and acting areas, as well as a lineup of foggy, self-involved characters groping to get on track in life.

Longtime couple Joseph (Eric Stoltz) and Sarah (Meg Tilly) decide to get married. This doesn't much change their L.A. lifestyle, however, as their extended family of friends continues to surround them. Joseph's best friend, Frank (Craig Sheffer), decides it's time to declare his overwhelming love for Sarah by kissing her in front of everyone at a dinner party. The fact that they have great sex in their one session together complicates matters considerably.

Conceived by Kelly and *Bodies* writer Roger Hedden, script is structured around several large-scale social events—some parties, a dinner and a couple of poker games—each of which was written by a different writer. A hilarious recurring riff by Quentin Tarantino, in which he delivers a convoluted but coherent interpretation of *Top Gun* as a gay film, packs more punch than anything else in the picture. Stoltz, Sheffer and Tilly are competent and amiable without being compelling.

•

SLEEPY HOLLOW
1999, 105 mins, US Ⓥ ⦿ col
Dir Tim Burton ***Prod*** Scott Rudin, Adam Schroeder ***Scr*** Andrew Kevin Walker ***Ph*** Emmanuel Lubezki ***Ed*** Chris Lebenzon ***Mus*** Danny Elfman ***Art*** Rick Heinrichs
Act Johnny Depp, Christina Ricci, Miranda Richardson, Michael Gambon, Casper Van Dien, Jeffrey Jones (Rudin/American Zoetrope/Mandalay/Paramount)

Tim Burton's *Sleepy Hollow* is an entertainingly eccentric horror tale that envelopes the audience in a dreamy and bloody nightmare. At the same time, Washington Irving's classic story about Ichabod Crane and the fearsome Headless Horseman has been radically reconceived [from a screen story by Kevin Yagher and scripter Andrew Kevin Walker] for the express purpose of maximizing the mayhem, a legitimate if very '90s ploy that puts the picture on a somewhat predictable and repetitive track.

In the opulence of a quasi-historical world mostly within studio confines, as well as its bloodthirstiness, *Sleepy Hollow* forcibly recalls [the 1992] *Dracula*, whose director, Francis Coppola, is one of the exec producers here.

Re-creating a small Hudson River community of exactly 200 years ago, in the fall of 1799, Burton and his outstanding collaborators have rigorously developed a monochromatic look that is broken only by intrusion of the color red.

New York City constable Crane (Johnny Depp) is sent on a two-day journey up the river to "detect" the murderer in three grisly beheadings in the vicinity of Sleepy Hollow, a mostly Dutch community haunted by a violent past. Welcomed at the home of the village's most affluent citizen, Baltus Van Tassel (Michael Gambon), Ichabod learns the story of the Hessian Horseman (Christopher Walken), a German mercenary who slew countless settlers on behalf of the English during the Revolutionary War before being killed himself.

Tousled, obstinate and resolute in his rationalism, Depp is engaging as the thoughtful outsider who takes on the literal demon of an insular community. Pic was shot in the U.K., with some follow-up lensing in New York.

1999: Best Art Direction

NOMINATIONS: Best Cinematography, Costume Design

•

SLENDER THREAD, THE
1965, 98 mins, US b/w
Dir Sydney Pollack ***Prod*** Stephen Alexander ***Scr*** Stirling Silliphant ***Ph*** Loyal Griggs ***Ed*** Thomas Stanford ***Mus*** Quincy Jones ***Art*** Hal Pereira, Jack Poplin
Act Sidney Poitier, Anne Bancroft, Telly Savalas, Steven Hill, Ed Asner, Indus Arthur (Athene/Paramount)

The Slender Thread, suggested by a May 29, 1964, *Life* article by Shana Alexander (wife of producer) of an actual occurrence, is supercharged with emotion and dramatic overtones. As a showy vehicle for talents of Sidney Poitier and Anne Bancroft, the production offers mounting tension, but good as the picture is it could have been improved through more lucid writing. Story is of a distraught woman who has taken an overdose of barbiturates and phones a clinic. Film takes its title from the telephone line which suddenly becomes a slender thread by means of Poitier, a college student volunteer who answers femme's call, must try to save her life without breaking the connection.

Poitier, who remains on the telephone almost the entire unreeling of the picture, delivers a compelling performance, matched by Bancroft as the tortured wife and mother who attempts suicide when she sees her marriage of 12 years going down the drain.

Film is kept on a realistic level. The two stars never meet, their sole contact strictly telephonic.

1965: NOMINATIONS: Best B&W Costume Design, B&W Art Direction

•

SLEUTH
1973, 138 mins, UK Ⓥ ⦿ col
Dir Joseph L. Mankiewicz ***Prod*** Morton Gottlieb ***Scr*** Anthony Shaffer ***Ph*** Oswald Morris ***Ed*** Richard Marden ***Mus*** John Addison ***Art*** Ken Adam
Act Laurence Olivier, Michael Caine (Palomar/20th Century Fox)

Joseph L. Mankiewicz's film version of *Sleuth* is terrific. Anthony Shaffer's topnotch screenplay of his legit hit provides Laurence Olivier and especially Michael Caine with two of their best roles.

Olivier is outstanding as the famed mystery novelist and society figure who is galled at the prospect of losing his wife to Caine. Latter is sensational as the lower-class tradesman (hairdresser) who eventually proves himself worthy of playing the game of cat-and-mouse with which Olivier seeks to avenge his honor.

Ken Adam's outstanding production design, replete with the automated gadgetry with which Olivier's character enjoys his private games, contributes mightily to the overall achievement.

1972: NOMINATIONS: Best Director, Actor (Michael Caine, Lawrence Olivier), Original Score

•

SLIDING DOORS
1998, 108 mins, UK/US Ⓥ ⦿ col
Dir Peter Howitt ***Prod*** Sydney Pollack, Philippa Braithwaite, William Horberg ***Scr*** Peter Howitt ***Ph*** Remi Adefarasin ***Ed*** John Smith ***Mus*** David Hirschfelder ***Art*** Maria Djurkovic
Act Gwyneth Paltrow, John Hannah, John Lynch, Jeanne Tripplehorn, Zara Turner, Douglas McFerran (Mirage/Miramax/Paramount)

Sliding Doors is a frothy, lightweight romantic comedy that strives to seem richer and more complex than it really is. Peter Howitt, a British actor making his bigscreen writing and directing debut, has whipped up a concoction with enough quick wit and charm, a solid star vehicle for Gwyneth Paltrow.

Before the opening reel is finished, saucy young Helen (Paltrow) is fired from her job, mugged by a purse-snatcher and jilted by her live-in boyfriend, Jerry (John Lynch). And while she is indeed being betrayed by Gerry, the latter turn of events is one Helen sees only in an alternative reality that is triggered when the sliding doors of a tube car close on her.

Pictures plays out on parallel tracks—what might have happened had she made the train [and what might have happened had she not. In the former,] Helen arrives home early to find Gerry in the sack with his former g.f., Lydia (Jeanne Tripplehorn); [in the latter] she only vaguely suspects something based on odd hints.

Entire picture is built around Paltrow, who sports a reasonable English accent and very nearly shines as a young career woman caught up short by professional and personal setbacks. Helen's pain at being betrayed is gradually offset by the amusing and increasingly amorous attentions of James (John Hannah), whom the actor makes almost impossibly charming and tactful.

Howitt proves himself a good writer of glib, bubbly dialogue, and the frequency of yocks is sufficient to keep most viewers happy.

•

SLING BLADE
1996, 136 mins, US Ⓥ ⦿ col
Dir Billy Bob Thornton ***Prod*** Brandon Rosser, David L. Bushell ***Scr*** Billy Bob Thornton ***Ph*** Barry Markowitz ***Ed*** Hughes Winborne ***Mus*** Daniel Lanois ***Art*** Clark Hunter
Act Billy Bob Thornton, Dwight Yoakam, J. T. Walsh, John Ritter, Lucas Black, Natalie Canderday (Shooting Gallery)

A slowly accruing character study of several Southern misfits that possesses the remorseless inevitability of a Greek tragedy, *Sling Blade* makes a forceful but uneven cut. Marked by some powerful scenes, fine performances and colorful dialogue, this talented directorial debut by actor-writer Billy Bob Thornton has its effectiveness diluted by serious overlength and a rather monotonous, unmodulated tone.

Project had its origins in a short, *Some Call It a Sling Blade*, directed by George Hickenlooper, that attracted favorable notice a couple of years back. It has basically been reshot to make up the opening reel of the feature, which takes off from there.

A patient in a mental hospital (a terrific J. T. Walsh) tells a few sex-obsessed stories to another patient, Karl Childers (Thornton), due to be released that day. Karl then tells how, when he was about 12, he took a sling blade and hacked up a neighbor and his own mother [who had been engaging in sex].

Karl takes up residence with an unhappy young boy (Lucas Black) and his widowed mother, Linda (Natalie Canderday). Here he comes into contact with another outcast, Vaughan (John Ritter), as well as Linda's boyfriend (country singer Dwight Yoakam). Slowly, the gears of Thornton's script start to turn toward the inexorable climax. Production values are decent for this pic, shot in Benton, AR.

1996: Best Screenplay Adaptation

NOMINATION: Best Actor (Billy Bob Thornton)

•

SLIPPER AND THE ROSE, THE
THE STORY OF CINDERELLA
1976, 146 mins, UK Ⓥ ▭ col
Dir Bryan Forbes ***Prod*** Stuart Lyons ***Scr*** Bryan Forbes, Richard M. Sherman, Robert B. Sherman ***Ph*** Tony Imi ***Ed*** Timothy Gee ***Mus*** Richard M. Sherman, Robert B. Sherman ***Art*** Raymond Simm
Act Richard Chamberlain, Gemma Craven, Annette Crosbie, Edith Evans, Christopher Gable, Michael Hordern (Paradine)

What script has managed to do so surprisingly well is first of all to modernize the classic Cinderella tale, making it entertaining and (almost) believable for adults while preserving basic pattern and texture of the original for the youngsters.

Richard Chamberlain makes a believable, feet-on-the-ground Prince, Gemma Craven is a pretty and very effective Cinderella.

Michael Hordern steals many a scene as the king, in a very good performance; Kenneth More has great moments as the chamberlain; while Edith Evans thefts the scenes she's in with some irresistible windup oneliners.

Physical facets, from eye-popping Pinewood Studio sets to the lushly romantic Austrian exteriors, are standout.

1977: NOMINATION: Best Adapted Score, Song

•

SLIPSTREAM
1989, 101 mins, UK Ⓥ ⦿ col
Dir Steven Lisberger ***Prod*** Gary Kurtz ***Scr*** Tony Kayden ***Ph*** Frank Tidy ***Ed*** Terry Rawlings ***Mus*** Elmer Bernstein ***Art*** Andrew McAlpine
Act Mark Hamill, Bob Peck, Bill Paxton, Kitty Aldridge, Ben Kingsley, F. Murray Abraham (Entertainment)

British-made sci-fi adventure romp *Slipstream* is one of those films that had potential, but unfortunately it doesn't make the grade.

Slipstream seems to be making some kind of ecological message; the film's version of Earth [from a story by Sam Clemens] is a place ruined by pollution with the planet washed clean by a river of wind called the "Slipstream."

Lawman Mark Hamill and his partner Kitty Aldridge capture Bob Peck, who's wanted for murder. When adventurer Bill Paxton discovers there is a price on Peck's head he snatches him and makes his escape down the Slipstream.

They come across a cult of religious fanatics who worship the wind, led by Ben Kingsley. One of the cult (Eleanor David) falls for Peck—even though it turns out he is an android.

Strong points are the stunning locations (Turkey and the Yorkshire moors), the performances by Hamill and Aldridge, plus impressive aircraft and technical effects. Kingsley and F. Murray Abraham have virtual walk-on parts.

•

SLITHER
1973, 98 mins, US Ⓥ col
Dir Howard Zieff ***Prod*** Jack Sher ***Scr*** W. D. Richter ***Ph*** Laszlo Kovacs ***Ed*** David Bretherton ***Mus*** Tom McIntosh ***Art*** Dale Hennesy
Act James Caan, Peter Boyle, Sally Kellerman, Louise Lasser, Allen Garfield, Richard B. Shull (M-G-M)

Slither is, in effect, an excellent, live-action, feature-length counterpart to a great old Warner Bros. cartoon. That is to say, a combination of physical and visual madness overlaid with satirical, throwaway sophistication which ends up its caper plot while nourishing it to the full.

W. D. Richter's first produced script is a smash achievement in structure and dialog. James Caan is superb as a likeable paroled car thief whose incidental friendship with Richard B. Shull, an embezzler, leads him into contact with a bizarre set of characters, some in search of a concealed fortune, others determined to thwart the treasure hunt.

The characters road-run over the countryside, where a couple of ominous black vans and several ordinary-looking businessmen create a mood of latent terror.

•

SLIVER
1993, 106 mins, US Ⓥ ⦿ ▭ col
Dir Phillip Noyce ***Prod*** Robert Evans ***Scr*** Joe Eszterhas ***Ph*** Vilmos Zsigmond, Michael A. Benson, Laszlo Kovacs ***Ed*** Richard Frances-Bruce, William Hoy ***Mus*** Howard Shore ***Art*** Paul Sylbert
Act Sharon Stone, William Baldwin, Tom Berenger, Polly Walker, Colleen Camp, Martin Landau (Paramount)

After ratings board strife and last-minute reshoots, *Sliver* proves all flash and no sizzle—a thriller that simply changes gender on the *Basic Instinct* formula to "did he or didn't he?"

Working from Ira Levin's novel, writer Joe Eszterhas and director Phillip Noyce have crafted a cold, inaccessible yarn about murder and voyeurism that's too leisurely about getting where it needs to go and doesn't fully develop what should be its core: a just-divorced woman (Sharon Stone) drawn into a kinky, voyeuristic relationship with mysterious younger man (William Baldwin).

Carly (Stone) is a book editor who moves into a new building and catches the eye of both Zeke (Baldwin), a computer whiz, and Jack (Tom Berenger), a burned-out writer who comes on strong right away. Carly discovers Zeke owns the building, has each unit wired with intrusive video cameras and that there's been a series of murders there—including a woman to whom she bears an unerring resemblance and who occupied her unit.

Blame it on the editing and reediting, but even the sex scenes aren't all that steamy, and the movie suffers from some choppy moments and highrise-size lapses in logic.

For Stone fans, the actress shows a lot less here, both literally and figuratively, than she did in her menacing and alluring turn in *Basic Instinct*. Baldwin brings the requisite creepy-yet-alluring quality to the role, while Berenger sleepwalks through an underdeveloped character.

•

SLOW DANCING IN THE BIG CITY
1978, 101 mins, US col
Dir John G. Avildsen ***Prod*** Michael Levee, John G. Avildsen ***Scr*** Barra Grant ***Ph*** Ralf Bode ***Ed*** John G. Avildsen ***Mus*** Bill Conti ***Art*** Henry Shrady
Act Paul Sorvino, Anne Ditchburn, Nicolas Coster, Anita Dangler, Hector Jaime Mercado, Thaao Penghlis (United Artists)

Slow Dancing in the Big City has so much heart John Avildsen's aorta is showing.

Barra Grant's story is a simple boy meets girl tale, or in this case, dancer meets columnist. Anne Ditchburn, a lovely dancer and choreographer, meets Paul Sorvino, the columnist.

Sorvino seems to do a good job in any picture under any conditions and he's just terrific here. Ditchburn is promising, but the post-production looping is downright dreadful and interferes not just with her performance but with the flow of the film.

A number of dancing scenes featuring Ditchburn—performances, rehearsals and a solo on the roof of a Manhattan apartment—are among the production's high points.

The film has two plots moving along side by side although the focus clearly is on the Ditchburn-Sorvino relationship. The second genuinely touching plot concerns a young ghetto kid Sorvino is writing about and his struggle to overcome the harsh city.

What's a shame about *Slow Dancing* is that somewhere on the cutting room floor probably is a fine film.

•

SLUMBER PARTY MASSACRE
(UK: SLUMBER PARTY MURDERS)
1982, 84 mins, US Ⓥ col
Dir Amy Jones ***Prod*** Amy Jones, Aaron Lipstadt ***Scr*** Rita Mae Brown ***Ph*** Steve Posey ***Ed*** Wendy Allan ***Mus*** Ralph Jones ***Art*** Pam Canzano
Act Michele Michaels, Robin Stille, Michael Villela, Andre Honore (Santa Fe)

Besides its obviously catchy title, *Slumber Party Massacre* is an entertaining terror thriller, with the switch that distaff filmmakers handle the "young women in jeopardy" format.

Set in Venice, CA, pic concerns high school girls having a sleep-over party, with "let's scare 'em" antics by the boyfriends. Meanwhile, a mad killer is in the vicinity, wasting kids of both sexes in bloody fashion with a portable drill and various wicked knives.

Out of traditional horror material consisting of red herrings, sudden shock movements into frame, etc., helmer Amy Jones develops some very stylish sequences. Notable is a complex mid-film montage mixing (with matched compositions) a horror film on TV, actual killings by the nut, and the sister chatting humorously on the phone.

•

SLUMBER PARTY MURDERS
SEE: SLUMBER PARTY MASSACRE

•

SMALL BACK ROOM, THE
(US: HOUR OF GLORY)
1949, 106 mins, UK b/w
Dir Michael Powell, Emeric Pressburger ***Prod*** Michael Powell, Emeric Pressburger ***Scr*** Michael Powell, Emeric Pressburger, Nigel Balchin ***Ph*** Christopher Challis ***Ed*** Clifford Turner, Reginald Mills ***Mus*** Brian Easdale ***Art*** Hein Heckroth
Act David Farrar, Kathleen Byron, Jack Hawkins, Cyril Cusack, Michael Gough, Leslie Banks (London/Archers)

Central character in the plot [from a novel by Nigel Balchin] is Sammy Rice, scientist and research worker, whose lame foot has made him a complex individual. Although becoming extremely unpopular by his frank and adverse comments on a new type of anti-tank gun, he redeems himself by dismantling a booby bomb which is the enemy's latest secret weapon. It is this latter scene which is by far the high spot of the production, and although it is a long time coming it is handled to extract every ounce of suspense from it. In scenes like that the drama becomes real and satisfying but the same reaction isn't forthcoming in the highly imaginative sequence in which the complex Sammy seeks solace in whisky.

•

SMALLEST SHOW ON EARTH, THE
(US: BIG TIME OPERATORS)
1957, 81 mins, UK Ⓥ b/w
Dir Basil Dearden ***Prod*** Michael Relph ***Scr*** William Rose, John Eldridge ***Ph*** Douglas Slocombe ***Ed*** Oswald Hafenrichter ***Mus*** William Alwyn ***Art*** Allan Harris
Act Bill Travers, Virginia McKenna, Leslie Phillips, Peter Sellers, Margaret Rutherford, Bernard Miles (British Lion)

William Rose, who scripted *Genevieve*, has fashioned a shrewd and bright comedy around the exhibition side of motion pictures. The center of interest is a small, derelict picture house inherited by a young struggling writer.

The theatre, in a small, smelly provincial town, is adjacent to the mainline railroad station. The staff comprises three ancients—Margaret Rutherford, who played the piano in the silent days, but now sits at the cash desk; Peter Sellers, the boothman with a weakness for whisky; and Bernard Miles, a doorman and general handyman.

When Bill Travers and Virginia McKenna inherit the theatre, their immediate reaction is to sell out to the opposition, who had made a substantial offer to the previous owner. But the offer now forthcoming would not even be adequate to meet the inherited debts, so they set about on a big bluff, pretending to re-open in the hope that the bids will be bettered.

The film is loaded with delightful touches, and there's one prolonged laughter sequence when the projectionist is on a drinking bout and Bill Travers takes over the booth.

•

SMALL FACES
1996, 102 mins, UK Ⓥ ⊙ col
Dir Gillies MacKinnon ***Prod*** Billy MacKinnon, Steve Clarke-Hall ***Scr*** Billy MacKinnon, Gillies MacKinnon ***Ph*** John de Borman ***Ed*** Scott Thomas ***Mus*** John Keane ***Art*** Zoe Macleod
Act Claire Higgins, Iain Robertson, Joseph McFadden, J. S. Duffy, Laura Fraser (Skyline/BBC)

The violent flipside to the swinging '60s is captured to powerful effect in *Small Faces*, a Scottish-set drama of restless hormones and teen confusion that reps a powerful return to roots by helmer Gillies MacKinnon after his Steve Martin starrer *A Simple Twist of Fate*.

Setting is Glasgow (MacKinnon's home town), 1968, where widow Lorna MacLean (Claire Higgins, good in a shaded performance) has her hands full with her three teenage kids: screwed-up Bobby (J. S. Duffy), who runs with the gang led by thug Charlie Sloan (Gerry Sweeney); sensitive Alan (Joseph McFadden), who just wants to go to art school; and 13-year-old midget Lex (Iain Robertson), a self-styled "genius" who's awed by all the "adult" action going on around him.

When Lex accidentally shoots the psycho leader of the feared Tongs gang, Malky Thompson (Kevin McKidd), in the head with his air gun, Lex gets drawn into the escalating violence that's the only escape valve for tenement youths in the north.

One of the pic's strengths is its gradual easing into the subject matter. Gang warfare and the much-feared Malky appear only halfway through, by which time we're fully acquainted with the main characters' dreams and aspirations. Though the violence, when it comes, is brutal and bloody, pic's overall tone is more irreal than grungily realistic. Performances are terrific down the line, with casting on the nose. As the girl in the middle of all the male bravado, Laura Fraser makes a considerable impression.

•

SMALL TIME CROOKS
2000, 94 mins, US Ⓥ ⊙ col
Dir Woody Allen ***Prod*** Jean Doumanian ***Scr*** Woody Allen ***Ph*** Zhao Fei ***Ed*** Alisa Lepselter ***Art*** Santo Loquasto
Act Woody Allen, Tracey Ullman, Tony Darrow, Hugh Grant, George Grizzard, John Lovitz, Elaine May, Michael Rappaport, Elaine Stritch (Sweetland/Dream Works)

After a first half-hour that's as lowbrow as anything Woody Allen has done, *Small Time Crooks* evolves into a pretty funny satire of the divide between the cultural poseurs and adamant anti-intellectuals.

Viewers who have been complaining for years about Allen's continued insistence upon casting himself opposite very young women will be pleased to note that here he's acting more his age, pairing himself opposite Tracey Ullman and Elaine May.

Initially *Crooks* seems aimed at the lowest common denominator—someone like Allen's character Ray Winkler, an aging loser and ex-con who wears ridiculous shorts and sneakers and concocts a crazy plan to rent a former pizza joint and tunnel underneath to rob the bank down the street. As a front, Ray and his yenta wife, Frenchy (Ullman), a former "exotic dancer," open a cookie store that unexpectedly becomes a New York sensation. A year later, Sunset Cookies has taken over the country, the Winklers are Manhattan's latest multimillionaires, and Frenchy is poised to make her move into high society. She latches on to elegant English art dealer David (Hugh Grant) to educate her in the finer things of life.

Some of the low comedy is mighty low indeed, and the dialogue could have been sharpened all the way through. But *Small Time Crooks* still satisfies in the way it moves from flat-out comedy to more multilayered storytelling. The fact that Allen himself plays the lowlife adds an intriguing element to the mix, and the provocation provided by Frenchy's upwardly mobile pretensions for once justifies his many harangues, which have been annoying elements in some of his recent work. Allen's most enjoyable performance in years may also have been spurred by working opposite Ullman, who is wonderful as the homely housewife who gets off putting on airs.

•

SMALL TOWN GIRL
1936, 95 mins, US b/w
Dir William A. Wellman ***Prod*** Hunt Stromberg ***Scr*** John Lee Mahin, Edith Fitzgerald ***Ph*** Charles Rosher ***Ed*** Blanche Sewell ***Mus*** Herbert Stothart, Edward Ward ***Art*** Cedric Gibbons, Arnold Gillespie
Act Janet Gaynor, Robert Taylor, Binnie Barnes, Lewis Stone, Andy Devine, James Stewart (M-G-M)

Small Town Girl is romance with nice comedy sequences and with a well balanced cast headed by Janet Gaynor and Robert Taylor.

Ben Ames Williams's novel gives a few neat twists to the ancient plot of the obscure Cinderella who marries into the wealthy family. All the time-tested and easy-to-foresee elements are present, including the hoity-toity sweetheart who is bad for the character and the career of the silver-spoon kid who is ultimately brought onto the right track by the wholesome influence exponent.

Picture has tempo and humanity. There is a skillful blending of the sentimentality and the giggles. On the acting end it's a smacko assignment for Gaynor and she displays considerable authority in her performance.

Taylor looks like the dames like him to look, and he acts like the boys can okay him. Binnie Barnes makes a provocative off-type vixen.

1953: NOMINATION: Best Song ("My Flaming Heart")

•

SMALL TOWN GIRL
1953, 93 mins, US Ⓥ col
Dir Leslie Kardos ***Prod*** Joe Pasternak ***Scr*** Dorothy Cooper, Dorothy Kingsley ***Ph*** Joseph Ruttenberg ***Ed*** Albert Akst ***Mus*** Andre Previn (dir.) ***Art*** Cedric Gibbons, Hans Peters
Act Jane Powell, Farley Granger, Ann Miller, S. Z. Sakall, Robert Keith, Bobby Van (M-G-M)

Small Town Girl packages an engaging round of light musical comedy and a plot [from a story by Dorothy Cooper] with just enough substance to hold the attention without wearing. Jane Powell and Farley Granger are the chief exponents of young love and both carry a major portion of the entertainment to excellent results. However, it is the spotlighting of young Bobby Van in a song-dance-comedy spot that impresses the most. However, Van doesn't grab all the dance footage. Shapely Ann Miller exposes her gams in two hot production pieces. "I've Gotta Hear That Beat," flashily staged by Busby Berkeley, and "My Gaucho," a piece of south-of-the-border rhythm that she makes pay off. Both tunes were written by Nicholas Brodszky and Leo Robin.

Granger is a rich playboy who makes the mistake of speeding through a small town in which Robert Keith is judge. He's jailed for 30 days, thus breaking up his elopement with showgirl Miller. Granger makes happy time, though, with Powell, Keith's daughter, even talking her and Chill Wills, jailer, into letting him out for a night in New York. She goes along to insure his return, and love blooms, breaking up the hopes of S. Z. Sakall that his son, Van, will eventually marry the gal and settle down to clerking job instead of dreaming of the N.Y. stage.

•

SMALL WORLD OF SAMMY LEE, THE
1963, 107 mins, UK b/w
Dir Ken Hughes ***Prod*** Frank Godwin ***Scr*** Ken Hughes ***Ph*** Wolfgang Suschitzky ***Ed*** Henry Richardson ***Mus*** Kenny Graham
Act Anthony Newley, Julia Foster, Robert Stephens, Wilfrid Brambell, Warren Mitchell, Miriam Karlin (British Lion/Bryanston Seven Arts)

Originally an award-winning teleplay by Ken Hughes the film has been pumped up to feature length, perhaps at overlength. Though highly overcoloured, it remains a sharp, snide commentary on the sleazy side of Soho, and emerges as a first-class vehicle for Anthony Newley.

Newley, a fugitive from the East End, is the smart-aleck emcee of a shabby strippery. Between churning out tired, near-blue gags and introducing the peelers, he is an inveterate poker and horse player. The story consists entirely of his efforts to raise $840 in five hours to pay off a gangster-bookie who is threatening to cut him up if he doesn't deliver the loot on time.

Hughes's uninhibited screenplay is incisive and tart while his direction has the deft assurance of a man who is reeling with his own idea and knows what he wants as the end product. His cameras stray restlessly around the seamier parts of Soho and the East End.

Newley gives a restless, intelligent and perceptive performance. Few of the supporting actors have much opportunity to make great impact but some register brilliantly, notably Warren Mitchell as Newley's East End delicatessen store-owner brother.

•

SMASHING TIME
1967, 96 mins, UK col
Dir Desmond Davis ***Prod*** Roy Millichip, Carlo Ponti ***Scr*** George Melly ***Ph*** Manny Wynn ***Ed*** Barry Vince ***Mus*** John Addison ***Art*** Ken Bridgeman
Act Rita Tushingham, Lynn Redgrave, Michael York, Anna Quayle, Irene Handl, Ian Carmichael (Paramount/Solmur)

Starring Rita Tushingham and Lynn Redgrave as a pair of girls from the north of England who go to London to explore its glittery side—and have themselves a smashing time—the writer and producers display an amazing memory of Hollywood film.

Femmes play Laurel and Hardy characters, Tushingham as the bewildered Stan, Redgrave the aggressive Oliver. George Melly's original screenplay might be the further misadventures of the Hollywood comics in change-of-sex garb.

Extensive use is made of a swinging London background, with many of its characters, particularly the fey. Desmond Davis's direction, when it isn't focusing on hoary routines, is fast in limning the conglomerate situations in which femmes are plunged, Lynn becoming a recording star, Rita a top fashion photographer's model. With their usual flair for disaster, both find themselves out.

•

SMASH PALACE
1981, 100 mins, New Zealand Ⓥ ⊙ col
Dir Roger Donaldson ***Prod*** Roger Donaldson ***Scr*** Roger Donaldson ***Ph*** Graeme Cowley ***Ed*** Mike Horton ***Mus*** Sharon O'Neill ***Art*** Reston Griffiths
Act Bruno Lawrence, Anna Jemison, Greer Robson, Keith Aberdein, Les Kelly (Aadvark)

Smash Palace is a thoroughly remarkable drama about a marital breakup which erupts into an impulsive kidnapping of a child by its father and a totally believable escalation to the brink of tragedy.

Roger Donaldson's handling of actors is excellent, and his visual control constantly enthralling. The eponymous location is a vast junk-yard of cars, established by Al Shaw's father, and now the panier of hope for Al, a former Grand Prix driver, returned to a remote New Zealand country town with a pregnant French wife.

However, his wife has, during the ensuing eight years, grown increasingly dissatisfied, and the early scenes economically establish the deeper reasons. The script's expositional sequences are neatly handled, making the character development logically part of the narrative.

With strong performances by both Bruno Lawrence and Anna Jemison to work with, the director has effectively created a reality to the tension that goes beneath the surface—or as it might be said: has re-created real life on film.

•

SMILE
1975, 113 mins, US Ⓥ col
Dir Michael Ritchie ***Prod*** Michael Ritchie ***Scr*** Jerry Belson ***Ph*** Conrad Hall ***Ed*** Richard Harris ***Mus*** Daniel Osborn, Leroy Holmes, Charles Chaplin
Act Bruce Dern, Barbara Feldon, Michael Kidd, Geoffrey Lewis, Nicholas Pryor, Colleen Camp (United Artists)

Smile is a hilarious but ultimately shallow putdown of teenage beauty contests. Jerry Belson's original script depicts the climactic days of a statewide beauty competition, where a group of adolescent girls get caught up in the melange of mercantilism, boosterism and backstage politics attendant to such tribal rites.

The uniformly excellent performances come from Bruce Dern, a compulsively upbeat smalltown mobile home dealer and chief judge of the contest; Barbara Feldon, perfect as an "active" woman whose marriage to Nicholas Pryor is in a shambles; Geoffrey Lewis, very effective as pageant president; and Michael Kidd, imported bigtime choreographer whose career is in a slump.

Titles employ Nat "King" Cole's old hit record of "Smile."

•

SMILES OF A SUMMER NIGHT
SEE: SOMMARNATTENS LEENDE

•

SMILING LIEUTENANT, THE
1931, 88 mins, US ⦿ b/w
Dir Ernst Lubitsch ***Prod*** Ernst Lubitsch ***Scr*** Ernest Vaida, Samson Raphaelson, Ernst Lubitsch ***Ph*** George Folsey ***Mus*** Oscar Straus
Act Maurice Chevalier, Claudette Colbert, Miriam Hopkins, Charles Ruggles, George Barbier (Paramount)

Ernst Lubitsch, Ernest Vajda and Samuel Raphaelson form a plenty smart trio working behind a camera. Any script or treatment springing from this source is bound to hold many things that are good and very few that are not.

The film's real weakness is not theirs. The drought is in the disappointing Oscar Straus score of four numbers.

Its story is a pert yarn of free morals and makes no attempt to be otherwise. Maurice Chevalier steals Claudette Colbert, a violinist, from Charles Ruggles. She moves in and stays until the officer becomes circumstantially embroiled with Miriam Hopkins as the unsophisticated and plain but willing princess whom he has to marry. Thereafter it's something of a contest to lure the lieutenant into the princess' chamber.

On performance Hopkins ranks equally with Colbert in doing the unattractive princess who sees her lieutenant and wants him at any cost. Colbert also plays well but lacks the opportunity to make the foremost impression. Neither of the girls seems happy when singing.

No question as to George Barbier's valiant assistance as the king. He makes everything count and handles many a laugh on his own.

1931/32: NOMINATION: Best Picture

•

SMILIN' THROUGH
1932, 96 mins, US b/w
Dir Sidney Franklin ***Scr*** Ernest Vajda, James Bernard Fagan ***Ph*** Lee Garmes ***Ed*** Margaret Booth ***Mus*** William Axt
Act Norma Shearer, Fredric March, Leslie Howard, O. P. Heggie, Ralph Forbes (M-G-M)

In interpretation, in acting and in the fine presentation of all its poetically romantic qualities, this version is a worthy successor to the earlier transcription, first the stage play by Jane Murfin and Jane Cowl, the 1922 silent screenplay with Norma Talmadge, and now with Norma Shearer, who reveals a fine feeling for this old-fashioned but perennial romantic role.

Story is about as sentimetal as it could be without spilling over, and the literary trick of casting the dialog in the love scenes in the patter of the day serves to emphasize by its very nonchalance the depth of the feeling it thus indirectly conveys.

The cutting has not been done as expertly as the other details. Many sequences are a bit overdone, for no good reason save that of pictorial effect and the episode of the tragic wedding is held a fatal instant too long.

1932/33: NOMINATION: Best Picture

•

SMOKE
1995, 112 mins, US col
Dir Wayne Wang ***Prod*** Greg Johnson, Peter Newman, Hisami Kuriowa ***Scr*** Paul Auster ***Ph*** Adam Holender ***Ed*** Maisie Hoy ***Mus*** Rachel Portman ***Art*** Kalina Ivanov
Act William Hurt, Harvey Keitel, Harold Perrineau, Jr., Forest Whitaker, Victor Argo, Erica Gimpel (Miramax/Nippon/Smoke)

There's plenty of smoke but not a great deal of fire in *Smoke*, which unites the talent of director Wayne Wang and cult novelist Paul Auster, who provides his first original screenplay. Basically a repeat of the *Short Cuts* formula, very specifically set in Brooklyn, and with an extremely interesting cast, episodic pic is pleasant but insubstantial. Auster, whose only previous screen work was the adaptation of his novel *The Music of Chance*, has written a script that flirts with interesting ideas and characters but contains too many loose ends and builds to an underwhelming is-that-all-there-is climax.

Most of the 15 or so characters in the film, which unfolds during the summer of 1990, hang out at the Brooklyn Cigar Store, which is managed by Auggie Wren (Harvey Keitel) on behalf of the owner, Vinnie (Victor Argo). Pic is divided into five chapters.

Chapter one, *Paul*, features William Hurt as a novelist saved from being hit by a truck by the intervention of a black teenager who calls himself Rashid (Harold Perrineau, Jr.). Paul is so grateful he offers the boy accommodation for a couple of nights.

In *Rashid*, Rashid tracks down his Father, Cyrus Cole (Forest Whitaker), who operates a run-down garage. Meanwhile, Auggie's ex, Ruby (Stockard Channing), turns up after more than 18 years' absence and informs him their daughter is a pregnant crack addict.

Chapter three, *Ruby*, has little to do with Ruby. Paul gets Rashid a job in Auggie's cigar store, but the youth carelessly allows $5,000 worth of Cuban cigars to be destroyed. Next comes *Cyrus*, in which Rashid reveals his true identity to his father, and finally *Auggie*, in which Auggie tells Paul a Christmas story involving a thief, a missing wallet and an old blind woman.

Hurt gives another subdued performance, but it's Keitel, extremely relaxed as Auggie who gives the film most of its charm.

[A companion pic, *Blue in the Face*, was shot immediately afterwards.]

•

SMOKEY AND THE BANDIT
1977, 96 mins, US Ⓥ ⦿ col
Dir Hal Needham ***Prod*** Mort Engelberg ***Scr*** James Lee Barrett, Charles Shyer, Alan Mandel ***Ph*** Bobby Byrne ***Ed*** Walter Hanneman, Angelo Ross ***Mus*** Bill Justis, Jerry Reed, Dick Feller ***Art*** Mark Mansbridge
Act Burt Reynolds, Sally Field, Jerry Reed, Jackie Gleason, Mike Henry, Paul Williams (Universal/Rastar)

Burt Reynolds stars as a bootlegger-for-kicks who, with Jerry Reed and Sally Field, outwit zealous sheriff Jackie Gleason.

The plot is simple: rich father-son team of blowhards Pat McCormick and Paul Williams offer a reward if Reynolds will truck a load of Coors beer from Texas to Georgia; Reynolds and buddy Reed race to meet the deadline: Field complicates matters as a not-yet-bride who flees beau Mike Henry, son of outraged Gleason, who then chases them all across the southeast.

There is a parade of roadside set pieces involving many different ways to crash cars. Overlaid is citizens band radio jabber (hence, the title) which is loaded with downhome gags. Field is the hottest element in the film.

•

SMOKEY AND THE BANDIT II
1980, 101 mins, US Ⓥ ⦿ col
Dir Hal Needham ***Prod*** Hank Moonjean ***Scr*** Jerry Belson, Brock Yates ***Ph*** Michael Butler ***Ed*** Donn Cambern, William Gordean ***Mus*** Snuff Garrett (sup.) ***Art*** Henry Bumstead
Act Burt Reynolds, Jackie Gleason, Sally Field, Dom DeLuise, Jerry Reed, Paul Williams (Universal/Rastar)

Sally Field tells Burt Reynolds in *Smokey and the Bandit II* that he is no longer having fun doing what used to come naturally. This stale sequel seems to be evidence of going through the motions for money instead of fun.

Smokey II [from a story by Michael Kane] concentrates on sluggish and mostly overdone attempts at roadside comedy skits, and it doesn't even bother to have Reynolds and Field play the same characters they played so engagingly in the original.

Here, Reynolds is hired to haul a pregnant elephant to the Republican convention. The heavy reliance on elephant gags quite literally slows down the film.

Ironically, the best part of the film is the unusual end credit sequence, which shows the actors having fun when they blow lines in outtakes.

•

SMOKEY AND THE BANDIT 3
1983, 88 mins, US Ⓥ ⦿ ▭ col
Dir Dick Lowry ***Prod*** Mort Engelberg ***Scr*** Stuart Birnbaum, David Dashev ***Ph*** James Pergola ***Ed*** Byron "Buzz" Brandt, David Blewitt, Christopher Greenbury ***Mus*** Larry Cansler ***Art*** Ron Hobbs
Act Jackie Gleason, Paul Williams, Pat McCormick, Jerry Reed, Mike Henry, Colleen Camp (Universal)

Filmmakers, including first-time theatrical director Dick Lowry, have wisely returned to the non-stop car-chasing destruction derby of the first movie. But the sense of fun in that original is missing and the countless smashups and near-misses are orchestrated randomly.

Result is a patchwork of arbitrary mayhem as Jackie Gleason's sheriff Budford T. Justice, who tires of retirement in Florida, pursues Jerry Reed and sidekick Colleen Camp through the South. Except for the closing and opening moments, film is so devoid of structure that reels could be shown in reverse order without any loss of coherence.

Gleason, in a testament to endurance, remains funny, and his dimwit son is still humorously parlayed by Mike Henry. All Reed has to do is grin a lot and he's fast becoming a parody of former film roles. Pat McCormick and Paul Williams, reprising their rich and nasty father-son combo, are tiresome caricatures.

•

SMOKING/NO SMOKING
1993, 135 mins, France Ⓥ ⦿ col
Dir Alain Resnais ***Prod*** Bruno Persey, Michel Seydoux ***Scr*** Jean-Pierre Bacri, Agnes Jaoui ***Ph*** Renato Berta ***Ed*** Albert Jurgenson ***Mus*** John Pattison ***Art*** Jacques Saulnier
Act Sabine Azema, Pierre Arditi (Arena/Camera One/France 2 Cinema)

Smoking and *No Smoking* light up the screen and rev up the intellect. In having the vision and audactiy to compress Alan Ayckbourn's variation-loaded octet of plays [*Intimate Exchanges*] into two freestanding but richly complementary feature films, Alain Resnais may have made the first self-regulating interactive movie. Gallic plexes are unspooling the pix simultaneously on different screens, leaving it to viewers to choose which they see first.

Plays were premiered at Ayckbourn's home base of Scarborough, England, in 1982 and were first staged in London In 1984. Screenwriters have dropped two of the plays, resulting in six tales with 12 potential conclusions.

The ingenious premise is to eavesdrop on the lives, loves, aspirations and disappointments of the nine characters (all played by versatile thesps Sabine Azema and Pierre Arditi). Each film flows from a similar opening sequence: faculty wife Celia Teasdale goes onto the terrace, eyes a pack of cigarettes and (according to pic's title) either lights up or doesn't. At about the 55-minute point, after recounting one story straight, each pic then asks "what if?" and explores a parallel universe peopled by the same characters.

Smoking emphasizes the tottering marriage of alcoholic school director Toby Teasdale and his insecure wife Celia; Celia's tentative relationship with cocky jack-of-all-trades Lionel Hepplewick; and the transformation of Eliza Doolittle-like punkette employee Sylvie Bell. *No Smoking* favors the tottering marriage between wimpish gentleman Miles Coombes and his hot-to-trot wife Rowena, and the friendship between Miles and Toby.

Both pix, though set exclusively in exteriors, were shot totally on soundstages.

•

SMUGGLERS, THE
SEE: THE MAN WITHIN

•

SMULTRONSTALLET
(WILD STRAWBERRIES)
1957, 90 mins, Sweden Ⓥ ⦿ b/w
Dir Ingmar Bergman ***Scr*** Ingmar Bergman ***Ph*** Gunnar Fischer ***Ed*** Oscar Rosander ***Mus*** Erik Nordgren ***Art*** Gittan Gustafsson
Act Victor Sjostrom, Bibi Andersson, Ingrid Thulin, Gunnar Bjornstrand, Folke Sundquist, Naima Wifstrand (Svensk Filmindustri)

Grim drama deals with an old man (Victor Sjostrom) who is on his way to get an honorary doctorate degree after 50 years as a doctor. He is accompanied by his daughter-in-law (Ingrid Thulin). The trip becomes a reliving of the old man's life as he realizes he led an empty life due to his stuffiness, egotism and inability to really love and feel.

Nightmares, dreams and reminiscences are expertly blended as space and time are broken to work on the various levels of the man's thoughts. Pic sometimes talks too much in philosophical asides, but it remains a searching pictorial analysis of a man's life. Expert directorial touches and notations of director Ingmar Bergman, and the dignified miming of old-time director Sjostrom, plus other fine thespic additions, make this an offbeat. It's a personal and profound work.

•

SNAKE EYES (1993)
SEE: DANGEROUS GAME

•

SNAKE EYES
1998, 99 mins, US Ⓥ ⊙ ▭ col
Dir Brian De Palma ***Prod*** Brian De Palma ***Scr*** David Koepp ***Ph*** Stephen H. Burum ***Ed*** Bill Pankow ***Mus*** Ryuichi Sakamoto ***Art*** Anne Pritchard
Act Nicolas Cage, Gary Sinise, John Heard, Carla Gugino, Stan Shaw, Kevin Dunn (DeBart)

Snake Eyes is snakebit. After a razzle-dazzle opening, this hyperactive thriller about a corrupt cop's investigation of a political assassination devolves into a mere excuse for a stylistic exercise by director Brian De Palma.

Something of a companion piece to De Palma's 1981 suspenser in the way it pieces together recorded evidence of a politically inspired killing, as well as its cynicism. New outing affords De Palma and his game cinematographer, Stephen H. Burum, the opportunity to show how dexterously cinematic they can be.

After a brief simulated TV newscast, the Steadicam gets 12 minutes to shine as De Palma covers an enormous amount of ground and action in a single, apparently uninterrupted take. The camera picks up Atlantic City homicide Det. Rick Santoro (Nicolas Cage) as he bounds through stadium hallways, stops at the dressing room of heavyweight boxer (Stan Shaw), takes a ringside seat next to his boyhood friend, Navy Cmdr. Kevin Dunne (Gary Sinise) and watches the first round of the title fight, which concludes with a sniper shooting of the U.S. Secretary of Defense sitting in the row behind Santoro.

But it doesn't take long for the film, which David Koepp wrote from a story he cooked up with the director, to flame out and fall into an ever-accelerating tailspin.

Although Dunne manages to nail the apparent assassin, Santoro has the stadium doors locked in hopes of finding other suspects among the 14,000 fight fans. His suspicions aroused when a videotape replay reveals that the champ went down after a phantom punch, Santoro begins listening to various witnesses' accounts of the moments surrounding the sniper fire.

Cage supplies beaucoup energy, but his hustler-cop character provides little else in which he can invest his talent. Sinise wears an increasingly grim demeanor in a part that comes to make no sense.

•

SNAKE PIT, THE
1948, 107 mins, US b/w
Dir Anatole Litvak ***Prod*** Anatole Litvak, Robert Bassler ***Scr*** Frank Partos, Millen Brand ***Ph*** Leo Tover ***Ed*** Dorothy Spencer ***Mus*** Alfred Newman ***Art*** Lyle R. Wheeler, Joseph C. Wright
Act Olivia de Havilland, Mark Stevens, Leo Genn, Celeste Holm, Helen Craig, Leif Erickson (20th Century-Fox)

The Snake Pit is a standout among class melodramas. Based on Mary Jane Ward's novel, picture probes into the processes of mental illness with a razor-sharp forthrightness, giving an open-handed display of the makeup of bodies without minds and the treatments used to restore intelligence. Clinical detail is stated with matter-of-fact clarity and becomes an important part of the melodramatics.

Olivia de Havilland is a young bride who goes insane and is committed to an institution for treatment. An understanding medico (Leo Genn) uses kindness and knowledge of mental ills to restore her. Just as a cure seems possible, she again plunges into a mental snake pit and starts all over on the road to insanity.

De Havilland's performance is top gauge. Genn goes about his part of the doctor with a quietness that gives it strength and Mark Stevens is excellent as De Havilland's husband.

1948: Best Sound Recording

NOMINATIONS: Best Picture, Director, Actress (Olivia de Havilland), Screenplay, Scoring of a Dramatic Picture

•

SNATCH
2000, 102 mins, UK/US Ⓥ ⊙ col
Dir Guy Ritchie ***Prod*** Matthew Vaughn ***Scr*** Guy Ritchie ***Ph*** Tim Maurice-Jones ***Ed*** John Harris, Les Healey ***Mus*** John Murphy ***Art*** Hugo Luczyc-Wyhowski
Act Benicio Del Toro, Dennis Farina, Vinnie Jones, Brad Pitt, Rade Sherbedgia, Jason Statham (Vaughn-SKA/Columbia)

Scripter-director Guy Ritchie, 31, and his even younger producer, Matthew Vaughn, 29, blow away the sophomore curse with a less flashy, considerably better written and more evenly cast crime serio-comedy than their surprise low-budget hit, *Lock, Stock and Two Smoking Barrels*. Pic shows the same delight in corkscrew plotting, but is far lighter in tone, sans the obsession with guns.

Though the largely London-set movie has three American faces (Brad Pitt, Dennis Farina, Benicio Del Toro), none of them dominate the action, with Pitt especially—as a scruffy, bearded gypsy with an incomprehensible Irish accent—melding seamlessly into the large ensemble cast.

Pic spins on the efforts of a bunch of low-life characters to retrieve a missing 84-carat stone stolen from an Antwerp jeweler. Turkish (Jason Statham), with his pal Tommy (Stephen Graham), makes a living as an amusement arcade owner and boxing promoter. They sign up Mickey (Pitt), an Irish gypsy with a knockout punch, to take a fall in a boxing match engineered by Brick Top (Alan Ford), a psychotic gang leader. Crazed Russian gangster Boris the Blade (Rade Sherbedgia) asks Jewish gangster Frankie Four Fingers (Del Toro) to place a bet for him at a bookie's and simultaneously arranges for pawnshop owner Sol (Lennie James), and his bumbling associates, Vinnie (Robbie Gee) and Tyrone (Ade), to rob the joint. And there's New Yorker Avi (Farina), who flies to London and hires Bullet Tooth Tony (former soccer personality Vinnie Jones, launched in *Lock, Stock*) to find Frankie when he comes up missing. Why? Frankie was transporting the stolen diamond to Gotham.

The way in which the script juggles these groups is both entertaining and clever. The dialogue—expletive-filled but far less offensively so than in many Brit gangster pics—is nimble on its feet, chucklesome, and written in the same kind of Cockney Runyonese that Ritchie aimed for in *Lock, Stock*. Effect here is less self-conscious and better integrated—as are the occasional speeded-up visual effects.

•

SNEAKERS
1992, 125 mins, US Ⓥ ⊙ col
Dir Phil Alden Robinson ***Prod*** Walter F. Parkes, Lawrence Lasker ***Scr*** Phil Alden Robinson, Lawrence Lasker, Walter F. Parkes ***Ph*** John Lindley ***Ed*** Tom Rolf ***Mus*** James Horner ***Art*** Patrizia von Brandenstein
Act Robert Redford, Dan Aykroyd, Ben Kingsley, Mary McDonnell, River Phoenix, Sidney Poitier (Universal)

A slick, hip, liberal, hi-tech, all-star buddy spy comic caper pic, *Sneakers* serves up a breezy good time in the vein of some of toplined Robert Redford's 1970s hits.

Film gets off to a good start with a mock break-in demonstrating the skill of Redford's company in cracking security systems. His gang of underpaid but fun-loving experts sports a full complement of shady backgrounds: Sidney Poitier was fired from the CIA, Dan Aykroyd is an ex-con, David Strathairn is a blind wiretapping and audio expert, and River Phoenix changed his school grades by computer.

Two alleged agents from the top-secret National Security Agency enlist Redford's services to recover a mysterious black box that turns out to contain a device that can penetrate the computer systems of vital services.

It turns out the boys are up against Redford's criminal college cohort Ben Kingsley, who sees the box as a way to accomplish their student dream of changing the world, and to take revenge on Redford in the bargain.

When issues grow into matters of life and death, viewer can be expected to take matters more seriously as well. Unfortunately, script's second half can't support a more sober examination, as too many issues are ignored or glossed over.

The film looks exceedingly expensive, and no doubt was. The big-time cast provides sterling company.

•

SNIPER
1993, 98 mins, US Ⓥ ⊙ col
Dir Luis Llosa ***Prod*** Robert L. Rosen ***Scr*** Michael Frost Beckner, Crash Leyland ***Ph*** Bill Butler ***Ed*** Scott Smith ***Mus*** Gary Chang, Mark Mancina, Hans Zimmer ***Art*** Herbert Pinter
Act Tom Berenger, Billy Zane, J. T. Walsh, Aden Young, Ken Radley, Reinaldo Arenas (Baltimore/Tri-Star)

Sniper is an expertly directed, yet ultimately unsatisfying psychological thriller. Luis Llosa's first-rate action direction is undermined by underdeveloped characters and pedestrian dialogue. Tom Berenger essays a Marine sniper, oddly named Thomas Beckett, on assignment in Panama. Pic quickly establishes sniping as a lonely profession shunned even by other gung-ho Marines. On his latest assignment he's accompanied by an ambitious young Washington bureaucrat, Richard Miller (Billy Zane), who is so green he doesn't really need camouflage.

The hostile interplay between the emotionally detached veteran and the cocky youngster is strictly textbook, as is their eventual male bonding. This would be okay if they weren't virtually the only characters in the film.

Action scenes—and there are a good number of them—range from good to edge-of-your-seat. Audiences will see the finale coming from a mile away, but the pace only flags when the characters stop to make sense of their actions.

The tropical forests of Queensland, Australia, stood in for Panama.

•

SNOOPY, COME HOME
1972, 80 mins, US Ⓥ ⊙ col
Dir Bill Melendez ***Prod*** Lee Mendelson, Bill Melendez ***Scr*** Charles M. Schulz ***Ph*** Dickson/Vasu ***Ed*** Robert T. Gillis, Charles McCann, Rudy Zamora, Jr. ***Mus*** Richard M. Sherman, Robert B. Sherman (Melendez)

Snoopy, a cartoon figure known to millions, comes full orbit to screen. This is the second cartoon feature based upon Charles M. Schulz's cartoon creations. Lee Mendelson and Bill Melendez, who produced *A Boy Named Charlie Brown*, focus most of their attention on the independent beagle who is the despair of his master, Charlie Brown.

Schulz has written the story of the adventures of Snoopy as he leaves home to try to find Lila, his original owner, who writes from the hospital that she needs him.

Snoopy is captured by a little girl who gives him some bad moments, he engages in a boxing match with Lucy, tries to snatch Linus's security blanket from that worthy, finally is able to make his way to Lila's hospital room.

•

SNOWS OF KILIMANJARO, THE
1952, 113 mins, US Ⓥ col
Dir Henry King ***Prod*** Darryl F. Zanuck ***Scr*** Casey Robinson ***Ph*** Leon Shamroy ***Ed*** Barbara McLean ***Mus*** Bernard Herrmann ***Art*** Lyle Wheeler, John DeCuir
Act Gregory Peck, Susan Hayward, Ava Gardner, Hildegarde Neff, Leo G. Carroll, Torin Thatcher (20th Century-Fox)

A big, broad screen treatment has been given to Ernest Hemingway's *The Snows of Kilimanjaro*. The script broadens the 1927 short story considerably without losing the Hemingway penchant for the mysticism behind his virile characters and lusty situations.

Ava Gardner makes the part of Cynthia a warm, appealing, alluring standout. Gregory Peck delivers with gusto the character of the writer who lies dangerously ill on the plain at the base of Kilimanjaro, highest mountain in Africa, and relives what he believes is a misspent life. Susan Hayward is splendid, particularly in the dramatic closing sequence, in the less colorful role of Peck's wife.

The location-lensed footage taken in Paris, Africa, the Riviera and Spain add an important dress to the varied sequences. The Paris street and cafe scenes, the music and noise, are alive. The African-lensed backgrounds are brilliant, as are those on the Riviera and in Spain.

1952: NOMINATIONS: Best Color Cinematography, Color Art Direction

•

SNOW WHITE AND THE SEVEN DWARFS
1937, 80 mins, US Ⓥ col
Dir David Hand ***Prod*** Walt Disney ***Scr*** Ted Sears, Otto Englander, Earl Hurd, Dorothy Ann Blank, Richard Credon, Dick Rickard, Merrill De Maris, Webb Smith ***Mus*** Frank Churchill, Paul Smith, Leigh Harline (arr.) ***Art*** Charles Philippi, High Hennesy, Terrell Stapp, McLaren Stewart, Harold Miles, Tom Codrick, Gustaf Tenggren, Kenneth Anderson, Kendall O'Connor, Hazel Sewell (Disney/RKO)

Walt Disney's *Snow White and the Seven Dwarfs*, seven reels of animated cartoon in Technicolor, unfolds an absorbingly interesting and, at times, thrilling entertainment.

More than two years and $1 million were required by the Disney staff, under David Hand's supervision, to complete the film. In a foreword Disney pays a neat compliment to animators, designers and musical composers whose united efforts have produced a work of art. No less than 62 staff names are flashed in the credit titles as being responsible for various divisions of the job.

The opening shows the cover of Grimm's book of tales. Soon all the characters assume lifelike personalities. Snow White is the embodiment of girlish sweetness and kindness, exemplified in her love for the birds and the small animals of the woods that are her friends and, as it subsequently develops, her rescuers. The queen is a vampish brunet, of homicidal instincts, who consorts with black magic and underworld forces of evil. And the seven little dwarfs, Doc, Grumpy, Dopey, Sleepy, Happy, Sneezy and Bashful, are the embodiments of their nametags, a merry crew of masculine frailities.

Pastel shades predominate in the Technicolor and there is an absence of garish, brilliant colorings.

Sound plays an important part in the production and the synchronization of words to the moving lips of the characters is worked out perfectly.

1937: NOMINATION: Best Score

1938: Special Award (significant screen innovation)

•

SOAPDISH

1991, 95 mins, US Ⓥ ⊙ col

Dir Michael Hoffman ***Prod*** Aaron Spelling, Alan Greisman ***Scr*** Robert Harling, Andrew Bergman ***Ph*** Ueli Steiger ***Ed*** Garth Craven ***Mus*** Alan Silvestri ***Art*** Eugenio Zanetti

Act Sally Field, Kevin Kline, Robert Downey, Jr., Cathy Moriarty, Whoopi Goldberg, Elizabeth Shue (Paramount)

Soapdish aims at a satiric target as big as a Macy's float and intermittently hits it. Sally Field and Kevin Kline play a feuding pair of romantically involved soap opera stars in this broad but amiable sendup of daytime TV.

Field, the reigning "queen of misery" on the sudser *The Sun Also Sets*, is at the peak of her glory but is going to pieces emotionally. Amazonian harpy Cathy Moriarty is scheming to take over the show by using her sexual wiles to convince the slimy producer (Robert Downey, Jr.) to have Field's character destroy her popularity by committing some unspeakable crime.

To drive Field even more off the edge, Downey surprises her by bringing back her long-ago flame, Kevin Kline, whom she had thrown off the show in 1973. Whoopi Goldberg, the show's jaded head writer, flips when told Kline is coming back because his character was written out by having him decapitated in a car crash.

Field works hard and shows an expert sense of comic timing, but the grittily down-to-earth acting persona Field has developed now makes her seem a bit too reasonable for the zany demands of this script [from a screen story by Robert Harling].

Kline is utterly marvelous as a sort of low-rent John Barrymore type, boozing and carousing his way through the ranks of worshipful young actresses. Moriarty, who acts as if she's been staying up late studying Mary Woronov pics, is a scream as Field's deep-voiced, hate-consumed rival.

•

S.O.B.

1981, 121 mins, US Ⓥ ⊙ ▭ col

Dir Blake Edwards ***Prod*** Blake Edwards, Tony Adams ***Scr*** Blake Edwards ***Ph*** Harry Stradling ***Ed*** Ralph E. Winters ***Mus*** Henry Mancini ***Art*** Rodger Maus

Act Julie Andrews, William Holden, Robert Webber, Larry Hagman, Robert Preston, Robert Vaughn (Paramount/Lorimar)

S.O.B. is one of the most vitriolic—though only occasionally hilarious—attacks on the Tinseltown mentality ever.

Taking its core from part of director Blake Edwards's own battle-weary Hollywood career, pic is structured as an arch fairy tale, spinning the chronicle of a top-grossing producer (Richard Mulligan) whose latest $30 million musical extravaganza is hailed by the world as the b.o. turkey of the century, relegating him to has-been status overnight.

With Julie Andrews as his pure-as-driven snow imaged wife prompted finally to leave him for good, while production chief Robert Vaughn plots how to salvage the pic by massive, contract-bending recutting, Mulligan tries several failed variations on the suicide route until a mid-orgy epiphany tells him to cut and reshoot the G-rated failure into an opulent softcore porno fantasy.

Black comedy is a tough commodity to sustain and, after a broad start, Edwards quickly finds a deft balance that paints a cockeyed, self-contained world that comfortably supports its exaggerated characters. Unhappily, about midway through the pic, the tone becomes less certain (especially when it strains for seriousness) and styles begin to switch back and forth.

•

SO BIG

1953, 101 mins, US b/w

Dir Robert Wise ***Prod*** Henry Blanke ***Scr*** John Twist ***Ph*** Ellsworth Fredericks ***Ed*** Thomas Reilly ***Mus*** Max Steiner ***Art*** John Beckman

Act Jane Wyman, Sterling Hayden, Nancy Olson, Steve Forrest, Elizabeth Fraser, Martha Hyer (Warner)

This is the third time around for Edna Ferber's Pulitzer Prize–winning novel. It was made as a silent film by First National back in 1925 and as a talker by Warner Bros. in 1932. Jane Wyman handles the emotional histrionics in this remake. *So Big* is big and sprawling, covering a period of some 25 years. Its basic flaw is that it attempts to cover too much, resulting in an episodic quality and in flat surface characters.

Wyman is superb in transition from the young girl with the aristocratic background to the widow of a Dutch truck farmer. Nothing stops Selina's nobility from the time she arrives in the Dutch community outside of Chicago as a young schoolteacher to the moment her son decides to return to his drawing board. She takes poverty, back-breaking farm work, widowhood and disappointment serenely, philosophically and with dignity. Sterling Hayden scores as the unlearned, rugged yet gentle farmer who wins the schoolteacher. Nancy Olson is appropriately flippant and understanding as the Paris-trained artist who values true creativeness over financial success. Steve Forrest, as Selina's architect-son, wrestles neatly with the money versus art problem.

Ellsworth Fredericks's camera has successfully captured the drudgery of the farm, the excitement of the market place, and the splendor and gaudiness of the rich in 1900 Chicago.

•

SO DARK THE NIGHT

1946, 71 mins, US b/w

Dir Joseph H. Lewis ***Prod*** Ted Richmond ***Scr*** Martin Berkeley, Dwight Babcock ***Ph*** Burnett Guffey ***Ed*** Jerome Thoms ***Mus*** Hugo Friedhofer ***Art*** Carl Anderson

Act Steven Geray, Micheline Cheirel, Eugene Borden, Ann Codee, Egon Brecher, Helen Freeman (Columbia)

Around the frail structure of a story [by Aubrey Wisberg] about a schizophrenic Paris police inspector who becomes an insane killer at night, a tight combination of direction, camerawork and musical scoring produce a series of isolated visual effects that are subtle and moving to an unusual degree.

Paradoxically, the film seems to collapse under the weight of its technical niceties as director Joseph H. Lewis continuously takes time out to make his points through the indirection of cinematic imagery rather than directly through the spoken word.

Settings for the pic, which unfolds in an obscure French village, are outstanding for their density and accuracy of detail. Despite the obvious budget limitations, the layout of the streets, interior decorations and landscape shots define France as it exists in our imagination.

Story revolves around the ill-fated romance between a middle-aged Parisian detective and a young country girl who is already betrothed to a neighboring farmer. On the wedding eve, the farmer in a well-portrayed dramatic encounter, threatens the detective and stalks out of the party, the girl following in a frenzy of mixed emotions. Several days later, both the girl and farmer are found to have been strangled to death.

•

SODOM AND GOMORRAH

1962, 153 mins, ITALY Ⓥ ⊙ ▭ col

Dir Robert Aldrich ***Prod*** Goffredo Lombardo, Joseph E. Levine ***Scr*** Hugo Butler, Giorgio Prosperi ***Ph*** Silvano Ippoliti, Mario Montuori, Cyril Knowles ***Ed*** Peter Tanner ***Mus*** Miklos Rozsa ***Art*** Ken Adam

Act Stewart Granger, Pier Angeli, Stanley Baker, Anouk Aimee, Rossana Podesta, Claudia Mori (20th Century-Fox/Titanus)

Director Robert Aldrich has said, "Every director ought to get one Biblical film out of his system, but there's not very much that you can do about this sort of picture." Too true. Net: *Sodom and Gomorrah* has many of the faults of the Biblical epic, but many good qualities.

Storyline concerns Lot's pilgrimage to the Valley of Jordan with the Hebrews. They set up camp in the valley but are almost immediately involved in a bitter clash between the Helamites, who covet the wealth of Sodom and Gomorrah, two cesspools of depravity, ruled over by the cold, beautiful, unscrupulous Queen Bera who, incidentally, is being doublecrossed for power by her scheming brother.

Stewart Granger makes a distinguished, solemn and sincere figure of Lot and Stanley Baker, as the treacherous Prince of Sodom, is sufficiently sneaky though he has only a couple of highspots in his role. Anouk Aimee is an impressively sinister Queen, Pier Angeli has some moments of genuine emotion as Lot's wife and Rosanna Podesta and Claudia Mori play the shadowy roles of Lot's daughters adequately.

•

SO FINE

1981, 91 mins, US Ⓥ col

Dir Andrew Bergman ***Prod*** Mike Lobell ***Scr*** Andrew Bergman ***Ph*** James A. Contner ***Ed*** Alan Helm ***Mus*** Ennio Morricone ***Art*** Santo Loquasto

Act Ryan O'Neal, Jack Warden, Mariangela Melato, Richard Kiel, Fred Gwynne (Warner)

So Fine is quite all right. Andrew Bergman, screenwriter on *Blazing Saddles* and *The In-Laws*, has come up with a somewhat less zany concoction this time but makes an impressively sharp directorial debut highlighted by some good bedroom farce.

Ryan O'Neal is a Shakespeare-spouting English professor implausibly recruited into his father Jack Warden's faltering dressmaking firm upon the unchallengeable demand of Big Eddie, played by the 7;pr2;dp Richard Kiel. Latter's petite wife, Mariangela Melato, quickly corrals O'Neal into the sack (while Kiel's in it too, no less) and, in his best bumbling manner, O'Neal inadvertantly hits upon a new fashion discovery—skin tight jeans with seethrough behinds.

Despite his smashing success in the garment district, O'Neal retreats to the world of academia but is pursued by Melato, who in turn is followed by the jealous Big Eddie. It all ends up in a slapstick, amateur-hour operatic production of Verdi's *Otello* remindful of, among other things, *A Night at the Opera*.

•

SOFT SKIN

SEE: LA PEAU DOUCE

•

SOFT TOP HARD SHOULDER

1993, 93 mins, UK Ⓥ ▭ col

Dir Stefan Schwartz ***Prod*** Richard Holmes ***Scr*** Peter Capaldi ***Ph*** Henry Braham ***Ed*** Derek Trigg ***Mus*** Chris Rea ***Art*** Sonja Klaus

Act Peter Capaldi, Elaine Collins, Frances Barber, Simon Callow, Phyllis Logan, Richard Wilson (Gruber Bros./Road Movies)

Scotland gets its first road movie with *Soft Top Hard Shoulder*, a wafer-thin but likable addition to the genre.

Gavin Bellini (scripter Peter Capaldi) is a crazy Italo-Scot trying to make it as an illustrator down south in London. Meeting his Uncle Sal (witty Richard Wilson) by chance, he learns he has 36 hours to make it to his father's surprise 60th birthday party in Glasgow if he's to collect a chunk of family money.

Hitting the highways in a bronchial old auto, he quickly meets kooky hitchhiker Yvonne (Elaine Collins), a resourceful Glaswegian. Rest of pic follows the familiar route of the pair's love-hate relationship, stopovers and breakdowns, capped by a happy ending.

Capaldi's script comes up with plenty of incident. When it's good, it's very good, with plenty of dry Scots humor, but other sections lack zing.

•

SO I MARRIED AN AXE MURDERER

1993, 93 mins, US Ⓥ ⊙ col

Dir Thomas Schlamme ***Prod*** Robert N. Fried, Cary Woods ***Scr*** Robbie Fox ***Ph*** Julio Macat ***Ed*** Richard Halsey, Colleen Halsey ***Mus*** Bruce Broughton ***Art*** John Graysmark

Act Mike Myers, Nancy Travis, Anthony LaPaglia, Amanda Plummer, Brenda Fricker, Charles Grodin (Tri-Star)

Don't expect to see gobs of gore in *So I Married an Axe Murderer*. Fueled by an anarchic style and a winning cast, the comedy is a hip slice of life about the dilemma of marital commitment with just a pinch of Hitchcock providing the cutting edge.

The San Francisco-set yarn finds poet Charlie Mackenzie (Mike Myers) glibly fashioning a verse concerning his umpteenth failed relationship. Both his weird Scottish family and his best friend, Tony (Anthony LaPaglia), understand Charlie's desperately in need of a strong centering influence.

So, by chance, his eye catches Harriet Michaels (Nancy Travis), a butcher at the not-too-elegant Meats of the World. Quicker than you can say "hae ya got any haggis?" they are kindred souls. But Charlie begins to believe that Harriet might be an uncaught husband killer.

Director Thomas Schlamme milks the ambiguity for all it's worth. Despite a few narrative lulls and some humor in questionable taste, the film has an oddball spirit of invention. It aspires to the deft deadpan style of Bill Forsyth with splashes of Monty Python and Grand Guignol. It's not surprising a few ingredients fail to jell.

•

SOLARIS

SEE: SOLYARIS

•

SOLDIER BLUE

1970, 112 mins, US Ⓥ ▭ col

Dir Ralph Nelson ***Prod*** Harold Loeb, Gabriel Katzka ***Scr*** John Gay ***Ph*** Robert Hauser ***Ed*** Alex Beaton ***Mus*** Roy Budd ***Art*** Frank Arrigo

Act Candice Bergen, Peter Strauss, Donald Pleasence, John Anderson, Jorge Rivero, Dana Elcar (Avco Embassy)

Screenplay, from Theodore V. Olsen's novel, *Arrow in the Sun*, deals with the attempt of U.S. soldier Honus Gant (Peter Strauss), the "soldier blue" of the title, and a white woman who had been captured by Indians two years before (Candice Bergen) to stay alive until they can reach an army outpost. The paymaster's party, with which they have been traveling, is ambushed and slaughtered by the Cheyennes.

The major portion of the film deals with the pair's trek. Their misadventures include encountering white man Isaac Cumber (Donald Pleasence) who is en route to the Cheyennes to sell them guns for the gold they stole from the paymaster and who takes the pair prisoner. Finally, Bergen goes on ahead for help when Strauss is wounded, but discovers the Army's plot to wipe out the Indians. She rides out to warn them.

The climax of the film makes the Army the complete villain and the Cheyennes the complete innocents. The seemingly handful of warriors are quickly wiped out, the women raped, children mutilated and, in many cases, murdered.

It would appear obvious that director Ralph Nelson is trying to correlate this allegedly historical incident with more contemporous events.

•

SOLDIER IN LOVE
SEE: FANFAN LA TULIPE

•

SOLDIER IN THE RAIN
1963, 87 mins, US Ⓥ b/w
Dir Ralph Nelson ***Prod*** Martin Jurow ***Scr*** Maurice Richlin, Blake Edwards ***Ph*** Philip Lathrop ***Ed*** Ralph E. Winters ***Mus*** Henry Mancini ***Art*** Phil Barber
Act Jackie Gleason, Steve McQueen, Tuesday Weld, Tony Bill, Tom Poston, Ed Nelson (Allied Artists/Cedars-Solar)

One might classify the film a fairy tale in khaki. The screenplay out of a novel by William Goldman relates the bittersweet tale of two modern army buddies—a smooth operating master sergeant (Jackie Gleason) who has found a home in the service, and his hero-worshipping protege (Steve McQueen), a supply sergeant who is about to return to civvies and hopes Gleason will join him in private enterprise on the outside.

There are several sudden, and vigorous, bursts of comedy dialog, principally exchanges between Gleason, who has a complex about his bulk, and Tuesday Weld, who plays a basically sweet but dumb and ingeniously tactless 18-year-old whose idea of a compliment is to refer to him as a "fat Randolph Scott." But such mirth is only spasmodic and is snowed under by a sentimental approach that misfires.

McQueen is a kind of southern-fried boob who reminds one of Clem Kadiddlehoffer. The style of portrayal is exaggerated and unnatural. Gleason fares better with a restrained approach, through which his natural endomorphic vitality seeps through. Weld is a standout with her convincing portrait of the classic dizzy blonde as a teenager. Tony Bill scores as McQueen's screwball sidekick.

•

SOLDIER OF FORTUNE
1955, 94 mins, US Ⓥ ⌴ col
Dir Edward Dmytryk ***Prod*** Buddy Adler ***Scr*** Ernest K. Gann ***Ph*** Leo Tover ***Ed*** Dorothy Spencer ***Mus*** Hugo Friedhofer ***Art*** Lyle Wheeler, Jack Martin Smith
Act Clark Gable, Susan Hayward, Michael Rennie, Gene Barry, Alex D'Arcy, Tom Tully (20th Century-Fox)

Clark Gable and Susan Hayward team advantageously in this thriller of mystery and intrigue in the Orient. There's plenty of action, a lacing of romance, and some spectacular photographic effects in CinemaScope to make it a well balanced show.

Hong Kong is the setting for all of the exteriors. Ernest K. Gann committed his own novel to screenplay form, and the writing, along with Edward Dmytryk's very able direction, keeps the high adventure of the plot always on a believable plane.

When Hayward's husband (Gene Barry) disappears on a photographic trip into Red China, she comes to Hong Kong to institute a search for him and runs the gamut of colorful types, most all of whom have their hands out for a quick buck. With British authorities and others no help, her path leads to Gable, soldier of fortune reaping just that with some smuggling enterprises.

Michael Rennie is extremely able and likeable as a Crown officer participating in the rescue and Barry shows up well in lesser footage. The standout photography by Leo Tover takes the audience on an intriguing tour of Hong Kong and its points of interest. In only one department does the storytelling slip—it skirts calling the Communist Chinese by name.

•

SOLDIER'S STORY, A
1984, 101 mins, US Ⓥ ⦿ col
Dir Norman Jewison ***Prod*** Norman Jewison, Ronald L. Schwary, Patrick Palmer ***Scr*** Charles Fuller ***Ph*** Russell Boyd ***Ed*** Mark Warner, Caroline Biggletaff ***Mus*** Herbie Hancock ***Art*** Walter Scott Herndon
Act Howard E. Rollins, Jr., Adolph Caesar, Dennis Lipscomb, Art Evans, Denzel Washington, Larry Riley (Caldix)

A Soldier's Story is a taut, gripping film which features many of the old-fashioned virtues of a good Hollywood production—brilliant ensemble acting, excellent production values, a crackling script (adapted from the Pulitzer Prize–winning *A Soldier's Play* [1981] by its author, Charles Fuller), fine direction and a liberal political message. Howard Rollins, Jr. plays Captain Davenport, a prideful black army attorney called into Fort Neal, LA, to investigate the murder of Sgt. Waters (Adolph Caesar). Rollins's arrival at this holding tank for black soldiers is cause for racial strife on both sides of the fence—the white officers are contemptuous and the black soldiers are proud. Film is structured around a series of flashbacks as Rollins interviews the team members who represent a variety of black experience and attitudes.

1984: NOMINATIONS: Best Picture, Supp. Actor (Adolph Caesar), Adapted Screenplay

•

SOLDIERS THREE
1951, 91 mins, US b/w
Dir Tay Garnett ***Prod*** Pandro S. Berman ***Scr*** Marguerite Roberts, Tom Reed, Malcolm Stuart Boylan ***Ph*** William Mellor ***Ed*** Robert J. Kern ***Mus*** Adolph Deutsch ***Art*** Cedric Gibbons, Malcolm Brown
Act Stewart Granger, Walter Pidgeon, David Niven, Robert Newton, Cyril Cusack, Greta Gynt (M-G-M)

Three scripters worked on the story, loosely based on Rudyard Kipling, but come up with nothing more than a string of incidents involving three soldiers in India (Stewart Granger, Robert Newton and Cyril Cusack).

Trio's off-limits antics, such as drunken brawling, add to the hot water in which their colonel (Walter Pidgeon) finds himself and do nothing to calm the colonel's aide (David Niven). Antics do, however, enliven the film's footage and save it from missing altogether.

Granger is very likeable in his comedy role, and his two cohorts, Newton and Cusack, do their full share in getting laughs. Niven also is good as the slightly stuffy aide who leads the pants-losing patrol. Pidgeon, as a colonel with worries, forgets his broad British bumbling occasionally, but this fits with general development.

•

SOLID GOLD CADILLAC, THE
1956, 99 mins, US col
Dir Richard Quine ***Prod*** Fred Kohlmar ***Scr*** Abe Burrows ***Ph*** Charles Lang ***Ed*** Charles Nelson ***Mus*** Cyril J. Mockridge ***Art*** Ross Bellah
Act Judy Holliday, Paul Douglas, Fred Clark, John Williams, Neva Patterson, Ralph Dumke (Columbia)

Original George S. Kaufman–Howard Teichmann Broadway script was changed to fit an older stage actress, Josephine Hull, and is now changed back in the Columbia film version for a younger comedienne, Judy Holliday. The satire on minority stockholder gadfly treatment of vested interests and pompous executives makes for hilarity.

It's a broad treatment of big corporation board members who get their comeuppance from a femme who owns only 10 shares of common in the company. As the dizzy blonde with some native, and naive, common sense, Holliday is a delight. The man's Paul Douglas, who does much to make the comedy click.

Fred Kohlmar's production achieves a plushy look without the use of colour or big-screen assists. There is a flash of color at the tale's wrapup to show off that creampuff auto of the title, but the comedy is such that no one will miss a dye job elsewhere.

Film has a narration by George Burns, although it serves no particular purpose as far as the comedy is concerned. In the stage original the late Fred Allen officiated similarly.

1956: Best B&W Costume Design

•

SOL MADRID
1968, 90 mins, US ⌴ col
Dir Brian G. Hutton ***Prod*** Hall Bartlett ***Scr*** David Karp ***Ph*** Fred Koenekamp ***Ed*** John McSweeney ***Mus*** Lalo Schifrin ***Art*** George W. Davis, Carl Anderson
Act David McCallum, Stella Stevens, Telly Savalas, Rip Torn, Pat Hingle, Ricardo Montalban (M-G-M)

Hard-hitting action compensates for certain confusing story elements, and plottage is sufficiently exciting and suspenseful to maintain interest. For pictorial values, there's the beauty of an Acapulco location.

Direction by Brian G. Hutton is a potent assist to film's unfoldment, in which David McCallum takes on the Mafia and drug smuggling across the Mexican border. Hutton, who draws strong performances from entire cast, specializes here in legitimately premised violence and hits a torrid pace.

Hall Bartlett as producer has dumped a flock of attractive physical values into the adaptation of Robert Wilder's novel, *Fruit of the Poppy*, and has smartly packaged the overall for a good audience feature. McCallum makes a good impression and gets handsome support from Stella Stevens as the former girlfriend, Telly Savalas as a heroin pusher, Ricardo Montalban as an Acapulco contact and Rip Torn, Mafia leader. Savalas is a particular standout.

•

SOLOMON AND SHEBA
1959, 141 mins, US Ⓥ ⦿ ⌴ col
Dir King Vidor ***Prod*** Ted Richmond ***Scr*** Anthony Veiller, Paul Dudley, George Bruce ***Ph*** Freddie Young ***Ed*** Otto Ludwig ***Mus*** Mario Nascimbene ***Art*** Richard Day, Alfred Sweeney, Luis Perez Espinosa
Act Yul Brynner, Gina Lollobrigida, George Sanders, Marisa Pavan, David Farrar, Harry Andrews (United Artists)

The tab for this expensive production was unexpectedly hiked when Tyrone Power died in mid-production (although insurance covered much) and the subsequent hiring of Yul Brynner necessitated new writing as well as new shooting. A figure of over $5 million, judging by the spectacle, color and location expenses in Spain seems a reasonable one.

The story [by Crane Wilbur] concerns the clash between Solomon and his brother Adonijah when King David crowns the poet-philosopher instead of the warrior. From then on it's political intrigue, with Egypt conniving with Sheba to bring down Israel, which is flourishing under the wise rule of Solomon, and the treacherous manner in which the Queen of Sheba undermines Solomon but falls in love with him in the process.

The fascinating clash between the two brothers is only spasmodically developed and, inevitably, plays second fiddle to the relationship between the queen and her infatuated target. Often what should have been a moving, gripping romance turns out to be little more than an affair between a couple of people at the local golf club.

There are some magnificent production scenes. Three startlingly effective battle sequences, the stoning of Sheba, her arrival in Jerusalem, the terrifying wrath of God which razes the Temple of Jehova and Sheba's God of Love, the scene where Solomon gives judgment over the baby, the sight of the plains of Israel made bleak and arid and, above all, the startling dance-ritual to the God of Love which develops into an orgy.

Gina Lollobrigida virtually portrays three different Shebas. First, the arrogant, fiery, ambitious Queen; then the voluptuous, wily, seductress; finally, the Sheba who involuntarily falls in love with the King and risks all by denouncing her own gods.

Lollobrigida not only looks stunning but shows the queen to be a woman of sharp brain as well as sensual beauty. Brynner, surprisingly subdued, also does a fine job in presenting a Solomon who credibly suggests a singer of songs, yet finally is a man of ordinary flesh and blood who cannot resist Sheba.

•

SO LONG AT THE FAIR
1950, 84 mins, UK b/w
Dir Terence Fisher, Antony Darnborough ***Prod*** Sidney Box ***Scr*** Anthony Thorne, Hugh Mills ***Ph*** Reginald Wyer ***Ed*** Gordon Hales ***Mus*** Benjamin Frankel
Act Jean Simmons, Dirk Bogarde, David Tomlinson, Honor Blackman, Cathleen Nesbitt, Felix Aylmer (Gainsborough/Rank)

The pic is a good workmanlike British thriller, not in the top bracket. Setting for the film is the Paris exhibition of 1889.

The story opens as Vicky Barton (Jean Simmons) arrives in Paris with her brother (David Tomlinson). After a festive first night, they return to their hotel eager to participate in the revels of the following day. But the next morning, the brother disappears. At the hotel they insist that the girl came alone and both the British consul and the chief of police find it hard to accept her story.

Despite the strong plot, the film never succeeds in developing a tense atmosphere. Picture has a good all-round cast. Simmons turns in a smooth performance. Dirk Bogarde displays a keen determination as the young artist who helps her unravel the mystery.

•

SOLYARIS
(SOLARIS)
1972, 168 mins, Russia Ⓥ ▭ col
Dir Andrei Tarkovsky ***Scr*** Friedrich Horenstein, Andrei Tarkovsky ***Ph*** Vadim Yusov ***Mus*** Enduard Artemyev ***Art*** Mikhail Romadin
Act Natalya Bondarchuk, Juri Jaarvet, Donatas Banionis, Anatoli Solonitsyn, Vladislav Dvoryetsky, Nikolai Grinko (Mosfilm)

Andrei Tarkovsky spins a strange, slow but absorbing parable on life and love in the guise of a sci-fi theme [from a book by Stanislas Lemm]. It seems to take place in a near future when there is a space station around a strange planet called Solaris, made up of viscous swirling waters, like an ocean but lensed to suggest an oozing mixture of sea and sky, which leads to apparent hallucinations by those up there. Solaris, in fact, may be a thinking mass which creates humans from man's secret needs or desires.

Film is a flashback by one astronaut who finds the place run-down. A videotape shows him a man who killed himself due to an apparition that had come from Solaris.

Space effects are not in spectacular vein but efficacious, and playing is intense and effective, as are the moral statements about love, life and humanity.

•

SOMEBODY LOVES ME
1952, 97 mins, US col
Dir Irving Brecher ***Prod*** William Perlberg ***Scr*** Irving Brecher ***Ph*** George Barnes ***Ed*** Frank Bracht ***Mus*** Emil Newman (dir.)
Act Betty Hutton, Ralph Meeker, Robert Keith, Adele Jergens, Billy Bird, Sid Tomack (Paramount)

The film acknowledges it was only suggested by the careers of Blossom Seeley and her husband, Benny Fields, and the semi-biopic treatment flows along conventional lines, highlighted by Betty Hutton's vivacity, song-selling talents and the memorable tunes of another era. Some 20 tunes are used, three being new cleffings by Jay Livingston and Ray Evans.

Ralph Meeker is not geared to portraying song and dance man Benny entirely, thus injecting the film's sole offkey note. (Meeker's offstage warbling was expertly done by Pat Morgan.)

The Seeley career is picked up in a Barbary Coast spot as the 1906 earthquake hits San Francisco. Then comes a try at vaude for the late D. J. Grauman. Passing years briefly depict her World War I work and then Broadway success as she continues to climb the show biz ladder.

•

SOMEBODY TO LOVE
1994, 103 mins, US Ⓥ col
Dir Alexandre Rockwell ***Prod*** Lila Cazes ***Scr*** Sergei Bodrov, Alexandre Rockwell ***Ph*** Robert Yeoman ***Ed*** Elena Maganini ***Mus*** Mader ***Art*** J. Rae Fox
Act Rosie Perez, Harvey Keitel, Anthony Quinn, Michael DeLorenzo, Steve Buscemi, Sam Fuller (Lumiere)

Rosie Perez shines as a spunky Latino taxi dancer with show biz in her eyes in *Somebody to Love*, but she's too often a lone beacon in a dramatically foggy and curiously unaffecting pic. Despite some treasurable moments, and a largely reliable cast, Alexandre Rockwell's first pic since his off-the-wall cult comedy *In the Soup* rarely fires on more than one cylinder at a time.

Rockwell wrote the main role of a dollar-a-dance babe in a tacky L.A. club with Perez in mind. Pic was inspired by the Giulietta Masina character in Fellini's *Nights of Cabiria* and carries a final dedication "In Memory of Federico and Giulietta."

Rockwell's movie is sufficiently rooted in a West Coast milieu for any comparisons to be meaningless. Mercedes (Perez) is a tough-talking Brooklyn transplant who spends her days being rejected at casting calls. Her lover, Harry (Harvey Keitel), also from the East Coast, is a passed-over star who's going through mid-age career and marital crises.

Enter Ernesto (Michael DeLorenzo), a dewy-eyed Latin kid who falls for Mercedes at the dance club and starts following her around like a faithful dog. Keen to make an impression on his new love, Ernesto takes a job as a runner for local racketeer Emilio (Anthony Quinn).

Given that Mercedes clearly is a loser and her relationship with Ernesto is a non-starter, pic's flat dialog draws down a movie that initially seemed to celebrate the wackier side of day-to-day life among the showbiz fringe of modern L.A.

The movie's one constant is Perez, who acquits herself well. Almost wearing a succession of tacky, figure-hugging clothes, she singlehandedly creates a character of superficial hopes and half-understood desires who deserves a sharper script and company than she gets.

•

SOMEBODY UP THERE LIKES ME
1956, 112 mins, US Ⓥ ⊙ b/w
Dir Robert Wise ***Prod*** Charles Schnee ***Scr*** Ernest Lehman ***Ph*** Joseph Ruttenberg ***Ed*** Albert Akst ***Mus*** Bronislau Kaper ***Art*** Cedric Gibbons, Malcolm Brown
Act Paul Newman, Pier Angeli, Everett Sloane, Eileen Heckart, Sal Mineo, Harold J. Stone (M-G-M)

Somebody Up There Likes Me is a superbly done, frank and revealing film probe of Rocky Graziano, the East Side punk who overcame a lawless beginning to win respect and position as middle-weight champion of the world.

Paul Newman's talent is large and flexible, revealing an approach to the Graziano character that scores tremendously.

In the latter half, when Norma Unger, played with beautiful sensitivity by Pier Angeli, comes into his life, the audience is back on his side, pulling for him to shake off the past, and literally cheering him on in that potently staged championship match with Tony Zale. Credit for this stirring climax and its authenticity must be shared by technical adviser Johnny Indrisano and Courtland Shepard, who fights like a true-to-life Zale.

Numbered among the featured and supporting cast are Everett Sloane, great as the manager Irving Cohen; Eileen Heckart, exceptionally fine as Graziano's mother; Harold J. Stone, almost uncomfortably real as the wine-sodden father; and Sal Mineo, excellent as the street chum who shared Graziano's early ways.

1956: Best B&W Cinematography, B&W Art Direction

NOMINATION: Best Editing

•

SOME CAME RUNNING
1958, 137 mins, US Ⓥ ⊙ ▭ col
Dir Vincente Minnelli ***Prod*** Sol C. Siegel ***Scr*** John Patrick, Arthur Sheekman ***Ph*** William H. Daniels ***Ed*** Adrienne Fazan ***Mus*** Elmer Bernstein ***Art*** William A. Horning, Urie McCleary
Act Frank Sinatra, Dean Martin, Shirley MacLaine, Martha Hyer, Arthur Kennedy, Nancy Gates (M-G-M)

The story is pure melodrama, despite the intention of the original novel's author, James Jones, to invest it with greater stature. But the integrity with which the film is handled by all its contributors lifts it at times to tragedy. Jones's novel has been stripped to essentials in the screenplay, and those are presented in hard clean dialog and incisive situations.

Frank Sinatra is an ex-serviceman and ex-novelist who returns to his hometown, unwitting and unwilling, when he gets drunk in Chicago and is shipped back unconscious on a bus. Accompanying him is Shirley MacLaine who is generally unwitting but never unwilling, a good-natured tart with no pretensions.

Sinatra can't stand his brother (Arthur Kennedy) or the brother's wife (Leora Dana) but he falls deeply in love with a friend of theirs (Martha Hyer). He meets a pal (Dean Martin) who becomes an ally, and he becomes involved in the personal life of his niece (Betty Lou Keim).

The title, incidentally, is taken from St. Mark, and is construed to mean that some have come running to find the meaning of life, but are prevented from finding it by obsession with materialism.

Sinatra gives a top performance, sardonic and compassionate, full of touches both instinctive and technical. It is not easy, either, to play a man dying of a chronic illness and do it with grace and humor, and this Martin does without faltering.

MacLaine isn't conventionally pretty. Her hair looks like it was combed with an eggbeater. But she elicits such empathy and humor that when she offers herself to Sinatra she seems eminently worth taking.

1958: NOMINATIONS: Best Actress (Shirley MacLaine), Supp. Actor (Arthur Kennedy), Supp. Actress (Martha Hyer), Costume Design, Song ("To Love and Be Loved")

•

SOME GIRLS
(UK: SISTERS)
1988, 94 mins, US Ⓥ col
Dir Michael Hoffman ***Prod*** Rick Stevenson ***Scr*** Rupert Walters ***Ph*** Ueli Steiger ***Ed*** David Spiers ***Mus*** James Newton Howard ***Art*** Eugenio Zanetti
Act Patrick Dempsey, Florinda Bolkan, Jennifer Connelly, Lance Edwards, Ashley Greenfield, Lila Kedrova (Oxford/Wildwood)

A cross-cultural teen sex farce with some good moments, *Some Girls* hinges on the deadpan comic timing of Patrick Dempsey, who plays Michael, an American student invited by his college sweetheart Gabby (Jennifer Connelly) to spend Christmas with her family in Quebec City. The architecturally stately city is presented as a snow-covered fairyland in the eyes of the Yank visitor.

Gabby informs Michael that she doesn't love him anymore and that sleeping arrangements will be separate. Fortunately for Michael, Gabby has two fetching sisters (Sheila Kelley, Ashley Greenfield) who each show more than a passing interest in him.

Eccentric spice is provided by the girls' father, a head-in-the-clouds scholar with a proclivity for working in the nude, portrayed by Andre Gregory in a little gem of a performance. There's also a sweet, batty grandmother (Lila Kedrova), who's convinced Michael is her long-dead husband.

Director and screenwriter have fun mixing and mismatching these comic elements and succeed in springing a few flashes of wacky hilarity.

•

SOME KIND OF HERO
1982, 97 mins, US Ⓥ ⊙ col
Dir Michael Pressman ***Prod*** Howard W. Koch ***Scr*** James Kirkwood, Robert Boris ***Ph*** King Baggot ***Ed*** Christopher Greenbury ***Mus*** Patrick Williams ***Art*** James L. Schoppe
Act Richard Pryor, Margot Kidder, Ray Sharkey, Ronny Cox, Lynne Moody, Olivia Cole (Paramount)

Some Kind of Hero is yet another example of how Richard Pryor can take a mediocre film and elevate it to the level of his extraordinary talents.

Something went awry in the adaptation of James Kirkwood's novel to the screen, for Pryor's performance is truly a class piece of acting, playing a likable enough fellow who loses everything but his sense of humor during five years in a Vietnamese prison camp.

During this tenure, he establishes a loving friendship with hot-tempered POW Ray Sharkey. When Sharkey becomes deathly ill, Pryor signs a denouncement of U.S. activities in the war to get the North Vietnamese to provide proper medical attention. Action then shifts to Pryor's return to the U.S., where the act comes back to haunt him.

Pryor's only luck is meeting Beverly Hills prostitute Margot Kidder, who gives him some loving encouragement and considers him something more than just another customer.

With Kidder's role almost as limited as Sharkey's, latter portion of the story pretty much falls apart as Pryor is torn between good and bad.

•

SOME KIND OF WONDERFUL
1987, 93 mins, US Ⓥ ⊙ col
Dir Howard Deutch ***Prod*** John Hughes ***Scr*** John Hughes ***Ph*** Jan Kiesser ***Ed*** Bud Smith, Scott Smith ***Mus*** Stephen Hague, John Musser ***Art*** Josan Russo
Act Eric Stoltz, Mary Stuart Masterson, Lea Thompson, Craig Sheffer, John Ashton, Elias Koteas (Paramount)

Some Kind of Wonderful is a simple, lovely and thoughtful teenage story that occasionally shines due to fine characterizations and lucid dialog. Writer-producer John Hughes and director Howard Deutch, who collaborated on *Pretty in Pink*, return here for an empathetic portrayal of dilemmas on such weighty matters as individuality, genuine friendship and love.

Film is set in L.A.'s San Pedro area and centers on high school senior Eric Stoltz, who is a sensitive young man struggling to develop his artistic talent while juggling school, part-time work as a car mechanic and the distraction of the immensely popular Lea Thompson that he can't quite pick up on the emotions of Mary Stuart Masterson, whom Stoltz dismisses early on as just a tomboy friend.

As Thompson fights with her wealthy and arrogant b.f. (Craig Sheffer), Stoltz manages to get her to accept a date amidst the furor and stage is set for the inevitable confrontation with Sheffer. It's especially satisfying to watch the bond deepen between Stoltz and longtime friend Masterson.

Masterson is so adept and appealing in her role that she becomes the most interesting character of all. Fortunately, however, Stoltz has the substance to maintain his lead role. Maddie Corman as one of his younger sisters is just precocious enough to avoid being unlikable.

•

SOME LIKE IT HOT
1959, 105 mins, US Ⓥ ⊙ b/w
Dir Billy Wilder ***Prod*** Billy Wilder ***Scr*** Billy Wilder, I. A. L. Diamond ***Ph*** Charles Lang, Jr. ***Ed*** Arthur P. Schmidt ***Mus*** Adolph Deutsch ***Art*** Ted Haworth
Act Marilyn Monroe, Tony Curtis, Jack Lemmon, George Raft, Pat O'Brien, Joe E. Brown (Ashton/Mirisch)

Some Like It Hot is a wacky, clever, farcical comedy [suggested by a story by R. Thoeren and M. Logan] that starts off like a firecracker and keeps on throwing off lively sparks till the very end.

Story revolves around the age-old theme of men masquerading as women. Tony Curtis and Jack Lemmon escape from a Chicago nightclub that's being raided, witness the St. Valentine's Day massacre and "escape" into the anonymity of a girl band by dressing up as feminine musicians. This leads to the obvious complications, particularly since Curtis meets Marilyn Monroe (ukulele player, vocalist and gin addict) and falls for her. Lemmon, in turn, is propositioned by an addle-brained millionaire (Joe E. Brown).

A scene on a train, where the "private" pullman berth party of Lemmon and Monroe in her nightie is invaded by guzzling dames, represents humor of Lubitsch proportions. And the alternating shots of Monroe trying to stimulate Curtis on a couch, while Lemmon and Brown live it up on the dance floor, rate as a classic sequence.

Marilyn has never looked better. Her performance as Sugar, the fuzzy blonde who likes saxophone players "and men with glasses," has a deliciously naive quality. It's a toss-up whether Curtis beats out Lemmon or whether it goes the other way round. Both are excellent.

Curtis has the upper hand because he can change back and forth from his femme role to that of a fake "millionaire" who woos Monroe. He employs a takeoff on Cary Grant, which scores with a bang at first, but tends to lose its appeal as the picture progresses.

Lemmon draws a choice assignment. Some of the funniest bits fall to him, such as his announcement that he's "engaged" to Brown.

But, in the final accounting, this is still a director's picture, and the Wilder touch is indelible. If the action is funny, the lines are there to match it.

1959: Best B&W Costume Design (Corry Kelly)

NOMINATIONS: Best Director, Actor (Jack Lemmon), Adapted Screenplay, B&W Cinematography, B&W Art Direction

•

SOME MOTHER'S SON

1996, 112 mins, Ireland/US Ⓥ col

Dir Terry George ***Prod*** Jim Sheridan, Arthur Lappin, Edward Burke ***Scr*** Terry George, Jim Sheridan ***Ph*** Geoffrey Simpson ***Ed*** Craig McKay ***Mus*** Bill Whelan ***Art*** David Wilson

Act Helen Mirren, Fionnula Flanagan, Aidan Gillen, David O'Hara, John Lynch, Tim Woodward (Hell's Kitchen/Castle Rock)

The troubles in Northern Ireland are given yet another spin in *Some Mother's Son*, which takes the point of view of the mothers whose IRA-affiliated sons were jailed by the British. This emotional perspective is designed to transcend mundane political details, but the fact remains that the action is dominated by the realities of domestic violence, prison life and a prolonged hunger strike. The directorial debut of Terry George, coscenarist of *In the Name of the Father* with present cowriter and producer Jim Sheridan, doesn't come within hailing distance of its predecessor artistically or commercially.

A fictional story centered on the events surrounding the death, during a hunger strike, of IRA member Bobby Sands, who was elected to Parliament while in an Ulster prison, pic takes off with newly elected Prime Minister Margaret Thatcher's get-tough policies against the IRA in 1979. Young Catholics Gerard Quigley (Aidan Gillen) and Frank Higgins (David O'Hara) are quickly apprehended.

Their mothers are drawn slowly together despite their vastly different political stances. Kathleen Quigley (Helen Mirren) is a schoolteacher adamantly opposed to violence who didn't even know her son was politically active. The tough-minded Annie Higgins (Fionnula Flanagan), however, lives for the day the Limeys leave the Emerald Isle for good.

As Kathleen is ever so slowly brought around to the necessity of political activism, the pic dwells at length on the protest schemes of the prisoners, who all adopt mangy Jesus Christ-like martyr looks and delight in upping the ante against the Brits. The film also focuses on the nasty machinations of the Thatcherites, personified by yuppie-scum functionary Farnsworth (Tom Hollander).

The pic has a vivid, realistic feel due to the location shooting, but George's direction is pretty cut-and-dried, devoted mostly to getting information across in the most straightforward manner possible.

•

SOMEONE ELSE'S AMERICA

1995, 96 mins, France/UK/Germany Ⓥ col

Dir Goran Paskaljevic ***Prod*** David Rose, Helga Baehr, Antoine de Clermont-Tonnerre ***Scr*** Gordon Mihic ***Ph*** Yorgos Arvanitis ***Ed*** William Diver ***Mus*** Andrew Dickson ***Art*** Wolf Seesselberg

Act Tom Conti, Miki Manojlovic, Mana Casares, Zorka Manojlovic, Sergej Trifunovic, Chia-ching Niu (Mact/Intrinsica/Lichtblick)

Proof of the Europudding is in *Someone Else's America*, a delightfully quirky, well-observed character comedy that viewers can digest sans cross-cultural burps. Directed and written by Serbs, lensed largely in a Hamburg studio by a Greek, produced by a Franco-British-German troika, and featuring a rich mix of international thesps, this fairy-tale-like study of a friendship between two Euro-bozos in Brooklyn is a charmer on every level.

Bayo (Miki Manojlovic) is a Montenegrin illegal in N.Y. who does construction gigs and works as a cleaner at the scuzzy Brooklyn bar of Alonso (Tom Conti), a shifty-eyed Spaniard who lives with his blind mother. Bayo also shares a room atop Alonso's bar with his pet rooster. Unknown to Bayo, his young daughter Savka (Andjela Stojkovic) is seriously ill back home in the mountains of Montenegro so the whole family decides to immigrate illegally to the U.S. to join the paterfamilias.

Their trek takes them via Mexico and the Rio Grande, where youngest kid Pepo is apparently swept away. When the rest of the family finally reaches Brooklyn, they adapt to the underbelly of the American Dream in various ways. Smartest off the blocks is eldest son Luka (Sergej Trifunovic), who smartens up Alonso's bar and zeroes in on a Chinese girl who just happens to have a green card.

Though the film centers on the volatile friendship between Alonso and Bayo, it's very much an ensemble piece, with a large cast and a narrative style that shows a Central European disregard for transitions and doesn't loiter on the sidewalk. Director Goran Paskaljevic's view of his characters is alert to their shortcomings, but film is done with a twinkle in the eye; even the self-centered Luka is ultimately portrayed in kindly terms.

A major assist in creating the pic's special flavor is the giant Brooklyn backstreets set built at Studio Hamburg, Germany. Actual location shooting (including Greece subbing for Montenegro) doesn't disturb the overall tone.

•

SOMEONE TO LOVE

1987, 109 mins, US Ⓥ ⊙ col

Dir Henry Jaglom ***Prod*** M. H. Simonsons ***Scr*** Henry Jaglom ***Ph*** Hanania Baer

Act Orson Welles, Henry Jaglom, Andrea Marcovicci, Michael Emil, Sally Kellerman, Oja Kodar (Rainbow)

Someone To Love represents Henry Jaglom's alternately engaging and chaotic rumination on loneliness and aloneness in the 1980s. A serio-comic psycho-drama in which the filmmaker calls upon his friends to explore why he and they have problems with commitment or finding the right mate, pic is blessed with an almost overwhelming final screen appearance by Orson Welles.

Jaglom plays himself, a director so frustrated at his girlfriend Andrea Marcovicci's unwillingness to settle down he decides to devote an entire feature to what he perceives as a general malaise of his generation. Without revealing his intentions, Jaglom invites many friends to a St. Valentine's Day party. They are somewhat taken aback by their host's desire to scrutinize their innermost feelings and insecurities with a camera, and some bow out.

Orson Welles, who appeared in Jaglom's first feature, *A Safe Place* (1971), returns here to act as the younger man's mentor and provocateur as he sits in the back of the theater smoking a cigar and delivering stunningly perceptive and intellectually far-ranging comments.

Also notable is Welles's longtime companion Oja Kodar, who portrays a visiting Yugoslavian woman with particularly sensitive and personal things to say about being a woman alone. Marcovicci gets to sing impressively and aggravate Jaglom, Sally Kellerman gives a vivid account of what one imagines Sally Kellerman to be like, and Michael Emil here gets his usual humorous philosophical ramblings thrown back in his face for a change.

•

SOMEONE TO WATCH OVER ME

1987, 106 mins, US Ⓥ ⊙ col

Dir Ridley Scott ***Prod*** Thierry de Ganay ***Scr*** Howard Franklin ***Ph*** Steven Poster ***Ed*** Claire Simpson ***Mus*** Michael Kamen ***Art*** Jim Bissell

Act Tom Berenger, Mimi Rogers, Lorraine Bracco, Jerry Orbach, John Rubinstein, Andreas Katsulas (Columbia)

Someone to Watch Over Me is a stylish and romantic police thriller which manages, through the sleek direction of Ridley Scott and persuasive ensemble performances, to triumph over several hard-to-swallow plot developments.

Tom Berenger portrays Mike Keegan, a happily married NY cop from the Bronx who has just been promoted to detective and finds himself assigned on the night shift to protect socialite Claire Gregory (Mimi Rogers), witness to a brutal murder.

Heinous killer Joey Venza, played with economical nuance and menace by Andreas Katsulas, tracks Gregory down at the Guggenheim Museum and terrorizes her in the ladies' room while Keegan is distracted. Though he subsequently chases Venza down and effects the collar, failure to read the goon his rights results in Venza back on the street and Gregory marked for death.

Berenger carries the film handily, utterly convincing as the working-class stiff out of his element accompanying Rogers through her elegant apartment or posh parties. Rogers is alluring as the romantic interest, recalling the sharpness and beauty of Laraine Day, while wife, Lorraine Bracco is fully sympathetic and easily has the viewer siding against the two leads during their hanky-panky segments.

•

SOME PEOPLE

1962, 93 mins, UK col

Dir Clive Donner ***Prod*** James Archibald ***Scr*** John Eldridge ***Ph*** John Wilcox ***Ed*** Fergus McDonell ***Mus*** Ron Grainer ***Art*** Reece Pemberton

Act Kenneth More, Ray Brooks, Annika Wills, Angela Douglas, David Andrews, David Hemmings (Anglo Amalgamated)

This one is something of a hybrid. It is designed as a feature entertainment film, a peek at the problems of modern youth in danger of becoming delinquents. As such it stands up as reasonable entertainment. But also planted firmly in the film, some unabashed propaganda for the Duke of Edinburgh's Award Scheme for Youth.

The pic is set in the industrial town of Bristol. Three lads are part of a gang of ton-up motorcyclists. Involved in an accident, they are banned from driving. Then, out of sheer boredom, they become potential young hoods. Luckily, they become involved with Kenneth More, playing a voluntary church choirmaster. He gives them the opportunity to rehearse their rock 'n' roll combo. And gradually, they become interested in the new pursuits that the Duke's scheme has to offer youngsters of initiative.

John Eldridge's storyline is loose. Clive Donner's direction is leisurely but affectionate.

More handles the role of the sympathetic choirmaster with his usual, easy charm. But the revelation is in the performances of some of the youngsters. Ray Brooks, David Andrews and David Hemmings play the three main teenagers with authority. Angela Douglas is pretty provocative as a young blonde who can handle a song and a boy with equal assurance.

•

SOMETHING FOR THE BOYS

1944, 87 mins, US col

Dir Lewis Seiler ***Prod*** Irving Starr ***Scr*** Robert Ellis, Helen Logan, Frank Gabrielson ***Ph*** Ernest Palmer ***Ed*** Robert Simpson ***Mus*** Cole Porter ***Art*** Lyle R. Wheller, Albert Hogsett

Act Carmen Miranda, Michael O'Shea, Vivian Blaine, Phil Silvers, Perry Como, Sheila Ryan (20th Century-Fox)

Screen adaptation of the [1943] musical play includes various amusing situations, but, taken as a whole, the story does not have particular punch in dialog or otherwise. Also, the comedy values are somewhat spotty, though, here and there, including among the slapstick stuff, some fairly good laughs are registered. Phil Silvers works hard on the comic end and, in one clowning number, provides several minutes of surefire nature.

Carmen Miranda, Vivian Blaine and Silvers are the three cousins who fall heir to the old plantation, only to learn that they are poorer by having acquired the debt-laden property. They get an idea, with cooperation of a nearby Army camp, to make it a home for army wives, and raise money to repair and maintain it through putting on shows and otherwise. This opens the way for the various song and dance numbers.

•

SOMETHING TO SING ABOUT

1937, 90 mins, US/UK Ⓥ ⊙ b/w

Dir Victor Schertzinger ***Prod*** Zion Myers ***Scr*** Austin Parker ***Ph*** John Stumar ***Ed*** Gene Milford ***Mus*** Constantin Bakaleinikoff ***Art*** Robert Lee, Paul Murphy

Act James Cagney, Evelyn Daw, William Frawley, Mona Barrie, Gene Lockhart, James Newill (Grand National)

James Cagney's second independently produced film for Grand National release is a first-class comedy with music. He sings, dances and plays a romantic juvenile. Having been a song-and-dance man originally, he does that well.

It is difficult to draw the line of commendation between Cagney and Victor Schertzinger, who wrote the original story, composed the music and lyrics of some tuneful numbers, and then cast and directed the piece with imagination.

Schertzinger's hero is a band leader from a New York café who is beguiled to take a fling at picture acting. There is the overnight sensational screen success, but the consequences are amusing and farcical.

Newcomer Evelyn Daw is given the supporting lead and does everything that Schertzinger demands. She sings four numbers and makes a good impression. William Frawley, as a studio press agent, has one of his best roles and gets laughs with a minimum of effort.

•

SOMETHING TO TALK ABOUT

1995, 106 mins, US Ⓥ ⊙ col

Dir Lasse Hallstrom ***Prod*** Anthea Sylbert, Paula Weinstein ***Scr*** Callie Khouri ***Ph*** Sven Nykvist ***Ed*** Mia Goldman ***Mus*** Hans Zimmer ***Art*** Mel Bourne

Act Julia Roberts, Dennis Quaid, Robert Duvall, Gena Rowlands, Kyra Sedgwick, Brett Cullen (Spring Creek/Warner)

Bland one moment and barbed the next, *Something to Talk About* dithers on like compulsive conversationalists who take twice as long as necessary to say what they want to say. This star-driven, comic take on the wages of infidelity displays much the same sisterly bonding against ratty men that marked Callie Khouri's far superior script for *Thelma & Louise*.

An affluent young wife and mother, Grace (Julia Roberts) is frantic, scattered and absent-minded, the Southern version of neurotic. She's quick to react when she spots her husband Eddie (Dennis Quaid) making out on the street with a flashy blonde, confronting him in front of a crowded bar.

None of this sits well with her dad, Wyly King (Robert Duvall), the wealthy, authoritarian owner of the snooty King Farms horse-breeding spread, where he lives with his compliant wife, Georgia (Gena Rowlands), and saucy second daughter, Emma Rae (Kyra Sedgwick). While licking her wounds back home, the distraught Grace manages to stir up trouble all around.

Modest yarn takes an unmotivated detour into *National Velvet* territory in the second half. By the time the picture winds its way back to resolving Grace's and Eddie's domestic dilemma, it has nothing more original to say on the subject than that only time and a forgiving attitude can mend such wounds.

As a vehicle for Roberts, this is a mixed bag. Sedgwick easily steals the show in a part that jumps out like a pop-up card, and Duvall loads his glances and line-readings with amusing doses of scorn and superiority. Quaid is rambunctious and credible enough as the unfaithful hubby.

•

SOMETHING WICKED THIS WAY COMES

1983, 94 mins, US Ⓥ ⊙ col

Dir Jack Clayton ***Prod*** Peter Vincent Douglas ***Scr*** Ray Bradbury ***Ph*** Stephen H. Burum ***Ed*** Argyle Nelson ***Mus*** James Horner ***Art*** Richard MacDonald

Act Jason Robards, Jonathan Pryce, Diane Ladd, Pam Grier, Royal Dano, Vidal Peterson (Walt Disney/Bryna)

Film version of Ray Bradbury's popular novel *Something Wicked This Way Comes* must be chalked up as something of a disappointment. Possibilities for a dark, child's view fantasy set in rural America of yore are visible throughout the $20 million production, but various elements have not entirely congealed into a unified achievement.

Location scenes shot in an astonishingly beautiful Vermont autumn stand-in for early 20th century Illinois, where two young boys are intrigued by the untimely arrival of a mysterious carnival troupe. By day, fairgrounds seem innocent enough, but by night they possess a strange allure that leads local inhabitants to fall victim to their deepest desires.

Thanks to the diabolical talents of carnival leader Mr. Dark, played by the suitably sinister Jonathan Pryce, these wishes can be granted, but at the price of becoming a member of the traveling freak show. Mr. Dark decides that little Will and Jim would make excellent recruits and pursues them vigilantly until the apocalyptic finale.

•

SOMETHING WILD

1986, 113 mins, US Ⓥ ⊙ col

Dir Jonathan Demme ***Prod*** Jonathan Demme, Kenneth Utt ***Scr*** E. Max Frye ***Ph*** Tak Fujimoto ***Ed*** Craig McKay ***Mus*** John Cale, Laurie Anderson ***Art*** Norma Moriceau

Act Jeff Daniels, Melanie Griffith, Ray Liotta, Margaret Colin, Tracey Walter, Dana Preu (Religioso Primitiva)

Conceptually and stylistically compelling under Jonathan Demme's sometimes striking direction, this offbeat thriller is about an unlikely couple on the run.

First-time screenwriter E. Max Frye's story sees superyuppie Jeff Daniels being picked up by hot number Melanie Griffith at a luncheonette, driven out to New Jersey and, before he knows what's happening, being handcuffed to a bed and ravished by this crazy lady.

Everything changes at her high school reunion, however, as Griffith's ex-con husband makes an unexpected appearance and proceeds to change the couple's joyride into a nightmare. From this point on, Demme and Frye adroitly tighten the screws as the focus shifts from Griffith to the showdown between the two utterly different men vying for her attention.

Daniels does a good job in transforming himself from straitlaced good boy to loosened up, wised-up man. Griffith is provocative enough, but falls a little short in putting across all the aspects of this complicated woman.

•

SOMETIMES A GREAT NOTION
(UK: NEVER GIVE AN INCH)

1971, 114 mins, US Ⓥ ▭ col

Dir Paul Newman ***Prod*** John C. Foreman ***Scr*** John Gay ***Ph*** Richard Moore ***Ed*** Bob Wyman ***Mus*** Henry Mancini ***Art*** Philip Jefferies

Act Paul Newman, Henry Fonda, Lee Remick, Michael Sarrazin, Richard Jaeckel, Linda Lawson (Universal)

Sometimes a Great Notion is a good, if plot-sprawling, outdoor action film set in Northwest lumber country, about a family of individualists fighting a town and a union. Paul Newman directs, produces, and stars as the crown prince to family patriarch Henry Fonda.

John Gay's adaptation of Ken Kesey's novel tries to balance the intellectual angles—Fonda's rigorous adherence to a principle, Newman's unending follow-through after disaster, and Michael Sarrazin's maturity from a self-indulgent drop-out. The result is rather good—a sort of contemporary "western" in the timber territory.

Fonda's performance is perhaps his first in a crotchety characterization; there is an artistic overrun, however, which makes the character seem semi-senile instead of rock-ribbed noble. Lee Remick is too chic and sophisticated for her nothing part as Newman's concerned wife.

Sarrazin and Newman come off the best, the latter again in the kind of believable melodramatic role that first made him a star, the former in a demanding role that begins with drop-out petulance mixed with fraternal enmity.

1971: NOMINATIONS: Best Supp. Actor (Richard Jaekel), Song ("All His Children")

•

SOMEWHERE I'LL FIND YOU

1942, 107 mins, US b/w

Dir Wesley Ruggles ***Prod*** Pandro S. Berman ***Scr*** Marguerite Roberts ***Ph*** Harold Rosson ***Ed*** Frank E. Hull ***Mus*** Bronislau Kaper

Act Clark Gable, Lana Turner, Robert Sterling, Patricia Dane, Reginald Owen, Lee Patrick (M-G-M)

Lana Turner is a sexy, torchy, clinging blonde. Clark Gable has seemingly always made the same impress on women. Tossing them both together, even if surrounding their clinches with but a specious story, provides an extremely potent brew.

The fact that the 1940 *Cosmopolitan* magazine serial [by Charles Hoffman] has been updated and given a rousingly patriotic finish will not once permit the audience to forget that a supposedly irresistible force (Gable) is in contact most of the 107 minutes with a very movable object.

Japan's invasion of the Philippines is overshadowed and even at the finish, when Gable is dictating the story of the fall of Bataan peninsula, the story seems to merely await the final showdown with Turner. Thus Gable could just as well have been a soldier, or a truck driver, rather than a go-getting, ruthless foreign correspondent for a N.Y. daily.

One of the picture's most ridiculous angles is having Gable, deep in the jungles of Bataan, dictating a story to a Filipino secretary.

•

SOMEWHERE IN EUROPE

SEE: VALAHOL EUROPABAN

•

SOMEWHERE IN TIME

1980, 103 mins, US Ⓥ ⊙ col

Dir Jeannot Szwarc ***Prod*** Stephen Deutsch ***Scr*** Richard Matheson ***Ph*** Isidore Mankofsky ***Ed*** Jeff Gourson ***Mus*** John Barry ***Art*** Seymour Klate

Act Christopher Reeve, Jane Seymour, Christopher Plummer, Teresa Wright, Bill Erwin, Sean Hayden (Universal/Rastar)

A charming, witty, passionate romantic drama about a love transcending space and time, *Somewhere in Time* is an old-fashioned film in the best sense of that term. Which means it's carefully crafted, civilized in its sensibilities, and interested more in characterization than in shock effects.

In the finely wrought screenplay by veteran fantasy writer Richard Matheson, based on his own novel *Bid Time Return*, Christopher Reeve is a young Chicago playwright who becomes mysteriously fascinated by a 1912 photo of a stage actress (Jane Seymour).

Reeve is drawn to a hotel on Mackinac Island in Michigan, where it transpires they actually did meet and have an affair at the time the photo was taken.

Seymour is lovely and mesmerizing enough to justify Reeve's grand romantic obsession with her.

1971: NOMINATION: Best Costume Design

•

SOMMARNATTENS LEENDE
(SMILES OF A SUMMER NIGHT)

1955, 108 mins, Sweden Ⓥ ⊙ b/w

Dir Ingmar Bergman ***Scr*** Ingmar Bergman ***Ph*** Gunnar Fischer ***Ed*** Oscar Rosander ***Mus*** Erik Nordgren ***Art*** P. A. Lundgren

Act Eva Dahlbeck, Ulla Jacobsson, Harriet Andersson, Margit Carlqvist, Jarl Kulle, Ake Fridell (Svensk Filmindustri)

Offbeat Swedish comedy of manners and passions has an unusual, lusty comedy manner. It details how a group of badly assorted couples are straightened out one summer night influenced by a strange elixir that makes people do what they want.

Clever, and at times ribald, it has a too ponderous touch to really light up the comedic aspects of this slightly overlong affair. It has top-notch acting and technical mounting, with Ingmar Bergman's direction knowing and agile.

•

SOMMERSBY

1993, 112 mins, US Ⓥ ⊙ ▭ col

Dir Jon Amiel ***Prod*** Arnon Milchan, Steven Reuther ***Scr*** Nicholas Meyer, Sarah Kernochan ***Ph*** Philippe Rousselot ***Ed*** Peter Boyle ***Mus*** Danny Elfman ***Art*** Bruno Rubeo

Act Richard Gere, Jodie Foster, Bill Pullman, James Earl Jones, William Windom, Maury Chaykin (Warner/Canal Plus/Regency/Alcor)

Sommersby is an unabashedly romantic and morally intricate Civil War-era tale splendidly acted by Richard Gere and Jodie Foster. It's one of those rare occasions that the Americanization of a foreign property (here Daniel Vigne's *The Return of Martin Guerre*) works as well as the original.

The missing-in-action and presumed dead Jack Sommersby (Gere) suddenly reappears two years after the end of the Civil War and attempts to start life anew with his wife Laurel (Foster) and young son. Foster breaks off her relationship with the righteous Orin (Bill Pullman) and tentatively resumes her place alongside her husband.

Sommersby returns a new man, as tender and committed to his wife as he had once been distant and cruel. Naturally, this arouses suspicion about his identity.

The movie keeps the question beautifully balanced in midair. Nicholas Meyer and Sarah Kernochan's screenplay (from Meyer and Anthony Shaffer's story) is cogent and elegantly literate. The film's ending is entirely appropriate, but will be much debated.

Foster is a compelling actress, telegraphing layer after layer of emotional subtext. But Gere, whose production company developed the film, comes close to stealing the picture.

•

SONG IS BORN, A

1948, 112 mins, US Ⓥ col

Dir Howard Hawks ***Prod*** Samuel Goldwyn ***Scr*** Harry Tugent ***Ph*** Gregg Toland ***Ed*** Daniel Mandell ***Mus*** Emil Newman, Hugo Friedhofer (dir) ***Art*** George Jenkins, Perry Ferguson

Act Danny Kaye, Virginia Mayo, Benny Goodman, Hugh Herbert, Steve Cochran, Louis Armstrong (RKO/Goldwyn)

Picture is a remake of Goldwyn's *Ball of Fire* (1941) starring Gary Cooper and Barbara Stanwyck. Most of Goldwyn's production crew worked on both films, including director, cameraman and editor. Charles Brackett and Billy Wilder screenplayed *Ball* from an original story, *From A to Z*, by Wilder and Thomas Monroe, but there's no screenplay credit given on *Song*.

While *Ball* dealt with a group of stodgy old professors writing a new dictionary and the way a burlesque stripper tossed a bombshell into their work, *Song* presents a similar group of professors, only this time they're compiling a history of music and the stripper is a nitery thrush. When Danny Kaye is working with them before the camera, in fact, the picture is standout entertainment. Last half of the picture, though, in which they get a semi-brushoff as Kaye becomes involved with a group of gangsters, drags by comparison.

Kaye himself does his usual neat thesping job as the youngest of the bachelor pendants, who gets his first intro to feminine wiles at the hands of a worldly-wise nitery singer, played engagingly by Virginia Mayo.

Script makes good use of the various musicians involved. They're spotlighted neatly at the beginning, as Kaye tours various Broadway niteries to get an idea of swing and jazz, which is completely unknown to the professorial group.

•

SONG OF BERNADETTE, THE
1943, 158 mins, US Ⓥ ⦿ b/w
Dir Henry King ***Prod*** William Perlberg ***Scr*** George Seaton ***Ph*** Arthur Miller ***Ed*** Barbara McLean ***Mus*** Alfred Newman ***Art*** James Basevi, William Darling
Act Jennifer Jones, Charles Bickford, Gladys Cooper, Vincent Price, Lee J. Cobb, Anne Revere (20th Century-Fox)

Song of Bernadette is an absorbing, emotional and dramatic picturization of Franz Werfel's novel. Film version is a warming and intimate narrative of godly visitation on the young girl of Lourdes that eventuated in establishment of the Shrine at Lourdes, a grotto for the divine healing of the lame.

Sensitively scripted and directed in best taste throughout, *Bernadette* unfolds in leisurely fashion with attention held through deft characterizations and incidents, rather than resort to synthetic dramatics. Many times during the extended running time there are sideline episodes inserted, but even these fail to lessen intense attention to the major theme.

Cast is expertly selected, and even the one-shot bits click solidly in fleeting footage. Jennifer Jones, in title role, delivers an inspirationally sensitive and arresting performance. Wistful, naive, and at times angelic, Jones takes command early to hold control as the motivating factor through the lengthy unfolding.

Despite the deeply religious tone of the dramatic narrative, theme is handled with utmost taste and reverence.

1943: Best Actress (Jennifer Jones), B&W Cinematography, B&W Interior Decoration, Score for a Dramatic Picture

NOMINATIONS: Best Picture, Director, Supp. Actor (Charles Bickford), Supp. Actress (Gladys Cooper, Anne Revere), Screenplay, Editing, Sound

•

SONG OF LOVE
1947, 117 mins, US Ⓥ b/w
Dir Clarence Brown ***Prod*** Clarence Brown ***Scr*** Ivan Tors, Irmgard von Cube, Allen Vincent, Robert Ardrey ***Ph*** Harry Stradling ***Ed*** Robert J. Kern ***Mus*** Bronislau Kaper (adapt.) ***Art*** Cedric Gibbons, Hans Peters
Act Katharine Hepburn, Paul Henreid, Robert Walker, Henry Daniell, Leo G. Carroll, Else Janssen (M-G-M)

Story of the lives, loves and music of Robert and Clara Schumann and Johannes Brahms, *Song of Love* has a good cast, entertaining tale and the usual top Metro production mountings.

Picture offers a goldmine of thesping opportunities to its three stars, Katharine Hepburn, Paul Henreid and Robert Walker, all of whom play it to the hilt. All three, moreover, show a surprising adeptness at pianistics, which is highly necessary despite the fact that Artur Rubinstein ghosted for them all.

Screenplay, based on a play by Bernard Schubert and Mario Silva, is overlong. Yarn picks up the young Clara Wieck as an already popular concert pianist in the early part of the last century, at the time of her marriage to Schumann, a struggling young composer. Duo promptly, by screen time, have seven children, for whose care Frau Schumann sacrifices her concert work. The young Brahms enters the household as a student and promptly complicates things by falling for Clara.

Hepburn is fine as Clara, showing in her work touches of the expert direction of Clarence Brown. She progresses neatly from emotion to emotion and registers solidly in both comedy and pathos. Henreid is a little too austere as Schumann, but comes off well in a role suited more to his talents than some of his recent films. Walker is surprisingly good as Brahms, underplaying the part and making it seem at all times authentic.

•

SONG OF NORWAY
1970, 138 mins, US Ⓥ ▭ col
Dir Andrew L. Stone ***Prod*** Andrew L. Stone, Virginia Stone ***Scr*** Andrew L. Stone ***Ph*** Davis Boulton ***Ed*** Virginia Stone ***Mus*** Roland Shaw (sup.) ***Art*** William Albert Havemeyer
Act Toralv Maurstad, Florence Henderson, Christina Schollin, Harry Secombe, Robert Morley, Edward G. Robinson (ABC)

Production and staging, the Robert Wright–George Forrest music and lyrics based on Norwegian composer Edvard Grieg's music, and wide-screen photography make *Song of Norway* a magnificent motion picture. Unfortunately, Andrew L. Stone's screenplay imparts a frequently banal, two-dimensional note featuring a wooden performance by Norwegian actor Toralv Maurstad in this musical biopic.

It is not another *Sound of Music*, but screenplay, even with its faults, is superior to the original stage play by Homer Curran.

Maurstad as Grieg, Florence Henderson as the cousin he marries and Frank Porretta as composer Rikard Nordraak, Grieg's closest friend, are primarily required to sing—not bring deep psychological sensitivity to their roles.

Stone shot *Song of Norway* totally on location in Europe at an announced cost of $3.9 million and scenes follow scenes with an irresistible richness. Choreographer Lee Theodore's staging of the musical numbers is smashing.

Harry Secombe gives a hearty, warm portrayal of the Norwegian playwright Bj;tOrnson, one of Grieg's early benefactors, displaying a rich, strong voice; Robert Morley imparts a delicate villainy to a role as Schollin's father; and Edward G. Robinson is kindly and concerned as the kindly and concerned old piano teacher.

•

SONG OF SCHEHERAZADE
1947, 105 mins, US col
Dir Walter Reisch ***Prod*** Edward Kaufman ***Scr*** Walter Reisch ***Ph*** Hal Mohr, William V. Skall ***Ed*** Frank Goss ***Mus*** Miklos Rozsa (adapt.) ***Art*** Jack Olterson
Act Yvonne De Carlo, Brian Donlevy, Jean-Pierre Aumont, Eve Arden, Philip Reed (Universal)

The music of Rimsky-Korsakov and eye value of brilliant color give *Song of Scheherazade* entertainment elements not otherwise found in the fluffy, ineptly directed and played story. Score contains 10 Rimsky-Korsakov tunes, ably adapted to the screen by Miklos Rozsa.

Basis for display of composer's muscle is his supposed escapades during a week in Spanish Morocco. Story has a comic-opera flavor, and Walter Reisch's direction of his own script often wavers in the treatment of plot elements and characters. Adding to ludicrous spots are a variety of accents, topped by the Broadwayese and 20th-century flippancy tossed into the 1865 period by Eve Arden. Plot purports to be based on an incident in Rimsky-Korsakov's life, when he was a midshipman in the Russian Navy, and is aimed at showing the influence the background had on his music.

Jean-Pierre Aumont plays the young composer. Yvonne De Carlo is the Spanish dancer with whom he falls in love during the week's adventuring. Brian Donlevy does a chain-smoking captain of the training ship who tries to make his students the pride of the Russian Navy.

•

SONG OF SONGS
1933, 83 mins, US b/w
Dir Rouben Mamoulian ***Prod*** Rouben Mamoulian ***Scr*** Leo Birinski, Samuel Hoffenstein ***Ph*** Victor Milner ***Mus*** Nat Finston (dir.)
Act Marlene Dietrich, Brian Aherne, Lionel Atwill, Alison Skipworth, Hardie Albright, Helen Freeman (Paramount)

What matter the beautiful panshots, idyllic scenes in the wildwood, the cinematic portrayal of the unsophisticated peasant girl's amorous outpourings if it doesn't entertain?

Marlene Dietrich is glamorous. She's an eyeful, but she has nothing but a Theatre Guild stager's directorial artistry to augment her innate qualities. There are long stretches of dreary talk and tedious detail until the obvious is attained.

The unsophisticated maiden, the artist and the craven colonel are a cinch formula, especially if the artist is Brian Aherne. Lionel Atwill makes the German colonel a lecherous a.k. character.

There are some excellent performances [in this adaptation of the story by Hermann Sudermann and play by Edward Sheldon]. Alison Skipworth's dipsomaniacal aunt is a gem in realism. But Atwill has so difficult an assignment that even this capable trouper permits it to get away from him in a couple of spots, such as that ten-twent-thirt leer on the bridal night. Aherne, debuting in flickers, does not connect as effectively as another debut performance, that of Helen Freeman, the Theatre Guild cofounder and a veteran legit actress.

•

SONG OF THE ISLANDS
1942, 73 mins, US Ⓥ ⦿ col
Dir Walter Lang ***Prod*** William Le Baron ***Scr*** Joseph Schrank, Robert Pirosh, Robert Ellis, Helen Logan ***Ph*** Ernest Palmer ***Ed*** Robert Simpson ***Mus*** Mack Gordon
Act Betty Grable, Victor Mature, Jack Oakie, Thomas Mitchell, Hilo Hattie (20th Century-Fox)

Song of the Islands is a spontaneous and breezy mixture of comedy, song, dance and romance—set in Hawaiian atmosphere.

There's plenty of color, a load of romance, and sufficient comedy ladled out in generally broad style to carry audience interest.

Story is only a light and fragile framework on which to hang the various sequences. Betty Grable is the daughter of Thomas Mitchell, philosophical Irish beachcomber, who owns a portion of a small island in the Hawaiian group and treats the natives with consideration.

Victor Mature sails in to visit his father's cattle ranch on the other side of the island, and immediately romance gets under way.

Liberal potions of surefire comedy are supplied by Jack Oakie, who has a field day in by-play with buxom native maid (Hilo Hattie). Fast-paced script is enhanced by consistently zippy direction by Walter Lang.

•

SONG O' MY HEART
1930, 85 mins, US Ⓥ b/w
Dir Frank Borzage ***Prod*** William Fox ***Scr*** Tom Barry, Sonya Levien ***Ph*** Chester Lyons, Al Brick, J. O. Taylor ***Ed*** Margaret V. Clancey ***Art*** Harry Oliver
Act John McCormack, Maureen O'Sullivan, John Garrick, J. M. Kerrigan, Tommy Clifford, Alice Joyce (Fox)

This is not merely a matter of John McCormack singing 11 songs. Fox has molded what might easily have become so much sentimental sop into a charming background for the Irish tenor.

The script [from a story by J. J. McCarthy] draws him as a prominent singer in his native land with an unsuccessful love affair, the subject of which, Mary, has wed elsewhere by command. Her death leaves him to look after her two children. The build-up to the "I Hear You Calling Me" climax comes when Mary dies and a cable so informs McCormack's accompanist as the tenor is in the midst of an American concert.

Meanwhile, there are the two village cronies—J. M. Kerrigan and Farrell MacDonald. Almost as good as Kerrigan's comedy is MacDonald's "straight." Between them it's superb. Maureen O'Sullivan and the lad, Tommy Clifford, impress favorably.

•

SONG TO REMEMBER, A
1945, 110 mins, US Ⓥ ⦿ col
Dir Charles Vidor ***Prod*** Sidney Buchman, Louis F. Edelman ***Scr*** Sidney Buchman ***Ph*** Tony Gaudio ***Ed*** Charles Nelson ***Mus*** Miklos Rozsa (adapt.) ***Art*** Lionel Banks, Van Nest Polglase
Act Paul Muni, Merle Oberon, Cornel Wilde, Stephen Bekassy, George Coulouris, Sig Arno (Columbia)

Based on the colorful—though brief—life of Polish composer Frederic Chopin, picture is a showmanly presentation of intimate drama and music.

Plot [from a story by Ernst Marischka] introduces Chopin as a prodigy at 11, with Paul Muni the old music master who easily recognizes his genius. When 22, the student and teacher flee to Paris after Chopin refuses to perform for the Russian governor. Young Franz Liszt befriends the newcomer and is directly responsible for getting him recognition.

Brilliant performances are generally turned in by the cast, with Muni provoking maximum interest with his portrayal of the music teacher. Cornel Wilde is spotlighted as Chopin and establishes himself as a screen personality. Merle Oberon clicks as the cold and calculating writer.

Jose Iturbi contributes importantly in the overall with his background playing of numerous Chopin compositions. Wilde does a fine job of keyboard manipulations, and the visual and sound components blend accurately for realist effect.

Reproduction of the piano passages is the best of its kind that has so far been accomplished, and credit for the achievement must go to John Livadary and the entire Columbia sound department.

1945: NOMINATIONS: Best Actor (Cornel Wilde), Original Story, Color Cinematography, Editing, Scoring of a Musical Picture, Sound

•

SONG WITHOUT END

1960, 145 mins, US col

Dir Charles Vidor, George Cukor ***Prod*** William Goetz ***Scr*** Oscar Millard ***Ph*** James Wong Howe ***Ed*** William A. Lyons ***Mus*** Harry Sukman (arr.) ***Art*** Walter Holscher

Act Dirk Bogarde, Capucine, Genevieve Page, Patricia Morison, Ivan Desny, Martita Hunt (Columbia)

Song Without End dramatizes the story of pianist-composer Franz Liszt. It is a must-see motion picture for music lovers, an enriching experience for family audiences, and a particularly compelling attraction for social security eligibles.

A complex central character, Liszt is depicted as a man tragically embroiled in overlapping romantic, religious and professional conflicts. His relations with the opposite sex are stormy, illicit and ill-fated. Discarding the irreligious mother of his two children, he discovers happiness and the germ of artistic fulfillment during his affair with the devout wife of a Russian prince, only to have it dissolve abruptly on the eve of their wedding.

Where the screenplay is never quite clear is in its concept of Liszt's creative ability. Peerless keyboard technician and interpreter of the genius of his contemporaries, he is regarded as a victim of his own virtuosity.

It is in the production itself that the film attains stature. It is a feast of sight and sound put together by a battery of expert cinema craftsmen. Lensman James Wong Howe zeroes in on the authentic settings with athletic dexterity. All these skills have been integrated into an impressive physical whole by directors Charles Vidor and George Cukor, but they were not as uniformly successful in commandeering a matching dramatic spirit from the cast.

Vidor died on June 4, 1959, having filmed about 15% of the picture. He got full director's title at request of Cukor who took a smaller screen credit.

1960: Best Scoring of a Musical Picture

•

SONGWRITER

1984, 94 mins, US Ⓥ ⦿ col

Dir Alan Rudolph ***Prod*** Sydney Pollack ***Scr*** Bud Shrake ***Ph*** Matthew Leonetti ***Ed*** Stuart Pappe ***Mus*** Larry Cansler ***Art*** Joel Schiller

Act Willie Nelson, Kris Kristofferson, Melinda Dillon, Rip Torn, Lesley Ann Warren, Richard C. Sarafian (Tri-Star)

Songwriter is a good-natured film that rolls along on the strength of attitudes and poses long ago established outside the picture by its stars, Willie Nelson and Kris Kristofferson, basically playing themselves disguised as fictional characters.

Brief opening collage establishes the younger days of Doc Jenkins (Nelson) and Blackie Buck (Kristofferson) as a performing duo before they go their semi-separate ways and revert to character.

Doc Jenkins is the saint of country music, loved and respected by everyone. Luckily Nelson has enough of a screen presence to support his deification. As Blackie Buck, Kristofferson is still the outlaw with a heart of gold, but who will probably never grow up and settle down.

Director Alan Rudolph, who took over for Steve Rash two weeks into the filming, is best at working with actors, and Lesley Ann Warren, in particular, is radiant as an up-and-coming, but reluctant country & western singer.

1984: NOMINATION: Best Original Song Score

•

SON OF DRACULA

1943, 79 mins, US Ⓥ ⦿ b/w

Dir Robert Siodmak ***Prod*** Ford Beebe ***Scr*** Eric Taylor ***Ph*** George Robinson ***Ed*** Saul Goodkind ***Mus*** Hans J. Salter

Act Lon Chaney, Robert Paige, Louise Allbritton, Evelyn Ankers, Frank Craven, J. Edward Bromberg (Universal)

This is another in the Universal series of *Dracula* horror features. It's a good entry of its type.

Plot, in detailing the legendary transformation of humans to vampire form at night through throat-bites by a previous victim, ships Dracula's son (Lon Chaney) to a small town where Louise Allbritton is an occult follower. There's the usual lonely manse with surrounding woods, and killings by the night-flying vampire to arouse the countryside. Allbritton marries Chaney, whom she believes to be a Hungarian count, and comes under his influence. Her affianced (Robert Paige) figures strange things going on, and compares notes with town doctor, Frank Craven, and psychologist J. Edward Bromberg.

•

SON OF FRANKENSTEIN

1939, 94 mins, US Ⓥ ⦿ b/w

Dir Rowland V. Lee ***Prod*** Rowland V. Lee ***Scr*** Willis Cooper ***Ph*** George Robinson ***Ed*** Ted Kent ***Mus*** Frank Skinner ***Art*** Jack Otterson, Richard H. Riedel

Act Basil Rathbone, Boris Karloff, Bela Lugosi, Lionel Atwill, Josephine Hutchinson, Donnie Dunagan (Universal)

Boris Karloff's man-made monster is revived in the castle of Frankenstein to provide material for another adventure of the ogre. Basil Rathbone, son of the scientist-creator, returns from America to the family estate, becomes intrigued with the dormant ogre and revives him with idea of changing the brute nature within.

There are secret passages and panels; surprise opening of doors; and well-timed sound effects to further create tense interest.

For offering of its type, picture is well mounted, nicely directed, and includes cast of capable artists. Karloff has his monster in former groove as the big and powerful brute who crushes and smashes victims. Bela Lugosi is the mad cripple who guides the monster on murder forays. Lionel Atwill is prominent as village inspector of police.

•

SON OF FURY
THE STORY OF BENJAMIN BLAKE

1942, 98 mins, US Ⓥ b/w

Dir John Cromwell ***Prod*** Darryl F. Zanuck ***Scr*** Philip Dunne ***Ph*** Arthur Miller ***Ed*** Walter Thompson ***Mus*** Alfred Newman ***Art*** Richard Day, James Basevi

Act Tyrone Power, Gene Tierney, George Sanders, Frances Farmer, Roddy McDowall, Elsa Lanchester (20th Century-Fox)

Set in England during the reign of King George III, the story [from the novel *Benjamin Blake* by Edison Marshall] is that of Benjamin Blake (Tyrone Power) who undergoes great hardships and reverses in an attempt, ultimately successful, to establish the birthright that had been snatched from him nefariously by a scheming uncle of the upper crust. However, on regaining title to the fortune that was rightfully his, he parcels it out to servants of the estate and others in order to return to the tropic isle where he made himself independently rich from oyster pearls and, in the process, met Gene Tierney.

Running time is a little long, with some sequences slowing the action down, but generally the story commands rapt attention and, on the whole, emerges as sound, compelling entertainment.

There is virtually no comic relief. It could have been used here and there to fine advantage because of the general heaviness of the action.

•

SON OF KONG, THE

1933, 69 mins, US Ⓥ ⦿ b/w

Dir Ernest B. Schoedsack ***Prod*** Merian C. Cooper (exec.) ***Scr*** Ruth Rose ***Ph*** Edward Linden, Vernon Walker, J. O. Taylor ***Ed*** Ted Cheesman ***Mus*** Max Steiner ***Art*** Van Nest Polglase, Al Herman

Act Robert Armstrong, Helen Mack, Frank Reicher, John Marston, Victor Wong, Ed Brady (RKO)

This is the sequel to and wash-up of the King Kong theme, consisting of salvaged remnants from the original production and rating as fair entertainment.

Story is by Ruth Rose who, with others, worked on the adaptation of the original. It is concerned mostly in building up the explorer's return to the island of prehistoric animals, which cuts down the actual running time of the trick stuff to perhaps less than 25% of the total footage.

His pop was one tough hombre, but young Kong is lots more friendly. The explorer saves him from destruction in quicksand, so he proceeds to reciprocate. He wrassles and kayoes some bad eggs among the beasts of the Stone Age jungle while protecting the visiting mortals. The senior Kong was around 50 feet high in his bare tootsies. Junior is a comparative shrimp, standing a mere 25 feet or so, but he can handle himself in a scrap.

Three of the principals, Robert Armstrong, Frank Reicher and Victor Wong, are holdovers from the original cast. Helen Mack is the girl this time, called upon to be a brave creature, in place of Fay Wray who was directed into doing nothing but screaming.

•

SON OF LASSIE

1945, 100 mins, US col

Dir S. Sylvan Simon ***Prod*** Samuel Marx ***Scr*** Jeanne Bartlett ***Ph*** Charles Schoenbaum ***Ed*** Ben Lewis ***Mus*** Herbert Stothart ***Art*** Cedric Gibbons, Hubert B. Hobson

Act Peter Lawford, Donald Crisp, June Lockhart, Nigel Bruce, Nils Asther, Leon Ames (M-G-M)

Theme is the same dog's-devotion-to-master that motivated *Lassie Come Home*, only this time it's Lassie's son, Laddie, who follows his young master into the war and a high-adventure trek across Nazi-occupied countries back to England after their plane is shot down. Suspense elements hit high peaks at times, offsetting the sticky sentiment, and flambuoyant adventures carry sufficient interest to move it along. Peter Lawford plays excellently and with restraint the character of Joe, whose younger version was portrayed by Roddy McDowall in *Lassie Come Home*. Donald Crisp is again seen as Joe's father, also excellent, and Nigel Bruce repeats his Duke of Rudling characterization to good effect.

•

SON OF PALEFACE

1952, 95 mins, US Ⓥ ⦿ col

Dir Frank Tashlin ***Prod*** Robert L. Welch ***Scr*** Frank Tashlin, Robert L. Welch, Joseph Quillan ***Ph*** Harry J. Wild ***Ed*** Eda Warren, Ellsworth Hoagland ***Mus*** Lyn Murray ***Art*** Hal Perira, Roland Anderson

Act Bob Hope, Jane Russell, Roy Rogers, Bill Williams, Lloyd Corrigan, Paul E. Burns (Paramount)

A freewheeling, often hilarious, rambunctious followup to *The Paleface*. It is the broadest kind of slapstick, drawing advantageously on the silent-day masters of the pratfall.

Plot finds Roy Rogers and Lloyd Corrigan, government agents, assigned to the case of running down "The Torch," a bandit and gang that is looting gold shipments and then mysteriously disappearing. The job is complicated by the appearance in the small western town of Sawbuck Pass of Hope, the Harvard grad son of the late Paleface Potter.

A supercilious, cowardly braggart, Hope complicates matters temporarily until the agents decide to use him to confirm their suspicions that Jane Russell, the long-legged, amorous keeper of the Dirty Shame saloon, is the leader of the robbers.

1952: NOMINATION: Best Song ("Am I in Love?")

•

SON OF THE PINK PANTHER

1993, 93 mins, US Ⓥ ⦿ col

Dir Blake Edwards ***Prod*** Tony Adams ***Scr*** Blake Edwards, Madeline Sunshine, Steve Sunshine ***Ph*** Dick Bush ***Ed*** Robert Pergament ***Mus*** Henry Mancini ***Art*** Peter Mullins

Act Roberto Benigni, Herbert Lom, Claudia Cardinale, Debrah Farentino, Jennifer Edwards, Robert Davi (United Artists)

Blake Edwards, Hollywood's one-time ingenious *farceur*, desperately tries to bounce back with *Son of the Pink Panther*, the eighth episode in the series that began in 1964. Starring Italian comedian Roberto Benigni as the new bumbling inspector, it is a tired pastiche of recycled sketches and gags.

This time around, twitching Commissioner Dreyfus (Herbert Lom) is investigating the disappearance of Princess Yasmin (Debrah Farentino), kidnapped by a nasty terrorist (Robert Davi). Also assigned to the case is Jacques Gambrelli (Benigni), a second-class gendarme who doesn't initially realize he's the illegitimate son of the famed Inspector Clouseau. Nor, to his dismay, does Lom.

Too bad that Edwards's speciality, the elaborate orchestration of sight gags with hilarious payoffs, is almost absent here, replaced by vulgar slapstick humor and a few effective gags. Benigni is the major asset, but his vast talents are underutilized.

•

SON OF THE SHEIK, THE

1926, 70 mins, US Ⓥ d b/w

Dir George Fitzmaurice ***Prod*** John W. Considine, Jr. ***Scr*** Frances Marion, Fred De Gresac, George Marion, Jr. ***Ph*** George Barnes ***Art*** William Cameron Menzies

Act Rudolph Valentino, Vilma Banky, George Fawcett, Montagu Love, Karl Dane, Agnes Ayres (Feature/United Artists)

In *The Son of the Sheik* Rudolph Valentino not only is the dashing youth of the Arabian plains but he also plays his father, the sheik. The double-exposure shots are not as clear as is possible. Naturally, the "son" is the predominant character, and in this role Valentino wins new laurels.

The Son is a sequel to *The Sheik* adapted by Frances Marion from the novel by E. M. Hull. It is best described as an interesting study in psychology, showing how a son of the desert inherited the love, passions and hate of his father.

Some exceptionally fine photography, especially the desert scenes, and the excellent acting of the supporting cast help to make *The Son of the Sheik* an outstanding success.

•

SONS AND LOVERS
1960, 99 mins, UK ▭ b/w
Dir Jack Cardiff ***Prod*** Jerry Wald ***Scr*** Gavin Lambert, T. E. B. Clarke ***Ph*** Freddie Francis ***Ed*** Gordon Pilkington ***Art*** Tom Morahan
Act Trevor Howard, Dean Stockwell, Wendy Hiller, Mary Ure, Heather Sears, William Lucas (20th Century-Fox)

Sons and Lovers is a well-made and conscientious adaptation of D. H. Lawrence's famed novel, smoothly directed by Jack Cardiff and superbly acted by a notable cast.

Gavin Lambert and T. E. B. Clarke collaborated in producing a literate screenplay, though not entirely recapturing the atmosphere of the Nottinghamshire mining village so vividly described in the original. Also there is a tendency to portray the mother as an overly selfish, possessive and nagging woman. Even Wendy Hiller's flawless performance cannot make her a sympathetic character.

Many of the exteriors were filmed on location outside Nottingham, and their authenticity is a plus factor. Against the background of the grimy mining village is unfolded the story of a miner's son with promising artistic talents who is caught up in continual conflict between his forthright father and possessive mother. He sacrifices a chance to study art in London, gives up the local farm girl he loves, and eventually becomes entangled with a married woman separated from her husband.

Easily the outstanding feature of the production is the powerful performance by Trevor Howard, as the miner. He gives a moving and wholly believable study of a man equally capable of tenderness as he is of being tough. He looks the character, too. Dean Stockwell puts up a good showing as the son and makes a valiant try to cope with the accent.

1960: Best B&W Cinematography

NOMINATIONS: Best Picture, Director, Actor (Trevor Howard), Supp. Actress (Mary Ure), Adapted Screenplay, B&W Art Direction

•

SONS OF KATIE ELDER, THE
1965, 120 mins, US Ⓥ ⦿ ▭ col
Dir Henry Hathaway ***Prod*** Hal Wallis ***Scr*** William H. Wright, Allan Weiss, Harry Essex ***Ph*** Lucien Ballard ***Ed*** Warren Low ***Mus*** Elmer Bernstein ***Art*** Hal Pereira, Walter Tyler
Act John Wayne, Dean Martin, Martha Hyer, Michael Anderson, Jr., Earl Holliman, Dennis Hopper (Paramount)

Talbot Jennings's story tells of four brothers—John Wayne a notorious gunslinger, Dean Martin a gambler—who return to their Texas home to attend their mother's funeral and remain to fight the town.

Two stars are joined by Earl Holliman and Michael Anderson, Jr., latter the kid brother, in family setup. The three older brothers are prodigals who left home years before. The mother is never shown, but her influence is felt throughout the film as the three seniors decide that the best monument they can erect for their mother is to send her last-born back to college.

Drama takes form as the brothers decide to stay long enough to learn who murdered their father six months previously, look into the situation of their mother losing her ranch to a townsman, and a grim young deputy sheriff learning Martin is wanted for murder and deciding to bring the brothers in.

Wayne delivers one of his customary rugged portrayals, a little old, perhaps, to have such a young brother as Anderson but not so old that he lacks the attributes of a gunman. Martin, who plays his part with a little more humor than the others, is equally effective in a hardboiled characterization.

•

SONS OF THE DESERT
1934, 68 mins, US Ⓥ ⦿ b/w
Dir William A. Seiter ***Prod*** Hal Roach ***Scr*** Frank Craven, Byron Morgan ***Ph*** Kenneth Peach ***Ed*** Bert Jordan
Act Stan Laurel, Oliver Hardy, Charlie Chase, Mae Busch, Dorothy Christy, Lucien Littlefield (Roach/M-G-M)

Announced as an original, this appears to be a blowup of a two-reel comedy, *We Faw Down*, in which the team was seen three or four years earlier. In the original the comedians used a visit to a vaudeville theatre as an alibi for their dalliance. They describe the performance at length to their wives only to be confronted with a newspaper telling of the destruction of the theatre by fire during the performance they were supposed to have witnessed. In the longer version it's a trip to a lodge convention, with a supposed voyage to Honolulu as a cover. They return home to find that the steamer on which they were supposed to have sailed, foundered and the passengers returned to the home port on another vessel.

Stretched to feature length, with no additional plot material, the story is thin to the point of attenuation but the idea is adhered to, which at least supplies a peg on which to hang the buildup. The latter, chiefly belly laughs with a bit of production in the middle: a pre-Code Hawaiian dance in a café set led by a highly personable young woman who knows it pays to advertise.

About the only injection of novelty is a slick bit in which Laurel hysterically breaks down and tells the truth. Which gets him a Japanese dressing gown and permission to smoke cigarettes, while Hardy is on the receiving end of the family china and tinware.

•

SOPHIE'S CHOICE
1982, 157 mins, US Ⓥ ⦿ col
Dir Alan J. Pakula ***Prod*** Alan J. Pakula, Keith Barish ***Scr*** Alan J. Pakula ***Ph*** Nestor Almendros ***Ed*** Evan Lottman ***Mus*** Marvin Hamlisch ***Art*** George Jenkins
Act Meryl Streep, Kevin Kline, Peter MacNicol, Rita Karin, Stephen D. Newman, Josh Mostel (ITC)

Sophie's Choice is a handsome, doggedly faithful and astoundingly tedious adaptation of William Styron's bestseller.

Set in 1947, tale has young aspiring writer Stingo (Peter MacNicol), a Southern lad, taking a room in a comfortable house in which also dwell Sophie (Meryl Streep), a Polish former Catholic, and her exuberant, changeable, Jewish lover, Nathan Landau (Kevin Kline). Three become best of friends, although at times Nathan turns on the other two, leaving Stingo to console Sophie and hear some of her painful confessions about her prewar life and incarceration by the Nazis.

Ever so slowly, it comes clear that Sophie has lied about many things, notably her father. After 90 minutes, film flips into a half-hour, subtitled, sepiatoned flashback to portray Sophie's tenure as secretary to the commanding officer at Auschwitz.

Streep, Kline and MacNicol all give it a good shot individually, but they never coalesce into the close, warm trio called for by the story.

1982: Best Actress (Meryl Streep)

NOMINATIONS: Best Screenplay Adaptation, Cinematography, Costume Design, Original Score

•

SO PROUDLY WE HAIL!
1943, 126 mins, US b/w
Dir Mark Sandrich ***Prod*** Mark Sandrich ***Scr*** Allan Scott ***Ph*** Charles Lang ***Ed*** Ellsworth Hoagland ***Mus*** Miklos Rozsa
Act Claudette Colbert, Paulette Goddard, Veronica Lake, George Reeves, Barbara Britton, Sonny Tufts (Paramount)

Mark Sandrich's *So Proudly We Hail!* is a saga of the war-front nurse and her heroism under fire. As such it glorifies the American Red Cross and presents the wartime nurse, in the midst of unspeakable dangers, physical and spiritual, in a new light.

Director-producer Sandrich and scripter Allan Scott have limned a vivid, vital story. It's backgrounded against a realistic romance of how a group of brave American Nightingales came through the hellfire to Australia and thence back to Blighty.

Done in flashback manner, with Claudette Colbert rapidly sinking physically, the saga of their travail pitches to the situation where, out of the past, a love letter from her officer-lover finally brings her back on the road to recovery. Paulette Goddard does a capital job as running mate, and Veronica Lake is the sullen nurse who finally sees the light.

Sonny Tufts walks off with the picture every time he's on. As Kansas, the blundering ex-footballer, he's Goddard's vis-á-vis. George Reeves isn't as effective as the romantic opposite to Colbert.

1943: NOMINATIONS: Best Supp. Actress (Paulette Goddard), Original Screenplay, B&W Cinematography, Special Effects

•

SORCERER
(U.K.: WAGES OF FEAR)
1977, 121 mins, US Ⓥ ⦿ col
Dir William Friedkin ***Prod*** William Friedkin ***Scr*** Walon Green ***Ph*** John M. Stephens, Dick Bush ***Ed*** Bud Smith ***Mus*** Tangerine Dream ***Art*** John Box
Act Roy Scheider, Bruno Cremer, Francisco Rabal, Amidou, Ramon Bieri, Peter Capell (Universal/Paramount)

William Friedkin's *Sorcerer* is a painstaking, admirable, but mostly distant and uninvolving suspenser based on the French classic *The Wages of Fear* [from the novel by Georges Arnaud]. Friedkin vividly renders the experience of several men driving trucks loaded with nitro through the South American jungle, yet the characters are basically functional. "Sorcerer" is merely the name of one of the trucks.

The first 70 minutes are devoted to establishing the violent backgrounds of the characters before the trucks roll, unlike the 1953 Henri-Georges Clouzot film, which took place entirely in the jungle. Production took 10 months, largely in the jungles of the Dominican Republic and central Mexico, but also in Paris, Jerusalem, New Jersey, and New Mexico. Reports are the film could have gone as high as $21 million.

The drivers are Roy Scheider, Bruno Cremer, Amidou and Francisco Rabal. The oil company boss hires the truckers because he needs the nitro to fight a well fire.

The story has a strong existential feeling, desperate men staking their lives on a suicidal mission because they have no other way of making a living. But despite the opening scenes—of Scheider involved in a New Jersey robbery, Cremer in a French bank scandal, and Amidou in an Arab terrorist incident—the film fails to bring them alive as people.

In the journey, the last 51 minutes of the film, one becomes enervated watching the agonizing progress of the trucks and the men's gradually increasing hysteria. Lensing is extraordinarily good, particularly the long sequences shot during torrential rainstorms.

[In the U.K., the film was retitled and cut to 92 mins., partly by eliminating the flashbacks.]

1977: NOMINATION: Best Sound

•

SORCERERS, THE
1967, 86 mins, UK Ⓥ col
Dir Michael Reeves ***Prod*** Patrick Curtis, Tony Tenser ***Scr*** Michael Reeves, Tom Baker ***Ph*** Stanley Long ***Ed*** Ralph Sheldon ***Mus*** Paul Ferris ***Art*** Tony Curtis
Act Boris Karloff, Catherine Lacey, Ian Ogilvy, Elizabeth Ercy, Victor Henry, Susan George (Tigon)

Boris Karloff brings his familiar adroit horror touch to the role of an aging somewhat nutty ex-stage mesmerist who aims to complete his experiments by dominating the brain of a young subject. Karloff himself is dominated by his wife (Catherine Lacey), who was his stage assistant.

Karloff persuades Ian Ogilvy, who plays a feckless, slightly moody youth, to become the subject for his experiments. Initial experiments work well as Karloff sees in the youth a tool who may be able to benefit mankind under his influence. But Karloff's wife, motivated by greed, insists that the lad should work for their benefit for a while.

•

SOROK PYERVI
(THE FORTY-FIRST)
1956, 90 mins, USSR col
Dir Grigori Chukhrai ***Scr*** G. Koltunov ***Ph*** Sergei Urusevsky ***Ed*** Zh. Lysenkova ***Mus*** Nikolai Kryukov ***Art*** V. Kamsky, K. Stepanov
Act Isolda Izvitskaya, Oleg Strizhenov, Nikolai Kryuchkov (Mosfilm)

Film reveals more destalinization and emerges an extremely well made adventure-love opus that has a taking mood and story despite the propaganda line.

A female sharpshooter, taking back a White Russian prisoner during the Revolution, is marooned on a desert isle with him. They fall in love, only to have it end in tragedy when she shoots him rather than be rescued by Czarist soldiers searching for him.

Well-acted, expertly mounted and with slick love tale, in spite of the hefty qualities of the girl, this is entertaining. [Pic is from the story by Boris Lavrenyov, previously filmed by Yakov Protazanov in 1927.]

•

SORROW AND THE PITY, THE
SEE: LE CHAGRIN ET LA PITIE

•

SORROWS OF SATAN, THE
1926, 117 mins, US ⊗ b/w
Dir D. W. Griffith ***Prod*** D. W. Griffith ***Scr*** Forrest Halsey, Julian Johnson, John Russell, George Hull ***Ph*** Harry Fischbeck, Arthur De Titta ***Ed*** Julian Johnson ***Art*** Charles M. Kirk
Act Adolphe Menjou, Ricardo Cortez, Carol Dempster, Lya De Putti, Ivan Lebedeff (Paramount)

D. W. Griffith again symbolizes good and evil, meanwhile out-DeMilling DeMille in sets and bacchanalian revels, plus liberal suggestiveness. For all of that, the picture is overshadowed in story and cast by its superb photography. Limited action comes very close to trying the patience more than once. There is the usual ruined young lady (Carol Dempster) after which comes the enticing of the poor lover (Ricardo Cortez) to the upper social stratum by Satan (Adolphe Menjou), masquerading as a fabulously wealthy prince, and later a broad display of passion by Lya De Putti when, as Princess Olga, she figuratively strips her soul before the prince.

And yet Harry Fischbeck's work at the camera dominates the film, especially in the latter footage. Illumination of a mammoth staircase so that just the tops of the stairs are in relief, and down which the figures come only picked out by a "pin" spot showing the last of the characters, rates as a great piece of work.

•

SORRY, WRONG NUMBER
1948, 89 mins, US Ⓥ b/w
Dir Anatole Litvak ***Prod*** Hal B. Wallis, Anatole Litvak ***Scr*** Lucille Fletcher ***Ph*** Sol Polito ***Ed*** Warren Low ***Mus*** Franz Waxman ***Art*** Hans Dreier, Earl Hedrick
Act Barbara Stanwyck, Burt Lancaster, Ann Richards, Wendell Corey, Ed Begley (Wallis/Paramount)

Sorry, Wrong Number is a real chiller. Film is a fancily dressed coproduction by Hal B. Wallis and Anatole Litvak. Pair has smoothly coordinated efforts to give strong backing to the Lucille Fletcher script, based on her radio play.

Plot deals with an invalid femme who overhears a murder scheme through crossed telephone lines. Alone in her home, the invalid tries to trace the call. She fails, and then tries to convince the police of the danger. She gradually comes to realize that it is her own death that is planned.

Barbara Stanwyck plays her role of the invalid almost entirely in bed. Her reading is sock, the actress giving an interpretation that makes the neurotic, selfish woman understandable. Same touch is used by Burt Lancaster to make audiences see through the role of the invalid's husband and how he came to plot her death.

Considerable emphasis is placed on the score by Franz Waxman to heighten the gradually mounting suspense. Sol Polito uses an extremely mobile camera for the same effect, sharpening the building terror with unusual angles and lighting.

1948: NOMINATION: Best Actress (Barbara Stanwyck)

•

S.O.S. ICEBERG
1933, 77 mins, US/Germany b/w
Dir Tay Garnett ***Prod*** Paul Kohner ***Scr*** Tom Reed, Edwin H. Knopf, Arnold Fanck ***Ph*** Hans Schneeberger, Richard Angst ***Ed*** Andrew Marton ***Mus*** Paul Desau
Act Rod La Rocque, Leni Reifenstahl, Sepp Rist, Gibson Gowland, Ernst Ujet (Universal)

Made chiefly in Greenland under the aegis of Knud Rasmussen, polar authority, deputized by the Danish government, Universal had the further advice of two members of the ill-fated Wegener expedition. The result is an authentic and authoritative series of polar pictures that scarcely need the pressbook assurance that no miniatures were used to supplement the straight shots.

Briefly, a young scientist seeks to recover the records of the lost Wegener expedition. He achieves his purpose with the aid of three friends, experienced ice men, and his financial backer, who goes along for the fun of the adventure and is driven mad by the awful perils. They are marooned on an iceberg. The hero's wife, a noted flier, goes to the rescue and crashes against the berg in landing.

The finest bit of acting is contributed by Gibson Gowland. Leni Reifenstahl, the one woman in the picture, bears the same relation to the story as the heroine in a standard Western. She supplies the alleged love interest while otherwise serving only to impede the story.

According to the inside, this picture was conceived and started by Germans and turned over to Universal when the originators were unable to carry it through. Interiors were made in Berlin and only the finished negative went to Hollywood.

•

SO THIS IS PARIS
1926, 80 mins, US ⊗ b/w
Dir Ernst Lubitsch ***Scr*** Hans Kraly ***Ph*** John Mescall
Act Monte Blue, Patsy Ruth Miller, Lilyan Tashman, Andre Beranger, Myrna Loy (Warner)

A highly laughable farce [based on the French comedy *Reveillon*] with the laughs heavy on situations, and humorous captions added to make an excellent total. There is unusual photography also. At one time Lubitsch plays continuous scenes in what actually amounts to close-ups.

Lubitsch handles a Parisian ball scene in a manner only equaled by a freaky shot or two of *Variety*. In the massive crowded ballroom, splendid in its own way, Lubitsch runs in a mass of mazy and hazy feet and heads, figures and legs, at times clear, at other times misty. Double exposures and a dozen other tricks are there.

The story develops several angles in complications with two married couples living opposite each other drawn into a mass of lies and deceptions. There is much gagging business, legitimately and logically fitted in. That is the strength of the picture. Hardly anything is foretold nor can it be guessed at.

•

SOUFFLE AU COEUR, LE
(MURMUR OF THE HEART; DEAREST LOVE)
1971, 118 mins, France/Italy Ⓥ ⊙ col
Dir Louis Malle ***Prod*** Vincent Malle, Claude Nedjar ***Scr*** Louis Malle ***Ph*** Ricardo Aronovich ***Ed*** Suzanne Baron
Act Lea Massari, Daniel Gelin, Michel Lonsdale, Benoit Ferreux, Marc Wincourt, Fabien Ferreux (NEF/Marianne/Vides)

Film is quintessentially French in its look at the awakening outlooks and sex imbroglios of a 14-year-old boy who likes to pass himself off as 15. Louis Malle lavishes insight, perhaps personal reminiscences, and unflagging rightness in atmosphere, character and observation to make this a richly comic, touching and incisive portrait of a young man in the French provincial city of Dijon in 1954.

A young Italian mother (Lea Massari) with a vital, free spirit, a conventional gynecologist father (Daniel Gelin) with hidebound outlooks, if flirting with more liberal outlooks, and two older brothers whose revolt is in horseplay and brash jokes surround the teenage hero, Laurent (Benoit Ferreux).

Suffering from a heart murmur, he is sent to a spa with his young mother who, he knows, has a young lover. This leads eventually to a sort of love bout with his mother that is to be a secret between them and never repeated.

Ferreux has the vulnerability, warmth and witty outlook that give his young protagonist a human and recognizable quality. His mother is excellently drawn by Massari, whose need for freedom will not allow her to give way to a demanding suitor. All others are excellent. In the background is the Indochina War and loss of the French colonies, and some youthful if unformed political revolt.

•

SOUL MAN
1986, 101 mins, US Ⓥ ⊙ col
Dir Steve Miner ***Prod*** Steve Tisch ***Scr*** Carol Black ***Ph*** Jeffrey Jur ***Ed*** David Finfer ***Mus*** Tom Scott ***Art*** Gregg Fonseca
Act C. Thomas Howell, Arye Gross, Rae Dawn Chong, James Earl Jones, Melora Hardin, Leslie Nielsen (Balcour/Tisch)

This social farce is excellently written, fast paced and intelligently directed.

Film is hilarious throughout as initial screenplay by Carol Black consistently engages via fablelike tale of a white man (C. Thomas Howell) darkening his skin in order to win a law-school scholarship intended for a black.

Director Steve Miner skillfully guides pic through visually compelling scenes, producing a comedic review of the state of America's racist attitudes.

Howell as the white-turned-black law student is just effective enough to be believable. As Howell's close buddy, Arye Gross delivers gifted and energized screen humor. Rae Dawn Chong is wholly natural and intellectually appealing. Her reluctant romantic involvement with Howell focuses his ultimate moral dilemma over the skin deception.

•

SOULS AT SEA
1937, 90 mins, US b/w
Dir Henry Hathaway ***Prod*** Henry Hathaway ***Scr*** Grover Jones, Dale Van Every ***Ph*** Charles Lang, Jr., Merritt Gerstad ***Ed*** Ellsworth Hoagland ***Mus*** W. Franke Harling, Milton Roder, Bernard Kaun ***Art*** Hans Dreier, Roland Anderson
Act Gary Cooper, George Raft, Frances Dee, Henry Wilcoxon, Harry Carey, Olympe Bradna (Paramount)

Souls at Sea is a good picture, second in the cycle of slaveship films.

Narrative opens with a courtroom trial and flashes back to recount the saga of Gary Cooper and George Raft as adventurous seamen, the latter frankly a slave-trader, but Cooper of finer and seemingly nobler antecedents.

Henry Hathaway's direction is bold, brave and sweeping. He paints the yarn [by Ted Lesser] with an indelible brush, particularly in the sequences on the seas leading up to and following the conflagration of the SS *William Brown*. Skillful film editing permits little that's extraneous. Human touch when little Virginia Weidler capsizes the kerosene lamp that fires the packet from Liverpool to Philadelphia is vividly translated to the audience.

Cooper and Raft are outstanding—the former up to his usual standard; Raft a bit of a surprise as a sympathetic player who meets his dramatic opportunities more than half way. Frances Dee is a bit above Olympe Bradna's opportunities in the principal, but relatively minor, femme roles.

•

SOUND AND THE FURY, THE
1959, 115 mins, US ▭ b/w
Dir Martin Ritt ***Prod*** Jerry Wald ***Scr*** Irving Ravetch, Harriet Frank, Jr. ***Ph*** Charles G. Clarke ***Ed*** Stuart Gilmore ***Mus*** Alex North
Act Yul Brynner, Joanne Woodward, Margaret Leighton, Stuart Whitman, Ethel Waters, Jack Warden (20th Century-Fox)

Considerable talents have gotten together to make *The Sound and the Fury* a work of cinematic stature. It is a mature, provocative and sensitively executed study of the decadent remnants of an erstwhile eminent family of a small southern town, from the William Faulkner allegorical novel.

The Compsons are two brothers, one a weak alcoholic and the other a mute idiot (John Beal and Jack Warden), and a sister (Margaret Leighton) who has a long history of promiscuity. Their father, before his own death, had taken on a stepson (Yul Brynner). Latter in turn has taken on the Compson name and rules as master over a decrepit estate and his wretched second-hand relatives.

Subject to his control also is Joanne Woodward, cast as Leighton's youthful, illegitimate daughter. A Negro servant family, headed by Ethel Waters, completes the cast of residents.

Woodward gives firm conviction to the part of the girl who, somewhat giddily, takes up with a crude mechanic (lecherous, bare-chested type) who's in town with a traveling carnival (Stuart Whitman).

Leighton is remarkably realistic as the washed-out hag. Brynner is every inch the household tyrant. The Mississippi settings are unusually effective in communicating atmosphere.

•

SOUND BARRIER, THE
(U.S.: BREAKING THE SOUND BARRIER)
1952, 118 mins, UK Ⓥ b/w
Dir David Lean ***Prod*** David Lean ***Scr*** Terence Rattigan ***Ph*** Jack Hildyard ***Ed*** Geoffrey Foot ***Mus*** Malcolm Arnold ***Art*** Vincent Korda
Act Ralph Richardson, Ann Todd, Nigel Patrick, John Justin, Dinah Sheridan, Joseph Tomelty (London/British Lion)

Technically, artistically and emotionally, this is a topflight British offering.

Dwarfing the individual performers, good though they are, are the magnificent air sequences, with impressive and almost breathtaking dives by the jet as it attempts to break the sound barrier.

The visionary in the film is superbly played by Ralph Richardson. His ambition to make the first faster-than-sound plane has brought him nothing but grief and disaster. He sees his only son killed on his first solo try; he accepts the estrangement of his daughter (Ann Todd) when his son-in-law (Nigel Patrick) crashes while making the first attempt to crash the barrier.

Ann Todd's portrayal of the daughter correctly yields the emotional angle.

David Lean's direction is bold and imaginative.

1952: Best Sound Recording (London Film Sound Dept.)

NOMINATION: Best Story & Screenplay

•

SOUNDER
1972, 105 mins, US Ⓥ ⊙ ▭ col
Dir Martin Ritt ***Prod*** Robert B. Radnitz ***Scr*** Lonne Elder III ***Ph*** John Alonzo ***Ed*** Sid Levin ***Mus*** Taj Mahal ***Art*** Walter Herndon
Act Cicely Tyson, Paul Winfield, Kevin Hooks, Carmen Mathews, Taj Mahal, Janet MacLachlan (20th Century Fox)

Sounder is an outstanding film. The superb production depicts the heart-warming and character-building struggles of a poor black sharecropper family in the Depression era. Martin Ritt's masterful direction, an excellent adaptation [from William H. Armstrong's novel], and a uniformly terrific cast make this a film that transcends space, race, age and time. Ritt's sensitive, gentle and delicate style is mated well with script and cast.

Appearing in his first major theatrical role is Kevin Hooks, excellent as the eldest son who assumes the challenges of manhood when his father (Paul Winfield) is sentenced to a year at hard labor for stealing some food for his family.

Winfield is a smash in combining youth and mature virility into a figure of parental authority and parental love. His scenes with Hooks are magnificent, as are his interactions with Cicely Tyson as his wife.

1972: NOMINATIONS: Best Picture, Actor (Paul Winfield), Actress (Cicely Tyson), Adapted Screenplay

•

SOUND OF MUSIC, THE
1965, 173 mins, US Ⓥ ⊙ ▭ col
Dir Robert Wise ***Prod*** Robert Wise ***Scr*** Ernest Lehman ***Ph*** Ted McCord, Paul Beeson ***Ed*** William Reynolds ***Mus*** Irwin Kostal (arr.) ***Art*** Boris Leven
Act Julie Andrews, Christopher Plummer, Eleanor Parker, Richard Haydn, Peggy Wood, Charmian Carr (20th Century-Fox)

The magic and charm of the Rodgers-Hammerstein-Lindsay-Crouse 1959 stage hit are sharply blended in this filmic translation. The Robert Wise production is a warmly pulsating, captivating drama set to the most imaginative use of the lilting R-H tunes, magnificently mounted and with a brilliant cast headed by Julie Andrews and Christopher Plummer.

Wise drew on the same team of creative talent associated with him on *West Side Story* to convert the stage property, with its natural physical limitations, to the more expansive possibilities of the camera.

For the story of the Von Trapp family singers, of the events leading up to their becoming a top concert attraction just prior to the Second World War and their fleeing Nazi Austria, Wise went to the actual locale, Salzburg, and spent 11 weeks limning his action amidst the pageantry of the Bavarian Alps.

Against such background the tale of the postulant at Nonnberg Abbey in Salzburg who becomes governess to widower Captain Von Trapp and his seven children, who brings music into a household that had, until then, been run on a strict naval office regimen, with no frivolity permitted, takes on fresh meaning.

Andrews endows her role of the governess who aspires to be a nun, but instead falls in love with Navy Captain Von Trapp and marries him, with fine feeling and a sense of balance that assures continued star stature. Plummer also is particularly forceful as Von Trapp, former Austrian Navy officer who rather than be drafted into service under Hitler prefers to leave his homeland.

Playing the part of the baroness, whom the captain nearly married, Eleanor Parker acquits herself with style.

1965: Best Picture, Director, Sound (20th Century-Fox Sound Dept.), Adapted Musical Scoring, Editing

NOMINATIONS: Best Actress (Julie Andrews), Supp. Actress (Peggy Wood), Color Cinematography (Ted McCord), Color Art Direction, Color Costume Design

•

SOUND OF TRUMPETS, THE
SEE: IL POSTO

•

SOURSWEET
1989, 110 mins, UK Ⓥ col
Dir Mike Newell ***Prod*** Roger Randall-Cutler ***Scr*** Ian McEwan ***Ph*** Michael Gerfath ***Ed*** Mick Audsley ***Mus*** Richard Hartley ***Art*** Adrian Smith
Act Sylvia Chang, Danny Dun, Jodi Long, Soon-Teck Oh, William Chow (First/British Screen/Zenith)

Soursweet is an aptly titled charmer about a Chinese family living in a dismal suburb of London. Pic sympathetically explores the insidious ways in which Chinese emigrants have to adapt to life in Britain after moving to London from Hong Kong.

Adapted from Timothy Mo's novel, the film opens with an elaborate wedding ceremony for a young couple (Sylvia Chang, Danny Dun) held on the outskirts of Hong Kong. Shortly after, the couple moves to London, where Dun finds work as a waiter in a crowded Chinatown restaurant. Dun goes through a period in which he becomes indebted to a seedy moneylender who works for one of the two gangs who seem to control the Chinatown underworld. The couple soon moves to the suburbs, where they start a modest Chinese restaurant in a rented house. After a slow start, the place prospers, and gradually friendly links are formed with the locals.

It's the small details that are most significant. The way a little boy discovers at school that the Chinese way of fighting, taught to him by his mother, is considered unfair. Or the way traditional Chinese customs give way in the face of British culture and lifestyle; french fries replace noodles.

•

SOUS LES TOITS DE PARIS
1930, 86 mins, France b/w
Dir Rene Clair ***Scr*** Rene Clair ***Ph*** Georges Perinal ***Ed*** Rene Le Henaff ***Mus*** Armand Bernard (arr.) ***Art*** Lazare Meerson
Act Albert Prejean, Pola Illery, Gaston Modot, Edmond Greville, Paul Ollivier, Bill Bocket (Tobis)

Director Rene Clair wrote the story himself. It is the simplest kind of yarn. A boy loves a girl. He is sent to jail for a short time. When he comes back he finds she has fallen in love with his best friend. They shake hands all around. Practically nothing else of importance happens, and yet the director has managed to wind together a film that holds and never lags.

Clair permits only occasional sequences with conversation. But the acting, the score and sound effects allow for perfect understanding of the action.

As an instance, two men are shown through the glass doors of a café. They are seen to be looking out at a girl passing by. Their faces show their thoughts to be alike. The girl is shown smiling at them. They start out, only to stop when they realize they are both going for the one girl. The two men start back toward the bar. They pick up a pair of dice and play. One starts out alone. All of which is a few minutes of plot development without talk.

Score is carefully written to hold interest. Most of it comes from dancehalls nearby or phonograph records. There are two songs, one being the same title as the picture and having a nice melody.

Albert Prejean does an excellent piece of acting as the boy, and Pola Illery is as good as the girl. Support parts are carefully played.

•

SOUTH CENTRAL
1992, 99 mins, US Ⓥ ⊙ col
Dir Steve Anderson ***Prod*** Janet Yang, William B. Steakley ***Scr*** Steve Anderson ***Ph*** Charlie Lieberman ***Ed*** Steve Nevius ***Mus*** Tim Truman ***Art*** David Brian Miller, Marina Kieser
Act Glenn Plummer, Byron Keith Minns, Lexie D. Bigham, Vincent Craig Dupree, LaRita Shelby, Kevin Best (Warner/Ixtlan)

As a cautionary tale about the nihilistic life of street gangs, *South Central* speaks eloquently to black kids desperately in need of straight talk. A profoundly moving story of a father's attempt to save his son from his own mistakes, Steve Anderson's film has performances by Glenn Plummer and young Christian Coleman that will touch any viewer.

Based on a novel by an L.A. teacher [Donald Bakeer's *Crips*], starting in 1981, pic picks up Plummer as a hardened gang leader getting out of jail and drifting back into the clutches of charismatic Deuces boss Byron Keith Minns, who wants to take over the local drug business from ruthless pusher/pimp Kevin Best.

Since Best has appropriated Plummer's PCP-addict wife (LaRita Shelby), Plummer is easily manipulated into murdering the pusher, which sends him to prison for 10 years. While in the slammer, Plummer is transformed into a man of reason and idealism by his Muslim cellmate (Carl Lumbly). The direction is suitably unobtrusive and tech credits are pro.

•

SOUTHERN COMFORT
1981, 100 mins, US Ⓥ ⊙ col
Dir Walter Hill ***Prod*** David Giler ***Scr*** Michael Kane, Walter Hill, David Giler ***Ph*** Andrew Laszlo ***Ed*** Freeman Davies ***Mus*** Ry Cooder ***Art*** John Vallone
Act Keith Carradine, Powers Boothe, Fred Ward, Franklyn Seales, T. K. Carter, Peter Coyote (20th Century-Fox)

An arresting exercise in visual filmmaking and a tautly told suspenser about men out of their depths in the Louisiana swamps, *Southern Comfort* is hardly a cinematic equivalent of the libation of the same name. It's an elemental drama of survival in a threatening environment, and the traditional themes of group camaraderie and mutual support are turned inside out.

Set in 1973, tale presents nine National Guard members, weekend soldiers, heading out into the bayou for practice maneuvers. They make the mistake of appropriating some canoes belonging to local Cajuns, and when the densest of the group commits the lunacy of firing (blanks) at some native pursuers the ill-prepared unit finds itself in a virtual state of war with forbidding area's inhabitants.

Pic is most exciting as a visual experience, as Walter Hill once again proves himself a consummate filmmaker with a great talent for mood, composition and action choreography. Also outstanding is Ry Cooder's unusual score, which makes use of spare, offbeat instrumentation as well as some authentic Cajun music. Acting-wise, this is an ensemble piece, and all hands contribute strongly.

•

SOUTHERNER, THE
1945, 91 mins, US Ⓥ b/w
Dir Jean Renoir ***Prod*** David L. Loew, Robert Hakim ***Scr*** Jean Renoir ***Ph*** Lucien Andriot ***Ed*** Gregg G. Tallas ***Mus*** Werner Janssen ***Art*** Eugene Lourie
Act Zachary Scott, Betty Field, Beulah Bondi, Percy Kilbride, J. Carrol Naish, Jay Gilpin, Charles Kemper (Producing Artists)

There is something distressing about the haphazards of the soil's human migrants, and all the squalor that one associates with their condition is brought to *The Southerner*. An adaptation [by Hugo Butler] from the George Sessions Perry novel, *Hold Autumn in Your Hand*, this film conjures a naked picture of morbidity. It may be trenchant realism, but these are times when there is a greater need. Escapism is the word.

The Southerner creates too little hope for a solution to the difficulties of farm workers who constantly look forward to the day when they can settle forever their existence of poverty with a long-sought harvest—a harvest that invariably never comes.

This is, specifically, the story of Sam and Nona, and their struggle to cultivate the rich earth of their Midwest farm. It is a farm beset by liabilities, of which lack of money and food are no small factors. Their home is a patchwork of sagging planks and misguided faith.

Zachary Scott and Betty Field give fine performances, as do Beulah Bondi, the grandmother, Percy Kilbride, Charles Kemper and J. Carrol Naish.

1945: NOMINATIONS: Best Director, Scoring of a Dramatic Picture, Sound

•

SOUTH PACIFIC
1958, 163 mins, US Ⓥ ⊙ ▭ col
Dir Joshua Logan ***Prod*** Buddy Adler ***Scr*** Paul Osborn ***Ph*** Leon Shamroy ***Ed*** Robert Simpson ***Mus*** Alfred Newman (dir.) ***Art*** Lyle R. Wheeler, John DeCuir
Act Rossano Brazzi, Mitzi Gaynor, John Kerr, Ray Walston, Juanita Hall, France Nuyen (20th Century-Fox/South Pacific Enterprises/Magna)

South Pacific is a compelling entertainment. The songs, perennial favorites, are mated to a sturdy James A. Michener story [from his *Tales of the South Pacific*]. Combination boffo.

Mitzi Gaynor is no Mary Martin but there are millions who never saw the original Nellie Forbush [in the 1949 Broadway production]. Rossano Brazzi may be no Ezio Pinza but the late, great Metropolitan Opera basso profundo hasn't the global b.o. impact of the Italian film-star-gone-Hollywood. Besides, Giorgio Tozzi's dubbed basso has been skillfully integrated into the Brazzi brand of romantic antics.

The histrionics are effective throughout and of high standard. John Kerr (vocally dubbed by Bill Lee) is the right romantic vis-á-vis for Eurasian beauty France Nuyen, daughter of the bawdy "Bloody Mary" whom Juanita Hall recreates for the screen. She's of the Broadway original and, like most of the other principals, has been given a vocal stand-in (Muriel Smith, but unbilled; Tozzi alone gets screen credit as Brazzi's ghost voice). Ray Walston is capital as the uninhibited Seabee Luther Billis, recreating the role he did in the road company and in London. Gaynor is uneven in her overall impact. She is in her prime with "Honey-Bun" in that captivating misfit sailor's uniform, and she is properly gay and buoyant and believable in "Wonderful Guy." In other sequences she is conventional. No dubbee she, Gaynor's song-and-dance is essentially very professional.

Brazzi is properly serious of mien and earnest in his love protestations. The Seabees are forthrightly dame-hungry; and there is enough cheesecake among the nurses corps to decorate the beachhead. Their treatment of "Nothing Like a Dame" is standout.

From "Some Enchanted Evening" to "My Girl Back Home," it's a surefire score. It's probably the greatest galaxy of popular favorites from a single show in the history of musical comedy. "Home" was originally in the legit score, was eliminated for show's length but, a favorite with R-H, reinstated into the film version.

All the other credits are topflight—the Alfred Newman baton, the Ken Darby musical assist, and all that goes with this $5 million spectacle. [Original roadshow presentations featured an intermission after 105 mins.]

1958: Best Sound (Todd-AO Sound Dept)

NOMINATIONS: Best Color Cinematography, Scoring of a Musical Picture

•

SOUTH PARK
BIGGER, LONGER & UNCUT
1999, 80 mins, US Ⓥ ⦿ col
Dir Trey Parker ***Prod*** Trey Parker, Matt Stone ***Scr*** Trey Parker, Matt Stone, Pam Brady ***Ed*** John H. Venzon ***Mus*** Marc Shaiman (Paramount/Warner)

Delivering on at least two-thirds of its title—commercial considerations evidently led co-creators Trey Parker and Matt Stone to cave in at the 11th hour [on the last adjective]—*South Park* brings cable TV's most objectionable tykes to the silver screen with considerable aplomb.

Pint-sized, third-grade protags Stan, Kyle, Cartman (the tantrum-prone fat kid) and Kenny (the fatal-accident-prone one whose dialogue is ever muffled by his parka hood) are thrilled to discover their TV faves, Canadian *fartistes* Terrence and Philip, have a movie (*Asses of Fire*) at the local 'plex. The boys emerge with a whole new graphic vocabulary to abet their already precocious "potty mouths."

Kyle's mom spearheads an anti-Canadian agitprop campaign and violent Canuck reprisal follows, with all thesping Baldwin brothers the first to be bombed. Soon both nations are on the brink of full-scale combat. Kyle, Stan and Cartman orchestrate La Resistance, a children's underground aimed at preventing North American war and possible biblical collapse.

Screenplay ladles out parodic high doses of xenophobia, knee-jerk patriotism, racism, homophobia and whatever else comes to mind. It's all really in service of an earnest pro-tolerance theme, however snarkily articulated.

Bigger preserves the TV series' "handmade" aesthetic to delightful bigscreen effect, adding tacky bits of digital imagery and live action. Show's voice talents [of Parker, Stone, Mary Kay Bergman and Isaac Hayes] stick to their willfully amateurish guns. George Clooney, Minnie Driver and Dave Foley make brief audio appearances.

1999: NOMINATIONS: Best Art Direction, Original Song

•

SOUTH RIDING
1938, 91 mins, UK Ⓥ b/w
Dir Victor Saville ***Prod*** Victor Saville ***Scr*** Ian Dalrymple, Donald Bull ***Ph*** Harry Stradling ***Ed*** Hugh Stewart, Jack Dennis ***Mus*** Richard Addinsell ***Art*** Lazare Meerson
Act Edna Best, Ralph Richardson, Edmund Gwenn, Ann Todd, John Clements, Marie Lohr (London)

There are enough requisites in this English melodrama [from a novel by Winifred Holtby] to excite attention. It is fairly familiar matter—the spoiled child whose father fears she will grow up to be like her stark-mad mother, the conniving contractor and real estate operator, and the country gentleman whose intense love of his estate nearly enables the crooked plot to hatch. But all of this has been heightened by original twirls of acting and direction.

Many incidental plot threads are dragged in at the sacrifice of more vital episodes. An example is the flashback to show how the estate owner's wife became demented, obviously to display Ann Todd's histrionics.

The affair the week-kneed councilman is supposed to have had with a country damsel is not obvious enough for average American audiences. Edna Best is tops in the film as the school teacher. Ralph Richardson contributes one of his finer thespian jobs as the country gentleman. John Clements, who resembles Gary Cooper, also is top flight as the ambitious young councilman. Glynis Johns, in the role of the headstrong daughter of the wealthy estate holder, shows promise.

Title of film, derives from a supposed judicial district. Actually there is no "South" Riding, the other divisions being East, West and North.

•

SOUTH SEA FURY
SEE: HELL'S ISLAND

•

SOUVENIR
1989, 93 mins, UK col
Dir Geoffrey Reeve ***Prod*** Tom Reeve, James Reeve ***Scr*** Paul Wheeler ***Ph*** Fred Tammes ***Ed*** Bob Morgan ***Mus*** Tom Kinsey
Act Christopher Plummer, Catherine Hicks, Michael Lonsdale, Christopher Casenove, Patrick Bailey, Lisa Daniely (Fancy Free)

A potentially dramatic story has been flattened out into a string of unconvincing confrontations and coincidences in *Souvenir*, an earnest but bland film about a former Nazi soldier's need to unburden himself of guilt 40 years after the war.

Based on David Hughes acclaimed novel *The Pork Butcher*, tale sees German native Christopher Plummer leaving his adopted country of the U.S. for the first time since the war to see his daughter in Paris. His real mission, however, is to return to the French village of Lascaud where, as a young recruit, he had an unforgettable love affair with a local girl and, as it turns out, played an unwitting part in the massacre of more than 100 townsfolk.

Unfortunately, most of the first half of the picture has his immature, unhappy, incredibly irritating daughter, played by Catherine Hicks, acting very intolerant and impatient with her old man. Furthermore, most of her dialogue consists of questions, designed to elicit expository ramblings from Plummer.

Shady Brit journalist Christopher Casenove turns up to interrogate the principals further, and to provide Hicks with some distraction while Plummer revisits the scenes of his youth and broods about his crimes and lost love.

Plummer looks appropriately tortured throughout, but Geoffrey Reeve, making the transaction from producer's desk to director's chair, never gets under his skin or draws the audience close to him.

•

SOYLENT GREEN
1973, 97 mins, US Ⓥ ⦿ ▭ col
Dir Richard Fleischer ***Prod*** Walter Seltzer, Russell Thatcher ***Scr*** Stanley R. Greenberg ***Ph*** Richard H. Kline ***Ed*** Samuel E. Boetley ***Mus*** Fred Myrow ***Art*** Edward C. Carfagno
Act Charlton Heston, Leigh Taylor-Young, Chuck Connors, Joseph Cotten, Brock Peters, Edward G. Robinson (M-G-M)

The somewhat plausible and proximate horrors in the story of *Soylent Green* carry the production over its awkward spots to the status of a good futuristic exploitation film.

The year is 2022, the setting N.Y. City, where millions of overpopulated residents exist in a smog-insulated police state, where the authorities wear strange-looking foreign uniforms (not the gray flannel suits which is more likely the case), and where real food is a luxury item. Charlton Heston is a detective assigned to the assassination murder of industrialist Joseph Cotten, who has discovered the shocking fact that the Soylent Corp, of which he is a director, is no longer capable of making synthetic food from the dying sea. The substitute—the reconstituted bodies of the dead.

The character Heston plays is pivotal, since he is supposed to be the prototype average man of the future who really swallows whole the social system. Edward G. Robinson, his investigative aide, reminisces about the old days—green fields, flowers, natural food, etc. But the script bungles seriously by confining Heston's outrage to the secret of Soylent Green.

•

SPACEBALLS
1987, 96 mins, US Ⓥ ⦿ ▭ col
Dir Mel Brooks ***Prod*** Mel Brooks ***Scr*** Mel Brooks, Thomas Meehan, Ronny Graham ***Ph*** Nick McLean ***Ed*** Conrad Buff IV, Nicholas C. Smith ***Mus*** John Morris ***Art*** Terence Marsh
Act Mel Brooks, John Candy, Rick Moranis, Bill Pullman, Daphne Zuniga, John Hurt, Dick Van Patten (M-G-M/Brooksfilms)

Mel Brooks will do anything for a laugh. Unfortunately, what he does in *Spaceballs*, a misguided parody of the *Star Wars* adventures, isn't very funny.

Pic features Bill Pullman as Lone Starr and Daphne Zuniga as Princess Vespa, former a composite of Harrison Ford and Mark Hamill, latter a Carrie Fisher clone. Pullman's partner is John Candy as Barf, a half-man, half-dog creature who is his own best friend. Equipped with a constantly wagging tale and furry sneakers, Barf is one of the better comic creations here.

The plot about the ruthless race of Spaceballs out to steal the air supply from the planet Druidia is more cliched than the original. Brooks turns up in the dual role of President Skroob of Spaceballs and the all-knowing, all-powerful Yogurt.

Brooks's direction is far too static to suggest the sweeping style of the *Star Wars* epics, and pic more closely resembles Flash Gordon programmers. Aside from a few isolated laughs *Spaceballs* is strictly not kosher.

•

SPACECAMP
1986, 107 mins, US Ⓥ ⦿ col
Dir Harry Winer ***Prod*** Patrick Bailey, Walter Coblenz ***Scr*** W. W. Wicket [= Clifford Green, Ellen Green], Casey T. Mitchell ***Ph*** William A. Fraker ***Ed*** John W. Wheeler, Timothy Board ***Mus*** John Williams ***Art*** Richard MacDonald
Act Kate Capshaw, Lea Thompson, Kelly Preston, Larry B. Scott, Tom Skerritt, Tate Donovan (ABC)

SpaceCamp is a youthful view of outer space set at the real-life United States Space Camp in Huntsville, Alabama for aspiring young astronauts. Pic [from a screen story by Patrick Bailey and Larry B. Williams] never successfully integrates summer camp hijinks with outer space idealism to come up with a dramatically compelling story.

Hampered by cliche-ridden dialog, performances suffer from a weightlessness of their own. Kate Capshaw as the instructor and one trained astronaut to make the flight neither looks nor acts the part of a serious scientist.

As for the kids, Tate Donovan as the shuttle commander-in-training is uninteresting and Lea Thompson as his would-be girlfriend is too young and naive for words, even the ones she's given.

•

SPACE COWBOYS
2000, 129 mins, US Ⓥ ⦿ ▭ col
Dir Clint Eastwood ***Prod*** Clint Eastwood, Andrew Lazar ***Scr*** Ken Kaufman, Howard Klausner ***Ph*** Jack N. Green ***Ed*** Joel Cox ***Mus*** Lennie Niehaus ***Art*** Henry Bumstead
Act Clint Eastwood, Tommy Lee Jones, Donald Sutherland, James Garner, James Cromwell, Marcia Gay Harden (Malpaso/Mad Chance/Warner)

"We've got three weeks to send four old farts into space," laments a NASA flight director about the central predicament in *Space Cowboys*, and the remark quite neatly expresses the breezy charm as well as the disarmingly devil-may-care attitude toward plausibility of Clint Eastwood's film.

Space Cowboys revels in a world of joking macho camaraderie and competitive mutual support among men with names like Tank and Hawk, takes its own sweet time as it dawdles over behavioral and attitudinal displays by its hardy thesps and sports an entirely beguiling disregard for the current fashion in filmmaking style.

All the same, Eastwood brands the picture as his own almost from the outset, first in the bitter antiauthoritarian streak his character exhibits even in encroaching old age, and shortly thereafter in the vibrant, unapologetic way in which he asserts the presence of both the adventurous little boy and the randy young man in males of advancing years.

Space Cowboys deftly pulls off the trick of being a thoroughly unrealistic picture set in a highly documented area of the real world. Frank Corvin (Eastwood) is the man approached by NASA when a giant Soviet-era satellite is breaking down and will fall out of orbit and crash to Earth. Mysteriously, its guidance system is identical to that of the old U.S. satellite designed by—who else?—Frank, the only man around who might remember the obsolete technology of the ancient spacecraft. The job offers Frank his long-lost chance at traveling in space. His condition is that he's accompanied by his old cohorts: Hawk (Tommy Lee Jones), now a joyride pilot and widower; Jerry O'Neill (Donald Sutherland), an astrophysicist, structural engineer and the real ladies' man of the bunch; and Tank Sullivan (James Garner), navigator-turned-Baptist preacher.

Some genuine excitement is stirred by the liftoff 80 minutes in; impact is facilitated by the seamless combination of actual space shuttle footage and outstanding special effects by Industrial Light & Magic that succeed in duplicating one's idea of what hovering above Earth's atmosphere is like based on actual photographs. Discovery of some significant surprises aboard the satellite push the proceedings into thriller mode, and an absorbing mix of perilous suspense, derring-do, personal courage and well-judged self-sacrifice propel the film swiftly through to its rousing and not entirely conventional wrap-up.

Eastwood, the actor, solid as ever, would appear to have taken considerable pleasure in working with his co-stars, all of whom seem in the most excellent of spirits.

•

SPACEHUNTER
ADVENTURES IN THE FORBIDDEN ZONE
1983, 90 mins, US Ⓥ ⦿ ▭ col
Dir Lamont Johnson ***Prod*** Don Carmody, John Dunning, Andre Link ***Scr*** Edith Rey, David Preston, Dan Goldberg, Len Blum ***Ph*** Frank Tidy ***Ed*** Scott Conrad ***Mus*** Elmer Bernstein ***Art*** Jackson DeGovia
Act Peter Strauss, Molly Ringwald, Ernie Hudson, Andrea Marcovicci, Michael Ironside, Beeson Carroll (Columbia/Delphi)

Columbia's big-budget ($12–13 million) 3-D entry is a muddled science fiction tale set in the mid-21st century on planet Terra Eleven of a double-star sysem, an Earth colony reduced to *Road Warrior*–style rubble by wars and a plague.

Weak story premise, lacking urgency of any sense of importance, has salvage ship pilot Wolff (Peter Strauss) and other "Earthers" including orphaned waif Niki (Molly Ringwald) and Wolff's former training school colleague, now sector chief Washington (Ernie Hudson), searching the planet for three shipwrecked, later kidnaped girls.

Episodic treatment pits them against many local dangers including a well-executed set of puffy monsters, en route to a showdown at the lair of local tyrant McNabb, known as Overdog (Michael Ironside, in skull-like makeup reminiscent of actor Reggie Nalder).

Technical highlights are the vast metal sculpture sets, plus impressive and well-matched miniatures and explosions. Director Lamont Johnson, who entered the picture midstream after original helmer Jean LaFleur [author of screen story with Stewart Harding] was bounced, handles the action scenes well, but editing opposes viewer involvement, taking one out of each hectic action scene before its impact can be enjoyed.

•

SPANISH GARDENER, THE

1957, 97 mins, UK Ⓥ col

Dir Philip Leacock ***Prod*** John Bryan ***Scr*** Lesley Storm, John Bryan ***Ph*** Christopher Challis ***Ed*** Reginald Mills ***Mus*** John Veale ***Art*** Maurice Carter

Act Dirk Bogarde, Jon Whiteley, Michael Hordern, Cyril Cusack, Maureen Swanson, Bernard Lee (Rank)

A. J. Cronin's novel of a minor diplomat with considerable academic qualifications, but without human understanding, translates into absorbing screen entertainment. It is a leisurely told story with colorful Spanish backgrounds.

Michael Hordern is the diplomat separated from his wife, continually passed up for promotion, who insists that his son is delicate, cannot join other children in games or at school and is denied every form of companionship. Dirk Bogarde is hired as a gardener and his friendly attitude to the kid sparks a violent jealousy in the father.

Bogarde gives a polished, restrained study as the Spanish gardener whose motives in befriending the boy are completely misunderstood. Jon Whiteley's moppet is a keenly sensitive portrayal. Cyril Cusack, as a sinister valet, and Maureen Swanson, as the gardener's girlfriend, top a good supporting cast.

•

SPANISH MAIN, THE

1945, 101 mins, US Ⓥ ⊙ col

Dir Frank Borzage ***Prod*** Robert Fellows ***Scr*** George Worthing Yates, Herman J. Mankiewicz ***Ph*** George Barnes ***Ed*** Ralph Dawson ***Mus*** Hanns Eisler ***Art*** Albert S. D'Agostino, Carroll Clark

Act Paul Henreid, Maureen O'Hara, Walter Slezak, Binnie Barnes, John Emery, Barton MacLane (RKO)

Robust saga of swaggering pirates and beautiful girls. Story concentrates on action melodrama, but occasionally takes a satirical slant on such high adventure doings, thus bringing nifty chuckles.

Plot [from an original story by Aeneas MacKenzie] concerns a group of Dutchmen whose ship is wrecked by a storm on the shore of Spanish-held Cartagena. Spanish governor orders the survivors into slavery and the ship's captain to be hung. The captain and several others escape and take up piracy against all Spanish ships. One ship seized is carrying the governor's betrothed, daughter of Mexico's viceroy. The captain-turned-buccaneer forces the girl into marriage, but reckons not of jealousy and treachery among his fellow pirates who fear marriage will result in Spaniards arising in force against Tortuga, the buccaneer colony.

Paul Henreid does well by the dashing Dutchman who becomes the Spaniards' sea-scourge and will please his following. Maureen O'Hara hasn't much opportunity to show off her acting ability, but fulfills the role's other requirements with lush beauty. Walter Slezak's cruel Spanish governor character is showy.

•

SPANISH PRISONER, THE

1997, 112 mins, US Ⓥ ⊙ ▭ col

Dir David Mamet ***Prod*** Jean Doumanian ***Scr*** David Mamet ***Ph*** Gabriel Beristain ***Ed*** Barbara Tulliver ***Mus*** Carter Burwell ***Art*** Tim Galvin

Act Campbell Scott, Rebecca Pidgeon, Steve Martin, Ricky Jay, Ben Gazzara, Felicity Huffman (Sweetlands)

David Mamet has a penchant for sleight-of-hand thrillers, and *The Spanish Prisoner* is his craftiest to date. Centered on a relentless cat's cradle of a business scam, the picture is a devilishly clever series of reversals that keeps you guessing to the very end.

Joe Ross (Campbell Scott) arrives at the fictional Caribbean isle of St. Estephe for a secret meeting to unveil a new invention. While taking photos with Susan (Rebecca Pidgeon), a company secretary, Joe is approached by Jimmy Dell (Steve Martin) and offered $1,000 for the camera. Later, a contrite Jimmy explains he's fearful Joe may have inadvertently have caught him on film in the midst of an illicit tryst.

Joe agrees to deliver a package to Jimmy's sister when he returns to Manhattan—a first edition of *Budge on Tennis*. Back in New York, Joe decides to buy a better-preserved edition, and that sets off a chain of action that kicks into the plot's many twists. The "friendship" that develops between the reserved Joe and mercurial Jimmy is the perfect frame for the Kafkaesque machinations. "The Spanish Prisoner," we're told by a seeming FBI agent, is the term for a classic confidence scam.

An elegant construct, the picture echoes the tone of Mamet's early film, *House of Games*. Scott and Martin are a deliciously effective pairing and the support players, especially Pidgeon, provide the sort of mixed messages that bring both the onscreen characters and audience to the brink.

•

SPARROWS CAN'T SING

1963, 94 mins, UK Ⓥ b/w

Dir Joan Littlewood ***Prod*** Donald Taylor ***Scr*** Stephen Lewis, Joan Littlewood ***Ph*** Max Greene, Desmond Dickinson ***Ed*** Oswald Hafenrichter ***Mus*** Stanley Black, James Stevens ***Art*** Bernard Sarron

Act James Booth, Barbara Windsor, Roy Kinnear, George Sewell, Avis Bunnage, Barbara Ferris (Carthage)

For her first essay in pix, Joan Littlewood plays fairly safe. The film is based on a play that she staged at the Theatre Workshop. She and the author of the play (Stephen Lewis) collaborated on the loose screenplay and Littlewood surrounds herself with most of the Workshop cast. She also operates almost entirely on location in the East End that she knows and clearly loves so well.

The story line is disarmingly slight. James Booth plays a tearaway merchant seaman who comes back to his East End home after two years afloat to find that his home had been torn down during replanning and his wife (Barbara Windsor) has found herself another nest with a local bus driver. His arrival strikes uneasiness in the hearts of the locals, who know his uncertain temper. But Booth sets out to find his wife and collect his conjugal rights.

This could have been played for drama or even tragedy. The screenplay writers and Littlewood's direction beckon to the brighter and breezier slant, and, though there is a sober side to the film, this is mostly played for yocks. Much of the dialog, which is rather salty, appears to have been made up off the cuff of the players. This shows up dangerously in the intimate scenes, but gives gusto to others.

Booth is a striking personality, a punchy blend of toughness, potential evil and irresistible charm. Barbara Windsor (who also chants the Lionel Bart title song) is a cute young blonde who teeters delightfully through her role, on stiletto heels and with a devastating sense of logic.

•

SPARTACUS

1960, 197 mins, US Ⓥ ⊙ ▭ col

Dir Stanley Kubrick, [Anthony Mann] ***Prod*** Edward Lewis ***Scr*** Dalton Trumbo ***Ph*** Russell Metty, Clifford Stine ***Ed*** Robert Lawrence ***Mus*** Alex North ***Art*** Alexander Golitzen

Act Kirk Douglas, Laurence Olivier, Jean Simmons, Charles Laughton, Peter Ustinov, Tony Curtis (Bryna/Universal)

It took a lot of moolah—U says $12 million—and two years of intensive work to bring *Spartacus* to the screen. Film justifies the effort. There is solid dramatic substance, purposeful and intriguingly contrasted character portrayals and, let's come right out with it, sheer pictorial poetry that is sweeping and savage, intimate and lusty, tender and bittersweet.

Director Stanley Kubrick had a remarkably good screenplay with which to work by Dalton Trumbo, whose name appears on the film for the first time in about a decade since he served a prison sentence for contempt of Congress because he refused to declare whether or not he was a member of the Communist party.

Spartacus is a rousing testament to the spirit and dignity of man, dealing with a revolt by slaves against the pagan Roman Empire [from the novel by Howard Fast]. In terms of spectacle the clash between the slave army led by Kirk Douglas and the Romans commanded by Laurence Olivier is nothing short of flabbergasting.

Douglas is the mainstay of the picture. He is not particularly expressive—in contrast with the sophisticated Olivier, the conniving parasite of a gladiator ring operator portrayed by Peter Ustinov, or the supple and subtle slave maiden represented by Jean Simmons. But Douglas succeeds admirably in giving an impression of a man who is all afire inside. Tony Curtis as the Italian slave, Antoninus, who serves as houseboy to Olivier before running away to join Spartacus, gives a nicely balanced performance.

Charles Laughton is superbly wily and sophisticated as a Republican senator who is outwitted by Olivier in attempting to gain control of Rome through sponsorship of the young Julius Caesar. John Gavin plays the latter adequately.

Some 8,000 Spanish soldiers became Roman legionnaires for the massive battle sequences filmed outside Madrid, but the rest of the picture was made in Hollywood. [Version reviewed was the complete one, before censor cuts. Initial release version ran for 192 minutes. Complete version was finally released in 1991.]

1960: Best Supp. Actor (Peter Ustinov), Color Cinematography, Color Art Direction, Color Costume Design (Valles, Bill Thomas)

NOMINATIONS: Best Editing, Scoring of a Dramatic Picture

•

SPAWN

1997, 97 mins, US Ⓥ ⊙ col

Dir Mark A. Z. Dippe ***Prod*** Clint Goldman ***Scr*** Alan McElroy ***Ph*** Guillermo Navarro ***Ed*** Michael N. Knue ***Mus*** Graeme Revell ***Art*** Philip Harrison

Act John Leguizamo, Michael Jai White, Martin Sheen, Theresa Randle, Melinda Clarke, Nicol Williamson (New Line)

Spawn is a moodily malevolent, anything-goes revenge fantasy that relies more upon special visual and digitally animated effects than any comics-derived sci-fier to date. Based on Todd McFarlane's enormously successful comic books, which have already spawned an HBO animated series and a thriving toy line, this narratively knuckleheaded, visually teeming $45 million film will appeal to the comics' abundant fan base.

On a mission to take out a North Korean biological weapons plant, U.S. government operative Al Simmons (Michael Jai White, star of HBO's *Tyson*) is blown to smithereens by his boss Jason Wynn (Martin Sheen), who takes possession of the germ material to establish his bid for world domination. Five years later, a horribly scarred Simmons is given the chance to return to Earth and see his beloved wife (Theresa Randle) and daughter, if he will lead the devil's army to conquer the world. To this end, he is influenced on behalf of the forces of darkness by the repellant, scabrously sarcastic Clown from hell (John Leguizamo, unrecognizable in billowing fat and costumes).

All of this is presented in a muddled way in Alan McElroy's screenplay [from a screen story by him and director Mark A. Z. Dippe], which has Simmons, transformed into the armor-plated, superhuman Spawn, get on the trail of the nefarious Wynn.

Thesps have all been seen to better advantage elsewhere, to say the least.

[A 98-min. Director's Cut was issued on homevideo in 1998.]

•

SPAWN OF THE NORTH

1938, 105 mins, US b/w

Dir Henry Hathaway ***Prod*** Albert Lewin ***Scr*** Jules Furthman, Talbot Jennings ***Ph*** Charles Lang ***Ed*** Ellsworth Hoagland ***Mus*** Dimitri Tiomkin

Act George Raft, Henry Fonda, Dorothy Lamour, Akim Tamiroff, John Barrymore, Louise Platt (Paramount)

Impressive scenes of the Alaskan waters, backgrounded by towering glaciers which drop mighty icebergs into the sea, imperiling doughty fishermen and their frail craft, lift *Spawn of the North* into the class of robust out-of-door films where the spectacular overshadows the melodrama.

The plot [story by Barrett Willoughby] recounts the battles between licensed fishermen and pirates who steal the catch from the traps that are set for salmon at spawning time. George Raft and Henry Fonda, boyhood friends, are members of opposing factions, the former having fallen in with Russian thieves.

Merit of the film is in the persuasive and authentic photographic record of Alaskan life and customs. Akim Tamiroff is a truly menacing pirate with a black heart and no regard for law and order. John Barrymore is an amusing small town editor and Lynne Overman makes a cynical role standout by his gruff humor.

1938: Special Award (special photographic and sound effects)

•

SPEAKING PARTS
1989, 92 mins, Canada Ⓥ ⊙ col
Dir Atom Egoyan ***Scr*** Atom Egoyan ***Ph*** Paul Sarossy ***Ed*** Bruce McDonald ***Mus*** Mychael Danna ***Art*** Linda Del Rosario
Act Michael McManus, Arsinee Khanjian, Gabrielle Rose, David Hemblen, Patricia Collins (Ego)

Speaking Parts, the third feature from Toronto's Atom Egoyan, is a brooding, personal effort, adroitly blending film and video, but with mixed results overall.

Hero cleans hotel rooms, sexually services female clients off screen on orders from the housekeeper, but seeks a speaking part in films after playing extra roles.

He spurns advances from an equally brooding hotel laundry worker and persuades a scriptwriter guest to advance him for the role as her dead brother in a forthcoming pic. That she does to a producer, who is seen almost throughout on a video screen communicating with his staff.

Meanwhile, the laundry worker replays videos of the would-be-actor's bit part scenes at home and attaches herself to a vidstore owner who tapes a sexual orgy and a wedding.

•

SPECIALIST, THE
1994, 109 mins, US Ⓥ ⊙ col
Dir Luis Llosa ***Prod*** Jerry Weintraub ***Scr*** Alexandra Seros ***Ph*** Jeffrey L. Kimball ***Ed*** Jack Hofstra ***Mus*** John Barry ***Art*** Walter P. Martishius
Act Sylvester Stallone, Sharon Stone, James Woods, Rod Steiger, Eric Roberts (Warner)

The Specialist delivers plenty of bright fireballs while agreeably dispensing with the genre cliché of mad bomber fighting iron-willed hero amid a terrified populace. But pic demonstrably fails to make good on the potential chemistry of Sylvester Stallone and Sharon Stone.

Story opens with a prologue in which CIA explosives specialists Ray Quick (Stallone) and Ned Trent (James Woods) come to blows while trying to assassinate a Columbian drug lord. Subsequent grudge feud moves to the back burner when tale shifts to present-day Miami. Ray, now apparently not connected with a government agency, makes phone contact with a potential client, May Munro (Stone), who is looking to eradicate three Cuban-American gangsters led by Tomas Leon (Eric Roberts).

She begins by making herself available to Tomas, capably incarnated by Roberts, who again proves his aptitude at oozing sleaze from every pore. The killer's affair transpires under the increasingly watchful eyes of his crime boss father, Joe Leon (Rod Steiger), and Ned, who now appears to be simultaneously employed by the Leon family and the Miami police. Ray finally agrees to execute May's wishes, but warns her, "If this is a setup, I'll kill you."

Director Luis Llosa, abetted by cinematographer Jeffrey Kimball, gives pic a polished look and handles the action scenes competently. He faces a thankless task, though, in trying to breathe life into Alexandra Seros's script (derived from the *Specialist* novels of John Shirley). Woods attacks his somewhat absurd part with exuberant, scenery-devouring gusto.

•

SPECIES
1995, 108 mins, US Ⓥ ⊙ ▭ col
Dir Roger Donaldson ***Prod*** Frank Mancuso, Jr., Dennis Feldman ***Scr*** Dennis Feldman ***Ph*** Andrzej Bartkowiak ***Ed*** Conrad Buff ***Mus*** Christopher Young ***Art*** John Muto
Act Ben Kingsley, Michael Madsen, Alfred Molina, Forest Whitaker, Marg Helgenberger, Natasha Henstridge (M-G-M)

A propulsive sci-fi actioner genetically engineered from spores of the *Alien* and *Terminator* series, *Species* provides a gripping if not overly original account of an extraterrestrial species attempting to overwhelm our own.

Experts recruited by scientist Xavier Fitch (Ben Kingsley) to track down the nonhuman include Press (Michael Madsen), a marine-trained tracker and assassin; Dan (Forest Whitaker), an "empath" who can read thoughts and feelings; Laura (Marg Helgenburger), a molecular biologist; and Arden (Alfred Molina), a Harvard anthropologist.

Sil, as the creature [designed by H. R. Giger] is known, was engineered from human DNA and a code received from outer space. She morphs into a strikingly gorgeous blonde (newcomer Natasha Henstridge, a Canadian model) whose mission is to reproduce as quickly as possible, fortunately in single-scene L.A.

Sex, mayhem and chases dominate tale's final hour. Thanks to high-velocity direction, lavishly realized effects [supervised by Richard Edlund] and sharp lensing, pic ends up an effective thrill machine.

•

SPECIES II
1998, 93 mins, US Ⓥ ⊙ col
Dir Peter Medak ***Prod*** Frank Mancuso, Jr. ***Scr*** Chris Brancato ***Ph*** Matthew F. Leonetti ***Ed*** Richard Nord ***Mus*** Edward Shearmur ***Art*** Miljen Kreka Kljakovic
Act Michael Madsen, Natasha Henstridge, Marg Helgenberger, Mykelti Williamson, George Dzundza, James Cromwell (FGM/M-G-M)

Species II, a half-baked rehash of the hit 1995 sci-fi shocker about a half-human, half-alien beauty with a murderous urge to mate, is an unsavory and unsatisfying blend of dumb plotting, leering lasciviousness and full-bore gore.

Natasha Henstridge is back as another half-breed, Eve, who's been cooked up in a top-secret government lab to help scientists develop a way to battle other evil extraterrestrials. Marg Helgenberger reprises her role as Dr. Laura Baker, one of the more humane scientists in the breeding program. And Michael Madsen encores as Press Lennox, a freelance assassin who's once again hired to seek and destroy a killer alien.

This time, Lennox's target is a male of the species. During the first manned mission to Mars, astronaut Patrick Ross (Justin Lazard) is infected with the same DNA that figured in the births of Sil [from *Species*] and Eve. Once Ross returns to Earth, he finds that each time he has sexual intercourse with a woman, he instantly impregnates her and each embryo rapidly develops to the size of a preschooler.

The L.A. cops are wondering who's behind all the female corpses with ruptured stomachs. Meanwhile, back in the lab, Dr. Laura figures out that Eve is telepathically connected with Ross—and they have an urge to merge.

Despite many messy deaths, some fairly impressive special effects and a surprising amount of softcore sexuality, *Species II* fails to generate much excitement. Madsen walks through his performance with all the enthusiasm of someone fulfilling a contractual obligation. Helgenberger is a great deal more lively—at times, too much so.

Henstridge and Lazard are fine physical specimens, but their characters appear far more animated when the actors are replaced by tentacled, animatronic monsters.

•

SPECTER OF THE ROSE
1946, 90 mins, US Ⓥ b/w
Dir Ben Hecht ***Prod*** Ben Hecht, Lee Garmes ***Scr*** Ben Hecht ***Ph*** Lee Garmes ***Ed*** Harry Keller ***Mus*** George Antheil
Act Judith Anderson, Michael Chekhov, Ivon Kirov, Viola Essen, Lionel Stander (Republic)

Ben Hecht, to say the least, has done the expected by coming up with the unusual. *Specter of the Rose* was obviously a conscious attempt by Hecht to prove on how small a budget he could produce an acceptable picture. Reports are that it cost in the neighborhood of $160,000. The serious defect productionwise is a general lack of polish that is at times disturbing.

Yarn concerns a ballet troupe in which the top male dancer has gone berserk. OK mentally for periods, he at times has hallucinations in which he hears music that forces him to dance the ballet *Spectre de la Rose* and, while terpin, he gets a desire to slit his wife's throat. This he has already done to one wife when the picture opens. One of the ballerinas is nevertheless in love with him and is sure she can cure him. She marries him, his mind remains clear and the ballet goes on. But, as is expected, the hallucinations suddenly return.

All this is against a serio-comic and satirical background of the ballet company's travails, financial and otherwise, in staging a tour. Judith Anderson is the troupe's mentor, Michael Chekhov the comic impresario, and two actual ballet dancers, Ivan Kirov and Viola Essen, the boy and girl. Stander is a Greenwich Village poet who seems to be in the film for no other reason than to mouth Hechtisms.

Hecht's direction and dialog give the acting a stylized artificiality that grows on the spectator as the picture progresses. Satire of the characterizations makes many of the film's people virtually caricatures.

•

SPEECHLESS
1994, 99 mins, US Ⓥ ⊙ col
Dir Ron Underwood ***Prod*** Renny Harlin, Geena Davis ***Scr*** Robert King ***Ph*** Don Peterman ***Ed*** Richard Francis-Bruce ***Mus*** Marc Shaiman ***Art*** Dennis Washington
Act Michael Keaton, Geena Davis, Christopher Reeve, Bonnie Bedelia, Ernie Hudson, Charles Martin Smith (M-G-M/Forge)

Likable but uneven, this romantic comedy about sparring speechwriters features appealing performances by Michael Keaton and Geena Davis. While much may be made of similarities to dueling campaign advisers James Carville and Mary Matalin, the filmmakers have stressed that Robert King's script predated those events.

Davis and Keaton play warring speechwriters (she's a Democrat, he's a Republican) who have a chance encounter before realizing they're on opposite sides of the same New Mexico Senate race. Concern about fraternizing with the enemy creates tension between the pair even though they're perfect for each other—both hyperactive insomniacs (they meet over a box of Nytol), though Davis's Julia is more the idealist, Keaton's Kevin the gun-for-hire.

Aside from the campaign's ebb and flow, played out in the relentless pursuit of TV news sound bites, another wrinkle gets thrown into the budding relationship when Julia's absentee boyfriend (Christopher Reeve) returns to try to sweep her away.

But *Speechless* never achieves the madcap hilarity of the '40s romantic comedies it seeks to emulate, and some of the dramatic moments feel a bit forced. Few of the supporting players get the opportunity to shine.

•

SPEED
1994, 115 mins, US Ⓥ ⊙ ▭ col
Dir Jan De Bont ***Prod*** Mark Gordon ***Scr*** Graham Yost ***Ph*** Andrzej Bartkowiak ***Ed*** John Wright ***Mus*** Mark Mancina ***Art*** Jackson De Govia
Act Keanu Reeves, Dennis Hopper, Sandra Bullock, Joe Morton, Jeff Daniels, Alan Ruck (20th Century-Fox)

Although it hits any number of gaping credibility potholes on its careening journey around Los Angeles, *Speed* still manages to deliver the goods as a non-stop actioner that scarcely pauses to take a breath.

Story by debuting screenwriter Graham Yost actually offers three disaster pictures rolled into one: 23-minute curtain raiser, which resembles a *Die Hard* offshoot, features passengers in a highrise elevator being terrorized; 67-minute main action is set on board a bus that's rigged to blow up if it slows to under 50 miles-per-hour; and 25-minute climax features the film debut of L.A.'s new, still-under-construction subway. Whatever the means of transportation, Yost has written a stuntman's delight.

Pic opens with an obviously demented Howard Payne (Dennis Hopper) imperiling a long-drop elevator with a powerful charge of dynamite. Demanding a large bundle of cash if the passengers are to be spared, the baddie is done in by the fearless aerialist maneuvers of LAPD SWAT daredevil Jack Traven (Keanu Reeves) and his partner Harry (Jeff Daniels). However, Payne is not dead. He soon announces to his nemesis, Jack, that he's wired a Santa Monica bus so that, once it hits 50 on the freeway, it will blow sky-high if its speed descends below that level.

Film's hallmark stunt—which will have audiences everywhere oohing and aahing—has the huge bus building up a big head of steam so that it can bridge a 50-foot gap in a freeway overpass.

First-time helmer Jan De Bont, the ace lenser of most of Paul Verhoeven's films as well as *Die Hard* and numerous other large-scale pix, handles the action with great nimbleness and dexterity. Reeves is surprisingly commanding in the sort of role he's never tackled before.

1994: Best Sound, Sound Effects Editing

NOMINATION: Best Film Editing

•

SPEED 2
CRUISE CONTROL
1997, 125 mins, US Ⓥ ⊙ ▭ col
Dir Jan De Bont ***Prod*** Jan De Bont ***Scr*** Randall McCormick, Jeff Nathanson ***Ph*** Jack N. Green ***Ed*** Alan Cody ***Mus*** Mark Mancina ***Art*** Joseph Nemec III, Bill Kenney
Act Sandra Bullock, Jason Patric, Willem Dafoe, Temuera Morrison, Brian McCardie, Christine Firkins (Blue Tulip/20th Century-Fox)

Hampered by a derivitive, cliche-ridden screenplay [from a screen story by director-producer Jan De Bont], the water-bound sequel to the 1994 smash hit is a serviceable action thriller that takes too long to deliver its anticipated goods. Sandra Bullock and Jason Patric, who replaces Keanu Reeves in the male lead, are more animated than in previous screen roles, but not enough to give the film the drive it needs.

In an effort to establish a link with *Speed*, Annie (Bullock) is presented as a woman whose big problem is her inability to maintain a decent relationship. Indeed, it takes some subtle maneuvering on the part of boyfriend, Alex (Patric)—and a pair of tickets for a Caribbean cruise—to pacify Annie. Unbeknownst to her, he is a member of an elite SWAT unit.

Yarn picks up some momentum once they get aboard the "world's most luxurious" cruise liner and secondary characters are thrown into the mix. John Geiger (Willem Dafoe), a mad computer mastermind, orchestrates a nasty takeover; most of the thrilling action scenes occur in the last 40 minutes, as a desperate effort is made to flood and slow down the liner so it won't crash into another ship.

Bullock and Patric don't generate much heat in their romantic scenes. Tech credits and special effects are proficient, though not as impressive as those of *Speed*.

•

SPELLBOUND

1945, 116 mins, US b/w

Dir Alfred Hitchcock ***Prod*** David O. Selznick ***Scr*** Ben Hecht, Angus MacPhail ***Ph*** George Barnes ***Ed*** William Ziegler, Hal C. Kern ***Mus*** Miklos Rozsa ***Art*** James Basevi, John Ewing

Act Ingrid Bergman, Gregory Peck, Rhonda Fleming, Leo G. Carroll, Norman Lloyd, Michael Chekhov (United Artists)

David O. Selznick devised unique production values for this Alfred Hitchcock–directed version of a psychological mystery novel [*The House of Dr. Edwardes*, written by Hilary St. George Saunders].

The story, employing as it does psychiatry and psychoanalysis in a murder mystery, would not lend itself for anything but a skillfully blended top budget production.

Gregory Peck, suffering from amnesia, believes that he committed a murder, but has no memory of the locale or circumstances surrounding the crime. Ingrid Bergman as a psychiatrist in love with Peck tries desperately to save him from punishment for the crime she is certain he could not have committed, and in doing so risks her career and almost her life.

Salvador Dali designed the dream sequence with all the aids of futurism and surrealism in his sets. The sets, chairs and tables have human legs and roofs slope at 45-degree angles into infinity.

Alfred Hitchcock handles his players and action in suspenseful manner and, except for a few episodes of much scientific dialogue, maintains a steady pace in keeping the camera moving.

1945: Best Score for a Dramatic Picture.

NOMINATIONS: Best Picture, Director, Supp. Actor (Michael Chekhov), B&W Cinematography, Special Effects

•

SPENCER'S MOUNTAIN

1963, 121 mins, US col

Dir Delmer Daves ***Prod*** [uncredited] ***Scr*** Delmer Daves ***Ph*** Charles Lawton ***Ed*** David Wages ***Mus*** Max Steiner ***Art*** Carl Anderson

Act Henry Fonda, Maureen O'Hara, James MacArthur, Donald Crisp, Wally Cox, Mimsy Farmer (Warner)

Delmer Daves chooses the majestic Grand Teton's to background a quite ordinary, but generally enjoyable and often emotionally moving comedy-drama about a large, simple, hardworking family and its joys and disappointments from the cradle to the grave.

Daves, working from a novel (set in Blue Ridge Mountain Country) by Earl Hamner, Jr., views the Spencers idealistically—the family that pulls together and walks straight.

Daves's script plays better than it sounds in synopsis for it is the interplay and incidents that spark humor and warmth, sentiment and a bit of boisterousness in the story that is motivated by the desire of uneducated parents to fulfill their son's desire for a college education when all that the father earns is required to keep food on the table for a brood of nine youngsters, plus husband-wife and grandparents.

With less ingratiating and expert performers than Henry Fonda and Maureen O'Hara as the central characters the chances are Daves might have found himself in trouble. Fonda, in particular, can take what easily could have been an ordinary hayseed and invest such a role with depth, purposefulness and dignity.

•

SPHERE

1998, 133 mins, US col

Dir Barry Levinson ***Prod*** Barry Levinson, Michael Crichton, Andrew Wald ***Scr*** Stephen Hauser, Paul Attanasio ***Ph*** Adam Greenberg ***Ed*** Stu Linder ***Mus*** Elliot Goldenthal ***Art*** Norman Reynolds

Act Dustin Hoffman, Sharon Stone, Samuel L. Jackson, Peter Coyote, Liev Schreiber, Queen Latifah (Baltimore/Constant/Warner)

Sphere is an empty shell. Derivative of any number of famous sci-fi movies and as full of false promises as the Wizard of Oz, this portentous underwater *Thing* swims along with reasonable good humor for its first hour, then descends into mechanical and routine "suspense" sequences that fail to deliver what genre fans demand.

Basically a chamber piece, but produced on the most lavish possible scale, this low-voltage Michael Crichton tale [adaptation by Kurt Wimmer] falls between several stools in the sci-fi arena: alien spaceship mystery, theological/philosophical inquiry, monster thriller, time travel adventure, close-quarters pressure cooker, and voyage into the mind. Scraps from genre classics abound.

Psychologist Dr. Norman Goodman (Dustin Goodman) is summoned to a remote Pacific site where group leader Barnes (Peter Coyote) throws him together with biochemist Beth Halperin (Sharon Stone), with whom Goodman has a past, mathematician Harry Adams (Samuel L. Jackson) and astrophysicist Ted Fielding (Liev Schreiber). A thousand feet down they view an amazing sight: a submerged spacecraft nearly half a mile long that must have crashed there 288 years before.

The main revelation is an enormous, shimmering, golden sphere seemingly made of liquid metal. Convinced there is life within the sphere, Harry devises to apparently enter it, and from then on takes on a distracted air, sleeping through emergencies and obsessively reading *20,000 Leagues Under the Sea*.

The only emotional component derives from the neurotic Beth still not having got over the way Norman treated her many years before, and her instability quickly becomes wearisome. Actors are all underused in shallow roles.

Pic was shot entirely on soundstages installed at the abandoned Mare Island Naval Shipyard at Vallejo in Northern California.

•

SPHINX

1981, 117 mins, US col

Dir Franklin J. Schaffner ***Prod*** Stanley O'Toole ***Scr*** John Byrum ***Ph*** Ernest Day ***Ed*** Robert E. Swink, Michael F. Anderson ***Mus*** Michael J. Lewis ***Art*** Terence Marsh

Act Lesley-Anne Down, Frank Langella, Maurice Ronet, John Gielgud, Saeed Jaffrey, John Rhys-Davies (Orion)

This film is an embarrassment. Contempo *Perils of Pauline* sees earnest, dedicated Egyptologist Lesley-Anne Down through countless situations of dire jeopardy as she travels from Cairo to Luxor's Valley of the Kings in pursuit of a mysterious tomb of riches, which also holds great interest for black marketeers.

Along the way, lovely Lesley-Anne is almost murdered after witnessing John Gielgud's demise, caught off guard not once, not twice, but three times in her hotel room, shot at as a matter of course, nearly raped by a prison guard, held at knifepoint, thrown into a dark dungeon inhabited by decomposed corpses, attacked by bats, chased by a car, shot at again and finally nearly buried as the tomb's ceiling comes crashing down. In all, she screams, gasps and exclaims "My God!" more often than any heroine since Jamie Lee Curtis in her collected horror films.

Franklin J. Schaffner's steady and sober style is helpless in the face of the mounting implausibilities.

•

SPICE WORLD

1997, 92 mins, UK col

Dir Bob Spiers ***Prod*** Uri Fruchtman, Barnaby Thompson ***Scr*** Kim Fuller, Jamie Curtis ***Ph*** Clive Tickner ***Ed*** Andrea MacArthur ***Mus*** Paul Newcastle ***Art*** Grenville Horner

Act The Spice Girls, Richard E. Grant, Alan Cumming, George Wendt, Claire Rushbrook, Roger Moore (Fragile/Spice Girls)

A bright and breezy movie that's as timely but evanescent as the Cool Britannia culture it celebrates, *Spice World* will delight the Fab Five's prepubescent fans and recall fond memories of the '60s to those who actually lived through them. Pic is more *Austin Powers*–like retro than the genuinely groundbreaking *A Hard Day's Night* it apes.

Picture is not so much a story as a series of musical opportunities dotted with celeb cameos, following the Spices through five days leading up to their first live gig in London's Royal Albert Hall. En route, the movie takes potshots at the tabloid press, the capital's glitterati and the media in general, as well as stirring in beaucoup filmic refs to amuse oldsters while the young 'uns are transfixed by the girls and their music.

This is '90s theme-park New Britain, with the Union Jack–painted Spicebus constantly passing London landmarks and the gals themselves a walking gallery of regional, blue-collar Blighty on the Move. Always on their trail is a photo-journalist (Richard O'Brien), hired by sleazoid Australian newspaper proprietor Kevin McMaxford (Barry Humphries), who's determined to bring the Spices down.

The question of whether the Spices can act—they can't, but neither could the Beatles—is largely irrelevant. None is allowed to dominate, though the sultry Victoria (Posh), constantly griping about her wardrobe, gets the best of a so-so bunch of quips. Roger Moore's Blofeld-like Chief is the classiest of the cameos.

Technically, the movie (shot totally in the U.K. in 43 days) is surprisingly modest and low-tech, eschewing widescreen and fancy musicvid visuals.

•

SPIES LIKE US

1985, 109 mins, US col

Dir John Landis ***Prod*** Brian Grazer, George Folsey, Jr. ***Scr*** Dan Aykroyd, Lowell Ganz, Babaloo Mandel ***Ph*** Robert Paynter ***Ed*** Malcolm Campbell ***Mus*** Elmer Bernstein ***Art*** Peter Murton

Act Chevy Chase, Dan Aykroyd, Steve Forrest, Donna Dixon, Bruce Davison, Bernard Casey (Paramount)

Teamed together for the first time in *Spies Like Us*, Chevy Chase and Dan Aykroyd need a subteen audience for their juvenile humor.

Spies is not very amusing. Though Chase and Aykroyd provide moments, the overall script thinly takes on eccentric espionage and nuclear madness, with nothing new to add.

Chase and Aykroyd are a couple of bumbling bureaucrats with aspirations for spy work, but no talent for the job. They unknowingly are chosen for a mission, however, because they will make expendable decoys for a real spy team headed by pretty Donna Dixon.

Much of the time, Aykroyd is fooling with gadgets, Chase is fooling with Dixon and director John Landis is fooling with half-baked comedy ideas.

•

SPINSTER

SEE: TWO LOVES

•

SPIRAL ROAD, THE

1962, 145 mins, US col

Dir Robert Mulligan ***Prod*** Robert Arthur ***Scr*** Neil Paterson, John Lee Mahin ***Ph*** Russell Harlan ***Ed*** Russell F. Schoengarth ***Mus*** Jerry Goldsmith ***Art*** Alexander Golitzen, Henry Bumstead

Act Rock Hudson, Burl Ives, Gena Rowlands, Geoffrey Keen, Neva Patterson, Will Kuvula (Universal)

Being uninspired, *The Spiral Road* is the uninspiring tale of an atheist's conversion to God. The picture, moreover, takes the devil's own time getting down to cases and the resolution; and of its numerous defects, prolonged length is a major infirmity of this chronicle of jungle medicine in Java as practiced by the Dutch.

A novel by Dutch author Jan de Hartog is the source for the flabby screenplay. It concerns an opportunist, gainsaying freshman medic (Rock Hudson) and his determination to ride to scientific fame on the research of a seasoned jungle physician (Burl Ives). Hudson's arrogance and cynicism are played against sundry goodhearts—his suffering wife (Gena Rowlands), the Salvation Army man (Geoffrey Keen), and high-minded types who constitute his superiors in the government medical mission.

•

SPIRAL STAIRCASE, THE

1946, 83 mins, US b/w

Dir Robert Siodmak ***Prod*** Dore Schary ***Scr*** Mel Dinelli ***Ph*** Nicholas Musuraca ***Ed*** Harry Marker, Harry Gerstad ***Mus*** Roy Webb ***Art*** Albert S. D'Agostino, Jack Okey

Act Dorothy McGuire, George Brent, Ethel Barrymore, Kent Smith, Rhonda Fleming, Elsa Lanchester (RKO)

This is a smooth production of an obvious, though suspenseful murder thriller, ably acted and directed. Mood and pace are well set, and story grips throughout.

Mel Dinelli has done a tight, authentic-sounding script of a mass-murder story [based on Ethel Lina White's novel, *Some Must Watch*] set in a small New England town of 1906. Director Robert Siodmak has retained a feeling for terror throughout the film by smart photography, camera angles and sudden shifts of camera emphasis, abetted in this job by a choice performance of his cast.

Film lacks the leaven of a little humor, but interest never wanes.

Dorothy McGuire's stature as actress is increased by her performance as a maidservant bereft of speech by a shock since childhood, and Ethel Barrymore's list of pic-portraits will get another gold-framer from her role of bedridden wealthy eccentric. McGuire's portrayal of a tongue-tied girl in love; the pathos of her dream wedding-scene; her terror when pursued by the murderer—are all etched sharply for unforgettable moments. Barrymore's awareness from her bedchamber of the insanity and murder going on about her is also acutely set, to give distinction to her part.

1946: NOMINATION: Best Supp. Actress (Ethel Barrymore)

•

SPIRIT OF ST. LOUIS, THE
1957, 135 mins, US Ⓥ ▭ col
Dir Billy Wilder ***Prod*** Leland Hayward ***Scr*** Billy Wilder, Wendell Mayes ***Ph*** Robert Burks, J. Peverell Marley ***Ed*** Arthur P. Schmidt ***Mus*** Franz Waxman ***Art*** Art Loel
Act James Stewart, Murray Hamilton, Patricia Smith, Bartlett Robinson (Warner)

Although lacking the elaborate production trappings that would automatically mirror a multimillion dollar budget, an extensive shooting schedule and painstaking care went into this picture. It's Class A picture-making yet doesn't manage to deliver entertainment wallop out of the story about one man in a single-engine plane over a 3,610-mile route.

Spirit is a James Stewart one-man show. He portrays Charles Lindbergh with a toned-down performance intended as consistent with the diffident (i.e. noncommunicative) nature of the famed aviator. The story development tends to focus on the personal side of the 1927 hero, as much as it does on the flight itself, and Stewart comes off with sort of an appropriate, shy amiability.

The flashback technique is used frequently to convey some of Lindbergh's background, such as his days as a mail pilot, an amusing bit re his first encounter with the air force, his barnstorming stunts, etc.

1957: NOMINATION: Best Special Effects

•

SPIRIT OF THE BEEHIVE, THE
SEE: EL ESPIRITU DE LA COLMENA

•

SPITFIRE
SEE: THE FIRST OF THE FEW

•

SPITFIRE
1934, 88 mins, US b/w
Dir John Cromwell ***Prod*** Merian C. Cooper, Pandro S. Berman ***Scr*** Lulu Vollmer, Jane Murfin ***Ph*** Edward Cronjager ***Ed*** William H. Morgan ***Mus*** Max Steiner ***Art*** Van Nest Polglase, Carroll Clark
Act Katharine Hepburn, Robert Young, Ralph Bellamy, Martha Sleeper, Louis Mason, Sara Haden (RKO)

Rather than a picture with Katharine Hepburn, this is Hepburn with a picture built around her and the part she plays, that of a backwoods mountain girl of the South.

The Lulu Vollimer play of secluded mountain life was a piece called *Trigger*. This is the name of the girl around whom the story is built, but for box office purposes the change was made to *Spitfire*.

Hepburn not only has to look the part of the hotly-tempered young mountain woman but match a difficult accent with it throughout. In both respects the performance is almost without flaw.

The girl in prayer, and the legend that springs up around the country as to her powers, furnishes the only melodramatic content of the story, and builds from a sequence in which the girl helps herself to a neighbor's baby. Her only thought is in giving it the care its parents are neglecting to bestow, but shortly after the child is returned to its native heath it dies.

This arouses the mountaineers to lynching frenzy from which they are partly scared and party spared by the intervention of one of Trigger's engineer friends (Ralph Bellamy) who, along with his dam-building partner, has become smitten by her. Development of the love interest follows an intriguing course.

Robert Young, also an engineer, figures more prominently in the love interest up to about the middle when Trigger discovers he has a wife and quickly dismisses his suit.

•

SPIVS, THE
SEE: I VITELLONI

•

SPLASH
1984, 111 mins, US Ⓥ ⦿ col
Dir Ron Howard ***Prod*** Brian Grazer ***Scr*** Lowell Ganz, Babaloo Mandel, Bruce Jay Friedman ***Ph*** Don Peterman ***Ed*** Daniel P. Hanley, Michael Hill ***Mus*** Lee Holdridge ***Art*** Jack T. Collis
Act Tom Hanks, Daryl Hannah, John Candy, Eugene Levy, Dody Goodman, Shecky Greene (Touchstone)

Touchstone Films takes the plunge with surprisingly charming mermaid yarn notable for winning suspension of disbelief and fetching by-play between Daryl Hannah and Tom Hanks.

Although film is a bit uneven, production benefits from a tasty look, an airy tone, and a delectable, unblemished performance from Hannah who couldn't be better cast if she were Neptune's daughter incarnate. Hanks, as a Gotham bachelor in search of love, makes a fine leap from sitcom land, and John Candy as an older playboy brother is a marvelous foil.

The mermaid's fin materializes into human legs when she leaves the water and, à la Lady Godiva, blonde tresses covering her breasts.

Screenplay is marred by some glaring loopholes in its inner structure but story is a sweet takeoff on the innocence mythology and sensuality associated with mermaids.

1984: NOMINATION: Best Original Screenplay

•

SPLENDOR
1935, 77 mins, US b/w
Dir Elliott Nugent ***Prod*** Samuel Goldwyn ***Scr*** Rachel Crothers ***Ph*** Gregg Toland ***Ed*** Margaret Clancey ***Mus*** Alfred Newman ***Art*** Richard Day
Act Miriam Hopkins, Joel McCrea, Paul Cavanaugh, Helen Westley, Billie Burke, David Niven (Goldwyn/United Artists)

Here is a rare combination of a well-written story, interpreted in skilled and sympathetic action under able and understanding direction. This is the film Rachel Crothers specially authored for Goldwyn on a royalty and guarantee basis.

Miriam Hopkins marries Joel McCrea while he is south on a business trip, and he proudly bring her home, not realizing that his ambitious mother (Helen Westley) is looking to a marriage with an heiress (Ruth Weston). Hopkins gets small welcome from her in-laws, and even McCrea is a bit impatient with her because of his own perplexities. His father and grandfather amassed money, apparently without effort. He doesn't seem able to realize why he cannot.

Paul Cavanaugh, a distant relative, takes an interest in the young wife and things become easier for her. The old lady looks to her to use her influence in behalf of McCrea. She virtually forces the girl into an affair.

Helen Westley, as the mother, is the dominant figure. Her cold-blooded, merciless nagging of the girl is as well played as it has been written. Hopkins is not altogether at ease as the sweet young thing in the first few scenes, but later she doesn't miss a chance. Paul Cavanaugh is admirable.

•

SPLENDOR IN THE GRASS
1961, 124 mins, US Ⓥ ⦿ col
Dir Elia Kazan ***Prod*** Elia Kazan ***Scr*** William Inge ***Ph*** Boris Kaufman ***Ed*** Gene Milford ***Mus*** David Amram ***Art*** Richard Sylbert
Act Natalie Wood, Warren Beatty, Pat Hingle, Audrey Christie, Barbara Loden, Fred Stewart (Warner)

Elia Kazan's production of William Inge's original screenplay covers a forbidding chunk of ground with great care, compassion and cinematic flair. Yet there is something awkward about the picture's mechanical rhythm. There are missing links and blind alleys within the story. Too much time is spent focusing on characters of minor significance.

Inge's screenplay deals with a young couple deeply in love but unable to synchronize the opposite polarity of their moral attitudes. Their tragedy is helped along by the influence of parental intervention. The well-meaning parents (his father, her mother, both of whom completely dominate their more perceptive mates), in asserting their inscrutable wills upon their children, lead them into a quandary. The children cannot consummate their relationship, either sexually or maritally.

Natalie Wood and Warren Beatty (whom the picture "introduces") are the lovers. Although the range and amplitude of their expression is not always as wide and variable as it might be, both deliver convincing, appealing performances. The real histrionic honors, though, belong to Audrey Christie, who plays Wood's mother, and Pat Hingle, as Beatty's father. Both are truly exceptional, memorable portrayals.

Barbara Loden does an interesting job in a role (Beatty's flapper sister) that is built up, only to be sloughed off at the apex of its development. Fred Stewart is excellent as Wood's father.

Exteriors for the picture were shot in New York state, and the countryside looks a little lush for Kansas, which is the setting of the drama. David Amram's romantic theme is hauntingly beautiful. There's an exceptional job of costuming by Anna Hill Johnstone. The clothes are not only faithful to the two eras (late 1920s, early 1930s) covered, but they are attractive on the people who wear them.

1961: Best Original Story & Screenplay

NOMINATION: Best Actress (Natalie Wood)

•

SPLITTING HEIRS
1993, 86 mins, UK/US Ⓥ ⦿ col
Dir Robert Young ***Prod*** Simon Bosanquet, Redmond Morris ***Scr*** Eric Idle ***Ph*** Tony Pierce-Roberts ***Ed*** John Jympson ***Mus*** Michael Kamen ***Art*** John Beard
Act Rick Moranis, Eric Idle, Barbara Hershey, Catherine Zeta Jones, John Cleese, Sadie Frost (Prominent/Universal)

Splitting Heirs is a minor royalty *King Ralph*, a breezy but lightweight comedy toplining Rick Moranis as a phony Yank heir to a Brit dukedom.

Moranis plays a motormouth Yank who becomes the 15th Duke of Bournemouth and head of the family bank when his father suddenly drowns. Unbeknownst to him, the real heir to the fortune is bank underling Eric Idle, who's become his best pal.

Source of the confusion is Idle's mom (Barbara Hershey) who left him in a restaurant during the Swinging Sixties and claimed the wrong baby at the police station. When Idle stumbles across the truth he tries every means to deep-six Moranis and claim his rightful fortune, in between fighting off the foxy Hershey who doesn't realise he's her son.

Even though it's short of true belly-laughs, the dumb-sounding storyline plays better than it reads, thanks to brisk pacing, all-out playing by the main leads, and some OK sight gags once the plot cranks up into revenge mode.

•

SPOILERS, THE
1942, 87 mins, US Ⓥ ⦿ b/w
Dir Ray Enright ***Prod*** Frank Lloyd ***Scr*** Lawrence Hazard, Tom Reed ***Ph*** Milton Krasner ***Ed*** Clarence Kolster ***Mus*** Hans J. Salter
Act Marlene Dietrich, Randolph Scott, John Wayne, Richard Barthelmess, William Farnum, Harry Carey (Universal)

The Spoilers in its present form is still a teeming, raw saga of Alaska in its 1898 gold rush days. It tells of Randolph Scott, as the crooked gold commissioner, an equally unscrupulous judge (Samuel S. Hinds) and their "legal" confiscation of the miners' claims. John Wayne plays a prospector who, through the crooked court, loses the mine he jointly owns with Harry Carey. Marlene Dietrich is the operator of a gin and gambling emporium. Dovetailed to this is the tempestuous romance between Wayne and Dietrich, with Scott as the bad third.

Of course, the big scene is the fight originally made one of the classic brawls of filmdom by Tom Santschi and William Farnum. The slugging match in the final reel between Wayne and Scott is something that apparently could be staged profitably at Madison Square Garden.

Performances are all uniformly good, with the stellar trio, of course, showing up best because of their prominent parts. Dietrich is excellent in a role suggesting it was designed for her. Scott and Wayne are typical of the great outdoors men for which the parts call.

•

SPRING AND PORT WINE
1970, 101 mins, UK col
Dir Peter Hammond ***Prod*** Michael Medwin ***Scr*** Bill Naughton ***Ph*** Norman Warwick ***Ed*** Fergus McDonell ***Mus*** Douglas Gamley ***Art*** Reece Pemberton
Act James Mason, Susan George, Diana Coupland, Rodney Bewes, Hannah Gordon, Len Jones (Memorial)

Set in the mill area of Lancashire and its moors (though lacking most of the cliché Lancashire gags and mannerisms), this is the story [from the play by Bill Naughton] of a generation clash in a small family and the points of view of both parents and children are fairly, compassionately and interestingly brought out.

James Mason plays the patriarch of the family, a kindly but stubborn man who brings up his family with a startling strictness. Remembering his own youth he is determined the house he reigns over shall not be such a mess.

Chief rebel is the high-spirited Susan George whose refusal to eat a herring for tea sparks off a handful of situations that remind Mason that "you can spend a lifetime creating a family and break it up in a weekend."

•

SPRINGFIELD RIFLE
1952, 92 mins, US Ⓥ col
Dir Andre de Toth ***Prod*** Louis F. Edelman ***Scr*** Charles Marquis Warren, Frank Davis ***Ph*** Edwin B. DuPar ***Ed*** Robert L. Swanson ***Mus*** Max Steiner ***Art*** John Beckman
Act Gary Cooper, Phyllis Thaxter, David Brian, Paul Kelly, Lon Chaney, Philip Carey (Warner)

The Springfield rifle and army counter-espionage are the bases for the plot of this Gary Cooper starrer.

Story is of how a foresighted Union officer masterminds a scheme to use counter-espionage to uncover the reasons why a Northern cavalry post is unable to supply the mounts needed to keep the government's army on the move in the Southern states. Every time the cavalry outpost tries to move a string of horses, renegades are tipped to the plan, ambush the soldiers and sell the horses to the Confederacy.

Cooper, Union officer, is the key to the counter-espionage plot. He's cashiered on charges bordering on cowardice in the scheme cooked up by Wilton Graff, Union colonel, and joins up with David Brian, leader of the herd raiders.

•

SPRING IN PARK LANE
1948, 91 mins, UK b/w
Dir Herbert Wilcox ***Prod*** Herbert Wilcox ***Scr*** Nicholas Phipps ***Ph*** Max Greene ***Ed*** F. Clarke ***Mus*** Robert Farnon ***Art*** Bill Andrews
Act Anna Neagle, Michael Wilding, Tom Walls, Peter Graves, Nicholas Phipps, Nigel Patrick (British Lion)

Great merit of the story is that it seems like a happy improvisation. None of the elaborate and necessary scaffolding is apparent, and when Michael Wilding as a younger son of a noble family, needing money for a return trip to New York, becomes a temporary footman in a Park Lane mansion, he is immediately accepted as such by the audience. And since Anna Neagle plays a secretary in the same house, everybody knows it will be love at first sight and that sooner or later the two will march altarwards.

It's a story in which the trimmings and incidentals are all-important. The gay harmless fun poked at the film stars, the dinner party bore, the housekeeper to whom bridge is a religion, the footman cutting in to dance or discussing art with his boss—incident upon incident carry merry laughter through the picture.

•

SPRINGTIME IN THE ROCKIES
1942, 90 mins, US Ⓥ ⦿ col
Dir Irving Cummings ***Prod*** William LeBaron ***Scr*** Walter Bullock, Ken Englund ***Ph*** Ernest Palmer ***Ed*** Robert Simpson ***Mus*** Alfred Newman
Act Betty Grable, John Payne, Carmen Miranda, Cesar Romero, Charlotte Greenwood, Edward Everett Horton (20th Century-Fox)

Story [based on a story by Philip Wylie, adapted by Jacques Thery] is a light framework on which to hang the various numbers and specialties. Betty Grable and John Payne, costars in a Broadway musical, are romantically inclined—but he has a weakness for pretty girls, which keeps them continually battling. When the show closes, Grable joins her former dancing partner Romero for a western tour, but Payne follows to Lake Louise to woo her back to a new Broadway show.

Script is studded with laugh lines that are well distributed among the cast. Picture sags considerably towards the end, when story has to devote extended amount of footage to the romantic interludes without interruption of any song or dance specialties. But this is minor in the overall content of entertainment provided.

•

SPY HARD
1996, 80 mins, US Ⓥ ⦿ col
Dir Rick Friedberg ***Prod*** Rick Friedberg, Doug Draizin, Jeffrey Konvitz ***Scr*** Rick Friedberg, Dick Chudnow, Jason Friedberg, Aaron Seltzer ***Ph*** John R. Leonetti ***Ed*** Eric Sears ***Mus*** Bill Conti ***Art*** William Creber
Act Leslie Nielsen, Nicollette Sheridan, Charles Durning, Marcia Gay Harden, Barry Bostwick, John Ales (Hollywood)

The picture that will test the durability of Leslie Nielsen's lowbrow franchise, *Spy Hard* sticks closely to the *Naked Gun* formula. Not only is the formula itself wearing thin, but the gags themselves feel recycled. Although the four screenwriters (including director Rick Friedberg) had the sense to include spoofs of *Mission Impossible* and *Speed*, they more often fall back on targets so tired they could be outtakes from previous *Naked Gun* scripts.

Title notwithstanding, the film is less a spoof of the ripe-for-parody *Die Hard*–style actioners than of the timeworn James Bonders (by way of *Get Smart*). Nielsen, ever reliable even when his material isn't, stars as Dick Steele, Agent WD-40. He's called out of retirement to hunt for his old nemesis, the evil Gen. Rancor (Andy Griffith), an armless madman with plans for global takeover. Joining Steele through various misadventures is agent Veronique Ukrinsky (Nicolette Sheridan), the beautiful love interest/sidekick.

Trying hard is Charles Durning as the Agency Director with a fondness for disguising himself as office furniture, Marcia Gay Harden as the lustful secretary Miss Cheevus, Barry Bostwick (with an unexplained Kennedy accent) as another agent and Carlos Lauchu as Steele's undercover chauffeur.

"Weird Al" Yankovic appears in (and wrote) the opening title sequence, a "Goldfinger" song parody that starts OK but takes too long to pay off.

•

SPY IN BLACK, THE
(U.S.: U-BOAT 29)
1939, 82 mins, UK Ⓥ ⦿ b/w
Dir Michael Powell ***Prod*** Irving Asher ***Scr*** Emeric Pressburger ***Ph*** Bernard Browne ***Ed*** William Hornbeck, Hugh Stewart ***Mus*** Miklos Rozsa ***Art*** Vincent Korda
Act Conrad Veidt, Sebastian Shaw, Valerie Hobson, Marius Goring, June Duprez, Mary Morris (Harefield/Korda)

The Spy in Black is a praiseworthy film on international espionage during World War I.

The plot [adapted by Roland Pertwee from a novel by J. Storer Clouston], while necessarily melodramatic, is always within the range of possibility. Conrad Veidt, as captain of a German submarine, receives instructions to proceed to the Orkney Islands, where he's to meet a woman spy, from whom he's to take orders. She instructs him to sink 15 British ships cruising off the coast of Scotland, and contacts him with a discharged traitorous lieutenant of the British Navy.

Veidt has a strong role for which he's admirably suited. Sebastian Shaw is excellent as the English naval officer. Valerie Hobson, as the other spy, is creditable.

•

SPYS
1974, 100 mins, UK/US Ⓥ col
Dir Irvin Kershner ***Prod*** Irwin Winkler, Robert Chartoff ***Scr*** Malcolm Marmorstein, Lawrence J. Cohen, Fred Freeman ***Ph*** Gerry Fisher ***Ed*** Robert Lawrence, Keith Palmer ***Mus*** John Scott [U.S. version: Jerry Goldsmith] ***Art*** Michael Seymour
Act Donald Sutherland, Elliott Gould, Zou Zou, Joss Ackland, Shane Rimmer, Vladek Sheybal (Dymphana/Chartoff-Winkler/American Film Properties)

Spys is a mess. The Irwin Winkler–Robert Chartoff production reteams Elliott Gould and Donald Sutherland, this time as a pair of bungling CIA agents. The script is tasteless, Irvin Kershner's direction is futile, and the whole effort comes across as vulgar, offensive and tawdry. Sutherland and Gould bungle the defection of Russian dancer Michael Petrovitch, so under a deal between CIA chief Martinson (Joss Ackland) and Russian counterpart (Vladek Sheybal), they are marked for extinction. In the course of evading lots of people, the two stars encounter revolutionaries (Zou Zou, Xavier Gelin, Pierre Oudry), urbane Lippet (Kenneth Griffith) and his dog, and a bird fancier (Jaques Marin).

The "fun" of international espionage is depicted by a series of bomb explosions, lavatory homicide, police torture, kinky sex, a car chase, a search through canine feces, and a disrupted church wedding ceremony. [Version reviewed was 87 min. U.S. one.]

•

SPY WHO CAME IN FROM THE COLD, THE
1966, 112 mins, UK Ⓥ ⦿ b/w
Dir Martin Ritt ***Prod*** Martin Ritt ***Scr*** Paul Dehn, Guy Trosper ***Ph*** Oswald Morris ***Ed*** Anthony Harvey ***Mus*** Sol Kaplan ***Art*** Hal Pereira, Tambi Larsen
Act Richard Burton, Claire Bloom, Oskar Werner, Sam Wanamaker, George Voskovec, Rupert Davies (Salem/Paramount)

The Spy Who Came in from the Cold is an excellent contemporary espionage drama of the Cold War that achieves solid impact via emphasis on human values, total absence of mechanical spy gimmickry, and perfectly controlled underplaying. Filmed at Ireland's Ardmore Studios and England's Shepperton complex, the production boasts strong scripting, acting, direction and production values.

Film effectively socks over the point that East-West espionage agents are living in a world of their own, apart from the day-to-day existence of the millions whom they are serving.

Other fictional spies operate with such dash and flair that the erosion of the spirit is submerged in picturesque exploits and intricate technology. Not so in this adaptation of John Le Carré's novel in which Richard Burton "comes in from the cold"—meaning the field operations—only to find himself used as a pawn in high-level counter-plotting.

Burton fits neatly into the role of the apparently burned-out British agent, ripe for cultivation by East German Communist secret police as a potential defector.

1965: NOMINATIONS: Best Actor (Richard Burton), B&W Art Direction

•

SPY WHO LOVED ME, THE
1977, 125 mins, UK Ⓥ ⦿ ⌑ col
Dir Lewis Gilbert ***Prod*** Albert R. Broccoli ***Scr*** Christopher Wood, Richard Maibaum ***Ph*** Claude Renoir ***Ed*** John Glen ***Mus*** Marvin Hamlisch ***Art*** Peter Lamont
Act Roger Moore, Barbara Bach, Curt Jurgens, Richard Kiel, Caroline Munro, Walter Gotell (United Artists/Eon)

As always, story and plastic character are in the service of comic-strip parody, an excuse to star the prop department, set designer, stunt arrangers, the optical illusion chaps, and such commercial suppliers as the maker of the sporty Lotus car, a lethal job that also converts to an underwater craft.

When British and Russian nuclear subs start to mysteriously vanish, two agents are assigned by their collaborating governments to jointly crack the case.

Curt Jurgens's arsenal includes the film's gimmick character, a monster human known as "Jaws," played with robotic finesse by Richard Kiel.

The big action sequences were shot on a specially-built stage with tank at Pinewood Studios outside London.

1977: NOMINATIONS: Art Direction, Original Score, Song ("Nobody Does It Better")

•

SPY WITH MY FACE, THE
1966, 86 mins, US col
Dir John Newland ***Prod*** Sam Rolfe ***Scr*** Clyde Ware, Joseph Calvelli ***Ph*** Fred Koenekamp ***Ed*** Joseph Dervin ***Mus*** Morton Stevens ***Art*** George W. Davis, Merrill Pye
Act Robert Vaughn, Senta Berger, David McCallum, Leo G. Carroll, Michael Evans, Sharon Farrell (M-G-M/Arena)

The Spy with My Face, new version of an old *Man from U.N.C.L.E.* episode, is perhaps most garbled, plotwise, of any entry in the [mid-1960s] spy melodrama cycle. Thrush, that band of murderous renegades that would rule the world and is constantly combating U.N.C.L.E., fixes up one of its agents to be the exact double of Napoleon Solo, the goodguy, and nearly succeeds in its purpose—whatever that is.

New footage was added to the original TV segment hour's length to bring it up to 86 minutes for theatrical release.

Film loses sight of story line, which has something to do with transporting a new combination to a vault in Switzerland containing a scientific secret of world import. Vaughn plays his double role straight, and Senta Berger is in as a beauteous she-spy. Femme honors, however go to Sharon Farrell as a cute sexpot. David McCallum appears in his familiar sidekick role, as does Leo G. Carroll as U.N.C.L.E. topper, and Michael Evans is the smooth heavy.

•

SQUEAKER, THE
1937, 79 mins, UK Ⓥ b/w
Dir William K. Howard ***Prod*** Alexander Korda ***Scr*** Edward O. Berkman ***Ph*** Georges Perinal ***Ed*** Jack Dennis, Russell Lloyd ***Mus*** Miklos Rozsa ***Art*** Vincent Korda
Act Edmund Lowe, Sebastian Shaw, Ann Todd, Tamara Desni, Robert Newton, Alastair Sim (London)

Typically fine Korda production, starring Edmund Lowe in an adaptation from the Edgar Wallace play. Despite the fact that Wallace's son Bryan is credited with the scenario, the screenplay is by Edward O. Berkman, and there now remains not a single line, joke or wisecrack by the original author.

Barest framework of Wallace Sr. remains, but it has been changed from a whodunit to a newer formula, that of revealing early the identity of the arch-criminal who for years baffled Scotland Yard, and interest in the film is wholly dependent on how the Yard unravels the crime.

Role of Inspector Barrabal has been built up into a romantic lead for Edmund Lowe, and he fulfills this purpose to a nicety. That of the villain, played by Sebastian Shaw, is not carried through convincingly. Audience is asked to believe that a ruthless criminal, who doesn't even stop at murder, breaks down and confesses in a cowering, hysterical manner when confronted with the corpse of his victim.

There are only two feminine roles of consequence in the cast. Ann Todd is the lead in a colorless part, and Tamara Desni is a cabaret singer in love with the murdered man.

Fine piece of character work on the part of Robert Newton, eventually murdered, is outstanding.

•

SQUEEZE, THE

1977, 106 mins, UK Ⓥ col

Dir Michael Apted ***Prod*** Stanley O'Toole ***Scr*** Leon Griffiths ***Ph*** Dennis Lewiston ***Ed*** John Shirley ***Mus*** David Hentschel ***Art*** William McCrow

Act Stacy Keach, Freddie Starr, Edward Fox, Stephen Boyd, David Hemmings, Carol White (Warner)

There's nothing to distinguish *The Squeeze* from routine crime drama in which retribution triumphs. Stacy Keach plays a busted cop fighting the booze habit and some murderous thugs at the same time.

Keach suffers some nasty lumps and sundry humiliations, all in the cause of Edward Fox as a security film exec whose wife and kid are hostages against a million-dollar-plus payoff. Carol White is the terrorized wife, with the complication that she's also Keach's former spouse.

Directed on locations in London by Michael Apted, pic has little in the way of style and no great surprises. It does, however, have a kind of gratuitous nasty tone, as evidenced when the thugs holding White captive force her to perform a strip.

•

SQUEEZE

1996, 100 mins, US Ⓥ col

Dir Robert Patton-Spruill ***Prod*** Ari Newman, Garen Topalian, Stephanie Danan, ***Scr*** Robert Patton-Spruill ***Ph*** Richard Moos ***Ed*** Richard Moos ***Mus*** Bruce Flowers ***Art*** Maxmillian Cutler

Act Tyrone Burton, Eddie Cutanda, Phuong Duong, Geoffrey Rhue, Russell G. Jones, Leigh Williams (Robbins/Cathartic Filmworks)

Squeeze represents the flowering of homegrown filmmaking in Boston. Shot entirely in and around the city's Dorchester neighborhood, this gritty debut film by writer-director Robert Patton-Spruill plays like a New England version of *Boyz N the Hood*.

Tyson (Tyrone Burton), Hector (Eddie Cutanda) and Bao (Phuong Duong) are three poor 14-year-olds trying to figure out where they fit into life on the streets. What follows is a series of episodes as the three adolescents try to make sense of the conflicting messages they get from drug dealers, relatives and officials. One source of help is J.J. (Geoffrey Rhue), a kind but tough-minded youth counselor who survived the era of fistfights and heroin, but finds himself working in a time of guns and crack.

Patton-Spruill draws standout performances from his young cast, all of whom worked in the Dorchester Youth Collaborative. Critical attention will go to Burton for his portrayal of a character squeezed to the brink of destruction. Pic boasts a surprisingly polished look given the reported $500,000 budget.

•

SQUIRM

1976, 93 mins, US Ⓥ col

Dir Jeff Lieberman ***Prod*** George Manasse ***Scr*** Jeff Lieberman ***Ph*** Joseph Mangine ***Ed*** Brian Smedley ***Mus*** Robert Prince ***Art*** Henry Shrady

Act John Scardino, Patricia Pearcy, R. A. Dow, Jean Sullivan, Peter MacLean, Fran Higgins (American International)

Squirm is an average shock meller about some rampaging sand worms in the Georgia sticks, claimed to be derived from an actual occurrence on September 29, 1975. Some genuine creepy special effects are offset by clumsy and amateurish low-budget location production, yet there is an admirable earnestness to the effort.

Story kicker is an electrical storm which downs power lines, with runaway juice charging the wet mud and driving out the 10-18-inch sand worms of the area. They are hungry and angry. They are also effective. City slicker John Scardino visits local Patricia Pearcy, eldest daughter of widow Jean Sullivan. Sheriff Peter MacLean doesn't believe in the worm plague, but becomes one of its victims.

•

STAGECOACH

1939, 95 mins, US Ⓥ ⊙ b/w

Dir John Ford ***Prod*** Walter Wanger ***Scr*** Dudley Nichols ***Ph*** Bert Glennon ***Ed*** Dorothy Spencer, Walter Reynolds ***Mus*** Leo Shuken, John Leipold, Richard Hageman, W. Franke Harling, Louis Gruenberg ***Art*** Alexander Toluboff

Act Claire Trevor, John Wayne, Andy Devine, Thomas Mitchell, George Bancroft, John Carradine (United Artists)

Directorially, production [based on Ernest Haycox's *Collier's* magazine story, *Stage to Lordsburg*] is John Ford in peak form, sustaining interest and suspense throughout, and presenting exceptional characterizations. Picture is a display of photographic grandeur. It's the adventures of a group aboard a stagecoach between two frontier settlements during the sudden uprising of the Apaches. Situation is a *Grand Hotel* on wheels.

There's Claire Trevor, dance hall gal forced to leave town; driver, Andy Devine; gambler, John Carradine; inebriated frontier medic, Thomas Mitchell; marshall, George Bancroft; wife of an army officer en route to his post, Louise Platt; whiskey salesman, Donald Meek, and absconding banker, Berton Churchill. John Wayne, recently escaped from prison, is picked up on the road shortly after the start.

In maintaining a tensely dramatic pace all the way, Ford still injects numerous comedy situations, and throughout sketches his characters with sincerity and humaneness. It's absorbing drama without the general theatrics usual to picturizations of the early West.

The running fight between the stagecoach passengers and the Apaches has been given thrilling and realistic presentation by Ford. In contrast, the hacienda sequence is an extremely tender episode.

1939: Best Score, Supp. Actor (Thomas Mitchell)

NOMINATIONS: Best Picture, Director, B&W Cinematography, Art Direction, Editing

•

STAGECOACH

1966, 114 mins, US ▭ col

Dir Gordon Douglas ***Prod*** Martin Rackin ***Scr*** Joseph Landon ***Ph*** William H. Clothier ***Ed*** Hugh S. Fowler ***Mus*** Jerry Goldsmith ***Art*** Jack Martin Smith, Herman A. Blumenthal

Act Ann-Margret, Red Buttons, Michael Connors, Alex Cord, Bing Crosby, Bob Cummings (Rackin/20th Century-Fox)

New version of *Stagecoach* derives from a 1939 Walter Wanger production for United Artists, written by Dudley Nichols from a 1937 short story by Ernest Haycox.

Film kicks off with a gory two-minute sequence establishing the brutality of Indians on the warpath, the menace which hangs over subsequent developments, after which the stagecoach starts loading its motley passenger crew. Ann-Margret is quite good as the saloon floozy badmouthed out of town under U.S. Army pressure by John Gabriel. Bing Crosby, the boozy medic, is a similar victim of Gabriel's incorrect evaluation of a drunken brawl.

Bob Cummings, the gutless bank clerk absconding with a large payroll, is excellent. Cummings delivers much depth, evoking pity and sympathy. He makes an excellent heavy.

To Alex Cord goes the choice John Wayne role of Ringo, framed into prison by landgrabbing Keenan Wynn. Cord underplays very well and conveys the stubborn determination to avenge his dead father and brother, killed by Wynn, which sustained him during a sadistic incarceration from which he has escaped to join the stage.

Artist Norman Rockwell, who designed pic's logo and painted the perceptive talent portraits used in end titles and exploitation, appears briefly in an early saloon scene.

•

STAGE DOOR

1937, 83 mins, US/UK Ⓥ b/w

Dir Gregory La Cava ***Prod*** Pandro S. Berman ***Scr*** Morrie Ryskind, Anthony Veiller ***Ph*** Robert de Grasse ***Ed*** William Hamilton ***Mus*** Roy Webb

Act Katharine Hepburn, Ginger Rogers, Adolphe Menjou, Gail Patrick, Constance Collier, Andrea Leeds (RKO)

It isn't *Stage Door*, as written [for the stage] by Edna Ferber and George S. Kaufman. Instead, it is a hall bedroom view of aspiring young actresses who live in a New York theatrical boarding house and vent their bitterness against the economic uncertainties of legit employment in sharp and cutting repartee. It is funny in spots, emotionally effective occasionally, and generally brisk and entertaining. Whether it was Gregory La Cava or Pandro S. Berman, the producer, who decided to throw away the play and write a new script on the old idea that there is a broken heart for every light on Broadway, is beside the point.

Story revolves around one of the minor characters, a talented young actress of promise unable to withstand the pressure of constant casting disappointment. Part is played for all it's worth by Andrea Leeds. Opening shows the inhabitants of a rooming house in the West 40s. They're a high strung, noisy bevy of showgirls, nightclub dancers and embryo dramatic timber. Dialog is caustic as they comment on each other and the passing world of show business. Ginger Rogers does a floor specialty in a night club which gives her an introduction to Adolphe Menjou, a hardboiled theatrical producer and femme despoiler.

Katharine Hepburn, stagestruck daughter of a wealthy westerner, becomes Ginger's roommate at the boarding house. Former's father, in the hope he can discourage her theatrical career, anonymously finances a Menjou dramatic production, with Hepburn in the lead.

Rogers has more to do than Hepburn, but her part is less clearly defined. As a sharpshooter with the snappy reply she scores heavily. Her dancing is limited to a short floor number.

1937: NOMINATIONS: Best Picture, Director, Supp. Actress (Andrea Leeds), Screenplay

•

STAGE DOOR CANTEEN

1943, 132 mins, US Ⓥ ⊙ b/w

Dir Frank Borzage ***Prod*** Sol Lesser ***Scr*** Delmer Daves ***Ph*** Harry Wild ***Ed*** Hal Kern ***Mus*** Freddie Rich

Act Cheryl Walker, William Terry, Marjorie Riordan, Lon McCallister, Margaret Early, Michael Harrison (United Artists)

What stood a good chance of emerging a "big short" under less skillful hands than Sol Lesser proves a sock film musical of great stature. It has a cast that reads like an out-of-this-world benefit, and a romance as simple as Elsie Dinsmore—and the blend is plenty boffo.

Stage Door Canteen is a skilful admixture by two casts, in itself a departure. One cast projects the simple love story—Eileen and her "Dakota"; Jean and her "California"; Ella Sue and her "Texas"; Mamie and her "Jersey." Another cast comprises the Stars of the Stage Door Canteen, and but few of them do walk-through parts.

Plausibly and smoothly, these stars are introduced into their natural habitat, the Stage Door Canteen on West 44th Street, just off Broadway, where Lunt and Fontanne and Vera Gordon, Sam Jaffe, George Raft and Allen Jenkins, Ned Sparks, Ralph Morgan and Hugh Herbert—these, among others, are shown doing their menial back-in-the-kitchen chores. Then, up front, performing for the visiting men in uniform, gobs, doughboys, marines—no officers—is paraded a galaxy of talent that's a super-duper, all-star array which reads like a casting agent's dream of paradise.

Thus are paraded six bands—Basie, Cugat, Goodman, Kyser, Lombardo and Martin, in sock specialties all.

And, to project the mechanics of the canteen, showing the officer-of-the-day, the senior hostesses, the dancing junior hostesses, or as part of the plot motivation (as with Katherine Cornell's skillful bit of *Romeo and Juliet*, and Paul Muni's part as rehearsing his own play), there are introduced another array of stars and legit personalities: Helen Hayes, Ina Claire, Tallulah Bankhead, Vinton Freedley, Merle Oberon, Brock Pemberton, Katherine Hepburn and the others are intertwined into the lonely-soldier-boy-meets-romantic-stage-girl plot. Scripter Delmer Daves does a deft writing job, and Frank Borzage's direction smoothly splices the sum total into a very palatable cohesive entity.

1943: NOMINATIONS: Best Scoring of a Musical Picture, Song ("We Mustn't Say Goodbye")

•

STAGE FRIGHT

1950, 110 mins, US/UK Ⓥ ⊙ b/w

Dir Alfred Hitchcock ***Prod*** Alfred Hitchcock ***Scr*** Whitfield Cook ***Ph*** Wilkie Cooper ***Ed*** Edward Jarvis ***Mus*** Leighton Lucas ***Art*** Terence Verity

Act Jane Wyman, Marlene Dietrich, Michael Wilding, Richard Todd, Kay Walsh, Alistair Sim (Warner/Associated British)

Alfred Hitchcock doesn't stress melodrama throughout. He plays a surprising number of sequences strictly for lightness. Also, he has a choice cast to put through its paces, and there's not a bad performance anywhere [in this adaption by Alma Reville of a novel by Selwyn Jepson]. The dialog has purpose, either for a chuckle or a thrill, and the pace is good.

Jane Wyman is a drama student who is sought out by a friend (Richard Todd) who is fleeing from the charge of murdering Marlene Dietrich's husband. Wyman and her father (Alistair Sim) hide Todd and attempt to prove Dietrich is guilty of the crime.

Wyman is delightful as embryo actress, but the choice femme spot goes to Dietrich. Michael Wilding clicks as a debonair detective.

•

STAGE STRUCK

1925, 70 mins, US ⊗ b/w

Dir Allan Dwan ***Scr*** Forrest Halsey, Sylvia La Varre, Frank R. Adams ***Ph*** George Webber ***Art*** Van Nest Polglase

Act Gloria Swanson, Lawrence Gray, Gertrude Astor, Marguerite Evans, Ford Sterling (Paramount)

Women will laugh and men will writhe at *Stage Struck* and Gloria Swanson. It's a fine piece of hoke. This Allan Dwan–directed comic is said to have been made in three weeks, whereby Dwan drew down a bonus. Famous players should have paid Dwan more if it had not been made at all.

Watching the picture after the second of the six reels, you try to figure how this ever got past for over two reels. It's one of the old-time Keystone models padded out.

One laugh is when Swanson tries to make up as an actress. And another after her prize fight when she jumps overboard to be saved from drowning by her pants catching on a nail on the side of the *Water Queen*, a riverboat.

At least the boat doesn't try to be funny. Next to the boat Lawrence Gray gives rather a good performance in the juvenile role, and, barring her material, Swanson is not at all bad as a comedienne.

●

STAGE STRUCK
1936, 90 mins, US Ⓥ b/w
Dir Busby Berkeley ***Scr*** Tom Buckingham, Pat C. Flick ***Ph*** Byron Haskin
Act Dick Powell, Joan Blondell, Warren William, Frank McHugh, Jeanne Madden, Carol Hughes (Warner)

Even though it makes an attempt to poke fun at the show-must-go-on thing, *Stage Struck* is cut from the same old pattern, gravitating between moments of sizzling comedy and long stretches of dull palaver. Picture takes a pretzel-like course in recounting the conventional yarn [by Robert Lord] about the unknown kid who makes good as the last-minute fill-in for the show's star. Musical interludes [songs by E. Y. Harburg and Harold Arlen] are kept down to the minimum.

With her material anything but surefire, Joan Blondell unlimbers a likable grade of comedy. Hers is the part of the dame whose only claim to fame is a penchant for drilling her troublesome boyfriends and the newsprint attention that goes with such incidents. She backs herself to the lead part in a musical show where Dick Powell functions as director. A clash of temperaments ends that venture and the pair meet again in her next bit of angeling. Paired with Powell for the romantic byplay, Jeanne Madden does okay for a starter.

●

STAGE STRUCK
1958, 95 mins, US Ⓥ ⊙ col
Dir Sidney Lumet ***Prod*** Stuart Millar ***Scr*** Ruth Goetz, Augustus Goetz ***Ph*** Franz Planer, Maurice Hartzband ***Ed*** Stuart Gilmore ***Mus*** Alex North ***Art*** Kim Edgar Swados
Act Henry Fonda, Susan Strasberg, Joan Greenwood, Herbert Marshall, Christopher Plummer, Patricia Englund (RKO)

Stage Struck weaves another variation on the well-worn tale of the eager young actress who can't persuade anyone on Broadway to give her a job until the star flounces out on the eve of opening night. The tyro steps into the star's shoes, knocks the audience right out of its red plush seats; veterans backstage murmur, "That's showbiz," and the camera pans slowly away from a solitary figure standing in the middle of an empty theatre; music up and out. It's a remake of *Morning Glory*, a yesteryear [1933] Katharine Hepburn starrer.

Susan Strasberg plays the would-be actress who hounds producer Henry Fonda for a chance. He is intrigued by the girl, but not as an actress, and turns her down. Not so his playwright (Christopher Plummer), who sees her both as actress and romantic opposite. When the star of their show (Joan Greenwood) makes a temperamental exit, Plummer has Strasberg set to take over her role, and she does with plot-predictable ease and success.

Strasberg occupies a major portion of the footage in this screenplay from a Zoe Akins play. She is not a conventional screen beauty, but her face is expressive and lively. Fonda plays with his customary quiet authority and disarming command and Herbert Marshall limns a warming portrait as a stage veteran. Greenwood gives the rampaging star the Bankhead bit and very funny she is. Plummer has considerable depth to his playing.

Camerawork is striking, notably in the Central Park scenes, a setting of a Greenwich Village street, dawn in Times Square, and the interiors of the theatre (actually the National on 41st Street).

●

STAIRCASE
1969, 101 mins, US Ⓥ ▭ col
Dir Stanley Donen ***Prod*** Stanley Donen ***Scr*** Charles Dyer ***Ph*** Christopher Challis ***Ed*** Richard Marden ***Mus*** Dudley Moore ***Art*** Willy Holt
Act Richard Burton, Rex Harrison, Cathleen Nesbitt, Beatrix Lehmann, Avril Angers, Stephen Lewis (20th Century-Fox)

Staircase, investigating lonely, desperate lives of two aging male homosexuals in a drab London suburb, comes uncomfortably close to being depressing. Caustic wit, splendid photography and fine direction serve only to point up weary plight of the middle-aged pair who cling to one another even while they clash.

Homosexuality, though predominant influence of storyline [from the play by Charles Dyer], is not central theme of screenplay. Its basis is urgent need of neurotic individuals for consolation.

Harrison as the flighty dagger-tongued roommate of fellow "hair stylist" Burton offers portrait of a bitter, disenchanted man living in terror of being alone. Burton, almost stoic, commands respect and, at the same time, sympathy. Harrison and Burton have dared risky roles and have triumphed.

●

STAIRWAY TO HEAVEN
SEE: A MATTER OF LIFE AND DEATH

●

STAKEOUT
1987, 115 mins, US Ⓥ ⊙ col
Dir John Badham ***Prod*** Jim Kouf, Cathleen Summers ***Scr*** Jim Kouf ***Ph*** John Seale ***Ed*** Tom Rolf, Michael Ripps ***Mus*** Arthur B. Rubinstein ***Art*** Philip Harrison
Act Richard Dreyfuss, Emilio Estevez, Madeleine Stowe, Aidan Quinn, Dan Lauria, Forest Whitaker (Touchstone)

Stakeout is a slick, sure-footed entertainment, one part buddy comedy and one part police actioner stitched together with a dash of romance.

Richard Dreyfuss is a reckless cop whose life is unraveling slowly. While he's on familiar ground talking his way out of tight spots and jousting with partner Emilio Estevez, when the plot calls for rough stuff, it's a stretch he doesn't make.

As the more stable, but still mischievous anchor of the pair, Estevez is likable, if a bit flat. He's not an actor with a great gift for comedy, and many of his exchanges with Dreyfuss lack chemistry.

As Seattle cops (the film was shot in Vancouver), the wisecracking duo is assigned to a routine stakeout where they are supposed to wait for an escaped con (Aidan Quinn) to contact his ex-girlfriend (Madeleine Stowe). Dreyfuss is not a man to wait around for something to happen and, as he barrels into the case, he falls in love with Stowe.

●

STALAG 17
1953, 119 mins, US Ⓥ ⊙ b/w
Dir Billy Wilder ***Prod*** Billy Wilder ***Scr*** Billy Wilder, Edwin Blum ***Ph*** Ernest Laszlo ***Ed*** George Tomasini ***Mus*** Franz Waxman ***Art*** Hal Pereira, Franz Bachelin
Act William Holden, Don Taylor, Otto Preminger, Robert Strauss, Harvey Lembeck, Peter Graves (Paramount)

The legit hit about GI internees in a Nazi prison camp during the Second World War is screened as a lusty comedy-melodrama, loaded with bold, masculine humor and as much of the original's uninhibited earthiness as good taste and the Production Code permit.

Producer-director Billy Wilder, who did the screen adaptation of the Donald Bevan–Edmund Trzcinski play with Edwin Blum, uses a suspense approach with plenty of leavening humorous byplay springing from the confinement of healthy young males. Nub of the plot is the uncovering of an informer among the GIs in a particular barracks, and up to the time his identity is revealed there is plenty of tenseness in the footage.

Opening shows the death of two GIs while attempting a well-plotted escape and the sudden realization there is an informer in their midst. Suspicion fastens on William Holden, a cynical character trying to make the best of his prison lot. When Don Taylor is temporarily moved into the barracks and just as quickly revealed as the American who blew up an ammunition train, the prisoners decide Holden is their man and beat him unmercifully.

Otto Preminger is the third star, playing the camp commander, with obvious relish for its colorful cruelty. Laugh standouts are Robert Strauss, the dumb Stosh of the play, and Harvey Lembeck as Harry, the only slightly brighter pal of Stosh.

1953: Best Actor (William Holden)

NOMINATIONS: Best Director, Supp. Actor (Robert Strauss)

●

STALKING MOON, THE
1969, 109 mins, US Ⓥ ▭ col
Dir Robert Mulligan ***Prod*** Alan J. Pakula ***Scr*** Alvin Sargent ***Ph*** Charles Lang ***Ed*** Aaron Stell ***Mus*** Fred Karlin ***Art*** Roland Anderson, Jack Poplin
Act Gregory Peck, Eva Marie Saint, Robert Forster, Noland Clay (National General/Stalking Moon)

The Stalking Moon seemingly was meant to be a chilling suspenser, framed in a western environment. It does not achieve this goal, because of clumsy plot structuring and dialog and limp direction, which produces tedious pacing.

Theodore V. Olsen's novel, scripted by Alvin Sargent, has Gregory Peck retiring as a vet Indian scout with the U.S. Army. In an Indian round-up, Eva Marie Saint appears, with son Noland Clay. Years before, she was kidnapped and impressed into squaw service by Nathaniel Narcisco. Peck takes her and the boy to his retirement ranch, but the Indian brave stalks them.

Forgetting the oater atmosphere (which is supposed to be secondary) film doesn't cut it as a suspenser. Saint, although perhaps as stolid as a frightened Indian slave-woman might be, is not able to project her determined flight from the range territory.

Kid Clay just stares at everything. Dialog is spare and vapid.

●

STAND BY ME
1986, 87 mins, US Ⓥ ⊙ col
Dir Rob Reiner ***Prod*** Bruce A. Evans, Raynold Gideon, Andrew Scheinman ***Scr*** Raynold Gideon, Bruce A. Evans ***Ph*** Thomas Del Ruth ***Ed*** Robert Leighton ***Mus*** Jack Nitzsche ***Art*** Dennis Washington
Act Wil Wheaton, River Phoenix, Corey Feldman, Jerry O'Connell, Richard Dreyfuss, Kiefer Sutherland (Act III)

Stand by Me falls somewhat short of being a first-rate "small" picture about adventurous small-town adolescent boys, although director Rob Reiner is to be lauded for coming close. Formerly titled *The Body*, based on a novella of the same name by Stephen King, it is the experiences of four youths on a two-day trek through the woods around their hometown of Castle Rock, Oregon, to find the yet-undiscovered body of a dead teenager reported missing for several days.

Film opens very slowly with the extraneous narration of grownup writer Richard Dreyfuss reminiscing on that certain summer of 1959 between sixth and seventh grades that he spent with three close buddies as they sought to become heroes in each other's and the town's eyes.

Scripters have written inspired dialog for this quartet of plucky boys at that hard-to-capture age when they're still young enough to get scared and yet old enough to want to sneak smokes and cuss.

Leading the cast is the introspective, sensitive "brain" of the bunch, Gordie Lachance (Wil Wheaton). His somber personality is matched by best friend Chris Chambers (River Phoenix), a toughie who is an abused child; Teddy Dechamp (Corey Feldman), the loony kid of an institutionalized father; and the perfectly named wimp, Vern Tessie, the chubby kid who everyone else enjoys poking fun at.

1986: NOMINATION: Best Adapted Screenplay

●

STAND-IN
1937, 90 mins, US Ⓥ b/w
Dir Tay Garnett ***Prod*** Walter Wanger ***Scr*** Gene Towne, Graham Baker ***Ph*** Charles Clarke ***Ed*** Otho Lovering, Dorothy Spencer ***Mus*** Rox Tommell ***Art*** Alexander Toluboff, Wade Rubottom
Act Leslie Howard, Joan Blondell, Humphrey Bogart, Alan Mowbray, Marla Shelton, C. Henry Gordon (United Artists)

Hollywood studios and the people who make films receive some good-natured ribbing in *Stand-In*. It leans far to the comedy side, and is good entertainment, chiefly because Leslie Howard and Joan Blondell mix up some very funny roughhouse with a dash of solid logic.

Howard is a bespectacled representative of New York bankers who control a Hollywood film producing company. Howard comes west with a briefcase, a college education, high respect for balance sheets and a total ignorance of motion pictures. He volunteers to straighten out the production difficulties and save Colossal Films for the stockholders.

Blondell, who is a stand-in for the big star, takes him to one side and gives him the lowdown on what it's all about. With Blondell as his secretary, Howard tackles the job as if he were running a shipbuilding plant. Finally, when things go from bad to worse, he bucks up and pulls the studio out of its difficulties.

Film is from a *Sat Eve Post* story by Clarence Budington Kelland (author of *Mr. Deeds Goes to Town*), and a screenscript possessing much originality by Gene Towne and Graham Baker.

Humphrey Bogart plays a producer who turns teetotaler; Alan Mowbray does a foreign director; Marla Shelton is a vampy film star, and C. Henry Gordon is a menacing stock jobber who tries to get control of the studio.

STANDING ROOM ONLY
1944, 83 mins, US b/w
Dir Sidney Lanfield ***Prod*** Paul Jones ***Scr*** Darrel Ware, Karl Tunberg ***Ph*** Charles Lang ***Ed*** William Shea ***Mus*** Robert Emmett Dolan ***Art*** Hans Dreier, Earl Hedrick
Act Fred MacMurray, Paulette Goddard, Edward Arnold, Roland Young, Anne Revere, Hillary Brooke (Paramount)

War-crowded Washington is the nucleus for a comedy based on the trouble people have in securing living accommodations and the red tape involved in getting in to see officials on business in the nation's capital.

This is a picture for all the family. All problems are dealt with in the light vein used by most predecessors based on similar themes. With the acting ability of Fred MacMurray and Paulette Goddard, ably abetted by Edward Arnold, Roland Young and Porter Hall, and the snappily paced direction of Sidney Lanfield, the film is escapist entertainment with many amusing sequences.

Script [based on a story by Al Martin] gives the two stars plenty of opportunities to prove their capabilities. MacMurray, as the butler, is especially funny in a scene where he drops a cherry from the fruit salad he is serving into the lap of one of the women and endeavors to snare the elusive condiment with a knife and spoon, while she continues her conversation with one of the guests.

STANLEY & IRIS
1990, 102 mins, US Ⓥ ⦿ ▭ col
Dir Martin Ritt ***Prod*** Arlene Sellers, Alex Winitsky ***Scr*** Harriet Frank, Jr., Irving Ravetch ***Ph*** Donald McAlpine ***Ed*** Sidney Levin ***Mus*** John Williams ***Art*** Joel Schiller
Act Jane Fonda, Robert De Niro, Swoosie Kurtz, Martha Plimpton, Harley Cross, Jamey Sheridan (Lantana/M-G-M)

The elements are in place but they don't add up to great drama in this well-meant effort to personalize the plight of illiterate people.

Project reunites director Martin Ritt with screenwriting team that produced the Oscar-winning *Norma Rae*, which also had a working-class setting and underdog social concern. *Stanley & Iris* [from the novel *Union Street* by Pat Barker] features Robert De Niro's plight as an illiterate cook, but proves too small for a feature film framework.

Jane Fonda plays Iris, a recent widow still struggling with grief while trying to support a whole household. She catches the eye of Stanley Cox, a cafeteria cook who at middle age has never learned to read or write.

Fired by his boss for being potentially dangerous, Stanley no longer can afford to care properly for the aging father who lives with him. When the old man dies, Stanley finally confronts his fears and asks Iris to teach him to read.

Fonda has some trouble evoking a woman whose life would have dropped her off at such a humble station. De Niro, as a quiet, prideful man who feels foolish and like "a big dummy" trying to learn, does in fact come across as self-consciously awkward and a tad silly, though his performance includes some muted, winning comedy.

STANLEY AND LIVINGSTONE
1939, 100 mins, US Ⓥ b/w
Dir Henry King ***Prod*** Darryl F. Zanuck ***Scr*** Philip Dunne, Julien Josephson ***Ph*** George Barnes ***Ed*** Barbara McLean ***Mus*** Louis Silvers (dir.)
Act Spencer Tracy, Nancy Kelly, Cedric Hardwicke, Richard Greene, Walter Brennan, Charles Coburn (20th Century-Fox)

Stanley and Livingstone is absorbing and adventurous drama, accentuated by outstanding performances by Spencer Tracy and Cedric Hardwicke in title spots respectively.

Fundamentally, it's lusty, pioneering adventure, detailing successful attempt of Tracy to find Hardwicke in the heart of Africa. Tracy gives persuasive portrayal as the reporter determined to get his story and inspired by love of Nancy Kelly. Kelly is a most adequate romantic interest; Walter Brennan is excellent as the Indian scout transposed to African plains.

Interweaving the dramatic production, in Hollywood, with sequences made for the picture more than year before when director Otto Brower headed an expedition to Africa to obtain background and atmosphere shots on the ground, is excellent.

STAR, THE
1952, 90 mins, US Ⓥ b/w
Dir Stuart Heisler ***Prod*** Bert E. Friedlob ***Scr*** Katherine Albert, Dale Eunson ***Ph*** Ernest Laszlo ***Ed*** Otto Ludwig ***Mus*** Victor Young ***Art*** Boris Levin
Act Bette Davis, Sterling Hayden, Natalie Wood, Warner Anderson, Minor Watson, June Travis (Friedlob/20th Century-Fox)

A strong performance by Bette Davis, in a tailor-made role, gives a lift to *The Star* that it might not have had otherwise.

There is a "tradey" feel to the story, as befits the backstage Hollywood plot. Opening finds Davis sulking outside an auction house that is selling her last possessions to pay her creditors. A meeting there with her agent-friend (Warner Anderson) and a pitch for him to get her another picture fails. She gets drunk, is arrested and bailed out by a boating man (Sterling Hayden).

Hayden tries to get her to forget a film career and become a normal, natural woman. She tries, but fails at holding a department store job, and wangles a screen test from a kindly producer.

With most of the footage concentrating on Davis's character, there isn't too much for the other players to do.

1952: NOMINATION: Best Actress (Bette Davis)

STAR!
(A.K.A: THOSE WERE THE HAPPY TIMES)
1968, 169 mins, US Ⓥ ⦿ ▭ col
Dir Robert Wise ***Prod*** Saul Chaplin ***Scr*** William Fairchild ***Ph*** Ernest Laszlo ***Ed*** William Reynolds ***Mus*** Lennie Hayton (arr.) ***Art*** Boris Leven
Act Julie Andrews, Richard Crenna, Michael Craig, Daniel Massey, Robert Reed, Bruce Forsyth (Wise/20th Century-Fox)

Julie Andrews's portrayal of the late, great music comedy idol, Gertrude Lawrence, occasionally sags between musical numbers, but the cast and team of redoubtable technical contributors have helped to turn out a pleasing tribute to one of the theatre's most admired stars.

It gives a fascinating coverage of Lawrence's spectacular rise to showbiz fame, and also a neatly observed background of an epoch now gone.

The film has, as its framework, the star sitting in with a TV producer watching a supposed black-and-white 1940 documentary of her career. It's a tricky but meaty role, but even those intimate with Lawrence's work and personality will quickly settle for accepting, in Andrews's carefully built-up performance, the illusion that they're watching Lawrence. Andrews, however, tends to overdo the cockney hoydenishness in the early stages.

Humor is more witty than boisterously funny, while the 16 musical numbers are staged in polished fashion [by Michael Kidd].

1968: NOMINATIONS: Best Supp. Actor (Daniel Massey), Cinematography, Costume Design, Art Direction, Adapted Musical Score, Song ("Star!"), Sound

STAR CHAMBER, THE
1983, 109 mins, US Ⓥ ⦿ ▭ col
Dir Peter Hyams ***Prod*** Frank Yablans ***Scr*** Roderick Taylor, Peter Hyams ***Ph*** Richard Hannah ***Ed*** Jim Mitchell ***Mus*** Michael Small ***Art*** Bill Malley
Act Michael Douglas, Hal Holbrook, Yaphet Kotto, Sharon Gless, James B. Sikking, Joe Regalbuto (20th Century-Fox)

Producer and director exhibit an excess of faith in today's educational system if they think the bulk of today's filmgoing audience will know the title's 15th-century derivation as an extra-judicial body.

Chamber does start out on an important note. The U.S. criminal justice system is not only collapsing but what's left has been perverted until the victims of crime have no hope of satisfaction nor protection.

As a decent, conscientious judge, Michael Douglas deals with the problem daily, forced by straining legal precedent to free the obviously "guilty."

Severely stricken by one event, Douglas turns to his friend and mentor, Hal Holbrook, who is secretly part of a group of judges who mete out their own fatal sentences on criminals who've been through their real courts and gone free.

Getting to this point in the film, there's a pleasure in rediscovering intelligent dialog, ably provided by Hyams and Roderick Taylor. But the talk is haunted by concern that this intellectual morass cannot be solved within the confines of cinema.

STAR DUST
1940, 84 mins, US b/w
Dir Walter Lang ***Prod*** Kenneth MacGowan ***Scr*** Robert Ellis, Helen Logan ***Ph*** Peverell Marley ***Ed*** Robert Simpson ***Mus*** Mack Gordon ***Art*** Richard Day, Albert Hogsett
Act Linda Darnell, John Payne, Roland Young, Charlotte Greenwood, William Gargan, Donald Meek (20th Century-Fox)

Ivan Kahn, talent digger-upper for 20th-Fox, was one of the coauthors of the original story, and no doubt he incorporated many of his experiences in seeking new film faces in the hinterlands. The yarn about Linda Darnell's experiences in getting a bid to Hollywood for a test, the resultant turndown because she is too young, and eventual connivance to stay and click in her first picture, closely parallels her experiences in real life.

Darnell displays a wealth of youthful charm and personality. She handles her assignment in top-notch style. John Payne surprises with a crackerjack performance as the grid star unearthed by the talent tractor and eventually scooted along for a test. He and Darnell are the romantic interest.

Roland Young, Charlotte Greenwood and Donald Meek effectively carry comedy assignments. Young is the faded film star turned talent scout, hitting the southwest college campuses. Greenwood provides a slick characterization of the dramatic coach. Meek is the studio casting director who tries to blow down the efforts of Young and Greenwood to put Darnell across.

The picture takes good-natured cracks at Darryl Zanuck's rapid-fire delivery while in story conference or deciding on a casting assignment. William Gargan, as the producing head, realistically imitates the striding and shortened mallet-swinging performances of Zanuck in one brief office sequence.

STARDUST
1974, 110 mins, UK Ⓥ col
Dir Michael Apted ***Prod*** David Puttnam, Sandy Lieberson ***Scr*** Ray Connolly ***Ph*** Tony Richmond ***Ed*** Mike Bradsell ***Mus*** Dave Edmunds, David Puttnam (arr.)
Act David Essex, Adam Faith, Larry Hagman, Ines Des Longchamps, Rosalind Ayres, Marty Wilde (EMI/Goodtimes)

Several members of the team that put together the highly successful *That'll Be the Day* [1973] are associated with this much more elaborate and ambitious follow-up.

Singer-guitarist Jim Maclaine (David Essex), seen on the verge of maturity and foretasting fame and fortune at the end of *Day*, is followed here on his rapid rise and fall as the eventual star of a heterogeneous pop group, the Stray Cats, as it makes it first in the nabes, then in the U.K., U.S. and the world.

En route, pic details the loves, joys and tribulations, hardships and achievements, jealousies, superficialities and hypocrisies, as well as—and importantly—the damning effect of drugs, of the music scene glimpsed from the lowest beginnings to number one position in the global charts.

STARDUST MEMORIES
1980, 89 mins, US Ⓥ ⦿ b/w
Dir Woody Allen ***Prod*** Robert Greenhut ***Scr*** Woody Allen ***Ph*** Gordon Willis ***Ed*** Susan E. Morse ***Art*** Mel Bourne
Act Woody Allen, Charlotte Rampling, Marie-Christine Barrault, Jessica Harper, Amy Wright, Tony Roberts (United Artists)

While Woody Allen teased with autobiography in *Manhattan* and *Annie Hall*, he drops all pretense here. No effort is made to pretend that his character of Sandy Bates is anybody but Allen himself—a filmmaker first adored for wacky comedies, then gradually appreciated as a cinematic genius.

But Bates-Allen thinks those who like his early comedies more than his later "deeper" pictures are buffoons; he thinks those who try to sift through the meaning of his later works are intellectual lamebrains and he makes clear that any attempt to analyze *Stardust Memories* itself would be the height of pompous pretension.

Though there are laughs along the way, this is a truly mean-spirited picture. Once a sympathetic nebbish, Allen here sees himself as a put-upon, embittered genius, disdainful of everything around him.

STAR 80
1983, 102 mins, US Ⓥ ⦿ col
Dir Bob Fosse ***Prod*** Wolfgang Glattes, Kenneth Utt ***Scr*** Bob Fosse ***Ph*** Sven Nykvist ***Ed*** Alan Helm ***Mus*** Ralph Burns ***Art*** Jack G. Taylor, Jr.
Act Mariel Hemingway, Eric Roberts, Cliff Robertson, Carroll Baker, Roger Rees, David Clennon (Ladd Company)

Bob Fosse takes another look at the underside of the success trip in *Star 80*, an engrossing, unsentimental and unavoidably depressing account of the short life and ghastly death of Playmate-actress Dorothy Stratten.

Stratten was a sweet, voluptuous blonde who became a popular Playmate of the Year in Playboy, appeared in a few films, all of which are forgettable except for Peter Bogdanovich's *They All Laughed* (1981), and was brutally killed by her estranged husband in a murder-suicide in 1980.

As played here by Mariel Hemingway, Stratten is a virginal, extremely insecure teenager—almost a baby, really—in Vancouver who is swooped down upon by small-time hustler Paul Snider. Although doubtlessly in love with his discovery, Snider uses Stratten as his ticket to the big time in L.A.

Give Stratten's passivity and pliability, histrionics fall to the Snider character, and Eric Roberts gives a startlingly fine performance as this pathetic loser.

•

STARGATE
1994, 120 mins, US Ⓥ ⊙ ▭ col
Dir Roland Emmerich ***Prod*** Joel Michaels, Oliver Eberle, Dean Devlin ***Scr*** Dean Devlin, Roland Emmerich ***Ph*** Karl Walter Lindenlaub ***Ed*** Michael Duthie, Derek Brechin ***Mus*** David Arnold ***Art*** Holger Gross
Act Kurt Russell, James Spader, Jaye Davidson, Viveca Lindfors, Alexis Cruz, Mili Avital (Canal Plus/Centropolis)

What this $60-70 million juvenile adventure has in spades is special effects and picturesque locations. What it lacks is an emotional link to make the Saturday afternoon he-man posturing palatable, or at least bearable.

The setup occurs in Giza, Egypt, circa 1928. An archeological expedition unearths a giant ring inscribed with hieroglyphs. We're promptly propelled into the present, where Egyptologist Dr. Daniel Jackson (James Spader) is telling a learned, if disbelieving, crowd that the pyramids could not possibly have been built by man. One listener offers him the job of translating an ancient stone lodged in a secret military complex. It is, of course, the piece seen at the beginning. The ring is a portal to another dimension.

Breaking the impenetrable code leads to a military probe commanded by former basket case Col. Jack O'Neil (Kurt Russell). Jackson tags along as interpreter. The inhabitants of this world are biblical-style slaves, the ruler a galactic hermaphrodite (Jaye Davidson). The oppressed workers, with the help of the soldiers and scientist, rise up to quell the evil oppressor.

Director Roland Emmerich pushes the obvious plot buttons, turns up the florid score and injects appropriate panoramas. O'Neil never truly confronts the dark past of a dead son, and Jackson's budding relationship with a slave (Mili Avital) is chaste beyond belief. [A 126 min. *Collector's Edition* was released on home video in 1996.]

•

STAR IS BORN, A
1937, 111 mins, US Ⓥ ⊙ col
Dir William A. Wellman ***Prod*** David O. Selznick ***Scr*** Robert Carson, Dorothy Parker, Alan Campbell ***Ph*** W. Howard Greene ***Ed*** Hal C. Kern ***Mus*** Max Steiner ***Art*** Lansing C. Holden
Act Janet Gaynor, Fredric March, Adolphe Menjou, May Robson, Andy Devine, Lionel Stander (Selznick/United Artists)

Although not the first film which has attempted to capitalize on the international reputation of Hollywood, it is unquestionably the most effective one yet made. The highly commendable results are achieved with a minimum of satiric hokum and a maximum of honest storytelling.

Film is photographed throughout in Technicolor. Several scenes impress on sheer beauty and composition—a view of the California desert backed by snow-capped mountains, a garden landscape with swans in the foreground, a Pacific sunset towards which the broken screen idol swims to his tragic death. Colors of the interiors are soft and subdued.

Story [by William A. Wellman, Robert Carson] relates the experiences of a young girl who rises to cinema fame while her husband, having touched the heights, is on a swift descent. Love is the heroine; alcohol, the villain.

Janet Gaynor gives to her role, the small town girl who makes good, a characterization of sustained loveliness. She is equally as good in the comedy passages.

The same, without reservation, may be said for Fredric March and the manner in which he plays the passe star, Norman Maine. He creates a finely drawn portrait of weakness without viciousness, a demoralization which reminds of George Hurstwood in Theodore Dreiser's novel *Sister Carrie*.

Others in the cast also are excellent, including Adolphe Menjou, who plays a producer; Lionel Stander, as a studio publicity man; Andy Devine, an assistant director, and May Robson.

1937: Best Original Story, Special Award (color cinematography)

NOMINATIONS: Best Picture, Director, Actor (Fredric March), Actress (Janet Gaynor), Screenplay, Assistant Director (Eric Stacey)

•

STAR IS BORN, A
1954, 154 mins, US Ⓥ ⊙ ▭ col
Dir George Cukor ***Prod*** Sidney Luft ***Scr*** Moss Hart ***Ph*** Sam Leavitt ***Ed*** Folmar Blangsted ***Mus*** Ray Heindorf (dir.) ***Art*** Malcolm Bert
Act Judy Garland, James Mason, Jack Carson, Charles Bickford, Tom Noonan, Lucy Marlow (Warner/Transcona)

A Star Is Born was a great 1937 moneymaker, and it's an even greater picture in its filmusical transmutation.

Unfolded in the showmanly adaptation is a strong personal saga which somehow becomes, in a sense, integrated into the celluloid plot. The reel- and the real-life values sometimes play back and forth, in pendulum fashion, and the unspooling is never wanting for heart-wallop and gutsy entertainment values.

Judy Garland glitters with that stardust which in the plot the wastrel star James Mason recognizes. And her loyalties are as Gibraltar amidst the house of cards which periodically seem to collapse around her and upon him.

From the opening drunken debacle at the Shrine benefit to the scandalous antics of a hopeless dipsomaniac when his wife (Garland) wins the Academy Award, there is an intense pattern of real-life mirrorings. Whatever the production delays, which allegedly piled up a near $5 million production cost, the end results are worth it.

[Version reviewed is the original 182-min. premiere one. Pic was subsequently cut to 154 mins. A 1983 partial restoration runs 170 mins.]

1954: NOMINATIONS: Best Actor (James Mason), Actress (Judy Garland), Color Costume Design, Color Art Direction, Scoring of a Musical Picture, Song ("The Man That Got Away")

•

STAR IS BORN, A
1976, 140 mins, US Ⓥ col
Dir Frank Pierson ***Prod*** Jon Peters ***Scr*** John Gregory Dunne, Joan Didion, Frank Pierson ***Ph*** Robert Surtees ***Ed*** Peter Zinner ***Art*** Polly Platt
Act Barbra Streisand, Kris Kristofferson, Paul Mazursky, Gary Busey, Oliver Clark, Vanetta Fields (Warner)

The new *A Star Is Born* has the rare distinction of being a superlative remake. Barbra Streisand's performance as the rising star is her finest screen work to date, while Kris Kristofferson's magnificent portrayal of her failing benefactor realizes all the promise first shown five years earlier in *Cisko Pike*.

Film rightfully credits the original William Wellman–Robert Carson story on which David O. Selznick mounted his 1937 version, the first to use this title. All the familiar plot turns are here, but updated to the spirit of the times.

Plot picks up Kristofferson past his rock superstar prime, unable or unwilling to make his tour commitments, raising hell and alienating people. His success has become a machine, supervised by Paul Mazursky (as a smooth rock music manager), kept in line by Gary Busey, and attended to by Sally Kirkland, Joanne Linville and others who typify the coterie that comes with fame.

Barbra Streisand is discovered in a tacky nitery, singing with Vanetta Fields and Clydie King. There's a lot of music in the film, mostly by Paul Williams and Kenny Ascher, and it's important to note that, while the material is better than the rest, in the context of the story it should be that way.

1976: Best Song ("Evergreen")

NOMINATIONS: Best Cinematography, Adapted Score, Sound

•

STARLIGHT HOTEL
1987, 93 mins, New Zealand Ⓥ ⊙ col
Dir Sam Pillsbury ***Prod*** Finola Dwyer, Larry Parr ***Scr*** Grant Hindin Miller ***Ph*** Warrick Attewell ***Ed*** Mike Horton ***Art*** Mike Beacroft
Act Peter Phelps, Greer Robson, Marshall Napier, The Wizard, Alice Fraser, Patrick Smyth (Challenge)

Starlight Hotel is a road movie [from Grant Hinden Miller's 1986 novel *The Dream Monger*] centering on the friendship between a man on the run from the law and a 13-year-old girl looking for her father. Setting is central South Island in 1930, with farmers forced to leave their land as the Depression bites. Kate (Greer Robson) runs away to try to find her father, who's looking for work in Wellington on the North Island.

She soon encounters Patrick (Peter Phelps), a man whose life was shattered by his experiences in the world war and later when his wife left him. He's wanted by the police for beating a repo man who was taking advantage during the Depression, and is trying to get to a port and then passage to Australia.

All the classic elements of this kind of film are here: jumping on trains, hiding out in barns, making friends and enemies along the way. The film benefits enormously from the charismatic performances in the leads. Phelps, an Aussie actor, gives a rugged, charming performance. Robson, the little girl in *Smash Palace*, has the required toughness and sensitivity for this role.

Title refers to the "hotel" where the runaways sleep: under the stars.

•

STARMAN
1984, 115 mins, US Ⓥ ⊙ ▭ col
Dir John Carpenter ***Prod*** Larry J. Franco ***Scr*** Bruce A. Evans, Raynold Gideon ***Ph*** Donald M. Morgan ***Ed*** Marion Rothman ***Mus*** Jack Nitzsche ***Art*** Daniel Lomino
Act Jeff Bridges, Karen Allen, Charles Martin Smith, Richard Jaeckel, Robert Phalen, Tony Edwards (Columbia-Delphi II)

There is little that is original in *Starman*, but at least it has chosen good models. As amalgam of elements introduced in *Close Encounters of the Third Kind*, *E.T.* and even *The Man Who Fell to Earth*, *Starman* shoots for the miraculous and only partially hits its target.

The Starman (Jeff Bridges) arrives much like E.T.—an alien in a hostile environment—but in an elaborate transformation scene he assumes human form. The body he chooses for his sojourn on Earth happens to belong to the dead husband of Jenny Hayden (Karen Allen) who lives alone in a remote section of Wisconsin.

Bridges and Allen set off on a trip across the country to Arizona where the Starman must make his connection to return home.

1984: NOMINATION: Best Actor (Jeff Bridges)

•

STAR OF MIDNIGHT
1935, 90 mins, US Ⓥ ⊙ b/w
Dir Stephen Roberts ***Prod*** Pandro S. Berman ***Scr*** Howard J. Green, Anthony Veiller, Edward Kaufman ***Ph*** J. Roy Hunt ***Ed*** Arthur Roberts ***Mus*** Max Steiner
Act William Powell, Ginger Rogers, Paul Kelly, Gene Lockhart, Ralph Morgan, Leslie Fenton (RKO)

Star of Midnight is a non-camouflaged follow-up on *The Thin Man* (1934), although made by a different producer [from the novel by Arthur Somers Roche]. It hits a similar merry comedy-drama stride and attains practically the same effectiveness as screen entertainment.

William Powell is once more the happy-go-lucky master sleuth, brought into the case against his wishes and better judgment, but solving it just the same. His romance this time is not so adult, but equally humorous, and, with Ginger Rogers opposite, always interesting.

The mystery is double-barrelled, concerning the disappearance of a show's leading woman and the killing of a Broadway columnist. Powell unravels both in the customary ingenious manner, to the consternation and despite the interference of the regularly assigned policemen. As did Myrna Loy in *Thin Man*, Rogers here helps him considerably. She looks like a million, troupes splendidly and wears a pictureful of class clothes.

Smart dialog containing a good share of genuine laughs keeps Powell and Rogers occupied most of the time when they are not mystery-solving or drinking.

•

STARS AND STRIPES FOREVER
1952, 89 mins, US Ⓥ col
Dir Henry Koster ***Prod*** Lamar Trotti ***Scr*** Lamar Trotti ***Ph*** Charles G. Clarke ***Ed*** James B. Clark ***Mus*** Alfred Newman (dir.)
Act Clifton Webb, Debra Paget, Robert Wagner, Ruth Hussey, Finlay Currie (20th Century-Fox)

As spirited as any march John Philip Sousa ever led, *Stars and Stripes Forever* registers as topnotch entertainment, a kaleidoscopically presented career of the bandmaster. Henry Koster's direction sharpens the nostalgia and emotional bits to be found in the episodic Ernest Vajda screen story based on Sousa's own *Marching Along*.

Enacting the late march king is Clifton Webb. It possibly might not be an accurate Sousa, but it is good Webb. Ruth Hussey is splendid as Mrs. Sousa, a woman who understands and loves a husband who leans to the eccentric.

Generously sprinkled through the footage is a parade of Sousa tunes that start the feet marching.

Story spans his career briskly and reveals his secret desire to create ballads, not marches.

•

STARSHIP TROOPERS
1997, 129 mins, US Ⓥ ⊙ col
Dir Paul Verhoeven ***Prod*** Jon Davison, Alan Marshall ***Scr*** Ed Neumeier ***Ph*** Jost Vacano ***Ed*** Mark Goldblatt, Caroline Ross ***Mus*** Basil Poledouris ***Art*** Allan Cameron
Act Casper Van Dien, Dina Meyer, Denise Richards, Jake Busey, Neil Patrick Harris, Clancy Brown (TriStar/Touchstone)

Human culture and insect culture duel to the death in *Starship Troopers*, a spectacularly gung-ho, sci-fi epic that delivers two hours of good, nasty fun. It is, in the end, a picture about teenagers and giant bugs, but one with enough visual exhiliration and narrative wit to keep one thoroughly on board.

Working from a long-celebrated (and very right-wing) novel by Robert A. Heinlein, *RoboCop* coscripter Ed Neumeier and director Paul Verhoeven start off with a teaser TV transmission from the planet Klendathu, where a military emergency has developed in the worldwide federal government army's battle with the resident arthropods.

Flashing back a year, attention alights upon several good-looking high school seniors. Rich boy Johnny Rico (Casper Van Dien) is disowned by his parents when he enlists in the Mobile Infantry; his girlfriend, Carmen Ibanez (Denise Richards), is heading for the Fleet Academy to become a pilot. Johnny finds himself in basic training with the sultry, ultra-fit Dizzy Flores (Dina Meyer), who has the permanent hots for him.

The federal government, while never described in detail, is clearly of a fascistic nature, underlined by the Nazi-style uniforms. At the one-hour point, the invasion of Klendathu begins, and pic shifts into fifth gear without ever looking back.

The first encounter is a disaster, with some 100,000 dead. The bugs have sucked the brains out of the defeated humans, thereby acquiring all their knowledge. The soldiers are shortly confronted with a blood-chilling spectacle, thousands of warrior bugs descending from the mountains with another brain-drain in mind. The sheer spectacle of the sequence recalls the beginning of the climactic battle in *Zulu*.

Main credit for the insect creations goes to Phil Tippett (*RoboCop*, *Jurassic Park*). The reputed $100 million budget decidedly shows on screen. Young and virtually unknown cast is serviceable, with Van Dien a stalwart lead and Meyer standing out as Dizzy.

1997: NOMINATION: Best Visual Effects

•

STARS LOOK DOWN, THE
1939, 104 mins, UK Ⓥ b/w
Dir Carol Reed ***Prod*** Isadore Goldsmith ***Scr*** J. B. Williams ***Ph*** Mutz Greenbaum ***Ed*** Reginald Beck ***Art*** James Carter
Act Michael Redgrave, Margaret Lockwood, Emlyn Williams, Nancy Price, Edward Rigby, Cecil Parker (Grafton/Grand National)

The Stars Look Down is a visual education on British mining. A picturization of a subject long an uncomfortable wedge in the English social-political scheme, *Stars* would merit laurels alone for a faithful and gripping treatment. But film goes for more; it is a splendid dramatic portrait of those who burrow for the black diamond in England's northland. Direction is of class standing and picture is mounted with exactness of detail and technique.

Adopted from A. J. Cronin's novel of the mining town from where two sons seek different roads to success, one returning to foster misery, the other to fight on for its alleviation, film unrolls at steady pace a wealth of dramatic incident.

There are some gaps where treatment is not on par with dramatic situation. The Emlyn Williams part, the focal point of the tragedy, is underdeveloped, but director Carol Reed has guided well a cast that exacts the utmost generally. Michael Redgrave, as son of the strike-leader (Williams), a ne'er-do-well, and Margaret Lockwood, as a slut, share the starring honors.

•

STAR SPANGLED RHYTHM
1943, 99 mins, US b/w
Dir George Marshall ***Prod*** Joseph Sistrom ***Scr*** Harry Tugend ***Ph*** Leo Tover ***Ed*** Arthur Schmidt ***Mus*** Robert Emmett Dolan
Act Victor Moore, Betty Hutton, Eddie Bracken, Anne Revere, Walter Abel (Paramount)

Except for a few gags and situations, *Rhythm* has essentially nothing new in it. But neither has a Christmas tree. Yet both bring good cheer because of the way they're dressed up. The whole thing, as Harry Tugend has written it and George Marshall directed it, is fresh, alive and full of bounce.

It's a gay and good-humored tune-pic, but on the grand scale, grand because of the personalities who wander in and out of the pic, because of the seven listenable tunes, because of the general lavishness of the production and because of the downright gaiety of the whole affair. Best of all, most of the flock of stars do much better than the usual smile and a couple of lines. Among the names whose contribution to the film deserves more than perfunctory billing are Bing Crosby, Bob Hope, Dorothy Lamour, Paulette Goddard, Veronica Lake, Mary Martin, Victor Moore, Betty Hutton and Eddie Bracken.

Scaffolding for this galaxy is the arrival at San Pedro of Bracken and a pile of his navy shipmates. Bracken's father (Victor Moore) is a former hoss opry star who's now a gateman at the Paramount lot. Rather than disclose this comedown to Bracken, Hutton convinces Moore that he should say he's head of the studio. Bracken thereupon brings his shipmates to the lot (promising each of them a 24-karat Par blonde) and Moore has to attempt to play the big-shot that his son has billed him.

1943: NOMINATIONS: Best Scoring of a Musical Picture, Song ("Black Magic")

•

STAR STRUCK
1982, 102 mins, Australia Ⓥ ⊙ col
Dir Gillian Armstrong ***Prod*** David Elfick, Richard Brennan ***Scr*** Stephen Maclean ***Ph*** Russell Boyd ***Ed*** Nicholas Beauman ***Mus*** Mark Moffatt ***Art*** Brian Thomson
Act Jo Kennedy, Ross O'Donovan, Pat Evison, Margo Lee, Max Cullen, Ned Lander (Palm Beach)

Picture is a raucous, "let's put on a show" musical with a punk rock beat. Story centers on an enterprising 14-year-old entrepreneur, Ross O'Donovan, who has big career plans for his cousin, singer Jo Kennedy. Grooming (?) her in the punk mode, O'Donovan has his sights on copping first prize on a New Year's television talent show.

However, he can't get the attention of a powerful Sydney disk jockey until he stages a daring balancing tightrope stunt for Kennedy. Suddenly, she's a media star quickly homogenized for home consumption.

Meanwhile, the family hotel-bar is on the verge of bankruptcy. The $25,000 talent prize becomes all-important to save the failing establishment.

Script is pure fantasy material offering director Gillian Armstrong the opportunity to send up the likes of Busby Berkeley and Garland-Rooney musicals. The film certainly doesn't lack energy. Camerawork by Russell Boyd is glossy and fluid, and song-and-dance routines are loud and splashy. Regrettably, the choreography is uninspired.

•

STARTING OVER
1979, 106 mins, US Ⓥ ⊙ col
Dir Alan J. Pakula ***Prod*** Alan J. Pakula ***Scr*** James L. Brooks ***Ph*** Sven Nykvist ***Ed*** Marion Rothman ***Mus*** Marvin Hamlisch ***Art*** George Jenkins
Act Burt Reynolds, Jill Clayburgh, Candice Bergen, Charles Durning, Frances Sternhagen, Austin Pendleton (Paramount/Brook)

Starting Over takes on the subject of marital dissolution from a comic point of view, and succeeds admirably, wryly directed by Alan J. Pakula, and featuring an outstanding cast.

In fact, *Starting Over* [from the novel by Dan Wakefield] favorably evokes the screwball comedies of the 1930s and the heyday of American screen comedy.

Burt Reynolds plays a mild-mannered writer unwillingly foisted into a "liberated" condition by spouse Candice Bergen, feeling her feminine oats as a songwriter. Fleeing to Boston and protection of relatives Charles Durning and Frances Sternhagen, he meets spinster schoolteacher Jill Clayburgh, and the off-and-on romance begins.

With unfailing comic timing Reynolds is the core of the film, and underplays marvellously.

1979: NOMINATIONS: Best Actress (Jill Clayburgh), Supp. Actress (Candice Bergen)

•

STAR TREK: FIRST CONTACT
1996, 110 mins, US Ⓥ ⊙ ▭ col
Dir Jonathan Frakes ***Prod*** Rick Berman ***Scr*** Brannon Braga, Ronald D. Moore ***Ph*** Matthew F. Leonetti ***Ed*** John W. Wheeler ***Mus*** Jerry Goldsmith ***Art*** Herman Zimmerman
Act Patrick Stewart, Jonathan Frakes, Brent Spiner, Gates McFadden, Marina Sirtis, Alice Krige (Paramount)

The Borgs are back, the future is in peril—and the *Star Trek* mythos proceeds apace. A smashingly exciting sci-fi adventure that ranks among the very best in the long-running Paramount franchise, this is one TV spinoff that does not require ticketbuyers to come equipped with an intimate knowledge of the small-screen original. It is also the first *Star Trek* movie to feature no one from the late Gene Roddenberry's original 1966-69 series.

Written with considerable input from producer and TV's *Star Trek—The Next Generation* veteran Rick Berman, *First Contact* actually is a sequel to *The Best of Both Worlds*, a popular two-part episode from *Next Generation*. Capt. Picard (Patrick Stewart) was captured and very nearly "assimilated" by the Borg, a marauding race of half-organic, half-robotic cyborgs, and as *First Contact* begins, he continues to be troubled by Borg bogeymen in his nightmares.

[After an opening battle,] several of the Borg escape and head to Earth, where they hope to gain control of the "present"—i.e., the 24th century—by sabotaging the past. Even more unfortunately, some other Borg manage to board the USS *Enterprise*, and set out to assimilate the entire crew for the greater good of their Borg Queen (Alice Krige).

More jarring is the way *First Contact* introduces horror-film elements to a traditional *Star Trek* plot. Much of the violence is heavily influenced by *Alien* and *Aliens*. Purists who recall Roddenberry's original vision of a less blood-soaked universe may be put off.

Stewart once again comports himself with all the gravity and panache you would expect from a Shakespearean-trained actor. Special-effects wizardry is by far the most elaborate seen in a *Star Trek* film.

1996: NOMINATION: Best Makeup (Michael Westmore, Scott Wheeler, Jake Garber)

•

STAR TREK V
THE FINAL FRONTIER
1989, 106 mins, US Ⓥ ⊙ ▭ col
Dir William Shatner ***Prod*** Harve Bennett ***Scr*** David Loughery ***Ph*** Andrew Laszlo ***Ed*** Peter Berger ***Mus*** Jerry Goldsmith ***Art*** Herman Zimmerman
Act William Shatner, Leonard Nimoy, DeForest Kelley, James Doohan, Nichelle Nichols, George Takei (Paramount)

Even die-hard Trekkies may be disappointed by *Star Trek V*. Coming after Leonard Nimoy's delightful directorial outing on *Star Trek IV*, William Shatner's inauspicious feature directing debut is a double letdown.

A major flaw in the story [by Shatner, Harve Bennett and David Loughery] is that it centers on an obsessive quest by a character who isn't a member of the Enterprise crew, a renegade Vulcan played by Laurence Luckinbill in Kabuki-like makeup. The crazed Luckinbill kidnaps the crew and makes them fly to a never-before-visited planet at the center of the galaxy in quest for the meaning of life.

Better they should have stayed home and watched reruns of the TV series, which had a lot more to say about the meaning of life.

Shatner rises to the occasion, however, in directing a dramatic sequence of the mystical Luckinbill teaching Nimoy and DeForest Kelley to re-experience their long-buried traumas. The re-creations of Spock's rejection by his father after his birth and Kelley's euthanasia of his own father are moving highlights.

•

STAR TREK IV
THE VOYAGE HOME
1986, 119 mins, US Ⓥ ⊙ ▭ col
Dir Leonard Nimoy ***Prod*** Harve Bennett ***Scr*** Harve Bennett, Steve Meerson, Peter Krikes, Nicholas Meyer ***Ph*** Don Peterman ***Ed*** Peter E. Berger ***Mus*** Leonard Rosenman ***Art*** Jack T. Collis
Act William Shatner, Leonard Nimoy, DeForest Kelley, James Doohan, Catherine Hicks, George Takei (Bennett)

Latest excursion is warmer, wittier, more socially relevant and truer to its TV origins than prior odysseys.

This voyage finds the crew earthbound, but they find the galaxy dark and messages from Earth distorted. Spock locates the source of the trouble in the bleating, eerie sounds of an unidentified probe and links them to a cry from the

Earth's past that has long been silenced. Scripters employ successful use of time travel.

Spock (Leonard Nimoy) and Kirk (William Shatner) play off each other in a sort of deadpan futuristic version of Hope and Crosby with Nimoy, surprisingly, as the awkward one relying on Shatner's smooth talking to win the help of a zealous save-the-whales biologist (Catherine Hicks) in capturing a couple of specimens.

●

STAR TREK
GENERATIONS

1994, 118 mins, US Ⓥ ⊙ ▭ col

Dir David Carson ***Prod*** Rick Berman ***Scr*** Ronald D. Moore, Brannon Braga ***Ph*** John Alonzo ***Ed*** Peter Berger ***Mus*** Dennis McCarthy ***Art*** Herman Zimmerman

Act Patrick Stewart, William Shatner, Malcolm McDowell, Jonathan Frakes, Brent Spiner, Whoopi Goldberg (Paramount)

It may not "boldly go where no one has gone before," but *Star Trek Generations* has enough verve, imagination and familiarity to satisfy three decades' worth of Trekkers raised on several incarnations of the television skein.

The story [by Rick Berman, Ronald D. Moore and Brannon Braga] begins at a PR-event maiden voyage of a "New" *Enterprise*, with Kirk (William Shatner), engineer Scott (James Doohan) and Chekov (Walter Koenig) aboard as honored guests and living relics of the Starfleet. (Leonard Nimoy opted out of this voyage.) When a distress signal summons the craft into action, the combination of an inexperienced captain and a not yet fully equipped craft add up to catastrophe and the end, albeit heroic, of Kirk.

Four generations after the disaster, the "Next" crew receives an emergency call to throw a lifeline to scientists on an experimental probe. A survivor, rec center barkeep Guinan (Whoopi Goldberg), tells Capt. Picard (Patrick Stewart) of the Nexus, a mysterious ribbon of energy. To regain its nirvana, fellow survivor Soran (Malcolm McDowell) is willing to do anything, including aligning with malevolent Klingons.

Star Trek Generations is primarily about stopping the proverbial mad scientist run amok. Its secondary concern, which makes Kirk's resuscitation necessary, is Picard's personal crisis in weighing duty against the need for family—blood-related and otherwise.

Shatner and Doohan have mastered the art of playing their roles while providing sly self-commentary. The others have not quite reached that level of acting enlightenment, but give them a few more voyages and they'll be able to make the Vulcan yellow pages entertaining.

Director David Carson, a small-screen *Trek* vet, does well, not brilliantly, in the widescreen arena. Carson scores best in capturing the *Star Trek* look, though he tends to linger too long in recording those achievements.

●

STAR TREK
INSURRECTION

1998, 100 mins, US Ⓥ ⊙ ▭ col

Dir Jonathan Frakes ***Prod*** Rick Berman ***Scr*** Michael Piller ***Ph*** Matthew F. Leonetti ***Ed*** Peter E. Berger ***Mus*** Jerry Goldsmith ***Art*** Herman Zimmerman

Act Patrick Stewart, Jonathan Frakes, Brent Spiner, Michael Dorn, F. Murray Abraham, Anthony Zerbe (Paramount)

The *Star Trek* feature franchise continues apace with a ninth installment aimed primarily at an audience of faithful fans. Entry is a distinct comedown after the smashingly exciting *First Contact* and plays less like a stand-alone sci-fi adventure than an expanded episode of *Star Trek—The Next Generation*.

The Ba'ku, peaceful inhabitants of an idyllic planet, are in clear and present danger of forced relocation, thanks to an ends-justify-means alliance between Federation leaders and their new allies, the aging Son'a. Capt. Jean-Luc Picard (Patrick Stewart) leads the *Enterprise* crew to the Ba'ku planet and discovers that the 600 or so inhabitants, thanks to metaphasic radiation, remain eternally youthful.

The age-reversal magic is a mixed blessing for the *Enterprise* crew. Cmdr. Riker (Jonathan Frakes) and Lt. Cmdr. Troi (Marina Sirtis) get frisky in a candlelit bath, while Picard is briefly seized with an uncontrollable urge to mambo. No kidding.

Ru'afro (F. Murray Abraham), the seriously hideous leader of the Son'a, wants to remove the Ba'ku from their planet so his people can gain control of the metaphasic radiation. Defying direct Federation orders, Picard leads the *Enterprise* officers in a defense of the Ba'ku.

Working from a serviceable script [from a screen story by coscripter Michael Piller and Rick Berman], director-actor Jonathan Frakes maintains a brisk pace and generates a satisfying amount of excitement. Unfortunately, it's not always easy to make sense of what people are doing—and how they're able to do it—during the frenzied hurly-burly of the final half-hour.

Even when things get most confusing, however, the lead players manage to easily carry the audience along. Tech values are in keeping with the franchise's high standards.

●

STAR TREK VI
THE UNDISCOVERED COUNTRY

1991, 109 mins, US Ⓥ ⊙ ▭ col

Dir Nicholas Meyer ***Prod*** Ralph Winter, Steven-Charles Jaffe ***Scr*** Nicholas Meyer, Denny Martin Flinn ***Ph*** Hiro Narita ***Ed*** Ronald Roose, William Hoy ***Mus*** Cliff Eidelman ***Art*** Herman Zimmerman

Act William Shatner, Leonard Nimoy, DeForest Kelley, Kim Cattrall, David Warner, Christopher Plummer (Paramount)

Weighed down by a midsection even flabbier than the long-in-the-tooth cast, director Nicholas Meyer still delivers enough of what *Trek* auds hunger for to justify the trek to the local multiplex.

Following a Chernobyl-like disaster, a Klingon leader seeks peace with the Federation, the Klingon economy and environment having been depleted by constant warring—a not-at-all-veiled parable for the end of the Cold War. Kirk and Co. are sent, reluctantly, to escort the leader to peace talks on earth, but conspirators seek to scuttle the détente by assassinating him and pinning the blame on the *Enterprise*.

Unfortunately, the murder is a rather tepid mystery and the ice planet to which Kirk and McCoy travel feels like a pale imitation of the *Star Wars* films. Pace and visual trappings pick up considerably in the final frames, when the Enterprise rides to the rescue of the peace talks, in the process dueling with a Klingon vessel.

Meyer and coscripter Denny Martin Flinn [working from a story by Leonard Nimoy, Lawrence Konner and Mark Rosenthal] also have loaded the film with sentimental touches. (Why Christian Slater turns up in an uncredited cameo is anybody's guess.) Cliff Eidelman's terrific score manages to stand on its own yet still evoke earlier work associated with the pics and series. Sappy ending provides a fitting send-off (and ridiculously literal sign-off) to the groundbreaking series and its rabid fans, reinforcing its humanistic messages and fairy-tale trappings. [Pic is dedicated to creator Gene Roddenberry who died in 1991.]

1991: NOMINATIONS: Best Sound Effects Editing, Makeup

●

STAR TREK
THE MOTION PICTURE

1979, 132 mins, US Ⓥ ⊙ ▭ col

Dir Robert Wise ***Prod*** Gene Roddenberry ***Scr*** Harold Livingston ***Ph*** Richard H. Kline ***Ed*** Todd Ramsay ***Mus*** Jerry Goldsmith ***Art*** Harold Michelson

Act William Shatner, Leonard Nimoy, DeForest Kelley, Stephen Collins, James Doohan, Persis Khambatta (Paramount)

Producer Gene Roddenberry and director Robert Wise have corralled an enormous technical crew, and the result is state-of-the-art screen magic. Screenplay [based on a screen story by Alan Dean Foster] makes the most of its audience's familiarity with the long-running TV series [1966-69, 78 episodes] in this tale of people and gadgetry.

The *Enterprise* has been completely reconditioned during a two-year drydock, but must be prematurely dispatched to intercept an earthbound attacker destroying everything in its wake. William Shatner's Kirk is told to lead the mission along with other show regulars.

Upshot is a search-and-destroy thriller that includes all of the ingredients the TV show's fans thrive on: the philosophical dilemma wrapped in a scenario of mind control, troubles with the space ship, the dependable and understanding Kirk, the ever-logical Spock, and suspenseful take with twist ending. Touches of romance and corn also dot this voyage, natch.

But the expensive effects (under supervision of Douglas Trumbull) are the secret of this film, and the amazing wizardry throughout would appear to justify the whopping budget. Jerry Goldsmith's brassy score is the other necessary plus.

[An extended TV and homevideo version runs 143 mins.]

1979: NOMINATIONS: Best Art Direction, Original Score, Visual Effects

●

STAR TREK III
THE SEARCH FOR SPOCK

1984, 105 mins, US Ⓥ ⊙ ▭ col

Dir Leonard Nimoy ***Prod*** Harve Bennett ***Scr*** Harve Bennett ***Ph*** Charles Correll ***Ed*** Robert F. Shugrue ***Mus*** James Horner, Alexander Courage ***Art*** John E. Chilberg II

Act William Shatner, DeForest Kelley, James Doohan, George Takei, Walter Koenig, Leonard Nimoy (Paramount)

Star Trek III is an emotionally satisfying science fiction adventure. Dovetailing neatly with the previous entry in the popular series, *Star Trek II*, film centers upon a quest to bring Spock (Leonard Nimoy), the noble science officer and commander who selflessly gave his life to save "the many," back to life.

Spock's friend, Admiral Kirk (William Shatner), is visited by Spock's Vulcan father (Mark Lenard), who informs him that Spock's living spirit may still be alive via a mind-meld with one of Kirk's crew and must be taken to the planet Vulcan to be preserved.

Kirk discovers who the "possessed" crew member is, and with his other shipmates, steals the *Enterprise* out of its dock and sets off for Vulcan.

1986: NOMINATIONS: Best Cinematography, Original Score, Sound, Sound Effects Editing

●

STAR TREK II
THE WRATH OF KHAN

1982, 113 mins, US Ⓥ ⊙ ▭ col

Dir Nicholas Meyer ***Prod*** Robert Sallin ***Scr*** Jack B. Sowards ***Ph*** Gayne Rescher ***Ed*** William P. Dornisch ***Mus*** James Horner, Alexander Courage ***Art*** Joseph R. Jennings

Act William Shatner, Leonard Nimoy, DeForest Kelley, Ricardo Montalban, James Doohan, Walter Koenig (Paramount)

Star Trek II is a very satisfying space adventure, closer in spirit and format to the popular TV series than to its big-budget predecessor.

Story is nominally a sequel to the TV episode *Space Seed*, with Starship *Reliant* Captain Terrell (Paul Winfield) and Commander Chekov (Walter Koenig) incorrectly landing on a planet on an exploration mission. This allows the evil Khan (Ricardo Montalban), who was marooned there with his family and crew 15 years before by Kirk (William Shatner), to take over the *Reliant* and vow revenge on Kirk.

Admiral Kirk is coaxed to take command once again of the Starship *Enterprise* on a training mission, travels to the Regula space station on a rescue mission. Dr. Carol Marcus (Bibi Besch) and her (and Kirk's) son David (Merritt Butrick) have been working there on the Genesis Project, to convert barren planets into Eden-like sources of life. Khan has stolen the Genesis Effect equipment.

Final reel is a classic of emotional manipulation: Spock unhesitatingly calculates that he must sacrifice himself to save the *Enterprise* crew.

●

STAR WARS

1977, 121 mins, US Ⓥ ⊙ ▭ col

Dir George Lucas ***Prod*** Gary Kurtz ***Scr*** George Lucas ***Ph*** Gilbert Taylor ***Ed*** Paul Hirsch, Marcia Lucas, Richard Chew ***Mus*** John Williams ***Art*** John Barry

Act Mark Hamill, Harrison Ford, Carrie Fisher, Peter Cushing, Alec Guinness, Anthony Daniels (20th Century-Fox)

Star Wars is a magnificent film. George Lucas set out to make the biggest possible adventure fantasy out of his memories of serials and older action epics, and he succeeded brilliantly. Lucas and producer Gary Kurtz assembled an enormous technical crew, drawn from the entire Hollywood production pool of talent, and the results equal the genius of Walt Disney, Willis O'Brien and other justifiably famous practitioners of what Irwin Allen calls "movie magic."

The story is an engaging space adventure that takes itself seriously while occasionally admitting an affectionate poke at the genre. The most immediate frame of reference is Flash Gordon, but it's more than that; it's an Errol Flynn escapist adventure.

The superb balance of technology and human drama is one of the many achievements: one identifies with the characters and accepts, as do they, the intriguing intergalactic world in which they live.

Carrie Fisher is delightful as the regal but spunky princess on a rebel planet who has been kidnapped by Peter Cushing, would-be ruler of the universe. Mark Hamill, previously a TV player, is excellent as a farm boy who sets out to rescue Fisher in league with Alec Guinness, last survivor of a band of noble knights. Harrison Ford is outstanding as a likeable mercenary pilot.

Both Guinness and Cushing bring the right measure of majesty to their opposite characters. One of Cushing's key aides is played by David Prowse, destined to a fatal duel with Guinness, with whom he shares mystical powers. Prowse's face is concealed behind frightening black armor. James Earl Jones, unbilled, provides a note of sonorous menace as

Prowse's voice. Anthony Daniels and Kenny Baker play a Mutt-and-Jeff team of kooky robots [C-3PO and R2-D2].

Locations in Tunisia, Death Valley, Guatemala and Africa were utilized, and interiors were shot at EMI's British studios where the terrific score was also recorded. But the technical effects were all done in California.

Lucas's first feature, *THX 1138*, was also futuristic in tone, but there the story emphasis was on machines controlling man. In *Star Wars* the people remain the masters of the hardware.

[In January 1997 an "improved" version was released theatrically in the U.S., with remixed sound, added digital effects and some brief extra scenes, including one showing Jabba the Hutt.]

1977: Best Art Direction, Sound, Original Score, Editing, Costume Design, Visual Effects, Special Achievement Award (sound effects)

NOMINATIONS: Best Picture, Supp. Actor (Alec Guinness), Original Screenplay

•

STAR WARS: EPISODE I THE PHANTOM MENACE
1999, 133 mins, US col
Dir George Lucas ***Prod*** Rick McCallum ***Scr*** George Lucas ***Ph*** David Tattersall ***Ed*** Paul Martin Smith ***Mus*** John Williams ***Art*** Gavin Bocquet
Act Liam Neeson, Ewan McGregor, Natalie Portman, Jake Lloyd, Pernilla August, Frank Oz (Lucasfilm/20th Century-Fox)

At heart a fanciful and fun movie for young boys, the first installment of George Lucas's three-part prequel to the original *Star Wars* trilogy is always visually diverting thanks to the technical wizardry. But it is neither captivating nor transporting, for it lacks any emotional pull, as well as the sense of wonder and awe that marks the best works of sci-fi/fantasy.

Action is set a generation prior to *Star Wars*, a period of weakness and bureaucratic squabbling in the Republic, and initial conflict is triggered by a ruthless decision by the enormous Trade Federation to invade the peaceful planet of Naboo, ruled by a teenage queen, Amidala (Natalie Portman).

Critical to Naboo's chances are the Jedi Master Qui-Gon Jinn (Liam Neeson) and his somewhat undisciplined apprentice, Obi-Wan Kenobi (Ewan McGregor), played by Alec Guinness in *Star Wars*. Rescuing the queen, the Jedi warriors become stranded on the desert planet of Tatooine, where they encounter a nine-year-old boy named Anakin Skywalker. The kid makes a profound impression upon Qui-Gon Jinn, who begins to suspect the boy is the Chosen One and will one day bring balance to the Force.

The layover on Tatooine includes, at roughly the film's halfway point, what is arguably its action/effects highlight, a pod race, the sci-fi equivalent of *Ben-Hur*'s chariot race. Effect is as comparable to a videogame as to a movie sequence.

As the story zigzags through its second hour, even more characters and creatures are introduced. The new CGI characters are notably lacking in charm or interest, other than on the design level.

Neeson's Zenlike samurai is a basically stolid guy with only moderate charisma. McGregor's Obi-Wan is relegated to second-banana status, but does register some subtle echoes of Guinness's vocal inflections.

1999: NOMINATIONS: Best Sound, Sound Effects Editing, Visual Effects

•

STATE AND MAIN
2000, 106 mins, US col
Dir David Mamet ***Prod*** Sarah Green ***Scr*** David Mamet ***Ph*** Oliver Stapleton ***Ed*** Barbara Tulliver ***Mus*** Theodore Shapiro ***Art*** Gemma Jackson
Act Alec Baldwin, Charles Durning, Philip Seymour Hoffman, Patti LuPone, William H. Macy, Sarah Jessica Parker, David Paymer, Rebecca Pidgeon (Green-Renzi/Fine Line)

With *State and Main*, his lucky seventh stint in the director's chair, David Mamet stands at the intersection of art-house and mainstream. A bona fide populist laffer in which a beleagured and obnoxiously frazzled film crew plays havoc with the citizens of a tiny New England burg—and vice versa—on the eve of a shoot, saucy and eccentric pic immediately joins the rarefied pantheon of fast-paced and salty screwball comedies about showbiz and the sort of person attracted to it, right up there with Preston Sturges' *Sullivan's Travels* and Billy Wilder's *Kiss Me Stupid*.

Fresh from being run out of their New Hampshire location after leading man Bob Barrenger (Alec Baldwin) is caught with another in a series of underaged girls ("Everybody needs a hobby," he explains with vacuous sincerity), no-nonsense vet helmer Walt Price (William H. Macy) and his pre-production crew land in the small, quasi-picturesque town of Waterford, Vermont, on the promise of an authentic structure to feature in their new opus, *The Old Mill*. Problem is, the mill burned down decades ago. Price leans on timid first-time screenwriter Joseph Turner White (Philip Seymour Hoffman) to alter the script, unaware that the idealistic scribbler, who got the job on the strength of a play he wrote called *Anguish*, lives up to that title.

White is nurtured through his *Barton Fink*-ish crisis by local bookseller Ann Black (Rebecca Pidgeon), a serenely spunky townie. Meanwhile, Price ensconces himself in the town's inn and begins making everyone around him miserable. He's soon joined in this alliance by vicious producer Marty Rossen (David Paymer).

Rich with situational humor and laced with a nonstop barrage of often out-of-nowhere barbs aimed at everything from dot-com startups and the electoral college to the true purpose of men's ties and the meaninglessness of the associate producer credit, Mamet's script takes the rat-a-tat dialogue he's known for and applies it to the tenets of screwball comedy, with spectacular results.

As with all inhabitants of the Mamet universe who aren't victims, these players are ruthless, insensitive cold-blooded monsters in single-minded pursuit of the next score or hustle. What's different is the sheer triviality of their enterprise here and the writer's obvious affection for it; White talks of the "quest for purity" at the heart of his material, when from all available evidence pic's well on its way to becoming a severely conflicted piece of Hollywood claptrap.

•

STATE FAIR
1933, 80 mins, US b/w
Dir Henry King ***Prod*** Winfield Sheehan ***Scr*** Paul Green, Sonya Levien ***Ph*** Hal Mohr ***Ed*** R. W. Bischoff ***Mus*** Ray Flynn ***Art*** Duncan Cramer
Act Will Rogers, Janet Gaynor, Lew Ayres, Sally Eilers, Norman Foster, Louise Dresser (Fox)

Based on Phil Stong's bestseller written around a country fair, Henry King has nicely caught the spirit of the simple story and has turned in a production that has the charm of naturalness and the virtue of sincerity.

No villain, little suspense, but a straightforward story of a rural family who find their great moments at the state fair, where paterfamilias captures the title for his prize hog, the mother makes a clean sweep in the pickle entries, the boy gets his first vicarious but satisfying taste of romance, and the girl finds a more lasting love.

Of chief interest is the debut of a new romance team in Janet Gaynor and Lew Ayres. His rather flippant style gives a needed tang to situations that sometimes in the past have been too saccharine. It is a charming romance between these two. There is interest, too, in the less wholesome romance of the boy with the girl of the acrobatic act. Norman Foster and Sally Eilers handle this capably, while there is just enough of Will Rogers's quaint humor and Louise Dresser's country dame to temper the more hectic moments.

For a moment Victor Jory steals the screen as the concession owner who gypped young Frake (Foster) the year before and smilingly prepares to repeat, only to find that his erstwhile victim has spent the twelve-month interval in practising to ring the prizes and is practically a dead shot. There is even a humorous twist to the porcine romance of Blue Boy, the prize hog, who comes to life only when he meets Esmeralda, the red-headed sow.

1932/33: NOMINATIONS: Best Picture, Adaptation

•

STATE FAIR
1945, 100 mins, US
Dir Walter Lang ***Prod*** William Perlberg ***Scr*** Oscar Hammerstein II ***Ph*** Leon Shamroy ***Ed*** J. Watson Webb ***Mus*** Alfred Newman, Charles Henderson (dirs.) ***Art*** Lyle R. Wheeler, Lewis Creber
Act Jeanne Crain, Dana Andrews, Dick Haymes, Vivian Blaine, Charles Winninger, Fay Bainter (20th Century-Fox)

The Philip Stong novel, which Oscar Hammerstein II authored for the latest screen version [adapted by Sonya Levien and Paul Green], is still a boy-meets-girl yarn that has lost none of the flavor of the years. And notably distinctive in the telling is the frequent punctuation of the story by the Rodgers-Hammerstein tunes [written specifically for the film]. Otherwise, the yarn is still the one of Midwest rustication, concerning mainly the hoopla attendant to the annual state fair, at which products, from pickles to hogs, are displayed for judging and prizes.

Jeanne Crain and Dick Haymes are the Frake progeny, and Dana Andrews is the newspaper reporter who covers the fair and is the other half of the Crain romantic attachment. Haymes and Blaine handle the other romantic situation. Fay Bainter is the mother.

The film's top tune is "That's for Me," featured by Vivian Blaine in a bandstand sequence. It's a sock ballad. Not too far behind is another, "It Might as Well Be Spring," sung by Crain. "It's a Grand Night for Singing," by Haymes, is another. The tunes are whammo from both lyrical and melody content, made evident by the allotment of one to each of the three singing principals.

1945: Best Song ("It Might as Well Be Spring")

NOMINATION: Best Scoring of a Musical Picture

•

STATE FAIR
1962, 118 mins, US col
Dir Jose Ferrer ***Prod*** Charles Brackett ***Scr*** Richard Breen ***Ph*** William C. Mellor ***Ed*** David Bretherton ***Mus*** Alfred Newman (arr.) ***Art*** Jack Martin Smith, Walter M. Simonds
Act Pat Boone, Bobby Darin, Pamela Tiffin, Ann-Margret, Tom Ewell, Alice Faye (20th Century-Fox)

This marks the third time around (1933, 1945) on the screen for this vehicle. To the five original R-H refrains retained in this version, five new numbers with both music and lyrics by Richard Rodgers have been added. The old songs are still charming, but they are not rendered with quite the zest and feeling of the 1945 cast.

Richard Breen's updated, reset (from Iowa to Texas) scenario isn't otherwise appreciably altered from the last time out. Same three love affairs are there (involving four people and two Hampshire hogs). Same brandy-spiked mince meat episode. Fairgrounds, however, have been switched to Dallas, and there's something crass and antisceptic about the atmosphere—a significant loss.

None of the four young stars comes off especially well. Pat Boone and Bobby Darin emerge rather bland and unappealing. Pamela Tiffin's range of expression seems rather narrow on this occasion. Of the four, Ann-Margret makes perhaps the most vivid impression, particularly during her torrid song-dance rendition of "Isn't It Kind of Fun," the film's big production number.

•

STATE OF GRACE
1990, 134 mins, US col
Dir Phil Joanou ***Prod*** Ned Dowd, Randy Ostrow, Ron Rotholz ***Scr*** Dennis McIntyre ***Ph*** Jordan Cronenweth ***Ed*** Claire Simpson ***Mus*** Ennio Morricone ***Art*** Patrizia Von Brandenstein, Doug Kraner
Act Sean Penn, Ed Harris, Gary Oldman, Robin Wright, John Turturro, Burgess Meredith (Cinehaus/Orion)

State of Grace is a handsomely produced, mostly riveting, but ultimately overlong and overindulgent gangster picture.

Sean Penn plays Terry, one of New York's Irish residents who grew up in Hell's Kitchen with his friends, brothers Frankie (Ed Harris) and Jackie (Gary Oldman) and their sister, Kathleen (Robin Wright), with whom he was once in love.

Terry's been away from New York for 12 years, but now he returns and signs up with the Irish mob headed by the ruthless Frankie. He also resumes his passionate relationship with Kathleen. Terry isn't all he seems, and in fact he's an undercover cop assigned to get the goods on Frankie.

Penn is excellent as Terry, who drinks too much and who ultimately gets too personally involved with his mission. Harris is a malevolent Frankie, who carries out his executions personally. Oldman is suitably manic as the unstable younger brother. Wright, though she gives a glowing performance as Kathleen, seems to belong to an altogether different movie.

•

STATE OF THE UNION
(U.K.: THE WORLD AND HIS WIFE)
1948, 121 mins, US b/w
Dir Frank Capra ***Prod*** Frank Capra ***Scr*** Anthony Veiller, Myles Connolly ***Ph*** George J. Folsey ***Ed*** William Hornbeck ***Mus*** Victor Young ***Art*** Cedric Gibbons, Urie McCleary
Act Spencer Tracy, Katharine Hepburn, Van Johnson, Angela Lansbury, Adolphe Menjou, Lewis Stone (M-G-M/Liberty)

The hit Broadway play by Howard Lindsay and Russel Crouse has been expanded somewhat in the screen adaptation, a broadening that makes the best use of screen technique. Dialog has headline freshness, and a stinging bite when directed at politicians, the normal voter and the election scene.

Plot deals with a power-mad femme newspaper publisher who picks up a self-made plane magnate and shoves him towards the White House to satisfy her own interests. The candidate begins to lose his common sense when the political malarkey soaks in and only is saved by his frank and honest wife.

Cast is loaded with stalwarts who deliver in top form. The fact is that it's pat casting only helps to insure the payoff. Spencer Tracy fits his personality to the role of the airplane manufacturer who becomes a presidential aspirant. It's a sock performance. Katharine Hepburn makes much of the role of Tracy's wife, giving it understanding and warmth that register big. Van Johnson shines as the columnist turned political press agent. It's one of his better performances.

Capra's direction punches over the pictorial exposé of U.S. politics and candidate manufacturers, the indifference of the average voter, and the need for more expression of true public opinion at the polls.

●

STATION SIX-SAHARA

1964, 97 mins, UK b/w

Dir Seth Holt ***Prod*** Victor Lyndon ***Scr*** Bryan Forbes, Brian Clemens ***Ph*** Gerald Gibbs ***Ed*** Alastair McIntyre ***Mus*** Ron Grainer ***Art*** Jack Stephens

Act Carroll Baker, Peter Van Eyck, Ian Bannen, Denholm Elliott, Jorg Felmy, Mario Adorf (Allied Artists)

Station Six-Sahara is a sex melodrama [from the play, *Men without a Past*, by Jacques Maret], filmed in the Libyan desert with Carroll Baker. Story premise of a sexpot arriving at an isolated desert oil pipeline station where five lonely men have only one thing in common—the nagging need for a woman—is generally well developed.

Good interest is early sustained despite fact that Baker does not appear for first forty-two minutes. Limited confines of the rude station settings puts emphasis strictly upon yarn unfoldment and permits director Seth Holt to display his helming mettle while audience awaits entrance of femme star, only woman in cast. With her entry into plot, when a car roars out of the night and eager hands, after it crashes, lift her seductive figure out of the wreckage, attention picks up perceptibly as the men react in varying degrees and kind to her presence.

Baker, in what amounts actually to a smaller role, feelingly delineates this key character and makes her work count. Peter Van Eyck, in charge of the station, which he operates with typical cold Teutonic efficiency, is smooth and convincing. Jorg Felmy, another German with icy self-control, underplays his role for excellent effect. Ian Bannen, a Scotsman with a sour sense of humor, and Denholm Elliott, a paper-spined Englishman who lives on memories of the desert war in World War II, persuasively portray their respective parts.

●

STAVISKY . . .

1974, 115 mins, France/Italy Ⓥ col

Dir Alain Resnais ***Prod*** Alexandre Mnouchkine, Georges Dancigers (exec.) ***Scr*** Jorge Semprun ***Ph*** Sacha Vierny ***Ed*** Albert Jurgenson ***Mus*** Stephen Sondheim ***Art*** Jacques Saulnier

Act Jean-Paul Belmondo, Francois Perier, Anny Duperey, Michel Lonsdale, Roberto Bisacco, Claude Rich (Cerito/Ariane/Euro International)

This is an elegant, arresting film about the times and charm of a swindler who actually existed and almost brought down the French Third Republic in the 1930s.

And it is the era that seems to fascinate Alain Resnais as he dotes on the shiny opulence, sensual modes of living, with the psychology of his successful but ultimately sacrificed hero or anti-hero being mirrored by those around him as their testimony at a governmental inquest committee after his suicide or murder is intercut within the film.

Political substance is there, for it was written by Jorge *(Z)* Semprun, but all is bathed in a study of a driving charm that turned an immigrant Jewish boy (Jean-Paul Belmondo) from a small-time embezzler with a prison record into the most dazzling of economic operators who was discarded by disclosures of some of his frauds.

Belmondo is excellent, Charles Boyer is efficient as a ruined nobleman who is his friend and frontman, and Anny Duperey gracefully reveals an almost archetypal embodiment of the beauties who became Paris centers of admiration and following.

●

STAY HUNGRY

1976, 102 mins, US Ⓥ ⊙ col

Dir Bob Rafelson ***Prod*** Harold Schneider ***Scr*** Charles Gaines, Bob Rafelson ***Ph*** Victor Kemper ***Ed*** John F. Link II ***Mus*** Bruce Langhorne ***Art*** Toby Carr Rafelson

Act Jeff Bridges, Sally Field, Arnold Schwarzenegger, R. G. Armstrong, Robert Englund, Helena Kallianiotes (United Artists)

Stay Hungry features an excellent Jeff Bridges as a spoiled but affable rich young Alabama boy who slums his way to maturity through relationships with street-smart characters.

Bridges gets involved in a big urban real estate scheme with Joe Spinell and cohorts, all buying up small plots for a major development. But R. G. Armstrong's second-rate gym can't be had, so Bridges decides to infiltrate.

There he falls for Sally Field and also is exposed to the barbell denizens who include real-life bodybuilding champ Arnold Schwarzenegger, good-natured staffer Robert Englund, uptight ladies instructor Helena Kallianiotes and amiable attendant Roger E. Mosely.

All these characters conflict with Bridges's family and social circle. But underneath it all is a lurching and poorly defined film concept.

●

STAYING ALIVE

1983, 96 mins, US Ⓥ ⊙ col

Dir Sylvester Stallone ***Prod*** Robert Stigwood, Sylvester Stallone ***Scr*** Sylvester Stallone, Norman Wexler ***Ph*** Nick McLean ***Ed*** Don Zimmerman, Mark Warner ***Mus*** The Bee Gees ***Art*** Robert F. Boyle

Act John Travolta, Cynthia Rhodes, Finola Hughes, Steve Inwood, Julie Bovasso, Frank Stallone (Stigwood/Paramount)

The bottom line is that *Staying Alive* is nowhere near as good as its 1977 predecessor, *Saturday Night Fever*.

When last heard from, John Travolta's Tony Manero had left Brooklyn for an uncertain future in Manhattan. Now, he's on the rounds of casting calls and auditions for Broadway dance shows.

He's also got a comfortable but uncommitted relationship going with fellow struggling dancer and sometime saloon singer Cynthia Rhodes, who loves him a lot. Nevertheless, Travolta doesn't think twice about her feelings when he spots alluring British dancer Finola Hughes and hooks up with her while winning a background role in a show in which she will be starring.

By close to showtime, Travolta and Hughes loathe each other, and she's none too pleased when this unknown upstart manages to replace her faltering costar in the male lead of the production. The show, entitled *Satan's Alley*, emerges as an opening night smash, and Tony Manero is a success at last.

●

STAYING TOGETHER

1989, 91 mins, US Ⓥ col

Dir Lee Grant ***Prod*** Joseph Feury ***Scr*** Monte Merrick ***Ph*** Dick Bush ***Ed*** Katherine Wenning ***Art*** W. Steven Graham

Act Sean Astin, Stockard Channing, Melinda Dillon, Jim Haynie, Levin Helm (Feury)

Staying Together, a sincerely made coming-of-age tale, serves up familiar homilies about family values in changing small-town America and the indomitable power of love.

In a bucolic town somewhere in South Carolina, Mr. and Mrs. McDermott and their three strapping sons run a self-named home-cooked-chicken restaurant. Mom is a tower of strength and a paragon of understanding; Dad is gruff but caring, and the brothers confine their red-blooded oats-sowing, boozing and pot-smoking to their off hours.

The yuppies have landed and Pop McDermott takes an offer he can't refuse for the restaurant and its choice land site.

Middle sibling Brian (essayed by Tom Cruise–John Travolta hybrid Tim Quill) has been having an affair with an older woman who's championing the developers' cause. When his dad decides to cash in, the hot-tempered kid denounces pop, leaves home and talks his way into a job on the condo construction site.

Lee Grant and screenwriter Monte Merrick push all the preprogrammed melodrama buttons, including prodigal son Brian's too-late-to-say-goodbye dash to the hospital.

●

STAY TUNED

1992, 87 mins, US Ⓥ ⊙ ▭ col

Dir Peter Hyams ***Prod*** James G. Robinson ***Scr*** Tom S. Parker, Jim Jennewein ***Ph*** Peter Hyams ***Ed*** Peter E. Berger ***Mus*** Bruce Broughton ***Art*** Philip Harrison

Act John Ritter, Pam Dawber, Jeffrey Jones, David Tom, Heather McComb, Bob Dishy (Morgan Creek)

Not diabolical enough for true black comedy and witless in its send-up of obsessive TV viewing, *Stay Tuned* is a picture with nothing for everybody. As a Seattle couple trapped in a hellish cable system run by the devil himself, John Ritter and Pam Dawber look glum for more than plot reasons. [Screen story by Tom S. Parker, Jim Jennewein, and Richard Siegel.]

Ritter is introduced as the ultimate couch potato, a depressed plumbing-supplies salesman who's a sucker for the suave Jeffrey Jones's free cable-tryout offer. The catch is that if he and Dawber don't survive 24 hours lost inside the alternative dimension, they forfeit (what else?) their souls.

The titles of the cable shows are the only (mildly) amusing things about them: *Sadistic Hidden Videos*, *Three Men and Rosemary's Baby*, *Autopsies of the Rich and Famous*, *Driving Over Miss Daisy*. The crudely executed skits tend to expire as soon as they are announced.

One brief respite from the overall inanity is a six-minute cartoon interlude by the masterful Chuck Jones, with Ritter and Dawber portrayed as mice menaced by a robot cat. The animation has grace and depth.

●

STEAL BIG, STEAL LITTLE

1995, 135 mins, US Ⓥ col

Dir Andrew Davis ***Prod*** Andrew Davis, Fred Caruso ***Scr*** Andrew Davis, Lee Blessing, Jeanne Blake, Terry Kahn ***Ph*** Frank Tidy ***Ed*** Don Brocha, Tina Hirsch ***Mus*** William Olvis ***Art*** Michael Haller

Act Andy Garcia, Alan Arkin, Rachel Ticotin, Joe Pantoliano, Ally Walker, David Ogden Stiers (Chicago Pacific/Savoy)

Filmmaker Andrew Davis spins a bloated fairy tale of two brothers—alternately good and greedy—in *Steal Big, Steal Little*. The tug of war and tug of hearts in this comedy might best be described as Capra-grotesque.

Ruben Martinez (Andy Garcia) is a dreamer with a big heart who, much to the chagrin of his slick, soulless twin brother Robby (also Garcia), inherits a vast spread in Santa Barbara from their wealthy stepmother. The bad bro has been skimming money from the estate and is in cahoots with local muck-a-mucks to create a sprawling real estate development.

Story is relayed in flashback, with Ruben telling a cable reporter how, through intimidation, bribery and chicanery, Robby and his monied minions pushed him and his extended family off the land.

Davis [who cowrote original story with Teresa Tucker-Davies and Frank Ray Perilli], steals big but reaps little from an arsenal of Capra greats of the 1930s. The new outing has neither the incisive social commentary nor the antic wit of those inspirations.

The large cast tries valiantly to elevate the material. About the only member of the cast to hit the right note is Alan Arkin, as an opportunist who weighs in with the underdogs and learns the true meaning of decency and friendship.

●

STEALING BEAUTY
(AKA: I DANCE ALONE)

1996, 118 mins, Italy/UK/France Ⓥ ⊙ ▭ col

Dir Bernardo Bertolucci ***Prod*** Jeremy Thomas ***Scr*** Susan Minot, Bernardo Bertolucci ***Ph*** Darius Khondji ***Ed*** Pietro Scalia ***Mus*** Richard Hartley ***Art*** Gianni Silvestri

Act Liv Tyler, Sinead Cusack, Donal McCann, Jeremy Irons, Jean Marais, Rachel Weisz (Fiction/Recorded Picture/UGC)

Bernardo Bertolucci returns to his native Italy after 15 years and an exotic epic trilogy with *Stealing Beauty*, a richly satisfying chamber piece that is both literary and utterly contemporary.

Liv Tyler plays Lucy Harmon, an American sent to Tuscany for the summer following her mother's suicide. The vacation is ostensibly to have her portrait done by her host, Ian Grayson (Donal McCann); he and his wife Diana (Sinead Cusack) were friends of her mother. Lucy's real motive is to follow through on an incipient romance from an earlier visit with handsome neighbor Niccolo (Roberto Zibetti).

Niccolo is away when Lucy arrives, leaving her at the mercy of the menagerie of expatriates camped out at the Grayson's hilltop farmhouse. These include Alex (Jeremy Irons), a playwright dying of a terminal illness, a half-mad French art dealer (Jean Marais, giving free rein to theatricality), Diana's spoiled daughter (Rachel Weisz) and her slick entertainment lawyer lover (D. W. Moffett).

Their discussions dissecting Lucy take on a zoolike curiosity when they learn that the ripely sensual girl is waiting before giving up her virginity. Niccolo's return looks set to end that wait.

Although the elite aesthetes and intellectuals surrounding Lucy send off a certain chilliness that may alienate some viewers, the villa and its assorted inhabitants constitute a playfully Chekhovian frame for this modern girl's emotional odyssey.

This is only the second Bertolucci feature in 25 years not to be shot by Vittorio Storaro, and, in his place, Darius Khondji (*Se7en*) again proves himself a major new talent. While never underselling the beauty of the Tuscan landscape (the pic was shot in the Chianti area near Siena), Khondji studiously avoids commonplace sun-drenched exteriors.

•

STEALING HEAVEN
1989, 110 mins, UK/Yugoslavia Ⓥ ⦿ col
Dir Clive Donner ***Prod*** Simon MacCorkindale, Andros Epaminondas ***Scr*** Chris Bryant ***Ph*** Mikael Salomon ***Ed*** Michael Ellis ***Mus*** Nick Bicat ***Art*** Voytek
Act Derek de Lint, Kim Thomson, Denholm Elliott, Bernard Hepton, Kenneth Cranham, Rachel Kempson (Amy/Jadran)

This handsome historical pageant attempts to tell the "true story" behind one of history's most famous romances, that of 12th-century French philosopher Pierre Abelard and his beloved Heloise which has survived through the ages in the exchange of letters between them, each of them shut off from the world in another convent.

Chris Bryant's script, based on Marion Meade's novel, pushes toward a sharp and witty, anticlerical, feminist tract. Abelard shuns emotional commitments as dangerous to his intellectual capacities. Fulbert, Heloise's uncle, is a mercenary bigot who looks for the best deal on his niece; and Heloise is the smart, intelligent and unconventional girl with the courage to assume responsibility for her feelings.

•

STEALING HOME
1988, 98 mins, US Ⓥ ⦿ col
Dir Steven Kampmann, Will Aldis ***Prod*** Thom Mount, Hank Moonjean ***Scr*** Steven Kampmann, Will Aldis ***Ph*** Bobby Byrne ***Ed*** Antony Gibbs ***Mus*** David Foster ***Art*** Vaughan Edwards
Act Mark Harmon, Blair Brown, Jodie Foster, Jonathan Silverman, Harold Ramis, John Shea (Mount)

For all the sadness and loss in *Stealing Home*, the story of how a privileged boy's love for playing baseball is gone with the sudden death of his father, the film remains too remote emotionally to elicit more than a sigh of relief at its conclusion.

In suburban Philadelphia of big homes and summer beach houses most of the kids are like Billy Wyatt (played at 10, teenage and 38 by Thacher Goodwin, William McNamara and Mark Harmon respectively) and his pal Alan Appleby (Jonathan Silverman, Harold Ramis). Around for valuable lessons on how to grow up fast is the wayward and rebellious Katie (Jodie Foster), the family friends' daughter and the irresponsible babysitter that becomes for Billy a mentor, lover and tragic figure.

For Billy, baseball takes priority. It's something he breathes for and something he cherishes sharing with his equally fanatical baseball-loving dad (John Shea).

Foster's complex and confused character would have been the better choice upon which to center this melodrama. The actress is perfect for the part and, along with Ramis's warm and funny short screen time as the adult Alan, brings whatever emotional energy there is to the proceedings.

•

STEAMBOAT BILL, JR.
1928, 65 mins, US Ⓥ ⦿ ⊗ b/w
Dir Charles Riesner ***Prod*** Joseph M. Schenck ***Scr*** Carl Harbaugh ***Ph*** Dev Jennings, Bert Haines
Act Buster Keaton, Ernest Torrence, Tom McGuire, Marion Byron, Tom Lewis (United Artists)

The last comedy Buster Keaton made under his United Artists contract, it was held back for several months, getting itself concerned in several wild rumors. Whatever may have been the real reason why United Artists took its time about releasing this one, it had nothing to do with quality, for it's a pip of a comedy. It's one of Keaton's best.

The story concerns the efforts of an old hard-boiled river captain (Ernest Torrence), to survive on the river in the face of opposition from a brand new modern rival boat, put in commission by his rival (Tom McGuire). The old-timer hasn't seen his son since he was an infant. The son (Keaton) arrives, and things begin to happen fast and furiously. The son falls in love with the daughter of the rival owner. Matters reach a climax when the old tub of Steamboat Bill is condemned. In a rage, he confronts his rival and accuses him of robbing him. A battle ensues.

An excellent cast gives Keaton and Torrence big league support. Tom Lewis as the first mate, McGuire as the rival owner and Marion Byron as the girl, contribute heavily. The windstorm is a gem and the river stuff interesting and colorful.

•

STEAMING
1985, 95 mins, UK Ⓥ col
Dir Joseph Losey ***Prod*** Paul Mills ***Scr*** Patricia Losey ***Ph*** Christopher Challis ***Ed*** Reginald Beck ***Mus*** Richard Harvey ***Art*** Maurice Fowler
Act Vanessa Redgrave, Sarah Miles, Diana Dors, Patti Love, Brenda Bruce, Felicity Dean (World Film Service)

On film, *Steaming* lacks the impact it had on stage. The ebullience and sheer fun of the original [play by Nell Dunn] have mostly disappeared and, although this is by no means an earnest women's lib tract, it's a lesser experience.

There's no opening out—all the action takes place in a run-down steam bath on ladies' day. Here we find the manager, Violet (Diana Dors), worried that the local council is going to close the place down; Josie (Patti Love), an ebullient type forever talking about her sex life; conservative Mrs. Meadows (Brenda Bruce) and her daughter, Dawn (Felicity Dean); and the upper-class Sarah (Sarah Miles) who introduces her friend, Nancy (Vanessa Redgrave), to the group.

Performances are all very strong, with Redgrave probably making the least impact in the rather tight-lipped role of Nancy. Miles positively glows as Sarah, while Love seizes all her opportunities in the flashiest role. Dors, who like director Joseph Losey, died soon after the film was completed, is quietly effective as the motherly Violet.

•

STEEL
1980, 99 mins, US Ⓥ col
Dir Steve Carver ***Prod*** Peter S. Davis, William N. Panzer ***Scr*** Leigh Chapman ***Ph*** Roger Shearman ***Ed*** David Blewitt ***Mus*** Michel Colombier ***Art*** Ward & Preston
Act Lee Majors, Jennifer O'Neill, Art Carney, George Kennedy, Harris Yulin (Davis-Panzer/New Line)

Steel began lensing in Lexington, Kentucky, in 1978 and during production famed stuntman A. J. Bakunis died doing a tricky maneuver (pic is dedicated to him).

Lee Majors stars and exec-produces, and his well-crafted, restrained portrayal as the leader of the constructioners provides a solid base for a series of involving relationships.

There is an explosion and George Kennedy, the good-hearted company owner, plunges to a tragic death. Daughter Jennifer O'Neill is then left to take on the task of completing the project. Kennedy's friend Art Carney suggests O'Neill search out Majors to coordinate the job, and he rounds up the most famous workers in the business.

What unravels is a rightly directed story and true-to-life character study of endearing personalities interacting against outside forces.

•

STEEL HELMET, THE
1951, 84 mins, US Ⓥ b/w
Dir Samuel Fuller ***Prod*** Samuel Fuller ***Scr*** Samuel Fuller ***Ph*** Ernest W. Miller ***Ed*** Philip Cahn ***Mus*** Paul Dunlap ***Art*** Theobald Holsopple
Act Gene Evans, Robert Hutton, Richard Loo, Steve Brodie, James Edwards, William Chun (Deputy/Lippert)

The Steel Helmet pinpoints the Korean fighting in a grim, hard-hitting tale that is excellently told.

A veteran top sergeant is the sole survivor of a small patrol bound and murdered by North Koreans. He and a young native boy, who freed him, start back for the lines. They are soon joined by a Negro medic, sole survivor of another group. Trio encounters a patrol of green GIs, helps them out of an ambush and goes along to establish an observation post in a Korean temple. There they help direct artillery fire and capture a North Korean major hiding out in the temple.

Film serves to introduce Gene Evans as the sergeant, a vet of World War II, a tough man who is interested in staying alive and hardened to the impact of warfare. Robert Hutton, conscientious objector in the last war but now willing to fight against communism; Steve Brodie, the lieutenant who used pull to stay out of combat previously; James Edwards, the Negro medic, and Richard Loo, a heroic Nisei, are the other principals who add to the rugged realism.

•

STEEL MAGNOLIAS
1989, 118 mins, US Ⓥ ⦿ ▭ col
Dir Herbert Ross ***Prod*** Ray Stark ***Scr*** Robert Harling ***Ph*** John A. Alonzo ***Ed*** Paul Hirsch ***Mus*** Georges Delerue ***Art*** Gene Callahan, Edward Pisoni
Act Sally Field, Dolly Parton, Shirley MacLaine, Daryl Hannah, Olympia Dukakis, Julia Roberts (Rastar/Tri-Star)

Robert Harling's play was set solely in the beauty parlor where his heroines—a group of the liveliest, warmest Southern women imaginable—gather to dish dirt, crack jokes, do hair and give one another some solid, post-feminist emotional support. In opening up his own play for the screen, Harling has made actual characters of the menfolk only talked about in the play.

As Sally Field's troubled yet ever-hopeful seriously diabetic daughter Julia Roberts has real freshness and charm of the sort that can't be faked.

As the beauty shop owner around whom all the action swirls, Dolly Parton is thoroughly in her element. Wisely she remains in character as a particular good ole gal—with the Dolly her fans love peeking out from underneath.

Shirley MacLaine is a nicely bridled caricature as the town curmudgeon. She looks a wreck, talks trash and obviously loves every minute of it. As her partner in hamming-as-an-art-form, Olympia Dukakis just about walks away with the picture, even though she's never the center of attention in any of the film's scenes.

Daryl Hannah, not unexpectedly, has her hands full keeping up with this company as a gawky, nerdish beautician's assistant.

Field does some spectacular underplaying through the bulk of the action, revealing layer after layer of the feelings of this kindly tempered, deeply worried mother.

1989: NOMINATION: Best Supp. Actress (Julia Roberts)

•

STEEL TRAP, THE
1952, 84 mins, US b/w
Dir Andrew L. Stone ***Prod*** Bert E. Friedlob ***Scr*** Andrew L. Stone ***Ph*** Ernest Laszlo ***Ed*** Otto Ludwig ***Mus*** Dimitri Tiomkin
Act Joseph Cotten, Teresa Wright, Eddie Marr, Aline Towne, Bill Hudson (Thor/20th Century-Fox)

Andrew Stone's direction of his own story emphasizes suspense that is leavened with welcome chuckles of relief in telling the improbable but entertaining events.

Joseph Cotten is a minor bank exec who succumbs to a larcenous impulse and lays plans to heist $1 million when the bank closes on Friday, take off via plane with his wife for Brazil, where there is no extradition treaty with the States. Suspense continues to mount as Cotten encounters such frustrating difficulties as passport trouble, delays in plane transportation from Los Angeles to New Orleans that cause him to miss the Saturday plane to Brazil and, finally, customs curiosity that reveals to his wife he is a thief.

Cotten is very good, and Wright is capable as the wife.

•

STEELYARD BLUES
1973, 92 mins, US Ⓥ col
Dir Alan Myerson ***Prod*** Tony Bill, Michael Phillips, Julia Phillips ***Scr*** David S. Ward ***Ph*** Laszlo Kovacs, Steven Larner ***Ed*** Donn Cambern, Robert Grovenor ***Mus*** Nick Gravenites, Paul Butterfield, David Shire ***Art*** Vincent Cresciman
Act Jane Fonda, Donald Sutherland, Peter Boyle, Garry Goodrow, Howard Hesseman, John Savage (Warner)

Steelyard Blues is an erratically amusing slapstick comedy about nonconformists.

Screenplay spotlights Donald Sutherland as ringleader of some dropouts who also include kid brother John Savage and Peter Boyle, who does a hilarious takeoff of Marlon Brando's *The Wild One* image. Jane Fonda is the town hooker whose customers include most of the city hall, including Sutherland's prime adversary, his older brother Howard Hesseman, a politically ambitious DA.

The dropouts focus their energies on restoring an old U.S. Navy amphibian plane, and their search for spare parts leads to a climactic raid on a nearby naval air station.

Like many other films, this one suffers from a lingering late 1960s social-protest plot fibre, the result being an odd combination of nostalgia and anachronism.

•

STELLA
1990, 114 mins, US Ⓥ ⦿ col
Dir John Erman ***Prod*** Samuel Goldwyn, Jr. ***Scr*** Robert Getchell ***Ph*** Billy Williams ***Ed*** Jerrold L. Ludwig ***Mus*** John Morris ***Art*** James Hulsey
Act Bette Midler, John Goodman, Trini Alvarado, Stephen Collins, Marsha Mason, Eileen Brennan (Touchstone/Goldwyn)

The semitragic *Stella Dallas* shows her years in this hopelessly dated and ill-advised remake.

The idea of a lower-class mother who selflessly sends her daughter off to her upper-crust dad and his new wife—all so daughter can land the right beau—must sound like nails on a blackboard to Equal Rights Amendment proponents, and Bette Midler's ballsy wit completely misses the redeeming lower-class yearning Barbara Stanwyck gave the 1937 role.

All of the significant changes in the story come early, as Stella (Midler) meets a young doctor (Stephen Collins) while tending bar and quickly gets pregnant by him. She refuses his half-hearted offer of marriage as well as any financial help, letting him run off to New York while she raises their daughter (Trini Alvarado) on her own.

Erman and writer Robert Getchell try to inject some levity into the maudlin proceedings. On that front they largely succeed, thanks primarily to the winning performance by John Goodman as Stella's long-suffering admirer Ed as well as Midler's natural comic flair.

•

STELLA DALLAS

1925, 108 mins, US Ⓥ d b/w

Dir Henry King ***Prod*** Samuel Goldwyn ***Scr*** Frances Marion ***Ph*** Arthur Edeson ***Ed*** Stuart Heisler ***Art*** Ben Carre

Act Belle Bennett, Ronald Colman, Alice Joyce, Jean Hersholt, Lois Moran, Douglas Fairbanks, Jr. (Goldwyn/United Artists)

A mother picture. Not a great picture, but a great mother picture. Its sentiment is terrific. Henry King tells his story simply and directly without dramatics, gauging the extent to which he can play upon such an emotional subject to a nicety. In this he is helped by two magnificent performances by Belle Bennett and Lois Moran.

If ever there were a two-character picture this is it. Both characters are women, mother and daughter. It tells of a mother who eliminates herself so that her child may enjoy the advantages of which the girl will not partake while knowing that her mother has no one to whom she can turn.

Moran convinces in what practically amounts to three roles, as she plays the daughter at 10, 13 and as a young woman. Excellent in each, her performance is something of a revelation. Bennett, makes something of a cinema comeback in this release.

Alice Joyce makes a splendid contrast, while Ronald Colman is limited in his activities. Jean Hersholt is prominent among the secondary players, with young Douglas Fairbanks, Jr., acquitting himself creditably in his brief footage.

•

STELLA DALLAS

1937, 104 mins, US Ⓥ ⊙ b/w

Dir King Vidor ***Prod*** Samuel Goldwyn ***Scr*** Harry Wagstaff Gribble, Gertrude Purcell ***Ph*** Rudolph Mate ***Ed*** Sherman Todd ***Mus*** Alfred Newman ***Art*** Richard Day

Act Barbara Stanwyck, John Boles, Anne Shirley, Barbara O'Neil, Alan Hale, Marjorie Main (Goldwyn/United Artists)

Producer Samuel Goldwyn made the film first in 1925 and did mighty well by the results. *Stella Dallas* is chiefly a tearjerker of A ranking.

In producing this picture Goldwyn pretty much followed his original, bringing it, however, a bit more up-to-date. Thus the sock scenes are still the same ones. These are, especially, a scene between Barbara Stanwyck and Anne Shirley in a train when the former has just heard playmates of the latter criticize the mother as a millstone around the child's head; a scene between the girl and her father, and the woman he wants to marry; and a scene between the mother and daughter at a birthday party to which no one has shown up because of one of the mother's indiscretions.

The story [from the novel by Olive Higgins Prouty] itself is a simple enough one, not so much of mother love as the difficulties of a young girl whose parents are at extremes in the social world. It isn't overdone.

There are few faults to be pointed. Only one that is obvious is that Stanwyck is permitted to go entirely too far in costuming in her latter scenes. Especially when it is considered that the mother makes all the daughter's clothes and these are in rare good taste.

1937: NOMINATIONS: Best Actress (Barbara Stanwyck), Supp. Actress (Anne Shirley)

•

STELLA MARIS

1918, 77 mins, US ⊗ b/w

Dir Marshall Neilan ***Scr*** Frances Marion ***Ph*** Walter Stradling

Act Mary Pickford, Conway Tearle, Camille Ankewich, Ida Waterman, Herbert Standing (Artcraft)

In *Stella Maris*, a screen adaption of the novel of the same title, originally written by William J. Locke, and pictur-ized by Frances Marion, Mary Pickford is given an opportunity to act that proves a revelation. There are two characters in Locke's story of great importance. One is Stella Maris and the other Unity Blake. Pickford plays them both.

In the former she is the sweet ingenue type one expects her to be, but in the latter she is a deformed little slatternly slavey. Stella Maris is a sweet child, an orphan, crippled in her nether limbs from birth. Her parents were wealthy and left her well provided for.

As Unity Blake she sees nothing but the harder side of the world's face, for Unity is also an orphan and the inmate of a home. John Risca (Conway Tearle) is the hero.

It is a production for which the director, Marshall Neilan, must receive unstinted credit. It is a revelation in exterior locations and interior settings and the titling is exceedingly clever.

•

ST. ELMO'S FIRE

1985, 108 mins, US Ⓥ ⊙ ▭ col

Dir Joel Schumacher ***Prod*** Lauren Shuler ***Scr*** Joel Schumacher, Carl Kurlander ***Ph*** Stephen H. Burum ***Ed*** Richard Marks ***Mus*** David Foster (sup.) ***Art*** William Sandell

Act Rob Lowe, Demi Moore, Andrew McCarthy, Judd Nelson, Ally Sheedy, Emilio Estevez (Columbia-Delphi IV/Channel)

St. Elmo's Fire is all about a group of recent college graduates in Washington who were always the best of friends but now are drifting apart as real life approaches, discovering various reasons why they are so individually obnoxious.

Rob Lowe is a saxophone player who refuses to assume any adult responsibility. The rest of the gang befriends him, especially virginal Mare Winningham, who's a social worker by trade anyway.

The other major problem is beautiful, coked-out Demi Moore who lives in a pink apartment, sleeps with her boss and calls her friends with wee-hour problems.

There's also yuppie Capitol Hill aide Judd Nelson, a Democrat turned Republican because the pay is better, and his live-in (Ally Sheedy) who won't marry him but has reason to resent his cheating.

Making them all look good by comparison is Emilio Estevez. He spots medical student Andie MacDowell and decides he must marry her despite her absolute lack of interest.

Beyond occasional mutterings of words like "love" and "beer," there's never any explanation in the dialog that would hint at motivation.

•

STEPFATHER, THE

1987, 98 mins, US Ⓥ ⊙ col

Dir Joseph Ruben ***Prod*** Jay Benson ***Scr*** Donald E. Westlake ***Ph*** John W. Lindley ***Ed*** George Bowers ***Mus*** Patrick Moraz ***Art*** James Newton Westport

Act Terry O'Quinn, Jill Schoelen, Shelley Hack, Stephen Shellen, Charles Lanyer (ITC)

The Stepfather is an engrossing suspense thriller that refreshingly doesn't cheat the audience in terms of valid clues and plot twists.

Terry O'Quinn toplines as a mild-looking guy who immediately is revealed to be a psychotic who has murdered his entire family. A year later he has started a new life as Jerry Blake, married to young Susan (Shelley Hack) who has a teenage daughter Stephanie (Jill Schoelen).

His past eventually catches up with him as his previous brother-in-law Jim (Stephen Shellen) is still researching the murder of his sister with the help of a reporter, the police and (independently) Stephanie's psychiatrist Dr. Bondurant (Charles Lanyer).

What makes *The Stepfather* work is its believability, as writer Donald Westlake [from a story by him, Carolyn Lefcourt and Brian Garfield] expertly injects clues that can trip up Blake's new identity. A most ingenious plot peg has Blake carefully planning out his new identity (quitting his job, finding a new home, etc.) each time before he goes completely over the edge and sets out to murder his family.

O'Quinn gives a measured, effective performance balancing the normalcy and craziness of the character, while Schoelen is powerfully empathetic as the young heroine. Helmer Joseph Ruben brings a lot more credibility to the film than his previous *Dreamscape* assignment.

•

STEPFATHER II

1989, 86 mins, US Ⓥ ⊙ col

Dir Jeff Burr ***Prod*** William Burr, Darin Scott ***Scr*** John Auerbach ***Ph*** Jacek Laskus ***Ed*** Pasquale A. Buba ***Mus*** Jim Manzie, Pat Regan ***Art*** Bernadette Disanto

Act Terry O'Quinn, Meg Foster, Caroline Williams, Jonathan Brandis, Henry Brown, Mitchell Laurance (ITC)

This dull sequel reduces the intriguing premise of the original *Stepfather* to the level of an inconsequential, tongue-in-cheek slasher film.

Terry O'Quinn as the murderous, average guy vainly trying to mimic the American Family ideal was killed off at the end of the first pic. Sequel opens with recap of previous finale (including brief footage of previous costars Shelley Hack and Jill Schoelen), followed by O'Quinn waking up in a Washington State asylum with several chest scars indicating his not-quite-fatal wounds.

This time, O'Quinn bamboozles the shrink (Henry Brown) at the asylum and escapes, lifts the identity of a deceased family therapist from the newspaper obituary, and moves into an L.A. suburb. He romances the pretty real estate divorcee who's his neighbor (Meg Foster).

Pic builds towards their impending marriage, but 13-year-old son Todd (Jonathan Brandis) is only a minor character who does not figure in the dramatics. It is another neighbor (Caroline Williams), the postal delivery woman, who is suspicious of O'Quinn.

Jeff Burr, who has horror pics under his belt, directs the piece claustrophobically and fails to whip up any atmosphere.

•

STEPFORD WIVES, THE

1975, 114 mins, US Ⓥ ⊙ col

Dir Bryan Forbes ***Prod*** Edgar J. Scherick ***Scr*** William Goldman ***Ph*** Owen Roizman ***Ed*** Timothy Gee ***Mus*** Michael Small ***Art*** Gene Callahan

Act Katharine Ross, Paula Prentiss, Peter Masterson, Nanette Newman, Patrick O'Neal, Tina Louise (Palomar/Columbia)

Bryan Forbes's film of Ira Levin's *The Stepford Wives* is a quietly freaky suspense-horror story.

Katharine Ross (in an excellent and assured performance), husband Peter Masterson and kids depart NY's urban pressures to a seemingly bovine Connecticut existence. Trouble is, Ross and new friend Paula Prentiss (also excellent) find all the other wives exuding sticky hairspray homilies and male chauvinist fantasy responses. When Prentiss finally changes her attitude, Ross panics but cannot escape.

Patrick O'Neal heads a local men's club that somehow is involved in the unseen, sluggishly developed but eventually exciting climax.

The black humor and sophistication of the plot is handled extremely well.

•

STEPKIDS

SEE: BIG GIRLS DON'T CRY . . . THEY GET EVEN

•

STEP LIVELY

1944, 86 mins, US Ⓥ b/w

Dir Tim Whelan ***Prod*** Robert Fellows ***Scr*** Warren Duff, Peter Milne ***Ph*** Robert de Grasse ***Ed*** Gene Milford ***Mus*** Ernst Matray ***Art*** Albert S. D'Agostino, Carroll Clark

Act Frank Sinatra, George Murphy, Adolphe Menjou, Gloria de Haven, Eugene Pallette, Walter Slezak (RKO)

The old George Abbott [produced] play, *Room Service* [by John Murray and Allen Boretz], has been resurrected for an RKO remake, with song trimming palpably designed to fit Frank Sinatra. As a tailor-made vehicle it's somewhat loosely fitted, but in the main it will please.

The hectic machinations of theatrical shoestringers have been given a thorough going-over. But as Warren Duff and Peter Milne have revamped it, under Tim Whelan's staccato direction, it is pleasant enough celluloid divertissement.

Outside of an opening audience number (bubble-bath routine) and the show-within-a-show, as part of the finale production, the production values are moderate. Director Whelan lets himself go in the finale, and some of the Oriental hoke (with George Murphy, et al) is bright, as is the black-and-white terp creation. (Plot-wise, this is a show supposedly put on in five days.)

•

STEPPENWOLF

1974, 105 mins, US Ⓥ ⊙ col

Dir Fred Haines ***Prod*** Melvin Fishman, Richard Herland ***Scr*** Fred Haines ***Ph*** Tomislav Pinter ***Ed*** Irving Lerner ***Mus*** George Gruntz ***Art*** Leo Karen

Act Max von Sydow, Dominique Sanda, Pierre Clementi, Carla Romanelli, Roy Bosier, Alfred Baillou (Sprague)

Four decades after publication, *Steppenwolf* sold some 1.5 million paperbacks to a young audience suddenly attracted to Hermann Hesse. Film remains just as subjective and essentially plotless as the book, but director Fred Haines seems fully in control.

Film has a rich appearance far beyond its $1.2 million budget. The weird effects produced from a sophisticated, electronic video mix allow Haines to translate Hesse's abstractions faithfully, if such a thing is at all possible.

Haines was equally careful in casting Max von Sydow as Harry Haller, the misanthrope who opts for one last try at life before reaching 50 and a preplanned suicide. Whether it's madness, drugs or love that envelopes him remains as mysterious in pic, but von Sydow makes the journey remarkable.

•

STEPPING OUT
1991, 106 mins, US Ⓥ ⦿ col
Dir Lewis Gilbert ***Prod*** Lewis Gilbert ***Scr*** Richard Harris ***Ph*** Alan Hume ***Ed*** Humphrey Dixon ***Mus*** Peter Matz ***Art*** Peter Mullins
Act Liza Minnelli, Shelley Winters, Bill Irwin, Ellen Greene, Julie Walters, Sheila McCarthy (Paramount)

It's Liza-as-you-love-her in *Stepping Out*, a modest heartwarmer about a bunch of suburban left-feeters getting it together for a charity dance spot. Fragile ensemble item often creaks under the Minnelli glitz, but results are likeable enough.

Adapted by Richard Harris from his 1984 award-winning play, action is switched from a London church hall to a Buffalo, NY, equivalent. Minnelli is a former pro hoofer who's now teaching amateur dance classes on the side.

Her current group includes a snooty Brit with a cleanliness fixation (Julie Walters), a shy plain Jane with a bossy husband (Sheila McCarthy), a pretty, disillusioned young nurse (Jane Krakowski) and a working-class pants-chaser (Robyn Stevan).

Minnelli's problems start when her grumpy accompanist (Shelley Winters) threatens to walk out. She's then invited to put together an amateur tap routine for a charity show.

Minnelli's lost none of her pizzazz. Looking as freshfaced and gamine as ever, and in good voice and shape, she provides the pic's emotional highs in a solo dance spot and the finale's John Kander–Fred Ebb title song, but as an actress, she's one-note perky. Technically, the Toronto-lensed pic is solid.

•

STEREO
1969, 63 mins, Canada b/w
Dir David Cronenberg ***Prod*** David Cronenberg ***Scr*** David Cronenberg ***Ph*** David Cronenberg ***Ed*** David Cronenberg
Act Ronald Mlodzik, Jack Messinger, Iain Ewing, Clara Mayer, Paul Mulholland, Ronald Mlodzik (Emergent)

Lensed for a paltry $3,500, *Stereo* is the initial feature film effort by David Cronenberg.

Shot in black-and-white without synch sound, *Stereo* carries built-in liabilities thanks to its technical limitations and aesthetic idiosyncracies. Basically a student effort (Cronenberg was 26), pic tests the viewer's patience and endurance even with its hour's running time due to its emphatically dry, scientific narration and deliberate emotional distancing.

Film abstractly examines the situation at the Canadian Academy for Erotic Inquiry, where eight individuals have been subjected to telepathic surgery. As the narrator drones on the operation, alternately strange and static scenes are presented that only occasionally bear any relation to the words being spoken.

•

STERILE CUCKOO, THE
(U.K.: POOKIE)
1969, 108 mins, US Ⓥ ⦿ col
Dir Alan J. Pakula ***Prod*** Alan J. Pakula ***Scr*** Alvin Sargent ***Ph*** Milton R. Krasner ***Ed*** Sam O'Steen, John W. Wheeler ***Mus*** Fred Karlin ***Art*** Roland Anderson
Act Liza Minnelli, Wendell Burton, Tim McIntire, Elizabeth Harrower, Austin Green (Paramount/Boardwalk)

The Sterile Cuckoo is a kook named Pookie, a wacky, wisecracking motherless, outrageously adorable, collegiate gamine [from a novel by Jack Nichols] who comes on like gangbusters. Liza Minnelli plays the role, and her fragile, funny freshman love affair with an undergraduate entomologist (Wendell Burton in his first screen role) is in a class by itself.

A first affair in a ramshackle upstate New York motel becomes high comedy with the hot-to-trot vamp Minnelli prodding the nervous-in-the-service Burton, who keeps his mackinaw buttoned up to the chin while she strips down.

It is Minnelli's one-woman show. The 21-year-old Burton is not so much her costar as her straight man.

1969: NOMINATIONS: Best Actress (Liza Minelli), Song ("Come Saturday Morning")

•

STEVIE
1978, 102 mins, UK Ⓥ col
Dir Robert Enders ***Prod*** Robert Enders ***Scr*** Hugh Whitemore ***Ph*** Freddie Young ***Ed*** Peter Tanner ***Mus*** Patrick Gowers ***Art*** Bob Jones
Act Glenda Jackson, Mona Washbourne, Alec McCowen, Trevor Howard (Bowden)

Stevie is a well-acted and literate, but also talky and claustrophobic screen biography of British poet and novelist Stevie Smith. Glenda Jackson stars in the title role and her performance—in fact, the entire style of the film—seems better suited to the stage than the big screen.

Robert Enders, who directed from Hugh Whitemore's script of his own play, has adopted a visual style better suited to a telefilm than a theatrical feature. Most of the picture takes place inside a suburban residence Smith shared with her aunt, portrayed by Mona Washbourne in a charming and sympathetic performance.

By limiting the action to that one setting the film becomes stifling. Too much of Smith's life is described by Jackson in reminiscences to her aunt, confessions into the camera, or recitations of her poetry, rather than re-enacted.

Only other characters are Alec McCowen as a boyfriend of Jackson and Trevor Howard as companion who also comments on the poet's life and work.

•

STICKY FINGERS
1988, 97 mins, US Ⓥ ⦿ col
Dir Catlin Adams ***Prod*** Catlin Adams, Melanie Mayron ***Scr*** Catlin Adams, Melanie Mayron ***Ph*** Gary Thieltges ***Ed*** Robert Reitano ***Mus*** Gary Chang ***Art*** Jessica Scott-Justice
Act Helen Slater, Melanie Mayron, Danitra Vance, Eileen Brennan, Carol Kane, Christopher Guest (Hightop)

Sticky Fingers is a snappy, offbeat urban comedy about two NY gal pals—starving artist types—who get caught up in the shopping spree of a lifetime. Too bad the money isn't theirs.

Story, cowritten by debut director Catlin Adams and Melanie Mayron, casts Mayron and Helen Slater as struggling musicians on the verge of eviction from their N.Y. walkup until a bagful of drug money—nearly a million bucks—lands in their laps. They've been asked to "mind it" for a spacey friend-of-a-friend (Loretta Devine) who's clearing out of town in a hurry.

Initially panicked, they wind up using it to pay their rent, then to replace their instruments. As days pass, the urge to spend becomes insatiable, and they give in with gusto.

Memorable supporting roles abound, including Danitra Vance as a fellow musician and Stephen McHattie as a tough but romantic undercover cop posing as a parking lot attendant across from their building.

Eileen Brennan is right on as the ailing landlady, and Carol Kane is delightful as her sister, who has a romance with the cop. Christopher Guest is near perfect as Mayron's uncertain boyfriend, a newly published novelist pursued by a spooky ex-girlfriend (Gwen Welles).

•

STIGMATA
1999, 103 mins, US Ⓥ ⦿ col
Dir Rupert Wainwright ***Prod*** Frank Mancuso, Jr. ***Scr*** Tom Lazarus, Rick Ramage ***Ph*** Jeffrey L. Kimball ***Ed*** Michael R. Miller, Michael J. Duthie ***Mus*** Billy Corgan, Elia Cmiral, Mike Garson ***Art*** Waldemar Kalinowski
Act Patricia Arquette, Gabriel Byrne, Jonathan Pryce, Nia Long, Thomas Kopache, Rade Sherbedgia (FGM/M-G-M)

Aggressively silly, this possession thriller starts out promising a good-time mix of unintentional laughs and Rupert Wainwright's visual hyperbole. Unfortunately, even those guilty pleasures soon pall under the dulling effect of a murky, rather uneventful scenario.

De rigueur Third World prologue is set in a Brazilian village, where Vatican investigator Father Kiernan (Gabriel Byrne) discovers the "miracle" of a blood-weeping Virgin Mary statue. A thief steals a rosary from a dead cleric's corpse and an American tourist mails it as a souvenir to her daughter.

The recipient is Frankie (Patrcia Arquette), a larky 23-year-old Pittsburgh stylist, who soon experiences spooky visions and seizures that leave her mutilated with Christ-on-the-cross-like wounds. Father Kiernan is dispatched by his antagonistic superior (Jonathan Pryce) to examine her once the attacks attract media attention.

Pic's eventual talky tedium is unfortunate, because in its early going *Stigmata* [from a screen story by co-scripter Tom Lazarus] whips up an entertaining hysteria of stylistic overkill, tittersome dialogue and giddily outlandish situations. The fashion-victim hipness of Frankie and her pals (including Nia Long), combined with commercials and musicvid vet Wainwright's hyperkinetic visual design, suggest this as a sort of *Romy and Michelle's Demonic Possession*. The fun doesn't last.

Arquette does just fine here as a party girl in incongruous peril. Byrne maintains an admirably straight face; other thesps get little to do. Splashy lensing and design effects conjure an atmosphere somewhere betwixt *Batman* Gothicism, MTV and fashion layout

•

STILL CRAZY
1998, 95 mins, UK Ⓥ col
Dir Brian Gibson ***Prod*** Amanda Marmot ***Scr*** Dick Clement, Ian La Frenais ***Ph*** Ashley Rowe ***Ed*** Peter Boyle, Niven Howie ***Mus*** Clive Langer ***Art*** Max Gottlieb
Act Stephen Rea, Billy Connolly, Jimmy Nail, Timothy Spall, Bill Nighy, Juliet Aubrey (Marmot Tandy/Columbia)

The *Full Monty* formula gets a fresh and inventive spin in *Still Crazy*, a chucklesome, warmly observed comedy about five middle-aged losers who reassemble their rock band that broke up in the '70s.

The script reaches back to Dick Clement and Ian La Frenais's background in British sitcoms, with the laughs coming from acute observation of the characters' foibles and weaknesses rather than from sending up the music industry per se (which is hardly dealt with). Film says far more in its own way about the '70s Brit-rock scene and its self-destructive qualities than the overhyped *Velvet Goldmine*.

Strange Fruit was a classic rock band, riven by drugs, booze, egos and sex, that was finished in 1977 when a bolt of lightning canceled an open-air gig. The son of the original fest promoter bumps into keyboard player Tony (Stephen Rea), now selling condoms in Spain, and suggests the Fruits hold a reunion concert.

In London, Tony contacts their former p.a. Karen (Juliet Aubrey), and the pair sets about rounding up the group. All are flat broke, with nothing more to lose.

Guts of the picture is the band's odyssey through a series of low-rent continental clubs, marked by embarrassing disasters, the resurgence of old friction between guitarist composer Les (Jimmy Nail) and addled lead singer Ray (Bill Nighy), and a growing re-attraction between Tony and Karen.

Pic's ambling style and humor takes a while to settle down but finds its focus with the second-reel appearance of Nighy, in an on-the-button portrait of a burned-out, middle-aged rocker whose brains are still fried by past excesses. The TV/legit actor's perf anchors the movie, with the rest of the fine cast essentially playing straight. Production values are modest.

•

STILL OF THE NIGHT
1982, 91 mins, US Ⓥ col
Dir Robert Benton ***Prod*** Arlene Donovan ***Scr*** Robert Benton ***Ph*** Nestor Almendros ***Ed*** Jerry Greenberg ***Mus*** John Kander ***Art*** Mel Bourne
Act Roy Scheider, Meryl Streep, Jessica Tandy, Joe Grifasi, Sara Botsford, Josef Sommer (United Artists)

It comes as almost a shock to see a modern suspense picture that's as literate, well-acted and beautifully made as *Still of the Night*. Despite its many virtues, however, Robert Benton's film [from a story by him and David Newman] has its share of serious flaws, mainly in the area of plotting.

Roy Scheider effectively plays an introspective New York shrink whose own life becomes endangered after one of his patients is found murdered. Prime suspect may well be Meryl Streep, the neurotic mistress of the dead man whose distressed, unpredictable behavior represents the source of most of the film's mystery.

Perpetually moving around physically, mentally and emotionally, Streep slowly insinuates herself into Scheider's relatively uneventful life.

Benton has fashioned as gorgeously crafted a suspense piece as one could ask for. High marks also go to supporting players, particularly Josef Sommer as the murdered man who appears in flashback, and Joe Grifasi as the persistent cop.

•

STING, THE
1973, 127 mins, US Ⓥ ⦿ col
Dir George Roy Hill ***Prod*** Tony Bill, Michael Phillips, Julia Phillips ***Scr*** David S. Ward ***Ph*** Robert Surtees ***Ed*** William Reynolds ***Mus*** Marvin Hamlisch (adapt.) ***Art*** Henry Bumstead
Act Paul Newman, Robert Redford, Robert Shaw, Charles Durning, Ray Walston, Eileen Brennan (Universal)

Paul Newman and Robert Redford are superbly reteamed as a pair of con artists in Chicago of the 1930s, out to fleece a big-time racketeer, brilliantly played by Robert Shaw.

Script establishes Redford as a novice con artist, apprentice to Robert Earl Jones who is murdered when one of their marks turns out to be a cash runner for Shaw's regional syndicate. Ambition plus revenge leads Redford to Newman, an acknowledged master of the con trade who rounds up Eileen Brennan, Harold Gould, Ray Walston and John Heffernan to fake a bookie joint operation to snare Shaw in a major bet.

The three stars make all the difference between simply a good film and a superior one. Newman's relationship with Brennan (in a sensational supporting role) rounds out his characterization of an old pro making his last big score. Redford really turns to and works superbly. Shaw's taciturn menace commands attention even when he is simply part of a master shot.

The film comes to a series of startling climaxes, piled atop one another with zest. In the final seconds the audience realizes it has been had, but when one enjoys the ride, it's a pleasure.

1973: Best Picture, Director, Original Story & Screenplay, Art Direction, Adapted Scoring, Editing, Costume Design (Edith Head)

NOMINATIONS: Best Actor (Robert Redford), Cinematography, Sound

•

STING II, THE

1983, 102 mins, US Ⓥ ⦿ col

Dir Jeremy Paul Kagan ***Prod*** Jennings Lang ***Scr*** David S. Ward ***Ph*** Bill Butler ***Ed*** David Garfield ***Mus*** Lalo Schifrin ***Art*** Edward C. Carfagno

Act Jackie Gleason, Mac Davis, Teri Garr, Karl Malden, Oliver Reed, Bert Remsen (Universal)

Stars Jackie Gleason and Mac Davis come nowhere close to evoking the charming on-screen qualities of Paul Newman and Robert Redford. Combined with the slow pace and overdone exposition, *The Sting II* is mostly just a chore to watch.

Though screenwriter David S. Ward concocts as viable a story as he did in the original, the trouble is there is still an original.

Gleason plays the master con man out to make a big score with the help of fellow huckster Davis. The chief patsy is tacky nightclub owner Karl Malden, while Oliver Reed does a less than distinctive turn as a mysterious gangster watching it all happen.

So much of the intricate plot is explained in dialog that the first half of the film often seems like someone reading an instruction book.

Exception is Teri Garr, who provides what little life there is as a slick, seasoned trickster who becomes involved in the scam.

The second half picks up a bit as the plan goes into effect, and this is where the performances come into play.

1983: NOMINATION: Best Adapted Score

•

STIR CRAZY

1980, 111 mins, US Ⓥ ⦿ col

Dir Sidney Poitier ***Prod*** Hannah Weinstein ***Scr*** Bruce Jay Friedman ***Ph*** Fred Schuler ***Ed*** Harry Keller ***Mus*** Tom Scott ***Art*** Alfred Sweeney

Act Gene Wilder, Richard Pryor, JoBeth Williams, Georg Stanford Brown, Craig T. Nelson, Barry Corbin (Columbia)

Story setup has down-on-their-luck New Yorkers Richard Pryor and Gene Wilder deciding to blow the city for what they think are the promising shores of California. Driving cross-country they land in a small town where they take a job dressing up as woodpeckers in a local bank in order to make some cash. Two baddies they meet in a bar use the woodpecker suits to rob the bank, leaving Pryor and Wilder 120-year prison sentences and no alibi.

Majority of the action focuses on the antics of prison life, with Pryor and Wilder at the center of a group of fairly stereotypical jail characters.

Director Sidney Poitier's chief role seems to be providing enough space for Pryor and Wilder to do their schtick without going too far afield from the scant storyline.

•

STIR OF ECHOES

1999, 110 mins, US Ⓥ ⦿ col

Dir David Koepp ***Prod*** Gavin Polone, Judy Hofflund ***Scr*** David Koepp ***Ph*** Fred Murphy ***Ed*** Jill Savitt ***Mus*** James Newton Howard ***Art*** Nelson Coates

Act Kevin Bacon, Kathryn Erbe, Illeana Douglas, Liza Weil, Kevin Dunn, Conor O'Farrell (Hofflund-Polone)

Screenwriter-turned-auteur David Koepp's sophomore effort as a multihyphenate (following *The Trigger Effect*) is a white-knuckle thriller [from Richard Matheson's novel *A Stir of Echoes*] propelled by Kevin Bacon's exceptional performance as a working-class Everyman who discovers dark secrets under his own roof after inadvertently gaining precognitive powers.

When Tom Witzky (Bacon) is momentarily distracted from bathing his young son, Jake (Zachary David Cope), moppet calmly converses with an unseen apparition. "Does it hurt to be dead?" Jake asks.

Shortly afterward, the focus shifts as Tom and his wife, Maggie (Kathryn Erbe), attend a neighborhood party, where Tom is outspoken in his teasing of Lisa (Illeana Douglas), his metaphysical-minded sister-in-law. Lisa insists she knows enough about hypnosis to plant a posthypnotic suggestion inside the mind of anyone, so Lisa lulls him into a trance and encourages him to be more "open" in his thinking.

Trouble is, being more "open" makes Tom receptive to bad vibes, and is especially upset by his vision of an unfamiliar teenage girl on his living room couch. Jake may be having the same vision.

Koepp does a masterful job of grounding his intimations of the supernatural in a persuasive, down-to-earth context. The verisimilitude is enhanced by Fred Murphy's moody lensing in three Chicago environs—Wicker Park, Polish Village and Brighton Park—which editor Jill Savitt seamlessly weaves into a single working-class neighborhood.

But the credibility quotient gets its biggest boost from Bacon's shrewdly detailed performance.

•

STITCH IN TIME, A

1963, 94 mins, UK b/w

Dir Robert Asher ***Prod*** Hugh Stewart ***Scr*** Jack Davies ***Ph*** Jack Asher ***Ed*** Gerry Hambling ***Mus*** Philip Green

Act Norman Wisdom, Edward Chapman, Jeanette Sterke, Jerry Desmonde, Jill Melford (Rank)

This gains by economizing on plot, but devises a string of farcical events that put the pint-sized Norman Wisdom through the full pratfalling routine. The thin thread linking the scenes has Wisdom as a hapless butcher's assistant causing constant commotion in a hospital, where his employer is undergoing surgery for a swallowed watch. He gets banned from the place by the hospital boss, Sir Hector (Jerry Desmonde), and the remainder of the running time is taken up by his bizarre attempts to regain entry.

The sketches follow each other thick and fast and leave no time to brood over their naivety. Jack Davies's script is the sixth for the comedian, and he knows the strength and limitations of the star. For sophisticated palates, Wisdom is mechanical, and he plays up the sentiment of the "little man" up against authority to cloying effect.

•

ST. IVES

1976, 93 mins, US Ⓥ col

Dir J. Lee Thompson ***Prod*** Pancho Kohner, Stanley Canter ***Scr*** Barry Beckerman ***Ph*** Lucien Ballard ***Ed*** Michael F. Anderson ***Mus*** Lalo Schifrin ***Art*** Philip M. Jefferies

Act Charles Bronson, John Houseman, Jacqueline Bisset, Maximilian Schell, Harry Guardino, Harris Yulin (Warner)

St. Ives merely confirms a point: eliminate gratuitous, offensive and overdone violence from a dull and plodding film story, and all you've got left is a dull and plodding film.

The production stars Charles Bronson as an ex-police reporter involved with wealthy crime dilettante John Houseman and partner Jacqueline Bisset. J. Lee Thompson's direction is functional.

Barry Beckerman wrote the script from an Oliver Bleeck novel, *The Procane Chronicle*. Plot injects Bronson as go-between in recovery for some stolen Houseman papers, but every time the ransom is to be delivered, somebody dies.

Plot progress is marred by lots of month-old red herrings. Film is careful to show that Bronson's character doesn't need pistols.

•

ST. LOUIS BLUES

1939, 90 mins, US b/w

Dir Raoul Walsh ***Prod*** Jeff Lazarus ***Scr*** John C. Moffitt, Malcolm Stuart Boylan, Virginia Van Upp ***Ph*** Theodor Sparkuhl ***Ed*** William Shea ***Mus*** W. C. Handy, Leo Robin, Sam Coslow, Hoagy Carmichael ***Art*** Hans Dreier

Act Dorothy Lamour, Lloyd Nolan, Tito Guizar, Jerome Cowan (Paramount)

St. Louis Blues, is behind-the-scenes Mississippi riverboat stuff in a modern setting, which is perhaps its most discordant note. It lacks the charm of the background that keynotes *Show Boat*.

There's quite a bit of stuff packed into this Jeff Lazarus production, ranging from the 52nd Street jitterbug motif (Maxine Sullivan) to Broadway injunction suits by Jerome Cowan against Dorothy Lamour. Latter eventually goes into her standard sarong routine as part of a South Seas sequence.

Story [based on an adaptation by Frederick Hazlitt Brennan of a story by Eleanore Griffin and William Rankin] is one o' those things sometimes. There's much ado about injunctions and the law, yet, for the climactic situation, Lamour flaunts the restraint order, appears on the showboat, seemingly nonplusses the cops by her vocal charm, and it winds up in an inconclusive clinch.

Raoul Walsh's direction was handicapped by the script.

•

STOLEN HOURS

1963, 100 mins, US Ⓥ col

Dir Daniel Petrie ***Scr*** Jessamyn West ***Ph*** Harry Waxman ***Ed*** Geoffrey Foote ***Mus*** Mort Lindsey ***Art*** Wilfried Shingleton

Act Susan Hayward, Michael Craig, Diane Baker, Edward Judd, Paul Rogers (Mirisch/Barbican)

Director Daniel M. Petrie has shaped a smooth and slick production out of the story of a woman facing death as the result of brain disease. A remake of the 1939 Bette Davis starrer *Dark Victory*, the film moves easily from discovery to predetermined conclusion and gives Hayward a chance to do some effective emoting.

Jessamyn West has written the screenplay for this made-in-Britain effort and has fortunately chosen not to go overboard on the bathos. The result is a picture that moves well, with fine photography and credible performances.

As the doctor, who Hayward eventually marries despite their mutual knowledge of her fate, Michael Craig does a solid job. Diane Baker is attractive and proves a capable actress as Hayward's sister, and Edward Judd is also strong as an ex-beau but still chum of the ailing socialite.

•

STOLEN KISSES

SEE: BAISERS VOLÉS

•

STOLEN LIFE, A

1946, 100 mins, US Ⓥ b/w

Dir Curtis Bernhardt ***Prod*** Bette Davis ***Scr*** Catherine Turney ***Ph*** Sol Polito, Ernest Haller ***Ed*** Rudi Fehr ***Mus*** Max Steiner ***Art*** Robert M. Haas

Act Bette Davis, Glenn Ford, Dane Clark, Walter Brennan, Charles Ruggles, Bruce Bennett (Warner/BD)

Story [from a novel by Karel J. Benes] unfolds leisurely in telling of a sister who assumes her twin's identity in order to find love.

Bette Davis appears as a sweet, sincere, artistic girl, and as this girl's man-crazy sister. When the latter, by trickery, marries man with whom former has fallen in love and is later drowned in a boating accident, the sweet girl takes on her sister's identity in a try for happiness. Script spends a great deal of footage establishing life in New England summer resorts. Since it is a woman's story, dialog hands plenty of clichés to male players, particularly to Glenn Ford as the man in love with both sisters.

Dane Clark appears briefly in role of rude artist. Role is difficult and not a fortunate one for Clark. Walter Brennan gives a good character reading to his part of a salty old Down-easter.

Special photography for dual role played by Davis is the best yet. At no time is double exposure or other tricks used to bring the characters together in scenes apparent. Credit for trick work goes to Willard Van Enger and Russell Collings.

1946: NOMINATION: Best Special Effects

•

STONE BOY, THE

1984, 93 mins, US Ⓥ col

Dir Christopher Cain ***Prod*** Joe Roth, Ivan Bloch ***Scr*** Gina Berriault ***Ph*** Juan Ruiz-Anchia ***Ed*** Paul Rubell ***Mus*** James Horner ***Art*** Joseph G. Pacelli

Act Robert Duvall, Jason Presson, Frederic Forrest, Glenn Close, Wilford Brimley, Gail Youngs (TLC)

Director Chris Cain, in only his second feature, draws a remarkably restrained and moving performance from debuting child actor Jason Presson, who plays central role of a 12-year-old brother who accidentally and tragically slays his older, beloved brother with a shotgun in the opening moments of the film.

Production's sorrowful subject matter as family is rendered dazed and grief-stricken by the death of the older son, while young responsible brother retreats behind a wall of guilt, never lapses into sentimentality or melodrama.

Robert Duvall unthinkingly compounds the misery of his son by fostering a family attitude that denies the boy communication.

The Stone Boy, in its inarticulate characters whose feelings tear them apart, is a singular and highly accessible film.

•

STONE KILLER, THE

1973, 95 mins, US Ⓥ ⦿ col

Dir Michael Winner ***Prod*** Michael Winner ***Scr*** Gerald Wilson ***Ph*** Richard Moore ***Ed*** Freddie Wilson ***Mus*** Roy Budd ***Art*** Ward Preston

Act Charles Bronson, Martin Balsam, David Sheiner, Norman Fell, Ralph Waite, Stuart Margolin (De Laurentiis)

The Stone Killer [from John Gardner's novel *A Complete State of Death*] is a confused, meandering crime potboiler, starring Charles Bronson as a tough detective who starts out on a low-level gangster case only to find upper Mafia echelon also are involved. The story and direction reach for so many bases that the end result is a lot of cinema razzle-dazzle without substance.

Bronson is discovered killing a N.Y. ghetto punk, his overkill enough to banish him to the L.A. Police Dept, a plot point which may strike some as unintentionally amusing. Eventually it becomes clear that Martin Balsam, a prototype hood of the Prohibition era, is planning massacre-revenge for a 40-year-old shootout that introduced non-Sicilian elements to organized crime.

•

STONEWALL

1995, 99 mins, US/UK Ⓥ col

Dir Nigel Finch ***Prod*** Ruth Caleb ***Scr*** Rikki Beadle Blair ***Ph*** Chris Seager ***Ed*** John Richards ***Mus*** Michael Kamen ***Art*** Therese DePrez

Act Guillermo Diaz, Fred Weller, Brendan Corbalis, Bruce MacVittie, Duane Boutte, Luis Guzman (Arena NY/BBC)

A fictionalized account of a subject widely covered in docu form, *Stonewall* takes its name from the legendary Greenwich Village gay bar and its dramatic cue from the 1969 riot in which drag queens took on New York cops during a raid on the premises, signaling the beginnings of the gay pride movement.

Factual basis for the film is Martin Duberman's social history *Stonewall*. The script strikes a winning balance between pathos and comedy, juicing things up via some campy musical interludes.

The story centers on Matty Dean (Fred Weller), a handsome country boy who hits New York expecting a free-thinking gay paradise. He hooks up with LaMiranda (Guillermo Diaz), a sassy young drag queen, and Ethan (Brendan Corbalis), a member of an ineffectual gay activist group. A third track follows neighborhood drag queen godmother Bustonia (Bruce MacVittie) and her secret relationship with the Stonewall's owner, Vinnie (Duane Boutte).

Characters are affectionately drawn, as is the sense of community and solidarity. The film's greatest strengths are its warmth and humor. The writing suffers mildly, however, from a second-act energy loss and is decidedly stronger in bringing the trash-glamour drag queen milieu to life.

Budgeted at less than $2 million, the pic is a resourceful, visually striking operation.

•

STOOGE, THE

1952, 100 mins, US b/w

Dir Norman Taurog ***Prod*** Hal Wallis ***Scr*** Fred F. Finklehoffe, Martin Rackin, Elwood Ullman ***Ph*** Daniel L. Fapp ***Ed*** Warren Low ***Mus*** Joseph J. Lilley (dir.)

Act Dean Martin, Jerry Lewis, Polly Bergen, Marion Marshall, Eddie Mayehoff, Richard Erdman (Paramount)

Dean Martin and Jerry Lewis venture into a straight story line comedy in *The Stooge* as a change of pace from their usual frenetic clowning.

Martin plays a crooning, accordion-playing comic who flunks as a single and only becomes a success when he acquires a dumb stooge to work with him from the audience. He is fortunate in landing Lewis as the patsy, and it isn't long before the act, still billed as a single at Martin's insistence, becomes a big success.

Lewis scores as the wistful ugly duckling who adores the man who gave him a chance in show business. He's particularly outstanding when he subs for Martin as a single during a vaude stand, and in the mirror sequence when he admires and fancies himself as a dashing hero.

•

STOP! OR MY MOM WILL SHOOT

1992, 87 mins, US Ⓥ ⦿ col

Dir Roger Spottiswoode ***Prod*** Ivan Reitman, Joe Medjuck, Michael C. Gross ***Scr*** Blake Snyder, William Osborne, William Davies ***Ph*** Frank Tidy ***Ed*** Mark Conte, Lois Freeman-Fox ***Mus*** Alan Silvestri ***Art*** Charles Rosen

Act Sylvester Stallone, Estelle Getty, JoBeth Williams, Roger Rees, Martin Ferrero, Gailard Sartain (Universal/Northern Lights)

Expertly produced in the mold of slick, juvenile action comedies like Ivan Reitman's *Kindergarten Cop*, this buddy cop picture casts budding comic actor Sylvester Stallone (*Oscar*) and proven laugh-getter Estelle Getty (TV's *Golden Girls*) as a beleaguered LA lawman and his aggravating mother.

Visiting from the east coast, the hyper-meddlesome Getty, as New Jersey widow Tutti Bomowski, proves second to none in embarassing the pants off her Joey (Stallone). Knowing that her visit will be brief is all that keeps Joey sane, but then his mother becomes a key witness in a drive-by shooting, and the cops ask her to stay on indefinitely. Before long she's pushed her way even further into Joey's business as his pistol-packing partner in some perilous escapades.

Stallone, in a slim, articulate and disciplined incarnation, is the model of the amiable, put-upon comic hero, while the tiny Getty, her familiar technique and timing honed to a cutting edge, is worth triple her weight in ticket stubs.

Director Roger Spottiswoode delivers purely pro product in his adept handling of both action and comedy scenes. JoBeth Williams is typically excellent in the light comic role of the precinct lieutenant who's also Joey's neglected flame.

•

STORK CLUB, THE

1945, 98 mins, US Ⓥ b/w

Dir Hal Walker ***Prod*** Buddy DeSylva ***Scr*** Buddy DeSylva, John McGowan ***Ph*** Charles Lang, Jr. ***Ed*** Gladys Carley ***Mus*** Robert Emmett Dolan (dir.) ***Art*** Hans Dreier, Earl Hedrick

Act Betty Hutton, Barry Fitzgerald, Don DeFore, Andy Russell, Iris Adrian, Robert Benchley (Paramount)

Much on the plus side is the fact that story is not restricted to being another Grand Hotel theme in a nitery setting. In fact, at one time one wonders what happened to the Stork Club part of the tale, since so much occurs in the penthouse where Betty Hutton has been mysteriously ensconced.

Interspersed is a blighted romance between the oldster Barry Fitzgerald and Mary Young, his wife of 40 years, who had walked out on the eccentric Irish millionaire in disgust over his pecuniary habits.

Robert Benchley is the deadpan lawyer who fronts for his eccentric client, further complicating the plot by not disclosing the facts when a romantic crisis occurs between the checkroom gal (Hutton) and her bandleader–ex-Marine (Don DeFore), who can't dope out her unaccustomed affluence.

Hutton is capital throughout, vocally and histrionically, while Fitzgerald is superb; he almost steals the picture from everything and everybody.

•

STORM, THE

1930, 76 mins, US b/w

Dir William Wyler ***Scr*** Wells Root ***Ph*** Alvin Wyckoff

Act Lupe Velez, Paul Cavanaugh, William Boyd, Alphonz Ethier, Ernie S. Adams (Universal)

The Storm served on two former occasions as a silent, in 1916 for Paramount and in 1922 for U. Lupe Velez is a French smuggler's daughter who is left with a friendly trapper by her father just before a bullet from a Mountie's gun lays him low. She plays with an accent that is a cross between Spanish and French, half the time doing a flashing Spanish señorita, the other half a piquant young demoiselle.

Story [from a play, *Men without Skirts*, by Langdon McCormick] is that of a trapper-miner and his best friend who develop a bad jealousy between each other for the girl ward left with the former. They both lean heavily toward the girl, finally hating each other.

Shots of the girl in the river attempting to rescue her father from Mounties are very cleverly done. The old man's leap from a cliff, and their race down the river until the canoe capsizes, is also fairly thrilling stuff expertly photographed.

•

STORM BOY

1976, 88 mins, Australia Ⓥ col

Dir Henri Safran ***Prod*** Matt Carroll ***Scr*** Sonia Borg ***Ph*** Geoff Burton ***Ed*** G. Turney-Smith ***Mus*** Michael Carlos ***Art*** David Copping

Act Greg Rowe, Peter Cummins, David Gulpilil, Judy Dick, Tony Allison, Michael Moody (SAFC)

Storm Boy is a gem of a film. Modestly and carefully made, it is a skillful adaptation of a kid's book by Colin Thiele.

Mike (Greg Rowe) is the 10-year-old son of Tom (Peter Cummins), a wifeless fisherman who inhabits a shanty on the beach and ekes out a living selling his catch to the fishmonger in the nearest town.

They live near a bird sanctuary, and a chance meeting with an aborigine (David Gulpilil) affects Mike's life and gives him the name Storm Boy.

Fingerbone Bill is also a rejector of society, his tribe has cast him out and he lives a nomadic life pretty much along the lines of his ancestors. And he has retained the mystical insights of his forebears.

Storm Boy is certainly a kid-flick, but it's one that'll get to the adults, too.

For a first feature, Paris-born director Henri Safran shows a sure hand. Final kudos to composer, Michael Carlos, for an evocative score.

•

STORM OVER THE NILE

1955, 107 mins, UK Ⓥ ▭ col

Dir Terence Young, Zoltan Korda ***Prod*** Zoltan Korda ***Scr*** R. C. Sherriff, Lajos Biro, Arthur Wimperis ***Ph*** Ted Scaife, Osmond Borradaile ***Ed*** Raymond Poulton ***Mus*** Benjamin Frankel ***Art*** Wilfrid Shingleton

Act Anthony Steel, Laurence Harvey, Mary Ure, Ronald Lewis, Ian Carmichael, James Robertson Justice (London)

The Four Feathers ranked high among Alexander Korda's prewar successes and, in this remake of the A. E. W. Mason story, his brother Zoltan assumes some producer credit as well as sharing the directorial chore with Terence Young.

Use of the wide-screen process is probably the main justification for the remake, particularly as it enhances the vivid battle scenes in which Kitchener's troops rout the native armies at Khartoum, while imprisoned British officers capture the enemy arsenal. These spectacular sequences are the main highlight of the picture, which in other ways is outmoded in spirit and story content. Battle sequences filmed in the Sudan have a convincing look.

Generally, the acting hardly matches the lavish and spectacular qualities of the production. Laurence Harvey as a fellow officer who gets blinded by an overdose of sun, appears miscast. Only James Robertson Justice, as a veteran of the Crimea and father of Anthony Steel's fiancée, fits happily into the story.

•

STORM WARNING

1950, 93 mins, US b/w

Dir Stuart Heisler ***Prod*** Jerry Wald ***Scr*** Daniel Fuchs, Richard Brooks ***Ph*** Carl Guthrie ***Ed*** Clarence Kolster ***Mus*** Daniele Amfitheatrof

Act Ginger Rogers, Ronald Reagan, Doris Day, Steve Cochran, Hugh Sanders, Lloyd Gough (Warner)

Storm Warning weaves a hard-hitting plot around violence, murder and the Ku Klux Klan.

Story points a probing finger at Klan. However, the well-written script never lets itself go overboard on the moral side.

Ginger Rogers visits overnight with her married sister. She finds the streets strangely deserted and while walking them inadvertently witnesses the brutal slaying of a newspaperman by Klansmen. Terrified and sick by the experience, she finds her sister and then discovers the husband is one of the killers.

Rogers does well as the model, and the county prosecutor is given a lot of sock by Ronald Reagan. Very good is the offbeat assignment of the sister, as done by Doris Day, and Steve Cochran scores soundly.

•

STORMY MONDAY

1988, 93 mins, UK Ⓥ ⦿ col

Dir Mike Figgis ***Prod*** Nigel Stafford-Clark ***Scr*** Mike Figgis ***Ph*** Roger Deakins ***Ed*** David Martin ***Mus*** Mike Figgis ***Art*** Andrew McAlpine

Act Melanie Griffith, Tommy Lee Jones, Sting, Sean Bean, Prunella Gee, Alison Steadman (Moving Picture)

The attempt to come up with a stylish British film noir in the vein of *Mona Lisa* comes a cropper in *Stormy Monday*. Debut theatrical pic for Mike Figgis is all visual flash and no script, with comatose performances to boot.

Melanie Griffith toplines as a sort of B-girl working for U.S. gangster/real estate magnate Tommy Lee Jones. Jones is in Newcastle to run an American Week promotion to boost U.S./U.K. business development and also is trying to run Sting out of business, operating a local jazz club.

Griffith soon becomes involved romantically with a handsome Irish lad (Sean Bean) who is doing odd jobs at Sting's club. Plot unfolds as a string of ridiculous coincidences, set in motion when Bean at lunch overhears two of Jones's hitmen plotting to do in Sting.

Jones walks through his idiotic role with barely hidden embarrassment. Griffith hasn't missed many meals, sporting an unbecoming figure resembling latter-day Anita Ekberg.

•

STORMY WEATHER
1943, 77 mins, US Ⓥ ⊙ b/w
Dir Andrew L. Stone ***Prod*** William LeBaron ***Scr*** Frederick Jackson, Ted Koehler ***Ph*** Leon Shamroy, Fred Sersen, Benny Carter ***Ed*** James B. Clark
Act Lena Horne, Bill Robinson, Fats Waller, Dooley Wilson, Cab Calloway, Katherine Dunham (20th Century-Fox)

Stormy Weather is chockful of the cream-of-the-crop colored talent, with a deft story skein to hold it together. Bill Robinson and Lena Horne top the cast. It's a tribute to the affection in which Bojangles is held that the story plot is glossed over in favor of all the other components.

Story nicely spans both wars. Lt. Jim Europe's band is marching up 5th Ave. in a riotous homecoming. Dooley Wilson, Robinson and the others have come back from the wars. The big Harlem hoopla thus projects Lena Horne, who takes a liking immediately to Robinson. Her partner (Babe Wallace) is the menace, a conceited professional.

Story is told via the flashback formula. A 25th anniversary number of *Theatre World* holds the plot together. The special edition is in tribute to the great trouper, Robinson. Surrounding him are the neighbors' children on his comfortable, handsome front porch.

Via the *Theatre World* anniversary number, Robinson continues crossing and re-crossing paths with Horne, in and out of shows, Hollywood filmusicals, etc., with Cab Calloway, Katherine Dunham and her expert troupe of ballet dancers, Fats Waller, the Nicholas Bros., plus others.

•

STORY OF ADELE H., THE
SEE: L'HISTOIRE D'ADELE H.

•

STORY OF DR. WASSELL, THE
1944, 136 mins, US col
Dir Cecil B. DeMille ***Prod*** Cecil B. DeMille ***Scr*** Alan LeMay, Charles Bennett ***Ph*** Victor Milner, William Snyder ***Ed*** Anne Bauchens ***Mus*** Victor Young ***Art*** Hans Dreier, Roland Anderson
Act Gary Cooper, Laraine Day, Signe Hasso, Dennis O'Keefe, Carol Thurston, Carl Esmond (Paramount)

Because this is the factual story of Dr. Wassell's heroic evacuation of 12 men, plus himself, from Java in earlier stages of the war, it packs more interest than otherwise might have been the case. The exploits of the by-now famed naval commander are brought to the screen on a lavish scale by Cecil B. DeMille, with an exceptionally fine cast and good comedy relief. The entertainment value, even had the scenario been fictional, is very strong.

There can be no quarrel with the cast. While Gary Cooper bears no particular resemblance to Commander Wassell himself, who was 60 and a weather-beaten type, the star imparts to the role much vigor, color and sympathetic interest. It's one of Cooper's best performances.

The story [by James Hilton] based upon facts as related by Commander Wassell [and 15 of the wounded sailors involved], through various cutbacks, takes Cooper from his early horse-and-buggy country doctor days in Arkansas through medical research in China before the war and, finally, to Australia after he has successfully transported wounded men to that point. Instead of being court-martialed there for having disobeyed orders to leave stretcher cases behind in Java, Dr. Wassell was awarded the Navy Cross, and his heroic deed made the subject of a broadcast by President Roosevelt.

1944: NOMINATION: Best Special Effects

•

STORY OF ESTHER COSTELLO, THE
1957, 104 mins, UK b/w
Dir David Miller ***Prod*** Jack Clayton ***Scr*** Charles Kaufman ***Ph*** Robert Krasker ***Ed*** Ralph Kemplen ***Mus*** Georges Auric ***Art*** George Provis, Tony Masters
Act Joan Crawford, Rossano Brazzi, Heather Sears, Lee Patterson, Ron Randell, Denis O'Dea (Romulus/Valiant)

Nicholas Monsarrat's poignant bestselling novel has been shaped into a glossy, highly effective screenplay, with David Miller's direction affording his powerful cast every opportunity for an all-out assault on the emotions.

Joan Crawford is a rich American socialite who, revisiting her Irish birthplace, finds a young girl, deaf, dumb and blind as a result of an explosion when she was a child. Joan rescues the girl from her evil surroundings, takes her to the U.S. and devotes her life to the girl's recovery. This mercy campaign sparks the interest of the world, but Crawford's estranged husband (played by Rossano Brazzi) and a slick exploitation guy turn it into a giant racket.

Apart from its gripping story, *Esther Costello* has an almost documentary quality in showing the patient way a mute can be taught to communicate with the world. So authentic are these scenes that Heather Sears, who portrays Esther, and Crawford as her tutor actually learned to "hand-talk."

The acting throughout is impeccable and is noteworthy for a remarkable debut by 21-year-old Heather Sears, who stands up notably to seasoned competition though faced with the tricky chore of conveying emotion without benefit of eye-play or dialog.

•

STORY OF G.I. JOE, THE
1945, 109 mins, US b/w
Dir William A. Wellman ***Prod*** Lester Cowan ***Scr*** Leopold Atlas, Guy Endore ***Ph*** Russell Metty ***Ed*** Otto Lovering, Albrecht Joseph ***Mus*** Ann Ronell, Louis Applebaum ***Art*** James Sullivan, David Hall
Act Burgess Meredith, Robert Mitchum, Freddie Steele, Wally Cassell (United Artists)

From where the civilian sits, this seems the authentic story of GI Joe—that superb, slugging human machine, the infantryman, without whom wars cannot be won. Add to authentic story handling a production that's superb, casting and directing that's perfect, and a sock star supported by a flawless group of artists.

From the moment the infantrymen are picked out by the camera at "blanket drill" in the African desert until the last shot on the open highway to Rome, it's the foot-slogging soldier who counts most in this film. Real-life GI diarist Ernie Pyle is there, very much. He is ever present. But as conceived by the scripters, directed by William A. Wellman, and acted by Burgess Meredith, Pyle is not the war but a commentary on it—which is as it should be.

Meredith, playing the simple little figure that's Pyle, is felt in every scene, his impact carrying over from the preceding sequences.

But without support, Meredith for all his worth could not have made this the great picture it is. Robert Mitchum is excellent as the lieutenant who, in the film, grows to a captaincy. Freddie Steele is tops as the tough sergeant who finally cracks up when he hears his baby's voice on a disc mailed from home. Wally Cassell as the Lothario of the company, and all the others—professionals as well as real-life GIs who helped make the pic—are excellent.

•

STORY OF LOUIS PASTEUR, THE
1936, 85 mins, US Ⓥ b/w
Dir William Dieterle ***Scr*** Sheridan Gibney, Pierre Collings ***Ph*** Tony Gaudio ***Ed*** Ralph Davison ***Mus*** Erich Wolfgang Korngold ***Art*** Robert Haas
Act Paul Muni, Josephine Hutchinson, Anita Louise, Donald Woods, Fritz Leiber, Henry O'Neill (Warner)

It couldn't have been an easy film to make, and the fact that it holds as much general interest as it does speaks volumes. But the producers couldn't avoid some dull stretches of scientific discourse.

Expert casting and splendid production are the points in the film's favor, primarily. Paul Muni in the title role is at his very top form.

Film starts out with Pasteur already somewhat established, skipping his early life and struggles. His wine and beer discoveries have already been accepted and he's propagandizing for sterilization of doctors and doctors' instruments in childbirth. Doesn't get him very far because of general medical opposition, and he turns to treatment of anthrax in sheep and cattle. Gets that over and is admitted into the French Academy, although still scoffed at by the majority of his confreres. Works on a cure for rabies and hydrophobia for the rest of the picture. His reward finally is general acclaim.

Josephine Hutchinson as Pasteur's wife is splendid and believable. Anita Louise as his daughter and Donald Woods as her fiancé are expected to handle the romance and almost do it. Fritz Leiber as Dr. Charbonnet, Pasteur's strongest enemy, turns in an outstanding performance.

1936: Best Actor (Paul Muni), Original Story & Screenplay

NOMINATION: Best Picture

•

STORY OF MANKIND, THE
1957, 99 mins, US col
Dir Irwin Allen ***Prod*** Irwin Allen ***Scr*** Irwin Allen, Charles Bennett ***Ph*** Nicholas Musuraca ***Ed*** Roland Gross, Gene Palmer ***Mus*** Paul Sawtell ***Art*** Art Loel
Act Ronald Colman, Vincent Price, Agnes Moorehead, Peter Lorre, Dennis Hopper, Virginia Mayo (Cambridge/Warner)

Hendrik Willem Van Loon's monumental *Story of Mankind* has been brought to the screen in a name-dropping production that provides a kaleidoscope of history from Pleistocene man to Plutonium man. In the process, however, producer-director Irwin Allen seems unable to decide whether to do a faithful history of man's development into a thinking being, a debate on whether man's good outweighs his evil, or a compilation of historical sagas with some humor dragged in for relief.

As a peg on which to hang the panorama, screenplay convokes the "High Tribunal of Outer Space" upon news that man has discovered the Super-H bomb 60 years too soon. The problem is whether to halt the scheduled explosion and thereby save mankind or let it go off and exterminate the human race. To reach a decision, the tribunal permits both the Devil and the Spirit of Man to give evidence as to man's fitness to continue.

In the dreary cataloguing of man's crimes against humanity, the Devil makes a much better case.

Best of the portrayals is Agnes Moorehead's Queen Elizabeth, and Cedric Hardwicke turns in a good performance as the High Judge. Ronald Colman is a dignified personification of the Spirit of Man and Vincent Price is the sophisticated, sneering embodiment of Old Scratch.

Peter Lorre brings some conviction to the role of Nero, Dennis Hopper is moodily appropriate as Napoleon and Virginia Mayo looks the part of Cleopatra. Hedy Lamarr is miscast as Joan (yes, of Arc) in one of the few other key parts, some of the "stars" being on and off the screen so rapidly as to go unrecognized.

•

STORY OF QIU JU, THE
SEE: QIUJU DA GUANSI

•

STORY OF ROBIN HOOD, THE
(AKA: THE STORY OF ROBIN HOOD AND HIS MERRIE MEN)
1952, 83 mins, UK Ⓥ ⊙ col
Dir Ken Annakin ***Prod*** Perce Pearce ***Scr*** Lawrence E. Watkin ***Ph*** Guy Green ***Ed*** Gordon Pilkington ***Mus*** Clifton Parker ***Art*** Carmen Dillon, Arthur Lawson
Act Richard Todd, Joan Rice, Peter Finch, James Hayter, James Robertson Justice, Martita Hunt (Walt Disney/RKO)

For his second British live-action production, Walt Disney took the legend of Robin Hood and translated it to the screen as a superb piece of entertainment, with all the action of a Western and the romance and intrigue of a historical drama.

Despite his modest stature, Richard Todd proves to be a first-rate Robin Hood, alert, dashing and forceful, equally convincing when leading his outlaws against Prince John as he is in winning the admiration of Maid Marian. Although a comparative newcomer to the screen, Joan Rice acts with charm and intelligence.

James Hayter as Friar Tuck, Martita Hunt as the queen, Peter Finch as the sheriff, James Robertson Justice as Little John, Bill Owen as the poacher, and Elton Hayes as the minstrel are in the front rank.

•

STORY OF RUTH, THE
1960, 132 mins, US Ⓥ ▭ col
Dir Henry Koster ***Prod*** Samuel G. Engel ***Scr*** Norman Corwin ***Ph*** Arthur E. Arling ***Ed*** Jack W. Holmes ***Mus*** Franz Waxman ***Art*** Lyle R. Wheeler, Franz Bachelin
Act Stuart Whitman, Tom Tryon, Peggy Wood, Viveca Lindfors, Jeff Morrow, Elana Eden (20th Century-Fox)

The Story of Ruth is a refreshingly sincere and restrained biblical drama, a picture that elaborates on the romantic, political and devotional difficulties encountered by the Old Testament heroine. Yet, for all its obvious high purpose, bolstered by several fine performances, there is a sluggishness that is disturbing.

The screenplay describes the heroine's activities from her youthful indoctrination as a Moabite priestess through her marriage to the Judean, Boaz. Along the way it dramatizes her romance with the kindly Mahlon, his violent death, her conversion to Judaism and flight with Mahlon's mother, Naomi, to Bethlehem, where she encounters religious persecution and becomes embroiled in a romantic triangle.

Although the screenplay wisely avoids archaic phrases, director Henry Koster has not always succeeded in sidestepping stereotyped biblical-pic posturing and mannerisms among his players, and is inclined to anticipate mysterious character knowledge in a few instances. But he has coaxed several very effective portrayals out of his principals.

The film introduces Elana Eden in the title role. She gives a performance of dignity, projecting an inner strength through a delicate veneer. The picture is helped by veteran Peggy Wood's excellent characterization of Naomi. Her timing is always sharp. Tom Tryon establishes a pleasing screen personality with a vigorous delineation of Mahlon. Franz Waxman's music is typically biblical in tone and tempo.

•

STORY OF THREE LOVES, THE

1953, 122 mins, US col

Dir Gottfried Reinhardt, Vincente Minnelli ***Prod*** Sidney Franklin ***Scr*** John Collier, Jan Lustig, George Froeschel ***Ph*** Charles Rosher, Harold Rosson ***Ed*** Ralph E. Winters ***Mus*** Miklos Rozsa ***Art*** Cedric Gibbons, Preston Ames, Edward Carfagno, Gabriel Scognamillo

Act Pier Angeli, Ethel Barrymore, Leslie Caron, Kirk Douglas, James Mason, Moira Shearer (M-G-M)

Metro has put some top stars into a beautifully dressed Technicolor combination of three yarns tied together by placing the key characters aboard an ocean liner. With a strong initial entry and a suspenseful finale [directed by Gottfried Reinhardt], picture's weakness lies in the middle [section, directed by Vincente Minnelli].

Opening episode, *The Jealous Lover* [scripted by John Collier] is easily the most effective. Moira Shearer plays an aspiring ballerina prevented from dancing by a serious heart condition. When James Mason, a famous choreographer, sees her improvising on an empty stage, he asks her to perform for him.

Both Mason and Shearer score, the latter especially in her beautiful terping to the music of Rachmaninoff's *Rhapsody on a Theme of Paganini*. Credit Sadler's Wells choreographer Frederick Ashton with some topnotch dance arrangements.

Second episode, *Mademoiselle*, a fantasy [scripted by Jan Lustig and George Froeschel, from a story by Arnold Phillips], is aimless in direction and lacking in interest. A boy (Ricky Nelson), in Rome with his parents, wishes he could grow up so as to be rid of his French governess (Leslie Caron). Ethel Barrymore, as an old lady believed by children to be a witch, grants him the wish for four hours, and as a man (Farley Granger) he falls in love with the governess.

Final episode [*Equilibrium*, scripted by Collier, from a story by Ladislas Vadja and Jacques Maret, adaptation by Lustig and Froeschel] has Kirk Douglas as a trapeze artist who's retired after being accused of killing his femme partner by giving her too risky a trick. After he fishes Pier Angeli, a lonely young widow, out of the Seine, he decides she would be a good partner, since she has no will to live. Story gets off to a slow start, but it builds suspense and thrills for a solid close.

•

STORY OF US, THE

1999, 94 mins, US Ⓥ ⊙ col

Dir Rob Reiner ***Prod*** Rob Reiner, Alan Zweibel, Jessie Nelson ***Scr*** Alan Zweibel, Jessie Nelson ***Ph*** Michael Chapman ***Ed*** Robert Leighton, Alan Edward Bell ***Mus*** Eric Clapton, Mark Shaiman ***Art*** Lilly Kilvert

Act Bruce Willis, Michelle Pfeiffer, Tim Matheson, Rob Reiner, Rita Wilson, Paul Reiser (Castle Rock/Universal)

The Story of Us is a seriocomic anatomy of the ups and downs of a 15-year marriage between two bright and attractive partners, credibly played by Michelle Pfeiffer and Bruce Willis. More somber than humorous, the tale is burdened by a complicated time scheme of flashbacks and flashforwards that will prevent audiences from being involved in—and entertained by—the endless bickering and occasional reconciliations of the central duo.

One gets the impression that the filmmakers believe they are conveying deep emotional and universal truths about how to survive a long-enduring marriage. But this is merely a small, tolerable film.

About to celebrate their 15th anniversary, Ben and Katie Jordan have grown apart. Emotionally drained by their frustrating, sexless relationship, they attempt a trial separation. Story unfolds as a series of brief reflections on their shared history, from their first, charming meeting in an office to the present, when each is in bed waiting for the other's call.

The ins and outs of the marriage are not related in chronological order, and for a while it's fun to deduce the era of a scene by the couple's clothes and hairdos. Problem is that the stylistic devices used, which recall early Woody Allen and Paul Mazursky, get increasingly tedious. There are too many voiceovers and flashbacks.

Drawing on her beauty and dramatic range, Pfeiffer delivers a compelling performance, though her big monologue at the end is not as effective as it should be. In a role reversal, as a man who's more emotionally demonstrative than his wife, Willis is also good.

•

STORY OF VERNON AND IRENE CASTLE, THE

1939, 96 mins, US Ⓥ ⊙ b/w

Dir H. C. Potter ***Prod*** George Haight ***Scr*** Richard Sherman ***Ph*** Robert de Grasse ***Ed*** William Hamilton ***Mus*** Victor Baravalle (dir.) ***Art*** Van Nest Polglase, Perry Ferguson

Act Fred Astaire, Ginger Rogers, Edna May Oliver, Walter Brennan, Lew Fields, Etienne Girardot (RKO)

The Story of Vernon and Irene Castle is top-flight cinematic entertainment. It's another switch on the backstage story, this time dealing with a much-in-love married pair of ballroomologists catapulted from dire straits in Paris into international acclaim and fortune.

The medley of some 40 yesteryear pops is the common denominator for all types of audiences.

Irene Castle technically-advised. Her published memoirs, *My Husband* and *My Memories of Vernon Castle*, are the story background [adapted by Oscar Hammerstein II and Dorothy Yost] of the film. Her personal life story has been seemingly transmuted into celluloid with considerable faithfulness and a minimum of bombast or heroics.

Their success story dates from the time that the shrewd Maggie Sutton (Edna May Oliver) gets them an audition at the Café de Paris. Comes the war, however, and Castle enlists in the Canadian Royal Flying Corps, and meets untimely death as a flying instructor.

Ginger Rogers and Fred Astaire are excellent as the Castles.

•

STORYVILLE

1992, 110 mins, US Ⓥ col

Dir Mark Frost ***Prod*** David Roe, Edward R. Pressman ***Scr*** Mark Frost, Lee Reynolds ***Ph*** Ron Garcia ***Ed*** B. J.Sears ***Mus*** Carter Burwell ***Art*** Richard Hoover

Act James Spader, Joanne Whalley-Kilmer, Jason Robards, Charlotte Lewis, Michael Warren, Michael Parks (Davis Entertainment/Pressman)

Storyville has a little trouble getting its story straight. A teeming cesspool of illicit sex, murder, suicide, family intrigue and political chicanery in exotic Louisiana, this would-be *Chinatown* is so overloaded with outrageous implausibilities that the temptation is very strong to consider it all a joke.

In his first big-screen direction, Mark Frost, a key force behind *Hill Street Blues* and David Lynch's partner on *Twin Peaks* for TV, has taken an Australian novel [*Juryman* by Frank Galbally and Robert Macklin] and relocated it in New Orleans, where just about anything goes.

James Spader plays Cray Fowler, a callow, good-looking kid trying to carry his rich, corrupt family's tradition of political service into a third generation. Encouraged by family patriarch Clifford Fowler (Jason Robards) in the old-boy-network school, Cray is divorcing his wife and seeking the support of black voters.

Cray is crazy enough to run off with the enticing Lee (Charlotte Lewis), a Vietnamese woman he's barely met. He is obliged to fight her maniacal father, who mysteriously winds up dead. When Lee is charged with the murder, Cray astoundingly offers his services as defense attorney. Opposing him will be a prosecutor (Joanne Whalley-Kilmer) who's his old flame.

Cray does so many apparently stupid things, and the many jaw-dropping loopholes and long-shots in the first half make the film systematically unconvincing. Whalley-Kilmer and Lewis are attractive in functional parts, and Robards serves up an old-school blowhard to a fare-thee-well.

•

STOWAWAY

1936, 87 mins, US Ⓥ b/w

Dir William A. Seiter ***Prod*** Earl Carroll, Harold Wilson (assoc.) ***Scr*** William Conselman, Arthur Sheekman, Nat Perrin ***Ph*** Arthur Miller ***Ed*** Lloyd Nosler ***Mus*** Louis Silvers (dir.) ***Art*** William Darling

Act Shirley Temple, Robert Young, Alice Faye, Eugene Pallette, Helen Westley, Arthur Treacher (20th Century-Fox)

In addition to her customary singing, dancing and exceptional line reading for a child her age, Shirley Temple this time goes in for talking Chinese, quoting Oriental proverbs, giving imitations of Jolson, Cantor and Fred Astaire and other departures. She even handles a tearful dramatic exit expertly.

But while the kid is on top at all times, *Stowaway* doesn't make the mistake of some other preceding pictures in permitting the story to run a bad second. This one [from a screen story by Samuel G. Engle], while no masterpiece, is competent in itself and constantly a reasonable basis for the Temple histrionics.

It opens and remains for a brief period ashore in China, then switches to an ocean vessel and remains there most of the way. Daughter of missionary parents who are slain by bandits, the kid meets up with a cruising American playboy in Shanghai and winds up marrying him off. The romantic leads are Robert Young and Alice Faye, both very good on performance, particularly Young, with Faye keeping abreast through her singing.

When Temple enters a Chinese amateur show, from the audience, she miraculously appears on the stage with a dummy for her Astaire-Rogers takeoff. But the amateur show itself is such a clever insertion and so well done that nobody will care about improbabilities.

Songs by Mack Gordon and Harry Revel were intended mostly for Temple, and while they fill the bill, none seems like a smash as presented.

Helen Westley does a bang-up job with a meddling mother-in-law role.

•

STRADA, LA

1954, 115 mins, Italy Ⓥ ⊙ b/w

Dir Federico Fellini ***Prod*** Carlo Ponti, Dino De Laurentiis ***Scr*** Federico Fellini, Ennio Flaiano, Tullio Pinelli ***Ph*** Otello Martelli ***Ed*** Leo Cattozzo ***Mus*** Nino Rota ***Art*** Mario Ravasco

Act Giulietta Masina, Anthony Quinn, Richard Basehart, Aldo Sivani, Marcella Rovena, Lidia Venturini (Ponti-De Laurentiis)

Story by Federico Fellini, who also directed this picture, and Tullio Pinelli tells of a blunt, brutal wandering carnie performer (Anthony Quinn) who "buys" a girl (Giulietta Masina) to serve as his assistant.

She's on the nutty side, but falls for him despite his many affairs with other women and his poor treatment of her. Her poetic conversations with a similarly dim-witted clown-trapezist (Richard Basehart) anger the brute, who finally accidentally kills his rival in a fist fight. The death completely unbalances the gal's mind, and the brute abandons her.

Many years later, alone and broken, he hears someone whistle a tune she used to play on trumpet and learns she is dead. That night after a violent drunk, alone on a deserted beach, he breaks down his lifelong reserve.

Story reads badly, but is filled with pathetic and poetic moments, and often is both very touching and extremely amusing. Acting by Quinn and Basehart is tops, but Masina, one of Italy's best performers, easily steals show with her clownish mimicry.

The on-the-road atmosphere, the slum area showbiz aspects typical of some parts of Italian life, are realistically pictured by Fellini's story and Otello Martelli's camera in this intelligent film.

1956: Best Foreign Language Film

•

STRAIGHT TIME

1978, 114 mins, US Ⓥ col

Dir Ulu Grosbard ***Prod*** Stanley Beck, Tim Zinnemann ***Scr*** Alvin Sargent, Edward Bunker, Jeffrey Boam ***Ph*** Owen Roizman ***Ed*** Sam O'Steen, Randy Roberts ***Mus*** David Shire ***Art*** Stephen Grimes

Act Dustin Hoffman, Theresa Russell, Gary Busey, Harry Dean Stanton, M. Emmet Walsh, Rita Taggart (First Artists/Sweetwall)

Straight Time is a most unlikeable film because Dustin Hoffman, starring as a paroled and longtime criminal, cannot overcome the essentially distasteful and increasingly unsympathetic elements in the character. Ulu Grosbard's sluggish direction doesn't help.

Apparent plot peg [from Edward Banker's novel *No Beast So Fierce*] is that a parolee suffers so many indignities that a return to crime is easier.

Viewers are asked initially to believe that M. Emmet Walsh, the assigned parole officer, is a sadistic person who delights in hassling his charges. But given the circumstances, he does not emerge as a heavy. Indeed, Hoffman's too-easy lapse into his old ways absolves any blame on the System. Hoffman's character would have defied the parole supervision of a saint.

Theresa Russell is very good as Hoffman's girl; Harry Dean Stanton is excellent as a reformed hood who (nobody explains why) is being suffocated in the life of a successful suburban businessman; Gary Busey is good as a weak ex-con who bungles a climactic robbery plan.

•

STRAIT-JACKET
1963, 93 mins, US Ⓥ b/w
Dir William Castle ***Prod*** William Castle ***Scr*** Robert Bloch ***Ph*** Arthur Arling ***Ed*** Edwin Bryant ***Mus*** Van Alexander ***Art*** Boris Leven
Act Joan Crawford, Diane Baker, Leif Erickson, Howard St. John, John Anthony Hayes, George Kennedy (Columbia)

Strait-Jacket could be summoned up as a chip off the old Bloch. Writer Robert Bloch's *Psycho*, that is. In crossing the basic plot design of that 1960 Bloch-buster with the instrument of murder (the axe) and at least one of the ramifications of the celebrated Lizzie Borden case, Bloch has provided the grisly ingredients for producer-director William Castle to concoct some marketable "chop" suey.

Heads really roll in this yarn, which commences with a dual hatchet job on a cheating husband and his lady friend who are discovered bedroominating by the wife (Joan Crawford), whose three-year-old daughter witnesses in horror the 40 some odd whacks per victim administered by her mother. Mom goes to the insane asylum, and daughter grows up into Diane Baker. They are reunited 20 years later when mom is released.

Crawford does well by her role, delivering an animated performance. Baker is pretty and histrionically satisfactory as her daughter. Some of Castle's direction is stiff and mechanical, but most of the murders are suspensefully and chillingly constructed.

•

STRANGE AFFAIR, THE
1968, 102 mins, UK ▭ col
Dir David Greene ***Prod*** Howard Harrison, Stanley Mann ***Scr*** Stanley Mann ***Ph*** Alex Thomson ***Ed*** Brian Smedley-Aston ***Mus*** Basil Kirchin ***Art*** Brian Eatwell
Act Michael York, Jeremy Kemp, Susan George, Jack Watson, David Glaisyer, Richard Vanstone (Paramount)

Michael York is the "Strange" involved in an affair that finds Scotland Yard detective Pierce (Jeremy Kemp) trying to nail a trio of dangerous criminals and drug peddlers.

Frustrated in various attempts at getting legal evidence, Kemp in desperation resorts to blackmailing Strange, who's been caught in a compromising situation with a girl, into planting a drug packet on one of the trio during a search.

Situation provides opportunities for some subsurface characterizations of the two men torn by different concepts of duty.

There are no lags in the action, with Stanley Mann's literate script [from a novel by Bernard Toms] ringing true all the way, just as it provides an amusing change of pace in the tryst linking Strange with an ebullient hippie played by Susan George.

York makes a very sympathetic person out of Strange. Kemp is suitably harassed and obsessed as the duty-first plainclothesman, while Jack Watson, David Glaisyer and Richard Vanstone are properly sneery as the baddies. It is, however, George who captures most attention in a very appealing performance.

•

STRANGE ALIBI
1941, 63 mins, US b/w
Dir D. Ross Lederman ***Scr*** Kenneth Gamet ***Ph*** Allen G. Siegler ***Ed*** Frank Magee
Act Arthur Kennedy, Joan Perry, Howard da Silva, Florence Bates (Warner/First National)

This rates high among the average run of B mellers. It's an evidence of Warners' crime-and-punishment actioners working at an all-out peak.

Everything in it has been seen before—particularly the sets—but the concoction has been tossed together again under director D. Ross Lederman to become a speedy and delectable dish.

Plot [from a story by Leslie T. White] is far from new. Unfortunately, Lederman has had to dive into the stock barrel for a load of trite court and prison stuff that bogs the picture right down in the center.

Arthur Kennedy plays a detective who arranges with his chief for a publicized break between them so that he can go over to the mob. Racket guys find out he's not playing them straight and kill the chief, planting the murder on Kennedy, who is sent up for life. He breaks from prison and very neatly squares himself for fade-out clinch.

Kennedy does a nice job when not stilted by the B-picture dialog.

•

STRANGE BEDFELLOWS
1964, 99 mins, US col
Dir Melvin Frank ***Prod*** Melvin Frank ***Scr*** Melvin Frank, Michael Pertwee ***Ph*** Leo Tover ***Ed*** Gene Milford ***Mus*** Leigh Harline ***Art*** Alexander Golitzen, Joseph Wright
Act Rock Hudson, Gina Lollobrigida, Gig Young, Edward Judd, Terry-Thomas, Arthur Haynes (Panama-Frank/Universal)

Strange Bedfellows is another of those romantic marital comedies, based primarily on misunderstandings. Critics for the thinking man may scoff at the plot, which derives much of its drama from ancient device of each character not quite understanding what the others are up to. But story line differs enough so that it isn't simple carbon of all the Rock Hudson–Tony Randall–Doris Day comedies.

Hudson is a trifle solemn as London-based U.S. oil executive who can rise to extreme top echelon if his corporate image is whitewashed. This means he must patch up seven-year marriage to Gina Lollobrigida, who more than compensates for Hudson's stuffiness by her enthusiastic rapport with zany causes.

But the unabashed comedians steal the show. Probably the funniest bit has Arthur Haynes and David King as taxi drivers with Hudson and Gina in their respective vehicles. The estranged lovers try to communicate with one another by way of two-way cab radio, with hilarity resulting from cabbies garbling of messages.

•

STRANGE CARGO
1940, 111 mins, US Ⓥ b/w
Dir Frank Borzage ***Prod*** Joseph L. Mankiewicz ***Scr*** Lawrence Hazard ***Ph*** Robert Planck ***Ed*** Robert J. Kern ***Mus*** Franz Waxman
Act Joan Crawford, Clark Gable, Ian Hunter, Peter Lorre, Paul Lukas, Albert Dekker (M-G-M)

Strange Cargo is a strange melodramatic concoction [from a book by Richard Sale] that endeavors to mix the adventures of an escaping group of convicts from a tropical island prison with religious preachment through inclusion of a mysterious stranger with Christ-like attributes. The attempt is not successful. Combined with this fault is a slow, ploddy technique on the directing side, overlong footage and many dragging passages.

In accentuating the individual spiritual redemptions of the various convict members of the escaping group, story builds up with some rather strong talk and ridicule of the Bible, its passages and teachings.

Story, in attempt to dovetail stark and dangerous adventure with a religious motif, does not jell to any degree of consistency. Shortly after establishing the prison setting, the convicts escape and struggle through jungle, swamp and sand to reach a hidden boat. Clark Gable saves Joan Crawford from the clutches of a designing miner en route and takes her along. It's a strange group aboard the small open sailboat, the stranger (Ian Hunter) dominating with his quiet though definite manner.

Crawford is provided with a particularly meaty role as the hardened dance hall gal who falls hard for the tough convict. Gable is vigorous in his portrayal of the self-appointed head of the escaping convicts, a far from sympathetic assignment, and he is overshadowed by the reserved but strong-willed Hunter as the redeemer of the tough souls assembled in the small boat.

•

STRANGE DAYS
1995, 145 mins, US Ⓥ ⊙ ▭ col
Dir Kathryn Bigelow ***Prod*** James Cameron, Steven-Charles Jaffe ***Scr*** James Cameron, Jay Cocks ***Ph*** Matthew F. Leonetti ***Ed*** Howard Smith ***Mus*** Graeme Revell ***Art*** Lilly Kilvert
Act Ralph Fiennes, Angela Bassett, Juliette Lewis, Tom Sizemore, Michael Wincott, Vincent D'Onofrio (Lightstorm/20th Century-Fox)

A very dark vision of the very near future, *Strange Days* is enough to make any Angeleno plan now to be out of town on New Year's Eve, 1999. A technical tour de force for director Kathryn Bigelow and her team, pic is less accomplished in putting over its characters, emotions and dubious sociopolitical agenda.

Pic presents L.A. as an urban inferno of many people's worst nightmares, full of random violence, burning vehicles, anarchic punks, rogue police, increasingly militant blacks and troops barely able to stem the tide of surging masses ready to torch what's left.

Black marketeer Lenny Nero (Ralph Fiennes), a lowlife hustler and former cop, offers customers "a piece of somebody's life" available on a small disk and viewable via a compact headpiece. For his own personal pleasure, Nero prefers to replay scenes of happier times, when the saucy singer Faith (Juliette Lewis) was his eager-to-please girlfriend.

Now, however, Faith has run off with the sadistic Philo Gant (Michael Wincott), a sinister gangster who manages radical black political leader and singer Jeriko One (Glenn Plummer). One of her friends, a hooker named Iris (Brigitte Bako), warns Faith she is in terrible danger.

At this, the increasingly pathetic Nero hooks up with an old friend, "Mace" Manson (Angela Bassett), an exclusive security agent/chauffer who has her own reasons for helping him out. Inevitably, all the major characters wind up at the mammoth party-to-end-all-parties in downtown L.A. to usher in the new millennium.

Long on action sequences, script by James Cameron, who also produced and penned the original story, and Jay Cocks is elemental in posting its emotional signals. Fiennes comes off as just too elegant and refined for the principled slime bag he plays. Bassett is nearly as pumped-up here as Linda Hamilton was in *Terminator 2*, and tougher-talking. Lewis fans will love her wanton ways here, both onstage and in the bedroom.

•

STRANGE HOLIDAY
1946, 62 mins, US b/w
Dir Arch Oboler ***Scr*** Arch Oboler ***Ph*** Robert Surtees ***Ed*** Fred Feitshans, Jr. ***Mus*** Gordon Jenkins
Act Claude Rains, Bobbie Stebbins, Barbara Bate, Paul Hilton, Gloria Holden, Milton Kibbee (Elite)

Strange Holiday is a converted commercial film, turned out in wartime to boost morale of General Motors workers.

Written and directed by Arch Oboler, film poses thought that America's liberty must be carefully guarded. Most of the burden falls on Claude Rains's shoulders, and he makes a good try at keeping piece alive. It's pure propaganda aimed at winning the peace now that the war is over, but poses no method of how it's to be done.

Message is hung on melodramatic plot that has John Stevenson (Rains) coming back to the city after a vacation in an isolated spot. He finds the Nazis have taken over, and he's kicked around, beaten and subjected to other totalitarian stunts to draw contrast of how great it is to live in a free United States.

Oboler's direction is not always forte, but the subject matter is not too easy to get across. Heavy and lengthy dialog that falls to Rains keeps general pace slow with little interest around. Gloria Holden plays Rains's wife. Lensing by Robert Surtees and score by Gordon Jenkins are favorable factors.

•

STRANGE INTERLUDE
(U.K.: STRANGE INTERVAL)
1932, 110 mins, US Ⓥ b/w
Dir Robert Z. Leonard ***Scr*** Bess Meredyth, C. Gardner Sullivan ***Ph*** Lee Garmes ***Ed*** Margaret Booth
Act Norma Shearer, Clark Gable, Alexander Kirkland, Ralph Morgan, Robert Young, May Robson (M-G-M)

Norma Shearer, who shoulders the brunt of the histrionic burden, somehow misses in a vacillating characterization that was made necessarily so, for censor purposes alone, if nothing else. As for Clark Gable, he is eclipsed by Alexander Kirkland as the weak husband of the heroine and Ralph Morgan as the mawk with the mother fixation.

Through their life's span, as the story proceeds into old age, when Nina Leeds (Shearer) sees her illegitimate son molded to conform with her life's ideas, the episodic, transitory cinematurgy is as much a credit to the hairdressers and the makeup staff on the Metro lot as to Shearer, Gable, Kirkland and Morgan. The makeup is excellent but the make-believe isn't.

No question that the devitalizing of the [1928–29 Pulitzer Prize play by Eugene] O'Neill has much to do with it. The formula cinematic contrivances employed to pitch emotions falsely, to misfit climaxes, are very apparent.

The O'Neill asides, in screen treatment, might be said to be somewhat of an improvement over the stage original. The actual words are uttered, and then the subconscious thoughts are voiced by the same player on the soundtrack (with a different inflection, of course).

•

STRANGE INTERVAL
SEE: STRANGE INTERLUDE

•

STRANGE LOVE OF MARTHA IVERS, THE
1946, 113 mins, US Ⓥ ⊙ b/w
Dir Lewis Milestone ***Prod*** Hal B. Wallis ***Scr*** Robert Rossen ***Ph*** Victor Milner ***Ed*** Archie Marshek ***Mus*** Miklos Rozsa ***Art*** Hans Dreier, John Meehan
Act Barbara Stanwyck, Van Heflin, Lizabeth Scott, Kirk Douglas, Judith Anderson, Darryl Hickman (Wallis/Paramount)

Story is a forthright, uncompromising presentation of evil, greedy people and human weaknesses. Characters are sharply drawn in the Robert Rossen script, based on Jack Patrick's original story [*Love Lies Bleeding*], and Lewis Milestone's direction punches home the melodrama for full suspense and excitement.

Prolog opening [in 1928] establishes the murder of a bullying aunt by her young niece. Deed is witnessed by the son of the girl's tutor, but is blamed on an unknown prowler. Cover-up moves the tutor and son into a position of power in the girl's household. Story then picks up 18 years later with the accidental return to the town of another of the girl's childhood friends. Return panics Barbara Stanwyck and Kirk Douglas, now grown-up and married, who fear the friend was also a witness of the early killing.

Character portrayed by Stanwyck is evil, and she gives it a high-caliber delineation. Douglas makes his weakling role interesting, showing up strongly among the more experienced players. Best performance honors, though, are divided between Heflin and Scott, latter as a Heflin pickup.

1946: NOMINATION: Best Original Story

•

STRANGER, THE
1946, 94 mins, US Ⓥ ⦿ b/w
Dir Orson Welles ***Prod*** S. P. Eagle [= Sam Spiegel] ***Scr*** Anthony Veiller, [John Huston, Orson Welles] ***Ph*** Russell Metty ***Ed*** Ernest Nims ***Mus*** Bronislau Kaper ***Art*** Perry Ferguson
Act Orson Welles, Edward G. Robinson, Loretta Young, Philip Merivale, Richard Long (RKO/International)

The Stranger is socko melodrama, spinning an intriguing web of thrills and chills. Director Orson Welles gives the production a fast, suspenseful development, drawing every advantage from the hard-hitting script from the Victor Trivas story. Plot moves forward at a relentless pace in depicting the hunt of the Allied Commission for Prosecution of Nazi War Criminals for a top Nazi who has removed all traces of his origin and is a professor in a New England school. Edward G. Robinson is the government man on his trail. Loretta Young is the New England girl who becomes the bride of the Nazi.

Story opens in Germany, where a Nazi is allowed to escape in belief he will lead the way to former head of a notorious prison camp. Chase moves across Europe to the small New England town where Welles is marrying Young. When the escaped Nazi contacts him, Welles strangles him and buries the body in the woods. From then on the terror mounts as Robinson tries to trap Welles into revealing his true identity.

A uniformly excellent cast gives reality to events that transpire. The three stars, Robinson, Young and Welles, turn in some of their best work, the actress being particularly effective as the misled bride.

1946: NOMINATION: Best Original Story

•

STRANGER AMONG US, A
(UK: CLOSE TO EDEN)
1992, 111 mins, US Ⓥ col
Dir Sidney Lumet ***Prod*** Steve Golin, Sigurjon Sighvatsson, Howard Rosenman ***Scr*** Robert J. Avrech ***Ph*** Andrzej Bartkowiak ***Ed*** Andrew Mondshein ***Mus*** Jerry Bock ***Art*** Philip Rosenberg

Director Sidney Lumet's fish-out-of-water mystery about a case-hardened WASP female cop investigating a murder in New York's cloistered Hasidic community tries to make up in local color what it lacks in dramatic plausibility.

Melanie Griffith stars as seen-it-all cop Eden who, after having killed a thug who stabbed her lover-partner, is assigned to the low-pressure case of a vanished Hasidic jewelry dealer. When this fellow turns up dead in his office with $720,000 in diamonds missing, Griffith moves in with the Brooklyn group's rebbe (Lee Richardson) and his adopted children Eric Thal—the next rebbe designate—and Mia Sara to penetrate the community in her search for the killer.

Plot is overloaded with hard-to-take factors, while the revelation of the killer is far from surprising. More importantly, the nature of the Hasidic community effectively prevents Griffith from conducting any kind of penetrating investigation.

Griffith is at her best in the role's moments of awakening, when she realizes she is no longer satisfied with the prosaic interests of her cop b.f. and that she may have a spiritual side that has never been acknowledged.

•

STRANGER IN THE HOUSE
1967, 104 mins, UK col
Dir Pierre Rouve ***Prod*** Dimitri de Grunwald ***Scr*** Pierre Rouve ***Ph*** Ken Higgins ***Ed*** Ernest Walter ***Mus*** John Scott ***Art*** Tony Woollard
Act James Mason, Geraldine Chaplin, Bobby Darin, Paul Bertoya, Ian Ogilvy, Brian Stanyon (Rank)

This yarn pinpoints the complete misunderstanding and lack of communication between many of the flip generation and their middle-aged parents. It is sparked by the suspicious, coldly antagonistic attitude of Geraldine Chaplin to her middle-aged father (James Mason), who was once a brilliant barrister. The idea is woven into a smooth, holding murder mystery, based on a story by Georges Simenon.

Chaplin plays one of a small, live-it-up discotheque and coffee-bar set that gets its kicks from whoop-it-up parties and drugs. A predatory, slightly nutty and blandly sinister young American ship's steward (Bobby Darin) infiltrates the group, and he's found murdered in the Mason home.

Mason's first-rate performance holds the pic together and it is a fine study of disillusionment, self-disgust and sly humor.

•

STRANGER ON THE THIRD FLOOR
1940, 67 mins, US Ⓥ b/w
Dir Boris Ingster ***Prod*** Lee Marcus ***Scr*** Frank Partos ***Ph*** Nicholas Musuraca ***Ed*** Harry Marker ***Mus*** Roy Webb ***Art*** Van Nest Polglase, Albert S. D'Agostino
Act Peter Lorre, John McGuire, Margaret Tallichet, Charles Waldron, Elisha Cook, Jr., Charles Halton (RKO)

Yarn concerns a stern newspaper reporter whose testimony proves the circumstantial evidence that convicts an innocent man. The familiar artifice of placing the scribe in parallel plight, with the newspaperman arrested for two slayings and only clearing himself because of his sweetheart's persistent search for the real slayer, is used.

Peter Lorre, cast as the maniacal murder, is not seen for nearly two reels. It is only in the final footage that he has much of anything to do. By that time, the picture has lost its momentum. Absence of action and humor is a further handicap.

Unknown from NY, John McGuire, as the newspaperman, needs considerably more grooming with the RKO stock company, while Margaret Tallichet is only passable. Charles Waldron makes an acceptable d.a. while Elisha Cook, Jr. is satisfying in the role of the innocent man railroaded to jail.

Boris Ingster's direction is too studied and, when original, lacks the flare to hold attention. It's a film too arty for average audiences and too humdrum for others.

•

STRANGERS
SEE: VIAGGIO IN ITALIA

•

STRANGERS IN THE CITY
1962, 80 mins, US Ⓥ b/w
Dir Rick Carrier ***Prod*** Rick Carrier ***Scr*** Rick Carrier ***Ph*** Rick Carrier ***Ed*** Stan Russell ***Mus*** Bob Prince
Act Robert Gentile, Camilo Delgado, Rosita De Triana, Creta Margos, Robert Corso (Embassy/Carrier)

A first film by Yank Rick Carrier, this shows a Puerto Rican family in a Manhattan slum. The father is a vain, proud man with a lack of understanding of America or his family—and he has just lost his job. His teenage son and daughter go to look for work but he orders his wife to stay home. The boy runs into local racism and general hoodlumism as a delivery boy while the girl, a beauty, is used by factory workers and then becomes a sort of call girl for a dressmaker.

It may sound overly melodramatic, but this has a neat insight into NY life, as this producer sees it. Though this pic shows mainly bigoted people, it also depicts how their own weaknesses help betray this family. Much of the wickedness is from plain ignorance.

Some of the acting in skimpy. But Robert Gentile, as the son; Creta Margos, as his pliant comely sister; Rosita De Triana, as the anguished mother and Robert Corso, as the foppish gang leader, are standout.

•

STRANGER'S KISS
1983, 94 mins, US Ⓥ col
Dir Matthew Chapman ***Prod*** Doug Dilge ***Scr*** Matthew Chapman, Blaine Novak ***Ph*** Mikail Suslov ***Ed*** William Carruth ***Mus*** Gato Barbieri
Act Peter Coyote, Victoria Tennant, Blaine Novak, Dan Shor, Richard Romanus, Linda Kerridge (White)

Stranger's Kiss is a glowing homage to 1950s melodrama set in the film world. Though shot on a modest budget, picture has a lush look aided by strong artistic and technical contributions.

The love triangle tale is mirrored in both the real life and film-within-a-film structure of the production. Principals are Carole Redding (Victoria Tennant), a young woman kept by a gangster (Richard Romanus) who agrees to finance the film's film and costar, Stevie Blake (Blaine Novak, who also cowrote the script), a hustler who soon becomes consumed by Carole's mysterious background.

Stanley (Peter Coyote), the director, keeps Stevie in the dark to capitalize on his emotions. Both stories concern a boxer and a dancehall girl who fall in love, but her past debt to a hoodlum threatens to destroy the relationship. Plot is reminiscent of Stanley Kubrick's *Killer's Kiss* and several other low budget items circa 1955, the setting of the picture.

Tennant is radiant as Carole with a genuine screen presence suited to her role. In sharp contrast, Novak has a forceful presence which demands our attention and eventually wins our affection.

•

STRANGERS MAY KISS
1931, 82 mins, US b/w
Dir George Fitzmaurice ***Scr*** John Meehan ***Ph*** William Daniels ***Ed*** Hugh Wynn
Act Norma Shearer, Robert Montgomery, Neil Hamilton, Marjorie Rambeau, Irene Rich, Hale Hamilton (M-G-M)

Strangers May Kiss is based on the bestseller by Ursula Parrott, whose *Ex-Wife* provided Metro and Norma Shearer with a previous release. The Metro star is back with a sweet film.

Story deals with a girl's unwavering love for a roving newspaperman and their intimate relations in the hope (by the girl) of ultimate marriage. The novel ended with the girl waiting so many years that she finally determined suicide as a better antidote than counting days on calendars. Writer John Meehan has changed this to a happy ending.

Here is a refined, thoroughly sophisticated picture. Shearer gives an extraordinarily fine performance. Only once does she overact, in a burst of hysteria.

Neil Hamilton gives a very good account of himself as the newspaperman-hero and Robert Montgomery is very good as the swain, long courting the girl against great odds. Montgomery plays his part for the comedy it contains and wrenches plenty from it as a good-natured man-about-town who's mostly always in his cups.

The picture moves around a lot, including locales in and about New York, Mexico and various sections of Europe. Director George Fitzmaurice cuts from one sequence or shot to a totally different one hardly without a dissolve, yet the continuity is always smooth.

•

STRANGERS ON A TRAIN
1951, 100 mins, US Ⓥ ⦿ b/w
Dir Alfred Hitchcock ***Prod*** Alfred Hitchcock ***Scr*** Raymond Chandler, Czenzi Ormonde ***Ph*** Robert Burks ***Ed*** William H. Ziegler ***Mus*** Dimitri Tiomkin ***Art*** Ted Haworth
Act Farley Granger, Robert Walker, Ruth Roman, Leo G. Carroll, Patricia Hitchcock, Laura Elliott (Warner)

Given a good basis for a thriller in the Patricia Highsmith novel [script adaption by Whitfield Cook] and a first-rate script, Hitchcock embroiders the plot into a gripping, palm-sweating piece of suspense.

Story offers a fresh situation for murder. Two strangers meet on a train. One is Farley Granger, separated from his tramp wife (Laura Elliott) and in love with Ruth Roman. The other is Robert Walker, a neurotic playboy who hates his rich father. Walker proposes that he will kill Elliott if Granger will do away with the father. Granger treats the proposal as a bad joke, but Walker is serious.

Latter stalks down Elliott in an amusement park and strangles her. He then starts chasing Granger to make him fulfill the other end of the bargain.

Performance-wise, the cast comes through strongly. Granger is excellent as the harassed young man innocently involved in murder. Roman's role of a nice, understanding girl is a switch for her, and she makes it warmly effective. Walker's role has extreme color, and he projects it deftly. Elliott stands out briefly as the victim, and Patricia Hitchcock (the director's daughter) also registers.

[In the U.K. pic was released in version two minutes longer, with a truncated ending but a longer sequence in which the men meet on the train.]

1951: NOMINATION: Best B&W Cinematography

•

STRANGER'S RETURN
1933, 88 mins, US b/w
Dir King Vidor ***Prod*** King Vidor ***Scr*** Brown Holmes, Phil Stong ***Ph*** William Daniels ***Ed*** Dick Fantl ***Art*** Frederic Hope
Act Lionel Barrymore, Miriam Hopkins, Franchot Tone, Stuart Erwin, Irene Hervey, Beulah Bondi (M-G-M)

It is the story [from the novel by Phil Stong] of a New York girl who goes west after she leaves her husband, finds a new love, but loses out when the hero leaves to avoid temptation since he does not want to injure his wife and son, despite his greater love for his new idol.

Supplementing, or rather overshadowing the love interest, is a rare well-written story of a somewhat eccentric old farmer plagued by his fortune-seeking relatives who hover about the farm awaiting the death of their prospective victim.

As the farmer, Lionel Barrymore has a role he fits. Even his false whiskers are forgiven. Barrymore carries the bulk of the story. Miriam Hopkins is not as fortunate. She is natural for the greater part, but fails at times in the lighter phases.

Franchot Tone is a likable hero, always in command of his scenes. No faulty performance in the entire cast.

•

STRANGERS WHEN WE MEET

1960, 117 mins, US Ⓥ ▭ col

Dir Richard Quine ***Prod*** Richard Quine ***Scr*** Evan Hunter ***Ph*** Charles Lang, Jr. ***Ed*** Charles Nelson ***Mus*** George Duning ***Art*** Ross Bellah

Act Kirk Douglas, Kim Novak, Ernie Kovacs, Barbara Rush, Walter Matthau, Virginia Bruce (Bryna-Quine/Columbia)

A pictorially attractive but dramatically vacuous study of modern-style infidelity, *Strangers When We Meet* is easy on the eyes but hard on the intellect. A bunch of maladjusted suburbanites are thrown together in Evan Hunter's screenplay (from his novel), and what comes out is an old-fashioned soap opera.

Brilliant architect Kirk Douglas is upset because his spouse (Barbara Rush) is overly concerned with balancing the family budget. Meanwhile, housewife Kim Novak is disturbed over being taken for granted by her undersexed mate (John Bryant). Out of this germ of marital instability, a feverishly passionate affair blossoms between Douglas and Novak via a series of trysts. But unstable, sharp-eyed neighbor Walter Matthau, putting two and two together and coming up with an odd number, decides to even things up by getting into the act.

It is a rather pointless, slow-moving story, but it has been brought to the screen with such skill that it charms the spectator into an attitude of relaxed enjoyment, much the same effect as that produced by a casual daydream fantasy. Douglas does well by his role, and Novak brings to hers that cool, style-setting attitude that is her trademark.

•

STRANGER THAN PARADISE

1984, 95 mins, US Ⓥ ⦿ b/w

Dir Jim Jarmusch ***Prod*** Sara Driver ***Scr*** Jim Jarmusch ***Ph*** Tom DiCillo ***Ed*** Jim Jarmusch, Melody London ***Mus*** John Lurie

Act John Lurie, Eszter Balint, Richard Edson, Cecilia Stark (Cinesthesia-Grokenberger)

Stranger than Paradise is a bracingly original avant-garde black comedy. Begun as a short that was presented under the same title at some earlier festivals, film has been expanded in outstanding fashion by young New York writer-director Jim Jarmusch.

Simple narrative starts with self-styled New York hipster Willie (John Lurie) being paid a surprise, and quite unwelcome, visit by Hungarian cousin Eva (Eszter Balint). But when she finally leaves after 10 days, there seems to be a strange sort of affection between them.

Since plot doesn't count for much here, the style takes over, and Jarmusch has made such matters as camera placement, composition (in stunning black-and-white) and structure count for a lot.

•

STRANGE VENGEANCE OF ROSALIE, THE

1972, 107 mins, US col

Dir Jack Starrett ***Prod*** John Kohn ***Scr*** Anthony Greville-Bell, John Kohn ***Ph*** Ray Parslow ***Ed*** Thom Noble ***Mus*** John Cameron ***Art*** Roy Walker

Act Bonnie Bedelia, Ken Howard, Anthony Zerbe (20th Century-Fox/Cinecrest)

The Strange Vengeance of Rosalie is an offbeat film, centered around the fascinating, although admittedly preposterous, situation of a lonely adolescent part-Indian girl (Bonnie Bedelia), naive and emotionally disturbed, who hitches a ride with a traveling salesman (Ken Howard) and leads him to her isolated ramshackle cabin in New Mexico, where she lets the air out of the tires of his car, breaks his leg and holds him captive.

Pic generally holds together on strength of engaging performances and a fair amount of tension throughout, but the mixture of serious suspenseful drama (tinged with an ever-present air of impending violence) and humorous repartee between the characters doesn't jell.

[Based on *Chicken* by Miles Tripp.]

•

STRANGE WOMAN, THE

1946, 100 mins, US Ⓥ b/w

Dir Edgar G. Ulmer ***Prod*** Hunt Stromberg ***Scr*** Herb Meadow ***Ph*** Lucien Andriot ***Ed*** James E. Newcom, John Foley, Richard G. Wray ***Mus*** Carmen Dragon ***Art*** Nicolai Remisoff

Act Hedy Lamarr, George Sanders, Louis Hayward, Gene Lockhart, Hillary Brooke, June Storey (United Artists)

Based on the Ben Ames William bestseller, story deals with strong willed Jenny Hager who uses men for personal pleasure and as stepping stones to wealth. It's told against a background of Bangor, Maine, in the 1840s, itself a lusty, brawling town in the throes of growing pains. Settings and costumes present a seemingly authentic picture of the period.

Hedy Lamarr scores as the scheming Hager. Two-sided character obtains plenty of realism in her hands. Her capacity of appearing as a tender, ministering angel and of mirroring sadistic satisfaction in the midst of violence bespeaks wide talent range.

Not so adept are her male costars, although Louis Hayward gets across the weakling son of Hager's first husband who is finally driven to suicide by the evil woman. George Sanders is out of his depths as a shy, backwoods character who becomes Lamarr's second husband.

•

STRANGLER, THE

1964, 89 mins, US Ⓥ b/w

Dir Burt Topper ***Prod*** Samuel Bischoff, David Diamond ***Scr*** Bill S. Ballinger ***Ph*** Jacques Marquette ***Ed*** Robert Eisen ***Mus*** Marlin Skiles ***Art*** Hal Pereira, Eugene Lourie

Act Victor Buono, David McLean, Diane Sayer, Davey Davison, Ellen Corby, Baynes Barron (Allied Artists)

Bill S. Ballinger's scenario describes the latter phases of the homicidal career of a paranoid schizophrenic (Victor Buono) whose hatred of women has been motivated by a possessive mother who has completely warped his personality. His fetish for dolls ultimately betrays him to the police just as he is in the act of applying the coup de grace to distaff victim No. 11.

Dramatically skillful direction by Burt Topper and a firm level of histrionic performances help *The Strangler* over some rough spots and keep the picture from succumbing to inconsistencies of character and contrivances of story scattered through the picture.

Bueno for Buono, a convincing menace all the way. There's always a place on the screen for a fat man who can act, and Buono has the avoirdupois field virtually to himself.

•

STRAPLESS

1990, 97 mins, UK Ⓥ ⦿ col

Dir David Hare ***Prod*** Rick McCallum ***Scr*** David Hare ***Ph*** Andrew Dunn ***Ed*** Edward Marnier ***Mus*** Nick Bicat ***Art*** Roger Hall

Act Blair Brown, Bruno Ganz, Bridget Fonda, Alan Howard, Michael Gough, Hugh Laurie (Granada)

Writer-director David Hare's third feature centers on the concerns of a middle-aged professional woman whose personal problems relate to wider political and social issues in Britain today.

This time the central character is an American, Dr. Lillian Hempel (Blair Brown), who's lived in Britain for 12 years. While on vacation in Portugal she meets an apparently wealthy stranger, Raymond Forbes (Bruno Ganz), who woos her but fails to get her into his bed.

Back in London, Forbes continues his courtship, begging Lillian to marry him. They marry secretly, and soon after he simply disappears. Lillian discovers he already has a wife and son, also abandoned.

Lillian's serious, well-ordered life is contrasted with her flighty younger sister Amy (Bridget Fonda), who has a series of Latin lovers and gets pregnant by one of them.

Meanwhile, Lillian gradually is being drawn toward political activism as the British government's health service cutbacks begin to hurt.

Strapless (so-named because both the sisters wind up with no visible means of support) is an intelligent, ironic, multilayered drama that's consistently intriguing. Performances are impeccable.

•

STRATEGIC AIR COMMAND

1955, 110 mins, US Ⓥ ⦿ ▭ col

Dir Anthony Mann ***Prod*** Samuel J. Briskin ***Scr*** Valentine Davies, Beirne Lay, Jr. ***Ph*** William Daniels, Thomas Tutwiler ***Ed*** Eda Warren ***Mus*** Victor Young ***Art*** Hal Pereira, Earl Hedrick

Act James Stewart, June Allyson, Frank Lovejoy, Barry Sullivan, Alex Nicol, Jay C. Flippen (Paramount)

SAC is at its best when off the ground. Two giant ships engaging in a refueling operation and sweeping views of a B36 with its jet engines skywriting long hyphens in blue smoke—this is visually stirring stuff.

Screenplay presents James Stewart as a hotshot third baseman for the St. Louis Cardinals who's beckoned back to the Air Force, this time with the nation's great, long-range striking force.

June Allyson scores as the wife, rebelling as the SAC takes hold on her mate and then showing sympathy and understanding. She's warm and appealing.

Anthony Mann's direction keeps *SAC* well on the move, seguing smoothly from ground operations to the high altitudes. For an actionful highlight, he wrings out good excitement from Stewart's forced pancake landing in Greenland when his big jet bomber catches fire.

•

STRAWBERRY AND CHOCOLATE

SEE: FRESA Y CHOCOLATE

•

STRAWBERRY BLONDE

1941, 98 mins, US Ⓥ b/w

Dir Raoul Walsh ***Prod*** William Cagney ***Scr*** Julius J. Epstein, Philip G. Epstein ***Ph*** James Wong Howe ***Ed*** William Holmes ***Mus*** Heinz Roemheld

Act James Cagney, Olivia de Havilland, Rita Hayworth, Jack Carson, Alan Hale, George Tobias (Warner)

Warners dips into the Gay Nineties period with this second film version of James Hagan's play, *One Sunday Afternoon*. Paramount turned out the original picture back in 1933 with Gary Cooper starred.

This entry of the Hagan play switches the locale to New York; otherwise it sticks close to the original. Story is told in retrospect. James Cagney is a struggling dentist with few patients, when an emergency call comes to pull a molar of his worst enemy and he figures to give the latter a good dose of gas. While waiting for the patient's arrival, yarn goes back 10 years, when Cagney was enamored of the neighborhood's "strawberry blonde."

Jilted, he conveniently marries the loving and understanding nurse (Olivia de Havilland), but through the years carries a hate for the man who victimized him and stole his first girl. But he again meets the girl of his memories, finds her a nagging nuisance, and figures his enemy has had sufficient punishment through the years. It's then that he realizes he has the perfect wife.

Cagney and de Havilland provide top-notch performances that do much to keep up interest in the proceedings. Rita Hayworth is an eyeful as the title character, while Jack Carson is excellent as the politically ambitious antagonist of the dentist.

1941: NOMINATION: Best Scoring of a Musical Picture

•

STRAW DOGS

1971, 118 mins, UK/US Ⓥ ⦿ col

Dir Sam Peckinpah ***Prod*** Daniel Melnick ***Scr*** David Zelag Goodman, Sam Peckinpah ***Ph*** John Coquillon ***Ed*** Roger Spottiswoode, Paul Davies, Tony Lawson ***Mus*** Jerry Fielding ***Art*** Ray Simm

Act Dustin Hoffman, Susan George, Peter Vaughan, T. P. McKenna, David Warner, Colin Welland (ABC/Talent Associates/Amerbroco)

Director Sam Peckinpah indulges himself in an orgy of unparalleled violence and nastiness with undertones of sexual repression in this production.

Dustin Hoffman appears as a quiet American mathematician who has married a lively, sexy English girl, played by Susan George, and goes to live on her isolated West Country farm. They get on reasonably well with a moronic assortment of locals, most of whom are heavy drinkers. Some are sexually repressed and the wife is seduced while her husband is hunting. When the village dolt accidentally kills a teenage mini-skirted flirt he takes refuge at the farm. Hoffman refuses to give him to the enflamed villagers. Count is lost of the gruesome killings and bestialities that ensue.

The script [from Gordon M. Williams' novel *The Siege of Trencher's Farm*] relies on shock and violence to tide it over weakness in development, shallow characterization and lack of motivation. Hoffman scores as the easygoing American who rises to heights of belligerence when he considers the dolt is being wronged.

1971: NOMINATION: Best Original Score

•

STREAMERS
1983, 118 mins, US Ⓥ ⦿ col
Dir Robert Altman ***Prod*** Nick J. Mileti, Robert Altman ***Scr*** David Rabe ***Ph*** Pierre Mignot ***Ed*** Norman Smith ***Mus*** Stephen Foster ***Art*** Wolf Kroeger
Act Matthew Modine, Michael Wright, Mitchell Lichtenstein, David Allen Grier, Albert Macklin, Guy Bond (United Artists Classics)

Streamers is a highly stylized set of theatricals describing an existentialist hell among a small group of men in a military barracks.

Apart from allowing the camera to occasionally peek through a curtain, writer David Rabe and director Robert Altman have their 1965 soldiers await orders to go to Vietnam and spending the waiting time either lying around on their bunks or returning drunk from saloon or whorehouse outings. They mostly taunt each other with tales of their own past history, but the taunts are socially, racially and sexually loaded, two of the soldiers being black, a third being an Ivy League homosexual and the fourth an intellectual "from the sticks."

Things explode in blood-gushing violence and general sadness when the possibilities have been exhausted in this overlong, overemphatic film.

•

STREET ANGEL
1928, 85 mins, US ⊗ b/w
Dir Frank Borzage ***Prod*** William Fox ***Scr*** Marion Orth, Katherine Hilliker, H. H. Caldwell, Philip Klein, Henry Roberts Symonds ***Ph*** Ernest Palmer ***Ed*** Barney Wolf ***Mus*** Erno Rapee
Act Janet Gaynor, Charles Farrell, Natalie Kingston, Henry Armetta, Guido Trento, Alberto Rabagliali (Fox)

Janet Gaynor is in the title role of *Street Angel* [from the play by Monckton Hoffe] and plays it all of the while, though none of the characters draws real sympathy. With the scene set in Italy and Naples for the opening, Gaynor is rescued from the police by a touring circus after receiving a year's sentence for soliciting to gain 20 lire to fill a prescription for her dying mother. Through that circumstance she meets a vagrant painter (Charles Farrell) who is showing in opposition to the little wagon oufit.

Secondary roles are well cast and played. Natalie Kingston as a streetwalker does very well, while there is real comedy in a quiet manner of Henry Armetta as the circus manager.

•

STREETCAR NAMED DESIRE, A
1951, 125 mins, US Ⓥ ⦿ b/w
Dir Elia Kazan ***Prod*** Charles K. Feldman ***Scr*** Oscar Saul ***Ph*** Harry Stradling ***Ed*** David Weisbart ***Mus*** Alex North ***Art*** Richard Day
Act Vivien Leigh, Marlon Brando, Kim Hunter, Karl Malden, Rudy Bond, Nick Dennis (Feldman)

Tennessee Williams's exciting Broadway stage play—winner of the Pulitzer Prize and New York Drama Critics award during the 1947–48 season—has been screenplayed into an even more absorbing drama of frustration and stark tragedy. With Marlon Brando essaying the part he created for the Broadway stage and Vivien Leigh as the morally disintegrated Blanche DuBois (originated on Broadway by Jessica Tandy), *A Streetcar Named Desire* is thoroughly adult drama, excellently produced and imparting a keen insight into a drama whose scope was, of necessity, limited by its stage setting.

Pic is a faithful adaptation from the original play. It is the story of Blanche DuBois, a faded Mississippi teacher, who seeks refuge with a sister in the old French Quarter of New Orleans. Because her presence intrudes on the husband-wife relationship, the husband, a crude brutal young Polish-American, immediately becomes hostile to the visitor. He also suspects she's lying about her past. It is this hostility that motivates the story's basic elements. Stanley Kowalski (Brando), the husband, embarks on a plan to force his sister-in-law from his home.

Leigh gives a compelling performance in telling the tragedy of Blanche DuBois. Brando at times captures strongly the brutality of the young Pole but occasionally he performs unevenly in a portrayal marked by frequent garbling of his dialog. Kim Hunter and Karl Malden are excellent as Blanche's sister and frantic suitor.

1951: Best Actress (Vivien Leigh), Supp. Actor (Karl Malden), Supp. Actress (Kim Hunter), B&W Art Direction

NOMINATIONS: Best Picture, Director, Actor (Marlon Brando), Screenplay, B&W Cinematography, B&W Costume Design, Scoring of a Dramatic Picture, Sound

•

STREETFIGHTER, THE
SEE: HARD TIMES

•

STREET FIGHTER
(AKA: STREET FIGHTER—THE ULTIMATE BATTLE)
1994, 97 mins, US Ⓥ ⦿ ▭ col
Dir Steven E. de Souza ***Prod*** Edward R. Pressman, Kenzo Tsujimoto ***Scr*** Steven E. de Souza ***Ph*** William A. Fraker ***Ed*** Dov Hoenig, Anthony Redman, Robert F. Shugrue, Ed Abroms, Donn Aron ***Mus*** Graeme Revell ***Art*** William Creber
Act Jean-Claude Van Damme, Raul Julia, Ming-na Wen, Damian Chapa, Kylie Minogue, Simon Callow (Capcom/Columbia)

Jean-Claude Van Damme takes a career step backward in *Street Fighter*, a messy, basically plotless big-screen rendition of the popular multimedia game [*Street Fighter II*]. Film suffers from the same problem that impaired *Super Mario Brothers*: it is noisy, overblown and effects-laden and lacks sustained action or engaging characters.

Van Damme plays Col. Guile, the military commander of the Allied Nations forces, assigned to defeat Gen. Bison (Raul Julia), the megalomaniac dictator of a country called Shadaloo, in order to rescue 63 kidnapped relief workers held hostage by the psychotic ruler. When the Allied Nations succumb to Bison's demands for a huge ransom, the protesting Guile is relieved of his command. But the fiesty fighter disobeys orders and leads a commando force of tough street fighters on a covert mission.

The two men, who play archetypes, are surrounded by some colorful characters who add flavor to the proceedings, such as attractive TV reporter Chun-li (Ming-na Wen), who has her personal agenda for wanting to destroy Bison; Sagat (Wes Studi), Bison's arms supplier, who controls the toughest gang in Southeast Asia; and Dhalsim (Roshan Seth), Bison's captive biophysicist.

Steven E. de Souza, a veteran of some functional action scripts (the *Die Hard* movies, *48HRS.*), makes an unimpressive directorial debut in this misconceived adventure. Van Damme disappears for long stretches, during which the action drags and meanders in too many directions.

[European prints had a brief extra scene, after the end credits, showing Bison coming back to life.]

•

STREET OF SORROW, THE
SEE: DIE FREUDLOSE GASSE

•

STREETS
1990, 83 mins, US Ⓥ col
Dir Katt Shea Ruben ***Prod*** Andy Ruben ***Scr*** Katt Shea Ruben, Andy Ruben ***Ph*** Phedon Papamichael ***Ed*** Stephen Mark ***Mus*** Aaron Davis ***Art*** Virginia Lee
Act Christina Applegate, David Mendenhall, Eb Lottimer, Patrick Richwood, Alan Stock (Concorde)

Despite its B-film framework involving a maniacal killer stalking street kids, *Streets* transcends its genre with a gritty and affecting portrait of a teenage throwaway struggling to exist in L.A.'s demimonde.

Director Katt Shea Ruben, who scripted with her producer-husband Andy Ruben, clearly had more ambitious things in mind than just another Concorde thriller in which nubile girls are stalked and murdered.

Christina Applegate's solid performance in her first starring feature as the jaded but still sensitive Dawn, who sells sex to survive and shoots up heroin to get through the day, speaks volumes about the scuzzy side of L.A. life. Working with a minimal budget and a 19-day shooting sked, Ruben conjures up an impressive, subtly fantastic atmosphere.

Yet since this is a Roger Corman-type production, neorealism isn't enough, and there has to be a psycho killer (vampirish policeman Eb Lottimer), who preys on street kids and becomes obsessed with eliminating Applegate. Although without much insight into the character of the killer, *Streets* has a compelling pattern of visual suspense.

•

STREET SCENE
1931, 80 mins, US Ⓥ b/w
Dir King Vidor ***Prod*** Samuel Goldwyn ***Scr*** Elmer Rice ***Ph*** George Barnes ***Ed*** Hugh Bennett ***Mus*** Alfred Newman ***Art*** Richard Day
Act Sylvia Sidney, William Collier, Jr., Estelle Taylor, Max Montor, David Landau, Russell Hopton (Goldwyn/United Artists)

Street Scene comes upon the screen in faithful reproduction of the stage play. Author Elmer Rice went to Hollywood and had a supervisory hand in the filming, and nearly a dozen of the characters are played by the same actors who appeared in the first New York production.

Principal setting is almost a reproduction of the stage locale, even to the scaffolding of the construction job adjoining the tenement house in the West 60s of New York.

Picture opens on a sequence of city life with the introduction of a crashing symphonic musical setting, rather in the Gershwin manner, symbolizing the breadth and scope of the subject.

Sylvia Sidney gives an even, persuasive performance in a role for which she is particularly fitted, typifying the tragedy of budding girlhood cramped by sordid surroundings. Even her lack of formal beauty intensifies the pathos of the character. Young William Collier, Jr., makes a splendid opposite to the heroine, playing his quieter scenes with true emphasis and rising to the swifter tempo with satisfying vigor.

In a purely acting sense the honors go to Beula Bondi, as the malicious scandalmonger of the tenement, playing the part she created on the stage and playing it to the hilt.

•

STREETS OF FIRE
1984, 94 mins, US Ⓥ ⦿ col
Dir Walter Hill ***Prod*** Lawrence Gordon, Joel Silver ***Scr*** Walter Hill, Larry Gross ***Ph*** Andrew Laszlo ***Ed*** Freeman Davies, Michael Ripps ***Mus*** Ry Cooder ***Art*** John Vallone
Act Michael Pare, Diane Lane, Rick Moranis, Amy Madigan, Willem Dafoe, Deborah Van Valkenburgh (Universal/RKO)

Assembled by the team that created *48HRS.* [1982], pic is a pulsing, throbbing orchestration careening around the rescue of a kidnapped young singer. The decor is urban squalor.

Movie has 10 original songs, and musically the movie is continually hot, with lyrics charting the concerns of the narrative line, simplistic as it is.

Film also has undeniable texture. Smoke, neon, rainy streets, platforms of elevated subway lines, alleys and warehouses create an urban inferno in an unspecified time and place.

Diane Lane, whose singing voice is dubbed, looks great and is cast expertly. So are Willem Dafoe and Lee Ving.

Briefly seen as a stripper-dancer in the Bombers's hangout is Marine Jahan, who was the uncredited dancer in *Flashdance*.

•

STREETS OF GOLD
1986, 95 mins, US Ⓥ col
Dir Joe Roth ***Prod*** Joe Roth ***Scr*** Heywood Gould, Richard Price, Tom Cole ***Ph*** Arthur Albert ***Ed*** Richard Chew ***Mus*** Jack Nitzsche ***Art*** Marcos Flaksman
Act Klaus Maria Brandauer, Adrian Pasdar, Wesley Snipes, Angela Molina (Ufland/Roth)

Streets of Gold is a likable, but hardly compelling story of not one, but two kids trying to box their way out of the slums.

Klaus Maria Brandauer is at the center of the ring, playing a Russian Jew and former boxing champion who was banned from competing for the Soviet team because of his religion—so he emigrated to the U.S. and now works as a dishwasher and gets drunk a lot.

A brash Irish tough named Timmy Doyle (Adrian Pasdar) is so impressed that this middle-aged and seemingly out-of-shape lunk can so easily humiliate an athlete half his age, he seeks him out the next day, and asks him to be his coach.

Streets of Gold is paved with credibly gritty scenes, but the end result comes off as a highbrow boxing training film.

•

STREET WITH NO NAME, THE
1948, 94 mins, US Ⓥ b/w
Dir William Keighley ***Prod*** Samuel G. Engel ***Scr*** Harry Kleiner ***Ph*** Joe MacDonald ***Ed*** William Reynolds ***Mus*** Lionel Newman (dir.) ***Art*** Lyle Wheeler, Chester Gore
Act Mark Stevens, Richard Widmark, Lloyd Nolan, Barbara Lawrence, Ed Begley, Donald Buka (20th Century-Fox)

A double-barreled gangster film, *The Street with No Name* ranks at the top of the list of documentary-type productions which have been rolling out of the 20th-Fox lot. This pic has a lean, tough surface wrapped around a nucleus of explosive violence. Beneath its documentary exterior there lies a straight melodrama that harks back to the great gangster films of the early 1930s.

Richard Widmark, who twitched his way to stardom with his performance in *Kiss of Death*, is the backbone of this film. As the leader of a gang of youngsters who operate with military science, Widmark commands complete interest with his interpretation of a psychotically ruthless character. His looks and personality have the latent menace of a loaded automatic.

In neat contrast to Widmark, Mark Stevens plays the role of an all-American boy who, as an agent of the FBI, becomes a gang member. His efforts to collect the evidence for the police while exposing himself to the fate of a stoolpigeon provide the basis for the plot structure and tension.

Along a continuous line of fresh details, film includes a crackerjack fight sequence between Stevens and a professional pug, a glimpse into the FBI machinery, and a slambang finale in which the cops and the hoodlums shoot it out in an industrial plant.

In a secondary role, Lloyd Nolan, playing the same Inspector Briggs of the FBI of *The House on 92nd Street*, delivers with his usual competence.

•

STRICTLY BALLROOM
1992, 92 mins, Australia Ⓥ ⊙ col
Dir Baz Luhrmann ***Prod*** Tristram Miall ***Scr*** Baz Luhrmann, Craig Pearce ***Ph*** Steve Mason ***Ed*** Jill Bilcock ***Mus*** David Hirschfelder ***Art*** Catherine Martin
Act Paul Mercurio, Tara Morice, Bill Hunter, Barry Otto, Pat Thomson, Gia Carides (M&A)

This bright, breezy and immensely likable musical-comedy is a remarkably confident film debut for cowriter/director Baz Luhrmann [based on an earlier screenplay by Luhrmann and Andrew Bovell, from an idea by the former]. A behind-the-scenes look at a contest for ballroom dancers, pic unfolds a classical tale of a young dance star, Scott, who wants to break the rules and the opposition he faces from the establishment.

Paul Mercurio (son of vet character actor Gus Mercurio) is a real find as Scott, a handsome leading man who, in addition, is obviously a top-flight dancer. Opposite him, Tara Morice shines as a plain Jane who turns from ugly duckling to swan when she's on the dance floor.

Scott, partnered with the lovely but waspish Liz (Gia Carides) blows the semifinals when he breaks federation rules by improvising on the floor. Enter Fran (Morice), a shy Spanish girl with bad skin and glasses. They work on a flamenco routine they know will be anathema to the federation honchos, but, this being a wish-fulfillment pic, everything turns out fine at fade-out.

•

STRICTLY DISHONORABLE
1951, 94 mins, US b/w
Dir Melvin Frank, Norman Panama ***Prod*** Melvin Frank, Norman Panama ***Scr*** Melvin Frank, Norman Panama ***Ph*** Ray June ***Ed*** Cotton Warburton ***Mus*** Lennie Hayton (dir)
Act Ezio Pinza, Janet Leigh, Millard Mitchell, Gale Robbins, Maria Palmer, Esther Minciotti (M-G-M)

Preston Sturges's by-now venerable legit comedy comes to the screen as an amusing celluloid treatment of the loves and life of a romantic opera star back in the speakeasy days. There is still life left in the play, and the production, direction and scripting of Melvin Frank and Norman Panama take advantage of it.

Plot reprise finds Ezio Pinza famous for his opera notes and amours. Into his life comes Janet Leigh, a wide-eyed innocent from Mississippi who has long worshipped him. She arrives just at the time Pinza is embroiled in a feud with Hugh Sanders's publisher, because he has nixed the singing efforts of the latter's wife (Gale Robbins).

Circumstance brings about a marriage of convenience between Pinza and Leigh, with both willing to make it more than that, and plot has the added threat of a breach-of-promise move by Maria Palmer, a lush countess who had been romanced by the singer.

Leigh is easy to take as the Southern girl, adding charm to the footage even though she has trouble maintaining her mushmouth drawl. Pinza does quite well by the light comedy. Millard Mitchell snaps over some good moments as Pinza's press agent.

•

STRIKE ME PINK
1936, 99 mins, US b/w
Dir Norman Taurog ***Prod*** Samuel Goldwyn ***Scr*** Frank Butler, Walter De Leon, Francis Martin, Philip Rapp ***Ph*** Gregg Toland, Merritt Gerstad, Ray Binger ***Ed*** Sherman Todd ***Mus*** Alfred Newman (dir.)
Act Eddie Cantor, Ethel Merman, Sally Eilers, William Frawley, Brian Donlevy (Goldwyn/United Artists)

Many and varied gags, majority of which land, combine with a set of good songs and individual performances to make this good entertainment. Picture doesn't look the cost of previous Cantor starrers. It is a little less lavish.

Cantor is aces all the way. In some instances he's actually cute, but he isn't singing so much in *Strike Me Pink*, having only two numbers, one with Merman atop a ferris wheel, the other (a production display) with Rita Rio, hotcha tapster and the girls. There are only four songs [by Harold Arlen and Lew Brown] and no reprises.

Other two numbers are for Ethel Merman alone in the nitery setting, where she's spotted as the particular weakness of the hick Cantor. Merman is tops.

Dances and ensembles were photographed by Gregg Toland, while Merman's first number, unusually well done, was cameraed by Merritt Gerstad and specially credited.

Story is the kind of comedy yarn which could have been done without the benefit of singing and dancing. Originally called *Dreamland*, it was intended for Harold Lloyd and would have made ideal material for this comedian. Going to Sam Goldwyn instead for the use of Cantor, rights to title *Strike Me Pink*, name of a musical comedy done several years earlier, were acquired.

Big-eyed comic plays a meek tailor to college campus trade whose efforts to overcome an inferiority complex land him quite by accident into the job of general manager for an amusement park that is trying to keep slot machines off the premises. Cantor's troubles with the racketeers behind the slot machines form the basis for most of the comedy situations.

•

STRIKE UP THE BAND
1940, 119 mins, US Ⓥ ⊙ b/w
Dir Busby Berkeley ***Prod*** Arthur Freed ***Scr*** John Monks, Jr., Fred Finklehoffe ***Ph*** Ray June ***Ed*** Ben Lewis ***Mus*** Arthur Freed, Roger Edens, George Gershwin
Act Mickey Rooney, Judy Garland, Paul Whiteman, June Preisser, William Tracy, Ann Shoemaker (M-G-M)

Strike Up the Band is Metro's successor to *Babes in Arms*, with Mickey Rooney, assisted by major trouping on the part of Judy Garland, dominating every minute of the extended running time.

Story details the enthusiastic musical talents of Rooney, who converts the high school band into a swing orchestra and then aims for a spot on the Paul Whiteman scholastic band broadcast.

The attention-arresting abilities of Rooney are forcibly demonstrated here. Young star is a socko personality, timing every movement for most effective reaction. In addition to a standout performance, he sings, dances and plays both piano and drums in talented style.

Despite the overall dominance of Rooney, Garland catches major attention for her all-around achievements. She's right there with Rooney in much of the story as his mentoring girlfriend, teams with him in the production numbers for both songs and dances, and rings the bell with several songs sold to the utmost.

Outstanding production number is a conga played by the school band and danced by a large student ensemble, with Rooney and Garland spotlighted prominently throughout. In contrast, a novel and ingenious little production number—with only Rooney and Garland participating—is one of the most original sequences ever devised for pictures. In bragging to Judy how he will arrange and lead the band for the contest, Rooney sets out the contents of a fruit dish on the table and starts his imaginary direction. The various pieces of fruit dissolve into small puppet musicians, playing their respective instruments in proper tempo.

Direction by Busby Berkeley deftly carries through the story side, despite script deficiencies, but he is in his element in the staging of the production and musical sequences.

1940: Best Sound Recording (Douglas Shearer)

NOMINATIONS: Best Score, Song ("Our Love Affair")

•

STRIPES
1981, 103 mins, US Ⓥ ⊙ col
Dir Ivan Reitman ***Prod*** Ivan Reitman, Dan Goldberg ***Scr*** Len Blum, Dan Goldberg, Harold Ramis ***Ph*** Bill Butler ***Ed*** Eva Ruggiero, Michael Luciano, Harry Keller ***Mus*** Elmer Bernstein ***Art*** James H. Spencer
Act Bill Murray, Harold Ramis, Warren Oates, Sean Young, John Candy, Judge Reinhold (Columbia)

Stripes is a cheerful, mildly outrageous and mostly amiable comedy pitting a new generation of enlistees against the oversold lure of a military hungry for bodies and not too choosy about what it gets. There's little in the way of art or comic subtlety here, but the film really seems to work.

Bill Murray, who worked under Ivan Reitman in *Meatballs*, is an aimless layabout whose Sad Sack life prompts him to consider the army as a last-ditch passport to the career, romances, travels and other delights painted in those glossy Federal commercials.

Predictably, after he cons buddy Harold Ramis into enlisting, the sexy ads quickly prove to be Madison Avenue fiction, with basic training—under the grizzled glare of drill sergeant Warren Oates—taking the place of fraternity hell week as Murray heads deeper into trouble, cued by his amiably arrogant smart-assedness.

Apart from Murray's focal presence, Ramis and obese John Candy are wildly funny, with Oates treading a good balance between grizzly humor and military convictions (which the film, surprisingly, winds up more honoring than knocking).

•

STRIPPER, THE
(U.K.: WOMAN OF SUMMER)
1963, 95 mins, US Ⓥ ▭ b/w
Dir Franklin J. Schaffner ***Prod*** Jerry Wald ***Scr*** Meade Roberts ***Ph*** Ellsworth Fredericks ***Ed*** Robert Simpson ***Mus*** Jerry Goldsmith ***Art*** Jack Martin Smith, Walter M. Simonds
Act Joanne Woodward, Richard Beymer, Claire Trevor, Carol Lynley, Robert Webber, Gypsy Rose Lee (20th Century-Fox)

This final film by Jerry Wald is an unsuccessful attempt to convert William Inge's 1959 Broadway flop, *A Loss of Roses*, into a substantial and appealing motion picture. Like the play, the film has its merits, but they are only flashes of magic in a lackluster package. Joanne Woodward's performance in a role expanded to focal prominence in the film is one of them.

The story is set in traditional Inge country—a small town in Kansas—more specifically the modest residence of two characters into those humdrum lives comes Woodward, stranded by the abrupt deterioration of the little magician's unit of which she is a part.

She is taken in by an old friend (Claire Trevor) now a widow who lives with her son (Richard Beymer), an ardent but inexperienced lad. There are attempts to make something of the mother-son relationship, but the two characters are never properly clarified and remain two-dimensional. At any rate, Beymer fancies himself in love with the visitor and has a one-night affair with the fading, desperately accommodating and romantically vulnerable would-be actress.

Histrionic honors go hands down to the animated Woodward, who rivets attention and compassion to herself throughout with a forceful and vivacious portrayal of the goodhearted but gullible girl. Beymer is adequate, little more, in the rather baffling role of the lad.

Lovely Carol Lynley is wasted in a thankless role which requires mostly a photogenic rear anatomy for walking away shots. Woodward's rear gets a big photographic play, too.

Franklin Schaffner's direction tends to be a bit choppy, uneven and, in spots, heavy-handed or unobservant. Jerry Goldsmith's score has sparkle and character and is obtrusive in a constructive manner—when a musical lift is needed to enliven the going.

1963: NOMINATION: Best B&W Costume Design

•

STRIPTEASE
1996, 115 mins, US Ⓥ ⊙ col
Dir Andrew Bergman ***Prod*** Mike Lobell ***Scr*** Andrew Bergman ***Ph*** Stephen Goldblatt ***Ed*** Anne V. Coates ***Mus*** Howard Shore ***Art*** Mel Bourne
Act Demi Moore, Armand Assante, Ving Rhames, Robert Patrick, Burt Reynolds, Paul Guilfoyle (Castle Rock/Columbia)

A dark comedy about sleaze, corruption and naughty behavior below the Bible Belt, *Striptease* doesn't quite come off. Writer-director Andrew Bergman has good fun sending up the weak morals, outrageous hypocrisy and trashy lifestyles of many of his characters, but his satirical aim is wobbly, the jibes and potshots falling short of their mark more often than not.

Based on Carl Hiaasen's novel *Strip Tease*, script jumps right in by showing Erin Grant (Demi Moore) being stripped of custody of her seven-year-old daughter, Angela (Moore's daughter Rumer Willis) in favor of her lowlife ex, Darrell (Robert Patrick). Erin takes up stripping at the Eager Beaver, a congenial enough club where the girls have good backstage camaraderie and tough black bouncer Shad (Ving Rhames) protects them with vigilance.

Sending everyone's lives into a different orbit is the arrival of Congressman David Dilbeck (Burt Reynolds), a sex fiend who regularly visits strip joints. Things spin further in crazy and unpredictable directions after Erin kidnaps her daughter from Darrell.

The star looks quite buff, with legs and butt that attest to hours on the Stairmaster and other attributes that are far from demi-class. After a teaser about 45 minutes in, Moore finally does her first full-fledged strip at the hour mark. Moore's dance routines have a rather overly calculated, too disciplined feel, but the actress otherwise delivers one of her more credible performances.

Rhames slowly develops a vastly amusing character, at first seeming like a gruntingly one-note thug but ultimately emerging as quite a tough-guy wit. Reynold's exaggerated turn as the shameless politico sort of sums up the pros and cons of the picture.

•

STRIPTEASE LADY
SEE: LADY OF BURLESQUE

•

STROMBOLI
SEE: STROMBOLI, TERRA DI DIO

•

STROMBOLI, TERRA DI DIO
(STROMBOLI)
1950, 107 mins, Italy/US Ⓥ b/w
Dir Roberto Rossellini ***Prod*** Ingrid Bergman, Roberto Rossellini ***Scr*** Roberto Rossellini, Art Cohn, Renzo Cesana, Sergio Amidei, Gianpaolo Callegari ***Ph*** Otello Martelli ***Ed*** Roland Gross, Jolanda Benvenuti ***Mus*** Renzo Rossellini
Act Ingrid Bergman, Mario Vitale, Renzo Cesana, Mario Sponzo (Be-Ro/RKO)

Director Roberto Rossellini purportedly denied responsibility for the film, claiming the American version was cut by RKO beyond recognition. Cut or not cut, the film reflects no credit on him. Given elementary-school dialog to recite and impossible scenes to act, Ingrid Bergman's never able to make the lines real nor the emotion sufficiently motivated to seem more than an exercise.

So many morally-questionable scenes apparently had to be removed that RKO found it necessary to insert a great deal of detail in other actions to stretch the film to its 81-minute length. [Version reviewed was U.S. one.]

The only visible touch of the famed Italian director is in the hard photography, which adds to the realistic, documentary effect of life on the rocky, lava-blanketed island. Rossellini's penchant for realism, however, does not extend to Bergman. She's always fresh, clean and well-groomed.

The story is of a girl (Bergman) in an Italian displaced persons camp who marries a native fisherman (Mario Vitale) of Stromboli so that she may be released. Miss Bergman hates it from the start, but she does grow to love her man.

Language of the pic is a bit confusing. Bergman, on an Italian isle, speaks English with a Swedish accent. Vitale's voice has been dubbed and there's little strain in deciphering his English. Renzo Cesana as the priest does the best thespic job in the pic.

•

STRONGEST MAN IN THE WORLD, THE
1975, 92 mins, US col
Dir Vincent McEveety ***Prod*** Bill Anderson ***Scr*** Joseph L. McEveety, Herman Groves ***Ph*** Andrew Jackson ***Ed*** Cotton Warburton ***Mus*** Robert F. Brunner ***Art*** John B. Mansbridge, Jack Senter
Act Kurt Russell, Joe Flynn, Eve Arden, Cesar Romero, Phil Silvers, Dick Van Patten (Walt Disney)

The students of Medfield College unintentionally zap the laws of nature with unexpected and sometimes hilarious results. Through a lab accident, they concoct a scientific formula which gives people superhuman strength, a spoof on vitality and energy claims of cereal companies.

The script rivets on situation of the school's reputation and financial stability tied in with sale of the formula to a cereal outfit and participating in an intercollegiate weight-lifting contest. The other team is sponsored by a rival cereal concern, acknowledgedly the No. 1 because of its previous success in out-publicizing the merits of its product.

Joe Flynn, who died just after pic was finished, is the sputtering college dean, faced with the threat by the college board that he's through unless he can create a financial turnaround, and Kurt Russell is the student responsible for the formula, and Cesar Romero cops a hand as the slick heavy.

•

STRONG MAN, THE
1926, 75 mins, US Ⓥ ⊙ ⊗ b/w
Dir Frank Capra ***Scr*** Arthur Ripley ***Ph*** Elgin Lessley, Glenn Kershner ***Ed*** Harold Young ***Art*** Lloyd Brierly
Act Harry Langdon, Priscilla Bonner, Gertrude Astor, William V. Mong, Robert McKim, Arthur Thalasso (Langdon/First National)

A whale of a comedy production that has a wealth of slapstick, a rough-and-tumble finish and in the earlier passages bits of pantomimic comedy that are notable.

Harry Langdon has a comic method distinct from other film fun makers. The quality of pathos enters into it more fully than the style of any other comedian with the possible exception of Chaplin. His gift of legitimate comedy here has a splendid vehicle.

There is one scene where the awkward hero is engaged in fighting off a bad cold while traveling in a crowded stagecoach. He earns the enmity of his fellow passengers and his pantomime display of helpless suffering mingled with indignation is an epic of laughable absurdity.

•

STUART LITTLE
1999, 92 mins, US Ⓥ ⊙ col
Dir Rob Minkoff ***Prod*** Douglas Wick ***Scr*** M. Night Shyamalan, Greg Brooker ***Ph*** Guillermo Navarro ***Ed*** Tom Finan ***Mus*** Alan Silvestri ***Art*** Bill Brzeski
Act Geena Davis, Hugh Laurie, Jonathan Lipnicki, Brian Doyle-Murray, Estelle Getty, Julia Sweeney (Columbia)

Given what a tricky proposition it is to adapt a classic children's book for the screen, this take on E. B. White's *Stuart Little* does a more-than-passable job of resurrecting the story for a new generation. Still, despite technically impressive animation, ample doses of humor and seamless special effects, the filmmakers have taken a slick, commercial approach to the material that turns White's magical 1945 tale into a labored feel-good movie.

Presumably, the birth of a rodent into a human family (the book's scenario) would have been difficult to explain, so in this version Mr. and Mrs. Little (played with earnest, eccentric charm by Hugh Laurie and Geena Davis) cheerfully trot off to a Gotham adoption agency, having promised to bring home a little brother for their son, George (Jonathan Lipnicki).

George is less than thrilled when his parents return from the orphanage with a mouse named Stuart (voiced with boyish glee by Michael J. Fox). Even more irked with the new arrival is family feline Snowbell (Nathan Lane). Though Snowbell initially mistakes Stuart for dinner, Mr. Little reminds the cat that Stuart is family, "and we don't eat family members." Appalled, Snowbell's alley cat pals insist the mouse must go, so they consult feline crime boss Smokey (a raspy Chazz Palminteri), who brings in a pair of wayward mice (Bruno Kirby, Jennifer Tilly) to pose as Stuart's long-lost biological parents.

The humans tend to serve as window dressing in support of the more interesting animated creatures. In all tech areas, *Stuart Little* is top-notch

1999: NOMINATION: Best Visual Effects

•

STUART SAVES HIS FAMILY
1995, 95 mins, US Ⓥ col
Dir Harold Ramis ***Prod*** Lorne Michaels, Trevor Albert ***Scr*** Al Franken ***Ph*** Lauro Escorel ***Ed*** Pembroke Herring, Craig Herring ***Mus*** Marc Shaiman ***Art*** Joseph T. Garrity
Act Al Franken, Laura San Giacomo, Vincent D'Onofrio, Shirley Knight, Harris Yulin, Lesley Boone (Paramount)

It isn't good enough, it isn't smart enough, and, doggone it, most people won't like *Stuart Saves His Family*. This feeble comedy isn't the worst pic ever to be spun off from a *Saturday Night Live* sketch—*It's Pat!* maintains a firm grip on that dubious distinction—but it is woefully lacking in the humor and charm needed to attract mainstream audiences.

Stuart Smalley, the lisping self-help specialist created and portrayed by Al Franken, simply isn't amusing or interesting enough to sustain a feature. And two-thirds of the way through, pic suddenly becomes a maudlin drama about Stuart's intervention on behalf on his hard-drinking father (Harris Yulin).

Loosely based on Franken's book of Stuart's daily affirmations, *Stuart* introduces the title character as an affable and vaguely androgynous New Ager who offers advice and affirmation on a Chicago public-access TV show. Unfortunately, even his most supportive sponsor, played with attractive sincerity by Laura San Giacomo, can't help Stuart when he goes home to Minnesota to "save" his highly dysfunctional family.

Franken gives a two-dimensional portrayal of a one-note character, which gets exceedingly tedious by pic's midway point. Tech values are better than they have to be.

•

STUD, THE
1978, 90 mins, UK Ⓥ col
Dir Quentin Masters ***Prod*** Ronald S. Kass ***Scr*** Jackie Collins, Dave Humphries, Christopher Stagg ***Ph*** Peter Hannan ***Ed*** David Campling ***Mus*** Biddu, John Cameron (arr.) ***Art*** Michael Bastow
Act Joan Collins, Oliver Tobias, Emma Jacobs, Sue Lloyd, Walter Gotell, Mark Burns (Brent Walker)

The Stud goes a long way toward transcending the softcore sexpo genre, but ultimately doesn't quite make it. It's a shame because the producers have obviously tried hard to avoid low-budget seediness of routine skinflicks.

Based on the novel by Jackie Collins (sister of Joan, who toplines) the $1 million production has Oliver Tobias in title role as a virile manager of a London nitery.

Joan Collins is the lady who pulls the strings to manipulate him as her own sexual marionette. Her husband (Walter Gotell) owns the nightclub, and if the stud wants to keep his perquisites he must toe the line and keep the lady happy. And quite a few others, too.

Tobias is short on sensitivity and would-be Lotharios seeking useful tips might be excused for wondering what, apart from rakish good looks, is the secret of his success in persuading so many eligibles into the sack. He, in fact, seems faintly embarrassed about the whole thing.

Collins sails through her part giving just what was demanded but adding no dimension.

•

STUDENT PRINCE, THE
1927, 105 mins, US Ⓥ ⊗ ▭ b/w
Dir Ernst Lubitsch ***Scr*** Hans Kraly, Marian Ainslee, Ruth Cummings ***Ph*** John Mescall ***Ed*** Andrew Marton ***Art*** Cedric Gibbons, Richard Day
Act Ramon Novarro, Norma Shearer, Jean Hersholt, Gustav von Seyffertitz, Philippe De Lacy (M-G-M)

Ernst Lubitsch took his tongue out of his cheek when he directed this special [based on the 1924 operetta by Dorothy Donnelly and Sigmund Romberg from the novel by Wilhelm Meyer-Forster]. He had to, and in doing so he also took any kick right out of the picture, if any were there in the script for him. It's not farce and it's not drama. Just a pretty love story of peaches and cream.

The Student Prince concerns an heir to a throne who is forced to give up his love for a tavern maid because of duty to his country. And on the point of the prince marrying the princess his dead uncle had selected, the film ends.

The claim is that it took a year to make this feature, yet this doesn't show. Productionally there are some rich interiors counterbalanced by a sprinkling of backdrops on exteriors.

But nothing can stand off Ramon Novarro's facial makeup. This is ghastly under certain lighting conditions and at no time allows him to completely spin the illusion of the character he is playing. Shearer's personal efforts are a highlight, and Jean Hersholt stands a good chance of outlasting both in the memory.

•

STUDENT PRINCE, THE
1954, 107 mins, US Ⓥ ▭ col
Dir Richard Thorpe ***Prod*** Joe Pasternak ***Scr*** William Ludwig, Sonya Levien ***Ph*** Paul C. Vogel ***Ed*** Gene Ruggiero ***Mus*** Georgie Stoll (dir.) ***Art*** Cedric Gibbons, Randall Duell
Act Ann Blyth, Edmund Purdom, John Ericson, Louis Calhern, Edmund Gwenn, Betta St. John (M-G-M)

The venerable operetta about a royal cutup in the beer gardens of Heidelberg has been given a brand new look in this classy Joe Pasternak production via CinemaScope and Ansco Color. This latest pic version is a fresh, beguiling musical, beautiful to hear and behold.

The voice personality of Mario Lanza doesn't jibe with the British starch of Edmund Purdom's physical appearance, but not many will mind because the latter's acting is good. Doing her own singing in a gracious, charming manner is Ann Blyth, who might not be everyone's idea of a barmaid who could charm a prince, but she's pert and pretty.

Richard Thorpe's direction keeps things moving at a likeable pace, whether the people are engaging in song, amour or duel.

To the Sigmund Romberg tunes for which Dorothy Donnelly did the original lyrics and Paul Francis Webster the revised ones used here, have been added three new songs by Webster and Nicholas Bredszky. They are "Beloved," "I'll Walk With God," that is given a standout staging, and "Summertime in Heidelberg."

Louis Calhern plays, with a flourish, the king who sends his grandson (Purdom) to Heidelberg to learn how to be a man. There the young prince falls in love with Blyth and is about to run away with her when the king's illness intervenes.

•

STUDS LONIGAN
1960, 103 mins, US Ⓥ b/w
Dir Irving Lerner ***Prod*** Philip Yordan ***Scr*** Philip Yordan ***Ph*** Arthur H. Feindel, Haskell P. Wexler ***Ed*** Verna Fields ***Mus*** Jerry Goldsmith ***Art*** Jack Poplin

Act Christopher Knight, Frank Gorshin, Helen Westcott, Dick Foran, Venetia Stevenson, Jack Nicholson (United Artists)

Compressing James T. Farrell's respected trilogy into a 103-minute film doesn't come off. *Studs Lonigan* is an earnest attempt gone wrong, principally through incoherent execution complicated by undisciplined histrionics.

Philip Yordan's scenario is quite faithful to Farrell's book, which centers its attention on the essentially decent hero who struggles against slum life of Chicago's South Side district in the 1920s.

Christopher Knight, as the hero, has a disquieting tendency toward facial contortion and responsive exaggeration. The role is an extremely demanding one for any actor, let alone a newcomer to the screen.

The three standouts in the large cast are Frank Gorshin, Helen Westcott and Dick Foran. Gorshin has an instinctive ability to generate a natural reaction. Westcott creates a figure of pathos and dimension, despite the fact that Yordan's screenplay leaves the character she is playing undeveloped and unexplored. Foran comes through admirably in the role of Stud's decent father. Lensman Arthur H. Feindel and special photographic consultant Haskell P. Wexler have chosen an unusual assortment of sharp, tilted angles at which to place the camera. In combination with some unusual shading effects, this emphasis on startling composition is clever, but frequently distracting.

•

STUFF, THE

1985, 93 mins, US Ⓥ col

Dir Larry Cohen *Prod* Paul Kurta *Scr* Larry Cohen *Ph* Paul Glickman *Ed* Armond Lebowitz *Art* Marleen Marta, George Stoll

Act Michael Moriarty, Andrea Marcovicci, Paul Sorvino, Scott Bloom, Garrett Morris, Danny Aiello (Larco/New World)

The Stuff is sci-fi with no hardware but lots of white goo. It's a certified Larry Cohen film that seems to fly right out of the 1950s horror genre. It also has an underlying humor about it, plays around with satirizing fast foods, and cloaks a sly little subtext about people who ingest stuff they know is not good for them.

What's not to like? The film enjoys a larky sense of innocence, some hideous gaping mouths full of a curdling, parasitic menace, and a fey performance by Michael Moriarty as an industrial saboteur who, along with Andrea Marcovicci and little Scott Bloom, tracks down the scourge of the countryside and the heavies.

It also benefits from a hilarious performance played straight by Paul Sorvino as a self-styled paramilitary nut. The 11-year-old Bloom is appealing, while Garrett Morris as a chocolate cookie mogul and Danny Aiello as Vickers lend flavor in support.

•

STUNT MAN, THE

1980, 129 mins, US Ⓥ ⊙ col

Dir Richard Rush *Prod* Richard Rush *Scr* Lawrence B. Marcus *Ph* Mario Tosi *Ed* Jack Hofstra, Caroline Ferriol *Mus* Dominic Frontiere *Art* James Schoppe

Act Peter O'Toole, Steve Railsback, Barbara Hershey, Allen Garfield, Alex Rocco, Sharon Farrell (Simon)

Offbeat tale, based on Paul Brodeur's 1970 novel, has Vietnam vet Steve Railsback on the lam and accepting refuge from both benevolent and sinister film director Peter O'Toole, who puts the fugitive through some highly dangerous paces as a stunt man while shielding him from the cops.

Lawrence B. Marcus and adaptor-director Richard Rush are least successful in making fully credible the relationship between Railsback and film-within-the-film star Barbara Hershey, with his disillusionment upon discovering that she once had a fling with O'Toole playing as particularly unconvincing.

O'Toole is excellent in his best, cleanest performance in years. He smashingly delineates an omnipotent, godlike type whose total control over those around him makes him seem almost unreal.

1980: NOMINATIONS: Best Director, Actor (Peter O'Toole), Adapted Screenplay

•

STUNTS

1977, 90 mins, US Ⓥ col

Dir Mark L. Lester *Prod* Raymond Lofaro, William Panzer *Scr* Dennis Johnson, Barney Cohen *Ph* Bruce Logan *Ed* Corky Ehlers *Mus* Michael Kamen

Act Robert Forster, Fiona Lewis, Joanna Cassidy, Darrell Fetty, Bruce Glover, Jim Luisi (New Line/Fleischman)

Robert Forster is excellent as an ace stuntman who thwarts a maniac stalking a film crew making a police actioner on an ocean-side location in San Luis Obispo, California.

This is a tight-lipped actioner about a male group involved in a dangerous trade, with sexy female camp followers admitted to the group once they accept the code of grace under pressure.

There is much emphasis on expertise, emotional control, and the details of the craft, which are shown in docu-like style. The action scenes alternate with more relaxed character interplay in a motel and a bar, where the concept of expertise is translated into personal relationships.

Fiona Lewis is the prime romantic interest, a groupie journalist who initially causes friction in the group.

•

ST. VALENTINE'S DAY MASSACRE, THE

1967, 100 mins, US Ⓥ ▭ col

Dir Roger Corman *Prod* Roger Corman *Scr* Howard Browne *Ph* Milton Krasner *Ed* William B. Murphy *Mus* Fred Steiner *Art* Jack Martin Smith, Philip Jeffries

Act Jason Robards, George Segal, Ralph Meeker, Jean Hale, Clint Ritchie, Frank Silvera (20th Century-Fox)

The film is a slam-bang, gutsy recreation of *The St. Valentine's Day Massacre*, a 1929 gangland sensation of Chicago. Well-written and presented in semi-documentary style, it features Jason Robards as Al Capone. Salty dialog and violence are motivated properly, and solid production values re-create a by-gone era.

Robards is excellent as Capone, and Ralph Meeker, as Moran, is equally chilling. A large cast spotlights George Segal, who with brother David Canary act as Meeker's ace gunmen.

Clint Ritchie, playing in very good fashion the ever-smiling, dapper Jack McGurn, one of Capone's key aides, is placed by his boss in charge of eliminating Moran and his mob. Latter—through a stroke of fate—escaped the bloodbath, and Capone was never proven the man behind it all.

•

SUBJECT WAS ROSES, THE

1968, 107 mins, US Ⓥ col

Dir Ulu Grosbard *Prod* Edgar Lansbury *Scr* Frank D. Gilroy *Ph* Jack Priestley *Ed* Jerry Greenberg *Mus* Lee Pockriss *Art* George Jenkins

Act Patricia Neal, Jack Albertson, Martin Sheen, Don Saxon, Elaine Williams (M-G-M)

Frank D. Gilroy's Pulitzer Prize legit drama of 1964 has been translated to the screen in an outstanding way by original producer Edgar Lansbury and stager Ulu Grosbard, all three making an impressive debut in films. Joining original stars Jack Albertson and Martin Sheen is Patricia Neal, in a triumphant return to pix after near-fatal illness.

An intimate, poignant and telling drama of a young World War II vet, returning to an unhappy home, film is superior in all departments. Neal and Albertson are outstanding as a married Bronx-Irish couple who, while not happy and loving, are not unloving either. Albertson, whose rising business star fell in the Depression, and Neal, whose overdependence on her unseen mother is a sore point with Albertson, have struggled along for years.

Return from war of only son Sheen brings the festering crisis to a head, partly by a title-inspiring gift of flowers which releases pent up emotions.

The terrific writing, which top-notch performances make more magnificent, displays a wide range of human emotions, without recourse to cheap sensationalism or dialog. Grosbard's perceptive direction keeps the bickering and banter from becoming shrill histrionics.

•

SUBSTITUTE, THE

1996, 114 mins, US Ⓥ col

Dir Robert Mandel *Prod* Morrie Eisenman, Jim Steele *Scr* Roy Frumkes, Rocco Simonelli, Alan Ormsby *Ph* Bruce Surtees *Ed* Alex Mackie *Mus* Gary Chang *Art* Ron Foreman

Act Tom Berenger, Ernie Hudson, Diane Venora, Marc Anthony, Glenn Plummer, Cliff De Young (Dinamo/H2/Live)

The premise of *The Substitute* places an out-of-work soldier of fortune in a tough-as-nails high school to clean up the joint. Though the setup is largely preposterous, the filmmakers go whole-hog for the idea and provide a kinetic entertainment.

Shale (Tom Berenger) washes ashore in Miami and camps out at the apartment of his girlfriend, Jane (Diane Venora). She teaches at Columbus High, a powder-keg environment largely run by the Latino gang Kings of Destruction.

Jane makes the mistake of crossing swords with gang honcho Juan Lacas (Marc Anthony), who has a goon bust her kneecap. When her substitute can't step in, Shale decides to have his team provide him with a new identity—James Smith—to get a bead on the gang. He takes charge in the classroom and, to his surprise, actually gets most of the kids to listen and learn.

Fueled by a sense of righteous justice, *The Substitute* goes into action with both barrels blazing. Berenger exacts revenge much in the style of the Man With No Name or the hero of *Death Wish*. It's a very satisfying fantasy scenario.

Pic is exceptionally well cast, with such vets as Hudson, Venora and mercenary team members Raymond Cruz and William Forsythe bringing humanity to genre archetypes.

•

SUBTERRANEANS, THE

1960, 89 mins, US ▭ col

Dir Ranald MacDougall *Prod* Arthur Freed *Scr* Robert Thom *Ph* Joseph Ruttenberg *Ed* Ben Lewis *Mus* Andre Previn *Art* George W. Davis, Urie McCleary

Act Leslie Caron, George Peppard, Janice Rule, Roddy McDowell, Anne Seymour, Jim Hutton (M-G-M)

Those who have suspected all along that beatniks are dull, have proof in Metro's *The Subterraneans*.

Jack Kerouac's novel is the basis for the screenplay, which pokes around the offbeaten path of San Francisco's North Beach and dredges up some bargain basement philosophy, B(eat)-girls and bed ruminations. Its hero (George Peppard), an ex-Olympic gold medal winner and Columbia honor grad now a nervous novelist, beats it when his mom chants the square cliché "you need a nice girl."

Cruising around the Bay Area in search of meaning, he finds his home-away-from-home with the local coffeehouse colony, and promptly develops a crush on its most mixed-up member (Leslie Caron), an analyst's darling whose Freudian slip shows every time she submits frigidly to the sexual advances of her pals.

Caron's fragile gamine charm is all but smothered under the character's unattractive, sickly veil. An apparent shortage of sensitivity makes handsome Peppard rather unsuitable for his role.

Among the assorted beatniks, flashiest work is performed by Roddy McDowall as a kind of benevolent Zen-mother who sleeps standing up, Janice Rule as a beat beaut with a complexion complex, and Arte Johnson as a paid-up member whose sizeable left bankroll stems from literary sales to Hollywood.

There is a lot of music in the picture, all of the modern jazz variety. Created by Andre Previn and interpreted by experts at the idiom such as Gerry Mulligan, Red Mitchell, Shelly Manne and Carmen McRae, it is the outstanding aspect of this film.

•

SUBURBAN COMMANDO

1991, 90 mins, US Ⓥ ⊙ col

Dir Burt Kennedy, Gary Davis *Prod* Howard Gottfried *Scr* Frank Cappello *Ph* Bernd Heinl, Ken Lambkin, Richard Clabaugh, Charlie Lieberman *Ed* Terry Stokes *Mus* David Michael Frank *Art* Ivo Cristante, C. J. Strawn

Act Terry "Hulk" Hogan, Christopher Lloyd, Shelley Duvall, Larry Miller, William Ball, Jack Elam (New Line)

Some funny gags enliven the stupid sci-fi spoof *Suburban Commando*. Lame vehicle for wrestler Hulk Hogan is a bad "high-concept" effort marrying two elements. Hogan is an intergalactic warrior who travels to earth for some r&r, instantly becoming a fish out of water boarding at suburbanites Christopher Lloyd and Shelley Duvall's house. Lloyd is a Casper Milquetoast architect who briefly becomes the title character by donning Hogan's muscle-enhancing power suit.

Special effects are OK in copying and spoofing the *Star Wars* films, with good stunts as Hogan battles two intergalactic bounty hunters sent to kill him. His final battle with his evil nemesis (William Ball) is an underwhelming anticlimax. Casting of top talent Lloyd and Duvall was a good idea, but both are underutilized.

•

SUBURBIA

1996, 118 mins, US Ⓥ ⊙ col

Dir Richard Linklater *Prod* Anne Walker-McBay *Scr* Eric Bogosian *Ph* Lee Daniel *Ed* Sandra Adair *Art* Catherine Hardwicke

Act Jayce Bartok, Amie Carey, Nicky Katt, Ajay Naidu, Parker Posey, Giovanni Ribisi (Castle Rock)

Writer-director teamings seldom mesh as smoothly or suggest so many creative affinities as does the one at the heart of *subUrbia*, a brooding, incisive comedy that blends the talents of helmer Richard Linklater and playwright Eric Bogosian.

Scripted by Bogosian from his [Off-Broadway hit] play, *subUrbia* fits Linklater naturally with its acidly amusing account of 20-year-old losers acting out their miseries on the night one of their high school chums returns to town as a neophyte rock star.

Pic focuses on three dyspeptic pals. Jeff (Giovanni Ribisi) is obviously the thinker in the bunch. Spinning his wheels in the rut between adolescence and adulthood, he's got apt company in Buff (Steve Zahn), a hedonistic goofball who works in a pizza joint, and Tim (Nicky Katt), a surly, tattooed hothead. The three rendezvous around nightfall in the parking lot of a 24-hour convenience store, where much of the pic's remainder transpires.

They're soon joined by Jeff's punkette g.f., Sooze (Amie Carey), and her friend Bee-Bee (Dina Spybey). Then Pony (Jayce Bartok) shows up as promised, ferried in a boat-size limo and accompanied by a sleek L.A. publicist, Erica (Parker Posey).

Bogosian's dialog is rich and flavorful, avid at capturing the pungent nuances of slang and the precise verbal textures of a world that seems like a giant invitation to "smoke a doob and hang out." Linklater's direction is fluid and almost classical.

Actors are all very good.

•

SUBWAY
1985, 104 mins, France Ⓥ ⦿ ▭ col
Dir Luc Besson ***Prod*** Luc Besson, Francois Ruggieri ***Scr*** Luc Besson, Pierre Jolivet, Alain Le Henry, Sophie Schmit, Marc Perrier ***Ph*** Carlo Varini ***Ed*** Sophie Schmit ***Mus*** Eric Serra ***Art*** Alexandre Trauner
Act Isabelle Adjani, Christophe Lambert, Richard Bohringer, Michel Galabru, Jean-Hugues Anglade, Jean Bouise (Gaumont/Films du Loup/TSF/TF1

Subway brings to mind Orson Welles's quip about the cinema being the greatest electric train set a boy could have. Its director, Luc Besson, only 26, showed resourcefulness and a sense of filmmaking fun with his 1982 low-budget sci-fier *Le dernier combat*. For his second feature, Gaumont (distrib of *Combat*) gave him over 15 million francs, Christophe Lambert and Isabelle Adjani as stars, and let him go play in the Paris Metro.

Result may disappoint some for its singular lack of ambition or purpose and its ragged narrative, but still proves a charmingly cartoonish escapade, strong on humor and rock rhythms.

Pic's hero is Lambert, a dynamite-toting, punk-coiffed eccentric who has stolen some compromising documents belonging to Adjani's influential husband. Lambert takes refuge in the subway at the moment of its early morning closing.

There he befriends some of the subterranean denizens—a young roller-skating purse-snatcher (Jean-Hugues Anglade), a shady flower-seller (Richard Bohringer) and a black muscleman who works out with spare subway car parts—and decides to realize his dream of managing a rock band by recruiting the Metro's itinerant musicians. In the meantime, he is sought by the thugs, the Paris transport police (headed by Michel Galabru), and Adjani.

Film went through heavy cutting in final editing stages, with forty minutes shorn away to get it down to average commercial length, which explains the lapses in plot and sometimes disjointed continuity. But the roughness feels right in a film that resolutely refuses to take itself seriously.

•

SUCCESS
SEE: THE AMERICAN SUCCESS COMPANY

•

SUCCESS IS THE BEST REVENGE
1984, 90 mins, UK/France Ⓥ col
Dir Jerzy Skolimowski ***Prod*** Jerzy Skolimowski ***Scr*** Jerzy Skolimowski, Michael Lyndon ***Ph*** Mike Fash ***Ed*** Barrie Vince ***Mus*** Stanley Myers, Hans Zimmer ***Art*** Voytek
Act Michael York, Joanna Szczerbic, Michael Lyndon, Michel Piccoli, Anouk Aimee, John Hurt (De Vere/Gaumont)

After *Moonlighting*, London-based, longtime Polish exile Jerzy Skolimowski stays with the exile theme in *Success is the Best Revenge*. Pic deals with how exile can become a trap, a temptation to coast along quite professionally on the artist-exile's most obvious obsession, and how the children of such exiles will sooner or later insist on exploring their roots.

Story is told on parallels between teenager Adam (Michael Lyndon), who secretly prepares for combined punkdom and flight to Warsaw, and his father, Alex Rodak (Michael York), a Polish stage director about to put on another exile show at a London West End theater.

The sad plight of the younger generation of refugees is a theme well worth exploring, but Skolimowski really has much more to say in a satirical way—about the older generation that has turned exile into business.

Rodak finally—against the wishes of his long-suffering wife (Joanna Szczerbic)—gets the money from a cynical millionaire (John Hurt) who has his own shady reasons for entering the game as a backer. He also has by his side Monique de Fontaine (Anouk Aimee) as a theater manager with possible off-stage designs on him.

Although mostly a shot-on-location film, production designer Voytek manages to make even its street scenes look like they were done in a studio. Film's title is a slight twist of the 1920s adage about living well being the best revenge.

•

SUDBA CHELOVYEKA
(DESTINY OF A MAN)
1959, 98 mins, USSR b/w
Dir Sergei Bondarchuk ***Scr*** Yuri Lukin, F. Shakhmagonov ***Ph*** Vladimir Monakhov ***Ed*** B. Bassner ***Mus*** V. Basnov
Act Sergei Bondarchuk, Zinaida Kirienko, Pavlik Boriskin, Yuri Averin, Pavel Volkov (Mosfilm)

This well-made, moving film details how a Russian prisoner of war (Sergei Bondarchuk) has only the thought of getting back alive to his family. After many adventures and privations he does find them, but all are dead. He adopts a homeless boy to give him the necessary love and reason to go on living.

Bondarchuk has served himself well [in his first film] as director except for some slow progression and overdone camera bravura. But it has an eye-catching style and depicts Nazi brutality.

[The official Soviet entry at the 1959 Cannes fest, pic was withdrawn at the request of the fest authorities because of its portrayal of Nazi atrocities. It was screened in a private theater and received plenty of press coverage.]

•

SUDDEN DEATH
1995, 110 mins, US Ⓥ ⦿ ▭ col
Dir Peter Hyams ***Prod*** Moshe Diamant, Howard Baldwin ***Scr*** Gene Quintano ***Ph*** Peter Hyams ***Ed*** Steven Kemper ***Mus*** John Debney ***Art*** Philip Harrison
Act Jean-Claude Van Damme, Powers Boothe, Raymond J. Barry, Whittni Wright, Ross Malinger, Dorian Harewood (Signature/Universal)

Van Damme's the man, but the man ain't the movie in *Sudden Death*, a whipcord-taut actioner that's bigger and better than its main star. Reuniting the Muscles from Brussels with *Timecop* helmer Peter Hyams, this *Die Hard in a Hockey Arena* scores low on originality but high on sheer oomph.

Pacey opening sets the tone, with Van Damme intro'd as Darren McCord, a (divorced) fire marshal at Pittsburgh's Civic Arena, whither he and his two sprigs go for a playoff game between the Pittsburgh Penguins and Chicago Blackhawks. Also due in the audience that evening is the U.S. vice president (Raymond J. Barry).

The action elements start appearing right after the main titles, with Hyams cutting back and forth between scenes of McCord collecting his kids, and various members of a gang led by smooth-talking psycho Joshua Foss (Powers Boothe) prepping for some kind of major hit.

Aforesaid hit takes place some 20 minutes in, as Foss & Co. take over the VP's box and hold its human contents ransom for a cool $1.7 billion currently held by the U.S. government in frozen foreign-country funds. Time limit for the transfer is the length of the ice hockey game.

Basically, this is straight action stuff with a vague martial arts riff in the fight scenes. Though the pic [based on a story by Karen Baldwin] is already a third over by the time Van Damme gets a chance to do any twirls, he's well served by director Hyams in the physical sequences.

The movie is a two-character affair, with Boothe spitting out sub-Alan Rickmanisms and Van Damme somewhat uneasily stuck between a failed family man and all-out action hero.

But as a straight-arrow, medium-budget actioner, *Sudden Death* more than delivers the goods, with a low-budget energy and humor that never lets up. Hyams's restless camera has as good an eye for close-up drama as for big visual moments like Van Damme's duel atop the arena's roof.

•

SUDDEN FEAR
1952, 110 mins, US b/w
Dir David Miller ***Prod*** Joseph Kaufman ***Scr*** Lenore Coffee, Robert Smith ***Ph*** Charles Lang, Jr. ***Ed*** Leon Barsha ***Mus*** Elmer Bernstein ***Art*** Boris Leven
Act Joan Crawford, Jack Palance, Gloria Grahame, Bruce Bennett, Virginia Huston, Touch Connors (RKO)

Sudden Fear is a suspense drama tailored for Joan Crawford. It allows the actress to experience a familiar gamut of emotions, encompassing ecstatic love, fear, hate and revenge. It is essentially a routine chiller [from a story by Edna Sherry], replete with more or less clever gimmicks, but mounted handsomely.

Crawford is presented as a playwright-heiress. Eminently successful at her craft, she falls in love and marries an actor whom she had considered unsuited for the lead in her play. The union is idyllic until she discovers accidentally, via a dictating machine, that her husband had only married her for her money and with the aid of an old flame is planning her murder.

Crawford scores in this type of role.

•

SUDDEN IMPACT
1983, 117 mins, US Ⓥ ⦿ ▭ col
Dir Clint Eastwood ***Prod*** Clint Eastwood ***Scr*** Joseph C. Stinson ***Ph*** Bruce Surtees ***Ed*** Joel Cox ***Mus*** Lalo Schifrin ***Art*** Edward Carfagno
Act Clint Eastwood, Sondra Locke, Pat Hingle, Bradford Dillman, Paul Drake, Audrie J. Neenan (Warner)

The fourth entry in the lucrative *Dirty Harry* series, *Sudden Impact* is a brutally hard-hitting policier which casts Clint Eastwood as audiences like to see him, as the toughest guy in town.

Sudden Impact sends Harry out of his normal jurisdiction in San Francisco to research a case with connections to coastal San Paulo. While there, he bumps into Sondra Locke, who is extracting her own brand of vengeance on a group of individuals who, some years back, savagely raped both her and her younger sister.

Local police chief Pat Hingle tries to bar Harry from behaving as usual in his community, but that doesn't prevent a slew of shootings.

This is the first entry in the series to have been directed by Eastwood himself, and action is put over with great force, if also with some obviousness. Locke looks astonishingly like Tippi Hedren did in Hitchcock's *Marnie* and, with the exception of a sympathetic black cop played by Albert Popwell, nearly everyone else in the cast represents a menace to Harry in one way or another.

•

SUDDENLY
1954, 75 mins, US Ⓥ b/w
Dir Lewis Allen ***Prod*** Robert Bassler ***Scr*** Richard Sale ***Ph*** Charles G. Clarke ***Ed*** John F. Schreyer ***Mus*** David Raksin ***Art*** Frank Sylos
Act Frank Sinatra, Sterling Hayden, James Gleason, Nancy Gates, Willis Bouchey, Kim Charney (Libra)

This slick exploitation feature twirls about a fantastic plot to assassinate the President of the U.S. Robert Bassler's first indie chore since ankling 20th-Fox comes through as a well-worked-out meller. Taking its title from the name of the California town where the action unfolds, the Richard Sale script carries sufficient theme novelty to whet the imagination. Frank Sinatra, as a professional gunman hired to kill the president as he debarks from his special train for a few days' fishing in neighboring mountains, is an offbeat piece of casting which pays off in lively interest.

Thesp inserts plenty of menace into a psycho character, never too heavily done, and gets good backing from his costar, Sterling Hayden, as sheriff, in a less showy role but just as authoritatively handled. Lewis Allen's direction manages a smart piece where static treatment easily could have prevailed.

Action occurs within a few hours' time on a Saturday afternoon in Suddenly, where nothing has happened for years. A group of Secret Service men, detailed to guard the president, precedes him to check the security of the station area. Almost simultaneously, John Baron (Sinatra) and two cohorts arrive and take over a house, overlooking the station, belonging to Benson (James Gleason), retired Secret Service operative, with the intention of using it as a sniper's post.

•

SUDDENLY IT'S SPRING
1947, 87 mins, US b/w
Dir Mitchell Leisen ***Prod*** Claude Binyon ***Scr*** Claude Binyon, P. J. Wolfson ***Ph*** Daniel L. Fapp ***Ed*** Alma Macrorie ***Mus*** Victor Young ***Art*** Hans Dreier, John Meehan
Act Paulette Goddard, Fred MacMurray, Macdonald Carey, Arleen Whelan, Lillian Fontaine (Paramount)

Socko escapist film fare, *Suddenly It's Spring* starts from foundation of a topnotch script, and has been aptly cast and directed.

Story concerns marital team of lawyers, husband and wife, who had agreed to separate before the war. World strife delays the divorce and script picks them up again just as the WAC wife is returning from overseas. The husband already has his discharge, has fallen for another gal and wants the divorce pronto. His wife has new ideas since her army service and would like to try again. Fun springs from Fred MacMurray's prodding of Paulette Goddard to get her to ink the necessary papers and her continual coy delay.

•

SUDDENLY, LAST SUMMER
1959, 112 mins, UK Ⓥ ⊙ b/w
Dir Joseph L. Mankiewicz ***Prod*** Sam Spiegel ***Scr*** Gore Vidal, Tennessee Williams ***Ph*** Jack Hildyard ***Ed*** William W. Hornbeck, Thomas G. Stanford ***Mus*** Buxton Orr, Malcolm Arnold ***Art*** Oliver Messel
Act Elizabeth Taylor, Katharine Hepburn, Montgomery Clift, Albert Dekker, Mercedes McCambridge, Gary Raymond (Horizon/Columbia)

Perversion and greed, Tennessee Williams's recurrent themes, are worked over again in *Suddenly Last Summer*. The play was concerned with homosexuality and cannibalism. The cannibalism has been dropped, or muted, in the film version. It has some very effective moments, but on the whole it fails to move.

Perhaps the reason is that what was a long one-act play has been expanded in the screenplay to a longish motion picture. Nothing that's been added is an improvement on the original; they stretch the seams of the original fabric without strengthening the seamy aspects of the story.

The story is that of a doting mother (Katharine Hepburn) and her son. The son was a homosexual and his mother his procuress. When she had passed the age when she could function effectively in this capacity, he enlisted the services of his beautiful cousin, Elizabeth Taylor. The question is whether Taylor is fancifully insane or ruthlessly sane. Hepburn wants a lobotomy performed on Taylor, to excise the memory of the son's death, by detaching a portion of the brain. It is the job of Montgomery Clift, as the neurosurgeon who would perform the operation, to decide if Taylor is deranged as Hepburn insists.

Hepburn is dominant, making her brisk authority a genteel hammer relentlessly crushing the younger woman. Taylor is most effective in her later scenes, although these have been robbed of their original theatricality. Clift is little more than straight man to the two ladies.

Although Joseph L. Mankiewiez's direction is inventive in giving the essentially static narrative some movement and rhythm, it must be faulted for blunting Taylor's final scene so it fails to match Hepburn's opening monolog. (The play was actually only two monologs of almost equal power and length.)

1959: NOMINATIONS: Best Actress (Katharine Hepburn, Elizabeth Taylor), B&W Art Direction

•

SUDDEN MANHATTAN
1996, 89 mins, US Ⓥ col
Dir Adrienne Shelly ***Prod*** Marcia Kirkley ***Scr*** Adrienne Shelly ***Ph*** Jim Deanult ***Ed*** Jack Halgas ***Mus*** Pal Irwin ***Art*** Teresa Mastropierro
Act Adrienne Shelly, Tim Guinee, Roger Rees, Louise Lasser, Hynden Walch, Chuck Montgomery (Kirkley)

Actress and first-time writer-director Adrienne Shelly, best known for her work in Hartley's *Trust*, has created a light, original and at times amusing urban fantasy in *Sudden Manhattan*. But while pic starts out searching for answers to life's Big Questions, it ends up settling for much less.

For the first hour, pic bops along in a breezy, self-assured way with nods to Hal Hartley's deadpan non sequiturs and the jokey mysticism of Woody Allen's *Alice*. In the last reel, though, pic degenerates into a kind of cut-rate surrealism à la *Twin Peaks*, and climaxes in a baffling finale that is neither funny nor satisfying.

Donna (Shelly) is a cute, single twenty-something woman living in the Village. Things take a turn for the weird when Donna starts hearing earthquakelike rumblings emanating from a plate of scrambled eggs and witnesses a series of identical murders on a quiet residential street. Unsure whether it's her or the world that's gone crazy, she seeks the guidance of Dorinda, a lugubrious gypsy soothsayer played with casual aplomb by Louise Lasser.

One by one, more characters are thrown into the self-consciously wacky mix. Once all the characters are introduced, however, Shelly doesn't seem to know what to do with them.

•

SUDDEN TERROR
SEE: EYEWITNESS

•

SUEZ
1938, 100 mins, US b/w
Dir Allan Dwan ***Prod*** Gene Markey ***Scr*** Philip Dunne, Julien Josephson ***Ph*** Peverell Marley ***Ed*** Barbara McLean ***Mus*** Louis Silvers ***Art*** Bernard Herzbrun, Rudolph Sternad
Act Tyrone Power, Loretta Young, Annabella, J. Edward Bromberg, Joseph Schildkraut, Henry Stephenson (20th Century-Fox)

Suez misses out on its epic aims. Film's shortcomings are chiefly psychological, although a lethargic pace in the forepart almost counts too heavily against it.

The fictional liberties taken with history come under acceptable Hollywood license. There's considerable theatrical abracadabra with the manner in which the young Ferdinand de Lesseps (Tyrone Power), with his dream of a big ditch from the Mediterranean into the Red Sea, wins over the Egyptian viceroy's heir—parlor magic, boxing and fencing lessons, horsemanship, etc.—and there's also the inconclusive relationship with the beauteous Countess Eugenie (Loretta Young), who forgets Power for Louis Bonaparte of France.

Annabella, costarred with Power and Young, is a child of the desert, enamored of the young Frenchman, a quondam hoyden in her Moroccan fez and general masculine attire, and at the same time some sort of a symbolic inspiration.

The sepia tinting and the general photography is splendid as are the arresting montage effects when called into play, notably, of course, that simoon that almost completely wrecks the well-nigh bankrupted de Lesseps. The desert storm is an unquestionable sock as are such other productional punctuations as the sabotage by the Turks, for example [battle sequences directed by Otto Brower].

•

SUGAR HILL
1993, 123 mins, US Ⓥ ⊙ col
Dir Leon Ichaso ***Prod*** Rudy Langlais, Gregory Brown ***Scr*** Barry Michael Cooper ***Ph*** Bojan Bazelli ***Ed*** Gary Karr ***Mus*** Terence Blanchard ***Art*** Michael Helmy
Act Wesley Snipes, Michael Wright, Theresa Randle, Clarence Williams III, Abe Vigoda, Larry Joshua (Beacon/South Street)

A self-indulgent drama about a Harlem drug kingpin trying to go straight, *Sugar Hill* plays like a dreary variation on *New Jack City*. Heavy on simplistic psychology and light on plausibility, pic exists in a netherworld between art and action films.

Riddled with flashbacks, the script by former journalist and *New Jack City* cowriter Barry Michael Cooper tells of two brothers with giant chips on their shoulders. Having witnessed their mother overdose and white mobsters shoot their addict father, Roemello and Raynathan Skuggs (Wesley Snipes, Michael Wright) long ago decided to get their own by becoming the biggest dealers in Harlem.

When not brooding in lonely luxury, Roemello persistently courts the beautiful young Melissa (Theresa Randle), a proper lady who wants nothing more to do with him when she discovers his metier, but who can't ignore him either. It all ends in predictably bloody violence.

Best known for his 1985 indie musical *Crossover Dreams*, director Leon Ichaso opts for a straightforward presentational approach utterly lacking in dynamics and excitement. Snipes invests little energy in his performance until the end.

•

SUGARLAND EXPRESS, THE
1974, 109 mins, US Ⓥ ▭ col
Dir Steven Spielberg ***Prod*** Richard D. Zanuck, David Brown ***Scr*** Hal Barwood, Matthew Robbins ***Ph*** Vilmos Zsigmond ***Ed*** Edward M. Abroms, Verna Fields ***Mus*** John Williams ***Art*** Joseph Alves, Jr.
Act Goldie Hawn, Ben Johnson, Michael Sacks, William Atherton, Gregory Walcott, Harrison Zanuck (Universal)

The Sugarland Express begins and plays for much of its length as a hilarious madcap caper chase comedy.

Goldie Hawn stars as a young mother who helps husband William Atherton escape from prison so they may rescue their baby from involuntary adoption. Unfortunately, the film degenerates in final reels to heavy-handed social polemic and sound-and-fury shootout.

Based on an actual event in Texas in 1969, the screenplay is by Hal Barwood and Matthew Robbins, from a story by them and feature-debuting director Steven Spielberg. Besides some excellent major characterizations—Michael Sacks as a patrol car officer whom they kidnap, and Ben Johnson, outstanding as a police captain—the comedic impact is enhanced by terrific visual staging.

•

SUICIDE SQUADRON
SEE: DANGEROUS MOONLIGHT

•

SUITABLE CASE FOR TREATMENT, A
(U.S.: MORGAN!; AKA: MORGAN (A SUITABLE CASE FOR TREATMENT))
1966, 97 mins, UK Ⓥ ⊙ b/w
Dir Karel Reisz ***Prod*** Leon Clore ***Scr*** David Mercer ***Ph*** Gerry Turpin, Larry Pizer ***Ed*** Tom Priestley ***Mus*** Johnny Dankworth ***Art*** Philip Harrison
Act Vanessa Redgrave, David Warner, Robert Stephens, Irene Handl, Bernard Bresslaw, Arthur Mullard (British Lion/Quintra)

Morgan follows the frequently funny, sometimes pathetic but relentlessly lunatic exploits of an eccentric artist to his eventual, though not inevitable, incarceration in an insane asylum. Although it is established that the title character, played with zest and skill by David Warner, was always engagingly dotty, his latest bizarre binge is triggered by his opposition to ex-wife's (Vanessa Redgrave) impending marriage to a sympathetic and likeable suitor.

Spare, straight-line plot follows Morgan's misguided but amusingly slapstick attempts to win back his mate, Leonie, who, though displaying a tolerance and protectiveness bordering on the saintly, longs for a less frenetic and wearying life with a "normal" husband. To director Karel Reisz's credit, the suitor, well played by Robert Stephens, is never cast as a villain.

Schizophrenia seems to have infected Reisz's direction. Instead of providing the subtle, gradually disintegrating character of Morgan, Reisz dwells on the comedic aspects of each prank, cunningly milked for maximum yaks, in the process ceding any hope of the observer taking Morgan seriously.

1966: NOMINATIONS: Best Actress (Vanessa Redgrave), B&W Costume Design

•

SULLIVANS, THE
1944, 111 mins, US Ⓥ b/w
Dir Lloyd Bacon ***Prod*** Sam Jaffe ***Scr*** Mary C. McCall, Jr. ***Ph*** Lucien Andriot ***Ed*** Louis Loeffler ***Mus*** Alfred Newman ***Art*** James Baseri, Leland Fuller
Act Anne Baxter, Thomas Mitchell, Ward Bond, Bobby Driscoll, Selena Royle, Addison Richards (20th Century-Fox)

The story is that of the five Sullivan boys who enlisted in the U.S. Navy immediately after Pearl Harbor and went down with their ship, later to be honored by the christening of a battlewagon named after them. That is fact, this being the true story of the Sullivans of Waterloo (IA). It has been done with assumed fidelity and as a documentary account of heroism by the Sullivan family of the small Midwestern town.

The first half deals with the five Sullivan lads as little boys, with much homey humor derived from their pranks and the worries they cause their folks. Skipping several years, the second half deals with the boys as adolescents, four of the Sullivans now working on various jobs, while the youngest, Al, is still in high school.

It is here that the romance between Al and Katherine Mary (Anne Baxter) develops, reaching full flower quickly and with a baby born to them. Since the boys had always stuck together through thick and thin, including all the fights they won as little boys, Al goes along with the other four when latter decide to enlist in the Navy.

Outstanding on performance is that of Bobby Driscoll, playing Al when he was a boy of perhaps five or six years old, although Thomas Mitchell, as the father, and others are transcendentally fine in their work.

•

SULLIVAN'S TRAVELS
1941, 90 mins, US Ⓥ ⊙ b/w
Dir Preston Sturges ***Prod*** Paul Jones ***Scr*** Preston Sturges ***Ph*** John Seitz ***Ed*** Stuart Gilmore ***Mus*** Leo Shuken, Charles Bradshaw ***Art*** Hans Dreier, Earl Hedrick
Act Joel McCrea, Veronica Lake, William Demarest, Franklin Pangborn, Porter Hall, Eric Blore (Paramount)

Sullivan's Travels is a curious but effective mixture of grim tragedy, slapstick of the Keystone brand and smart, trigger-fast comedy. It is written and directed by Preston Sturges, who springs a flock of surprises as he flits from slapstick to stark drama, from high comedy to a sequence of the

Devil's Island prison type of stuff, into romantic spells, some philosophy and, in effect, all over the place without warning.

He ties it all together neatly, however, and keeps his audience on the go and on edge. Sturges's dialog is trenchant, has drive, possesses crispness and gets the laughs where that is desired.

Hollywood director Joel McCrea, anxious to produce *Oh, Brother, Where Art Thou?*, an epic of hard times and troubles, disguises himself as a hobo and goes out to look for troubles, finding plenty for himself. He picks up Veronica Lake on the way and they travel the rails together, she in boy's clothes.

A fine cast has been assembled around McCrea and Lake. Latter supplies the sex appeal and does a good acting job. McCrea, in the lap of luxury as a Hollywood director one minute, and a bum the next, turns in a swell performance.

•

SULT
(HUNGER)
1966, 111 mins, Denmark/Sweden/Norway Ⓥ b/w
Dir Henning Carlsen ***Scr*** Henning Jensen, Peter Seeberg ***Ph*** Henning Kristiansen ***Ed*** Anja Breien
Act Per Oscarsson, Gunnel Lindblom, Birgitte Federspiel, Sigrid Horne-Rasmussen, Knud Rex, Hans W. Petersen (Carlsen/Sandrews/Svenska/Filminstitutet/Studio ABC)

First Scandinavian coproduction is a fine mixture of an adaptation of a book by a noted Norwegian writer, the long-dead Nobel prize–winner Knut Hamsun, two Swedish thesps and a Danish director and adapter.

Pic is a taut tour de force about a time of hunger and near breakdown of a talented writer in turn-of-the-century Norway. Its relentless dwelling on anguish, plus the brilliant playing of Per Oscarsson, keep this from ever being stilted or repetitive.

Oscarsson is a scrawny, black-clad young man waiting for a reaction from an editor on an article he has written. He is reduced to eating paper, pawning his things, succumbing to hallucination, but still refusing to ask for help. A brief interlude with a girl who spurns him puts the last touch on his resistance.

The director, Henning Carlsen, holds a firm visual rein on the proceedings and creates the period, eschewing sentimentality and didacticism. Gunnel Lindblom is enticing and unpredictable as the girl.

•

SUMMER AND SMOKE
1961, 120 mins, US Ⓥ ⊙ ▭ col
Dir Peter Glenville ***Prod*** Hal Wallis ***Scr*** James Poe, Meade Roberts ***Ph*** Charles Lang, Jr. ***Mus*** Elmer Bernstein ***Art*** Hal Pereira, Walter Tyler
Act Laurence Harvey, Geraldine Page, John McIntire, Una Merkel, Rita Moreno, Thomas Gomez (Paramount)

Peter Glenville, who guided Tennessee Williams's play in Britain, gives this pic version a solid delineation, effectively guiding his cast, and giving several scenes heightened impact by cutting them off short, allowing effect to follow into next sequence. Throughout most of the first half, he has also successfully disengaged film from its stage format.

Performances are almost uniformly excellent, though Geraldine Page walks off with top honors in a repeat of her 1952 stage role as Alma Winemiller, the repressed spinster. Laurence Harvey, perhaps a bit young to play her opposite number, John, perhaps a bit too continental as a bayou boy, is nevertheless very good, and gives a solid and believeable rendering of the ne'er-do-well who reforms.

Una Merkel (again a repeat of her stage role) cuts herself a memorable cameo in a relatively small part, while Rita Moreno as the dance hall girl, Thomas Gomez as her father, John McIntire as the boy's pa, all give their supporting roles an effective reading. Earl Holliman is standout in a brief one-sequence appearance as the traveling salesman in the finale. An extra nod must go also to Pamela Tiffin, who as Nellie adds a pro flair to dazzling youthful beauty. It's her first screen role.

1961: NOMINATIONS: Best Actress (Geraldine Page), Supp. Actress (Una Merkel), Color Art Direction, Scoring of a Dramatic Picture

•

SUMMERFIELD
1977, 95 mins, Australia col
Dir Ken Hannam ***Prod*** Pat Lovell ***Scr*** Cliff Green ***Ph*** Mike Molloy ***Ed*** Sarah Bennet ***Mus*** Bruce Smeaton ***Art*** Grace Walker
Act Nick Tate, John Walters, Elizabeth Alexander, Michelle Jarman, Charles Tingwell, Geraldine Turner (Clare Beach)

A good-looking mystery, *Summerfield* is not unlike an Australian version of Hitchcock's *The Birds* in the opening sequences. It starts slowly, introducing the characters while at the same time establishing an undefined menace in the locale—a remote island community off the coast of Victoria.

Nick Tate is the replacement schoolteacher—his successor has disappeared in strange circumstances—and he unravels the intricacies of the local society. The atmosphere is heavy with xenophobic responses by the denizens of the area, and there is a generally overpowering feeling of mendacity and tightly inbred cover-up.

Gradually he picks up clues to what everybody is not talking about. And, of course, once he starts, his curiosity gets the better of him and impetus takes over.

•

SUMMER HOLIDAY
1948, 92 mins, US Ⓥ col
Dir Rouben Mamoulian ***Prod*** Arthur Freed ***Scr*** Frances Goodrich, Albert Hackett, Irving Brecher, Jean Holloway ***Ph*** Charles Schoenbaum ***Ed*** Albert Akst ***Mus*** Harry Warren, Ralph Blane ***Art*** Cedric Gibbons, Jack Martin Smith
Act Mickey Rooney, Gloria de Haven, Walter Huston, Frank Morgan, Agnes Moorehead, Marilyn Maxwell (M-G-M)

The Eugene O'Neill play, *Ah, Wilderness* with its account of a turn-of-the-century small town New England family, provides admirable setting, story, color and mood for the musical numbers and script. The musical numbers, tastefully chosen and skillfully staged, are not spotted arbitrarily, but stem naturally from the situations.

For example, the film is introduced by a song called "It's Our Home Town." Walter Huston sings the first chorus, as the newspaper publisher, with the other characters taking it up to identify themselves and plant the general storyline.

The story emphasizes the puppy-love romance between the publisher's son and girl across the street. Respectively Mickey Rooney and Gloria de Haven. Except for some laughable mugging by the former, they make an appealing pair, and their musical numbers are nicely done.

Huston is fine as the understanding Nat Miller, the boy's father. Frank Morgan achieves a nice blend of comedy and pathos as Uncle Sid.

Mamoulian's direction has style, is well paced and without sacrificing story credibility makes the songs stand out.

•

SUMMER HOLIDAY
(U.S.: Swingers in Paradise)
1963, 107 mins, UK Ⓥ ▭ col
Dir Peter Yates ***Prod*** Kenneth Harper ***Scr*** Peter Myers, Ronald Cass ***Ph*** John Wilcox ***Ed*** Jack Slade ***Mus*** Stanley Black (dir.) ***Art*** Syd Cain
Act Cliff Richard, Lauri Peters, Melvyn Hayes, Una Stubbs, Teddy Green, Pamela Hart (Ivy/Elstree)

Peter Myers and Ronald Cass have provided a screenplay that is short on wit but anyway is simply a valid excuse for a lighthearted jaunt through sunny Europe. Cliff Richard and three mechanic buddies set out for a European holiday in a borrowed double-decker London bus. They pick up (in quite the nicest way) three stranded girls, a cabaret act en route to Athens. The boys decide to make Athens their objective. They also encounter a troupe of wandering entertainers and a stowaway in the shape of a young boy. "He" turns out to be an American girl tele singer, fleeing from the professional demands of her dragon of a mother and her agent.

From this thin thread of yarn, songs, situations and dance routines arise fairly naturally. Even when dragged in, they add a lot to the excitement. Richard has a warm presence and sings and dances more than adequately.

Lauri Peters is pleasant as the young Yank heroine and romantic interest, and Melvyn Hayes has a sharp comic talent.

Highlighted throughout are production sequences which are put over shrewdly by director Peter Yates and into which choreographer Herbert Ross pumps an exuberant American expertise.

Myers and Cass have written seven numbers and others including Richard have contributed another nine. Filmed largely in France and Greece, the editing and backgrounds give an impression of a continuous trip across Europe.

•

SUMMER MADNESS
(U.S.: SUMMERTIME)
1955, 100 mins, UK/US Ⓥ ⊙ col
Dir David Lean ***Prod*** Ilya Lopert ***Scr*** H. E. Bates, David Lean ***Ph*** Jack Hildyard ***Ed*** Peter Taylor ***Mus*** Alessandro Cicognini ***Art*** Vincent Korda
Act Katharine Hepburn, Rossano Brazzi, Isa Miranda, Darren McGavin, Mari Aldon, Jeremy Spenser (Lopert/London)

Summer Madness, made in Venice during the summer of 1954, is a loose adaptation of Arthur Laurents's stage play, *The Time of the Cuckoo*. With Katharine Hepburn in the role originated by Shirley Booth and with the scenic beauties of the canal city, the film stacks up as promising entertainment—with some reservations. There is a lack of cohesion and some abruptness in plot transition without a too-clear buildup. Lesser characterizations, too, are on the sketchy side.

Covering these flaws is a rich topsoil of drama as the proud American secretary who hits Venice as a tourist falls for and is disillusioned by the middle-aged Italian charmer.

Rossano Brazzi, as the attractive vis-à-vis, scores a triumph of charm and reserve. Hepburn turns in a feverish acting chore of proud loneliness.

1955: NOMINATIONS: Best Director, Actress (Katharine Hepburn)

•

SUMMER OF '42
1971, 102 mins, US Ⓥ ⊙ col
Dir Robert Mulligan ***Prod*** Richard A. Roth ***Scr*** Herman Raucher ***Ph*** Robert Surtees ***Ed*** Folmar Blangsted ***Mus*** Michel Legrand ***Art*** Albert Brenner
Act Jennifer O'Neill, Gary Grimes, Jerry Houser, Oliver Conant, Katherine Allentuck, Christopher Norris (Warner)

The emotional and sexual awakening of teenagers is a dramatic staple. Robert Mulligan's *Summer of '42* has a large amount of charm and tenderness; it also has little dramatic economy and much eye-exhausting photography which translates to forced and artificial emphasis on a strung out story.

Script tells of that long-ago summer, way out on Long Island, when Gary Grimes had his first sexual-romantic experience with war-widowed Jennifer O'Neill. His two pals (Jerry Houser and Oliver Conant), begin and end the film not yet matured. For Houser, the easy charms of Christopher Norris still suffice, but the younger Conant literally disappears from the plot when the prospects of action instead of talk presents itself.

The three boys come across well, particularly Grimes. Houser's character is more coarse, even obnoxious at times, and he plays it well to help set off Grimes's more introspective nature. O'Neill is wooden and stilted, though her lines are few so the handicap does not unduly mar the film.

1971: Best Original Score

NOMINATIONS: Best Story & Screenplay, Cinematography, Editing

•

SUMMER OF SAM
1999, 142 mins, US Ⓥ ⊙ col
Dir Spike Lee ***Prod*** John Kilik, Spike Lee ***Scr*** Victor Colicchio, Michael Imperioli ***Ed*** Barry Alexander Brown ***Mus*** Terence Blanchard ***Art*** Therese DePrez
Act John Leguizamo, Adrien Brody, Mira Sorvino, Jennifer Esposito, Anthony LaPaglia, Bebe Neuwirth (40 Acres & a Mule/Touchstone)

A hard-driving, combustible, collagelike drama about a notorious serial killer's traumatic effect on New York City in summer '77, *Summer of Sam* is never less than absorbing, but feels a bit like yesterday's news. As vibrant, assaultive, loud and in-your-face as the city itself, Spike Lee's ambitious picture is rather too reminiscent of his best film, *Do the Right Thing*.

Lee's first film with a nearly all-white and Latino cast is positioned as a period piece at the outset, as newspaper columnist Jimmy Breslin explains to contempo viewers that the story is about "a different time and a different place." The killing spree is taking place in the Bronx, and the many, largely Italian, characters are brought onstage with relative dispatch.

Vinny and Dionna (John Leguizamo, Mira Sorvino) are stylish young marrieds; however, the highly priapic Vinny philanders compulsively. Ritchie (Adrien Brody) is a neighborhood boy who shocks his buddies by suddenly materializing as a London-style, spike-haired punk. Ritchie hooks up with lusty local Ruby (Jennifer Esposito).

Son of Sam, as the murderer has been dubbed, arrives as a force of terror in Gotham. He quickly kills again, and tempers soar with the temperature as a blackout occurs and riots ensue. Tension reaches its peak on July 29, when the maniac [later identified as David Berkowitz] is expected to strike again.

Ensemble cast fits together snugly, with nominal leads convincing as working-class types. Disco-heavy '70s soundtrack is a major mood-setting force.

SUMMER PLACE, A
1959, 130 mins, US Ⓥ ⊙ col
Dir Delmer Daves ***Prod*** Delmer Daves ***Scr*** Delmer Daves ***Ph*** Harry Stradling ***Ed*** Owen Marks ***Mus*** Max Steiner
Act Richard Egan, Dorothy McGuire, Sandra Dee, Arthur Kennedy, Troy Donahue, Constance Ford (Warner)

A Summer Place is one of those big, emotional, slickly produced pictures that bite off a great deal more than they can chew and neatly dispose of their intense, highly dramatic melange by dropping their characters into slots clearly marked "good" and "bad."

In his capacity as writer [from the novel by Sloan Wilson] and director, Delmer Daves has missed the mark by a mile. His characters, anguished most of the time, are unreal and totally devoid of depth. The film runs at least 20 minutes too long and has a tendency to use dialog to preach what should be implied.

Millionaire Richard Egan, his wife (Constance Ford) and daughter (Sandra Dee) arrive on a small island off the New England coast where, twenty years ago, Egan was a lifeguard and had an affair with Dorothy McGuire, who subsequently married Arthur Kennedy, the impoverished owner of a summer mansion. Egan has an affair with McGuire, which is discovered, and divorces result. Meanwhile, Dee and Kennedy's son (Troy Donahue) have fallen in love, but are broken up by Dee's mother.

With the single exception of McGuire, who comes through with a radiant performance and is lovely to look at, the cast does an average job.

•

SUMMER RENTAL
1985, 88 mins, US Ⓥ ⊙ col
Dir Carl Reiner ***Prod*** George Shapiro ***Scr*** Jeremy Stevens, Mark Reisman ***Ph*** Ric Waite ***Ed*** Bud Molin ***Mus*** Alan Silvestri ***Art*** Peter Wooley
Act John Candy, Rip Torn, Richard Crenna, Karen Austin, Kerri Green, John Larroquette (Paramount)

Amusing in spots, *Summer Rental* is more a collection of bits about taking the family to the shore for the summer than a coherent story. John Candy manages to elevate some of those bits to the hilarious and therein lies the film's appeal.

With three kids, dog and a U-Haul, family sets off for r&r at the Florida shore. Things don't go as planned and Candy finds himself sunburned and with an injured leg. Script also is lame and dreams up only the most pedestrian domestic catastrophes, from a young daughter's (Kerri Green) budding interest in boys to a gay divorcee's interest in Candy's wife (Karen Austin). After an hour meandering around the beach and environs, Candy locks horns with local denizen and resident sailing champ Richard Crenna.

Best bits in the film are supplied by Candy's wardrobe. As a modern-day pirate with a heart of gold, Rip Torn demonstrates once again that he can make any role believable regardless of how silly it is.

•

SUMMER'S TALE, A
SEE: CONTE D'ÉTÉ

•

SUMMER STOCK
(U.K.: IF YOU FEEL LIKE SINGING)
1950, 108 mins, US Ⓥ ⊙ col
Dir Charles Walters ***Prod*** Joe Pasternak ***Scr*** George Wells, Sy Gomberg ***Ph*** Robert Planck ***Ed*** Albert Akst ***Mus*** Johnny Green, Saul Chaplin (dirs.) ***Art*** Cedric Gibbons, Jack Martin Smith
Act Judy Garland, Gene Kelly, Eddie Bracken, Gloria de Haven, Marjorie Main, Phil Silvers (M-G-M)

Summer Stock showcases M-G-M's two top musical stars, Judy Garland and Gene Kelly. It has a light, gay air, including nine tunes [chiefly by Harry Warren and Mack Gordon], some used for dance numbers [staged by Nick Castle]. Story portion is never allowed to intrude much.

The background is a New England farm setting. Garland is the farmerette. Her younger sister (Gloria de Haven) brings a troupe of would-be thespians to the farm and they take over the barn to stage a new musical written by Kelly. Not only is Garland upset at such an invasion, so is the whole village of New Englanders.

Setup [story by Sy Gomberg] provides ample excuse for ringing in most of the musical numbers, although not justifying the finale that sees a production that would do credit to Broadway being staged in a barn by a group of impoverished actors.

•

SUMMER STORM
1944, 103 mins, US Ⓥ b/w
Dir Douglas Sirk ***Prod*** Seymour Nebenzal ***Scr*** Rowland Leigh, Robert Thoeren ***Ph*** Archie J. Stout ***Ed*** Gregg Tallas ***Mus*** Karl Hajos ***Art*** Rudi Feld
Act George Sanders, Linda Darnell, Anna Lee, Edward Everett Horton, Hugo Haas, Lori Lahner (United Artists)

Summer Storm is a carefully made drama of people and passion adapted from a Chekhov drama [*The Shooting Party*].

Russian background of the Kharkov district displays intimate study in contrasts of various persons—local judge, George Sanders; young and impetuous siren, Linda Darnell, who's determined to have wealth and finery; flustery and decadent Edward Everett Horton, land-owning aristocrat; estate superintendent, Hugo Haas; and Anna Lee, engaged to Sanders. All become engulfed in tragedy when Darnell marries Haas and immediately embarks on an affair with Sanders, while slyly playing Horton for the finery and jewels he can supply.

Darnell is spotlighted with her particularly effective performance. Sanders is excellent, sharing supporting prominence with Horton, Lori Lahner scores as the maid who protects Sanders's secret; Lee, Haas, and John Philliber are strong in support.

Script, with adaptation credited to Michael O'Hara, is particularly effective despite details of characters and carefully etched situations which consume plenty of footage and tend to slow down the tempo.

1944: NOMINATION: Best Scoring of a Dramatic Picture

•

SUMMER STORY, A
1988, 95 mins, UK/US Ⓥ col
Dir Piers Haggard ***Prod*** Danton Rissner ***Scr*** Penelope Mortimer ***Ph*** Kenneth MacMillan ***Ed*** Ralph Sheldon ***Mus*** Georges Delerue ***Art*** Leo Austin
Act Imogen Stubbs, James Wilby, Kenneth Colley, Sophie Ward, Susannah York, Jerome Flynn (ITC)

A Summer Story is a beautifully made pastoral romance, skillfully adapted from a John Galsworthy story, "The Apple Tree."

Screen version is set in Devon in 1902, portraying the ill-fated romance one summer between weak-willed young barrister Ashton (James Wilby, perfectly cast) and a lovely country lass, Megan (newcomer Imogen Stubbs).

Holed up at a country farm on holiday due to a sprained ankle, Ashton procrastinates, delaying his departure due to a crush on Megan. Shortly after they consummate the relationship, he heads for home via the resort of Torquay and procrastinates again, lolling with a beautiful sister (Sophie Ward) of an old school chum he meets there rather than returning quickly to fetch Megan as promised.

Stage actress Stubbs is a real find as the heartbroken heroine, bringing a modern strength to the period role, while Wilby is a sympathetic version of the archetypal weak young aristocrat.

•

SUMMERTIME
SEE: SUMMER MADNESS

•

SUMMER WISHES, WINTER DREAMS
1973, 87 mins, US Ⓥ col
Dir Gilbert Cates ***Prod*** Jack Brodsky ***Scr*** Stewart Stern ***Ph*** Gerald Hirschfeld ***Ed*** Sidney Katz ***Mus*** Johnny Mandel ***Art*** Peter Dohanos
Act Joanne Woodward, Martin Balsam, Sylvia Sidney, Dori Brenner, Tresa Hughes (Columbia/ Rastar)

Summer Wishes, Winter Dreams begins with idle chatter between Joanne Woodward and her mother, Sylvia Sidney, about lunch and tea. Fifteen minutes later the two are still debating whether to have broiled chicken and fritters. And 80 minutes later—long after mother is gone with a heart attack—Woodward and husband Martin Balsam are reminiscing about the macaroons in Atlantic City.

After one of her routine days is interrupted by the sudden death of mother, Woodward takes off for Europe with Balsam. Now the focus shifts from her woes to his as he searches for the only place his life had drama: 28 years earlier at Bastogne. He recalls the horror of two frightened days under attack, staring at the bodies of three young Germans he had killed, and the abandoned prayer he made that he would never be ungrateful for life if allowed to hold onto it.

Performances by Woodward, Balsam and Sidney (her first pic in 17 years) are first-rate, and they create genuinely tender moments. But only those past 40 and approaching 50 or more are likely to feel the depth.

1973: NOMINATIONS: Best Actress (Joanne Woodward), Supp. Actress (Sylvia Sidney)

•

SUN ALSO RISES, THE
1957, 129 mins, US ▭ col
Dir Henry King ***Prod*** Darryl F. Zanuck ***Scr*** Peter Viertel ***Ph*** Leo Tover ***Ed*** William Mace ***Mus*** Hugo Friedhofer ***Art*** Lyle R. Wheeler, Mark-Lee Kirk
Act Tyrone Power, Ava Gardner, Mel Ferrer, Errol Flynn, Eddie Albert, Juliette Greco (20th Century-Fox)

In undertaking the transmutation into screen fare of the novel which first escalatored Ernest Hemingway to renown, producer Darryl F. Zanuck doesn't gloss over key plot twist that Tyrone Power plays an impotent newspaperman in frustrated love with Ava Gardner, who plays Lady Brett Ashley. But the script drags along their "love affair" instead of propelling it. Thus the yarn never comes off either as a love story or a definitive study of the "lost generation."

Performances are mixed. Power is on the wooden side, his character never wholly believable. Gardner turns in a far more sympathetic and credible performance. Mel Ferrer never quite achieves the hangdog aspect required of his role. Errol Flynn and Eddie Albert turn in topflight characterizations as drunken members of the gambling expatriates. Flynn registers especially well.

•

SUNA NO ONNA
(WOMAN IN THE DUNES; WOMAN OF THE DUNES)
1964, 127 mins, Japan Ⓥ b/w
Dir Hiroshi Teshigahara ***Scr*** Kobo Abe ***Ph*** Hiroshi Segawa ***Ed*** F. Susui ***Mus*** Toru Takemitsu
Act Eiji Okada, Kyoko Kishida, Koji Mitsui, Hiroko Ito, Sen Yano (Teshigahara)

A basically simple tale [from Kobo Abe's novel] takes on two profound and symbolic sides as to the very meaning of life and mankind, yet can be accepted on its own grounds as an offbeat adventure that befalls an entomologist while hunting insects in a barren, sand-dune part of the country.

Some townspeople let him down to a house set in the side of a dune cliff. Here he finds a woman living alone. But next morning the ladder he came down on has been pulled up and he is told he cannot go up but must help this woman to fill lowered buckets with sand every night.

Then the film shows the man's attempts to escape, his rage at the woman and his finally giving in and even becoming her lover.

No matter what the meanings may be, director Hiroshi Teshigahara displays a flawless feel for texture and observation. Underneath is a pulsating, if sometimes gritty, compassion for man's general fate and the state of his so-called liberty.

Eliji Okada is exemplary as the civilized man caught in a trap he eventually adapts to, while Kyoko Kishida is touching, annoying, beguiling or irritating in turn as the simple woman who accepts her lot and can only give of herself. The sharp, contrasting black-and-white photography is perfect for the tale.

•

SUNBURN
1979, 99 mins, US Ⓥ col
Dir Richard C. Sarafian ***Prod*** John Daly, Gerald Green ***Scr*** John Daly ***Ph*** Alex Phillips, Jr. ***Ed*** Geoff Foot ***Mus*** John Cameron ***Art*** Ted Tester
Act Farrah Fawcett, Charles Grodin, Art Carney, Joan Collins, Eleanor Parker, Keenan Wynn (Paramount)

Sunburn exists for no other reason than to provide a vehicle for Farrah Fawcett.

Confection [from the book *The Bind* by Stanley Ellin] has Fawcett as a Gotham model posing as Charles Grodin's wife as he sleuths around chic Acapulco settings investigating the mysterious death of an industrialist on behalf of an insurance company stuck with a $5 million claim.

Scenes devoted to real plot movement are few and far between in script's first hour, since Fawcett's character is mostly irrelevant and has to be given something to do, like being scared by a lizard entering her bedroom.

Grodin works overtime to carry the picture and does so marvelously, displaying a savvy low-key comedy style. Grodin and Joan Collins share a farcical seduction scene that's a small comic gem.

•

SUNCHASER, THE
1996, 122 mins, US Ⓥ ▭ col
Dir Michael Cimino ***Prod*** Arnon Milchan, Michael Cimino, Larry Spiegel ***Scr*** Charles Leavitt ***Ph*** Doug Milsome ***Ed*** Joe D'Augustine ***Mus*** Maurice Jarre ***Art*** Victoria Paul

Act Woody Harrelson, Jon Seda, Anne Bancroft, Alexandra Tydings, Matt Mulhern, Talisa Soto (Regency/Warner)

The Sunchaser, Michael Cimino's return to filmmaking after a six-year layoff, is a conceptually bold tale marked, in its execution, both by visceral intensity and dramatic sloppiness. This is a film with a number of things on its mind, including issues related to the widely varied mind-sets that exist within American society, Western medical practices vs. ancient treatments, and practical materialistic values contrasted with more mystical, spiritual ones.

Dr. Michael Reynolds (Woody Harrelson) is a fastidious UCLA medic defined by his brand-new Porsche, his table at Morton's and the $2 million house he's about to buy for his trophy wife. Brandon "Blue" Monroe (Jon Seda), on the other hand, is a born loser, a 16-year-old, shaven-headed half-Navajo from the 'hood, whose muscular body is marked by tattoos and bullet wounds and who is in the pen for killing his stepfather. He also has an abdominal tumor, for which he needs to be examined by Dr. Reynolds.

The two, of course, are instantly at odds, and when Blue learns his cancer is inoperable and he's only got a month or two to live, he manages to kidnap the doc and, at gunpoint, force him to drive toward the Navajo reservation in Arizona.

The two briefly encounter a leftover hippie (Anne Bancroft) with whom they discuss different approaches to healing. Finally committed to helping his abductor, Reynolds manages to whisk Blue up the mountain to his destination, where a mystical and rather too unspecific fate awaits the ailing young man.

To really work, pic would need to have had Reynolds undergo a true transformation, and neither the script nor Harrelson's sincere but constrained performance achieves the desired depth. Seda doesn't quite pass as a 16-year-old, but his imposing looks and forceful presence bump up the energy quotient considerably.

•

SUNDAY BLOODY SUNDAY
1971, 110 mins, UK Ⓥ ⦿ col
Dir John Schlesinger ***Prod*** Joseph Janni ***Scr*** Penelope Gilliatt ***Ph*** Billy Williams ***Ed*** Richard Marden ***Art*** Norman Dorme
Act Glenda Jackson, Peter Finch, Murray Head, Peggy Ashcroft, Maurice Denham, Vivian Pickles (United Artists)

John Schlesinger's *Sunday Bloody Sunday* is a low-keyed, delicately poised recital of triangular love in which Glenda Jackson and Peter Finch share the affections of AC-DC Murray Head. The visible sexplay, however, is diffident, the storyline sparse. Observation and character are all.

The story's bi-sexual triangle differs in that it's not ménage-à-trois stuff. Head goes from one pad to the other. Scripter Penelope Gilliatt, with nice economy of dialog, is herein observing the emotional incompleteness of people and how they try to cope.

Jackson is a career femme on the rebound (separated from husband), Finch is a Jewish doctor, and Head, youngest of the trio, is a sculptor-designer oscillating between homo and hetero affairs and career.

Sequence after vignette after sequence, larded with deft little touches, all add to this story's cumulative message, namely that half a loaf is often better than none.

1971: NOMINATIONS: Best Director, Actor (Peter Finch), Actress (Glenda Jackson), Original Story and Screenplay

•

SUNDAY IN NEW YORK
1963, 105 mins, US col
Dir Peter Tewksbury ***Prod*** Everett Freeman ***Scr*** Norman Krasna ***Ph*** Leo Tover ***Ed*** Fredric Steinkamp ***Mus*** Peter Nero ***Art*** George W. Davis, Edward Carfagno
Act Rod Taylor, Jane Fonda, Cliff Robertson, Robert Culp, Jim Backus, Jo Morrow (M-G-M)

Norman Krasna's screenplay, from his Broadway legiter, doesn't really get rolling until it has virtually marked time for almost an hour, but once it gets up this head of steam the entire complexion of the picture seems to change.

The story has to do with the sudden arrival at her brother's apartment in New York of an Albany maiden (Jane Fonda) who's fretting over that age-old puzzler—should a girl before marriage? By now, she has alienated herself from a well-heeled hometown beau (Robert Culp) upon whom she had matrimonial designs. Big brother (Cliff Robertson), an airline pilot, lauds the virtuous life, but when sis subsequently discovers flimsy negligee in his closet, she impulsively attempts to seduce the nearest male (Rod Taylor), a young newspaperman.

The entire cast is equal to the challenge. Best of the lot is Taylor, who delivers a warm, flexible and appealing performance as the young journalist. Fonda, showing more becoming restraint on this outing, scores comedically and romantically as the forward-thinking lass. Robertson is convincing and chips in some highly amusing reactions as her generally befuddled pilot-brother.

•

SUNDAYS AND CYBELE
SEE: LES DIMANCHES DE VILLE D'AVRAY

•

SUNDAY TOO FAR AWAY
1975, 90 mins, Australia Ⓥ col
Dir Ken Hannam ***Prod*** Gil Brealey, Matt Carroll ***Scr*** John Dingwall ***Ph*** Geoff Burton ***Ed*** Rod Adamson ***Mus*** Patrick Flynn
Act Jack Thompson, Max Cullen, Reg Lye, John Ewart, Robert Bruning, Peter Cummins (SAFC)

Sheep shearers are journeymen who go about to the sheep farms, and, through a contractor, skim off the wool in backbreaking, dreary work. This, of course, leads to a sort of rivalry to remove some of the strain.

Foley (Jack Thompson) is a solid chap who would like to quit after his present job. But apparently that is not to be. The cutting of prices for shearers leads to a strike after the odyssey of their last contract. They finally win it.

Pic [set in 1955] may have resemblances to oaters in its place and hardbitten characters, the brawls and the landscapes. But this has a directorial ease that gets over a rather flat intro to create an extraordinary insight into men at work.

•

SUNDOWN
1941, 90 mins, US Ⓥ b/w
Dir Henry Hathaway ***Prod*** Walter Wanger ***Scr*** Barre Lyndon ***Ph*** Charles Lang ***Ed*** Dorothy Spencer ***Mus*** Miklos Rozsa ***Art*** Alexander Golitzen
Act Gene Tierney, Bruce Cabot, George Sanders, Harry Carey, Joseph Calleia, Reginald Gardiner (Wanger/United Artists)

An adventurous melodrama, unfolded in a colonial outpost of British East Africa, *Sundown* is an interesting tale of its type. Locale is cinematically fresh, the Kenya country near the Abyssinian border. Barre Lyndon's screenplay of own *Sat Eve Post* story neatly mixes informative material with interesting drama of conditions on East African front; while Henry Hathaway directs in straight line to hold audience attention, and accentuate the dramatic highlights en route. Story details the British administration of colonies, and the far-reaching efforts of Nazi agents to foment native uprisings against the British. Bruce Cabot is local commissioner of Manieka, being joined by army officer George Sanders, who is detailed to uncover gun-running plot to natives. Carl Esmond, secret Nazi agent, arrives posing as mining engineer; also Gene Tierney, operator of large caravans and network of native trading posts.

1941: NOMINATIONS: Best B&W Cinematography, B&W Art Direction, Scoring of a Dramatic Picture

•

SUNDOWNERS, THE
(UK: THUNDER IN THE DUST)
1950, 65 mins, US Ⓥ col
Dir George Templeton ***Prod*** Alan LeMay ***Scr*** Alan LeMay ***Ph*** Winton C. Hoch ***Ed*** Jack Ogilvie ***Mus*** Al Colombo
Act Robert Preston, Robert Sterling, Chill Wills, John Litel, Cathy Downs, John Barrymore, Jr. (Eagle Lion/LeMay-Templeton)

Story pits brother against brother to bring to a conclusion its account of a feud between rival cattlemen. Before that finale, tension is kept alive by cattle raids, gun battles and the constant fight of wills between a brother trying to carve a ranch and home from his section of Texas land and an older brother who dominates.

Interesting is the film debut of John Barrymore, Jr. He does well by his role of a kid who idolizes his bad, eldest brother but is held in line by the middle kin (Robert Sterling). Latter makes his footage count. Robert Preston gets his teeth into the colorful role of the daring, dashing eldest member of the Cloud family, and will be liked despite his bad ways.

•

SUNDOWNERS, THE
1960, 133 mins, UK Ⓥ col
Dir Fred Zinnemann ***Prod*** Gerry Blattner ***Scr*** Isobel Lennart ***Ph*** Jack Hildyard ***Ed*** Jack Harris ***Mus*** Dimitri Tiomkin ***Art*** Michael Stringer
Act Deborah Kerr, Robert Mitchum, Peter Ustinov, Glynis Johns, Dina Merrill, Chips Rafferty (Warner)

Jon Cleary's novel is the basic source from which director Fred Zinnemann's inspiration springs. Between Cleary and Zinnemann lies Isobel Lennart's perceptive, virile screenplay, loaded with bright, telling lines of dialog and gentle philosophical comment. But, fine as the scenario is, it is Zinnemann's poetic glances into the souls of his characters, little hints of deep longings, hidden despairs, indomitable spirit that make the picture the achievement it is.

On paper, the story sounds something short of fascinating. It tells of a 1920s Irish-Australian sheepdrover (Robert Mitchum) whose fondness for the freedom of an itinerant existence clashes with the fervent hope of settling down shared by his wife (Deborah Kerr) and his son (Michael Anderson, Jr.). The wife, in an effort to raise funds for a down payment on a farm, persuades her husband to accept stationary employment as a shearer.

Mitchum's rugged masculinity is right for the part. There are moments when he projects a great deal of feeling with what appears to be a minimum of effort. Kerr gives a luminous and penetrating portrayal of the faithful wife, rugged pioneer stock on the outside, wistful and feminine within. There is one fleetingly eloquent scene at a train station, in which her eyes meet those of an elegant lady traveller, that ranks as one of the most memorable moments ever to cross a screen.

Peter Ustinov, as a whimsical, learned bachelor who joins the family and slowly evolves into its "household pet," gives a robust, rollicking performance. Glynis Johns is a vivacious delight as a hotelkeeper who sets her sights on matrimonially evasive Ustinov.

Art, photographic and technical skills are extremely well represented by the craftsmen assembled in the bush country of Australia and at Elstree Studios in London.

1960: NOMINATIONS: Best Picture, Director, Actress (Deborah Kerr), Supp. Actress (Glynis Johns), Screenplay Adaptation

•

SUNFLOWER
1970, 105 mins, Italy/France Ⓥ col
Dir Vittorio De Sica ***Prod*** Carlo Ponti, Arthur Cohn ***Scr*** Antonio Guerra, Cesare Zavattini, Gheorghij Mdivani ***Ph*** Giuseppi Rotunno ***Ed*** Adriana Novelli ***Mus*** Henry Mancini ***Art*** Piero Poletto
Act Sophia Loren, Marcello Mastroianni, Ludmila Savelyeva, Galina Andreeva, Anna Carena (Champion/Concordia)

Sunflower is the tragedy of an ill-starred love destroyed by the horrors of war.

Sophia Loren reaches a new high of mature, dramatic expression, particularly in contrast with Ludmila Savelyeva's briefer but beautifully contained portrait of a Russian woman who saves an Italian soldier (Marcello Mastroianni) on the Stalingrad front, to become his wife and mother of his child. The climactic confrontation between Loren, the wife Mastroianni left behind, and Savelyeva is a sterling credit to both femme performers.

Also creditable is the glimpse of postwar Moscow and Russia, grimly objective of life there, during and post-Stalin. The Soviets cooperated in providing the loosely integrated but spectacular battlefield action.

It's a heart-clutcher and a four-handkerchief hit, abetted at every turn by a Henry Mancini theme of lyric substance that quietly penetrates every mournful moment. Giuseppe Rotunno's color camerawork is first-rate.

•

SUNNY
1941, 97 mins, US b/w
Dir Herbert Wilcox ***Prod*** Herbert Wilcox ***Scr*** Sig Herzig ***Ph*** Russell Metty ***Ed*** Elmo Williams ***Mus*** Jerome Kern
Act Anna Neagle, Ray Bolger, John Carroll, Edward Everett Horton (RKO)

Sunny, the third successive picturization of a musical comedy by the English team of producer-director Herbert Wilcox and star Anna Neagle, is a typical operetta Cinderella tale.

Despite the limitations imposed on producer-director Wilcox by transference of lightly molded musical comedy plot, he gets the maximum out of the dancing abilities of Ray Bolger, who scores in three solo routines and teams up with Neagle for a pair of numbers.

The Cinderella adventures of *Sunny* are set in New Orleans during Mardi Gras festivities. Neagle is the star of a streamlined circus. She meets, falls in love and becomes engaged to John Carroll, heir to an auto fortune. Ditching the circus, she accompanies him to the family mansion to meet the relatives, especially gruff and eccentric auntie (Helen Westley). Wedding ceremony is blown up by premature arrival and celebration of the bride's circus friends.

More important than Neagle's standard performance in the title spot is the sterling performance of John Carroll, who gaily romps through as the young millionaire.

•

SUNNY SIDE UP
1929, 80 mins, US Ⓥ ⊙ col
Dir David Butler ***Scr*** David Butler, Buddy DeSylva, Lew Brown, Ray Henderson ***Ph*** Ernest Palmer, John Schmitz ***Mus*** Howard Jackson, Arthur Kay (dir)
Act Janet Gaynor, Charles Farrell, El Brendel, Marjorie White, Frank Richardson, Sharon Lynn (Fox)

Buddy DeSylva, Lew Brown and Ray Henderson have turned out an average Cinderella story for Janet Gaynor, and she plays it. And sings it. David Butler in direction does so well by Gaynor that you even believe she has a voice.

The ace songsters pile up likeable songs so fast they have to be sung over again in the picture to decide which is the best. And here it's "If I Had a Talking Picture of You." But for delivery Gaynor's "I'm a Dreamer—Aren't We All?" leads.

"Turn on the Heat" is a cooch by 36 gals. And what a cooch! As the hot dance proceeds, the snow melts, trees and palms grow, and all of this while 36 coochers go the limit. There's a bit of hinted color in this scene.

Picture is one of those sidewalk of New York tales, but switches on the Cinderella end to Southampton. Plenty of comedy. Some of it by Joe Brown as an undertaker acting as m.c. for a block party on the East Side. Down at Southampton the garden party gives its affair on a stage fronted by a large lake.

•

SUNRISE—A SONG OF TWO HUMANS
1927, 95 mins, US Ⓥ ⊙ ⊗ b/w
Dir F. W. Murnau ***Scr*** Carl Mayer, Katherine Hilliker, H. H. Caldwell ***Ph*** Charles Rosher, Karl Struss ***Ed*** [Katherine Hilliker, H. H. Caldwell, Harold Schuster] ***Mus*** [Hugo Riesenfeld] ***Art*** [Rochus Gliese]
Act George O'Brien, Janet Gaynor, Margaret Livingston, Bodil Rosing, J. Farrell McDonald, Ralph Sipperly (Fox)

Sunrise is a distinguished contribution to the screen, made in this country, but produced after the best manner of the German school. In its artistry, dramatic power and graphic suggestion it goes a long way toward realizing the promise of this foreign director in his former works, notably *Faust*.

What director F. W. Murnau has tried to do is to crystallize in dramatic symbolism those conflicts, adjustments, compromises and complexities of man-and-woman mating experiences that ultimately grow into an enduring union.

Many elements enter into the success of this ambitious effort. Murnau reveals a remarkable resourcefulness of effects; the playing of George O'Brien and Janet Gaynor and their associates is generally convincing.

The incidental music blends smoothly, suggesting the mood of the scene, but without intruding into the conscientiousness. In many scenes (honking autos, when dreaming lovers block a street, is a case in point) sound effects are introduced. This has been managed with skill.

All these things lie upon a story [based on a short story by Herman Sudermann, *"Die Reise nach Tilsit"/ "The Trip To Tilsit"*] as simple as it is human. The Woman from the City (Margaret Livingston) snares a young farmer (O'Brien). Under her hypnotism he listens to a plan to drown the young wife (Gaynor), sell the farm and go off to the city.

1927/28: Best Actress (Janet Gaynor), Cinematography, Artistic Quality of Production

NOMINATION: Best Art Direction

•

SUNRISE AT CAMPOBELLO
1960, 144 mins, US Ⓥ ⊙ col
Dir Vincent J. Donehue ***Prod*** Dore Schary ***Scr*** Dore Schary ***Ph*** Russell Harlan ***Ed*** George Boemler ***Mus*** Franz Waxman ***Art*** Edward Carrere
Act Ralph Bellamy, Greer Garson, Hume Cronyn, Jean Hagen, Ann Shoemaker, Tim Considine (Warner)

In the journey from stage to screen this chapter from the life of Franklin Delano Roosevelt loses none of its poignant and inspirational qualities, none of its humor and pathos. Dore Schary, as author-producer of the play and the film, can take just pride in this grand-slam feat. And this satisfaction is to be shared also by Ralph Bellamy, whose brilliant portrayal of Roosevelt, and Vincent J. Donehue, the director, clicked so resoundingly on Broadway.

The period is 1921, when polio shatters a joyous family vacation on the island retreat of Campobello, to 1924, when Roosevelt re-emerged in public to put in Al Smith's name as a presidential hopeful at the Democratic convention and in the process, lit his own political star.

Campobello opened a new career for Schary as a playwright in 1958, shortly after he exited as production head of M-G-M. The film is also a brilliant new showcase for Greer Garson. She comes through as Eleanor Roosevelt with a deeply moving, multifaceted characterization.

There is a third tower of strength in the person of Hume Cronyn as Louis Howe, the wizened, asthmatic, devoted friend and political Svengali to Roosevelt. There is, considering the sober nature of the subject, a surprising amount of humor in *Campobello* and a good measure of it is deftly generated by Cronyn.

Franz Waxman's score makes a big contribution, notably to the convention sequence. Pic begins with an overture, about eight minutes, of melodious old-timers.

1960: NOMINATIONS: Best Actress (Greer Garson), Color Costume Design, Color Art Direction, Sound

•

SUNSET
1988, 106 mins, US Ⓥ ⊙ ⌑ col
Dir Blake Edwards ***Prod*** Tony Adams ***Scr*** Blake Edwards ***Ph*** Anthony B. Richmond ***Ed*** Robert Pergament ***Mus*** Henry Mancini ***Art*** Rodger Maus
Act Bruce Willis, James Garner, Malcolm McDowell, Mariel Hemingway, Kathleen Quinlan, Jennifer Edwards (Hudson Hawk/Tri-Star)

Sunset is a silly Hollywood fiction, unconvincing in all but a couple of its details. Premise of teaming up righteous cowboy star Tom Mix and real-life lawman Wyatt Earp to solve an actual murder case may have looked good on paper, but it plays neither amusingly nor excitingly. Despite the tough-guy charm he has exhibited elsewhere, Bruce Willis is one of the least likely choices imaginable to play Mix, perhaps the top Western star of the 1920s.

That's just the beginning of the film's lack of plausibility, even on its own terms. The notion of English, Chaplin-like former star (Malcolm McDowell) becoming the venal head of a studio bears no resemblance to anything that ever occurred in Hollywood, while the idea of multiple murders taking place at the first Academy Awards ceremony is nasty and far-fetched.

Fortunately, there is James Garner as Earp as relief from all the nonsense around him. In fact, the man from Tombstone seems a little too sophisticated and at ease in Tinseltown, but the actor's natural charm and fine sense of one-upmanship wins the day in virtually all his scenes.

1988: NOMINATION: Best Costume Design

•

SUNSET BLVD.
1950, 110 mins, US Ⓥ ⊙ b/w
Dir Billy Wilder ***Prod*** Charles Brackett ***Scr*** Charles Brackett, Billy Wilder, D. M. Marshman, Jr. ***Ph*** John F. Seitz ***Ed*** Arthur Schmidt ***Mus*** Franz Waxman ***Art*** Hans Dreier, John Meehan
Act William Holden, Gloria Swanson, Erich von Stroheim, Nancy Olson, Cecil B. DeMille, Buster Keaton (Paramount)

Sunset Blvd. is a backstage melodrama using a filmland, instead of a legit, locale. It is tied in with a pseudo-exposé of Hollywood. The exposé of the land of the swimming pool opens with a shot of a dead man floating in the plunge of a Beverly Hills mansion. The voice of the dead man then narrates the story, going back six months to explain why he eventually reached such a sorry state.

He is a young writer with a few minor credits and many creditors. He finds refuge in what he believes to be an abandoned mansion. It is occupied by a former great femme star. She takes a fancy to the young man, employs him to write a script that will return her to past glory. The association segues into an affair.

Performances by the entire cast, and particularly William Holden and Gloria Swanson, are exceptionally fine. Swanson, returning to the screen after a very long absence, socks hard with a silent-day technique to put over the decaying star she is called upon to portray. Erich von Stroheim, as her butler and original discoverer, delivers with excellent restraint.

The other performer rating more than a mention is Cecil B. DeMille. He plays himself with complete assurance in one of the few sympathetic roles.

1950: Best Story & Screenplay, B&W Art Direction, Score for a Dramatic Picture

NOMINATIONS: Best Picture, Director, Actor (William Holden), Actress (Gloria Swanson), Supp. Actor (Erich von Stroheim), Supp. Actress (Nancy Olson), B&W Cinematography, Editing

•

SUNSHINE BOYS, THE
1975, 111 mins, US Ⓥ col
Dir Herbert Ross ***Prod*** Ray Stark ***Scr*** Neil Simon ***Ph*** David M. Walsh ***Ed*** Margaret Booth, John F. Burnett ***Mus*** Harry V. Lojewski (sup.) ***Art*** Albert Brenner
Act Walter Matthau, George Burns, Richard Benjamin, Lee Meredith, Carol Arthur, Rosetta Le Noire (M-G-M)

The Sunshine Boys is an extremely sensitive and lovable film version of Neil Simon's play, with Walter Matthau and George Burns outstanding in their starring roles as a pair of long-hostile vaudeville partners.

Matthau, with some complex makeup artistry atop his own brilliant talent, gives the Willy Clark character its full dimension of rascality, stubbornness, heart, pride and, eventually, humility. Burns, returning to pix, provides in his standout performance the right complementing aspects to the pair's love-hate relationship spanning 43 years. Richard Benjamin, the nephew-agent who is the catalyst of their reconciliation, serves to ventilate audience responses to the principals' behavior while simultaneously creating an independent characterization all his own.

Apart from the incidental title music, there is no score, which seems the proper decision. Matthau, Burns, Benjamin and the story need no musical accent.

1975: Best Supp. Actor (George Burns)

NOMINATIONS: Best Actor (Walter Matthau), Screenplay Adaptation, Art Direction

•

SUN SHINES BRIGHT, THE
1953, 90 mins, US Ⓥ b/w
Dir John Ford ***Prod*** John Ford, Merian C. Cooper ***Scr*** Laurence Stallings ***Ph*** Archie Stout ***Ed*** Jack Murray ***Mus*** Victor Young ***Art*** Frank Hotaling
Act Charles Winninger, Arleen Wheelan, John Russell, Stepin Fetchit, Russell Simpson, Ludwig Stossel (Argosy/Republic)

This is a lightweight comedy-drama, poorly plotted and overlong. Three Irvin S. Cobb short stories ["The Sun Shines Bright," "The Mob from Massac" and "The Lord Provides"] have been spliced together. Characters are such stereotype figures as julep-drinking Southerners, comic-opera darkies and bigoted poor white trash. Script and John Ford's direction attempt to cloak these hackneyed types with a generous dose of schmaltz and a theme of "good triumphing over evil" but it fails to come off with any impact.

Charles Winninger makes as much as possible of his Judge Priest character, the principal figure. It's election time in Fairfield, KY, a sleepy Southern town back in 1905, and an upstart Yankee state's attorney (Milburn Stone) is threatening to unseat the judge. Depite the damage it may do to his political future, the judge goes his easy-going humane way.

He talks down a mob threatening to lynch a colored boy falsely accused of rape; aids a woman who keeps a house of ill fame on the outskirts of town; and leads the town's few substantial, right-thinking citizens in the funeral march for another fallen woman.

Players go through their chores in routine fashion.

•

SUPER COPS, THE
1974, 95 mins, US Ⓥ col
Dir Gordon Parks ***Prod*** William Belasco ***Scr*** Lorenzo Semple, Jr. ***Ph*** Dick Kratina ***Ed*** Harry Howard ***Mus*** Jerry Fielding ***Art*** Stephen Hendrickson
Act Ron Leibman, David Selby, Sheila Frazier, Pat Hingle, Dan Frazer, Joseph Sirola (M-G-M)

The Super Cops is essentially the real-life story of two N.Y. police officers who brought their effective and original brand of justice to a crime-ridden section of Brooklyn. As produced from the book by L. H. Whittemore, and enacted by Ron Leibman and David Selby as the two tough cops, the finished result is a gem of realism. Highlighted by smashing violence, storyline, though episodic, punches over its theme in first-rate fashion.

Narrative builds strongly from the day the two rookies are sworn into the Police Academy through their ferreting in the filth of the ghettos to combat the sale of drugs and their constant harassment by the police themselves.

Leibman and Selby as the most controversial cops in the department sock over their roles.

•

SUPERFLY
1972, 96 mins, US Ⓥ col
Dir Gordon Parks, Jr. ***Prod*** Sig Shore ***Scr*** Phillip Fenty ***Ph*** James Signorelli ***Ed*** Bob Brady ***Mus*** Curtis Mayfield
Act Ron O'Neal, Carl Lee, Sheila Frazier, Julius W. Harris, Charles McGregor, Nate Adams (Warner)

Best that can be said for this quickie is its unpretentiousness in not seeking any pseudo-sociological meaning or theme, or assuming any airs that one is supposed to be enriched or provoked by it all. It's strictly action-adventure, alternating, like clockwork, drugs-sex-violence for its duration with hardly a plot line to hold it together.

Cast handles the simple characterizations adequately, with Ron O'Neal heading as Superfly, sluggin', lovin', needlin' and philosophizing his way through the tale of the pusher with heart of gold, wanting to get out—but only after making his easy $1 million. Supporting convincingly are Carl Lee, Julius W. Harris as Scatter and Charles McGregor as Fat Freddie.

Sheila Frazier and Polly Niles offer the sex interests, including a breast or two when things get otherwise dull.

●

SUPERGIRL

1984, 117 mins, UK Ⓥ ⊙ ▭ col

Dir Jeannot Szwarc ***Prod*** Timothy Burrill ***Scr*** David Odell ***Ph*** Alan Hume ***Ed*** Malcolm Cooke ***Mus*** Jerry Goldsmith ***Art*** Richard MacDonald

Act Faye Dunaway, Helen Slater, Peter O'Toole, Hart Bochner, Peter Cook, Brenda Vaccaro (Artistry/Cantharus)

Supergirl is Kara, Superman's cousin, who journeys from her home on the planet of Argo to Earth to recover the missing Omegahedron Stone, life-force of her world, which has fallen into the clutches of the evil Selena (Fay Dunaway), a power-hungry sorceress.

Landing near an exclusive boarding school for young ladies, Kara quickly adopts the name of Linda Lee and finds herself rooming with Lois Lane's kid sister, Lucy (Maureen Teefy).

Rest of pic represents a struggle between the good of Supergirl and the evil of Selena with, as is usually the case, evil being a lot more fun.

Dunaway has a ball as Selena, and her enjoyably over-the-top handling of the part could merit cult attention. She's ably backed by Brenda Vaccaro as her incredulous assistant, and Peter Cook as her sometime lover and math teacher at the girls' school.

Peter O'Toole makes a modest impression as Supergirl's friend and mentor, while Mia Farrow and Simon Ward, as her parents, have even smaller roles than Susannah York and Marlon Brando in the first *Superman*.

Helen Slater is a find: blonde as Supergirl, dark-haired as Linda Lee, she's an appealing young heroine in either guise. Screenplay is filled with witty lines and enjoyable characters, but Jeannot Szwarc's direction is rather flat.

●

SUPERMAN

1978, 143 mins, US Ⓥ ⊙ ▭ col

Dir Richard Donner ***Prod*** Pierre Spengler ***Scr*** Mario Puzo, David Newman, Leslie Newman, Robert Benton ***Ph*** Geoffrey Unsworth ***Ed*** Stuart Baird ***Mus*** John Williams ***Art*** John Barry

Act Marlon Brando, Gene Hackman, Christopher Reeve, Margot Kidder, Ned Beatty, Glenn Ford (Warner/Salkind)

Magnify James Bond's extraordinary physical powers while curbing his sex drive and you have the essence of *Superman*, a wonderful, chuckling, preposterously exciting fantasy.

Forget Marlon Brando, who tops the credits. As Superman's father on the doomed planet Krypton, Brando is good but unremarkable.

As both the wholesome man of steel and his bumbling secret identity Clark Kent, Christopher Reeve is excellent. As newswoman Lois Lane, Margot Kidder plays perfectly off both of his personalities.

Tracing the familiar cartoon genesis, film opens with spectacular outer-space effects and the presentation of life on Krypton where nobody believes Papa Brando's warnings of doom. So he and wife Susannah York ship their baby son on his way to Earth.

Striking terra firma, the baby is found by Glenn Ford and Phyllis Thaxter who take him for their own. But the time must ultimately come when Superman's powers for good are revealed to the world and his debut becomes a wild night, beginning with Lane's rescue from a skyscraper, the capture of assorted burglars and the salvation of the president's airplane.

Lurking in wacky palatial splendor in the sewers beneath Park Ave., supercriminal Gene Hackman views this caped arrival as a superthreat befitting his evil genius.

1978: Special Achievement Award (visual effects)

NOMINATIONS: Best Editing, Original Score, Sound

●

SUPERMAN IV
THE QUEST FOR PEACE

1987, 89 mins, US Ⓥ ⊙ ▭ col

Dir Sidney J. Furie ***Prod*** Menahem Golan, Yoram Globus ***Scr*** Lawrence Konner, Mark Rosenthal ***Ph*** Ernest Day ***Ed*** John Shirley ***Mus*** John Williams ***Art*** John Graysmark

Act Christopher Reeve, Gene Hackman, Jackie Cooper, Mariel Hemingway, Jon Cryer, Margot Kidder (Cannon/Warner)

Opening sequence shows Superman has picked up the spirit of glasnost as he flies into space to rescue an imperiled cosmonaut and utters his first lines of the picture in Russian.

Superman's newly assumed mission sees him addressing the United Nations to tell the world he personally is going to remove all nuclear weapons from the face of the earth.

Meanwhile, Lex Luthor (Gene Hackman) has created an evil clone of Superman called Nuclear Man, who wreaks havoc with famous landmarks around the world and does savage battle with the hero on the face of the moon until Superman discovers his nemesis' single flaw.

The earlier films in the series were far from perfect, but at their best they had some flair and agreeable humor, qualities this one sorely lacks. Hackman gets a few laughs, but has less to work with than before, and everyone else seems to be just going through the motions and having less fun doing so.

●

SUPERMAN III

1983, 123 mins, UK Ⓥ ⊙ ▭ col

Dir Richard Lester ***Prod*** Pierre Spengler ***Scr*** David Newman, Leslie Newman ***Ph*** Robert Paynter ***Ed*** John Victor Smith ***Mus*** Ken Thorne ***Art*** Peter Murton

Act Christopher Reeve, Richard Pryor, Robert Vaughn, Annette O'Toole, Annie Ross, Margot Kidder (Salkind/ Dovemead)

Superman III emerges as a surprisingly soft-cored disappointment. Putting its emphasis on broad comedy at the expense of ingenious plotting and technical wizardry, it has virtually none of the mythic or cosmic sensibility that marked its predecessors.

The film begins with a hilarious pre-credits sequence in which Richard Pryor, an unemployed "kitchen technician," decides to embark on a career as a computer programmer. Robert Vaughn, a crooked megalomaniac intent on taking over the world economy, dispatches Pryor to a small company subsid in Smallville, where he programs a weather satellite to destroy Colombia's coffee crop (and make a market-cornering killing for Vaughn). Foiled by Superman (Christopher Reeve), Pryor uses the computer to concoct an imperfect form of Kryptonite—using cigarette tar to round out the formula. The screenplay opts for the novelty of using the Kryptonite to split the Clark Kent/Superman persona into two bodies, good and evil.

Most of the action relies on explosive pyrotechnics and careening stuntpersons. At the romantic level, the film does paint a nice relationship between Reeve (as Kent) and his onetime crush Annette O'Toole.

●

SUPERMAN II

1981, 127 mins, UK Ⓥ ⊙ ▭ col

Dir Richard Lester ***Prod*** Pierre Spengler ***Scr*** Mario Puzo, David Newman, Leslie Newman ***Ph*** Geoffrey Unsworth, Robert Paynter ***Ed*** John Victor-Smith ***Mus*** Ken Thorne ***Art*** John Barry, Peter Murton

Act Christopher Reeve, Gene Hackman, Margot Kidder, Ned Beatty, Terence Stamp, Sarah Douglas (IFP/Salkind)

For all the production halts, setbacks, personnel changeovers and legal wrangling that paved its way to the screen, *Superman II* emerges as a solid, classy, cannily constructed piece of entertainment which gets down to action almost immediately.

Although original plans called for lensing the first two *Superman* features simultaneously, the sequel is reportedly 80% newly shot footage.

The film does an especially good job of picking up the strings of unexplored characters and plot seeds left dangling from the first pic, taking its core plot from the three Kryptonian villains—Terence Stamp, Jack O'Halloran and Sarah Douglas—briefly glimpsed in the first pic. Here, they're liberated from perpetual imprisonment in a bizarre time-warp by an H-bomb explosion in outer space.

The film builds quickly to a climactic battle between Christopher Reeve and the three supervillains in midtown Manhattan.

●

SUPER MARIO BROS.

1993, 104 mins, US Ⓥ ⊙ ▭ col

Dir Rocky Morton, Annabel Jankel ***Prod*** Jake Eberts, Roland Joffe ***Scr*** Parker Bennett, Terry Runte, Ed Solomon ***Ph*** Dean Semler ***Ed*** Mark Goldblatt ***Mus*** Alan Silvestri ***Art*** David L. Snyder

Act Bob Hoskins, John Leguizamo, Dennis Hopper, Samantha Mathis, Fisher Stevens, Fiona Shaw (Hollywood Pictures/Lightmotive/Allied Filmmakers)

The task of converting a non-narrative Nintendo videogame [and characters created by Shigeru Miyamoto and Takashi Tezuka] into a $50 million motion picture was too much for a trio of scripters, a pair of (married) directors and a couple of high-profile producers. What set them in motion was obviously the success of the *Teenage Mutant Ninja Turtles* movies, which *Mario* imitates when it's not into *Star Wars* riffs or *Batman* pastiche.

Awkwardly constructed pic, featuring two prologues and two epilogues, starts with the premise of a parallel world to New York created 65 million years ago by a meteorite that also killed off the dinosaurs. A miscast (he's not the only one) Dennis Hopper is intent upon retrieving a meteorite fragment and a young princess (Samantha Mathis) sent with it to our world.

Mathis is kidnapped by Hopper's bumbling assistants and pursued into his world by the Mario Bros., two Brooklyn plumbers. If you're over the age of five and can believe that Bob Hoskins and John Leguizamo are brothers, let alone Italian, the rest of the film's leaps of faith are child's play.

As stiffly directed by Annabel Jankel and Rocky Morton, *Mario* occasionally attempts to careen along like a videogame with chases, fireballs and narrow escapes. However, the action is generally photographed in unexciting closeups and telephoto shots.

●

SUPERNATURAL

1933, 65 mins, US b/w

Dir Victor Halpern ***Prod*** Edward Halpern ***Scr*** Harvey Thew, Brian Marlow ***Ph*** Arthur Martinelli

Act Carole Lombard, Allan Dinehart, Vivienne Osborne, Randolph Scott, H. B. Warner, Beryl Mercer (Paramount)

A 65-minute ghost story [by Garnett Weston] that dies after the first half hour. Up to the turning point there's some excitement, but the authors and director fall into the usual traps and put too much pressure on a frail plot. Once the grip on audience interest is relaxed, the picture never recovers.

Carole Lombard, featured, is pitted against a role that needs more expert handling in acting and direction than it receives. She's called on to change from a nice to a bad girl when the spirit of a dead murderess takes full possession of her. Her Jekyll-Hyde transposition in the femme gender is crudely done, forced as it is to depend on such flimsy devices as fainting spells, smirks, she-devil facial expressions and double exposures.

The villain is a phoney spiritualist (Alan Dinehart), and he's painted with a pretty broad brush all the way. On the other hand, there's a prominent scientist whose ideas are equally far-fetched, but he's accepted as a legitimate person.

After getting her revenge, the spirit murderess scrams, leaving Lombard as her nice self again. That's the cue for Lombard and Randolph Scott to clinch, the ghost playing cupid.

●

SUPERNOVA

2000, 90 mins, US Ⓥ ⊙ col

Dir Thomas Lee [= Walter Hill] ***Prod*** Ash R. Shah, Daniel Chuba, Jamie Dixon ***Scr*** David Campbell Wilson ***Ph*** Lloyd Ahern II ***Ed*** Michael Schweitzer, Melissa Kent ***Mus*** David Williams ***Art*** Marek Dobrowolski

Act James Spader, Angela Bassett, Robert Forster, Lou Diamond Phillips, Peter Facinelli, Robin Tunney, Wilson Cruz (Screenland/Hammerhead/M-G-M)

A standard-issue intergalactic actioner, pic was directed by Walter Hill, who removed his name after the proverbial creative differences ("Thomas Lee" perhaps aims to avoid the blatancy of "Alan Smithee"); editing was reportedly completed by the likewise uncredited Francis Coppola. Whatever the appropriate divvying of credit or blame, pic is an embarrassment to no one, but neither is it a feather in any cap.

Tale [story by William Malone] kicks off in the early 22nd century aboard a small, medical-rescue spaceship. Attention centers on co-pilot Nick Vanzant, who has recently emerged from rehab and is played by a newly bulked-up, deep-voiced and dark-haired James Spader. The other crew members are Capt. A. J. Marley (Robert Forster), gruff medical officer Kaela Evers (Angela Bassett), engineer Benj (Wilson Cruz), medical tech Yerzy (Lou Diamond Phillips) and paramedic Danika (Robin Tunney).

One small novelty here is the understated paralleling of cosmic energies and sexual interplay. Yerzy and Danika are getting it on as tale opens, and Nick and Kaela soon taste the pleasures of zero-gravity whoopee. Crew members doff their clothes whenever the spaceship's "dimension-jumping."

Crew and ship dimension-jump to what seems to be a standard rescue situation but soon grows strange and perilous. At the site, the only person they find alive is an odd young man named Karl (Peter Facinelli). Karl is more lethal than bereft. Endowed with powers from the ninth dimension, the interloper makes love to Danika, then starts picking off crew members, growing more youthful and muscular as he does. The battle from there is energetic but thoroughly predictable in its shape and outcome, which leaves pic feeling competent but programmatic.

•

SUPERVIXENS

1975, 105 mins, US Ⓥ col

Dir Russ Meyer ***Prod*** Russ Meyer ***Scr*** Russ Meyer ***Ph*** Russ Meyer ***Ed*** Russ Meyer ***Mus*** William Loose ***Art*** Michael Levesque

Act Shari Eubank, Charles Pitts, Charles Napier, Uschi Digard, Henry Rowland, Christy Hartburg (September 19)

Russ Meyer's *Supervixens* is an overlong and overly violent skin pic whose interest lies in its pretentions to be more than a skin film. The story involves a gas-station attendant, Clint (Charles Pitts), whose foul-mouthed girlfriend is successively stabbed, beaten, drowned and electrocuted by a brutish cop (Charles Napier) with Clint getting the blame. Fleeing town, he has sexual encounters with a succession of busty amazons, then falls for Supervixen (Shari Eubank), whom he must eventually rescue from a sick cop (Napier again). It's all very low on camp and high on blood.

The film is technically slick and the acting is competent.

•

SUPPORT YOUR LOCAL GUNFIGHTER

1971, 92 mins, US Ⓥ col

Dir Burt Kennedy ***Prod*** Bill Finnegan ***Scr*** James Edward Grant ***Ph*** Harry Stradling ***Ed*** Bill Gulick ***Mus*** Jack Elliot, Allyn Ferguson ***Art*** Phil Barber

Act James Garner, Suzanne Pleshette, Jack Elam, Joan Blondell, Harry Morgan, Marie Windsor (Cherokee/Brigade)

Burt Kennedy's follow-up to *Support Your Local Sheriff* has James Garner escaping from the clutches of Marie Windsor, only to become mistaken by competing mine-owners Harry Morgan and John Dehner for a hired gun, played in finale cameo by Chuck Connors. Jack Elam again is excellent in role of a befuddled but willing accomplice to Garner's maneuvers. Joan Blondell is good as a bordello queen, and Henry Jones scores as a nosy gossip.

Suzanne Pleshette starts out a bit too strong as a tomboy, but eventually settles in. There are a few hefty laughs, many chuckles, a few smiles, and some cold gags.

A. D. Flowers's special explosive effects punch up some of the action sequences, and Elam's curtain-narration speech, where he describes how he went on to become a big star of Italian westerns, brings the 92 minutes to a good finish.

•

SUPPORT YOUR LOCAL SHERIFF

1969, 96 mins, US Ⓥ col

Dir Burt Kennedy ***Prod*** William Bowers ***Scr*** William Bowers ***Ph*** Harry Stradling ***Ed*** George Brooks ***Mus*** Jeff Alexander ***Art*** Leroy Coleman

Act James Garner, Joan Hackett, Walter Brennan, Harry Morgan, Jack Elam, Bruce Dern (United Artists/Cherokee)

Support Your Local Sheriff uses as the basis for its comedy the many clichés that have become part and parcel of the Western genre.

Whether it's the town dominated by a tyrant, the never-missing gunfighter, the absolutely pure hero, the chaste but unchased maiden, the growth of the territory—they're all dealt with and done under, by demolishing dialogue or just enough exaggeration to point up the ridiculous in even the most respectable circumstances.

James Garner is delightful as the "stranger" riding into town on his way to Australia, so modest, yet so perfect in his various abilities—never missing a shot, turning the town derelict into his deputy, outthinking the Danbys (a superb quartet of villains), outwitting the attempts of the mayor's daughter to land him until he's ready.

The action almost never moves beyond the tiny town's limits, and the community itself seems just enough exaggerated to let the audience know that it's not to be taken seriously.

•

SUPPOSE THEY GAVE A WAR AND NOBODY CAME

1970, 113 mins, US Ⓥ col

Dir Hy Averback ***Prod*** Fred Engel ***Scr*** Don McGuire, Hal Captain ***Ph*** Burnett Guffey ***Ed*** John F. Burnett ***Mus*** Jerry Fielding ***Art*** Jack Poplin

Act Brian Keith, Tony Curtis, Ernest Borgnine, Suzanne Pleshette, Tom Ewell, Bradford Dillman (ABC)

A meandering comedy about three old-time army tankmen in a non-combatant missile base at war with the Southern redneck town in which it is located.

Main problem is that Hy Averback's direction and the screenplay [from a story by Hal Captain], both of which have their moments, never focus and decide if it is a comedy, serious drama or farce.

Ernest Borgnine is the heavy-handed Southern sheriff. Tony Curtis keeps it lighthearted, but nevertheless convincing, as "a middle-aged, paunchy garrison soldier who thinks he is Warren Beatty."

Suzanne Pleshette, a wise-cracking, self-proclaimed "beer hustler," is very real, and her handling of tough snappy dialog makes her appearances some of the best scenes in the film, especially in those with Curtis.

•

SURE THING, THE

1985, 94 mins, US Ⓥ ⊙ col

Dir Rob Reiner ***Prod*** Roger Birnbaum ***Scr*** Steven L. Bloom, Jonathan Roberts ***Ph*** Robert Elswit ***Ed*** Robert Leighton ***Mus*** Tom Scott ***Art*** Lilly Kilvert

Act John Cusack, Daphne Zuniga, Boyd Gaines, Tim Robbins, Lisa Jane Persky, Viveca Lindfors (Embassy/Monument)

The Sure Thing is at heart a sweetly old-fashioned look at the last lap of the coming-of-age ordeal in which the sure thing becomes less important than the real thing. Realization may not be earth shattering, but in an era of fast food and faster sex, return to the traditional is downright refreshing.

Gib (John Cusack) is a beer guzzling junk-food devotee with a flair for the outrageous, but he is not having much luck with the opposite sex in his freshman year at an eastern Ivy League college. One of the women he strikes out with is Alison (Daphne Zuniga), a prim and proper coed who thinks that spontaneity is a social disease.

The plot thickens as they both arrange a ride, unbeknownst to each other, with a California-bound couple for the Christmas break. Gib is off to score with the sure thing (Nicollette Sheridan) while Alison is visiting her boorish boyfriend (Boyd Gaynes). Stranded together, the two travelers mix like oil and water, volatile at first and gradually realizing that their different personalities complement each other.

Chemistry between Cuzack and Zuniga is a plus as they change and grow together as the film progresses. Off-key serenade of showtunes from Tim Robbins and Lisa Jane Persky in the car heading west supplies the same daffy humor director Rob Reiner brought to his mock documentary, *This Is Spinal Tap.*

•

SURF NAZIS MUST DIE

1987, 80 mins, US Ⓥ ⊙ col

Dir Peter George ***Prod*** Robert Tinnell ***Scr*** Jon Ayre ***Ph*** Rolf Kestermann ***Ed*** Craig Colton ***Mus*** Jon McCallum ***Art*** Bernadette Disanto

Act Barry Brenner, Gail Neely, Michael Sonye, Dawn Wildsmith, Tom Shell, Bobbie Bresee (Troma/Institute)

A sort of *Clockwork Orange* meets *Mad Max* on the beach, pic hasn't one redeeming feature. Time is the near future and California's social fabric has been torn apart by a devastating earthquake. It's hell out there on the beaches.

Striving for supremacy are the Surf Nazis, who live in a beach bunker, own beweaponed surf boards, bristle with knives and swastika tattoos and are fueled by a surfing Fuhrer—Adolf—who has a dream of owning the "new beach."

Not much else is clear until a revenge-seeking mother takes on the Nazis after they kill her son; prior to this there are various and often bloody fights between the Nazis and the other gangs, and there's even regular surf footage interspersed. The hulking mother, played by Bobbie Bresee, turns out to be quite a handful and wreaks gory retribution on each of the nasty Nazis.

Pic looks like most of its budget went on its titles, a not unlikeable score, and a surprisingly punchy and facetious trailer.

•

SURF NINJAS

1993, 86 mins, US Ⓥ ⊙ col

Dir Neal Israel ***Prod*** Evzen Kolar ***Scr*** Dan Gordon ***Ph*** Arthur Albert, Victor Hammer ***Ed*** Tom Walls ***Mus*** David Kitay ***Art*** Michael Novotny

Act Ernie Reyes, Jr., Rob Schneider, Nicolas Cowan, Leslie Nielsen, Tone Loc, Ernie Reyes, Sr. (New Line)

Surf Ninjas is a juvenile comedy-action pic. Action is relatively mild for the genre and, unfortunately, so are the jokes.

Two California surfing dudes (Ernie Reyes, Jr., Nicolas Cowan) discover they are long-lost crown princes of the obscure nation of Patu San after a royal family retainer (Ernie Reyes, Sr.) arrives to inform them of their true identities. To regain the throne, they must overthrow the dictator (Leslie Nielsen, looking like a cross between a samurai and *Star Trek*'s Borg). Joining them on their adventure is a spaced-out friend (Rob Schneider), an L.A. cop (rap star Tone Loc) and a prospective bride (Kelly Hu).

While the martial arts choreography by Reyes, Sr., can't be totally dismissed, the PG target ensures it's pretty tame stuff. Reyes, Jr., was a stunt double in *Teenage Mutant Ninja Turtles* and then got his own role in the sequel.

•

SURRENDER

1987, 95 mins, US Ⓥ ⊙ col

Dir Jerry Belson ***Prod*** Aaron Spelling, Alan Greisman ***Scr*** Jerry Belson ***Ph*** Juan Ruiz Anchia ***Ed*** Wendy Greene Bricmont ***Mus*** Michel Colombier ***Art*** Lilly Kilvert

Act Sally Field, Michael Caine, Steve Guttenberg, Peter Boyle, Jackie Cooper, Julie Kavner (Cannon)

Surrender is a '50s sitcom dressed up in modern clothes. The issues are somewhat updated but the characters still think like Doris Day and Rock Hudson. As the confused lovers, Michael Caine and Sally Field are good for a couple of laughs along the way, but production runs out of steam early.

Caine is a casualty of too many marriages and too much success as a pop novelist. Field is a would-be artist who takes the easy way out in the form of a rich and indulgent but unchallenging boyfriend (Steve Guttenberg).

Opening skirmish is love at first fight. But once they've coupled, the series of complications concocted by writer-director Jerry Belson can only lead to an inevitable happy ending. Things at least move fast and Belson does have an ear for modern courtship and the silly things people say to each other.

Although their acting styles don't quite mesh and there isn't a great deal of chemistry between them, both Caine and Field are strong enough presences to make them entertaining to observe.

•

SURVIVORS, THE

1983, 102 mins, US Ⓥ ⊙ col

Dir Michael Ritchie ***Prod*** William Sackheim ***Scr*** Michael Leeson ***Ph*** Billy Williams ***Ed*** Richard A. Harris ***Mus*** Paul Chihara ***Art*** Gene Callahan

Act Walter Matthau, Robin Williams, Jerry Reed, James Wainwright, Kristen Vigard, Annie McEnroe (Delphi/Rastar)

An aimless, unfocused social comedy, *The Survivors* misfires on just about every level, finding what laughs it has to offer solely in the personal performing talents of Walter Matthau and Robin Williams.

Exec Williams and gas station owner Matthau both become unemployed at the outset, and through a bizarre coincidence are thrown together as intended victims of professional hitman Jerry Reed.

Confronted with the threat of another attack by Reed, Williams becomes a maniacal gun enthusiast and joins a survival-training unit run in the snowy mountains by James Wainwright.

It feels as though the script, such as it was, was tossed out the window once action moves to the New Hampshire compound. All of Williams's dialog from this point on sounds like lifts from crazed comic monologs he might deliver onstage. Matthau at least makes things watchable thanks to his masterful comic timing.

•

SUSAN AND GOD

(UK: THE GAY MRS TREXEL)

1940, 115 mins, US Ⓥ b/w

Dir George Cukor ***Prod*** Hunt Stromberg ***Scr*** Anita Loos ***Ph*** Robert Planck ***Ed*** William H. Terhune ***Mus*** Herbert Stothart ***Art*** Cedric Gibbons, Randall Duell

Act Joan Crawford, Fredric March, Ruth Hussey, John Carroll, Rita Hayworth, Nigel Bruce (M-G-M)

Film version of Rachel Crothers's play, with Joan Crawford in the role played by Gertrude Lawrence on the stage, is smartly cast, deftly directed and elaborately mounted. In contrast to the original piece, picture builds up parts of the husband (Fredric March) and young daughter (Rita Quigley) to the equals of Susan (Crawford). In fact, when everything is over, sympathy tends strongly to the former pair rather than the latter.

Crawford returns from abroad a shallow and scatter-brained disciple of a "new thought," or Oxford, movement. In expounding her views strongly amongst her socialite friends, she upsets several happy couples; but is faced with reconstructing her own marital happiness through personal practice of her tenets. Persistence of her husband to keep her in line and sincerity of the couple's youngster finally bring her to reason.

Crawford provides a strong portrayal of Susan—a mature matron characterization, which is a marked departure for the player. March provides a polished and capital presentation of the bewildered husband who battles through to reestablish happiness in his household. Quigley, as the daughter, is excellent.

George Cukor's direction highlights the characterizations he unfolds, and his weakness in piloting can be attributed to the slow pace at which he develops the story.

•

SUSAN LENOX: HER FALL AND RISE
1931, 75 mins, US Ⓥ b/w
Dir Robert Z. Leonard ***Scr*** Wanda Tuchock, Zelda Sears, Leon Gordon, Edith Fitzgerald ***Ph*** William Daniels ***Ed*** Margaret Booth
Act Greta Garbo, Clark Gable, Jean Hersholt, John Miljan, Alan Hale (M-G-M)

Not the least of this film's assets is the title, carrying the prestige of a novel that was a sensation upon its publication. What David Graham Phillips wrote as a protest against narrow-minded respectability has evolved in the filming into a hot romance based on sexual antagonism. The picture provides Greta Garbo with the role of destiny-hounded woman, not altogether unlike her Anna Christie, and adds to the Garbo gallery another impressive portrait.

The Garbo Susan is a glamorous figure, a vital Swedish immigrant girl who flees her ignorant, self-righteous foster parents in a raging storm to take refuge with a prepossessing young engineer (Clark Gable). The young pair fall in love. Out of the curious sexual antagonism that seems to be generated by their passion she goes her errant way to become a famous courtesan, while he sinks from bad to worse to the finality of a South Seas beachcomber.

Teaming with the great Garbo, of course, marks the peak of Gable's vogue. He appears to excellent purpose here, playing with agreeable urbanity and giving a performance that blends effectively into the whole atmosphere.

•

SUSAN SLADE
1961, 116 mins, US col
Dir Delmer Daves ***Prod*** Delmer Daves ***Scr*** Delmer Daves ***Ph*** Lucien Ballard ***Ed*** William Ziegler ***Mus*** Max Steiner ***Art*** Leo K. Kuter
Act Troy Donahue, Connie Stevens, Dorothy McGuire, Lloyd Nolan, Bert Convy (Warner)

Susan Slade, though slickly produced and attractively peopled, weighs in as little more than a plodding and predictable soap opera. It is, however, a telling showcase for Connie Stevens.

The screenplay by Delmer Daves, who also produced and directed as is his custom, is from the novel by Doris Hume. Yarn has a chicken way of evading its real issues by ushering in devastatingly convenient melodramatic swerves at key moments.

Stevens enacts the innocent, virginal daughter of a devoted family man and engineer (Lloyd Nolan) who returns with his brood to luxury in the States after 10 years of service on a project in remote Chile. The girl promptly falls madly in love and finds herself with child but without husband.

The family then tries a fake by moving to Guatemala, where Nolan dies and his wife (Dorothy McGuire) supposedly bears the child. The story returns to the U.S. and boils down to the inevitable triangle. Who is worthy of Stevens' love—junior tycoon Bert Convy or poor stable operator Troy Donahue?

Pretty Stevens comes on like gangbusters, and Lucien Ballard's misty, flattering close-up photography is her ally from start to finish. Donahue gives a wooden performance. Veterans Nolan and McGuire emote with sincerity.

The film was lensed in dazzlingly scenic places such as the Carmel coastline and San Francisco.

•

SUSAN SLEPT HERE
1954, 97 mins, US Ⓥ ⦿ col
Dir Frank Tashlin ***Prod*** Harriet Parsons ***Scr*** Alex Gottlieb ***Ph*** Nicholas Musuraca ***Ed*** Harry Marker ***Mus*** Leigh Harline ***Art*** Albert S. D'Agostino, Carroll Clark
Act Dick Powell, Debbie Reynolds, Anne Francis, Alvy Moore, Glenda Farrell, Horace McMahon (RKO)

Some 97 minutes of well-farced escapism is offered in *Susan Slept Here*. Romantic comedy is imaginatively developed, brightly trouped under Frank Tashlin's smart direction most of the way. Alex Gottlieb script, based on Gottlieb–Steve Fisher play [*Susan*], involves Hollywood writer Dick Powell with juve delinquent Debbie Reynolds in sort of May-October romantic affair.

Tashlin handling, and players, score strongest in scenes played strictly for pantomime. One sure laugh-getter scene is Powell watching old movie he dialoged on television. Other has Debbie watching home movies, grimacing cattily at love rival Anne Francis.

Some of material approaches frankness of *Moon Is Blue*. Some chuckles are sly type since battle-of-sexes stuff is open to assorted interpretations. For [Production] Code purposes, Debbie remains pure through all (her delinquency only that of being left homeless by mother gone off to remarry). She manages to spoil Francis's courtship of Powell and gets him for herself.

1954: NOMINATIONS: Best Song ("Hold My Hand"), Sound

•

SUSPECT, THE
1944, 85 mins, US b/w
Dir Robert Siodmak ***Prod*** Islin Auster ***Scr*** Bertram Millhauser ***Ph*** Paul Ivano ***Ed*** Arthur Hilton ***Mus*** Frank Skinner ***Art*** John B. Goodman, Martin Obzina
Act Charles Laughton, Ella Raines, Rosalind Ivan, Stanley C. Ridges (Universal)

Film is a murder mystery lacking much mystery but with all the suspense of a super-whodunnit. More than that, this production actually is a keen character study of a man whose married life has been a hell-on-earth and who sacrifices all to protect the one happiness in his middle age, a sensible young stenographer who later becomes his wife.

In Charles Laughton's accomplished hands, this character becomes fascinating. Withal, he makes him a typical home-loving storekeeper accustomed to the simple things in London of the gaslight era.

There is less of the bluster and none of the villainy of Laughton's previous vehicles. He gives an impeccable performance as the kindly, law-abiding citizen. Matching his deft portrayal is Ella Raines as the youthful steno he weds after his wife's demise.

•

SUSPECT
1987, 121 mins, US Ⓥ ⦿ col
Dir Peter Yates ***Prod*** Daniel A. Sherkow ***Scr*** Eric Roth ***Ph*** Billy Williams ***Ed*** Ray Lovejoy ***Mus*** Michael Kamen ***Art*** Stuart Wurtzel
Act Cher, Dennis Quaid, Liam Neeson, John Mahoney, Joe Mantegna, Philip Bosco (Tri-Star)

Art imitates art—and not very well—in Peter Yates's gimmicky suspense drama sabotaged by a flimsy script full of cliches. Dennis Quaid valiantly struggles to breathe life into the matter, but comes up short when a surprise ending packs little punch because the audience knows in the first five minutes the prime suspect can't be guilty.

Cher stars as Kathleen Riley, a hard-working Washington, D.C. public defender unlike any ever seen before. A day before taking a long-needed vacation, she's given a defendant charged with the brutal murder of a Justice Dept. staffer. Carl Wayne Anderson (Liam Neeson) has everything working against him: a Vietnam vet, he was rendered deaf and speechless by the psychological toll of the war, and he's homeless—he *has* to be innocent.

Just when it seems the entire film is going to be suffocated by liberal piety, Quaid shows up as Dairy State lobbyist Eddie Sanger, so persuasive that he's "dangerous." Sanger is called in for jury duty and sparks begin to fly when he faces off against Cher in the courtroom. Scenes with the two of them are the best in the film, but there aren't enough.

•

SUSPICION
1941, 102 mins, US Ⓥ ⦿ b/w
Dir Alfred Hitchcock ***Prod*** [Alfred Hitchcock] ***Scr*** Samson Raphaelson, Joan Harrison, Alma Reville ***Ph*** Harry Stradling ***Ed*** William Hamilton ***Mus*** Franz Waxman ***Art*** Van Nest Polglase, Carroll Clark
Act Cary Grant, Joan Fontaine, Cedric Hardwicke, Nigel Bruce, May Whitty, Isabel Jeans (RKO)

Alfred Hitchcock's trademarked cinematic development of suspenseful drama, through mental emotions of the story principals, is vividly displayed in *Suspicion*, a class production [from the novel *Before the Fact* by Francis Iles] provided with excellence in direction, acting and mounting.

Joan Fontaine successfully transposes to the screen her innermost emotions and fears over the wastrel and apparently murderous antics of her husband. Cary Grant turns in a sparkling characterization as the bounder who continually discounts financial responsibilities and finally gets jammed over thefts from his employer.

Unfolded at a leisurely pace, Hitchcock deftly displays the effect of occurrences on the inner emotions of the wife. Protected girl of an English country manor, Fontaine falls in love and elopes with Grant, an impecunious and happy-go-lucky individual, who figured her family would amply provide for both of them. Deeply in love, she overlooks his monetary irresponsibilities until discovery that he has stolen a large sum from an estate, and prosecution and exposure loom.

1941: Best Actress (Joan Fontaine)

NOMINATIONS: Best Picture, Scoring of a Dramatic Picture

•

SUTURE
1993, 96 mins, US Ⓥ ▭ b/w
Dir Scott McGehee, David Siegel ***Prod*** Scott McGehee, David Siegel ***Scr*** Scott McGehee, David Siegel ***Ph*** Greg Gardiner ***Ed*** Lauren Zuckerman ***Mus*** Cary Berger ***Art*** Kelly McGehee
Act Dennis Haysbert, Mel Harris, Sab Shimono, Dina Merrill, Michael Harris, David Graf (Kino-Korsakoff)

Suture is an exceedingly smart and elegant American indie in a very unusual vein. Part mystery thriller, part psychological investigation and part avant-garde experiment, first feature from the team of Scott McGehee and David Siegel was shot in black-and-white 'scope.

A brilliant, attention-getting opening tersely presents the lead-up to a dramatic confrontation between a white intruder and a black man hiding with a shotgun, all to the disorienting accompaniment of narration concerning memory and amnesia.

Suddenly jumping back in time, the narrative introduces Vincent Towers (Michael Harris), a wealthy but cold white man living in an opulent home in Phoenix. Vincent has initiated a reunion with his half-brother, Clay Arlington (Dennis Haysbert), who's black. Vincent plots to blow up his own car with Clay in it, and assumes a new identity after having planted his own papers with Clay. Clay survives the explosion, and attempts to rebuild his memory from scraps of assorted evidence.

Handling of the story is intelligent and precise, although the pacing is too static and the plotting too elliptical for those not attuned to art films. Performances are functionally low key. Steven Soderbergh came aboard as exec. producer after lensing was completed to help navigate the film through post-production.

•

SVENGALI
1931, 79 mins, US Ⓥ ⦿ b/w
Dir Archie Mayo ***Scr*** J. G. Alexander ***Ph*** Barney McGill ***Art*** Anton Grot
Act John Barrymore, Marian Marsh, Bramwell Fletcher, Donald Crisp, Lumsden Hare, Carmel Myers (Warner)

Formerly well known as *Trilby* via famed novel [by George Du Maurier] and stage interpretations, the studio renamed it to designate the villainous hypnotist as the leading character.

Story, of course, is well known, but Svengali (John Barrymore) here makes it clear that Trilby (Marian Marsh), the model has been the house guest of several artists so that her desire to become legally attached to the pursuing young Englishman is not going to be without family difficulties. He hypnotizes her into running away with him and also into a career as a concert star.

Barrymore's playing is interesting, sterling and in broad strokes. Marsh takes a change for the better on looks in the late footage, but flashes nothing unusual histrionically.

1930/31: NOMINATIONS: Best Cinematography, Art Direction

•

SWALLOWS AND AMAZONS
1974, 92 mins, UK Ⓥ col
Dir Claude Whatham ***Prod*** Richard Pilbrow ***Scr*** David Wood ***Ph*** Denis Lewiston ***Ed*** Michael Bradsell ***Mus*** Wilfred Josephs ***Art*** Simon Holland,
Act Virginia McKenna, Ronald Fraser, Brenda Bruce, Jack Woolgar, John Franklyn-Robbins, Simon West (EMI/Theatre Projects)

This charming, delightful, beautifully made film for both adults and children is faithfully based on the 1929 children's classic by Arthur Ransome. In the deft screenplay by David Wood, the essential plot involving four children (the Swallows) on holiday in the Lake District, and their friendly rivalry with two tomboy girls (the Amazons) is simple but absorbing, and captures the spirit of the period.

Their activities take place on and around the water, with the picturesque landscape caught in pastel shades by Denis Lewiston.

Virginia McKenna and Ronald Fraser are seen briefly but register well, especially Fraser as the peppery but sympathetic uncle, living on a houseboat. The main burden is carried by the child actors, who all enter into the spirit of the proceedings with naturalness and enthusiasm.

●

SWAMP THING
1982, 90 mins, US Ⓥ ⦿ col
Dir Wes Craven ***Prod*** Benjamin Melniker, Michael E. Uslan ***Scr*** Wes Craven ***Ph*** Robin Goodwin ***Ed*** Richard Bracken ***Mus*** Harry Manfredini ***Art*** Robb Wilson King
Act Louis Jourdan, Adrienne Barbeau, Ray Wise, David Hess, Nicholas Worth, Don Knight (United Artists)

Writer-director Wes Craven's adaptation of the DC Comics book *Swamp Thing* to live-action feature filming is a childish programmer, short on thrills and laughs.

Sci-fi premise has scientist Alec Holland (Ray Wise) working with his sister in a lab in the bayous on a secret government project. He's developing a vegetable cell with an animal nucleus. With government agent Alice Cable (Adrienne Barbeau) inspecting the operation, all hell breaks loose when evil genius Arcane (Louis Jourdan) has his henchmen break in to steal the scientific formula. The green mixture is accidentally poured on Holland who, catching fire (in pic's best special effects scene), runs off into the swamp, later emerging as a big, green dude in a rubber suit, the Swamp Thing (Dick Durock). Pic disintegrates at this point into a series of contrived chases, pitting Arcane vs. Cable in a battle to obtain the formula and the creature.

Craven tries in vain, through old-fashioned characters and dialog, to re-create the '50s B-monster movie. The film's only asset for adult audiences is Barbeau, who is thoroughly believable and a feisty, rough 'n' tumble heroine, able to beat up most bad guys or outrun them through the swamp.

●

SWAMP WATER
(UK: THE MAN WHO CAME BACK)
1941, 90 mins, US b/w
Dir Jean Renoir ***Prod*** Irving Pichel ***Scr*** Dudley Nichols ***Ph*** Peverell Marley ***Ed*** Walter Thompson ***Mus*** David Buttolph
Act Walter Brennan, Walter Huston, Anne Baxter, Dana Andrews, Virginia Gilmore, John Carradine (20th Century-Fox)

Too bad that this picture's story does not match its excellent cast. Another of the hillbilly dramas, *Swamp Water* is an unflattering reflection upon Dudley Nichols's usually facile pen. The scenarist has failed to spark Vereen Bell's *Sat Eve Post* serial.

French director Jean Renoir's first job for an American company, it's something less than an auspicious beginning. Giving him a story dealing with a segment of the U.S. population with whom not even many Americans are familiar appears open to debate. The background is the Georgia swamps.

All the ingredients of an oldtime meller have been thrown into the plot. Story has Walter Brennan hiding in a swamp after escaping hanging for a murder. Dana Andrews, Huston's son by a previous marriage, finds him while searching for his dog. Brennan first threatens to kill the boy, but then convinces the kid of his innocence. They enter a fur-trapping partnership, the boy to give Brennan's share to the latter's daughter. But the lad's girl gets hep to what's going on and in a fit of jealousy gives the secret away.

●

SWAN, THE
1956, 107 mins, US Ⓥ ⌑ col
Dir Charles Vidor ***Prod*** Dore Schary ***Scr*** John Dighton ***Ph*** Joseph Ruttenberg, Robert Surtees ***Ed*** John Dunning ***Mus*** Bronislau Kaper
Act Grace Kelly, Alec Guinness, Louis Jourdan, Agnes Moorehead, Jessie Royce Landis, Brian Aherne (M-G-M)

Delightful make-believe of Ferenc Molnar's venerable play *The Swan* makes for a genteel picture about genteel people in a never-never world of crowns, titles and luxury living. There's subtle humor and broad humor, and several scenes that reach right into the heart.

Co-starring with Grace Kelly is Alec Guinness, who adds the correct, modified comedy touch to his role of the crown prince who, regardless of what audiences might want, must end up with the princess, and Louis Jourdan, who adds a feeling romantic flavor to his character of the commoner-tutor who dares to love the princess. Kelly shines right along with her male stars as the princess.

A standout romantic sequence occurs during a ball welcoming the crown prince. The tutor and Kelly fall in love right before your eyes as they dance to "The Swan Waltz."

Abetting the star trio with sock support in featured roles are Jessie Royce Landis, Kelly's mother; Brian Aherne, as the monk; Estelle Winwood, the pixilated, not-bright old maid sister of Landis and Agnes Moorehead, the strident queen mother.

●

SWANN IN LOVE
SEE: UN AMOUR DE SWANN

●

SWARM, THE
1978, 116 mins, US Ⓥ ⌑ col
Dir Irwin Allen ***Prod*** Irwin Allen ***Scr*** Stirling Silliphant ***Ph*** Fred J. Koenekamp ***Ed*** Harold F. Kress ***Mus*** Jerry Goldsmith ***Art*** Stan Jolley
Act Michael Caine, Katharine Ross, Richard Widmark, Richard Chamberlain, Olivia de Havilland, Ben Johnson (Warner)

Killer bees periodically interrupt the arch writing, stilted direction and ludicrous acting in Irwin Allen's disappointing and tired non-thriller.

Stirling Silliphant gets writing credit, based on an Arthur Herzog novel. It's the kind of screenplay where characters who supposedly are familiar with certain technical work spend most of their time explaining it to each other.

Then there's the sub-plot romance between schoolmarm Olivia de Havilland (with the worst phony Southern accent imaginable) and either Fred MacMurray or Ben Johnson.

Michael Caine heads the cast as a scientist who must contend with killer bees as well as with Richard Widmark, once again playing one of those cardboard military officers. Lots of other familiar names crop up. Allen was smarter on *The Towering Inferno* to have a partner handling the dramatic sequences. By the time the bees get to Houston, and the city is torched, few will care.

1978: NOMINATION: Best Costume Design

●

SWASHBUCKLER
(UK: THE SCARLET BUCCANEER)
1976, 101 mins, US Ⓥ ⦿ ⌑ col
Dir James Goldstone ***Prod*** Jennings Lang ***Scr*** Jeffrey Bloom ***Ph*** Philip Lathrop ***Ed*** Edward A. Biery ***Mus*** John Addison ***Art*** John Lloyd
Act Robert Shaw, James Earl Jones, Peter Boyle, Genevieve Bujold, Beau Bridges, Anjelica Huston (Universal)

An uneven picture which is splotchy in the form it tries to emulate and vacuous in the substance.

Jeffrey Bloom is given sole screenplay credit and Paul Wheeler sole story credit, for the coloring-book plot and formula characters as follows: genial lead pirates, Robert Shaw and James Earl Jones; wicked colonial governor, Peter Boyle; wronged noblelady, Genevieve Bujold; wronged noblelady's noble father, Bernard Behrens; and foppish soldier, Beau Bridges.

There's no sincerity in *Swashbuckler*. There's not even a consistent approach. This tacky pastepot job can't make up its mind whether it is serious, tongue-in-cheek, satirical, slapstick, burlesque, parody or travesty; but be assured it's all of the above.

●

SWEENEY!
1977, 97 mins, UK Ⓥ col
Dir David Wickes ***Prod*** Ted Childs ***Scr*** Ranald Graham ***Ph*** Dusty Miller ***Ed*** Chris Burt ***Mus*** Denis King ***Art*** Bill Alexander
Act John Thaw, Dennis Waterman, Barry Foster, Ian Bannen, Colin Welland, Diane Keen (Euston)

Regular TV series topliners John Thaw and Dennis Waterman as two cops drift through Ranald Graham's occasionally witty screenplay with no special flair, following the unlikely storyline.

Oil and its sway on the world's political and economic situation is the plot. Ian Bannen plays a steely-eyed alcoholic government minister and easily gives the best performance of the pic, while Barry Foster, an English actor, is unconvincing as an American press agent whose accent-slip is constantly showing.

David Wickes's direction and Chris Burt's editing produce a dull package. The TV show [created by Ian Kennedy Martin] packed a certain authenticity. This theatrical version must put the concept back into the realms of the fairy story class.

●

SWEENEY 2
1978, 108 mins, UK Ⓥ col
Dir Tom Clegg ***Prod*** Ted Childs ***Scr*** Troy Kennedy Martin ***Ph*** Dusty Miller ***Ed*** Chris Burt ***Mus*** Tony Hatch ***Art*** Bill Alexander
Act John Thaw, Dennis Waterman, Denholm Elliott, Georgina Hale, Nigel Hawthorne, Lewis Fiander (Euston)

Sweeney 2 is excellent British cops and robbers stuff in which a special squad of Scotland Yard detectives ultimately crack and demolish a gang of bank robbers whose hallmarks include goldplated shotguns. Good action well spaced and paced; good characterization played with finesse; a witty script and stylish direction all lend the production a degree of distinction.

Thesping is good to excellent. John Thaw is credible and appealing as the hardbitten cop who leads the police team on the case. Also notably fine are Denholm Elliott as a corrupt police officer who lands in the jug, Dennis Waterman as Thaw's number two, and Georgina Hale as a pickup promoted by the unattached Thaw.

●

SWEET ADELINE
1935, 85 mins, US Ⓥ b/w
Dir Mervyn LeRoy ***Prod*** Edward Chodorov ***Scr*** Erwin S. Gelsey ***Ph*** Sol Polito ***Ed*** Harold McLernon ***Mus*** Leo Forbstein (dir.) ***Art*** Robert Haas
Act Irene Dunne, Donald Woods, Hugh Herbert, Ned Sparks, Joseph Cawthorn, Winifred Shaw (Warner)

As a production *Sweet Adeline* is in the big-time-musical class, but strictly on merit it rates no better than fair. Except for the fact that the girl leaves her father's Hoboken beer garden to go on the stage against parental objections, Jerome Kern and Oscar Hammerstein II, who wrote the [1929] stage original, wouldn't know their Addie anymore.

She's not a very convincing or interesting person as rebuilt in Erwin S. Gelsey's adaptation.

Adeline (Irene Dunne) and Sid (Donald Woods) have a love spat over some unknown issue early in the picture and spend more than an hour of footage scowling at each other. When they stop scowling the picture is over.

That he's got to smirk most of the time makes it tough for Woods, who is no singer. There are two male voices in the show, but neither pertinent to the story. Noah Beery, hardly recognizable behind whiskers while doing a basso in the rehearsal scene, and Phil Regan, leading two production numbers. Dunne, in fine voice, is comely as Adeline, and effective, also, despite that she's not suited to torch songs. "Here Am I" and "Why Was I Born?" are retained from the original score, but the music otherwise is mostly new.

●

SWEET AND LOWDOWN
1999, 95 mins, US Ⓥ ⦿ ⌑ col
Dir Woody Allen ***Prod*** Jean Doumanian ***Scr*** Woody Allen ***Ph*** Zhao Fei ***Ed*** Alisa Lepselter ***Mus*** Dick Hyman ***Art*** Santo Loquasto
Act Sean Penn, Samantha Morton, Uma Thurman, Brian Markinson, Anthony LaPaglia, Gretchen Mol (Magnolia/Sweetland)

Woody Allen is in a mellow mood with *Sweet and Lowdown*, the fictionalized biopic of a supposedly legendary American jazz guitarist of the '30s. With Sean Penn in formidable form in the leading role, and beautiful turns from Samantha Morton and Uma Thurman as two contrasted women in his life, pic offers the filmmaker a wonderful showcase for presenting some of the great jazz standards he loves so much.

An opening title declares that the film will deal with Emmet Ray (Penn), a little-known jazz guitarist considered by aficionados to be second only to the great Django Reinhardt. Ray is a bombastic, self-centered extrovert with an ego a mile high. His dealings with women are shabby. Nonetheless, he finds himself touched by Hattie (Morton), a mute, orphaned laundress he meets on the boardwalk in Atlantic City.

At first he considers her just a "mute half-wit," but somehow they stay together for a year. Then, abruptly, we learn (from one of the narrators) he's walked out on her and married Blanche (Thurman), a sultry, elegant writer.

The usual Allen one-liners are in short supply; generally the mood is reflected by the film's apt title. Penn gives a winning performance as the brash, mostly unlikably Ray, who is redeemed only by the beautiful music he makes. British thesp Morton essays the touching character of Hattie with great distinction, conveying volumes of dialogue without a word. Thurman is sardonically amusing as the bitchy Blanche. Look and feel of the period are deftly caught.

1999: NOMINATIONS: Best Actor (Sean Penn), Supp. Actress (Samantha Morton)

●

SWEET BIRD OF YOUTH
1962, 120 mins, US Ⓥ ⊙ ▭ col
Dir Richard Brooks ***Prod*** Pandro S. Berman ***Scr*** Richard Brooks ***Ph*** Milton Krasner ***Ed*** Henry Berman ***Mus*** Harold Gelman (sup.) ***Art*** George W. Davis, Urie McCleary
Act Paul Newman, Geraldine Page, Shirley Knight, Ed Begley, Rip Torn, Mildred Dunnock (M-G-M)

Sweet Bird of Youth is a tamer and tidied but arresting version of Tennessee Williams's Broadway play. It's a glossy, engrossing hunk of motion picture entertainment, slickly produced by Berman.

In altering the playwright's Dixie climax (castration of the hero) Brooks has slightly weakened the story by damaging character consistency and emotional momentum. But he has accomplished this revision as if winking his creative eye at the "in" audience.

Four members of the original Broadway cast re-create their roles: Newman, Page, Torn and Sherwood. Newman brings thrust and vitality to the role, but has some overly-mannered moments that distract.

But this is Page's picture. She draws the best, wittiest and most acid lines and the most colorful character and what she does with this parley is a lesson in the art of acting. Her portrayal of the fading actress seeking substitute reality in drink, sex and what have you to offer is a histrionic classic. Shirley Knight is sympathetic and attractive as the distraught daughter of a corrupt political boss, and Ed Begley is outstanding in a perceptive portrayal of the latter.

1962: Best Supp. Actor (Ed Begley)

NOMINATIONS: Best Actress (Geraldine Page), Supp. Actress (Shirley Knight)

•

SWEET CHARITY
1969, 148 mins, US Ⓥ ⊙ ▭ col
Dir Bob Fosse ***Prod*** Robert Arthur ***Scr*** Peter Stone ***Ph*** Robert Surtees ***Ed*** Stuart Gilmore ***Mus*** Joseph Gershenson (sup.), Ralph Burns (orch.) ***Art*** Alexander Golitzen, George C. Webb
Act Shirley MacLaine, John McMartin, Ricardo Montalban, Sammy Davis, Jr., Chita Rivera, Paula Kelly (Universal)

Sweet Charity is, in short, a terrific musical film. Based on the 1966 legituner [by Neil Simon, Cy Coleman and Dorothy Fields, based on Federico Fellini's film, *Nights of Cabiria*], extremely handsome and plush production accomplishes everything it sets out to do.

Elements of comedy, drama, pathos and hope blend superbly with sure-fire entertainment values, stylishly and maturely planned and executed.

The story involves a gullible woman, of relatively low station in life, who refuses to believe that tomorrow does not hold a promise of happiness. [Pic was made available with both "sad" and "happy" endings.] Shirley MacLaine is a dance-hall hostess who, at the outset, has just been sloughed off by a gigolo. An accidental encounter with an Italian screen idol, played superbly by Ricardo Montalban, precedes a blossoming romance with John McMartin.

MacLaine's unique talents as a comic tragedienne are set off to maximum impact.

The film strikes the correct balance between escapist fantasy and hard reality. MacLaine's working environment is sleazy, but romantic adventures occur in believable settings—a lavish apartment, a street, a rooftop, a restaurant, a discotheque. Fosse's staging of the musical numbers is outstanding. Atop his remembered style is a brilliant, film-oriented appreciation of the emphasis possible only with camera and movieola.

1969: NOMINATIONS: Best Costume Design, Art Direction, Adapted Musical Score

•

SWEET DREAMS
1985, 115 mins, US Ⓥ ⊙ col
Dir Karel Reisz ***Prod*** Bernard Schwartz, Charles Mulvehill ***Scr*** Robert Getchell ***Ph*** Robbie Greenberg ***Ed*** Malcolm Cooke ***Mus*** Charles Gross ***Art*** Albert Brenner
Act Jessica Lange, Ed Harris, Ann Wedgeworth, David Clennon, James Staley, Gary Basaraba (HBO/Silver Screen)

Clearly the *Coal Miner's Daughter*'s cousin by both birthright and ambition, *Sweet Dreams* upholds the family honor quite well, with Jessica Lange's portrayal of country singer Patsy Cline certainly equal to Sissy Spacek's Oscar-winning re-creation of Loretta Lynn.

The film slants Cline's biography toward romance as likeable redneck Harris meets Lange at a roadside inn and their initially blissful marriage tackles the rough, upward climb to stardom, with many a shabby way-stop. Apart from the deftly interwoven singing sequences, most of Cline's career takes place off-camera.

Instead, *Dreams* deals with what could have been any marriage of its time and place: an ambitious, independent wife—a bit too sassy and sharp-tongued at times—versus an essentially loving working stiff, whose macho insecurities inspire him to too much booze, a little infidelity and boorish brutality.

1985: NOMINATION: Best Actress (Jessica Lange)

•

SWEET HEREAFTER, THE
1997, 110 mins, Canada Ⓥ ⊙ ▭ col
Dir Atom Egoyan ***Prod*** Atom Egoyan, Camelia Frieberg ***Scr*** Atom Egoyan ***Ph*** Paul Sarossy ***Ed*** Susan Shipton ***Mus*** Mychael Danna ***Art*** Phillip Barker
Act Ian Holm, Sarah Polley, Bruce Greenwood, Tom McCamus, Arsinee Khanjian, Alberta Watson (Ego/Alliance)

Canadian writer-director Atom Egoyan's most ambitious work to date, *The Sweet Hereafter* is a rich, complex meditation on the impact of a terrible tragedy on a small town.

Working from a memorable novel by Russell Banks, Egoyan shies away from the obvious tearjerker elements in this story of a bus crash that kills 14 children, and the film's power comes from his skillful ability to keep the anger and sorrow simmering just below the surface of the tale.

Egoyan has turned Mitchell Stephens (Ian Holm) into the central character, a big-city lawyer who arrives to mount a class-action suit targeting the city authorities, the bus manufacturer and anyone else who can be made to pay for the accident. Stephens has also lost a child—in his case, to drugs. The one man staunchly opposed to Stephens's efforts is Billy Ansell (Bruce Greenwood), a world-weary widower who lost his two kids in the disaster.

Pic has few of the visual quirks that Egoyan is known for, but it is shot with no small amount of style.

1997: NOMINATIONS: Best Director, Screenplay Adaptation

•

SWEETIE
1989, 97 mins, Australia Ⓥ ⊙ col
Dir Jane Campion ***Prod*** John Maynard, William MacKinnon ***Scr*** Jane Campion, Gerard Lee ***Ph*** Sally Bongers ***Ed*** Veronika Haussler ***Mus*** Martin Armiger ***Art*** Peter Harris
Act Genevieve Lemon, Karen Colston, Tom Lycos, Jon Darling, Dorothy Barry (Arenafilm)

Sweetie is an original, audacious tragicomedy about two sisters, one who's afraid of trees but believes in fortune tellers, the other who's plump and plain and eager to make her mark in showbiz.

At the beginning, focus is on Kay (Karen Colston) who works in an undefined factory in the inner city. She becomes convinced that a man described by a fortune teller as the man of her life is Louis (Tom Lycos), who just became engaged to a workmate. Kay sets about seducing him (in the factory parking lot) and before long they're living together in a rundown house in an unfashionable part of town.

Enter Dawn (Genevieve Lemon), known as Sweetie, Kay's sister, who with her drugged-out boyfriend Bob (Michael Lake) simply breaks into the house and moves into the spare room.

Genevieve Lemon is so good as the overweight, slow-witted Sweetie that her part seems too small. Karen Colston is fine as the sensitive, constantly nervous Kay. As Sweetie's tacky, somnolent boyfriend, Michael Lake steals his scenes.

•

SWEET LIBERTY
1986, 107 mins, US Ⓥ ⊙ col
Dir Alan Alda ***Prod*** Martin Bregman ***Scr*** Alan Alda ***Ph*** Frank Tidy ***Ed*** Michael Economou ***Mus*** Bruce Broughton ***Art*** Ben Edwards
Act Alan Alda, Michael Caine, Michelle Pfeiffer, Bob Hoskins, Lise Hilboldt, Lillian Gish (Universal)

Comedic potential is too rarely realized in this story of a college professor who watches filming of his historical tome become bastardized by Hollywood into a lusty romp.

Playing their true ages are Alan Alda as college professor Michael Burgess who teaches history of the American Revolution, and Michael Caine as box-office draw Elliot James.

When the film company arrives on location in bucolic Sayeville, Alda falls for leading lady Faith Healy (Michelle Pfeiffer), at the same time stringing along girlfriend Gretchen Carlsen (Lise Hilboldt).

The Hollywood cast and crew look and act the part, notably the macho stuntmen out to strut their stuff, as do the townsfolk who appear eager to do something other than endure another stifling Southern summer.

•

SWEET MOVIE
1974, 99 mins, France/Canada Ⓥ col
Dir Dusan Makavejev ***Scr*** Dusan Makavejev ***Ph*** Pierre Lhomme ***Ed*** Yann Dedet ***Mus*** Manos Hadjidakis
Act Carole Laure, Pierre Clementi, Anna Pruchnal, Sami Frey, Jane Mallet, John Vernon (VM/Mojack)

Sweet Movie is literally sweet, with lovemaking in a bed of sugar and a girl being bathed in chocolate for advertising purposes. But it also has an underpinning of scatology and a zany look at sensuality. Neither hard- nor softcore. Yugoslav filmmaker Dusan Makavejev's first pic in the West is provocative but also arbitrary.

It begins as broad funny satire on the richest man in the world looking for a virgin to marry and then goes into the girl's hegira as she finds personal sensual liberation with a revolutionary-type woman who plows the rivers in a boat called *Survival* with a giant head of Karl Marx on its prow.

The virgin, played with winsome innocence and then phlegmatism and eventual awakening by Carole Laure, finds her rich husband has a golden phallus.

•

SWEET NOVEMBER
1968, 114 mins, US col
Dir Robert Ellis-Miller ***Prod*** Jerry Gershwin, Elliott Kastner ***Scr*** Herman Raucher ***Ph*** Daniel L. Fapp ***Ed*** James Heckett ***Mus*** Michel Legrand ***Art*** John Lloyd
Act Sandy Dennis, Anthony Newley, Theodore Bikel, Burr DeBenning, Sandy Baron, Marj Dusay (Warner/Seven Arts)

Sweet November is a love story with a charming, almost fragile and slightly nebulous premise.

Sandy Dennis and Anthony Newley are the stars and each is outstanding in a strongly characterized role. They are called upon to engage in what some may regard as an overabundance of dialog, which lends more an aspect of a stage play than a motion picture, but this fits the mood and the tenor of the plot. Plot itself, which deals with a quixotic Brooklyn girl, is curiously motivated but interesting in its fulfillment.

Herman Raucher's original screenplay focuses on the girl, who takes to her heart—and her flat—for a month at a time some man with a problem. In doing so, she seeks to ease her own troubles, which may mean the end of her life at any time, but the man always leaves her as a changed human being.

Dennis is delightful in role of the kindly femme and Newley shades his performance with subtle comedy.

•

SWEET RIDE, THE
1968, 111 mins, US ▭ col
Dir Harvey Hart ***Prod*** Joe Pasternak ***Scr*** Tom Mankiewicz ***Ph*** Robert B. Hauser ***Ed*** Philip W. Anderson ***Mus*** Pete Rugolo ***Art*** Jack Martin Smith, Richard Day
Act Anthony Franciosa, Michael Sarrazin, Jacqueline Bisset, Bob Denver, Michael Wilding, Michael Carey (20th Century-Fox)

The Sweet Ride could sum up as *Hell's Angels' Bikini Beach Party in Valley of the Dolls Near Peyton Place.* Though well-mounted and interesting in the spotlighting of Michael Sarrazin and Jacqueline Bisset, overall result is a flat programmer, with ragged scripting, papier mache characters and routine direction.

Tony Franciosa is a beach-bum tennis hustler who is a sort of god to Malibu pad-mates Sarrazin and draft-dodging musician Bob Denver. Their life is a ball, we are told, interrupted only by neighbor Lloyd Gough, who keeps yelling about the decline of morals.

Enter Bisset, who has a running, masochistic affair with producer Warren Stevens. She takes to Sarrazin, though Charles Dierkop, a recurring motorcycle bum, gets an inordinate amount of attention from Bisset.

William Murray's novel has been adapted by Tom Mankiewicz into a contrived, unbelievable script about the Malibu-Hollywood young set, which supposedly "tells it like it is." It succeeds both in talking down to young people, and talking up to older folks.

•

SWEET ROSIE O'GRADY
1943, 76 mins, US col
Dir Irving Cummings ***Prod*** William Perlberg ***Scr*** Ken Englund ***Ph*** Ernest Palmer ***Ed*** Robert Simpson ***Mus*** Alfred Newman, Charles Henderson (dir.)
Act Betty Grable, Robert Young, Adolphe Menjou, Virginia Grey, Phil Regan (20th Century-Fox)

Everything about this William Perlberg production is showmanly appealing. The casting is tiptop, with Robert Young, as the *Police Gazette* reporter, the romantic vis-a-vis after forcing Betty Grable to jilt Reginald Gardiner, cast as an honorably enamored English duke whom she had met in London. Adolphe Menjou is the volatile *Gazette* ed, but the rest of the cast is also-ran save for Virginia Grey as the star's pal and Phil Regan, marking his cinematic comeback effectively in a songsmithing role.

Apart from Maude Nugent's classic title song, and sundry other excerpts such as the opener, "Here Am I Waiting at the Church," the tunes by Mack Gordon and Harry Warren are zestful and certain of popularity. They fit the action well, and in the person of pseudo-songwriting Regan, who does handsomely while tenoring the tunes he has "just written," they are given excellent demonstration throughout.

A saucy title that "if you think the Gay '90s were gay, get a load of the 1880s"—or words to that effect—sets the pace well.

●

SWEET SMELL OF SUCCESS
1957, 96 mins, US Ⓥ ⊙ b/w
Dir Alexander Mackendrick ***Prod*** James Hill ***Scr*** Clifford Odets, Ernest Lehman ***Ph*** James Wong Howe ***Ed*** Alan Crosland, Jr. ***Mus*** Elmer Bernstein ***Art*** Edward Carrere
Act Burt Lancaster, Tony Curtis, Susan Harrison, Marty Milner, Sam Levene, Barbara Nichols (Norma-Curtleigh/United Artists)

James Hill's production, locationed in Manhattan, captures the feel of Broadway and environs after dark. It's a no-holds-barred account of the sadistic fourth estater played cunningly by Burt Lancaster [from the novelette *Tell Me About It* by Ernest Lehman].

Failure to comply with his wishes means a broken career. Breaks in his column sustain the press agent but for the mentions there are certain favors to be granted. To the p.a., the columnist's dictates are law; if the favors include framing a young musician on a narcotics rap, that's all right, too.

Flaw in *Success* concerns the newspaperman's devotion to his sister. It's not clear why he rebels at her courtship with a guitarist, who appears to be a nice kid.

Tony Curtis as the time-serving publicist comes through with an interesting performance, although somehow the character he plays is not quite all the heel as written.

Susan Harrison is "introduced" in the picture and comes off well as the sister. She has a fetching beauty and shows easiness in handling the assignment.

●

SWEET SWEETBACK'S BAAD ASSSSS SONG
1971, 97 mins, US Ⓥ ⊙ col
Dir Melvin Van Peebles ***Prod*** Melvin Van Peebles, Jerry Gross ***Scr*** Melvin Van Peebles ***Ph*** Bob Maxwell ***Ed*** Melvin Van Peebles ***Mus*** Melvin Van Peebles ***Art*** [uncredited]
Act Brer Soul [= Melvin Van Peebles], Simon Chuckster, Hubert Scales, John Dullaghan, West Gale, Niva Rochelle (Yeah)

Melvin Van Peebles produced this film, edited it, wrote the screenplay, composed the music and played the leading role. He comes out ahead in all but one category: there are some serious problems with his screenplay.

Sweetback, who presumably derives his name from his prowess in the sack, is first seen, aged 12, in the arms of an accommodating older woman, and soon thereafter as the adult lead performer in a sexual circus. By chance, he's selected by his employer to go along with a couple of white detectives who need an arrest for the evening, and on the way he's witness to a ghetto riot in which his friendly captors brutally beat a young black revolutionary.

The moment of decision at hand, Sweetback smashes the detectives—and his own place in "the system." Thereafter, it's one long chase, and one long parable of the white man's brutality and duplicity.

Most of the many vignettes are absorbing in themselves, notably an encounter with a white motorcycle gang. Van Peebles has used every technical trick in the book to jazz up the sameness of the chase, but endless shots of Sweetback running through city and countryside can't help being boring.

●

SWEET WILLIAM
1980, 92 mins, UK Ⓥ col
Dir Claude Whatham ***Prod*** Jeremy Watt, Don Boyd ***Scr*** Beryl Bainbridge ***Ph*** Les Young ***Ed*** Peter Coulson ***Art*** Eileen Diss
Act Sam Waterston, Jenny Agutter, Anna Massey, Tim Pigott-Smith, Geraldine James, Arthur Lowe (Kendon)

Nice, ordinary English girl Jenny Agutter meets wild, romantic Scots divorcee Sam Waterston. Sadly for her—though the tone is never more than just slightly bitter-sweet—his romantic nature includes having a wildly on-off relationship with the truth. He's a wolf with two not-so-ex-wives, and a compulsion to bed down her friends, neighbors and anything else he sees move.

Adapted from her own novel by Beryl Bainbridge, the screenplay is diligent without being distinguished. The same goes for Claude Whatham's direction, which tends to prefer lingering realism to dramatic pace, and thus to set up apparent significance where there is none.

Agutter is well cast, and good in that her seduction by the outlandish Waterston is entirely believable.

●

SWELL GUY
1946, 96 mins, US b/w
Dir Frank Tuttle ***Prod*** Mark Hellinger ***Scr*** Richard Brooks ***Ph*** Tony Gaudio ***Ed*** Edward Curtiss ***Mus*** David Tamkin ***Art*** John B. Goodman
Act Sonny Tufts, Ann Blyth, Ruth Warrick, Thomas Gomez, Millard Mitchell (Universal)

Swell Guy is an ironical handle for drama content of this Mark Hellinger production. Based on the old play *The Hero* by Gilbert Emery, but with a modern background, picture deals with a heel hero who doesn't reform. Hellinger has given it smooth production polish, a number of noteworthy touches and a casting surprise. Sonny Tufts plays the title role, a departure from his usual casting. That he doesn't always fulfill demands of part doesn't diminish interest that casting twist generates.

Story concerns stir caused in a small California town when a war correspondent comes to visit his family and how his lack of scruples and inability to do the right thing affect all he meets.

Ann Blyth, co-starred, comes through with a highly effective performance as the spoiled rich girl who is taken in by the phoney hero.

●

SWIMMER, THE
1968, 94 mins, US Ⓥ ⊙ col
Dir Frank Perry ***Prod*** Frank Perry, Roger Lewis ***Scr*** Eleanor Perry ***Ph*** David L. Quaid, Michael Nebbia ***Ed*** Sidney Katz, Carl Lerner, Pat Somerset ***Mus*** Marvin Hamlisch ***Art*** Peter Dohanos
Act Burt Lancaster, Janet Landgard, Janice Rule, Marge Champion, Kim Hunter, Joan Rivers (Columbia/Horizon)

Burt Lancaster stars as a suburban bum who, in retracing his steps from pool to pool, illuminates the causes of his downfall. The stylized, episodic, moody film, based on John Cheever's dramatic fantasy, is something of a minor triumph in collaborative filmmaking.

Lancaster, in swim trunks throughout, pops up on a sunny Sunday morning at a suburban poolside, miles away from his house, and decides to "swim" home by visiting at each neighbor's house. Each self-contained sequence adds indirect light to Lancaster himself; he is compulsively gregarious, compulsively youthful, compulsively sexual, compulsively self-deluded.

Film is the story of a moral hangover, with the sobered-up bewildered man retracing his steps to see what he has done.

Without detailing the large cast, suffice it to say that performances, direction and writing hit the target. Lancaster emerges with a strong achievement, that of a pitiable middle-aged Joe College.

●

SWIMMING TO CAMBODIA
1987, 87 mins, US Ⓥ ⊙ col
Dir Jonathan Demme ***Prod*** R. A. Shafransky ***Scr*** Spalding Gray ***Ph*** John Bailey ***Ed*** Carol Littleton ***Mus*** Laurie Anderson ***Art*** Sandy McLeod
Act Spalding Gray (Demme)

Witnessed in its original SoHo incarnation as a staged monolog, Spalding Gray's free-associating recollection of his experiences in Thailand during the making of *The Killing Fields* had an exhilarating immediacy which is mostly absent in this compressed filmed performance of *Swimming to Cambodia*.

Addressing a live audience from a seat at a bare table, the emotionally expansive, anti-heroic raconteur skillfully fosters an illusion of spontaneous, confessional intimacy.

Recreating a dislocating culture-shocked odyssey that takes him from the surreal fleshpots of Bangkok to a nearly suicidal quest for a "perfect moment" at a spectacularly paradisical Thai beach, Gray elicits compassion and universal recognition for his serio-comic search for self.

●

SWIMMING WITH SHARKS
(AKA: THE BUDDY FACTOR)
1995, 93 mins, US Ⓥ ⊙ col
Dir George Huang ***Prod*** Steve Alexander, Joanne Moore ***Scr*** George Huang ***Ph*** Steven Finestone ***Ed*** Ed Marx ***Mus*** Tom Heil ***Art*** Veronika Merlin, Cecil Gentry
Act Kevin Spacey, Frank Whaley, Michelle Forbes, Benicio Del Toro, Jerry Levine, Roy Dotrice (Cineville)

Borrowing a page from *The Player* with a tip of the hat to *Reservoir Dogs*, George Huang's sharp first feature is a revenge fantasy in which a much put-upon flunky gets some of his own back when he holds his insufferable boss hostage and tortures him over all "the indignities and hardships" he's suffered. Pic charts a recent Hollywood arrival's quick trip from idealism to murderous mefirstism.

Film school grad Guy (Frank Whaley) gets lucky in town right away, landing a fast-track job as personal assistant to high-powered studio production exec Buddy Ackerman (Kevin Spacey), a man known for reveling in power, babes and abuse of employees. Not only does Buddy humiliate the naive Guy in front of other workers, he even prevents the kid from ever taking lunch, which means Guy must meet foxy young producer Dawn (Michelle Forbes) one evening. She does it mostly to improve her position with Buddy so he'll move on her new project.

Intercut with the office action are "current" scenes in which an enraged Guy, having tied up Buddy in the latter's house, forces him to confront his own childish sadism, all the while torturing him and threatening worse. Escalating face-off is climaxed by an unexpected arrival, and surprise ending truly does *The Player* one better in its evaluation of how self-centered, amoral and insular Hollywood can be.

Within its very limited range, pic has verve, a fine control of tone and a stylish look given its low budget and three-week sked. Spacey dominates, but Whaley makes a convincing transition from goody-goody to icy insider, and Forbes manages well despite being forced to flip-flop on command between sarcastic bitchiness and softer intimacy.

[Pic was reviewed from the 1994 Telluride fest under the title *The Buddy Factor*, but was retitled for general release.]

●

SWINDLE, THE
SEE: IL BIDONE

●

SWINGER, THE
1966, 81 mins, US col
Dir George Sidney ***Prod*** George Sidney ***Scr*** Lawrence Roman ***Ph*** Joseph Biroc ***Ed*** Frank Santillo ***Mus*** Marty Paich ***Art*** Hal Pereira, Walter Tyler
Act Ann-Margret, Anthony Franciosa, Robert Coote, Yvonne Romain, Horace McMahon, Barbara Nichols (Paramount)

The Swinger is a very amusing original screen comedy which satirizes nudie books and magazines. The colorful, tuneful George Sidney production utilizes outstanding post-production skills to enhance impact of hip scripting and good performances.

Ann-Margret's best screen work derives from Sidney's direction, which herein spotlights her singing-dancing talents. She is an aspiring mag writer who, unable to sell straight material, fakes her autobiog in the form of a mish-mash of lurid paperback plots. Tony Franciosa, the editor, swallows the bait and tries to reform her, while nudie mag publisher Robert Coote seeks to exploit the gal.

A two-minute terp scene by Ann-Margret, to a rhythmic title tune by Andre and Dory Previn, precedes main title. Pic then opens with a hilarious tour of L.A., featuring non-sequitur narration by Coote to some jazzy picture editing. David Winters choreographed the terp sequences, one of which is a rather sexy bit in which Ann-Margret, in a fake orgy, rolls about on canvas with her body covered with paint.

●

SWINGERS IN PARADISE
SEE: SUMMER HOLIDAY (1963)

●

SWING HIGH, SWING LOW
1937, 92 mins, US Ⓥ b/w
Dir Mitchell Leisen ***Prod*** Arthur Hornblow, Jr. ***Scr*** Virginia Van Upp, Oscar Hammerstein II ***Ph*** Ted Tetzlaff ***Ed*** Eda Warren ***Mus*** Boris Morros (dir.)
Act Carole Lombard, Fred MacMurray, Charles Butterworth, Jean Dixon, Dorothy Lamour, Franklin Pangborn (Paramount)

Swing High, Swing Low is a switch on the old George Manker Watters–Arthur Hopkins play, *Burlesque*. Instead of the burlesque comic, Skid Johnson, of the putty nose, whom the late Hal Skelly glorified in the Broadway original and in the first filmization (called *Dance of Life*, 1929), the switch to a Panama honky-tonk and a class

N.Y. cafe is as ultra-modern as the sweet-hot trumpeting which is the keynote of Fred MacMurray's expert performance.

As an ex-Canal Zone soldier who can toot a mean horn, which carries him from Mama Murphy's Panama joint to the Hollywood version of an El Morocco–type of class place, MacMurray, ably foiled by Carole Lombard, does much to sustain a story, which, in spots, looms as a bit dated. Sagas about kings of the nite clubs who, when they start to skid, go down fast, have become a bit familiar, as has also the basic triangle situation when MacMurray goes the whoopee route and Lombard ultimately comes back to resurrect him from the sloughs. However, expert trouping by both more than sustains the story requirements.

MacMurray's off-screen hot lips are two boys from Victor Young's band, Frank Zinziv and William Candreva, and their triple-tongue and other horn intricacies are somethin'! Young with Phil Boutelje, of the Par musical corps, does an expert job on the arrangements.

•

SWING KIDS
1993, 112 mins, US Ⓥ col
Dir Thomas Carter ***Prod*** Mark Gordon, John Bard Manulus ***Scr*** Jonathan Marc Feldman ***Ph*** Jerzy Zielinski ***Ed*** Michael R. Miller ***Mus*** James Horner ***Art*** Allan Cameron
Act Robert Sean Leonard, Christian Bale, Frank Whaley, Barbara Hershey, Kenneth Branagh, Tushka Bergen (Hollywood Pictures)

A fascinating footnote to WWII Nazi Germany is trivialized and sanitized in this odd concoction of music and politics.

Screenplay plays fast and loose with historical fact and chronology as it chronicles the development of a trio of young men whose passion for such American pop music favorites as Benny Goodman, Artie Shaw and Count Basie puts them in the unusual dilemma of embracing officially forbidden "decadent art."

Peter's (Robert Sean Leonard) situation provides the narrative line. His family lives under a cloud of suspicion only relieved by the intervention of a seemingly generous SS official (an uncredited Kenneth Branagh) who has romantic intentions on Peter's mother (Barbara Hershey).

The more upwardly mobile Thomas (Christian Bale) finds his musical ardor dampened after joining the Hitler Youth. Initially, he signs up to pal around with Peter (who was forced to join after committing a petty crime), but Thomas soon gives way to total conformity. The third, the physically crippled Arvid (Frank Whaley), remains unrepentant: the least capable of standing against the tide, he is the fiercest in devotion to jazz.

•

SWING SHIFT
1984, 100 mins, US Ⓥ ⊙ col
Dir Jonathan Demme ***Prod*** Jerry Bick ***Scr*** Rob Morton [= Ron Nyswaner, Bo Goldman, Nancy Dowd, Robert Towne] ***Ph*** Tak Fujimoto ***Ed*** Craig McKay ***Mus*** Patrick Williams ***Art*** Peter Jamison
Act Goldie Hawn, Kurt Russell, Christine Lahti, Fred Ward, Ed Harris, Holly Hunter (Lantana/Warner)

With all the heartwarming heroics to choose from on the homefront in World War II, *Swing Shift* tries instead to twist some consequence out of a tawdry adulterous tryst by a couple of self-centered sneaks. But the writing and acting are too flat for the challenge.

Goldie Hawn and Ed Harris are your basic nice young couple living modestly in a Santa Monica cottage until Pearl Harbor demands he immediately volunteer. Hawn fretfully sees him off to war and somewhat timidly goes to work at an aircraft factory where she draws the immediate romantic interest of Kurt Russell.

Bearded by Hawn's neighbor/coworker Christine Lahti, the lovers spend the war having loads of fun, dancing, smooching, bedding and riding with the top down.

But Harris eventually comes home for a happy ending.

1984: NOMINATION: Best Supp. Actress (Christine Lahti)

•

SWING TIME
1936, 103 mins, US Ⓥ ⊙ b/w
Dir George Stevens ***Prod*** Pandro S. Berman ***Scr*** Howard Lindsay, Allan Scott ***Ph*** David Abel ***Ed*** Henry Berman ***Mus*** Nathaniel Shilkret (dir.) ***Art*** Van Nest Polglase, Carroll Clark
Act Fred Astaire, Ginger Rogers, Victor Moore, Helen Broderick, Eric Blore, Betty Furness (RKO)

Swing Time is another winner for the Fred Astaire–Ginger Rogers combo. It's smart, modern, and impressive in every respect, from its boy-loses-girl background to its tunefulness, dancipation, production quality and general high standards.

There are six Jerome Kern tunes (Dorothy Fields's clever lyrics don't retard the motivation, either) and while perhaps a bit more sprightly in general tenor than the quasi-operetta score of Kern's previous *Roberta* (1935) for the same team, the tunes as usual have substance and quality. "The Way You Look Tonight" is the ballad outstander, although not overplugged and first introduced in her boudoir after Astaire and his pop (Victor Moore) are shown picketing Ginger Rogers and Helen Broderick's rooms as being "unfair" to them.

Finale number, after the pash maestro (Georges Metaxa) seemingly breaks up the romance, is "Never Gonna Dance," perhaps the best tune of the score, with its sweet-swing tempo.

This is George Stevens's first directorial chore for Astaire-Rogers and also his first film musical on the RKO lot. Young megger (nephew of Ashton Stevens, the Chicago dramatic critic) does a highly competent job considering everything. He's also credited for suggesting the *Swing Time* title which Astaire's personal endorsement finally clinched after *Never Gonna Dance* was agreed upon, more or less officially, as the release title.

1936: Best Song ("The Way You Look Tonight')

NOMINATION: Best Dance Direction ("Bo Jangles")

•

SWISS FAMILY ROBINSON
1960, 126 mins, US Ⓥ ⊙ ▭ col
Dir Ken Annakin ***Prod*** Bill Anderson ***Scr*** Lowell S. Hawley ***Ph*** Harry Waxman ***Ed*** Peter Boita ***Mus*** William Alwyn ***Art*** John Howell
Act John Mills, Dorothy McGuire, James MacArthur, Janet Munro, Sessue Hayakawa, Cecil Parker (Walt Disney)

The rather modest 1813 Johann Wyss tale has been blown up to prodigious proportions. The essence and the spirit of the simple, intriguing story of a marvelously industrious family is all but snuffed out, only spasmodically flickering through the ponderous approach.

The Robinson family seems to be enjoying a standard of living that would be the envy of an average modern family. Their famous tree house is almost outrageously comfortable (running water, no less), and seems to pop up overnight with virtually no effort. In fact, the element of time and realistic effort, so vital to the overall perspective, is consistently vague in this version. It seems to be happening in a matter of days, not decades. The climactic scrape with a band of Oriental buccaneers is the crushing blow to any semblance of credulity.

Photographically, it is a striking achievement. Through Harry Waxman's lens have been captured some compelling views of Tobago island in the West Indies. Several sequences have a heap of genuine excitement, particularly the opening raft scene in which the family battles treacherous ocean currents to get from wrecked ship to island. These aspects add excitement and interest but don't make up for the all-important loss of the story's basic values. The acting is generally capable, but hardly memorable.

•

SWITCH
1991, 103 mins, US Ⓥ ⊙ ▭ col
Dir Blake Edwards ***Prod*** Tony Adams ***Scr*** Blake Edwards ***Ph*** Dick Bush ***Ed*** Robert Pergament ***Mus*** Henry Mancini ***Art*** Rodger Maus
Act Ellen Barkin, Jimmy Smits, JoBeth Williams, Lorraine Bracco, Tony Roberts, Lysette Anthony (Beco/HBO)

Switch is a faint-hearted sex comedy that doesn't have the courage of its initially provocative convictions. Undemanding audiences will get a few laughs from the notion of a man parading around in Ellen Barkin's body. Ladykiller Steve Brooks (Perry King) accepts an invitation for a hot tub frolic with three of his old girlfriends, only to be murdered by them for his innumerable emotional crimes against women over the years. Steve is given a chance to escape a fiery fate by returning to Earth and finding just one woman who genuinely likes him. Only catch is that he will henceforth inhabit the body of a woman, and that of an uncommonly sexy one.

Masquerading as the disappeared man's long-lost half-sister, "Amanda" manages to hold on to Steve's old job at a high-powered ad agency, hangs out with Steve's best friend Jimmy Smits and intimidates the murder ringleader, JoBeth Williams, into assisting her in dressing.

Things look like they'll shift into high gear when Amanda meets cosmetics queen Lorraine Bracco, a lesbian, and decides to seduce her into transferring her big account to the agency. Unfortunately, pic chickens out from this point on, to dismaying ends.

Barkin is clearly game for anything the director wants her to do, including extensive physical clowning, but mugs and overdoes the grimacing and macho posturing. Smits and Bracco are smooth enough.

•

SWITCHING CHANNELS
1988, 105 mins, US Ⓥ ⊙ col
Dir Ted Kotcheff ***Prod*** Martin Ransohoff ***Scr*** Jonathan Reynolds ***Ph*** Francois Protat ***Ed*** Thom Noble ***Mus*** Michel Legrand ***Art*** Anne Pritchard
Act Kathleen Turner, Burt Reynolds, Christopher Reeve, Ned Beatty, Henry Gibson, Al Waxman (Tri-Star)

Switching Channels is a broad, sometimes silly transfer of *The Front Page* or, more specifically, *His Girl Friday*, from the old world of smoke-filled newspaper offices to the gleaming modern setting of a satellite TV news station. This is the least-distinguished rendition of the classic Ben Hecht–Charles MacArthur piece on record.

Ace anchorwoman Kathleen Turner leaves Chicago for a much-needed Canadian vacation and is swept off her feet by the dashing and obscenely rich Christopher Reeve. Upon her return, Turner announces to her crafty, manipulative boss (Burt Reynolds) that she is through with the news game and intends to settle down in New York with her new love.

Reynolds also is her ex-husband and, though he'd never admit it, still is in love with her, so he launches into a frantic campaign to keep her on the station. As in *The Front Page*, this involves her in covering the scheduled execution of a hapless man, played in a nice touch by Henry Gibson, who escapes just as his electrocution is about to be covered live.

Reynolds is good at his part's sardonic insincerity, but isn't really intimidating. Reeve comes off as the last word in confident swank in the seduction scenes. Unfortunately, he turns into a wimp almost from the moment he meets Reynolds, making it no contest. Turner suits her superstar news-hen role to a T.

Lensed mostly in Toronto, production looks a little thin around the edges and makes the setting, Chicago, look more like a suburb than a metropolis.

•

SWOON
1992, 90 mins, US Ⓥ b/w
Dir Tom Kalin ***Prod*** Christine Vachon ***Scr*** Tom Kalin, Hilton Als ***Ph*** Ellen Kuras ***Ed*** Tom Kalin ***Mus*** James Bennett ***Art*** Therese Deprez
Act Daniel Schlachet, Craig Chester, Ron Vawter, Michael Kirby, Michael Stumm (Intolerance)

A dramatization of the 1924 Leopold and Loeb murder case unlike any before it, *Swoon* is a studied, ultra-arty look at a notorious crime as seen through a thick filter of sexual politics.

Sensational story revolves around Nathan Leopold, Jr., and Richard Loeb, two wealthy, brilliant, Jewish teenage lovers whose crime spree culminated in the murder of a kidnaped boy in their native Chicago. Having left behind a trail of evidence, pair was quickly caught and later convicted in a massively publicized trial. Tale previously inspired Alfred Hitchcock's *Rope* and Richard Fleischer's *Compulsion*.

Tom Kalin, in his first feature after making short films and videos, has taken another tack entirely, one specifically informed by gay politics, essentially equating gayness with outlaw status in a hostile society. Kalin mixes in archival footage with his staged material and has used actual texts (diary entries, courtroom testimony and the like) for a substantial portion of the script.

•

SWORD AND THE SORCERER, THE
1982, 100 mins, US Ⓥ ⊙ col
Dir Albert Pyun ***Prod*** Brandon Chase, Marianne Chase, Tom Karnowski ***Scr*** Albert Pyun, Tom Karnowski, John Stuckmeyer ***Ph*** Joseph Mangine ***Ed*** Marshall Harvey ***Mus*** David Whitaker ***Art*** George Costello
Act Lee Horsley, Kathleen Beller, Simon MacCorkindale, George Maharis, Richard Lynch, Nina Van Pallandt (Chase)

Combine beaucoup gore and an atrocity-a-minute action edited in fast-pace style. Then, toss in a scantily clad cast of none-too-talented performers mouthing dimwitted dialog and garnish with a touch of medieval gibberish. The result would be something resembling *The Sword and the Sorcerer*.

The plot is needlessly complicated by a truly lackluster script. Stripped to essentials, which the cast often does in this pseudo epic, *Sword* is about the retaking by a group of rag-tag medievalists of a once peaceable kingdom sadistically ruled by an evil knight named Cromwell.

Lee Horsley grins a lot as the leader of the rebels, who turns out to be the long-banished son of the old and virtuous king. Simon MacCorkindale grimaces a good deal as a royal pretender.

For trivia fans, Nina Van Pallandt plays the good queen who's dispatched quickly and mercifully since her performance is nothing to boast of.

•

SWORD IN THE STONE, THE
1963, 75 mins, US Ⓥ ⦿ col
Dir Wolfgang Reitherman ***Scr*** Bill Peet ***Ed*** Donald Halliday ***Mus*** George Bruns (Walt Disney)

Bill Peet, artist—writer and longtime member of the Walt Disney production company, has chosen a highly appropriate fable, the 1938 T. H. White book of the same title, for screen adaptation for the youngsters. It emerges as a tasty confection.

The feature-length cartoon demonstrates anew the magic of the Disney animators and imagination in character creation. But one might wish for a script which stayed more with the basic storyline rather than taking so many twists and turns which have little bearing on the tale about King Arthur as a lad.

Key figures are the boy who is to become king of England because he alone has the strength to remove the sword embedded in a stone in a London churchyard (he goes by the name of Wart), and Merlin, a magician and prophet, who's alternately wise and somewhat nutty. Others include the villainess Mad Madam Mim, who turns out to be a nice old dame, an English nobleman, a kind—hearted owl, flora & fauna, etc.

The songs by Richard M. and Robert B. Sherman are in the familiar Disney cartoon groove with such titles as "Higitus—Figitus," "Mad Madam Mim" and "The Legend of the Sword in the Stone." They're agreeable tunes and go along nicely with the animated action.

•

SWORD OF LANCELOT
SEE: LANCELOT AND GUINEVERE

•

SYLVIA
1965, 115 mins, US b/w
Dir Gordon Douglas ***Prod*** Martin H. Poll ***Scr*** Sydney Boehm ***Ph*** Joseph Ruttenberg ***Ed*** Frank Bracht ***Mus*** David Raksin ***Art*** Hal Pereira, Roland Anderson
Act Carroll Baker, George Maharis, Joanne Dru, Peter Lawford, Viveca Lindfors, Edmond O'Brien (Paramount)

Sylvia is the story of a prostitute who turns to decency. The production is episodic until its closing reels, covering a period of 14 to 15 years as a private investigator digs into her obscure past to learn who she really is; consequently, considerable dramatic impact is lost due to film's rambling flashback treatment.

Carroll Baker is joined in stellar spot by George Maharis as the private eye who ultimately falls in love with the woman he is tracing. Actually, although hers is the motivating character, top honours go to Maharis for a consistently restrained performance which builds, while actress suffers somewhat from the spotty nature of her haphazard part.

Under Gordon Douglas's telling direction of Sydney Boehm's screenplay, based on the E. V. Cunningham novel, sequences limning title character's part are generally individually strongly etched.

Ann Sothern is a definite standout; Viveca Lindfors likewise scores as a Pittsburgh librarian.

•

SYLVIA SCARLETT
1936, 90 mins, US Ⓥ ⦿ b/w
Dir George Cukor ***Prod*** Pandro S. Berman ***Scr*** Gladys Unger, John Collier, Mortimer Offner ***Ph*** Joseph August ***Ed*** [Jane Loring] ***Mus*** Roy Webb (dir) ***Art*** Van Nest, Polglase, Sturges, Carne
Act Katharine Hepburn, Cary Grant, Brian Aherne, Edmund Gwenn, Natalie Paley, Dennie Moore (RKO)

Sylvia Scarlett is puzzling in its tangents and sudden jumps, plus the almost poetic lines that are given to Katharine Hepburn. At moments the film [from the novel by Compton MacKenzie] skirts the border of absurdity.

Mistake seems to have been in not sticking to a broad vein of comedy. In the serious passages, notably the half-crazy jealousy of the father (Edmund Gwenn) for his young and helter-skelter wife (Dennie Moore) there is little preparation in the audience's mind for anything so serious as a suicide.

Perhaps it is not valid to ask whether anybody would really fail to suspect the true sex of such a boy as Hepburn looks and acts. But while carrying this off well enough, she shines brightest and is most likeable in the transition into womanhood inspired by her meeting with an artist (Brian Aherne).

Cary Grant, doing a petty English crook with a Soho accent, practically steals the picture. This is especially true in the earlier sequences. A scene in an English mansion to which Hepburn, Grant and Gwenn have gone for purposes of robbery is dominated by Grant.

The picture is half-whimsical, almost allegorical, and with the last half having a dream-worldish element that's hard to define, and equally hard to understand.

•

SYMPHONY OF SIX MILLION
(UK: MELODY OF LIFE)
1932, 92 mins, US b/w
Dir Gregory La Cava ***Prod*** David O. Selznick, Pandro S. Berman ***Scr*** Bernard Schubert, J. Walter Ruben, James Seymour ***Ph*** Leo Tover ***Ed*** Archie Marshek ***Mus*** Max Steiner ***Art*** Carroll Clark
Act Irene Dunne, Ricardo Cortez, Gregory Ratoff, Anna Appel, Lita Chevret, Noel Madison (RKO)

This is a story [by Fannie Hurst] of a brilliant Jewish surgeon who loses his nerve when his family virtually forces him to operate on his father for a brain tumor. The father dies on the table and the boy goes to pieces, vowing he will never touch an instrument again. His faith in himself is restored when he successfully performs a delicate spinal operation on the girl he loves. She has deliberately endangered her own life to force him to action.

It is an all-Jewish film which could have stood more attention as to racial contrasts for general appeal. Only now and then do the characters become human, but all have at least one fine moment of sincerity. Gregory Ratoff gets his big chance in the scene of the redemption of the firstborn. Anna Appel, as the mother, gets her scene early in the play when she persuades her son to move uptown to a fashionable practice and wealth.

Ricardo Cortez is generally good as the young surgeon. Irene Dunne is meaningless, appearing but seldom and then always in forced and unreal situations.

•

SYNANON
(UK: GET OFF MY BACK)
1965, 105 mins, US b/w
Dir Richard Quine ***Prod*** Richard Quine ***Scr*** Ian Bernard, S. Lee Pogostin ***Ph*** Harry Stradling ***Ed*** David Wages ***Mus*** Neal Hefti
Act Edmond O'Brien, Chuck Connors, Stella Stevens, Alex Cord, Richard Conte, Eartha Kitt (Columbia)

Synanon is a fictionized semi-documentary of a rehabilitation home for drug addicts on the beachfront of Santa Monica, Calif., where almost miraculous cures are said to be achieved. As backdrop for a dramatic story it is grim, hard-hitting and sometimes shocking.

Producer-director Richard Quine moved his cameras to the actual locale to ensure authenticity in this story of Synanon House, established by Charles E. Dederich, an ex-alcoholic, in 1958.

Edmond O'Brien enacts the character of Dederich (who acted as technical advisor), plagued by debts and civil opposition as he goes about his seemingly thankless task of trying to bring lives back from the brink.

O'Brien's performance is smooth and convincing and lends strength to the character he portrays. Cord registers decisively in an unsympathetic role, and Stella Stevens is persuasive as a hooker, with a great love for her five-year-old son.

•

SYSTEM, THE
(US: THE GIRL-GETTERS)
1964, 90 mins, UK b/w
Dir Michael Winner ***Prod*** Kenneth Shipman ***Scr*** Peter Draper ***Ph*** Nicolas Roeg ***Ed*** Fred Burnley ***Mus*** Stanley Black ***Art*** Geoffrey Tozer
Act Oliver Reed, Jane Merrow, Barbara Ferris, Harry Andrews, Julia Foster, David Hemmings (Shipman/Bryanston)

The System is a slight anecdote, not explored as fully as it might have been, but made worthwhile by some bright direction, lensing and acting from young, eager talent.

Screenplay concerns the activities of a bunch of local lads at a seaside resort who every summer work a system by which they "take" the holidaying femmes for a lighthearted emotional ride. There's nothing vicious about it. It's simply young men in search of goodtime romances that will have to make do in their memories during the dreary offseason winter months.

Tinker (Oliver Reed), a young beach photographer, is leader of the "come up and see my pad" gang. The film tells how, one summer, he himself gets taken. He falls heavily in love with a well-loaded, well-stacked fashion model (Jane Merrow), and that's against the "rules," even when the girl reciprocates.

This thin yarn is an adroitly spun concoction of comedy, sentiment and pathos which, however, needs a strong subplot to sustain interest. Scripter Peter Draper has decked out his situations with some neat dialog, mostly of the flip-talk variety, but there are one or two moments of genuine emotional depth between the young lovers.

•

SZEGENYLEGENYEK
(THE ROUND-UP)
1966, 94 mins, Hungary b/w
Dir Miklos Jancso ***Scr*** Gyula Hernadi ***Ph*** Tamas Somlo ***Ed*** Zoltan Farkas ***Art*** Tamas Banovich
Act Janos Gorbe, Tibor Molnar, Andras Kozak, Gabor Agardy, Zoltan Lastinovits, Bela Barsi (Mafilm)

Fable concerns Hungary of 1848, when the country's most notorious gang of highwaymen joined the war of independence sparked by Kossuth. After the defeat of the revolution, they became outlaws again, and even snowballed in strength.

Finally the government decided to exterminate the outlaws and turned over the job to Count Gedeon Raday, who swung into action, giving no quarter. It is at this point that Miklos Jancso's film takes up the story.

This is not a romantic adventure pic, crammed with galloping horsemen, wild chases and gunmen biting the dust. Action is pinned down to a single locale. Gendarmes pen up several hundred suspects in a stockade. They have proof that one of the men is guilty of a double murder, and promise him a pardon if he will finger a bigger fry. Scared out of his wits, Janos Gajdor (Janos Gorbe) makes a try.

This is a psycho pic, an anatomy of betrayal. Long focusing and ingenious camerawork build up tension. Closest thing to violence is a scene where a girl runs the gauntlet of interrogators.

Emotional strength is given to the plot by the desolate horizon of the Hungarian lowlands, minus any natural beauty.

•

SZERELEM
(LOVE)
1971, 92 mins, Hungary b/w
Dir Karoly Makk ***Prod*** Peter Bacso ***Scr*** Tibor Dery ***Ph*** Janos Toth ***Ed*** Gyorgy Sivo ***Mus*** Andras Mihaly ***Art*** Jozsef Romvari
Act Lili Darvas, Mari Torocsik, Ivan Darvas, Tibor Bitskey, Eszter Szakacs, Erzsi Orsolya (Mafilm 1)

In a firm classical mold, yet with a fragmented flair in construction, director Karoly Makk has worked out a touching but never sentimental tale of three people set in 1953, when there was some attempt to throw off the Stalinist yoke [in Hungary].

Lili Darvas, widow of playwright Ferenc Molnar, who has lived in the U.S. for 30 years, was called back by Makk to play the dying octagenarian mother. It is a stroke of perfect casting.

Enthroned in an old house, she is demanding without being shrewish or senile. She accepts the whopping letters of her son (Ivan Darvas) making a film in America and other outlandish things her daughter-in-law (Mari Torocsik) cooks up. Whether she ever suspects anything is left ambiguous.

Torocsik's only fragments of the past are the arrest of her husband, in prison for political matters. He is suddenly freed and comes home, during the aftermath of the death of Stalin.

Written by a leading Magyar writer, Tibor Dery [from his two short stories "Two Women" and "Love"], this intense, subtly atmospheric film has literary insights that are well worked into a visual pattern by Makk, all handled with poise, pace and balance.

TABLE FOR FIVE
1983, 122 mins, US Ⓥ ⊙ col
Dir Robert Lieberman ***Prod*** Robert Schaffel ***Scr*** David Seltzer ***Ph*** Vilmos Zsigmond ***Ed*** Michael Kahn ***Mus*** Miles Goodman, John Morris ***Art*** Robert F. Boyle
Act Jon Voight, Richard Crenna, Marie-Christine Barrault, Millie Perkins, Roxana Zal, Robby Kiger (CBS Theatrical)

Well-written drama concerns an errant father who takes his three children on an ocean voyage in an effort to close the gap that's grown between them. Pic earns most of its emotional points honestly and will touch most anyone who's ever taken the responsibilities of parenting seriously, either in fact or theoretically.

At the opening, Jon Voight's kids have lived with their mother (Millie Perkins) and her new man, attorney Richard Crenna, for several years. Voight swoops into New York to take the moppets off on a luxurious sea cruise with the promise of a new-found sense of responsibility. But Voight quickly realizes that he really doesn't know how to communicate with the kids who, for their part, resent the fact he's more interested in chasing blondes in the bar than hanging out with them.

Despite the attempted interference of his sharp daughter, Voight manages to initiate a shipboard romance with a sympathetic French woman, Marie-Christine Barrault.

•

TABU
1931, 81 mins, US Ⓥ ⊙ b/w
Dir F. W. Murnau ***Prod*** Robert J. Flaherty, F. W. Murnau ***Scr*** Robert J. Flaherty, F. W. Murnau ***Ph*** Floyd Crosby, Robert J. Flaherty ***Mus*** Hugo Riesenfeld
Act Reri, Matahi, Hitu, Jean, Jules, Kong Ah (Paramount)

A strong love story in a South Seas background, with South Sea natives rather than regular actors.

The title, *Tabu*, means death. It's the fate that hangs over the romantic leads who flee from a distant isle and its barbaric customs after the girl has been handed over to Tabu, ruler of one of the islands, as "the chosen one." Along with her goes the dictum, "no man must touch her or cast eyes of desire upon her."

Matahi rescues the girl, Reri, from a schooner at the propitious moment, just as she is to be taken away. They flee to an island that flourishes in the pearl trade and has been penetrated to a greater extent by white men. Here Matahi becomes famous as a pearl diver, but finally Tabu turns up to claim the girl, threatening the Tabu sign (or death) on Matahi if she doesn't come along with him.

About 90% of the footage is devoted to the romantic leads, their happiness, troubles, heartaches, etc. Against this, there is a little native life—fishing, diving, waterfalls, mode of living, etc., as was shown, but to a far greater extent, in *Moana*.

Tabu is a silent, with synchronization and sound effects, but difficult to figure out whether some of the effects and the singing, as well as native music, were dubbed over or not.

1930/31: Best Cinematography

•

TAI-PAN
1986, 127 mins, US Ⓥ ⊙ ▭ col
Dir Daryl Duke ***Prod*** Raffaella De Laurentiis ***Scr*** John Briley, Stanley Mann ***Ph*** Jack Cardiff ***Mus*** Maurice Jarre ***Art*** Tony Masters
Act Bryan Brown, Joan Chen, John Stanton, Tom Guinee, Bill Leadbitter, Russell Wong (De Laurentiis)

Tai-Pan is a historical epic [from James Clavell's novel] lost somewhere between 19th-century Hong Kong and 20th-century Hollywood. Despite flashes of brilliance and color, *Tai-Pan* fails to evoke a mysterious and moving world as a backdrop to its romantic drama. Director Daryl Duke and his team have made an attractive shell but failed to put in any heart.

As the Tai-Pan, or trade leader of the European community, first in Canton and then later in Hong Kong, Aussie thesp Bryan Brown looks the part well enough, but lacks charisma.

Within the exotic setting the story is actually rather conventional. Brown is opposed by arch villains Brock (John Stanton) and his son Gorth (Bill Leadbitter) for the control of the trading rights. At the same time there is considerable politicking going on with the Chinese over the opium trade and the British over trade regulations.

Film presents a good deal of romancing between Brown and his lovely Chinese concubine May-May (Joan Chen) and several other women who seem to have a bottomless supply of revealing costumes.

•

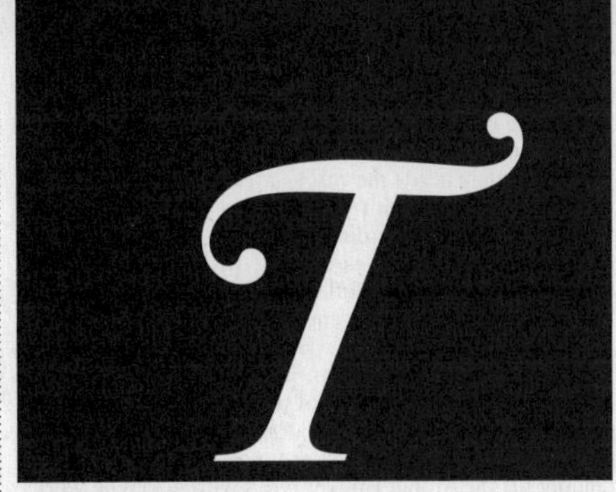

TAKE A GIRL LIKE YOU
1970, 101 mins, UK Ⓥ col
Dir Jonathan Miller ***Prod*** Hal Chester ***Scr*** George Melly ***Ph*** Dick Bush ***Ed*** Jack Harris ***Mus*** Stanley Myers
Act Noel Harrison, Oliver Reed, Hayley Mills, Sheila Hancock, John Bird, Aimi MacDonald (Columbia)

Take a movie like this. It's about a virgin (Hayley Mills) and a guy (Oliver Reed) who is trying to make her, can't and is obsessed about it. That's all there is to it.

Basically, it is not a bad little English kitchen-sink drama with some strong but low-key performances, but a lack of sense of humor, generally wearisome development and a downbeat ending.

At the core of George Melly's script, based on Kingsley Amis's novel, is the whole dreary ritual of a boy and girl in conflict about sex.

Jonathan Miller's direction is competent, not without its occasional humor and bright spots, but they are too occasional, and what should be a comedy is essentially heavy and melodramatic.

•

TAKE A HARD RIDE
1975, 103 mins, US Ⓥ col
Dir Anthony M. Dawson [= Antonio Margheriti] ***Prod*** Harry Bernsen ***Scr*** Eric Bercovici, Jerry Ludwig ***Ph*** Riccardo Pallotini ***Ed*** Stanford C. Allen ***Mus*** Jerry Goldsmith ***Art*** Julio Molina
Act Jim Brown, Lee Van Cleef, Fred Williamson, Catherine Spaak, Jim Kelly, Barry Sullivan (20th Century-Fox)

Take a Hard Ride is a poly-formula period western dual-bill item for the popcorn belt. Jim Brown heads cast as a wrangler hunted for the $86,000 in cash he is returning to his late employer's widow. Lots and lots of people get killed in Harry Bernsen's location production shot in the Canary Islands.

The script mixes several potboiler genres: Brown, gambler Fred Williamson and mute Jim Kelly contribute black and karate elements; Lee Van Cleef provides the Italoater menace as a callous bounty hunter; Catherine Spaak is briefly encountered and dropped on the trail, not before adding a Continental touch; crooked sheriff Barry Sullivan and Dana Andrews, in a cameo as Brown's boss, are in more conventional oater roles.

Second unit director and stunt boss, Hal Needham, jazzes up the pace with several offbeat highlights.

•

TAKE HER, SHE'S MINE
1963, 98 mins, US ▭ col
Dir Henry Koster ***Prod*** Henry Koster ***Scr*** Nunnally Johnson ***Ph*** Lucien Ballard ***Ed*** Marjorie Fowler ***Mus*** Jerry Goldsmith ***Art*** Jack Martin Smith, Malcolm Brown
Act James Stewart, Sandra Dee, Audrey Meadows, Robert Morley, Philippe Forquet, John McGiver (20th Century-Fox)

The screen version of *Take Her, She's Mine* is an improvement over the Phoebe and Henry Ephron stage play from which it springs, even though several of the revisions and additions dreamed up by scenarist Nunnally Johnson are contrived and far from fresh.

The difficulty encountered by an older generation in comprehending the behavior of a younger generation is the business explored in this comedy. More specifically, one father's (James Stewart) trials and tribulations when he packs his precious daughter (Sandra Dee) off to college and observes, in long-distance dismay with an occasional globe-trot for closer inspection, her transition from adolescent to young woman.

An occasional dash of the *Tammy* whammy seeps into Dee's characterization, but on the whole she's effective. Audrey Meadows, a gifted comedienne, is wasted in the bland and barren role of Stewart's wife. Robert Morley, though in the somewhat irrelevant role of a jaded Britisher, has some of the best lines in the film. Jerry Goldsmith contributes a whimsical score, especially helpful in a costume party sequence that needs all the help it can get.

•

TAKE ME OUT TO THE BALL GAME
(UK: EVERYBODY'S CHEERING)
1949, 83 mins, US Ⓥ ⊙ col
Dir Busby Berkeley ***Prod*** Arthur Freed ***Scr*** Harry Tugend, George Wells ***Ph*** George Folsey ***Ed*** Blanche Sewell ***Mus*** Adolph Deutsch (dir.) ***Art*** Cedric Gibbons, Daniel B. Cathcart
Act Frank Sinatra, Esther Williams, Gene Kelly, Betty Garrett, Edward Arnold, Jules Munshin (M-G-M)

Take Me Out to the Ball Game, backgrounded by an early-day baseball yarn, is short on story, but has some amusing moments—and Gene Kelly. Aided by Technicolor, Esther Williams is an eyeful, and Frank Sinatra cavorts pleasantly as shortstop Kelly's second baseman. Jules Munshin and Betty Garrett are the comedy relief, and the overall combination of talents is actually worthier of better material.

The yarn [by Kelly and Stanley Donen, who both staged the musical numbers] is about a couple of singing-dancing major league ballplayers and the complications in which they become involved when they meet some gamblers and Williams, owner of the club. There is no pretense that *Ball Game* is anything more than a romp for Kelly's virtuosity.

•

TAKE ME TO TOWN
1953, 80 mins, US col
Dir Douglas Sirk ***Prod*** Ross Hunter ***Scr*** Richard Morris ***Ph*** Russell Metty ***Ed*** Milton Carruth ***Mus*** Joseph Geshenson ***Art*** Alexander Golitzen, Hilyard Brown
Act Ann Sheridan, Sterling Hayden, Philip Reed, Lee Patrick, Lee Aaker, Phyllis Stanley (Universal)

Ann Sheridan and Sterling Hayden head the competent players who, under Douglas Sirk's direction, run through the antics with likeable results. Film goes about its business of being a good, folksy offering in an unpretentious manner and sprinkles in several songs.

Sheridan is a lady with a past who is hiding out from the Federals in a northwest lumber town. When the law, in the person of Larry Gates, gets close to her trail, she takes advantage of a proposition from three engaging young tykes who think she would make a good mother to look after them while their father (Hayden) is busy in the big timber. Papa gets wind of the situation from a jealous widow (Phyllis Stanley), who has set her own cap for him, and returns home. It doesn't take him long to see that his kids had the right idea, and it's only a matter of convincing Miss Sheridan and winning over the straitlaced members of the community, for which he is part-time preacher.

Since Sheridan is a saloon singer, there is ample reason for the sight values of the costumes she wears for display purposes. She does justice to them, as well as furnishing the situations and dialog with a well-charged humorous worldliness that's a big help to the picture. Hayden is excellent as the logger-preacher.

•

TAKE THE HIGH GROUND
1953, 100 mins, US col
Dir Richard Brooks ***Prod*** Dore Schary ***Scr*** Millard Kaufman ***Ph*** John Alton ***Ed*** John Dunning ***Mus*** Dimitri Tiomkin ***Art*** Cedric Gibbons, Edward Carfagno
Act Richard Widmark, Karl Malden, Elaine Stewart, Russ Tamblyn, Carleton Carpenter, Steve Forrest (M-G-M)

Take the High Ground is an absorbing study of the training that makes tough, fighting GIs out of raw civilians. It has meticulous attention to detail and authenticity of incident.

There's the strictly general-issue top sergeant intent on making fighting men out of callow youths; the non-com who uses a softer, more the understanding good fellow, approach to the fresh recruits; the mixed-up girl whose drinking covers a great sorrow; and the assorted trainee types—brash, shy, cowardly.

In the script treatment and under Brooks's direction, however, these standard forms take on new life and become interesting people whose careers through the plot attract the attention and hold it.

Richard Widmark comes over very strongly as the tough top sarg. Karl Malden is the understanding sergeant and he too gives the character life and feeling. Elaine Stewart is the mixed-up girl and, as the only credited femme in the cast, makes much of her part.

1953: Best Story & Screenplay

•

TAKE THE MONEY AND RUN
1969, 85 mins, US Ⓥ ⊙ col
Dir Woody Allen ***Prod*** Charles H. Joffe ***Scr*** Woody Allen, Mickey Rose ***Ph*** Lester Shorr ***Ed*** Ralph Rosenblum, James T. Heckert ***Mus*** Marvin Hamlisch ***Art*** Fred Harpman

Act Woody Allen, Janet Margolin, Marcel Hillaire, Jacquelyn Hyde, Lonny Chapman (Palomar)

A few good laughs in an 85-minute film do not a comedy make. Woody Allen's *Take the Money and Run*, basically a running gag about hero Allen's ineptitude as a professional crook, scatters its fire in so many directions it has to hit at least several targets. But satire on documentary coverage of criminal flop is overextended and eventually tiresome.

Bright spots are interviews with parents-in-disguise Ethel Sokolow and Henry Leff; Janet Margolin, as wife, and prison psychiatrist Don Frazier also deliver yocks.

Margolin turns in a neat performance as Allen's wife. Allen, both as director and actor, sustains his own characterization. In such scenes as robbery when he can't convince bank personnel they are being robbed, or in chain gang's visit to farmhouse, he creates genuinely funny moments.

•

TAKING CARE OF BUSINESS
(UK: FILOFAX)

1990, 103 mins, US Ⓥ ⦿ col

Dir Arthur Hiller ***Prod*** Geoffrey Taylor ***Scr*** Jill Mazursky, Jeffrey Abrams ***Ph*** David M. Walsh ***Ed*** William Reynolds ***Mus*** Stewart Copeland ***Art*** Jon Hutman

Act James Belushi, Charles Grodin, Anne DeSalvo, Loryn Locklin, Veronica Hamel, Hector Elizondo (Hollywood)

Charles Grodin and James Belushi come together too late in the plot to prevent a poky start for *Taking Care of Business*, but their mutual chemistry eventually kicks in some jovial jousting. Brash Belushi and befuddled Grodin are perfect casting for yarn about a likable escaped con who assumes the identity of a stuffy, overworked ad agency exec.

At the start, Belushi is still in county jail, and there's some fun as he high-fives it with fellow inmates and torments warden Hector Elizondo. Mostly familiar schtick. Ditto Grodin's intro as he fusses with his workload and neglects wife, Victoria Hamel. Though Belushi is set for release in days, he can't wait to see the World Series so he escapes just as Grodin arrives in L.A. to pitch his agency to a Japanese tycoon.

At the airport, Grodin loses his time-planning book—*Business* is one long commercial itself for a particular brand (Filofax, as pic is titled in the U.K.)—and Belushi finds it. Setting himself up in a Malibu mansion, Belushi proceeds to live Grodin's life just the opposite of how the businessman would do it, romancing the boss's daughter (played with sexy feistiness by Loryn Locklin), beating the potential client (Mako) at tennis, criticizing his products and making sexist remarks to fierce, feminist exec (Gates McFadden).

Inevitably, Grodin catches up with Belushi and the farcical convolutions multiply with the arrival of Hamel. As the action picks up, so does the dialog.

•

TAKING OFF

1971, 92 mins, US Ⓥ col

Dir Milos Forman ***Prod*** Alfred W. Crown ***Scr*** Milos Forman, John Guare, Jean-Claude Carriere ***Ph*** Miroslav Ondricek ***Ed*** John Carter ***Art*** Robert Wightman

Act Lynn Carlin, Buck Henry, Linnea Heacock, Georgia Engel, Tony Harvey, Audra Lindley (Universal)

Taking Off is a very compassionate, very amusing contemporary comedy about a N.Y. couple whose concern for a dropout daughter is matched by her astonishment at their social mores. Milos Forman's first U.S.-made film shows him to be a director who can depict the contradictions of human nature while avoiding tract, harangue and polemics.

The plot peg is the flight to Greenwich Village of Linnea Heacock, who's seeking something not provided in her home life. Lynn Carlin and Buck Henry (as the parents) enliven the many motivated and developing sequences: initial search for the girl conducted with friends Tony Harvey and Georgia Engel; a large meeting of discarded parents where Vincent Schiavelli turns them all on to marijuana; and a funny strip poker game at home which ends abruptly when the runaway girl calmly appears from her bedroom.

Henry tackles his first big screen role and achieves superb results. Carlin seems not an actress in a part, but a real mother, caught by candid camera, who doesn't know whether to laugh or cry about a family crisis.

•

TAKING OF PELHAM ONE TWO THREE, THE

1974, 104 mins, US Ⓥ ⦿ ⌴ col

Dir Joseph Sargent ***Prod*** Gabriel Katzka, Edgar J. Scherick ***Scr*** Peter Stone ***Ph*** Owen Roizman ***Ed*** Jerry Greenberg ***Mus*** David Shire ***Art*** Gene Rudolf

Act Walter Matthau, Robert Shaw, Martin Balsam, Hector Elizondo, Earl Hindman, James Broderick (Palomar/Palladium)

The Taking of Pelham One Two Three is a good action caper about a subway car heist under the streets of Manhattan. Walter Matthau heads the cast as a Transit Authority detective matching wits with the hijackers headed by Robert Shaw. Joseph Sargent's direction is fast, but the major liability is Peter Stone's screenplay [from novel by John Godey] which develops little interest in either Matthau or Shaw's gang, nor the innocent hostages.

Shaw, Martin Balsam, Hector Elizondo and Earl Hindman seize a subway car, named for the starting station on the line and its time of departure, and demand $1 million. Matthau is on duty at subway communications h.q. and deals with Shaw over voice radio, all the while fending off the Archie Bunker types with whom he works.

A sidebar characterization is that of Lee Wallace as the mayor, a travesty of a role played for silly laughs.

Shaw is superb in another versatile characterization.

•

TALENTED MR. RIPLEY, THE

1999, 139 mins, US Ⓥ ⦿ col

Dir Anthony Minghella ***Prod*** William Horberg, Tom Sternberg ***Scr*** Anthony Minghella ***Ph*** John Seale ***Ed*** Walter Murch ***Mus*** Gabriel Yared ***Art*** Roy Walker

Act Matt Damon, Gwyneth Paltrow, Jude Law, Cate Blanchett, Philip Seymour Hoffman, Jack Davenport (Mirage/Timnick/Miramax/Paramount)

The Talented Mr. Ripley is a mostly intoxicating and involving tale of intrigue and crime that loses its stride somewhat in the home stretch. This highly scenic adaptation of Patricia Highsmith's classic murder meller is splendidly served by a beautiful cast headed by Matt Damon, Gwyneth Paltrow and Jude Law, and proves a fine follow-up by writer-director Anthony Minghella to his Oscar-winning *The English Patient.*

Well-filmed in 1960 by French director Rene Clement as *Plein soleil* (*Purple Noon*) with Alain Delon, Highsmith's 1955 novel, the first in her Ripley series, is an eerie tale of a young man trying to acquire what another has by murdering him.

Tom Ripley (Damon) is a nice kid from New York who's paid by shipbuilding tycoon Herbert Greenleaf (James Rebhorn) to fetch back his wastrel son, Dickie (Law). Quickly managing to ingratiate himself with the son and his beautiful writer girlfriend, Marge (Paltrow), Tom becomes a happy hanger-on in their idyllic seaside town south of Naples.

On a boat ride, however, Tom suddenly erupts, finishing off the friend he has envied and obsessed over since he arrived in Italy. Once he's discovered what he's capable of, a new life opens up for the young American, one that includes trying to assume the indentity (and bank account) of Dickie.

Scenes are played out in a classical fashion that elicits many nuances from the actors, and full value is extracted from the already rich material. Performances are aces top to bottom.

1999: NOMINATIONS: Best Adapted Screenplay, Supp. Actor (Jude Law), Art Direction, Original Score, Costume Design

•

TALE OF TWO CITIES, A

1936, 121 mins, US Ⓥ b/w

Dir Jack Conway ***Prod*** David O. Selznick ***Scr*** W. P. Lipscomb, S. N. Behrman ***Ph*** Oliver T. Marsh ***Ed*** Conrad A. Nervig ***Mus*** Herbert Stothart ***Art*** Cedric Gibbons, Frederic Hope, Edwin B. Willis

Act Ronald Colman, Elizabeth Allan, Edna May Oliver, Reginald Owen, Basil Rathbone, Blanche Yurka (M-G-M)

Metro achieves in *A Tale of Two Cities* a screen classic. The two yawning pitfalls of spectacle and dialog have been adroitly evaded. The fall of the Bastille [directed by Val Lewton and Jacques Tourneur] is breathtaking, but it is given no greater valuation than its influence on the plot [from the novel by Charles Dickens] warrants.

The rabble at the guillotine is blood-chilling in its ferocity, but not for a moment does it overlie the principals, waiting in the shadow of the bloody platform for their turn to come. In the dialog the lines are neither the often stilted phrases of the book, nor yet the colloquial language of today.

Ronald Colman makes his Carton one of the most pathetic figures in the screen catalog. Gone are his drawing-room mannerisms, shaved along with his moustache. Henry B. Walthall is good as Manette and Blanche Yurka magnificent as the vengeful Mme. De Farge.

The others all are good, each in proportion to assignment, with Elizabeth Allan suffering somewhat from necessity for being so typically a Dickens heroine.

1936: NOMINATIONS: Best Picture, Editing

•

TALE OF TWO CITIES, A

1958, 117 mins, UK Ⓥ b/w

Dir Ralph Thomas ***Prod*** Betty E. Box ***Scr*** T.E.B. Clarke ***Ph*** Ernest Steward ***Ed*** Alfred Roome ***Mus*** Richard Addinsell ***Art*** Carmen Dillon

Act Dirk Bogarde, Dorothy Tutin, Cecil Parker, Marie Versini, Stephen Murray, Athene Seyler (Rank)

Set against the storming of the Bastille, *Cities* is primarily a character study of a frustrated young lawyer who fritters his life away in drink until the moment when he makes everything worthwhile by a supreme sacrifice for the girl he loves. Dirk Bogarde brings a lazy charm and nonchalance to the Sydney Carton role but tends to play throughout in a surprisingly minor key.

Leading femme is Dorothy Tutin, whose role does not strain her thesping ability. Cecil Parker, as a banker; Athene Seyler, as Tutin's fussy companion; and Stephen Murray, as Dr. Manette, all have meaty portrayals which they handle with authority.

But it is among some of the other characterizations that there is most to admire, notably new young actress Marie Versini. Playing a young servant girl who becomes a victim of Madame Guillotine, Versini brings a beautiful restraint and appeal to her task.

Among other standout performances are those by Donald Pleasence, as an unctuous spy; Christopher Lee, as a sadistic aristocrat; and Duncan Lamont, as one of the leaders of the revolution. Rosalie Crutchley also makes notable impact with a brilliant study in malevolence as his vengeful wife.

•

TALES AFTER THE RAIN
SEE: UGETSU MONOGATARI

•

TALES FROM THE CRYPT PRESENTS DEMON KNIGHT
SEE: DEMON KNIGHT

•

TALES FROM THE DARKSIDE—THE MOVIE

1990, 93 mins, US Ⓥ ⦿ col

Dir John Harrison ***Prod*** Richard P. Rubinstein, Mitchell Galin ***Scr*** Michael McDowell, George A. Romero ***Ph*** Robert Draper ***Ed*** Harry B. Miller ***Mus*** Donald A. Rubinstein, Jim Manzie, Pat Regan, Chaz Jankel, John Harrison ***Art*** Ruth Ammon

Act Deborah Harry, Christian Slater, Rae Dawn Chong, James Remar, David Johansen, Steve Buscemi (Paramount)

Tales from the Darkside is significantly gorier than its namesake TV series, and has better production values.

Structure is a lift from Scheherazade in *1,001 Nights*; as Deborah Harry prepares to cook little boy Matthew Lawrence, he delays his fate by telling her a trio of horror stories.

Most ambitious segment, *Beetlejuice* writer Michael McDowell's "Lover's Vow," is saved for last: Gotham artist James Remar witnessing a barman's extremely gory murder by a gargoyle come to life. To save his skin he vows to the gargoyle not to tell anyone what happened, but after meeting beautiful Rae Dawn Chong and romancing and marrying her 10 years later, he spills the beans with tragic results. Sexy and sinister Chong is a delight in this one.

Middle segment is more routine. George A. Romero's adaptation of a Stephen King story is punched up by casting David Johansen as a hit man assigned to kill a black cat by drug tycoon William Hickey.

Curtain raiser is a corny but effective tale from the creator of Sherlock Holmes: college student Steve Buscemi bringing an ancient mummy back to life for revenge with ironic results.

•

TALES FROM THE HOOD

1995, 97 mins, US Ⓥ col

Dir Rusty Cundieff ***Prod*** Darin Scott ***Scr*** Rusty Cundieff, Darin Scott ***Ph*** Anthony Richmond ***Ed*** Charles Bornstein ***Mus*** Christopher Young ***Art*** Stuart Blatt

Act Clarence Williams III, Joe Torry, Wings Hauser, Anthony Griffith, Michael Massee, Tom Wright (40 Acres and a Mule/Savoy)

Rusty Cundieff's *Tales From the Hood* is a smart and sassy horror anthology that mixes blunt shocks and sharp satire.

As its title implies, pic is a clever commingling of elements from *Boyz N the Hood* and *Tales From the Crypt*. Script by producer Darin Scott (*Menace II Society*) and director Cundieff (*Fear of a Black Hat*) is singularly audacious, and perhaps controversial. The filmmakers take dead-serious subjects—racism, child abuse, police brutality, gang violence—and lace them with dark comedy and supernatural horror. Result is a genre-bending pic that is fearsome and ferociously funny as well as socially conscious.

The framing device for the four tales is a late-night visit by three street toughs (Joe Torry, De'Aundre Bonds, Samuel Monroe, Jr.) to the inner-city funeral home of Mr. Simms (Clarence Williams III). While the hoods impatiently wait for the mortician to turn over a drug stash, Mr. Simms entertains them with spooky tales about his "clients."

First story has Anthony Griffith playing a black rookie policeman who isn't able to stop three crooked white cops (led by an over-the-top Wings Hauser) from beating, and ultimately killing, a black community leader (Tom Wright). In true E.C. Comics fashion, the victim rises from the grave and wreaks havoc.

Second tale, the most discomforting, is about an abused youngster who claims a "monster" is responsible for his bruises. It turns out that the boy (well played by Brandon Hammond) and his helpless mother (Paula Jai Parker) are regularly victimized by the boy's brutal stepfather (David Alan Grier). Seg is quite simply one of the most terrifyingly realistic depictions of domestic violence ever seen in a feature film.

The third segment is a *Twilight Zone*–style parable featuring Corbin Bernsen as an ex—Ku Klux Klansman who runs for governor of an unnamed Deep South state. The plot involves the grisly revenge of a legendary voodoo queen and her homicidal dolls.

Cundieff takes off the gloves for his fourth tale and hammers home his message with earnest zeal. Crazy K (Lamont Bentley), a violent gang-banger, refuses to reform even after he's nearly killed by well-armed rivals. Arrested and convicted, he volunteers for a "behavioral modification" experiment and is briefly imprisoned near a homicidal white supremacist. The irony, of course, is that the white supremacist thinks Crazy K is "cool," since both men have a penchant for killing black people.

•

TALES OF BEATRIX POTTER
(AKA: PETER RABBIT AND TALES OF BEATRIX POTTER)
1971, 90 mins, UK Ⓥ col
Dir Reginald Mills ***Prod*** John Brabourne, Richard Goodwin ***Scr*** Richard Goodwin, Christine Edzard ***Ph*** Austin Dempster ***Ed*** John Rushton ***Mus*** John Lanchbery ***Art*** John Howell
Act Frederick Ashton, Alexander Grant, Ann Howard, Wayne Sleep, Michael Coleman, Lesley Collier (M-G-M/EMI)

The production partners John Brabourne and Richard Goodwin and director Reginald Mills, conceived the happy notion of having Beatrix Potter's animals represented by members of the Royal Ballet and the result is 90 minutes of style, fun and enchantment.

Film's opener introduces Erin Geraghty as the introverted young Beatrix in her gloomy Victorian home. But then the animals take over. There's little point in detailing the various stories—the adventures of The Bad Mice, the jaunty capers of Jeremy Fisher, how Jemima Puddle-Duck escapes a fate worse than death at the paws of The Fox, etc. The point is that the episodes skip merrily along, the choreography by Frederick Ashton blends splendidly with Reginald Mills's direction and John Lanchbery's bright, if tinkly, music has the right lilting note. But the whole thing might have fallen apart but for the lifelike masks designed by Rostislav Doboujinsky and Christine Edzard's gay costumes.

•

TALES OF HOFFMAN, THE
1951, 138 mins, UK Ⓥ ⦿ col
Dir Michael Powell, Emeric Pressburger ***Prod*** Michael Powell, Emeric Pressburger ***Scr*** Michael Powell, Emeric Pressburger ***Ph*** Christopher Challis ***Ed*** Reginald Mills ***Art*** Arthur Lawson
Act Moira Shearer, Robert Rounseville, Robert Helpmann, Pamela Brown, Frederick Ashton, Leonide Massine (Archers/London)

Michael Powell and Emeric Pressburger follow up their sock *Red Shoes* ballet picture with as distinguished an opera-ballet film in *Tales of Hoffman*. The Jacques Offenbach fantasy opera has been transformed to the screen with great imagination and taste, with an unusual amount of inventiveness and effects, for a lush, resplendent production that's a treat to eye and ear.

Hoffman is a better picture than *Shoes*, with more imagination and story structure. But the storylines in the second and third episodes are confusing, except perhaps to the inveterate operagoer. *Hoffman* lacks the everyday romance of *Shoes*, is sung throughout instead of having spoken dialog, and lacks humor.

Film is a brilliant integration of dance, story and music. Fantastic nature of its story is brought out more sharply by the excellent use of Technicolor.

Prolog has Hoffman (Robert Rounseville) watching a ballet and in love with the prima ballerina, Stella (Moira Shearer), who appears to him as the embodiment of his past loves. When he thinks Stella has spurned him, he moons in a tavern, and relates to a group of students "the three tales of my folly of love."

One concerns the time, in Paris, when he fancied himself in love with Olympia (Shearer), who turned out to be a life-size doll created by a magician. Second act, set in Venice, has Hoffman bewitched by a beautiful courtesan, Giulietta (Ludmilla Tcherina), whose master is trying to acquire Hoffman's soul through the girl. Third act, set on a Grecian isle, has Hoffman in love with Antonia (Ann Ayars), daughter of a singer and conductor, who is in danger of dying from consumption if she herself attempts to sing.

Shearer, Robert Helpmann, Ludmilla Tcherina and Leonide Massine, all of them dancers who appeared in *Red Shoes*, are distinguished again here.

1951: NOMINATIONS: Color Costume Design, Color Art Direction

•

TALES OF MANHATTAN
1942, 117 mins, US b/w
Dir Julien Duvivier ***Prod*** Boris Morros, S. P. Eagle [= Sam Spiegel] ***Scr*** Ben Hecht, Ferenc Molnar, Donald Ogden Stewart, Samuel Hoffenstein, Alan Campbell, Ladislas Fodor, L. Vadnai, L. Gorog, Lamar Trotti, Henry Blankfort ***Ph*** Joseph Walker ***Ed*** Robert Bischoff ***Mus*** Sol Kaplan ***Art*** Richard Day, Boris Leven
Act Charles Boyer, Rita Hayworth, Ginger Rogers, Henry Fonda, Charles Laughton, Edward G. Robinson (20th Century-Fox)

In *Tales of Manhattan* the hero is an expensive dress coat, which bears a curse, and the film recounts the fortunes and misfortunes of those who wear or come in possession of it. It was originally made for Charles Boyer, playing a Broadway matinee idol, and winds up as scarecrow on a poor old Negro's farm.

The expanse of acting and writing talent may have been too much for Julien Duvivier, a fine foreign director, for he comes up with very few original touches in this picture. Some of the sequences he appears to have permitted to go along on their momentum.

Despite the plenitude of costly stars, featured players and writers, Boris Morros and S. P. Eagle [= Sam Spiegel] brought the film in for slightly more than $1 million, not high considering all the credits.

•

TALES OF ORDINARY MADNESS
1981, 107 mins, Italy Ⓥ col
Dir Marco Ferreri ***Prod*** Jacqueline Ferreri ***Scr*** Sergio Amidei, Marco Ferreri, Anthony Foutz ***Ph*** Tonino Delli Colli ***Ed*** Ruggero Mastroianni ***Mus*** Philippe Sarde ***Art*** Dante Ferretti
Act Ben Gazzara, Ornella Muti, Susan Tyrrell, Tanya Lopert, Roy Brocksmith, Katia Berger (23 Giugno/Ginis)

Marco Ferreri, the anarchically inclined "Italo" filmmaker who has delved into the human psyche often in its mainly frustrated, exploited aspects in today's world, seems to have found a kindred spirit in the stories of the 1960s Yank subculture writer-poet Charles Bukowski. Film [shot in English, and adapted from Bukowski's book *Erections, Ejaculations, Exhibitions, and General Tales of Ordinary Madness*] is a distillation of Ferreri's themes.

Ben Gazzara, in a knowing characterization of a poet (Charles) searching for the essence of love though primarily self-destructive and half believing in its redemptive powers, is first seen giving a philosophical comic talk in some foreign university on a tour. Going back to a dressing room, he finds a Lolita-like runaway who steals his money when he falls asleep.

He goes back to L.A. to write, drink and keep searching for women in a sort of adventurous series of escapades reminiscent of Henry Miller but not as self-indulgent and sex-for-its-own-sake as the writings of Miller.

One day a sexy-looking blonde catches his eye in the street and he follows her. He finds her house and goes in, to be suddenly devoured by her sexually but then turned over to the police for molesting her. Susan Tyrrell is effective in her sexual quirkiness.

Charles is freed and joins the tramp wino world for a while. Then home again to write and dry out. He also comments on the action along the way.

•

TALK OF THE TOWN
1942, 110 mins, US Ⓥ ⦿ b/w
Dir George Stevens ***Prod*** George Stevens ***Scr*** Irwin Shaw, Sidney Buchman ***Ph*** Ted Tetzlaff ***Ed*** Otto Meyer ***Mus*** Frederick Hollander ***Art*** Lionel Banks, Rudolph Sternad
Act Cary Grant, Jean Arthur, Ronald Colman, Edgar Buchanan, Glenda Farrell, Rex Ingram (Columbia)

Case of Cary Grant, the outspoken factory-town, soapbox "anti" worker, being tried for arson and the death of factory foreman in the blaze, serves as a vehicle to introduce a pert schoolteacher (Jean Arthur) and a law school dean (Ronald Colman) in a procession of comedy dissertations on law, in theory and practice. Plot has Grant escaping before his trial is completed and seeking refuge in the schoolmarm's home.

Story [from one by Sidney Harmon, adapted by Dale Van Every] doesn't give Grant quite enough to do, with plenty of meaty lines and situations handed Colman, who manages the transition from the stuffy professor to a human being with the least amount of implausibility.

George Stevens's direction is top-flight for the most part. Transition from serious or melodramatic to the slap-happy and humorous sometimes is a bit awkward, but in the main it is solid escapist comedy.

1942: NOMINATIONS: Best Picture, Original Story & Screenplay, B&W Cinematography, B&W Art Direction, Editing, Scoring of a Dramatic Picture

•

TALK RADIO
1988, 110 mins, US Ⓥ ⦿ col
Dir Oliver Stone ***Prod*** Edward R. Pressman, A. Kitman Ho ***Scr*** Eric Bogosian, Oliver Stone ***Ph*** Robert Richardson ***Ed*** David Brenner ***Mus*** Stewart Copeland ***Art*** Bruno Rubeo
Act Eric Bogosian, Alec Baldwin, Ellen Greene, Leslie Hope, John C. McGinley, John Pankow (Cineplex Odeon/Ten Four)

Talk Radio casts a spotlight on the unpalatable underside of American public opinion, and turns up an unlimited supply of anger, hatred and resentment in the process.

Known in theatrical circles as a monologist and performance artist, Eric Bogosian debuted the initial incarnation of *Talk Radio* in Portland, Ore., in 1985. For the screenplay, he and director Oliver Stone worked in material relating to Alan Berg, the Denver talk-show host murdered by neo-Nazis in 1984, and also created a flashback to illuminate their antihero's personal background and beginnings in the radio game. Most of the film, however, unfolds in the modern studio of KGAB, a Dallas station from which the infamous Barry Champlain (Bogosian) holds forth. Young, caustic, rude, insulting, grandstanding, flippant and mercilessly cruel, the talk-show host spews vitriol impartially on those of all races, colors and creeds and spares the feelings of no one. Champlain draws out the nighttime's seamiest denizens from under their rocks, fringe characters with access to the airwaves.

A dramatic structure has been imposed on the proceedings by the arrival of a radio syndicator who wants to take Champlain's show nationwide. At the same time, Champlain's ex-wife Ellen (Ellen Greene) arrives in town, which occasions a look back at the man's origins.

Bogosian commands attention in a patented tour-de-force. Supporting performances are all vividly realized, notably Michael Wincott's drug-crazed Champlain fan invited to the studio for a tête-à-tête with the host.

•

TALL GUY, THE
1989, 92 mins, UK Ⓥ ⦿ col
Dir Mel Smith ***Prod*** Paul Webster ***Scr*** Richard Curtis ***Ph*** Adrian Biddle ***Ed*** Dan Rae ***Mus*** Peter Brewis ***Art*** Grant Hicks
Act Jeff Goldblum, Emma Thompson, Rowan Atkinson, Emil Wolk, Geraldine James, Anna Massey (LWT/Virgin)

The Tall Guy is a cheery, ingratiating romantic comedy with Jeff Goldblum putting in a stellar performance as a bumbling American actor in London whose career and romantic tribulations are suddenly transformed into triumphs.

At the outset, Yank thesp Goldblum has been performing in the West End for several years as straight man to popular comic Rowan Atkinson. The insecure goof-ball is earning a living but going nowhere fast when he comes under the care of hospital nurse Emma Thompson.

Immediately smitten, Goldblum spends the time between weekly visits for injections desperately concocting ways to ask her out.

Throughout the entire film, the relationship evolves winningly, with so much believable give-and-take, mutual ribbing and support that one roots for it heavily.

As soon as he has discovered domestic bliss, however, Goldblum is sacked by Atkinson, who resents anyone else in his show getting a laugh, and is thrust into the forbidding world of the unemployed actor.

The fresh, alert performances add enormously to the polished sparkle of the script. Goldblum is in splendid form as the eternally naive American abroad. Thompson makes a wonderfully poised foil for her leading man's volubility. British favorite Atkinson has a great time enacting the most vain and mean-spirited of stars, and Hugh Thomas elicits quite a few laughs in his brief appearance as a wild-eyed medic.

•

TALL IN THE SADDLE
1944, 84 mins, US Ⓥ ⦿ b/w
Dir Edwin L. Marin *Prod* Robert Fellows *Scr* Michael Hogan, Paul Fix *Ph* Robert de Grasse *Ed* Philip Martin *Mus* Roy Webb *Art* Albert S. D'Agostino, Ralph Berger
Act John Wayne, Ella Raines, Audrey Long, George "Gabby" Hayes, Ward Bond, Elisabeth Risdon (RKO)

Tall in the Saddle is exciting and adventurous drama in the best western tradition. Picture, mounted with fine scenic backgrounds for the action, combines all the regulation ingredients of wild stagecoach rides, rough-and-tumble fights, gunplay and chases. Story carries unusual twists from regulation formula to provide top interest as strictly exciting escapist entry.

John Wayne shows up at the cattle town to take a job as cowhand, only to find out his employer has been murdered recently. He refuses position with Audrey Long, grandnieceheiress at the ranch, instead joining up with tempestuous Ella Raines, who operates adjoining layout. Woman-hating Wayne is caught in middle between the two girls while he antagonizes several of the town's tough guys and supposedly respectable citizens. He gradually traces clues to the murder.

•

TALL MEN, THE
1955, 122 mins, US Ⓥ ▭ col
Dir Raoul Walsh *Prod* William A. Bacher, William B. Hawks *Scr* Sydney Boehm, Frank Nugent *Ph* Leo Tover *Ed* Louis Loeffler *Mus* Victor Young *Art* Lyle Wheeler, Mark-Lee Kirk
Act Clark Gable, Jane Russell, Robert Ryan, Cameron Mitchell, Emile Meyer, Harry Shannon (20th Century-Fox)

They must have had *The Tall Men* in mind when they invented CinemaScope. It's a big, robust western that fills the wide screen with a succession of panoramic scenes of often incredible beauty.

This is the Clark Gable of old in a role that's straight up his alley—rough, tough, quick on the draw and yet with all the "right" instincts. The vet actor seems to enjoy himself thoroughly and he is equally at ease in the saddle as in his swap-a-quip dialog with Jane Russell.

There's no use quibbling about Russell. She goes through most of the film taunting both Gable and Robert Ryan. It's probably only fair to assume that her pancake-flat acting is a secondary consideration. She does show a sense of comedy in a couple of scenes and the pic benefits from it.

Story [from the novel by Clay Fisher] has brothers Gable and Cameron Mitchell working for Ryan, and they become partners in a venture that calls for them to drive a large herd of cattle from Texas to Montana. On the way south, the trio runs into Russell, and Gable saves her from an Indian attack.

•

TALL T, THE
1957, 78 mins, US Ⓥ col
Dir Budd Boetticher *Prod* Randolph Scott, Harry Joe Brown *Scr* Burt Kennedy *Ph* Charles Lawton, Jr. *Ed* Al Clark *Mus* Heinz Roemheld *Art* George Brooks
Act Randolph Scott, Richard Boone, Maureen O'Sullivan, Arthur Hunnicutt, Skip Homeier, Henry Silva (Columbia)

An unconventional western, *The Tall T* passes up most oater clichés. There's a wealth of suspense in the screenplay based on a story ["The Captives"] by Elmore Leonard. From a quiet start the yarn acquires a momentum which explodes in a sock climax.

Modest and unassuming, Randolph Scott is a rancher who's been seized by a trio of killers led by Richard Boone. Also captured are newlyweds Maureen O'Sullivan and John Hubbard. Originally the outlaws planned a stage robbery, but are urged privately by the craven Hubbard to hold his heiress-wife for ransom in the hope that this move might save his skin.

Under Budd Boetticher's direction the story develops slowly, but relentlessly toward the action-packed finale. Scott impresses as the strong, silent type who ultimately vanquishes his captors. Boone is crisply proficient as the sometimes remorseful outlaw leader. His psychopathic henchmen are capably delineated by Skip Homeier and Henry Silva.

•

TALL TALE
1995, 96 mins, US Ⓥ ▭ col
Dir Jeremiah Chechik *Prod* Joe Roth, Roger Birnbaum *Scr* Steven L. Bloom, Roger Rodat *Ph* Janusz Kaminski *Ed* Richard Chew *Mus* Randy Edelman *Art* Eugenio Zanetti
Act Patrick Swayze, Oliver Platt, Roger Aaron Brown, Nick Stahl, Scott Glenn, Stephen Lang (Walt Disney/Caravan)

Tall Tale is a lavishly produced, robustly entertaining Old West fantasy that is unlike anything else in recent memory. Pic is impressively larger than life, both in physical scale and heroic action. And while the pacing could be brisker during its slightly flabby midsection, it works its way up to a dandy crowd-pleasing climax.

Nick Stahl is well cast as Daniel Hackett, a plucky young farm boy. Scott Glenn is the darkly sinister villain of the piece, a black-hatted rogue who's employed by business interests to gobble up all the homesteads in the territory. When Nick's dad (Stephen Lang) refuses to sell, he's nearly killed by a bad guy's bullet. Nick takes off to parts unknown, hoping he can hide the deed to the family farm far from the greedy land-grabbers.

Magically, he finds himself transported to a sun-baked desert. And that's where he meets Pecos Bill (Patrick Swayze), one of the many heroes in his father's tall tales. In the course of their travels, they rope logger Paul Bunyan (Oliver Platt) and steer driver John Henry (Roger Aaron Brown) into their battle with the land-grabbers. Glenn makes a splendidly wicked villain, and Swayze is everything any kid could want in a two-fisted, hard-drinking, pistol-packing whirlwind-rider.

Director Jeremiah Chechik strives for a look and feel of slightly exaggerated grandeur, at once celebrating and gently tweaking the traditions of the Old West.

•

TAMARIND SEED, THE
1974, 123 mins, UK Ⓥ ▭ col
Dir Blake Edwards *Prod* Ken Wales *Scr* Blake Edwards *Ph* Freddie Young *Ed* Ernest Walter *Mus* John Barry *Art* Harry Pottle
Act Julie Andrews, Omar Sharif, Anthony Quayle, Dan O'Herlihy, Sylvia Syms, Oscar Homolka (ITC/Jewel/Lorimar)

Blake Edwards, whose forte usually is comedy, has turned Evelyn Anthony's novel *The Tamarind Seed* into what some will see as a love story against an espionage background and others as an excellent spy effort involving two people in love.

Julie Andrews as a British civil servant on vacation in the Caribbean meets and becomes fond of (but keeps at arm's length) a handsome Russian (Omar Sharif), also on leave. The Russian also has thoughts of enlisting her as an agent.

Sharif's importance lessens and he's slated for recall to Moscow, so he decides to defect. His bargaining point is the disclosure of a Britisher of high rank who is a Russian spy.

A major strong point of the film is the convincing performances of Andrews and Sharif as a pair of unlikely romantics.

•

TAMING OF THE SHREW, THE
1929, 63 mins, US Ⓥ ⦿ b/w
Dir Sam Taylor *Scr* Sam Taylor *Ph* Karl Struss
Act Mary Pickford, Douglas Fairbanks, Edwin Maxwell, Joseph Cawthorn, Clyde Cook, Dorothy Jordan (United Artists)

Mary Pickford and Douglas Fairbanks in a vastly extravagant burlesque of Bill Shakespeare's best laugh. The two stars often turn that into a howl.

Fairbanks and Pickford go to it knock-about. And Pickford takes the pratfalls. Two and each good. One lands her in a bridal gown while it rains in the mud with the pigs. The other is you-slap-me-and-I'll-slap-you, and again Pickford goes kerflop, clear across the room to land on a feather bed this time.

Fairbanks skeletonizes the scheme when first meeting Katherine, the hell-raising daughter. He says, "Howdy, Kate." She says, "Katherine to you, mug," or something near, and the warrior answers, "Kate, d'ya hear, plain Kate." Then to show her it stands, he and Katie roll down a flight of stairs.

While there is plenty of romance and dialog, slapstick and mud, there's no dirt, so that part of Pickford's career remains as clean as ever.

Splendid settings in the Fairbanks massive-production manner.

•

TAMING OF THE SHREW, THE
1967, 122 mins, UK/Italy Ⓥ ⦿ ▭ col
Dir Franco Zeffirelli *Prod* Richard Burton, Elizabeth Taylor *Scr* Paul Dehn, Suso Cecchi D'Amico, Franco Zeffirelli *Ph* Oswald Morris, Luciano Trasatti *Ed* Peter Taylor, Cario Fabianelli *Mus* Nino Rota *Art* Renzo Mongiardino, John F. De Cuir
Act Richard Burton, Elizabeth Taylor, Michael York, Michael Hordern, Victor Spinetti, Cyril Cusack (Columbia/Royal Films International/F.A.I.)

The Taming of the Shrew offers the interesting situation of Richard Burton fictionally taming Elizabeth Taylor, although the version is a boisterous, often overstagey frolic. It will strike many as a fair compromise for mass audiences between the original Shakespeare and, say, *Kiss Me Kate*.

Screenwriters have done neat job, infusing dialog without rocking Bard's memory overmuch. The two stars pack plenty of wallop, making their roles meaty and flamboyant with a larger-than-life Burton playing for plenty of sly laughs in the uninhibited wife-beating lark.

Taylor tends to overexploit an "earthy" aspect in early footage and switch to the subdued attitude comes too abruptly. But against that she's a buxom delight when tamed. Comedy is sustained in witty wedding ceremony.

Shrewd casting of experienced players pays off with Michael Hordern, Victor Spinetti, Cyril Cusack, Alfred Lynch and Giancarlo Cobelli standouts.

1967: NOMINATIONS: Best Costume Design, Art Direction

•

TAMPOPO
1986, 114 mins, Japan Ⓥ ⦿ col
Dir Juzo Itami *Prod* Yasushi Tamaoki, Seigo Hosogoe *Scr* Juzo Itami *Ph* Masaki Tamura *Ed* Akira Suzuki *Art* Takeo Kimura
Act Ken Watanabe, Nobuko Miyamoto, Tsutomu Yamazaki, Koji Yakusho, Rikiya Yasuoka, Kinzo Sakura (Itami)

Former actor Juzo Itami's second feature, after the success of *The Funeral* (1985), is a thoroughly offbeat but most enjoyable comedy on the subject of food. Main plotline is pretty slight: a truck driver (Ken Watanabe) and his friend take pity on a pretty widow (Nobuko Miyamoto) who operates a rundown noodle shop, and undertake to teach her how to make a success of her business.

Along the way, Itami takes dozens of sidetracks, all of them on the theme of food. Pic actually opens with a gangster addressing the cinema audience and telling them not to eat noisy food during the screening. Later on, the gangster and his moll do some pretty erotic things with food, especially the yolk of an egg.

The viewer learns how to make noodle soup in three minutes flat, and how to make the best turtle soup. This is a film that's as informative as it is funny.

Pic is certainly a bit too long but deserves attention for its superb filmcraft (with great lensing by Masaki Tamura) and cheerfully loony obsession with all things gastronomical. Title [which means *Dandelion*] is the name of its heroine and her restaurant.

•

TANGO & CASH
1989, 98 mins, US Ⓥ ⦿ ▭ col
Dir Andrei Konchalovsky, [Albert Magnoli] *Prod* John Peters, Peter Guber, Larry Franco *Scr* Randy Feldman *Ph* Donald E. Thorin *Ed* Huber De La Bouillerie, Robert Forretti *Mus* Harold Faltermeyer *Art* David Klassen, Richard Berger
Act Sylvester Stallone, Kurt Russell, Teri Hatcher, Jack Palance, Brion James, Michael J. Pollard (Guber-Peters/Warner)

Tango & Cash is a mindless buddy cop pic, loaded with nonstop action that's played mostly for laughs and delivers too few of them. Inane and formulaic, the film relies heavily on whatever chemistry it can generate between Sylvester Stallone and Kurt Russell, who repeatedly trade wisecracks while facing life-or-death situations.

Jack Palance re-creates down to each gasp his role from *Batman* as a snarling crime boss who decides to bring down the two cops who have separately plagued his drug-dealing schemes.

Framed and sent to prison, the two rival cops (named Tango and Cash) become a reluctant team to exonerate themselves. Along the way, they hitch up with Tango's bombshell sister (Teri Hatcher), who happens to be an exotic dancer at some *Star Wars*-esque nightspot.

The thinking seems to be if you're going to be ridiculous you might as well go at it full throttle, and director Andrei Konchalovsky does just that. Albert Magnoli, helmer of *Purple Rain*, directed the final two weeks of lensing after Konchalovsky quit in a dispute over pic's ending.

•

TANG SHAN DAXIONG
(THE BIG BOSS; FISTS OF FURY)
1971, 100 mins, Hong Kong Ⓥ ▭ col
Dir Lo Wei *Prod* Raymond Chow *Scr* Lo Wei, Ni Kuan *Ph* Chen Ching-chu *Ed* Fan Chia-ken *Mus* Wang Fu-ling *Art* Chien Hsin
Act Bruce Lee, Maria Yi, Nora Miao, James Tien, Han Yingchieh, Liu Yung (Golden Harvest)

Mixture is much the same as for others in the genre, which for sheer mindlessness competes favorably with the early '60s spear-and-sandal cycle and the late '60s Italian westerns. This time around, Bruce Lee is compelled to avenge the deaths of friends and cousins who have been murdered for discovering that their employer trafficks in drugs and prostitution.

Despite the silly plot, dreadful supporting cast and prim morality (or perhaps because of them), *Fists of Fury* is sometimes entertaining, with most of the credit due to Lee. Besides his seemingly endless displays of athletic skill and grace, he manages to affect a sneer that often looks addressed to the material rather than his on-screen foes. He's an irrepressible mugger, but the results are often inanely entertaining.

•

TANK

1984, 113 mins, US Ⓥ ⦿ col

Dir Marvin Chomsky ***Prod*** Irwin Yablans ***Scr*** Dan Gordon ***Ph*** Don Brinkrant ***Ed*** Donald R. Rede ***Mus*** Lalo Schifrin ***Art*** Bill Kenney

Act James Garner, G. D. Spradlin, Shirley Jones, C. Thomas Howell, James Cramwell, Jenilee Harrison (Lorimar)

The audience appeal of loners-against-corruption is here refashioned with the hero inside a marauding Sherman tank, taking on a maniacal southern sheriff in defense of integrity and family.

James Garner's persona gives the events a soft, human, and at times bemused edge.

First 10 minutes, showing Garner's arrival on an army base, are terribly slow; relationship is ploddingly established with wife, Shirley Jones, and teenage son, C. Thomas Howell.

Pace finally picks up when Garner gets in trouble for bashing a deputy who had slapped around a prostitute in a bar. The action triggers outrage by the local sheriff, another signature role by G. D. Spradlin, who gets even with Garner by framing his son and sending the boy to a despicable work farm.

•

TANK GIRL

1995, 104 mins, US Ⓥ ⦿ col

Dir Rachel Talalay ***Prod*** Richard B. Lewis, Pen Densham, John Watson ***Scr*** Tedi Sarafian ***Ph*** Gale Tattersall ***Ed*** James R. Symons ***Mus*** Graeme Revell ***Art*** Catherine Hardwicke

Act Lori Petty, Malcolm McDowell, Ice-T, Naomi Watts, Don Harvey, Jeff Kober (Trilogy/United Artists)

Coming to save the world in 2033 is that wild, wacky and energetic *Tank Girl*. But the movie version of the graphic comic book is a classic case of kitchen-sink filmmaking, in which the principals have thrown everything into the stew, hoping enough will stick to the audience. There are dazzling pyrotechnics, state-of-the-art makeup, a lavish song-and-dance production, nifty animation reflecting pic's comic book origins and a thumping rock soundtrack. What's missing from the mix is an engaging story to bind together its intriguing bits. And Lori Petty as Tank Girl, aka Rachel Buck, has the spunk but, sadly, not the heart of the post-apocalyptic heroine.

The planet is a massive desert ruled by the tyrannical military-industrial Water & Power Co. and its chief exec, Kesslee (Malcolm McDowell). Renegades, including the title character's band, poach the precious fluid. Rachel is taken captive and put to work in the W&P mines. But Kesslee wants her to flush out the Rippers, a ferocious strain—part man, part kangaroo—created in some warped biolab experiment. Escaping with the aid of fellow drone Jet Girl (Naomi Watts), Rachel hijacks a tank and sets off in search of the Rippers.

Director Rachel Talalay has culled the loudest and most obvious elements associated with her comic book hero. It's a biff-bam approach. Petty's take on her character favors brash, physical elements. Lost is the humor and ingenious nature that might have spawned a series.

•

TAP

1989, 110 mins, US Ⓥ ⦿ col

Dir Nick Castle ***Prod*** Gary Adelson, Richard Vane ***Scr*** Nick Castle ***Ph*** David Gribble ***Ed*** Patrick Kennedy ***Mus*** James Newton Howard ***Art*** Patricia Norris

Act Gregory Hines, Suzzanne Douglas, Sammy Davis, Jr., Savion Glover, Joe Morton, Terrence McNally (Tri-Star)

Tap is a surprisingly rich and affecting blend of dance and story that transcends its respectful deference toward the great hoofers of a bygone era to deliver plenty of glowing contemporary entertainment.

Impassioned by the twin personal commitments of writer-director Nick Castle (whose father choreographed Fred Astaire and Gene Kelly) and star Gregory Hines (whose tap career began at five at Harlem's Apollo Theater), project benefits from a dream cast and crew.

Hines plays Max, an ex-con torn between the high style and fast money of his former career as a jewel thief and the more deeply felt pleasures of tap dance, learned from his dead father. Trying to spark up an old romance with a dance teacher (Suzzanne Douglas), whose father, Lil Mo (Sammy Davis, Jr.), was his dad's pal, Max gets pulled unwillingly into the world of the oldtime hoofers, who occupy the exalted third floor of Sonny's, a dance studio and shabby shrine to the all-but-forgotten form.

Much like blues music, the dancing in this pic seems a heartfelt and exuberant response to urban struggle. Another big asset is pic's introduction in final dance seg of Tap-Tronics, a blend of tap and electric rock in which dancer's taps are connected with synthesizers that allow him to make both rhythmic and melodic music.

•

TAPS

1981, 118 mins, US Ⓥ col

Dir Harold Becker ***Prod*** Stanley R. Jaffe, Howard B. Jaffe ***Scr*** Darryl Ponicsan, Robert Mark Kamen ***Ph*** Owen Roizman ***Ed*** Maury Winetrobe ***Mus*** Maurice Jarre ***Art*** Stan Jolley, Alfred Sweeney

Act George C. Scott, Timothy Hutton, Ronny Cox, Sean Penn, Tom Cruise, Brendan Ward (20th Century-Fox/Jaffe)

A heavy dramatic portrait of military school education with a disturbing shoot 'em up climax, *Taps* labors at an unbearably slow pace to an inevitable, depressing conclusion.

Plot [based on Devery Freeman's novel *Father Sky*, adapted by James Lineberger] centers on a military academy whose students are angered that their school and its traditions are being sold out from under them in order to build a bunch of condominiums.

Timothy Hutton tries to lend some humanity to the headstrong cadet who leads his fellow students in forcibly taking over the school (weapons and all) in a last-ditch effort to save it, but he just appears too nice a guy. George C. Scott makes a brief but convincing appearance as a slightly deranged general.

Much of the supporting cast fare better, especially Sean Penn as Hutton's humane best friend, Tom Cruise as a trigger-happy cadet and Ronny Cox as the reasonable colonel who tries to talk Hutton out of his mission.

•

TARANTULA

1955, 80 mins, US Ⓥ b/w

Dir William Alland ***Prod*** Jack Arnold ***Scr*** Robert M. Fresco, Martin Berkeley ***Ph*** George Robinson ***Ed*** William M. Morgan ***Mus*** Henry Mancini ***Art*** Alexander Golitzen, Alfred Sweeney

Act John Agar, Mara Corday, Leo G. Carroll, Nestor Paiva, Ross Elliott, Clint Eastwood (Universal)

A tarantula as big as a barn puts the horror into this well-made program science-fictioner and it is quite credibly staged and played, bringing off the far-fetched premise with a maximum of believability.

Some scientists, stationed near Desert Rock, Ariz., are working on an automatically stabilized nutritional formula that will feed the world's ever-increasing population when the natural food supply becomes too small. Through variously staged circumstances, a tarantula that has been injected with the yet unstabilized formula escapes and, while continuously increasing in size, starts living off cattle and humans.

Leo G. Carroll is excellent in his scientist role, while John Agar, young town medico, and Mara Corday carry off the romantic demands very well.

•

TARAS BULBA

1962, 123 mins, US Ⓥ ⦿ ▭ col

Dir J. Lee Thompson ***Prod*** Harold Hecht ***Scr*** Waldo Salt, Karl Tunberg ***Ph*** Joseph MacDonald ***Ed*** William Reynolds, Gene Milford, Eda Warren, Folmar Blangsted ***Mus*** Franz Waxman ***Art*** Edward Carrere

Act Tony Curtis, Yul Brynner, Christine Kaufmann, Sam Wanamaker, Brad Dexter, Guy Rolfe (United Artists)

For many minutes of the two hours it takes director J. Lee Thompson to put Gogol's tale of the legendary Cossack hero on the screen, the panorama of fighting men and horses sweeping across the wide steppes (actually the plains of Argentina) provides a compelling sense of pageantry and grandeur.

As powerful as they are, the spectacular features of *Taras Bulba* do not quite render palatable the wishy-washy subplot, seemingly devised to give Tony Curtis as much screen time as the far more colorful title role of Yul Brynner.

Curtis, an excellent actor when properly supervised or motivated, was seemingly neither inspired nor irritated sufficiently by his talented credits-sharer to do more than kiss and kill on cue.

Brynner's Taras Bulba is an arrogant, proud, physically powerful Cossack chief. Even though the actor follows the habit of running his lines together, his actions are always unmistakably clear. He's allowed plenty of space in which to chew the scenery and there's precious little of it in which he doesn't leave teethmarks.

The battle sequences and, to a lesser extent, the Cossack camp scenes are the picture's greatest assets. Some of cameraman Joseph MacDonald's long shots of hordes of horsemen sweeping across the plains, as countless others pour over every hillside, are breathtakingly grand and fully utilize the wide screen. Franz Waxman's score, Russian derived, for the battles and his czardaslike themes for the Cossacks are among his best work.

1962: NOMINATION: Best Original Music Score

•

TARGET

1985, 117 mins, US Ⓥ ⦿ col

Dir Arthur Penn ***Prod*** Richard D. Zanuck, David Brown ***Scr*** Howard Berk, Don Petersen ***Ph*** Jean Tournier ***Ed*** Stephen A. Rotter, Richard P. Cirincione ***Mus*** Michael Small ***Art*** Willy Holt

Act Gene Hackman, Matt Dillon, Gayle Hunnicutt, Victoria Fyodorova, Josef Sommer, Guy Boyd (CBS)

Target is a spy thriller that's not only completely understandable and involving throughout, but also continually surprising along the way. It also strangely contains a few scenes of dreadful writing, acting and direction.

Gene Hackman is a seemingly dull lumberyard owner in Dallas and Matt Dillon is his sporty roughneck son. Loving but a bit bored, too, mother Gayle Hunnicutt finally has decided to vacation in Paris alone because Hackman has an odd aversion to visiting Europe. While away, she hopes the two will make an effort to get to like each other. Then comes news that Mom has been kidnapped.

Although there are the obligatory preposterous auto chases, the action overall is supportive of the plot rather than a substitute. Ditto bloodshed and pyromania.

•

TARGETS

1968, 90 mins, US Ⓥ col

Dir Peter Bogdanovich ***Prod*** Peter Bogdanovich ***Scr*** Peter Bogdanovich ***Ph*** Laszlo Kovacs ***Ed*** [uncredited] ***Art*** Polly Platt

Act Boris Karloff, Tim O'Kelly, Nancy Hsueh, James Brown, Peter Bogdanovich (Saticoy)

A good programmer, within low-budget limitations, about a sniper and his innocent victims. A separate, concurrent subplot features Boris Karloff as a horror film star who feels he is washed up. Both plotlines converge in an exciting climax.

Peter Bogdanovich has made a film of much suspense and implicit violence. It opens with a typical horror pic finale, which in a neat switcheroo turns out to be just that, as producer Monte Landis o.o.'s the film. Karloff declares he is through with films and exits. A sidewalk scene introduces Tim O'Kelly, all-American boy who has drawn a bead on Karloff from a nearby gun shop.

Plot then picks up O'Kelly, a gun-loving, disturbed youth who "had everything to live for." One night, his mind snaps. He hides in the screen tower of a drive-in theater, whence he terrorizes the audience. A press stunt has drawn Karloff to the ozoner for the climax.

As any newspaper or TV newsreel shows, mass murderers look just like anyone else. O'Kelly's projection of blandness is most appropriate to the suspense.

Aware of the virtue of implied violence, Bogdanovich conveys moments of shock, terror, suspense and fear.

•

TARNISHED ANGELS, THE

1957, 87 mins, US ▭ b/w

Dir Douglas Sirk ***Prod*** Albert Zugsmith ***Scr*** George Zuckerman ***Ph*** Irving Glassberg ***Ed*** Russell F. Schoengarth ***Mus*** Frank Skinner ***Art*** Alexander Golitzen, Alfred Sweeney

Act Rock Hudson, Robert Stack, Dorothy Malone, Jack Carson, Robert Middleton, Troy Donahue (Universal)

The Tarnished Angels is a stumbling entry. Characters are mostly colorless, given static reading in drawn-out situations, and storyline is lacking in punch. Film is designed as a follow-up to *Written on the Wind*, to take advantage of the principals both before and behind the camera.

The production is based on William Faulkner's novel *Pylon*, and screenplay carries an air circus setting. Rock

Hudson is intro'd as a seedy, but idealistic, New Orleans reporter covering a barnstorming show in that city. He falls for Dorothy Malone, trick parachutist-wife of Robert Stack, speed flyer and World War I ace, still living in his past glory as he and his small unit cruise about the country participating in air events.

Hudson appears in an unrealistic role to which he can add nothing and Stack spends most of the time with eagles in his eyes.

•

TARNISHED LADY

1931, 80 mins, US b/w

Dir George Cukor ***Prod*** Walter Wanger ***Scr*** Donald Ogden Stewart ***Ph*** Larry Williams ***Ed*** Barry Royan

Act Tallulah Bankhead, Clive Brook, Phoebe Foster, Alexander Kirkland, Osgood Perkins, Elizabeth Patterson (Paramount)

This weepy and ragged melo about two society women, their lovers and how all cross each other's paths, has little outside its cast to be recommended. Tallulah Bankhead has personality, charm and a voice loaded with s.a.

In the story, after she has left her husband and is on the downgrade, upon finding her former lover is having an affair with her rival girlfriend, the many speaks Bankhead visits would even surprise prohibition officers.

Cast, as a whole, comports in a manner suggesting they were under orders to give way before Bankhead. Clive Brook suffers the most. Ordinarily a fine actor, he slumps here in trying to get over some of the silly dialog. Phoebe Foster, who plays the femme nemesis, and in a totally unsympathetic role, gives an even performance.

•

TARZAN

1999, 88 mins, US Ⓥ ⊙ col

Dir Kevin Lima, Chris Buck ***Prod*** Bonnie Arnold ***Scr*** Tab Murphy, Bob Tzudiker, Noni White, David Reynolds, Jeffrey Stepakoff ***Ed*** Gregory Perler ***Mus*** Mark Mancina ***Art*** Daniel St. Pierre (Disney)

Disney's *Tarzan* swings, even if it doesn't always soar. This first animated treatment of one of the screen's great perennial characters is always engaging, although it doesn't measure up to Disney's top-level animated features on several counts.

Tarzan always seemed like a natural for the animated screen, even to author Edgar Rice Burroughs himself, who in the '30s cautioned only that "the cartoon must be good. It must approximate Disney excellence." As it happened, all 47 previous Tarzan features have been live-action.

Screenplay makes most of its obvious p.c. points right away ("Why am I so different?" the lad asks his "mom"), as it lays the groundwork for the more important psychological issues that will surface later, when Tarzan has to figure out whether he's more at home among men or beasts.

The tyke Tarzan neatly transforms into the ripply adult version (voiced by Tony Goldwyn) in the middle of one of Phil Collins's typically throbbing and propulsive songs, in a show-off sequence in which Tarzan slips and slides through the jungle in the manner of a human roller coaster. Encores of the "thrill-ride" approach are part of pic's tendency toward in-your-face overkill.

Tone shortly becomes more serious as the party of late-Victorian Brits begin teaching the deeply curious Tarzan about civilization via projected engravings and other means, and the well-behaved wild man begins sensing that Jane (Minnie Driver), the spirited daughter of nutty Professor Porter (Nigel Hawthorne), may be of interest to him in a way that no monkey ever has been.

Voicings are first class all round. Animation work is richly detailed and colorfully conceived.

1999: Best Original Song

•

TARZAN AND HIS MATE

1934, 92 mins, US Ⓥ ⊙ b/w

Dir Cedric Gibbons ***Scr*** Howard Emmett Rogers, Leon Gordon, James Kevin McGuinness ***Ph*** Charles Clarke, Clyde De Vinna

Act Johnny Weissmuller, Maureen O'Sullivan, Neil Hamilton, Paul Cavanagh, Forrester Harvey, Nathan Curry (M-G-M)

In *Tarzan and His Mate*, second of the Metro series with Johnny Weissmuller, the monkeys do everything but bake cakes and the very human elephants always seem on the verge of sitting down for a nice, quiet game of chess; yet the picture has a strange sort of power that overcomes the total lack of logic.

Tarzan No. 1 ended with Tarz and the white girl from England at peace in their jungle kingdom. They're again at peace as No. 2 ends, but in the 92 minutes between the two fade-outs they're almost in pieces, several times. Trouble starts soon as the domain of Mr. and Mrs. Tarzan (Weissmuller and Maureen O'Sullivan) is trespassed upon by Neil Hamilton and Paul Cavanagh, a couple of heels from Mayfair. Boys are after the fortune in ivory which lies in a pachyderm graveyard.

Tarzan and his mate spend most of their time swinging through the branches. The Tarzans also do some fancy swimming, particularly during a tank sequence when Weissmuller and a lady swimmer doubling for O'Sullivan perform some artistic submarine formations. The lady is brassiere-less, but photographed from the side only.

•

TARZAN AND THE AMAZONS

1945, 76 mins, US b/w

Dir Kurt Neumann ***Prod*** Sol Lesser ***Scr*** John Jacoby, Marjorie L. Pfaelzer ***Ph*** Archie Stout ***Ed*** Robert O. Crandall ***Mus*** Paul Sawtell ***Art*** Phil Paradise

Act Johnny Weissmuller, Brenda Joyce, Johnny Sheffield, Henry Stephenson, Maria Ouspenskaya, Barton MacLane (Champion/RKO)

The usual Tarzan adventures have been screened in an African setting with the three stars doing a good job, and the supporting cast performing competently.

Story concerns Tarzan's efforts to keep faith with mysterious Palmyrians whose valley hideout is peopled only by women. Queen of the Amazons (Maria Ouspenskaya) trusts Tarzan (Johnny Weissmuller), knowing he will never reveal her secret.

Unwittingly, the Tarzan household chimpanzee, Cheetah, reveals to group of Europeans that Palmyrians are somewhere in the neighborhood. Group, composed of scientists and a couple of greedy traders, are led to the hideout by Tarzan's son (Johnny Sheffield). In denouement, Europeans war against the women.

Photography is good, and African wildlife is pictured smoothly. All three stars do some good swimming, and Cheetah is very engaging.

•

TARZAN AND THE GREAT RIVER

1967, 88 mins, US ▭ col

Dir Robert Day ***Prod*** Sy Weintraub ***Scr*** Bob Barbash ***Ph*** Irving Lippman ***Ed*** Anthony Carras, Edward Mann, James Nelson, Donald H. Wolfe ***Mus*** William Loose ***Art*** Herbert Smith

Act Mike Henry, Jan Murray, Manuel Padilla, Jr., Diana Millay, Rafer Johnson, Paulo Grazindo (Weintraub/Paramount)

Tarzan goes into upper reaches of the Amazon for his latest escapades, marking the first time that this location has been utilized for the Apeman series. Beautifully photographed against striking and often magnificent scenery, the production is strictly run of the mill in story content, often clumsily scripted.

Mike Henry is the umpteenth thesp to portray the title character; his physique is better than his acting, but he's doing well enough by the few demands of the role. In Rio de Janeiro, he's called upon to break an ancient killer cult which has been revived in the jungle by a vicious native leader (Rafer Johnson).

Zoologists probably will be a bit startled to learn that African maned lions roam the Brazilian jungles, as well as hippos who splash in the Amazon. Robert Day's direction is as good as the script [from a screen story by Bob Barbash and Lewis Reed] will permit.

Starring with Henry is Jan Murray, as a convincing river skipper in for too much out-of-place comedy. Manuel Padilla, Jr. plays his small Indian charge, who travels up and down the river with him. Diana Millay portrays a doctor who wants to help the natives, looking like she just stepped out of a beauty parlor.

•

TARZAN AND THE GREEN GODDESS

1938, 72 mins, US b/w

Dir Edward Kull ***Scr*** Charles F. Royal ***Ph*** [uncredited]

Act Herman Brix, Ula Holt, Frank Baker, Don Castello, Lew Sargeant, Jack Mower (Burroughs-Tarzan)

Limpid direction makes this sequel to [*The New Adventures of Tarzan*, 1935, taken from a 12-episode serial] fall way short of even the limited possibilities of an independent production. Herman Brix, who still gets billing as an Olympic champ, is at home in the Tarzan role, but even his robust endeavors fail to lift this production.

Quest of the Major Martling (Frank Baker) expedition for a legendary "green goddess," containing a valuable munitions formula, is glossed over lightly, travelog clips and foggy distant shots developing to the point where the inevitable enemy party headed by Raglan (Don Castello) starts using devious methods to grab the much desired formula.

This rings in the fights between natives, ambushes, captures, fist battles, and always the colossal deeds of Tarzan. If he isn't able to defeat 12 men at a clip, it is an off-day.

Despite these episodes, told in oldtime serial fashion, and a comparatively realistic storm at sea, the new Tarzan story seldom impresses or even proves exciting. Jungle scenes, supposed to be Guatemalan wildland, are fair. Ula Holt, as the heroine who goes on the expedition's party, is mediocre. Dialog is elementary. Edward Kull directs with a heavy hand.

•

TARZAN AND THE HUNTRESS

1947, 72 mins, US b/w

Dir Kurt Neumann ***Prod*** Sol Lesser ***Scr*** Jerry Gruskin, Rowland Leigh ***Ph*** Archie Stout ***Ed*** Merrill White ***Mus*** Paul Sawtell ***Art*** Paul Paradise

Act Johnny Weissmuller, Brenda Joyce, Johnny Sheffield, Patricia Morison, Barton MacLane, John Warburton (Lesser/RKO)

Some 16 Tarzan films have ground through the hopper since National broke the ice in 1918 with *Tarzan of the Apes*. Sol Lesser, releasing through RKO, has turned out five of the jungle epics in the past four years. His latest shapes up as a moderately entertaining adventure film. Apeman this time flexes his muscles to repel the depredations of a zoological expedition which seeks to capture scores of animals for various zoos. Huntress Tanya (Patricia Morison) is a leader of the safari, along with Weir (Barton MacLane) and Marley (John Warburton). Fauna quota set by native king Farrod (Charles Trowbridge) dampens the hunters' prospects. Weir, along with sinister Prince Ozira (Ted Hecht), a nephew of the king, arranges for the potentate's elimination in a hunting "accident."

Story's modeled after the countless plots found in any juvenile's library. Acting is also singularly undistinguished. Johnny Weissmuller's lines are confined to monosyllabic utterances and his still striking physique remains his top asset. Kurt Neumann could have directed at a faster pace.

•

TARZAN AND THE JUNGLE BOY

1968, 90 mins, US ▭ col

Dir Robert Gordon ***Prod*** Robert Day ***Scr*** Steven Lord ***Ph*** Ozen Sermet ***Ed*** Milton Mann, Reg Browne ***Mus*** William Loose ***Art*** Herbert Smith

Act Mike Henry, Rafer Johnson, Alizia Gur, Steve Bond, Ed Johnson, Ronald Gans (Banner/Paramount)

Tarzan is up to his customary brand of jungle antics in the latest entry in the Apeman series, which celebrates its 50th year on the screen. Lensed on location in South America, the production lacks the finish of early Tarzan mellers but nonetheless, after a confused opening, unspools along regulation lines for a fairly fast windup.

Tarzan helps a femme journalist, Myrna Claudel (Alizia Gur), and her associate locate a supposed wild jungle boy (Ronald Gans) whose American father was drowned seven years before and lad, then only about four, managed to survive. Search takes them into forbidden Zagunda country.

Mike Henry, one of the more muscular Tarzans, is okay in part but isn't called upon to do much fraternizing with wild animals, nor are there any battles of the sort Johnny Weissmuller used to engage in with lions et al. Rafer Johnson makes a good native heavy.

Direction by Robert Gordon is only as good as the screenplay, which doesn't give him much latitude, but color photography by Ozen Sermet is outstanding.

•

TARZAN AND THE LEOPARD WOMAN

1946, 75 mins, US b/w

Dir Kurt Neumann ***Prod*** Sol Lesser ***Scr*** Carroll Young ***Ph*** Karl Struss ***Ed*** Robert O. Crandall ***Mus*** Paul Sawtell ***Art*** Phil Paradise

Act Johnny Weissmuller, Brenda Joyce, Johnny Sheffield, Acquanetta, Edgar Barrier, Dennis Hoey (Lesser/RKO)

Tarzan is growing old. After all these years of swinging through the trees and giving out with an occasional bloodcurdling yell to thrill the kids in the front row, he's finally showing signs of age. Latest Tarzan film is bogged down by stock situations, unimaginative production and direction indicating Sol Lesser, producer of the series since he purchased the rights from Metro, is having difficulty keeping up the standard.

Story has Tarzan out to break up a belligerent tribe of natives who dress up in leopard skins with iron claws—the situation found in quickie serials. Apeman doesn't give out with his famous call once during the picture and, instead of bringing in the herd of elephants that used to get Tarzan out of trouble in the old days, story falls back on another cliché to let the hero free himself in the nick.

Brawny Johnny Weissmuller still makes a presentable Tarzan but he, too, shows signs of age, with a growing waistline and a minimum of athletic antics. Brenda Joyce is a decorative Jane, and little Johnny Sheffield does some good work as Boy. Acquanetta wears a beautiful sarong as the high priestess of the leopard clan. Leopard men's dances, staged by Lester Horton, resemble a high school gym class warming up. Karl Struss's camerawork and Paul Sawtell's score, however, belong on the credit side.

•

TARZAN AND THE LOST SAFARI

1957, 80 mins, UK/US col

Dir H. Bruce Humberstone ***Prod*** John Croydon ***Scr*** Montgomery Pittman, Lillie Hayward ***Ph.*** C. R. Pennington-Richards, Miki Carter ***Ed*** Bill Lewthwaite ***Mus*** Clifton Parker ***Art*** Paul Sheriff

Act Gordon Scott, Robert Beatty, Yolande Donlan, Betta St. John, Wilfred Hyde White, George Coulouris (Croydon/Lesser)

Tarzan, perennial screen hero in black-and-white, here takes to color. Along with the tint treatment, Tarzan takes to authentic jungle backgrounds, and the antics come off entertainingly under H. Bruce Humberstone's actionful direction. Listed as a British production by John Croydon for the Sol Lesser presentation banner, film is the first Tarzan to wear the Metro release label in some 15 years. The combination of African footage lensed in Technicolour by Miki Carter and the matching studio-staged sequences by C. R. Pennington-Richards adds excellent sight values to go with the standard adventuring.

Gordon Scott has the physique for the title role and does acceptably by it. This one was lensed about a year ago.

The script finds the hero guiding a party of bored upper-crust socialites out of the jungle after its plane has crashed. To give the hero obstacles to overcome, plot introduces "Tusker" Hawkins (Robert Beatty), hunter who has a deal to turn over some white sacrifices to a native chief (Orlando Martins) as payment for a vast hoard of ivory.

Distaff roles fall to Yolande Donlan and Betta St. John, members of the party, and both come through nicely. Beatty is a good heavy.

•

TARZAN AND THE MERMAIDS

1948, 68 mins, US b/w

Dir Robert Florey ***Prod*** Sol Lesser ***Scr*** Carroll Young ***Ph*** Jack Draper, Gabriel Figueroa, Raul Martinez Solares ***Ed*** Merrill White ***Mus*** Paul Sawtell

Act Johnny Weissmuller, Brenda Joyce, Linda Christian, John Laurenz, Fernando Wagner, Edward Ashley (Lesser/RKO)

Tarzan and the Mermaids is standard Johnny Weissmuller, differing only from other jungle epics in that this one was produced in Mexico. Also, it introduces Linda Christian to U.S. audiences and is faster moving than others in the Tarzan group.

Sol Lesser moved his company into the Churubusco Studios just outside of Mexico City to film the picture. They also went on location at Acapulco, Mexico's west coast watering resort, for many exteriors and the hair-raising diving shots. Newcomer Christian, native-born Mexican, hints possibilities. She's comely and has the physical attributes to measure up for the screen.

This story is strictly one of those things about a forbidden island in mythical Aquatania where a white trader and his undercover cutthroat employ a fake tribal god to keep the natives subjugated in order to grab pearls. The crooks want Mara (Christian) as a bride for this god, but she has other ideas.

Here's where Tarzan comes in. He fishes her out of the river accidentally and tells his wife (Brenda Joyce) he has bagged a mermaid. Tarzan ultimately unfrocks the phoney tribal priest and his helper.

Two [Mexican] photographers helped Jack Draper on the lensing. Result is some spectacular camerawork, probably the best on any Tarzan film.

•

TARZAN AND THE SHE-DEVIL

1953, 75 mins, US b/w

Dir Kurt Neumann ***Prod*** Sol Lesser ***Scr*** Karl Kamb, Carroll Young ***Ph*** Karl Struss ***Ed*** Leon Barsha ***Mus*** Paul Sawtell ***Art*** Carroll Clark

Act Lex Barker, Joyce MacKenzie, Raymond Burr, Monique Van Vooren, Tom Conway, Michael Grainger (Lesser/RKO)

A much tamer Tarzan than heretofore cavorts in *Tarzan and the She-Devil*, resulting in film being a tedious affair for a goodly portion of its 75 minutes. Keeping the hero a tied-up captive for a long stretch wasn't hep scripting.

Yarn pits Tarzan against a group of ivory thieves. The baddies want the apeman's help in rounding up a large herd of elephants, and when he refuses they try to capture his wife, Jane. She escapes into the jungle, however. When he sees their tree home burnt to the ground, Tarzan thinks Jane has been killed. The fight is out of him and he's captured.

Lex Barker looks like a Tarzan should, and consequently comes across okay in the lead, while Joyce MacKenzie is acceptable as his vis-a-vis. Raymond Burr is good as one of the heavies, as is Tom Conway as another. Monique Van Vooren presents sex allure and nothing more as the gal who finances the ivory hunters.

Kurt Neumann's direction is on the slow side, but then he wasn't given much to work with. Karl Struss's camerawork is average.

•

TARZAN AND THE SLAVE GIRL

1950, 74 mins, US b/w

Dir Lee Sholem ***Prod*** Sol Lesser ***Scr*** Hans Jacoby, Arnold Belgard ***Ph*** Russell Harlan ***Ed*** Christian Nyby ***Mus*** Paul Sawtell ***Art*** Harry Horner

Act Lex Barker, Vanessa Brown, Robert Alda, Denise Darcel, Hurd Hatfield, Arthur Shields (RKO/Lesser)

Lex Barker, as Tarzan, takes to the jungle on the trail of some femme natives who are being held prisoners by a group of lost tribesmen [led by Hurd Hatfield]. With him on the trek are a doctor (Arthur Shields), searching for the source of a jungle disease; a comely half-breed nurse with a yen for men; a drunken jungle beachcomber (Robert Alda), and sundry native carriers. Enroute, the safari fights off natives disguised as bushes and armed with deadly blowguns.

Vanessa Brown makes her bow in the Jane role and fills the bill on all counts. Denise Darcel is the nurse, adding plenty of s.a. spice.

•

TARZAN ESCAPES

1936, 90 mins, US Ⓥ b/w

Dir Richard Thorpe ***Prod*** Sam Zimbalist (assoc.) ***Scr*** Cyril Hume ***Ph*** Leonard Smith ***Ed*** W. Donn Hayes ***Mus*** [uncredited] ***Art*** Elmer Sheeley

Act Johnny Weissmuller, Maureen O'Sullivan, John Buckler, Benita Hume, William Henry, Herbert Mundin (M-G-M)

This plot permits Tarzie's idyllic romance with his mate (Maureen O'Sullivan) to be rudely interrupted by a couple of the missus' relatives from London. Mrs. Tarzan has unknowingly become the heir to a late uncle's large fortune, and the relatives try to bring her back to civilization so that she may grab the coin and help them grab some of it also.

It so happens, however, that their jungle guide is a dastardly rat who sees in Tarzan a cinch freak show attraction for up north, and it takes not only Tarz himself but also a big zoo full of animal friends to clear up the mess, save the lives of the white folks, give the villain his just dues, and restore Tarzan's mate to Tarzan.

Johnny Weissmuller once again looks good as the jungle boy. And O'Sullivan is also okay once more as the loving wife, but considerably more covered up in clothing this time. A female ape called Cheetah is the Tarzans' pet and houseworker, and some expert handling of the monk provides the picture with its most legitimately comical and best moments.

•

TARZAN FINDS A SON!

1939, 81 mins, US Ⓥ b/w

Dir Richard Thorpe ***Prod*** Sam Zimbalist ***Scr*** Cyril Hume ***Ph*** Leonard Smith ***Ed*** Frank Sullivan, Gene Ruggiero ***Art*** Cedric Gibbons, Urie McCleary

Act Johnny Weissmuller, Maureen O'Sullivan, Johnny Sheffield, Ian Hunter, Laraine Day, Frieda Inescort (M-G-M)

Tarzan Finds a Son carries more credulity and believable jungle adventure than the long list of preceding Tarzan features.

Tarzan and the Missus save a baby in plane that crashes in the jungle. Tarzan is proudly teaching his accepted son the jungle lore, when a searching party arrives to establish death of the baby, who has come into heavy inheritance. Ian Hunter and Frieda Inescort are out to grab the inheritance for themselves, and start plotting death of Tarzan and snatch of the youngster.

Johnny Weissmuller athletically runs and swims through as the apeman in okay fashion. Maureen O'Sullivan is the jungle wife, and gets in some good dramatic work in battling against herself to give up the youngster. Tarzan's boy, little Johnny Sheffield, does nicely and performs his athletic chores satisfactorily.

•

TARZAN GOES TO INDIA

1962, 88 mins, UK/US col

Dir John Guillermin ***Prod*** Sy Weintraub ***Scr*** Robert Hardy Andrews, John Guillermin ***Ph*** Paul Beeson ***Ed*** Max Benedict ***Mus*** Ken Jones ***Art*** George Provis

Act Jock Mahoney, Jai, Leo Gordon, Mark Dana, Feroz Khan, Simi (Weintraub/M-G-M)

Name's the same, but the character is counterfeit. Widespread appeal of the original primitive apeman will never be duplicated by his jet-age descendant, an articulate, subdued, businesslike troubleshooter in the jungles of the world. Still, the 36th in the venerable screen series that began in 1918, and the first to be endowed with CinemaScope, has a large-scale production sheen and exotic faraway flavor—it was filmed entirely in India.

Loin-clothed hero aids a young elephant boy in the rescue of a pack of pachyderms callously doomed to be submerged under the waters of a giant new jungle reservoir. To do this, Tarzan must battle, tooth, nail and tusk, the uncooperative dispositions of both elephant and man, latter in the form of inflexibly cruel construction interests.

Jock Mahoney, who had a secondary role in the last edition (*Tarzan the Magnificent*), has graduated to the title character, a role he endows with admirable physique, dexterity and personality. A long-time film stunt man, Mahoney is the best Tarzan in years. Jai, the [real-life] Elephant Boy, a pint-sized modern variation of the '30s Sabu, scores in a prominent role. Feroz Khan and Simi carry off a minor romantic interest.

Pic has been impressively produced. Cameraman Paul Beeson and art director George Provis have used the exotic picturesque locales and views of India's Mysore Province to advantage.

•

TARZAN OF THE APES

1918, 130 mins, US Ⓥ b/w

Dir Scott Sidney ***Ed*** Isidor Bernstein

Act Elmo Lincoln, Gordon Griffith, True Boardman, Colin Kenny, Enid Markey, Bessie Toner (National)

Edgar Rice Burroughs's story *Tarzan of the Apes*, as a 10-reel screen feature produced by the National Film Corporation, lacks much of the pep of the original. When Tarzan first appeared as a serial in the *Evening World* there was no thought that the story would have so widespread an appeal, but it attracted universal attention, republished in a popular fiction magazine and later in book form. The occasional touches of the extraordinary are the film's greatest asset, and listed among these will have to be the work of Gordon Griffith, as Tarzan, a 10-year-old boy. *Tarzan* in film is divided into three chapters. The [five-minute] intermission occurs after the first two chapters which consume approximately one hour and 20 minutes.

The early sections are almost wholly devoted to planting the underlying theme of the story, which in the original was of a secondary nature. Much time is devoted to the reason for the parents of Tarzan going to South Africa; also tremendous footage is held by the succeeding holder of the title of Lord Greystoke (Colin Kenny), his escapades, marriage to a bar maid (Bessie Toner) and subsequent heir.

Lord and Lady Greystoke (True Boardman, Kathleen Kirkham) are in England in 1897, and all South Africa is in an uproar over the slave trade. Greystoke is delegated to ferret out the inside of the slave trade. The final stage of his journey is on a sailing vessel, ruled by three brutal officers. Then a mutiny and the final disposition of the Greystokes by the crew. This is followed by their Robinson Crusoe existence; the birth of their child; the death of the parents and the adoption of the baby by an ape.

The film jumps 10 years. This is the second chapter, about equally divided between the development of the ape boy and the rearing of the son of the successor to the title in England. Then there is another leap [to the third chapter], and Tarzan is 20. He has become King of the Apes, while in England the heir apparent is a dissipated youth. [When news comes] that a son of the Greystoke who went to Africa is living, an expedition is organized, and in Africa Tarzan is brought on the scene again.

The ape family has been achieved by the medium of a flock of acrobats in skins and very foolishly a number of closeups are shown which kill the illusion. Otherwise from a production angle the picture is passable. Elmo Lincoln as Tarzan at 20 is all that could be asked for. Enid Markey [as the rich American, Jane Porter] fails to register effectively. Picture needs cutting in the first hour and a half. [Film was shown on U.S. TV in a 55-min. version.]

•

TARZAN'S DEADLY SILENCE

1970, 88 mins, US col

Dir Robert L. Friend ***Prod*** Leon Benson ***Scr*** Lee Edwin, Jack A. Robinson, John Considine, Tim Considine ***Ph*** Abraham Vialla ***Ed*** Gabriel Torres ***Mus*** Walter Greene

Act Ron Ely, Jock Mahoney, Woody Strode, Manuel Padilla, Jr., Gregorio Acosta, Nichelle Nichols

Old Tarzans don't disappear, they just end up in later Tarzan pix as villains. At least, that's the jump Jock Mahoney made from 1962's *Tarzan Goes to India* to this patchwork of three TV shows, in which he plays a jungle dictator. Although no longer the lead, Mahoney nabs pic's best line—and heartiest laugh. As efforts fail to rescue a cohort sinking fast in quicksand, he shouts, "Chico, get out of there."

Excepting that bright moment, film (second of such tube adaptations, other being *Tarzan's Jungle Rebellion*) painfully corroborates just how drab TV techniques can be when subjected to the concentration level of a theatre. Every action or piece of dialog is redundantly reiterated (broadcast style) as the grenade-deafened apeman (Ron Ely) attempts escape from the evil "Colonel" (Mahoney) plus accomplice or two.

Area is a patch of jungle apparently no larger than Central Park Zoo. No wonder, as the cliché-bound script explains, Tarzan "knows this jungle like the back of his hand."

•

TARZAN'S DESERT MYSTERY

1943, 70 mins, US b/w

Dir William Thiele ***Prod*** Sol Lesser ***Scr*** Edward T. Lowe ***Ph*** Harry Wild, Russell Harlan ***Ed*** Ray Lockert ***Mus*** Paul Sawtell ***Art*** Hans Peters, Ralph Berger

Act Johnny Weissmuller, Nancy Kelly, Johnny Sheffield, Otto Kruger, Joe Sawyer, Lloyd Corrigan (Lesser/RKO)

Tarzan's Desert Mystery doesn't miss a thing with its quota of Nazi agents and gruesome animals, plus the usual Tarzan jungle scenes. Picture [from a screen story by Carroll Young] opens with Tarzan (Johnny Weissmuller), Boy (Johnny Sheffield) and the chimp Cheetah setting out across a desert to find a cure-all herb ordered by Mrs. Tarzan in London. On the way they run into Connie Bryce (Nancy Kelly), an American vaude performer who is on her way to warn a local sheik that Hendrix (Otto Kruger) and Karl (Joe Sawyer) are a couple of Nazi agents trying to stir up trouble. Things look tough for Tarzan and his crew when he is accused of stealing a stallion intended for the sheik, and Connie is framed on a murder charge and sentenced to be hanged.

Kelly turns in a workmanlike performance as an American magician. Weissmuller, young Sheffield and Cheetah are per usual. Kruger just dosen't belong as the Nazi. Film is nicely paced and photography highly effective.

•

TARZAN'S FIGHT FOR LIFE

1958, 86 mins, US col

Dir H. Bruce Humberstone ***Prod*** Sol Lesser ***Scr*** Thomas Hal Phillips ***Ph*** William Snyder ***Ed*** Aaron Stell ***Mus*** Ernest Gold

Act Gordon Scott, Eve Brent, Rickie Sorensen, Jil Jarmyn, James Edwards, Woody Strode (Lesser/M-G-M)

Metro is putting a big push behind *Tarzan's Fight for Life*. The current Sol Lesser production has handsome color, capable acting and able direction. If the campaign is to be carried through, however, the approach and writing will have to be lifted above the current level, which is persistently juvenile.

This chapter has Tarzan involved with a medical outpost headed by Dr. Sturdy (Carl Benton Reid). The natives are wary of the scientific experiments and their natural superstition is given a healthy assist by witch doctor Futa (James Edwards), eager to stir them up for reasons of his own.

Gordon Scott again plays the title role and makes a good Tarzan. He makes the athletic stunts believable and possible and he also handles the few romantic scenes with Eve Brent with acceptable finesse.

H. Bruce Humberstone's direction gets all possible action and excitement out of the script, and camera work is effective. The 16mm African photography by Miki Carter [who also worked on the previous *Tarzan and the Lost Safari*] does not contain any particularly new or exciting material, although it is visually appealing.

•

TARZAN'S GREATEST ADVENTURE

1959, 90 mins, UK col

Dir John Guillermin ***Prod*** Sy Weintraub ***Scr*** Berne Giler, John Guillermin ***Ph*** Ted Scaife ***Ed*** Bert Rule ***Mus*** Douglas Gamley ***Art*** Michael Stringer

Act Gordon Scott, Anthony Quayle, Sara Shane, Niall MacGinnis, Sean Connery, Scilla Gabel (Solar)

Tarzan finally steps away from Hollywood's process screens to pound his chest amid authentic terrors in the heart of Africa. Death and trauma are the stars, and the supporting players are bullets, arrows, knives, hatchets, dynamite, neck-choking paraphernalia, crocodiles, lions, snakes, spiders, boulders, spikes, pits, quicksand and prickly cactus. It's a furious affair, with an exciting chase or two.

Tarzan (Gordon Scott) is a modern he-man, still adorned in loincloth but more conversational than Edgar Rice Burroughs pictured him. Scott puts little emotion into his greatest adventure, but he swings neatly from tree to tree, takes good care of a crocodile, even if it does appear dead from the start, deciphers with ease the sounds of his animal friends and, more than anything else, looks the part.

Film's storyline [by Les Crutchfield] has Tarzan and another white man as mortal enemies. The antagonist (Anthony Quayle) is leading a five-member boat expedition to get rich in diamonds, and Tarzan, knowing of his bestial attitude, follows in hot pursuit. An approximately beautiful female (Sara Shane) drops out of the sky to tag along with Tarzan and turns out to be quite handy in helping the apeman through a bad time or two.

Quayle is excellent as the scarfaced villain, and Niall MacGinnis as a nearly blind diamond expert is equally fine. Sean Connery and Al Mulock, the two other male members of the expedition, are okay, and Scilla Gabel, looking like a miniature Sophia Loren, is easy to look at.

•

TARZAN'S HIDDEN JUNGLE

1955, 72 mins, US b/w

Dir Harold Schuster ***Prod*** Sol Lesser ***Scr*** William Lively ***Ph*** William Whitney ***Ed*** Leon Barsha ***Mus*** Paul Sawtell ***Art*** William Flannery

Act Gordon Scott, Vera Miles, Peter Van Eyck, Jack Elam, Charles Fredericks, Richard Reeves (Lesser/RKO)

Tarzan's Hidden Jungle is a stock entry in the Edgar Rice Burroughs apeman marathon and serves to introduce a new title hero. Gordon Scott, succeeding Lex Barker who last played the character, is a well-muscled man but seldom convincing in the part.

A pair of hunters (Jack Elam, Charles Fredericks), who have a contract to deliver fats, skins, heads and ivory, are the heavies and they receive rough justice when an elephant stampede tramples them to death. Intervening footage shows them accompanying a United Nations doctor (Peter Van Eyck) who thinks they are cameramen, into savage country where he is the only white allowed. Their purpose is to drive the vast number of animals out of this territory so they can slaughter them without fear of the natives. Tarzan defeats this intention, simultaneously saving the doctor and the latter's nurse (Vera Miles).

Harold Schuster's direction rarely rises above the script deficiencies, and the insertion of stock animal footage fails to match the quality of the footage proper. Zippy, a new Cheetah, and another chimp, Lucky, are the real cuties of this show.

•

TARZAN'S MAGIC FOUNTAIN

1949, 73 mins, US b/w

Dir Lee Sholem ***Prod*** Sol Lesser ***Scr*** Curt Siodmak, Henry Chandlee ***Ph*** Karl Struss ***Ed*** Merrill White ***Mus*** Alexander Laszlo ***Art*** Phil Paradise

Act Lex Barker, Brenda Joyce, Albert Dekker, Evelyn Ankers, Charles Drake, Alan Napier (Lesser/RKO)

The tenth screen Tarzan makes his appearance in *Tarzan's Magic Fountain* in the person of Lex Barker. Since Edgar Rice Burroughs's character is practically foolproof in the hands of any male with the proper heft, Barker seems earmarked for a long career of swinging through cimematic jungles.

A mythical fountain of youth is the springboard for adventure in this one, and all the stock ingredients are there to supply the chimerical thrills. As important to *Fountain* as the humans is the spotlighting of Cheetah, the chimp, and her ape pal. For humor that jells, there's little that can match the human antics of the anthropoids.

Plot has Tarzan rescuing an aviatrix (Evelyn Ankers), lost for 20 years in a mythical jungle valley where the residents never grow old. Greed of two traders (Albert Dekker, Charles Drake) and their efforts to learn the secret of eternal life keep Tarzan in hot water and supply most of the motivation.

Brenda Joyce is back again as Tarzan's mate, Jane, and does okay by the role. Lee Sholem's direction has a number of slow spots, particularly in dialog scenes between the humans, but otherwise furnishes a good pace to the action.

•

TARZAN'S NEW YORK ADVENTURE

1942, 70 mins, US Ⓥ b/w

Dir Richard Thorpe ***Prod*** Frederick Stephani ***Scr*** William R. Lipman, Myles Connolly ***Ph*** Sidney Wagner ***Ed*** Gene Ruggiero ***Mus*** David Snell ***Art*** Cedric Gibbons, Howard Campbell

Act Johnny Weissmuller, Maureen O'Sullivan, John Sheffield, Virginia Grey, Charles Bickford, Paul Kelly (M-G-M)

Like others of its series, this is in the groove for the juves and holds little for adults. Maybe even less this time, considering the extraordinary amount of footage the director gave—and the cutter permitted to remain—to the antics of the trained chimp.

Seventy minutes of jungle hoss opry is interspliced with Mr. and Mrs. Tarzan's adventures in N.Y. regaining their adopted son, carried off by an unscrupulous hunter who figured he could clean up with the kid in a circus. Charles Bickford plays that menace and Cy Kendall is his sidekick, as owner of a one-ring show. Chill Wills and Paul Kelly are involved with them, but they go to the aid of the jungle parents when the latter pull the rescue in the metropolis.

All the situations are trite, even including Tarzan's 200-foot dive off the Brooklyn Bridge to escape some cops who just don't understand the jungle-man. In the end, of course, everything works out right for the Tarzan family and back they go to dear old darkest Africa.

There's all the usual swinging-from-the-trees and animal stuff, and the photography and direction are standard. Performances ditto, with Johnny Weissmuller not improving as an actor, but pretty Maureen O'Sullivan, as his missus, and John Sheffield, as the junior Tarzan, compensate for him to a great extent. [Screen story by Myles Connolly.]

•

TARZAN'S PERIL

1951, 79 mins, US b/w

Dir Byron Haskin, Phil Brandon ***Prod*** Sol Lesser ***Scr*** Samuel Newman, Francis Swann, John Cousins ***Ph*** Karl Struss, Jack Whitehead ***Ed*** Jack Murray ***Mus*** Michel Michelet ***Art*** John Meehan

Act Lex Barker, Virginia Huston, George Macready, Douglas Fowley, Glenn Anders, Dorothy Dandridge (Lesser/ RKO)

This latest entry in the *Tarzan* series has the familiar ingredients of jungle adventure, plus good background footage actually lensed in Africa.

Lex Barker is a capable hero in his Tarzan character. Script could have made him even more of a superman, but otherwise does not let down the fans of the Edgar Rice Burroughs creation.

Tarzan is called upon to mete out jungle justice to a gunrunner who supplies forbidden weapons to a tribe of would-be warriors. The script has the hero swinging through trees, swimming rivers, surviving a plunge over a waterfall and taking on a whole tribe in battle before establishing peace and quiet again in his native heath.

Virginia Huston has only a few scenes as Tarzan's mate, Jane, in the footage. There's more emphasis on Dorothy Dandridge, queen of a tribe that is saved by Tarzan from its warring rivals. George Macready is the able villain.

•

TARZAN'S REVENGE

1938, 70 mins, US Ⓥ b/w

Dir D. Ross Lederman ***Prod*** Sol Lesser ***Scr*** Robert Lee Johnson, Jay Vann ***Ph*** George Meehan ***Ed*** Eugene Milford ***Mus*** Hugo Riesenfeld ***Art*** Lewis J. Rachmil

Act Glenn Morris, Eleanor Holm, George Barbier, C. Henry Gordon, Hedda Hopper, George Meeker (Principal/20th Century-Fox)

Screen's new Tarzan, Glenn Morris, and the swimmer Eleanor Holm romp, swim, run and swing through trees in another of Edgar Rice Burroughs's fables about the kid's hero who grew up with the animals. There are a few laughs, intentional and otherwise, to strengthen the entertainment value for adult trade.

A minor fault of the picture is that it's too long, frequently becoming draggy through repetition and lack of dramatic variation. Menace is an ever-present factor, however, and the suspense is at times rather well maintained. Both human and animal dangers coat the action as it follows a safari across a part of Africa to the hidden mansion of a villainous king who's after the girl.

Morris's feats on ropes between trees and elsewhere, including in the water, make him a highly acceptable Tarzan. His physique is what the fiction hero calls for. Cast in support includes George Barbier as the American Babbitt who's looking for trophies; his wife, played well by Hedda Hopper; the spoiled-type hunter, George Meeker, and C. Henry Gordon as the native ruler.

•

TARZAN'S SAVAGE FURY

1952, 81 mins, US b/w

Dir Cy Endfield ***Prod*** Sol Lesser ***Scr*** Cyril Hume, Hans Jacoby, Shirley White ***Ph*** Karl Struss ***Ed*** Frank Sullivan ***Mus*** Paul Sawtell ***Art*** Walter Keller

Act Lex Barker, Dorothy Hart, Patric Knowles, Charles Korvin, Tommy Carlton (Lesser/RKO)

A series of unexciting jungle heroics are offered in *Tarzan's Savage Fury*. The long-lived film series introduces a sort of

Tarzan, Jr., in the person of young Joey (Tommy Carlton), a jungle boy taken in by Tarzan and Jane (Lex Barker, Dorothy Hart). Moppet tags along when the jungle lord and ride lead a party into dangerous Wazuri country on a diamond hunt.

Tarzan has been sold a bill of goods by Rokov (Charles Korvin) and Edwards (Patric Knowles), latter posing as Tarzan's English cousin, that the diamonds are for England's war industry. Trek through jungle and over desert and mountains is dragged out very slowly by Cy Endfield's direction.

Carlton is introduced while being used as crocodile bait by some native hunters. Kid's muscular physique fits in with the demands of the series. Technical credits are standard.

●

TARZAN'S SECRET TREASURE

1941, 82 mins, US b/w

Dir Richard Thorpe ***Prod*** B. P. Fineman ***Scr*** Myles Connolly, Paul Gangelin ***Ph*** Clyde De Vinna ***Ed*** Gene Ruggiero ***Mus*** David Snell ***Art*** Cedric Gibbons, Howard Campbell

Act Johnny Weissmuller, Maureen O'Sullivan, Johnny Sheffield, Reginald Owen, Barry Fitzgerald, Tom Conway (M-G-M)

Picture is a par entry in the series. Early section of the yarn displays the usual animal stuff, with comedy antics of the pet simian, Cheetah, providing elemental laughs.

The secret treasure turns out to be gold, which is plentiful among the rocks of the high escarpment on which the Tarzan group lives. After Tarzan saves a band of explorers and scientists from the nearby savage tribe, greedy members of the band figure to move in on the golden hill. Picture swings into straight meller for the second half, with several sequences devoted to miraculous escapes by Tarzan from death.

Weissmuller adequately handles the Tarzan role in his usual style, with Maureen O'Sullivan as his jungle mate and Johnny Sheffield their offspring. O'Sullivan carries quite an English accent into the jungle, which is apparent throughout. Direction by Richard Thorpe injects a good pace to the script.

●

TARZAN'S THREE CHALLENGES

1963, 92 mins, UK/US ▭ col

Dir Robert Day ***Prod*** Sy Weintraub ***Scr*** Berne Giler, Robert Day ***Ph*** Ted Scaife ***Ed*** Fred Burnley ***Mus*** Joseph Horovitz ***Art*** Wilfrid Shingleton

Act Jock Mahoney, Woody Strode, Tsuruko Kobayashi, Earl Cameron, Jimmy Jamal, Anthony Chinn (Weintraub/M-G-M)

In an effort to prevent Tarzan from becoming a ludicrous anachronism in a world looking to space geography for its new mysteries and exotic characters of fantasy, producer Sy Weintraub and his creative unit have gradually converted the character from the simple apeman to a globetrotting troubleshooter, a kind of one-man Peace Corps in loincloth. But, in thus broadening the scope, they have stripped the character of much of its distinguishing identity. Tarzan is a man without a country and with only a shred of his former personality. In *Tarzan's Three Challenges*, he has been transplanted to Thailand to escort a young spiritual heir (Ricki Der) from a monastery to his rightful throne at the head of an ancient land. To protect his charge, Tarzan must ward off the challenge of the brother, Kahn Tarim (Woody Strode), of the dying ruler.

Some interesting socio-political ramifications of the power struggle between the brother, who represents the radical younger faction of the tribe, and the young heir-apparent, who represents tradition, are touched upon but eventually submerged by the requirements of physical action.

For the purists and the kiddies, there are vines in the Thailand jungle for Tarzan to go tree-hopping on. Strode is a most impressive figure as the antagonist, and also briefly enacts the role of the dying chieftain. The production is notable for a smattering of culture.

●

TARZAN THE APE MAN

1932, 70 mins, US Ⓥ b/w

Dir W. S. Van Dyke ***Prod*** [uncredited] ***Scr*** Cyril Hume, Ivor Novello ***Ph*** Harold Rosson, Clyde De Vinna ***Ed*** Ben Lewis, Tom Held ***Mus*** [uncredited] ***Art*** Cedric Gibbons

Act Johnny Weissmuller, Maureen O'Sullivan, Neil Hamilton, C. Aubrey Smith, Doris Lloyd, Forrester Harvey (M-G-M)

A jungle and stunt picture, done in deluxe style, with tricky handling of fantastic atmosphere, and a fine, artless performance by the Olympic athlete that represents the absolute best that could be done with the character [created by Edgar Rice Burroughs].

Footage is loaded with a wealth of sensational wild animal stuff. Suspicion is unavoidable that some of it is cut-in material left over from the same producer's *Trader Horn* (by the same director).

Some of the stunt episodes are grossly overdone, but the production skill and literary treatment in other directions compensates. Tarzan (Johnny Weissmuller) is pictured as achieving impossible feats of strength and daring. One of them has him battling single-handed, and armed only with an inadequate knife, not only with one lion but with a panther and two lions, and saved at the last minute from still a third big cat only by the friendly help of an elephant summoned by a call of distress in jungle language.

Story that introduces the Tarzan character is slight. An English trader (C. Aubrey Smith) and his young partner (Neil Hamilton) are about to start in search of the traditional elephants' graveyard where ivory abounds, when the elder man's daughter from England (Maureen O'Sullivan) appears at the trading post and insists upon going along. The adventures grow out of their travels.

●

TARZAN, THE APE MAN

1959, 82 mins, US col

Dir Joseph Newman ***Prod*** Al Zimbalist ***Scr*** Robert Hill ***Ph*** Paul C. Vogel ***Ed*** Gene Ruggiero ***Mus*** Shorty Rogers ***Art*** Hans Peters, Malcolm Brown

Act Denny Miller, Cesare Danova, Robert Douglas, Joanna Barnes, Thomas Yangha (M-G-M)

Metro has remade its 1932 Johnny Weissmuller–Maureen O'Sullivan starrer, *Tarzan the Ape Man*, and the story is even more implausible than it was 27 years earlier.

In recent years Tarzan has encountered everything from Amazons and slave girls to mermaids and she-devils, but never has he met anything quite like Jane. He meets her, falls in love with her, wins her love and ultimately takes her as his wife. It's quite a feat considering he's unable to mutter even "Me Tarzan!"

To be sure, there will be snickers when Jane, the rapacious but gentle Englishwoman, gives up the riches of ivory to spend her life in a paradise of crocodiles. But producer Al Zimbalist has made sure the adventure along the way is furious enough and the dangers overpowering enough to result in an entertaining, fast-moving film.

Denny Miller has his first to-do with the Tarzan character and is able to get by without revealing whether or not he is as strong an actor as he is a tree-swinger. Joanna Barnes makes a fetching Jane, proving herself to be a better actress than the part demands. Cesare Danova is fine as a rather ruthless fortune seeker, and Robert Douglas is very good as Jane's father. Zimbalist apparently has garnered his jungle footage from a myriad of sources.

Not quite so effective, however, are black-and-white cut-ins from previous jungle films, and one underwater fight looks suspiciously like another Tarzan, perhaps Weissmuller himself.

The musical score was composed and conducted by contemporary artist Shorty Rogers. His sound is a whole lot more modern than the film's period, but the interest overcomes the anachronism.

●

TARZAN THE APE MAN

1981, 112 mins, US Ⓥ ⊙ col

Dir John Derek ***Prod*** Bo Derek ***Scr*** Tom Rowe, Gary Goddard ***Ph*** John Derek, Wolfgang Dickmann ***Ed*** James B. Ling ***Mus*** Perry Botkin ***Art*** Alan Roderick-Jones

Act Bo Derek, Richard Harris, John Phillip Law, Miles O'Keeffe, Wilfrid Hyde White (M-G-M/Svengali)

This endless romp through the jungle, lacking any focus, fun or excitement (sexual or otherwise), seems to exist merely as a reason for husband John to find another 1001 ways to photograph wife, Bo, in varying stages of undress.

With about three minutes shaved as a result of a court decision stating that the Dereks and M-G-M went beyond the remake rights bought from the Burroughs estate, this opus will disappoint both Tarzan fans and Bo admirers.

A supposed remake of the 1932 *Tarzan the Ape Man*, the Derek version has less to do with the jungle man (who doesn't show his face until halfway through the picture) than it does in dealing with Jane's (Bo's) rediscovery of her long-lost explorer father, Richard Harris. The father-daughter relationship doesn't have a chance here with Bo's wooden recitation of her lines and Harris's ranting through any number of dreary, confusing speeches.

Although John Derek's direction remains loose and uninspired (the few action shots of Tarzan are ruined with corny slow-motion footage), he does know how to shoot pretty pictures of Sri Lanka and, more particularly, Bo. If *Tarzan* were a magazine layout, he'd probably be nominated for something.

●

TARZAN THE FEARLESS

1933, 60 mins, US Ⓥ b/w

Dir Robert Hill, William Lord Wright ***Prod*** Sol Lesser ***Scr*** Basil Dickey, George Plympton, Walter Anthony ***Ph*** Harry Neuman, Joe Brotherton ***Ed*** Carl Himm

Act Buster Crabbe, Jacqueline Wells, E. Alyn Warren, Edward Woods, Philo McCullough, Mischa Auer (Lesser/Principal)

Episode is loaded with shots clipped from hunt films and burdened with forced situations and yard after yard of Buster Crabbe doing his daily dozen in the jungle gym. Same old chimp whispers secrets in his ear and the same old lion tries to put a little spirit into a man-and-lion wrestle that has become boresome to him. This time the lion has two bouts with Crabbe and a prelim with one of the heavies, all inside of 60 minutes.

Crabbe also has a struggle with a crocodile, this sequence being hurt by the fact that a prop animal is towed in the scenes in which the girl is shown. Crabbe does his rough and tumble with a real croc.

Plot concerns Tarzan's interest in the daughter, Mary (Jacqueline Wells), of a scientist, Dr. Brooks (E. Alyn Warren), who is looking for the people of Zar and is made prisoner. His safari is guided by a couple of scoundrels who are after the emeralds which tradition ascribes to Zar.

Action ends rather abruptly with Tarzan admiring the girl in his cave. For all the audience knows, they set up light housekeeping there. [Pic was designed as a feature-length first chapter of a serial, to be followed by eight two-reelers, though this was not explained at the New York public showing the reviewer attended.]

Story is haltingly told in poor dialog and no one in the cast gets a chance with the material at hand.

●

TARZAN THE MAGNIFICENT

1960, 82 mins, UK/US col

Dir Robert Day ***Prod*** Sy Weintraub, Harvey Hayutin ***Scr*** Berne Giler, Robert Day ***Ph*** Ted Scaife ***Ed*** Bert Rule ***Mus*** Ken Jones ***Art*** Ray Simm

Act Gordon Scott, Jock Mahoney, Betta St. John, John Carradine, Lionel Jeffries, Alexander Stewart (Weintraub/Paramount)

In updating *Tarzan* to fit what they seem to feel are modern specifications, producers have taken most of the charm and vigor out of the character. Their jet-age *Tarzan* has lost his identity, and emerges anything but "The Magnificent" in this film. Instead, audiences will discover a rather glum, earthbound, unexciting version of the ape man in a slow-moving picture.

Also a victim of jet-age accessibility is the once fascinating and mysterious, primitive appeal of the Dark Continent. It has become the setting for a routine chase that might, save for an occasional lion or crocodile, just as easily have occurred in a western. It is concerned with Tarzan's efforts to bring a criminal to justice through treacherous jungle terrain, pursued by the criminal's evil family and slowed up by the haggling of his own entourage, which includes a cowardly Britisher (Lionel Jeffries) whose unstable wife (Betta St. John) is sexually attracted to the captive. Only briefly, near the climax, does the reckless, tree-swinging Tarzan of old emerge.

The acting surpasses the material, although Gordon Scott, as Tarzan, seems uncomfortable in the role and brings it little more than an ample physique. There is good work from Jock Mahoney as the captive. Director Day hasn't made things easy on his cast. In striving for realism he has immersed them neck-deep in swamp mud during several passages.

●

TARZAN TRIUMPHS

1943, 76 mins, US b/w

Dir William Thiele ***Prod*** Sol Lesser ***Scr*** Roy Chanslor, Carroll Young ***Ph*** Harry Wild ***Ed*** Hal Kern ***Mus*** Paul Sawtell ***Art*** Harry Horner

Act Johnny Weissmuller, Johnny Sheffield, Frances Gifford, Stanley Ridges, Sig Ruman, Philip Van Zandt (Principal/RKO)

This is the first of at least two Tarzan features that Sol Lesser will turn out for RKO release, after Metro wound up its interest in the jungleman's adventures last fall [with *Tarzan's New York Adventure*]. Virtually all jungle stuff, *Tarzan Triumphs* [from a screen story by Carroll Young] has good portion of stock animal shots and includes a hidden city for convenient takeover by a squad of Nazi paratroops and subsequent battle in which Tarzan, with the aid of the subjugated natives, knocks off the invaders and restores peace in the jungle territory.

Usual tree-swinging, dashes through the jungle undergrowth, and other familiar Tarzanian ingredients are again on display. Also Boy (little Johnny Sheffield), the chimp Cheetah and the small elephant. Inability to obtain Maureen

O'Sullivan for this picture switches script for her to be visiting in England, with Frances Gifford filling in as the girl from the hidden city.

Weissmuller and Sheffield run around as usual without necessity of displaying much acting ability. Direction by William Thiele hits usual standard for the Tarzan features.

•

TASK FORCE
1949, 116 mins, US Ⓥ col
Dir Delmer Daves ***Prod*** Jerry Wald ***Scr*** Delmer Daves ***Ph*** Robert Burks, Wilfrid M. Cline ***Ed*** Alan Crosland, Jr. ***Mus*** Franz Waxman
Act Gary Cooper, Jane Wyatt, Wayne Morris, Walter Brennan, Julie London, Bruce Bennett (Warner)

Starring Gary Cooper, *Task Force* glorifies the birth and development of the American aircraft carrier, up to the part it played in the Second World War.

This is a story about a handful of naval air heroes who, in the early 1920s, seek to assert naval air power but are stymied for years by Washington politics and navy protocol. Eventually, through the aircraft carrier, they're able to whip the rubber-stamp admirals by proving themselves in the Pacific during the war.

Cooper is forthright as the naval hero, and Jane Wyatt is properly sacrificing as his wife.

•

TASTE OF HONEY, A
1961, 100 mins, UK Ⓥ b/w
Dir Tony Richardson ***Prod*** Tony Richardson ***Scr*** Shelagh Delaney, Tony Richardson ***Ph*** Walter Lassally ***Ed*** Antony Gibbs ***Mus*** John Addison ***Art*** Ralph Brinton
Act Dora Bryan, Rita Tushingham, Robert Stephens, Murray Melvin, Paul Danquah (Woodfall)

Shelagh Delaney's play, which clicked both in the West End and on Broadway, has an earthy gusto and sincerity that lift its somewhat downbeat theme and drab surroundings. It has humor, understanding and poignance. Oddly enough the dialog, though pointedly couched in the semi-illiterate vernacular of the lower-class North Country working folk, achieves at times a halting and touching form of poetry.

The film faithfully follows the narrative of the play. But the camera effectively gets into the streets and captures the gray drabness of the locals as well as the boisterous vulgarity of Blackpool, saloons and dance-halls. Yarn primarily concerns five people and their dreams, hopes and fears. They are Jo (Rita Tushingham); her flighty, sluttish neglectful mother; the fancy man her mother marries; a young Negro ship's cook with whom Jo has a brief affair which leaves her pregnant; and a sensitive young homosexual who gives her the tenderness and affection lacking in her relationship with her mother.

Film introduces 19-year-old Rita Tushingham as the 16-year-old schoolgirl. She plays with no makeup, her hair is untidy, her profile completely wrong by all accepted standards; but her expressive eyes and her warm, wry smile are haunting.

Dora Bryan tackles the role of the flighty, footloose mother with confidence and zest. The three men in the lives of daughter and mother are also played with keen insight by Robert Stephens, Paul Danquah and Murray Melvin. Perhaps the most difficult role is that of Melvin. He repeats the success he made of the part of the young homosexual in the play.

•

TASTE THE BLOOD OF DRACULA
1970, 95 mins, UK Ⓥ col
Dir Peter Sasdy ***Prod*** Aida Young ***Scr*** John Elder [= Anthony Hinds] ***Ph*** Arthur Grant ***Ed*** Chris Barnes ***Mus*** James Bernard ***Art*** Scott MacGregor
Act Christopher Lee, Linda Hayden, Anthony Corlan, Geoffrey Keen, Gwen Watford, Peter Sallis (Hammer)

The setting is in Victorian England, on London's fringes, and concerns three hypocritical, erotic old buffers who, sated by their dingy little orgies in the East End, look for bigger, more lustful thrills. They get entangled with one of Dracula's disciples and, with the aid of the blood of Dracula and some of his "props," sold to them by a wise peddler, they start to dabble in Black Mass and Satanic ritual. They bump off Dracula's messenger in terror and Dracula swears to dispose of the three men.

From then on, it's the old routine of Dracula causing death and disaster, upsetting the families by abducting daughters and turning one of them into a vampire and generally making himself a thundering evil nuisance.

•

TAXI!
1932, 70 mins, US b/w
Dir Roy Del Ruth ***Prod*** [uncredited] ***Scr*** Kubec Glasmon, John Bright ***Ph*** James Van Trees ***Ed*** James Gibbon ***Mus*** Leo F. Forbstein (dir.) ***Art*** Esdras Hartley
Act James Cagney, Loretta Young, George E. Stone, Guy Kibbee, Leila Bennett, Dorothy Burgess (Warner)

An hour's entertainment for the boys in the now established golden-hearted-hoodlum manner of James Cagney.

Foundation of the tale [from the play by Kenyon Nicholson] is the strife of the independent taxi owner whom the syndicates run off the most desirable corner stands. This leads to the girl's father drawing a jail sentence when he shoots the truck driver he knows has purposely smashed his cab because he defied the leader of the strong arm squad. She's on her own after that, first battling with Cagney, then marrying him and finally trying to save him from killing this same leader.

Taxi! speeds along interestingly until near the finish, where the script cheats Cagney of his revenge and thereby saves him from prison. It's a scenario compromise which will leave the majority of fans unsatisfied. Weaving through the plot are George E. Stone and Leila Bennett, as friends of the lovers, with Bennett doing an exceptionally good piece of work as a dumb, prattling waitress. Further player support is unimportant, although Dorothy Burgess convinces in doing the menace's moll.

Loretta Young does better than usual as the orphaned miss. At least there is more solidity to her portrayal than is generally so in her case.

The dialog is distinctly in the vernacular of the characters, director Roy Del Ruth has given it pace, and Cagney jauntily carries the major burden.

The director, incidentally, has also given the film a corking laugh start in Cagney conversationally rescuing a well-played old Hebrew from a cop.

•

TAXI DRIVER
1976, 113 mins, US Ⓥ ⊙ col
Dir Martin Scorsese ***Prod*** Michael Phillips, Julia Phillips ***Scr*** Paul Schrader, [Julia Cameron] ***Ph*** Michael Chapman ***Ed*** Marcia Lucas, Tom Rolf, Melvin Shapiro ***Mus*** Bernard Herrmann ***Art*** Charles Rosen
Act Robert De Niro, Cybill Shepherd, Jodie Foster, Peter Boyle, Albert Brooks, Leonard Harris, Harvey Keitel (Columbia)

Assassins, mass murderers and other freakish criminals more often than not turn out to be the quiet kid down the street. *Taxi Driver* is Martin Scorsese's frighteningly plausible case history of such a person. It's a powerful film and a terrific showcase for the versatility of star Robert De Niro.

The pic has a quasi-documentary look, and Bernard Herrmann's final score is superb (a final credit card conveys "Our gratitude and respect"). Paul Schrader's original screenplay is in fact a sociological horror story. Take a young veteran like Travis Bickle. A night cabbie, he prowls the N.Y. streets until dawn, stopping occasionally for coffee, killing offduty time in porno theatres.

What prods Travis are a series of rejections: among others by Cybill Shepherd, adroitly cast as the tele-heroine lookalike working for the presidential campaign of Leonard Harris, and by Jodie Foster, teenage prostitute.

In a climactic sequence, the madman exorcises himself. It's a brutal, horrendous and cinematically brilliant sequence, capped by the irony that he becomes a media hero for a day.

De Niro gives the role the precise blend of awkwardness, naïveté and latent violence.

1976: NOMINATIONS: Best Picture, Actor (Robert De Niro), Supp. Actress (Jodie Foster), Original Score

•

TAXING WOMAN, A
SEE: MARUSA NO ONNA

•

TAZA, SON OF COCHISE
1954, 79 mins, US col
Dir Douglas Sirk ***Prod*** Ross Hunter ***Scr*** George Zuckerman, Gerald Drayson Adams ***Ph*** Russell Metty ***Ed*** Milton Carruth ***Mus*** Frank Skinner
Act Rock Hudson, Barbara Rush, Gregg Palmer, Bart Roberts, Morris Ankrum, Gene Iglesias (Universal)

Taza, Son of Cochise is a colorful 3-D Indian–U.S. Cavalry entry alternating between hot action and passages of almost pastoral quality. The spectacular scenery of Moab, Utah, furnishes a particularly apropos background for unfoldment of the script, and Douglas Sirk's direction is forceful, aimed at making every scene an eye-filling experience.

This is the story of the great Apache chief's son, who promises at his father's death bed he will try to keep the peace that Cochise so painstakingly made with the whites. He is opposed here by his younger brother, who attempts to win the tribe over to Geronimo and take to the warpath again.

Rock Hudson suffices in action demands of his role of Taza, but character is none too believable. Barbara Rush, co-starring as the daughter of Morris Ankrum, one of Geronimo's followers, is in for romantic purposes and handles part well.

Jeff Chandler, who was Cochise in studio's *Battle at Apache Pass*, repeats character for the single death-bed scene, without screen credit.

•

TEA AND SYMPATHY
1956, 122 mins, US Ⓥ ⊙ ⌑ col
Dir Vincente Minnelli ***Prod*** Pandro S. Berman ***Scr*** Robert Anderson ***Ph*** John Alton ***Ed*** Ferris Webster ***Mus*** Adolph Deutsch ***Art*** William A. Horning, Edward Carfagno
Act Deborah Kerr, John Kerr, Leif Erickson, Edward Andrews, Darryl Hickman, Norma Crane (M-G-M)

This is the story of a youngster regarded by fellow students as "not regular" (i.e., not manly). The spotlight is on clearly implied homosexuality.

Robert Anderson's adaptation of his own legiter keeps the essentials in proper focus. The pivotal role of the misunderstood sensitive boy is an excellently drawn characterization. The part is played with marked credibility by John Kerr. The housemaster's wife is a character study of equal sensitivity and depth. Deborah Kerr gives the role all it deserves.

The housemaster part, played with muscle-flexing exhibitionism by Leif Erickson, loses some of its meaning in the tone-down. On the stage his efforts at being "manly" carried the suggestion that he was trying to compensate a fear of a homo trend in his own makeup. The suggestion is diluted to absence in the picture.

Edward Andrews, as John Kerr's father, is the brash and understanding parent who would prefer to see his son carry on with the town tart to erase his "sister-boy" reputation.

•

TEACHERS
1984, 106 mins, US Ⓥ ⊙ col
Dir Arthur Hiller ***Prod*** Aaron Russo ***Scr*** W. R. McKinney ***Ph*** David M. Walsh ***Ed*** Don Zimmerman ***Mus*** Sandy Gibson (sup.) ***Art*** Richard MacDonald
Act Nick Nolte, JoBeth Williams, Judd Hirsch, Ralph Macchio, Lee Grant, Richard Mulligan (United Artists)

Teachers stars Nick Nolte as a burned-out teacher who's drawn back to his ideals. Social drama and irreverent, often broad comedy underscore this story of a zoolike urban high school that's run like an asylum. Pic makes stinging, important points about the mess of secondary public education, but those points are diluted gradually by an overload of comic absurdity.

Catalyst to dark comedy is a lawsuit brought against the school district for awarding a diploma to a student who can't read or write. JoBeth Williams plays the attorney serving notice on the school.

Filmmakers engaged a large cast of well-known performers: Lee Grant as calculating, ruthless school superintendent; Allen Garfield as a teacher afraid of his students but who turns heroic; Royal Dano as a glum disciplinarian; and, in the central student role, Ralph Macchio as a street-smart but illiterate kid who triggers Nolte's reemergence. Nolte nicely captures the image of a rather shaggy 10-year veteran of the classroom, and Williams is okay as his zealous nemesis.

Script was written by 27-year-old debuting screenwriter W. R. McKinney from a story conceived by producer Aaron Russo and his brother and exec producer Irwin Russo. Latter capitalized on his 10 years' experience as a teacher in New York.

•

TEACHER'S PET
1958, 120 mins, US Ⓥ ⊙ b/w
Dir George Seaton ***Prod*** William Perlberg ***Scr*** Fay Kanin, Michael Kanin ***Ph*** Haskell Boggs ***Ed*** Alma Macrorie ***Mus*** Roy Webb ***Art*** Hal Pereira, Earl Hedrick
Act Clark Gable, Doris Day, Gig Young, Mamie Van Doren, Nick Adams, Vivian Nathan (Perslea/Paramount)

There is rich new life and liveliness, and even a fresh approach with humor and heartiness, in Fay and Michael Kanin's original screenplay. Clark Gable is one of those crusty, old-line newspapermen who believes that nothing good comes out of colleges, certainly not out of schools of journalism. When he is invited to lecture by journalism professor Doris Day, he discovers his ideas about female professors were wrong.

For various reasons he must pretend he is not a city editor but a pupil. In trying to get this straightened out, his emotional relations with Day become more involved and they finally arrive at the expected conclusion.

This is the straight storyline, but the Kanins have decorated the framework with some hilarious comedy lines and scenes which director George Seaton has set up with skill and delivered with gusto. There is the sequence of Gable's reactions to a strip-tease by Mamie Van Doren; another between Gable and his rival for Day, Gig Young, where Young is suffering from the grandfather of all hangovers. These and a dozen other bright gags spark the story. It runs long (two hours) for a comedy but it holds up.

Gable frankly mugs through many of his comedy scenes and it is effective low comedy. Day is as bright and fresh as a newly set stick of type. Young gives the picture its funniest moments, milking the scenes with the expertness of a master.

1958: NOMINATIONS: Best Supp. Actor (Gig Young), Original Story and Screenplay

•

TEA FOR TWO

1950, 97 mins, US Ⓥ ⊙ col

Dir David Butler ***Prod*** William Jacobs ***Scr*** Harry Clork ***Ph*** Wilfrid M. Cline ***Ed*** Irene Morra ***Mus*** Ray Heindorf (dir.) ***Art*** Douglas Bacon

Act Doris Day, Gordon MacRae, Gene Nelson, Eve Arden, Billy De Wolfe, S. Z. Sakall (Warner)

A generous sprinkling of songs, dances and comedy makes *Tea for Two* the type of beguiling musical nonsense that practically always finds a ready reception. It wears its Technicolor dress well, the nostalgic numbers from the 1929 *No, No, Nanette* and other cleffing of the period listen well, the pacing is smooth and the cast able.

Suggested by the *Nanette* book by Frank Mandel, Otto Harbach, Vincent Youmans and Emil Nyitray, the script is spiced with dialog and situations that permit easy introduction of the variety of dance numbers [directed by LeRoy Prinz, staged by Eddie Prinz and Al White].

Flashback technique to get 1929 period on the screen has the capable help of S. Z. Sakall, playing Doris Day's uncle, who is telling the story to the children of the two singers.

•

TEAHOUSE OF THE AUGUST MOON, THE

1956, 123 mins, US Ⓥ ⊙ ▭ col

Dir Daniel Mann ***Prod*** Jack Cummings ***Scr*** John Patrick ***Ph*** John Alton ***Ed*** Harold F. Kress ***Mus*** Saul Chaplin, Kikuko Kanai ***Art*** William A. Horning, Eddie Imazu

Act Marlon Brando, Glenn Ford, Machiko Kyo, Eddie Albert, Paul Ford, Harry Morgan (M-G-M)

Teahouse retains the basic appeal that made it a unique war novel and a legit hit. There is some added slapstick for those who prefer their comedy broader. Adding to its prospects are some top comedy characterizations, notably from Glenn Ford, plus the offbeat casting of Marlon Brando in a comedy role.

In transferring his play based on the Vern Sneider novel to the screen, John Patrick has provided a subtle shift in the focal interest. Deft screenplay provides an interesting fillip in retaining the stage device of a narrative prolog and epilog by Brando, and the warmly humorous verbiage has been left intact. Storyline also is unsullied as the film unspools the tribulations of Ford, the young army officer assigned to bring the benefits of democracy and free enterprise to the little Okinawan town of Tobiki.

The role of Capt. Fisby represents a romp for Glenn Ford, who gives it an unrestrained portrayal that adds mightily to the laughs. Brando is excellent as the interpreter, limning the rogueish character perfectly. Physically, he seems a bit too heavy for the role.

Japanese actress Machiko Kyo is easy on the eyes as the geisha girl and there is excellent support from Eddie Albert, who sparkles as the psychiatrist who yearns to be an agricultural expert.

•

TEENAGE MUTANT NINJA TURTLES

1990, 93 mins, US Ⓥ ⊙ col

Dir Steve Barron ***Prod*** Kim Dawson, Simon Fields, David Chan ***Scr*** Todd W. Langen, Bobby Herbeck ***Ph*** John Fenner ***Ed*** William Gordean, Sally Menke, James Symons ***Mus*** John Du Prez ***Art*** Roy Forge Smith

Act Judith Hoag, Elias Koteas, Raymond Serra, Michael Turney, James Saito, Jay Patterson (Golden Harvest/Limelight)

While visually rough around the edges, sometimes sluggish in its plotting and marred by overtones of racism in its use of Oriental villains, the wacky live-action screen version of the *Teenage Mutant Ninja Turtles* cartoon characters [created by Kevin Eastman and Peter Laird] scores with its generally engaging tongue-in-cheek humor.

Supposedly mutated by radioactive goop, the turtles live in the sewers, eat pizza, dance to rock music, play Trivial Pursuit and casually toss around such words as "awesome," "bodacious" and "gnarly."

The screenplay makes all four of the green guys seem like clones, differentiated mostly by their variegated colored headbands. The plot is nothing more than some nonsense about the turtles and a handful of human sidekicks trying to stop the Foot Clan from terrorizing N.Y. streets.

A bit too much time is devoted to the peculiar romance of unbelievably funky TV newswoman Judith Hoag and her off-the-wall vigilante b.f. Elias Koteas, who join forces with the creatures and misunderstood j.d. Michael Turney.

The martial-arts set pieces are amusingly outlandish, with the screen populated by hordes of attackers whom the nonchalant, graceful turtles have little trouble vanquishing as they toss off streams of surfer-lingo wisecracks.

•

TEENAGE MUTANT NINJA TURTLES II: THE SECRET OF THE OOZE

1991, 88 mins, US Ⓥ ⊙ col

Dir Michael Pressman ***Prod*** Thomas K. Gray, Kim Dawson, David Chan ***Scr*** Todd W. Langen ***Ph*** Shelly Johnson ***Ed*** John Wright, Steve Mirkovich ***Mus*** John Du Prez ***Art*** Roy Forge Smith

Act Paige Turco, David Warner, Michelan Sisti, Leif Tilden, Kenn Troum, Mark Caso (Golden Harvest/Propper)

Though *Turtles II* suffers from a lack of novelty and an aimless screenplay, the bottom line is that the pic won't disappoint its core subteen audience. It gives more footage to Michelangelo, Donatello, Raphael, Leonardo and their giant rat master Splinter than the original did, and adds two hilarious childlike monsters, Rahzar and Tokka, who virtually steal the show.

The murky lighting, uninteresting human characters and violence of the original have been modified in the more amiable sequel, mostly to good effect.

Subtitle's promise that the ooze secret will be revealed doesn't pay off. David Warner, as the sympathetic and eccentric scientist who invented the stuff and now is trying to dispose of it, doesn't have much to do.

Paige Turco takes over the lead human role of Gotham TV newswoman April O'Neil from Judith Hoag, and while Turco is more glamorous, the character still seems unfocused and overly ditzy.

Ernie Reyes, Jr., has a winning role as a youthful pizza deliveryman/martial arts expert who wangles his way into the turtles' company and helps them in their neverending battle with the Foot Clan.

•

TEENAGE MUTANT NINJA TURTLES III: THE TURTLES ARE BACK . . . IN TIME

1993, 95 mins, US Ⓥ ⊙ col

Dir Stuart Gillard ***Prod*** Thomas Gray, Kim Dawson, David Chan ***Scr*** Stuart Gillard ***Ph*** David Gurfinkel ***Ed*** William Gordean, James Symons ***Mus*** John Du Prez ***Art*** Roy Forge Smith

Act Elias Koteas, Paige Turco, Stuart Wilson, Vivian Wu, Sab Shimono, Henry Hayashi (Golden Harvest)

Bow-wow-abunga! The third installment of *Teenage Mutant Ninja Turtles* is a decided case of diminishing returns. On a story and craft level it borders on the unforgivably bad.

The new episode is a time travel yarn in which the four amphibian heroes and their pal, reporter April O'Neil (Paige Turco), switch places with five 17th-century samurai warriors. This is all effected with questionable scientific aplomb and a device that resembles a vintage streetlamp.

In feudal Japan, they become embroiled in a struggle between two dynasties: Lord Norinaga (Sab Shimono) seeks to quash the rebel faction led by Mitsu (Vivian Wu) by enlisting the aid of the English mercenary and gunrunner Walker (Stuart Wilson).

Writer-director Stuart Gillard inappropriately paces the action at tortoise speed. Virtually every department fires wide. Performances range from competent to just plain embarrassing.

•

TEEN AGENT

SEE: IF LOOKS COULD KILL

•

TEEN WOLF

1985, 91 mins, US Ⓥ ⊙ col

Dir Rod Daniel ***Prod*** Mark Levinson, Scott Rosenfelt ***Scr*** Joseph Loeb III, Matthew Weisman ***Ph*** Tim Suhrstedt ***Ed*** Lois Freeman-Fox ***Mus*** Miles Goodman ***Art*** Rosemary Brandenberg

Act Michael J. Fox, James Hampton, Scott Paulin, Susan Ursitti, Jerry Levine, Jim Mackrell (Wolfkill/Atlantic)

Lightweight item is innocuous and well intentioned but terribly feeble, another example of a decent idea yielding the least imaginative results conceivable.

The Beacontown Beavers have the most pathetic basketball team in high school history, and pint-sized Michael J. Fox is on the verge of quitting when he notices certain biological changes taking place. Heavy hair is growing on the backs of his hands; his ears and teeth are elongating.

Instead of turning into a horrific teen werewolf, however, Fox takes to trucking around school halls in full furry regalia, becoming more successful with the ladies and, most importantly, winning basketball games.

Fox is likeable enough in the lead, something that cannot be said for the remainder of the lackluster cast.

•

TELEFON

1977, 103 mins, US Ⓥ col

Dir Don Siegel ***Prod*** James B. Harris ***Scr*** Peter Hyams, Stirling Silliphant ***Ph*** Michael Butler ***Ed*** Douglas Stewart ***Mus*** Lalo Schifrin ***Art*** Ted Haworth

Act Charles Bronson, Lee Remick, Tyne Daly, Donald Pleasence, Alan Badel, Sheree North (M-G-M)

Pleasant escapism, Don Siegel's film stars Charles Bronson and Lee Remick as two spies trying to stop a diehard Stalinist (Donald Pleasence) from upsetting detente by triggering a war between the U.S. and USSR.

Walter Wager's novel was adapted into a screenplay that is credited to Peter Hyams (once involved as a prospective director when Martin Elfand was the producer before he went to Warners) and Stirling Silliphant.

Intriguing premise is that old-line cold warriors in Russia are resisting detente and have activated some deep cover spies planted in the U.S. two decades ago under drug-induced hypnosis, ready to blow up key military sites on telephonic code cue.

Dalchimsky (Pleasence) escapes to the U.S. from a round-up of the Stalinists ordered by secret police toppers (Patrick Magee, Alan Badel). Borzov (Bronson) is recruited to come to the U.S. to eliminate the potential bombers before Dalchimsky triggers their response. Barbara (Remick) is supposedly a Russian agent.

Tyne Daly is notable as a CIA staffer. Remick's teaming with Bronson is a graceful one for both players.

•

TELL ME LIES
A FILM ABOUT LONDON

1968, 118 mins, UK/US col

Dir Peter Brook ***Prod*** Peter Brook ***Scr*** Denis Cannan ***Ph*** Ian Wilson ***Ed*** Ralph Sheldon ***Mus*** Richard Peaslee ***Art*** Sally Jacobs

Act Mark Jones, Pauline Munro, Robert Lloyd, Glenda Jackson, Paul Scofield, Kingsley Amis (Ronorus)

Tell Me Lies depicts a wide range of attitudes toward the war in Vietnam. It's loosely based on Peter Brook's theatrical success-de-scandale *US*.

While Brook's emotional concern about the war seems unquestionable, his artistic sincerity is open to examination. *Tell Me Lies* suggests an aesthetic bankruptcy resulting from the director's debts to Bertolt Brecht, Joan Littlewood (*Oh! What a Lovely War*) and Jean-Luc Godard.

Color and black-and-white footage is haphazardly alternated to no effect. Musical numbers are shouted-sung in a cacophonic manner that only underscores the lyrics' vacuity. Staged discussions are juxtaposed with cinema-verité encounters with British parliamentarians, Maoists and black-power advocate Stokely Carmichael.

Verbal material is splayed in subtitles at the bottom of the screen, overlapped on sequences or subliminally injected word by word within a continuous segment. It's all pretty ugly.

•

TELL ME THAT YOU LOVE ME, JUNIE MOON

1970, 112 mins, US col

Dir Otto Preminger ***Prod*** Otto Preminger ***Scr*** Marjorie Kellogg ***Ph*** Boris Kaufman ***Ed*** Henry Berman, Dean O. Ball ***Mus*** Philip Springer ***Art*** Morris Hoffman

Act Liza Minnelli, Ken Howard, Robert Moore, James Coco, Kay Thompson, Ben Piazza (Paramount)

Otto Preminger has given this tale [from Marjorie Kellogg's novel] of a trio of handicapped, scarred, emotionally and psychologically marred humans a somewhat bland mounting to miss the poetics inherent in the tale.

Liza Minnelli is Junie Moon, who has had acid poured over her face and arm by a perverted date when she laughs at him for making her undress in a cemetery for weird kicks. Robert Moore is a young man brought up by a queer (Leonard Frey) and wounded in an accident on a hunting trip with a friend at whom he made a pass. Ken Howard had been sent to homes as retarded.

They've met in the hospital and, being orphans in a sense, decide to live together afterwards. Moore is the brains, Minnelli the heart and spunk, and Howard the apparent breadwinner.

Pic reaches for such symbols as blacks being also handicapped in the social system, with the apparently gay cripple having his first woman via a lovely intellectual black girl (beautifully played by Emily Yancy).

All this is well mounted and lensed but sans the right dramatic flourishes to get human depth, melodramatic gusto or humane symbolism into the right focus.

•

TELL THEM WILLIE BOY IS HERE
1969, 97 mins, US Ⓥ ▭ col
Dir Abraham Polonsky ***Prod*** Jennings Lang ***Scr*** Abraham Polonsky ***Ph*** Conrad Hall ***Ed*** Melvin Shapiro ***Mus*** Dave Grusin ***Art*** Alexander Golitzen, Henry Bumstead
Act Robert Redford, Katharine Ross, Robert Blake, Susan Clark, Barry Sullivan, John Vernon (Universal)

A powerful unfoldment of a particular incident in U.S. history, the film becomes, by extension, a deeply personal and radical vision of the past and future.

Film [from the book *Willie Boy . . . A Desert Manhunt* by Harry Lawton] tells the story of the tracking-down of a renegade Indian in California in 1909. Although Robert Blake is the title character, the film is really about Robert Redford, Coop, the deputy sheriff whose assignment it is to track down Willie.

Abraham Polonsky, who was blacklisted for 20 years, is not a director who works through his actors. Thesps are simple tools of his vision—their presence more than their abilities are used. Nobody's going to win any acting awards for their work herein. Still, Redford's "presence" is magnificent, always suggesting the classically structured, powerful-but-weak American.

•

TEMP, THE
1993, 95 mins, US Ⓥ ⦿ col
Dir Tom Holland ***Prod*** David Permut, Tom Engelman ***Scr*** Kevin Falls ***Ph*** Steve Yaconelli ***Ed*** Scott Conrad ***Mus*** Frederic Talgorn ***Art*** Joel Schiller
Act Timothy Hutton, Lara Flynn Boyle, Dwight Schultz, Oliver Platt, Steven Weber, Faye Dunaway (Columbus Circle)

If this *Temp* were applying for a full-time position, she wouldn't get the job. Moronic, derivative, artificial and pointless are just the first adjectives that come to mind to describe this concoction [screen story by Kevin Falls and Tom Engelman].

Lara Flynn Boyle temps for Timothy Hutton, a junior executive at the Mrs. Appleby baked goods firm in Portland, run by the sleekly ruthless Faye Dunaway. Job uncertainty pits worker against worker, but provides room for Boyle to slither up the corporate ladder through stealth and, depending upon what you choose to believe, murder. Boyle doesn't disguise her interest in Hutton.

Tom Holland's directorial style consists of making everyone appear busy by moving them around at twice normal speed and shoving Steadicams down every available hallway. Every cast member has been seen to better effect.

•

TEMPEST, THE
1979, 96 mins, UK Ⓥ col
Dir Derek Jarman ***Prod*** Guy Ford, Mordecai Schreiber ***Scr*** Derek Jarman ***Ph*** Peter Middleton ***Ed*** Leslie Walker ***Mus*** Wavemaker ***Art*** Yolanda Sonnaband
Act Heathcote Williams, Karl Johnson, Jack Birkett, Toyah Willcox, Elisabeth Welch (Boyd's)

British helmer Derek Jarman's third feature, a film version of Shakespeare's most fanciful play, is definitely one of a kind. Its greatest strength is its "look." That offsets the director-adaptor's generally limp control of the narrative.

Although heavily cut and reorganized, the Bard's lines are used virtually throughout. The plot remains intact. Jarman's biggest liberty is the insertion of a wedding feast at the end, complete with dancing sailor boys, and blues singer Elisabeth Welch crooning "Stormy Weather" as a kind of diva ex machina.

Most successful innovation is Toyah Willcox's assault on the usually vacuous role of Miranda. Plump and punkish, her reaction to the first eligible male she has ever seen is more lusty than wide-eyed, and thoroughly believable.

•

TEMPTATION
1946, 98 mins, US b/w
Dir Irving Pichel ***Prod*** Edward Small ***Scr*** Robert Thoeren ***Ph*** Lucien Ballard ***Ed*** Ernest Nims ***Mus*** Daniele Amfitheatrof ***Art*** Bernard Herzbrun
Act Merle Oberon, George Brent, Charles Korvin, Paul Lukas, Lenore Ulric, Ludwig Stossel (Universal)

Production is well stacked with solid values in every department except for the screenplay, which falls short in its attempt to stretch an unsubstantial storyline over so long a running time.

Pulling the full weight of the pic practically single-handedly, Merle Oberon in the central role of the femme fatale scores a personal triumph.

Two male vis-a-vis register less successfully. George Brent, playing the part-time husband and full-time Egyptologist, walks through his part with a wooden gait and frozen expression that fails to evoke the needed sympathy. Charles Korvin, as the Egyptian roue, complete with fez and corny romantic patter, lacks the polish and assurance for his role, and too frequently substitutes a sophomoric leer for heartbreak brutality. In a minor role as family doctor and adviser, Paul Lukas contributes heavily.

Story [based on Robert Hichens's novel *Bella Donna*] is located in Egypt, where Brent, newly married to Oberon, is engaged in a British museum expedition. Overcome by boredom while her husband is out digging for a mummy, Oberon, already with a shady past containing several divorces, gets mixed up with an Egyptian dandy in a full-blown love affair.

•

TEMPTRESS, THE
1926, 95 mins, US ⊗ b/w
Dir Fred Niblo ***Scr*** Dorothy Farnum, Marian Ainslee ***Ph*** Tony Gaudio, William Daniels ***Ed*** Lloyd Nosler ***Art*** Cedric Gibbons, James Basevi
Act Greta Garbo, Antonio Moreno, Roy D'Arcy, Marc MacDermott, Lionel Barrymore, Virginia Brown Faire (Cosmopolitan/M-G-M)

A sumptuously produced picture, one unbroken succession of pictorial surprises in beauty. No better handling of background and composition has been seen.

This flawlessness is unfortunately not matched by selection of story or star. Greta Garbo does not make the woman of sinister passion created by [novelist Blasco] Ibanez. She is scarcely the screen type of aggressive vitality the character demands.

The story starts at a masquerade ball in Paris, a remarkable bit of staging. Elena, unhappy wife (as later develops) of a Paris fop, and Robledo, Spanish engineer on leave from a vast irrigation work in the Argentine, meet and fall in love, Elena vowing she is free.

Elena's married state is disclosed. When it is further revealed that she was the mistress of a rich banker whom she ruined and drove to suicide Robledo breaks away, returning to South America. Thither Elena follows with her husband. One after another the white men in charge of the big work fall under her fatal fascination and go down to wreck, while Robledo alone holds aloof.

•

TEMPTRESS MOON
SEE: FENG YUE

•

10
1979, 122 mins, US Ⓥ ⦿ ▭ col
Dir Blake Edwards ***Prod*** Blake Edwards, Tony Adams ***Scr*** Blake Edwards ***Ph*** Frank Stanley ***Ed*** Ralph E. Winters ***Mus*** Henry Mancini ***Art*** Rodger Maus
Act Dudley Moore, Julie Andrews, Bo Derek, Robert Webber, Brian Dennehy, Dee Wallace (Orion/Geoffrey)

Blake Edwards's *10* is a shrewdly observed and beautifully executed comedy of manners and morals.

10 is theoretically the top score on Dudley Moore's female ranking system, although he raves that his dream girl is an "11" after he first spots her. Frustrated in his song writing and in his relationship with g.f. Julie Andrews, diminutive Moore, 40-ish, four-time Oscar winner, decides to pursue the vision incarnated by Bo Derek despite fact that she's on her honeymoon with a jock type seemingly twice Moore's size.

Long build-up to Moore's big night with Derek is spiced with plenty of physical comedy which displays both Moore and Edwards in top slapstick form.

1979: NOMINATIONS: Best Original Score, Song ("It's Easy to Say")

•

TENANT, THE
1976, 125 mins, France Ⓥ col
Dir Roman Polanski ***Scr*** Roman Polanski, Gerard Brach ***Ph*** Sven Nykvist ***Ed*** Francoise Bonnot ***Mus*** Philippe Sarde ***Art*** Pierre Guffroy
Act Roman Polanski, Isabelle Adjani, Melvyn Douglas, Jo Van Fleet, Bernard Fresson, Lila Kedrova (Marianne)

A tale of a paranoid breakdown of a little bureaucratic clerk that wastes no time in trying to be clinical. It has a humorous tang, underlying the macabre.

Director Roman Polanski plays the little man himself, a naturalized Frenchman of Polish origin, who expertly combines a deceptive internal resiliency to his outward timidity that makes him pathetic.

He goes to look at an apartment he has heard of. A girl who has it threw herself out the window. He is told he may have it only if she does not come back. Polanski calls the hospital and learns the girl is dead. He moves in but mysterious things begin to happen.

There is an effective atmosphere and it does create a feeling of personal anguish. Thus not achieving a balance of humor and suspense.

•

TEN COMMANDMENTS, THE
SEE: DEKALOG

•

TEN COMMANDMENTS, THE
1923, 160 mins, US Ⓥ ⊗ col
Dir Cecil B. DeMille ***Prod*** Cecil B. DeMille ***Scr*** Jeanie MacPherson ***Ph*** Bert Glennon, Peverell Marley, Archie Stout, J. F. Westerberg, Ray Rennahan ***Ed*** Anne Bauchens ***Mus*** Hugo Riesenfeld ***Art*** Paul Iribe
Act Theodore Roberts, Charles De Roche, Estelle Taylor, Richard Dix, Rod La Rocque, Edythe Chapman (Paramount)

The opening Biblical scenes of *The Ten Commandments* are irresistible in their assembly, breadth, color and direction; they are enormous and just as attractive. Cecil B. DeMille puts in a thrill here with the opening of the Red Sea for Moses to pass through with the Children of Israel. This section is in color, and there are often big scenes besides that one. They are immense and stupendous, so big the modern tale after that seems puny. The story is of two sons, one his mother's boy and the other a harum-scarum atheist. Cheating as a contractor, the atheist's defects in building material result in the collapse of a partly built church's wall, with the mother killed by the falling debris.

The best performance is given by Rod La Rocque as the atheist son, Dan McTavish. La Rocque really doesn't get properly started until called upon for plenty of emotion toward the finish. Theodore Roberts as Moses is but required to stride majestically, something he can do perhaps a little better than anyone else, while Charles De Roche as Rameses (Pharaoh) always appears in a genteel, thoughtful mood as though wondering what it is all about.

The women do no better. Leatrice Joy wears a hat that may have been of the period of Moses; anyway it is an awful hat and her acting is strong enough to make you forget it.

•

TEN COMMANDMENTS, THE
1956, 219 mins, US Ⓥ ⦿ col
Dir Cecil B. DeMille ***Prod*** Cecil B. DeMille ***Scr*** Aeneas MacKenzie, Jesse L. Lasky, Jr., Fredric M. Frank, Jack Gariss ***Ph*** Loyal Griggs ***Ed*** Anne Bauchens ***Mus*** Elmer Bernstein ***Art*** Hal Pereira, Walter Tyler, Albert Nozaki
Act Charlton Heston, Yul Brynner, Anne Baxter, Edward G. Robinson, Yvonne De Carlo, Debra Paget (Paramount)

Cecil B. DeMille's super-spectacular about the Children of Israel held in brutal bondage until Moses, prodded by the God of Abraham, delivers them from Egyptian tyranny is a statistically intimidating production: the negative cost was $13.5 million and 25,000 extras were employed. DeMille remains conventional with the motion picture as an art form. The eyes of the onlooker are filled with spectacle. Emotional tug is sometimes lacking.

Commandments is too long. More than two hours pass before the intermission and the break is desperately welcome. Scenes of the greatness that was Egypt, and Hebrews by the thousands under the whip of the taskmasters, are striking. But bigness wearies. There's simply too much.

Commandments hits the peak of beauty with a sequence that is unelaborate, this being the Passover supper wherein Moses is shown with his family while the shadow of death falls on Egyptian first-borns. The creeping shadow of darkness that destroyed the Egyptian first-borns, the trans-composition of Moses's staff into a serpent, the changeover of the life-giving water into blood, flames to engulf the land and the parting of the Red Sea—these are shown. The effect of all these special camera devices is varying, however, and does not escape a certain theatricality.

Performances meet requirements all the way but exception must be made of Anne Baxter as the Egyptian princess Nefretiri. Baxter leans close to old-school siren histrionics and this is out of sync with the spiritual nature of *Commandments*.

Charlton Heston is an adaptable performer as Moses, revealing inner glow as he is called by God to remove the chains of slavery that hold his people. Yvonne De Carlo is Sephora, the warm and understanding wife of Moses. Yul Brynner is expert as Rameses, who inherits the Egyptian throne and seeks to battle Moses and his God until he's forced to acknowledge that "Moses's God is the real God."

1956: Best Special Effects.

NOMINATIONS: Best Picture, Color Cinematography, Color Costume Design, Color Art Direction, Editing, Sound

•

TEN DAYS THAT SHOOK THE WORLD

SEE: OKTYABR

•

TENDER COMRADE

1943, 103 mins, US Ⓥ b/w

Dir Edward Dmytryk ***Prod*** David Hempstead ***Scr*** Dalton Trumbo ***Ph*** Russell Metty ***Ed*** Roland Gross ***Mus*** Leigh Harline ***Art*** Albert S. D'Agostino, Carroll Clark

Act Ginger Rogers, Robert Ryan, Ruth Hussey, Patricia Collinge, Mady Christians, Kim Hunter (RKO)

Centered around five women, all of whom have their men in the services and all of whom are contributing to the war effort in one way or another, *Tender Comrade* is a preachment for all that democracy stands for.

It is a picture of considerable charm despite its terrific emotional effects. And if the emotional impact is sometimes achieved with what may seem to be overdone dramatics, then it's to be marked off to what one can assume to be an enactment of what is actually real-life drama.

Ginger Rogers gives an unrestrained performance throughout, and where several scenes are almost dawdling she perks it up with neat bits of business. Ruth Hussey, Kim Hunter and Patricia Collinge also give excellent portrayals.

Dalton Trumbo contributes a screenplay compact and replete with plenty of excellent dialog. A notably big factor in the film's pace is Edward Dmytryk's direction of the sometimes slow but never tedious story.

•

TENDER IS THE NIGHT

1962, 146 mins, US ▭ col

Dir Henry King ***Prod*** Henry T. Weinstein ***Scr*** Ivan Moffat ***Ph*** Leon Shamroy ***Ed*** William Reynolds ***Mus*** Bernard Herrmann ***Art*** Jack Martin Smith, Malcolm Brown

Act Jennifer Jones, Jason Robards, Joan Fontaine, Tom Ewell, Cesare Danova, Jill St. John (20th Century-Fox)

A combination of attractive, intelligent performances and consistently interesting, De Luxecolorful photography of interiors and exteriors—mostly the French Riviera—provide big plus qualities in this 20th-Fox adaptation of *Tender Is the Night*. This may not be a 100-proof distillation of F. Scott Fitzgerald. But *Tender Is the Night* is nonetheless on its own filmic terms a thoughtful, disturbing and at times absorbing romantic drama.

Novel and film depict the decay and deterioration of a brilliant and idealistic psychiatrist (Jason Robards), whose love for and marriage to a wealthy patient (Jennifer Jones) ultimately consumes, dissipates and destroys him by engulfing him in the meaningless motives and glamorous leisure of upper-social-class Americans adrift in Europe in the prosperous 1920s. Moffat's screenplay emphasizes the point of transference of strength from doctor to patient, traces the reverse process in which heroine and hero travel in emotionally opposite directions as a result of their tragic relationship.

Jones emerges a crisply fresh, intriguing personality and creates a striking character as the schizophrenic Nicole. Robards, whose non-matinee-idol masculinity makes him an ideal choice for the role of the ill-fated doctor-husband, Dick Diver, plays with intelligence and conviction. Joan Fontaine is convincing as Nicole's shallow older sister, performing with the right manifestation of frivolity and bite that her part requires.

1962: NOMINATION: Best Song ("Tender Is the Night")

•

TENDER MERCIES

1983, 89 mins, US/UK Ⓥ ⊙ col

Dir Bruce Beresford ***Prod*** Philip S. Hobel, Mary Ann Hobel ***Scr*** Horton Foote ***Ph*** Russell Boyd ***Ed*** William Anderson ***Mus*** George Dreyfus ***Art*** Jeannine Claudia Oppewall

Act Robert Duvall, Tess Harper, Allan Hubbard, Betty Buckley, Ellen Barkin, Wilford Brimley (Antron Media/EMI)

Robert Duvall is Mac Sledge, a down-and-out ex-country and western singer on the skids since his marriage to fellow C&W warbler Dixie (Betty Buckley) broke up.

Out on a drunken binge one night, he winds up in a small motel in Texas prairie country, and next morning accepts an offer of work from Rosa Lee (Tess Harper), the young widow who runs the place. Rosa Lee's husband had been killed in Vietnam, and she is having trouble keeping the motel and gas station going, and at the same time looking after her small son (Allan Hubbard).

Sledge stays on, the couple fall in love and marry. When tragedy unexpectedly touches his life, he finds he now has the strength to keep going and achieves new peace of mind.

Tender Mercies is, in the best sense, an old-fashioned film. There's no sex, no violence. Duvall is dignified and moving as Sledge; Harper is most affecting as the widow he loves and marries; Hubbard almost steals the film as her inquiring son.

1983: Best Actor (Robert Duvall), Original Screenplay

NOMINATIONS: Best Picture, Director, Original Song ("Over You")

•

TENDER TRAP, THE

1955, 110 mins, US Ⓥ ⊙ ▭ col

Dir Charles Walters ***Prod*** Lawrence Weingarten ***Scr*** Julius Epstein ***Ph*** Paul C. Vogel ***Ed*** Jack Dunning ***Mus*** Jeff Alexander

Act Frank Sinatra, Debbie Reynolds, David Wayne, Celeste Holm, Lola Albright, Carolyn Jones (M-G-M)

This film version of the legit comedy [by Max Shulman and Robert Paul Smith] is a fairly diverting, but considerably overlong, takeoff on the romantic didoes of bachelors and gals. Picture has been given a plushy look.

Into the lives of Frank Sinatra, bachelor theatrical agent, and David Wayne, his married friend from Indiana, visiting Manhattan sans spouse, enters Debbie Reynolds, a determined girl who already has set the date for her wedding even without having found the right man. After some preliminaries she decides Sinatra is it.

Remainder of the footage details his capture, but not before he finds himself engaged to both her and Celeste Holm, an impossible situation that rights itself following a humdinger of a drunken party that segues into the morning-after comedy highlight of the footage.

The title tune gets some consistent plugging in the film. It's good cleffing by Sammy Cahn and James Van Heusen.

1955: NOMINATION: Best Song ("(Love Is) The Tender Trap")

•

TEN GENTLEMEN FROM WEST POINT

1942, 104 mins, US Ⓥ b/w

Dir Henry Hathaway ***Prod*** William Perlberg ***Scr*** Richard Maibaum, George Seaton ***Ph*** Leon Shamroy ***Ed*** James B. Clark ***Mus*** Alfred Newman

Act George Montgomery, Maureen O'Hara, John Sutton, Laird Cregar, Victor Francen, Ward Bond (20th Century-Fox)

This tells of the establishment of West Point as a military academy in the early 1800s, and the experiences of the original class of cadets. After a brief prolog in which Congress is shown debating and then passing an appropriation for maintenance of the military training school, picture swings to the old fort and the arrival of the first class.

The cadets are considered intruders by the regular bombardier company quartered at West Point, and are rousingly hazed by the commanding major.

There's a fair amount of dramatic incident, and some comedy injected to keep up audience interest—but overall the picture drops too many times into the doldrums. Only the patriotic angle helps it survive.

Major difficulty encountered by scripter Richard Maibaum [working from an idea by Malvin Ward] seems to be the requirement of jelling dramatic episodes with factual history—and, as is usually the case, the problem was too great for Maibaum to solve for sustained entertainment purposes.

•

TEN LITTLE INDIANS

1966, 92 mins, UK Ⓥ b/w

Dir George Pollock ***Prod*** Harry Alan Towers ***Scr*** Peter Yeldham ***Ph*** Ernest Steward ***Ed*** Peter Boita ***Mus*** Malcolm Lockyer ***Art*** Frank White

Act Hugh O'Brian, Shirley Eaton, Fabian, Leo Genn, Stanley Holloway, Wilfrid Hyde White (Tenlit)

Second film version [after *And Then There Were None*] of Agatha Christie's endurable variation on the old idea of putting a group of disparate characters into a confined situation and letting them be killed one by one shapes up as a good suspenser. The film was made entirely in Ireland, although the setting has been changed to what appears to be a solitary schloss in the Austrian Alps.

Director George Pollock, despite a script with complicated credits (screenplay by Peter Yeldham, based on a script by Dudley Nichols, and adapted by Peter Welbeck, based on the Christie novel and play *Ten Little Niggers*), works quite a bit of suspense into the restricted action, successfully hiding identity of the tenth Indian without resorting to too many "red herrings."

One major switch, an unfortunate one, has the first victim, originally an eccentric prince, changed to an American rock 'n' roll singer (Fabian, in an embarrassingly bad performance).

A one-minute "whodunit break" is inserted near the end when the action is suspended while the audience is encouraged to guess the murderer's identity.

•

TEN LITTLE INDIANS

1975, 105 mins, Italy/W. Germany/France/Spain Ⓥ col

Dir Peter Collinson ***Scr*** Enrique Llovet, Erich Krohnke ***Ph*** Fernando Arritas ***Mus*** Bruno Nicolai ***Art*** Jose Maria Tapiador

Act Oliver Reed, Elke Sommer, Richard Attenborough, Gert Frobe, Stephane Audran, Herbert Lom (Talia/Coralta/Corona/Comeci)

Remake of Agatha Christie's whodunit classic, in which ten suspects find themselves incommunicado 300 kilometers from the nearest town in a luxurious hotel in the middle of a desert in Iran. The invitees accept this, and thereupon make only the feeblest of efforts to seek a way of escaping. Dressed in tuxedos and evening gowns, they resign themselves to being eliminated one by one.

The murders are all committed in the most discreet, unspectacular ways, and cause only the mildest of trepidations among the remaining "Indians."

Thesping consists of the usual cameos typical of the copro genre. Charles Aznavour manages to get in a song before nonchalantly drinking his poison and the others dutifully plod through their parts.

•

TEN NORTH FREDERICK

1958, 102 mins, US Ⓥ ▭ b/w

Dir Philip Dunne ***Prod*** Charles Brackett ***Scr*** Philip Dunne ***Ph*** Joe MacDonald ***Ed*** David Bretherton ***Mus*** Leigh Harline ***Art*** Lyle R. Wheeler, Addison Hehr

Act Gary Cooper, Diane Varsi, Geraldine Fitzgerald, Tom Tully, Suzy Parker, Stuart Whitman (20th Century-Fox)

Ten North Frederick is a fairly interesting study of a man who is the victim of his own virtues. But because of the psychological intricacies involved, the screen telling of the John O'Hara novel sacrifices detail and explanation at some loss to audience satisfaction.

The politics section has been so telescoped as to be puzzling. The question of whether the protagonist actually entertains the dream of the presidency or jollies his wife on the point is never clear. And it is crucial to conviction. Joe Chapin (Gary Cooper) is a regional lawyer, rich but not apparently otherwise distinguished. Most of all he is a gentleman and from this fact flow his troubles.

The vaguest part of the screen version is the hometown attitude toward the hero, although at his 50th birthday party he is twitted by a philanderer with being a dull and slow fellow. Nonetheless the story gets on and after his series of disillusionments, including his beloved daughter's forced marriage, subsequent miscarriage, annullment and leaving home, the lawyer moves to his bitter-sweet romance in New York with a younger woman.

Told in flashback, the story opens at the 1945 funeral of the lawyer and shows the hypocrites gathered afterwards in his home. The greatest hypocrite of all is the widow, played with iceberg selfishness by Geraldine Fitzgerald.

By the time the story is played out the thesis makes sense—Joe Chapin has indeed been hopelessly handicapped in life by being a gentleman. It is convincing in the end and in Cooper's performance, and it is also sad.

•

10 RILLINGTON PLACE

1971, 111 mins, UK Ⓥ ⊙ col

Dir Richard Fleischer ***Prod*** Martin Ransohoff, Leslie Linder ***Scr*** Clive Exton ***Ph*** Denys Coop ***Ed*** Ernest Walter ***Mus*** John Dankworth ***Art*** Martin Cooper

Act Richard Attenborough, Judy Geeson, John Hurt, Pat Heywood, Isobel Black, Robert Hardy (Columbia)

In 1944, a woman was gassed, strangled and ravished by John Christie, the first of several victims of a seemingly quiet, respectable man living in a drab London district.

Richard Fleischer has turned out an authenticated documentary-feature which is an absorbing and disturbing picture. But the film has the serious flaw of not even attempting to probe the reasons that turned a man into a monstrous pervert.

Could be that Fleischer, like most other people, found more interest in the other central figure in the case, Timothy Evans. He was an illiterate who, with his young wife and baby, was Christie's lodger. Mrs. Evans and their daughter became death victims of Christie. The bewildered lad, duped by Christie, confessed and was executed. Several years later Christie was arrested for the murder of his own wife, confessed to the murder of seven women, including Mrs. Evans, but vigorously denied strangling the child. Some 12 years later Evans was pardoned. All this is dealt with in the Ludovic Kennedy book from which Clive Exton has written a factual, interesting but not particularly moving or emotional screenplay.

Though Richard Attenborough, playing the killer, is the central character, the acting honors are firmly wrapped up by John Hurt as Evans. He gives a remarkably subtle and fascinating performance as the bewildered young man who plays into the hands of both the murderer and the police.

●

TEN SECONDS TO HELL
1959, 93 mins, UK b/w
Dir Robert Aldrich ***Prod*** Michael Carreras ***Scr*** Robert Aldrich, Teddi Sherman ***Ph*** Ernest Laszlo ***Ed*** James Needs, Henry Richardson ***Mus*** Kenneth V. Jones ***Art*** Ken Adam
Act Jeff Chandler, Jack Palance, Martine Carol, Wesley Addy, Virginia Baker, Richard Wattis (Hammer)

Hazardous job of deactivating dud bombs after World War II appears sound material for a melodramatic and suspenseful film. But curiously *Ten Seconds to Hell* emerges as a downbeat picture.

Based on Lawrence P. Bachmann's novel *The Phoenix*, the screenplay seldom draws sympathy for any of its characters. Of six former German soldiers who form a bomb disposal unit in Berlin at the war's end, three are quickly killed in performance of their duties.

Jack Palance, self-styled leader of the unit, is a man of courage and conviction. But he's a moody individual who appears to be continually wrestling with inner problems. Ruthless and egotistical is Jeff Chandler who has regard for no one except himself. Martine Carol, in an unglamorous role, runs a boarding house, where Palance and Chandler reside.

With the film shot on location in Berlin, cameraman Ernest Laszlo has provided some realistic backgrounds.

●

TENSION
1950, 91 mins, US b/w
Dir John Berry ***Prod*** Robert Sisk ***Scr*** Allen Rivkin ***Ph*** Harry Stradling ***Ed*** Albert Akst ***Mus*** Andre Previn ***Art*** Cedric Gibbons, Leonid Vasian
Act Richard Basehart, Audrey Totter, Cyd Charisse, Barry Sullivan, Tom D'Andrea (M-G-M)

Tension lives up to its title. It's a tight, tersely stated melodrama that holds the attention.

Plot has Richard Basehart, drugstore manager married to wicked Audrey Totter, plotting a perfect murder to do away with his wife's lover (Lloyd Gough). He creates himself a new identity and carefully shapes his crime so that no suspicion will be cast on him.

Script [from a story by John Klorer] wraps smart dialog and situations around the plot to make it play very well, and Berry's direction keeps it always on the move and the cast showing to advantage.

Cyd Charisse is charming as the girl whom Basehart meets during the establishment of his new identity.

●

TENSION AT TABLE ROCK
1956, 93 mins, US col
Dir Charles Marquis Warren ***Prod*** Sam Wiesenthal ***Scr*** Winston Miller ***Ph*** Joseph Biroc ***Ed*** Harry Marker, Dean Harrison ***Mus*** Dimitri Tiomkin ***Art*** Albert S. D'Agostino, John B. Mansbridge
Act Richard Egan, Dorothy Malone, Cameron Mitchell, Billy Chapin, Royal Dano, Angie Dickinson (RKO)

There's more "mood" than pace in this western entry, but it comes off with a fair classification for the regular outdoor situation because of a number of good action scenes. Script from the Frank Gruber novel *Bitter Sage* abets the slow moodiness and takes quite a while to set the characters.

Wes Tancred (Richard Egan) is on the run after having killed in self-defense the leader of a robber gang he is riding with. Main action takes place in Table Rock, where Egan brings a small boy (Billy Chapin) after the latter's dad has been killed by some holdup men. He finds the town prepping for the arrival of Texas trailherders and the sheriff (Cameron Mitchell) frightened. The sheriff's wife (Dorothy Malone) could go for Egan.

Performances are all competent. Dimitri Tiomkin provides an okay background score. Malone and Angie Dickinson seem a bit too well dressed for the prairie femmes they play.

●

TEN TALL MEN
1951, 97 mins, US col
Dir Willis Goldbeck ***Prod*** Harold Hecht ***Scr*** Roland Kibbee, Frank Davis ***Ph*** William Snyder ***Ed*** William Lyon ***Mus*** David Buttolph ***Art*** Carl Anderson
Act Burt Lancaster, Jody Lawrance, Gilbert Roland, Kieron Moore, George Tobias, John Dehner (Norma/Columbia)

Yarn [from a story by James Warner Bellah and Willis Goldbeck] is tailor-made for the burly Burt Lancaster. Cast as a Foreign Legion sergeant, he picks up a tip while in jail that the Riffs plan an invasion of the city. With nine fellow prisoners he volunteers to harass the would-be invaders.

Mission succeeds all expectations when the group manages to seize a sheik's daughter (Jody Lawrance), a key to the whole attack.

Proceedings come off at a crisp pace under Willis Goldbeck's breezy direction. Lancaster, Lawrance and a lengthy list of supporting players handle their roles broadly, which at times achieves almost a satiric effect. Whether that was intentional or not is tough to determine.

●

10 THINGS I HATE ABOUT YOU
1999, 97 mins, US Ⓥ ⦿ col
Dir Gil Junger ***Prod*** Andrew Lazar ***Scr*** Karen McCullah Lutz, Kirsten Smith ***Ph*** Mark Irwin ***Ed*** O. Nicholas Brown ***Mus*** Richard Gibbs ***Art*** Carol Winstead Wood
Act Heath Ledger, Julia Stiles, Joseph Gordon-Levitt, Larisa Oleynik, David Krumholtz, Andrew Keegan (Mad Chance/Janet/Touchstone)

Turning *The Taming of the Shrew* into a teen comedy sounds like a high-concept no-brainer, until you realize the play's extremely crusty plot mechanics make it even less likely a modern school transplant than, say, *Titus Andronicus. 10 Things I Hate About You* thus doesn't take much time before ditching its pitch idea in favor of a mishmash of newer formulas, never quite settling on a cogent game plan or directorial tone. Tyro co-writers simply ignore the no-longer-p.c. parts of the play.

It's less funny-ha-ha than funny-queasy when divorced Walter Stratford (Larry Miller) won't let his younger daughter, Bianca (Larisa Oleynik), date until his eldest, Kat (Julia Stiles), finds a beau, ostensibly because as a doctor he's seen too many unwanted teen pregnancies.

Everybody wants to date Padua sophomore Bianca, because she's pretty and popular and bubbleheaded. Kat, however, is into grrl rock, feminist theory and other interests that in pic's strained reasoning somehow preclude the hormonal urge. But so long as she's dateless in Seattle (story's setting), so is hot-to-trot Bianca. Ergo two would-be boyfriends—noxiously vain Joey (Andrew Keegan) and dweebish nice guy Cameron (Joseph Gordon-Levitt)—each plot to fix up the standoffish sis with whoever's willing. This search turns up only mysterious new kid in town Patrick (Heath Ledger), reputedly a very bad boy.

Sitcom vet Gil Junger's feature bow is high on energy, low on cohesion. Gag reel under closing credits hints at better, loopier comedy than *10 Things* can muster. Cast is decent, with fast-rising Stiles and Aussie transplant Ledger an assured lead duo.

●

10:30 P.M. SUMMER
1966, 85 mins, US col
Dir Jules Dassin ***Prod*** Jules Dassin, Anatole Litvak ***Scr*** Jules Dassin, Marguerite Duras ***Ph*** Gabor Pogany ***Ed*** Roger Dwyre ***Mus*** Christobal Halffter ***Art*** Enrique Alarcon
Act Melina Mercouri, Romy Schneider, Peter Finch, Julian Mateos, Isabel Maria Perez, Beatriz Savon (Dassin-Litvak)

Jules Dassin's *10:30 P.M. Summer* is only 85 minutes long but seems longer. Dassin's direction is uncertain, frequently illogical and, for the most part, plodding; Melina Mercouri's thesping is in a similar vein. There's reason to believe that the major fault is in the script of Dassin and novelist Marguerite Duras and, beyond that, in the novella of Duras on which the script is based.

The thread of a plot (a married couple and a female friend, traveling together in Spain, are under a mounting tension that is touched off by an incident with a fugitive in a village) may have made a moody and effective short story but as the basis of an intelligent screenplay it is less than satisfactory.

There's some possibility of exploitation in the frankly erotic scenes of lovemaking between Romy Schneider (the reluctant guest) and Peter Finch (the husband).

An even more grievous shortcoming is the absence of any explanation as to the reason for her condition. Alcoholism is, evidently, only a part of her tragedy, as is a suggested latent homosexual feeling towards Schneider.

Gabor Pogany's camerawork overcomes the necessary low-key lighting (most of the film takes place at night) to give a technical gloss to the proceedings.

●

10 TO MIDNIGHT
1983, 100 mins, US Ⓥ ⦿ col
Dir J. Lee Thompson ***Prod*** Pancho Kohner, Lance Hool ***Scr*** William Roberts ***Ph*** Adam Greenberg ***Ed*** Peter Lee-Thompson ***Mus*** Robert O. Ragland ***Art*** Jim Freiburger
Act Charles Bronson, Lisa Eilbacher, Gene Davis, Andrew Stevens, Geoffrey Lewis, Wilford Brimley (Golan-Globus/City)

A sexually deranged killer slices up five young women like melons. The killer (well enough played by Gene Davis) is literally getting away with murder because of bureaucratic red tape and a pending insanity plea. As cop Charles Bronson puts it: "I remember when legal meant lawful. Now it means loophole." So Bronson takes matters into his own hands.

William Roberts's screenplay, while it sags in the middle, is damnably clever at dropping in its vicious vigilante theme without being didactic, and J. Lee Thompson's direction, borrowing from Hitchcock's editing in *Psycho*, creates the full horror of blades thrusting into naked bellies without the viewer ever actually seeing it happen.

Lisa Eilbacher plays Bronson's daughter and the beautiful, major target of the killer. Geoffrey Lewis is very good as a self-serving defense attorney who tells his warped client to be cool because "you'll walk out of a crazy house alive."

●

TENUE DE SOIREE
(MENAGE; EVENING DRESS)
1986, 81 mins, France Ⓥ ▭ col
Dir Bertrand Blier ***Prod*** Rene Cleitman ***Scr*** Bertrand Blier ***Ph*** Jean Penzer ***Ed*** Claudine Merlin ***Mus*** Serge Gainsbourg ***Art*** Theo Meurisse
Act Gerard Depardieu, Michel Blanc, Miou-Miou, Bruno Cremer, Jean-Pierre Marielle, Jean-Francois Stevenin (Hachette Premiere/Dussart/Cine Valse/DD

There's nothing like a good shot of insolence for getting one's flagging career out of a rut. After the failure of his two previous films (*My Best Friend's Girl* and *Our Story*), writer-director Bertrand Blier finally has recovered the abrasive imagination and tonic bad taste that fired some of his early films, notably *Les Valseuses*.

Tenue de soiree is a tart black comedy of sexuality in which, among other things, Blier energetically turns the French star system on its head. Despite his impressive range, one did not quite expect to see robust Gerard Depardieu falling for another man, especially somebody so nebbishy as Michel Blanc. Blier charges what could have been little more than a clever gay variation on the romantic triangle with a bulldozing wit and cynicism, and his talent for writing raw, bristling, strangely lyrical dialog is exhilarating.

Depardieu, a burglar whose sexual tastes have undergone a change in prison, meets a down-and-out couple (Blanc and Miou-Miou), and drags them into a series of housebreakings with promises of lucre and a new life. Blanc is hopelessly in love with his now-contemptuous mate, and naturally is disturbed when their new friend begins making advances—at him. He's even more unsettled when he finds himself slowly giving in to Depardieu's husky wooing. They become lovers and shack up together, with Depardieu secretly paying off a pimp to take the now intrusive wife off their hands.

●

TEOREMA
(THEOREM)
1968, 100 mins, Italy Ⓥ col
Dir Pier Paolo Pasolini ***Prod*** Franco Rossellini, Manolo Bolognini ***Scr*** Pier Paolo Pasolini ***Ph*** Giuseppe Ruzzolini ***Ed*** Nino Baragli ***Mus*** Ennio Morricone ***Art*** Luciano Puccini
Act Silvana Mangano, Terence Stamp, Massimo Girotti, Anne Wiazemsky, Laura Betti, Ninetto Davoli (Aetos)

Teorema is an allegory in two acts which merges eros and religion in an up-to-date context. Pier Paolo Pasolini, ever sensitive to religion, eroticism, homosexuality and social forces, employs all these elements to detail his premise that a sudden revelation of possible human self-fulfilment can permanently mar the upper strata of society and exalt its sub-strata.

With a simple, mathematical design, he systematically pursues this proposition with the device of guesting an unknown in an upper-bourgeois household. The visitor (Terence Stamp) is a university student with a heavenly divining rod enabling him to offer fulfilment and authenticity through physical love.

For the provincial maid Emilia (Laura Betti) the sexual experience becomes a holy illumination. The deviate son, Pietro (Jose Cruz), is solaced. His mother (Silvana Mangano), disrobes on the country estate to partake of the visitor's magic. Teenage daughter Odette (Anne Wiazemsky) invites him to her room for her first connubial fling. The father, Paolo (Massimo Girotti), a captain of industry, discovers his true and radically different personality in the arms of his supernatural guest.

The narrative, almost silent in the first half, is unusually clear for a film by Pasolini. Performances by all members of the cast are praiseworthy, though Stamp dominates the first half and Betti, the second.

•

TEQUILA SUNRISE
1988, 116 mins, US Ⓥ ⊙ col
Dir Robert Towne ***Prod*** Thom Mount ***Scr*** Robert Towne ***Ph*** Conrad L. Hall ***Ed*** Claire Simpson ***Mus*** Dave Grusin ***Art*** Richard Sylbert
Act Mel Gibson, Michelle Pfeiffer, Kurt Russell, Raul Julia, J. T. Walsh, Arliss Howard (Mount/Warner)

There's not much kick in this cocktail, despite its mix of quality ingredients. Casually glamorous South Bay is the setting for a story of little substance as writer-director Robert Towne attempts a study of friendship and trust but gets lost in a clutter of drug dealings and police operations.

Mel Gibson plays Dale "Mac" McKussic, a former big-time drug operator who's attempting to go straight just about the time his high school pal, cop Nick Frescia (Kurt Russell), is required to bust him. Frescia tries to dodge the duty by pressuring his friend to get out, but Mac owes one last favor to an old friend who's a Mexican cocaine dealer (Raul Julia).

Russell and Gibson are pushed into a cat-and-mouse game, complicated by their attraction to high-class restaurant owner Jo Ann Vallenari (Michelle Pfeiffer).

Gibson projects control skating atop paranoia, and is appealing as a man you'd want to trust. Russell is fine as the slick cop who's confused by his own shifting values, and Pfeiffer achieves a rather touching quality with her gun-shy girl beneath the polished professional.

1988: NOMINATION: Best Cinematography

•

TERESA
1951, 101 mins, US b/w
Dir Fred Zinnemann ***Prod*** Arthur M. Loew ***Scr*** Stewart Stern ***Ph*** William J. Miller ***Ed*** Frank Sullivan ***Mus*** Louis Applebaum ***Art*** Leo Kerz
Act Pier Angeli, John Ericson, Patricia Collinge, Bill Mauldin, Peggy Ann Garner, Ralph Meeker (M-G-M)

Bright news of *Teresa* is the American introduction of Pier Angeli, as the Italian war bride of the mixed-up John Ericson. There's enough of the waif in her appearance to generate a tremendous audience sympathy.

Fred Zinnemann is too consciously documentary in the directorial handling of the story, and the Stewart Stern screenplay [from an original story by him and Alfred Hayes] does not support such treatment.

Opening finds Ericson muddling his way through post-war life, resisting all aid, although wanting it. A flashback takes the plot to Italy, where he is a green replacement GI. During a stay in a small mountain village he meets and falls in love with Angeli.

On his first patrol, Ericson cracks up even before combat when the sergeant on whom he leans is absent. After a hospital confinement for treatment, he returns to the village, marries Angeli then goes to the States to await her arrival. When she does arrive, they make their home in cramped tenement quarters with his parents, and it is gradually brought out that his trouble is caused by a dominant mother and a false conception of his father.

1951: NOMINATION: Best Motion Picture Story

•

TERMINAL VELOCITY
1994, 100 mins, US Ⓥ ⊙ col
Dir Deran Sarafian ***Prod*** Scott Kroopf, Tom Engelman ***Scr*** David Twohy ***Ph*** Oliver Wood ***Ed*** Frank J. Urioste, Peck Prior ***Mus*** Joel McNeely ***Art*** David L. Snyder
Act Charlie Sheen, Nastassja Kinski, James Gandolfini, Christopher McDonald, Gary Bullock, Melvin Van Peebles (Hollywood/Interscope/PFE)

Terminal Velocity is a snappy, thrill-packed political espionage/heist picture, set in the spectacularly cinematic world of skydiving.

Pic starts in high gear, with an intrigue involving damsels in distress and midnight landings of jumbo jets in a desolate Arizona desert. Faster than you can yell "Jump!" skydiving instructor Ditch Brodie (Charlie Sheen) is taking a winsome novice jumper named Chris (Nastassja Kinski) on a danger-filled leap into post–Cold War politics, murder and a bounty of tongue-in-cheek homages to Hitch and Ian Fleming.

Sheen finds himself a classically Hitchcockian wrong man, employed as the ultimate fall guy (pun intended) for Kinski's earnest KGB agent, who's trying to save Russia from a massive hit on its already shaky treasury. The unlikely scenario is no obstacle to a rousing good time: As Ditch and Chris chase the evildoers and in turn are chased by same, pic is filled with punchy gag-filled dialog and sensational action bits, both in the air and on the ground.

Deran Sarafian's sharp, lean direction is perfectly matched to David Twohy's clever, well-paced script. Romantic leads are in on the jokes and up to pic's physical demands.

•

TERMINATOR, THE
1984, 108 mins, US Ⓥ ⊙ col
Dir James Cameron ***Prod*** Gale Anne Hurd ***Scr*** James Cameron, Gale Anne Hurd, William Wisher, Jr. ***Ph*** Adam Greenberg ***Ed*** Mark Goldblatt ***Mus*** Brad Fiedel ***Art*** George Costello
Act Arnold Schwarzenegger, Michael Biehn, Linda Hamilton, Paul Winfield, Lance Henriksen, Rick Rossovich (Hemdale)

The Terminator is a blazing, cinematic comic book, full of virtuoso moviemaking, terrific momentum, solid performances and a compelling story.

The clever script, cowritten by director James Cameron and producer Gale Anne Hurd, opens in a post-holocaust nightmare, A.D. 2029, where brainy machines have crushed most of the human populace. From that point, Arnold Schwarzenegger as the cyborg Terminator is sent back to the present to assassinate a young woman named Sarah Connor (Linda Hamilton) who is, in the context of a soon-to-be-born son and the nuclear war to come, the mother of mankind's salvation.

A human survivor in that black future (Michael Biehn) also drops into 1984 to stop the Terminator and save the woman and the future.

The shotgun-wielding Schwarzenegger is perfectly cast in a machinelike portrayal that requires only a few lines of dialog.

•

TERMINATOR 2: JUDGMENT DAY
1991, 136 mins, US Ⓥ ⊙ ▭ col
Dir James Cameron ***Prod*** James Cameron ***Scr*** James Cameron, William Wisher ***Ph*** Adam Greenberg ***Ed*** Conrad Buff, Mark Goldblatt, Richard A. Harris ***Mus*** Brad Fiedel ***Art*** Joseph Nemec III
Act Arnold Schwarzenegger, Linda Hamilton, Edward Furlong, Robert Patrick, Earl Boen, Joe Morton (Carolco/Pacific Western)

As with *Aliens*, director James Cameron has again taken a first-rate science fiction film and crafted a sequel that's in some ways more impressive—expanding on the original rather than merely remaking it. This time he's managed the trick by bringing two cyborgs back from the future into the sort-of present (the math doesn't quite work out) to respectively menace and defend the juvenile John Connor (Edward Furlong)—leader of the human resistance against machines that rule the war-devastated world of 2029.

Arnold Schwarzenegger is more comfortable and assured here than the first time around, reprising a role so perfectly suited to the voice and physique that have established him as a larger-than-life film persona.

The story finds Connor living with foster parents, his mother Sarah (Linda Hamilton) having been captured and committed to an asylum for insisting on the veracity of events depicted in the first film. The machines who rule the future dispatch a new cyborg to slay him while the human resistance sends its own reprogrammed Terminator back—this one bearing a remarkable resemblance to the evil one that appeared in 1984.

The film's great innovation involves the second cyborg: an advanced model composed of a liquid metal alloy that can metamorphose into the shape of any person it contacts and sprout metal appendages to skewer its victims.

Script by Cameron and William Wisher at times gets lost amid all the carnage. Hamilton's heavy-handed narration also is at times unintentionally amusing, though through her Cameron again offers the sci-fi crowd a fiercely heroic female lead, albeit one who looks like she's been going to Madonna's physical trainer.

If the reported $100 million budget is a study in excess, at least a lot of it ended up on the screen.

[In 1993 a *Special Edition* was issued on laserdisc, running 153 mins.]

1991: Best Sound, Visual Effects, Sound Effects Editing, Makeup

NOMINATIONS: Best Cinematography, Editing

•

TERM OF TRIAL
1962, 130 mins, UK b/w
Dir Peter Glenville ***Prod*** James Woolf ***Scr*** Peter Glenville ***Ph*** Oswald Morris ***Ed*** James Clark ***Mus*** Jean-Michel Demase ***Art*** Wilfrid Shingleton
Act Laurence Olivier, Simone Signoret, Sarah Miles, Terence Stamp, Thora Hird, Hugh Griffith (Warner-Pathe/Romulus)

Here Olivier's an idealistic, but seedily unsuccessful schoolmaster in a small mixed school in the North of England. He has had to settle for this inferior teaching job because as a pacifist during the war he went to jail. He's afflicted with a sense of inferiority, a nagging scold of a wife and a taste for hard liquor.

He also suffers from a suspicious headmaster and a class which, inevitably, contains the school bully, played with remarkable assurance by Terence Stamp. Olivier is delighted when he sees a desire to learn in a young 15-year-old girl (Sarah Miles) but, rather naively, fails to see that she is precociously sexually aroused by him.

The "crush" comes to a head when he takes some of the pupils on a school trip to Paris. She then feeds her mother with the tale that she has been indecently assaulted and he lands in the courtroom.

There are several loose ends, which could have emerged from the writing or the editing. But overall the characters are well drawn, the situations dramatic and the thesping all round is tops.

•

TERMS OF ENDEARMENT
1983, 130 mins, US Ⓥ ⊙ col
Dir James L. Brooks ***Prod*** James L. Brooks ***Scr*** James L. Brooks ***Ph*** Andrzej Bartkowiak ***Ed*** Richard Marks ***Mus*** Michael Gore ***Art*** Polly Platt
Act Shirley MacLaine, Debra Winger, Jack Nicholson, Jeff Daniels, John Lithgow, Danny DeVito (Paramount)

Teaming of Shirley MacLaine and Jack Nicholson at their best makes *Terms of Endearment* an enormously enjoyable offering, adding bite and sparkle when sentiment and seamlessness threaten to sink other parts of the picture [from the novel by Larry McMurtry].

At the core are mother MacLaine and daughter Debra Winger, fondly at odds from the beginning over the younger's impending marriage to likeable, but limited, Jeff Daniels. Literally, it's just one cut to the next; then Winger is a mother and moving away from Texas to Iowa, where she becomes a mother a couple of more times; talks to MacLaine every day, carries on an affair with John Lithgow while Daniels dallies at college with Kate Charleson.

Plotwise, MacLaine and Nicholson are first introduced as she watches him come home next door drunk. Then it's several more years before the film finds them together again as he makes a stumbling pass at her over the fence. Then it's several more years before they're together again and she finally agrees to go out to lunch.

Early on, MacLaine tells Winger, "You aren't special enough to overcome a bad marriage." But *Terms of Endearment* is certainly special enough to overcome its own problems.

1983: Best Picture, Director, Actress (Shirley MacLaine), Supp. Actor (Jack Nicholson), Adapted Screenplay

NOMINATIONS: Best Actress (Debra Winger), Supp. Actor (John Lithgow), Art Direction, Editing, Original Score, Sound

•

TERRA TREMA, LA EPISODIO DEL MARE
1948, 127 mins, Italy Ⓥ b/w
Dir Luchino Visconti ***Prod*** Salvo D'Angelo ***Scr*** Luchino Visconti ***Ph*** G. R. Aldo ***Ed*** Mario Serandrei ***Mus*** Luchino Visconti, Willy Ferrero (co-ord.)
(Universalia)

La Terra Trema, Luchino Visconti's second directorial effort (after *Ossessione*), is a ponderous, fragmentary tale of Sicilian fishermen and their troubles [inspired by Giovanni Verga's novel *I malavoglia*].

Artistically and technically the film is an important achievement. There is unnecessary caricaturization and certain lack of logic with which Visconti points up class antagonisms, plus a confusing fragmentary quality.

Visconti's direction of the Sicilian fisherfolk is a magnificent job; the entire cast is well chosen and he's captured the grim and joyful sides of their daily lives with stark realism, aided by G. R. Aldo's superb lensing (which includes the first functional use of deep-focus photography in Italy), and by an impressive soundtrack recorded on the spot.

•

TERROR IN A TEXAS TOWN
1958, 80 mins, US b/w
Dir Joseph H. Lewis ***Prod*** Frank N. Seltzer ***Scr*** Ben L. Perry ***Ph*** Ray Rennahan ***Ed*** Frank Sullivan, Stefan Arnsten ***Mus*** Gerald Fried ***Art*** William Ferrari
Act Sterling Hayden, Sebastian Cabot, Carol Kelly, Eugene Martin, Ned Young, Victor Millan (Seltzer)

Handicapped by a slow-moving story, *Terror in a Texas Town* shapes up as a routine filler for the duals.

Ben L. Perry's yarn, which he also screenplayed, revives the time-honored incident where the unscrupulous land-grabber attempts to toss the squatters off their property by hook or crook. In this case Sebastian Cabot is the No.1 heavy who carries on a campaign of intimidation with the aid of gunman Ned Young and several other cohorts. There's oil under them thar fields and Cabot aims to get it. But he fails to reckon with Hayden, a seafaring Swede who comes on the scene after his farmer father has been shot down by Young.

Hayden isn't too convincing as the hero and either the story, Joseph H. Lewis's direction or both could be listed as the culprits. Young is amply sinister as the top killer and Carol Kelly is good as the moll who eventually gives him the air.

Producer Frank N. Seltzer evidently guided this one with an eye to economy for, while there are many scenes in a hotel and one on the town's street, seldom is anyone seen with exception of the immediate principals.

•

TERRORISTS, THE
SEE: RANSOM

•

TERROR TRAIN
1980, 97 mins, Canada/US Ⓥ ⦿ col
Dir Roger Spottiswoode ***Prod*** Harold Greenberg ***Scr*** T. Y. Drake ***Ph*** John Alcott ***Ed*** Anne Henderson ***Mus*** John Mills-Cockell ***Art*** Glenn Bydwell
Act Ben Johnson, Jamie Lee Curtis, Hart Bochner, David Copperfield (Astral-Bellevue-Pathe)

Roger Spottiswoode, vet editor who co-authored a respected book on the subject with Karel Reisz, makes a competent directing debut here.

As in Jamie Lee Curtis's other shocker pix, she limns the feisty survivor character in a group of young people menaced by a psychotic while having a wild party on a train. Her acting fits a narrow groove. But it must be said in young thesp's favor that she has not been given the most challenging material.

Efficient screenplay quickly sets up the premise by showing a repulsive sick joke being perpetrated by college med students on a sensitive youth who goes insane as a result. Three years later the kids all take a train excursion to celebrate their graduation, and the chickens come home to roost.

•

TERRY FOX STORY, THE
1983, 96 mins, Canada Ⓥ col
Dir R. L. Thomas ***Prod*** Robert Cooper ***Scr*** Edward Hume ***Ph*** Richard Ciupka ***Ed*** Ron Wisman ***Mus*** Bill Conti ***Art*** Gavin Mitchell
Act Robert Duvall, Eric Fryer, Michael Zelniker, Chris Makepeace, Rosalind Chao, Elva Mai Hoover (Astral)

The Terry Fox Story chronicles the heroic life of the young Canadian man whose 1980 Marathon of Hope resulted in raising more than $20 million for cancer research.

Eric Fryer plays the title role with tremendous conviction. The story [by John and Rose Kastner] opens in Vancouver in 1977, prior to the time Fox lost his right leg to cancer. In short order, the film dispenses with the diagnosed malignancy, Fox's convalescence, the fitting of a prosthetic leg and his decision to run across Canada to raise money for cancer research.

Despite initial parental and medical opposition, Fox's dream begins in April 1980. He enlists the aid of his friend Doug Alward (Michael Zelniker) to drive a camper and watch his progress but cannot convince his girlfriend, Rika (Rosalind Chao), to leave her job and join the marathon.

Fryer, an acting newcomer and himself an amputee, shows no rough edges in his performance. Robert Duvall as Vigars has another accomplished, gutsy role.

•

TESS
1979, 180 mins, France/UK Ⓥ ⦿ ▭ col
Dir Roman Polanski ***Prod*** Claude Berri ***Scr*** Roman Polanski, Gerard Brach, John Brownjohn ***Ph*** Geoffrey Unsworth, Ghislain Cloquet ***Ed*** Alastair McIntyre ***Mus*** Philippe Sarde ***Art*** Pierre Guffroy
Act Nastassja Kinski, Leigh Lawson, Peter Firth, John Collin, David Markham, Carolyn Pickles (Renn/Burrill)

Tess is a sensitive, intelligent screen treatment of a literary masterwork. Roman Polanski has practiced no betrayal in filming Thomas Hardy's 1891 novel, *Tess of the d'Urbervilles*, and his adaptation often has that infrequent quality of combining fidelity and beauty.

Tess Durbeyfield is an uncommonly beautiful peasant girl whose derelict father learns of the family's descent from once noble Norman ancestry, the d'Urbervilles. Learning of the existence of a rich family bearing this name, Tess's parents induce the girl to present herself as a distant relation in the hope of reaping profit from the family tree.

The young rakish master of the d'Urbervilles, Alec, gives her employment and seduces her. Tess returns home and bears a child who dies after a short time.

She meets and falls in love with Angel Clare. They marry but, on the wedding night, Tess reveals her past. Angel reacts horribly and leaves her.

First-rate contributions are the color photography of Geoffrey Unsworth (who died during the shooting and was succeeded by Ghislain Cloquet) and the superb production design of Pierre Guffroy.

1980: Best Cinematography, Art Direction, Costume Design (Anthony Powell)

NOMINATIONS: Best Picture, Director, Original Score

•

TESS OF THE STORM COUNTRY
1914, 60 mins, US ⊗ b/w
Dir Edwin S. Porter ***Scr*** Edwin S. Porter
Act Mary Pickford, Harold Lockwood, Olive Golden (Famous Players)

In *Tess of the Storm Country*, Grace Miller White's human heart story, little Mary Pickford comes into her own. As the little, expressive-eyed tatterdemalion of the Lake Cayuga shores, Pickford sticks another feather in her movie crown.

There are some big scenes—big moments—that give the picture k.o. wallop. The theft of the Bible from the mission, the fight with the real murderers of the gamekeeper, getting milk by desperate methods for the baby, the struggle in the courtroom crowd, the hut fight with the shore bully, the break with her sweetheart and the big situation in the church where Tess, realizing the baby is dying, makes a superhuman effort to have the kidlet baptized so that it can enter the Kingdom of Heaven, are all well staged.

The photography in the first part is somewhat indistinct, but the excellent filming which follows makes up for all shortcomings in this respect.

•

TESS OF THE STORM COUNTRY
1922, 110 mins, US ⊗ b/w
Dir John S. Robertson ***Scr*** Elmer Harris ***Ph*** Charles Rosher ***Art*** Frank Ormston
Act Mary Pickford, Lloyd Hughes, Gloria Hope, David Torrence, Forrest Robinson, Jean Hersholt (Pickford/United Artists)

Mary Pickford fans will revel with her in *Tess of the Storm Country* [based on the novel by Grace Miller White]. It's Mary Pickford all of the time. Pickford acts with her head, hands and feet; she pantomimes and plays the part all of the while, with the titles often lending an additional but quiet though effective amusing touch.

Naught to be said against the least item in the film. Everything has been done well, particularly the photography by Charles Rosher and the direction.

After Pickford, the finest performance is that of Ben Letts by Jean Hersholt. Hersholt makes his villainous character real, of the seafaring sort, shaggy and bearded, uncouth and rough. In contrast is the Teola Graves of Gloria Hope, carrying a miserable whining countenance that cannot bring her sympathy in a sympathetic role.

•

TESTAMENT
1983, 89 mins, US Ⓥ ⦿ col
Dir Lynne Littman ***Prod*** Jonathan Bernstein, Lynne Littman ***Scr*** John Sacret Young ***Ph*** Steven Poster ***Ed*** Suzanne Pettit ***Mus*** James Horner ***Art*** David Nichols
Act Jane Alexander, William Devane, Ross Harris, Roxana Zal, Lukas Haas, Kevin Costner (Entertainment Events/American Playhouse)

Testament is an exceptionally powerful film dealing with the survivors of a nuclear war. Debuting director Lynne Littman brings an original approach to the grim material.

Based on Carol Amen's magazine story "The Last Testament," pic depicts a normal, complacent community in the small California town of Hamlin. The town's calm is shattered when a TV newscast announces that nuclear devices have exploded in New York and on the east coast, with the film proper suddenly going to yellow and whiteout, indicating blasts on the west coast as well. Ham radio operator Henry Abhart (Leon Ames) becomes Hamlin's communications link to the outside world.

Isolated, Hamlin's residents attempt to survive, but within a month over 1,000 people have died from radiation sickness. A young couple (Rebecca DeMornay and Kevin Costner), whose baby has died, drive off in search of "a safe place."

Holding it all together as a tower of strength is actress Jane Alexander as Carol Wetherby, coping with the deaths of her family and friends in truly heroic fashion via an understated performance.

1983: NOMINATION: Best Actress (Jane Alexander)

•

TESTAMENT DES DR. MABUSE, DAS
(THE TESTAMENT OF DR. MABUSE; THE LAST WILL OF DR. MABUSE; THE CRIMES OF DR. MABUSE)
1933, 118 mins, Germany Ⓥ b/w
Dir Fritz Lang ***Prod*** Seymour Nebenzal ***Scr*** Thea von Harbou, [Fritz Lang] ***Ph*** Fritz Arno Wagner, Karl Vash ***Art*** Karl Vollbrecht, Emil Hasler
Act Rudolf Klein-Rogge, Otto Wernicke, Oscar Beregi, Gustav Diessl, Vera Liessem, Karl Meixner (Nero)

This sequel to the silent picture and the novel, which both had enormous successes more than 12 years earlier, certainly shows the influence of American mystery pictures. The story is very long-winded, and even an ingenious director like Fritz Lang could not prevent its being rather slow-moving in places.

Dr. Mabuse (Rudolf Klein-Rogge), great scientist and greater criminal, is confined in a lunatic asylum when the tale begins. Yet the mysterious crimes committed in his own style continue and their perpetrators cannot be traced. Mabuse's gang receive their instructions from a mysterious source against which they are unable to put up any resistance. Detective Chief Lohmann (Otto Wernicke) is trying to get at the bottom of the mystery.

The crimes continue after the death of Mabuse. A doctor at the asylum finds the testament of Mabuse, with plans of crimes committed since his death, on the table of Dr. Baum (Oscar Beregi), the alienist who treated Mabuse and made a special study of his case. This doctor dies before he can speak of his discovery, the detective on the track of the mystery goes crazy, and other mysterious tragedies appear.

Baum's difficult double part, that of the alienist and of a maniac hypnotically obsessed, is played admirably by Beregi. Klein-Rogge, in the figure of Mabuse, is very suggestive.

[As the pic was banned by the Nazi authorities, its first showing was in Paris in 1933 (in the French version). World preem of the German version was in Budapest the same year. Above review is of that showing.]

•

TESTAMENT D'ORPHEE, LE
(THE TESTAMENT OF ORPHEUS)
1960, 80 mins, France b/w
Dir Jean Cocteau ***Prod*** Jean Thuillier ***Scr*** Jean Cocteau ***Ph*** Roland Pontoiseau ***Ed*** Marie-Josephe Yoyotte ***Mus*** Jacques Metehan ***Art*** Pierre Guffroy
Act Jean Cocteau, Edouard Dermit, Henri Cremieux, Maria Casares, Francois Perier, Jean-Pierre Leaud (Editions Cinematographiques)

A great deal of the money for this film was raised from friends and well-wishers. The combo patronage-industry pic allows Jean Cocteau, 70, poet-writer-playwright filmmaker, to try to explain the meaning of a poet's life and, incidentally, his own. Playing himself as an errant poet who roams through the ages, this is distinctly offbeat fare.

Cocteau subtitles his pic *And Don't Ask Me Why*. He still has a flair for provoking strange moods in ordinary landscapes, as well as utilizing simple trick effects effectively and judiciously. He ribs himself at times but is quite clear in his summation that a poet is rarely recognized in his time.

Popping up throughout are familiar local actors, plus Yul Brynner, Picasso, Serge Lifar, Luis Dominguin and others. This is Cocteau's final film fling.

•

TESTAMENT OF DR. MABUSE, THE
SEE: DAS TESTAMENT DES DR. MABUSE

•

TESTAMENT OF ORPHEUS, THE
SEE: LE TESTAMENT D'ORPHEE

•

TESTIMONY
1987, 157 mins, UK ▭ col
Dir Tony Palmer ***Prod*** Tony Palmer ***Scr*** David Rudkin, Tony Palmer ***Ph*** Nic Knowland ***Ed*** Tony Palmer ***Art*** Tony Palmer
Act Ben Kingsley, Sherry Baines, Magdalen Asquith, Mark Asquith, Terence Rigby, Ronald Pickup (Isolde/Film Four)

Testimony is quite an undertaking. Long, muddled and abstract at times, but ultimately a beautifully conceived and executed art film with fine topline performances, it makes fascinating viewing.

In essence the pic [based on *The Memoirs of Dmitri Shostakovich*, edited by Solomon Volkov] follows the life of the Russian composer, played by Ben Kingsley sporting a dubious wig, but especially focuses on his relationship with Stalin.

Testimony traces the young Shostakovich who had success after success until Stalin took a dislike to the opera *Lady Macbeth*, and in a marvelous scene at the Extraordinary Conference of Soviet Musicians his work is denounced, but still he apologizes.

Later Stalin pours on further humiliation by sending him to an International Peace Congress in New York, where he is forced to denounce his fellow musicians, such as Stravinsky, who had fled Russia.

Ronald Pickup is excellent as Kingsley's friend Tukhachevsky and Robert Urquhart puts in a telling—though small—appearance as the journalist who quizzes Kingsley at the U.S. peace conference.

Helmer Tony Palmer utilizes stunning technical skill to tell his story though at times seems to be a bit too clever for his own good. Technical credits are excellent, and Shostakovich's music suitably stirring.

•

TEST PILOT
1938, 120 mins, US Ⓥ b/w
Dir Victor Fleming ***Prod*** Louis D. Lighton ***Scr*** Vincent Lawrence, Waldemar Young ***Ph*** Ray June ***Ed*** Tom Held ***Mus*** Franz Waxman (dir.) ***Art*** Cedric Gibbons
Act Clark Gable, Myrna Loy, Spencer Tracy, Lionel Barrymore, Samuel S. Hinds, Marjorie Main (M-G-M)

Test Pilot is an actioner against a new approach to the aviation theme, fortified by a strong romance.

Spencer Tracy is Clark Gable's ground aide—the Gunner. Gable as a crack but arrogant pilot is forced down on a Kansas farm, where Myrna Loy is introduced as a romance interest. Ensuing action, backgrounded by ultra-modern aviation tests and experiments, plus a military note attendant to the U.S. aviation service, vividly portrays the strong Loy–Gable romance.

Her disposition to understand the peculiar ways of the men with wings, and the pilot's appreciation of this understanding, have been artfully limned by director Victor Fleming. Three stars are capital in their assignments, particularly Gable, because it's a tailor-made role.

Story bespeaks authority in detail, obviously explained by the fact that Capt. Frank Wead, who authored the original, has had practical aviation background.

1938: NOMINATIONS: Best Picture, Original Story, Editing

•

TEX
1982, 103 mins, US Ⓥ ⊙ col
Dir Tim Hunter ***Prod*** Tim Zinnemann ***Scr*** Charlie Haas, Tim Hunter ***Ph*** Ric Waite ***Ed*** Howard Smith ***Mus*** Pino Donaggio ***Art*** Jack T. Collis
Act Matt Dillon, Jim Metzler, Meg Tilly, Bill McKinney, Ben Johnson, Emilio Estevez (Walt Disney)

What *Tex* will probably best be remembered for is breaking new ground at Disney Studios in representing some of the real problems confronting today's young people. The teenagers are put in the milieu of drugs, alcohol, sex and violence. Family life is not necessarily rosy and well scrubbed.

Where the picture ironically goes awry is in trying to tackle all of these problems in the space of 103 minutes. Writers Charlie Haas and Tim Hunter (latter making his directing debut) seem intent on incorporating every conceivable adolescent and adult trauma into their script [from the novel by S. E. Hinton], thus leaving the film with a very overdone, contrived feeling.

Story primarily centers on 15-year-old Oklahoma farm boy Tex, played admirably by Matt Dillon. Growing up with his older brother, while his father is "traveling" with the rodeo, he must deal with family skeletons, school, friends, class distinctions, drugs, love, sex, death, responsibility, etc.

•

TEXAN, THE
1930, 79 mins, US b/w
Dir John Cromwell ***Prod*** Jesse L. Lasky, Adolph Zukor ***Scr*** Oliver H. P. Garrett, Daniel N. Rubin ***Ph*** Victor Milner ***Ed*** Verna Willis
Act Gary Cooper, Fay Wray, Emma Dunn, Oscar Apfel, James Marcus (Paramount)

Most of the action centers in South America in a setting of rich Spanish ancestral life. The turn the story [based on "A Double-Dyed Deceiver" by O. Henry] takes is a wide one after the first reel, which devotes itself to the Llano Kid, wanted bandit, and some of his operations in the southwest.

An agent of a rich widow in South America has been commissioned to find her long-lost son. Making a deal with the Llano Kid, who speaks Spanish and is possessed of Hispanic features sufficient to fool the rich widow below the Caribbean, the two set out on their strange deception for dough.

Fay Wray, as a cousin of the long-lost son, lends a pleasing touch to both eye and ear. Gary Cooper is a great type as the Llano Kid. He turns in an A1 performance, registering by turn steely coldness, brutality, amazement, uneasiness and tenderness.

•

TEXANS, THE
1938, 92 mins, US b/w
Dir James Hogan ***Prod*** Lucien Hubbard ***Scr*** Bertram Millhauser, Paul Sloane, William Wister Haines ***Ph*** Theodor Sparkuhl ***Ed*** LeRoy Stone ***Mus*** Gerard Carbonara
Act Joan Bennett, Randolph Scott, May Robson, Walter Brennan, Robert Cummings, Robert Barrat (Paramount)

More western than anything else, basically *The Texans* is a story of the Reconstruction period and carpetbaggers following the Civil War. It is another of a long line of pictures which adopts a strong pro-Southern attitude in dealing with this period of American history.

Plot [story by Emerson Hough] deals with the plight of an old Texas family of ranchers which escapes from the homeland with 10,000 head of cattle to avoid onerous taxation levied by the landgrabbers, scalawags and carpetbaggers of the days following the War between the States. Most of the action covers the long and treacherous drive of the cattle through wild country up to the nearest railroad point in Kansas.

Camera crew get some beautiful outdoor shots on the cattle push from Texas to Kansas. Blizzard is realistically shot, also the prairie fire sequence and the night scene when the caravan is camping.

Joan Bennett is too much the Fifth Avenue debbie in a cow-hat to impart the desired touch. Someone should have mussed her up a little now and then. Randolph Scott, paired with Bennett for romantic interest, shepherds the flock (men and cattle) through to Kansas and finally edges out Robert Cummings, who also figures on the romantic end, but unsympathetically. Scott gives an even performance and looks much more the pioneer type than the star opposite him.

•

TEXAS ACROSS THE RIVER
1966, 100 mins, US Ⓥ ▭ col
Dir Michael Gordon ***Prod*** Harry Keller ***Scr*** Wells Root, Harold Greene, Ben Starr ***Ph*** Russell Metty ***Ed*** Gene Milford ***Mus*** Frank DeVol ***Art*** Alexander Golitzen, William D. DeCinces
Act Dean Martin, Alain Delon, Rosemary Forsyth, Joey Bishop, Tina Marquand, Peter Graves (Universal)

Texas Across the River is a rootin', tootin' comedy-western with no holds barred. It's a gag-man's dream, an uninhibited spoof of the early frontier packed with a choice assemblage of laughs, many of the belly genre.

Writers have developed a situation of a gallant Spanish innocent set down in a world he can never quite understand. That he is a nobleman, too, with courtly ethics, makes him all the more improbable as a character who takes in stride wild Comanches and wilder longhorns, and finds Dean Martin, as a Texan, the most perplexing of all.

Michael Gordon's direction juggles the misadventuress of Alain Delon, in Spanish role, and Martin with a mission of transporting guns across Comanche territory and Delon on his hands. Both Indians and the cavalry are satirized with countless slick touches.

•

TEXAS CARNIVAL
1951, 76 mins, US Ⓥ col
Dir Charles Walters ***Prod*** Jack Cummings ***Scr*** Dorothy Kingsley ***Ph*** Robert Planck ***Ed*** Adrienne Fazan ***Mus*** David Rose (dir.) ***Art*** Cedric Gibbons, William Ferrari
Act Esther Williams, Red Skelton, Howard Keel, Ann Miller, Paula Raymond, Keenan Wynn (M-G-M)

Plenty of laugh diversion, dressed up to treat the eye and ear, is offered in *Texas Carnival*. Material provides Red Skelton with several surefire comedy sequences. In the eye department film offers Esther Williams in a bathing suit and one imaginative dream swim number, as well as the talented terping and physical charms of Ann Miller. For tunes it has Howard Keel as a virile cowpoke baritoning his way through the footage and two of the four Harry Warren–Dorothy Fields songs.

Williams and Skelton are a carnival team struggling along until proud Texan Keenan Wynn, in an alcoholic moment, takes a fancy to Skelton. Latter goes to a swank hotel to meet Wynn but, instead, is mistaken for the rich Texan himself. Life of ease being lived by Skelton during Wynn's absence wears easy on his conscience even though it troubles Williams plenty. Appearance of Keel, foreman of Wynn's ranch, adds some complications.

•

TEXAS CHAIN SAW MASSACRE, THE
1974, 83 mins, US Ⓥ ⊙ col
Dir Tobe Hooper ***Prod*** Tobe Hooper ***Scr*** Kim Henkel, Tobe Hooper ***Ph*** Daniel Pearl, Tobe Hooper ***Ed*** Sallye Richardson, Larry Carroll ***Mus*** Tobe Hooper, Wayne Bell ***Art*** Robert A. Burns
Act Marilyn Burns, Allen Danziger, Paul A. Partain, William Vail, Teri McMinn, Gunnar Hansen (Vortex)

Despite the heavy doses of gore in *The Texas Chain Saw Massacre*, Tobe Hooper's pic is well made for an exploiter of its type. The script by Hooper and Kim Henkel is a takeoff on the same incident which inspired Robert Bloch's novel (and later Alfred Hitchcock's film) *Psycho*.

In 1957, Plainfield, Wis., authorities arrested handyman Ed Gein after finding dismembered bodies and disinterred corpses strewn all over his farmhouse.

When a dozen graves are found violated in a rural Texas cemetery, Marilyn Burns visits her father's grave to make sure it is unmolested. Disaster strikes on a side trip to her deserted family home. A family of graverobbers, led by saw-wielding Gunnar Hansen, butcher everyone but Burns, who makes a narrow escape.

Though marred by thin, washed-out color, pic otherwise has a professional look, with skillful and frequent use of dolly shots for atmospheric effect. Sharp sense of composition and careful accumulation of detail also help enliven the crude plot, and the acting is above par for this type of film.

•

TEXAS CHAIN SAW MASSACRE PART 2, THE
1986, 95 mins, US Ⓥ ⊙ col
Dir Tobe Hooper ***Prod*** Menahem Golan, Yoram Globus ***Scr*** L. M. Kit Carson ***Ph*** Richard Kooris ***Ed*** Alain Jakubowicz ***Mus*** Tobe Hooper, Jerry Lambert ***Art*** Cary White
Act Dennis Hopper, Caroline Williams, Bill Johnson, Jim Siedow, Bill Moseley, Lou Perry (Cannon)

Success of the low-budget *Chain Saw* in 1974 spawned a generation of splatter films which largely have lost the power to shock and entertain. Not so *Chain Saw 2*. Director Tobe Hooper is back on the Texas turf he knows.

Also a big help is L. M. Kit Carson's tongue-in-cheek script. In truth the story is basically a setup for a series of gory confrontations. The family is just an ordinary American hard-luck story—butchers who have fallen on hard times and take their resentment out on the human race.

Although Dennis Hopper gets top billing his role is surprisingly limited, climaxing in a chainsaw duel to the death with Leatherface (Bill Johnson). Performances of the family are fine, especially Jim Siedow and a crazed Bill Moseley, but the real star here is carnage.

•

TEXASVILLE
1990, 123 mins, US Ⓥ ⦿ col
Dir Peter Bogdanovich ***Prod*** Barry Spikings, Peter Bogdanovich ***Scr*** Peter Bogdanovich ***Ph*** Nicholas von Sternberg ***Ed*** Richard Fields ***Art*** Phedon Papamichael
Act Jeff Bridges, Cybill Shepherd, Annie Potts, Timothy Bottoms, Cloris Leachman, Randy Quaid (Nelson)

Peter Bogdanovich's sequel to *The Last Picture Show* is long on folksy humor and short on plot. In adapting Larry McMurtry's 1987 follow-up novel (predecessor was penned in 1965, filmed in 1971), Bogdanovich uses an impending county centennial celebration as the weak spine for this slice of small-town Texas life.

Set in 1984, film revolves around the nonadventures of oil tycoon Jeff Bridges. He's $12 million in debt and his loyal assistant (Cloris Leachman) is ready to quit.

Bogdanovich has rounded up many of the first film's players (notably absent are Oscar-winner Ben Johnson, whose character died, Ellen Burstyn, Clu Gulager, Sam Bottoms and John Hillerman), but the plum role goes to Annie Potts as Bridges's domineering wife.

Less successful is Cybill Shepherd, whose career was launched with the 1971 pic. Making a delayed entrance as Bridges's old flame who's brooding over the death of her son, Shepherd adopts a no-makeup look and is unflatteringly photographed.

Apart from a few set pieces involving the Archer County pageant parade celebrating Texasville, pic is static and poorly lensed.

•

THANKS A MILLION
1935, 85 mins, US Ⓥ b/w
Dir Roy Del Ruth ***Prod*** Darryl F. Zanuck ***Scr*** Nunnally Johnson ***Ph*** Peverell Marley ***Ed*** Allen McNeil ***Mus*** Arthur Lange (dir.) ***Art*** Jack Otterson
Act Dick Powell, Ann Dvorak, Fred Allen, Patsy Kelly, Raymond Walburn, Paul Whiteman (20th Century-Fox)

Thanks a Million is corking entertainment. Film unquestionably establishes Fred Allen for the screen. It also takes Paul Whiteman and his orchestra, including Ramona, the Yacht Club Boys and Rubinoff and his violin, and shows 'em at their best.

Allen's radio rep as a pungent comedy deliverer is well capitalized here as the manager of the near-stranded unit which includes Ann Dvorak and Patsy Kelly as a sister team; an anonymous band, presumably maestroed by Dave Rubinoff, who gets in a couple of violin solos (including a pash personality); the Yacht Club Boys, who, like Rubinoff, also have lines besides two corking specialties; and Benny Baker, who's an indeterminate stooge throughout the footage.

Nunnally Johnson's script [from a story by Melville Crossman, nom de plume of Darryl F. Zanuck] deserves some sort of an award as a sample of celluloid writing. It's made to order for Allen's dead-pan comedy. Punchy, pithy and punctuated with a flock of telling nifties, the comedy wordage doesn't sacrifice the story. The title song is the best of Gus Kahn–Arthur Johnston's five numbers; "Pocket Full of Sunshine" and "High on a Hill Top," along with "Thanks a Million," are handled by Dick Powell.

1935: NOMINATION: Best Sound

•

THANK YOU, MR. MOTO
1938, 68 mins, US b/w
Dir Norman Foster ***Prod*** Sol M. Wurtzel (exec.) ***Scr*** Willis Cooper, Norman Foster ***Ph*** Virgil Miller ***Ed*** Irene Morra, Nick DeMaggio ***Mus*** Samuel Kaylin (dir.) ***Art*** Bernard Herzbrun, Albert Hoggsett
Act Peter Lorre, Thomas Beck, Pauline Frederick, Jayne Ryan, Sidney Blackmer, John Carradine (20th Century-Fox)

Moto wriggles through another mass of Oriental-Occidental intrigue in the Far East for the second [from a story by John P. Marquand] of 20th-Fox's rival series to the well-established Charlie Chans. Moto string bears a marked resemblance to the Chans, even to the use of several characters.

Peter Lorre is ideal for role of the sly Oriental who watches the smuggling outfits who try to steal his country's art treasures, and whose appearance anywhere is the immediate signal for adventure. Moto is adept in the manly arts—can use his fists, his feet, his gun or his knife, which makes colorful film material.

Thank You, Mr. Moto gives Jayne Ryan, Fox stock contractee from St. Louis, her first chance, and she's a striking looker. Works opposite Thomas Beck, whose one constant demand seems to be that he appear in a white suit. Pauline Frederick, never handed too great material in films, disappears behind a daub of clay and becomes an expressionless Chinese mother who is killed midway trying to save the honor of her house.

•

THANK YOUR LUCKY STARS
1943, 127 mins, US Ⓥ ⦿ b/w
Dir David Butler ***Prod*** Mark Hellinger ***Scr*** Norman Panama, Melvin Frank ***Ph*** Arthur Edison ***Ed*** Irene Morra ***Mus*** Arthur Schwartz, Frank Loesser
Act Eddie Cantor, Dinah Shore, Joan Leslie, Dennis Morgan, Edward Everett Horton, S. Z. Sakall (Warner)

As an Eddie Cantor vehicle this is topped by some of his previous efforts but it's chiefly due to the banjo-eyed comedian that the thing is pulled together during its sagging moments. As such it's a triumph for Cantor. Film has long stretches that are under par; the musical and star participation interludes are dovetailed together by a story that often gets lost in the shuffle and is something less than inspiring; a few of the star bits have dubious entertainment value. But even the most captious will admit to its many moments of diversion.

In novelty, *Stars* packs a wallop. The idea of a dual Cantor role, on the one hand a film star portrayed strictly as a heel, with a crush on any Cantor gag, and the other a film colony bus guide whose affliction is that he can't land a picture job because he looks "too much like that Cantor guy" has solid merit in itself. But that idea goes astray too. For novelty there's also Bette Davis being tossed around in a swank nitery by a frenzied jitterbug, lamenting her fate of resorting to a.k.'s and adolescent pups in a vocalization of Arthur Schwartz's sock tune, "They're Either Too Young or Too Old." Or Errol Flynn as a cockney sailor singing a sea shanty, with Gilbertian overtones, only to emerge in the finale reprise by kidding the dubbed vocal.

Stars marks Dinah Shore's film debut.

•

THAT CERTAIN AGE
1938, 100 mins, US b/w
Dir Edward Ludwig ***Prod*** Joe Pasternak ***Scr*** Bruce Manning ***Ph*** Joseph Valentine ***Ed*** Bernard W. Burton ***Mus*** Charles Previn (dir.) ***Art*** Jack Otterson, John Ewing
Act Deanna Durbin, Melvyn Douglas, Jackie Cooper, Irene Rich, Nancy Carroll, John Halliday (Universal)

That Certain Age is brimful of substantial entertainment, carrying all of the charm and wholesomeness which characterizes Deanna Durbin's previous pictures. Universal brilliantly bridges the adolescent period at one crack, and launches her into the broader fields of youthful romance and adventure.

Original story by F. Hugh Herbert provides sufficient foundation for a sparkling script.

Durbin develops a romantic crush for Melvyn Douglas's globetrotting reporter, when her father, John Halliday's newspaper publisher, brings him to the country estate to prepare a series of articles. Girl tosses aside Jackie Cooper, her loyal puppy-love admirer, and by her attentions keeps Douglas amused and away from social affairs, for which he is grateful.

Douglas turns in a sterling performance. Cooper clicks resoundingly. Particularly effective is his scene with Douglas when the youngster congratulates the latter for his conquest of the girl—and talking "man-to-man." It's a standout.

•

THAT CERTAIN FEELING
1956, 102 mins, US Ⓥ col
Dir Norman Panama, Melvin Frank ***Prod*** Norman Panama, Melvin Frank ***Scr*** Norman Panama, Melvin Frank, I.A.L. Diamond, William Altman ***Ph*** Loyal Griggs ***Ed*** Tom McAdoo ***Mus*** Joseph J. Lilley
Act Bob Hope, Eva Marie Saint, George Sanders, Pearl Bailey, David Lewis, Al Capp (Paramount)

Overall what's fashioned here is amusingly frothy, with a touch of heart occasionally to add depth to the adaptation of legiter *The King of Hearts* by Jean Kerr and Eleanor Brooke.

Bob Hope's femme costar is Eva Marie Saint in her first film since *On the Waterfront*. What she does in the change of pace casting is all to the good.

A big asset is Pearl Bailey, maid in the household of renowned cartoonist George Sanders, for whom Saint is secretary-fiancée and Hope is ghost "stripper." Bailey's wow personality adds a most engaging comedy touch.

Sanders has himself a free-wheeling ball as the sophisticated cartoonist who has lost the common touch and calls in ghoster Hope, a neurotic who wants to upchuck every time he tries to stand up to the boss. Complicating his employment is the fact that Saint's his ex-wife.

There's a nepotism note to the uncredited casting. One of Hope's sons does well as a playmate to young Mathers; and three other Hope offspring are in amusement park bits.

•

THAT CERTAIN WOMAN
1937, 91 mins, US b/w
Dir Edmund Goulding ***Prod*** Robert Lord ***Scr*** Edmund Goulding ***Ph*** Ernest Haller ***Ed*** Jack Killifer ***Mus*** Max Steiner ***Art*** Max Parker
Act Bette Davis, Henry Fonda, Ian Hunter, Anita Louise, Donald Crisp, Hugh O'Donnell (Warner)

Appeal is aimed strictly at the emotions, as the plot is another variation of self-sacrificing mother love. The film is a remake of *The Trespasser*, which Edmund Goulding earlier wrote and directed for Gloria Swanson in 1929.

Film relates the adventures of a self-reliant young woman (Bette Davis), who as a girl of 16 married a gangster, since deceased, after a bootleg altercation. She becomes the secretary of a prominent lawyer, an unhappily married man, who falls in love with her but keeps his distance. She falls in love with a wealthy young wastrel and marries him.

His father compels the young woman to reveal her past. The marriage is annulled, and the girl returns to her job. A son is born. Much later a scandal brings back the wastrel youth, now reformed, to help his one-time wife.

It's a synthetic tale that does not stand up under too close analysis. The story deficiencies are not so important, however, because the characters are made credible by Davis and the cast, and by Goulding's smooth direction. Ian Hunter as the girl's employer and Henry Fonda as the boy in the case are excellent.

•

THAT COLD DAY IN THE PARK
1969, 115 mins, Canada Ⓥ col
Dir Robert Altman ***Scr*** Gillian Freeman ***Ph*** Laszlo Kovacs ***Mus*** Johnny Mandel
Act Sandy Dennis, Michael Burns, Susanne Benton, Luana Anders, John Garfield, Jr. (Factor-Altman-Mirell)

A pretty, reserved, rich spinster in Vancouver, B.C., spots a teenager sitting in the park in the rain. She invites the boy to her apartment and a strange relationship starts that ends in breakdown and tragedy. Sandy Dennis is strikingly effective, if her character's veering into madness is a bit abrupt. Michael Burns is good as the cherubic youth, with Susanne Benton displaying a fine feel for character as his freewheeling, slightly nympho sister.

This mixing of themes and social strata [from the book by Richard Miles] is too literary to get a true insight into the many layers involved. It tries to bring in too much and waters down the interesting personal relations, turning the denouement into grand guignol, rather than perceptive dramatic and psychological progression.

•

THAT FORSYTE WOMAN
1950, 112 mins, US Ⓥ col
Dir Compton Bennett ***Prod*** Leon Gordon ***Scr*** Jan Lustig, Ivan Tors, James B. Williams, Arthur Wimperis ***Ph*** Joseph Ruttenberg ***Ed*** Frederick Y. Smith ***Mus*** Bronislau Kaper
Act Errol Flynn, Greer Garson, Walter Pidgeon, Robert Young, Janet Leigh, Harry Davenport (M-G-M)

Metro has fashioned a long, elaborate and costly class feature out of John Galsworthy's writings about his Victorian family, the Forsytes. Compton Bennett's direction unfolds it at a measured pace, in keeping with the quaintness of the Victorian English setting, as it tells the story of an outsider femme who marries into the Forsyte family, then falls in love with a man engaged to one of the Forsyte women, bringing discord into an ordered, dull way of life.

Greer Garson's playing, and that of her co-stars Errol Flynn, the cold, proper Forsyte whom she marries; Walter Pidgeon, the Forsyte black sheep; and Robert Young, the man with whom she falls in love; approach the characters with all the dignified stuffiness that distinguishes Galsworthy's people.

The script is based on Book One of Galsworthy's *The Forsyte Saga*.

1950: NOMINATION: Best Color Costume Design

•

THAT HAMILTON WOMAN
(UK: LADY HAMILTON)
1941, 124 mins, US Ⓥ ⦿ b/w
Dir Alexander Korda ***Prod*** Alexander Korda ***Scr*** Walter Reisch, R. C. Sherriff ***Ph*** Rudolph Mate ***Ed*** William Hornbeck ***Mus*** Miklos Rozsa ***Art*** Vincent Korda

Act Vivien Leigh, Laurence Olivier, Alan Mowbray, Sara Allgood, Gladys Cooper, Henry Wilcoxon (Korda Inc./United Artists)

Alexander Korda dips into the files of British history for this biographical drama of Lady Hamilton and her amorous affair with naval hero Lord Nelson.

Korda makes out a sympathetic case for the scandalous (of the period) romance between the wife of a British ambassador and the great Lord Nelson. Utilizing the retrospect story device, the haggish Lady Hamilton is tossed in the Calais jail for stealing, and tells her tale to a girl of the streets.

Vivien Leigh hits the peaks with her delineation of Lady Hamilton, a vivacious girl who is pictured as a victim of men but whose ingenuity in statecraft saves the Empire. She dominates the picture throughout with her reserved love for Nelson and her determination to aid his success. Laurence Olivier's characterization of Nelson carries the full dignity and reserve of the historical figure.

Picture shows plenty of production outlay with its series of elaborate settings. Battle of Trafalgar sequence carries intercut of cannon broadsides from the English men-of-war with too obvious miniatures of the two fleets in action.

1941: Best Sound Recording

NOMINATIONS: Best B&W Cinematography, B&W Art Direction, Special Effects

•

THAT'LL BE THE DAY
1973, 90 mins, UK Ⓥ ⦿ col
Dir Claude Whatham *Prod* David Puttnam, Sandy Lieberson *Scr* Ray Connolly *Ph* Peter Suschitzky *Ed* Michael Bradsell *Mus* Neil Aspinall, Keith Moon (sup.)
Act David Essex, Ringo Starr, Rosemary Leach, James Booth, Billy Fury, Keith Moon (Anglo-EMI/Goodtimes)

Here is a nice bit of nostalgia (late 1950s): a serious, loving, but not sticky-sweet probe of a youngster's torment in finding himself, complete with parental problems, friendships gained and lost (ditto jobs), puppy love hangups and first sex; in short, the lot.

Script is a big assist, and it rings true without being cloying. Another major asset is having David Essex as its star and key ingredient, as well as in being able to hark back to so colorful a period in which to have him grow up. Essex copes well enough with the few dramatic requirements of the role. Ringo Starr is excellent as his sometime sidekick.

Technically, pic is a superior job, nicely paced by director Claude Whatham with a superior period feel.

•

THAT LUCKY TOUCH
1975, 93 mins, UK Ⓥ col
Dir Christopher Miles *Prod* Dimitri de Grunwald *Scr* John Briley *Ph* Douglas Slocombe *Mus* John Scott *Art* Tony Masters
Act Roger Moore, Susannah York, Shelley Winters, Lee J. Cobb, Jean-Pierre Cassel, Raf Vallone (Rank)

This contemporary light comedy of love-against-the-odds, which evokes the Hollywood genre of the 1930s, falls short of its target.

The film aims to extract some classy fun from the entanglements of an arms dealer (Roger Moore) and a leftist women's libber (Susannah York), covering NATO war games for the *Washington Post*.

Moore just about copes as the assertive, high-living gun merchant, but where moments of finesse are called for he is merely game and/or workmanlike. York makes the best of her chances as the aggressive, sex-shunning pacifist.

Lee J. Cobb's harassed and world-weary U.S. Army general is a gem of resigned bewilderment when coping with his wife (Shelley Winters) or her prickly journalistic pal (York).

•

THAT MIDNIGHT KISS
1949, 96 mins, US col
Dir Norman Taurog *Prod* Joe Pasternak *Scr* Bruce Manning, Tamara Hovey *Ph* Robert Surtees *Ed* Gene Ruggiero
Act Kathryn Grayson, Mario Lanza, Jose Iturbi, Ethel Barrymore, Keenan Wynn, J. Carrol Naish (M-G-M)

The film introduces tenor Mario Lanza, recruited from grand opera. His voice, when he's singing opera, is excellent. He's no great actor but handles his thesping chores adequately.

Original screenplay has Ethel Barrymore as a wealthy Philly blueblood, who attempts to compensate for her own operatic frustrations by financing a civic company to star her granddaughter, Kathryn Grayson. Jose Iturbi, as the maestro, agrees to audition Lanza after Grayson discovers him. When the temperamental tenor originally booked to co-star with Grayson quits, she convinces Iturbi to give Lanza the big chance.

Producer Joe Pasternak had some innocuous stilted lyrics written for a theme from Tchaikovsky's Fifth Symphony. Staging and scoring are both static, which doesn't do either Lanza or Grayson any good.

•

THAT NIGHT IN RIO
1941, 90 mins, US col
Dir Irving Cummings *Prod* Fred Kohlmar *Scr* George Seaton, Bess Meredyth, Hal Long, Samuel Hoffenstein *Ph* Leon Shamroy, Ray Rennahan *Ed* Walter Thompson *Mus* Alfred Newman
Act Alice Faye, Don Ameche, Carmen Miranda, J. Carrol Naish, S. Z. Sakall, Curt Bois (20th Century-Fox)

This successor to *Down Argentine Way* is a close carbon copy of *Folies Bergere* which 20th turned out six years earlier, but with locale switch from Paris to Rio de Janeiro. Embellished with lavish production, brilliant Technicolor and several tuneful songs, it's peak entertainment.

Lightweight story [from a play by Rudolph Lothar and Hans Adler] provides Don Ameche with the dual role of a breezy American night club m.c. performing in Rio and a native financier. Resemblance beween the pair is so close the former's sweetheart (Carmen Miranda) and the financier's wife (Alice Faye) cannot tell them apart. When a business crisis arrives, the tycoon's associates secure the entertainer to impersonate the absent Baron, with the stand-in innocently completing a deal that prevents financial ruin.

Ameche is very capable in a dual role, and Faye is eye-appealing, but it's the tempestuous Miranda who really gets away to a flying start from the first sequence.

•

THAT OBSCURE OBJECT OF DESIRE
SEE: CET OBSCUR OBJET DU DESIR

•

THAT'S DANCING!
1985, 105 mins, US Ⓥ ⦿ ▭ col
Dir Jack Haley, Jr. *Prod* David Niven, Jr., Jack Haley, Jr. *Scr* Jack Haley, Jr. *Ph* Andrew Laszlo, Paul Lohmann *Ed* Bud Friedgen, Michael J. Sheridan *Mus* Henry Mancini
Act Gene Kelly, Sammy Davis, Jr., Mikhail Baryshnikov, Liza Minnelli, Ray Bolger (M-G-M)

For anyone who wants to see big-screen terpsichorean art at its top, *Dancing* is definitive. M-G-M has not only dipped into its own generous collection, but borrowed judiciously from most of the other studios that were in brisk competition during the golden years of movie musicals.

For openers from the early days, there is a lot of Busby Berkeley, plus Ruby Keeler and Dick Powell, followed by the wonderful work of Fred Astaire and Ginger Rogers and on through an absolutely complete list of the greats.

Much is made of a Ray Bolger–Judy Garland dance number from *The Wizard of Oz*, omitted from the final cut of the original. It's interesting to see, but also easy to see (contrary to the gushing narration) why it was left out: the technique is a bit tacky and hardly up to the quality of what was released.

•

THAT'S ENTERTAINMENT!
1974, 132 mins, US Ⓥ ⦿ ▭ col
Dir Jack Haley, Jr. *Prod* Jack Haley, Jr. *Scr* Jack Haley, Jr. *Ph* Gene Polito, Ernest Laszlo, Russell Metty, Ennio Guarnieri, Allan Green *Ed* Bud Friedgen, David E. Blewitt *Mus* Henry Mancini (adapt.)
Act Fred Astaire, Bing Crosby, Gene Kelly, Frank Sinatra, Liza Minnelli, Donald O'Connor (M-G-M)

Metro-Goldwyn-Mayer celebrated its 50th anniversary with *That's Entertainment!*, an outstanding, stunning, sentimental, exciting, colorful, enjoyable, spirit-lifting, tuneful, youthful, invigorating, zesty, respectful, dazzling and richly satisfying feature documentary commemorating its filmusicals.

As Liza Minnelli puts it in her narrated segment (among 11 names appearing in new footage and film clip voiceover), "Thank God for film. It can capture and hold a performance forever."

From the musical library, about 100 films were selected from the 1929–58 era, enough to satisfy nearly every memory. Each segment has a particular theme (usually film highlights of a particular star); and each has its narrator. Minnelli appears in the portion devoted to her mother, Judy Garland.

•

THAT'S ENTERTAINMENT, PART II
1976, 133 mins, US Ⓥ ⦿ ▭ col
Dir Gene Kelly *Prod* Saul Chaplin, Daniel Melnick *Scr* Leonard Gershe *Ph* George Folsey *Ed* Bud Friedgen, David Blewitt, David Bretherton, Peter C. Johnson *Mus* Nelson Riddle (sup.) *Art* John DeCuir
Act Fred Astaire, Gene Kelly (M-G-M)

That's Entertainment, Part II is a knockout. The very handsome and polished sequel to *That's Entertainment!* transforms excerpts from perhaps $100 million worth of classic Metro library footage into a billion dollars worth of fun, excitement, amusement, escapism, fantasy, nostalgia and happiness.

In addition, Fred Astaire and Gene Kelly shine in sharp bridging footage, well directed by Kelly.

There are approximately 100 remembered players to be seen in segments of about 75 films.

Bulk of the footage is Metro musicals. However, in a good pace change there are periodic brief collages including The Marx Brothers, Spencer Tracy–Katharine Hepburn, Clark Gable, Laurel & Hardy and Buster Keaton.

•

THAT'S ENTERTAINMENT! III
1994, 110 mins, US Ⓥ ⦿ col
Dir Bud Friedgen, Michael J. Sheridan *Prod* Bud Friedgen, Michael J. Sheridan *Scr* Bud Friedgen, Michael J. Sheridan *Ph* Howard A. Anderson III *Ed* Bud Friedgen, Michael J. Sheridan *Mus* Marc Shaiman (arr.)
Act Cyd Charisse, Lena Horne, Gene Kelly, Ann Miller, Debbie Reynolds, Esther Williams (M-G-M)

By searching a little further into unfamiliar corners and outtake cans, resourceful filmmakers Bud Friedgen and Michael J. Sheridan, who edited the first two anthologies, have come up with a bang-up third anthology of golden-era musical highlights that capably holds its own with its predecessors. Metro was reportedly the only major studio to systematically save its outtakes.

Format is the same as before, as legendary stars from M-G-M's musical heyday introduce different chapters in the story, which encompasses 62 musical numbers culled from more than 100 films.

June Allyson, Cyd Charisse, Lena Horne, Howard Keel, Ann Miller, Debbie Reynolds, Mickey Rooney and Esther Williams reminisce, mostly in genteel fashion, how it was in the glory days.

Buffs will be drawn by the numerous outtakes, beginning with two by Reynolds, one a rendition of "You Are My Lucky Star" cut from *Singin' in the Rain*, another an alternate version of "A Lady Loves" from *I Love Melvin*.

Horne is repped by a deleted tune, "Ain't It the Truth," which she sang in a bubble bath for *Cabin in the Sky*, and her electrifying "Can't Help Lovin' Dat Man," shown after two versions of Ava Gardner performing the same song from *Show Boat*.

Judy Garland's "I'm an Indian Too," lensed before she was fired from *Annie Get Your Gun*, proves rather sloppy, shrill and vaguely embarrassing, but her "March of the Doagies" from *The Harvey Girls* was a giant production number to have been dropped. Another previously unseen performance, her rendition of "Mr. Monotony" shot for *Easter Parade*, is a stunner.

A version of the song "Two Faced Woman," with a sizzling Charisse, is shown here for the first time and is great, but was cut from *The Band Wagon*.

[A longer version of the pic was subsequently released on laserdisc.]

•

THAT SINKING FEELING
1979, 80 mins, UK Ⓥ col
Dir Bill Forsyth *Prod* Bill Forsyth *Scr* Bill Forsyth *Ph* Michael Coulter *Ed* John Gow *Mus* Colin Tully *Art* Adrienne Atkinson
Act Robert Buchanan, John Hughes, Billy Greenlees, Douglas Sannachan, Alan Love, John Gordon Sinclair (Minor Miracle)

The first wholly Scottish feature for many a year proves debuting filmmaker Bill Forsyth has an entertaining touch.

Forsyth's screenplay, largely set in Glasgow's dank demolition areas, plots a motley bunch of unemployed lads, amiably led by Robert Buchanan, who heist a hundred stainless steel sinks in a boisterous bid to embark on an essentially light-hearted life of crime.

The central joke—the absurdity of seeing sinks as likely hot sellers—is hardly strong enough to carry a full-length film. But Forsyth's incidental observations, and the generally high standard of playing by nonprofessionals, help to offset the fact that most scenes could be pruned to advantage. Technical credits are remarkable considering the almost invisible production budget.

•

THAT'S LIFE!

1986, 102 mins, US Ⓥ ⊙ ▭ col

Dir Blake Edwards ***Prod*** Tony Adams ***Scr*** Milton Wexler, Blake Edwards ***Ph*** Anthony Richmond ***Ed*** Lee Rhoads ***Mus*** Henry Mancini ***Art*** Tony Marando

Act Jack Lemmon, Julie Andrews, Sally Kellerman, Robert Loggia, Jennifer Edwards, Rob Knepper (Paradise Cove/Ubilam)

Personal virtually to the point of being a home movie, film proves thoroughly absorbing and entertaining and benefits enormously from a terrific lead performance by Jack Lemmon.

Story opens with Lemmon's wife, played by director Blake Edwards's wife, Julie Andrews, leaving a hospital and knowing she'll have to wait all weekend to learn the results of a biopsy.

For his part, Lemmon dreads the arrival of his 60th birthday, can't face the big party planned for him over the weekend, is fretting because he can't perform sexually these days and can't stand the idea of becoming a grandfather.

Andrews responds beautifully to Lemmon's sweaty, nerve-racked state, betraying years of love and understanding of her mate, but doesn't receive equal dramatic opportunities.

1986: NOMINATION: Best Song ("Life in a Looking Glass")

•

THAT THING YOU DO!

1996, 110 mins, US Ⓥ ⊙ col

Dir Tom Hanks ***Prod*** Gary Goetzman, Jonathan Demme ***Scr*** Tom Hanks ***Ph*** Tak Fujimoto ***Ed*** Richard Chew ***Mus*** Howard Shore ***Art*** Victor Kempster

Act Tom Everett Scott, Liv Tyler, Johnathon Schaech, Steve Zahn, Ethan Embry, Tom Hanks (Clinica Estetico/20th Century-Fox)

That Thing You Do! is an immensely likable, sweet-natured tale of the quick rise to fame, and just as quick demise, of a small-town rock band. Set in 1964, this end-of-innocence film provides a sanitized, *Gump*ish look at a semi-mythical period, when boys were boys and girls were girls, with almost no intimations of the sex-drug-music subculture soon to burst upon the American scene.

The best thing to be said about Tom Hanks's directing debut is that it bears all the elements that have made him a movie star: boyish charm, natural ease, comic precision and, above all, generosity of spirit.

In Erie, PA, Guy (Tom Everett Scott) helps his very conservative dad sell TV sets, washing machines and vacuum cleaners. But his heart has been set on music ever since he listened to a jazz album by Del Paxton (Bill Cobbs). Opportunity knocks when a local drummer breaks his arm and Guy is approached by songwriter Jimmy (Johnathon Schaech), guitarist Lenny (Steve Zahn) and the energetic bass player (Ethan Embry) to replace him.

What follows is an episodic chronicle that is as shallow as it is engaging, a collective portrait of the white boys in the band from the early days to their ultimate collapse—all in a matter of months. Dramatic turning point occurs when the band is introduced to Mr. White (Hanks), a tough but savvy record executive.

Score consists entirely of original songs, some written by Hanks. Adam Schlesinger's winningly melodic title song was reportedly selected out of more than 300 submissions.

1996: NOMINATION: Best Original Song ("That Thing You Do")

•

THAT TOUCH OF MINK

1962, 99 mins, US Ⓥ ▭ col

Dir Delbert Mann ***Prod*** Stanley Shapiro, Martin Melcher ***Scr*** Stanley Shapiro, Nate Monaster ***Ph*** Russell Metty ***Ed*** Ted Kent ***Mus*** George Duning ***Art*** Alexander Golitzen, Robert Clatworthy

Act Cary Grant, Doris Day, Gig Young, Audrey Meadows, John Astin, Dick Sargent (Universal)

The recipe is potent: Cary Grant and Doris Day in the old cat-and-mouse game. The gloss of *That Touch of Mink*, however, doesn't obscure an essentially threadbare lining. In seeming to throw off a sparkle, credit performance and pace as the key virtues. The rest of it is commonplace.

In this particular arrangement of coy *he-she-nanigans*, the comedy is premised on the conflict of her inexperience and his old-pro suavity. He's a company-gobbling financier; she's a trim chick legging it through Manhattan canyons in search of a job. It starts when his limousine splatters her with puddle water. Fortuitous meeting and mating maneuvers follow, with the action shuttling between Gotham and Bermuda or Gotham and New Jersey suburbia.

Although Grant gives his tycoon the advantage of long seasoning at this sort of gamey exercise, he's clearly shaded in the laugh-getting allotment. As written, Day's clowning has the better of it; and she, by the way, certifies herself an adept farceuse with this outing. But not surprisingly, the featured bananas make the best comedic score.

1962: NOMINATIONS: Best Original Story & Screenplay, Color Art Direction, Sound

•

THAT UNCERTAIN FEELING

1941, 89 mins, US Ⓥ b/w

Dir Ernst Lubitsch ***Prod*** Sol Lesser, Ernst Lubitsch ***Scr*** Walter Reisch ***Ph*** George Barnes ***Ed*** William Shen ***Mus*** Werner Heymann

Act Merle Oberon, Melvyn Douglas, Burgess Meredith, Alan Mowbray, Olive Blakeney, Harry Davenport (United Artists)

Premised on the assumption that when a husband doesn't pay his wife enough attention someone else is going to do it for him, Ernst Lubitsch's *That Uncertain Feeling* tackles the problem in a light and singularly satirical vein. The famed Lubitsch touch is there but the entertainment value isn't.

Merle Oberon and Melvyn Douglas are the apparently happily married Bakers. Husband is a prosperous insurance man who is settled in his home life in a routine way, but unconsciously fails to fulfill the more romantic duties expected of a spouse. Lubitsch, with characteristic subtlety, suggests that this is what causes the hiccups from which the wife suffers and ultimately lands her in a psychoanalyst's office.

By stages she begins to have suspicions concerning the widespread impressions that they are the happy Bakers, and into her life, under slightly absurd circumstances, comes a wacky pianist. He's Burgess Meredith, not the great-lover type, and he has a strange, impudent dislike for a lot of things.

Taking the picture as a whole it is tiring, very slow generally and embraces numerous situations that are basically weak.

1941: NOMINATION: Best Scoring of a Dramatic Picture

•

THAT WAS THEN . . . THIS IS NOW

1985, 102 mins, US Ⓥ ⊙ col

Dir Christopher Cain ***Prod*** Gary R. Lindberg, John M. Ondor ***Scr*** Emilio Estevez ***Ph*** Juan Ruiz-Anchia ***Ed*** Ken Johnson ***Mus*** Keith Olsen, Bill Cuomo ***Art*** Chester Kaczenski

Act Emilio Estevez, Craig Sheffer, Kim Delaney, Jill Schoelen, Barbara Babcock, Frank Howard (Media Ventures/Belkin)

God save the kids who live in an S. E. Hinton novel. They're firecrackers waiting to go off. Hinton's is a very peculiar vision where adults are basically in the background and kids are left on their own to battle their way into an adulthood that promises them even less.

Most troubled of the kids here is Emilio Estevez as Mark Jennings, a lonely, brooding child anxious to be through with his adolescence. Title refers to his youthful bond with Bryon Douglas (Craig Sheffer). To Mark's dismay, the friendship is falling apart as Bryon takes on a girlfriend and starts to accept some adult responsibility.

Estevez also wrote the screenplay, and as a writer he fails to raise the pronouncements and revelations of youth beyond the mundane. Dark tone is reinforced by cinematographer Juan Ruiz-Anchia, who captures well the look of the street, but that's all one sees. It's an oppressive world without being particularly insightful.

Central relationship between Estevez and Sheffer does have some touching moments. Kim Delaney is perfectly likeable as Sheffer's girlfriend.

•

THAT WONDERFUL URGE

1948, 82 mins, US b/w

Dir Robert B. Sinclair ***Prod*** Fred Kohlmar ***Scr*** Jay Dratler ***Ph*** Charles G. Clarke ***Ed*** Louis Loeffler ***Mus*** Cyril J. Mockridge ***Art*** Lyle R. Wheeler, George Davis

Act Tyrone Power, Gene Tierney, Reginald Gardiner, Gene Lockhart (20th Century-Fox)

Mounted in a slick production, the screenplay is another variation of the poor-little-rich-girl theme against a newspaper background. But Jay Dratler dresses up the script with enough new twists and smart dialog to give an old chestnut the flavor of a brand-new soufflé.

Tyrone Power makes the most of his comedy chances as a cynical reporter assigned to assassinate the character of a grocery chain heiress. Posing as a lover to get the inside story for his series, he becomes tangled in his own line and bait when the gal (Gene Tierney) snaps back and turns him into a national laughing stock.

This is also one of Tierney's most successful performances. Costumed to highlight her natural charms and rigged with peppery lines, she polishes off her role with considerable grace.

•

THEATRE OF BLOOD

1973, 104 mins, US/UK Ⓥ ⊙ col

Dir Douglas Hickox ***Prod*** John Kohn, Stanley Mann ***Scr*** Anthony Greville-Bell ***Ph*** Wolfgang Suschitzky ***Ed*** Malcolm Cooke ***Mus*** Michael J. Lewis ***Art*** Michael Seymour

Act Vincent Price, Diana Rigg, Ian Hendry, Harry Andrews, Coral Browne, Robert Coote (Harbor/Cineman)

Theatre of Blood is black comedy played for chills and mood and emerges a macabre piece of wild melodramatics.

Douglas Hickox manages neatly in his direction to catch the spirit of a demented Shakespearean actor's (Vincent Price) revenge on eight members of the London Critics' Circle who he believes denied him a Best Actor of the Year award. Situation [from an idea by producers Stanley Mann and John Kohn] allows for some good old-fashioned suspense and high comedy, such as the sequence in which Price saws off the head of one critic while his spouse, needled into unconsciousness, sleeps beside him. Price uses gory Shakespeare-inspired deaths to systematically murder each of the offending critics.

Price delivers with his usual enthusiasm and Diana Rigg is good as his daughter. Ian Hendry heads the list of critics, and Diana Dors is in briefly as Jack Hawkins's wife, whom he smothers to death in a moment of jealousy.

•

THELMA & LOUISE

1991, 128 mins, US Ⓥ ⊙ ▭ col

Dir Ridley Scott ***Prod*** Ridley Scott, Mimi Polk ***Scr*** Callie Khouri ***Ph*** Adrian Biddle ***Ed*** Thom Noble ***Mus*** Hans Zimmer ***Art*** Norris Spencer

Act Susan Sarandon, Geena Davis, Harvey Keitel, Michael Madsen, Christopher McDonald, Brad Pitt (Pathe/Main)

Thelma & Louise is a thumpingly adventurous road pic about two regular gals who shoot down a would-be rapist and wind up on the lam in their 1966 T-bird. Even those who don't rally to pic's fed-up feminist outcry will take to its comedy, momentum and dazzling visuals.

Arkansas housewife Thelma (Geena Davis) and waitress Louise (Susan Sarandon) set out for a weekend fishing trip away from the drudgery of their lives and the indifference of their men; they stop at a roadside honkytonk to blow off steam, and things turn ugly. A guy tries to rape Thelma; Louise can't take it so she plugs the creep with a .38. Then they hit the highway, dazed and in trouble.

Sarandon is the big sister, more feminine, more focused, smoldering with a quiet determination. Davis is more loosely wrapped; she goes with the flow, follows her whims into trouble. The journey into recklessness is exhilarating, which gives the film its buoyant pull. In an indelible final image, it maintains the sense of reckless exhilaration to the end.

Despite some delectably funny scenes between the sexes, Ridley Scott's pic isn't about women vs. men. It's about freedom, like any good road picture. In that sense, and in many others, it's a classic.

California and southern Utah locales stand in for Arkansas, Oklahoma and Texas.

1991: Best Original Screenplay

NOMINATIONS: Best Director, Actress (Geena Davis, Susan Sarandon), Cinematography, Editing

•

THEM!

1954, 93 mins, US Ⓥ ⊙ b/w

Dir Gordon Douglas ***Prod*** David Weisbart ***Scr*** Ted Sherdeman ***Ph*** Sid Hickox ***Ed*** Thomas Reilly ***Mus*** Bronislau Kaper ***Art*** Stanley Fleischer

Act James Whitmore, Edmund Gwenn, Joan Weldon, James Arness, Onslow Stevens, Sean McClory (Warner)

This science-fiction shocker has a well-plotted story [by George Worthington Yates, adapted by Russell Hughes], expertly directed and acted in a matter-of-fact style.

The title monsters are mutations caused by radiation from the 1945 detonation of an atomic bomb in the desert. Over the intervening years the tiny insects affected by the lingering radiation have become fantastic creatures, ranging in size from nine to 12 feet. James Whitmore, sergeant in the New Mexico State Police, first gets on the track of the incredible beings. Into the picture then come Edmund Gwenn and Joan Weldon, entomologists, and James Arness, FBI man.

With the aid of air force officers Onslow Stevens and Sean McClory, the little group attempts to wipe out the nest of the mutated monsters with flame throwers and gas. Two of the newly born queen ants escape, however. It's a real chiller-diller finale.

Whitmore, Gwenn, Weldon and Arness wrap up the acting chores in first-rate fashion. Fess Parker and Olin Howlin show up very well, the first as a pilot booby-hatched for his "flying saucer" story, and the other as a happy drunk. Sid Hickox's photography gets plenty of menace into the fantastic monsters.

1954: NOMINATION: Best Special Effects

•

THEODORA GOES WILD

1936, 94 mins, US b/w

Dir Richard Boleslawski ***Prod*** Everett Riskin ***Scr*** Sidney Buchman ***Ph*** Joseph Walker ***Mus*** Morris Stoloff

Act Irene Dunne, Melvyn Douglas, Thomas Mitchell, Spring Byington, Elisabeth Risdon, Margaret McWade (Columbia)

A comedy of steady tempo and deepening laughter. Irene Dunne takes the hurdle into comedy with versatile grace.

Theodora may superficially be compared to the *Mr. Deeds Goes to Town* (1936) character in that both come from small New England villages. Quaint and eccentric figures and customs are exploited for laughs and background in both cases. And the experiences of the small-town character when hitting Manhattan form the main content of the story [from the novel by Mary McCarthy].

Painstaking direction of Richard Boleslawski brings out the nuances. His direction and Dunne's playing of the first New York escapade of Theodora in a dashing blade's apartment is a high point of light-and-shade farce.

Melvyn Douglas is an excellent romantic partner for Dunne. She, rather than he, gets the real acting chances but he is consistently intelligent.

1936: NOMINATIONS: Best Actress (Irene Dunne), Editing

•

THEOREM

SEE: TEOREMA

•

THERE'S A GIRL IN MY SOUP

1971, 94 mins, UK Ⓥ col

Dir Roy Boulting ***Prod*** Mike Frankovich, John Boulting ***Scr*** Terence Frisby ***Ph*** Harry Waxman ***Ed*** Martin Charles ***Mus*** Mike D'Abo ***Art*** John Howell

Act Peter Sellers, Goldie Hawn, Tony Britton, Nicky Henson, John Comer, Diana Dors (Columbia)

There's a Girl in My Soup is a delightful surprise: a rather simple legit sex comedy (by Terence Frisby) transformed into breezy and extremely tasteful screen fun.

Peter Sellers is a TV personality whose roving eye misses few femme specimens. Accidental encounter with Goldie Hawn, who is having some free-love domestic problems with mate Nicky Henson, blossoms into unexpected love and compassion between the unlikely pair.

Henson is excellent in giving depth to the limited part, and adds immeasurably to the general moral tone. In superior support also are Tony Britton as Sellers's publisher-confidant; John Comer as Sellers's envious doorman; and Diana Dors in a good offbeat character casting as Comer's shrewish wife.

•

THERE'S ALWAYS A WOMAN

1938, 81 mins, US b/w

Dir Alexander Hall ***Prod*** William Perlberg ***Scr*** Gladys Lehman ***Ph*** Henry Freulich ***Ed*** Viola Lawrence ***Mus*** Morris Stoloff

Act Joan Blondell, Melvyn Douglas, Mary Astor, Frances Drake, Jerome Cowan (Columbia)

This one is a briskly paced, battle-of-the-sexes comedy against a background of a murder mystery. Smart production and, notably, the direction of Alexander Hall have imbued a basically incredible plot [by Wilson Collison] with the tempo and animation necessary to make people either believe or forget to disbelieve.

Melvyn Douglas and Joan Blondell are man and wife. He professionally a detective; she an amateur ditto who gums up the works repeatedly. Plenty of slapstick in the *Thin Man* tradition. Laughs come pretty steadily. Many of these are cleverly planted as surprise twists.

Two leads have the only roles of consequence. Everything else and everybody else is a passing panorama for their antics and clashes as they crazily progress toward the solution of a not-very-obtuse mystery situation.

•

THERESE DESQUEYROUX

1962, 109 mins, France b/w

Dir Georges Franju ***Prod*** Eugene Lepicier ***Scr*** Francois Mauriac, Claude Mauriac, Georges Franju ***Ph*** Christian Matras ***Ed*** Gilbert Natot ***Mus*** Maurice Jarre ***Art*** Jacques Chalvet

Act Emmanuelle Riva, Philippe Noiret, Edith Scob, Sami Frey, Renee Devillers, Lucien Nat (Filmel)

This is one of those rare films, a social and psychological drama that remains taut and absorbing throughout due to a rare combination of observant direction, expert thesping and an insight into the personages.

A woman has tried to poison her husband in a provincial section of France. She is freed when he does not press charges. But on her way back to him she thinks over what led to it. She is a sensitive almost exalted girl who marries the son of a rich, landed family. But the man is direct, stuffy and incapable of awakening any feeling or love in her. She becomes frigid, dissatisfied and disenchanted.

Emmanuelle Riva has a way of overcoming her ordinary looks by an intense projection of internal sincerity, and etches a brilliant picture of this fragile tragic woman almost destroyed by human pettiness, pride and indifference. Others all limn their parts well.

Director Georges Franju keeps this [adaptation of Francois Mauriac's novel] from being literary, in spite of a commentary, by a controlled feel for visual detail, and a pace and rhythm that build this probing drama into a film of strength and originality.

•

THERESE RAQUIN

1953, 110 mins, France b/w

Dir Marcel Carne ***Scr*** Charles Spaak ***Ph*** Roger Hubert ***Ed*** Henri Rust ***Mus*** Maurice Thiriet ***Art*** Paul Bertrand

Act Simone Signoret, Raf Vallone, Jacques Duby, Roland Lesaffre, Sylvie (Paris/Lux)

Marcel Carne has conceived a brilliant but curiously cold film. Story of illicit love in a lower-class bourgeois setting is done with a care that removes its melodramatic aspects and makes it an alternately absorbing and lagging film.

A modernization of the Emile Zola period piece, this evokes the infatuation and love between a manly truck driver and the wife of his officious, petty and sickly superior. The affair leads to the murder of the husband and the final destruction of the lovers.

Carne's direction builds a heavy, brooding atmosphere of the self-indulgent, dreary life of the woman whose attempt at escape and gratification leads to her eventual destruction.

Simone Signoret is adequate as the browbeaten wife who finally breaks with her drab environment, but her sudden surrender to the bourgeois codes does not hold up. Raf Vallone, as the truck driver, adds an intense presence, but even he is betrayed by the overelaborate unfoldment. Newcomers Jacques Duby, cast as the husband, and Roland Lesaffre, the oily witness, provide fine backing for the stars.

Lensing is brilliant and matches the heavy atmosphere of the bleak Lyon streets to the studio reconstructions.

•

THERE'S NO BUSINESS LIKE SHOW BUSINESS

1954, 117 mins, US Ⓥ ⦿ ▭ col

Dir Walter Lang ***Prod*** Sol C. Siegel ***Scr*** Phoebe Ephron, Henry Ephron ***Ph*** Leon Shamroy ***Ed*** Robert Simpson ***Mus*** Alfred Newman, Lionel Newman (dirs.) ***Art*** Lyle Wheeler, John DeCuir

Act Ethel Merman, Donald O'Connor, Marilyn Monroe, Dan Dailey, Johnnie Ray, Mitzi Gaynor (20th Century-Fox)

Lamar Trotti's original, from which Phoebe and Henry Ephron fashioned the screenplay, is palpably a script primed to point up the "heart" of showfolk.

Ethel Merman and Dan Dailey are capital as the vaudeville Donahues who bring out first one, then two, then three of their offspring for that extra bow, with a running gag, as the vaude annunciator cards change to the three Donahues, the four and finally the five Donahues.

Robert Alton rates a big bend along with producer Sol C. Siegel and director Walter Lang on those lavish musical routines. From Irving Berlin's viewpoint, they're all a song-plugger's delight.

Ethel Merman is boffo. She's a belter of a school of song stylists not to be found on every stage or before every mike. *Show Business* gets the works in every respect. The orchestral-vocal treatments of the Berlin standards are so richly endowed as to give them constantly fresh values.

1954: NOMINATIONS: Best Motion Picture Story, Color Costume Design, Scoring of a Musical Picture

•

THERE'S SOMETHING ABOUT MARY

1998, 118 mins, US Ⓥ ⦿ col

Dir Peter Farrelly, Bobby Farrelly ***Prod*** Frank Beddor, Michael Steinberg, Charles B. Wessler, Bradley Thomas ***Scr*** Ed Decter, John J. Strauss, Peter Farrelly, Bobby Farrelly ***Ph*** Mark Irwin ***Ed*** Christopher Greenbury ***Mus*** Jonathan Richman ***Art*** Arlan Jay Vetter

Act Cameron Diaz, Matt Dillon, Ben Stiller, Lee Evans, Chris Elliott, Lin Shaye (20th Century-Fox)

Crudely made, somewhat overlong and larded with plenty of things that don't work, pic stands as proof positive that a comedy can be far from perfect and still hit the bull's-eye if it delivers when it counts in its big scenes. And deliver it does, in episodes and a general outlook of spectacular irreverence, rudeness and cheek.

Twenty-minute, 1985-set prolog intros Ted (Ben Stiller), a geeky teen in smalltown Rhode Island who is asked by class knockout Mary (Cameron Diaz) [grateful for him defending her retarded brother] to the senior prom. But Ted and Mary never make it to the dance. Instead, Ted has the gross misfortune of catching his private parts in his pants zipper.

Thirteen years later, a depressed Ted hires a sleazy private dick, Pat Healy (Matt Dillon), to find her. But when Pat lays eyes on Mary in Miami and sees that she's not only a sexy babe who loves sports but is unattached, he reports back to Ted that his inamorata now weighs 200 pounds and is confined to a wheelchair, and sets his sights on her himself.

Mary begins falling for the connelster, but when Ted hears that Mary is still a fox after all he heads for Miami to check her out for himself.

Much of the silliness [in the screen story by scripters Ed Decter and John J. Strauss] is of a physically brutal, Three Stooges variety and involves crossing many lines of expectation and taste. But the sense of violation becomes explosively liberating in audience terms, which would seem to be the secret of the writer-director Farrelly brothers' success (*Dumb & Dumber*).

Diaz is dazzling throughout. Sexy, insouciant and always a good sport, her character will be all the more appealing to many guys because she's a jock who at one point asks her date, "Hey, you want to go upstairs and watch SportsCenter?" What a gal.

•

THERE WAS A CROOKED MAN

1960, 90 mins, UK ▭ b/w

Dir Stuart Burge ***Prod*** John Bryan ***Scr*** Reuben Ship ***Ph*** Arthur Ibbetson ***Ed*** Peter Hunt ***Mus*** Kenneth V. Jones

Act Norman Wisdom, Alfred Marks, Andrew Cruickshank, Reginald Beckwith, Susannah York, Jean Clarke (Knightsbridge)

Stuart Burge, a TV director making his debut in feature films, does a good job, considering the many traps that Reuben Ship's ingenious, though far-fetched, screenplay lays. Ship has overloaded his storyline but has produced an idea which holds interest.

Norman Wisdom is a down-and-out who runs into a gang of crooks who want his help because he is a demolitions expert. Rather naively he is conned into assisting the mob into cracking a bank vault. He alone is caught holding the loot, and goes to jail. When he's let out after five years, he goes to take up a job in a Northern seaside factory. He soon finds out that the town is under the control of a swindler (Andrew Cruickshank) who is persuading everybody to buy up shares in the town's future. Wisdom enlists the help of his crook friends on a wild enterprise to outwit Cruickshank.

There are so many holes in this yarn that it's like a fishing net, but the result is amiable comedy. The robbery, in which Wisdom and his pals pose as surgeons and tunnel from the operating theatre into the next-door bank, is wildly funny. Wisdom getting caught up in a wool sorting machine, avoiding the cops and finally blowing up the town has good clowning moments.

•

THERE WAS A CROOKED MAN . . .

1970, 128 mins, US Ⓥ ▭ col

Dir Joseph L. Mankiewicz ***Prod*** Joseph L. Mankiewicz ***Scr*** David Newman, Robert Benton ***Ph*** Harry Stradling, Jr. ***Ed*** Gene Milford ***Mus*** Charles Strouse

Act Kirk Douglas, Henry Fonda, Hume Cronyn, Warren Oates, Burgess Meredith, Arthur O'Connell (Warner)

There Was a Crooked Man . . . has a crooked plot that is neither comedy nor convincing drama. Kirk Douglas,

Henry Fonda, Hume Cronyn, Warren Oates and Burgess Meredith are the formidable elements that don't jell in this picaresque tale set in a bleak western desert prison. It is the type of action drama in which neither the actors nor director appear to believe the script or characters.

Douglas is the crooked man of title, who steals $500,000 from Arthur O'Connell and is caught in a bordello literally with his pants down when voyeur O'Connell recognizes him through the peephole.

Fonda plays it straight as the saintly sheriff who becomes an idealistic prison reformer, only to have his principles literally blow up in his face when Douglas organizes a riot and break-out.

•

THESE ARE THE DAMNED
SEE: THE DAMNED

•

THESE THREE
1936, 90 mins, US Ⓥ ⊙ b/w
Dir William Wyler ***Prod*** Samuel Goldwyn ***Scr*** Lillian Hellman ***Ph*** Gregg Toland ***Ed*** Danny Mandell ***Mus*** Alfred Newman ***Art*** Richard Day
Act Miriam Hopkins, Merle Oberon, Joel McCrea, Catherine Doucet, Alma Kruger, Bonita Granville (Goldwyn/United Artists)

A thoroughly fine cinematic transmutation of Lillian Hellman's dramatic Broadway smash *The Children's Hour* is her own scenarization, reedited and retitled for Haysian purposes as *These Three*. Stripped of its original theme [of lesbianism], it is fortified by a socko trio in Miriam Hopkins, Merle Oberon and Joel McCrea.

Parring the tungsten threesome, however, are two adolescents, Bonita Granville as the hateful Mary Tilford, and Marcia Mae Jones as the subjected, inhibited child. Theirs are inspired performances.

Hellman, if anything, has improved upon the original in scripting the triangle as a dramatis personae of romantic frustration, three basically wholesome victims of an unwholesome combination of circumstance.

McCrea was never better in translating a difficult assignment intelligently and sympathetically. The well-bred restraint of Hopkins and Oberon in their travail with the mixture of juvenile emotions at their boarding school is likewise impressive. Oberon is the sympathetic Karen; Hopkins has the assignment of unrequited love.

1936: NOMINATION: Best Supp. Actress (Bonita Granville)

•

THEY ALL KISSED THE BRIDE
1942, 84 mins, US b/w
Dir Alexander Hall ***Prod*** Edward Kaufman ***Scr*** P. J. Wolfson ***Ph*** Joseph Walker ***Ed*** Viola Lawrence ***Mus*** Werner Heymann
Act Joan Crawford, Melvyn Douglas, Roland Young, Billie Burke, Helen Parrish, Allen Jenkins (Columbia)

Picture is adult entertainment—liberally spotted with episodes and lines of explosive and intimate nature—that veers from the general run of pictures of its type sufficiently to get audience attention.

Originally, Carole Lombard was set for the starring spot, but her untimely death projected Joan Crawford in as replacement.

Crawford is in command of the vast business interests left by her father, and shaken by the writings of Melvyn Douglas, a happy-go-lucky scribbler of sorts who takes a crack at the family personal and business skeletons.

In addition to a spotlight performance by Crawford, Douglas clicks solidly as the writer and principal romanticist. Script is studded with amusing dialog of most intimate and double entendre content.

Alexander Hall's direction is snappy and speedy all along the line, and he contrives laugh toppers to every episode.

•

THEY ALL LAUGHED
1981, 115 mins, US Ⓥ ⊙ col
Dir Peter Bogdanovich ***Prod*** George Morfogen, Blaine Novak ***Scr*** Peter Bogdanovich ***Ph*** Robby Muller ***Ed*** Scott Vickrey ***Mus*** Douglas Dilge ***Art*** Kert Lundell
Act Audrey Hepburn, Ben Gazzara, John Ritter, Colleen Camp, Dorothy Stratten, Patti Hansen (20th Century-Fox/Time-Life)

Rarely does a film come along featuring such an extensive array of attractive characters with whom it is simply a pleasure to spend two hours. Nothing of great importance happens in a strict plot sense, but this *La Ronde*–like tale is intensely devoted to the sexual and amorous sparks struck among some unusually magnetic people.

In fact, pic could be considered a successful, non-musical remake of *At Long Last Love*, as the dynamics of the partner changes are virtually identical.

It takes a little while to figure out just where the story is headed, but basic framework has Ben Gazzara, John Ritter and Blaine Novak working for the Odyssey Detective Agency, which is truthfully advertised by the line "We never sleep." Gazzara's been assigned to track Gotham visitor Audrey Hepburn by her husband, while Ritter and Novak trail Dorothy Stratten as she slips away from her husband to rendezvous with young Sean Ferrer.

Hepburn doesn't have a line to speak for the entire first hour (much of the film is devoted to vaguely voyeuristic pursuit and observation on the part of the detectives), but ultimately she emerges winningly as the most mature and discreet character in the group.

Certain plot contrivances bear eerie resemblances to the cirumstances leading up to Stratten's real-life 1980 murder, as she too, had been followed by a detective hired by a husband suspicious of her fidelity. A palm reading sequence in which Ritter predicts that her marriage will come to a quick end—and she wonders if she has much time left—is chilling for those familiar with the Stratten case.

•

THEY CALL ME MISTER TIBBS!
1970, 108 mins, US Ⓥ col
Dir Gordon Douglas ***Prod*** Herbert Hirschman ***Scr*** Alan R. Trustman, James R. Webb ***Ph*** Gerald Perry Finnerman ***Ed*** Bud Molin ***Mus*** Quincy Jones ***Art*** Addison Hehr
Act Sidney Poitier, Martin Landau, Barbara McNair, Anthony Zerbe, Edward Asner, Jeff Corey (Mirisch)

A Nob Hill prostitute is murdered in her $300-a-month apartment. Last seen leaving the apartment is Martin Landau, a politically involved minister in the midst of an activist campaign to pass a ballot measure to reform local government. Landau is a close personal friend of Sidney Poitier, who is assigned to investigate the case.

The detective is a tough, ruthlessly efficient cop, and the portrayal, realistic as it is, might be dramatically deadly. However script switches back and forth between the case and the cop's everyday domestic problems with wife, Barbara McNair, 11-year-old son, George Spell, and six-year-old daughter, Wanda Spell.

The father all too frequently must also be a cop to his son and it is in the relationship with the boy that Poitier's character paradoxically is given flesh and blood.

•

THEY CAME FROM WITHIN
SEE: SHIVERS

•

THEY CAME TO CORDURA
1959, 123 mins, US Ⓥ ⊙ ▭ col
Dir Robert Rossen ***Prod*** William Goetz ***Scr*** Ivan Moffat, Robert Rossen ***Ph*** Burnett Guffey ***Ed*** William A. Lyon ***Mus*** Elie Siegmeister
Act Gary Cooper, Rita Hayworth, Van Heflin, Tab Hunter, Richard Conte, Michael Callan (Columbia)

A bitter and realistic drama of the wry twists life can work on men when they are thrown into situations beyond their control—in this case the 1916 border action between U.S. troops and Pancho Villa's Mexican rebels.

The screenplay, from Glendon Swarthout's book, takes its theme from the title. Cordura is the name of the Texas town the principals are bound for. It is also the Spanish word for courage. The moral is that what's called courage is sometimes a question of interpretation, of accident, or of momentary aberration.

Gary Cooper is the U.S. Army officer detailed to lead five Medal of Honor candidates back from the front lines of the war. Cooper has been made Awards Officer after showing cowardice in battle. The son of an army general and himself a career officer, Cooper is desperately interested in the five heroes because they have what he lacks—or so he thinks. Also on the party is Rita Hayworth, the disillusioned and dissolute daughter of a disgraced politician.

Gary Cooper is very good as the central figure, although he is somewhat too old for the role. Hayworth, looking haggard, drawn and defeated, gives the best performance of her career. If she shows only half the beauty she usually does, she displays twice the acting.

Van Heflin does a brilliantly evil job as one of the "heroes," and Richard Conte, as his malevolent sidekick, is almost equally impressive.

•

THEY DIED WITH THEIR BOOTS ON
1941, 140 mins, US Ⓥ ⊙ b/w
Dir Raoul Walsh ***Prod*** Hal B. Wallis (exec.) ***Scr*** Wally Kline, Aeneas MacKenzie ***Ph*** Bert Glennon ***Ed*** William Holmes ***Mus*** Max Steiner ***Art*** John Hughes
Act Errol Flynn, Olivia de Havilland, Arthur Kennedy, Charley Grapewin, Gene Lockhart, Anthony Quinn (Warner)

They Died with Their Boots On is the Custer story, full of action, Indians and anachronisms, with Olivia de Havilland co-starred.

Warner studio provided generously for the picture, in terms of a good supporting cast, hundreds of horsemen and outdoor locations. Raoul Walsh directed and brought to the screen all the pageantry and adventure that the biography provides.

They're a long time getting to the tragic engagement in the Black Hills when Custer (Errol Flynn) with a third of his command, numbering 264 members of the 7th Cavalry, fell into ambush and were slaughtered by the Sioux.

The liberties which the screenwriters have taken with well-established and authenticated facts are likely to be a bit trying in spots. But the test of the yarn is not its accuracy, but its speed and excitement. Of these it has plenty.

When Flynn is ordered to command of a frontier post, disorders with Indians require immediate and drastic action. Custer is the man for the emergency. There is a period of armistice. Then the civilian traders and land grabbers move in. Trouble with the redskins rides with every covered wagon.

•

THEY DRIVE BY NIGHT
1940, 93 mins, US Ⓥ ⊙ b/w
Dir Raoul Walsh ***Prod*** Mark Hellinger ***Scr*** Jerry Wald, Richard Macaulay ***Ph*** Arthur Edeson ***Ed*** Thomas Richards ***Mus*** Adolph Deutsch ***Art*** John Hughes
Act George Raft, Ann Sheridan, Humphrey Bogart, Ida Lupino, Gale Page, Alan Hale (Warner)

Fast-moving and actionful melodrama of long-haul trucking biz, *They Drive* clicks with plenty of entertainment content. Story, off the beaten track, divides into two sections, but with a neat dovetail to weld it together. First half is adventure of George Raft and Humphrey Bogart as brothers operating a freelance highway truck, culminating with an asleep-at-the-wheel wreck in which Bogart loses an arm and his desire for further highway adventures. Second half is devoted to the triangle melodrama, with Raft on the receiving end of persistent amorous advances of the married Ida Lupino.

Raoul Walsh provides deft direction that accentuates dramatic moments and maintains a zippo tempo throughout. Script is decidedly workmanlike with numerous snappy and at times spicily double-entendre lines interwoven.

Raft holds the spotlight as the vigorous and determined trucking indie battling against adversities to consummate a dream of owning his own fleet. He turns in a topnotch performance. Equal in importance is Lupino, who turns on her dramatic talents for an exceptionally outstanding portrayal, unsympathetic though it is. Bogart is excellent as the hard-working driver and Raft's brother. Ann Sheridan is okay, mainly for love interest, overshadowed by the stellar performance of Lupino.

•

THEY GOT ME COVERED
1943, 96 mins, US Ⓥ ⊙ b/w
Dir David Butler ***Prod*** Samuel Goldwyn ***Scr*** Harry Kurmitz, Frank Fenton, Lynn Root ***Ph*** Rudolph Mate ***Ed*** Daniel Mandell ***Mus*** Leigh Harline
Act Bob Hope, Dorothy Lamour, Lenore Aubert, Otto Preminger, Eduardo Ciannelli, Marion Martin (RKO/Goldwyn)

Samuel Goldwyn took top comedy writers, a top comedy director and top comic and distilled them into a farce of the broadest stripe. Sometimes it takes and sometimes it doesn't.

An apparent endeavor by the writers to be super-funny has certainly resulted in a barrage of entertaining gags and situations, although lacking spontaneity. It's just too clear how hard the boys were trying.

Bob Hope is pictured as a newspaperman who's just been fired as a Moscow correspondent for completely missing the German invasion of Russia. He returns and goes to Washington in the hope of re-establishing his rep.

No asset to the film is the quality of much of the acting, particularly that of Dorothy Lamour, whose flat delivery of her lines makes Hope work twice as hard to sell his gags.

Director David Butler succeeds in keeping the film moving, although it is sometimes a battle against the episodic construction of the situation gags.

•

THEY LIVE
1988, 93 mins, US Ⓥ ⦿ ▭ col
Dir John Carpenter ***Prod*** Larry Franco ***Scr*** Frank Armitage [= John Carpenter] ***Ph*** Gary B. Kibbe ***Ed*** Gib Jaffe, Frank E. Jimenez ***Mus*** John Carpenter, Alan Howarth ***Art*** William J. Durrell, Jr., Daniel Lomino
Act Roddy Piper, Keith David, Meg Foster, George "Buck" Flower, Peter Jason (Carolco/Alive)

Conceived on 1950s B-movie sci-fi terms, *They Live* is a fantastically subversive film, a nifty little confection pitting us vs. them, the haves vs. the have-nots.

Screenplay by "Frank Armitage" (presumably another Carpenter pseudonym as was "Martin Quatermass"), based on a Ray Nelson short story ["Eight O'Clock in the Morning"], takes the clever premise that those in control of the global economic power structure are secretly other-worldly aliens.

His leading character, pretentiously named Nada (Roddy Piper), is a heavily muscled working Joe, a wanderer who makes his way to Justiceville, a shantytown settlement for the homeless in the shadows of downtown's skyscrapers.

Nada happens upon some sunglasses which, when worn, reveal a whole alternate existence, in which certain individuals—the ruling class—are instantly recognizable due to their hideously decomposed, skeletal faces.

Nada becomes an outlaw, picking off aliens wherever he can. He seeks an accomplice, first in Meg Foster, who unwillingly rescues him from the police, and then in black coworker Keith David, another bodybuilder whom he has to fight seemingly forever before getting him to try on the glasses.

Pro wrestler Piper comes across quite adequately as the blue-collar Everyman, and remainder of the cast is okay.

•

THEY LIVE BY NIGHT
(AKA: THE TWISTED ROAD)
1948, 95 mins, US Ⓥ ⦿ b/w
Dir Nicholas Ray ***Prod*** John Houseman ***Scr*** Charles Schnee ***Ph*** George E. Diskant ***Ed*** Sherman Todd ***Mus*** Leigh Harline ***Art*** Albert S. D'Agostino, Al Herman
Act Cathy O'Donnell, Farley Granger, Howard da Silva, Jay C. Flippen, Helen Craig, Will Wright (RKO)

Underneath *They Live by Night* is a moving, somber story of hopeless young love. There's no attempt at sugar-coating a happy ending, and yarn moves towards its inevitable, tragic climax without compromise.

A gifted team of young players stands out in making the performances thoroughly realistic. Farley Granger and Cathy O'Donnell are in the lead roles, selling the portrayals with a sock.

The script by Charles Schnee is based on Edward Anderson's novel, *Thieves Like Us*, and tells the story of a young escaped convict who falls in love and marries a girl whose circumstances are little better than his own.

Nicholas Ray adapted the novel and directed, demonstrating a complete understanding of the characters. It's a first-rate job of moody storytelling. Howard da Silva clicks as a ruthless, one-eyed bank robber, and Jay C. Flippen is equally top-notch for his delineation of a criminal.

•

THEY LOVED LIFE
SEE: KANAL

•

THEY MET IN BOMBAY
1941, 92 mins, US b/w
Dir Clarence Brown ***Prod*** Hunt Stromberg ***Scr*** Edwin Justus Mayer, Anita Loos, Leon Gordon ***Ph*** William Daniels ***Ed*** Blanche Sewell ***Mus*** Herbert Stothart
Act Clark Gable, Rosalind Russell, Peter Lorre, Reginald Owen, Matthew Boulton, Jessie Ralph (M-G-M)

This is an actionful adventure yarn [based on a story by John Kafka] unfolded in a Far East setting.

Story picks up Clark Gable and Rosalind Russell in Bombay, both bent on lifting a famous jewel during Empire Day celebration. Pair meet, Gable tabs girl's purpose immediately, and then proceeds to let her grab the gem so he can conveniently take it from her after the theft. But his scheming is discovered by Russell, and pair take it on the lam in front of Scotland Yard pursuers, grabbing a tramp steamer bound for Hong Kong.

Logic prevails in the early episodes which present much rapid-fire and sparkling by-play between Gable and Russell. But when the pair reach Hong Kong, story strays through fields of corn in an attempt to reform the pair.

Gable is swaggering, resourceful and adventurous to the danger point—and capably gets over these phases of the character. Russell is fine in the early section, but drops into a groove in the second half. Clarence Brown directs at a consistent pace, and manages to hold attention throughout.

•

THEY MIGHT BE GIANTS
1971, 91 mins, US Ⓥ col
Dir Anthony Harvey ***Prod*** John Foreman ***Scr*** James Goldman ***Ph*** Victor J. Kemper ***Ed*** Gerald Greenberg ***Mus*** John Barry ***Art*** John Robert Lloyd
Act George C. Scott, Joanne Woodward, Jack Gilford, Lester Rawlins, Rue McClanahan, Ron Weyand (Universal)

They Might Be Giants starts off splendidly and hilariously, with George C. Scott at his intense and imposing best as a former jurist who thinks he's Sherlock Holmes, and Joanne Woodward charmingly harried as the psychiatrist who's delighted to encounter a "classic paranoid," and who just happens to be named Dr. (Mildred) Watson.

After that it's all downhill. It's not only unfunny, but increasingly preachy and sentimental—hammering at the clichéd tale of the good-hearted nut who's basically saner, and certainly nicer, than the pack of meanies who attempt to defeat him.

Scott and Woodward battle the script valiantly. Scott has the easier time of it by virtue of his character's self-contained system. But both are buried eventually under a pile of loose ends, and they're not helped much either by Anthony Harvey's visually unimaginative direction.

•

THEY'RE A WEIRD MOB
1966, 109 mins, Australia/UK Ⓥ col
Dir Michael Powell ***Prod*** Michael Powell ***Scr*** Richard Imrie ***Ph*** Arthur Grant ***Ed*** Gerald Turney-Smith ***Mus*** Laurence Leonard, Alan Boustead ***Art*** Dennis Gentle
Act Walter Chiari, Clare Dunne, Chips Rafferty, Alida Chelli, Ed Devereaux, Slim de Grey (Williamson/Powell International)

Italian import Walter Chiari scores in a role that seems tailor-made—an Italian journalist who emigrates to Australia to write for an Italian journal in Sydney edited by his cousin. He arrives very green, and much amusement is caused by his taking too literally some of the Aussie slang.

Chiari finds his cousin has fled. He has left a very irate young lady, Clare Dunne, who has put money into the journal. Chiari gets a job as a bricklayer and ultimately makes the grade with his fellow Aussie workmen. Determined to repay his cousin's debts in installments, Chiari seeks Dunne on Sydney's beaches and elsewhere, but is rebuffed all the way.

Apart from Chiari, Chips Rafferty (who gives an outstanding performance as Dunne's father) and Ed Devereaux as the main bricklayer, most of the cast seems self-conscious before the cameras. For the first half, the film [from the bestselling novel *Down Under* by John O'Grady] strives too hard to be funny and concentrates too much upon the strange Aussie lingo. Once it settles down to telling a story and forgetting about this, it is stronger entertainment.

•

THEY SHOOT HORSES, DON'T THEY?
1969, 129 mins, US Ⓥ ⦿ ▭ col
Dir Sydney Pollack ***Prod*** Irwin Winkler, Robert Chartoff ***Scr*** James Poe, Robert E. Thompson ***Ph*** Philip H. Lathrop ***Ed*** Fredric Steinkamp ***Mus*** John Green ***Art*** Harry Horner
Act Jane Fonda, Michael Sarrazin, Susannah York, Gig Young, Red Buttons, Bonnie Bedelia (Palomar/ABC)

Horace McCoy's 1935 grimy novel of a depression-era dance marathon, which sold a forgettable 3,000 copies as a book, is a film with Jane Fonda as a hard-as-nails babe. It becomes, in a re-created old ballroom, a sordid spectacle of hard times, a kind of existentialist allegory of life.

Gig Young is the promoter-emcee, the barker for a cheap sideshow attraction with an endless patter of clichés on pluck, luck, courage, true grit and the American Way. Puffy-eyed, unshaven, reeking of stale liquor, sweat and cigarettes, Young has never looked older or acted better.

Fonda, as the unremittingly cynical loser, the tough and bruised babe of the Dust Bowl, gives a dramatic performance that gives the film a personal focus and an emotionally gripping power.

Pollack turns the marathon into a vulgar, sleazy, black microcosm of life in 1932.

1969: Best Supp. Actor (Gig Young)

NOMINATIONS: Best Actress (Jane Fonda), Supp. Actress (Susannah York), Screenplay Adaptation, Costume Design, Art Direction, Editing, Adapted Music Score

•

THEY WERE EXPENDABLE
1945, 135 mins, US Ⓥ ⦿ b/w
Dir John Ford ***Prod*** John Ford ***Scr*** Frank Wead ***Ph*** Joseph H. August ***Ed*** Frank E. Hull, Douglass Biggs ***Mus*** Herbert Stothart ***Art*** Cedric Gibbons, Malcolm F. Brown
Act Robert Montgomery, John Wayne, Donna Reed, Cameron Mitchell, Ward Bond, Leon Ames (M-G-M)

They Were Expendable, dealing with the Japs' overrunning of the Philippines [from the book of the same name by William L. White], primarily concerns the part played by the U.S. torpedo boats in their use against the Japs.

Robert Montgomery and his buddy (John Wayne) are naval lieutenants in command of P-T boats. Montgomery from the start has faith in the little destroyers but Wayne is slow to appreciate their value.

While the squadron of P-T tubs stationed at Manila Bay prior to Pearl Harbor were looked upon doubtfully by naval officers, invasion by the Japs gave them their chance to show what they could do. Most of the rest of the picture vividly portrays the big job the little boats did.

The battle scenes in which the P-Ts go after Jap cruisers and supply ships were exceptionally well directed, John Ford aided by James C. Havens, captain of the U.S. Marine Corps Reserves.

Love interest is built around Wayne and an army nurse, played appealingly by Donna Reed. It develops at an early stage but is dropped as Wayne and Reed lose each other through assignments that separate them.

1945: NOMINATIONS: Best Sound, Special Effects

•

THEY WON'T FORGET
1937, 95 mins, US Ⓥ b/w
Dir Mervyn LeRoy ***Prod*** Mervyn LeRoy ***Scr*** Abem Kandel, Robert Rosson ***Ph*** Arthur Edeson ***Ed*** Thomas Ricards ***Mus*** Adolph Deutsch ***Art*** Robert Haas
Act Claude Rains, Edward Norris, Allyn Joslyn, Linda Perry, Cy Kendall, Clinton Rosemond (Warner Bros.)

The film [from the novel *Death in the Deep South* by Ward Greene] pulls no punches, indicting lynch law and mob fury with scalpellike precision.

The locale is the Deep South. A young business-school student is assaulted and murdered in the institution's building on Confederate Memorial Day, after classes are out. Only circumstantial evidence is available to the district attorney (Claude Rains) and the two most likely guilty individuals are a Negro janitor (Clinton Rosemond) and a young Yankee professor (Edward Norris) at the school.

The d.a., driven by unswerving political ambition, and taunted by a news-hungry reporter (Allyn Joslyn), decides by a hair's breadth ("Anyone can convict a Negro in the South") that the young teacher, recently transplanted from the North, is the better bait.

Finally a w.k. lawyer (Otto Kruger) goes South to defend the indicted man. In the punch-packed courtroom scenes, the film really implants its wallop.

The cast, while not boasting any names of much marquee magnetism, is uniformly fine. Rains especially stands out.

•

THIEF, THE
1952, 85 mins, US Ⓥ b/w
Dir Russell Rouse ***Prod*** Clarence Greene ***Scr*** Russell Rouse, Clarence Greene ***Ph*** Sam Leavitt ***Ed*** Chester Schaeffer ***Mus*** Herschel Burke Gilbert ***Art*** Joseph St. Amand
Act Ray Milland, Rita Gam, Martin Gabel, Harry Bronson, Rex O'Malley, Rita Vale (Fran/United Artists)

This has an offbeat approach to film storytelling (a complete absence of dialog), a good spy plot and a strong performance by Ray Milland.

The film is not soundless. The busy hum of a city is a cacophonous note, a strident-sounding telephone bell plays an important part and, overall, there's the topnotch musical score by Herschel Gilbert, sometimes used almost too insistently to build a melodramatic mood and in other spots softly emphasizing and making clear the dumb action of the players.

Missed in the story is the reason why Milland, a respected scientist in the field of nuclear physics, should turn traitor to his country and deliver its nuclear secrets to foreign agents.

Film introduces Rita Gam, N.Y. actress, and in her three scenes as a temptress her personality impresses.

1952: Scoring of a Dramatic Picture

•

THIEF
1981, 122 mins, US Ⓥ ⊙ col
Dir Michael Mann ***Prod*** Jerry Bruckheimer, Ronnie Caan ***Scr*** Michael Mann ***Ph*** Donald Thorin ***Ed*** Dov Hoenig ***Mus*** Tangerine Dream ***Art*** Mel Bourne
Act James Caan, Tuesday Weld, Willie Nelson, James Belushi, Robert Prosky, Tom Signorelli (United Artists)

Michael Mann proves to be a potent triple threat as exec producer-director-writer on *Thief*. Although there are points where he gets bogged down in the technical aspects of thievery, the film is a slick Chicago crime-drama with a well-developed sense of pathos running throughout. James Caan comes up with a particularly convincing portrait of the central figure, and superior soundtrack from Tangerine Dream adds immeasurably to the action.

Mann, who won awards for his work on the critically acclaimed telefilm *The Jericho Mile*, has woven a fine story around a highly honorable man who just happens to be an expert thief with an extensive prison record.

Caan plays the thief, a victim of an unfortunate childhood who lands in jail and is hardened with his unsavory environment, with an incredible vulnerability.

In terms of story, Caan is a highly successful crook who takes great pains to maintain his professional independence. Against his better judgment he gives in to "godfather"-type Robert Prosky's request to join forces, mostly in an effort to provide personal stability.

The basic story centers on Caan's work, which becomes increasingly complicated by his new association. Oddly enough, Mann's major flaw is being a bit too meticulous in delineating the process Caan must go through in order to make a big score.

[A *Special Director's Edition*, trimming some scenes and adding others, was released on home video in 1995. Running time is also 122 mins.]

•

THIEF AND THE COBBLER, THE
SEE: ARABIAN NIGHT

•

THIEF OF BAGDAD, THE
1924, 155 mins, US Ⓥ ⊙ ⊗ b/w
Dir Raoul Walsh ***Prod*** Douglas Fairbanks ***Scr*** Lotta Woods, Elton Thomas [= Douglas Fairbanks] ***Ph*** Arthur Edeson ***Ed*** William Nolan ***Mus*** Mortimer Wilson ***Art*** William Cameron Menzies
Act Douglas Fairbanks, Snitz Edwards, Julanne Johnston, Anna May Wong, Charles Belcher, Sojin (Fairbanks/United Artists)

Douglas Fairbanks comes forth with an absorbing, interesting picture, totally different than any of its predecessors. Nearly all of it is fairytalelike or fantasy, and so well is it done that the picture carries its audience along in the spirit of the depiction. *The Arabian Nights* are classic stories in book form. *The Thief of Bagdad* is a classic in pictures.

There is a magic rope thrown into the air up which the thief climbs high walls. There is a magic carpet upon which he sails with his princess away into the land of happiness. There is a magic chest which the favored one retrieves after heroic struggles through the valley of fire, the vale of dragons, even to the depths of the seas. It is the thief, now a prince, who returns at the coming of the seventh moon to win his princess against the wiles of Oriental potentates seeking her hand. He wraps her in his invisible cloak and whisks her away.

The cast has been brightly selected. At the head of those players is Sojin in the role of the Mongol prince, a really fine characterization. Anna May Wong, as the little slave girl who is a spy for the Mongol prince, proves herself a fine actress. Julanne Johnston as the princess is languorous, being more decorative than inspiring.

•

THIEF OF BAGDAD, THE
AN ARABIAN FANTASY
1940, 106 mins, UK/US Ⓥ ⊙ col
Dir Ludwig Berger, Michael Powell, Tim Whelan, Geoffrey Boothby, Charles David, [Zoltan Korda, William Cameron Menzies, Alexander Korda] ***Prod*** Alexander Korda ***Scr*** Lajos Biro, Miles Malleson ***Ph*** Georges Perinal, Osmond Borradaile ***Ed*** William Hornbeck, Charles Crichton ***Mus*** Miklos Rozsa ***Art*** Vincent Korda
Act Conrad Veidt, Sabu, June Duprez, John Justin, Rex Ingram, Miles Malleson (Korda)

The Thief of Bagdad is a colorful, lavish and eye-appealing spectacle. It's an expensive production accenting visual appeal, combining sweeping panoramas and huge sets, amazing special effects and process photography and vivid magnificent Technicolor. These factors completely submerge the stolid, slow and rather disjointed fairytale, which lacks any semblance of spontaneity in its telling.

Alexander Korda retains only the Bagdadian background and title in presenting his version of the picture first turned out by Douglas Fairbanks in 1924. But while Fairbanks presented dash and movement to his story, to have the latter dominate his spectacular settings, Korda uses the reverse angle. As result, audience interest is focused on the production and technical displays of the picture, and the unimpressive story and stagey acting of the cast fail to measure up to the general production qualities.

The story combines many imaginative incidents culled from *Arabian Nights* fables. There's the mechanical horse that flies through the air; the giant genie of the bottle; the huge spider that guards the all-seeing eye; the six-armed dancing doll; the evil magic of the villain; and the famous magic carpet.

Korda spent two years in preparation and production of *Thief of Bagdad*. All of the large sets, including the city of Bagdad and seaport of Basra, were shot in England, in addition to most of the dramatic action. With the war stopping production in England Korda moved to Hollywood to complete the picture, substituting the American desert and the Grand Canyon for sequences that he originally intended to shoot in Arabia and Egypt.

Conrad Veidt is most impressive as the sinister grand vizier, sharing honors with Sabu, who capably carries off the title role.

1940: Best Color Cinematography, Color Interior Decoration (Vincent Korda), Special Effects (Lawrence Butler, Jack Whitney)

NOMINATION: Best Original Score

•

THIEF WHO CAME TO DINNER, THE
1973, 105 mins, US Ⓥ col
Dir Bud Yorkin ***Prod*** Bud Yorkin ***Scr*** Walter Hill ***Ph*** Philip Lathrop ***Ed*** John C. Horger ***Mus*** Henry Mancini ***Art*** Polly Platt
Act Ryan O'Neal, Jacqueline Bisset, Warren Oates, Jill Clayburgh, Charles Cioffi, Ned Beatty (Tandem/Warner)

The Thief Who Came to Dinner has a good title and a helpful supporting cast. Otherwise it is a tepid caper comedy, starring Ryan O'Neal as a computer-age society gem burglar, Jacqueline Bisset as his girl, and Warren Oates as a befuddled insurance detective.

Using a Terrence Lore novel, adapter Walter Hill structured an episodic script focusing on O'Neal, who blackmails magnate Charles Cioffi for entree into rich circles where he can plot his heists.

The film, which exudes the lethargy of a project where some talent commitments are being exercised, uses as a running gag O'Neal's heist signature of a chess move, leading to a newspaper promotion with chess editor Austin Pendleton becoming frustrated at the thief's computer-aided expertise.

•

THIEVES' HIGHWAY
1949, 93 mins, US b/w
Dir Jules Dassin ***Prod*** Robert Bassler ***Scr*** A. I. Bezzerides ***Ph*** Norbert Brodine ***Ed*** Nick DeMaggio ***Mus*** Alfred Newman ***Art*** Lyle Wheeler, Chester Gore
Act Richard Conte, Valentina Cortese, Lee J. Cobb, Jack Oakie, Millard Mitchell (20th Century-Fox)

Script stresses realism and Jules Dassin's direction further carries out that emphasis in the no-holds-barred love sequences between Richard Conte and Hollywood newcomer Valentina Cortese, and the high-action trucking scenes and barroom fight finale. A. I. Bezzerides did the screenplay from his novel, *Thieves' Market*. It's guttily dialoged and plays fast under Dassin's helming.

Conte depicts a trucker whose father has lost his legs in an accident staged by heavy Lee J. Cobb, produce commission man. Conte goes out for revenge, aided by Millard Mitchell, in an attempt to beat Cobb at his own game of thievery.

Cortese is introduced as a prostitute, hired by Cobb to lure Conte from his revenge game. She and Conte make the most of the meaty assignments.

•

THIEVES LIKE US
1974, 123 mins, US Ⓥ ⊙ col
Dir Robert Altman ***Prod*** Jerry Bick ***Scr*** Calder Willingham, Joan Tewkesbury, Robert Altman ***Ph*** Jean Boffety ***Ed*** Lou Lombardo
Act Keith Carradine, Shelley Duvall, John Schuck, Bert Remsen, Louise Fletcher, Tom Skerritt (United Artists)

Thieves Like Us proves that when Robert Altman has a solid story and script, he can make an exceptional film, one mostly devoid of clutter, auterist mannerism and other cinema chic. It's a better film than Nicholas Ray's first jab at the story in 1948 [*They Live by Night*], the mid-1930s tale of lower-class young love and Dixie bank-robbing.

Edward Anderson's novel of the same name has, this time, been adapted into a no-nonsense screenplay. Keith Carradine heads the cast as a young prison trustee who escapes with John Schuck to join Bert Remsen in a spree of small-town bank heists. Shelley Duvall and Carradine fall in love, their romance clearly destined for tragedy as the robberies inevitably lead to murders and eventual police capture.

•

THIN BLUE LINE, THE
1988, 106 mins, US Ⓥ ⊙ col
Dir Errol Morris ***Prod*** Mark Lipson ***Ph*** Stefan Czapsky, Robert Chappell ***Ed*** Paul Barnes ***Mus*** Philip Glass ***Art*** Ted Bafaloukos
(American Playhouse/Third Floor)

Errol Morris's *The Thin Blue Line* constitutes a mesmerizing reconstruction and investigation of a senseless murder. It employs strikingly original formal devices to pull together diverse interviews, filmclips, photo collages and recreations of the crime from many points of view.

Case in question centers upon the 1976 murder of a Dallas policeman. Late one night, Officer Robert Wood and his partner pulled over a car that was traveling without its headlights on. When Wood approached the driver's window, he was shot five times and killed.

Some time later, David Harris, 16, was arrested in Vidor, Texas, after having bragged to friends that he'd killed a Dallas cop. Harris later insisted his boasting was only meant to impress his buddies, and that the real murderer was a hitchhiker he'd picked up earlier in the day, one Randall Adams.

Despite Harris's extensive criminal history and Adams's unblemished past, the teenager got off scot-free, while the older man was convicted and sentenced to death (later committed to life imprisonment).

Morris first introduces the two men via freshly filmed, straightforward interviews, then stages the crime for the camera from a variety of angles and at an assortment of speeds.

Title refers to the police, said by the judge here to be the only thing that separates the public from the rule of anarchy.

•

THING, THE
1982, 108 mins, US Ⓥ ⊙ col
Dir John Carpenter ***Prod*** David Foster, Lawrence Turman ***Scr*** Bill Lancaster ***Ph*** Dean Cundey ***Ed*** Todd Ramsay ***Mus*** Ennio Morricone ***Art*** John J. Lloyd
Act Kurt Russell, A. Wilford Brimley, T.K. Carter, David Clennon, Keith David, Richard Dysart (Universal/Turman-Foster)

If it's the most vividly gruesome monster ever to stalk the screen that audiences crave, then *The Thing* is the thing. On all other levels, however, John Carpenter's remake of Howard Hawks's 1951 sci-fi classic comes as a letdown.

Strong premise of a group of American scientists and researchers posted at an isolated station in Antarctica. A visit to a decimated Norwegian encampment in the vicinity reveals that a space ship, which had remained buried in ice for as many as 100,000 years, has been uncovered, and that no survivors were left to tell what was found.

First manifestation of The Thing arrives in the form of an escaped dog from the Scandinavian camp. It soon becomes clear that The Thing is capable of ingesting, then assuming the bodily form of, any living being.

What the old picture delivered—and what Carpenter has missed—was a sense of intense dread, a fear that the loathed creature might be lurking around any corner or behind any door.

Kurt Russell is the nominal hero, although suicidal attitude adopted towards the end undercuts his status as a center-screen force.

•

THING CALLED LOVE, THE
1993, 116 mins, US Ⓥ ⊙ col
Dir Peter Bogdanovich ***Prod*** John Davis ***Scr*** Carol Heikkinen ***Ph*** Peter James ***Ed*** Terry Stokes ***Mus*** G. Marq Roswell (sup.) ***Art*** Michael Seymour
Act River Phoenix, Samantha Mathis, Dermot Mulroney, Sandra Bullock, K. T. Oslin, Anthony Clark (Paramount)

A fairly typical tale of young talent on the rise in Nashville is given nicely nuanced treatment in *The Thing Called Love*. Perhaps there's not much new to say about the dues and disappointments involved in breaking into the country music scene, but the scenes are fresh and the emotions real in Peter Bogdanovich's tune-laden, mixed-mood drama.

Debuting screenwriter Carol Heikkinen's story seems familiar from the outset, as cute aspiring singer-songwriter Miranda Presley (Samantha Mathis) Greyhounds from New York City to Nashville in search of her dream. Moving in with the buoyantly untalented Linda Lue Linden (Sandra Bullock), Miranda attracts the attention of two good-looking dudes, the moody, gifted James Wright (River Phoenix) and soulful Kyle Davidson (Dermot Mulroney), who writes better than he sings.

Characters hit the crossroads at a big country dance to which Kyle brings Miranda, but loses her after James, who is unexpectedly performing that night, invites her up onstage to join in one of his numbers.

Brought on to replace another director on relatively short notice, Bogdanovich hasn't been able to transcend such fundamental script problems as its predictability and the conventional, thinly conceived secondary characters. But, like good country songwriters and singers, he and his leading actors have been able to locate authentic emotion in a standard format.

•

THING FROM ANOTHER WORLD, THE
1951, 89 mins, US Ⓥ ⊙ b/w
Dir Christian Nyby ***Prod*** Howard Hawks ***Scr*** Charles Lederer ***Ph*** Russell Harlan ***Ed*** Roland Gross ***Mus*** Dimitri Tiomkin ***Art*** Albert S. D'Agostino, John J. Hughes
Act Margaret Sheridan, Kenneth Tobey, Robert Cornthwaite, Douglas Spencer, Dewey Martin, James Arness (Winchester/RKO)

Strictly offbeat subject matter centers around a weird, outlandish interplanetary space-hopper (see title) which descends upon earth in what's referred to as a flying saucer.

Christian Nyby's direction sustains a mood of tingling expectancy as a small group of U.S. airmen and scientists stationed near the North Pole learn that a new, mysterious element is playing tricks with their compass-readings, etc. Tension develops effectively as the expedition takes off to reckon with the unearthly intruder. Hawks's production also scores in its depiction of the bleak, snow-swept Arctic region. The background layout, shot in Montana, conveys an air of frigid authenticity.

But the resourcefulness shown in building the plot groundwork is lacking as the yarn gets into full swing. Cast members, headed by Margaret Sheridan and Kenneth Tobey, fail to communicate any real terror as the "Thing" makes its appearance and its power potential to destroy the world is revealed.

Screenplay, based on the story "Who Goes There?" by John W. Campbell, Jr., shows strain in the effort to come up with a cosmic shocker in the name of science fiction.

•

THINGS CHANGE
1988, 100 mins, US Ⓥ ⊙ col
Dir David Mamet ***Prod*** Michael Hausman ***Scr*** David Mamet, Shel Silverstein ***Ph*** Juan Ruiz-Anchia ***Ed*** Trudy Ship ***Mus*** Alaric Jans ***Art*** Michael Merritt
Act Don Ameche, Joe Mantegna, Robert Prosky, J. J. Johnston, Ricky Jay, Mike Nussbaum (Filmhaus/Columbia)

David Mamet's *Things Change* is a dry, funny and extremely intelligent comedy about an innocent mistaken for a Mafia don.

Pic opens in Chicago as the elderly Gino (Don Ameche), a shoeshine boy, is "invited" to meet a Mafia boss who he physically resembles. He wants Gino to confess to a murder and take the rap and as a reward he can have his heart's desire.

Gino is handed over to Jerry (Joe Mantegna), a very junior member of the Mafia clan. All Jerry has to do is coach Gino in his story for two days, then deliver him to the law. Instead, Jerry decides to give the oldster a final fling and takes him to Lake Tahoe where, unknown to him, a Mafia convention is about to take place.

Gino is instantly mistaken for a senior Don and given royal treatment. He's also invited to meet the local Mafia kingpin (Robert Prosky) with whom he instantly strikes up a close rapport while Jerry sees himself getting into deeper and deeper trouble.

This comedy of mistaken identity centers around a beautifully modulated starring performance from Ameche as the poor but painfully upright and honest Gino. As the dimwitted Jerry, Mantegna is consistently funny and touching.

•

THINGS OF LIFE, THE
SEE: LES CHOSES DE LA VIE

•

THINGS TO COME
1936, 97 mins, UK Ⓥ b/w
Dir William Cameron Menzies ***Prod*** Alexander Korda ***Scr*** H. G. Wells ***Ph*** Georges Perinal ***Ed*** William Hornbeck, Charles Crichton, Francis Lyon ***Mus*** Arthur Bliss ***Art*** Vincent Korda
Act Raymond Massey, Cedric Hardwicke, Edward Chapman, Ralph Richardson, Margaretta Scott, Maurice Braddell (London)

This is England's first $1 million picture. It's an impressive but dull exposition of a bad dream.

H. G. Wells's idea is that in 1946 there will be a new and disastrous world war. It will last for 30 years and, at the end of that time, civilization will be reduced to nothingness, disease having scourged the world. In exile a group of engineers and aviators, however, think things over and decide that the ravages and wastes of war, properly harnessed and channeled, can be used for the world's salvation.

They take things over, do away with the petty little fascistic countries that have sprung up, do away with their petty little fascistic leaders, and create a new world of steel and glass, radio and television, artificial light and heat. It is all very pictorial, very imaginative, very artificial and it runs on and on.

William Cameron Menzies directs with a firm hand and even manages to inject some power into the fantasy. Where his characters are allowed to live, he sees to it that they also breathe. Georges Perinal's photography is tops. Garlands are also due Harry Zech for trick photography and Ned Mann for special effects.

Raymond Massey is tops as John Cabal, leader of the new world. Ralph Richardson does a splendid job as the Boss, a sort of combo Hitler-Mussolini.

•

THINGS TO DO IN DENVER WHEN YOU'RE DEAD
1995, 114 mins, US Ⓥ ⊙ col
Dir Gary Felder ***Prod*** Cary Woods ***Scr*** Scott Rosenberg ***Ph*** Elliot Davis ***Ed*** Richard Marks ***Mus*** Michael Convertino ***Art*** Nelson Coates
Act Andy Garcia, Christopher Lloyd, William Forsythe, Bill Nunn, Treat Williams, Jack Warden (Miramax/Woods Entertainment)

Tartly written and vividly performed by a fine ensemble cast, Gary Felder's bracingly entertaining first feature covers familiar ground in a fresh, breezy way.

Jimmy the Saint (Andy Garcia) is a smooth-talking, sharp-dressing hipster who has retired from the life and started up an "afterlife advice" video company that tapes dying people's testimonies for the benefit of their survivors. Jimmy is in the midst of launching a promising romance with a gorgeous young woman, Dagney (Gabrielle Anwar), when he is paged by his former boss (Christopher Walken), an ailing criminal kingpin, who asks him to do a small favor in return for a big payday.

The "action" requested is for Jimmy to put a scare into the new boyfriend of the boss's son's ex-girlfriend and make it clear he's not to enter Denver. To this end, Jimmy rounds up his old gang: Franchise (William Forsythe), a tough biker type who's now got a weird wife and brood of kids; Critical Bill (Treat Williams), a hair-trigger psycho; Pieces (Christopher Lloyd), a disfigured porn theater projectionist; and Easy Wind (Bill Nunn), a hulking black man who has shifted from human to insect extermination.

Due to a bit of mistaken judgment on Jimmy's part and typical rashness on Critical Bill's, the "action" goes awry, pushing the big boss into issuing death warrants for all the boys, to be executed by hit man Mr. Shhh (Steve Buscemi).

Some of writer Scott Rosenberg's conceits are too precious and cute by half, and the film's eagerness to please may put some viewers off. But this is far outweighed by the pic's constant inventiveness, the bright, original dialog and the vibrancy of direction that can be felt in the excitingly alert performances as well as the dynamic visual style.

•

THINGS YOU CAN TELL JUST BY LOOKING AT HER
2000, 106 mins, US Ⓥ ⊙ col
Dir Rodrigo Garcia ***Prod*** Jon Avnet, Lisa Lindstrom, Marsha Oglesby ***Scr*** Rodrigo Garcia ***Ph*** Emmanuel Lubezki ***Ed*** Amy E. Duddleston ***Mus*** Edward Shearmur ***Art*** Jerry Fleming
Act Glenn Close, Cameron Diaz, Calista Flockhart, Kathy Baker, Amy Brenneman, Valeria Golino, Holly Hunter (Avnet-Franchise/United Artists/M-G-M)

A Southern California ensembler similar in format to *Short Cuts* and *Magnolia* but quite different in tone, not to mention length, this marks a promising directorial debut by Rodrigo Garcia. A collection of five femme-oriented vignettes that are not intricately linked dramatically but overlap characters, this observant, emotionally acute drama is distinguished by a pronounced poetic sensibility in its writing and visual style. Garcia is the son of novelist Gabriel Garcia Marquez as well as being an experienced cinematographer.

Segments run from 15 to 27 minutes and there isn't a stinker among them; they all sustain interest through unpredictable storytelling and nuanced characterization as they study San Fernando Valley women who are unfulfilled in one way or another.

This film gets started in muted but insinuating fashion with *This Is Dr. Keener* in which the accomplished titular physician (Glenn Close), while looking after her invalid mother for a day, is brought up short by the devastatingly accurate comments of a tarot card reader (Calista Flockhart). In *Fantasies About Rebecca*, a sexy and winningly self-confident Holly Hunter stars as a bank manager who, at age 39, becomes pregnant for the first time. Mood lightens with the third tale, *Someone for Rose*, in which a middle-aged author of children's books (Kathy Baker) becomes romantically curious about a well-spoken dwarf (Danny Woodburn). Episode hinges upon the emotional and sexual emptiness Rose feels when she learns that her hipster 15-year-old son (Noah Fleiss) is sexually active, and upon the notion of the unpredictability of sexual attraction.

Good Night Lilly, Good Night Christine marks the reappearance of Flockhart's character, Christine, who is revealed to be the lover of the seriously ill Lilly (Valeria Golino). Garcia's skill with dialogue comes to the fore here; brief episode plays like a short theater piece as the women cope with their unknown future together.

Final episode, *Love Waits for Kathy*, centers upon the strong relationship between sisters Kathy (Amy Brenneman), a doctor who has put her romantic life on hold, and the blind Carol (Cameron Diaz), who enjoys a healthy sex life that seems like a natural extension of her boisterous, and amusingly self-deprecating, approach to life. At this point, assorted other characters from earlier segments are neatly dropped into the mix. Ending too softly acknowledges the numerous intriguing themes that have been engagingly introduced.

•

THIN ICE
1937, 78 mins, US b/w
Dir Sidney Lanfield ***Prod*** Raymond Griffith ***Scr*** Boris Ingster, Milton Sperling ***Ph*** Robert Planck, Edward Cronjager ***Ed*** Robert Simpson ***Mus*** Louis Silvers (dir.)
Act Sonja Henie, Tyrone Power, Arthur Treacher, Raymond Walburn, Joan Davis, Sig Ruman (20th Century-Fox)

Sonja Henie is the skating and skiing instructress at an Alpine hotel, meeting place of a group of European diplomats concerned about the political status quo. Tyrone Power is a young prince, sent on by his prime minister to play dumb. While affairs of nations are being discussed he slips out with his skis and his dark snow glasses. Sliding down a glacier at 40 miles an hour, he meets Sonja traveling in the same direction. There's a lot of plot about mistaken identities, threatened international complications and old-fashioned romance [from the play *Der Komet* by Attila Orbok].

Power does some duet skiing but stays off the ice. Just as well that he does. On ice Henie is a virtuoso. The only thing which can keep up with her is the music. Outdoor scenes were taken at Mt. Ranier and are lovely landscapes.

Production wallop is the staging of three elaborate ice ballets [staged by Harry Losee], engaging a skating corps of 100 men and women. Troupe is beautifully costumed and photographed from angles which bring out grace, speed and skill.

•

THINK FAST, MR. MOTO
1937, 66 mins, US b/w
Dir Norman Foster ***Prod*** Sol M. Wurtzel (exec.) ***Scr*** Howard Ellis Smith, Norman Foster ***Ph*** Harry Jackson ***Ed*** Alex Troffey ***Mus*** Samuel Kaylin (dir.) ***Art*** Lewis Creber
Act Peter Lorre, Virginia Field, Thomas Beck, Sig Ruman, Murray Kinnell, John Rogers (20th Century-Fox)

Peter Lorre's new characterization, that of an educated Japanese merchant and amateur sleuth, gets away from the grim villainy of his previous film efforts. He no longer is a bogey man. When he smiles, it is not a wry, warped grimace.

In *Mr. Moto* he carries the title role, as a San Francisco importer who decides to run down a vast ring of gem smugglers, operating between Shanghai and the U.S. port. His identity is skillfully masked till the pay-off scene. Aboard a liner bound for the Chinese seaport metropolis, Moto begins unraveling the skeins of a Frisco murder mystery [from a story by John P. Marquand] and identity of a mysterious beauty who boards the steamer at Honolulu.

Lorre is surrounded by a capable cast, with Virginia Field and Sig Ruman as diinct assets. She is the gang's unwilling undercover operative who tries to warn the wealthy youth with whom she falls in love. Ruman plays the cabaret owner and king of the smugglers.

•

THIN MAN, THE
1934, 80 mins, US Ⓥ ⊙ b/w
Dir W. S. Van Dyke ***Prod*** Hunt Stromberg ***Scr*** Albert Hackett, Frances Goodrich ***Ph*** James Wong Howe ***Ed*** Robert J. Kern ***Mus*** William Axt ***Art*** Cedric Gibbons, David Townsend, Edwin B. Willis
Act William Powell, Myrna Loy, Maureen O'Sullivan, Nat Pendleton, Minna Gombell, Porter Hall (M-G-M/Cosmopolitan)

The Thin Man was an entertaining novel, and now it's an entertaining picture. In the Dashiell Hammett original there was considerable material not suited by nature to pictures. That this has been cut without noticeable loss of story punch or merit is high commendation for the adapters.

They capture the spirit of the jovial, companionable relationship of the characters, Nick, retired detective, and Nora, his wife. Their very pleasant manner of loving each other and showing it is used as a light comedy structure upon which the screen doctors perform their operation on the Hammett novel.

The comedy as inserted, and also as directed by W. S. Van Dyke and played by William Powell and Myrna Loy, carries the picture along during its early moments and gives it an impetus which sweeps the meat of the mystery story through to a fast finish.

No changes made in the basic plot nor in the murder mystery developments.

1934: NOMINATIONS: Best Picture, Director, Actor (William Powell), Writing Adaptation

•

THIN MAN GOES HOME, THE
1944, 100 mins, US Ⓥ ⦿ b/w
Dir Richard Thorpe ***Prod*** Everett Riskin ***Scr*** Robert Riskin, Dwight Taylor ***Ph*** Karl Freund ***Ed*** Ralph E. Winters ***Mus*** David Snell ***Art*** Cedric Gibbons, Edward Carfagno
Act William Powell, Myrna Loy, Gloria de Haven, Anne Revere, Harry Davenport, Edward Brophy (M-G-M)

Based on the characterizations originally created by Dashiell Hammett, the story emerges as a neatly fashioned whodunit. Richard Thorpe paces the plot nicely, overcoming, before too long, the hurdles of a rather slow opening.

Production as a whole, however, lacks much of the sophistication and smartness which characterized the early *Thin Man* films. Deficiency is mainly in the dialog and other business provided for the two leads.

Yarn deals with an espionage ring working for a foreign power. Involves a battle of wits to secure a group of paintings which leads to a couple of killings.

Myrna Loy, while graceful and piquant for the most part, photographs unattractively in a number of sequences.

•

THIN RED LINE, THE
1964, 90 mins, US ▭ b/w
Dir Andrew Marton ***Prod*** Sidney Harmon ***Scr*** Bernard Gordon ***Ph*** Manuel Berenguer ***Ed*** Derek Parsons ***Mus*** Malcolm Arnold ***Art*** Jose Alguero
Act Keir Dullea, Jack Warden, James Philbrook, Ray Daley, Robert Kanter, Merlyn Yordan (Allied Artists)

Aficionados of the action-packed war film will savor the crackling, combat-centered approach of *The Thin Red Line*, an explosive melodramatization of the Yank assault on Guadalcanal in World War II.

Bernard Gordon's scenario, turbulently gleaned from James Jones's novel, focuses its characterization gaze at two figures prominently implicated in the taking of that small but significant piece of Pacific real estate. One is a resourceful private (Keir Dullea), the other a war-wise, sadistic sergeant (Jack Warden).

The two quickly become enemies but it is no surprise when, ultimately, one dies in the other's arms after saving the other's life. Dullea and Warden are colorful antagonists, former's intensity contrasting sharply with the latter's easygoing air. In addition to this pivotal intramural conflict, there are other hostilities, including the one between Japan and the United States.

•

THIN RED LINE, THE
1998, 170 mins, US Ⓥ ⦿ ▭ col
Dir Terrence Malick ***Prod*** Robert Michael Geisler, John Roberdeau, Grant Hill ***Scr*** Terrence Malick ***Ph*** John Toll ***Ed*** Billy Weber, Leslie Jones, Saar Klein ***Mus*** Hans Zimmer ***Art*** Jack Fisk
Act Sean Penn, Adrien Brody, Jim Caviezel, Ben Chaplin, George Clooney, John Cusack (Geisler-Roberdeau/Phoenix/Fox 2000)

Terrence Malick's much anticipated return to the film scene after a 20-year hiatus is a complex, highly talented work that will captivate some critics and serious viewers by an abstract nature, emotional remoteness and a lack of dramatic focus that will frustrate mainstream audiences.

Malick's previous pictures, *Badlands* (1973) and *Days of Heaven* (1978), were never more than cult hits, but they were sufficiently distinctive for the reclusive writer-director to parlay them into legendary status during his two decades of Garboesque silence.

WWII buffs and fans of the James Jones novel may be brought up short by the lack of political, strategic and military nuts and bolts vis-a-vis the battle of Guadalcanal. However, it is clear that Malick has things on his mind other than the specifics of what it took to turn the tide of war in the Pacific. Things like the Garden of Eden, Milton's *Paradise Lost*, mankind as a collective embodiment of the two extremes of nature, and other lofty notions.

Surprised to encounter no initial resistance on the lush green island, the Americans are forced to pursue the Japanese up toward their dug-in positions in the hills, resulting in some fierce action.

Structurally, the film is lumpy, with confrontations and climaxes coming and going abruptly, and a final 45 minutes in which the dramatic momentum slides noticeably downhill. Characters are given special attention and then disappear for lengths of time—Sean Penn's stand-apart sergeant is a particular victim of this choppiness. The full meaning of the pic is realized only in the extensive voiceover commentaries.

Physically, the film is ravishing, and Malick's ability to build dense, multilayered sequences proves as supple as ever. A limited amount of shooting was done at Guadalcanal, but for the most part the Daintree Rain Forest in Queensland, Australia, has filled in beautifully.

•

THIRD DAY, THE
1965, 119 mins, US ▭ col
Dir Jack Smight ***Prod*** Jack Smight ***Scr*** Burton Wohl, Robert Presnell, Jr. ***Ph*** Robert Surtees ***Ed*** Stefan Arnsten ***Mus*** Percy Faith ***Art*** Edward Carrere
Act George Peppard, Elizabeth Ashley, Roddy McDowall, Arthur O'Connell, Mona Washbourne, Herbert Marshall (Warner)

The Third Day shapes up as an interesting and sometimes suspenseful drama revolving around a man fighting amnesia and faced with a manslaughter rap. The production is adapted from Joseph Hayes's novel. A chief weakness lies in the lack of script development of how George Peppard, who has lost all recollection of a 24-hour period during which a young woman meets her death, regains his memory.

Film opens on Peppard climbing a steep bank from a river into which he obviously plunged, but he cannot remember what happened or who he is. He learns he's married to a beautiful aristocrat whom he's about to lose because he's a drunk, and is about to be talked into selling the family business.

Peppard delivers an expert enactment and Elizabeth Ashley, as his wife, lends a colorful note as she handles a well-played role. Roddy McDowall socks over a conniving character and a standout performance is offered by Mona Washbourne in a warm and understanding characterization, perhaps the most memorable delineation of the picture.

•

THIRD FINGER, LEFT HAND
1940, 96 mins, US b/w
Dir Robert Z. Leonard ***Prod*** John W. Considine, Jr. ***Scr*** Lionel Houser ***Ph*** George Folsey ***Ed*** Elmo Vernon ***Mus*** David Snell ***Art*** Cedric Gibbons, Paul Groesse
Act Myrna Loy, Melvyn Douglas, Raymond Walburn, Lee Bowman, Bonita Granville, Felix Bressart (M-G-M)

Third Finger, Left Hand is sufficiently light and fluffy in its farcical setup to provide diverting entertainment. Story is of mild texture, and obvious from the opening reel. Although lacking sustained pace, it still displays several corking comedy episodes.

Myrna Loy is presented as a magazine editor, who—on assuming the post—invents a fictitious husband to insure her job against the jealous forays of the boss's wife. But she soon meets Melvyn Douglas, a roaming artist who's quick on the thinker, and the pair fall in love. After discovering status of her illusionary mate, he moves into her home as the missing husband, and from there on it's a melange of by-play and provoking situations until the windup.

Robert Z. Leonard directs with a capable hand and does much to overcome the lightweight script. Loy is in the comedienne vein similar to the *Thin Man* pictures, with excellent results. Douglas is okay as the artist who takes advantage of the situation. Felix Bressart adds much to the comedy side with a slick characterization of a fidgety photographer.

•

THIRD MAN, THE
1949, 93 mins, UK Ⓥ ⦿ b/w
Dir Carol Reed ***Prod*** Carol Reed ***Scr*** Graham Greene ***Ph*** Robert Krasker ***Ed*** Oswald Hafenrichter ***Mus*** Anton Karas ***Art*** Vincent Korda, John Hawkesworth, Joseph Bato
Act Joseph Cotten, Alida Valli, Orson Welles, Trevor Howard, Bernard Lee, Wilfrid Hyde White (London)

This is a full-blooded, absorbing story adapted from book by Graham Greene. Locale is postwar Vienna, which is controlled by combined military force of the four occupying powers, and revolves around the black market and all its unsavory ramifications.

Holly Martins, a young American writer, arrives to join his friend Harry Lime, who has promised him a job. He just gets to him in time to attend his funeral. Suspicious of conflicting evidence and with a strong hunch that Harry was murdered, Holly decides to unravel the mystery.

Orson Welles manifests as the "corpse" of the opening shots, and his contribution is mainly in dodging through back streets.

Joseph Cotten makes a pleasing personality of the loyal friend, and Trevor Howard, as the detached, cool British officer, displays just the right amount of human sympathy and understanding.

1950: Best B&W Cinematography

NOMINATIONS: Best Director, Editing

•

THIRD SECRET, THE
1964, 103 mins, UK ▭ b/w
Dir Charles Crichton ***Prod*** Robert L. Joseph ***Scr*** Robert L. Joseph ***Ph*** Douglas Slocombe ***Ed*** Freddie Wilson ***Mus*** Richard Arnell ***Art*** Tom Morahan
Act Stephen Boyd, Jack Hawkins, Richard Attenborough, Diane Cilento, Pamela Franklin, Paul Rogers (Hubris)

When a renowned psychoanalyst is deemed a suicide, the puzzle surrounding his sudden and unaccountable death, as it is put together piece by piece by one of his agitated patients, is the plot pursued by *The Third Secret*, an engrossing, if not altogether convincing, mystery melodrama of the weighty psychological school.

Stephen Boyd, as the inquisitive patient of the deceased analyst, conducts a private investigation to determine whether the death was actually a suicide (contradicting everything the noted doctor stood for) or a murder committed by one of his patients, of whom there were only four, according to the analyst's daughter (Pamela Franklin). The investigation leads Boyd—an American telenewscaster living in England—from patient to patient, a fruitless path until he unearths "the third secret."

A lack of animation in spots is evident in Boyd's performance, but there are moments when he catches the spark of the character. Franklin does a highly professional job as the daughter. The three ex-patients visited by Boyd are Jack Hawkins as a judge, Diane Cilento as a secretary and Richard Attenborough as an art gallery owner.

•

THIRTEEN CHAIRS, THE
SEE: 12 PLUS 1

•

THIRTEEN DAYS
2000, 145 mins, US Ⓥ ⦿ col
Dir Roger Donaldson ***Prod*** Armyan Bernstein, Peter O. Almond, Kevin Costner ***Scr*** David Self ***Ph*** Andrzej Bartkowiak ***Ed*** Conrad Buff ***Mus*** Trevor Jones ***Art*** Dennis Washington
Act Kevin Costner, Bruce Greenwood, Steven Culp, Dylan Baker, Michael Fairman, Henry Strozier (Beacon/New Line)

The Cuban missile crisis, which in bringing the East and West to the brink of nuclear conflict represented the tensest moment of the Cold War, has been turned into a solid historical thriller [based on the book *The Kennedy Tapes: Inside the White House During the Cuban Missile Crisis*, edited by Ernest R. May, Philip D. Zelikow] that puts presidential aide Kenny O'Donnell (Kevin Costner) into the center of the action. O'Donnell, a member of the Kennedy "Irish Mafia" who had been a Harvard classmate of Bobby's and had worked on JFK's Senate campaigns, was especially trusted by the president on military matters and, if not a decision maker per se, was a valued adviser and tough-minded problem solver. While placing O'Donnell in the orbit of critical events, script, fortunately, isn't intent upon inflating him with undue importance, and positioning such a figure in the foreground puts the Kennedy brothers in relief in a way that helpfully removes some of their iconic aura.

In rather too-insistent fashion, extensive footage of nuclear explosions is used to set the context for the standoff that began Oct. 16, 1962, when U.S. spy plane photographs revealed that the USSR had smuggled medium-range ballistic missiles into Cuba and was within a couple of weeks of making operational nuclear weapons that could reach the American capital within five minutes. For six days American officials managed to keep the news a secret while they scrambled to develop a proper response that the president, for one, hoped could stop short of a military strike that would likely trigger an all-out war.

In workmanlike fashion that maintains a judicious, unfrenzied focus on the personal jockeying among JFK's Cabinet members and advisers against the backdrop of monumental events, director Roger Donaldson steadily lays out the drama's many twists and turns while adroitly slipping many characters into the mix. On the one side are the hawks who fairly drool at this golden opportunity to blow up "the red bastards." On the other side are liberal doves whose natural inclination toward diplomacy and negotiation has the stench of timid appeasement to everyone else.

Most of the drama consists of men in suits and uniforms arguing tactics and mulling things over in well-upholstered rooms. But the way in which they wrestle with agonizing issues, largely maintain their cool and finally land on their feet proves very absorbing, and the entire episode makes one grateful that, on this occasion, at least, the U.S. government was in good hands.

Given the memorable looks and distinctive vocal qualities of JFK and RFK, portraying them is always a dicey enterprise, but Bruce Greenwood and Steven Culp, respectively, pull it off. Costner is in possession of a Boston accent that's less reliable than those assumed by Greenwood and Culp. One stops dwelling on the vicissitudes of the regional accent after the initial scenes, and Costner ends up giving a low-key, unshowy performance that blends effectively with the ensemble.

•

13 RUE MADELEINE

1946, 95 mins, US Ⓥ b/w

Dir Henry Hathaway ***Prod*** Louis de Rochemont ***Scr*** John Monks, Jr., Sy Bartlett ***Ph*** Norbert Brodine ***Ed*** Harmon Jones ***Mus*** David Buttolph ***Art*** James Basevi, Maurice Ransford

Act James Cagney, Annabella, Richard Conte, Frank Latimore, Walter Abel, Sam Jaffe (20th Century-Fox)

Utilizing the same off-screen documentary exposition as he did in *The House on 92nd Street* producer Louis de Rochemont, himself an alumnus of the *Time-Life* technique, reemploys the stentorian *March of Time* commentary to set his theme. Thereafter it evolves into a Nazi-Allies cops-and-robbers tale of bravery and bravado, honest histrionics and hokum.

When he is one of the strategic services' masterminds, on U.S. or British soil, James Cagney is effectively the mature training officer engaged in the important branch of the service having to do with strategy. When he essays the role of a brave young soldier-spy, to pit himself against Richard Conte, the crack Gestapo agent who had insinuated himself into the American espionage school as a means to learn our invasion plans, Cagney suffers comparison. Conte as Bill O'Connell, né Wilhelm Kuncel of the Nazi espionage, emerges as the cast's outstander.

The training methods, as indoctrinated into the plot's development, are arresting stuff. *Madeleine* was shot wholly away from Hollywood, utilizing New England and Quebec sites in the main, but there is nothing about the film that doesn't indicate super-Hollywood standards.

•

THIRTEENTH FLOOR, THE

1999, 120 mins, US Ⓥ ⊙ ▭ col

Dir Josef Rusnak ***Prod*** Roland Emmerich, Ute Emmerich, Marco Weber ***Scr*** Josef Rusnak, Ravel Centeno-Rodriguez ***Ph*** Wedigo von Schultzendorff ***Ed*** Henry Richardson ***Mus*** Harald Kloser ***Art*** Kirk M. Petrucelli

Act Craig Bierko, Armin Mueller-Stahl, Gretchen Mol, Vincent D'Onofrio, Dennis Haysbert, Steven Schub (Centropolis)

The makers of the pic, quite loosely based on Daniel Galouye's '60s sci-fi novel *Simulacron 3,* are clearly entranced with the notion of a supercomputer designed to provide the user with simulated time travel, but never figured out how to build a dramatically intriguing story around the concept.

Prologue is set in a sepia-toned 1937 Los Angeles, where dapper Fuller (Armin Mueller-Stahl) gives an important letter about "the awful truth" to hotel barkeep Ashton (Vincent D'Onofrio) with instructions that it is only for the eyes of Douglas Hall (Craig Bierko). Fuller zaps himself back into the present, but he's made the last trip in the machine he's invented, since he's murdered soon after phoning Hall.

LAPD Det. McBain (Dennis Haysbert) is increasingly suspicious of Hall, who stands to inherit the company fortune. Hall, in turn, is intrigued by Jane Fuller (Gretchen Mol), who arrives claiming to be Fuller's daughter. With the help of longhaired assistant Whitney (also D'Onofrio), Hall turns from computer mogul into cyber-sleuth as he zaps back into Fuller's simulated 1937 reality to uncover the truth behind the murder.

Pic's highlight is an astonishing re-creation of a bygone City of the Angels, stuffed with such period detail as a view of southbound La Cienega Boulevard from Sunset Boulevard, cutting through undeveloped land forested with nothing but oil derricks.

Innocent-looking but bland, Bierko is continually upstaged by his heftier comrades, especially the classily subdued Mueller-Stahl and versatile D'Onofrio. Mol has the ideal '30s look, but with nothing going on inside.

•

13TH LETTER, THE

1951, 85 mins, US b/w

Dir Otto Preminger ***Prod*** Otto Preminger ***Scr*** Howard Koch ***Ph*** Joseph LaShelle ***Ed*** Louis Loeffler ***Mus*** Alex North ***Art*** Lyle Wheeler, Maurice Ransford

Act Linda Darnell, Charles Boyer, Michael Rennie, Constance Smith, Francoise Rosay (20th Century-Fox)

Well-made and with an offbeat location site, film is an interesting account of the effects of poison pen letters on a small Quebec village [from a story and screenplay *Le corbeau* by Louis Chavance, directed by Henri-Georges Clouzot in 1943].

Plot deals principally with Michael Rennie, as a doctor; Charles Boyer, an older doctor, and his young wife (Constance Smith). The small Quebec village in which they live becomes a gossip mill when poison pen letters, indicating Rennie and Smith are having an affair, are widely distributed. Letters go on to bring in other people, eventually causing a wounded war hero to commit suicide.

Linda Darnell heads the star list as a crippled, romance-starved girl on whom suspicion falls briefly. However, cleared she and Rennie become the story's one valid romance. Her playing is excellent.

Charles Boyer slips into the character of the elderly French-Canadian doctor with wonderful ease. Smith, a British import, displays emotional talent.

•

13TH WARRIOR, THE

1999, 103 mins, US Ⓥ ⊙ ▭ col

Dir John McTiernan ***Prod*** John McTiernan, Michael Crichton, Ned Dowd ***Scr*** William Wisher, Warren Lewis ***Ph*** Peter Menzies, Jr. ***Ed*** John Wright ***Mus*** Jerry Goldsmith ***Art*** Wolf Kroeger

Act Antonio Banderas, Diane Venora, Dennis Storhoi, Vladimir Kulich, Omar Sharif, Anders T. Andersen (Touchstone)

The 13th Warrior emerges from a couple of years on the shelf as a bloody but anemic story of he-men with broadswords and long ships fighting off marauding cannibals dressed in bear skins.

Although produced in 1997—before director John McTiernan's *The Thomas Crown Affair* [released a month earlier]—and the subject of reported significant reworking by co-producer Michael Crichton, *Warrior* shows only limited signs of postproduction surgery. Yarn moves along in orderly three-act fashion and delivers the expected quotient of blood and guts.

What this adaptation of Crichton's 1976 novel *Eaters of the Dead* also serves up, however, is an odd combo of civilized rather than primitive-minded talk, some vaguely conceived mumbo jumbo about unmentionable flesh-eating beasts, and a promising but finally unrealized contrasting of Western and Eastern cultures, circa the 10th century.

The hero is Ahmed Ibn Fahdlan (Antonio Banderas), a cultured poet from Baghdad who is exiled to a distant land for coveting the wrong woman, but is soon coerced into joining a band of mostly blond fellows who require a non-Nordic 13th warrior to help them fight rampaging fiends who are terrorizing their land.

On the visual side, pic is not all it might have been: The compositions of McTiernan and lenser Peter Menzies, Jr., lack boldness and true epic stature. Banderas cuts a fine figure with his black robes and white horse. Heavily wooded British Columbian locations substitute plausibly for northern Euro settings.

•

30 IS A DANGEROUS AGE, CYNTHIA

1968, 85 mins, UK Ⓥ col

Dir Joseph McGrath ***Prod*** Walter Shenson ***Scr*** Dudley Moore, Joseph McGrath, John Wells ***Ph*** Billy Williams ***Ed*** Bill Blunden ***Mus*** Dudley Moore ***Art*** Brian Eatwell

Act Dudley Moore, Eddie Foy, Jr., Suzy Kendall, John Bird, Duncan MacRae (Columbia)

Generously endowed with the better comedic elements of satire, knockabouts, subtleties, pie-in-the-face, etc, film is almost a virtuoso performance by Dudley Moore. He stars, is credited with the original story, composed and conducted music—played by the Dudley Moore Trio. Close to his 30th birthday Moore, with an amazing spurt of energy, launches a desperation drive to achieve two ambitions, writing a successful musical comedy and getting married.

From this plot establishment, Moore and friends take off on a romp that involves a false broken arm, getting away from it all, losing girl, finishing musical and so on, with such a sense of camp that audiences are bound to be laughing long after the last frame.

Moore's versatility is central focus with a remarkably underplayed performance that sets pace and keeps it on track; his storyline is a single joke that undoubtedly grew during the filming, and his music and lyrics are like early Noel Coward set in rock idiom.

•

39 STEPS, THE

1935, 86 mins, UK Ⓥ ⊙ b/w

Dir Alfred Hitchcock ***Prod*** Michael Balcon ***Scr*** Charles Bennett, Alma Reville, Ian Hay ***Ph*** Bernard Knowles ***Ed*** Derek Twist ***Mus*** Louis Levy (dir.) ***Art*** Oscar Werndorff, Albert Jullion

Act Robert Donat, Madeleine Carroll, Godfrey Tearle, Peggy Ashcroft, Lucie Mannheim, Wylie Watson (Gaumont-British)

Gaumont has a zippy, punchy, romantic melodrama in *The 39 Steps*. Story is by John Buchan. It's melodrama and at times far-fetched and improbable, but the story twists and spins artfully from one high-powered sequence to another while the entertainment holds like steel cable from start to finish.

Story places a Canadian rancher (Robert Donat) in the centre of an English military secret plot. He is simultaneously flying from a false accusation of murder and hunting down the leader of the spies, of whom he has learned from a lady who becomes a corpse early in the story. In the course of his wanderings through Scotland's hills and moors he has a series of spectacular escapes and encounters.

It's a creamy role for Donat and his performance, ranging from humor to horror, reveals acting ability behind that good-looking facade. Teamed with Madeleine Carroll, who enters the footage importantly only toward the latter quarter section of the film, the romance is given a light touch which nicely colors an international spy chase.

•

39 STEPS, THE

1959, 93 mins, UK Ⓥ col

Dir Ralph Thomas ***Prod*** Betty Box, Ralph Thomas ***Scr*** Frank Harvey ***Ph*** Ernest Steward ***Ed*** Alfred Roome ***Mus*** Clifton Parker

Act Kenneth More, Taina Elg, Brenda de Banzie, Barry Jones, Reginald Beckwith, James Hayter (Rank)

Though somewhat altered from Alfred Hitchcock's original, the main idea remains unchanged and the new version of John Buchan's novel stands up very well.

When a strange young woman is stabbed to death in his flat, Kenneth More finds himself involved in a mysterious adventure involving espionage and murder. Before her death the girl tells him that she is a secret agent and gives him all the clues she knows about a spy organization seeking to smuggle some important plans out of the country. All he knows is that the top man is somewhere in Scotland and that the tangle is tied up with strange words told him by the victim—"The 39 Steps." Suspected of the murder of the girl, More has just 48 hours to find out the secret of the 39 Steps, expose the gang and so clear himself of the murder rap.

Film starts off brilliantly with tremendous tension and suitably sinister atmosphere. After a while that mood wears off as the pic settles down to an exciting and often amusing chase yarn, set amid some easy-on-the-eye Scottish scenery.

More's performance is a likeable mixture of humor and toughness while Taina Elg is appealing as the pretty schoolmistress who is dragged into the adventure against her will. Then there are Barry Jones, as a sinister professor; Brenda de Banzie, as a fake spiritualist who, with her eccentric husband (Reginald Beckwith) helps More's getaway; James Hayter as a vaude "memory man" who is a tool of the gang; and Faith Brook, whose murder sparks off the drama, all pitch in splendidly in a well-acted picture.

•

THIRTY-NINE STEPS, THE

1978, 102 mins, UK Ⓥ ⊙ col

Dir Don Sharp ***Prod*** Greg Smith ***Scr*** Michael Robson ***Ph*** John Coquillon ***Ed*** Eric Boyd-Perkins ***Mus*** Ed Welch ***Art*** Harry Pottle

Act Robert Powell, David Warner, Eric Porter, Karen Dotrice, John Mills, George Baker (Rank/Norfolk)

The Thirty Nine Steps is an okay period suspense, directed with a smooth but unremarkable touch by Don Sharp.

For the short of memory, *Steps* is the melodramatic tale of a man on the run from Prussian assassins plotting World War I. It was first a classic novel by John Buchan, then a classic film by Alfred Hitchcock [1935], with Robert Donat as the elusive hero and Madeleine Carroll as the romantic interest. This third version has attractive young Robert Powell and Karen Dotrice, but nothing like the Donat-Carroll chemistry or flourish.

John Mills is very good as the British agent trying to persuade the government of the momentous plot and its dire consequences. Also effective are David Warner as the topmost villain and Eric Porter as a police official.

•

THIRTY SECONDS OVER TOKYO
1944, 138 mins, US Ⓥ b/w
Dir Mervyn LeRoy ***Prod*** Sam Zimbalist ***Scr*** Dalton Trumbo ***Ph*** Harold Rosson, Robert Surtees ***Ed*** Frank Sullivan ***Mus*** Herbert Stothart ***Art*** Cedric Gibbons, Paul Groesse
Act Van Johnson, Robert Walker, Phyllis Thaxter, Tim Murdock, Robert Mitchum, Spencer Tracy (M-G-M)

Lt. Col. James Doolittle mapped his blitz on Japan 131 days after Pearl Harbor. There is suspense as the flyers prepare themselves for their long-range training in anticipation of the secret mission. [Script is based on the book and *Collier's* magazine story by Cpt. Ted W. Lawson and Robert Considine.] More or less relegated but capital as the bulwark of the entire mission is Spencer Tracy's conception of Doolittle. Van Johnson is Ted Lawson and Phyllis Thaxter his wife. It's an inspired casting.

Prominent in Johnson's crew are Tim Murdock, a standout as the co-pilot; Don DeFore as the navigator; Gordon McDonald as the bombardier; and Robert Walker, who is particularly effective as the wistful gunner-mechanic.

Their plane, the *Ruptured Duck*, and its pleasant little family become the focal attention henceforth. After Doolittle finally tells them of their mission to bomb Japan, the war becomes a highly personalized thing through the actions of these crew members.

1944: Best Special Effects

NOMINATION: Best B&W Cinematography

•

37°2 LE MATIN
(BETTY BLUE)
1986, 120 mins, France Ⓥ ⊙ col
Dir Jean-Jacques Beineix ***Prod*** Claude Ossard (exec.) ***Scr*** Jean-Jacques Beineix ***Ph*** Jean-Francois Robin ***Ed*** Monique Prim ***Mus*** Gabriel Yared ***Art*** Carlos Conti
Act Jean-Hugues Anglade, Beatrice Dalle, Gerard Darmon, Consuelo de Haviland, Clementine Celarie, Vincent Lindon (Gaumont/Constellation/Cargo)

Director Jean-Jacques Beineix has adapted a novel by Philippe Djian, considered an *enfant terrible* of the new literary generation. It's another feverish tale of *amour fou*.

Film begins with the animal attraction between Zorg (Jean-Hugues Anglade), a young man living off odd jobs in a coastal bungalow colony, and Betty (Beatrice Dalle), a waitress. The carnal links soon deepen into stronger bonds, particularly for Betty, who comes across a stashed-away manuscript that reveals Zorg's long-suppressed literary ambitions.

They move into a Paris suburban house shared by a girlfriend of Betty's (Consuelo de Haviland) and her mate (Gerard Darmon). Betty sends off Zorg's manuscript to numerous publishers, but what little response there is is negative. They try to settle down, but Betty's failed pregnancy and her unrealized hopes of stability push her into madness.

Though Beineix hasn't abandoned his esthetic preoccupations (notable here in the preponderant use of primary colours in clothing and decors), he has concentrated on his two actors, who are extraordinarily genuine. Dalle, a model, makes a moving debut as the desperate baby-doll who fails to mold reality to her own conceptions of happiness. Anglade is more introvertedly affecting as the lucidly casual, but devoted Zorg.

•

36 HOURS
1964, 115 mins, US/W. Germany ▭ b/w
Dir George Seaton ***Prod*** William Perlberg ***Scr*** George Seaton ***Ph*** Philip Lathrop ***Ed*** Adrienne Fazan ***Mus*** Dimitri Tiomkin ***Art*** George W. Davis, Edward Carfagno
Act James Garner, Eva Marie Saint, Rod Taylor, Werner Peters, John Banner, Alan Napier (M-G-M/Perlberg-Seaton/Cherokee)

36 Hours is a fanciful war melodrama limning an incident during that crucial number of hours immediately preceding D-Day. The production takes its title from the span of time allotted a German psychiatrist to learn from a captured U.S. intelligence officer fully briefed on the oncoming Allied invasion the exact point of landing.

Based on Roald Dahl's *Beware of the Dog* and a story of Carl K. Hittleman and Luis H. Vance, it provides a behind-the-scenes glimpse of high military intelligence at work.

James Garner plays the American sent to Lisbon to confirm through a German contact that the Nazis expect the Allies to land in the Calais area rather than the secretly planned Normandy beach. Drugged, he's flown under heavy sedation by the Germans to an isolated resort in Bavaria where upon regaining consciousness he's led to believe he has been an amnesia victim for six years.

Rod Taylor registers most effectively in the offbeat role of the German, playing it for sympathy and realistically. Garner in a derring-do part is okay and up to his usual sound brand of histrionics. Eva Marie Saint also delivers strongly as the nurse drafted by the Nazis from a concentration camp and promised help by Taylor if she plays her part well—in the masquerade with Garner.

•

THIRTY-TWO SHORT FILMS ABOUT GLENN GOULD
1993, 93 mins, Canada col
Dir Francois Girard ***Prod*** Niv Fichman ***Scr*** Francois Girard, Don McKellar ***Ph*** Alain Dostie ***Ed*** Gaetan Huot ***Art*** Charles Dunlop, John Rubino
Act Colin Feore, Gale Garnett, Katya Ladan, David Hughes, Gerry Quigley, Carlo Rota (Max)

Thirty-Two Short Films About Glenn Gould is a thirtysomething, impressionistic approach to the life and times of the iconoclastic classical pianist. An assured melange of dramatic recreation, archival material and interviews, it is a uniquely entertaining venture.

Apart from the requisite biographical details, the so-called short films run the gamut. There are a couple of Gould's nonmusical ventures for radio and a segment of his film collaboration with the animator Norman MacLaren. There's also dramatic reconstruction of key events in his life, including his last live performance. Woven into an already rich tapestry are a handful of recollections, often bland, from real-life colleagues and friends.

The personal qualities that made Gould unique and a seminal force are never fully defined. But in this instance that proves a satisfying tact; any conclusion about the driven, chronically unwell artist who died at 50 undoubtedly would have been glib and banal.

Though arguably a one-man show for actor Colin Feore, an army of performers tramp through the life story providing memorable turns, particularly Gale Garnett and David Hughes.

•

THIS ABOVE ALL
1942, 110 mins, US b/w
Dir Anatole Litvak ***Prod*** Darryl F. Zanuck ***Scr*** R. C. Sherriff ***Ph*** Arthur Miller ***Ed*** Walter Thompson ***Mus*** Alfred Newman ***Art*** Richard Day, Joseph Wright
Act Tyrone Power, Joan Fontaine, Thomas Mitchell, Henry Stephenson, Nigel Bruce, Gladys Cooper (20th Century-Fox)

This Above All is a tale of England in that tense interval between Dunkirk and the London blitz of September 1940. It tells of the romance between a beauteous daughter of the aristocracy and a lowly born soldier who has deserted after fighting honorably through the shattering battle of Flanders and the tragic evacuation of Dunkirk.

Although the screen adaptation softens certain aspects of Eric M. Knight's novel, such as toning down the love affair during the couple's stay at the Dover inn, or eliminating the complication of the soldier's brain injury, it has not weakened the story.

In some ways the yarn is even improved. For one thing, the whole involved subject of the democratic aims in the war, problem of the conflict of social classes, or the question of pacifism against duty to one's country are expertly focused in personal terms.

1942: Best B&W Art Direction (Richard Day, Joseph Wright)

NOMINATIONS: Best B&W Cinematography, Editing, Sound

•

THIS BOY'S LIFE
A TRUE STORY
1993, 115 mins, US Ⓥ ⊙ col
Dir Michael Caton-Jones ***Prod*** Art Linson ***Scr*** Robert Getchell ***Ph*** David Watkin ***Ed*** Jim Clark ***Mus*** Carter Burwell ***Art*** Stephen J. Lineweaver
Act Robert De Niro, Ellen Barkin, Leonardo DiCaprio, Jonah Blechman, Eliza Dushku, Chris Cooper (Warner)

This Boy's Life is a nicely acted but excessively bland coming-of-age memoir about a young man's escape from domestic turmoil and abuse, with numerous potent scenes of conflict between the central teenager and his violent step-father.

Tale is based on Tobias Wolff's acclaimed 1989 book of the same name and is duly narrated in writerly style by young Toby (Leonardo DiCaprio). Hitting the road in 1957 with his working class mother, Caroline (Ellen Barkin), Toby begins hanging out with a bad crowd once they settle in Seattle.

Then mom meets Dwight (Robert De Niro), a man's man with a crewcut. Even before Dwight and Caroline marry, Toby is sent to live with Dwight in Concrete, WA, where Dwight devotes himself to cutting the sullen "hotshot" down to size.

Unfortunately, after a relatively promising warmup, pic actually proceeds to flatten out the characters in the latter sections. Film's strength lies in its portrait of the father-stepson struggle, how each pushes the other toward even worse behavior.

De Niro brings both a rough charm and ferocious power to Dwight. Centerscreen almost throughout, DiCaprio is excellent as Toby. Barkin weighs in with plenty of spirit until her character dries up.

•

THIS DAY AND AGE
1933, 82 mins, US b/w
Dir Cecil B. DeMille ***Prod*** Cecil B. DeMille ***Scr*** Bartlett Cormack ***Ph*** J. Peverell Marley ***Ed*** Anne Bauchens ***Mus*** Howard Jackson, L. W. Gilbert, Abel Baer
Act Charles Bickford, Judith Allen, Richard Cromwell, Eddie Nugent, Ben Alexander (Paramount)

A Cecil B. DeMille spectacle of modern time employing for mob effect the crusading student body of a high school which, aroused by racketeering activities and a system of law and order that permits it, sets out to deal justice in its own way. A highly improbable and fantastic story.

Except for the racketeering element and a few others, the cast is preponderately collegiate. Charles Bickford supplies the major menace as a gunman who starts the first reel off with a couple of ruthless murders. Trying to exact tribute from tailors, Bickford makes the mistake of murdering a high-school pants presser who's beloved by the students. About the same time, in connection with a Boy's Week, local politicians deputize boys as district attorney, municipal court judge, chief of police, etc. At the sides of these law-enforcing gentlemen, the boys get a first hand idea of how easy it is for a racketeer to get away with his game.

The girl who inveigles the racketeer's bodyguard into her company under dangerous circumstances is the only feminine member of the cast in the spotlight. Through her a mild love interest is created. She's Judith Allen.

Principal student assignment goes to Richard Cromwell, lessers being Eddie Nugent, Ben Alexander and Lester Arnold, all well cast. Bickford turns in one of his best performances as the heavy.

•

THIS EARTH IS MINE
1959, 123 mins, US ▭ col
Dir Henry King ***Prod*** Casey Robinson, Claude Heilman ***Scr*** Casey Robinson ***Ph*** Winton Hoch, Russel Metty ***Ed*** Ted J. Kent ***Mus*** Hugo Friedhofer
Act Rock Hudson, Jean Simmons, Dorothy McGuire, Claude Rains, Kent Smith, Anna Lee (Universal/Vintage)

This film is almost completely lacking in dramatic cohesion. It is verbose and contradictory, and its complex plot relationships from Alice Tisdale Hobart's novel, *The Cup and the Sword* begin with confusion and end in tedium.

The setting is the Napa Valley wine country in the waning years of Prohibition. The basic plot is a conflict between generations—the older, European-born vintners, headed by Claude Rains, with traditions of dedication to the craft, and the younger men, represented by Rock Hudson, who are interested in selling their crop to the highest bidders, even if it means their grapes will be made into bootleg liquor.

Some of the scenes are pure bathos, such as the one where Rock Hudson learns that he is actually the son of his uncle (Kent Smith). What's lacking mostly in the script, and not supplemented in the direction, is an overall intelligence that would have appraised these complexities.

Hudson gives a sympathetic portrayal, but not a satisfying one, because his characterization is riddled by inconsistencies. Jean Simmons achieves involvement but little sympathy because her motivations are so sketchy and superficial. Claude Rains fares best.

•

THIS GUN FOR HIRE
1942, 86 mins, US Ⓥ ⦿ b/w
Dir Frank Tuttle ***Prod*** Richard M. Blumenthal ***Scr*** Albert Maltz, W. R. Burnett ***Ph*** John Seitz ***Ed*** Archie Marshek ***Mus*** David Buttolph
Act Veronica Lake, Robert Preston, Laird Cregar, Alan Ladd, Tully Marshall, Mikhail Rasumny (Paramount)

The idea of presenting Veronica Lake as the heroine of an exciting melodrama has its merits. But the material selected is distinctly unsuited to her. It is a very involved yarn by Graham Greene which deals with international intrigue and treason, having to do with the sale of a secret chemical formula to the Japanese. Albert Maltz and W. R. Burnett wrote the screenplay, which is a succession of gunplay scenes in which Lake becomes the unwilling accomplice of a young killer. He is Alan Ladd.

Other players in the film had difficult assignment trying to give some credence to an improbable story. Robert Preston plays a policeman, who is too easily outwitted to deserve Lake in the end. Laird Cregar is an interesting heavy, and Tully Marshall a reprobate of the worst kind.

•

THIS HAPPY BREED
1944, 116 mins, UK Ⓥ col
Dir David Lean ***Prod*** Noel Coward, Anthony Havelock-Allan ***Scr*** Ronald Neame, David Lean, Anthony Havelock-Allan ***Ph*** Ronald Neame ***Ed*** Jack Harris ***Mus*** Muir Mathieson (dir.) ***Art*** C. P. Norman
Act Robert Newton, Celia Johnson, John Mills, Kay Walsh, Stanley Holloway, Amy Veness (Two Cities/Cineguild)

Based on Noel Coward's London legit hit, film soundly captures the spirit of the 1920s and 1930s reviving the era of the British general strike, the jazz dress style, the Charleston, and the depression. It touches on the troubled sphere of the class struggle and labor strife, although it has a dubious note once or twice, such as in an apparent defense of strike-breaking. But it is so much more the history of an average British family, with its pleasures and pains, to make this the paramount interest.

Film is a bit episodic and choppy at the start, as it unwinds in cavalcadish fashion, but it settles down soon to an absorbing chronicle. Film's excellence comes mainly in the performances. Celia Johnson, as the mother of three grown children and the rock around which the family revolves, presents a masterful, poignant portrayal.

Robert Newton, who has almost as important a role as the head of the house, is also a superb presentation as the steady, earth-bound but intelligent Britisher. Kay Walsh, as the flighty daughter dissatisfied with her lot; John Mills, as the loyal sailor in love with the errant daughter; and Stanley Holloway, as the next-door neighbor, give fine support.

•

THIS IS ELVIS
1981, 88 mins, US Ⓥ col
Dir Malcolm Leo, Andrew Solt ***Prod*** Malcolm Leo, Andrew Solt ***Scr*** Malcolm Leo, Andrew Solt ***Ph*** Gil Hubbs ***Ed*** Bud Friedgen, Glenn Farr ***Mus*** Walter Scharf ***Art*** Charles Hughes
Act Johnny Harra, David Scott, Paul Boensch III, Lawrence Koller, Rhonda Lyn (Warner)

A real curiosity item, *This Is Elvis* is a fast-paced gloss on Presley's life and career packed with enough fine music and unusual footage to satisfy anyone with an interest in the late singing idol. An imaginative combination of docu-footage, home movies and docu-drama re-creations of more private moments has been bolstered with a double album's worth of top tunes to good effect.

Pic opens with day of Presley's death at 42 and subsequent funeral mob scene, and is thereafter narrated by uncanny Elvis soundalike Ral Donner in fashion of William Holden telling tale of *Sunset Boulevard*, even though character is dead.

Much of the docu-material has been kept under wraps by Col. Tom Parker for years only to be released here through his participation as technical adviser.

Included are glimpses of the 1950s sensation in his earliest television appearance, some previously unseen press conference footage, harsh, often racist, anti-rock 'n' roll diatribes by bluenoses of the period, the celebrated Ed Sullivan performance, extensive coverage of his army indoctrination and stint in Germany, comeback appearance with Frank Sinatra, clips of a few feature films and a look at his smash 1968 TV special.

Elvis's bloated condition by 1977 is genuinely shocking, effect being akin to seeing Robert De Niro in middle-age in *Raging Bull*. Narration has Elvis from above intoning, "If only I coulda seen what was happening to me, I mighta done something about it."

•

THIS ISLAND EARTH
1955, 87 mins, US Ⓥ ⦿ ▭ col
Dir Joseph M. Newman ***Prod*** William Alland ***Scr*** Franklin Coen, Edward G. O'Callaghan ***Ph*** Clifford Stine ***Ed*** Virgil Vogel ***Mus*** Herman Stein ***Art*** Alexander Golitzen, Richard H. Riedel
Act Jeff Morrow, Faith Domergue, Rex Reason, Lance Fuller, Russell Johnson, Douglas Spencer (Universal)

Plot motivation in the screenplay is derived from the frantic efforts of the men of the interstellar planet, Metaluna, to find on Earth a new source of atomic energy. For the accomplishment of this goal, the outstanding scientists in the field have been recruited by a character named Exeter, who has set up a completely equipped laboratory in Georgia.

One of the most thrilling sequences occurs as huge meteors attack the space ship as it is working its way to Metaluna. Ingeniously constructed props and equipment, together with strange sound effects also are responsible for furthering interest, which is of the edge-of-the-seat variety during the latter half of the film. For an added fillip, there's a mutant, half human, half insect, which boards the ship as it escapes from Metaluna.

•

THIS IS MY AFFAIR
SEE: I CAN GET IT FOR YOU WHOLESALE

•

THIS IS MY LIFE
1992, 105 mins, US Ⓥ col
Dir Nora Ephron ***Prod*** Lynda Obst ***Scr*** Nora Ephron, Delia Ephron ***Ph*** Bobby Byrne ***Ed*** Robert Reitano ***Mus*** Carly Simon ***Art*** Barbra Matis
Act Julie Kavner, Samantha Mathis, Gaby Hoffmann, Carrie Fisher, Dan Aykroyd, Danny Zorn (20th Century-Fox)

A schlepper turns star but finds that when your kids still need you, success is all very complicated in *This Is My Life*, a deftly accomplished directorial debut from scripter Nora Ephron. Glib urban sensibility that informed Ephron's screenplay for *When Harry Met Sally . . .* is toned down this time in favor of humbler, texture-of-life comedy coscripted with sister Delia.

Julie Kavner stars as a New Jersey divorcee who hams it up in her cosmetics counter selling placenta extract and exfoliating wax to Jewish mavens, then shares her excess comic energy with her 16- and 10-year-old daughters (Samantha Mathis, Gaby Hoffmann) as they dream of her comedy breakthrough.

When an aunt leaves Kavner some start-up money, she packs the kids up for Manhattan, and before long her dreams do start to come true. But it's more than the teenage daughter, who's introverted and dependent, can handle.

Based on a novel [of the same name] by Meg Wolitzer, pic moves along quite briskly. Comedienne Kavner gives a zesty and touching perf as the mom coming into her own, and both girls, particularly Mathis as the confused, hypercritical teen, are quite skillful. Carrie Fisher contributes a deft and savory turn as a glib and chummy agent.

•

THIS IS SPINAL TAP: A ROCKUMENTARY BY MARTIN DIBERGI
1984, 82 mins, US Ⓥ ⦿ col
Dir Rob Reiner ***Prod*** Karen Murphy ***Scr*** Christopher Guest, Michael McKean, Harry Shearer, Rob Reiner ***Ph*** Peter Smokler ***Ed*** Kent Beyda, Kim Seerisf ***Art*** Dryan Jones
Act Rob Reiner, Michael McKean, Christopher Guest, Harry Shearer, R. J. Parnell, David Kaff (Spinal Tap)

For music biz insiders, *This Is Spinal Tap* is a vastly amusing satire of heavy metal bands. Director Rob Reiner has cast himself as Marty DiBergi, a filmmaker intent upon covering the long-awaited American return of the eponymous, 17-year-old British rock band. Pic then takes the form of a cinema-verité documentary, as Reiner includes interviews with the fictional musicians, records their increasingly disastrous tour and captures the internal strife which leads to the separation of the group's two founders.

Reiner and cowriters have had loads of fun with the material, creating mock 1960s TV videotapes of early gigs and filling the fringes with hilariously authentic music-biz types, most notably Fran Drescher's label rep and Paul Shaffer's cameo as a Chicago promo man.

•

THIS IS THE ARMY
1943, 120 mins, US Ⓥ col
Dir Michael Curtiz ***Prod*** Jack L. Warner ***Scr*** Casey Robinson, Claude Rinyon ***Ph*** Bert Glennon, Sol Polito ***Ed*** George Amy ***Mus*** Ray Heindorf (arr.) ***Art*** John Hughes, John Koenig
Act George Murphy, Joan Leslie, Ronald Reagan, George Tobias, Julie Oshins, Una Merkel (Warner)

It's a dynamic linking of World War I and II with its respective soldier shows—*Yip Yip Yaphank* and *This Is the Army*, both by Irving Berlin. It's showmanship and patriotism combined to a super-duper Yankee Doodle degree.

Skillfully linked are both generations, with George Murphy capital as the yesteryear musicomedy star who suffers a leg injury, which doesn't curb his skill as a theatrical impresario post-1918, and Ronald Reagan, as Johnny Jones, his son, who carries the romance interest in World War II. George Tobias and Julie Oshins are father-and-son to span both periods, and Joan Leslie is the 1943 femme offspring of Charles Butterworth, another of the "Yip Yip Yaphankers." She is the romantic vis-a-vis to Reagan.

But putting the story aside, the socko Berlin songs—17 of them—tie the whole package together.

Under the Jack Warner-Hal Wallis production supervision and with Mike Curtiz's expert direction—all of whom donated their services, along with the rest of it—*This Is the Army* looks like a $3 million Technicolor production instead of the $1.4 million it cost to bring it in.

1943: Best Scoring of a Musical Picture

NOMINATIONS: Best Color Art Direction, Sound

•

THIS LAND IS MINE
1943, 103 mins, US Ⓥ ⦿ b/w
Dir Jean Renoir ***Prod*** Jean Renoir, Dudley Nichols ***Scr*** Dudley Nichols ***Ph*** Frank Redman ***Ed*** Frederic Knudtson ***Mus*** Lothar Perl ***Art*** Eugene Lourie
Act Charles Laughton, Maureen O'Hara, George Sanders, Walter Slezak, Kent Smith, Una O'Connor (RKO)

Turned out by the ace director-writer combination of Jean Renoir and Dudley Nichols, *This Land* is a steadily engrossing film based on the inner drama of character rather than the exciting physical action of some war films. Its theme is the invincibility of ideas over brute force, and its story is of how circumstances and the realization of responsibility turn a craven weakling into a heroic champion of freedom. That is epic subject matter and it is given sincere, dignified and eloquent treatment.

Not that the picture is by any means perfect. Some of its incidents tax belief, and the presentation at times is ultra-obvious, possibly to clarify the meaning for the broadest possible audience. Similarly, although such scenes as Charles Laughton's courtroom espousal of the cause of patriotism, civil disobedience and even of sabotage, or his defiant schoolroom reading of "The Rights of Man," are suspiciously theatrical, the speeches themselves are magnificent.

As usual when a picture has such compulsion and distinction, the individual roles are rewarding and the performances impressive. As the blubbering coward who rises to heroism in a crisis, Charles Laughton gives a shrewdly conceived and developed portrayal, although he occasionally mugs a bit. Maureen O'Hara is believably intense as the lovely, tragic patriot school teacher. George Sanders proper projects the mental turmoil of the traitorous informer, while Walter Slezak turns in an acting gem in the rich role of the Nazi major.

1943: Best Sound Recording (Stephen Dunn)

•

THIS LOVE OF OURS
1945, 90 mins, US b/w
Dir William Dieterle ***Prod*** Howard Benedict ***Scr*** Bruce Manning, John Klorer, Leonard Lee ***Ph*** Lucien Ballard ***Ed*** Frank Gross ***Mus*** Hans J. Salter ***Art*** John B. Goodman, Robert Clatworthy
Act Merle Oberon, Charles Korvin, Claude Rains, Carl Esmond, Sue England, Ralph Morgan (Universal)

Most commendable feature is the plot's originality. Charles Korvin plays a famous doctor whose young daughter (Sue England) has sanctified the memory of her presumably dead mother. Visiting a Chicago nitery while attending a doctors' convention, Korvin meets Merle Oberon who, it turns out, is his "dead" wife. She is working as accompanist for Claude Rains, an artist who does flash sketches of the bistro's patrons. She tries suicide after the meeting and Korvin saves her through an intricate operation.

Film could have been a trite tear-jerker but Dieterle's expert handling prevents that. Korvin seems to be just what the doctor ordered for the lonely hearts club, and both he and Oberon do well with their roles. Supporting cast is outstanding, with Rains and the diminutive England as the sensitive daughter, especially commendable.

•

THIS PROPERTY IS CONDEMNED
1966, 110 mins, US Ⓥ ⦿ col
Dir Sydney Pollack ***Prod*** John Houseman ***Scr*** Francis Coppola, Fred Coe, Edith Sommer ***Ph*** James Wong Howe ***Ed*** Adrienne Fazan ***Mus*** Kenyon Hopkins ***Art*** Hal Pereira
Act Natalie Wood, Robert Redford, Charles Bronson, Kate Reid, Mary Badham, Alan Baxter (Seven Arts/Stark)

This is a handsomely mounted, well-acted Depression-era drama about the effect of railroad retrenchment on a group of boardinghouse people. Derived from a Tennessee Williams one-acter, the production is adult without being sensational, touching without being maudlin.

Francis Coppola, Fred Coe and Edith Sommer are credited with the script, "suggested" from an earlier Williams play in which two young kids chat about the past.

Natalie Wood stars as the young Dixie belle, older daughter of Kate Reid, latter playing a sleazy landlady to some railroad men. Wood dreams of another life while she flirts up a storm, acting as the shill for her mother.

Robert Redford gives an outstanding performance as the railroad efficiency expert sent to town to lay off most of the crew. Plot-wise, the role is thankless and heavy, but Redford, through voice, expression and movement—total acting—makes the character sympathetic.

Charles Bronson is excellent as the earthy boarder.

•

THIS RECKLESS AGE
1932, 63 mins, US b/w
Dir Frank Tuttle ***Scr*** Joseph L. Mankiewicz ***Ph*** Henry Sharp
Act Charles "Buddy" Rogers, Richard Bennett, Peggy Shannon, Charles Ruggles, Frances Dee, Frances Starr (Paramount)

Film is pretty completely lacking in anything resembling dramatic force, and what plot is present is largely synthetic, particularly in the closing sequence, but in the place of drama there is an abundance of sentimentality in the relations of a sometimes rowdy, but always honest and courageous pair of adolescents toward their parents, who in turn deal with them with large and affectionate tolerance.

It is in the sympathetically drawn family picture that the punch of the story lies. There is the mother role engagingly played by Frances Starr, a mother who is borne along through life by an abiding affection for her husband and a splendid faith and happiness in the integrity of her two children, boy and girl.

Story [by Lewis Beach] is expertly told within its modest comedy limits and the playing by the cast is flawless.

Young "Buddy" Rogers does one of the neatest, if least important, bits of juvenile playing of his career, while the two younger women of the cast (Peggy Shannon and Frances Dee) make two contrasting examples of the flap type, the former a rather conventional figure and the latter a sometimes scatter-brained hoyden.

•

THIS SPORTING LIFE
1963, 134 mins, UK Ⓥ b/w
Dir Lindsay Anderson ***Prod*** Karel Reisz ***Scr*** David Storey ***Ph*** Denys Coop ***Ed*** Peter Taylor ***Mus*** Roberto Gerhard ***Art*** Alan Withy
Act Richard Harris, Rachel Roberts, Alan Badel, William Hartnell, Colin Blakely, Arthur Lowe (Independent Artists)

Set in the raw, earthy mood of *Saturday Night and Sunday Morning, Taste of Honey* and *Room at the Top* this has a gutsy vitality. Karel Reisz who directed *Saturday Night*, produced this one and his influence can clearly be seen. Lindsay Anderson, making his debut as a feature director, brings the keen, observant eye of a documentary man to many vivid episodes without sacrificing the story line.

Based on a click novel by David Storey, who also scribed the screenplay, the yarn has a sporting background in that it concerns professional rugby football. Richard Harris plays miner Frank Machin who, at first, resents the hero-worship heaped on players of the local football team. But he has second thoughts. He gets a trial and soon becomes the skillful, ruthless star of his team. He revels in his new prosperity, and preens at the adulation that's showered on his bullet head. He doesn't realize that he is being used by local businessmen opportunists.

Anderson has directed with fluid skill and sharp editing keeps the film moving, even at its more leisurely moments, Denys Coop's lensing is graphic and the atmosphere of a northern town is captured soundly. Among the varied sequences which impress are a horrifying quarrel between Harris and Rachel Roberts, a hospital death scene, a poignant interlude at a wedding when Harris first approaches the moment of truth, a rowdy Christmas party and a countryside excursion when Harris plays with the widow's two youngsters. The football scenes have a live authenticity.

Harris gives a dominating, intelligent performance as the arrogant, blustering, fundamentally simple and insecure footballer. Roberts as a repressed widow, brings commendable light and shade as well as poignance to a role that might have been shadowy and overly downbeat.

1963: NOMINATIONS: Best Actor (Richard Harris), Actress (Rachel Roberts)

•

THIS STRANGE PASSION
SEE: EL

•

THIS THING CALLED LOVE
1940, 98 mins, US b/w
Dir Alexander Hall ***Prod*** William Perlberg ***Scr*** George Seaton, Ken Englund, P. J. Wolfson ***Ph*** Joseph Walker ***Ed*** Viola Lawrence ***Mus*** Werner Heymann
Act Rosalind Russell, Melvyn Douglas, Binnie Barnes, Allyn Joslyn, Gloria Dickson, Lee J. Cobb (Columbia)

Here is fun with a capital F. It is adult, it is amusing, it has sparkle, and it has vim. Basically, there is very little difference in story here from *My Favorite Wife, Doctor Takes a Wife* and other pix of that genre. The couple are married to begin with, and all their troubles consist of trying to fulfill or avoid their marital relationships.

Rosalind Russell and Melvyn Douglas are the couple this time who, though legally wedded, don't know what to do about sex. Or, rather, to be specific, only one of them (at a time) knows what to do, while the other is coy. Roz starts off by having a theory: they will test their love by a three-month abstainment period. Douglas can't see that at all and decides to break her down.

Alexander Hall pilots the picture with considerable spirit and a furious pace; so much so that it seems a bit overlong, and some of the biz is repetitious.

Really topnotch bow (more so than in most recent films) belongs to the Werner Heymann scoring job. Music is used here as an intrinsic and basic film element. The way a certain tune keeps popping up every time Douglas repeats a certain piece of pantomimic business (looking at himself in a mirror reflectively) is positively inspired. It is as much a laugh-getter as any of the acting business or any of the dialog. And the triumphant military march motive played very much forte as Russell walks towards Douglas's bedroom for the fadeout is a roar.

Both are about evenly divided on the acting honors, managing to point up their laughs beautifully, although a top scene in which Douglas does a rumba as a coverup for scratching (having contracted oak poisoning) is outstanding.

•

THIS WOMAN IS DANGEROUS
1952, 97 mins, US b/w
Dir Felix Feist ***Prod*** Robert Sisk ***Scr*** Geoffrey Homes, George Worthington Yates ***Ph*** Ted McCord ***Ed*** James C. Moore ***Mus*** David Buttolph ***Art*** Leo K. Kuter
Act Joan Crawford, Dennis Morgan, David Brian, Richard Webb, Mari Aldon, Philip Carey (Warner)

As the mastermind of a holdup gang, and the sweetheart of David Brian, a violent killer-type, Joan Crawford turns in the type of character and performance that especially suits her sophisticated appearance.

Story by Bernard Girard deals with a woman who, after the holdup of a New Orleans gambling house, goes off to the hospital for a dangerous operation to restore her failing sight. She leaves behind a violent, jealous lover, plus a slight clue that tips the FBI she might have been in on the robbery.

Her medico is Dennis Morgan and the forced association with him leads to an unwilling romance. Suspicious of her overlong hospital stay, Brian puts a private eye on her trail to protect his romantic interest when he cannot contact her.

•

THOMAS CROWN AFFAIR, THE
1968, 102 mins, US Ⓥ ⦿ col
Dir Norman Jewison ***Prod*** Norman Jewison ***Scr*** Alan R. Trustman ***Ph*** Haskell Wexler ***Ed*** Hal Ashby, Ralph Winters, Byron Brandt ***Mus*** Michel Legrand ***Art*** Robert Boyle
Act Steve McQueen, Faye Dunaway, Paul Burke, Jack Weston, Yaphet Kotto, Biff McGuire (United Artists/Mirisch)

The Thomas Crown Affair is a refreshingly different film which concerns a Boston bank robbery, engineered by a wealthy man who is romantically involved with the femme insurance investigator sent to expose him.

Free of social-conscious pretensions, the Norman Jewison film tells a crackerjack story, well-tooled, professionally crafted and fashioned with obvious meticulous care.

Boston attorney Alan R. Trustman, who never before wrote for films, is responsible for an excellent story. Steve McQueen is a rich young industrialist who masterminds a bank heist. Paul Burke delivers an excellent performance as a detective who works with Faye Dunaway, an insurance company bounty hunter whose job is to trap McQueen.

Jewison adds a showmanly touch in the use of split- and multiple-screen images.

McQueen is neatly cast as the likeable, but lonely heavy. Dunaway makes an excellent detective who gradually develops a conflict of interests regarding her prey. The only message in this film is: enjoy it.

1968: Best Song ("The Windmills of Your Mind")

NOMINATION: Best Original Score

•

THOMAS CROWN AFFAIR, THE
1999, 111 mins, US Ⓥ ⦿ ▭ col
Dir John McTiernan ***Prod*** Pierce Brosnan, Beau St. Clair ***Scr*** Leslie Dixon, Kurt Wimmer ***Ph*** Tom Priestley ***Ed*** John Wright ***Mus*** Bill Conti ***Art*** Bruno Rubeo
Act Pierce Brosnan, Rene Russo, Denis Leary, Ben Gazzara, Frankie Faison, Fritz Weaver (Irish DreamTime/M-G-M)

This redo of Norman Jewison's 1968 Steve McQueen–Faye Dunaway hit is an ultrasleek and slick thriller that attempts to justify its existence by shifting the focus from the caper elements to the psychological and emotional factors that compel two hard-shelled professional adversaries to risk a romantic entanglement.

A considerable overhaul was definitely in order if Alan R. Trustman's original script was going to be made to fit the '90s. In an unusual move, Leslie Dixon was hired to write the personal scenes, while Kurt Wimmer was engaged to pen the heist sequences. Combo works seamlessly.

Pre-credits teaser has playboy tycoon Thomas Crown (Pierce Brosnan) nonchalantly revealing his Achilles' heel to his shrink, played in a super-reflexive homage by Dunaway. Crown is a self-made man who can never imagine settling down with a woman because he can't open himself up enough to trust anyone.

This time out, title character pulls not a bank job but the theft of a $100 million Monet from New York's Metropolitan Museum of Art. Insurance company investigator Catherine Banning (Rene Russo) is positive that Crown is the culprit.

The twists and turns of their relationship are not without interest—especially because Russo takes seriously her rare opportunity at a part more substantial than her usual superstar pairings. When one of them is the victim of turned tables, the result is momentarily affecting. Brosnan's Thomas Crown is carved out of ice and, unfortunately, thesp's charisma is insufficient to melt it much.

•

THOMAS L'IMPOSTEUR
(THOMAS THE IMPOSTER)
1965, 93 mins, France b/w
Dir Georges Franju ***Prod*** Eugene Lepicier ***Scr*** Jean Cocteau, Georges Franju, Michel Worms, Raphael Cluzel ***Ph*** Marcel Fradetal ***Ed*** Gilbert Natot ***Mus*** Georges Auric ***Art*** Jacques Metehen
Act Emmanuelle Riva, Fabrice Rouleau, Jean Servais, Sophie Dares, Rosy Varte, Michel Vitold (Filmel)

The late Jean Cocteau worked on the script of his early book with director Georges Franju several years earlier. Put off often, this was finally made a year after Cocteau's death. It is a poetic film about a teenage boy impersonating an officer during the First World War. It also embodies a gentle love story and a biting feel for war's horrors, as well as its strangeness.

A headstrong, noble widow princess (Emmanuelle Riva) gets up a caravan to go to the front to pick up wounded men and bring them back to her chateau near Paris for treatment. Stymied by red tape, she is helped by a 16-year-old boy (Fabrice Rouleau) in an officer's uniform who says he is the nephew of a noted general.

The boy becomes indispensable to the princess who feels a strange attachment for him. Her teenage daughter (Sophie Dares) falls in love with the lad, and the woman finally feels she has no place in the war. So she gives up her work. But the youth gets attached to a canteen on the farflung northern lines.

Franju is true to the poetic, artful world of Cocteau but adds his own talent for imbuing the narrative with an underlying strangeness that makes it constantly eye-filling and sometimes disturbing. A horse running wildly through a street with its mane on fire, a priest giving communion to a dead soldier by prying his mouth open with a knife, a party with the Germans supposedly advancing on Paris, and other scenes build an offbeat, worldly commentary on war. Casting is also excellent.

•

THOMAS THE IMPOSTER
SEE: THOMAS L'IMPOSTEUR

•

THOROUGHLY MODERN MILLIE
1967, 138 mins, US Ⓥ ⦿ col
Dir George Roy Hill ***Prod*** Ross Hunter ***Scr*** Richard Morris ***Ph*** Russell Metty ***Ed*** Stuart Gilmore ***Mus*** Elmer Bernstein ***Art*** Alexander Golitzen, George C. Webb
Act Julie Andrews, James Fox, Mary Tyler Moore, Carol Channing, John Gavin, Beatrice Lillie (Hunter/Universal)

The first half of *Thoroughly Modern Millie* is quite successful in striking and maintaining a gay spirit and pace. There are many recognizable and beguiling satirical recalls of the flapper age and some quite funny bits.

Liberties taken with reality, not to mention period, in the first half are redeemed by wit and characterization. But the sudden thrusting of the hero, played by James Fox in horn-rimmed glasses, into a skyscraper-climbing, flagpole-hanging acrobat, à la Harold Lloyd, has little of Lloyd but the myth. This sequence is forced all the way.

Musically *Millie* is a melange. Standards such as "Baby Face" mingle with specials by Jimmy Van Heusen and Sammy Cahn. All is part of Elmer Bernstein's score, as arranged and conducted by Andre Previn.

Julie Andrews is very much like the leading lady of the story but hardly more than a bystander when Carol Channing commands the scene and at such times it is seldom that a star has been so static so long in a film.

Mary Tyler Moore serves the plot in that she is essentially a prototype of a sweet, long curls and rather dumb rich girl.

1967: Best Original Score

NOMINATIONS: Best Supp. Actress (Carol Channing), Costume Design, Scoring of Music, Song ("Thoroughly Modern Millie"), Sound

•

THOSE MAGNIFICENT MEN IN THEIR FLYING MACHINES
OR HOW I FLEW FROM LONDON TO PARIS IN 25 HOURS 11 MINUTES
1965, 131 mins, UK Ⓥ ⦿ ▭ col
Dir Ken Annakin ***Prod*** Stan Margulies ***Scr*** Jack Davies, Ken Annakin ***Ph*** Christopher Challis ***Ed*** Gordon Stone ***Mus*** Ron Goodwin ***Art*** Tom Morahan
Act Stuart Whitman, Sarah Miles, James Fox, Alberto Sordi, Robert Morley, Gert Frobe (20th Century-Fox)

As fanciful and nostalgic a piece of clever picture-making as has hit the screen in recent years, this backward look into the pioneer days of aviation, when most planes were built with spit and bailing wire, is a warming entertainment experience.

A newspaper circulation gimmick serves nicely as the story premise, with a London newspaper publisher offering a £10,000 prize to winner of an event which will focus worldwide attention on the fledgling sport of flying—circa 1910—subsequently attracting a flock of international contestants.

While there is naturally a plotline, and a nice romance, the planes themselves, a startling collection of uniquely designed oddities, which actually fly, probably merit the most attention.

Top characters are played by Stuart Whitman, as an American entrant; James Fox, an English flier who interests publisher Robert Morley in the race to promote aviation; Sarah Miles, publisher's daughter understood to be the intended of Fox (arrangement with father) but beloved by Whitman. Terry-Thomas is a dastardly English lord not above the most abject skullduggery to win the race. Alberto Sordi as an Italian count with a worrying wife and immense family, Gert Frobe a German cavalry officer intent upon bringing glory to the Fatherland, Jean-Pierre Cassel, a whimsical Frenchman, are the chief Continental contestants.

[Original roadshow version of the pic featured a musical overture.]

1965: NOMINATION: Best Story & Screenplay

•

THOSE WERE THE HAPPY TIMES
SEE: STAR!

•

THOUSAND CLOWNS, A
1965, 117 mins, US Ⓥ ⦿ b/w
Dir Fred Coe ***Prod*** Fred Coe ***Scr*** Herb Gardner ***Ph*** Arthur J. Ornitz, Joe Coffey ***Ed*** Ralph Rosenblum, Edward Beyer ***Mus*** Don Walker ***Art*** Burr Smidt
Act Jason Robards, Barbara Harris, Martin Balsam, Gene Saks, William Daniels, Barry Gordon (Harrell/United Artists)

A Thousand Clowns depicts a happy-go-lucky nonconformist who attains some maturity when a child welfare board threatens to take away his young resident nephew.

Key personnel of the long-running 1962–3 Broadway legiter have followed through with the pic. They include playwright-adapter Herb Gardner, producer-director Coe, and Jason Robards as the ex-vidscripter living it up in a littered NY pad while trying to prevent nephew Barry Gordon (also encoring) from becoming one of the "dead people," meaning conformists.

Terrif dialog to match Robards's scenery-chewing create a sock impact as he lectures the 12-year-old (a hip juve, wiser than unk), ignores the pleas of brother-agent Martin Balsam to return to work, and pierces the outstanding social worker bureaucratic shell of Barbara Harris and original cast member William Daniels, who've arrived to check the kid's home life.

All performances present three-dimensional, identifiable characters underneath the yocks.

1965: Best Supp. Actor (Martin Balsam)

NOMINATIONS: Best Picture, Screenplay Adaptation, Adapted Music Score

•

THOUSANDS CHEER
1943, 124 mins, US Ⓥ ⦿ col
Dir George Sidney ***Prod*** Joseph Pasternak ***Scr*** Paul Jarrico, Richard Collins ***Ph*** George Folsey ***Ed*** George Boemler ***Mus*** Herbert Stothart (dir.)
Act Kathryn Grayson, Gene Kelly, Mary Astor, John Boles, Jose Iturbi, Frances Rafferty (M-G-M)

Comparison of *Thousands Cheer* to *Stage Door Canteen* is inevitable and natural. Both have the same format. Kathryn Grayson is the colonel's (John Boles) daughter who puts on a super-duper camp show which not only reintroduces Jose Iturbi as part of the entertainment—the eminent pianist-maestro is already made part of the regular plot—but it brings forth Mickey Rooney, Judy Garland, Red Skelton, Eleanor Powell and others.

Paramount keynote of this expert filmusical is the tiptop manner in which young George Sidney has marshalled his multiple talents so that none trips over the other. It's a triumph for Sidney on his first major league effort.

Paul Jarrico and Richard Collins supplied a smooth story to carry the mammoth marquee values. Casting Kathryn Grayson as herself, a click diva, making her longhair farewell at an Iturbi concert, is as plausible as it is appealing. Her idea to move with papa Boles to his camp, in an endeavor to reconcile him and Mary Astor (the mother), is well interlarded with romance and basic Americanism.

Judy Garland's "Joint Is Jumpin' Down at Carnegie Hall" (unbilled specialty) is the cue for Iturbi to boogie-woogie; and his Steinwaying straight or barrelhouse, is something for the cats.

1943: NOMINATIONS: Best Color Cinematography, Color Art Direction, Scoring of a Musical Picture

•

THREE AGES, THE
1923, 67 mins, US ⊗ b/w
Dir Buster Keaton, Edward Cline ***Prod*** Joseph M. Shenck ***Scr*** Jean Havez, Joseph A. Mitchell, Clyde Bruckman ***Ph*** William McGann, Elgin Lessley ***Art*** Fred Gabowie
Act Buster Keaton, Margaret Leahy, Wallace Beery, Lillian Lawrence, Joe Roberts, Horace "Cupid" Morgan, Oliver Hardy (Schenck/Metro)

The three periods are the Stone Age, the pompous days of Rome, and the modern. The three parallel stories are held together by a brief foreword explaining that, although customs and times change, lovemaking and loving are always the same.

First we have the young lover of the Stone Age up to a certain point in his courtship; then the Roman dandy up to the same point; and finally the modern swain in a like cross section of his love affair.

In all three cases the situation is about the same—a humble, but faithful lover (Buster Keaton) struggling for his lady fair against the unscrupulous unworthy adventurer (Wallace Beery) and in his efforts stumbling into all sorts of scrapes.

Some of the settings are rather pretentious, particularly in the Roman episodes, and the stories are worked out with the most ingenious incidents.

There's a lot of rich fun also in the Stone Age incident of The Boy dictating to a stone age stenographer.

The modern instance where the hero pursues his sweetheart into an up-to-date cabaret is a mine of knockabout comedy and the wedding scene is packed with solid laughs.

•

¡THREE AMIGOS!
1986, 105 mins, US Ⓥ ⦿ col
Dir John Landis ***Prod*** Lorne Michaels, George Folsey, Jr. ***Scr*** Steve Martin, Lorne Michaels, Randy Newman ***Ph*** Ronald W. Browne ***Ed*** Malcolm Campbell ***Mus*** Elmer Bernstein ***Art*** Richard Sawyer
Act Chevy Chase, Steve Martin, Martin Short, Patrice Martinez, Alfonso Arau, Joe Mantegna (LA Films/Orion)

A few choice morsels of brilliant humor can't save *¡Three Amigos!* from missing the whole enchilada.

Film is a takeoff of *The Magnificent Seven*, but also tries perhaps too hard to parody the style of a number of other classic westerns.

It also has three funny guys, Steve Martin, Chevy Chase and Martin Short, playing the three wimpy matinee idols known as the "Three Amigos," each doing his particular brand of shtick that is priceless in some scenes but not at all amusing in others.

Martin does clever slapstick, Chase does goofy slapstick and Short doesn't do slapstick, but plays off the other two with a certain wide-eyed innocence.

These singing cowboy stars of the silent screen have just been fired by the flamboyant Goldsmith Studios mogul Harry Flugelman (Joe Mantegna) when they get a cryptic telegram from a Mexican woman (Patrice Martinez) offering them 100,000 pesos to come to her dusty desert town of Santa Poco. It turns out she's hired them under the mistaken belief that they are as macho in real life as on screen.

•

THREE CABALLEROS, THE
1945, 71 mins, US Ⓥ ⦿ col
Dir Norman Ferguson ***Prod*** Walt Disney ***Ph*** Ray Rennahan ***Ed*** Don Holliday ***Mus*** Edward Plumb, Paul J. Smith, Charles Wolcott (dir.)
Act Aurora Miranda, Carmen Molina, Dora Luz (RKO/Walt Disney)

Walt Disney in *The Three Caballeros* reveals a new form of cinematic entertainment wherein he blends live action with animation into a socko feature production.

It's a gay, colorful, resplendent conceit. Neatly conceived, it ties in many Pan-American highlights through the medium of irascible Donald Duck, the wiseguy Joe Carioca (first introduced in *Saludos Amigos*), and a lovable character in Panchito, the little South American boy.

It's DD's birthday and on Friday-the-13th he gets three huge packages of gifts from his friends in Latin America. What he unwraps as his "gifts" are transplanted to this live action-animation feature. The off-screen narration is so skillfully blended with the dialog between Donald, Joe Carioca, et al, and it's all so smoothly cut and edited, one is only casually conscious of where one stops and the other begins.

1945: NOMINATIONS: Best Scoring of a Musical Picture, Sound

•

THREE CAME HOME
1950, 106 mins, US Ⓥ b/w
Dir Jean Negulesco ***Prod*** Nunnally Johnson ***Scr*** Nunnally Johnson ***Ph*** Milton Krasner ***Ed*** Dorothy Spencer ***Mus*** Hugo Friedhofer ***Art*** Lyle Wheeler, Leland Fuller
Act Claudette Colbert, Patric Knowles, Sessue Hayakawa, Florence Desmond (20th Century-Fox)

Agnes Newton Keith's deeply affecting autobiog of hardships in a Jap prison camp [in Borneo] has been turned from print to celluloid without any easing of the book's harrowing impact.

Many of the scenes are tearjerkers in the better sense of the word. Particularly effective is the sequence which portrays the principal character, an American woman (Claudette Colbert) married to a British administrator, crawling wretchedly under barbed wire and through the jungle to keep a tryst with her husband.

The rigid, implacable conduct of the jailers is related convincingly. There are brutal Japs and there are others just doing a job. That is the import of the pic. The colonel in command is brilliantly delivered by the old-time, silent star, Sessue Hayakawa.

•

THREE COINS IN THE FOUNTAIN
1954, 101 mins, US Ⓥ ⦿ ▭ col
Dir Jean Negulesco ***Prod*** Sol C. Siegel ***Scr*** John Patrick ***Ph*** Milton Krasner ***Ed*** William Reynolds ***Mus*** Victor Young ***Art*** Lyle Wheeler, John De Cuir

Act Clifton Webb, Dorothy McGuire, Jean Peters, Louis Jourdan, Maggie McNamara, Rossano Brazzi (20th Century-Fox)

Once before, in *How to Marry a Millionaire*, director Jean Negulesco CinemaScoped a trio of feminine beauties into a lucrative attraction. In *Three Coins in the Fountain* he repeats this feat but obviously has gained some experience. The film has warmth, humor, a rich dose of romance and almost incredible pictorial appeal.

For those who aren't satisfied feasting their eyes on the stunning backgrounds and the plush interior sets, there is another trio of femme stars—Dorothy McGuire, Jean Peters and Maggie McNamara—in smart and expensive-looking clothes. As their male counterparts they have Clifton Webb, debonnaire and fun as always; Rossano Brazzi, an appealing young Italian and suave Louis Jourdan, appealing as the romantic lead.

Story [from a novel by John H. Secondari] introduces to Rome McNamara, an American coming to take a secretarial job. She's met by Peters and later introduced to her third roommate in their sumptuous apartment, McGuire. They all toss a coin in the fountain, and it grants them their wish.

1954: Best Color Cinematography, Song ("Three Coins in the Fountain")

NOMINATION: Best Picture

•

THREE COLORS: BLUE

SEE: TROIS COULEURS: BLEU

•

THREE COLORS: RED

SEE: TROIS COULEURS: ROUGE

•

THREE COLORS: WHITE

SEE: TROIS COULEURS: BLANC

•

THREE COMRADES

1938, 100 mins, US b/w

Dir Frank Borzage ***Prod*** Frank Borzage ***Scr*** F. Scott Fitzgerald, Edward E. Paramore ***Ph*** Joseph Ruttenberg ***Ed*** Frank Sullivan ***Mus*** Franz Waxman

Act Robert Taylor, Margaret Sullavan, Franchot Tone, Robert Young, Guy Kibbee, Lionel Atwill (M-G-M)

There must have been some reason for making this picture, but it certainly isn't in the cause of entertainment. It provides a dull interlude, despite the draught of the star names.

Someone passed producer-director Frank Borzage a novel of postwar Germany by Erich Maria Remarque which deals with the psychological subtleties of German youth lately released from the World War armies; of the internal political struggle in establishing the republic; of the futility of the army-bred boys to cope with civilian connivance; and finally the tragedy of a love affair between one of the youths and a young woman dying of tuberculosis (Margaret Sullavan).

It is a film of characterization, rather than plot. Writers string together an interminable thread of unimportant incident to show the deep affection which exists among three young German officers. The titular comrades are Robert Taylor, Franchot Tone and Robert Young. After Young is killed in a street riot, the other two look forward to a dark, unhappy and lonely future.

That's it, and all the poetry in the dialog about falling leaves and the approaching winter only further confuses.

1938: NOMINATION: Best Actress (Margaret Sullavan)

•

THREE DAYS OF THE CONDOR

1975, 117 mins, US Ⓥ ⦿ ▭ col

Dir Sydney Pollack ***Prod*** Stanley Schneider ***Scr*** Lorenzo Semple, Jr., David Rayfiel ***Ph*** Owen Rolgman ***Ed*** Fredric Steinkamp, Don Guidice ***Mus*** Dave Grusin ***Art*** Stephen Grimes

Act Robert Redford, Faye Dunaway, Cliff Robertson, Max von Sydow, John Houseman, Addison Powell (Paramount)

James Grady's book, *Six Days of the Condor*, underwent a time-compression title change in this adaptation by Lorenzo Semple, Jr., and David Rayfiel. Robert Redford, working in a CIA front, discovers all his associates massacred. He runs, pants, thinks, schemes, evades and ultimately exposes an agency insider who has been plotting on the side, so to speak. Disenchanted with the world as he wants it, Redford walks into a newspaper to expose the whole thing.

The film is a perfect contemporary example of an old studio formula approach to filmmaking. Basically a B, it has been elevated in form—but not in substance—via four bigger names, location shooting and more production values. Sometimes the trick works, but not here.

1975: NOMINATION: Best Editing

•

THREE FACES OF EVE, THE

1957, 91 mins, US Ⓥ ▭ b/w

Dir Nunnally Johnson ***Prod*** Nunnally Johnson ***Scr*** Nunnally Johnson ***Ph*** Stanley Cortez ***Ed*** Marjorie Fowler ***Mus*** Robert Emmett Dolan ***Art*** Lyle R. Wheeler, Herman A. Blumethal

Act Joanne Woodward, David Wayne, Lee J. Cobb, Edwin Jerome, Alena Murray, Nancy Kulp (20th Century-Fox)

Three Faces of Eve is based on a true-life case history recorded by two psychiatrists—Corbett H. Thigpen and Hervey M. Cleckley—and which was a popular-selling book. It is frequently an intriguing, provocative motion picture, but director Nunnally Johnson's treatment of the subject matter makes the film neither fish nor foul. Johnson shifts back and forth—striving for comedy at one point and presenting a documentary case history at another.

However, it is notable for the performance of Joanne Woodward as the woman with the triple personality. The three personalities Woodward is called on to play are (1) a drab, colorless Georgia housewife, (2) a mischievous, irresponsible sexy dish, and (3) a sensible, intelligent and balanced woman.

The psychiatric sessions, while possibly authentic, could readily confuse the layman. The manner in which the doctor (Lee J. Cobb) can hypnotize and alter his patient's personality seems so easy and pat as to appear hard to believe.

That Johnson had no intention of treating the film entirely seriously is tipped off in an opening tongue-in-cheek narration by the urbane and erudite Alistair Cooke.

1957: Best Actress (Joanne Woodward)

•

THREE FUGITIVES

1989, 96 mins, US Ⓥ ⦿ col

Dir Francis Veber ***Prod*** Lauren Shuler-Donner ***Scr*** Francis Veber ***Ph*** Haskell Wexler ***Ed*** Bruce Green ***Mus*** David McHugh ***Art*** Rick Carter

Act Nick Nolte, Martin Short, Sarah Rowland Doroff, James Earl Jones, Alan Ruck, Kenneth McMillan (Touchstone)

Three Fugitives marks the Hollywood helming debut of French director Francis Veber, remaking his own 1986 comedy *Les fugitifs* American-style.

Clever premise starts pic off on a roll, as master bankrobber Lucas (Nick Nolte) gets out of the slammer determined to go straight, only to get involved in another heist in the very first bank he enters. This time, he's an innocent bystander taken hostage by a hysterically inept gunman (Martin Short). But who's going to believe that?

Short, once he figures out Nolte's predicament, blackmails him into aiding and abetting his escape from the country. To make things even stickier, Short's got an emotionally withdrawn little girl (Sarah Rowland Doroff) who latches onto Nolte like a stray kitten.

As for the Nolte-Short pairing, it'll do, but it's no chemical marvel. Nolte, not really a comic natural, gruffs and grumbles his way through as hunky straight man to Short's calamitous comedian. Short runs with the slapstick style.

•

300 SPARTANS, THE

1962, 108 mins, US ▭ col

Dir Rudolph Mate ***Prod*** George St. George, Rudolph Mate ***Scr*** George St. George ***Ph*** Geoffrey Unsworth ***Ed*** Jerome Webb ***Mus*** Manos Hadjidakis ***Art*** Arrigo Equini

Act Richard Egan, Ralph Richardson, Diane Baker, Barry Coe, David Farrar, Donald Houston (20th-Century Fox)

The hopeless but ultimately inspiring defense of their country by a band of 300 Spartan soldiers against an immense army of Persian invaders in 480 B.C.—known to history as the Battle of Thermopylae—is the nucleus around which George St. George's screenplay is constructed [based on original story material of Ugo Liberatori, Remigio Del Grosso, Giovanni Deramo, Gian Paolo Callegari]. The inherent appeal and magnitude of the battle itself virtually dwarfs and sweeps aside all attempts at romantic byplay.

An international cast has been assembled for the enterprise, primarily populated with Britishers, Greeks and Americans. Richard Egan, as King Leonidas of Sparta, is physically suitable for the character, but the heroic mold of his performance is only skin deep—more muscle than corpuscle. Ralph Richardson, as might be expected, does the best acting in the picture, but no one is going to list this portrayal as one of the great achievements in his career.

Diane Baker is glaringly miscast. The fragile actress has been assigned the part of a Spartan girl who knocks two large men off their feet, bodily. As written, it's a role that required an actress of at least Lorenesque proportions.

•

THREE IN THE ATTIC

1968, 90 mins, US Ⓥ col

Dir Richard Wilson ***Prod*** Richard Wilson ***Scr*** Stephen Yafa ***Ph*** J. Burgi Contner ***Ed*** Richard C. Meyer, Eve Newman ***Mus*** Chad Stuart ***Art*** William S. Creber

Act Yvette Mimieux, Christopher Jones, Judy Pace, Maggie Thrett, Nan Martin, John Beck (American International)

Three in the Attic apparently starts out to be a tragicomedy about physical sex versus love. It is littered with padding optical effects, hampered by uneven dramatic concept, and redundant in its too-delicious sex teasing.

Author Stephen Yafa disowned the pic. Screenplay tells of Christopher Jones, a college campus lover type, who gets hung up on Yvette Mimieux. He won't admit he loves her (that is, beyond the physical aspects), and adds Judy Pace, a Negro charmer, and Maggie Thrett, a Jewish hippie, to his harem.

The gals learn of the bed rotation plan and lock Jones in an attic, where they attempt to exhaust him with regular, clock-timed sex visits.

Acting is amateurish, save for Mimieux, who tries and slightly succeeds.

•

3 INTO 2 WON'T GO

1969, 93 mins, UK col

Dir Peter Hall ***Prod*** Julian Blaustein ***Scr*** Edna O'Brien ***Ph*** Walter Lassally ***Ed*** Alan Osbiston ***Mus*** Francis Lai ***Art*** Peter Murton

Act Rod Steiger, Claire Bloom, Judy Geeson, Peggy Ashcroft, Paul Rogers (Universal)

Superb British film, *3 into 2 Won't Go* is an examination of a shattered marriage between career-oriented Rod Steiger, who is an appliance salesman, and his childless, schoolteacher-wife, Claire Bloom. Judy Geeson, 19-year-old hitchhiker with no particular social or moral ties, seduces Steiger on one of his overnight sales trips.

With dialog that has the banal sound of realistic human exchanges, Edna O'Brien's script [from a novel by Andrea Newman] investigates all sorts of suggestions and shifts in audience reaction.

With all technical credits at top level and director Peter Hall getting top performances from all involved, especially the well-controlled Steiger, film is brisk and emotionally stirring.

•

THREE KINGS

1999, 115 mins, US Ⓥ ⦿ ▭ col

Dir David O. Russell ***Prod*** Charles Roven, Paul Junger Witt, Edward L. McDonnell ***Scr*** David O. Russell ***Ed*** Robert K. Lambert ***Mus*** Carter Burwell ***Art*** Catherine Hardwicke

Act George Clooney, Mark Wahlberg, Ice Cube, Spike Jonze, Nora Dunn, Jamie Kennedy (Coast Ridge/Atlas/Warner)

Just the second Hollywood feature, after *Courage Under Fire*, to take on the 1991 Gulf War, *Three Kings* does so in an impudently comic, stylistically aggressive and, finally, very thoughtful manner.

Using a *Kelly's Heroes*–like heist of enemy loot as a point of departure, David O. Russell's individualistic first studio picture discharges black humor, startling action, genre subversion, anarchic attitude and barbed political commentary on its way to making cogent points about the cynically expedient nature of war and, specifically, America's role as the world's policeman.

In the deliberately grainy, bleached-out, almost digital look of this widescreen adventure, any sense of heroism is canceled, military grandeur is neutered and desert beauty is not allowed.

Special Forces Capt. Archie Gates (George Clooney), a seen-it-all career officer, discovers that three GIs (Mark Wahlberg, Ice Cube, Spike Jonze) have a map that seems to identify an enormous stash of gold bullion snatched from Kuwait by Saddam's army. But the four men encounter a confusing situation at their destination, welcomed with open arms by the Iraqi civilians whom the soldiers treat brusquely in their single-minded quest to grab the gold bricks.

Underlying it all are sentiments concerning the amorality and lack of consistent principles in American foreign policy. The sobering final impression is that, unless the world's most powerful country defines what it stands for, it will stand for nothing other than the threat of brute action and economic coercion.

Clooney, Cube and, particularly, Wahlberg deliver rugged and well-considered turns, and Nora Dunn has some strong moments as a pushy journo.

•

THREE LITTLE WORDS
1950, 100 mins, US Ⓥ ⊙ col
Dir Richard Thorpe ***Prod*** Jack Cummings ***Scr*** George Wells ***Ph*** Harry Jackson ***Ed*** Ben Lewis ***Mus*** Andre Previn (dir.)
Act Fred Astaire, Red Skelton, Vera-Ellen, Arlene Dahl, Keenan Wynn, Debbie Reynolds (M-G-M)

A biopic of the songwriting team of Harry Ruby and Bert Kalmar, the picture is a charmful, entertaining cavalcade of show business which spans their years together. Yarn, while doing the usual glossy job on its subjects, sticks closely to the Kalmar-Ruby careers.

Toplined by Fred Astaire as Kalmar and Red Skelton as Ruby, the entire cast does fine work under the skillful direction of Richard Thorpe.

Vera-Ellen matches Astaire tap for tap in their terping duets, which is no mean achievement, and looks to be possibly the best partner he's ever had. Her singing, too, gets by and, as Jessie Brown, Kalmar's vaude partner, she emotes competently.

Arlene Dahl plays Eileen Percy and also turns in a standout performance.

1950: NOMINATION: Best Scoring of a Musical Picture

•

THREE LOVES HAS NANCY
1938, 70 mins, US b/w
Dir Richard Thorpe ***Prod*** Norman Krasna ***Scr*** Bella Spewack, Samuel Spewack, George Oppenheimer, David Hertz ***Ph*** William Daniels ***Ed*** Frederick Y. Smith ***Mus*** William Axt
Act Janet Gaynor, Robert Montgomery, Franchot Tone, Guy Kibbee, Claire Dodd, Reginald Owen (M-G-M)

Three Loves Has Nancy is a completely daffy, reasonably entertaining romp by Janet Gaynor, Robert Montgomery, Franchot Tone and a group of familiar supporting players.

Story is one of the trivialities about a semi-conscious smalltown gal who gets stranded in New York and becomes the object of a furious set-to between a flighty author and his hell-raising publisher. On that slender framework have been scribbled all the balmy situations, crackpot gags and slapstick whimsy that six frenzied scripters [story by Lee Loeb and Mort Braus] could concoct.

Director Richard Thorpe and the cast play it with broad relish. As the naive little menace from the sticks, Gaynor gives an admirably straight-faced performance, her intense seriousness contrasting sharply with the wild and woolly clowning of Montgomery and Tone. Latter two, as the author and publisher, respectively, pull all the acting stops.

•

3 MEN AND A BABY
1987, 102 mins, US Ⓥ ⊙ col
Dir Leonard Nimoy ***Prod*** Ted Field, Robert W. Cort ***Scr*** James Orr, Jim Cruickshank ***Ph*** Adam Greenberg ***Ed*** Michael A. Stevenson ***Mus*** Marvin Hamlisch ***Art*** Peter Larkin
Act Tom Selleck, Steve Guttenberg, Ted Danson, Nancy Travis, Margaret Colin, Celeste Holm (Touchstone/Interscope)

3 Men and a Baby is about as slight a feature comedy as is made—while at the same time it's hard to resist Tom Selleck, Ted Danson and Steve Guttenberg shamelessly going goo-goo over caring for an infant baby girl all swaddled in pink.

This is an Americanized version of the 1985 French sleeper hit *3 hommes et un couffin* and parallels the original's storyline almost exactly. The lives of three confirmed bachelors—the studly sort who live, play and scheme on voluptuous women together—is thrown into confusion when a baby is left at their front door. As it happens, actor and suspected father of the infant (Danson) is conveniently out of town on a shoot, leaving architect and super pushover Peter (Selleck) and cartoonist Michael (Guttenberg) all in a quandary what to do with the precious little thing.

Big macho men tripping all over themselves trying to successfully feed, diaper and bathe a bundle of innocence and helplessness is ripe for comic development, and it certainly helps that these three are having a blast seeing it through.

Film is a good showcase for the comic abilities of this threesome, all of whom seem to have their one-liner timing down pat.

•

3 MEN AND A CRADLE
SEE: 3 HOMMES ET UN COUFFIN

•

3 MEN AND A LITTLE LADY
1990, 100 mins, US Ⓥ ⊙ col
Dir Emile Ardolino ***Prod*** Ted Field, Robert W. Cort ***Scr*** Charlie Peters ***Ph*** Adam Greenberg ***Ed*** Michael A. Stevenson ***Mus*** James Newton Howard ***Art*** Stuart Wurtzel
Act Tom Selleck, Steve Guttenberg, Ted Danson, Nancy Travis, Robin Weisman, Christopher Cazenove (Touchstone/Interscope)

Back in their places for this two-dimensional sequel are the three bachelor dads of the waif who landed on their doorstep in part one: vain actor Ted Danson and biological dad, and architect Tom Selleck and illustrator Steve Guttenberg, the honorary dads.

What's new is that Selleck has fallen in love with the baby's mom, Sylvia (Nancy Travis), the actress who shares their new apartment, though he hasn't admitted it to her or himself.

Crisis occurs when baby turns five and enrolls in preschool, thereby encountering other children. Mom decides she must marry. She accepts a proposal from her director friend, Edward (Christopher Cazenove), and plans to move to England with little Mary (Robin Weisman), all because bachelor No. 2 (Selleck) is too confused to pop the question.

Rest of the pic is standard romantic comedy. Script [story by Sara Parriott and Josann McGibbon] spoonfeeds the audience with a plodding script that seems based more on demographic research than on any wisp of a creative impulse. Emile Ardolino directs with the same degree of competent but calculated non-risk. As for the actors, they have nothing to play.

•

THREE MEN ON A HORSE
1936, 85 mins, US b/w
Dir Mervyn LeRoy ***Prod*** Mervyn LeRoy ***Scr*** Laird Doyle ***Ph*** Sol Polito ***Ed*** Ralph Dawson
Act Frank McHugh, Joan Blondell, Guy Kibbee, Carol Hughes, Allen Jenkins, Sam Levene (Warner)

Mervyn LeRoy, producing this screen version of the legit hit [by John Cecil Holm and George Abbott], adhered pretty closely to the original. There are practically no alterations and only a few additions, and whatever was added is on the profit side. Instead of the radio broadcast finish, the screen permits carrying the action direct to the racetrack, which opens the way for some extra comedy business. About the only other new sequence is a hospital bit.

Another improvement is the handling of the lead, "Oiwin," by Frank McHugh. He does splendidly in the sap assignment without changing the character (of the timid man who always picks winners). Other cast standouts include two of the boys from the legit cast, Sam Levene and Teddy Hart. Levene's wise guy and Hart's soft-hearted chiseler are both highly enjoyable.

Joan Blondell, Allen Jenkins and Guy Kibbee, of the Warner comedy stock company, are all capable, as usual.

•

THREE MUSKETEERS, THE
1921, 140 mins, US ⊗ b/w
Dir Fred Niblo ***Prod*** Douglas Fairbanks ***Scr*** Edward Knoblock, Lotta Woods ***Ph*** Arthur Edeson ***Ed*** Nellie Mason ***Mus*** Louis F. Gottschalk ***Art*** Edward M. Langley
Act Douglas Fairbanks, Leon Bary, George Siegmann, Eugene Pallette, Marguerite De La Motte, Adolphe Menjou (Fairbanks/United Artists)

The story of Dumas has been ideally approximated in this screen version. There is a flare and sweep about the film, with the assembling, cutting and continuity seeming spotlessly correct. Douglas Fairbanks and D'Artagnan are a happy combination.

Of the interpretations, that of Nigel de Brulier as Richelieu developed a real creation. Excepting only the star, he dominates the picture. Adolphe Menjou does excellently in a role not actor-proof by any manner of means. His Louis XIII evidences both sides of the king, gaining sympathetic response where in most instances the opposite is the case. The companions of D'Artagnan, Athos, Porthos and Aramis find apt treatment by Leon Bary, George Siegmann and Eugene Pallette. Marguerite De La Motte is a sweet and winsome Constance.

•

THREE MUSKETEERS, THE
1931, 97 mins, US Ⓥ ⊙ b/w
Dir Rowland V. Lee ***Prod*** Cliff Reid ***Scr*** Dudley Nichols, Rowland V. Lee ***Ph*** Peverell Marley ***Mus*** Max Steiner
Act Walter Abel, Paul Lukas, Margot Grahame, Heather Angel, Ian Keith, Moroni Olsen (RKO)

The impotency of the sound medium in the field of romantic adventure comedy, when inexpertly handled, is revealed with melancholy effect in the unreeling of this famous Dumas story, remade with dialog. *The Three Musketeers* is dull entertainment.

Walter Abel, a young, competent, and well-regarded player from Broadway, is unsuited in nearly every respect for the role of D'Artagnan. If the tempo of the film were faster and the acting more flamboyant in the spirit of the story, Abel might have fared better.

From the title to the final fade there is an almost continuous struggle between the dialog and the musical score as to which will finally capture the ear.

The three men in the title parts are Paul Lukas as Athos, Moroni Olsen as Porthos, and Onslow Stevens as Aramis. Nigel de Brulier is convincing as Richelieu, the same role he played in the 1921 Fairbanks picture. Ian Keith, as the villainous de Rochefort, is excellent, as always, in a costume role which requires acting in the grand manner.

•

THREE MUSKETEERS, THE
1939, 71 mins, US b/w
Dir Allan Dwan ***Prod*** Raymond Griffith ***Scr*** M. M. Musselman, William A. Drake, Sam Hellman ***Ph*** Peverell Marley ***Ed*** Jack Dennis ***Mus*** David Buttolph (dir.) ***Art*** Bernard Herzbrun, David Hall
Act Don Ameche, Ritz Bros, Binnie Barnes, Lionel Atwill, Pauline Moore (20th Century-Fox)

Utilizing the broadest strokes of comedy technique, this version of Dumas's romantic adventure presents Don Ameche as a rather personable D'Artagnan, and the Ritz Bros as a helter-skelter trio hopping in and out frequently to perform their standard screwball antics.

There is little seriousness or suspense generated in the slender story, and not much interest in the adventures of D'Artagnan and his pals to regain the queen's brooch in the possession of the Duke of Buckingham. Main excuse for the yarn apparently is to provide Ameche with an opportunity to be a dashing hero while the freres Ritz clown through the footage as phoney musketeers.

Romance between Ameche and Pauline Moore is sketchily presented, developing little interest or sincerity.

•

THREE MUSKETEERS, THE
1948, 126 mins, US Ⓥ ⊙ col
Dir George Sidney ***Prod*** Pandro S. Berman ***Scr*** Robert Ardrey ***Ph*** Robert Planck ***Ed*** Robert J. Kern, George Boemler ***Mus*** Herbert Stothart ***Art*** Cedric Gibbons, Malcolm Brown
Act Gene Kelly, Lana Turner, June Allyson, Van Heflin, Angela Lansbury, Vincent Price (M-G-M)

The Three Musketeers is a swaggering, tongue-in-cheek treatment of picturesque fiction, extravagantly presented.

The fanciful tale is launched with a laugh, and quickly swings into some colorful and exciting sword duels as the pace is set for the imaginative adventures that feature the lives and loves of D'Artagnan and his three cronies. It is the complete Dumas novel.

There are acrobatics by Gene Kelly that would give Douglas Fairbanks pause. His first duel with Richelieu's cohorts is almost ballet, yet never loses the feeling of swaggering swordplay. It is a masterful mixture of dancing grace, acroagility and sly horseplay of sock comedic punch.

Lana Turner is a perfect visualization of the sexy, wicked Lady de Winter, sharply contrasting with the sweet charm of June Allyson as the maid Constance. The three king's musketeers of the title are dashingly portrayed by Van Heflin, Gig Young and Robert Coote as Athos, Porthos and Aramis. They belt over their parts in keeping with the style Kelly uses for D'Artagnan.

Another aid in making the film top commercial entertainment is the telling score by Herbert Stothart, using themes by Tchaikovsky. Score bridges any gap in movement without intruding itself.

1948: NOMINATION: Best Color Cinematography

•

THREE MUSKETEERS, THE
1993, 105 mins, US Ⓥ ⊙ ⊏⊐ col
Dir Stephen Herek ***Prod*** Joe Roth, Roger Birnbaum ***Scr*** David Loughery ***Ph*** Dean Semler ***Ed*** John F. Link ***Mus*** Michael Kamen ***Art*** Wolf Kroeger
Act Charlie Sheen, Kiefer Sutherland, Chris O'Donnell, Oliver Platt, Tim Curry, Rebecca DeMornay (Walt Disney)

Fifth major screen version of Alexandre Dumas's classic swashbuckling saga is a handsome but pallid affair aimed squarely at a young Disney audience.

Although filmed on beautiful locations in Austria and elsewhere, pic has an Americanized slant, with the good guys all speaking in Yank vernacular and the baddies sporting British accents. No doubt the straightest and possibly most faithful rendition of the perennial favorite, it is quite tame compared with Richard Lester's wild and woolly 1974 version.

Set in 16th century France, yarn begins as the noble Musketeers, guardians of the king, are disbanded by Cardinal Richelieu (Tim Curry), who is conniving to wrest the throne from the weak teenaged monarch. Dashing D'Artagnan (Chris O'Donnell) is hoping to join their ranks, but the only ones left are renegades Aramis (Charlie Sheen), Athos (Kiefer Sutherland) and Porthos (Oliver Platt).

D'Artagnan is captured, but upon his rescue is able to inform his friends about Richelieu's dastardly plot to form an alliance with Britain. Chased to Calais, they intercept His Eminence's messenger, the crafty Milady (Rebecca De-Mornay), and eventually return to Paris to disrupt Richelieu's plans.

Curry steals the film as the evil Richelieu, bringing lip-smacking glee to his naughty deeds and pronouncements. Also aces is Platt, always the one to watch when all the young Turks are working in ensemble. A bit portly and unusual looking, Platt has the sense of relish, experience and tossed-off humor that defines a Musketeer.

•

THREE MUSKETEERS, THE
THE QUEEN'S DIAMONDS
1973, 105 mins, PANAMA/SPAIN Ⓥ col
Dir Richard Lester ***Prod*** Alexander Salkind, Brian Eatwell ***Scr*** George MacDonald Fraser ***Ph*** David Watkin ***Ed*** John Victor Smith ***Mus*** Michel Legrand
Act Oliver Reed, Charlton Heston, Raquel Welch, Faye Dunaway, Richard Chamberlain, Michael York (Fox Film Trust)

The Three Musketeers take very well to Richard Lester's provocative version that does not send it up but does add comedy to this adventure tale [by Alexandre Dumas].

Here D'Artagnan, played with brio by Michael York, is a country bumpkin; the musketeers themselves are more interested in money, dames and friendship than undue fidelity to the King, a simple-minded type, and their fight scenes are full of flailing, kicks and knockabout. They are not above starting a fight at an inn to steal victuals when they run out of money.

Behind it, however, is a look at an era of poverty and virtual worker slavery to fulfill the King's flagrantly rich whims.

Musketeers are played with panache by Richard Chamberlain as the haughty ladies' man, Oliver Reed as the gusty one and Frank Finlay as the dandyish type. Raquel Welch has comedic timing as the maladroit girl of D'Artagnan while Faye Dunaway has less to do as the perfidious Milady, but makes up for the lack in the sequel [*The Four Musketeers*] quietly made at the same time.

•

3 NINJAS
1992, 84 mins, US Ⓥ ⊙ col
Dir Jon Turteltaub ***Prod*** Martha Chang ***Scr*** Edward Emanuel ***Ph*** Richard Michalak, Chris Faloona ***Ed*** David Rennie ***Mus*** Rick Marvin ***Art*** Kirk Petruccelli
Act Victor Wong, Michael Treanor, Max Elliott Slade, Chad Power, Rand Kingsley, Alan McRae (Global Venture Hollywood)

Though there aren't any name actors in the chopsocky comedy and the plot [from Kenny Kim's story] is thin and formulaic, the gracefully choreographed spectacle of three little boys outfighting hordes of evil adult ninjas is a surefire juve crowd-pleaser.

Borrowing liberally from *The Karate Kid* and *Home Alone*, the filmmakers tap knowingly into kids' fantasies by showing little guys Michael Treanor, Max Elliott Slade and Chad Power hurling baddies through the air and flattening the massive, seemingly invincible Toru Tanaka. Director Jon Turteltaub and editor David Rennie keep things zipping along, wisely not wasting much time with the ninjas' arms dealer boss, sneering Steven Seagal clone Rand Kingsley, or with his antagonist, the boys' blandly inattentive FBI agent father (Alan McRae).

When taken hostage, the Southern California boys have to rely on the martial arts lessons learned from their grandfather (the charming Victor Wong), who has shadowy past connections with Kingsley but takes their side in the battle royal.

•

3 NINJAS KICK BACK
1994, 99 mins, US Ⓥ ⊙ col
Dir Charles T. Kanganis ***Prod*** James Kang, Martha Chang, Arthur Leeds ***Scr*** Mark Saltzman ***Ph*** Christopher Faloona ***Ed*** Jeffrey Reiner, David Rennie ***Mus*** Richard Marvin ***Art*** Hiroyuki Takatsu, Gregory Martin
Act Victor Wong, Max Elliott Slade, Sean Fox, Evan Bonifant, Caroline Junko King, Sab Shimono (Sheen)

Set mostly in Japan and adding a female ninja to the three boys, this high-spirited sequel to Disney's 1992 sleeper succeeds in conveying the positive and fun elements of both Japanese and American cultures. [Pic was actually shot after the real sequel, *Three Ninjas Knuckle Up*, but released second in the series.]

The new adventure [from a screenplay by Simon Sheen, a.k.a. South Korean director Shin Sang-okk] engages its three cute ninjas, Rocky (Sean Fox), Colt (Max Elliott Slade) and Tum Tum (Evan Bonifant), in two missions. Resourceful siblings have to help Grandpa Mori (Victor Wong) return to Japan to present a ceremonial dagger he had won half a century ago to the new winner of the Ninja tournament. And they have to return to LA on time to aid their baseball team, the Dragons, against the rival Mustangs.

In pursuit of the dagger, which is a key to a secret gold cave, Grandpa's old enemy Koga (Sab Shimono) recruits a trio of spaced-out heavy-metal rockers. A young girl, Miyo (Caroline Junko King), teaches the boys a lesson or two in the ninja arts.

Charles T. Kanganis, who has directed a number of serviceable actioners, knows that the crucial factors in such adventures are comic energy and swift tempo.

•

3 NINJAS KNUCKLE UP
1995, 85 mins, US Ⓥ col
Dir Simon S. Sheen ***Prod*** Martha Chang ***Scr*** Alex S. Kim ***Ph*** Eugene Shlugleit ***Ed*** Pam Choules ***Mus*** Gary Stevan Scott ***Art*** Don Day
Act Victor Wong, Charles Napier, Michael Treanor, Max Elliott Slade, Chad Power, Crystle Lightning (Sheen)

The third time isn't the charm for this latest adventure of the pint-size chopsocky heroes. *3 Ninjas Knuckle Up* actually was filmed before *3 Ninjas Kick Back*, sequel to the 1992 sleeper hit *3 Ninjas*. (That explains why Michael Treanor and Chad Power—the two child actors who appeared in the first pic were replaced in *Kick Back*—reappear in this outing.)

Knuckle Up (which bears a 1992 copyright date) is thoroughly second-rate in all regards, with slapdash production values, cartoonish performances, by-the-numbers scripting and ridiculous martial-arts fight scenes. Korean—born helmer Simon S. Sheen [aka Shin Sang-okk] tries to liven up the sequel with a lot of Three Stooges-style slapstick. But the silliness is strained and witless.

Once again, brothers Rocky (Treanor), Tum Tum (Power) and Colt (Max Elliot Slade, the only youngster to appear in all three pix), spend an eventful summer vacation with their Grandpa Mori (Victor Wong), a sage martial arts instructor. Alex S. Kim's formulaic script has the young heroes defending a Native American tribe against a ruthless businessman (Charles Napier) who's dumping toxic waste on their land.

•

THREE OF HEARTS
1993, 102 mins, US Ⓥ col
Dir Yurek Bogayevicz ***Prod*** Joel B. Michaels, Matthew Irmas ***Scr*** Adam Greenman, Mitch Glazer ***Ph*** Andrzej Sekula ***Ed*** Dennis M. Hill ***Mus*** Joe Jackson ***Art*** Nelson Coates
Act William Baldwin, Kelly Lynch, Sherilyn Fenn, Joe Pantoliano, Gail Strickland, Cec Verrell (New Line)

Most American comic triangles involve two men in love with the same woman. But *Three of Hearts* offers a male prostitute and a lesbian nurse enamored of a seemingly bisexual woman. The film [from a screen story by Adam Greenman] gets off to a good start, when Sherilyn Fenn dumps g.f. Kelly Lynch in Washington Square Park. The heartbroken Lynch, who intended to officially come out at her sister's wedding by bringing Fenn, hires William Baldwin, a good-looking hustler, to accompany her. Before long—with the help of a silly suspense subplot—Baldwin moves into Lynch's apartment and a new friendship is formed to win Fenn back.

For viewers willing to suspend disbelief, this aspiring screwball is immensely likable. As he demonstrated in *Anna*, Yurek Bogayevicz is a director with sensitivity for texture. Baldwin delivers a knockout performance in film's richest role. Lynch also shines as a droll, slightly obsessive lesbian.

[Version reviewed was a work-in-progress shown at 1993 Sundance Film Festival.]

•

THREE ON A WEEKEND
SEE: BANK HOLIDAY

•

THREEPENNY OPERA, THE
SEE: DIE DREIGROSCHENOPER

•

3 RING CIRCUS
1954, 103 mins, US ▭ col
Dir Joseph Pevney ***Prod*** Hal B. Wallis ***Scr*** Don McGuire ***Ph*** Loyal Griggs ***Ed*** Warren Low ***Mus*** Walter Scharf ***Art*** Hal Pereira, Tambi Larsen
Act Dean Martin, Jerry Lewis, Joanne Dru, Zsa Zsa Gabor, Elsa Lanchester, Wallace Ford (Paramount)

Circus background of this expensively mounted Hal Wallis production gives Dean Martin and Jerry Lewis slick opportunity to disport themselves along familiar lines.

The script projects comics straight from army uniform to the circus, where Lewis reports as a lion tamer's assistant in the hope he'll get to be a clown. Martin tags along, catching the eye of the beautiful but temperamental trapeze artist (Zsa Zsa Gabor), who makes him her "assistant." He takes over circus owner Joanne Dru's place when she leaves the circus—she's in love and keeps fighting with him—but all is later happiness again.

Comics as a team are somewhat less zany than in previous productions. Dru and Gabor supply plenty of flash and femme splendor. Wallace Ford is tops as the barking but sympathetic circus manager.

•

THREE SAILORS AND A GIRL
1953, 94 mins, US col
Dir Roy Del Ruth ***Prod*** Sammy Cahn ***Scr*** Roland Kibbee, Devery Freeman ***Ph*** Carl Guthrie ***Ed*** Owen Marks ***Mus*** Ray Heindorf (dir.) ***Art*** Leo K. Kuter
Act Jane Powell, Gordon MacRae, Gene Nelson, Sam Levene, George Givot, Veda Ann Borg (Warner)

Jane Powell, Gordon MacRae and Gene Nelson co-star and are the chief exponents of the songs and dances that occupy much of the footage in the Sammy Cahn production. Cahn also doubled from his producer chores to co-cleff the songs with Sammy Fain and the music listens easily. The big production finale is a dressed up, tuneful affair with Powell and MacRae doing "Home Is Where the Heart Is" before Nelson takes over the terping with line dancers.

The film [based on the play *The Butter and Egg Man* by George S. Kaufman] deals with a group of submarine sailors who put their savings into a musical being promoted by Sam Levene. The three sailors are babes in the woods on B'way, but soon learn the ropes and a flop show is turned into a hit with the boys starring with Powell after its hambone leading man (George Givot) has ankled the setup.

LeRoy Prinz staged and directed the musical numbers for sight appeal.

•

THREE SMART GIRLS
1937, 86 mins, US b/w
Dir Henry Koster ***Prod*** Joseph Pasternak ***Scr*** Adele Comandini ***Ph*** Joseph Valentine ***Ed*** Ted J. Kent ***Mus*** Charles Previn (dir.)
Act Deanna Durbin, Binnie Barnes, Alice Brady, Ray Milland, Charles Winninger, Mischa Auer (Universal)

Film is a sentimental comedy and has that rare quality of making an audience feel better for having seen it. In 14-year-old diva Deanna Durbin, U has an engaging girl who—established via Eddie Cantor's radio programs—more than matches expectations.

Both director Henry Koster (Herman Kosterlitz) and Joseph Pasternak, the associate producer, were a U production team when Laemmle was making films in Germany. But when Nate Manheim, U's foreign sales chief, shut up U's shop over there Manheim insisted that the Koster(litz)-Pasternak team be given a crack in Hollywood.

Story merely tells of three girls' attempts to reconcile their estranged parents. Durbin is the prime schemer, the other two daughters find future husbands as the action progresses and it all ends on a happy tear as the younger reintroduces her mother to her dad. As presented it's wholesome, funny, and very satisfying.

Durbin stands out not only as "a darling child" personality, but as a winsome little dramatic actress whose talents do not end with an ability to hit the high registers. This is also one of Charles Winninger's best performances while Binnie Barnes's light vamp is not overdone. Alice Brady, as the mamma with an eye to a bankroll, just skirts dangerous shoals in overplaying.

1936: NOMINATIONS: Best Picture, Original Story, Sound

•

THREESOME
1994, 93 mins, US Ⓥ ⊙ col
Dir Andrew Fleming ***Prod*** Brad Krevoy, Steve Stabler ***Scr*** Andrew Fleming ***Ph*** Alexander Gruszynski ***Ed*** William C. Carruth ***Mus*** Thomas Newman ***Art*** Ivo Cristante
Act Lara Flynn Boyle, Stephen Baldwin, Josh Charles, Alexis Arquette, Martha Gehman, Mark Arnold (Motion Picture Corp. of America)

Cute, sexy and funny, *Threesome* also manages to deftly capture the working out of personality and sexual identity that is part and parcel of the college years. Pic should establish writer-director Andrew Fleming (*Bad Dreams*) as a talent to watch.

Because of a silly technicality involving her male-sounding name, sharp-looking Alex (Lara Flynn Boyle) is assigned a room in the same UCLA dorm suite already shared by hot-looking party boy Stuart (Stephen Baldwin) and handsome intellectual Eddy (Josh Charles).

Characters' close physical proximity quickly leads to emotional ties and eruptions. The first to surface is Alex's infatuation with Eddy, who instantly backs off and soon must acknowledge that he's actually attracted to Stuart, not Alex. Stuart tries to seduce Alex, but she spurns him, still distracted by Eddy's sexual ambivalence and intent upon molding him into a heterosexual.

Before long the trio is almost constantly locked in three-way embraces and gropings, supplemented by separate sessions between Alex and the two young men.

Baldwin, the third of the talented brothers to break through notably on the screen, expands corners of his character in a rambunctiously sexy and thoroughly winning performance. Flynn Boyle rebounds here with some spirited, spunky, passionate work.

•

THREE STRANGERS
1946, 91 mins, US b/w
Dir Jean Negulesco ***Prod*** Wolfgang Reinhardt ***Scr*** John Huston, Howard Koch ***Ph*** Arthur Edeson ***Ed*** George Amy ***Mus*** Adolph Deutsch ***Art*** Ted Smith
Act Sydney Greenstreet, Peter Lorre, Geraldine Fitzgerald, Joan Lorring, Robert Shayne, Marjorie Riordan (Warner)

Three Strangers carries a rather complicated episodic plot, depending mostly on the fine cast performances to carry it.

Not only the three stars, Sydney Greenstreet, Geraldine Fitzgerald and Peter Lorre, but various supporting players command special attention. Greenstreet overplays to some extent as the attorney who has raided a trust fund, but he still does a good job. Lorre is tops as a drunk who gets involved in a murder of which he's innocent, while Fitzgerald rates as the victim.

Along with Greenstreet and Lorre, Fitzgerald has an equal share in a sweepstakes ticket. They are strangers. All three win on the ticket but Greenstreet murders the girl in a fit of rage, in Lorre's presence, thus leaving the latter, also a loser, since he cannot risk trying to cash the ticket because it would involve him in the killing.

Story jumps around uncertainly but Jean Negulesco's direction is satisfactory.

•

3:10 TO YUMA
1957, 92 mins, US Ⓥ ⦿ b/w
Dir Delmer Daves ***Prod*** David Heilweil ***Scr*** Halsted Welles ***Ph*** Charles Lawton, Jr. ***Ed*** Al Clarke ***Mus*** George Duning ***Art*** Frank Hotaling
Act Glenn Ford, Van Heflin, Felicia Farr, Leora Dana, Henry Jones, Richard Jaeckel (Columbia)

Aside from the fact that this is an upper-drawer western, *3:10 to Yuma* will strike many for its resemblance to *High Noon*. That the climax fizzles must be laid on doorstep of Halsted Welles, who adapts Elmore Leonard's story quite well until that point.

Glenn Ford portrays the deadly leader of a slickly professional outlaw gang, which holds up a stagecoach. Van Heflin, impoverished neighborhood rancher, helps capture Ford when the latter lags behind his gang, to dally with lovely, lonely town barmaid Felicia Farr.

But Ford's gang is too strong for local lawmen to handle. Stagecoach owner Robert Emhardt promises a large reward to Heflin and the town drunk (Henry Jones). Idea is to hold Ford in another town, unknown to his gang, until daily train (3:10 of title) can take him to Yuma for trial. Here, story cleaves closely to *High Noon* formula.

Ford's switch-casting, as the quietly sinister gang leader, is authoritative, impressive and successful. Heflin measures up fully and convincingly to the rewarding role of the proud and troubled rancher. Farr's contribution is a short one, but she registers with a touching poignancy and a delicate beauty.

Title song by Ned Washington and George Duning, sung by Frankie Lane under credits and by Norma Zimmer during the picture, is a well-written tune.

•

THREE VIOLENT PEOPLE
1956, 100 mins, US col
Dir Rudolph Mate ***Prod*** Hugh Brown ***Scr*** James Edward Grant ***Ph*** Loyal Griggs ***Ed*** Alma Macrorie ***Mus*** Walter Scharf
Act Charlton Heston, Anne Baxter, Gilbert Roland, Tom Tryon, Forrest Tucker, Bruce Bennett (Paramount)

This one is elephant's eye high above most westerns. The story opens trite: demobilized Confederate soldiers are being taunted and abused by Yankee soldiers and carpetbaggers in Texas. The proud-as-sin captain, now mellowed from four years of war and retreating, holds his temper and his gunfire.

The tangent which refreshes the proceedings has to do with the precipitate marriage of the proud-as-sin Texan to the not-too-proud-to-sin fille de nuit. A member of the nasty occupation army camp-followers spots the gal and spills the chili beans all over the ranch porch.

Anne Baxter has the requisite sauciness combined with essential sincerity to make the woman's part stand up. Her interrelatedness to and with Charlton Heston, a rugged and believable characterization, gives the production its underpinning.

Westerns have many a beguiling and lovable and sturdy-souled Mexican. This one comes equipped with Gilbert Roland, whose loyalties and warmth build the human side which redeems *Three Violent People* from being just another giddyap.

Early in the film, legit's Elaine Strich makes an acidy blondine madame arouse interest.

•

THREE WISE GIRLS
1932, 67 mins, US b/w
Dir William Beaudine ***Scr*** Agnes C. Johnson, Robert Riskin ***Ph*** Ted Tetzlaff ***Ed*** Jack Dennis
Act Jean Harlow, Mae Clarke, Walter Byron, Marie Prevost, Andy Devine, Natalie Moorhead (Columbia)

Three small-town girls come to New York. One gets an apartment on Park Ave, with a banker paying the bills. When he goes back to his wife she shuffles off. The second girl addresses envelopes for a living and marries a chauffeur. The third goes back home disgusted because the boyfriend can't get a divorce from his wife, but he gets his freedom and comes after her.

Jean Harlow has the lead—the girl who keeps straight. She does her best to suggest the innocent young thing and does better than might be expected. But she fails to be convincing and Mae Clarke takes the acting honors from her, even with her stilted speeches. Marie Prevost struggles gamely with the comedy. Natalie Moorhead has one brief scene, which adds another good name to the cast. Walter Byron carries himself nicely as the sincere lover, and Jameson Thomas keeps just this side of overacting the heavy.

•

THREE WOMEN
1924, 82 mins, US ⊗ b/w
Dir Ernst Lubitsch ***Prod*** Ernst Lubitsch ***Scr*** Hans Kraly ***Ph*** Charles J. Van Enger ***Art*** Svend Gade
Act May McAvoy, Pauline Frederick, Lew Cody, Marie Prevost, Willard Louis (Warner Bros)

Three Women is a pretty piece of direction. For this Ernst Lubitsch is to be credited. Pauline Frederick playing mother to May McAvoy is something of a shock at first glance, but not so great after one has seen the picture.

The heavy is handled by Lew Cody, who appears as a penniless Don Juan and lays siege to the heart of the $3 million widow (Pauline Frederick). She is strikingly bedecked in jewels and Cody, with his creditors hounding him, before long manages to lay a touch for $100,000, which is pretty heavy lover stuff, even with a $3 million widow.

He is not aware that she has a daughter until the night he makes the heavy touch. The young girl returns from school unawares and steps right into her mother's romance. When Cody hears that the daughter is to receive half of the family fortune on her marriage he lays plans to win her; in fact, he compromises her, which makes the marriage a necessity. As soon as the ceremony is set he starts playing around on the outside and sets up a second establishment, which is where the third woman comes in. She is Marie Prevost; but hers is little better than a bit in the picture.

Lubitsch does not resort to one written title to convey the story of the young daughter's downfall in the entire sequence. That is direction. Everything is suggestion in facial expression.

•

THREE WOMEN
1977, 122 mins, US ▭ col
Dir Robert Altman ***Prod*** Robert Altman ***Scr*** Robert Altman ***Ph*** Chuck Rosher ***Ed*** Dennis Hill ***Mus*** Gerald Busby ***Art*** James D. Vance
Act Shelley Duvall, Sissy Spacek, Janice Rule, Robert Fortier, Ruth Nelson, John Cromwell (20th Century-Fox)

Absorbing moody and often compelling story about psychological dependence and transference.

Robert Altman had a dream which he used as the basis for his original screenplay, set in the desert where Shelley Duvall works as an attendant in an old-folks' health center and new staffer Sissy Spacek becomes her roommate.

Janice Rule is the mural-painting wife of retired stuntman Robert Fortier, the two of them being important catalysts to the changing relationship between Spacek and Duvall.

Duvall is magnificent as a girl whose inner unhappiness is masked by dialog straight out of smart-set magazines and fast-snack recipe folders. Spacek, at the outset adoring and subservient, gets all the sympathy.

Spacek matches in complementing excellence Duvall's performance. Rule registers well.

•

THREE WORLDS OF GULLIVER, THE
1960, 98 mins, UK Ⓥ ⦿ col
Dir Jack Sher ***Prod*** Charles H. Schneer ***Scr*** Arthur Ross, Jack Sher ***Ph*** Wilkie Cooper ***Ed*** Raymond Poulton ***Mus*** Bernard Herrmann ***Art*** Gil Parrendo, Derek Barrington
Act Kerwin Mathews, Jo Morrow, June Thorburn, Basil Sydney, Gregoire Aslan, Lee Patterson (Columbia)

Jonathan Swift's 18th-century stinging satire has been considerably softened and drastically romanticized, but enough of its telling caustic comment remains.

The original four-part work has been trimmed to the more familiar twosome of Lilliput, land of little people, and Brobdingnag, where the natives are as tall in proportion to Gulliver as the Lilliputians are short. The hero's wife and family of Swift's tome have been dropped in favor of a fiery fiancée who shares his misadventure in Brobdingnag. Gulliver, thankfully, still goes it alone in Lilliput, according to the film.

The picture is notable for its visuo-cinematic achievements and its bold, bright and sweeping score by Bernard Herrmann. Special visual effects expert Ray Harryhausen, whose Superdynamation process makes the motion pictured Gulliver plausible and workable, rates a low bow for his painstaking, productive efforts.

Kerwin Mathews, generally reserved and persuasive, makes a first-rate Gulliver. Among the more arresting performances are those of Basil Sydney as the pompous emperor of Lilliput, Martin Benson as its conniving minister of finance, Marian Spencer as the vain empress, Mary Ellis and Gregoire Aslan as king and queen of Brobdingnag.

•

THRESHOLD
1981, 106 mins, Canada Ⓥ col
Dir Richard Pearce ***Prod*** Jon Slan, Michael Burns ***Scr*** James Salter ***Ph*** Michael Brault ***Ed*** Susan Martin ***Mus*** Mickey Erbe, Mary-Beth Solomon
Act Donald Sutherland, John Marley, Sharon Ackerman, Jeff Goldblum, Mare Winningham, Michael Lerner (Paragon)

Donald Sutherland takes the central role of a heart specialist involved in the development of a mechanical heart for transplant purposes. The device is the brainchild of medical biologist Jeff Goldblum, a fanatic who is certain his radical conception will revolutionize surgical techniques.

When all current practices fail on patient Mare Winningham, Sutherland decides to defy the board and bring out the miracle device. The controversial operation immediately generates media attention and Sutherland nervously waits out the consequence of his action.

Writer James Salter and director Richard Pearce have strenously avoided taking a melodramatic approach to the material. What emerges is virtually a visualized medical journal filled with the tedium and monotony facing a dedicated surgeon incorporated along with the excitement of venturing into new medical frontiers. At times one wishes the film had opted for a more dramatic tone.

Sutherland gives a cooly effective performance. The stability of Sutherland's surgeon is in sharp contrast to Goldblum's erratic inventor, providing the film with a keen sense of humor.

•

THRILL OF IT ALL
1963, 108 mins, US Ⓥ col
Dir Norman Jewison ***Prod*** Ross Hunter, Martin Melcher ***Scr*** Carl Reiner ***Ph*** Russell Metty ***Ed*** Milton Carruth ***Mus*** Frank DeVol ***Art*** Alexander Golitzen, Robert Boyle
Act Doris Day, James Garner, Arlene Francis, Edward Andrews, ZaSu Pitts, Reginald Owen (Universal/Arwin)

Carl Reiner's scenario, from a story he wrote in collaboration with Larry Gelbart, is peppered with digs at various institutions of American life. Among the targets of his fairly subtle but telling assault with the needle are television, Madison Avenue, the servant problem and such specific matters as the sharp points at the rear extremities of the modern Cadillac and the maitre d' who has immediate seating for celebrities only.

But these nuggets and pinpricks of satiric substance are primarily bonuses. Ultimately it is in the design and engineering of cumulative sight gag situations that *Thrill of It All* excels. In addition to a running gag about a suspiciously similar weekly series of live TV dramas, there is a scene in which a swimming pool saturated with soap gives birth to a two-story-high mountain of suds and another in which James Garner, coming home from work one evening, drives his convertible into his backyard and straight into a pool that wasn't there in the morning.

Doris Day scores as the housewife with two children who is suddenly thrust into an irresistible position as an $80,000-a-year pitch woman for an eccentric soap tycoon who is impressed by her unaffected quality. Bearing the brunt of these soap operatics is Garner as the gynecologist whose domestic tranquillity is shattered by his wife's sudden transition to career girl.

Arlene Francis and Edward Andrews are spirited in the key roles of a middle-aged couple suddenly expectant parents. ZaSu Pitts does all she can with some ridiculous shenanigans as a fretful maid.

•

THRONE OF BLOOD
SEE: KUMONOSU-JO

•

THROUGH A GLASS DARKLY
SEE: SASOM I EN SPEGEL

THROW MOMMA FROM THE TRAIN
1987, 88 mins, US Ⓥ ⦿ col
Dir Danny DeVito ***Prod*** Larry Brezner ***Scr*** Stu Silver ***Ph*** Barry Sonnenfeld ***Ed*** Michael Jablow ***Mus*** David Newman ***Art*** Ida Random
Act Danny DeVito, Billy Crystal, Anne Ramsey, Kim Greist, Kate Mulgrew, Annie Ross (Orion)

Throw Momma from the Train is a fun and delightfully venal comedy. Very clever and engaging from beginning to end, pic builds on the notion that nearly everyone—at least once in life—has the desire to snuff out a relative or nemesis, even if 99.9% of us let the urge pass without ever acting on it.

Here, it's the idle death threats of a frustrated writer and flunky junior college professor (Billy Crystal) against his ex-wife that are overheard by one of his dimwitted and very impressionable students (Danny DeVito).

DeVito's limited creative abilities are further stifled by his crazy, overbearing momma (Anne Ramsey), a nasty, jealous old bag whom he loathes and fears. He seeks out Crystal for help on his writing and instead is told to go see Alfred Hitchcock's *Strangers on a Train*, which he does—coming away with a ridiculous scheme on the film's plot to kill Crystal's wife and then ask for a like favor in return.

Crystal's talent as a standup comic comes through as it appears he got away with a fair amount of ad-libbing. His tirades on his ex-wife, a routine he does several times, get funnier with each delivery and are a good counterbalance for DeVito's equally comical dumb-impish schtick.

If there were to be a first place prize for scene stealing, however, it would to to Ramsey, whose horrible looks and surly demeanor are sick and humorous at the same time.

1987: NOMINATION: Best Supp. Actress (Anne Ramsey)

THUNDER AND LIGHTNING
1977, 93 mins, US Ⓥ col
Dir Corey Allen ***Prod*** Roger Corman ***Scr*** William Hjortsberg ***Ph*** James Pergola ***Ed*** Anthony Redman ***Mus*** Andy Stein
Act David Carradine, Kate Jackson, Roger C. Carmel, Sterling Holloway, Ed Barth, Ron Feinberg (20th Century-Fox)

Thunder and Lightning has just about everything in the action department but Dracula loping after Frankenstein's monster, packing thrills and fast movement as stunt drivers have their day in some wild pic mileage.

Film picks up in tempo and ends on a socko note as David Carradine, an irrepressible booze runner, competes with girlfriend Kate Jackson's pop in his chosen field.

Script laces comedy with the action, and director Corey Allen expertly maneuvers his chase sequences with stunting both with Everglade buggies and fast cars on the highways.

Carradine shows he has the stuff of which action stars are made, and distaffer Jackson lends a distracting note as an actress who doesn't mind getting her hair mussed.

•

THUNDERBALL
1965, 130 mins, UK Ⓥ ⦿ ▭ col
Dir Terence Young ***Prod*** Kevin McClory ***Scr*** Richard Maibaum, John Hopkins ***Ph*** Ted Moore ***Ed*** Peter Hunt ***Mus*** John Barry ***Art*** Ken Adam
Act Sean Connery, Claudine Auger, Adolfo Celi, Luciana Paluzzi, Rik Van Nutter, Bernard Lee (McClory)

Sean Connery plays his indestructible James Bond for the fourth time in the manner born, faced here with a $280 million atomic bomb ransom plot. Action, dominating element of three predecessors, gets rougher before even the credits flash on. Richard Maibaum (who coscripted former entries) and John Hopkins's screenplay [based on an original screenplay by Jack Whittingham, from the original story by Kevin McClory, Whittingham and Ian Fleming] is studded with inventive play and mechanical gimmicks. There's visible evidence that the reported $5.5 million budget was no mere publicity figure; it's posh all the way. Underwater weapon-carrying sea sleds provide an imaginative note, as does a one-man jet pack used by Bond in the opening sequence, reminiscent of the one-man moon vehicle utilized by Dick Tracy in the cartoon strip.

Connery is up to his usual stylish self as he lives up to past rep, in which mayhem is a casual affair.

Adolfo Celi brings dripping menace to part of the swarthy heavy who is nearly as ingenious—but not quite—as the British agent, whom, among other means, he tries to kill with man-eating sharks.

Terence Young takes advantage of every situation in his direction to maintain action at fever-pitch.

1965: Best Visual Effects (John Stears)

THUNDER BAY
1953, 103 mins, US Ⓥ col
Dir Anthony Mann ***Prod*** Aaron Rosenberg ***Scr*** Gil Doud, John Michael Hayes ***Ph*** William Daniels ***Ed*** Russell Schoengarth ***Mus*** Frank Skinner ***Art*** Alexander Golitzen, Richard H. Riedel
Act James Stewart, Joanne Dru, Gilbert Roland, Dan Duryea, Jay C. Flippen, Marcia Henderson (Universal)

A modern plot that deals with offshore oil drilling gives this regulation outdoor actioner an interesting switch.

James Stewart and Dan Duryea, as a couple of ex-GIs with a dream of extracting oil from the bottom of the Gulf of Mexico off the coast of Louisiana, carry the principal story load. Having talked Jay C. Flippen, head of an oil company, into backing the offshore exploration, the two adventurers plunge into their work against the wishes of the shrimp fishermen, who see their livelihood ruined.

Stewart moves easily through his role as the stalwart, steadfast member of the adventuring pair. Duryea supplies likeable color to his wise-cracking heroics and comes over strongly. Joanne Dru's character as the daughter of fisherman Antonio Moreno needed more clarity to be effective.

Anthony Mann's direction manages considerable action to balance a script tendency towards talkiness. The water sequences have punch.

•

THUNDERBOLT AND LIGHTFOOT
1974, 114 mins, US Ⓥ ⦿ ▭ col
Dir Michael Cimino ***Prod*** Robert Daley ***Scr*** Michael Cimino ***Ph*** Frank Stanley ***Ed*** Ferris Webster ***Mus*** Dee Barton ***Art*** Tambi Larsen
Act Clint Eastwood, Jeff Bridges, George Kennedy, Geoffrey Lewis, Catherine Bach, Gary Busey (United Artists)

Thunderbolt and Lightfoot is an overlong, sometimes hilariously vulgar comedy-drama, about the restaging of a difficult safecracking heist. Debuting director Michael Cimino obtains superior performances from Clint Eastwood, George Kennedy, Geoffrey Lewis and especially Jeff Bridges.

Cimino's story picks up Eastwood as a cowtown preacher, his longtime refuge from Kennedy, a survivor of an earlier caper where the loot was hidden and never found. A Kennedy henchman uncovers Eastwood, who meets Bridges (also on the lam from a car theft), then Kennedy and Lewis. The secret hiding place of the loot, an old schoolhouse, has been replaced by a new structure. Uneasily, the group decides to pull the job all over again.

1974: NOMINATION: Best Supp. Actor (Jeff Bridges)

•

THUNDERHEAD— SON OF FLICKA
1945, 78 mins, US col
Dir Louis King ***Prod*** Robert Bassler ***Scr*** Dwight Cummins, Dorothy Yost ***Ph*** Charles Clarke ***Ed*** Nick De Maggio ***Mus*** Cyril J. Mockridge ***Art*** Lyle R. Wheeler
Act Roddy McDowall, Preston Foster, Rita Johnson, Diana Hale (20th Century-Fox)

Thunderhead—Son of Flicka, 20th-Fox's sequel to *Flicka*, is a worthy successor. A simple outdoor idyll of a ranch lad and his horse, it has the same refreshing quality of its predecessor and a similar appeal. Story, like *Flicka*, is filmed on open ranges of Utah and Oregon, with its rolling country, gorges and hills.

Shots, too, of herds of horses roaming the range, always intrigue, as do brief scenes of a horse warily nosing a porcupine or violently killing a rattler. Though story [from a novel by Mary O'Hara] is a simple one of a boy rearing a colt in hopes of making him a racer, pic contains drama throughout, as in various stages of breaking in the horse or the hunt for an equine killer.

Roddy McDowall again plays the rancher's son, as in *Flicka*, with shy appeal, exhibiting, however, more of the practical rancher than the kid dreamer in this film in trying to tame Thunderhead. Preston Foster plays the rancher father with warmth. Rita Johnson is again the understanding mother.

•

THUNDERHEART
1992, 118 mins, US Ⓥ ⦿ col
Dir Michael Apted ***Prod*** Robert De Niro, Jane Rosenthal, John Fusco ***Scr*** John Fusco ***Ph*** Roger Deakins ***Ed*** Ian Crafford ***Mus*** James Horner ***Art*** Dan Bishop
Act Val Kilmer, Graham Greene, Sam Shepard, Sheila Tousey, Fred Ward, Fred Dalton Thompson (Tribeca/Waterhorse)

Dances with the Evidence could be the title of this pic about a young, part-Indian FBI hotdog whose loyalties are tested when he discovers the power of his roots during a murder probe on a Sioux reservation.

Reasonably engrossing as a mystery-thriller despite its overburdened plot, *Thunderheart* succeeds most in its captivating portrayal of mystical Native American ways.

Val Kilmer stars as a sharp but surly and guarded young fed whose crewcut bristles when he learns he's expected to use his long-suppressed Indian heritage to help quell violence on a South Dakota reservation. Partnered with a crack FBI vet (Sam Shepard), he travels 'cross the lone prairie to the Res, where the two city sharpies excel at shockingly insensitive behavior.

Befriended by a wary but compassionate Sioux sheriff (Graham Greene, in a standout portrayal), he's introduced to tribal spiritual elder (Chief Ted Thin Elk), who points him toward his true self.

Set among the tinderbox tensions of the late 1970s, when militant Indians waged bloody battles to take back their culture and lands, pic finds a lively platform for its essential view that the old ways were far wiser and better. Kilmer holds the screen strongly in an intense young Turk role, but when script calls for him to transform into a mythical Indian savior, he doesn't quite fill the moccasins.

•

THUNDERING HERD, THE
1925, 70 mins, US ⊗ b/w
Dir William K. Howard ***Scr*** Lucien Hubbard ***Ph*** Lucien Andriot
Act Jack Holt, Lois Wilson, Noah Beery, Raymond Hatton, Col. Tim McCoy, Eulalie Jensen (Paramount)

Here is the greatest western picture since *The Covered Wagon* and if anything it is as great, if not greater, than that western epic, at least from the standpoint of thrills. The credit for the wallop goes to the director, William K. Howard. Howard's composition stands out. He has achieved groupings and scenes that rival the best that that great artist of the west, Frederic Remington, has done.

Heading the cast are Jack Holt, Lois Wilson, Noah Beery and Raymond Hatton. This quartet stand out wonderfully well in their characterizations. But it isn't the cast, the director, the story or the photography that makes *The Thundering Herd* a truly great picture. It is the thrills.

•

THUNDER IN THE CITY
1937, 86 mins, UK Ⓥ b/w
Dir Marion Gering ***Prod*** Alexander Erway ***Scr*** Robert Sherwood, Aben Kandel, Akos Tolnay ***Ph*** Al Gilks ***Ed*** Arthur Hilton ***Mus*** Miklos Rozsa ***Art*** David Ramon
Act Edward G. Robinson, Luli Deste, Nigel Bruce, Constance Collier, Ralph Richardson, Arthur Wontner (Atlantic/Columbia)

For a long time, Edward G. Robinson wanted to do something lighter than eye-gouging racketeers and went to London for that purpose after getting an offer to appear in this picture. He wasn't so wrong in wanting to try his hand at something different such as this, except that, as a romantic lead opposite Luli Deste, he is a bit awkward.

Robinson plays an American ballyhoo artist who invades the staid calm of business methods in England and, backed by a lot of nerve, much luck and fictional situations, promotes a metal mine in Africa into a big proposition. Robinson's rival ties him up under patents and it looks as though the Horatio Algerian hero is stymied.

Three writers have written much smart dialog into the picture and provided numerous comedy situations which are ably maneuvered by director Marion Gering.

Deste is a Viennese with a pleasant but very slight accent. She looks to have the goods besides having the looks. Two who contribute much are Nigel Bruce and Constance Collier, who play a duke and duchess, respectively. Ralph Richardson renders a good job as a British banker.

•

THUNDER IN THE DUST

SEE: THE SUNDOWNERS

•

THUNDER ROCK

1942, 110 mins, UK b/w

Dir Roy Boulting ***Prod*** John Boulting ***Scr*** Jeffrey Dell, Bernard Miles ***Ph*** Mutz Greenbaum ***Mus*** Hans May

Act Michael Redgrave, Barbara Mullen, James Mason, Lilli Palmer, Finlay Currie, Frederick Valk (M-G-M/Charter)

Thunder Rock is a remarkable piece of technical work. Its treatment of the subject [a newspaperman gains new hope through visions of drowned people] is realistic.

A more felicitous job of casting would have been difficult. Acting credits are headed by Michael Redgrave, who enacted the same role in the stage play [by Robert Ardrey].

•

THX 1138

1971, 88 mins, US Ⓥ ⦿ ▭ col

Dir George Lucas ***Prod*** Lawrence Sturhahn ***Scr*** George Lucas, Walter Murch ***Ph*** Dave Meyers, Albert Kihn ***Ed*** George Lucas ***Mus*** Lalo Schifrin ***Art*** Michael Haller

Act Robert Duvall, Donald Pleasence, Don Pedro Colley, Maggie McOmie, Ian Wolfe, Sid Haig (American Zoetrope)

THX 1138 is a psychedelic science fiction horror story about some future civilization regimented into computer-programmed slavery.

Film is a feature-length expansion of George Lucas's student film. In that brief form, the story of one man's determination to crash out of his worldly prison was exciting; the expansion by director-editor Lucas with Walter Murch [who is also credited with "sound montages"] succeeds in fleshing out the environment, but falls behind in constructing a plotline to sustain interest. Robert Duvall heads cast as the defector after his mate Maggie McOmie is programmed into the cell of Donald Pleasence, a corrupt computer technician. Don Pedro Colley is another fugitive, who helps Duvall reach his freedom.

•

TIARA TAHITI

1962, 100 mins, UK Ⓥ col

Dir Ted Kotcheff ***Prod*** Ivan Foxwell ***Scr*** Geofrey Cotterell, Ivan Foxwell ***Ph*** Otto Heller ***Ed*** Anthony Gibbs ***Mus*** Phil Green ***Art*** Alex Vetchinsky

Act James Mason, John Mills, Claude Dauphin, Herbert Lom, Rosenda Monteros, Jacques Marin (Rank)

Action stems from Germany, just after the war. A jumped up, pompous lieutenant-colonel with a king size inferiority complex (Mills) clashes with a sophisticated, carefree junior officer (Mason). Mills stops Mason when he tries to smuggle loot back to London, and Mason is cashiered. He finds a life of dissolute ease and enchantment in Tahiti, with a native girl and no worries. Mills, well after the war, arrives to negotiate a deal to build a hotel in Tahiti, comes across Mason and finds to his intense irritation that Mason still has the same effect on him, that of reducing him to fumbling ineptitude and humility.

The two male stars in this pic have a field day. Mason is fine as the mocking wastrel while Mills is equally good in a more difficult role that could have lapsed into parody.

These two carry the main burden of the film but get affectionate alliance from a string of people. As Mason's girlfriend, Monteros is attractive. Herbert Lom (skillfully made up as a Chinese) has a serio-comic role as the local tradesman who is the frustrated rival for the affections of Monteros, and does it up brown.

•

TIE ME UP! TIE ME DOWN!

SEE: ¡ATAME!

•

TIE THAT BINDS, THE

1995, 98 mins, US Ⓥ col

Dir Wesley Strick ***Prod*** David Madden, Patrick Markey, John Morrissey ***Scr*** Michael Auerback ***Ph*** Bobby Bukowski ***Ed*** Michael N. Knue ***Mus*** Graeme Revell ***Art*** Marcia Hinds-Johnson

Act Daryl Hannah, Keith Carradine, Moira Kelly, Vincent Spano, Julia Devin, Cynda Williams, (Interscope/PolyGram/Hollywood)

A nasty and violent take on the real versus adoptive parents issue, *The Tie That Binds* is simply dull for most of its running time before turning downright nauseating. From three of the same producers as *The Hand That Rocks the Cradle* and presumably partly inspired by that creepy hit, new effort just sits there generating disgust rather than suspense.

Tyro screenwriter Michael Auerbach and first-time helmer Wesley Strick plod through a tale that has outlaw team of John and Leann Netherwood (Keith Carradine, Daryl Hannah) forced to flee a crime scene, leaving their young daughter, Janie (Julia Devin), behind. Taken in by professional couple Russell and Dana Clifton (Vincent Spano, Moira Kelly) with an eye to eventual adoption, little Janie slowly begins to adapt to her new surroundings.

Naturally, her white trash parents aren't about to let their sprig become a yuppie kid, so they set out, not just to recapture their daughter, but to murder everyone who had anything to do with the separation, including a cop and an adoption official.

Director Strick indulges in a parade of gratuitous crane and over-head shots that only call attention to themselves in their pointlessness. Characters are all one-dimensional.

•

TIGER AND THE PUSSYCAT, THE

1967, 105 mins, Italy/US Ⓥ col

Dir Dino Risi ***Prod*** Mario Cecchi Gori ***Scr*** Incrocci Agenore, Furio Scarpelli, Dino Risi ***Ph*** Sandro D'Eva ***Ed*** Marcello Malvestiti ***Mus*** Fred Buongusto ***Art*** Luciano Ricceri

Act Vittorio Gassman, Ann-Margret, Eleanor Parker (Fair/Embassy)

Screenwriters take a timeworn three-point relationship and bulwark it with many physical gag situations and flash comic inserts. But they depend on the more basic cleavage between parents and offspring to underscore the extra-marital fling between a middle-age captain of industry (Vittorio Gassman) and a 20-year-old Bohemian ball of fire (Ann-Margret). Eleanor Parker plays the abused wife with suave dignity.

For about two-thirds of the film *The Tiger* is a swiftly paced romp of gay deceit for the male partner and a purposeful drive for sexual plentitude on the distaff side. Slowdown occurs with Gassman's dilemma. Prodded by his young mistress to give up wife and family (his career by this time is practically shot anyway), the charm and tempo slacken while Gassman weighs a choice that distills the joy of a seven-inning stretch.

Gassman is on the scene almost every minute of the film. It's an unfair load to bear with such a slight story in support but he's first-rate until the action sags. Parker is standout as the attractive, understanding wife and mother of two grown-up children.

•

TIGER BAY

1959, 105 mins, UK Ⓥ b/w

Dir J. Lee Thompson ***Prod*** Julian Wintle, Leslie Parkyn ***Scr*** John Hawkesworth, Shelley Smith ***Ph*** Eric Cross ***Ed*** Sidney Hayers ***Mus*** Laurie Johnson

Act John Mills, Horst Buchholz, Hayley Mills, Yvonne Mitchell, Megs Jenkins, Anthony Dawson (Rank)

A disarming, snub-nosed youngster makes her debut in *Tiger Bay*, and registers a sock impact. She is Hayley Mills, 12-year-old daughter of actor John Mills, star of the film. Young Mills gives a lift to a pic which, anyway, stacks up as a lively piece of drama.

The story concerns a Polish seaman who, returning from a voyage, finds that his mistress has moved in with another man. In a burst of anger he kills her. The slaying is witnessed by the child, who also rescues the gun. She is a lonely youngster whose attachment for the killer seriously complicates police investigations.

Mills is authoritative as the detective while Horst Buchholz brings charm to a role which could easily have been played by a British actor. Lee Thompson and cameraman Eric Cross capture the dockland area of Cardiff arrestingly. The screenplay by John Hawkesworth and Shelley Smith is taut and literate.

•

TIGERLAND

2000, 109 mins, US Ⓥ ⦿ col

Dir Joel Schumacher ***Prod*** Arnon Milchan, Steven Haft, Beau Flynn ***Scr*** Ross Klavan, Michael McGruther ***Ph*** Matthew Libatique ***Ed*** Mark Stevens ***Mus*** Nathan Larsen ***Art*** Andrew Laws.

Act Colin Farrell, Matthew Davis, Clifton Collins Jr., Thomas Guiry, Shea Whigham, Russell Richardson (Haft/New Regency/20th Century-Fox)

Though it doesn't break much new ground thematically, Joel Schumacher's Vietnam War movie is a tautly focused, well-executed drama that represents his most coherent and satisfying work since 1993's *Falling Down*.

Tigerland belongs to a cycle of Vietnam movies that focus on the internal psychology of a small fighting unit, most notably *Platoon, Full Metal Jacket* and *Hamburger Hill*. Set in 1971, the intense narrative centers on the group dynamics within an infantry platoon in its last phase of basic training. The novel point of the well-honed script is its setting: Story begins at Fort Lake, Louisiana, then switches to Tigerland, a wilderness designated by the army for jungle combat simulation—the very last stop before Vietnam.

Schumacher's decision to use unknown actors has paid off: The faces are fresh and innocent as they should be. Each of the 10 or so actors is given at least one big dramatic scene, but the film does not feel theatrical at all. From the very first scene, audience sympathy is with Colin Farrell, who shines as the subversive yet basically decent lad whose cynicism may be the only sane reaction to an insane situation. The entire ensemble is excellent, from Matthew Davis's would-be writer to Shea Whigham's Wilson, whose insecurities and zeal to kill lead to horrific consequences.

Assisted by the inventive lenser Matthew Libatique, Schumacher employs a semi-documentary style, keeping his dynamic camera close to the action, always reflecting reality from the grunts' p.o.v. Pic's overall impact derives in no small measure from helmer's choice to avoid tripod and dolly in favor of handheld 16mm camera.

•

TIGER MAKES OUT, THE

1967, 94 mins, US col

Dir Arthur Hiller ***Prod*** George Justin ***Scr*** Murray Schisgal ***Ph*** Arthur J. Ornitz ***Ed*** Robert C. Jones ***Mus*** Milton "Shorty" Rogers ***Art*** Paul Sylbert

Act Eli Wallach, Anne Jackson, Bob Dishy, John Harkins, Ruth White, Roland Wood (Columbia)

Beware of the one-act play with apparent screen possibilities. *The Tiger Makes Out* was adapted by Murray Schisgal from his 1963 two-character comedy-drama *The Tiger* into a distended, uneven pic.

Filmed in New York, the George Justin production stars Eli Wallach and Ann Jackson, encoring their legit roles. Good performances, production and yeoman directorial effort by Arthur Hiller buoy up interest.

The play concerned the (offstage) kidnapping of Jackson, a suburban housefrau, by frustrated mailman Wallach, after which some genuinely tender dialog brings together the two spirits.

The kidnapping itself is not detailed; on film, however, it is, and, while necessary, the act itself is not a laugh-getter.

•

TIGER SHARK

1932, 78 mins, US b/w

Dir Howard Hawks ***Prod*** [uncredited] ***Scr*** Wells Root ***Ph*** Tony Gaudio ***Ed*** Thomas Pratt ***Mus*** Leo F. Forbstein (dir.) ***Art*** Jack Okey

Act Edward G. Robinson, Richard Arlen, Zita Johann, Leila Bennett, J. Carrol Naish, Vince Barnett (First National)

A strong and exceedingly well-played and directed sea drama [from the story *Tuna* by Houston Branch]. After losing his hand to a tiger shark in a realistic underwater shot, Edward G. Robinson, as Capt. Mike Mascarenhas, replaces the lost member with a steel hook. The shady lady who marries him bears no love, but only appreciation for his kindness. It's to be expected that she should fall for the personable best friend of her husband (Richard Arlen). From friendship, the captain's feelings toward his first mate turn to hatred when the boy and the missus are caught in a clinch.

No human villains in the cast. All the dirty work is assigned to the sharks. When they're not biting off the captain's hand they're chewing up luckless fishermen who fall into the water.

The tuna fishing moments are the big thrills. One big scene shows a haul of countless tunas by hook and line. Sharks enter the picture with each fishing sequence, and disaster to one of the crew always follows.

•

TIGHT LITTLE ISLAND

SEE: WHISKY GALORE!

•

TIGHTROPE
1984, 117 mins, US Ⓥ ⊙ col
Dir Richard Tuggle ***Prod*** Clint Eastwood, Fritz Manes ***Scr*** Richard Tuggle ***Ph*** Bruce Surtees ***Ed*** Joel Cox ***Mus*** Lennie Niehaus ***Art*** Edward Carfagno
Act Clint Eastwood, Genevieve Bujold, Dan Hedaya, Alison Eastwood, Jennifer Beck, Marco St. John (Malpaso/Warner)

Tightrope sees Clint Eastwood comfortably in the role of a big city homicide cop, but also as a vulnerable, hunted man, a deserted husband, father of two daughters, a man whose taste for seamy sex nearly brings him down.

Written and directed by Richard Tuggle, pic trades extensively on the theme of guilt transference from killer to presumed hero which for so long was the special domain of Alfred Hitchcock.

Surface action is highly familiar, as an anonymous killer, stalks prostitutes and massage parlor girls in New Orleans's French Quarter. Eastwood has been accustomed to taking his pleasure with the very sort of women upon whom the murderer is preying.

A fair amount of running time is given over to Eastwood's relationship with his growing daughters (older of whom is played by his real-life offspring, Alison).

It all leads up to a rather predictable assault on the cop's home and daughters, and some sweating and soul-searching on his part.

Overall, however, action is well-handled, as Tuggle demonstrates ample storytelling talent and draws a multitude of nuances from his cast.

●

TILLIE AND GUS
1933, 58 mins, US b/w
Dir Francis Martin ***Prod*** Douglas MacLean ***Scr*** Walter DeLeon, Francis Martin ***Ph*** Ben Reynolds ***Art*** Hans Dreier, Harry Oliver
Act W. C. Fields, Alison Skipworth, Baby LeRoy, Jacqueline Wells, George Barbier, Clarence Wilson (Paramount)

This is an effort to stretch a brief idea to feature length with horseplay and mechanical punch which doesn't quite register. Chief handicap is a lack of spontaneity and swiftness of movement. Basic idea is good, the big time slickers who beat the country amateur, but this rich vein is scarcely uncovered.

W. C. Fields and Alison Skipworth are a married couple who have gone their separate ways but reunite when called to the old home for a presumed legacy. Local bad boy is trying to hog the fortune and oust the young couple from their inheritance. Last thing to be picked up is a ferry franchise, and that's whipped into a race between the old boat and the new contender.

In between it's some of Fields's old vaude gags, frequent references to wet babies and such bits as the $1,000 vase being dropped to catch the one dollar cane. Comedy not helped any by efforts to inject a dramatic story.

●

TILLIE'S PUNCTURED ROMANCE
1914, 70 mins, US Ⓥ ⊙ ⊗ b/w
Dir Mack Sennett ***Scr*** Hampton Del Ruth ***Ph*** Frank D. Williams
Act Marie Dressler, Charles Chaplin, Mabel Nornand, Mack Sennett, Mack Swain, Keystone Kops (Keystone)

Tillie's Punctured Romance came from the title role Marie Dressler played in *Tillie's Nightmare*. She is splendidly supported by the Keystone Company, including Charles Chaplin, Mabel Normand, Mack Sennett, Mack Swain and others. Dressler is the central figure, but Chaplin's camera antics [as a city slicker who tries to steal an inheritance from country girl Dressler] are an essential feature in putting the picture over.

Mack Sennett directs the picture right well. Dressler wears clothes that make her appear ridiculous. Furthermore she makes gestures and distorts her face in all directions, which help all the more. The picture runs a trifle too long, but the hilarious, hip-hurrah comedy finale is worth waiting for.

●

TILL THE CLOUDS ROLL BY
1946, 120 mins, US Ⓥ ⊙ col
Dir Richard Whorf, [George Sidney, Vincente Minnelli] ***Prod*** Arthur Freed ***Scr*** Myles Connolly, Jean Holloway ***Ph*** Harry Stradling, George J. Folsey ***Ed*** Albert Akst ***Mus*** Lennie Hayton (dir.) ***Art*** Cedric Gibbons, Daniel B. Cathcart
Act Robert Walker, Judy Garland, Lucille Bremer, Joan Wells, Van Heflin, Dorothy Patrick (M-G-M)

Why quibble about the story? It's notable that the Jerome Kern saga [from a screen story by Guy Boton, adaptation by George Wells] reminds of the Cole Porter *Night and Day*—both apparently enjoyed a monotonously successful life. No early-life struggles, no frustrations, nothing but an uninterrupted string of Broadway and West End show success. Nearest thing to travail is Kern's contretemps with turn-of-the-century Broadway impresario Charles Frohman, who was apparently a rabid Anglophile—"no good songsmith in America; the only good ones come from Europe."

Of the basic cast, Robert Walker is completely sympathetic as Kern. Van Heflin plays Jim Hessler, the arranger-composer-confidant, whose life story parallels Kern's in a Damon-and-Pythias plot. (Some real-life counterpart may be the veteran arranger, Frank Sadler.)

Picture actually opens with *Show Boat*, a 1927 whammo. There is virtually a tabloid version of that operetta utilized for the opener, a play-within-a-play and the rest of the story is virtually a success-story flashback. [Musical numbers staged and directed by Robert Alton.]

●

TILL THERE WAS YOU
1991, 93 mins, Australia Ⓥ col
Dir John Seale ***Prod*** Jim McElroy ***Scr*** Michael Thomas ***Ph*** Geoffrey Simpson ***Ed*** Jim Bilcock ***Mus*** Graeme Revell ***Art*** George Liddle
Act Mark Harmon, Deborah Unger, Jeroen Krabbe, Shane Briant (Ayer/Five Arrow/AFFC)

By Australian standards, top cinematographer John Seale's first pic as a director is an expensive, high-concept affair that falls between several categories.

The serviceable, if familiar, plot has Mark Harmon playing a New York sax player who wings off to a Pacific island on his brother's invitation. When he arrives he discovers his brother has been killed, and that he's not very welcome on the island.

Although Harmon does his best with his undemanding role, Canadian-born Aussie thesp Deborah Unger is miscast as the sultry wife of the dead brother's friend. Unger is far too down-to-earth for the role.

Furthermore, there's no chemistry between her and Harmon. As her seemingly charming husband, Jeroen Krabbe brings a touch of menace to a conventional character.

Camerawork on little-seen island locations is often spectacular. A plane crash in the jungle is superbly staged, and the local Vanuatans, mostly from Pentecost Island, prove to be natural actors.

●

TILL WE MEET AGAIN
1944, 85 mins, US b/w
Dir Frank Borzage ***Prod*** Frank Borzage ***Scr*** Lenore Coffee ***Ph*** Theodor Sparkuhl ***Ed*** Elmo Veron ***Mus*** David Buttolph ***Art*** Hans Dreier, Robert Usher
Act Ray Milland, Barbara Britton, Walter Slezak, Mona Freeman, Lucile Watson, Vladimir Sokoloff (Paramount)

For all its underground intrigue, Nazi brutality and Machiavellian Gestapo methods, film is a different sort of war romance. For one thing, its heroine is a novitiate nun and Ray Milland is an almost too happily married albeit dashing American aviator, forced down in occupied France.

Sometimes Milland's love-hunger for his wife and child is a bit sticky, but it gets over a wholesome message of the American standard of love and marriage to the young French convent girl. To her it's a new-found litany of love that awakens a new perspective on the mundane world as she accompanies Milland—as his pseudo-wife—in order to aid his escape with valuable secret papers from the French Underground for London.

Barbara Britton, a newcomer, is compelling as the beauteous but unworldly church disciple.

●

'TIL WE MEET AGAIN
1940, 99 mins, US b/w
Dir Edmund Goulding ***Prod*** Hal B. Wallis, David Lewis ***Scr*** Warren Duff, Robert Lord ***Ph*** Tony Gaudio ***Ed*** Ralph Dawson
Act Merle Oberon, George Brent, Pat O'Brien, Geraldine Fitzgerald, Binnie Barnes, Frank McHugh (Warner)

This remake of *One Way Passage* still has plenty of sock left. The WB original, back in 1932, had William Powell and Kay Francis in the top roles, but the present combination, George Brent and Merle Oberon, do an excellent job. Oberon's sincere and eye-filling performance equals that of her predecessor in the role, while Brent comes within at least a shade of Powell's superb portrayal. Frank McHugh repeats his performance as the conman passenger.

Warren Duff's screenplay varies little from the 1932 adaptation of Robert Lord's original by Wilson Mizner and Joseph Jackson. Story opens in Hong Kong with Oberon falling for Brent, a total stranger, in a bar. She meets him again on the ship bound for the United States and chases after him in a manner that is just as implausible as in their original meeting. Brent is being returned to San Quentin to hang for murder, while Oberon is in final stages of cardiac ailment.

Pat O'Brien is considerably superior to Warren Hymer who played the police officer returning the prisoner to the U.S. in the original, although the part is built up somewhat in the present version. Geraldine Fitzgerald, strangely heavy, is an exuberant and sympathetic tourist while Binnie Barnes, with a French accent, is a phony countess who plays for O'Brien in an effort to help Brent escape. Eric Blore is as usual strong as the "branch of the Bank of England" who falls for McHugh's wily ways.

●

TIM BURTON'S THE NIGHTMARE BEFORE CHRISTMAS
SEE: THE NIGHTMARE BEFORE CHRISTMAS

●

TIME AFTER TIME
1980, 112 mins, UK Ⓥ ⊙ ▭ col
Dir Nicholas Meyer ***Prod*** Herb Jaffe ***Scr*** Nicholas Meyer ***Ph*** Paul Lohmann ***Ed*** Donn Cambern ***Mus*** Miklos Rozsa ***Art*** Edward C. Carfagno
Act Malcolm McDowell, David Warner, Mary Steenburgen, Charles Cioffi, Patti D'Arbanville, Corey Feldman (Warner/Orion)

Time After Time is a delightful, entertaining trifle of a film that shows both the possibilities and limitations of taking liberties with literature and history. Nicholas Meyer has deftly juxtaposed Victorian England and contemporary America in a clever story, irresistible due to the competence of its cast.

H. G. Wells and Jack The Ripper abandon London circa 1893 in Wells's famous time machine. Their arrival in 1979 San Francisco is played for all the inevitable anachronisms, with results that are both witty and pointed.

Thanks to Meyer's astute scripting [from a screen story by Karl Alexander and Steve Hayes] and direction, and superb performances by Malcolm McDowell as Wells, David Warner as the mythical killer, and Mary Steenburgen as the woman in between, there's plenty of mileage in *Time*.

●

TIME BANDITS
1981, 110 mins, UK Ⓥ ⊙ col
Dir Terry Gilliam ***Prod*** Terry Gilliam ***Scr*** Michael Palin, Terry Gilliam ***Ph*** Peter Biziou ***Ed*** Julian Doyle ***Mus*** Mike Moran ***Art*** Milly Burns
Act John Cleese, Sean Connery, Shelley Duvall, Ralph Richardson, David Warner, Michael Palin (Handmade)

When you can count the laughs in a comedy on the fingers of one hand, it isn't so funny. *Time Bandits*, is a kind of potted history of man, myth and the eternal clash between good and evil as told in the inimitable idiom of Monty Python.

Not that the basic premise is bad, with an English youngster and a group of dwarfs passing through time holes on assignment by the Maker to patch up the shoddier parts of His creation. What results, unfortunately, is a hybrid neither sufficiently hair-raising or comical.

The plot's grand tour ranges from ancient Greece and other parts to the Titanic to the Fortress of Ultimate Darkness, the latter gothic region presided over by a costume-heavy David Warner as one of nine above-title and mostly cameo parts. Of which the funniest, near pic's conclusion, is the Maker Himself as none other than Ralph Richardson in business suit.

John Cleese as Robin Hood, Ian Holm as Napoleon, Sean Connery as a Greek warrior-ruler with a passion for magic, and Michael Palin as a plummy English upperclass type all acquit well enough in the limited circumstances.

●

TIMECODE
2000, 97 mins, US Ⓥ ⊙ col
Dir Mike Figgis ***Prod*** Mike Figgis, Annie Stewart ***Scr*** Mike Figgis ***Ph*** Patrick Alexander Stewart ***Mus*** Mike Figgis, Anthony Marinelli ***Art*** Charlotte Malmlof
Act Salma Hayek, Jeanne Tripplehorn, Saffron Burrows, Kyle MacLachlan, Stellan Skarsgard, Holly Hunter (Red Mullet/Screen Gems)

He's tried and tried again, but this time Mike Figgis has finally done it: The form *is* the content in *Timecode*, a fascinating, sometimes exhilarating, experiment in which four continuous shots—that's *four separate feature-length takes*—occupy the screen throughout, as an ensemble cast's dialogue-improvised multiple story lines overlap and criss-cross. It puts digital video technology at last to a (relatively) mainstream commercial use that's innovative technically and artistically.

Reasonably enough, given both the possibilities and hair-raising logistical demands inherent in this project, Figgis has chosen to set his creative bungee jump smack in the middle of the Sunset Strip. There, he tracks 20-odd primary characters, all of whom have some direct or indirect relation to the film industry.

Sans the absorbing novelty of its presentation, *Timecode* might well look like the emperor's new (or old) clothes. Yet if the satire feels familiar, and the dramatics often contrived, there's rarely a moment here when something funny, intense or cleverly interconnected, doesn't keep one's synapses firing on overdrive. Perfs are all over the map, making for a delectable goulash of emotional tenors and acting styles.

In a sense, the full *Timecode* experience won't be available until its DVD release, when viewers will be able to focus on one audio track throughout, or create their own, everchangeable mix.

Dialogue was entirely improvised by the cast within a time-specific story outline designed to hit various dramatic marks (particularly the earthquakes) in synch. Pic was shot over two weeks' time in 15 90-minute takes, with the release version consisting of the last takes from each of the four cameras. Handheld camerawork, live sound recording and other tech factors perfectly exploit the equation's precarious immediacy.

•

TIMECOP
1994, 98 mins, US Ⓥ ⊙ col
Dir Peter Hyams ***Prod*** Moshe Diamant, Sam Raimi, Robert Tapert ***Scr*** Mark Verheiden ***Ph*** Peter Hyams ***Ed*** Steven Kemper ***Mus*** Mark Isham ***Art*** Philip Harrison
Act Jean-Claude Van Damme, Mia Sara, Ron Silver, Bruce McGill, Gloria Reuben, Scott Bellis (Largo/Signature/Renaissance/Dark Horse)

Despite a marketable concept and first-rate production values, director Peter Hyams delivers a curiously flat sci-fi comic-book actioner starring the ever limber Jean-Claude Van Damme. Like most time-travel stories, this one must grapple with the usual absurdities and contradictions about changing the past to affect the present.

Van Damme plays Max Walker, a D.C. cop whose wife (Mia Sara) is apparently murdered in an explosion. Ten years later, in 2004, we find Walker functioning as a "timecop," policing those who have gone back in time to strike it rich or influence the course of history. He discovers the real mastermind behind the time-crime wave is the U.S. Senator (Ron Silver) responsible for overseeing the enforcement program—a slick operator seeking to use his ill-gotten gains to finance a run for the presidency.

That crisscrossing, cat-and-mouse chase through time has its moments, but the script by comic creator Mark Verheiden (from a story crafted with exec producer Mike Richardson) has a hard time connecting the strands. Strictly in terms of the action, Hyams also milks the fight scenes too long.

Van Damme acquits himself well, though the more acting he gets to do the more violence his accent inflicts on the English language. Silver proves a glib but not particularly menacing villain through no fault of his own.

•

TIME FOR ACTION
SEE: TIP ON A DEAD JOCKEY

•

TIME LOST AND TIME REMEMBERED
SEE: I WAS HAPPY HERE

•

TIME MACHINE, THE
1960, 103 mins, US Ⓥ ⊙ col
Dir George Pal ***Prod*** George Pal ***Scr*** David Duncan ***Ph*** Paul C. Vogel ***Ed*** George Tomasini ***Mus*** Russell Garcia ***Art*** George W. Davis, William Ferrari
Act Rod Taylor, Alan Young, Yvette Mimieux, Sebastian Cabot, Tom Helmore, Whit Bissell (M-G-M/Galaxy)

In utilizing contemporary knowledge to update H. G. Wells's durable novel, scenarist David Duncan has brought the work into modern focus. The point-of-view springs properly from 1960 rather than from the turn of the century. The social comment of the original has been historically refined to encompass such plausible eventualities as the physical manifestation of atomic war weapons. But the basic spirit of Wells's work has not been lost.

The film's chief flaw is its somewhat palsied pace. Forging its way through vital initial exposition, it perks to a fascinating peak when the Time Traveller (Rod Taylor) plants himself in his machine and begins his enviable tour of time. His "visits" to World Wars I, II, and III, and the way in which the passage of time is depicted within these "local" stops give the picture its most delightful moments.

But things slow down to a walk when Taylor arrives at the year 802,701 and becomes involved generally with a group of tame, antisocial towheads (the Eloi) and specifically with their loveliest and most sociable representative (Yvette Mimieux), with whom he falls in love.

Taylor's performance is a gem of straightforwardness, with just the proper sensitivity and animation. A standout in support is Alan Young, in a gentle, three-ply role. Mimieux is well cast. Innocent vacancy gleams beautifully in her eyes.

1960: Best Special Effects

•

TIME OF THEIR LIVES, THE
1946, 82 mins, US Ⓥ b/w
Dir Charles T. Barton ***Scr*** Val Burton, Walter De Leon, Bradford Ropes ***Ph*** Charles Van Enger ***Ed*** Philip Cahn ***Mus*** Milton Rosen ***Art*** Jack Otterson, Richard Riedel
Act Lou Costello, Bud Abbott, Marjorie Reynolds, Binnie Barnes, Gale Sondergaard (Universal)

This one's a picnic for Abbott and Costello fans, replete with trowelled-on slapstick, corned-up gags and farcical plot.

Shot by mistake as a traitor in the American Revolutionary War and doomed to remain an earthbound ghost until proved innocent, Costello turns up in 1946 still looking for the evidence. In a similar fix, Marjorie Reynolds floats through the film like a Sears-Roebuck model ghost, but Costello can't quite make the smoothie grade. It's good for laughs.

Abbott, who early in the picture plays a 1780 heel, turns up in modern times as a psychiatrist, house-guesting in the mansion Costello and his girlfriend are haunting. Latter wreak their revenge via a series of invisible-man stunts that drive the brain specialist out of his mind. This gimmick is worked to the limit, and beyond.

•

TIME OF YOUR LIFE, THE
1948, 108 mins, US Ⓥ b/w
Dir H. C. Potter ***Prod*** William Cagney ***Scr*** Nathaniel Curtis ***Ph*** James Wong Howe ***Ed*** Walter Hannemann, Truman K. Wood ***Mus*** Carmen Dragon ***Art*** Wiard B. Ihnen
Act James Cagney, William Bendix, Wayne Morris, Jeanne Cagney, Broderick Crawford, Ward Bond (United Artists/William Cagney)

The Time of Your Life is as full of guffaw-type humor and entertainment as the frothiest of comedies. The catch is that it is presented in the unconventional and more-or-less formless pattern of William Saroyan's stage writing.

Saroyan-lovers will find that the play has been tampered with to the minimum extent consistent with transference from one medium to another. The heavy Saroyan philosophy has been partly excised (not so much that the playwright's "I love the common people" theme doesn't remain perfectly clear) and the comedy has been pointed up.

Major switch has been in the ending. After shooting a Johnston-office version of the original finale, it was discovered in sneak previews that it didn't play. The heavy Saroyanism left audiences bewildered. As a result, $300,000 was added to the original $1.7 million budget to retake the closing scenes. The result is a more pat and conventional fadeout, but one that retains much of the beauty of the original.

The difference between *Life* and the standard film is that this one has no story in the accepted sense of the term. It merely introduces, one by one, a series of "characters." It doesn't even delve deeply into what makes them tick, but presents their amusing exterior sides as they spout the Saroyan views on life and living.

•

TIME, THE PLACE AND THE GIRL, THE
1946, 105 mins, US col
Dir David Butler ***Prod*** Alex Gottlieb ***Scr*** Francis Swann, Agnes Christine Johnston, Lynn Starling ***Ph*** William V. Skall, Arthur Edeson ***Ed*** Irene Morra ***Mus*** Arthur Schwartz, Leo Robin ***Art*** Hugh Reticker
Act Dennis Morgan, Jack Carson, Janis Paige, Martha Vickers (Warner)

The Time the Place and the Girl is snappy tom-foolery, tunefully embroidered.

Score contains six numbers by Leo Robin and Arthur Schwartz. All are tuneful. Dennis Morgan, Jack Carson, Janis Paige and Martha Vickers vocal the songs. A standout is Carmen Cavallaro's spot with "Thousand Dreams."

David Butler's direction punches over the comedy, getting the most from bright lines and situations in the script. Plot is thin but neatly put together in the writing to carry through as support for musical sequences. Butler gives it broad treatment and cast responds for laughs. Story line has Morgan and Carson trying to put on a musical show against the opposition of Florence Bates, old-time opera star, and her priggish manager, Donald Woods.

•

TIME TO KILL, A
1996, 150 mins, US Ⓥ ⊙ ▭ col
Dir Joel Schumacher ***Prod*** Arnon Milchan, Michael Nathanson ***Scr*** Akiva Goldsman, ***Ph*** Peter Menzies, Jr. ***Ed*** William Steinkamp ***Mus*** Elliot Goldenthal ***Art*** Larry Fulton
Act Sandra Bullock, Samuel L. Jackson, Matthew McConaughey, Kevin Spacey, Brenda Fricker, Oliver Platt (Warner)

Although it has its share of implausibilities, *A Time to Kill* is generally the most satisfying of the John Grisham screen adaptations to date. An absorbing tale of racial tension as seen through the prism of a highly controversial murder case, this sweaty Southern courtroom drama is well served by a stellar cast. Just as much of a synthetic fabrication as other Grisham yarns, this one emerges as more substantial due to the social fabric.

Blood-boiling opening has two bad ol' boys grabbing a 10-year-old black girl, and beating her within an inch of her life. The girl's father, Carl Lee Hailey (Samuel L. Jackson), guns down the goons as they are being led through the county courthouse. With little going for him other than the moral support of his disbarred and drunken former law professor (Donald Sutherland), secretary (Brenda Fricker) and lawyer buddy (Oliver Platt), young, good-looking Jake Brigance (Matthew McConaughey) takes on the murder case.

The case inspires a revival of the largely dormant Klu Klux Klan in Canton, Mississippi, a movement led by the brother (Kiefer Sutherland) of one of the murdered men. Arriving from left field, both dramatically and politically, is perky rich-girl law student Ellen Roark (Sandra Bullock), who keeps pestering Brigance to let her pitch in with the defense.

McConaughey possesses traditional movie-star good looks and is up to the varied demands of the central role. In the film's most riveting performance, Jackson capitalizes on his role's potent dramatic opportunities. Although she receives top billing, Bullock plays a somewhat peripheral character.

•

TIME TO LOVE AND A TIME TO DIE, A
1958, 133 mins, US Ⓥ ▭ col
Dir Douglas Sirk ***Prod*** Robert Arthur ***Scr*** Orin Jannings ***Ph*** Russell Metty ***Mus*** Miklos Rozsa ***Art*** Alexander Golitzen, Alfred Sweeney
Act John Gavin, Lilo Pulver, Keenan Wynn, Erich Maria Remarque, Thayer David, Jock Mahoney (Universal)

A Time to Love and a Time to Die is less a panorama of the battle horrors of the Second World War, though these are implicit, than a poignant telling of the anguish of being in love while civilian bombings rage, and decency is held hostage to vicious character traits. In unfolding the Erich Maria Remarque novel, producer and director have been long on "heart" and "sentiment" and the result is a bitter-sweet love story.

The story is somewhat slow in development. Orin Jannings opens his screenplay with the hero (John Gavin) on the Russian front under the cloud of defeat in 1944. The wretchedness of modern war, the compassion and pity felt by the better type of German soldier, is established before the boy gets his long-delayed furlough and goes off to his native town, only to find his home is rubble and his parents disappeared. Nearly all the action comprises the experiences of the furloughed soldier: with the townspeople, the Nazis and the Gestapo as counterpoint to his budding romance and hurry-up marriage to the girl (Lilo Pulver) and the denouement comes back at the Russian front.

The film may be remembered more for types than performances. There is a mad air-raid warden (Alexander Engel), a Jew hiding in a Catholic church tower (Charles Regnier) and a Teutonic hellion (Dorothea Wieck).

1958: NOMINATION: Best Sound

•

TINA
WHAT'S LOVE GOT TO DO WITH IT
SEE: WHAT'S LOVE GOT TO DO WITH IT

•

TIN CUP
1996, 93 mins, US Ⓥ ⊙ ▭ col
Dir Ron Shelton ***Prod*** Gary Foster, Ron Shelton ***Scr*** John Norville, Ron Shelton ***Ph*** Russell Boyd ***Ed*** Paul Seydor, Kimberly Ray ***Mus*** William Ross ***Art*** James Bissell
Act Kevin Costner, Rene Russo, Cheech Marin, Linda Hart, Don Johnson, Dennis Burkley (Regency/Warner)

It's taken a long time for anyone to dare use golf as the focus of a major Hollywood movie, but Ron Shelton has managed to make the sight of grown men hitting a little ball around kind of fun in *Tin Cup*. Amiable and constantly amusing rather than uproarious, this mangy tale of a ne'er-do-well's fitful assault on personal and professional respectability benefits greatly from Kevin Costner's ingratiatingly comic star turn, his most appealing work in years.

With more armadillos than customers at his dilapidated desert range outside of Salome, Texas, Rod McAvoy (Costner) swigs beers with the boys and hits a bucket or two when he feels like it. But life is passing him by when Dr. Molly Griswold (Rene Russo) turns up for a lesson. What this foxy lady is doing in these godforsaken parts is never really explained.

When Roy's old college partner, David Simms (a credible Don Johnson), now a top pro, comes around to ask him to caddy for him in a celebrity tourney, Roy accepts the humiliating job. When he learns that Molly happens to be David's girlfriend, Roy uses this as added inspiration to make it to the U.S. Open, where nearly the final hour of the film takes place.

Playing an easy-to-identify-with Everyman with all too much unrealized potential, Costner gives a movie star performance in the best sense, aware of what he's good at and ready to give it in smartly judged doses. The teasing and flirting between Costner and Russo is appealing enough, but the quirks of her neurotic psychologist quickly grow a bit wearisome.

Pic runs a bit long for what it is, and appears rather untidy directorally, with mismatched shots and less than totally coherent coverage at times.

•

TIN DRUM, THE

SEE: DIE BLECHTROMMEL

•

TIN MEN

1987, 112 mins, US Ⓥ ⦿ col

Dir Barry Levinson ***Prod*** Mark Johnson ***Scr*** Barry Levinson ***Ph*** Peter Sova ***Ed*** Stu Linder ***Mus*** David Steele, Andy Cox ***Art*** Peter Jamison

Act Richard Dreyfuss, Danny DeVito, Barbara Hershey, John Mahoney, Jackie Gayle, Stanley Brock (Touchstone)

The improbable tale of a pair of feuding aluminum siding salesmen, *Tin Men* winds up as bountiful comedy material in the skillful hands of writer-director Barry Levinson.

Film is packed with laughs, thanks to taut scripting and superb character depictions by Richard Dreyfuss, Danny DeVito and a fascinating troupe of sidekicks. These fast-buck hustlers collectively fashion a portrait of superficial greed so pathetic it soars to a level of black humor.

Central storyline finds Dreyfuss and DeVito tangling from the start after an accident damages both of their Cadillacs. Conflict between the two strangers—who don't find out until later they're both tin men—escalates to the point where Dreyfuss seeks to get even by making DeVito's unhappy wife (Barbara Hershey) into bed.

While each of the tin men is revealed as a compelling, off-center type in his own right, the one played by Jackie Gayle especially shines.

•

TIN PAN ALLEY

1940, 94 mins, US b/w

Dir Walter Lang ***Prod*** Kenneth Macgowan (assoc.) ***Scr*** Robert Ellis, Helen Logan ***Ph*** Leon Shamroy ***Ed*** Walter Thompson ***Mus*** Alfred Newman (dir.) ***Art*** Richard Day, Joseph C. Wright

Act Alice Faye, Betty Grable, Jack Oakie, John Payne, Allen Jenkins, Esther Ralston (20th Century-Fox)

Tyrone Power and Don Ameche were originally set for the top honors with Alice Faye, but casting assignments necessitated shifts of Jack Oakie and John Payne into the Power-Ameche slots, and addition of Betty Grable. Hays Office also stepped in and required extended cutting of the harem number, nixing what was claimed a too vivid display of showgirls' torsos. Particularly efficient job of cutting in this sequence retains all of the entertainment, and speeds things up in what might have developed into a slowdown spot.

Story [by Pamela Harris] carries background of the noisy but colorful stretch of 46th Street and 8th Avenue, headquartering successful and shoestring song publishers in 1915. Oakie is a typical breezy ex-vaudevillian, teamed with tunesmith-ambitious Payne in a publishing venture. The impecunious pair hit the jackpot with a pop tune, and swing into swank offices, with main song-plugging end handled by Faye, half of a sister act who warms up to Payne. But there's the inevitable romantic split. Faye hops to London to become a music hall sensation with Grable.

In addition to infectious and solid entertainment factors, *Tin Pan Alley* focuses attention on the Edgar Leslie-Archie Gottler hit of 1917, "America I Love You." Other old favorites brought back for renewed interest include "Goodbye Broadway, Hello France," "K-K-Katy," "Moonlight Bay," "Honeysuckle Rose" and "Shiek of Araby." New tune "You Say the Sweetest Things (Baby)," by Mack Gordon and Harry Warren, is enhanced by extended production montage.

Oakie provides a standout characterization as the free-and-easy vaudevillian, generating plenty of laughs with his mugging lines and situations that highlight his abilities. Faye is highlighted as the senior member of the sister act, and carries most of the singing burden to topmost effect. Grable displays her shapeliness in a series of abbreviated and eyeful costumes, although the camera in other respects is sometimes none too flattering; and Payne catches attention with his serious-minded portrayal of the ambitious song publisher and suitor in the romantic sequences.

1940: Best Score

•

TIN STAR, THE

1957, 92 mins, US Ⓥ b/w

Dir Anthony Mann ***Prod*** William Perlberg, George Seaton ***Scr*** Dudley Nichols ***Ph*** Loyal Griggs ***Ed*** Alma Macrorie ***Mus*** Elmer Bernstein ***Art*** Hal Pereira, J. MacMillan Johnson

Act Henry Fonda, Anthony Perkins, Betsy Palmer, Michael Ray, Neville Brand, John McIntire (Perlsea/Paramount)

The Tin Star is a quality western that unfolds interestingly under the smooth direction of Anthony Mann, who draws top performances from cast. Screenplay [from a story by Barney Slater and Joel Kane] centers around Anthony Perkins's insistence upon keeping his sheriff's badge despite the pleading of his sweetheart to abandon hazards of the job, and Henry Fonda, a former lawman turned human bounty hunter, reluctantly teaching him the tricks of the trade.

Fonda gives his character telling authority as he waits in a small western town for a reward check, then stays on to help the over-anxious young sheriff. Perkins asserts himself forcibly, his nemesis being Neville Brand, capable as a gun-handy bully who nearly forces him to back down in his authority.

1957: NOMINATION: Best Original Story & Screenplay

•

TIP ON A DEAD JOCKEY

(UK: TIME FOR ACTION)

1957, 98 mins, US ▭ b/w

Dir Richard Thorpe ***Prod*** Edwin H. Knopf ***Scr*** Charles Lederer ***Ph*** George J. Folsey ***Ed*** Ben Lewis ***Mus*** Miklos Rozsa ***Art*** William A. Horning, Hans Peters

Act Robert Taylor, Dorothy Malone, Gia Scala, Martin Gabel, Marcel Dalio, Jack Lord (M-G-M)

Once this *Jockey* spurs up momentum, film shapes as a solid, satisfactory action picture. However, plots dealing with war-weary pilots who have lost their nerve have an overfamiliar ring and smart, updated dialog by Charles Lederer, in adapting Irwin Shaw's *New Yorker* tale, doesn't entirely dispel the familiar.

In brittle, cosmopolitan expatriate society of Madrid, Robert Taylor is an ex-pilot, afraid of emotional entanglements because his war job was sending pilots to their deaths. He's now eking out a precarious existence on the fringes of Spain's precarious economy. Offbeat title reflects this, when he loses his entire bankroll on a horse-race in which his jockey is killed in a spill.

Dorothy Malone is his wife, fighting to regain his love after he requests a divorce. To help raise coin for war buddy Jack Lord, and Lord's lovely Spanish wife (Gia Scala) Taylor undertakes a currency-smuggling caper proposed by sinister Martin Gabel. Here, film picks up tempo, especially in chase sequences involving various Mediterranean police authorities.

•

TIREZ SUR LE PIANISTE

(SHOOT THE PIANO PLAYER; SHOOT THE PIANIST)

1960, 80 mins, France Ⓥ ⦿ ▭ b/w

Dir Francois Truffaut ***Scr*** Francois Truffaut, Marcel Moussy ***Ph*** Raoul Coutard ***Ed*** Claudine Bouche ***Mus*** Jean Constantin ***Art*** Jacques Mely

Act Charles Aznavour, Nicole Berger, Marie Dubois, Michele Mercier, Albert Remy, Claude Mansard (Pleiade)

Francois Truffaut's second film [from the novel *Down There* by David Goodis] is done with the same freewheeling, inventive quality as his *400 Blows*. But with adult heroes, the plot is less clear and has a tendency to skirt its theme. Story line, too, goes off in too many directions and moods.

Charlie (Charles Aznavour) is a pianist in a little bar. The waitress, who loves him, reveals she knows he was once a noted concert pianist before his inability to forgive his wife, who had had an affair with his sleazy impresario. He is content to play in the bar until his brother brings in two gangsters whom he has doublecrossed.

The gangsters take out after Charlie and eventually slay the waitress. Charlie also inadvertently kills his boss in self-defense. He goes back to his piano and a new serving girl after it is all over.

Truffaut leaves too much that is not clear as he concentrates on individual scenes. Using a CinemaScope-like process, Dyaliscope, he still manages to give this a terse quality in keeping with the hero's own prison he has created within himself. But the meandering script only intermittently makes its point. Aznavour is excellent as the pianist.

•

TITANIC

1953, 97 mins, US b/w

Dir Jean Negulesco ***Prod*** Charles Brackett ***Scr*** Charles Brackett, Walter Reisch, Richard Breen ***Ph*** Joe MacDonald ***Ed*** Louis Loeffler ***Mus*** Sol Kaplan ***Art*** Lyle R. Wheeler, Maurice Ransford

Act Clifton Webb, Barbara Stanwyck, Robert Wagner, Audrey Dalton, Thelma Ritter, Richard Basehart (20th Century-Fox)

The sinking of HMS *Titanic* in 1912 provides a factual basis for this screen drama reenacting the tragic voyage. Story line is built around fictional characters aboard the supposedly unsinkable British luxury liner when it started its maiden voyage from Southampton to N.Y. on April 11, 1912.

During the first half the film is inclined to dawdle and talk, but by the time the initial 45 or 50 minutes are out of the way, the impending disaster begins to take a firm grip on the imagination and builds a compelling expectancy.

Jean Negulesco's direction and the script really shine after the ship's bottom is opened by a jagged iceberg spur, bringing out the drama that lies in the confusion of shipwreck and passengers' reaction to certain doom. The records show that of the 2,229 persons aboard, only 712 escaped before the ship plunged to the bottom of the North Atlantic at 2:30 A.M., April 15, 1912.

Barbara Stanwyck and Clifton Webb do well by the principal roles in the fictional story. She is a wife trying to take her two children (Audrey Dalton and Harper Carter) away from the spoiling influence of a husband interested only in a superficial society life. A shipboard romance between Robert Wagner, a student returning to the States, and Dalton offer some pleasant, touching moments. Brian Aherne is excellent as the ship's captain. Richard Basehart, a de-frocked priest addicted to the bottle, makes his few moments stand out.

1953: Best Story & Screenplay.

NOMINATION: Best B&W Art Direction

•

TITANIC

1997, 194 mins, US Ⓥ ⦿ ▭ col

Dir James Cameron ***Prod*** James Cameron, Jon Landau ***Scr*** James Cameron ***Ph*** Russell Carpenter ***Ed*** Conrad Buff, James Cameron, Richard A. Harris ***Mus*** James Horner ***Art*** Peter Lamont

Act Leonardo DiCaprio, Kate Winslet, Billy Zane, Kathy Bates, Frances Fisher, Gloria Stuart (Lightstorm/Paramount/20th Century-Fox)

This *Titanic* arrives at its destination. A spectacular demonstration of what modern technology can contribute to dramatic storytelling, James Cameron's $200 million-plus romantic epic, the biggest roll of the dice in film history, will send viewers in search of synonyms for the title to describe the film's size and scope. The dynamic of the central love story is as effective as it is corny.

Capitalizing on the 1985 discovery of the *Titanic*'s remains 2+ miles beneath the surface, Cameron frames the period drama with contemporary action in which American explorer/opportunist Brock Lovett (Bill Paxton) turns up an intriguing drawing of a young nude woman wearing a fabulous necklace and dated April 14, 1912. This discovery comes to the attention of a 102-year-old woman, Rose (Gloria Stuart, a leading lady of the early sound era), the woman in the portrait, who tells her story as it happened 84 years before.

Cameron's camera swoops up, down and around, taking in the masses from all classes crowding on board, but takes an immediate interest in two people: Rose DeWitt Bukater (Kate Winslet), a haughty society girl returning to Philadelphia to marry her rich snob fiancé, Cal Hockley (Billy Zane), and penniless, devil-may-care American Jack Dawson (Leonardo DiCaprio).

As soon as they are under way, Rose does everything she can to rebel against her fiancé and class-obsessed mother (Frances Fisher). Finally, she is rescued from jumping overboard by none other than Jack. And so it goes with their schematic romance.

The *Titanic* hits the iceberg 100 minutes into the film, and the next 80 minutes represent uninterrupted excitement and spectacle. Even at this point, however, Cameron piles on even more complications for Jack and Rose, as the latter must discover where her vengeful fiancé has had him locked up. The film misses a suspenseful beat by largely ignoring the presence of other boats in the vicinity and why they never made it to the *Titanic*.

The ship's final plunge is utterly stunning and effectively places the viewer in the jaws of death. The integration of digital special effects into the live filming is seamless.

DiCaprio and Winslet deliver all and more of what might have been expected of them. Others, however, are stuck with stock characterizations.

Hollywood first gave the *Titanic* story a go in 1953 in Fox's *Titanic*, with the British *A Night to Remember* following to general acclaim in 1958.

1997: Best Picture, Director, Cinematography, Editing, Original Dramatic Score, Original Song ("My Heart Will Go On"), Art Direction, Costume Design (Deborah L. Scott), Sound, Sound Effects Editing, Visual Effects

NOMINATIONS: Best Actress (Kate Winslet), Supp. Actress (Gloria Stuart), Makeup

•

TITFIELD THUNDERBOLT, THE

1953, 84 mins, UK Ⓥ col

Dir Charles Crichton ***Prod*** Michael Truman ***Scr*** T.E.B. Clarke ***Ph*** Douglas Slocombe ***Ed*** Seth Holt ***Mus*** Georges Auric ***Art*** C. P. Norman

Act Stanley Holloway, George Relph, Naunton Wayne, John Gregson, Godfrey Tearle, Hugh Griffith (Ealing)

Titfield is a small English village which gets worked up when the government decides to close the unprofitable branch railway line. The vicar and the squire are both railway enthusiasts and are heartbroken at the news. The only ones cheered by the decision are the partners of a transport company who can see big profits by organizing a bus service. The railway enthusiasts, however, persuade the village tippler to provide the cash by telling him he will be able to start drinking far earlier if they install a buffet car on the train.

The *Thunderbolt* is the railway engine involved in the story. Once the basic situation is accepted, the entire yarn concentrates on the feuding between the rival factions with the opposition stopping at nothing to block the train service.

Stanley Holloway gives a polished performance as the village soak. George Relph does a fine job as the vicar, Naunton Wayne's contribution as the town clerk is in typical vein while John Gregson does nicely as the earnest squire. A gem from Godfrey Tearle as the bishop and a powerful performance by Hugh Griffith are among the strong characterizations.

•

TITUS

1999, 162 mins, Italy/Japan/US Ⓥ ⊙ ▭ col

Dir Julie Taymor ***Prod*** Jody Patton, Conchita Airoldi, Julie Taymor ***Scr*** Julie Taymor ***Ph*** Luciano Tovoli ***Ed*** Francoise Bonnot ***Mus*** Elliot Goldenthal ***Art*** Dante Ferretti

Act Anthony Hopkins, Jessica Lange, Alan Cumming, Colm Feore, James Frain, Laura Fraser (Urania/NDF/Clear Blue Sky/Fox Searchlight)

Gutsily grappling with one of Shakespeare's least performed and most gruesomely melodramatic plays, the lauded director of Broadway's *The Lion King* makes this wild tale of a savage cycle of revenge in imperial Rome accesible and exceedingly vivd, distinguished by some outstanding thesping and an arresting stylistic approach that successfully mixes ancient [c. 400 A.D.] '30s fascist and modern motifs.

The great General Titus Andronicus (Anthony Hopkins) has spent years in the north fighting the Goths and has triumphantly returned with their beautiful Queen, Tamora (Jessica Lange). Titus sets the bloody ball rolling by selecting Tamora's eldest son for sacrifice. The enraged Tamora vows revenge, and she is soon afforded the opportunity when she becomes the wife of Rome's new emperor, the shifty Saturninus (Alan Cumming), first seen riding through the streets of Rome in a flashy white T-Bird.

Aaron (Harry Lennix), a Moor who is the queen's secret lover, engineers the murder of Saturninus' brother, Bassianus (James Frain). He then turns the latter's wife, Lavinia (Laura Fraser), Titus' only daughter, over to Tamora's punk sons Chiron and Demetrius (Jonathan Rhys Meyers, Matthew Rhys), who rape her. The aging general's personal revenge against Tamora is in a word, delicious.

Dante Ferretti's sensational production design and Milena Canonero's madly creative costume design mix with the Italian settings (including parts of Hadrian's villa and Mussolini's fascist government center) and some Croatian locations to give the film a strikingly harsh look.

Along with Hopkins, the standout thesp is Lennix. Lange, bedecked in gold braids, makeup, armor and tattoos, enthusiastically enters into the spirit of the piece, while Cumming is the picture of a depraved emperor.

1999: NOMINATION: Best Costume Design

•

T-MEN

1947, 91 mins, US Ⓥ ⊙ b/w

Dir Anthony Mann ***Prod*** Aubrey Schenck ***Scr*** John C. Higgins ***Ph*** John Alton ***Ed*** Alfred De Gaetano, Fred Allen ***Mus*** Paul Sawtell ***Art*** Edward C. Jewell

Act Dennis O'Keefe, Mary Meade, Charles McGraw, Alfred Ryder, Wally Ford, June Lockhart (Reliance/Small)

Producer Edward Small has taken a closed case out of the Treasury Dept. files, reenacted it in documentary fashion, and the result is *T-Men*—an entertaining action film. *March-of-Time* technique in the early reels flavors the footage with pungent realism that builds up to a suspenseful finish at the final fadeout.

Location scenes in Detroit, Los Angeles and several of its beach suburbs, may have cost a little more but the effect they achieve in verity can't be denied.

Preceded by a brief foreword delivered by a Treasury official, plot [suggested by a story by Virginia Kellogg] unfolds at a slow pace in its early stages. Later, however, it's obvious why the opening scenes were so carefully and meticulously outlined. Solution of every crime depends upon the most minute clues. When assembled in the proper sequence there's a crashing denouement. And so it is with *T-Men*. The final reel is a corker.

Dennis O'Keefe's characterization of the Treasury agent is finely drawn. He's almost Jimmy Cagneyish at times. Cast as his partner is Alfred Ryder. They're undercover agents assigned to break the "Shanghai Paper Case." Masquerading as mobsters they join a ring of liquor cutters in Detroit who are known to be using phony revenue stamps.

1947: NOMINATION: Best Sound

•

TOAST OF NEW YORK, THE

1937, 93 mins, US Ⓥ ⊙ b/w

Dir Rowland V. Lee ***Prod*** Edward Small ***Scr*** Dudley Nichols, John Twist, Joel Sayre ***Ph*** Peverell Marley ***Ed*** George Hively, Samuel Beetley ***Mus*** Nathaniel Shilkret (dir.) ***Art*** Van Nest Polglase, Caroll Clark

Act Edward Arnold, Cary Grant, Frances Farmer, Jack Oakie, Donald Meek, Clarence Colb (RKO)

Here is the life of Jim Fisk, Wall Street operator of the 1880s, told in ragtime. It's absurd biography but good entertainment despite its inanities, extravagances and exaggerations.

With such material from which to weave a screenplay, drawing also from recent bestsellers, *Robber Barons* [by Matthew Josephson] and *Book of Daniel Drew* [by Bouck White], the writers have fashioned a broad burlesque. Edward Arnold takes the principal role of Fisk, and other leaders in the cast are Frances Farmer, as his actress-protegee Josie Mansfield; Cary Grant and Jack Oakie, as his business partners; Donald Meek, as Daniel Drew; and Clarence Kolb, as the senior Cornelius Vanderbilt, who is portrayed as the friend of the oppressed and Fisk's nemesis.

Fisk and his stooges, Boyd and Luke, are introduced as medicine show fakers in the South just before the start of the Civil War. When hostilities commence, the trio engage in unlawful smuggling of raw cotton across the frontier for New England mills. They make a fortune, which is soon lost and won again in the purchase and sale of steamships. Thereafter, on the floor of the New York stock exchange, Fisk devises various schemes which culminate in a struggle with Vanderbilt for control of the Erie railroad.

Arnold plays Fisk in an expansive, lighthearted sort of way. Jack Oakie is in there strictly for laughs and gets plenty. Farmer conveys innocence as the love interest, having very little to do.

•

TOBACCO ROAD

1941, 91 mins, US b/w

Dir John Ford ***Prod*** Darryl F. Zanuck ***Scr*** Nunnally Johnson ***Ph*** Arthur Miller ***Ed*** Barbara McLean ***Mus*** David Buttolph ***Art*** Richard Day, James Basevi

Act Charley Grapewin, Marjorie Rambeau, Gene Tierney, William Tracy, Elizabeth Patterson, Dana Andrews (20th Century-Fox)

Tobacco Road as a motion picture falls far short of its promises. The sensational pulling elements of the 1933 play by Jack Kirkland from Erskine Caldwell's saga—the dialog and the low-life manners of its people—have been deleted, altered or attenuated to the point of dullness. What remains of the story is a back-in-the-hills comedy of shiftless folk.

Tobacco Road emerges with a trite comedy theme about the dubious efforts, chiefly larcenous, by which old Jeeter hopes, through act of Providence or dishonest opportunity, to raise $100 for the annual rent of the old farm.

For all of its dehydration *Tobacco Road* is told with a canny camera. Ford is more intent on story telling than in his recent productions. Chief load of the acting falls on Charley Grapewin, whose Jeeter is a fine characterization within the revised limitations. He plays the old fellow for comedy and sympathy, revealing also a lazy shrewdness. Elizabeth Patterson is Ma Ada, and brings out the sullen hopelessness of the role.

•

TO BEGIN AGAIN

SEE: VOLVER A EMPEZAR

•

TO BE OR NOT TO BE

1942, 99 mins, US Ⓥ b/w

Dir Ernst Lubitsch ***Prod*** Ernst Lubitsch ***Scr*** Edwin Justus Mayer ***Ph*** Rudolph Mate ***Ed*** Dorothy Spencer ***Mus*** Werner R. Heymann ***Art*** Vincent Korda

Act Carole Lombard, Jack Benny, Robert Stack, Felix Bressart, Lionel Atwill, Stanley Ridges (Korda)

To Be or Not to Be, co-starring Carole Lombard and Jack Benny, under expert guidance of Ernst Lubitsch, is absorbing drama with farcical trimmings. It's an acting triumph for Lombard, who delivers an effortless and highly effective performance that provides memorable finale to her brilliant screen career.

To Be is typically Lubitsch in dramatic setup and satirical by-play. He's responsible for the producer-director and original writer chores [with Melchior Lengyel], dovetailing all into a solid piece of entertainment. Story recounts the adventures of a legit stock company in Warsaw, before and during the Nazi invasion, from August 1939 to December 1941. Lombard is the femme lead, with husband Jack Benny a hammy matinee idol with penchant for playing *Hamlet*.

Lubitsch's guidance provides a tense dramatic pace with events developed deftly and logically throughout. The farcical episodes display Lubitsch in best form.

1942: NOMINATION: Best Scoring of a Dramatic Picture

•

TO BE OR NOT TO BE

1983, 108 mins, US Ⓥ ⊙ col

Dir Alan Johnson ***Prod*** Mel Brooks ***Scr*** Thomas Meehan, Ronny Graham ***Ph*** Gerald Hirschfeld ***Ed*** Alan Balsam ***Mus*** John Morris ***Art*** Terence Marsh

Act Mel Brooks, Anne Bancroft, Tim Matheson, Charles Durning, Jose Ferrer, George Gaynes (Brooksfilms)

With the solid farcical underpinning of Ernst Lubitsch's 1942 *To Be or Not to Be*, Mel Brooks's glossy remake of the original Carole Lombard-Jack Benny starrer is very funny stuff indeed.

Maintaining some of the dramatic core of the original, but played mostly for Brooks-style laughs, the convoluted tale of a Warsaw theatrical troupe that winds up saving the Polish underground during the Nazi occupation does have some potential hurdles to clear. Cute Nazis and roly-poly Gestapo officers hardly have universal lure.

Brooks sustains, with varying success, a full-fledged role as Frederick Bronski, vainglorious head of a tawdry theatrical company whose shows run the spectrum from cheap vaudeville turns to *Highlights from Hamlet*. Mainstay of the film is a superbly sustained comic performance by Anne Bancroft, as Bronski's wife, in the real-life Brooks couple's first tandem co-starring acting job.

Charles Durning is a standout as the buffoonish Gestapo topper and Bancroft's pseudo-seduction of him, and Nazi hireling Jose Ferrer, are among the pic's highpoints. Bancroft's sustained delights are not matched by Brooks, who seems to be trying too hard.

1983: NOMINATION: Best Supp. Actor (Charles Durning)

•

TOBRUK

1967, 107 mins, US Ⓥ ▭ col

Dir Arthur Hiller ***Prod*** Gene Corman ***Scr*** Leo V. Gordon ***Ph*** Russell Harlan ***Ed*** Robert C. Jones ***Mus*** Bronislau Kaper ***Art*** Alexander Golitzen, Henry Bumstead

Act Rock Hudson, George Peppard, Nigel Green, Guy Stockwell, Jack Watson, Norman Rossington (Gibraltar/Universal)

Tobruk is a colorful, hard-hitting World War II melodrama with plenty of guts and suspense to hold the action buff. Rock Hudson heads the four-name star roster but actually comes out third best to George Peppard and Nigel Green in interesting characterizations.

Screenplay has a serviceable plot twist as it projects the protagonists on a suicidal mission in the North African war of 1942. Daring plan calls for a British column of 90, composed of commandos and German-born Jews who have come over to the Allies, to form a special attack unit to cross the Libyan Desert to Tobruk, Mediterranean seaport in the hands of 50,000 German and Italian troops. Once there, they are to hold its key fortified positions pending arrival of a British naval force, and blow up the gigantic German fuel bunkers upon which Rommel depends for his push to the Suez canal.

Arthur Hiller's realistic direction makes the most of the premise, both in the eight-day desert trek and approach and invasion of Tobruk.

1967: NOMINATION: Best Sound Effects

•

TO CATCH A THIEF

1955, 103 mins, US Ⓥ ⦿ col

Dir Alfred Hitchcock ***Prod*** Alfred Hitchcock ***Scr*** John Michael Hayes ***Ph*** Robert Burks ***Ed*** George Tomasini ***Mus*** Lyn Murray ***Art*** Hal Pereira, Joseph MacMillan Johnson

Act Cary Grant, Grace Kelly, Jessie Royce Landis, John Williams, Charles Vanel, Brigitte Auber (Paramount)

Cary Grant is a reformed jewel thief, once known as "The Cat," but now living quietly in a Cannes hilltop villa. When burglaries occur that seem to bear his old trademark, he has to catch the thief to prove his innocence, a chore in which he is assisted by Grace Kelly, rich American girl, her mother, Jessie Royce Landis, and insurance agent John Williams. While a suspense thread is present, director Alfred Hitchcock doesn't emphasize it, letting the yarn play lightly for comedy more than thrills.

Grant gives his role his assured style of acting, meaning the dialog and situations benefit. Kelly, too, dresses up the sequences in more ways than one.

Support from Landis and Williams is firstrate, both being major assets to the entertainment in their way with a line or a look.

1955: Best Color Cinematography

NOMINATIONS: Best Color Costume Design, Color Art Direction

•

TO DIE FOR

1995, 103 mins, US Ⓥ ⦿ col

Dir Gus Van Sant ***Prod*** Laura Ziskin ***Scr*** Buck Henry ***Ph*** Eric Alan Edwards ***Ed*** Curtiss Clayton ***Mus*** Danny Elfman ***Art*** Missy Stewart

Act Nicole Kidman, Matt Dillon, Joaquin Phoenix, Casey Affleck, Illeana Douglas, Alison Folland (Rank/Columbia)

A quirky comic study of the criminals-as-celebrities syndrome and a very individualized look at the Andy Warhol 15-minutes-of-fame phenomenon, Gus Van Sant's *To Die For* delivers continuous pinpricks of irreverent humor and subversive cultural commentary.

Although this is Van Sant's first film for a major studio, as well as his initial outing with a script by a major screenwriter (other than himself), the picture [based on the book by Joyce Maynard] fully retains the highly idiosyncratic, charmingly ragged feel of his previous, lower-budget productions.

Presented in faux-docu style, pic is narrated straight-to-camera by multiple parties acquainted with the sordid murder of Larry Maretto (Matt Dillon), the working-class husband of glamorous Suzanne Stone (Nicole Kidman) who, it is clear from the outset, has been charged with the crime.

Tending bar in his family Italian restaurant, Larry Maretto is dumbstruck by the awesome blond beauty of Suzanne. The cutest boy in town, he marries her despite the disapproval of his spunky sister Janice (Illeana Douglas), who sees through this China doll from the outset.

Suzanne is a modern monster, a big-timer dabbling with small-timers, a woman who believes that something is important only if it's seen on the tube. It's a tough part to play, but Kidman rises to the occasion, displaying great facility at conveying a winning personality, seductiveness, sincerity and utter heartlessness. Van Sant's mixed-media roughhewn style is inelegant but full of texture. Film was shot in Canada.

•

TO DIE IN MADRID

SEE: MOURIR A MADRID

•

TODO SOBRE MI MADRE (ALL ABOUT MY MOTHER)

1999, 99 mins, Spain/France Ⓥ ⦿ col

Dir Pedro Almodóvar ***Prod*** Agustin Almodóvar ***Scr*** Pedro Almodóvar ***Ph*** Affonso Beato ***Ed*** José Salcedo ***Mus*** Alberto Iglesias ***Art*** Antxón Gómez

Act Cecilia Roth, Eloy Azorín, Marisa Paredes, Penélope Cruz, Candela Peña, Antonia San Juan (El Deseo/Renn/France 2)

Women on the edge of nervous breakdowns are at the heart of Pedro Almodóvar's 13th outing, an emotionally satisfying and brilliantly played take on the ups and (mostly) downs of a group of less-than-typical female friends. The energetic kitsch of his early work has largely given way to thought-provoking melodrama (dubbed "Almodrama" by local crits) and a profound empathy with offbeat characters who were once little more than vehicles for comedy.

Almodóvar vet Cecilia Roth plays Manuela, a single mother in her late 30s who raised Esteban (Eloy Azorín), a Truman Capote fan and would-be novelist. After a theater visit, he runs into the street to get the autograph of actress Huma Rojo (Marisa Paredes) and is killed by a passing car.

Wanting to get back in touch with Esteban's father (Toni Canto)—who, in the interim, has become a transvestite called Lola, La Pionera—Manuela returns to Barcelona. When she goes in search of work, she meets Huma, who's playing Blanche in *A Streetcar Named Desire*; Huma's junkie g.f., Nina (Candela Pena); innocent do-gooder nun Sister Rosa (Penelope Cruz); and her hysterical mother (Rosa Maria Sarda). All the women have some emotional burden to bear.

The emotional tone is predominantly dark and confrontational, with death, pain and disease just around the corner. But thanks to a sweetly paced and genuinely witty script, pic doesn't become depressing. Roth binds it all together with a nice perf as a woman with powerful maternal instincts locked into a struggle against grief.

1999: Best Foreign Language Film

•

TO EACH HIS OWN

1946, 122 mins, US b/w

Dir Mitchell Leisen ***Prod*** Charles Brackett ***Scr*** Charles Brackett, Jacques Thery ***Ph*** Daniel L. Fapp ***Ed*** Alma Macrorie ***Mus*** Victor Young ***Art*** Hans Dreier, Roland Anderson

Act Olivia de Havilland, Mary Anderson, Roland Culver, John Lund, Philip Terry, Griff Barnett (Paramount)

Charles Brackett, who wrote and produced, injected a human quality in the script, and Mitchell Leisen makes full use of it in his direction. Start and finish of story are laid against a wartime London background, but flashes back to World War I and a small-town locale. It depicts the love and sacrifices of an unwed mother for her son, born out of a one-night romance with a war hero in 1918. It carries her through the years to London where, the relationship still unacknowledged, she waits to catch a brief glimpse of the young man as he comes to town on leave.

Artistry of Olivia de Havilland as the mother is superb. From the eager young girl whose first romance ends when her hero is killed before marriage, through to the cold, brusque business woman, her performance doesn't miss a beat.

•

TOGETHER AGAIN

1944, 93 mins, US b/w

Dir Charles Vidor ***Prod*** Virginia Van Upp ***Scr*** Virginia Van Upp, F. Hugh Herbert ***Ph*** Joseph Walker ***Ed*** Otto Meyer ***Mus*** Werner Heymann ***Art*** Stephen Goosson, Van Nest Polglase

Act Irene Dunne, Charles Boyer, Charles Coburn, Mona Freeman, Elizabeth Patterson (Columbia)

Plot is a light affair, displaying Irene Dunne as the widow of the former mayor of a small town in Vermont, who carries the elective office on her shoulders as a family obligation rather than from choice. She goes to New York to hire a sculptor to make a statue of her late husband for the town square, hires Charles Boyer, is mistaken for a striptease artist in a nightclub while at dinner, and fires the sculptor. He shows up in town later to do the job, and carry his romantic pitches to the mayoress.

Story, developed in broad farcical vein, romps along at a good clip and—although at times the script reaches pretty far to generate laughs—it's so generally crazy-quilt that the overall effect is far on the credit side in entertainment values. Dunne and Boyer competently team in the top spots—she as the pursued and he as the pursuer in the love match. Charles Coburn clicks for prominent attention with his constant conniving and manipulations to develop the romance.

•

TO HAVE AND HAVE NOT

1944, 100 mins, US Ⓥ ⦿ b/w

Dir Howard Hawks ***Prod*** Howard Hawks ***Scr*** Jules Furthman, William Faulkner ***Ph*** Sidney Hickox ***Ed*** Christian Nyby ***Mus*** Leo Forbstein (dir.) ***Art*** Charles Novi

Act Humphrey Bogart, Walter Brennan, Lauren Bacall, Dolores Moran, Hoagy Carmichael, Marcel Dalio (Warner)

With an eye to the lucrative box-office of its *Casablanca*, the brothers Warner turned out another epic of similar genre in a none-too-literal adaptation of Ernest Hemingway's novel *To Have and Have Not*. There are enough similarities in both films to warrant more than cursory attention, even to the fact that Humphrey Bogart is starred in each, though this story of Vichy France collaborationism is not up to Warner's melodramatic story standards.

Though *Have Not* was one of Hemingway's inferior novels—whose theme of rum-running was certainly antithetical to the film's story of French collaboration—it affords considerable picture interest because of some neat characterizations. And it introduces Lauren Bacall, in her first picture. She's an arresting personality. She can slink, brother, and no fooling!

Yarn deals with the intrigue centering around the Caribbean island of Martinique, owned by France, and the plotting that ensued there prior to its ultimate capitulation to Allied pressure. Bogart is an American pressure skipper there who hires out his boat to anyone who has the price. When he becomes involved in the local Free French movement, the story's pattern becomes woven around him, at times in cops-and-robbers fashion.

Warners give the pic its usually nifty productional accoutrements, and that includes casting, musical scoring and Howard Hawks's direction but the basic story is too unsteady.

Bogart is in his usual metier, a tough guy who, no less, has the facility of making a dame go for him, instead of he for her. That's where Bacall comes in. Walter Brennan, as Bogart's drunken sidekick; Dolores Moran, as the film's second looker; and songwriter Hoagy Carmichael have lesser roles that they handle to advantage.

•

TO HELL AND BACK

1955, 106 mins, US Ⓥ ⦿ col

Dir Jesse Hibbs ***Prod*** Aaron Rosenberg ***Scr*** Gil Doud ***Ph*** Maury Gertsman ***Ed*** Edward Curtiss ***Mus*** Joseph Gershenson (sup.) ***Art*** Alexander Golitzen, Robert Clatworthy

Act Audie Murphy, Marshall Thompson, Charles Drake, Jack Kelly, Gregg Palmer, David Janssen (Universal)

This biopic on the World War II exploits that made Audie Murphy the most decorated soldier in American history is gripping drama with the original playing himself. The picturization of Murphy's autobiography has no blustering heroics for the sake of derring-do and the action shown is that of a modest, unassuming young man.

He gets into the army in 1942 at 18. In 1943, Murphy became a replacement in Company B, 15th Infantry Regiment, Third Division, 7th Army, in North Africa, and served with the unit throughout the war in Tunisia, Italy, France, Germany and Austria. During that time he rose from PFC to company commander, was wounded three times, personally killed 240 Germans, and was one of the only two soldiers left in the original company at the end of the war. His decorations total 24, from the Congressional Medal of Honor on down.

Among some of the more outstanding sequences are the knocking out of a Nazi machine-gun nest from a farmhouse near Anzio, the crazed attack on another Nazi emplacement in France after one of his buddies has been killed, and Murphy's almost single-handed blasting of a German tank group.

Aside from the fighting, footage works in some touching moments between battles during too-short leaves.

•

TO KILL A MOCKINGBIRD

1962, 129 mins, US Ⓥ ⦿ b/w

Dir Robert Mulligan ***Prod*** Alan J. Pakula ***Scr*** Horton Foote ***Ph*** Russell Harlan ***Ed*** Aaron Stell ***Mus*** Elmer Bernstein ***Art*** Henry Bumstead

Act Gregory Peck, Mary Badham, Phillip Alford, John Megna, Robert Duvall, Brock Peters (Universal)

Harper Lee's highly regarded first novel has been artfully and delicately translated to the screen. Horton Foote's trenchant screenplay, Robert Mulligan's sensitive and instinctively observant direction and a host of exceptional performances are all essential threads in the rich, provocative fabric.

As it unfolds on the screen, *To Kill a Mockingbird* bears with it, oddly enough, alternating overtones of Faulkner, Twain, Steinbeck, Hitchcock and an *Our Gang* comedy. A telling indictment of racial prejudice in the Deep South, it is also a charming tale of the emergence of two youngsters from the realm of wild childhood fantasy to the horizon of maturity, responsibility, compassion and social insight.

It is the story of a wise, gentle, soft-spoken Alabama lawyer (Gregory Peck) entrusted with the formidable dual chore of defending a Negro falsely accused of rape while raising his own impressionable, imaginative, motherless children in a hostile, terrifying environment of bigotry and economic depression.

For Peck, it is an especially challenging role, requiring him to project through a veneer of civilized restraint and resigned, rational compromise the fires of social indignation and humanitarian concern that burn within the character. He not only succeeds, but makes it appear effortless, etching a portrayal of strength, dignity, intelligence. But by no means is this entirely, or even substantially, Peck's film. Two youngsters just about steal it away, although the picture marks their screen bows. Both nine-year-old Mary Badham and 13-year-old Phillip Alford, each of whom hails from the South, make striking debuts as Peck's two irrepressible, mischievous, ubiquitous, irresistibly childish children.

There are some top-notch supporting performances. Especially sharp and effective are Frank Overton, Estelle Evans, James Anderson and Robert Duvall. Brock Peters has an outstanding scene as the innocent, ill-fated Negro on trial for his life.

1962: Best Actor (Gregory Peck), Adapted Screenplay, B&W Art Direction

NOMINATIONS: Best Picture, Director, Supp. Actress (Mary Badham), B&W Cinematography, Original Music Score

•

TO KILL A PRIEST

1988, 116 mins, France/US Ⓥ ⊙ ▭ col

Dir Agnieszka Holland ***Prod*** Jean-Pierre Alessandri (exec.) ***Scr*** Agnieszka Holland, Jean-Yves Pitoun ***Ph*** Adam Holender ***Ed*** Herve de Luze ***Mus*** Georges Delerue, Zbigniew Preisner ***Art*** Emile Ghigo

Act Christopher Lambert, Ed Harris, Joanne Whalley-Kilmer, Joss Ackland, David Suchet, Tim Roth (JP/FR3/Columbia)

Polish by subject and director, French by official production and shooting locations, American by soundtrack and partial financing, and transatlantic in casting, *To Kill a Priest* is an ambitious political thriller emptied of substance by its heterogeneous components and hybrid dramaturgy.

Backed by Columbia under the brief David Puttnam regime, this is a fictional recreation of the murder of Polish priest Jerzy Popieluszko by security police in 1984. But exiled Polish helmer Agnieszka Holland's recreation on French soil of her homeland under the banner of Solidarity and the boot of martial law lacks a sense of time and place, a socio-political density.

Central weakness is the casting of France's linguistically versatile Christopher Lambert, playing a rather bland "charismatic" priest and Solidarity apostle, and America's Ed Harris, not quite the right stuff as the Polish militia officer who engineers and executes the plot to assassinate him. The Cain and Abel theme is spelled out literally in Joan Baez's bookending theme song.

Film picks up some steam and dramatic interest in the second half, though by this time one's empathy or antipathy for the principals of the story has been severely tried.

•

TOKYO JOE

1949, 87 mins, US Ⓥ ⊙ b/w

Dir Stuart Heisler ***Prod*** Robert Lord ***Scr*** Cyril Hume, Bertram Millhauser ***Ph*** Charles Lawton, Jr. ***Ed*** Viola Lawrence ***Mus*** George Antheil

Act Humphrey Bogart, Alexander Knox, Florence Marley, Sessue Hayakawa (Columbia/Santana)

Tokyo Joe has been given a documentary flavor by much process footage shot in Tokyo. This authetic touch serves as an excellent background for the unfolding of the plot's meller elements, and Stuart Heisler's direction develops a neat air of anticipation that climaxes in a gripping, exciting fight finale.

Story [from one by Steve Fisher, adapted by Walter Doniger] opens with Bogart returning to Tokyo, where he owns a night club, after service in the war. He finds the wife he had left has married another. Out to win her back, Bogart starts a small freight airline, and soon becomes involved in smuggling war criminals back into Japan.

Alexander Knox is quietly effective as the man who replaces Bogart as Florence Marly's husband. Marly does an adequate job of her role.

•

TOL'ABLE DAVID

1930, 78 mins, US b/w

Dir John G. Blystone ***Scr*** Benjamin Glazer ***Ph*** Ted Tetzlaff ***Ed*** Glenn Wheeler ***Art*** Edward Jewell

Act Richard Cromwell, Noah Beery, Joan Peers, Henry B. Walthall, Tom Keene (Columbia)

In his first picture Richard Cromwell does surprisingly well. He looks the part and John Blystone, directing, covers him up splendidly by curtailing his lines to a minimum.

Columbia execs and Blystone must have sat through the [1921] silent print time after time as there's an absolute parallel between the two interpretations. The studio evidently made up its mind it couldn't improve on Henry King's superb silent job.

The story [from Joseph Hergesheimer's of the same name] borders on the feud theme and is localed in the Virginia hills. Young David, chafing at being the youngest of the family, finally comes into his own when his elder brother is crippled and his father dies as he is about to launch a vengeance campaign.

Beery does excellently as the uncouth villain while Peter Richmond [John Carradine] makes the small part of the halfwit brother count.

•

TO LIVE

SEE: IKIRU

•

TO LIVE

SEE: HUOZHE

•

TO LIVE AND DIE IN L.A.

1985, 116 mins, US Ⓥ ⊙ col

Dir William Friedkin ***Prod*** Irving H. Levin ***Scr*** William Friedkin, Gerald Petievich ***Ph*** Robby Muller ***Ed*** Bud Smith, Scott Smith ***Mus*** Wang Chung ***Art*** Lilly Kilvert

Act William L. Petersen, Willem Dafoe, John Pankow, Debra Feuer, John Turturro, Darlanne Fluegel (United Artists/New Century/SLM)

To Live and Die in L.A. looks like a rich man's *Miami Vice*. William Friedkin's evident attempt to fashion a West Coast equivalent of his [1971] *The French Connection* is engrossing and diverting enough on a moment-to-moment basis but is overtooled.

Friedkin leaves no doubt about his technical abilities, as he has created another memorable car chase and, with the considerable assistance of cinematographer Robby Muller, has offered up any number of startling and original shots of the characters inhabiting weirdly ugly-beautiful L.A. cityscapes.

William L. Petersen plays a highly capable Secret Service agent who decides to nail a notorious counterfeiter responsible for the murder of his partner.

Petersen's search leads him into the kinky, high-tech world of Willem Dafoe, a supremely talented and self-confident artist whose phony $20 bills look magnificent and whose tentacles reach into surprising areas of the criminal underworld, both high and low-class.

Friedkin keeps dialog to a minimum, but what conversation there is proves wildly overloaded with streetwise obscenities, so much so that it becomes something of a joke. [Pic is based on the novel by Gerald Petievich, who co-scripted.]

•

TOM & VIV

1994, 125 mins, UK/US Ⓥ ⊙ ▭ col

Dir Brian Gilbert ***Prod*** Marc Samuelson, Harvey Kass, Peter Samuelson ***Scr*** Michael Hastings, Adrian Hodges ***Ph*** Martin Fuhrer ***Ed*** Tony Lawson ***Mus*** Debbie Wiseman ***Art*** Jamie Leonard

Act Willem Dafoe, Miranda Richardson, Rosemary Harris, Tim Dutton, Nickolas Grace, Philip Locke (Samuelson/Kass/IRS Media)

Passion of only the driest and most cerebral kind peeks through the lace curtains of *Tom & Viv*, a handsomely appointed but overly starchy love story that attains real clout only in the final reel. Intense but tight-jawed playing by Willem Dafoe as Yank poet T. S. Eliot and an eccentric perf by Miranda Richardson that doesn't jell until its latter stages mark this as a well-meaning but noble failure.

Michael Hastings's original play started life at London's Royal Court Theatre in February 1984, with Julie Covington and Tom Wilkinson in the leads. In December 1992, the play was broadcast by BBC Radio 3, with Richardson bowing as Viv and John Duttine as Tom.

Tale opens in 1914, with spoiled socialite Vivienne Haigh-Wood (Richardson) visiting Merton College, Oxford, with her soppy brother, Maurice (Tom Dutton), to see American student Tom Eliot (Dafoe). Following a whirlwind affair, the couple marry, but Viv's wild mood swings continue, even in public or when with friends. Tom finally has her committed to an asylum.

From the first of Viv's attacks, pic essentially becomes a catalog of her breakdowns and public embarrassments, with Tom an increasingly clench-jawed bystander. With little feel for Eliot's growing rep as a poet, it's hard to get a handle on Viv's obsessive belief in his talent.

Dafoe gives one of his most desiccated, emotionally withdrawn performances. Richardson's performance is even more eccentric, with a seemingly deliberate decision to play Viv's mood swings in a semi-comedic vein. However, in her final scenes, in superb, measured dialog describing Viv's love for Eliot, Richardson gives a glimpse of the emotion *Tom & Viv* attempts to describe but which remains out of reach.

1994: NOMINATIONS: Best Actress (Miranda Richardson), Supp. Actress (Rosemary Harris)

•

TOMB OF LIGEIA, THE

1965, 80 mins, UK/US Ⓥ ⊙ ▭ col

Dir Roger Corman ***Prod*** Pat Green ***Scr*** Robert Towne ***Ph*** Arthur Grant ***Ed*** Alfred Cox ***Mus*** Kenneth V. Jones ***Art*** Colin Southcott

Act Vincent Price, Elizabeth Shepherd, John Westbrook, Oliver Johnston, Derek Francis, Richard Vernon (American International/Alta Vista)

More Poe but no go about sums up *The Tomb of Ligeia*, a tedious and talky addition to American International's series of chillpix based on tales by the 19th century U.S. author. Roger Corman produced and directed a script that resists analysis and lacks credibility, with all performances blah monotones and color lensing of no help. Widescreen pic tries serious supernatural approach minimizing gore angles, but it doesn't jell.

Amid ruins of English abbey lives widower Vincent Price, near grave of first wife, Ligeia, buried under strange circumstances some years before. Price disappoints in attempt to project character's inner struggle to escape spell since no one knows why he acts kooky. Elizabeth Shepherd vacillates between too-stiff patrician elegance and unconvincing terror in role of second wife who is subjected to endless repetitions of brief, ineffective horror bits involving black cat, saucer of milk, and dead fox.

•

TOM BROWN'S SCHOOL DAYS (AKA: ADVENTURES AT RUGBY)

1940, 88 mins, US Ⓥ b/w

Dir Robert Stevenson ***Prod*** Gene Towne, Graham Baker ***Scr*** Walter Ferris, Frank Cavett, Gene Towne, Graham Baker ***Ph*** Nicholas Musuraca ***Ed*** William Hamilton ***Mus*** Anthony Collins ***Art*** Van Nest Polglase

Act Cedric Hardwicke, Freddie Bartholomew, Jimmy Lydon, Josephine Hutchinson, Billy Halop, Polly Moran (The Play's The Thing/RKO)

Much can be said for the treatment in this edition of the Thomas Hughes yarn. While remaining faithful to the spirit of the original, it contrives to vitalize the action and humanize the characters. Thus young Tom's confused terror among the milling cruelties of the young hellions on his first time away from home is understandable and compelling. The terrible seriousness of his scrapes, his fights and youthful crises are immediate and vivid.

Although *Tom Brown* is not a lavish production, it is sympathetically and skillfully made, with many touching moments and an excellent cast. It alters the emphasis somewhat from the development of the boy to the character of the headmaster, Arnold. But that should bother only a few purists. It probably results in a better picture, since Cedric Hardwicke, who plays the wise and kindly teacher, is much better qualified to carry a story than is any Hollywood prodigy.

Hardwicke's performance is one of the best he has ever given on the screen. While maintaining the schoolmaster's surface severity, he clearly indicates the underlying sympathy, tolerance, quiet humor and steadfast courage. In the title part, Jimmy Lydon is believable and moving in the early portions, but too young for the final moments.

Freddie Bartholomew is sincere and convincing as Tom's sidekick, while Josephine Hutchinson's lustrous quality makes the role of the headmaster's wife seem too brief. Billy Halop is a properly sadistic bully.

•

TOM BROWN'S SCHOOL DAYS

1951, 96 mins, UK Ⓥ b/w

Dir Gordon Parry ***Prod*** George Minter ***Scr*** Noel Langley ***Ph*** C. Pennington-Richards, Raymond Sturgess ***Ed*** Kenneth Heeley-Ray ***Mus*** Richard Addinsell ***Art*** Frederick Pusey

Act John Howard Davies, Robert Newton, Diana Wynyard, Francis De Wolff, Kathleen Byron, Hermione Baddeley (Renown)

England's classic story of public school life is acted with great sincerity by a name cast, but script and direction go all out to emphasize the obvious emotional tearjerker angles.

Almost the entire script hinges on the popular angle of the new boy versus the bully. John Howard Davies makes Tom Brown a lovable and sympathetic youngster without a shade of priggishness. Robert Newton as the reforming headmaster, Dr. Arnold, fills his role with commendable restraint.

The plot, of course, is dominated by the schoolboys, and there is a standout performance by John Forrest as the sneering, bullying Flashman. Special facilities having been granted to film this in Rugby School, the authenticity of the background cannot be questioned.

•

TOMBSTONE
1994, 127 mins, US Ⓥ ⊙ ▭ col
Dir George Pan Cosmatos ***Prod*** James Jacks, Sean Daniel, Bob Misiorowski ***Scr*** Kevin Jarre, [John Fasano] ***Ph*** William A. Fraker ***Ed*** Frank J. Urioste, Roberto Silvi, Harvey Rosenstock ***Mus*** Bruce Broughton ***Art*** Catherine Hardwicke
Act Kurt Russell, Val Kilmer, Michael Biehn, Powers Boothe, Dana Delaney, Sam Elliott (Hollywood/Cinergi)

A decent addition to the current cycle of screen and TV Westerns, *Tombstone* is a tough-talking but soft-hearted tale that is entertaining in a sprawling, old-fashioned manner. Hollywood Pictures won the race to be the first to offer a 1990s version of the oft-told adventures of legendary Wyatt Earp and Doc Holliday, against Lawrence Kasdan's Warner Bros. release starring Kevin Costner.

As written by Kevin Jarre, who was replaced as director early in the shoot by George P. Cosmatos, *Tombstone* is not so much a revisionist view of the Old West as a retelling of the famous story that blends drama, comedy, action and romance the way 1950s movies did.

Story begins in 1879, when Wyatt Earp (Kurt Russell), retired marshall of Dodge City, arrives in the lawless boomtown of Tombstone, Arizona, determined to settle down into domesticity with his wife (Dana Wheeler-Nicholson) and open a business with his brothers Virgil (Sam Elliott) and Morgan (Bill Paxton). But Earp is soon forced to drop his ideology of non-involvement, as the town is terrorized by a bunch of fearless, corrupt villains, headed by the McLaurys and Clantons. Earp is assisted by the unpredictable Doc Holliday (Val Kilmer).

Cosmatos opts for the more operatic, gritty style of Sergio Leone, particularly in his cutting and use of megacloseups during the legendary gunfight at OK Corral. After a weak initial half-hour, Cosmatos judiciously finds the most audience-appealing dimensions of his tale. Pic's chief virtue is that its handsome actors show a gleaming pleasure in being cast against type.

Excepting Bruce Broughton's bombastic music, production values are accomplished. Filmed on location around Tucson, AZ, where the story's major incidents occurred, *Tombstone* boasts the visuals of an epic thanks to William A. Fraker's luminous widescreen lensing.

•

TOM, DICK AND HARRY
1941, 85 mins, US Ⓥ ⊙ b/w
Dir Garson Kanin ***Prod*** Robert Sisk ***Scr*** Paul Jarrico ***Ph*** Merritt Gerstad ***Ed*** John Sturges ***Mus*** Roy Webb
Act Ginger Rogers, George Murphy, Alan Marshal, Burgess Meredith, Phil Silvers, Jane Seymour (RKO)

Director Garson Kanin cleverly steers his tale through a series of spontaneous episodes—taking advantage of every laugh opportunity—to deliver a surprise finish. Original story and screenplay by Paul Jarrico is a cleverly contrived version of a modern Cinderella with punchy script and dialog.

Ginger Rogers, telephone operator, aims for romance with a millionaire but accepts the proposal of breezy and ambitious auto-salesman George Murphy. Mistaking Burgess Meredith for her rich Romeo, she nonchalantly becomes engaged to him also. Then she meets the young millionaire (Alan Marshal) and neatly wangles a proposal from him—but eventually has to decide among the three.

Rogers again hits the peak in her performance of the working girl dizzily confused by the romantic profusion that enters her life. While Murphy, as the ambitious and personable auto salesman, and Marshal, the millionaire candidate, both deliver solidly in their respective assignments, it's Meredith who stands out most prominently with a sterling and lightsome performance as the happy-go-lucky and lazy individual.

•

TOM HORN
1980, 98 mins, US Ⓥ ▭ col
Dir William Wiard, [James William Guercio] ***Prod*** Fred Weintraub ***Scr*** Thomas McGuane, Bud Shrake ***Ph*** John Alonzo ***Ed*** George Grenville ***Mus*** Ernest Gold ***Art*** Ron Hobbs
Act Steve McQueen, Richard Farnsworth, Linda Evans, Billy Green Bush, Slim Pickens, Elisha Cook (Warner/First Artists)

Steve McQueen's *Tom Horn* is a sorry ending to the once high hopes of the star-studded founding of First Artists Prods.

If rumor be true, McQueen did not want to do *Horn* as his third pic to fulfill his founder's commitment, but was forced into it. True or not, he certainly looks like he's walking through the part.

Imagine a film that opens up with dialog that can't be heard at all, then proceeds to build up to a fistfight that's never seen, that cuts away to sunsets to fill in other scenes that have no dramatic point, and you have just the beginning of what's wrong with *Tom Horn*.

Pic [from Horn's *Life of Tom Horn, Government Scout and Interpreter*] takes up in the final days of the life of the legendary Western hero. And the only plus at all is a couple of good, bloody shoot-out sequences.

•

TOM JONES
1963, 128 mins, UK Ⓥ ⊙ col
Dir Tony Richardson ***Prod*** Tony Richardson ***Scr*** John Osborne ***Ph*** Walter Lassally ***Ed*** Antony Gibbs ***Mus*** John Addison ***Art*** Ralph Brinton
Act Albert Finney, Susannah York, Hugh Griffith, Edith Evans, Joan Greenwood, Diane Cilento (Woodfall)

Based on Henry Fielding's enduring novel, story is set in Somerset, a West Country lush county, and in London during the 18th century. Hero is Tom Jones (Albert Finney), born in suspicious circumstances, with a maidservant dismissed because she is suspected of being his unwed mother. He is brought up by Squire Allworthy (George Devine) and leads a rollicking life in which women play a prominent part before he finally escapes the gallows after a frameup.

The somewhat sprawling, bawdy and vivid screenplay of John Osborne provides some meaty acting opportunities and the thesps grasp their chances with vigorous zest. Finney slips through his adventures with an ebullient gusto that keeps the overlong film on its toes for most of the time. Hugh Griffith and Edith Evans as Squire Western and his sister ham disarmingly. Evans has some of the choicer cameos in the film.

Director Tony Richardson has occasionally pressed his luck with some over-deliberate arty camera bits. The music of John Addison is a trifle obtrusive and lacking in period style. An added bonus is Micheal MacLiammoir putting over occasional narration with smooth wit and perception.

1963: Best Picture, Director, Adapted Screenplay, Original Music Score

NOMINATIONS: Best Actor (Albert Finney), Supp. Actor (Hugh Griffith), Supp. Actress (Diane Cilento, Dame Edith Evans, Joyce Redman), Color Art Direction

•

TOMMY
1975, 111 mins, UK Ⓥ ⊙ col
Dir Ken Russell ***Prod*** Robert Stigwood ***Scr*** Ken Russell ***Ph*** Dick Bush ***Ed*** Stuart Baird ***Mus*** Pete Townshend, John Entwistle, Keith Moon ***Art*** John Clark
Act Ann-Margret, Oliver Reed, Roger Daltrey, Elton John, Eric Clapton, Jack Nicholson (Columbia)

Ken Russell's filmization of *Tommy* is spectacular in nearly every way. The enormous appeal of the original 1969 record album by The Who has been complemented in a superbly added visual dimension.

Young Tommy, traumatized when he sees his real father, Robert Powell, accidentally killed in an argument with stepfather Oliver Reed as mother Ann-Margret watches in horror, grows up amid an atmosphere of cruel exploitation and abuse. Even his miraculous recovery, and subsequent delusions of grandeur, simply extend the ripoff.

Among the cameo players, Elton John plays the pinball wizard and Eric Clapton is well featured as a preacher and Tina Turner virtually rips the screen apart with her animalistic Acid Queen.

1975: NOMINATIONS: Best Actress (Ann-Margret), Adapted Score

•

TOMMY THE TOREADOR
1959, 90 mins, UK col
Dir John Paddy Carstairs ***Prod*** George H. Brown ***Scr*** George H. Brown, Patrick Kirwan ***Ph*** Gilbert Taylor ***Ed*** Peter Bezencenet ***Mus*** Stanley Black
Act Tommy Steele, Janet Munro, Sidney James, Bernard Cribbins, Kenneth Williams, Eric Sykes (Associated-British/Fanfare)

Tailored for the talents of Tommy Steele, *Tommy the Toreador* emerges as a brisk, disarming little comedy. Steele plays a young seaman who gets stranded in Spain and through a string of highly fortuitous circumstances gets conned into making a one-performance-only appearance as a toreador.

Janet Munro is Steele's girlfriend in the picture. She has little to do that's demanding but she has a fresh, likable personality and strikes up a happy partnership with Steele. Major disappointment is Sidney James. This time he has little opportunity and, saddled with a broken Spanish accent, he seems justifiably unhappy with his role of a bullfight promoter. However, his partner, Bernard Cribbins, scores a distinct success.

Steele puts over half a dozen cheerful songs written by Lionel Bart, Michael Pratt and Jimmy Bennett.

•

TOMORROW IS FOREVER
1946, 102 mins, US Ⓥ b/w
Dir Irving Pichel ***Prod*** David Lewis ***Scr*** Lenore Coffee ***Ph*** Joseph Valentine ***Ed*** Ernest Nims ***Mus*** Max Steiner ***Art*** Wiard B. Ihnen
Act Claudette Colbert, Orson Welles, George Brent, Lucille Watson, Richard Long, Natalie Wood (RKO/International)

International Pictures takes its audience through a deep emotional bath in this moving filmization of Gwen Bristow's magazine serial and novel. Yarn is a variation of the *Enoch Arden* theme.

It goes back to World War I, with Orson Welles and Claudette Colbert virtual newlyweds when the bugle's note separates them. Badly disfigured and crippled, Welles allows himself to be mistakenly declared dead and makes a new life for himself in Austria under another name. Colbert, meantime, marries George Brent and is happily married until shortly before World War II, when Welles returns to the States to work as a chemist in Brent's plant and he and Colbert again come face-to-face.

First half of the film goes from one heart-shaking sequence to another but, unfortunately Lenore Coffee in her screenplay has been unable to build to great climaxes.

Cast is solid throughout, director Irving Pichel even holding his children pretty well in check on precocity. Colbert gives an honest and sincere performance, while Welles, with beard, limp, cane and cough, has a tailored role for his brand of thespics. He certainly doesn't underplay the part, but neither does he push it too heavily.

•

TOMORROW NEVER DIES
1997, 119 mins, UK/US Ⓥ ⊙ ▭ col
Dir Roger Spottiswoode ***Prod*** Michael G. Wilson, Barbara Broccoli ***Scr*** Bruce Feirstein ***Ph*** Robert Elswit ***Ed*** Dominique Fortin, Michel Arcand ***Mus*** David Arnold ***Art*** Allan Cameron
Act Pierce Brosnan, Jonathan Pryce, Michelle Yeoh, Teri Hatcher, Joe Don Baker, Judi Dench (Eon/United Artists)

There is plenty of bang-bang but very little kiss-kiss in this solid but somewhat by-the-numbers 18th entry in the James Bond cycle.

However, scenarist Bruce Feirstein, who cowrote *GoldenEye*, has done his best work here in cooking up a delicious and easy-to-hate villain for the post–Cold War '90s, a megalomaniacal communications tycoon, Elliot Carver (Jonathan Pryce), whose network of satellites enables him to reach nearly every corner of the globe.

Carver sinks a British naval vessel in the South China Sea in a way that pins the blame on the Chinese. With tensions rising between East and West, the Brits send Bond to Hamburg to infiltrate a huge party Carver is throwing, and it just so happens that Bond is an old playmate of Carver's wife, Paris (Teri Hatcher). Bond also makes the acquaintance of a striking Chinese woman, Wai Lin (Malaysian–Hong Kong favorite Michelle Yeoh), whose journalistic credentials are as transparent as Bond's as a banker.

Action then shifts to Southeast Asia, where, just by coincidence, Bond runs into Wai Lin scuba diving in the sunken remains of the British naval ship. The two secret agents [eventually] reunite to prevent World War III by locating Carver's stealth ship, from which a cruise missile is about to be launched toward Beijing.

Action finale recalls any number of earlier Bond pics in its giant industrial hardware setting. Filmmakers have steered almost exclusively toward action at the expense of sex, humor or jet-set glamor.

Yeoh proves a worthy equal partner to Bond, displaying snappy martial arts moves and not falling into the compliant-bimbo mode.

•

TOMORROW THE WORLD
1944, 96 mins, US b/w
Dir Leslie Fenton ***Prod*** Lester Cowan ***Scr*** Ring Lardner, Jr., Leopold Atlas ***Ph*** Henry Sharp ***Ed*** Anne Bauchens ***Mus*** Louis Applebaum ***Art*** James Sullivan
Act Fredric March, Betty Field, Agnes Moorehead, Skip Homeier, Joan Carroll, Boots Brown (United Artists)

Reformation of Nazi youth, a problem forcefully projected in *Tomorrow the World* on Broadway [in the play by James Gow and Arnaud D'Usseau], is dealt with no less assiduously in Lester Cowan's screen presentation of the same story.

It's a vivid story of a youngster brought to America from Germany into the home of a college professor whose philosophies have been governed by those of the boy's father, a well-known liberal killed by the Nazis because of his views.

The boy has been geared in the Nazi way, taught that his father had been a traitor to the Third Reich. Repudiation of the American concept and an attempt to inculcate Nazi fears into the minds of his American schoolfellows almost succeed. He would also break up the impending marriage between the professor and his Jewish fiancée, and this, too, is almost realized.

Fredric March and Betty Field both give dignity to the parts of the professor and his bride-to-be. But the main accolade must go to Skippy Homeier, as the young Nazi.

•

TOM SAWYER
1930, 82 mins, US Ⓥ b/w
Dir John Cromwell ***Prod*** Louis D. Lighton ***Scr*** Sam Mintz, Grover Jones, William Slavens McNutt ***Ph*** Charles Lang ***Ed*** Alyson Shaffer ***Art*** Bernard Herzbrun, Robert O'Dell
Act Jackie Coogan, Junior Durkin, Mitzi Green, Lucien Littlefield, Tully Marshall, Clara Blandick (Paramount)

The Mark Twain classic has been shrewdly molded to the screen. It somehow crystallizes the essence of a work that is timeless in its human appeal.

The picture is a real achievement for its director, John Cromwell, one of the stage directors who crashed Hollywood. Cromwell had a wild desire to do *Tom Sawyer* and the finished work has all the marks of a labor of love.

Picture was originally designed as the first of a series to bring the younger generation back to the talking screen. Story is splendidly acted by a great group of youngsters. Young Jackie Coogan plays Tom to the life but the secondary role of Junior Durkin as Huckleberry Finn is also appealing. Little Mitzi Green is rather lost in the child part of Becky Thatcher, built up somewhat for the film.

•

TOM SAWYER
1973, 100 mins, US Ⓥ col
Dir Don Taylor ***Prod*** Arthur P. Jacobs ***Scr*** Robert B. Sherman, Richard M. Sherman ***Ph*** Frank Stanley ***Ed*** Marion Rothman ***Mus*** Robert B. Sherman, Richard M. Sherman ***Art*** Philip Jefferies
Act Johnny Whitaker, Celeste Holm, Warren Oates, Jeff East, Jodie Foster, Lucille Benson (Reader's Digest/United Artists)

The strikingly handsome $2.5 million production, directed with discreet and appealing folksiness by Don Taylor, boasts an excellent cast, including Johnny Whitaker as Sawyer and Celeste Holm just sensational as Aunt Polly. Robert B. and Richard M. Sherman's script, music and lyrics maintain an all-age interest.

Jeff East is most effective as Huck Finn, making of that character an intriguing and contrasting personality. Jodie Foster is great as Becky Thatcher.

Holm returns to the screen in personal triumph. Few actresses project so well warmth-with-backbone, and a ladylike gentility not immune to kicking up the heels occasionally.

Also superbly cast is Warren Oates as Muff Potter, the likeable boozy philosopher. Oates and Holm keep the film together for older audiences.

1973: NOMINATIONS: Best Costume Design, Art Direction, Adapted Score

•

TOM THUMB
1958, 92 mins, US Ⓥ col
Dir George Pal ***Prod*** George Pal ***Scr*** Ladislas Fodor ***Ph*** Georges Perinal ***Ed*** Frank Clarke ***Mus*** Douglas Gamley, Ken Jones ***Art*** Elliot Scott
Act Russ Tamblyn, Alan Young, Terry-Thomas, Peter Sellers, Jessie Matthews, June Thorburn (M-G-M)

The only thing lower case about this production is the Metro spelling of *tom thumb*. Otherwise, film is top-drawer, a comic fairy tale with music that stacks up alongside some of the Disney classics. It is really a musical comedy. It has five good songs, two of them by Peggy Lee.

The screenplay, from the Grimm Bros fairly tale, is as simple as it can be. A childless couple (Bernard Miles and Jessie Matthews) get a miniature son (Russ Tamblyn) when wood-cutter Miles spares a special tree in the forest surrounding their home, and is rewarded by the Forest Queen (June Thorburn).

Complications in the story come from tom's size, only five and one-half inches. There are villains (Terry-Thomas and Peter Sellers) attempting to use tom for their own evil purposes. There is romance between Alan Young, a neighbor, and Thorburn, finally unbewitched from a fairy queen to a real, live girl.

Highlights of the production are the musical numbers and the special effects. Alex Romero staged the dance numbers, in which Tamblyn does some of the most athletic and exciting dancing he has had a chance at since *Seven Brides for Seven Brothers*. Georges Perinal's photography, with special effects by Tom Howard, catches all the fun and liveliness of the staging. The miniature work was done in Hollywood, based on George Pal's Puppetoon figures, and the life-size work in London.

1958: Best Special Effects

•

TONGNIAN WANGSHI
(THE TIME TO LIVE AND THE TIME TO DIE)
1985, 137 mins, Taiwan col
Dir Hou Hsiao-hsien ***Prod*** Lin Teng-fei ***Scr*** Chu Tien-wen, Hou Hsiao-hsien ***Ph*** Li Ping-pin ***Ed*** Wang Chi-yang ***Mus*** Wu Chu-chu ***Art*** Lin Chung-wen
Act Tien Feng, Mei Fang, Tang Ju-yun, Yu An-shun, Hsiao Ai, Hsin Shu-fen (CMPC)

After the success reaped by his *Summer at Grandpa's*, Hou Hsiao-hsien is back with another beautifully controlled and highly nostalgic picture of childhood, based on his own boyhood, a period coinciding with the last years of the Chinese revolution and establishment of an independent Taiwanese identity.

Not that politics have anything to do directly with this film. What the script is mostly concerned with is growing up in a lower middle-class family, culturally bridging between the ancient superstitions and the new modern ways of education. It is also about the economic struggle to keep afloat in those difficult years.

Mostly episodic in nature, the film impresses by its exquisite camerawork which suggests perfectly framed paintings.

Time is one of the essential elements of the story, the changing seasons contributing to establish moods and the passing years indicating a change in mentality. Time, however, may also be one of the film's drawbacks, overlong at 137 minutes.

•

TONI
1935, 80 mins, France Ⓥ b/w
Dir Jean Renoir ***Prod*** Marcel Pagnol (exec.) ***Scr*** Jean Renoir, Carl Einstein ***Ph*** Claude Renoir ***Ed*** Marguerite Renoir, Suzanne de Troeye ***Mus*** Eugene Bozza ***Art*** Bourelly
Act Charles Blavette, Celia Montalvan, Jenny Helia, Edouard Delmont, Max Dalban (Films d'Aujourd'hui)

Full of atmosphere, intensely tragic, studded with artistic touches of direction, acting and photography, it's the filming of the story behind a rural police case [from an idea by J. Levert]. Takes place in the south of France and was filmed on the spot, with a sound truck. Not a single scene made in a studio.

Actors are all unknown but highly competent. Director Jean Renoir says he chose them obscure, not only for economy, but because unknown people can act the way they like and the script requires.

Locale is a region not far from Marseilles where there are a lot of Italian and Spanish laborers who work in quarries and till the soil. Leading character, Toni (Charles Blavette), is Italian. He gets entangled with a girl who keeps his boarding house. Marie (Jenny Helia) loves him but he falls in love with a young Spanish girl, Josepha (Celia Montalvan). She loves him but is taken away by the quarry foreman, Albert (Max Dalban), a Belgian with some education. Toni goes to live in the woods from where he can see Josepha's house. There things come to a climax.

Fine guitar music, always apropos, provides relief and augmentation of the drama. There are no slow spots: tragedy is deliberately and regularly developed. Pic is all in dialect, a combination of Italian and Spanish accents and the Provencal accent of the part of France in which it was shot.

•

TONIGHT AND EVERY NIGHT
1945, 89 mins, US Ⓥ col
Dir Victor Saville ***Prod*** Victor Saville ***Scr*** Lesser Samuels, Abem Finkel ***Ph*** Rudolph Mate ***Ed*** Viola Lawrence ***Mus*** Morris Stoloff (dir.) ***Art*** Rudolph Sternad, Stephen Goosson, Lionel Banks
Act Rita Hayworth, Lee Bowman, Janet Blair, Marc Platt, Florence Bates, Shelley Winters (Columbia)

Tonight and Every Night has plenty of pace in its backstage tale [from the play *Heart of the City* by Lesley Storm], which gets slightly away from regulation formula to carry adequately the many showmanly production numbers.

Setting is a five-a-day music hall in London, which carries on with daily performances during the blitz through the courage of the performers, headed by American-born Rita Hayworth and the persistence of impresario Florence Bates. Romance is quickly developed between Hayworth and RAF pilot Lee Bowman.

Comedy specialty handled by Hayworth and Janet Blair, in twin bed setting and with both attired in woolen underwear, is neatly contrived and excellently presented by the two performers.

Marc Platt, plucked by Columbia from his featured role in the Broadway *Oklahoma*, makes a sensational debut and his finale stepping to a haranguing speech by Hitler is a showstopper.

•

TONIGHT FOR SURE
1962, 69 mins, US Ⓥ col
Dir Francis Coppola ***Prod*** Francis Coppola ***Scr*** Francis Coppola ***Ph*** Jack Hill ***Mus*** Carmine Coppola ***Art*** Albert Locatelli, Barbara Cooper
Act Don Kenney, Karl Schanzer, Virginia Gordon, Marti Renfro, Sandy Silver, Linda Gibson (Searchlight)

Francis Coppola's first feature film effort, the nudie pic *Tonight for Sure*, was released by Premier Pictures in 1962, thus preceding director's "official" first film, *Dementia 13*, by at least a year. There are really only two ways to approach viewing such a piece of juvenalia: to look for precocious signs of talent in the then-22-year-old filmmaker, and to consider its position in the late, unlamented "nudie" genre.

Surprisingly, unlike most of the long-forgotten "adults only" features of the period, *Tonight for Sure* is chock full of nudity.

Storyline is ridiculous, to be sure. Two definitive dirty old men who fashion themselves as moral crusaders slip into a Hollywood burlesque house to plot the cessation of the lewd, indecent behavior transpiring therein.

In the meantime, they relate how they've each arrived at their righteous beliefs. Two yarns are cut in with stripteases being performed at the club. Predictably, it all ends with forces of puritanism raiding the joint.

•

TONIGHT WE SING
1953, 109 mins, US col
Dir Mitchell Leisen ***Prod*** George Jessel ***Scr*** Harry Kurnitz, George Oppenheimer ***Ph*** Leon Shamroy ***Ed*** Dorothy Spencer ***Mus*** Alfred Newman (dir.) ***Art*** Lyle R. Wheeler, George W. Davis
Act David Wayne, Ezio Pinza, Roberta Peters, Tamara Toumanova, Anne Bancroft, Isaac Stern (20th Century-Fox)

This is a topflight musical drama, based on the career of Sol Hurok, a renowned impresario in the concert field. Mitchell Leisen's direction recognizes the need to cloak the music with a human touch, and his handling points up this aspect in the screenplay based on a book by Hurok and Ruth Goode.

No particular attempt is made at a chronological revealing of the Hurok career. In essence, it establishes Hurok's early love for music, though he has no talent to express it through instrument or voice, and which later becomes a determination to bring the world's top artists to the common working man as well as the top-hatted music-lover. From his native Russia he comes to America and, with the backing and encouragement of his wife and a few friends, he achieves his goal.

As the basso Feodor Chaliapin, with a passion for playing jokes, and for rich foods and drink, Ezio Pinza deftly lards humor into the footage. Pinza, Isaac Stern and Roberta Peters and Tamara Toumanova also lend their considerable musical and dance talents to the film. David Wayne gives an earnest, pleasing portrayal to the role of Hurok, and Anne Bancroft impresses favorably as Mrs Hurok.

•

TONY ROME
1967, 110 mins, US Ⓥ ▭ col
Dir Gordon Douglas ***Prod*** Aaron Rosenberg ***Scr*** Richard L. Breen ***Ph*** Joseph Biroc ***Ed*** Robert Simpson ***Mus*** Billy May ***Art*** Jack Martin Smith, James Roth

Act Frank Sinatra, Jill St. John, Richard Conte, Gena Rowlands, Simon Oakland, Jeffrey Lynn (20th Century-Fox/Arcola-Millfield)

Tony Rome is a flip gumshoe on the Miami scene, with a busy, heavily populated script, zesty Gordon Douglas direction, and solid production values.

Marvin H. Albert's novel, *Miami Mayhem*, is scripted into a fast-moving whodunit which, per se, is far less intriguing than the individual scenes en route to climax. Credit Frank Sinatra's excellent style, and the production elements, for pulling it off.

Apart from some inside gags, including an overplugging of the beer with which Sinatra has a blurb tie-in, there is an abundance of double-entendre dialog which in reality can be taken only one way.

●

TOO BEAUTIFUL FOR YOU
SEE: TROP BELLE POUR TOI

●

TOO HOT TO HANDLE
SEE: THE MARRYING MAN

●

TOO HOT TO HANDLE
1938, 106 mins, US Ⓥ b/w
Dir Jack Conway *Prod* Lawrence Weingarten *Scr* Laurence Stallings, John Lee Mahin *Ph* Harold Rosson *Ed* Frank Sullivan *Mus* Franz Waxman *Art* Cedric Gibbons, Daniel B. Cathcart, Edwin B. Willis
Act Clark Gable, Myrna Loy, Walter Pidgeon, Walter Connolly, Leo Carrillo, Marjorie Main (M-G-M)

Adventures of a newsreel cameraman are the basis for this Clark Gable-Myrna Loy co-starrer. It's a blazing action thriller aimed as a follow-up to same pair's click in *Test Pilot* (1938). It has driving excitement, crackling dialog, glittering performances and inescapable romantic pull.

The story is one of those familiar Hollywood triangle affairs, with Gable and Walter Pidgeon as the sizzling rival newsreelers and Loy the he-man's ideal who entangles their already frenzied competition. When Gable hijacks Pidgeon's girl and they both land in the doghouse through Pidgeon's efforts to get even, the girl goes to South America to search for her long-lost aviator brother.

Strange angle of the picture's implausibilities is that the story was written by Len Hammond, an executive of Fox Movietone newsreel, while Laurence Stallings, co-author of the screenplay, is a former employee of the same outfit.

Best parts are the early sequences, all the way up to the sequence of a shipload of dynamite exploding directly underneath a tiny plane. Metro gives the picture one of its typically slick productions. Gable and Loy zoom through the leading parts with glittering persuasion.

●

TOO LATE BLUES
1962, 100 mins, US b/w
Dir John Cassavetes *Prod* John Cassavetes *Scr* Richard Carr, John Cassavetes *Ph* Lionel Lindon *Ed* Frank Bracht *Mus* David Raksin *Art* Hal Pereira, Tambi Larsen
Act Bobby Darin, Stella Stevens, Everett Chambers, Cliff Carnell, Seymour Cassel, Marilyn Clark (Paramount)

John Cassavetes's first Hollywood-made project shows a tendency to force casebook psychology on the characters at a loss of spontaneity. Thus an idealistic small-time jazz pianist and composer (Bobby Darin) loses his way when he is left by his girl due to a physically cowardly act. Used in an explanatory way there may be something psychologically right in this but it is somewhat too flat and contrived for acceptance in a film. Same goes for the flashy, good-looking would-be singer, Stella Stevens.

Darin's group is shown playing engagements in orphanages and in a park where nobody comes. A chance for a record date is blown sky-high when Darin's early insistence on doing what he wants is compromised by his girl's quitting him after his cowardly actions in a pool room brawl. He becomes the gigolo of an aging woman but finds his spark dampened. He finally seeks out his old girl, now a tramp.

Film never makes it clear whether the Darin character truly has talent or whether he should accept what he has and do his best at it. Ambiguity also robs the pic of a lot of punch. Cassavetes shows at his best in party scenes where characters are deftly blocked in good natured "getting-to-love-you" scenes.

Too Late Blues includes a neat jazz score by David Raksin. Dubbing for the musician-impersonating actors are Shelly Manne, Red Mitchell, Benny Carter, Uan Ramsey, Jimmy Bowles.

●

TOO LATE THE HERO
1970, 133 mins, US Ⓥ ▭ col
Dir Robert Aldrich *Prod* Robert Aldrich *Scr* Robert Aldrich, Lukas Heller *Ph* Joseph Biroc *Ed* Michael Luciano *Mus* Gerald Fried
Act Michael Caine, Cliff Robertson, Henry Fonda, Ian Bannen, Harry Andrews, Denholm Elliott (ABC/Palomar)

An okay World War II melodrama [from a story by Robert Aldrich and Robert Sherman], featuring Michael Caine and Cliff Robertson as antagonists who come to respect each other in the course of destroying a Japanese radio transmitter.

Robertson is introduced as a lazy Navy officer, specializing in Japanese translation. The British group, somewhat battle-weary and jaded in spirit, is headed by Harry Andrews, who outlines the mission to Robertson. The patrol, which must cross a sort of no-man's land where both Japanese and Allied soldiers occasionally exchange fire, comprises Robertson plus Denholm Elliott, as a weak, stupid, but curiously brave officer when it counted, and 12 enlisted men.

●

TOO MANY CHEFS
SEE: WHO IS KILLING THE GREAT CHEFS OF EUROPE?

●

TOO MANY HUSBANDS
1940, 80 mins, US b/w
Dir Wesley Ruggles *Prod* Wesley Ruggles *Scr* Claude Binyon *Ph* Joseph Walker *Ed* Otto Meyer, William Lyon *Mus* Frederick Hollander
Act Jean Arthur, Fred MacMurray, Melvyn Douglas, Harry Davenport, Dorothy Peterson, Edgar Buchanan (Columbia)

Too Many Husbands is a light, fluffy and amusing triangle with complications set up when a woman finds herself with two husbands on her hands as the first turns up after reportedly drowning a year previously in a boat cruise. Picture is studded with explosive dialog and situations, with the two husbands pitted against each other in highly amusing episodes, while the wife becomes bewildered while enjoying the love and attention showered on her from two sides.

Husbands is very light in texture but keeps going at a merry pace mainly through deft direction by Wesley Ruggles and intimate dialog and situations provided by scripter Claude Binyon [from play by W. Somerset Maugham]. Finish is rather inconclusive with windup unable to provide a climax to the merry mad mixup of dual husbands displayed throughout.

Jean Arthur, Fred MacMurray and Melvyn Douglas are excellent in the three leads, each taking advantage of individual opportunities to score. Harry Davenport is fine as the wife's father, while Melville Cooper is a bewildered butler.

●

TOOTSIE
1982, 116 mins, US Ⓥ ⦿ ▭ col
Dir Sydney Pollack *Prod* Sydney Pollack, Dick Richards *Scr* Larry Gelbart, Murray Schisgal, [Elaine May] *Ph* Owen Roizman *Ed* Fredric Steinkamp, William Steinkamp *Mus* Dave Grusin *Art* Peter Larkin
Act Dustin Hoffman, Jessica Lange, Teri Garr, Dabney Coleman, Charles Durning, Bill Murray (Mirage/Punch/Columbia)

Tootsie is a lulu. Remarkably funny and entirely convincing, film pulls off the rare accomplishment of being an in-drag comedy [from a story by Don McGuire and Larry Gelbart] which also emerges with three-dimensional characters.

Dustin Hoffman portrays a long-struggling New York stage actor whose "difficult" reputation has relegated him to employment as a waiter and drama coach.

Brash but appealing actor's solution: audition for a popular soap opera as a woman. Becoming a hit on the show, "Dorothy Michaels" develops into a media celebrity thanks to her forthright manner and "different" personality. Hoffman finds it hard to devote much time to sort-of-girlfriend Teri Garr, and all the while is growing more deeply attracted to soap costar Jessica Lange.

Hoffman triumphs in what must stand as one of his most brilliant performances. His Dorothy is entirely plausible and, physically, reasonably appealing. But much more importantly, he gets across the enormous guts and determination required of his character to go through with the charade.

1982: Best Supp. Actress (Jessica Lange)

NOMINATIONS: Best Picture, Director, Actor (Dustin Hoffman), Supp. Actress (Teri Garr), Original Screenplay, Cinematography, Editing, Original Song ("It Might Be You"), Sound

●

TOPAZ
1969, 126 mins, US Ⓥ ⦿ col
Dir Alfred Hitchcock *Prod* Alfred Hitchcock *Scr* Samuel Taylor *Ph* Jack Hildyard *Ed* William H. Ziegler *Mus* Maurice Jarre *Art* Henry Bumstead
Act Frederick Stafford, Dany Robin, John Vernon, Karin Dor, Michel Piccoli, John Forsythe (Universal)

Topaz tends to move more solidly and less infectiously than many of Alfred Hitchcock's best remembered pix. Yet Hitchcock brings in a full quota of twists and tingling moments.

Story [set in 1962], from Leon Uris's heavily plotted novel, centers around high politics, with intrigue and trickery involving French, American, Russian and Cuban security. Action is triggered by defection of a Russian scientist in Copenhagen to the Americans.

The director has a comparatively little known, but impeccable cast, with Frederick Stafford scoring as the French security investigator and with neat work by Philippe Noiret and Michel Piccoli as two French Quislings. John Vernon is a powerful Cuban political leader.

Hitchcock concentrates less than usual on his cool, blonde heroine, and it's Karin Dor as a Cuban spy and mistress of Stafford who steals most of the thunder.

●

TOP GUN
1986, 110 mins, US Ⓥ ⦿ ▭ col
Dir Tony Scott *Prod* Don Simpson, Jerry Bruckheimer *Scr* Jim Cash, Jack Epps, Jr. *Ph* Jeffrey Kimball *Ed* Billy Weber *Mus* Harold Faltermeyer *Art* John F. DeCuir
Act Tom Cruise, Kelly McGillis, Val Kilmer, Anthony Edwards, Tom Skerritt, Meg Ryan (Paramount)

Set in the world of naval fighter pilots, pic has strong visuals and pretty young people in stylish clothes and a non-stop soundtrack. Cinematographer Jeffery Kimball and his team have assembled some exciting flight footage.

Tom Cruise is Maverick, a hot-shot fighter pilot with a mind of his own and something to prove, assigned to the prestigious Top Gun training school.

Along for the ride as a romantic interest is Kelly McGillis, a civilian astrophysicist brought in to teach the boys about negative Gs and inverted flight tanks. Cruise, however, has his sights set on other targets.

McGillis is blessed with an intelligent and mature face that doesn't blend that well with Cruise's one-note grinning. There is nothing menacing or complex about his character. Tom Skerritt turns in his usual nice job as the hardened but not hard flight instructor.

1986: Best Song ("Take My Breath Away")

NOMINATIONS: Best Editing, Sound, Sound Effects Editing

●

TOP HAT
1935, 101 mins, US Ⓥ ⦿ b/w
Dir Mark Sandrich *Prod* Pandro S. Berman *Scr* Dwight Taylor, Allan Scott *Ph* David Abel *Ed* William Hamilton *Mus* Max Steiner (dir.) *Art* Van Nest Polglase, Carroll Clark
Act Fred Astaire, Ginger Rogers, Edward Everett Horton, Erik Rhodes, Helen Broderick, Eric Blore (RKO)

This one can't miss and the reasons are three—Fred Astaire, Irving Berlin's 11 songs and sufficient comedy between numbers to hold the film together.

Astaire's sock routines are up forward starting with "No Strings." He does this alone. It is the hot ditty of the batch, then "Isn't it a Lovely Day?" with Ginger Rogers for probably the best dance they've ever done together, trailed in turn by the title item, "Top Hat, White Tie and Tails," the boy number. It is the same number Astaire did in his Ziegfield show *Smiles*, practically the only change being the melody.

But the danger sign is in the story and cast. Substitute Alice Brady for Helen Broderick and it's the same lineup of players as was in *The Gay Divorcee* (1934). Besides which the situations in the two scripts parallel each other closely.

For the rest of the cast, Edward Everett Horton bears the brunt and is the secondary pillar around which the story revolves. His is the comedy burden which he splits with Eric Blore, his valet, and Erik Rhodes as a dress designer.

Rogers never opens her mouth vocally until the concluding "Piccolino." She is again badly dressed while her facial makeup and various coiffeurs give her a hard appearance.

1935: NOMINATIONS: Best Picture, Art Direction, Song ("Cheek to Cheek"), Dance Direction ("Top Hat," "Piccolino")

•

TOPKAPI
1964, 120 mins, US Ⓥ col
Dir Jules Dassin ***Prod*** Jules Dassin ***Scr*** Monja Danischewsky ***Ph*** Henri Alekan ***Ed*** Roger Dwyre ***Mus*** Manos Hadjidakis ***Art*** Max Douy
Act Melina Mercouri, Peter Ustinov, Maximilian Schell, Robert Morley, Akim Tamiroff, Gilles Segal (United Artists/Filmways)

Jules Dassin has taken a minor novel by Eric Ambler [*The Light of Day*] and turned it into a delightful and suspenseful comedy spoof of his own *Rififi*.

The band of thieves whose adventures make *Topkapi* are a motley crew indeed. Besides Melina Mercouri, it includes Maximilian Schell, master thief; Robert Morley, Gilles Segal and Jess Hahn. Added later, although it takes him some time and a bit of adventure to realize it, Peter Ustinov is an unwitting accomplice.

The basically simple plot, which is rich in detail and background, has the gang attempting to steal a fabulous jeweled dagger from the Topkapi Palace museum in Istanbul. The actual theft is depicted in a long sequence reminiscent of the one in *Rififi* but with a bit more levity.

Mercouri has a holiday in a role that asks her to be equally enamored of gems and males. Schell, surprisingly, plays his role somewhat tongue-in-cheek, never evidencing more than a surface interest in anything (including Mercouri), other than his work. Ustinov has probably the meatiest part in the film and one that allows him to use many of the unsubtleties in dominating scenes he has at his command.

1964: Best Supp. Actor (Peter Ustinov)

•

TOPPER
1937, 98 mins, US Ⓥ ⦿ b/w
Dir Norman Z. McLeod ***Prod*** Milton H. Bren (assoc.) ***Scr*** Jack Jevne, Eric Hatch, Eddie Moran ***Ph*** Norbert Brodine ***Ed*** William Terhune ***Mus*** Arthur Morton (arr.) ***Art*** Arthur I. Royce
Act Cary Grant, Constance Bennett, Roland Young, Billie Burke, Alan Mowbray, Eugene Pallette (Roach/M-G-M)

With the assistance of Norman McLeod, as director, Hal Roach has produced a weird and baffling tale of spiritualism. It is entitled *Topper*, from the novel by Thorne Smith. It is carefully made, excellently photographed, and adroitly employs mechanical illusions and trick sound effects.

Story is about the adventures, among living persons, of a young married couple, George and Marion Kerby, who are killed in an automobile smashup as the climax of a wild night of drinking and carousing. Their astral bodies rise from the ruins, and they agree that until they have done someone a good deed they are likely to remain indefinitely in a state of double exposure.

Reviewing the possibilities for charitable action, they decide that their friend, Cosmo Topper, a hen-pecked bank president, who has lived a dull, routine life, shall have the benefit of their assistance.

Performances are usually good. Cary Grant and Constance Bennett, as the reincarnated Kerbys, do their assignments with great skill. Roland Young carries the brunt of the story and does it well. In the title role, he is the docile, good citizen until the transformation of his personality changes him into a dashing man about town.

1937: NOMINATION: Best Sound

•

TOPPER RETURNS
1941, 95 mins, US Ⓥ b/w
Dir Roy Del Ruth ***Prod*** Hal Roach ***Scr*** Jonathan Latimer, Gordon Douglas, Paul Gerard Smith ***Ph*** Norbert Brodine ***Ed*** James Newcom ***Mus*** Werner R. Heymann ***Art*** Nicolai Remisoff
Act Joan Blondell, Roland Young, Carole Landis, Billie Burke, Dennis O'Keefe, Patsy Kelly (Roach/United Artists)

This is the third feature film which Hal Roach has produced from the strikingly original ideas and characters conceived by Thorne Smith in his use of astral bodies to motivate the hilarious and nonsensical actions of living persons. Roland Young again appears as Topper, the mild-mannered suburbanite whose quiet way of life is rudely upset by his strange affinity for spirits that lead him into weird complications. Billie Burke is his flighty wife, and the newcomers are Joan Blondell and Carole Landis.

This time the innocent Young is dragged into the midst of a murder mystery, in the solving of which he has able and amusing assistance from Eddie "Rochester" Anderson, who just about steals the picture from the other players.

Blondell is murdered by a hooded mysterious character, having been mistaken for her friend, the blonde Landis. Thereupon, Blondell, in shadowy form, appeals to Young for aid in capturing the villain and saving the life of the intended victim. Film begins to miss out when the story veers from its own premise to the level of a conventional mystery farce. Direction by Roy Del Ruth is uneven and lacking in improvisations.

•

TOPPER TAKES A TRIP
1938, 80 mins, US Ⓥ b/w
Dir Norman Z. McLeod ***Prod*** [Hal Roach] ***Scr*** Eddie Moran, Jack Jevne, Corey Ford ***Ph*** [Norbert Brodine] ***Ed*** [William Terhune] ***Mus*** [Edward Powell, Hugo Friedhofer] ***Art*** [Charles D. Hall]
Act Constance Bennett, Roland Young, Billie Burke, Alan Mowbray, Veree Teasdale, Franklin Pangborn (Roach/United Artists)

A delightful, very entertaining comedy [from the novel by Thorne Smith] built around several of the characters who appear in *Topper*, of which this is a sequel.

Roland Young, as Topper, is in court trying to offer a dubious defense in a divorce case Billie Burke has brought against him because he had a woman in his room. Thereafter, with the action shifting to Europe, where Burke has gone to get her divorce, the living spirit of Constance Bennett and her dog Skippy remain to keep him company. Bennett is still trying to reconcile Young and Burke.

Norman McLeod's adroit direction throughout keeps the film at a nice pace. Pantomime takes care of much of the footage, with just the proper but pungent amount of dialog to suit for story-telling and comedy purposes.

1939: NOMINATION: Best Special Effects

•

TOP SECRET!
1984, 90 mins, US Ⓥ ⦿ col
Dir Jim Abrahams, David Zucker, Jerry Zucker ***Prod*** Jon Davison, Hunt Lowry ***Scr*** Jim Abrahams, David Zucker, Jerry Zucker, Martyn Burke ***Ph*** Christopher Challis ***Ed*** Bernard Gribble ***Mus*** Maurice Jarre ***Art*** Peter Lamont
Act Val Kilmer, Lucy Gutteridge, Christopher Villiers, Omar Sharif, Peter Cushing, Jeremy Kemp (Paramount)

Top Secret! is another bumptious tribute to all that was odd in old movies. Followers of the *Airplane!* writer-director trio will probably be happy and satisfied with this effort, yet short of overjoyed.

The attempted target this time is a combination of the traditional spy film and Elvis Presley musical romps, which in and of itself is funny to start with. And Val Kilmer proves a perfect blend of staunch hero and hothouse heartthrob.

But in a deliberate effort to do something different, the directors have unfortunately discarded the cast of matinee idols so closely identified with the originals.

Other than that, *Secret!* shares the same wonderful wacky attitude that allows just about any kind of gag to come flowing in and out of the picture at the strangest times, given a full framework of Kilmer as an American pop idol drawn into a plot to reunite Germany under one rule.

And how all of this gets started on the beach with "skeet surfing" is a bit beyond easy description, along with the parachuting fireplace, a magniloquent minuet and the unexpected sexual delights in dressing up like a cow.

•

TORA! TORA! TORA!
1970, 144 mins, US Ⓥ ⦿ ▭ col
Dir Richard Fleischer, Toshio Masuda, Kinji Fukasaku ***Prod*** Elmo Williams ***Scr*** Larry Forrester, Hideo Oguni, Ryuzo Kikushima ***Ph*** Charles F. Wheeler, Sinsaku Himeda, Masamichi Satch, Osami Furuya ***Ed*** James E. Newcom, Pembroke J. Herring, Inoue Chikaya ***Mus*** Jerry Goldsmith ***Art*** Jack Martin Smith, Yoshiro Muraki, Richard Day, Taizoh Kawashima
Act Martin Balsam, Soh Yamamura, Joseph Cotten, Tatsuya Mihashi, E. G. Marshall, Takahiro Tamura (20th Century-Fox)

Lavish ($25 million) and meticulous restaging of the Japanese airborne attack on Pearl Harbor on December 7, 1941, constitutes a brilliant logistics achievement which is not generally matched by the overall artistic handling of the accompanying dramatic narrative.

Effect of the story [from *Tora! Tora! Tora!* by Gordon W. Prange and *The Broken Seal* by Ladislas Farago] seems to prove that the Japanese government, while somewhat divided internally, at least had some unity of purpose in its expansion plans.

Both overall director Richard Fleischer and his Japanese counterparts do a dull job, and the monotonously low-key tone of scene after scene almost suggests that each was filmed without a sense of ultimate slotting in the finished form.

1970: Best Special Visual Effects (A. D. Flowers, L. B. Abbot)

NOMINATIONS: Best Cinematography, Art Direction, Editing, Sound

•

TORCHLIGHT
1984, 91 mins, US Ⓥ ⦿ col
Dir Tom Wright ***Prod*** Joel Douglas ***Scr*** Pamela Sue Martin, Eliza Moorman ***Ph*** Alex Phillips ***Mus*** Michael Cannon ***Art*** Craig Stearns
Act Pamela Sue Martin, Steve Railsback, Ian McShane, Al Corley, Rita Taggart, Arnie Moore (UCO)

Torchlight is largely a family affair. Pamela Sue Martin, who costars with Steve Railsback and Ian McShane, is cowriter of the screenplay, as well as taking associate producer credit, while her husband, Manuel Rojas, is executive producer. Between them they've fashioned a film which opens on a deceptively lighthearted note but develops in downbeat style.

In its opening sequences, the plot depicts the love-at-first-sight romance and marriage of Martin and Railsback. Enter McShane, a sinister and larger than life pusher, and Railsback's downfall progresses until he becomes a physical and mental wreck, left without wife or home.

Martin has written for herself a role which allows her to reach the highs and lows of elation and despair. Railsback has a demanding role and mainly fills it convincingly, but McShane as the sinister pusher is a grossly overdrawn character.

•

TORCH SONG
1953, 89 mins, US Ⓥ ⦿ col
Dir Charles Walters ***Prod*** Henry Berman, Sidney Franklin, Jr. ***Scr*** John Michael Hayes, Jan Lustig ***Ph*** Robert Planck ***Ed*** Albert Akst ***Mus*** Adolph Deutsch (dir.) ***Art*** Cedric Gibbons, Preston Ames
Act Joan Crawford, Michael Wilding, Gig Young, Marjorie Rambeau, Henry Morgan, Dorothy Patrick (M-G-M)

M-G-M has supplied Joan Crawford with a strong starring vehicle in *Torch Song*, and she makes it her show all the way, as well as a topnotch woman's picture. There are striking gowns, high-styled but not extreme, class background settings and an overall polish that goes well with the story and its characters. Script is based on a story by I.A.R. Wylie.

The picture tells a backstage story of Jenny Stewart, a successful musical comedy star on Broadway. The career drive has left her a lonely woman, but too self-sufficient to acknowledge needs outside of herself. This tough veneer begins to crack when Tye Graham (Michael Wilding), a war-blinded pianist, substitutes for her regular vocal arranger and accompanist. Her reluctant interest in this man builds to a tremendous scene in which she, alone in her bedroom, simulates blindness to discover what it must be like to live in a world of darkness.

The simulated blindness scene and several others come over with a sock dramatic impact, and there are little touches throughout, such as the growling dislike Wilding's seeing-eye dog has for the actress, that maintain audience interest even when the pace has a tendency to falter.

The musical star character has four songs, several rating reprises. "Tenderly," one of the four, also themes the background score which is ably directed by Adolph Deutsch. "Two Faced Woman," by Arthur Schwartz and Howard Dietz, is spotlighted in the picture's big high—yellow production number. Crawford's terp chores and the production number were staged by director Charles Walters, who also cut himself in as her dance partner.

Gig Young is somewhat lost in the role of a shallow, tippling young man in the star's entourage.

•

TORCH SONG TRILOGY
1988, 117 mins, US Ⓥ ⦿ col
Dir Paul Bogart ***Prod*** Howard Gottfried ***Scr*** Harvey Fierstein ***Ph*** Mikael Salomon ***Ed*** Nicholas C. Smith ***Mus*** Peter Matz ***Art*** Richard Hoover
Act Anne Bancroft, Matthew Broderick, Harvey Fierstein, Brian Kerwin, Karen Young, Charles Pierce (New Line)

Harvey Fierstein repeats his Tony Award–winning performance as Arnold Beckoff, a flamboyant drag queen looking for love and respect. Originated as separately staged one-acts, the play, when finally mounted as a unified work in 1982, proved bracing in its frank depiction of gay sex life, both promiscuous and committed.

Nervous, mannered, gravelly voiced, overly sensitive, campy and with a taste for eye-rolling rivaled only by Groucho Marx in modern showbiz annals, Arnold appears a bit gun-shy of romance, but allows himself to be picked up in a gay bar by Ed (Brian Kerwin), a good-looking, straight-seeming fellow who openly announces his bisexuality. This doesn't stop Arnold from falling head over heels for his Middle American catch, but causes him endless pain when he discovers Ed with a young woman, Laurel (Karen Young).

In what is effectively Act Two, Arnold meets Alan (Matthew Broderick), to him an impossibly good-looking kid who used to be a hustler and actively seeks out Arnold for his human, as opposed to superficial, qualities.

Act Three, the most conventional of the sections, is given over to Arnold's efforts to handle an adopted teenage son and sort out his strained relations with his mother (Anne Bancroft).

•

TORN CURTAIN
1966, 126 mins, US Ⓥ ⊙ col
Dir Alfred Hitchcock ***Prod*** Alfred Hitchcock ***Scr*** Brian Moore ***Ph*** John F. Warren ***Ed*** Bud Hoffman ***Mus*** John Addison ***Art*** Hein Heckroth
Act Paul Newman, Julie Andrews, Lila Kedrova, Hansjoerg Felmy, Tamara Toumanova, Wolfgang Kieling (Universal)

Torn Curtain is an okay Cold War suspenser with Paul Newman as a fake defector to East Germany in order to obtain Communist defense secrets. Julie Andrews is his femme partner. Alfred Hitchcock's direction emphasizes suspense and ironic comedy flair but some good plot ideas are marred by routine dialog, and a too relaxed pace contributes to a dull overlength.

Brian Moore scripted from his original story about a top U.S. physicist who essays a public defection in order to pick the brains of a Communist wizard. Writing, acting and direction make clear from the outset that Newman is loyal, although about one-third of pic passes before this is made explicit in dialog. This early telegraphing diminishes suspense.

Hitchcock freshens up his bag of tricks in a good potpourri which becomes a bit stale through a noticeable lack of zip and pacing.

•

TORRENT, THE
1926, 68 mins, US ⊙ ⊗ b/w
Dir Monta Bell ***Scr*** Dorothy Farnum, Katherine Hilliker, H. H. Caldwell ***Ph*** William Daniels ***Ed*** Frank Sullivan ***Art*** Cedric Gibbons, Merrill Pye
Act Ricardo Cortez, Greta Garbo, Gertrude Olmstead, Edward Connelly, Martha Mattox (Cosmopolitan/MGM)

Greta Garbo, making her American debut as a screen star, has everything with looks, acting ability and personality. When one is a Scandinavian and can put over a Latin characterization with sufficient power to make it most convincing, need there be any more said regarding her ability? She makes *The Torrent* worthwhile.

The Torrent is a picturization of the Blasco Ibanez novel of the same name. It is evident that the great scene of the rush of waters was counted on to carry the picture, but a bursting dam doesn't mean anything in a picture except as an incident. It is the story itself that carries here. The tale of the unrequited love of the little Spanish peasant girl who develops into a great operatic star will hold because of its love twist.

•

TORTILLA FLAT
1942, 105 mins, US Ⓥ col
Dir Victor Fleming ***Prod*** Sam Zimbalist ***Scr*** John Lee Mahin, Benjamin Glazer ***Ph*** Karl Freund ***Ed*** James E. Newcom ***Mus*** Franz Waxman
Act Spencer Tracy, Hedy Lamarr, John Garfield, Frank Morgan, Akim Tamiroff, Donald Meek (M-G-M)

From John Steinbeck's book of related stories, *Tortilla Flat* (presented as a Broadway play in the winter of 1937–38 which was a failure) Metro has made a sincere, tender, beguiling and at times exalting picture. It is sympathetically and adroitly adapted, handsomely produced, expertly directed and eloquently acted. Film is sepia-colored.

Steinbeck's stories have been compressed into a single narrative, with dramatic form, steadily heightening interest and a fairly moving, if obvious, climax. Not only does the camera's increased scope help the yarn, but the characters have sharper definition and Steinbeck's compassionate feeling for his humble subject has been skillfully transmitted to the screen.

Title refers to a locale near Monterey, in northern California, and the story deals with the *paisanos*, lowly descendants of early Spanish settlers.

Spencer Tracy is superb as the strong-headed leader of the group, somehow retaining sympathy for the character even when he's behaving with shameless selfishness. Hedy Lamarr not only looks stunning as the Portuguese girl, but gives easily her best dramatic performance to date.

•

TORTURE GARDEN
1968, 92 mins, UK Ⓥ col
Dir Freddie Francis ***Prod*** Max S. Rosenberg, Milton Subotsky ***Scr*** Robert Bloch ***Ph*** Norman Warwick ***Ed*** Peter Elliott ***Mus*** Don Banks ***Art*** Bill Constable
Act Jack Palance, Burgess Meredith, Beverly Adams, Peter Cushing, Michael Bryant, Barbara Ewing (Amicus)

Robert Bloch penned the episodic script in which Burgess Meredith is a sideshow mystic, who gives a special after-hours show to five patrons. Jack Palance is an Edgar Allen Poe buff who, it turns out, will do almost anything to achieve eminence in his hobby.

Michael Bryant's sequence involves a man-eating house cat with whom he tangles after greed induces him to permit the death of a supposedly wealthy relative.

The situations are developed economically and inventively, both from script and Freddie Francis's very good direction. Cast is competent, considering the apparent fast shooting sked and limited productions coin. In latter regard, sets range from well-thought-out to skimpy.

•

TO SIR, WITH LOVE
1967, 104 mins, UK Ⓥ ⊙ col
Dir James Clavell ***Prod*** James Clavell ***Scr*** James Clavell ***Ph*** Paul Beeson ***Ed*** Peter Thornton ***Mus*** Ron Grainer ***Art*** Tony Woollard
Act Sidney Poitier, Christian Roberts, Judy Geeson, Suzy Kendall, Lulu, Ann Bell (Columbia)

To Sir, With Love is a well-made, sometimes poignant, drama [from the 1959 E. R. Braithwaite novel] about a Negro teacher, working in a London slum, who transforms an unruly class into a group of youngsters better prepared for adult life. Sidney Poitier stars in an excellent performance.

Poitier, after gauging the rebellious mood of his class, scraps the formal agenda and institutes what he rightly calls "survival training." Students include Christian Roberts, very good as the natural class leader; Judy Geeson, a looker who gets a crush on teacher; Christopher Chittell, another reformed punk; and Lulu, an engaging personality with substantial acting ability.

•

TOTAL ECLIPSE
1996, 110 mins, France/UK/Belgium Ⓥ col
Dir Agnieszka Holland ***Prod*** Ramsey Levi ***Scr*** Christopher Hampton ***Ph*** Yorgos Arvanitis ***Ed*** Isabel Lorente ***Mus*** Jan A. P. Kaczmarek ***Art*** Dan Weil
Act Leonardo DiCaprio, David Thewlis, Romane Bohringer, Domonique Blanc (Fit/Portman/SFP/K2)

A good biographical film about artists should, at the very least, inspire the viewer to learn more about its subjects and the work they created. *Total Eclipse* has totally the opposite effect, of making one never want to hear about its protagonists again.

This misbegotten look at the mutually destructive relationship between the 19th-century French poets Arthur Rimbaud and Paul Verlaine is a complete botch in all respects. Christopher Hampton adapted his screenplay from a play he wrote at 18, presumably when he was infatuated with the rebellious artistic posturings of the equally youthful Rimbaud.

Pic is in trouble from the outset, as it is only much later explained how the boyish country lad Rimbaud (Leonardo DiCaprio) comes to enter the well-appointed Paris household of Verlaine (David Thewlis) and his pregnant wife, Mathilde (Romane Bohringer). Verlaine is hopelessly smitten by his fine-featured protégé, setting him up in an atelier, tolerating his rudeness to his friends at top literary salons and taking seriously Rimbaud's arrogant stance that he is too good to be published. The two also become lovers and the poets' ugly sado-masochistic seesawing is intercut with interludes in which a drunken, guilt-ridden Verlaine returns to ingratiate himself with his wife. Kissing and sodomy scenes between the two men are photographed in frankly embarrassing close-up.

DiCaprio cuts an acceptable, if still rather childlike, figure as the burning artist. Thewlis has had his head unattractively shorn and is made to look like a young, degenerate Ralph Richardson. The ever-voluptuous Bohringer is encouraged to show off her body as much as possible.

•

TOTAL RECALL
1990, 113 mins, US Ⓥ ⊙ col
Dir Paul Verhoeven ***Prod*** Buzz Feitshans, Ronald Shusett ***Scr*** Ronald Shusett, Dan O'Bannon, Gary Oldman ***Ph*** Jost Vacano ***Ed*** Frank J. Urioste ***Mus*** Jerry Goldsmith ***Art*** William Sandell
Act Arnold Schwarzenegger, Rachel Ticotin, Sharon Stone, Ronny Cox, Michael Ironside, Marshall Bell (Carolco)

Estimates of the cost of this futuristic extravaganza range from $60 to $70 million making it one of the most expensive pics ever made. There are gargantuan sets repping Mars and a futuristic Earth society, grotesque creatures galore, genuinely weird and mostly seamless visual effects, and enough gunshots, grunts and explosions to keep anyone in a high state of nervous exhilaration.

The story [by Ronald Shusett, Dan O'Bannon and John Povill] is actually a good one, taking off from Phillip K. Dick's celebrated sci-fi tale *We Can Remember It for You Wholesale*.

Arnold Schwarzenegger's character, a working stiff in the year 2084, keeps having these strange nightmares about living on Mars, and it transpires that he once worked in the colony as an intelligence agent before rebelling against dictator Ronny Cox. Schwarzenegger had most, but not quite all, of his bad memories erased and was sent to Earth to work on a construction crew, with a sexy but treacherous wife (Sharon Stone).

A visit to a mind-altering travel agency named Rekall Inc. alerts Schwarzenegger to the truth, setting him off on a rampage through Earth and Mars with the help of equally tough female sidekick Rachel Ticotin.

The fierce and unrelenting pace, accompanied by a tongue-in-cheek strain of humor in the roughhouse screenplay, keeps the film moving like a juggernaut.

1990: Special Achievement Award (visual effects)

NOMINATION: Best Sound

•

TO THE DEVIL A DAUGHTER
1976, 92 mins, UK/W. Germany Ⓥ col
Dir Peter Sykes ***Prod*** Roy Skeggs ***Scr*** Chris Wicking ***Ph*** David Watkin ***Ed*** John Trumper ***Art*** Don Picton
Act Richard Widmark, Christopher Lee, Honor Blackman, Denholm Elliott, Michael Goodliffe, Nastassja Kinski (Hammer/Terra)

To the Devil a Daughter is lacklustre occult melodrama in which Christopher Lee is up to his old tricks as an excommunicated priest who takes up satan's cause in order to save the world from its own decadent folly.

Based on a novel by English author Dennis Wheatley, the picture makes a few too many pretensions to serious exploration of the occult, that hamper the flow.

Lee is ever-dependable in this sort of menace routine, Richard Widmark turns in a serviceable job, ditto Honor Blackman and Anthony Valentine as pals who aid and abet him at mortal cost. Nastassja Kinski is moderately appealing as the child-woman novitiate and Denholm Elliott turns on the requisite anguish as the fearful father who originally signed the girl over to Lee in order to spare his own hide.

•

TOTO LE HEROS
(TOTO THE HERO)
1991, 89 mins, Belgium/France/Germany Ⓥ ⊙ col
Dir Jaco van Dormael ***Prod*** Pierre Drouot, Dany Geys ***Scr*** Jaco van Dormael ***Ph*** Walther van den Ende ***Ed*** Susana Rossberg ***Mus*** Pierre van Dormael ***Art*** Hubert Pouille
Act Michel Bouquet, Jo De Backer, Mireille Perier, Sandrine Blancke, Peter Boehlke, Fabienne Loriaux, Fabienne Loriaux (Iblis/Dussart/Metropolis)

Toto the Hero, debut pic by Belgian helmer Jaco van Dormael, is a winning blend of kid's fantasy and adult comedy that's as fresh as a hot croissant. Multilayered plot kicks off in rollercoaster style with Thomas van Hasebroeck (Michel Bouquet) soliloquizing in a hospital bed about childhood buddy Alfred Kant "stealing" his life. Thomas reckons he was given to the wrong family because of chaos during a hospital fire. The Kant family went on to become rich and famous, while Thomas was stuck with a workaday middle-class upbringing in a dull Belgian nabe.

Especially in its early stages, with kid Thomas's screwy view of life, pic often plays like a Euro version of *The World According to Garp*. The tempo slows in the long central section dominated by the adult Thomas's affair with Evelyne (Mireille Perier), who may or may not be his sister; but the pacey final reels rediscover the opening's elan and spring some neat twists in the bargain.

Former clown and children's theater director Van Dormael unravels the complex skein with much assurance and shows a sharp talent for absurdist comedy. Technically it's fine all round, with perky use of the w.k. Charles Trenet song "Boum."

•

TOTO THE HERO
SEE: TOTO LE HEROS

•

TO TRAP A SPY
1966, 92 mins, US col
Dir Don Medford ***Prod*** Norman Felton ***Scr*** Sam Rolfe ***Ph*** Joseph Biroc ***Ed*** Henry Berman ***Mus*** Jerry Goldsmith ***Art*** George W. Davis, Merrill Pye
Act Robert Vaughn, Luciana Paluzzi, Patricia Crowley, Fritz Weaver, William Marshall, David McCallum (M-G-M)

To Trap a Spy is an elaborated version of MGM-TV's *The Man From U.N.C.L.E.* pilot, originally lensed in color but telecast in black-and-white to tee off series on September 23, 1964. Additional footage was shot to bring total running time now to 92 minutes.

Patently released to cash in on current espionage mania, much of the new footage is devoted to build Robert Vaughn, the agent from U.N.C.L.E., into a glamor boy with a roving eye for beautiful femmes. Whatever plot there is revolves around efforts to prevent the assassination of a visiting African dignitary, but the refurbished entry isn't much better than the original.

Vaughn tries hard and with some success through plot holes, and gets capable support from Patricia Crowley, Luciana Paluzzi and Fritz Weaver. His sidekick in teleseries, David McCallum, is in only two scenes.

•

TOUCH, THE
1971, 113 mins, Sweden/US Ⓥ col
Dir Ingmar Bergman ***Prod*** Ingmar Bergman ***Scr*** Ingmar Bergman ***Ph*** Sven Nykvist ***Ed*** Siv Kanaly-Lundgren ***Mus*** Jan Johannson
Act Bibi Andersson, Elliott Gould, Max von Sydow, Sheila Reid, Steffan Hallerstram, Maria Nolgard (ABC/Persona)

Shot in English with occasional Swedish dialog and splendidly acted and lensed, *The Touch* is both a romantic film of great poignancy and strength and an example of masterful cinema honed down to deceptively simple near-perfection.

In telling what is basically a straight triangle tale (bored wife, busy husband, "interesting" and available friend) Bergman seems to be appealing to and aiming primarily at the emotions rather than the intellect.

Not unexpectedly, Bergman's cast is superb. Bibi Andersson walks away with pic thanks to one of those immense, bigger-than-life performances. Rarely has the moving anguish of a trysting woman been so stirringly caught. Elliott Gould is a perfect choice as the somewhat neurotic foreign archeologist who, despite oafish manners, selfishness and instability, fascinates and attracts her. Max von Sydow does expected wonders with the normally unplayable role of the silently strong husband.

•

TOUCH AND GO
1986, 101 mins, US Ⓥ ⦿ col
Dir Robert Mandel ***Prod*** Stephen Friedman ***Scr*** Alan Ormsby, Bob Sand, Harry Colomby ***Ph*** Richard H. Kline ***Ed*** Walt Mulconery ***Mus*** Sylvester Levay ***Art*** Charles Rosen
Act Michael Keaton, Maria Conchita Alonso, Ajay Naidu, Maria Tucci, Max Wright, Jere Burns (Tri-Star)

Touch and Go mixes humor, heart and considerable hokum in an engaging story matching an unusually serious Michael Keaton and zesty Latin star Maria Conchita Alonso as lovers in spite of themselves.

Pic features Keaton as a hot-shot hockey jock with the Chicago Eagles. His regimen gets disrupted one night when a punk kid (Ajay Naidu) acts as the innocent front for his thug friends as they try to mug the sports star. Keaton fends the rascals off and he's left throttling the 11-year-old. But the kid's a charmer and Keaton returns him home to his slummy neighborhood and to Mom (Alonso) for discipline, opening the way for romance. Rapport between the disrespectful kid and Keaton unfolds immediately.

•

TOUCHEZ PAS AU GRISBI
1954, 95 mins, France/Italy b/w
Dir Jacques Becker ***Scr*** Jacques Becker, Albert Simonin, Maurice Griffe ***Ph*** Pierre Montazel ***Ed*** Marguerite Renoir ***Mus*** Jean Wiener ***Art*** Jean D'Eaubonne
Act Jean Gabin, Rene Dary, Paul Frankeur, Lino Ventura, Jeanne Moreau, Dora Doll (Del Duca/Silver/Antares)

Jacques Becker, who did such a fine job in painting the turn-of-the-century apache milieu in *Casque D'Or*, brings the same care and psychological overtones to a film on the modern racketeer element.

Max the Liar (Jean Gabin) is an aging racketeer who has made a big haul in gold bullion and wants to retire. However, friendship, gang codes and women mess up this dream when Max's best friend (Rene Dary) gets kidnapped by a rival gang, who will only release him in return for the gold.

The usual gilding of pretty girls, nitery scenes, gunfights and milieu talk abound in the film, but the element of keen insight into gang behavior puts this into a measured pacing which crescendos in a final well-staged gunfight. Becker brings this off in spite of a puffy story and some thumbnail characterizations.

Gabin brings all his authority and experience to bear in making Max a sturdy, noble crook whose code carries him through a logical series of actions, though Max the man is left a bit shadowy. Jeanne Moreau turns in a neat bit as a moll and Dary as the inarticulate aging Romeo friend is memorable.

•

TOUCH OF CLASS, A
1973, 106 mins, UK Ⓥ ▭ col
Dir Melvin Frank ***Prod*** Melvin Frank ***Scr*** Melvin Frank, Jack Rose ***Ph*** Austin Dempster ***Ed*** Bill Butler ***Mus*** John Cameron ***Art*** Terry Marsh
Act George Segal, Glenda Jackson, Paul Sorvino, Hildegard Neil, Cec Linder, K. Callan (Brut)

A Touch of Class is sensational. Director, writer and producer Melvin Frank has accomplished precisely what Peter Bogdanovich did in *What's Up, Doc?*—revitalizing, updating and invigorating an earlier film genre to smash results.

George Segal herein justifies superbly a reputation for comedy ability while Glenda Jackson's full-spectrum talent is again confirmed. An accidental London meeting between Segal and Jackson leads to a casual pass by Segal, thence (through a series of hilarious complications, including wife, in-laws, and old friends) to a frustrated rendezvous in a Spanish resort. Pair's romance flourishes into a full-blown affair at home, with Segal wearing himself out dashing between two beds.

The visual and verbal antics are supported by just enough underlying character depth to keep the film on a solid credible basis, setting up the plot for its tender, bittersweet climax.

1973: Best Actress (Glenda Jackson)

NOMINATIONS: Best Picture, Story & Screenplay, Original Dramatic Score, Song ("All That Love Went to Waste")

•

TOUCH OF EVIL
1958, 95 mins, US Ⓥ ⦿ b/w
Dir Orson Welles, Harry Keller ***Prod*** Albert Zugsmith ***Scr*** Orson Welles ***Ph*** Russell Metty ***Ed*** Virgil M. Vogel, Aaron Stell, [Edward Curtiss] ***Mus*** Henry Mancini ***Art*** Alexander Golitzen, Robert Clatworthy
Act Charlton Heston, Janet Leigh, Orson Welles, Joseph Calleia, Akim Tamiroff, Joanna Moore (Universal)

Touch of Evil smacks of brilliance but ultimately flounders in it. Taken scene by scene, there is much to be said for this filmization of Whit Masterson's novel, *Badge of Evil*. Orson Welles's script contains some hard-hitting dialog; his use of low key lighting is effective, and Russell Metty's photography is fluid and impressive; and Henry Mancini's music is poignant. But *Touch of Evil* proves it takes more than good scenes to make a good picture.

Welles portrays an American cop who has the keen reputation of always getting his man. Before you know it, he's hot on the trail of those scoundrels who blew to smithereens the wealthy "owner" of a small Mexican border town. Charlton Heston, a bigwig in the Mexican government, just happens to be around with his new American bride (Janet Leigh) and gets himself rather involved in the proceedings, feeling the dynamiting has something to do with a narcotics racket he's investigating.

Off his rocker since his wife was murdered years ago, Welles supposedly is deserving of a bit of sympathy. At least, there's a hint of it in dialog, even though it isn't seen in his characterization. Aside from this, he turns in a unique and absorbing performance. Heston keeps his plight the point of major importance, combining a dynamic quality with a touch of Latin personality. Leigh, sexy as all get-out, switches from charm to fright with facility in a capable portrayal. Dennis Weaver, as the night man, is fine though exaggerated.

Spicing up the production are a single close-up of Zsa Zsa Gabor as a non-stripped stripper, a word or two from Joseph Cotton, who's slipped in without screen credit and a provocative few minutes with gypsy-looking Marlene Dietrich. Dietrich is rather sultry and fun to watch, even though it's somewhat incongruous to see her walk into the Mexican darkness at the picture's finish, turn to wave, then wail, "Adios."

[In 1998 a "restored version" of Welles's "original" was released, featuring minor changes to picture and soundtrack.]

•

TOUCH OF LOVE, A
1969, 102 mins, UK Ⓥ col
Dir Waris Hussein ***Prod*** Max J. Rosenberg, Milton Subotsky ***Scr*** Margaret Drabble ***Ph*** Peter Suschitzky ***Ed*** Bill Blunden ***Mus*** Michael Dress ***Art*** Tony Curtis
Act Sandy Dennis, Ian McKellen, Michael Coles, John Standing, Eleanor Bron (Palomar)

Sharply scripted by Margaret Drabble from her novel [*The Millstone*], story deals with a well-educated philosophy student whose first all-the-way seduction by a chance acquaintance leaves her pregnant, while each of her steady but platonic suitors thinks his rival is the father.

Pic details girl's solo battle against society and herself to decide whether to keep the child and bring it up sans a father.

Key factor, aside from a fine script, trim direction by newcomer Waris Hussein and moody lensing, lies in the Sandy Dennis performance, which is pin-point accurate in conveying the tremendous inner strength which helps her character win through against hostile—or disinterested—society and family.

She gets very strong support here from Ian McKellen as the unknowing father.

•

TOUCH OF ZEN, A
SEE: XIA NU

•

TOUGH GUYS
1986, 104 mins, US Ⓥ ⦿ ▭ col
Dir Jeff Kanew ***Prod*** Joe Wizan ***Scr*** James Orr, Jim Cruickshank ***Ph*** King Baggot ***Ed*** Kaja Fehr ***Mus*** James Newton Howard ***Art*** Todd Hallowell
Act Burt Lancaster, Kirk Douglas, Charles Durning, Alexis Smith, Dana Carvey, Darlanne Fluegel (Touchstone/Silver Screen/Bryna)

Tough Guys is unalloyed hokum that proves a sad waste of talent on the parts of co-stars Burt Lancaster and Kirk Douglas.

The two venerable thesps, both 70-ish and looking fit and alert, turn up here as Harry Doyle and Archie Long, two gentleman crooks celebrated in the annals of American crime for having been the last outlaws to rob a train.

Pic pokes along with Lancaster provoking havoc at his old folks' home and Douglas quitting a series of jobs in disgust until scripters decide that perhaps a plot would be nice, so the guys get together and—surprise—decide to rob the train again.

It's all silly, meaningless and vaguely depressing, since the awareness lingers throughout that both actors are capable of much, much more than is demanded of them here.

•

TOUGH GUYS DON'T DANCE
1987, 108 mins, US Ⓥ ⦿ col
Dir Norman Mailer ***Prod*** Menahem Golan, Yoram Globus ***Scr*** Norman Mailer ***Ph*** John Bailey ***Ed*** Debra McDermott ***Mus*** Angelo Badalamenti ***Art*** Armin Ganz
Act Ryan O'Neal, Isabella Rossellini, Debra Sandlund, Wings Hauser, John Bedford Lloyd, Frances Fisher (Cannon/Zoetrope)

Tough Guys is part parody and part serious with a nasty streak running right down the middle.

Set in a small coastal town in Massachusetts in the sort of place where everyone knows everyone else's business, and for Tim Madden (Ryan O'Neal) business is bad. Story has something to do with a botched drug deal, men who love the wrong women and women who love the wrong men.

In the course of playing its hand, Madden's wealthy wife (Debra Sandlund), a washed up porno star (Frances Fisher), a suicidal Southerner (John Bedford Lloyd), a gay sugar daddy (R. Patrick Sulliva) and a corrupt police chief (Wings Hauser) all get blown away.

Film is at its best when it's tongue-in-cheek and it's fun to listen to the guys talk tough. And the biggest, baddest, nastiest one of them all is Lawrence Tierney as O'Neal's father, a man who won't dance for anyone.

•

TOVARICH
1937, 94 mins, US b/w
Dir Anatole Litvak ***Prod*** [Robert Lord] ***Scr*** Casey Robinson ***Ph*** Charles Lang ***Ed*** Henri Rust ***Mus*** Max Steiner ***Art*** Anton Grot
Act Claudette Colbert, Charles Boyer, Basil Rathbone, Anita Louise, Melville Cooper, Isabel Jeans (Warner)

With a distinguished record in legit theatres, both here and abroad, [Jacques Deval's play] *Tovarich* emerges from its Warner filming [of the English version by Robert E. Sherwood] as a piece of popular entertainment, plus the very considerable drawing value of Claudette Colbert and Charles Boyer. Story changes are not radical (one or two modifications being prompted by censorship restrictions).

Boyer's diction is difficult to comprehend in several places. His accent is enhanced by the fact that only he, of all the players, speaks rapidly. Only in brief moments does Colbert convey the dignity, bearing and fine humor of a Russian imperial princess.

Litvak seems imbued with the idea that he had to make *Tovarich* look like a big picture, whereas the story of the royal refugee couple, who enter domestic service in the household of a Paris banker, is a yarn of charming and finely shaded characterizations.

Of the supporting cast Melville Cooper, as the banker, and Basil Rathbone, as a commissar, contribute splendid characterizations.

•

TOWERING INFERNO, THE
1974, 165 mins, US Ⓥ ⊙ ▭ col
Dir John Guillermin, Irwin Allen ***Prod*** Irwin Allen ***Scr*** Stirling Silliphant ***Ph*** Fred Koenekamp, Joseph Biroc ***Ed*** Harold F. Kress, Carl Kress ***Mus*** John Williams ***Art*** William Creber
Act Steve McQueen, Paul Newman, William Holden, Faye Dunaway, Fred Astaire, Richard Chamberlain (20th Century-Fox/Warner)

The Towering Inferno is one of the greatest disaster pictures made, a personal and professional triumph for producer Irwin Allen. The $14 million cost has yielded a truly magnificent production which complements but does not at all overwhelm a thoughtful personal drama.

The strategy of casting expensive talent pays off handsomely. Steve McQueen, as the fireman in charge of extinguishing the runaway fire in a 130-story San Francisco building; Paul Newman, as the heroic and chagrined architect of the glass and concrete pyre; William Holden as its builder; and Faye Dunaway, as Newman's fiancée, get and deserve their star billing.

Both 20th and WB pooled their finances and their separate but similar book acquisitions—Richard Martin Stern's *The Tower* and *The Glass Inferno*, by Thomas N. Scortia and Frank M. Robinson—to effect a true example of synergy.

1974: Best Cinematography, Song ("We May Never Love Like This Again"), Editing

NOMINATIONS: Best Picture, Supp. Actor (Fred Astaire), Art Direction, Original Dramatic Score, Sound

•

TOWER OF LIES, THE
1925, 80 mins, US ⊗ b/w
Dir Victor Seastrom ***Scr*** Agnes Christine Johnson, Max Marcin ***Ph*** Percy Hilburn ***Art*** Cedric Gibbons, James Basevi
Act Norma Shearer, Lon Chaney, Ian Keith, Claire McDowell, William Haines, David Torrence (M-G-M)

The thread of fantasy in the theme is well planted by the director and the acting of Lon Chaney goes a long way toward making it bearable, but the theme itself is ponderous and advanced largely by means of subtitles. The fault with the whole thing is that it isn't a movie story by any stretch of the imagination.

The locale is apparently some Scandinavian country. Jan, a rough farmer, finds love playing an important part in his life when a baby daughter is born. She grows to be his pride but when the nephew of their former landlord gets bad over back rents, the girl goes to the city to make money.

Primarily, the fault with the story itself [from Selma Lagerlof's novel *The Emperor of Portugallia*] is its illogical explanation of how the girl went wrong. That a woman, well bred, with parental love always about her, would turn prostitute for purely pecuniary reasons is silly. Furthermore, if she had gone into the business for that purpose she would have stopped immediately had she raised enough dough to raise the mortgage on the old homestead.

The acting is aces and the direction masterful. But with all this, *Tower of Lies* can never be anything more than a soggy picture made bearable by the leavening forces of director Victor Seastrom, Chaney and Norma Shearer.

•

TOWER OF LONDON
1939, 92 mins, US Ⓥ b/w
Dir Rowland V. Lee ***Prod*** Rowland V. Lee ***Scr*** Robert N. Lee ***Ph*** George Robinson ***Ed*** Ed Curtiss ***Mus*** Charles Previn (dir.) ***Art*** Jack Otterson, Richard H. Riedel
Act Basil Rathbone, Boris Karloff, Vincent Price, Barbara O'Neill, Ian Hunter, Nan Grey (Universal)

Setting the 15th-century torture devices in the London Tower amid the court intrigue of that period, *Tower of London* emerges as a spine-chiller with accent on gruesomeness of the several deaths depicted along the line.

Reminiscence of the Frankenstein series is present here, with Boris Karloff a clubfooted and misshapen giant who is chief executioner and torturor for the conniving Basil Rathbone.

Story, based on historical fact, delves into the continual court intrigues during the reign of King Edward IV. Everyone seems to be indulging in undercover manipulations except the king, with latter's brother, Richard, Duke of Gloucester (Rathbone) the mainspring of a long-range plot to eventually become ruler.

•

TOWN LIKE ALICE, A
(US: THE RAPE OF MALAYA)
1956, 117 mins, UK Ⓥ ⊙ b/w
Dir Jack Lee ***Prod*** Joseph Janni ***Scr*** W. P. Lipscomb, Richard Mason ***Ph*** Geoffrey Unsworth ***Ed*** Sidney Hayers ***Mus*** Matyas Seiber ***Art*** Alex Vetchinsky
Act Virginia McKenna, Peter Finch, Marie Lohr, Renee Houston, Jean Anderson, Maureen Swanson (Rank/Vic)

Filmed largely on location in Malaya and Australia, story is based on Nevil Shute's novel of the same name. Film describes how a handful of women and children were force-marched through Malaya at the hands of the Japanese. For months on end they tramped from one camp to another, through swamp and storm, through dust and heat. Many died on the roadside, but the few survivors eventually found refuge in a village after their guard had succumbed.

During the period of their cross-country march the women and kids are befriended by a couple of Australian POWs who have been assigned to truck-driving duties for the Japs, and over a shared cigarette and an exchange of minor confidence, a bond develops between Virginia McKenna and Peter Finch.

The subject matter is necessarily grim, but wherever possible the script and direction endeavor to infuse a touch of lighter relief. The focus, however, is almost constantly on the trials of the women and children as they fight against famine and disease.

•

TOWN WITHOUT PITY
1961, 112 mins, US b/w
Dir Gottfried Reinhardt ***Prod*** Gottfried Reinhardt ***Scr*** Silvia Reinhardt, Georg Hurdalek ***Ph*** Kurt Hasse ***Ed*** Hermann Haller ***Mus*** Dimitri Tiomkin ***Art*** Rolf Zehetbauer
Act Kirk Douglas, E. G. Marshall, Robert Blake, Richard Jaeckel, Christine Kaufmann, Frank Sutton (United Artists/Mirisch/Gloria)

At face value, *Town Without Pity* appears to be a straight courtroom drama treatment of a gang rape case and its repercussions on a German community incensed over the fact that the rapists are American GIs and the victim a local girl. But the production attempts to go much deeper than that.

The screenplay, based on an adaptation by Jan Lustig of Manfred Gregor's novel *The Verdict*, dramatizes the story of a military defense attorney who, in attempting to properly perform his task, must against his will bring about the destruction of an innocent (the raped girl), victim of her own human fallibility and the fallibility of German witnesses whose pride, hatreds and insecurities lead them to lie, exaggerate or conceal on the stand.

A picture that raises important moral and judicial questions must do so in terms of rounded, dimensional characters if it is to register with impact. *Town Without Pity* fails in this regard.

Kirk Douglas does an able job as the defense attorney. Likewise E. G. Marshall as the prosecutor. There is an especially earnest and intense portrayal of one of the defendants by Robert Blake. The others—less prominent—are skillfully delineated by Richard Jaeckel, Frank Sutton and Mal Sondock. Christine Kaufmann, a rare combination of sensual beauty and sensitivity, handles her assignment—the victim—with sincerity and animation.

1961: NOMINATION: Best Song ("Town Without Pity")

•

TO WONG FOO, THANKS FOR EVERYTHING! JULIE NEWMAR
1995, 108 mins, US Ⓥ ⊙ col
Dir Beeban Kidron ***Prod*** G. Mac Brown ***Scr*** Douglas Carter Beane ***Ph*** Steve Mason ***Ed*** Andrew Mondshein ***Mus*** Rachel Portman ***Art*** Wynn Thomas
Act Wesley Snipes, Patrick Swayze, John Leguizamo, Stockard Channing, Blythe Danner, Arliss Howard (Amblin/Universal)

To Wong Foo, Thanks for Everything! Julie Newmar, the long-awaited American response to *The Adventures of Priscilla, Queen of the Desert*, is not as outrageous or funny as the Aussie pic, but it still offers some rewards as mainstream entertainment, toplined by macho actors Wesley Snipes and Patrick Swayze and up-and-comer John Leguizamo, who look hilarious as drag queens in fabulous costumes.

"Ready or not, here comes mama," says Vida Boheme (Swayze) in the film's first line, as preparations for a N.Y. drag queen beauty pageant begin. A tie is declared between Vida and Noxeema Jackson (Snipes). The prize: two airline tickets, destination Hollywood.

Plans change, however, after the pair meet Chi Chi Rodriguez (Leguizamo), a poor Hispanic queen who all his life has been dreaming of winning something. The trio buy a '67 Cadillac convertible (with the help of an uncredited Robin Williams) and hit the open road. As a good luck charm, they take a celebrity portrait, autographed by Julie Newmar (hence the title).

It takes about a reel for the film to find its center and settle into an amiable melodrama. This happens when the car breaks down in the middle of nowhere and the trio find themselves stuck in Snydersville, a reactionary Midwestern town. Over the course of one long weekend, the three end up performing miracles.

There are some fairly amusing gags along the way before the entire affair sinks into predictable soap opera conflicts and resolutions. The most entertaining parts in *Priscilla* were the musical numbers, which were integral to the plot; here, there are not enough opportunities for music and for flaunting outrageous wigs and dresses.

British helmer Beeban Kidron (*Antonia and Jane*, *Used People*) is obviously attracted to comedies about eccentrics, but *To Wong Foo* suffers from problems similar to those of her former outings. The movie unfolds at a rather deliberate and unvarying pace, but the material is too thin to merit such extended treatment.

•

TOXIC AVENGER, THE
1985, 100 mins, US Ⓥ ⊙ col
Dir Michael Herz, Samuel Weil ***Prod*** Lloyd Kaufman, Michael Herz ***Scr*** Joe Ritter, Lloyd Kaufman, Gay Terry, Stuart Strutin ***Ph*** James London, Lloyd Kaufman ***Ed*** Richard W. Haines ***Mus*** Marc Katz (consult.) ***Art*** Barry Shapiro, Alexandra Mazur
Act Andree Maranda, Mitchell Cohen, Jennifer Baptist, Cindy Manion, Robert Prichard, Mark Torgl (Troma)

This madcap spoof on *The Incredible Hulk* is an outlandish mix of gory violence and realistic special effects.

The story concerns Melvin, a 90-pound weakling who works in a body building club pushing around a mop, and who is hated by the muscular and healthy types that flaunt their bodies before him and the audience. Following some rather pointless shenanigans in which Melvin is humiliated by the bodybuilders, he jumps out of a window and lands in a truck carrying toxic waste. This transforms him into a hulking monster, but one seeking only to right wrongs in his town and persecute the meanies.

•

TOXIC AVENGER, PART II, THE
1989, 95 mins, US Ⓥ ⊙ col
Dir Lloyd Kaufman, Michael Herz ***Prod*** Lloyd Kaufman, Michael Herz ***Scr*** Gay Partington Terry ***Ph*** James London ***Ed*** Michael Schweitzer ***Mus*** Barrie Guard ***Art*** Alex Grey
Act Ron Fazio, John Altamura, Phoebe Legere, Rick Collins, Rikiya Yasuoka, Lisa Gaye (Troma)

Even die-hard Troma fans will have a hard time stomaching *The Toxic Avenger, Part II*. A weak script [from a story by Lloyd Kaufman] and sluggish direction turn this sequel to the 1985 spoof into a seemingly endless, stultifying mess.

Toxic II finds 90-pound weakling Melvin suffering from emotional problems. It seems he was unable to save a home for the blind from an evil drug magnate who razed the center and killed its inhabitants in his march to conquer Tromaville. The only thing that will help his depression is a trip to Japan to find his father, Big Mac, who turns out to be a fish peddler who is really an underworld coke peddler.

Because each limited spoof is telegraphed and laboriously executed, this toxic sequel can be hazardous to your health.

•

TOYS
1992, 121 mins, US Ⓥ ⦿ col
Dir Barry Levinson ***Prod*** Mark Johnson, Barry Levinson ***Scr*** Valerie Curtin, Barry Levinson ***Ph*** Adam Greenberg ***Ed*** Stu Linder ***Mus*** Hans Zimmer, Trevor Horn ***Art*** Ferdinando Scarfiotti
Act Robin Williams, Michael Gambon, Joan Cusack, Robin Wright, LL Cool J, Donald O'Connor (20th Century-Fox/Baltimore)

Only a filmmaker with Barry Levinson's clout would have been so indulged to create such a sprawling, seemingly unsupervised mess as *Toys*, a painful exercise that makes *Hudson Hawk* look like a modest throwaway.

The slow-developing story has aging toymaker Kenneth Zevo (a cameo by Donald O'Connor) leave his factory to his army-general brother (Michael Gambon), fearing that his two children (Robin Williams and Joan Cusack) are too immature for the job.

Rendered obsolete by the end of the Cold War, the General goes about converting the plant into a factory producing war toys and machines of war, sinisterly training toddlers to operate them through the use of videogames.

Levinson, a director most at home with slice-of-life portraits relating to his Baltimore roots, tries his hand here at a darkly satiric fable and ends up doing an extremely poor impression of Terry Gilliam.

Williams and Cusack, the supposed spirits of innocence, are for the most part annoying—particularly Cusack's adult-as-child antics. Through sheer energy Williams generates a few laughs. The movie's real star, production designer Ferdinando Scarfiotti (*The Last Emperor*), nevertheless deserves enormous credit.

1992: NOMINATIONS: Best Art Direction, Costume Design

•

TOYS IN THE ATTIC
1963, 88 mins, US Ⓥ ▭ b/w
Dir George Roy Hill ***Prod*** Walter Mirisch ***Scr*** James Poe ***Ph*** Joseph F. Biroc ***Ed*** Stuart Gilmore ***Mus*** George Duning ***Art*** Cary Odell
Act Dean Martin, Geraldine Page, Yvette Mimieux, Wendy Hiller, Gene Tierney, Frank Silvera (United Artists)

Toys in the Attic is a somewhat watered-down version of Lillian Hellman's play, but enough of the original emotional savagery has been retained to satisfy those who prefer their melodramatic meat raw and chewy. *Toys* is laid in the Deep South and liberally crammed with such sick-sick cargo as incest, adultery, imbecility, lust and a few other popular folk pleasantries.

Principal tampering scenarist James Poe has done with Hellman's neatly constructed, momentum-gathering play about a New Orleans household shattered by latent incest and corrosive possessiveness is in altering the ending.

Hellman's heavyweight drama examines the tragedy that transpires as a result of a spinster sister's secret lust for her younger brother, whose monetarily motivated marriage to a simple-minded girl sets in operation the mechanism for his ultimate disaster. The new ending is thoroughly artificial. Otherwise, Poe's additions and subtractions are sound.

George Roy Hill has made an error or two along the way, but generally his direction is taut, progressive and fast-paced considering this is a very talky, confined piece. The performances are fine.

1963: NOMINATION: Best B&W Costume Design

•

TOY SOLDIERS
1991, 112 mins, US Ⓥ ⦿ col
Dir Daniel Petrie, Jr. ***Prod*** Jack E. Freedman, Wayne S. Williams, Patricia Herskovic ***Scr*** David Koepp, Daniel Petrie, Jr. ***Ph*** Thomas Burstyn ***Ed*** Michael Kahn ***Mus*** Robert Folk ***Art*** Chester Kaczenski
Act Sean Astin, Wil Wheaton, Keith Coogan, Andrew Divoff, Louis Gossett, Jr., Denholm Elliott (Tri-Star)

Toy Soldiers is a very entertaining action film that updates 1981's sleeper hit *Taps*. Pic is unrelated to the 1984 *Toy Soldiers*, wherein Jason Miller and Cleavon Little led a bunch of Beverly Hills kids (including Tim Robbins in an early role) on a hostage rescue mission against terrorists in Colombia.

The new picture [from William P. Kennedy's novel] presents the reverse situation of rich kids at a Virginia prep school who have to develop some backbone and defend themselves against Andrew Divoff's group of Colombian terrorists who take over their school and hold them hostage. Seeing Sean Astin (son of John Astin and Patty Duke) and his pranksters turn into commandos who wipe out the nasty invaders makes for purely escapist, crowd-pleasing pleasure.

In his feature directing debut, Daniel Petrie, Jr., gets maximum mileage out of the derring-do of the final reels while emphasizing comic relief earlier on. Young villain Divoff is terrific at creating a brutal figure of hate.

Remaining in the end credits is Tracy Brooks Swope, but she doesn't appear on screen; in fact there are no women's roles other than bit parts.

•

TOY STORY
1995, 80 mins, US Ⓥ ⦿ col
Dir John Lasseter ***Prod*** Ralph Guggenheim, Bonnie Arnold ***Scr*** Joss Whedon, Andrew Stanton, Joel Cohen, Alec Sokolow ***Ed*** Robert Gordon, Lee Unkrich ***Mus*** Randy Newman ***Art*** Ralph Eggleston (Pixar/Walt Disney)

Walt Disney continues its long tradition of cutting-edge animation with the computer-generated *Toy Story*. The very good news is that, in addition to stylistic innovation, the film sports a provocative and appealing story that's every bit the equal of this technical achievement.

Actually the brainchild of Pixar—the Northern California animation unit that made the Oscar short *Tin Toy*—the film is a modern parable [from a screen story by John Lasseter, Peter Docter, Andrew Stanton and John Ranft] that effortlessly masks its serious side with a fun house full of colorful characters and thrilling adventures.

The core story involves a group of toys owned by a boy named Andy. They spring to life to form a rag-tag community when the human element departs the scene. Woody, a cowboy marionette, has been the boy's longtime, sentimental favorite. He takes a leadership role among his peers, which include a slinky doll, a piggy bank, Rex the dinosaur, Bo Peep and Mr. Potato Head.

As the film opens, he's put to the test with the arrival of Buzz Lightyear, a galactic superhero with an arsenal of flashy gadgets. The new resident is a gung ho type with an annoyingly good nature and helpful attitude.

The camera loops and zooms in a dizzying fashion that fairly takes one's breath away. But if the film were merely an exercise in style, it soon would become tiresome. Rather, the filmmakers display and dispense with the most dazzling elements of computer-generated graphics and concentrate on telling an effective story.

The filmmakers, led by director John Lasseter, have corralled a first-rate voice cast with wonderful character turns from the likes of Wallace Shawn as a timorous T-Rex and Don Rickles as a gruff spud. Tom Hanks as Woody and Tim Allen as Buzz lend full bodied performances to visually agile renderings.

1995: NOMINATIONS: Best Original Screenplay, Original Musical or Comedy Score. Original Song ("You've Got a Friend")

•

TOY STORY 2
1999, 92 mins, US Ⓥ ⦿ col
Dir John Lasseter, Lee Unkrich, Ash Brannon ***Prod*** Helene Plotkin, Karen Robert Jackson ***Scr*** Andrew Stanton, Rita Hsiao, Doug Chamberlin, Chris Webb ***Ph*** Sharon Calahan ***Ed*** Edie Bleiman, David Ian Salter, Lee Unkrich ***Mus*** Randy Newman ***Art*** William Cone, Jim Pearson (Pixar/Walt Disney)

In the realm of sequels, *Toy Story 2* is to *Toy Story* what *The Empire Strikes Back* was to its predecessor—a richer, more satisfying film in every respect [from a screen story by John Lasseter, Pete Docter, Ash Brannon and Andrew Stanton].

Brisk setup sees the affable Woody (voiced by Tom Hanks) eagerly anticipating being taken to a summer Cowboy Camp by his owner, Andy (John Morris). But excitement quickly turns to disappointment when a "broken" arm causes Woody to be left behind.

Woody's nightmare of being flung into the trash heap of broken toys comes true when he inadvertently lands in a yard-sale 25¢ bin, from which he's kidnapped by the greedy Al McWhiggin (Wayne Knight), owner of the local Al's Toy Barn, who knows something that Woody himself doesn't—that Woody was a big TV star back in the '50s.

Stashed in a downtown building, Woody meets cowgirl Jessie (Joan Cusack), Stinky Pete the Prospector (Kelsey Grammer) and a horse named Bullseye and, in a wonderfully entertaining interlude, learns of his long-ago celebrity. Now Woody is safely in hand, Al plans to cash in by selling the whole set to a museum in Japan. It's up to spaceman Buzz Lightyear (Tim Allen) and Andy's other toys, including Rex the Dinosaur (Wallace Shawn), Hamm the Pig (John Ratzenberger), Mr. Potato Head (Don Rickles) and Slinky Dog (Jim Varney), to mount a rescue expedition.

A sense of spirited invention permeates the proceedings from top to bottom. Added to this spirit are the outstanding voicings by a stellar cast.

1999: NOMINATION: Best Original Song

•

TRACK OF THE CAT
1954, 102 mins, US ▭ col
Dir William A. Wellman ***Prod*** Robert Fellows ***Scr*** A. I. Bezzerides ***Ph*** William H. Clothier ***Ed*** Fred MacDowell ***Mus*** Roy Webb
Act Robert Mitchum, Teresa Wright, Diana Lynn, Tab Hunter, Beulah Bondi, Philip Tonge (Warner)

The novelty of lensing, in color, a picture designed to reproduce black-and-white is rather dissipated in this production. If there had been some entertainment impact to go with the photographic treatment, the combination might have paid off strongly.

William A. Wellman is responsible for the novelty idea and directs in a manner to achieve some rather startling effects. Only color seen is the flesh tones of the characters, the green of trees on the snow-covered Mt. Rainier location site, a red and black mackinaw and a light-colored blouse. It gives the right "mood" to the Walter Van Tilburg Clark novel, which is a "moody" piece, at best.

Story deals with a farm family of three brothers, an old-maid sister, a drunken father and a Bible-reading mother, plus a girl from a neighboring farm. As the melodrama unfolds, first the older brother, William Hopper, is killed by a mountain lion. Then the middle brother, Robert Mitchum, dies while looking for the "cat."

The lion symbolizes the "cat" every man must throw off before he is a man.

•

TRACKS
1976, 90 mins, US Ⓥ ⦿ col
Dir Henry Jaglom ***Prod*** Howard Zuker ***Scr*** Henry Jaglom ***Ph*** Paul Glickman ***Ed*** George Folsey, Jr.
Act Dennis Hopper, Taryn Power, Dean Stockwell, Topo Swope, Alfred Ryder, Michael Emil (Rainbow)

Henry Jaglom abandons the poseur excesses that marred his first film, *A Safe Place*. This time it's an incisive, revelatory film about a returning war veteran from Vietnam transporting the body of a friend across the U.S. for burial.

Dennis Hopper gives an excellent rendering of this prosoldier probably needing tenderness but hiding it until he finds it with a headstrong but knowing girl, played with authority by Tyrone Power's daughter, Taryn, who shows an offbeat beauty and presence.

Sometimes uneasy on its rails, film has perceptive personages and works on the level of reality and hallucination as they interact to give a feel of the U.S. Film takes place mostly on the train.

•

TRACK 29
1988, 86 mins, UK Ⓥ col
Dir Nicolas Roeg ***Prod*** Rick McCallum ***Scr*** Dennis Potter ***Ph*** Alex Thomson ***Ed*** Tony Lawson ***Mus*** Stanley Myers ***Art*** David Brockhurst
Act Theresa Russell, Gary Oldman, Sandra Bernhard, Christopher Lloyd, Colleen Camp, Seymour Cassel (HandMade)

Though clearly of above-average quality in direction, psychology and Theresa Russell's 3-D performance as a childless housewife with a dark secret in the closet, *Track 29* is connected closely to the classic American smalltown horror film.

Screenplay is set in a Southern town where strange things happen every day. Linda (Russell) and husband Henry (Christopher Lloyd) are at odds over Linda's burning desire for a child and Henry's preference for his model trains. He also enjoys being spanked by Nurse Stein (Sandra Bernhard).

Into this world of normal absurdity arrives a stranger. Young Martin (Gary Oldman) convinces Linda he's her baby boy born out of wedlock and taken from her at birth, but viewer begins to have doubts that the appearing-disappearing weirdo isn't a figment of her imagination.

Perverse humor is the keynote of the Oedipal complexed duo, who spend a long day going to bars, exchanging unplatonic caresses, and acting out their traumas. Russell and Oldman are consummate thesps able to reach the edge of frenzy (and beyond) while remaining fun and original.

•

TRADER HORN
1931, 123 mins, US b/w
Dir W. S. Van Dyke ***Scr*** Richard Schayer, Cyril Hume, Dale Van Every, J. T. Neville ***Ph*** Clyde De Vinna ***Ed*** Ben Lewis ***Mus*** Charles Maxwell
Act Harry Carey, Edwina Booth, Duncan Renaldo, Mutia Omoolu, Olive Golden, C. Aubrey Smith (M-G-M)

A good-looking animal picture. The story doesn't mean anything other than a connecting link for a series of sequences which, at one point, become nothing more than an out-and-out lecture tour, as various herds of animals are described by the voice of Harry Carey, in the title role. Studio has simply interpreted the original novel [by Aloysius Horn and Ethelreda Lewis] as it saw fit, lifting a couple of characters therefrom and putting them through a succession of narrow escapes from four-footed enemies and a cannibal tribe.

Light love vein is introduced between Carey's young companion, Duncan Renaldo, and Edwina Booth as the queen of a tribe from whom she and the men escape when her followers turn on her after she countermands an order of death by torture for Carey, Renaldo and Rencharo, the former's native gun boy.

Booth, very easy to look at, prances through the jungle in scanty raiment, knowing only the gutteral language of the blacks. The escape of the quartet immediately goes into a chase, during which Carey doubles back to act as decoy so the boy and girl can get away. Finish is the successful reaching of a river settlement where the youth and former tribal queen board a small river steamer bound for civilization, while Carey, as Trader Horn, prepares to go back into the jungle.

Sound effects are outstanding. Andy Anderson, the sound man, accompanied director W. S. Van Dyke's unit to Africa. The camera work is also swell marksmanship.

1930/31: NOMINATION: Best Picture

•

TRADING PLACES
1983, 106 mins, US Ⓥ ⊙ col
Dir John Landis ***Prod*** Aaron Russo ***Scr*** Timothy Harris, Herschel Weingrod ***Ph*** Robert Paynter ***Ed*** Malcolm Campbell ***Mus*** Elmer Bernstein ***Art*** Gene Rudolf
Act Dan Aykroyd, Eddie Murphy, Ralph Bellamy, Don Ameche, Denholm Elliott, Jamie Lee Curtis (Paramount)

Trading Places is a light romp geared up by the schtick shifted by Dan Aykroyd and Eddie Murphy. Happily, it's a pleasure to report also that even those two popular young comics couldn't have brought this one off without the contributions of three veterans—Ralph Bellamy, Don Ameche and the droll Englishman, Denholm Elliott.

Aykroyd plays a stuffy young financial wizard who runs a Philadelphia commodities house for two continually scheming brothers, Bellamy and Ameche.

Conversely, Murphy has grown up in the streets and lives on the con, including posing as a blind, legless veteran begging outside Aykroyd's private club.

On a whim motivated by disagreement over the importance of environment versus breeding, Bellamy bets Ameche that Murphy could run the complex commodities business just as well as Aykroyd, given the chance. Conversely, according to the bet, Aykroyd would resort to crime and violence if suddenly all friends and finances were stripped away from him.

So their scheme proceeds and both Aykroyd and Murphy are in top form reacting to their new situations.

The only cost, however, is a mid-section stretch without laughs, still made enjoyable by the presence of Jamie Lee Curtis as a good-hearted hooker who befriends Aykroyd.

1983: NOMINATION: Best Adapted Score

•

TRAFFIC
2000, 147 mins, US Ⓥ ⊙ col
Dir Steven Soderbergh ***Prod*** Edward Zwick, Marshall Herskovitz, Laura Bickford ***Scr*** Stephen Gaghan ***Ph*** Peter Andrews [Steven Soderbergh] ***Ed*** Stephen Mirrione ***Mus*** Cliff Martinez ***Art*** Philip Messina
Act Michael Douglas, Don Cheadle, Benicio Del Toro, Luiz Guzman, Dennis Quaid, Catherine Zeta-Jones (Bedford Falls-Bickford/USA)

Enormously ambitious and masterfully made, *Traffic* represents docudrama-style storytelling at a very high level. A powerful overview of the contemporary drug culture that is both panoramic and specific, the multistrand story bears some traces of its origins in a five-hour 1989 miniseries [*Traffik*, created by Simon Moore] from Britain's Channel 4.

While its three principal story lines don't presume to constitute a comprehensive account of North American drug trade and consumption, the shrewd choices of characters and locales manage to illuminate an excitingly diverse range of participants, from government officials and traffickers (sometimes the same thing) to earnest enforcement officers, users and incidental victims on both sides of the Mexican border and at all stations on the class scale. The various threads have been interwoven and balanced with extraordinary skill so that the tension and power keep steadily building, until close to the end of this nearly 2½ hour film.

First glimpsed, in bleached-out sepia tones, are Tijuana-based cops Javier Rodriguez (Benicio Del Toro) and Manolo Sanchez (Jacob Vargas), who intercept an airborne coke drop-off in the desert but are then themselves apprehended by army general Salazar (Tomas Milian), who seizes the stash. In Stateside scenes drenched in bluish hues, Ohio State Supreme Court Justice Robert Wakefield (Michael Douglas) is about to be appointed the nation's new drug czar, just as his bright 16-year-old daughter, Caroline (Erika Christensen), is moving from recreational drugs into heavier stuff.

In bold color, determined and resourceful DEA agents Montel Gordon (Don Cheadle) and Ray Castro (Luis Guzman) are conducting a sting operation on San Diego–based dealer Eduardo Ruiz (Miguel Ferrer), whom they hope will help them nail local kingpin Carlos Ayala (Steven Bauer), whose pregnant society wife, Helena (Catherine Zeta-Jones), doesn't know the nature of her husband's business.

Once these story lines are effectively set up, Soderbergh pushes deeper to show how the pervasiveness of drugs has poisoned the lives of everyone concerned, even if most of the characters don't actually use drugs themselves.

The film accepts that there are no easy answers to the gigantic problem that drugs pose for society, but it also is animated by the underlying suggestion that the status quo is unacceptable. Although the filmmakers apparently didn't care to cross the line from implicit critique into advocacy, they have still fumbled by not working more sting and irony into the picture's concluding section.

Lensing the film himself under the *nom de camera* of Peter Andrews, Soderbergh has given the film tremendous texture as well as a vibrant immediacy through constant handheld operating, mostly using available light, and manipulating the look both in shooting and in the lab.

•

TRAIL OF THE LONESOME PINE, THE
1916, 70 mins, US ⊗ b/w
Dir Cecil B. DeMille ***Prod*** Jesse L. Lasky ***Scr*** Jeanie MacPherson ***Ph*** Alvin Wychoff ***Art*** Wilfred Buckland
Act Charlotte Walker, Theodore Roberts, Earle Foxe, Thomas Meighan (Lasky)

The Trail of the Lonesome Pine is a remarkable motion picture reproduction of the play which Eugene Walter adapted from the novel by John Fox. Charlotte Walker, who was the star of the original stage production, is seen in the picture version, but to Theodore Roberts, who plays the role of Judd Tolliver, the aged head of the clan of Tollivers who make their headquarters in the lonesome by-ways of the Tennessee Mountains, must go the credit for giving the star performance.

Walker portrays the role of June, and Thomas Meighan is the young revenue officer with whom she falls in love. Earle Foxe as the cousin of June, and in love with her, gives a most capable performance. Scenically the picture is wonderful.

A wonderful vista, with a single giant pine stuck right in the center of it, is the introduction to the picture. Then the four principal characters are brought into view, one at a time. The sheriff of the county in which the Tollivers hold sway is certain that they are running a still for the production of illicit whiskey, but he cannot obtain the evidence. So he applies to the federal authorities and John Hale (Meighan) is sent into the mountains to assist the sheriff and run down the case.

•

TRAIL OF THE LONESOME PINE, THE
1936, 100 mins, US col
Dir Henry Hathaway ***Prod*** Walter Wanger ***Scr*** Grover Jones, Harvey Thew, Horace McCoy ***Ph*** W. Howard Greene, Robert C. Bruce ***Ed*** Robert Bischoff ***Mus*** Hugo Friedhofer, Gerard Carbonara ***Art*** Alexander Toluboff
Act Sylvia Sidney, Henry Fonda, Fred MacMurray, Fred Stone, Nigel Bruce, Beulah Bondi (Paramount)

The Trail of the Lonesome Pine is a good show, the first all-Technicolor feature produced 100 percent outdoors.

Director Henry Hathaway has sympathetically dealt with the ignorance of the mountaineer folk. His dialogicians, following the John Fox, Jr., original play, have faithfully preserved the reticent, curt mien of the feuding Tolliver and Falin clans.

Sylvia Sidney's performances as the 'billy looker is uncompromising in every detail. After a brief spell of schooling in Louisville, where Fred MacMurray has sent her, she reverts to type. Upon hearing how Buddy (Spanky McFarland) has been murdered, she too cries for a Falin's blood.

Henry Fonda, as her mountaineer vis-à-vis, is equally consistent in his scowling hate for the Falin clan, as well as for the advent of the city engineer (MacMurray). Latter is capital in his dealings with the ignorant hillbillies and his affection for June Tolliver (Sidney).

1936: NOMINATION: Best Song ("A Melody from the Sky")

•

TRAIL OF THE PINK PANTHER
1983, 97 mins, UK Ⓥ ⊙ ▭ col
Dir Blake Edwards ***Prod*** Blake Edwards, Tony Adams ***Scr*** Frank Waldman, Tom Waldman, Blake Edwards, Geoffrey Edwards ***Ph*** Dick Bush ***Ed*** Alan Jones ***Mus*** Henry Mancini ***Art*** Peter Mullins
Act Peter Sellers, David Niven, Herbert Lom, Richard Mulligan, Joanna Lumley, Capucine (Titan)

A patchwork of out-takes, reprised clips and new connective footage, *Trail of the Pink Panther* is a thin, peculiar picture unsupported by the number of laughs one is accustomed to in this series. Stitched together after Peter Sellers's death, this is by a long way the slightest of the six Inspector Clouseau efforts.

Story's structure is strange, to say the least. The fabulous Pink Panther gem is stolen yet again from its vulnerable resting place in an Arab museum, which sparks immediate interest from the haplessly effective French detective.

Opening two reels are devoted to supposed out-take footage of Sellers trying on a disguise and on attempting to relieve himself in an airplane lavatory despite the encumbrance of an ungainly cast.

After about 40 minutes, Clouseau's Lugash-bound plane is reported missing. French television reporter Joanna Lumley sets out to interview many of those who had known the inspector in earlier pics, including David Niven, Capucine (looking great), Burt Kwouk, Graham Stark and Andre Maranne, as well as his father, Richard Mulligan, and a Mafia kingpin, Robert Loggia.

•

TRAIN, THE
1965, 140 mins, US/France/Italy Ⓥ b/w
Dir John Frankenheimer ***Prod*** Jules Bricken ***Scr*** Franklin Coen, Frank Davis, [Walter Bernstein, Ned Young, Howard Infell] ***Ph*** Walter Wottitz, Jean Tournier ***Ed*** David Bretherton ***Mus*** Maurice Jarre ***Art*** Willy Holt
Act Burt Lancaster, Paul Scofield, Jeanne Moreau, Michel Simon, Suzanne Flon, Wolfgang Preiss (Artistes Associes/Ariane/Dear)

After a slow start, *The Train* picks up to become a colorful, actionful big-scale adventure opus. Made in French and English in France, it was entirely lensed in real exteriors with unlimited access to old French rolling stock of the last war.

Pic [from the novel *Le front de l'art* by Rose Valland] concerns an elaborate railroad resistance plot to keep a train full of French art treasures from being shipped to Germany near the end of the war. An earthy station master (Burt Lancaster), if in the resistance, is reluctant to sacrifice men for paintings, especially with the war nearing its end. But he finally gives in when an old engineer, almost his foster father, is killed by the Germans for trying to hold up the art train. An elaborate plot is put into action. Lancaster himself is made to drive the train by the fanatic German colonel (Paul Scofield) to whom the art has become bigger than the war itself.

Jeanne Moreau has a small but telling cameo bit as does Michel Simon as the dedicated old engineer who swings Lancaster into line to go all out for saving the train. But above all it is the railroad bustle, the trains themselves and some bang-up special effects of bombing attacks and accidents that give the pic its main points.

1965: Best Original Story & Screenplay

•

TRAIN OF EVENTS
1949, 89 mins, UK b/w
Dir Sidney Cole, Charles Crichton, Basil Dearden ***Prod*** Michael Balcon ***Scr*** Basil Dearden, T.E.B. Clarke, Ronald

Millar, Angus MacPhail *Ph* Lionel Banes, Paul Beeson, Chic Waterson *Ed* Bernard Gribble *Mus* Leslie Bridgewater
Act Jack Warner, Valerie Hobson, John Clements, Peter Finch, John Gregson, Susan Shaw (Ealing)

This is an absorbing human drama on the multiple plot system. This one concerns a train wreck and the lives of four sets of people immediately prior to their presence on the doomed train. There is sufficient light and shade to preclude top-heaviness, but accent is more on the grave than gay.

Valerie Hobson handles the role of a musician's wife with delightful nonchalance with John Clements exuding charm and temperament as her errant spouse. Joan Dowling and Lawrence Payne make a pathetic pair of fugitives and Jack Warner's guard is characterized with his usual unerring touch.

Acting plum falls to Peter Finch. His tense overwrought emotions, depicting how war can turn a harmless nonentity into a murderer, are convincingly and forcefully portrayed.

•

TRAIN ROBBERS, THE
1973, 92 mins, US Ⓥ ⦿ ▭ col
Dir Burt Kennedy *Prod* Michael Wayne *Scr* Burt Kennedy *Ph* William H. Clothier *Ed* Frank Santillo *Mus* Dominic Frontiere *Art* Ray Moyer, Alfred Sweeney
Act John Wayne, Ann-Margret, Rod Taylor, Ben Johnson, Christopher George, Bobby Vinton (Batjac)

The Train Robbers is an above-average John Wayne actioner, written and directed by Burt Kennedy with suspense, comedy and humanism not usually found in the formula.

The plot peg is simple. Wayne recruits a group to recover gold stolen from a train by Ann-Margret's deceased outlaw husband, so her name and that of her child can be clear. However, Kennedy has provided a series of rich, deep individual characterizations, plus some intriguing red-herring plot twists.

Most important, for example, is the exposition of the Wayne character. Instead of the cardboard superman, he is given the added dimension of a man who actually could fall for a woman. Ann-Margret is most convincing in a role which requires that she be of her hardy environment, but above it enough to be credible as a lady-like, attractive widow.

•

TRAINSPOTTING
1996, 94 mins, UK Ⓥ ⦿ col
Dir Danny Boyle *Prod* Andrew Macdonald *Scr* John Hodge *Ph* Brian Tafano *Ed* Masahiro Hirakubo *Art* Kave Quinn
Act Ewan McGregor, Ewen Bremner, Johnny Lee Miller, Kevin McKidd, Robert Carlyle, Kelly Macdonald (Figment/Channel 4)

Scabrous, brutal and hip, *Trainspotting* is a *Clockwork Orange* for the '90s. This inventive pic version of U.K. author Irvine Welsh's cult 1993 novel, set among a group of self-destructive no-hopers and junkies in Edinburgh's underbelly, shares only the visual invention and buccaneering spirit of the same team's explosive debut, the black comedy *Shallow Grave*.

Welsh's book—more a collection of p.o.v. episodes, written in different styles, than a conventional novel—has already been translated to London's off–West End stage. For the film, scripter John Hodge has centered the action on Mark Renton (Ewan McGregor), an on-off junkie who acts as a funnel to the surreal world of his four "friends." Like Alex in Kubrick's 1971 pic (to which there's a brief homage), Mark regales the audience with his anti-middle-class values and idiosyncratic philosophy of life, finally achieving a liberation that's more a temporary escape than a real shift in perception.

There's Begbie (Robert Carlyle), a knife-carrying, "sensory-addicted," foul-mouthed psycho who "only does people," not drugs; Sick Boy (Johnny Lee Miller), a philandering self-obsessive; way-out Spud (Ewen Bremner), who dates Gail (Shirley Henderson); and Tommy (Kevin McKidd), who dates Lizzy (Pauline Lynch) and claims he never takes drugs or tells lies.

The tone is set by the rough, self-deprecating Scottish humor delivered in heavy accents. Film's most striking accomplishment is the way it takes a bunch of goal-less losers and turns the material into a sustained piece of cinema that's often wildly funny and, at a character level, extremely involving. Unstated is the fact that the story is set in the Thatcherite '80s.

Performances are terrific at all levels. Dominating the film, however, is Carlyle, who turns in a genuinely terrifying perf as the psychopathic Begbie, a walking time bomb who's halfway to hell.

Though set in Edinburgh, pic was shot almost entirely in Glasgow.

1996: NOMINATION: Best Adapted Screenplay

•

TRANCERS
(AKA: FUTURE COP)
1985, 85 mins, US Ⓥ ⦿ col
Dir Charles Band *Prod* Charles Band *Scr* Paul De Meo, Danny Bilson *Ph* Mac Ahlberg *Mus* Mark Ryder, Phil Davies
Act Tim Thomerson, Helen Hunt, Michael Stefani, Art La Fleur, Biff Manard, Anne Seymour (Empire)

Trancers works out of a central idea closely akin to *The Terminator*. That is where resemblances end. This film in no way can match the Arnold Schwarzenegger vehicle—in gritty action, wit and technical knowhow.

Plot centers on Angel City 2247 AD. The ruins of L.A, as it exists today, lie below the sea following a catastrophic earthquake. A sinister mystic, Martin Whistler (Michael Stefani), threatens the peace with his legion of controlled trancers.

Whistler retreats in time to L.A. 1985 with a plan to murder the ancestors of the rulers of Angel City, thus ensuring that the rulers cease to exist. Trooper Jack Deth (Tim Thomerson) is sent back to stop him. He is aided by Leena (Helen Hunt), his guide in the "strange world" of today.

Only Hunt in the femme role breaks through a script that rarely rings new.

•

TRANSYLVANIA TWIST
1989, 82 mins, US col
Dir Jim Wynorski *Prod* Alida Camp *Scr* R. J. Robertson *Ph* Zoran Hochstatter *Ed* Nina Gilberti *Mus* Chuck Cirino *Art* Gary Randall
Act Robert Vaughn, Teri Copley, Steve Altman, Monique Gabrielle, Angus Scrimm, Ace Mask (Concorde)

Transylvania Twist is an occasionally hilarious horror spoof notable for the range of its comical targets. Filmmakers let all the stops out in silliness worthy of Mel Brooks.

Immediately with the teaser opening of perennial Jim Wynorski starlet Monique Gabrielle (uncredited though in a big role) being stalked through the woods by Jason, Freddy Krueger and Leatherface, pic applies a scattershot approach delving into other genres as well.

Robert Vaughn is delightful as a Dracula-styled vampire pronouncing the end of his last name Orlock with relish. His beautiful niece Teri Copley is an American singing star who travels to his castle in Transylvania upon the death of her father, accompanied by wise-cracking sidekick Steve Altman.

Mixed into the comic stew are many delightful reflexive bits: tracking camera that gets sidetracked on bodacious women passing by; a black-and-white sequence when star visits a set that looks left over from *The Honeymooners*; and a terrifically edited appearance by Boris Karloff.

•

TRAP, THE
1966, 106 mins, UK Ⓥ ▭ col
Dir Sidney Hayers *Prod* George H. Brown *Scr* David Osborn *Ph* Robert Krasker *Ed* Tristam Cones *Mus* Ron Grainer *Art* Harry White
Act Rita Tushingham, Oliver Reed, Rex Sevenoaks, Barbara Chilcott, Linda Goranson, Blain Fairman (Rank)

This Anglo-Canadian get-together deals with an earthy adventure yarn, a struggle for survival, and an offbeat battle of the sexes.

Story is set in the mid-1890s when British Columbia was wild and untamed and only the strong came out on top. Jean La Bete (Oliver Reed), a huge, lusty French-Canadian trapper, returns to the trading post too late for the once-a-year "auction" of harlots, thieves and femme riff-raff sent away from civilization for this purpose. So he settles for a young mute orphan, a servant in the trader's house, sold to him by the grasping wife.

He hauls the protesting girl into a canoe and sets off for the wastes. There follows an edgy *Taming of the Shrew* situation as the hunter tries to win her affection by cajoling, bullying, threatening, and occasionally sweet-talking.

Reed is larger-than-life as the crude, brawling trapper yet also has moments of great sensitivity with his co-star. Tushingham, sans benefit of dialog has to depend on her famous eyes, and wistful mouth to put over a tricky role embracing many emotions, from spitfire to waif, and she does marvels.

•

TRAPEZE
1956, 106 mins, US Ⓥ ▭ col
Dir Carol Reed *Prod* James Hill *Scr* James R. Webb *Ph* Robert Krasker *Ed* Bert Bates *Mus* Malcolm Arnold *Art* Rino Mondellini
Act Burt Lancaster, Tony Curtis, Gina Lollobrigida, Katy Jurado, Thomas Gomez, Minor Watson (Susan/United Artists)

Trapeze is a high-flying screen entertainment equipped with circus thrills and excitement, a well-handled romantic triangle and a cast of potent marquee names. Cirque d'Hiver, Paris's famed one-ring circus, provides the authentic, colorful, exciting setting.

Reed's direction loads the aerial scenes with story suspense for even more thrill effect, and male stars Burt Lancaster and Tony Curtis simulate the bigtop aristocrats realistically.

The well-plotted script, from Liam O'Brien's adaptation of Max Catto's novel *The Killing Frost*, tells how Curtis, son of an aerialist, comes to Paris to learn from Lancaster, one of the few fliers able to achieve the triple somersault, a feat which had left him crippled. Together, they start to work up an act when the tumbler moves in, using her wiles on the young man but loving the older.

Gina Lollobrigida, justly famed for her curves, proves she can act, giving the necessary touch of flamboyance without going overboard. Katy Jurado lights up what scenes she has.

•

TRASH
1970, 103 mins, US Ⓥ col
Dir Paul Morrissey *Prod* Andy Warhol *Scr* Paul Morrissey *Ph* Paul Morrissey *Ed* Jed Johnson
Act Joe Dallesandro, Holly Woodlawn, Jane Forth, Michael Sklar, Geri Miller, Andrea Feldman (Warhol)

Andy Warhol surfaces from the camp underground with *Trash*, the most comprehensible, and least annoying of a long line of quasi-porno features from *Chelsea Girls* to *Lonesome Cowboys*.

As with earlier *Flesh*, director here is Paul Morrissey who has the Warhol gift of attracting gregarious grotesque and eliciting no-holds improvisations within loosely structured dramatic situations.

Once again, stud-in-residence is Joe Dallesandro, this time as a strung-out heroin addict unable to function sexually despite numerous provocations. He displays both a forceful screen presence and ease in front of the camera that cannot be hastily dismissed.

•

TRAVELING EXECUTIONER, THE
1970, 94 mins, US Ⓥ ▭ col
Dir Jack Smight *Prod* Jack Smight *Scr* Garrie Bateson *Ph* Philip Lathrop *Ed* Neil Travis *Mus* Jerry Goldsmith *Art* George W. Davis, Edward Carfagno
Act Stacy Keach, Marianna Hill, Bud Cort, Graham Jarvis, James J. Sloyan, M. Emmet Walsh (M-G-M)

The Traveling Executioner is a macabre, tastefully seamy comedy-drama about bayou prison life, circa 1918. The original Garrie Bateson screenplay stars Stacy Keach in an outstanding performance as an infectious con-man.

Bateson's first screenplay, written as a University of Southern California student, is dominated by Keach, the professional executioner who makes $100 per client. He's a promoter from the word go, but an underlying, disarming sincerity about the job makes the character believable and sympathetic. Keach's talents convey the whole spectrum of his role.

A literal description of the story does injustice to the whole; there are some gritty elements and some broad comedy elements—earthy enough to anchor the story in its proper context.

•

TRAVELLING NORTH
1987, 96 mins, Australia Ⓥ col
Dir Carl Schultz *Prod* Ben Gannon *Scr* David Williamson *Ph* Julian Penny *Ed* Henry Dangar *Mus* Alan John *Art* Owen Paterson
Act Leo McKern, Julia Blake, Graham Kennedy, Henri Szeps, Michelle Fawdon, Diane Craig (View)

This superbly crafted adaptation of David Williamson's popular stage play is a mature, frequently funny and ultimately most moving story of old age and retirement.

Leo McKern plays Frank, a rather cantankerous ex-Communist and civil engineer who retires from work at age 70. A widower, he has persuaded his close friend, Frances (Julia Blake), a widow but not as old as he, to accompany him north, to subtropical northern Queensland.

After many happy days fishing, reading and listening to

music (and enjoying the sexual side of the relationship), Frank's health begins to deteriorate and Frances starts to yearn to see her family again.

Australian-born McKern, in his first Australian film, gives a remarkable performance as the crotchety, yet endearing, Frank. It's a hugely enjoyable portrayal. As Frances, Blake positively glows; she plays a patient, loving woman with a determination of her own, and it's a rich characterization.

•

TRAVELS WITH MY AUNT

1972, 109 mins, UK ▭ col

Dir George Cukor ***Prod*** Robert Fryer, James Cresson ***Scr*** Jay Presson Allen, Hugh Wheeler ***Ph*** Douglas Slocombe ***Ed*** John Bloom ***Mus*** Tony Hatch ***Art*** John Box

Act Maggie Smith, Alec McCowen, Lou Gossett, Robert Stephens, Cindy Williams, Robert Flemyng (M-G-M)

Travels with My Aunt is the story [based on the Graham Greene bestseller] of an outrageous femme of indeterminate years cavorting in a set of outrageous situations which spell high comedy. Of course, it may also be regarded as utter nonsense in a hammed-up set of overly contrived circumstances.

Maggie Smith plays the title role in an overdrawn but thoroughly delightful manner. Film opens quietly enough at the funeral services of her nephew's mother, but the disrupting arrival of the over-dressed, over-cosmeticked Aunt Augusta sets the stage for a comedy spree.

George Cukor's direction is quite up to meeting the demands of the script, and he is responsible for a tempo attuned to his unusual characters. Alec McCowen's characterization of the nephew is subtle and expansive as he gradually withdraws from his former stuffy, priggish, ex-bank manager style.

1972: Best Costume Design (Anthony Powell)

NOMINATIONS: Best Actress (Maggie Smith), Cinematography, Art Direction

•

T. R. BASKIN

(UK: A DATE WITH A LONELY GIRL)

1971, 89 mins, US Ⓥ col

Dir Herbert Ross ***Prod*** Peter Hyams ***Scr*** Peter Hyams ***Ph*** Gerald Hirschfield ***Ed*** Maury Winstrobe ***Mus*** Jack Elliott ***Art*** Albert Brenner

Act Candice Bergen, Peter Boyle, James Caan, Marcia Rodd, Erin O'Reilly, Howard Platt (Paramount)

T. R. Baskin makes a few good comedy comments on modern urban existence, but these are bits of rare jewelry lost on a vast beach of strung-out, erratic storytelling. Candice Bergen is featured in title role of a rural girl who is, or is not, worth caring about in the big city. Told in flashback, Peter Hyams's debut production is handsomely mounted, but his screenplay is sterile, superficial and inconsistent. Peter Boyle is an out-of-towner who called Bergen for sex, but instead suffers through her equivocal talk-therapy.

Bergen's screen presence is too sophisticated for the role, and both her acting, direction and dialog result in confusion. One moment she is to be pitied; the next she is fouling up her own chances with people.

Boyle, whose contribution is little more than a foil, tries to get some depth into the role of a square salesman.

James Caan, looking more mature, is another professional victim, as a divorced man who ends a perfect night with Bergen by offering her some money. He isn't the only one who isn't sure what she is.

•

TREASURE ISLAND

1934, 105 mins, US Ⓥ b/w

Dir Victor Fleming ***Prod*** Hunt Stromberg ***Scr*** John Lee Mahin ***Ph*** Ray June, Clyde De Vinna, Harold Rosson ***Ed*** Blanche Sewell ***Mus*** Herbert Stothart ***Art*** Cedric Gibbons, Merrill Pye, Edwin B. Willis

Act Wallace Beery, Jackie Cooper, Lionel Barrymore, Otto Kruger, Lewis Stone, Nigel Bruce (M-G-M)

It's pretty dangerous to put an old classic as popular as this Robert Louis Stevenson yarn on the screen. It is hard to imagine anyone else in the Long John Silver role than Wallace Beery. It is hard to think of anyone who might have replaced Jackie Cooper as Jim Hawkins. Yet neither of the two completely convinces.

Best performance honors are really split between Lionel Barrymore and Chic Sale. Former, as Billy Bones, and latter as Ben Gunn, seem most thoroughly to have caught the Stevenson spirit. They overact almost to mugging but it's in keeping with the manner of the story.

Treasure Island as a story is a grand, blood-curdling adventure yarn. In portions where it is so played it's genuinely thrilling and good entertainment.

•

TREASURE ISLAND

1950, 96 mins, UK Ⓥ ⊙ col

Dir Byron Haskin ***Prod*** Perce Pearce ***Scr*** Lawrence E. Watkin ***Ph*** Freddie Young ***Ed*** Alan Jaggs ***Mus*** Clifton Parker ***Art*** Tom Morahan

Act Bobby Driscoll, Robert Newton, Basil Sydney, Walter Fitzgerald, Denis O'Dea, Finlay Currie (RKO/Walt Disney)

Treasure Island, Robert Louis Stevenson's classic, has been handsomely mounted by Walt Disney. Settings are sumptuous and a British cast headed by American moppet Bobby Driscoll faithfully recaptures the bloodthirsty 18th-century era when pirates vied for the supremacy of the seas. It was made in Britain with Disney and RKO frozen pounds.

Stevenson yarn revolves around a squire and a doctor who fit out a ship to search for South Seas treasure on the strength of a chart obtained from a dying pirate.

Robert Newton racks up a virtual tour de force as Long John Silver. Likewise, Driscoll smashes across with a vital portrayal of Jim Hawkins, the saloonkeeper's son who falls heir to a map leading the way to pirate treasure.

There's no dearth of action in the footage.

•

TREASURE OF THE GOLDEN CONDOR

1953, 93 mins, US Ⓥ col

Dir Delmer Daves ***Prod*** Jules Buck ***Scr*** Delmer Daves ***Ph*** Edward Cronjager ***Ed*** Robert Simpson ***Mus*** Sol Kaplan ***Art*** Lyle R. Wheeler, Albert Hogsett

Act Cornel Wilde, Constance Smith, Finlay Currie, Walter Hampden, Anne Bancroft, Fay Wray (20th Century-Fox)

A moderate round of entertainment is offered in this adventure-swashbuckler that lays its action against Technicolored backgrounds in early France and Guatemala. Ancient Mayan ruins, particularly the earthquake-wrecked city of Antigua, supply a picturesque touch to the physical values. Action scenes are good.

Plot, from a novel by Edison Marshall, deals with Wilde's efforts to oust a cruel uncle (George Macready) who has usurped his French estates and title. Needing money to prove his rights, Wilde joins forces with Finlay Currie, possessor of a map to a fabulous Mayan treasure, and his daughter (Constance Smith). Back in France his plans are exposed by Anne Bancroft, a selfish girl he hopes to wed.

Wilde is likeable as the dashing hero and has some good swashbuckling moments in the latter portions of the footage. Smith and Bancroft both look good in their costumes. Fay Wray has only a few brief scenes as Macready's suffering wife.

•

TREASURE OF THE SIERRA MADRE, THE

1948, 124 mins, US Ⓥ ⊙ b/w

Dir John Huston ***Prod*** Henry Blanke ***Scr*** John Huston ***Ph*** Ted McCord ***Ed*** Owen Marks ***Mus*** Max Steiner ***Art*** John Hughes

Act Humphrey Bogart, Walter Huston, Tim Holt, Bruce Bennett, Barton MacLane (Warner)

Sierra Madre, adapted from the popular novel by B. Traven, is a story of psychological disintegration under the crushers of greed and gold. The characters here are probed and thoroughly penetrated, not through psychoanalysis but through a crucible of human conflict, action, gesture and expressive facial tones.

Huston, with an extraordinary assist in the thesping department from his father, Walter Huston, has fashioned this standout film with an unfailing sensitivity for the suggestive detail and an uncompromising commitment to reality, no matter how stark ugly it may be.

Except for some incidental femmes who have no bearing on the story, it's an all-male cast headed by Bogart, Huston and Tim Holt. They play the central parts of three gold prospectors who start out for pay dirt in the Mexican mountains as buddies, but wind up in a murderous tangle at the finish.

Lensed for most part on location, the film has, at least, a physical aspect of rugged beauty against which is contrasted the human sordidness.

Bogart comes through with a performance as memorable as his first major film role in *The Petrified Forest*. In a remarkable controlled portrait, he progresses to the edge of madness without losing sight of the subtle shadings needed to establish persuasiveness.

1948: Best Director, Best Supp. Actor (Walter Huston), Screenplay

NOMINATION: Best Picture

•

TREE GROWS IN BROOKLYN, A

1945, 132 mins, US Ⓥ ⊙ b/w

Dir Elia Kazan ***Prod*** Lovis D. Lighton ***Scr*** Tess Slesinger, Frank Davis ***Ph*** Leon Shamroy ***Ed*** Dorothy Spencer ***Mus*** Alfred Newman ***Art*** Lyle R. Wheeler

Act Dorothy McGuire, Joan Blondell, James Dunn, Lloyd Nolan, Peggy Ann Garner (20th Century-Fox)

The earthy quality of Brooklyn tenement squalor, about which Betty Smith wrote so eloquently in the bestseller novel *A Tree Grows in Brooklyn*, has been given a literal translation to the screen by 20th-Fox to become an experiment in audience restraint. This is the story of the poverty-ridden Nolan family.

Tree recalls an absorbing period of a colorful tribe, of a Brooklyn neighborhood that was tough in its growing-up, where kids fought, where on Saturday nights fathers and husbands loped uncertainly from the corner quenchery.

Some of this might have acquired the tinge of travesty in hands less skilled than those of Smith—or director Elia Kazan—but never does the serio-comic intrude on a false note; never does this story become maudlin.

To Dorothy McGuire went the prize part of Katie Nolan. It is a role that she makes distinctive by underplaying. James Dunn plays excellently. Peggy Ann Garner is the teenaged Francie, and the young actress performs capitally.

Where *Tree* is frequently slow, it is offset by the story's significance and pointed up notably by the direction of Elia Kazan.

1945: Best Supp. Actor (James Dunn)

NOMINATION: Best Screenplay

•

TREES LOUNGE

1996, 94 mins, US Ⓥ col

Dir Steve Buscemi ***Prod*** Kelley Forsyth, Sarah Vogel, Brad Wyman, ***Scr*** Steve Buscemi ***Ph*** Lisa Rinzler ***Ed*** Kate Williams ***Mus*** Evan Lurie ***Art*** Steve Rosenzweig

Act Steve Buscemi, Mark Boone, Jr., Chloe Sevigny, Michael Buscemi, Anthony LaPaglia, Elizabeth Bracco (Live)

A serio-comedy about a ne'er-do-well barfly, *Trees Lounge* reps a modest, agreeable directorial debut by indie acting stalwart Steve Buscemi. Pic takes a rueful, kaleidoscopic look at the petty feuds and minimal ambitions that dominate people's lives in a working-class New York suburb.

Buscemi has said that his first outing as a filmmaker can be taken as a speculative autobiography, a projection of what his life might have been like had he never left the Long Island village of Valley Stream and gone into acting.

Tommy (Buscemi) is a joker, an alcoholic and, at 31, a loser. He spends amost of his time downing drinks at the neighborhood watering hole, the Trees Lounge, and conveniently lives above the '50s-style establishment. Plenty of people pass through the bar and Tommy's life. Mike (Mark Boone, Jr.) is a family man with big problems at home. Uncle Al (Seymour Cassel) ups and dies, bringing diverse family members together. Debbie (Chloe Sevigny) is a hot little 17-year-old with a big crush on Tommy. It leads to an ill-advised night together that Debbie's hot-headed father (Danny Baldwin) won't let Tommy live down.

Neither the comedy nor the melodrama of these situations is punched up in a manipulative way, as Buscemi, seemingly taking his cue from indie pioneer John Cassavetes, roots everything in his characters and actors. Tech contributions on the low-budgeter are modest but solid.

•

TREMORS

1990, 96 mins, US Ⓥ ⊙ col

Dir Ron Underwood ***Prod*** S. S. Wilson, Brent Maddock ***Scr*** S. S. Wilson, Brent Maddock ***Ph*** Alexander Gruszynski ***Ed*** O. Nicholas Brown ***Mus*** Ernest Troost ***Art*** Ivo Cristante

Act Kevin Bacon, Fred Ward, Finn Carter, Michael Gross, Reba McEntire, Bobby Jacoby (No Frills)

An affectionate send-up of schlocky 1950s monster pics, but with better special effects, *Tremors* has a few clever twists but ultimately can't decide what it wants to be—flat-out funny, which it's not, or a scarefest.

In this case, the threat comes in the form of four house trailer-sized worm-creatures, with multiple serpent-like tongues, that tunnel underground before bursting up to devour human prey.

All the conventions of the genre are here: a small town in the middle of nowhere isolated from outside help, with a scientist on hand to study strange seismic phenomena. After that, however, the scripters begin to play with those clichés. The scientist, for example, is a pretty young woman (Finn Carter) who doesn't know where the monsters come from or understand why everyone keeps asking her to explain, while the heroes—handyman types Kevin Bacon and Fred Ward—carry on like Curly and Larry in search of Moe.

The pacing and action improve considerably as the film goes on, maintaining a tongue-in-cheek approach while the situation becomes more dire.

•

TRESPASS

1992, 101 mins, US Ⓥ ⦿ col

Dir Walter Hill ***Prod*** Neil Canton ***Scr*** Bob Gale, Robert Zemeckis ***Ph*** Lloyd Ahern ***Ed*** Freeman Davies ***Mus*** Ry Cooder ***Art*** Jon Hutman

Act Bill Paxton, Ice T, William Sadler, Ice Cube, Art Evans, De'voreaux White (Universal)

Throw together *The Treasure of the Sierra Madre* and *Rio Bravo*, bring in the Ice crew, inject a noxious dose of racial hatred and stir in some sharp action direction and you've got *Trespass*.

Originally called *Looters*, pic underwent a title change, a delay and some alterations after the L.A. riots in spring '92. Understandably so: the level of racial tension depicted here is way past the boiling point. After a brief prolog, the film is entirely set in one location, a huge abandoned factory in East St. Louis, IL. Learning that a huge stash of gold is supposedly buried somewhere in the bombed-out building, good ol' boy firemen Bill Paxton and William Sadler drive to the eerily underpopulated area with the idea of recovering the loot.

Unfortunately for them, the two Arkansas crackers stumble on to a gangland murder and instantly become marked men. Pursued by some tough, well-armed blacks led by a resplendent Ice T, Paxton and Sadler manage to nab T's brother (De'voreaux White). Holed up in one room, the white guys squabble about what to do with the gold.

Director Walter Hill's handling of the action is fluid and kinetic, making the film a pleasure to watch for the expertness of its craft. Ice T and Ice Cube strut their stuff in impressively forceful, if one-dimensional, fashion. Paxton and Sadler come off as decent but unremarkable. Technically, film is tops. Buildings in Atlanta and Memphis were employed for the single location.

•

TRESPASSER, THE

1929, 120 mins, US b/w

Dir Edmund Goulding ***Prod*** Joseph P. Kennedy ***Scr*** Edmund Goulding

Act Gloria Swanson, Robert Ames, Purnell Pratt, William Holden, Henry B. Walthall (United Artists)

The Trespasser has superior direction by Edmund Goulding, taking a conventional tale to make it stand up very high by twisting it about. Likely there is no picture with as many anti-climaxes as *The Trespasser* contains. At least four times the film goes to a finish, as one might suspect, to take another interesting tack. That is one of the novelties of the story. Three others are Gloria Swanson, her voice and clothes. Speaking and singing, she is okay, with a soft and clear diction which does not grate. Dialog is good and snappy, and steers well clear of melo, with William Holden having plenty of strong lines. Robert Ames does not quite get over, being out-trouped and outspoken by Swanson in most of his scenes.

Marion Donnell (Swanson), stenog to Hector Ferguson (Purnell Pratt), elopes with Jack Merrick (Ames), rich man's son, and a few days after father Merrick (Holden) horns in and persuades Jack that annulment to be followed by building up of Marion through publicity and remarriage later is socially essential.

The pic is framed to carry a sob at the close of every sequence and with a luscious part for Swanson.

•

TRIAL AND ERROR

SEE: THE DOCK BRIEF

•

TRIAL BY JURY

1994, 92 mins, US Ⓥ ⦿ col

Dir Heywood Gould ***Prod*** James G. Robinson, Chris Meledandri, Mark Gordon ***Scr*** Jordan Katz, Heywood Gould ***Ph*** Frederick Elmes ***Ed*** Joel Goodman ***Mus*** Terence Blanchard ***Art*** David Chapman

Act Joanne Whalley-Kilmer, Armand Assante, Gabriel Byrne, William Hurt, Kathleen Quinlan, Ed Lauter (Morgan Creek/Warner)

Even charismatic top-rank stars like William Hurt, Gabriel Byrne and Joanne Whalley-Kilmer can't resuscitate this leaden-paced legal thriller.

The script's troubles begin immediately, when the key government witness in the murder and racketeering trial of John Gotti–like crime boss Rusty Pirone (Armand Assante) is murdered in an unbelievable fashion. The only saving grace at the outset is Kathleen Quinlan's nice 'n' nasty turn as Wanda, a hard-bitten hooker/contract killer. That her character is never developed beyond her leather mini, tattoos and stiletto is only one of the pic's wasted assets.

Trying hard to put Pirone away is Byrne's U.S. Attorney Daniel Graham, laboring in a stock role as a crusading good boy from the same bad neighborhood as Pirone.

Valerie Alston (Whalley-Kilmer) strolls into the trial, an idealistic single mom who runs an antique clothing store in Manhattan. She wakes up to the possibility that sending a mob boss to the gas chamber could be hazardous to her health only after disgraced ex-cop Tommy Vesey (Hurt) kidnaps her in broad daylight. The plan is to scare Alston into hanging up the jury. An unrequited love story of sorts develops between Vesey and Alston, and Pirone also falls for the pert brunette.

With cinematographer Frederick Elmes's atmospheric lensing, Hurt and Quinlan's dark turns as menacing mob torpedoes, and enough laughable dialog to fill a camp film festival, all *Jury* needed was a director willing to take the film all the way into the realm of courtroom-thriller parody. Director Heywood Gould, the writer behind the Tom Cruise starrer *Cocktail*, apparently didn't see the possibilities.

•

TRIAL OF BILLY JACK, THE

1974, 170 mins, US Ⓥ ▭ col

Dir Frank Laughlin [= Tom Laughlin] ***Prod*** Joe Cramer ***Scr*** Frank Christina [= Tom Laughlin], Teresa Christina [= Delores Taylor] ***Ph*** Jack A. Marta ***Ed*** Tom Rolf, Michael Economou, George Grenville, Michael Karr, Jules Nayfack ***Mus*** Elmer Bernstein ***Art*** George W. Troast

Act Tom Laughlin, Delores Taylor, Victor Izay, Teresa Laughlin, William Wellman, Jr, Russell Lane (Taylor-Laughlin)

The Trial of Billy Jack is a violent, sometimes-explosive, anti-Establishment sequel to *Billy Jack* [1971]. Like its predecessor, starring the same two principals, it pinpoints community prejudices against the refusal of many to accept the American Indian.

Trial takes up as *Billy* ended, when Tom Laughlin as the half-breed Billy Jack was arrested for murder. Told in flashback by Delores Taylor, whose earlier rape was avenged by Billy Jack, and now he is sentenced to prison much of the footage unfolds at the Freedom School, a reservation institution headed by white femme.

The production enjoys extraordinary pictorial interest through having been photographed in Arizona's Monument Valley. But it is only when Laughlin is on-camera that the picture picks up.

•

TRIAL OF JOAN OF ARC, THE

SEE: PROCES DE JEANNE D'ARC

•

TRIAL OF SERGEANT RUTLEDGE

SEE: SERGEANT RUTLEDGE

•

TRIAL OF THE CATONSVILLE NINE, THE

1972, 85 mins, US Ⓥ col

Dir Gordon Davidson ***Prod*** Gregory Peck ***Scr*** Daniel Berrigan, Saul Levitt ***Ph*** Haskell Wexler ***Ed*** Aaron Stell ***Mus*** Shelley Manne ***Art*** Peter Wexler

Act Gwen Arner, Ed Flanders, Barton Heyman, Richard Jordan, Nancy Malone, Donald Moffat (Melville)

Gregory Peck has produced a film version of *The Trial of the Catonsville Nine* which shapes intelligent, well-acted filmed theatre and is potent in its look at the reasons behind burning of draft records and the trial that followed.

Film begins with a reenactment of burning of the records and the nine waiting for the police, to call attention to their outlooks. Though based on a play by Father Daniel Berrigan, and with high-flown passages of talk, it reportedly draws heavily on the actual court proceedings. But Berrigan tries to delve into the backgrounds, reasons and outlooks of those involved, their attempts to explain their actions by what they thought was wrong with the participation in the Vietnam War.

Theatrical, but fluidly controlled, direction by Gordon Davidson gives this a dramatic impetus despite static qualities and literary dialog.

•

TRIALS OF OSCAR WILDE, THE

(US: THE MAN WITH THE GREEN CARNATION)

1960, 123 mins, UK ▭ col

Dir Ken Hughes ***Prod*** Harold Huth ***Scr*** Ken Hughes ***Ph*** Ted Moore ***Ed*** Geoffrey Foot ***Mus*** Ron Goodwin ***Art*** Ken Adam

Act Peter Finch, Yvonne Mitchell, James Mason, Nigel Patrick, Lionel Jeffries, John Fraser (Warwick)

Color and wide screen are a sock asset to *The Trials of Oscar Wilde* and, on balance, it has greater stellar appeal [than the b&w version, *Oscar Wilde*, released at virtually the same time].

Main difference in the two films is the color job starts where the scandalous friendship is well established and spends more time setting the atmosphere of the time of the turn of the century.

Trials [from John Furnald's play *The Stringed Lute* and Montgomery Hyde's book *The Trials of Oscar Wilde*] also introduces Wilde's re-trial and, in one brilliant scene at Brighton, shows Wilde's anguish when he first realizes that he is merely being used by his young friend as a weapon in his vindictive struggle with his brutal father.

Peter Finch gives a moving and subtle performance as the ill-starred playwright. Before his downfall he gives the man the charm that he undoubtedly had. The famous Wilde epigrams could well have been thought up by Finch.

John Fraser as handsome young Lord Alfred Douglas is suitably vain, selfish, vindictive and petulant and the relationship between the two is more understandable.

Where *Trials* suffers in comparison with the b&w film is in the remarkable impact of the libel case court sequence. James Mason never provides the strength and bitter logic necessary for the dramatic cut-and-thrust when Wilde is in the witness box.

•

TRIAL, THE

1962, 115 mins, France/W. Germany/Italy Ⓥ ⦿ b/w

Dir Orson Welles ***Prod*** Alexander Salkind ***Scr*** Orson Welles ***Ph*** Edmond Richard ***Ed*** Fritz H. Mueller ***Mus*** Jean Ledrut ***Art*** Jean Mandaroux

Act Anthony Perkins, Jeanne Moreau, Romy Schneider, Elsa Martinelli, Akim Tamiroff, Orson Welles (Paris-Europa/Hisa/FICIT)

Written and directed by himself from the "nightmare" novel by Franz Kafka, Orson Welles's film may well delight film buffs and startle or irritate many others.

A young white-collar worker, Joseph K, wakes up one morning to find a sinister police inspector and two seedy detectives in his room. He is technically under arrest but he is not told why. He accepts the fact after various attempts at rationalizing.

Then the film gets progressively more expressionistic and surreal as he is caught up completely in his impending trial and neglects work, one woman next door who promised adventure, and gets deeper into the complex setup of the law. The geography of the film becomes inextricably bound up with dusty file rooms, waiting rooms full of supposedly guilty men not knowing why they are there and K's final attempt to revolt.

Anthony Perkins as K is on screen practically all the time. His boyishness is oft pedaled to turn him into a timid but priggish type who faces up to an impersonal court. It shapes as a knowing, incisive screen performance.

Jeanne Moreau, Elsa Martinelli and others have fleeting parts that are adequately done. Most outstanding is Romy Schneider as the lawyer's nurse who is irresistibly drawn to accused men.

Welles has given slight intimations that this could be a totalitarian nation or one of over-automation. And it also may be a man's awakening to consciousness and finding himself alienated in the world and rejecting its aspects one by one.

So pic is uneven and sometimes filled with arid talk, but has enough visual vitality to keep it engrossing in its first part.

•

TRIAL, THE

1993, 118 mins, UK Ⓥ col

Dir David Jones ***Prod*** Louis Marks ***Scr*** Harold Pinter ***Ph*** Phil Meheux ***Ed*** John Stothart ***Mus*** Carl Davis ***Art*** Don Taylor

Act Kyle MacLachlan, Anthony Hopkins, Jason Robards, Jean Stapleton, Polly Walker, Juliet Stevenson (BBC/Europanda)

The Trial is just that. Despite a fine cast, superior Prague locations and a faithful Harold Pinter screenplay, this second film adaptation of Kafka's landmark 1913 novel is dull, lifeless and strictly TV-bound in its aesthetics.

Up against the brick wall of an authoritarian regime and an unknowable Law, K (Kyle MacLachlan) has experiences that are positively illogicial and evocative of modern man's absurd status in the universe.

There are sexual skirmishes with another boarder (Juliet Stevenson) and his lawyer's mistress (Polly Walker), encounters with various men who possess passing knowledge of aspects of the Law (uncle Robert Lang, attorney Jason Robards, court painter Alfred Molina) and assorted odd characters, such as a washerwoman (Catherine Neilson) who submits sexually to her detested boyfriend in front of hundreds of people at K's hearing.

But, as structured, the script evolves as a tedious series

of mostly two-character scenes. Performances are perfectly acceptable without being at all electrifying.

•

TRIBUTE

1980, 123 mins, Canada Ⓥ ⊙ col

Dir Bob Clark *Prod* Joel B. Michaels, Garth B. Drabinsky *Scr* Bernard Slade *Ph* Reginald H. Morris *Ed* Richard Halsey *Mus* Ken Wannburg *Art* Trevor Williams

Act Jack Lemmon, Robby Benson, Lee Remick, Kim Cattrall, Colleen Dewhurst, John Marley (20th Century-Fox)

When Jack Lemmon opened *Tribute* on Broadway, people said it would be impossible to imagine any other actor in the role and sure enough the show shuttered when he departed. The complex role of Scottie Templeton has been tailored for Lemmon's oft-proclaimed talents for both comedy and heavy drama. Working from his own stage script, and with an able assist from director Bob Clark, writer Bernard Slade uses film to deepen and enrich Templeton's story, which begins with his learning of his fatal illness just as the young son he hasn't seen for several years arrives for a visit.

Robby Benson is excellent in the equally complex part of the intellectual, introspective boy, both repelled by his father's superficial, even pimpish existence as a broadway press agent and attracted, as everyone is, to his charm. Most of all he's resentful of the years lost since father divorced mother (Lee Remick).

In the smallest of the three major parts, Remick nonetheless turns a solid performance as the ex-wife who still loves him but learned long ago he wasn't worth putting up with. Kim Cattrall adds a lot as the young girl involved closely with father and son; Colleen Dewhurst is strong as Lemmon's doctor-friend and John Marley catches fire in the second half of the film as Lemmon's partner and defender.

•

TRIBUTE TO A BAD MAN

1956, 95 mins, US ▭ col

Dir Robert Wise *Prod* Sam Zimbalist *Scr* Michael Blankfort *Ph* Robert Surtees *Ed* Ralph E. Winters *Mus* Miklos Rozsa *Art* Cedric Gibbons, Paul Groesse

Act James Cagney, Don Dubbins, Stephen McNally, Irene Papas, Vic Morrow, Lee Van Cleef (M-G-M)

A rugged frontier drama of the early west, played off against the scenically striking Colorado Rockies, *Tribute to a Bad Man* is a sight to behold, using the location sites for full visual worth. Irene Papas, Greek actress, in her Hollywood debut comes off well.

Critically, *Bad Man* is both fast- and slow-paced. Latter, in part, results from a feeling of repetition in some of the story points as scripted from a Jack Schaefer short story, and in some scene-prolonging beyond the point of good dramatic return by Robert Wise's direction.

The title is somewhat of a misnomer. The man portrayed so well by Cagney is a hard-bitten pioneer who must enforce his own law on the limitless range he controls. The picture of him is seen through the eyes of young Don Dubbins, eastern lad come west to make his fortune and who tarries awhile in Cagney's employ.

The stay is long enough for him to fall in love with Papas and almost win her away from Cagney when she rebels at the latter's arrogant justice of the rope for breakers of his laws.

•

TRICK OR TREAT

1986, 97 mins, US Ⓥ col

Dir Charles Martin Smith *Prod* Michael S. Murphey, Joel Soisson *Scr* Michael S. Murphey, Joel Soisson, Rhet Topham *Ph* Robert Elswit *Ed* Jane Schwartz *Mus* Christopher Young, Fastway *Art* Curt Schnell

Act Marc Price, Tony Fields, Lisa Orgolini, Ozzy Osbourne (De Laurentiis)

Like a relatively dark street on Halloween night, *Trick or Treat* is ripe for howls and hoots, but only manages to deliver a choice handful of them when the festivities are just about over.

A recently killed rock star named Sammi Curr (Tony Fields, made up like a member of KISS), comes back to life when his last, awful unreleased record is played backwards. He's determined to seek revenge on his most ardent critics.

The thing is, the satanic rocker takes himself seriously in reincarnation and ends up acting out all those evil acts he's been singing about for years—drawing his power from the megawatts that surge through his guitar.

There's a geeky high-school kid, Eddie (Marc Price), who idolizes the rocker and is responsible for his appearances. Price is cast perfectly as the dismayed rock worshipper.

•

TRIO

1950, 91 mins, UK Ⓥ b/w

Dir Ken Annakin, Harold French *Prod* Antony Darnborough *Scr* W. Somerset Maugham, R. C. Sherriff, Noel Langley *Ph* Reginald Wyer, Geoffrey Unsworth *Ed* Alfred Roome *Mus* John Greenwood *Art* Maurice Carter

Act James Hayter, Anne Crawford, Nigel Patrick, Jean Simmons, Michael Rennie, Kathleen Harrison (Gainsborough)

The success of *Quartet*, in which four unrelated Somerset Maugham short stories were strung together in a single picture, encouraged the producers to repeat the formula.

The only connecting link between the three yarns is a pithy Maugham foreword. The first two vignettes, *The Verger* and *Mr. Knowall* [directed by Ken Annakin], between them occupy roughly half the screen time. *Sanatorium* [directed by Harold French] deals with the treatment of tuberculosis.

The first two are bright. The longer piece strikes a happy note between sentiment and laughter.

In *The Verger*, James Hayter is warm and colorful and Kathleen Harrison is typically cast.

Nigel Patrick dominates *Mr. Knowall* while Jean Simmons and Michael Rennie in *Sanatorium* play their roles with distinctive charm.

1950: NOMINATION: Best Sound

•

TRIP, THE

1967, 85 mins, US Ⓥ col

Dir Roger Corman *Prod* Roger Corman *Scr* Jack Nicholson *Ph* Arch Dalzell *Ed* Ronald Sinclair *Mus* Electric Flag

Act Peter Fonda, Susan Strasberg, Bruce Dern, Dennis Hopper, Salli Sachse, Katherine Walsh (American International)

Jack Nicholson's script opens with Peter Fonda, a director of TV commercials, shooting on a beach and being confronted by wife, Susan Strasberg, who is about to divorce him. Distressed by his personal life, he goes off with friend Bruce Dern to the hippie, weirdly painted house of a pusher, played by Dennis Hopper, to buy LSD.

Guarded by Dern, Fonda's trip begins. Scenes rapidly cut from Fonda climbing lofty sand dunes, being chased by two black hooded horsemen through forests, as well as being the sacrificial victim at a dark medieval rite in a torchlit cave. Unconnected scenes begin to spin off the screen with increasing speed and with no attempt at explanation.

Fonda comes across very well, establishing the various moods needed to further the visual effects. Strasberg is on only briefly, and Hopper is okay, except in a dream sequence in which he plays a weirdo high priest, but that whole scene is sophomoric.

•

TRIPLE CROSS

1966, 140 mins, France/UK Ⓥ col

Dir Terence Young *Prod* Jacques-Paul Bertrand *Scr* Rene Hardy, William Marchant, Terence Young *Ph* Henri Alekan *Ed* Roger Dwyre *Mus* Georges Gavarentz *Art* Tony Roman

Act Christopher Plummer, Yul Brynner, Romy Schneider, Claudine Auger, Trevor Howard, Gert Frobe (Cineurop)

Though based on a true story of a British safecracker who worked as a double spy during the Second World War, *Triple Cross* is made in the standard spy pattern of having him a ladies' man, fast with his mitts, glib and shrewd, and with overloaded and obvious suspense bits thrown in to rob this of the verisimilitude needed to give it a more original fillip.

Director Terence Young plays this slightly tongue-in-cheek and it actually emerges as a sort of mini-Bond. Christopher Plummer is first seen cracking a series of safes and is finally arrested in Jersey. Along comes war and the Germans take over the island. He bluffs his way into getting a hearing with some top German undercover people.

He manages to gull them into letting him work for them and is finally entrusted with a mission. Once in Britain he goes to the British security people, finally convinces them and goes to work for them for a big sum and a promise to wipe out his criminal record.

Plummer walks through his role and does not quite have the impassive mask for the pro criminal or the needed lightness to give the romantic dash it calls for.

•

TRIPLE ECHO, THE

1972, 102 mins, UK Ⓥ col

Dir Michael Apted *Prod* Graham Cottle *Scr* Robin Chapman *Ph* Mark Wilkinson *Ed* Barrie Vince *Mus* Denis Lewiston *Art* Edward Marshall

Act Glenda Jackson, Oliver Reed, Brian Deacon, Anthony May, Gavin Richards, Jenny Lee Wright (Hemdale/Senta)

Story is set on an English farm in 1943. Alice (Glenda Jackson) has been living alone in the country, since her husband was taken a prisoner by the Japanese a half-year earlier. One day a young soldier, Barton (Brian Deacon), comes along and during a tender moment she invites him in for tea. When time comes for Barton to rejoin his regiment, he decides to go AWOL and stay with Alice. So as not to be discovered he starts donning female clothes.

Just as Barton is becoming tired of his equivocal role, a stray tank comes rolling down the hill with a sergeant (Oliver Reed) in it. Next day he's back again, trying to catch a glimpse of Barton, whom he believes to be Alice's sister. At length he does see the "sister" and announces he's going to take her out dancing.

Aside from the contrived ending, the slow pacing through most of the pic up to the time Reed appears, one never really gets into the motivations of the two main characters.

•

TRIP TO BOUNTIFUL, THE

1985, 106 mins, US Ⓥ ⊙ col

Dir Peter Masterson *Prod* Sterling Van Wagenen, Horton Foote *Scr* Horton Foote *Ph* Fred Murphy *Ed* Jay Freund *Mus* J.A.C. Redford *Art* Neil Spisak

Act Geraldine Page, John Heard, Carlin Glynn, Richard Bradford, Rebecca DeMornay, Kevin Cooney (FilmDallas/Bountiful Film Partners)

The Trip to Bountiful is a superbly crafted drama featuring the performance of a lifetime by Geraldine Page. She plays Mrs. Watts, a woman whose determination to escape the confines of life in a small Houston apartment with her selfless son, Ludie (John Heard), and his domineering wife, Jessie Mae (Carlin Glynn), leads her on a moving and memorable journey across the Gulf Coast to return to Bountiful, the town where she was born and raised.

Adapted by Horton Foote from his 1953 teleplay that enjoyed theatrical success on Broadway, the 1947-set film recalls the days of scripts with real plots and dialog.

Life for Mrs. Watts with Ludie and Jessie Mae is a claustrophobic and harsh existence of forced politeness, petty battles and demanded apologies. Heard is excellent as the downtrodden Ludie burdened with keeping the peace while contending with money problems and self doubts. Glynn likewise puts in a strong performance, giving a human edge and depth to what could have been an otherwise nagging wife stereotype. Page's work is excellent throughout.

1985: Best Actress (Geraldine Page)

NOMINATION: Best Screenplay Adaptation

•

TRISTANA

1970, 105 mins, Spain/Italy/France Ⓥ ⊙ col

Dir Luis Bunuel *Scr* Luis Bunuel, Julio Alejandro *Ph* Jose F. Aguayo *Ed* Pedro del Rey *Mus* [none] *Art* Enrique Alarcon

Act Catherine Deneuve, Fernando Rey, Franco Nero, Lola Gaos, Antonio Casas, Jesus Fernandez (Epoca/Talia/Selenia/Corona)

Luis Bunuel based his pic on an obscure novel by Spain's prolific, realistic, humorless literary giant, Benito Perez Galdos, who, throughout his life, showed a penchant for liberalism, a taste for analyses of Spanish life at all levels, and a strong involvement with the multifold problems of his country. [He died in 1920.]

Those seeking the Bunuel touches of black humor, digs at Church and Establishment, irreverence and criticism, and an overall condemnation of Spanish mores and hypocrisy, will find a modicum of scenes here to titillate their palates. Yet Bunuel, despite occasional digs, has remained more or less respectful.

Much of the pic [which deals with the love-hate relationship between an orphaned girl and her elder protector] is rather somber. Shots are limited to a few key locations: the local cafe, the house of Don Lope, several of the streets of Toledo, an artist's studio, a belfry, etc. Weighing upon all these scenes is a vision of life in Spain in the 1920s.

As Don Lope, Fernando Rey is superb. He seems completely at ease in the part. Catherine Deneuve, though she brings considerable acting talents to the title role, cannot hide the fact that she is a foreigner, though her voice is skillfully dubbed. Franco Nero (also non-Spanish) plays the role of a young artist competently.

•

TRIUMPH OF THE SPIRIT

1989, 120 mins, US Ⓥ ⊙ col

Dir Robert M. Young *Prod* Arnold Kopelson, Shimon Arama *Scr* Andrzej Krakowski, Laurence Heath *Ph* Curtis Clark *Ed* Arthur Coburn *Mus* Cliff Eidelman *Art* Jerzy Maslowski

Act Willem Dafoe, Edward James Olmos, Robert Loggia, Wendy Gazelle, Kelly Wolf, Costas Mandylor (Nova/Arama/Kopelson)

An event as oft-dramatized as the Holocaust becomes difficult to portray anew, a circumstance that blunts the impact of *Triumph of the Spirit*. Film's *raison d'etre*—its true story of a Greek boxing champ who survived life-or-death bouts in the ring at Auschwitz—is murkily underplayed within the harrowing chronicle of death-camp suffering.

Producer Arnold Kopelson (*Platoon*), bucking indifference from the studios, spent seven years bringing the story [by Shimon Arama and Zion Haen] to the screen.

In conveying the experience of the Greek middleweight boxer Salamo Arouch (Willem Dafoe), writers were hamstrung by history, as Arouch did not take part in the film's climactic event—an uprising that leads to the blowing up of the crematorium (and the death of most of the conspirators). Focus is therefore spread among Arouch's family and friends, including his love interest, Allegra (Wendy Gazelle).

Arouch's fights don't commence until 45 minutes into a very slow film. For the most part, screen time is devoted to retelling the Holocaust story in a version that, lacking distinctive characters, relies heavily on images chosen by director Robert M. Young. Film is notably short on dialog. Dafoe finds little to do; like the others he just tries to exude sorrowful stamina.

•

TROIS COULEURS BLANC
(THREE COLORS WHITE)

1994, 89 mins, France/Switzerland/Poland Ⓥ ⊙ col

Dir Krzysztof Kieslowski **Prod** Marin Karmitz **Scr** Krzysztof Piesiewicz, Krzysztof Kieslowski **Ph** Edward Klosinski **Ed** Urszula Lesiak **Mus** Zbigniew Preisner **Art** Halina Dobrowolska, Claude Lenoir

Act Zbigniew Zamachowski, Julie Delpy, Janusz Gajos, Jerzy Stuhr, Florence Pernel, Juliette Binoche (MK2/Cab/Tor)

The entertaining second seg of Krzysztof Kieslowski's *Three Colors* trilogy, *White* is involving, bittersweet and droll. A fine lead perf from Zbigniew Zamachowski anchors an ingenious rags-to-riches tale of revenge filtered through abiding love. Pic is mostly in Polish, with a smattering of French.

Although mostly set in Warsaw, pic begins in a Paris law court where cruel French beauty Dominique (Julie Delpy) is finalizing her divorce from somewhat bumbling Polish hubby, Karol (Zamachowski). Karol is offered a lucrative job by fellow countryman Mikolaj (Janusz Gajos) of killing an unnamed Pole. He declines, but the two become friendly and Mikolaj agrees to smuggle Karol back home as "checked baggage."

Karol gets a rude introduction to the new Poland in which anything and everything can be bought and sold. At the pinnacle of his career, Karol hatches a plot to fake his own death and leave his financial empire to his ex-wife.

As the resourceful underdog, Karol ("Charles") is meant as an homage to Chaplin, with the worldly Mikolaj a perfect friend and foil to the Little Tramp. Although Delpy is fine as the wife, the pic is Zamachowski's through and through.

•

TROIS COULEURS BLEU
(THREE COLORS BLUE)

1993, 97 mins, France/Switzerland/Poland Ⓥ ⊙ col

Dir Krzysztof Kieslowski **Prod** Marin Karmitz **Scr** Krzysztof Piesiewicz, Krzysztof Kieslowski, Agnieszka Holland, Edward Zebrowski, Slawomir Idziak **Ph** Slawomir Idziak **Ed** Jacques Witta **Mus** Zbigniew Preisner **Art** Claude Lenoir

Act Juliette Binoche, Benoit Regent, Florence Pernel, Charlotte Very, Emmanuelle Riva, Hugues Quester (MK2/CED/France 3/CAB/Tor)

The first installment in Kryzsztof Kieslowski's trilogy inspired by the French tricolor falls short of the mystical perfection that characterized *The Decalogue*, but boasts a riveting central performance by a carefully controlled, lovingly lit Juliette Binoche.

Dramatic tale of a woman who streamlines her life after surviving the accident that kills her young daughter and composer husband, retains traces of the puzzle-piece serendipity that distinguishes helmer's most captivating work. But in this outing (as, to a lesser extent, in *The Double Life of Veronique*) Kieslowski's French characters are watered-down icons compared to their Polish counterparts.

Post-accident, bereaved but businesslike Julie (Binoche) instructs her lawyer to sell every last shred of property. But is she truly at liberty to discard the *Concerto for Europe* that her late husband left unfinished?

Julie wants only to blend into Paris, but a sex-attuned neighbor (Charlotte Very, as a sensitive sinner) and her late husband's assistant (Benoit Regent) exert a pull on her.

Zbigniew Preisner's music, whose thundering chords evoke memory, limn loss and hail the tenuous promise of European unity, is a character in its own right, making up in expressiveness what taciturn Julie seems to lack. Binoche goes from banged-up to smashing, but rarely smiles or sheds her reserve.

•

TROIS COULEURS ROUGE
(THREE COLORS RED)

1994, 99 mins, France/Switzerland/Poland Ⓥ ⊙ col

Dir Krzysztof Kieslowski **Prod** Marin Karmitz **Scr** Krzysztof Piesiewicz, Krzysztof Kieslowski **Ph** Piotr Sobocinski **Ed** Jacques Witta **Mus** Zbigniew Preisner **Art** Claude Lenoir

Act Irene Jacob, Jean-Louis Trintignant, Frederique Feder, Jean-Pierre Lorit, Juliette Binoche, Julie Delpy (MK2/France 3/Cab/Tor)

Red, the beautifully spun and splendidly acted tale of a young model's decisive encounter with a retired judge, is another deft, deeply affecting variation on Krzysztof Kieslowski's recurring theme that people are interconnected in ways they can barely fathom.

Swiss law student and judge-to-be Auguste (Jean-Pierre Lorit) lives across the street from fashion model Valentine (Irene Jacob), who communicates via telephone with her boyfriend in England. Auguste is in love with Karin (Frederique Feder), who runs a "personalized weather service," dispensing tailor-made forecasts by telephone. Auguste and Valentine pass each other on countless occasions but have never noticed each other.

Valentine meets a former judge (Jean-Louis Trintignant), who listens in on his neighbors' telephone conversations. The innocent, faintly troubled young woman and the resigned older man explore the implications of extending a fraternal hand.

Location lensing in Geneva is aces. The title color is ever present, from a glass of wine to a bowling ball, from a transit ticket to an automobile. Jacob has never been so radiant as in her work with Kieslowski. Trintignant is fascinating as a man who recalibrates his moral compass thanks to Jacob. Zbigniew Preisner's score, augmented by soaring vocals, is a fine ally throughout.

1994: NOMINATIONS: Best Director, Original Screenplay, Cinematography

•

3 HOMMES ET UN COUFFIN
(3 MEN AND A CRADLE)

1985, 104 mins, France Ⓥ ⊙ col

Dir Coline Serreau **Prod** Jean-Francois Lepetit **Scr** Coline Serreau **Ph** Jean-Yves Escoffier **Ed** Catherine Renault **Art** Yvan Maussion

Act Roland Giraud, Michel Boujenah, Andre Dussollier, Philippine Leroy Beaulieu, Dominique Lavanant, Marthe Villalonga (Flach/Soprofilms/TF1)

Coline Serreau's comedy about three hardened bachelors saddled with a newborn baby, produced on a modest budget and without bankable talent, is warm, hilarious and well-made. Serreau's direction is bright and confident, avoiding the saccharine pitfalls of the material.

Most of the story is set in the sprawling Paris apartment that serves as the macho sanctuary of the three liberty-loving bucks. The baby is the unannounced deposit of a girl whom airline pilot Jacques (Andre Dussollier) has already bedded and forgotten (he is the alleged father), and who has taken off for the States for several months.

With Jacques away for the time being, Pierre (Roland Giraud) and Michel (Michel Boujenah) react with the expected panic and their calamitous first attempts to take care of their new ward are chronicled with a sure sense of farce pacing by Serreau. Added complications arise in the form of a small package of heroin, which the trio has been unwittingly harboring, and which is sought by both its dealers and the police drug squad.

Film marks the full-fledged screen debut of Boujenah, an exuberant young Tunisian Jewish stand-up comic who has enjoyed success with his one-man shows. Giraud, who has already shown deft comic abilities in previous films, hits full stride under Serreau's direction. Dusollier comes across with skillful aplomb.

•

TROJAN WOMEN, THE

1971, 111 mins, Greece/US Ⓥ col

Dir Michael Cacoyannis **Prod** Michael Cacoyannis, Anis Nohra **Scr** Michael Cacoyannis **Ph** Alfio Contini **Ed** Russell Woolnough **Mus** Mikis Theodorakis **Art** Nicholas Georgiadis

Act Katharine Hepburn, Genevieve Bujold, Vanessa Redgrave, Irene Papas, Brian Blessed, Patrick Magee (Shaftel)

Michael Cacoyannis has come up with a version of Euripides's *The Trojan Women*, which he did successfully off-Broadway in New York. Pic has a surface resonance and not enough of the tragic sweep and force its outcry against war and oppression call for.

It has a solid cast. There is Katharine Hepburn as the proud but fallen Queen of Troy, Hecuba, whose husband and sons have been killed. Only a daughter, mad Cassandra, and Andromache, the wife and child of her son, Hector, are alive. She valiantly tries to lament, dirge and stand up to the fates in dignity, but the force and the needed tragic depth elude her laudatory attempt.

Vanessa Redgrave is lacking in passion as Andromache. Her tragic lamentations do not get to the core of loss. Nor is Genevieve Bujold, as Cassandra, up to the frenzy and needed steely quality of her preachments on man's warring nature and her prophecies on her future demise.

Irene Papas, probably the true tragedienne among them, plays Helen, abducted by Paris, Hecuba's son, on a visit to Sparta, causing the Greeks to attack Troy, sack it, kill the men and send the women, including Hecuba, off to slavery, then burning the city.

•

TROLL

1986, 86 mins, US Ⓥ ⊙ col

Dir John Carl Buechler **Prod** Albert Band **Scr** Ed Naha **Ph** Romana Albani **Ed** Lee Percy **Mus** Richard Band **Art** Gayle Simon

Act Noah Hathaway, Michael Moriarty, Shelley Hack, Jenny Beck, Sonny Bono, June Lockhart (Empire)

Troll is a predictable, dim-witted premise executed for the most part with surprising style. Horror-fantasy of a universe of trolls taking over a San Francisco apartment house is far-fetched even for this genre. Creatures designed by John Buechler, who also directed, are a repulsive assortment of hairy, fanged, evil-looking elves but the plot is pure shlock.

No sooner does the Potter family move into an ordinary looking building than the young daughter (Jenny Beck) is possessed by the troll. Where the film rises above the ordinary is in the domestic scenes when, thanks to her acquired personality, young Beck can flout all the conventions of how a good girl should act. Performances by the kids are convincing.

•

TROLLENBERG TERROR, THE
(US: THE CRAWLING EYE)

1958, 85 mins, UK Ⓥ ⊙ b/w

Dir Quentin Lawrence **Prod** Robert S. Baker, Monty Berman **Scr** Jimmy Sangster **Ph** Monty Berman **Ed** Henry Richardson **Mus** Stanley Black **Art** Duncan Sutherland

Act Forrest Tucker, Laurence Payne, Janet Munro, Jennifer Jayne, Warren Mitchell, Andrew Faulds (Eros)

Based on a successful TV serial by Peter Key, the yarn concerns a creature from outer space secreted in a radioactive cloud on the mountain of Trollenberg in Switzerland. The mysterious disappearance of various climbers brings Forrest Tucker to the scene as a science investigator for UNO. He and a professor at the local observatory set out to solve the problem.

During investigations, two headless corpses are discovered and a couple of ordinary citizens go berserk and turn killers. Main object of the two is Janet Munro who is one of a sister mind-reading act and obviously presents a threat to the sinister visitor.

The taut screenplay extracts the most from the situations and is helped by strong, resourceful acting from a solid cast. Tucker tackles the problem with commendable lack of histrionics and Munro adds considerably to the film's interest with an excellent portrayal of the girl whose mental telepathy threatens the creature's activities and draws her into danger.

•

TROLOSA
(FAITHLESS)

2000, 154 mins, Sweden Ⓥ ⊙ col

Dir Liv Ullmann **Prod** Kaj Larsen **Scr** Ingmar Bergman **Ph** Jorgen Persson **Ed** Sylvia Ingemarsson **Art** Goran Wassberg

Act Lena Endre, Erland Josephson, Krister Henriksson, Thomas Hanzon, Michelle Gylemo, Juni Dahr (SVT Drama)

Admirers of the great Swedish director Ingmar Bergman will find much to enjoy in this personal and revelatory film about the destructive forces unleashed by thoughtless sexual misbehavior. Bergman's script, which is structured around the efforts of a film director to write a screenplay based on his experiences, is filled with references to his films as a director and, perhaps, to his life; Liv Ullmann, directing her second Bergman screenplay, extracts every nuance from the tantalizing material.

The story is simple enough. Marianne Vogler (the name resonates with the names of past Bergman characters), beautifully played by Lena Endre, is a successful actress, happily married to Markus (Thomas Hanzon), an orchestra conductor much in demand, and devoted to her young daughter, Isabelle (Michelle Gylemo). The family's best friend is David (Krister Henriksson), a film director with a reckless attitude toward money, family and relationships. Marianne has an affair with David that destroys her marriage and brings grief to all concerned, with the innocent Isabelle suffering most of all. Augmenting this straightforward premise, screenwriter Bergman has constructed a framing device in which an elderly film director named Bergman, played by Erland Josephson, is attempting to write a screenplay about infidelity and marital breakup.

Ullmann, one of Bergman's most luminous collaborators and the mother of one of his children, does a solid job behind the camera, though is perhaps a bit too reverential with the material, which merits judicious pruning.

For many viewers, the stumbling block may be the performance of Henriksson as David. The actor is far less charismatic than Hanzon, who plays the husband, making it a bit of a mystery what Marianne sees in him. Beyond that, David is given some extremely unpleasant character traits—violent jealousy, for one—and is, essentially, unlikable. Maybe that's the point: Bergman, seeing himself in the role of the reckless lover, imbues David with the ugliest characteristics as a comment on his own behavior.

•

TRON
1982, 96 mins, US Ⓥ ⊙ ▭ col
Dir Steven Lisberger ***Prod*** Donald Kushner ***Scr*** Steven Lisberger ***Ph*** Bruce Logan ***Ed*** Jeff Gourson ***Mus*** Wendy Carlos ***Art*** Dean Edward Mitzner
Act Jeff Bridges, Bruce Boxleitner, David Warner, Cindy Morgan, Barnard Hughes, Dan Shor (Walt Disney)

Tron is loaded with visual delights but falls way short of the mark in story and viewer involvement. Screenwriter-director Steven Lisberger has adequately marshalled a huge force of technicians to deliver the dazzle, but even kids (and specifically computer game freaks) will have a difficult time getting hooked on the situations.

After an awkward "teaser" intro the story unfolds concisely: Computer games designer Kevin Flynn (Jeff Bridges) has had his series of fabulously successful programs stolen by Ed Dillinger (David Warner). Dillinger has consequently risen to a position of corporate power and with his Master Control Program (MCP) has increasingly dominated other programmers and users.

Flynn must obtain the evidence stored in computer's memory proving that Dillinger has appropriated his work. His friend Alan Bradley (Bruce Boxleitner) is concurrently working on a watchdog program (called Tron) to thwart the MCP's growing control. The MCP scientifically transforms Flynn into a computer-stored program, bringing the viewer into the parallel world inside the computer.

Computer-generated visuals created by diverse hands are impressive but pic's design work and execution consistently lack the warmth and humanity that classical animation provides.

1982: NOMINATIONS: Best Costume Design, Sound

•

TROP BELLE POUR TOI
(TOO BEAUTIFUL FOR YOU)
1989, 93 mins, France Ⓥ ⊙ ▭ col
Dir Bertrand Blier ***Scr*** Bertrand Blier ***Ph*** Philippe Rousselot ***Ed*** Claudine Merlin ***Art*** Theo Meurisse
Act Gerard Depardieu, Josiane Balasko, Carole Bouquet, Roland Blanche, Francios Cluzet, Myriam Boyer (Cine Valse/DD)

Bertrand Blier, whose films usually have made sardonic fun of such staple themes as friendship and sexual relationships, has come up with a new charmer in *Too Beautiful for You*, this time bringing fresh insight to the old, old story of marital infidelity.

Gerard Depardieu plays a successful car dealer married to a sublimely beautiful woman (Carole Bouquet) to the envy of all his friends. Perversely, he falls passionately in love with a temporary secretary who comes to work for him—a plump, somewhat plain, middle-aged woman who would seem to be the least likely type to woo him away from his family. Josiane Balasko plays the sweet, sensual mistress with a warmth which makes Depardieu's passion acceptable.

The plot is simple enough, but Blier keeps his audience in a constant state of surprise, and delight, with the complex but frequently funny way he tells his essentially banal story. Blier gleefully takes every cliché and turns it on its head, juggling time, allowing his characters to address the audience and including such genuinely charming scenes as one in which the blissful Balasko shares her happiness with a complete stranger at a railway station, telling him she's been making love for the last three hours.

Two scenes in which the wife and the mistress meet, once in the office and again in the motel, are exquisitely written and acted emotional encounters. Another highlight is a complex flashback to the Depardieu/Bouquet wedding which is intercut with a dinner party they give for friends in the present.

•

TROU, LE
(THE HOLE)
1960, 145 mins, France/Italy b/w
Dir Jacques Becker ***Prod*** Serge Silberman (exec.) ***Scr*** Jacques Becker, Jose Giovanni, Jean Aurel ***Ph*** Ghislain Cloquet ***Ed*** Marguerite Renoir, Genevieve Vaury ***Mus*** [none] ***Art*** Rino Mondellini
Act Michel Constantin, Jean Keraudy, Philippe Leroy, Raymond Meunier, Marc Michel (PlayArt/Filmsonor/Titanus)

The late Jacques Becker [who died Feb. 21, 1960, a few weeks before release of *Le Trou*] left behind a solidly built film, based on a true story [authored by Jose Giovanni] of a jailbreak. Using non-actors, picture tells a tale of human endeavor and cooperation that transcends its actual locale. It is taut sans trying for any untowards suspense gambits because of its feeling for its people, place and motivations.

Five men awaiting sentence break through their cell floor, enter the insides of the prison, and get to the sewer system from where they can break into the regular sewage setup and freedom. But the best-laid plans are foiled by a newcomer who turns them in.

The intricate break and digging aspects are dynamically detailed. The rugged sets have the feel of a cement-and-iron prison. The acting is uncannily clear for non-actors, and gives an added quality to the pic. In spite of the lack of background, the prisoners are all well depicted and acceptable. Becker, sans music, holds the tension firmly in hand.

•

TROUBLE ALONG THE WAY
1953, 109 mins, US Ⓥ ⊙ b/w
Dir Michael Curtiz ***Prod*** Melville Shavelson ***Scr*** Melville Shavelson, Jack Rose ***Ph*** Archie Stout ***Ed*** Owen Marks ***Mus*** Max Steiner ***Art*** Leo K. Kuter
Act John Wayne, Donna Reed, Charles Coburn, Tom Tully, Sherry Jackson, Marie Windsor (Warner)

A delightful comedy-drama of a Catholic college that saves itself from bankruptcy with a football team. The lines, a principal factor in carrying the film, are zinged home by the performers under the neat directorial timing of Michael Curtiz, who also mixes in a nice touch of sentiment.

John Wayne is completely at home in a role that, while action-ful in most phases, leans towards a humorous lightness. Charles Coburn wallops dialog lines delightfully incongruous to the priest character he plays. Donna Reed gives her role as a probation officer all that it needs. Other standout in casting is young Sherry Jackson, as Wayne's little daughter.

Coburn heads the bankrupt St. Anthony's College in New York, which has been ordered closed because he's $170,000 in debt. Searching for an out, the rector decides a football team is needed. His scouting uncovers Wayne, a cynical ex-coach who had been kicked out of most of the big college leagues, not from lack of ability but from being unable to conform. Wayne spurns Coburn's offer until he sees the job as a sanctuary to defeat the threats of his ex-wife, Marie Windsor, to take custody of their daughter.

•

TROUBLE IN MIND
1985, 111 mins, US Ⓥ ⊙ col
Dir Alan Rudolph ***Prod*** Carolyn Pfeiffer, David Blocker ***Scr*** Alan Rudolph ***Ph*** Toyomichi Kurita ***Ed*** Tom Walls ***Mus*** Mark Isham ***Art*** Steven Legler
Act Kris Kristofferson, Keith Carradine, Lori Singer, Genevieve Bujold, Joe Morton, Divine (Island Alive)

Trouble in Mind is a stylish urban melodrama instantly recognizable as an Alan Rudolph picture. It is peopled by a strange collection of off-center characters living in a stylish, almost-real location.

Set in RainCity, action could be taking place in the 1950s, 1980s or 1990s, so stylized is the production design. The good people of RainCity are like a microcosm of the larger world seen through the lens of 1940s gangster pictures with several other influences thrown in for good measure.

At the core of the film is a not-so-classic romantic triangle involving Hawk (Kris Kristofferson), Georgia (Lori Singer) and her boyfriend, Coop (Keith Carradine).

Center of this emotional landscape is Wanda's cafe, owned and operated by Wanda (Genevieve Bujold), a former lover of Hawk's and the woman for whom he committed a murder.

Rudolph stirs all the ingredients around—love, crime, friendship, responsibility—and ties them together with a charged score by Mark Isham.

•

TROUBLE IN PARADISE
1932, 81 mins, US ⊙ b/w
Dir Ernst Lubitsch ***Prod*** Ernst Lubitsch ***Scr*** Samson Raphaelson, Grover Jones ***Ph*** Victor Milner ***Mus*** W. Franke Harling
Act Miriam Hopkins, Kay Francis, Herbert Marshall, Charles Ruggles, Edward Everett Horton, C. Aubrey Smith (Paramount)

Despite the Lubitsch artistry, much of which is technically apparent, it's not good cinema in toto. For one thing, it's predicated on a totally meretricious premise. Herbert Marshall is the gentleman crook. Miriam Hopkins is a light-fingered lady. Kay Francis is a rich young widow who owns the largest parfumerie in Paris. She's decidedly on the make for Marshall, and his appointment as her "secretary" inspires beaucoup gossip.

Rest becomes a proposition of cheating cheaters as the well-mannered rogue exposes C. Aubrey Smith, the parfumerie's general manager, at the same time climaxing into a triangle among the two attractive femmes and Marshall.

The dialog is bright [from the play *The Honest Finder* by Laszlo Aladar] and the Lubitsch montage is per usual tres artistique, but somehow the whole thing misses.

There's some good trouping by all concerned, plus the intriguing Continental atmosphere of the Grand Hotel on the Grand Canal, Venice, plus ultra-modern social deportment in smart Parisian society.

•

TROUBLE IN STORE
1953, 85 mins, UK Ⓥ b/w
Dir John Paddy Carstairs ***Prod*** Maurice Cowan ***Scr*** John Paddy Carstairs, Maurice Cowan, Ted Willis ***Ph*** Ernest Steward ***Ed*** Peter Seabourne, Geoffrey Foot ***Mus*** Mischa Spoliansky ***Art*** Alex Vetchinsky, John Gow
Act Norman Wisdom, Margaret Rutherford, Moira Lister, Derek Bond, Lana Morris, Jerry Desmonde (Two Cities)

This British piece of slapstick marks the debut of Norman Wisdom. He clowns his way through the whole thing, playing in his inimitable way the most humble member of a big department store who falls foul of his new boss. But he gets his girl and also rounds up some gangsters.

Apart from one or two brief exteriors, the entire action is in the department store, but there is plenty of movement and an ample slice of broad comedy. Margaret Rutherford has some nice comedy scenes as an inveterate shoplifter and Moira Lister is a very lush manageress who's in league with the gangsters led by Derek Bond. Lana Morris pleasantly offers the romantic interest. Jerry Desmonde is little more than a comedy stooge, as the boss, but plays the role for all it is worth.

•

TROUBLE WITH ANGELS, THE
1966, 111 mins, US Ⓥ ⊙ col
Dir Ida Lupino ***Prod*** William Frye ***Scr*** Blanche Hanalis ***Ph*** Lionel Lindon ***Ed*** Robert C. Jones ***Mus*** Jerry Goldsmith ***Art*** John Beckman
Act Rosalind Russell, Hayley Mills, Binnie Barnes, Gypsy Rose Lee, Camilla Sparv, June Harding (Columbia)

The trouble with *The Trouble with Angels* is hard to pinpoint. An appealing story idea—hip Mother Superior nun who outfoxes and matures two rebellious students in a Catholic girls' school—has lost impact via repetitious plotting and pacing, plus routine direction.

Jane Trahey's book, *Life with Mother Superior*, was adapted by Blanche Hanalis into an episodic screenplay.

Story takes the extrovert Hayley Mills and pal, sensitive, introverted June Harding, through three full years of school under the watchful eye of Rosalind Russell. Graduation finds Mills in character switcheroo to which Catholic audiences will long since be alerted.

Russell gives appropriate spiritual depth to her part, although eventually is shot down by excess chatter and exposition. Latter also affects two younger femme principals in achieving character development.

The large supporting cast fares far better, simply from less exposure.

•

TROUBLE WITH HARRY, THE
1955, 96 mins, US Ⓥ ⦿ col
Dir Alfred Hitchcock *Prod* Alfred Hitchcock *Scr* John Michael Hayes *Ph* Robert Burks *Ed* Alma Macrorie *Mus* Bernard Herrmann *Art* Hal Pereira, John Goodman
Act Edmund Gwenn, John Forsythe, Shirley MacLaine, Mildred Natwick, Mildred Dunnock, Royal Dano (Paramount)

This is a blithe little comedy, produced and directed with affection by Alfred Hitchcock, about a bothersome corpse that just can't stay buried.

Edmund Gwenn is a delight as a retired "sea" captain who stumbles on Harry's corpse while rabbit hunting. In the belief he did the killing, he decides to bury the cadaver on the spot. Harry goes in and out of the ground three or four times, is responsible for two romances and not a little consternation and physical exercise.

During the course of events Gwenn and Mildred Natwick, a middle-aged spinster who thinks she did Harry in, find love, as do John Forsythe, local artist, and Shirley MacLaine, young widow of the in-and-out Harry.

Natwick pairs perfectly with Gwenn, and the script from the novel by Jack Trevor Story provides them with dialog and situations that click.

•

TRUCK STOP WOMEN
1974, 82 mins, US Ⓥ ▭ col
Dir Mark L. Lester *Prod* Mark L. Lester *Scr* Mark L. Lester, Paul Deason *Ph* John A. Morrill *Ed* Marvin Wallowitz *Mus* Big Mack & The Truckstoppers *Art* Tom Hassen
Act Claudia Jennings, Lieux Dressler, John Martino, Dennis Fimple, Dolores Dorn, Gene Drew (Lester)

Truck Stop Women spoofs the mindless sensationalism involved in films of its type while it also exploits sex and violence.

Localed in New Mexico, pic deals with bloody territorial warfare between Mafia hit man John Martino and indie gang leader Lieux Dressler over Dressler's lucrative theft and prostitution operation, conducted out of a highway truck stop with henchpersons including her daughter, Claudia Jennings.

A ludicrous string of murders occurs as the rivalry unfolds, with Jennings lured to the opposite side by money-waving Martino. Plenty of flesh is on display.

Mark L. Lester's direction is highly uneven, with many scenes run through in perfunctory fashion and others handled with care and skill. There is a stunning semidocumentary montage of trucks on the highway half an hour into the film, and action scenes are done with flair.

•

TRUE COLORS
1991, 111 mins, US Ⓥ ⦿ col
Dir Herbert Ross *Prod* Herbert Ross, Laurence Mark *Scr* Kevin Wade *Ph* Dante Spinotti *Ed* Robert Reitano, Stephen A. Rotter *Mus* Trevor Jones *Art* Edward Pisoni
Act John Cusack, James Spader, Imogen Stubbs, Mandy Patinkin, Richard Widmark, Dina Merrill (Paramount)

True Colors represents a cloyingly schematic attempt to portray the political and moral bankruptcy of the 1980s in a neat little package. Pic condemns but doesn't begin to analyze the corrupted values of the Reagan years, leaving one feeling soiled but unenlightened.

Paired off at law school at the University of Virginia in 1983, James Spader is a rich boy with the daughter of U.S. senator Richard Widmark as a girlfriend, while John Cusack is a pretender, a social climber whose lower-class roots are quickly exposed.

Cusack, a bluffer and something of a charmer, resolves to be elected to Congress within 10 years. He launches a political career based upon trickery, blackmail and betrayal, and receives backing from interests represented by oily developer Mandy Patinkin.

Personal relationships fall by the wayside like roadkill. Having scooped Spader's g.f. (Imogen Stubbs) out from under him, Cusack then loses her when he stupidly threatens her powerful father.

Cusack does what he can, but the character is simply weighed down with too much symbolic baggage. Yet again playing a privileged preppie type, Spader is likable but suffers from his character being pushed to the side midstream.

•

TRUE CONFESSIONS
1981, 108 mins, US Ⓥ ⦿ col
Dir Ulu Grosbard *Prod* Irwin Winkler, Robert Chartoff *Scr* John Gregory Dunne, Joan Didion *Ph* Owen Roizman *Ed* Lynzee Klingman *Mus* Georges Delerue *Art* Stephen S. Grimes
Act Robert De Niro, Robert Duvall, Charles Durning, Burgess Meredith, Cyril Cusack, Rose Gregorio (United Artists)

Given the powerhouse topline casting combo and provocative theme, *True Confessions* has to be chalked up as something of a disappointment. Adaptation of John Gregory Dunne's bestseller, which was inspired by L.A.'s legendary Black Dahlia murder case of the late 1940s, features corrupt cops, whores, pimps, sibling rivalry, pornography and political intrigue within the Roman Catholic Church, but still comes off as relatively mild fare which fails to pack a dramatic or emotional wallop.

For at least the first hour, it's hard to tell where the drama's headed. Bookended by years-later scenes in which brothers, Robert De Niro and Robert Duvall, both white-haired, play out mutual climax to their radically different lives at the former's pathetic desert parish, main body of pic flip-flops between police detective Duvall handling two bizarre deaths and ambitious Monsignor De Niro negotiating the delicate waters of church diplomacy.

Unfortunately, nowhere near the full weight of these considerations is ever felt in Ulu Grosbard's muted, unmuscular telling of the sordid, fateful events. Script is deliberately structured to build to a big dramatic pay-off, but this never comes, leaving audience frustrated that careful groundwork has been laid to little avail.

Failings cannot be attributed to the actors, all of whom have clearly immersed themselves in their roles. Duvall is excellent as an unsentimental dick working a tough beat which irrevocably poisons his personal life. Charles Durning's portrait of a big-time phony is right on target.

•

TRUE CRIME
1999, 127 mins, US Ⓥ ⦿ col
Dir Clint Eastwood *Prod* Clint Eastwood, Richard D. Zanuck, Lili Fini Zanuck *Scr* Larry Gross, Paul Brickman, Stephen Schiff *Ph* Jack N. Green *Ed* Joel Cox *Mus* Lennie Niehaus *Art* Henry Bumstead
Act Clint Eastwood, Isaiah Washington, Denis Leary, Lisa Gay Hamilton, James Woods, Bernard Hill

The struggles of individuals to rise above their profound weaknesses and those of the society they've created receive absorbingly dramatic treatment in *True Crime*. A capital-punishment yarn that is much more concerned with character issues than with moral or legal matters, Clint Eastwood's picture boasts tight storytelling, sharp acting and an eye for unexpected, enlivening detail.

Confined to a 24-hour period and constructed on parallel tracks to follow the fortunes of two men, black inmate Frank Beachum (Isaiah Washington) scheduled for execution at midnight and white newspaper reporter Steve Everett (Eastwood) who becomes convinced at the 11th hour that the prisoner is innocent, solid script [from the novel by Andrew Klavan] is plotted in conventional beat-the-clock suspense fashion.

Pic's understated contrasting of the husband-wife-daughter relationships within Steve and Frank's respective families reps one of its strongest points. Steve, who's free, repeatedly throws it all away through his irresponsibility and selfishness; Frank is doomed, but exhibits unlimited love and care for his family and impressive moral rigor while staring death in the face.

Eastwood takes evident delight in applying fine brush strokes to his portrait of a sympathetic but amoral scoundrel. Washington mainly must keep himself tightly coiled, but does a fine job with this. James Woods is enjoyably showy as an editor who loves to hear himself talk. Shot in deliberately ordinary East Bay locations, pic is solid technically.

•

TRUE GRIT
1969, 128 mins, US Ⓥ ⦿ col
Dir Henry Hathaway *Prod* Hal B. Wallis *Scr* Marguerite Roberts *Ph* Lucien Ballard *Ed* Warren Low *Mus* Elmer Bernstein *Art* Walter Tyler
Act John Wayne, Glen Campbell, Kim Darby, Jeremy Slate, Robert Duvall, Dennis Hopper (Paramount)

Story centers on young girl (Kim Darby) of the 1830s starting out from Arkansas to avenge the murder of her father with the aid of Wayne, whom she pays, and Texas Ranger Glen Campbell, who wants to claim the murderer (Jeff Corey) for a reward. Men develop instant mutual loathing, but girl recognizes they can get her father's murderer because they have grit, true grit.

Darby is refreshingly original. If at times she seems restrained, she sticks relentlessly to the strong character of Mattie.

Campbell, less successful as an actor than as a singer-performer, still holds his own as a foil for Wayne. But it's mostly Wayne all the way. He towers over everything in the film—actors, script [from Charles Portis's novel], even the magnificent Colorado mountains. He rides tall in the saddle in this character role of "the fat old man."

1969: Best Actor (John Wayne)

NOMINATION: Best Song ("True Grit")

•

TRUE HEART SUSIE
1919, 72 mins, US ⊗ b/w
Dir D. W. Griffith *Prod* D. W. Griffith *Scr* D. W. Griffith, Marion Fremont *Ph* Billy Bitzer *Ed* James E. Smith
Act Lillian Gish, Loyola O'Connor, Robert Harron, Wilber Higby, Clarine Seymour, Kate Bruce (Artcraft)

The production, in a screen foreword, is dedicated to "the plain woman." It pans the paint-and-powder girls, and then goes right ahead and shows how the paint-and-powder ladies snare the men, while the real true-hearted, but plain and unbeautiful ones are left in the lurch.

To relate his story, Griffith took Lillian Gish for the role of plain little country girl and Robert Harron as the "boy across the road." There is an early love affair and the girl sacrifices part of her farm to send the boy to college. On his return he falls in love with a milliner from Chicago and marries her.

She leads him a decidedly merry life and slips out on an evening or two to do a little stepping with the boys.

The story in itself is one that embraces all of the elementals of successful comedy drama. It carries a role of tremendous sympathy in *True Heart Susie*, which Gish portrays most successfully.

Griffith has handled the picture in the same masterly way that he usually has things done. The idea of fading out at the end of the picture, with a cut-back to the second reel, is a novelty in itself. The comedy elements are splendidly handled, and there are any number of real laughs in the action.

•

TRUE LIES
1994, 141 mins, US Ⓥ ⦿ col
Dir James Cameron *Prod* James Cameron, Stephanie Austin *Scr* James Cameron *Ph* Russell Carpenter *Ed* Mark Goldblatt, Conrad Buff, Richard A. Harris *Mus* Brad Fiedel *Art* Peter Lamont
Act Arnold Schwarzenegger, Jamie Lee Curtis, Tom Arnold, Bill Paxton, Tia Carrere, Art Malik (Lightstorm/20th Century-Fox)

A reunion of *Terminator 2* star Arnold Schwarzenegger and writer/director James Cameron creates obvious expectations, and this 2½-hour $100 million-plus action comedy tries way too hard to live up to them. Providing its share of fun in stretches, pic ultimately overstays its welcome with a level of mayhem that will simply feel like too much for any marginal fan of the genre.

In its best moments, *True Lies* comes closest to Schwarzenegger's earlier vehicle, *Commando*, which also mixed plenty of humor with a cartoonish level of destruction. Yet even with its ribald laughs and spectacular action sequences, the movie gets mired in a comedic midsection that wears the audience down, sapping their energy before a chaotic third act that doesn't know when to quit.

Lies is really two movies in one. An impressive Bondian opening sequence introduces us to secret agent Harry Tasker (Schwarzenegger), who infiltrates a heavily guarded compound, mixes it up with partygoers (among them the stunning Tia Carrere) and then beats a sensational retreat.

Tasker, it turns out, leads a double life, having convinced his wife (Jamie Lee Curtis) and teenage daughter (Eliza Dushku) that he's a staid computer salesman. Back in Washington, Harry and sidekick Gib (Tom Arnold) get on the trail of an Arab terrorist (Art Malik) who's acquired four nuclear weapons.

So far, so good, until the script (based very loosely on the 1991 French film *La totale!* [written by Claude Zidi, Simon Michael, and Didier Kaminka, starring Thierry Lhermitte and Miou-Miou]) veers into a periodically amusing but staggeringly drawn-out tangent that has Harry suspecting his wife of infidelity and using all his agenting wiles to investigate. Roughly an hour long on its own, this foray into romantic comedy offers some crowd-pleasingly broad flourishes—including an over-the-top turn by Bill Paxton—but doesn't jibe with what precedes or follows it.

Curtis is provided some juicy moments as the buttoned-up, soon-to-be-awakened wife, while Arnold launches his solo career with a scene-stealing performance as Harry's affable and foul-mouthed sidekick.

There's plenty of jaw-dropping stuntwork, terrific fight choreography and breathtaking use of the Florida Keys as a background locale; but there are also some noteworthy glitches, including easily spotted doubles during a few chase sequences.

1994: NOMINATION: Best Visual Effects

•

TRUE LOVE
1989, 104 mins, US col
Dir Nancy Savoca ***Prod*** Richard Guay, Shelley Houis ***Scr*** Nancy Savoca, Richard Guay ***Ph*** Lisa Rinzler ***Ed*** John Tintori ***Art*** Lester W. Cohen
Act Annabella Sciorra, Ron Eldard, Star Jasper, Aida Turturro, Roger Rignack, Michael J. Wolfe (Forward)

True Love is anything but traditional, even though it's solidly rooted in the Bronx working-class Italian community. The bride (wonderfully played by newcomer Annabella Sciorra) and her bridesmaids know enough four-letter words to easily supply all the "something blue" needed for the wedding preparations.

Sciorra and her friends aren't too starry-eyed about the men available for matrimony. Certainly, her fiancé (well-acted by Ron Eldard in his feature debut) is no bargain, except perhaps in bed. For most of the picture, Sciorra frets about why she's marrying the immature, self-centered lout and never comes up with a good reason, except he's good-looking and says he loves her even though he doesn't act like it.

True Love is very much a story about family and neighborhood and Nancy Savoca obviously has an eye for the several generations. This is Savoca's first feature, with first-rate perfomances out of neophytes.

•

TRUE ROMANCE
1993, 116 mins, US col
Dir Tony Scott ***Prod*** Bill Unger, Steve Perry, Samuel Hadida ***Scr*** Quentin Tarantino ***Ph*** Jeffrey Kimball ***Ed*** Michael Tronick, Christian Wagner ***Mus*** Hans Zimmer ***Art*** Benjamin Fernandez
Act Christian Slater, Patricia Arquette, Dennis Hopper, Gary Oldman, Brad Pitt, Christopher Walken (Morgan Creek/Warner)

The footprints of dozens of classic thrillers are imprinted on the slick, violent and energetic *True Romance*. One of the endless variations on the couple-on-the-run subgenre, yarn provides some amazing encounters, bravura acting turns and gruesome carnage. But it doesn't add up to enough.

The odd couple here are Clarence (Christian Slater) and Alabama (Patricia Arquette), a young man working in a comic-book store and a gal on the job on the streets of Detroit. Their not-so-chance encounter blossoms into true love and marriage.

Clarence, on the pretense of picking up Alabama's suitcase, walks into the lair of her former pimp, Drexl (Gary Oldman). Clarence kills Drexl and grabs his wife's suitcase—except it's the wrong one. Opening the Pandora's box reveals a fortune in uncut cocaine. The young man foolishly believes he can skip town, sell the stash and escape to some remote paradise—in this case, Hollywood.

True Romance rides along largely on the power of its colorful rogues' gallary. Besides Oldman's gleeful incarnation of evil, there's dopey fun in Brad Pitt's space cadet and Saul Rubinek as a Hollywood producer whose ego transcends morality, law and common sense. Slater and Arquette lend the proceedings a charged sexuality, elevating the essentially inane material.

Movie mavens have a veritable field to plow in the Quentin Tarantino screenplay. Tony Scott's slick style is visually arresting if too obvious.

[On laserdisc and outside the U.S. theatrically, pic was released in its full 120-min. version, with more violence.]

•

TRUE STORIES
A FILM ABOUT A BUNCH OF PEOPLE IN VIRGIL TEXAS
1986, 90 mins, US col
Dir David Byrne ***Prod*** Gary Kurfirst ***Scr*** David Byrne, Beth Henley, Stephen Tobolowsky ***Ph*** Ed Lachman ***Ed*** Caroline Biggerstaff ***Mus*** David Byrne, Talking Heads ***Art*** Barbara Ling
Act David Byrne, John Goodman, Swoosie Kurtz, Spalding Gray, Alix Elias, Annie McEnroe (True Stories)

In more than 10 years with the Talking Heads, David Byrne received well-earned if often slavishly uncritical praise for his distinctive marriage of polyrhythmic pop-rock with an archly skewed perspective on mechanistic modern life. *True Stories* was a natural progression into film.

In his feature directorial debut, Byrne takes a bemused and benevolent view of provincial America's essential goodness in a loosely connected string of vignettes that amount to sophisticated music video concepts dressed up as film-making.

Byrne uses the surreal, cartoonish conceit of examining life in the hypothetical town of Virgil, Texas, with the human interest perspective of a supermarket tabloid feature. Affecting a trusting innocence as easily as he slips into natty Western duds, Byrne drives into Virgil during its sesquicentennial "celebration of specialness" for a series of close encounters with the town's peculiar denizens.

•

TRUE STORY OF JESSE JAMES, THE
(UK: THE JAMES BROTHERS)
1957, 92 mins, US col
Dir Nicholas Ray ***Prod*** Herbert B. Swope, Jr. ***Scr*** Walter Newman ***Ph*** Joe MacDonald ***Ed*** Robert Simpson ***Mus*** Leigh Harline ***Art*** Lyle R. Wheeler, Addison Hehr
Act Robert Wagner, Jeffrey Hunter, Hope Lange, Agnes Moorehead, Alan Hale, John Carradine (20th Century-Fox)

On celluloid Jesse James has had more lives than a cat, and *The True Story of Jesse James* suggests it's time screenwriters let him roll over and play dead for real and reel. In past reworkings of the 19th-century delinquent's shoddy career just about every angle was covered. There's nothing new in this glorification. It's a routine offering for the outdoor market.

The attempt to view the James character through the eyes of pro and con contemporaries only makes for confusion, depriving an audience of clear-cut plotline that might keep it interested. Dialog, too, is poor, continually veering from period to modern idioms in the script, based on Nunnally Johnson's screenplay for the 1939 *Jesse James*.

Nicholas Ray directs in stock fashion, adding little of substance to the picture. As Jesse and Frank James, respectively, Robert Wagner and Jeffrey Hunter go through the motions of telling why the former took up the gun when Northern sympathizers made it difficult for them to live in Missouri after the War between the States. Both are adequate to the demands of script and direction, as is Hope Lange, playing Zee, the girl who married Jesse.

•

TRUE TO LIFE
1943, 94 mins, US b/w
Dir George Marshall ***Prod*** Paul Jones ***Scr*** Don Hartman, Harry Tugend ***Ph*** Charles Lang, Jr. ***Mus*** Victor Young
Act Mary Martin, Franchot Tone, Dick Powell, Victor Moore, William Demarest, Ernest Truex (Paramount)

Taking the premise, in an audible intro title that "life should mirror the movies, instead of the movies reflecting life," the escapist theme of *True to Life* is quickly set. It treats radio family serials with tongue-in-cheek but utilizes the radio soap opera appeal for the plot bulwark of a frothy film. Franchot Tone and Dick Powell are the all-written-out radio scripters on the verge of losing their $1,000-a-week jobs because their *Kitty Farmer* serial has become too phoney. Powell, in search for down-to-the-peasants material, runs into hash-house waitress Mary Martin whose real-life family in Sunnyside, a suburb of NY, and their zany behaviorisms provide the authors with almost literal libretto.

Action shuttles between the bourgeois Sunnyside family menage and the lush apartment and slick Radio City environment of the Powell-Tone team. Three songs, all good, are skillfully interwoven and the finale is a madcap radio pickup of how things right themselves. Well-paced direction by George Marshall and some excellent scripting do much to hold the madcap proceedings together.

•

TRULY MADLY DEEPLY
(AKA: CELLO)
1991, 105 mins, UK col
Dir Anthony Minghella ***Prod*** Robert Cooper ***Scr*** Anthony Minghella ***Ph*** Remi Adefarasian ***Ed*** John Stothart ***Mus*** Barrington Pheloung ***Art*** Barbara Gosnold
Act Juliet Stevenson, Alan Rickman, Bill Paterson, Michael Maloney, Jenny Howe, Stella Maris (BBC)

This sharply scripted study of a bereaved woman who literally wishes her partner back from the grave is an impressive directorial bow by British playwright Anthony Minghella. Despite surface similarities with *Ghost* pic has a different feel and theme.

Nina (Juliet Stevenson) is still cut up about losing her longtime partner, virtuoso cellist Jamie (Alan Rickman). She still feels his presence in her tiny London flat, where plumbing's gone bananas and rats are moving in.

One day, while she's doodling at the piano, Jamie literally reappears and thereon it's a matter of reliving their idyllic relationship until it's time for both to move on—he to a higher plane, she to a growing friendship with young social worker Mark (Michael Maloney) who can give her the child Jamie never wanted.

Sans special effects, pic manages to suspend belief through fine ensemble playing and sheer strength of the main performances. It's Stevenson's movie through and through (project was in the works for some years and was penned for her), and although she sometimes overdoes the histrionics, as in scenes with her shrink, it's a tour de force of sustained playing. Rickman gives subtle support, with a nice line in po-faced comedy.

[Pic was reviewed in original 16mm version premiered at 1990 London Film Festival as *Cello*. For 35mm theatrical release, and subsequent TV airing, title was changed to *Truly Madly Deeply*.]

•

TRUMAN SHOW, THE
1998, 102 mins, US col
Dir Peter Weir ***Prod*** Scott Rudin, Andrew Niccol, Edward S. Feldman, Adam Schroeder ***Scr*** Andrew Niccol ***Ph*** Peter Biziou ***Ed*** William Anderson, Lee Smith ***Mus*** Burkhard Dallwitz, Philip Glass ***Art*** Dennis Gassner
Act Jim Carrey, Laura Linney, Noah Emmerich, Natascha McElhone, Holland Taylor, Ed Harris (Rudin/Paramount)

A gemlike picture crafted with rare and immaculate precision, *The Truman Show* amusingly and convincingly presents a nuclear community as a vast television studio. An outstandingly successful change of pace for comic star Jim Carrey and a tour de force for director Peter Weir, this clever commentary on media omnipotence is unusual enough to be perceived as daringly offbeat for a major Hollywood studio production.

A fable about a man whose entire life, unbeknownst to him, has been the subject of a staggeringly popular, 24-hour-per-day TV show, pic trades in issues of personal liberty vs. authoritarian control, safe happiness vs. the excitement of chaos, manufactured emotions, the penetration of media to the point where privacy vanishes, and the fascination of fabricated images over plain sight.

But as lucid and concentrated as the film's point-making is, its saving grace is its lightness, its assumption that modern audiences are just as savvy about the media as are its practitioners and don't need to have lessons hammered home.

Pic's first half-hour presents excerpts from day 10,909 in the life of Truman Burbank (Carrey), a virtual caricature of a clean-cut, "normal" guy. Married to the perenially perky Meryl (Laura Linney), Truman lives in the immaculate planned community of Seahaven, an antiseptic island "paradise" where people are forever cheery and nothing untoward ever happens.

In the course of things, however, slight cracks appear in his life's perfect veneer that arouse his suspicion. Once the curtain has been raised on the wizardry behind Truman's existence, those around him go into panicky damage-control mode and the hand of Truman's "inventor" and manipulator, Christof (Ed Harris), becomes increasingly evident. Above all, Truman must not escape.

Shooting at Seaside, FL, Weir and his ace team reveal a veritable velvet coffin under glass, a "safe" haven that the self-styled benevolent fascist Christof can convincingly argue is "the best place on Earth." Carrey delivers an impressively disciplined performance that is always engaging.

•

TRUST
1990, 103 mins, US/UK col
Dir Hal Hartley ***Prod*** Bruce Weiss ***Scr*** Hal Hartley ***Ph*** Michael Spiller ***Ed*** Nick Gomez ***Mus*** Phil Reed ***Art*** Daniel Ouellette
Act Adrienne Shelly, Martin Donovan, Merritt Nelson, John MacKay, Edie Falco, Marko Hunt (True Fiction/Zenith)

Long Island filmmaker Hal Hartley progresses from his debut feature, *The Unbelievable Truth* to this bleak, off-center comedy about dysfunctional families in working class suburbia.

When Maria (Adrienne Shelly) gets pregnant by the high school quarterback, she's dropped by her boyfriend, drops out of school, and her father drops dead of a heart attack. Maria's hard-bitten mother treats her like a pariah.

Meanwhile, Matthew (Martin Donovan), an intellectually inclined reform school graduate with a talent for fixing things, quits his mind-numbing job assembling computers. Matthew wanders the streets, encounters Maria, and takes the shattered girl to his home.

This sets the stage for a tale of uneasy love and spiritual anomie in sterile precincts of middle America. Donovan is excellent as the brooding misfit, and Shelly is tangibly right as the suburban brat. Also very good are Merritt Nelson as Maria's emotionally alienated mother and John MacKay as Matthew's bullying father.

•

TRUTH, THE
SEE: LA VERITE

•

TRUTH ABOUT CATS AND DOGS, THE
1996, 97 mins, US col
Dir Michael Lehmann ***Prod*** Cari-Esta Albert ***Scr*** Audrey Wells ***Ph*** Robert Brinkman ***Ed*** Stephen Semel ***Mus*** Howard Shore ***Art*** Sharon Seymour

Act Uma Thurman, Janeane Garofalo, Ben Chaplin, Jamie Fox, James McCaffrey, Richard Coca (Noon Attack/20th Century-Fox)

Yet another modern riff on the *Cyrano de Bergerac* theme, this thinly conceived comedy climbs above its material thanks to charming performances by the three principals (as well as a wildly expressive dog named Hank) and a genial tone.

Director Michael Lehman tries his hand at an utterly conventional comedy scripted by first-time writer (and former disc jockey) Audrey Wells. The premise is sheer simplicity, with a touch of screwball farce that Lehmann can't quite maintain.

Janeane Garofalo plays Abby, host of a radio talkshow about pets who talks a caller, dreamy photographer Brian (Ben Chaplin, making his U.S. debut after roles in a number of British films, among them *The Remains of the Day*), through a threatening experience with a dog he's acquired for a photo shoot. Brian suggests the two meet, yet when asked what she looks like, Abby describes her model neighbor, Noelle (Uma Thurman)—a 5-foot, 10-inch blonde who can literally stop traffic. A confusing situation is made worse when both women become interested in Brian.

Because there's virtually no suspense about how things will turn out, the pic drags somewhat before its conclusion as the courtship period is padded before Brian inevitably discovers what a chump he's been.

What really makes the pic special in places is Garofalo's dry, self-effacing wit and Thurman's ditzy, old-style Hollywood glamour.

•

TRUTH OR DARE
IN BED WITH MADONNA
(UK/AUSTRALIA: IN BED WITH MADONNA)

•

TRYGON FACTOR, THE

1967, 87 mins, UK col

Dir Cyril Frankel *Prod* Brian Taylor *Scr* Derry Quinn, Stanley Munroe *Ph* Harry Waxman *Ed* Oswald Hafenrichter *Mus* Peter Thomas *Art* Roy Stannard

Act Stewart Granger, Susan Hampshire, Robert Morley, Cathleen Nesbitt, Brigitte Horney, James Robertson Justice (Warner/Seven Arts/Rialto)

The Trygon Factor, its title totally meaningless, is a complicated Scotland Yard whodunit which the spectator will find taxing to follow. Stewart Granger, as the Yard superintendent investigating a rash of unsolved robberies, is assigned to a large country house where a gang is operating under the cloak of respectability: its mistress, a member of an old English family who has turned to crime to save her family estate from ruin.

She has installed in her house a phony order of nuns who actually are in on the various crimes, and who receive and ship stolen goods to Morley's warehouse.

Script is pocketed with story loopholes and attempts to confuse, plus certain motivations and bits of business impossible to fathom. Granger still makes a good impression.

•

TSUBAKI SANJURO
(SANJURO)

1962, 96 mins, Japan Ⓥ ⊙ ⌑ b/w

Dir Akira Kurosawa *Prod* Tomoyuki Tanaka, Ryuzo Kikushima (execs.) *Scr* Ryuzo Kikushima, Hideo Oguni, Akira Kurosawa *Ph* Fukuzo Koizumi *Mus* Masaru Sato *Art* Yoshiro Muraki

Act Toshiro Mifune, Yuzo Kayama, Tatsuya Nakadai, Keiju Kobayashi, Reiko Dan, Takashi Shimura (Kurosawa/Toho)

Roughly the Japanese equivalent of an American Western, *Sanjuro* brings to the screen an epic hero far more formidable than the celebrated tall men and top guns of the 19th century Yankee frontier. The charm of this fascinating Toho production, stylishly directed by Akira Kurosawa, is the personality of the hero, powerfully played by Toshiro Mifune.

Story [from *Hibi heian* by Shugoro Yamamoto] is set in the turbulent mid-1800s, and describes the remarkable manner in which one man, the warrior Sanjuro, destroys the wretched machinery of a corrupt ruling faction. He is endowed with an incredible sense of logic—a Gestaltian way of reasoning, invariably correct in drawing the simplest, most natural conclusions when others have jumped to theirs emotionally and illogically.

As usual, Kurosawa doesn't compromise in the battle and brutality area. This one features a rousing climactic duel between the title roleist and his chief adversary that outdoes the average Western showdown by a dramatic mile.

•

TSUI KUN
(DRUNK MONKEY IN THE TIGER'S EYES; DRUNKEN MASTER)

1978, 110 mins, Hong Kong Ⓥ col

Dir Yuen Woo-ping *Prod* Ng See-yuen *Scr* Siu Lung, Ng See-yuen *Ph* Cheung Hoi *Ed* Poon Hung *Mus* Chow Fuk-leung *Art* Ting Yuen-tai

Act Jackie Chan, Simon Yuen, Hwang Jeong-ri, Sek Tin, Tsui Ha, Lam Ying (Seasonal)

This is the new trendmaker in current local kung fu films. It made nearly HK$7 million in Hong Kong alone [on initial release] and imitations mushroomed immediately like Chinese restaurants. Variations and revivals of old Jackie Chan movies are in the offing.

Pic like its unique title is kung fu with a big difference, in the sense that unusual drunken martial arts techniques are mixed with high Cantonese comedy. Lead star Jackie Chan (contract player of Lo Wei Prod.) has found fame at last by freelancing outside where his talents were properly utilized.

Chan, an excellent acrobat, has the stamina and movements of an experienced kung fu specialist. His charming boyish appeal and talent for comedy routines help in captivating audiences. In fact, he makes a very human hero as he doesn't win all the fights, with the exception of the required finale battle.

Highlights include practice sessions with an eccentric teacher (Simon Yuen). The idea of having a couple of drinks prior to fighting add an off-beat touch to the disciplined art of kung fu. The storyline as can be expected is practically nil but the humour is universal enough.

•

TUCKER
THE MAN AND HIS DREAM

1988, 111 mins, US Ⓥ ⊙ ⌑ col

Dir Francis Coppola *Prod* Fred Roos, Fred Fuchs *Scr* Arnold Schulman, David Seidler *Ph* Vittorio Storaro *Ed* Priscilla Nedd *Mus* Joe Jackson *Art* Dean Tavoularis

Act Jeff Bridges, Joan Allen, Martin Landau, Frederic Forrest, Dean Stockwell, Lloyd Bridges (Lucasfilm/Zeotrope)

The true story of a great American visionary who was thwarted, if not destroyed, by the established order, *Tucker* represents the sunniest imaginable telling of an at least partly tragic episode in recent history.

Tucker's life and career present so many parallels to Coppola's own it is easy to see why he coveted his project for so long. Industry-ites will nod in recognition of this story of a self-styled genius up against business interests hostile to his innovative ideas, but also will note the accepting, unbelligerent stance adopted toward the terms of the struggle.

After World War II, seemingly on the strength of his enthusiasm alone, Tucker got a small core of collaborators to work on his dream project, which he called "the first completely new car in 50 years." With a factory in Chicago, Tucker managed to turn out 50 of his beauties, but vested interests in Detroit and Washington dragged him into court on fraud charges, shutting him down and effectively ending his automobile career. As his moneyman tells him, "You build the car too good."

Flashing his charming smile and ouzing cocky confidence, Jeff Bridge's Tucker is inspiring because he won't be depressed or defeated by anything.

1988: NOMINATIONS: Best Supp. Actor (Martin Landau), Art Direction, Costume Design

•

TUFF TURF

1985, 112 mins, US Ⓥ ⊙ col

Dir Fritz Kiersch *Prod* Donald Borchers *Scr* Jette Rinck *Ph* Willy Kurant *Ed* Marc Grossman *Mus* Jonathan Elias *Art* Craig Stearns

Act James Spader, Kim Richards, Paul Mones, Robert Downey, Matt Clark, Claudette Nevins (New World)

This modestly budgeted youth pic is a poor man's and partially musicalized *Rebel Without a Cause* with a touch of *The Warriors* thrown in. Rebellious newcomer James Spader is the James Dean character and saucy gang moll Kim Richards is the Natalie Wood character.

They go through social and romantic hell for each other and, in the process, a large slice of suburban L.A. and uncomprehending parenthood embellish a story that is deceptively compelling despite, in this case, a distracting mix of comedy and music. Latter, which includes on-screen appearances by the L.A. band Jack Mack and Heart Attack and rocker Jim Carroll, gives the production a socking sound.

The on-screen music, however, lurches the film off balance, especially combined with unexpected and dramatically jarring numbers by the two stars (Spader materializing as a balladeer in a country club and Richards whirling into an aerodynamic disco dancer).

Robert Downey is a fresh surprise in a nice sidekick role, and Olivia Barash and Catya Sassoon (the daughter of Vidal Sassoon) lend able teen support.

•

TUGBOAT ANNIE

1933, 85 mins, US b/w

Dir Mervyn LeRoy *Prod* Harry Rapf *Scr* Zelda Sears, Eve Greene, Norman Reilly Raine *Ph* Gregg Toland *Ed* Blanche Sewell *Art* Merrill Pye

Act Marie Dressler, Wallace Beery, Robert Young, Maureen O'Sullivan, Willard Robertson, Tammany Young (M-G-M)

Tugboat Annie, while weak in many respects, is on the whole perfectly suited to the Dressler-Beery requirements. In the hands of the co-starring couple its deficiencies are barely noticeable.

Making Marie Dressler the femme skipper of a harbor tugboat, Wallace Beery her shiftless, soused but likeable husband, and giving them a son of whom to be proud, was giving Dressler-Beery a blueprint and then going home.

Beery is always stewed and Dressler constantly trying to keep him dry. That provides the comedy. Beery is getting the family into all sorts of jams—stupidly, drunkenly, tragically, but unintentionally. That provides the pathos.

Robert Young and Maureen O'Sullivan are the juves, and just juves, with no chance to be anything more. It's a Dressler-Beery picture [from the *Saturday Evening Post* series by Norman Reilly Raine].

•

TUMBLEWEEDS

1925, 76 mins, US Ⓥ ⊙ ⊗ b/w

Dir King Baggot *Prod* William S. Hart *Scr* C. Gardner Sullivan, Hal G. Evarts *Ph* Joseph August

Act William S. Hart, Barbara Bedford, Lucien Littlefield, J. Gordon Russell, Richard R. Neill (Hart/United Artists)

Tumbleweeds marks Bill Hart's return to the screen following his long lapse through a disagreement with Famous Players over policy. It's a welcome return. Bill Hart is seen here under a new banner, a new hat and on a new horse.

This is a typical Hart western, although the story carries something of a different angle on the open country. Its punch is a stampede of homesteaders to claim-stake the Cherokee Strip, an area undoubtedly famed in the annals of the Old West, as Hart is fastidious on the authenticity of his pictures.

The heroine, not getting into any serious difficulties, has eliminated the need of any ultra-heroic measures to save her and for that matter the love theme of the tale may be said to be secondary to its historical interest.

•

TUNE IN TOMORROW
(UK: AUNT JULIA AND THE SCRIPTWRITER)

1990, 102 mins, US Ⓥ ⊙ col

Dir Jon Amiel *Prod* John Fielder, Mark Tarlov *Scr* William Boyd *Ph* Robert Stevens *Ed* Peter Boyle *Mus* Wynton Marsalis *Art* Jim Clay

Act Barbara Hershey, Keanu Reeves, Peter Falk, Hope Lange, Peter Gallagher, Elizabeth McGovern (Polar)

Tune in Tomorrow, Jon Amiel's screen version of Mario Vargas Llosa's acclaimed novel *Aunt Julia and the Scriptwriter*, is lusty and full of zany characters, but cluttered and overdone.

Aunt Julia (Barbara Hershey), a double divorcee, returns to New Orleans in 1951 at age 36 to find a rich third husband. Instead, she finds her 21-year-old nephew by marriage (Keanu Reeves), a local radio station newswriter, who falls in love with her. The aunt succumbs, incurring her family's anger. On top of that plot is the more complicated story of a disheveled writer (Peter Falk), who's new in town.

Falk's Pedro Carmichael creates a successful radio soap opera laced with incest and anti-Albanian sentiment. While actors read their lines on the air, different ones, including John Larroquette, Hope Lange, Peter Gallagher and Elizabeth McGovern, act out the scenes in dramatic soap style. Falk manipulates the nephew-aunt relationship, and, to Reeves's anger, reproduces the couple's arguments in his soap.

There's enough in William Boyd's sprawling script for three films. And while the action is fun for much of the first half, the storylines ultimately smother each other. Hershey and Reeves are outstanding and Falk is delightfully melodramatic.

•

TUNES OF GLORY
1960, 105 mins, UK Ⓥ ⦿ col
Dir Ronald Neame ***Prod*** Colin Lesslie ***Scr*** James Kennaway ***Ph*** Arthur Ibbetson ***Ed*** Anne V. Coates ***Mus*** Malcolm Arnold
Act Alec Guinness, John Mills, Dennis Price, John Fraser, Susannah York, Kay Walsh (United Artists)

Both Alec Guinness and John Mills are cast as colonels, the former a man of humble origin who has risen from the ranks, the other a product of Eton, Oxford and a classy military academy. It is the clash of personalities between the two that provides the main story thread.

Tunes is the story of a Scottish regiment in peacetime commanded by Guinness. He's reasonably popular with his fellow officers, though a few appear to resent his rough-and-ready behavior in the mess. His is only an acting command, and when he is superseded by Mills (whose grandfather had commanded the same regiment), the clash is inevitable.

The struggle between the two reaches its climax when Guinness finds his daughter in a public house with a young corporal, and strikes the soldier. That's a serious offense under military law, and though Mills has the power to deal with the case, he chooses to submit a report to higher authority, which would inevitably lead to a courtmartial.

Ronald Neame's crisp and vigorous direction keeps the main spotlight on the two central characters. Guinness, as always, is outstanding, and his performance is as forthright as it is subtle. He assumes an authentic Scottish accent naturally, and never misses a trick to win sympathy, even when he behaves foolishly. It's a tough assignment for Mills to play against Guinness, particularly in a fundamentally unsympathetic role, but he is always a match for his co-star.

1960: NOMINATION: Best Adapted Screenplay

•

TUNNEL OF LOVE, THE
1958, 98 mins, US ⌑ b/w
Dir Gene Kelly ***Prod*** Joseph Fields, Martin Melcher ***Scr*** Joseph Fields ***Ph*** Robert Bronner ***Ed*** John McSweeney, Jr. ***Art*** William A. Horning, Randall Duell
Act Doris Day, Richard Widmark, Gig Young, Gia Scala, Elisabeth Fraser, Elizabeth Wilson (M-G-M)

The Broadway hit on which this is based has been transferred virtually intact to the screen.

Richard Widmark is a would-be cartoonist for a *New Yorker*–type magazine, whose gags are good but whose drawings are not. He and his wife (Doris Day) want a child and cannot catch. They live in a remodeled barn (naturally) adjacent to the home of their best friends (Gig Young and Elisabeth Fraser) whom they envy in many ways. Young is an editor of the magazine Widmark aspires to crack, and is a parent. Young adds to his and Fraser's brood as regularly as the seasons, Widmark and Day are planning to adopt a baby.

Meantime, back at the barn, Young, whose homework has been stimulated by extracurricular activities, urges his system on Widmark. With this suggestion in the back of his mind, Widmark is visited by an adoption home investigator (Gia Scala). When he wakes up in a motel after a night on the town with her, he assumes the thought has been father to the deed in more ways than one.

Day and Widmark make a fine comedy team, working as smoothly as if they had been trading gags for years. They are ably abetted by Young, one of the greatest flycatchers in operation, and Scala, who displays a nice and unexpected gift for comedy.

This is the first time Gene Kelly has operated entirely behind the camera, and he emerges as an inventive and capable comedy director.

•

TUNTEMATON SOTILAS
(THE UNKNOWN SOLDIER)
1955, 181 mins, Finland b/w
Dir Edvin Laine ***Prod*** T. J. Sarkka ***Scr*** Juha Nevalainen ***Ph*** Pentti Unho, Osmo Harkimo, Olavi Tuomi, Antero Ruuhonen ***Ed*** Armas Vallasuvo ***Mus*** Jean Sibelius, Ahti Sonninen ***Art*** Aarre Kolvisto
Act Kosti Klemela, Jussi Jurkka, Heikki Savolainen, Matti Ranin, Reino Tolvanen, Veikko Sinisalo (SF)

Film, based on the same-titled bestseller by Vaino Linna, has actually no plot and may be better classified as a documentary report. It is a recklessly open and hard-hitting production about victory and defeat and life and death of Finnish soldiers during the last war. The camera follows a group of soldiers and shows via very impressive scenes how they go through the murderous phase of modern warfare.

There is perhaps a bit too much of war battling in this. The constant battling becomes monotonous and even dull towards the end. The acting is honest and often very powerful, although some of the players tend to exaggeration.

Direction by Edvin Laine is very good and praiseworthy, particularly in view of the fact that he never seeks the exterior effect which easily might have cheapened the good overall impression. Technical credits are of amazingly high quality. Camerawork utilizes newsreel footage with remarkable skill. The fine score by Jean Sibelius and Ahti Sonninen greatly adds to the mood.

[Review is of the 133-min. version for foreign release.]

•

TURK 182!
1985, 98 mins, US Ⓥ ⌑ col
Dir Bob Clark ***Prod*** Ted Field, Rene DuPont ***Scr*** James Gregory Kingston, Denis Hamill, John Hamill ***Ph*** Reginald H. Morris ***Ed*** Stan Cole ***Mus*** Paul Zaza ***Art*** Harry Pottle
Act Timothy Hutton, Robert Urich, Kim Cattrall, Robert Culp, Darren McGavin, Steven Keats (20th Century-Fox)

Taking aim squarely at the popular theme of the working man's struggle against the inequities in the system, *Turk 182!*, a cleverly conceived story [by James Gregory Kingston] of a mystery rebel in New York City whose popularity reaches almost mythic proportions, convincingly hits its mark.

Timothy Hutton plays a 20-year-old who defends the honor of his older brother (Robert Urich), a fireman who, when off-duty in a bar, responds to a plea for help and risks his life by going into a burning building to save a young girl. Urich is severely injured but the city refuses to come to his aid, maintaining that he should not have entered the premises in his intoxicated state.

That's when Hutton takes his plea on his brother's behalf through the city bureaucracy to no avail, including a forced confrontation with the mayor (Robert Culp). Hutton begins a one-man quest to embarrass and discredit the mayor.

Besides its compelling storyline, *Turk 182!* features outstanding performances across the board, with Hutton perfect in the role of the determined unassuming hero.

•

TURNER & HOOCH
1989, 100 mins, US Ⓥ ⦿ col
Dir Roger Spottiswoode ***Prod*** Raymond Wagner ***Scr*** Dennis Shryack, Michael Blodgett, Daniel Petrie, Jr., Jim Cash, Jack Epps, Jr. ***Ph*** Adam Greenberg ***Ed*** Garth Craven, Paul Seydor, Mark Conte, Kenneth Morrisey, Lois Freeman-Fox ***Mus*** Charles Gross ***Art*** John DeCuir, Jr.
Act Tom Hanks, Mare Winningham, Craig T. Nelson, Reginald Veljohnson, Scott Paulin, J. C. Quinn (Touchstone)

Until its grossly miscalculated bummer of an ending, *Turner & Hooch* is a routine but amiable cop-and-dog comedy enlivened by the charm of Tom Hanks and his homely-as-sin canine partner.

Hanks plays a fussy small-town California police investigator whose life is disreputed by a messy junkyard dog with a face only a furry mother could love.

In the numbingly unoriginal plot [by Dennis Shryack and Michael Blodgett], the dog named Hooch (delightfully played by Beasley), witnesses a double murder and is Hanks's only means of catching the drug smugglers responsible for the slayings. The rather mechanical style of director Roger Spottiwoode (who took over the film after original director Henry Winkler departed) fails to enliven the stereotypical criminal proceedings.

•

TURNING POINT, THE
1952, 85 mins, US col
Dir William Dieterle ***Prod*** Irving Asher ***Scr*** Warren Duff ***Ph*** Lionel Lindon ***Ed*** George Tomasini ***Mus*** Irving Talbot ***Art*** Hal Pereira, Joseph McMillan Johnson
Act William Holden, Edmond O'Brien, Alexis Smith, Tom Tully, Ed Begley, Ray Teal (Paramount)

Paramount trains its cameras on a fictional crime syndicate in *The Turning Point*. Armed with a college education and a law degree, Edmond O'Brien tackles his new job of a crime committee chairman with a youthful enthusiasm. Also on hand is Alexis Smith, his girl Friday, and William Holden, a cynical reporter who warns O'Brien of the pitfalls that lie ahead.

Occasionally, the movement of the script tends to lag in a rash of superfluous dialog. This is especially apparent at the midway point. However, the action accelerates thereafter and the closing reels are highlighted by a suspenseful hunt for an "all-important" femme witness, plus Holden's frantic efforts to escape from an assassin in the concrete cavern of a fight stadium.

•

TURNING POINT, THE
1977, 119 mins, US Ⓥ col
Dir Herbert Ross ***Prod*** Herbert Ross, Arthur Laurents ***Scr*** Arthur Laurents ***Ph*** Robert Surtees ***Ed*** William Reynolds ***Mus*** John Lanchbery ***Art*** Albert Brenner
Act Anne Bancroft, Shirley MacLaine, Mikhail Baryshnikov, Leslie Browne, Tom Skerritt, Martha Scott (20th Century-Fox)

The Turning Point is one of the best films of its era. It's that rare example of synergy in which every key element is excellent and the ensemble is an absolute triumph.

Anne Bancroft and Shirley MacLaine, starring as long-time friends with unresolved problems, are magnificent.

The intricate plotting introduces Bancroft as a ballet star just reaching that uneasy age where a lot of Eve Harringtons (male and female) are beginning to move in.

MacLaine, her best friend, long ago abandoned a similar career to marry Tom Skerritt and now their teenage daughter (Leslie Browne) shows real promise as a dancer. This is the incident which triggers an explosion of new and old conflicts.

Pic ranks as one of MacLaine's career highlights, ditto for Bancroft. They have a climactic showdown scene which filmgoers will remember for decades.

1977: NOMINATIONS: Best Picture, Director, Actress (Anne Bancroft, Shirley MacLaine), Supp. Actor (Mikhail Baryshnikov), Supp. Actress (Leslie Browne), Original Screenplay, Cinematography, Art Direction, Editing, Sound

•

12 ANGRY MEN
1957, 95 mins, US Ⓥ ⦿ b/w
Dir Sidney Lumet ***Prod*** Henry Fonda, Reginald Rose ***Scr*** Reginald Rose ***Ph*** Boris Kaufman ***Ed*** Carl Lerner ***Mus*** Kenyon Hopkins ***Art*** Robert Markel
Act Henry Fonda, Lee J. Cobb, Ed Begley, E. G. Marshall, Jack Warden, Martin Balsam (Orion-Nova)

The *12 Angry Men* are a jury, a body of peers chosen to decide the guilt or innocence of a teenager accused of murdering his father. They have heard the arguments of the district attorney and the defense lawyer. They have received instructions from the presiding judge. Now they are on their own. What will they do?

Rose has a lot to say about the responsibility of citizens chosen to serve on a jury. He stresses the importance of taking into account the question of "reasonable doubt." It is soon evident that the majority of the men regard the assignment as a chore. To most of them, it is an open and shut case. The boy is guilty and they demand a quick vote. On the first ballot it is 11 to 1 for a conviction. Henry Fonda is the lone holdout.

Most of the action takes place in the one room on a hot summer day. The effect, rather than being confining, serves to heighten the drama. It's not static, however, for Sidney Lumet, making his bow as a film director, has cleverly maneuvered his players in the small area. Perhaps the motivations of each juror are introduced too quickly and are repeated too often before each changes his vote. However, the film leaves a tremendous impact.

1957: NOMINATIONS: Best Picture, Director, Screenplay Adaptation

•

TWELVE CHAIRS, THE
1970, 94 mins, US Ⓥ ⦿ col
Dir Mel Brooks ***Prod*** Michael Hertzberg ***Scr*** Mel Brooks ***Ph*** Djordje Nikolic ***Ed*** Alan Heim ***Mus*** John Morris ***Art*** Mile Nikolic
Act Ron Moody, Frank Langella, Dom DeLouise, Mel Brooks, Andreas Voutsinas, David Lander (UMC/Crossbow)

The Twelve Chairs is a nutty farce, frequently slapstick and often tongue-in-cheek. Mel Brooks, who directed, scripted, plays a leading role and authored a song, has turned a search for jewels into a cornpop—circa 1927, Russia, when all men were comrades—and the result is a delightful adventure-comedy.

Based on the novel by Ilf and Petrov, exteriors were lensed in Yugoslavia, which provides some novel and picturesque backdrops. The steps in Dubrovnik, vistas of the Dalmatian coast and mountains in the interior lend fascinating atmosphere.

Simple story thread is of three men trying to locate 12 dining-room chairs, once owned by a wealthy woman who confesses separately to her son-in-law and village priest on her deathbed that years before she had secreted all her jewels in the upholstery of one of them. Voila, the plot.

•

TWELVE MONKEYS
1995, 131 mins, US Ⓥ ⦿ col
Dir Terry Gilliam ***Prod*** Charles Roven ***Scr*** David Peoples, Janet Peoples ***Ph*** Roger Pratt ***Ed*** Mick Audsley ***Mus*** Paul Buckmaster ***Art*** Jeffrey Beecroft
Act Bruce Willis, Madeleine Stowe, Brad Pitt, Christopher Plummer, Jon Seda, Joseph Melito (Atlas/Classico/Universal)

A dark and somber sci-fier in the mold of *Blade Runner*, Terry Gilliam's *Twelve Monkeys* is a spectacular mess, an excessively complicated film that attempts to be timely by blending a "virus" thriller with a post-apocalyptic anti-science drama. Gilliam's seventh feature is neither as visually compelling as *Brazil* nor as emotionally gripping as *The Fisher King*.

Pic's inspiration is Chris Marker's *La Jetee*, a landmark 1962 French New Wave film that ran a mere 27 minutes. Its impressive black-and-white imagery, grim voiceover narration and dense texture perfectly conveyed the gloomy post-apocalyptic tale of a young man obsessed with an eerie image from the past, though he's never sure if this image is dream or reality.

Story is set in a subterranean nether world in 2035, following the eradication of 99 percent of the Earth's population. To reverse their fate, the survivors turn to time travel as their only hope. A group of scientists living beneath Philadelphia "volunteer" prisoner James Cole (Bruce Willis) to embark on a dangerous trip back to 1996.

Back in time, Cole lands in a mental institution under the supervision of Dr. Kathryn Railly (Madeleine Stowe), an expert in madness and prophecy. Another inmate is Jeffrey Goines (Brad Pitt), unstable son of a renowned scientist, Dr. Goines (Christopher Plummer).

Cole himself questions his sanity. Nonetheless, two bizarre clues continue to torment him: airport memory and some puzzling symbols from a group called the Army of the 12 Monkeys. In the course of an overly long and convoluted plot, Dr. Railly falls for the tortured man.

Unfortunately, the stellar cast can't overcome the cartoonish nature of their characters. The few joys to be had are in observing the majestic peculiarities of Gilliam's ever-fanciful universe.

1995: NOMINATIONS: Best Supporting Actor (Brad Pitt), Costume Design

•

TWELVE O'CLOCK HIGH
1949, 132 mins, US Ⓥ ⦿ b/w
Dir Henry King ***Prod*** Darryl F. Zanuck ***Scr*** Sy Bartlett, Beirne Lay, Jr. ***Ph*** Leon Shamroy ***Ed*** Barbara McLean ***Mus*** Alfred Newman ***Art*** Lyle Wheeler, Maurice Ransford
Act Gregory Peck, Hugh Marlowe, Gary Merrill, Millard Mitchell, Dean Jagger, Robert Arthur (20th Century-Fox)

Picture treats its story [from the novel by Beirne Lay, Jr. and Sy Bartlett] from the high brass level, i.e., a general's concern for his men's morale while establishing the man-killing daylight bombing raids back in 1942.

As a drama, *High* deals soundly and interestingly with its situations. It gets close to the emotions in unveiling its plot and approaches it from a flashback angle so expertly presented that the emotional pull is sharpened.

Gregory Peck heads up the operations of a bombing squadron from a base in Chelveston, England. Peck gives the character much credence as he suffers and sweats with his men.

There are a number of what amount to "surprise" performances in the male cast. Standout among them is Dean Jagger as a retread still determined to do his bit. Story comes to life through his eyes as he revisits the Chelveston base in 1948.

1949: Best Supp. Actor (Dean Jagger), Sound Recording (20th Century-Fox Sound Dept.)

NOMINATIONS: Best Picture, Actor (Gregory Peck)

•

12 PLUS 1
(US: THE THIRTEEN CHAIRS)
1970, 95 mins, Italy/France Ⓥ col
Dir Nicholas Gessner ***Prod*** Claude Giroux ***Scr*** Marc Behm, Nicholas Gessner ***Ph*** Giuseppe Ruzzolini ***Ed*** Giancarlo Cappelli ***Mus*** Piero Poletto, David Whitaker
Act Vittorio Gassman, Sharon Tate, Orson Welles, Vittorio De Sica, Terry-Thomas, Mylene Demongeot (CEF/COFCI)

Film is mainly of interest as being the last of the tragically fated Sharon Tate. It is a sort of madcap romantic comedy in the form of a chase for treasure hidden in a chair left by a recluse, with some added fashionable sex tidbits and some way-out extravagant interludes by such stalwarts as Orson Welles and Vittorio De Sica.

Tate has charm and grace as a rather hardbitten American girl abroad who puts money before romance. Gassman is a Yank barber who is supposedly left an estate in Britain by an eccentric aunt. But he finds only a rundown house and some antique chairs that he immediately sells to get the fare back.

He finds a note from his aunt saying a fortune is hidden in one of the chairs. So the chase begins. Tate, who works in the gallery he sold the chairs to, teams up with him for a share of the loot. The chase leads to a bordello, an Afro embassy in Paris and a villa in Rome plus a zany interlude in a grand guignol theater run by Welles.

Pic has some good moments, but overall misses the light touch and forward propelling zest to keep this comedy from lagging. Producer Claude Giroux changed title from original *13 Chairs* (from the old Russo tale) after the Tate murder.

•

TWENTIETH CENTURY
1934, 91 mins, US Ⓥ b/w
Dir Howard Hawks ***Prod*** Howard Hawks ***Scr*** Ben Hecht, Charles MacArthur ***Ph*** Joseph August ***Ed*** Gene Havlick
Act John Barrymore, Carole Lombard, Walter Connolly, Roscoe Karns, Etienne Girardot, Ralph Forbes (Columbia)

John Barrymore, who stars, is quoted as saying, "I've never done anything I like as well . . . a role that comes once in an actor's lifetime." It's Barrymore's picture, no doubt of that, with something left over for Carole Lombard, who manages to shine despite practically stooging.

Lily Garland (Lombard) walks out on producer Oscar Jaffe (Barrymore) to go Hollywood shortly after he makes her, double, and that happens early in the picture [from the play *Napoleon of Broadway* by Charles Bruce Milholland]. From then on it's a chase. Jaffe goes broke trying to land another Lily Garland and Lily goes big in Hollywood. The way Jaffe and his boys try to frame Lily into coming back into the legit fold paves the road for some crazy trouping.

Lombard, looking very well, must take Barrymore's abuse as his mistress and handmade star for the first few hundred feet, but when she goes temperamental herself she's permitted to do some head-to-head temperament punching with him.

•

28 DAYS
2000, 103 mins, US Ⓥ ⦿ col
Dir Betty Thomas ***Prod*** Jenno Topping ***Scr*** Susannah Grant ***Ph*** Declan Quinn ***Ed*** Peter Teschner ***Mus*** Richard Gibbs ***Art*** Marcia Hinds-Johnson
Act Sandra Bullock, Viggo Mortensen, Dominic West, Diane Ladd, Elizabeth Perkins, Steve Buscemi (Tall Trees/ Columbia)

A sort of *Lost Weekend Lite, 28 Days* plays like a "Rehab Is Good For You" promo feature offering the audacious suggestion that it's preferable to live life with a clear head than with addictions and hangovers. Watching the ever-likable Sandra Bullock ride a predictable roller coaster from substance-abusing party girl to scornful rehab cynic to sober reformed citizen gives this smoothly made picture whatever appeal it possesses, but it's a superficial, no-rough-edges account of a process that's got to be a lot tougher than the month-in-the-country picnic depicted herein.

A major problem is the lack of distinction developed in the numerous supporting characters. Unlike a classic such as *One Flew Over the Cuckoo's Nest* or even the recent, so-so *Girl, Interrupted*, both of which featured numerous inmate characters who made quick impressions and subsequently achieved some depth, *28 Days* is remarkable for how one-dimensional almost everyone but the lead remains. The casting of Steve Buscemi as the no-nonsense rehab supervisor at first seems like an inspired stroke, given the baggage of excess and weirdness the actor carries from previous roles. But the part never emerges as an important one, giving Buscemi no chance to color it in a personal way.

A bit more substantial in the end is Viggo Mortensen, appealingly underplaying the plausible part of a star baseball pitcher, accustomed to boundless adoration and sexual opportunity, who's got to do time in rehab before returning to the game.

Bullock is required to hit more varied notes here than usual, and she shifts gear with apparent ease. All the same, the script never asks her to go deep, and director Betty Thomas, herself changing pace after a series of hit comedies, demonstrates a constant desire to please rather than to push the material into the rough and dangerous waters that would have made it bracing, illuminating and worth one's time.

•

TWENTY-ONE
1991, 101 mins, US Ⓥ ⦿ col
Dir Don Boyd ***Prod*** Morgan Mason, John Hardy ***Scr*** Zoe Heller, Don Boyd ***Ph*** Keith Goddard ***Ed*** David Spiers ***Mus*** Phil Sawyer ***Art*** Roger Murray Leach
Act Patsy Kensit, Jack Shepherd, Patrick Ryecart, Rufus Sewell, Sophie Thompson, Maynard Eziashi (Anglo International)

Twenty-One mirrors the character of its cheeky protagonist: bored, cynical and operating chiefly for self-amusement. Director/co-writer Don Boyd [who also wrote the screen story] depicts the uncensored experience of a worldly young Brit (Patsy Kensit) who ankles her life in London for a fresh start in New York.

Boyd employs a direct-to-camera technique in which the frank, salty-tongued heroine talks while having her facial, tending to nature's call and so on. If only she were more compelling. This rather vapid lass hasn't much on her mind, and her intimate revelations are forgettable. Kensit tells the audience she was doing all right in London, bouncing from job to job and having an affair with a married man (Patrick Ryecart) until she fell for a lovely Scot (Rufus Sewell). He proved to be a junkie.

Camera also operates in pic's spirit (with flash and style, and no real purpose). Fans of Kensit get plenty of her; her lovely face and form are always the center of attention. The cool control with which she executes the role is admirable.

•

20,000 LEAGUES UNDER THE SEA
1954, 120 mins, US Ⓥ ⦿ ⌑ col
Dir Richard Fleischer ***Prod*** Walt Disney ***Scr*** Earl Fenton ***Ph*** Franz Planer ***Ed*** Elmo Williams ***Mus*** Paul Smith ***Art*** John Meehan
Act Kirk Douglas, James Mason, Paul Lukas, Peter Lorre, Robert J. Wilke, Carleton Young (Walt Disney)

Walt Disney's production of *20,000 Leagues Under the Sea* is a very special kind of picture, combining photographic ingenuity, imaginative storytelling and fiscal daring. Disney went for a bundle (say $5 million in negative costs) in fashioning the Jules Verne classic.

The story of the "monster" ship *Nautilus*, astounding as it may be, is so astutely developed that the audience immediately accepts its part on the excursion through Captain Nemo's underseas realm.

James Mason is the captain, a genius who had fashioned and guides the out-of-this-world craft. Kirk Douglas is a free-wheeling, roguish harpoon artist. Paul Lukas is a kind and gentle man of science and Peter Lorre is Lukas's fretting apprentice.

But it is the production itself that is the star. Technical skill was lavished in fashioning the fabulous *Nautilus* with its exquisitely appointed interior. The underwater lensing is remarkable on a number of counts, among them being the special designing of aqualungs and other equipment to match Verne's own illustrations.

Story opens in San Francisco where maritime men have been terrorized by reports of a monstrous denizen of the seas which has been sinking their ships. An armed frigate sets out in pursuit and is itself destroyed, with Lukas, Douglas and Lorre the survivors.

1954: Best Color Art Direction, Special Effects

NOMINATION: Best Editing

•

20,000 YEARS IN SING SING
1932, 78 mins, US b/w
Dir Michael Curtiz ***Prod*** [uncredited] ***Scr*** Wilson Mizner, Brown Holmes ***Ph*** Barney McGill ***Ed*** George Amy ***Mus*** [Bernhard Kaun] ***Art*** Anton Grot
Act Spencer Tracy, Bette Davis, Arthur Byron, Lyle Talbot, Warren Hymer, Louis Calhern (First National)

Interesting film material comes from warden Lewis E. Lawes's book of memoirs of prison administration [adapted by Courtenay Terrett and Robert Lord]. While it may take some liberties and overstep bounds of conviction, it's still good entertainment.

Sing Sing's warden can have no complaint against the Warner picture. He extended WB every cooperation in the filming and permitted cameras within his prison for actual scenes, including prisoners in the mob scenes.

Of pictures having inside of penal institutions as their locale, this one is the best. It builds up its interest strongly through that alone, covering a lot of routine that's unknown to most outsiders. Finally, it begins to appear Sing Sing wouldn't be a bad place at all to spend a vacation over the Depression. Arthur Byron's paternal smile as the warden, his anxiety to create reform and allow plenty of leeway even to tuff ones among his charges, would make it quite a resort.

Though let out to visit the dying gal friend and committing murder meanwhile, convict Tom Connors (Spencer Tracy) returns, putting the warden's honor system to the strongest test imaginable. In the end it's the chair for the reformed bad boy whose only regret seems to be his parting from the warden's shelter and benevolence.

Far-fetched, but it sells. Considerable comedy dots the action. Tracy and Warren Hymer, teamed in *Up the River* for Fox, are again together. Bette Davis is the convict's moll who does him dirt in one breath and shoots to kill for him in another. She's not particularly impressive here.

•

TWICE IN A LIFETIME

1985, 117 mins, US Ⓥ ⦿ col

Dir Bud Yorkin ***Prod*** Bud Yorkin ***Scr*** Colin Welland ***Ph*** Nick McLean ***Ed*** Robert Jones ***Mus*** Pat Metheny ***Art*** William Creber

Act Gene Hackman, Ann-Margret, Ellen Burstyn, Amy Madigan, Ally Sheedy, Stephen Lang (Yorkin)

An edgy, shifty-eyed 50th birthday tribute for hero Harry Mackenzie gets this midlife-crisis film off to a risky, sentimental start, and from there on out it's Ellen Burstyn, the abandoned wife, versus Gene Hackman, the not-unsympathetic-but-risk-taking husband, vying for audience affections.

Burstyn claims the film as Kate, who has to cope with her own life and family, and some rather mediocre lines. Hackman is stalwart and determined in his resolve to make a new life with Ann-Margret, but she is far too sexy and he far too underdeveloped for anybody to understand what she sees in him.

The pic is loaded with jock humor and incidental comments that allow the characters' frustrations to seep out. Audiences will love Burstyn's warm wrinkles and visit with her daughters to a male strip joint, as well as Hackman's workmanlike heroism.

1985: NOMINATION: Best Supp. Actress (Amy Madigan)

•

TWILIGHT

1998, 94 mins, US Ⓥ ⦿ col

Dir Robert Benton ***Prod*** Arlene Donovan, Scott Rudin ***Scr*** Robert Benton, Richard Russo ***Ph*** Piotr Sobocinski ***Ed*** Carol Littleton ***Mus*** Elmer Bernstein ***Art*** David Gropman

Act Paul Newman, Susan Sarandon, Gene Hackman, Reese Witherspoon, Stockard Channing, James Garner (Cinehaus/Paramount)

Twilight is an autumnal murder mystery awash in rueful intimations of mortality. As a suspenser, Robert Benton's return to the L.A. detective genre more than two decades after *The Late Show* reps a sometimes clunky and unconvincing recycling of standard private detective conventions dating back to Raymond Chandler. But the truly stellar cast ensures that whatever is happening onscreen, however incredible, will still be worth watching.

Paul Newman plays longtime cop and, more recently, private dick Harry Ross, who, in the Puerto Vallarta–set prolog, is accidentally shot in the groin by 17-year-old Mel Ames (Reese Witherspoon). Two years later, the divorced, broke and formerly alcoholic Harry is reduced to living above the garage on the estate of his movie star friends Jack and Catherine Ames (Gene Hackman, Susan Sarandon). Pouty blond Mel, it turns out, is their daughter.

Plot jerks into motion when Harry encounters a gunshot old man (M. Emmet Walsh) who empties his pistol at him before expiring. The detective in him is reawakened by his discovery that the dead man was investigating the disappearance of Catherine's first husband 20 years before.

Harry suddenly manages to seduce Catherine the very next time they're alone together. Yarn becomes even more far-fetched when Harry is attacked by Mel's former lover (Giancarlo Esposito).

Writers conscientiously connect the dots by directly explaining almost everyone's motivations at one point or another, and *Twilight* is similarly explicit about its meanings. "It looks like we all run out of luck in the end," Harry's old colleague Raymond Hope (James Garner) exclaims between bursts of dirty-old-man horniness.

Newman's work is sly, stealthy and subtle, and his rapport with his co-stars is a pleasure to watch. Writing for the younger characters is not so good.

•

TWILIGHT FOR THE GODS

1958, 120 mins, US col

Dir Joseph Pevney ***Prod*** Gordon Kay ***Scr*** Ernest K. Gann ***Ph*** Irving Glassberg ***Ed*** Tony Martinelli ***Mus*** David Raksin ***Art*** Alexander Golitzen, Eric Orborn

Act Rock Hudson, Cyd Charisse, Arthur Kennedy, Leif Erickson, Charles McGraw, Richard Haydn (Universal)

Twilight for the Gods emerges as a routine sea adventure drama, bolstered by the marquee names of Rock Hudson and Cyd Charisse. Novelist Ernest Gann, who also wrote the screenplay, has employed the familiar technique [from his successful *The High and the Mighty*] of assembling a group of passengers of different personalities and backgrounds, including several with shady pasts, and studies their reactions to the dangers encountered during a long sea voyage.

There's Hudson, a court-martialed ship's captain fighting alcoholism, as the skipper of the battered sailing ship; Charisse as a Honolulu call girl running away from the authorities; Arthur Kennedy as a bitter and treacherous second mate; Leif Erickson as a down-and-out showman; Judith Evelyn as a has-been opera singer; Vladimir Sokoloff and Celia Lovsky as an elderly refugee couple; Ernest Truex as a missionary, and Richard Haydn as a British beachcomber.

Filmed on location in the Hawaiian islands, the photography is a delight to the eyes as it captures the sailing ship in motion, a sea village, various beaches and sites on a chain of islands, Honolulu harbor, and Waikalulu Falls.

•

TWILIGHT OF HONOR

1963, 105 mins, US ▭ b/w

Dir Boris Sagal ***Prod*** William Perlberg, George Seaton ***Scr*** Henry Denker ***Ph*** Philip Lathrop ***Ed*** Hugh S. Fowler ***Mus*** John Green ***Art*** George W. Davis, Paul Groesse

Act Richard Chamberlain, Joey Heatherton, Nick Adams, Claude Rains, Joan Blackman, James Gregory (M-G-M)

Twilight of Honor casts Richard Chamberlain in his first starring role, as a court-appointed defense attorney who takes on an entire New Mexico town, at the risk of his career, to save his client from the gas chamber.

Frank and often startling treatment is made of a section in New Mexico's criminal code—No. 12–24—which provides that a husband is innocent if he kills another man whom he discovers in the act of adultery with his wife. Henry Denker's polished script, based upon the novel by Al Dewlen, brings out that Chamberlain's client killed the town's most respected citizen after he found him in bed with his trampish teenage spouse.

Dexterity which writer displays is matched by the shrewd, moving direction of Boris Sagal, who is particularly proficient in his realistic courtroom sequences. Chamberlain turns in a smooth and persuasive performance. He is surrounded by a thoroughly experienced cast to help him over the rough spots. One of highlights of pic is introduction of Joey Heatherton, a sexpot from the eastern stage and television making her film bow. In the part of the two-timing wife of the man up for murder she registers impressively.

1963: NOMINATIONS: Best Supp. Actor (Nick Adams), B&W Art Direction

•

TWILIGHT'S LAST GLEAMING

1977, 146 mins, US/W. Germany Ⓥ ⦿ col

Dir Robert Aldrich ***Prod*** Merv Adelson ***Scr*** Ronald M. Cohen, Edward Huebsch ***Ph*** Robert Hauser ***Ed*** Michael Luciano ***Mus*** Jerry Goldsmith ***Art*** Rolf Zehetbauer

Act Burt Lancaster, Richard Widmark, Charles Durning, Melvyn Douglas, Paul Winfield, Burt Young (Lorimar-Bavaria/Geria)

Robert Aldrich's *Twilight's Last Gleaming* is intricate, intriguing and intelligent drama. Filmed in Munich, the setting is the U.S.

Burt Lancaster stars as a cashiered U.S. Air Force officer who seizes a nuclear missile site to force public disclosure of secret Vietnam war policy goals. Charles Durning is outstanding as a U.S. president who must respond to the challenge.

A Walter Wager novel, *Viper Three*, has been adapted into a suspenseful and taut confrontation.

Outside, Richard Widmark mobilizes for the forcible recapture of the base, while in the White House, Durning assembles his top military and Cabinet advisors to ponder Lancaster's demands.

•

TWILIGHT ZONE THE MOVIE

1983, 102 mins, US Ⓥ ⦿ col

Dir John Landis, Steven Spielberg, Joe Dante, George Miller ***Prod*** Steven Spielberg, John Landis ***Scr*** John Landis, George Clayton Johnson, Richard Matheson, Josh Rogan ***Ph*** Steve Larner, Allen Daviau, John Hora ***Ed*** Malcolm Campbell, Michael Kahn, Tina Hirsch, Howard Smith ***Mus*** Jerry Goldsmith ***Art*** James D. Bissell

Act Dan Aykroyd, Albert Brooks, Vic Morrow, Scatman Crothers, Kathleen Quinlan, John Lithgow (Warner)

Twilight Zone, feature film spinoff from Rod Serling's perennially popular 1960s TV series, plays much like a traditional vaudeville card, what with its tantalizing teaser opening followed by three sketches of increasing quality, all building up to a socko headline act.

Pic consists of prolog by John Landis as well as vignettes, none running any longer than original TV episodes, by Landis, Steven Spielberg, Joe Dante and George Miller. Dante and Miller manage to shine the brightest in this context.

Landis gets things off to a wonderful start with a comic prolog starring Dan Aykroyd and Albert Brooks.

Landis's principal episode, however, is a downbeat, one-dimensional fable about racial and religious intolerance. An embittered, middle-aged man who has just been passed over for a job promotion, Vic Morrow sports a torrent of racial epithets aimed at Jews, Blacks and Orientals while drinking with buddies at a bar. Upon exiting, he finds himself in Nazi-occupied Paris as a suspected Jew on the run from the Gestapo.

This is the only sequence in the film not derived from an actual TV episode, although it does bear a thematic resemblance to a 1961 installment titled *A Quality of Mercy*.

Spielberg's entry is the most down-to-earth of all the stories. In a retirement home filled with oldsters living in the past, spry Scatman Crothers encourages various residents to think young and, in organizing a game of kick the can, actually transforms them into their childhood selves again.

Most bizarre contribution comes from Dante. Outsider Kathleen Quinlan enters the Twilight Zone courtesy of little Jeremy Licht, who lords it over a Looney-Tune household by virtue of his power to will anything into existence except happiness.

But wisely, the best has been saved for last. Miller's reworking of *Nightmare at 20,000 Feet*, about a man who sees a gremlin tearing up an engine wing of an airplane, is electrifying from beginning to end.

•

TWIN PEAKS FIRE WALK WITH ME

1992, 135 mins, US Ⓥ ⦿ col

Dir David Lynch ***Prod*** Gregg Fienberg ***Scr*** David Lynch, Robert Engels ***Ph*** Ron Garcia ***Ed*** Mary Sweeney ***Mus*** Angelo Badalamenti ***Art*** Patricia Norris

Act Sheryl Lee, Ray Wise, Moira Kelly, Chris Isaak, Kyle MacLachlan, Kiefer Sutherland (Lynch-Frost/CiBy)

A feature prequel to the celebrated but short-lived TV series, pic is like an R-rated episode embodying both the pros and cons of the intriguingly offbeat TV program. It's a detailing of the final week in the life of the quasi-legendary Laura Palmer, with plenty of digressions and artistic doodlings, as well as the occasional striking sequence.

After a 33-minute prolog detailing the FBI's investigation of the Portland murder of a woman named Teresa Banks, action then cuts to one year later in Twin Peaks, where Laura (Sheryl Lee) prepares for class by snorting some coke. Events largely center on Laura's downward spiral of drug use, promiscuity and crime, up to the moment of her killing, which leaves things off where they all started on TV.

Suspense is clearly lacking in this story with a preordained outcome. Another significant drawback is that long before the climax Laura has become a tiresome teen.

Many of the show's familiar performers (Lara Flynn Boyle, Sherilyn Fenn, Richard Beymer and Joan Chen just for starters) aren't on view here. Performances are solid but unremarkable across the board, and craft contributions are very attractively similar to what was accomplished on the small screen.

•

TWINS

1988, 112 mins, US Ⓥ ⦿ col

Dir Ivan Reitman ***Prod*** Ivan Reitman ***Scr*** William Davies, William Osborne, Timothy Harris, Herschel Weingrod ***Ph*** Andrzej Bartkowiak ***Ed*** Sheldon Kahn, Donn Cambern ***Mus*** Georges Delerue, Randy Edelman ***Art*** James D. Bissell

Act Arnold Schwarzenegger, Danny DeVito, Kelly Preston, Chloe Webb, Bonnie Bartlett, Trey Wilson (Universal)

Director Ivan Reitman more than delivers on the wacky promise of *Twins* in this nutty, storybook tale of siblings separated at birth and reunited at age 35.

Arnold Schwarzenegger plays Julius Benedict, a perfect specimen of a man in both body and soul, raised as an orphan in pristine innocence on a tropical isle. Created in a genetic experiment, he has a twin brother on the mainland. Lionhearted Julius, filled with familiar longing, rushes off to L.A. to search for bro—only to discover he'd have found him faster by looking under rocks.

Danny DeVito's Vincent Benedict is a major creep, a guy you wouldn't mind seeing get hit by a car. To him, Julius is a dopey nut who makes a good bodyguard. They finally set out to locate their mother, but Vincent is still on his incorrigible path.

Schwarzenegger is a delightful surprise in this perfect transitional role to comedy. So strongly does he project the tenderness, nobility and puppy-dog devotion that make Julius tick that one is nearly hypnotized into suspending disbelief.

DeVito is a blaze of energy and body language as Vince, articulating the part as though he's written it himself.

•

TWINS OF EVIL

1971, 87 mins, UK Ⓥ ⦿ col

Dir John Hough ***Prod*** Harry Fine, Michael Style ***Scr*** Tudor Gates ***Ph*** Dick Bush ***Ed*** Spencer Reeve ***Mus*** Harry Robinson ***Art*** Roy Stannard

Act Peter Cushing, Madelaine Collinson, Mary Collinson, Kathleen Byron, Dennis Price, Damien Thomas (Hammer)

Blood flows and thunder roars as Mary and Madelaine Collinson, attractive identical twins playing orphans, come to live with their witch-hunting, godfearing uncle (Peter Cushing), in the shadow of dreaded Karnstein Castle.

One is good and timid while the other is bold and brazen. The latter cannot wait to find out more about the castle and the handsome young count (Damien Thomas). He is one of the undead and soon she is his victim. The question becomes, which twin is the vampire?

John Hough has given Tudor Gates's script [based on a characters created by J. Sheridan Le Fanu] a good pace and directed so that audiences can take it as straight horror or as a slight send-up. Settings, production values, camerawork and acting are all of a high standard.

•

TWISTED NERVE

1968, 118 mins, UK Ⓥ col

Dir Roy Boulting ***Prod*** George W. George, Frank Granat ***Scr*** Roy Boulting, Leo Marks ***Ph*** Harry Waxman ***Ed*** Martin Charles ***Mus*** Bernard Herrmann ***Art*** Albert Witherick

Act Hayley Mills, Hywel Bennett, Billie Whitelaw, Phyllis Calvert, Frank Finlay, Barry Foster (British Lion)

Twisted Nerve has Hayley Mills involved in some fairly gruesome *Psycho*-like proceedings.

She's a bit shocked when the young anti-hero (Hywel Bennett) catches her off guard and kisses her fiercely; she's sweetly reasonable when he suddenly turns to her stark naked; and she eventually faces near-rape and imminent murder with displeasure, but non-Disney-like aplomb. There's a firm, if unwitting, implication of a link between Down's syndrome and homicidal madness. This dangerous untruth is likely to be offensive to many.

This angle was not necessary. Stripped of it the film could still stand up as a reasonably tough, chilling suspenser giving a compelling study of a warped young psychopath. Bennett, with his babyface and pageboy-bobbed hairstyle, is compelling, his performance being an effectively blended piece of menace.

Roy Boulting lacks the subtleties of a Hitchcock but manages to bring some brooding menace into his direction, woven with some neat dialog and brash humor.

•

TWISTED ROAD, THE

SEE: THEY LIVE BY NIGHT

•

TWISTER

1989, 94 mins, US Ⓥ ⦿ col

Dir Michael Almereyda ***Prod*** Wieland Schulz-Keil ***Scr*** Michael Almereyda ***Ph*** Renato Berta ***Ed*** Roberto Silvi ***Mus*** Hans Zimmer ***Art*** David Waso

Act Harry Dean Stanton, Suzy Amis, Crispin Glover, Dylan McDermott, Jenny Wright, Lois Chiles (Vestron)

Twister is an oddball family drama about some Kansas nuts who bounce off the walls of their mansion while a storm brews outside. Appealing for its ambition to achieve a unique tone and for its wildly disparate cast, pic never entirely comes together.

Harry Dean Stanton is a retired soda pop tycoon who casually presides over a brood consisting of his layabout daughter, Suzy Amis; the latter's eight-year-old daughter; his pretentious would-be *artiste* son, Crispin Glover; the latter's fiancée, Jenny Wright; unconventional black maid Charlaine Woodard and his own fiancée, children's TV evangelist, Lois Chiles.

Trying to work his way back under the same roof is Dylan McDermott, father of Amis's child, a ne'er-do-well who seems like too nice a guy for the fruitcakes populating Stanton's family.

Although it's impossible to see what first-time writer-director Michael Almereyda, working from a novel [*OH!*] by Mary Robison, is trying to get at, he doesn't at this point display the powers to unify the set of performances or to consistently control the tone. Novelist William Burroughs puts in a brief appearance.

•

TWISTER

1996, 114 mins, US Ⓥ ⦿ ▭ col

Dir Jan De Bont ***Prod*** Kathleen Kennedy, Ian Bryce, Michael Crichton ***Scr*** Michael Crichton, Anne-Marie Martin ***Ph*** Jack N. Green ***Ed*** Michael Kahn ***Mus*** Mark Mancina ***Art*** Joseph Nemec III

Act Helen Hunt, Bill Paxton, Cary Elwes, Jami Gertz, Lois Smith, Alan Ruck (Amblin/Warner/Universal)

Another theme park ride of a movie without an ounce of emotional credibility to it, *Twister* succeeds on its own terms by taking the audience somewhere it has never been before: into a tornado's funnel. Even more than with most of Michael Crichton's concoctions, this one conveys the overwhelming impression of a mechanical entertainment, a very high concept in which the characters and their problems seem like utterly arbitrary creations. Despite the spunky work of Helen Hunt and Bill Paxton, the time between tornadoes is just dead air.

A ragtag group, headed by scientist Jo Harding (Hunt), is attempting to place sensors directly inside a funnel, which would give the outfit unequaled status in the meteorological world. Unfortunately, this is easier said than done, since someone needs to place the sensors' satellite-like container—nicknamed "Dorothy" in honor of the picture with the most famous twister to date—directly in harm's way.

Jo's hard-driving almost-ex, Bill (Paxton), who was the group leader before opting for the soft life as a broadcast weatherman, turns up in the middle of the Oklahoma farmlands as bad weather is brewing to obtain his divorce papers, so anxious is he to marry his princess fiancée, Melissa (Jami Gertz).

Bill has his buttons pushed further when the competition, in the guise of hotshot Dr. Jonas Miller (Cary Elwes) and his corporate-sponsored caravan of black vans, roar onto the scene with their own sensors to launch.

Pic never lets up, even in the so-called quiet scenes, which are generally filled with argumentative bickering and characters shouting to be heard over either the weather or one another. The effects set a new standard in their field.

1996: NOMINATIONS: Best Sound, Visual Effects

•

TWO BITS

1995, 85 mins, US Ⓥ col

Dir James Foley ***Prod*** Arthur Cohn ***Scr*** Joseph Stefano ***Ph*** Juan Ruiz-Anchia ***Ed*** Howard Smith ***Mus*** Jane Musky ***Art*** Jane Musky

Act Jerry Barone, Mary Elizabeth Mastrantonio, Al Pacino, Joe Grifasi, Joanna Merlin, Andy Romano (Connexion)

A mild, nostalgic Depression-era memoir, *Two Bits* has the impact of a sweet little short story or one-act play rather than a thoroughly fleshed-out drama. Joseph Stefano's reminiscence of childhood on the streets of South Philadelphia in 1933 serves up some briefly poignant monologues and episodes, but the whole undertaking, shot in 1993, is just too slight. Grizzled and rumpled, sitting in an overgrown garden and dispensing advice in a rough, muted voice, an elderly Italian gent (Al Pacino) announces that this summer day will be his last. Of more pressing concern to his 12-year-old grandson Gennaro (Jerry Barone) is how he's going to raise the 25¢ he needs to attend the opening day of the new local movie palace, La Paloma. He takes to the streets in an attempt to earn the two bits any way he can.

These escapades comprise the bulk of the picture, as the kid tries a range of gambits of varying legitimacy and precariousness.

The best moments are purely theatrical in nature, notably the one-set scene in which Gennaro visits the woman from his grandfather's distant past, and a beautifully delivered monologue by Mary Elizabeth Mastrantonio.

A great deal of loving care clearly has gone into production designer Jane Musky's re-creation of a long-vanished incarnation of South Philly, but it's so prettified and idealized as to go over the top.

•

TWO ENGLISH GIRLS

SEE: DEUX ANGLAISES ET LE CONTINENT

•

TWO-FACED WOMAN

1941, 94 mins, US Ⓥ b/w

Dir George Cukor ***Prod*** Gottfried Reinhardt ***Scr*** S. N. Behrman, Salka Viertel, George Oppenheimer ***Ph*** Joseph Ruttenberg ***Ed*** George Boemler ***Mus*** Bronislau Kaper ***Art*** Cedric Gibbons, Daniel B. Cathcart

Act Greta Garbo, Melvyn Douglas, Constance Bennett, Ruth Gordon, Roland Young, Frances Carson (M-G-M)

In a daring piece of showmanship, Metro presents the one-time queen of mystery in a wild, and occasionally very risque, slap farce entitled *Two-Faced Woman*. That the experiment of converting Greta Garbo into a comedienne is not entirely successful is no fault of hers. Had the script writers and the director, George Cukor, entered into the spirit of the thing with as much enthusiasm, lack of self-consciousness and abandon as the star, the result would have been a smash hit.

There is no holding back Garbo when she steps down from the serious dramatic pedestal and has her fling with broad comedy. Melvyn Douglas is an excellent foil. Much of the action takes place in bedrooms, boudoirs and the psychological proximities of both.

The story, which was taken from a play by Ludwig Fulda, is one of those naturalized importations from the Continent wherein the wife masquerades during most of the film as her own twin-sister just to test the fibre of her husband's adoration. There's a double entendre to nearly everything that is said between the two, and nearly everything is said.

•

TWO FLAGS WEST

1950, 92 mins, US b/w

Dir Robert Wise ***Prod*** Casey Robinson ***Scr*** Casey Robinson ***Ph*** Leon Shamroy ***Ed*** Louis Loeffler ***Mus*** Hugo Friedhofer

Act Joseph Cotten, Linda Darnell, Jeff Chandler, Cornel Wilde, Dale Robertson, Jay C. Flippen (20th Century-Fox)

The Civil War is carried into the west for Indian-fighting, giving *Two Flags West* an interesting premise for solid action and fast pace. Factual basis for the plot (from a story by Frank S. Nugent and Curtis Kenyon), laid in 1864, is the recruiting of Confederate prisoners to man western army outposts under the Union flag. Joseph Cotten, Confederate colonel, and a group of his soldiers accept the deal to escape prison existence and because they see in it an opportunity eventually to get back to fighting for the South.

The motley crew is taken west under the guidance of Colonel Wilde, Union officer, to the fort commanded by Jeff Chandler, a bitter, brooding man crippled in his first clash of arms.

•

TWO FOR THE ROAD

1967, 112 mins, UK Ⓥ ⦿ ▭ col

Dir Stanley Donen ***Prod*** Stanley Donen ***Scr*** Frederic Raphael ***Ph*** Christopher Challis ***Ed*** Richard Marden, Madeleine Gug ***Mus*** Henry Mancini ***Art*** Willy Holt

Act Audrey Hepburn, Albert Finney, Eleanor Bron, William Daniels, Claude Dauphin, Georges Descrieres (20th Century-Fox)

As far as producer, director, femme lead and screenwriter are concerned, this attempt to visually analyze the bits and pieces that go into making a marriage, and then making it work, is successful. If it drags a bit here and there, blame it on the stodgy performance of actor Albert Finney who is unable to convey the lightness, gaiety and romanticism needed.

In the story, the same married couple make basically the same trip, from London to the Riviera, at three different stages of their life with continual crosscutting and flashing backwards and forwards from one period to the other.

The credibility of the changes in periods is left, except for changes of costume and vehicular equipment, to the two leads. Finney remains the same throughout but Audrey Hepburn is amazing in her ability to portray a very young girl, a just pregnant wife of two years, and a beginning-to-be-bored wife of five years.

1967: NOMINATION: Best Original Story & Screenplay

•

TWO FOR THE SEESAW

1962, 119 mins, US ▭ b/w

Dir Robert Wise ***Prod*** Walter Mirisch ***Scr*** Isobel Lennart ***Ph*** Ted McCord ***Ed*** Stuart Gilmore ***Mus*** Andre Previn ***Art*** Boris Leven

Act Robert Mitchum, Shirley MacLaine, Edmon Ryan, Elisabeth Fraser, Eddie Firestone, Billy Gray (United Artists)

There is a fundamental torpor about *Seesaw* that is less troublesome on stage than it is on screen, a medium of motion that exaggerates its absence, that emphasizes the slightest hint of listlessness. On film, it drags. It drags in spite of the charm, insight, wit and compassion of William Gibson's play, the savvy and sense of scenarist Isobel Lennart's mild revisions and additions, the infectious friskiness of Shirley

MacLaine's performance and the consummate care taken by those who shaped and mounted the film reproduction.

The basic flaws appear to be the play's innate talkiness and the unbalance of the two-way "see-saw." The selection of Robert Mitchum for the role of Jerry Ryan proves not to have a been a wise one. The strong attraction Gittel is supposed to feel for Jerry becomes less plausible because of Mitchum's lethargic, droopy-eyed enactment. Something more appealing and magnetic is needed to make this love affair ring true.

MacLaine's performance in the meaty role of the disarmingly candid, stupendously kindhearted Gittel Mosca, is a winning one. Her handling of the Yiddish dialect and accompanying mannerisms is sufficiently reserved so that it does not lapse into a kind of gittal-gitterless caricature.

1962: NOMINATIONS: Best B&W Cinematography, Song ("Second Chance")

•

TWO GENTLEMEN SHARING
1969, 106 mins, UK col
Dir Ted Kotcheff ***Prod*** J. Barry Kulick ***Scr*** Evan Jones ***Ph*** Billy Williams ***Ed*** Derek York ***Mus*** Stanley Myers ***Art*** Ken Bridgeman
Act Robin Phillips, Judy Geeson, Esther Anderson, Hal Frederick, Norman Rossington, Rachel Kempson (American International)

Film boasts a solid and well-chosen cast, strong physical values for such a medium-scaled item, and a racial story [from a novel by David Stuart Leslie] delivered with unhysterical acumen and, at times, with considerable barbed humor.

The two "gentlemen" who share the London pad in question are a young, white ad exec with a liberal outlook and a certain disgust—or mistrust—for his middle-class background, and a black lawyer with a youthfully unblunted hope of making a go of things in his profession on his own merits.

Robin Phillips has just the right naive physique as the well-meaner who bears the major brunt of film's thematics and manages to convince as the white member of the temporary duo, while Hal Frederick is generally very good.

•

TWO GIRLS AND A SAILOR
1944, 124 mins, US Ⓥ ⦿ b/w
Dir Richard Thorpe ***Prod*** Joe Pasternak ***Scr*** Richard Connell, Gladys Lehman ***Ph*** Robert Surtees ***Ed*** George Boemler ***Mus*** George Stoll ***Art*** Cedric Gibbons, Paul Groesse
Act Van Johnson, June Allyson, Gloria DeHaven, Jimmy Durante, Lena Horne, Jose Iturbi (M-G-M)

Weakness of story, a very thin one in this instance, reduces *Two Girls and a Sailor* to little more than a salmagundi of band numbers by Harry James and Xavier Cugat, with their soloists, plus Jimmy Durante, of whom there isn't enough, and various other specialties ranging from Lena Horne to the concert pianist Jose Iturbi. It is too long and generally slow.

June Allyson and Gloria DeHaven play a sister act, featured in a few short numbers. Headliners at a nightclub with the James and Cugat orchestras, they turn their home into a place where servicemen may be entertained after they're through with their nightly chores.

Allyson turns in a very fine performance despite the poorness of the script, which also is true of Van Johnson, opposite her as the sailor boy.

1944: NOMINATION: Best Original Screenplay

•

TWO-HEADED SPY, THE
1958, 93 mins, UK b/w
Dir Andre de Toth ***Prod*** Bill Kirby ***Scr*** James O'Donnell ***Ph*** Ted Scaife ***Ed*** Raymond Poulton ***Mus*** Gerard Schurmann ***Art*** Ivan King
Act Jack Hawkins, Gia Scala, Erik Schumann, Alexander Knox, Felix Aylmer, Donald Pleasence (Sabre)

Based on a real-life story, this pursues a fairly pedestrian beat but it builds its tension excellently and without too blatant use of the usual cloak-and-dagger methods. Director Andre de Toth has sought to get his effects by showing the mental strain of Jack Hawkins in his dilemma rather than by stress on too much physical danger.

Hawkins, a British spy in both wars and therefore an exile in Germany between the two conflicts, has built up confidence as an astute, loyal and resourceful member of the Nazi machine. At the same time he is feeding the Allies invaluable information through a British agent, neatly played by Felix Aylmer, disguised as an antique-clock seller.

When Aylmer is arrested and murdered, suspicion falls on Hawkins through his aide, a member of the Gestapo. But he manages to brush off this suspicion and continues his espionage through his new contact, a beautiful singer.

Hawkins plays the role of the general with his usual reliability.

•

200 MOTELS
1971, 98 mins, UK Ⓥ ⦿ col
Dir Frank Zappa, Tony Palmer ***Prod*** Jerry Good, Herb Cohen ***Scr*** Frank Zappa, Tony Palmer ***Ph*** Tony Palmer ***Ed*** Rich Harrison ***Mus*** Frank Zappa ***Art*** Leo Austin
Act The Mothers of Invention, Theodore Bikel, Ringo Starr, Janet Ferguson, Lucy Offerall, Pamela Miller (United Artists)

Frank Zappa's *200 Motels*, featuring his group, The Mothers of Invention, plus Theodore Bikel and Ringo Starr, is the zaniest. The film is a series of surrealistic sequences allegedly inspired by the experiences of a rock group on the road. The incidents are often outrageously irreverent. The comedy is fast and furious, both sophisticated and sophomoric.

The story proceeds on many different levels. Bikel appears to superior advantage in several characterizations: a TV MC, an officious military bureaucrat, and something resembling a British secret agent or banker. Starr's okay cameo has him dressed up like Zappa. Group member Jimmy Carl Black is excellent as a redneck cowboy; Keith Moon is in nun's drag; Janet Ferguson and Lucy Offerall are a smash as two jaded groupies; and leather-costumed Pamela Miller scores as an underground news hen.

Film is the first theatrical release to have been shot in the color vidtape-to-film process of Technicolor's vidtronics subsid. The seven-day shooting sked (on a reported $600,000 budget) was followed by 11 days of editing.

•

TWO IF BY SEA
1996, 96 mins, US Ⓥ col
Dir Bill Bennett ***Prod*** James G. Robinson ***Scr*** Denis Leary, Mike Armstrong ***Ph*** Andrew Lesnie ***Ed*** Bruce Green ***Mus*** Nick Glennie-Smith, Paddy Moloney ***Art*** David Chapman
Act Denis Leary, Sandra Bullock, Stephen Dillane, Yaphet Kotto, Wayne Robson, Jonathan Tucker (Morgan Creek/Warner)

An inert tale of a criminal couple, *Two if by Sea* is suitable for incarceration, provided the jailer loses the key.

Denis Leary receives first billing in and co-wrote this vanity piece about a petty thief, Frank, who backs into the theft of a Matisse painting. Frank decides to swipe the painting three days earlier than planned and spend the extra time vacationing in a tiny, remote New England enclave with his long-suffering girlfriend, Roz (Sandra Bullock).

The FBI, led by the obsessive O'Malley (Yaphet Kotto), is convinced this is the work of a seasoned professional. The islanders are equally problematic. New neighbor Evan Marsh (Stephen Dillane) takes a shine to Roz, while obnoxious preteen Todd (Jonathan Tucker) proves a thorn in Frank's side.

Director Bill Bennett is far from the acclaim and distinction of his Australian work. It's as if his understanding of the American milieu (though the Canadian coastline subs for Boston and environs) went overboard.

Leary's work feels much like catching a seasoned comic on a bad night. Bullock, playing dumb but good-hearted and groomed to look bad, displays none of the qualities that propelled her to recent stardom.

•

TWO JAKES, THE
1990, 138 mins, US Ⓥ ⦿ ▭ col
Dir Jack Nicholson ***Prod*** Robert Evans, Harold Schneider ***Scr*** Robert Towne ***Ph*** Vilmos Zsigmond ***Ed*** Anne Goursaud ***Mus*** Van Dyke Parks ***Art*** Jeremy Railton, Richard Sawyer
Act Jack Nicholson, Harvey Keitel, Meg Tilly, Madeleine Stowe, Eli Wallach, Frederic Forrest (Paramount)

Following a trek to the big screen almost as convoluted as its plot, this oft-delayed sequel proves a jumbled, obtuse yet not entirely unsatisfying follow-up to *Chinatown*, rightly considered one of the best films of the 1970s. Like much of the film noir of the 1940s, *Jakes* simply spins a web of intrigue so thick its origins become imperceptible.

Picking up in 1948, 11 years after the events in *Chinatown*, Jake Gittes (Jack Nicholson) has become a prosperous and respected private investigator, though he still makes his living spying on an unfaithful wife (Meg Tilly) for her suspicious husband, Jake Berman (Harvey Keitel).

When the name of Katherine Mulwray turns up on an audiotape of the couple in bed together, it revives Gittes's ghosts of events that occurred in *Chinatown*, linking sex, murder and deceit to the role of precious resources—*Chinatown*, water; here, oil—in a developing Southern California. The film then takes on a dual structure, with Gittes in the eye of the hurricane as holder of the incriminating tape while seeking to unravel its connection to Mulwray, the memorable product of the coupling of father and daughter in Roman Polanski's earlier film.

A few scenes do carry tremendous power, especially Gittes's confrontation with detective Loach (David Keith) and, from a comic standpoint, his encounter with the murdered man's not-so-grieving widow, Lillian (Madeleine Stowe). Still, Nicholson the director (working from Robert Towne's script) provides too few moments of that stripe for Nicholson the star.

•

TWO-LANE BLACKTOP
1971, 102 mins, US ▭ col
Dir Monte Hellman ***Prod*** Michael S. Laughlin ***Scr*** Rudolph Wurlitzer, Will Corry ***Ph*** Jack Deerson ***Ed*** Monte Hellman ***Mus*** Bill James (sup.)
Act James Taylor, Warren Oates, Laurie Bird, Dennis Wilson, Harry Dean Stanton, Alan Vint (Universal/Laughlin)

The strange and sometimes pathetic world of barnstorming, hustling, street-racing is explored with feeling by director-editor Monte Hellman in *Two-Lane Blacktop*. The production, shot on cross-country locations, shapes up as an excellent combination of in-depth contemporary storytelling and personality casting.

Will Corry's story, scripted by Rudolph Wurlitzer and Corry, establishes James Taylor as a modern dropout, living on winnings from impromptu pavement racing challenges. Dennis Wilson is his expert mechanic. En route to nowhere in particular, they are latched on to by Laurie Bird. The strong and compelling plot fibre is supplied by the writing, direction and performing of Warren Oates's role. He's an older man, a failure in some Establishment profession, now roaming the country in a souped-up Detroit vehicle. When Oates challenges Taylor to a cross-country run, with vehicle ownership the payoff, the story becomes a superior interplay of basic human nature.

Much of the story's import is on Oates's back, and he carries it like a champion in an outstanding performance.

•

TWO LEFT FEET
1965, 93 mins, UK Ⓥ b/w
Dir Roy Ward Baker ***Prod*** Roy Ward Baker, Leslie Gilliat ***Scr*** Roy Baker, John Hopkins ***Ph*** Wilkie Cooper ***Ed*** Michael Hart ***Mus*** Phil Green
Act Michael Crawford, Nyree Dawn Porter, Julia Foster, Michael Craze, David Hemmings, Dilys Watling (British Lion)

Whatever attracted producers in David Stuart Leslie's novel must have been lost in the transition to the screen because this is a very flyweight trite pic. It explores in only the most superficial terms the dilemma of a gauche youth whose ham-handed attempts to cope with his early sex problems are not highly satisfactory.

A callow youth is infatuated with a teasing waitress but his attempt to seduce her ends in disaster. She turns to brighter young men at a jazz club and he finds consolation in a naive young shop assistant. Undertones of homosexuality between two of the youths are only hinted at and the sex lark is more talked about than acted upon. An attempt to satirize an appalling suburban wedding party becomes more of a caricature. Director Baker seems to have been unable to pull together a limp script.

Nyree Dawn Porter plays the waitress with exaggerated sex appeal. Michael Crawford handles the role of the gauche lad likeably. But much of the dialog is out of step with the minus-confidence character he is playing. Julia Foster, as the simple, goodhearted wench with whom he feels at ease, is pleasant, but unexciting.

•

TWO LOVES
(UK: SPINSTER)
1961, 100 mins, US ▭ col
Dir Charles Walters ***Prod*** Julian Blaustein ***Scr*** Ben Maddow ***Ph*** Joseph Ruttenberg ***Ed*** Fredric Steinkamp ***Mus*** Bronislau Kaper ***Art*** George W. Davis, Urie McCleary
Act Shirley MacLaine, Laurence Harvey, Jack Hawkins, Juano Hernandez, Norah Howard, Nobu McCarthy (M-G-M)

Frigidity is the subject broached by *Two Loves*, a story of the reawakening of a spinster American schoolteacher in New Zealand. Based on Sylvia Ashton-Warner's novel *Spinster*, it also takes a passing swipe at U.S. morality, examines the vigorous, spontaneous way-of-life of the Maori natives and utilizes the "civilized" point-of-view of western-white values as a frame of reference. Unfortunately, the personal story emerges less lucid than its broader overtones.

Shirley MacLaine plays a dedicated schoolteacher who has found her way to an isolated settlement in northern New Zealand from Pennsylvania, although how and why is never clearly established. Her dogged innocence is threatened by the amorous advances of Laurence Harvey, a rather irrational and immature fellow teacher unhappy with his lot but unable to rise above it. Influenced by the primitive but practical morality of the Maoris, she seems on the verge of giving her all to Harvey when he (rather conveniently) comes to a violent end in a motorcycle mishap. On the rebound, she is coaxed out of self-guilt pangs by senior school inspector Jack Hawkins.

MacLaine, although not ideally suited to the role, manages for the most part to rise above the miscasting and deliver an earnest, interesting portrayal. But there is a degree of gravity and warmth missing in her delineation, making it slightly difficult to understand Harvey's passion and Hawkins's tender affection for her. Nobu McCarthy comes through with flying colors as a 15-year-old Maori girl delighted to bear Harvey's children out of wedlock.

•

TWO-MINUTE WARNING
1976, 115 mins, US Ⓥ ⦿ ⌑ col
Dir Larry Peerce ***Prod*** Edward S. Feldman ***Scr*** Edward Hume ***Ph*** Gerald Hirschfeld ***Ed*** Eve Newman, Walter Hannemann ***Mus*** Charles Fox ***Art*** Herman A. Blumenthal
Act Charlton Heston, John Cassavetes, Martin Balsam, Beau Bridges, Marilyn Hassett, David Janssen (Universal)

An off-the-beaten-track story (based on the novel by George La Fountaine) of a football stadium crowd menaced by a sniper, combined with above-average plotting, acting and direction.

The sniper is introduced intriguingly via subjective camera, but later is seen (Warren Miller) in teasing long shots, blurred closed-circuit pans and other clever devices which keep him all the more menacing.

Among the prominent players, all of whom take seriously their roles, are stadium manager Martin Balsam and assistant Brock Peters; unmarried but longtime lovers David Janssen and Gena Rowlands (she can convey a reel of characterization in 10 seconds of film); and unemployed young father Beau Bridges, trying to show his and wife Pamela Bellwood's children a good time.

1976: NOMINATION: Best Editing

•

TWO MOON JUNCTION
1988, 104 mins, US Ⓥ ⦿ col
Dir Zalman King ***Prod*** Donald P. Borchers ***Scr*** Zalman King ***Ph*** Mark Plummer ***Ed*** Marc Grossman ***Mus*** Jonathan Elias ***Art*** Michelle Minch
Act Sherilyn Fenn, Richard Tyson, Louise Fletcher, Kristy McNichol, Martin Hewitt, Burl Ives (DDM/Lorimar)

Two Moon Junction is a bad hick version of *Last Tango in Paris* down to the poor imitative scoring by Jonathan Elias. Sexual obsession might be the aim, but the result is anything but hot.

In the Maria Schneider role is Madonna-clone Sherilyn Fenn who decides to give her virginity to a guy who works at the traveling midway (Richard Tyson) instead of her fiancé (Martin Hewitt). She wears white all the time and acts pure when on her home turf.

Plot has all the ingredients of a 1940s meller with the obvious exception that poor little rich girl Fenn unabashedly defrocks at the drop of a hat while Tyson manages to never bare much more than his chest.

Kristy McNichol appears as a midway groupie whose subtle bisexual scenes dancing with Fenn have more electricity than Fenn's encounters with Tyson.

Shot in and around Los Angeles pic seldom looks like Alabama.

•

TWO MRS CARROLLS, THE
1947, 100 mins, US Ⓥ b/w
Dir Peter Godfrey ***Prod*** Mark Hellinger ***Scr*** Thomas Job ***Ph*** Peverell Marley ***Ed*** Frederick Richards ***Mus*** Franz Waxman ***Art*** Anton Grot
Act Humphrey Bogart, Barbara Stanwyck, Alexis Smith, Nigel Bruce, Isobel Elsom (Warner)

The Two Mrs Carrolls, adapted from the Martin Vale legiter, is more stage play than motion picture. Overladen with dialog as action substitute, it talks itself out of much of the suspense that should have developed. There is some femme appeal, however, in the Humphrey Bogart character as hero-villain.

Production format hugs stage technique in settings and carrying out story. Backgrounds never seem realistic but rather appear as grouped on stage. Bogart, Barbara Stanwyck and Alexis Smith feel the burden of dialog and unnatural characters but, under Peter Godfrey's direction, manage to give material an occasional lift.

Plot deals with married artist who meets a new love while vacationing in Scotland. He returns to London, murders his wife by methodical poisoning and marries the new flame. Second marriage works okay until another attractive girl appears.

•

TWO MUCH
1995, 115 mins, Spain Ⓥ ⌑ col
Dir Fernando Trueba ***Prod*** Cristina Huete ***Scr*** Fernando Trueba, David Trueba ***Ph*** Jose Luis Alcaine ***Ed*** Nena Bernard ***Mus*** Michel Camilo ***Art*** Juan Botella
Act Melanie Griffith, Antonio Banderas, Daryl Hannah, Danny Aiello, Joan Cusack, Eli Wallach (Andres Vicente Gomez/Interscope/PFE)

Antonio Banderas amply proves himself as a romantic lead, injecting charm, energy and comedic skill into uneven material in *Two Much*, an English-language feature from Spanish helmer Fernando Trueba (*Belle Epoque*).

The film provides Banderas with perhaps the best mainstream showcase yet for his Latin-lover charisma, and the off-camera romance between Banderas and co-star Melanie Griffith earned the couple royalty status in the Spanish gossip press.

Banderas plays Art Dodge, a failed painter and now the brash owner of an unprofitable modern-art gallery in Miami. A scam fails to fool shady businessman Gene Paletto (Danny Aiello). Threatened by the man's thugs during Paletto senior's funeral, Art escapes by hiding in the convertible of Paletto's impulsive ex-wife, Betty (Griffith).

Closer acquaintance between the sheets follows, and Betty immediately hears wedding bells. Matters are complicated when Art meets and is attracted to Betty's more level-headed sis, Liz (Daryl Hannah). To assist in his courtship of Liz, Art invents a brother, Bart, who also proves handy in escaping Paletto and his henchmen.

Banderas reveals himself to be remarkably adept at physical comedy, giving the slapstick antics considerably more vigor than they might otherwise have mustered. One of the weak links is Griffith, whose character is established in only the flimsiest terms. Hannah's character has a little more edge; consequently, her scenes function better.

•

TWO MULES FOR SISTER SARA
1970, 116 mins, US Ⓥ ⌑ col
Dir Don Siegel ***Prod*** Martin Rackin, Carroll Case ***Scr*** Albert Maltz ***Ph*** Gabriel Figueroa ***Ed*** Robert F. Shugrue ***Mus*** Ennio Morricone ***Art*** Jose Rodriguez Granada
Act Shirley MacLaine, Clint Eastwood, Manolo Fabregas, Alberto Morin, Armando Silvestre, John Kelly (Universal/Malpaso)

Two Mules for Sister Sara might have worked. But with Clint Eastwood as one of the mules, an American mercenary looking for a fast peso in old French-occupied Mexico, Shirley MacLaine as a scarlet sister disguised in a nun's habit, and Don Siegel's by-the-old-book direction, it doesn't.

Screenplay based on a story by Budd Boetticher, needed a Lee Marvin, or a portrayal like Humphrey Bogart's in *The African Queen* to work. MacLaine is literally unbelievable as a nun, and the story's main thread of tension, the relationship between her and Eastwood, simply dissipates.

Siegel and Mexican cameraman Gabriel Figueroa use the Mexican locations to great advantage, with sweeping panoramics of the brutal countryside and intriguing settings.

•

TWO OF A KIND
1983, 87 mins, US Ⓥ ⦿ col
Dir John Herzfeld ***Prod*** Roger M. Rothstein, Joe Wizan ***Scr*** John Herzfeld ***Ph*** Fred Koenekamp ***Ed*** Jack Hofstra ***Mus*** Patrick Williams ***Art*** Albert Brenner
Act John Travolta, Olivia Newton-John, Charles Durning, Beatrice Straight, Scatman Crothers, Oliver Reed (20th Century-Fox)

Aside from the presence of the two stars, *Two of a Kind* has all the earmarks of a bargain-basement job. Sets are as constricted as those for live, three-camera sitcoms, and many of the so-called New York location scenes possess an obvious back-lot look.

Script's only vaguely amusing conceit presents itself at the beginning, when God returns from a vacation and, finding the world gone to seed in the interim, announces to four of his angels that he's going to wipe out the human race and start over again. The angels urge him to reconsider his decision based on whether or not a random man can prove himself possible of genuine goodness.

So John Travolta, a self-styled inventor of such inane items as edible sunglasses, is selected as the guinea pig, just in time to find him robbing a bank in order to pay off a debt to the mob. Bank teller Olivia Newton-John, fired for flirting with the stick-up man, actually makes off with the dough. She is saved by Travolta after being taken hostage by a gunman.

•

TWO PEOPLE
1973, 100 mins, US col
Dir Robert Wise ***Prod*** Robert Wise ***Scr*** Richard DeRoy ***Ph*** Henri Decae ***Ed*** William Reynolds ***Mus*** David Shire ***Art*** Henry Michelson
Act Peter Fonda, Lindsay Wagner, Estelle Parsons, Alan Fudge, Philippe March, Frances Sternhagen (Filmakers/Universal)

Two People is a major disappointment. Producer-director Robert Wise's film clearly aimed to develop a love-at-first-sight romance, in the form of a "road" film, between two characters whose different lifestyles parallel in brief encounter. However, sluggish pacing and ludicrous dialog turn the film into a travesty of its own form.

Script finds Peter Fonda, a repentant Vietnam field deserter, tired of running and ready to return to the U.S. to face his court martial and punishment. In Marrakech, Fonda meets Lindsay Wagner, a fashion model in the tow of her editor (Estelle Parsons) and her live-in lover (Geoffrey Horne), father of their child (Brian Lima) stashed in Manhattan with her mother, Frances Sternhagen.

The film's pacing turns the desired audience wish—that the couple make physical love—into barely concealed impatience.

•

TWO RODE TOGETHER
1961, 108 mins, US Ⓥ ⦿ col
Dir John Ford ***Prod*** Stan Shpetner ***Scr*** Frank Nugent ***Ph*** Charles Lawton, Jr. ***Ed*** Jack Murray ***Mus*** George Duning ***Art*** Robert Peterson
Act James Stewart, Richard Widmark, Shirley Jones, Linda Cristal, Andy Devine, John McIntire (Columbia)

John Ford's western is a story (from the novel by Will Cook) of the ill-advised attempt to haul white prisoners back to civilized society in the 1880s after they have spent a decade or more suffering the slings and arrows of Comanche Indian captivity. This is fairly fresh sagebrush fiction, invading and surveying a relatively untapped corner of American history. But somehow the production misfires in the process.

Whereas parts of the film zoom into the heavy, psychological sphere of the modern western, others revert to the outmoded innocence and directness of a 1930s sagebrush style, as if intended as parody. There are, however, compensations. Not the least is the unusually practical, non-heroic nature of the central character, most disarmingly and authoritatively enacted by James Stewart. He far and away cops histrionic honors.

•

TWO SISTERS FROM BOSTON
1946, 112 mins, US b/w
Dir Henry Koster ***Prod*** Joe Pasternak ***Scr*** Myles Connolly ***Ph*** Robert Surtees ***Ed*** Douglas Biggs ***Mus*** Sammy Fain, Ralph Freed ***Art*** Cedric Gibbons, Daniel B. Cathcart
Act Kathryn Grayson, June Allyson, Lauritz Melchior, Jimmy Durante, Peter Lawford (M-G-M)

Two Sisters from Boston is both an operatic and a low comedy treat, Kathryn Grayson and Lauritz Melchior carry the straight chirping, Jimmy Durante is at his peak with an equally legit role in that he's an integral character in the plot. June Allyson is the other sister from Hubtown, good running mate to her impetuous cinematic kin, Grayson. Latter tees off as "High C Susie," a hotsy chirper who's quite a click in a Bowery joint until her staid Back Bay family descends on N.Y. and with the somewhat outlandish assistance of Spike (Durante), the diamond-in-the-rough pianist-impressario of the Bowery bistro, does make the Met.

Starting in the Bowery atmosphere it segues into staid Boston. Thence the pyrotechnics to keep Grayson's shame from her family, until she makes good on her own in the Met. In between, Melchior indulges in temperamental outbursts. There's a close-up on the prehistoric method of His Master's Voice recording (old phonograph horn, etc), a great sequence; and also some good turn-of-the-century song hokum, viz, "There Are Two Sides to Every Girl" to carry the action along.

•

TWO STAGE SISTERS
SEE: WUTAI JIEMEI

•

2001: A SPACE ODYSSEY
1968, 139 mins, UK/US Ⓥ ⦿ ⌑ col
Dir Stanley Kubrick ***Prod*** Stanley Kubrick ***Scr*** Stanley Kubrick, Arthur C. Clarke ***Ph*** Geoffrey Unsworth, John Al-

cott *Ed* Ray Lovejoy *Art* Tony Masters, Harry Lange, Ernest Archer

Act Keir Dullea, Gary Lockwood, William Sylvester, Daniel Richter, Douglas Rain, Leonard Rossiter (M-G-M)

When Stanley Kubrick and sci-fi specialist Arthur C. Clarke first conceived the idea of making a Cinerama film, neither had any idea that it would run into a project of several years. Shooting actually began late December 1965 in England and continued, if one counts added footage and retakes, until early 1968. Actor Keir Dullea completed another film (*The Fox*) and did a Broadway play (*Dr. Cook's Garden*) between completion of his role in *2001* and its release [in April 1968].

A major achievement in cinematography and special effects, *2001* lacks dramatic appeal and only conveys suspense after the halfway mark; Kubrick must receive all the praise—and take all the blame.

The plot, so-called, uses up almost two hours in exposition of scientific advances in space travel and communications, before anything happens. The surprisingly dull prolog deals with the "advancement of man," centering on a group of apes. A huge black monolith is shown briefly (to reappear light years later as the key to possible life on planets other than Earth).

The little humor is provided by introducing well-known commercial names which are presumably still operational during the space age: the Orbiter Hilton hotel, refreshments by Howard Johnson, picture phones by Bell, and Pan Am space ships. A computer named HAL that can talk (voiced by Douglas Rain, although originally done by Martin Balsam) is one of the film's best effects and surprisingly acceptable.

Dullea and Gary Lockwood, as the two principal astronauts, are not introduced until well along. Their complete lack of emotion becomes rather implausible during scenes where they discover, and discuss, the villainy of the computer.

Kubrick and Clarke have kept dialog to a minimum, frequently inserting lengthy passages where everything is told visually. Scientific advances appear much further along than would seem possible for 2001. Incongruously, Earth citizens are shown [on monitors] dressed and acting 1968 while the scientists (even in their casual attire) wear stylized space-age garb.

Film ends on a confused note, never really tackling the "other life" situation and evidently leaving interpretation up to the viewer. The tremendous centrifuge which makes up the principal set (in which the two astronauts live and travel) reportedly cost $750,000 and looks every bit of it. Ray Lovejoy's editing, generally good, too often holds views to the point of losing interest while other scenes are chopped abruptly. The over-long 160-minute running time could have been shortened by some slicing in the lengthy introduction. [Pic was cut to 139 mins. by Kubrick after the premiere.]

2001 compares with, but does not best, previous efforts at science fiction, lacking the humanity of *Forbidden Planet*, the imagination of *Things to Come* and the simplicity of *Of Stars and Men*. It actually belongs to the technically slick group previously dominated by George Pal and the Japanese.

1968: Special Visual Effects

NOMINATIONS: Best Director, Original Story & Screenplay, Art Direction

•

2010

1984, 114 mins, US Ⓥ ⦿ ⊏⊐ col

Dir Peter Hyams *Prod* Peter Hyams *Scr* Peter Hyams *Ph* Peter Hyams *Ed* James Mitchell *Mus* David Shire *Art* Albert Brenner

Act Roy Scheider, John Lithgow, Helen Mirren, Bob Balaban, Keir Dullea, Douglas Rain (M-G-M)

As the title proclaims, *2010* begins nine years after something went wrong with the Jupiter voyage of Discovery. On Earth, politicians have brought the U.S. and Russia to the brink of war, but their scientists have united in a venture to return to Jupiter to seek an answer to Discovery's fate and the significance of the huge black monolith that orbits near it. American crew is headed by Roy Scheider, John Lithgow and Bob Balaban. The Soviets want them along mainly for their understanding of HAL 9000, whose mutiny remains unexplained. If revived in the salvage effort, can HAL still be trusted?

In Peter Hyams's hands [working from a novel by Arthur C. Clarke], the HAL mystery is the most satisfying substance of the film and handled the best. Unfortunately, it lies amid a hodgepodge of bits and pieces.

1984: NOMINATIONS: Best Costume Design, Art Direction, Sound, Visual Effects, Makeup

•

TWO WAY STRETCH

1960, 87 mins, UK Ⓥ b/w

Dir Robert Day *Prod* M. Smedley Aston *Scr* John Warren, Len Heath, Alan Hackney *Ph* Geoffrey Faithfull *Ed* Bert Rule *Mus* Ken Jones *Art* John

Act Peter Sellers, Wilfrid Hyde White, David Lodge, Bernard Cribbins, Maurice Denham, Lionel Jeffries (British Lion/Shepperton)

Peter Sellers gives another deft, very funny performance in *Two Way Stretch*. The thin story line concerns a free-and-easy prison run by a governor who is more interested in gardening than discipline. Occupying a cell, which is far more like a luxury bedsitting room, are three partners in crime—Sellers, David Lodge and Bernard Cribbins. They have the prison completely sewn up.

Posing as a clergyman, an outside partner arrives with a scheme for stealing $5 million in diamonds. It needs the trio to break jail the night before their release, pull off the job, return to prison with their loot, and next morning walk out free men and with a perfect alibi. The arrival of a tough new chief warden frustrates their plans.

Much of the dialog was supplied by Alan Hackney and, almost certainly, by Sellers himself. Success of this film depends largely on the actors and Robert Day's brisk direction. Sellers has himself a ball as the leader of the crafty trio of crooks while Lodge and Cribbins make perfectly contrasted partners. A long list of tried, handpicked performers chip in when required.

•

TWO WEEKS IN ANOTHER TOWN

1962, 106 mins, US Ⓥ ⦿ ⊏⊐ col

Dir Vincente Minnelli *Prod* John Houseman *Scr* Charles Schnee *Ph* Milton Krasner *Ed* Adrienne Fazan, Robert J. Kern, Jr. *Mus* David Raksin *Art* George W. Davis, Urie McCleary

Act Kirk Douglas, Edward G. Robinson, Cyd Charisse, George Hamilton, Daliah Lavi, Claire Trevor (M-G-M)

Two Weeks in Another Town [from the novel by Irwin Shaw] is not an achievement about which any of its creative people are apt to boast. Kirk Douglas stars as an unstable actor, fresh off a three-year hitch in sanitariums, who goes to Rome to rejoin the director (Edward G. Robinson) with whom, years earlier, he's scored his greatest triumphs. In the course of a series of shattering incidents, Douglas comes to discover that it is upon himself alone that he must rely for the stability and strength of character with which he can fulfill his destiny.

Douglas emotes with his customary zeal and passion, but labors largely in vain to illuminate an unbelievable character. Even less believable is the character of his ex-wife, a black-as-night, hard-as-nails seductress exotically overplayed by Cyd Charisse.

Only remotely lifelike characters in the story are Robinson and Claire Trevor as an ambiguous married couple whose personalities transform under the secretive cover of night.

There is a haunting score by David Raksin. A considerable amount of footage from *The Bad and the Beautiful* is cleverly incorporated into the drama. As a matter of fact, the portion of the film-within-a-film is livelier than just about anything else in the film.

•

TWO YEARS BEFORE THE MAST

1946, 96 mins, US b/w

Dir John Farrow *Prod* Seton I. Miller (assoc.) *Scr* Seton I. Miller, George Bruce *Ph* Ernest Laszlo *Ed* Eda Warren *Mus* Victor Young *Art* Hans Dreier, Franz Bachelin

Act Alan Ladd, Brian Donlevy, William Bendix, Barry Fitzgerald, Howard da Silva, Esther Fernandez (Paramount)

Chief credit for this one [based on Richard Henry Dana, Jr.'s novel] belongs to director John Farrow. With the emphasis on action throughout, Farrow keeps his cast thesping to the hilt and achieves several little bits of suspense.

Although Alan Ladd and the other stars top the cast, it's Howard da Silva, as the pitiless ship's captain, who walks off with the blue ribbon.

Rest of cast, from leads to minor bit parts perform excellently. Ladd does a nice job as the fop who finds his regeneration while fighting to get human treatment for the merchant seamen of that day. Bendix gives a restrained reading to his role as the tough but necessarily sympathetic first mate, and Barry Fitzgerald adds the comedy touches as the ship's cook.

•

TYSTNADEN
(THE SILENCE)

1963, 95 mins, Sweden Ⓥ ⦿ b/w

Dir Ingmar Bergman *Scr* Ingmar Bergman *Ph* Sven Nykvist *Ed* Ulla Ryghe *Art* P. A. Lundgren

Act Ingrid Thulin, Gunnel Lindblom, Jorgen Lindstrom, Hakan Jahnberg, Birger Malmsten, Eduardo Gutierrez (Svensk Filmindustri)

Unlike previous pictures in which he investigated the human mind and looking for God, Ingmar Bergman turns his attention in *The Silence* exclusively to the body and its passions.

The story is simple: Two lonely sisters—Ann and Ester—traveling home to Sweden, make a stay in the strange town of Timuku in a fictitious country. The town is full of soldiers, tanks, crowded cafe halls. The sisters, together with Ann's seven-year-old son, Johan, are installed in an old hotel with stuffy majestic rooms, deep beds and mile-long corridors.

The older, Ester (Ingrid Thulin), is a masculine type, intellectual with a lesbian fixation to Ann (Gunnel Lindblom), a seductive, sex-hungry animal. Instead of caring for her son, Ann is more interested in adventures in the town. Distressed by the antics of her amorous sister, Ester despairs and undertakes to forget her love in alcohol and degredation.

There is not much dialog, almost no music, but the sex scenes have vigor and primitive power, to say the least. Technical credits are all excellent, with a special mention of the camerawork and the birth of a new star, Lindblom. She has the fury of an Anna Magnani and the beauty of a Sophia Loren; for the first time she has a big role in a Bergman picture.

U-BOAT 29
SEE: THE SPY IN BLACK

•

U-571
2000, 116 mins, US Ⓥ ⊙ ▭ col
Dir Jonathan Mostow ***Prod*** Dino De Laurentiis, Martha De Laurentiis ***Scr*** Jonathan Mostow, Sam Montgomery, David Ayer ***Ph*** Oliver Wood ***Ed*** Wayne Wahrman ***Mus*** Richard Marvin ***Art*** Wm. Ladd Skinner, Gotz Weidner
Act Matthew McConaughey, Bill Paxton, Harvey Keitel, Jon Bon Jovi, Jake Weber, David Keith (De Laurentiis/Universal)

The submarine goes deep but the story never does in *U-571*, a good, old-fashioned World War II picture that is exciting in only the most superficial way. A fictionalized account of the Allied (but, historically speaking, mostly British) effort to break the Nazis' Enigma code by capturing an enemy submarine with one of the coding machines on board, the film's story unfolds in an exceedingly mechanical way, as if written in strict adherence to nuts-and-bolts principles taught in a screenwriting course. The picture gets the job done where it counts for the modern public, in terms of the instant gratification provided by the special effects, technical verisimilitude, multiple climaxes and even politically correct elements. But it has no emotional or moral weight at all, leaving it leagues behind the classic it clearly means to emulate and, in some instances, explicitly imitates, Wolfgang Petersen's *Das Boot*.

This is one of those movies, very much of the old school, in which the bad guys' aim is always off but the good guys invariably hit the target, however difficult, with a single shot. The Americans seem to survive more close calls than Indiana Jones did in all of his adventures rolled together in what's meant to be a basically realistic picture.

•

UGETSU
SEE: UGETSU MONOGATARI

•

UGETSU MONOGATARI
(UGETSU; TALES AFTER THE RAIN)
1953, 96 mins, Japan Ⓥ b/w
Dir Kenji Mizoguchi ***Prod*** Masaichi Nagata ***Scr*** Matsutaro Kawaguchi, Yoshikata Yoda ***Ph*** Kazuo Miyagawa ***Mus*** Fumio Hayasaka ***Art*** Kisaku Itoh
Act Machiko Kyo, Masayuki Mori, Kinuyo Tanaka, Sakae Ozawa, Mitsuko Mito (Daiei)

Tale of two men in seething 16th-century Japan has a color and panorama which makes this absorbing film fare. The trials of the two men, one a potter (Masayuki Mori) who gets involved with a phantom princess (Machiko Kyo) and the other a merchant (Sakae Ozawa) who yearns to be a Samurai warrior, is unfolded on the teeming tile of the clan wars.

One man finally breaks the hold of the phantom princess, who has created a romantic paradise for him, when his longing for his wife and child gets too strong. The other gives up his military armor and glory when he finds his wife (Mitsuko Mito) has been reduced to a prostitute during his absence.

Lensing is rich in tone and resembles old Japanese prints in composition. Direction of Kenji Mizoguchi keeps the complicated proceedings coherent. Editing is fine. Acting is good right down the line. Mori, as the bedeviled potter, and Kyo, as the princess, are excellent. Production value of period settings, mob scenes and eye-catching architecture and costuming are other top assets.

•

UGLY AMERICAN, THE
1963, 120 mins, US Ⓥ col
Dir George Englund ***Prod*** George Englund ***Scr*** Stewart Stern ***Ph*** Clifford Stine ***Ed*** Ted J. Kent ***Mus*** Frank Skinner ***Art*** Alexander Golitzen, Alfred Sweeney
Act Marlon Brando, Eiji Okada, Sandra Church, Arthur Hill, Pat Hingle, Jocelyn Brando (Universal)

Some of the ambiguities, hypocrisies and perplexities of Cold War politics are observed, dramatized and, to a degree, analyzed in *The Ugly American*. It is a thought-provoking but uneven screen translation taken from, but not in a literal sense based upon, the popular novel by William J. Lederer and Eugene Burdick.

Focal figure of the story is an American ambassador (Marlon Brando) to a Southeast Asian nation who, after jumping to conclusions in the course of dealing with an uprising of the natives of that country against the existing regime and what they interpret as Yankee imperialism comes to understand that there is more to modern political revolution than meets the casual or jaundiced bystander's

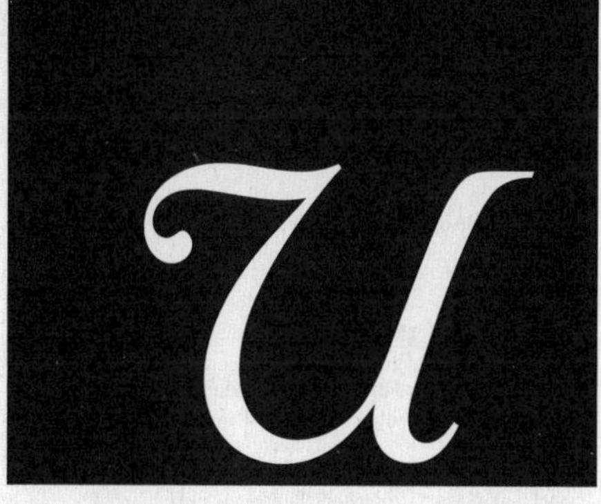

eye. As a result of his experience, he senses that Americans "can't hope to win the Cold War unless we remember what we're for as well as what we're against."

Although skillfully and often explosively directed by George Englund and well played by Brando and others in the cast, the film tends to be overly talkative and lethargic in certain areas, vague and confusing in others. Probably the most jarring single flaw is the failure to clarify the exact nature of events during the ultimate upheaval.

Brando's performance is a towering one; restrained, intelligent and always masculine. Japanese actor Eiji Okada of *Hiroshima, mon amour* renown, makes a strong impression.

Mass riot scene near the outset of the picture is frighteningly realistic. Art direction is outstanding, with a convincing replica of a Southeast Asian village on the Universal backlot.

•

UGLY DACHSHUND, THE
1965, 93 mins, US Ⓥ col
Dir Norman Tokar ***Prod*** Walt Disney, Winston Hibley ***Scr*** Albert Aley ***Ph*** Edward Colman ***Ed*** Robert Stafford ***Mus*** George Bruns ***Art*** Carroll Clark, Marvin Aubrey Davis
Act Dean Jones, Suzanne Pleshette, Charles Ruggles, Kelly Thordsen, Farley Baer, Robert Kino (Walt Disney)

Walt Disney, who knows his way with a dog as well as a family, has turned out a rollicking piece of business in this comedy about a Great Dane which thinks he's a dachshund.

Dean Jones and Suzanne Pleshette are the two principals, a young married couple faced with the fancy cut-ups of four Dachs and a Dane raised with the low-slung pups. The Fritzels are hers, the Dane his, and actually the Albert Aley screenplay builds to trying to sell the Dane—named Brutus—that he actually is a Dane.

Action is light and airy as the couple go their own way with their respective pets, Suzanne insisting that Dean rid himself of the clumsy big-foot while her spouse stoutly maintains that his Dane has a rightful place in the household.

•

ULEE'S GOLD
1997, 111 mins, US Ⓥ ⊙ col
Dir Victor Nunez ***Prod*** Victor Nunez ***Scr*** Victor Nunez ***Ph*** Virgil Marcus Mirano ***Ed*** [uncredited] ***Mus*** Charles Engstrom ***Art*** Robert (Pat) Garner
Act Peter Fonda, Patricia Richardson, Jessica Biel, J. Kenneth Campbell, Christine Dunford, Steven Flynn (Clinica Estetico)

A gem of rare emotional depth and integrity, *Ulee's Gold* is the cinematic equivalent of a wonderful old backwater town, a community bypassed by the interstate of the mainstream American film industry that possesses virtues and knowledge that travelers in the fast lane never stop to appreciate. Graced by a performance from Peter Fonda that is the best of his career, pic is a richly realized drama about a man reawakening to his family responsibilities.

Ulysses (Ulee) Jackson (Fonda) is a middle-aged Vietnam War vet living modestly in a rural area of the Florida panhandle. Devastated by the death of his wife six years before and the long-term imprisonment of his son, Jimmy (Tom Wood), Ulee has put most of his attention into his work as a beekeeper, hard and solitary labor, making him a distinctly endangered species.

But since his daughter-in-law, Helen (Christine Dunford), has disappeared, Ulee is obliged to look after his two granddaughters, teenage Casey (Jessica Biel) and the younger Penny (Vanessa Zima). Their quiet, mundane lives suddenly change, however, when Jimmy asks his father to go fetch Helen and he is confronted with two low-rent criminals (Steven Flynn, Dewey Weber) who demand, at gunpoint, that Ulee produce the $100,000 Jimmy has hidden from them.

Writer-director Victor Nunez (*Ruby in Paradise*) achieves a rare emotional depth that rewards the moderate demands he makes on contemporary viewers' short attention spans. His focus on the essentials among life's priorities—family, work and honorable values—is ennobling without being sticky or sanctimonious. Fonda responds splendidly, with work that is reserved yet revealing; it is impossible not to compare the actor here to his father.

1997: NOMINATION: Best Actor (Peter Fonda)

•

ULTIMATE SOLUTION OF GRACE QUIGLEY, THE
(AKA: GRACE QUIGLEY)
1984, 102 mins, US Ⓥ col
Dir Anthony Harvey ***Prod*** Menahem Golan, Yoram Globus ***Scr*** A. Martin Zweiback ***Ph*** Larry Pizer ***Ed*** Bob Raetano ***Mus*** John Addison
Act Katharine Hepburn, Nick Nolte, Elizabeth Wilson, Chip Zien, Kit Le Fever, William Duell (Cannon/Northbrook)

In this black comedy dealing with voluntary euthanasia by the Geritol set, casting Katharine Hepburn as the spry, entrepreneurial mother figure who arranges for her peers' demise and Nick Nolte as the gruff, hard-bitten and sarcastic hitman she hires, the two actors impart a lighthearted and whimsical tone to otherwise unpleasant subject matter.

Pic opens with Hepburn as a lonely and economically strapped pensioner who lost her immediate family in a prewar auto accident, but who has a zestful embrace for life nonetheless. Sitting across from her apartment one day, she inadvertently witnesses Nolte put a bullet into her money-grubbing landlord, and subsequently enlists him in her scheme to provide a "service" for her aging compatriots who wish to meet the hereafter ahead of schedule.

There are some marvelous supporting performances by Elizabeth Wilson as the spinster who can't get arrested trying to get Nolte to put her out of her misery, William Duell as the nerdy neighbor of Hepburn, and Kit Le Fever as Nolte's girlfriend hooker.

•

ULYSSES
1954, 104 mins, Italy Ⓥ col
Dir Mario Camerini ***Prod*** Carlo Ponti, Dino De Laurentiis ***Scr*** Mario Camerini, Franco Brusati, Ben Hecht, Irwin Shaw, Hugh Gray, Ennio De Concini ***Ph*** Harold Rosson ***Ed*** Leo Catozzo ***Mus*** Alessandro Cicognini ***Art*** Flavio Mogherini
Act Kirk Douglas, Silvana Mangano, Anthony Quinn, Rossana Podesta, Jaques Dumesnil (Lux/Ponti-De Laurentiis)

A lot, perhaps too much, money went into the making of *Ulysses*, but expense shows. Besides the epic Homeric peg, pic has an internationally balanced cast, with Yank, French and Italian elements predominant.

Only a few of the w.k. Homeric episodes have been included in the already lengthy pic, and are told in flashback form as remembered by the hero. Featured are his love for Nausicaa; the cave of Polyphemus, the one-eyed monster; the Siren Rocks; the visit to Circe's Island cave and the return to Penelope. But material covered makes for plenty of action, dominated by a virile performance by Kirk Douglas.

Others include costar Silvana Mangano, a looker, as both Circe and Penelope, but unfortunately limited by both parts to expressing monotonous unhappiness until the finale. Anthony Quinn handles his bits well. For a spectacle, the pic runs too many closeups, with longish stretches of dialog between the two principals, or soliloquized.

•

ULYSSES
1967, 140 mins, Ireland Ⓥ ⊙ ▭ b/w
Dir Joseph Strick ***Prod*** Joseph Strick ***Scr*** Joseph Strick, Fred Haines ***Ph*** Wolfgang Suschitzky ***Ed*** Reginald Mills ***Mus*** Stanley Myers ***Art*** Graham Probst
Act Barbara Jefford, Milo O'Shea, Maurice Roeves, T. P. McKenna, Martin Dempsey, Sheila O'Sullivan (Continental/Walter Reade)

Ulysses [from James Joyce's novel] is a healthy, promising cinematic piece of flora, nightblooming and carnivorous. Filmed entirely in Ireland, with a cast almost entirely Irish, the picture concentrates on the trio of primary characters—Leopold and Molly Bloom and student Stephen Dedalus. Although their tales overlap, the primary emphasis is on the two males leaving the last 20 or 30 minutes to Molly's famous libidinous soliloquy.

Barbara Jefford's Molly is handsomely overblown, a wasted garden of a woman who yearns for a man with a passion that almost causes the screen to pulsate yet depriving Leopold of his marital rights because she so abhors another possibility of pregnancy. Milo O'Shea's Leopold Bloom is a realized example of the degraded, dejected husband—his dignity rapidly fading, but still capable of dreaming of lost sexual prowess. Maurice Roeves's Stephen Dedalus might have been more impressive had some of the many flashbacks been used to better fill in his past—viewers are only told that he comes from an unhappy home, with a failure of a father.

1967: NOMINATION: Best Adapted Screenplay

•

ULZANA'S RAID
1972, 103 mins, US Ⓥ ⊙ col
Dir Robert Aldrich ***Prod*** Carter De Haven ***Scr*** Alan Sharp ***Ph*** Joseph Biroc ***Ed*** Michael Luciano ***Mus*** Frank DeVol ***Art*** James D. Vance
Act Burt Lancaster, Bruce Davison, Jorge Luke, Richard Jaeckel, Joaquin Martinez, Lloyd Bochner (Universal)

Ulzana's Raid is the sort of pretentious U.S. Army-vs-Indians period potboiler that invites derision from its own dialog and situations. However, suffice it to say that the production is merely ponderous in its formula action-sociology-violence, routine in its acting and direction, and often confusing in its hokey storytelling.

Screenplay finds a weathered old frontier scout (Burt Lancaster) saddled with a super-naive greenhorn young army officer-who-matures-under-pressure, etc. (Bruce Davison) as the patrol attempts to round up some marauding Apaches.

Whatever the film's aspirations, the effect is simply another exploitation western which crassly exploits the potentials in physical abuse, and in which plot suspense is not what is going to happen, but how bestial it can be.

•

UMBERTO D.
1952, 82 mins, Italy Ⓥ ⊙ b/w
Dir Vittorio De Sica ***Scr*** Vittorio De Sica, Cesare Zavattini ***Ph*** G. R. Aldo ***Ed*** Eraldo Da Roma ***Mus*** Alessandro Cicognini
Act Carlo Battisti, Maria Pia Casilio, Lina Gennari (Dear)

In telling a simple tale of a poor pensioner's search for friendship and a means of sustenance, both director Vittorio De Sica and writer Cesare Zavattini have ample opportunity to embroider with sharp and poignant bits of life as it can be, of humanity, or the lack thereof.

Umberto D., played by Carlo Battisti (in real life a university professor), has only two friends in the world: the maid in the apartment in which he boards, and his dog. It is the dog, and the problem of its disposal, variously attempted, which finally persuade him to give up his tragic idea of committing suicide. The ending is happy, but the general effect of the film is disturbing, so compelling is De Sica's description of a man's solitude.

Film is at its warmest in scenes showing the pensioner's attempts to beg against his will, or in such vivid observations of life as the morning awakening in the apartment, the maid's kitchen routine, the noises and sights associated with his apartment life. The performances, especially that of the maid, Maria Pia Casilio, are real and compelling.

•

UMBRELLAS OF CHERBOURG, THE
SEE: LES PARAPLUIES DE CHERBOURG

•

UNBEARABLE LIGHTNESS OF BEING, THE
1988, 171 mins, US Ⓥ ⊙ col
Dir Philip Kaufman ***Prod*** Saul Zaentz ***Scr*** Jean-Claude Carriere, Philip Kaufman ***Ph*** Sven Nykvist ***Ed*** Walter Murch, B. J. Sears, Vivien Hillgrove Gilliam, Stephen A. Rotter ***Mus*** Mark Adler ***Art*** Pierre Guffroy
Act Daniel Day-Lewis, Juliette Binoche, Lena Olin, Derek de Lint, Erland Josephson, Donald Moffat (Zaentz)

Milan Kundera's 1984 international bestseller of love and erotica set against the Russian invasion of Czechoslovakia has been regarded as essentially unfilmable by many observers, so Philip Kaufman has pulled off a near-miracle in creating this richly satisfying adaptation.

Tomas, a top surgeon and compulsive ladies' man in Prague, takes in and eventually marries a lovely country girl, Tereza. He continues his womanizing, however, particularly with his voluptuous mistress, Sabina, an artist who takes off for Geneva as soon as Russian tanks put a halt to the Prague Spring of 1968.

The sexuality which drenches the entire film possesses a great buoyancy and spirit in the first act, set during the exciting liberalization of communism under Alexander Dubcek. Second act, in Geneva, is comparatively somber and spare, but is punctuated by Sabina's new affair with a married man and by the growing friendship between Sabina and Tereza.

As played by Juliette Binoche and Lena Olin, the two women are absolutely enchanting; Binoche is adorably doll-like while Olin is simply striking as a woman who lives her sexual and artistic lives just as she pleases.

Attractive in some ways, Tomas is irritatingly uncommunicative and opaque at others, and Daniel Day-Lewis at times overdoes the self-consciously smug projection of his own appeal.

1988: NOMINATIONS: Best Adapted Screenplay, Cinematography

•

UNBELIEVABLE TRUTH, THE
1989, 98 mins, US Ⓥ col
Dir Hal Hartley ***Prod*** Bruce Weiss, Hal Hartley ***Scr*** Hal Hartley ***Ph*** Michael Spiller ***Ed*** Hal Hartley ***Mus*** Jim Coleman ***Art*** Carla Gerona
Act Adrienne Shelly, Robert Burke, Christopher Cooke, Julia McNeal, Gary Sauer, Mark Bailey (Action)

The Unbelievable Truth is a promising, reasonably engaging first feature of the art school film variety. Very consciously designed and stylized in all departments, pic has a minor-key feel to it.

Narrative has Josh, a good-looking, taciturn guy, showing up in his small New York hometown after a spell in the slammer. Josh manages to land a job in a garage owned by Vic, whose daughter Audry is a 17-year-old sexpot due to enter Harvard at summer's end.

Audry drops her longtime boyfriend, moans about the impending end of the world, resists going to college, then shocks everyone by going materialistic and hitting it big as a model in Manhattan, where she shacks up with a photographer she detests. She also makes passes at Josh, and the eventual sexual suspicions and permutations nearly take on the dimensions of a French farce.

All this is told by way of an acting style that could be described as heightened naturalism, the broadness of which constantly provokes a tickling humor while simultaneously emphasizing the banality of what is being said.

Framing the middle-class melodrama is director Hal Hartley's manipulative artistry, which uses such devices as orchestrated color schemes, highly unrealistic sound, Godardian intertitles, repeated motifs and careful scoring.

•

UNBREAKABLE
2000, 107 mins, US Ⓥ ⊙ ▭ col
Dir M. Night Shyamalan ***Prod*** M. Night Shyamalan, Barry Mendel, Sam Mercer ***Scr*** M. Night Shyamalan ***Ph*** Eduardo Serra ***Ed*** Dylan Tichenor ***Mus*** James Newton Howard ***Art*** Larry Fulton
Act Bruce Willis, Samuel L. Jackson, Robin Wright Penn, Charlayne Woodard, Spencer Treat Clark, Eamonn Walker (Blinding Edge-Mendel/Touchstone)

M. Night Shyamalan, singular writer-director of *The Sixth Sense*, delivers much of the same: same star, same preoccupation with telepathic and quasi-supernatural/religious powers, same hushed tone and deliberate pace, same sense of absolute control. But there are also serious differences: a weaker story, increased pretentiousness, some ill-advised narrative zigzags and a "surprise" ending that can't begin to compare with the one in his previous picture.

David Dun (Bruce Willis) is sitting on a train. When an attractive young woman, Kelly (Leslie Stefanson), sits down next to him, he quietly chats her up, only to see her get up and move when he pushes too far. He stares outside at the onrushing scenery until it becomes apparent that the train is moving too fast, at which point a cut to David's son (Spencer Treat Clark) flipping TV channels reveals the news of a terrible derailment. Sequence establishes a sense of total confidence that one is in the hands of a master storyteller.

David turns out to be the sole survivor of the wreck. Now a minor local celebrity, he agrees with his wife Audrey (Robin Wright Penn) to use his good fortune to give their dried-up relationship a new lease of life, but otherwise returns to his normal routine as a security guard.

Elijah Price (Samuel L. Jackson) is preoccupied with strength and heroism due to his own lifelong debility. David, he suspects, could be the man he's long been searching for—invulnerable, impervious to disease, an individual who "could protect us." David, Elijah rightly suspects, has a sixth sense, as it were, for sniffing out evil. Superhero angle, which seems a bit odd when introduced, eventually feels all wrong, especially when invested with supernatural and spiritual dimensions that seem like holdovers from *The Sixth Sense*.

The presence of pop culture refs via comics makes quite notable the absence of any humor of sense of fun, just as it makes it pretentions to deep meaning and self-importance all the more specious. All the same, Shyamalan's handling of individual sequences is often extremely impressive. In subdued, subtle form, Willis gently conveys the essence of a working-class man victimized mostly by his own refusal to realize his true potential.

•

UNCENSORED
1944, 82 mins, UK Ⓥ b/w
Dir Anthony Asquith ***Prod*** Edward Black ***Scr*** Rodney Ackland, Terence Rattigan ***Ph*** Arthur Crabtree ***Ed*** R. E. Dearing ***Mus*** Hanns May ***Art*** Alex Vetchinsky
Act Eric Portman, Phyllis Calvert, Griffith Jones, Irene Handl, Peter Glenville, Walter Hudd (Gainsborough)

Efforts of the Belgian underground to thwart the Nazi grip form the basis for this thrilling melodrama, which often reaches the melodramatic heights of *39 Steps*. Picture contains about an hour of suspenseful action.

Director Anthony Asquith has done much to develop the yarn. Whole action centers about the efforts of Belgium's patriots to maintain regular publication of an underground paper as a constant thorn to the Nazi occupational troops. Scripters have taken Wolfgang Wilhelm's story and framed it around the apparently unpatriotic Eric Portman, who quietly continues his underground operations while entertaining nightly at a cabaret for Nazi toppers. Walter Hudd is the editor of paper while at the same time turning out material for the Nazi publication, at a fee. Portman, slightly reminiscent of Cary Grant, contributes a standout performance. Phyllis Calvert, as the wistful, but faithful Belgian worker, provides several romantic interludes with Portman.

•

UNCERTAIN GLORY
1944, 102 mins, US Ⓥ b/w
Dir Raoul Walsh ***Prod*** Robert Buckner ***Scr*** Laszlo Vadnay, Max Brand ***Ph*** Sid Hickox ***Ed*** George Amy ***Mus*** Adolph Deutsch ***Art*** Robert M. Haas
Act Errol Flynn, Paul Lukas, Jean Sullivan, Lucile Watson, Faye Emerson, Douglass Dumbrille (Warner)

France under the Nazis is again being portrayed in *Uncertain Glory*, a psychological, melodramatic study that is lengthy and frequently tedious.

Glory is more a yarn of two people than any group of people, it is scattered in its development of both narrative and characters; it is slow-paced and possessive of little action. Lack of action, perhaps, might be excusable in melodrama—providing that there is the omniscient thought of impending action. Story is involved, dealing with a Surete inspector and the object of his longtime chase (Errol Flynn).

The film's opening finds Flynn being led to the guillotine for murder. A British flying squadron bombs the prison, upsetting the execution and leading to Flynn's escape. Then follows once again the chase by Paul Lukas, the capture and the subsequent plan by Flynn, at first for escape reasons, to give himself up as a saboteur so that 100 French hostages could go free. The idea is that thus he would be doing the only redeeming thing in his life.

•

UNCLE, THE
1966, 87 mins, UK b/w
Dir Desmond Davis ***Prod*** Leonard Davis, Robert Goldston ***Scr*** Desmond Davis, Margaret Abrams ***Ph*** Manny Wynn ***Ed*** Brian Smedley-Aston
Act Rupert Davies, Brenda Bruce, Robert Duncan, William Marlowe, Ann Lynn, Maurice Denham (British Lion/Lenart)

A dispute ensued after completion of this excellent British film [based on the book by Margaret Abrams] between director Desmond Davis and producer Leonard Davis (no relation), because of editing and other changes made by the producer without the "permission" of the director. The producer's version indicates that the changes were not sufficient to damage the film.

The director creates a cinematic essay on the life of a seven-year-old who finds himself in a catastrophic situation. Totally unprepared for the position, he finds being an uncle of a nephew the same age presents many difficulties. The entire film is done from the attitude of the pint-sized hero.

Most of *The Uncle* deals with the "loss of innocence" of a small boy, Gus (Robert Duncan), over one summer.

Although the firm control of director Davis is evident throughout, he has been fortunate in having a cast that is entirely excellent, particularly young Robert Duncan as Gus (only a British child could look so profound at seven) and Rupert Davies and Brenda Bruce as his parents.

•

UNCLE BUCK
1989, 100 mins, US Ⓥ ⊙ col
Dir John Hughes ***Prod*** John Hughes, Tom Jacobson ***Scr*** John Hughes ***Ph*** Ralf D. Bode ***Ed*** Lou Lombardo, Tony Lombardo, Peck Prior ***Mus*** Ira Newborn, Matt Dike, Michael Ross ***Art*** John W. Corso

Act John Candy, Amy Madigan, Jean Louisa Kelly, Gaby Hoffman, Macaulay Culkin, Elaine Bromka (Universal)

John Hughes unsuccessfully tries to mix a serious generation gap message between the belly laughs in *Uncle Buck*, a warm-weather John Candy vehicle.

On paper the rotund Second City veteran seems ideal for the title role: a ne'er-do-well, coarse black sheep of the family suddenly pressed into service when his relatives (Elaine Bromka, Garrett M. Brown), a suburban Chicago family, have to rush off to visit Bromka's dad, stricken with a heart attack.

Enter Uncle Buck, put in charge of the three youngsters for an indefinite period. The kids wear down Buck's rough edges and he teaches them some seat-of-the-pants lessons about life.

Unfortunately, Candy is too likable to give the role any edge. When called upon to be tough or mean he's unconvincing, as in the slapstick dealings with the precociously oversexed boyfriend, Bug (Jay Underwood), of eldest daughter, Jean Louisa Kelly.

Kelly's performance is technically okay but the character is so unsympathetic and Hughes's dialog so cruel that the picture stops dead for each of her big scenes. There's a thankless role for Amy Madigan, miscast as Candy's long suffering g.f. Young kids Gaby Hoffman and Macaulay Culkin are supportive, particularly Culkin in *Dragnet*-voices routine with the star.

•

UNCOMMON VALOR
1983, 105 mins, US Ⓥ ⊙ col
Dir Ted Kotcheff ***Prod*** John Milius, Buzz Feitshans ***Scr*** Joe Gayton ***Ph*** Stephen H. Burum ***Ed*** Thom Noble, Mark Melnick ***Mus*** James Horner ***Art*** James L. Schoppe
Act Gene Hackman, Robert Stack, Fred Ward, Reb Brown, Randall "Tex" Cobb, Patrick Swayze (Paramount)

All of the top talent involved—especially Gene Hackman—is hardly needed to make *Uncommon Valor* what it is, a very common action picture. Hackman does as much as he can as a grieving father obsessed with the idea that his son remains a prisoner 10 years after he was reported missing-in-action in Vietnam. Financed by oil tycoon Robert Stack, whose son is also missing, Hackman puts together his small invasion force and two-thirds of *Valor* is consumed introducing the characters and putting them through various practice drills for the rescue which will predictably be tougher than they planned on.

True to a long tradition of war films, by the time the tough really get going it's only a question of who won't come back from the dangerous mission. But at least each of the main characters in *Valor* does his best to make you care whether it's him.

•

UNCONQUERED
1947, 135 mins, US col
Dir Cecil B. DeMille ***Prod*** Cecil B. DeMille ***Scr*** Charles Bennett, Fredric M. Frank, Jesse Lasky, Jr. ***Ph*** Ray Rennahan ***Ed*** Anne Bauchens ***Mus*** Victor Young ***Art*** Hans Dreier, Walter Tyler
Act Gary Cooper, Paulette Goddard, Howard da Silva, Boris Karloff, Ward Bond, Cecil Kellaway (Paramount)

Cecil B. DeMille's *Unconquered* is a $4 million Technicolor spectacle; it's a pre-Revolutionary western with plenty of Injun stuff which, for all the vacuousness and shortcomings, has its gripping moments.

The redskins are ruthless scalpers and the British colonials alternatively naive and brave, patriotic and full of skullduggery to give substance to the melodramatic heroics and knavery of the most derring-do school.

Howard da Silva is the arch-knave whose marriage to Injun chief Boris Karloff's daughter (Katherine DeMille) puts him plenty in the black with the redskins on fur-trading and the like. Paulette Goddard is the proud slave-girl whose freedom Gary Cooper purchases on the British slaveship, only to cross paths with the heavy (da Silva) and his No. 2 menace (Mike Mazurki).

It's not generally known that in that 1763 period English convicts had the alternative of being sold into limited slavery in the American colonies. Although a bond slave, Goddard spurns da Silva and sufficiently attracts Cooper to make for a romantic angle.

Despite the ten-twenty-thirty melodramatics and the frequently inept script [based on Neil H. Swanson's novel], the performances are convincing, a great tribute to the cast because that dialog and those situations try the best of troupers.

1947: NOMINATION: Best Special Effects

•

UNDEFEATED, THE
1969, 118 mins, US Ⓥ ⊙ ▭ col
Dir Andrew V. McLaglen ***Prod*** Robert L. Jacks ***Scr*** James Lee Barrett ***Ph*** William Clothier ***Ed*** Robert Simpson ***Mus*** Hugo Montenegro ***Art*** Carl Anderson
Act John Wayne, Rock Hudson, Tony Aguilar, Roman Gabriel, Marian McCargo, Lee Meriwether (20th Century-Fox)

John Wayne plays Old-Tall-in-the-Saddle in a film based on a story by Stanley L. Hough. Film has a basic storyline, character elements and dialog for what might have been a superior drama and possibly a great western. But Andrew McLaglen's direction, seems to consist of splicing together clichés, static camera work and Central Casting of the bit parts.

Wayne is the leader of the ragtail remnants of a troop of Union cavalry who make a bloody charge against a thin line of Confederate soldiers, only to find after the massacre that the war has been over for three days.

Basically wrong is the whole uneven mood of the film. Neither Wayne nor Hudson seems to know whether they are in a light comedy or a serious drama. They are, to use the word in an exact sense, simply unbelievable.

•

UNDER CAPRICORN
1949, 116 mins, UK Ⓥ ⊙ col
Dir Alfred Hitchcock ***Prod*** Alfred Hitchcock, Sidney Bernstein ***Scr*** James Bridie ***Ph*** Jack Cardiff, Paul Beeson ***Ed*** A. S. Bates ***Mus*** Richard Addinsell
Act Ingrid Bergman, Joseph Cotten, Michael Wilding, Margaret Leighton, Cecil Parker (Transatlantic)

Under Capricorn is overlong and talky, with scant measure of the Alfred Hitchcock thriller tricks.

Time of the plot is 1831, in Sydney, NSW, during that period when a convict, after serving his time, could start life anew with a clean slate. Such a man is Joseph Cotten, former groom and now Ingrid Bergman's husband. Cotten has become a man of wealth, but is not accepted socially.

That fact, along with his past crime—the killing of his wife's brother, a deed committed by Bergman but for which he took the blame—are the motives stressed as causing the wife's addiction to the bottle.

•

UNDERCOVER BLUES
1993, 89 mins, US Ⓥ ⊙ col
Dir Herbert Ross ***Prod*** Mike Lobell ***Scr*** Ian Abrams ***Ph*** Donald E. Thorin ***Ed*** Priscilla Nedd-Friendly ***Mus*** David Newman ***Art*** Ken Adam
Act Kathleen Turner, Dennis Quaid, Fiona Shaw, Stanley Tucci, Larry Miller, Tom Arnold (M-G-M)

The moderately enjoyable *Undercover Blues* plays like a big-screen, big-budget pilot for a TV series.

Former spies Jane and Jeff Blue (Kathleen Turner, Dennis Quaid) are relaxing in New Orleans with their 11-month-old baby when they're lured back into the espionage business to help foil an international terrorist ring led by Novacek (Fiona Shaw), who's a cross between Cruella de Vil and Lotte Lenya in *From Russia with Love*.

The film spends about four of its 89 minutes on plot, with the rest devoted to comic scenes of Quaid and Turner playing kissy-face and cooing over their baby, fending off attackers, sidestepping the New Orleans police and brushing aside the assaults of persistent street mugger Muerte (Stanley Tucci, who garners the lion's share of laughs).

Script by first-timer Ian Abrams doesn't cover any new ground, but aims at one of the most difficult targets—lighthearted fun—and hits it. Story occasionally wanders off on tangents, like Quaid foiling a bank robbery, but has some good scenes, such as Turner and Quaid interrogating Saul Rubinek, and Tucci in the alligator pit at the zoo.

•

UNDERCOVER GIRL
1950, 83 mins, US b/w
Dir Joseph Pevney ***Prod*** Aubrey Schenck ***Scr*** Harry Essex ***Ph*** Carl Guthrie ***Ed*** Russell Schoengarth ***Mus*** Joseph Gershenson (dir.)
Act Alexis Smith, Scott Brady, Richard Egan, Gladys George, Royal Dano, Regis Toomey (Universal)

Undercover Girl, by its very title, suggests a conventional melodrama with a twist in that a girl is the gangsters' foil. Which is exactly what it is.

Alexis Smith has the part of Christine Miller, who interrupts her police training in New York to go to California to avenge the death of her policeman father, killed by a narcotics ring. Working with the Los Angeles police, she gets into the confidence of the gang, posing as a dope-buyer.

Love interest is provided by Smith and Scott Brady, who is in charge of the police detail working on the case, and there is an exciting windup in a hide-and-seek sequence in a deserted house.

Smith's role is routine but she makes the most of it, especially in a couple of sequences dealing with the small-fry of the gang.

•

UNDERCOVER MAN, THE
1949, 80 mins, US b/w
Dir Joseph H. Lewis ***Prod*** Robert Rossen ***Scr*** Sydney Boehm, Malvin Wald ***Ph*** Burnett Guffey ***Ed*** Al Clark ***Mus*** George Duning ***Art*** Walter Holscher
Act Glenn Ford, Nina Foch, James Whitmore, Barry Kelley, David Wolfe, Frank Tweddell (Columbia)

Narrated in a straightforward, hardhitting documentary style, *The Undercover Man* is a good crime-busting saga. Standout features are the pic's sustained pace and its realistic quality. Fresh, natural dialog help to cover up the formula yarn, while top-notch performances down the line carry conviction. Joseph H. Lewis's direction also mutes the melodramatic elements but manages to keep the tension mounting through a series of violent episodes [based on an article, "Undercover Man: He Trapped Capone," by Frank J. Wilson and a story outline by Jack Rubin].

Glenn Ford plays a Government Treasury agent on the trail of an underworld czar. Aiming to nail the racketeer on a tax-evasion rap, Ford attempts to contact some stool-pigeons but the syndicate knocks them off before they can squeal.

Ford bolsters his conventional part with a sincere, matter-of-fact performance.

•

UNDERCURRENT
1946, 111 mins, US Ⓥ b/w
Dir Vincente Minnelli ***Prod*** Pandro S. Berman ***Scr*** Edward Chodorov, Marguerite Roberts, [George Oppenheimer] ***Ph*** Karl Freund ***Ed*** Ferris Webster ***Mus*** Herbert Stothart ***Art*** Cedric Gibbons, Randall Duell
Act Katharine Hepburn, Robert Taylor, Robert Mitchum, Edmund Gwenn, Marjorie Main, Jayne Meadows (M-G-M)

Undercurrent is heavy drama with femme appeal. Picture [from Thelma Strabel's novel *You Were There*] deals with psychology angle in which a weak, uncertain man uses lies, theft and even murder to obtain power and acclaim.

Appeal lies in romance between Katharine Hepburn and Robert Taylor and uncertainty as to how it will work out. Taylor, war-made industrialist, marries Hepburn, daughter of a scientist, after a whirlwind courtship. After marriage, the bride begins to discover odd incidents in her husband's past, including his brother's mysterious disappearance and the fear that dogs and other animals have for the man.

Hepburn sells her role with usual finesse and talent. Robert Mitchum, as the missing brother, has only three scenes but makes them count for importance.

•

UNDER FIRE
1983, 100 mins, US Ⓥ ⊙ col
Dir Roger Spottiswoode ***Prod*** Jonathan Taplin ***Scr*** Ronald Shelton, Clayton Frohman ***Ph*** John Alcott ***Ed*** John Bloom, Mark Conte ***Mus*** Jerry Goldsmith ***Art*** Agustin Ytuarte, Toby Rafelson
Act Nick Nolte, Gene Hackman, Joanna Cassidy, Jean-Louis Trintignant, Ed Harris, Richard Masur (Lion's Gate)

The American media are strongly taken to task in *Under Fire*. This is the story of two correspondents (one working for *Time*, the other Public Radio) and an on-the-scenes war photographer. The action [story by Clayton Frohman] begins in the African bush of Chad, then moves on to Nicaragua—and a feature-film rehearsal of that tragic televised killing of the ABC correspondent by a Somoza government soldier in the late 1970s as he was covering the fighting with the winning Sandinista rebels.

Three individuals cover the Chad conflict in the late 1970s: the 30-year-old photog, Russell Price (Nick Nolte); the 50-year-old senior correspondent for *Time* mag, Alex Grazier (Gene Hackman); and the circa 40-year-old radio newslady, Claire Stryder (Joanna Cassidy). All are tough professionals.

There's a fourth individual who surfaces now and then: he's a hired mercenary, a killer by trade, whom lenser Nolte meets from time to time, first in Chad and later in Nicaragua.

In the course of covering the events Nolte and Cassidy opt to search for a certain rebel leader named Rafael among the revolutionary Sandinistas, for Rafael has never been photographed nor interviewed by the American press.

Further, Nolte's photos of the rebels play into the hands of a double-agent, the Frenchman (Jean-Louis Trintignant), who uses them to hunt down and kill the key Sandinista leaders. Moral factors like these are the core of the action.

Thesping is on the plus side, particularly Nolte in a role cut to his proportions. Director Roger Spottiswode, after a couple of earlier actioners, has great potential.

1983: NOMINATION: Best Original Score

●

UNDERGROUND

1941, 95 mins, US b/w

Dir Vincent Sherman ***Prod*** William Jacobs ***Scr*** Edwin Justus Mayer, Oliver H. P. Garrett ***Ph*** Sid Hickox ***Ed*** Thomas Pratt ***Mus*** Adolph Deutsch

Act Jeffrey Lynn, Philip Dorn, Kaaren Verne, Mona Maris, Frank Reicher, Martin Kosleck (Warner)

In essence, *Underground* is merely another violent attack on the barbarism of Nazism, with elements of the chase, minor romance and a gleam of hope at the finale. It has the urgency of an overpowering subject, with the usual Warner punch. It's a potent picture.

Yarn deals with the underground anti-Nazi movement in the Reich, specifically, with the outlaw shortwave radio stations that help to spread the voice of truth and freedom and thus keep Nazi officialdom in a state of frenzy. It's a story of brother-against-brother, of a forbidden love between a young, idealistic Nazi zealot and a girl member of the underground movement, and of a tragic death of several leaders of the group serving to open the eyes of the hero to the real evil of Nazism.

From a scripting, production, direction and acting standpoint, *Underground* is a sincere effort. It has the integrity that indicates its makers believed in what they were doing. Jeffrey Lynn, Philip Dorn and Kaaren Verne are undeniably persuasive as the young leads.

●

UNDERGROUND

1995, 178 mins, France/Germany/Hungary Ⓥ col

Dir Emir Kusturica ***Prod*** Pierre Spengler ***Scr*** Dusan Kevacevic, Emir Kusturica ***Ph*** Vilko Filac ***Ed*** Branca Ceperac ***Mus*** Goran Bregovic ***Art*** Miljen Kljakovic

Act Miki Manojlovic, Lazar Ristovski, Mirjana Jokevic, Slavko Stimac, Ernst Stotzner, Srdan Todorovic (Ciby 2000/Pandora/Novo)

If Fellini had shot a war movie, it might bear a resemblance to *Underground*. Emir Kusturica's epic black comedy about Yugoslavia from 1941 to 1992 is a three-hour steamroller circus that leaves the viewer dazed and and exhausted, but mightily impresssed.

Accompanied by a band of tuba and horn players whose rollicking gypsy music is reprised throughout the film, pic kicks off to a wild and joyous start. Leading the band is Marko (Miki Manojlovic), dancing and whoring his way through 1941 Belgrade. He and his best pal, Blacky (Lazar Ristovski), are at the same time patriots and gangsters, directing a black market operation from a warren of underground tunnels, where Marco also holds on-the-run Communist Party meetings.

Though the Gestapo is after them, Blacky and Marko continue partying. They hide their families in a cellar, where refugees have put together an underground munitions factory. After his wife dies in childbirth, Blacky begins courting headstrong actress Natalija (Mirjana Jokovic). When she rejects him in favour of Nazi officer Franz (Ernst Stotzner), Blacky shoots Franz, but the Nazi survives and throws Blacky in a torture chamber. Marko stages a farcical rescue dressed as a doctor and smuggles Blacky out.

While Blacky recuperates in the cellar, Marko seduces Natalija. As Allied bombers destroy what the Nazis have left of Belgrade, Marko completes his betrayal: He makes the refugees in the cellar believe the war is still going on.

Twenty years later, Marko has become an important party boss. In the cellar, Blacky and the others keep manufacturing arms while they wait for Tito's call to "the final battle." Though they eat dog food and their lives are a lie the cellar's inhabitants believe they are living the good life. The metaphor obviously relates to how Yugoslavs saw themselves under Tito's rule.

Pic's final section *The War* takes place in 1992. Ivan learns the truth about his brother's treachery, and the fate of the country he knew as Yugoslavia. Kusturica presents the conventional view that the conflict is a civil war in which all parties are guilty: The breakup of Yugoslavia is the great tragedy, and violence comes from all sides.

[Version reviewed was 192-min. one preemed at the 1995 Cannes fest. Director subsequently prepared a 178-min. version for international release, first shown in October 1995.]

●

UNDER MILK WOOD

1971, 90 mins, UK Ⓥ col

Dir Andrew Sinclair ***Prod*** Jules Buck, Hugh French ***Scr*** Andrew Sinclair ***Ph*** Bob Huke ***Ed*** Willy Kemplen ***Mus*** Brian Gascoigne

Act Richard Burton, Elizabeth Taylor, Peter O'Toole, Glynis Johns, Vivien Merchant, Sian Philips (Timon)

Screen adaptations of hard-to-slot items such as Dylan Thomas's *Under Milk Wood*, have long been tricky affairs, so it's a tribute to the makers of this pic that it's come off this well.

Writer-director Andrew Sinclair has a wonderful feel for his material, and a happy hand in matching it to its setting. Normal screen conventions are broken as Sinclair chooses to follow Thomas instead in his dissection of a Welsh seaside village and its inhabitants, done with caustically keen and boisterously, earthily humorous pen.

Peter O'Toole plays the blind but still all-seeing Captain Cat, with a (sometimes distracting) assist from makeup on the surface and a fine and oft-moving limn underneath. Richard Burton is fully at ease in a physical walk-through of a village day, and he speaks the bulk of Thomas's voice-over lines with feeling and obvious love. Through him principally, the purr and the occasional soar of the poet's phrase flows and satisfies. Elizabeth Taylor, glimpsed all too briefly, has rarely been more beautiful. A very distinguished roster of featured players.

●

UNDERNEATH, THE

1995, 99 mins, US Ⓥ ▭ col

Dir Steven Soderbergh ***Prod*** John Hardy ***Scr*** Sam Lowry, Daniel Fuchs ***Ph*** Elliot Davis ***Ed*** Stan Salfas ***Mus*** Cliff Martinez ***Art*** Howard Cummings

Act Peter Gallagher, Alison Elliott, William Fichtner, Adam Trese, Joe Don Baker, Elisabeth Shue (Populist/Gramercy)

Steven Soderbergh attempts to navigate a tense story of a criminal heist into the uncustomarily deep waters of emotional, psychological and philosophical exploration in *The Underneath*, with intriguing results. A remake of the superb 1949 film noir *Criss Cross*, new entry downplays the boilerplate genre elements in favor of something akin to a meditation on personal responsibility and culpability.

Pic follows the basic plotline of *Criss Cross*, derived from Don Tracy's novel, quite closely. After a considerable absence, Michael Chambers (Peter Gallagher) arrives back home in Austin, TX, to attend the wedding of his mother (Anjanette Gomer) to a nice older fellow, Ed Dutton (Paul Dooley). But his ulterior motive is to see what's cooking with his former flame, the slinky Rachel (Alison Elliott), whom he tracks down at the Ember, a nightclub owned by Rachel's snaky new beau, Tommy Dundee (William Fichtner).

From the outset, storytelling adroitly fragments along three chronological fronts: real time, which sees Michael and Rachel beginning to reignite their romance; flashbacks, which sketch in Michael's reckless gambling habits and his abrupt abandonment of Rachel; and the near future, which shows Michael, now an armored-truck driver, heading for a pickup in the company of his new stepfather.

All of these plot strands are deftly orchestrated. At the same time, however, Soderbergh has curiously crimped the story's most exploitable genre ingredients, i.e., the sex and violence, from what they were in the 1949 telling. The original ending has been entirely reworked.

●

UNDER SIEGE

1992, 102 mins, US Ⓥ ⊙ col

Dir Andrew Davis ***Prod*** Arnon Milchan, Steven Seagal, Steven Reuther ***Scr*** J. F. Lawton ***Ph*** Frank Tidy ***Ed*** Robert A. Ferretti, Denis Virkler, Don Brochu, Dov Hoenig ***Mus*** Gary Chang ***Art*** Bill Kenney

Act Steven Seagal, Tommy Lee Jones, Gary Busey, Erika Eleniak, Patrick O'Neal, Nick Mancuso (Warner)

Warners has the right stuff with *Under Siege*, an immensely slick, if also old-fashioned and formulaic, entertainment. Steven Seagal fans and action buffs should eat this up.

Seagal plays a cook on the USS *Missouri*, the Navy's largest and most powerful battleship. En route to decommission, a quiet, calm journey turns out to be volatile and dangerous when two corrupt psychopaths, both top military experts, hijack the ship and steal its nuclear arsenal.

Seagal's rebellious cook is actually a decorated Navy Seal. He is contrasted with the lethal and hot-tempered William Strannix (Tommy Lee Jones), a former covert CIA operative, and Commander Krill (Gary Busey), a frustrated officer. Motivated by revenge, both men feel they have good reasons to execute their diabolical plot.

An attractive actress (*Playboy* and *Baywatch* alum Erika Eleniak), hired to perform at a farewell party, is thrown into the all-male adventure, and later functions as Seagal's resourceful mate and quasi-romantic interest.

In between battles, blasts and explosions, scripter J. F. Lawton (*Pretty Woman*) has shrewdly placed the funny one-liners, delivered by Seagal in his customary cool, tongue-in-cheek style.

1992: NOMINATION: Best Sound, Sound Effects Editing

●

UNDER SIEGE 2: DARK TERRITORY

1995, 100 mins, US Ⓥ ⊙ col

Dir Geoff Murphy ***Prod*** Steven Seagal, Arnon Milchan, Steve Perry ***Scr*** Richard Hatem, Matt Reeves ***Ph*** Robbie Greenberg ***Ed*** Michael Tronick ***Mus*** Basil Poledouris ***Art*** Albert Brenner

Act Steven Seagal, Eric Bogosian, Katherine Heigl, Everett McGill, Nick Mancuso, Brenda Bakke (Warner/Regency/Nasso)

The second Steven Seagal *Under Siege* foray is a true victim of the terrible twos. It's muscle-bending, mind-numbing action at high-decibel levels for the lowest and least discerning common denominator.

Pic once again adopts the "wrong guy at the right time" premise. This time, Seagal's former CIA black op, Casey Ryback, just happens to be on a train that just happens to get hijacked by wacko terrorists with diabolical plans for world devastation. Travis Dane (Eric Bogosian) is a disaffected strategic arms techno genius who wants a cool billion not to set off missiles from a covert, orbiting death star he created prior to being fired for nuttiness.

Thankfully, for the world, Ryback is also aboard, escorting his teenage niece (Katherine Heigl) to L.A. for the funeral of her father. When the Uzis come out, he goes into combat mode.

The script by Richard Hatem and Matt Reeves cribs mercilessly from the structure devised by Jon Lawton in the original. Once again there are a civilian sidekick, eccentric bad guys and spectacular stunts. But the writing duo effect a cut-and-paste job in which the actors battle to maintain some dignity while delivering stilted dialog.

The exception is Seagal, who strides through the wreckage with the self-knowledge of his standing as a movie star. Unfortunately, he's betrayed every time he opens his mouth or is called upon to display an emotion other than pain.

Bogosian provides some much-needed comic relief to the slogging tale. Director Geoff Murphy handles the action with the precision of a good traffic cop.

●

UNDER SUSPICION

1991, 99 mins, UK Ⓥ ⊙ ▭ col

Dir Simon Moore ***Prod*** Brian Eastman ***Scr*** Simon Moore ***Ph*** Vernon Layton ***Ed*** Tariq Anwar ***Mus*** Christopher Gunning ***Art*** Tim Hutchinson

Act Liam Neeson, Laura San Giacomo, Kenneth Cranham, Alphonsia Emmanuel, Stephen Moore, Maggie O'Neill (Carnival)

Writer-director Simon Moore makes a stylish bow with *Under Suspicion*, an old-fashioned murder mystery flawed by wobbly playing from Irish actor Liam Neeson.

Tense prolog, set in Brighton, 1957, has a cop (Neeson) caught with his pants down with the wife (Maggie O'Neill) of a gangster he's trailing. Two years later, Neeson is a down-at-the-heels private investigator arranging phoney divorce evidence. O'Neill, now his wife, poses as the other woman in hotel setups to get photographic court evidence. During one of these setups, she ends up with her brain splattered on the sheets next to an equally dead client.

Enter the hotel stiff's mysterious American mistress (Laura San Giacomo) who quickly heads the police list of suspects. She hires Neeson to investigate her lover's murder.

Pic plays like a loving tribute to every film noir in the book. But despite vague parallels to Fritz Lang's *Beyond a Reasonable Doubt*, it's more like a rainy-day Brit cross between *Jagged Edge* and *Body Heat*.

Former TV scripter Moore, keeps the dialog taut and the red herrings coming, but he skimps on electricity between the two leads. Production design is polished, exactly catching the story's setting on the borderline of the more liberated 1960s.

●

UNDER THE CHERRY MOON

1986, 98 mins, US Ⓥ ⊙ b/w

Dir Prince ***Prod*** Robert Cavallo, Joseph Ruffalo, Steven Fargnoli ***Scr*** Becky Johnston ***Ph*** Michael Ballhaus ***Ed*** Eva Gardos ***Mus*** Clare Fischer ***Art*** Richard Sylbert

Act Prince, Steven Berkoff, Francesca Annis, Kristin Scott Thomas, Jerome Benton, Alexandra Stewart (Warner)

In *Under the Cherry Moon*, Prince tries to direct too, giving himself a lot of closeups kissing but hardly any of him singing. What is left is a trite story about a rich girl and a poor musician (Prince) that's set on the Riviera and shot in, of all things, black and white.

Before shooting began, Prince reportedly fired director Mary Lambert (who has retained the dubious distinction of having credit as "creative consultant") and took over the set.

Story has less plot than the average music video, featuring Prince as a pianist at a Nice hotel and Revolution backup singer, Jerome Benton, as his friend Tricky. After a half-hearted rendezvous with a wealthy woman (Francesca Annis), Prince sets his sights on meeting a young, wealthy woman.

Through the newspaper, he finds out that young, beautiful Mary Sharon (Kristin Scott Thomas) is about to turn 21 and come into her $50 million trust fund. He meets her, they fall in love, and Dad (Steven Berkoff) gets his thugs to rid his sheltered daughter of Prince.

Film was shot in color (at the insistence of Warner Bros.) with prints in black and white (at the insistence of Prince) on location in Nice, and comes out looking about as flat and uninteresting as a newsreel from the 1930s about vacationing in the south of France.

•

UNDER THE CLOCK
SEE: THE CLOCK

•

UNDER THE RED ROBE
1937, 80 mins, UK Ⓥ b/w
Dir Victor Seastrom ***Prod*** Robert T. Kane ***Scr*** Lajos Biro, Philip Lindsay, J. L. Hodson, Arthur Wimperis ***Ph*** James Wong Howe, Georges Perinal ***Ed*** James B. Clark ***Mus*** Arthur Benjamin ***Art*** Frank Wells
Act Conrad Veidt, Annabella, Raymond Massey, Romney Brent, Sophie Stewart, F. Wyndham Goldie (20th Century-Fox)

Considering its only moderate success as a legit show [by Edward Hope, from the novel by Stanley J. Weyman] and that it may be automatically and erroneously tabbed as a costume production, *Under the Red Robe* turns out to be surprisingly fine entertainment.

Annabella photographs superbly, acts like a trouper of the first water, and only in her lightly intoned speeches is there any difficulty about understanding her English. Both in her love sequences and her dramatic moments, the comely French actress comes through with few flaws.

Direction never wastes a move, going directly to the point, holding proper suspense and mixing droll comedy with the exciting and dramatic moments.

Conrad Veidt, the "black death" and chief undercover killer for Cardinal Richelieu (Raymond Massey), starts on his quest of corralling the elusive duke and rebel without delay. Once in the duke's castle, he immediately starts weaving the romantic thread which eventually leads to the duke's capture and the sudden termination of their love affair.

Annabella has plenty tough competition from Conrad Veidt for spotlight honors, because he turns in one of his most polished portrayals. Greatest test of his ability comes in his love scenes because the girl, sister of the duke, is obviously much younger than he, while his character is scarcely that of a Robert Taylor.

•

UNDER THE VOLCANO
1984, 109 mins, US Ⓥ ⊙ col
Dir John Huston ***Prod*** Moritz Borman, Wieland Schulz-Kiel ***Scr*** Guy Gallo ***Ph*** Gabriel Figueroa ***Ed*** Roberto Silvi ***Mus*** Alex North ***Art*** Gunther Gerzso
Act Albert Finney, Jacqueline Bisset, Anthony Andrews, Ignacio Lopez Tarzo, Katy Jurado, James Villiers (Ithaca-Conacine)

Although it's said John Huston has wanted to film British author Malcolm Lowry's autobiographical masterpiece *Under the Volcano* for some 30 years, it was always a project fraught with difficulties.

Story unfolds over a 24-hour period in November 1938 in the Mexican village of Cuernavaca where the former British Consul, Geoffrey Firmin (Albert Finney), guilt-ridden over the past and abandoned by his wife, is drinking himself to death. It's a time of celebration, the Day of the Dead, a day when death is celebrated.

After a drunken night, Firmin returns home to discover that Yvonne (Jacqueline Bisset), the wife he so desperately yearned for, has unexpectedly returned. The occasion provides only a momentary interval from hard liquor, however.

Although this voyage into self-destruction won't be to the taste of many, there will be few unmoved by Finney's towering performance as the tragic Britisher, his values irretrievably broken down, drowning himself in alcohol and practically inviting his own death.

1984: NOMINATIONS: Best Actor (Albert Finney), Original Score

•

UNDER THE YUM YUM TREE
1963, 110 mins, US col
Dir David Swift ***Prod*** Frederick Brisson ***Scr*** Lawrence Roman, David Swift ***Ph*** Joseph Biroc ***Ed*** Charles Nelson ***Mus*** Frank DeVol ***Art*** Dale Hennesy
Act Jack Lemmon, Carol Lynley, Dean Jones, Edie Adams, Imogene Coca, Paul Lynde (Columbia)

The screen version of Lawrence Roman's hit stage play is concerned with an experiment wherein two young people in love (Carol Lynley and Dean Jones) agree to determine their "character compatibility" prior to marriage by living together platonically. The project is complicated by the intrusion of the lecherous landlord (Jack Lemmon) of the apartment building in which they have chosen to reside.

As engineered by director David Swift, the film's cardinal error is its lack of restraint. There is a tendency to embellish, out of all proportion, devices and situations that, kept simple, would have served the comic purposes far more effectively.

Exaggeration has also spilled over into the area of production design. Having Lemmon's apartment fully equipped for romantic pursuits is one thing, but some of the props, notably a pair of pop-up, mechanical violins, strain credulity.

For Lemmon, the role of amorous landlord is a tour de farce, and he plays it to the hilt. Lynley is a visual asset and does a satisfactory job as the somewhat ingenuous ingenue. Jones, who played the rather gullible boyfriend on Broadway, effectively repeats his characterization on screen.

•

UNDER TWO FLAGS
1936, 111 mins, US b/w
Dir Frank Lloyd ***Prod*** Darryl F. Zanuck ***Scr*** W. P. Lipscomb, Walter Ferris ***Ph*** Ernest Palmer ***Ed*** Ralph Dietrich ***Mus*** Louis Silvers (dir.) ***Art*** William Darling
Act Ronald Colman, Claudette Colbert, Victor McLaglen, Rosalind Russell, Gregory Ratoff, Nigel Bruce (20th Century-Fox)

The classic *Under Two Flags*, in book [by Ouida], play and through two silent filmizations [1916 and 1922], is still sturdy fare, talkerized. A pioneer saga of the Foreign Legion, Darryl Zanuck and 20th Century-Fox have further fortified it by a four-ply marquee ensemble (Ronald Colman, Claudette Colbert, Victor McLaglen and Rosalind Russell).

Not the tempestuous Cigarette of the Theda Bara vintage [1916 version] when *Under Two Flags* was a highlight in that silent film vamp's career, Colbert nonetheless makes the somewhat bawdy cafe hostess stand up. It's not exactly in her metier. Twixt the native Cigarette and Rosalind Russell as the English lady, Colman does all right on the romance interest, with the desert as a setting.

Victor McLaglen turns in an expert chore as the scowling Major Doyle, lovesick for and jealous of Cigarette's two-timing. Gregory Ratoff is planted well for comedy relief with his plaint that he's already forgotten just what he joined the Legion to forget.

The production highlight is the pitched battle on the desert [directed by Otto Brower, photographed by Sidney Wagner] between the marauding Arabs and the handful of legionnaires defending the fort.

•

UNDERWATER!
1955, 98 mins, US Ⓥ ⊙ ⌑ col
Dir John Sturges ***Prod*** Harry Tatelman ***Scr*** Walter Newman ***Ph*** Harry J. Wild ***Ed*** Stuart Gilmore, Frederic Knudtson ***Mus*** Roy Webb ***Art*** Albert S. D'Agostino, Carrol Clark
Act Jane Russell, Gilbert Roland, Richard Egan, Lori Nelson, Robert Keigh, Joseph Calleia (RKO)

While Jane Russell is the main cast attraction as far as name value goes, the story (by Hugh King and Robert C. Bailey) is slanted towards Richard Egan, her husband, and Gilbert Roland, adventurer, who are diving for the treasure aboard a sunken galleon. Russell is a fetching sight, whether plumbing the depths or lounging comfortably aboard ship.

Egan and Roland handle the masculine spots easily, both having the kind of muscles that look good when bared. Robert Keith, good as a priest with a knowledge of sunken treasure, and Lori Nelson, scantly used but good to look at, are the other principals in the treasure-questing group. On the surface the treasure-hunters are threatened by Cuban shark fisherman (Joseph Calleia) and his crew.

Sturges's direction is hampered for the first half by more dialog than the picture's pace can comfortably assimilate, but once the unnecessary talk and extraneous sequences are out of the way, the pace tightens and thrills are consistent.

Film is RKO's first SuperScope release. The 2-to-1 aspect ratio produces a big picture excellently proportioned to show off the pictorial splendors achieved by Harry J. Wild's lensing above the water and Lamar Boren's under the ocean.

•

UNDERWORLD
1927, 75 mins, US ⊗ b/w
Dir Josef von Sternberg ***Prod*** Hector Turnbull ***Scr*** Ben Hecht, Robert N. Lee, George Marion, Jr., Charles Furthman ***Ph*** Bert Glennon ***Art*** Hans Dreier
Act George Bancroft, Clive Brook, Evelyn Brent, Larry Semon, Fred Kohler (Paramount)

Underworld, without mentioning Chicago as the scene of the ensuing machine-gun warfare between the crooks and cops, evidently is a page out of Ben Hecht's underworld acquaintance with the Cicero and South Side gun mob.

There's a wallop right through and yet the film retains romance, clicks not a little on comedy (through the medium of Larry Semon) and even whitewashes itself with a "moral" that banditry cannot successfully defy the law and that the wages of sin are death.

Hecht could have made *Underworld* a true biography of Cicero with the "alky" gun mob, with a little switching of the motivation, but instead of bootlegging, our hero is a jewelry store sampler. George Bancroft as Bull Weed, a sympathetic crook, explains why Paramount re-signed him by his performance in *Underworld*. Clive Brook, cast as the regenerated drunkard and Evelyn Brent, as Bancroft's girl, complete the outstanding trio.

•

UNDERWORLD INFORMERS
SEE: THE INFORMERS

•

UNDERWORLD, U.S.A.
1961, 98 mins, US Ⓥ b/w
Dir Samuel Fuller ***Prod*** Samuel Fuller ***Scr*** Samuel Fuller ***Ph*** Hal Mohr ***Ed*** Jerome Thoms ***Mus*** Harry Sukman ***Art*** Robert Peterson
Act Cliff Robertson, Dolores Dorn, Beatrice Kay, Paul Dubov, Richard Rust, Larry Gates (Globe/Columbia)

Underworld, U.S.A. is a slick gangster melodrama made to order for filmgoers who prefer screen fare explosive and uncomplicated. In this picture, the "hero" sets out on a four-ply vendetta of staggering proportions and accomplishes his mission with the calculation and poise of a pro bowler racking up a simple four-way spare.

The yarn follows the wicked career of supposedly decent but hate-motivated, revenge-consumed fellow who, as a youngster, witnessed in horror the gangland slaying of his father by four budding racketeers.

As the central figure, Cliff Robertson delivers a brooding, virile, finely balanced portrayal. It's a first-rate delineation atop a cast that performs expertly. Dolores Dorn supplies romantic interest with sufficient sincerity, and Beatrice Kay is persuasive as the decent, compassionate woman whose fervent, but unfulfilled, desire for motherhood gives rise to a vague mother-son relationship with Robertson.

Director Samuel Fuller's screenplay [from the *Saturday Evening Post* articles by Joseph F. Dinneen] has its lags, character superficialities and unlikelihoods, but it is crisp with right-sounding gangster jargon and remains absorbing.

•

UNFAITHFULLY YOURS
1948, 105 mins, US Ⓥ ⊙ b/w
Dir Preston Sturges ***Prod*** Preston Sturges ***Scr*** Preston Sturges ***Ph*** Victor Milner ***Ed*** Robert Fritch ***Mus*** Alfred Newman ***Art*** Lyle R. Wheeler, Joseph C. Wright
Act Rex Harrison, Linda Darnell, Barbara Lawrence, Rudy Vallee, Lionel Stander, Edgar Kennedy (20th Century-Fox)

Unfaithfully Yours misses that stamp of originality which marked the scripting and direction of Preston Sturges's previous films. The fabric of stale ideas and antique gags out of which this pic was spun is just barely hidden by its glossy production casing.

The yarn is too slight to carry the long running time. It's a takeoff on the suspicious husband–beautiful wife formula, which is stirred up into a frothy pastry only on occasion.

With Rex Harrison playing a symphony orch leader, Sturges executes some amusing highjinks with serious music, but the humor is mild and unsustained.

The yarn unfolds via three long revenge fantasies which race through Harrison's brain while he batons his way through a concert. During a frenzied number by Rosini, there's a gruesome sequence in which Harrison slashes his wife, Linda Darnell, with a razor and then pins the rap on her supposed lover. Against a background of Wagnerian music, he daydreams of nobly renouncing his wife in favor of the other man. Finally, against a Tchaikovsky number, he imagines playing Russian roulette with his rival in a test of passion.

Stylization of the fantasies would have given these sequences that comic energy which is lacking.

•

UNFAITHFULLY YOURS
1984, 96 mins, US Ⓥ ⊙ col
Dir Howard Zieff ***Prod*** Marvin Worth, Joe Wizan ***Scr*** Valerie Curtin, Barry Levinson, Robert Klane ***Ph*** David M. Walsh ***Ed*** Sheldon Kahn ***Mus*** Bill Conti ***Art*** Albert Brenner
Act Dudley Moore, Nastassja Kinski, Armand Assante, Albert Brooks, Cassie Yates, Richard Libertini (20th Century-Fox)

Unfaithfully Yours is a moderately amusing remake of Preston Sturges's wonderful comedy which, it might be remembered, was a commercial bust upon its release in 1948.

Lavishly mounted and astutely cast farce features Dudley Moore in the role of a big-time orchestra conductor who has just taken a much younger Italian screen star, Nastassja Kinski, as his bride. Moore suspects her of fooling around with dashing concert violinist Armand Assante. The core of the film consists of a fantasy in which Moore murders his wife, but makes it look as though Assante did it. He then tries to pull off such a scheme, with predictably incompetent results.

Moore is right at home on the podium or behind the piano, and his comic invention results in a delightful performance.

•

UNFAITHFUL WIFE
SEE: LA FEMME INFIDELE

•

UNFINISHED BUSINESS
1984, 99 mins, Canada col
Dir Don Owen ***Prod*** Annette Cohen, Don Owen ***Scr*** Don Owen ***Ph*** Douglas Kiefer ***Ed*** Peter Dale, David Nicholson ***Mus*** Patricia Cullen ***Art*** Barbara Tranter, Ann Pepper
Act Isabelle Mejias, Peter Spence, Leslie Toth, Peter Kastner, Julie Biggs, Chuck Shamata (Zebra Films/NFBC)

Don Owen's *Unfinished Business* continues the story the filmmaker began in *Nobody Waved Goodbye* [1964], a ground-breaking Canadian feature. Sequel picks up with the original young couple, now divorced, experiencing the travails of parents with a rebellious 17-year-old daughter.

A high school senior, Izzy (Isabelle Mejias) is days away from her finals yet balks at the prospect of completing her education. She finds diversions in dope, friends, a rock club and a group of antinuke activists. The clash between pressures from her parents and the seemingly more meaningful pursuits of the radicals sends her into the streets for a different kind of education.

Although a common enough story, *Unfinished Business* has a raw energy which is touching and deeply felt.

•

UNFINISHED SYMPHONY, THE
1934, 90 mins, UK/Germany b/w
Dir Willy Forst, Anthony Asquith ***Prod*** Arnold Pressburger ***Scr*** Walter Reisch, Benn W. Levy ***Ph*** Franz Planer ***Mus*** Willy Schmidt-Gentner (adapt.)
Act Helen Chandler, Marta Eggerth, Hans Jaray, Ronald Squire, Beryl Laverick, Brember Wills (Gaumont-British/UFA)

A thing of arresting beauty in pictorial and musical conception, *The Unfinished Symphony* should garner attention from the musically appreciative. Particularly those for whom the melodies of Franz Schubert have always been in the upper brackets of their enjoyment.

What emotional appeal there is is not derived from the acting but from the instrumentation of Schubert's *Unfinished Symphony*, and the reproduction in voice and orchestra of a number of his other compositions. They're all brilliantly woven into the fine costume mosaic turned out by director Willy Forst.

Story has been aptly cast, even if the players constitute a babel of dialects. Striking case in point is that of Marta Eggerth and Beryl Laverick, who are cast as sisters. The former's accent is German and the latter's a precise Oxonian. Like Hans Jaray, Eggerth did the same part in the UFA version of *Unfinished Symphony* which Forst also directed.

•

UNFORGETTABLE
1996, 116 mins, US Ⓥ ⊙ col
Dir John Dahl ***Prod*** Dino De Laurentiis, Martha De Laurentiis ***Scr*** Bill Geddie ***Ph*** Jeffrey Jar ***Ed*** Eric L. Beason, Scott Chestnut ***Mus*** Christopher Young ***Art*** Rob Pearson
Act Ray Liotta, Linda Fiorentino, Peter Coyote, Christopher McDonald, Kim Cattrall, Kim Coates (De Laurentiis/Spelling)

Unforgettable doesn't linger in the memory. Cult modern noir-meister John Dahl's yarn of a forensic scientist obsessed with discovering his wife's murderer packs an explosive punch in its opening reels but becomes progressively less impressive as the twists and body count mount.

Aside from unconvincing casting of Linda Fiorentino as a plain-Jane scientist, pic also suffers from being a slave to plotting that's not much better than an average whodunit.

The first few reels, however, are stunners, as the camera roams over the bloody corpses in a Seattle drugstore massacre, and hotshot medical examiner David Krane (Ray Liotta) arrives to hunt for clues. At the crime scene, he discovers a rolled-up matchbook that exactly matches one found at his wife's murder, for which he was initially the prime suspect but later acquitted because of inadmissible evidence.

Krane subsequently meets Martha Briggs (Fiorentino), a neurobiologist who's been working on memory transference by injecting a cocktail of brain fluid and a special carrier solution into rats. Possessed by a wild idea, Krane steals some of his dead wife's brain fluid and Martha's solution, and shoots up at home in the den where his wife was murdered. As he suspected, he's able to relive his wife's murder through her memories of the event.

•

UNFORGIVEN, THE
1960, 125 mins, US Ⓥ ▭ col
Dir John Huston ***Prod*** James Hill ***Scr*** Ben Maddow ***Ph*** Franz Planer ***Ed*** Hugh Russell Lloyd ***Mus*** Dimitri Tiomkin
Act Burt Lancaster, Audrey Hepburn, Audie Murphy, John Saxon, Charles Bickford, Lillian Gish (James/United Artists)

There are many aspects of *The Unforgiven* that elicit comparison with *Shane*, particularly in regard to the composition of the scenes and the photography. Director John Huston and cameraman Franz Planer have teamed to provide an intelligent use of the medium for eye-pleasing effects, filmed in Mexico.

The screenplay from a novel by Alan Le May—although many parts are better than the whole—provides a good framework for the talents of Huston and his performers. Audrey Hepburn gives a shining performance as the foundling daughter of a frontier family. As her foster brother, obviously desperately in love with his "sister," Burt Lancaster is fine as the strong-willed, heroic family spokesman and community leader.

The scene is the Texas Panhandle immediately after the Civil War at a time of unbending hatred between the white settlers and the local Kiowa Indians. The antagonism is marked by senseless massacres and excesses on the part of both sides. In the midst of this tension, it's discovered that Hepburn is actually a full-blooded Indian. The desire of the Indians to recover their own "blood," the resentment of the settlers in having an "enemy" in their midst, and the determination to hold on to the girl who has been a member of the family almost since birth provides the crux of the conflict.

Lillian Gish, a silent film favorite, is okay as the mother who guards the secret of her foundling daughter. However, she has a tendency to over-react emotionally. There are good performances by Charles Bickford, as the head of another frontier family; June Walker, as his wife; Albert Salmi, as his son who courts Hepburn; Kipp Hamilton, as his daughter, and Doug McClure, as Lancaster's youngest brother. Audie Murphy is surprisingly good as Lancaster's hotheaded brother whose hatred of Indians causes him to abandon his family.

•

UNFORGIVEN
1992, 130 mins, US Ⓥ ⊙ ▭ col
Dir Clint Eastwood ***Prod*** Clint Eastwood ***Scr*** David Webb Peoples ***Ph*** Jack N. Green ***Ed*** Joel Cox ***Mus*** Lenny Niehaus ***Art*** Henry Bumstead
Act Clint Eastwood, Gene Hackman, Morgan Freeman, Richard Harris, Jaimz Woolvett, Saul Rubinek (Warner/Malpaso)

Unforgiven is a classic Western for the ages. In his 10th excursion into the genre that made him a star more than 25 years earlier, Clint Eastwood has crafted a tense, hard-edged, superbly dramatic yarn that is also an exceedingly intelligent meditation on the West, its myths and heroes.

Eastwood has dedicated the film "to Sergio and Don," references to Sergio Leone and Don Siegel. The salute signals Eastwood's intention to reflect upon the sort of terse, tough, hard-bitten characters he became famous for in their pictures, a man described here as being "as cold as the snow."

Eastwood's Bill Munny can be seen as a hypothetical portrait of the Man With No Name in his sunset years. When a hotshot named the "Schofield Kid" (Jaimz Woolvett) turns up offering to split a $1,000 reward being offered for the hides of two men who gruesomely sliced up a prostitute, Munny reluctantly straps on his holster for the first time in more than a decade.

To the kid's annoyance, Munny insists upon bringing along his former partner in crime (Morgan Freeman). Beating this group to their destination of Big Whiskey is railroad gunman English Bob (Richard Harris), an arrogant mythomaniac traveling with a biographer (Saul Rubinek) who memorializes his bloody accomplishments in dime novels.

Outlaws and bounty hunters around Big Whiskey face a problem by the name of Sheriff Little Bill Daggett (Gene Hackman), a brutal ex-badman who allows no one to carry guns in town. Resolution comes not in an expected, standard showdown, but much more complexly, in a series of alternately tragic and touching confrontations.

Recurring Eastwood themes involving humiliation and physical pain are present, and a strong feminist streak runs through the center of the story. A close-knit group of hookers defy Sheriff Daggett in the first place and put up the reward money for their mutilated co-worker.

Playing a stubbly, worn-out, has-been outlaw who can barely mount his horse at first, Eastwood, unafraid to show his age, is outstanding in his best clipped, understated manner. Hackman deliciously realizes the two sides of the sheriff's quicksilver personality, the folksy raconteur and the vicious sadist.

Lenser Jack Green's wide-screen images have a natural, unforced beauty that imaginatively make use of the mostly flat expanses of the Alberta locations.

1992: Best Picture, Director, Supp. Actor (Gene Hackman), Editing

NOMINATIONS: Best Actor (Clint Eastwood), Original Screenplay, Cinematography, Art Direction, Sound

•

UNHOLY ROLLERS, THE
1972, 88 mins, US Ⓥ col
Dir Vernon Zimmerman ***Prod*** John Prizer, Jack Bohrer ***Scr*** Howard R. Cohen ***Ph*** Mike Shea ***Ed*** George Trirogoff, Yeu-Bun Yee ***Mus*** Bobby Hart ***Art*** Spencer Quinn
Act Claudia Jennings, Louis Quinn, Betty Anne Rees, Roberta Collins, Alan Vint, Candice Roman (American International)

Unholy Rollers is another gander into the rough, tough world of the femme roller derby, a folo-up to Metro's *Kansas City Bomber* on same subject. Same type of violence and near-mayhem highlight this story of the rise and fall of a skating star.

While script by Howard R. Cohen concentrates more on the violence of the track than straight story line, there's sufficient propelling narrative to keep audience amply rewarded.

Yarn focuses on Claudia Jennings, who leaves her factory job to win a place on a roller team and almost immediately become its star through her departure from the routinely planned phony action of opponents on the track and plays for real.

Jennings does yeoman service with role which necessitates her taking plenty of lumps.

•

UNION CITY
1980, 87 mins, US Ⓥ ⊙ col
Dir Mark Reichert ***Prod*** Graham Belin ***Scr*** Mark Reichert ***Ph*** Ed Lachman ***Ed*** Lana Tokel, J. Michaels ***Mus*** Chris Stein ***Art*** George Stavrinos
Act Dennis Lipscomb, Deborah Harry, Irina Maleeva, Everett McGill, Sam McMurray, Pat Benatar (Kinesis)

Cornell Woolrich's dark and fetishistic [1937 story *The Corpse Next Door*] is both a source of strength and the undoing of *Union City*. His story is similar to Poe's *The Telltale Heart* in structure and while indie helmer Mark Reichert exploits its strangeness very well, he fails to flesh out the short, one actor sketch into a full-length feature.

Pic concerns a paranoid businessman (Dennis Lipscomb), obsessed with catching the mysterious culprit who steals a drink out of his milk bottle that is delivered every morning. His plain, vapid wife, Lillian (Deborah Harry, in her screen debut), puts up with his increasingly bizarre behavior.

Ultimately, he captures a young war vet vagrant (Sam McMurray) in the act and releases his pent-up anger and frustration by beating the man's head bloodily on the floor. The Hitchcockian body removal footage provides fine black humor as Lipscomb hides the corpse in a Murphy bed in the vacant apartment next door.

•

UNION DEPOT
1932, 66 mins, US b/w
Dir Alfred E. Green ***Scr*** Kenyon Nicholson, Walter DeLeon, Kubec Glasmon, John Bright ***Ph*** Sol Polito ***Ed*** Jack Killifer
Act Douglas Fairbanks, Jr., Joan Blondell, Guy Kibbee, Alan Hale, George Rosener, David Landau (First National)

A bing-bing, action melodrama [from a play by Joe Laurie, Jr., Gene Fowler and Douglas Durkin].

Opening is a capital bit of technique, being a series of brief shots establishing the bustling serio-comic atmosphere that is characteristic of a big railway terminal—a series of thumbnail sketches of human types.

Into this bustling scene strides Chic (Douglas Fairbanks, Jr.), careless and carefree knight of the road and the rods, and his older hobo pal. The windfall of a forgotten handbag in the washroom gives Chic good clothes and a heaven-sent bankroll, and he starts out to roll 'em high and handsome. The too-easy flaps he throws aside with cynical brusqueness, but for Ruth (Joan Blondell), the stranded chorus girl, on her uppers and desperate, he falls with the complete sangfroid of a sophisticated drifter.

Meanwhile the police have been closing in on a counterfeiter gang. A few turns of fate and the spurious fortune is in Chic's hands, just as the police begin to close in from all sides.

The limpid-eyed Blondell does an interesting piece of work in a role a little different from her wont. She's a knowing young thing, but not the hard-boiled type and it is just that degree of feminine helplessness that makes her here romantically possible.

•

UNION PACIFIC
1939, 133 mins, US Ⓥ b/w
Dir Cecil B. DeMille ***Prod*** Cecil B. DeMille ***Scr*** Walter DeLeon, C. Gardner Sullivan, Jesse Lasky, Jr. ***Ph*** Victor Milner, Dewey Wrigley ***Ed*** Anne Bauchens ***Mus*** George Antheil
Act Barbara Stanwyck, Joel McCrea, Akim Tamiroff, Robert Preston, Brian Donlevy, Anthony Quinn (Paramount)

Basically, the production a super-western, cowboys and Injuns backgrounded by the epochal building of the Union Pacific. It's a post–Civil War saga [from an adaptation by Jack Cunningham of an original by Ernest Haycox], with Henry Kolker enacting the banker menace who foments the sabotage that would favor the competitive Central Pacific.

Joel McCrea comes on the scene as a trouble-shooter. Barbara Stanwyck sustains the femme interest in a sometimes unprepossessing manner, which is chiefly the script's fault rather than her own. Basically she more than impresses as the railroad engineer's daughter.

The clash in realistic values comes through the pauses in the melodramatics between genial badman Preston and trouble-shooter McCrea. Preston does a standout job through a consistently affable albeit frankly renegade role.

1939: NOMINATION: Best Special Effects

•

UNION STATION
1950, 81 mins, US Ⓥ b/w
Dir Rudolph Mate ***Prod*** Jules Schermer ***Scr*** Sydney Boehm ***Ph*** Daniel L. Fapp ***Ed*** Ellsworth Hoagland ***Mus*** Irvin Talbot ***Art*** Hans Dreier, Earl Hedrick
Act William Holden, Nancy Olson, Barry Fitzgerald, Lyle Bettger, Jan Sterling, Allene Roberts (Paramount)

Union Station [from a story by Thomas Walsh] is a melodrama that locales its thrills in a big city railway terminal and spins off a tale of kidnapping.

William Holden, while youthful in appearance to head up the railway policing department of a metropolitan terminal, is in good form. Kidnapping is revealed when a femme passenger arriving at the terminal reports two suspicious characters. The passenger is Nancy Olson, secretary to a rich man and his blind daughter (Allene Roberts). Events prove Roberts has been kidnapped and the terminal is to be used as the payoff location.

The production catches the feel of a large terminal and its constantly shifting scenes of people arriving and departing.

•

UNIVERSAL SOLDIER
1992, 104 mins, US Ⓥ ⊙ ⌴ col
Dir Roland Emmerich ***Prod*** Allen Shapiro, Craig Baumgarten, Joel B. Michaels ***Scr*** Richard Rothstein, Christopher Leitch, Dean Devlin ***Ph*** Karl Walter Lindenlaub ***Ed*** Michael J. Duthie ***Mus*** Christopher Franke ***Art*** Holger Gross
Act Jean-Claude Van Damme, Dolph Lundgren, Ally Walker, Ed O'Ross, Jerry Orbach, Leon Rippy (Carolco/IndieProd)

Despite its not-insignificant production values, the story feels like a late-night sci-fi movie patched together with a mix of elements from *RoboCop* and *The Terminator*, with a dash of Captain America comic books. The result is almost as many derisive laughs as dead bodies.

A crazed Vietnam platoon leader (Dolph Lundgren) and his thickly accented subordinate (Jean-Claude Van Damme) waste each other prior to the opening credits during a 1969 My Lai–type massacre, only to pop up 23 years later as reanimated corpses, brought back by the Defense Dept. to act as an elite terrorism-fighting unit.

Something goes wrong, however, and Van Damme begins to recover his memory, taking off accompanied by a pretty reporter (Ally Walker), with Lundgren, his mind still addled with 'Nam hysteria, and other brigade members in hot pursuit.

The film is on the wrong foot from the get-go, since it's difficult to have much empathy for walking corpses with superhuman strength whose flesh regenerates when punctured.

After his rendition of twin brothers in *Double Impact*, Van Damme offers nothing new here other than baring a little more of his physique than had been his norm. Lundgren remains an imposing presence who hasn't been properly used since *Rocky IV*, though he'll probably score points with some moviegoers thanks to his character's morbid penchant for collecting victims' ears. Walker is the modern damsel-in-distress blend of tomboy tough and conveniently available.

•

UNIVERSAL SOLDIER THE RETURN
1999, 82 mins, US Ⓥ ⊙ col
Dir Mic Rodgers ***Prod*** Craig Baumgarten, Allen Shapiro, Jean-Claude Van Damme ***Scr*** William Malone, John Fasano ***Ph*** Michael A. Benson ***Ed*** Peck Prior ***Mus*** Don Davis ***Art*** David Chapman
Act Jean-Claude Van Damme, Michael Jai White, Heidi Schanz, Xander Berkeley, Justin Lazard, Kiana Tom (Baumgarten Prophet/Tri-Star)

Lightning fails to strike twice for Jean-Claude Van Damme in this underwhelming follow-up to one of the career-stalled action star's better efforts. *Return* picks up a few years later, reintroducing Luc Deveraux—the last bionic UniSol standing at the end of the first pic—as a kinder, gentler and appreciatively more human hero. He's a widowed father with a cute kid.

Deveraux and his employers at a Dallas research facility try to perfect a new breed of UniSol—stronger, smarter and, presumably, less likely to annihilate innocent bystanders.

The real brain of the outfit is a super-duper computer: the Self-Evolving Thought Helix, aka SETH. Think of HAL 2000 from *2001: A Space Odyssey* with an army of buff and badass cyborgs at his disposal, and you've got the basic setup.

Van Damme struggles mightily to inject a touch of soulfulness into his macho-man heroics, but he ends up looking faintly ridiculous each time he gets all teary-eyed over a casualty.

Vet stunt director Mic Rodgers (*Braveheart, Payback*) makes a less-than-promising debut as a feature director. He places great emphasis on frenetic action and deafening explosions, but fails to instill a sense of urgency in the routine and occasionally incoherent goings-on.

Most of the repetitious action is set in and around the research facility, as Deveraux and an obnoxious TV reporter (embarrassingly overplayed by Heidi Schanz) dodge bullets and seek hiding places. Editor Peck Prior proves to be the production's most valuable player by skillfully enhancing the rough stuff.

•

UNKNOWN, THE
1927, 55 mins, US ⊗ b/w
Dir Tod Browning ***Scr*** Tod Browning, Waldemar Young, Joe Farnham ***Ph*** Merritt Gerstad ***Ed*** Harry Reynolds, Errol Taggart ***Art*** Cedric Gibbons, Richard Day
Act Lon Chaney, Norman Kerry, Joan Crawford, Nick De Ruiz, John George, Frank Lanning (M-G-M)

A good Lon Chaney film that might have been great. The tale concerns an armless fakir in a gypsy circus who loves the proprietor's daughter. The girl has come to detest all men for their constant pawing, hence the welcome companionship of Alonzo (Chaney). None of the circus troupe knows that the latter is physically normal, except his helper. Alonzo fakes by strapping his arms to his sides.

Director Tod Browning has chopped to the bone in the cutting room. And that's smart, too, because it crams the picture with action and interest. Sweet photography and production all the way, while Joan Crawford never looked better in her life. Both she and Norman Kerry turn in neat support, as do the others in this small-cast feature.

•

UNKNOWN SOLDIER, THE
SEE: TUNTEMATON SOTILAS

•

UNLAWFUL ENTRY
1992, 111 mins, US Ⓥ ⊙ col
Dir Jonathan Kaplan ***Prod*** Charles Gordon ***Scr*** Lewis Colick, [Ken Friedman] ***Ph*** Jamie Anderson ***Ed*** Curtiss Clayton ***Mus*** James Horner ***Art*** Lawrence G. Paull
Act Kurt Russell, Ray Liotta, Madeleine Stowe, Roger E. Mosley, Ken Lerner, Deborah Offner (Largo)

Although it exists primarily to send an audience into a bloodthirsty frenzy, and has major credibility problems in the bargain, *Unlawful Entry* still works as an effective victimization thriller.

Tense opening scene has a black intruder breaking into the lovely L.A. home of attractive married couple Kurt Russell and Madeleine Stowe. The man escapes after a scuffle with Russell and holding a knife to Stowe's throat; the policemen (Ray Liotta and Roger E. Mosley) are the picture of helpfulness and encouragement.

Problem is that Liotta becomes excessively solicitous, arranging for the installation of topnotch security system in the couple's home and eagerly accepting an invitation to dinner. After speaking nicely to a class at the elementary school where Stowe and her friend Deborah Offner teach, Liotta comes on to Stowe in a quiet but insidious way, and from this point will stop at nothing to get Russell out of the way and have Stowe for himself.

Had the Liotta character been presented as an essentially decent cop gone wrong, story [by George D. Putnam, John Katchmer and Lewis Colick] might have achieved genuinely chilling dimensions. Instead, fact that he's clearly off-base and demented from the beginning gets everyone off the hook.

Liotta effectively conveys both the nice and nasty sides of his character but true sexual tension between him and Stowe is absent, and he tips his hand too early regarding the man's instability. Russell is solid as the husband, while Stowe is opaque as the wife.

•

UNMAN, WITTERING AND ZIGO
1971, 100 mins, UK col
Dir John Mackenzie ***Prod*** Gareth Wigan ***Scr*** Simon Raven ***Ph*** Geoffrey Unsworth ***Ed*** Fergus McDonnell ***Mus*** Michael J. Lewis ***Art*** Bill McCrow
Act David Hemmings, Carolyn Seymour, Douglas Wilmer, Hamilton Dyce, Anthony Haygarth, Donald Gee (Mediarts)

Unman, Wittering and Zigo are on the roster at Chantry, a British school for teenage boys, which looks down treacherously on ocean-splashed rocks. The three are students, but Zigo is constantly marked absent, for reasons unexplained.

Unman, Wittering and the rest of the class are present and they make for a sinister lot, blatantly threatening their new teacher, David Hemmings, with the same kind of death-on-the-rocks that has befallen his predecessor, unless he eases up on the scholastic schedule and runs their bets with the local bookmaker. The viewer may be both intrigued and puzzled, for while film is a compelling piece of dramatics about innocent-looking terrorists, it asks a great deal of credence.

Director John Mackenzie, working with a screenplay by Simon Raven, which in turn was fashioned from a television show by Giles Cooper, has in large part captured the viciousness. But why these youths are this way goes unexplained.

•

UNMARRIED WOMAN, AN
1978, 124 mins, US Ⓥ col
Dir Paul Mazursky ***Prod*** Paul Mazursky, Tony Ray ***Scr*** Paul Mazursky ***Ph*** Arthur Ornitz ***Ed*** Stuart H. Pappe ***Mus*** Bill Conti ***Art*** Pato Guzman
Act Jill Clayburgh, Alan Bates, Michael Murphy, Cliff Gorman, Pat Quinn, Kelly Bishop (20th Century-Fox)

Paul Mazursky's excellent screenplay presents Jill Clayburgh in a most demanding role where she is torn between conflicting forces following the surprise confession of weak-willed husband, Michael Murphy, that he has fallen in love with another woman.

Daughter Lisa Lucas needs her mother's support just as she herself is coming on to adolescent love; Clayburgh's girlfriends, Pat Quinn, Kelly Bishop and Linda Miller, offer well-meaning advice not necessarily of the best calibre; blind date Andrew Duncan's premature pass falls flat; therapist Penelope Russianoff's probing strikes raw nerves; neighborhood stud Cliff Gorman, in an excellent though brief role, comes to realize that the only thing worse than not getting what you want can be getting it.

Finally, artist Alan Bates arrives in Clayburgh's life. A thoughtful and deep attachment evolves which survives the early resentment of the daughter and the lover's increasing demands on her time. Resolution avoids the pat but portents for happiness are strong.

1978: NOMINATIONS: Best Picture, Actress (Jill Clayburgh), Original Screenplay

•

LES UNS ET LES AUTRES
(US: BOLERO)
1981, 184 mins, France Ⓥ col
Dir Claude Lelouch ***Prod*** Claude Lelouch ***Scr*** Claude Lelouch ***Ph*** Jean Boffety ***Ed*** Claude Lelouch ***Mus*** Francis Lai, Michel Legrand ***Art*** Jean-Louis Poveda, Stuart Wurtzel
Act Robert Hossein, Nicole Garcia, Geraldine Chaplin, Jacques Villeret, James Caan, Evelyne Bouix (Films 13/TF1)

In *Toute une vie* Claude Lelouch covered the whole 20th century with a foray into the future to boot. He did it in two and a half hours. Here he covers only 45 years and it drags on for over three hours. This surface album of criss-crossed destinies is heavy-footed, innocent, syrupy thumbnail history.

There is a couple in Russia, one in Germany, one in France, with a few other characters, and one in the U.S. It begins in 1936 and they all have something in common, music, which allows for wholesale working in of ballet numbers, Folies Bergeres extracts, the Lido, big bands, and later rock shows or film musical scenes.

The time is 1936, and soon comes the war and all are, of course, embroiled. The Russian couple has the man die but she has a son; the German (Daniel Olbrychski), a conductor, loses his son; the French couple (Robert Hossein, Nicole Garcia) are deported to a concentration camp but leave their son along the railroad with a note; and the Yank couple are patterned on Glenn Miller.

James Caan comes through the war after bringing swing to liberated Paris but his wife (Geraldine Chaplin) dies in an accident. Chaplin soon remerges, playing the grown daughter who becomes a singer though beset by drugs, drink, tobacco and cancer. The German conductor meanwhile finds himself giving a concert in NY, where the house is empty. The Russian boy turns out to be Nureyev. The French Vietnam and Algerian Wars are passed over, as is the U.S. Vietnam debacle. Film is reportedly part of a French TV miniseries. That may explain many holes in the lives and growth of the many characters.

[Original showings of the film featured an intermission at 115 mins, following the defection of the Russian dancer.]

•

UNSINKABLE MOLLY BROWN, THE
1964, 128 mins, US Ⓥ ⦿ ▭ col
Dir Charles Walters ***Prod*** Lawrence Weingarten ***Scr*** Helen Deutsch ***Ph*** Daniel L. Fapp ***Ed*** Fredric Steinkamp ***Mus*** Robert Armbruster (dir.) ***Art*** George W. Davis, Preston Ames
Act Debbie Reynolds, Harve Presnell, Ed Begley, Jack Kruschen, Hermione Baddeley, Martita Hunt (M-G-M)

The Unsinkable Molly Brown is a rowdy and sometimes rousing blend of song and sentiment, a converted stage tuner.

The film is adorned with the music and lyrics of Meredith Willson, although a number of his songs for the legiter have been excised and one new production number ("He's My Friend") has been added. The dramatic story remains virtually intact.

It relates the adventures of Molly Brown, a hillbilly heroine who rises from poverty to become one of the richest and most celebrated women of her time. Shortly after her marriage to Leadville Johnny Brown he strikes it rich, and the rest of the picture depicts her feverish efforts to cut the mustard with snooty Denver society.

In essence, it's a pretty shallow story since the title character, when you get right down to it, is obsessed with a very superficial, egotistical problem beneath her generous, razzamatazz facade. On top of that, Wilson's score is rather undistinguished.

Debbie Reynolds thrusts herself into the role with an enormous amount of verve and vigor. At times her approach to the character seems more athletic than artful.

Harve Presnell, who created the role on Broadway in 1960, makes a generally auspicious screen debut as the patient Johnny. His fine, booming voice and physical stature make him a valuable commodity for Hollywood.

1964: NOMINATIONS: Best Actress (Debbie Reynolds), Color Cinematography, Color Costume Design, Color Art Direction, Adapted Music Score

•

UNSTRUNG HEROES
1995, 94 mins, US Ⓥ ⦿ col
Dir Diane Keaton ***Prod*** Susan Arnold, Donna Roth, Richard LaGravenese ***Scr*** Richard LaGravenese ***Ph*** Phedon Papamichael ***Ed*** Lisa Churgin ***Mus*** Thomas Newman ***Art*** Gareth Stover
Act Andie MacDowell, John Turturro, Michael Richards, Maury Chaykin, Nathan Watt, Kendra Krull (Hollywood)

A coming-of-age piece that is slight to the point of anaemia, *Unstrung Heroes* sports a wilful eccentricity that almost immediately becomes annoying. Diane Keaton's debut dramatic feature aims for a distinctively offbeat tone that never really gels, and the movie's emotional power, stemming from personal growth through family tragedy, falls short of the goal as well.

Set in middle-class Los Angeles in 1962, yarn [from the book by Franz Lidz] focuses on 12-year-old Steven Lidz (Nathan Watt), a bright kid whose life at home becomes too much to take. Father Sid (John Turturro), a genius inventor, has always been a bit around the bend, forever imposing his rigorous scientific standards and weird contraptions on Steven and his little sister, Sandy (Kendra Krull).

After Mom Selma (Andie MacDowell) becomes ill, Steven feels compelled to run away to the home of his seriously goofy uncles Danny (Michael Richards) and Arthur (Maury Chaykin). Home, in this case, consists of a newspaper-and-tchotchke-infested apartment in a skid-row hotel.

Richards and Chaykin command the interest whenever they're around, but Turturro brings little feeling to a man who, at least on paper, would seem to be tormented by the craziness in his family, his inability to communicate with his son and the knowledge that he will soon lose his wife. MacDowell floats through it all in a nearly blissful daze.

1995: NOMINATION: Original Musical or Comedy Score

•

UNSUITABLE JOB FOR A WOMAN, AN
1982, 94 mins, UK Ⓥ col
Dir Christopher Petit ***Scr*** Elizabeth McKay, Brian Scobie, Christopher Petit ***Ph*** Martin Schafer ***Ed*** Mick Audsley ***Mus*** Chas Jankel, Philip Bagenal, Peter Van Hooke ***Art*** Anton Furst
Act Pippa Guard, Billie Whitelaw, Paul Freeman, Dominic Guard, Dawn Archibald, David Horovitch (Boyd's/NFE)

Cordelia Gray (Pippa Guard) comes to work one day where she is assistant to a shabby gumshoe. She finds him in his office with his veins cut and a big bowl of blood next to him. A posthumous tape asks her to take over. After the burial an intense middle-aged woman (Billie Whitelaw) asks her to take on a case, the suicide of her boss's son.

Obsession is the keynote of this case. Gray is fascinated by the dead boy as she finds out more about him. It develops he was first found hanging dressed and made up as a woman but someone had changed that. She almost hangs herself imitating the way the dead boy did it, gets thrown into a well but muddles through as the English do. Perhaps it is unfair to unravel this tale [from the novel by P. D. James] which is handled from a distance by director Christopher Petit, robbing it of a more forceful narration, timing and revelation.

•

UNSUSPECTED, THE
1947, 103 mins, US b/w
Dir Michael Curtiz ***Prod*** Charles Hoffman ***Scr*** Ranald MacDougall ***Ph*** Woody Bredell ***Ed*** Frederick Richards ***Mus*** Franz Waxman ***Art*** Anton Grot
Act Joan Caulfield, Claude Rains, Audrey Totter, Constance Bennett, Hurd Hatfield, Michael North (Warner)

Director Michael Curtiz packs yarn with plenty of rugged action thrills, despite society setting. Two chase sequences are especially humdingers for audience chills. Story deals with suave mayhem, with murderer Claude Rains known from the opening crime.

Plot workings are not as clear as they could have been but motivation of principal characters is followable, as scripted from a Bess Meredyth adaptation of the Charlotte Armstrong story. Rains is seen as radio narrator of murder mysteries who's not above making his stories actually true. An apparently suave, kindly soul, he's unsuspected in the death of his secretary, niece and latter's husband.

Rains pulls out all his thesping tricks to sustain the character, and makes it believable. Joan Caulfield is good as the rich, troubled niece who believes in her uncle's goodness. Audrey Totter and Hurd Hatfield show up well as the murdered pair, and Constance Bennett peps up assignment as a radio producer.

•

UNTAMED HEART
1993, 102 mins, US Ⓥ ⦿ col
Dir Tony Bill ***Prod*** Tony Bill, Helen Buck Bartlett ***Scr*** Tom Sierchio ***Ph*** Jost Vacano ***Ed*** Mia Goldman ***Mus*** Cliff Eidelman ***Art*** Steven Jordan
Act Christian Slater, Marisa Tomei, Rosie Perez, Kyle Secor, Willie Garson (M-G-M)

Appealing lead performances elevate this modestly scaled romantic tearjerker, from a first script by Tom Sierchio. Marisa Tomei plays a Minneapolis waitress who is assaulted one night by two creeps from the local diner, only to be rescued by Christian Slater, an introverted, almost nonverbal busboy enamored of her.

An awkward and unlikely romance develops, Tomei slowly penetrating Slater's protective shell, put up due to the orphaned youth's congenital heart ailment, which has kept him at arm's distance from people throughout his life. He also clings to a fairy tale about his heart coming from a baboon king after the death of his father (the pic's working title was *Baboon Heart*).

The story sometimes seems like an excuse to get out the can opener and serve up the corn. But Sierchio's script possesses some strong romantic flourishes and director Tony Bill takes advantage of them. The perfs prove so earnest the movie largely works on its own terms, particularly for those looking for a traditional "good cry."

•

UNTIL SEPTEMBER
1984, 95 mins, US Ⓥ col
Dir Richard Marquand ***Prod*** Michael Gruskoff ***Scr*** Janice Lee Graham ***Ph*** Philippe Welt ***Ed*** Sean Barton ***Mus*** John Barry ***Art*** Hilton McConnico
Act Karen Allen, Thierry Lhermitte, Christopher Cazenove, Marie Catherine-Conti, Hutton Cobb, Michael Mellinger (M-G-M/United Artists)

Set in Paris, plot centers on a young American woman stranded in the City of Light when she becomes separated from a tour group headed for Eastern Bloc countries. Frustrated by airline and diplomatic red tape, Mo Alexander (Karen Allen), takes refuge in a modest hotel.

Temporary setback is put aright when a neighbor, suave banker Xavier de la Perouse (Thierry Lhermitte), checks on the woman's story for verification. It doesn't take much to guess that the two tenants are destined to hit it off romantically, even if there are some initial awkward moments.

However, filmmakers are not intent on making another "woman involved with a married man" or "doomed love affair" saga. Instead a fanciful, unconvincing "love conquers all" scenario emerges.

•

UNTIL THE END OF THE WORLD
1991, 158 mins, Germany/France/Australia Ⓥ ⦿ col
Dir Wim Wenders ***Prod*** Jonathan Taplin, Anatole Dauman ***Scr*** Peter Carey, Wim Wenders ***Ph*** Robby Muller ***Ed*** Peter Przygodda ***Mus*** Graeme Revell ***Art*** Thierry Flamand
Act William Hurt, Solveig Dommartin, Sam Neill, Max von Sydow, Rudiger Vogler, Jeanne Moreau (Road Movies/Agos/Village Roadshow)

A dream project about allowing other people to see one's dreams, *Until the End of the World* is a dream partly realized and partly still in the head of the director. Described by director Wim Wenders as "the ultimate road movie," the $23 million production was intended to shoot in 65mm in 17 countries, but the format proved too unwieldy for all the location work and budget limitations forced a cutback to nine nations.

Film conveys the feeling of an abridgment, as narration by Sam Neill wallpapers the gaps in the globetrotting of William Hurt, Solveig Dommartin and other characters. Set in 1999, script by Wenders and Aussie writer Peter Carey [from an idea by Wenders and Dommartin] presents a world threatened by a nuclear satellite careening toward Earth. Party girl Claire Tourneur (Dommartin) is given stolen money by some bank robbers and, for kicks, she picks up a stranger, Trevor McPhee (Hurt), while transporting the loot to Paris.

Pursuing Trevor to Lisbon, Claire gets him into bed, but he takes off again. One step behind him to Berlin, Moscow,

China and Japan, with the assisitance of detective Philip Winter (Wenders regular Rudiger Vogler), Claire finally wins Trevor's trust and learns his true agenda. Detouring to San Francisco, pic comes to a rest after 78 minutes in Australia's outback.

In the logistically taxing effort to get all this on screen, Wenders has sacrificed some of his customary poetry. And the grand emotion and obsession needed to carry the two lovers around the world isn't apparent in Hurt and Dommartin. Pair strike no sparks, and Hurt seems blank most of the time.

[Version reviewed ran 178 mins.]

•

UNTOUCHABLES, THE

1987, 119 mins, US Ⓥ ⦿ ▭ col

Dir Brian De Palma ***Prod*** Art Linson ***Scr*** David Mamet ***Ph*** Stephen H. Burum ***Ed*** Jerry Greenberg, Bill Pankow ***Mus*** Ennio Morricone ***Art*** William A. Elliott

Act Kevin Costner, Sean Connery, Charles Martin Smith, Andy Garcia, Robert De Niro, Richard Bradford (Linson/Paramount)

The Untouchables is a beautifully crafted portrait of Prohibition-era Chicago.

Director Brian De Palma sets the tone in a lavish overhead opening shot in which Robert De Niro's Al Capone professes to be just "a businessman" giving people the product they want. That such business often required violent methods is immediately depicted as prelude to arrival of idealistic law enforcer Eliot Ness (Kevin Costner).

While the dichotomy of values is thus established between these two adversaries, it is the introduction of street cop Jim Malone (Sean Connery) that truly gives the film its momentum.

Connery delivers one of his finest performances. It is filled with nuance, humor and abundant self-confidence. Connery's depth strongly complements the youthful Costner, who does grow appreciably as Ness overcomes early naivete to become just hard-bitten enough without relinquishing the innocence of his personal life.

De Palma has brought his sure and skilled hand to a worthy enterprise. His signature for this film is an intense scene involving a baby carriage. Filmmakers liken it to the Odessa Steps montage from 1925's *The Battleship Potemkin* by Sergei Eisenstein.

1987: Best Supp. Actor (Sean Connery)

NOMINATIONS: Best Costume Design, Art Direction, Original Music Score

•

UNVANQUISHED, THE

SEE: APARAJITO

•

UP!

1976, 80 mins, US col

Dir Russ Meyer ***Prod*** Russ Meyer ***Scr*** B. Callum ***Ph*** Russ Meyer ***Ed*** Russ Meyer ***Mus*** William Loose, Paul Ruhland ***Art*** Michele Levesque

Act Robert McLane, Edward Schaaf, Mary Gavin, Elaine Collins, Su Ling, Janet Wood (RHM)

Director Russ Meyer's trademark is the casting of the most incredibly endowed actresses who bounce and jiggle through a primitive world, driving men to violence and murder for their favors.

The men in Meyer's pix are rarely a match for the women, though Meyer has equipped his actors with "marital aids" (to be polite) so they can compete with the ladies in long shots.

The violence, like much of the sex, is too outrageous to be believable. At one point, an axe is buried in a man's back, but he pulls it out and buries it in turn in his attacker's chest who then pulls it out and finishes the job with a buzzsaw to the groin. Fun stuff.

•

UP CLOSE AND PERSONAL

1996, 124 mins, US Ⓥ ⦿ col

Dir Jon Avnet ***Prod*** Jon Avnet, David Nicksay, Jordan Kerner ***Scr*** Joan Didion, John Gregory Dunne ***Ph*** Karl Walter Lindenlaub ***Ed*** Debra Neil-Fisher ***Mus*** Thomas Newman ***Art*** Jeremy Conway

Act Robert Redford, Michelle Pfeiffer, Stockard Channing, Joe Mantegna, Kate Nelligan, Glenn Plummer (Touchstone)

Up Close and Personal is *A Star Is Born* meets *The Way We Were*. The story of an attractive, ambitious young woman's romance with her boss, who grooms her into a pro TV newscaster, is a pleasing fairy tale with a charismatic cast and lush surroundings and music.

Sally Atwater (Michelle Pfeiffer) is fresh out of Reno. The demo tape she's sent to dozens of stations has landed her a job in Miami, where she arrives overdressed and over-eager. A teleprompter glitch has Sally re-christened "Tally."

Her debut's a catastrophe, but her boss—Warren Justice (Robert Redford), a former network White House correspondent—admires her spunk and makes her an on-air reporter. Warren takes her under his wing, and she begins to improve.

Loosely based on writer Alanna Nash's Jessica Savitch bio, *Golden Girl*, pic only distantly recalls the tragic rise and fall of Savitch, the late NBC reporter; Tally is considerably more wholesome and accessible. Nonetheless, Savitch's specter looms over the proceedings, threatening to turn this love story into a saga of the American Dream gone wrong. It also offers some delicious and brief star turns for the likes of Stockard Channing, Kate Nelligan and Noble Willingham. Otherwise, it's basically a two-character piece bolstered by the chemistry of Pfeiffer and Redford.

Director Jon Avnet does a fair job of substituting pace and scenery for logic. This piece of recycled goods isn't nearly as accomplished as its inspiration, but, regrettably, it's the best Hollywood currently has to offer in the heartstring-pulling genre.

1996: NOMINATION: Best Original Song ("Because You Loved Me")

•

UP IN ARMS

1944, 100 mins, US Ⓥ col

Dir Elliott Nugent ***Prod*** Samuel Goldwyn ***Scr*** Don Hartman, Allen Boretz, Robert Pirosh ***Ph*** Ray Rennahan ***Ed*** Daniel Mandell, James Newcom ***Mus*** Louis Forbes, Ray Heindorf (dir.) ***Art*** Perry Ferguson

Act Danny Kaye, Dinah Shore, Dana Andrews, Constance Dowling, Louis Calhern, Elisha Cook, Jr. (RKO/Goldwyn)

Expertly showcasing the comedic talents of Danny Kaye in his first film starrer, *Up in Arms* is a filmusical that's expensively mounted in Technicolor and in the best Samuel Goldwyn tradition of elaborateness. Character portrayed by Kaye is a wacky hypochondriac who's inducted by the army for a series of wild misadventures. At start, before Kaye is drafted, yarn [based on Owen Davis's play *The Nervous Wreck*] introduces him as reticent suitor for Constance Dowling, while Dinah Shore has designs on snagging Kaye and Dana Andrews is in love with Dowling.

While Kaye and Andrews go into service together, the girls enlist as army nurses. On transport going to the South Pacific, quartet are thrown together for further episodes to hold thread of yarn together, with main routine on shipboard being a wild chase evolving from Kaye's efforts to hide stowaway Dowling.

Kaye has great sense of timing in putting over his comedy for maximum effect. He also smartly delivers three song specialities especially written by Sylvia Fine (Mrs. Kaye) and Max Liebman.

•

UP IN SMOKE

1978, 86 mins, US Ⓥ ⦿ col

Dir Lou Adler ***Prod*** Lou Adler, Lou Lombardo ***Scr*** Tommy Chong, Cheech Marin ***Ph*** Gene Polito ***Ed*** Lou Lombardo, Scott Conrad ***Art*** Leon Ericksen

Act Cheech Marin, Tommy Chong, Stacy Keach, Edie Adams, Tom Skerritt, Strother Martin (Paramount)

Up in Smoke is essentially a drawn-out version of the drug-oriented comedy routines of Tommy Chong and Cheech Marin.

Script by the two comedians has hippie rich-kid Chong teaming up with barrio boy Cheech in a confused search for some pot to puff on, presumably to aid them in putting together a rock band. Pursuit takes them to Tijuana, where they end up driving back a van constructed out of treated marijuana called "fibreweed."

In diligent pursuit is narcotics detective Stacy Keach, saddled with the usual crew of incompetent assistants. The trail eventually leads to popular L.A. nitery, The Roxy, (in which Adler is partnered) where the dopers' band engages in a punk rock marathon. They take top prize when the high-grade van, catching on fire, inundates the club with potent smoke.

What's lacking in *Up in Smoke* is a cohesiveness in both humor and characterization. Once the more obvious drug jokes are exhausted, director Lou Adler lets the film degenerate into a mixture of fitful slapstick and toilet humor.

•

UP THE DOWN STAIRCASE

1967, 120 mins, US Ⓥ col

Dir Robert Mulligan ***Prod*** Alan J. Pakula ***Scr*** Tad Mosel ***Ph*** Joseph Coffey ***Ed*** Folmar Blangsted ***Mus*** Fred Karlin ***Art*** George Jenkins

Act Sandy Dennis, Patrick Bedford, Eileen Heckart, Ruth White, Jean Stapleton (Warner)

Based on the novel of the same title by Bel Kaufman, *Up the Down Staircase* concerns troubles of a beginning teacher in a tough city high school. And it is very good, almost in spite of itself.

With only one major star (Sandy Dennis) and virtually a single setting, this pic is nevertheless thoroughly cinematic and completely engrossing. This is mainly because it is well acted, carefully scripted and directed and finely photographed. Director Robert Mulligan has for the most part avoided sentimentalism and presents his story honestly and directly.

As pretty young Miss Barrett, fresh from a purely theoretical college training as an English teacher, Dennis is plopped into impersonal Calvin Coolidge High School, a multiracial institution where most of the teachers feel they are successful if they manage to keep their classrooms fairly civilized. Though many of the characters are familiar stock ones their treatment is generally successful.

•

UP THE JUNCTION

1968, 119 mins, UK col

Dir Peter Collinson ***Prod*** Anthony Havelock-Allan, John Brabourne ***Scr*** Roger Smith ***Ph*** Arthur Lavis ***Ed*** John Trumper ***Mus*** Mike Hugg, Manfred Mann ***Art*** Ken Jones

Act Suzy Kendall, Dennis Waterman, Adrienne Posta, Maureen Lipman, Michael Gothard, Alfie Bass (British Home Entertainment)

Up the Junction began its much-publicized life as a TV play which caused a flurry of controversy about its outspokenness. This feature pic is no sense a film version of the tele adaptation [of the book by Nell Dunn].

Story concerns an affluent girl (Suzy Kendall) who goes to live in Battersea, [then] a seedy area of London. There she works in a factory and falls for a good-looking van driver.

The irony implicit in this relationship is that the boy wants the lush life she's left behind, and she is quite unsympathetic, feeling that life is more real when it is underprivileged.

But, in practically every respect, pic fails. The treatment introduces an air of patronage into what was honest reportage, and turns it into a condescending class-conscious view of the British working classes.

Kendall, while a looker, hasn't the versatility to encompass a role that demands a plus of personality to make it convincing. She is continuously blank and subdued. Dennis Waterman is quite pleasing as the boyfriend.

•

UP THE RIVER

1930, 90 mins, US b/w

Dir John Ford ***Scr*** Maurine Watkins ***Ph*** Joseph August ***Ed*** Frank E. Hull ***Art*** Duncan Cramer

Act Spencer Tracy, Claire Luce, Warren Hymer, Humphrey Bogart, William Collier, Sr., Joan Lawes (Fox)

A comedy prison picture. The love portion of this Maurine Watkins story is played underneath the comedy. Spencer Tracy and Warren Hymer, as the laugh team, take the picture all of the time, along with William Collier, Sr., though much of their comic material is based on the love plot.

Funny idea has two escaped prisoners returning of their own volition just in time to save the big ball game against an opposition jail. Thought is said to have come from a Fox studio publicity man, Joe Shea.

Humphrey Bogart and Claire Luce are also in the prison, but really don't belong. The boy's respectable New England folks think he's in China. The girl was framed by a crooked stock salesman. The way the couple romance is interesting. They must do it with their backs turned and the prison fence between them.

This is Tracy's first talker, and he easily makes the grade. Joan Lawes, daughter of the noted warden of Sing Sing, plays just that part in this picture, and competently.

•

UP THE SANDBOX

1972, 97 mins, US Ⓥ col

Dir Irvin Kershner ***Prod*** Robert Chartoff, Irwin Winkler ***Scr*** Paul Zindel ***Ph*** Gordon Willis ***Ed*** Robert Lawrence ***Mus*** Billy Goldenberg ***Art*** Harry Horner

Act Barbra Streisand, David Selby, Jane Hoffman, John C. Becher, Jacobo Morales, Iris Brooks (First Artists)

Forget the euphemisms, *Up the Sandbox* is an untidy melange of overproduced, heavy-handed fantasy concerning a married woman's identity crisis, and laced with boring gallows humor about how bad life is in Manhattan.

The novel by Anne Richardson Roiphe has been adapted into a screenplay with very few genuine laughs but an awful lot of straining for cheap guffaws. Barbara Streisand, married to Prof. David Selby, is harried by two children and fears the effect on herself and her marriage of accommodating the birth of a third child.

Resolution is as inarticulate as the development. Were Streisand to have been working off some old contractual commitment, there would be much sympathy. But this is not the case, since the star is the producer.

•

U-TURN
1997, 125 mins, US Ⓥ ⊙ col
Dir Oliver Stone ***Prod*** Dan Halsted, Clayton Townsend ***Scr*** John Ridley ***Ph*** Robert Richardson ***Ed*** Hank Corwin, Thomas J. Nordberg ***Mus*** Ennio Morricone ***Art*** Victor Kempster
Act Sean Penn, Nick Nolte, Jennifer Lopez, Powers Boothe, Claire Danes, Jon Voight (Illusion/Phoenix/TriStar)

A sun-baked film noir related in the style of a demented fever dream, *U-Turn* lives almost as dangerously as its wild characters, and gets away with it. Exceedingly raw, imaginative, daring and energized, this rare straight genre exercise by Oliver Stone is loaded with twisted motives, brazen amorality, double dealing, incestuous relationships, subversive intent and hilarious surreal asides.

Adapted by young crime writer John Ridley from his novel *Stray Dogs*, tale features a hapless fellow becoming ensnared in a treacherous web of passion and deceit, with an alluring black widow spider at the center.

Jump-cutting and free-associating to its heart's content, film lands two-bit criminal Bobby Cooper (Sean Penn) in god-forsaken Superior, AZ, with an overheated engine. Leaving his old red Mustang convertible with mechanic Darrell (Billy Bob Thornton, hilariously rendering the definitive take on white trash), Bobby bops through downtown, where he succeeds in picking up Grace (Jennifer Lopez), a looker in a tight red dress who invites the drifter up to her well-appointed home.

Who should walk in but Grace's gruff husband, Jake (Nick Nolte), who kicks him out. Moments, later, however, Jake picks Bobby up on the road and asks him if he'd care to murder his wife for a price. Attempting the deed is complicated for Bobby by continuing hassles with the local sheriff (Powers Boothe), a wise-ass "blind Indian" (Jon Voight) and repeated assaults by a tough-guy (Joaquin Phoenix) who imagines Bobby is trying to make time with his tarty girlfriend (Claire Danes).

Pic could easily be mistaken for the work of an adventurous artist making his first or second film. Few directors with as many films under their belt are displaying this kind of stylistic urgency, without the slightest speck of Hollywood complacency. In addition, there are enormous pleasures to be taken from the performances.

•

UPTOWN SATURDAY NIGHT
1974, 104 mins, US Ⓥ col
Dir Sidney Poitier ***Prod*** Melville Tucker ***Scr*** Richard Wesley ***Ph*** Fred J. Koenekamp ***Ed*** Pembroke J. Herring ***Mus*** Tom Scott ***Art*** Alfred Sweeney
Act Sidney Poitier, Bill Cosby, Harry Belafonte, Flip Wilson, Richard Pryor, Rosalind Cash (First Artists)

Uptown Saturday Night is an uneven black melodramatic comedy. Its assets include an unwavering ragamuffin charm and some amusing bits by Bill Cosby, Harry Belafonte, Flip Wilson, Richard Pryor and Roscoe Lee Browne. Its debits stem from (1) a helter-skelter screenplay; (2) Sidney Poitier's lifeless performance; and (3) Poitier's unimaginative comic direction.

Factory worker Poitier and cabdriver Cosby take a night off from their wives (Rosalind Cash, Ketty Lester) to visit an after-hours gambling club, where the customers are held up by four stocking-hooded thieves. When Poitier later realizes that a $50,000 winning lottery ticket was in his stolen wallet, he and Cosby decide to track down the holdup men. They seek help from gumshoe Pryor.

•

UPTURNED GLASS, THE
1947, 86 mins, UK b/w
Dir Lawrence Huntington ***Prod*** Sydney Box, James Mason ***Scr*** J. P. Monaghan, Pamela Kellino ***Ph*** Reginald Wyer ***Ed*** Alan Osbiston ***Mus*** Bernard Stevens ***Art*** Andrew Mazzer
Act James Mason, Rosamund John, Pamela Kellino, Jane Hylton, Ann Stephens, Henry Oscar (Sydney Box)

Some will condemn the interminable narrative—even though it's admirably spoken through clenched teeth by James Mason.

Some will dislike the unnecessary flashbacks and the actual repetition of one incident. Many will squirm at two operations performed on children, sparing the audience nothing. Michael, a brilliant young surgeon, falls in love with Emma (Rosamund John), whose child he has saved from total blindness. The husband is abroad and her sheltered life is disturbed only by a jealous, widowed sister-in-law, Kate (Pamela Kellino). But Emma decides she cannot endanger the child's future nor shirk her responsibilities to her husband, and she and Michael agree to say goodbye.

Then with tragic suddenness Michael learns that Emma is dead, having fallen from a high window in her country house. Suspicious of foul play, his notions are confirmed at the inquest, and he realizes that Kate has killed her sister-in-law. He decides to murder Kate, begins an affair with her, eventually takes her to the house and the very room where Emma was killed and murders Kate in a similar manner, throwing her from the window.

That's the skeleton of the story and most of it is related by Michael to a class of students as the case history of an anonymous surgeon.

The part has been tailored to fit Mason, and he gives it complete credibility. John has never looked better nor played better, and Kellino is the perfect shrew.

•

URBAN COWBOY
1980, 135 mins, US Ⓥ ⊙ ▭ col
Dir James Bridges ***Prod*** Robert Evans, Irving Azoff ***Scr*** James Bridges, Aaron Latham ***Ph*** Ray Villalobos ***Ed*** Dave Rawlins ***Mus*** Ralph Burns ***Art*** Stephen Grimes
Act John Travolta, Debra Winger, Scott Glenn, Madolyn Smith, Barry Corbin, Bonnie Raitt (Paramount)

Director James Bridges has ably captured the atmosphere of one of the most famous chip-kicker hangouts of all: Gilley's Club on the outskirts of Houston.

Enter John Travolta, fresh from a West Texas farm and working his first job in an oil refinery, quickly learning that Gilley's is where everybody heads after work. Try as you might, it's hard to completely accept Travolta as a redneck and his Texas accent is not quite right.

Debra Winger is outstanding as a fetching little slut who marries Travolta only to lose him almost to Madolyn Smith.

Winger leaves Travolta to move in with Scott Glenn while Smith moves in with Travolta.

In one way or another, the quadrangle revolves around Gilley's mechanical bucking bull, a menacing device that tests the courage of all the would-be cowboys.

•

USED CARS
1980, 113 mins, US Ⓥ ⊙ col
Dir Robert Zemeckis ***Prod*** Bob Gale ***Scr*** Robert Zemeckis, Bob Gale ***Ph*** Donald M. Morgan ***Ed*** Michael Kahn ***Mus*** Patrick Williams ***Art*** Peter M. Jamison
Act Kurt Russell, Jack Warden, Frank McRae, Gerrit Graham, Deborah Harmon, Joseph P. Flaherty (Columbia)

What might have looked like a great idea on paper has been tackled by filmmakers who haven't expanded it much beyond the one joke inherent in the premise.

Plot has fat-cat car dealer Jack Warden desperate to knock out competition provided by a brother also portrayed by Warden. Latter dies early on but operator Kurt Russell and partners Gerrit Graham and Frank McRae disguise the fact to prevent their slimey neighbor from inheriting the property.

Scripters have provided very little context or societal texture for their unmodulated tale, which disagreeably seeks to find humor in characters' humiliation, embarrassment and even death.

Nonetheless Robert Zemeckis directs with undeniable vigor, if insufficient control and discipline.

•

USED PEOPLE
1992, 115 mins, US Ⓥ ⊙ col
Dir Beeban Kidron ***Prod*** Peggy Rajski ***Scr*** Todd Graff ***Ph*** David Watkin ***Ed*** John Tintori ***Mus*** Rachel Portman ***Art*** Stuart Wurtzel
Act Shirley MacLaine, Kathy Bates, Jessica Tandy, Marcello Mastroianni, Marcia Gay Harden, Sylvia Sidney (Largo/20th Century-Fox)

A modern, absurdist sensibility informs the soap opera *Used People* [from Todd Graff's *The Grandma Plays*], which harks back to '50s weepies.

Set in 1969 in the Sunnyside section of Queens, NY, film limns the colorful family life of a Jewish matriarchy centered around Shirley MacLaine, whose husband (Bob Dishy) has just died. Key characters include her protective mom (Jessica Tandy), dysfunctional children (Kathy Bates and Marcia Gay Harden), both of whom have been divorced, and Tandy's best friend (Sylvia Sidney).

Enter Marcello Mastroianni, MacLaine's secret admirer who uses the family's sitting shiva after Dishy's funeral as his occasion to make his platonic affections for her manifest.

The family's rejection of Mastroianni and cross-cultural antics between them and Mastroianni's Italian-American clan make for some effective comedy in the middle reels but Graff's work is built around highly dramatic confrontation scenes, in particular, a heartrending fight between MacLaine and daughter Bates.

MacLaine's precise acting is laudatory and balanced by a very sympathetic turn by twinkle-eyed Mastroianni, in his best English-language role by far. The support ensemble is excellent.

•

U.S. MARSHALS
1998, 133 mins, US Ⓥ ⊙ ▭ col
Dir Stuart Baird ***Prod*** Arnold Kopelson, Anne Kopelson ***Scr*** John Pogue ***Ph*** Andrzej Bartkowiak ***Ed*** Terry Rawlings ***Mus*** Jerry Goldsmith ***Art*** Maher Ahmad
Act Tommy Lee Jones, Wesley Snipes, Robert Downey, Jr., Kate Nelligan, Joe Pantoliano, Irene Jacob (Kopelson-Barish/Warner)

The charismatic presence of Harrison Ford in *The Fugitive*, and the gravity he brought to his role as a wrongly convicted man, are very much missed in *U.S. Marshals*, a disappointing sequel to the 1993 blockbuster that represented Hollywood craftsmanship at its best. Stuart Baird's new thriller is inferior to the Andrew Davis movie in every respect: script, acting, rhythm and even tech credits.

Routine, uninvolving story is credited to John Pogue, who's described in the production notes as one of Hollywood's most successful unproduced screenwriters.

Tommy Lee Jones reprises his Oscar-winning role as chief deputy marshal Sam Gerard, a dogged pursuer who this time around is chasing the ruthless and mysterious Sheridan (Wesley Snipes), accused of murdering two top agents in a Gotham parking lot.

Filmmakers have come up with a hodge-podge yarn that offers parallel setpieces. Instead of the terrifically produced train crash in the 1993 movie, this one features a plane crash, which enables Sheridan to escape. In lieu of the glorious overhead shot that depicted Ford diving into a waterfall, Snipes jumps from the roof of a skyscraper onto a moving train.

Gerard's elite law enforcement crew is newly joined by Cooper (Latanya Richardson), a black female, and John Royce (Robert Downey, Jr.), a cocky special agent who's not completely trustworthy. The interaction between Gerard and Royce provides some humor.

In the first reel, not much info is provided about Sheridan, who remains enigmatic throughout the film. Second problem is that an hour into the movie, almost everything is disclosed, which means the story has nowhere to go.

Considering that Baird (*Executive Decision*) is a former editor, what's most dissatisfying about *U.S. Marshals* is its lack of calibrated rhythm—pic is burdened with the kind of tempo that allows viewers too much time to think about the fraudulent plot. Production values are vastly uneven.

•

U.S.S. TEAKETTLE
1951, 92 mins, US b/w
Dir Henry Hathaway ***Prod*** Fred Kohlmar ***Scr*** Richard Murphy ***Ph*** Joe MacDonald ***Ed*** James B. Clark ***Mus*** Cyril Mockridge ***Art*** Lyle Wheeler, J. Russell Spencer
Act Gary Cooper, Jane Greer, Millard Mitchell, Eddie Albert, John McIntire, Ray Collins (20th Century-Fox)

The misadventures of a group of landlubbers in charge of a navy craft is rib-tickling filmfare as presented in *U.S.S. Teakettle*. Richard Murphy concocted his screenplay from a *New Yorker* article by John W. Hazard.

Gary Cooper is a 90-day wonder assigned to a craft to conduct trials with an experimental steam engine. He's given the chore simply because he studied engineering in college years before, not because of any nautical knowledge, of which he has none. Crew of the craft, with the exception of Navy vet Millard Mitchell, is in the landlubber class.

String of incidents developed around such a situation are run off smartly and help to disguise fact that there's practically no plot.

Cooper does excellently by his assignment, sharpening up the entertainment values. Jane Greer, as his wife, who joins the WAVES, doesn't have much footage but makes what she does have very pleasant to view. Mitchell's boatswain's mate chore is chuckful of salty humor that he plays to the hilt. Eddie Albert, Jack Webb, Richard Erdman, Harvey Lembeck, Henry Slate, Charles Bronson, Lee Marvin and Jack Warden are among the motley crew.

•

USUAL SUSPECTS, THE
1995, 105 mins, US Ⓥ ⊙ ▭ col
Dir Bryan Singer ***Prod*** Bryan Singer, Michael McDonnell ***Scr*** Christopher McQuarrie ***Ph*** Newton Thomas Sigel ***Ed*** John Ottman ***Mus*** John Ottman ***Art*** Howard Cummings

Act Stephen Baldwin, Gabriel Byrne, Chazz Palminteri, Kevin Pollak, Pete Postlethwaite, Kevin Spacey (Blue Parrot/Bad Hat Harry/PFE/Spelling)

Like a contemporary *The Asphalt Jungle*, *The Usual Suspects* is an ironic, bang-up thriller about the wages of crime. A terrific cast of exciting actors socks over this absorbingly complicated yarn that's been spun in a seductively slick fashion by director Bryan Singer.

Singer was the controversial co-winner of the grand prize at Sundance in 1993 for his *Public Access*, an intriguing but muddled account of a stranger who comes to stir up trouble in a small town. What he's done with *The Usual Suspects* represents one of the most impressive qualitative jumps in memory from a first to a second film.

The pleasures begin from the opening moments, as John Ottman's resplendant classical score backdrops some eye-popping Panavision images of an unseen man shooting Gabriel Byrne and starting a huge fire dockside in San Pedro. Pic then jumps back in time six weeks.

A blown hijacking of a gun-running truck in New York results in a police roundup of suspects who include corrupt cop-turned-thief Keaton (Byrne), the hot-headed McManus (Stephen Baldwin), the impudent Hockney (Kevin Pollak), the unpredictable Latin Fenster (Benicio Del Toro) and a crippled squealer appropriately named Verbal (Kevin Spacey). Christopher McQuarrie's ingeniously structured script then begins cutting back and forth between Gotham and the events leading up to the shipboard inferno. Singer provides what are sometimes called real movie-movie moments, scenes filled with live-wire acting, dramatic confrontations, startling action and surprising twists. His widescreen compositions are bold and muscular, and pic moves along at just the right pace. Every one of the thesps playing gang members makes a strong impression.

1995: Best Supp. Actor (Kevin Spacey), Original Score

NOMINATION: Best Original Screenplay

•

UTU

1983, 120 mins, New Zealand Ⓥ col

Dir Geoff Murphy ***Prod*** Geoff Murphy, Don Blakeney ***Scr*** Geoff Murphy, Keith Aberdein ***Ph*** Graeme Cowley ***Ed*** Michael Horton, Ian John ***Mus*** John Charles ***Art*** Ron Highfield

Act Anzac Wallace, Bruno Lawrence, Kelly Johnson, Wi Kuki Kaa, Tim Elliott, Ilona Rodgers (Glitteron)

In a NZ western of the North American Indian–white settler school, Geoff Murphy has fashioned a fast-moving visual tale of archetypal passion and action. "Utu" is the Maori word for "revenge."

Central figure is rebel leader Te Wheke (Anzac Wallace) during the wars between European settlers and the native Maoris in the late 19th century.

At first sympathetic to the European (pakeha) cause, Te Wheke turns guerrilla when his village is wiped out by British soldiers protecting the settlers. He retaliates in kind while recruiting supporters. As his actions become more despotic and cruel, he is hunted, captured and finally shot.

Murphy has produced powerful images and strong performances, particularly from Wallace, Wi Kuki Kaa (as Wirimu) and a big cast of Maori actors. Action sequences, special effects, and visual exploitation of a rugged, high country location in central New Zealand are superb.

•

U2 RATTLE AND HUM

1988, 99 mins, US Ⓥ col

Dir Phil Joanou ***Prod*** Michael Hamlyn ***Ph*** Robert Brinkmann, Jordan Cronenweth ***Ed*** Phil Joanou (Midnight)

Visionary Irish rock band U2 has not sold itself short with *U2 Rattle and Hum*, a deeply felt cinematic treatment of band's music and concern infused with striking visual style and electric momentum.

Film follows the band throughout the landscape of American-roots music, encountering street musicians in Harlem, collaborating with a gospel choir, performing with bluesmaster B. B. King and recording "Angel of Harlem," a poignant remembrance of Billie Holiday at Sun Studios in Memphis.

There also is plenty of homage paid to the 1960s, with covers of Bob Dylan, the Beatles and Jimi Hendrix. None of it takes away from the riveting performances of U2's own music, captured mostly at concert venues in Denver, Fort Worth and Arizona.

Director Phil Joanou films mostly in black and white save one color concert sequence, using grainy blowups of 16mm footage to create a gritty texture for the "street" segs and a startling mixture of silhouette and shadow for the concert footage.

VACANCES DE MONSIEUR HULOT, LES
(MR. HULOT'S HOLIDAY)
1953, 90 mins, France Ⓥ ⦿ b/w
Dir Jacques Tati ***Scr*** Jacques Tati, Henri Marquet, P. Aubert, Jacques Lagrange ***Ph*** Jacques Mercanton, Jean Mousselle ***Ed*** Suzanne Baron, Charles Bretoneiche, Grassi ***Mus*** Alain Romans ***Art*** Roger Briaucourt, Henri Schmitt
Act Jacques Tati, Nathalie Pascaud, Louis Perrault, Michele Rolla, Andre Dubois, Valentine Camax (Cady/Discina/Eclair Journal)

Jacques Tati, whose comic talents were revealed in *Jour de Fete*, confirms them in his second pic. Though not as funny as *Fete*, due to a lesser story peg, this one generates a load of yocks, with fine observation of types at a vacation resort.

All the types are there, from the robust English spinster to the beach strong-boy, henpecked husband, frustrated, martyred waiter, ingenue, and a host of other characters that give this a rounded, comic feel. Tati builds his gags with sureness, and clever timing and pantomime bring most of them off.

Tati is the semi-articulate, blundering but well-meaning clown, reminiscent of the early Mack Sennett types. Whether he is being chased by dogs, setting off a cabin full of fireworks, or blundering into a staid funeral, he is a very funny man. He has a weird broken-down car that is also a good source of gags.

•

VAGABOND KING, THE
1930, 100 mins, US col
Dir Ludwig Berger ***Scr*** Herman J. Mankiewicz ***Ph*** Henry Gerrard ***Ed*** Merrill White ***Mus*** Rudolph Friml ***Art*** Hans Dreier
Act Dennis King, Jeanette MacDonald, O. P. Heggie, Lillian Roth, Warner Oland (Paramount)

This ornate operetta, a pageant of bright fabrics, big sets and milling mobs, is founded upon *If I Were King*, a story [by Justin Huntly McCarthy] which has been done three or four times earlier in pictures. Protagonist this time of Francois Villon is Englishman Dennis King. Musically, only the one number, "Song of the Vagabonds," stands out. *Vagabond King*, as an operetta, retards itself as a melodrama. Touches of grim realism are sapped of their power by girls in tights as pages in the royal court and dwarfs turning cartwheels.

At least one case of miscasting is also a handicap. Lillian Roth has neither the necessary age nor emotional maturity to play the passionate Huguette.

Despite its weaknesses, *Vagabond King* is always interesting. It's a treat for the optics with some of the color effects of arresting beauty.

Jeanette MacDonald's performance supplies the requisite aroma of glamor.

1929/30: NOMINATION: Best Art Direction

•

VAGHE STELLE DELL'ORSA
(SANDRA; OF A THOUSAND DELIGHTS)
1965, 95 mins, Italy b/w
Dir Luchino Visconti ***Prod*** Franco Cristaldi ***Scr*** Luchino Visconti, Suso Cecchi D'Amico, Enrico Medioli ***Ph*** Armando Nannuzzi ***Ed*** Mario Serandrei
Act Claudia Cardinale, Michael Craig, Jean Sorel, Marie Bell, Renzo Ricci, Fred Williams (Vides)

An admitted steal from *Electra*, Luchino Visconti's modernized story is set in a small Italian town where Sandra (Claudia Cardinale) brings her new husband, Andrew (Michael Craig), for a visit to the old family palazzo. Family's disintegration, not to say degeneracy, emerges in rapid strokes, via an explicitly told tale of a far from chilled love affair between Sandra and her brother, Gianni (Jean Sorel), plus their mother's near-insanity, their father's mysterious death at Auschwitz, and the new and fairly sinister presence of their mother's second husband, Gilardini (Renzo Ricci).

Ambiguity prevails in many of Visconti's situation developments, and while this may irk some, it does confer an air of mystery and suspense on a feature which might otherwise be merely morbid. The brother-sister sex relationship is depicted graphically, though actual seduction is left slightly ambiguous.

Cardinale makes a striking Sandra/Electra, rising to impactful heights in her near-finale scenes with Sorel, whose limning of frere Gianni/Orestes, should win him plenty of international attention.

Craig's part as the husband is of more limited range, but he puts in an accomplished, sympathetic stint.

Visconti's own musical selections consist mainly of a Cesar Frank potpourri, strangely effective in keying moods.

•

VALACHI PAPERS, THE
1972, 123 mins, Italy Ⓥ col
Dir Terence Young ***Prod*** Dino De Laurentiis ***Scr*** Stephen Geller ***Ph*** Aldo Tonti ***Ed*** Johnny Dwyre ***Mus*** Riz Ortolani ***Art*** Mario Garbuglia
Act Charles Bronson, Lino Ventura, Jill Ireland, Walter Chiari, Joseph Wiseman, Gerald S. O'Loughlin (Columbia/De Laurentiis)

The Valachi Papers, based upon the revelations of the mobster [and a book by Peter Maas] who disclosed details of Cosa Nostra organized crime in the U.S., is a hard-hitting, violence-ridden documented melodrama of the underworld covering more than three decades.

Joseph Valachi was the Brooklyn gangster who, while serving a life sentence for his crimes, was induced by a Federal agent to reveal the inside structure of the Cosa Nostra.

Flashback technique is utilized as Charles Bronson, as Valachi, recounts to the Federal agent the innermost secrets of the mob, of which he was a constant but unimportant "soldier."

Terence Young, who directs forcefully, hits a shock note in this latter sequence which climaxes numerous scenes of brutality, including Anastasia's famed cutdown in Park Central Hotel barber shop chair.

•

VALAHOL EUROPABAN
(SOMEWHERE IN EUROPE)
1948, 85 mins, Hungary b/w
Dir Geza Radvanyi ***Scr*** Bela Balazs, Geza Radvanÿi, Judit Fejer, Felix Mariassy ***Ph*** Barnabas Hegyi ***Ed*** Felix Mariassy ***Mus*** Denes Buday ***Art*** Jozsef Pan, Miklos Benda
Act Arthur Somlay, Miklos Gabor, Zsuzsa Banki, Gyorgy Bardi, Laszlo Horvath, Laszlo Kemeny (Mafirt)

Picture, fourth produced in Hungary since the war's end, and first in the past two years, is a good, artistic attempt. Geza Radvanyi, director who made many films in Italy during the war, has touched with great skill and ability on many of the most important problems of Europe, that of children who were lost in the welter of World War II.

Story starts a bit slowly, showing children of various origin forced to roam the highways. They formed a gang, and due to mistreatment, are forced to rob for food.

Kids find a ruined castle and decide to live there. However, its not deserted as they thought; an elderly pianist living there too wants to escape from the world into this asylum. First they rob him, get drunk and want to hang him, but Hosszu (Miklos Gabor), their leader, saves him. The artist later begins to lead them back to the right way, and battles local officials who want to get rid of them.

The kids are played by boys picked up on the streets. Camerawork of Barnabas Hegyi is outstanding.

•

VALDEZ IS COMING
1971, 90 mins, US Ⓥ ⦿ col
Dir Edwin Sherin ***Prod*** Ira Steiner ***Scr*** Roland Kibbee, David Rayfiel ***Ph*** Gabor Pogany ***Ed*** James T. Heckart ***Mus*** Charles Gross ***Art*** Jose Maria Tapiador
Act Burt Lancaster, Susan Clark, Jon Cypher, Barton Heyman, Richard Jordan, Hector Elizondo (United Artists)

Valdez Is Coming is a sluggish [Spanish-shot western] meller starring Burt Lancaster. Story collapses from premise of a man attempting to right a wrong, to reels of boring mayhem. Legit stager Edwin Sherin's film directorial debut is unimpressive.

The Elmore Leonard novel is about an ethnic southwestern constable (Lancaster) who accidentally kills suspected murderer Lex Monson. Latter has been tracked into a corner by Jon Cypher, who also happens to have stolen away Susan Clark, wife of the man Monson is wrongfully suspected of having killed. Cypher has Lancaster brutally beaten. Latter's vengeance comprises the main story thrust.

In supporting parts are Richard Jordan, flashy but shallow as a young psychotic killer; Barton Heyman as Cypher's gang boss who comes to respect Lancaster's guts; and the late Frank Silvera as a friend to Lancaster and therefore hassled by Cypher.

•

VALENTINO
1951, 103 mins, US col
Dir Lewis Allen ***Prod*** Edward Small ***Scr*** George Bruce ***Ph*** Harry Stradling ***Ed*** Daniel Mandell ***Mus*** Heinz Roemheld
Act Anthony Dexter, Eleanor Parker, Richard Carlson, Patricia Medina, Joseph Calleia, Lloyd Gough (Small/Columbia)

Valentino is a full-blown romantic drama that makes little pretense of accurately biographing the screen star's life, but has the gimmick of his name and likeness. Anthony Dexter bears a remarkably true resemblance to the man he impersonates.

Director Lewis Allen gets the story underway with a meeting between Dexter and Eleanor Parker on board ship enroute to New York from Naples. Parker is a film star traveling incognito and Dexter is a member of a dance troupe headed by Donna Drake.

Stranded in the big city, Dexter has a period of dishwashing and gigoloing before he again finds Parker and, through her and a director (Richard Carlson) gets his first taste of film work. Plot again contrives to separate Dexter and Parker, he goes to Hollywood and works as an extra until successfully crashing a party and winning the gaucho role in *Four Horsemen of the Apocalypse*, a part that skyrocketed Valentino to fame in real life.

Story re-creates scenes from a number of Valentino's subsequent successes, such as *The Sainted Devil*, *Blood and Sand*, *The Eagle* and others, although they are not presented in real-life sequence. Parker brings to her star role a quiet warmth and quality that helps to make Dexter look better than he actually is.

•

VALENTINO
1977, 132 mins, UK Ⓥ col
Dir Ken Russell ***Prod*** Robert Chartoff, Irwin Winkler ***Scr*** Ken Russell, John Byrum ***Ph*** Peter Suschitzky ***Ed*** Stuart Baird ***Art*** Philip Harrison
Act Rudolf Nureyev, Leslie Caron, Michelle Phillips, Carol Kane, Felicity Kendal, Seymour Cassel (United Artists)

Director Ken Russell seems less interested in nostalgia and early Hollywood days than in trying to find the essence of a certain charisma that can be turned into a sort of world sex symbol. Casting of Kirov defector ballet dancer Rudolf Nureyev as Valentino works despite the elimination of the Latino darkness and smoldering looks.

Nureyev's pic bow is impressive as he manages to avoid being ridiculous in certain scenes by sheer grace and aplomb. And using him also excuses the film a slavish need to hue to Valentino's factual life. Yet Russell has now and then opted for the lyric, even the outrageous.

Early part of the pic does not quite come alive but with the start of his film career it perks up for some bravura scenes that capture the strength, vulnerability and appeal of this tragic figure.

•

VALERIE
1957, 81 mins, US b/w
Dir Gerd Oswald ***Prod*** Hal R. Makelim ***Scr*** Leonard Heideman, Emmett Murphy ***Ph*** Ernest Laszlo ***Ed*** David Bretherton ***Mus*** Albert Glasser ***Art*** Frank Smith
Act Sterling Hayden, Anita Ekberg, Anthony Steel, Peter Walker (United Artists)

Tale, briskly and imaginatively directed by Gerd Oswald, is laid in the west, but is by no means a western. Rather, it is a gothic and sombre psychological tale which repeats the same theme three times, each time from the viewpoint of a different character. Save for a preposterously melodramatic finale, which doesn't fit, it's a well-told tale and a work of solid craftsmanship.

Story starts with bloody shooting fray, in which Sterling Hayden and his henchmen wipe out the family of his estranged wife (Anita Ekberg) and seriously wounds her. At the trial, sympathy is on his side, since he's a leading citizen, a war hero (Civil War), and Ekberg supposedly was running away with handsome preacher Anthony Steel.

But Steel's testimony, related in backflash, relates another version—that he was helping an ill and neglected parishioner by taking her to her parents. Hayden's story, also told in flashback, is that she was a loose wanton, only interested in his money, who had seduced his younger brother (Peter Walker) and was carrying on an affair with Steel.

But Ekberg, supposedly near death, regains consciousness and gives her testimony.

Hayden turns in one of his best chores in years, while Ekberg impresses as an actress as well as a scenic wonder.

•

VALLEY GIRL
1983, 95 mins, US Ⓥ ⦿ col
Dir Martha Coolidge ***Prod*** Wayne Crawford, Andrew Lane ***Scr*** Wayne Crawford, Andrew Lane ***Ph*** Frederick Elmes ***Ed*** Eva Gardos, Scott Wolk, Marc Levinthal ***Art*** Marya Delia Javier
Act Nicolas Cage, Deborah Foreman, Elizabeth Daily, Michelle Meyrink, Colleen Camp, Frederic Forrest (Valley 9000/Atlantic)

Valley is very good simply because director Martha Coolidge obviously cares about her two lead characters and is privileged to have a couple of fine young performers, Nicolas Cage and Deborah Foreman, to make the audience care.

As the title suggests, she's a definitive valley girl, mouthing all the nonsensical catch phrases recently popularized in song and book. He's a Hollywood punker who normally wouldn't venture over the hills into the square valley, except to crash a party where they meet.

Their blazing romance, which shocks her high-school friends, ultimately becomes too socially threatening for Foreman and she cuts it off.

For a change, there aren't any cartoon problem adults on hand as there often are in these pictures.

•

VALLEY OF DECISION, THE
1945, 118 mins, US b/w
Dir Tay Garnett ***Prod*** Edwin H. Knopf ***Scr*** John Meehan, Sonya Levien ***Ph*** Joseph Ruttenberg ***Ed*** Blanche Sewell ***Mus*** Herbert Stothart ***Art*** Cedric Gibbons, Paul Groesse
Act Greer Garson, Gregory Peck, Donald Crisp, Lionel Barrymore, Preston Foster, Dan Duryea (M-G-M)

The Marcia Davenport novel of the same title contained enough material for any number of pictures, but no reader of the book will be able to quarrel with the film's results.

Plot picks up the Scott clan, a Pittsburgh pioneer steel family, at the time Irish Mary Rafferty comes to join it as in-between maid. The tale of unfulfilled love between the servant girl and young Paul Scott, one of the family's sons, is movingly dealt with.

Casting is of uniform excellence, topped by Greer Garson. It is only in the initial scenes that Garson doesn't quite fit the picture of the young Irish girl, but as characters and the story mature she rises to every demand. Gregory Peck, playing opposite as Paul Scott, is standout. He has the personality and ability to command attention in any scene.

•

VALLEY OF THE DOLLS
1967, 123 mins, US Ⓥ ⦿ ▭ col
Dir Mark Robson ***Prod*** David Weisbart ***Scr*** Helen Deutsch, Dorothy Kingsley ***Ph*** William H. Daniels ***Ed*** Dorothy Spencer ***Mus*** John Williams ***Art*** Jack Martin Smith, Richard Day
Act Barbara Parkins, Patty Duke, Paul Burke, Sharon Tate, Tony Scotti, Susan Hayward (20th Century-Fox/Red Lion)

Plot meanders between New England country girl Barbara Parkins, who comes to the big city and eventually is seduced by urban social patterns; Patty Duke, rising young singing star who gets hung up on pills, and Sharon Tate, playing a big-breasted, untalented, but basically sensitive girl who never finds happiness. Parkins and Tate, the latter particularly good, suffer from under-emphasis in early reels, and corny plot resolution.

Main body of the story [from Jacqueline Susann's novel] concerns the rise, plateau and erratic performance of Duke's character. For her, this is a very good role.

Susan Hayward, who replaced Judy Garland in cast, does an excellent job in giving acting depth to the role of the older legit star, ever alert to remove threats to her supremacy.

Five songs, including title theme, by Andre and Dory Previn are interpolated nicely, and logically, into plot. Dionne Warwick regularly warbles title tune.

1967: NOMINATION: Best Adapted Music Score

•

VALLEY OF THE KINGS
1954, 85 mins, US col
Dir Robert Pirosh ***Prod*** [uncredited] ***Scr*** Robert Pirosh, Karl Tunberg ***Ph*** Robert Surtees ***Ed*** Harold F. Kress ***Mus*** Miklos Rozsa ***Art*** Cedric Gibbons, Jack Martin Smith
Act Robert Taylor, Eleanor Parker, Carlos Thompson, Samia Gamal, Kurt Kasznar, Victor Jory (M-G-M)

Spectators are given a tour of the land of the Nile in this suspense drama, and the backgrounds offer more freshness to the film than does the routine story, dealing with robbers of the tombs of the Pharaohs, with a side angle having to do with the establishment that Old Testament accounts of Joseph in Egypt are literally true.

Robert Taylor plays a rugged American archaeologist who agrees to help Eleanor Parker, married to Carlos Thompson, search for the tomb of the Pharaoh, Ra-hotep. She wants to prove that her late father was right in believing the tomb will prove his theory about Joseph in Egypt. A mysterious gang, seemingly headed by sinister Kurt Kasznar, puts obstacles in the way of the search.

Plot period is 1900 and ageless wonders of the land of the Nile fit perfectly. Parker and Taylor are a good lead team for the drama, but Thompson comes off only fair. The script was suggested by historical data in *Gods, Graves and Scholars* by C. W. Ceram.

1989: NOMINATION: Best Costume Design

•

VALMONT
1989, 137 mins, France/UK Ⓥ ⦿ ▭ col
Dir Milos Forman ***Prod*** Paul Rassam, Michael Hausman ***Scr*** Jean-Claude Carriere ***Ph*** Miroslav Ondricek ***Ed*** Alan Heim, Nena Danevic ***Mus*** Christopher Palmer, John Strauss ***Art*** Pierre Guffroy
Act Colin Firth, Annette Bening, Meg Tilly, Fairuza Balk, Sian Phillips, Jeffrey Jones (Renn/Burrill)

Milos Forman's meticulously produced *Valmont* is an extremely well-acted period piece that suffers from stately pacing and lack of dramatic high points.

Plot of Choderlos de Laclos's 1782 novel is quite familiar due to Stephen Frears's 1988 hit film, *Dangerous Liaisons*, from Christopher Hampton's 1987 play. Forman has met the challenge of breathing new life into the material, but key plot twists and revelations are robbed of their novelty.

Basic story revolves around a bet by two 18th-century French aristocrats, Valmont (Colin Firth) and his old flame Marquise de Merteuil (Annette Bening). She wants Valmont to seduce 15-year-old Cecile (Fairuza Balk) to cuckold Cecile's fiancé, Gercourt (Jeffrey Jones), who is Merteuil's unfaithful lover.

Valmont counters with the bet that he can bed timid married lady Madame de Tourvel (Meg Tilly). If he wins Merteuil must submit to his lust as well.

What keeps the film interesting, if not riveting, is the generally on target casting and resulting topnotch interpretations.

•

VALSEUSES, LES
(GOING PLACES; MAKING IT)
1974, 118 mins, France Ⓥ ⦿ col
Dir Bertrand Blier ***Prod*** Paul Claudon ***Scr*** Bertrand Blier, Philippe Dumarcay ***Ph*** Bruno Nuytten ***Ed*** Kenout Peltier ***Mus*** Stephane Grappelli ***Art*** Jean-Jacques Caziot
Act Gerard Depardieu, Miou-Miou, Patrick Dewaere, Jeanne Moreau, Jacques Chailleux, Isabelle Huppert (CAPAC/UPF/Prodis)

A rather raunchy tale of two drifters who live off the land, women and small-time extortion and theft. Maybe a French road film, sometimes gritty, sometimes funny and even touching.

Longhaired, a bit ragged, the jovial and sometimes menacing duo, one 23, one 25, are first seen terrorizing a middle-aged woman and running off with her bag, with irate citizens in pursuit. Then they take a joyride in a car. The owner has a gun and threatens to take them in, but they manage to escape with his girl, who becomes part of their group from time to time.

Earthy at times but held from trying to shock for its own sake. An older woman is played with a mixture of weariness and appetite by Jeanne Moreau. She has an interlude with the two, who have gotten robbed in the store of the man whose car they took.

The girl is done with placid charm by Miou-Miou, and [as the two drifters] Gerard Depardieu and Patrick Dewaere appear promising.

Director Bertrand Blier [adapting his own novel] also shows a sure hand, and a brio and anarchic bounce.

•

VAMP
1986, 94 mins, US Ⓥ ⦿ col
Dir Richard Wenk ***Prod*** Donald P. Borchers ***Scr*** Richard Wenk ***Ph*** Elliot Davis ***Ed*** Marc Grossman ***Mus*** Jonathan Elias ***Art*** Alan Roderick-Jones
Act Chris Makepeace, Sandy Baron, Robert Rusler, Dedee Pfeiffer, Gedde Watanabe, Grace Jones (New World)

Vamp is an extremely imaginative horror film styled as jet black comedy.

Richard Wenk [co-writer of original story, with producer Donald P. Borchers] opens the film deceptively with the format of a teenage sex comedy. Fraternity pledges Keith (Chris Makepeace) and A. J. (Robert Rusler) agree to find a stripper for the frat party that night. They team up with Duncan (Gedde Watanabe), who significantly has a car. Upon their arrival in the big city, film quickly makes a permanent detour into *The Twilight Zone* when their car skids and comes out of a lengthy spin with bright daylight suddenly turned to spooky nighttime. Trio heads for the After Dark Club, which turns out to be a den of vampires.

Picture benefits immensely from the casting of disco star turned actress Grace Jones as the leader of the vampires. She has no dialog in the film, but expresses herself sexily in several scary scenes.

•

VAMPIRA
(US: OLD DRACULA)
1975, 89 mins, UK Ⓥ col
Dir Clive Donner ***Prod*** Jack H. Wiener ***Scr*** Jeremy Lloyd ***Ph*** Tony Richmond ***Ed*** Bill Butler ***Mus*** David Whittaker ***Art*** Phillip Harrison
Act David Niven, Teresa Groves, Peter Bayliss, Jennie Linden, Nicky Henson, Linda Hayden (World)

David Niven goes the way of Vincent Price in *Vampira*. Screenplay is set in the present day, and has Dracula reading *Playboy*, sleeping in an automated coffin, and giving tours of his castle as a means of luring fresh victims.

Niven smoothly incarnates the old-style rake, while magazine writer Nicky Henson, one of his victims, repellently typifies the hip young stud.

All of this might have made a good high-comedy satire, instead of sporadically amusing camp, if the dialog were sharper and if the plot didn't revolve around Niven's attempts to revive his long-dead mate Vampira, played witlessly by Teresa Graves.

•

VAMPIRE IN BROOKLYN
1995, 101 mins, US Ⓥ ⦿ col
Dir Wes Craven ***Prod*** Eddie Murphy, Mark Lipsky ***Scr*** Charles Murphy, Michael Lucker, Chris Parker ***Ph*** Mark Irwin ***Ed*** Patrick Lussier ***Mus*** J. Peter Robinson ***Art*** Gary Diamond, Cynthia Charette
Act Eddie Murphy, Angela Bassett, Allen Payne, Kadeem Hardison, John Witherspoon, Zakes Mokae (Paramount)

Striking a good balance between horror and comedy (with the emphasis tilted to the former), this contemporized vampire tale flits along in entertaining fashion before making like a ghoul and falling apart at the end.

Maximillian (Eddie Murphy) is the last of a breed of Caribbean vampires, descending on Brooklyn in search of a half-human, half-vampire woman who's unaware of her lineage to be his bride. Rita (Angela Bassett) and her partner Justice (Allen Payne) are cops investigating the murder spree Maximillian has caused, with furtive romantic interest between the two partners complicated by Rita's attraction to Maximillian.

Stealing scenes as the Renfield of the piece is Kadeem Hardison as Julius, whom Maximillian turns into his ghoulish assistant, and his foulmouthed uncle Silas (John Witherspoon), who's unconcerned about having a vampire in his building so long as the rent gets paid.

Helmer Wes Craven keeps the action [from a screen story by Murphy, Vernon Lynch, Jr., and Charles Murphy] moving despite some detours allowing Murphy to play other characters as he did in *Coming to America*. Murphy proves effective and menacing as the vampire in a rather brave departure from what might be expected. Bassett looks great once she gets vampired-up. The vampire effects and makeup are also impressive.

•

VAMPIRE LOVERS, THE
1970, 91 mins, UK/US Ⓥ ⦿ col
Dir Roy Ward Baker ***Prod*** Harry Fine, Michael Style ***Scr*** Tudor Gates ***Ph*** Moray Grant ***Ed*** James Needs ***Mus*** Harry Robinson ***Art*** Scott MacGregor
Act Ingrid Pitt, George Cole, Kate O'Mara, Peter Cushing, Ferdy Mayne, Dawn Addams (Hammer/American International)

The vampire/anti-heroine, played by Ingrid Pitt, has distinct lesbian tendencies. She prefers sinking her fangs into the bosoms of comely young women, though when required she's not averse to giving the works to an interfering local doctor and a manservant.

Not much of a story, but the screenplay [from an adaptation by Harry Fine, Tudor Gates and Michael Style of

J. Sheridan Le Fanu's story *Carmilla*] has all the needed ingredients. Dank interiors, eerie exteriors and stagecoaches, plenty of blood, a couple of unconvincing decapitations, stakes in the vampire's heart, the sign of the Cross, etc. Fairly flat dialog doesn't provide much of the unconscious humor that usually gives a lift to this type of entertainment.

•

VAMPIRES
(AKA: JOHN CARPENTER'S VAMPIRES)
1998, 104 mins, US Ⓥ ⊙ ▭ col
Dir John Carpenter ***Prod*** Sandy King ***Scr*** Don Jacoby ***Ph*** Gary B. Kibbe ***Ed*** Edward A. Warschilka ***Mus*** John Carpenter ***Art*** Thomas A. Walsh
Act James Woods, Daniel Baldwin, Sheryl Lee, Thomas Ian Griffith, Tim Guinee, Maximilian Schell (Storm King/ Largo/Film Office)

The pleasures are modest but consistent in *Vampires*, a part-Western, part-horror flick [based on John Steakley's novel *Vampire$*] that doesn't aim too high but nails the range it occupies. A tale of parallel quests in the photogenic American Southwest, the film centers on a vampire slayer on the Vatican payroll who's intent on destroying a 600-year-old master vampire before the already superhuman creature gets his hands on a secret weapon that will afford 24-hour mobility.

In New Mexico, Jack Crow (James Woods) and his team of specially equipped mercenaries attack a vampire "nest." Forget garlic, forget crosses: it takes a lot of aggressive pummeling and blasting to subdue a vampire enough to get him out of a dark shelter. No-nonsense Crow, who lost his parents to fanged critters, is fearless and married to his work.

At the aptly named Sun God Motel, Master Vampire Valek (Thomas Ian Griffith, very tall, very gothic) literally breaks up the party along with the chests and spines of most of the revelers. Only ones to get out alive are Jack, his buddy Montoya (Daniel Baldwin) and Katrina (Sheryl Lee), a hooker Valek has already bitten. Their plan is to use Katrina as a sort of diving-rod-cum-bait to find Valek, who's been on the loose since a botched "inverse exorcism" in the 1300s rendered him unstoppable.

Vampires taps into an appealing mix of anti-clerical sentiment, unsentimental rebel codes and gung-ho gouging and splattering. Unlike garlic, Carpenter's humor-leavened handling of evil doesn't leave a bad taste in the mouth.

Woods is a laconic delight, and Baldwin is OK as the lunk whose feelings for Katrina lead to a satisfyingly bittersweet conclusion. Lee harnesses a certain look in her eyes to convey a striking range of conflicted emotions.

[Due to the initial lack of a U.S. distribution, the film premiered in France in April and only opened later that year in North America.]

•

VAMPIRE'S KISS
1988, 103 mins, US Ⓥ ⊙ col
Dir Robert Bierman ***Prod*** Barry Shils, Barbara Zitwer ***Scr*** Joseph Minion ***Ph*** Stefan Czapsky ***Ed*** Angus Newton ***Mus*** Colin Towns ***Art*** Christopher Nowak
Act Nicolas Cage, Maria Conchita Alonso, Jennifer Beals, Elizabeth Ashley, Kasi Lemmons, Bob Lujan (Magellan)

Nicolas Cage is Peter Loew, a New York literary agent who works hard and plays hard. Only indications that all is not OK are his sessions with his shrink (Elizabeth Ashley). One night his latest pickup (Jennifer Beals) exposes her fangs. She keeps him alive so that she may continue to feed. As a result he starts getting the urge for blood himself, becoming even more manic at work and taking it out on his beleaguered secretary (Maria Conchita Alonso).

The film then takes a major U-turn, suddenly getting deadly serious as it appears that Loew is not turning into a vampire at all, but is becoming a full-blown psychotic. Latter portion of the film shows him raping, murdering and pleading with people to kill him.

Problem is that Cage's over-the-top performance generates little sympathy for the character, so it's tough to be interested in him as his personality disorder worsens. The supporting cast is given little to work with, as Alonso mostly cowers and Beals mostly bites Cage. Ashley fares best as the psychiatrist, particularly in a fantasy sequence at the end in which she tells Cage's character what he wants to hear.

•

VAN, THE
1996, 105 mins, UK Ⓥ col
Dir Stephen Frears ***Prod*** Lynda Myles ***Scr*** Roddy Doyle ***Ph*** Oliver Stapleton ***Ed*** Mick Audsley ***Mus*** Eric Clapton ***Art*** Mark Geraghty
Act Colm Meaney, Donal O'Kelly, Ger Ryan, Caroline Rothwell, Neili Conroy, Ruaidhri Conroy (Deadly/BBC)

The Van is the third film [after *The Commitments* and *The Snapper*] set in the now familiar suburbs of North Dublin, as seen from the perspective of author Roddy Doyle. Unfortunately, the new film turns out to be a minor affair that tries hard but fails to recapture the wild humor of the earlier outings. It's essentially a small story expanded to feature length.

Pic unfolds in 1989–90, when unemployment was rife in the Barrytown area (as it was in much of Ireland). Larry (Colm Meaney) has become used to being on welfare; best friend Bimbo (Donal O'Kelly) has, until now, held down a job in a bakery. The discovery of a filthy, abandoned fast-food van in a back yard spurs Bimbo to a bold idea: If he and Larry can refurbish the van, they can cook fish and chips, hamburgers and other delights for sporting crowds. The timing is right, because Ireland is in the finals of the World Cup soccer competition.

Members of the families pitch in and, after much effort, the grease-stained vehicle is more or less clean. The lads overcome a few minor setbacks and eventually open for business, which is soon brisk. But despite their success, the relationship between the friends becomes more strained. There are plenty of amusing moments in *The Van*, but ultimately the jokes remain anecdotal and don't build into a satisfying narrative. Meaney and O'Kelly give robust, larger-than-life performances, but they have an unfortunate tendency to shout at one another.

•

VANGELO SECONDO MATTEO, IL
(THE GOSPEL ACCORDING TO ST. MATTHEW)
1964, 142 mins, Italy/France Ⓥ ⊙ b/w
Dir Pier Paolo Pasolini ***Prod*** Alfredo Bini ***Scr*** Pier Paolo Pasolini ***Ph*** Tonino Delli Colli ***Ed*** Nino Baragli ***Mus*** Luis Bacalov (arr.)
Act Enrique Irazoqui, Margherita Caruso, Susanna Pasolini, Marcello Morante, Mario Socrate, Otello Sestili (Arco/Lux)

Offbeat, almost neorealistic film version of the St. Matthew Gospel, pic has many talking points and effective moments. Pier Paolo Pasolini has made a pic poles apart from the many which have told the story of Christ—though remaining faithful in its development and spoken text. It's probably the first instance in which a Marxist has tangled with this subject matter on film.

Pic was filmed in Southern Italy, and the faces are deliberately those of Italians. Costumes are a simplification of tradition, and settings are also different from those "usually" seen or visualized. Thesps are all non-actors, and Enrique Irazoqui is a find as the man who plays Christ. Faces have the craggy, unglamorous, rugged look of the working man or peasant. The music is similarly offbeat, containing Negro spirituals (*Motherless Child*, sung in Russian for example), Russo folk songs, etc.

Lensing by Tonino Delli Colli is a fine standout feature with its grey tone giving it a certain timelessness in keeping with Pasolini's choice of bleakly beautiful settings.

•

VANISHING, THE
1993, 110 mins, US Ⓥ ⊙ col
Dir George Sluizer ***Prod*** Larry Brezner, Paul Schiff ***Scr*** Todd Graff ***Ph*** Peter Suschitzky ***Ed*** Bruce Green ***Mus*** Jerry Goldsmith ***Art*** Jeannine C. Oppewall
Act Jeff Bridges, Kiefer Sutherland, Nancy Travis, Sandra Bullock, Maggie Linderman, Lisa Eichhorn (20th Century-Fox)

Some last-reel thrills and cathartic violence provide commercial oomph to the otherwise tedious thriller *The Vanishing*. Dutch director George Sluizer had the rare chance to remake his own 1988 *Spoorloos* in America. Unfortunately this version, scripted by Todd Graff, is schematic and unconvincing.

Film introduces Jeff Bridges as the villain at the outset, rehearsing methods of chloroforming victims and plotting kidnappings. He's a happily married schoolteacher but with a Nietzschean complex. Parallel story has Kiefer Sutherland and g.f. Sandra Bullock on vacation from Seattle driving past Mount St. Helens when, after a row that hints at possibilities of a break-up, she suddenly disappears from a rest stop. Sutherland goes crazy looking for her; the police don't help as there's no evidence of foul play. Fade out to three years later and Sutherland's obsession with finding her has continued.

The ultimate chilling climax of the original is repeated in the remake, but with 25 minutes to go and with very little impact. Unlike the subtle acting of Bernard-Pierre Donnadieu in the original, Bridges adopts an odd gait, curious manner, and an on-and-off accent that are distracting and spoil his performance. Sutherland comes off as a wimp.

•

VANISHING POINT
1971, 107 mins, US Ⓥ ⊙ col
Dir Richard C. Sarafian ***Prod*** Norman Spencer ***Scr*** Guillermo Cain ***Ph*** John A. Alonzo ***Ed*** Stefan Arnsten ***Mus*** Jimmy Bowen ***Art*** Glen Daniels
Act Barry Newman, Cleavon Little, Charlotte Rampling, Dean Jagger, Victoria Medlin, Paul Koslo (Cupid)

If the viewer believes what Guillermo Cain's screenplay is trying to say in this lowercase action effort, the "wasteland" between Denver and the California border is peopled only with uniformed monsters, aided and abetted by an antagonistic citizenry with the only "good" people the few hippies, motorcycle gangs and dope pushers.

The action is almost entirely made up of one man driving a car at maximum speed from Denver to, hopefully, San Francisco, against various odds, from the police who try to intercept him, to the oddball individuals he meets along the way.

Barry Newman is the ex-Marine who tackles the 15-hour drive sans rest or reason, kept awake by pep pills. A Negro disk jockey (Cleavon Little), tucked away on a tiny radio station in what is close to being a ghost town becomes his collaborator, warning him over the radio when he's near a police trap. This leads, naturally, to the now screen cliché of his being attacked and beaten by racists.

Also seen briefly is Dean Jagger as a Death Valley prospector who tries to befriend Newman and, very briefly, Charlotte Rampling, as a hitchhiker with whom Newman beds down for the night.

•

VANYA ON 42ND STREET
1994, 119 mins, US Ⓥ ⊙ col
Dir Louis Malle ***Prod*** Fred Berner ***Scr*** David Mamet ***Ph*** Declan Quinn ***Ed*** Nancy Baker ***Mus*** Joshua Redman ***Art*** Eugene Lee
Act Wallace Shawn, Julianne Moore, Brooke Smith, Larry Pine, George Gaynes, Lynn Cohen (Berner)

The performances are precise, the language is alive and well spoken and the setting is striking, but *Vanya on 42nd Street* still suffers rather heavily from the limitations of filmed theater.

Reuniting with Andre Gregory 13 years after their surprise success *My Dinner with Andre*, Louis Malle has unobtrusively recorded a theater piece that Gregory and this cast rehearsed and performed, on and off, for more than four years. Working from an adaptation of Chekov's classic drama done by David Mamet from a literal translation, Gregory and his actors continued to explore the depths of the timeless work through periodic rehearsals, improvisations and informal performances before limited audiences at the decaying Victory Theater off Times Square. To make the film, the company moved to the nearby New Amsterdam Theater, the former home of the *Ziegfeld Follies*.

Wallace Shawn is the 47-year-old Vanya, who vainly pursues the affections of the beautiful Yelena (Julianne Moore), who is faithfullly married to aging scientist and writer Serybryakov (George Gaynes). Latter's daughter by his first marriage, Sonya (Brooke Smith), pines for a frequent visitor to the estate, Dr Astrov (Larry Pine), while other members of the family and staff have their say about the unhappy goings-on at key moments along the way.

Mamet's dialog, while not as modern as that of his own plays, spills nicely out of the mouths of these actors, all of whom seem quite at home with their characters. Shot in two weeks in May '94, film looks and sounds good.

•

VELVET GOLDMINE
1998, 123 mins, UK/US Ⓥ ⊙ col
Dir Todd Haynes ***Prod*** Christine Vachon ***Scr*** Todd Haynes ***Ph*** Maryse Alberti ***Ed*** James Lyons ***Mus*** Carter Burwell ***Art*** Christopher Hobbs
Act Ewan McGregor, Jonathan Rhys Meyers, Toni Collette, Christian Bale, Eddie Izzard, Emily Woof (Zenith/Killer)

Iconoclastic American indie filmmaker Todd Haynes takes a highly personal look at the British glam rock scene of the early '70s in *Velvet Goldmine*, a constantly imaginative, stylistically lively but dramatically inert chronicle of cultural and sexual rebellion. Self-consciously structured as a *Citizen Kane*–like investigation into the life and career of a vanished superstar rocker and his intimates, boldly conceived film [from a screen story by Haynes and editor James Lyons] boasts an arresting first half but bogs down thereafter.

Film comes into focus as megastar glam rocker Brian Slade (Jonathan Rhys Meyers) is seemingly shot dead during a concert. When the killing is exposed to have been a hoax, Slade's career slides right down the chute. Ten years later, in a very grim 1984, Brit newspaper reporter Arthur Stuart (Christian Bale), who was a big Slade fan, is assigned to write a "Whatever Happened to Brian Slade" feature.

Arthur first visits the man who discovered Slade, Cecil (Michael Feast). Cecil covers the star's early life and his career-altering encounter with the outlandish American singer Curt Wild (Ewan McGregor), whose audacious act makes Slade realize he's seen the future.

The narrative baton is passed to Mandy Slade (Toni Collette), the popster's American ex-wife who, in the most explicit *Kane* reference, gives her interview to Arthur while drinking in a dark, empty nightclub. No one will have any trouble identifying David Bowie as the inspiration for Slade.

Pic is loaded with music, much of it excitingly staged and performed. Musician and glam rock fans will have their say on how the sound has been re-created through a combo of actual tunes from the period by the likes of Bryan Ferry, Lou Reed, Brian Eno and Gary Glitter, covers of vintage songs and some new compositions.

Performances are functional rather than deep or psychologically telling. McGregor seems vaguely off the mark as the unhinged but inspired American performer.

•

VENETIAN AFFAIR, THE
1967, 92 mins, US ▭ col
Dir Jerry Thorpe ***Prod*** Jerry Thorpe, E. Jack Neuman ***Scr*** E. Jack Neuman ***Ph*** Milton Krasner, Enzo Serafin ***Ed*** Henry Berman ***Mus*** Lalo Schifrin ***Art*** George W. Davis, Leroy Coleman
Act Robert Vaughn, Elke Sommer, Felicia Farr, Karl Boehm, Ed Asner, Boris Karloff (M-G-M)

The Venetian Affair is a tepid programmer about international espionage in Venice. Pacing is tedious and plotting routine, but the production is enlivened by some actual footage of Venice.

E. Jack Neuman adapted a Helen MacInnes novel into a routine script, dotted generally with prototype spy types. Vaughn, ex-CIA agent now a reporter, is sent to Venice after a diplomatic meeting has been bombed. Ed Asner, CIA boss there, once canned Vaughn because latter's then wife, Elke Sommer, was a Communist agent. Now she has disappeared.

Pot boils slowly under Thorpe's casual direction. What was meant as an underplayed approach becomes awkward, meaningless pause, reinforced by dull dialog.

•

VENGEANCE IS MINE
SEE: FUKUSHU SURE WA WARE NI ARI

•

VENICE/VENICE
1992, 92 mins, US Ⓥ col
Dir Henry Jaglom ***Prod*** Judith Wolinsky ***Scr*** Henry Jaglom ***Ph*** Hanania Baer ***Ed*** Henry Jaglom
Act Nelly Alard, Henry Jaglom, Melissa Leo, Suzanne Bertish, Daphna Kastner, David Duchovny (International Rainbow)

Venice/Venice represents the definition of a vanity production. Sliding way over the line between personal cinema and egotism, Henry Jaglom's ninth feature lacks either the colorful characters or innately interesting subject matter of his better films, telling essentially a non-story in slight, schematic fashion.

Portraying the director of the only American film in competition at the Venice Film Festival, Jaglom announces at the outset that he is a maverick: "I am the representative of the anti-establishment."

Jaglom builds a fragile little story about his curious relationship with attractive French journalist Nelly Alard, who is obsessed with his work. Jaglom gives her a sort-of interview that allows him to expound upon his own talents, pursue her a bit at lunch and around the pool and finally make out with her during a scenic gondola ride.

After an hour, setting shifts to Venice, CA, as Alard wanders in on a party Jaglom is throwing. Nothing much happens here except for some auditions in which Jaglom is looking for a woman to play his wife in an upcoming film, *Happy Endings*.

Seemingly given their heads in the dialog department, thesps seem at a loss where to take the scenes.

•

VENOM
1982, 93 mins, UK Ⓥ col
Dir Piers Haggard ***Prod*** Martin Bregman ***Scr*** Robert Carrington ***Ph*** Gil Taylor ***Ed*** Michael Bradsell ***Mus*** Michael Kamen ***Art*** Tony Curtis
Act Klaus Kinski, Oliver Reed, Nicol Williamson, Sarah Miles, Sterling Hayden, Susan George (Venom/Paramount)

Venom is an engrossing traditional suspense thriller [from a novel by Alan Scholefield] about a kidnapping, hypoed by the genuinely frightening plot gimmick of a deadly black mamba snake on the loose.

Klaus Kinski toplines as Jacmel, a German criminal who kidnaps a young American boy (Lance Holcomb) living in London, aided in the inside job by the boy's servants (Oliver Reed and Susan George). Unbeknownst, the boy has accidentally acquired a poisonous snake intended for toxicologist Dr. Marion Stowe (Sarah Miles) and the lethal reptile gets loose in the house.

With old-fashioned lines beween good guys and bad guys sharply drawn, film satisfyingly metes out snake-delivered justice to the evildoers. Combo of Kinski's quiet, dominant menace and Reed's explosive, brutish violence makes for a memorable ensemble of villains.

•

VENUS PETER
1989, 92 mins, UK Ⓥ col
Dir Ian Sellar ***Prod*** Christopher Young ***Scr*** Ian Sellar, Christopher Rush ***Ph*** Gabriel Beristain ***Ed*** David Spiers ***Mus*** Jonathan Dove ***Art*** Andy Harris
Act Gordon R. Strachan, Ray McAnally, David Hayman, Sinead Cusack, Caroline Paterson, Peter Caffrey (BFI)

Ian Sellar's first feature, shot in the windswept Orkney Islands, north of Scotland, is a film about childhood which moves very slowly to a quite moving climax.

Central character is young Peter who lives with his mother and fisherman grandfather; he's not certain where his father is, but imagines him to be a ship's captain. Much of the film is taken up with Peter's observations: family scenes, scenes in a church and at school, the discovery of a stranded whale. Then the father returns, and it seems he'd simply tired of island life and gone to the mainland.

The evocative background of the Orkneys is a major asset to the film, as is the unaffected performance of young Gordon R. Strachan, an Orkney schoolboy, as Peter. Professional players, like Ray McAnally as the grandfather and David Hayman as the local priest, work generously alongside the youthful tyro.

•

VERA CRUZ
1954, 94 mins, US Ⓥ ▭ col
Dir Robert Aldrich ***Prod*** James Hill ***Scr*** Roland Kibbee, James R. Webb ***Ph*** Ernest Laszlo ***Ed*** Alan Crosland, Jr. ***Mus*** Hugo Friedhofer
Act Gary Cooper, Burt Lancaster, Denise Darcel, Cesar Romero, Sarita Montiel, George Macready (United Artists)

Vera Cruz, the first release in SuperScope, stresses mostly the violence and suspenseful action bred during Mexico's revolutionary period when the Juaristas were trying to free the country of the French-supported Emperor Maximilian.

Gary Cooper, ex-Confederate major from New Orleans, joins forces with Burt Lancaster, western outlaw, and his gang of choice pug-uglies to escort a countess from the court of Maximilian in Mexico City to the port at Vera Cruz. It's more than the simple guard job indicated, since secretly the countess has a load of gold to be used in Europe to bring more troops to Maximilian's aid.

Besides the more obvious advantages of their star teaming, Cooper and Lancaster come through with actionful and colorful performances. Sarita Montiel, of the Mexican film industry, is film-introduced stateside in this, and shows up well in her U.S. debut.

•

VERBOTEN!
1959, 86 mins, US Ⓥ b/w
Dir Samuel Fuller ***Prod*** Samuel Fuller ***Scr*** Samuel Fuller ***Ph*** Joseph Biroc ***Ed*** Philip Cahn ***Mus*** Harry Sukman ***Art*** John Mansbridge
Act James Best, Susan Cummings, Tom Pittman, Paul Dubov, Harold Daye, Dick Kallman (Globe/RKO)

The photographic record of Nazi atrocities which Samuel Fuller has incorporated in *Verboten!* is timeless horror and piercing documentation of the low point in modern history. Fuller wrote, produced and directed the film and has created an interesting picture of a German city in the first days of U.S. occupation following World War II.

The initial scenes build a troubled romance between a warm GI (James Best) and a sympathetic German girl (Susan Cummings), with the latter part of the film being devoted to the thought-provoking resurgence of the Hitler youth into a "Werewolf" band—a kind of ersatz ratpack—which loots, kills, aids escaped war criminals and generally poses intolerable trouble to the American Military Government. Key to the band's destruction is the girls' 15-year-old brother, a member of the gang, who becomes disillusioned upon attending the Nuremberg War Criminal Trials and seeing the captured German film of Nazi horrors.

Fuller's production is excellent, having the look and feel of a film more costly than it likely was. His direction is good, often excellent, and his cast responds adeptly. Best is forceful in his determination to love in the days when it, as so many things, was forbidden. Cummings is very good throughout, growing steadily with the film coming across expertly in the final sequences. The late Tom Pittman has introductory billing in the film, and, as the leader of the wild youth, showed fine style and sound talent.

•

VERDICT, THE
1946, 86 mins, US b/w
Dir Don Siegel ***Prod*** William Jacobs ***Scr*** Peter Milne ***Ph*** Ernest Haller ***Ed*** Thomas Reilly ***Mus*** Frederick Hollander ***Art*** Ted Smith
Act Sydney Greenstreet, Peter Lorre, Joan Lorring, George Coulouris, Arthur Shields, Rosalind Ivan (Warner)

Stock mystery tale with period background, *The Verdict* aims at generating suspense and thrills, succeeding modestly. Sydney Greenstreet creates character of a Scotland Yard superintendent who is fired when he convicts and hangs a man on circumstantial evidence. To show up the Yard and the man who replaced him, Greenstreet commits the perfect crime. Only the conviction of an innocent man for the murder makes Greenstreet reveal how the killing was done and the reason for it.

Script by Peter Milne, from a novel by Israel Zangwill, is peopled with the usual number of suspects in order to divert suspicion from the real killer and Don Siegel's direction does well with his material. Peter Lorre, macabre artist friend of Greenstreet's is the prime suspect and turns in a good job to match latter's performance.

•

VERDICT, THE
1982, 122 mins, US Ⓥ ⦿ col
Dir Sidney Lumet ***Prod*** Richard D. Zanuck, David Brown ***Scr*** David Mamet ***Ph*** Andrzej Bartkowiak ***Ed*** Peter Frank ***Mus*** Johnny Mandel ***Art*** Edward Pisoni
Act Paul Newman, Charlotte Rampling, Jack Warden, James Mason, Milo O'Shea, Edward Binns (20th Century-Fox/Zanuck-Brown)

There are many fine performances and sensitive moral issues contained in *The Verdict* but somehow that isn't enough to make it the compelling film it should be. David Mamet's script [from a novel by Barry Reed] offers little out of the ordinary.

Paul Newman is a cloudy-headed boozer who was at one time clearly a top junior lawyer but has been reduced to soliciting clients at funerals. Colleague Jack Warden hands him the case that could put him back on the straight and narrow.

A young woman lies in a respected Boston hospital—a vegetable thanks to a dose of anesthesia she received from doctors while delivering a baby. Her sister wants to sue the hospital and Catholic Church (which owns the facility) for a sum of money large enough to enable her to start a new life.

Newman becomes convinced the church and hospital have conspired to cover up medical malpractice.

While Newman's drunk is a little difficult to take at the outset, he manages to weave an extraordinarily realistic portrayal by the film's completion. He gets especially solid support from Warden and James Mason.

1982: NOMINATIONS: Best Picture, Director, Actor (Paul Newman), Supp. Actor (James Mason), Screenplay Adaptation

•

VERITE, LA
(THE TRUTH)
1960, 130 mins, France/Italy b/w
Dir Henri-Georges Clouzot ***Prod*** Raoul J. Levy ***Scr*** Henri-Georges Clouzot, Jerome Geronimi, Simone Drieu, Michele Perrein, Christiane Rochefort ***Ph*** Armand Thirard ***Ed*** Albert Jurgenson ***Art*** Jean Andre
Act Brigitte Bardot, Charles Vanel, Paul Meurisse, Louis Segnier, Marie-Jose Nat, Sami Frey (Iena/CEIAP)

Using the background of a murder trial, director Henri-Georges Clouzot gives a series of slice-of-life sketches, via flashbacks, detailing a young provincial girl's adventures in Paris and the eventual murder of her lover and her own suicide. It stars Brigitte Bardot, forced into one of her most dramatic roles.

Bardot is a dissatisfied smalltown girl who goes to Paris. Instead of working, she sinks into a Bohemian life and first affairs with intellectual characters. Her sister's boyfriend falls for her but she is capable of having other affairs while theirs is on. They finally fight and part. But she tries to come back to him.

Bardot is her morally blind, pleasure-ridden sexy self in most of the production and is then called on to have big dramatic moments. Though they are mainly outbursts, she seems to have been whipped into shape by Clouzot. She has some savvily done nude and love scenes.

VERTICAL LIMIT
2000, 126 mins, US Ⓥ ⊙ col
Dir Martin Campbell *Prod* Lloyd Phillips, Robert King, Martin Campbell *Scr* Robert King, Terry Hayes *Ph* David Tattersall *Ed* Thom Noble *Mus* James Newton Howard *Art* Jon Bunker
Act Chris O'Donnell, Bill Paxton, Robin Tunney, Scott Glenn, Izabella Scorupco, Temuera Morrison (Columbia)

Cliffhanger meets *The Wages of Fear* in *Vertical Limit*, a high-altitude thriller that remains exciting as long as it stays on the mountains, which is most of the time. Once again proving his skill with straightforward, physical filmmaking, director Martin Campbell clearly relishes sequences that demand inventive visual solutions for the staging of intensely dangerous situations. Wasting no time, he delivers one right off the bat, an eight-minute prologue that will put many viewers' hearts in their throats. On the sheer red cliffs of a towering butte in Monument Valley, bro and sis Peter and Annie Garrett (Chris O'Donnell, Robin Tunney) are doing some technical climbing with their expert climber dad, Royce (Stuart Wilson). In a horrible accident, Royce demands that his son cut him loose to have any hope of saving himself and his sister.

Three years later, Peter is a *National Geographic* lenser who has abandoned mountaineering, while Annie has become a hotshot climber whose current gig has her accompanying billionaire entrepreneur Elliot Vaughn (Bill Paxton) on a rapid ascent of K2. The arrogantly confident Elliot has surrounded himself with the best team that his limitless money can buy, including expert climber Tom McLaren (Nicholas Lea). At 26,000 feet when severe weather hits, Elliot, Annie and Tom end up inside a deep cavern that shortly becomes sealed by an avalanche. A galvanized Peter takes charge of the rescue attempt, quickly assembling a team of diverse and sometimes strange characters including enigmatic hard case Montgomery Wick (Scott Glenn). Not only does this bunch have to rush up what may be the world's most perilous mountain, but must do so carrying canisters of nitroglycerin to blast through the snow and rock that enshroud the trio. Just the slightest undue jostling or contact will make nitro blow, and the very idea that climbers could imagine carrying the stuff is merely the unlikeliest of the story's numerous hokey elements.

But all the narrative contortions exist to enable Campbell to do what he does best, which is to ratchet up tension and put across scenes of intense peril and imminent death with visceral impact. That the rescue attempt itself comes at the last possible minute is a given, and the resolutions of certain significant story strands are outfitted with some pat but sweet ironies. Pic has virtually no flab and action-suspense scenes in particular have been cut to maximum effect.

VERTIGO
1958, 126 mins, US Ⓥ ⊙ col
Dir Alfred Hitchcock *Prod* Alfred Hitchcock *Scr* Alec Coppel, Samuel Taylor *Ph* Robert Burks *Ed* George Tomasini *Mus* Bernard Herrmann *Art* Hal Pereira, Henry Bumstead
Act James Stewart, Kim Novak, Barbara Bel Geddes, Tom Helmore, Henry Jones, Ellen Corby (Paramount)

Vertigo is prime though uneven Hitchcock. James Stewart, on camera almost constantly, comes through with a startlingly fine performance as the lawyer-cop who suffers from acrophobia. Kim Novak, shopgirl who involves Stewart in what turns out to be a clear case of murder, is interesting under Hitchcock's direction and nearer an actress than in the earlier *Pal Joey* or *Jeanne Eagles*.

Unbilled is the city of San Francisco, photographed extensively and in exquisite color. Through all of this runs Alfred Hitchcock's directorial hand, cutting, angling and gimmicking with mastery. Unfortunately, even that mastery is not enough to overcome one major fault—that the film's first half is too slow and too long. This may be because: (1) Hitchcock became overly enamored with the vertiginous beauty of Frisco; or (2) the screenplay (from the novel *D'entre les morts* by Pierre Boileau and Thomas Narcejac) just takes too long to get off the ground.

Film opens with a rackling scene in which Stewart's acrophobia is explained: He hangs from top of a building in midst of chasing a robber over rooftops and watches a police buddy plunge to his death. But for the next hour the action is mainly psychic, with Stewart hired by a rich shipbuilder to watch the shipowner's wife (Novak) as she loses her mental moorings, attempts suicide and immerses herself in the gloomy maunderings of her mad great-grandmother. Stewart goes off his rocker and winds up in a mental institution. When he comes out, still a trifle unbalanced, he keeps hunting for a girl who resembles Novak.

Supporting players are all excellent, with Barbara Bel Geddes, in limited role of Stewart's down-to-earth girlfriend, standout for providing early dashes of humor.

Frisco location scenes—whether of Nob Hill, interior of Ernie's restaurant, Land's End, downtown, Muir Woods, Mission Dolores or San Juan Bautista—are absolutely authentic and breathtaking.

1958: NOMINATIONS: Best Art Direction, Sound

VERY SPECIAL FAVOR, A
1965, 105 mins, US col
Dir Michael Gordon *Prod* Stanley Shapiro *Scr* Stanley Shapiro, Nate Monaster *Ph* Leo Tover *Ed* Russell F. Schoengarth *Mus* Vic Mizzy *Art* Alexander Golitzen, Walter Simonds
Act Rock Hudson, Leslie Caron, Charles Boyer, Walter Slezak, Dick Shawn, Larry Storch (Universal)

The beautifully mounted feature draws its title from Rock Hudson, as American oilman who bests French lawyer Charles Boyer in a Paris court case simply by romancing the femme judge, admitting to Boyer on a plane en route back to U.S. that he feels he owes him a favor by beating him at his own national sport, which he'll grant anytime latter requests.

Boyer, in NY to see a daughter for first time in 25 years, sees in her, although a highly successful psychologist, a spinster with the spirit of an old maid, a woman nearly 30 who has never tasted the life her French father thinks every femme should know. He calls on Hudson to make good his offer.

Script develops along expected lines, with Hudson posing to Leslie Caron, the psychologist, as a man with a disturbing problem—he's irresistible to women who pursue him and he's a love toy.

Hudson delivers one of his customary light characterizations, and Boyer as usual is suave. Most outstanding work in pic, however, is contributed by Nita Talbot, a switchboard operator infatuated with Hudson, and Larry Storch, a hardboiled taxi-driver.

VEUVE DE SAINT-PIERRE, LA
(THE WIDOW OF SAINT-PIERRE)
2000, 112 mins, France Ⓥ ⊙ ▭ col
Dir Patrice Leconte *Prod* Gilles Legrand, Frederic Brillion *Scr* Claude Faraldo *Ph* Eduardo Serra *Ed* Joelle Hache *Mus* Pascal Esteve *Art* Ivan Maussion
Act Juliette Binoche, Daniel Auteuil, Emir Kusturica (Epithete)

An unconventional love story told with delicacy and power, *The Widow of Saint-Pierre* is a sweeping costumer shot through with issues and considerations that are as pertinent today as they were 150 years ago. Based on true events, pic recounts the strange and wonderful triangle formed by a military officer, his beloved wife and the convicted murderer she endeavors to redeem via kindness and trust.

Story is set in 1849 and 1850 on the French-run island of St. Pierre, off the southern coast of Newfoundland. The local captain (Auteuil) and his wife (Binoche) are childless. She is referred to simply as Madame La, as calling a woman Madame La Capitaine would be unseemly. Life on St. Pierre is disrupted when two visiting sailors murder a local resident and are sentenced to death. One dies in an accident, leaving only Neel Auguste (Yugoslav helmer Emir Kusturica, in his screen debut). In a French territory subject to French regulations, all executions must be carried out via guillotine—"widow" in 19th-century slang—but St. Pierre doesn't have one, so the contraption has to be sent from faroff Paris.

Convinced that no men are all bad, Madame La suggests that Neel could do useful work such as gardening and roof repair in the meantime. The captain, who can refuse his wife nothing, allows Neel to move freely, which is the beginning of a treacherous chess game between the stubborn officer and the increasingly intransigent bigwigs of local government. If the prisoner were to escape, the captain would be required to take his place on the guillotine.

Pacing is slow by Hollywood standards, but there's always something going on as pic explores the ramifications of civil disobedience and the death penalty. In a vividly delineated world of firm decisions and ineluctable consequences, it is a heady experience witnessing the bold speech and decisive actions of people who have the courage of their convictions.

Binoche is called upon to be both kindhearted and radiant, and her features seem to lend themselves to an admiring camera that could hail from the silent era. Auteuil is terrific as the enigmatic, serenely self-assured officer whose wife and whose word are sacred. With his halting, accented French and imposing demeanor, Kusturica is excellent as the initially oafish outsider who becomes a cherished member of the tight-knit community.

VIAGGIO IN ITALIA
(VOYAGE TO ITALY ; STRANGERS; THE LONELY WOMAN)
1954, 100 mins, Italy Ⓥ b/w
Dir Roberto Rossellini *Scr* Roberto Rossellini, Vitaliano Brancati *Ph* Enzo Serafin *Ed* Jolanda Benvenuti *Mus* Renzo Rossellini *Art* Piero Filippone
Act Ingrid Bergman, George Sanders, Leslie Daniels, Natalia Ray, Anna Proclemer, Maria Mauban (Sveva/Junior)

Story tells of an English couple, coldly moving close to divorce because of mutual incomprehension, who inherit a house near Naples. Planning to sell it, they begin suddenly to warm to the southern climate and the boisterous humanity about them. Film as a whole alternates brilliant bits with long stretches of so-so. [Version reviewed was the original Italian one. Overseas, pic was distributed in a 75-min. version.]

Rapid change from grit to grin, especially in George Sanders, who plays Ingrid Bergman's husband, mars the effect of the warmup process by overspeeding. Tale is unevenly told, has some unhappy bits of dialog and sometimes shows the roughout form, which for its director is the final version.

Editing, for example, is characteristically abrupt. Whereas Bergman's character, given more footage, appears much clearer in delineation, Sanders lacks the needed definition enabling proper audience participation. For instance, his interlude with a prostitute begins promisingly, but the idea is not followed through. Others in cast fill in well.

VICE SQUAD
1953, 88 mins, US b/w
Dir Arnold Laven *Prod* Jules V. Levy, Arthur Gardner *Scr* Lawrence Roman *Ph* Joseph F. Biroc *Ed* Arthur H. Nadel *Mus* Herschel Burke Gilbert *Art* Carroll Clark
Act Edward G. Robinson, Paulette Goddard, K. T. Stevens, Porter Hall, Adam Williams, Mary Ellen Kay (United Artists/Sequoia)

The workaday world of a police captain, complete with murder, bank robbery and sundry other major and minor crimes, is basis for this okay melodrama. Because of the semidocumentary style, the picture has a tendency to be repetitious in detailing police work.

Edward G. Robinson does the expected competent job of playing the police captain who arrives at work one morning to find his men looking for the gunmen who killed a cop during the early hours. The killing is tied in with a planned bank robbery, a scheme thwarted by police vigilance, but which doesn't prevent the desperate kidnaping of a femme bank clerk as a shield.

Paulette Goddard is used as the head of an escort bureau whose girls sometimes furnish the police valuable leads. She plays it colorfully. Pic is based on Leslie T. White's novel, *Harness Bull*, and Los Angeles is the scene of the action.

VICE VERSA
1988, 98 mins, US Ⓥ ⊙ col
Dir Brian Gilbert *Prod* Dick Clement, Ian La Frenais *Scr* Dick Clement, Ian La Frenais *Ph* King Baggot *Ed* David Garfield *Mus* David Shire *Art* Jim Schoppe
Act Judge Reinhold, Fred Savage, Corinne Bohrer, Swoosie Kurtz, David Proval, Jane Kaczmarek (Columbia)

Vice Versa finds Judge Reinhold, a tony Chicago department store exec named Marshall, and his junior high school age son, Charlie (Fred Savage), ending up with each other's personalities after they both touch a mystical oriental skull.

Reinhold is in his element acting like an 11-year-old more interested in heavy metal rock and his pet frog than girls and other yucky things. The store's chief honcho is ready to fire him, but his fellow execs, all coveting his job, are relishing his antics.

Things get a bit too sappy, though, with his lovestruck girlfriend, Sam (Corinne Bohrer); the more immature he acts, the more enamored she becomes.

It is really Savage, best known for his role as the little boy in *The Princess Bride*, who is particularly winsome as the smart-alecky Dad stuck in his kid's pint-size body. Except for the overuse of profanity for Savage's character, this is fun family fare.

VICTIM
1961, 100 mins, UK Ⓥ ⊙ b/w
Dir Basil Dearden *Prod* Michael Relph *Scr* Janet Green, John McCormick *Ph* Otto Heller *Ed* John D. Guthridge *Mus* Philip Green *Art* Alex Vetchinsky

Act Dirk Bogarde, Sylvia Syms, Dennis Price, Anthony Nicholls, Peter McEnery, Nigel Stock (Allied Film Makers)

Producer Michael Relph, director Basil Dearden and writers Janet Green and John McCormick (the team which produced *Sapphire*, involving racial prejudice) adopt a similar technique with *Victim*. They provide a taut, holding thriller about blackmailers latching on to homosexuals and at the same time take several critical swipes at the British law which encourages the blackmailing by making homos criminal outcasts.

Dirk Bogarde plays a successful barrister who is on the verge of becoming a Queen's Counsel. He is happily married to a wife (Sylvia Syms) who knew of his homo leanings when she married him but has successfully helped him to lead a normal life. He refuses to see a youth (Peter McEnery) with whom he previously has had association because he fears possible blackmail. Instead the boy is trying to protect the barrister from blackmail. The youth commits suicide, Bogarde is caught up in enquiries by the cops and, from remorse, sets out to break the blackmailers even though he knows that if the facts come out it will ruin his marriage and his career.

The homosexuals involved are not caricatures but are shown as varying human beings. There are a philanthropist peer, an actor, an aging barber, a hearty car salesman from a good family, a photographer, a bookseller and a factory clerk.

Bogarde is subtle, sensitive and strong. Syms handles a difficult role with delicacy and there is one memorable scene when the two quarrel after she forces him to admit what she doesn't want to hear. This is telling, moving stuff.

•

VICTOIRE EN CHANTANT, LA
(BLACK AND WHITE IN COLOR)

1976, 100 mins, France/W. Germany/Ivory Coast Ⓥ ⦿ col

Dir Jean-Jacques Annaud ***Prod*** Arthur Cohn, Jacques Perrin, Giorgio Silvagni ***Scr*** Georges Cauchon, Jean-Jacques Annaud ***Ph*** Claude Agostini, Eduardo Serra, Manamoudou Magasouba ***Ed*** Jean-Claude Huguet, Monique Laurent, Christine Giretnet ***Mus*** Pierre Bachelet

Act Jean Carmet, Jacques Dufilho, Catherine Rouvel, Jacques Spiesser, Dora Doll, Maurice Barrier (Raggane/SFP/FR3/Smart/Societe Ivorienne de Cinema)

A cutting crucible pic dealing in racism, colonialism, imperialism and that great leveler of them all, war. Film takes place in a remote corner of Africa during World War I when a handful of bored Frenchmen belatedly find they are at war with Germany and decide to attack the neighboring Germans in another European colony nearby.

Each has little military power, but they press natives into their armies who do the fighting and dying for no reason. Finally an English group moves in and tells them the war is over.

The film manages to avoid overdoing its satirical thrust and is a sort of moral fable or philosophical tale about man's general inhumanity to man, especially those below them.

Director Jean-Jacques Annaud, coming from ad pic making, gives this a good local color, never forces the farcical aspects, and keeps the actors in line. He does not indulge in the technical hijinks usually revealed in first pix by ad makers who have to grab attention fast. Acting rightfully keeps itself flamboyant but rarely slops over into stereotype or hamming.

1976: Best Foreign Language Film

•

VICTORIA THE GREAT

1937, 112 mins, UK b/w & col

Dir Herbert Wilcox ***Prod*** Herbert Wilcox ***Scr*** Miles Malleson, Charles de Grandcourt ***Ph*** Freddie Young, William V. Skall ***Ed*** James Elmo Williams, Jill Irving ***Mus*** Anthony Collins ***Art*** L. P. Williams

Act Anna Neagle, Anton Walbrook, Walter Rilla, Mary Morris, H. B. Warner, Felix Aylmer (Imperator)

Not cloak-and-cocked-hat historical tedium of pageantry and fancy dramatics, *Victoria the Great* travels a long way toward a full and clarified explanation of the most popular ruler England ever had. Her career, both public and private, is traced from June 20, 1837, when she ascended the throne, until the day of her 60th anniversary as queen, shortly before her demise.

Anna Neagle, in the title role, gives an unwavering performance throughout. Anton Walbrook as Albert, the Prince Consort, is superb.

The film wisely puts its prime focus on the private life of Victoria, her romance, marriage, and personal characteristics. Backgrounded is her public life, and her gradual rise to such high estimation of her people.

Victoria the Great is done with a lavish hand—the closing sequence is in Technicolor [shot by William V. Skall]. The tinting isn't too good, but serves effectively as a pointer-up for the climax.

This is the very first pic made after the Crown permitted a dramatization to be presented within the Empire dealing with Victoria.

•

VICTORS, THE

1963, 175 mins, US b/w

Dir Carl Foreman ***Prod*** Carl Foreman ***Scr*** Carl Foreman ***Ph*** Christopher Challis ***Ed*** Alan Osbiston ***Mus*** Sol Kaplan ***Art*** Geoffrey Drake

Act George Hamilton, George Peppard, Eli Wallach, James Mitchum, Romy Schneider, Jeanne Moreau (Highroad/Columbia)

Carl Foreman tells his tale of war in terms of vignettes, concentrating on homesickness, woman-hunger, civilian starvation, the "nice" girls who shack up with the GI smoothies for food, cigarettes and kicks. One of these is played by Romy Schneider. Her indifference to the decent soldier (George Hamilton) and ultimate bumming around with the slicker is underplayed, but it's part of the mosaic of the decent GI's own ultimate hardening.

The story is properly told in black and white photography. Foreman has incorporated a lot of newsreel footage. He has designed his narrative with great filmmaking skill and considerable daring, recalling the early 1940s both for nostalgia and irony.

In general Foreman has had the wisdom to underplay his scenes, leave many an incident without the sequel which seems, but is not, mandatory. In his alter ego as adaptor he has taken his story from [the book *The Human Factor* by] an English writer, Alexander Baron, to whom all proper honor. There will be a plausible temptation to call this a director's picture, which it is, but all is made possible in the end by a good script.

•

VICTOR/VICTORIA

1982, 133 mins, UK Ⓥ ⦿ ▭ col

Dir Blake Edwards ***Prod*** Blake Edwards, Tony Adams ***Scr*** Blake Edwards ***Ph*** Dick Bush ***Ed*** Ralph E. Winters ***Mus*** Henry Mancini ***Art*** Rodger Maus

Act Julie Andrews, James Garner, Robert Preston, Lesley Ann Warren, Alex Karras, John Rhys-Davies (M-G-M/Peerford/Artista)

Victor/Victoria is a sparkling, ultra-sophisticated entertainment from Blake Edwards. Based on a 1933 German film comedy [*Viktor und Viktoria*, written and directed by Rheinhold Schunzel] which was a big hit in its day, pic sees Edwards working in the Lubitsch-Wilder vein of sly wit and delightful sexual innuendo.

Set in Paris of 1934, gorgeously represented by Rodger Maus's studio-constructed settings, tale introduces Julie Andrews as a down-on-her-luck chanteuse. Also suffering a temporary career lapse is tres gai nightclub entertainer Robert Preston, who remakes her as a man who in short order becomes celebrated as Paris' foremost female impersonator. Enter Windy City gangster James Garner, with imposing bodyguard Alex Karras and dizzy sexpot Lesley Ann Warren in tow. Not knowing he's in one of "those" clubs, the tough guy falls hard for Andrews, only to experience a severe blow to his macho ego when it become's apparent she's a he.

While the central thrust of the story rests in Andrews-Garner covergence, everyone in the cast is given the chance to shine. Most impressive of all is Preston, with a shimmering portrait of a slightly decadent "old queen." Andrews is able to reaffirm her musical talents.

Garner is quizzically sober as the story's straight man, in more ways than one.

1982: Best Original Song Score

NOMINATIONS: Best Actress (Julie Andrews), Supp. Actor (Robert Preston), Supp. Actress (Lesley Ann Warren), Screenplay Adaptation, Costume Design, Art Direction

•

VICTORY

1940, 77 mins, US b/w

Dir John Cromwell ***Prod*** Anthony Veiller ***Scr*** John L. Balderston ***Ph*** Leo Tover ***Ed*** William Shea ***Mus*** Frederick Hollander

Act Fredric March, Betty Field, Cedric Hardwicke, Jerome Cowan, Sig Rumann, Rafaela Ottiano (Paramount)

This film version of Joseph Conrad's novel impresses with several strongly individual performances rather than with the basic movement of the story itself.

Story unfolds at a most leisurely pace, script deviating from regulation picture formula and tempo, and filled with long stretches of dialog to highlight development of characters displayed. Fredric March is the recluse living on a small East Indian Island seeking happiness away from the world. Under his protection comes Betty Field, a stranded musician, and when March finds himself falling in love with the girl he prepares to ship her away on a trading schooner. Cedric Hardwicke and his outlaw companions arrive to rob and kill March for his buried fortune.

March capably carries the lead with restrained action to put over transformation of his original weakling, golden-rule character to one of strength, physically and mentally. Field registers with an unusual performance as the English girl musician who falls in love with the recluse. Jerome Cowan clicks with a meritorious performance as Hardwicke's Cockney assistant in outlawry; while Hardwicke handles his assignment with usual ability.

Direction by John Cromwell, in retaining all of the character etchings displayed in Conrad's book, employs a stagey technique with burdensome dialog and slow pace until the final episodes, which pick up dramatic interest.

•

VICTORY
(UK: ESCAPE TO VICTORY)

1981, 117 mins, US Ⓥ ⦿ ▭ col

Dir John Huston ***Prod*** Freddie Fields ***Scr*** Evan Jones, Yabo Yablonsky ***Ph*** Gerry Fisher ***Ed*** Roberto Silvi ***Mus*** Bill Conti ***Art*** J. Dennis Washington

Act Sylvester Stallone, Michael Caine, Max von Sydow, Pele, Daniel Massey, Carole Laure (Lorimar/Victory)

Victory amounts to a frankly old-fashioned World War II morality play, hinging on soccer as a civilized metaphor for the game of War.

Though set in a German POW camp in 1943, *Victory* is barely a "war movie" by any stretch. Plot hinges on a morality-building ploy by a genteel propaganda officer (Max von Sydow) who once played for Germany to pit a team of Allied prisoners (including officer Michael Caine, a onetime British soccer pro, Brazil's legendary Pele, and Yank badboy Sylvester Stallone) against the local German troops.

When his superiors get wind of the plan, they quickly see the worldwide propaganda potential and insist on expanding the plan to square off a POW "all-star" team drawn from imprisoned footballers throughout Europe, against the German national team.

Script [from a story by Yabo Yablonsky, Djordje Milicevic and Jeff Maguire] spends so much effort extolling man's basic goodness and the values of selflessness, teamwork and fair play, that it frequently softens the action. Fortunately, director John Huston has such a firm grip on the dramatic line that does exist—and works some very good performances from the cast, particularly Caine—that the pic (lensed entirely in Hungary) survives intact.

•

VICTORY AT SEA

1954, 97 mins, US Ⓥ b/w

Prod Henry Salomon, Robert W. Sarnoff ***Scr*** Henry Salomon, Richard Hanser ***Ed*** Isaac Kleinerman ***Mus*** Richard Rodgers (NBC Film Division)

Originally presented on NBC as a 26-part filmed documentary of World War II naval history, the television *Victory at Sea* was compressed to 97 minutes for theatrical release. But despite the loss of many fine scenes of the original, the edited print is still a forceful pictorial chronicle of the Allies's global sea campaigns against the Axis Powers.

Sea covers the period from the Axis's 1939 ascendancy to its defeat in 1945. Among key points captured by the cameras are the Japanese attack on Pearl Harbor, the Allied invasion of Normandy, the sweep of the U.S. fleets through the Pacific, the North African invasion, the atomic bombing of Japan and the liberation of the prisoners of Dachau, Buchenwald and other infamous concentration camps.

Alexander Scourby's narration of the commentary written by Henry Salomon and Richard Hanser is unobtrusive and never detracts from the screen movement. Quality of the print is good considering the varied origin and age of the footage.

•

VICTORY THROUGH AIR POWER

1943, 65 mins, US col

Dir H. C. Potter, Clyde Geronimi, Jack Kinney, James Algar ***Prod*** Walt Disney ***Scr*** Alexander P. de Seversky, T. Hee, Erdman Penner, William Cottrell, Jim Bodrero, George Stallings, Jose Rodriguez ***Ph*** Ray Rennahan ***Ed*** Jack Dennis ***Mus*** Edward Plumb, Paul J. Smith, Oliver Wallace ***Art*** Richard Irvine

Act Alexander P. de Seversky (Walt Disney)

Historically, albeit kaleidoscopically, Disney and Major Alexander P. de Seversky trace the progress of aviation in 65 snappy minutes, a combination of super-animation, all in color, plus Technicolored photography with the major himself participating.

It flashes back from the prophetic Gen. Billy Mitchell—to whom the film is dedicated—to 1903 when the Wright Bros first succeeded in lifting a heavier-than-air craft off the ground.

In cartoon and narration is traced the Luftwaffe's exploits, plus the concluding arguments by de Seversky of how to beat Hitler in his Fortress Europa and how to overcome the Japs' air-based advantages.

Disney and his battalion of artists, animators and backgrounders have not permitted the seriousness of the theme to completely dwarf their humor. There are the usual imaginative complement of Disneyisms in his cartoonics, and an excellent musical score to point it up.

1943: NOMINATION: Best Scoring of a Dramatic Picture

●

VIDEODROME

1983, 88 mins, Canada Ⓥ col

Dir David Cronenberg ***Prod*** Claude Heroux ***Scr*** David Cronenberg ***Ph*** Mark Irwin ***Ed*** Ronald Sanders ***Mus*** Howard Shore ***Art*** Carol Spier

Act James Woods, Sonja Smits, Deborah Harry, Peter Dvorsky, Les Carlson, Jack Creley (Filmplan)

Story concerns a small-time cable TV outlet in Toronto. The quasi-clandestine operation is run by Max Renn (James Woods) who's ever on the lookout for offbeat and erotic material.

He becomes fascinated with a program called Videodrome, picked up from a satellite by a station technician. The show appears to be little more than a series of torture sequences, primarily involving women. Renn pursues the program but is blocked at every turn. One of his suppliers warns him that the activities on the show are not staged. However, he perseveres, making contact with a McLuhanesque media guru named Brian O'Blivion (Jack Creley).

Film is dotted with video jargon and ideology which proves more fascinating than distancing. And Cronenberg amplifies the freaky situation with a series of stunning visual effects.

Woods aptly conveys Renn's obsession and eventual bondage to the television nightmare. Sonja Smits is an alluring and mysterious femme fatale and Deborah Harry seems just right as Renn's girlfriend who thrives on and is undone by Videodrome's games cruelty.

●

VIE DEVANT SOI, LA
(MADAME ROSA)

1977, 105 mins, France Ⓥ col

Dir Moshe Mizrahi ***Prod*** Ralph Baum (exec.) ***Scr*** Moshe Mizrahi ***Ph*** Nestor Almendros ***Ed*** Sophie Coussein ***Mus*** Philippe Sarde ***Art*** Bernard Evein

Act Simone Signoret, Claude Dauphin, Samy Ben Youb, Gabriel Jabbour, Michal Bat-Adam, Constantin Costa-Gavras (Lira)

Based on a book [by Emile Ajar] that won the top literary prize in '75, film weaves a series of anecdotes about the relationship between an aging, ailing old Jewish woman who cares for the children of prostitutes and one of her charges, an Arab boy. Direction is unobstrusive and leaves the film to its actors, which works, due to the canny, insightful playing of Simone Signoret as the old woman.

Though unfolding mainly in the milieu of prostitutes and pimps in the Arab and Jewish worker section of Paris, it is never sordid. There is a tangy, salty humanity that never gets mawkish or bathetic.

Rose (Signoret), once in a concentration camp and a prostitute for 35 years, is very ill. One of her charges is a handsome, brooding boy who loves her, but whose stifled tenderness makes him unruly. When she dies, he stays with her for weeks, going out to eat, helped with money from a goodhearted transsexual joy girl. He spreads toilet water to kill the smell but firemen finally break in and take him away.

Director Moshe Mizrahi is Israeli of Moroccan origins and has lived in France for 10 years. Fine lensing by Nestor Almendros and a potent musical score by Philippe Sarde also help.

1977: Best Foreign Language Film

●

VIETNAM, TEXAS

1990, 85 mins, US Ⓥ col

Dir Robert Ginty ***Prod*** Robert Ginty, Ron Joy ***Scr*** Tom Badal, C. Courtney Joyner ***Ph*** Robert M. Baldwin, Jr. ***Ed*** Jonathan P. Shaw ***Mus*** Richard Stone ***Art*** Kate J. Sullivan

Act Robert Ginty, Haing S. Ngor, Tim Thomerson, Kiev Chinh, Tamlyn Tomita (Epic)

Good intentions are roughly served in this uneven actioner that displays some compassion for the stateside Vietnam community while exploiting its violent elements.

Robert Ginty, who also directed, stars as Father Thomas McCain, a Vietnam vet turned priest who still suffers guilt about the Vietnamese woman he abandoned—pregnant with his child—when he returned to the States. Fifteen years later, he tracks them down in Houston's Little Saigon and forces himself into their lives, despite the fact that his former flame Mailan (Kieu Chinh) is now comfortably established as the wife of a vicious drug runner, Wong (Haing S. Ngor).

Ginty hooks up with his old soldier buddy Max (Tim Thomerson), now a dissolute bar owner, and they set out to reach Mailan and her teenage daughter, Lan (Tamlyn Tomita), setting off beatings and murders as they run up against Wong's henchmen.

Among its plusses, pic features numerous Asian roles, with Tomita a standout as the spirited teenage daughter. Ngor (*The Killing Fields*) is suitably chilling as Wong.

●

VIEW TO A KILL, A

1985, 131 mins, UK Ⓥ ⦿ ⌑ col

Dir John Glen ***Prod*** Albert R. Broccoli, Michael G. Wilson ***Scr*** Richard Maibaum, Michael G. Wilson ***Ph*** Alan Hume ***Ed*** Peter Davies ***Mus*** John Barry ***Art*** Peter Lamont

Act Roger Moore, Christopher Walken, Tanya Roberts, Grace Jones, Patrick Macnee, Fiona Fullerton (Eon/United Artists)

Bond's adversary this time is the international industrialist Max Zorin (Christopher Walken) and his love-hate interest, May Day (Grace Jones). Bond tangles with them at their regal horse sale and uncovers a profitable scheme in which microchips are surgically implanted in the horse to assure an easy victory.

Horse business is moderately entertaining, particularly when Patrick Macnee is on screen as Bond's chauffeur accomplice. Action, however, jumps abruptly to San Francisco to reveal Zorin's true motives. He's hatching some master plan to pump water from the sea into the San Andreas fault causing a major earthquake, destroying the Silicon Valley and leaving him with the world's microchip monopoly.

While Bond pics have always traded heavily on the camp value of its characters, *A View to a Kill* almost attacks the humor, practically winking at the audience with every move.

As for Roger Moore, making his seventh [and final] appearance as Bond, he is right about half the time. He still has the suave and cool for the part, but on occasion he looks a bit old and his womanizing seems dated.

●

VIGIL

1984, 90 mins, New Zealand Ⓥ col

Dir Vincent Ward ***Prod*** John Maynard ***Scr*** Vincent Ward, Graeme Tetley ***Ph*** Alun Bollinger ***Ed*** Simon Reece ***Mus*** Jack Body ***Art*** Kai Hawkins

Act Penelope Stewart, Frank Whitten, Bill Kerr, Fiona Kay (Film Investment/NZFC)

Central figure is 11-year-old Toss (Fiona Kay), on the threshold of womanhood and caught in the tragedy of the death of her father and the coincidental arrival of a stranger, Ethan (Frank Whitten). It is primarily through her eyes, actions and interpretation of events, that the impact of Ethan's presence upon the household is registered.

While Toss is fascinated by Ethan's mysterious aura, her mother, Elizabeth (Penelope Stewart), is reawakened from a joyless marriage, and her grandfather Birdie (Bill Kerr) finds a comrade for his eccentric pranks and grandiose mechanical inventions.

The remarkable quality of the film is the way it gives fresh resonance to universal themes.

●

VIKINGS, THE

1958, 114 mins, US Ⓥ ⌑ col

Dir Richard Fleischer ***Prod*** Jerry Bresler ***Scr*** Calder Willingham ***Ph*** Jack Cardiff ***Ed*** Elmo Williams ***Mus*** Mario Nascimbene ***Art*** Harper Goff

Act Kirk Douglas, Tony Curtis, Ernest Borgnine, Janet Leigh, Alexander Knox, Frank Thring (United Artists/Bryna)

The Vikings is spectacular, rousing and colorful. Blood flows freely as swords are crossed and arrows meet their mark in barbarian combat. And there's no hesitance about throwing a victim into a wolf pit or a pool of crabs.

There is some complication at the start, however, as the various characters are brought into view—as the Viking army of 200 raids the Kingdom of Northumbria, in England, and elements of mystery and intrigue are brought into the story. But it is not too long before the screenplay [from the novel by Edison Marshall] and director Richard Fleischer have their people in clear focus.

History is highly fictionalized. It starts with the raid, the death of the English leader, the succession to the throne of Frank Thring who's strictly the heavy. The queen is with child, the father being Ernest Borgnine, head of the marauding Vikings. To escape the new king's wrath she flees to another land and with the proper passage of time the child, now a young man (Tony Curtis), turns up in the Viking village as a slave whose identity is not known.

It is at this point that Curtis encounters Kirk Douglas, latter as heir to the Viking throne. Neither is aware of the fact that the other is his brother. They clash. Janet Leigh participates as daughter of the king of Wales who is to be taken as a bride by the sadistic English king.

Douglas falls for Leigh in a big way but she comes to favor Curtis, and thus is established the romantic triangle.

It's the production that counts and producer Jerry Bresler, working with Douglas's indie outfit, has done it up big and with apparent authenticity. Lensing was in the Norse fjord area and various parts of Europe, including the Bavarian Studios.

Douglas, doing a bang-up, freewheeling job as the ferocious and disfigured Viking fighter, fits the part splendidly. Borgnine's Viking chief is a conqueror of authority.

●

VIKTOR UND VIKTORIA

1933, 90 mins, Germany b/w

Dir Reinhold Schunzel ***Prod*** Eduard Kubat ***Scr*** Reinhold Schunzel ***Ph*** Konstantin Irmen-Tschet ***Ed*** [uncredited] ***Mus*** Franz Doelle ***Art*** Benno von Arent, Artur Gunther

Act Renate Muller, Hermann Thimig, Hilde Hildebrand, Friedel Pisetta, Fritz Odemar, Aribert Wascher (UFA)

Most successful musical comedy in this season and by far the best. Real fast comedy put over with pace and pleasant lightness.

Setting gives ample space for backstage atmosphere and revue fillings with a Spanish taint. The whole is a splendid vehicle for Renate Muller in trousers who develops extraordinary talents in the nonchalent representation of a would-be unconcerned aristocrat. She sings with a small but natural and pleasant voice. Hermann Thiming plays the fool wherever the plot gives him a chance in the part of the original "Viktoria," and he has lots of chances, overdoing it at times.

Reinhold Schunzel leaves no laugh possibilities unused and supplies a long footage of laughter with lots of novel ideas and hardly any empty spaces. Adolf Wohlbruck, the "suspecting" lover, plays with agreeable unobtrusiveness. A good song is "Do Come Along with Me to Madrid," by Franz Doelle.

●

VILLAGE OF THE DAMNED

1960, 77 mins, US Ⓥ b/w

Dir Wolf Rilla ***Prod*** Ronald Kinnoch ***Scr*** Stirling Silliphant, Wolf Rilla, George Barclay ***Ph*** Geoffrey Faithfull ***Ed*** Gordon Hales ***Mus*** Ron Goodwin ***Art*** Ivan King

Act George Sanders, Barbara Shelley, Michael Gwynn, Laurence Naismith, John Phillips, Richard Vernon (M-G-M)

Plot kicks around what is not an uninteresting idea. A little British village comes under the spell of some strange, supernatural force which first puts everybody out for the count. Then the villagers come to and find that every woman capable of being pregnant is.

Snag is that all the children are little monsters. They all look alike—fair-haired, unblinking stare and with intellects the equivalent of adults, plus the knack of mental telepathy. George Sanders, a physicist, is intimately involved, since his wife is the mother of the leader of the little gang of abnormal moppets. Sanders decides to probe the mystery.

If there had happend to be any hint of why this remarkable business should have occurred, the film [from the novel *The Midwich Cuckoos* by John Wyndham] would have been slightly more plausible. As it is, this just tapers off from a taut beginning into soggy melodrama. Wolf Rilla's direction is adequate, but no more.

●

VILLAGE OF THE DAMNED

1995, 98 mins, US Ⓥ ⦿ ⌑ col

Dir John Carpenter ***Prod*** Michael Preger, Sandy King ***Scr*** David Himmelstein ***Ph*** Gary B. Kibbe ***Ed*** Edward A. Warschilka ***Mus*** John Carpenter, Dave Davies ***Art*** Rodger Maus

Act Christopher Reeve, Kirstie Alley, Linda Kozlowski, Michael Pare, Meredith Salenger, Mark Hamill (Alphaville/Universal)

Village of the Damned is a risible remake of the British 1960 sci-fi classic.

M-G-M produced the original low-budget, black-and-white quickie about malevolent children mysteriously born at the same time who employ superior cerebral skills and mental telepathy to gain the upper hand over adults. Thirty-five years ago, tale was read as an allegory for a sinister Communist takeover, and the Catholic Church was so incensed by the plot element of virgin birth that it condemned the picture.

But unlike, for instance, the subversively anti-Reaganite undercurrents in Carpenter's 1988 *They Live*, there are no unsettling frissons here to lend any dimension to the minimal surface thrills.

Setup is moderately effective, as the town of Midwich, a small Northern California community (lensed in Inverness and Point Reyes, where Carpenter previously shot *The Fog* is hit by a mysterious force that knocks out the entire population for six hours. Soon thereafter, 10 women in town turn up pregnant, resulting in a mass birthing supervised by local medic Alan Chaffee (Christopher Reeve) and brash outside scientist Dr. Susan Verner (Kirstie Alley).

By the time they are a few years old, the kids—who sport platinum hair and dour expressions—begin sticking together, walking two-by-two in formation, being taught in special classes and exercising practice sessions in domination. Ringleader Mara (Lindsey Haun) is Chaffee's daughter.

Pic's one notable adjustment lies in shifting more importance to the women in the story, which would have been a fine idea were it not for the silly roles and atrocious dialog.

•

VILLAIN

1971, 98 mins, UK Ⓥ col

Dir Michael Tuchner ***Prod*** Alan Ladd, Jr., Jay Kanter ***Scr*** Dick Clement, Ian La Frenais ***Ph*** Christopher Challis ***Ed*** Ralph Sheldon ***Mus*** Jonathan Hodge ***Art*** Maurice Carter

Act Richard Burton, Ian McShane, Nigel Davenport, Donald Sinden, Fiona Lewis, T. P. McKenna (Anglo-EMI)

Dick Clement and Ian La Frenais's screenplay, adapted by Al Lettieri, and based on a James Barlow novel [*The Burden of Proof*], uses a frayed shoestring plot of a payroll stickup to flesh out the sadistic actions of Richard Burton as a onetime nightclub bouncer with a handy razor who has become one of the major figures of the London underworld. It isn't just a penchant for cutting and slicing that makes our man tick. He has an entire assortment of quirks.

Tied to a dying mother (Cathleen Nesbitt) by a silver cord stronger than steel cable, he also is a homosexual but no run-of-the-subway version. He has a thing about a petty criminal (Ian McShane) that makes him beat him up, then bed down with him. His bête noir, however, is a dedicated police inspector (Nigel Davenport) whose sole duty is to pin something on him.

Support is strong with top honors going to Joss Ackland as a thief with an ulcer; Donald Sinden, as a Member of Parliament with not quite standard sexual demands which, naturally, makes him an ideal blackmail prospect; and T. P. McKenna, as another gang leader.

•

VILLAIN, THE

1979, 93 mins, US Ⓥ col

Dir Hal Needham ***Prod*** Mort Engelberg ***Scr*** Robert G. Kane ***Ph*** Bobby Byrne ***Ed*** Walter Hannemann ***Mus*** Bill Justis ***Art*** Carl Anderson

Act Kirk Douglas, Ann-Margret, Arnold Schwarzenegger, Paul Lynde, Ruth Buzzi, Jack Elam (Columbia/Rastar)

Idea for the satire must have looked great on paper. Why not take all the standard sagebrush types—the handsome stranger, the décolleté femme, the evil outlaw, etc.—and put them through a parody of their usual paces?

The answer no one came up with was that without any depth of characterization, and only the flimsiest plot structure, a take-off has nowhere to go. Hal Needham, again dazzles audiences with some eye-popping stunts but the film gets lost in the dust.

With Kirk Douglas in the title role, Arnold Schwarzenegger as the good guy, and Ann-Margret as the lascivious girl who loves being fought over, *The Villain* becomes even more of a disappointment. Rarely has so much talent been used to so little purpose.

•

VILLA RIDES

1968, 125 mins, US Ⓥ ▭ col

Dir Buzz Kulik ***Prod*** Ted Richmond ***Scr*** Robert Towne, Sam Peckinpah ***Ph*** Jack Hildyard ***Ed*** David Bretherton ***Mus*** Maurice Jarre ***Art*** Ted Haworth

Act Yul Brynner, Robert Mitchum, Grazia Buccella, Charles Bronson, Robert Viharo, Herbert Lom (Paramount)

Villa Rides is a pseudo-biopic of a portion of the bandit career of Mexico's folk hero, Pancho Villa, with Yul Brynner in title role. Ted Richmond's handsome exterior production, filmed in 1967 in Spain, is competently, if leisurely and routinely, directed with the accent on violent death.

Script [based on the book *Pancho Villa* by William Douglas Lansford, adapted by the author] fails to establish clearly the precise political framework, while over-developing some lesser details. This, plus overlength, adds up to dramatic tedium.

Film concerns itself with Villa's own aggressive acts. With the aid of Charles Bronson and Robert Viharo, Brynner is responsible for the onscreen deaths of literally dozens of men, most explicitly detailed.

Brynner makes Villa sympathetic at times, as a man fighting for human rights, though that's a bit hard to swallow since his philosophy does not get spelled out for 105 minutes into the film. His rationalization is rather facile and specious: those he killed were "traitors," by his convenient self-excusing definition.

•

VINCENT & THEO

1990, 138 mins, UK/France/Netherlands/Italy Ⓥ col

Dir Robert Altman ***Prod*** Ludi Boeken ***Scr*** Julian Mitchell ***Ph*** Jean Lepine ***Ed*** Francoise Coispeau, Geraldine Peroni ***Mus*** Gabriel Yared ***Art*** Stephen Altman

Act Tim Roth, Paul Rhys, Jip Wijngaarden, Johanna Ter Steege, Jean-Pierre Cassel, Anne Canovas (Belbo/Central/La Sept/Telepool/RAI Uno/Vara/Sofica Valor)

A study of Van Gogh's last years as seen through his tortured relationship with his brother, *Vincent & Theo* paradoxically is one of Robert Altman's most cinematically conventional films as well as one of his most deeply personal. Bearing little resemblance to the glamorized, overheated Vincente Minnelli 1956 biopic *Lust for Life*, this masterwork operates in the intimate, thoughtful vein of the great BBC bios of artistic figures.

Altman and his incisive scripter Julian Mitchell focus on Vincent's obsessive devotion to his craft and the failure of his overly timid art-dealer brother to win him acceptance in an art world that scorned his idiosyncratic genius.

The heart of the film is its exploration of the destructive, unacknowledged but important relationship between artist and patron. Paul Rhys skillfully inhabits a character even more wretchedly unhappy than his brother, who at least has the consolation of his art, and Theo's own incipient madness gives the film much of its unsettling tone.

Tim Roth powerfully conveys Vincent's heroic, obsessive concentration on his work, and then resultant loneliness and isolation.

•

VINCENT, FRANCOIS, PAUL . . . ET LES AUTRES
(VINCENT, FRANCOIS, PAUL AND THE OTHERS)

1974, 118 mins, France/Italy Ⓥ col

Dir Claude Sautet ***Prod*** Raymond Danon, Roland Girard, Jean Bolvary ***Scr*** Jean-Loup Dabadie, Claude Neron, Claude Sautet ***Ph*** Jean Boffety ***Ed*** Jacqueline Thiedot ***Mus*** Philippe Sarde ***Art*** Theo Meurisse

Act Yves Montand, Michel Piccoli, Serge Reggiani, Gerard Depardieu, Stephane Audran, Marie Dubois (Lira/President)

Claude Sautet seems to be turning into the chronicler of middle-class, middle-aged manners and mores. Sautet is quintessentially French in treating these still-boyish almost-fiftyish characters [from co-scripter Claude Neron's novel *La grande narrade*] caught up in the mode of friendship consisting of Sundays at one's country home or meetings in town.

Character is etched fleetingly, with Vincent (Yves Montand) most developed since he is losing his business as well as separated from his wife and drifting away from a young mistress Francois (Michel Piccoli), a doctor is also losing his wife while Paul (Serge Reggiani), a failed writer, has a woman who loves him. A young friend, Jean (Gerard Depardieu), a boxer, gives the film its final burst of action as all assist at his victory.

Pic has an insistent feel for the ordinary, is well played, but misses a transcending dramatic insight to make the fates of these old-time friends more revealing of themselves and their milieu. The women either bear with or leave these guileless old-time chums.

Montand is developing into a character actor of shrewd range, with Piccoli his usual effective self and Reggiani excellent as the more good natured, more settled member of the gang.

•

VINCENT, FRANCOIS, PAUL AND THE OTHERS
SEE: VINCENT, FRANCOIS, PAUL . . . ET LES AUTRES

•

VINCENT: THE LIFE AND DEATH OF VINCENT VAN GOGH

1987, 103 mins, Australia/Netherlands Ⓥ col

Dir Paul Cox ***Prod*** Tony Llewellyn-Jones ***Scr*** Paul Cox ***Ph*** Paul Cox ***Ed*** Paul Cox ***Mus*** Norman Kaye ***Art*** Neil Angwin (Illumination/Look/Ozfilms/Dasha)

This very special art film is neither documentary nor fiction. Paul Cox, one of Australia's foremost directors, was born in Holland and has made an exquisite, timeless tribute to Vincent Van Gogh using as his text simply the letters Vincent wrote to his brother, Theo, letters beautifully read by John Hurt.

Van Gogh worked as a painter for only 10 years, and during that period produced about 1,800 works, but when he killed himself at 37 in 1890 he had only sold one of them, and was unknown and impoverished. Cox's film covers those last 10 years but, save for one brief moment at the end, when Van Gogh's funeral is depicted, the central character of the drama is never seen. His thoughts and philosophies are enunciated superbly on the soundtrack.

Cox traveled to the places Van Gogh knew, lived and worked. The images accompanying the text are of trees and fields and birds in flight, and the inevitable sunflowers. And, of course, there are the paintings themselves.

•

VIOLENT PLAYGROUND

1958, 108 mins, UK b/w

Dir Basil Dearden ***Prod*** Michael Relph ***Scr*** James Kennaway ***Ph*** Reginald Wyer ***Ed*** Arthur Stevens ***Mus*** Philip Green ***Art*** Maurice Carter

Act Stanley Baker, Anne Heywood, David McCallum, Peter Cushing, John Slater, Clifford Evans (Rank)

Violent Playground brings a sincere semi-documentary touch to the matter of juve delinquency. James Kennaway's human and literate screenplay is convincingly acted against authentic Liverpool backgrounds. Result is an absorbing film that works up to an overlong but tense climax.

Film concerns an experiment made in Liverpool in 1949. Policemen have become Juvenile Liaison Officers whose job is to keep an eye on mischievous youngsters and steer them away from crime. Stanley Baker gives a vigorous and sympathetic performance as a cop who is taken off the investigation of a series of unexplained fires for this work. He becomes particularly involved with one family and discovers who is responsible for the arson.

There are a number of other very creditable performances, notably David McCallum as the young delinquent, Peter Cushing as a very serious but wholehearted priest, Clifford Evans as a schoolmaster and in her first big chance, as David McCallum's elder sister, Anne Heywood.

•

VIOLENT SATURDAY

1955, 90 mins, US ▭ col

Dir Richard Fleischer ***Prod*** Buddy Adler ***Scr*** Sydney Boehm ***Ph*** Charles G. Clarke ***Ed*** Louis Loeffler ***Mus*** Hugo Friedhofer

Act Victor Mature, Richard Egan, Stephen McNally, Virginia Leith, Lee Marvin, Sylvia Sidney (20th Century-Fox)

Lensed on location in Arizona in a modern-day setting, the film concerns the bank robbery planned by a cool trio played by Stephen McNally, Lee Marvin and J. Carrol Naish.

As their preparations for the holdup unfold, several subplots are set up.

Purpose of all the subplots is to set the stage for the holdup, where they all fall into place and are solved by the events of the holdup and what follows. They're highly contrived and unconvincing, but they do serve the purpose of giving the film a greater sense of scope and power.

Climax comes with the robbery itself and the getaway. It's here that the screen version of the William L. Heath novel strips the action of the nonessentials and turns on the heat in a powerful windup that's worth the waiting.

•

VIOLENT STRANGER
SEE: WETHERBY

•

V.I.P.S, THE

1963, 119 mins, UK ▭ col

Dir Anthony Asquith ***Prod*** Anatole de Grunwald ***Scr*** Terence Rattigan ***Ph*** Jack Hildyard ***Ed*** Frank Clarke ***Mus*** Miklos Rozsa

Act Elizabeth Taylor, Richard Burton, Louis Jourdan, Margaret Rutherford, Maggie Smith, Rod Taylor (M-G-M)

This has suspense, conflict, romance, comedy and drama. Its main fault is that some of the characters and the byplots are not developed enough. But that is a risk inevitable in any film in which a number of strangers are flung together, each with problems and linked by a single circumstance.

In this case the setting is London Airport and the basic problem is the necessity for at least four of the Very Important Passengers bound for the States to get out of the country pronto. Their plans go haywire when a thick fog grounds all planes overnight.

Terence Rattigan's screenplay juggles these situations and does not neglect many of the star performers. The script has literate, witty and sometimes touching dialog and Anthony Asquith has directed skillfully, in that though there is the sense of bustle inseparable from any international airport he has retained a sympathetic feeling of intimacy for all his characters.

Principal story, that of the business tycoon who has taken his wife for granted and now looks set to lose her, is played out by Elizabeth Taylor, Richard Burton and Louis Jourdan as the lover. Maybe Taylor needs a sabbatical but there is a feeling of ordinariness about her thesping.

Burton, however, gives a top-league performance as the business chief who eventually regains his wife but only after a few hours of taut misery, humiliating and self-enlightenment. Jourdan is also excellent as the would-be lover and he has one scene with Burton which is a little masterpiece of dual virtuosity.

1963: Best Supp. Actress (Margaret Rutherford)

•

VIRGIN AND THE GYPSY, THE

1970, 95 mins, UK Ⓥ col

Dir Christopher Miles ***Prod*** Kenneth Harper ***Scr*** Alan Plater ***Ph*** Bob Huke ***Ed*** Paul Davies ***Mus*** Patrick Gowers ***Art*** Terence Knight

Act Joanna Shimkus, Franco Nero, Honor Blackman, Mark Burns, Maurice Denham, Fay Compton (De Grunwald)

D. H. Lawrence's last unpolished novella, *The Virgin and the Gypsy* is about a young English girl's awakening to adult life in northern England, circa 1921. While faithful perhaps to the author, film is a stilted period piece.

Joanna Shimkus and Harriett Harper are two rural sisters returning from a French school to a provincial environment, ruled by Grandmother Fay Compton. Puppets in the household include rector-Father Maurice Denham, Aunt Kay Walsh, Uncle Norman Bird, and maid Janet Chappell.

Shimkus (whose mother abandoned her family's stultifying influence) grows restive, and finds a sexual stirring under Franco Nero's gaze, plus sympathetic adult companionship from Honor Blackman and Mark Burns, who are living together and evoking prissy clucks from the townsfolk.

•

VIRGINIA CITY

1940, 123 mins, US Ⓥ b/w

Dir Michael Curtiz ***Prod*** Hal B. Wallis (exec.) ***Scr*** Robert Buckner ***Ph*** Sol Polito ***Ed*** George Amy ***Mus*** Max Steiner ***Art*** Ted Smith

Act Errol Flynn, Miriam Hopkins, Randolph Scott, Humphrey Bogart, Frank McHugh, Alan Hale (Warner)

On the theory, perhaps, that one good western deserves another, Warner Bros follows up *Dodge City*, starring Errol Flynn, with another saga of the land of the blazing sunsets entitled *Virginia City*. As a shoot 'em up, the picture is first class; as a bit of cinematic history telling, it is far short of the possibilities indicated by the title and cast.

It's about the cache of $5 million in gold bullion which Confederate sympathizers are reported to have offered to the cause of the Southern states during the Civil War. The catch, of course, is how to get the gold out of Nevada and through Union scouting lines.

Flynn is first shown as a Union captive in Libby prison, from which he and companions escape, later to be assigned to travel across the plains and thwart the conspiracy by which the Confederacy hoped to come in possession of all that gold from the Nevada hills. Miriam Hopkins is a singer in a Virginia City saloon and travels west on the stage with Flynn. She is a rebel spy, fresh from a meeting with Jeff Davis. There's the romance.

En route, the stage is held up by John Murrell, outlaw, who is really Humphrey Bogart behind a slick-waxed mustache. There's the chase. And in Virginia City is Randolph Scott, secretly planning the removal of the gold, which is to be taken south in a wagon train. Scott also is much in love with Hopkins, who leans heavily towards Flynn. She betrays Flynn into a trap, thus placing patriotism ahead of love. There's the drama.

Michael Curtiz, the director, has taken all this and steamed it up with some noisy trigger work, charging cavalry, dance-hall intimacies and the burning sands of the desert to concoct a bustling western, which is replete with action, although short on credulity.

•

VIRGINIAN, THE

1929, 92 mins, US Ⓥ b/w

Dir Victor Fleming ***Scr*** Howard Estabrook

Act Gary Cooper, Walter Huston, Mary Brian, Chester Conklin, Eugene Pallette, E. H. Calvert (Paramount)

This Paramount production takes the old play dirt of ancient plains pictures, shuffles it around a bit, and makes of the Owen Wister and Kirk La Shelle story 92 minutes of drama and comedy.

There's an anticlimax toward the middle, one of the most harrowing and vivid sequences ever before the lenses. It is when the silent and lanky Virginian (Gary Cooper) is forced to give the signal which sends his pal, Steve (Richard Arlen), along with three other cattle rustlers, galloping to their death in nooses.

Trampas (Walter Huston), the menace, is saved from the hanging to bait along the story for the vengeance climax.

The school mam, played by the pretty Mary Brian, doesn't fly at the neck of the tall backwoodsman. She teases him, letting him use the old gag of rescuing her from a frightened cow and then promptly bawling him out. This provides Cooper with a chance for a bit of byplay and wise-cracking with Arlen as a sincere but out-for-easy-dough Steve.

•

VIRGINIAN, THE

1946, 83 mins, US col

Dir Stuart Gilmore ***Prod*** Paul Jones ***Scr*** Frances Goodrich, Albert Hackett ***Ph*** Harry Hallenberger ***Ed*** Everett Douglas ***Mus*** Daniele Amfitheatrof ***Art*** Hans Dreier, John Meehan

Act Joel McCrea, Brian Donlevy, Sonny Tufts, Barbara Britton, Fay Bainter, Henry O'Neill (Paramount)

The Virginian stands up pretty well over the years. First filmed in 1914 for the silents, then in 1929 (by Par), the present version of the Owen Wister novel is still a pleasant, flavorsome western, with much of the old charm of a daguerreotype.

Although story is a little dated as well as a mite slow, the yarn is still a satisfactory romance, with enough shooting and suspense to offset the plodding pace. Yarn hasn't been changed much, still being the story of the little schoolmarm from Vermont and the cowboy from Virginia, who meet in Montana and wed, after the hero has disposed of a few troublesome cow rustlers.

Costumes of the eastern 1870s, the early-type railroads, the horse riding and cow roundups, the rolling Montana hills, all help in the nostalgic flavor.

Joel McCrea follows soundly in footsteps of Dustin Farnum and Gary Cooper as The ("When You Call Me That, Smile") Virginian, with a straightforward characterization. Barbara Britton is pert and pretty as the schoolteacher. Brian Donlevy, as the rustler, and Sonny Tufts, in his first western role as a misguided cowhand, head an okay supporting cast.

•

VIRGIN SOLDIERS, THE

1969, 96 mins, UK Ⓥ col

Dir John Dexter ***Prod*** Leslie Gilliat, Ned Sherrin ***Scr*** John Hopkins, Ian La Frenais ***Ph*** Ken Higgins ***Ed*** Thelma Connell ***Mus*** Peter Greenwell ***Art*** Frank White

Act Lynn Redgrave, Hywel Bennett, Nigel Davenport, Nigel Patrick, Rachel Kempson, Jack Shepherd (Columbia/Foreman)

Much of the irony and subtlety of Leslie Thomas's novel have been ironed out in favor of a broader approach to the humor. Nevertheless, *The Virgin Soldiers* comes out as a bright and affectionate peek at the trials and tribulations of young National Service rookies.

Though the writers have concentrated mainly on making the film ruefully funny, the serious side has not been neglected. The smell of death is often just around the corner and violence in the jungle and streets of terrorist-infested Malaya is in striking, effective contrast to the boisterous, bawdy, barrack-room atmosphere.

Acting all around is first rate, though only a few characters are allowed to develop.

Redgrave as the sulky heroine has her moments but creates no sympathy and, in fact, is mainly dull, but Tsai Chin makes joyful capital out of her small but lively role as the local prostie.

•

VIRGIN SPRING, THE

SEE: JUNGFRUKALLAN

•

VIRIDIANA

1961, 90 mins, Spain/Mexico Ⓥ b/w

Dir Luis Bunuel ***Prod*** Ricardo Munoz Suay (exec.) ***Scr*** Luis Bunuel, Julio Alejandro ***Ph*** Jose F. Aguayo ***Ed*** Pedro del Rey ***Mus*** Gustavo Pitaluga (dir.) ***Art*** Francisco Canet

Act Silvia Pinal, Fernando Rey, Francisco Rabal, Margarita Lozano, Victoria Zinny, Teresa Rabal (Uninci/Films 59/Alatriste)

Brilliantly carpentered offbeat pic is sure to be controversial. Theme is about charity and its uses and misuses, coupled with an insight into human reasons.

A girl, who is about to take her vows to be a nun, pays a visit to a rich uncle. He sees in her an image of his dead wife who died on their wedding night. He begs her to be his wife, then drugs her and almost makes advances to her. He finally hangs himself, leaving his large estate to her and a son.

The would-be nun tries to become a useful saintly creature by bringing in a flock of poor derelicts. But they almost rape her, and she finally decides to try and become a human being first before trying to be a selfless saint.

Director Luis Bunuel returned to Spain for the first time since 1938 to make this film. Atmosphere is invoked by a fluid feel for incidents. Symbols abound but are never superfluous or unclear. Bunuel has welded the thesping into a perfect whole that defies singling out any for special praise.

[Pic was reviewed at its world premiere at the Cannes festival, having been banned in Spain.]

•

VIRTUOSITY

1995, 105 mins, US Ⓥ ⊙ col

Dir Brett Leonard ***Prod*** Gary Lucchesi ***Scr*** Eric Bernt ***Ph*** Gale Tattersall ***Ed*** B. J. Sears, Rob Kobrin ***Mus*** Christopher Young ***Art*** Nilo Rodis

Act Denzel Washington, Kelly Lynch, Russell Crowe, Stephen Spinella, William Forsythe, Louise Fletcher (Paramount)

A futuristic actioner set in a world where computer-generated killers can come to life, *Virtuosity* exhibits the perils of putting technology ahead of virtues like emotion and character. Pic offers only the evanescent thrills of a videogame, despite a profusion of flashy effects and high-velocity pacing.

Parker Barnes (Denzel Washington), an ex-cop now doing prison time for an act of revenge, is taking part in a Virtual Reality simulation designed to train police officers for violent situations. He returns to the slammer only to be thrust into a fight with a white-supremacist convict. Barnes's real nemesis, it turns out, is the VR fabrication he chased in the first scene. Sid 6.7 (Russell Crowe) has been designed by computer whiz Lindenmeyer (Stephen Spinella) to combine the least savory character traits of Hitler, Manson and 181 other psychopath poster boys, including the serial killer who offed Barnes's family.

Predictably enough, Sid 6.7 escapes into the real world, in a cyber-body that makes him virtually immune to conventional modes of extermination, and Barnes is chosen to hunt him down with the assistance of police psychologist Madison Carter (Kelly Lynch).

What follows is a tautly mounted but relentlessly conventional chase through L.A. locales that include a futuristic nightclub (the year is 1999), a wrestling arena and a shopping mall. Like too many other such movies, pic climaxes with a battle atop a tall building. Helmer Brett Leonard's handling is competent but undistinctive.

•

VISIONS OF EIGHT

1973, 110 mins, US Ⓥ col

Dir Milos Forman, Kon Ichikawa, Claude Lelouch, Yuri Ozerov, Arthur Penn, Michael Pfleghar, John Schlesinger, Mai Zetterling ***Prod*** Stan Margulies ***Ph*** Arthur Wooster, Igor Slabnevich, Rune Ericson, Ernst Wild, Walter Lassally, Masuo Yamaguchi, Daniel Bocly, Jorgen Persson ***Ed*** Robert Lambert, Jim Clark, Edward Roberts, Dede Allen, Margot von Schlieffen, Catherine Bernard, Lars Hagstrom ***Mus*** Henry Mancini (Wolper)

Producer David Wolper recruited eight (originally 10) name directors to choose a segment of the 1972 Munich Olympics and give his/her view of the event on a smaller plane.

The problem is that many of the sketches sometimes forget the idea of sport and competition itself, to indulge in ideas. But the flurry, crowds and human endeavor are there, and in the background the tragic terrorist events that led to the massacre of Israeli athletes by Arab terrorists.

Russo filmmaker Yuri Ozerov starts the ball rolling with *The Beginning*. Mai Zetterling looks at weightlifters in *The Strongest*, a mannered seg but quite funny and well edited. Arthur Penn has a stylized look at pole-vaulting in *The*

Highest. Michael Pfleghar devoted himself to women in various events.

Kon Ichikawa, who helmed the remarkable *Tokyo Olympiad* [1965], delves into the 300-meter dash, stretching it in time. Claude Lelouch concentrates on losers, and gets some laughable and even pathetic insights at times. Milos Forman lenses the harsh decathlon to milk comic relief from it. John Schlesinger winds it with a sentimental homage to a British marathon runner who loses.

•

VISITEURS DU SOIR, LES
(THE DEVIL'S ENVOYS)
1942, 118 mins, France b/w
Dir Marcel Carne ***Prod*** Andre Paulve ***Scr*** Jacques Prevert, Pierre Laroche ***Ph*** Roger Hubert ***Ed*** Henri Rust ***Mus*** Maurice Thiriet, Joseph Kosma ***Art*** Alexandre Trauner, Georges Wakhevitch
Act Arletty, Jules Berry, Marie Dea, Fernand Ledoux, Alain Cuny, Gabriel Gabrio (Superfilm)

The story is romantic legend and the theme is classic morality, about two damned souls who return to earth to corrupt the human race, but remain long enough for one to be saved by a girl's love.

Film's story is based on an old French legend. It is a sort of love-conquers-all version of the Good-versus-Evil theme, but isn't too well pointed or paced in the script. The early scenes, in which the Devil's two disciples arrive at the castle in time to entertain the banquet guests and presently disrupt the household, are promising. Some of the Devil's later scenes are amusing, too. But the yarn itself is slow and the direction further retards it. Technically, the picture is about average for a French-made.

Arletty plays an enigmatic femme fatale, handling the assignment with skill and poise. Jules Berry, as Satan, gives a standout performance, revealing excellent range, flexibility and personal impact. The others are less notable, though Alain Cuny is acceptable as the lost soul saved by a girl's devotion, and Marie Dea is dramatically satisfactory as the mortal heroine.

•

VISKNINGAR OCH ROP
(CRIES AND WHISPERS)
1973, 91 mins, Sweden Ⓥ col
Dir Ingmar Bergman ***Prod*** Ingmar Bergman ***Scr*** Ingmar Bergman ***Ph*** Sven Nykvist ***Ed*** Siv Lundgren ***Art*** Marik Vos
Act Harriet Andersson, Kari Sylwan, Ingrid Thulin, Liv Ullmann, Erland Josephson, Henning Moritzen (Cinematograph)

Ingmar Bergman's dark vision of the human condition has focused on individuals incapable of real interpersonal communications except on the most primitive level. Crying for help in a world they can neither cope with nor comprehend, his characters confront a silent universe inhabited by a God whose attitude is at best uncaring, at worst malignant. How the individual adjusts to his plight remains Bergman's central concern, and in *Cries and Whispers* he provides a bravado portrait of four women in this barren emotional landscape.

Two sisters (Ingrid Thulin and Liv Ullmann) return to their family home to await the death of a third (Harriet Andersson), a spinster long cared for by a peasant housekeeper (Kari Sylwan). The women represent varying degrees of alienation, ranging from Thulin's suicidal despair to Sylwan's benign acceptance of God's will.

The atmosphere of imminent death cues memories of past events which occurred in the house. Andersson recalls a lonely childhood in which she failed to make contact with her mother, the housekeeper remembers the death of her young daughter, Ullmann is reminded of an extramarital affair which caused her husband to attempt suicide, and, in the film's most bizarre sequence, Thulin relives the night she mutilated her vagina with broken glass to avoid her dreaded conjugal duties.

Bergman's lean style, his use of lingering close-ups, fades to red and a soundtrack echoing with the ticking of clocks, the rustle of dresses and the hushed cries of the lost gives pic a hypnotic impact.

•

VITAL SIGNS
1990, 103 mins, US Ⓥ ⊙ col
Dir Marisa Silver ***Prod*** Laurie Perlman, Cathleen Summers ***Scr*** Larry Ketron, Jeb Stuart ***Ph*** John Lindley ***Ed*** Robert Brown, Danford B. Greene ***Mus*** Miles Goodman ***Art*** Todd Hallowell
Act Adrian Pascar, Diane Lane, Jimmy Smits, Norma Aleandro, Jack Gwaltney, Laura San Giacomo (20th Century-Fox)

Vital Signs is a strikingly well-done ensemble piece about a pivotal year in the lives of a group of medical students, with polished script, direction and performances.

As a gifted doctor-to-be who oozes charm and good looks, Adrian Pasdar is the focus of this group of serious strivers navigating their tough third year at L.A. Central's med school. Diane Lane is the crisp but compassionate fellow student he falls in love with. Jack Gwaltney plays the blander, grimmer fellow from a less-advantaged background who's determined not to let Pasdar surpass him.

Interesting subplots are played out in the relationship of Gwaltney and his neglected wife (Laura San Giacomo, in an effective but unexciting plain-Jane turn), and the amusing discomfort of best pals Jane Adams and Tim Ransom after they cross into romantic involvement.

Director Marisa Silver does a good job of getting across characters' emotional lives, making these mainstream twentysomething types absorbing, and fashions a crisply moving story.

•

VITELLONI, I
(THE SPIVS; THE YOUNG AND THE PASSIONATE)
1953, 105 mins, Italy/France ▭ b/w
Dir Federico Fellini ***Prod*** Lorenzo Pegoraro ***Scr*** Federico Fellini, Ennio Flaiano ***Ph*** Otello Martelli, Luciano Trasatti, Carlo Carlini ***Ed*** Rolando Benedetti ***Mus*** Nino Rota ***Art*** Mario Chiari
Act Alberto Sordi, Franco Interlenghi, Franco Fabrizi, Leopoldo Trieste, Eleonora Ruffo, Riccardo Fellini (PEG/Cite)

Federico Fellini, long a scripter, in his second feature film satirizes the "wastrels," the do-nothing sons of middle-class Italian provincials whose life ranges from schoolroom to poolroom. Beyond lies the big city, a thing they eternally dream of, but few ever see. Work is strictly taboo, and they spend their lives avoiding it.

Fellini has mirrored this atmosphere and its characters sharply [from an original story by him, Ennio Flaiano and Tullio Pinelli]. Such sequences as the carnival ball, the visit to the village of the broken-down vaude troupe, and many others are good entertainment. Scenes of Alberto's drunken wanderings is a classic of the genre. Thesping throughout points up the strong direction.

Development of story concerning Fausto (Franco Fabrizi) and his wife (Eleonora Ruffo) is weak, with the ending hurried and a bit too pat. Alberto Sordi stands out as Alberto while other "wastrels" perform capably in various colorful roles. Ruffo is okay as the wife.

Nino Rota's music makes for good backdropping to the action. Three cameramen worked on the pic, which was held up variously for refinancing, but switches are not noticeable.

•

VIVACIOUS LADY
1938, 90 mins, US Ⓥ b/w
Dir George Stevens ***Prod*** George Stevens ***Scr*** P. J. Wolfson, Ernest Pagano ***Ph*** Robert de Grasse ***Ed*** Henry Berman ***Mus*** Roy Webb (dir.) ***Art*** Van Nest Polglase
Act Ginger Rogers, James Stewart, James Ellison, Beulah Bondi, Charles Coburn, Frances Mercer (RKO)

Vivacious Lady is entertainment of the highest order and broadest appeal. Story by I.A.R. Wylie tells the romantic adventures and tribulations of a New York cabaret singer and a youthful college professor.

It is a case of love at first sight, a speedy wooing and hasty marriage. Then the young man takes his bride to the small town and introduces her to his family and associates. Prejudice and stern respectability resist the invasion. Manner in which approval of the marriage is won from the boy's parents is amusingly accomplished.

In their predicament of living apart until the conventional amenities of proper introduction into society are observed, Ginger Rogers and James Stewart undergo a series of connubial disappointments, interruptions ad interferences.

Beulah Bondi is the understanding mother-in-law and Charles Coburn is excellent as the father of the bridegroom.

1938: NOMINATIONS: Best Cinematography, Sound

•

VIVA KNIEVEL!
1977, 104 mins, US Ⓥ ▭ col
Dir Gordon Douglas ***Prod*** Stan Hough ***Scr*** Antonio Santillan ***Ph*** Fred Jackman ***Ed*** Harold Kress ***Mus*** Charles Bernstein
Act Evel Knievel, Gene Kelly, Marjoe Gortner, Lauren Hutton, Leslie Nielsen, Red Buttons (Warner/Corwin)

In the most daring feat of his career, Evel Knievel leaps over a mountain of blazing clichés and a cavernous plot, somehow landing upright to the predictable cheers of his legions of fans.

Actually, Evel the actor emerges from the wreck in better shape than the bent careers of his veteran co-stars, Gene Kelly, Marjoe Gortner, Red Buttons, Lauren Hutton and Leslie Nielsen. For him, it's a chance to show he can be fairly natural in front of the camera when the demands are minimal; for them, it's a credit best forgotten.

Plot: Evil Leslie Nielsen will lure the leaper to Mexico where he'll kill Knievel and steal his red-white-and-blue truck, substituting an identical red-white-and-blue truck whose sides are packed with illegal white powder.

•

VIVA LAS VEGAS
(UK: LOVE IN LAS VEGAS)
1964, 85 mins, US Ⓥ ⊙ ▭ col
Dir George Sidney ***Prod*** Jack Cummings, George Sidney ***Scr*** Sally Benson ***Ph*** Joseph Biroc ***Ed*** John McSweeney ***Mus*** George Stoll ***Art*** George W. Davis, Edward Carfagno
Act Elvis Presley, Ann-Margret, Cesare Danova, William Demarest, Nicky Blair, Jack Carter (Cummings/M-G-M)

The sizzling combination of Elvis Presley and Ann-Margaret is enough to carry *Viva Las Vegas* over the top. The picture is fortunate in having two such commodities for bait, because beyond several flashy musical numbers, a glamorous locale and one electrifying auto race sequence, the production is a pretty trite and heavyhanded affair, puny in story development and distortedly preoccupied with anatomical oomph.

The film is designed to dazzle the eye, assault the ear and ignore the brain. Vegas, of course, is the setting of Sally Benson's superficial contrivance about an auto racing buff (Presley) trying to raise funds to purchase an engine for the racer with which he hopes to win the Grand Prix. His main obstacle is a swimming instructress (A-M) who doesn't approve of his goal, but ultimately softens.

Hackneyed yarn provides the skeletal excuse for about 10 musical interludes, a quick tour of the U.S. gambling capital and that one slam-bang climactic sequence that lifts the film up by its bootstraps just when it is sorely in need of a lift.

•

VIVA MARIA!
1965, 120 mins, France/Italy Ⓥ ⊙ ▭ col
Dir Louis Malle ***Prod*** Oscar Dancigars, Louis Malle ***Scr*** Jean-Claude Carriere, Louis Malle ***Ph*** Henri Decae ***Ed*** Kenout Peltier, Suzanne Baron ***Mus*** Georges Delerue ***Art*** Bernard Evein
Act Jeanne Moreau, Brigitte Bardot, George Hamilton, Claudio Brooks, Gregor Von Rezzoni, Carlos Lopez Moctezuma (NEF/Artistes Associes/Vides)

Big Bertha pic has B. B. in her best form since *And God Created Woman*, and brilliantly matched by Jeanne Moreau. They are backed by a rollicking, comic adventure opus impeccably brought off by director Louis Malle.

Bardot is the daughter of a lifelong anarchist who has spent her life blowing up bridges and police stations. She finds herself hunted in some Latino country in 1910 when she has to blow up papa and a bridge. She is taken up by Moreau, a dancer in a traveling music hall cum circus. The two, both named Maria, team up.

There follow some knowing take-offs on the songs of the era, with Bardot unwittingly seeming to invent the striptease when her skirt falls off in one show.

The fine scripting takes advantage of the land, color, Panavision and outdoor shooting in Mexico as the tale gets the circus involved in a local revolution. Bardot is an innocent who suddenly discovers love, and just uses it like a pure little animal. Moreau is the more knowing and wry one who is still the more romantic.

Big scale extra scenes and mob fighting are also spectacular, with bright gags interlarded.

•

VIVA MAX
1969, 92 mins, US/UK Ⓥ col
Dir Jerry Paris ***Prod*** Mark Carliner ***Scr*** Elliott Baker ***Ph*** Henri Persin ***Ed*** Bud Molin, David Berlatsky ***Mus*** Hugo Montenegro, Ralph Dino, John Sembello ***Art*** James Hulsey
Act Peter Ustinov, Pamela Tiffin, Jonathan Winters, John Astin, Keenan Wynn, Harry Morgan (Commonwealth United)

This satirical saga of a ragtail platoon of Mexican soldiers who recapture the Alamo in 1969 is a captivatingly original idea, well produced but questionably cast with Peter Ustinov in the lead. Screenplay, based on James Lehrer's novel, carries a perfectly plausible but inherently comic idea to its logical absurdities.

Ustinov is the Mexican general who leads his small band of grousing, shuffling troops across the border on the pretext of marching in a Washington's Birthday parade in Laredo. Both he and John Astin, as his tough sergeant, do yeoman work, but have that vague aura of embarrassment of good actors who wonder what the director has wrought. The film has a little something to offend a wide variety of groups—Texans, the National Guard, right-wing paramilitary groups, and even the Alamo defender, John Wayne.

Cameraman Henri Persin makes excellent use of the locations in San Antonio, and his matching of shots makes it impossible to tell at first viewing what was shot in Texas and what at Rome's Cinecitta Studios.

•

VIVA VILLA!

1934, 112 mins, US b/w

Dir Jack Conway ***Prod*** David O. Selznick ***Scr*** Ben Hecht ***Ph*** James Wong Howe, Charles G. Clarke ***Ed*** Robert J. Kern ***Mus*** Herbert Stothart ***Art*** Harry Oliver

Act Wallace Beery, Leo Carrillo, Fay Wray, Donald Cook, Joseph Schildkraut, Stuart Erwin (M-G-M)

Viva Villa! is a corking western. It's a big, impressive production which sets out to make Wallace Beery's Pancho Villa appear as a somewhat sympathetic and quasi-patriotic bandit.

But Beery's characterization, apart from the basic screen material [suggested by the book by Edgcumb Pinchon and O. B. Stade], lets Pancho down too much. His Villa is a hybrid dialectician, neither Mex nor gringo, with a vacillating accent that suffers alongside of Leo Carrillo's charming dialect or the contra-renegade version as done by Joseph Schildkraut as Pascal. Both impart an unction and a style to their cruelties that makes Beery's boorish Villa show up too sadly.

The two principal femmes are well handled by Fay Wray as the sympathetic aristocrat who is brutally assaulted and assassinated by Villa; and Katherine DeMille (Cecil's daughter, who manifests much talent) likewise stands out. Latter's s.a. personality registers as one of Villa's casual "brides" whom sotted newspaperman Johnny Sykes (Stuart Erwin) abracadabras in mock-marriage ritual in order to appease the requirements for ceremonials by both principals.

There is no denying the mass-movement impressiveness of the production in toto. The handling of the mob scenes on field of battle was no mean task.

1934: Best Assistant Director

NOMINATIONS: Best Picture, Writing Adaptation, Sound

•

VIVA ZAPATA!

1952, 112 mins, US Ⓥ ⦿ b/w

Dir Elia Kazan ***Prod*** Darryl F. Zanuck ***Scr*** John Steinbeck ***Ph*** Joe MacDonald ***Ed*** Barbara McLean ***Mus*** Alex North ***Art*** Lyle Wheeler, Leland Fuller

Act Marlon Brando, Jean Peters, Anthony Quinn, Joseph Wiseman, Arnold Moss, Margo (20th Century-Fox)

The story of Emiliano Zapata, a lesser-known Mexican revolutionary, is a picture that records a hard, cruel, curiously unemotional account of Mexican banditry and revolt against oppressive government. Elia Kazan's direction strives for a personal intimacy but neither he nor the John Steinbeck scripting achieves in enough measure.

Convenient use is made of historical fact as the script plays hop-skip-and-jump in spanning the nine years that Zapata was a controversial figure in Mexican political life just prior to and during the earlier part of World War I.

Marlon Brando brings to the Zapata character the same type of cold objectivity noted in script and direction. Jean Peters is the girl who becomes his bride and forsees his violent end.

There's a stark quality to the photography by Joe MacDonald that suggests the raw, hot atmosphere of Mexico.

1952: Best Supp. Actor (Anthony Quinn)

NOMINATIONS: Best Actor (Marlon Brando), Story & Screenplay, Art Direction, Scoring of a Dramatic Picture

•

VIVRE POUR VIVRE
(LIVE FOR LIFE)

1967, 120 mins, France col

Dir Claude Lelouch ***Prod*** Alexandre Mnouchkine, Georges Danciger ***Scr*** Claude Lelouch, Pierre Uytterhoeven ***Ph*** Claude Lelouch, Patrick Pouget ***Ed*** Claude Barrois ***Mus*** Francis Lai

Act Yves Montand, Annie Girardot, Candice Bergen, Irene Tunc, Uta Taeger, Anouk Ferjac (Ariane/Artistes Associes/Vides)

Claude Lelouch's previous *A Man and a Woman* copped first prize at the Cannes film festival, won Oscars for best foreign-language film and original screenplay, and earned a phenomenal $3 million in U.S. rentals. *Live for Life* is very similar in subject matter and style but lacks the lyric sweep and charm of its predecessor, and even falters technically despite a sizable budget.

The hero (Yves Montand), a married man whose ritualized adulteries unexpectedly culminate in a serious love affair, is self-absorbed and emotionally sterile. The young American girl (Candice Bergen) whom he loves is equally immature, much given to pouting and aimless tear-ridden sessions in which she berates him for not leaving his spouse.

Montand's acting generally consists of who-cares shrugs, downturned mouth, eyebrows raised in a perpetual state of boredom, and tired line readings. Bergen has seemingly been asked to improvise many of her scenes, but she lacks the spontaneity and experienced self-confidence. Much better is Annie Girardot in the hazily defined role of Montand's long-suffering wife.

Hero is a TV reporter whose job takes him to Africa, Vietnam, and other inflamed sections of the world. Trouble is that these sidetrips don't connect to the narrative or develop the main theme but seem entirely gratuitous.

Most debatable, insofar as taste is concerned, is a sequence near the film's end: Montand in a realistically bloody Vietnam battle, Girardot watching TV, and Bergen walking through wintry Central Park are crosscut to the accompaniment of a vapid love ballad.

•

VIVRE SA VIE: FILM EN DOUZE TABLEAUX
(MY LIFE TO LIVE; IT'S MY LIFE)

1962, 80 mins, France Ⓥ ⦿ b/w

Dir Jean-Luc Godard ***Prod*** Pierre Braunberger ***Scr*** Jean-Luc Godard ***Ph*** Raoul Coutard ***Ed*** Agnes Guillemot ***Mus*** Michel Legrand ***Art*** [uncredited]

Act Anna Karina, Saddy Rebbot, Andre Labarthe, G. Schlumberger, Gerard Hoffman, Monique Messine (Braunberger)

As he looked at a young, cynical hoodlum in *Breathless*, director Jean-Luc Godard brings his dispassionate outlook to a pretty girl who slips into prostitution. Nothing sentimental here but a knowing series of episodes that skillfully probe the girl's character and life.

Godard eschews his jump cutting and brittle pacing of the past to make a well sustained, non-sensational look at a girl adrift in Paris. She is depicted via 12 little episodes, each getting a title on the screen. First she breaks with a rather weak, self-indulgent boyfriend (Andre Labarthe). The girl gets locked out of her apartment, leaves her job and finally goes into prostitution. She ends up with a procurer (Saddy Rebot). When she tries to break with him for a young man she is sold to another group, only to be shot down when they fight over money.

Godard mixes titles, unusual use of sound, and long scenes of dialog. He is brilliantly served by his wife, Anna Karina, in this film. Karina gives the girl a ring of truth and depth.

•

V. I. WARSHAWSKI

1991, 89 mins, US Ⓥ ⦿ col

Dir Jeff Kanew ***Prod*** Jeffrey Lurie ***Scr*** Edward Taylor, David Aaron Cohen, Nick Thiel ***Ph*** Jan Kiesser ***Ed*** C. Timothy O'Meara, Debra Neil ***Mus*** Randy Edelman ***Art*** Barbara Ling

Act Kathleen Turner, Jay O. Saunders, Charles Durning, Angela Goethals, Nancy Paul, Frederick Coffin (Hollywood/Chestnut Hill)

You can't be much worse-offski than to sit through *V. I. Warshawski*. Klutzy murder mystery [from a screen story by Edward Taylor] was obviously intended to be the first in a hoped-for series about the eponymous femme detective impersonated by Kathleen Turner.

Somewhere behind the vast underachievement here, one can discern that there was screen promise in the blue collar female dick of Sara Paretsky's novels. The daughter of a cop and a habitue of sports bars on Chicago's North Side, this salty, sexy, streetwise straight-shooter clearly could have represented a refreshing new twist on the standard issue private investigator.

The story has Warshawski getting involved in dirty business among three warring brothers. One brother, the good-looking Boom-Boom Grafalk, a former hockey player for whom V. I. has eyes, is killed in a suspicious dockside explosion. Warshawski also is responsible for Boom-Boom's 13-year-old daughter, Kat (Angela Goethals), for whom she was babysitting when the girl's father was sent into permanent slumber.

From a filmmaking point of view, it is all uninspired and perfunctory, utterly lacking in a sense of style that might have made this punchy fun. Center screen throughout, Turner would seem to have been perfectly cast in such a sassy, confident part, but even she can't drive a totally rusty vehicle.

[For pic's U.K. release the handle *Detective in High Heels* were added to posters.]

•

VIXEN!

1968, 71 mins, US col

Dir Russ Meyer ***Prod*** Russ Meyer ***Scr*** Robert Rudelson ***Ph*** Russ Meyer ***Ed*** Russ Meyer ***Mus*** Igo Kantor ***Art*** Wilfred Kues

Act Erica Gavin, Harrison Page, Garth Pillsbury, Michael O'Donnell, Vincene Wallace, Robert Aiken (Eve/Coldstream)

Russ Meyer's film is another of his technically polished sexplicit dramas, this time free of physical violence and brutality, and hyped with some awkwardly developed draft-dodging and patriotism angles. Vixen is a girl who can't say no, and she proves it every seven minutes. She finds time for her husband, too.

There is a frankness to Meyer's sex scenes, in that they are unabashed in their frequent amorality, motivated without hypocrisy, and executed with dispatch. No tortured rationalizing here (Meyer's budget—$70,000—couldn't afford it anyway), nor any sophisticated gloss-over. His people simply meet, rut a bit, then move along. Often the sequences are hilarious in their unbelievability.

Erica Gavin is featured in title role, and besides the ample visual aspect, carries off the dramatic moments to okay effect. Garth Pillsbury is her square husband, Jon Evans her motorcycle hood brother, and Peter Carpenter the passing Mountie with whom she passes the first few minutes.

•

VOGUES OF 1938

1937, 108 mins, US Ⓥ col

Dir Irving Cummings ***Prod*** Walter Wanger ***Scr*** Bella Spewack, Samuel Spewack ***Ph*** Ray Rennahan ***Ed*** Otho Lovering, Dorothy Spencer ***Mus*** Boris Morros (dir.) ***Art*** Alexander Toluboff

Act Warner Baxter, Joan Bennett, Helen Vinson, Mischa Auer, Alan Mowbray, Jerome Cowan (Wanger/United Artists)

A distinct departure from routine picture producing, *Vogues of 1938* has an ingenious script, of surprising elasticity. It has a group of superlative floor-show specialties. It introduces a dozen of the country's famous fashion models. And it is photographed throughout in some of the loveliest Technicolor so far projected.

The Spewacks's screenplay is more of a libretto than a tightly knit story. Of interest is the exposure of the inner workings of the fashion racket, the rivalry for latest Paris designs and models, the methods of exploiting styles, and the salesmanship necessary to convince fickle women they must buy only what the establishments have for sale.

Production numbers are incorporated in the annual public showings of new styles in costumes, furs and lingerie.

Warner Baxter plays the proprietor of the House of Curson and goes about his manifold duties with the air of a diplomat and with serene good humor. When Joan Bennett's society girl pleads with him to delay delivery of her wedding costume, he refuses to fall down on an order, but he hires her as a model after she does a walkout.

Helen Vinson does a neat bit of wifely villainy, Mischa Auer displays temperament as a rival designer, and Alma Kruger contributes a warm characterization of a hard-working general manager of seamstresses and girlish models.

•

VOLCANO

1997, 102 mins, US Ⓥ ⦿ col

Dir Mick Jackson ***Prod*** Neal H. Moritz, Andrew Z. Davis ***Scr*** Jerome Armstrong, Billy Ray ***Ph*** Theo van de Sande ***Ed*** Michael Tronick, Don Brochu ***Mus*** Alan Silvestri ***Art*** Jackson DeGovia

Act Tommy Lee Jones, Anne Heche, Gaby Hoffmann, Don Cheadle, Jacqueline Kim, Keith David (Shuler Donner-Donner/Moritz Original/20th Century-Fox)

A furiously paced popcorn picture whose outrageous implausibility is somewhat amusing, *Volcano* is neither appreciably better or worse than *Dante's Peak* [released two months earlier, in February]. Although running time has been kept laudably economical, pic never generates a head of true excitement, partly because the characters remain constructs to perform designed functions.

Filmmakers waste no time with exposition or scene-setting, starting the fireworks with a nerve-jangling morning earthquake that puts city workers on alert. Chief among them is Mike Roark (Tommy Lee Jones), director of L.A.'s Office of Emergency Management, which takes remarkably efficient control of the increasingly chaotic situation. Soon turning up to help out is crack seismologist Dr. Amy Barnes (Anne Heche).

Less than a half-hour in, the Big One hits. Most unexpected result is a fiery geyser that erupts from the La Brea

Tar Pits, sending meteor-like lava bombs skyrocketing and finally producing a lava flow that heads right onto Wilshire Boulevard alongside the L.A. County Museum of Art (fortunately, in the opposite direction from the offices of *Variety*, just a block to the east). Remaining hour is occupied by the frantic battle to stem the molten tide.

Allegedly weighing in at around $100 million, or a third more than *Dante's Peak*, production delivers the goods on the physical side. An 80% full-size replica of Wilshire between the tar pits and Fairfax Avenue (reputedly the largest set ever constructed in the U.S.) was put up in Torrance and then destroyed on-camera. Effects are all quite convincing, although lava is not the most exciting of the destructive natural forces to watch onscreen.

•

VOLUNTEERS
1985, 106 mins, US Ⓥ ⦿ col
Dir Nicholas Meyer ***Prod*** Richard Shepherd, Walter F. Parkes ***Scr*** Ken Levine, David Isaacs ***Ph*** Ric Waite ***Ed*** Ronald Roose, Steven Polivka ***Mus*** James Horner ***Art*** James Schoppe
Act Tom Hanks, John Candy, Rita Wilson, Tim Thomerson, Gedde Watanabe, George Plimpton (HBO)

Volunteers is a very broad and mostly flat comedy [from a story by Keith Critchlow] about hijinx in the Peace Corps, circa 1962. Top-lined Tom Hanks gets in a few good zingers as an upperclass snob doing time in Thailand, but promising premise and opening shortly descend into unduly protracted tedium.

Hanks plays Lawrence Bourne III, an arrogant, snide rich boy from Yale who trades places with an earnest Peace Corps designate when his gambling debts land him in danger at home. Once ensconced in a remote village, contentious couple Hanks and cohort Rita Wilson and ultra do-gooder John Candy set out to build a bridge across a river. Kidnapped and brainwashed by the commies, the gung-ho Candy disappears for a long stretch.

With Candy absent most of the time, Hanks's one-note, if sometimes clever, attitudinizing wears out its welcome after a while. He also is deprived of anyone effective to play off.

Lensed in Mexico, pic features a muddy, truly ugly look. Also present is the most offensively blatant plug for Coca-Cola yet seen in the new era of Coke-owned entertainment companies.

•

VOLVER A EMPEZAR
(TO BEGIN AGAIN; BEGIN THE BEGUINE)
1982, 90 mins, Spain col
Dir Jose Luis Garci ***Prod*** Jose Esteban Alenda, Angel Llorente (execs.) ***Scr*** Jose Luis Garci, Angel Llorente ***Ph*** Manuel Rojas ***Ed*** Miguel Gonzales Sinde ***Art*** Gil Parrondo
Act Antonio Ferrandis, Encarna Paso, Jose Bodalo, Agustin Gonzalez, Pablo Hoyo, Marta Fernandez Muro (Nickel Odeon)

Pic recounts a story of utter simplicity, or at least it seems simple in its plot and characterizations; in fact, it is buoyed by outstanding performances all around, a script which is sensitive, eloquent and pointed, and flawless direction, cinematography and editing.

Story concerns an exiled Spanish novelist and Nobel Prize–winner reminiscent of Ramon Sender who returns to his native town (Gijon, a coastal city in northern Asturias province) after 40 years for a two-day trip into the past. The reason is that he's terminally ill.

The writer pensively walks about the town, looks up an old girlfriend from the prewar days who's now running an art gallery, watches a soccer game, and is showered with honors. He and the now aged lady reminisce about a dance where they met while the band played "Begin the Beguine."

Though subject is maudlin and once or twice director Jose Luis Garci veers rather close to the lachrymose, helmer succeeds in keeping the story upbeat, partly through use of some nicely limned comic releif via an obsequious hotel clerk.

1982: Best Foreign Language Film

•

VON RYAN'S EXPRESS
1965, 114 mins, US Ⓥ ▭ col
Dir Mark Robson ***Prod*** Saul David ***Scr*** Wendell Mayes, Joseph Landon ***Ph*** William H. Daniels ***Ed*** Dorothy Spencer ***Mus*** Jerry Goldsmith ***Art*** Jack Martin Smith, Hilyard Brown
Act Frank Sinatra, Trevor Howard, Raffaella Carra, Brad Dexter, Sergio Fantoni, John Leyton (20th Century-Fox)

Mass escape of 600 American and British prisoners-of-war across 1943 Nazi-controlled Italy lends colorful backing to this fast, suspenseful and exciting Second World War tale. Mark Robson has made realistic use of the actual Italian setting of the David Westheimer novel in garmenting his action in hard-hitting direction and sharply drawn performances.

Frank Sinatra and Trevor Howard co-star as leaders of the escape, who, under former's initiative, seize a freight train which is bearing prisoners for delivery to the Germans in Austria and divert it across northern Italy in an attempt to find haven in Switzerland. Sinatra plays a hardboiled American Air Force colonel named Ryan, shot down by Italians and imprisoned in the camp where Howard, an equally tough British major, is senior officer.

Robson depends heavily on suspense and accompanying thrills after Sinatra and Howard take over the train.

1965: NOMINATION: Best Sound Effects

•

VOYAGE OF THE DAMNED
1976, 155 mins, UK Ⓥ col
Dir Stuart Rosenberg ***Prod*** Robert Fryer ***Scr*** Steve Shagan, David Butler ***Ph*** Billy Williams ***Ed*** Tom Priestley ***Mus*** Lalo Schifrin ***Art*** Wilfrid Shingleton
Act Faye Dunaway, Max von Sydow, Oskar Werner, Malcolm McDowell, Orson Welles, James Mason (ITC/Associated General)

Voyage of the Dammed is a sluggish melodrama, loaded with familiar film names who flesh out the diverse formula characters involved in this story about a ship carrying Jews away from Nazi Germany.

Based on the book by Gordon Thomas and Max Morgan-Witts, screenplay follows the form of a prototype "ark" film, introducing the specimen couples, herein Jews deliberately loaded aboard a ship to which Cuba will deny entry permit, thereby fulfilling a Nazi propaganda plan. Max von Sydow, a non-Nazi German, is skipper of the ship.

Fact that the story is based on an actual, and shocking, incident makes all the more disappointing its transfer to the screen. The action zigs and zags between the cluttered set of characters.

1976: NOMINATIONS: Best Supp. Actress (Lee Grant), Adapted Screenplay, Original Score

•

VOYAGER
1991, 117 mins, Germany/France Ⓥ col
Dir Volker Schlondorff ***Prod*** Eberhard Junkersdorf ***Scr*** Volker Schlondorff, Rudy Wurlitzer ***Ph*** Yorgos Arvanitis, Pierre Lhomme ***Ed*** Dagmar Hirtz ***Mus*** Stanley Myers ***Art*** Nicos Perakis
Act Sam Shepard, Julie Delpy, Barbara Sukowa, Dieter Kirchlechner, Traci Lind, Deborra-Lee Furness (Bioskop/Action)

Equal parts road movie and Greek tragedy, Volker Schlondorff's latest literary adaptation (of Max Frisch's German classic *Homo Faber*) makes good use of fine material.

In this moral tale without a moral, Walter Faber (Swiss in the book, Yank in pic) is an inveterate traveler, an engineer and pragmatist approaching middle age in the not-yet-defined postwar Europe of the 1950s. Sam Shepard is ideal as Faber, the quintessentially cool cowboy-loner-businessman.

Via black & white flashbacks, Faber recalls his days as a student in Zurich before the war: He was in love with Hanna, a German Jew pregnant with his child. Waiting for a flight to Venezuela, Faber learns that his friend Joachim married Hanna, and they had a daughter but divorced shortly afterward.

Back in New York, he decides to travel to Paris by ship. On board he meets Sabeth (Julie Delpy), 20ish and returning home after studying in the States. Faber initially ignores her until her charm and almost unbearably fragile beauty begin to take effect. Is it love or a protective, paternal instinct?

A well-told tale, with a fine cast and good tech credits.

•

VOYAGE TO ITALY
SEE: VIAGGIO IN ITALIA

•

VOYAGE TO THE BOTTOM OF THE SEA
1961, 105 mins, US Ⓥ ⦿ ▭ col
Dir Irwin Allen ***Prod*** Irwin Allen ***Scr*** Irwin Allen, Charles Bennett ***Ph*** Winton C. Hoch ***Ed*** George Boemler ***Mus*** Paul Sawtell, Bert Shefter ***Art*** Jack Martin Smith, Herman A. Blumenthal
Act Walter Pidgeon, Joan Fontaine, Barbara Eden, Peter Lorre, Robert Sterling, Frankie Avalon (Windsor/20th Century-Fox)

Voyage is a crescendo of mounting jeopardy, an effervescent adventure in an anything-but-Pacific Ocean.

The way the story goes, this brilliant admiral (Walter Pidgeon), commander of a marvelous atomic sub that resembles a smiling Moby Dick, devises a scheme to save mankind when life on earth is suddenly threatened by a girdle of fire caused when the Van Allen Belt of Radiation encircling the globe goes berserk and erupts. Trouble is mankind does not seem to want to be saved and unable to contact the U.S. prez (golfing?), skipper Pidgeon heads for a spot near the Marianas where he plans to orbit a Polaris and explode the heavenly blaze out into space.

Actually the title is somewhat misleading. Customers who expect a kind of advanced course in oceanography will discover only an occasional giant squid and a lot of rubbery vegetation. For the most part, *The Bottom* of director Irwin Allen's *Sea* is merely the setting for the kind of emotional calisthenics that might just as easily break out 100 feet from the tip of Mount Everest.

The acting is generally capable, about the best it can be under the trying dramatic circumstances.

•

VOYNA I MIR I: ANDREI BOLKONSKY
(WAR AND PEACE, PART I)
1966, 140 mins, Russia Ⓥ ▭ col
Dir Sergei Bondarchuk ***Scr*** Vasili Solovyov, Sergei Bondarchuk ***Ph*** Anatoli Petritsky ***Ed*** Tatyana Likhacheva ***Mus*** Vyacheslav Ovchinnikov ***Art*** Mikhail Bogdanov, Gennadi Myasnikov
Act Lyudmila Savelyeva, Sergei Bondarchuk, Vyacheslav Tikhonov, Anatoli Ktorov, Boris Smirnov, Kira Ivanova-Golovko (Mosfilm)

More than three years in the making, *War and Peace* is a sumptuous and lavish spectacular, making brilliant use of the 70mm screen. Sergei Bondarchuk has kept to his intention of making a faithful filmization of Leo Tolstoy's famous novel. That may have been a worthy decision, but not necessarily the wisest one, as the film suffers occasionally from being too "literary."

At its best, the production is superb. Bondarchuk is a master at controlling crowds, and the two great battle scenes in the first part are nothing short of breathtaking. There is an unforgettable moment as the Russian and French armies march defiantly toward each other, and the moment of impact is spectacularly exciting. Something like 10,000 extras are used in these scenes. Equally spectacular is the subsequent Battle of Austerlitz.

But in his determination to translate the novel literally, Bondarchuk tries also to be too poetic, and overdoes it with an endless succession of shots of clouds, trees and the countryside.

On the other hand he's not been afraid to use old-fashioned techniques where he believes it helps the picture, such as split screens and gimmicky camera angles.

One of the surprises is Bondarchuk's own performance in the demanding role of the shy, tongue-tied Pierre. His thesping range is quite remarkable, from a drunk scene with fellow officers in the opening stages to his embarrassed proposal to the beautiful Helene (Irina Skobtseva).

•

VOYNA I MIR II: NATASHA ROSTOVA
(WAR AND PEACE, PART II)
1966, 90 mins, Russia Ⓥ ▭ col
Dir Sergei Bondarchuk ***Scr*** Vasili Solovyov, Sergei Bondarchuk ***Ph*** Anatoli Petritsky ***Ed*** Tatyana Likhacheva ***Mus*** Vyacheslav Ovchinnikov ***Art*** Mikhail Bogdanov, Gennadi Myasnikov
Act Lyudmila Savelyeva, Sergei Bondarchuk, Vyacheslav Tikhonov, Anastasia Vertinskaya, Vladislav Strzhelchik, Irina Skobtseva (Mosfilm)

The spectacle in *War and Peace* is not confined to the two battle sequences [in Part I]. In *Natasha Rostova*, there is a superbly staged and photographed ballroom scene, and a magnificent hunt, which comes to a brilliant climax as the hounds grapple with the wolf.

Lyudmila Savelyeva, the Leningrad ballerina who plays the part of Natasha, is an absolute find and a joy to behold. She's a beauty, and she can act. All the fresh, impetuous eagerness of youth comes out in her performance, and it comes out naturally. There's an incandescent glow whenever she's on screen. Her dance of joy toward the end is as charming as it is sincere.

Another imposing performance comes from Vyacheslav Tikhonov as Prince Andrei Bolkonsky. It is he who proposes to Natasha—a delicate and touching piece of filmmaking, truly in keeping with the character of the novel.

•

VOYNA I MIR III: 1812 GOD
(WAR AND PEACE, PART III)
1967, 85 mins, Russia Ⓥ ▭ col
Dir Sergei Bondarchuk ***Scr*** Vasili Solovyov, Sergei Bondarchuk ***Ph*** Anatoli Petritsky ***Ed*** Tatyana Likhacheva ***Mus***

Vyacheslav Ovchinnikov ***Art*** Mikhail Bogdanov, Gennadi Myasnikov
Act Lyudmila Savelyeva, Sergei Bondarchuk, Vyacheslav Tikhonov, Boris Zakhava, V. Stanitsyn, Vladislav Strzhelchik (Mosfilm)

Part III deals with the death of Prince Andrei's father; Pierre's visit to the young Natasha; and his visit to the battlefield of Borodino, where he wanders amidst the carnage, bombast and explosiveness of hand-to-hand combat and its skirmishes, cannons and the mingling of flesh, horses, earth and sky.

The film remains posey, conventional and more often opting for tableaus, rather than the more personal and interpretive look at the Napoleonic wars and their effect on the Russian people and country. But its sheer size soon casts a spell; that, and the dinning sound of battle. The camera will suddenly zoom up from the field, disclosing thousands of scurrying men, horses and battle gear, or it will watch one character face death near a sizzling bomb, or climb dizzily among the trees.

Sergei Bondarchuk has stayed completely with the Tolstoy novel and translated it ambitiously to the screen. It sometimes, therefore, appears literary but has an epic drive that manages to overcome its academic trappings.

A man's leg shot off, and his quizzical look as awareness dawns; horses hurtling off their feet; cannon exploding; men rallying, running, withdrawing, going on again. All this begins to take on a hypnotic quality, and somehow the logistics of battle are clear. Napoleon, in the midst of hundreds of bodies, brooding, is the final shot as a series of frozen stills front for a stentorian voice extolling the victory of the Russian moral drive over the French will of conquest.

•

VOYNA I MIR IV: PYER BEZUKHOV
(WAR AND PEACE, PART IV)

1967, 95 mins, Russia Ⓥ ⌑ col
Dir Sergei Bondarchuk ***Scr*** Vasili Solovyov, Sergei Bondarchuk ***Ph*** Anatoli Petritsky ***Ed*** Tatyana Likhacheva ***Mus*** Vyacheslav Ovchinnikov ***Art*** Mikhail Bogdanov, Gennadi Myasnikov
Act Lyudmila Savelyeva, Sergei Bondarchuk, Vyacheslav Tikhonov, Boris Zakhava, Vladislav Strzhelchik (Mosfilm)

Fourth and final part of the massive Russo costumer is an impressive windup to this super spec. It shows that it has a cumulative force which overcomes some of its academic and posey qualities.

This entry has a written prolog to set up the fortunes of its main characters during a time of peace and then the Napoleonic Wars. It blocks out the main characters—Pierre's bad marriage, growing love for a young noble girl, his travails during the war, and the destinies of the girl and a prince she loved—as a microcosm of the destinies of a whole people in war and peace.

Part IV deals with Pierre's capture and near-execution when the Napoleonic troops invade and burn Moscow, the death of the prince, and Pierre's final uniting with the girl after the disastrous retreat of Napoleon's troops in the terrible Russo winter. It reaches grandiose proportions and an operatic, almost ecstatic, quality that is in keeping with the book via Tolstoy's cosmic vision.

The burning of Moscow and the frenzy of pillage and arbitrary executions get a dizzying mounting. Pierre's near-execution awakens an almost mystic feel of his realization that he is a part of everything.

The camera zooming through a burning building, Pierre's rage at soldier inhumanity, the prince's death, a mother's mourning, the young girl's anguish—all work as comments on man's prevailing end and overcome the sentimentality and overdone aspects in some of the earlier segs.

[The entire film was first shown in the U.S. in 1968, and the U.K. in 1969, in a 357-min. dubbed version, in two parts, each with an intermission.]

1968: Best Foreign Language Film

WABASH AVENUE
1950, 90 mins, US col

Dir Henry Koster ***Prod*** William Perlberg ***Scr*** Harry Tugend, Charles Lederer ***Ph*** Arthur E. Arling ***Ed*** Robert Simpson ***Mus*** Lionel Newman (dir.)

Act Betty Grable, Victor Mature, Phil Harris, James Barton, Reginald Gardiner, Margaret Hamilton (20th Century-Fox)

Plot is a satisfactory backdrop for the deluge of tunes that run through the footage. There's nothing in the writing to tax the dramatic skill of the players, and they romp along neatly.

It's Betty Grable's picture, viewed strictly from the angle of physical attractions which she uses to the fullest. But she is abetted by some strong personalities in the male department. Background music score totals 26 oldies.

Phil Harris and Victor Mature portray friendly enemies, out to beat each other with a smile. It's all good fun as long as they cheat each other at cards, win and lose their various business enterprises. It's a more serious thing, though, when they compete for Grable and skullduggery runs high.

•

WAGES OF FEAR
SEE: SORCERER

•

WAGES OF FEAR, THE
SEE: LE SALAIRE DE LA PEUR

•

WAGNER
1983, 300 mins, UK/Austria/Hungary Ⓥ ⊙ col

Dir Tony Palmer ***Prod*** Alan Wright ***Scr*** Charles Wood ***Ph*** Vittorio Storaro, Nic Knowland ***Ed*** Tony Palmer, Graham Bunn ***Art*** Kenneth E. Carey

Act Richard Burton, Vanessa Redgrave, Gemma Craven, Marthe Keller, John Gielgud, Ralph Richardson (London Trust Cultural)

There's nothing particularly intimate or revelatory about this five-hour (plus intermission) biopic of the German 19th-century composer.

The film begins in Dresden in 1848 when Richard Wagner (Richard Burton) was beginning to gain notoriety for his compositions and grand, heroic operas. He was also actively involved in the movement for a unified Germany.

So begins a 40-year trek across Europe for the most part as a stateless artist. Brunt of the first part deals with his self-imposed exile with part two beginning with his introduction to Ludwig II who becomes his patron. Along the way there are mounting bills, political scandals and Faustian pursuits.

Burton's performance as Wagner presents an almost entirely unsympathetic picture. Vanessa Redgrave and Gemma Craven as Wagner's wives have largely thankless roles. For buffs, the film's biggest draw is watching England's acting knights—Laurence Olivier, John Gielgud, Ralph Richardson—working together for the first time on screen.

Chief attraction remains the visual components of the film which beautifully capture the era.

•

WAGON MASTER
1950, 85 mins, US Ⓥ ⊙ b/w

Dir John Ford ***Prod*** John Ford, Merian C. Cooper ***Scr*** Frank Nugent, Patrick Ford ***Ph*** Bert Glennon ***Ed*** Jack Murray ***Mus*** Richard Hageman ***Art*** James Basevi

Act Ben Johnson, Harry Carey, Jr., Ward Bond, Joanne Dru, Alan Mowbray, Jane Darwell (RKO/Argosy)

Wagon Master is a good outdoor action film, done in the best John Ford manner. That means careful character development and movement, spiced with high spots of action, good drama and leavening comedy moments. Pic has some of the best cross-country chases

Site of the story and the filming is Utah, and the rugged locale supplies fresh backgrounds for the action. The story deals with a wagontrain of Mormons seeking a rich valley in which to locate. They are led by Ward Bond and he hires horsetraders Ben Johnson and Harry Carey, Jr., to guide the pioneers to the new land.

Johnson sits his saddle mighty easily and gives the same kind of a performance, natural and likeable. Carey and Bond also come over in fine style.

•

WAGONS EAST!
1994, 106 mins, US Ⓥ col

Dir Peter Markle ***Prod*** Gary Goodman, Barry Rosen, Robert Newmyer, ***Scr*** Matthew Carlson ***Ph*** Frank Tidy ***Ed*** Scott Conrad ***Mus*** Michael Small ***Art*** Vince J. Cresciman

Act John Candy, Richard Lewis, John C. McGinley, Ellen Greene, Robert Picardo, Ed Lauter (Carolco/Outlaw)

Wagons East! records John Candy's final hours spent before the cameras, and, unfortunately, they were far from his finest. Everyone's creative burners were on low heat for this woeful outing [from a screen story by Jerry Abrahamson].

Gag here is completely related by the title: a bunch of Old West pioneers who have had enough of bank robbers, cattle rustlers, drunken boors and intolerant know-nothings decide to head back from whence they came. To guide them east, they hire wagonmaster James Harlow (Candy), who has a pretty shaky sense of direction.

In ultra-politically correct fashion, the Indians are only too happy to oblige and escort the palefaces out of their territory, but the trek is vehemently opposed by the big-money rail interests, who fear bad publicity if word of the malcontents gets around. Fat cats hire an inept gunslinger and, finally, the Cavalry to make sure the bumbling crew doesn't make it back.

The dialog and the characters' neuroses are insistently contemporary, with colloquialisms and '90s urban lingo cascading out of everyone's mouth. Candy looks heavier than ever and seems rather listless.

•

WAGONS ROLL AT NIGHT, THE
1941, 83 mins, US b/w

Dir Ray Enright ***Prod*** Harlan Thompson ***Scr*** Fred Niblo, Jr., Barry Trivers ***Ph*** Sid Hickox ***Ed*** Frederick Richards ***Mus*** Heinz Roemheld

Act Humphrey Bogart, Sylvia Sidney, Eddie Albert, Joan Leslie, Sig Ruman, Cliff Clark (Warner)

The Wagons Roll at Night is a fast-moving meller. Background is supplied by a traveling carnival operated by the tough and calloused Humphrey Bogart who succeeds in evading successive sheriffs to keep the show moving.

Yarn uses the carny atmosphere casually, sticking directly to the melodramatics of the story for audience attention throughout. There are several exciting episodes in which Eddie Albert works the troupe of lions in the cage of the one-ring tent.

Bogart delivers his usually capable characterization, putting plenty of zest into his role of the carny operator. Albert is excellent as the bumpkin, providing plenty of lightness and humor to the part.

Ray Enright's direction focuses attention on the drama and excitement and keeps things moving at a consistently fast pace.

•

WAG THE DOG
1997, 97 mins, US Ⓥ ⊙ col

Dir Barry Levinson ***Prod*** Jane Rosenthal, Robert De Niro, Barry Levinson ***Scr*** Hilary Henkin, David Mamet ***Ph*** Robert Richardson ***Ed*** Stu Linder ***Mus*** Mark Knopfler ***Art*** Wynn Thomas

Act Dustin Hoffman, Robert De Niro, Anne Heche, Woody Harrelson, Denis Leary, Willie Nelson (Tribeca/Baltimore/Punch)

Glib cynicism isn't a tremendously appealing quality, but in *Wag the Dog* it at least has the benefit of comic precision and polished handling. Pic satirizes media culture in a way that hardly delivers real insight or pungency, but shrewdly flatters the educated viewer's knowingness. That, plus welcome concision and a deftly hilarious turn by Dustin Hoffman.

Wag was shot in under a month for $15 million by the production companies of stars Hoffman and Robert De Niro and helmer Barry Levinson.

Pic's premise, adapted from Larry Beinhart's novel *American Hero*, contains an obvious timeliness. Two weeks before he's up for re-election, the president (Michael Belson) is accused of accosting a Girl Scout in the Oval Office. Before the news reaches the media, his advisors, led by Winifred Ames (Anne Heche), call in a mysterious political consultant, Conrad Brean (De Niro), who specializes in near-impossible image rescues. His ruse is to buy time by whipping up an aura of impending national crisis.

Brean jets off to Hollywood and the mansion of producer Stanley Motss (Hoffman), a caricature come to life with his carefully cultivated tan, tennis togs and upswept hairdo. Motss jumps at orchestrating a patriotic campaign aimed against the enemy du jour picked rather impulsively by Brean: Albania.

De Niro seems to hang back to let his costar have a clear field. Heche, who also has a lot of screen time, is De Niro's opposite; where he's too relaxed and vague, she's too tightly wound and brittle.

1997: NOMINATIONS: Best Actor (Dustin Hoffman), Screenplay Adaptation

•

WAITING TO EXHALE
1995, 121 mins, US Ⓥ ⊙ col

Dir Forest Whitaker ***Prod*** Ezra Swerdlow, Deborah Schindler ***Scr*** Terry McMillan, Ronald Bass ***Ph*** Toyomichi Kurita ***Ed*** Richard Chew ***Mus*** Kenneth (Babyface) Edmonds ***Art*** David Gropman

Act Whitney Houston, Angela Bassett, Loretta Devine, Lela Rochon, Gregory Hines, Dennis Haysbert (20th Century-Fox)

Like a meeting of Douglas Sirk and Barry White, *Waiting to Exhale* smoothly combines the elan and emotional luxuriance of old-fashioned women's mellers with a modern black-pop sensibility. Adapted from the bestseller by Terry McMillan, this tale of four women beset by romantic perplexities comes to life thanks to an appealing cast and skilled and imaginative direction by Forest Whitaker.

Atypical among recent screen blacks, the four friends here are well-off Southwestern suburbanites whose only want is romantic: all complain of the dearth of black men able to forge long-term commitments.

Bernadine (Angela Bassett) has perhaps the worst case. Her tycoon husband left her for his white book-keeper. Her friend Savannah (Whitney Houston), obliged to choose between a handsome freeloader and a former flame who's unhappily married, has to wonder if being single isn't her destiny.

For Robin (Lela Rochon), the chances for amour are numerous, but she has yet to find a mate among the sex partners. For Gloria (Loretta Devine), such chances are now mostly history until Marvin (Gregory Hines), a new neighbor, sets her dreaming again.

Briskly paced, pic deftly interweaves stories of the four women over a year, using their friendship mainly as the glue that binds the individual tales.

Assigned the pic's meatiest (and perhaps largest) role, Bassett again proves her gifts with a performance at once fiery and delicate. Houston follows her *Bodyguard* debut with another glamorous turn, while Rochon's spunky charm and Devine's earthy aplomb round out the quartet of well-matched perfs.

Even more striking, though, is the opulent look Whitaker applies, which recalls vintage studio pics in its deliberately unreal orchestration of rich colors, operatic lighting and picture-book interiors.

•

WAIT UNTIL DARK
1967, 107 mins, US Ⓥ col

Dir Terence Young ***Prod*** Mel Ferrer ***Scr*** Robert Carrington, Jane-Howard Carrington ***Ph*** Charles Lang ***Ed*** Gene Milford ***Mus*** Henry Mancini ***Art*** George Jenkins

Act Audrey Hepburn, Alan Arkin, Richard Crenna, Efrem Zimbalist, Jr., Jack Weston, Samantha Jones (Warner)

Wait until Dark, based on Frederick Knott's legit hit, emerges as an excellent suspense drama, effective in casting, scripting, direction and genuine emotional impact. Audrey Hepburn stars as the not-so-helpless blind heroine, in a superior performance.

Plot turns on a supposedly hapless femme protagonist, an accident-blinded Hepburn. Hubby Efrem Zimbalist, Jr., has made his wife self-sufficient and reasonably able to fend for herself in their apartment home.

Zimbalist accidentally plays into the hands of heroin-smuggling Samantha Jones who plants a dope-loaded doll in his possession. Alan Arkin disposes of Jones, then hires Richard Crenna and Jack Weston to intimidate Hepburn into surrendering the doll.

1967: NOMINATION: Best Actress (Audrey Hepburn)

•

WAKE ISLAND
1942, 87 mins, US Ⓥ b/w

Dir John Farrow ***Prod*** Joseph Sistrom ***Scr*** W. R. Burnett, Frank Butler ***Ph*** Theodor Sparkuhl ***Ed*** LeRoy Stone ***Mus*** David Buttolph

Act Brian Donlevy, Robert Preston, Macdonald Carey, Albert Dekker, Barbara Britton, William Bendix (Paramount)

The heroic defense of Wake Island in December 1941 by some 385 U.S. Marines has not only been reproduced as a screen feature almost minutely faithful to the facts but without stooping to cheapness in any way.

Wake Island makes it clear those men didn't fight and die in vain. True, the Japs took Wake, but the Marines took the Japs for at least four warships and hundreds of men.

Brian Donlevy is excellent as the ever-going and unexcitable major who commanded the post, while coming nearest to stealing personal glory away from the story itself are Robert Preston and William Bendix as a kind of Quirt and Flagg combination. Albert Dekker overdoes things just a bit as a tough construction superintendent, while Macdonald Carey shows fine restraint as a flier who is trying to even the score for the death of his wife in the Pearl Harbor attack.

Par obtained a very faithful reproduction of Wake on the shores of the Salton Sea in the California desert. It has all the desolateness of the real thing.

1942: NOMINATIONS: Best Picture, Director, Supp. Actor (William Bendix), Original Screenplay

•

WAKE OF THE RED WITCH

1949, 106 mins, US Ⓥ b/w

Dir Edward Ludwig ***Prod*** Edmund Grainger (assoc.) ***Scr*** Harry Brown, Kenneth Gamet ***Ph*** Reggie Lanning ***Ed*** Richard L. Van Enger ***Mus*** Nathan Scott ***Art*** James Sullivan

Act John Wayne, Gail Russell, Gig Young, Luther Adler, Adele Mara, Eduard Franz (Republic)

Wake of the Red Witch, with its Polynesian locale, is replete with action, drama and adventure. Story is a gripping account of deadly rivalry between two men. Struggle between John Wayne, an impetuous sea captain, and his employer—shipping tycoon Luther Adler—should have been stressed more fully.

As master of the square rigger, *Red Witch*, Wayne has a score to settle with the ship's owner, Adler. He chooses to do it by scuttling the bullion-laden vessel on an uncharted reef.

Gail Russell appears miscast among the South Pacific flora and fauna. Her romantic scenes with Wayne never achieve an aura of realism.

•

WAKE UP AND LIVE

1937, 91 mins, US b/w

Dir Sidney Lanfield ***Prod*** Darryl F. Zanuck, Kenneth Macgowan ***Scr*** Harry Tugend, Jack Yellen ***Ph*** Edward Cronjager ***Ed*** Robert Simpson ***Mus*** Louis Silvers (dir.)

Act Walter Winchell, Ben Bernie and His Band, Alice Faye, Patsy Kelly, Ned Sparks, Jack Haley (20th Century-Fox)

Both Alice Faye and Jack Haley are capital as the love interest, former never looking better and handling light emotional scenes with conviction. Walter Winchell and bandleader Ben Bernie play Winchell and Bernie, and are swell. Any modifications of Winchell the newspaperman into Winchell the actor therefore are few and mild enough not to be noticed. The Winchell-Bernie backbiting is brittle. This duel holds up in the picture, especially since it's deftly tied with the story. Patsy Kelly, as Winchell's Girl Friday, and Ned Sparks, as his chief spy, are corking comedy support. Grace Bradley is a looker and cast as a light menace. Leah Ray whams with her personality in a brief rhumba interlude.

Production and technical niceties are plentiful. They range from the ultra-modern dialog to the corking Mack Gordon and Harry Revel songs, of which there are nine. The radio background, with its deft digs at the military austerity and the honor of being a Radio Centre guide, makes *Wake Up and Live* the first really good satire on radio [from a story by Curtis Kenyon based on Dorothy Brande's book of the same title].

The whammo off-screen singing of radio's Buddy Clark for Jack Haley will impress. There's no billing for Clark, of course, under contract to CBS.

•

WALKABOUT

1971, 95 mins, UK Ⓥ ⊙ col

Dir Nicolas Roeg ***Prod*** Si Litvinoff ***Scr*** Edward Bond ***Ph*** Nicolas Roeg ***Ed*** Antony Gibbs, Alan Patillo ***Mus*** John Barry ***Art*** Brian Eatwell

Act Jenny Agutter, Lucien John, David Gulpilil, John Meillon, John Illingsworth (Raab-Litvinoff)

Walkabout is a tepid artistic effort about two children, lost in the Australian wilds, who are befriended by an aborigine. Nicolas Roeg directed and photographed on authentic locations. Roeg's bag is photography, but pretty pictures alone cannot sustain—and, in fact, inhibit—this fragile and forced screen adaptation of a James Vance Marshall novel.

Apparent intent was to begin the film with jarring montage of urban life, so as to contrast better with the later wasteland footage. Jenny Agutter and Lucien John (Roeg's own son) find themselves alone in the desert after father John Meillon tries to kill the boy and then shoots himself after setting fire to his car.

On the kids' long trek in search of civilization, they encounter David Gulpilil, an aborigine who guides them toward rescue.

In an effort to pump up the plot, Roeg resorts to ad nauseam inserts of insects, reptiles and assorted wild beasts, in varying stages of life and decay.

•

WALK A CROOKED MILE

1948, 90 mins, US b/w

Dir Gordon Douglas ***Prod*** Edward Small ***Scr*** George Bruce ***Ph*** George Robinson ***Ed*** James E. Newcom ***Mus*** Paul Sawtell ***Art*** Rudolph Sternad

Act Louis Hayward, Dennis O'Keefe, Louise Allbritton, Raymond Burr, Onslow Stephens (Columbia)

The documentary technique gives a factual gloss to the high melodramatics of *Walk a Crooked Mile*. A Southern California atomplant is losing its top secrets and the FBI and Scotland Yard, in the respective persons of Dennis O'Keefe and Louis Hayward, join forces to run down the criminals. Action swings to San Francisco and back to the southland, punching hard all the time under the knowledgeable direction of Gordon Douglas. On-the-site filming of locales adds authenticity.

George Bruce has loaded his script with nifty twists that add air of reality to the meller doings in the Bertram Millhauser story. Dialog is good and situations believably developed, even the highly contrived melodramatic finale. Documentary flavor is forwarded by Reed Hadley's credible narration chore.

•

WALK DON'T RUN

1966, 114 mins, US Ⓥ ⊙ ▭ col

Dir Charles Walters ***Prod*** Sol C. Siegel ***Scr*** Sol Saks ***Ph*** Harry Stradling ***Ed*** Walter Thompson, James Wells ***Mus*** Quincy Jones ***Art*** Joe Wright

Act Cary Grant, Samantha Eggar, Jim Hutton, John Standing, Miiko Taka, Ted Hartley (Columbia/Granley)

Walk Don't Run is a completely entertaining, often hilarious romantic comedy spotlighting as a matchmaker a deliberately mature Cary Grant at the peak of his comedy prowess. The fast-moving and colorful production pegs its laughs on a Tokyo housing shortage during the 1964 Olympics [from a screen story by Robert Russell and Frank Ross].

Grant is outstanding as the middle-aged and distinguished English industrialist who arrives two days before his Tokyo hotel suite will be available. Noting an apartment-to-share sign, he finds it to be the diggings of prim, schedule-conscious Samantha Eggar. She is engaged to a stuffy embassy functionary, played by John Standing, with whom Grant has already had a run-in.

Jim Hutton, a member of the U.S. Olympic walking team (hence the title), is also awaiting quarters, so he, too, winds up in Eggar's pad.

•

WALKER

1987, 95 mins, US Ⓥ col

Dir Alex Cox ***Prod*** Lorenzo O'Brien ***Scr*** Rudy Wurlitzer ***Ph*** David Bridges ***Ed*** Carlos Puente Ortega, Alex Cox ***Mus*** Joe Strummer ***Art*** Bruno Rubeo

Act Ed Harris, Marlee Matlin, Peter Boyle, Bianca Guerra, Richard Masur, Rene Auberjonois (Incine/Universal)

The potentially fascinating story of an American adventurer who installed himself as president of Nicaragua 132 years ago, *Walker* unfortunately exists for one reason and one reason only—for director Alex Cox to vent his spleen about continued American interference with the Central American country. The comic, idiosyncratic approach has merit in theory, but the result onscreen is a virtual fiasco.

With the financial backing of tycoon Cornelius Vanderbilt, Walker led a mercenary band of 58 men to Nicaragua in 1855 and ruled the tiny nation with an increasingly heavy hand for two years until being kicked out.

Cox makes a muddled attempt at the outset to paint Walker as an idealist who becomes fatally twisted after the premature death of his strong-willed fiancée (played in a very brief appearance by Marlee Matlin). From then on, however, Walker is ramrod stiff and impenetrable, a man given to self-seriously strutting about and delivering platitudes such as, "One must act with severity, or perish."

•

WALKING AND TALKING

1996, 83 mins, US/UK Ⓥ col

Dir Nicole Holofcener ***Prod*** Ted Hope, James Schamus ***Scr*** Nicole Holofcener ***Ph*** Michael Spiller ***Ed*** Alisa Lepselter ***Mus*** Billy Bragg ***Art*** Anne Stuhler

Act Catherine Keener, Anne Heche, Todd Field, Liev Schreiber, Kevin Corrigan, Randall Batinkoff (Good Machine/Zenith)

Walking and Talking is a glibly observant comedy about the anxieties of romance and the evolution of a female friendship. Written and cut with an eye more toward jokes than on developing much emotional depth, writer-director Nicole Holofcener's first feature is boosted by uniformly droll lead performances as well as by impressively confident filmmaking savvy.

Zippy script charts the worst of times in the relationship of best friends Amelia (Catherine Keener) and Laura (Anne Heche), young Manhattan professionals. Placing them at odds is Laura's upcoming marriage to Frank (Todd Field), which gives Laura much less time to counsel Amelia about her romantic woes.

Having broken up with Andrew (Liev Schreiber), who's recently gotten into phone sex, Amelia reluctantly goes out with video-store geek and horror-film devotee Bill (Kevin Corrigan). But when this liaison lasts only one night, Amelia becomes more insecure than ever.

Pic is loaded with delightfully fresh, disarmingly frank moments of its characters' intimate lives. The two young actresses have been seen to favorable advantage before but haven't had such an opportunity to fly until now. The men are secondary but solid as well. The clean images of Hal Hartley regular Michael Spiller gives the film an accessible and appealing look.

•

WALKING DEAD, THE

1936, 62 mins, US Ⓥ b/w

Dir Michael Curtiz ***Scr*** Lillie Hayward, Robert Andrews, Ewart Adamson, Peter Milne ***Ph*** Hal Mohr ***Ed*** Tommy Pratt ***Art*** Hugh Reticker

Act Boris Karloff, Ricardo Cortez, Edmund Gwenn, Marguerite Churchill, Warren Hull, Barton MacLane (Warner)

Those with a yen for shockers will get limited satisfaction from the story that has been wrapped around Boris Karloff's initial stalking piece under the Warner banner.

Karloff plays a sensitive-souled musician who twice gets himself into prison by the railroad route. After his original discharge from the bastille he artlessly becomes embroiled with a racketeering gang and in the murder of the judge that had sent him away. Karloff protests his innocence but the governor's pardon doesn't get to the prison until after the first electric shock has been applied to Karloff.

An operation brings the executed man back to life. In place of a personality and subconscious the living dead man has acquired a supernatural power. He is able to recognize his enemies and to track them down one by one.

As the head menace, Ricardo Cortez is loaded down with no easy assignment. About all he can do is look wise, keep a sneer well oiled and give the living dead man stare for stare. Edmund Gwenn plays the soul-probing scientist true to traditional screen requirements.

•

WALKING DEAD, THE

1995, 89 mins, US ▭ col

Dir Preston A. Whitmore II ***Prod*** George Jackson, Douglas McHenry, Frank Price ***Scr*** Preston A. Whitmore II ***Ph*** John L. Demps Jr ***Ed*** Don Brochu, William C. Carruth ***Mus*** Gary Chang ***Art*** George Costello

Act Allen Payne, Eddie Griffin, Joe Morton, Vonte Sweet, Roger Floyd (Price)

Playing tribute to the black combat soldier, *The Walking Dead* is an earnest, socially conscious pic that is not terribly effective as an actioner or personal drama. It doesn't really explore their ethnic backgrounds or racial and class tensions.

Set in 1972, tale centers on Sgt. Barkley (Joe Morton) and his fellow Marines as they are assigned their last mission, which involves evacuating all remaining survivors from a p.o.w. camp abandoned by the Viet Cong. Only two Marines have combat experience: Hoover Branche (Eddie Griffin), a 22-year-old cynic who has survived two tours of duty, and Pippins (Roger Floyd), a former criminal whose toughness and "ease" with killing borders dementia.

But for the other soldiers, it's their first bloody journey: Cole Evans (Allen Payne) is a devoted father, and Joe Brookes (Vonte Sweet) is a naive youngster who joined the Marines to achieve manhood and secure a better future.

Helmer Preston A. Whitmore II lacks the technical savvy and visual style that an action film requires—the combat sequences are poorly staged and roughly integrated into the story. But Whitmore coaxes decent performances from his talented cast, headed by Morton.

Pic was shot in Orlando and Chuluota, FL, and physical location is not particularly convincing.

●

WALKING HILLS, THE
1949, 78 mins, US col
Dir John Sturges ***Prod*** Harry Joe Brown ***Scr*** Alan Le May, Virginia Roddick ***Ph*** Charles Lawton, Jr. ***Ed*** William Lyon ***Mus*** Arthur Morton
Act Randolph Scott, Ella Raines, Arthur Kennedy, John Ireland, William Bishop, Edgar Buchanan (Columbia)

An intriguing theme, good cast and tight direction combine to make *The Walking Hills* an out-of-the-way westerner.

Opening in a Mexican border town, yarn introduces eight men who accidentally stumble on some information pointing to the location in the desert of a 100-year-old wagon train loaded with bullion.

Major portion of the film concerns the digging for the treasure and developing hatreds among the men.

Screenplay's attempt to handle the cross-currents of greed for gold and a three-way romantic tangle is not fully successful due to a slightly hazy plot structure. But the main outlines of a sharp human conflict are made to emerge nonetheless. Mainly responsible for this are John Sturges's controlled and modulated direction and standout performances.

●

WALKING STICK, THE
1970, 100 mins, UK ▭ col
Dir Eric Till ***Prod*** Alan Ladd, Jr. ***Scr*** George Bluestone ***Ph*** Arthur Ibbetson ***Ed*** John Jympson ***Mus*** Stanley Myers ***Art*** John Howell
Act David Hemmings, Samantha Eggar, Emlyn Williams, Phyllis Calvert, Ferdy Mayne, Dudley Sutton (Winkast/M-G-M)

The Walking Stick is notable for outstanding performances by David Hemmings and Samantha Eggar, and excellent direction by Eric Till. Story concerns a physically handicapped girl who finds love, then betrayal in a jewel robbery involvement.

George Bluestone adapted the Winston Graham novel about an introverted girl who blossoms under the patient love of a vagabond artist.

Hemmings suddenly emerges as a tool of Emlyn Williams, an art dealer whose night acquisitions come via robbery. Eggar, who works in a gallery, is pressured into the heist.

Her dilemma—should she give up her happiness by reporting to the police, or keep a gnawing silence?—is resolved in a somewhat melodramatic way.

●

WALK IN THE CLOUDS, A
1995, 103 mins, US Ⓥ ⦿ col
Dir Alfonso Arau ***Prod*** Gil Netter, David Zucker, Jerry Zucker ***Scr*** Robert Mark Kamen, Mark Miller, Harvey Weitzman ***Ph*** Emmanuel Lubezki ***Ed*** Don Zimmerman ***Mus*** Maurice Jarre ***Art*** David Gropman
Act Keanu Reeves, Aitana Sanchez-Gijon, Anthony Quinn, Giancarlo Giannini, Angelica Aragon, Evangelina Elizondo (Zucker/20th Century-Fox)

Trying to transfer the Latino magic of his arthouse smash *Like Water for Chocolate* to a U.S. setting, Mexican helmer Alfonso Arau has turned out a glossy, fairy-tale romance that's longer on wishfulness than believability.

Pic's source Alessandro Blasetti's *Quattro passi fra le nuvole (Four Steps in the Clouds)*, a 1942 Italian film regarded as a forerunner of Neorealism, is a modest but sharply mounted comedy/melodrama about an unhappily wed chocolate salesman who briefly poses as a young woman's husband to help her escape the ire of her rural family, then returns to his domestic misery. Arau's Americanized, happy-ending version opens at the end of World War II.

Plagued by memories of combat horrors, returning vet Paul Sutton (Keanu Reeves) is on a business trip when a series of train and bus mishaps leaves him stranded roadside with a beautiful fellow traveler, Victoria (Aitana Sanchez-Gijon). She's pregnant by a departed lover and Paul gallantly agrees to appear as her husband.

Surprised by the couple's unheralded marriage, Alberto Aragon (Giancarlo Giannini) at first spurns his supposed son-in-law. Paul, though, is welcomed by the rest of the clan, especially gregarious patriarch Don Pedro (Anthony Quinn).

Arau stages all this with a determined gusto that at least has the virtue of consistency, and involves winning perfs from Giannini, Quinn and Spanish actress Sanchez-Gijon. It's hardly her fault that the drama founders on a lack of electricity between the two lovers, because Reeves offers more in the way of looks and presence than thesping savvy.

●

WALK IN THE SHADOW
SEE: LIFE FOR RUTH

●

WALK IN THE SPRING RAIN, A
1970, 98 mins, US Ⓥ ▭ col
Dir Guy Green ***Prod*** Sterling Silliphant ***Scr*** Sterling Silliphant, [Frank Hummert, Anne Hummert] ***Ph*** Charles B. Lang ***Ed*** Ferris Webster ***Mus*** Elmer Bernstein ***Art*** Malcolm C. Bert
Act Anthony Quinn, Ingrid Bergman, Fritz Weaver, Katherine Crawford, Tom Fielding, Virginia Gregg (Columbia)

Rachel Maddux wrote the basic novella, adapted by Sterling Silliphant, with an uncredited bow to Frank and Anne Hummert. Ingrid Bergman and story hubby, Fritz Weaver, go on sabbatical from campus to the Tennessee mountain country so he can write a law text. Between the frigid winter and the verdant spring rains, Bergman finds love beating again in her bosom. The reason is Anthony Quinn a Spanish desdendant, Zorba-like hillbilly.

Quinn is not without his own responsibilities. He has a cackling wife, played terribly by Virginia Gregg. He also has a son, played by Tom Fielding in the style of a Method actor satire. At least he doesn't even bother faking a Dixie accent.

Cast is rounded out by Katherine Crawford, the selfish daughter.

●

WALK IN THE SUN, A
1945, 117 mins, US Ⓥ ⦿ b/w
Dir Lewis Milestone ***Prod*** Lewis Milestone ***Scr*** Robert Rossen ***Ph*** Russell Harlan ***Ed*** Duncan Mansfield ***Mus*** Frederic Efrem Rich ***Art*** Max Bertisch
Act Dana Andrews, Richard Conte, John Ireland, Norman Lloyd, Lloyd Bridges, Huntz Hall (20th Century-Fox)

As a film *Walk* is not so sunny. It is distinguished for some excellent, earthy GI dialog, but the author has failed to achieve a proper fusing of dialog and situation. Too frequently he is given to spieling the colorful talk of the enlisted man, and thus allows his yarn to flounder. He is content, seemingly, to allow GI talk to encompass all else.

Film [from a novel by Harry Brown] concerns an operation by a platoon of American soldiers after they hit the beach at Salerno. They're detailed to wipe out a farmhouse and its Nazi occupants. That's the major element of the story, such as it is, and the rest of the pic is mostly concerned with reactions of the GIs to the conditions under which they're fighting, their thoughts, and so forth.

Dana Andrews gives one of his invariably forthright performances as a sergeant, and the rest of the impressive cast know their way around a script. And that holds particularly true of Richard Conte, who, perhaps, has the best lines.

●

WALK LIKE A DRAGON
1960, 95 mins, US b/w
Dir James Clavell ***Prod*** James Clavell ***Scr*** James Clavell, David Mainwaring ***Ph*** Loyal Griggs ***Ed*** Howard Smith ***Mus*** Paul Dunlop ***Art*** Hal Pereira, Ronald Anderson
Act Jack Lord, Nobu McCarthy, James Shigeta, Mel Torme, Benson Fong (Paramount)

In attempting to dramatize the unarguable doctrine that slavery is an ugly, unwelcome visitor in a free society, producer-director-writer James Clavell has somehow wound up with the curious message that clannish conformity is the logical path to peaceful coexistence for foreigners to pursue in America. Since Clavell wisely has set his story in the conveniently unprovocative and usefully primitive atmosphere of the old west, and has utilized some interesting, offbeat historical data in the process, the film fits snugly into the "adult western" genre.

A maze of incomplete, often contradictory, character motivations gnaws away destructively at the roots of the screenplay. It is based on a three-ply conflict, an interracial romantic triangle consisting of one tall, strapping American (Jack Lord); one proud, rebellious Chinaman (James Shigeta); and one frail, would-be Chinese slave girl (Nobu McCarthy). Rescuing the latter from the perils of enforced prostitution, Lord promptly bumps into mass discrimination and an emotional duel with Shigeta when he brings the girl to live in his home.

Although shackled with a superficially-drawn role, Lord constructs a sympathetic characterization. McCarthy, an attractive actress, lacks the subtle variety required for her role. Shigeta, too, manages only a shallow, one-note portrayal of the defiant Oriental. Mel Torme, cast as a guntotin', scripture-spoutin' "deacon," plays the offbeat role with a flourish, but appears bewildered by the nebulous nature of the character.

As director, Clavell is adept in his handling of the film's more provocative moments, notably a scene where the heroine is stripped to the waist in the slave market. But his overall approach tends to form predictably repetitive patterns such as following each soft, tender sequence with an explosion of gunfire to open the next one.

●

WALK ON THE WILD SIDE
1962, 114 mins, US Ⓥ b/w
Dir Edward Dmytryk ***Prod*** Charles K. Feldman ***Scr*** John Fante, Edmund Morris ***Ph*** Joe MacDonald ***Ed*** Harry Gerstad ***Mus*** Elmer Bernstein ***Art*** Richard Sylbert
Act Laurence Harvey, Capucine, Jane Fonda, Anne Baxter, Barbara Stanwyck, Joanna Moore (Columbia)

It's obvious that in their treating of prostitution and lesbianism the filmmakers did not want to be offensive to anyone. The result is a somewhat watered-downing of the Nelson Algren story of the Doll House in New Orleans and the madame's affection for one of the girls.

Laurence Harvey plays a drifter in search of his lady, Capucine. He does it well but not strikingly. Capucine, it turns out, is a member of the Doll House, showing a classic, Garbo-type beauty but somehow limited as to range in emotionality via script and/or direction.

Jane Fonda cops the show with her hoydenish behavior as another member of the House and Just-Lucky-I-Guess Alumnus of the freighter transportation circuit. Barbara Stanwyck is steely as the madame who looks to Capucine for the "affection" she cannot find in her maimed husband.

Dmytryk maintains a nice pace in direction—that is, a steady pace—but more forcefulness in both his direction and the writing might have provided more dramatic impact.

1962: NOMINATION: Best Song ("Walk on the Wild Side")

●

WALK WITH LOVE AND DEATH, A
1969, 90 mins, US col
Dir John Huston ***Prod*** Carter De Haven ***Scr*** Dale Wasserman ***Ph*** Ted Scaife ***Ed*** Russell Lloyd ***Mus*** Georges Delerue ***Art*** Wolfgang Witzemann
Act Anjelica Huston, Assaf Dayan, Anthony Corlan, John Hallam, Robert Lang, Michael Gough (20th Century-Fox)

A Walk with Love and Death, set in the framework of the Middle Ages, is an unrelenting examination of France when human life was valueless, social order unbending and individual outloook bleak. Filmed in Austria, director John Huston tells his story [from a novel by Hans Koningsberger] unhurriedly, lingering over details of style and torture with equal unsparing lenses.

His young hero, Assaf Dayan, obeying a mystic call from the sea, leaving Paris and studies behind, begins journey on foot through the war-scarred French countryside. His meeting with Anjelica Huston, daughter of a nobleman, is the beginning of the end for the scholar and the lady.

The slow pace and gloomy atmosphere tend to dull viewer interest. High flown speech, confusion of action undermine even as Huston builds.

●

WALL STREET
1987, 124 mins, US Ⓥ ⦿ col
Dir Oliver Stone ***Prod*** Edward R. Pressman, A. Kitman Ho ***Scr*** Oliver Stone, Stanley Weiser ***Ph*** Robert Richardson ***Ed*** Claire Simpson ***Mus*** Stewart Copeland ***Art*** Stephen Hendrickson
Act Michael Douglas, Charlie Sheen, Daryl Hannah, Martin Sheen, Terence Stamp, Sean Young (Pressman/American Entertainment/20th Century-Fox)

Watching Oliver Stone's *Wall Street* is about as wordy and dreary as reading the financial papers accounts of the rise and fall of an Ivan Boesky–type arbitrageur.

The lure of making a bundle on Wall Street by the young broker (Charlie Sheen) totally seduced by the power and financial stature of such a megalomaniacal arbitrageur as Gordon Gekko (Michael Douglas) is as good a contemporary story as there is in the real world of takeovers and mergers.

Douglas is a nasty enough manipulator barking orders to buy, sell and run his competitors into the ground or delivering declamatory speeches on how greed is what makes America great.

Trouble is, Sheen comes off as a pawn in Douglas's corporate raider game and as the easily duped sort doesn't elicit much sympathy. Martin Sheen as his father, the airplane mechanic, is the only person worth caring about.

1987: Best Actor (Michael Douglas)

•

WALTZ OF THE TOREADORS
1962, 104 mins, UK Ⓥ col
Dir John Guillermin ***Prod*** Peter de Savigny ***Scr*** Wolf Mankowitz ***Ph*** John Wilcox ***Ed*** Peter Taylor ***Mus*** Richard Addinsell ***Art*** Wilfrid Shingleton
Act Peter Sellers, Dany Robin, Margaret Leighton, John Fraser, Cyril Cusack, Prunella Scales (Rank/Independent Artists)

A considerably broadened version of Jean Anouilh's ironic stage comedy results in a capital acting opportunity for Peter Sellers. Pic is handsomely mounted, and it's directed with zest and pace by John Guillermin. But too many moods jostle for it to be a complete success. Slapstick, farce, high comedy, drama and tragedy are all there but they don't always make easy companions.

Mankowitz has transferred the yarn from France to Sussex. Briefly, it concerns an elderly general, about to retire before World War I. He is a man with a roving eye for the girls, trapped by a neurotic, shrewish, sham-invalid of a wife and two unprepossessing daughters. For 17 years, he has had a platonic romance with a French woman, never having a real opportunity to consummate their love. She turns up at his castle determined that this sad state of affairs should end.

Sellers extracts laughs and compassionate pity with equal ease, whether he is being caught up in a drunken party at a tavern, conducting a riotous mock duel with his local doctor (Cyril Cusack), taking charge of a court martial, leching after his maids, facing up to the fact that he is a failure or, in the more tragic moments, stripping his soul bare as he struggles in his hateful scenes with his wife.

•

WANDA
1970, 105 mins, US col
Dir Barbara Loden ***Prod*** Harry Shuster ***Scr*** Barbara Loden ***Ph*** Nicholas T. Proferes ***Ed*** Nicholas T. Proferes
Act Barbara Loden, Michael Higgins (Foundation for Filmakers)

Wanda is a wanderer, a loser somewhere in a heavily industrialized part of the U.S. Barbara Loden shows a calm, dispassionate feel for direction and an insight into the psyche of an inarticulate, ill-educated but non-despairing woman as the protagonist of this probing pic about a cultural wasteland alongside affluence.

Loden dramatizes an oft-treated social theme about people drifting into crime and prostitution and does not force blame on anyone but denotes the growing conflicts between puritanism and promiscuity, poverty within plenty and ignorance alongside the more educated that grows in observation, insight and impact as it goes along.

Loden has the vulnerability, negation and yet inner resiliency that keeps her character from being a drudge.

•

WANDERER, THE
SEE: LE GRAND MEAULNES

•

WANDERERS, THE
1979, 113 mins, US Ⓥ col
Dir Philip Kaufman ***Prod*** Martin Ransohoff ***Scr*** Rose Kaufman, Philip Kaufman ***Ph*** Michael Chapman ***Ed*** Ronald Roose, Stuart H. Pappe ***Art*** Jay Moore
Act Ken Wahl, John Friedrich, Karen Allen, Linda Manz, Toni Kalem, Tony Ganios (Orion)

Despite an uneasy blend of nostalgia and violence, *The Wanderers* is a well-made and impressive film. Philip Kaufman, who also co-scripted with his wife, Rose [from the novel by Richard Price], has accurately captured the urban angst of growing up in the 1960s.

Thesping is first-rate from the largely unknown cast, with Ken Wahl, John Friedrich and especially Tony Ganios delivering well-rounded and believable characterizations. Also outstanding are Toni Kalem as a gum-popping flirt, and Karen Allen as her more serious, soulful counterpart.

Disturbing elements in *The Wanderers* crop up in the explicitly violent episodes, including those involving the symbolic Ducky Boys, a murderous pint-sized gang, and the Fordham Baldies, bald behemoths.

•

WANDERING JEW, THE
1923, 111 mins, UK ⊗ b/w
Dir Maurice Elvey ***Scr*** Alicia Ramsey
Act Matheson Lang, Hutin Britton, Malvina Longfellow, Isobel Elsom, Florence Sanders, Shayle Gardner (Stoll)

With this Stoll picture Matheson Lang established a right to be regarded as a screen star. Throughout, his impersonation of the Jew—condemned to wander through the ages, arrogant, proud, though brokenhearted, ever within reach of happiness, but always overtaken by disaster just as he is about to grasp his heart's desire—is masterly.

The story follows the Temple Thurston play fairly close. In the opening scenes we see the Jew, Matathias, and his lover, Judith, his reviling of the Savior on His way to Calvary and the dreadful outlawry which sent him into the world a wanderer. Thirteen hundred years pass and he is among the Crusaders; again a lovely woman loves him, but again fate stands between him and happiness, and so the story goes down the years until at last the Inquisition gives him the peace and eternal rest which before have always been denied him.

Spectacularly, the production is very fine and the subject is treated with great reverence by Maurice Elvey.

•

WANDERING JEW, THE
1933, 110 mins, UK b/w
Dir Maurice Elvey ***Prod*** Julius Hagen ***Scr*** H. Fowler Mear ***Ph*** Sydney Blythe ***Ed*** Jack Harris ***Art*** James Carter
Act Conrad Veidt, Marie Ney, Anne Grey, Joan Maude, Peggy Ashcroft (Twickenham/Gaumont-British)

The film is based on Temple Thurston's play of the same name, and the adaptation is divided into four episodes. The first is Jerusalem on the day of the Crucifixion; the second, Antioch in the time of the first crusade; third, Palermo, Sicily, in 1290; and fourth, Seville in 1560, during the Inquisition.

It is a massive, artistic and well-acted filming, flavored perhaps by an overplus of scenes, and more detail than is necessary.

Conrad Veidt in the first half of the picture is guilty of scene-chewing. All this is counteracted before the finish by a restrained, moving dignity which he contributes to the wanderer of centuries.

Maria Ney, Anne Grey and Joan Maude are the three women in the first three episodes, and do nothing to distinguish themselves; Peggy Ashcroft as the Magdalene in the fourth phase, who is converted by the Christlike nobility of Battadios (Veidt), offers a fine characterization rich in feeling. The inquisitors are Francis L. Sullivan, Felix Aylmer and Ivor Barnard, all of them vividly Machiavellian.

•

WANTON CONTESSA, THE
SEE: SENSO

•

WAR, THE
1994, 125 mins, US Ⓥ ⊙ col
Dir Jon Avnet ***Prod*** Jon Avnet, Jordan Kerner ***Scr*** Kathy McWorter ***Ph*** Geoffrey Simpson ***Ed*** Debra Neil ***Mus*** Thomas Newman ***Art*** Kristi Zea
Act Elijah Wood, Kevin Costner, Mare Winningham, Lexi Randall, Christine Baranski, Raynor Scheine (Island World/Universal)

Director Jon Avnet's attempt to recapture the flavor of his *Fried Green Tomatoes* comes out of the oven a bit squishy in *The War*, an earnest but overcooked stew. The main ingredient is actually a big slice of *Stand by Me*, but there are sprinkles from various Vietnam War movies and even *Places in the Heart*.

Despite Kevin Costner's presence *The War* really belongs to its child cast, headed by Elijah Wood and newcomer Lexi Randall. The parallel between the Vietnam War and the children's feud with a local clan of kids feels heavy-handed and attempts to infuse the narrative with a sense of spirituality are blatantly manipulative.

Set in Mississippi during the summer of 1970, the story focuses on a poor family whose patriarch (Costner) has returned from Vietnam bearing emotional scars that make it difficult for him to hold a job. His wife (Mare Winnigham) struggles to keep the family afloat, while the kids set about the task of building a tree fort, all the while feuding with the despised Lipnickis—an almost feral family of dirt-poor bullies. The filmmakers invest too much time demonizing the Lipnickis to allow for the sort of pat ending they've devised.

Wood remains a gifted child actor and also proves to be about the only cast member who doesn't find himself stumbling over his Southern drawl. Some of the children's speech is so thick that many who live north of the Mason-Dixon line or west of Galveston will find themselves in need of a translator. Costner proves earnest and sincere in his good ol' boy performance.

•

WAR AND PEACE
1956, 208 mins, US/Italy Ⓥ ⊙ col
Dir King Vidor ***Prod*** Dino De Laurentiis ***Scr*** Bridget Boland, Robert Westerby, King Vidor, Mario Camerini, Ennio De Concini, Ivo Perilli, [Irwin Shaw] ***Ph*** Jack Cardiff, Aldo Tonti ***Ed*** Stuart Gilmore, Leo Catozzo ***Mus*** Nino Rota ***Art*** Mario Chiari, Franz Bachelin
Act Audrey Hepburn, Henry Fonda, Mel Ferrer, Vittorio Gassman, John Mills, Anita Ekberg (Ponti-De Laurentiis/Paramount)

Hollywood and Italian know-how, some $6 million capital investment, and between 5,000 and 6,000 Italian troops doubling as celluloid soldiers, have produced a visual epic.

The classic Tolstoy novel which requires weeks and, more often, months to read is digested into three-and-a-half hours of vivid cinematic magic.

The wonder of the production is that it has maintained cohesiveness and fluidity of story and also has given fullest accent to the size and sweep of Bonaparte's armies at Austerlitz and Borodino. Life among the Russian aristocracy with its passion for good living and innate respect for the church in time of stress is brought into sharp focus.

Audrey Hepburn is the epitome of wholesome young love under benevolent aristocratic rearing. Henry Fonda, the confused young liberal who apes the French as so many Russians did, is perhaps sometimes too literally the confused character.

Other than the above and the moody but compelling performance by Mel Ferrer, the rest are lesser roles but almost wholly effective.

The film's scripting credits are a strangely multiple thing in light of Irwin Shaw's request to remove his billing when director Vidor reportedly rewrote so many scenes on his own.

1956: NOMINATIONS: Best Director, Color Cinematography, Color Costume Design

•

WAR AND PEACE, PART I
SEE: VOYNA I MIR I: ANDREI BOLKONSKY

•

WAR AND PEACE, PART II
SEE: VOYNA I MIR II: NATASHA ROSTOVA

•

WAR AND PEACE, PART III
SEE: VOYNA I MIR III: 1812 GOD

•

WAR AND PEACE, PART IV
SEE: VOYNA I MIR IV: PYER BEZUKHOV

•

WAR BETWEEN MEN AND WOMEN, THE
1972, 105 mins, US col
Dir Melville Shavelson ***Prod*** Danny Arnold ***Scr*** Melville Shavelson, Danny Arnold ***Ph*** Charles F. Wheeler ***Ed*** Frank Bracht ***Mus*** Marvin Hamlisch Art Dir Stan Jolley
Act Jack Lemmon, Barbara Harris, Jason Robards, Herb Edelman, Severn Darden, Lisa Eilbacher (Cinema Center)

The love affair Melville Shevelson and Danny Arnold originally had with the works of the late James Thurber, in their Emmy-winning *My World and Welcome to It* series, continues in this amusing clambake of a Thurber-like character portrayed by Jack Lemmon. *The War Between Men and Women* comes off as a first-rate comedy peopled by some delicious humans, as well as a pregnant pooch.

A longer fantasy sequence dramatizes Thurber's *The Last Flower*. Insertions are logically introduced and considerably enliven the action as a novelty device.

Lemmon is an acerbic and grumpy NY writer and cartoonist whose failing eyesight and unflattering way of dealing with women in his works make him a natural for arousing the interest of Barbara Harris. Her children, even the dog, are unfriendly, and further problems arise when the near-bride's former spouse arrives during the marriage ceremony and stays on.

•

WAR GAME, THE
1966, 50 mins, UK Ⓥ b/w
Dir Peter Watkins ***Scr*** Peter Watkins ***Ph*** Peter Bartlett ***Art*** Michael Bradsell (BBC-TV)
The War Game was originally made by BBC-TV for showing on TV, but corporation brass had second thoughts after it had been completed, decided it was unsuitable for mass audiences, and ordered it to be kept off the airwaves. As a result of political and press agitation, it was eventually agreed to make it available for theatrical release through the British Film Institute.

A wholly imaginary picture of what could happen immediately before, during and after a nuclear attack on Britain, *The War Game* is grim, gruesome, horrific and realistic. It is not a pleasant picture to watch, but yet it is one that needs to be shown as widely as possible.

The attack itself is predictably grim, but the most telling part is the aftermath of the bomb—the severely burned are killed off and their bodies burned, and looters face the firing squad.

Watkins, who left the BBC in protest when it was banned, does an excellent and imaginative job, based on considerable research.

1966: Best Feature Documentary

●

WARGAMES
1983, 110 mins, US Ⓥ ⊙ col
Dir John Badham ***Prod*** Harold Schneider ***Scr*** Lawrence Lasker, Walter F. Parkes ***Ph*** William A. Fraker ***Ed*** Tom Rolf ***Mus*** Arthur B. Rubinstein ***Art*** Angelo P. Graham
Act Matthew Broderick, Dabney Coleman, John Wood, Ally Sheedy, Barry Corbin, Dennis Lipscomb (United Artists)

Although the script has more than its share of short circuits, director John Badham solders the pieces into a terrifically exciting story charged by an irresistible idea: An extra-smart kid can get the world into a whole lot of trouble that it also takes the same extra-smart kid to rescue it from.

Matthew Broderick is on the mark as the bright teenager, bored by traditional high school subjects like biology, but brilliant with computers. Unfortunately, thinking he's sneaking an advance look at a new line of video games, he taps into the country's Norad missile-defense system to challenge its computer to a game of global thermonuclear warfare.

WarGames's weakness, sad to say, is that the adult side of the yarn is not peopled with very realistic characters, although the performances are fine.

Ally Sheedy is perfectly perky as Broderick's girlfriend; Dabney Coleman brings his usual dissonance to the role of the computer-reliant defense specialist; but John Wood's large talents aren't fully used in a somewhat confusing part as the misanthropic eccentric who designed the computer.

1983: NOMINATIONS: Best Original Screenplay, Cinematography, Sound

●

WAR IS OVER, THE
SEE: LA GUERRE EST FINIE

●

WARLOCK
1989, 102 mins, US Ⓥ ⊙ col
Dir Steve Miner ***Prod*** Steve Miner ***Scr*** David Twohy ***Ph*** David Eggby ***Ed*** David Finfer ***Mus*** Jerry Goldsmith ***Art*** Roy Forge Smith
Act Richard E. Grant, Julian Sands, Lori Singer, Kevin O'Brien, Richard Kuse, Mary Woronov (New World)

Warlock is an attempt to concoct a pic from a pinch of occult chiller, a dash of fantasy thriller and a splash of "stalk 'n' slash." But what could have been a heady brew falls short, despite some gusto thesping from Richard E. Grant and Lori Singer.

Pic opens in the Massachusetts Bay colony in 1691 where a contemptuous warlock (Julian Sands) is being readied for execution. But with a bit of nifty hocus-pocus, both he and witch-hunter Grant are sent to 1988 L.A. Sands soon gets back to his nasty habits—including chopping off a finger, gouging out eyes and skinning a child—as he pursues the magical book the *Grand Grimoire*.

Waitress Lori Singer meets Sands when he crashes through a window into her house. After he puts an aging spell on her, she teams up with Grant to try to kill the warlock.

Director Steve Miner directs ably but doesn't pull away from some of the horror clichés.

●

WARLOCK: THE ARMAGEDDON
1993, 93 mins, US Ⓥ ⊙ col
Dir Anthony Hickox ***Prod*** Peter Abrams, Robert Levy ***Scr*** Kevin Rock, Sam Bernard ***Ph*** Gerry Lively ***Ed*** Chris Cibelli ***Mus*** Mark McKenzie ***Art*** Steve Hardie
Act Julian Sands, Chris Young, Paula Marshall, Steve Kahan, Charles Hallahan, R. G. Armstrong (Trimark/Tapestry)

Julian Sands remains unrepentantly evil as he assails familiar territory in *Warlock: The Armageddon*. Though not specifically linked to the earlier horror thriller, the new outing echoes the first foray sufficiently to satisfy fans of hokum-filled good-and-evil conflict.

The current mumbo jumbo involves the struggle for control of six 17th-century Druidic rune stones. The baubles not only have the ability to summon Satan's emissary but also have the power to quell his nefarious activities.

The Warlock's path leads to a Northern California hamlet that is one of the last known enclaves of the virtually extinct sect. The descendants sense the coming of evil but remain secure in the knowledge they have two warriors in their midst. The problem is that the young designated defenders—Kenny (Chris Young) and Samantha (Paula Marshall)—are neither aware of nor trained in their chosen roles.

Dramatically, these scrubbed, wholesome teens are bland beside Sands' sinister histrionics. Director Tony Hickox, too, seems more at home with the bad guy.

●

WAR LORD, THE
1965, 120 mins, US Ⓥ ⊙ ▭ col
Dir Franklin J. Schaffner ***Prod*** Walter Seltzer ***Scr*** John Collier, Millard Kaufman ***Ph*** Russell Metty ***Ed*** Folmar Blangsted ***Mus*** Jerome Moross ***Art*** Alexander Golitzen, Henry Bumstead
Act Charlton Heston, Richard Boone, Rosemary Forsyth, Maurice Evans, Guy Stockwell, Niall MacGinnis (Universal/Court)

The War Lord digs back into the 11th century against a Druid setting in ancient Normandy for unfoldment of its generally fast action. Producer Walter Seltzer has given his picturization of Leslie Stevens's play *The Lovers*—finely lensed to lend realism and pictorial beauty—elaborate mounting and clash battle movement.

Franklin Schaffner's direction, while not always overcoming deficiencies of convincing dialog and Charlton Heston's sometimes vacillating characterization, in the main projects the proper spirit of a derring-do, days-of-yore melodrama. His battle scenes, utilizing the weapons and tactics of the period are particularly well handled.

Script presents Heston as war lord of the Duke of Normandy, detailed to oversee a primitive Druid village on a barren shore of the North Sea, whose inhabitants are constantly harassed by invaders from the north. With him are his brother (Guy Stockwell) and Richard Boone, his faithful aide in 20 years of warring. Plottage dwells on his mad passion for a village girl, claiming her on her wedding night according to custom of "droit de seigneur"—a lord's right of the first night.

Heston is more convincing in his battle scenes than in romancing Rosemary Forsyth, but nevertheless delivers a hard-hitting performance. Top acting honors, however, go to Stockwell, as the young knight.

●

WARLORDS OF ATLANTIS
1978, 96 mins, UK Ⓥ col
Dir Kevin Connor ***Prod*** John Dark ***Scr*** Brian Hayles ***Ph*** Alan Hume ***Ed*** Bill Blunden ***Mus*** Mike Vickers ***Art*** Elliot Scott
Act Doug McClure, Peter Gilmore, Shane Rimmer, Lea Brodie, Michael Gothard, Cyd Charisse (EMI)

In *Warlords of Atlantis*, Doug McClure and several other earthlings suffer a close encounter with Cyd Charisse and Daniel Massey who rule over the legendary lost city. More terrifying are their brushes with various species of marine monsters on periodic rampages. And a good thing, too, in an otherwise skimpy reworking of the hoary Atlantis legend.

Donald Bisset and Peter Gilmore are appealing as a British father-son scientific team in quest of Atlantis. McClure is the Yank who made the diving bell that plumbs the sea and implausibly manages to resurface.

The one not inconsiderable virtue of the script is that it keeps the pot boiling. Direction by Kevin Connor and the editing keep the eye-filling pace brisk. The clichéd characters are played in workmanlike fashion by all hands.

●

WARLORDS OF THE 21ST CENTURY
SEE: BATTLETRUCK

●

WAR LOVER, THE
1962, 105 mins, US Ⓥ ⊙ b/w
Dir Philip Leacock ***Prod*** Arthur Hornblow, Jr. ***Scr*** Howard Koch ***Ph*** Bob Huke ***Ed*** Gordon Hales ***Mus*** Richard Addinsell ***Art*** Bill Andrews
Act Steve McQueen, Robert Wagner, Shirley Anne Field, Gary Cockrell, Michael Crawford, Jerry Stovin (Columbia)

This production of John Hersey's novel *The War Lover* is accomplished in all respects save one: lack of proper penetration into the character referred to by the title. The scenario seems reluctant to come to grips with the issue of this character's unique personality—a "war lover" whose exaggerated shell of heroic masculinity covers up a psychopathic inability to love or enjoy normal relationships with women.

The story transpires in 1943 England and focuses on B-17 bombing raids over Germany, with the title character (Steve McQueen) a pilot of one of the planes.

That the central character emerges more of an unappealing symbol than a sympathetic flesh-and-blood portrait is no fault of McQueen, who plays with vigor and authority, although occasionally with two much eyeball emotion. Robert Wagner and Shirley Anne Field share the film's secondary, but interesting, romantic story. Wagner does quite well, and Field has a fresh, natural quality.

Outside of his central failure director Philip Leacock does a sound job. Scenes of the bombing raids and accompanying aerial incidents are adroitly and authentically executed.

●

WARNING SHOT
1967, 100 mins, US col
Dir Buzz Kulik ***Prod*** Buzz Kulik ***Scr*** Mann Rubin ***Ph*** Joseph Biroc ***Ed*** Archie Marshek ***Mus*** Jerry Goldsmith ***Art*** Hal Pereira, Roland Anderson
Act David Janssen, Ed Begley, Keenan Wynn, Sam Wanamaker, Lillian Gish, Stefanie Powers (Paramount)

Warning Shot is a police drama in which fine production, direction and performances overcome a sometimes flawed script. David Janssen toplines as a cop accused of being trigger-happy.

Mann Rubin has adapted Whit Masterson's novel, *711—Officer Needs Help*, in which a cop is accused of poor judgment in killing an apparently innocent medic. His superiors, the d.a. and the public turn on him, and only hope of vindication is proving the existence of a missing gun, and the discovery of evidence to prove the medic was breaking the law.

Filmed smoothly on L.A. locations, with technical assist from the police department, pic has the immediacy of headlines about police brutality, irresponsibility, etc. Scripting incorporates some cliché, unnecessary angles which detract from a very viable story line; namely, that cops are fallible human beings who drink, smoke, make mistakes—just like every one else.

●

WAR OF THE BUTTONS
SEE: LA GUERRE DES BOUTONS

●

WAR OF THE BUTTONS
1994, 90 mins, UK/France Ⓥ col
Dir John Roberts ***Prod*** David Puttnam ***Scr*** Colin Welland ***Ph*** Bruno De Keyzer ***Ed*** Jim Clark, David Freeman ***Mus*** Rachel Portman ***Art*** Jim Clay
Act Liam Cunningham, Gregg Fitzgerald, Colm Meaney, John Coffey, Eveanna Ryan, Paul Batt (Enigma/Hugo)

Though no one seems to have stopped and asked if the world really needs it, this remake of the 1962 Gallic kid pic about warring tykes is a light, often charming transplant to Irish soil that's old-fashioned in the best sense and manages to avoid almost every obstacle that time and changing values can throw in its path.

Original director/co-scripter Yves Robert, who owned the rights to Louis Pergaud's novel [*La guerre des boutons*], reportedly resisted all offers for a remake for a long time. Producer David Puttnam and writer Colin Welland's ingenious solution of setting it deep in rural Ireland, in an unspecified period, and virtually excluding all signs of modern, everyday, adult life, gives the movie a sense of timelessness and (for non-Irish auds) a slightly whimsical edge that just about makes the goings-on acceptable. Interestingly, the reworking is much softer than the Gallic B&W original.

Standing in for the rural Brittany of the original is a sleepy corner of southwest Ireland, where two villages, Carrickdowse and Ballydowse, straddle a stretch of tidal water. Welland's adaptation is framed as a v.o. reminiscence by the adult Marie, a girl once attached to the "Ballys" gang and, it turns out, stuck on its young leader (Gregg Fitzgerald). The scruffy Ballys are engaged in a permanent kids' war with the neighboring "Carricks," whose leader is the more upscale-looking Geronimo (John Coffey).

To the movie's credit, any allegory to the present Irish troubles is simply there for the taking rather than being forced onto center stage.

●

WAR OF THE ROSES, THE
1989, 116 mins, US Ⓥ ⊙ col
Dir Danny DeVito ***Prod*** James L. Brooks, Arnon Milchan ***Scr*** Michael Leeson ***Ph*** Stephen H. Burum ***Ed*** Lynzee Klingman ***Mus*** David Newman ***Art*** Ida Random

Act Michael Douglas, Kathleen Turner, Danny DeVito, Marianne Sagebrecht, Sean Astin, Heather Fairfield (Gracie/20th Century-Fox)

What Michael Douglas does to the fish at Kathleen Turner's dinner party in *The War of the Roses*, director Danny DeVito does to the audience. Piddling notions of humor are the least of this misanthropic comedy's offenses, however. Trying to wring yocks from a deranged couple locked in mortal combat over possession of their house is more suited to film noir than black comedy.

Everything beautiful on screen in this glossily photographed film, from the house to Douglas's antique sportscar to the couple's china figurines to the ravishingly leonine Turner herself, is thoroughly trashed by DeVito, whose sicko humor will wind up alienating everyone in the audience.

The aptly intense Douglas is a workaholic Washington, DC, lawyer on the rise in the early years of his marriage to Turner, a saucy former college gymnast who channels her fierce energies into raising two children and remodeling their stately old house. Once her work is completed, she realizes the marriage is a shell, but Douglas refuses to change his ways and causes her to seek a divorce.

In outline, up to this point, the adaptation of the Warren Adler novel follows predictable lines, with Douglas's rampant sexism challenged by Turner's burgeoning feminism. What keeps it fresh are the sexually charged performances of the two attractive leads and the sarcastic twists DeVito and scripter Michael Leeson pull from the material.

•

WAR OF THE WORLDS, THE

1953, 85 mins, US Ⓥ col

Dir Byron Haskin ***Prod*** George Pal ***Scr*** Barre Lyndon ***Ph*** George Barnes ***Ed*** Everett Douglas ***Mus*** Leith Stevens ***Art*** Hal Pereira, Albert Nozaki

Act Gene Barry, Ann Robinson, Les Tremayne, Lewis Martin, Robert Cornthwaite, Jack Kruschen (Paramount)

War of the Worlds is a socko science-fiction feature, as fearsome as a film as was the Orson Welles 1938 radio interpretation of the H. G. Wells novel. Gene Barry, as a scientist, is the principal in this story of an invasion of the earth by weird, spider-like characters from Mars, against whom the world's most potent weapons, even the atom bomb are of no avail.

Into this setup, the special effects group headed by Gordon Jennings loosens a reign of screen terror, of futile defense, demolished cities, charred landscapes and people burned to ashes by the invaders' weapons.

While following closely the plot laid down in Wells's novel, the film transfers the first invasion to a small town in Southern California. What is believed to be a huge meteor lands near a small town but it turns out to be a Martian machine that raises itself on pulsating beams and promptly turns deadly heatwaves on humans, buildings and anything else that comes within range.

In the siege of terror, the story finds opportunity to develop a logical love story between Barry and Ann Robinson. Both are good and others seen to advantage include Les Tremayne as a general; Lewis Martin, a pastor who faces the invaders with a prayer and is struck down. An ominous commentary is spoken by Cedric Hardwicke.

1953: Best Special Effects

NOMINATIONS: Best Editing, Sound

•

WAR PARTY

1988, 99 mins, US Ⓥ ⊙ col

Dir Franc Roddam ***Prod*** John Daly, Derek Gibson, Bernard Williams ***Scr*** Spencer Eastman ***Ph*** Brian Tufano ***Ed*** Sean Barton ***Art*** Michael Bingham

Act Billy Wirth, Kevin Dillon, Tim Sampson, Jimmy Ray Wales, Kevin Major Howard, M. Emmet Walsh (Hemdale)

A lethal contemporary game of Cowboys and Indians is played out in this revisionist western whose thesis is that, deep down, old hatreds never die. British director Franc Roddam comes down firmly on the side of the Native Americans in this downbeat action pic.

Opening scene is the aftermath of a massacre that took place 100 years ago: A camera pan following runaway horses brings us, without a cut, to present-day Montana and a small town with a large Indian population. The (white) mayor has planned, as a Labor Day tourist attraction, a reenactment of that old battle; but racial hatreds run deep, and a drunken white boy shoots and kills an Indian youth whose pals quickly avenge him. Pic then develops into a manhunt as five Indian youths take off on horseback.

It's to the credit of Roddam, and the late screenwriter Spencer Eastman (to whom the pic is dedicated), that the present-day world of the West's Indians is so thoughtfully and seriously presented. Yet despite its interesting depiction of modern Indian life, *War Party* is basically just another pursuit movie, no better or worse than the average. Billy Worth and Kevin Dillon impress as the two young Indian leaders.

•

WARRENDALE

1967, 105 mins, Canada col

Dir Allan King ***Prod*** Allan King ***Scr*** Allan King ***Ph*** William Brayne ***Ed*** Peter Moseley (King)

This pic is a shattering documentary look at a home, Warrendale, for disturbed children and adolescents in Canada. It deals with a group of young, dedicated workers who stay with these emotionally mixed-up youngsters and emerges as engrossing, stark film.

The people involved seem unaware of the camera except when the filmmaker is mentioned by one of the workers. It is the treatment in this institution that is the thing in this psychologically absorbing, well-made and incisive truth pic. Death of a beloved cook is one of the main segs of the film as it details the reactions of the patients who had become attached to her.

•

WAR REQUIEM

1988, 85 mins, UK Ⓥ col

Dir Derek Jarman ***Prod*** Don Boyd ***Scr*** Derek Jarman ***Ph*** Richard Greatrex ***Ed*** Rick Elgood ***Art*** Lucy Morahan

Act Nathaniel Parker, Tilda Swinton, Laurence Olivier, Patricia Hayes, Rohan McCullough, Nigel Terry (Anglo International/BBC)

As well as being a stunning visual and serious music treat, *War Requiem* is probably avant garde British director Derek Jarman's most mature effort. Pic is a visualization of Benjamin Britten's oratorio and was financed through the BBC's Independent Planning Unit on a budget of just £650,000. It was shot and released in the U.K. within a staggeringly short three-month period.

War Requiem has no dialog, though it opens with Laurence Olivier reciting Wilfred Owen's poem "Strange Meeting." Olivier also appears in cameo as an old soldier tended by a young nurse (Tilda Swinton). The live-action footage is intercut with documentary footage from the Imperial War Museum.

Pic uses the story of Owen's experiences in World War I, up to his death by a sniper bullet one week before the war ended, as its structure, while a nurse and unknown soldier are introduced to supplement Britten's musical scenarios. Nathaniel Parker as tortured poet Owen and Swinton (a Jarman regular) as the nurse are excellent. The soundtrack is the original recording of the work, composed for the reopening of Coventry Cathedral in 1962.

•

WARRIORS, THE

1979, 90 mins, US Ⓥ ⊙ col

Dir Walter Hill ***Prod*** Lawrence Gordon ***Scr*** David Shaber, Walter Hill ***Ph*** Andrew Laszlo ***Ed*** David Holden ***Mus*** Barry DeVorzon ***Art*** Don Swanson, Bob Wightman

Act Michael Beck, James Remar, David Patrick Kelly, Deborah Van Valkenburgh, Mercedes Ruehl, Brian Tyler (Paramount)

Theme of the pic, based on Sol Yurick's 1965 novel, is a variation on countless westerns and war films.

Update the setting to modern-day New York, and the avenues of escape to graffiti-emblazoned subway cars, and that's *The Warriors*.

The slaying of a hood (Roger Hill) is pinned on a Coney Island gang, the Warriors of the title, and the word soon goes out that the group's members are to be eliminated. It's a long subway ride to Coney Island, so for at least 70 of the film's 90 minutes, the boys in this band experience a variety of macho passage rites.

As with his previous pix, *Hard Times* and *The Driver*, director Walter Hill demonstrates an outstanding visual sense here, with the gaudy "colors" of the gang members, the desolation of nighttime NYC, and the cavernous subway platforms where much of the action takes place.

•

WAR ROOM, THE

1993, 94 mins, US Ⓥ ⊙ col

Dir D.A. Pennebaker, Chris Hegedus ***Prod*** R. J. Cutler, Wendy Ettinger, Frazer Pennebaker ***Ph*** Nick Doob, D. A. Pennebaker, Kevin Rafferty ***Ed*** Chris Hegedus, Erez Laufer, D. A. Pennebaker

Act James Carville, George Stephanopolous (Pennebaker)

If *The War Room* were a fictional feature, it would be a sure-fire star-making vehicle for James Carville. President Clinton's crafty, straight-talking campaign manager dominates this absorbing but basically unrevelatory behind-the-scenes look at the former Arkansas governor's long push for the presidency.

With Clinton as a sort of secondary character who pops in periodically, pic charts the nine-month pregnancy of his battle for the White House from the perspective of his key strategists, Carville and communications director George Stephanopoulos.

From frigid New Hampshire to the inner sanctum of their Little Rock h.q. on election night, the two young men and their staffs could almost as easily pass for grad students plotting a campus event as professionals whose hunches and whims will profoundly mark the world political landscape.

With his country boy Cajun accent, fast thinking and frank talking, Carville is a disarming presence from the get-go. Sneering that "I think of an old calendar when I look at George Bush's face," Carville is usually seen on the phone or addressing his troops.

Cinema verite pioneer Pennebaker, whose early work included the landmark political docus *Crisis* and *Primary*, has, with his wife, Hegedus, and their collaborators, valuably added to the official record with this fresh angle on the US political process.

1993: NOMINATION: Best Documentary Feature

•

WAR WAGON, THE

1967, 100 mins, US Ⓥ ⊙ ▭ col

Dir Burt Kennedy ***Prod*** Marvin Schwartz ***Scr*** Clair Huffaker ***Ph*** William H. Clothier ***Ed*** Harry Gerstad ***Mus*** Dimitri Tiomkin ***Art*** Alfred Sweeney

Act John Wayne, Kirk Douglas, Howard Keel, Robert Walker, Keenan Wynn, Bruce Cabot (Universal)

The War Wagon is an entertaining, exciting western drama of revenge, laced with action and humor. Strong scripting, performances and direction are evident, enhanced by terrif exterior production values. Kirk Douglas also stars in an excellent performance.

Clair Huffaker's novel, *Badman*, has been adapted by the author into a very fine screenplay which is a neat blend of always-advancing plot, the right amount of good-natured grousing, and two-fisted action, all building to a strong climax. Burt Kennedy directs with an eye for panorama, as well as intimate, personal interaction.

John Wayne, framed into prison by Bruce Cabot who then seized his land to make a fortune in gold, returns for revenge. He teams with Kirk Douglas, a hired gun used earlier by Cabot. Together they plan a heist of Cabot's armored gold wagon.

•

WATCHER IN THE WOODS, THE

1980, 100 mins, UK col

Dir John Hough ***Prod*** Ron Miller ***Scr*** Brian Clemens, Harry Spalding, Rosemary Anne Sisson ***Ph*** Alan Hume ***Ed*** Geoffrey Foot ***Mus*** Stanley Myers ***Art*** Alan Cassie

Act Bette Davis, Carroll Baker, David McCallum, Ian Bannen, Lynn-Holly Johnson, Kyle Richards (Walt Disney)

Although Bette Davis has star billing there's not much reason for it as the film revolves around teenager Lynn-Holly Johnson who just happens to resemble the long-lost daughter of Davis.

Johnson's family (Carroll Baker, David McCallum and Kyle Richards) rent the huge country house belonging to Davis, who lives in a nearby cottage and depends on the big-house rentals for income. The pretitle sequences establish the house and woods (which actually appear to encroach on the house at times) with being something less than fun city. Whatever is out there, however, remains undiscovered even after the film has ended.

The acting and writing are barely professional but the art direction, especially Alan Hume's stunning camerawork, gives the pic a gloss.

•

WATCH ON THE RHINE

1943, 109 mins, US Ⓥ b/w

Dir Herman Shumlin ***Prod*** Hal B. Wallis ***Scr*** Dashiell Hammett ***Ph*** Merritt Gerstad, Hal Mohr ***Ed*** Rudi Fehr ***Mus*** Max Steiner

Act Bette Davis, Paul Lukas, Geraldine Fitzgerald, George Coulouris, Lucile Watson, Beulah Bondi (Warner)

Watch on the Rhine is a distinguished picture. It is even better than its powerful original stage version. It expresses the same urgent theme, but with broader sweep and in more affecting terms of personal emotion. The film more than retains the vital theme of the original play. It actually carries the theme further and deeper, and it does so with passionate conviction and enormous skill. There is no compromise on controversial matters. Fascists are identified as such and, although the point is not brought home as it might have been, the industrial-financial support that makes fascism possible is also mentioned.

Just as he was in the play, Paul Lukas is the outstanding star of the film. Anything his part may have lost in the transfer of key lines to Bette Davis is offset by the projective value of the camera for closeups. His portrayal of the heroic German has the same quiet strength and the slowly gathering force that it had on the stage, but it now seems even better defined and carefully detailed, and it has much more vitality.

In the lesser starring part of the wife, Davis gives a performance of genuine distinction.

1943: Best Actor (Paul Lukas)

NOMINATIONS: Best Picture, Supp. Actress (Lucile Watson), Screenplay

•

WATCH YOUR STERN

1960, 88 mins, UK b/w

Dir Gerald Thomas ***Prod*** Peter Rogers ***Scr*** Alan Hackney, Vivian A. Cox ***Ph*** Ted Scaife ***Ed*** John Shirley ***Mus*** Bruce Montgomery ***Art*** Carmen Dillon

Act Kenneth Connor, Eric Barker, Leslie Phillips, Joan Sims, Hattie Jacques, Spike Milligan (Anglo Amalgamated)

The team responsible for the clicko *Carry On* series are up to their profitable yock-raising larks with *Watch Your Stern*. There is a stronger story line [from Earle Couttie's play *Something About a Sailor*], characters are developed more roundly and director Gerald Thomas does not rely on a string of largely disconnected gags and situations.

The yarn concerns a top secret test on an acoustic torpedo which, when fired, upsets arrangements by doubling in its tracks, missing the target raft and blowing up the firing ship. An Admiralty boffin is detailed to modify the torpedo, the plan gets destroyed, a copy mislaid and the destroyer's officers manage to bluff the admiral with the plans of the ship's refrigeration plant.

Acting is on a firstclass farcical comedy level, with Kenneth Connor scoring heavily in his two disguises, especially when as a "woman scientist," he has to cope with the attentions of the amorous admiral. Sidney James, guest-starring as a chief petty officer, enlivens his scenes as always and there are standout cameos by Spike Milligan and Eric Sykes as a couple of gabby electricians.

•

WATER

1985, 95 mins, UK Ⓥ col

Dir Dick Clement ***Prod*** Ian La Frenais ***Scr*** Dick Clement, Ian La Frenais ***Ph*** Douglas Slocombe ***Ed*** John Victor Smith ***Mus*** Mike Moran ***Art*** Norman Garwood

Act Michael Caine, Valerie Perrine, Brenda Vaccaro, Billy Connolly, Leonard Rossiter, Maureen Lipman (HandMade)

A British satire of political muddle in Caribbean island, *Water* is a frenetic mishmash. Michael Caine is fine as a laidback British governor who is aptly described as "the Patty Hearst of the British diplomatic corps," but he can't salvage a production that's top heavy with multinational plots threatening the island's harmony.

Those include a singing revolutionary (Billy Connolly) backed by Cubans, mindless British officials (a nice turn by the late Leonard Rossiter and a Margaret Thatcher send-up by Maureen Lipman), some fuzzy French-German intruders, and a U.S. industrialist (Fred Gwynne) who's exploiting the island's underground reserves of mineral water.

The British filmmakers, who shot on the island of St. Lucia, obviously were targeting the invasions of Grenada and the Falkland Islands as subjects of satire.

Playing Caine's hysterical South American wife, Brenda Vaccaro hits the nadir of her career in a performance that is one unrelieved shriek.

•

WATER BABIES, THE

1979, 93 mins, UK Ⓥ col

Dir Lionel Jeffries ***Prod*** Peter Shaw ***Scr*** Michael Robson ***Ph*** Ted Scaife ***Ed*** Peter Weatherley ***Mus*** Phil Coulter, Bill Martin ***Art*** Herbert Westbrook

Act James Mason, Billie Whitelaw, Bernard Cribbins, Joan Greenwood, David Tomlinson, Samantha Gates (Pethurst/Production Associates/Ariadne)

The musical screen version of *The Water Babies*, Charles Kingsley's children's novel, tells the story of innocence-versus-evil more or less straight. The slim $2 million production budget combines live action footage and—for the underwater sequences—animation.

Screenplay plots the adventures of a 12-year-old apprentice chimneysweep, wrongly accused of theft, who dives into a pool to escape his pursuers. Trapped below the surface, he meets a succession of human stereotypes, jokily animated as underwater creatures, and has a battle to free the water babies, who normally inhabit an eternal playground in mid-ocean but have been captured by a shark and an electric eel.

Animated sequences by Cuthbert Cartoons in London, and movement synchronized by Miroslaw Kijowicz in Poland to a prerecorded soundtrack, are garish but effective.

•

WATERBOY, THE

1998, 88 MINS, US Ⓥ ⊙ col

Dir Frank Coraci ***Prod*** Robert Simonds, Jack Giarraputo ***Scr*** Tim Herlihy, Adam Sandler ***Ph*** Steven Bernstein ***Ed*** Tom Lewis ***Mus*** Alan Pasqua ***Art*** Perry Andelin Blake

Act Adam Sandler, Kathy Bates, Henry Winkler, Fairuza Balk, Jerry Reed, Larry Gilliard, Jr. (Touchstone)

After amiable crossover vehicle *The Wedding Singer*, Adam Sandler scrambles back to his SNL Cajun Boy persona for *The Waterboy*, a formulaic mix of mirth and mayhem aimed way down the MTV food chain.

The big laughs come from a ragtag football team that's so poor its players share a single protective cup, so demoralized the cheerleaders and mascot get tanked every game. As for Sandler, he remains an acquired (lack of) taste. His stammering simp and recycled Jerry Lewis shtick would test the patience of even the French.

Sandler, again teamed with *Wedding Singer* director Frank Coraci and writer Tim Herlihy, plays Bobby Boucher, your proverbial water/whipping boy for Louisiana U.'s football team. Bobby is used as tackling dummy by the coach (Jerry Reed) and players.

Fired for fighting back, Bobby returns to Mama Boucher's (Kathy Bates) arms and then signs on with the underdog Mud Dogs, led by a hallucinating coach (Henry Winkler). He transfers his pent-up anger to the opposing team and, following the formula, overcomes 11th-hour adversity to lead his team to victory in the Big Game.

Besides Bates, who gets into the spirit of things and mugs throughout, pic has cameos by Rob Schneider, NFL personalities and a number of ABC Sports announcers. Fairuza Balk is sexy and funny as Bobby's bad-girl girlfriend, and Winkler underplays nicely as the coach who sports a tattoo of Roy Orbison on his tush.

Tech credits are what you'd expect of a low-grade genre entry. Those that are a notch above include f/x supervisor David Fogg's morphing game faces (when Bobby projects his anger) and production designer Perry Andelin Blake's swamp cabin, decorated in road-kill provincial.

•

WATERDANCE, THE

1992, 106 mins, US Ⓥ ⊙ col

Dir Neal Jimenez, Michael Steinberg ***Prod*** Gale Anne Hurd, Marie Cantin ***Scr*** Neal Jimenez ***Ph*** Mark Plummer ***Ed*** Jeff Freeman ***Mus*** Michael Convertino ***Art*** Bob Ziembicki

Act Eric Stoltz, Helen Hunt, William Forsythe, Wesley Snipes, Elizabeth Pena (JBW)

Co-directing debut of writer Neal Jimenez (*River's Edge*, *For the Boys*) with Michael Steinberg is a smashing success, the writer's semi-autobiographical story of a young man's struggle to avoid despair after a crippling accident.

Set in a hospital for paralyzed men where a young novelist (Eric Stoltz) lands after a hiking accident, pic is about his coming to terms with the fate he shares with others in the ward; among them, a hostile white redneck biker (William Forsythe) and a restless, fast-talking black man (Wesley Snipes).

Script unfolds with a spirit and sparkle devoid of self-indulgence, and Stoltz plays the lead with lightness, wit and balance, as well as a measure of despair and denial. Much of the pic concerns the anguish of these young men at losing sexual ability, and this aspect of paralysis is covered with a frankness heretofore unseen.

•

WATERHOLE #3

1967, 95 mins, US Ⓥ ▭ col

Dir William Graham ***Prod*** Joseph T. Steck ***Scr*** Joseph T. Steck, R. R. Young ***Ph*** Robert Burks ***Ed*** Warren Low ***Mus*** Dave Grusin ***Art*** Fernando Carrere

Act James Coburn, Carroll O'Connor, Maggie Blye, Claude Akins, Timothy Carey, Bruce Dern (Paramount)

Waterhole #3 is a slow-building, deliberate oater comedy blending satire, slapstick and double entendre dialog for laughs.

Distended story line turns on two gags: gold heist by crooked army sergeant Claude Akins, grounting outlaw Timothy Carey and unwilling hostage Harry Davis; and casual seduction by gambler James Coburn of Carroll O'Connor's daughter, Margaret Blye.

O'Connor is far more interested in Coburn's theft of a prize horse, and this gag is milked for all it is worth. Joan Blondell has a bright role as a madame, ditto James Whitmore as a cliché frontier Army officer.

Coburn, O'Connor and Blye (whose voice and projection are perfect) handle their roles in very good fashion, while rest of cast offers good support.

•

WATERLAND

1992, 95 mins, UK/US Ⓥ ⊙ ▭ col

Dir Stephen Gyllenhaal ***Prod*** Katy McGuinness, Patrick Cassavetti ***Scr*** Peter Prince ***Ph*** Robert Elswit ***Ed*** Lesley Walker ***Mus*** Carter Burwell ***Art*** Hugo Luczyc-Wyhowski

Act Jeremy Irons, Ethan Hawke, Sinead Cusack, John Heard, Cara Buono, Grant Warnock (Palace/Fine Line)

High-school teacher Jeremy Irons walks his students through the physical and emotional landscapes of his troubled life in *Waterland*, a talented but terminally parched piece of literary cinema [from the novel by Graham Swift].

This twisted, inbred yarn is not the sort of thing normally associated with British accents, scarfed pipe-smokers and memory flashbacks. At heart, tale is a Southern gothic of sordid family secrets.

Seeing that his Pittsburgh students find little relevance in his lectures about the French Revolution, teacher Tom Crick (Irons) begins telling them about his own upbringing in the odd area called the Fens, bleak, flat marshlands in East Anglia on the North Sea.

At 16, he and his sweetheart, Mary, used to have feverish sex in private train compartments. Mary in the present is a barren woman in her 40s with a pathological desire for a child, someone clearly off the deep end who finally kidnaps a baby, insisting, "I got him from God."

Irons does his best to carry the project through thick and thin, but he can't entirely break through its fundamental reediness. As his wife, Irons's real-life mate Sinead Cusack seems utterly possessed.

•

WATERLOO

1970, 132 mins, Italy/Russia Ⓥ ▭ col

Dir Sergei Bondarchuk ***Prod*** Dino De Laurentiis ***Scr*** H.A.L. Craig, Sergei Bondarchuk, Vittorio Bonicelli ***Ph*** Armando Nannuzzi ***Ed*** Richard C. Meyer, E.V. Michajlova ***Mus*** Nino Rota ***Art*** Mario Garbuglia

Act Rod Steiger, Christopher Plummer, Orson Welles, Jack Hawkins, Virginia McKenna, Dan O'Herlihy (De Laurentiis/Mosfilm)

Directed by Russia's Sergei Bondarchuk, who made *War and Peace*, and filmed on location in Italy and Russia, with interiors at De Laurentiis's Rome studios, the long-nursed Dino De Laurentiis project has an international flavor. Despite the fact that the battle is the focal point, and a striking din-laden affair it is, the film is raised from being just another historical war epic by the performances of Rod Steiger as Napoleon and Christopher Plummer as Wellington.

Story begins with Europe entirely opposed to the ambitious, flamboyant Napoleon and the French, scared of overwhelming odds, forcing him to abdicate and retire to the island of Elba. But barely has the film started than he's back again.

Steiger gives a remarkably powerful portrayal of Napoleon. It's a Method performance, with his sudden blazes of rage highlighting his moody introspection.

Others stand out, too. Dan O'Herlihy as Marshal Ney, devoted, loyalist to Napoleon, and Orson Welles, making much of two minor but memorable moments as Louis XVIII.

•

WATERLOO BRIDGE

1940, 103 mins, US Ⓥ ⊙ b/w

Dir Mervyn LeRoy ***Prod*** Sidney Franklin ***Scr*** S. N. Behrman, Hans Rameau, George Froeschel ***Ph*** Joseph Ruttenberg ***Ed*** George Boemler ***Mus*** Herbert Stothart ***Art*** Cedric Gibbons, Urie McCleary

Act Vivien Leigh, Robert Taylor, Lucile Watson, Virginia Field, Maria Ouspenskaya, C. Aubrey Smith (M-G-M)

Elaborating on the basic premise of Robert Sherwood's play, and doing a slick job of cleansing to conform to present regulations of the Hays code, this is a persuasive and compelling romantic tragedy.

Story steers a leisurely path in delineating the romantic tragedy of a love affair which is launched on Waterloo Bridge during World War I. Vivien Leigh, a sweet, vivacious and unsophisticated ballet dancer, meets and falls in love with British officer Robert Taylor on eve of his departure for the front. There's a whirlwind romance with immediate marriage delayed until his first furlough. Fate intervenes, and erroneous report of his death eventually sends her onto the streets, but Taylor returns, meets her at the station where she is soliciting, and the romance flares again for an instant.

Leigh demonstrates outstanding ability as an actress. Her transition from the virginal ingenue of the early passages to the hardened prostie later is a standout performance. Taylor, in a straight romantic role, provides an arresting characterization.

There's plenty of strength in the supporting cast. Virginia Field is excellent as Leigh's chum, who takes the first step along the easiest way to provide food for the pair. Lucile Watson is a perfect grand dame as the aristocratic mother of Taylor; Maria Ouspenskaya is a stern ballet mistress; and C. Aubrey Smith is an army colonel.

1940: NOMINATIONS: Best B&W Cinematography, Original Score

•

WATERLOO ROAD
1945, 76 mins, UK b/w
Dir Sidney Gilliat ***Prod*** Edward Black ***Scr*** Sidney Gilliat ***Ph*** Arthur Crabtree ***Ed*** Alfred Roome ***Mus*** Bob Busby ***Art*** Alex Vetchinsky
Act John Mills, Stewart Granger, Alastair Sim, Joy Shelton, Beatrice Varley, George Carney (Gainsborough)

Played against the drab, bomb-shattered background of a London slum, story is the familiar triangle theme with use of the flashback technique not adding to its originality. But it's acted with such sincerity and is so true-to-life in its characterization that the picture grips throughout. There is a terrific climax in which the two men (John Mills and Stewart Granger) fight for one woman as the bombs thunder down.

A soldier deserts when he learns his wife is receiving attentions from another man. Story depicts his day spent in pursuit of the pair, finally confronting them in a sports arcade.

Entire cast is adequate, but particular praise goes to Alastair Sim as the neighborhood doctor and George Carney's role of pigeon fancier.

Picture [from a story by Val Valentine] is a striking example of how sound an English production can be if it keeps to the medium it interprets best, that of the middle-class character.

•

WATERWORLD
1995, 135 mins, US Ⓥ ⊙ col
Dir Kevin Reynolds ***Prod*** Charles Gordon, John Davis, Kevin Costner ***Scr*** Peter Radar, David Twohy ***Ph*** Dean Semler ***Ed*** Peter Boyle ***Mus*** James Newton Howard ***Art*** Dennis Gassner
Act Kevin Costner, Dennis Hopper, Jeanne Tripplehorn, Tina Majorino, Michael Jeter, Gerard Murphy (Universal/Gordon/Davis/Licht-Mueller

Because of the inevitable attention on the film's all-time record $175 million pricetag, the problem-plagued shoot and the falling out of the two Kevins—director Kevin Reynolds and producer/star Costner—the unfortunate temptation for critics and public alike will be to review the budget rather than the picture. The short answer is that, no, the $1.3 million-per-minute cost isn't really on the screen.

Putting all that aside, Waterworld is a not-bad futuristic actioner with three or four astounding sequences, an unusual hero, a nifty villain and less mythic and romantic resonances than might be delivered. Pic owes more than a passing debt to the *Mad Max* movies.

Pic's opening gambit is among its most clever: the premise of a world whose land masses have been entirely covered by water. Like a quintessential Western wanderer without a name the Mariner (Costner) sails the endless seas and has developed survival instincts to the point where tiny gills behind his ears allow him to breathe under water and webbed feet enable him to swim like a dolphin.

The Mariner pulls into a floating scrap-metal island whose folks represent easy prey for the savage Smokers who take orders from the maniacal Deacon played with full-tilt relish by a bald-headed, eye-patched Dennis Hopper.

In an incredible 12-minute assault sequence, the Smokers overtake the atoll but the Mariner manages to escape, reluctantly taking with him Helen (Jeanne Tripplehorn), as well as her feisty adopted daughter, Enola (Tina Majorino) on whose back is tatooed a sunlike symbol that may indicate the whereabouts of the mythical Dryland. It's little Elona who the Deacon really covets.

The story has a sort of grim obsessiveness about it. The humor that might have helped the film could have derived from the central male-female relationship. But Tripplehorn provides a terribly serious, overwrought woman quite unable to leaven Kevin.

The sets, costumes and many of the effects are stupendous.

1995: NOMINATION: Best Sound

•

WAY AHEAD, THE
(US: IMMORTAL BATTALION)
1944, 115 mins, UK Ⓥ b/w
Dir Carol Reed ***Prod*** Norman Walker, John Sutro ***Scr*** Eric Ambler, Peter Ustinov ***Ph*** Guy Green ***Ed*** Fergus McDonell ***Mus*** William Alwyn ***Art*** David Rawnsley
Act David Niven, Raymond Huntley, Billy Hartnell, Stanley Holloway, James Donald, Leo Genn (Two Cities)

There is no story in the accepted sense, and no love interest. There are momentary shots of femmes, chiefly wives, but no pin-up girls. This heightens the documentary value of this wartime slice of English life. Slickness of cutting should be enough to put this among notable British films, but there is additional cleverness in keeping David Niven far less obtrusive than his star's status might seem to justify. He's a subaltern in command of a platoon.

Covering the period from early 1939 to the Tunisian campaign of 1943, *The Way Ahead* shows how a totally unprepared, peace-loving people were suddenly catapulted into war; how a score of widely different individuals reacted to it.

Direction by Carol Reed is competent, and undoubtedly accounts for the underlying genuineness of the picture as a semi-documentary. Reed's job was made relatively easy by the solid script turned in by Eric Ambler and Peter Ustinov [from Ambler's original story].

•

WAY DOWN EAST
1920, 150 mins, US Ⓥ ⊗ b/w
Dir D. W. Griffith ***Prod*** D. W. Griffith ***Scr*** Anthony Paul Kelly, Joseph R. Grismer, D. W. Griffith ***Ph*** Billy Bitzer, Hendrik Sartov ***Ed*** James E. Smith, Rose Smith ***Mus*** William Frederick Peters ***Art*** Charles O. Sessel, Clifford Pember
Act Lillian Gish, Richard Barthelmess, Lowell Sherman, Burr McIntosh, Creighton Hale, Kate Bruce (Griffith/United Artists)

Way Down East by D. W. Griffith is a film poem. Without the aid of any especially spectacular or stupendous mechanical effects such as were utilized in *Intolerance*, or the employment of a large ensemble of mob scenes as in the same picture and *The Birth of a Nation*, *Judith of Bethulia*, etc., with the gathering together of a relatively small cast and less than half a dozen stellar film artists, D. W. has taken a simple, elemental, old-fashioned, bucolic melodrama and milked it for 12 reels of absorbing entertainment.

First honors for acting belong to Lillian Gish, who had to court comparison with the preconceived characterization of Anna Moore, which had always been played by a much larger woman in the spoken productions [of the play by Lottie Blair Parker]. Hers is a materially different conception of the role, and she reveals hitherto unsuspected emotional powers. Richard Barthelmess, as David, has little to do until almost the finish, when he rescues Anna from an ice floe about to be precipitated over a rapidly moving, seething waterfall.

•

WAYNE'S WORLD
1992, 95 mins, US Ⓥ ⊙ ▭ col
Dir Penelope Spheeris ***Prod*** Lorne Michaels ***Scr*** Mike Myers, Bonnie Turner, Terry Turner ***Ph*** Theo Van de Sande ***Ed*** Malcolm Campbell ***Mus*** J. Peter Robinson ***Art*** Gregg Fonseca
Act Mike Myers, Dana Carvey, Rob Lowe, Tia Carrere, Lara Flynn Boyle, Colleen Camp (Paramount)

Wayne's World weakly transfers the popular *Saturday Night Live* TV sketch to the big screen . . . NOT! *SNL* regular Mike Myers created the characters of two overage heavy metal teens fronting a cable access TV show in Aurora, IL. Like Weird Al Yankovic's flop pic *UHF*, the film satirizes various genres using TV as a starting point.

Ostensible plot has Rob Lowe as a slimy opportunist who buys the heroes' *Wayne's World* show and re-structures it to plug Brian Doyle-Murray's video arcade business. Wayne (Myers) falls in love with beautiful Hong Kong rock singer Tia Carrere and has to worry about womanizer Lowe stealing her away.

Director Penelope Spheeris, with her first major studio assignment (and eight-figure budget), delivers a colorful but uneventful picture. As with *Clue*, picture features three alternate endings, played back to back like the *Clue* video.

Guest stars add almost nothing to the proceedings, including Dan Aykroyd's wife Donna Dixon as Carvey's beautiful dream girl, Ione Skye as Lowe's girlfriend, Meat Loaf as a bouncer and Ed O'Neill as a nutty donut shop manager.

•

WAYNE'S WORLD 2
1993, 94 mins, US Ⓥ ⊙ col
Dir Stephen Surjik ***Prod*** Lorne Michaels ***Scr*** Mike Myers, Bonnie Turner, Terry Turner ***Ph*** Francis Kenny ***Ed*** Malcolm Campbell ***Mus*** Carter Burwell ***Art*** Gregg Fonseca
Act Mike Myers, Dana Carvey, Christopher Walken, Tia Carrere, Ralph Brown, Kim Basinger (Paramount)

The latest chapter in the saga of Aurora, IL, twosome Wayne and Garth is a puerile, misguided and loathsome effort . . . NOT! The *SNL* icons of vapid youth have come up with an exceedingly clever mixture of pure juvenilia and hip, social comedy for *Wayne's World 2*.

Since the last episode, Wayne Campbell (Mike Myers) and Garth Algar (Dana Carvey) have graduated or been turfed out of high school and have entered the big world. Wayne is visited in his dreams by a Native American guide who leads him into the desert where he encounters late rock star Jim Morrison (Michael Nickles). The singer tells him to put on a concert. He sagely advises, "If you book them, they will come." Thus is born Waynestock.

The mad pursuit to put on the show fuels subplots, asides, digressions and 100 percent, unadulterated non sequiturs. The stream of conscious unconsciousness includes Wayne's anxiousness about girlfriend Cassandra's (Tia Carrere) growing attachment to record producer Bobby Cahn (Christopher Walken) and Garth's initiation into manhood by hungry housewife Honey Hornee (Kim Basinger).

The incredible sleight of hand is largely accomplished thanks to a deft script and extremely shrewd casting. Walken and Basinger, for instance, know how to use the extremes of their screen personae without succumbing to caricature.

•

WAY OF ALL FLESH, THE
1927, 90 mins, US ⊗ b/w
Dir Victor Fleming ***Scr*** Jules Furthman ***Ph*** Victor Milner
Act Emil Jannings, Belle Bennett, Phyllis Haver, Donald Keith, Fred Kohler (Paramount)

No specific punch to this initial made-in-the-USA Emil Jannings release. It really amounts to a study by the star of a middle class character who succumbs, just once, to the feminine and must forever after live in hiding while his family believes him dead and enjoys prosperity through one of the sons' violin concerts. Starting in 1910, the story weaves its way up to the present year, giving opportunity to display three characterizations in as many makeups.

First as the bewhiskered gruff and trusted cashier of a Milwaukee bank, second as under the influence of a demimondaine, thereby shorn of his facial growth, and finally as a broken example of indiscretion cleaning up park playgrounds and peddling chestnuts.

In substance the story revolves around the incident of Schilling (Jannings) being entrusted with valuable bonds to be sold in Chicago. On the train he meets Mayme (Phyllis Haver), obviously attired for the character, who ultimately leads him to a drunken sleep in a hotel where she rifles him of his consignment.

Most of the production is studio made, although there are theatre and amusement park sequences, the last named inviting various camera angles, one or two of which stand out.

As regards Jannings, this, is first domestic made picture, is assuredly creditable.

1927/28: Best Actor (Emil Jannings)

NOMINATION: Best Picture

•

WAY OF THE DRAGON, THE
SEE: MENG LONG GUO JIANG

•

WAY OUT WEST
1937, 64 mins, US Ⓥ ⊙ b/w
Dir James W. Horne ***Prod*** Hal Roach, Stan Laurel ***Scr*** Charles Rogers, Felix Adler, James Parrott ***Ph*** Art Lloyd, Walter Lundin ***Ed*** Bert Jordan ***Mus*** Marvin Hatley (dir.) ***Art*** Arthur I. Royce
Act Stan Laurel, Oliver Hardy, Sharon Lynn, James Finlayson, Stanley Fields, Vivian Oakland (M-G-M)

Manner in which this comedy falters and stumbles along is probably due both to formula direction and scripting. Three are credited with the scenario and two [Jack Jevne and Charles Rogers] for the original story. Seemingly too many took a hand; plot reads that way.

In general pattern the Laurel & Hardy entry follows closely the old methods used on their feature shorts. There's too much driving home of gags.

They sing and dance in this one, both to neat returns. The two boys are commissioned to deliver a deed to a gold mine. They find out, after handing it over, that the valuable paper has been given to the wrong girl. Hence, the mad race to readjust matters. On this thin framework hang all of the quips. And Oliver Hardy falls into a pool of water for the third time as the eventual fadeout arrives.

James Finlayson again is cast as villain-straight man, which further slows up the action. Rosina Lawrence, heroine who's supposed to inherit the gold mine, appears only for fleeting glimpses.

1937: NOMINATION: Best Score

•

WAY TO THE STARS, THE
(US: JOHNNY IN THE CLOUDS)
1945, 107 mins, UK b/w
Dir Anthony Asquith ***Prod*** Anatole de Grunwald ***Scr*** Terence Rattigan ***Ph*** Derrick Williams ***Ed*** Fergus McDonell ***Mus*** Nicholas Brodzsky ***Art*** Paul Sheriff, Carmen Dillon
Act John Mills, Michael Redgrave, Douglass Montgomery, Trevor Howard, Rosamund John, Stanley Holloway (Two Cities)

This straight tale of what happened to an RAF airdrome when it was taken over by the 8th USAAF is outstanding. It's the nearest thing to a Yank's letter home from wartime England ever to reach the screen. Not the least interesting thing is the camera technique. Instead of many aerial shots, the camera is grounded entirely. Except for a few necessary runway shots and snatches of formation flying as seen from the ground, the camera concentrates on how the forces lived on terra firma.

Despite technically perfect performances by the three male principals—Michael Redgrave, John Mills and Douglass Montgomery—Rosamund John actually walks away with the acting honors in a part as devoid of glamor as it is rich in femme charm.

Several sequences showing the British aces imitating the Yanks, and the Yanks imitating the Englishmen, are guaranteed belly laughs.

Direction by Anthony Asquith is underlined with sincerity and imagination while the script by Terence Rattigan [based on a scenario by him and Richard Sherman] is strong.

•

WAY WEST, THE
1967, 122 mins, US Ⓥ ▭ col
Dir Andrew V. McLaglen ***Prod*** Harold Hecht ***Scr*** Ben Maddow, Mitch Lindemann ***Ph*** William H. Clothier ***Ed*** Otho Lovering ***Mus*** Bronislau Kaper ***Art*** Ted Haworth
Act Kirk Douglas, Robert Mitchum, Richard Widmark, Lola Albright, Jack Elam, Sally Field (United Artists)

A. B. Guthrie, Jr., wrote the Pulitzer Prize novel on which Ben Maddow and Mitch Lindemann have based a rambling screenplay. Story takes a group of Missouri farmers, under martinet Kirk Douglas, to the promised land of Oregon. Robert Mitchum is the trail scout who leads them despite fading eyesight, and Richard Widmark an irascible member of the party.

Project probably looked good on paper, but washed out in scripting, direction and pacing. Incidents do not build to any climax; excepting the first and last reels, any others could be shown out of order with no apparent discontinuity.

The three male stars all could have phoned in their acting. Douglas, the stern disciplinarian, at one point orders Negro slave Roy Glenn to whip him; this incident, as written, is crude, and instead of indicating a Spartan attempt at self-control, it comes across as unmotivated masochism.

•

WAY WE WERE, THE
1973, 118 mins, US Ⓥ ⦿ ▭ col
Dir Sydney Pollack ***Prod*** Ray Stark ***Scr*** Arthur Laurents ***Ph*** Harry Stradling ***Ed*** Margaret Booth, John F. Burnett ***Mus*** Marvin Hamlisch ***Art*** Stephen Grimes
Act Barbra Streisand, Robert Redford, Bradford Dillman, Patrick O'Neal, Viveca Lindfors, Lois Chiles (Columbia/Rastar)

The film version of Arthur Laurents's book is a distended, talky, redundant and moody melodrama, combining young love, relentless 1930s and 1940s nostalgia, and spiced artifically with Hollywood Red–hunt pellets. The major positive achievement is Barbra Streisand's superior dramatic versatility, but Robert Redford has too little to work with in the script.

The story follows the stars from the late 1930s—on a college campus where Streisand is a young Communist activist, and Redford a casual, shallow type—through World War II civilian and military service, finally to Hollywood where liberal activities lead to blacklisting and marriage breakup.

The overemphasis on Streisand makes the film just another one of those Streisand vehicles where no other elements ever get a chance. Redford's role is another instance of waste of his talent. Supporting players are virtual cameos.

1973: Best Original Score, Song ("The Way We Were")

NOMINATIONS: Best Actress (Barbra Streisand), Cinematography, Costume Design, Art Direction

•

WEB, THE
1947, 87 mins, US b/w
Dir Michael Gordon ***Prod*** Jerry Bresler ***Scr*** William Bowers, Bertram Milhauser ***Ph*** Irving Glassberg ***Ed*** Russell Schoengarth ***Mus*** Hans J. Salter ***Art*** Bernard Herzbrun, James Sullivan
Act Ella Raines, Edmond O'Brien, William Bendix, Vincent Price, Maria Palmer (Universal-International)

There are no Freudian angles cluttering up *The Web*'s melodrama. Picture presents a crook who kills because he wants money and power and not because of some psycho-quirk springing from a past incident.

Top-notch performances by majority of cast carry the melodramatics along in forthright style. The pace is tight and fast, accentuating intrigue and excitement. Standout is Edmond O'Brien as the hero who becomes enmeshed in Vincent Price's scheme to hold on to a stolen million dollars. Another honor-garnerer is William Bendix as an honest cop whose lack of faith in things being as they appear is responsible for eventual downfall of Price. Latter gives a compelling reading to the role of a treacherous, suave big-business man. Ella Raines co-stars as heroine and secretary to Price who awakens romantic interest in O'Brien.

Plot deals with efforts of a young attorney and the police to trap Price into confession of two murders and theft of the million bucks. As his first screen directing chore, former stage director Michael Gordon makes an effective first try that gets the best from the suspense ingredients.

•

WEDDING, A
1978, 125 mins, US Ⓥ ▭ col
Dir Robert Altman ***Prod*** Robert Altman ***Scr*** John Considine, Patricia Resnik, Allan Nicholls, Robert Altman ***Ph*** Charles Rosher ***Ed*** Tony Lombardo ***Mus*** Tom Walls
Act Carol Burnett, Mia Farrow, Lillian Gish, Howard Duff, Geraldine Chaplin, Lauren Hutton (Lion's Gate)

If *Nashville* is ensemble Altman at its best—and it is—then *A Wedding* is the other extreme. Altman's loose, seemingly unstructured style backfires in this comedy-drama.

The title is self-descriptive: The picture is a day in the life of a wedding between the daughter of a nouveau rich Southern family and the son of old midwestern money. The setting is rife with conventions—marriage, religion, wealth.

Unlike *Nashville*, the film lacks a core. Nothing builds; the characters, except for Lillian Gish as the old money matriarch and Mia Farrow as the silent sister of the bride, are uninteresting and unsympathetic. They pop in and out of the film and when they pop out, who cares if they return?

Altman's idea of humor comes off as puerile and dated. John Cromwell plays a senile bishop who performs the wedding ceremony. He forgets how to conduct the service and is too near-sighted to know that at one point he's talking to a corpse. That's hardly sharp-edged satire.

•

WEDDING BANQUET, THE
SEE: XI YAN

•

WEDDING BELLS
SEE: ROYAL WEDDING

•

WEDDING MARCH, THE
1928, 115 mins, US Ⓥ col
Dir Erich von Stroheim ***Prod*** Pat Powers ***Scr*** Erich von Stroheim, Harry Carr ***Ph*** Ben Reynolds, Hal Mohr ***Ed*** Josef von Sternberg ***Mus*** J.B. Zamencnik, Louis de Francesco ***Art*** Erich von Stroheim, Richard Day
Act Erich von Stroheim, Fay Wray, George Fawcett, George Nichols, ZaSu Pitts, Maude George (Paramount)

Left of all the footage on *Wedding March* are 10 reels, with the finish where intermission would have been had the picture come in for $2 with the rest of it. Also remaining is a ponderous slow moving production and some beautiful photography telling a very familiar story, the tip off on which is the lead title, "Vienna 1914." It's fair but hardly brilliant program material which the boys salvaged from a regiment of reels. Scissors to the right and left, leaving most of the picture still in cans, cut the story to the well-known blue-blooded Austrian army officer having his fling with the country maiden and then wedding a limping heiress as the seduced rural miss promises marriage to pacify the browbeating butcher who has threatened the life of the hit-and-run lieutenant.

Fay Wray appeals and convinces as the shy, pretty-faced and innocent victim, while Stroheim's scoundrel is interesting, despite the half-hearted attempt to soften the character. George Fawcett and George Nichols make conventional fathers. Maude George will startle the peasants with her cigar-smoking mother of Nicki. ZaSu Pitts is the crippled princess, giving the role legitimate interpretation.

Getting *Wedding March* to a screen took something like two years and over $1 million. Main defect is that deletion has not added pace. Synchronized score is excellent and shows judgment in the use of minor effects.

•

WEDDING NIGHT, THE
1935, 81 mins, US b/w
Dir King Vidor ***Prod*** Samuel Goldwyn ***Scr*** Edith Fitzgerald ***Ph*** Gregg Toland ***Ed*** Stuart Heisler ***Mus*** Alfred Newman ***Art*** Richard Day
Act Gary Cooper, Anna Sten, Helen Vinson, Ralph Bellamy, Sig Ruman, Esther Dale (Goldwyn/United Artists)

Story [by Edwin Knopf] is irritating in many ways. Gary Cooper is a young author who sells a piece of his land to a Polish tobacco grower, who wants it as a dowry for his daughter. He goes to the farmhouse to make the sale. He is received with hospitality and made welcome at the meal which turns out to be a betrothal feast.

Author returns home, announcing that he has just found the theme for his new book in the family he has just left. The Polish girl becomes first interested in the man and then flattered by the novel in which she, the heroine, works the spiritual regeneration of the author, who frankly divorces his wife—on paper—to take on the new love.

King Vidor, in his direction, handles the incidents with fine touch, keeping each character whole and consistent and developing a fluid action which moves easily from the American to the Polish home and back again.

Anna Sten is more fortunately cast than in *Nana* (1934). She is exotic, but her still-marked accent fits the character and she gives a finely sensitive performance.

She is handicapped in a way by the more showy personality of Helen Vinson, as the author's wife; hard as nails, but realizing eventually she loves her man and is willing to fight for him. Cooper contibutes an easy character drawing which by its charm almost blinds to the havoc he works. Ralph Bellamy is capital as the destined husband.

•

WEDDING PARTY, THE
1969, 90 mins, US Ⓥ b/w
Dir Cynthia Munroe, Brian De Palma, Wilford Leach ***Prod*** Cynthia Munroe, Brian De Palma, Wilford Leach ***Scr*** Cynthia Munroe, Brian De Palma, Wilford Leach ***Ph*** Peter Powell ***Ed*** Cynthia Munroe, Brian De Palma, Wilford Leach ***Mus*** John Herbert McDowell
Act Jill Clayburgh, Charles Pflugar, Valda Setterfield, Ray McNally, Robert De Niro, Judy Thomas (Ondine)

Story dwells on a young man who, accompanied by two friends, arrives at the island estate of his soon-to-be-bride.

The individual scenes come off as a kind of practiced improvisation. Apparently a script was employed but the dialog itself was produced by taping ad-libbed scenes.

The film suffers from this technique. Each scene is only loosely connected with what went before and what comes after. And tightness and direction of the dialog is sacrificed for a certain spontaneity that is seldom forthcoming.

The cast includes professional actors combined with Sarah Lawrence College workshop students.

Film was actually completed [in 1963]. De Palma worked in collaboration with then fellow student Cynthia Munroe and faculty member Wilford Leach when all three were at Sarah Lawrence College.

•

WEDDING SINGER, THE
1998, 96 mins, US Ⓥ ⦿ col
Dir Frank Coraci ***Prod*** Robert Simonds, Jack Giarraputo ***Scr*** Tim Herlihy ***Ph*** Tim Suhrstedt ***Ed*** Tom Lewis ***Mus*** Teddy Castellucci ***Art*** Perry Andelin Blake
Act Adam Sandler, Drew Barrymore, Christine Taylor, Allen Covert, Matthew Glave, Ellen Albertini Dow (New Line)

The aptly names Robbie Hart (Adam Sandler) is good at what he does—singing the hits of the '80s and elevating the fun level at weddings, bar mitzvahs and other celebrations. *The Wedding Singer* captures that joie de vivre in an unabashedly romantic comedy that has hit written all over it. Picture serves up Sandler and Drew Barrymore in a new way that enhances their most winning qualities.

Julia Sullivan (Barrymore) shares Robbie's open, ingenuous quality. A waitress at events where Robbie performs, she's hardly a world beater. She believes in love and family and has convinced herself that marriage to Glen (Matthew Glave)—a boorish womanizer—will fulfill her life. After Robbie is stood up at his own wedding, all doubt is erased that these two are the right people with the wrong mates.

Director Frank Coraci and scripter Tim Herlihy work in concert to maintain a quality of farce rooted in human comedy. Structurally it's like a series of syncopated opening and closing doors. The skill is in the filmmakers' ability to camouflage the mechanical parts by means of digression, red herrings and simple sleight of hand.

The trump card, however, is the performers. Sandler is a revelation playing a character with innate decency. Barrymore also covers new ground as a light comic actress, making the most of the opportunity to play a vulnerable and appealing character.

The film, set in 1985, allows for a pallette of Day Glo colors artfully employed by cameraman Tim Suhrstedt to accentuate the garish side to otherwise quite ordinary events.

•

WE DIVE AT DAWN
1943, 92 mins, UK Ⓥ b/w
Dir Anthony Asquith ***Prod*** Edward Black ***Scr*** J. B. Williams, Val Valentine ***Ph*** Jack Cox ***Ed*** R. E. Dearing ***Mus*** Louis Levy (dir.) ***Art*** Walter Murton
Act Eric Portman, John Mills, Reginald Purdell, Niall MacGinnis, Jack Watling, Leslie Watson (Gainsborough)

The submarine *Sea Tiger* is sent out to sink a Nazi battleship which is due to leave Bremerhaven for the Kiel Canal, en route to the Baltic. The sub's instructions are to intercept her off the German coast before she enters the canal. Too late for this, the lieutenant in charge decides to brave the dangers of the Baltic and attack the battleship when she emerges at the other end of the canal. Owing to depth charges from accompanying destroyers, the attack results in a leakage in the sub's oil tanks and the Britisher decides to blow her up and escape to Denmark.

One of the seamen remembers there is a port on a nearby Danish island where there may be a tanker in dock. Donning the uniform of a dead German airman, he lands on the island, finds a tanker and signals to his ship to come in shore. They refuel and return home, and only then discover they have sunk the German vessel they were after.

John Mills enacts the lieutenant with not only requisite dignity, but with a human touch. But it is Eric Portman, as the seaman, who has the outstanding role and scores best. Rest of the cast gives excellent performances, while direction and production are above par.

•

WEEK-END
(WEEKEND)
1968, 95 mins, France/Italy Ⓥ col
Dir Jean-Luc Godard ***Scr*** Jean-Luc Godard ***Ph*** Raoul Coutard ***Ed*** Agnes Guillemot
Act Mireille Darc, Jean Yanne, Jean-Pierre Kalfon, Valerie Lagrange, Paul Gegauff, Jean Eustache (Copernic/Ascot Cineraid)

No doubt about it, Jean-Luc Godard is still the "enfant terrible" of French films. For his third pic [shot in 1967,] he looks at the collective hysteria of weekend drivers. But he also laces it with his personalized symbols of the consumer world, the class battle, guerilla warfare, growing human violence, pettiness and meanness. It all adds up to a grating, disturbing, funny, witty, and controversial film package that just tackes too much but has enough plus aspects and sheer talent to make for the usual pros and cons.

The sharp and fluid color camera of Raoul Coutard is a help, together with the adroit editing. Godard also uses an established star, comely and lissome Mireille Darc, but shapes her in his own image and does away with her usual roles of the free-loving young woman.

First, she is seen confessing to a psychoanalyst, who might also be her lover, at home. The husband is calling a mistress and also sees some motorists outside fighting, after rubbing fenders. This sets the scene for a trip the couple take to see his dying father. On the road, there is a tremendous traffic jam that turns into what looks like the end of the world. But after this promising first part, pic turns into a series of adventures. They meet figures from the French Revolution and then they are captured by a gang of revolutionary hippie-beatniks.

Besides Darc, who is raped, attacked, beaten and smeared with mud throughout, Jean Yanne is right as her flippant, mean husband.

•

WEEKEND AT BERNIE'S
1989, 97 mins, US Ⓥ ⦿ col
Dir Ted Kotcheff ***Prod*** Victor Drai ***Scr*** Robert Klane ***Ph*** Francois Protat ***Ed*** Joan E. Chapman ***Mus*** Andy Summers ***Art*** Peter Jamison
Act Andrew McCarthy, Jonathan Silverman, Catherine Mary Stewart, Terry Kiser, Don Calfa, Catherine Parks (Gladden)

As shlepping-the-stiff pics go, *Weekend at Bernie's* ranks below the classic black comedy of *The Trouble with Harry* and *S.O.B.*, but there's enough farcical fun. Terry Kiser steals the show as the corpse hauled around by frantic Andrew McCarthy and Jonathan Silverman.

When Gotham insurance company go-getters McCarthy and Silverman show up for a weekend in the Hamptons with slimy boss Kiser, only to find him bumped off by the mob, it's a scream for a few minutes before the gags become repetitive.

Gross caricatures abound as Kiser's decadent party guests fail to notice their host is much more laid-back than usual. For reasons which are not made totally credible, the boys feel they have to keep Bernie's demise a secret from everyone, and only their hilarious attempts to get the stiff off the island put the film back on track.

Script comes up with the occasional outrageous invention, such as a scene in which Kiser's sex-crazed mistress engages him in strenuous lovemaking, causing McCarthy to lament that Bernie does better dead than he's been doing alive.

•

WEEKEND AT BERNIE'S II
1993, 90 mins, Italy/US Ⓥ ⦿ col
Dir Robert Klane ***Prod*** Victor Drai ***Scr*** Robert Klane ***Ph*** Edward Morry III ***Ed*** Peck Prior ***Mus*** Peter Wolf ***Art*** Michael Bolton
Act Andrew McCarthy, Jonathan Silverman, Terry Kiser, Tom Wright, Steve James, Troy Beyer (Artimm/Drai)

Hitching a routine rehash of the first installment's cavorting cadaver antics to a frantic hunt for the defunct's cash stash, writer-director Robert Klane delivers a mildly diverting farcical caper in *Weekend at Bernie's II*.

Story picks up ambitious insurance company stooges Andrew McCarthy and Jonathan Silverman, back in Gotham to check boss Bernie (Terry Kiser) into the morgue and return to work as heroes after uncovering his $2 million plunder. But instead of a promotion, they get fired, with company snoop Barry Bostwick tailing them to track down the missing loot.

Also after the cash are Kiser's mob cohorts, now in cahoots with a Virgin Islands voodoo queen. She dispatches a bumbling duo (Tom Wright and Steve James) to NY to resurrect Kiser and bring him back.

Plot complications are troweled on with varying degrees of plausibility, but serve mainly as a stage for Klane's endless succession of well-timed setups. But Klane pays scant attention to connecting scenes, which despite the affable mugging of McCarthy and Silverman, fail to keep things buoyant.

•

WEEKEND AT THE WALDORF
1945, 130 mins, US Ⓥ b/w
Dir Robert Z. Leonard ***Prod*** Arthur Hornblow, Jr. ***Scr*** Sam Spewack, Bella Spewack ***Ph*** Robert Planck ***Ed*** Robert J. Kern ***Mus*** Johnny Green ***Art*** Cedric Gibbons, Daniel B. Cathcart
Act Ginger Rogers, Lana Turner, Walter Pidgeon, Van Johnson, Edward Arnold, Keenan Wynn (M-G-M)

The origin of *Waldorf in Grand Hotel* is apparent from the start. In fact, with tongue-in-cheek one of the characters reprises a scene from the play based on the Vicki Baum novel, and Ginger Rogers recognizes it as being from *Grand Hotel*—and says so as part of the dialog.

Everything happens during this particular weekend at the famed Park Ave hostelry. Bob Benchley's scottie has pups; a benevolent tycoon lets a honeymooning couple utilize his apartment while he weekends in the country; Edward Arnold tries to gyp a visiting Egyptian bey; stenographer Lana Turner falls in love with the war-wounded Van Johnson; Phyllis Thaxter solves her own romance; Keenan Wynn, reporter, gets his scoop; and movie star Ginger Rogers and cynical war correspondent Walter Pidgeon find a throbbing romance.

Never a dull moment in this weekend. In between, Van Johnson lands a coast-to-coast plug for a pal's song from Xavier Cugat. The Starlight Roof puts on a little floor show that would do credit to the Roxy; Cugie acts sage and handles lines as well as his baton.

•

WEEKEND WITH KATE
1990, 95 mins, Australia Ⓥ col
Dir Arch Nicholson ***Prod*** Phillip Emanuel ***Scr*** Henry Tefay, Kee Young ***Ph*** Dan Burstall ***Ed*** Rose Evans ***Mus*** Bruce Rowland ***Art*** Larry Eastwood
Act Colin Friels, Catherine McClements, Jerome Ehlers, Helen Mutkins (Emanuel)

The well-constructed script indicates a knowledge of romantic comedies of another era. Setup has journalist turned rock music promoter Colin Friels torn between beautiful wife, Catherine McClements, who wants to have a baby, and his ambitious mistress, Helen Mutkins, who wants Friels. He decides to tell his wife he's leaving her during a weekend they plan to spend alone at her family's beach house. She has decided to use the intimacy of the weekend to get pregnant. Both plans go astray when British rock idol Jerome Ehlers arrives and moves in for a peaceful weekend of fishing.

The sexual adventures are exuberantly captured on screen. Dialog is sharp and witty, direction is brisk and well-timed, and performances are top notch. Friels is fine as the errant, ambitious husband, and is nicely contrasted with Ehlers as the lanky, self-centered rock star. McClements is a joy as Kate.

Principal photography was completed by spring 1989, with additional shooting taking place several months later to provide a new ending and bridging scenes.

•

WEE WILLIE WINKIE
1937, 105 mins, US Ⓥ b/w
Dir John Ford ***Prod*** Gene Markey ***Scr*** Julien Josephson ***Ph*** Arthur Miller ***Ed*** Walter Thompson ***Mus*** Alfred Newman
Act Shirley Temple, Victor McLaglen, C. Aubrey Smith, June Lang, Michael Whalen, Cesar Romero (20th Century-Fox)

Shirley Temple is growing up to be a big little girl. The dimple in the cheek is still there but those knees are losing their contour.

Darryl Zanuck and 20th-Fox recognized the need of transition. Temple is surrounded but not submerged by Academy prizewinners. She comes up smiling through her tears.

The Rudyard Kipling story is an adventure yarn about a young American widow and her daughter who journey to India and the paternal protection of the child's grandfather, a colonel of a Highland regiment stationed on the frontier. The menace of native insurrection and massacre provides melodramatic suspense.

When open warfare is threatened, the little girl on a peace-pleading mission is delivered into enemy hands. She is the means of reconciling the two factions.

Victor McLaglen as a tough segeant-major creates a splendid characterization of a vigorous warrior whose heart is softened when he becomes the friend and guide of Shirley.

•

WEIGHT OF WATER, THE
2000, 113 mins, US ⦿ ▭ col
Dir Kathryn Bigelow ***Prod*** Janet Yang, Sigurjon Sighvatsson, A. Kitman Ho ***Scr*** Alice Arlen, Christopher Kyle ***Ph*** Adrian Biddle ***Ed*** Howard E. Smith ***Mus*** David Hirschfelder ***Art*** Karl Juliusson
Act Catherine McCormack, Sarah Polley, Sean Penn, Josh Lucas, Elizabeth Hurley, Katrin Cartlidge, Vinessa Shaw (Manifest/Palomar/Miracle)

Artistically speaking, Kathryn Bigelow's first film in five years is her richest, most ambitious and personal work to date. Boasting a multilayered narrative, this psychological thriller [from the novel by Anita Shreve] interweaves a contempo tale of a marriage breakdown with the story of a brutal double murder in 1873. Pic benefits from a superlative femme-centered cast, headed by Sarah Polley and Catherine McCormack.

At the center of *Weight of Water* are five riveting women, each struggling in her own way with sexual politics and personal identity. Loosely based on a true case, the story begins with a court trial in which Louis Wagner (Ciaran Hinds) is accused of murdering two Norwegian immigrants with an ax. Identified by Maren Hontvedt (Polley) as the murderer, Wagner is sentenced to death.

Cut to a modern-day setting that introduces Jean (McCormack), a photographer who arrives on Smuttynose Island, off the coast of New Hampshire, to research the century-old crime. Jean is accompanied by her poet husband Thomas (Sean Penn), his handsome brother (Josh Lucas) and the latter's sexy girlfriend, Adaline (Elizabeth Hurley).

Deeply immersing herself in the case's details to the point of obsession, Jean finds herself undergoing a precarious emotional journey that shakes the very foundation of her marriage and her life. Her suspicion that Thomas is having an affair with the alluring Adaline burgeons into jealousy and distrust, setting in motion a series of crises with horrific consequences.

Both the period and modern tales are imbued with suspense, benefiting from Bigelow's penchant for creating a visual sense of menace and an atmosphere of fear. The earlier tale, replete with Freudian psychology in relating the women's repression, jealousy and rage, suffers from being overly explicit, spelling out every element and emotion. In contrast, the modern tale is more ambiguous and subtle, relying less on dialogue than looks and gestures.

•

WEIRD SCIENCE

1985, 94 mins, US Ⓥ ⊙ col

Dir John Hughes ***Prod*** Joel Silver ***Scr*** John Hughes ***Ph*** Matthew F. Leonetti ***Ed*** Mark Warner, Christopher Lebenzon, Scott Wallace ***Mus*** Ira Newborn ***Art*** John W. Corso

Act Anthony Michael Hall, Kelly Le Brock, Ilan Mitchell-Smith, Bill Paxton, Suzanne Snyder, Robert Downey, Jr. (Universal)

Starting with the delectable premise of two high school nerds who create a woman through some inexplicable computer hocus-pocus, *Weird Science* veers off into a typical coming-of-age saga without exploring any of the psychological territory it lightly sails over in the early going.

Helplessly horny chums Gary (Anthony Michael Hall) and Wyatt (Ilan Mitchell-Smith), in an act of creative frustration, put their brains together and create the answer to their fantasies—the beautiful and very available Lisa (Kelly Le Brock). The trouble is the boys hardly use her.

Although clearly not grounded in reality, the film really goes nowhere with its central conceit, opting instead for a more ordinary approach. Director John Hughes never capitalizes on the idea that Lisa is a creation of 15-year-old psyches or examines the intriguing question of who controls whom in this relationship.

Hughes's true gift is at capturing the naturalistic rhythms and interaction between the boys with a great ear for dialog. Le Brock is just right as the film's calm but commanding center.

•

WELCOME HOME

1989, 87 mins, US Ⓥ col

Dir Franklin J. Schaffner ***Prod*** Martin Ransohoff ***Scr*** Maggie Kleinman ***Ph*** Fred J. Koenekamp ***Ed*** Bob Swink ***Mus*** [uncredited] ***Art*** Dan Yarhi

Act Kris Kristofferson, JoBeth Williams, Brian Keith, Sam Waterston, Trey Wilson, Thomas Wilson Brown (Columbia/Rank)

A fine opportunity to explore the emotional conflict and military-political hush-hush regarding the unexpected reappearance of U.S. soldiers recorded as dead in Vietnam and Cambodia is missed almost totally in Franklin J. Schaffner's *Welcome Home*.

Kris Kristofferson looks suitably haggard and tired as Lt. Jake Robbins, who returns to Vermont after 17 years in Cambodia. He was shot down there and put in POW camp. Jake later settled down to married village life with Cambodian Leang (Kieu Chinh Nguyen) who bore him two children. It is not until he wakes up in a New York State Air Force hospital that Jake remembers that he had just married his American sweetheart, Sarah (mournfully played by JoBeth Williams), before he set out on his Far East tour of duty. He is told that she is now remarried and lives happily in Vermont with her second husband (Sam Waterston) and 17-year-old son (Thomas Wilson Brown), who is actually Jake's.

Jake, however, feels he must at least see his son, so he bungles on to the Vermont scene where he upsets everybody.

An uninspired screenplay does not help Schaffner in making the film move forward more than sluggishly. The plot flounders is shallow waters.

•

WELCOME HOME ROXY CARMICHAEL

1990, 98 mins, US Ⓥ ⊙ col

Dir Jim Abrahams ***Prod*** Penney Finkelman Cox ***Scr*** Karen Leigh Hopkins ***Ph*** Paul Elliott ***Ed*** Bruce Green ***Mus*** Thomas Newman ***Art*** Dena Roth

Act Winona Ryder, Jeff Daniels, Laila Robins, Thomas Wilson Brown, Joan McMurtrey, Frances Fisher (ITC)

Fans of Winona Ryder will definitely want to catch her in an offbeat role as the town rebel in this teen-oriented small-town saga; unfortunately, the rest of the production doesn't quite match up.

Ryder plays 15-year-old Dinky Bossetti, a moody, glowering misfit who scribbles poetry, wears baggy black clothes and doesn't comb her hair. Her nowhereville hometown of Clyde, OH, is all in a dither about the impending return of legendary local Roxy Carmichael, and Dinky, being adopted, decides that Roxy must have been her real mother.

Also certain that Roxy is coming back for him is Jeff Daniels as Denton, formerly the teenaged boyfriend with whom she had a baby, now a married man with a family. As all gossip turns to Roxy and her precocious local deeds, Denton's wife (Joan McMurtrey) gets fed up with the situation and leaves him.

Meanwhile the socially reviled Dinky is being pursued by a nerdy guidance counselor who wants to put her in a school for misfits, and a rather blank-slated surfer-looking dude (Thomas Wilson Brown) who wants to be her boyfriend.

Ryder's performance has a subtle glow and maturity that mesmerizes. Her keenly observed creation of the spooky, androgynous Dinky, with her low voice and deadpan delivery, injects her scenes with a natural comedy far more satisfying than the more hysterical efforts being made around her.

•

WELCOME TO BLOOD CITY

1977, 96 mins, UK/Canada Ⓥ col

Dir Peter Sasdy ***Prod*** Marilyn Stonehouse ***Scr*** Stephen Schneck, Michael Winder ***Ph*** Reginald Morris C.S.C. ***Ed*** Keith Palmer ***Mus*** Roy Budd ***Art*** Tony Hall

Act Jack Palance, Keir Dullea, Samantha Eggar, Barry Morse, Hollis McLaren, Chris Wiggins (EMI/Herberman)

An anonymous totalitarian organization kidnaps Keir Dullea. Via computer electronics, he is mentally transported to a fantasized oater settlement (Blood City) where a person's status accrues according to the number of people he/she can murder. Sheriff Jack Palance is classified as Immortal, having 20 killings to his score.

Dullea's progress through the city is monitored by program technicians Samantha Eggar (who also inexplicably lives in Blood City) and John Evans.

Although the film's initial conception may have held traces of intelligence, Swiss-cheese script strains coherence and interest with each development. Consequently, neither in their interdependence or individuality do the film's sci-fi or western elements emerge as generically satisfying.

•

WELCOME TO HARD TIMES

1967, 103 mins, US col

Dir Burt Kennedy ***Prod*** Max E. Youngstein, David Karr ***Scr*** Burt Kennedy ***Ph*** Harry Stradling, Jr. ***Ed*** Aaron Stell ***Mus*** Harry Sukman ***Art*** George W. Davis, Carl Anderson

Act Henry Fonda, Janice Rule, Keenan Wynn, Janis Paige, Warren Oates, Fay Spain (M-G-M)

Welcome to Hard Times is more than an oater title; it is a pretty fair evaluation of this production. Burt Kennedy's direction is as inept as his script, an adaptation of E. L. Doctorow's novel about sadistic tough Aldo Ray who burns down a western town. Cowardly (or is he?) mayor Henry Fonda inspires town to rebuild.

Janice Rule is unsatisfactory as the woman who taunts Fonda for a whole year, then cues a bloody climax. She plays it with an Irish accent, effect being a sort of Method school version of Maureen O'Hara.

Keenan Wynn, with wife Janis Paige and three saloon babes, offer some low comedy relief. Edgar Buchanan comes off best as a territorial officer. Presence of many pro names—Lon Chaney, Elisha Cook, Paul Fix, etc.—only serves to emphasize the lack of depth and perception in script and direction.

•

WELCOME TO L.A.

1976, 103 mins, US Ⓥ col

Dir Alan Rudolph ***Prod*** Robert Altman ***Scr*** Alan Rudolph ***Ph*** Dave Myers ***Ed*** William A. Sawyer, Tom Walls ***Mus*** Richard Baskin

Act Keith Carradine, Sally Kellerman, Geraldine Chaplin, Harvey Keitel, Lauren Hutton, Viveca Lindfors (United Artists)

The banal point of *Welcome to L.A.* is pretty much summed up in the closing song by Richard Baskin, in which Keith Carradine sings of the city "where the air is thick and yellow with the stale taste of decay."

The film has a studied, calculated, over-designed look that drains the vitality from the cast as director Alan Rudolph puts them through their predictable paces in a *Nashville*-like amorphous story which has something to do with the music industry.

Welcome to L.A. has lots of aimless driving around town, gloomy sex encounters, mumbled dialog, and showy camera movements.

Carradine sings a few songs, guzzles booze without feeling it, and exerts a mysterious attraction on every woman in sight.

•

WELCOME TO SARAJEVO

1997, 101 mins, UK/US Ⓥ ⊙ ▭ col

Dir Michael Winterbottom ***Prod*** Graham Broadbent, Damian Jones ***Scr*** Frank Cottrell Boyce ***Ph*** Daf Hobson ***Ed*** Trevor Waite ***Mus*** Adrian Johnston ***Art*** Mark Geraghty

Act Stephen Dillane, Woody Harrelson, Marisa Tomei, Emira Nusevic, Kerry Fox, Emily Lloyd (Dragon Pictures/Channel 4/Miramax)

Like a Sidewinder missile, *Welcome to Sarajevo* creeps up on you when you're least expecting it. Seen through the eyes of a cool British war journo who becomes emotionally attached to his subject, this multilayered portrait of a city that miraculously keeps going, even with both hands tied behind its back, hits a whole range of emotional buttons.

Based on the chronicled experiences [in the book *Natasha's Story*] of ITN reporter Michael Nicholson, this is clearly a movie by British filmmakers, in which much is left unsaid and unshown rather than ladled across the screen in large helpings. The city itself is an active participant in the drama, and it's the revival of its communal soul that pic celebrates at the end.

On the periphery are Flynn (Woody Harrelson), a spaced-out U.S. TV journalist who's more famous than the news he's covering, and Annie (Emily Lloyd), a freelancer covering her first war. At the center is hot-spot hotshot Michael Henderson (Stephen Dillane) and his team: cameraman Gregg (James Nesbitt), producer Jane (Kiwi actress Kerry Fox) and their local driver (Croat actor Goran Visnjic).

In the course of a routine news hunt, Henderson and company happen on an orphanage near the front lines. Henderson becomes obsessed with the story of the orphanage, and makes plans to take one of the children, Emira (Emira Nusevic), illegally back to England, with the help of an American aid worker (Marisa Tomei).

The film's persistent skimming from one vantage point to another, with no dominant dramatic line until midway through, will unsettle audiences expecting something on which to hook their emotions over the long term. But the movie unquestionably delivers in its final half-hour and especially during Henderson's return to Sarajevo.

The $9 million film, which also used locations in Croatia and Macedonia, shot in the summer of 1996, only a few months after the January cease-fire.

•

WELCOME TO THE DOLLHOUSE

1995, 87 mins, US Ⓥ col

Dir Todd Solondz ***Prod*** Ted Skillman, Todd Solondz ***Scr*** Todd Solondz ***Ph*** Randy Drummond, Gabor Szitanyi ***Ed*** Alan Oxman ***Mus*** Jill Wisoff ***Art*** Susan Block

Act Heather Matarazzo, Darina Kalinina, Matthew Faber, Angela Pietropinto, Bill Buell, Brendan Sexton, Jr. (Suburban)

Since few people saw or even heard about Todd Solondz's first feature, the 1989 *Fear, Anxiety and Depression*, his impressive sophomore effort, *Welcome to the Dollhouse*, will effectively count as his real entry into the movie world, a stark, often funny and always poignant comedy about how to survive junior high school and life in the 'burbs. The protagonist is 11-year-old Dawn Wiener (Heather Matarazzo), the middle child of a Jewish family in suburban New Jersey. Life is one continuous struggle for the unattractive, slump-shouldered girl, who wears thick glasses and the tackiest clothes.

As a seventh-grader in Benjamin Franklin Junior High, Dawn is tortured and humiliated by both the boys and girls of her class. Her little sister, Missy (Daria Kalinina), a ballerina who's always dressed in a pink tutu, is clearly her mother's favorite, and she also suffers in comparison to her older brother, Mark (Matthew Faber), a computer whiz who has his own garage band.

Solondz explores an idea that is seldom depicted in American films—i.e., that parents are expected to but might not really love their children equally. He also shows that sisters can actually hate each other with passion.

The narrative unfolds as a catalog of Dawn's (mis)adventures and mishaps, and every creepy detail encountered by children in this difficult transitional phase is conveyed with stark accuracy. Shot in West Caldwell, NJ, the production has an alert intelligence.

•

WE LIVE AGAIN

1934, 85 mins, US b/w

Dir Rouben Mamoulian ***Prod*** Samuel Goldwyn ***Scr*** Maxwell Anderson, Leonard Praskins, Preston Sturges ***Ph*** Gregg Toland ***Ed*** Otho Lovering ***Mus*** Alfred Newman (dir.) ***Art*** Richard Day, Sergei Soudeikin

Act Anna Sten, Fredric March, Jane Baxter, C. Aubrey Fish, Sam Jaffe, Jessie Ralph (Goldwyn)

We Live Again is a fine, artistic production which further impresses Anna Sten as a celluloid satellite, vividly displaying her histrionic talents, with Fredric March equally effective. It is Tolstoy's *Resurrection* beautifully re-created in dialog and endowed with lavish Goldwynesque artistry.

The film itself opens almost as a scenic, showing the peasants tilling the soil for benefit of a tyrannical nobility, and winds up something of a spec, with the orgy of secular splendor at the 8–10 minute Easter service and the extra-curricular maneuvers between the student officers and the ballerinas from the czar's subsidized ballet.

The nobleman March portrays is well depicted to illustrate how the youth's natural instincts are sated by power and pleasure to the degree that he betrays the peasant girl (Sten) with whom he had been reared in equal companship.

March's resurrection and regeneration is handled with unusual restraint. Director Rouben Mamoulian has held him in fine check, at the same time not sacrificing Sten. Her blonde beauty is enhanced by a highly effective native histrionism which the camera angles and the lighting further emphasize.

•

WELL, THE

1951, 84 mins, US Ⓥ b/w

Dir Russell Rouse, Clarence Greene ***Prod*** Harry M. Popkin ***Scr*** Clarence Greene, Russell Rouse ***Ph*** Ernest Laszlo ***Ed*** Chester Schaeffer ***Mus*** Dimitri Tiomkin

Act Richard Rober, Gwendolyn Laster, Maidie Normon, George Hamilton, Ernest Anderson, Dick Simmons (Popkin/United Artists)

High drama and suspense are embodied strongly in this production. Writers took the [true-life] Kathy Fiscus episode, in which a California child was trapped in an old well, and used this as a story hook for a tense and gripping screenplay. For purposes of drama, they have made this key character a Negro child, and added the Negro problem in build-up of plot. It's unusually well handled.

Plot has for its motivation the measures taken by Negro populace of a small town, after a white man comes under suspicion of having kidnapped the girl.

Considerable editing during the early rescue sequences would speed action and lift interest, which is pretty static here, but in the main production is progressively suspenseful.

Cast, headed by Richard Rober, as sheriff in charge of settling threatened mob violence and rescue of the child, is uniformly strong.

•

WE'LL SMILE AGAIN

1942, 93 mins, UK b/w

Dir John Baxter ***Prod*** John Baxter ***Scr*** Bud Flanagan, Austin Melford, Barbara Emary ***Ph*** James Wilson, Arthur Grant ***Mus*** Kennedy Russell

Act Bud Flanagan, Chesney Allen, Phyllis Stanley, Peggy Dexter (British National)

Anglo-American Film Corp "announces proudly that no expense has been spared to save money on this production." With that nifty this Flanagan and Allen starring vehicle opens with a bellylaugh, forerunner of plenty more during the 93 minutes these erstwhile members of the Crazy Gang do their stuff against a background of Nazi spies at work in a British film studio.

The chief fault is in the mis-casting of the two principal females. Phyllis Stanley, as a film star and a leader of the spy gang, is not only almost a head taller than Chesney Allen but she has a poor singing voice, cannot dance, and is sadly lacking in the required glamor. As Googie, an extra girl supposed to have what it takes, Peggy Dexter acts much too much like an extra suddenly shoved into a part worthy of a Barbara Stanwyck.

•

WENT THE DAY WELL? *(US: 48 HOURS)*

1942, 93 mins, UK b/w

Dir Alberto Cavalcanti ***Prod*** Michael Balcon ***Scr*** John Dighton, Diana Morgan, Angus MacPhail ***Ph*** Wilkie Cooper ***Ed*** Sidney Cole ***Mus*** William Walton ***Art*** Tom Morahan

Act Leslie Banks, Basil Sydney, Frank Lawton, Elizabeth Allan, Valerie Taylor, John Slater (Ealing)

This Ealing Studios tale [from a story by Graham Greene] of 72 hours of the life of Bramley End, a tiny hamlet in the heart of the English countryside, is introduced by an old grave-digger playing straight into the camera. Dealing with an attempt at an airborne invasion of a sparsely peopled part of England, as contrasted with the well-defended key cities, this picture achieves considerable interest.

Settings, exterior and interior, smack of the real thing, from the 13th-century church to the village grocery whose proprietress is also postmistress and telephone exchange operator.

Direction by Alberto Cavalcanti is workmanlike, but to the men of the Gloucestershire Regiment (cast as both German invaders and members of the local Home Guard) must go chief credit for the realistic note underlying the film, which is almost as factual as a propaganda short.

•

WE OF THE NEVER NEVER

1982, 136 mins, Australia Ⓥ ▭ col

Dir Igor Auzins ***Prod*** Greg Tepper ***Scr*** Peter Schreck ***Ph*** Gary Hansen ***Ed*** Clifford Hayes ***Mus*** Peter Best ***Art*** Josephine Ford

Act Angela Punch McGregor, Arthur Dignam, Tony Barry, Tommy Lewis, Lewis Fitz-Gerald, Martin Vaughan (Adams Packer/FCWA)

We of the Never Never is a stirring historical drama which explores a number of themes—racism, women's emancipation, and man's struggle to come to terms with an alien environment.

Pic is hindered, although not severely, by the casting of Arthur Dignam in the lead role. He lacks the authority and ruggedness to be credible as a turn-of-the-century explorer and adventurer who can run a 4,000-acre cattle station and control unruly stockmen and nomadic Aborigines. Compensating for that weakness is the topline performance of Angela Punch McGregor, an actress with a commanding presence.

Based on a classic Australian novel [by Mrs Aeneas Gunn], film concerns a 30-year-old city-bred woman, Jeannie, who is forced to make the transition from civilized Melbourne to the barren outback of the Northern Territory when she marries station owner Aeneas Gunn.

Director Igor Auzins, helming only his second feature, has created a big, bold and magnificently scenic picture. Gary Hansen's photography eloquently captures the paradoxical beauty and harshness of the outback.

•

WE'RE BACK!: A DINOSAUR'S STORY

1993, 72 mins, US Ⓥ ⦿ col

Dir Dick Zondag, Ralph Zondag, Phil Nibbelink, Simon Wells ***Prod*** Stephen Hickner ***Scr*** John Patrick Shanley ***Ed*** Sim Evan-Jones, Nick Fletcher ***Mus*** James Horner ***Art*** Neil Ross (Amblin/Universal)

In spite of narrative problems in this adaptation of the children's book by Hudson Talbott, the film's chief appeal is its central conceit—that giant prehistoric monsters can be transformed into intelligent, talking tourists who like to play with children. (*Jurassic Park* is even plugged on a marquee as the lumbering creatures pass by.)

The source of this miracle is a special cereal invented by Captain NewEyes (voice of Walter Cronkite), who brings Rex (John Goodman) and his friends to New York so that children who want to see a real dinosaur can have their wish come true. Problems ensue when the addled Dr. Bleeb (Julia Child) fails to meet them and they instead are trapped by the Captain's evil brother, Professor ScrewEyes (Kenneth Mars).

Film gets off to a slow start, first with a framing story and then the back story of how the dinosaurs make it to New York. Eventually things click, especially in the film's best sequence, in which the dinosaurs pretend to be floats in Macy's Thanksgiving Day Parade.

The animation is a bravura mix of traditional cel animation and computer-generated material.

•

WE'RE NO ANGELS

1955, 105 mins, US Ⓥ ⦿ ▭ col

Dir Michael Curtiz ***Prod*** Pat Duggan ***Scr*** Ranald MacDougall ***Ph*** Loyal Griggs ***Ed*** Arthur Schmidt ***Mus*** Frederick Hollander ***Art*** Hal Pereira, Roland Anderson

Act Humphrey Bogart, Aldo Ray, Peter Ustinov, Joan Bennett, Basil Rathbone, Leo G. Carroll (Paramount)

Paramount has fashioned a breezy 105-minute VistaVision feature. Light antics swing around three convicts of Devil's Island who find themselves playing Santa Claus to a family they came to rob.

At times proceedings are too consciously cute and stage origin of material [a play by Albert Husson] still clings since virtually all scenes are interiors with characters constantly entering and exiting. However, Michael Curtiz's directorial pacing and topflight performances from Humphrey Bogart, Aldo Ray and Peter Ustinov help minimize the few flaws.

Screenplay uses great deal of conversation, mostly amusingly flavored, to tell how convicts descend on store-home operated by Leo G. Carroll and his wife (Joan Bennett), planning robbery that would finance journey to France. Trio, all lifers, Bogart for forgery, others for murder, find family in difficulties unbecoming Christmas Eve spirit.

•

WE'RE NO ANGELS

1989, 108 mins, US Ⓥ ⦿ col

Dir Neil Jordan ***Prod*** Art Linson ***Scr*** David Mamet ***Ph*** Philippe Rousselot ***Ed*** Mick Audsley, Jake van Wijk ***Mus*** George Fenton ***Art*** Wolf Kroeger

Act Robert De Niro, Sean Penn, Demi Moore, Wallace Shawn, Ray McAnally, James Russo (Paramount)

Described by its producer as "very loosely based on some of the ideas" in the eponymous 1955 movie about convicts on the lam, *We're No Angels* is precisely about a pair of jailbirds on the run. The year is 1935 and Robert De Niro and Sean Penn are hard-timers in a hellish north country penitentiary that may be a metaphor for Depression-era America.

The late, great Ray McAnally, reduced here to a caricature of cruelty as the Big House warden, forces the heroes to witness the electocution of a remorseless murderer. But the condemned con and two heroes pull an improbable breakout and head for the Canadian border.

De Niro and Penn reach a remote border town renowned for a shrine of "the weeping Madonna" and a monastery. The town is swarming with police on their trail, but the cons are happily mistaken for visiting ecclesiastical scholars. Director Neil Jordan and screenwriter David Mamet thus set the stage for a parable about virtue, wisdom, faith and redemption.

Pug-faced, slack-jawed and marble-mouthed, De Niro and Penn mug their semiarticulate proles with relish, but as religioso fish out of water their con game becomes a tiresome joke.

•

WE'RE NOT DRESSING

1934, 80 mins, US b/w

Dir Norman Taurog ***Prod*** Benjamin Glazer ***Scr*** Horace Jackson, Francis Martin, George Marion, Jr. ***Ph*** Charles Lang

Act Bing Crosby, Carole Lombard, George Burns, Gracie Allen, Ethel Merman, Leon Errol (Paramount)

We're Not Dressing in plot is an unofficial remake of Par's *Male and Female* (nee James Barrie's *The Admirable Crichton*). Where it's light and familiar on the story it's heavy on sturdy croonology by Bing Crosby, who makes the footage a vocal delight. There's also no small amount of comedy via the combined efforts of Burns and Allen, Leon Errol and a comedy bear that motivates the action.

Plot is one of those familiar patterns of the fabulously rich heiress on whose yacht Bing is a gob. His particular chore is to exercise the furry pet of the femme owner. Comes the wreck and strangely enough none of the crew survives but this particular sailor (Crosby), although somehow all the less expert passengers—Carole Lombard, Errol, that clown princeling pair, and Ethel Merman—manage to reach shore safely. Burns and Allen are introduced as a botanical explorer and his wife who thinks flora and fauna are a vaudeville team. The Crichton stuff naturally fast asserts itself, with the gob alone knowing how to wrest food and comforts from the natural sources, thus making the proud heiress capitulate.

Mack Gordon and Harry Revel do a notably good job of the songs, in that they're patterned to conform with the plot action.

Lombard is negligible and not impressive opposite Crosby. She is eclipsed in the femme division both by Allen and Merman, latter working with Errol.

•

WES CRAVEN'S NEW NIGHTMARE

1994, 112 mins, US Ⓥ ⦿ col

Dir Wes Craven ***Prod*** Marianne Maddalena ***Scr*** Wes Craven ***Ph*** Mark Irwin ***Ed*** Patrick Lussier ***Mus*** J. Peter Robinson ***Art*** Cynthia Charette

Act Robert Englund, Heather Langenkamp, Miko Hughes, David Newsom, Tracy Middendorf, John Saxon (New Line)

Freddy Krueger is alive and well and raising hell one more time in *Wes Craven's New Nightmare*, an ingeniously conceived and devilishly clever opus that proves *Freddy's Dead* wasn't so aptly named after all.

Craven's audacious conceit is that his first *Nightmare* (1984) and the five sequels were works of fiction that inadvertently summoned, and briefly contained, a real supernaturally evil force. After Krueger was decisively killed in the series' finale, the evil force was freed to wreak havoc on an unsuspecting world. For that reason, Craven explains while playing himself in the pic's most darkly comical sequence, he simply *must* make another *Nightmare* pic.

Heather Langenkamp, star of the first *Nightmare*, returns to star as Heather Langenkamp, an actress who has a devoted cult following for her performance in *Nightmare on Elm Street*. She's still on good terms with her *Nightmare* sequel, despite lucrative offers made by real-life New Line Cinema exec Robert Shaye and producer Sara Risher.

Unfortunately, even though she wants no part of another Freddy pic, Freddy just won't stay out of her life. And her dreams. When Langenkamp seeks help from Craven, the writer/director admits he is transforming those nightmares into a new script.

Englund once again is in bravura form as Freddy, playing as much for nasty laughs as unnerving shocks. Langenkamp proves she is still one of cinema's most resourceful scream queens.

●

WEST 11

1963, 93 mins, UK b/w

Dir Michael Winner ***Prod*** Daniel M. Angel ***Scr*** Keith Waterhouse, Willis Hall ***Ph*** Otto Heller ***Ed*** Bernard Gribble ***Mus*** Stanley Black, Acker Bilk

Act Alfred Lynch, Kathleen Breck, Eric Portman, Diana Dors, Harold Lang (Associated-British)

The writing team of Keith Waterhouse and Willis Hall have done little to uplift this adaptation of a novel called *The Furnished Room*.

This is only hackneyed drama about a young man (Alfred Lynch) who is a layabout, a misfit, a self-pitier ("I'm an emotional leer," he says, profoundly). He gets involved with chicks, can't keep a job and gets mixed up with jazz clubs and seedy parties. Turning point in his life is when he meets up with Richard Dyce (Eric Portman), an ex-army con-man. He is talked into an association with Portman, who wants his aunt bumped off.

It has its merits. The sleazy London locations are very authentically shown. Perhaps too authentically. Lynch is an intelligent actor but, in this instance, he fails to induce any pity. Probably the fault of the script. Kathleen Breck, his girlfriend, copes reasonably. It's her first film part after a small experience in stock.

●

WESTERNER, THE

1940, 97 mins, US Ⓥ ⦿ b/w

Dir William Wyler ***Prod*** Samuel Goldwyn ***Scr*** Jo Swerling, Niven Busch ***Ph*** Gregg Toland ***Ed*** Daniel Mandell ***Mus*** Dimitri Tiomkin ***Art*** James Basevi

Act Gary Cooper, Walter Brennan, Doris Davenport, Fred Stone, Forrest Tucker, Lillian Bond (Goldwyn/United Artists)

Although Gary Cooper is starred, Walter Brennan commands major attention with a slick characterization of Judge Roy Bean, the dispenser of law at Vinegaroon—west of the Pecos. Supplied with a particularly meaty role, of which he takes fullest advantage, Brennan turns in a socko job that does much to hold together a not too impressive script. The story [by Stuart N. Lake], of cattlemen's resentment against the migration of settlers to Texas in the post–Civil War days, is a rather familiar one cinematically. But producer Samuel Goldwyn has invested his version with plenty of production assets—good cast topped by Cooper; extended shooting schedule under direction of William Wyler; and eye-filling scenic backgrounds that are accentuated by expert photography.

Cooper is a wandering cowhand charged with horse-stealing who comes before the two-gun judge, and convicted by the jury that brings in verdicts according to the ideas of Brennan. But the latter is a worshipper of actress Lily Langtry, and when Cooper professes intimate acquaintance with the lady, sentence is suspended while the judge gets some anecdotes about the beauteous "Jersey Lily."

A strange friendship develops between the cantankerous old judge and the cowboy. In the midst of the battle between the homesteaders and the cattlemen, Cooper mediates the trouble by convincing the judge to declare peace between the factions. Then Cooper falls in love with Doris Davenport, daughter of a rancher, to cement him closer to the settlers.

Cooper provides a satisfactory portrayal of the roaming westerner, although he has handled the same type of role many times. Davenport, a newcomer from the extra field, delivers satisfactorily as the rancher's daughter.

1940: Best Supp. Actor (Walter Brennan)

NOMINATIONS: Best Original Story, B&W Art Direction

●

WESTERN UNION

1941, 93 mins, US Ⓥ col

Dir Fritz Lang ***Prod*** Harry Joe Brown ***Scr*** Robert Carson ***Ph*** Edward Cronjager ***Ed*** Robert Bischoff ***Mus*** David Buttolph

Act Robert Young, Randolph Scott, Dean Jagger, Virginia Gilmore, Barton MacLane, John Carradine (20th Century-Fox)

Western Union is another epic of the early American frontier. This time the stringing of telephone lines in the 1860s, between Omaha and Salt Lake City, provides the background for adventures and excitement in empire building. Hewing to a straight line in telling the story of pioneering the west, *Western Union* is a lusty and actionful offering. Mounted with expansiveness as a super-western of upper-budget proportions, the picture displays some eyeful exterior panoramas. The tinting photography has some of the finest outdoor scenes which were photographed in the colorful Utah park country.

Randolph Scott, an ex-outlaw who joins the expedition as a scout, turns in a strongly persuasive characterization. Dean Jagger is the company engineer in charge of construction; Robert Young a dudish easterner who toughens up under western ways; and Barton MacLane is the renegade outlaw whose band continually harasses the camp. Virginia Gilmore is minor as the romantic interest for conflict between Scott and Young in the early reels.

●

WEST OF ZANZIBAR

1928, 70 mins, US b/w

Dir Tod Browning ***Scr*** Elliott Clawson, Waldemar Young ***Ph*** Percy Hilburn ***Ed*** Harry Reynolds ***Art*** Cedric Gibbons

Act Lon Chaney, Lionel Barrymore, Warner Baxter, Mary Nolan, Jane Daly, Roscoe Ward (M-G-M)

West of Zanzibar will satisfy Lon Chaney fans who like their color regardless of the way it is daubed.

Lionel Barrymore captures the magician's bride, just after Chaney has subtitled his affection for her. The latter part is dully played and given scant meaning. She passes out of the picture too soon thereafter for the magician to believe that the competition is the kid's dad.

Then, for no particular reason, the action is transferred to another world. Chaney, too hurriedly, is shown as an ivory robber and just as mysteriously Barrymore suddenly develops to have quit the stage and become a white trader in Africa.

With the same unexplainable rapidity, Chaney is revealed to have started his revenge by training the babe in the ways of tropical fleshpots. Mary Nolan as the grown daughter does not make the matriculation of a prostitute any too vivid. Rather, a blonde saint in Chaney's eerie jungle den is the reaction. Jungle scenes with crocodiles oozing through slime and a score or so of vaselined black extras doing their dances and attending to their funeral pyres are what get this by.

●

WEST POINT STORY, THE
(UK: FINE AND DANDY)

1950, 106 mins, US b/w

Dir Roy Del Ruth ***Prod*** Louis F. Edelman ***Scr*** John Monks, Jr., Charles Hoffmann, Irving Wallace ***Ph*** Sid Hickox ***Ed*** Owen Marks ***Mus*** Ray Heindorf (dir.)

Act James Cagney, Virginia Mayo, Doris Day, Gordon MacRae, Gene Nelson, Alan Hale, Jr. (Warner)

Fresh treatment and new twists to the musical formula make *The West Point Story* worthwhile entertainment.

James Cagney sparkplugs the fun and frolic among a group of players who press him hard for top honors. Another big assist in putting this one over is Virginia Mayo. She bolsters the comedy and wallops the eyes with her array of s.a.

There are several production numbers in keeping with the cadet background of the story.

The story has Cagney as a brash Broadway director down on his luck who accepts the assignment to stage the annual West Point show, "100th Night." Gordon MacRae, a cadet, wrote the show's book and tunes, and his producer uncle wants it and the young man for a Broadway staging.

1950: NOMINATION: Best Score of a Musical Picture

●

WEST SIDE STORY

1961, 153 mins, US Ⓥ ⦿ ▭ col

Dir Robert Wise, Jerome Robbins ***Prod*** Robert Wise ***Scr*** Ernest Lehman ***Ph*** Daniel L. Fapp ***Ed*** Thomas Stanford ***Mus*** Johnny Green (dir.) ***Art*** Boris Leven

Act Natalie Wood, Richard Beymer, Russ Tamblyn, Rita Moreno, George Chakiris, Simon Oakland (Mirisch/Beta)

West Side Story is a beautifully mounted, impressive, emotion-ridden and violent musical. This powerful and sometimes fascinating translation of the [1957] Broadway musical is said to have cost $6 million.

The Romeo and Juliet theme, propounded against the seething background of rival Puerto Rican and American gangs (repping the Montagues and the Capulets) on the Upper West Side of Manhattan, makes for both a savage and tender admixture of romance and war-to-the-death.

Even more notable, however, is the music of Leonard Bernstein and most of all the breathtaking choreography of Jerome Robbins. Bernstein's score, with Stephen Sondheim's expressive lyrics, accentuates the tenseness that constantly builds.

Ernest Lehman's screenplay, based upon Arthur Laurents's solid and compelling book in the Broadway production, is a faithful adaptation in which he reflects the brutality of the juve gangs which vent upon each other the hatred they feel against the world. Plottage focuses on the romance of a young Puerto Rican girl with a mainland boy, which fans the enmity between the two gangs and ultimately leads to the "rumble" which leaves both gang leaders dead of knife wounds.

Natalie Wood offers an entrancing performance as the Puerto Rican who falls in love with Richard Beymer, forbidden by strict neighborhood ban against group intermingling, and latter impresses with his singing. Most colorful performance, perhaps, is by George Chakiris, leader of Puerto Rican gang the Sharks, and brother of femme lead, who appeared in London company in same role portrayed here by Russ Tamblyn, leader of the white Jets gang. Tamblyn socks over his portrayal and scores particularly with his acrobatic terping. Rita Moreno, in love with Chakiris, presents a fiery characterization and also scores hugely.

Singer Marni Nixon dubs Wood's voice. Film, opening with a three-minute orchestral overture, has been expertly lensed by Daniel L. Fapp, whose aerial prolog, looking straight down upon Gotham as camera flies from the Battery uptown and swings to West Side, provides impressive views. Johnny Green conducts music score, which runs 51½ minutes; Saul Bass is responsible for novel presentation of titles and credits; Irene Sharaff, who designed costumes for Broadway, repeats here.

1961: Best Picture, Directors, Supp. Actor (George Chakiris), Supp. Actress (Rita Moreno), Color Cinematography, Color Art Direction, Sound (Todd-AO Sound Dept, Samuel Goldwyn Sound Dept), Scoring of a Musical Picture, Editing, Color Costume Design

NOMINATION: Best Adapted Screenplay

●

WESTWARD THE WOMEN

1951, 116 mins, US Ⓥ b/w

Dir William A. Wellman ***Prod*** Dore Schary ***Scr*** Charles Schnee ***Ph*** William Mellor ***Ed*** James E. Newcom ***Mus*** Jeff Alexander ***Art*** Cedric Gibbons, Daniel B. Cathcart

Act Robert Taylor, Denise Darcel, Hope Emerson, John McIntire, Julie Bishop, Lenore Lonergan (M-G-M)

The femmes who helped settle the west didn't chase the sun via cozy streamliners or luxury planes. Showing just what the hardships of such a crossing were and the valiant spirit of the women who braved them is the purpose of this production.

The picture [from a story by Frank Capra] depicts them graphically, if redundantly, over a somewhat lengthy 116-minute course. John McIntire's California settler conceives the idea of going east to Chicago and picking up a group of women who will be brought west as wives for the mateless men peopling his rich valley. He hires Robert Taylor, a rough, tough trail guide, to lead the women into the sun. The long trek is started from Independence, MO.

The junket battles Indians, further decimating the original 140, and this elimination continues in encounters with the elements: snow, rain, sand, bitter cold and searing heat, and in hazardous crossing of mountains, rivers and deserts.

Taylor does an excellent job of getting over the rugged facets of his character. Hope Emerson, a giant, salty, New Englander, commands a large share of the better scenes.

●

WESTWORLD

1973, 88 mins, US Ⓥ ⦿ ▭ col

Dir Michael Crichton ***Prod*** Paul N. Lazarus III ***Scr*** Michael Crichton ***Ph*** Gene Polito ***Ed*** David Bretherton ***Mus*** Fred Karlin ***Art*** Herman Blumenthal

Act Yul Brynner, Richard Benjamin, James Brolin, Alan Oppenheimer, Victoria Shaw, Dick Van Patten (M-G-M)

Westworld is an excellent film, which combines solid entertainment, chilling topicality, and superbly intelligent serio-comic story values. Michael Crichton's original script is as superior as his direction. Crichton's Westworld is one of three gigantic theme parks built in what is left of the American outdoors; the others are Romanworld and Medievalworld. For $1,000 a day, flown-in tourists may indulge their highest and lowest appetities. Automated robots move about as real people. These automatons may be raped, shot to death, befriended, betrayed, etc. They never strike back.

To this world come Richard Benjamin and James Brolin. They have picked the western-themed park, where they switch to Levi's, pack revolvers and live out the screen life depicted by John Wayne, Clint Eastwood, and other actioner stars. Yul Brynner plays a black-clothed bad guy whom Benjamin kills in a saloon confrontation. All the while supervisor Alan Oppenheimer oversees the entire world and its creatures.

But suddenly things begin to go wrong. An unidentified computer casualty begins to spread like a plague. The automatons strike back.

•

WETHERBY
(AKA: VIOLENT STRANGER)
1985, 97 mins, UK Ⓥ col
Dir David Hare ***Prod*** Simon Relph ***Scr*** David Hare ***Ph*** Stuart Harris ***Ed*** Chris Wimble ***Mus*** Nick Bicat ***Art*** Hayden Griffin
Act Vanessa Redgrave, Ian Holm, Judi Dench, Stuart Wilson, Tim McInnerny, Suzanna Hamilton (Greenpoint/Film Four)

The title refers to a small town in the northeastern county of Yorkshire. Jean Travers (Vanessa Redgrave) has lived here all her life; she's a lonely schoolteacher, tormented by the memory of a teenage love affair with a boy who was senselessly murdered while on air force duty in Malaya.

The film opens with a dinner party hosted by Jean in her little cottage. Present are two couples, close friends, and a young stranger, John Morgan, whom Jean assumes came with one of the couples, while they in turn assume he is her guest. Next day, Morgan returns to the cottage, and while Jean is making tea, he pulls out a gun and kills himself.

The skill of Hare's approach is that he initially allows us to assume, via normal cinema techniques, that what we saw of the dinner party was the whole story. Gradually, however, we realize we only saw a highly selected part of that evening, and as we return to it again and again, the whole story takes on a different complexion.

Performances are uniformly excellent. Joely Richardson (real-life daughter of Redgrave and Tony Richardson) portrays Redgrave in her youth with great conviction.

•

WE WERE STRANGERS
1949, 106 mins, US b/w
Dir John Huston ***Prod*** S. P. Eagle [= Sam Spiegel] ***Scr*** Peter Viertel, John Huston ***Ph*** Russell Metty ***Ed*** Al Clark ***Mus*** George Antheil
Act Jennifer Jones, John Garfield, Pedro Armendariz, Gilbert Roland, Ramon Novarro (Columbia/Horizon)

In *We Were Strangers*, John Huston has come up with a finished job of directing that edges close to his best films. It's chiefly a suspenseful and hard-driving adaptation of Robert Sylvester's novel, *Rough Sketch*. While relating the overthrow of the Machado dictatorship on the Carribean island, *Strangers'* distillation of political and social overtones are worked mainly as a foil to the revolutionary stalwarts vs. state gestapo duelling that makes up the body of the film.

Its strongpoint and weakness too is the chief dramatic device employed—the tunnelling by a secret band to the center of Havana's big cemetery where the conspirators plan to blow up most of the politicos gathered at a state funeral.

Film could have packed considerably more documentary wallop if the revolt, which did in fact occur, had been woven into the main story.

•

WHALE MUSIC
1994, 100 mins, US Ⓥ col
Dir Richard J. Lewis ***Prod*** Raymond Massey, Steven DeNure ***Scr*** Paul Quarrington, Richard J. Lewis ***Ph*** Vic Sarin, Craig Ibbotson ***Ed*** Richard Martin ***Mus*** George Blondheim ***Art*** Rex Raglan
Act Maury Chaykin, Cyndy Preston, Jennifer Dale, Kenneth Walsh, Paul Gross, Blu Mankuma (Alliance/Cape Scott)

The oddball saga of a burned-out rock star and the tough runaway who invades his tumbledown estate, *Whale Music* is an offbeat, tuneful romance just a shade too quirky to swim in the mainstream.

Somewhere in the Pacific Northwest, Desmond Howl (Maury Chaykin) has retreated from the grind of recording studios and concert tours. The childlike music genius has installed a state-of-the-art recording studio and devotes himself to creating a masterwork—a symphonic piece for whales. The ramshackle harmony threatens to come undone with the arrival of Claire (Cyndy Preston), a rather frank young woman on the run from the law.

The film painstakingly details not only the evolution of Howl's composition, but also the growing attachment between two seemingly unsuited people. The potential union is muddied by the myriad demons who haunt Desmond. They include Fay (Jennifer Dale), his ex-wife bent on getting him to sell the house, and Kenneth (Kenneth Walsh), the recording exec who owns every note he creates. Most disturbing is an unresolved problem between Howl and his brother (Paul Gross), his singing partner who died in an auto accident that may or may not have been a suicide.

Chaykin is a particular standout in a role that literally and figuratively strips him naked for the camera. But even Chaykin cannot overcome several shortcomings. The film's song score just isn't of a quality to convince viewers Howl is a major talent. The filmmaker also feels compelled to give inordinate weight to secondary concerns.

•

WHALES OF AUGUST, THE
1987, 90 mins, US Ⓥ ⊙ col
Dir Lindsay Anderson ***Prod*** Carolyn Pfeiffer, Mike Kaplan ***Scr*** David Berry ***Ph*** Mike Fash ***Ed*** Nicolas Gaster ***Mus*** Alan Price ***Art*** Jocelyn Herbert
Act Bette Davis, Lillian Gish, Vincent Price, Ann Sothern, Harry Carey, Jr., Frank Grimes (Alive)

Muted but engrossing tale about the balance of power between two elderly sisters boasts superior lead performances from two of the screen's most legendary actresses, Bette Davis and Lillian Gish. Adapted by David Berry from his 1981 play, story has two sisters living alone in a comfortable but basic home they have occupied for decades on the striking coast of Maine. Sarah (Gish) is a doting busybody who is obliged to care for her sister Libby (Davis), because the latter is blind.

Trouble rears its head in the form of Vincent Price, a White Russian of considerable charm and gentlemanliness who for decades has lived as a "houseguest" of numerous ladies.

Wearing long, pure-white hair, Davis looks gaunt, grim and disturbed, but her performance is restrained in such a way that may even increase its power. Gish is a delight throughout.

A black-&-white prolog, in which Mary Steenburgen, Tisha Sterling and Margaret Ladd appear as the women in their youth, gets the film off to a nice start.

1987: NOMINATION: Best Supp. Actress (Ann Sothern)

•

WHAT ABOUT BOB?
1991, 99 mins, US Ⓥ ⊙ col
Dir Frank Oz ***Prod*** Laura Ziskin ***Scr*** Tom Schulman ***Ph*** Michael Ballhaus ***Ed*** Anne V. Coates ***Mus*** Miles Goodman ***Art*** Les Dilley
Act Bill Murray, Richard Dreyfuss, Julie Hagerty, Charlie Korsmo, Kathryn Erbe, Tom Aldredge (Touchstone Pacific Partners I)

Bill Murray finds a real showcase for his oft-shackled talent in this manic comedy. Originally discussed as a pairing of Murray and Woody Allen, pic ended up with Richard Dreyfuss in the role of the tightly wound, egotistical psychiatrist whose life is disrupted by "multiphobic" new patient Bob Wiley (Murray), the human equivalent of gum on the bottom of one's shoe.

Dreyfuss's Dr. Leo Marvin gets irked when the persistent patient follows him to a rustic New Hampshire retreat, then grows increasingly outraged as Bob proceeds to win over his family. He helps the doc's death-obsessed son (Charlie Korsmo, kid in *Dick Tracy*) to learn to enjoy life and shows compassion to his daughter (Kathryn Erbe) and unappreciated wife (Julie Hagerty).

Murray has a field day with the character, which allows him to act like a little kid while occasionally lapsing into other aspects from his *Saturday Night Live* days, from his smarmy lounge singer to the nerd. Dreyfuss generally reprises the role he played in *Down and Out in Beverly Hills*: domineering, nouveau-riche family man whose stolid existence is turned upside down by unwelcome intruder.

•

WHAT A MAN
SEE: NEVER GIVE A SUCKER AN EVEN BREAK

•

WHAT A WAY TO GO!
1964, 111 mins, US ▭ col
Dir J. Lee Thompson ***Prod*** Arthur P. Jacobs ***Scr*** Betty Comden, Adolph Green ***Ph*** Leon Shamroy ***Ed*** Marjorie Fowler ***Mus*** Nelson Riddle ***Art*** Jack Martin Smith, Ted Haworth
Act Shirley MacLaine, Paul Newman, Robert Mitchum, Dean Martin, Gene Kelly, Dick Van Dyke (Apjac/Orchard/20th Century-Fox)

What a Way to Go! is a big, gaudy, gimmicky comedy which continually promises more than it delivers by way of wit and/or bellylaffs. The screenplay, based on a story by Gwen Davis, is, at its very promising basis, the sad, sad story of a little poor girl from Ohio, who, though she wants only true love, is married and widowed in succession by four diverse types who eventually make her the richest woman in the world. It's a sort of ironic *True Story*, related in flashbacks from a psychiatrist's couch.

Essentially, the film is a series of blackout sketches, enlivened from time to time as Shirley MacLaine tells of her marriages in styles of various types of films. Thus, in recalling her life with a Thoreau-reading idealist (Dick Van Dyke), she sees it in the jerky, exaggerated terms of a silent movie romance; her life with a beatnik, abstract-impressionist painter (Paul Newman), in Paris, is viewed as a sexy French film complete with English subtitles; and her life with tycoon Robert Mitchum is remembered as an overdressed Ross Hunter production.

Some of these parodies are very funny but there often isn't much difference between the style of the parody and that of the encasing flashback.

Picture is gaudily, expensively mounted. There are a couple of songs by Jule Styne, including an hilarious production number (choreographed by Gene Kelly) which might have come out of *Follow the Fleet*.

1964: NOMINATIONS: Best Color Costume Design, Best Color Art Direction

•

WHAT A WIDOW!
1930, 90 mins, US b/w
Dir Allan Dwan ***Prod*** Joseph P. Kennedy ***Scr*** James Gleason, James Seymour ***Ph*** George Barnes ***Ed*** Viola Lawrence ***Mus*** Vincent Youmans ***Art*** Paul Nelson
Act Gloria Swanson, Owen Moore, Lew Cody, Margaret Livingston, William Holden (Kennedy/United Artists)

Gloria Swanson is a youthful widow, innocent in the world's ways, who is left $5 million when her sixty-year-old husband passes on. Seemingly New York isn't big enough for the corking-looking widow. So she switches to Paris, to the dress and hat shops, the masseurs, the rest of it that's there when the dough is also.

Into all of this come three men. The American is done by Owen Moore. He is a member of the widow's legal firm and coincidentally is on the same boat for Paris, entrusted with the mission of looking after her. Other two are a couple of gigs, one a Russian violinist and the second a Spanish piano-playing warbler.

Director Allan Dwan has given an unusually fast tempo to the entire direction. He weaves everything in and out. Swanson, as the joy-seeking widow, has plenty of scope for airy playing. Moore does a good show.

•

WHAT DID YOU DO IN THE WAR, DADDY?
1966, 115 mins, US ▭ col
Dir Blake Edwards ***Prod*** Blake Edwards ***Scr*** William Peter Blatty ***Ph*** Philip Lathrop ***Ed*** Ralph E. Winters ***Mus*** Henry Mancini ***Art*** Fernando Carrere
Act James Coburn, Dick Shawn, Sergio Fantoni, Aldo Ray, Giovanna Ralli, Carroll O'Connor (United Artists/Mirisch)

What Did You Do in the War, Daddy? carries an engaging title but after dreaming it up the writers promptly forgot all about it and launched into a thinly devised comedy without much substance.

Blake Edwards, who directs, also collabed on original story with Maurice Richlin. Set against a World War II backdrop—Sicily, 1943—the screenplay dwells on a single situation which holds promise but is never sufficiently realized.

Basic idea has a war-weary American company, commanded by a by-the-book officer, being detailed to take a town held by a large Italian force, and their welcome reception by the Italians who are agreeable to surrendering willingly. But first, they must hold their wine festival. No festival, no surrender.

Edwards has packed his action with a flock of individual gags and routines but frequently the viewer isn't too certain what's happening. Director draws good comedy portrayals from a talented cast headed by James Coburn and Dick Shawn, both delivering bangup performances.

•

WHATEVER HAPPENED TO AUNT ALICE?
1969, 101 mins, US Ⓥ col
Dir Lee H. Katzin ***Prod*** Robert Aldrich ***Scr*** Theodore Apstein ***Ph*** Joseph Biroc ***Ed*** Frank J. Urioste ***Mus*** Gerald Fried ***Art*** William Glasgow
Act Geraldine Page, Ruth Gordon, Rosemary Forsyth, Robert Fuller, Mildred Dunnock (Palomar/Associates & Aldrich)

Fresh story, using old-hat scare tricks combined with highly skillful acting.

Widow Geraldine Page hits upon ingenious method of building up unencumbered women as companions, to take their life savings and then bash their heads in. Trouble starts when she eliminates wistful Mildred Dunnock. Suspicious Ruth Gordon, former employer of Dunnock, appears on the scene in the guise of yet another housekeeper.

Page as a high-and-mighty wealthy eccentric delivers a bravura performance. Gordon, working crisply, offers a remarkable portrait of a brave woman. The two ladies play off each other relentlessly and audience reaps the rewards.

Grim humor and superior dialog, as well as night prowling, barred doors, disconnected phones, an unexplained wheelchair, wigs and maniacal laughter total up to fine tale [from the novel *The Forbidden Garden* by Ursula Curtiss] of suspense rounded off with a twist ending.

•

WHAT EVER HAPPENED TO BABY JANE?
1962, 132 mins, US Ⓥ ⊙ b/w
Dir Robert Aldrich ***Prod*** Robert Aldrich ***Scr*** Lukas Heller ***Ph*** Ernest Haller ***Ed*** Michael Luciano ***Mus*** Frank DeVol ***Art*** William Glasgow
Act Bette Davis, Joan Crawford, Victor Buono, Marjorie Bennett, Anna Lee (Seven Arts-Associates)

Teaming Bette Davis and Joan Crawford now seems like a veritable prerequisite to putting Henry Farrell's slight tale of terror on the screen. Although the results heavily favor Davis (and she earns the credit), it should be recognized that the plot, of necessity, allows her to run unfettered through all the stages of oncoming insanity.

Crawford gives a quiet, remarkably fine interpretation of the crippled Blanche, held in emotionally by the nature and temperament of the role. Physically confined to a wheelchair and bed through the picture, she has to act from the inside and has her best scenes (because she wisely underplays with Davis) with a maid and those she plays alone.

The slight basic tale is of two sisters, complete opposites. As children, Jane is *Baby Jane*, a vaudeville star and the idol of the public. Offstage, she's a vicious brat, domineering her plain, inhibited sister and preening parents. Eventually both girls go into films, where the dark, mousey Blanche blossoms into a beauty and fine actress, and becomes Hollywood's top star.

As a result of an accident, hazily presented, Blanche is permanently crippled. Jane, dependent on her sister for her livelihood, is forced to care for her, her hate growing with the years. So, also, does the "Baby Jane" illusion until, living it daily, she determines to get rid of Blanche and return to vaudeville.

Advertising for an accompanist, the sole applicant is a huge, ungainly lout (a superb off-beat performance by Victor Buono), who sizes up the situation's opportunities and goes along, planning to get enough money to enable him to break the tarnished-silver cord binding him to a possessive mother.

The chain of circumstances grows, violence creating violence. Once the inept, draggy start is passed, the film's pace builds with ever-growing force.

1962: Best B&W Costume Design

NOMINATIONS: Best Actress (Bette Davis), Supp. Actor (Victor Buono), B&W Cinematography, Sound

•

WHAT EVERY WOMAN KNOWS
1934, 90 mins, US b/w
Dir Gregory La Cava ***Scr*** Monckton Hoffe, John Meehan, James Kevin McGuinness ***Ph*** Charles Rosher ***Mus*** Herbert Stothart
Act Helen Hayes, Brian Aherne, Madge Evans, Lucile Watson, Dudley Digges, Donald Crisp (M-G-M)

The theme is by no means new, but the idea is ever popular. Paramount first presented it as a silent back in 1921. In 1926 Helen Hayes and Kenneth MacKenna made a season of the same James M. Barrie play on Broadway. It's the "lil woman" all over again, the helpmeet who humbly does her quiet bit in balancing impulsive man's judgments or, rather, misjudgments.

This Barrie version brings the egotistical but knowledge-hungry young barrister (Brian Aherne) out of Scotland into Parliament, where he thinks he finds new romance with power, but is actually catapulted into even greater glory by the brainy Maggie (Hayes), who types and edits his MP speeches.

Aherne is a vigorous zealot who makes his upstartishness respected and even liked by the Scots community (and the audience), for none can deny his sincerity.

Madge Evans is out of her usual groove as a light menace, but she makes it as likeable as circumstances warrant. Lucile Watson as the comtesse is a gallant lady, while Dudley Digges is particularly impressive as the somewhat numb Jamie.

•

WHAT HAPPENED WAS
1994, 91 mins, US Ⓥ ⊙ col
Dir Tom Noonan ***Prod*** Robin O'Hara, Scott Macaulay ***Scr*** Tom Noonan ***Ph*** Joe DeSalvo ***Ed*** Richmond Arrley ***Mus*** Lodovico Sorret ***Art*** Dan Ouelette
Act Karen Sillas, Tom Noonan (Good Machine/Genre)

Off-Broadway actor Tom Noonan emerges as a talented writer and director in *What Happened Was*, an intriguing, often mysterious drama about a date between two lonely misfits. This intense chamber piece for two features strong performances, particularly by Karen Sillas.

It's Friday night and Jackie (Sillas), a secretary in a law firm, leaves work early to prepare for a dinner date at her New York loft with paralegal colleague Michael (Noonan).

It doesn't help much that Jackie and Michael know each other from work, for when he arrives at the door, it's a new ball game with a new set of rules.

Jumping from one topic to another, Michael tells Jackie he has been engaged in writing an exposé about the firm. Jackie reveals she has written children's fairy tales. Dealing with child abuse, violence and terror, her story disturbs Michael.

There are plenty of shocking role reversals and twists, but the script's most illuminating insights show how potentially pleasurable encounters can turn disastrous as a result of differing expectations. Though based on a play [by Noonan], there's nothing theatrical or claustrophobic about the narrative. Production values are first-rate, particularly Dan Ouelette's remarkable production design of the loft, the film's single locale.

•

WHAT LIES BENEATH
2000, 126 mins, US Ⓥ ⊙ ▭ col
Dir Robert Zemeckis ***Prod*** Steve Starkey, Robert Zemeckis, Jack Rapke ***Scr*** Clark Gregg ***Ph*** Don Burgess ***Ed*** Arthur Schmidt ***Mus*** Alan Silvestri ***Art*** Rick Carter, Jim Teegarden
Act Harrison Ford, Michelle Pfeiffer, Diana Scarwid, Miranda Otto, James Remar, Joe Morton (Image Movers/Dream Works-20th Century Fox)

The imposing shadow of Hitchcock looms large over a thriller that tries aggressively but not entirely successfully to deliver the goods of three genres—suspense, supernatural and horror—for the price of one movie. Revisiting the turf of stylish thrillers, in which an upscale yuppie couple is haunted by mistakes of the past, story centers on a genius researcher and his loving wife, played by Harrison Ford and Michelle Pfeiffer, whose seemingly happy marriage and stable life are utterly shaken by mysterious events that spiral out of control.

Topflight talent on both sides of the camera can't quite disguise the B-quality of Clark Gregg's script [from his and Sarah Kernochan's story], a patchwork composed of bits and pieces from Hitchcock's suspensers, the Gothic "haunted house" tradition, *Fatal Attraction*-like cheap-thrill sensations, creepy supernatural mysteries like *The Sixth Sense* and so on.

All along, the feeling is that the filmmakers don't trust the core material and try to compensate with a complicated story line and overbaked production. Directing a thriller for the first time, Zemeckis succeeds in creating a swirl of Hitchcockian suspense, which means that you can expect a nasty fright every time a door opens, a shock when the family dog appears out of nowhere, a scare when the bathtub gets filled with water with no human presence in sight and so on. But something is amiss: Sophisticated technology can't substitute for intriguing characters, which are lacking here.

Though he gets star billing, Ford actually plays a supporting role—he's hardly present in the first hour. Ford employs his customary "Rock of Gibraltar" strength, but despite twists and turns his role isn't particularly rewarding. Credibly cast as his vulnerable wife, Pfeiffer almost succeeds in holding the picture together with her beautiful presence. However, what both stars desperately need is help from a larger, more colorful gallery of secondary characters—pic is vastly underpopulated, particularly in its second half.

•

WHAT LOLA WANTS
SEE: DAMN YANKEES

•

WHAT PRICE GLORY?
1926, 116 mins, US ⊗ b/w
Dir Raoul Walsh ***Prod*** William Fox ***Scr*** James T. O'Donohoe, Malcolm Stuart Boylan ***Ph*** Barney McGill, Jack Marta, John Smith ***Ed*** Rose Smith ***Art*** William Darling
Act Victor McLaglen, Edmund Lowe, Dolores Del Rio, William V. Mong, Phyllis Haver, Leslie Fenton (Fox)

It's a picture [from the play by Maxwell Anderson and Laurence Stallings] that has everything except an out-and-out love story of the calibre of the one in *The Big Parade*. But where it lacks in that, it certainly makes up in sex stuff and comedy.

There is a wallop right at the beginning in the two short sequences showing both Flagg and Quirt as sergeants of the marines in China and the Philippines. Right here the conflict between the two men, whose trade is soldiering, over women is set down, yet with a light touch of comedy.

Victor McLaglen stands out bigger than he ever has. He is the hardboiled Capt. Flagg, and his role gets far greater sympathy than that of Sergeant Quirt, which Edmund Lowe plays.

As for the Charmaine of Dolores Del Rio, she registers like a house afire. It is no wonder that she had the whole army after her.

To Raoul Walsh a great deal of credit will have to go. His handling of the war stuff is little short of marvelous.

•

WHAT PRICE GLORY?
1952, 110 mins, US Ⓥ col
Dir John Ford ***Prod*** Sol C. Siegel ***Scr*** Phoebe Ephron, Henry Ephron ***Ph*** Joe MacDonald ***Ed*** Dorothy Spencer ***Mus*** Alfred Newman ***Art*** Lyle Wheeler, George W. Davis
Act James Cagney, Dan Dailey, Corinne Calvet, William Demarest, Robert Wagner, Marisa Pavan (20th Century-Fox)

The durable heroics of *What Price Glory?* undergo a comedic treatment in Technicolor for this fresh version of the Maxwell Anderson-Laurence Stallings stage drama.

James Cagney, a corpulent Captain Flagg who looks like he'll bust out of his britches any minute, and Dan Dailey, the braggard Sergeant Quirt, enact the top male roles as rivals for gals and glory with amusing emphasis on frenetics. Both are inclined to mumble or shout their dialog.

Corinne Calvet's charms are freely displayed as the ever-loving Charmaine, ready and willing to give any masculine ally of France aid and comfort.

Story scatters itself among episodes dealing with the marines in World War I and the professional and amatory rivaly of Cagney and Dailey.

Over the entire production is a feeling that any second the picture will break into a musical number. This doesn't happen, but it still serves as a subconscious distraction.

•

WHAT PRICE HOLLYWOOD?
1932, 87 mins, US Ⓥ ⊙ b/w
Dir George Cukor ***Prod*** Pandro S. Berman (assoc.) ***Scr*** Gene Fowler, Rowland Brown, Jane Murfin, Ben Markson ***Ph*** Charles Rosher ***Ed*** [Jack Kitchen] ***Mus*** Max Steiner (dir.) ***Art*** Carroll Clark
Act Constance Bennett, Lowell Sherman, Neil Hamilton, Gregory Ratoff, Brooks Benedict (RKO)

It's a fan-magazineish interpretation of Hollywood plus a couple of twists. A waitress becomes a picture star, marries a wealthy playboy, loses him and gets him back when her screen career founders on the suicide of the director who gave her a start.

Director George Cukor tells it interestingly. Story [by Adela Rogers St. John] has its exaggerations, but they can sneak under the line as theatrical license. In any case, there's Constance Bennett floating around smartly costumed for street or boudoir; Neil Hamilton is more pleasant than usual as the juvenile; Gregory Ratoff is closer to some film producers in his portrayal than the average audience will realize; and Lowell Sherman is again to the front with a fine interpretation of a derelict director.

1931/32: NOMINATION: Best Original Story

•

WHAT'S EATING GILBERT GRAPE?
1993, 118 mins, US Ⓥ ⊙ col
Dir Lasse Hallstrom ***Prod*** Meir Teper, Bertil Ohlsson, David Matalon ***Scr*** Peter Hedges ***Ph*** Sven Nykvist ***Ed*** Andrew Mondshein ***Mus*** Alan Parker, Bjorn Isfalt ***Art*** Bernt Capra

Act Johnny Depp, Juliette Lewis, Mary Steenburgen, Leonardo DiCaprio, Darlene Cates, Laura Harrington (Matalon-Teper-Ohlsson)

What's Eating Gilbert Grape? is an offbeat middleweight charmer that is lent a measure of substance by its astute performances and observational insight.

Based on playwright and actor Peter Hedges's 1991 novel, small-scale film depicts the Grapes, a rural family that has every right to qualify as dysfunctional. However, the family copes reasonably well due to the princely, self-sacrificial ministrations of eldest son, Gilbert (Johnny Depp), who carries on a discreet affair with an older woman and can't even think of leaving due to how much Momma (Darlene Cates) and Arnie (Leonardo DiCaprio) depend upon him.

Becky (Juliette Lewis), with her grandmother, pitches tent outside town in a shiny trailer. More worldly and sophisticated than the local rubes, Becky gently entices the reticent, unassertive Gilbert into a tentative romantic relationship just as his lover (Mary Steenburgen) is moving away.

This sort of quirky, low-key material could have veered in numerous objectionable directions. But Swedish director Lasse Hallström and his fine cast have endowed the story with a good deal of behavioral truth and unstressed comedy. Set in Iowa but lensed in central Texas, pic has an unassuming look.

1993: NOMINATION: Best Supp. Actor (Leonardo DiCaprio)

•

WHAT'S LOVE GOT TO DO WITH IT
(UK/AUSTRALIA: TINA: WHAT'S LOVE GOT TO DO WITH IT)

1993, 118 mins, US Ⓥ ⊙ col

Dir Brian Gibson ***Prod*** Doug Chapin, Barry Krost ***Scr*** Kate Lanier ***Ph*** Jamie Anderson ***Ed*** Stuart Pappe ***Mus*** Stanley Clarke ***Art*** Stephen Altman

Act Angela Bassett, Larry Fishburne, Vanessa Bell Calloway, Jenifer Lewis, Phyllis Yvonne Stickney, Khandi Alexander (Touchstone)

This immensely enjoyable biography of songstress Tina Turner [from her and Kurt Loder's book *I, Tina*] is a passionate personal and professional drama that hits both the high and low notes of an extraordinary career.

Young Tina, a.k.a. Anna Mae Bullock (Angela Bassett), is first seen as a precocious youngster. She is left in the care of her grandmother after her mother (Jenifer Lewis) goes off to the big city.

It's also in St. Louis, circa 1958, that she encounters charismatic R&B singer-songwriter Ike Turner (Laurence Fishburne). Part of his act involves coaxing comely women to the mike. When Anna Mae lets loose, Ike sees a potent meal ticket.

Nothing in Bassett's earlier repertoire suggested the consummate skill she brings to the part. It is a full-bodied, nuanced portrayal. Fishburne as Ike Turner is also pitch perfect.

1993: NOMINATIONS: Best Actor (Laurence Fishburne), Actress (Angela Bassett)

•

WHAT'S NEW, PUSSYCAT?

1965, 108 mins, US Ⓥ ⊙ col

Dir Clive Donner ***Prod*** Charles K. Feldman ***Scr*** Woody Allen ***Ph*** Jean Badal ***Ed*** Fergus McDonell ***Mus*** Burt Bacharach ***Art*** Jacques Saulnier

Act Peter Sellers, Peter O'Toole, Romy Schneider, Capucine, Paula Prentiss, Woody Allen (Famous Artists/Famartists)

What's New, Pussycat? is designed as a zany farce, as wayout as can be reached on the screen. It's all that, and more . . . it goes overboard in pressing for its goal and consequently suffers from over-contrived treatment.

The Charles K. Feldman production is peopled exclusively by mixed-up characters. Peter Sellers is a Viennese professor to whom Peter O'Toole, editor of a Parisian fashion magazine, goes for psychiatric help in solving his women problems, which keep piling up as he finds more pretty girls. On his part, Sellers has a jealous wife and a roving eye which keeps getting him into trouble.

Original screenplay by Woody Allen—who plays an undresser for strippers at the Crazy Horse Saloon and similarly afflicted with girl troubles—provides a field day for gagmen, who seldom miss a trick in inserting a sight gag.

Two top stars come off none too happily in their characterizations. Sellers's nuttiness knows no bounds as he speaks with a thick German accent, and O'Toole proves his forte is drama rather than comedy. Trio of femmes who chase O'Toole have the proper looks and furnish as much glamour as any one man can take.

1965: NOMINATION: Best Song ("What's New Pussycat")

•

WHAT'S THE MATTER WITH HELEN?

1971, 101 mins, US col

Dir Curtis Harrington ***Prod*** George Edwards ***Scr*** Henry Farrell ***Ph*** Lucien Ballard ***Ed*** William H. Reynolds ***Mus*** David Raksin ***Art*** Eugene Lourie

Act Debbie Reynolds, Shelley Winters, Dennis Weaver, Agnes Moorehead, Micheal MacLiammoir, Sammee Lee Jones (Filmways/Raymax)

What's the Matter with Helen? is an okay exploitation shocker starring Debbie Reynolds and Shelley Winters as two Hollywood types of the early sound era caught up in mayhem and mutual suspicion. The good red-herring script is hindered from maximum impact by director Curtis Harrington, who raises the interest and excitement level too early and lets the film coast to less-than-tense resolution.

Film opens with an excellent title sequence using period newsreel clips ending with a midwest Loeb-Leopold-type juve murder trial, where the femmes are mothers of the two slayers. Threatening phone calls spur pair to Hollywood, where they open a terp studio for would-be Shirley Temple carbons.

Reynolds finds romance with Dennis Weaver, the father of one of her pupils (Sammee Lee Jones). His Texas millionaire accent is a few feet too thick. Winters, mentally hassled by mysterious strangers across the street and unnerved by friends, turns more to the radio preachings of Agnes Moorehead, excellent in hard-sell evangelist role.

•

WHAT'S UP, DOC?

1972, 94 mins, US Ⓥ ⊙ col

Dir Peter Bogdanovich ***Prod*** Peter Bogdanovich ***Scr*** Buck Henry, Robert Benton, David Newman ***Ph*** Laszlo Kovacs ***Ed*** Verna Fields ***Mus*** Artie Butler ***Art*** Polly Platt

Act Barbra Streisand, Ryan O'Neal, Kenneth Mars, Austin Pendleton, Sorrell Booke, Stefan Gierasch (Saticoy/Warner)

Peter Bogdanovich's *What's Up, Doc?* is a contemporary comedy [from his own original story] in the screwball 1930s style, with absolutely no socially relevant values. This picture is a total smash.

The script and cast are excellent; the direction and comedy staging are outstanding; and there are literally reels of pure, unadulterated and sustained laughs.

Gimmick is a quartet of identical suitcases that of course get into the wrong hands. Barbra Streisand is discovered conning some food out of a hotel, where Ryan O'Neal and fiancée (Madeline Kahn) are attending a musicologists' convention. There is an unending stream of opening and closing doors, perilous balcony walks, and two terrific chases through San Francisco streets.

The humor derives much from the tradition of Warner Bros. cartoons, with broad visuals amid sophisticated ideas. One of the hilarious car chases is virtually a *Road Runner* storyboard, and there's absolutely nothing wrong about that.

•

WHAT'S UP, TIGER LILY?

1966, 79 mins, US Ⓥ ⊙ ▭ col

Dir Woody Allen ***Prod*** Henry G. Saperstein (exec.) ***Scr*** Woody Allen ***Ph*** Kazuo Yamada ***Ed*** Richard Krown ***Mus*** The Lovin' Spoonful

Act Woody Allen, Tatsuya Mihashi, Mie Hama, Akiko Wakabayashi, Tadao Nakamura, Susumu Korobe (American International/Benedict)

Take a Toho Films (Japan) crime meller [directed by Senkichi Taniguchi], fashioned in the James Bond tradition for the domestic market there, then turn loose Woody Allen and associates to dub and re-edit in camp-comedy vein, and the result is *What's Up, Tiger Lily?* The production has one premise—deliberately mismatched dialog—which is sustained reasonably well through its brief running time.

Film opens cold with over three minutes of straightforward Japanese meller and chase footage until Allen pops up, explaining the format to follow. The Samurai posturing, to the non-sequitur dialog, is relieved regularly by stop-motion and other effects.

Allen's cohorts, both in writing and dubbing, are Frank Buxton, Len Maxwell, Louise Lasser, Mickey Rose, Julie Bennett and Bryna Wilson.

•

WHAT WOMEN WANT

1998, 133 mins, US Ⓥ ⊙ ▭ col

Dir Barry Levinson ***Prod*** Barry Levinson, Michael Crichton, Andrew Wald ***Scr*** Stephen Hauser, Paul Attanasio ***Ph*** Adam Greenberg ***Ed*** Stu Linder ***Mus*** Elliot Goldenthal ***Art*** Norman Reynolds

Act Dustin Hoffman, Sharon Stone, Samuel L. Jackson, Peter Coyote, Liev Schreiber, Queen Latifah (Baltimore/Constant/Warner)

Sphere is an empty shell. Derivative of any number of famous sci-fi movies and as full of false promises as the Wizard of Oz, this portentous underwater *Thing* swims along with reasonable good humor for its first hour, then descends into mechanical and routine "suspense" sequences that fail to deliver what genre fans demand.

Basically a chamber piece, but produced on the most lavish possible scale, this low-voltage Michael Crichton tale [adaptation by Kurt Wimmer] falls between several stools in the sci-fi arena: alien spaceship mystery, theological/philosophical inquiry, monster thriller, time travel adventure, close-quarters pressure cooker, and voyage into the mind. Scraps from genre classics abound.

Psychologist Dr. Norman Goodman (Dustin Goodman) is summoned to a remote Pacific site where group leader Barnes (Peter Coyote) throws him together with biochemist Beth Halperin (Sharon Stone), with whom Goodman has a past, mathematician Harry Adams (Samuel L. Jackson) and astrophysicist Ted Fielding (Liev Schreiber). A thousand feet down they view an amazing sight: a submerged spacecraft nearly half a mile long that must have crashed there 288 years before.

The main revelation is an enormous, shimmering, golden sphere seemingly made of liquid metal. Convinced there is life within the sphere, Harry devises to apparently enter it, and from then on takes on a distracted air, sleeping through emergencies and obsessively reading *20,000 Leagues Under the Sea*.

The only emotional component derives from the neurotic Beth still not having got over the way Norman treated her many years before, and her instability quickly becomes wearisome. Actors are all underused in shallow roles.

Pic was shot entirely on soundstages installed at the abandoned Mare Island Naval Shipyard at Vallejo in Northern California.

•

WHAT WOMEN WANT

2000, 126 mins, US Ⓥ ⊙ col

Dir Nancy Meyers ***Prod*** Nancy Meyers, Bruce Davey, Matt Williams, Susan Cartsonis, Gina Matthews ***Scr*** Josh Goldsmith, Cathy Yuspa ***Ph*** Dean Cundey ***Ed*** Stephen A. Rotter, Thomas J. Nordberg ***Mus*** Alan Silvestri ***Art*** Jon Hutman

Act Mel Gibson, Helen Hunt, Marisa Tomei, Mark Feuerstein, Lauren Holly, Alan Alda (Icon-Wind Dancer/Paramount)

With a manic Mel Gibson starring in his first romantic comedy, playing an incorrigible seducer who temporarily becomes endowed with the ability to hear women's uncensored thoughts, Nancy Meyers's second directorial outing has sheer energy and audience allure to burn, even if numerous speed bumps cause many of the comic possibilities to go tumbling overboard.

Nick Marshall (Gibson) is a hotshot ad exec with an ex-wife (Lauren Holly) and a 15-year-old daughter, Alex (Ashley Johnson), whose top priority is losing her virginity. Fully expecting a promotion at work, Nick is taken aback when his boss (Alan Alda) informs him that he's instead hired the estimable Darcy Maguire (Helen Hunt).

Asked by Darcy to come up with suggestions for a new, femme-slanted campaign, Nick gets drunk in his penthouse apartment, dances around and immerses himself in what it's like to be a woman by waxing his legs, polishing his nails and trying on pantyhose and a WonderBra—only to be caught by an aghast Alex and her b.f. Sequence is shameless, to be sure, but sets off gales of laughter due to the way it plays off of Gibson's ultra-macho image—and simply because the star is so game.

Episode concludes in the *Twilight Zone*-ish bathroom accident that sets up the big gimmick: To his initial dismay but eventual delight, Nick finds, "I hear what women think." The dismay, as it turns out, is pretty superficial, taking the form of Nick's learning that there are actually some women out there who think he's a jerk. The delight, of course, is much more profound, as a shrink (Bette Midler in an uncredited cameo) for some reason has to explain to him, "If you know what women want, you can rule."

Before long, Nick is putting his advantage to good use, throwing Darcy off-guard by telling her exactly what she's thinking, and by almost literally picking her brain for creative ideas. Nick's finally able to break down the resistance of vibrant coffee-shop girl Lola (Marisa Tomei), while he also becomes attentive to the plight of office wallflower Erin (Judy Greer). And then there's one of the film's funniest gags, in which Nick waits to discern the inner thoughts of his two zaftig assistants (Delta Burke and Valerie Perrine).

Meyers underlines, boldfaces and italicizes every scene, then applies a high-gloss finish so that no one in the audience could possibly miss a single line, effect or intention. But Gibson seems all but inflated with helium throughout, which contagiously lifts everyone else around him, and Hunt's more earthbound pragmatism plays well off of her co-star's buoyancy. Tomei shoots off some amusingly unpredictable sparks.

•

WHEN A MAN LOVES A WOMAN
1994, 124 mins, US Ⓥ ⦿ col
Dir Luis Mandoki ***Prod*** Jordan Kerner, Jon Avnet ***Scr*** Ronald Bass, Al Franken ***Ph*** Lajos Koltai ***Ed*** Garth Craven ***Mus*** Zbigniew Preisner ***Art*** Stuart Wurtzel
Act Andy Garcia, Meg Ryan, Lauren Tom, Philip Seymour Hoffman, Tina Majorino, Ellen Burstyn (Touchstone)

There's something terribly askew and misleading in the very title *When a Man Loves a Woman* (*Significant Other*, its original name, is no better). This contempo tale of alcoholism and substance abuse does have an underlying tenderness, but its core is sober, vivid and gut-wrenching.

Michael (Andy Garcia) and Alice (Meg Ryan) Green are the seeming paradigm of the yuppie lifestyle. He's an airplane pilot and she's a high school guidance counselor. They have a snug little San Francisco home and two well-adjusted, preteen girls.

But the cracks in the veneer soon become obvious. Alice cannot face a social situation without at least one drink too many. After a near-fatal boating incident on a Mexican vacation, she promises to reform—meaning only that she will hide her drinking problem more ferociously.

The ambition of the screenplay is often staggering. It's more a case study than a traditional three-act movie fable. The film takes on the logic of a bar crawl, veering toward the conventional only in Luis Mandoki's direction and with some much appreciated excursions into levity.

Ryan has one of those rollercoaster roles that demands attention. Garcia, as the unexpected villain of the piece, is capable of inflicting enormous damage under the veil of good intentions.

•

WHEN A STRANGER CALLS
1979, 97 mins, US Ⓥ ⦿ col
Dir Fred Walton ***Prod*** Doug Chapin, Steve Feke ***Scr*** Steve Feke, Fred Walton ***Ph*** Don Peterman ***Ed*** Sam Vitale ***Mus*** Dana Kaproff ***Art*** Elayne Barbara Ceder
Act Carol Kane, Charles Durning, Colleen Dewhurst, Tony Beckley, Rachel Roberts, Ron O'Neal (Columbia/Simon-Krost)

Thanks to a fine cast, a rich and atmospheric score by Dana Kaproff, and astute direction by cowriter Fred Walton, *Stranger* is unquestionably a scary film. Bridging two distinct storylines: one the standard frightened baby-sitter alone in a dark house, and the other the subsequent manhunt for an escaped killer, script has chills a-plenty.

But something seems lacking overall. By the film's end, the deficiency seems clear—key actions and motivations just don't make sense. Carol Kane, who disappears for almost 70 of the film's 97 minutes, is quite good as the terrified sitter who grows up to have the same chilling chain of events begin all over again.

More than anything else, *When a Stranger Calls* resembles a good, old-fashioned grade-B thriller.

•

WHEN DINOSAURS RULED THE EARTH
1970, 100 mins, UK Ⓥ ⦿ col
Dir Val Guest ***Prod*** Aida Young ***Scr*** Val Guest ***Ph*** Dick Bush ***Ed*** Peter Curran ***Mus*** Mario Nascimbene ***Art*** John Blezard
Act Victoria Vetri, Robin Hawdon, Patrick Allen, Sean Caffrey, Magda Konopka, Imogen Hassall (Hammer)

This is one of those simple sci-fi prehistoric films which do no harm. Normally, they're taken either dead seriously or as send-ups. This one quite deftly combines the two angles.

What the story (mainly shot in the Canary Islands) is all about is subject to doubt since Val Guest, who both directed and wrote the original screenplay, has elected to invent a "prehistoric" lingo for the dialog.

Story concerns a huge upheaval in the sun at the dawn of history, resulting in a fiery, sullen appearance of the moon. A blonde (Victoria Vetri) is blamed for this, her golden tresses having suspectedly insulted the sun. She's condemned to death, but is rescued by a neighboring Sand Tribe. The rest consists largely of fisherman Tara (Robin Hawdon) falling for the cutie, which irritates his girlfriend (Imogen Hassall).

Amid the animals, special effects, and tribal rituals (and saddled with noncommunicative language) the human thesps don't stand much chance of scoring. There are a lot of very nubile, scantily clad dames.

•

WHEN EIGHT BELLS TOLL
1971, 94 mins, UK Ⓥ ▭ col
Dir Etienne Perier ***Prod*** Elliott Kastner ***Scr*** Alistair MacLean ***Ph*** Arthur Ibbetson ***Ed*** John Shirley ***Mus*** Wally Stott ***Art*** Jack Maxsted
Act Anthony Hopkins, Robert Morley, Nathalie Delon, Jack Hawkins, Corin Redgrave, Derek Bond (Winkast)

Alistair MacLean's two-fisted, no-holds-barred adventure yarns are a natural for the screen. *When Eight Bells Toll* brings in more slugging, quick action twists, sharp dialog, amusing acting than many pix twice its length.

Anthony Hopkins has a role that creates a character full of resource, courage, cheek and personality. A kind of James Bond, without the latter's trademarks. Character is a naval secret service agent assigned to find out how millions of pounds in gold bullion are being pirated. He starts his explorations in the bleakness of the Western Highlands of Scotland. Hopkins and his pal (Corin Redgrave) posing as marine biologists find mystery and hostility among the natives and the obvious suspect is a suave, rich Greek tycoon (Jack Hawkins) whose luxury yacht guests some odd characters.

Main femme appeal comes from Nathalie Delon as the mystery woman who is allegedly Hawkins's wife but apparently goes over to the Hopkins camp. Hawkins himself as the Greek tycoon retains his usual stature and his voice (lost to throat cancer) is very shrewdly dubbed [by Charles Gray]. Comedy relief comes from Robert Morley, as Hopkins's snobbish, stuffy chief.

•

WHEN FATHER WAS AWAY ON BUSINESS
SEE: OTAC NA SLUZBENOM PUTU

•

WHEN HARRY MET SALLY . . .
1989, 95 mins, US Ⓥ ⦿ col
Dir Rob Reiner ***Prod*** Rob Reiner, Andrew Scheinman ***Scr*** Nora Ephron ***Ph*** Barry Sonnenfeld ***Ed*** Robert Leighton ***Mus*** Marc Shaiman ***Art*** Jane Musky
Act Billy Crystal, Meg Ryan, Carrie Fisher, Bruno Kirby, Steven Ford, Lisa Jane Persky (Castle Rock/Nelson)

Can a man be friends with a woman he finds attractive? Can usually acerbic scripter Nora Ephron sustain 95 minutes of unrelenting cuteness? Can the audience sit through 11 years of emotional foreplay between adorable Billy Crystal and Meg Ryan?

Abandoning the sour, nasty tone of some of her previous writing about contemporary sexual relationships, Ephron cuddles up to the audience in this number about the joys and woes of (mostly) platonic friendship. Two characters who seem to have nothing on their minds but each other (even though they won't admit it), Harry and Sally are supposed to be a political consultant and a journalist, but it's hard to tell from the evidence presented.

Rob Reiner directs with deftness and sincerity, making the material seem more engaging than it is, at least until the plot mechanics begin to unwind and the film starts to seem shapeless. The only thing that's unpredictable about the story is how long it takes Harry and Sally to realize they're perfect for each other.

1989: NOMINATION: Best Original Screenplay

•

WHEN I FALL IN LOVE
SEE: EVERYBODY'S ALL-AMERICAN

•

WHEN LADIES MEET
1933, 73 mins, US b/w
Dir Harry Beaumont ***Prod*** Lawrence Weingarten ***Scr*** John Meehan, Leon Gordon ***Ph*** Ray June ***Ed*** Hugh Wynn
Act Ann Harding, Robert Montgomery, Myrna Loy, Alice Brady, Frank Morgan, Luis Alberni (M-G-M)

Few stage plays reach the screen with the author's idea. But here the adapters have preserved the savor of the original [by Rachel Crothers] while producing a generally mobile atmosphere.

Story gets off to a typical picture start, which will lead those unfamiliar with the drama to fear another of those wild-life-in-society yarns, but it soon steadies down into nicely paced action punctuated by plenty of laughs that arise from the lines instead of horseplay.

When the big scene between the two women (Ann Harding and Myrna Loy) does arrive, the spectator is so intrigued by the characters that it is not necessary to frantically angle to conceal the fact that the chat runs what might be overlong. It's interesting and holds quiet attention, which is unusual.

The script is nicely planned with much of the original dialog apparently preserved, and Harry Beaumont does an exceptional job of direction.

In addition to Harding's fine playing, Loy does an excellent chore with the nominal heroine as the ambitious young writer who has fallen in love with her publisher. She plays sincerely and naturally. Robert Montgomery does not quite get into his character. On the other hand Alice Brady, in a fat part as a socialite is dangerously close to running away with the film now and then, and is responsible for the major portion of laughs.

1932/33: NOMINATION: Best Art Direction

•

WHEN LADIES MEET
1941, 103 mins, US Ⓥ b/w
Dir Robert Z. Leonard ***Prod*** Robert Z. Leonard, Orville O. Dull ***Scr*** S. K. Lauren, Anita Loos ***Ph*** Robert Planck ***Ed*** Robert J. Kern ***Mus*** Bronislau Kaper ***Art*** Cedric Gibbons, Randall Duell
Act Joan Crawford, Robert Taylor, Greer Garson, Herbert Marshall, Spring Byington, Rafael Storm (M-G-M)

Second picturization of Rachael Crothers's play carries excellence in directing, acting and mounting, all combined in a carefully charted production. But being a close translation of the stage piece, it's long on talk and slim on action, with plot unfolding entirely via the dialog route.

Joan Crawford is Mary Howard, a young authoress, admired and loved by Jimmy Lee (Robert Taylor), who launches a romance with book publisher Woodruff (Herbert Marshall). Deciding that the affair has gone far enough, Lee introduces Woodruff's wife to Howard, with both women unaware of their triangle corners. After the wife does some frank talking on marriage and husbands, in a boudoir chat, the respective positions of wife and other women are unveiled.

Sterling performances by the cast principals do much to overcome the talky atmosphere generated by the stagey unfolding. Greer Garson is outstanding as the wife, catching major honors. Crawford is fine in the role of the writer who is confronted with a love triangle in both her new book and real life. Taylor lightly carries the assignment of the young man who sets up the dramatic climax.

Spring Byington, who was in the 1932 stage original, adds moderate portions of comedy as the flustery matron who becomes bewildered by the mixup.

•

WHEN SATURDAY COMES
1996, 97 mins, UK Ⓥ col
Dir Maria Giese ***Prod*** James Daly, Christopher Lambert, Meir Teper ***Scr*** Maria Giese ***Ph*** Gerry Fisher ***Ed*** George Akers ***Mus*** Anne Dudley ***Art*** Hugo Luczyc-Wyhowski
Act Sean Bean, Emily Lloyd, Pete Postlethwaite, John McEnery, Ann Bell, Melanie Hill (Capitol)

A strong British cast adds dramatic tone to familiar material in *When Saturday Comes*, a northern working-class drama about a young guy trying to better himself and break his ne'er-do-well father's family jinx. In a role Albert Finney would have played in the early '60s, Sean Bean adds another strongly drawn character to his portfolio.

Making her feature bow, American writer-director Maria Giese bases her script on the early life of her husband, Sheffield-born producer James Daly (*Highlander II* and its sequel). The low-budgeter is clearly a labor of love for all concerned, including Bean, who's also from Sheffield.

Jimmy Muir (Bean) still lives at home, with his younger brother Russell (Craig Kelly), embittered father (John McEnery) and downtrodden mom (Ann Bell). His dream is to make it as a professional soccer player with Sheffield United. Jimmy starts making headway with the perky Annie (Emily Lloyd), an Irish girl who's just started at his factory. The big time beckons Jimmy with an invitation to try out for Sheffield United, but he suddenly blows his chances on all fronts.

What surprises the pic presents come almost entirely from the performances, with Bean playing his part to the hilt, and Lloyd making quite a mark as the sassy, self-possessed Annie.

•

WHEN STRANGERS MARRY
(AKA: BETRAYED)
1944, 67 mins, US b/w
Dir William Castle ***Prod*** Maurice King, Franklin King ***Scr*** Philip Yordan, Dennis J. Cooper ***Ph*** Ira Morgan ***Ed*** Martin G. Cohn ***Mus*** Dimitri Tiomkin ***Art*** F. Paul Sylos
Act Dean Jagger, Kim Hunter, Robert Mitchum, Neil Hamilton, Lou Lubin, Milt Kibbee (Monogram)

Only thing wrong with this film is its misleading title. Tag, *When Strangers Marry*, suggests another of the problem plays of newlyweds when in reality pic is a taut psychological thriller about a murderer and a manhunt full of suspense and excitement.

Film has smart, fresh handling throughout, in scripting, direction and especially photography. Some neat angle shots, montages and other mood-instilling camera bits are worked in for proper effect without disrupting flow of narrative [from an original story by George Moscov]. Psych mood is cleverly sustained throughout for good atmosphere.

Two strangers are married after three meetings and immediately separated. The girl goes off to find her man. Then begins another type of manhunt, the police on the trail of a killer who to all intents and purposes is the disappearing husband. Girl finds her man in hiding, and the two continue dodging the cops.

Dean Jagger has the soft menacing air that befits the suspect. Kim Hunter, a comparative newcomer, is attractive as well as immensely appealing as the distraught but loyal wife. Robert Mitchum has a breezy quality to fit his role of boyfriend, and Neil Hamilton plays the police lieutenant quietly and with dignity.

•

WHEN THE BOYS MEET THE GIRLS

1965, 97 mins, US ⦿ ⌑ b col

Dir Alvin Ganzer ***Prod*** Sam Katzman ***Scr*** Robert E. Kent ***Ph*** Paul C. Vogel ***Ed*** Ben Lewis ***Mus*** Fred Karger

Act Connie Francis, Harve Presnell, Herman's Hermits, Louis Armstrong, Sam The Sham and the Pharoahs, Sue Ane Langdon (Four Leaf/M-G-M)

When the Boys Meet the Girls is the third film to be based specifically on the 1930–1 legituner, *Girl Crazy*. This production is a spotty comedy film, loaded with often extraneous tunes, also limited to some okay performances and gags.

Top-featured Connie Francis and Harve Presnell (seemingly cast more from contractual commitments than suitability) are adequate; she as the backwoods Nevada U.S. mailwoman saddled with pop Frank Faylen, a chronic gambler, while Presnell is the big city playboy exiled to the boondocks to avoid a breach-of-promise suit by chorine Sue Ane Langdon.

Joby Baker is Presnell's buddy who eventually pairs with a rather mute Susan Holloway, and Fred Clark is good as the neighboring rancher who hitches up with Hortense Petra. Langdon remains the most impressive of the principals; she makes a first-rate shrew.

Among the 11 tunes are five vintage Gershwin numbers, including "I Got Rhythm," subject of which is the big production number.

•

WHEN THE WHALES CAME

1989, 99 mins, UK Ⓥ ⦿ col

Dir Clive Rees ***Prod*** Simon Channing Williams ***Scr*** Michael Morpurgo ***Ph*** Robert Paynter ***Ed*** Andrew Boulton ***Mus*** Christopher Gunning ***Art*** Bruce Grimes

Act Paul Scofield, David Thelfall, Helen Mirren, David Suchet, Helen Pearce, Jeremy Kemp (Golden Swan/Central)

When the Whales Came is a slight story beautifully dressed to give the appearance of more substance. Performances, direction and design are all first-rate, but there is the overwhelming sensation that there is a lot less there then meets the eye.

Film [from the novel *Why the Whales Came* by Michael Morpurgo] opens on the island of Samson in the Scilly Isles in 1844 where locals leave the island they believe cursed. Then in 1914 on the neighbouring island of Bryher, youngsters Daniel (Max Rennie) and Gracie (Helen Pearce) play on the beach, watched by the mysterious Birdman (Paul Scofield).

Though warned against Birdman by other villagers, they make friends with him and he warns them about never going to Samson. When a tusked whale (a narwhal) is beached on the shore, it seems the curse of Samson will strike Bryher.

Paul Scofield's portrayal of the deaf Birdman has the quality of sadness and pride that only he can give a role. Most endearing performance is by radiant young Pearce. A non-actor, she is a resident of Bryher (where pic is set) and was only found when she turned up for work as an extra.

•

WHEN WILLIE COMES MARCHING HOME

1949, 82 mins, US b/w

Dir John Ford ***Prod*** Fred Kohlmar ***Scr*** Mary Loos, Richard Sale ***Ph*** Leo Tover ***Ed*** James B. Clark ***Mus*** Alfred Newman ***Art*** Lyle Wheeler, Chester Gore

Act Dan Dailey, Corinne Calvet, Colleen Townsend, William Demarest, Mae Marsh (20th Century-Fox)

Dan Dailey, in the title role, carries most of the picture alone as a small-town lad who becomes a hero when he is first to enlist after Pearl Harbor. Immediately after his basic training, though, he is shipped back to a newly opened air base in the same hometown and the population turns against him when he is held there for over two years as a gunnery instructor.

Dailey is finally tagged as a last-minute replacement for an ailing B-17 gunner.

Credit for the laugh-fest can be spread among Dailey and the rest of the cast, the excellent script [based on a story by Sy Gomberg] and all connected with the production. But the major share goes to John Ford. Ford turns to comedy for the first time and demonstrates that a laugh-film can also be his forte.

•

WHEN WORLDS COLLIDE

1951, 81 mins, US Ⓥ ⦿ col

Dir Rudolph Mate ***Prod*** George Pal ***Scr*** Sydney Boehm ***Ph*** John F. Seitz, W. Howard Greene ***Ed*** Doane Harrison, Arthur Schmidt ***Mus*** Leith Stevens ***Art*** Hal Pereira, Albert Nozaki

Act Richard Derr, Barbara Rush, Peter Hanson, John Hoyt, Larry Keating, Judith Ames (Paramount)

Top honors for this interplanetary fantasy rest with the cameramen and special effects technicians rather than with performances of the non-name cast. Process photography and optical illusions are done with an imaginativeness that vicariously sweeps the spectator into space.

Story is predicated upon the findings of a scientist (Hayden Rorke) that a planet, Zyra, will pass so close to the earth a year hence and oceans will be pulled from their beds. Moreover, 19 days after this catastrophe, the star, Bellus, will collide with whatever remains of the world.

Unfortunately, scripter Sydney Boehm who fashioned the screenplay [from a novel by Edwin Balmer and Philip Wylie], chose to work in a romance between Barbara Rush, daughter of astronomer Larry Keating, and Richard Derr, a plane pilot. His love rival is Peter Hanson, a doctor.

Departure, actual flight and landing upon Zyra represent the highpoint of the picture. Somewhat of a puzzle, however, is the fact that although the ship lands upon an ice-covered valley, its occupants step out into a verdant paradise when opening the craft's door.

1951: Best Special Effects

NOMINATION: Best Color Cinematography

•

WHERE ANGELS FEAR TO TREAD

1991, 112 mins, UK Ⓥ col

Dir Charles Sturridge ***Prod*** Derek Granger ***Scr*** Tim Sullivan, Derek Granger, Charles Sturridge ***Ph*** Michael Coulter ***Ed*** Peter Coulson ***Mus*** Rachel Portman ***Art*** Simon Holland

Act Helena Bonham Carter, Judy Davis, Rupert Graves, Giovanni Guidelli, Barbara Jefford, Helen Mirren (Sovereign)

A turn-of-the-century costumer about cold-blooded Brits thawing out in sunny Italy, *Where Angels Fear to Tread* is a far more rewarding dip into the E. M. Forster tub than some of its predecessors. Paralleling the 1905 book's light, seriocomic tone, pic has none of the top-heaviness of David Lean's *A Passage to India* or the starchiness of Merchant-Ivory's *A Room with a View*.

Feisty widow Lilia (Helen Mirren) goes to Italy for some R&R with younger companion Caroline (Helena Bonham Carter) and tangles with Tuscan boytoy Gino (Giovanni Guidelli). When news reaches home, Lilia's bossy mother-in-law, Mrs. Herriton (Barbara Jefford), dispatches milquetoast son Philip (Rupert Graves) to buy off the hot-blooded Italo. That idea goes down the tubes when the pair reveal they're already hitched.

Pic's strength is the way in which characters come in and out of focus. Lilia, it turns out, is simply a catalyst: true love affair is a sexually blurred triangle of Philip, Caroline and Gino.

Helmer Charles Sturridge tweaks what could have been a talky telepic into a proper theatrical product. Like his previous *A Handful of Dust*, pic plays well on the big screen, with tasty Italian vistas, sharp pacing and (apart from a few static interiors) sequences that really move.

Bonham Carter, who gives her strongest performance to date as the repressed Caroline, is ably supported by Graves. Duo's final scene, a *Brief Encounter*–like meet in a station, packs real emotional clout.

•

WHERE EAGLES DARE

1969, 158 mins, UK/US Ⓥ ⦿ ⌑ col

Dir Brian G. Hutton ***Prod*** Elliott Kastner ***Scr*** Alistair MacLean ***Ph*** Arthur Ibbetson ***Ed*** John Jympson ***Mus*** Ron Goodwin ***Art*** Peter Mullins

Act Richard Burton, Clint Eastwood, Mary Ure, Michael Hordern, Patrick Wymark, Anton Diffring (M-G-M/Winkast)

Alistair MacLean wrote an original screenplay that was treated with respect for the writer's unusual abilities as a master of actionful suspense. The resulting film is highly entertaining, thrilling and rarely lets down for a moment.

It's basically a tale of rescuing a captured American general from a German stronghold in Bavaria during World War II by a hand-picked team of experts. There are so many twists and turns that the viewer is seldom able to predict the next scene.

Richard Burton, a British agent, and Clint Eastwood, an OSS "assassin," head the crew which includes femme agent Mary Ure, who works at the spy bit.

Although the film is replete with killings and explosions, they're so integrated into the story that they never appear overdone. It's more of a saga of cool, calculated courage, than any glorification of war. Burton never treats his role, though full of clichés, as anything less than *Hamlet*. Eastwood seems rather wooden in the early scenes, but snaps out of it when action starts piling up.

•

WHERE LOVE HAS GONE

1964, 111 mins, US Ⓥ ⌑ col

Dir Edward Dmytryk ***Prod*** Joseph E. Levine ***Scr*** John Michael Hayes ***Ph*** Joseph MacDonald ***Ed*** Frank Bracht ***Mus*** Walter Scharf ***Art*** Hal Pereira, Walter Tyler

Act Susan Hayward, Bette Davis, Michael Connors, Joey Heatherton, Jane Greer, DeForest Kelley (Paramount)

Sooner or later it was bound to happen—a film based on the celebrated one-time Hollywood scandal of the daughter of a film star stabbing to death her mother's paramour. Picture takes its cue in close detail from this incident and patently was inspiration for the Harold Robbins novel. Scene is changed from Hollywood to San Francisco, and the mother now is a society woman with a bent for sculpture.

Sufficient ingenuity and shock value in character delineation have been interwoven into the screenplay to maintain high-tempoed interest as the yarn revolves around a bitter divorced couple come together again briefly to save their daughter after the fifteen-year-old girl kills her mother's lover.

Susan Hayward and Bette Davis share top honors in impressive performances, former as the daughter whose life is a story of indiscretions. Davis, smart in a white wig, plays the autocratic mother, who always sees that the family name is protected at any price, a scheming woman of unscrupulous methods and seemingless inexhaustible means. Picture is a brilliant showcase for both actresses and projects them in roles which will find much comment. As the mixed-up teenager who never knew domestic happiness, Joey Heatherton is ideally cast and delivers a compelling portrayal.

1964: NOMINATION: Best Song ("Where Love Has Gone')

•

WHERE NO VULTURES FLY *(US: IVORY HUNTER)*

1951, 106 mins, UK col

Dir Harry Watt ***Prod*** Michael Balcon, Leslie Norman ***Scr*** W. P. Lipscomb, Ralph Smart, Leslie Norman ***Ph*** Paul Beeson ***Ed*** Gordon Stone ***Mus*** Alan Rawsthorne

Act Anthony Steel, Dinah Sheridan, Harold Warrender, Meredith Edwards, William Simons, Orlando Martins (Ealing)

Excellent Technicolor photography and a few thrilling wild animal sequences are the highlights of *Where No Vultures Fly*. On the whole, it's a soundly made film, lensed in the attractive East African setting of the Kenya National Park.

Merely as a peg for the fine location work, there is tagged on an insignificant though basically true story of a game warden who starts the National Park after fighting local prejudice, hunters and ivory poachers. Plot is of little consequence. Main entertainment is derived from some of the exciting animal sequences.

Harry Watt's direction of the game sequences is top grade, but he tends to flounder when handling human characters. Notwithstanding this, Anthony Steel does an excellent and spirited job as the warden, but Dinah Sheridan is never anything but demure as his wife.

•

WHERE'S JACK?

1969, 113 mins, UK col

Dir James Clavell ***Prod*** Stanley Baker ***Scr*** Rafe Newhouse, David Newhouse ***Ph*** John Wilcox ***Ed*** Peter Thornton ***Mus*** Elmer Bernstein ***Art*** Cedric Dawe

Act Tommy Steele, Stanley Baker, Fiona Lewis, Alan Badel, Dudley Foster, Noel Purcell (Paramount/Oakhurst)

Where's Jack, story of Jack Sheppard, notorious eighteenth-century London highwayman, does not move speedily or with tremendous dramatic climaxes, but it has an authentic sense of atmosphere, and provides a holding battle of wits between the two leading protagonists.

Tommy Steele and Stanley Baker are supported by a competent cast of character actors.

Steele turns in a good acting performance. Unfortunately, the script does not give him much chance to give the role any depth.

Where's Jack? could well have been a more impressive picture about a colorful era in bawdy, criminal, corrupt London [of 1724]. But film has settled for a single adventure and, despite occasional lagging in inventiveness, is a simple and holding yarn.

●

WHERE SLEEPING DOGS LIE

1992, 89 mins, US Ⓥ col

Dir Charles Finch **Prod** Mario Sotela **Scr** Yolande Turner, Charles Finch **Ph** Monty Rowan **Ed** B. J. Sears, Gene M. Gemaine **Mus** Hans Zimmer, Mark Mancina **Art** Eve Cauley

Act Dylan McDermott, Tom Sizemore, Sharon Stone, Mary Woronov, David Combs, Shawne Rowe (Sotela)

A clash of two dissimilar personalities is examined with mixed success in the thriller *Where Sleeping Dogs Lie*. Dylan McDermott portrays an unsuccessful writer in Hollywood who's frustrated by the commercial need to write blood-and-guts stories. His agent, Sharon Stone, puts on the pressure, and he decides to write a detailed novel about a mass killer. McDermott moves into the creepy old mansion his day-job real estate boss (Ron Karabatsos) has ordered him to sell. Gimmick is that he uses the house for inspiration, basing his novel on a notorious murder case that took place there. Before the film can turn into a haunted house suspenser, Tom Sizemore shows up as a twitchy boarder.

Director Charles Finch (son of the late actor Peter Finch) and his mother, coscripter Yolande Turner, get good mileage from the insidious relationship that develops between the two protagonists, reminiscent of the classic *The Servant*. Stone is perfect in a small role as the bitchy agent. Rest of the cast has mere walk-ons in a film that reportedly was heavily trimmed to reach its release version.

●

WHERE'S POPPA?

1970, 83 mins, US Ⓥ ⦿ col

Dir Carl Reiner **Prod** Jerry Tokofsky, Marvin Worth **Scr** Robert Klane **Ph** Jack Priestly **Ed** Bud Molin, Chic Ciccolini **Mus** Jack Elliott **Art** Warren Clymer

Act George Segal, Ruth Gordon, Ron Liebman, Trish Van Devere, Barnard Hughes, Vincent Gardenia (United Artists)

Where's Poppa? is an insane movie, a black comedy with George Segal as a young lawyer with an active death wish for his old Jewish mother, played by Ruth Gordon, whose senile eccentricities are ruining his career, sex life and health.

Robert Klane's screenplay, adapted from his novel, is very close to tragedy, except that he, director Carl Reiner and an exceptional cast work from the firm conviction that everyone, at least everyone living in New York City, is insane.

Gordon, as the widowed mother, is in senile dementia, constantly asking "Where's Poppa?" and scaring off nurses and Segal's girlfriends with her bawdy eccentricities.

In her mental lapses she can't remember her son is a grown man, and when he brings home Trish Van Devere, the mother suddenly describes the size of her son's sex organs as if he were a child.

Van Devere as a prospective nurse looks like the Angel of Mercy with her sweet pure face framed in a white cap, but she is also a little insane.

●

WHERE THE BOYS ARE

1960, 99 mins, US Ⓥ ⦿ ▭ col

Dir Henry Levin **Prod** Joe Pasternak **Scr** George Wells **Ph** Robert Bronner **Ed** Fredric Steinkamp **Mus** George Stoll **Art** George W. Davis, Preston Ames

Act Dolores Hart, George Hamilton, Yvette Mimieux, Jim Hutton, Barbara Nichols, Paula Prentiss (M-G-M)

The Boys of today, according to the screenplay out of Glendon Swarthout's novel, are generally in irresponsible sexual orbit and it is up to the girls of today to bring them down to earth.

The scenario is set in Fort Lauderdale, Florida, site of an annual spring invasion by Easter-vacationing collegians from all over the East and Midwest, most of the males apparently from the Halls of Ivy (or "Yalies," as they are precociously referred to once too often here). Most of the girls manage to avoid the primitive passion, but there is an occasional casualty, in this case Yvette Mimieux, who winds up walking the white line on a Florida highway after getting in too deep with a pair of these unscrupulous "Yalies."

Mimieux, in a demanding role, gets by dramatically. Visually she is a knockout, and has a misty quality. Paula Prentiss, making her screen debut, is of the Rosalind Russell–Eve Arden mold. Recording star Connie Francis also makes her screen debut.

Jim Hutton is affable, Barbara Nichols flashy (as a dumb blonde in an exaggerated swimming-tank sequence), Frank Gorshin animated and amusing, and Chill Wills effective. Dolores Hart and George Hamilton make beautiful music together.

●

WHERE THE BUFFALO ROAM

1980, 96 mins, US Ⓥ col

Dir Art Linson **Prod** Art Linson **Scr** John Kaye **Ph** Tak Fujimoto **Ed** Christopher Greenbury **Mus** Neil Young **Art** Richard Sawyer

Act Peter Boyle, Bill Murray, Bruno Kirby, Rene Auberjonois, R. G. Armstrong, Leonard Frey (Universal)

Where the Buffalo Roam is based on the self-described antics of flip journalist Hunter S. Thompson, who cooperated as "executive consultant." Pic features a number of amusing set-pieces of irreverent lunacy, but lack of serious substance renders film too frivolous and detached from reality.

Film establishes its tone in the opening scene, as writer tries to finish a piece while downing full glasses of Wild Turkey.

Only things fortifying Thompson here are drink, drugs and the search for the insane in American culture.

Sole exceptional element is Bill Murray's clearly studied but provocatively off-beat performance as Thompson, which rings absolutely true.

●

WHERE THE DAY TAKES YOU

1992, 92 mins, US Ⓥ ⦿ col

Dir Marc Rocco **Prod** Paul Hertzberg **Scr** Michael Hitchcock, Kurt Voss, Marc Rocco **Ph** King Baggott **Ed** Russel Livingstone **Art** Kirk Petrucelli

Act Dermont Mulroney, Lara Flynn Boyle, Balthazar Getty, Sean Astin, James LeGros, Kyle MacLachlan (Cintel)

Attempting a hard-hitting pic on the grimy realities of Hollywood Boulevard street life, and blessed with a cast bursting with up-and-comer names and a technically adept cameraman, *Where the Day Takes You* inevitably winds up giving the runaway's life the kind of romantic-tragic scope that appeals to troubled teens.

A goateed and tattooed Dermot Mulroney, in a very charismatic turn, plays King, a twenty-one-year-old parolee who returns to his position as a natural leader of street dwellers. He has his hands full watching a gun-happy youth (Balthazar Getty) with an itch for violence and a middle-class runaway (Sean Astin) who stays totally "tweaked" on speed.

In between profiling himself in social work sessions with a sultry-voiced interviewer (Laura San Giacomo), King takes up with the newest and prettiest chick off the bus from Chicago (a bra-less Lara Flynn Boyle), and shows her off round the streets.

Director Mark Rocco shapes some very fine performances, particularly from Mulroney, Boyle and Getty, while Steven Tobolowsky turns in a memorably chilly perf as a wealthy gay man who pays Getty for titillation. An uncredited Christian Slater turns up in a brief cameo as a social worker.

●

WHERE THE HEART IS

1990, 94 mins, US Ⓥ ⦿ col

Dir John Boorman **Prod** John Boorman **Scr** John Boorman, Telsche Boorman **Ph** Peter Suschitzky **Ed** Ian Crafford **Mus** Peter Martin **Art** Carol Spier

Act Dabney Coleman, Uma Thurman, Joanna Cassidy, David Hewlett, Suzy Amis, Christopher Plummer (Touchstone/Silver Screen Partners IV)

Film is a companion piece to John Boorman's little-seen *Leo the Last*, in which Marcello Mastroianni was an aristocrat who learns about life from ghetto denizens in London. This time it's tycoon Dabney Coleman who gets the message when he and his family end up in a Brooklyn tenement. Predictable plotting has tyrannical buildings demolitions expert Coleman getting fed up with his spoiled, grown-up kids. He throws them out of the mansion and (unconvincingly) orders them to live in a Brooklyn tenement.

Kids, led by Uma Thurman, are determined to make it on their own. Her sister (Suzy Amis) gets a gig doing a calendar for an insurance company, with Thurman the chief nude model for her body-painting and photography artwork.

Film's most successful element is the series of spectacular *trompe d'oeil* artworks by Timna Woollard, personified by Thurman. Combined with the all-nighter atmosphere of the delapidated Brooklyn house, pic succeeds in capturing a 1960s ambience.

Beside Thurman, who is perfectly cast as a sexy kook, Amis makes a very good impression as her artistic, romantic sister.

●

WHERE THE MONEY IS

2000, 90 mins, US Ⓥ ⦿ col

Dir Marek Kanievska **Prod** Ridley Scott, Charles Weinstock, Chris Zarpas, Christopher Dorr **Scr** E. Max Frye, Topper Lilien, Carroll Cartwright **Ph** Thomas Burstyn **Ed** Sam Craven, Garth Craven, Dan Lebental **Mus** Mark Isham **Art** Andre Chamberland

Act Paul Newman, Linda Fiorentino, Dermot Mulroney, Susan Barnes, Anne Pioniak, Bruce MacVittie (Scott Free-IMF/Gramercy)

Dominating every frame, Paul Newman's charismatic, multishaded performance as a legendary bank robber elevates this hodgepodge caper comedy a couple of notches above its preposterous plotting and self-consciously movie-ish texture. The uneven screenplay consciously echoes various roles in Newman's rich career, particularly that of "Fast Eddie" Felson in *The Hustler* and its sequel, *The Color of Money*, with further motifs and subplots borrowed from *Butch Cassidy and the Sundance Kid* and *The Sting*.

The mute and unresponsive Henry Manning (Newman) is delivered by prison guards to a nursing home, where the apparent stroke victim is placed under the care of Carol (Fiorentino), a nurse who's utterly bored by her job and her marriage to the none-too-ambitious Wayne (Dermot Mulroney). Throughout, text effectively conveys the notion of life as a prison, in ways both realistic (for Henry) and figurative (for Carol and Wayne).

Carol suspects that there's more to the feeble and helpless man in the wheelchair than meets the eye. She orchestrates an audacious and irresponsible act, dumping Henry into the river. Henry emerges from the water intact and under his own power, and his trick is revealed: He faked a stroke in order to get out of prison.

Most exciting reel details the intimate, secretive bond that develops between the con man and the nurse. It's a tribute to Newman's still-handsome looks and abundant charm that he effortlessly generates an erotic charge with a woman who is young enough to be his daughter. Hubby Wayne, of course, gets jealous.

Henry consents to instruct Carol and the initially reluctant Wayne in the art of bank robbing, dispensing with great panache his accumulated wisdom. Yarn then proceeds none too convincingly with a heist that can only be described as a bargain-basement re-creation of Newman's earlier screen escapades. Story's crucial problem is not that it rehashes ideas from better films, but that it tries to play it both ways, moral and immoral, mythic and realistic. This is particularly true of the crowd-pleasing ending. The major entertainment in this slight film is Newman's performance.

●

WHERE THE RIVER BENDS

SEE: BEND OF THE RIVER

WHERE THE RIVER RUNS BLACK

1986, 100 mins, US Ⓥ ⦿ ▭ col

Dir Christopher Cain **Prod** Joe Roth, Harry Ufland **Scr** Peter Silverman, Neal Jimenez **Ph** Juan Ruiz-Anchia **Ed** Richard Chew **Mus** James Horner **Art** Marcos Flaksman

Act Charles Durning, Alessandro Rabelo, Ajay Naidu, Peter Horton, Conchata Ferrell, Dana Delany (M-G-M)

Where the River Runs Black is a beautifully simple film that celebrates an innocent boy's peaceful coexistence with nature while subtly despairing about man's abuse of it.

Film revolves around a boy with roots in modern civilization being raised by Amazon tribespeople without the knowledge he is the child of two very distinct worlds.

Scripters Peter Silverman and Neal Jimenez have taken David Kendall's novel, *Lazaro*, and crafted a screenplay where the few words of dialog spoken speak worlds of meaning.

Much is said in silence and most effectively told through the movements of ten-year-old Rabelo, a waiflike Brazilian swimmer perfectly cast to portray the physically and emotionally confused dolphin boy traumatized by competing forces. Charles Durning is a natural as a fatherly Irish priest, letting his heart—not the fact that he wears a collar—determine the ultimate fate of the orphan boy.

●

WHERE THE SIDEWALK ENDS
1950, 95 mins, US b/w
Dir Otto Preminger ***Prod*** Otto Preminger ***Scr*** Ben Hecht ***Ph*** Joseph LaShelle ***Ed*** Louis Loeffler ***Mus*** Cyril J. Mockridge ***Art*** Lyle Wheeler, J. Russell Spencer
Act Dana Andrews, Gene Tierney, Gary Merrill, Karl Malden, Tom Tully, Ruth Donnelly (20th Century-Fox)

Story, by Ben Hecht [adapted by Victor Trivas, Frank P. Rosenberg and Robert E. Kent from the novel *Night City* by William Stuart], unwinds with a maximum of suspense and swiftly paced action and is featured by an excellent performance by Dana Andrews. Picture is also notable for better-than-average character portrayals and costar Gene Tierney.

Andrews, while he is on the carpet for slugging too many hoodlums before he has criminal evidence against them, accidentally kills a man in a fistic battle, in self-defense. Victim is Craig Stevens, former war hero and ne'er-do-well estranged husband of Gene Tierney, a lush model.

Otto Preminger, director, does an excellent job of pacing the story and of building sympathy for Andrews.

•

WHERE THE SPIES ARE
1966, 113 mins, UK col
Dir Val Guest ***Prod*** Val Guest, Steven Pallos ***Scr*** Wolf Mankowitz, Val Guest ***Ph*** Arthur Grant ***Ed*** Bill Lenny ***Mus*** Mario Nascimbene ***Art*** John Howell
Act David Niven, Francoise Dorleac, Cyril Cusack, John Le Mesurier, Nigel Davenport, Eric Pohlmann (M-G-M)

David Niven stars as a mild-mannered English doctor pressed into Middle East espionage. The production carries suspense, after a slow and talky start, and action, even if a bit on the contrived side, is fast-paced once story gets underway. Locale is Beirut, where troupe locationed to come up with interesting authenticity of background.

Based on James Leasor's thriller, *Passport to Oblivion*, Guest, who also directs and collabed with Wolf Mankowitz on script, concentrates on the dangers confronting a secret agent. Niven, who once figured in some fancy undercover work for British Intelligence, is sent to Lebanon to try to learn what urgent information the agent there had uncovered before he was bumped off by the Russians.

Niven delivers one of his customary competent performances, stuffy at times but able to cope with the melodramatic demands of the character. Teaming with Niven as a French mam'selle playing both sides as a secret agent and supposedly his contact is Francoise Dorleac, lushly effective.

•

WHERE WERE YOU WHEN THE LIGHTS WENT OUT?
1968, 90 mins, US col
Dir Hy Averback ***Prod*** Everett Freeman, Martin Melcher ***Scr*** Everett Freeman, Karl Tunberg ***Ph*** Ellsworth Fredricks ***Ed*** Rita Roland ***Mus*** Dave Grusin ***Art*** George W. Davis, Urie McCleary
Act Doris Day, Robert Morse, Terry-Thomas, Patrick O'Neal, Lola Albright, Jim Backus (M-G-M)

An okay Doris Day comedy, well cast with Robert Morse and Terry-Thomas. On November 9, 1965, large parts of the eastern U.S. were blacked out. Almost six months later, this film was announced. Some fifteen months later, it rolled. And over thirty months after the event, it was released. How's that for reacting to events?

In this script [based on a play by Claude Magnier], the blackout is less than a prop for a routine marital mixup. Day, as a legit actress employed by producer Thomas, is married to architect Patrick O'Neal. Latter lingers a bit too long with sexy magazine interviewer Lola Albright, cueing Day's stormy exit to Connecticut hideaway. Simultaneously, Morse, aced out of being made president of his company by nepotism, steals a pile of money.

Averback's comedy direction lifts things a bit out of a well-plowed rut, making for an amusing, while never hilarious, film.

•

WHILE THE CITY SLEEPS
1956, 99 mins, US Ⓥ b/w
Dir Fritz Lang ***Prod*** Bert Friedlob ***Scr*** Casey Robinson ***Ph*** Ernest Laszlo ***Ed*** Gene Fowler Jr ***Mus*** Herschel Burke Gilbert ***Art*** Carroll Clark
Act Dana Andrews, Ida Lupino, Rhonda Fleming, George Sanders, Vincent Price, Howard Duff (RKO)

The old-fashioned "stop the presses" newspaper yarn has been updated with intelligence and considerable authenticity, and further brightened with crisp dialog from the pen of Casey Robinson. His screen adaptation of Charles Einstein's novel [*The Bloody Spur* weaves several story lines together. Among them are the murderous activities of a homicidal maniac, played by John Barrymore, Jr.; a scramble for power among the top brass of a newspaper empire; and a good-natured love story between the paper's top reporter, played by Dana Andrews, and Sally Forrest, the secretary of one of the contestants.

When the empire's chieftain, played by Robert Warwick, dies, his son, Vincent Price, decides to set up a new top exec post for grabs.

Contenders are: Thomas Mitchell, editor of the keystone paper; George Sanders, head of the empire's wire service; and James Craig, dapper photo bureau chief.

Price lets it be known that the one to crack the wave of murders being committed by Barrymore gets the job. Sanders and Mitchell commence heartily to cut each other's throats, while Craig puts the pressure, literally and figuratively, on Fleming.

Plot intricacies are deftly interwoven, with director Fritz Lang doing a topflight job of balancing the ingredients without dragging the pace.

•

WHILE YOU WERE SLEEPING
1995, 103 mins, US Ⓥ ⊙ col
Dir Jon Turteltaub ***Prod*** Joe Roth, Roger Birnbaum ***Scr*** Daniel G. Sullivan, Fredric Lebow ***Ph*** Phedon Papamichael ***Ed*** Bruce Green ***Mus*** Randy Edelman ***Art*** Garreth Stover
Act Sandra Bullock, Bill Pullman, Peter Gallagher, Peter Boyle, Jack Warden, Glynis Johns (Hollywood)

While You Were Sleeping, a clear descendent of the Cornell Woolrich story *I Married a Dead Man* (filmed earlier as *No Man of Her Own* in 1950 and in 1983), has all the trappings of a lighthearted romantic comedy. Woolrich's tale involved a woman who took the identity of another who'd been killed on her way to meeting in-laws for the first time. The new film's complete embrace of love's ability to break through all barriers is undeniably infectious.

Lucy (Sandra Bullock) is alone and lonely in Chicago, working as a toll-taker for the Chicago Transit Authority. Her dreamboat is a handsome guy in a camelhair coat (Peter Gallagher) who's never so much as said hello. Nonetheless, she knows they will meet.

That momentous day arrives around Christmas, when she sees him jostled, mugged and pushed off the train platform. She struggles to get the unconscious man out of the path of a speeding train, and succeeds. A series of misunderstandings result in Lucy's being presented as the comatose man's fiancée, as well as his savior. His loud, eccentric family thinks that's just great. And, after some mild trepidation, so does Lucy.

The twist that keeps the audience off balance is the budding but unresolvable romance between the poseur and Mr. Coma's brother Jack (Bill Pullman). *While You Were Sleeping* is as fragile as a house of cards. Its success is a true testament to its cast and to director Jon Turteltaub's keen sense of balance.

Bullock's first romantic starring vehicle reveals a high likability quotient in her role as a smart, if vulnerable, woman. Pullman, rarely used effectively onscreen, takes great relish in his plum role. He's a delight.

•

WHIRLPOOL
1949, 97 mins, US b/w
Dir Otto Preminger ***Prod*** Otto Preminger ***Scr*** Ben Hecht, Andrew Solt ***Ph*** Arthur Miller ***Ed*** Louis Loeffler ***Mus*** David Raksin
Act Gene Tierney, Richard Conte, Jose Ferrer, Charles Bickford, Barbara O'Neil, Fortunio Bonanova (20th Century-Fox)

Whirlpool is a highly entertaining, exciting melodrama that combines the authentic features of hypnosis.

Ben Hecht and Andrew Solt have tightly woven a screenplay [from a novel by Guy Endore] about the effects of hypnosis on the subconscious, but they, and Otto Preminger in his direction, have eliminated the phoney characteristics that might easily have allowed the picture to slither into becoming just another eerie melodrama.

Their subject is a young wife of a prominent psychiatrist who, since adolescence, has been plagued by kleptomania.

As the young wife, Gene Tierney gives a plausible performance, though at times she fails to achieve the intensity that the entranced woman should have. Richard Conte, as her husband, is a little out of his metier here. The acting honors go to Jose Ferrer as the blackguard hypnotist.

•

WHISKY GALORE!
(US: TIGHT LITTLE ISLAND)
1949, 82 mins, UK Ⓥ b/w
Dir Alexander Mackendrick ***Prod*** Michael Balcon ***Scr*** Compton Mackenzie, Angus MacPhail ***Ph*** Gerald Gibbs, Chick Waterson ***Ed*** Joseph Sterling ***Mus*** Ernest Irving ***Art*** Jim Morahan
Act Basil Radford, Joan Greenwood, Gordon Jackson, James Robertson Justice, Bruce Seaton, Gabrielle Blunt (Ealing)

Compton Mackenzie's novel, on which the pic is based, is unfolded on a Hebridean island in 1943. Only sign of the war is the local Home Guard, but a major disaster occurs when the island runs out of whisky. After some days, a freighter with 50,000 cases of Scotch runs aground off the island. The natives organize a midnight expedition and lay in a tremendous store for future consumption.

Sustained comedy treatment successfully carries the film forward to the point where the islanders outwit the Home Guard captain who regards the adventure as the worst type of looting.

Basil Radford gives a flawless performance of the misunderstood Home Guard chief whose zealousness leads to trouble in high quarters. Bruce Seton and Joan Greenwood, as well as Gabrielle Blunt and Gordon Jackson, provide the slight romances of the film.

•

WHISPERERS, THE
1966, 103 mins, UK b/w
Dir Bryan Forbes ***Prod*** Michael S. Laughlin, Ronald Shedlo ***Scr*** Bryan Forbes ***Ph*** Gerry Turpin ***Ed*** Anthony Harvey ***Mus*** John Barry ***Art*** Ray Sims
Act Edith Evans, Eric Portman, Nanette Newman, Gerald Sim, Avis Bunnage, Ronald Fraser (United Artists)

Low-budgeter [from a novel by Robert Nicolson] centers around an old woman, estranged from her husband, who lives alone in a broken-down, tiny flat in a slummy outskirt of a British town. Her imaginary dream of sudden riches due her from a relative unexpectedly comes true one day when her son hides the haul of a robbery in her spare room, and she finds it.

Few other films have attacked the unglamorous but poignant theme of old-age loneliness with such understated feeling and unsentimental taste and discretion.

It has in Edith Evans's great performance an invaluable asset. Her portrayal of the ageing woman, now living on the near edge of insanity but unbowed by other physical hazards, determinedly struggling ahead in her waning fight for life, but head high, without complaints, makes the film.

1967: NOMINATION: Best Actress (Edith Evans)

•

WHISPERS IN THE DARK
1992, 102 mins, US Ⓥ ⊙ col
Dir Christopher Crowe ***Prod*** Martin Bregman, Michael S. Bregman ***Scr*** Christopher Crowe ***Ph*** Michael Chapman ***Ed*** Bill Pankow ***Mus*** Thomas Newman ***Art*** John Jay Moore
Act Annabella Sciorra, Jamey Sheridan, Anthony LaPaglia, Jill Clayburgh, John Leguizamo, Deborah Unger (Paramount)

A turn-off psycho-sexual thriller, *Whispers in the Dark* grows steadily more absurd by the reel until literally stumbling into the ocean at its climax.

Looking pale and vulnerable, Annabella Sciorra essays a meek Gotham shrink who begins getting turned on by tales of bondage and great sex confided by her patient Deborah Unger, a disturbing development she confides to her professional mentor (Alan Alda).

Ending a relationship with b.f. Anthony Heald, Sciorra begins falling for straight-arrow pilot Jamey Sheridan, but then discovers Sheridan is the sex partner Unger so deliciously describes. In a tiff, Unger makes off with some of Sciorra's private files and tapes but, before you can say ropes and handcuffs, Sciorra finds Unger murdered in her gallery.

Detective Anthony LaPaglia develops a thing for Sciorra while investigating the case, and it all devolves into a guessing game over which of these men killed Unger and may or may not be threatening Sciorra.

Some initial interest is generated by the intensely erotic performance of Unger, and by the unavoidable voyeuristic appeal of the numerous private sexual revelations. But a succession of psychiatric sessions do not a plot make, and writer-director Christopher Crowe nudges the picture along a very narrow track without coupling the viewer to the train.

•

WHISTLE BLOWER, THE
1987, 104 mins, UK Ⓥ ⊙ col
Dir Simon Langton ***Prod*** Geoffrey Reeve ***Scr*** Julian Bond ***Ph*** Fred Tammes ***Ed*** Robert Morgan ***Mus*** John Scott ***Art*** Morley Smith
Act Michael Caine, James Fox, Nigel Havers, Felicity Dean, John Gielgud, Gordon Jackson (Portreeve)

The Whistle Blower [from John Hale's novel] is a highly charged conspiracy theory drama. A murdered man, played by Nigel Havers, worked as a Russian translator at the top-secret listening center, GCHQ, in Cheltenham.

Michael Caine is excellent as his father, a role rather similar to that played by Jack Lemmon in *Missing*—a non-political, middle-aged man who's driven to radical action as a result of what the government he once trusted has done to his son.

The central sections, as Caine doggedly insists on finding out who killed his son and why, are tautly handled, creating considerable tension. Unfortunately, the film ends rather lamely, almost as if the writer wasn't sure how to finish it.

•

WHISTLE DOWN THE WIND
1961, 99 mins, UK Ⓥ b/w
Dir Bryan Forbes ***Prod*** Richard Attenborough ***Scr*** Keith Waterhouse, Willis Hall ***Ph*** Arthur Ibbetson ***Ed*** Max Benedict ***Mus*** Malcolm Arnold ***Art*** Ray Simm
Act Hayley Mills, Alan Bates, Bernard Lee, Norman Bird, Elsie Wagstaff, John Arnatt (Rank/Allied Film Makers)

Whistle Down the Wind takes a modern, sentimental-religious subject and treats it with care, taste, sincerity, imagination and good humor. The film was shot entirely on location in the bleak, raw countryside around Burnley in Lancashire, superbly caught by Arthur Ibbetson's camerawork. Based on Mary Hayley Bell's novel, it is a slight but human story of faith seen through the eyes of children.

Three small children, leading a lonely life on their father's farm, stumble on a ragged, unshaven man taking refuge in their barn. Startled when a terrified Hayley Mills asks who he is, the stranger is so relieved at finding the intruder is merely a child that he involuntarily swears "Jesus . . . Christ." The children take the remark literally. In fact, the man is a murderer on the run.

There are many pieces of New Testament symbolism but they arise naturally from the action. For instance, the betrayal is innocently done by a child at a birthday party. The local bully twists a smaller boy's arm and three times makes him deny that the fugitive is, indeed, Jesus Christ. Finally, when the police close in and frisk him, he stands with arms raised quite naturally, but the implication of the Crucifixion is clear in the pose.

Bryan Forbes in his debut as a director coaxes some outstanding performances from a bunch of local kids. Only their leader, young Mills, ever saw a script before. Result is complete authenticity.

•

WHISTLE STOP
1946, 84 mins, US Ⓥ b/w
Dir Leonide Moguy ***Prod*** Seymour Nebenzal ***Scr*** Philip Yordan ***Ph*** Russell Metty ***Ed*** Gregg Tallas ***Mus*** Dimitri Tiomkin ***Art*** Rudi Feld
Act George Raft, Ava Gardner, Victor McLaglen, Tom Conway (United Artists)

Heavy melodrama, adapted from the Maritta M. Wolff novel of same title, is somber melodrama, vignetting a seamy side of life in a small town. Production and playing are excellent and the direction strong, although latter is given to occasional arty tone.

Characters are all little people and not very nice. Story opens with Ava Gardner returning to the whistle-stop town of Ashbury to renew her romance with the shiftless George Raft. Pair had broken off two years previous because he refused to change his habits. Pair fight continually, and romance is getting nowhere until a prosperous rival, Tom Conway, owner of the town's hotel and saloon, starts to move in.

Under Leonide Moguy's direction Raft does a capable job of the small-timer. Gardner displays her best work to date as the girl who must have her man. McLaglen hits top form as the not-too-bright bartender, and Conway is smooth as the heavy. Score is an aid in projecting the somber mood.

•

WHITE BUFFALO, THE
1977, 97 mins, US Ⓥ col
Dir J. Lee Thompson ***Prod*** Pancho Kohner ***Scr*** Richard Sale ***Ph*** Paul Lohmann ***Ed*** Michael F. Anderson ***Mus*** John Barry ***Art*** Tambi Larsen
Act Charles Bronson, Jack Warden, Will Sampson, Kim Novak, Clint Walker, Stuart Whitman (De Laurentiis)

Charles Bronson stars as Wild Bill Hickok, returned to the West to hunt down an albino buffalo that haunts his dreams. Will Sampson is an Indian who also must purge himself of some dishonor.

Production features arch scripting by Richard Sale (from his novel), stilted acting by the cast and forced direction by J. Lee Thompson. The title beast looks like a hung-over carnival prize despite attempts at camouflage via hokey sound track noise, busy John Barry scoring, murky photography and fast editing.

The buffalo trackdown is actually more of a cheap writing hook, on which to hang a lot of dubious sociological gab between the players, than an outdoor adventure story.

•

WHITE CARGO
1942, 89 mins, US b/w
Dir Richard Thorpe ***Prod*** Victor Saville ***Scr*** Leon Gordon ***Ph*** Harry Stradling ***Ed*** Frederick Y. Smith ***Mus*** Bronislau Kaper
Act Hedy Lamarr, Walter Pidgeon, Frank Morgan, Richard Carlson, Reginald Owen (M-G-M)

This is the first American-made version of the sensational stage hit produced in 1923 by Earl Carroll in Greenwich Village, NY. From that downtown area Carroll moved the Leon Gordon play [from a novel by Ida Vera Simonton] to Broadway for a box-office mop up. The very fact that the entire action revolved around the passion of a white man, disintegrating in a tropical English colony, for a half-breed made it surefire for the then jazz and flapper era.

Playwright Leon Gordon adapted his own play for the screen and he hews closely to the original, even to holding off Tondelayo's first entrance until the film is 30 minutes old.

Walter Pidgeon plays well the part of the tough English magistrate of the colony who has to wet-nurse a succession of novices from the home country. Hedy Lamarr as the only femme in the film does her best acting to date.

•

WHITE CHRISTMAS
1954, 120 mins, US Ⓥ ⊙ col
Dir Michael Curtiz ***Prod*** Robert Emmett Dolan ***Scr*** Norman Krasna, Norman Panama, Melvin Frank ***Ph*** Loyal Griggs ***Ed*** Frank Bracht ***Mus*** Joseph J. Lilley ***Art*** Hal Pereira, Roland Anderson
Act Bing Crosby, Danny Kaye, Rosemary Clooney, Vera-Ellen, Dean Jagger, Mary Wickes (Paramount)

Bing Crosby and Danny Kaye, along with VistaVision, keep the entertainment going in this fancifully staged production, clicking well. The directorial handling by Michael Curtiz gives a smooth blend of music (thirteen numbers plus snatches of others) and drama, and in the climax creates a genuine heart tug that will squeeze tears.

The plot holding the entire affair together has Crosby and Kaye, two army buddies, joining forces after the war and becoming a big musical team. They get together with the girls and trek to Vermont for a white Christmas. The inn at which they stay is run by Dean Jagger, their old general, and the boys put on a show to pull him out of a financial hole. Crosby wraps up his portion of the show with deceptive ease, shuffling a mean hoof in the dances and generally aquitting himself like a champion. Kaye takes in his stride the dance, song and comedy demands of his assignment, keeping Crosby on his toes at all times.

1954: NOMINATION: Best Song ("Count Your Blessings Instead of Sheep")

•

WHITE CLIFFS OF DOVER, THE
1944, 126 mins, US b/w
Dir Clarence Brown ***Prod*** Sidney Franklin ***Scr*** Claudine West, Jan Lustig, George Froeschel ***Ph*** George Folsey ***Ed*** Robert J. Kern ***Mus*** Herbert Stothart ***Art*** Cedric Gibbons, Randall Duell
Act Irene Dunne, Alan Marshall, Frank Morgan, Roddy McDowall, Van Johnson, Peter Lawford (M-G-M)

The White Cliffs of Dover is the saga [based on Alice Duer Miller's poem] of an American girl who went to England for a vacation in 1914, fell in love with a title, learned to love Britain and remained there to go through the First World War and see the coming of the Second.

As the story opens, Irene Dunne, a Red Cross supervisor in an English army hospital, is awaiting the arrival of casualties from what ostensibly was the Dieppe raid. At her desk, prepared for a heavy load of injured soldiers, she begins to muse about the white cliffs and the first time she saw them as a young girl on her arrival in England back in 1914.

From this, the action cuts back to that time and carries Dunne through her marriage to Sir John Ashwood (Alan Marshal), her grief over his loss in World War I, and finally to the second which claims their son.

Dunne gives an excellent performance, as does Alan Marshal, playing her husband, while Roddy McDowall stands out sharply as their son.

•

WHITE DAWN, THE
1974, 109 mins, US Ⓥ ⊙ col
Dir Philip Kaufman ***Prod*** Martin Ransohoff ***Scr*** James Houston, Tom Rickman ***Ph*** Michael Chapman ***Ed*** Douglas Stewart ***Mus*** Henry Mancini
Act Warren Oates, Timothy Bottoms, Lou Gossett, Simonie Kopapik, Joanasie Salomone, Pilitak (Paramount)

James Houston's 1971 book, subtitled *An Eskimo Saga*, is the springboard for this production. Both limn the tale of how a trio of whaleboaters, stranded in the late 1890s near the North Pole, interact with and nearly destroy the band of Eskimos who saved their lives. But while the book had a logic and sensitivity of its own, the film version emerges as a static narrative.

Essentially, the three whalers bring familiar baggage to the pristine setting of the Eskimo village—they find ways of making booze, they gamble, they take advantage of village women, they steal, etc. Although each member of the trio is by no means uniform in his misconduct—Billy (Warren Oates) is easily the most nefarious—collective behaviour is at first accepted by the Eskimos, then tolerated and then viewed with a deepseated displeasure.

Oates is properly blustery as the roistering older sea hand.

•

WHITE DOG
1982, 90 mins, US Ⓥ col
Dir Samuel Fuller ***Prod*** Jon Davison ***Scr*** Samuel Fuller, Curtis Hanson ***Ph*** Bruce Surtees ***Ed*** Bernard Gribble ***Mus*** Ennio Morricone ***Art*** Brian Eatwell
Act Kristy McNichol, Paul Winfield, Burl Ives, Jameson Parker, Lynne Moody, Marshall Thompson (Paramount)

White Dog is an unusual, often powerful study of racism in the guise of a man vs. animal suspenser. Too unevenly balanced and single-minded to work completely, Samuel Fuller's first Hollywood picture in 18 years nevertheless packs a provocative punch.

Curtis Hanson and Fuller have fashioned an intense yarn about an up-and-coming L.A. actress (Kristy McNichol) who takes in a German shepherd after she hits it with her car, only to discover that her new pet is a deadly White Dog, trained from birth to hate anyone with black skin.

Pic really gets down to business when McNichol takes the dog to Burl Ives's Noah's Ark animal compound, where scientist-trainer Paul Winfield quickly becomes obsessed with the idea of curing the beast of its racism. Set in an enormous cage reminiscent of a gladiatorial arena, Winfield's very physical attempts to wear the dog down are effectively elemental.

McNichol is very fine as a modern gal who becomes devoted to the dog, as well as Winfield's cause, in a totally unsentimental way.

•

WHITE FANG
1936, 70 mins, US b/w
Dir David Butler ***Prod*** Bogart Rogers ***Scr*** Gene Fowler, Hal Long, S. G. Duncan ***Ph*** Arthur Miller ***Ed*** Irene Morra ***Mus*** Hugo Friedhofer, Charles Maxwell
Act Michael Whalen, Jean Muir, Slim Summerville, Charles Winninger, John Carradine, Jane Darwell (20th Century-Fox)

This is a sequel to [the 1935 release] *The Call of the Wild*, from a Jack London bestseller. While *White Fang* hasn't got the name that *Call* had, and does not equal it in screen strength, it pleases and, for those who lean towards yarns of the north country, will satisfy.

What *Fang* lacks in names, it makes up for in good production and the element of comedy which, in its case, is both very good and important. Charles Winninger [as Doc McFane] and Slim Summerville [as Slats] concede nothing to nobody in view of the fine job they do at tickling the ribs. They are given pretty free rein by the scenario and the director.

Michael Whalen [as Weedon Scott] isn't altogether a sympathetic character, especially after trying to cheat the girl out of the mine her uncle left her up in Yukon. She not only forgives him for this but refuses to believe that he murdered her own brother. Girl is Jean Muir, a rather brittle type for the tough north country.

Excellent heavy is John Carradine. Much more in her place up in the arctic country than Muir is the hotel keeper (Jane Darwell), a rugged lady.

•

WHITE FANG
1990, 107 mins, US Ⓥ ⊙ col
Dir Randal Kleiser ***Prod*** Markay Powell ***Scr*** Jeanne Rosenberg, Nick Thiel, David Fallon ***Ph*** Tony Pierce-Roberts ***Ed*** Lisa Day ***Mus*** Basil Poledouris, Fiachra Trench ***Art*** Michael Bolton
Act Klaus Maria Brandauer, Ethan Hawke, Seymour Cassel, Susan Hogan, James Remar, Bill Moseley (Hybrid/Walt Disney)

Disney's workmanlike remake of Jack London's adventure *White Fang* boasts enough nature footage and a strong central performance by Ethan Hawke to win over small fry.

20th Century-Fox first filmed the book in 1936 as a programmer follow-up to its London-derived hit *Call of the Wild*, notable for John Carradine's performance as the villain. Italian horror maestro Lucio Fulci directed an excellent remake in 1973 toplining Franco Nero and Virna Lisi.

Hawke plays a would-be prospector who heads to the Alaska gold rush just before the turn of the century to find and work his late father's claim. After a scenic, "cast of 100s" climb up a mountain, Hawke teams up with veteran miner Klaus Maria Brandauer and his Gabby Hayes–esque sidekick Seymour Cassel to trek across the snow.

Hampered by a choppy screenplay that reduces earthy star Brandauer's dialog to near pidgin English, pic never adds up to more than a series of individual moments. The majestic beauty of Tony Pierce-Roberts's cinematography and Basil Poledouris's score are highlights.

•

WHITE FANG 2
MYTH OF THE WHITE WOLF
1994, 106 mins, US Ⓥ ⊙ col
Dir Ken Olin ***Prod*** Preston Fischer ***Scr*** David Fallon ***Ph*** Hiro Narita ***Ed*** Elba Sanchez-Short ***Mus*** John Debney ***Art*** Cary White
Act Scott Bairstow, Charmaine Craig, Al Harrington, Anthony Michael Ruivivar, Victoria Racimo, Alfred Molina (Walt Disney)

Even though Jack London wouldn't recognize any of it, *White Fang 2* should attract a respectable percentage of the family audience that made Disney's *White Fang* (1992) a noteworthy b.o. performer.

Ethan Hawke, who starred as young prospector Jack Conroy in the previous pic, shows up here only for a brief, unbilled cameo at the start to plausibly introduce Henry Casey (Scott Bairstow) as the new human companion of the titular half-dog, half-wolf. When Casey and White Fang nearly drown while paddling upriver for supplies, Casey is saved by a Haida Indian princess, Lily Joseph (Charmaine Craig).

Even after he's dubbed White Wolf, Casey insists he is just a regular guy who happens to keep a wolf as a pet. But tribal leader Moses Joseph (Al Harrington) calmly contends that Casey is indeed the one who will help his hunger-ravaged community by finding out why the caribou no longer graze nearby.

There wasn't much time for lovey-dovey stuff in the first *White Fang*, but the sequel develops a chaste romance between Casey and Lily, and even allows White Fang to find a mate. Actor-turned-director Ken Olin (*thirtysomething*) handles these elements with the same sure hand he applies to the action scenes in his feature helming debut.

•

WHITE FEATHER
1955, 102 mins, US ▭ col
Dir Robert D. Webb ***Prod*** Leonard Goldstein ***Scr*** Delmer Daves, Leo Townsend ***Ph*** Lucien Ballad ***Ed*** George Gittens ***Mus*** Hugo Friedhofer
Act Robert Wagner, John Lund, Debra Paget, Jeffrey Hunter, Eduard Franz, Noah Beery (Panoramic/20th Century-Fox)

Screenplay, based on a John Prebble story about the Cheyenne Indians circa 1877 when they were being pushed out of Wyoming by the Federals, is grippingly unfolded in colorful CinemaScope.

Plot depicts Robert Wagner as Josh Tanner, a surveyor who is with the vanguard of the government party (U.S. Cavalry and all) about to sweep west from Fort Cheyenne. They are stalled until the Cheyennes agree to move from their hunting grounds to some southern area. Scripters apparently slipped up when they pointed up that gold had been found. Film builds to climax when the big chief's son and his young fighter pal challenge (via the arrow with white feather attached) the whole cavalry contingent to pitched battle. It is only through the successful intervention of Tanner and Indian girl Appearing Day (Debra Paget) that a needless slaughter is averted.

Produced by the late Leonard Goldstein and directed by Robert D. Webb, the characters are all well portrayed by Wagner, Paget and Jeffrey Hunter, last as the chief's son. Eduard Franz is superb as the venerable Indian chief, Broken Hand, while Hugh O'Brian is well chosen as Hunter's warrior pal, American Horse. Noah Beery does one of his better thespian jobs as a cavalry lieutenant.

•

WHITE HEAT
1949, 114 mins, US Ⓥ ⊙ b/w
Dir Raoul Walsh ***Prod*** Louis F. Edelman ***Scr*** Ivan Goff, Ben Roberts ***Ph*** Sid Hickox ***Ed*** Owen Marks ***Mus*** Max Steiner ***Art*** Edward Carrere
Act James Cagney, Virginia Mayo, Edmond O'Brien, Steve Cochran, Margaret Wycherly, John Archer (Warner)

The tight-lipped scowl, the hunched shoulders that rear themselves for the kill, the gargoyle speech, the belching gunfire of a trigger-happy paranoiac—one with a mother complex, no less—these are the standard and still-popular ingredients that constitute the James Cagney of *White Heat*. All that is missing is the grapefruit in a dame's physiog.

White Heat [suggested by a story by Virginia Kellogg] specifically is about a killer over whom only his mother can wield any influence. He heads a western gang, with his mother and his double-dealing wife along for company.

Cagney has an excellent supporting cast. Steve Cochran makes a good-looking, double-crossing mobster's aide whose ambition for the gang leadership, and the leader's wife, ends in a rain of bullets. It's a capable performance. Virginia Mayo has little to do except look sexy as the wife.

1949: NOMINATION: Best Motion Picture Story

•

WHITE HUNTER, BLACK HEART
1990, 110 mins, US Ⓥ ⊙ col
Dir Clint Eastwood ***Prod*** Clint Eastwood ***Scr*** Peter Viertel, James Bridges, Burt Kennedy ***Ph*** Jack N. Green ***Ed*** Joel Cox ***Mus*** Lennie Niehaus ***Art*** John Graysmark
Act Clint Eastwood, Jeff Fahey, George Dzundza, Alun Armstrong, Marisa Berenson, Timothy Spall (Malpaso/Rastar/Warner)

Clint Eastwood's film isn't an African adventure epic, as those unaware of Peter Viertel's 1953 book may surmise from the title. It's an intelligent, affectionate study of an obsessive American film director who, while working on a film in colonial Africa, becomes sidetracked by his compulsion to hunt elephants.

Though the end credits note that this is "a work of fiction," this is clearly a story about John Huston and the preproduction period for *The African Queen* (called *The African Trader* here). Eastwood plays the Huston character with obvious appreciation of the man: he wears Huston clothes and hats, assumes Huston mannerisms, smokes Huston cigars and speaks with the characteristic Huston timbre.

The first 20 minutes of the pic unfold in England, where Wilson is living in a splendid old stately home as if he were a country squire. It's here that Wilson welcomes Pete Verrell (Jeff Fahey), his biographer, and it's from Verrell's perspective that the events unfold. Once the film crew moves to Africa, it becomes clear that Wilson's interest in making the film takes second place to his impractical passion for big-game hunting.

•

WHITE LIGHTNING
1973, 100 mins, US Ⓥ col
Dir Joseph Sargent ***Prod*** Arthur Gardner, Jules V. Levy ***Scr*** William Norton ***Ph*** Edward Rosson ***Ed*** George Nicholson ***Mus*** Charles Bernstein ***Art*** [uncredited]
Act Burt Reynolds, Jennifer Billingsley, Ned Beatty, Bo Hopkins, Matt Clark, Diane Ladd (United Artists)

Cast as an expert auto driver doing time in a Southern state prison for running bootleg whiskey, Burt Reynolds makes a deal with U.S. Treasury agents to help them trap a gang of bootleggers on income tax evasion. Pitch for his freedom to act as an undercover man is made after he learns that a sheriff on the take is the probable murderer of his brother.

He's helped by another undercover man (Matt Clark) and a daredevil driver (Bo Hopkins), from whom Reynolds proceeds to steal his gal (Jennifer Billingsley).

Joseph Sargent's direction is particularly effective in the light and auto-chasing sequences, latter a field day for stunt drivers and occasionally incorporating humorous bits of biz. Reynolds is quite up to all the demands of his smashing role.

•

WHITE LINE FEVER
1975, 89 mins, US/Canada Ⓥ ⊙ col
Dir Jonathan Kaplan ***Prod*** John Kemeny ***Scr*** Ken Friedman, Jonathan Kaplan ***Ph*** Fred Koenekamp ***Ed*** O. Nicholas Brown ***Mus*** David Nichtern ***Art*** Sydney Litwack
Act Jan-Michael Vincent, Kay Lenz, Slim Pickens, L. Q. Jones, Don Porter, Sam Laws (Columbia/International Cinemedia)

White Line Fever is a good action drama starring Jan-Michael Vincent as a young truck driver fighting corruption.

Air Force vet Vincent returns home to marriage with Kay Lenz and starting in as an independent trucker. He soon finds smuggling to be endemic to the career, and is repeatedly and violently hassled when he refuses to go along.

What seems missing from the film is more depth and logical transition: Vincent passes too rapidly from a stubborn, honest lone wolf to practically a union leader.

With stunt experts Carey Loftin, Nate Long and Joe Hooker creating some powerful action footage, Vincent and Lenz experience assaults, fires, beatings and other troubles sent their way by L. Q. Jones and others, all under orders from Don Porter.

•

WHITE MAN'S BURDEN
1995, 89 mins, US/France Ⓥ ⊙ col
Dir Desmond Nakano ***Prod*** Lawrence Bender ***Scr*** Desmond Nakano ***Ph*** Willy Kurant ***Ed*** Nancy Richardson ***Mus*** Howard Shore ***Art*** Naomi Shohan
Act John Travolta, Harry Belafonte, Kelly Lynch, Margaret Avery, Tom Bower, Carrie Snodgress (A Band Apart/UGC)

Imagining an American society in which the wealthy, privileged classes are predominantly black, and whites have exclusive domain over the lower strata, *White Man's Burden* very cogently places the shoe on the other foot for audiences of both skin tones. The film's shortcoming is that, once this challenging food for thought is on the table, debuting writer-director Desmond Nakano fails to make a substantial meal of it.

John Travolta plays Louis Pinnock, a hard-working factory hand employed at a chocolate manufacturing plant owned by Thaddeus Thomas (Harry Belafonte). When Pinnock makes a well-deserved bid for a soon-to-be vacant foreman's job, he finds himself accused of being a peeping Tom and fired instead.

Humiliated and turfed out by the landlord and two lawmen, his wife (Kelly Lynch) and two young kids go to stay with her unsympathetic mother (Carrie Snodgress). Robbed of his livelihood, home and family, Pinnock is driven to drastic measures. He hijacks Thomas at gunpoint, demanding the money he feels is due him for his years of undeclared overtime.

The changes undergone by the two men during their enforced association of not much more than twenty-four hours provide interesting human drama, impressively played by the two actors. As the unlikely pair get to know each other better, the film's tone often digresses pleasurably into something more gentle and amusing.

But the feeling remains that both talented actors have been denied the chance to take their roles in more interesting directions. In underwritten parts, Lynch and Avery (as Thomas's wife) have little do do. Nakano's lack of a strong visual sense keeps it largely within the realm of a performance piece.

•

WHITE MISCHIEF
1987, 107 mins, UK Ⓥ ⊙ col
Dir Michael Radford ***Prod*** Simon Perry ***Scr*** Michael Radford, Jonathan Gems ***Ph*** Roger Deakins ***Ed*** Tom Priestley ***Mus*** George Fenton ***Art*** Roger Hall
Act Greta Scacchi, Charles Dance, Sarah Miles, Joss Ackland, John Hurt, Trevor Howard (Columbia/Nelson/Goldcrest/Umbrella)

White Mischief goes back into Africa with a vengeance. It glossily portrays the flip side of colonial life, exposing the opulent and lush—but downright debauched—lifestyle of the British "Happy Valley" crowd in Kenya during the war years [from the book by James Fox].

Pic opens in 1940 with newlyweds "Jock" Broughton (Joss Ackland) and Diana (Greta Scacchi) about to leave England for the British colony in Nairobi. He needs a wife and she wants the money and a title, but when Diana meets handsome Erroll (Charles Dance) in Nairobi, the scene is set for some philandering.

With stoical British reserve, Broughton seemingly accepts the affair, even suggesting a celebratory dinner for the couple when they announce their plans to go away together. Later that night Erroll is shot through the head while in his car. Suspects for the murder are plentiful and the scandal means the end of the Happy Valley set and their dalliances. In real life the Erroll murderer was never found.

Dance and Scacchi are fine in the lead roles, with Scacchi certainly looking desirable and elegant bedecked in stunning costumes and sporting a seemingly endless collection of sunglasses.

•

WHITE NIGHTS
1985, 135 mins, US Ⓥ ⦿ col
Dir Taylor Hackford ***Prod*** Taylor Hackford, William S. Gilmore ***Scr*** James Goldman, Eric Hughes ***Ph*** David Watkin ***Ed*** Fredric Steinkamp, William Steinkamp ***Mus*** Michel Colombier ***Art*** Philip Harrison
Act Mikhail Baryshnikov, Gregory Hines, Jerzy Skolimowski, Helen Mirren, Geraldine Page, Isabella Rossellini (Columbia-Delphi V/New Visions)

At its core *White Nights* is a political thriller about the dilemma of a famous Russian defector who, after a plane crash, finds himself trapped back in his mother country. However, pic shies away from the world of classical dance, personified by leading man Mikhail Baryshnikov, in favor of Gregory Hines's "improvography" and assorted modern stuff in blatant music-video contexts.

Mix all this in with KGB intrigue, racial tensions, numerous emotional breakdowns and several suspense sequences, all played at the broadest levels of melodrama, and one has quite a mish-mash indeed.

Without so much as an interrogation by the KGB, Baryshnikov is moved to the dingy Siberian residence of Hines, a black American tap dancer who jumped to the other side during Vietnam, and his Russian wife, Isabella Rossellini.

The trio is installed in Baryshnikov's luxurious old apartment in Leningrad, and the dancer is expected to begin preparations for a triumphant homecoming at the Kirov. Inevitably, an escape attempt is the climax.

Hines plays a bitter, ornery man with a quick trigger. Rossellini, in her Hollywood film debut, has disappointingly little to do.

1985: Best Song ("Say You, Say Me")

NOMINATION: Best Song ("Separate Lives")

•

WHITE OF THE EYE
1987, 110 mins, UK Ⓥ col
Dir Donald Cammell ***Prod*** Cassian Elwes, Brad Wyman ***Scr*** Donald Cammell, China Cammell ***Ph*** Alan Jones, Larry McConkey ***Ed*** Terry Rawlings ***Mus*** George Fenton (sup.), Nick Mason, Rick Fenn
Act David Keith, Cathy Moriarty, Art Evans, Alan Rosenberg, Alberta Watson, Michael Greene (Kastner/Cannon)

White of the Eye is an intriguing thriller [from the novel *Mrs. White* by Margaret Tracy].

Beneath the layers of flashbacks and at times almost subliminal imagery is a conventional storyline. Sound expert Paul White (David Keith), living in a small Arizona town, is having marital problems with frau Joan (Cathy Moriarty). Circumstantial evidence points strongly at Keith, with cop Mendoza (Art Evans) in from Phoenix to hound him in the case of a serial murder who mutilates the corpses of his wealthy housewife victims.

With lots of clues and red herrings introduced in the early reels (including a heavy emphasis on ten years earlier 16mm blow-up flashbacks of Moriarty first meeting Keith while trekking westward with her boyfriend Alan Rosenberg), picture maintains considerable suspense. Moriarty is quite forceful here. Keith likewise creates a powerful figure, until the mystery is fully out of the bag.

•

WHITE PALACE
1990, 104 mins, US Ⓥ ⦿ col
Dir Luis Mandoki ***Prod*** Mark Rosenberg, Amy Robinson, Griffin Dunne ***Scr*** Ted Tally, Alvin Sargent ***Ph*** Lajos Koltai ***Ed*** Carol Littleton ***Mus*** George Fenton ***Art*** Jeannine Claudia Oppewall
Act Susan Sarandon, James Spader, Jason Alexander, Kathy Bates, Eileen Brennan, Steven Hill (Universal/Mirage)

Outstanding performances by Susan Sarandon and James Spader, working from a relentlessly witty script, make *White Palace* one of the best films of its kind since *The Graduate* (1967).

Sarandon is Nora, a forty-three-year-old fast-food worker who gets involved with a twenty-seven-year-old advertising exec—the same sort of character Spader played in *Pretty in Pink*, now mellowed and matured. Both have experienced terrible loss—Max (Spader) is a widower; Nora's child has died—and they share a magnetic sexual attraction.

Their *Odd Couple* differences, however, include class, religion and hygiene (he's a buttoned-down neat freak; she's a gregarious slob) in addition to the Mrs. Robinson–esque age discrepancy.

The ferocity that director Luis Mandoki brings to the pair's early love scenes helps establish how two people can fall into lust and worry about love later.

Raunchy yet vulnerable, Sarandon carefully avoids the clichés that might have been associated with Nora. Spader continues to establish himself as star material, especially when it comes to playing self-conscious yuppies.

•

WHITE PARADE, THE
1934, 80 mins, US b/w
Dir Irving Cummings ***Prod*** Jesse L. Lasky ***Scr*** Sonya Levien, Ernest Pascal ***Ph*** Arthur Miller
Act Loretta Young, John Boles, Dorothy Wilson, Muriel Kirkland, Astrid Allwyn, Frank Conroy (Fox)

The White Parade is a woman's picture, but also for general appeal. The stern curriculum which goes toward the moulding of the "white parade," the present-day Florence Nightingales who are dedicated to the service of humankind, and all the other details that go toward the schooling of the modern nurse are deftly, graphically, punchily and sometimes heart-throbbingly depicted [from the novel by Rian James, adapted by James and Jesse L. Lasky, Jr.].

Loretta Young is altogether convincing as the sympathetic femme novitiate who has consecrated herself to her profession. Dorothy Wilson is a fine little actress. Muriel Kirkland in a more hoydenish role registers, as do Astrid Allwyn as a light heavy, and Joyce Compton in one of those Una Merkel Dixie drawleries.

Frank Conroy is given the toughest male assignment as the mature medico of stern mien who must make some of his hyper-solemnous lines read convincingly. John Boles, though the featured vis-à-vis, is handicapped and limited by his role. Polo-playing Boston playboys who fall for nurses are tough to make real, but he manages quite well.

1934: NOMINATION: Best Picture

•

WHITE SANDS
1992, 101 mins, US Ⓥ ⦿ ▭ col
Dir Roger Donaldson ***Prod*** William Sackheim, Scott Rudin ***Scr*** Daniel Pyne ***Ph*** Peter Menzies, Jr. ***Ed*** Nicholas Beauman ***Mus*** Patrick O'Hearn ***Art*** John Graysmark
Act Willem Dafoe, Mary Elizabeth Mastrantonio, Mickey Rourke, Samuel L. Jackson, M. Emmet Walsh, Mimi Rogers (Morgan Creek)

The plot shifts as often as the desert in *White Sands*, an absorbing, tightly coiled thriller not always easy to follow, with a fine cast, no-fat direction by Roger Donaldson, and nasties belonging to the all-purpose CIA-FBI consortium of evil.

Willem Dafoe sets himself up for plenty of abuse when, after finding a dead Indian with $500,000 in cash in the middle of nowhere, he takes on the victim's identity in an effort to solve the case. He is quickly beaten and robbed of the loot by two babes and then abducted by the FBI. Latter demands that the stash be recovered and Dafoe keeps an appointment in Santa Fe with mysterious Mickey Rourke, who introduces him to another shadowy character, spoiled rich girl Mary Elizabeth Mastrantonio.

Pic builds tautly to a powerful first-act peak. Intensity dwindles a bit, however, when Dafoe pairs off with Mastrantonio, to whom he appeals for the extra coin.

Some thrillers have gone down as classics despite the lack of total narrative coherence, and while *White Sands* doesn't rate that high, it can hold its own with Donaldson's *No Way Out* as an audience-pleasing cliffhanger. An uncredited Mimi Rogers appears briefly at the outset as Dafoe's wife.

•

WHITE SISTER, THE
1933, 105 mins, US b/w
Dir Victor Fleming ***Scr*** Donald Ogden Stewart ***Ph*** William Daniels ***Ed*** Margaret Booth ***Mus*** Herbert Stothart
Act Helen Hayes, Clark Gable, Lewis Stone, Louise Closser Hale, May Robson, Edward Arnold (M-G-M)

Helen Hayes is the sorrowing Angela, as solid and satisfying a bit of acting as comes to the screen in a blue moon. Clark Gable is a gallant soldier hero and leaves nothing to be desired.

The studio has given the story [from the play by Walter Hackett, from the novel by E. Marion Crawford] a superlative production, making the most of the setting in Rome with the background of the church's pomp and pageantry; a background, too, which colors the sentimental quality of the whole tale and gives it emotional grip.

Midway there are war sequences involving nicely handled airplane battles, and later the hero's escape from an enemy prison camp, which give the action substance, although side issues of the central theme. This, of course, is the separation of the lovers, a parting which sends the girl, believing her lover is dead, into a nunnery, from which, upon his return, she cannot bring herself to depart.

•

WHITE SQUALL
1996, 127 mins, US Ⓥ ⦿ col
Dir Ridley Scott ***Prod*** Mimi Polk Gitlin, Rocky Lang ***Scr*** Todd Robinson ***Ph*** Hugh Johnson ***Ed*** Gerry Hambling ***Mus*** Jeff Rona ***Art*** Peter J. Hampton
Act Jeff Bridges, Caroline Goodall, John Savage, Scott Wolf, Jeremy Sisto, Ryan Phillippe (Scott Free/Hollywood)

Call it *Floating Poets Society*, or perhaps *Dead Sailors Society*, but this coming-of-age story, circa 1960, has much the same feel as that earlier release, with a group of teenage boys undergoing a rite of passage—under the tutelage of a stern mentor—by sailing around the Caribbean for a year. Director Ridley Scott's lavish production isn't totally satisfying, coasting aimlessly at times before suddenly leaping to a more intense dramatic plane.

Scott Wolf is Chuck Gieg, a high-school senior through whose eyes the audience sees the boat's stern skipper (Jeff Bridges) and his other, sometimes troubled classmates aboard the *Albatross*. Pic takes plenty of time introducing its attractive young cast as they bond while sailing around the Caribbean, before erupting into the storm sequence that claims several lives. It's worth the wait—a staggering, if at times confusing, sequence in which the boat is sunk and various members of the crew are lost.

That, in turn, is followed by a brief, anticlamactic courtroom tribunal—a sort of poor man's *The Caine Mutiny* that, true story or not, feels a bit forced and contrived.

Each of the young men is plagued by his own demons, including Frank (Jeremy Sisto), who struggles against a domineering father; Gil (Ryan Phillippe), whose fear of heights stems from an earlier tragedy; and Dean (Eric Michael Cole), whose bullying ways hide insecurity about his academic skills.

Tech credits are impressive, with Sts. Vincent, Sts. Lucia and Grenada providing the principal locales.

•

WHITE TOWER, THE
1950, 98 mins, US Ⓥ col
Dir Ted Tetzlaff ***Prod*** Sid Rogell ***Scr*** Paul Jarring ***Ph*** Ray Rennahan ***Ed*** Samuel E. Beetley ***Mus*** Roy Webb
Act Glenn Ford, Alida Valli, Claude Rains, Oscar Homolka, Cedric Hardwicke, Lloyd Bridges (RKO)

Magnificent scenic Swiss backgrounds and a gripping yarn are welded together in *The White Tower* for a powerful emotional impact. Out of James Ramsey Ullman's novel, scripter Paul Jarring has fashioned a pictorial theme with elemental appeal—the struggle of man to conquer nature.

Plot opens in a peasant village, where a small group of Europeans and one American (Glenn Ford) have gathered. The dominating passion of the group is to lick the forbidding heights of a nearby summit.

The pic may be resented for its attempt to define various national characteristics. In the case of the German member of the party (Lloyd Bridges), the pic frankly exploits the opportunity to blast the cold brutality and superman pretensions of the Herrenvolk.

•

WHO?
1974, 93 mins, UK/W. Germany Ⓥ col
Dir Jack Gold ***Prod*** Barry Levinson ***Scr*** John Gould ***Ph*** Petrus Schloemp ***Ed*** Norman Wanstall ***Mus*** John Cameron ***Art*** Peter Scharff
Act Elliott Gould, Trevor Howard, Joseph Bova, Ed Grover, James Noble, Lyndon Brook (Lion International/Hemisphere)

Adapted from Algis Budrys's novel by British playwright John Gould, *Who?* is an action-espionage thriller examining, from a science fiction perspective, the nature of identity.

Joe Bova gives a beautiful, underplayed performance as diminutive U.S. scientist Martino, whose face and arm are remade of metal after an accident in Berlin. The film's mystery-suspense plot derives from iterated flashbacks showing Martino grilled and/or indoctrinated by East German intelligence officer Azarin (Trevor Howard).

Once back in the U.S., Martino is subjected to gruelling questioning and investigation by FBI operative Rogers (Elliott Gould) to check his new security clearance for continuing a top-secret research project in Florida. Gould examines the reactions of Martino's old associates to his transformed, robotlike appearance.

Gould brings humor to the assignment. Howard is seen only in the flashbacks.

•

WHO DARES WINS
1982, 125 mins, UK Ⓥ col
Dir Ian Sharp ***Prod*** Euan Lloyd ***Scr*** Reginald Rose ***Ph*** Phil Meheux ***Ed*** John Grover ***Mus*** Roy Budd ***Art*** Syd Cain
Act Lewis Collins, Judy Davis, Richard Widmark, Edward Woodward, Robert Webber, Tony Doyle (Rank)

Who Dares Wins is pulp fare about the politics of terrorism in which the anti-war movement is discredited as prone to reckless murder in the ironic name of peace. In this case, provocative premise is no substitute for classy drama.

The simple-minded plot [from an original story by George Markstein] has a militant anti-nuke organization take over a U.S. diplomatic facility in London with its glitzy bunch of hostages, and demanding the wipeout of a U.S. sub base in Scotland by a nuclear missile. Wiped out instead, by a crack British commando team, are the peaceniks. All characters are stereotyped rather than clichéd.

Performing standout is Judy Davis as the "terrorist" leader. Lewis Collins offers pleasing virile projection as an undercover agent who shacks up with Davis.

•

WHO FRAMED ROGER RABBIT
1988, 103 mins, US Ⓥ ⦿ col
Dir Robert Zemeckis ***Prod*** Robert Watts, Frank Marshall ***Scr*** Jeffrey Price, Peter S. Seaman ***Ph*** Dean Cundey ***Ed*** Arthur Schmidt ***Mus*** Alan Silvestri ***Art*** Elliot Scott, Roger Cain
Act Bob Hoskins, Christopher Lloyd, Joanna Cassidy, Stubby Kaye, Alan Tilvern (Touchstone/Amblin/Silver Screen Partners III)

Years in the planning and making, *Who Framed Roger Rabbit* is an unparalleled technical achievement where animation is brilliantly integrated into live action. Yet the story amounts to little more than inspired silliness about the filmmaking biz where cartoon characters face off against cartoonish humans.

Pic opens appropriately enough with a cartoon, a hilarious, overblown, calamitous scene where Roger Rabbit, a famous contract Toon player (as in car*toon*) for Maroon Studios, is failing in his attempt to keep Baby Herman (voice by Lou Hirsch) from the cookie jar.

Things aren't going well for poor Roger. Ever since he became estranged from his voluptuous human character Toon wife Jessica (sultry, uncredited voice courtesy of Kathleen Turner, and Amy Irving for the singing) he just can't act.

This is the context from which scripters, in adapting Gary Wolf's story, try to work up a Raymond Chandler-style suspenser where Roger becomes an innocent murder suspect, with a disheveled, alcoholic private eye (Bob Hoskins) being his only hope to help him beat the rap.

The real stars are the animators, under British animation director Richard Williams, who pull off a technically amazing feat of having humans and Toons seem to be interacting with one another. It is clear from how well the imagery syncs that a lot of painstaking work [two years] went into this production—and clearly a lot of money [$35 million].

1988: Best Editing, Sound Effects Editing, Visual Effects

NOMINATIONS: Best Cinematography, Art Direction, Sound

•

WHO IS KILLING THE GREAT CHEFS OF EUROPE?
(UK: TOO MANY CHEFS)
1978, 112 mins, US/W. Germany Ⓥ col
Dir Ted Kotcheff ***Prod*** William Aldrich ***Scr*** Peter Stone ***Ph*** John Alcott ***Ed*** Thom Noble ***Mus*** Henry Mancini ***Art*** Rolf Zehetbauer
Act George Segal, Jacqueline Bisset, Robert Morley, Jean-Pierre Cassel, Philippe Noiret, Jean Rochefort (Aldrich/Lorimar)

Who Is Killing the Great Chefs of Europe? is a happy combination of the macabre and the merry. It's a fast-moving, witty film, beautifully cast with a large group of international professionals who give full justice to Peter Stone's adaptation of Nan and Ivan Lyons's novel, *Someone Is Killing the Great Chefs of Europe*.

While George Segal and Jacqueline Bisset carry star billing and, indeed, provide the romantic and plot evolution, it is Robert Morley as a massive, dedicated gourmet who provides the film's finest moments. The series of murders is made the responsibility of some of France and Italy's most outstanding character actors. It's touch and go who excels but Philippe Noiret underplays in a manner that gives him a slight edge over the more voluble Italians, although Stefano Satta Flores's unabashed description of how he'll romance Bisset, given the opportunity, is Italian macho comedy at its finest.

The other endangered chef is Jean-Pierre Cassel, while Jean Rochefort is a red herring who'll fool no one. These are the principal roles but Madge Ryan as Morley's dedicated secretary is also a key figure.

•

WHOLE TOWN'S TALKING, THE
(UK: PASSPORT TO FAME)
1935, 95 mins, US b/w
Dir John Ford ***Prod*** [Lester Cowan] ***Scr*** Jo Swerling, Robert Riskin ***Ph*** Joseph H. August ***Ed*** Viola Lawrence ***Mus*** [uncredited] ***Art*** [uncredited]
Act Edward G. Robinson, Jean Arthur, Wallace Ford, Arthur Hohl, Donald Meek, Etienne Girardot (Columbia)

Robert Riskin and Jo Swerling put the scenario together [from a story by W. R. Burnett]. It's a model in the expert manipulation of such hokum as the office worm thrust into danger by coincidence and emerging with fame, fortune and the girl.

Edward G. Robinson plays a dual role. He is a softie in one part and tough in the other. Plot twist to the worm-turning is that the softie bookkeeper is a dead ringer for a gangster wanted by the police. Police have orders to shoot on sight, and when picking up the hoodlum's counterpart, and third-degreeing him, they are confronted with a dilemma: what to do to protect an innocent citizen from the police. So the bookkeeper gets a pass identifying him as okay. Real criminal, of course, shows up and quietly takes over the passport as a shield to continue his activities.

Robinson's characterization of the submerged, over-polite and indecisive office worker is human and believable.

Second in unusualness among the cast is Jean Arthur. She's gone blonde and fresh. She's more individualistic, more typically the young American, self-reliant, rather sassy, stenog.

•

WHOLE WIDE WORLD, THE
1996, 111 mins, US Ⓥ ⦿ ▭ col
Dir Dan Ireland ***Prod*** Carl-Jan Colpaert, Dan Ireland, Vincent D'Onofrio, ***Scr*** Michael Scott Myers ***Ph*** Claudio Rocha ***Ed*** Luis Colina ***Mus*** Harry Gregson-Williams, Hans Zimmer ***Art*** John Frick
Act Vincent D'Onofrio, Renee Zellweger, Ann Wedgeworth, Harve Presnell, Benjamin Mouton, Helen Cates (Kushner-Locke)

Essentially a two-hander superbly acted by Vincent D'Onofrio and Renee Zellweger, this well-appointed indie production recounts the largely platonic but deep true-life relationship between a small-town Texas schoolteacher and Robert E. Howard, creator of *Conan the Barbarian* and other 1930s pulp-fiction classics.

Tale, beginning in 1933, is related from the p.o.v. of Novalyne Price, upon whose recent memoir (*One Who Walked Alone*) the film is based. Price (Zellweger), a proper young Texas woman, teaches school but aspires to be a writer herself, and so arranges to be introduced to Howard (D'Onofrio), a rather mysterious and wild figure. Both cocky and awkward, Howard is endlessly egotistical about his own abilities. Pic has no dramatic aspirations other than to chart the course of the pair's three-year relationship. There is no suggestion they ever slept together.

While Price's character is fully fleshed out, film's main drawback is that it can never truly get under the skin of Howard's weirdness. All the same, the decidedly offbeat relationship has been examined by Myers and director Dan Ireland, a former film festival exec and producer making his directorial debut, in fine detail.

•

WHO'LL STOP THE RAIN
(UK: DOG SOLDIERS)
1978, 125 mins, US Ⓥ ⦿ col
Dir Karel Reisz ***Prod*** Herb Jaffe, Gabriel Katzka ***Scr*** Judith Roscoe, Robert Stone ***Ph*** Richard H. Kline ***Ed*** John Bloom ***Mus*** Laurence Rosenthal
Act Nick Nolte, Tuesday Weld, Michael Moriarty, Anthony Zerbe, Richard Masur, Ray Sharkey (United Artists)

British filmmaker Karel Reisz for his second American film has come up with a corking couple-on-the-run adventure pic, given depth in its focus on the personal disarray, the growing governmental corruption and the effects of that most unpopular, divisive Vietnam war on America.

Michael Moriarty, a journalist and photog during the Vietnam War, suffers a trauma under a deadly enemy barrage and the mayhem around him. He decides to try to smuggle heroin to the U.S.

Moriarty brings in an old Marine buddy (Nick Nolte), who is now in the Merchant Marines. Nolte is to get in touch with Moriarty's wife (Tuesday Weld) and wait for him, Moriarty, to get back. But back in the U.S. Nolte is followed. He and Weld go on the lam after sending Weld's little girl off to relatives for safekeeping.

Based on a bestseller by Robert Stone, film has a hard-nose progression and solidity in its characterizations. Nolte earns his star stripes here, displaying presence and perceptiveness in socking home his character, while Weld and Moriarty are also effective.

•

WHORE
1991, 84 mins, US Ⓥ ⦿ col
Dir Ken Russell ***Prod*** Dan Ireland, Ronaldo Vasconcellos ***Scr*** Ken Russell, Deborah Dalton ***Ph*** Amir Mokri ***Ed*** Brian Tagg ***Mus*** Michael Gibbs ***Art*** Richard Lewis
Act Theresa Russell, Benjamin Mouton, Antonio Fargas, Sanjay, Elizabeth Moorehead, Michael Crabtree (Trimark)

Given the infinite possibilities afforded by the subject matter, *Whore* features little of the kinkiness and bravura stylistics one normally expects from director Ken Russell, and no compensating psychological or documentary insight into the lead character or her lifestyle.

Project is based on a British play by David Hines, a London cabbie who nightly picked up prostitutes in Kings Cross and began writing down their stories they told him about their work. Due to financing requirements, the setting is shifted to Los Angeles, where the consummately vulgar Liz (Theresa Russell) plies her trade on thinly populated downtown streets.

Flashbacks make up a substantial portion of the brief running time, as Liz covers her initial tricks, hook-up with her pimp and sometime boyfriend, Blake (Benjamin Mouton), and failed marriage and hopeless stint as a mother.

Overriding problem is a pervasive feeling of utter inauthenticity. Russell's strident, stops-out performance sets the tone for the entire picture. She's all over the place, occasionally hitting a responsive note, but more often flailing about. Director puts in an unbilled cameo appearance as a waiter in a snooty restaurant.

•

WHO'S AFRAID OF VIRGINIA WOOLF?
1966, 131 mins, US Ⓥ ⦿ b/w
Dir Mike Nichols ***Prod*** Ernest Lehman ***Scr*** Ernest Lehman ***Ph*** Haskell Wexler ***Ed*** Sam O'Steen ***Mus*** Alex North ***Art*** Richard Sylbert
Act Elizabeth Taylor, Richard Burton, George Segal, Sandy Dennis (Warner)

The naked power and oblique tenderness of Edward Albee's incisive, inhuman drama have been transformed from legit into a brilliant motion picture. Keen adaptation and handsome production by Ernest Lehman, outstanding direction by Mike Nichols in his feature debut, and four topflight performances score an artistic bull's-eye.

Elizabeth Taylor earns every penny of her reported $1 million plus. Her characterization is at once sensual, spiteful, cynical, pitiable, loathsome, lustful and tender.

Richard Burton delivers a smash portrayal. He evokes sympathy during the public degradations to which his wife subjects him, and his outrage, as well as his deliberate vengeance, are totally believable.

Provoking the exercise in exorcism is the late-night visit of Dennis and Segal. Latter is the all-American boy type who, in the course of one night, is seduced by his hostess, exposed by his host, but enlightened as to more mature aspects of love and marriage. Segal is able to evoke sympathy, then hatred, then pity, in a first-rate performance.

Dennis makes an impressive screen debut as the young bride, her delivery rounded with the intended subtlety of a not-so-Dumb Dora.

1966: Best Actress (Elizabeth Taylor), Supp. Actress (Sandy Dennis), B&W Cinematography, B&W Art Direction, B&W Costume Design (Irene Sharaff)

NOMINATIONS: Best Picture, Director, Actor (Richard Burton), Supp. Actor (George Segal), Screenplay Adaptation, Editing, Original Music Score, Sound

•

WHO'S BEEN SLEEPING IN MY BED?
1963, 103 mins, US ▭ col
Dir Daniel Mann ***Prod*** Jack Rose ***Scr*** Jack Rose ***Ph*** Joseph Ruttenberg ***Ed*** George Tomasini ***Mus*** George Duning
Act Dean Martin, Elizabeth Montgomery, Martin Balsam, Jill St. John, Carol Burnett, Macha Meril (Paramount)

Dean Martin is seemingly right for the part of an actor who appears on television as a doctor, such as Kildare or Ben Casey, and then moonlights into the field of psychiatric advice (and perhaps romantic stimulation) for the glamorous dames married to his TV-business associates.

But there's the slip between cup and lip. The slip makes the difference between what might have been mischievous, zesty comedy and what is a sometimes laughable frolic that in a couple of instances is permitted to sink in its quest for sophisticated hilarity.

This is unfortunate because a substantial part of *Who's Been Sleeping in My Bed*? plays sparkingly well. Martin is an amiable performer in light comedy and does fine with the material at hand.

•

WHOSE LIFE IS IT ANYWAY?

1981, 118 mins, US Ⓥ ▭ col

Dir John Badham ***Prod*** Lawrence P. Bachmann ***Scr*** Brian Clark, Reginald Rose ***Ph*** Mario Tosi ***Ed*** Frank Morriss ***Mus*** Arthur B. Rubinstein ***Art*** Gene Gallahan

Act Richard Dreyfuss, John Cassavetes, Christine Lahti, Bob Balaban, Kenneth McMillan, Kaki Hunter (M-G-M)

Director and scripters have done a masterly job in the rather difficult screen adaptation of Brian Clark's legit drama. Richard Dreyfuss delivers a sensitive portrait of the animated young sculptor who is cut down in an automobile accident at the height of his life and recovers only to be paralysed from the neck down.

Although John Badham directed Dreyfuss in an actual stage version in Massachusetts for two weeks, he succeeds in opening up the story far beyond the confines of a proscenium. There is an opening sequence establishing his idyllic relationship with dancer Janet Eilber; scenes throughout the hospital with hard-crusted chief of staff John Cassavetes, soft-hearted doctor Christine Lahti and light-hearted, humane nurse trainee and orderly Kaki Hunter and Thomas Carter; and glimpses at Dreyfuss's "former" life, most particularly through his artist's studio.

All the action leads to the unresolvable issue of who has the power to decide the fate of the patient—the hospital or the patient. Dreyfuss demands a legal hearing in his fight to be rid of all life-sustaining methods.

•

WHO'S HARRY CRUMB?

1989, 98 mins, US Ⓥ ⊙ col

Dir Paul Flaherty ***Prod*** Arnon Milchan ***Scr*** Robert Conte, Peter Martin Wortmann ***Ph*** Stephen M. Katz ***Ed*** Danford B. Greene ***Mus*** Michel Colombier ***Art*** Trevor Williams

Act John Candy, Jeffrey Jones, Annie Potts, Tim Thomerson, Barry Corbin, Shawnee Smith (Tri-Star/NBC/Frostbacks)

Foolishness in the right hands can be sublimely funny, and combo of star John Candy and director Paul Flaherty (former SCTV cohorts) puts the perfect spin on *Who's Harry Crumb?*, a *Naked Gun*–style farce about a bumbling private eye who succeeds in spite of himself.

Candy plays Crumb, a complete idiot who's related by birth to a line of crack detectives and finally gets assigned to a lucrative kidnapping case—but only because his beady-eyed boss (Jeffrey Jones), who's the kidnapper, doesn't want it solved.

At stake is Jones's lust for the golddigging newlywed wife (maliciously and deliciously played by Annie Potts) of a benign, trusting multimillionaire (Barry Corbin). The plot is to get $10 million ransom for the return of Corbin's slinky daughter (Renee Coleman), and use the riches to pry Potts away from her main meal-ticket.

Candy seems to have picked up some tricks from Dan Aykroyd and Steve Martin (both former costars) that he applies to good effect to achieve the attitude of a winning but moronic wiseguy in this pic. Director Flaherty peppers the action with goofy business.

•

WHO'S MINDING THE STORE?

1963, 90 mins, US col

Dir Frank Tashlin ***Prod*** Paul Jones ***Scr*** Frank Tashlin, Harry Tugend ***Ph*** W. Wallace Kelley ***Ed*** John Woodcock ***Mus*** Joseph J. Lilley ***Art*** Hal Pereira, Roland Anderson

Act Jerry Lewis, Jill St. John, Agnes Moorehead, John McGiver, Ray Walston, Francesca Bellini (Paramount/York/Lewis)

Frank Tashlin directs with full emphasis on the madcap nonsense [from a screen story by Harry Tugend] and Jerry Lewis has a field day playing it all out in his uninhibited (meaning zany) style. It's fun.

The filmmaker also has gotten in an abundance of commercial display for appliances, other household items, as Lewis goes to work in a department store and wrecks it department by department.

He has an especially attractive romantic vis-à-vis in Jill St. John who takes a job as elevator operator to hide the fact she's really the daughter of the store's owner. Agnes Moorehead plays the owner's domineering wife, who regards Lewis as an idiot, Frank McGiver is the owner, and Ray Walston is a dame-chasing manager.

They all romp through with accent on the broad comedy and, of course, with the spotlight mainly on havoc-wreaking Lewis.

•

WHO'S THAT GIRL?

1987, 94 mins, US Ⓥ ⊙ col

Dir James Foley ***Prod*** Rosilyn Heller, Bernard Williams ***Scr*** Andrew Smith, Ken Finkleman ***Ph*** Jan De Bont ***Ed*** Pembroke Herring ***Mus*** Stephen Bray, Patrick Leonard ***Art*** Ida Random

Act Madonna, Griffin Dunne, Haviland Morris, John McMartin, Bibi Besch, John Mills (Warner)

Griffin Dunne reprises his role as the crazed, overwrought straight man while Madonna lays on a thick New Yawk bimbette act in this frenetic and ridiculously reworked *After Hours–Arthur* combination.

The Material Girl plays a just-out-of-jail, back-talking petty thief who's bent on avenging the thugs who made her take the rap for a murder she didn't commit. Weak-kneed lawyer type Dunne is sent by his megabucks soon-to-be-father-in-law (John McMartin) to pick her up and make sure she's on the next bus home. All this occurs on the eve of his wedding to McMartin's ice princess daughter (Haviland Morris).

Madonna bamboozles Dunne into doing what she wants to do, turning him into a near nutcase bashing up his future mother-in-law's Corniche, buying stolen goods in Harlem, stealing right and left, and so on.

Fortunately, Dunne's playful personality eventually counter-balances Madonna's shrillness, and their adventures together, while completely farfetched, finally become involving. What's lacking is pure and simple good humor.

•

WHO'S THAT KNOCKING AT MY DOOR

1968, 90 mins, US Ⓥ b/w

Dir Martin Scorsese ***Prod*** Joseph Weill, Betzi Manoogian, Haig Manoogian ***Scr*** Martin Scorsese, Betzi Manoogian ***Ph*** Michael Wadley, Richard Coll ***Ed*** Thelma Schoonmaker ***Mus*** [uncredited] ***Art*** Vic Magnotte

Act Zina Bethune, Harvey Keitel, Lennard Kuras, Ann Collette, Michael Scala, Harry Northup (Trimod)

This independent effort, two years in the making, is the handiwork of, for the most part, film teacher Haig Manoogian and his students. These include Martin Scorsese, who's reponsible for both the script and the direction (with some "additional dialog" credited to Betzi (Mrs. Haig) Manoogian). In addition, Joseph Weill, a practising attorney who's also a student, is listed as one of the producers.

The tale, apparently, is the inner struggle of a young Italian-American, J. R., torn between a Roman Catholic upbringing and the temptations of modern life. Unfortunately, he's portrayed as a crude, carousing lout who seemingly never works, but devotes most of his time to drinking and drifting or spending time with a "good" girl (until he finds that she's not the virgin he imagined). Zina Bethune, as the girl, is believable, but Harvey Keitel, as the anti-hero, is alternatively boorish or bewildered. Scorsese occasionally brings the film to life, as in a weekend drive by J. R. and two buddies to an upstate village where the camera shows up their "big city" shallowness in comparison to the townspeople.

Generally, however, his script and direction lack any dramatic value and give far too much exposure to sexual fantasies on the part of the boy.

•

WHO WAS THAT LADY?

1960, 116 mins, US b/w

Dir George Sidney ***Prod*** Norman Krasna ***Scr*** Norman Krasna ***Ph*** Harry Stradling ***Ed*** Viola Lawrence ***Mus*** Andre Previn

Act Tony Curtis, Dean Martin, Janet Leigh, James Whitmore, John McIntire, Barbara Nichols (Ansark/Columbia)

Who Was That Lady? is perhaps not the rouser it might have been, but it is an often hilarious romp made somewhat sedate only in a compromise between farce and romantic comedy.

The story [from Norman Krasna's play *Who Was That Lady I Saw You With?*] is concerned with Tony Curtis as an assistant professor of chemistry, whose chief extracurricular interest is biology. When Curtis's wife, Janet Leigh, catches him kissing a pretty student, she threatens divorce. In his desperation for an acceptable alibi, Curtis turns to a friend (Dean Martin), a television writer.

The film follows the play closely, except for greater stress on the romance of husband Curtis and wife Leigh. They make a handsome couple. It also slows down the pace and throws off the timing.

Curtis and Martin work nicely together, and much of the film depends upon their teamwork. James Whitmore, not ordinarily thought of as a comedian, gets the film's biggest single laughs, mostly on reaction shots of no lines, just looks.

•

WICKED LADY, THE

1945, 102 mins, UK Ⓥ b/w

Dir Leslie Arliss ***Prod*** R.J. Minney ***Scr*** Leslie Arliss, Gordon Glennon, Aimee Stuart ***Ph*** Jack Cox ***Ed*** Terence Fisher ***Mus*** Hans May ***Art*** John Bryan

Act Margaret Lockwood, James Mason, Patricia Roc, Griffith Jones, Michael Rennie, Felix Aylmer (Gainsborough)

Producers claim that this story is "set in the days of Charles II." Sets, costumes and a comely bunch of femmes bear out the claim. But the period atmosphere is not convincing.

James Mason as a Robin Hood–type highwayman manages to suggest the swaggering love-'em-and-leave-'em rascal of an earlier day. He scores in spite of the weak script [from the novel *The Life and Death of the Wicked Lady Skelton* by Magdalen King-Hall]. The other performance lending credibility to the period comes from Felix Aylmer as an old retainer who tumbles to the villainy of Margaret Lockwood in the title role, and dies at her fair hands.

The Wicked Lady as a title is a characteristic English understatement. The way Lockwood shoots, poisons and betrays all who get in her way makes that taboo name a modest one. Between murders, she steals the fiancé of her best girlfriend and then grabs the bridal chamber for herself.

•

WICKED LADY, THE

1983, 98 mins, US Ⓥ col

Dir Michael Winner ***Prod*** Menahem Golan, Yoram Globus ***Scr*** Michael Winner, Leslie Arliss ***Ph*** Jack Cardiff ***Ed*** Arnold Crust [= Michael Winner] ***Mus*** Tony Banks ***Art*** John Blezard

Act Faye Dunaway, Alan Bates, John Gielgud, Denholm Elliott, Prunella Scales, Oliver Tobias (Cannon)

Sex, humor and even a facsimile of style distinguish Michael Winner's entertaining remake of *The Wicked Lady* as a comedy-drama of rogue-ridden 17th-century England, with Faye Dunaway an effective title star. Winner, who coauthored the piece with [director of the 1945 version] Leslie Arliss [based on *The Life and Death of the Wicked Lady Skelton* by Magdalen King-Hall], has pumped some amusing life and typically brisk pace into a basically tired old (and even campy) story about an alluring high society dame for whom seduction, highway robbery and even murder are all in a day's work.

After marrying Denholm Elliott for his money, Dunaway turns to a life of nocturnal crime, solo at first, but later in cahoots with legendary stagecoach robber Alan Bates.

Dunaway performs her dominating role with satisfying conviction, straight face and all. Ditto Elliott as her scorned and cuckolded husband. Bates makes for a charming but all-too-brief rogue, while John Gielgud as a God-fearing retainer has a marvelous deadpan time of it kidding himself.

•

WICKER MAN, THE

1973, 87 mins, UK Ⓥ col

Dir Robin Hardy ***Prod*** Peter Snell ***Scr*** Anthony Shaffer ***Ph*** Harry Waxman ***Ed*** Eric Boyd-Perkins ***Mus*** Paul Giovanni ***Art*** Seamus Flannery

Act Edward Woodward, Britt Ekland, Diane Cilento, Ingrid Pitt, Christopher Lee, Roy Boyd (British Lion/Brut)

The Wicker Man was lensed entirely on location in Scotland and is possessed of a weird and paganistic story. Anthony Shaffer penned the screenplay which, for sheer imagination and near-terror, has seldom been equalled.

Frightening aspects build one upon the other as a Scottish police sergeant arrives on a little offshore island to investigate the disappearance of a young girl. He finds, under the regime of an all-powerful, benevolent and suave despot, a sinister situation dating back to the days of pagan practices and fertility rites.

Edward Woodward plays role of the sergeant who arrives to find a conspiracy of silence and is forced into a fatal part in the paganistic rituals. Christopher Lee is the cultured feudal Lord Summerisle, lord of the island. Both score in their roles.

•

WIDE SARGASSO SEA

1993, 96 mins, Australia Ⓥ ⊙ col

Dir John Duigan ***Prod*** Jan Sharp ***Scr*** Jan Sharp, Carole Angier, John Duigan ***Ph*** Geoff Burton, Gabriel Beristain ***Ed*** Anne

Goursaud, Jimmy Sandoval ***Mus*** Stewart Copeland ***Art*** Franckie D
Act Karina Lombard, Nathaniel Parker, Rachel Ward, Michael York, Martine Beswick, Claudia Robinson (Laughing Kookaburra)

An exotic and erotic melodrama bearing notable literary pedigrees, *Wide Sargasso Sea* is an uneven but ultimately engrossing feature. Aussie director John Duigan has filmed British novelist Jean Rhys's novel with stunning location photography in Jamaica and the north of England, but the editing looks like the film was put through a shredder.

The initially confusing storyline concerns a mad French woman (Rachel Ward) in Jamaica who marries an Englishman (Michael York). Her daughter (lovely model Karina Lombard) is stuck in a marriage arranged by her uncle to Englishman Edward Rochester (Nathaniel Parker), the brooding hero of Charlotte Brontë's *Jane Eyre*.

The couple's erotic tangles in and out of love are set against a backdrop of superstition in which the local form of voodoo seems to hold each of them in thrall.

Lombard is a hauntingly beautiful heroine, well-matched to shirt-ad-handsome Parker. Their acting is not really up to some dramatic scenes, particularly those in which they may be operating under the influence of voodoo. Thesping honors go to Claudia Robinson as Lombard's sharp-tongued black nanny.

•

WIDOW OF SAINT-PIERRE, THE
SEE: VEUVE DE SAINT-PIERRE, LA

•

WIDOWS' PEAK
1994, 102 mins, UK/US Ⓥ ⊙ col
Dir John Irvin ***Prod*** Jo Manuel ***Scr*** Hugh Leonard ***Ph*** Ashley Rowe ***Ed*** Peter Tanner ***Mus*** Carl Davis ***Art*** Leo Austin
Act Mia Farrow, Joan Plowright, Natasha Richardson, Adrian Dunbar, Jim Broadbent, Anne Kent (Rank/Fine Line)

There's more old-fashioned blarney on show in *Widows' Peak* than at a shamrock-growers' convention. One-two-three teaming of Mia Farrow, Joan Plowright and Natasha Richardson manages to keep the dramatically rickety craft afloat through star power alone.

Irish scribe Hugh Leonard's story was written years earlier for Maureen O'Sullivan and her daughter, Mia Farrow. Farrow ends up playing her mom's role, Richardson Farrow's role, and the whole shebang was shot in County Wicklow, home ground for O'Sullivan and familiar turf for Farrow.

Yarn is set during the mid-'20s in the spa resort of Kilshannon, a stuffy, parochial, middle-class enclave socially ruled by a Mrs. Doyle Counihan (Plowright), high priestess of a section dubbed Widows' Peak, whose members also include penurious spinster Miss O'Hare (Farrow), a Brit-hater with a murky past.

Enter American of Brit descent Edwina Broome (Richardson), a superglam World War I widow who soon has D. C.'s son, Godfrey (Adrian Dunbar), dancing on a string, but is seemingly loathed by the dowdy O'Hare. There's a sudden clanking of dramatic gears 70 minutes in, when all this whimsy takes on a darker edge. Each woman learns the dark truth about the other's background—until a final double-twist that's not entirely unexpected.

Forty years earlier, *Widows' Peak* would have been shot on an M-G-M backlot with studio interiors. Here, belief is suspended by the sound of Plowright and Farrow grappling with Irish accents, and Richardson with an American accent. Pic needs a sharper script and pacier direction to counter the earthbound realism of locations on display here.

•

WIFE VS. SECRETARY
1936, 88 mins, US b/w
Dir Clarence Brown ***Prod*** Hunt Stromberg ***Scr*** Norman Krasna, Alice Duer Miller, John Lee Mahin ***Ph*** Ray June ***Ed*** Frank E. Hull ***Mus*** Herbert Stothart, Edward Ward ***Art*** Cedric Gibbons, William A. Horning
Act Clark Gable, Jean Harlow, Myrna Loy, May Robson, Hobart Cavanaugh, James Stewart (M-G-M)

Here Jean Harlow is no siren. She is a perfectly competent secretary, very much in love with her job and her boss, but she does not go on the make for him. Myrna Loy, as the wife, is much in love with Clark Gable, and he with her. They are an ideal couple until his mother plants the seeds of suspicion, which are watered and fertilized by other women friends.

The blow-off comes when Gable refuses to take his wife to Havana on a business trip, but has his secretary fly down with some important data on the deal he has gone to close. Loy calls up and Harlow answers the phone. Loy decides to go to Europe and forget it all.

The script has been excellently handled, with the dialog held to a naturalness seldom achieved on the screen.

Gable gets a part which might have been tailored to his order and differentiates skillfully between his impulsive love for his wife and his friendly appreciation of his stenographer's merits. Loy gets a part which suits her, but it is Harlow who profits most. She clicks in every scene without going spectacular as to costume.

•

WILBY CONSPIRACY, THE
1975, 101 mins, UK Ⓥ col
Dir Ralph Nelson ***Prod*** Martin Baum ***Scr*** Rod Amateau, Harold Nebenzal ***Ph*** John Coquillon ***Ed*** Ernest Walter ***Mus*** Stanley Myers ***Art*** Harold Pottle
Act Sidney Poitier, Michael Caine, Nicol Williamson, Prunella Gee, Persis Khambatta, Saeed Jaffrey (United Artists)

The Wilby Conspiracy [from Peter Driscoll's novel] is a good action melodrama about apartheid in South Africa. It was made in Kenya. The stars Sidney Poitier and Michael Caine are relentlessly stalked by Nicol Williamson, superb as a coldly dedicated and brutal policeman out after racial agitators.

Poitier is linked by fate with Caine, an Englishman accidently enmeshed in South African segregation discrimination through his girl (Prunella Gee), who as Poitier's lawyer has him freed from a decade in prison for racial agitation.

Williamson, almost too chillingly realistic as a bigot, permits the two to escape an early police confrontation, so as to let Poitier lead him to Joseph De Fraf, the title character and a political guerrilla partner to Poitier. En route to the good climax, one encounters Persis Khambatta, a most attractive Indian actress, and Rutger Hauer, Gee's playboy-type husband.

But somehow the story comes out too much of a potboiler undeserving of the fine work that Williamson, Caine and Poitier put into it.

•

WILD AND THE WILLING, THE
(US: YOUNG AND WILLING)
1962, 123 mins, UK b/w
Dir Ralph Thomas ***Prod*** Betty E. Box ***Scr*** Nicholas Phipps, Mordecai Richler ***Ph*** Ernest Steward ***Ed*** Alfred Roome ***Mus*** Norrie Paramor ***Art*** Alex Vetchinsky
Act Virginia Maskell, Paul Rogers, Ian McShane, Samantha Eggar, Catherine Woodville, John Hurt (Rank)

The Wild and the Willing, adapted from *The Tinker*, a play by Laurence Dobie and Robert Sloman which didn't make the grade in the West End, has nothing much new to say on its chosen theme—youth trying to find its place in society. The screenplay is lucid and the background of a provincial university authentic.

It concerns a brilliant young student from a poor working-class family who is acutely class-conscious and rebels against the university, its professors and the opportunities they offer. He does not know where he is going and is arrogantly content to drift along raising cain, drinking beer, playing football and pawing his girl friend, another student. He is a leading light in the university with a particular influence on his roommate, a shyer, more introspective lad.

Throughout there is a complete air of realism. The students, the professors and the townsfolk are real people about whose problems audiences will care. Ralph Thomas has directed with tact and has brought out some surprisingly sure performances from his inexperienced actors. Ian McShane, with a broad Manchester accent, came straight from drama school to play this leading role. He is a virile, good-looking young man with authority who is a real discovery, as is John Hurt, also a first-timer, who plays his sensitive roommate.

•

WILD ANGELS, THE
1966, 83 mins, US Ⓥ ▭ col
Dir Roger Corman ***Prod*** Roger Corman ***Scr*** Charles B. Griffith ***Ph*** Richard Moore ***Ed*** Monte Hellman ***Mus*** Mike Curb ***Art*** Leon Ericksen
Act Peter Fonda, Nancy Sinatra, Bruce Dern, Diane Ladd, Michael J. Pollard, Gayle Hunnicutt (American International)

The foreword to this well-turned-out Roger Corman production is its tipoff: "The picture you are about to see will shock and perhaps anger you. Although the events and characters are fictitious, the story is a reflection of our times."

For thematic motivation, Corman, who produces in almost documentary style, chooses the marauding of the Hell's Angels. Pinpointed here, the Angels, in vicious stride and without regard for law and order, operate in a Southern California beach community, and it is upon this particular segment that Corman directs his clinical eye in dissecting their philosophical (?) rebellion.

Corman tackles the assignment with realism, taking apart the cult and giving its members an in-depth study as he follows a gang headed by Peter Fonda in their defiancé of common decencies.

Fonda lends credence to character, voicing the creed of the Angels in "wanting to do what we want to do" without interference, and is well-cast in part.

•

WILD AT HEART
1990, 127 mins, US Ⓥ ⊙ ▭ col
Dir David Lynch ***Prod*** Monty Montgomery, Steve Golin, Joni Sighvatsson ***Scr*** David Lynch ***Ph*** Fred Elmes ***Ed*** Duwayne Dunham ***Mus*** Angelo Badalamenti ***Art*** Patricia Norris
Act Nicolas Cage, Laura Dern, Diane Ladd, Willem Dafoe, Isabella Rossellini, Harry Dean Stanton (Polygram/Propaganda)

Joltingly violent, wickedly funny and rivetingly erotic, David Lynch's *Wild at Heart* [based on the novel by Barry Gifford] is a rollercoaster ride to redemption through an American gothic heart of darkness.

The brutal opening signals that this film is not for the faint of heart. Sailor (Nicolas Cage), an Elvis-acolyte whose snakeskin jacket proclaims his "duality and individuality," and his seethingly sexy 18-year-old girlfriend, Lula (Laura Dern), are waylaid leaving a dance hall somewhere in the Carolinas. Sailor literally cracks open the assassin with his bare hands. He does two years for manslaughter in "Pee Dee" state pen. Sailor breaks parole and absconds with Lula to New Orleans, pursued by private eye Johnnie Farragut (Harry Dean Stanton) who's hired by Lula's insanely obsessive mother Marietta (Dern's real-life mother, Diane Ladd) his sometime lover.

His rival for this psychotic witch's affections are mobster Marcello Santos (J. E. Freeman), also unleashed on the lovers' trail as a precaution by Mama. Santos tabs a bordello-dwelling hit-man to annihilate Stanton in a bayou-style ritual murder. It's not the storyline's first or last doublecross.

1990: NOMINATION: Best Supp. Actress (Diane Ladd)

•

WILD BILL
1995, 97 mins, US Ⓥ ⊙ col
Dir Walter Hill ***Prod*** Richard D. Zanuck, Lili Fini Zanuck ***Scr*** Walter Hill ***Ph*** Lloyd Ahern ***Ed*** Freeman Davies ***Art*** Joseph Nemec III
Act Jeff Bridges, Ellen Barkin, John Hurt, Diane Lane, David Arquette, Christina Applegate (Zanuck/United Artists)

Wild Bill is an art Western that manages to shoot itself in both feet. Walter Hill's third oater represents a case of diminishing returns in the genre for the director, after skillfully taking on several famous outlaw clans in *The Long Riders* and rather too reverentially approaching the legend of Geronimo years ago.

Although less flamboyant and showbizzy, this awkwardly structured look at one of the West's most famous gunmen stands as an artistic companion piece to Robert Altman's dud *Buffalo Bill and the Indians* in its preoccupation with myth and legend and its at least partial basis in a play [Thomas Babe's 1978 *Fathers and Sons*, plus Pete Dexter's novel *Deadwood*].

As impersonated with great physical conviction by Jeff Bridges, this Wild Bill is one ornery, sore-headed s.o.b. In the film's weird initial 20 minutes, this rattlesnake cuts down a succession of men in an elongated montage that spans nine years up to 1876 and locations from Abilene to Cheyenne to New York City.

In Deadwood Gulch in the Dakota Territory, Bill resumes his old quasi-romance with Calamity Jane (Ellen Barkin), suffers an opium-induced crisis of conscience and faces a recurring challenge from green would-be assassin Jack McCall (David Arquette), who, it appears, may be Wild Bill's son.

The druggy dreams and romantic pangs prompt a series of flashbacks done in parched, high-contrast black-and-white that further reveal Bill's murderousness as well as his lost love for Jack's mother, Susannah (Diane Lane). The problem is that these regrets have no seeming effect on the dubious hero's character. Pic comes to a near dead-stop, in the final stretch, as Wild Bill, Calamity Jane and Jack's band of killers sit around all night in a saloon while Jack decides whether or not to kill his nemesis.

Bridges acquits himself honorably, snarling meanly and attempting to search a soul that is void. Barkin is game, but doesn't really ring true as Calamity Jane, while Lane is one of the dreamiest visions to hit the territories since Claudia Cardinale in *Once Upon a Time in the West.*

•

WILD BUNCH, THE
1969, 145 mins, US Ⓥ ⦿ ▭ col
Dir Sam Peckinpah ***Prod*** Phil Feldman ***Scr*** Walon Green, Sam Peckinpah ***Ph*** Lucien Ballard ***Ed*** Lou Lombardo ***Mus*** Jerry Fielding ***Art*** Edward Carrere
Act William Holden, Ernest Borgnine, Robert Ryan, Edmond O'Brien, Warren Oates, Jaime Sanchez (Warner/Seven Arts)

Plot concerns a small band of outlaws headed by William Holden who hijack a U.S. ammunition train crossing the border into Mexico in 1913 to supply the revolutionary army of Pancho Villa.

Actually, the story is two-pronged. Holden and his men go their way of outlawry, and Robert Ryan, a former member of Holden's gang and temporarily released convict, tracks down his former chief to "buy" his freedom from jail.

Screenplay, based on a story by Walon Green and Roy N. Sickner, builds suspensefully when action finally starts about the middle of film. Sam Peckinpah's forceful direction is a definite asset, particularly in later sequences in which Holden deals with a vicious Mexican general over the hijacked guns and ammo.

Holden goes into character for his role and handles assignment expertly. Ernest Borgnine delivers his usual brand of acting as former's aide.

1969: NOMINATIONS: Best Original Story & Screenplay, Original Music Score

•

WILDCATS
1986, 107 mins, US Ⓥ ⦿ col
Dir Michael Ritchie ***Prod*** Anthea Sylbert ***Scr*** Ezra Sacks ***Ph*** Donald E. Thorin ***Ed*** Richard A. Harris ***Mus*** Hawk Wolinski, James Newton Howard ***Art*** Boris Leven
Act Goldie Hawn, James Keach, Swoosie Kurtz, Nipsey Russell, Bruce McGill, M. Emmet Walsh (Warner)

When Goldie Hawn tangles with high school varsity coach Bruce McGill, anyone can foresee the final confrontation.

Sure enough, when McGill has her appointed football coach at the unspeakable ghetto school, Central High, it's an inevitable collision course. Along the way crises pop up at carefully placed intervals, the first being winning the confidence of the rag-tag collection of players.

Michael Ritchie's direction lacks his usual bite and eye for detail. There is nothing spontaneous about the action and football footage is also surprisingly dull.

Hawn, seemingly on screen for the entire film, is fun to watch as she runs her team through aerobics and mugs for the camera, but even better is Nipsey Russell as the rough-hewn high school principal with a word for all occasions.

•

WILD CHILD
SEE: L'ENFANT SAUVAGE

•

WILDE
1997, 115 mins, UK Ⓥ ⦿ ▭ col
Dir Brian Gilbert ***Prod*** Marc Samuelson, Peter Samuelson ***Scr*** Julian Mitchell ***Ph*** Martin Fuhrer ***Ed*** Michael Bradsell ***Mus*** Debbie Wiseman ***Art*** Maria Djurkovic
Act Stephen Fry, Jude Law, Vanessa Redgrave, Jennifer Ehle, Gemma Jones, Judy Parfitt (Samuelson)

Big, bold and burnished—*Wilde* is the full monty on Oscar. Toplining British comedian/wit Stephen Fry in a once-in-a-lifetime role as the brilliant, acerbic playwright, and mounted with a care and affection in all departments that squeezes the most from its $10 million budget, movie is a tony biopic that manages to combine an upfront portrayal of the scribe's gayness with an often moving examination of his broader emotions and artistic ideals.

Pic is the first to go the whole enchilada on Wilde's homosexuality, with reasonably forthright, though far from full-frontal, sex scenes replacing the lingering looks by Peter Finch and Robert Morley, respectively, in the two 1960 versions, *The Trials of Oscar Wilde* and *Oscar Wilde.*

Script, from the revealing biography [*Oscar Wilde*] by Richard Ellman, equally addresses Wilde's love for his wife and children, the nervousness behind his outward courage as a convention-breaker, as well as his higher, Platonic ideals of beauty and youth.

It's when Wilde is introduced to the upper-crust Alfred (Bosie) Douglas (Jude Law) at the triumphant opening-night party of *Lady Windermere's Fan* that Fry's perf really kicks in. Behind the man's overweening arrogance lies a real sadness that his affection for the kamikaze-like Bosie, prone to childish tantrums and sexual philandering, is to be the vehicle for his eventual downfall.

Brian Gilbert, till now only a journeyman director, brings to the picture most of the qualities that were memorably absent in his previous costumer, *Tom & Viv*—visual fluency, deep-seated emotion and first-rate playing from his cast. Up-and-coming young actor Law makes an alternately likable and infuriating Bosie. Jennifer Ehle is excellent as Wilde's wife, Constance, giving quiet substance to a potentially token role.

•

WILDER NAPALM
1993, 109 mins, US Ⓥ ⦿ col
Dir Glenn Gordon Caron ***Prod*** Mark Johnson, Stuart Cornfeld ***Scr*** Vince Gilligan ***Ph*** Jerry Hartleben ***Ed*** Artie Mandelberg ***Mus*** Michael Kamen ***Art*** John Muto
Act Debra Winger, Dennis Quaid, Arliss Howard, M. Emmet Walsh, Jim Varney, Mimi Lieber (Tri-Star)

If nothing else, *Wilder Napalm* deserves a special mention in the history books as the first and only pyrokinetic romantic comedy-drama. Beyond that, there's little to recommend in the slow-moving, fuzzy-minded yarn.

The Foudroyant brothers—Wallace (Dennis Quaid) and Wilder (Arliss Howard)—have that oh-so-special gift of thinking real hard and making things explode in flames. Wallace has managed to incorporate such shenanigans into a clown act he performs in a low-grade traveling carnival.

Wilder works quietly and alone in one of those shopping mall film-processing joints. Yet he's married to the spunky, brash Vida (Debra Winger). There's mysterious bad blood involving a prank Wallace inflicted on his brother, and deeply ingrained tension over Vida's affections. But that might change when the carnival arrives in town and parks itself in the very mall where Wilder plies his trade.

If this all sounds like gobbledygook, one can only say that the filmmakers have worked diligently at rendering the material incomprehensible. The moral really isn't any more brilliant than "Don't play with matches."

Winger and Quaid appear at a loss to make sense of their characters and it's painful to watch such gifted actors struggling to maintain their dignity.

•

WILD GEESE, THE
1978, 132 mins, UK Ⓥ ⦿ col
Dir Andrew V. McLaglen ***Prod*** Euan Lloyd ***Scr*** Reginald Rose ***Ph*** Jack Hildyard ***Ed*** John Glen ***Mus*** Roy Budd
Act Richard Burton, Roger Moore, Richard Harris, Hardy Kruger, Stewart Granger, Jack Watson (Rank)

Euan Lloyd's uppercase actioner, centered on a caper by mercenaries in Africa, attempts to be a cornucopia of tried box-office hooks but ultimately fails to meld its comedy, adventure, pathos, violence, heroics—or even its political message—into a credible whole.

Reginald Rose's adaptation of Daniel Carney's story—about mercenary tough guys who parachute into the African bush to snatch a deposed African president for reinstatement to suit British business interests—is routinely predictable and, in the end, cornily incredible.

Roger Moore's shootouts with the Mafia in London and Hardy Kruger's neat killing of three sentries with cyanide-tipped arrows is good "traditional" escapism. Then, as if to contemporize the film, Peckinpah-fashion, the screen's suddenly filled with bloody graphics and four-letter words.

Winston Ntshona is well cast as the deposed president, Limbani, though much of his "message" dialog is unnecessarily and unpalatably heavy for what's presumably designed as a riproaring blood-and-guts actioner.

•

WILD GEESE II
1985, 125 mins, UK Ⓥ ⦿ col
Dir Peter Hunt ***Prod*** Euan Lloyd ***Scr*** Reginald Rose ***Ph*** Michael Reed ***Ed*** Keith Palmer ***Mus*** Roy Budd ***Art*** Syd Cain
Act Scott Glenn, Barbara Carrera, Edward Fox, Laurence Olivier, Robert Webber, Robert Freitag (Thorn-EMI/Frontier)

Script [from the book *The Square Circle* by Daniel Carney] has a promising basic premise. An American TV station commissions mercenary John Haddad (Scott Glenn) to kidnap the nonagenarian Nazi leader Rudolf Hess from the impregnable Spandau prison in Berlin, but the follow-through never arrives. A routine car ambush is substituted for the impossible jailbreak. The liberated Hess just doesn't want to play games with history by revealing the Watergate-style story supposedly underlying Hitler's rise to power.

Despite these structural problems, film contains a wealth of incident. Haddad is the object of numerous assassination attempts organized by the German Heinrich Stroebling (Robert Freitag), who is in league with the Russians and Palestinian terrorists. The British are after Hess too. There's also a supporting role for members of the Irish Republican Army and the kidnap of Yank journalist Kathy Lukas (Barbara Carrera) occasions a major shootout.

Edward Fox plays Colonel Faulkner with comic zest. Unintentionally, perhaps, Laurence Olivier also extracts laughs from his Hess cameo. By contrast, Glenn and Carrera take their parts more seriously than the script merits.

•

WILD HEART, THE
SEE: GONE TO EARTH

•

WILD IN THE COUNTRY
1961, 112 mins, US Ⓥ ▭ col
Dir Philip Dunne ***Prod*** Jerry Wald ***Scr*** Clifford Odets ***Ph*** William C. Mellor ***Ed*** Dorothy Spencer ***Mus*** Kenyon Hopkins ***Art*** Jack Martin Smith, Preston Ames
Act Elvis Presley, Hope Lange, Tuesday Weld, Millie Perkins, John Ireland, Gary Lockwood (20th Century-Fox)

Dramatically, there simply isn't substance, novelty or spring to this wobbly and artificial tale of a maltreated country boy (Elvis Presley) who, supposedly, has the talent to become a great writer, but lacks the means, the emotional stability and the encouragement until he comes in contact with a beautiful psychiatric consultant (Hope Lange) who develops traumas of her own in the process.

The complications occur when the two spend an innocent night in a motel, innocent on the strength of their May (he)-December (she) respect for each other. The gap in romantic seasons is quickly bridged when their one-night relationship is misinterpreted by some of the incredibly foul and mischievous people who live in the town. Clifford Odets penned the screenplay, from the novel *The Lost Country* by J. R. Salamanca. The writing has its occasional rewards.

Presley, subdued, uses what dramatic resources he has to best advantage in this film. Lange, for the most part, plays intelligently and sensitively. Tuesday Weld contributes a flashy and arresting portrait of a sexy siren enamored of Mr. P.

Story, set in the Shenandoah Valley, was filmed in the Napa Valley. Sans wiggle, Presley croons four or five songs. Guitars rather mysteriously keep turning up on the premises, but E. P. leaves the plunking to Weld.

•

WILD IN THE STREETS
1968, 96 mins, US Ⓥ col
Dir Barry Shear ***Prod*** Burt Topper ***Scr*** Robert Thom ***Ph*** Richard Moore ***Ed*** Fred Feitshans, Eve Newman ***Mus*** Les Baxter
Act Shelley Winters, Christopher Jones, Diane Varsi, Ed Begley, Hal Halbrook, Millie Perkins (American International)

An often chilling political science-fiction drama, with comedy, the production considers the takeover of American government by the preponderant younger population. Good writing and direction enhance the impact of a diversified cast headed by Shelley Winters.

Christopher Jones plays a rock'n'roll hero who, as a result of a request from would-be U.S. Senator Hal Holbrook, exceeds the bounds of electioneering help by mobilizing teenagers into legalized voters. Winters plays his sleazy, selfish mother, whose purported emasculation of dad Bert Freed years before cued Jones's running away from home. Holbrook projects perfectly the bright young politico who exploits the young crowd, only to be turned on by those whose help he seeks.

Actual footage from real-life demonstrations was shot for pic, some of it matched quite well with internal drama. What comes off as a partial documentary flavor makes for a good artistic complement to the not-so-fictional hypothesis, the logical result of an over-accent on youth.

1968: NOMINATION: Best Editing

•

WILD IS THE WIND
1957, 110 mins, US b/w
Dir George Cukor ***Prod*** Hal Wallis ***Scr*** Arnold Schulman ***Ph*** Charles Lang, Jr. ***Ed*** Warren Low ***Mus*** Dimitri Tiomkin ***Art*** Hal Pereira, Tambi Larsen
Act Anna Magnani, Anthony Quinn, Anthony Franciosa, Dolores Hart, Joseph Calleia, Lili Valenty (Paramount)

Top grade performances, some unusual film sequences and expert production highlight *Wild Is the Wind*, a story of earthy passion. Screenplay, from a story by Vittorio Nino Novarese, is a good one, particularly in its delineation of the characters. It's an unusual switch in that it starts off on a comedy level before abruptly switching to the dramatic problem and long early portions of it are almost entirely in Italian.

Anthony Quinn is a wealthy sheep rancher in Nevada and goes back to the old country to wed the sister of his long-dead wife. He brings her home to a promise of happiness, but the shadow of the first wife is constantly between them. Her urgent need to be loved makes her mistake the growing attraction between herself and Anthony Franciosa, a young Basque sheepherder who had been raised by Quinn.

George Cukor directs with taste and imagination and his skillful handling is evident in many scenes, particularly the sequence showing a film audience how a lamb is dropped, or one in which Franciosa trains sheep dogs, and in his handling of the affair between Magnani and Franciosa.

1957: NOMINATIONS: Best Actor (Anthony Quinn), Actress (Anna Magnani), Song ("Wild Is the Wind")

•

WILD ONE, THE

1953, 79 mins, US Ⓥ ⦿ b/w

Dir Laslo Benedek ***Prod*** Stanley Kramer ***Scr*** John Paxton ***Ph*** Hal Mohr ***Ed*** Al Clark ***Mus*** Leith Stevens ***Art*** Walter Holscher

Act Marlon Brando, Mary Murphy, Robert Keith, Lee Marvin, Jay C. Flippen, Hugh Sanders (Columbia)

Inspired by an episode when a mob of youths on motorcycles terrorized a Californian town for an entire evening, this feature is long on suspense, brutality and sadism. Marlon Brando contributes another hard-faced "hero" who never knew love as a boy and is now plainly in need of psychoanalysis.

The young cyclists are a motley mob of jivesters, some carrying their own female cargo. Much given to showoff antics and mimicry, they also drink beer in vast quantities and incessantly deposit nickels in jukeboxes. Reckless, impudent, cruel and knife-carrying, they break and borrow things and drive motorcycles into and through saloons.

However intolerable and barbarian the cyclists are, nothing they do is as vicious and vindictive as the "vigilante" spirit which develops among the merchants of the village. Big bruisers twice the size of the young cyclists, these adults readily and joyously beat Brando to a pulp and then later try to frame him by their silence for a manslaughter rap. Picture [from a story by Frank Rooney] was made some time before its release and had three titles in succession, *Cyclists Raid*: *The Wild One* and *Hot Blood*. All performances are highly competent. A second band of ruffians comes along later led by a colorful young character named Lee Marvin.

The femme interest is intelligently managed by Mary Murphy. Robert Keith is excellent as the mush-soft village constable. The county sheriff is the nicest guy in the film, and nearly the only one. He's impersonated with professional sincerity by the old vaudeman Jay C. Flippen.

•

WILD ORCHID

1990, 100 mins, US Ⓥ ⦿ col

Dir Zalman King ***Prod*** Mark Damon, Tony Anthony, Howard North ***Scr*** Zalman King, Patricia Louisianna Knop ***Ph*** Gale Tattersall ***Mus*** Geoff MacCormack, Simon Goldenberg

Act Mickey Rourke, Jacqueline Bisset, Carre Otis (Vision)

If *Wild Orchid* aims to grab audiences with a hot-house atmosphere of erotica, it mainly teases until a pay-off in the last sequence.

Claudia (Jacqueline Bisset) is a wired jet-set businesswoman who hires tyro lawyer Emily (Carre Otis) to help her close a deal. Prim Emily, a Midwest farm girl still wet under the collar—but highly attractive—is dazed to find herself on a plane to Rio. There she meets Claudia's old flame Wheeler (Mickey Rourke), a self-made millionaire with perverse sexual tastes. Hypnotizing Emily with his original personality (?), he forces her to forget her good-girl upbringing and do liberating things. What doesn't work is the hold Rourke is supposed to have over Otis. Looking pudgy and puffy-faced, with a little gold earring, he is anything but an appetizing sex object.

As Emily, Otis really is hypnotically attractive, but she plays the still-waters-run-deep country beauty with expressionless immobility. Bisset, always a class act, here bubbles over with caricatured *joie de vivre*.

As for eros, only when Emily breaks through Wheeler's reserve/impotence in the last sequence does pic deliver in a torrid, highly choreographed but equally explicit bedroom session between the two.

•

WILD PARTY, THE

1975, 100 mins, US Ⓥ col

Dir James Ivory ***Prod*** Ismail Merchant ***Scr*** Walter Marks ***Ph*** Walter Lassally ***Ed*** Kent McKinney ***Mus*** Laurence Rosenthal ***Art*** David Nichols

Act James Coco, Raquel Welch, Perry King, Tiffany Bolling, Royal Dano, David Dukes (American International)

The Wild Party is an extremely handsome, overly talky musical drama starring James Coco as a faded 1920s' film comic whose disastrous premiere houseparty for a comeback film leads to murder.

Based on a long-ago poem by Joseph Moncure March, the film is a magnificent showpiece for Coco's talents. He successfully covers a spectrum from silly comedy, warm humor, sober anger, maddening frustration and drunken psychosis. Holding her own as his mistress is Raquel Welch, registering very strongly.

Key featured players include Perry King, very good as a current film heartthrob; Tiffany Bolling, his femme counterpart; and Royal Dano, quite good as Coco's loyal valet.

•

WILD RIVER

1960, 115 mins, US ⊏⊐ col

Dir Elia Kazan ***Prod*** Elia Kazan ***Scr*** Paul Osborn ***Ph*** Ellsworth Fredericks ***Ed*** William Reynolds ***Mus*** Kenyon Hopkins ***Art*** Lyle R. Wheeler, Herman A. Blumenthal

Act Montgomery Clift, Lee Remick, Jo Van Fleet, Albert Salmi, Jay C. Flippen, Barbara Loden (20th Century-Fox)

Wild River is an important motion picture. In studying a slice of national socio-economic progress (the Tennessee Valley Authority of the early 1930s) in terms of people (those who enforced vs. those who resisted), it catches something timeless and essential in the human spirit and shapes it in the American image.

Sturdy foundation for director Elia Kazan's artistic indulgences and a number of exceptional performances is Paul Osborn's thought-provoking screenplay, erected out of two novels, *Mud on the Stars* by William Bradford Huie, and *Dunbar's Cove* by Borden Deal. It is the tragic tale of an 80-year-old "rugged individualist" (Jo Van Fleet) who refuses to give ground (a small island on the Tennessee River smack dab in TVA's dam-building path) to an understanding, but equally firm, TVA agent (Montgomery Clift).

In the process of successfully separating the grand old lady from her precious, but doomed, slice of real estate, Clift gets into several scrapes with the local Tennessee bigots over his decent treatment of Negroes and squeezes sufficient romance into his tight schedule to wind up the spouse of the old woman's pretty granddaughter (Lee Remick).

Where the film soars is in its clean, objective approach to the basic conflict between progress and tradition ("electricity and souls," as Osborn puts it). Through this gentle veil of objectivity, a point-of-view unmistakably stirs, but never emerges to the point where it takes sides just to be taking sides. The result is that rare element of tragedy, in the truly classical sense of the word, where an indomitable individual eventually must fall helpless prey to an irresistible, but impersonal edict designed for universal good.

•

WILD ROVERS

1971, 110 mins, US Ⓥ ⊏⊐ col

Dir Blake Edwards ***Prod*** Blake Edwards, Ken Wales ***Scr*** Blake Edwards ***Ph*** Philip Lathrop ***Ed*** John F. Burnett ***Mus*** Jerry Goldsmith ***Art*** George W. Davis, Addison Hehr

Act William Holden, Ryan O'Neal, Karl Malden, Lynn Carlin, Tom Skerritt, Joe Don Baker (M-G-M)

William Holden and Ryan O'Neal, two cowboys who decide to rob a bank, and Karl Malden, their employer, star in a technically superior film.

Film tells a sentimental story about an aging cowpoke and a younger buddy whose dreams of crashing out of their rut lead to violence and death.

Emphasis is on Holden and O'Neal, and there are a few touching moments as the older man imparts some wisdom to the younger. The mood is broken regularly with pratfall humor, also some dehumanizing slow-motion ballets of death. O'Neal's character is not always well defined, since the boyish naivete also exhibits some jarring evidence of cruelty, thereby limiting empathy for his ultimate downfall.

Large supporting cast is lost in throwaway parts. Even Malden has little to do except plot-motivate the dispatch of sons Tom Skerritt and Joe Don Baker to join the posse. Skerritt overacts, and Baker's abilities are smothered in a second banana line-throwing part.

•

WILD STRAWBERRIES

SEE: SMULTRONSTALLET

•

WILD THINGS

1998, 108 mins, US Ⓥ ⦿ ⊏⊐ col

Dir John McNaughton ***Prod*** Rodney Liber, Steven A. Jones ***Scr*** Stephen Peters ***Ph*** Jeffrey L. Kimball ***Ed*** Elena Maganini ***Mus*** George S. Clinton ***Art*** Edward T. McAvoy

Act Kevin Bacon, Matt Dillon, Neve Campbell, Theresa Russell, Denise Richards, Bill Murray (Columbia/Mandalay)

In the blue-chip Florida enclave of Blue Bay, the sex is as steamy as the climate. Sly, torrid and original, *Wild Things* captures the passions of the area's haves and have-nots and gives them a wicked comic spin. Imagine *Double Indemnity* cast young, *Twin Peaks* basked in sunshine and a lethal *Grosse Pointe Blank*.

On the surface, it's about high-nosed teen socialite Kelly Van Ryan (Denise Richards) discovering her sexuality and finding out she can't get whatever she wants: her moves on guidance counselor Sam Lombardo (Matt Dillon) have been met with indifference. But that doesn't stop her from crying rape.

The social-climbing Lombardo is forced to enlist personal-injuries lawyer Ken Bowden (Bill Murray), who proves more shrewd than the army of legal eagles Kelly's mother—and Sam's former lover (Theresa Russell)—employs to destroy the teacher. It looks grim when another teen, trailer-trash Suzie Toller (Neve Campbell), comes forward with a carbon-copy tale of Sam's advances. Still, the story demands further explanation for both the audience and local investigating cop Ray Duquette (Kevin Bacon).

Wild Things really gets cooking once it begins unraveling "facts" to get at the truth. Even the most detailed road map of the story will lead one hopelessly off course.

Director John McNaughton casts his four principals against type. Dillon is the picture of duplicity, while Bacon is a dumb cop with a good gut. The young women, the good girls of *Scream* and *Starship Troopers* become the wanton wenches from both sides of the tracks. There's not a wrong note struck by the game group of players.

Generally associated with grittier fare, McNaughton stretches his reach with a high-sheen package.

•

WILD WILD WEST

1999, 107 mins, US Ⓥ ⦿ col

Dir Barry Sonnenfeld ***Prod*** Jon Peters, Barry Sonnenfeld ***Scr*** S. S. Wilson, Brent Maddock, Jeffrey Price, Peter S. Seaman ***Ph*** Michael Ballhaus ***Ed*** Jim Miller ***Mus*** Elmer Bernstein ***Art*** Bo Welch

Act Will Smith, Kevin Kline, Kenneth Branagh, Salma Hayek, Ted Levine, M. Emmet Walsh (Peters/Sonnenfeld-Josephson/Warner)

Some very talented people stub their collective toes quite elaborately and expensively in *Wild Wild West*.

As refittings of old TV shows go, this one is neither the best nor the worst from a conceptual p.o.v., turning the 1964–68 Robert Conrad–Ross Martin series into a Jules Verne–like 19th-century quasi-sci-fier equipped with hip refs and contempo attitude. The notions here are to make a futuristic romp from the perspective of the film's setting in 1869, and pit a black hero against a Southern white villain driven by revenge for the losses he suffered during the Civil War.

Special government agents James West (Will Smith) and Artemus Gordon (Kevin Kline), temperamentally opposed, are thrown together by President Grant (Kline again) to thwart Confederate Gen. "Bloodbath" McGrath (Ted Levine), who is allegedly developing a highly advanced "weapons system" that threatens the Union. However, it becomes evident that their real foe is Dr. Arliss Loveless (Kenneth Branagh), a paraplegic mounted on a motorized cart, who has kidnapped all the top scientists, one of whom is supposedly the father of Rita Escobar (Salma Hayek), a beauteous saloon "entertainer" who keeps West and Gordon at odds over her amorous intention.

Smith is hardly at his most inspired or amusing. Kline has fun with his multitude of disguises but also fights an uphill battle with undernourished dialogue. Branagh supplies all the vinegar he can to his Prussian-style villain, while Hayek is all sauciness and pulchritude as the ever-elusive Rita.

•

WILLARD
1971, 95 mins, US Ⓥ ⦿ col
Dir Daniel Mann *Prod* Mort Briskin *Scr* Gilbert A. Ralston *Ph* Robert B. Hauser *Ed* Warren Low *Mus* Alex North *Art* Howard Hollander
Act Bruce Davison, Ernest Borgnine, Elsa Lanchester, Sondra Locke, Michael Dante, Jody Gilbert (BCO)

Neat little horror tale, shrewdly organized from Stephen Gilbert's novel, *Ratman's Notebooks*, capitalizes on human repugnance for rodents as Bruce Davison unleashes his trained rats on obstacles. Some good jump moments and at least two stomach-churning murders committed by the rats with tight direction of Daniel Mann develop pic into sound nail-chewer.

Davison, working for wheeler-dealer Ernest Borgnine, who took foundry over from Davison's dead father, lives with invalid, unrelenting mother Elsa Lanchester. Their old mansion gone to seed, loner Davison makes friends with resident rats, who learn to obey his commands. Davison, after death of his mother, killing of one of chief rats at Borgnine's hands, and receipt of pink slip from Borgnine, begins to fight back. Davison supplies nicely controlled characterization as he fiddles with his rats, puts up with his mother and her friends and finally loses patience. Borgnine is first rate as he confronts subordinates. Lanchester is highly credible as the demanding mama.

•

WILLIAM SHAKESPEARE'S A MIDSUMMER NIGHT'S DREAM
SEE: MIDSUMMER NIGHT'S DREAM, A

•

WILLIAM SHAKESPEARE'S ROMEO + JULIET
SEE: ROMEO + JULIET

•

WILLIE & PHIL
1980, 116 mins, US Ⓥ col
Dir Paul Mazursky *Prod* Paul Mazursky, Tony Ray *Scr* Paul Mazursky *Ph* Sven Nykvist *Ed* Donn Cambern *Mus* Claude Bolling, Georges Delerue *Art* Pato Guzman
Act Michael Ontkean, Margot Kidder, Ray Sharkey, Jerry Hall, Natalie Wood, Tom Brennan (20th Century-Fox)

Willie & Phil is an amiable and humane film about a *menage-a-trois* spanning the 1970s. Director Paul Mazursky's compassionate eye for character and his wry wit balance out a tendency to overromanticize and sentimentalize his characters.

Michael Ontkean and Ray Sharkey play the title characters (roles once intended for Woody Allen and Al Pacino) and Margot Kidder completes the romantic triangle, which forms in Greenwich Village at the beginning of the 1970s and winds up in Malibu nine years later. Along the way, Mazursky deftly traces changing sexual mores and other social values while portraying the trio as typical representatives of their generation's hopes and confusions.

Beginning rather coyly with the two men meeting at a Bleecker Street Cinema screening of Truffaut's classic 1962 film about a *menage-a-trois*, *Jules et Jim*, Mazursky then has the two become friends so inseparable that they have trouble deciding who should board with Kidder.

It's all handled in very civilized and low-key fashion by Mazursky and his characters.

•

WILLOW
1988, 125 mins, US Ⓥ ⦿ ▭ col
Dir Ron Howard *Prod* Nigel Wooll *Scr* Bob Dolman *Ph* Adrian Biddle *Ed* Daniel Hanley, Michael Hill *Mus* James Horner *Art* Allan Cameron
Act Val Kilmer, Joanne Whalley-Kilmer, Warwick Davis, Patricia Hayes, Jean Marsh, Billy Barty (Lucasfilm)

Willow is medieval mishmash from George Lucas [executive producer who wrote the original story], a sort of tenth-century *Star Wars* tossed together with a plethora of elements taken from numerous classic fables. There's a baby princess, an evil queen, trolls, fairies, little people, warriors, sorcerers and a community of midgets called Nelwyns. Willow is a Nelwyn.

They are saving their kingdom from an evil queen (Jean Marsh) who makes her crusade to kill every newborn in the land to ensure that baby Elora Danan, a princess, never ascends to the throne. Willow gets a loving send-off, baby on his back papoose-style. Along the way, he teams up with a wisecracking Han Solo renegade warrior named Madmartigan (read: Mad Max), played well enough by Val Kilmer.

Dialog waivers from the truly banal—Willow himself is very earnest and boring—to some very clever interplay between the secondary characters, including a delightful scene between Madmartigan, dusted with love sparkles, and the object of his desire, Sorsha (real-life wife, Joanne Whalley), the evil queen's daughter.

Ron Howard directed, but only Lucasness shows up on the screen, particularly toward the end when the special effects start to come on at full bore. *Willow* was lensed in England, Wales and New Zealand. It's not surprising the overall flavor of the production looks familiar. Production designer Allan Cameron (*Aliens*) and cinematographer Adrian Biddle (*Aliens, The Princess Bride*) have put their stamp on the film. Industrial Light & Magic wizards, too numerous to mention, are up to usual Lucasfilm standards of excellence.

1988: NOMINATIONS: Best Sound Effects Editing, Visual Effects

•

WILL PENNY
1968, 108 mins, US Ⓥ ⦿ col
Dir Tom Gries *Prod* Fred Engel, Walter Seltzer *Scr* Tom Gries *Ph* Lucien Ballard *Ed* Warren Low *Mus* David Raksin *Art* Hal Pereira, Roland Anderson
Act Charlton Heston, Joan Hackett, Donald Pleasence, Lee Majors, Bruce Dern, Ben Johnson (Paramount)

Will Penny is not a straight out-and-out Western but more a character study of an aging cowpoke who for the first time feels the stirrings of romance.

There is beautiful range and mountain scenery but basically interest rests on the man, and his gropings, which at times aren't overly clear, rather than on Western action all too often slowed by characterization.

Charlton Heston in title role is persuasively effective as the cowpoke who finally rides away from romance. Joan Hackett is quietly commanding as the woman, traveling across the plains with her young son to join her farmer-husband in Oregon, willing to renounce that marriage to wed the penniless range rider.

Donald Pleasence is a scavenging rawhider who, with his three sons, would rather murder than not. Given these elements, a story takes form which displays thoughtful conception. This is not a story of the wild West but the West as lived in by real-life characters.

•

WILL SUCCESS SPOIL ROCK HUNTER?
(UK: OH! FOR A MAN)
1957, 93 mins, US Ⓥ ⦿ ▭ col
Dir Frank Tashlin *Prod* Frank Tashlin *Scr* Frank Tashlin *Ph* Joseph MacDonald *Ed* Hugh Fowler *Mus* Cyril J. Mockridge *Art* Lyle R. Wheeler, Leland Fuller
Act Jayne Mansfield, Tony Randall, Betsy Drake, Joan Blondell, John Williams, Henry Jones (20th Century-Fox)

In converting the stageplay *Will Success Spoil Rock Hunter?* to his purposes, Frank Tashlin turns out a vastly amusing comedy. Picture bears comparatively little resemblance to the George Axelrod original.

Tony Randall's second excursion into the big-screen realm from TV and the stage shows he's a fellow who knows timing, and his clowning has a slightly sophisticated touch that hits bull's-eye. Jayne Mansfield does a socko job as the featherbrained, sex-motivated movie star.

Tashlin fashions a funny opening for the credits, which are introed by Randall. There's also an "intermission," with Randall coming out to comfort those who are used to TV commercials. In the end, Groucho Marx comes on for a briefy.

Story has Randall as a TV commercial writer about to be fired because his agency is threatened with the loss of its big lipstick account. He saves the situation by getting the endorsement from a famous movie star. Supporting roles are all very well cast. Betsy Drake is cute and displays a strong sense for comedy as Randall's fiancée; Henry Jones, ad-agency v.p., coaxes from the sidelines and delivers some rather lengthy speeches; Joan Blondell is standout in a small part and Mickey Hargitay is properly pompous as the Tarzan he-man who triggers Randall's troubles.

•

WILLY/MILLY
1986, 90 mins, US Ⓥ col
Dir Paul Schneider *Prod* M. David Chilewich *Scr* Walter Carbonne, Carla Reuben *Ph* Dominique Chapuis *Ed* Michael Miller *Mus* David McHugh *Art* Nora Chavooshian
Act Pamela Segall, Eric Gurry, Mary Tanner, Patty Duke, John Glover, Seth Green (Cinema)

The rather silly title *Willy/Milly* caps this charming and substantial kidpic about sex roles.

Rather than face the trauma of crossing the threshold of womanhood, fourteen-year-old Milly (Pamela Segall) turns into a boy under the effect of a magic spell she tries out during an eclipse. The matter-of-fact reaction of Milly is captured when she spins the first letter of her name upside-down and decides to try out Willy, effectively turning her entire world upside-down.

The effects of the kid's crossover are explored on all fronts, going beyond locker-room humor and capturing the kinds of expectations that spark the war between the sexes at all ages.

Film's biggest asset is in the performances of the unknown adolescent actors.

•

WILLY WONKA AND THE CHOCOLATE FACTORY
1971, 98 mins, US Ⓥ ⦿ col
Dir Mel Stuart *Prod* Stan Margulies, David L. Wolper *Scr* Roald Dahl *Ph* Arthur Ibbetson *Ed* David Saxon *Mus* Walter Scharf (arr.) *Art* Harper Goff
Act Gene Wilder, Jack Albertson, Peter Ostrum, Roy Kinnear, Julie Dawn Cole, Leonard Stone (Wolper/Quaker)

Based on a Roald Dahl children's book, *Willy Wonka and the Chocolate Factory* is an okay family musical fantasy featuring Gene Wilder as an eccentric candymaker who makes a boy's dreams come true. Handsomely produced in partnership with Quaker Oats, the film has a fair score by Leslie Bricusse and Anthony Newley.

Dahl himself adapted his book, *Charlie and the Chocolate Factory*, and his dialog is better than the structure. Plot hook is a merchandising gimmick by Wilder who puts five golden tickets into a candy bar run, and tests the honesty of the winners. Inhibiting the sustaining of interest among those who are not familiar with the book is that Wilder's character is rather cynical and sadistic until virtually the end of the film. Ultimately Peter Ostrum, the kids' hero, and Grandpa Jack Albertson pass the honesty test.

Sidebar incidents and dialog are the sharpest elements, particularly the running satire on TV news-programming cliché.

1971: NOMINATION: Best Adapted Score

•

WILSON
1944, 136 mins, US col
Dir Henry King *Prod* Darryl F. Zanuck *Scr* Lamar Trotti *Ph* Leon Shamroy *Ed* Barbara McLean *Mus* Alfred Newman *Art* Wiard B. Ihnen, James Basevi
Act Alexander Knox, Charles Coburn, Geraldine Fitzgerald, Thomas Mitchell, Cedric Hardwicke, Vincent Price (20th Century-Fox)

The production is said to cost over $3 million and looks it. When there are crowds in the senate, at the sundry political conventions, in the Palmer Stadium, on the campus, they are there in staggering, sizable numbers.

When the period of 1912–20 is recreated in Technicolor, it is as authentic as it is splendiferous. All the detail of the White House decor of the Wilson administration; all the local color of the era and the day are faithfully brought to the canvas in a nostalgic, authentic fashion.

In fact, that is the keynote of *Wilson*—authority, warmth, idealism, a search for a better world. Through it all stalks a potent personality in Alexander Knox, a newborn star, supported by a flawless cast.

1944: Best Original Screenplay, Color Cinematography, Color Art Direction, Editing, Sound

NOMINATIONS: Best Picture, Director, Actor (Alexander Knox), Scoring of a Dramatic Picture, Special Effects

•

WILT
1989, 91 mins, UK Ⓥ col
Dir Michael Tuchner *Prod* Brian Eastman *Scr* Andrew Marshall, David Renwick *Ph* Norman Langley *Ed* Chris Blunden *Mus* Anne Dudley *Art* Leo Austin
Act Griff Rhys Jones, Mel Smith, Alison Steadman, Diana Quick, Jeremy Clyde (Carnival/LWT)

There is a good deal of enjoyment to be derived from *Wilt* [based on Tom Sharpe's novel], mainly thanks to a uniformly excellent cast and unpretentious, straightforward direction by Michael Tuchner, as well as the charmingly honest urban provincial settings.

Griff Rhys Jones is the title character, a disillusioned college lecturer, who spends his spare time walking his dog and dreaming about murdering his domineering wife (Alison Steadman).

She has made friends with upwardly mobile couple Diana Quick and Jeremy Clyde. When Steadman and Rhys Jones attend a party at their posh country home, Rhys Jones gets dead-drunk and, due to Quick's machinations, finds himself locked in a naked passionate embrace with a life-size inflatable doll named Angelique.

He drunkenly roams the town trying to get rid of the doll. The next day, Steadman goes missing and Rhys Jones's nocturnal activities are noted—especially by ambitious inspector Mel Smith.

The most amusing scenes are those with Rhys Jones and Smith indulging in the banter they are known for from their TV appearances.

●

WINCHESTER '73

1950, 92 mins, US Ⓥ ⊙ b/w

Dir Anthony Mann ***Prod*** Aaron Rosenberg ***Scr*** Robert L. Richards, Borden Chase ***Ph*** William Daniels ***Ed*** Edward Curtiss ***Mus*** Joseph Gershenson

Act James Stewart, Shelley Winters, Dan Duryea, Stephen McNally, Rock Hudson, Tony Curtis (Universal)

Story [by Stuart N. Lake] is centered on a manhunt, the search of Lin McAdam (James Stewart) for the cowardly murderer of his father. Film opens with Lin and his friend, High Spade (Millard Mitchell), riding into Dodge City in time for a 4 July celebration. Big event is a rifle match, with first prize a priceless "one of a 1,000" 1873 model Winchester rifle.

Lin's brother Dutch (Stephen McNally), however, makes off with the precious rifle.

Stewart brings real flavor and appeal to the role of Lin, in a lean, concentrated portrayal. McNally is hard and unbending as the runaway brother. Mitchell lends warmth as Stewart's loyal henchman and friend. Shelley Winters is just sufficiently hard-bitten and cynical as the dancehall girl.

●

WIND, THE

1928, 70 mins, US Ⓥ ⊙ d b/w

Dir Victor Seastrom ***Scr*** Frances Marion, John Colton ***Ph*** John Arnold ***Ed*** Conrad A. Nervig ***Art*** Cedric Gibbons, Edward Withers

Act Lillian Gish, Lars Hanson, Montagu Love, Dorothy Cumming, Edward Earle, William Orlamond (M-G-M)

Some stories are just naturally poison for screen purposes and Dorothy Scarborough's novel here shows itself a conspicuous example. Everything a high-pressure, lavishly equipped studio, expert director and reputable star could contribute was showered on this production. Everything about the picture breathes quality. Yet it flops dismally.

Tragedy on the high winds, on the desolate desert prairies, unrelieved by that sparkling touch of life that spells human interest, is what this picture has to offer. It may be a true picturization of life on the prairie, but it still remains lifeless—and unentertaining.

The story opens with an unknown girl, Letty (Lillian Gish), from Virginia, train-bound for her cousin's ranch, which she describes as beautiful to the stranger, Roddy (Montagu Love), who has made her acquaintance informally.

Roaring, blinding wind and sandstorms immediately frighten the girl. She remains in a semiconscious state of fright throughout, except at the close of the picture.

At Beverly's (Edward Earle) ranch the girl becomes too popular with Cora's (Dorothy Cummings) children and is forced to leave. The girl then accepts a proposal from Lige (Lars Hanson), whom she had laughed at the night before. During a round-up of wild horses, brought down by a fierce northern gale, Roddy forces his way into Lige's home and stays there for the night with Letty.

●

WIND

1992, 125 mins, US/Japan Ⓥ ⊙ col

Dir Carroll Ballard ***Prod*** Mata Yamamoto, Tom Luddy ***Scr*** Rudy Wurlitzer, Mac Gudgeon ***Ph*** John Toll ***Ed*** Michael Chandler ***Mus*** Basil Poledouris ***Art*** Laurence Eastwood

Act Matthew Modine, Jennifer Grey, Stellan Skarsgard, Rebecca Miller, Cliff Robertson, Jack Thompson (American Zoetrope/Filmlink)

The elements prove far more stimulating than the people in *Wind*, a sail-racing saga that could have used a great deal more dramatic rigging.

In his two previous narrative pics (*The Black Stallion*, *Never Cry Wolf*), maverick director Carroll Ballard had subjects that suited his tendency to make Mother Nature the main character. Unfortunately, the crew members here are stick figures of no emotional or psychological interest.

Three-act script is credited to the distinctive writer Rudy Wurlitzer and Aussie scribe Mac Gudgeon, with three others [Jeff Benjamin, Roger Vaughan, Kimball Livingston] receiving story credit. But several other scenarists reportedly had a hand in this unimaginatively fictional telling of the U.S. losing, for the first time, then winning back the America's Cup.

Uncompelling protagonists are Matthew Modine, a young sailor with a knack for choking when things get tough, and Jennifer Grey, his spunky g.f., who is seemingly a sailing genius, but is kept off the crew due to sexism.

Having lost the race and his lady, Modine turns up six months later at Deadman's Flat, NV, where Grey and new b.f./engineering whiz Stellan Skarsgard are designing aircraft. Modine convinces them to develop a new yacht to compete in the next America's Cup race, more than three months hence.

Final 40 minutes go Down Under and downhill, with a *Rocky* underdog mood taking hold.

●

WIND ACROSS THE EVERGLADES

1958, 91 mins, US col

Dir Nicholas Ray ***Prod*** Stuart Schulberg ***Scr*** Budd Schulberg ***Ph*** Joseph Brun ***Ed*** George Klotz, Joseph Zigman ***Art*** Richard Sylbert

Act Burl Ives, Christopher Plummer, Gypsy Rose Lee, George Voskovec, Emmett Kelly, Peter Falk (Warner)

Wind Across the Everglades is a worthy attempt to make a picture about early efforts of the Audubon Society to preserve the bird wildlife of Florida. It is an "interesting" picture, with some impressive backgrounds of the Everglades country (where it was shot), but it is not consistently engrossing. It should have been far better.

The screenplay fictionalizes the struggle of the Audubon Society to end the slaughter of Florida's plume birds, whose feathers were so highly prized around the turn of the century for women's hats. The action revolves around the almost single-handed efforts of an agent (Christopher Plummer) to stop the mass killings, and in particular his battle with the leader of one band of bird-hunters (Burl Ives).

There are some good shots of the egrets and other fowl, some with spectacular effect, and satisfactory simulated scenes of the birds' slaughter. Plummer does a good job as the idealistic bird warden, although not much motivation is ever given for his dedication. Ives, looking remarkably like Henry VIII in a red beard, eyebrows and hair, does a characteristically intense job, and his character, as a free-booting, civilization-hating rugged individualist, makes sense if not sympathy. Gypsy Rose Lee has some good comedy scenes, which she handles adroitly while displaying some startling cleavage.

●

WIND AND THE LION, THE

1975, 119 mins, US Ⓥ ⊙ ▭ col

Dir John Milius ***Prod*** Herb Jaffe ***Scr*** John Milius ***Ph*** Billy Williams ***Ed*** Robert L. Wolfe ***Mus*** Jerry Goldsmith ***Art*** Gil Parrondo

Act Sean Connery, Candice Bergen, Brian Keith, John Huston, Geoffrey Lewis, Steve Kanaly (M-G-M)

The Wind and the Lion is generally literate and very commercial period action drama, well written and better directed by John Milius. Film stars Sean Connery as an upstart independent Berber chieftain who in 1904 kidnaps Candice Bergen and children, provoking Brian Keith (as Theodore Roosevelt) into dramatic power politics, which confound European moves into North Africa.

The quasi-fictional story gives full exposition to the black, white and gray personal and political elements involved, providing focal points of empathy and criticism for all.

The film sustains itself throughout, the first hour carefully laying out the diverse attitudes and motivations of the principals, and the second depicting the ultimate and daring rescue ploy which frees both Bergen and Connery, while sparking Keith's own political career.

Connery scores one of his major screen impressions, while Bergen handles with assured excellence the subtleties of a woman first outraged at her captor, then later his benefactor after a multinational doublecross. Keith's performance is marvelous.

Milius, armed with an expert crew of action specialists, has crafted a superior film, enhanced even further by Jerry Goldsmith's outstanding score.

1975: NOMINATIONS: Best Original Score, Sound

●

WIND CANNOT READ, THE

1958, 115 mins, UK col

Dir Ralph Thomas ***Prod*** Betty E. Box ***Scr*** Richard Mason ***Ph*** Ernest Steward ***Ed*** Freddie Wilson ***Mus*** Angelo Lavagnino ***Art*** Maurice Carter

Act Dirk Bogarde, Yoko Tani, Ronald Lewis, John Fraser, Anthony Bushell, Michael Medwin (Rank)

Richard Mason's novel shapes up as a useful romantic drama. The pic is a love story [set in India in 1943] told against a Burma war background. Scenery pluses include the doll-like good looks of the young Japanese actress, Yoko Tani. She and Dirk Bogarde hold the acting side together in what is an almost uninterrupted Cupid duolog.

Bogarde is a grounded flyer sent to learn Japan ese in order to be able to interrogate Japan ese POWs. He falls for Tani, one of the instructors, marries her in secret and is then sent off to the front where he is captured, tortured and humiliated before escaping.

The gradual falling in love of the two stars is written with trite dialog but is directed charmingly. Then, when the action moves to the front, the prison torture scenes are put over with stark realism.

●

WINDOM'S WAY

1957, 108 mins, UK Ⓥ col

Dir Ronald Neame ***Prod*** John Bryan ***Scr*** Jill Craigie ***Ph*** Christopher Challis ***Ed*** Reginald Mills ***Mus*** James Bernard ***Art*** Michael Stringer

Act Peter Finch, Mary Ure, Natasha Parry, Robert Flemyng, Michael Hordern, Gregoire Aslan (Rank)

Peter Finch is a dedicated doctor working in the village of Selim, on a Far East island. He is loved and trusted by the villagers and finds himself involved in their political problems. Mary Ure is his estranged wife who comes out for a trial reconciliation at a time when the locality is in a state of unrest. Finch's ideals are such that he tries to prevent the villagers from getting up in arms against the local police and plantation manager.

The acting throughout this drama is first class, with Finch particularly convincing. Ure has little chance in the colorless role of his wife, but Natasha Parry as a native nursing sister, in love with Finch, is warm, sensitive and technically very sound.

Jill Craigie has provided a slow-moving, but literate script, from a novel by James Ramsey Ullman. Ronald Neame's direction brings out qualities of dignity and credibility.

●

WINDOW IN THE SKY

SEE: THE OTHER SIDE OF THE MOUNTAIN

●

WINDY CITY

1984, 102 mins, US Ⓥ ⊙ col

Dir Armyan Bernstein ***Prod*** Alan Greisman ***Scr*** Armyan Bernstein ***Ph*** Reynaldo Villalobos ***Ed*** Clifford Jones ***Mus*** Jack Nitzsche ***Art*** Bill Kenney

Act John Shea, Kate Capshaw, Josh Mostel, Jim Borrelli, Jeffrey DeMunn, Eric Pierpoint (CBS)

Windy City marks writer Armyan Bernstein's (*One from the Heart*) maiden voyage as director of his own tales, and while the endeavor isn't always smooth sailing, the heartfelt nature of his subject is generally strong enough to weather the awkwardness of this story of romance, friendship and shattered dreams.

Focus is Danny Morgan (John Shea), the most obvious victim of failed ambition among a group of seven men. He's a writer forced to take odd jobs, including delivering mail. In the latter capacity he meets Emily (Kate Capshaw), the woman who finally accelerates his maturation which ironically forces their estrangement.

Cast is very strong, although Shea is saddled with too much voice-over narration at top of picture.

●

WINGED SERPENT, THE

SEE: Q

●

WINGED VICTORY

1944, 130 mins, US b/w

Dir George Cukor ***Prod*** Darryl F. Zanuck ***Scr*** Moss Hart ***Ph*** Glen MacWilliams ***Ed*** Barbara McLean ***Mus*** David Rose ***Art*** Lyle R. Wheeler, Lewis Creber

Act Mark Daniels, Lon McCallister, Don Taylor, Red Buttons, Edmond O'Brien, Jeanne Crain (20th Century-Fox)

This is no story of any specific segment of Americana; it is, rather, the tale of Main Street and Broadway, of Texas and Brooklyn, of Christian and Jew—of American youth fighting for the preservation of American ideals. This is a documentation of American youth learning to fly for victory—a winged victory—and though it's fashioned in the manner of fictional entertainment, all the boys listed are bona fide members of the AAF—acting real-life roles.

The story of six boys from diverse parts of America, and how they leave behind wives and sweethearts and mothers to join the AAF, *Victory* is an honest understanding of American youth with the insatiable urge to ride the clouds.

The narrative follows them through basic training, the rigorous aptitude tests, and then the news on whether they had passed or were washed out. The solo flights—from which one of the sextet fails to return—and, ultimately, graduation day, followed by their assignments as either pilots, navigators or bombardiers, are all significantly told.

•

WINGS
1927, 139 mins, US Ⓥ ⊙ ⊗ b/w
Dir William A. Wellman ***Prod*** Lucien Hubbard ***Scr*** Hope Loring, Louis D. Lighton ***Ph*** Harry Perry ***Ed*** E. Lloyd Sheldon ***Mus*** (sound version) J. S. Zamecnik
Act Clara Bow, Charles "Buddy" Rogers, Richard Arlen, Jobyna Ralston, Gary Cooper, El Brendel (Paramount)

When the action [from a story by John Monk Saunders] settles on terra firma, there is nothing present that other war supers haven't had, some to a greater degree. But nothing has possessed the graphic descriptive powers of aerial flying and combat that have been poured into this effort.

Some of the Magnascope battle scenes in the air are in color. Not natural, but with sky and clouds deftly tinted, plus spouts of flame shooting from planes that dive, spiral and even zoom as they supposedly plunge to earth in a final collapse.

Richard Arlen goes through the picture minus make-up. At least the cameras register him that way. Consequently he looks the high-bred, high-strung youngster who would dote on aviation and backs it up with a splendid performance that never hints of the actor. Charles Rogers's effort is also first rate, the important point here being that these two boys team well together. There not being so much of Clara Bow in the picture, she gives an all around corking performance. El Brendel's comedy is spasmodic and mostly early in the first half, while Gary Cooper is on and off within half a reel.

The most planes counted in the air at once are 18. But there are the pursuit and bombing machines, captive balloons, smashes and crashes of all types, with some of the shots of these "crack-ups" remarkable. Fake stuff and double photography, too, although no miniatures in regard to the air action are discernible if used.

1927/28: Best Picture, Engineering Effects

•

WINGS OF DESIRE
SEE: DER HIMMEL UEBER BERLIN

•

WINGS OF THE APACHE
SEE: FIRE BIRDS

•

WINGS OF THE DOVE, THE
1997, 101 mins, UK/US Ⓥ ⊙ ▭ col
Dir Iain Softley ***Prod*** David Parfitt, Stephen Evans ***Scr*** Hossein Amini ***Ph*** Eduardo Serra ***Ed*** Tariq Anwar ***Mus*** Gabriel Yared ***Art*** John Beart
Act Helena Bonham Carter, Linus Roache, Alison Elliott, Elizabeth McGovern, Charlotte Rampling, Michael Gambon (Renaissance Dove/Miramax)

This handsomely produced release renders one of Henry James's lesser novels into a mostly satisfying romantic melodrama, with colorful settings in London and Venice soon after the turn of this century. The character of the willful Kate, born to the nobility but romantically attached to a member of the lower classes, gives Helena Bonham Carter one of her best opportunities in a while, looking vibrant and totally convincing.

It's 1910, and Kate is taken in hand by her deeply conservative aunt Maud (Charlotte Rampling), who is determined to find her a place in high society. Kate, however, is in love with Merton Densher (Linus Roache), an impoverished journalist.

The arrival of Millie (Alison Elliott), a fabulously wealthy and beautiful young orphaned American touring Europe, offers the clandestine lovers new opportunities. Discovering that Millie is terminally ill, Kate decides, during a trip to Venice, to push Merton into the sick woman's arms in order to make him, eventually, a widower of social standing.

Hossein Amini's adaptation of the book seems geared as far as possible to popular taste; the characters are driven by very contemporary needs and passions, and the bitter climax is carefully prepared. Bonham Carter captures with considerable precision the shifting moods of her character. Roache makes Merton rather too vacillating and feeble a character; it's hard to figure what makes him so attractive to the two stunning women.

British director Iain Softley's handling of several key elements, including an unusually frank love scene in the later stages, is always inventive.

1997: NOMINATIONS: Best Actress (Helena Bonham Carter), Screenplay Adaptation, Cinematography, Costume Design

•

WINNING
1969, 123 mins, US Ⓥ ▭ col
Dir James Goldstone ***Prod*** John Foreman ***Scr*** Howard Rodman ***Ph*** Richard Moore ***Ed*** Edward A. Biery, Richard C. Meyer ***Mus*** Dave Grusin ***Art*** Alexander Golitzen, John J. Lloyd, Joe Alves
Act Paul Newman, Joanne Woodward, Robert Wagner, Richard Thomas, David Sheiner, Clu Gulager (Universal)

Winning, a love story set against an auto-racing background, stars Paul Newman and Joanne Woodward. Overly long, it nevertheless carries socko appeal in suspenseful racing sequences and its principals in a realistically developed marital romance score strongly.

Newman underplays his part throughout, resulting in one of his better performances. He is ideally cast as the racer, and those sequences in which he is racing are convincingly portrayed. There is a compelling authority, too, about his scenes with his femme costar.

Woodward, who makes no attempt at glamor or any other goal except as Newman's earthy wife, turns in a ringingly effective characterization, lacking in color but packing dramatic punch. Robert Wagner, who costars with other two, is the heavy, lending credibility to role.

•

WINNING OF BARBARA WORTH, THE
1926, 90 mins, US ⊗ b/w
Dir Henry King ***Prod*** Samuel Goldwyn ***Scr*** Frances Marion ***Ph*** George Barnes ***Ed*** Viola Lawrence ***Art*** Karl Oscar Borg
Act Ronald Colman, Vilma Banky, Charles Lane, Gary Cooper (Goldwyn/United Artist)

The Winning of Barbara Worth in novel form sold around 2.8 million copies. Samuel Goldwyn figured that if he spent around $1 million on a story that had this circulation, he was making a good investment. Originally this story was to have been brought to the screen by Sol Lesser and Mike Rosenberg of Principal Pictures. They had had the release all set with UA. Henry King came along and told Goldwyn he thought this epic of the reclamation of the desert lands was a highly dramatic incident for interpretation on the screen by him, and Goldwyn paid over $125,000 to Lesser and Rosenberg for the story.

Instead of going to Arizona and making his picture, he went into the arid lands of Nevada, and instead of choking off and holding down the cost of production to a minimum, with the idea that the Harold Bell Wright name would carry it, he put every dollar necessary into the production.

Taking a story of this sort and injecting, besides the author's purport, entertainment, is no child's task. King has performed a miraculous task. The telling of the story, of course, was the big thing. Putting over the fine points of the yarn by showing a desert sandstorm and then showing the progress of reclamation work and the destruction done by faulty construction was a mountainous job, well executed.

For massiveness of production, this film is incomparable in telling a new angle of the development of the West. Goldwyn paid heavy for the making of the flood stuff. He had to wipe out his towns in Nevada and then had to use miniatures to convey the destructive theme of the story.

•

WINSLOW BOY, THE
1948, 117 mins, UK Ⓥ b/w
Dir Anthony Asquith ***Prod*** Anatole de Grunwald ***Scr*** Terence Rattigan, Anatole de Grunwald ***Ph*** Freddie Young ***Ed*** Gerald Turney Smith ***Mus*** William Alwyn ***Art*** Andre Andrejew
Act Robert Donat, Margaret Leighton, Cedric Hardwicke, Basil Radford, Kathleen Harrison, Francis L. Sullivan (British Lion/London)

Terence Rattigan's story, based on an actual incident that occurred just before the First World War, is a simple story of a thirteen-year-old naval cadet, expelled from school for the alleged theft of a postal order. The boy's father is certain of his innocence and when he fails to have the case reopened, invokes the whole machinery of British democracy by arranging a full-scale parliamentary debate and subsequently bringing a successful action against the King.

It's more the father's conviction of his son's innocence, rather than the incident itself, which forms the background of this well-knit story, with sufficient emphasis on the emotional angles to make it a sure tearjerker. From its brisk opening the plot quickly develops the main theme, building up the fight for justice through a series of incidents which are highlighted by the interview between Robert Morton, MP and famous attorney, and the boy before he decides to accept the brief. A flawless cast portrays the principal characters to perfection, and minor roles have been painstakingly filled.

•

WINSTANLEY
1975, 95 mins, UK b/w
Dir Kevin Brownlow, Andrew Mollo ***Scr*** Kevin Brownlow, Andrew Mollo ***Ph*** Ernest Vincze ***Ed*** Sarah Ellis ***Art*** Andrew Mollo
Act Miles Halliwell, Jerome Wills (BFI)

The very opposite of the typical, commercial costume drama, *Winstanley* [based on the novel *Comrade Jacob* by David Caute] depicts the hardships and political turmoil in 17th-century England following the Civil War and the victory of the Puritans.

Winstanley was a leader of one of those dissident religious sects which sprang up in plentitude after the first wave of the Protestant Reformation. His was known as the Diggers, a commune set up in Surrey to proclaim equality and the right to work "free" land.

The parson, upon whose land the Diggers squatted, takes a different view and sends ruffians to destroy their crops, beat them and burn down the makeshift hovels. Winstanley's writing and preaching wins him favor, but the arrival of less idealistic members of the commune undermines the movement.

•

WINTER KILLS
1979, 97 mins, US Ⓥ ⊙ ▭ col
Dir William Richert ***Prod*** Fred Caruso ***Scr*** William Richert ***Ph*** Vilmos Zsigmond ***Ed*** David Bretherton ***Mus*** Maurice Jarre ***Art*** Robert Boyle
Act Jeff Bridges, John Huston, Anthony Perkins, Sterling Hayden, Eli Wallach, Elizabeth Taylor (Avco Embassy)

If there's a decent film lurking somewhere in *Winter Kills*, writer-director William Richert doesn't want anyone to see it in his Byzantine version of a presidential assassination conspiracy [from a book by Richard Condon].

Tale of wealthy family patriarch John Huston, whose elder son was a president slain nineteen years before the pic's beginning, and younger sibling Jeff Bridges, now after his brother's killer(s), is an exercise in methodical obfuscation.

Huston gives a powerhouse performance, and Bridges, always likeable, runs through his repertoire of facial expressions and grimaces, but it's a lost cause.

Elizabeth Taylor has a wordless cameo as a procuress for the late president, but contractual provisions prevent her name from being used in connection with *Winter Kills*. The rest of the cast should have been so lucky.

[Pic was re-released in 1983 in a re-edited version and with original ending.]

•

WINTER PEOPLE
1989, 110 mins, US Ⓥ ⊙ ▭ col
Dir Ted Kotcheff ***Prod*** Robert H. Solo ***Scr*** Carol Sobieski ***Ph*** Francois Protat ***Ed*** Thom Noble ***Mus*** John Scott ***Art*** Ron Foreman
Act Kurt Russell, Kelly McGillis, Lloyd Bridges, Mitchell Ryan, Amelia Burnette (Nelson/Columbia)

The wages of sin are forever up in the old North Carolina hills, especially when they concern clans carrying on a blood feud. That's the backdrop for *Winter People*, a grimly unappetizing melodrama that forwards themes and concerns as remote as its time and place.

Adaptation of John Ehle's novel is set in 1934. Widower Kurt Russell decamps from his native town with little daughter in tow and alights at the remote cabin of Kelly McGillis, who has an illegitimate baby son. An old-fashioned, unassertive type, Russell has to prove himself to McGillis's three brothers by joining them on a bear hunt, and wins the approval of her pa (Lloyd Bridges) by designing and building a clock tower for the little community.

But the demented Campbell clan lives across the river, and McGillis's dark secret is then revealed.

Continual histrionic demands are placed upon McGillis, who is not necessarily always up to them, and Russell is stuck with the Richard Barthlemess role of the earnest do-gooder forced to lower himself to the occasion of taking on brutal thugs.

•

WINTERTIME
1943, 82 mins, US b/w
Dir John Brahm *Prod* William Le Baron *Scr* E. Edwin Moran, Jack Jevne, Lynn Starling *Ph* Joe MacDonald *Ed* Louis Loeffler
Act Sonja Henie, Jack Oakie, Cornel Wilde, Cesar Romero, Carole Landis, S. Z. Sakall (20th Century-Fox)

Story revolves about a Norwegian refugee and his daughter (Sonja Henie), whose destination is the Chateau Frontenac, Quebec. Jack Oakie, who, in partnership with Cornel Wilde, operates a small, shabby hostelry called the Chateau Promenade, detours the party to his own place in order to build trade through the presence of the distinguished refugees. Romantic interest is woven in via the familiar triangle motif, with Henie chasing Wilde, who temporarily devotes himself to a gal, representing a sports magazine with large circulation, in order to grab space for his hotel. Cesar Romero, as a frivolous Casanova, loses out, following a slapstick bit where he runs through the hotel in long underwear.

Henie's blade sequences, solo and with a partner, enhanced by gorgeous settings, are socko as always.

•

WIRED
1989, 108 mins, US Ⓥ ⊙ col
Dir Larry Peerce *Prod* Edward S. Feldman, Charles P. Meeker *Scr* Earl Mac Rauch *Ph* Tony Imi *Ed* Eric Sears *Mus* Basil Poledouris *Art* Brian Eatwell
Act Michael Chiklis, Ray Sharkey, J. T. Walsh, Patti D'Arbanville, Lucinda Jenney, Alex Rocco (F/M/Lion)

In a brief but outstanding career on TV and in pics, John Belushi was an engaging personality. His drug overdose death further enthralled the public. *Wired*, however, told in episodes, flashbacks and dream sequences, is relentlessly offputting.

In a fanciful, less-than-successful effort to string together the events in Belushi's tragicomic life, *Wired* begins after Belushi (Michael Chiklis) has died. He rises, dressed in an autopsy gown to join another "spirit," Angel Valesquez (Ray Sharkey), in a cab ride down memory lane. The professional benchmarks in Belushi's life are there: the Blues Bros., the comic performances on *Saturday Night Live*, his Hollywood films. One episode is interrupted by others, including graphic glimpses of Belushi's cocaine habit and the devastating effect it has on his confidantes and colleagues.

Somehow, Chiklis ekes out an estimable performance as the doomed comic actor, sweating flashes of Belushi's intensity and vulnerability.

•

WISE BLOOD
1979, 108 mins, US/W. Germany Ⓥ col
Dir John Huston *Prod* Michael Fitzgerald, Kathy Fitzgerald *Scr* Benedict Fitzgerald, Michael Fitzgerald *Ph* Gerry Fisher *Ed* Roberto Silvi *Mus* Alex North
Act Brad Dourif, Ned Beatty, Harry Dean Stanton, Dan Shor, Amy Wright, John Huston (Ithaca/Anthea)

John Huston, with uncluttered direction and expert handling of actors, has fashioned a disturbing tale of the fringe side of overzealous religious preachers in the deep South.

Taken from a short novel by Flannery O'Connor, film is grim and Gothic in feeling, but balanced by an underlying tenderness for these fringe people.

Brad Dourif is effective as a young man home from the wars, probably World War II. He visits his now boarded-up house in the country and then doffs his uniform to buy clothes making him look like a preacher. He goes to a city where he is attracted by a blind preacher with a teenage daughter who gives him lubricious looks. Flashbacks reveal Dourif as the grandson of a fire-and-brimstone preacher, played by Huston himself.

•

WISH YOU WERE HERE
1987, 91 mins, UK Ⓥ ⊙ col
Dir David Leland *Prod* Sara Radclyffe *Scr* David Leland *Ph* Ian Wilson *Mus* Stanley Myers *Art* Caroline Amies
Act Emily Lloyd, Tom Bell, Clare Clifford, Barbara Durkin, Geoffrey Hutchings, Jesse Birdsall (Zenith/Working Title)

Set in a thoroughly uptight, provincial British seaside resort in the 1950s, this touching account of a girl's growing pains marks the directorial debut of director-scripter David Leland.

What makes it interesting is the character of the heroine; her refreshing rudeness disconcerts those around her. By focusing on a spunky but troubled sixteen-year-old girl named Lynda (played with exasperating charm by newcomer Emily Lloyd), Leland squeezes out more poignancy than would have been possible had the central character been the typical gawky male youth of most films about sexual awakening.

What makes the girl troubled is the fact that her mother died when she was eleven—and no one has replaced that essential loss. Lynda's reaction to her plight is to shock people with her rudeness and to taunt the opposite sex. This makes for some verbally sharp and occasionally visually eloquent scenes.

Lynda's rebelliousness eventually leads to a potentially sinister liaison with a seedy older man (played with taciturn intensity by Tom Bell), as much a misfit as she is. Their scenes together, though quite limited, are highly charged.

•

WITCHCRAFT
SEE: HAXAN

•

WITCHCRAFT THROUGH THE AGES
SEE: HAXAN

•

WITCH DOCTOR
SEE: MEN OF TWO WORLDS

•

WITCHES, THE
1966, 91 mins, UK col
Dir Cyril Frankel *Prod* Anthony Nelson Keys *Scr* Nigel Kneale *Ph* Arthur Grant *Ed* James Needs, Chris Barnes *Mus* Richard Rodney Bennett *Art* Bernard Robinson
Act Joan Fontaine, Kay Walsh, Alec McCowen, Ann Bell, Gwen Ffrangcon-Davies, Ingrid Brett (Hammer)

Despite a very professional cast, this Nigel Kneale script [from Peter Curtis's novel *The Devil's Own*] doesn't spark off enough horror and tension to make the picture more than routine entertainment. This one has the air of a film that has lost its way.

Joan Fontaine is a schoolmistress who endures a horrible traumatic witch-doctor experience in an African mission. She seeks a new, peaceful life in a British village as headmistress of the local school, but she realizes that the village is under some strange spell.

Cyril Frankel has directed the slightly phony script with skill. But, mainly, it is the acting that keeps this pic alive. Fontaine brings a sensitive air to her thesping, but there's not enough fiber in her role to give her full scope. Kay Walsh is excellent as an enigmatic journalist, and Gwen Ffrangcon-Davies, making one of her rare screen appearances, is dominating as the grandmother.

•

WITCHES, THE
1990, 92 mins, US Ⓥ ⊙ col
Dir Nicolas Roeg *Prod* Mark Shivas *Scr* Allan Scott *Ph* Harvey Harrison *Ed* Tony Lawson *Mus* Stanley Myers *Art* Andrew Sanders
Act Anjelica Huston, Mai Zetterling, Jasen Fisher, Rowan Atkinson, Bill Paterson, Jane Horrocks (Lorimar/Henson)

The wizardry of Jim Henson's Creature Shop and a superbly over-the-top performance by Angelica Huston gives *The Witches* a good deal of charm and enjoyment.

Pic opens in Norway where grandmother Helga (Mai Zetterling) is telling her nine-year-old grandson Luke (Jasen Fisher) about witches and their wicked ways. His parents die in a car crash, and Luke and grandmother travel to England for a holiday.

They go to a stark Cornish hotel. Also checking in is the annual ladies' meeting of the Royal Society for the Prevention of Cruelty to Children; in actual fact a meeting of the British witches, due to be addressed by the Grand High Witch, Huston. Young Luke accidentally overhears the meeting where Huston announces her grand plan to feed poisoned chocolate to all British children, which will turn them into mice.

In a tight black dress and vampish haircut, Huston seems to enjoy herself as the evil chief witch, and the pic seems to be merely plodding along until she arrives on the scene.

•

WITCHES OF EASTWICK, THE
1987, 118 mins, US Ⓥ ⊙ ▭ col
Dir George Miller *Prod* Neil Canton, Peter Gruber, Jon Peters *Scr* Michael Cristofer *Ph* Vilmos Zsigmond *Ed* Richard Francis-Bruce, Hubert C. de la Bouillerie *Mus* John Williams *Art* Polly Platt
Act Jack Nicholson, Cher, Susan Sarandon, Michelle Pfeiffer, Veronica Cartwright, Richard Jenkins (Warner/Guber-Peters/Kennedy Miller)

The Witches of Eastwick [from the novel by John Updike] is a brilliantly conceived metaphor for the battle between the sexes that literally poses the question: must a woman sell her soul to the devil to have a good relationship?

With a no-holds-barred performance by Jack Nicholson as the horny Satan, it's a very funny and irresistible set-up for anyone who has ever been baffled by the opposite sex.

Sukie Ridgemont (Michelle Pfeiffer), a writer for the local newspaper, is the intellectual; Jane Spofford (Susan Sarandon), a high school music teacher, is the woman of feeling; and Alexandra Medford (Cher), a sculptress, represents the sensuous side. They're all divorced and they're all looking for a Mr. Right.

Enter Daryl Van Horn (Jack Nicholson), the answer to their collective longing for a man of wit, charm and intelligence. For Nicholson it's the role of a lifetime, the chance to seduce these women and be cock of the roost.

Spectacle of the film is really Nicholson. Dressed in eccentric flowing robes, odd hats and installed in a lush mansion, he is larger than life, as indeed the devil should be. The witches, lovely though they are, exist more as types than distinct personalities.

1987: NOMINATIONS: Best Original Score, Sound

•

WITCHFINDER GENERAL
(US: THE CONQUEROR WORM)
1968, 88 mins, UK Ⓥ ⊙ col
Dir Michael Reeves *Prod* Louis M. Heyward, Philip Waddilove, Arnold Miller *Scr* Michael Reeves, Tom Baker, Louis M. Heyward *Ph* John Coquillon *Ed* Howard Lanning *Mus* Paul Ferris *Art* Jim Morahan
Act Vincent Price, Ian Ogilvy, Rupert Davies, Hilary Dwyer, Robert Russell, Nicky Henson (Tigon)

Story [from Ronald Bassett's novel] is all about witchcraft, inquisitions and executions as performed by Vincent Price and his thuggish henchman (Robert Russell) during the days when Cromwell was deposing the King of England. Ian Ogilvy is the soldier-hero who stops them after lots of bloody executions and the rape of his sweetheart (Hilary Dwyer).

Price is an excellent heavy, but while sometimes he seems to piously believe he is rooting out witches, most of the time he's simply killing for the fun of it, and some money. Russell's character is similarly ambiguous. He's brutal, but isn't properly set up to display cowardice while fighting with Ogilvy in the film's only really good action scene. Ogilvy is somewhat dashing, but has a one-note hero's role to play. Dwyer gives evidence of acting talent, but she and all principals are hampered by Michael Reeves's mediocre script and ordinary direction.

•

WITH A FRIEND LIKE HARRY
SEE: HARRY, UN AMI QUI VOUS VEUT DU BIEN

•

WITH A SONG IN MY HEART
1952, 116 mins, US col
Dir Walter Lang *Prod* Lamar Trotti *Scr* Lamar Trotti *Ph* Leon Shamroy *Ed* J. Watson Webb, Jr. *Mus* Alfred Newman (dir.) *Art* Lyle Wheeler, Joseph C. Wright
Act Susan Hayward, Rory Calhoun, David Wayne, Thelma Ritter, Robert Wagner, Helen Westcott (20th Century-Fox)

The story of one of show business' courageous figures—Jane Froman—comes to the screen. Froman, a songbird who started her rise to fame in 1936 as a penny-ante singer of radio commercials, does her own chirping on twenty-three songs in this film version of her career.

In the first half, the pattern is the rather pat one of an unknown coming into prominence. The next 60 minutes, however, have the ring of sincere dramatics from the time Froman was nearly fatally injured in the Lisbon plane crash of February 23, 1943, while enroute to entertain servicemen overseas. Her fight back to life and only partial recovery of the use of her limbs, the birth of a new love, the resumption of a career to pay the enormous medical bills, come over on the screen as heartening drama.

While not entirely at home in the dancing accompaniment to some of the production numbers [staged by Billy Daniel], Susan Hayward punches over the straight vocal-simulation and deftly handles the dramatic phases.

1952: Best Scoring of a Musical Picture

NOMINATIONS: Best Actress (Susan Hayward), Supp. Actress (Thelma Ritter), Color Costume Design, Sound

•

WITHNAIL & I
1986, 108 mins, UK Ⓥ ⊙ col
Dir Bruce Robinson ***Prod*** Paul M. Heller ***Scr*** Bruce Robinson ***Ph*** Bob Smith ***Ed*** Alan Strachan ***Mus*** David Dundas ***Art*** Michael Pickwoad
Act Richard E. Grant, Paul McGann, Richard Griffiths, Ralph Brown, Michael Elphick (HandMade)

Withnail & I is about the end of an era. Set in 1969 England, it portrays the last throes of a friendship mirroring the seedy demise of the hippie period, delivering some comic gems along the way.

It's the tale of two city boys stuck in a dilapidated country cottage in the middle of nowhere. The humor is both brutal and clever, and the acting uniformly excellent.

Pic opens with a pan round the disgusting London flat of out-of-work actors Withnail and Marwood (the "I" of the title). Marwood (Paul McGann) is the nervous type trying to look like John Lennon, while Withnail (Richard E. Grant) is gaunt, acerbic, and never without a drink in his hand.

Marwood declares the need to "get into the countryside and rejuvenate." A visit to Withnail's Uncle Monty secures them the loan of his country cottage, and the two head off into the night. They eventually arrive at the remote cottage, only to discover there is no light, no heat, and no water.

Uncle Monty (a standout performance by the portly Richard Griffiths) arrives with a twinkle in his eye when he is sidling up closer to Marwood. Monty's ardor and a telegram from his agent with news of a job are enough to convince Marwood that home is where the heart is, and he and Withnail retreat back to London. The two realize their friendship is coming to an end.

•

WITHOUT LOVE
1945, 111 mins, US b/w
Dir Harold S. Bucquet ***Prod*** Lawrence A. Weingarten ***Scr*** Donald Ogden Stewart ***Ph*** Karl Freund ***Ed*** Frank Sullivan ***Mus*** Bronislau Kaper ***Art*** Cedric Gibbons, Harry McAfee
Act Spencer Tracy, Katherine Hepburn, Keenan Wynn, Gloria Grahame, Patricia Morison, Lucille Ball (M-G-M)

Competent trouping and topflight production make *Without Love* a click. But there's no gainsaying the general obviousness of it all, along with a somewhat static plot basis [from a play by Philip Barry].

There is a lack of conviction despite the adult trouping of the lady scientist who aids the gentleman scientist. It's a foregone conclusion that behind their mutual shells of yesteryear amours they'll clinch eventually. Hers was the idyllic love, too shortlived, but a perfect two years, until his death; and Spencer Tracy's love life is something out of a Parisian past.

Interspersed is an intelligent pooch who has been trained to curb Tracy's somnambulism, which is planted early for boudoir usage later. Somehow this is inconsistent with so stoic a character as Tracy, but somehow, also, it's made acceptable, as is the squabbling Keenan Wynn-Patricia Morison business, and the rest of it. All of which is wholly to the cast's credit.

•

WITHOUT RESERVATIONS
1946, 107 mins, US Ⓥ ⊙ b/w
Dir Mervyn LeRoy ***Prod*** Jesse L. Lasky ***Scr*** Andrew Solt ***Ph*** Milton Krasner ***Ed*** Jack Ruggiero ***Mus*** Roy Webb ***Art*** Albert S. D'Agostino, Ralph Berger
Act Claudette Colbert, John Wayne, Don DeFore, Dona Drake, Louella Parsons, Thurston Hall (RKO)

Plot concerns what happens to a femme author when she meets the real-life counterpart of her tome's hero. The misadventures that befall her, her hero and his pal as they make a cross-country trip together are guaranteed hilarity. Claudette Colbert, the writer, is tripping west to adapt her book to the screen. On a crowded train she is picked up by two Marine fliers, John Wayne and Don DeFore. Without realizing her identity, boys proceed throughout the footage to impress her with how wrong the book's slant on life, love, returned heroes, etc., actually is.

Around this theme scripter Andrew Solt, working from a Jane Allen-Mae Livingston novel, has built delightful scenes and characters that, despite their laugh intentions, are a great deal closer to actual reality than most more serious writing. Mervyn LeRoy's direction doesn't miss a bet in underlying the laughs with a solid feeling of reality, and the players troupe the roles to the hilt. Colbert and Wayne prove particularly facile in building to a solid laugh.

Surprise walk-ons are in the footage, such as Jack Benny approaching Colbert in a railway station and asking for an autograph; Cary Grant dancing with the writer; LeRoy himself dining with her. Louella Parsons plays herself as an air chatterer who breathlessly brings breathless news to fans about the doings of the novelist and Hollywood.

•

WITHOUT YOU I'M NOTHING
1990, 90 mins, US Ⓥ col
Dir John Boskovich ***Prod*** Jonathan D. Krane ***Scr*** Sandra Bernhard, John Boskovich ***Ph*** Joseph Yacoe ***Ed*** Pamela Malouf-Cundy ***Mus*** Patrice Rushen ***Art*** Kevin Rupnik
Act Sandra Bernhard, Steven Antin, Lu Leonard (MCEG)

Sandra Bernhard's screen adaptation of her one-woman show is a rigorous, experimental examination of performance art. Stepping back from comedy per se, Bernhard and her collaborator, director John Boskovich, have fashioned a remote, self-absorbed and often cryptic picture.

Most ambitious device here is a failure: except for brief interstitial footage of "witnesses" such as Steven Antin (as himself) or Lu Leonard (portraying Bernhard's manager) addressing the camera, film unfolds in performance on stage at a large, ersatz night club before a predominantly black audience. Crowd reacts only with silent, quizzical expressions or files out, apparently not enjoying the show.

Pic's highlight underscores the material's emphasis on roleplaying and androgyny: a 1978-set "I Feel Real" monolog/song with Bernhard pretending to be two guys in a disco, one of whom gets turned on by a black man and comes out of the closet. With helmer Boskovich letting loose his camera for once from its slow, monotonous pirouetting, scene is a showstopper.

•

WITNESS
1985, 112 mins, US Ⓥ ⊙ col
Dir Peter Weir ***Prod*** Edward S. Feldman ***Scr*** Earl W. Wallace, William Kelley ***Ph*** John Seale ***Ed*** Thom Noble ***Mus*** Maurice Jarre ***Art*** Stan Jolley
Act Harrison Ford, Kelly McGillis, Josef Sommer, Lukas Haas, Danny Glover, Alexander Godunov (Paramount)

Witness is at times a gentle, affecting story of star-crossed lovers limited within the fascinating Amish community. Too often, however, this fragile romance is crushed by a thoroughly absurd shoot-'em-up, like ketchup poured over a delicate Pennsylvania Dutch dinner.

Australian director Peter Weir is obviously awed by the Amish, the quaint agrarian sect which maintains a seventeenth-century lifestyle, forsaking all modern conveniences while maintaining intense religious vows, including a pacifism most pertinent here.

Venturing outside the community on a trip to see her sister, recently widowed Kelly McGillis is drawn unfortunately into the twentieth century when her young son, (Lukas Haas), witnesses a murder in the men's room at the train station.

Enter gruff, foul-mouthed, streetwise detective Harrison Ford, whom the writers [story by William Kelley, Pamela Wallace, Earl W. Wallace] must somehow get out into the countryside as soon as possible so the cross-cultural romance can begin.

Witness warms up as the attraction builds between Ford, McGillis and Haas—all performing excellently through this portion. Admirable, too, is Ford's growing admiration for the people he's been thrown among.

1985: Best Original Screenplay, Editing

NOMINATIONS: Best Picture, Director, Actor (Harrison Ford), Cinematography, Art Direction, Original Score

•

WITNESS FOR THE PROSECUTION
1957, 114 mins, US Ⓥ ⊙ b/w
Dir Billy Wilder ***Prod*** Arthur Hornblow ***Scr*** Billy Wilder, Harry Kurnitz ***Ph*** Russell Harlan ***Ed*** Daniel Mandell ***Mus*** Matty Malneck ***Art*** Alexandre Trauner
Act Tyrone Power, Marlene Dietrich, Charles Laughton, Elsa Lanchester, Una O'Connor, Ian Wolfe (United Artists)

A courtroom meller played engagingly and building evenly to a surprising and arousing, albeit tricked-up, climax, *Witness for the Prosecution* has been transferred to the screen (from the Agatha Christie click play) with competence [adaptation by Larry Marcus].

Under Billy Wilder's direction, *Prosecution* unfolds realistically, generating a quiet and steady excitement.

Cleverly worked out is the story line which has defense attorney Charles Laughton, along with the audience, wholly convinced that the likeable chap played by Tyrone Power is innocent, that he couldn't have murdered the rich widow who had taken a fancy to him. A disturbing note, however, is the unexpected attitude taken by Power's wife (Marlene Dietrich) who, as it turns out, is not legally married to him and thus is not restrained from testifying against him.

Laughton, sage of the courtroom and cardiac patient who's constantly disobeying his nurse's orders, plays out the part flamboyantly and colorfully. His reputation for scenery chewing is unmarred via this outing.

1957: NOMINATIONS: Best Picture, Director, Actor (Charles Laughton), Supp. Actress (Elsa Lanchester), Editing, Sound

•

WITTGENSTEIN
1993, 71 mins, UK Ⓥ col
Dir Derek Jarman ***Prod*** Tariq Ali ***Scr*** Derek Jarman, Terry Eagleton, Ken Butler ***Ph*** James Welland ***Ed*** Budge Tremlett ***Mus*** Jan Latham-Koenig ***Art*** Annie Lapaz
Act Karl Johnson, Michael Gough, Tilda Swinton, John Quentin, Kevin Collins, Clancy Chassay (Channel 4/BFI/Bandung)

Shot on legit-like minimalist sets, this gabby but sophisticated riff on the tortured life of Austrian-born philosopher Ludwig Wittgenstein is an immaculately lensed, intellectual jape that's more a divertissement than a substantial addition to Derek Jarman's quirky oeuvre.

Pic's opening, with young Ludwig (confidently played by twelve-year-old Clancy Chassay) introducing the members of his ill-fated family, promises a Ken Russell–like irreverence that never really develops. With the appearance of the adult Wittgenstein (Karl Johnson), things settle down into a series of talky tableaux against black backdrops. Born into a rich Viennese family in 1889, Wittgenstein quickly fled to Britain, establishing his rep at Cambridge, where he fell in with other thinkers like Bertrand Russell (Michael Gough) and economist John Maynard Keynes (John Quentin). He died in 1951 of cancer.

Philosophical sparring between the trio takes up much of the running time, with light relief provided by Russell's snooty mistress, Lady Ottoline Morrell (Jarman regular Tilda Swinton in top histrionic form). Running parallel with the intellectual stuff is an exploration of Wittgenstein's repressed homosexuality, per his friendship with a handsome, working-class student (Kevin Collins) and Keynes, portrayed as a flouncing gay.

•

WIVES AND LOVERS
1963, 102 mins, US b/w
Dir John Rich ***Prod*** Hal Wallis ***Scr*** Edward Anhalt ***Ph*** Lucien Ballard ***Ed*** Warren Low ***Mus*** Lyn Murray ***Art*** Hal Pereira, Walter Tyler
Act Janet Leigh, Van Johnson, Shelley Winters, Martha Hyer, Ray Walston, Claire Wilcox (Paramount)

Failure to be consistent with itself mars *Wives and Lovers*, an otherwise highly polished and pleasurable sophisticated comedy about a couple whose happy marriage is nearly shattered in the wake of the husband's sudden professional success.

The film excels in one area. Edward Anhalt's scenario, from Jay Presson's stage play, *The First Wife*, contains some of the sharpest, wittiest, most perceptive comedy dialog to pop out of a soundtrack in some time.

Story relates the marital misadventure that materializes when an unsuccessful writer (Van Johnson), who for three years has been lovingly and uncomplainingly supported by his wife (Janet Leigh) while he pens a novel, suddenly hits the book-of-the-month jackpot. In a flash, the couple and their precocious tot have moved from a cramped Gotham cold-water flat to the luxury living of the fashionable Connecticut suburbs. In the process of converting his prose into a Broadway play, Johnson becomes entangled in an affair with his glamorous agent (Martha Hyer). In retaliation Leigh apparently gets herself voluntarily seduced by the star (Jeremy Slate) of her husband's play.

The acting is pleasing and skillful. Occasional mechanical inconsistencies tarnish John Rich's otherwise bright and breezy direction in his first major feature assignment.

1963: NOMINATION: Best B&W Costume Design

•

WIZ, THE
1978, 133 mins, US Ⓥ ⊙ col
Dir Sidney Lumet ***Prod*** Rob Cohen ***Scr*** Joel Schumacher ***Ph*** Oswald Morris ***Ed*** Dede Allen ***Mus*** Quincy Jones (adapt.) ***Art*** Tony Walton
Act Diana Ross, Michael Jackson, Nipsey Russell, Lena Horne, Richard Pryor, Ted Ross (Motown)

Frank Baum [author of book *The Wonderful Wizard of Oz*] would never recognize his simple little story in this fantastically blown-up version [of William F. Brown's play, with music and lyrics by Charlie Smalls], but the heart of his tale—that a person must find what he's searching for within himself—is still there.

The cast is virtually flawless but, when all is said and done, it's the combination of Oswald Morris's cinematography, the special visual effects of Albert Whitlock and Tony Walton's production design and costumes that linger longest in the memory.

Director Sidney Lumet has created what amounts to a love letter to the city of New York, which he equates with Oz.

Diana Ross, believable as a twenty-four-year-old Harlem school teacher, is always in key with the mood, whether it calls for shyness, gaiety, courage or simply cutting up. Vocally, she's superb but, surprise, she also dances with all the abandon of an Alvin Ailey protegée.

Of the supporting players and, despite their billing, that's what they amount to—Richard Pryor's Wiz (very briefly seen), Ted Ross's Lion and Mabel King's Evillene make the heaviest impressions. Nipsey Russell is fun as the Tin Man, but Michael Jackson, though vocally great, needs more acting exposure.

1978: NOMINATIONS: Best Cinematography, Costume Design, Art Direction, Adapted Score

•

WIZARD OF OZ, THE

1939, 100 mins, US Ⓥ ⦿ col

Dir Victor Fleming, [King Vidor] ***Prod*** Mervyn LeRoy ***Scr*** Noel Langley, Florence Ryerson, Edgar Allan Woolf, [E.Y. Harburg, John Lee Mahin] ***Ph*** Harold Rosson, Allen Davey ***Ed*** Blanche Sewell ***Mus*** Herbert Stothart (adapt.) ***Art*** Cedric Gibbons, William A. Horning

Act Judy Garland, Frank Morgan, Ray Bolger, Bert Lahr, Jack Haley, Billie Burke (M-G-M)

The Wizard of Oz springs from Metro's golden bowl (production cost reported close to $3 million). Except for opening and closing stretches of prolog and epilog, which are visioned in a rich sepia, the greater portion of the film is in Technicolor.

Such liberties that have been taken with the original story [from the book by L. Frank Baum, adaptation by Noel Langley] vest the yarn with constructive dramatic values. Underlying theme of conquest of fear is subtly thrust through the action. Fairy stories must teach simple truths.

What is on the screen is an adventure story about a small girl who lives on a Kansas farm. She and her dog, Toto, are caught in twister and whisked into an eerie land in which she encounters strange beings, good and evil fairies, and prototypes of some of the adults who comprised her farm world.

Then ensues the long trek to the mighty wizard's castle, where she and her companions seek fulfillment of desire. Dorothy wishes only to return home. The plot is as thin as all that.

In the playing of it, however, Judy Garland as the little girl is an appealing figure as the wandering waif. Her companions are Ray Bolger, as the Scarecrow; Jack Haley, as the Tinman; and Bert Lahr as the cringing lion. Frank Morgan appears in sundry roles as the wizard, and the good and evil fairies are Billie Burke and Margaret Hamilton.

1939: Best Original Score, Song ("Over the Rainbow")

NOMINATIONS: Best Picture, Art Direction, Special Effects

•

WOLF

1994, 125 mins, US Ⓥ ⦿ col

Dir Mike Nichols ***Prod*** Douglas Wick ***Scr*** Jim Harrison, Wesley Strick ***Ph*** Giuseppe Rotunno ***Ed*** Sam O'Steen ***Mus*** Ennio Morricone ***Art*** Bo Welch

Act Jack Nicholson, Michelle Pfeiffer, James Spader, Kate Nelligan, Richard Jenkins, Christopher Plummer (Columbia)

Wolf is a decidedly upscale horror film, a tony werewolf movie in which a full roster of fancy talents tries to mate with unavoidably hoary, not to say hairy, material. Offspring of this union is an intriguing thriller more enjoyable for its humor and sophistication than for its scare quotient.

No expense has been spared in outfitting this reportedly $70 million-plus project, which bears comparison to such perennials as *Dr. Jekyll and Mr. Hyde, Beauty and the Beast* and many mangier monster epics turned out over the decades. But no matter how snazzy the trappings, this is still, at heart, a werewolf picture.

Opening sequence has Will Randall (Jack Nicholson) hitting a wolf with his car on a lonely Vermont road. The animal suddenly revives and bites him on the hand before lighting out into the woods. Back in New York, Will is facing the dread midlife prospect of being ousted from his position as editor in the wake of a takeover by billionaire tycoon Raymond Alden (Christopher Plummer). At a swank dinner party at the latter's estate, he also has a chance meeting with Raymond's edgy, beautiful daughter, Laura (Michelle Pfeiffer).

Will's discovery that two-faced former protegé, Stewart Swinton (James Spader), whom Raymond has promoted into Will's former job, is also having an affair with his wife (Kate Nelligan), prompts him to seek solace with Laura. Fact that the Will-Laura relationship has no resonance delivers the picture a body blow that may not knock it out, but does put it on the ropes.

Script by Jim Harrison and Wesley Strick, which bears no relation to Harrison's novel *Wolf*, tries hard to make this shaggy story play plausibly as a modern piece. Nicholson begins his performance in a low key and cranks it up only by degrees. By contrast, Pfeiffer's Laura comes across as hard and brittle.

•

WOLFEN

1981, 114 mins, US Ⓥ ▭ ⦿ col

Dir Michael Wadleigh ***Prod*** Rupert Hitzig ***Scr*** David Eyre, Michael Wadleigh ***Ph*** Gerry Fisher ***Ed*** Chris Lebenzon, Dennis Dolan, Martin Bram, Marshall M. Borden ***Mus*** James Horner ***Art*** Paul Sylbert

Act Albert Finney, Diane Venora, Edward James Olmos, Gregory Hines, Tom Noonan, Dick O'Neill (Orion)

Wolfen is consistently more interesting than it is thrilling. Policeman Albert Finney is confronted with a series of baffling, grisly murders, gradually realizing they are not the work of mere mortals. As always in the best of pictures like this, the buildup is the most fun.

Initially, director Michael Wadleigh creates an exceedingly chilling atmosphere, especially as Finney and Gregory Hines, excellent as a space-case coroner, deal matter-of-factly with the dismembered dead.

Wadleigh creates a surreal point-of-view for the killers that works effectively, accented by handy digital sound. Overall, Paul Sylbert's production design is also a major plus. Add to that a splendid performance by Finney and a solid film debut for Diane Venora as his psychologist sidekick.

Film [from a novel by Whitley Strieber] was reportedly recut several times (four editors are credited) and a couple of bad cuts are clearly evident; a few scenes are awkward, too.

•

WOLF MAN, THE

1941, 69 mins, US Ⓥ ⦿ b/w

Dir George Waggner ***Prod*** George Waggner ***Scr*** Curt Siodmak ***Ph*** Joseph Valentine ***Ed*** Ted Kent ***Mus*** Charles Previn

Act Lon Chaney, Claude Rains, Ralph Bellamy, Bela Lugosi, Maria Ouspenskaya (Universal)

The legendary English werewolf provides basis for another cinematic adventure into the horrific chiller-diller realm. *The Wolf Man* is a compactly knit tale of its kind, with good direction and performances by an above-par assemblage of players, but dubious entertainment.

Young Lon Chaney (who drops the Jr. in films for the first time here) returns to the family's English castle after long absence in America, to stand in line as heir to the estate. According to legend, a person bitten by a werewolf assumes the dual personality of the latter—and Chaney is the victim of a bite.

Young Chaney gives a competent performance, both straight and under makeup for the dual role. Script stresses the tenseness of the fabled tale in both action and dialog, with George Waggner piloting in okay manner.

•

WOLVES OF WILLOUGHBY CHASE, THE

1989, 93 mins, UK Ⓥ ⦿ col

Dir Stuart Orme ***Prod*** Mark Forstater ***Scr*** William M. Akers ***Ph*** Paul Beeson ***Ed*** Martin Walsh ***Mus*** Colin Towns ***Art*** Christopher Hobbs

Act Stephanie Beacham, Mel Smith, Emily Hudson, Aleks Darowska, Geraldine James, Richard O'Brien (Zenith)

The Wolves of Willoughby Chase is a thoroughly enjoyable children's fantasy-adventure.

Pic has a suitable Dickensian feel, set during the imaginary reign of King James III some time in the last century in a snowbound part of North Yorkshire where wolves seem to rule the countryside. Based on Joan Aiken's children's novel, it has an attractively sinister quality and centers on the fight by two young girls to foil a dastardly plot hatched by the their evil governess, Slighcarp.

Tyro theatrical helmer Stuart Orme handles his chores well; they must have been doubly hard since pic was shot at the Barrandov Studios in Prague and on location around snowy Czechoslovakia in early 1988.

Emily Hudson and Aleks Darowska are excellent as the plucky youngsters, but best of all is Stephanie Beacham who outdoes herself as the wicked Slighcarp. The excellent cast is boosted by tongue-in-cheek performances from Mel Smith and Geraldine James.

•

WOMAN CHASES MAN

1937, 71 mins, US b/w

Dir John G. Blystone ***Prod*** Samuel Goldwyn ***Scr*** Joseph Anthony, Manuel Seff, David Hertz ***Ph*** Gregg Toland ***Ed*** Daniel Mandell ***Mus*** Alfred Newman

Act Miriam Hopkins, Joel McCrea, Charles Winninger, Erik Rhodes, Ella Logan, Broderick Crawford (Goldwyn/United Artists)

The Radio City Music hall first-night audience laughed with approval of this picture for the first three-quarters of its running, and then the giggles stopped. Laughs ceased when the action on the screen became so insanely illogical, and dull, that the amazed disappointment of the house expressed itself in chilly silence. It sums up as just a fair feature.

Three topflight players, Miriam Hopkins, Joel McCrea and Charles Winninger, simply run out of material [story by Lynn Root and Franklyn Fenton]. Towards the end of the film, the first two literally find themselves, somewhat inebriated, up a tree.

As a comedienne, Hopkins displays exceptional skill, charm and resource. She is effective and amusing so long as she has something to do. She brings to Winninger, as the father, a set of architectural plans of her own designing, which will turn his suburban development into a success if he can save his venture by obtaining a $100,000 loan to hold off creditors.

McCrea, as the son, has the money but not the inclination to invest. Hopkins volunteers to persuade him, and eventually does. She plays on the boy's weakness for drink and obtains his signature to a contract. It isn't much funnier than it reads, but that's *Woman Chases Man*.

•

WOMAN IN A DRESSING GOWN

1957, 98 mins, UK b/w

Dir J. Lee Thompson ***Prod*** Frank Godwin, J. Lee Thompson ***Scr*** Ted Willis ***Ph*** Gil Taylor ***Ed*** Richard Best ***Mus*** Louis Levy (arr.) ***Art*** Robert Jones

Act Yvonne Mitchell, Sylvia Syms, Anthony Quayle, Andrew Ray, Carole Lesley, Olga Lindo (Godwin-Willis)

The principal character in Ted Willis's screenplay is reminiscent of the Shirley Booth role in *Come Back, Little Sheba*. Yvonne Mitchell plays an endearing slut on the verge of losing her husband to a younger, more attractive and more wholesome girl. The uncanny depth of her portrayal lifts the story from a conventional rut and gives it a classy stature.

Mitchell plays the wife who is never able to keep pace with the demands of life. Every day she tries in vain to make her home attractive for her husband and son, but the odds are always overwhelming. Inevitably, her husband (Anthony Quayle) is attracted to a girl in the office (Sylvia Syms), but at the moment of crisis cannot make the break.

Astute writing and adroit direction help to retain sympathy for the leading character, although her tiresome behavior rarely justifies it. There's one moving scene in which she persuades her husband to bring the other girl to the house, so that the three of them can talk it over as adults.

Mitchell's performance is the walk-away highlight of the production, but Anthony Quayle does a solidly reliable job as the husband. J. Lee Thompson's crisp direction sets the pattern for the okay technical credits.

•

WOMAN IN RED, THE

1984, 87 mins, US Ⓥ ⦿ col

Dir Gene Wilder ***Prod*** Victor Drai ***Scr*** Gene Wilder ***Ph*** Fred Schuler ***Ed*** Christopher Greenburg ***Mus*** John Morris ***Art*** David L. Snyder

Act Gene Wilder, Charles Grodin, Joseph Bologna, Judith Ivey, Michael Huddleston, Kelly Le Brock (Orion)

The woman in red is simply a very sexy contemporary (Kelly Le Brock), hired as a model by a San Francisco city agency, bringing her into contact with a mundane bureaucrat, Gene Wilder, heretofore a contented family man.

But one look at Le Brock, and Wilder is ready to risk all for illicit romance: he is not very adept at adultery.

The laughs roll along readily as Wilder tries one idea after another to sneak out on wife Judith Ivey and family to rendevous with Le Brock.

A wonderful diversion through all of this is Gilda Radner, a relatively plain fellow office worker who initially thinks she's the object of Wilder's wanderlust and is bitterly—and vigorously—disappointed when she finds out she isn't. [Pic is based on 1976 French film, *Pardon Mon Affaire*, directed by Yves Robert.]

1984: Best Song ("I Just Called to Say I Love You")

•

WOMAN IN THE DUNES
SEE: SUNA NO ONNA

•

WOMAN IN THE WINDOW, THE
1945, 90 mins, US Ⓥ ⦿ b/w
Dir Fritz Lang ***Prod*** Nunnally Johnson ***Scr*** Nunnally Johnson ***Ph*** Milton Krasner ***Ed*** Marjorie Johnson ***Mus*** Arthur Lange ***Art*** Duncan Cramer
Act Edward G. Robinson, Joan Bennett, Raymond Massey, Dan Duryea, Edmond Breon, Robert Blake, Thomas E. Jackson (RKO/International)

Nunnally Johnson whips up a strong and decidedly suspenseful murder melodrama in *Woman in the Window*. Producer, who also prepared the screenplay [from the novel *Once off Guard* by J. H. Wallis] continually punches across the suspense for constant and maximum audience reaction. Added are especially fine timing in the direction by Fritz Lang and outstanding performances by Edward G. Robinson, Joan Bennett, Raymond Massey and Dan Duryea.

Opening sequence suggests that tragedies spring from little things, and anyone can become involved in a murder or criminal action. That's just what happens to Robinson, a staid and middle-aged college professor whose wife and children depart for vacation in Maine. He pauses and admires a painting on exhibition in store window adjoining his club. Later he again glances at the girl's portrait and finds the model standing beside him.

Robinson visits her apartment to look over other sketches; a stranger breaks in to accuse the girl of infidelity and attacks Robinson, who stabs the visitor in self-protection. Sidetracking initial impulse to call the police, he connives with the girl to dispose of the body in the country woods. Finish is a surprise for smash climax.

1945: NOMINATION: Best Scoring of a Dramatic Picture

•

WOMAN IS A WOMAN, A
SEE: UNE FEMME EST UNE FEMME

•

WOMAN OF AFFAIRS, A
1929, 90 mins, US Ⓥ b/w
Dir Clarence Brown ***Scr*** Bess Meredyth, Hugh Wynn ***Ph*** William Daniels ***Art*** Cedric Gibbons
Act Greta Garbo, John Gilbert, Lewis Stone, John Mack Brown, Douglas Fairbanks, Jr., Dorothy Sebastian (M-G-M)

A sensational array of screen names and the intriguing nature of the story (*The Green Hat*) from which it was made, together with some magnificent acting by Greta Garbo, carries through this vague and sterilized version of Michael Arlen's erotic play. Superb technical production counts in its favor.

But the kick is out of the material and, worse yet, John Gilbert has an utterly blah role. Most of the footage he merely stands around rather sheepishly.

So here is a woman who, disappointed in her first love, plunges into an orgy of amorous adventures from Calais to Cairo.

Garbo saves an unfortunate situation throughout by a subtle something in her playing that suggests just the erotic note that is essential to the whole theme and story.

Production is noteworthy for its beauty of setting and atmosphere.

Lewis Stone plays a wise and kindly old counsellor of the madcap heroine that is made to order for his suave and sophisticated style of playing. Dorothy Sebastian manages to register real personality as the wife.

•

WOMAN OF DISTINCTION, A
1950, 89 mins, US Ⓥ ⦿ b/w
Dir Edward Buzzell ***Prod*** Buddy Adler ***Scr*** Charles Hoffman ***Ph*** Joseph Walker ***Ed*** Charles Nelson ***Mus*** Werner R. Heymann
Act Ray Milland, Rosalind Russell, Edmund Gwenn, Janis Carter, Mary Jane Saunders, Francis Lederer (Columbia)

A Woman of Distinction is a loosely tied grabbag of screwball and nonsensical doings about two warring-but-loving pedagogues. Sans much logic, the Rosalind Russell-Ray Milland teamwork is good for more laughs than not, and the gags overcome a yarn [by Hugo Butler and Ian McLellan Hunter] that lacks sound motivation.

Featured is a running duel between Russell, the woman of distinction too busy for romance, and Prof. Milland, who is dragged into a faked news-headlined affair with the dean of a women's college through the connivings of an overly diligent press agent.

Russell pitches in with nice change of pace. Milland pieces together the necessary ingredients of genteel sobriety, confusion and indignation.

•

WOMAN OF PARIS, A
1923, 84 mins, US Ⓥ d b/w
Dir Charles Chaplin ***Prod*** Charles Chaplin ***Scr*** Charles Chaplin ***Ph*** Rollie Totheroh, Jack Wilson ***Ed*** Monta Bell ***Art*** Arthur Stibolt
Act Edna Purviance, Adolphe Menjou, Carl Miller, Lydia Knott, Charles K. French, Clarence Geldert (United Artists)

A Woman of Paris is a serious, sincere effort, with a bang story subtlety of idea-expression.

If the sentimental Charlie Chaplin made one outstanding error he did it in casting Edna Purviance, his leading woman of many classic comedies, for the central and stellar role in his first legitimate picture. She is not a sensation. She looks and acts well enough, but she falls short of the fine pace set by the rest of the endeavor.

However, this is not a conspicuous drag on *A Woman of Paris*. Chaplin, on the other hand, straying far from his haunts of yore, comes forth as a new genius both as a producer and a director.

The finish is as brilliant and as memorable as the Mexico-line finale of *The Pilgrim*. After the girl has gone through all the vicissitudes of Paris high and low life, her rich ex-lover, driving in the country, passes her on the road as she sits on the back of a farmer's cart with a little orphan. He just whizzes by—that's all. And it tells more than if he had the conventional breakdown.

•

WOMAN OF STRAW
1964, 117 mins, UK col
Dir Basil Dearden ***Prod*** Michael Relph ***Scr*** Robert Muller, Stanley Mann ***Ph*** Otto Heller ***Ed*** John D. Gutheridge ***Mus*** Muir Mathieson (arr.) ***Art*** Ken Adam
Act Gina Lollobrigida, Sean Connery, Ralph Richardson, Johnny Sekka, Laurence Hardy, Danny Daniels (United Artists)

Director Basil Dearden seems, here, to have temporarily misplaced the vigorous insight that has earned him some top credits. Best that can be said of *Straw* [from the novel by Catherine Arley] is that it looks handsome. But the film gets bogged down by stilted dialog and by the situations.

Ralph Richardson is a multimillionaire, an ill-mannered, sour tycoon condemned to spend his life in a wheelchair. He takes it out on anybody handy. These include his nephew-secretary (Sean Connery), his major-domo, colored houseboy, his yacht skipper and his dogs.

He even tosses some well-considered snarls in the direction of Gina Lollobrigida, who is hired by the nephew as the old man's nurse. As a result of all this humiliation there are several people who are not unhappy when he is found dead in the bunk of his yacht.

Interplay in the relationship and emotions of the characters involved make fair picture-going in the early stages. But when the plot gets down to the mystery of whether he died from natural causes or whether he was the victim of mayhem, then it descends into under-average mishmash.

Richardson manages to extract what fun there is out of the desultory proceedings. Lollobrigida is out of her depth, while the well-dressed Connery wanders around with the air of a man who can't wait to get back to being James Bond again.

•

WOMAN OF SUMMER
SEE: THE STRIPPER

•

WOMAN OF THE DUNES
SEE: SUNA NO ONNA

•

WOMAN OF THE YEAR
1942, 112 mins, US Ⓥ ⦿ b/w
Dir George Stevens ***Prod*** Joseph L. Mankiewicz ***Scr*** Ring Lardner, Jr., Michael Kanin ***Ph*** Joseph Ruttenberg ***Ed*** Frank Sullivan ***Mus*** Franz Waxman ***Art*** Cedric Gibbons, Randall Duell
Act Spencer Tracy, Katharine Hepburn, Fay Bainter, Reginald Owen, William Bendix, Dan Tobin (M-G-M)

Woman of the Year is an entertaining film with superb work by Katharine Hepburn and Spencer Tracy. There are very few palms due writers Ring Lardner, Jr. and Michael Kanin, who reputedly received the sum of $100,000 for the original screenplay. Director George Stevens likewise merits small praise.

Lardner and Kanin had an amusing starting point—a sports writer and a young and beautiful counterpart of Dorothy Thompson spatting, then falling in love and marrying—but wend it tortuously through every hackneyed and expected plot device without a surprise at any turn. Director Stevens lets it get out of hand completely with minutes on end devoted to a few tired situation gags. Picture runs 112 minutes and frequently seems every moment of that. Tracy and Hepburn go a long way toward pulling the chestnut out of the fire.

1942: Best Original Screenplay

NOMINATION: Best Actress (Katharine Hepburn)

•

WOMAN ON PIER 13, THE
SEE: I MARRIED A COMMUNIST

•

WOMAN ON THE BEACH, THE
1947, 71 mins, US b/w
Dir Jean Renoir ***Prod*** Jack J. Gross ***Scr*** Frank Davis, Jean Renoir ***Ph*** Leo Tover, Harry Wild ***Ed*** Roland Gross, Lyle Boyer ***Mus*** Hanns Eisler ***Art*** Albert S. D'Agostino, Walter E. Keller
Act Joan Bennett, Robert Ryan, Charles Bickford (RKO)

Film is more mood than meaning. On the surface, it is a confusion of logic, a narrative drawn with invisible lines around characters without motivation in a plot only shadowily defined. But beneath, the cinematic elements are brilliantly fused by Jean Renoir into an intense and compelling emotional experience.

Thesping is uniformly excellent with the cast from top to bottom responding to Renoir's controlling need for a surcharged atmosphere. In subtle counterpoint to the film's surface vagueness, the settings are notably realistic in their size and quality. Choice camerawork sustains the film's overall impact, while sweeping through the entire production is a magnificent score by Hanns Eisler which heightens all of the film's pictorial values.

Basically, the yarn [based on the novel, *None So Blind* by Mitchell Wilson] is a variation of the eternal triangle theme, but it unfolds elusively through implication and suggestion, only occasionally emerging to the level of full clarity. In the film's center, Charles Bickford plays the role of a blind artist, brutally strong and madly jealous of his wife. As the latter, Joan Bennett is a callous tart tied to her husband only through guilt arising from her accidental blinding of Bickford early in their marriage.

Third part is played by Robert Ryan, a coast guard officer stationed near the blind man's home in a desolate spot on the ocean front. He is recovering from a mental shock obtained in naval combat during the war.

•

WOMAN'S FACE, A
1941, 105 mins, US Ⓥ b/w
Dir George Cukor ***Prod*** Victor Saville ***Scr*** Donald Ogden Stewart, Elliot Paul ***Ph*** Robert Planck ***Ed*** Frank Sullivan ***Mus*** Bronislau Kaper ***Art*** Cedric Gibbons, Wade B. Rubottom
Act Joan Crawford, Melvyn Douglas, Conrad Veidt, Osa Massen, Reginald Owen, Albert Bassermann (M-G-M)

There's a rather intriguing dramatic quality to this American version of an original Swedish production (from a French play, Francis de Croisset's *Il etait une fois*) which had Ingrid Bergman as star. It's a story of a woman's handicap and final regeneration.

Opening with the court trial of Joan Crawford for murder, the story is developed through various stages by the testimony of several witnesses—and finally the defendant herself. Dramatic suspense is maintained by keeping the victim's identity well hidden for a surprise climax.

Crawford is the victim of a childhood accident which left her face distorted and disfigured. Case-hardened and calloused, shunning people generally, she drops into a criminal career. Romantic approach of Conrad Veidt is the first she has had and she accepts his flattery with love-hungry adoration.

She meets plastic surgeon Melvyn Douglas, whose offer of an operation is gladly accepted. Veidt then persuades her to take a job as governess on his uncle's estate—and to murder the child-heir that stands in his path to wealth inheritance.

Crawford has a strongly dramatic and sympathetic role, despite her hardened attitude, which she handles in top-notch fashion.

•

WOMAN'S SECRET, A
1949, 84 mins, US Ⓥ b/w
Dir Nicholas Ray ***Prod*** Herman J. Mankiewicz ***Scr*** Herman J. Mankiewicz ***Ph*** George Diskant ***Ed*** Sherman Todd ***Mus***

Frederick Hollander *Art* Albert S. D'Agostino, Carroll Clark
Act Maureen O'Hara, Melvyn Douglas, Gloria Grahame, Bill Williams, Victor Jory, Jay C. Flippen (RKO)

There's too much unintended mystery about *A Woman's Secret* for it to be anything but spotty entertainment.

Story [from Vicki Baum's novel *Mortgage on Life*] opens with Maureen O'Hara confessing to the shooting of Gloria Grahame, a trollop-minded chirp she has coached into the big time. O'Hara's friend (Melvyn Douglas) doesn't believe she did the shooting, and picture then goes into a confusing flashback account of her life as told by Douglas to a police detective (Jay C. Flippen). Footage moves constantly from the present to the past as Douglas tries to justify his belief in Miss O'Hara's innocence.

O'Hara gives a straightforward account of herself. Grahame carries handicap of bad makeup and unbecoming hairdress, and Douglas is too coy as the piano-playing friend. Flippen is topnotch as the detective, lifting his scenes, as does Mary Phillips as his amateur private-eye wife.

•

WOMAN'S TALE, A

1991, 93 mins, Australia Ⓥ col
Dir Paul Cox *Prod* Paul Cox, Santhana Naidu *Scr* Paul Cox, Barry Dickens *Ph* Nino G. Martinetti *Ed* Russell Hurley *Mus* Paul Grabowski *Art* Neil Angwin
Act Sheila Florance, Gosia Dobrowolska, Norman Kaye, Chris Haywood, Myrtle Woods, Ernest Gray (Illumination)

Sensitive and controversial themes about treatment of the aged and terminally ill are tackled with distinction in Paul Cox's *A Woman's Tale*, which bears all the director's hallmarks. Pic is structured around one of Cox's favourite actresses, veteran Sheila Florance, who carries the film on her frail shoulders. Her Martha is terminally ill yet fiercely determined to hold on to her independence. She lives alone in a small city apartment with her cat, canary and memories.

A nurse, Anna, visits her every day and Martha even lets her use her apartment for afternoon trysts with her married lover. Gosia Dobrowolska plays the nurse with sweetness and sensitivity.

Living in the next-door apartment is the equally old and even frailer Billy (Norman Kaye, in a tremendously touching performance). Anna also visits Billy, but is unamused when he makes pathetic sexual advances towards her.

These characters, and others, are, however, marginal. As Martha, Florance dominates the film and is in almost every scene. It's no secret Florance was seriously ill during production.

•

WOMAN'S WORLD

1954, 94 mins, US ▭ col
Dir Jean Negulesco *Prod* Charles Brackett *Scr* Claude Binyon, Mary Loos, Richard Sale, Howard Lindsay, Russel Crouse *Ph* Joe MacDonald *Ed* Louis Loeffler *Mus* Cyril J. Mockridge *Art* Lyle Wheeler, Mark-Lee Kirk
Act Clifton Webb, June Allyson, Van Heflin, Lauren Bacall, Fred MacMurray, Arlene Dahl (20th Century-Fox)

Woman's World is Hollywood at its commercial best, a highly polished product, technically and story-wise. Basic story premise is the behind-the-scenes scramble for the top job of a gigantic industrial firm. Clifton Webb, as president of Gifford Motors, brings three of his district managers to New York for a firsthand observation to select a successor to the recently deceased sales manager. He invites their wives along, since he believes that the right wife is just as important as the right man for the job.

There's June Allyson and Cornel Wilde from Kansas City, Lauren Bacall and Fred MacMurray from Philadelphia, and Arlene Dahl and Van Heflin from Dallas. All the men in Webb's estimation are equally capable of handling the No. 1 post. The final decision rests on their wives. Allyson is a hayseed from K.C., extremely devoted to her husband and three children. Bacall is bitter and disillusioned and at the point of separation from her ambitious husband. Dahl is a pushy glamor gal, not unwilling to throw her sex around to gain her aims.

The choice, of course, is left to the very end and will come as a surprise to many. Unlike Metro's *Executive Suite*, in which the audience could quickly put its finger on the chosen man, *World* keeps 'em guessing. The entire cast, under Jean Negulesco's fine direction, contribute performances as polished as the entire production.

•

WOMAN TIMES SEVEN

1967, 99 mins, US Ⓥ col
Dir Vittorio De Sica *Prod* Arthur Cohn *Scr* Cesare Zavattini *Ph* Christian Matras *Ed* Teddy Darvas, Victoria Spiri-Mercanton *Mus* Riz Ortolani
Act Shirley MacLaine, Peter Sellers, Alan Arkin, Rossano Brazzi, Michael Caine, Vittorio Gassman (Embassy)

Woman Times Seven means a seven-segment showcase for the talents of Shirley MacLaine, playing in tragicomedy and dramatic fashion a variety of femme types. MacLaine is spotted in many different adult situations, and largely convinces with each switcheroo.

With Peter Sellers, she is the bereaved widow, trailing her late husband in funeral procession, as Sellers puts the make on her. Then, as a wife who surprises hubby Rossano Brazzi in bed with a neighbor, MacLaine shifts to the enraged female, determined on revenge. The major tour de force segment finds MacLaine and Alan Arkin alone in a flophouse room, plotting suicide together.

•

WOMAN UNDER THE INFLUENCE, A

1974, 155 mins, US Ⓥ ⊙ col
Dir John Cassavetes *Scr* John Cassavetes *Ph* Mitch Breit *Ed* Bob Heffernan *Mus* Bo Harwood *Art* Phedon Papamichael
Act Peter Falk, Gena Rowlands, Matthew Cassel, Matthew Laborteaux, Christina Grisanti, Katherine Cassavetes (Faces International)

This is a disturbing portrait of a slightly mad housewife. Its serious treatment of a downbeat subject is hypoed by a fine performance from Peter Falk and a bravura one from Gena Rowlands.

Rowlands plays a lower-middle-class L.A. housewife whose sense of identity is so impoverished she defines herself only in terms of her husband's love and the devotion of her children.

Rowlands's performance in the title role is one of those tour de force numbers available only to screen players of alcoholics and lunatics. Falk is outstanding in a role which calls for him to be loving and callous at the same time. He, too, retains audience sympathy.

Film is technically superior to any of John Cassavetes's previous works.

1974: NOMINATIONS: Best Director, Actress (Gena Rowlands)

•

WOMEN, THE

1939, 132 mins, US Ⓥ ⊙ col
Dir George Cukor *Prod* Hunt Stromberg *Scr* Anita Loos, Jane Murfin *Ph* Oliver T. Marsh, Joseph Ruttenberg *Ed* Robert J. Kern *Mus* Edward Ward, David Snell *Art* Cedric Gibbons, Wade B. Rubottom
Act Norma Shearer, Joan Crawford, Rosalind Russell, Paulette Goddard, Joan Fontaine, Hedda Hopper (M-G-M)

As in the play [by Clare Boothe], no man appears—it's a field day for the gals to romp intimately in panties, scanties and gorgeous gowns. Most of the members of the cast (studio claims 135 speaking parts) deport themselves in a manner best described by Joan Crawford at the end. "There's a name for you ladies, but it's not used in high society outside of kennels."

Story is essentially lightweight and trivial, and covers a wide range of fem conversations—barbed shafts at friends, whisperings of husbands' indiscretions, maligning gossip and catty asides. Script basically maintains structure of the play, but directs more sympathetic appeal to the marital problem of Norma Shearer.

Picture however holds passages that slow movement down to a walk.

•

WOMEN IN LOVE

1969, 130 mins, UK Ⓥ ⊙ col
Dir Ken Russell *Prod* Larry Kramer, Martin Rosen *Scr* Larry Kramer *Ph* Billy Williams *Ed* Michael Bradsell *Mus* Georges Delerue *Art* Luciana Arrighi
Act Alan Bates, Oliver Reed, Glenda Jackson, Jennie Linden, Eleanor Bron, Vladek Sheybal (Brandywine/United Artists)

Directed with style and punch by Ken Russell, this is an episodic but challenging and holding pic. D. H. Lawrence's pungent thoughts about love and marriage, and the attitudes of the two sexes toward them, are not highly original but are shrewdly put over.

Russell's direction dominates the film, but he has the benefit of four excellent performances. The rough, tough coal-mining area of the Midlands is effectively evoked.

The story is fragmentary. Two sisters are wooed and won by two men and the film concerns their relationships. One settles down to a marriage on happy but uneasy terms. The other, more questing, has an equally uneasy yet gleeful romance which ends in tragedy.

Glenda Jackson gives a vital performance with punch and intelligence. Jennie Linden settles for married life with Alan Bates.

1970: Best Actress (Glenda Jackson)

NOMINATIONS: Best Director, Screenplay Adaptation, Cinematography

•

WOMEN ON THE VERGE OF A NERVOUS BREAKDOWN

SEE: MUJERES AL BORDE DE UN ATAQUE DE NERVIOS

•

WOMEN'S PRISON

1955, 80 mins, US b/w
Dir Lewis Seiler *Prod* Bryan Foy *Scr* Crane Wilbur, Jack DeWitt *Ph* Lester H. White *Ed* Henry Batista *Mus* Mischa Bakaleinikoff (dir.) *Art* Cary Odell
Act Ida Lupino, Jan Sterling, Cleo Moore, Audrey Totter, Phyllis Thaxter, Howard Duff (Columbia)

Psychological aspects of life behind bars, particularly as far as femmes are concerned, get a generous probing in *Women's Prison* [from a screen story by Jack DeWitt]. Villain of the piece is Amelia (Ida Lupino), supervisor of a women's prison which adjoins a jail for men. A "borderline psychopath" who's never been able to hit it off socially with men, she takes it out on her femme inmates, who apparently have done better with the opposite sex. Among the objects of her ire are Helene (Phyllis Thaxter), in for automobile manslaughter; Joan (Audrey Totter), doing time for a gun possession charge and wife of convict Glen (Warren Stevens), forger Brenda (Jan Sterling), et al.

Lupino, in portraying the heavy, makes herself intensely disliked. Howard Duff is an easy-going physician, patient and sympathetic despite his problems. Sterling scores nicely as a tough moll. Cleo Moore is a typical femme inmate and Vivian Marshall, as an ex-stripteaser gone wrong, shines in some amusing impersonations.

•

WONDER BOYS

2000, 112 mins, US Ⓥ ⊙ ▭ col
Dir Curtis Hanson *Prod* Scott Rudin, Curtis Hanson *Scr* Steve Kloves *Ph* Dante Spinotti *Ed* Dede Allen *Mus* Christopher Young *Art* Jeannine Oppewall
Act Michael Douglas, Tobey Maguire, Frances McDormand, Robert Downey Jr., Katie Holmes, Richard Thomas, Rip Torn, Philip Bosco (Rudin-Hanson/Paramount-Mutual)

It's refreshing to see a campus comedy populated largely by grown-ups. Unlike most coming-of-age sagas, *Wonder Boys* chronicles the rites of passage of a middle-aged man. Pushing 50, Grady Tripp (Michael Douglas), an English professor who was once the wonder boy and darling of the literati, is unable to finish his new novel. Consumed with fear that it will fail to live up to his masterpiece, published seven years earlier, he toys with various endings while the new book sits, waiting to be rescued. In the first scene, a sensitive student in Grady's writing class (Tobey Maguire) reads from his work. Grady immediately recognizes James's talent, but what he cannot realize is the crucial role the boy will play in his career and emotional life. In a marvelous twist on the convention of heterosexual couples in screwball comedy, the picture centers the narrative on a new type of a romantic (though not gay) duo: a distressed professor and his suicidal student, who may be a pathological liar.

When the story begins, Grady's wife has left him, and soon after, he is informed by his lover, college chancellor Sara Gaskell (Frances McDormand), whose husband (Richard Thomas) is the head of the English department and thus Grady's boss, that she is pregnant. Increasing Grady's anxieties is the university's literary festival, which brings the commercial interests into the insular ivory-tower academic environment. It's crisis time, accentuated by the presence of Q (Rip Torn), the older, self-satisfied writer who serves as the symbol of success that Grady once had.

Wonder Boys could be described as a comedy about the gallantry of defeat. Steve Kloves' faithful rendition of Michael Chabon's novel maintains the author's wicked, sharp-tongued humor. Boasting a crazy kind of sweetness, pic exudes tremendous charm, a result of impeccable timing, right tone and flawless performances. What comes through in each role is an improbable, almost romantic affection for the character that sets the mood for the whole movie.

•

WONDERFUL LIFE

1964, 113 mins, UK ▭ col
Dir Sidney J. Furie *Prod* Kenneth Harper *Scr* Peter Myers, Ronald Cass *Ph* Kenneth Higgins *Ed* Jack Slade *Mus* Stanley Black *Art* Stanley Dorfman
Act Cliff Richard, Walter Slezak, Susan Hampshire, The Shadows, Una Stubbs, Melvyn Hayes (Elstree/Ivy)

Film musicals often get by on shaky storylines but these are usually decked out with lively jokes and badinage and Peter Myers and Ronald Cass [who wrote the songs], prove themselves somewhat sparing in this department. It puts an unfair onus on Cliff Richard to expect his personality to buck several slack passages and remarkably unwitty wordage.

Richard, the Shadows group and comedians Melvyn Hayes and Richard O'Sullivan are merchant sailors stranded in the Canaries where they come across Walter Slezak directing a diabolical *Beau Geste* epic. Caught up in this mish mash, leading lady, Susan Hampshire is having a rough time. For love of the young lady the lads decide to boost her confidence by making an off-the-cuff musical version of the director's film.

The happiest flight of fancy is a sequence which sends up films down the ages. Richard, Hampshire, and the rest show a pleasing sense of mimicry and satire as they josh such favorites as Valentino, the Marx Brothers, the Mack Sennett Cops, Shirley Temple, Garbo, Grable, Boyer, Fairbanks, Sr., Bogart, Dick Powell, Tarzan and others right up to James Bond.

•

WONDERFUL WORLD OF THE BROTHERS GRIMM, THE

1962, 135 mins, US col

Dir Henry Levin, George Pal ***Prod*** George Pal ***Scr*** David P. Harmon, Charles Beaumont, William Roberts ***Ph*** Paul C. Vogel ***Ed*** Walter Thompson ***Mus*** Leigh Harline ***Art*** George W. Davis, Edward Carfagno

Act Laurence Harvey, Karl Boehm, Claire Bloom, Walter Slezak, Yvette Mimieux, Russ Tamblyn (M-G-M/Cinerama)

Grimm is a delightful, refreshing entertainment. Pal himself shares directorial credit with Levin, as the producer also is responsible for directing the Fairy Tales sequences. Pal and Grimm are sympatico, although he permitted Jim Backus as the King to sound too much like Mr. Magoo in *The Dancing Princess* sequence.

This traditional fairy tale of the princess who finds her true love in the humble woodsman is interestingly choreographed by Alex Romero and charmingly interpreted by Yvette Mimieux and Russ Tamblyn.

As far as acting honors go, Harvey is dominant, for in addition to playing Wilhem Grimm, he also enacts, and with touching warmth offset by a trace of irrascibility, the title role in *The Cobbler and the Elves*. This sequence, with its Christmas setting and assortment of orphans and puppets, which perform a miracle in the cobbler's shop overnight, is entirely enchanting.

The Singing Bone dealing with a titanic encounter involving a supercilious aspiring knight and his servant with a fire-spouting dragon, is full of exaggerated chills and wry humor. Buddy Hackett (who reminds one of the late Lou Costello) as the humble servant who finally emerges as the shining knight over his dastardly master, is enchanting. And Terry-Thomas also is excellent as the master whose cowardice ultimately strips him of honor and glory.

1962: Best Color Costume Design (Mary Wills)

NOMINATIONS: Best Color Cinematography, Color Art Direction, Scoring of Music

•

WONDERLAND

1999, 108 mins, UK col

Dir Michael Winterbottom ***Prod*** Michele Camarda, Andrew Eaton ***Scr*** Laurence Coriat ***Ph*** Sean Bobbitt ***Ed*** Trevor Waite ***Mus*** Michael Nyman ***Art*** Mark Tildesley

Act Shirley Henderson, Gina McKee, Molly Parker, Ian Hart, John Simm, Stuart Townsend (Kismet/Revolution/PolyGram/BBC)

Michael Winterbottom's ironically titled *Wonderland* is a wonderfully acted and emotionally rewarding slice of London life in which the versatile director enters Mike Leigh territory with considerable success. The entire film is shot with a handheld camera, only available light is used, and there is the occasional scene in which events are speeded up or slowed down. Winterbottom's complete control over these devices ensures that they add to the intensely immediate feel of the material.

Script unfolds over four days in November for an examination of a family in crisis. Nadia (Gina McKee) meets men via a dating agency, usually with disappointing results; she goes to bed with Tim (Stuart Townsend), but it's clear that to him she's just another conquest. Nadia's older sister, Debbie (Shirley Henderson), is separated from her oafish husband, Dan (Ian Hart). Molly (Molly Parker), the youngest sister, is nine months pregnant and her partner, Eddie (John Simm), leaves [after an argument]. The sisters' parents (Kika Markham, Jack Shepherd) are unhappy as well.

The film is suffused with stoic humor and ends on a note of guarded optimism; there's no sense of defeat or despair. Performances by the ensemble cast are just about flawless. McKee's vulnerable Nadia, with her air of awkwardness, is a genuinely moving character. Parker is achingly lovely as the pregnant woman terrified that her lover, too, may not afford the stability she needs.

The counterpoint created by the combination of Michael Nyman's out-front music and the film's pervasive realism brings an exciting edge to the material.

•

WONDER MAN

1945, 95 mins, US col

Dir H. Bruce Humberstone ***Prod*** Samuel Goldwyn ***Scr*** Don Hartman, Melville Shavelson, Philip Rapp ***Ph*** Victor Milner, William Snyder ***Ed*** Daniel Mandell ***Mus*** Louis Forbes (dir.), Ray Heindorf (arr.) ***Art*** Ernst Fegte, McClure Capps

Act Danny Kaye, Virginia Mayo, Vera-Ellen, Steve Cochran, Huntz Hall, Donald Woods (Goldwyn)

Niftily Technicolored and expensive-looking all the way, *Wonder Man* finds Kaye in a dual role, as twins; one being a nitery performer bumped off by yeggs because of information he was going to give the district attorney; the other as a mild-mannered, studious type who, after his brother's slaying, is belabored by the latter's "spirit" into taking his place and thus help run down the thugs.

The complications, notably on the romance, frequently get too unwieldy for comfort. Several of the comedy situations are rewrites of oldies, but Kaye makes them capital. [Script is from an original story by Arthur Sheekman, adaptation by Jack Levine and Eddie Moran.] There is, in particular, a final-reel scene in which Kaye seeks refuge as a costumed singer during the midst of an operatic performance. It's boilerplate comedy but Kaye makes it belly-laugh fun.

If this sounds like all Kaye, there's no mistaking that without him this film would be decidedly commonplace. He has a good supporting cast, namely the beauteous Virginia Mayo, as the main romantic link, and Vera-Ellen, out of the Broadway musicals, who is the secondary love interest.

The blonde Mayo screens like the couple of millions that are indicated to have been spent by Goldwyn on the pic, and Vera-Ellen is a fine young hoofer who can handle lines well, too.

1945: Best Special Effects

NOMINATIONS: Best Scoring of a Musical Picture, Song ("So in Love"), Sound

•

WOODEN HORSE, THE

1950, 101 mins, UK b/w

Dir Jack Lee ***Prod*** Ian Dalrymple ***Scr*** Eric Williams ***Ph*** C. Pennington-Richards ***Ed*** John Seabourne Sr, Peter Seabourne ***Mus*** Clifton Parker ***Art*** William Kellner

Act Leo Genn, David Tomlinson, Anthony Steel, Bryan Forbes, David Greene, Peter Finch (London/Wessex)

A commendable degree of documentary fidelity is established in this picturization of the escape of three prisoners-of-war from a German camp. The long and torturous period of preparation is faithfully recaptured.

Yarn traces the exploits of three officers who, after receiving approval from the camp's "escape committee," cover up their tunnel-digging by means of a vaulting horse.

Some of the best drama in the film comes after the prison break, where the two ex-airmen, with forged papers, make for a port and finally board a boat for Copenhagen on their last drive for freedom.

Thesping standard is universally good all round. Eric Williams's screenplay from his own novel is a workman-like job.

•

WOODSTOCK

1970, 183 mins, US col

Dir Michael Wadleigh ***Prod*** Bob Maurice ***Ph*** Michael Wadleigh, David Myers, Richard Pearce, Donald Lenzer, Al Wertheimer ***Ed*** Thelma Schoonmaker, Martin Scorsese, Stan Warnow, Jere Huggins, Yeu-Bun Yee (Warner)

Woodstock, brilliantly made by Michael Wadleigh, is a virtually perfect record of the music festival held in Bethel, NY, in summer 1969.

As a documentary feature, the film is a milestone in artistic collation of raw footage into a multipanel, variable-frame, dazzling montage that engages the senses with barely a let-up.

From countless thousands of feet of exposed stock, Wadleigh has superbly orchestrated on film the mass intimacy of pop music and its latter-day relationship to self and environment. *Woodstock* is an absolute triumph in its marriage of cinematic technology to reality.

Of no mean help, of course, are the outstanding musical talents. They do their own things, while the individual and collective effect is spine-tingling.

[In 1994 a 225-min. director's cut was released on home video.]

1970: Best Feature Documentary

NOMINATIONS: Best Editing, Sound

•

WORDS AND MUSIC

1948, 119 mins, US col

Dir Norman Taurog ***Prod*** Arthur Freed ***Scr*** Fred Finklehoffe ***Ph*** Charles Rosher, Harry Stradling ***Ed*** Albert Akst, Ferris Webster ***Mus*** Lennie Hayton (dir.) ***Art*** Cedric Gibbons, Jack Martin Smith

Act Tom Drake, Mickey Rooney, Betty Garrett, Ann Sothern, Janet Leigh, Marshall Thompson (M-G-M)

The saga of Rodgers and Hart itself is neither very interesting nor exceptional, unless it be in their early and continued success at turning out words and music for one top Broadway and Hollywood musical hit after another. Fred Finklehoffe, therefore, in preparing his screenplay [from a story by Guy Bolton and Jean Holloway, adapted by Ben Feiner, Jr.], acted wisely in reducing the biographical aspects to almost a minimum, using them only as a rack around which to weave production numbers, terp routines and lyric assignments [staged and directed by Robert Alton].

Tom Drake plays the serious, businesslike and home-loving Rodgers, the melodist of the pair. Mickey Rooney plays Hart, giving the role at least some partial physical verisimilitude in that his tiny stature was a near-tragedy in the lyricist's life.

Biog, as a matter of fact, sticks to truth about as closely as can be presented on the screen. While details are freely reshuffled, the yarn is strikingly sound from an overall psychological view, catching Hart's early zest for life and its gradual change to a tragic chase after a happiness he couldn't achieve, a chase that led to his death in 1943 at the age of forty-seven.

Hart, who never married, but bounded about the world, was, of course, the more colorful of the pair and the camera faithfully catches that. Rooney plays Rooney, however, rather than Hart, almost turning the role into a burlesque. Drake imbues Rodgers with the dignity and modesty of a Rodgers—if not with the spark. Film doesn't go into the break between the pair, two years before Hart's death. It was at this time Rodgers teamed with Oscar Hammerstein II.

•

WORKING GIRL

1988, 113 mins, US col

Dir Mike Nichols ***Prod*** Douglas Wick ***Scr*** Kevin Wade ***Ph*** Michael Ballhaus ***Ed*** Sam O'Steen ***Mus*** Carly Simon ***Art*** Patrizia Von Brandenstein

Act Sigourney Weaver, Harrison Ford, Melanie Griffith, Joan Cusack, Alec Baldwin, Philip Bosco (20th Century-Fox)

Working Girl is enjoyable largely due to the fun of watching scrappy, sexy, unpredictable Melanie Griffith rise from Staten Island secretary to Wall Street whiz. She's the kind with an eye for stock figures—the numeral kind and the real kind (Harrison Ford).

Griffith stands apart, both for her eagerness to break out of her clerical rut and her tenacity in dealing with whoever seems to be thwarting her, at first a lecherous brokerage house exec, whom she very cleverly and humorously exposes, and then a much more formidable and disarming opponent, femme boss Sigourney Weaver.

Just because they're both "girls" trying to make their way amidst a sea of men doesn't, however, make them friends.

This is not a laugh-out-loud film, though there is a light-hearted tone that runs consistently throughout, Griffith's innocent, breathy voice being a major factor.

1988: Best Song ("Let the River Run")

NOMINATIONS: Best Picture, Director, Actress (Melanie Griffith), Supp. Actress (Joan Cusack, Sigourney Weaver)

•

WORKING GIRLS

1986, 90 mins, US col

Dir Lizzie Borden ***Prod*** Lizzie Borden, Andi Gladstone ***Scr*** Lizzie Borden ***Ph*** Judy Irola ***Ed*** Lizzie Borden ***Mus*** David Van Tiegham ***Art*** Kurt Ossenfort

Act Louise Smith, Ellen McElduff, Amanda Goodwin, Marusia Zach, Janne Peters, Helen Nicholas (Alternative Current)

Working Girls is a simulated docu-style feature that allows audiences to be invisible guests for one day and part of the evening in a Manhattan brothel staffed by about 10 whores working two shifts and charging $50 per half hour when special services of limited scope ("mild dominance" is undertaken by some of the girls) are not required. When their shifts are over, the girls go home to private life with or without husbands or boyfriends.

Centering on Molly (Louise Smith), director Lizzie Borden neither glamorizes, romanticizes nor condemns anything or anybody connected to the brothel.

Borden sugars her pill with clean, crisp, often witty recording of brothel action and shop-talk. All acting is credible and the camerawork is smooth, the nonaction a bit on the long-winded side.

•

WORK IS A FOUR LETTER WORD

1968, 93 mins, UK col

Dir Peter Hall ***Prod*** Thomas Clyde ***Scr*** Jeremy Brooks ***Ph*** Gil Taylor ***Ed*** Jack Harris ***Mus*** Guy Woolfenden ***Art*** Philip Harrison

Act David Warner, Cilla Black, Elizabeth Spriggs, Zia Mohyeddin, David Waller, Alan Howard (Cavalade/Universal)

Work Is a Four Letter Word is based on Henry Livings' unconventional and not wholly satisfactory play *Eh?* A difficult theme for a film, *Work* is a wayout comedy fantasy.

There is an irritating air of improvisation about much of the picture which shows up particularly in the editing, Jack Harris clearly having difficulty in keeping Jeremy Brooks's wayward screenplay within coherent bounds.

The thin storyline visualizes man's struggle against automation, something of a hark back to Chaplin's *Modern Times*. Overwhelmed by the DICE organization which makes such horrors as plastic daffodils, and whose skyscraper offices and factories are automated to a point of frenzy, one young man holds out against the system.

The plot and message are merely hooks for a series of off-beat situations, some very funny and others over-reminiscent and over-stressed. Director Peter Hall often hangs on to a point just long enough to blunt it.

•

WORLD ACCORDING TO GARP, THE

1982, 136 mins, US Ⓥ col

Dir George Roy Hill ***Prod*** George Roy Hill, Robert L. Crawford ***Scr*** Steve Tesich ***Ph*** Miroslav Ondricek ***Ed*** Stephen A. Rotter ***Mus*** David Shire (adapt.) ***Art*** Henry Bumstead

Act Robin Williams, Mary Beth Hurt, Glenn Close, John Lithgow, Hume Cronyn, Jessica Tandy (Pan Arts)

George Roy Hill's film adaptation of [John Irving's novel] *The World According to Garp* has taste, intelligence, craft and numerous other virtues going for it.

Tale is that of young Garp, bastard son of independent-minded nurse Jenny Fields, who, at midlife, becomes a media celebrity upon the publication of her autobiographical tome, *A Sexual Suspect*.

Garp grows up in a placid academic environment, and the grown man in the person of Robin Williams appears only after 25 minutes. He meets and marries Mary Beth Hurt, raises his family, fitfully pursues his writing while she teaches, has skirmishes with the feminists at his mother's mansion, and all the while tries to avoid the "undertoad," the unseen, pervasive threat which lurks everywhere and strikes without warning.

Physically, Williams is fine, but much of the performance is hit-and-miss. Otherwise, casting is superior. Hurt is excellent as Garp's wife. Glenn Close proves a perfect choice as Jenny Fields, a woman of almost ethereal simplicity. Best of all, perhaps, is John Lithgow as Roberta Muldoon, a former football player, now a transsexual.

1982: NOMINATIONS: Best Supp. Actor (John Lithgow), Supp. Actress (Glenn Close)

•

WORLD AND HIS WIFE, THE

SEE: STATE OF THE UNION

•

WORLD APART, A

1988, 113 mins, UK Ⓥ ⦿ col

Dir Chris Menges ***Prod*** Sarah Radclyffe ***Scr*** Shawn Slovo ***Ph*** Peter Biziou ***Ed*** Nicolas Gaster ***Mus*** Hans Zimmer ***Art*** Brian Morris

Act Barbara Hershey, Jodhi May, David Suchet, Jeroen Krabbe, Paul Freeman, Tim Roth (British Screen/Working Title)

A World Apart provides a sharp glimpse of what it was like to be politically contrary in the early 1960s in South Africa. It is mostly told from the p.o.v. of a thirteen-year-old girl, Molly (Jodhi May), whose life becomes dramatically disrupted as a result of her parents' subversive activities.

Set in 1963, story is described as a fictionalized account of what happened to young Shawn Slovo, the writer, and her family when the authorities began cracking down on them. Pic traces the growing emotional and political awareness of the youngster, but also represents a daughter's critique of what she perceives as her mother's selfish absorption in concerns she condescendingly considers above her offspring's head.

The casual cruelties and injustices of the South African system are displayed as part of life's fabric, but what's really going on with Molly's parents, as well as the friendly blacks who often visit the house, remains unclear and out of reach to the girl.

Barbara Hershey (as the mother) represents a solid central figure for the film. Nevertheless, the limited, daughter's viewpoint restricts one's access to the woman's inner self, the source of her political beliefs and her self-image.

Happily, May is at all times engaging as Molly, sustaining the film with no problem. Performances throughout are uniformly naturalistic and believable, and pic, which was shot in Zimbabwe, possesses a rich, luminous look despite a limited budget.

•

WORLD IN HIS ARMS, THE

1952, 104 mins, US col

Dir Raoul Walsh ***Prod*** Aaron Rosenberg ***Scr*** Borden Chase, Horace McCoy ***Ph*** Russell Metty ***Ed*** Frank Gross ***Mus*** Frank Skinner ***Art*** Bernard Herzbrun, Alexander Golitzen

Act Gregory Peck, Ann Blyth, Anthony Quinn, John McIntire, Andrea King, Carl Esmond (Universal)

Rex Beach's novel of romance and adventure in early-day Alaska comes to the screen as a hearty, salty, action film well-trouped by a good cast headed by Gregory Peck.

Action spills over into mob fights, good-humored tests of strength between male principals, and even winds up with a finale horse chase, hand-to-hand duel and the explosion of a Russian gunboat for good measure.

Peck, as daring sea captain, sails his ship into San Francisco Harbor with a load of seal pelts taken in the waters off Russian-owned Alaska. He meets Ann Blyth, a Russian countess fleeing from a Czar-arranged marriage and trying to get to her uncle in Sitka.

Love blooms quickly between the two, but on the day they are to be married, the pursuing Russian prince arrives, carts her off on his gunboat and leaves Peck believing he has been jilted.

•

WORLD IS FULL OF MARRIED MEN, THE

1979, 107 mins, UK Ⓥ col

Dir Robert Young ***Prod*** Malcolm Fancey ***Scr*** Jackie Collins, Terry Howard ***Ph*** Ray Parslow ***Ed*** David Campling ***Mus*** Frank Musker, Dominic Bugatti ***Art*** Tony Curtis

Act Anthony Franciosa, Carroll Baker, Sherrie Cronn, Paul Nicholas, Gareth Hunt, Georgina Hale (New Realm/Married Men)

Set in a glossy world of penthouses and charge accounts, the medium for Jackie Collins's first (1968) novel's message is sexploitation melodrama which, cunningly, will titillate both sexes.

Anthony Franciosa brings a mercifully light touch to the central antihero, an errant advertising executive who trips over one floozie too many and falls in love. Carroll Baker works creditably hard as Franciosa's oft-betrayed spouse who—in a suspiciously convenient dramatic move—finds affection in the back of a limousine with a teen-idol some fifteen years her junior. Paul Nicholas in that role is uncharismatic.

Collins's manipulative technique does not allow for in-depth characterization, so cameos tend to come off best. Georgina Hale is routine (for her) but effective as a laconic wife who's come to terms with the sexcess scene.

•

WORLD IS NOT ENOUGH, THE

1999, 125 mins, UK/US Ⓥ ⦿ ⊏⊐ col

Dir Michael Apted ***Prod*** Michael G. Wilson, Barbara Broccoli ***Scr*** Neal Purvis, Robert Wade, Bruce Feirstein ***Ph*** Adrian Biddle ***Ed*** Jim Clark ***Mus*** David Arnold ***Art*** Peter Lamont

Act Pierce Brosnan, Sophie Marceau, Robert Carlyle, Denise Richards, Robbie Coltrane, Judi Dench (Eon/M-G-M)

The World Is Not Enough, and neither is this new entry in the James Bond cycle. Although not without its moments, particularly an exciting pre-credits high-speed boat chase and some solid work by the nicely matched Pierce Brosnan and Sophie Marceau, the 19th assignment of Bond's 37-year screen career sees 007 undone by villainous scripting [from a screen story by Neal Purvis and Robert Wade] and misguided casting in a couple of key secondary roles. Daft, over-crammed plotting is a shame, because Brosnan grows noticeably more comfortable in the role with each outing.

Story launch has Bond (Brosnan) in Bilbao, Spain, to collect a large stash of money recovered from a killed MI6 agent. He returns to London with the loot, only to see the rightful owner blown up. The man with the money was a wealthy industrialist whose daughter, Elektra (Marceau), also has a history with Bond's boss, M (Judy Dench).

Bond heads for the picturesquely ugly oil fields of Azerbaijan to protect her, but just as James and Elektra find each other, her old tormentor, the terrorist Renard (Robert Carlyle), turns up. The gifted Carlyle is saddled with a role that is more annoying than imposing.

Much further beyond the pale, however, is *Starship Troopers* and *Wild Things* bimbette Denise Richards, as high-level nuclear weapons expert. Prancing around a rugged work site in regulation nuke scientist shorts and midriff-revealing shirt, Richards looks the token Yank in the cast, unable to hold her own with her more mature co-stars.

Action grows murky and rather tiresome in the second half, with at least one setpiece too many.

•

WORLD MOVES ON, THE

1934, 90 mins, US b/w

Dir John Ford ***Prod*** Winfield Sheehan ***Scr*** Reginald C. Berkeley ***Ph*** George Schneiderman ***Mus*** Hugo Friedhofer ***Art*** William Darling

Act Madeleine Carroll, Franchot Tone, Lumsden Hare, Raul Roulien, Reginald Denny, Sig Rumann (Fox)

A pacifist tale concluding with a religious aspect. More frail as to story than the message which it carries, *The World Moves On* is a big production with an imposing cast, some of whom do little more than bits. It also holds six minutes of graphic war stuff from *Crosses of Wood*, a Pathe-Natan (French) release which Fox bought a few years earlier.

That this war passage is both the feature's strength and weakness is the paradox forged by the story. The first half hour is undeniably slow and to follow such war action is not easy. To do so, John Ford had his hands full and hasn't entirely succeeded.

It is not entirely fair to blame Madeleine Carroll for the shortcoming, for of the two principal parts, hers is the weaker. The role is not overboard on color in the first place, and the result is a pleasant if tepid performance. Franchot Tone takes his war stuff with a pipe and three fingers of reserve.

Story starts at New Orleans in 1825, with the reading of a will which combines the Girard and Warburton families through business.

Establishment of branches of the Girards in France and Germany paves the way to the complex situation brought on by the war.

•

WORLD OF APU, THE

SEE: APAR SANSAR

•

WORLD OF HENRY ORIENT, THE

1964, 115 mins, US Ⓥ ⦿ ⊏⊐ col

Dir George Roy Hill ***Prod*** Jerome Hellman ***Scr*** Nora Johnson, Nunnally Johnson ***Ph*** Boris Kaufman, Arthur J. Ornitz ***Ed*** Stuart Gilmore ***Mus*** Elmer Bernstein ***Art*** James Sullivan

Act Peter Sellers, Paula Prentiss, Angela Lansbury, Tippy Walker, Merrie Spaeth, Tom Bosley (Pan Arts)

Producer Jerome Hellman guided this production through many harrowing days as an all–New York try. Despite the problems, which included craft union hassles incident to being the first film ever lensed in its entirety at Michael Myerberg's Long Island Studios, as well as scheduling problems involving Peter Sellers's other commitments, *Orient* has come off an often-funny and always fetching production, the first feature to be made by the indie Pan Arts Co.

Nora and Nunnally Johnson's screenplay, based on Nora Johnson's novel, deals with the adventures of two young schoolgirls in Manhattan and their infatuation with a nutty avant garde pianist named Henry Orient (Sellers). One of the girls (Tippy Walker), the daughter of wealthy parents, is given to wild fights of fancy and her imagination is what first drums up the crush on Orient. At a ritzy Eastside private school she befriends a more stable youngster, (Merrie Spaeth), who is captivated by her pal's vicarious and actual adventures and the two become best friends.

Pic traces the duo in their often-relentless pursuit of Orient, whose talent at the piano is less than distinctive but whose ardor for ladies, especially married ones, is unbounded. The young femmes soon develop the knack of showing up constantly at just the wrong time.

Although it is primarily the girls' picture (probably the first time anyone has "stolen" a pic from Sellers), several others contribute fine performances. As Walker's selfish mother, Angela Lansbury delivers skillfully the epitome of the dominating wealthy wife. Paula Prentiss overplays as an object of Orient's amorous intentions.

•

WORLD OF SUZIE WONG, THE

1960, 130 mins, US Ⓥ ⊙ col

Dir Richard Quine ***Prod*** Ray Stark ***Scr*** John Patrick ***Ph*** Geoffrey Unsworth ***Ed*** Bert Bates ***Mus*** George Duning ***Art*** John Box

Act William Holden, Nancy Kwan, Sylvia Syms, Michael Wilding, Jacqui Chan, Laurence Naismith (Paramount)

The advantage of on-the-spot geography does a great deal for the screen version of *The World of Suzie Wong*. The ultra-picturesque environment of teeming Hong Kong brings a note of ethnic charm to the production, and amounts to a major improvement over the legit translation by Paul Osborn of Richard Mason's novel.

Suzie Wong is the story of an artist (William Holden) who has come to Hong Kong to devote one year to "learning something about painting and something about myself." Before long, he is also learning a great deal about Suzie (Nancy Kwan), a kind of titular leader of a band of lovable, warm-hearted prostitutes (are there any other kind?). After resisting temptations of the flesh and giving her the brush for an admirable period, Holden eventually succumbs to the yen. Complications ensue when it develops Kwan has a child.

The love story makes much more sense with the substitution of the mature Holden for the younger hero of the play. That and the scenery are the major improvements.

On the decidedly negative side are three passages in which realism is virtually abandoned for theatrical effect. (1) Kwan, beaten up by a sailor, proudly displays her bloody lip to the girls as a token of Holden's jealousy, (2) Kwan and Holden dine on salad dressing so as not to reveal her illiteracy to a "stuck-up" waiter, and (3) Holden impulsively tears Kwan's dress off when she turns up in his room looking like the western version of what she is.

Holden gives a first-class performance, restrained and sincere. He brings authority and compassion to the role. Kwan is not always perfect in her timing of lines (she has a tendency to anticipate) and appears to lack a full range of depth or warmth, but on the whole she manages a fairly believable portrayal. Michael Wilding is capable in a role that has been trimmed down. Jacqui Chan is convincing as a B-girl sans sex appeal, only one of the group (outside of the heroine) left with an identity in the screen translation.

•

WORLD'S GREATEST ATHLETE, THE

1973, 92 mins, US Ⓥ col

Dir Robert Scheerer ***Prod*** Bill Walsh ***Scr*** Gerald Gardner, Dee Caruso ***Ph*** Frank Phillips ***Ed*** Cotton Warburton ***Mus*** Marvin Hamlisch ***Art*** John B. Mansbridge, Walter Tyler

Act Tim Conway, Jan-Michael Vincent, John Amos, Roscoe Lee Browne, Dayle Haddon, Billy De Wolfe (Walt Disney)

The World's Greatest Athlete features Jan-Michael Vincent in title role of a jungle boy transplanted to an American campus, where he becomes a one-man track squad. Emphasis is on visual comedy, from the sublime to the camp.

Coach John Amos and assistant Tim Conway, with a terrible record behind them in all sports and alumnus Billy De Wolfe on their backs, discover Vincent during a trip to Africa. Vincent's godfather, witchdoctor Roscoe Lee Browne, is tricked into letting him go back with Amos and Conway, who proceed to enter Vincent as the solo contender for a slew of inter-college field awards.

Vincent provides beefcake and little else, since the script keeps him in the status of the bewildered alien.

•

WORLD'S GREATEST LOVER, THE

1977, 89 mins, US Ⓥ col

Dir Gene Wilder ***Prod*** Gene Wilder ***Scr*** Gene Wilder ***Ph*** Gerald Hirschfeld ***Ed*** Anthony A. Pellegrino ***Mus*** John Morris ***Art*** Steve Sardanis

Act Gene Wilder, Carol Kane, Dom DeLuise, Fritz Feld, Carl Ballantine, Michael Huddleston (20th Century-Fox)

The World's Greatest Lover is a good period comedy starring Gene Wilder competing in a Hollywood studio talent search of fifty years ago to be a rival of Rudolph Valentino. Wilder also functions as writer-producer-director on his second personal film project, ably assisted by Carol Kane, as his wife, and Dom DeLuise, as a prototype madhatter studio czar.

The individual sketch pieces—Wilder trapped on a bakery assembly line; swimming in a flooded sunken living room, seducing his own wife in Valentino disguise after tutoring by the great lover himself, freaking out at his screen test, emerge as varyingly humorous episodes strung out on a skimpy storyline.

DeLuise and Michael Huddleston repeatedly bring up the laugh level.

•

WORLD TEN TIMES OVER, THE
(US: PUSSYCAT ALLEY)

1963, 93 mins, UK b/w

Dir Wolf Rilla ***Prod*** Michael Luke ***Scr*** Wolf Rilla ***Ph*** Larry Pizer ***Ed*** Jack Slade ***Mus*** Edwin Astley ***Art*** Peggy Gick

Act Sylvia Syms, Edward Judd, June Ritchie, William Hartnell (Cyclops/Associated-British)

Wolf Rilla's screenplay explores in one day's fairly busy activity—the aimlessness, insecurity and heartaches of nightclub hostesses. The result is overdramatic but provides opportunities for deft thesping. Nightclub and location sequences in London have a brisk authenticity.

Story concerns two girls, euphemistically called nightclub hostesses, who share an apartment. One (June Ritchie) is a flighty, young extrovert who is having an affair with the married son of a property tycoon. The other (Sylvia Syms) is an older girl, daughter of a country schoolmaster, who is disgusted with her job but cannot break away from it.

Syms gives an intelligent and often moving performance. Her scenes with her father (William Hartnell) are excellent. Hartnell, playing the unworldly, scholarly father who has no contact with his daughter, also gives an observant study. The other two principals are more phonily drawn characters. Edward Judd seems strangely uneasy in his role, and Ritchie, despite many first-rate moments, sometimes appears as if she is simply jumping through paper hoops.

•

WORLD, THE FLESH AND THE DEVIL, THE

1959, 95 mins, US Ⓥ ⊙ ▭ b/w

Dir Ranald MacDougall ***Prod*** Sol C. Siegel ***Scr*** Ranald MacDougall ***Ph*** Harold J. Marzorati ***Ed*** Harold F. Kress ***Mus*** Miklos Rozsa

Act Harry Belafonte, Inger Stevens, Mel Ferrer (M-G-M/Har-Bel)

This is a provocative three-character story dealing with some pertinent issues (racism, atomic destruction) in a frame of suspense melodrama.

Ranald MacDougall, who directed his own screenplay (based on an ancient novel by M. P. Shiel), leaves a few holes in his story, but deliberately. Harry Belafonte is a coal miner who fights his way out of a wrecked Pennsylvania shaft to find himself apparently alone in a devastated world. After about a third of the film, Inger Stevens turns up, spared because she was in a decompression chamber when the bombs burst. Near the ending, in the last half-hour or so, Mel Ferrer arrives in a small power boat from a fishing expedition.

Although overall the film is engrossing, it gets curiously less effective as additional survivors turn up. When Belafonte is entirely alone on the screen for the first one-third of the film, and virtually alone for the first half, the semi-documentary style keeps the film crisp and credible.

It is not clear in the relationship between Belafonte and Stevens whether they are kept apart by her prejudice or his unfounded fear that such an attitude might exist. Ferrer's character is unsatisfying. He seems to be a racist of sorts, but how virulent isn't entirely clarified.

MacDougall shot a great deal of the film in Manhattan, and the realism (and the pains taken to achieve it) pay off. New Yorkers might complain that their geography is a little mixed up, but this is of small consequence.

•

WRATH OF GOD, THE

1972, 111 mins, US ▭ col

Dir Ralph Nelson ***Scr*** Ralph Nelson ***Ph*** Alex Phillips, Jr. ***Ed*** J. Terry Williams, Richard Bracken, Albert Wilson ***Mus*** Lalo Schifrin ***Art*** John S. Poplin Jr

Act Robert Mitchum, Frank Langella, Rita Hayworth, John Colicos, Victor Buono, Ken Hutchison (M-G-M)

The Wrath of God is a good solid action-adventure film, starring Robert Mitchum as a renegade priest who frees a Latin-American town of fear and terror during a rebellion of the 1920 era. Ralph Nelson's film has hard action, offsetting character-comedy relief, excellent production, and an outstanding cast of principals.

James Graham's novel has been adapted by Nelson into a screenplay which, apart from some sporadic dialog cliché, neatly establishes and steadily develops a set of constantly interesting characters.

With Victor Buono and Ken Hutchison, both outstanding as likeable freebooters and soldiers of fortune, Mitchum is forced by army colonel John Colicos to attempt the assassination of Langella, who rules his mountain retreat with vicious authority, largely implemented by Gregory Sierra.

•

WRECKING CREW, THE

1969, 105 mins, US Ⓥ col

Dir Phil Karlson ***Prod*** Irving Allen ***Scr*** William McGivern ***Ph*** Sam Leavitt ***Ed*** Maury Winetrobe ***Mus*** Hugo Montenegro ***Art*** Joe Wright

Act Dean Martin, Elke Sommer, Sharon Tate, Nancy Kwan, Nigel Green, Tina Louise (Columbia/Meadway-Claude)

Fourth in the Matt Helm series, *The Wrecking Crew* emerges as a very entertaining, relaxed spy comedy. It features Dean Martin, Elke Sommer, Nancy Kwan and Sharon Tate, the latter in a delightful comedy performance.

Nigel Green is the heavy, as mastermind of a gold theft. Sommer and Kwan are his principal aides, while Tate is a British agent in support of Martin's work. You wouldn't know it, though, because Tate keeps aborting Martin's plans and intimate rendezvous.

Film rolls along pleasantly for its 105 minutes, featuring the recurring music of Hugo Montenegro and a song by Mack David and Frank DeVol.

•

WRECK OF THE MARY DEARE, THE

1959, 105 mins, US ▭ col

Dir Michael Anderson ***Prod*** Julian Blaustein ***Scr*** Eric Ambler ***Ph*** Joseph Ruttenberg ***Ed*** Eda Warren ***Mus*** George Duning

Act Gary Cooper, Charlton Heston, Michael Redgrave, Emlyn Williams, Richard Harris, Ben Wright (M-G-M)

The mystery of a "ghost" ship looming suddenly out of the night, with only a crazed and battered captain aboard, is solved skillfully and with a good deal of suspense in *The Wreck of the Mary Deare*, from the Hammond Innes novel originally published in the *Saturday Evening Post* in 1956. It's the kind of adventure yarn which, thanks to intelligent treatment and topnotch photography, comes off with a bang.

Gary Cooper is Gideon Patch, the captain who's been the victim of foul play but stands accused himself of negligence. And Charlton Heston plays the skipper of a salvage boat who becomes innocently involved in the mystery of the *Mary Deare* and, in the end, helps solve it. Both men are perfectly cast in rugged roles and Cooper particularly conveys a surprising range of emotion and reaction.

In the smaller (almost bit) parts, Michael Redgrave and Emlyn Williams are very British as they participate in the London Court of Inquiry. Richard Harris is the snarling villain. Ben Wright is comfortable as Heston's partner.

There's a letdown in pace at the middle of the film when the Court of Inquiry appears stacked against Cooper. But the climax comes off with bangup effects.

•

WRESTLING ERNEST HEMINGWAY

1993, 122 mins, US Ⓥ ⊙ col

Dir Randa Haines ***Prod*** Todd Black, Joe Wizan ***Scr*** Steve Conrad ***Ph*** Lajos Koltai ***Ed*** Paul Hirsch ***Mus*** Michael Convertino ***Art*** Waldemar Kalinowski

Act Robert Duvall, Richard Harris, Shirley MacLaine, Sandra Bullock, Nicole Mercurio, Piper Laurie (Warner)

A poignant tale of intimate friendship between two elderly, eccentric men, *Wrestling Ernest Hemingway* serves mostly as a showcase for its two stars, Robert Duvall and Richard Harris. Set in a small Florida town, this bittersweet, often lyrical story is based on the age-old theory that opposites attract.

Duvall, a retired Cuban barber, and Harris, a flamboyant ex-sea captain, accidentally meet in a public park in what turns out to be a fateful encounter that will change their lives. The two men are dissimilar, but they share two characteristics: aging and loneliness.

Shy, dignified and gentlemanly, Duvall leads a quiet, orderly life marked by the absence of women—or friends. He's secretly enamored of a much younger waitress (Sandra Bullock). The often-married Harris is still an amorous daredevil, who tries to make it with his motel manager (Shirley MacLaine) and in a local movie house with a proudly reticent woman (Piper Laurie). Harris exhaustingly relishes telling the story of how as a youngster he wrestled Ernest Hemingway.

Script has a few inspired scenes and some poignant dialogue, but not enough to conceal the clanky machinery of the schematic plot.

•

WRITTEN ON THE WIND
1956, 99 mins, US Ⓥ col
Dir Douglas Sirk ***Prod*** Albert Zugsmith ***Scr*** George Zuckerman ***Ph*** Russell Metty ***Ed*** Russell F. Schoengarth ***Mus*** Frank Skinner ***Art*** Alexander Golitzen, Robert Clatworthy
Act Rock Hudson, Lauren Bacall, Robert Stack, Dorothy Malone, Robert Keith, Grant Williams (Universal)

This outspoken drama probes rather startlingly into the morals and passions of an uppercrust Texas oil family. Intelligent use of the flashback technique before and during the title credits' runoff builds immediate interest and expectancy without diminishing plot punch. Tiptop scripting from the Robert Wilder novel, dramatically deft direction by Douglas Sirk and socko performances by the cast give the story development a follow-through.

Rock Hudson, Lauren Bacall, Robert Stack and Dorothy Malone, aptly cast in the star roles, add a zing to the characters that pays off in audience interest. Hudson scores as the normal, lifelong friend of profligate Stack. The latter, in one of his best performances, draws a compelling portrait of a psychotic man ruined by wealth and character weaknesses.

Bacall registers strongly as a sensible girl swept into the madness of the oil family when she marries Stack, while Malone hits a career high as the completely immoral sister.

1956: Best Supp. Actress (Dorothy Malone)

NOMINATIONS: Best Supp. Actor (Robert Stack), Song ("Written on the Wind")

•

WR: MISTERIJE ORGANIZMA
(WR: MYSTERIES OF THE ORGANISM)
1971, 80 mins, Yugoslavia col
Dir Dusan Makavejev ***Prod*** Svetozar Udovicki (exec.) ***Scr*** Dusan Makavejev ***Ph*** Pega Popovic, Aleksandar Petkovic ***Ed*** Ivanka Vukasovic ***Art*** Dragoljub Ivkov
Act Milena Dravic, Jagoda Kaloper, Ivica Vidovic, Zoran Radmilovic, Miodrag Andric, Tuli Kupferberg (Neoplanta)

Yugoslav filmmaker Dusan Makavejev has brought off a most unusual film built around the late Wilhelm Reich, proponent of cosmic life, the energy of love, and the power of the orgasm. It is handled with shrewd association, charm and sheer fun.

Makavejev interviewed some Reichian practitioners in the U.S., including his own daughter and son, and also filmed some touch sessions, breathing trauma displays, plus listening to a U.S. transvestite talking about his first homosexual affair, and a Yank painter of masturbation scenes.

Tale centers on a Yugoslav beautician, who harangues her household about the need for sex that would cure all the ills of repression. She develops a crush on a Russian champion skater and literally loses her head over him.

Makavejev fills the 80 minutes with much brash and even sly wit, dynamic dialectics, excerpts from a Russo cult film, intercut with Nazi films showing backward or deranged people.

•

WR: MYSTERIES OF THE ORGANISM
SEE: WR: MISTERIJE ORGANIZMA

•

WRONG ARM OF THE LAW, THE
1963, 94 mins, UK Ⓥ b/w
Dir Cliff Owen ***Prod*** Aubrey Baring ***Scr*** Ray Galton, Alan Simpson, John Antrobus ***Ph*** Ernest Steward ***Ed*** Tristam Cones ***Mus*** Richard Rodney Bennett ***Art*** Harry White
Act Peter Sellers, Lionel Jeffries, Bernard Cribbins, Bill Kerr, Davy Kaye, Nanette Newman (Romulus)

A slight-weight cops-and-robbers idea is pepped up into a briskly amusing farce thanks to a combo of deft direction, thesping and writing. Written by the authors of Tony Hancock's original TV series, with the assistance of "Goon" writer John Antrobus, the screenplay [from a screenplay by John Warren and Len Heath; original story by Ivor Jay and William Whistance Smith] has a fair turn of wit and a number of excellent whacky situations.

Peter Sellers runs a top-league West End dress salon as Monsieur Jules. But that's only a front. As Pearly Gates, he is the Cockney King of the Underworld. His own gang he runs on Welfare State lines, with free luncheon vouchers, bubbly on Sundays, holidays with pay on the Costa Brava.

Everything's going fine until the police swoop on the gang job after job. Sellers realizes that an IPO (Impersonating Police Officers) mob is in town. He calls an extraordinary general meeting of London's crime syndicates, negotiates with Scotland Yard and arranges for a twenty-four-hour crime truce so that the police can concentrate on running in the IPO gang.

Sellers has a fat part as the gangster with modern methods (for instance, he makes his gang attend evenings of educational films such as *Rififi*). And he brings his usual alert intelligence to the role. He is surrounded with some sharp talent.

•

WRONG BOX, THE
1966, 110 mins, UK Ⓥ col
Dir Bryan Forbes ***Prod*** Bryan Forbes ***Scr*** Larry Gelbart, Burt Shevelove ***Ph*** Gerry Turpin ***Ed*** Alan Osbiston ***Mus*** John Barry ***Art*** Ray Simm
Act John Mills, Ralph Richardson, Michael Caine, Peter Cook, Dudley Moore, Peter Sellers (Columbia/Salamander)

Robert Louis Stevenson's macabre Victorian yarn has been impressively mounted by producer-director Bryan Forbes. He has lined up an impeccable cast of Britain's character comedian actors and brought his usual intelligent flourish to the film. But it might have improved this Columbia release had he written the script for *The Wrong Box* himself, instead of using the uneven work of Larry Gelbart and Burt Shevelove.

Storyline concerns a macabre lottery in which 20 parents each toss some money into a kitty for their children, the last survivor to draw the loot. Eventual survivors are two brothers who haven't seen each other for 40 years. One of them (John Mills) makes ineffective attempts to bump off his brother (Ralph Richardson), and their offspring take a more than casual interest in the proceedings.

Mills amusingly hams his way through two or three sequences as one of the dying brothers. Richardson, bland, imperturable old bore, is superb. He and Wilfrid Lawson, portraying a decrepit butler, virtually carry away the acting honors.

•

WRONG IS RIGHT
(UK: THE MAN WITH THE DEADLY LENS)
1982, 117 mins, US Ⓥ ⊙ col
Dir Richard Brooks ***Prod*** Richard Brooks ***Scr*** Richard Brooks ***Ph*** Fred J. Koenekamp ***Ed*** George Grenville ***Mus*** Artie Kane ***Art*** Edward Carfagno
Act Sean Connery, George Grizzard, Robert Conrad, Katharine Ross, G. D. Spradlin, John Saxon (Columbia)

Wrong Is Right represents Richard Brooks's shriek of protest at what he sees as the insane, downward spiral of world history over the past decade. Part political satire, part doomsday melodrama and part intellectual graffiti scribbled on the screen, film is impossible to pigeon-hole.

In a style simultaneously literal and surreal, Brooks takes potshots at the CIA, the FBI, presidents Nixon, Carter and Reagan, the military, the Arabs, the oil crisis, international terrorists and television, among many targets.

Sean Connery plays a sort of combination Edward R. Murrow and James Bond, a globe-trotting television commentator who enjoys total access to world leaders of all persuasions.

Basic situation involves an Arab king who seems ready to turn over two mini-atom bombs to a Khaddafi-like revolutionary leader, with the devices to be detonated in Israel, and later New York, unless the U.S. president, who has admitted ordering the killing of the king, resigns from office.

Wild proceedings are packed with convoluted intrigue involving such characters as CIA agents John Saxon and Katharine Ross, maniacal Pentagon rep Robert Conrad, international arms dealer Hardy Kruger and an array of suicidal terrorists who delight in blowing themselves up, as long as it's covered on television.

•

WRONG MAN, THE
1958, 110 mins, US Ⓥ ⊙ b/w
Dir Alfred Hitchcock ***Prod*** Alfred Hitchcock ***Scr*** Maxwell Anderson, Angus MacPhail ***Ph*** Robert Burks ***Ed*** George Tomasini ***Mus*** Bernard Herrmann ***Art*** Paul Sylbert, William L. Kuehl
Act Henry Fonda, Vera Miles, Anthony Quayle, Harold J. Stone, Charles Cooper, Richard Robbins (Warner)

Alfred Hitchcock draws upon real-life drama for this gripping piece of realism [from the *Life* magazine story *The True Story of Christopher Emmanuel Balestrero* by Maxwell Anderson]. He builds the case of a NY Stork Club musician falsely accused of a series of holdups to a powerful climax, the events providing director a field day in his art of characterization and suspense.

Subject here is Manny Balestrero, the bass fiddle player whose story hit Gotham headlines in 1953 when he was arrested for crimes he did not commit. In a case of mistaken identity, he was not freed until the actual culprit was found during his trial. Not, however, before the musician, a family man with a wife and two young sons, went through the harrowing ordeal of being unable to prove his innocence.

Hitchcock drains the dramatic possibilities with often frightening overtones, as the spectator comes to realize that the very same could happen to him, if he fell into such a situation. The musician, played with a stark kind of impersonation by Fonda, is positively identified by several of the holdup victims, and other circumstances arise which seem to prove his guilt.

•

WRONG MAN, THE
1993, 110 mins, US Ⓥ ⊙ col
Dir Jim McBride ***Prod*** Alan Beattie, Chris Chesser ***Scr*** Michael Thoma ***Ph*** Affonso Beato ***Ed*** Lisa Churgin ***Mus*** Los Lobos ***Art*** Jeannine Oppewall
Act Rosanna Arquette, Kevin Anderson, John Lithgow, Jorge Cervera, Jr., Ernesto Laguardia, Robert Harper (Viacom)

A sultry sex-suspenser about gringos on the run south of the border, *The Wrong Man* teeters back and forth over the line between good, dirty genre fun and outright silliness.

A blue-eyed Yank in a white suit (Kevin Anderson) is in the wrong place at the wrong time, standing in a grubby room with a gun in his hand over a dead man who robbed him of his wallet. Rosanna Arquette and older hubby, John Lithgow, agree to let him hitch a ride, and Arquette immediately gets their guest heated up by frolicking topless in the surf. It's only a matter of time until they ignite.

Michael Thoma's script, from a story by Roy Carlson, is low on believability and high on goofy contrivance; there's so little realistically at stake that no tension is generated.

These deficiencies make it incumbent upon director Jim McBride to goose up matters however he can, which he does through a heavy dose of colorfully seedy atmosphere.

•

WUSA
1970, 114 mins, US ▭ col
Dir Stuart Rosenberg ***Prod*** Paul Newman, John Foreman ***Scr*** Robert Stone ***Ph*** Richard Moore ***Ed*** Bob Wyman ***Mus*** Lalo Schifrin ***Art*** Philip Jefferies
Act Paul Newman, Joanne Woodward, Anthony Perkins, Laurence Harvey, Pat Hingle, Don Gordon (Paramount)

WUSA has some serious liabilities, but for all of them it's a breath of fresh air.

Title derives from call letters of New Orleans radio station which spews forth the type propaganda regularly disciplined in real life by the Federal Communications Commission.

Script is not always lucid and director Stuart Rosenberg's pacing is numbed by needless Newman-Woodward scenes which drag pic.

The cynical profession of crowd manipulation and psychology is the primary plot line of Robert Stone's adaptation of his novel, *A Hall of Mirrors*, original title of film. Newman is a drifter with radio experience. His buddy, Laurence Harvey, a con-man mission preacher, sends him to the radio station dedicated to exposing "welfare chiselers" and other social evils.

As Newman's star rises, his affair with Woodward becomes strained; she, too, is a drifter but there was a chance of some happiness between the two.

•

WUTAI JIEMEI
(TWO STAGE SISTERS)
1965, 114 mins, China col
Dir Xie Jin ***Scr*** Lin Gu, Xu Jin, Xie Jin ***Ph*** Zhou Daming, Chen Zhenxiang ***Ed*** Zhang Liqun ***Mus*** Huang Zhun ***Art*** Ge Shicheng
Act Xie Fang, Cao Yindi, Feng Ji, Gao Yuansheng, Shen Fengjuan, Shangguan Yunzhu (Tianma)

Story spans fifteen years in the relationship of two young actresses. As a way of eluding authorities, one girl joins a group of traveling players and soon develops a close, sisterly, friendship with the daughter of troupe's manager.

After the manager's death, the young women go to Japanese-occupied Shanghai in 1941 and quickly become well-regarded thesps. By 1944, however, a rift occurs, with one coming under the influence of corrupt, Western-style gangster types and the other beginning to display revolutionary awareness. It all ends up in court as the two former friends confront each other and agonizingly let the truth come out.

Tale then jumps to the revolutionary China of 1950. One actress tracks down the other in the provinces and, after their emotional, remorseful reunion, pair makes a joint resolve in a classic final line—"Let us remold ourselves and always perform revolutionary operas."

Last section is fortunately the only one with overt political content, as all that comes before plays as respectable, reasonably complex drama sparked by occasional stylistic flourishes from director Xie Jin. Film is a mix of excellent location lensing and highly atmospheric interiors.

•

WUTHERING HEIGHTS
1939, 103 mins, US Ⓥ ⦿ b/w
Dir William Wyler ***Prod*** Samuel Goldwyn ***Scr*** Ben Hecht, Charles MacArthur ***Ph*** Gregg Toland ***Ed*** Daniel Mandell ***Mus*** Alfred Newman ***Art*** James Basevi
Act Merle Oberon, Laurence Olivier, David Niven, Flora Robson, Geraldine Fitzgerald, Donald Crisp (United Artists/Goldwyn)

Emily Brönte's novel tells a haunting tale of love and tragedy. Samuel Goldwyn's film version retains all of the grim drama of the book. It's heavy fare throughout.

Merle Oberon has two loves—a pash for stableboy Laurence Olivier and love of the worldly things David Niven can provide. After unsuccessfully goading Olivier to make something of himself, girl turns to Niven. Olivier disappears, to return several years later with a moderate fortune. Oberon keeps her smouldering passions under control, and Olivier marries Niven's sister (Geraldine Fitzgerald) for spite. Story is unfolded through retrospect narration by Flora Robson, housekeeper in the early-Victorian mansion of Yorkshire.

Direction by William Wyler is slow and deliberate, accenting the tragic features of the piece.

1939: Best B&W Cinematography

NOMINATIONS: Best Picture, Director, Actor (Laurence Olivier), Supp. Actress (Geraldine Fitzgerald), Screenplay, Art Direction, Original Score

•

WUTHERING HEIGHTS
1971, 105 mins, UK/US Ⓥ col
Dir Robert Fuest ***Prod*** James H. Nicholson, Samuel Z. Arkoff ***Scr*** Patrick Tilley ***Ph*** John Coquillon ***Ed*** Ann Chegwidden ***Mus*** Michel Legrand ***Art*** Philip Harrison
Act Anna Calder-Marshall, Timothy Dalton, Julian Glover, Ian Ogilvy, Hilary Dwyer, Judy Cornwell (American International)

Wuthering Heights is a competent, tasteful, frequently even lovely re-adaption of Emily Brönte's Gothic, mystical love story. But the brooding tension, the electric passion of two lovers compelled to an inevitable tragedy is not generated.

Anna Calder-Marshall as Catherine is quite good, giving the role a wild young animal look and spirit. Timothy Dalton is also a technically capable actor, with a dark gypsy brooding look that is appropriate for Heathcliff. But his sullen, almost sulking portrayal is often that of a hurt boy rather than a man seething with resentment and a frustrated passion, a powder keg ready to explode.

Director Robert Fuest and cameraman John Coquillon compose striking and beautiful pictures, but without creating the sort of mood and tension the film needs.

•

WUTHERING HEIGHTS
1992, 105 mins, UK/US Ⓥ ⦿ col
Dir Peter Kosminsky ***Prod*** Mary Selway ***Scr*** Anne Devlin ***Ph*** Mike Southon ***Ed*** Tony Lawson ***Mus*** Ryuichi Sakamoto ***Art*** Brian Morris
Act Juliette Binoche, Ralph Fiennes, Janet McTeer, Sophie Ward, Simon Shepherd, Simon Ward (Paramount)

U.K.-lensed *Wuthering Heights* is a by-the-numbers telling of the Emily Bronte classic that's as cool as a Yorkshire moor, weakened by a wobbly central perf by Gallic thesp Juliette Binoche.

Third big-screen outing of the yarn lacks the visual stylization and intense performances of the 1939 classic, and the believability of the 1970 British remake. It serves up the full work (unlike the truncated 1939 version) but misses out on atmosphere and passion.

Halting in her delivery, and with an accent that's every which way, Binoche misses the spontaneity and feeling at the heart of the twin roles. Screen newcomer Ralph Fiennes makes a good stab at the Heathcliff part, more successful in the later scenes as the embittered power player than in the early ones as the glowering bad boy.

Sprawling story, set across two generations, moves at quite a clip to get everything in. Pacing, as well as look, is more akin to an edited-down TV miniseries than a developed feature. Filmmakers seem over-bound by fidelity to the novel and unwilling to take risks: a late-on fantasy sequence of Heathcliff reunited with the dead Cathy has some of the romantic panache badly missing elsewhere.

•

W. W. AND THE DIXIE DANCEKINGS
1975, 91 mins, US col
Dir John G. Avildsen ***Prod*** Steve Shagan ***Scr*** Thomas Rickman ***Ph*** James Crabe ***Ed*** Richard Halsey, Robbe Roberts ***Mus*** Dave Grusin ***Art*** Larry Paull
Act Burt Reynolds, Conny Van Dyke, Jerry Reed, Ned Beatty, James Hampton, Don Williams (20th Century-Fox)

Burt Reynolds stars as a 1950s con artist who turns straight through an odyssey with a country music band. The script establishes Reynolds as a footloose character, generating money by suave robberies of gas stations, where he divides the loot with the underpaid attendants in return for their giving phony descriptions.

Sherman G. Lloyd, redneck oil magnate, concludes that a devil is amok, so he recruits Art Carney, a lawman turned fundamentalist preacher, to find the evil spirit. This plot angle alternates with Reynolds's growing attachment to the Dixie Dancekings, a c&w band headed by Jerry Reed.

•

WYATT EARP
1994, 189 mins, US Ⓥ ⦿ ▭ col
Dir Lawrence Kasdan ***Prod*** Jim Wilson, Kevin Costner, Lawrence Kasdan ***Scr*** Dan Gordon, Lawrence Kasdan ***Ph*** Owen Roizman ***Ed*** Carol Littleton ***Mus*** James Newton Howard ***Art*** Ida Ransom
Act Kevin Costner, Dennis Quaid, Gene Hackman, Jeff Fahey, Mark Harmon, Michael Madsen (Tig/Kasdan/Warner)

Wyatt Earp is a stately, handsome, grandiose gentleman's Western that evenhandedly but too doggedly tries to tell more about the famous Tombstone lawman than has ever before been put onscreen.

Tale of the laconic, steel-nerved marshal who prevailed in the legendary gunfight at the OK Corral has always been a screen natural. By contrast with Disney's brassily entertaining *Tombstone*, which came out six months earlier, this new picture is serious and self-important. Everything that could be implied is underlined, especially by the bombastic, faux ennobling score.

After losing his pregnant young wife to typhoid, Wyatt (Kevin Costner) instantly goes into a drunken, criminal downward spin. With his father's help, he pulls himself out of his stupor, and lands in Wichita, where he almost inadvertently becomes a lawman.

From here on, pic begins treading on somewhat more familiar territory, as Bat and Ed Masterson enter the story, followed by Doc Holliday (Dennis Quaid), the gunslinging dentist and "sporting man" who forms an unlikely partnership with the brothers Earp in trying to tame lawlessness in the boom towns Dodge City and Tombstone.

The showdown between the Earps and Holliday on one side and the Clantons and McLaurys on the other is staged with a brutal, startlingly realistic quickness.

Standout performance, in what is invariably a showy role, comes from Quaid as Doc Holliday. Pic jumps to life whenever he's around.

[In 1995, a 212-min. special expanded version was issued on home video.]

1994: NOMINATION: Cinematography

X
(UK: THE MAN WITH THE X-RAY EYES)

1963, 80 mins, US Ⓥ col

Dir Roger Corman ***Prod*** Roger Corman ***Scr*** Robert Dillon, Ray Russell ***Ph*** Floyd Crosby ***Ed*** Anthony Carras ***Mus*** Les Baxter ***Art*** Daniel Haller

Act Ray Milland, Diana van der Vlis, Harold J. Stone, Don Rickles, John Hoyt (American International/Alta Vista)

Basically it's the plot where the scientist tampers with the unknown and is severely punished in the end. Ray Milland is a doctor who has devised a drug that he thinks will allow men's eyes to see infinitely more.

He tries it on himself when he is refused a grant to continue experiments on animals. He at first is put out of commission by a blinding light, but then can see inside human tissue and through clothes. This permits him to visit a party where the women are nude to him. Things get worse as he kills a friend inadvertently, forcing the doctor to hide out in a carnival as a mindreader. A girl who believes in him tries to help and they go off to work on some antidote.

There are many interesting comic, dramatic and philosophical ideas touched on, but treated only on the surface. However, director Roger Corman keeps this moving and Ray Milland is competent as the doomed man. Special effects on his prism-eye world, called Spectarama, are good if sometimes repetitive.

•

XANADU

1980, 92 mins, US Ⓥ ⊙ col

Dir Robert Greenwald ***Prod*** Lawrence Gordon ***Scr*** Richard Christian Danus, Marc Reid Rubel ***Ph*** Victor J. Kemper ***Ed*** Dennis Virkler ***Mus*** Barry DeVorzon ***Art*** John W. Corso

Act Olivia Newton-John, Gene Kelly, Michael Beck (Universal)

Xanadu is truly a stupendously bad film whose only salvage is the music. Olivia Newton-John plays a muse, first seen with her eight sisters painted on a wall. Suddenly, they all come alive, with glowing stuff all around them, singing and zipping hither and yon, apparently looking for a script that will never be found.

Newton-John's task is to inspire Michael Beck in his work as an artist. For this she stops glowing and he thinks she's a real girl, despite the sun dress she wears with roller skates and rags around both ankles.

But love is threatening and Newton-John decides it's best if she goes back into the painting on the wall, so she starts glowing again and bids Beck farewell. But he gets up a head of steam and skates into the wall after her and winds up somewhere near Mount Olympus.

•

X-FILES, THE

1998, 120 mins, US Ⓥ ⊙ ▭ col

Dir Rob Bowman ***Prod*** Chris Carter, Daniel Sackheim ***Scr*** Chris Carter ***Ph*** Ward Russell ***Ed*** Stephen Mark ***Mus*** Mark Snow ***Art*** Christopher Nowak

Act David Duchovny, Gillian Anderson, Martin Landau, Armin Mueller-Stahl, Blythe Danner, William B. Davis (Ten Thirteen/20th Century-Fox)

One of the few television-derived films to hit the bigscreen while the show is still on the air, *The X-Files* falls somewhere in between standing on its own feet as a real movie and merely being a glorified TV episode refitted for theaters. [Despite] the $60 million budget and $25 million-plus marketing ticket, film [from a screen story by producer-creator Chris Carter and Frank Spotnitz] lacks the excitement, scope and style expected from event movies.

Made largely by hands with long experience on the five-year program, pic begins in TV-teaser fashion with three startling suspense scenes. Initial sequence reveals a ferocious creature killing a caveman; second hook shows a young boy falling into a pit and being infected by a black goo that gets under his skin and darkens his eyes. Third and most elaborate deals with the discovery of a bomb at the Federal Building in Dallas.

FBI agent Fox Mulder (David Duchovny) is approached in a bar by a conspiracy theorist (Martin Landau) who

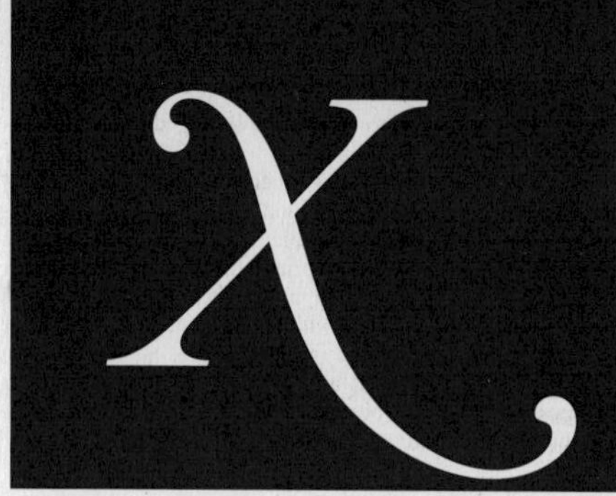

claims the explosion was triggered by powerful interests desirous of covering up the actual causes of death of the black-eyed boy and four infected rescue workers. Later, he hints at the existence of a "secret government" poised to take over after it unleashes a plague upon the world.

Thus resumes Mulder and Scully's (Gillian Anderson) ongoing probe into the presence of aliens on Earth. Director Rob Bowman knows his way around *X-Files* territory after helming 25 episodes, but he relies far too much on dark alleys and rain-slicked streets for atmospherics, and on shocks achieved by quick cutting, out-of-the-blue attacks and blasts of sound. Climax, set in a vast chamber under the Antarctic ice, unfolds as a rather routine action finale with unfulfilled James Bondian aspirations.

Duchovny and Anderson's appeal carries over intact to bigscreen, and the real threat of the team's separation, as well as their near-miss in the bedroom, will provide apprehension and tingles for their devoted fans.

•

XIA NU
(A TOUCH OF ZEN)

1969, 177 mins, Taiwan col

Dir King Hu ***Prod*** Hsia Wu Liang-fang ***Scr*** King Hu ***Ph*** Hua Hui-ying, Chou Yeh-hsing ***Ed*** King Hu ***Mus*** Wu Ta-chiang ***Art*** Chen Shang-lin

Act Hsu Feng, Shih Chun, Pai Ying, Tien Peng, Hsueh Han, Roy Chiao (Union)

Kung fu gets its just recognition as a genre that can be used in a serious, thoughtful film and have its exciting, dynamic effects and drive undiminished. Taking place in the fourteenth-century Ming Dynasty, tale is of a few people fighting the tyranny of a vicious secret police who have supreme power without any recourse to law.

Measured, leisurely tale [from the short story *The Gallant Girl* in the collection *Strange Tales from a Chinese Studio* by Pu Sung-ling] first sets up the atmosphere in a small town where the local scribe and artist gets mixed up in the intrigues of the higher echelons when he befriends a girl living near him who turns out to be the daughter of a tortured and murdered nobelman killed by the secret police.

Into this comes a police spy who finds the girl, but is bested in combat, for she learned the martial arts while living in a Buddhist monastery when first saved from police henchmen. The battles, with their swirling airborne bodies, swishing sounds and balletic grace, serve as codas to this tale of love and tyranny.

Its grace, visual beauty and feeling for time and place evoke memories of when the Japan ese films of Kenji Mizgoguchi were unveiled at film fests. Add the use of symbolic violence as a metaphor for the life cycle to invoke filmmaker Akira Kurosawa too.

[Pic was originally released in Taiwan in two parts, in 1970 and 1973. Above review is of combined version first shown in competition at Cannes in 1975.]

•

XI YAN
(THE WEDDING BANQUET)

1993, 107 mins, Taiwan Ⓥ ⊙ col

Dir Ang Lee ***Prod*** Ted Hope, James Schamus, Ang Lee ***Scr*** Ang Lee, Neil Feng, James Schamus ***Ph*** Jong Lin ***Ed*** Tim Squyres ***Mus*** Mader ***Art*** Steve Rosenzweig

Act Winston Chao, May Chin, Mitchell Lichtenstein, Sihung Lung, Ah-leh Gua (CMPC)

A slickly mounted Gotham comedy about two gays who try to hoodwink the Chinese partner's parents with a phony marriage, *The Wedding Banquet* slides down easily even if it doesn't leave much aftertaste. The Taiwan-funded pic is a shallower work than helmer Ang Lee's first feature, *Pushing Hands*.

Central couple are Wai-tung (Winston Chao), a Taiwanese with a comfy lifestyle in Manhattan from real estate investments, and his white U.S. lover Simon (Mitchell Lichtenstein). To fend off his overseas mom's nagging to get married, Wai-tung agrees to a green-card deal with one of his tenants, ambitious but broke Wei-wei (May Chin), an illegal immigrant from Shanghai.

The proverbial hits the fan when Wai-tung's parents suddenly fly over from Taiwan to attend the marriage. A planned quickie at City Hall becomes a full-blown wedding banquet to satisfy Mom and Dad's expectations.

Most of this is smoothly done and scripted with plenty of incident, especially in the setpiece of the enormous wedding banquet (complete with Chinese rituals). Where the movie is less satisfying is in giving the characters enough depth for the climax to pay emotional dividends.

Chin, a popular singer/TV thesp in her native Taiwan, adds color and shape to an initially unsympathetic role. Newcomer Chao, a former model and flight attendant, is okay as the pig-in-the-middle.

•

X-MEN

2000, 104 mins, US Ⓥ ⊙ ▭ col

Dir Bryan Singer ***Prod*** Lauren Shuler-Donner, Ralph Winter ***Scr*** David Hayter ***Ph*** Newton Thomas Sigel ***Ed*** Steven Rosenblum, Kevin Stitt, John Wright ***Mus*** Michael Kamen ***Art*** John Myhre

Act Hugh Jackman, Patrick Stewart, Ian McKellen, Famke Janssen, James Marsden, Halle Berry, Anna Paquin, Rebecca Romijn-Stamos (Donners' Co/Bad Hat Harry/20th Century Fox)

When Marvel Comics mastermind Stan Lee (co-creator of Spider-Man, the Fantastic Four, Incredible Hulk, etc.) first cooked up the *X-Men* series in 1963, its mutants vs. normals conflict was a provocative, usually serious-minded commentary on concurrent civil rights struggles. The anti-bias message seems less novel, if no less relevant, now, and with relatively little insight into mainstream society here (this "near future" looks pretty much like right now), the intended atmosphere of paranoia and prejudice doesn't come across vividly.

Unlike, say, Tim Burton's *Batman* films, *X-Men* lacks directorial and visual design cohesion, and a singular, haunted emotional center to make its brooding tenor more than just a fashionable attitude. Much of this is due to the X-Men concept itself. Since there appears no clear rhyme, reason or limitation to the mutants' all-over-the-map gifts, they seem much less an oppressed minority than a jumble of comic-book conceits. Aussie thesp Hugh Jackman gets enough screen time to create an admirably cynical, melancholy character. But Anna Paquin has little to do except whimper for help, while the other Xs (most notably Halle Berry and James Marsden) are highlighted so little their individual powers scarcely register.

Patrick Stewart and Ian McKellen exercise their RSC-trained perfect diction but little else; casting of these routine nemeses could have been switched with no discernible loss or gain. Visually, most striking figure is Rebecca Romijn-Stamos' memorably sexy, lethal vixen.

Though fast paced and reasonably entertaining, pic never exhilarates or finds a distinctive style in successive action segs, which range from straight-up road chases to f/x extravaganzas. Whether large scale or small, effects are well handled but their technological crazy quilt (morphing, animation, models, etc.) underlines the overall lack of stylistic/narrative focus. Most dismaying misstep is the so-what conclusion, which provides zero resolution or lingering suspense.

•

X, Y AND ZEE
SEE: ZEE & CO.

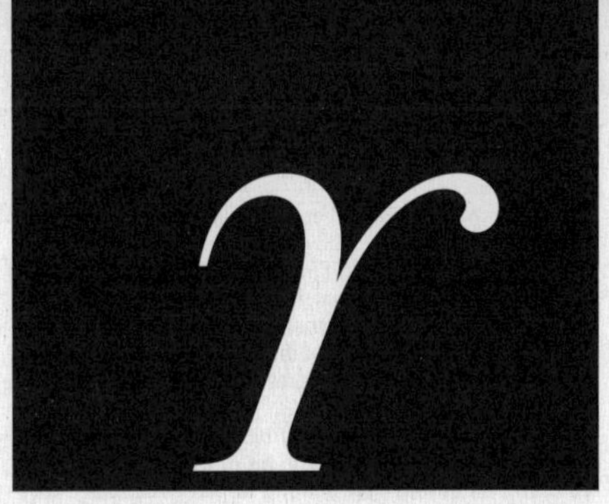

YAKUZA, THE
1975, 112 mins, US Ⓥ ⦿ ▭ col
Dir Sydney Pollack ***Prod*** Sydney Pollack ***Scr*** Paul Schrader, Robert Towne ***Ph*** Okazaki Kozo, Duke Callaghan ***Ed*** Fredric Steinkamp, Thomas Stamford, Don Guidice ***Mus*** Dave Grusin ***Art*** Stephen Grimes
Act Robert Mitchum, Ken Takakura, Brian Keith, Herb Edelman, Richard Jordan, Kishi Keiko (Warner)

The Yakuza is a confused and diffused film which bites off more than it can artfully chew. Robert Mitchum stars as a private eye returning to Japan to unravel some international crime matters, as well as his long-ago love affair.

The result is an uneasy and incohesive combination of an oriental Mafia story overlaid on a formula international business swindle, mixed up with a twenty-years-later update of *Sayonara*.

Mitchum is hired by old World War II army buddy Brian Keith, now a successful shipping executive, to rescue daughter Lee Chirillo from some Japanese hoods holding her for an alleged default on a business deal.

Ken Takakura, who owes Mitchum a favor from a generation back, must honor the request to infiltrate the mob.

•

YANGTSE INCIDENT
THE STORY OF H.M.S. AMETHYST
(US: BATTLE HELL)
1957, 113 mins, UK Ⓥ b/w
Dir Michael Anderson ***Prod*** Herbert Wilcox ***Scr*** Eric Ambler ***Ph*** Gordon Dines ***Ed*** Basil Warren ***Mus*** Leighton Lucas ***Art*** Ralph Brinton
Act Richard Todd, William Hartnell, Akim Tamiroff, Donald Houston, Keye Luke, Sophie Stewart (Everest)

Story [based on the book by Lawrence Earl and an idea by associate producer Franklin Gollings] is of the *Amethyst*, which, battered though not beaten, broke the Chinese Communist blockade and rejoined the British fleet. The *Amethyst* is shown sailing up the Yangtse, headed for Nanking on a lawful mission delivering supplies to the British Embassy. Suddenly, without warning, the Red shore batteries open fire and the frigate, after a heavy engagement, is grounded in the mud.

All attempts to persuade the British to issue an apology for "unprovoked aggression" are resolutely turned down, and both sides play a waiting game until the British commander decides to run for it.

Vivid battle scenes have been magnificently handled. The on-board scenes are genuine enough too, as the *Amethyst* was reprieved from the breaker's yard to allow producer Herbert Wilcox to use it in the film.

There's a high standard of acting by an all-round cast, led by Richard Todd as the commander who takes over after the captain is killed in the first engagement.

•

YANK AT OXFORD, A
1938, 100 mins, UK b/w
Dir Jack Conway ***Prod*** Michael Balcon ***Scr*** Malcolm Stuart Boylan, Walter Ferris, George Oppenheimer ***Ph*** Harold Rosson ***Ed*** Margaret Booth, Charles Frend ***Mus*** Hubert Bath, Edward Ward
Act Robert Taylor, Maureen O'Sullivan, Lionel Barrymore, Vivien Leigh, Edmund Gwenn, Griffith Jones (M-G-M)

Robert Taylor brings back from Oxford an entertaining rahrah film which is full of breathless quarter-mile dashes, heartbreaking boat race finishes and surefire sentiment—Metro's first British-made film under Hollywood supervision and with Hollywood principals and director.

Some of the opening sequences were made on the West Coast and pasted to what was shot in England. Taylor, Lionel Barrymore, Maureen O'Sullivan, Harold Rosson, cameraman, and Jack Conway and his directorial crew crossed the Atlantic. Their efforts were supported by British film and stage players, and Michael Balcon, formerly production head of Gaumont-British, acted as producer.

It is reported that the film players never were permitted within the sacred precincts of Oxford university, which is unimportant from a picture viewpoint as the architectural reproductions have been carefully and effectively photographed.

What Conway has caught is the humor of student life at the university. This is the background for Taylor's adventures, the wall against which a cocky Yank bounces his somewhat enlarged head, eventually regaining his poise a better and tamed human being. [Original story by Leon Gordon, Sidney Gilliatt and Michael Hogan, based on an idea by John Monk Saunders.]

Teamed to these sometimes hilarious adventures is a sentimental story which tells of Taylor's liking for O'Sullivan, whose brother is a rival in undergraduate affairs.

Edmund Gwenn as the Dean of Cardinal College, one of the Oxford group, does a standout. Griffith Jones is an English boy, and gives a sincere and earnest performance. O'Sullivan and her diction fit nicely into ensemble, and Vivien Leigh, as a college vamp, has looks and a way about her.

•

YANKEE DOODLE DANDY
1942, 126 mins, US Ⓥ ⦿ b/w
Dir Michael Curtiz ***Prod*** Hal B. Wallis (exec.) ***Scr*** Robert Buckner, Edmund Joseph ***Ph*** James Wong Howe ***Ed*** George Amy ***Mus*** Ray Heindorf (arr) ***Art*** Carl Jules Weyl
Act James Cagney, Joan Leslie, Walter Huston, Richard Whorf, Irene Manning, Jeanne Cagney (Warner)

Yankee Doodle Dandy is rah-rah, no matter how you slice it. It's a tribute to a grand American gentleman of the theatre—George M. Cohan—whose life and songs are glorified by Warner Bros.; and it's a tribute, perhaps even more so, to all show business.

James Cagney does a Cohan of which the original George M. might well be proud.

That [original story writer] Robert Buckner, and his coscripter, Edmund Joseph, jazzed up a little of the latter-day chronology is beside the point. That Cohan was cocky and conceited as the kid star of *Peck's Bad Boy*, in which he clicked at thirteen; that he remained close to Jerry Cohan, Nellie Cohan and sister Josie (so well played by the star's real-life sister, Jeanne Cagney); that his string of successes never upset this lovely and loving picture, are all part of a human, appealing story of one of the great theatrical families of all times.

1942: Best Actor (James Cagney), Scoring of a Musical Picture, Sound Recording

NOMINATIONS: Best Picture, Director, Supp. Actor (Walter Huston), Original Story, Editing

•

YANKEE IN KING ARTHUR'S COURT, A
SEE: A CONNECTICUT YANKEE IN KING ARTHUR'S COURT

•

YANK IN LONDON, A
SEE: I LIVE IN GROSVENOR SQUARE

•

YANK IN THE R.A.F., A
1941, 97 mins, US Ⓥ b/w
Dir Henry King ***Prod*** Darryl F. Zanuck ***Scr*** Darrell Ware, Karl Tunberg ***Ph*** Leon Shamroy ***Ed*** Barbara McLean ***Mus*** Alfred Newman (dir.) ***Art*** Richard Day, James Basevi
Act Tyrone Power, Betty Grable, John Sutton, Reginald Gardiner, Donald Stuart, Morton Lowry (20th Century-Fox)

Picture neatly mixes the adventures of cocky and carefree Tyrone Power, former airline pilot, with the inner workings and flights of the RAF squadrons during the hectic times of the German blitz against the Low countries and France. Producer Darryl F. Zanuck (who also authored the original as "Melville Crossman") sidesteps overloading the picture with flying sequences and bombing expeditions [photographed in England by Ronald Neame, Jack Whitehead and Otto Kanturek; directed by Herbert Mason].

In flying a training ship to Canada, Power enlists as pilot to ferry bombers to England. On his first trip, he meets former sweetheart (Betty Grable) a Texas girl performing in a night club and member of the ambulance reserve. Power pursues his former attention, and enlists in the RAF for fighter duty.

Power clicks solidly as the happy-go-lucky American pilot sure of his abilities with both planes and women. He handles the role with a lightly nonchalant attitude which will catch wide audience attention. Grable grooves excellently as the girl who fully realizes Power's inconsistencies, but finally breaks down.

1941: NOMINATION: Best Special Effects

•

YANKS
1979, 141 mins, UK Ⓥ ⦿ col
Dir John Schlesinger ***Prod*** Joseph Janni, Lester Persky ***Scr*** Colin Welland, Walter Bernstein ***Ph*** Dick Bush ***Ed*** Jim Clark ***Mus*** Richard Rodney Bennett ***Art*** Brian Morris
Act Richard Gere, Lisa Eichhorn, Vanessa Redgrave, William Devane, Rachel Roberts, Annie Ross (CIP/Universal)

Director John Schlesinger has done a beautiful job with both cast and craft in *Yanks*, a multiple love story set in England in World War II. Yet little that's exciting ever happens in the picture.

The British director, working with his own and the personal recollections of writers Colin Welland [original story writer] and Walter Bernstein, vividly recreates the atmosphere in a small English village inundated by thousands of American troops prepping for the invasion of Europe.

At one end of the extreme, Vanessa Redgrave and William Devane struggle to maintain a platonic friendship while both are deprived of their spouses. At the other, Chick Vennera and Wendy Morgan rush to bed immediately, with little initial concern for what lies beyond the war. The lovers and both parents are played excellently and Schlesinger and crew have created an extravagantly authentic period setting.

•

YAO A YAO YAO DAO WAIPO QIAO
(SHANGHAI TRIAD)
1995, 108 mins, China/France Ⓥ ⦿ col
Dir Zhang Yimou ***Prod*** Jean-Louis Piel ***Scr*** Bi Feiyu ***Ph*** Lu Yue ***Ed*** Du Yuan ***Mus*** Zhang Guangtian ***Art*** Cao Jiuping
Act Gong Li, Li Baotian, Li Xuejian, Shun Chun, Wang Xiaoxiao, Jiang Baoying (Shanghai/Alpha/UGC Images/La Sept

In its bold take on a subgenre that's every bit as resonant as '30s U.S. gangster pix, Zhang Yimou's seventh feature is as assured and attention-grabbing as his 1988 bow *Red Sorghum*. Poised somewhere between the visual flamboyance of that movie and the interior tension of the later *Raise the Red Lantern*, *Triad* oozes a confidence that carries the viewer almost without pause to its shocking climax and ironic close.

The picture—a stylized but gripping portrait of mob power play and lifestyles in 1930 Shanghai—went through a tortuous production history, sparked by the uproar over Zhang's *To Live*—competing in 1994 at Cannes without Peking's official "permission." With Zhang temporarily banned from making offshore-funded pix, *Triad* was officially reclassified as a local production for filming to proceed.

The script, originally a straightforward version of Li Xiao's novel *Gang Law*, also went through various changes. Those included actress Gong Li's role being beefed up and a change of perspective in which events are viewed through the eyes of a young kid.

Covering eight days in the fortunes of Shanghai's most powerful triad, yarn starts with the arrival from the countryside of young Tang Shuisheng (Wang Xiaoxiao), a naive member of the Tang clan who's placed under the care of Uncle Liu (Li Xuejian).

In his first day, Shuisheng sees almost every aspect of the closed, violent world—from a gang execution in a warehouse, through a visit to the family's nightclub where songbird Xiao (Gong), mistress of the triad boss (Li Baotian), is strutting her stuff, to a tour of the boss's mansion during a major gang powwow, and finally to the house where Xiao lives and Shuisheng is to work.

The script's boldest move is to go for a seemingly lopsided approach that makes big production numbers out of events that have little bearing on the main storyline. As in Greek tragedies, all the important events are actually taking place offstage—as we finally learn with a wallop at the end.

In her seventh movie for Zhang, Gong more than holds her own as the tramp-cum-singer, directly aping acting styles of the period.

•

YEARLING, THE
1946, 134 mins, US Ⓥ ⦿ col
Dir Clarence Brown ***Prod*** Sidney Franklin ***Scr*** Paul Osborn ***Ph*** Charles Rosher, Leonard Smith, Arthur Arling ***Ed*** Harold F. Kress ***Mus*** Herbert Stothart ***Art*** Cedric Gibbons, Paul Groesse
Act Gregory Peck, Jane Wyman, Claude Jarman, Jr., Chill Wills, Forrest Tucker, Margaret Wycherly (M-G-M)

Marjorie Kinnan Rawlings's 1938 Pulitzer prizewinning novel is the heartwarming story of good earth, family ties and the love of the eleven-year-old Jody Baxter for the faun which he is compelled to put out of his life as it becomes a yearling.

The Florida scrub country is the locale of the Baxters, and the story focuses on Gregory Peck and Jane Wyman in the fight for their very existence, while raising meagre patches of crops and also their offspring Jody (Claude Jarman, Jr.). The lad becomes a man, for all his meagre years, in a great love and effort to ward off destruction of his pet yearling, albeit it be at the kindly hands of his parents.

All done in a minor key, the underplaying is sometimes too static but, just as the interest lags, director Clarence Brown injects another highlight. The underlying power is impressive.

1946: Best Color Cinematography, Art Direction, Honorary (Claude Jarman, Jr., outstanding child actor)

NOMINATIONS: Best Picture, Director, Actor (Gregory Peck), Actress (Jane Wyman), Editing

•

YEAR MY VOICE BROKE, THE
1987, 103 mins, Australia Ⓥ ⦿ col

Dir John Duigan ***Prod*** George Miller, Doug Mitchell, Terry Hayes ***Scr*** John Duigan ***Ph*** Geoff Burton ***Ed*** Neil Thumpston ***Mus*** Christine Woodruff (co-ord.) ***Art*** Roger Ford

Act Noah Taylor, Loene Carmen, Ben Mendelsohn, Graeme Blundell, Lynette Curran, Bruce Spence (Kennedy Miller)

Setting is a small country town (pic was shot in Braidwood, NSW) in 1962. Danny (Noah Taylor) and Freya (Loene Carmen) have been friends from childhood: his parents run the local pub, hers the local cafe. Danny is confused and troubled because Freya, though she's the same age he is, is maturing far more rapidly. She falls heavily for Trev (Ben Mendelsohn), an older, hyperactive football coach.

Things turn out badly: Freya gets pregnant, Trev gets into trouble with the law. Danny tries to help his friends, but an old scandal involving Freya's mother, who died giving birth to her, surfaces, causing more distress.

All of this is handled by John Duigan, who penned the original screenplay, with insight and understatement. The characters are memorable ones, and beautifully played by the three young newcomers, with Noah Taylor especially effective as the lovesick Danny. Supporting roles are played by a fine roster of familiar Aussie thesps.

•

YEAR OF LIVING DANGEROUSLY, THE
1982, 114 mins, Australia/US Ⓥ ⦿ ▭ col

Dir Peter Weir ***Prod*** Jim McElroy ***Scr*** David Williamson, Peter Weir, C. J. Koch ***Ph*** Russell Boyd ***Ed*** Bill Anderson ***Mus*** Maurice Jarre ***Art*** Herbert Pinter

Act Mel Gibson, Sigourney Weaver, Linda Hunt, Michael Murphy, Bill Kerr, Noel Ferrier (McElroy & McElroy/M-G-M)

Peter Weir's *The Year of Living Dangerously*, is a $6 million adaptation of Christopher Koch's novel, set in Indonesia in 1965 in the turbulent months leading to the fall of the Sukarno government.

Mel Gibson limns a young Australian journalist on his first posting as a foreign correspondent. Wide-eyed and innocent, he is befriended by an astute Chinese-Australian cameraman, a dwarf who seeks to manipulate people as deftly as he handles shadow puppets.

Here is an astonishing feat of acting by New Yorker Linda Hunt, cast by Weir because he could not locate a short male actor to fit the bill. A bizarre, yet touching, romantic triangle develops between Gibson, Hunt, and Sigourney Weaver as a British Embassy official.

Having laid the groundwork, Weir hits the action button. Gibson learns that the Communists are bringing in arms for a coup against Sukarno and in broadcasting the story blows a confidence from Weaver, who rejects him.

Filming in the Philippines, and then Sydney, where the crew was forced to repair after receiving threats from the Islamic community, Weir and his crew expertly recreate the squalor, poverty, noise, heat and emotion of the pressure cooker that was Indonesia in 1965.

1983: Best Supp. Actress (Linda Hunt)

•

YEAR OF THE COMET
1992, 89 mins, US Ⓥ ⦿ ▭ col

Dir Peter Yates ***Prod*** Peter Yates, Nigel Wooll ***Scr*** William Goldman ***Ph*** Roger Pratt ***Ed*** Ray Lovejoy ***Mus*** Hummie Mann ***Art*** Anthony Pratt

Act Penelope Ann Miller, Timothy Daly, Louis Jourdan, Art Malik, Ian Richardson, Ian McNeice (Castle Rock)

Harvested from the same field as *Romancing the Stone*, this wine-soaked comedy-adventure never really ferments, in part due to a lack of chemistry between its romantic leads. William Goldman's first original script since *Butch Cassidy and the Sundance Kid* and his first collaboration with director Peter Yates since the 1972 *Hot Rock*, the film's problems begin with its title, a reference to the vintage of an invaluable 150-year-old bottle of wine that sounds more like a sci-fi thriller.

That bottle brings together a wine auctioneer's daughter (Penelope Ann Miller), who discovers it, and a Texan millionaire's troubleshooter (Tim Daly), assigned to bring it back to his boss. Unfortunately, Miller has the bad luck of finding the bottle in a Scottish castle where a trio of researchers, led by Louis Jourdan, are inconveniently torturing a scientist to obtain a secret formula, putting them in pursuit of the bottle.

Miller finds herself stranded by Goldman's screenplay, in which her character is a little bit of everything (spinster, repressed, ambitious) yet nothing in particular. Daly doesn't fare much better as a dapper leading man, who proves full of surprises.

•

YEAR OF THE DRAGON
1985, 136 mins, US Ⓥ ⦿ ▭ col

Dir Michael Cimino ***Prod*** Dino De Laurentiis ***Scr*** Oliver Stone, Michael Cimino ***Ph*** Alex Thomson ***Ed*** Francoise Bonnot ***Mus*** David Mansfield ***Art*** Wolf Kroeger

Act Mickey Rourke, John Lone, Ariane, Leonard Termo, Ray Barry, Caroline Kava (De Laurentiis)

Year of the Dragon [based on the novel by Robert Daley] is never as important as director Michael Cimino thinks it is, but there's a fair amount of solid action and gunplay, all set securely in the intricate, mysterious enigma of New York's Chinatown and its ties to worldwide drug-dealing.

Unquestionably, Cimino's eye for detail and insistence thereon has paid off in his impressive recreation of Chinatown at producer Dino De Laurentiis's studios in North Carolina. Crammed with an array of interesting characters, including the extras in the background, *Dragon* brims with authenticity.

Assigned to Chinatown to clear up a problem of murderous youth gangs, Mickey Rourke quickly proves to be one of those lone renegade cops that fiction favors more than real-life. Beyond the teen toughs, Rourke wants to undo a criminal system rooted in a culture for thousands of years.

Beyond the color and the corpses, though, Cimino fails to focus on an idea and stick with it. He ends up playing with significant thoughts in between awkward lessons in Chinese history, losing most of them as they filter through half-baked resentments Rourke has left over from the Vietnam war. Performances, though, are generally excellent and *Dragon* certainly never drags.

•

YEAR OF THE GUN
1991, 111 mins, US Ⓥ ⦿ col

Dir John Frankenheimer ***Prod*** Edward R. Pressman ***Scr*** David Ambrose ***Ph*** Blasco Giuarto ***Ed*** Lee Percy ***Mus*** Bill Conti ***Art*** Aurelio Crugnola

Act Andrew McCarthy, Valeria Golino, Sharon Stone, John Pankow, Mattia Sbragia, George Murcell (Pressman)

Year of the Gun is a competent but routine thriller [based on Michael Mewshaw's book] about a young American novelist in 1978 Rome who accidentally hits upon a terrorist kidnaping plot.

Andrew McCarthy plays an expatriate U.S. journalist who's doing quite nicely in Rome with a rich Italian g.f. (Valeria Golino) and the insistent attentions of a beautiful and nervy American photojournalist (Sharon Stone). Trouble is, Stone wants in on a book she believes he's writing about the Red Brigades terrorists, and McCarthy knows he can't pull the book off unless it stays a secret. Stone leaks it to a mutual friend (John Pankow), a university prof who leaks it to the Red Brigades, and suddenly the two Yanks are imperiled.

Stone adds some interest as the provocative photographer, though one never knows what makes her character such a maniacal careerist. McCarthy is merely servicable in the lead. Director John Frankenheimer and cinematographer Blasco Giuarto do a standout job with the taut, hysterical action scenes.

•

YEARS WITHOUT DAYS
SEE: CASTLE ON THE HUDSON

•

YELLOW BALLOON, THE
1953, 80 mins, UK b/w

Dir J. Lee Thompson ***Prod*** Victor Skutezky ***Scr*** Anne Burnaby, J. Lee Thompson ***Ph*** Gilbert Taylor ***Ed*** Richard Best ***Mus*** Philip Green ***Art*** Robert Jones

Act Andrew Ray, Kathleen Ryan, Kenneth More, Bernard Lee, William Sylvester, Sydney James (Associated British/Marble Arch)

This British pic is a depressing study of an innocent child who falls into the clutches of a modern Fagin and is forced to steal from his own parents before being used as a decoy in an holdup which leads to murder. J. Lee Thompson directs, with entire dramatic content focussed on the youngster (Andrew Ray). The boy plays the part almost on a single key but his almost static expression captures the story's spirit.

With most of the screen time allotted to the youngster, the adult cast members have comparatively minor roles. The roles of the kid's parents are effectively sustained by Kathleen Ryan and Kenneth More, while William Sylvester does a smooth job as the crook. Lesser roles are distinctively filled, with Sydney James giving a rich performance as a cockney trader.

•

YELLOW CANARY, THE
1943, 95 mins, UK b/w

Dir Herbert Wilcox ***Prod*** Herbert Wilcox ***Scr*** Miles Malleson, DeWitt Bodeen ***Ph*** Max Green

Act Anna Neagle, Richard Greene, Nova Pilbeam, Albert Lieven, Margaret Rutherford (Imperator)

Direction, cast, production and camerawork are so good it is a pity the suspensive story [from an original by D. M. Bower] is not on the same plane of excellence. There is smart comedy dialog and plenty of action throughout. It has a "mystery" start with red herring trails that lead up blind alleys, necessitating the return each time to a new start. The result is an overplus of the aforesaid "mystery."

Anna Neagle plays Sally Maitland, daughter of an aristocratic British family. She has achieved notoriety for her prewar association with the Nazis. Public antagonism to her is so violent that she is practically forced to leave Britain. It is a role altogether different from her previous film appearances. Her costar is Richard Greene, and principal support comes from Nova Pilbeam, Lucie Mannheim and Albert Lieven.

•

YELLOW CANARY, THE
1963, 93 mins, US ▭ b/w

Dir Buzz Kulik ***Prod*** Maury Dexter ***Scr*** Rod Serling ***Ph*** Floyd Crosby ***Ed*** Jodie Copelan ***Mus*** Kenyon Hopkins ***Art*** Walter Simmonds

Act Pat Boone, Barbara Eden, Steve Forrest, Jack Klugman, Jesse White, Steve Harris (20th Century-Fox)

Hero of the piece is Pat Boone, a surly singing idol whose apparently loose ways have him on the brink of divorce with his wife (Barbara Eden), who remains only for the sake of their infant. The baby is suddenly kidnapped and three people are needlessly murdered by the kidnapper, who turns out to be one of Boone's sycophants, his psychotic bodyguard (Steve Forrest).

Rod Serling's screenplay, from Whit Masterson's novel, *Evil Come, Evil Go*, is reasonably strong in dramatic anatomy, but limp and fuzzy in character definition. The characters are thrust at the audience, with little or no attempt to illustrate the nature of their odd dispositions toward society and each other.

Boone warbles several old standards pleasantly. Eden is her usual curvaceous self, and gets off a number of very convincing screams and shrieks. Forrest is an okay heavy, Jack Klugman likable as a frustrated gendarme. Kenyon Hopkins has composed a racy, pulsating score to underline the action.

•

YELLOW EARTH
SEE: HUANG TUDI

•

YELLOW ROLLS-ROYCE, THE
1964, 122 mins, US ▭ col

Dir Anthony Asquith ***Prod*** Anatole de Grunwald ***Scr*** Terence Rattigan ***Ph*** Jack Hildyard ***Ed*** Frank Clarke ***Mus*** Riz Ortolani ***Art*** Elliot Scott, Vincent Korda, William Kellner

Act Rex Harrison, Jeanne Moreau, Shirley MacLaine, George C. Scott, Ingrid Bergman, Omar Sharif (M-G-M)

With a sizzling international cast, the team of Anatole de Grunwald, Anthony Asquith and Terence Rattigan have produced a sleek piece of entertainment in *The Yellow Rolls-Royce*. It is handsomely tinted, lushly lensed and though leisurely in its approach, this has style, humor and some effective thesping.

Film consists of three separate anecdotes, linked only by ownership of the elegant Phantom II Rolls-Royce auto.

First one concerns Lord Frinton (Rex Harrison), a Foreign Office big shot who buys the car as an anni gift for his wife (Jeanne Moreau) and discovers her and a Foreign Office minion (Edmund Purdom) in a passionate embrace in its backseat.

Much mileage later, in the 1930s, the car is bought in Italy by gangster George C. Scott as a present for his current moll, hatcheck gal Shirley MacLaine. The dame falls for a street photographer (Alain Delon) and again the comfortable, accommodating back seat of the Rolls is pressed into service for l'amour.

Finally, in 1942, the Phantom II is acquired by Ingrid Bergman playing a hectoring American woman. Hitler is attacking Yugoslavia and she becomes involved when she finds that she has smuggled an archpatriot (Omar Sharif) across the border.

•

YELLOW ROSE OF TEXAS, THE

1944, 69 mins, US Ⓥ b/w

Dir Joseph Kane ***Scr*** Jack Townley ***Ph*** Jack Marta ***Ed*** Tony Martinelli ***Mus*** Morton Scott (dir.) ***Art*** Russ Kimball

Act Roy Rogers, Dale Evans, Grant Withers, Harry Shannon (Republic)

Roy Rogers is a secret investigator for an insurance company trying to locate a payroll stolen five years ago. He obtains a job singing on the showboat *Yellow Rose of Texas* from Betty Weston (Dale Evans), whose father was convicted and imprisoned for the robbery. When Sam Weston (Harry Shannon) breaks jail to clear himself of the framed charge, Rogers helps get the evidence that traps the real culprit.

The musical sequences are pleasant and well staged, enhanced by some good singing and dancing, and there is enough action to satisfy those who like excitement in their westerns.

Rogers acts and sings in his usually accomplished style, and Evans makes a decorative addition to the film with her fine singing and dancing, while Bob Nolan and the Sons of the Pioneers do well with their numbers. Rest of the cast is competent.

•

YELLOW SKY

1948, 99 mins, US b/w

Dir William A. Wellman ***Prod*** Lamar Trotti ***Scr*** Lamar Trotti ***Ph*** Joe MacDonald ***Ed*** Harmon Jones ***Mus*** Alfred Newman ***Art*** Lyle R. Wheeler, Albert Hogsett

Act Gregory Peck, Anne Baxter, Richard Widmark, Robert Arthur, John Russell, Harry Morgan (20th Century-Fox)

Setting for the story is the West of 1867 and the outdoor locations have been magnificently lensed as a telling backdrop for the dramatics. Lamar Trotti has put together an ace screenplay from a story by W. R. Burnett, given it dialog that rings true, and then proceeded with showmanly production guidance to make *Sky* a winner.

The direction by William A. Wellman is vigorous, potently emphasizing every element of suspense and action, and displaying the cast to the utmost advantage. There's never a faltering scene as sequence after sequence is unfolded at a swift pace.

Plot outline traces a group of outlaws who rob a bank, flee across a desert and seek refuge in a ghost mining town. There they find a girl and her grandfather, learn they have gold and seek to steal it.

There's many an earthy touch in the script and an understanding of the hungers of men; some for gold, some for women, and some for love and understanding.

Peck shines as the outlaw leader and matching dramatic stride for stride with him is Baxter as the ghost-town girl. Widmark steps out in another of his coldblooded killer delineations as Peck's doublecrossing partner in crime.

•

YELLOWSTONE KELLY

1959, 91 mins, US col

Dir Gordon Douglas ***Prod*** [uncredited] ***Scr*** Burt Kennedy ***Ph*** Carl Guthrie ***Ed*** William Ziegler ***Mus*** Howard Jackson ***Art*** Stanley Fleischer

Act Clint Walker, Edward Byrnes, John Russell, Ray Danton, Andra Martin, Claude Akins (Warner)

Yellowstone Kelly is a well-made Western.

The story [from the book by Clay Fisher] concerns a fabled fur trapper, Kelly, who is on good terms with the Sioux Indians. He refuses to help the U.S. Cavalry's punitive expedition of 1876, but ultimately has to help the arrogant white men after they have been trounced by the righteous red men.

Director Gordon Douglas moves the story along with a speed sufficient to cover up weak plot points and extracts some solid characterizations not implicit in the script: Clint Walker, as Kelly the trapper, is a laconic, gargantuan woodsman; John Russell is a magnetically powerful and believable chief; Ray Danton's a handsome swine of a brave; Andra Martin is fetchingly and helplessly lovely as the Indian girl; and Edward Byrnes enlists sympathy as the tenderfoot.

•

YELLOW SUBMARINE

1968, 89 mins, UK Ⓥ ⊙ col

Dir George Dunning ***Prod*** Al Brodax ***Scr*** Lee Minoff, Al Brodax, Jack Mendelsohn, Erich Segal ***Mus*** The Beatles ***Art*** Heinz Edelmann (Apple/King/Subafilms)

This is a full-length animated cartoon in which the prime factor is the appearance of the Beatles in caricature form. Here are all the ingredients of a novel entertainment.

Story consists of a fantastic voyage in a yellow submarine thru sky and sea, manned by the skipper, and The Beatles, to Pepperland where the inhabitants are up against thugs known as the Blue Meanies.

Time travel, science fiction, outer space, monsters, war and their own idiom of pop music are all taken for a ride in figments of fevered imaginations during which the Beatles come up against some odd specimens and situations.

The Beatles's flat Merseyside tones make good contrast to the surrounding frenzy. Dialog is mostly puns and throwaway gags. It remains deliberately corny at times and never ventures out of its depth in flirtations with time, space and philosophy.

Unlike Disney, the film makes no concession to sentiment. Characters are mostly matter-of-fact, grotesque and antiheroic and tend to be harsh, angular and intro'd for shock effect rather than any winsome qualities.

•

YENTL

1983, 134 mins, US Ⓥ ⊙ col

Dir Barbra Streisand ***Prod*** Barbra Streisand, Rusty Lemorande ***Scr*** Jack Rosenthal, Barbra Streisand ***Ph*** David Watkin ***Ed*** Terry Rawlings ***Mus*** Michel Legrand ***Art*** Roy Walker

Act Barbra Streisand, Mandy Patinkin, Amy Irving, Nehemiah Persoff, Steven Hill, Allan Corduner (Barwood/United Artists)

Based on a short story by Isaac Bashevis Singer, *Yentl* tells the tale of a young Eastern European woman, circa 1904, who disguises herself as a boy in order to pursue her passion for studying holy scripture, an endeavor restricted exclusively to men in orthodox Jewish culture.

Moving from her native village and passing as a pubescent boy, Yentl has no problem in the scholarly world, but tragi-comic results stem from the romantic situation her presence creates. Befriended by her brash, attractive fellow student Avigdor, wonderfully played by Mandy Patinkin, Yentl falls in love with him.

When Avigdor is prevented from marrying his lovely fiancée Hadass (a china doll Amy Irving) through a technicality of religious law, Avigdor pushes Yentl to marry Hadass in his stead.

Songs by Michel Legrand, with lyrics by Alan and Marilyn Bergman, have been carefully planned as interior monologues for Yentl.

In league with ace cinematographer David Watkin, Streisand has created a fine-looking period piece, working on Czech locations and in English studios.

1983: Best Original Song Score

NOMINATIONS: Best Supp. Actress (Amy Irving), Art Direction, Song ("Papa, Can You Hear Me?", "The Way He Makes Me Feel")

•

YESTERDAY, TODAY AND TOMORROW

SEE: IERI, OGGI, DOMANI

•

YEUX SANS VISAGE, LES

(EYES WITHOUT A FACE; THE HORROR CHAMBER OF DR. FAUSTUS)

1959, 90 mins, France Ⓥ ⊙ b/w

Dir Georges Franju ***Prod*** Jules Borkon ***Scr*** Jean Redon, Georges Franju, Claude Sautet, Pierre Boileau, Thomas Narcejac, Pierre Gascar ***Ph*** Eugen Schufftan ***Ed*** Gilbert Natot ***Mus*** Maurice Jarre ***Art*** Auguste Capelier

Act Pierre Brasseur, Alida Valli, Edith Scob, Francois Guerin, Juliette Mayniel, Beatrice Altariba (Champs-Elysees/Lux)

Ambitious horror pic [from the novel by Jean Redon] depends on clinical operation scenes and the showing of deformed faces for its effect. It has some queasy scenes, but unclear progression and plodding direction give this an old-fashioned air.

Plastic surgeon daughter's face is destroyed in an accident. He gets young girls, lured in by a woman whose face he has saved, and tries to transpose their faces to that of his daughter. The operations fail.

Director Georges Franju has given this some suspense and not spared any shock details. But the stilted acting, asides to explain characters and motivations, and a repetition of effects lose the initial impact.

Lensing is excellent and technical effects okay. The editing is too leisurely and lacking in snap for this type of film.

•

YIELD TO THE NIGHT

(US: BLONDE SINNER)

1956, 100 mins, UK Ⓥ b/w

Dir J. Lee Thompson ***Prod*** Kenneth Harper ***Scr*** John Cresswell, Joan Henry ***Ph*** Gilbert Taylor ***Ed*** Richard Best ***Mus*** Ray Martin ***Art*** Robert Jones

Act Diana Dors, Yvonne Mitchell, Michael Craig, Marie Ney, Geoffrey Keen, Liam Redmond (Associated British)

Diana Dors plays a heavy dramatic role in *Yield to the Night*, which calls for a drastic de-glamorizing treatment.

The actual killing which leads the star to the death cell is depicted before the credit titles appear on the screen, but the events which led her to shoot at point-blank range at the woman who forced her lover to suicide are shown in a series of flashbacks.

Main footage is concentrated inside the condemned cell and the script illustrates the anguished mind of the girl, the wardresses who guard her night and day, the members of her family and the husband whom she deserted.

The script [from a novel by Joan Henry] succeeds in maintaining strong suspense.

In the main, Dors rises to the occasion and shows up as a dramatic actress better than anticipated. Yvonne Mitchell strikes the right sympathetic note as one of the wardresses, Michael Craig reveals a good presence as the lover and Marie Ney shows proper dignity and restraint as the prison governor.

•

YINGHUNG BUNSIK

(A BETTER TOMORROW)

1986, 98 mins, Hong Kong Ⓥ ⊙ col

Dir John Woo ***Prod*** Tsui Hark (exec.) ***Scr*** John Woo, Chan Hing-kai, Leung Suk-wah ***Ph*** Wong Wing-hang ***Ed*** Kam Ma ***Mus*** Joseph Koo ***Art*** Bennie Lui

Act Ti Lung, Leslie Cheung, Chow Yun-fat, Emily Chu, Waise Lee, Kent Tseng (Cinema City)

A contemporary cop-and-gangster action drama burdened with an excess of practically everything except sex, *A Better Tomorrow* is a contrived bang-bang thriller with overdone violence and bloodshed.

Chow Yun-fat, the glamor boy who's no longer afraid of being ugly, and perennial teenager Leslie Cheung, who at thirty looks like an overaged spoiled youth imprisoned in a mature body, both overact in this one. But Ti Lung shines in his comeback role as he maintains a silent masculine presence and believably underplays his portrayal of a reformed ex-gangster. He has laced his portrayal with inner strength and vulnerability, despite his overdressed look. The trio make a formidable team of urban misfits.

It's a fine vehicle for the return from Taiwan of ex-Golden Harvest contract director John Woo, who evidently has changed his style from light comedy to the "macho" genre. Film is about two brothers in conflicting roles, the outlaw and the cop. Kit (Cheung) is a dedicated policeman who blames his elder brother (Ti Lung) for their father's death and for obstructing his career in the police force.

Mark (Chow) is Ti Lung's ex-associate also betrayed by jealous subordinate Waise Lee in the counterfeit syndicate. After serving a jail term in Taiwan, repentant Ti Lung returns to Hong Kong to lead a new life. He realizes soon enough a man with a past will have difficulties adjusting to a normal life.

•

YINGHUNG BUNSIK II

(A BETTER TOMORROW II)

1987, 103 mins, Hong Kong Ⓥ ⊙ col

Dir John Woo ***Prod*** Tsui Hark (exec.) ***Scr*** John Woo ***Ph*** Wong Wing-hang ***Ed*** [uncredited] ***Mus*** Joseph Koo ***Art*** Andy Lee

Act Dean Shek, Ti Lung, Leslie Cheung, Chow Yun-fat, Kwan San, Emily Chu (Film Workshop/Cinema City/Golden Princess)

This is a highly commercial, overblown but entertaining followup to the 1986 attraction that broke box-office records and reaffirmed the gangster genre's popularity in Cantonese cinema.

Superb actor Chow Yun-fat (his character Mark died in the last reel of Part I), returns as a twin brother called Ken, who lives in New York. Kid brother of Ti Lung, young cop Leslie Cheung is still stubborn as ever and dies a hero's death.

This time Ti Lung is forced by circumstances to join an international counterfeit syndicate, his way out from prison. His brother (Cheung) is secretly assigned to collect evidence by the police department against the illegal activities of the Lung Ship Building Co. headed by Dean Shek.

Villain Ko plans to have Shek murdered to take over his shipyard and full control of the profitable trading. Somehow, Shek is saved from assassination attempts and smuggled to New York, where Chow is running a Chinese restaurant.

The on-location Manhattan scenes are interesting. A deep friendship is developed between catatonic Shek and Ken, who both return to Hong Kong to set things right.

●

YINGHUNG BUNSIK III
TSIKYEUNG TSI GO
(A BETTER TOMORROW III; AKA: LOVE AND DEATH IN SAIGON)

1989, 108 mins, Hong Kong Ⓥ ⊙ col

Dir Tsui Hark ***Prod*** Tsui Hark (exec.) ***Scr*** Leung Yiu-ming, Tai Fu-ho ***Ph*** Wong Wing-hang ***Ed*** Tsui Hark, David Wu, Mak Tse-sin ***Mus*** Lowell Lo ***Art*** Luk Tse-fung

Act Chow Yun-fat, Anita Mui, Tony Leung Kar-fai, Saburo Tokito, Shek Kin, Maggie Cheung (Film Workshop/Golden Princess)

Admirers of John Woo's Hong Kong gangster blockbusters undoubtedly will be satisfied by this exotic prequel, though Tsui Hark has taken the series in a somewhat surprising direction with this entry, scaling down the action and tossing in a romantic subplot.

As the alternate title, *Love and Death in Saigon*, suggests, pic takes place in Vietnam (for the most part) during the chaotic withdrawal of U.S. troops in 1974. This ambitious setting gives Hark the opportunity to enlarge his canvas significantly and move away from the claustrophobic milieu of warring gangster clans defined in the first two films. Pic's basic plot follows the efforts of amiable yet deadly Hong Hong hustler Mark (Chow Yun-fat), who travels to Saigon to secure exit visas for his uncle and cousin. Needless to say, he doesn't accomplish this by standing in long lines at the customs office. Requiring large sums of cash for bribery, he becomes involved in smuggling U.S. currency with his cousin Mun (Tony Leung) and black-market temptress Kitty Chow (Anita Mui).

This scheme leads to the film's most spectacular action sequence when the trio is doublecrossed by a sleazy North Vietnamese Army sergeant and required to outgun what seems to be a full regiment of soldiers. Only cognoscenti of Hong Kong–style screen carnage can accurately imagine the outlandish scope of the violence that ensues.

In many ways, Mui emerges as the most memorable performer in the film. Even in her love scenes, she seems almost invulnerable. Topliner Chow is unusually subdued in this outing. The action scenes are subtle in comparison to the kill-fest that capped *A Better Tomorrow II*.

●

YINSHI NANNU
(EAT DRINK MAN WOMAN)

1994, 123 mins, Taiwan Ⓥ col

Dir Ang Lee ***Prod*** Hsu Li-kung ***Scr*** Ang Lee, James Schamus, Wang Hui-ling ***Ph*** Lin Jong ***Ed*** Tim Squyres ***Mus*** Mader ***Art*** Lee Fu-hsiung

Act Sihung Lung, Yang Kuei-mei, Wu Chien-lien, Gua Ah-leh, Sylvia Chang, Winston Chao (CMPC)

On the heels of the international success of *The Wedding Banquet*, Ang Lee has directed the ambitious and entertaining *Eat Drink Man Woman*. Again his focus is the family.

New tale centers on Chu (Sihung Lung), a master chef who's literally lost his sense of taste. The widower lives in Taipei with his three adult daughters—each of whom, consciously or otherwise, is just itching to leave the nest. Add to this Chu's seemingly inevitable marriage to Madame Liang (Gua Ah-leh) next door, and the tangle of relationships becomes extremely dense.

As one of the daughters notes, "We communicate by eating." In fact, the ritual of preparing food is a means to avoid interaction. That's been the father's modus operandi for years.

The technical sheen and visual assurance of Lee's third film is a quantum leap from earlier credits. He also elicits deeper, more textured performances from his actors.

1994: NOMINATION: Best Foreign Language Film

●

YOJIMBO
(THE BODYGUARD)

1961, 110 mins, Japan Ⓥ ⊙ ▭ b/w

Dir Akira Kurosawa ***Prod*** Tomoyuki Tanaka, Ryuzo Kikushima (execs.) ***Scr*** Ryuzo Kikushima, Akira Kurosawa ***Ph*** Kazuo Miyagawa ***Mus*** Masaru Sato ***Art*** Yoshiro Muraki

Act Toshiro Mifune, Eijiro Tono, Tatsuya Nakadai, Isuzu Yamada, Daisuke Kato, Kamatari Fujiwara (Kurosawa/Toho)

Rousing, good story, told with vigor and visual excitement by Akira Kurosawa, and splendidly acted by Toshiro Mifune, this has ideal remake material for a Yank company. [Pic was in fact remade by an Italian company, as *Fistful of Dollars*, 1964.]

Tale set in 1800s concerns a wandering samurai who arrives in a village split into two rival and warring factions. He offers his services to one, then to the other gang leader. Lured by a big pay-off, he almost joins one side, only to learn they want to kill him once he's won the battle for them. Going over to the rivals, he starts a series of fights, duels, kidnappings, until he unselfishly frees some prisoners giving them his money.

Though this lacks the epic stature of *Seven Samurai*, Kurosawa here again shows his mastery of the medium. His choice of backdrop characters is also adroit and colorful, as is his ever-exciting use of the camera. Music by Masaru Sato rates a special nod for the way it keys the serio-comic tone of various sequences.

●

YOLANDA AND THE THIEF

1945, 108 mins, US Ⓥ ⊙ col

Dir Vincente Minnelli ***Prod*** Arthur Freed ***Scr*** Irving Brecher ***Ph*** Charles Rosher ***Ed*** George White ***Mus*** Lennie Hayton (dir.) ***Art*** Cedric Gibbons, Jack Martin Smith

Act Fred Astaire, Lucille Bremer, Frank Morgan, Mildred Natwick, Mary Nash, Leon Ames (M-G-M)

Metro has a musical story of virtue and the Divine in *Yolanda and the Thief*, but the result is not all it might have been. Arthur Freed produced with lavishness, and the casting, topped by Fred Astaire, Lucille Bremer and Frank Morgan, has an eye towards marquee values, but the basic yarn doesn't lend itself toward the screen.

This is the story of a Latin-American heiress who, after being brought up in a convent, assumes charge of her fortune upon coming of age. Her childhood, naturally one that saw her sheltered from the outer world, makes her easy prey for a fraud that a young American and his elderly confederate would play upon her to relieve her of her millions.

There's an idea in this yarn, but it only suggests itself. It becomes too immersed in its musical background, and the story is too leisurely in pace. A musical production number attempts to be symbolic, but only serves to waste too many moments of the over-long film. And the story itself, the way it's done, strains credibility.

●

YOU AND ME

1938, 90 mins, US b/w

Dir Fritz Lang ***Prod*** Fritz Lang ***Scr*** Virginia Van Upp ***Ph*** Charles Lang, Jr. ***Ed*** Paul Weatherwax ***Mus*** Boris Morros (dir.) ***Art*** Hans Dreier, Ernst Fegte

Act Sylvia Sidney, George Raft, Robert Cummings, Barton MacLane, Roscoe Karns, Harry Carey (Paramount)

Fritz Lang's *You and Me* is a curious cinematic adventure. Basically, it's boy-meets-girl [from an original story by Norman Krasna]. There's quite a bit of Rene Clair in *You and Me*. Lang tries to blend dramatic music with melodramatic action more than heretofore. It's a sort of cinematic Mercury theater, by way of Marc Blitzstein–Orson Welles, with European flavoring, also.

Opening montages dramatically discourse, in Kurt Weill's music with Sam Coslow's lyrics, that "You can't get something for nothing" and that "you've got to pay for it." The montage shots of jewels, perfumes, travelog impressions or epicurean delicacies visually illustrate the premise.

Then it pans into Morris' department store which Harry Carey, as Morris, runs on a rehabilitation basis. Some 50 of his 2,500 employees are ex-convicts, out on parole, getting their comeback chance from Morris.

George Raft is one, and finally his parole is clear; he may even marry. He does. Sylvia Sidney is the girl. She too is a paroled penitentiary inmate, but Raft never knew that.

Raft's performance manifests a yen for restraint that's almost too restrained. It's a stoicism that doesn't quite jibe with the rest of it. Sidney's performance is competent in its earnestness to shield her past and not shatter the real amorous spark.

●

YOU BELONG TO ME

1941, 93 mins, US b/w

Dir Wesley Ruggles ***Prod*** Wesley Ruggles ***Scr*** Claude Binyon ***Ph*** Joseph Walker ***Ed*** Viola Lawrence ***Mus*** Frederick Hollander

Act Barbara Stanwyck, Henry Fonda, Edgar Buchanan, Roger Clark, Ruth Donnelly, Melville Cooper (Columbia)

Before the studio settled on this title, the film bore the far more descriptive, if not as romantic, caption *The Doctor's Husband*. As a spinner of comic notions, the theme suggested by the latter tag is a natural. They've been laughing at gags about the doctor and his jealous wife since way back and in this case the wife is the doctor to give it a reverse twist. So long as the story [by Dalton Trumbo] sticks to its comedy angle it beats a pleasant tattoo. But it veers off on a socio-economic tangent, the result being a sharp shift in mood and letdown in entertainment.

The performances of Barbara Stanwyck and Henry Fonda merit fulsome praise. Their strokes are keen and deft regardless of whether they're playing farce, romance, or the film's more serious moments.

Fonda, cast as a rich playboy who suffers a skiing fall and recovers with a medical wife, proves again that he is endowed with a high flair for comedy. He is equally surefire in the romantic passages, and there are enough of these to go around.

●

YOU CAN COUNT ON ME

2000, 109 mins, US Ⓥ ⊙ col

Dir Kenneth Lonergan ***Prod*** John Hart, Jeff Sharp, Larry Meistrich, Barbara De Fina ***Scr*** Kenneth Lonergan ***Ph*** Stephen Kazmierski ***Ed*** Anne McCabe ***Mus*** Lesley Barber ***Art*** Michael Shaw

Act Laura Linney, Mark Ruffalo, Rory Culkin, Matthew Broderick, Jon Tenney, Kenneth Lonergan (Shooting Gallery)

Writer-director Kenneth Lonergan's remarkably perceptive *You Can Count on Me* is a sensitive, intimate, enormously touching drama that explores the intricate bond between two adult siblings, orphaned as children when their parents were killed in a car accident.

Sammy's (Laura Linney) existence is conditioned by all the securities and limitations of small-town life, here defined by the chores of being a single mom and by the spiritual guidance provided by the church. Married and divorced at a young age, she's an overprotective mother to her 8-year-old son, Rudy (Rory Culkin). Sammy conceals from her son any info about his absentee father, but the curious, susceptible boy stubbornly harbors romantic notions about him. Her emotional involvement with Bob (Jon Tenney), a good-hearted but not terribly exciting man, only partially fulfills her needs as a woman.

In contrast, brother Terry (Mark Ruffalo) leads a troubled, nomadic existence. Leaving a pregnant girlfriend behind, Terry comes home to borrow money. Essence of drama is the complex yet intimate friendship that wild Terry strikes with his lonely nephew. Against Sammy's instructions, Terry takes Rudy to the local bar to play pool, goes fishing with him and shares secrets with him.

The beauty of Lonergan's multilayered script lies in its subtle depiction of how Terry's presence inspires his sister to break out of her dull routines. Sammy throws herself into an adulterous affair with her stiff new bank manager, Brian (Matthew Broderick), uses foul language, smokes dope with Terry and confides in the priest (played by helmer) about her reckless escapades. In brief scenes that have strong cumulative power, director shows variations on traditional role-playing as well as role reversals, suggesting that the real child in the family is not Rudy but Uncle Terry. Refusing to take a moralistic approach, Lonergan allows all of his characters to stumble and then learn the consequences of their lapses in judgment.

The work and sex scenes between Sammy and her boss are schematic and don't always ring true, and Broderick's rigid interpretation (the film's only weak performance) makes things worse. While some of pic's secondary male roles are not as well developed as they could be, when the central triangle is center stage, which is most of the time, this deftly observed drama is utterly engaging, thanks to flawless turns by Linney, Ruffalo and Culkin.

●

YOU CAN'T HAVE EVERYTHING

1937, 100 mins, US Ⓥ b/w

Dir Norman Taurog ***Prod*** Laurence Schwab ***Scr*** Harry Tugend, Jack Yellen, Karl Tunberg ***Ph*** Lucien Andriot ***Ed*** Hansen Fritch ***Mus*** David Buttolph (dir.)

Act Alice Faye, Ritz Bros., Don Ameche, Charles Winninger, Gypsy Rose Lee, Rubinoff (20th Century-Fox)

Those Ritz Bros. are let loose in a wild and hilarious filmusical, one of the best of the series of this type which 20th Century-Fox has turned out. There are others in it too—Alice Faye, Don Ameche, Charles Winninger, Arthur Treacher, Tony Martin, Rubinoff and Louise Hovick (Gypsy Rose Lee, all dressed up).

Another backstage story and all the principals are familiar types of the theatre. This time the heroine (Faye) is not the prima donna, but a young dramatist of serious plays, who sells a script because of her good looks. Ameche is the successful Broadway librettist who persuades Winninger to make the investment. When her serious play is made the basis for a satiric musical, Faye returns to town to protest, and discovers herself the author of a hit.

The Ritz Bros. sing and dance in their underwear; they disguise themselves as scrub women and do a routine in the YWCA; they do a good floor number with Louis Prima, and his band; and they give Hovick excellent support in some amusing blackouts.

Five numbers are contributed by Mack Gordon and Harry Revel.

•

YOU CAN'T SLEEP HERE
SEE: I WAS A MALE WAR BRIDE

•

YOU CAN'T TAKE IT WITH YOU
1938, 126 mins, US Ⓥ ⦿ b/w
Dir Frank Capra ***Prod*** Frank Capra ***Scr*** Robert Riskin ***Ph*** Joseph Walker ***Ed*** Gene Havlick ***Mus*** Dimitri Tiomkin ***Art*** Stephen Goosson, Lionel Banks
Act Jean Arthur, Lionel Barrymore, James Stewart, Edward Arnold, Mischa Auer, Ann Miller (Columbia)

A strong hit on Broadway, *You Can't Take It with You* [by George S. Kaufman and Moss Hart] is also a big hit on film. This is one of the highest priced plays to be bought in history, Columbia having taken the rights for $200,000. Production brought negative cost to around a reported $1.2 million.

The comedy is wholly American: wholesome, homespun, human, appealing, and touching in turn. The wackier comedy side contrasts with a somewhat serious, philosophical note which may seem a little overstressed on occasion.

The Vanderhoff tribe is played appealingly but screwily, the antics of the polyglot combination of grandpa, daughter, son-in-law, grandchildren and hangers-on, including a meek adding-machine operator turned inventor, and a ballet teacher, being basically for creation of fun.

The romance between James Stewart and Jean Arthur is the keystone of the comedy. Other comedy elements are registered at the expense of Edward Arnold, the stuff-shirt banker, and his wife, played excellently by Mary Forbes. The link that is formed between the modest, homey Vanderhoff coterie and the very rich Kirbys, created principally through the romance of the Arthur-Stewart pair, is a bit unbelievable, but for the purposes of entertainment has license.

Arthur acquits herself creditably. Stewart is not a strong romantic lead opposite her, but does satisfactorily in the love scenes. Others are tops from Lionel Barrymore down.

1938: Best Picture, Director

NOMINATIONS: Best Supp. Actress (Spring Byington), Screenplay, Cinematography, Editing, Sound

•

YOU LIGHT UP MY LIFE
1977, 90 mins, US Ⓥ col
Dir Joseph Brooks ***Prod*** Joseph Brooks ***Scr*** Joseph Brooks ***Ph*** Eric Saarinen ***Ed*** Lynzee Klingman ***Mus*** Joseph Brook ***Art*** Tom Rasmussen
Act Didi Conn, Joe Silver, Michael Zaslow, Stephan Nathan, Melanie Mayron, Amy Letterman (Brooks)

You Light Up My Life has all the virtues and all the liabilities of a low-budget effort. There's an earnest sincerity in the story of washed-up juvenile comedienne Didi Conn working out an adult identity. There's also a lot of cutesy, cornball, convenient and compacted plotting.

As the burnt-out child of stage-father Joe Silver (both of them doing very well in characterization), she is headed for a dull marriage to Stephan Nathan when film producer Michael Zaslow sponsors her first breakthrough into the field of pop music. She falls for Zaslow, but his mind is on his own career.

Along the way, there are some "slices-of-life" scenes involving the teleblurb business (whence came producer-director Joseph Brooks), Jewish weddings, and also interactions between Conn and the men in her life which border on treacle. Production credits are okay.

•

YOU'LL LIKE MY MOTHER
1972, 93 mins, US col
Dir Lamont Johnson ***Prod*** Mort Briskin ***Scr*** Jo Heims ***Ph*** Jack A. Marta ***Ed*** Edward M. Abroms ***Mus*** Gil Melle ***Art*** William D. De Cinces
Act Patty Duke, Rosemary Murphy, Richard Thomas, Sian Barbara Allen, Dennis Rucker, Harold Congdon (Crosby/Universal)

You'll Like My Mother is a quietly intense thriller spotlighting excellent performances by Patty Duke and Rosemary Murphy. The film avoids explicit physical gore, instead stimulating intellectual and unseen menace.

The novel by Naomi A. Hintze has been adapted into a moody atmosphere script which carefully and logically piles puzzle and confusion on Duke, a pregnant widow who comes for a first-time visit to her mother-in-law (Murphy). The latter's cold, gushing and blasé attitude, compounded by a winter blizzard, a mentally retarded girl played by Sian Barbara Allen, and the presence of Richard Thomas, cast as a deranged rape-murderer relative, add up to a situation which finds an audience rooting for Duke and her nursing infant.

•

YOU'LL NEVER GET RICH
1941, 87 mins, US Ⓥ ⦿ b/w
Dir Sidney Lanfield ***Prod*** Samuel Bischoff ***Scr*** Michael Fessier, Ernest Pagano ***Ph*** Phillip Tannura ***Ed*** Otto Meyer ***Mus*** Morris Stoloff (dir.)
Act Fred Astaire, Rita Hayworth, Robert Benchley, John Hubbard, Osa Massen, Frieda Inescort (Columbia)

Story has Fred Astaire as a stager of a musical show for producer Robert Benchley. Latter, in making a pitch for affections of Rita Hayworth, gets in a jam with his wife, and has Astaire get him out of the predicament. Girl, with a crush on Astaire, is somewhat disillusioned by the proceedings, and gives him the heave-ho.

When Astaire is inducted into the selective service camp, Benchley makes a deal to conduct rehearsals and stage a show for the boys—in order to obtain services of Astaire in putting it on. There's plenty of serious and humorous by-play around the camp, with Astaire a permanent resident of the guardhouse, but it all works out when the show finally goes on.

Script is studded with humorous lines and situations, and despite a somewhat familiar ring, it's all sufficiently refurbished by Sidney Lanfield's direction to get over in good style. Lanfield keeps things moving consistently, and the song-and-dance routines are neatly spotted.

1941: NOMINATIONS: Best Scoring of a Musical Picture, Song ("Since I Kissed My Baby Goodbye")

•

YOUNG AMERICANS, THE
1993, 103 mins, UK Ⓥ ⦿ ▭ col
Dir Danny Cannon ***Prod*** Paul Trijbits, Alison Owen ***Scr*** Danny Cannon, David Hilton ***Ph*** Vernon Layton ***Ed*** Alex Mackie ***Mus*** David Arnold ***Art*** Laurence Dorman
Act Harvey Keitel, Iain Glen, John Wood, Terence Rigby, Keith Allen, Viggo Mortensen (PFE/Live/Working Title/Trijbits-Worrell

Harvey Keitel hits the mean, mixed-race streets of London in *The Young Americans*, a high-octane, in-your-face cop thriller that's got everything going for it except a well-rounded script. Director Danny Canon, 25, landed the movie on the strength of his 65-minute film school grad work, *Strangers*, shot in L.A. for $20,000 with aid from Propaganda Films.

Tone is set straightaway with a moody pre-credits sequence of mysterious young punks blowing away two mobsters outside the back-streets Temple nightclub. Enter NY-out-of-L.A. cop John Harris (Keitel), who's been seconded from the DEA as an "adviser" to London's boys in blue on the current spate of London clubland killings.

Harris suspects the real villain is psychotic Yank drugster Frazer (Viggo Mortensen), whom he's been trailing from the U.S. and who is trying to move in on the London drug scene. Harris persuades a young bartender at the Temple, Chris (Craig Kelly), to help him.

Pic's strength is its vivid sense of place and identity. Thanks to a reined-back perf, Keitel blends into rather than dominates the Brit ambience of gruff cops, multicolored youth and grungy, back-streets villainy. Where the pic's reach exceeds its grasp is in the script department.

•

YOUNG AND THE DAMNED, THE
SEE: LOS OLVIDADOS

•

YOUNG AND THE PASSIONATE, THE
SEE: I VITELLONI

•

YOUNG AND WILLING
SEE: THE WILD AND THE WILLING

•

YOUNG BESS
1953, 111 mins, US col
Dir George Sidney ***Prod*** Sidney Franklin ***Scr*** Jan Lustig, Arthur Wimperis ***Ph*** Charles Rosher ***Ed*** Ralph E. Winters ***Mus*** Miklos Rozsa ***Art*** Cedric Gibbons, Urie McCleary
Act Jean Simmons, Stewart Granger, Deborah Kerr, Charles Laughton, Kay Walsh, Guy Rolfe (M-G-M)

Margaret Irwin's fine book on the life and times of the girl who was to become England's Queen Elizabeth has been made into a remarkably engrossing motion picture. *Young Bess* is a romantic drama told against a Tudor setting. It is a human story, sensitively written, directed and played. Romance phases are rich in emotion; court intrigue conjures suspense, and there is a suggestion of action throughout.

The four-star bracketing of Jean Simmons, in the title role; Stewart Granger, the dashing, heroic Lord Admiral, Thomas Seymour; Deborah Kerr, the beautiful Catherine Parr; and Charles Laughton, the gross, pompous Henry VIII, insures splendid trouping.

Main story gets underway after opening sequence, a gem in itself, sets the stage for a flashback to the unhappy childhood of young Bess. It is not until gracious Catherine becomes queen that young Bess, now fifteen, takes up a more or less permanent residence in the palace, finding love and happiness with the queen and her little stepbrother, the sickly Edward. When Henry dies and the queen marries the Lord Admiral, young Bess conceals her own infatuation for the dashing hero, but her feelings are found out and used by the evil Ned Seymour, the admiral's brother. Miklos Rozsa's music score is fine, never once intruding too strongly on a dramatic scene, and it is full of little identifying melodies for the humorous touches in the script.

1953: NOMINATIONS: Best Color Costume Design, Color Art Direction

•

YOUNG BILLY YOUNG
1969, 89 mins, US col
Dir Burt Kennedy ***Prod*** Max E. Youngstein ***Scr*** Burt Kennedy ***Ph*** Harry Stradling, Jr. ***Ed*** Otho Lovering ***Mus*** Shelly Manne ***Art*** Stan Jolley
Act Robert Mitchum, Angie Dickinson, Robert Walker, David Carradine, Jack Kelly, John Anderson (Talbot-Youngstein/United Artists)

Standard western plot undergoes generally good polishing in this production, costarring Robert Mitchum and Angie Dickinson. Plenty of gunplay heightens appeal and Robert Walker joins stars in turning in realistic performances.

Burt Kennedy, who directed and scripted [from the novel *Who Rides with Wyatt* by Will Henry], could have tightened film for better effect. His climax lacks the suspense it should have carried and confrontation misses. On the whole, however, film progresses satisfactorily.

Narrative unfolds mostly in Lordsburg, where Mitchum takes on a marshal's job after he learns that his quarry may be found there. Walker, an ornery youngster who wants his way, is with him, leaving Mitchum to his own devices until he discovers that a dozen gunmen have arrived to mow down the marshal.

•

YOUNGBLOOD
1986, 109 mins, US Ⓥ ⦿ col
Dir Peter Markle ***Prod*** Peter Bart, Patrick Wells ***Scr*** Peter Markle ***Ph*** Mark Irwin ***Ed*** Stephen E. Rivkin, Jack Hofstra ***Mus*** William Orbit, Torchsong ***Art*** Alicia Keywan
Act Rob Lowe, Cynthia Gibb, Patrick Swayze, Ed Lauter, Jim Youngs, Fionnula Flannagan (United Artists/Guber-Peters)

Picture has a simple premise: Rob Lowe desperately wants to leave the hard life on his father's farm to join a minor league Canadian hockey team where he believes he will be the star player. His half-blind brother (Jim Youngs), who once played for the same team before he was injured, tells their dad (Eric Nesterenko) he'll do double-duty so Lowe can be free to try and fulfill his dreams.

Dad agrees and Lowe takes off. He is an innocent who, after less than a week, is seduced by his landlady (Fionnula Flanagan), ridiculed by his teammates and enamored of the first girl he meets (Cynthia Gibb)—the coach's daughter who becomes his girlfriend. Scenes on the ice look great and Lowe truly looks like the fast and accurate son-of-a-gun hockey player he's supposed to be.

•

YOUNG CASSIDY
1965, 107 mins, US col

Dir Jack Cardiff, John Ford **Prod** Robert D. Graff, Robert Emmett Ginna **Scr** John Whiting **Ph** Ted Scaife **Ed** Anne V. Coates **Mus** Sean O'Riada
Act Rod Taylor, Julie Christie, Edith Evans, Michael Redgrave, Flora Robson, Maggie Smith (M-G-M)

Young Cassidy, biopic of Irish playwright Sean O'Casey in his sprouting years based on his autobiography, *Mirror in My House*, is notable principally for the top-rating performance of Rod Taylor in title role. Story of a rebel who rises to literary greatness, like the majority of screen bio narratives, is episodic; in attempting to cover the many facets of career, film consequently lacks the cohesion necessary for a full dramatic enactment of a historic personality.

Originally started under John Ford's direction, but taken over in midstream by Jack Cardiff when illness forced Ford to withdraw, pic opens in 1911 Dublin during the troubled times of opposition to the British. It is a period when Cassidy—name given himself by O'Casey in his third-person writing—was feeling the stirrings of a talent which was to elevate him ultimately to the position of one of Ireland's great playwrights.

Taylor delivers a fine, strongly etched characterization, believable both in his romantic scenes and as the writer who comes up the hard way. Splendid support is afforded particularly by Maggie Smith, as his one love, but who leaves him so he can progress better without her.

•

YOUNG DOCTORS, THE

1961, 103 mins, US b/w
Dir Phil Karlson **Prod** Stuart Millar, Lawrence Turman **Scr** Joseph Hayes **Ph** Arthur J. Ornitz **Ed** Robert Swink **Mus** Elmer Bernstein **Art** Richard Sylbert
Act Fredric March, Ben Gazzara, Dick Clark, Ina Balin, Eddie Albert, Phyllis Love (Drexel/Millar-Turman)

The Young Doctors is an enlightening motion picture executed with restraint and clinical authenticity.

The screenplay, based on a novel by Arthur Hailey, is a generally brisk, literate and substantial piece of writing marked by a few soaring bursts of thought-provoking philosophical wisdom as regards life, death and love.

Essentially the story represents an idealistic clash between two pathologists, one (Fredric March) the vet department head whose ideals and perspective have been mellowed and blunted somewhat by years of red tape and day-to-day frustration; the other (Ben Gazzara), his new assistant, young, aggressive, up-to-date and meticulous in his approach to the job. The conflict is dramatically illustrated via two critical cases in which both are pretty intimately involved.

Veteran March creates a character of dimension and compassion. Gazzara plays with great reserve and intensity, another fine portrayal. Dick Clark is persuasive as a young intern, Eddie Albert outstanding as a dedicated obstetrician. Ina Balin experiences a few uncertain moments as a gravely ill young nurse in love with life in general and Gazzara in particular, but she comes through in the more demanding passages. Camerawork by Arthur J. Ornitz is pretty bold stuff.

•

YOUNG EINSTEIN

1988, 89 mins, Australia Ⓥ ⊙ col
Dir Yahoo Serious **Prod** Yahoo Serious, Warwick Ross, David Roach **Scr** David Roach, Yahoo Serious **Ph** Jeff Darling **Ed** Yahoo Serious **Mus** William Motzing, Martin Armiger, Tommy Tycho **Art** Steve Marr, Laurie Faen, Colin Gibson, Ron Highfield
Act Yahoo Serious, Odile Le Clezio, John Howard, Pee Wee Wilson, Su Cruickshank (Serious)

This wild, cheerful, off-the-wall comedy showcases the many talents of Australian satirist Yahoo Serious, who not only directed and plays the leading role, but also cowrote (from his own original story), coproduced, edited and handled the stunts. Quite a lot to take on for a first-time filmmaker.

Pic posits young Einstein as the only son of eccentric apple farmers from Australia's southern island, Tasmania. He has a fertile mind, and is forever discovering things: it's not his fault that, by 1905 when the film's set, gravity has already been discovered by someone else.

According to the film, Einstein discovers accidentally how to split the atom while experimenting methods of injecting bubbles into home-brewed beer. He sets off for mainland Australia (a comically lengthy journey) to patent his invention, and meets French genius Marie Curie (Odile Le Clezio) on a train; he also meets villain and patents stealer Preston Preston (John Howard), scion of a family of Perth entrepreneurs.

The entire production rests on the shoulders of its director/star. Fortunately Serious (born Greg Pead), a long-haired gangly clown, exhibits a brash and confident sense of humor, endearing personality, and a fondness for sight gags.

YOUNGER AND YOUNGER

1993, 99 mins, US Ⓥ ⊙ col
Dir Percy Adlon **Prod** Percy Adlon, Eleonore Adlon, Aziz Ojjeh **Scr** Percy Adlon, Felix O. Adlon **Ph** Bernd Heinl **Ed** Suzanne Fenn **Mus** Hans Zimmer, Bob Telson **Art** Steven Legler
Act Donald Sutherland, Lolita Davidovich, Brendan Fraser, Julie Delpy, Sally Kellerman, Linda Hunt (Pelemele/BR/Duckster/Leora

The iconoclastic oeuvre of Percy Adlon expands by another unusual human comedy with *Younger and Younger*. Superficially a family drama of an errant, philandering father, the yarn spins out from its simple premise into fantasy, music, black comedy and innumerable offbeat digressions. It's a mad, wild souffle served up by actors at the top of their form. While the film isn't quite a bull's-eye, it is chockablock with intriguing elements and echoes of Adlon's earlier *Bagdad Cafe*. His latest American microcosm is set in a storage facility where the forgotten and marginal mingle with the hoi polloi.

Jonathan Younger (Donald Sutherland) is the titular overseer of the activity, comporting himself in the manner of some exiled European royal. The real work falls upon his dowdy, badly neglected wife, Penelope (Lolita Davidovich). Jonathan seems to care only about their son, Winston (Brendan Fraser), who is studying economics in England. He dreams of Winston's graduation and subsequent return to carry on the family business.

Adlon, who cowrote the script with his son Felix, dots the story with numerous subplots and colorful characters. Sally Kellerman and Julie Delpy pop up as a mother and daughter who are the subject of media scrutiny when Kellerman's husband dies under curious circumstances. There is also considerable attention given a pipe organ located in the bowels of the establishment, rabbits and other flights of fancy.

•

YOUNG FRANKENSTEIN

1974, 108 mins, US Ⓥ ⊙ b/w
Dir Mel Brooks **Prod** Michael Gruskoff **Scr** Gene Wilder, Mel Brooks **Ph** Gerald Hirschfeld **Ed** John Howard **Mus** John Morris **Art** Dale Hennesy
Act Gene Wilder, Peter Boyle, Marty Feldman, Madeline Kahn, Cloris Leachman, Gene Hackman (20th Century-Fox)

Young Frankenstein emerges as a reverently satirical salute to the 1930s horror film genre.

The screenplay features Gene Wilder as the grandson of Baron Victor Frankenstein, creator of the monster. Wilder, an American medical college teacher, is lured back to Transylvania by old family retainer Richard Haydn. Wilder's assistant, the namesake descendant of Igor, is played by Marty Feldman.

Teri Garr is a curvaceous lab assistant, while Cloris Leachman is a mysterious housekeeper composite of Una O'Connor and Mrs. Danvers. Wilder's fussy fiancée Madeline Kahn turns up importantly in the final reels. Peter Boyle is the monster, an artistically excellent blend of malice, pity and comedy.

1974: NOMINATIONS: Best Adapted Screenplay, Sound

•

YOUNG GIRLS OF ROCHEFORT, THE

SEE: LES DEMOISELLES DE ROCHFORT

•

YOUNG GUNS

1988, 107 mins, US Ⓥ ⊙ col
Dir Christopher Cain **Prod** Joe Roth, Christopher Cain **Scr** John Fusco **Ph** Dean Semler **Ed** Jack Hofstra **Mus** Anthony Marinelli, Brian Banks **Art** Jane Musky
Act Emilio Estevez, Kiefer Sutherland, Lou Diamond Phillips, Charlie Sheen, Jack Palance, Terence Stamp (Morgan Creek)

Young Guns is a lame attempt at a brat pack *Wild Bunch*, executed without style or feel for the genre.

Meager efforts at offbeat characterization are made at the outset, as British gang ring-leader Terence Stamp seeks to better the lot of his renegade boys by encouraging them to read and call each other "gentlemen."

Stamp's early murder by town bigshots prompts quick retaliation by the trigger-happy kids, who are briefly deputized, but whose irresponsibility and inclination toward gunplay brands them as outlaws and sets in motion an irreversible chain of violence that inevitably leads to a fateful confrontation.

What this film has that few, if any, Westerns ever have had before is a hard-rock score. Music's every appearance on the scene throws one right out of the scene and serves to remind that this is a high-tech artifact of the late 1980s.

As Billy the Kid, Emilio Estevez is the nominal star here, but no one really shines.

•

YOUNG GUNS II

(UK: YOUNG GUNS II—BLAZE OF GLORY)

1990, 103 mins, US Ⓥ ⊙ ▭ col
Dir Geoff Murphy **Prod** Paul Schiff, Irby Smith **Scr** John Fusco **Ph** Dean Semler **Ed** Bruce Green **Mus** Alan Silvestri **Art** Gene Rudolf
Act Emilio Estevez, Kiefer Sutherland, Lou Diamond Phillips, Christian Slater, William Petersen, James Coburn (Morgan Creek)

Although it's more ambitious than most sequels, *Young Guns II* exhausts its most inspired moment during the opening credits and fades into a copy of its 1988 predecessor—a slick, glossy MTV-style western.

Even the film's one surprise—a wizened horseman emerging from the desert, circa 1950, to recount the tale of Billy the Kid—feels lifted from Arthur Penn's 1970 classic *Little Big Man*, all the way down to Emilio Estevez's hoarse, whispering narration.

Oater follows a stripped-to-the-bone storyline that picks up the adventures of Billy Bonney's Lincoln County gang a few years after the events in 1988's *Young Guns*. Told in flashback, the story essentially involves the gang's hell-bent rush toward the perceived safety of Mexico with a band of government men—headed by ally-turned-adversary Pat Garrett (William Petersen)—in hot pursuit.

Estevez, Kiefer Sutherland and Lou Diamond Phillips are back, but the rest of the gang is new, and the other characterizations prove disappointingly thin. Christian Slater has a nice recurring bit as a Gun with an inferiority complex over his lack of notoriety; Petersen cuts a striking figure as Garrett without providing much insight into his motives.

1990: NOMINATION: Best Song ("Blaze of Glory")

•

YOUNG HEARTS

SEE: PROMISED LAND

•

YOUNG IN HEART, THE

1938, 91 mins, US Ⓥ b/w
Dir Richard Wallace **Prod** David O. Selznick **Scr** Paul Osborn, Charles Bennett **Ph** Leon Shamroy **Ed** Hal C. Kern **Mus** Franz Waxman **Art** Lyle Wheeler
Act Janet Gaynor, Douglas Fairbanks, Jr., Paulette Goddard, Roland Young, Billie Burke, Richard Carlson (Selznick/United Artists)

This is a beautiful and deeply touching picture, skillfully adapted from I.A.R. Wylie's poignant magazine story.

Selznick originally sought Maude Adams for this film, and when that deal fell through, recruited Minnie Dupree from legit to make her screen debut as the gentle, endearing old heroine of the story.

The original ending of the picture was the same as in the Wylie story, with the death of the kindly old spinster. But it drew unfavorable audience reaction at several sneak previews on the West Coast, so Selznick called back the cast to make a happier denouement.

The Young in Heart takes its title from the little old woman whose pathetic eagerness for companionship touches the affections of a conniving and indolent family. When she meets them on a Paris train after they have been exposed and expelled from a Riviera resort, she is captivated by their tall tales of troubles and delighted with their courage in their predicament.

Under Richard Wallace's direction, the fragile story is never permitted to lapse into bathos. Acting of the entire cast is superb. Janet Gaynor and Douglas Fairbanks, Jr. sparkle as the pseudo-thick-skinned children of the worthless family, while Roland Young and Billie Burke are brilliant as the parents who are soft-hearted in spite of their worst intentions. Paulette Goddard hasn't much acting to do as a clear-eyed girl in love with Fairbanks, but she is an eye-filler.

•

YOUNG LIONS, THE

1958, 167 mins, US Ⓥ ⊙ ▭ b/w
Dir Edward Dmytryk **Prod** Al Lichtman **Scr** Edward Anhalt **Ph** Joe MacDonald **Ed** Dorothy Spencer **Mus** Hugo Friedhofer **Art** Lyle R. Wheeler, Addison Hehr
Act Marlon Brando, Montgomery Clift, Dean Martin, Hope Lange, May Britt, Barbara Rush (20th Century-Fox)

The Young Lions is a canvas of the Second World War of scope and stature. It's a king-sized credit to all concerned, from Edward Anhalt's skillful adaptation of Irwin Shaw's novel to Edward Dmytryk's realistic direction, and the highly competent portrayals of virtually everyone in the cast.

Marlon Brando's interpretation of Anhalt's modified conception of the young Nazi officer; Montgomery Clift, the drafted G.I. of Jewish heritage; Dean Martin as a frankly would-be draft-dodger until the realities of war catch up with him are standout all the way.

Hope Lange gives a sensitive performance as the New England girl opposite Clift, and Barbara Rush is properly more resourceful as Martin's romantic vis-à-vis. Even more vivid are the performances of Sweden's May Britt, making her U.S. film debut in the role of the cheating wife of the Nazi officer, latter capitally played by Switzerland's Maximilian (young brother of Maria) Schell, also making his Hollywood bow.

Dmytryk effectively highlights the human values on both the German and American home-fronts. It gravitates from the boot camp in the States to the fall of France, the North African campaign, the deterioration of the Third Reich, the smirking obsequiousness to the invading Yanks by the Bavarian town mayor when the G.I.s liberate the inhuman concentration camp, and the gradual disillusionment of the once ardent Nazi as symbolized by Brando.

The Anhalt screenplay captures shade and nuance of the role in the pithy, pungent dialog. The accent on romance is as strong as the war stuff. Underplaying is the keynote of virtually all the performances.

1958: NOMINATIONS: Best B&W Cinematography, Scoring of a Dramatic Picture, Sound

•

YOUNG LOVERS, THE

1954, 95 mins, UK b/w

Dir Anthony Asquith ***Prod*** Anthony Havelock-Allan ***Scr*** Robin Estridge, George Tabori ***Ph*** Jack Asher ***Ed*** Freddie Wilson ***Mus*** Benjamin Frankel ***Art*** John Howell, John Box

Act Odile Versois, David Knight, David Kossoff, Joseph Tomelty, Theodore Bikel, Paul Carpenter (Group)

The political conflict between East and West is brought home poignantly in this moving, sensitive romantic drama, directed with a sympathetic hand by Anthony Asquith and delicately interpreted by Odile Versois and newcomer David Knight.

It is a development of the elementary boy-meets-girl theme. In this case, however, the boy works in the code room of the American Embassy in London; the girl is the daughter of and secretary to the minister of an Iron Curtain legation. The girl finds she's being followed; the boy's telephone messages are being intercepted. Both the embassy and the legation fear that confidential information is getting into the hands of the wrong people, so the girl is ordered home and the boy is placed under arrest.

The plot unfolds tenderly by pinpointing the emotions of the young lovers without indulging in unnecessary politics, using rare touches of humor to relieve a tense situation with great skill.

Under Asquith's polished direction, the two leading players bring a genuine freshness to their roles and give point to the arty touches used by the megger to bring home the sensitive side of the story. [Script is credited to Robin Estridge and George Tabori, from an "original screenplay" by Tabori.]

•

YOUNG LOVERS, THE

1964, 110 mins, US b/w

Dir Samuel Goldwyn, Jr. ***Prod*** Samuel Goldwyn, Jr. ***Scr*** George Garrett ***Ph*** Joseph Biroc, Ellsworth Fredericks ***Ed*** William A. Lyon ***Mus*** Sol Kaplan ***Art*** Frank Wade

Act Peter Fonda, Sharon Hugueny, Nick Adams, Deborah Walley, Beatrice Straight, Malachi Throne (M-G-M)

Samuel Goldwyn, Jr.'s *The Young Lovers* has a lot of things going for it. While the story [from novel by Julian Halevy] about young, unwed parents-to-be is no shocker, the talk is frank and switch is on problems mainly of unwed father, rather than of mother.

Most awkward parts come during opening scenes, as love affair between college students Peter Fonda and Sharon Hugueny is slowly built up. Fonda has uncomfortable moments as an art student who intends to live free, bachelor life, and his voice doesn't carry conviction in several scenes. How much of this is attributable to direction (film is producer Goldwyn's first as a director as well) rather than lack of acting experience is difficult to assess.

Hugueny also suffers acting lapses, but scores by making apparent her three-step transition from shy teenager to passionate lover, and on to wiser, more mature young adult.

YOUNG MAN OF MUSIC

SEE: YOUNG MAN WITH A HORN

•

YOUNG MAN WITH A HORN
(UK: YOUNG MAN OF MUSIC)

1950, 111 mins, US b/w

Dir Michael Curtiz ***Prod*** Jerry Wald ***Scr*** Carl Foreman, Edmund H. North ***Ph*** Ted McCord ***Ed*** Alan Crosland, Jr. ***Mus*** Ray Heindorf (dir.)

Act Kirk Douglas, Lauren Bacall, Doris Day, Hoagy Carmichael, Juano Hernandez (Warner)

For the jazz devotee this is nearly two hours of top trumpet notes. For the regular filmgoer, it is good drama.

Kirk Douglas's single-minded concentration on a horn and the notes that come from it sets the character up for an eventual downfall, but after events carry him down to alcoholic skidrow, a happy ending rounds out the film.

Topnotch scripting job adapts the Dorothy Baker novel, and Michael Curtiz's direction misses no bets in walloping over all the drama and heart-tugs.

Douglas falls for Lauren Bacall and when the marriage that results falls apart, he hits the bottle and winds up a drunk, only to be saved by the wholesome affection that band canary Doris Day has had for him over the years.

•

YOUNG MR. LINCOLN

1939, 101 mins, US b/w

Dir John Ford ***Prod*** Darryl F. Zanuck ***Scr*** Lamar Trotti ***Ph*** Bert Glennon ***Ed*** Walter Thompson ***Mus*** Alfred Newman ***Art*** Richard Day, Mark-Lee Kirk

Act Henry Fonda, Alice Brady, Marjorie Weaver, Arleen Whelan, Richard Cromwell, Donald Meek (20th Century Fox/Cosmopolitan)

As the title implies, this deals with the Great Emanicipator's early days in New Salem, Ill., emphasizing the Civil War president's then penchant for inherent honesty, fearlessness, shrewdness, plus such homely qualities as being a champ rail-splitter mixed with an avid hunger for book larnin'.

As motion-picture entertainment, however, *Young Mr. Lincoln* is something else again. Fundamentally it resolves itself down to a courtroom drama. He's called upon to extricate Richard Cromwell and Eddie Quillan, as Matt and Adam Clay, following a murder rap.

Henry Fonda is capital in the highlight scenes where he languorously addresses the small group in front of the little Berry-Lincoln general store in New Salem, Ill.

With judicious eye to authenticity and dignity the major shortcoming of this Lincoln film is at the altar of faithfulness, hampered by the rather lethargic production and direction.

1939: NOMINATION: Best Original Story

•

YOUNG MR. PITT, THE

1942, 110 mins, UK b/w

Dir Carol Reed ***Prod*** Edward Black ***Scr*** Sidney Gilliatt, Frank Launder, Viscount Castlerosse ***Ph*** Freddie Young ***Mus*** Charles Williams

Act Robert Donat, Robert Morley, Phyllis Calvert, John Mills, Max Adrian, Felix Aylmer (20th Century-Fox)

There is so much to acclaim and so little with which to find fault in this production. There are over 150 speaking parts, all of them praiseworthily handled, and the overly generous 18th-century period details have seldom been better reproduced. It's a costly production all the way.

Story is based on the political career of William Pitt, Jr. (Robert Donat), who was Prime Minister of England at 24.

Robert Morley, who so frequently steals the show, again towers above the rest of the excellent cast. In the stellar role, Donat acts with meticulous earnestness and sincerity, but seemingly lacks inspiration. One seems to detect the mechanics of fine acting—a sort of straining to be convincing. In sharp contrast, John Mills, in a relatively minor role, is impressive without resorting to heroics.

•

YOUNG ONE, THE

1961, 94 mins, US/Mexico b/w

Dir Luis Bunuel ***Prod*** George P. Werker ***Scr*** Luis Buñuel, H. B. Addis [= Hugo Butler] ***Ph*** Gabriel Figueroa ***Ed*** Carlos Savage ***Mus*** Jesus Zarzosa ***Art*** Jesus Bracho

Act Zachary Scott, Key Meersman, Bernie Hamilton, Crahan Denton, Claudio Brook (Werker/Olmeca)

The Young One is an odd, complicated and inconclusive attempt to interweave two sizzling themes—race prejudice in the deep South and an almost *Lolita*-like sex situation with Tennessee Williams's overtones—into an engrossing melodramatic fabric. The offbeat project was lensed in Mexico.

"Travelin' Man," a short story by Peter Matthiessen, is the origin of the screenplay. The story takes place on an island wild-game preserve off South Carolina occupied by an unsavory gamekeeper (Zachary Scott) and a 13- or 14-year-old orphan girl whose handyman-grandfather has just expired. Into this potentially explosive scene drifts a hip-talking Negro (Bernie Hamilton) falsely accused of rape and on the run.

Scott is convincingly unpleasant, Hamilton equally believable and sympathetic. Key Meersman cuts a rather pitiful figure as the innocent, nymphet-like nature-girl creature involved helplessly in the emotional turmoil.

Luis Buñuel does an alert, perceptive job of directing, succeeding in getting the Carolina geographical flavor out of the Mexican location. But his vigorous efforts are lamentably diluted by the unsatisfactory nature of the story.

•

YOUNG ONES, THE
(US: IT'S WONDERFUL TO BE YOUNG)

1962, 108 mins, UK col

Dir Sidney J. Furie ***Prod*** Kenneth Harper ***Scr*** Peter Myers, Ronald Cass ***Ph*** Douglas Slocombe ***Ed*** Jack Slade ***Mus*** Stanley Black (dir.) ***Art*** John Howell

Act Cliff Richard, Robert Morley, Carole Gray, Richard O'Sullivan, Melvyn Hayes, The Shadows (Associated British)

Producer Kenneth Harper signed up a twenty-eight-year-old Canadian director, Sidney Furie; a slick choreographer, Herbert Ross; and Cliff Richard to play the hero.

The songs [mostly by Peter Myers and Ronald Cass], dancing and Furie's nimble direction keep the screenplay on zestful enough plane. Richard is the leader of a youth club whose humble little clubhouse is endangered when a millionaire property tycoon buys the land on which it is situated. Unbeknown to the other teenagers, the tycoon is Richard's father. They decide to fight him and this involves raising $4,000 to challenge the lease. It's decided the best way to do this is by taking over a derelict theatre to stage a show.

The choreography of Ross is agile and sharp. Musical supervisor Stanley Black has made best use of the musical side. Main fault of the film is that the screenplay and dialog are uneven.

However, Robert Morley, as the tycoon, does an impressive job in bringing some adult wit and irony to the screen. Richard is inexperienced as an actor, but has a pleasant charm and sings well within his range.

New dancing girl Carole Gray is a youthful delight, though she too is happier when enjoying the exuberance of the numbers than when having to act. Melvyn Hayes and Richard O'Sullivan offer some pleasantly shrewd comedy.

•

YOUNG POISONER'S HANDBOOK, THE

1995, 106 mins, UK/Germany col

Dir Benjamin Ross ***Prod*** Sam Taylor ***Scr*** Jeff Rawle, Benjamin Ross ***Ph*** Hubert Taczanowski ***Ed*** Anne Sopel ***Mus*** Robert Lane, Frank Strobel ***Art*** Maria Djurkovic

Act Hugh O'Conor, Antony Sher, Ruth Sheen, Roger Lloyd Pack, Charlotte Coleman, Paul Stacey (Mass/Kinowelt/Haut & Court)

An expressive piece of grotesquerie, *The Young Poisoner's Handbook* takes a darkly comic look at a sinister British lad who, in the 1960s, pursued "a career as a poisoner." Based on a true story, the film has a lively sense of style and is cuttingly satiric about established norms of British life and medical practise.

Fourteen-year-old chemistry genius Graham Young (Hugh O'Conor) lives with his father, step-mother and sister, all of whom are caricatured to the nth degree of hideousness. The dispassionate youngster slowly murders his stepmother with poisoned chocolates.

After poisoning his uncle as well, Graham is finally convicted of murder, landing him in a hospital for the criminally insane. There, the psychopath specialist Dr. Zeigler (Antony Sher) believes that Graham's outstanding intellect makes him a prime candidate for salvation. The parole board reintroduces him to society where in short order he resumes his "career" on a wider scale than before.

The true story has apparently been altered and reshaped in many particulars save for the basic essentials, but first-time director Benjamin Ross's intentions are the opposite of realistic. He displays considerable talent for waspish caricature, speedy point-making and sustaining focus. Acting is all at the service of Ross's cartoon-like approach.

•

YOUNG SAVAGES, THE

1961, 103 mins, US b/w

Dir John Frankenheimer ***Prod*** Pat Duggan ***Scr*** Edward Anhalt,

J. P. Miller **Ph** Lionel Lindon **Ed** Eda Warren **Mus** David Amram **Art** Burr Smidt
Act Burt Lancaster, Dina Merrill, Shelley Winters, Edward Andrews, Larry Gates, Telly Savalas (United Artists)

The Young Savages is a kind of non-musical East Side variation on *West Side Story*. It is a sociological crossword puzzle, a twisted riddle aimed at detection of the true motivation for juvenile crime, as set against the backdrop of New York's teeming East Harlem district in which neighborhood nationalities mobilize into youthful raiding parties at the drop of a psychotic frustration.

The picture is inventively, arrestingly directed by John Frankenheimer, with the aid of cameraman Lionel Lindon. Together they have manipulated the lens to catch the wild fury of gang pavement warfare; twisting, tilting, pulling way back, zeroing in and composing to follow and frame the excitement.

But there is nothing Frankenheimer can do to make the yarn itself—concocted out of a novel by Evan Hunter, *A Matter of Conviction*—stand tall as screen fiction. The story is that of three Italian lads (of 15, 16 and 17) who murder a blind Puerto Rican boy of 15, who is regarded as a top warlord of a rival gang. The case for the prosecution is taken over by scrupulous d.a.'s asst. Burt Lancaster, whose search for truth and justice, and familiarity with the law of the asphalt jungle (he grew up there) leads him to make a valiant courtroom stand on behalf of the boys he is supposed to be trying to convict.

•

YOUNG SCARFACE
SEE: BRIGHTON ROCK

•

YOUNG SHERLOCK HOLMES
(UK: YOUNG SHERLOCK HOLMES AND THE PYRAMID OF FEAR)

1985, 109 mins, US Ⓥ ⦿ col
Dir Barry Levinson **Prod** Mark Johnson **Scr** Chris Columbus **Ph** Stephen Goldblatt **Ed** Stu Linder **Mus** Bruce Broughton **Art** Norman Reynolds
Act Nicholas Rowe, Alan Cox, Sophie Ward, Anthony Higgins, Susan Fleetwood, Freddie Jones (Amblin/Paramount)

Young Sherlock Holmes is another Steven Spielberg film corresponding to those lamps made from driftwood and coffee tables from redwood burl and hatch covers. It's not art, but they all serve their purpose and sell by the millions.

The formula this time is applied to the question of what might have happened had Sherlock Holmes and John Watson first met as teenage students.

As usual, Spielberg's team—this time led by director Barry Levinson—isn't really as interested in the answer as it is in fooling around with the visual effects possibilities conjured by George Lucas's Industrial Light & Magic shop.

Nicholas Rowe as Holmes and Alan Cox as Watson maturely carry off their roles, assisted by Sophie Ward as the necessary female accomplice. The adults are just there to fill in the spaces.

1985: NOMINATION: Best Visual Effects

•

YOUNG STRANGER, THE
1956, 83 mins, US Ⓥ ⦿ b/w
Dir John Frankenheimer **Prod** Stuart Millar **Scr** Robert Dozier **Ph** Robert Planck **Ed** Robert Swink, Edward Biery, Jr. **Mus** Leonard Rosenman **Art** Albert S. D'Agostino, John B. Mansbridge
Act James MacArthur, Kim Hunter, James Daly, James Gregory, Whit Bissell, Jeff Silver (RKO)

A story of conflict between youth and parents, the plot indulges in "one-note" dramatics that provide very little shading between the black and white of the problem, yet which are effective within the entertainment aim. Juvenile delinquency is not necessarily an issue. Rather, the plot purpose is to show how a father should give more time and understanding to his son.

Film marks the feature picture break-in of several younger talents. James MacArthur, teenage son of Helen Hayes and the late Charles MacArthur, gets his first prominent picture casting as the youthful star and delivers promisingly. He is seen as the rebellious son of picture producer James Daly and Kim Hunter. Filmmaking keeps the father too busy to give much time to his son, but he realizes the error after the son is arrested for socking a theatre manager and a cop.

Picture is young Stuart Millar's first full producership after production apprenticeship with William Wyler. Debuting as a theatrical film director is John Frankenheimer, from TV, and he handles the switch neatly. For Robert Dozier, son of RKO production veepee William Dozier, film is his first screenplay [from his TV play *Deal a Blow*].

•

YOUNG TOM EDISON
1940, 85 mins, US b/w
Dir Norman Taurog **Prod** John W. Considine, Jr. **Scr** Bradbury Foote, Dore Schary, Hugo Butler **Ph** Sidney Wagner **Ed** Elmo Vernon **Mus** Edward Ward
Act Mickey Rooney, Fay Bainter, George Bancroft, Virginia Weidler, Eugene Pallette (M-G-M)

When Metro originally planned to produce the biography of Thomas A. Edison, intention was to combine his boyhood and manhood in the one picture. But research provided so much material that two productions are necessary to adequately cover the life of the wizard of Menlo Park.

Young Tom Edison covers the inventor's life as a boy in Port Huron, Michigan, around 1863. It details his inquisitiveness on chemicals and labor-saving gadgets, and his disregard for school curriculum and rules. Split up of the life of Edison into two parts marks the first time that such a procedure has been followed by any company. *Edison, the Man*, with Spencer Tracy starred as the inventor in his years of real accomplishment, is the second part [released three months later].

Story points up the courage and eventual triumph of a typical American youth. No attempt is made to paint him as a youthful genius. He's an all-American boy, an inventive opportunist.

Picture is rich in youthful adventure, and human, homey qualities. Mickey Rooney plays the young inventor with sympathetic restraint. There are no obvious stunts or gags; no overplaying of the dreamy, though deeply serious boy who is laying the foundation for his later achievements.

Story revolves around the home life of the Edison family. There's the lovable and protecting mother (Fay Bainter), the stern father (George Bancroft) who fails to understand his son, and a younger sister (Virginia Weidler) continually sympathetic to her brother and his problems.

•

YOUNG WINSTON
1972, 157 mins, UK Ⓥ ▭ col
Dir Richard Attenborough **Prod** Carl Foreman **Scr** Carl Foreman **Ph** Gerry Turpin **Ed** Kevin Connor **Mus** Alfred Ralston **Art** Geoffrey Drake, Don Ashton
Act Simon Ward, Robert Shaw, Anne Bancroft, Jack Hawkins, Ian Holm, Anthony Hopkins (Columbia/Open Road)

Rate this biopic of Winston Churchill's early years as both a brilliant artistic achievement and a fascinating, highly enjoyable film—a combination not always obtained.

It's a richly multifaceted scrapbook [from Churchill's book *My Early Life*] which is unfolded, touching on his lonely childhood and only occasional contact with his politician father and a socially much-involved American mother, early school experience, first combat and war correspondent stints in India and the Sudan, and on to first political defeat and ultimate vindication as—after a headline-grabbing Boer War exploit—he makes an early political mark in an impassioned House of Commons' speech.

Far from a sycophantic paean to a great man in the bud, pic manages a believable portrait of an ambitious and sometimes arrogant young man.

1972: NOMINATIONS: Best Original Story & Screenplay, Costume Design, Art Direction

•

YOU ONLY LIVE ONCE
1937, 85 mins, US Ⓥ b/w
Dir Fritz Lang **Prod** Walter Wanger **Scr** Gene Towne, Graham Baker **Ph** Leon Shamroy **Ed** Daniel Mandell **Mus** Alfred Newman (dir.) **Art** Alexander Toluboff
Act Sylvia Sidney, Henry Fonda, Barton MacLane, Jean Dixon, William Gargan, Warren Hymer (Wanger/United Artists)

Fritz Lang follows up his *Fury* (1936) with another wallop. *You Only Live Once* is full of stark and bitter moments, but these bite no more deeply than deftly wrought scenes of tenderness. The self-sacrificing love of the girl for the ex-convict reaches a high level of heart-tugging during their flight as fugitives from the law.

Lang's penchant for mob scenes receives indulgence in only one sequence staged outside the courthouse after Henry Fonda has been found guilty of causing the death of six men in a holdup. On the spectacular side are the gas bombing of money-truck guards in a one-man robbery, the guile used by Fonda in getting out of the death house, and the bartering which goes on between the escaped convict and the warden just inside the prison gates.

Sylvia Sidney counts strongly. Turning in telling support are Barton MacLane, as the public defender, who, despite his love for Sidney, befriends Fonda, and Jean Dixon, as Sidney's critical but loyal sister.

•

YOU ONLY LIVE TWICE
1967, 117 mins, UK Ⓥ ⦿ ▭ col
Dir Lewis Gilbert **Prod** Albert R. Broccoli, Harry Saltzman **Scr** Roald Dahl **Ph** Freddie Young **Ed** Peter Hunt **Mus** John Barry **Art** Ken Adam
Act Sean Connery, Akiko Wakabayashi, Tetsuro Tamba, Mie Hama, Karin Dor, Donald Pleasence (United Artists/Eon)

Film begins with a prolog in which a U.S. astronaut's space walk is interrupted by another spacecraft that, crocodile-style, opens its jaws and swallows the capsule. U.S. government is peeved at what it assumes to be a Russian attempt to foil space exploration, and 007 is assigned by helpful British intelligence to locate the missing rocket before full-scale war breaks out between the two nuclear powers.

Film's title refers to Bond's "murder," which precedes the credits. Ensconced with the first in a long line of Japanese beauties, he is abruptly gunned down and pronounced dead in her bed by officials.

Sean Connery plays 007 with his usual finesse. Rest of cast in the $9.5 million film is strictly secondary, although Akiko Wakabayashi and Tetsuro Tamba register well as Bond's Japanese cohorts. Donald Pleasence makes a suitably menacing German heavy who appears in film's final scenes. [Additional story material by Harold Jack Bloom.]

•

YOU'RE A BIG BOY NOW
1966, 98 mins, US Ⓥ col
Dir Francis Coppola **Prod** Phil Feldman **Scr** Francis Coppola **Ph** Andy Laszlo **Ed** Aram Avakian **Mus** John Sebastian **Art** Vassili Fotopoulos
Act Elizabeth Hartman, Geraldine Page, Julie Harris, Peter Kastner, Rip Torn, Michael Dunn (Seven Arts)

You're a Big Boy Now [from the novel by David Benedictus] has a simple premise—a virginal young man growing into manhood, not so much through his own efforts as those about him—which has been expanded glowingly in a sophisticated approach. Francis Coppola has drawn top-flight performances from his talented cast.

Peter Kastner plays a roller-skating stack boy in a NY public library and somewhat of a dreamer. The father (Rip Torn) decides the best way for his son to grow up would be to move out of the family home on his own. Straightaway, lad becomes ensconced in a rooming house run by Julie Harris.

With the help of his library, dope-inclined pal (Tony Bill) and a pretty library assistant (Karen Black), the boy is launched on his road to manhood, which takes him into the arms of a sexy, way-out, Greenwich Village discotheque dish (Elizabeth Hartman). Frequent laughs spark his career toward full-blossomed virility, with amusing bumps along the way.

Kastner turns in a slick portrayal, endowing role with just the proper emphasis upon youth in the wondering stage. Both Geraldine Page as the mother and Harris as the landlady go all-out in hilarious roles and Torn, too, delivers a socko performance as the father who has difficulty understanding his son.

1966: NOMINATION: Best Supp. Actress (Geraldine Page)

•

YOU'RE IN THE ARMY NOW [1937]
SEE: O.H.M.S.

•

YOU'RE IN THE ARMY NOW
1941, 79 mins, US b/w
Dir Lewis Seiler **Prod** Ben Stoloff **Scr** Paul Gerard Smith, George Beatty **Ph** Arthur Todd **Ed** Frank Magee
Act Jimmy Durante, Jane Wyman, Phil Silvers, Regis Toomey, George Meeker, Donald MacBride (Warner)

Though it is a bit corny in spots and lays the slapstick on heavily, with some gag sequences stretched too far, here is a comedy of soldier life that completely entertains.

Jimmy Durante goes to town on the clowning, slapstick and other means of comedy, but while he's busy as a bee, many others contribute importantly to the numerous laugh-producing sequences. Among these is Phil Silvers. Durante and Silvers, trying to interest a recruiting officer in a vacuum cleaner, accidentally get themselves enlisted. As buck privates, they become guardhouse regulars as result of getting themselves into one jam after another.

The story job by Paul Gerard Smith, an old hand at the vaudeville-writing game, and George Beatty, is excellent and, if some of the gag situations are stretched a little too far or the slapstick gets out of hand, it may be the fault of the director, Lewis Seiler. Dialog is surefire all the way.

•

YOU'RE MY EVERYTHING
1949, 94 mins, US col
Dir Walter Lang ***Prod*** Lamar Trotti ***Scr*** Lamar Trotti, Will H. Hays, Jr. ***Ph*** Arthur E. Arling ***Ed*** J. Watson Webb, Jr. ***Mus*** Alfred Newman (dir.) ***Art*** Lyle Wheeler, Leyland Fuller
Act Dan Dailey, Anne Baxter, Anne Revere, Buster Keaton, Stanley Ridges, Alan Mowbray (20th Century-Fox)

You're My Everything is practically a synthesis of all the backstage musicals ever filmed, including the songs. The direction doesn't perceptibly freshen the material [based on a story by George Jessel].

Dan Dailey is presented as a hoofer who meets and marries Anne Baxter when his show is playing the Hub. As an inductee into the chorus, she's an enthusiastic wife, but when he's screen tested, she's drafted for a love scene opposite him, thereby getting the picture contract and becoming the hotcha sensation of the 1920s.

By this time the young hoofer is a nitery star, but the arrival of talkies ends the wife's career.

As the hoofer, Dailey is properly brash, and not only manages to read the lines with apparent conviction, but succeeds in being likable throughout.

•

YOU'RE NEVER TOO YOUNG
1955, 102 mins, US col
Dir Norman Taurog ***Prod*** Paul Jones ***Scr*** Sidney Sheldon ***Ph*** Daniel L. Fapp ***Ed*** Archie Marshek ***Mus*** Walter Scharf (arr.)
Act Dean Martin, Jerry Lewis, Diana Lynn, Nina Foch, Raymond Burr (Paramount)

In *You're Never Too Young*, Dean Martin and Jerry Lewis have one of their funniest pictures. Sidney Sheldon's screenplay [suggested by a play by Edward Childs Carpenter from a story by Fannie Kilbourne] is inconsequential, but who cares as long as it provides Lewis with the skeleton for his madcap antics.

Lewis has a field day as a barber's apprentice who unknowingly obtains possession of a stolen diamond. He gets the chance to disguise himself as an eleven-year-old, wears an outlandish kid's sailor suit, and shares a train bedroom, innocently of course, with Diana Lynn. He romps around a girls' school, falls in a pool, vies with Martin for Lynn's affections, runs from the jewel thief, disrupts a faculty meeting, does a takeoff of Humphrey Bogart, and upsets Martin in an unmanageable barber's chair.

•

YOU'RE ONLY YOUNG ONCE
1938, 77 mins, US b/w
Dir George B. Seitz ***Scr*** Kay Van Riper ***Ph*** Lester White ***Ed*** Adrienne Fazan ***Mus*** David Snell
Act Lewis Stone, Cecilia Parker, Mickey Rooney, Fay Holden, Frank Craven, Ann Rutherford (M-G-M)

First of the series involving the Hardy family is *You're Only Young Once*.

Lewis Stone replaces Lionel Barrymore as the head of the family, the latter having the job in *Wilderness* and in *Family Affair*.

Characters of the piece were ideaed by Aurania Rouverol. There's the kindly judge, the daughter suffering all the exquisite torture of young love, the son in his first long pants and getting away from the mumblety-peg period in a series of blushes, the mother who rules in fact, the old maiden aunt with a few ideas, etc.

Fairly well blessed with a bank balance, the judge (Lewis Stone) maneuvers his family into a trip to Catalina, where he wants to catch a swordfish to further clutter his study at home. Daughter Cecilia Parker wants to go where she can be near her boyfriend, Mickey Rooney, where girlfriend Ann Rutherford is sunning on the lakes, the mother to visit relatives—but the judge smooths the course to Catalina.

There Rooney encounters pash-lipped Eleanor Lynn and almost becomes a man. Parker vacation romances with Ted Pearson, a life guard, who has a wife already, and the judge has a patience-disturbing time wih the fish toying but not grabbing on.

Mickey Rooney will be chalked up by most seers for the film's honor-theft, although edging but slightly over Stone and Parker.

•

YOU'RE TELLING ME
1934, 66 mins, US b/w
Dir Erle C. Kenton ***Scr*** J. P. McEvoy, Walter DeLeon, Paul M. Jones ***Ph*** Alfred Gilks ***Ed*** Otho Lovering ***Mus*** Arthur Johnston ***Art*** Hans Dreier, Robert Odell
Act W. C. Fields, Joan Marsh, Buster Crabbe, Adrienne Ames, Louise Carter, Kathleen Howard (Paramount)

The kind of comedy that Chaplin used to do in two reels, but stretched out to run an even six. Thanks chiefly to J. P. McEvoy's dialog and the sustained pantomiming of W. C. Fields, it's a passable comedy as comedies go.

Main object of the scenarists seems to have been to lead up plausibly to Fields's standard golf bit. The build-up is a frail structure on which Fields's butter-finger style of panto and McEvoy's chatter are strung. Fields is a dumb but likeable guy who invents things and doubles in ruining his daughter's social chances by getting stewed and taking off his shoes in the parlor. A princess steps in to straighten things out for both father and daughter. Papa's big invention is a puncture-proof tire that finally nets him a million. When one scripter asked the other scripter, "Little man, what now?" they called in the caddie (Tammany Young) with the squeaky shoes and on went the golf bit. It manages to save the picture.

•

YOURS, MINE AND OURS
1968, 111 mins, US Ⓥ ⊙ col
Dir Melville Shavelson ***Prod*** Robert F. Blumofe ***Scr*** Melville Shavelson, Mort Lachman ***Ph*** Charles Wheeler ***Ed*** Stuart Gilmore ***Mus*** Fred Karlin ***Art*** Arthur Lonergan
Act Lucille Ball, Henry Fonda, Van Johnson, Tom Bosley, Jennifer Leak, Timothy Matheson (United Artists/Desilu-Walden)

To put it simply, *Yours, Mine and Ours* is socko family entertainment. Based on actual characters, the film is marked by uniform excellence. Literate scripting, excellent performances, and superior direction are underscored by topnotch production.

Based on the human interest story of the early 1960s when Frank Beardsley, naval officer and widower with ten children, married Helen North, a widow with eight kids, director Shavelson and Mort Lachman have fashioned a first-rate script which intermingles adroitly the amusing, as well as dramatic, angles of mature second love, raising a family, and adolescence.

Lucille Ball plays the widow, old enough to know her responsibilities, but young enough to want male companionship. Henry Fonda is cast perfectly as the widower.

Thereafter, the sometimes-awkward, always-loving, melding of the two families proceeds, and many of the children come to the fore. In particular, Ball's eldest daughter, Jennifer Leak, and Fonda's eldest son, Timothy Matheson, project admirably.

•

YOU'VE GOT MAIL
1998, 119 mins, US Ⓥ ⊙ col
Dir Nora Ephron ***Prod*** Nora Ephron, Lauren Shuler Donner ***Scr*** Nora Ephron, Delia Ephron ***Ph*** John Lindley ***Ed*** Richard Marks ***Mus*** George Fenton ***Art*** Dan Davis
Act Tom Hanks, Meg Ryan, Parker Posey, Greg Kinnear, Jean Stapleton, Steve Zahn (Warner)

The long-awaited reteaming of the *Sleepless in Seattle* combo of Tom Hanks and Meg Ryan and director Nora Ephron puts a fine contempo spin on the time-tested premise first used onscreen in Ernst Lubitsch's *The Shop Around the Corner* (1940) and reworked for the musical *In the Good Old Summertime* (1949), the story of anonymous, affectionate pen pals who dislike each other in person.

In many ways, new pic is the most successful version yet of this familiar premise, originally penned as a play, *Parfumerie*, by Nikolaus (Miklos) Laszlo. Hanks and Ryan show why they are two of Hollywood's most bankable and, in many ways, most traditional stars. Hanks meshes the boyish charm of Jimmy Stewart with the earthy integrity of Spencer Tracy, and Ryan blends Kate Hepburn's determined sensibility with the infectious ebullience of a Jean Arthur.

Corporate heir Joe Fox (Hanks) and shop owner Kathleen Kelly (Ryan) wend their ways to work on the Upper West Side, mere footsteps and yet worlds apart. Joe is planning to open a mammoth book store a la Barnes & Noble, while Kathleen runs a tiny children's bookshop. When they meet, romantic sparks fly, but when she later learns he's about to steamroll her shop, her appreciation of his quick-witted charm gives way to disapproval of his soulless guile. Both are involved in dull relationships (Greg Kinnear, Parker Posey).

Unwittingly, however, Joe and Kathleen are each other's cyber soul mates, exchanging daily E-mail under pseudonymous screen names ("NY152" and "Shopgirl"). When she tells him in general terms that she's facing a professional crisis, Joe advises her to "go to the mattress" and attack the enemy.

Pic makes a good point about the difference between public personae and private selves, indicating correctly how we can be more open with people we barely know. It's also extremely timely for the late '90s era of online dating.

Tech aspects are tops and just right for the genre.

•

YOU WERE NEVER LOVELIER
1942, 98 mins, US Ⓥ ⊙ b/w
Dir William A. Seiter ***Prod*** Louis F. Edelman ***Scr*** Michael Fessier, Ernest Pagano, Delmer Daves ***Ph*** Ted Tetzlaff ***Ed*** William Lyon ***Mus*** Jerome Kern
Act Fred Astaire, Rita Hayworth, Adolphe Menjou, Larry Parks, Xavier Cugat, Leslie Brooks (Columbia)

A Jerome Kern–Johnny Mercer score, Fred Astaire and Rita Hayworth on the dancing and singing end, and Xavier Cugat's crack rhumba band for the musical didoes are certainly an excellent combination of entertainment vitamins.

In a nutshell, the yarn concerns the efforts of hotel magnate Menjou to get his daughter (Rita Hayworth) interested in romance. His eldest daughter has already been married and until the next in line, Hayworth, takes the plunge, his two lovesick youngest girls must wait.

This is purely escapist screen fare—a song here, a dance there and Buenos Aires for a background. There isn't even a hint of the war, and that is some compensation for the few slow spots in the story's unfolding.

Hayworth has never been portrayed lovelier or more talented than she is here.

•

YUKINOJO HENGE
(AN ACTOR'S REVENGE; YUKINOJO'S REVENGE)
1963, 113 mins, Japan Ⓥ ▭ col
Dir Kon Ichikawa ***Prod*** Masaichi Nagata ***Scr*** Natto Wada ***Ph*** Setsuo Koba ***Mus*** Yasushi Akutagawa ***Art*** Yoshinobu Nishioka
Act Kazuo Hasegawa, Fujiko Yamamoto, Ayako Wakao, Raizo Ichikawa, Shintaro Katsu, Ganjiri Nakamura (Daiei)

A stylized film [from a novel by Otokichi Mikami], *An Actor's Revenge* mixes Kabuki theatre with ritual, action, humor and derring-do that jell into an entertaining opus. The hero is an actor who impersonates females, for there are no women in Kabuki. But he carries his female impersonations into real life, too.

The actor has sworn vengeance on those who ruined his father's business and drove him to suicide. The daughter of one falls for the actor, and he decides to use her to get to the others. There is also a Robin Hood-ish character who spies the goings-on and decides to help the actor.

Director Kon Ichikawa has done a sort of play-within-a-play pic. Outdoor shots are staged on sets which add to the ambiguity but are a visual delight of the film. Kazuo Hasegawa is extraordinary as the actor.

Hasegawa began his career as an *oyama* (actors who played female roles in classic Japanese theater), and actually played the same role in an earlier pic version of this tale.

•

YUKINOJO'S REVENGE
SEE: YUKINOJO HENGE

Z

1969, 126 mins, France/Algeria Ⓥ ⦿ col

Dir Constantin Costa-Gavras ***Prod*** Jacques Perrin, Ahmed Rachedi (exec.) ***Scr*** Jorge Semprun, Constantin Costa-Gavras ***Ph*** Raoul Coutard ***Ed*** Francoise Bonnot ***Mus*** Mikis Theodorakis ***Art*** Jacques D'Ovidio

Act Yves Montand, Irene Papas, Jean-Louis Trintignant, Jacques Perrin, Francois Perrier, Charles Denner (Reganne/ONCIC)

Z is a punchy political pic [from the novel by Vassilis Vassilikos] that mixes action, violence, and conspiracy on a robust, lavish scale. Originally subtitled "the anatomy of a political assassination," it is based on the murder of a noted progressive Greek political figure some years earlier, but also makes references to [the right-wing military junta governing Greece at the time of the pic's release]. All this is masked in setting it in a Southern-looking country that is never named. [Pic was shot in Algeria.]

Characters are firmly and quickly blocked out as types. There is an idealistic professor called "Z" fighting against A-bombs (Yves Montand), his wife who fears for his safety (Irene Papas), a young judge (Jean-Louis Trintignant) put on the case on the theory he will not upset things after the professor is killed, and a battery of others.

An ambitious newsman, fired by sensationalism rather than any nobility, finds a witness who can identify the killer and the young judge on the case turns out to be surprisingly strong and obdurate.

Director Costa-Gavras seems influenced by dynamically paced Yank pix of this sort, but manages not to exploit violence and political innuendo for its own sake. Players are all convincing in this political maelstrom, and Montand, with a small role, shows strength, dedication and dignity.

1969: Best Foreign Language Film

•

ZABRISKIE POINT

1970, 112 mins, US Ⓥ ⦿ ▭ col

Dir Michelangelo Antonioni ***Prod*** Carlo Ponti ***Scr*** Michelangelo Antonioni, Fred Gardner, Sam Shepard, Tonino Guerra, Clare Peploe ***Ph*** Alfino Contini ***Ed*** Franco Arcalli ***Art*** Dean Tavoularis

Act Mark Frechette, Daria Halprin, Paul Fix, G. D. Spradlin, Bill Garaway, Kathleen Cleaver (M-G-M)

Michelangelo Antonioni makes the U.S. social scene, and despite the imbalance in his concept, distills from his notes some arresting photographic moments. Antonioni has sought to bring into the focus of his own insights, the student vs. establishment conflict. He is on foreign terrain. His off-camera presence is sensed in each pictorial move.

Probably the most compelling footage of *Zabriskie Point* is the finis wrap up, in which things representative of the ultra "haves" go up in imagined explosions.

The special effects are magnificent as the remnants of modern architectured big business, including mod edifices, and billboards which had been planted by power corporations, hit the sky, piece by piece, and hang in a dangling collage of symbolism.

•

ZANDY'S BRIDE

1974, 116 mins, US ▭ col

Dir Jan Troell ***Prod*** Harvey Matofsky ***Scr*** Marc Norman ***Ph*** Jordan Cronenweth ***Ed*** Gordon Scott ***Mus*** Michael Franks ***Art*** Al Brenner

Act Gene Hackman, Liv Ullmann, Eileen Heckart, Susan Tyrrell, Sam Bottoms, Joe Santos (Warner)

Zandy's Bride is a good period frontier-romantic melodrama starring Gene Hackman as a gruff cattle rancher and Liv Ullmann as the mail-order bride who softens him up. Star performances sustain Jan Troell's delicate but placid direction.

Marc Norman's spare screenplay was adapted from a 1942 novel, *The Stranger*, by Lillian Bos Ross. Set in 1870 in upstate California's rugged Big Sur mountain and sea interface, story takes Hackman from a crude, thoughtless hermit to a loving husband and father. The going is rough, however, Ullmann's unexpectedly strong spirit overcomes his stiffness, learned at the back of the hand of father Frank Cady, a cruel patriarch who has reduced wife Eileen Heckart to serf status. The plot line is thin but sufficient.

•

ZARDOZ

1974, 104 mins, UK/US Ⓥ ⦿ ▭ col

Dir John Boorman ***Prod*** John Boorman ***Scr*** John Boorman ***Ph*** Geoffrey Unsworth ***Ed*** John Merritt ***Mus*** David Munrow ***Art*** Anthony Pratt

Act Sean Connery, Charlotte Rampling, Sara Kestelman, John Alderton, Sally Anne Newton, Niall Buggy (20th Century-Fox)

Zardoz is a futuristic, metaphysical and anthropological drama testing John Boorman in three creative areas. The results: direction, good; script, a brilliant premise which unfortunately washes out in climactic sound and fury; and production, outstanding, particularly special visual effects which belie the film's modest cost. Sean Connery heads the cast as a 23rd-century Adam.

The story, set in 2293, postulates a world society which this century's runaway technology forced into being. The highest-order beings are an elitist group of effete aesthete, eternally youthful on a spiritual plane. Connery rises from the lower ranks to overthrow the new order and recycle mankind into its older pattern.

Connery manifests well the brooding duality of man's nature, emerging from mechanical breeding to eventually tear down the system that created him.

•

ZAZA

1939, 83 mins, US b/w

Dir George Cukor ***Prod*** Albert Lewin ***Scr*** Zoe Akins ***Ph*** Charles Lang, Jr. ***Ed*** Edward Dmytryk ***Mus*** Frederick Hollander ***Art*** Hans Dreier, Earl Hedrick

Act Claudette Colbert, Herbert Marshall, Bert Lahr, Helen Westley, Constance Collier, Genevieve Tobin (Paramount)

In the third presentation of the play [following versions in 1915 and 1923], Paramount has retained basic fundamentals of the original [play by Pierre Berton and Charles Simon], but adaptation injects new treatment of the early 1900 story to freshen it up materially.

Zaza is a mischievous and flirtatious vaude soubrette in France. Forcing introduction with Herbert Marshall, pair fall in love and launch an affair.

Claudette Colbert hits a sincere and scintillating portrayal of the frivolous and tempestuous Zaza. Her coy flirtation with Marshall, and later dramatic passages are a finely tempered characterization. Marshall capably handles the role of the husband.

Play does not lend itself to fast-paced picture technique, and director George Cukor wisely steers away from trying to make such a radical change.

•

ZAZIE DANS LE METRO

1959, 92 mins, France Ⓥ ⦿ col

Dir Louis Malle ***Prod*** Irenee Leriche ***Scr*** Louis Malle, Jean-Paul Rappeneau ***Ph*** Henri Raichi ***Ed*** Kenout Peltier ***Mus*** Fiorenzo Carpi ***Art*** Bernard Evein

Act Catherine Demongeot, Philippe Noiret, Carla Marlier, Vittorio Caprioli, Hubert Deschamps, Jacques Dufilho (Nouvelles Editions)

After his stylized, sensual *The Lovers*, which was quite a hit, director Louis Malle essays his first comedy, which is a sort of intellectual slapstick entry [from the novel by Raymond Queneau]. It has some risible bits but is, in all, somewhat diffuse.

Zazie (Catherine Demongeot) is a twelve-year-old girl whose mother leaves her with an uncle (Philippe Noiret) when she comes into Paris from the country for a day with her latest lover. Zazie has never seen the subway and wants to ride in it, but it's on strike. Next morning she is off on a round of adventures in a weird, colorful Paris.

Her uncle is a pompous, self-indulgent type who dances in a nitery in travesty. Pic has obviously been influenced in style by the better Yank animated pix and Mack Sennett comedies. Malle shows a wealth of invention and uses color artfully. Traffic jams, a visit to the Eiffel Tower, and chase sequences are expertly manned.

Demongeot is a sassy, pert character. Vehicle moves at whirlwind pace.

•

ZED AND TWO NOUGHTS, A

1985, 115 mins, UK/Netherlands Ⓥ col

Dir Peter Greenaway ***Prod*** Kees Kasander, Peter Sainsbury ***Scr*** Peter Greenaway ***Ph*** Sacha Vierny ***Ed*** John Wilson ***Mus*** Michael Nyman ***Art*** Ben van Os

Act Andrea Ferreol, Brian Deacon, Eric Deacon, Frances Barber, Joss Ackland, Gerard Thoolen (Artificial Eye/BFI/Channel Four/Allarts/VPRO

Despite its visual pyrotechnics and an impressively woven texture of intellectual allusions, Peter Greenaway's feature fails to engage the audience's sympathies.

In the end, it remains the work of a highly talented British eccentric who hasn't managed to thresh out his private fantasies and obscurantist intellectual preoccupations to connect with major concerns or touch the emotions.

The action centers on a zoo (its letters making up the zed and two noughts of the title). In this lurid arena Greenaway is intent on upturning the seamier, humiliating side of animal existence in captivity (including that of homo sapiens).

Meanwhile, lots of pseudo-philosophical conundrums are tossed at the audience like peanuts to hungry caged animals. Is a zebra a white horse with black stripes or a black one with white? etc. Needless to say, the resulting stilted dialog does not make the acting much of a treat.

•

ZEE & CO.

(US: X, Y & ZEE)

1972, 110 mins, UK Ⓥ col

Dir Brian G. Hutton ***Prod*** Jay Kanter, Alan Ladd, Jr. ***Scr*** Edna O'Brien ***Ph*** Billy Williams ***Ed*** Jim Clark ***Mus*** Stanley Myers ***Art*** Peter Mullins

Act Elizabeth Taylor, Michael Caine, Susannah York, Margaret Leighton, John Standing, Mary Larkin (Columbia)

Not in years have three people more deserved the star billing they get in this *Love Story* for adults. Elizabeth Taylor and Susannah York both turn in performances that fully capture the excellently conceived characters of Edna O'Brien's original screenplay. Michael Caine keeps up beautifully with the pace set by his femme costars.

The script has Taylor, the "Zee" of the title, and Caine as a long-married couple, whose relationship has turned into a love-hate affair that leads into Caine's affair with York.

After a half-hearted suicide attempt, Zee recognizes the possibility of an actual break but, by accident finding that her rival has her own private Achilles' heel, makes a final, desperate move which may answer one problem but presents another.

•

ZELIG

1983, 84 mins, US Ⓥ ⦿ b/w

Dir Woody Allen ***Prod*** Robert Greenhut ***Scr*** Woody Allen ***Ph*** Gordon Willis ***Ed*** Susan E. Morse ***Mus*** Dick Hyman ***Art*** Mel Bourne

Act Woody Allen, Mia Farrow, Garreth Brown, Stephanie Farrow, Will Holt, Sol Lomita (Rollins-Joffe/Orion)

Lampooning documentary tradition by structuring the entire film as a meticulously crafted bogus docu, Woody Allen tackles some serious stuff en route (namely the two-edged sword of public and media celebrityhood), but manages to avoid the self-oriented seriousness that's alienated many of his loyalists. More positively, *Zelig* is consistently funny, though more academic than boulevardier.

Allen plays the eponymous Leonard Zelig, subject of the "documentary" that traces this onetime legend of the 1920s–30s, whose weak personality and neurotic need to be liked caused him to become the ultimate conformist.

Through the use of doctored photos and staged black-and-white footage cannily—and usually undetectably—matched with authentic newsreels and stock footage of the period, Allen is seen intermingling with everyone from the Hearst crowd at San Simeon, Eugene O'Neill and Fanny Brice to the likes of Pope Pius XI and even Adolf Hitler.

The narrative that does emerge limns the efforts of a committed psychiatrist (played with tact and loveliness by Mia Farrow) to give Zelig a single self, a relationship that blossoms, predictably, to love by fadeout.

1983: NOMINATIONS: Best Cinematography, Costume Design

•

ZENOBIA

1939, 71 mins, US b/w

Dir Gordon M. Douglas ***Prod*** Hal Roach ***Scr*** Corey Ford ***Ph*** Karl Struss ***Ed*** Bert Jordan ***Mus*** Marvin Hatley ***Art*** Charles D. Hall

Act Oliver Hardy, Harry Langdon, Billie Burke, Alice Brady (United Artists)

Hal Roach introduces Oliver Hardy in straight comedy. Teamed with Harry Langdon—drafted to replace Stan Laurel—Hardy gives out with a minimum of slapstick antics and knockabout stunts. A few of Hardy's double-takes remain, but the rest is a straight portrayal.

Slender story provided [by Walter De Leon and Arnold Belgard] does not warrant the amount of footage. Script is a series of incidents tied together in not too compact form.

As the doctor in a Mississippi town of the 1870s, Hardy is called on to treat Zenobia, an elephant belonging to a carnival pitchman (Langdon). Pachyderm gratefully follows Hardy around, through buildings and into a reception for his daughter. Matter winds up in court, with Langdon suing Hardy for alienation of the beast's affections.

•

ZENTROPA
SEE: EUROPA

•

ZEPPELIN
1971, 97 mins, UK/US Ⓥ ▭ col
Dir Etienne Perier ***Prod*** Owen Crump ***Scr*** Arthur Rowe, Donald Churchill ***Ph*** Alan Hume ***Ed*** John Shirley ***Mus*** Roy Budd ***Art*** Bert Davey
Act Michael York, Elke Sommer, Peter Carsten, Marius Goring, Anton Diffring, Andrew Keir (Getty & Fromkess/Warner)

Zeppelin settles for being just another wartime melodrama, with some good aerial sequences and a powerful, brisk raid sequence in the finale.

Story [by producer Owen Crump] deals with Britain's concern about German's new World War I weapon, the Zeppelin, the monstrous, looming aircraft that made Britain vulnerable. Indication that the Germans have perfected a new and even more effective Zeppelin jerks the British highups into swift action.

A young Scottish lieutenant, of Anglo-German parentage, who had left Germany and eventually joined the British Army (Michael York), looks the perfect spy. Worked on by an attractive German Mata Hari (Alexandra Stewart), he is softened up and when called on to "volunteer" to "defect" to the Germans and dig out the secrets of the new Zeppelin, he reluctantly agrees.

Many Germans are suspicious of his sudden switch back to the homeland. But only one appears to be convinced that he's a spy. She (Elke Sommer) is the wife of the aircraft designer (Marius Goring) and she's more concerned with helping to prepare the Zepp for its final trial run than in exposing York.

•

ZIEGFELD FOLLIES
1945, 116 mins, US Ⓥ ⊙ col
Dir Vincente Minnelli, [George Sidney, Norman Taurog, Robert Lewis, Roy Del Ruth, Lemuel Ayers] ***Prod*** Arthur Freed ***Scr*** [George White, David Freedman, William K. Wells, Al Lewis, Robert Alton, Kay Thompson, Roger Edens, Irving Brecher] ***Ph*** George Folsey, Charles Rosher, [Ray June] ***Ed*** Albert Akst ***Mus*** Lennie Hayton (dir.) ***Art*** Cedric Gibbons, Jack Martin Smith, Merrill Pye, [Lemuel Ayers]
Act Fred Astaire, Lucille Ball, Judy Garland, Gene Kelly, Esther Williams, William Powell (M-G-M)

Looking down from a very lush heaven, as Florenz Ziegfeld (William Powell) does in prolog of this film super, the Great Zieggy would be dazzled by color, sets and routines far above the capacities of his day. But despite the glory of Technicolor, Ziegfeld would have missed his nudes, his pleasantly risque interludes and a certain heartwarming which came with the old productions.

Those shining above all others in the generous cast of Metro stars are Fred Astaire, agile and gay; Judy Garland, who has perfected an ironic touch; sultry Lena Horne; graceful Esther Williams; comic Fanny Brice; and sweet-warbling Lucille Bremer.

Pic opens with dreamland set out of which Powell emerges, apparently comfortably fixed in celestial heights a la Ziegfeld. As the great producer, he reflects on his successes—*Rosalie*, *Rio Rita*, *Show Boat*, the various *Follies*.

It's all stupendous, terrific, colossal, practically everyone would agree. Even Zieggy.

•

ZIEGFELD GIRL
1941, 135 mins, US Ⓥ ⊙ b/w
Dir Robert Z. Leonard, Busby Berkeley ***Prod*** Pandro S. Berman ***Scr*** Marguerite Roberts, Sonya Levien ***Ph*** Ray June ***Ed*** Blanche Sewell ***Mus*** Herbert Stothart ***Art*** Cedric Gibbons, Daniel B. Cathcart
Act James Stewart, Judy Garland, Hedy Lamarr, Lana Turner, Tony Martin, Jackie Cooper (M-G-M)

The attempt to balance three parallel dramas of the lives of three Ziegfeld showgirls makes for continual switching from one tale to the other. Interpolation of two extended displays of Ziegfeldian production sequences, with parades of the glorified girls, prevents smooth unfolding of the piece [from an original story by William Anthony McGuire] and results in several dull passages.

Smart casting provides vivid contrast in the Ziegfeld selections for his showgirl ensemble. There's Judy Garland, youthful but veteran trouper, with showmanship, personality and talent; Hedy Lamarr, wife of a pecunious musical genius, with her striking and reserved beauty; and the sexy Lana Turner who succumbs to the easiest way for a brief fling at luxury.

Director Robert Z. Leonard provides a most capable directorial job. It's one of the top negative outlays of the studio, running approximately $1,900,000 in total outlay. The expenditure is apparent in every foot of unreeling.

•

ZIMLYA
(EARTH)
1930, 63 mins, USSR ⊙ ⊗ b/w
Dir Aleksandr Dovzhenko ***Scr*** Aleksandr Dovzhenko ***Ph*** Danylo Demutsky ***Art*** Vasili Krichevsky
Act Semyon Svashenko, Stepan Shkurat, Mikola Nademsky, Yelena Maksimova, Pyotr Masokha (VUFKU)

Earth was the sixth of Aleksandr Dovzhenko's eleven productions, and it embodies the quintessence of his philosophy of life: that the tenets of the Marxist are related to the attachment of simple men to the land of their forefathers.

Showing how the machines come to help the collectivization of farms in the Ukraine, *Earth* is well known for its simplicity, lyricism and deep feeling for humanity and nature. It remains one of the finest examples of the poetic cinema of the silent period.

[Pic was reviewed at a retrospective screening at the Montreal festival in 1962.]

•

ZOMBIES
SEE: DAWN OF THE DEAD

•

ZOO IN BUDAPEST
1933, 82 mins, US b/w
Dir Rowland V. Lee ***Prod*** Jesse L. Lasky ***Scr*** Dan Totheroh, Louise Long, Rowland V. Lee ***Ph*** Lee Garmes ***Mus*** Hugo Friedhofer
Act Loretta Young, Gene Raymond, O. P. Heggie, Wally Albright, Paul Fix (Fox)

Seemingly what producer Jesse Lasky has tried to do is to make a picture which has in it something of the strange fascination of romance and atmosphere of *Liliom*, and at the same time an element of Hollywood punch. He has gotten both things and they don't blend.

Besides the warring elements of a *Liliom* theme and a dramatic finish, the story [by Melville Baker and Jack Kirkland] has still another facet, the development of a submotif of bitter social satire in symbolic suggestions of similarities between the animals in the zoo and some of the people that cross the screen. This slant is but vaguely suggested and is never worked out satisfactorily.

However, there can be no two views of the picture's pictorial beauty. There are several sequences of night falling over a lake in the zoo peopled with strange creatures, where an escaped orphan girl is hiding as the evening mists gather, that are knockouts.

Playing by the two leads is eminently good. Role of the terror-stricken orphanage refugee proves a happy one for Loretta Young's talents, while the opposite character, that of a wild youngster brought up in a big-town menagerie, friend and play-fellow of the beasts of the cages, turns out to be one of those once-in-a-blue-moon for Gene Raymond, a newcomer from legit of only one or two pictures.

•

ZORBA THE GREEK
1964, 142 mins, US Ⓥ ⊙ b/w
Dir Michael Cacoyannis ***Prod*** Michael Cacoyannis ***Scr*** Michael Cacoyannis ***Ph*** Walter Lassally ***Ed*** Alex Archambault ***Mus*** Mikis Theodorakis ***Art*** Vassili Fotopoulos
Act Anthony Quinn, Alan Bates, Irene Papas, Lila Kedrova, George Foundas, Eleni Anousaki (20th Century-Fox)

To one who has not read Nikos Kazantzakis's widely praised novel, it appears that producer-director-scenarist Michael Cacoyannis may have tried to be too faithful to the original.

Zorba the Greek is a paean to life in all its diverse aspects, ranging from the farcical to the tragic, and as epitomized by the lusty title character. This Zorba, beautifully played by Anthony Quinn, is a wise and aging peasant, a free soul who is totally committed to life, no matter what it holds.

To dramatize this theme, Cacoyannis has written a screenplay which is so packed with incidents of varying moods that some of the more important ones cannot be developed fully. The story takes place in a remote section of the island of Crete, where Zorba has come as the self-appointed aide-de-camp to a young, inhibited Englishman of Greek parentage, played by Alan Bates. Latter, who describes himself as a writer who hasn't written anything in a long, long time, intends to reopen an old lignite mine he has inherited. Their subsequent adventures—rather loosely connected and wherein Bates finally learns to live a la Zorba—comprise the body of the film.

Quinn is excellent, and Bates, in a less flamboyant role, is equally good. Irene Papas is strikingly effective as a doomed widow, a role without dialog. Lila Kedrova plays the aging courtesan with all stops out, always halfway between laughter and tears.

1964: Best Supp. Actress (Lila Kedrova), B&W Cinematography, B&W Art Direction

NOMINATIONS: Best Picture, Director, Actor (Anthony Quinn), Adapted Screenplay

•

ZORRO, THE GAY BLADE
1981, 93 mins, US Ⓥ col
Dir Peter Medak ***Prod*** George Hamilton, C. O. Erickson ***Scr*** Hal Dresner ***Ph*** John A. Alonzo ***Ed*** Hillary Jane Kranze ***Mus*** Ian Fraser ***Art*** Herman A. Blumenthal
Act George Hamilton, Lauren Hutton, Brenda Vaccaro, Ron Leibman, Donovan Scott, James Booth (20th Century-Fox/Simon)

Despite an inspired, offbeat performance by George Hamilton, *Zorro, the Gay Blade* doesn't have nearly enough gags to sustain its 93 minutes. For the most part this is a Zorro with a very dull edge.

Although there is no time frame, film is obviously set years ago (in California) where Don Diego Vega, offspring of the legendary Zorro, is called upon to pick up his father's sword after the elder's death.

The hook here is that Hamilton's Vega, who is at first sight righting the wrongs of the poor villagers against leader Ron Leibman (who shouts unbearably through his entire role opposite equally brassy spouse Brenda Vaccaro), soon injures his foot and can no longer carry on his heroic deeds. Luckily his long-lost lookalike Englishman brother appears out of nowhere and takes on the Zorro persona.

The contrast between the two Zorros is initially quite funny, but there is nothing intriguing or original through the rest of the action. Pic climaxes at a snail's pace to Hamilton getting the girl (Lauren Hutton as a rather bland would-be political activist).

•

ZULU
1964, 135 mins, UK Ⓥ ⊙ ▭ col
Dir Cy Endfield ***Prod*** Stanley Baker, Cy Endfield ***Scr*** John Prebble, Cy Endfield ***Ph*** Stephen Dade ***Ed*** John Jympson ***Mus*** John Barry ***Art*** Ernest Archer
Act Stanley Baker, Jack Hawkins, Ulla Jacobsson, James Booth, Michael Caine, Nigel Green (Paramount/Diamond)

Joseph E. Levine makes an impressive debut in British film production with *Zulu*, a picture that allows ample scope for his flamboyant approach to showmanship.

Based on a famous heroic exploit, when a handful of British soldiers withstood an onslaught by 4,000 Zulu warriors, the production is distinguished by its notable on-screen values, which are enhanced by top-quality lensing by Stephen Dade. It also has an intelligent screenplay [suggested by an article written by co-scripter John Prebble] which avoids most of the obvious clichés. It keeps the traditional British stiff-upper-lip attitudes down to the barest minimum.

The defense of the garrison at Rorke's Drift took place on January 22, 1879. At the time the garrison heard the news that the 4,000 Zulu braves were on the way, reports had just come in that a far larger garrison had been completely wiped out, and there was no prospect of help from any other source.

One of the more obvious clichés in this type of yarn is apt to be the malingerer who displays great heroism in a moment of crisis. There is such a situation in *Zulu*, but the cliché is avoided, largely because of the excellent performance by James Booth. Indeed, the high all-round standard of acting is one of the notable plus features. Stanley Baker, a solid and reliable performer, turns in a thoroughly convincing portrayal as the resolute Royal Engineers officer, with an effective contrasting study by Michael Caine as a supercilious lieutenant. Richard Burton contributes a brief and dignified narration.

•

ZULU DAWN
1979, 117 mins, UK Ⓥ ⊙ col
Dir Douglas Hickox ***Prod*** Nate Kohn ***Scr*** Cy Enfield, Anthony Storey ***Ph*** Ousama Rawi ***Ed*** Malcolm Cook ***Mus*** Elmer Bernstein ***Art*** John Rosewarne ***Act*** Burt Lancaster, Peter O'Toole, Simon Ward, John Mills, Nigel Davenport, Denholm Elliott (Lamitas/Samarkand)

The subject of *Zulu Dawn* is the Battle of Islandlhwana wherein some 1,500 redcoats were slaughtered by 16 times their number of Zulu warriors led by legendary chief Cetshwayo.

The film is, in fact, a sort of "prequel" to the 1964 picture *Zulu*, which dealt with an heroic stand at Rorke's Drift by a small band of British soldiers in 1879.

The action sequences are superbly handled, as are the scenes in which the men and material are assembled and manoeuvered. For sheer scope and numbers of people being manipulated for the cameras, *Zulu Dawn* is positively DeMillesque in scale.

Such banality as there is, thankfully, confined to the expositional sequences which are quickly gotten out of the way to allow the army to get on the march.

DIRECTORS INDEX

Dawn; Journey, The; Long Night, The; Night of the Generals; Sisters, The; Snake Pit, The; Sorry, Wrong Number; This Above All; Tovarich
Llosa, Luis *Anaconda; Sniper; Specialist, The*
Lloyd, Cedric *Hardwicke, Frank Forever and a Day*
Lloyd, Frank *Berkeley Square; Blood on the Sun; Cavalcade; East Lynne; If I Were King; Mutiny on the Bounty; Sea Hawk, The; Under Two Flags*
Loach, Ken *Black Jack; Carla's Song; Family Life; Fatherland; Hidden Agenda; Kes; Ladybird Ladybird; Land and Freedom; Looks and Smiles; Poor Cow; Raining Stones; Riff Raff*
Locke, Sondra *Impulse; Ratboy*
Loden, Barbara *Wanda*
Logan, Bob *Repossessed*
Logan, Joshua *Bus Stop; Camelot; Fanny; Paint Your Wagon; Picnic; Sayonara; South Pacific*
Lommel, Ulli *BrainWaves*
Loncraine, Richard *Brimstone & Treacle; Full Circle; Missionary, The; Richard III*
London, Jerry *Rent-a-Cop; Shogun*
London, Roy *Diary of a Hit Man*
Lonergan, Kenneth You Can Count On Me
Longo, Robert *Johnny Mnemonic*
Lopez, Temistocles *Chain of Desire*
Lord, Peter *Chicken Run*
Lorentz, Pare *River, The*
Losey, Joseph *Accident; Assassination of Trotsky, The; Big Night, The; Boom; Boy with Green Hair, The; Damned, The; Doll's House, A; Eve; Figures in a Landscape; Go-Between, The; King & Country; Lawless, The; M; Modesty Blaise; Prowler, The; Romantic Englishwoman, The; Secret Ceremony; Servant, The; Steaming*
Lounsbery, John *Rescuers, The*
Lourie, Eugene *Beast from 20,000 Fathoms, The; Colossus of New York, The*
Louzil, Eric *Class of Nuke 'Em High, Part II: Subhumanoid Meltdown*
Loventhal, Charlie *First Time, The*
Lovitt, Bert *Prince Jack*
Lowry, Dick *Smokey and the Bandit, Part 3*
Lubin, Arthur *Buck Privates; In the Navy; Keep 'em Flying; Phantom of the Opera; Ride 'em Cowboy*
Lubitsch, Dorothy Arzner, Victor Heerman, Ernst *Paramount on Parade*
Lubitsch, Ernst *Angel; Bluebeard's Eighth Wife; Cluny Brown; Design for Living; Heaven Can Wait; Kiss Me Again; Lady Windermere's Fan; Love Parade, The; Man I Killed, The; Merry Widow, The; Monte Carlo; Ninotchka; One Hour with You; Patriot, The; Shop around the Corner, The; Smiling Lieutenant, The; So This Is Paris; Student Prince, The; That Uncertain Feeling; Three Women; To Be or Not to Be; Trouble in Paradise*
Lucarelli, Jack *Gift from Heaven, A*
Lucas, George *American Graffiti; Star Wars; Star Wars: Episode 1 - The Phantom Menace; THX-1138*
Ludwig, Edward *Big Jim McLain; That Certain Age; Wake of the Red Witch*
Luhrmann, Baz *Romeo + Juliet; Strictly Ballroom*
Lumet, Sidney *Anderson, Tapes, The; Appointment, The; Bye Bye Braverman; Child's Play; Daniel; Deadly Affair, The; Deathtrap; Dog Day Afternoon; Equus; Fail Safe; Family Business; Fugitive Kind, The; Garbo Talks; Group, The; Guilty As Sin; Hill, The; Long Day's Journey into Night; Lovin' Molly; Morning After, The; Murder on the Orient Express; Network; Offence, The; Pawnbroker, The; Power; Prince of the City; Q&A; Running on Empty; Sea Gull, The; Serpico; Stage Struck; Stranger Among Us, A; 12 Angry Men; Verdict, The; Wiz, The*
Lupino, Ida *Hard, Fast and Beautiful; Outrage; Trouble with Angels, The*
Luraschi, Tony *Outsider, The*
Luske, Hamilton *Alice in Wonderland; Cinderella; Lady and the Tramp; Make Mine Music; One Hundred and One Dalmations; Peter Pan; Pinocchio; Reluctant Dragon, The*
Lustig, William *Maniac Cop; Maniac Cop 2; Relentless*
Lynch, David *Blue Velvet; Dune; Elephant Man, The; Eraserhead; Lost Highway; Twin Peaks Fire Walk with Me; Wild at Heart*
Lynch, Jennifer *Chambers Boxing Helena*
Lynch, Paul *Prom Night*
Lyne, Adrian *Fatal Attraction; Flashdance; Foxes; Indecent Proposal; Jacob's Ladder; Lolita; Nine 1/2 Weeks*
Lynn, Jonathan *Clue; Distinguished Gentleman, The; Greedy; My Cousin Vinny; Nuns on the Run; Sgt. Bilko*

•

Maas, Dick *De Lift*
MacArthur, Charles *Crime without Passion; Scoundrel, The*
Macdonald, David *Cairo Road; Christopher Columbus; Petticoat Pirates*
Macdonald, Hettie *Beautiful Thing*
Macdonald, Mace *Neufeld Saint, The*
Macdonald, Peter *Mo' Money; Neverending Story III, The; Rambo III*
MacDougall, Ranald *Go Naked in the World; Man on Fire; Subterraneans, The; World, the Flesh and the Devil, The*
MacFadden, Hamilton *Charlie Chan Carries On*
MacGrath, Jospeh *Bliss of Mrs. Blossom, The*
Machaty, Gustav *Extase*
Mack, Willard *Broadway to Hollywood*
Mackendrick, Alexander *Don't Make Waves; High Wind in Jamaica, A; Ladykillers, The; 'Maggie', The; Mandy; Man in the White Suit, The; Sammy Going South; Sweet Smell of Success; Whisky Galore!*
Mackenzie, John *Fourth Protocol, The; Honorary Consul, The; Last of the Finest, The; Long Good Friday, The; Ruby; Unman, Wittering and Zigo*
MacKinnon, Gillies *Playboys, The; Simple Twist of Fate, A; Small Faces*
Madden, David *Separate Lives*
Madden, John *Mrs. Brown; Shakespeare in Love*
Maddow, Ben *Savage Eye, The*
Magnoli, Albert *Purple Rain; Tango & Cash*
Mailer, Norman *Tough Guys Don't Dance*
Makavejev, Dusan *Coca-Cola Kid, The; Nevinost Bez Zastite; Sweet Movie; WR: Misterije Organizma*
Makin, Kelly *Brain Candy; Mickey Blue Eyes; National Lampoon's Senior Trip*
Makk, Karoly *Szerelem*
Malick, Terrence *Badlands; Days of Heaven; Thin Red Line, The*
Malle, Louis *Alamo Bay; Les Amants; Atlantic City; Au Revoir, Les Enfants; Crackers; Damage; Lacombe Lucien; My Dinner with Andre; Pretty Baby; Le Souffle au Coeur; Vanya on 42nd* Street; Viva Maria!; Zazie Dans Le Metro
Mallon, Jim *Mystery Science Theater 3000: The Movie*
Malmuth, Bruce *Hard to Kill; Nighthawks*
Malone, Mark *Killer*
Malone, William *House on Haunted Hill*
Mamet, David *Homicide; House of Games; Oleanna; State and Main; Spanish Prisoner, The; Things Change*
Mamoulian, Rouben *Applause; Becky Sharp; Blood and Sand; City Streets; Dr. Jekyll and Mr. Hyde; Gay Desperado, The; High, Wide and Handsome; Love Me Tonight; Mark of Zorro, The; Queen Christina; Rings on Her Fingers; Silk Stockings; Song of Songs; Summer Holiday; We Live Again*
Manchevski, Milcho *Before the Rain*
Mandel, Robert *F/X; Independence Day; Substitute, The; Touch and Go*
Mandoki, Luis *Born Yesterday; When a Man Loves a Woman; White Palace*
Manduke, Joseph *Gumshoe Kid, The*
Mangold, James *Cop Land; Girl, Interrupted*
Mankiewicz, Joseph L. *All about Eve; Barefoot Contessa, The; Cleopatra; Dragonwyck; 5 Fingers; Ghost and Mrs. Muir, The; Guys and Dolls; Honey Pot, The; House of Strangers; Julius Caesar; Letter to Three Wives, A; No Way Out; People Will Talk; Quiet American, The; Sleuth; Suddenly, Last Summer; There Was a Crooked Man . . .*
Mankiewicz, Tom *Delirious; Dragnet*
Mann, Anthony *Bend of the River; Border Incident; Cimarron; Dandy in Aspic, A; Desperate; Devil's Doorway; El Cid; Fall of the Roman Empire, The; Far Country, The; Furies, The; Glenn Miller Story, The; God's Little Acre; Heroes of Telemark, The; Man from Laramie, The; Man of the West; Men in War; Naked Spur, The; Spartacus; Strategic Air Command; Thunder Bay; Tin Star, The; T-Men; Winchester '73*
Mann, Daniel *Butterfield 8; Come Back, Little Sheba; Dream of Kings, A; Five Finger Exercise; For Love of Ivy; I'll Cry Tomorrow; Judith; Last Angry Man, The; Our Man Flint; Rose Tattoo, The; Teahouse of the August Moon, The; Who's Been Sleeping in My Bed?; Willard*
Mann, Delbert *Bachelor Party, The; Dark at the Top of the Stairs, The; David Copperfield; Desire under the Elms; Fitzwilly; Gathering of Eagles, A; Jane Eyre; Kidnapped; Lover Come Back; Marty; Night Crossing; Separate Tables; That Touch of Mink*
Mann, Farhad *Lawnmower Man 2 Beyond Cyberspace*
Mann, Michael *Heat; Insider, The; Keep, The; Last of the Mohicans, The; Manhunter; Thief*
Marcus, Adam *Jason Goes to Hell The Final Friday*
Margheriti, Antonio *Take a Hard Ride*
Marin, Edwin L. *Abilene Town; Everybody Sing; Johnny Angel; Listen, Darling; Nocturne; Paris Calling; Tall in the Saddle*
Maris, Peter *Hangfire*
Marker, Chris *Le Joli Mai*
Markle, Fletcher *Incredible Journey, The*
Markle, Peter *BAT 21; Personals, The; Wagons East!; Youngblood*
Marks, Arthur *Friday Foster*
Marks, Ross Kagan *Homage*
Marquand, Richard *Eye of the Needle; Hearts of Fire; Jagged Edge; Legacy, The; Return of the Jedi; Until September*
Marshall, Frank *Alive; Arachnophobia; Congo*
Marshall, Gary *Beaches; Exit to Eden; Flamingo Kid, The; Frankie and Johnny; Overboard; Pretty Woman; Runaway Bride*
Marshall, George *Blue Dahlia, The; Boy, Did I Get a Wrong Number!; Destry; Destry Rides Again; Fancy Pants; Gazebo, The; Goldwyn Follies, The; Houdini; How The West Was Won; Incendiary Blonde; In Old Kentucky; It Started with a Kiss; Mating Game, The; Millionare for Christy, A; Monsieur Beaucaire; Murder, He Says; Never a Dull Moment; Off Limits; Pack up Your Troubles; Perils of Pauline, The; Riding High; Savage, The; Scared Stiff; Star Spangled Rhythm; True to Life; Variety Girl*
Marshall, Noel *Roar*
Marshall, Penny *Awakenings; Big; Jumpin' Jack Flash; League of Their Own, A; Preacher's Wife; Renaissance Man*
Martin, Darnell *I Like It Like That*
Martin, Francis *Tillie and Gus*
Martinson, Leslie *Batman; Fathom*
Marton, Andrew *Africa—Texas Style; Ben-Hur; Crack in the World; Devil Makes Three, The; 55 Days at Peking; Green Fire; King Solomon's Mines; Longest Day, The; 7 Wonders of the World; Thin Red Line, The*
Maselli, Francesco *Fine Pair, A*
Masters, Quentin *Stud, The*
Masterson, Peter *Blood Red; Trip to Bountiful, The*
Masuda, Toshio *Tora! Tora! Tora!*
Mate, Rudolph *Branded; Dark Past, The; D.O.A.; Mississippi Gambler, The; 300 Spartans, The; Three Violent People; Union Station; When Worlds Collide*
Matthau, Charles *Grass Harp, The*
Mattinson, Burny *Great Mouse Detective, The*
Maxwell, Ronald F. *Gettysburg; Little Darlings*
May, Elaine *Heartbreak Kid, The; Ishtar; Mikey and Nicky; New Leaf, A*
May, Joe *Invisible Man Returns, The*
Mayfield, Les *Encino Man; Flubber; Miracle on 34th Street*
Mayo, Archie *Adventures of Marco Polo, The; Angel on My Shoulder; Black Legion, The; Bordertown; Charley's Aunt; Crash Dive; Go into Your Dance; Great American Broadcast, The; It's Love I'm After; Moontide; Night in Casablanca, A; Svengali*
Mayo, Archie L. *Petrified Forest, The*
Mayron, Melanie *Baby-sitters Club, The*
Maysles, Albert *Gimme Shelter*
Maysles, David *Gimme Shelter*
Mazursky, Paul *Alex in Wonderland; Blume in Love; Bob & Carol & Ted & Alice; Down and Out in Beverly Hills; Enemies A Love Story; Harry and Tonto; Moon over Parador; Moscow on the Hudson; Next Stop, Greenwich Village; Pickle, The; Scenes from a Mall; Unmarried Woman, An; Willie & Phil*
McBride, Jim *Big Easy, The; Breathless; Great Balls of Fire!; Wrong Man, The*
McCall, Rod *Paper Hearts*
McCarey, Leo *Affair to Remember, An; Awful Truth, The; Belle of the Nineties; Bells of St. Mary's, The; Duck Soup; Going My Way; Good Sam; Indiscreet; Love Affair; Make Way for Tomorrow; Milky Way, The; Once upon a Honeymoon; Rally 'Round the Flag, Boys!; Ruggles of Red Gap; Satan Never Sleeps*
McCarey, Raymond *Pack up Your Troubles*
McCowan, George *Frogs*
McEveety, Vincent *Herbie Goes to Monte Carlo; Strongest Man in the World, The*
McGaugh, W. F. *New Adventures of Tarzan, The*
McGehee, Scott *Suture*
McGrath, Douglas *Emma*
McGrath, Joseph *Cynthia; Magic Christian, The; 30 Is a Dangerous Age*
McGrath, Robert Parrish, Joseph *Casino Royale*
McHenry, Doug *House Party 2*
McKay, Jim *Girls Town*
McLaglen, Andrew V. *Bandolero!; Cahill, United States Marshal; Chisum; Devil's Brigade, The; Last Hard Men, The; McLintock!; Monkeys, Go Home!; North Sea Hijack; Rare Breed, The; Sahara; Sea Wolves, The; Last Charge of the Calcutta Light Horse, The; Shenandoah; Undefeated, The; Way West, The; Wild Geese, The*
McLeod, Norman Z, *Horse Feathers; It's a Gift; Kid from Brooklyn, The; Lady Be Good; Let's Dance; Merrily We Live; Monkey Business; My Favorite Spy; Paleface, The; Road to Rio; Secret Life of Walter Mitty, The; Topper; Topper Takes a Trip*
McLeod, Stephen Roberts, Norman Z. *If I Had a Million*
McLoughlin, Tom *Jason Lives Friday the 13th Part VI*
McNally, David *Coyote Ugly*
McNaughton, John *Henry Portrait of a Serial Killer; Mad Dog and Glory; Wild Things*
McTiernan, John *13th Warrior, The; Die Hard; Die Hard with a Vengeance; Hunt for Red October, The; Last Action Hero; Medicine Man; Nomads; Predator; Thomas Crown Affair, The*
Meador, Bob Cormack, Josh *Make Mine Music*
Medak, Peter *Changeling, The; Day in the Death of Joe Egg, A; Krays, The; Let Him Have It; Men's Club, The; Pontiac Moon; Romeo Is Bleeding; Ruling Class, The; Species II; Zorro, the Gay Blade*
Medford, Don *Hunting Party, The; Organization, The; To Trap a Spy*
Megahey, Leslie *Hour of the Pig, The*
Mehta, Deepa *Camilla*
Meins, Gus *Babes in Toyland*
Meisel, Myron *It's All True*
Mekas, Adolfas *Hallelujah The Hills*
Melendez, Bill *Snoopy, Come Home*
Melford, George *Sheik, The*
Melkonian, James *Jerky Boys, The*
Melville, Jean-Pierre *Bob Le Flambeur; Le Deuxieme Souffle; Les Enfants Terribles; Leon Morin, Pretre; Le Samourai*
Menaul, Christopher *Feast of July*
Mendes, Lothar *Jew Suss; Moonlight Sonata*
Mendes, Sam *American Beauty*
Menendez, Ramon *Money for Nothing*
Menges, Chris *Criss Cross; Second Best; World Apart, A*
Menotti, Gian-Carlo *Medium, The*
Menshov, Vladimir *Moskva Slezam Ne Verit*